The Seven Deadly

1. Pride
2 Covetousness
3. Wrath
4 Envy
5. Gluttony
6. Sloth
7. Lechery

— Marlowe, Dr. Faustus, Scene 6

Cruden's
COMPLETE CONCORDANCE

Cruden's
COMPLETE CONCORDANCE
to the Old and New Testaments

By ALEXANDER CRUDEN, A.M.

Edited By

A. D. ADAMS, M. A.
C. H. IRWIN, M.A., D.D.
S. A. WATERS

*Notes and Biblical Proper Names
Under One
Alphabetical Arrangement
Plus a List of Proper Names with a
Foreword by Dr. Walter L. Wilson*

ZONDERVAN PUBLISHING HOUSE
GRAND RAPIDS, MICHIGAN 49506

This printing — 1968

Printed in the United States of America

FOREWORD

THE STUDY of the Word of God can best be facilitated by a wise and constant use of this Concordance. Here you will find almost every word of the whole Bible arranged alphabetically, so that at any time the student may find the location of any passage that he may desire. By this means also, the student will discover that many statements are incorrectly quoted from the Bible. Sometimes quotations are made which are not found in the Bible in any form. This may be discovered by consulting your Concordance and looking for any of the prominent words used in that quotation.

By means of this Concordance the student may study any subject desired. For instance, you might wish to study the subject of trees. Find the word "tree" in the Concordance, and then notice every place where the word occurs, and what is the subject under consideration. You will find that the "oak tree" is usually mentioned in connection with death. The "fig tree" is usually connected with political Israel, etc.

If you wish to study the subject of "grace," or "horses," or of the "blood," or of the "coming of Christ," or of the "judgments," or any other subject, just find that word in your Concordance and look up the various Scriptures in which that word occurs. By this means you will become well acquainted with your Bible, and with God's Truth.

If you hear a verse of Scripture quoted, and you do not know where it is found, seek the prominent word in the Concordance, follow down the Scriptures that are listed there, and you will find the verse that you desire to locate.

This Concordance is a library of instruction. It is a lexicon of explanation. It is a source of inspiration and knowledge which is indispensable to the Bible student. Permit me to encourage every student of the Word of God to own a copy of this wonderful and valuable book.

WALTER L. WILSON, M.D., L.H.D.

Kansas City, Missouri

INTRODUCTION

Cruden's Complete Concordance has long been considered the most practical and usable Concordance on the market. This clear-type edition was developed with the average Bible reader and student in mind. The key words in bold face type, easily discernible, and references following have been set up in a type face scientifically analyzed as the most readable.

It is a great pleasure and privilege for the publishers to continue making this edition of *Cruden's Complete Concordance* available to God's people in this and succeeding generations. The additional helps included in this edition are also selected with the Bible student in mind, for they provide information nowhere else available in such concise and usable form.

May your use of this Concordance make your own study of the Bible and related subjects more meaningful and effective.

THE PUBLISHERS

PREFACE

FOR nearly two hundred years "Cruden's Concordance" has been a household word wherever the English language is spoken and the English Bible read.

Its author, Alexander Cruden, was born in 1701 at Aberdeen, where he was educated at the grammar school and Marischal College. He was intended for the Presbyterian ministry, but ill-health, which for a time affected his mind, led him to take up teaching at the age of twenty-one. After some years spent in private tutorships, he came to London, where in 1732 he opened a bookseller's shop in the Royal Exchange and was appointed bookseller to Queen Caroline. He died at Camden Place, Islington, in 1770, and was buried in Southwark in a burial-ground now said to be included in the premises of a well-known brewery. A bursary provided by him and bearing his name is among the prizes of Aberdeen University.

The first edition of Cruden's Concordance was published in 1737. It won for him special honors at the Universities of Oxford and Cambridge. Two further editions of the Concordance appeared in Cruden's lifetime in 1761 and 1769 respectively. Since that time numerous editions have been published with some claim to revision but have varied slightly from the original text and repeated many inaccuracies which appeared in the early editions.

The present edition may justly claim to be the most accurate and complete Cruden's Concordance to the Old and New Testaments. It contains upwards of 220,000 references. Every quotation and reference in this new Concordance has received careful scrutiny. The result is that many inaccuracies which appeared in the original editions and others which have from time to time crept in have now been corrected. The explanatory notes, while mainly in the language of Cruden, have embodied the latest Scriptural interpretations and the results of the most recent discoveries of archeology. The work has the advantage of being edited on both sides of the Atlantic and the fruits of the work of the American revisers of the Bible will be especially found in the explanatory notes.

The text quoted throughout is that of the Authorised Version of 1611, known in America as the "King James's Version," and its spelling and punctuation have generally been followed. Where the Revised

Version of 1881 has altered the sense or made the meaning clearer, this is indicated by an asterisk [*]. Where such alteration has been made by the American Revision, this is indicated by a dagger [†].

The grouping of Proper Names and the general Concordance under one Alphabetical arrangement will greatly facilitate the use of the volume. In the Appendix will be found a list of Proper Names seldom mentioned in Scripture and not included in the body of the Concordance. Every endeavour has been made, in the necessarily shortened quotations, to include the most essential word, and to preserve the true meaning of the text.

The quotation occupies the first position in the column, followed by the main reference, and then by reference to other passages where the principal word is used. The principal word quoted is indicated by its *initial letter in italics*. A colon between the figures (1:6) divides chapter and verse; a semicolon (Isa 9:6; John 3:16, 17) divides the main reference from succeeding references; while a comma divides verses in the same chapter.

Thus, under the heading *Aaron:*

A. shall bear their.   Ex 28:12; 29:30

A. shall burn sweet incense.   30:7

A. lighteth the lamps at even.   8

A. shall make an atonement once.   10

In the first line there are two passages quoted with chapter and verse; in the second line one chapter and verse, while the third and fourth lines have the verse only, being a verse of chapter 30 quoted in the preceding lines.

Every modern mechanical facility was employed in the preparation of this edition. The type which was cast expressly for the work combines clearness with compactness. The black face type is restful to the eye. The special type arrangement is an aid to ready reference. Therefore in fulness of contents, clearness of type and logical arrangement, this edition is superior to any other edition of Cruden's Concordance previously published and is especially adapted for school and general use.

And now this new edition is sent forth with the prayer that it may be blessed to the men and women of to-day as it has been blessed in the past, in the fuller, clearer understanding of the Holy Scriptures and the enrichment thereby of Christian character and service.

A COLLECTION OF THE NAMES AND TITLES GIVEN TO JESUS CHRIST

ADAM. *1 Cor* 15:45
Advocate. *1 John* 2:1
Alpha and Omega. *Rev* 1:8, 11; 21:6; 22;13
Amen. *Rev* 3:14
Angel. *Isa* 63:9; *Mal* 3:1
Ancient of Days. *Dan* 7:22
Anointed. *Ps* 2:2; 45:7
Apostle. *Heb* 3:1
Author and Finisher of our faith. *Heb* 12:2
Babe. *Luke* 2:16
Beginning of Creation of God. *Rev* 3:14
Begotten of the Father. *John* 1:14
Beloved. *S of S* 1:13; *Eph* 1:6
Bishop. *1 Pet* 2:25
Blessed. *1 Tim* 6:15
Branch of Righteousness. *Zech* 3:8
Bread of Life. *John* 6:48, 51
Bridegroom. *Mat* 9:15
Bright and Morning Star. *Rev* 22:16
Brightness of the Father's Glory. *Heb*. 1:3
Captain. *Heb* 2:10
Chief Corner stone. *Eph* 2:20; *1 Pet* 2:7
Child. *Isa* 9:6
Chosen. *Mat* 12:18; *Luke* 23:35
Christ. *Mat* 1:16; 2:4
Consolation of Israel. *Luke* 2:25
Covenant. *Isa* 42:6
Counsellor. *Isa* 9:6
Covert. *Isa* 32:2
Creator. *Isa* 43:15
David. *Jer* 30:9; *Ezek* 37:24, 25; *Hos* 3:5
Daysman. *Job* 9:33
Day star. *2 Pet* 1:19
Deliverer. *Rom* 11:26
Desire of all Nations. *Hag* 2:7
Dew. *Hos* 14:5
Diadem. *Isa* 62:3
Door of Sheep. *John* 10:7
Eagle. *Deut* 32:11
Elect. *Isa* 42:1
Emmanuel. *Isa* 7:14; *Mat* 1:23
Everlasting Father. *Isa* 9:6

Express Image. *Heb* 1:3
Faithful Witness. *Rev* 1:5; 3:14; 19:11
Feeder. *Isa* 40:11
First begotten. *Rev* 1:5
Firstfruits. *1 Cor* 15:23
First and Last. *Rev* 2:8
Foundation. *Isa* 28:16
Fountain. *Zech* 13:1
Forerunner. *Heb* 6:20
Friend of Sinners. *Mat* 11:19
Gift of God. *2 Cor* 9:15
God. *John* 1:1; *Rom* 9:5; *1 Tim* 3:16; *1 John* 5:20
Governor. *Mat* 2:6
Gracious. *1 Pet* 2:3
Habitation. *Ps* 91:9
Harmless. *Heb* 7:26
Head of the Church. *Col* 1:18
Heir of all Things. *Heb* 1:2
High Priest. *Heb* 3:1; 7:1
Holy One of God. *Mark* 1:24
Holy Child. *Acts* 4:30
Hope. *Acts* 28:20; *1 Tim* 1:1
Image of God. *Heb* 1:3
Immanuel. *Isa* 7:14; *Mat* 1:23
Immortal. *1 Tim* 1:17
Invisible. *1 Tim* 1:17
Jesus. *Mat* 1:21; *1 Thes* 1:10
Judge. *Acts* 10:42
King. *Mat* 21:5; 25:34
Lamb. *John* 1:29; *Rev* 5:6
Leader. *Isa* 55:4
Light. *John* 1:9; 8:12; 12:46
Life. *John* 14:6
Lion of the Tribe of Judah. *Rev* 5:5
Lord. *Rom* 1:3; *Rev* 17:14
Man. *Acts* 17:31; *1 Tim* 2:5
Master. *Mat* 8:19; 23:8
Mediator. *1 Tim* 2:5
Merciful. *Heb* 2:17
Messiah. *Dan* 9:25; *John* 1:41
Mighty God. *Isa* 9:6
Minister. *Heb* 8:2
Morning star. *Rev* 2:28; 22:16
Nazarene. *Mat* 2:23
Offspring of David. *Rev* 22:16
Only begotten. *John* 1:14

Passover. *1 Cor* 5:7
Potentate. *1 Tim* 6:15
Prince. *Acts* 3:15; 5:31
Prophet. *Luke* 4:19; *Acts* 3:22
Propitiation. *1 John* 2:2; 4:10
Power of God. *1 Cor* 1:24
Purifier. *Mal* 3:3
Physician. *Mat* 9:12
Priest. *Heb* 4:14; 7:26
Prince of Peace. *Isa* 9:6
Ransom. *1 Tim* 2:6
Reaper. *Rev* 14:15
Redeemer. *Isa* 59:20; 60:16
Resurrection. *John* 11:25
Refiner. *Mal* 3:3
Righteousness. *Jer* 23:6
Rock. *1 Cor* 10:4
Rod and Branch. *Isa* 11:1
Root of David. *Rev* 22:16
Ruler in Israel. *Mi* 5:2
Sacrifice. *Eph* 5:2
Sanctification. *1 Cor* 1:30
Saviour *Luke* 2:11 etc.
Seed of Abraham. *Gal* 3:29
Seed of the Woman. *Gen* 3:15
Seed of David. *2 Tim* 2:8
Second Man. *1 Cor* 15:47
Servant. *Isa* 42:1, 19; 44:21
Shepherd. *John* 10:11; *Heb* 13:2C
Shiloh. *Gen* 49:10
Son of God. *Mat* 4:3; 8:29
Son of man. *Mat* 8:20
Sower. *Mat* 13:3
Spirit. *1 Cor* 15:45; *Heb* 9:14
Stone refused. *Mat* 21:42
Sun of Righteousness. *Mal* 4:2
Surety. *Heb* 7:22
Teacher. *John* 3:2
Testator. *Heb* 9:16, 17
Truth. *John* 14:6
Vine. *John* 15:1
Way. *Isa* 35:8; *John* 14:6
Wisdom of God. *1 Cor* 1:24
Witness. *Rev* 1:5; 3:14
Wonderful. *Isa* 9:6
Word of God. *Rev* 19:13
Worthy. *Heb* 3:3; *Rev* 5:12

A COLLECTION OF THE TITLES AND DESCRIPTIONS GIVEN TO THE CHURCH OF GOD IN THE SCRIPTURES

ADOPTED Sons. *Gal* 4:5
Angels. *Luke* 20:36
Assembly of Saints. *Heb* 10:25
Believers. *Acts* 5:14
Beloved of God. *Ps* 60:5; 108:6
Blessed. *Ps* 2:12; 32:1
Blameless. *Phil* 2:15
Body of Christ. *Eph* 1:23
Branches of Righteousness. *John* 15:5
Brethren. *Rom* 8:29; 12:1
Bride. *Rev* 21:2, 9; 22:17
Building of God. *1 Cor* 3:9
Called. *Isa* 62:12; *Rom* 8:28
Candlestick. *Rev* 1:12; 2:5
Cedars. *Ps* 92:12; *Ezek* 31:8
Children of the Kingdom. *Mat* 13:38
Christians. *Acts* 11:26; *1 Pet* 4:16
Church of the Firstborn. *Heb* 12:23
Church of God. *1 Cor* 1:2
Circumcision. *Phil* 3:3
City of God. *Heb* 12:22; *Rev* 3:12
Citizens. *Eph* 2:19
Complete. *Col* 2:10
Congregation of Saints. *Ps* 149:1
Contrite. *Isa* 57:15; 66:2
Converts. *Isa* 1:27
Daughter of the King. *Ps* 45:13
Dearly Beloved. *Jer* 12:7
Disciples. *Isa* 8:16; *Mat* 5:1
Elect. *Isa* 45:4; *Mat* 24:22
Election. *Rom* 9:11; 11:5, 7
Excellent. *Ps* 16:3; *Pr* 12:26
Faithful. *Eph* 1:1; *Col* 1:2
Family of God. *Eph* 3:15
Fearful. *Isa* 35:4
Firstfruits. *Jas* 1:18

Flock of God. *Acts* 20:28
Firstborn. *Heb* 12:23
Fold of Christ. *John* 10:16
Followers of God. *Eph* 5:1
Friends of God. *Jas* 2:23
Fruitful. *Col* 1:10
Fulness of Christ. *Eph* 1:23
Gathered. *Isa* 56:8
General Assembly. *Heb* 12:23
Generation of the Upright. *Ps* 112:2
Glory of God. *Isa* 46:13
Glorious. *Ps* 45:13
Grapes. *Hos* 9:10
Habitation of God. *Eph* 2:22
Heirs of God. *Rom* 8:17
Heritage of God. *Jer* 12:7
Hidden Ones. *Ps* 83:3
Holy. *1 Cor* 3:17; *Eph* 1:4
House of God. *1 Tim* 3:15
Husbandry of God. *1 Cor* 3:9
Image of God. *Rom* 8:29
Inhabitants of Zion. *Isa* 12:6
Israel of God. *Gal* 6:16
Jacob. *Ps* 14:7; 147:19
Jerusalem above. *Gal* 4:29—heavenly. *Heb* 12:22—holy. *Rev* 21:10
Jewels of the Lord. *Mal* 3:17
Joy of the whole Earth. *Ps* 48:2
Justified. *Acts* 13:39
Kings. *Rev* 1:6; 5:10
Lamb's Wife. *Rev* 21:9
Light of the World. *Mat* 5:14
Lively Stones. *1 Pet* 2:5
Lot of God's Inheritance. *Deut* 32:9
Lowly. *Ps* 138:6; *Pr* 3:34
Members of Christ. *Eph* 5:30

Merciful. *Mat* 5:7
Mighty. *Ps* 112:2; *Acts* 18:24
Mount Sion. *Heb* 12:22
Obedient. *1 Pet* 1:14
Palaces. *Ps* 45:15; 48:3, 13
Palm tree. *Ps* 92:12
Peaceable. *Gen* 34:21
Peculiar People. *1 Pet* 2:9
Perfect. *2 Tim* 3:17; *Heb* 12:23
Pilgrims. *Heb* 11:13
Pillar of Truth. *1 Tim* 3:15
Portion of the Lord. *Deut* 32:9
Precious. *Ps* 116:15; *Isa* 43:4
Pure in Heart. *Mat* 5:8
Ransomed. *Isa* 45:10; 51:11
Redeemed. *Isa* 51:11; 62:12
Sanctified. *1 Cor* 1:2; 6:11
Saved of the Lord. *Deut* 33:29
Sheep. *John* 10:3, 4; 21:16
Sincere. *Phil* 1:10
Stones. *1 Pet* 2:5
Sons of God. *Rom* 8:14
Spiritual. *Gal* 6:1; *1 Pet* 2:5
Strangers. *Ps* 39:12; 119:9
Temple of God. *1 Cor* 3:16
Treasure of God. *Ps* 135:4
Vessels of Mercy. *Rom* 9:23
Vineyard. *Isa* 5:1; 27:2
Wise Men. *1 Cor* 6:5
Woman. *Rev* 12:1
Worshippers. *Heb* 10:2
Worthy to walk with Christ. *Rev* 3:4
Written in Heaven. *Heb* 12:23
Zealous of good works. *Tit* 2:14
Zion. *Ps* 69:35; 76:2; 87:2

CONTENTS

Foreword

Introduction

Preface

A Collection of the Names and Titles Given to Jesus

A Collection of the Titles and Descriptions Given to the Church of God in the Scriptures

Cruden's Complete Concordance

Cruden's
COMPLETE CONCORDANCE

CRUDEN'S
COMPLETE CONCORDANCE

NOTE.—*A list of Proper Names is included in this Concordance under one alphabetical arrangement.*

An asterisk [*] *following a reference means that the Revised Versions have altered the sense of the verse or have made the meaning clearer.*

A dagger [†] *following a reference means that the American Revision alone has made this change.*

No mark is found where the Revisions are not materially different.

A

Aaron
is not *A.* the Levite thy ?   *Ex* 4:14
they met Moses and *A.* who.   5:20
A. took Elisheba . . . to wife.   6:23
and *A.* thy brother shall be thy.   7:1
but *A.* rod swallowed up their.   12
A. laid up the pot of manna.   16:34
and *A.* and Hur stayed up.   17:12
shalt come up, thou and *A.*   19:24
and behold *A.* and Hur are.   24:14
A. shall bear their.   28:12; 29:30
A. shall burn sweet incense.   30:7
A. lighteth the lamps at even.   8
A. shall make an atonement once.   10
they made the calf, which *A.*   32:35
Moses and *A.* and his sons.   40:31
he poured oil on *A.* head.   *Lev* 8:12
he sprinkled blood on *A.* and.   30
A. blessed them.   9:22
A. held his peace.   10:3
thus shall *A.* come into the holy.   16:3
A. shall cast lots.   8
A. shall lay his hands on the.   21
A. shall order it.   24:3
A. shall number them by.   *Num* 1:3
what is *A.* that ye murmur ?   16:11
they, and *A.* to-morrow.   16
Moses and *A.* came before the.   43
write *A.* name upon the rod.   17:3
A. rod again before the testimony. 10
thou and *A.* thy brother speak.   20:8
A. died there in the top of the mount.
  28; 33:38; *Deut* 32:50
A. was 123 years old.   *Num* 33:39
was very angry with *A.*   *Deut* 9:20
I sent Moses and *A.*   *Josh* 24:5
  1 Sam 12:8 ; *Mi* 6:4
advanced Moses and *A. 1 Sam* 12:6
A. and Moses.   *1 Chr* 6:3; 23:13
people by Moses and *A.*   *Ps* 77:20
Moses and *A.* among his.   99:6
they envied *A.* the saint.   106:16
O house of *A.* trust in the.   115:10
Lord will bless the house of *A.*   12
house of *A.* say, his mercy.   118:3
ran down upon *A.* beard.   133:2
the Lord, O house of *A.*   135:19
was of the daughters of *A. Luke* 1:5
saying to *A.* make us gods to.
  Acts 7:40
called of God, as was *A.*   *Heb* 5:4
called after the order of *A.*   7:11
A. rod that budded and tables.   9:4
Sons of **Aaron,** *see* **Abihu** *and* **Nadab**

Aaronites
was leader of the *A.*   *1 Chr* 12:27
Zadok was the ruler of the *A.* 27:17

Abaddon
the bottomless pit is *A.*   *Rev* 9:11

Abagtha
A. was chamberlain to.   *Esth* 1:10

Abana
(*Revised Version,* Abanah)
are not rivers *A.* and.   *2 Ki* 5:12

Abarim
get thee up into this mount *A.*
  Num 27:12; *Deut* 32:49
in the mountains of *A. Num* 33:47

abase
(*To bring low, usually in spirit; to humble*)
proud, and *a.* him.   *Job* 40:11
lion will not *a.* himself.   *Isa* 31:4
and *a.* him that is high.   *Ezek* 21:26
in pride, is able to *a.*   *Dan* 4:37

abased
shall exalt himself shall be *a.*
  Mat 23:12; *Luke* 14:11; 18:14
I know how to be *a.*   *Phil* 4:12

abasing
an offence in *a.* myself.   *2 Cor* 11:7

abated
(*Decreased*)
the waters were *a.*   *Gen* 8:3, 11
a. from thy estimation.   *Lev* 27:18
Moses' natural force *a. Deut* 34:7
anger was *a.* toward him.   *Judg* 8:3

abba
a. Father, all things are. *Mark* 14:36
whereby we cry, *a.* Father. *Rom* 8:15
into your hearts crying *a.*   *Gal* 4:6

Abda
Adoniram son of *A.* was.   *1 Ki* 4:6
A. was for thanksgiving. *Neh* 11:17

Abdi
Kish the son of *A.*   *2 Chr* 29:12
A. of them that married. *Ezra* 10:26

Abdon
A. judged Israel.   *Judg* 12:13
A. died.   15
commanded *A.* to inquire. *2 Chr* 34:20

Abed-nego
Azariah the name of *A.*   *Dan* 1:7
the king set *A.* over.   2:49; 3:30
A. fell down bound into the.   3:23

Abel, *person, place.*
Lord had respect to *A.*   *Gen* 4:4
stone of *A.* whereon.   *1 Sam* 6:18*
ask counsel at *A.*   *2 Sam* 20:18
blood of *A. Mat* 23:35; *Luke* 11:51
A. offered more excellent. *Heb.* 11:4
things than the blood of *A.*   12:24

Abel-beth-maachah
captains smote *A.*   *1 Ki* 15:20
came and took *A.*   *2 Ki* 15:29

Abel-maim
Ijon, and Dan, and *A.*   *2 Chr* 16:4

Abel-meholah
fled to the border of *A.*   *Judg* 7:22
son of Shaphat of *A.*   *1 Ki* 19:16

Abel-mizraim
name of it was called *A. Gen* 50:11

abhor
[1] *To loath or detest,* Job 42:6.
[2] *To despise or neglect,* Ps. 22:24;
Amos 6:8. [3] *To reject or cast off,*
Ps. 89:38.
my soul shall not *a.* you. *Lev* 26:11
or if your soul *a.* my judgments. 15
destroy, and my soul shall *a.*   30
nor will I *a.* them, to destroy.   44
utterly *a.* it, a cursed.   *Deut* 7:26
a. an Edomite, an Egyptian.   23:7
his people to *a.* him.   *1 Sam* 27:12
own clothes shall *a.* me.   *Job* 9:31
they *a.* me, they flee far.   30:10
I *a.* myself, and repent.   42:6
Lord will *a.* the bloody man. *Ps.* 5:6
I hate and *a.* lying.   119:163
nations shall *a.* him.   *Pr* 24:24
do not *a.* us.   *Jer* 14:21
a. him that speaketh.   *Amos* 5:10
I *a.* the excellency of Jacob.   6:8
hear, ye that *a.* judgment.   *Mi* 3:9
a. that which is evil.   *Rom* 12:9

abhorred
made our saviour to be *a.*   *Ex* 5:21
therefore I *a.* them.   *Lev.* 20:23
their soul *a.* my statutes.   26:43
Lord saw it, he *a.*   *Deut.* 32:19
for men *a.* the offering. *1 Sam* 2:17
art *a.* of thy father.   *2 Sam* 16:21
Hadad *a.* Israel.   *1 Ki* 11:25
inward friends *a.* me.   *Job* 19:19
nor *a.* the affliction of.   *Ps* 22:24
and greatly *a.* Israel.   78:59
thou hast cast off and *a.*   89:38*
he *a.* his own inheritance.   106:40
a. of the Lord shall fall.   *Pr* 22:14
Lord hath *a.* his sanctuary. *Lam* 2:7
thy beauty to be *a.*   *Ezek* 16:25*
and their soul also *a.* me. *Zech* 11:8

abhorrest
the land that thou *a.*   *Isa* 7:16
thou that *a.* idols, dost. *Rom* 2:22

abhorreth
life *a.* bread, and his soul. *Job* 33:20
covetous, whom the Lord *a.* *Ps* 10:3*
mischief on his bed, he *a.* not evil.
  36:4
soul *a.* all manner of meat.   107:18
nation *a.* to a servant.   *Isa* 49:7

abhorring
be an *a.* to all flesh.   *Isa* 66:24

1

Abia, Abiah
Samuel's second son was A.
1 Sam 8:2
A. Hezron's wife. *1 Chr 2:24*
Rehoboam was A. 3:10; *Mat 1:7*
sons of Becher, A. *1 Chr 7:8*

Abi-albon
A. was one of David's. *2 Sam 23:31*

Abiathar
A. escaped and fled. *1 Sam 22:20*
A. son of Ahimelech fled. 23:6
David said to A. bring. 9; 30:7
Ahimelech son of A. *2 Sam 8:17*
Zadok and A. were the priests.
20:25 ; *1 Ki 4:4*
kingdom for him and A. *1 Ki 2:22*
so Solomon thrust out A. 27
house of G. in days of A. *Mark 2:26*

Abib
in the month A. *Ex 13:4; 34:18*
the feast of unleavened bread in the
month A. 23:15; 34:18 ; *Deut 16:1*

Abidan
A. son of Gideoni. *Num 1:11; 2:22*
A. of Benjamin offered. 7:60, 65

abide
[1] *To stay,* Gen 22:5. [2] *To
dwell or live in a place,* Gen 29:19;
Ps 15:1. [3] *To bear or endure,*
Jer 10:10; Joel 2:11. [4] *To continue,* Eccl 8:15; John 14:16. [5]
To wait for, Acts 20:23. [6] *To
rest,* Pr 19:23. [7] *To stand firm,*
Ps 119:90; 125:1.

a. in the street all night. *Gen 19:2*
a. you here with the ass, and I. 22:5
damsel a. with us a few days. 24:55
I give her to thee, a. with me. 29:19
a. instead of the lad. 44:33
a. ye every man. *Ex 16:29*
therefore a. at the door. *Lev 8:35*
wages of him hired shall not a. 19:13
shall a. to the death. *Num 35:25*
a. here fast by my maidens. *Ruth 2:8*
before the Lord, and a. *1 Sam 1:22*
ark of God shall not a. 5:7
a. thou with me, fear not. 22:23
made to a. at brook Besor. 30:21
and with him will I a. *2 Sam 16:18*
nor a. in the paths of. *Job 24:13*
and a. in the covert to lie. 38:40
unicorn be willing to a. by. 39:9
shall a. in thy tabernacle ? *Ps 15:1*
I will a. in thy tabernacle. 61:4
he shall a. before God for ever. 7
shall a. under the shadow of. 91:1
feet a. not in her house. *Pr 7:11*
he that hath it shall a. 19:23
a. with him of his labour. *Eccl 8:15*
nations not able to a. his. *Jer 10:10*
if ye a. in this land I. 42:10
no man shall a. 49:18, 33; 50:40
shalt a. for me many days. *Hos 3:3*
sword shall a. on his cities. 11:6*
is terrible, who can a. it ? *Joel 2:11*
they shall a. for now shall. *Mi 5:4*
who can a. in the fierceness. *Nah 1:6*
a. the day of his coming ? *Mal 3:2*
there a. *Mat 10:11; Mark 6:10*
Luke 9:4
I must a. at thy house. *Luke 19:5*
a. with us, for it is towards. 24:29
not a. in darkness. *John 12:46*
Comforter that he may a. 14:16
a. in me and I in you, except ye a. in
me. 15:4, 7
if a man a. not in me, he is cast. 6
ye shall a. in my love, and a. 10
it pleased Silas to a. *Acts 15:34*
come into my house and a. 16:15
bonds and afflictions a. me. 20:23
except these a. in ship. 27:31
if any man's work a. he. *1 Cor 3:14*
it is good for them if they a. 7:8
man a. in the same calling. 20
she is happier if she a. after. 40
to a. in the flesh is more *Phil 1:24*
I know that I shall a. with. 25
I besought thee to a. *1 Tim 1:3*
let that a. in you which. *1 John 2:24*
ye shall a. in him. 27
children a. in him. 28

abideth
Ziba said, behold he a. *2 Sam 16:3*
man being in honour a. *Ps 49:12*
hear, even he that a. of. 55:19
the earth, and it a. 119:90
mount Zion, which a. for ever. 125:1
heareth reproof, a. *Pr 15:31*
but the earth a. for ever. *Eccl. 1:4*
he that a. in this city. *Jer 21:9*
but the wrath of God a. *John 3:36*
servant a. not, but the son a. 8:35
corn of wheat die, it a. 12:24
we have heard that Christ a. 34
he that a. in me bringeth. 15:5
a. faith, hope, charity. *1 Cor 13:13*
yet he a. faithful. *2 Tim 2:13*
Melchizedec a. a priest. *Heb 7:3*
word of God which a. *1 Pet 1:23*
that saith he a. in him. *1 John 2:6*
he that loveth his brother a. in. 10
and the word of God a. in you. 14
he that doeth the will of God a. 17
anointing a. in you and teacheth. 27
whosoever a. in him sinneth not. 3:6
loveth not his brother a. in death. 14
we know that he a. in us. 24
whoso a. not in the doctrine of Christ
hath not God, he that a. hath the.
2 John 9

abiding
Balaam saw Israel a. *Num 24:2*
a. in the inheritance. *1 Sam 26:19**
shadow, there is none a. *1 Chr 29:15*
shepherds a. in the field. *Luke 2:8*
not his word a. in you. *John 5:38*
no murderer hath eternal life a.in him.
1 John 3:15

Abiezer
lot for the children of A. *Josh 17:2*
A. was gathered after. *Judg 6:34*
better than the vintage of A. 8:2
A was one of David's. *2 Sam 23:27*

Abi-ezrite
pertained to Joash the A. *Judg.* 6:11

Abigail
of Nabal's wife was A. *1 Sam 25:3*
with his two wives, Ahinoam and A.
27:3; 30:5; *2 Sam 2:2*
sisters were Zeruiah and A.
1 Chr. 2:16

Abihail
Rehoboam took A. *2 Chr* 11:18
Esther the daughter of A. *Esth* 2:15
9:29

Abihu
Aaron's sons Nadab and A. Ex 6:23;
28:1; Lev 10:1; Num 3:2; 26:60;
1 Chr 6:3; 24:1.
come up, A. *Ex 24:1*
then A. went up. 9
A. died before. *Num 3:4; 26:61*

Abijah, Abijam
A. the son of Jeroboam. *1 Ki 14:1*
A. the son of Rehoboam. 31; 15:1, 7
eighth lot came forth to A.
1 Chr 24:10
mother's name was A. *2 Chr* 29:1
those that sealed were A. *Neh* 10:7
went up with Zerubbabel A. 12:4
of A. Zichri. 17

ability
his a. that vowed, priest. *Lev* 27:8
they gave after their a. *Ezra* 2:69
we after our a. redeemed. *Neh* 5:8
a. to stand in the king's. *Dan* 1:4
each according to his a. *Mat* 25:15
a. determined to send. *Acts* 11:29
as of the a. God giveth. *1 Pet* 4:11*

Abimelech
A. king of Gerar sent. *Gen* 20:2
A. and Phichol spake to. 21:22
Isaac went unto A. 26:1
A. said, go from us. 16
concubine bare him A. *Judg* 8:31
A. the son of Jerubbaal went. 9:1
A. son of Jerubbesheth. *2 Sam* 11:21
Zadok and A. were. *1 Chr* 18:16

Abinadab
ark into the house of A. *1 Sam* 7:1
Jesse called A. made him. 16:8
A. followed Saul to the. 17:13
A. son of Saul. 31:2; *1 Chr* 10:2

ark on new cart. it out of the house
of A. *2 Sam* 6:3; *1 Chr* 13:7
A. had Solomon's daughter.
1 Ki 4:11

Abinoam, *see* Barak

Abiram
Dathan and A. the sons. *Num* 16:1
26:9
sent to call Dathan and A. 12
he did to Dathan and A. *Deut* 11:6
laid the foundation in A. *1 Ki* 16:34
the company of A. *Ps* 106:17

Abishag
and A. ministered to. *1 Ki* 1:15
and why dost thou ask A. 2:22

Abishai
A. said, I will go. *1 Sam* 26:6
sons of Zeruiah there, Joab, A. and
Asahel. *2 Sam* 2:18; *1 Chr* 2:16
fled also before A. *2 Sam* 10:14
king charged thee, and A. 18:12
A. succoured him and smote. 21:17
A. was chief. 23:18; *1 Chr* 11:20
A. slew of the Edomites. *1 Chr* 18:12

Abiud
Zerobabel begat A. and A. *Mat* 1:13

abjects
the a. gathered together. *Ps* 35:15

able
provide out of all the people a. men.
Ex 18:21, 25
pigeons, such as he is a. *Lev* 14:22
31
a. to go to war *Num* 1:3, 20, 22, 24,
26, 28, 30, 32, 34, 36, 38, 40, 42,
45; 26:2.
are well a. to overcome it. 13:30
shall give as he is a. *Deut* 16:17
no man hath been a. tu. *Josh* 23:9
a. to stand before this. *1 Sam* 6:20
a. to judge so great a. *1 Ki* 3:9
is a. to build him. *2 Chr* 2:6
none is a. to withstand thee. 20:6
is a. to give thee much more. 25:9
who then is a. to stand. *Job* 41:10
a. to stand before envy. *Pr* 27:4
offering shall be as he is a.
Ezek 46:11
God whom we serve is a. *Dan* 3:17
thy God is a. to deliver. 6:20
God is a. of these stones to raise up
children. *Mat* 3:9; *Luke* 3:8
believe ye that I am a. to. *Mat* 9:28
a. to destroy soul and body. 10:28
he that is a. to receive it, let. 19:12
are ye a. to drink of the cup. 20:22
no man was a. to answer. 22:46
spake he, as they were a. *Mark* 4:33
no man is a. to pluck. *John* 10:29
yoke our fathers nor we a.
Acts 15:10
his grace, a. to build you. 20:32
among you are a. go down. 25:5*
he was a. to perform. *Rom* 4:21
for God is a. to graff them in. 11:23
God is a. to make him stand. 14:4
ye are a. also to admonish. 15:14
a. nor yet now are ye a. *1 Cor* 3:2
tempted above that ye are a. 10:13
made us a. ministers. *2 Cor* 3:6*
God is a. to make all grace. 9:8
a. to do abundantly above. *Eph.* 3:20
he is a. to subdue all. *Phil* 3:21
he is a. to keep that I. *2 Tim* 1:12
a. to come to the knowledge. 3:7
holy scriptures a. to make wise. 15
he is a. to succour them. *Heb* 2:18
to him that was a. to save him. 5:7
a. to save to the uttermost. 7:25
God was a. to raise him up. 11:19
the word which is a. to. *Jas* 1:21
a. also to bridle the whole. 3:2
one lawgiver a. to save. 4:12
to him that is a. to keep. *Jude* 24
a. to open the book nor. *Rev* 5:3
a. to make war with the. 13:4
a. to enter into the temple. 15:8

be able
himself be a. to redeem. *Lev* 25:26
man be a. to stand. *Deut* 7:24
11:25
be a. to stand before. *Josh* 1:5

I shall *be a.* to drive.   *Josh* 14:12
if he *be a.* to fight with.   *1 Sam* 17:9
be a. to offer willingly.   *1 Chr* 29:14
God should *be a.* to.   *2 Chr* 32:14
thou shalt *be a.* to.   *Isa* 47:12
righteous *be a.* to live.   *Ezek* 33:12
be a. with 10,000 to.   *Luke* 14:31
be a. to separate us from. *Rom* 8:39
ye may *be a.* to bear.   *1 Cor* 10:13
be a. to comprehend.   *Eph* 3:18*
be a. to stand against the.   6:11
ye shall *be a.* to quench.   16
be a. to teach others.   *2 Tim* 2:2
be a. by sound doctrine.   *Tit* 1:9
be a. after my decease.   *2 Pet* 1:15
who shall *be a.* to stand ?   *Rev* 6:17

not be able
not be a. to deliver.   *2 Ki* 18:29
   Isa 36:14
shall *not be a.* to rise.   *Ps* 36:12
shall he *not be a.* to find. *Eccl* 8:17
not be a. to put it off.   *Isa* 47:11
not be a. to escape.   *Jer* 11:11
not be a. to hide.   49:10
not be a. to deliver.   *Ezek* 7:19
seek, *not be a.*   *Luke* 13:24
not be a. to gainsay.   21:15

not able
not a. to bring a lamb.   *Lev* 5:7
I am *not a.* to bear all.   *Num* 11:14
not a. to go up against.   13:31
Lord was *not a.*   14:16; *Deut* 9:28
not a. to go to Tarshish. *2 Chr* 20:37
not a. to stand without.   *Ezra* 10:13
not a. to build the wall.   *Neh* 4:10
they were *not a.* to rise.   *Ps* 18:38
they are *not a.* to perform.   21:11
hold on me, so that I am *not a.* 40:12
land is *not a.* to bear.   *Amos* 7:10
not a. to do the thing.   *Luke* 12:26
foundation, and is *not a.* to.   14:29
not a. to draw it for the fishes.
   John 21:6
not a. to resist the wisdom. *Acts* 6:10

Abner
Ner father of *A.* was.   *1 Sam* 14:51
Saul said to *A.* whose son ?   17:55
A. and the people lay round.   26:7
cried, answerest thou not, *A.* ?   14
A. said, let young men.   *2 Sam* 2:14
Jacob said, thou knowest *A.*   3:25
Joab and Abishai his brother slew *A.*
   30
buried *A.* in Hebron, king wept.   32
king said, died *A.* as a fool ?   33
was not of the king to slay *A.*   37
when Saul's son heard that *A.*   4:1
buried Ish-bosheth's head in *A.*   12
what Joab did to *A.*   *1 Ki* 2:5
that *A.* had dedicated.   *1 Chr* 26:28
Jaasiel son of *A.* ruler of.   27:21

aboard
ship sailing, we went *a.*   *Acts* 21:2

abode, *substantive*
but I know thy *a.*   *2 Ki* 19:27*
   Isa 37:28*
make our *a.* with him.   *John* 14:23

abode, *verb*
Jacob *a.* with him the.   *Gen* 29:14
but his bow *a.* in strength.   49:24
glory of the Lord *a.* on Sinai.
   Ex 24:16
cloud *a.* Israel.   *Num* 9:17, 18, 21
a. in their tents.   20, 22
and *a.* at Hazeroth.   11:35
a. in Kadesh.   20:1; *Judg* 11:17
princes *a.* with Balaam.   *Num* 22:8
a. in Kadesh many.   *Deut* 1:46
we *a.* in the valley.   3:29
I *a.* in the mount.   9:9
they *a.* in their places.   *Josh* 5:8
they *a.* between Bethel and Ai.   8:9
Gilead *a.* beyond Jordan, Asher continued on the sea-shore, and *a.*
   Judg 5:17
Levite *a.* with him three.   19:4
a. in the rock Rimmon.   20:47
woman *a.* and gave.   *1 Sam* 1:23
ark *a.* in Kirjath-jearim.   7:2
Saul and Jonathan *a.*   13:16
Saul! *a.*   22:6*
David *a.*   23:14, 25; 26:3

David *a.* in wood.   *1 Sam* 23:18
a. at Ziklag.   *2 Sam* 1:1
Uriah *a.* in Jerusalem.   11:12
while I *a.* at Geshur.   15:8
to a loft where he *a.*   *1 Ki* 17:19
Jeremiah *a.* in the court.   *Jer* 38:28
while they *a.* in Galilee.   *Mat* 17:22
Mary *a.* with her.   *Luke* 1:56
nor *a.* in any house, but in.   8:27
Spirit, and it *a.* upon.   *John* 1:32
they came and *a.* with him.   39
words he *a.* in Galilee.   7:9
murderer, and *a.*   8:44*
a. two days still in the place.   11:6
upper room where *a.*   *Acts* 1:13
long time *a.* they speaking.   14:3
Paul *a.* with them and.   18:3
a. with the brethren one day.   21:7
house of Philip and *a.* with him.   8
I went and *a.* with Peter.   *Gal.* 1:18

abode *there* or *there* abode
days that ye *a. there.*   *Deut* 1:46
and *a. there* 3 days.   *Josh* 2:22
the people *a. there* till.   *Judg* 21:2
there a. we in tents.   *Ezra* 8:15
Jerusalem and *a. there* three.   32
Jesus *a. there* two days.   *John* 4:40
first baptized, and *there a.*   10:40
Cesarea, and *there a.*   *Acts* 12:19*
there they *a.* long time.   14:28
Silas and Timotheus *a. there.*   17:14

abodest
why *a.* thou among the.   *Judg* 5:16*

abolish
idols he shall utterly *a.*   *Isa.* 2:18*

abolished
righteousness shall not be *a. Isa* 51:6
your works may be *a.*   *Ezek* 6:6
end of that which is *a.*   *2 Cor* 3:13*
a. in his flesh the enmity.   *Eph* 2:15
Christ, who hath *a.* death.
   2 Tim 1:10

abominable
touch any *a.* unclean.   *Lev* 7:21
shall not make yourselves *a.*   11:43
any of these *a.* customs.   18:30
on the third day, it is *a.*   19:7
shall not make your souls *a.*   20:25
not eat any *a.* thing.   *Deut* 14:3
king's word was *a.*   *1 Chr* 21:6
Asa put away the *a.* idols. *2 Chr* 15:8
much more *a.* and filthy.   *Job* 15:16
they have done *a.* works.   *Ps* 14:1
and have done *a.* iniquity.   53:1
out like an *a.* branch.   *Isa* 14:19
broth of *a.* things is in.   65:4
carcases of their *a.*   *Jer* 16:18
O, do not this *a.* thing that.   44:4
nor came *a.* flesh into.   *Ezek* 4:14
saw and behold *a.* beasts.   8:10
thy sins committed more *a.*   16:52
scant measure that is *a.*   *Mi* 6:10
and I will cast *a.* filth.   *Nah* 3:6
works deny him, being *a.*   *Tit* 1:16
walked in *a.* idolatries.   *1 Pet* 4:3
unbelieving, and the *a.*   *Rev* 21:8

abominably
Ahab did very *a.*   *1 Ki* 21:26

abomination
[1] *A thing hateful and detestable,*
Gen 43:32; Pr 29:27.   [2] *An idol,*
2 Ki 23:13; Isa 44:19.
an *a.* to the Egyptians.   *Gen* 43:32
every shepherd is an *a.*   46:34
sacrifice the *a.* of Egyptians. *Ex* 8:26
shall be an *a.*   *Lev* 7:18; 11:41, 42
shall be an *a.* to.   11:10, 12, 20, 23
womankind it is *a.*   18:22; 20:13
a. to the Lord.   *Deut* 7:25; 17:1
bring an *a.* into thy house.   7:26
every *a.* they have done to.   12:31
such *a.* is wrought.   13:14; 17:4
these things are an *a.*   18:12; 22:5
are an *a.* to the Lord.   23:18
an *a.* before the Lord.   24:4
unrighteously are an *a.* to.   25:16
the man that maketh *a.*   27:15
in *a.* with Philistines.   *1 Sam* 13:4
Milcom the *a.*   *1 Ki* 11:5, 7
Chemosh the *a.* of Moab.   7
Ashtaroth the *a.* of the.   *2 Ki* 23:13
thou hast made me an *a.*   *Ps* 88:8

the froward is an *a.* to.   *Pr* 3:32
seven things are an *a.* to him.   6:16
wickedness is an *a.* to my lips.   8:7
a false balance is an *a.* to.   11:1
they of a froward heart are an *a.*   20
lying lips are *a.* to.   12:22
a. to fools to depart.   13:19
of the wicked is an *a.*   15:8; 21:27
way of the wicked is an *a.* to.   15:9
thoughts of the wicked are an *a.*   26
is proud in heart is an *a.*   16:5
it is an *a.* to kings to commit.   12
both are an *a.* to the Lord.   17:15
both of them are alike *a.* to.   20:10
divers weights are an *a.* to the.   23
the scorner is an *a.* to men.   24:9
his prayer shall be *a.*   28:9
is an *a.* to the just, and he that is
   upright in the way, is *a.*   29:27
incense is an *a.* to me.   *Isa* 1:13
an *a.* is he that chooseth you.   41:24
the residue thereof an *a* ?   44:19
eating swine's flesh, and the *a.* 66:17
ye made my heritage an *a.*   *Jer* 2:7
they committed *a.*   6:15; 8:12
do this *a.* to cause Judah.   32:35
and committed *a.*   *Ezek* 16:50
eyes to idols and committed *a.* 18:12
a. with his neighbour's wife.   22:11
your sword and ye work *a.*   33:26
a. that maketh desolate. *Dan.* 11:31
a. that maketh desolate set.   12:11
a. is committed in Israel. *Mal* 2:11
ye see *a.* of desolation.   *Mat* 24:15
   Mark 13:14
men is *a.* with God.   *Luke* 16:15
enter that worketh *a.*   *Rev* 21:27

abominations
not learn to do after the *a.*
   Deut 18:9
with *a.* provoked they him to. 32:16
according to all *a.*   *1 Ki* 14:24
through fire according to *a.*
   2 Ki 16:3; *2 Chr* 28:3
Manasseh did evil after the *a.* of the
   heathen.   *2 Ki* 21:2; *2 Chr* 33:2
a. spied did Josiah put.   *2 Ki* 23:24
   2 Chr 34:33
Jehoiakim and his *a.*   *2 Chr* 36:8
people transgressed after all *a.*   14
for there are seven *a.* in.   *Pr* 26:25
could not bear for the *a.*   *Jer* 44:22
for all the evil *a.* of.   *Ezek* 6:11
seest thou the great *a.* of Israel, but
   thou shalt see greater *a.*   8:6
   13, 15
behold the wicked *a.* that they do. 9
light thing to commit *a.* here ?   17
sigh and cry for all the *a.*   9:4
take away all the *a.* thereof.   11:18
your faces from all your *a.*   14:6
cause Jerusalem to know her *a.* 16:2
righteous doth according to all *a.*
   18:24
cause them to know the *a.*   20:4
cast ye away every man the *a.*   7
they did not cast away the *a.*   8
shalt shew her all her *a.*   22:2
loathe yourselves for all your *a.*
   36:31
it suffice you of all your *a.*   44:6
broken my covenant for all your *a.* 7
the overspreading of *a.*   *Dan* 9:27
a. from between his teeth. *Zech* 9:7
cup in her hand full of *a.*   *Rev* 17:4
mother of harlots and *a.* of.   5

their abominations
not to do after all *their a.*
   Deut 20:18
seen *their a.* and *their.*   29:17
doing according to *their a.* *Ezra* 9:1
their a. which have filled.   11
soul delighteth in *their a.*   *Isa* 66:3
their a. in the house.
   Jer 7:30; 32:34
committed in all *their a.*   *Ezek* 6:9
made the images of *their a.*   7:20
heart walketh after *their a.*   11:21
may declare all *their a.*   12:16
thou not done after *their a.*   16:47
ye whoredom after *their a.*   20:30
yea, declare to them *their a.*   23:36
desolate because of all *their a.* 33:29

defiled my holy name by *their a.*
Ezek 43:8
bear their shame and *their a.* 44:13
their a. were according. Hos 9:10

these abominations
commit any of *these a.* Lev 18:26
all *these a.* have the men of. 27
shall commit any of *these a.* 29
because of *these a.* the. Deut 18:12
Manasseh . . . *these a.* 2 Ki 21:11
affinity with people of *these a.*
Ezra 9:14
delivered to do all *these a.* Jer 7:10
these a. shall surely die. Ezek 18:13

thine or *thy* **abominations**
wilt put away *thine a.* Jer 4:1
seen *thine a.* on the hills. 13:27
I have not, because of *thine a.*
Ezek 5:9
defiled my sanctuary with *thy a.* 11
on thee all *thine a.* 7:3, 4, 8, 9
all *thine a.* thou has not. 16:22
with all the idols of *thine a.* 36
lewdness above all *thine a.* 43
multiplied *thine a.* 51
hast borne *thine a.* saith. 58

abound
the faithful man shall *a.* Pr 28:20
because inquity shall *a.* Mat 24:12*
that the offence might *a.* Rom 5:20
in sin, that grace may *a.?* 6:1
that ye may *a.* in hope through. 15:13
sufferings *a.* so consolation.
2 Cor 1:5
a. in every thing, see that ye *a.* 8:7
God is able to make all grace *a.* 9:8
your love may *a.* more. Phil 1:9
I know how to *a.* both to *a.* 4:12
but I desire fruit that may *a.* 17*
but I have all and *a.* I am full. 18
Lord make you to *a.* 1 Thes 3:12
so ye would *a.* more and more. 4:1
things be in you and *a.* 2 Pet 1:8

abounded, -eth, -ing
fountains *a.* with water. Pr 8:24
man *a.* in transgression. 29:22
truth of God hath more *a.* Rom 3:7
grace by Jesus Christ hath *a.* 5:15
sin *a.* grace did much more *a.* 20
always *a.* in the work. 1 Cor 15:58
poverty *a.* to the riches. 2 Cor 8:2
wherein he hath *a.* toward. Eph 1:8
therein with thanksgiving. Col 2:7
towards each other *a.* 2 Thes 1:3

about
a. three months after. Gen 38:24
shewed Pharaoh what he is *a.* 41:25
turned himself *a.* from them. 42:24
trade hath been *a.* cattle. 46:34*
a. midnight will I go out. Ex 11:4
God led the people *a.* through. 13:18
set bounds *a.* the mount. 19:23
fell that day *a.* 3000 men. 32:28
that *a.* which he hath. Lev 6:5
a. the tabernacle of. Num 16:24
a. and instructed him. Deut 32:10
to go down *a.* a day. Josh 10:13
a. which thou cursedst. Judg 17:2
and it was *a.* an ephah of. Ruth 2:17
was come *a.* Hannah. 1 Sam 1:20
the ark of God be carried *a.* 5:8
came to pass, *a.* the spring. 9:26
women have been kept from us *a.*
21:5
to fetch *a.* this form. 2 Sam 14:20*
kingdom is turned *a.* 1 Ki 2:15
a. going down of sun. 22:36
2 Chr 18:34
a. this season according. 2 Ki 4:16
which I am *a.* to build 2 Chr 2:9
employed *a.* this matter. Ezra 10:15*
is *a.* to fill his belly. Job 20:23
bind them *a.* thy. Pr 3:3; 6:21
that goeth *a.* as a tale-bearer. 20:19
heap of wheat set *a.* S of S 7:2
compass yourselves *a.* Isa 50:11
why gaddest thou *a.* so. Jer 2:36
how long wilt thou go *a.* 31:22*
people cast *a.* and returned. 41:14
doings have beset them *a.* Hos 7:2
went out *a.* the third. Mat 20:3
not so much as *a.* the. Mark 2:2

set an hedge *a.* it, and. Mark 12:1
a. my Father's business. Luke 2:49*
Jesus began to be *a.* thirty. 3:23
loins be girded *a.* and. 12:35
a question *a.* purifying. John 3:25
why go ye *a.* to kill me ? 7:19*
of the men was *a.* 5000. Acts 4:4
when Paul was *a.* to open. 18:14
a. to flee out of the ship. 27:30*
he was *a.* 100 years old. Rom 4:19
going *a.* to establish their own. 10:3*
power to lead *a. a.* 1 Cor 9:5
bearing *a.* in the body. 2 Cor 4:10
loins girt *a.* with truth. Eph 6:14
wandering *a.* from house. 1 Tim 5:13
when he was *a.* to make. Heb 8:5
silence *a.* the space of half. Rev. 8:1
I was *a.* to write, and I. 10:4

see **gone, him, me, thee, them,
round, stood, this, time, went.**

above
[1] *Aloft, high,* Gen 6:16; Pr 8:28.
[2] *More than,* Gen 3:14; 48:22;
2 Cor 1:8. [3] *Upwards,* Ex 30:14;
Lev 27:7. [4] *A higher state or
rank,* Num 16:3; Deut 28:13. [5]
Heaven, or the highest place, Job
3:4; Rom 10:6. [6] *Things that
relate to heaven,* Gal 4:26; Col 3:1.
[7] *God,* Jas 1:17.
waters *a.* the firmament. Gen 1:7
fowl that may fly *a.* the earth. 20
cursed *a.* all cattle, *a.* beast. 3:14
shalt thou finish the ark *a.* 6:16
and the ark was lifted up *a.* 7:17
one portion *a.* thy brethren. 48:22
prevailed *a.* the blessings of. 49:26
I will commune from *a.* Ex 25:22
a. the curious girdle of. 28:27, 28
from twenty years old and *a.* 30:14
1 Chr 23:27
which have legs *a.* their. Lev 11:21
from sixty years old and *a.* 27:7
a. the congregation. Num 16:3
heart be not lifted up *a.* Deut 17:20
lest if he should beat him *a.* 25:3
be *a.* only, and not beneath. 28:13
multiply thee *a.* thy fathers. 30:5
come down from *a.* Josh 3:13, 16
blessed shall she be *a.* women.
Judg 5:24
sent from *a.* 2 Sam 22:17; Ps 18:16
covered ark *a.* 1 Ki 8:7 ; 2 Chr 5:8
a. the throne of kings. 2 Ki 25:28
Jer 52:32
Judah prevailed *a.* his. 1 Chr 5:2
Benaiah was mighty and *a.* 27:6
Hananiah feared God *a.* Neh 7:2
up *a.* the house of David. 12:37
not God regard it from *a.* Job 3:4
a. shall his branch be cut. 18:16
price of wisdom is *a.* rubies. 28:18
portion of God is there from *a.* ? 31:2
have denied the God that is *a.* 28
thy judgments are *a.* out. Ps 10:5
liftest me *a.* those that rise. 18:48
head be lifted up *a.* enemies. 27:6
oil of gladness *a.* 45:7; Heb 1:9
the clouds from *a.* Ps 78:23
commandments *a.* gold. 119:127
that stretched out the earth *a.* 136:6
if I prefer not Jerusalem *a.* 137:6
send thine hand from *a.* rid. 144:7
his glory is *a.* the earth. 148:13
established the clouds *a.* Pr 8:28
way of life is *a.* to the wise. 15:24
for her price is far *a.* rubies. 31:10
man hath no pre-eminence *a.*
Eccl 3:19
mountain shall be exalted *a.* Isa 2:2
a. it stood the seraphims, each. 6:2
the depth or in the height *a.* 7:11
widows increased *a.* sand. Jer 15:8
from *a.* hath he sent fire. Lam 1:13
appearance of a man *a.* Ezek 1:26
God was over them *a.* 10:19 ;11:22
exalt itself any more *a.* the. 29:15
Daniel was preferred *a.* Dan 6:3
king magnify himself *a.* 11:36
destroyed his fruit from *a.* Amos 2:9
multiplied thy merchants *a.*
Nah 3:16
disciple not *a.* Mat 10:24; Luke 6:40

remained over and *a.* John 6:13
from *a.* ye are of this world. 8:23
it were given him from *a.* 19:11
man was *a.* forty years. Acts 4:22
I saw a light *a.* the brightness. 26:13
bring Christ down from *a.* Rom 10:6
esteemeth one day *a.* another. 14:5
not to think of men *a.* 1 Cor 4:6
you to be tempted *a.* that ye. 10:13
was seen of *a.* 500 brethren. 15:6
out of measure *a.* strength. 2 Cor 1:8
more, in stripes *a.* measure. 11:23
a. fourteen years ago, whether. 12:2
lest any man should think of me *a.* 6
Jerusalem which is *a.* Gal 4:26
given him a name *a.* Phil 2:9
seek those things which are *a.* Col 3:1
set your affection on things *a.* not. 2
servant, but *a.* a servant. Philem 16
a. when he said, sacrifice. Heb 10:8
perfect gift is from *a.* Jas 1:17
wisdom descendeth not from *a.* 3:15

above all
is cursed *a.* all cattle. Gen 3:14
very meek *a.* all the men. Num 12:3
blessed *a.* all people. Deut 7:14
he chose you *a.* all people, as. 10:15
a. all the nations. 14:2; 26:19 ; 28:1
done evil *a.* all that were. 1 Ki 14:9
provoked *a.* all that their. 22
Ahab did evil *a.* all that. 16:30
done wickedly *a.* all the. 2 Ki 21:11
over and *a.* all I have. 1 Chr 29:3
art exalted as head *a.* all. 11
Maachah *a.* all his. 2 Chr 11:21
for Ezra was *a.* all. Neh 8:5
king loved Esther *a.* all. Esth 2:17
Lord art high *a.* all the. Ps 97:9
is high *a.* all people. 99:2; 113:4
magnified thy word *a.* all thy. 138:2
a. all that were in Jerusalem.
Eccl 2:7
heart is deceitful *a.* all. Jer 17:9
this lewdness *a.* all. Ezek 16:43
his height was exalted *a.* all. 31:5
magnify himself *a.* all. Dan 11:37
added yet this *a.* all. Luke 3:20
sinners *a.* all the Galileans. 13:2, 4
from heaven is *a.* all. John 3:31
far *a.* all principality and. Eph 1:21
a. all that we ask. 3:20
one God *a.* all. 4:6
a. all taking the shield of faith. 6:16
a. all these things put on. Col 3:14
a. all that is called God. 2 Thes 2:4
a. all things, my brethren. Jas 5:12
a. all things have fervent. 1 Pet 4:8
I wish *a.* all things that. 3 John 2:1
above *all gods, see* **gods** ; **above**
heaven, see **heaven** ; *stood*
above, *see* **stood** ; **above** *me,*
him, them, see **him, me, them.**

Abram, Abraham
Lord said to *A.* get out. Gen 12:1
A. went down into Egypt to. 10
A. went up out of Egypt, he. 13:1
A. dwelt in land of Canaan, and. 12
A. came and dwelt in the plain. 18
A. armed his trained servants. 14:14
fear not, *A.* I am thy. 15:1
Lord made a covenant with *A.* 18
thy name shall be *A.* 17:5
1 Chr 1:27; Neh 9:7
A. hastened into the tent. Gen 18:6
shall I hide from *A.* that thing. 17
but *A.* stood yet before the Lord. 22
A. said of Sarah his wife, she. 20:2
and *A.* planted a grove in. 21:33
God did tempt *A.* and said. 22:1
out of heaven, and said, *A. A.* 11
Sarah died, and *A.* came to. 23:2
A. bought the field of. 17; 49:30
50:13
the Lord had blessed *A.* in all. 24:1
A. said, put thy hand under my. 2
Eliezer said, I am *A.* servant. 34
God of my master *A.* prosper. 42
they sent away Rebekah and *A.* 59
and *A.* gave all that he had. 25:5
the days of the years of *A.* life. 7
Hagar the Egyptian bare to. 12
that was in the days of *A.* 26:1
because *A.* obeyed my voice, kept. 5

multiply thy seed for A.   Gen 26:24
give thee the blessing of A.   28:4
except the God of A. had.   31:42
which he sware to A.   50:24
Ex 33:1; Num 32:11; Deut 1:8
   6:10; 30:20
I am the God of A.   Ex 3:6, 15, 16
  4:5; Mat 22:32; Mark 12:26
Luke 20:37; Acts 3:13; 7:32
remember his Isaac.   Ex 32:13
   Deut 9:27
people of the God of A.   Ps 47:9
covenant he made with A.   105:9
remembered his promise, and A. 42
Lord, who redeemed A.   Isa 29:22
art our father, though A. be.   63:16
A. was one, and he.   Ezek 33:24
perform the mercy to A.   Mi 7:20
son of David, the son of A.   Mat 1:1
raise up children unto A.   3:9
   Luke 3:8
sit down with A.   Mat 8:11
was the son of A. son.   Luke 3:34
shall see A. in the kingdom.   13:28
his eyes, and seeth A.   16:23
as he also is the son of A.   19:9
this did not A.   John 8:40
A. is dead.   52
hast thou seen A?   57
before A. was, I am.   58
of the stock of A.   Acts 13:26
A. were justified by works. Rom 4:2
A. believed God, and it was counted.
   3, 9; Gal 3:6; Jas 2:23
faith are the children of A.   Gal 3:7
preached before the gospel to A.   8
faith are blessed with faithful A.   9
God gave the inheritance to A.   18
A. had two sons, the one by a.   4:22
God made promise to A.   Heb 6:13
who met A. returning from.   7:1
say, Levi payed tithes in A.   9
A. obeyed.   11:8
by faith A. offered up Isaac.   17

Abraham with *father*
oath to A. thy *father*.   Gen 26:3
God of A. thy *father*.   24; 28:13
O God of my *father* A. and.   32:9
I took your *father* A.   Josh 24:3
look to A. your *father*.   Isa 51:2
A. to our *father*. Mat 3:9; Luke 3:8
he sware to our *father* A. Luke 1:73
he said, *father* A. have mercy. 16:24
nay, *father* A. but if one went.   30
to him A. is our *father*.   John 8:39
greater than our *father* A.?   53
your *father* A. rejoiced to see.   56
appeared to our *father* A.   Acts 7:2
say that A. our *father*.   Rom 4:1
of that faith of our *father* A.   12
faith of A. who is the *father*.   16
was not A. our *father* justified?
   Jas 2:21
Abraham with *seed*
gavest it to *seed* of A.   2 Chr 20:7
O ye *seed* of A. his.   Ps 105:6
Israel, the *seed* of A.   Isa 41:8
rulers over the *seed* of A. Jer 33:26
spake to A. and his *seed*. Luke 1:55
we be A. *seed* and were. John 8:33
I know ye are A. *seed* but ye.   37
was not to A. or his *seed*. Rom 4:13
they are *seed* of A.   9:7
of the *seed* of A. 11:1; 2 Cor 11:22
to A. and his *seed* were   Gal 3:16
be Christ's, then are ye A. *seed*   29
took on him the *seed* of A. Heb 2:16

abroad
ought of the flesh a.   Ex 12:46
a leprosy break out a.   Lev 13:12
be born at home or a.   18:9
shall he go a. out of.   Deut 23:10
wilt ease thyself a. shalt dig.   13
took daughters from a.   Judg 12:9
borrow thee vessels a.   2 Ki 4:3
it to carry it out a.   2 Chr 29:16
the commandment came a.   31:5
queen shall come a.   Esth 1:17
wandereth a. for bread.   Job 15:23
he goeth a. he telleth it.   Ps 41:6
fountains be dispersed a.   Pr 5:16
spreadeth a. the earth.   Isa 44:24
it out on the children a.   Jer 6:11*

---

a. the sword bereaveth.   Lam 1:20
began to blaze a. the.   Mark 1:45
but that it should come a.   4:22*
sayings were noised a.   Luke 1:65
made known a. the saying.   2:17
this was noised a. the.   Acts 2:6*
love of God is shed a. in.   Rom 5:5
for your obedience is come a. 16:19
see **cast**, **spread**, **stand**, **scatter**,
went.

Absalom
A. the son of. 2 Sam 3:3; 1 Chr 3:2
A. spake to Amnon neither.
   2 Sam 13:22
A. had sheep-shearers in.   23
saying, A. hath slain all the.   30
longed to go forth to A.   39
Joab arose and brought   14:23
to be so much praised as A.   25
A. said, O that I were made a. 15:4
A. stole the hearts of the men of.   6
among the conspirators with A.   31
A. went in unto his father's   16:22
Ahithophel's counsel pleased A. 17:4
Lord might bring evil upon A.   14
and when A. servants came to.   20
A. passed over Jordan.   24
A. pitched in Gilead.   26
deal gently for my sake with A. 18:5
I saw A. hanged in an oak.   10
darts through the heart of A.   14
it is called unto this day A.   18
is young man A. safe?   29, 32
O my son A.   33
if A. had lived, and all we had. 19:6
I fled because of A.   1 Ki 2:7
Adonijah, though not after A.   28
Maacah daughter of A. 2 Chr 11:20

absence
to betray him in a. of.   Luke 22:6
more in my a. work.   Phil 2:12

absent
when we are a. one.   Gen 31:49
I verily as a. in body.   1 Cor 5:3
at home in body are a.   2 Cor 5:6
to be a. from the body, present.   8
whether present or a.   9
being a. am bold toward you.   10:1
are by letters when we are a.   11
being a. now I write to.   13:2, 10
I come, or else be a.   Phil 1:27
though I be a. in the flesh.   Col 2:5

abstain
a. from pollutions of.   Acts 15:20
that ye a. from meats offered.   29
that ye should a. from.   1 Thes 4:3
a. from all appearance of evil.   5:22
commanding to a. from.   1 Tim 4:3
a. from fleshly lusts.   1 Pet 2:11

abstinence
after long a. Paul.   Acts 27:21*

abundance
God for the a. of all.   Deut 28:47
they shall suck of the a. of.   33:19
out of the a. of my.   1 Sam 1:16
no more such a. of spices. 1 Ki 10:10
sycamore-trees for a. 27; 2 Chr 1:15
sound of a. of rain.   1 Ki 18:41
of spices great a.   2 Chr 9:9
a. of waters. Job 22:11; 38:34
shall be a. of peace.   Ps 72:7
nor he that loveth a.   Eccl 5:10
the a of the rich will not suffer.   12*
a. of milk he shall eat.   Isa 7:22
the a. they have gotten.   15:7
great a. of thy enchantments. 47:9
a. of the sea shall be.   60:5
delighted with the a. of her.   66:11
I will reveal to them a.   Jer 33:6
a. of idleness was in.   Ezek 16:49*
of the a. of his horses.   26:10
silver, and apparel in great a.
   Zech 14:14
a. of the heart.   Mat 12:34
   Luke 6:45
shall have more a. Mat 13:12; 25:29
cast in of their a.   Mark 12:44*
   Luke 21:4*
receive a. of grace.   Rom 5:17
a. of their joy abounded.   2 Cor 8:2
your a. a supply, their a. a.   14
exalted through the a. of the.   12:7*
waxed rich thro' the a. of. Rev 18:3*

---

in **abundance**
spoil of the city *in* a.   2 Sam 12:30
slain oxen *in* a.   1 Ki 1:19, 25
prepared brass *in* a. 1 Chr 22:3, 14
trees *in* a. marble *in* a.   4; 29:2
workmen with thee *in* a. 1 Chr 22:15
they offered sacrifices *in* a.   29:21
me timber *in* a.   2 Chr 2:9
all these vessels *in* great a.   4:18
Sheba brought gold *in* a.   9:1
gave his sons victuals *in* a.   11:23
sheep and camels *in* a.   14:15
fell to Asa out of Israel *in* a.   15:9
to Jehoshaphat, and he had riches
   17:5; 18:1
sheep for Jehoshaphat *in* a.   18:2
Jehoshaphat found spoil *in* a. 20:25
they gathered money *in* a.   24:11
the burnt-offerings were *in* a. 29:35
Israel brought *in* a. first-fruits. 31:5
made darts and shields *in* a.   32:5
cities and possessions *in* a.   29
and fruit-trees *in* a.   Neh 9:25
them royal wine *in* a.   Esth 1:7
he giveth meat *in* a.   Job 36:31
delight themselves *in* a.   Ps 37:11
trusted *in* the a. of his riches.   52:7
brought forth frogs *in* a.   105:30
life consisteth not *in* a.   Luke 12:15
man blame us *in* this a. 2 Cor 8:20*

abundant
Lord God a. in goodness.   Ex 34:6
day, and much more a.   Isa 56:12*
Babylon, a. in treasures.   Jer 51:13
bestow more a. honour. 1 Cor 12:23
having given more a. honour to.   24
a. grace might redound. 2 Cor 4:15*
his inward affection is more a.   7:15
for the administration is a.   9:12*
in labours more a. in stripes.   11:23
rejoicing may be more a.   Phil 1:26
Lord was exceeding a.   1 Tim 1:14
according to his a. mercy. 1 Pet 1:3*

abundantly
waters bring forth a.   Gen 1:20, 21
breed a. in the earth.   8:17
bring forth a. in the earth.   9:7
Israel increased a.   Ex 1:7
river shall bring forth frogs a.   8:3*
the water came out a.   Num 20:11
oil, oxen, and sheep a. 1 Chr 12:40
so David prepared a. before.   22:5
thou hast shed blood a. and made. 8
brought they in a.   2 Chr 31:5
hand God bringeth a.   Job 12:6
drop, and distil upon man a. 36:28
they shall be a. satisfied.   Ps 36:8
waterest the ridges thereof a. 65:10
I will a. bless her provision. 132:15
shall a. utter the memory.   145:7*
drink a. O beloved.   S of S 5:1
shall howl, weeping a.   Isa 15:3
it shall blossom a. and rejoice. 35:2
our God, for he will a. pardon. 55:7
have life more a.   John 10:10
I laboured more a.   1 Cor 15:10
conversation, and more a. to.
   2 Cor 1:12
love I have more a. to you.   2:4
according to our rule a.   10:15
though the more a. I love you. 12:15
that is able to do exceeding a.
   Eph 3:20
endeavoured more a. to see.
   1 Thes 2:17*
he shed on us a. through Jesus.
   Tit 3:6*
God willing more a. to.   Heb 6:17
be ministered to you a. 2 Pet 1:11*

abuse, -ed
a. her all the night.   Judg 19:25
lest uncircumcised a. me.
   1 Sam 31:4; 1 Chr 10:4
I a. not my power in.   1 Cor 9:18*

abusers, -ing
nor a. of themselves.   1 Cor 6:9
use this world as not a. it.   7:31*

accept
[1] *To receive favourably*, Gen
4:7; Job 42:9; Mal 1:10, 13;
Acts 10:35. [2] *To show partiality*, Job 13:10; 32:21; Pr 18:5.

[3] *To regard or value,* 2 Cor 8:12.
[4] *To highly esteem,* Luke 4:24.
peradventure he will *a.*   *Gen* 32:20
and the owner shall *a.*   *Ex* 22:11
a. of the punishment.   *Lev* 26:41, 43
bless and *a.* the work.   *Deut* 33:11
let him *a.* an offering.   *1 Sam* 26:19
the L., thy God *a.* thee. *2 Sam* 24:23
will ye *a.* his person ?   *Job* 13:8
if ye do secretly *a.* persons.   10
not *a.* any man's person.   32:21
pray for you, for him will I *a.*   42:8
and *a.* thy burnt-sacrifice.   *Ps* 20:3
a. the persons of the wicked.   82:2
a. I beseech thee the free-.   119:108
not good to *a.* the person.   *Pr* 18:5
the Lord doth not *a.* them. *Jer* 14:10
I will not *a.* them.   12; *Amos* 5:22
there will I *a.* them.   *Ezek* 20:40
a. you with your sweet savour.   41
and I will *a.* you, saith the.   43:27
will he be pleased, or *a.* ?   *Mal* 1:8
nor will I *a.* an offering at your.   10
should I *a.* this of your hands ?   13
a. it always, and in all.   *Acts* 24:3

acceptable
Often has the stronger meaning of
well-pleasing, Rom 14:18; Eph 5:10.
shall not be *a.* for you.   *Lev* 22:20
Asher be *a.* to his.   *Deut* 33:24
meditation of my heart be *a.*
   Ps 19:14
thee, O Lord, in an *a.* time.   69:13
righteous know what is *a. Pr* 10:32
justice and judgment is more *a.* 21:3
preacher sought out *a.*   *Eccl* 12:10
in an *a.* time have I heard. *Isa* 49:8
call this an *a.* day to the ?   58:5
to proclaim the *a.* year of.   61:2†
burnt-offerings are not *a. Jer* 6:20
O king, let my counsel be *a.*
   Dan 4:27
to preach the *a.* year of. *Luke* 4:19
living sacrifice, holy, *a.*   *Rom* 12:1
is that good and *a.* will of God.   2
a. to God and approved of.   14:18
of the Gentiles might be *a.*   15:16
proving what is *a.* unto.   *Eph* 5:10
sacrifice *a.* well-pleasing. *Phil* 4:18
this is *a.* in the sight.   *1 Tim* 2:3
is good and *a.* before God.   5:4
sacrifices *a.* to God.   *1 Pet* 2:5
this is *a.* with God.   20

acceptably
we may serve God *a.*   *Heb* 12:28

acceptance
with *a.* on mine altar.   *Isa* 60:7

acceptation
saying worthy of all *a.*   *1 Tim* 1:15
   4:9

accepted
well, shalt thou not be *a.*   *Gen* 4:7
have *a.* thee concerning this.   19:21
they may be *a.* before.   *Ex* 28:38
offering shall be *a. Lev* 1:4; 22:27
it shall not be *a.*   7:18; 19:7
   22:23, 25
should it have been *a.* in.   10:19*
shall be perfect, to be *a.*   22:21
shall wave the sheaf to be *a.* 23:11
he was *a.* in the sight. *1 Sam* 18:5*
David said, see I have *a.*   25:35
a. of the multitude of.   *Esth* 10:3
the Lord also *a.* Job.   *Job* 42:9
sacrifice shall be *a.* on.   *Isa* 56:7
let my supplication be *a. Jer* 37:20
out supplication be *a.* before.   42:2
no prophet is *a.* in his.   *Luke* 4:24
worketh righteousness is *a.*
   Acts 10:35
my service may be *a.* of. *Rom* 15:31
present, we may be *a.*   *2 Cor* 5:9
time *a.* now is the *a.* time.   6:2
is *a.* according to that a man.   8:12
for indeed he *a.* the exhortation.   17
gospel which ye have not *a.*   11:4
made us *a.* in the beloved. *Eph* 1:6*

acceptest
neither *a.* thou the person.
   Luke 20:21

accepteth
him that *a.* not persons.   *Job* 34:19
eat with joy, for God now *a.*
   Eccl 9:7
sacrifice, but the Lord *a.*   *Hos* 8:13
God *a.* no man's person.   *Gal* 2:6

accepting, *see* deliverance.

access
also we *a.* by faith.   *Rom* 5:2
through him we both have *a.* to.
   Eph 2:18
have boldness and *a.* by faith.   3:12

Accho
drive out inhabitants of *A. Judg* 1:31

accompanied
brethren from Joppa *a.*   *Acts* 10:23
these six brethren *a.* me.   11:12
Sopater of Berea *a.* Paul.   20:4
and they *a.* him unto the ship.   38

accompany, *see* salvation.

accomplish
(*To perform, finish, or fulfil.*)
sacrifice to *a.* his vow.   *Lev* 22:21
a. my desire in giving.   *1 Ki* 5:9
a. as an hireling his day.   *Job* 14:6
they *a.* a diligent search.   *Ps* 64:6
shall *a.* that which I.   *Isa* 55:11
surely *a.* your vows.   *Jer* 44:25
thus will I *a.* my fury.   *Ezek* 6:12
now will I *a.* mine anger upon.   7:8
I *a.* my wrath upon the wall.   13:15
my fury to *a.* my anger.   20:8, 21
would *a.* seventy years.   *Dan* 9:2
a. at Jerusalem.   *Luke* 9:31

accomplished
by Jeremiah might be *a. 2 Chr* 36:22
of purification were *a.*   *Esth* 2:12
   Luke 2:22
shall be *a.* before his.   *Job* 15:32
the desire *a.* is sweet.   *Pr* 13:19
that her warfare is *a.*   *Isa* 40:2
when seventy years are *a. Jer* 25:12
   29:10
your dispersions are *a.*   25:34*
my words shall be *a.* before.   39:16
the Lord hath *a.* his fury. *Lam* 4:11
punishment of thine iniquity is *a.* 22
when hast *a.* them, lie on. *Ezek* 4:6
thus shall mine anger be *a.*   5:13
till the indignation be *a. Dan* 11:36
a. to scatter the power of the. 12:7*
his ministration were *a. Luke* 1:23
days were *a.* that she should.   2:6
days were *a.* for circumcising.   21
am I straitened till it be *a.*   12:50
the Son of man, shall be *a.*   18:31
must yet be *a.* in me.   22:37*
all things were now *a. John* 19:28*
we had *a.* those days.   *Acts* 21:5
same afflictions are *a.* in. *1 Pet* 5:9

accomplishing, *see* service.

accomplishment
signify the *a.* of days of. *Acts* 21:26

accord
groweth of its own *a.*   *Lev* 25:5
with Israel with one *a.*   *Josh* 9:2
all continued with one *a. Acts* 1:14
all with one *a.* in one place.   2:1*
daily with one *a.* in temple.   46
their voice to God with one *a.* 4:24
one *a.* in Solomon's porch.   5:12
ran upon Stephen with one *a.* 7:57
people with one *a.* gave heed.   8:6
opened to them of his own *a.* 12:10
they came with one *a.* to him.   20
being assembled with one *a.* 15:25
with one *a.* made insurrection. 18:12
with one *a.* into the theatre.   19:29
forward of his own *a.*   *2 Cor* 8:17
being of one *a.* of one.   *Phil* 2:2

according
done *a.* as thou badest.   *Gen* 27:19
a. as Joseph had said.   41:54
the Lord will give *a.*   *Ex* 12:25
be great, *a.* as thou.   *Num* 14:17
inheritance *a.* as God.   *Deut* 10:9
a. as the Lord thy God.   16:10
a. as he walked before.   *1 Ki* 3:6
to find *a.* to his ways.   *Job* 34:11
   Jer 17:10; 21:14 ; 32:19
went and did *a.* as the Lord. *Job* 42:9

judge me, O God, *a.* to my.   *Ps* 7:8
the Lord *a.* to his righteousness.   17
a. to thy mercy remember thou me.
   25:7; 51:1; 106:45; 109:26
   119:124
a. to their deeds, and *a.*   28:4
mercy be on us *a.* as we.   33:22
judge me, O God, *a.* to thy.   35:24
a. to thy name, so is thy.   48:10*
renderest to every man *a.*   62:12
   Pr 24:12, 29
a. to the greatness of thy. *Ps* 79:11
a. to thy fear, so is thy wrath. 90:11
rewarded us *a.* to our.   103:10
a. to thy word.   119:25, 28, 41, 58
   65, 76, 107, 116, 154, 169, 170
quicken me *a.* to. 119:159; *Isa* 63:7
praise him *a.* to his excellent.*Ps* 150:2
speak not *a.* to this word.   *Isa* 8:20
joy *a.* to the joy in harvest.   9:3
a. to all that the Lord has.   63:7
recompense her *a.* to her. *Jer* 50:29
shall rule, and do *a.*   *Dan* 11:3
a. to the love of the Lord. *Hos* 3:1
the Lord will punish Jacob *a.*   12:2
a. to the days of thy coming.
   Mi 7:15*
a. to your faith be it.   *Mat* 9:29
he will reward every man *a.* to.
   16:27; *Rom* 2:6; *2 Tim* 4:14
   Rev 2:23
nor did *a.* to his will.   *Luke* 12:47
judge not *a.* to the.   *John* 7:24
made to every man *a.* as. *Acts* 4:35
seed of David *a.* to the flesh.
   Rom 1:3
called *a.* to his purpose.   8:28
gifts differing *a.* to the grace. 12:6
to be like-minded *a.*   15:5
Christ died *a.* to the.   *1 Cor* 15:3
man *a.* as he purposeth. *2 Cor* 9:7
end shall be *a.* to their works. 11:15
who gave himself *a.* to.   *Gal* 1:4
Abraham's seed, and heirs *a.* 3:29
a. as he hath chosen us in him.
   Eph 1:4
a. to good pleasure.   5
a. to riches of his grace.   7
predestinated *a.* to the purpose. 11
a. to the power that worketh. 3:20
a. to the working.   *Phil* 3:21
God shall supply our need *a.*   4:19
not *a.* to our works.   *2 Tim* 1:9
a. to his mercy he saved us. *Tit* 3:5
not *a.* to the covenant.   *Heb* 8:9
a. to his mercy hath.   *1 Pet* 1:3
live *a.* to God in the Spirit.   4:6
a. as his divine power.   *2 Pet* 1:3*
we *a.* to his promise look.   3:13
judged *a.* to their works. *Rev* 20:12
   13
I come to give *a.* as his work. 22:12

according *to all, see* all.

according *to that*
obey my voice *a.* to that.   *Gen* 27:8
do to me *a.* to that.   *Judg* 11:36
slew not *a.* to that which. *2 Ki* 14:6
a. to that which was.   *2 Chr* 35:26
Tatnai did *a.* to that Darius.
   Ezra 6:13
a. to that which was spoken.
   Rom 4:18
a. to that he hath done.   *2 Cor* 5:10
a. to that a man hath, not *a.* to that.
   8:12

accordingly, *see* repay.

account
your *a.* for the lamb.   *Ex* 12:4
that passeth the *a.*   *2 Ki* 12:4*
number put in the *a.*   *1 Chr* 27:24
number of these *a.*   *2 Chr* 26:11*
for he giveth not *a.*   *Job* 33:13
man that thou makest *a.*   *Ps* 144:3
one to find out the *a.*   *Eccl* 7:27
the princes might give *a.*   *Dan* 6:2
give *a.* thereof in the day. *Mat* 12:36
take *a.* of his servants.   18:23*
a. of thy stewardship.   *Luke* 16:2
we may give an *a.* of.   *Acts* 19:40
every one shall give *a.*   *Rom* 14:12.
may abound to your *a.*   *Phil* 4:17
put that on mine *a.*   *Philem* 18

they watch as they that must give *a.*
    Heb 13:17
who shall give *a.* to him. *1 Pet* 4:5

account, -ed
which also were *a.* giants. *Deut* 2:11
that also was *a.* a land of giants. 20
Solomon shall be *a.*   *1 Ki* 1:21
silver was nothing *a.* of.   10:21
    2 Chr 9:20
be *a.* to the Lord for a. *Ps* 22:30*
wherein is he to be *a.* of ? *Isa* 2:22
a. to rule over Gentiles. *Mark* 10:42
a. worthy to obtain. *Luke* 20:35
should be *a.* the greatest.   22:24
we are *a.* as sheep for. *Rom* 8:36
let a man so *a.* of us as. *1 Cor* 4:1
a. to him for righteousness. *Gal* 3:6*
a. that the long-suffering *2 Pet* 3:15

accounting
a. that God was able to. *Heb* 11:19

accursed
[1] *Devoted to destruction,* Josh
6:17, etc. [2] *Separated from the
church,* Rom 9:3; Gal 1:8, 9.
  (*Anathema*)
is hanged, is *a.* of God. *Deut* 21:23
city shall be *a.* it and. *Josh* 6:17
any wise keep from the *a.* thing. 18
a. thing; Achan took of *a.*   7:1
even taken of the *a.* thing. 11
because they were *a.* except ye
  destroy the *a.*   12
there is an *a.* thing in the midst. 13
that is taken with the *a.* thing. 15
commit trespass in *a.* thing. 22:20
in the thing *a.*   *1 Chr* 2:7
100 years old shall be *a.* *Isa* 65:20
I could wish myself *a.* *Rom* 9:3
Spirit, calleth Jesus *a.* *1 Cor* 12:3
gospel, let him be *a.* *Gal* 1:8, 9

accusation
wrote they to him an *a.* *Ezra* 4:6
set over his head his *a.* *Mat* 27:37
  Mark 15:26
they might find an *a.* *Luke* 6:7
taken any thing by false *a.* 19:8*
what *a.* bring ye against ? *John* 18:29
they brought no *a.* as. *Acts* 25:18
elder receive not an *a.* *1 Tim* 5:19
bring not a railing *a.* *2 Pet* 2:11*
durst not bring a railing *a. Jude* 9*

accuse
a. not a servant to his. *Pr* 30:10*
a. him.   *Mat* 12:10; *Mark* 3:2
nor *a.* any falsely, and be. *Luke* 3:14
they began to *a.* him, saying. 23:2
those things whereof ye *a.* him. 14
will *a.* you to the Father. *John* 5:45
that they might have to *a.* him. 8:6
Tertullus began to *a.* him. *Acts* 24:2
of all things whereof we *a.* 8
prove things whereof they *a.* me. 13
go down with me, and *a.* 25:5
none of those whereof these *a.* 11
ought to *a.* my nation of. 28:19
falsely *a.* your good. *1 Pet* 3:16*

accused
near, and *a.* the Jews. *Dan* 3:8
them which had *a.* Daniel. 6:24
a. he answered nothing. *Mat* 27:12
priests *a.* him.   *Mark* 15:3
  Luke 23:10
a. that he had wasted. *Luke* 16:1
certainty wherefore he was *a.*
  Acts 22:30
cause whereof they *a.* him. 23:28
be *a.* of questions of their law. 29
is *a.* have the accusers. 25:16
things whereof I am *a.* 26:2
for which hope's sake I am *a.* of 7
faithful children, not *a.* of. *Tit.* 1:6
who *a.* them before our. *Rev* 12:10

accuser, *see cast down*

accusers
where are those thine *a.* ? *John* 8:10*
commandment to his *a.* *Acts* 23:30
hear thee when thine *a.* are. 35
commanding his *a.* to come. 24:8*
before he have the *a.* face. 25:16
against whom, when the *a.* 18
natural affection, false *a. 2 Tim* 3:3*
a. not given to much wine. *Tit* 2:3*

---

accuseth, -ing
that *a.* you, even Moses. *John* 5:45
thoughts *a.* or excusing. *Rom* 2:15

accustomed, *see do evil.*

aceldama, *see field*

Achaia
was the deputy of *A.* *Acts* 18:12
disposed to pass into *A.*   27
it pleased them of *A.* to. *Rom* 15:26
Epenetus, the first-fruits of *A.* 16:5
Stephanus, first-fruits of *A.*
  1 Cor 16:15
that *A.* was ready a year. *2 Cor* 9:2
stop me in the regions of *A.* 11:10
ensamples to all in *A.* *1 Thes* 1:7
the word sounded not only in *A.* 8

Achaicus
glad of the coming of *A. 1 Cor* 16:17

Achan, *or* **Achar**
A. of the tribe of Judah. *Josh* 7:18
did not *A.* son of Zerah commit
  22:20
A. the troubler of Israel. *1 Chr* 2:7

Achim
Sadoc begat *A.* and *A.* *Mat* 1:14

Achish
fled and went to *A.* *1 Sam* 21:10
  27:2
was afraid of *A.*   21:12
A. gave him Ziklag.   27:6
on in the rereward with *A.* 29:2
A. said, I know thou art good in. 9
Shimei went to Gath to *A. 1 Ki* 2:40

Achmetha
was found at *A.* a roll. *Ezra* 6:2

Achor
called the valley of *A.* *Josh* 7:26
valley of *A.* a place. *Isa* 65:10
give the valley of *A.* for. *Hos* 2:15

Achsah
will give *A.* to wife. *Josh* 15:16
  Judg 1:12

Achshaph
Jabin sent to king of *A.* *Josh* 11:1
king of *A.* one.   12:20
their border *A.*   19:25

Achzib
lot from the coast to *A.* *Josh* 19:29
the houses of *A.* shall be. *Mi* 1:14

acknowledge
[1] *To own, or confess,* Gen 38:26;
Ps 32:5. [2] *To esteem and
respect,* Isa 61:9; 1 Cor 16:18.
[3] *To approve of,* Cor 1:13;
Philem 6. [4] *To worship,* Dan
11:39.
a. the son of the hated. *Deut* 21:17
nor did he *a.* his brethren. 33:9
I *a.* my sin.   *Ps* 32:5
I *a.* my transgression. 51:3
in all thy ways *a.* him, he. *Pr* 3:6
are near, *a.* my might. *Isa* 33:13
that see them, shall *a.* them. 61:9
father, though Israel *a.* us not. 63:16
only *a.* thine iniquity. *Jer* 3:13
a. O Lord, our wickedness. 14:20
a. them that are carried. 24:5*
god whom he shall *a.* *Dan* 11:39
I will go, till they *a.* *Hos* 5:15
let him *a.* the things. *1 Cor* 14:37*
therefore *a.* ye them that are. 16:18
a. and I trust myself. *2 Cor* 1:13

acknowledged
Judah *a.* them, and said. *Gen* 38:26
also you have *a.* us in. *2 Cor* 1:14

acknowledgeth
a. the Son hath the Father.
  1 John 2:23

acknowledging
(*Revised Version,* knowledge)
the *a.* of the truth. *2 Tim* 2:25
a. the truth which is after. *Tit* 1:1
by the *a.* every good thing. *Philem* 6

acknowledgment
a. of the mystery of God. *Col* 2:2*

acquaint, -ed, -ing
a. thyself with him and. *Job* 22:21
thou art *a.* with all my. *Ps* 139:3
a. my heart with wisdom. *Eccl* 2:3
of sorrows, and *a.* with. *Isa* 53:3

---

acquaintance
let priests take it, every man of his *a.*
  2 Ki 12:5
no more money of your *a.* 7
a. are estranged from me. *Job* 19:13
all that had been of his *a.* 42:11
and a fear to mine *a.* *Ps* 31:11
mine equal, and mine *a.* 55:13*
put away mine *a.* far from me. 88:8
lover put from me, and my *a.* 18
sought him among their *a. Luke* 2:44
a. stood afar off, beholding. 23:49
forbid none of his *a.* to. *Acts* 24:23*

acquit
not *a.* me from mine iniquity.
  Job 10:14
the Lord will not at all *a.* the *Nah.* 1:3

acre, -s
half an *a.* of land. *1 Sam* 14:14
ten *a.* of vineyard shall. *Isa* 5:10

act
pass his *a.* his strange *a. Isa* 28:21
the *a.* of violence is in their. 59:6
in adultery, in the very *a. John* 8:4

actions
the Lord *a.* are weighed. *1 Sam* 2:3

activity
if knowest any man of *a.* *Gen* 47:6

acts
a. which he did in Egypt. *Deut* 11:3
eyes have seen the great *a.* of. 7
rehearse the righteous *a. Judg* 5:11
reason of all righteous *a. 1 Sam* 12:7
Benaiah the son . . . who had done
  many *a. 2 Sam* 23:20; *1 Chr* 11:22
report I heard of thy *a.* *1 Ki* 10:6
a. of Solomon, are they not written in
  the book of the *a.* 11:41; *2 Chr* 9:5
the *a.* of Jehu, and all. *2 Ki* 10:34
according to all the *a.* he had. 23:19
the *a.* of Josiah and all that he. 28
the *a.* of David, first. *1 Chr* 29:29
behold the *a.* of Asa. *2 Chr* 16:11
the *a.* of Jehoshaphat, first. 20:34
the *a.* of Hezekiah. 32:32; *2 Ki* 20:20
all the *a.* of his power. *Esth* 10:2
a. to the children of Israel. *Ps* 103:7
who can utter the mighty *a.* 106:2
declare thy mighty *a.* 145:4, 6, 12
praise him for his mighty *a.* 150:2

Adam
A. gave names to all cattle. *Gen* 2:20
and called their name *A.* 5:2
separated the sons of *A. Deut* 32:8
my transgressions as *A.* *Job* 31:33
death reigned from *A.* to. *Rom* 5:14
for as in *A.* all die. *1 Cor* 15:22
first man *A.* the last *A.* 45
for *A.* was first formed. *1 Tim* 2:13
and *A.* was not deceived, but. 14
Enoch the seventh from *A. Jude* 14

Adam
the city *A.* that is beside. *Josh* 3:16

adamant
a. have I made thy forehead.
  Ezek 3:9
their hearts as an *a.* stone. *Zech* 7:12

Adar
finished on third day of *A. Ezra* 6:15
lot till the twelfth month *A. Esth* 3:7
13th day of month *A.* 13; 8:12
  9:1, 17
gathered on the 14th day of *A.* 9:15
Jews made 14th day of *A.* a day. 19
14th and 15th days of *A.* yearly. 21

add
[1] *To join or put to,* Deut 4:2;
Acts 2:41; 2 Pet 1:5. [2] *To increase,* Pr 16:23. [3] *To give, or
bestow,* Gen 30:24; Mat 6:33.
a. to me another son. *Gen* 30:24
he shall *a.* a fifth part. *Lev* 5:16
  6:5; 27:13, 15, 19, 27, 31; *Num* 5:7
to cities of refuge *a.* forty-two.
  Num 35:6
not *a.* to the word. *Deut* 4:2; 12:32
thou shalt *a.* three cities. 19:9
to *a.* drunkenness to thirst. 29:19*
the Lord thy God to. *2 Sam* 24:3
I will *a.* to your yoke. *1 Ki* 12:11
  14; *2 Chr* 10:14

I *a.* to thy days. *2 Ki* 20:6; *Isa* 38:5
mayest *a.* thereto. *1 Chr* 22:14
ye intend to *a.* more to. *2 Chr* 28:13
a. iniquity to their iniquity. *Ps* 69:27
peace shall they *a.* to thee. *Pr* 3:2
a. thou not to his words, lest. 30:6
a. ye year to year, let. *Isa* 29:1
that they may *a.* sin to sin. 30:1
a. one cubit to his. *Mat* 6:27
Luke 12:25
supposing to *a.* affliction. *Phil* 1:16*
this *a.* to your faith. *2 Pet* 1:5
any *a.* God shall *a.* to him. *Rev.* 22:18

added
voice, and he *a.* no more. *Deut* 5:22
a. to all our sins this. *1 Sam* 12:19
were *a.* besides many like words.
Jer 36:32
the Lord hath *a.* grief to my. 45:3
majesty was *a.* to me. *Dan* 4:36
a. to you. *Mat* 6:33; *Luke* 12:31
Herod *a.* yet this above. *Luke* 3:20
they heard, he *a.* and. 19:11
day there were *a.* 3000. *Acts* 2:41
the Lord *a.* to the church daily. 47
believers were the more *a.* to. 5:14
much people were *a.* to the. 11:24
somewhat, *a.* nothing to. *Gal* 2:6
a. because of transgressions. 3:19

adder
Dan shall be an *a.* in. *Gen* 49:17
they are like the deaf *a.* *Ps* 58:4
tread on the lion and *a.* 91:13
a. poison is under their lips. 140:3
last stingeth like an *a.* *Pr* 23:32

addeth
a. rebellion to his sin. *Job* 34:37
and he *a.* no sorrow. *Pr* 10:22
heart of the wise *a.* learning. 16:23
disannulleth or *a.* thereto. *Gal* 3:15

Addi
was the son of *A.* son. *Luke* 3:28

addicted
a. themselves to the. *1 Cor* 16:15*

additions
(*Revised Version*, wreaths)
certain *a.* were made. *1 Ki* 7:29
molten at the side of every *a.* 30
he graved cherubims, and *a.* 36

adjure
[1] *To bind under the penalty of a feqrful curse*, Josh 6:26. [2] *To charge earnestly by word or oath*, 1 Ki 22:16; Mat 26:63.

how many times shall I *a.* thee to
tell. *1 Ki* 22:16; *2 Chr* 18:15
I *a.* thee by the living. *Mat* 26:63
I *a.* thee by God, thou. *Mark* 5:7
we *a.* you by Jesus. *Acts* 19:13

adjured
Joshua *a.* them at that. *Josh* 6:26
for Saul had *a.* the. *1 Sam* 14:24

Admah
Shinab king of *A.* *Gen* 14:2
like the overthrow of *A. Deut* 29:23
shall I make thee as *A?* *Hos* 11:8

administered
(*Revised Version*, ministered)
a. by us to the glory of. *2 Cor* 8:19
in this abundance which is *a.* 20

administration, -s
(*Revised Version*, ministration)
are differences of *a.* *1 Cor* 12:5
for the *a.* of this service. *2 Cor* 9:12

admiration
having men's persons in *a. Jude* 16*
I wondered with great *a. Rev* 17:6*

admired
to be *a.* in all them. *2 Thes* 1:10*

admonish, -ed
who will no more be *a. Eccl* 4:13
by these, my son, be *a.* 12:12
that I have *a.* you. *Jer* 42:19
now past, Paul *a.* them. *Acts* 27:9
also to *a.* one another. *Rom* 15:14
a. one another in psalms. *Col* 3:16
you in Lord, and *a.* you. *1 Thes* 5:12
a. him as a brother. *2 Thes* 3:15
as Moses was *a.* of God. *Heb* 8:5

admonition
are written for our *a.* *1 Cor* 10:11
bring them up in the *a.* of. *Eph* 6:4
the first and second *a.* *Tit* 3:10

ado
why make ye this *a.?* *Mark* 5:39*

Adoni-Bezek
they found *A.* in Bezek. *Judg* 1:5

Adonijah
A. the son of. *2 Sam* 3:4; *1 Chr* 3:2
then *A.* exalted himself. *1 Ki* 1:5
hast thou not heard that *A.?* 11
God save the king *A.* 25
A. feared. 50, 51
let Abishag be given to *A.* 2:21
A. shall be put to death this day. 25
Joab had turned after *A.* though. 28
sent Levites to teach *A.* *2 Chr* 17:8
sealed, *A.* and Adin. *Neh* 10:16

Adonikam
the children of *A.*, 666. *Ezra* 2:13
Neh 7:18

adoption
[1] *A legal action by which a person takes into his family a child not his own, and usually of no kin to him, with the purpose of treating him as, and giving him all the privileges of, an own son. So Moses was adopted by Pharaoh's daughter,* Ex 2:10, *and Esther by Mordecai,* Esth 2:7, 15. *The custom was not common among the Jews, but was so among the Romans, with whom, as with us, an adopted child is legally entitled to all rights and privileges of a natural-born child.*
[2] *The custom, being well-known where Rome held sway, is used in the New Testament to refer: (a) to the choice by Jehovah of Israel to be his special people,* Rom 9:4; *(b) the special sense in which all true Christians are the sons of God,* Gal 4:5; Eph 1:4, 5; *and (c) the final redemption of the body,* Rom 8:23.

received the spirit of *a.* *Rom* 8:15
for the *a.* the redemption of 23
to whom pertaineth the *a.* 9:4
might receive the *a.* of sons. *Gal* 4:5
us to the *a.* of children. *Eph* 1:5

adorn, -ed, -eth, -ing
as a bride *a.* herself with. *Isa* 61:10
be again *a.* with tabrets. *Jer* 31:4
the temple was *a.* with. *Luke* 21:5
women *a.* in modest. *1 Tim* 2:9
a. the doctrine of God. *Tit* 2:10
whose *a.* let it not be that outward *a.*
1 Pet 3:3
women who trusted in God *a.* 5
a bride *a.* for her husband. *Rev* 21:2

Adrammelech
burnt children to *A.* *2 Ki* 17:31
A. and Sharezer. 19:37; *Isa* 37:38

Adramyttium
entering into a ship of *A. Acts* 27:2

Adria
driven up and down in *A. Acts* 27:27

Adriel
given unto *A.* to wife. *1 Sam* 18:19
she brought up for *A.* *2 Sam* 21:8

Adullam
the cave *A. 1 Sam* 22:1; *1 Chr* 11:15
came to David to *A.* *2 Sam* 23:13
come to *A.* the glory of. *Mi* 1:15

adulterer, -s
a. shall surely be put. *Lev* 20:10
the eye of the *a.* waiteth. *Job* 24:15
been partaker with *a.* *Ps* 50:18
seed of *a.* and the whore. *Isa* 57:3
they be all *a.* an assembly. *Jer* 9:2
for the land is full of *a.* for. 23:10
they are all *a.* as an oven. *Hos* 7:4
swift witness against the *a. Mal* 3:5
others, extortioners, *a. Luke* 18:11
neither *a.* shall inherit. *1 Cor* 6:9
whoremongers and *a.* *Heb* 13:4
ye *a.* know ye not that the. *Jas* 4:4

adulteress, -es
a. shall surely be put. *Lev* 20:10
the *a.* will hunt for the. *Pr* 6:26

shall judge them as *a.* *Ezek* 23:45
love a woman, yet an *a.* *Hos* 3:1
she is no *a.* though she be. *Rom* 7:3

adulterous
way of an *a.* woman. *Pr* 30:20
an *a.* generation. *Mat* 12:39;16:4
be ashamed in this *a.* *Mark* 8:38

adultery, -ies
[1] *Natural,* Mat 5:28; Mark 10:
11. [2] *Spiritual, which is idolatry,* Jer 3:9; Ezek 23:37.

thou shalt not commit *a.* *Ex* 20:14
Deut 5:18; *Mat* 5:27; 19:18
Rom 13:9
committeth *a.*, even he that committeth *a.* shall surely be. *Lev* 20:10
commits *a.* lacketh. *Pr* 6:32
Israel committed *a.* *Jer* 3:8
committed *a.* with stones and. 9
then they committed *a.* 5:7
steal, murder, and commit *a.* 7:9
I have seen thine *a.* and. 13:27
they commit *a.* and walk in. 23:14
they have committed *a.* 29:23
wife that committeth *a.* *Ezek* 16:32
have they committed *a.* 23:37
said I to her that was old in *a.* 43
put away her *a.* between. *Hos* 2:2
by lying and committing *a.* 4:2
your spouses shall commit *a.* 13
them when they commit *a.* 14
hath committed *a.* in. *Mat* 5:28
her that is divorced committeth *a.*
32; 19:9; *Luke* 16:18
heart proceed *a.* *Mat* 15:19
Mark 7:21
marry another, committeth *a.*
Mark 10:11; *Luke* 16:18
do not commit *a.* *Mark* 10:19
Luke 18:20; *Jas* 2:11
a woman taken in *a.* *John* 8:3, 4
should not commit *a.* *Rom* 2:22
the flesh are manifest, *a.* *Gal* 5:19
having eyes full of *a.* *2 Pet* 2:14
cast them that commit *a.* *Rev* 2:22

advanced
Lord that *a.* Moses. *1 Sam* 12:6*
Ahasuerus *a.* Haman the. *Esth* 3:1
told him how he had *a.* him. 5:11
whereto the king *a.* 10:2

advantage, -ed, -eth
what *a.* will it be to thee. *Job* 35:3
is a man *a.* if he gain. *Luke* 9:25
what *a.* then hath the Jew. *Rom* 3:1
a. it me if the dead? *1 Cor* 15:32
Satan should get an *a.* *2 Cor* 2:11
in admiration, because of *a. Jude* 16

adventure, -ed
not *a.* to set the sole. *Deut* 28:56
father sought and *a.* his. *Judg* 9:17
that he would not *a.* *Acts* 19:31

adversaries
lest their *a.* should. *Deut* 32:27
render vengeance to his *a.* 43
for us, or for our *a.?* *Josh* 5:13
the *a.* of the Lord. *1 Sam* 2:10
this day be *a.* to me. *2 Sam* 19:22
when *a.* of Judah and. *Ezra* 4:1
our *a.* said, they shall not. *Neh* 4:11
evil for good, are my *a.* *Ps* 38:20
mine *a.* are all before thee. 69:19
confounded that are *a.* to. 71:13
my hand against their *a.* 81:14
the right hand of his *a.* 89:42
for my love they are my *a.* 109:4
let this be the reward of my *a.* 20
let my *a.* be clothed with shame. 29
I will ease me of my *a.* *Isa* 1:24
shall set up the *a.* of Rezin. 9:11
the *a.* of Judah shall be. 11:13*
he will repay fury to his *a.* 59:18
our *a.* have trodden down. 63:18
thy name known to thine *a.* 64:2
all thine *a.* shall go into. *Jer* 30:16
he may avenge him of his *a.* 46:10
their *a.* said, we offend not. 50:7
her *a.* are the chief. *Lam* 1:5
the *a.* saw her, and did mock. 7
his *a.* should be round about him. 17
hath set up the horn of thine *a.* 2:17
shall be lifted up upon thy *a. Mi* 5:9
take vengeance on his *a.* *Nah* 1:2

all his *a.* were ashamed. *Luke* 13:17
your *a.* shall not be able. 21:15
and there are many *a.* *1 Cor* 16:9
terrified by your *a.* *Phil* 1:28
which shall devour the *a.* *Heb* 10:27

adversary
an *a.* to thine adversaries. *Ex* 23:22
an *a.* against Balaam. *Num* 22:22
her *a.* also provoked her. *1 Sam* 1:6*
in the battle he be an *a.* to us. 29:4
is neither *a.* nor evil. *1 Ki* 5:4
Lord stirred up an *a.* to 11:14, 23
was an *a.* to Israel all the days. 25
the *a.* and enemy is this. *Esth* 7:6
a. had written a book. *Job* 31:35
shall the *a.* reproach? *Ps* 74:10
who is mine *a.* let him. *Isa* 50:8
the *a.* hath spread out. *Lam* 1:10
with his right hand as an *a.* 2:4
the *a.* should have entered. 4:12
an *a.* shall be round. *Amos* 3:11
agree with thine *a.* quickly, lest at
any time the *a.* deliver. *Mat* 5:25
goest with thine *a.* *Luke* 12:58
saying, avenge me of mine *a.* 18:3
no occasion to the *a.* *1 Tim* 5:14
a. the devil as a roaring. *1 Pet* 5:8

adversity, -ies
saved you out of all *a.* *1 Sam* 10:19
my soul out of all *a.* *2 Sam* 4:9
did vex them with all *a.* *2 Chr* 15:6
I shall never be in *a.* *Ps* 10:6
thou hast known my soul in *a.* 31:7
but in my *a.* they rejoiced. 35:15
rest from the days of *a.* 94:13
brother is born for *a.* *Pr* 17:17
if thou faint in day of *a.* 24:10
but in the day of *a.* *Eccl* 7:14
give you the bread of *a.* *Isa* 30:20
them which suffer *a.* *Heb* 13:3*

advertise (*To notify, or warn*)
I will *a.* thee, what. *Num* 24:14
I thought to *a.* thee. *Ruth* 4:4*

advice
take *a.* and speak your. *Judg* 19:30
give here your *a.* and counsel. 20:7
blessed be thy *a.* *1 Sam* 25:33*
that our *a.* should. *2 Sam* 19:43
what *a.* give ye, that. *2 Chr* 10:9
after the *a.* of young men. 14
king Amaziah took *a.* and. 25:17
with good *a.* make war. *Pr* 20:18
and herein I give my *a.* *2 Cor* 8:10

advise, -ed
a. and see. *2 Sam* 24:13; *1 Chr* 21:12
how do ye *a.* that. *1 Ki* 12:6
with the well-*a.* is wisdom. *Pr* 13:10
a. to depart thence also. *Acts* 27:12

advisement
the lords upon *a.* sent. *1 Chr* 12:19

advocate
we have an *a.* with. *1 John* 2:1

Æ.—(*For proper names beginning
with Æ, see* E)

afar, *usually joined with* **off**
[1] *The distance between place and
place.* Gen 37:18. [2] *Estrange-
ment from another,* Ps 38:11
saw the place *a. off.* *Gen* 22:4
brethren saw Joseph *a. off.* 37:18
and worship ye *a.* *Ex* 24:1
pitch the tabernacle *a. off.* 33:7
be in a journey *a. off.* *Num* 9:10
man of God saw her *a. off.* *2 Ki* 4:25
noise was heard *a. off.* *Ezra* 3:13
Jerusalem was heard *a. off.*
Neh 12:43
my knowledge from *a.* *Job* 36:3
a man may behold it *a. off.* 25
and her eyes behold *a. off.* 39:29
them that are *a. off.* *Ps* 65:5
proud he knoweth *a. off.* 138:6
my thoughts *a. off.* 139:2
her food from *a.* *Pr* 31:14
shall carry her *a. off.* *Isa* 33:7
escape to the isles *a. off.* 66:19
and not a God *a. off?* *Jer* 23:23
save thee from *a.* 30:10; 46:27
declare it in the isles *a. off.* 31:10
get you *a. off,* dwell. 49:30
remember the Lord *a. off.* 51:50

rebuke strong nations *a. off.* *Mi* 4:3
Peter followed him *a. off.* *Mat* 26:58
Mark 14:54; *Luke* 22:54
beholding *a. off.* *Mat* 27:55
Mark 15:40
saw Jesus *a. off,* he. *Mark* 5:6
and seeing a fig-tree *a. off.* 11:13
seeth Abraham *a. off.* *Luke* 16:23
to all that are *a. off.* *Acts* 2:39
preached peace to you which were *a.
off,* and to them that. *Eph* 2:17
seen the promises *a. off.* *Heb* 11:13
and cannot see *a. off.* *2 Pet* 1:9

see far, stand, stood

affairs
to God, and *a.* of the. *1 Chr* 26:32
he will guide his *a.* *Ps* 112:5*
Shadrach over *a.* of the. *Dan* 2:49
Jews whom thou set over *a.* 3:12
ye also may know my *a.* *Eph* 6:21
that ye might know our *a.* 22*
I may hear of your *a.* *Phil* 1:27
himself with the *a.* of life. *2 Tim* 2:4

affect, -ed, -eth
mine eye *a.* my heart. *Lam* 3:51
minds evil *a.* against. *Acts* 14:2
a. you, that ye might *a.* *Gal* 4:17*
good to be zealously *a.* in *a.* 18*

affection
a. to the house of God. *1 Chr* 29:3
natural *a.* *Rom* 1:31; *2 Tim* 3:3
a. is more abundant. *2 Cor* 7:15
set your *a.* on things. *Col* 3:2*
fornication, inordinate *a.* 5

affectionately
so being *a.* desirous of. *1 Thes* 2:8

affectioned
kindly *a.* one to another. *Rom* 12:10

affections
gave them up to vile *a.* *Rom* 1:26
the flesh with the *a.* *Gal* 5:24

affinity
Solomon made *a.* with. *1 Ki* 3:1
Jehoshaphat joined in *a.* *2 Chr* 18:1
should we join in *a.* *Ezra* 9:14

affirm
To maintain the truth of a thing,
Acts 25:19; Tit 3:8.
as some *a.* that we say. *Rom* 3:8
nor whereof they *a.* *1 Tim* 1:7
things I will that thou *a.* *Tit* 3:8

affirmed
an hour after another *a.* *Luke* 22:59
Rhoda constantly *a.* that. *Acts* 12:15
and of Jesus, whom Paul *a.* 25:19

afflict, -est
shall *a.* them 400 years. *Gen* 15:13
if thou shalt *a.* my daughters. 31:50
task-masters to *a.* them. *Ex* 1:11
ye shall not *a.* any widow. 22:22
if thou *a.* them in any wise, and. 23
ye shall *a.* your souls. *Lev* 16:29
31; 23:27, 32; *Num* 29:7
Chittim shall *a.* Ashur. *Num* 24:24
binding oath to *a.* the soul. 30:13
we bind him to *a.* him. *Judg* 16:5
mightest be bound to *a.* thee. 6
to *a.* him, and his strength went. 19
of wickedness *a.* them. *2 Sam* 7:10
will for this *a.* the seed. *1 Ki* 11:39
thou dost *a.* *2 Chr* 6:26; *1 Ki* 8:35
we might *a.* ourselves. *Ezra* 8:21*
Almighty, he will not *a.* *Job* 37:23
how thou didst *a.* the. *Ps* 44:2
God shall hear and *a.* them. 55:19*
son of wickedness *a.* him. 89:22
O Lord, they *a.* thine heritage. 94:5
all them that *a.* my soul. 143:12
did more grievously *a.* her. *Isa* 9:1*
the hand of them that *a.* thee. 51:23
day for a man to *a.* his soul? 58:5
O Lord, wilt thou *a.* us? 64:12
to destroy and to *a.* *Jer* 31:28
the Lord doth not *a.* *Lam* 3:33
they *a.* the just, they. *Amos* 5:12
shall *a.* you from Hemath. 6:14
have afflicted, I will *a.* *Nah* 1:12
will undo all that *a.* thee. *Zeph* 3:19

afflicted
more have *a.* the more. *Ex* 1:12
shall not be *a.* that day. *Lev* 23:29

hast thou *a.* thy? *Num* 11:11*
the Egyptians *a.* us. *Deut* 26:6
the Almighty hath *a.* me. *Ruth* 1:21
and the *a.* people thou. *2 Sam* 22:28
a. in all . . . my father was *a.*
1 Ki 2:26
rejected Israel and *a.* *2 Ki* 17:20
to him that is *a.* pity. *Job* 6:14*
loosed my cord, and *a.* me. 30:11
heareth the cry of the *a.* 34:28
wilt save the *a.* people. *Ps* 18:27
affliction of the *a.* 22:24
me, for I am desolate and *a.* 25:16
do justice to the *a.* and needy. 82:3
hast *a.* me with all thy waves. 88:7
am *a.* and ready to die from my. 15
days wherein thou hast *a.* us. 90:15
of their iniquities, are *a.* 107:17
I was greatly *a.* 116:10
before I was *a.* 119:67
for me that I have been *a.* 71
thou in faithfulness hast *a.* me. 75
I am *a.* very much, quicken me. 107
they *a.* me from youth. 129:1, 2
maintain the cause of the *a.* 140:12
all the days of the *a.* are. *Pr* 15:15
oppress the *a.* in the gate. 22:22
hateth those that are *a.* 26:28*
pervert the judgment of the *a.* 31:5
when at first he lightly *a.* *Isa* 9:1*
Lord will have mercy on his *a.* 49:13
hear now this, thou *a.* and. 51:21
him smitten of God and *a.* 53:4
he was oppressed, and was *a.* 7
O thou *a.* tossed with. 54:11
have we *a.* our souls? 58:3
if thou satisfy the *a.* soul. 10
sons of them that *a.* thee. 60:14
in all their affliction he was *a.* 63:9
sigh, her virgins are *a.* *Lam* 1:4
prosper, for the Lord hath *a.* her. 5
wherewith the Lord hath *a.* me. 12
gather her that I have *a.* *Mi* 4:6
I have *a.* I will afflict. *Nah* 1:12
leave in thee an *a.* people. *Zeph* 3:12
deliver you up to be *a.* *Mat* 24:9*
whether we be *a.* it is for. *2 Cor* 1:6
she have relieved the *a.* *1 Tim* 5:10
being destitute, *a.* and. *Heb* 11:37
be *a.* and mourn, and. *Jas* 4:9
is any among you *a.?* let. 5:13*

affliction
[1] *Adversity, trouble, or distress,*
Job 5:6; Jonah 2:2. [2] *Outward
oppression,* Ex 3:7; 14:31; Mark
4:17; Heb 10:32. [3] *Correction
from God.*
Lord hath heard thy *a.* *Gen* 16:11
hath looked upon my *a.* 29:32
God hath seen mine *a.* and. 31:42
fruitful in the land of *a.* 41:52
a. of my people. *Ex* 3:7; *Acts* 7:34
bring you out of the *a.* of. *Ex* 3:17
he had looked on their *a.* 4:31
eat even the bread of *a.* *Deut* 16:3
1 Ki 22:27; *2 Chr* 18:26
looked on our *a.* *Deut* 26:7
indeed look on my *a.* *1 Sam* 1:11
Lord will look on my *a.* *2 Sam* 16:12*
for the Lord saw the *a.* *2 Ki* 14:26
cry to thee in our *a.* *2 Chr* 20:9
Manasseh was in *a.* and. 33:12*
remnant are in great *a.* *Neh* 1:3
didst see the *a.* of our fathers. 9:9
though *a.* cometh not forth. *Job* 5:6
confusion, see-thou mine *a.* 10:15
the days of *a.* have taken. 30:16
the days of *a.* prevented me. 27
they be holden in cords of *c.* 36:8
he delivereth the poor in his *a.* 15
hast thou chosen rather than *a.* 21
my *a.* and pain, forgive. *Ps* 25:18
and forgettest our *a.* and. 44:24
thou laidst *a.* upon our loins. 66:11*
mournest by reason of *a.* 88:9
he regarded their *a.* 106:44*
being bound in *a.* and iron. 107:10
they are brought low through *a.* 39*
he the poor on high from *a.* 41
this is my comfort in my *a.* 119:50
then have perished in mine *a.* 92
consider mine *a.* and deliver me. 153
give you water of *a.* *Isa* 30:20

thee in the furnace of *a*.   *Isa* 48:10
in all their *a*. he was afflicted.   63:9
publisheth *a*. from mount. *Jer* 4:15*
thee well in the time of *a*.   15:11
my refuge in the day of *a*.   16:19
why criest thou for thine *a*. ? *30*:15*
Moab's calamity is near, and *a*. 48:16
captivity because of *a*.   *Lam* 1:3
remembered in the days of her *a*. 7
O Lord, behold mine *a*.   9
I am the man that hath seen *a*. 3:1
remembering my *a*. and my.   19
in their *a*. they will seek.   *Hos* 5:15
grieved for the *a*. of.   *Amos* 6:6
have looked on their *a*.   *Ob* 13
cried by reason of my *a*. *Jonah* 2:2
a. shall not rise up the.   *Nah* 1:9
tents of Cushan in *a*.   *Hab* 3:7
helped forward the *a*.   *Zech* 1:15
or came in, because of *a*.   8:10*
pass through the sea with *a*. 10:11
when *a*. ariseth for the. *Mark* 4:17*
for in those days shall be *a*. 13:19*
a dearth, and great *a*.   *Acts* 7:11
out of much *a*. I wrote. *2 Cor* 2:4
our light *a*. which is but for. 4:17
how that in a great trial of *a*. 8:2
supposing to add *a*. to.   *Phil* 1:16
with me in my *a*.   4:14
the word in much *a*. *1 Thes* 1:6
over you in all our *a*.   3:7
to suffer *a*. with people. *Heb* 11:25
the fatherless in their *a*. *Jas* 1:27
for an example of suffering *a*. 5:10*

afflictions

many are the *a*. of.   *Ps.* 34:19
David, and all his *a*.   132:1
him out of all his *a*.   *Acts* 7:10
saying, that bonds and *a*.   20:23
in much patience, in *a*. *2 Cor* 6:4
behind of the *a*. of Christ. *Col* 1:24
be moved by these *a*. *1 Thes* 3:3
be partakers of the *a*. *2 Tim* 1:8*
known the *a*. which came to. 3:11*
watch in all things, endure *a*. 4:5*
a great fight of *a*.   *Heb* 10:32*
were made a gazing-stock by *a*. 33
same *a*. accomplished *1 Pet* 5:9*

affording

garners full, *a*. all.   *Ps* 144:13

affright, -ed

shalt not be *a*. at them. *Deut* 7:21
with a loud voice to *a*. *2 Chr* 32:18
that went before were *a*. *Job* 18:20
at fear, and is not *a*.   39:22*
panted, fearfulness *a*. me. *Isa* 21:4
burnt, and men of war *a*. *Jer* 51:32
they were *a*. *Mark* 16:5*; *Luke* 24:37
be not *a*. ye seek Jesus. *Mark* 16:6*
the remnant were *a*.   *Rev* 11:13

afoot

many ran *a*. thither out. *Mark* 6:33
minding himself to go *a*. *Acts* 20:13*

afore

a. Isaiah was gone out. *2 Ki* 20:4
which withereth *a*. it. *Ps* 129:6
a. the harvest when the. *Isa* 38:15
a. he that was escaped. *Ezek* 33:22
which he had promised *a*. *Rom* 1:2
he had *a*. prepared unto glory. 9:23
mystery, as I wrote *a*. in. *Eph* 3:3

aforehand

come *a*. to anoint my. *Mark* 14:8

aforetime

and *a*. I was as a tabret. *Job* 17:6*
my people went down *a*. *Isa* 52:4
also shall be as *a*.   *Jer* 30:20
his God, as he did *a*. *Dan* 6:10
brought him that *a*. *John* 9:13
things were written *a*. *Rom* 15:4

afraid

money, they were *a*. *Gen* 42:35
they were *a*. to come. *Ex* 34:30
make you *a*. *Lev* 26:6; *Job* 11:19
why not *a*. to speak ? *Num* 12:8
people of whom thou art *a*.
  Deut 7:19
whosoever is fearful and *a*. *Judg* 7:3
the Philistines were *a*. *1 Sam* 4:7
Saul was yet the more *a*. of. 18:29
now wast thou not *a*. to *2 Sam* 1:14

people have made me *a*. *2 Sam* 14:15
come on him, and make him *a*. 17:2
men made me *a*.   22:5; *Ps* 18:4
they all made us *a*. saying. *Neh* 6:9
I am *a*. of all my sorrows. *Job* 9:28
none shall make thee *a*.   11:19
his excellency make you *a*. ? 13:11
let not thy dread make me *a*. 21
anguish shall make him *a*. 15:24
terrors shall make him *a*. on. 18:11
when I remember, I am *a*. 21:6*
when I consider, I am *a*. 23:15
terror shall not make thee *a*. 33:7
a. as a grasshopper.   39:20*
himself, the mighty are *a*. 41:25
what time I am *a*. I will. *Ps* 56:3
that dwell are *a*. at thy tokens. 65:8
saw thee, and they were *a*. 77:16
make them *a*. with thy storm. 83:15
I am *a*. of thy judgments. 119:120
none shall make them *a*. *Isa* 17:2
  Ezek 34:28; *Mi* 4:4; *Zeph* 3:13
the sinners in Zion are *a*. *Isa* 33:14
ends of the earth were *a*. 41:5*
of whom hast thou been *a*. 57:11
none shall make him *a*. *Jer* 30:10
yet they were not *a*. nor. 36:24
Zedekiah said, I am *a*. of 38:19
men, of whom thou art *a*. 39:17
made them *a*. *Ezek* 39:26; *Nah* 2:11
dream, which made me *a*. *Dan* 4:5
mariners were *a*. *Jonah* 1:5, 10
made them *a*. because of. *Hab* 2:17
mind, were *a*. *Mark* 3:15 ; *Luke* 8:35
understood not, and were *a*.
  Mark 9:32
followed, they were *a*. 10:32
any thing, for they were *a*. 16:8
they being *a*. wondered. *Luke* 8:25
they were all *a*. of Saul. *Acts* 9:26
me saw the light, and were *a*. 22:9*
I am *a*. of you, lest I. *Gal* 4:11
not *a*. of the king's. *Heb* 11:23
are not *a*. with any. *1 Pet* 3:6
are not *a*. to speak evil. *2 Pet* 2:10*

be afraid

neither be *a*. of. *Deut* 1:29; 31:6
behold we be *a*. here in. *1 Sam* 23:3
be *a*. out of close. *2 Sam* 22:46*
  Ps 18:45*
hired that I should be *a*. *Neh* 6:13
thou be *a*. of destruction. *Job* 5:21
be ye *a*. of the sword, for. 19:29
of whom shall I be *a*. ? *Ps* 27:1
their fear, nor be *a*. *Isa* 8:12 ; 44:8
maketh mention, shall be *a*. 19:17
that thou shouldest be *a*. 51:12
which is evil, be *a*. *Rom* 13:4

not be afraid

not be *a*. of the face of. *Deut* 1:17
thou shalt not be *a*. 7:18; 18:22
I will *not* be *a*. of ten. *Ps* 3:6
I will *not* be *a*. what man can. 56:11
thou shalt *not* be *a*. for the. 91:5
he shall *not* be *a*. of evil. 112:7
is established, he shall *not* be *a*. 8
liest down, shalt *not* be *a*. *Pr* 3:24
will trust and *not* be *a*. *Isa* 12:2
will *not* be *a*. of their voice. 31:4
and people *not* be *a*. *Amos* 3:6
wilt thou then *not* be *a*. ? *Rom* 13:3

be not afraid

be *not a*. of them. *Deut* 20:1
  Josh 11:6; *Neh* 4:14; *Jer* 10:5
  Ezek 2:6; *Luke* 12:4
Saul said, be *not a*. *1 Sam* 28:13
go down, be *not a*. *2 Ki* 1:15
be *not a*. when one is. *Ps* 49:16
be *not a*. of sudden fear. *Pr* 3:25
voice, lift it up, be *not a*. *Isa* 40:9
be *not a*. of their faces. *Jer* 1:8
son of man be *not a*. *Ezek* 2:6
it is I, be *not a*. *Mat* 14:27
  Mark 6:50; *John* 6:20
arise, be *not a*. *Mat* 17:7
be *not a*. go tell my brethren. 28:10
saith to the ruler, be *not a*.
  Mark 5:36
be *not a*. but speak, and. *Acts* 18:9
be *not a*. of their terror. *1 Pet* 3:14

sore afraid

and men were *sore a*. *Gen* 20:8
marched, they were *sore a*. *Ex* 14:10

Moab was *sore a*. of. *Num* 22:3
therefore we were *sore a*. *Josh* 9:24
Goliath, and were *sore a*.
  1 Sam 17:24
on the earth, and was *sore a*. 28:20
was *sore a*. 31:4; *1 Chr* 10:4
sorrow, and was very *sore a*. *Neh* 2:2
say, for they were *sore a*. *Mark* 9:6
and they were *sore a*. *Luke* 2:9

was afraid

thy voice, and I was *a*. *Gen* 3:10
I laughed not, for she was *a*. 18:15
then Jacob was greatly *a*. and 32:7
Moses hid his face, was *a*. *Ex* 3:6
I was *a*. of the anger. *Deut* 9:19
midnight the man was *a*. *Ruth* 3:8
Saul was *a*. *1 Sam* 18:12, 15*
Ahimelech was *a*. at the. 21:1*
host of Philistines, he was *a*. 28:5
David was *a*. *2 Sam* 6:9; *1 Chr* 13:12
not go, for he was *a*. *1 Chr* 21:30
which I was *a*. of, is come. *Job* 3:25
I was *a*. and durst not shew. 32:6*
Urijah heard it, he was *a*. *Jer* 26:21
when he came, was *a*. *Dan* 8:17
thy speech, and was *a*. *Hab* 3:2
was *a*. before my name. *Mal* 2:5*
Joseph was *a*. to go. *Mat* 2:22
the wind boisterous, was *a*. 14:30
I was *a*. and hid thy talent. 25:25
heard, he was the more *a*. *John* 19:8
Cornelius looked, he was *a*. *Acts* 10:4

afresh

crucify the Son of God *a*. *Heb* 6:6

after

a. I am waxed old. *Gen* 18:12
three months *a*. it was told. 38:24
ye seek *a*. your. *Num* 15:39
not go *a*. other gods. *Deut* 6:14
that before it, or *a*. *Josh* 10:14
turned again *a*. Saul. *1 Sam* 15:31
a. whom is the king come out ? *a*. a
  dog. 24:14
and *a*. make for thee. *1 Ki* 17:13
opened till *a*. the sabbath. *Neh* 13:19
thou inquirest *a*. mine. *Job* 10:6
cried *a*. them, as *a*. a thief. 30:5
give them *a*. the work of. *Ps* 28:4
that shall come *a*. *Eccl* 1:11
judge *a*. the sight of eyes. *Isa* 11:3
a. it shall return to the. *Ezek* 46:17*
shall walk *a*. the Lord. *Hos* 11:10
a. I am risen again, I. *Mat* 26:32
which had seen him *a*. *Mark* 16:14
so then *a*. the Lord had spoken. 19
on the second sabbath *a*. *Luke* 6:1*
a. a little while another. 22:58
space of an hour *a*. another. 59
he might bear it *a*. Jesus. 23:26
a. the sop Satan entered. *John* 13:27
space of three hours *a*. *Acts* 5:7
which was 430 years *a*. *Gal* 3:17
to those that *a*. should. *2 Pet* 2:6*

after that

and *a*. that he will let. *Ex* 3:20
her *a*. that she is defiled. *Deut* 24:4
avenged, and *a*. that I. *Judg* 15:7
a. that God was intreated for.
  2 Sam 21:14
a. that I have spoken, *Job* 21:3
and *a*. that they go to the. *Eccl* 9:3
a. that I was turned. *Jer* 31:19
a. that have no more. *Luke* 12:4
a. that thou shalt cut it. 13:9*
a. that which is lost, until he. 15:4
a. that shall they come. *Acts* 7:7
a. that he was seen of. *1 Cor* 15:6
and *a*. that he must be. *Rev* 20:3

after this

a. this Abraham buried. *Gen* 23:19
a. this David enquired. *2 Sam* 2:1
a. this I will return. *Acts* 15:16

afternoon

they tarried till *a*. and. *Judg* 19:8*

afterward, -s

a. he will let you go. *Ex* 11:1
a. shalt thou be gathered. *Num* 31:2
a. shall thy hands be. *Judg* 7:11
the sacrifice, *a*. they eat. *1 Sam* 9:13
a. David's heart smote him. 24:5
and *a*. we will speak. *Job* 18:2
guide me, and *a*. receive. *Ps* 73:24

deceit is sweet, but *a.*   *Pr* 20:17
prepare thy work, and *a.*   24:27
a. shall find more favour.   28:23
wise man keepeth it in till *a.* 29:11*
a. shall the children of.   *Hos* 3:5
a. I will pour out my Spirit. *Joel* 2:28
a. an hungered. *Mat* 4:2; *Luke* 4:2
seen it, repented not *a.*   *Mat* 21:32
a. Jesus findeth him in.   *John* 5:14
but thou shalt follow me *a.*   13:36
a. they that are Christ's. *I Cor* 15:23
the faith that should *a.*   *Gal* 3:23
would not *a.* have spoken. *Heb* 4:8
a. it yieldeth the peaceable.   12:11
a. when he would have inherited. 17
a. destroyed them that.   *Jude* 5

Agabus
one of them, named *A.*   *Acts* 11:28
a prophet named *A.*   21:10

Agag
shall be higher than *A.*   *Num* 24:7
the people spared *A.*   *I Sam* 15:9
Samuel hewed *A.* in pieces.   33

Agagite, see Haman

again
I will not *a.* curse, nor *a.* *Gen* 8:21
but they shall come hither *a.*   15:16
a. feed and keep thy flock.   30:31
Judah knew her *a.* no more.   38:26
I will see *a.* thy face no.   *Ex* 10:29
ye shall see them *a.* no more.   14:13
surely bring it back to him *a.*   23:4
will yet *a.* leave them in. *Num* 32:15
circumcise *a.* the children. *Josh* 5:2
and *a.* whom should.   *2 Sam* 16:19
child came into him *a.*   *1 Ki* 17:22
shall yet *a.* take root.   *2 Ki* 19:30
a. break thy commandments.
         Ezra 9:14
if ye do so *a.* I will lay. *Neh* 13:21
man die, shall he live *a.* ? *Job* 14:14
revive us *a.* that thy.   *Ps* 85:6
a. they minished and.   107:39
that they rise not up *a.*   140:10
that go to her return *a.*   *Pr* 2:19
deliver him, thou must do it *a.* 19:19
a. there be wicked men. *Eccl.* 8:14
thou never be found *a.* *Ezek* 26:21
will not *a.* pass by.   *Amos* 7:8; 8:14
shall fall, and never rise up *a.*   8:14
choose Jerusalem *a.*   *Zech* 2:12
this water shall thirst *a.* *John* 4:13
spirit of bondage *a.* to.   *Rom* 8:15
rejoice in the Lord, *a.* I.   *Phil* 4:4
a. I will be to him *a.*   *Heb* 1:5
and *a.* I will put my trust in.   2:13
begotten us *a.* to a lively. *1 Pet* 1:3
see **born, bring, brought, come,
turn, turned.**

against
hand will be *a.* every.   *Gen* 16:12
river's brink *a.* he come.   *Ex* 7:15*
set my face *a.* *Lev* 20:3; *Deut* 29:20
Urijah made it *a.* king.   *2 Ki* 16:11
a. whom hast thou exalted.   19:22
have pronounced *a.* it.   *Jer* 25:13
I am *a.* your pillows.   *Ezek* 13:20
a. his father. *Mat* 10:35; *Luke* 12:53
not with me, is *a.* me.   *Mat* 12:30
which shall be spoken *a.* *Luke* 2:34
a. him with 20,000 to.   14:31
cannot be spoken *a.*   *Acts* 19:36*
sect is every where spoken *a.* 28:22
see **another, God, him, Jerusalem, Israel, Lord, me, over,
thee, them, us, you.**

Agar
bondage, which is *A.*   *Gal* 4:24
A. is mount Sinai in Arabia.   25

agate, -s
an *a.* an amethyst. *Ex* 28:19; 39:12
make thy windows of *a.* *Isa* 54:12
in thy fairs with *a.* *Ezek* 27:16*

age
[1] *The whole continuance of a
man's life,* Gen 47:28. [2] *Times
past, present, or to come,* Eph 2:7;
3:5.

the whole *a.* of Jacob.   *Gen* 47:28
eyes of Israel were dim for *a.*   48:10
from the *a.* of 50 years. *Num* 8:25

---

die in the flower of their *a.* *1 Sam* 2:33
were set by reason of *a.*   *1 Ki* 14:4
from the *a.* of 30.   *1 Chr* 23:3
from the *a.* of twenty years and. 24
that stooped for *a.*   *2 Chr* 36:17*
thy grave in a full *a.*   *Job* 5:26
I pray thee, of the former *a.*   8:8
thy *a.* shall be clearer than. 11:17*
my *a.* is as nothing before. *Ps* 39:5
my *a.* is departed and. *Isa* 38:12†
man with his staff for *a.* *Zech* 8:4
a. of 12 years. *Mark* 5:42; *Luke* 8:42
was of a great *a.*   *Luke* 2:36
to be about 30 years of *a.*   3:23
he is of *a.* ask him. *John* 9:21, 23
pass the flower of her *a.* *1 Cor* 7:36
belongs to them of full *a.* *Heb* 5:14*
delivered when she was past *a.* 11:11

see old, stricken

aged
was a very *a.* man.   *2 Sam* 19:32
the understanding of *a.* *Job* 12:20
grey-headed and very *a.* men. 15:10
and the *a.* arose and stood up. 29:8
neither do the *a.* understand. 32:9
a. with him that is full. *Jer* 6:11
the *a.* men be sober, grave. *Tit* 2:2
the *a.* women, that they be.   3
such an one as Paul the *a.* *Philem* 9

ages
in the *a.* to come he might. *Eph* 2:7
in other *a.* was not made.   3:5*
in the church through all *a.* 21*
which hath been hid from *a. Col* 1:26

ago
were lost three days *a.* *1 Sam* 9:20
heard long *a.* *2 Ki* 19:25; *Isa* 37:26
builded many years *a.* *Ezra* 5:11
that fashioned it long *a.* *Isa* 22:11
repented long *a.*   *Mat* 11:21
         Luke 10:13
long *a.* since this came. *Mark* 9:21
4 days *a.* I was fasting. *Acts* 10:30
how that a good while *a.*   15:17
be forward a year *a.*   *2 Cor* 8:10
Achaia was ready a year *a.*   9:2
a man above fourteen years *a.* 12:2

agone
(*Revised Version,* ago)
three days *a.* I fell sick. *1 Sam* 30:13

agony
being in an *a.* he prayed. *Luke* 22:44

agree, -ed, -eth
[1] *To bargain with,* Mat 20:2, 13.
[2] *To approve, or give consent to,*
Acts 5:40. [3] *To be like,* Mark
14:70. [4] *To conspire, or resolve,*
John 9:22.

together except they be *a. Amos* 3:3
a. with thine adversary. *Mat* 3:25
if two of you shall *a.* on.   18:19
when he had *a.* with labourers. 20:2
not *a.* with me for a penny?   13
a. not together.   *Mark* 14:56, 59
art a Galilean, and thy speech *a.* 70*
out of the new, *a.* not. *Luke* 5:36
Jews had *a.* already. *John* 9:22
is it that ye have *a.* to. *Acts* 5:9
to him they *a.* and when they.   40
to this *a.* the words of the.   15:15
Jews have *a.* to desire.   23:20
when they *a.* not among.   28:25
blood, these *a.* in one. *1 John* 5:8
a. to give their kingdom. *Rev* 17:17

agreement
make an *a.* by *a.*   *2 Ki* 18:31
         Isa 36:16*
said, with hell are we at *a. Isa* 28:15
your *a.* with hell shall not stand. 18
of the north, to make an *a. Dan* 11:6
what *a.* hath the temple. *2 Cor* 6:16

Agrippa
A. and Bernice came to. *Acts* 25:13
A. said, I would also hear the. 22
specially before thee, O king *A.* 26
for which hope's sake, king *A.* 26:7
A. believest thou the prophets? 27
A. said almost thou persuadest. 28

aground
met, they ran the ship *a. Acts* 27:41

---

ague
(*Revised Version,* fever)
terror and the burning *a.* *Lev* 26:16

Agur
the words of *A.* the son of. *Pr* 30:1

ah
nor say, *a.* so would.   *Ps* 35:25*
a. sinful nation, a people. *Isa.* 1:4
a. I will ease me of mine.   24
said I, *a.* Lord God, I.   *Jer* 1:6
a. Lord God, thou hast.   4:10
a. Lord God, the prophets.   14:13
a. brother, *a.* sister, *a.* Lord, *a.*
         22:18
a. Lord, thou hast made the. 32:17
lament thee, saying, *a.* Lord. 34:5
a. Lord, my soul hath not. *Ezek* 4:14
a. Lord, wilt thou destroy the. 9:8
a. Lord, wilt thou make a full. 11:13
a. Lord, they say of me, doth. 20:49
a. the sword is made bright, it. 21:15
a. thou that destroyest. *Mark* 15:29*

aha
they said, *a.* our eye.   *Ps* 35:21
desolate, that say unto me *a.* 40.15
turned back that say *a. a.*   70:3
a. I am warm, I have.   *Isa* 44:16
a. against my sanctuary. *Ezek.* 25:3
because Tyrus hath said, *a.*   26:2
a. the ancient places are ours. 36:2

Ahab
A. did evil above all.   *1 Ki* 16:30
A. did more to provoke Lord. 33
Elijah, go shew thyself to *A.* 18:1
A. went one way, and Obadiah. 6
deliver me into the hand of *A.* 9
so *A.* went up to eat and to drink. 42
Elijah ran before *A.* to the. 46
there came a prophet to *A.* 20:13
A. came to his house heavy. 21:4
I will cut off from *A.* him that. 21
there was none like *A.* who did. 25
seest thou how *A.* humbleth. 29
persuade *A.* that he may go up and
  fall at?   22:20; *2 Chr* 18:19
so *A.* slept with his fathers. *I Ki* 22:40
after death of *A.*   *2 Ki* 1:1; 3:5
Jeroboam walked as did the house of
  A. for the daughter of *A.* 8:18, 27
thou shalt smite the house of *A.* 9:7
for the whole house of *A.* shall. 8
when I and thou rode after *A.* 25
slew all that remained of *A.* 10:11
Manasseh did as *A.* king of. 21:3
the plummet of house of *A.* 13
of the house of *A.*   *2 Chr.* 21:13
saith the Lord of *A.* son. *Jer* 29:21
the Lord make thee like *A.* 22
works of the house of *A.*   *Mi* 6:16

Ahasuerus
in the reign of *A.* wrote.   *Ezra* 4:6
this is *A.* which reigned. *Esth* 1:1
Esther was taken unto king *A.* 2:16
to lay hand on the king *A.* 21; 6:2
in the name of *A.* was it. 3:12; 8:10
A. gave to Esther the house. 8:1
the Jew was next to king *A.* 10:3
first year of Darius son of *A. Dan* 9:1

the river that runneth to *A. Ezra* 8:15
a fast at *A.*   21
then we departed from *A.*   31

Ahaz
A. was twenty years old when he
  began to.   *2 Ki* 16:2; *2 Chr* 28:1
made an altar against *A.* *2 Ki* 16:11
in the dial of *A.*   20:11; *Isa* 38:8
the altars of *A.* did Josiah. *2 Ki* 23:12
Micah, Pithon, *A.* *1 Chr* 8:35; 9:41
Judah low, because of *A. 2 Chr* 28:19
this is that king, *A.*   22
A. gathered vessels.   24
the vision in days of *A.*   *Isa* 1:1
         Hos 1:1; *Mi* 1:1
go forth to meet *A.*   *Isa* 7:3
the Lord spake to *A.*   10

Ahaziah
A. reigned in. *1 Ki* 22:40; *2 Ki* 8:24
A. fell through a lattice.   *2 Ki* 1:2
A. king of Judah went down. 8:29
A. there is treachery, O *A.* 9:23

A. fled, and Jehu followed. *2 Ki 9:*27
we are the brethren of *A.*   10:13
did join with *A.*   *2 Chr 20:*35
destruction of *A.* was of God.   22:7
house of *A.* had no power to keep. 9

Ahiah
A. son of Ahitub, the.   *1 Sam 14:*3
Saul said to *A.* bring hither the.   18
Elihoreph and *A.* were.   *1 Ki 4:*3

Ahijah
the prophet *A.* found.   *1 Ki 11:*29
his saying, which the Lord spake by
   A.   12:15; *2 Chr 10:*15
there is *A.* which told me I. *1 Ki 14:*2
wife came to the house of *A.*   4
it was so, when *A.* heard the.   6
Baasha son of *A.* conspired   15:27
Jerahmeel, Hezron, *A.*   *1 Chr 2:*25
David's valiant men, *A.* the.   11:36
over treasury of Levites *A.*   26:20
Solomon in prophecy of *A. 2 Chr 9:*29
sealed the covenant, *A.*   *Neh 10:*26

Ahikam
commanded *A.* the son of Shaphan.
   *2 Ki 22:*12; *2 Chr 34:*20
Gedaliah the son of *A.*   *2 Ki 25:*22
the hand of *A.* was with.   *Jer 26:*24
to Gedaliah the son of *A.*   40:6
   see **Gedaliah**

Ahimaaz
was the daughter of *A. 1 Sam 14:*50
Jonathan and *A.* staid. *2 Sam 17:*17
is like the running of *A.* son.   18:27
A. was in Naphtali, the.   *1 Ki 4:*15
begat Zadok, and Zadok *A. 1 Chr 6:*8

Ahiman
A. was of the children.   *Num 13:*22
Judah slew *A.*   *Judg 1:*10
porters, *A.*   *1 Chr 9:*17

Ahimelech
A. was afraid at the.   *1 Sam 21:*1
the son of Jesse coming to *A.*   22:9
thou shalt surely die, *A.*   16
David said to *A.* who will go?   26:6
Zadok and *A.* priests.   *2 Sam 8:*17
   *1 Chr 18:*16
A. of the sons of Ithamar. *1 Chr 24:*3
scribe wrote them before *A.*   6
in the presence of David and *A.*   31

Ahinoam
Saul's wife was *A.*   *1 Sam 14:*50
David also took *A.* of Jezreel. 25:43
   see **Abigail**

Ahio
A. drave the cart.   *2 Sam 6:*3
   *1 Chr 13:*7

Ahisamach
both he and the son of *A. Ex 35:*34

Ahithophel
Absalom sent for *A. 2 Sam 15:*12
Lord, turn the counsel of *A.* into. 31
thou defeat the counsel of *A.*   34
to Jerusal, and *A.* with him.   16:15
counsel of *A.* was as if a man.   23
the counsel of *A.* is not good.   17:7
thus did *A.* counsel Absalom.   15
A. saw that his counsel was not. 23
A. was the king's.   *1 Chr 27:*33

Ahitub
hear now, thou son of *A. 1 Sam 22:*12
son of *A. 2 Sam 8:*17; *1 Chr 18:*16

Aholah, Aholibah
is *A.* Jerusalem Aholibah. *Ezek 23:*4
judge *A.* and Aholibah?   36

Aholiab
wrought Bezaleel and *A. Exod 36:*1

Aholibamah
Esau took to wife *A.*   *Gen 36:*2
A. bare Jeush.   5

Ai, or Hai
between Beth-el and *A.*   *Gen 13:*3
fled before the men of *A.*   *Josh 7:*4
go up to *A.*   8:1
Gibeon was greater than *A.*   10:2
men of Beth-el and *A.*   *Ezra 2:*28
   *Neh 7:*32
howl, O Heshbon, for *A.*   *Jer 49:*3

Aiath
he is come to *A.* he is.   *Isa 10:*28

---

aided
a. him in the killing of.   *Judg 9:*24

ailed, -eth
what *a.* thee, Hagar?   *Gen 21:*17
to Micah, what *a.* thee? *Judg 18:*23
a. the people to weep? *1 Sam 11:*5
said, what *a. 2 Sam 14:*5; *2 Ki 6:*28
what *a.* thee, O sea, that? *Ps 114:*5
what *a.* thee now, that.   *Isa 22:*1

air
nor birds of the *a.* to.   *2 Sam 21:*10
no *a.* can come between.   *Job 41:*16
way of an eagle in the *a.*   *Pr 30:*19
bird of the *a.* shall carry. *Eccl 10:*20
the birds of the *a.* have.   *Mat. 8:*20*
the birds of the *a.* come and lodge in.
   13:32*; *Mark 4:*32*; *Luke 9:*58*
they threw dust into the *a. Acts 22:*23
I, not as one that beateth the *a.*
   *1 Cor 9:*26
for ye shall speak into the *a.*   14:9
prince of the power of the *a. Eph 2:*2
meet the Lord in the *a. 1 Thes 4:*17
the sun and the *a.* were.   *Rev 9:*2
poured out his vial into the *a.*   16:17
   see **fowls**

Ajalon
moon, in the valley of *A. Josh 10:*12

alabaster
having an *a.* box.   *Mat 26:*7
   *Mark 14:*3

alarm
blow an *a.* then the.   *Num 10:*5, 6
blow, but shall not sound an *a.*   7
go to war, then ye shall blow an *a.* 9
trumpets to cry an *a. 2 Chr 13:*12
O my soul, the *a.* of war. *Jer 4:*19
day is come, I will cause an *a.* 49:2
sound an *a.* in my holy.   *Joel 2:*1
a day of *a.* against the.   *Zeph 1:*16

alas
Aaron said to Moses, *a. Num 12:*11
a. who shall live when God?   24:23
Joshua said, *a.* O Lord,   *Josh 7:*7
a. because I have seen an. *Judg 6:*22
a. daughter, thou hast brought. 11:35
mourned over him, *a.*   *1 Ki 13:*30
a. that the Lord hath.   *2 Ki 3:*10
he cried. *a.* master, for it was.   6:5
servant said, *a.* my master, how. 15
a. for that day is great.   *Jer 30:*7
with thy foot, and say *a. Ezek 6:*11
a. for the day, for the.   *Joel 1:*15
say in the highways, *a.*   *Amos 5:*16
a. a. that great city, Babylon
   Rev. 18:10*, 16, 19*

albeit
the Lôrd saith, *a.* I have. *Ezek 13:*7
a. I say not, how thou.   *Philem 19*

Alexander
Simon the father of *A. Mark 15:*21
Annas, Caiaphas, *A.* were. *Acts 4:*6
they drew *A.* out of the.   19:33
is Hymeneus and *A.*   *1 Tim 1:*20
A. the copper smith did. *2 Tim 4:*14

Alexandria, -ans
of the Libertines and *A.*   *Acts 6:*9
named Apollos, born at *A.*   18:24
centurion found a ship of *A.*   27:6

alien, -s
an *a.* in a strange land.   *Ex 18:*3
mayest sell it to an *a. Deut 14:*21
I am an *a.* in their sight. *Job 19:*15
a. to my mother's children. *Ps 69:*8
sons of the *a.* shall be.   *Isa 61:*5
houses are turned to *a. Lam 5:*2
a. from the commonwealth. *Eph 2:*12
flight the armies of *a. Heb 11:*34

alienate, -ed
her mind was *a.* from.   *Ezek 23:*17
mind was *a.* from her as from.   18
from whom thy mind is *a.*   22, 28
they shall not *a.* the first fruits. 48:14
a. from the life of God. *Eph 4:*18
sometimes *a.* enemies.   *Col 1:*21

alike
and clean eat *a. Deut 12:*22; 15:22
they shall part *a.*   *1 Sam 30:*24
they shall lie down *a.* in. *Job 21:*26
fashioneth their hearts *a. Ps. 33:*15*

---

and light are both *a.*   *Ps 139:*12
both are *a.* abomination to. *Pr 20:*10
a contentious woman are *a.*   27:15
all things come *a.* to all.   *Eccl 9:*2
they both shall be *a.* good.   11:6
esteemeth every day *a.*   *Rom 14:*5

alive
[1] *Naturally,* Gen 43:27. [2]
*Supernaturally, being raised from
the dead,* Luke 24:23. [3] *Spiritually,* Rom 6:11.
Noah only remained *a.*   *Gen 7:*23
kill me, and save thee *a.*   12:12
day, to save much people *a.*   50:20
the men children *a.*   *Ex 1:*17, 18
every daughter ye shall save *a.*   22
theft be found in his hand *a.*   22:4
Aaron's sons left *a.*   *Lev 10:*16
command to take two birds *a.*   14:4
scapegoat shall be presented *a.* 16:10
are left *a.* of you, I will send. 26:36
they went down *a.* into.   *Num 16:*33
Og, till there was none left *a.* 21:35
slain thee, and saved her *a.*   22:33
ye saved all the women *a.* ?   31:15
are *a.* every one of you.   *Deut 4:*4
who are all of us *a.* here this.   5:3
he might preserve us *a.*   6:24
a. nothing that breatheth.   20:16
and I make *a.*   32:39; *1 Sam 2:*6
will save *a.* my father.   *Josh 2:*13
saved Rahab the harlot *a.*   6:25
the king of Ai they took *a.*   8:23
Lord hath kept me *a.* as he.   14:10
if ye had saved them *a.* I. *Judg 8:*19
which they had saved *a.*   21:14
Agag the king of Amalek *a.*
   *1 Sam 15:*8
left neither man nor woman *a.* 27:9
horses and mules *a.*   *1 Ki 18:*5
peace or war take them *a.*   20:18
Naboth is not *a.* but dead.   21:15
God, to kill and make *a.* ? *2 Ki 5:*7
if they save us *a.* we shall live. 7:4
out we shall catch them *a.*   12
a. and they took them *a.*   10:14
ten thousand left *a.*   *2 Chr 25:*12
thou hast kept me *a.*   *Ps 30:*3
let us swallow them up *a.*   *Pr 1:*12
fatherless I will preserve *a. Jer 49:*11
will ye save the souls *a.* ? *Ezek 13:*18
save the souls *a.* that should.   19
right, he shall save his soul *a.* 18:27
whom he would, he kept *a. Dan 5:*19
heard that he was *a.*   *Mark 16:*11
was dead and is *a. Luke 15:*24, 32
angels who said he was *a.*   24:23
shewed himself *a.* after his. *Acts 1:*3
the widows, presented her *a.*   9:41
they brought the young man *a.* 20:12
whom Paul affirmed to be *a.*   25:19
a. to God through Christ. *Rom 6:*11
God, as those that are *a.* from.   13
for I was *a.* without the law.   7:9
so in Christ shall all be made *a.*
   *1 Cor 15:*22
are *a.* and remain. *1 Thes 4:*15, 17
and behold I am *a.* for.   *Rev 1:*18
last, which was dead, and is *a.* 2:8
both cast *a.* into a lake of fire. 19:20

keep alive, see keep

yet alive
is your father *yet a.* ?   *Gen 43:*7
is he *yet a.* ?   27
he is well, he is *yet a.*   28
saying, Joseph is *yet a.*   45:26, 28
die, because thou art *yet a.*   46:30
see whether they be *yet a. Ex 4:*18
I am *yet a.* with you.   *Deut 31:*27
child was *yet a. 2 Sam 12:*18; 21, 22
while he was *yet a.* in the.   18:14
is he *yet a.* ? he is my.   *1 Ki 20:*32
living which are *yet a.*   *Eccl 4:*2
although they were *yet a. Ezek 7:*13
said, while he was yet *a. Mat 27:*63

all
surely die, thou and *a.*   *Gen 20:*7
to him hath he given *a.* that.   24:36
Laban said, *a.* that thou.   31:43
Jacob loved Joseph more than *a.*
   37:3

Lord made *a.* he did to. *Gen* 39:3
we are *a.* one man's sons, we. 42:11
lest thou and *a.* thou hast. 45:11
the God which fed me *a.* my. 48:15
earth, sea, and *a.* in them. *Ex* 20:11
I will make *a.* my goodness. 33:19
a. that come into the tent. *Num* 19:14
and shalt not see them *a.* 23:13
are *a.* of us here alive. *Deut* 5:3
days shalt thou labour and do *a.* 13
ye stand *a.* of you before the ? 29:10
a. came to pass. *Josh* 21:45; 23:14
plague was on you *a.* 1 *Sam* 6:4
I will tell thee *a.* that is in. 9:19
Samuel said, are here *a.* thy ? 16:11
and without fail recover *a.* 30:8
are *a.* that pertained to. 2 *Sam* 16:4
away dung till it be *a.* 1 *Ki* 14:10
Omri did worse than *a.* before. 16:25
lord, I am thine, and *a.* that. 20:4
the son of Uzzi, *a.* of. 1 *Chr* 7:3
is against *a.* that forsake. *Ezra* 8:22
thou preservest them *a.* and. *Neh* 9:6
comforters are ye *a.* *Job* 16:2
for they *a.* are the work of. 34:19
a. gone aside, *a.* become. *Ps* 14:3
a. my bones, they stare upon. 22:17
delivereth him out of them *a.* 34:19
Lord, *a.* my desire is before. 38:9
a. this is come upon us, yet. 44:17
mine adversaries are *a.* 69:19
these wait *a.* on thee, that. 104:27
they continue, for *a.* are thy. 119:91
cast in thy lot, let us *a* have. *Pr* 1:14
Lord is the maker of them *a.* 22:2
a. are of dust, *a.* turn to. *Eccl* 3:20
behold, see, we are *a.* thy. *Isa* 64:9
a. adulterers. *Jer* 9:2; *Hos* 7:4
a. of them mourning. *Ezek* 7:16
a. of them in the land shall. 20:40
king shall be king to them *a.* 37:22
son of man, declare *a.* that. 40:4
shew them *a.* the forms, *a.* the. 43:11
among them *a.* none. *Dan* 1:19
been a rebuker of them *a.* *Hos* 5:2
cut them in the head *a.* *Amos* 9:1
city, it is *a.* full of lies. *Nah* 3:1
have we not *a.* one Father. *Mal* 2:10
bring *a.* the tithes into the. 3:10*
pass from the law till *a.* *Mat* 5:18
sisters, are they not *a.* 13:56
she be, for they *a.* had her. 22:28
than *a.* burnt-offerings. *Mark* 12:33
cast in *a.* even *a.* 44; *Luke* 21:4
thou worship me, *a.* shall. *Luke* 4:7
looking round about on them *a.* 6:10
they were *a.* waiting for him. 8:40
except ye repent, ye shall *a.* 13:3
he said, son *a.* that I have is. 15:31
ye, when ye have done *a.* say. 17:10
sell *a.* that thou hast, and. 18:22
of his fulness have *a.* we. *John* 1:16
woman said, he told me *a.* 4:39
saith, ye are clean, but not *a.* 13:10
that they *a.* may be one, as. 17:21
grace was upon them *a.* *Acts* 4:33
we are *a.* here present before 10:33
he exhorted them *a.* to cleave. 11:23
do thyself no harm, we are *a.* 16:28
zealous towards God, as ye *a.* 22:3
but also *a.* that hear me this. 26:29
thanks in presence of them *a.* 27:35
through Jesus Christ for you *a.*
 Rom 1:8
delivered him up for us *a.* 8:32
a. are yours, and ye. 1 *Cor* 3:22
more abundantly than they *a.* 15:10
concluded *a.* under sin. *Gal* 3:22
but I have *a.* and abound. *Phil* 4:18
that they *a.* might be. 2 *Thes* 2:12
out of them *a.* the Lord. 2 *Tim* 3:11
they not *a.* ministering. *Heb* 1:14
chastisement, whereof *a.* are. 12:8
be ye *a.* of one mind. 1 *Pet* 3:8
that *a.* should come to. 2 *Pet* 3:9
that they were not *a.* of. 1 *John* 2:19

above all, *see* **above**

according to all
Noah did *ac.* to *a.* *Gen* 6:22; 7:5
according to the Lord. *Ex* 31:11
 36:1; 39:32, 42; 40:16; *Num* 2:34
 8:20; 9:5; 29:40; *Deut* 1:3, 41
took the land *ac.* to *a.* *Josh* 11:23

given rest *ac. to a.* that. 1 *Ki* 8:56
shalt reign *ac. to a.* that thy. 11:37
ac. to a. his father had done. 22:53
 2 *Ki* 23:32, 37; 24:9, 19
 2 *Chr* 26:4; 27:2
done *ac. to a.* that was. 2 *Ki* 10:30
ac to a. David. 18:3; 2 *Chr* 29:2
ac. to a. these words, *ac. to a.* this.
 1 *Chr* 17:15
think . . . for good, *ac. to a.* *Neh* 5:19
ac. to a. his wondrous. *Jer* 21:2
ac. to a. that the Lord shall. 42:20
ac. to a. that Babylon hath. 50:29
ac. to a. that he hath. *Ezek* 24:24
ac. to a. thy righteousness. *Dan* 9:16

after **all**
not to do *after a.* their. *Deut* 20:18
the word to do *after a.* 2 *Chr* 34:21
after a. that is come on. *Ezra* 9:13
after a. thy wickedness. *Ezek* 16:23
after a. these things do. *Mat* 6:32
for he longed *after* you *a.* *Phil* 2:26

at **all**
delivered thy people *at a.* *Ex* 5:23
afflict, and they cry *at a.* to. 22:23
if he will *at a.* redeem. *Lev* 27:13*
I now any power *at a.* *Num* 22:38
if thou do *at a.* forget. *Deut* 8:19*
if thy father *at a.* miss. 1 *Sam* 20:6
if ye shall *at a.* turn. 1 *Ki* 9:6*
not save them *at a.* *Jer* 11:12
mind shall not be *at a.* *Ezek* 20:32
most High, none *at a.* *Hos* 11:7
weep ye not *at a.* roll. *Mi* 1:10
Lord will not *at a.* acquit. *Nah* 1:3
have no power *at a.* *John* 19:11
his will was not *at a.* 1 *Cor* 16:12
him is no darkness *at a.* 1 *John* 1:5
be found no more *at a.* *Rev* 18:21
shall be heard no more *at a.* 22

before **all**
before a. that went in at. *Gen* 23:18
before a. the people I will. *Lev* 10:3
I have chosen *before a.* 2 *Chr* 33:7
an honour *before a.* *Jer* 33:9
denied *before a.* them *a.* *Mat* 26:70
to Peter *before* them *a.* *Gal* 2:14
sin rebuke *before* *a.* that. 1 *Tim* 5:20

for **all**
Levites *for a.* first-born. *Num* 8:18
for a. that do so. *Deut* 22:5; 25:16
hide my face in that day *for a.* 31:18
for a. his enemies. *Ps* 10:5
for a. this they sinned still. 78:32
what render to the Lord *for a.* 116:12
profit of the earth is *for a.* *Eccl* 5:9
for a. these God will bring thee. 11:9
hath received double *for a.* *Isa* 40:2
alas *for a.* the evil. *Ezek* 6:11
loathe yourselves *for a.* 20:43
and in it was meat *for a.* *Dan* 4:21
for a. the evils Herod. *Luke* 3:19
God of the living, *for a.* live. 20:38
for a. have sinned and. *Rom* 3:23
if one died *for a.* then. 2 *Cor* 5:14
for a. seek their own, not. *Phil* 2:21
himself a ransom *for a.* 1 *Tim* 2:6
for a. shall know me. *Heb* 8:11
the body of Christ once *for a.* 10:10

from **all**
redeemed me *from a.* *Gen* 48:16
be clean *from a.* your. *Lev* 16:30
and delivered me *from a.* *Ps* 34:4
from a. lands whither he. *Jer* 16:15
diverse *from a.* the beasts. *Dan* 7:7
seventh day *from a.* works. *Heb* 4:4

in **all**
in *a.* that Sarah hath said. *Gen* 21:12
God is with thee *in a.* that thou. 22
ye may prosper *in a.* *Deut* 29:9
obeyed my voice *in a.* *Josh* 22:2
thirty and seven *in a.* 2 *Sam* 23:39
thou mayest prosper *in a.* 1 *Ki* 2:3
afflicted *in a.* my father was. 26
Zerah, five of them *in a.* 1 *Chr* 2:6
just *in a.* that is brought. *Neh* 9:33
God is not *in a.* his. *Ps* 10:4
in a. thy ways acknowledge. *Pr* 3:6
nothing *in a.* his dominion. *Isa* 39:2
in a. their afflictions he was. 63:9
have done evil *in a.* they. *Jer* 38:9
in a. your doings your. *Ezek* 21:24

in a. my labours shall find. *Hos* 12:8
in a. in the ship 276 souls. *Acts* 27:37
in a. these more than. *Rom* 8:37
God worketh all *in a.* 1 *Cor* 12:6
that God may be all *in a.* 15:28
him that filleth all *in a.* *Eph* 1:23
but Christ is all and *in a.* *Col* 3:11
to be admired *in a.* 2 *Thes* 1:10
is honourable *in a.* *Heb* 13:4
as also *in a.* his epistles. 2 *Pet* 3:16

all night, *see* **night**

of **all**
took them wives of *a.* *Gen* 6:2
him tithes of *a.* 14:20; *Heb* 7:2
of *a.* that thou shalt give. *Gen* 28:22
nothing die of *a.* that is. *Ex* 9:4
not a word of *a.* which *Josh* 8:35
of *a.* I said to the. *Judg* 13:13
shall hands of *a.* with. 2 *Sam* 16:21
Jehu said, to which of *a.* 2 *Ki* 9:5
let nothing fail of *a.* thou. *Esth* 6:10
so are the paths of *a.* that. *Job* 8:13
he wanteth nothing of *a.* *Eccl.* 6:2
if they be ashamed of *a.* *Ezek* 43:11
you only have I known of *a.* *Amos* 3:2
be servant of *a.* *Mark* 9:35 ; 10:44
of *a.* which hath given. *John* 6:39
Christ, he is Lord of *a.* *Acts* 10:36
of *a.* judged of *a.* 1 *Cor* 14:24
heir, though he be lord of *a.* *Gal* 4:1
God who is Father of *a.* *Eph.* 4:6
to God the Judge of *a.* *Heb* 12:23
one point, he is guilty of *a.* *Jas* 2:10

on or *upon* **all**
of the Lord was *upon a.* *Gen* 39:5
for *upon a.* the glory shall. *Isa* 4:5
set thy heart *upon a.* that. *Ezek* 40:4
unto all, and *upon a.* them. *Rom* 3:22
might have mercy *upon a.* 11:32
execute judgment *upon a.* *Jude* 15
temptation shall come *upon a.*
 Rev 3:10

over **all**
mayest reign *over a.* 2 *Sam* 3:21
and thou reignest *over a.* 1 *Chr* 29:12
kingdom ruleth *over a.* *Ps* 103:19
ruler *over a.* *Mat* 24:47; *Luke* 12:44
given him power *over a.* *John* 17:2
who is *over a.* God blessed. *Rom* 9:5
the same Lord *over a.* is rich. 10:12

all, *that he had*
him and *a. that he had.* *Gen* 12:20
of Egypt, and *a. that he had.* 13:1
Abraham gave *a. that he had.* 25:5
Jacob fled with *a. that he had.* 31:21
a. that he had he put into. 39:4
Lord was on *a. that he had.* 5
sold, *a. that he had.* *Mat* 18:25
spent *a. that she had.* *Mark* 5:26
cast in *a. that she had.* 12:44
 Luke 21:4

all *these*
he took to him *a. these.* *Gen* 15:10
Jacob said, *a. these* things. 42:36
a. these are the twelve tribes. 49:28
God spake *a. these* words. *Ex.* 20:1
not that in *a. these.* *Deut* 12:9
for *a. these* nations are. *Jer* 9:26
shall not *a. these* take. *Hab* 2:6
a. these shall. *Mat* 6:33; *Luke* 12:31
a. these are the beginning. *Mat* 24:8
a. these evil things. *Mark* 7:23
are not *a. these* which. *Acts* 2:7
a. these worketh that. 1 *Cor* 12:11
now you put off *a. these.* *Col* 3:8
a. these died in faith, not. *Heb* 11:13

all *the while*
a. the while David. 1 *Sam* 22:4
nothing missing *a. the while.* 25:7
manner *a. the while* he. 27:11
a. the while my breath is. *Job* 27:3*

all *this*
hath shewed thee *a. this.* *Gen* 41:39
Lord hath not done *a. this.*
 Deut 32:27
is *a. this* befallen us ? *Judg* 6:13
knew nothing of *a. this.* 1 *Sam* 22:15
hand of Joab in *a. this* ? 2 *Sam* 14:19
a. this the Lord made. 1 *Chr* 28:19
after *a. this* the Lord. 2 *Chr* 21:18
a. this continued till the. 29:28
a. this was a burnt-. *Ezra* 8:35

because of *a. this* we.   *Neh* 9:38
yet *a. this* availeth me.   *Esth* 5:13
a. this Job sinned.   *Job* 1:22; 2:10
lo, mine eye hath seen *a. this.*   13:1
a. this is come upon us, yet. *Ps* 44:17
for *a. this* they sinned still.   78:32
a. this have I proved by.   *Eccl* 7:23
a. this have I seen, and applied. 8:9
a. this I considered in my heart, to
  declare *a. this.*   9:1
for *a. this* his anger is not. *Isa* 5:25
  9:12, 17, 21; 10:4
thou hast heard, see *a. this.*   48:6
a. this came upon.   *Dan* 4:28
though thou knewest *a. this.*   5:22
asked him the truth of *a. this.* 7:16
nor seek him for *a. this.*   *Hos* 7:10
of Jacob is *a. this.*   *Mi* 1:5
a. this was done that the prophets
  might be. *Mat* 1:22; 21:4; 26:56
a. this there is a gulf. *Luke* 16:26
besides *a. this* to-day is.   24:21

to or unto all

the Lord is good *to a.* and. *Ps* 145:9
event happeneth *to a.*   *Eccl* 2:14
  9:3, 11
things come alike *to a.* one.   9:2
so is Pharaoh *to a.* that.   *Isa* 36:6
I say *unto a.* watch.   *Mark* 13:37
to us, or even *to a.?*   *Luke* 12:41
the promise is *to a.* that. *Acts* 2:39
manifest *to a.* that dwell in.   4:16
Lord is rich *unto a.* that. *Rom* 10:12
render therefore *to a.* their.   13:7
myself a servant *unto a.* *1 Cor* 9:19
profiting may appear *to a.* *1 Tim* 4:15

with all

with a. that appertain.   *Num* 16:30
Lord *with a.* thy heart, *with a.* thy.
  Deut 6:5; 11:13; *Mat* 22:37
with a. the children of.   *2 Chr* 25:7
with a. thy getting, get.   *Pr* 4:7
feared God *with a.* Acts *10*:2; 16:34
with a. that in every place. *1 Cor* 1:2
and continue *with* you a.   *Phil* 1:25
I joy and rejoice *with* you a.   2:17

all *ye*

a. ye assemble yourselves. *Isa* 48:14
behold *a. ye* that kindle a.   50:11
be glad with her, *a. ye* that.   66:10
hear the word, *a. ye* that. *Jer* 29:20
it nothing to you, *a. ye?*   *Lam* 1:12
come to me, *a. ye* that.   *Mat* 11:28
one is your master; and *a. ye.* 23:8
a. ye shall be.   26:31; *Mark* 14:27
a. ye that dwell at.   *Acts* 2:14

see further other usual substan-
tives : **congregation, day, earth,**
Israel, men, people, things, *etc.*

alleging

a. Christ must needs.   *Acts* 17:3

allegory

which things are an *a.* for. *Gal* 4:24

allelujah

(*Revised Version,* hallelujah)
I heard a great voice, saying. *a.*
  Rev 19:1, 3, 4, 6

allied

Eliashib the priest was *a.* *Neh* 13:4

allow

that ye *a.* the deeds. *Luke* 11:48*
they themselves as *a.* *Acts* 24:15*
that which I do, I *a.* not. *Rom* 7:15*

allowance

his *a.* was a continual *a.* *2 Ki* 25:30

allowed, -eth

(*Revised Version,* approved, -eth)
that thing which he *a.*   *Rom* 14:22
but as we were *a.* of.   *1 Thes* 2:4

allure

I will *a.* and bring her into. *Hos* 2:14
they *a.* through the lusts. *2 Pet* 2:18

almighty

I am the *a.* God, walk.   *Gen* 17:1
God *a.* bless thee, and make.   28:3
I am God *a.* be fruitful and.   35:11
God *a* give you mercy before. 43:14
God *a.* appeared to me at Luz. 48:3
by the *a.* who shall bless thee. 49:25

Abram by the name God *a.*   *Ex* 6:3
the vision of the *a.*   *Num* 24:4, 16
for the *a.* hath dealt.   *Ruth* 1:20
seeing the *a.* hath afflicted me.   21
the chastening of the *a.*   *Job* 5:17
for the arrows of the *a.* are.   6:4
he forsaketh the fear of the *a.*   14
or doth the *a.* pervert justice ?   8:3
make thy supplication to the *a.*   5
canst thou find out the *a.?*   11:7
surely I would speak to the *a.*   13:3
himself against the *a.*   15:25
what is the *a.* that we ?   21:15
drink of the wrath of the *a.*   20
is it any pleasure to the *a.?*   22:3
which said, what can the *a.* do ?   17
if thou return to the *a.* thou shalt. 23
yea, the *a.* shall be thy defence.   25
thou have thy delight in the *a.*   26
my heart soft, and the *a.*   23:16
times are not hid from the *a.*   24:1
and the *a.* who hath vexed my. 27:2
will he delight himself in the *a.?* 10
with the *a.* will I not conceal.   11
which they shall receive of the *a.* 13
when the *a.* was yet with me.   29:5
what inheritance of the *a.?*   31:2
my desire is, that the *a.* would. 35
inspiration of the *a.* giveth.   32:8
and the breath of the *a.* hath. 33:4
far be it from the *a.* to.   34:10
neither will the *a.* pervert.   12
the *a.* will not regard vanity. 35:13
touching the *a.* we cannot.   37:23
contendeth with the *a.* instruct. 40:2
when the *a.* scattered.   *Ps* 68:14
under the shadow of the *a.*   91:1
as destruction from the *a.* *Isa* 13:6
the voice of the *a.* *Ezek* 1:24; 10:5
as destruction from the *a. Joel* 1:15
sons, saith the Lord *a.*   *2 Cor* 6:18
was, and is to come, the *a. Rev* 1:8
Lord God *a.* which was. 4:8; 11:17
Lord *a.* just and true are. 15:3; 16:7
of that great day of God *a.*   16:14
wine-press of wrath of the *a.*   19:15
God *a.* and the Lamb are.   21:22

almond, -s

spices, myrrh, nuts, and *a. Gen* 43:11
made like to *a.*   *Ex* 25:33*, 34*
  37:19, 20*
Aaron for Levi yielded *a. Num* 17:8
when the *a.* tree shall.   *Eccl* 12:5
I see a rod of an *a.* tree .   *Jer* 1:11

almost

they be *a.* ready to stone.   *Ex* 17:4
me, my feet were *a.* gone. *Ps* 73:2
soul had *a.* dwelt in silence. 94:17*
they had *a.* consumed me.   119:87
I was *a.* in all evil in the.   *Pr* 5:14*
came *a.* the whole city. *Acts* 13:44
only at Ephesus, but *a.*   19:26
seven days were *a.* ended.   21:27
a. thou persuadest me to.   26:28*
were both *a.* and altogether.   29*
a. all things by the law. *Heb* 9:22

alms

that ye do not your *a.*   *Mat* 6:1*
therefore when thou doest thine *a.* 2*
that thine *a.* may be in secret, and. 4
give *a.* of such things. *Luke* 11:41
sell that ye have, and give *a.* 12:33
they laid, to ask *a.* of.   *Acts* 3:2
seeing Peter and John, asked an *a.* 3
that it was he which sat for *a.*   10
Cornelius gave much *a.* to the. 10:2
a. are come up for a memorial. 4, 31
I came to bring *a.* to my.   24:17

almsdeeds

Dorcas full of *a.* which. *Acts* 9:36

almug-trees

Ophir plenty of *a.*-trees. *1 Ki* 10:11
a.-tree pillars, there came no such
  a.-trees.   12

aloes

thy garments smell of *a.*   *Ps* 45:8
perfumed my bed with *a.*   *Pr* 7:17
myrrh, *a.* with all the.   *S of S* 4:14
brought a mixture of *a. John* 19:39

alone

that man should be *a.*   *Gen* 2:18
perform it thyself *a.*   *Ex* 18:18

Moses *a.* shall come near.   *Ex* 24:2
leper dwell *a.* without.   *Lev* 13:46
to bear all this people *a. Num* 11:14
  Deut 1:9, 12
thou bear it not thyself *a. Num* 11:17
the people shall dwell *a.* not.   23:9
so the Lord *a.* did lead. *Deut* 32:12
then shall dwell in safety *a.* 33:28*
Achan perished not *a.*   *Josh* 22:20
a man running *a.*   *2 Sam* 18:24, 26
if he be *a.* there is tidings in his. 25
they two were *a.* in.   *1 Ki* 11:29
art the God *a. 2 Ki* 19:15; *Isa* 37:16
  Ps 86:10
Solomon, whom *a.* God. *1 Chr* 29:1
lay hands on Mordecai *a. Esth* 3:6
escaped *a.* to tell. *Job* 1:15, 16, 17, 19
God who *a.* spreadeth out the. 9:8
to whom *a.* the earth was.   15:19
eaten my morsel myself *a. ?* 31:17
thou whose name *a.* is.   *Ps* 83:18
watch and am as a sparrow *a.* 102:7
who *a.* doth great wonders.   136:4
for his name *a.* is excellent. 148:13
is one *a.* and there is not . *Eccl* 4:8
but woe to him that is *a.* when he. 10
Lord *a.* shall be exalted. *Isa* 2:11, 17
none shall be *a.* in his.   14:31*
I called him *a.* and blessed.   51:2*
have trodden the wine-press *a.* 63:3
he sitteth *a.* and keepeth. *Lam* 3:28
I Daniel *a.* saw the vision. *Dan* 10:7
to Assyria, a wild ass *a.*   *Hos* 8:9
live by bread *a. Mat* 4:4; *Luke* 4:4
come, he was *a.*   *Mat* 14:22
  Luke 9:18
between thee and him *a. Mat* 18:15
when they were *a.* he.   *Mark* 4:34
was in midst of sea, and he *a.* 6:47
forgive sins but God *a.?* *Luke* 5:21
to eat, but for the priests *a.*   6:4
came to pass, as Jesus was *a.* 9:18
voice was past, Jesus was found *a.* 36
sister hath left me to serve *a.* 10:40
into a mountain *a.*   *John* 6:15
disciples were gone away *a.*   22
for I am not *a.* but I. 8:16; 16:32
neither pray I for these *a.*   17:20
and hear that not *a.*   *Acts* 19:26
written for his sake *a.*   *Rom* 4:23
have rejoicing in himself *a. Gal* 6:4
went the high-priest *a.*   *Heb* 9:7
not works is dead, being *a. Jas* 2:17*

left alone

Jacob *left a.* and there.   *Gen* 32:24
dead, and he is *left a.* 42:38*; 44:20
I was *left a.* these where. *Isa* 49:21
I was *left a.* and saw this. *Dan* 10:8
and Jesus was *left a.*   *John* 8:9
the Father hath not *left* me *a.* for. 29
I am *left a.* and they.   *Rom* 11:3

let alone

let us *a.* that we may serve. *Ex* 14:12
let me *a.* that my wrath may. 32:10
let me *a.* that I may.   *Deut* 9:14
let me *a.* two months.   *Judg* 11:37
let him *a.* let him curse. *2 Sam* 16:11
let her *a.* her soul is.   *2 Ki* 4:27
let the work of this . . . *a.*   *Ezra* 6:7
let me *a.* that I may.   *Job* 10:20
hold your peace *let* me *a.* that. 13:13
joined to idols, *let* her *a.*   *Hos* 4:17
let them *a.* they be blind. *Mat* 15:14
let us *a.* what have we to do with
  thee ?   *Mark* 1:24*; *Luke* 4:34*
Jesus said, *let* her *a.* why ? *Mark* 14:6
let us see whether.   15:36*
Lord, *let* it *a.* this year. *Luke* 13:8
if we *let* him *a.* all men. *John* 11:48
let her *a.* against the day of my. 12:7*
from these men, *let* them *a. Acts* 5:38

along

will go *a.* by the king's.   *Num* 21:22
kine went *a.* the highway. *1 Sam* 6:12
then Saul fell all *a.* on the.   28:20*
went with her *a.*   *2 Sam* 3:16*
Shimei went *a.* cursing, and.   16:13
went, weeping all *a.*   *Jer* 41:6

aloof

my friends stand *a.* from. *Ps* 38:11

aloud, *see* **cry, cried, sing**

Alpha

A. and Omega. *Rev* 1:8; 21:6; 22:13

Alpheus

James the son of A.   *Mat* 10:3
  Mark 3:18; Luke 6:15; Acts 1:13
he saw Levi the son of A. *Mark* 2:14

already

Joseph was in Egypt a.   *Ex* 1:5
it hath been a. of old.   *Eccl* 1:10
I have cursed them a.   *Mal* 2:2
unto you, Elias is come a. *Mat* 17:12
not is condemned a.   *John* 3:18
in spirit, have judged a.   *1 Cor* 5:3
whereto we have a.   *Phil* 3:16
are a. turned aside .   *1 Tim* 5:15
but that which ye have a. *Rev* 2:25

also

man, for that he a. is flesh. *Gen* 6:3
ye the priesthood a.?   *Num* 16:10
Saul answered, God do so and more
  a. *1 Sam* 14:44; *2 Sam* 3:35; 19:13
if we sit still here, we die a. *2 Ki* 7:4
yea, for the rebellious a.   *Ps* 68:18
ye weary my God a.?   *Isa* 7:13
of hosts I will go a.   *Zech* 8:21
heart be a.   *Mat* 6:21; *Luke* 12:34
surely thou art a. one of. *Mat* 26:73
I may preach there a.   *Mark* 1:38
Son of man is Lord a.   2:28*
                   Luke 6:5*
thou reproachest us a.   *Luke* 11:45
what he doth, these a.   *John* 5:19
where I am, there shall a.   12:26
where I am, there ye may be a. 14:3
proceeded to take Peter a. *Acts* 12:3
many, and of myself a.   *Rom* 16:2*
not the law the same a.   *1 Cor* 9:8
last of all, he was seen of me a. 15:8
persuaded that in thee a. *2 Tim* 1:5
without works is dead, a.   *Jas* 2:26
God, love his brother a. *1 John* 4:21

altar

*Literally, any structure on which
sacrifices were offered. In speaking of spiritual worship the word is
used figuratively as a symbol easily
understood by both Jew and Gentile.*

Noah builded an a. to.   *Gen* 8:20
Abraham built an a. to.   12:7; 22:9
Beth-el, and make there an a.   35:1
Beth-el, I will make there an a.   3
built an a. Jehovah-nissi. *Ex* 17:15
an a. of earth shalt thou make.20:24
shalt take him from mine a.   21:14
sanctify it, it shall be an a.   29:37
sanctify the tabernacle and a.   44
a. of incense.   30:27
a. of burnt-offering.   40:10
the fire of the a. shall.   *Lev* 6:9
the dedication of the a.   *Num* 7:84
they shall not come nigh the a. 18:3
of Gad called the a. Ed. *Josh* 22:34
throw down the a. of Baal. *Judg* 6:25
because one hath cast down his a. 31
not cut off mine a.   *1 Sam* 2:33
go up, rear an a. to the. *2 Sam* 24:18
against the a. O. a.   *1 Ki* 13:2
Elijah repaired the a. of the. 18:30
and the water ran about the a.   35
before this a. *2 Ki* 18:22; *Isa* 36:7
so will I compass thine a.   *Ps* 26:6
will I go to the a. of God, to.   43:4
a. to the Lord in the.   *Isa* 19:19
stones of the a. as chalk-stones. 27:9
sacrifices be accepted on mine a. 56:7
Lord hath cast off his a.   *Lam* 2:7
the porch and a. 25 men. *Ezek* 8:16
howl, ye ministers of the a. *Joel* 1:13
weep between the porch and a. 2:17
to pledge by every a.   *Amos* 2:8
polluted bread on mine a.   *Mal* 1:7
nor do kindle fire on mine a.   10
covering the a. of the Lord.   2:13
thou bring thy gift to the a. *Mat* 5:23
whoso shall swear by the a.   23:18
the temple and a.   35; *Luke* 11:51
I found an a. with this. *Acts* 17:23
the a. partakers with a.   *1 Cor* 9:13
                   10:18
gave attendance at the a. *Heb* 7:13
we have an a. whereof they.   13:10

I saw under the a. the.   *Rev* 6:9
it with prayers on the golden a.   8:3
voice from horns of the golden a. 9:13
     see **built**

altars

shall destroy their a.   *Ex* 34:13
        Deut 7:5; 12:3
build here seven a.   *Num* 23:1
thrown down thine a. *1 Ki* 19:10, 14
bones of priests on the a. *2 Chr* 34:5
thine a. O Lord of hosts.   *Ps* 84:3
he shall not look to the a.   *Isa* 17:8
graven on horns of the a.   *Jer* 17:1
their children remember their a.   2
your a. shall be desolate. *Ezek* 6:4
made a. to sin, a. shall be. *Hos* 8:11
thistle shall come on their a.   10:8
a. are as heaps in the furrows. 12:11
I will also visit the a. of. *Amos* 3:14
digged down thine a.   *Rom* 11:3

alter

he shall not a. it, a good. *Lev* 27:10
that whosoever shall a.   *Ezra* 6:11
all that put their hand to a. this. 12
nor a. the thing gone out. *Ps* 89:34

altered

be not a. that Vashti.   *Esth* 1:19
his countenance was a.   *Luke* 9:29

altereth

the law which a. not.   *Dan* 6:8, 12

although

a. that was near, for God. *Ex* 13:17
a. my house be not so. *2 Sam* 23:5*
a. thou movedst me.   *Job* 2:3
a. I was an husband unto. *Jer* 31:32
a. I have cast them far. *Ezek* 11:16*
a. the fig-tree shall not.   *Hab* 3:17
a. all shall be offended. *Mark* 14:29

altogether

make thyself a.   *Num* 16:13*
which is a. just shalt.   *Deut* 16:20
are a. become filthy. *Ps* 14:3; 53:3
of the Lord are righteous a.   19:9
man at his best state is a.   39:5
that I was a. such a one as.   50:21
O Lord, thou knowest it a.   139:4
sweet, yea, he is a.   *S of S* 5:16
thou wast a. born in.   *John* 9:34
almost a. such as.   *Acts* 26:29*
a. with the fornicators. *1 Cor* 5:10+
or saith he it a. for our sakes? 9:10

alway, always

keep my commands a.   *Deut* 5:29
keep his commandments a.   11:1
learn to fear the Lord a.   14:23
it, I would not live a.   *Job* 7:16
will he a. call upon God?   27:10*
I have set the Lord a.   *Ps* 16:8
he will not a. chide, nor keep. 103:9
to perform thy statutes a.   119:112*
I was by him, rejoicing a.   *Pr* 8:30
neither will I be a. wroth. *Isa* 57:16
I am with you a. to the. *Mat* 28:20
ye have not a. *Mark* 14:7; *John* 12:8
I do a. those things.   *John* 8:29
I know that thou hearest me a. 11:42
Cornelius prayed to God a. *Acts* 10:2
God, who a. causeth us. *2 Cor* 2:14
in every prayer of.   *Phil* 1:4
as a. so now also, Christ shall.   20
as ye have a. obeyed, not.   2:12
rejoice in the Lord a. and.   4:4
to fill up their sins a.   *1 Thes* 2:16
a. in remembrance.   *2 Pet* 1:15*

am I

am I my brother's keeper? *Gen* 4:9
am I in God's stead, who?   30:2
am I God, to kill and?   *2 Ki* 5:7
am I come up.   18:25; *Isa* 36:10
am I a God at hand.   *Jer* 23:23
there am I in the midst. *Mat* 18:20
yet a little while am I.   *John* 7:33
am I not an apostle? am I not free?
                 1 Cor 9:1
weak, then am I strong. *2 Cor* 12:10

I am

amongst whom I am.   *Num* 11:21
there that being as I am.   *Neh* 6:11
he is not a man as I am.   *Job* 9:32
say to my soul, I am thy.   *Ps* 35:3
I may know how frail I am.   39:4

O Israel, I am God, even.   *Ps* 50:7
destroy them, for I am thy.   143:12
I am the first, I am the.   *Isa* 44:6
                   48:12
I am, and none.   47:8; *Zeph* 2:15
and he shall say, here I am. *Isa* 58:9
men say that I the Son of man am?
  Mat 16:13; *Mark* 8:27; *Luke* 9:18
God, ye say that I am. *Luke* 22:70
Jesus said, I am the bread. *John* 6:35
I am the light of the world.   8:12
before Abraham was, I am.   58
where I am there shall my.   12:26
may be with me where I am.   17:24
altogether such as I am. *Acts* 26:29
angel of God, whose I am, and. 27:23
I am what I am.   *1 Cor* 15:10
as I am, for I am.   *Gal* 4:12
learned in what state I am. *Phil* 4:11
I am he that liveth, I am. *Rev* 1:18
see thou do it not, I am thy.   19:10

I am that I am

I am that I am hath sent.   *Ex* 3:14
here am I, or here I am, *see* **here**

Amalek

to Eliphas Esau's son A. *Gen* 36:12
then came A. and fought.   *Ex* 17:8
out the remembrance of A.   14
sworn he will have war with A.   16
when he looked on A. . . . parable and
  said, A. was.   *Num* 24:20
what A. did. *Deut* 25:17; *1 Sam* 15:2
the remembrance of A. *Deut* 25:19
was a root against A.   *Judg* 5:14
smite A.   *1 Sam* 15:3
Saul came to the city of A.   5
not execute his wrath on A.   28:18
Gebal, Ammon, A. are.   *Ps* 83:7

Amalekite, -s

the A. came down and. *Num* 14:45
Israel had sown the A.   *Judg* 6:3
Midianites and A. lay like.   7:12
the A. did oppress you, and. 10:12
Saul smote the A. *1 Sam* 14:48; 15:7
get you from among A.   15:6
I have utterly destroyed the A.   20
and his men invaded the A.   27:8
the A. had invaded the south. 30:1
from the slaughter of A. *2 Sam* 1:1
answered him, I am an A.   8, 13
smote the rest of the A. *1 Chr* 4:43

Amana

look from the top of A. *S of S* 4:8

Amasa

Absalom made A. captain of the host,
  which A. was the. *2 Sam* 17:25
Joab took A. by the beard to.   20:9
A. wallowed in blood in the.   12
what Joab did to A.   *1 Ki* 2:5, 32
Abigail bare A. the.   *1 Chr* 2:17
A. son of Hadlai stood. *2 Chr* 28:12

amazed

of Benjamin were a.   *Judg* 20:41*
were a. they answered.   *Job* 32:15
be a. one at another.   *Isa* 13:8
many people a. at thee. *Ezek* 32:10
were exceedingly a.   *Mat* 19:25
all a. and glorified God. *Mark* 2:12
                   Luke 5:26
began to be sore a. and. *Mark* 14:33
all a. and spake among. *Luke* 4:36
were all a. at the mighty.   9:43
that heard Saul were a. *Acts* 9:21

amazement

filled with a. at what had. *Acts* 3:10
are not afraid with any a. *1 Pet* 3:6*

Amaziah

A. his son reigned.   *2 Ki* 12:21
                   2 Chr 24:27
fought against A. *2 Ki* 13:12; 14:15
A. would not hear, therefore. 14:11
father A. had done. 15:3; *2 Chr* 26:4
of Merari. A. the son.   *1 Chr* 6:45
after A. did turn from. *2 Chr* 25:27
A. priest of Beth-el sent. *Amos* 7:10

ambassador

but a faithful a. is health. *Pr* 13:17
an a. sent to the heathen. *Jer* 49:14
                   Ob 1
which I am an a. in bonds. *Eph* 6:20

ambassadors
as if they had been a.   Josh 9:4
the business of the a. 2 Chr 32:31
he sent a. what have I to.   35:21
that sendeth a. by the sea. Isa 18:2
princes at Zoan, his a. came. 30:4
a. of peace shall weep bitterly 33:7
rebelled in sending a. Ezek 17:15
then we are a. for Christ. 2 Cor 5:20

ambassage
sendeth an a. and.   Luke 14:32

amber, *see* **colour**

ambush, -es
lay thee an a. for the.   Josh 8:2
watchmen, prepare the a. Jer 51:12

ambushment, -s
caused an a. the a. was. 2 Chr 13:13
Lord set a. against Ammon. 20:22

amen
*The Hebrew means true, faithful,
certain. It is used in the end of
prayer as an earnest wish to be
heard; amen, so be it, so shall it be.
The word amen is used in many
languages.*
woman shall say a. a.   Num 5:22
the people shall say a. Deut 27:15
Benaiah answered a. the. 1 Ki 1:36
people said a. and.   1 Chr 16:36
to everlasting; a. and a. Ps 41:13
with his glory; a. and a.   72:19
Lord for evermore. a. and a. 89:52
and let all the people say a. 106:48
prophet Jeremiah said a. Jer 28:6
the glory for ever, a.   Mat 6:13
of the unlearned, say a. 1 Cor 14:16
in him are yea and a. 2 Cor 1:20
am alive for evermore, a. Rev 1:18
write these things, saith the a. 3:14
four beasts said a.   5:14; 19:4
come quickly, a. even so, 22:20

amend
a. ways, and doings.   Jer 7:3, 5
    26:13; 35:15
hour when he began to a. John 4:52

amends
(Revised Version, restitution)
make a. for the harm. Lev 5:16

amerce
(Punish by fine)
a. him in an 100 shekels. Deut 22:19

amethyst, *see* **agate** *and* **Jacinth**

amiable
how a. are thy tabernacles. Ps 84:1

amiss
sinned, we have done a. 2 Chr 6:37*
speak any thing a. against. Dan 3:29
man hath done nothing a. Luke 23:41
not, because ye ask a. Jas 4:3

Ammah
were come to the hill A. 2 Sam 2:24

Ammi
unto your brethren, A. Hos 2:1

Amminadab
Elisheba daughter of A. Ex 6:23
A. begat. Ruth 4:20 ; Mat 1:4

Ammi-nadib
me like the chariots of A. S of S 6:12

Ammon
father of children of A. Gen 19:38
I deliver you from A. ? Judg 10:11
the children of A. made war. 11:4
the land of the children of A. 15
thus the children of A. were. 33
if the children of A. be too strong for
  thee. 2 Sam 10:11; 1 Chr 19:12
children of A. saw that. 2 Sam 10:14
with sword of children of A. 14
all children of A. 31; 1 Chr 20:3
the abomination of the children of A.
   1 Ki 11:7; 2 Ki 23:13
god of the children of A. 1 Ki 11:33
had married wives of A. Neh 13:23
Gebal and A. confederate. Ps 83:7
the children of A. shall. Isa 11:14
punish the children of A. Jer 9:26
made children of A. to drink. 25:21
bring again the captivity of A. 49:6
escape, the chief of A. Dan 11:41
children of A. shall be as. Zeph 2:9

Ammonite, -s
A. not enter. Deut 23:3; Neh 13:1
slew the A. till the. 1 Sam 11:11
loved women of the A. 1 Ki 11:1
and the A. gave gifts. 2 Chr 26:8
to the abomination of A. Ezra 9:1
send to the king of A. Jer 27:3
to be heard in Rabbah of A. 49:2
make A. a couchingplace. Ezek 25:5
A. may not be remembered. 10

Amnon
David's first-born was A.
   2 Sam 3:2; 1 Chr 3:12
A. vexed, fell sick for. 2 Sam 13:2
I pray thee, let my brother A. 26
when I say, smite A. then kill. 28
Shimon, A. Rinnah. 1 Chr 4:20

Amon
back to A. 1 Ki 22:26; 2 Chr 18:25
A. reigned.   2 Ki 21:18
his servants slew A.   23
A. sacrificed to carved. 2 Chr 33:22
captivity children of A. Neh 7:59
Manasses begat A. and A. Mat 1:10

among
thou, Lord, art a. them. Num 14:14
a. the sons of the priests. Ezra 10:18
yet a. many nations. Neh 13:26
an interpreter, one a. Job 33:23
their life is a. the unclean. 36:14
evil common a. men. Eccl 6:1
one a. 1,000, but a woman a. 7:28
chiefest a. ten thousand. S of S 5:10
a. my people are found. Jer 5:26
there is none upright a. Mi 7:2
blessed art thou a. Luke 1:28*
I send you forth as lambs a. 10:3
what are they a. so many ? John 6:9

Amorite, -s
iniquity of the A. is not. Gen 15:16
which I took from A. with. 48:22
utterly destroy the A. Deut 20:17
fail drive out the A. Josh 3:10
the Lord delivered up A. 10:12
or gods of A. in whose land. 24:15
not the gods of the A. Judg 6:10
God hath dispossessed the A. 11:23
between Israel and the A. 1 Sam 7:14
Gibeonites were of the A. 2 Sam 21:2
abominably as did the A. 1 Ki 21:26
above all the A. did. 2 Ki 21:11
father an A. mother. Ezek 16:3, 45
yet destroyed I the A. Amos 2:9

Amos, or, Amoz
Isaiah the son of A. 2 Ki 19:2, 20
  20:1; 2 Chr 26:22; 32:20, 32
Isa. 1:1; 2:1; 13:1; 20:2; 37:2
   21; 38:1
then A. said, I was no. Amos 7:14
which was the son of A. Luke 3:25

Amphipolis
had passed through A. Acts 17:1

Amplias
greet A. my beloved in. Rom 16:8

Amram
of Kohath, A. Ex 6:18; Num 3:19
Dishon, A. and Eshban. 1 Chr 1:41
the children of A. Aaron. 6:3
sons of Bani, Maadai, A. Ezra 10:34

Anah
this was that A. that. Gen 36:24

Anak
saw the children of A. Num 13:28, 33
before the children of A. Deut 9:2
Caleb drove thence the three sons of
  A. Josh 15:14; Judg 1:20

Anakims
and tall as the A. Deut 2:10; 9:2
none of the A. were left. Josh 11:22
was a great man among the A. 14:15

Anammelech
Adrammelech, A. gods. 2 Ki 17:31

Ananias
A. hearing these words. Acts 5:5
seen in a vision A. 9:12; 22:12
high-priest A. commanded. 23:2
A. the priest descended with. 24:1

Anathema
him be a. maran-atha. 1 Cor 16:22

Anatnoth
of Benjamin, A. with her suburbs,
  Almon. Josh 21:18; 1 Chr 6:60
get thee to A. to. 1 Ki 2:26
the sons of Becher A. 1 Chr 7:8
A. and Nebai sealed. Neh 10:19
up thy voice, O poor A. Isa 10:30
evil on the men of A. Jer 11:23
not reproved Jeremiah of A. 29:27
my field that is in A. 32:7, 8

ancestors
the covenant of their a. Lev 26:45

anchor
they would have cast a. Acts 27:30
hope we have as an a. Heb 6:19

ancient
[1] Old, of former time, 1 Chr 4:22.
[2] Very old men, Job 12:12. [3]
Men of former times, 1 Sam 24:13
[4] Elders of the people Jer 19:1.
the chief things of the a. Deut 33:15
a. river, the river Kishon. Judg 5:21
of a. times. 2 Ki 19:25; Isa 37:26
and these are a. things. 1 Chr 4:22
were a. men, and had. Ezra 3:12*
with the a. is wisdom. Job 12:12*
remove not the a. land-. Pr 22:28
prudent and a. the Lord. Isa 3:2*
the a. and honourable, he. 9:15*
say ye, I am the son of a. ? 19:11
whose antiquity is of a. days. 23:7
since I appointed the a. people. 44:7
upon the a. hast thou laid thy. 47:6*
of the Lord, as in the a. days. 51:9*
to stumble from a. paths. Jer 18:15
then they began at the a. Ezek 9:6
the a. of days did sit. Dan 7:9
the Son of man came to a. of. 13
till the a. of days came, and. 22

ancients
(Revised Version, usually, elders)
the proverb of the a. 1 Sam 24:13
more than the a. Ps 119:100
into judgment with the a. Isa 3:14
Lord shall reign before his a. 24:23
a. of the people and a. of. Jer 19:1
shall perish from the a. Ezek 7:26
hast thou seen what the a. do? 8:12
the a. of Gebal were in thee. 27:9

ancle bones
a. bones received strength. Acts 3:7

ancles
the waters were to the a. Ezek 47:3

Andrew
into the house of A. Mark 1:29
James, John, and A. asked. 13:3
which heard was A. John 1:40
of Bethsaida the city of A. 44
Philip telleth A. and A. told. 12:22
Peter, John, James, and A. Acts 1:13

Andronicus
salute A. and Junia my. Rom 16:7

Aner
A. Eshcol, let them take. Gen 14:24
half tribe of Manasseh, A. 1 Chr 6:70

angel
Literally 'messenger': [1] A celestial
being, a messenger of God, Gen
24:7; Dan 3:28; Acts 12:8. [2]
A minister or pastor of a church,
Rev 2:1. [3] An evil, or fallen
angel, Mat 25:41.
a. of the Lord said. Gen 22:11
send his a. before thee. 24:7, 40
the a. who redeemed me. 48:16
send a. before thee. Ex 23:20, 23
   32:34; 33:2
sent an a. and brought. Num 20:16
the a. did wondrously. Judg 13:19
the a. stretched out his hand, the a.
  that. 2 Sam 24:16; 1 Chr 21:15
spake . . . saw the a. 2 Sam 24:17
a. spake to me by the. 1 Ki 13:18
an a. touched Elijah and said. 19:5
God sent an a. to. 1 Chr 21:15
turned back, and saw the a. 20
the Lord commanded the a. and. 27
the Lord sent an a. 2 Chr 32:21
nor say before the a. Eccl 5:6
the a. of his presence. Isa 63:9
God who hath sent a. and. Dan 3:28

God hath sent his *a.* and. *Dan* 6:22
he had power over the *a.* *Hos* 12:4
a. talked with me said. *Zech* 1:9; 4:5
Lord answered the *a.* that. 1:13
a. that communed with me said. 14
a. that talked. 19; 4:4; 5:10; 6:4
a. that talked . . . and another *a.* 2:3
and stood before the *a.* 3:3
a. that talked with me, went. 5:5
a. answered, these are the four. 6:5
a. answered the woman. *Mat* 28:5
the *a.* said, fear not. *Luke* 1:13
the *a.* answered and said, I am. 19
in the sixth month the *a.* Gabriel. 26
a. said to her, fear not, Mary. 30
a. answered, Holy Ghost shall. 35
a. said to the shepherds, fear. 2:10
suddenly there was with the *a.* 13
so named of the *a.* before he was. 21
an *a.* strengthening him. 22:43
an *a.* went down at a. *John* 5:4*
others said, an *a.* spake to. 12:29
been the face of an *a.* *Acts* 6:15
hands of the *a.* that appeared. 7:35
in the wilderness with the *a.* 38
a. which spake to Cornelius. 10:7
from God by an holy *a.* to send. 22
how he had seen an *a.* in his. 11:13
the *a.* said to Peter, bind on. 12:8
true which was done by the *a.* 9
forthwith the *a.* departed from. 10
the Lord hath sent his *a.* and. 11
then said they, it is his *a.* 15
Sadducees say, neither *a.* 23:8
if a spirit or an *a.* hath spoken to. 9
into an *a.* of light. *2 Cor* 11:14
an *a.* from heaven preach. *Gal* 1:8
he signified it by his *a.* *Rev* 1:1
a. of the church. 2:1, 8, 12, 18
3:1, 7, 14
I saw a strong *a.* proclaiming. 5:2
I saw another *a.* ascending. 7:2
another *a.* came and stood. 8:3
ascended before God out of the *a.* 4
the *a.* took the censer, and filled. 5
the first *a.* sounded. 7
second *a.* sounded. 8
third *a.* sounded. 10
fourth *a.* sounded. 12
I heard an *a.* flying through. 13*
fifth *a.* sounded. 9:1
the *a.* of the bottomless pit. 11
sixth *a.* sounded. 13
to the sixth *a.* loose the four *a.* 14
I saw another *a.* 10:1; 18:1; 20:1
the *a.* which I saw stand on. 10:5
days of the voice of the seventh *a.* 7
the book in the hand of the *a.* 8
I took the book. 10
and the *a.* stood, saying. 11:1*
seventh *a.* sounded, and there. 15
I saw another *a.* fly in. 14:6
another *a.* followed saying. 8
third *a.* followed. 9
another *a.* came. 15, 17, 18
and the *a.* thrust in his sickle in. 19
a. poured out. 16:2, 3, 4, 8, 10, 12, 17
and I heard the *a.* of the waters. 5
a. said, wherefore didst thou. 17:7
mighty *a.* took up a stone. 18:21
and I saw an *a.* standing in. 19:17
of a man, that is of the *a.* 21:17
to worship before the feet of an *a.* 22:8
I Jesus have sent mine *a.* to. 16

angel of God
a. of God who went. *Ex* 14:19
countenance of an *a.* of God.
Judg 13:6
sight, as an *a.* of God. *1 Sam* 29:9
as an *a.* of God. *2 Sam* 14:17; 19:27
the wisdom of an *a.* of God. 14:20
this night the *a.* of God. *Acts* 27:23
me as an *a.* of God. *Gal* 4:14

angel of the Lord
a. of the L. found Hagar. *Gen* 16:7
the *a.* of the L. said. 9, 10, 11; 22:11
Num 22:32, 35; *Judg* 13:18
2 Ki 1:3, 15
a. of the L. called. *Gen* 22:11, 15
ass saw the *a.* of the L. *Num* 22:23
25:27
a. of the L. stood in a path. 22:24, 26
Balaam saw *a.* of the L. standing. 31

Balaam said to *a.* of the L. *Num* 22:34
a. of the L. said to Balaam, go. 35
a. of the L. came up. *Judg* 2:1
1 Ki 19:7; *Acts* 12:7
when *a.* of the L. spake. *Judg* 2:4
Meroz, said the *a.* of the L. 5:23
came an *a.* of the L. and sat. 6:11
a. of the L. appeared to Gideon. 12
the *a.* of the L. put forth the. 21
perceived he was an *a.* of the L. 22
a. of the L. appeared to the. 13:3
knew not he was an *a.* of the L. 16
a. of the L. ascended in the flame. 20
a. of the L. was by threshing.
2 Sam 24:16; *1 Chr* 21:15
a. of the L. smote. *2 Ki* 19:35
Isa 37:36
a. of the L. destroying. *1 Chr* 21:12
a. of the L. commanded Gad to. 18
the sword of *a.* of the L. 30
a. of the L. encampeth. *Ps* 34:7
let *a.* of the L. chase them. 35:5
let *a.* of the L. persecute them. 6
answered the *a.* of the L. *Zech* 1:11
a. of the L. answered, wilt thou. 12
a. of the L. stood by Joshua. 3:5
a. of the L. protested. 6
of David is the *a.* of the L. 12:8
a. of the L. *Mat* 1:20; 2:13, 19
Joseph did as the *a.* of the L. 1:24
for the *a.* of the L. descended. 28:2
Zacharias an *a.* of the L. *Luke* 1:11
a. of the L. came upon them. 2:9
a. of the L. by night. *Acts* 5:19
a. of the L. spake to Philip. 8:26
a. of the L. smote Herod. 12:23

angels

there came two *a.* to. *Gen* 19:1
when the morning arose, the *a.* 15
lower than the *a.* *Ps* 8:5*; *Heb* 2:7, 9
of God are thousands of *a.* *Ps* 68:17*
man did eat *a.* food, he sent. 78:25*
and trouble, by sending evil *a.* 49
a. came and. *Mat* 4:11; *Mark* 1:13
the reapers are the *a.* *Mat* 13:39
the *a.* shall come forth and sever. 49
their *a.* always behold the. 18:10
in heaven. 24:36; *Mark* 13:32
Son of man, and all the holy *a.* with.
Mat 25:31
more than twelve legions of *a.* 26:53
Son of man . . . of his Father with
the holy *a.* *Mark* 8:38; *Luke* 9:26
marry, but are as the *a.* *Mark* 12:25
as the *a.* were gone. *Luke* 2:15
and was carried by the *a.* 16:22
they are equal unto the *a.* 20:36
had also seen a vision of *a.* 24:23
seeth two *a.* in white. *John* 20:12
law by disposition of *a.* *Acts* 7:53
a. able to separate us. *Rom* 8:38
to the world, to *a.* and. *1 Cor* 4:9
not that we shall judge *a.*? 6:3
on her head, because of the *a.* 11:10
with tongues of men and *a.* 13:1
it was ordained by *a.* in. *Gal* 3:19
you in worshipping of *a.* *Col* 2:18
heaven with mighty *a.* *2 Thes* 1:7
seen of *a.* preached to. *1 Tim* 3:16
before God and the elect *a.* 5:21
so much better than the *a.* *Heb* 1:4
the *a.* said he at any time. 5, 13
a. he saith, who maketh his *a.* 1:7
if the word spoken by *a.* was. 2:2
a. hath he not put in subjection. 5
him the nature of *a.* but seed. 16
innumerable company of *a.* 12:22
for some have entertained *a.* 13:2
which things the *a.* *1 Pet* 1:12
a. and powers being made. 22
if God spared not the *a.* *2 Pet* 2:4
whereas *a.* greater in power and. 11
a. who kept not their first. *Jude* 6
seven stars, *a.* of the. *Rev* 1:20
the voice of many *a.* about. 5:11
I saw four *a.* standing on the. 7:1
with a loud voice to the four *a.* 2
all the *a.* stood round about the. 11
trumpet of the three *a.* which. 8:13
loose the four *a.* which are. 9:14
the *a.* were loosed, which were. 15
in presence of the holy *a.* 14:10
and at the gates twelve *a.* 21:12

angels of God
a. of God ascend and descend.
Gen 28:12; *John* 1:51
and *a.* of God met him. *Gen* 32:1
as *a.* of God. *Mat* 22:30; *Mark* 12:25
confess before *a.* of God. *Luke* 12:8
be denied before the *a.* of God. 9
the presence of the *a.* of God. 15:10
all the *a.* of God worship. *Heb* 1:6

his **angels**
and *his a.* he charged with. *Job* 4:18
give *his a.* charge. *Ps* 91:11
Mat 4:6; *Luke* 4:10
ye *his a.* which excel in. *Ps* 103:20
his a. spirits. 104:4*; *Heb* 1:7
all *his a.* praise. *Ps* 148:2
man shall send forth *his a.* *Mat* 13:41
glory of his Father with *his a.* 16:27
send *his a.* with a great sound. 24:31
Mark 13:27
for the devil and his. *Mat* 25:41
before my Father and *his a.* *Rev* 3:5
his a. the dragon, and *his a.* 12:7
dragon was cast out, and *his a.* 9

anger, verb
foolish nation I will *a.* *Rom* 10:19

anger
till thy brother's *a.* turn. *Gen* 27:45
and let not thine *a.* burn. 44:18
cursed be their *u.* for it was. 49:7
dancing, Moses' *a.* waxed. *Ex* 32:19
Aaron said, let not the *a.* of my. 22
I was afraid of the *a.* and. *Deut* 9:19
from the fierceness of his *a.* 13:17
Josh 7:26
heat of this great *a.*? *Deut* 29:24
then their *a.* was abated. *Judg* 8:3
Ahasuerus his *a.* burned. *Esth* 1:12
will not withdraw his *a.* *Job* 9:13
oven in the time of thine *a.* *Ps* 21:9
a. endureth but a moment. 30:5
cease from *a.* and forsake. 37:8
my flesh because of thine *a.* 38:3
let thy wrathful *a.* take hold. 69:24
why doth thy *a.* smoke. 74:1
and *a.* also came up against. 78:21
many a time turned he his *a.* 38
on them the fierceness of his *a.* 49
he made a way to his *a.* he. 50
and cause thine *a.* towards us to. 4
the fierceness of thine *a.* 85:3
we are consumed by thine *a.* 90:7
knoweth the power of thine *a.* 11
nor will he keep his *a.* for. 103:9
Jer 3:5
grievous words stir up *a.* *Pr* 15:1
of a man deferreth his *a.* 19:11
a gift in secret pacifieth *a.* 21:14
the rod of his *a.* shall fail. 22:8
wrath is cruel, and *a.* is. 27:4
a. resteth in the bosom of. *Eccl* 7:9
for all this his *a.* is not turned away.
Isa 5:25; 9:12, 17, 21; 10:4
fear not, for the *a.* of Rezin. 7:4
O Assyrian, the rod of mine *a.* 10:5
shall cease, and my *a.* in their. 25
thou wast angry, thine *a.* 12:1
the Lord cometh with fierce *a.* 13:9
day of his fierce *a.* 13; *Lam* 1:12
Lord cometh burning with *a.* *Isa* 30:27
shew the indignation of his *a.* 30
poured on him the fury of *a.* 42:25
sake will I defer mine *a.* 48:9
will come to render his *a.* 66:15
surely his *a.* shall turn. *Jer* 2:35
mine *a.* to fall on you, I am merciful,
and I will not keep mine *a.* 3:12
were broken down by his *a.* 4:26
mine *a.* shall be poured on. 7:20
them in the time of thine *a.* 18:23
desolate because of his *a.* 25:38
as a provocation of mine *a.* 32:31
great is the *a.* the Lord hath. 36:7
as mine *a.* hath been poured. 42:18
wherefore mine *a.* was poured. 44:6
on them, my fierce *a.* 49:37
his footstool in the day *a.* *Lam* 2:1
in the indignation of his *a.* 6
them in the day of thine *a.* 21
in the day of the Lord's *a.* none. 22
thou hast covered with *a.* and. 3:43
he hath poured out his fierce *a.* 4:11

2

mine *a*. be accomplished. *Ezek* 5:13
I will send mine *a*. upon thee.   7:3
accomplish mine *a*. on. 8; 20:8, 21
Edom, according to mine *a*.   25:14
even do according to thine *a*.   35:11
thine *a*. be turned away.   *Dan* 9:16
the fierceness of mine *a*.   *Hos* 11:9
for mine *a*. is turned away.   14:14
a. did tear perpetually.   *Amos* 1:11
turn from his fierce *a*.   *Jonah* 3:9
he retained not his *a*. for.   *Mi* 7:18
abide . . . fierceness of his *a*.? *Nah* 1:6
a. against the rivers?   *Hab* 3:8
them all my fierce *a*.   *Zeph* 3:8
looked on them with *a*.   *Mark* 3:5
all *a*. be put.   *Eph* 4:31; *Col* 3:8

anger *of the Lord*
fierce *a*. of *the Lord* may. *Num* 25:4
augment the *a*. of *the Lord*.   32:14
a. of *the Lord* shall.   *Deut* 29:20
a. of *the Lord* against Israel.
       Judg 2:14, 20; 3:8; 10:7
through the *a*. of *the Lord* it came to
   pass.   2 *Ki* 24:20; *Jer* 52:3
fierce *a*. of *the Lord* is not. *Jer* 4:8
fierce *a*. of *the Lord*.   12:13; 25:37
a. of *the Lord* shall not. 23:20; 30:24
from the fierce *a*. of *the Lord*.   51:45
a. of *the Lord* hath.   *Lam* 4:16
before the fierce *a*. of *the Lord*.
       Zeph 2:2
be hid in the day of *a*. of *the Lord*. 3

in **anger**
for *in* their *a*. they slew. *Gen* 49:6
out from Pharaoh *in a*.   *Ex* 11:8
Lord overthrew *in a*.   *Deut* 29:23
them out of the land *in a*.   28
rose from the table *in a*. *1 Sam* 20:34
home *in* great *a*.   2 *Chr* 25:10
overturneth them *in* his *a*.   *Job* 9:5
he teareth himself *in* his *a*.   18:4
distributeth sorrows *in* his *a*.   21:17
not so, he hath visited *in* his *a*. 35:15
me not *in* thy *a*. *Ps* 6:1; *Jer* 10:24
arise, O Lord, *in* thine *a*. lift. *Ps* 7:6
put not thy servant away *in a*.   27:9
in thine *a*. cast down the.   56:7
hath he *in a*. shut up his?   77:9
called my mighty ones *in a*. *Isa* 13:3
he that ruled the nations *in a*.   14:6
tread them *in* mine *a*.   63:3, 6
against you, even *in a*.   *Jer* 21:5
have driven them *in* mine *a*.   32:37
whom I have slain *in* mine *a*.   33:5
Zion with a cloud *in* his *a*. *Lam* 2:1
he hath cut off *in a*. all the horn. 3:8
and destroy them *in a*.   3:66
judgments in thee *in a*.   *Ezek* 5:15
overflowing shower *in* mine *a*. 13:13
gather you *in* mine *a*. and.   22:20
have consumed them *in* mine *a*. 43:8
destroyed, neither *in a*.   *Dan* 11:20
thee a king *in* mine *a*.   *Hos* 13:11
execute vengeance *in a*.   *Mi* 5:15
thresh the heathen *in a*.   *Hab* 3:12

anger *kindled*
a. of Jacob was *k*. against. *Gen* 30:2
a. of *the Lord* was *k*. against Moses.
       Ex 4:14
a. of *the Lord* was *k*. *Num* 11:1, 10
       12:9; 22:22
Balaam's *a*. was *k*. and he.   22:27
Balak's *a*. was *k*. against.   24:10
the *a*. of *the Lord* was *k*. against
   Israel.   25:3; 32:13; *Josh* 7:1
       2 *Sam* 24:1; 2 *Ki* 13:3
Lord's *a*. was *k*. the same. *Num* 32:10
lest the *a*. of *the Lord* be *k*. against
   thee.   *Deut* 6:15
so will the *a*. of *the Lord* be *k*.   7:4
the *a*. of *the Lord* was *k*. against this
   land.   29:27
mine *a*. shall be *k*. 31:17; *Josh* 23:16
fire is *k*. in *a*. *Deut* 32:22; *Jer* 15:14
Zebul's *a*. was *k*.   *Judg* 9:30
Samson's *a*. *k*. and he went.   14:19
Saul heard, his *a*. was *k*. *1 Sam* 11:6
Eliab's *a*. was *k*. against.   17:28
Saul's *a*. was *k*. against.   20:30
a. of Lord *k*. against Uzzah.
       2 *Sam* 6:7; *1 Chr* 13:10
David's *a*. was *k*. against the.
       2 *Sam* 12:5

wherewith his *a*. was *k*. 2 *Ki* 23:26
their *a*. was *k*. against.   2 *Chr* 25:10
a. of *the Lord* was *k*. against Amaziah.   15
the *a*. of *the Lord* was *k*. against his
   people.   *Isa* 5:25
have *k*. a fire in mine *a*.   *Jer* 17:4
mine *a*. is *k*. against them. *Hos* 8:5
mine *a*. was *k*. against the shepherds.
       Zech 10:3

provoke or *provoked to* **anger**
to *pr*. him *to a*.   *Deut* 4:25; 9:18
   31:29; 2 *Ki* 17:17; 21:6; 23:19
       2 *Chr* 33:6
abominations *pr*. *to a*.   *Deut* 32:16
pr. me *to a*. I will *pr*. them *to a*.   21
and *pr*. the Lord *to a*.   *Judg* 2:12
images to *pr*. *to a*. *1 Ki* 14:9; 15:30
groves *pr*. Lord *to a*. 14:15; 16:7, 13
to pr. me *to a*. with their sins.   16:2
       2 *Ki* 17:11; *Jer* 11:17; 32:29, 32
       Ezek 16:26
Ahab did *pr*. the Lord *to a*. *1 Ki* 16:33
thou hast *pr*. me *to a*.   22:53
Ahaz *pr*. *to a*. the Lord God.   22:53
pr. me *to a*. since the day. 2 *Ki* 21:15
that they might *pr*. me *to a*.   22:17
       2 *Chr* 34:25; *Jer* 25:7
pr. *to a*. the Lord God. 2 *Chr* 28:25
have *pr*. thee *to a*. before. *Neh* 4:5
pr. him *to a*. with. *Ps* 78:58; 106:29
whoso *pr*. him *to a*. sinneth. *Pr* 20:2
pr. the Holy One . . . *to a*. *Isa* 1:4*
a people that *pr*. me *to a*.   65:3*
may *pr*. me *to a*.   *Jer* 7:18
do they *pr*. me *to a*.   19
why have they *pr*. *to a*.   8:19
pr. me not *to a*.   25:6
Israel have *pr*. me *to a*.   32:30
their wickedness to *pr*. me *to a*. 44:3
       Ezek 8:17
Ephraim *pr*. him *to a*.   *Hos* 12:14
pr. not your children *to a*. *Col* 3:21*

slow to **anger**
ready to pardon, *slow to a*. *Neh* 9:17
slow to a. plenteous. *Ps* 103:8; 145:8
he that is *slow to a*.   *Pr* 15:18
he that is *slow to a*. better.   16:32
slow to a. of great.   *Joel* 2:13
       Jonah 4:2
the Lord is *slow to a*. great. *Nah* 1:3

angered
they *a*. him at the waters. *Ps* 106:32

angle
they that cast *a*. shall.   *Isa* 19:8
up all of them with the *a*. *Hab* 1:15

angry
let not the Lord be *a*. *Gen* 18:30, 32
be not *a*. with yourselves that. 45:5
and Moses was *a*. with.   *Lev* 10:16
a. with me for you. *Deut* 1:37; 4:21
Lord was *a*. with you to have.   9:8
the Lord was very *a*. with Aaron. 20
lest *a*. fellows run upon. *Judg* 18:25
wherefore be ye *a*. for. 2 *Sam* 19:42
be *a*. with them. *1 Ki* 8:46; 2 *Ch* 6:36
Lord was *a*. with Solomon. *1 Ki* 11:9
therefore the Lord was *a*. 2 *Ki* 17:18
wouldst thou not be *a*.   *Ezra* 9:14
I was very *a*. when I.   *Neh* 5:6
kiss the Son, lest he be *a*.   *Ps* 2:12
God is *a*. with the wicked.   7:11
stand when once thou art *a*.?   76:7
wilt thou be *a*.?   79:5; 80:4; 85:5
he that is soon *a*. dealeth.   *Pr* 14:17
wilderness, than with an *a*.   21:19*
friendship with an *a*. man.   22:24
a. countenance, a backbiting.   25:23
a. man stirreth up strife, and. 29:22
wherefore should God be *a*.? *Eccl* 5:6
be not hasty in thy spirit to be *a*. 7:9
mother's children were *a*. *S of S* 1:6
though thou wast *a*. with.   *Isa* 12:1
and will be no more *a*.   *Ezek* 16:42
this cause the king was *a*. *Dan* 2:12
and he was very *a*.   *Jonah* 4:1
Doest thou well to be *a*.?   4:4, 9
he said, I do well to be *a*. even.   9
whosoever is *a*. with his.   *Mat* 5:22
of the house being *a*.   *Luke* 14:21
he was *a*. and would not.   15:28
are ye *a*. at me because.   *John* 7:23

be *a*. and sin not, let not.   *Eph* 4:26
be blameless, not soon *a*.   *Tit* 1:7
the nations were *a*. thy.   *Rev* 11:18

anguish
in that we saw the *a*.   *Gen* 42:21*
hearkened not to Moses for *a*. *Ex* 6:9
tremble, and be in *a*.   *Deut* 2:25
slay me, for *a*. is come. 2 *Sam* 1:9
I will speak in the *a*. of my. *Job* 7:11
trouble and *a*. shall make him. 15:24
trouble and *a*. have.   *Ps* 119:143
when distress and *a*. come.   *Pr* 1:27
and behold dimness of *a*.   *Isa* 8:22
into the land of trouble and *a*. 30:6
a. as of her that bringeth.   *Jer* 4:31
a. hath taken.   6:24; 49:24; 50:43
no more her *a*. for joy.   *John* 16:21
tribulation and *a*. upon.   *Rom* 2:9
for out of much *a*. of heart. 2 *Cor* 2:4

anise
ye pay tithe of mint, *a*.   *Mat* 23:23

Anna
A. a prophetess daughter. *Luke* 2:36

Annas
A. and Caiaphas being.   *Luke* 3:2
A. was father in law to.   *John* 18:13
A. had sent Jesus bound to.   24

anoint
[1] *To pour oil upon with the idea
of consecrating the person or thing
to God, or to set him apart for
an office,* Gen 31:13; Ex 28:41.
*Since kings and priests were
persons most frequently anointed on
taking office, they were frequently
spoken of as God's anointed,* 2 Sam
23:1; Isa 45:1. *In like manner
Jesus Christ as King and Priest, was
so termed,* Acts 10:38. [2] *Anointing with various preparations was
one of the principal methods of
healing in the small knowledge of
medicine in Palestine in Bible
times,* Jas 5:14. *The word is so
used of Jesus in healing the eyes of
the blind,* John 9:6, 11.

a. and consecrate.   *Ex* 28:41; 30:30
       40:15
oil and *a*. him.   29:7; 40:13
thou shalt *a*. the altar. 29:36; 40:10
a. the tabernacle.   30:26; 40:9
thou shalt *a*. the laver and.   40:11
priest whom he shall *a*.   *Lev* 16:32
but thou shalt not *a*.   *Deut* 28:40
the trees went to *a*. a king. *Judg* 9:8
if in truth ye *a*. me king over.   15
thyself therefore and *a*.   *Ruth* 3:3
a. him to be captain.   *1 Sam* 9:16
Lord sent me to *a*. thee king.   15:1
thou shalt *a*. him whom I name. 16:3
the Lord said, arise, *a*. him, this. 12
a. not thyself but this.   2 *Sam* 14:2
let Zadok *a*. him king.   *1 Ki* 1:34
a. Hazael king.   19:15
a. Jehu, *a*. Elisha.   16
arise ye princes, and *a*.   *Isa* 21:5
seal up the vision, and *a*. *Dan* 9:24
neither did I *a*. myself at all.   10:3
a. themselves with the.   *Amos* 6:6
the olives, but not *a*.   *Mi* 6:15
when thou fastest *a*. thine. *Mat* 6:17
is come to *a*. my body.   *Mark* 14:8
spices that they might *a*. him.   16:1
with oil thou didst not *a*. *Luke* 7:46
a. thine eyes with eye-.   *Rev* 3:18

anointed
sons after him, to be *a*.   *Ex* 29:29
if the priest that is *a*. do sin. *Lev* 4:3
of Aaron, when he is *a*.   6:20
in the day that he *a*. them.   7:36
a. the tabernacle.   8:10
a. the altar.   11; *Num* 7:1
oil on Aaron's head, and *a*. *Lev* 8:12
sons of Aaron *a*.   *Num* 3:3
offered after it was *a*.   7:10, 84, 88
Lord *a*. thee captain.   *1 Sam* 10:1
a. Saul.   15:17
a. David.   16:13; 2 *Sam* 2:4, 7
       5:3, 17; 12:7; 2 *Ki* 9:3, 6, 12
       1 Chr 11:3; 14:8
house of Judah have *a*.   2 *Sam* 2:7
day weak, though *a*. king.   3:39

from the earth, and *a.* *2 Sam* 12:20
David the *a.* of the God of. 23:1
the Lord hath *a. Isa* 61:1; *Luke* 4:18
thou art the *a.* cherub. *Ezek* 28:14
kissed his feet and *a.* *Luke* 7:38
but this woman hath *a.* my feet. 46
he *a.* the eyes of the blind. *John* 9:6
Jesus made clay, and *a.* mine. 11
it was that Mary which *a.* the. 11:2
took Mary ointment and *a.* 12:3
Jesus, whom thou hast *a. Acts* 4:27
how God *a.* Jesus of Nazareth. 10:38
which hath *a.* us is God. *2 Cor* 1:21

anointed ones
are the two *a.* ones. *Zech* 4:14

his anointed
and exalt horn of *his a. 1 Sam* 2:10
me before the Lord and *his a.* 12:3
the Lord and *his a.* is witness. 5
sheweth mercy to his *a. 2 Sam* 22:51
　　　　　　　　　　　　Ps 18:50
the Lord, and against *his a. Ps* 2:2
that the Lord saveth *his a.* 20:6
the saving strength of *his a.* 28:8
thus saith the Lord to *his a. Isa* 45:1

Lord's anointed
surely the *Lord's a.* is. *1 Sam* 16:6
to my master, the *Lord's a.* 24:6
my lord, for he is the *Lord's a.* 10
his hand against the *Lord's a.* 26:9
ye have not kept the *Lord's a.* 16
not afraid to destroy the *Lord's a.?*
　　　　　　　　　　　　2 Sam 1:14
because he cursed the *Lord's a.* 19:21
the *a. of Lord* was taken. *Lam* 4:20

mine anointed
walk before *mine a.* *1 Sam* 2:35
not *mine a. 1 Chr* 16:22; *Ps* 105:15
a lamp for *mine a.* *Ps* 132:17

anointed with oil
priest *a.* with holy *oil. Num* 35:25
had not been *a. with oil. 2 Sam* 1:21
God *a.* thee *with oil* of. *Ps* 45:7
　　　　　　　　　　　　Heb 1:9
with my holy *oil* have I *a.* *Ps* 89:20
I shall be *a. with* fresh *oil.* 92:10

thine anointed
O Lord God, turn not away the face
of *thine a. 2 Chr* 6:42; *Ps* 132:10
look on face of *thine a.* *Ps* 84:9
been wroth with *thine a.* 89:38
the footsteps of *thine a.* 51
for salvation with *thine a.* *Hab* 3:13

anointedst
of Beth-el where thou *a. Gen* 31:13
a. my head with oil, my. *Ps* 23:5

anointing
their *a.* be an everlasting. *Ex* 40:15
destroyed because of the *a. Isa* 10:27
but the *a.* which ye have received of
him as the same *a.* *1 John* 2:27

anointing oil
he made the holy *a. oil.* *Ex* 37:29
he poured of the *a. oil.* *Lev* 8:12
for the *a. oil* of the Lord is. 10:7
'on whose head the *a. oil* was 21:10
Eleazar pertaineth *a. oil. Num* 4:16
a. him with *oil* in the. *Jas* 5:14

anon
(*Revised Version*, straightway)
heareth, and *a.* with joy. *Mat* 13:20
mother lay sick, and *a.* *Mark* 1:30

another
appointed me *a.* seed. *Gen* 4:25
Lord shall add to me *a.* son. 30:24
asked us, have ye *a.* brother? 43:7
thing, which *a.* challengeth. *Ex* 22:9*
Caleb, because he had *a. Num* 14:24
a generation that knew. *Judg* 2:10
be weak, and be as *a.* man. 16:7
shalt be turned into *a. 1 Sam* 10:6
was so, that God gave him *a.* 9
give her royal estate to *a. Esth* 1:19
shall behold and not *a. Job* 19:27†
not a secret to *a.* *Pr* 25:9
let *a.* praise thee, and not thy. 27:2
will I not give to *a. Isa* 42:8; 48:11
a. shall call himself by the. 44:5
hast discovered thyself to *a.* 57:8
call his servants by *a.* name. 65:15
shalt not be for *a.* man. *Hos* 3:3*

man strive nor reprove *a.* *Hos* 4:4*
or do we look for *a.* ? *Mat* 11:3
is it I ? *a.* said, is it I ? *Mark* 14:19
said he to *a.* how much. *Luke* 16:7
faithful in that which is *a.* man's. 12
a. Jesus, a. Spirit, or *a.* *2 Cor* 11:4*
which is not *a.* but there be. *Gal* 1:7
rejoicing in himself and not in *a.* 6:4*
exhort one *a.* while. *Heb* 3:13; 10:25
not have spoken of *a.* day. 4:8

one another, see love

one against another
one man sin *against a. 1 Sam* 2:25
dash them *one against a. Jer* 13:14
puffed up *one against a. 1 Cor* 4:6
grudge not *one against a. Jas* 5:9

one for another
to eat, tarry *one for a. 1 Cor* 11:33
have same care *one for a.* 12:25
pray *one for a.* that ye may. *Jas* 5:16

answer
[1] *To reply,* Pr 26:4. [2] *To
begin to speak, when no question is
asked,* Dan 2:26; Acts 5:8. [3] *To
witness,* Gen 30:33. [4] *To grant
what one desires in prayer,* Ps 27:7;
86:7; Isa 65:24.

Pharaoh an *a.* of peace. *Gen* 41:16
the city make thee an *a. Deut* 20:11
see what *a.* I shall. *2 Sam* 24:13
return Mordecai this *a. Esth* 4:15
and he gave me no *a.* *Job* 19:16
because they found no *a.* 32:3
cry, but none giveth *a.* 35:12
a soft *a.* turneth away. *Pr* 15:1
a man hath joy by the *a.* of his. 23
the *a.* of the tongue is from. 16:1
his lips that giveth a right *a.* 24:26
him, but he gave me no *a. S of S* 5:6
the lips, for there is no *a.* *Mi* 3:7
they marvelled at his *a. Luke* 20:26
that we may give *a.* to. *John* 1:22
thou ? Jesus gave him no *a.* 19:9
what saith the *a.* of God ? *Rom* 11:4
mine *a.* to them that do. *1 Cor* 9:3
my first *a.* none stood. *2 Tim* 4:16*
be ready to give an *a.* *1 Pet* 3:15
a. of a good conscience towards. 21

answers
in your *a.* remaineth. *Job* 21:34
because of his *a.* for wicked. 34:36
were astonished at his *a. Luke* 2:47

answer, *verb*
my righteousness *a.* for. *Gen* 30:33
all the people shall *a. Deut* 27:15
voice, nor any to *a.* *1 Ki* 18:26
thou, and I will *a.* and *a. Job* 13:22
the words that he would *a.* me. 23:5
visiteth, what shall I *a.* him ? 31:14
a. thee, God is greater. 33:12; 35:4
that reproveth God, let him *a.* 40:2
mercy also on me, and *a.* *Ps* 27:7
things in right, wilt thou *a.* us. 65:5
thee, for thou wilt *a.* me. 86:7
the day when I call, *a.* me. 102:2
thy right hand, and *a.* me. 108:6
O Lord, in thy faithfulness *a.* 143:1
the righteous studieth to *a. Pr* 15:28
thou mightest *a.* the words. 22:21*
a. a fool according to his folly. 26:5
what shall one then *a. Isa* 14:32
was there none to *a.* ? 50:2; 66:4
thou call, and the Lord will *a.* 58:9
are not careful to *a.* thee. *Dan* 3:16
yea the Lord will *a.* and. *Joel* 2:19
what I shall *a.* when I. *Hab* 2:1
no man was able to *a.* *Mat* 22:46
heaven or of men ? *a. Mark* 11:30
wist they what to *a.* him. 14:40
he from within shall *a. Luke* 11:7
how or what thing ye shall *a.* 12:11
he shall *a.* I know you not. 13:25
before what ye shall *a.* 21:14
more cheerfully *a.* for myself.
　　　Acts 24:10*; 25:16*; 26:2*
have somewhat to *a.* *2 Cor* 5:12
know how ye ought to *a.* *Col* 4:6

I will answer
call, *I will a.* *Job* 13:22; 14:15
　　　　　　　　　Ps 91:15; *Jer* 33:3
before they call *I will a.* *Isa* 65:24
I the Lord *will a.* him. *Ezek* 14:4

not answer
brethren could *not a.* him. *Gen* 45:3
he could *not a.* Abner. *2 Sam* 3:11
was, *a.* not. *2 Ki* 18:36; *Isa* 36:21
a. him one of a thousand. *Job* 9:3
but I will *not a.* *Pr* 1:28
a. not a fool according to his. 26:4
understand, he will *not a.* 29:19*
I called, ye did *not a.* *Isa* 65:12
but they will *not a.* thee. *Jer* 7:27
they could *not a.* him. *Luke* 14:6
if I ask, you will *not a.* nor. 22:68

answerable
a. to the hangings of the. *Ex* 38:18

answered
(*Revised Version, frequently,* said)
Penuel *a.* as ... of Succoth *a. Judg* 8:8
and he *a.* here am I. *1 Sam* 3:4, 16
the women *a.* one another as. 18:7*
men of Judah *a.* the. *2 Sam* 19:42
and thus he *a.* me. *1 Ki* 2:30
king *a.* people. 12:13; *2 Chr* 10:13
no voice, nor any that *a. 1 Ki* 18:26
the man of God *a.* the. *2 Chr* 25:9
multitude of words be *a.* ? *Job* 11:2
I *a.* O Lord God, thou. *Ezek* 37:3
Daniel *a.* with counsel. *Dan* 2:14
Balaam the son of Beor *a.* *Mi* 6:5
accused he *a.* nothing. *Mat* 27:12
　　14; *Mark* 14:61; 15:5; *Luke* 23:9
perceiving that he had *a. Mark* 12:28
when Jesus saw that he *a.* 34
held their peace, James *a. Acts* 15:13
I *a.* who art thou, Lord ? and. 22:8
he *a.* for himself. 25:8*; 26:1*

answered, *referring to God*
who *a.* me in the day of. *Gen* 35:3
Moses spake, and God *a. Ex* 19:19
and the Lord *a.* it is. *2 Sam* 21:1
he *a.* him from heaven. *1 Chr* 21:26
that the Lord had *a.* him. 28
a. thee in the secret place. *Ps* 81:7
the Lord, and he *a.* them. 99:6
the Lord *a.* me, and set me. 118:5
a. till the cities be wasted. *Isa* 6:11
what hath the Lord *a. Jer* 23:35, 37
the Lord *a.* me, write the. *Hab* 2:2
the Lord *a.* the angel. *Zech* 1:13
he *a.* one of them and. *Mat* 20:13
his lord *a.* and said, thou. 25:26

answered not
she *a.* not, nor did she. *1 Sam* 4:20
he *a.* him *not* that day. 14:37; 28:6
a. them *not. 2 Sam* 22:42; *Ps* 18:41
people *a.* him *not* a word. *1 Ki* 18:21
　　　　　　2 Ki 18:36; *Isa* 36:21
you, but ye *a. not. Jer* 7:13; 35:17
but he *a.* her *not* a word. *Mat* 15:23

answered *and said*
Moses *a.* and said, will not. *Ex* 4:1
servants *a.* and said, let. *2 Ki* 7:13
then *a.* I them and said. *Neh* 2:20
Job *a.* and said. *Job* 6:1; 9:1
　　　　　　　　12:1; 16:1; 19:1
a. and said, Babylon is. *Isa* 21:9
then *a.* I *and said,* so be it. *Jer* 11:5

answeredst
thou *a.* them, O Lord our. *Ps* 99:8
day when I cried thou *a.* me. 138:3

answerest
David cried, *a.* thou ? *1 Sam* 26:14
thee, that thou *a.* ? *Job* 16:3
a. thou nothing ? *Mat* 26:62
　　　　　　　　　Mark 14:60; 15:4
a. thou the high-priest ? *John* 18:22

answereth
God is departed and *a. 1 Sam* 28:15
let the God that *a.* by. *1 Ki* 18:24
on God, and he *a.* him. *Job* 12:4
that *a.* a matter before. *Pr* 18:13
the poor intreat, but the rich *a.* 23
as face *a.* to face, so the. 27:19
God *a.* him in the joy of. *Eccl* 5:20
maketh merry, but money *a.* 10:19
and *a.* to Jerusalem that. *Gal* 4:25

answering
the other *a.* rebuked. *Luke* 23:40
be obedient, not *a.* again. *Tit* 2:9

ant, -s
go to the *a.* thou sluggard . *Pr* 6:6
the *a.* are a people not strong. 30:25

Antichrist, -s

A. will come, now there are many A.
1 John 2:18
he is A. that denieth the Father. 22
this is that spirit of A. whereof. 4:3
this is a deceiver and an A. 2 John 7

Antioch

travelled as far as A. Acts 11:19, 22
when they were come to A. spake. 20
were called Christians first in A. 26
they came to A. in Pisidia. 13:14
from Attalia they sailed to A. 14:26
of their own company to A. 15:22
Barnabas continued in A. 35
when Peter was come to A. Gal 2:11
which came to me at A. 2 Tim 3:11

Antipas, see Martyr

Antipatris

Paul by night to A. Acts 23:31

antiquity

joyous city, whose a. is of. Isa 23:7

anvil

him that smote the a. Isa 41:7

any

against a. of the children. Ex 11:7
sin against a. of the commandments.
Lev 4:2, 13, 22, 27; 5:17
lieth, in a. of all these that a. 6:3
nor a. that can deliver. Deut 32:39
word with a. 2 Sam 7:7; 1 Chr 17:6
yet a. left of the house? 2 Sam 9:1
was no voice, nor a. 1 Ki 18:26
he looketh, and if a. say. Job 33:27*
who will shew us a. good? Ps 4:6
turneth not away for a. Pr 30:30
no God, I know not a. Isa 44:8
shall say, is there yet a. Amos 6:10
nor go nor tell it to a. in. Mark 8:26*
if ye have ought against a. 11:25
nor could be healed of a. Luke 8:43
if he found a. of this way. Acts 9:2
brought under power of a. 1 Cor 6:12
if a. lack wisdom, let him. Jas 1:5
not willing that a. should. 2 Pet 3:9
if there come a. and bring. 2 John 10

see further, God, man, more,
thing, time, while, wise.

apace, see flee, fled

apart

shalt set a. all that open. Ex 13:12
shall be put a. seven. Lev 15:19*
approach, as long as she is a. 18:19*
the Lord hath set a. him. Ps 4:3
a. their wives a. Zech 12:12, 14
into a desert place a. Mat 14:13
into a mountain a. 23; 17:1
the disciples to Jesus a. 17:19
come ye yourselves a. Mark 6:31
lay a. all filthiness. Jas 1:21

Apelles

salute A. approved in. Rom 16:10

Aphek

pitched in A. 1 Sam 4:1; 29:1
the rest fled to A. there. 1 Ki 20:30
smite the Syrians in A. 2 Ki 13:17

apes, see peacocks

apiece

five shekels a. by poll. Num 3:47
spoons weighing ten shekels a. 7:86
their princes gave him a rod a. 17:6
eighteen cubits high a. 1 Ki 7:15
nor have two coats a. Luke 9:3
two or three firkins a. John 2:6

Apollonia

had passed through A. Acts 17:1

Apollos

certain Jew named A. Acts 18:24
I am of A. 1 Cor 1:12; 3:4
who is A.? 3:5
I have planted, A. watered, God. 3:6
in a figure transferred to A. 4:6
bring Zenas and A. on. Tit 3:13

Apollyon

tongue, his name is A. Rev 9:11

apostle

Literally, one sent forth. Used
as referring [1] chiefly to one of the
12 disciples of Christ, Matt. 10:2; or

[2] to any of various other followers
of Christ who did evangelistic
work, Rom 1:1.
called to be an a. Rom 1:1; 1 Cor 1:1
inasmuch as I am the a. Rom 11:13
am I not an a.? 1 Cor 9:1, 2
meet to be called an a. 15:9
an a. of Jesus. 2 Cor 1:1; Eph 1:1
Col 1:1; 1 Tim 1:1; 2 Tim 1:1
Gal 1:1
signs of an a. were. 2 Cor 12:12
ordained an a. 1 Tim 2:7; 2 Tim 1:11
Paul a servant of God, and a. Tit 1:1
the a. and high-priest. Heb 3:1

apostles

names of the 12 a. Mat 10:2
a. gathered themselves. Mark 6:30
whom he named a. Luke 6:13
a. when they were returned. 9:10
send them prophets and a. 11:49
a. said to the Lord, increase. 17:5
and the twelve a. with him. 22:14
told these things to the a. 24:10
with the eleven a. Acts 1:26
were done by the a. 2:43; 5:12
down at the a. feet. 4:35, 37; 5:2
laid their hands on the a. and. 5:18
scattered abroad, except the a. 8:1
of note among the a. Rom 16:7
set forth us the a. last. 1 Cor 4:9
God hath set first a. 12:28
are all a.? 29
for I am the least of the a. 15:9
behind the chiefest a. 2 Cor 11:5
12:11
false a. deceitful workers. 11:13
them that were a. before. Gal 1:17
but other of the a. saw I none. 19
now revealed to his holy a. Eph 3:5
some a and some prophets. 4:11
burdensome as the a. 1 Thes 2:6
commandment of us the a. 2 Pet 3:2
words spoken before of the a. Jude 17
them which say they are a. Rev 2:2
rejoice over her, ye holy a. 18:20

apostleship

(The office of the apostles)
he may take part of this a. Acts 1:25
have received grace and a. Rom 1:5
the seal of mine a. are ye. 1 Cor 9:2
effectually in Peter to the a. Gal 2:8

apothecary

(Revised Version, perfumer)
compounded after art of a. Ex 30:25
after the art of the a. 35; 37:29
the ointment of the a. Eccl 10:1

apparel

arose and changed his a. 2 Sam 12:20
the attendance of his ministers, and
their a. 1 Ki 10:5; 2 Chr 9:4
the changeable suits of a. Isa 3:22*
and wear our own a. 4:1
that is glorious in his a. 63:1
are clothed in strange a. Zeph 1:8
stood by them in white a. Acts 1:10
coveted no man's silver or a. 20:33
themselves in modest a. 1 Tim 2:9
if a man come in goodly a. Jas 2:2
gold, or putting on a. 1 Pet 3:3

see royal

apparelled

virgins, were a. 2 Sam 13:18
which are gorgeously a. Luke 7:25

apparently

(Revised Version, manifestly)
I speak even a. and not. Num 12:8

appeal, -ed

I a. unto Caesar. Acts 25:11, 21
liberty, if he had not a. to. 26:32
I was constrained to a. to. 28:19

appear

God said, let the dry land a. Gen 1:9
and none shall a. before me empty.
Ex 23:15; 34:20; Deut 16:16
the year all males shall a. Ex 23:17
when thou shalt go to a. 34:24
Israel is come to a. Deut 31:11
when shall I come and a.? Ps 42:2
thy work a. to thy servants. 90:16
flowers a. on the earth. S of S 2:12*
a flock of goats that a. 4:1*; 6:5
when ye come to a. Isa 1:12

that thy shame may a. Jer 13:26
doings your sins do a. Ezek 21:24
that they may a. to men. Mat 6:16
so ye outwardly a. righteous. 23:28
then shall a. the sign of the. 24:30
as graves which a. not. Luke 11:44
kingdom of God should a. 19:11
in which I will a. to thee. Acts 26:16
but sin, that it might a. Rom 7:13
we must all a. before. 2 Cor 5:10*
who is our life shall a. then. Col 3:4
that thy profiting may a. 1 Tim 4:15
now to a. in the presence. Heb 9:24
to them shall he a. the second. 28
not made of things which do a. 11:3
ungodly and sinner a.? 1 Pet 4:18
when the chief Shepherd shall a. 5:4
when he shall a. we may. 1 John 2:28
it doth not yet a. what we shall . . .
know that when he shall a. we. 3:2
thy nakedness do not a. Rev 3:18

appear, referred to God

to-day the Lord will a. to. Lev 9:4, 6
I will a. in the cloud on the. 16:2
did I plainly a. to the. 1 Sam 2:27
that night did God a. 2 Chr 1:7
build up Zion, he shall a. Ps 102:16
he shall a. to your joy. Isa 66:5*
in the which I will a. Acts 26:16

appearance

as the a. of fire. Num 9:15, 16
looketh on the outward a. 1 Sam 16:7
as the a. of a man. Dan 8:15; 10:18
his face as the a. of lightning. 10:6
not according to the a. John 7:24
which glory in a. and. 2 Cor 5:12
things after the outward a.? 10:7*
abstain from all a. of. 1 Thes 5:22*

appeared

a. to Abram. Gen 12:7; 17:1; 18:1
Lord a. to Isaac, and said. 26:2, 24
Jacob said, God Almighty a. to. 48:3
angel of the Lord a. in. Ex 3:2
the Lord hath a. to thee. 4:1
I a. to Abraham by name of. 6:3
returned when the morning a. 14:27
channels of the sea a. 2 Sam 22:16
which had a. to Solomon. 1 Ki 11:9
there a. a chariot of fire. 2 Ki 2:11
the work till the stars a. Neh 4:21
the Lord hath a. of old to. Jer 31:3
what time the star a. Mat 2:7
the blade sprang, then a. the. 13:26
a. to them Moses. 17:3; Mark 9:4
holy city, and a. to many. Mat 27:53
Jesus a. first to Mary. Mark 16:9
after that he a. in another form to. 12
after he a. to the eleven as they. 14
there a. to him an angel. Luke 1:11
who a. in glory, and spake. 9:31
there a. an angel to him. 22:43
Lord is risen indeed, and a. 24:34
there a. to them cloven. Acts 2:3
the God of glory a. to our. 7:2
even Jesus, that a. to thee. 9:17
I have a. to thee for this. 26:16
neither sun nor stars a. 27:20
the grace of God hath a. Tit 2:11
love of God toward man a. 3:4
in the end hath he a. to. Heb 9:26
there a. a great wonder. Rev 12:1, 3

appeareth

as the leprosy a. in the. Lev 13:43
deliver him. as a. this. Deut 2:30*
every one of them in Zion a. Ps 84:7
the hay a. and the tender. Pr 27:25*
for evil a. out of the north. Jer 6:1
shall stand when he a.? Mal 3:2
is even as a vapour that a. Jas 4:14

appearing

commandment till a. 1 Tim 6:14
made manifest by the a. 2 Tim 1:10
the quick and dead at his a. 4:1
all them also that love his a. 8
looking for glorious a. of. Tit 2:13
found to praise at the a. 1 Pet 1:7

appease

I will a. him with the. Gen 32:20

appeased, -eth

Ahasuerus a. he. Esth 2:1
slow to anger a. strife. Pr 15:18
town-clerk had a. the. Acts 19:35

appertain
them, with all that a. *Num* 16:30
fear, for to thee doth it a. *Jer* 10:7
see **pertain**

appertained
men that a. to Korah. *Num* 16:32, 33

appertaineth, -ing
give it to him to whom it a. *Lev* 6:5
Abraham, our father, as a. *Rom* 4:1

appetite
wilt thou fill the a. of the. *Job* 38:39
if thou be a man given to a. *Pr* 23:2
all labour for mouth, yet a. *Eccl* 6:7
awaketh, and his soul hath a. *Isa* 29:8

Appii-forum
meet us as far as A. *Acts* 28:15

apple of the eye
(*The eyeball*)
as the a. of his eye. *Deut* 32:10
keep me as the a. of the eye. *Ps* 17:8
law as the a. of thine eye. *Pr* 7:2
let not the a. of thine eye. *Lam* 2:18
toucheth the a. of his eye. *Zech* 2:8

apples
like a. of gold in pictures. *Pr* 25:11
comfort me with a. for I. *S of S* 2:5
and smell of thy nose like a. 7:8

apple-tree
as the a.-tree among. *S of S* 2:3
raised thee up under the a.-tree. 8:5
palm-tree and a.-tree. *Joel* 1:12

applied
I a. my heart to know. *Eccl* 7:25*
I a. my heart to every work. 8:9
when I a. mine heart to know. 16

apply
we may a. our hearts. *Ps* 90:12*
and a. thine heart to. *Pr* 2:2
hear words, a. thine heart to. 22:17
a. thine heart to instruction. 23:12

appoint
(*To establish, to set apart for an office, or to decree*)
a. me thy wages, and I. *Gen* 30:28
let Pharaoh a. officers over. 41:34
I will a. over you terror. *Lev* 26:16
Aaron and his sons a. *Num* 4:19
to a. me ruler over the. *2 Sam* 6:21
I will a. a place for my people. 7:10
that thou wouldest a. me. *Job* 14:13
salvation will God a. for. *Isa* 26:1
a. them that mourn in Zion. 61:3
a. over them four kinds. *Jer* 15:3
chosen man that I had a. over her ?
who will a. me ? 49:19; 50:44
the kingdoms a. a captain. 51:27
a. these two ways. *Ezek* 21:19
a. a way that. 20
they shall a. themselves. *Hos* 1:11
a. him his portion with the. *Mat* 24:51
a. him his portion with. *Luke* 12:46
I a. you a kingdom, as my. 22:29
seven men whom we a. *Acts* 6:3

appointed
she that thou hast a. for. *Gen* 24:14
passover in a. seasons. *Num* 9:2, 3
an offering, but at an a. season. 7
brought not offering in a. season. 13
these were the cities a. *Josh* 20:9
was an a. sign between. *Judg* 20:38
not within the days a. *1 Sam* 13:11
Samuel standing as a. over. 19:20*
Lord had a. to defeat. *2 Sam* 17:14
I have a. him to be ruler. *1 Ki* 1:35
let go a man whom I had a. 20:42*
thou hast a. prophets to. *Neh* 6:7
their rebellion a. a captain to. 9:17
wearisome nights are a. to. *Job* 7:3
thou hast a. his bounds, that. 14:5
and the heritage a. to him. 20:29
to death, and to the house a. 30:23
hast given us like sheep a. *Ps* 44:11
a. a law in Israel, which he. 78:5
those that are a. to die. 79:11
to loose those that are a. to. 102:20
come home at the day a. *Pr* 7:20*
when he a. the foundations of. 8:29
cause of all such as are a. to. 31:8*
new-moons and your a. *Isa* 1:14

who, since I a. the ancient. *Isa* 44:7†
he reserveth the a. weeks. *Jer* 5:24
sea-shore, there hath he a. 47:7
I have a. thee each day. *Ezek* 4:6
the rod, and who hath a. it. *Mi* 6:9
field, as the Lord a. *Mat* 27:10
more than what is a. you. *Luke* 3:13
after these the Lord a. other. 10:1
kingdom, as my Father hath a. 22:29
they a. two, Joseph and. *Acts* 1:23*
he hath a. a day in which. 17:31
apostles last, a. to death. *1 Cor* 4:9*
you know that we are a. *1 Thes* 3:3
God hath not a. us to wrath. 5:9
whereunto I am a. a. *2 Tim* 1:11
elders in every city, as I a. *Tit* 1:5
faithful to him that a. *Heb* 3:2
as it is a. to men once to die. 9:27
also they were a. *1 Pet* 2:8

appointed *time* and *times*
at the *time* a. will I. *Gen* 18:14
Lord a. a set *time*, saying. *Ex* 9:5
unleavened bread in *time* a. 23:15
the set *time* Samuel a. *1 Sam* 13:8
into the field at the *time* a. 20:35
the set *time* a. him. *2 Sam* 20:5
to their a. *time* every. *Esth* 9:27
is there not an a. *time* to ? *Job* 7:1*
the days of my a. *time* will. 14:14*
trumpet in the *time* a. *Ps* 81:3*
be alone in his a. *times*. *Isa* 14:31
heaven knoweth her a. *times*. *Jer* 8:7
he hath passed the *time* a. 46:17
for at the *time* a. the end. *Dan* 8:19
thing was true, but the *time* a. 10:1*
end shall be at the *time* a. 11:27
time a. shall return, and come. 29
because it is yet for a *time* a. 35
vision is yet for an a. *time*. *Hab* 2:3
times before a. *Acts* 17:26
under tutors, until the *time* a. *Gal* 4:2

appointeth
he a. over it whomsoever. *Dan* 5:21*

appointment
at the a. of Aaron and. *Num* 4:27*
by the a. of Absalom. *2 Sam* 13:32
wheat, salt according to a. *Ezra* 6:9*
had made an a. together. *Job* 2:11

apprehend
(*To seize or take prisoner*)
garrison desirous to a. *2 Cor* 11:32*
I may a. that for which. *Phil* 3:12

apprehended
when he a. Peter, he put. *Acts* 12:4
I am a. of Christ Jesus. *Phil* 3:12
not myself to have a. but. 13

approach
[1] *To draw nigh, or come near,*
2 Sam 11:20; *Ps* 65:4; *Isa* 58:2.
[2] *To contract marriage with,*
Lev 18:6.
none of you shall a. to. *Lev* 18:6
not a. to offer the bread. 21:17, 18
ye a. this day to battle. *Deut* 20:3
behold, thy days a. that thou. 31:14
make his sword to a. *Job* 40:19†
man whom thou causeth to a. *Ps* 65:4
a. to me, for who is this that engaged
his heart to a. to me ? *Jer* 30:21
light no man can a. unto. *1 Tim* 6:16

approached
wherefore a. ye so ? *2 Sam* 11:20
the king a. to the altar. *2 Ki* 16:12

approacheth, -ing
they take delight in a. to. *Isa* 58:2
where no thief a. nor. *Luke* 12:33
more as ye see the day a. *Heb* 10:25

approve
(*To like or commend*)
yet their posterity a. *Ps* 49:13
whom you shall a. by. *1 Cor* 16:3
that ye may a. things. *Phil* 1:10

approved
Jesus, a man a. of God. *Acts* 2:22
acceptable to God, and a. *Rom* 14:18
salute Apelles a. in Christ. 16:10
are a. may be made. *1 Cor* 11:19
in all things you have a. *2 Cor* 7:11
commendeth himself is a. 10:18
not that we should appear a. but. 13:7
study to shew thyself a. *2 Tim* 2:15

approvest, -eth
a man, the Lord a. not. *Lam* 3:36
a. the things that are. *Rom* 2:18

approving
but in all things a. *2 Cor* 6:4

apron, -s
fig-leaves together, and made a.
Gen 3:7
brought to the sick a. *Acts* 19:12

apt
a. for war, king of. *2 Ki* 24:16
be a. to teach. *1 Tim* 3:2; *2 Tim* 2:24

Aquila
a certain Jew named A. *Acts* 18:2
when A. and Priscilla heard. 26
greet A. and Priscilla. *Rom* 16:3
2 Tim 4:19
A. and Priscilla salute. *1 Cor* 16:19

Ar
consumed A. of Moab. *Num* 21:28
I have given A. to the. *Deut* 2:9
in the night A. of Moab is. *Isa* 15:1

Arabia
kings of A. *1 Ki* 10:15; *2 Chr* 9:14
A. shall lodge in A. *Isa* 21:13
all the kings of A. *Jer* 25:24
I went into A. and. *Gal* 1:17
Agar is mount Sinai in A. 4:25

Arabian, -s
the A. brought. *2 Chr* 17:11
helped Uzziah against the A. 26:7
nor shall the A. pitch tent. *Isa* 13:20
thou sattest for them as A. *Jer* 3:2
Cretes and A. we do hear. *Acts* 2:11

Aram
sons of Shem, Lud, A. *Gen* 10:22
1 Chr 1:17
Moab brought me from A. *Num* 23:7
Esrom begat A. *Mat* 1:3
A. begat Aminadab. 4:4
which was the son of A. *Luke* 3:33
see **Padan**

Ararat
on the mountains of A. *Gen* 8:4
her the kingdoms of A. *Jer* 51:27

Araunah
the threshing-place of A. *2 Sam* 24:16
all these did A. as a king give. 23

Arba
A. was a great man. *Josh* 14:15

Arba
gave them A. which city. *Josh* 21:11

archangel
with the voice of the a. *1 Thes* 4:16
Michael the a. when. *Jude* 9

archer, -s
grew and became an a. *Gen* 21:20
the a. have sorely grieved. 49:23
a. hit him. *1 Sam* 31:3; *1 Chr* 10:3
his a. compass me round. *Job* 16:13
they are bound by the a. *Isa* 22:3
bendeth let a. bend bow. *Jer* 51:3

arches
narrow windows to the a. *Ezek* 40:16

Archelaus
heard that A. did reign. *Mat* 2:22

Archippus
say to A. take heed to. *Col* 4:17
Paul to A. fellow-soldier. *Philem* 2

Arcturus
which maketh A. Orion and. *Job* 9:9
or canst thou guide A. with ? 38:32

Areopagite
was Dionysius the A. *Acts* 17:34

Areopagus
and brought him to A. *Acts* 17:19

Aretas
the governor under A. *2 Cor* 11:32

Argob
region of A. *Deut* 3:4; 13:14
1 Ki 4:13

arguing
doth your a. reprove ? *Job* 6:25*

arguments
would fill my mouth with a. *Job* 23:4

Ariel

sent for Eliezer and *A.*   *Ezra* 8:16
woe to *A.* the city where.   *Isa* 29:1
A. it shall be to me as *A.*   2
nations that fight against *A.*   7

aright

his conversation *a.*   *Ps* 50:23
that set not their heart *a.*   78:8
the wise useth knowledge *a. Pr* 15:2
wine, when it moveth itself *a.* 23:31
but they spake not *a.*   *Jer* 8:6

Arimathea

Joseph of *A.* who was.   *Mat* 27:57
Mark 15:43; *Luke* 23:51
John 19:38

Arioch

in the days of *A.* king of.   *Gen* 14:1
then *A.* brought in Daniel. *Dan* 2:25

arise

[1] *To proceed from*, Acts 20:30.
[2] *To be raised and comforted*,
Amos 7:2.

now *a.* get thee out of.   *Gen* 31:13
a. go up to Beth-el, and.   35:1
if there *a.* among you a.   *Deut* 13:1
then shalt thou *a.* and get.   17:8
now therefore *a.* go over.   *Josh* 1:2
a. Barak, lead thy.   *Judg* 5:12
let the young men *a.*   2 *Sam* 2:14
I will *a.* and gather all Israel.   3:21
so be that the king's wrath *a.* 11:20
after thee shall any *a.*   1 *Ki* 3:12
make Jehu *a.* from.   2 *Ki* 9:2
a. be doing, the Lord.   1 *Chr* 22:16
we his servants will *a.*   *Neh* 2:20
a. too much contempt.   *Esth* 1:18
then shall enlargement *a.* to.   4:14
when shall I *a.* and night? *Job* 7:4
whom doth not his light *a.* ?   25:3
a. O Lord, save me, O my. *Ps* 3:7
a. O Lord, in thine anger lift.   7:6
now will I *a.* saith the Lord, I. 12:5
a. for our help, and redeem.   44:26
let God *a.* let his enemies be.   68:1
shall the dead *a.* and praise? 88:10
when the waves of sea *a.* thou. 89:9
thou shalt *a.* and have mercy. 102:13
when wilt thou *a.* out of.   *Pr* 6:9
a. my love, my fair one. *S of S* 2:13
a. ye princes, and anoint. *Isa* 21:5
my dead body shall they *a.*   26:19
kings shall *a.* princes shall.   49:7
a. shine, for thy light is come.   60:1
but the Lord shall *a.* upon thee.   2
in trouble they will say. *a. Jer* 2:27
shall they fall and not *a.* ?   8:4
a. ye, let us go up to Zion to.   31:6
a. cry out in the night.   *Lam* 2:19
after thee shall *a.*   *Dan* 2:39
whom shall Jacob *a.*   *Amos* 7:2*, 5
a. aye and depart.   *Mi* 2:10
a. and thresh, O daughter of.   4:13
enemy, when I fall I shall *a.*   7:8
saith to the dumb stone *a. Hab* 2:19
Sun of righteousness *a.*   *Mal* 4:2
say *a.* and walk? *Mat* 9:5; *Mark* 2:9
there shall *a.* false Christs. *Mat* 24:24
say to these *a. Mark* 5:41; *Luke* 8:54
man, I say to thee *a.*   *Luke* 7:14
I will *a.* and go to my father.   15:18
and why do thoughts *a.* in?   24:38
even so I do, *a.* let us.   *John* 14:31
body said, Tabitha, *a.*   *Acts* 9:40
selves shall men *a.* speaking. 20:30
why tarriest thou? *a.* and be. 22:16
a. from the dead, and.   *Eph* 5:14
till the day-star *a.* in.   2 *Pet* 1:19

see rise

ariseth

behold, there *a.* a little.   1 *Ki* 18:44
to the upright *a.* light in.   *Ps* 112:4
a. to shake terribly the. *Isa* 2:19, 21
when persecution *a.*   *Mat* 13:21
Mark 4:17
for out of Galilee *a.*   *John* 7:52
the similitude of Melchizedec *a.*
Heb 7:15

see sun

Aristarchus

caught Gaius and *A.*   *Acts* 19:29
A. accompanied Paul into.   20:4
one *A.* a Macedonian being.   27:2

A. fellow-prisoner.   *Col* 4:10
Philem 24

Aristobulus

that are of *A.* household. *Rom* 16:10

ark

[1] *A chest or coffer to keep
things sure or secret*, Ex 2:3.
[2] *The great vessel in which Noah
and his family were preserved during the flood*, Gen 6:14, 15; Heb
11:7. [3] *That chest wherein the
two tables of the law, Aaron's rod,
and the pot of manna were kept*,
Ex 37:1; Heb 9:4.

an *a.* of gopher-wood.   *Gen* 6:14
and the *a.* went on the face of. 7:18
she took for him an *a.* of.   *Ex* 2:3
put into the *a.* the testimony which I
shall give thee. 25:16, 21; 40:3, 20
made the *a.* of shittim-wood.   37:1
charge shall be the *a.*   *Num* 3:31
a. of the Lord.   *Josh* 4:11; 6:12
1 Sam 4:6; 6:1; *2 Sam* 6:9
they looked into *a.*   *1 Sam* 6:19
the *a.* and Israel abide. *2 Sam* 11:11
thou barest the *a.* of.   *1 Ki* 2:26
was nothing in the *a.* save the.   8:9
after that the *a.* had.   *1 Chr* 6:31
let us bring again the *a.* of.   13:3
put forth his hand to hold the *a.*   9
prepared a place for the *a.*   15:1
and *a.* of thy strength.   *2 Chr* 6:41
Ps 132:8
whereunto the *a.* hath.   *2 Chr* 8:11
Noah entered the *a.*   *Mat* 24:38
Luke 17:27
of God prepared an *a.*   *Heb* 11:7
waited while the *a* was. *1 Pet* 3:20
seen in his temple the *a. Rev* 11:19

before the ark

altar of gold *before the a.*   *Ex* 40:5
were cut off *before the a.*   *Josh* 4:7
earth on his face *before the a.*   7:6
his face *before the a.*   *1 Sam* 5:3
left *before the a.* Asaph. *1 Chr* 16:37
assembled *before the a.*   *2 Chr* 5:6

ark *of the covenant*

a. of covenant of Lord.   *Num* 10:33
inside of *a.* of covenant. *Deut*. 31:26
off before *a.* of covenant.   *Josh* 4:7
a. of covenant of God.   *Judg* 20:27
the *a.* of the covenant of. *1 Sam* 4:3
bearing *a.* of covenant. *2 Sam* 15:24
a. of covenant remained. *1 Chr* 17:1
more, the *a.* of covenant.   *Jer* 3:16
had the *a.* of the covenant. *Heb* 9:4

ark *of God*

where the *a.* of God was. *1 Sam* 3:3
the *a.* of God was taken. 4:11; 17:22
if ye send away the *a.* of God.   6:3
died before the *a.* of God. *2 Sam* 6:7
but the *a.* of God dwelleth.   7:2
carry back the *a.* of God into. 15:25
I bring the *a.* of God.   *1 Chr* 13:12
ought to carry the *a.* of God.   15:2

arm

*Literally, for the part of the body so
called*, 2 Sam 1:10. [2] *Figuratively for power or strength*, Ps
10:15; Jer 27:5; Isa 53:1; John
12:38.

by greatness of thine *a.*   *Ex* 15:16
he teareth the *a.* with.   *Deut* 33:20
I will cut off thine *a.*   *1 Sam* 2:31
that was on his *a.*   2 *Sam* 1:10
with him is an *a.* of.   *2 Chr* 32:8
savest thou the *a.* that.   *Job* 26:2
a. fall from my shoulder.   31:22*
cry out by reason of the *a.* of.   35:9
the high *a.* shall be broken.   38:15
hast thou an *a.* like God?   40:9
break thou the *a.* of the.   *Ps* 10:15
own *a.* save them, but thy *a.*   44:3
hast with thy *a.* redeemed.   77:15
thou hast a mighty *a.* strong. 89:13
mine *a.* also shall strengthen him. 21
his holy *a.* hath gotten him.   98:1
set me as a seal on thine *a. S of S* 8:6
man the flesh of his *a.*   *Isa* 9:20
thou their *a.* every morning.   33:2
God will come, and his *a.* shall. 40:10
gather the lambs with his *a.*   11

---

a. shall judge the people, the isles . . .
me, and on my *a.*   *Isa* 51:5
put on strength, O *a.* of the Lord.   9
hath made bare his holy *a.*   52:10
believed our report? and to whom is
the *a.* of the?   53:1; *John* 12:38
a. brought salvation. *Isa* 59:16; 63:5
Lord hath sworn by the *a.* of.   62:8
led them with his glorious *a.*   63:12
that maketh flesh his *a.*   *Jer* 17:5
fight against you with a strong *a.* 21:5
and thine *a.* shall be.   *Ezek* 4:7
I have broken *a.* of Pharaoh.   30:21
into hell that where his *a.*   31:17
retain the power of the *a.* *Dan* 11:6
sword be on his *a.* his *a. Zech* 11:17
strength with his *a.*   *Luke* 1:51
with an high *a.* brought.   *Acts* 13:17

arm, *verb*

a. some of yourselves to.   *Num* 31:3
a. yourselves with the.   *1 Pet* 4:1

stretched-out arm

you with a *stretched-out a.*   *Ex* 6:6
nation with *stretched-out a.*
Deut 4:34
thee out thence with a *stretched-out
a.*   5:15; 7:19; 26:8; *Jer* 32:21
not seen *stretched-out a. Deut* 11:2
come for thy *stretched-out a.*
2 Chr 6:32
with a *stretched-out a.* *Ps* 136:12
my *stretched-out a. Jer* 27:5; 32:17
with a *stretched-out a.* *Ezek* 20:33
with a *stretched-out a.* and fury. 34

Armageddon

them together to *A.*   *Rev* 16:16

armed

Abram *a.* his trained.   *Gen* 14:14
tribe, twelve thousand *a. Num* 31:5
ourselves will go ready *a.* 32:17, 32
pass over *a. Deut* 3:18; *Josh* 1:14
let him that is *a.* pass on.   *Josh* 6:7
so the *a.* men left the.   2 *Chr* 28:14
he goeth on to meet the *a. Job* 39:21
of Ephraim being *a.*   *Ps* 78:9
want as an *a.* man.   *Pr* 6:11; 24:34
when a strong man *a.*   *Luke* 11:21

Armenia

into land of *A.* 2 *Ki* 19:37; *Isa* 37:38

arm-holes

rags under thy *a.-holes. Jer* 38:12
sew pillows to *a.-holes. Ezek* 13:18

armies

(*Used frequently in the sense of
hosts, great numbers*)

and bring forth my *a.*   *Ex* 7:4
same day I brought your *a.*   12:17
went forth with their *a.*   *Num* 33:1
captains of the *a.* to lead. *Deut* 20:9
I defy the *a.* of Israel. *1 Sam* 17:10
that he should defy the *a.* of the. 26
name of the God of the *a.* of.   45
there any number of his *a.* ? *Job* 25:3
not forth with our *a.*   *Ps* 44:9
kings of *a.* did flee apace, she. 68:12
the company of two *a. S of S* 6:13
his fury upon all their *a.*   *Isa* 34:2
he sent forth his *a.* and.   *Mat* 22:7
compassed with *a.*   *Luke* 21:20
who turned to flight the *a. Heb* 11:34
and the *a.* in heaven.   *Rev* 19:14
kings of the earth and their *a.*   19

armour

[1] *Weapons or instruments of war*,
1 Sam 17:54. [2] *Those things in
which one trusts for protection*,
Luke 11:22; Rom 13:12; Eph 6:11.

David put Goliath's *a.*   1 *Sam* 17:54
and take thee his *a.*   2 *Sam* 2:21
they washed his *a.*   1 *Ki* 22:38*
all able to put on *a.*   2 *Ki* 3:21
have a fenced city also and *a.*   10:2
silver and gold, the house of his *a.*
20:13; *Isa* 39:2
look in that day to *a.* of.   *Isa* 22:8
taketh his *a.* wherein he. *Luke* 11:22
and let us put on the *a. Rom* 13:12
approving by the *a.* of.   2 *Cor* 6:7
put on the *a.* of God to.   *Eph* 6:11
take to you the whole *a.* of God.   13

armour-bearer
called his a.-b., saying. Jud 9:54
a.-b. said, do all that is. 1 Sam 14:7
David, and he became his a.-b. 16:21
his three sons, and his a.-b. 31:6

armoury
of David builded for an a. S of S 4:4
the Lord hath opened his a. Jer 50:25

arms
the a. of his hands were. Gen 49:24
are the everlasting a. Deut 33:27
brake them from his a. Judg 16:12
steel is broken by mine a.
   2 Sam 22:35; Ps 18:34
Jehoram between his a. 2 Ki 9:24
the a. of the fatherless. Job 22:9
the a. of the wicked shall. Ps 37:17
strengtheneth her a. Pr 31:17
with strength of his a. Isa 44:12
bring thy sons in their a. 49:22
and my a. shall judge the. 51:5
tear them from your a. Ezek 13:20
will break Pharaoh's a. 30:22, 24
will strengthen the a. of king. 24, 25
breast and his a. of silver. Dan 2:32
a. and feet like to polished. 10:6
the a. of the south shall not. 11:15
with the a. of a flood shall they. 22
and a. shall stand on this part. 31
and strengthened their a. Hos 7:15
to go, taking them by their a. 11:3
taken him in his a. he. Mark 9:36
them up in his a. put his hands. 10:16
took Christ in his a. Luke 2:28

army
what he did to the a. of. Deut 11:4
give bread to thine a. Judg 8:6
he said, increase thine a. 9:29
of Benjamin out of a. 1 Sam 4:12
Philistines had put a. against a. 17:21
thee an a. like the a. 1 Ki 20:25
praise before the a. 2 Chr 20:21
O king, let not the a. of Israel. 25:7
his brethren, and the a. Neh 4:2
I dwelt as a king in the a. Job 29:25
as an a. with banners. S of S 6:4, 10
up for fear of Pharaoh's a. Jer 37:11
caused his a. to serve. Ezek 29:18
up an exceeding great a. 37:10
to his will in the a. of. Dan 4:35
his voice before his a. Joel 2:11
locust, my great a. which I sent. 25
house, because of the a. Zech 9:8
then came I with an a. Acts 23:27
the number of the a. of. Rev 9:16
that sat on horse and his a. 19:19

see **Chaldeans**

Arnon
he did in the brooks of A. Num 21:14
met Balaam in the border of A. 22:36
and pass over the river A. Deut 2:24
dwelt by the coasts of A. Judg 11:26
Moab shall be at fords of A. Isa 16:2
tell ye it in A. that Moab is. Jer 48:20

Aroer
children of Gad built A. Num 32:34
a present to them in A. 1 Sam 30:28
Jordan and pitched in A. 2 Sam 24:5
Bela, who dwelt in A. 1 Chr 5:8
cities of A. are forsaken. Isa 17:2
O inhabitant of A. stand. Jer 48:19

arose
perceived not when she a. Gen 19:33
lo my sheaf a. and. 37:7
a. up a new king. Ex 1:8; Acts 7:18
a. a generation that knew. Judg 2:10
till I Deborah a. till I a. 5:7
all the people a. as one man. 20:8
they a. early. 1 Sam 9:26; Isa 37:36
when he a. against me. 1 Sam 17:35
neither after him a. 2 Ki 23:25
the wrath of the Lord a. 2 Chr 36:16
young men hid, aged a. Job 29:8
when God a. to judgement. Ps 76:9
to his place where he a. Eccl 1:5
king a. early and went. Dan 6:19
a. and took the young. Mat 2:14, 21
a. and ministered. 8:15; Luke 4:39
he a. and rebuked the winds and the
  Mat 8:26; Mark 4:39; Luke 8:24
a. and followed. Mat 9:9, 19
   Mark 2:14

the hand, and the maid a. Mat 9:25
bodies of saints which slept a. 27:52
lifted up, and he a. Mark 9:27
flood a. the stream beat. Luke 6:48
he a. and came to his father. 15:20
persecution which a. Acts 11:19
there a. no small stir about. 19:23
said there a. dissension. 23:7, 10

see **rose**

arose *and went*
Samuel a. and went to. 1 Sam 3:6
Jonathan a. and went to David. 23:16
David a. and went to. 25:1
Elisha a. and went after. 1 Ki 19:21
Jonah a. and went to. Jonah 3:3
then Peter a. and went. Acts 9:39

Arpad, Arphad
gods of A. 2 Ki 18:34; Isa 36:19
where is the king of A. ? 2 Ki 19:13
   Isa 37:13
is not Hamath as A. ? Isa 10:9
is confounded and A. Jer 49:23

Arphaxad
the son of Shem A. Gen 10:22
   11:10; 1 Chr 1:17
who was the son of A. Luke 3:36

array
[1] To put on apparel, Esth 6:9;
Rev. 7:13. [2] To put an army in a
fit posture to fight. 2 Sam 10:9.
that they may a. the man. Esth 6:9
a. thyself with glory. Job 40:10
shall a. himself with the. Jer 43:12
adorn, not with costly a. 1 Tim 2:9

array
Joab put the choice in a. 2 Sam 10:9
God set themselves in a. Job 6:4
yourselves in a, against. Jer 50:14

see **battle**
arrayed
Pharaoh a. Joseph in fine. Gen 41:42
captives, with spoil a. 2 Chr 28:15
not a. like. Mat 6:29; Luke 12:27
his men of war a. Christ. Luke 23:11
Herod a. in royal apparel. Acts 12:21
are these that are a. in ? Rev 7:13
the woman was a. in purple. 17:4
her was granted to be a. in fine. 19:8

arrived
they a. at the country of. Luke 8:26
and the next day we a. Acts 20:15

arrogancy
not a. come out of your. 1 Sam 2:3
pride and a. and the evil. Pr 8:13
cause the a. of the proud. Isa 13:11
Moab, his loftiness, his a. Jer 48:29

arrow
[1] Literally, a dart used for
pleasure or in war. 1 Sam 20:20;
Jer 51:11. [2] Figuratively, any
word or judgement which pierces the
mind or the soul as does an arrow
the flesh, Job 6:4; Ps 64:3; 2 Sam
22:15.
Jonathan shot an a. 1 Sam 20:36
and the a. went out at. 2 Ki 9:24
a. of Lord's deliverance from. 13:17
shoot an a. there. 19:32; Isa 37:33
a. cannot make him flee. Job 41:28
they make ready their a. Ps 11:2
with an a. suddenly shall. 64:7
afraid for the a. that flieth. 91:5
false witness is a sharp a. Pr 25:18
their tongue is as an a. shot. Jer 9:8
set me as a mark for the a. Lam 3:12
his a. shall go forth as. Zech 9:14

arrows
them through with his a. Num 24:8
I will spend mine a. Deut 32:23
I will make mine a. drunk with. 42
I will shoot three a. on. 1 Sam 20:20
he sent out a. and scattered them.
   2 Sam 22:15; Ps 18:14
a. took to him bow and. 2 Ki 13:15
take the a. and smite upon the. 18
the a. of the Almighty are. Job 6:4
he ordaineth a. against the. Ps 7:13
shalt make ready thine a. 21:12
for thine a. stick fast in me. 38:2
thine a. are sharp in the heart. 45:5
whose teeth are spears and a. 57:4

bendeth his bow to shoot his a. Ps 58:7
bows to shoot their a. even. 64:3
brake he the a. of the bow, the. 76:3
clouds poured, thine a. also. 77:17
sharp a. of the mighty, with. 120:4
as a. are in the hand of a. 127:4
shoot out thine a. and destroy. 144:6
mad man who casteth a. Pr 26:18
whose a. are sharp and. Isa 5:28
with a. and bows shall men. 7:24
their a. shall be as of an. Jer 50:9
shoot at Babylon, spare no a. 14
make bright the a. gather the. 51:11
hath caused the a. of his. Lam 3:13
I shall send the evil a. Ezek 5:16
he made his a. bright, he. 21:21
I will cause thy a. to fall out. 39:3
go forth, and burn bows and a. 9
at the light of thine a. Hab 3:11

art, *verb*
to Adam, where a. thou ? Gen 3:9
from the place where thou a. 13:14
whose daughter a. thou ? 24:23, 47
and he said a. thou my very ? 27:24
whose a. thou ? whither goest ? 32:17
thee, because thou a. his wife. 39:9
discreet and wise as thou a. 41:39
die because thou a. yet alive. 46:30
a bloody husband thou a. Ex 4:26
a. thou for us, or our ? Josh 5:13
they answered, as thou a. Judg 8:18
the men said to him, a. thou ? 12:5
a. thou the man that spakest ? 13:11
stand by where thou a. 1 Sam 19:3
a prophet also as thou a. 1 Ki 13:18
said, I am as thou a. 22:4; 2 Ki 3:7
a. not thou our God. 2 Chr 20:7
hurt a man as thou a. Job 35:8
a. thou also become... ? a. Isa 14:10
a. not thou he, O Lord our ? Jer 14:22
a. thou he that should ? Luke 7:19
Rabbi, thou a. the Son of. John 1:49
a. not thou that Egyptian ? Acts 21:38
the captain said, tell me, a ? 22:27
a. and wast, and a. Rev 11:17; 16:5

art, -s, *substantive*
ointment after the a. of. Ex 30:25
spices prepared by a. 2 Chr 16:14
like stones graven by a. Acts 17:29
of them which used curious a. 19:19

Artaxerxes
in the days of A. wrote. Ezra 4:7
to the commandment of A. 6:14
in the reign of A. Ezra. 7:1; 8:1
the copy of a letter that A. gave. 7:11
I, even I A. the king do make a. 21
in 20th year of A. wine was. Neh 2:1
from 20th to 32nd year of A. 5:14

Artemas
when I shall send A. to. Tit 3:12

artificer
an instructor of every a. Gen 4:22
captain and the cunning a. Isa 3:3

artificers
of works made by a. 1 Chr 29:5
to a. and builders gave. 2 Chr 34:11

artillery
Jonathan gave his a. 1 Sam 20:40

as
ye shall be a. gods. Gen 3:5
behold the man is become a. 22
the Lord seeth not a. 1 Sam 16:7
he did evil a. did the. 2 Ki 8:27
had made in the temple, a. 24:13
a. thou hast said, so. Ezra 10:12
a. for such a. turn aside. Ps 125:5
say not, I will do to him a. Pr 24:29
a. with the people, a. Isa 24:2
a. his master, servant a. Mat 10:25
love thy neighbour a. thyself. 19:19
   Rom 13:9
the glory a. of the only-. John 1:14
ye resist Holy Ghost, a. Acts 7:51
but a. of sincerity, but a. 2 Cor 2:17
be a. I am, for I am a. ye. Gal 4:12
a. ye have received Christ. Col 2:6

even as
even as the Lord gave to. 1 Cor 3:5
so love his wife even a. Eph 5:33
even a. Christ forgave you. Col 3:13
even a. I received of my. Rev 2:27

Asa
A. did what. *1 Ki* 15:11; *2 Chr* 14:2
A. heart. *1 Ki* 15:14; *2 Chr* 15:17
A. took the silver. *1 Ki* 15:18
         2 Chr 16:2
Berechiah the son of A. *1 Chr* 9:16
A. cried to the Lord. *2 Chr* 14:11
Azariah went out to meet A. 15:2
no war to the 35th year of A. 19
A. was wroth . . . A. oppressed. 16:10
the pit was it which A. had. *Jer* 41:9
Abia begat A. *Mat* 1:7
A. begat Josaphat. 8

Asahel
sons of Zeruiah, Joab, A. *2 Sam* 2:18
         1 Chr 2:16
A. would not turn aside. *2 Sam* 2:21
they took up A. and buried him. 32
Abner died for the blood of A. 3:27
A. was one of the thirty. 23:24
         1 Chr 11:26
Levites, Zebadiah, A. *2 Chr* 17:8
Jehiel, Nahath and A. were. 31:13
son of A. was employed. *Ezra* 10:15

Asaiah
Jeshohaiah and A. *1 Chr* 4:36
sons of Merari, Haggiah, A. 6:30
Shilonites, A. the first-born. 9:5
king Josiah sent A. to. *2 Chr* 34:20

Asaph
Joah the son of A. the recorder.
   2 Ki 18:18, 37; *Isa* 36:3, 22
A. son of Berechiah. *1 Chr* 6:39
         9:15; 15:17
delivered first this psalm to A. 16:7
of the sons of A. 25:1, 2; 26:1
   2 Chr 5:12; 20:14; 29:13; 35:15
   Ezra 2:41; 3:10; *Neh* 7:44; 11:17
   22, 12:35.
first lot came forth for A. *1 Chr* 25:9
to sing with words of A. *2 Chr* 29:30
to the commandment of A. 35:15
a letter to A. keeper of the. *Neh* 2:8
in the days of A. were songs. 12:46

ascend
[1] *To climb up*, Josh 6:5. [2]
To go up to heaven, Eph 4:9, 10.

the people shall a. up. *Josh* 6:5
a. into the hill of the Lord, and shall
   stand in? *Ps* 24:3; *Rom* 10:6
he causeth vapours to a. *Ps* 135:7
       Jer 10:13; 51:16
if I a. up into heaven, thou. *Ps* 139:8
hast said, I will a. *Isa* 14:13. 14
thou shalt a. and come. *Ezek* 38:9
see the Son of man a. up. *John* 6:62
a. to my Father, and your. 20:17
beast shall a. out of the. *Rev* 17:8

ascended
the angel of the Lord a. *Judg* 13:20
thou hast a. up on high. *Ps* 68:18
who hath a. up into heaven. *Pr* 30:4
no man hath a. to heaven. *John* 3:13
touch me not, I am not yet a. 20:17
David is not yet a. into. *Acts* 2:34
when he a. up on high, he. *Eph* 4:8
now that he a. 9
is the same also that a. 10
the smoke of the incense a. *Rev* 8:4
they a. up to heaven in a cloud. 11:12

ascendeth
the beast that a. out of. *Rev* 11:7
the smoke of their torment a. 14:11

ascending
the angels of God a. and. *Gen* 28:12
said, I saw gods a. out. *1 Sam* 28:13
he went before, a. up to. *Luke* 19:28
of God a. and descending. *John* 1:51
I saw another angel a. from. *Rev* 7:2

ascent
up by the a. of Olivet. *2 Sam* 15:30
and his a. by. *1 Ki* 10:5; *2 Chr* 9:4

ascribe
a. ye greatness to our. *Deut* 32:3
I will a. righteousness to. *Job* 36:3
a. ye strength to God, his. *Ps* 68:34

ascribed
a. to David 10,000, to me a. but.
         1 Sam 18:8

Asenath
A. daughter of. *Gen* 41:45, 50; 46:20

ash
he planteth an a. the rain. *Isa* 44:14*

ashamed
*(The American Revision frequently
changes this word to* confounded *or
put to shame)*
and his wife were not a. *Gen* 2:25
tarried till they were a. *Judg* 3:25
the men were greatly a. *2 Sam* 10:5
         1 Chr 19:5
being a. steal away. *2 Sam* 19:3
urged him till he was a. *2 Ki* 2:17
his countenance till he was a. 8:11
the Levites were a. *2 Chr* 30:15
a. to require of the king. *Ezra* 8:22
a. and blush to lift up my face. 9:6
came thither, and were a. *Job* 6:20
shall no man make a.? 11:3
are not a. to make yourselves. 19:3
their faces were not a. *Ps* 34:5
not the oppressed return a. 74:21
she that maketh a. is as. *Pr* 12:4
shall be a. of Ethiopia. *Isa* 20:5
the sun shall be a. when the. 24:23
all a. of a people that could. 30:5
earth mourneth, Lebanon is a. 33:9
as the thief is a. when he. *Jer* 2:26
a. ? they were not at all a. 6:15; 8:12
the wise men are a. they are. 8:9
plowmen were a. they covered. 14:4
a. of Chemosh, as Israel was a. 48:13
of the Philistines are a. *Ezek* 16:27
with terror they are a. of. 32:30
his adversaries were a. *Luke* 13:17
I cannot dig, to beg I am a. 16:3
I am not a. of the gospel. *Rom* 1:16
hope maketh not a. because the. 5:5
things whereof ye are now a. 6:21
anything, I am not a. *2 Cor* 7:14
nevertheless I am not a. *2 Tim* 1:12
Onesiphorus was not a. of my. 16
he is not a. to call them. *Heb* 2:11
God is not a. to be called. 11:16

ashamed *and* confounded, *see* be ashamed
it to her, lest we *be* a. ̃ *Gen* 38:23
let all my enemies *be* a. and. *Ps* 6:10
wait on thee *be* a. let them *be* a. who
   transgress without cause. 25:3
put my trust, let me never *be* a. 31:1
be a. let the wicked *be* a. 17; 35:26
let not them that wait *be* a. 69:6
hate me, may see it and *be* a. 86:17
they arise. let them *be* a. 109:28
let proud *be* a. for they. 119:78
for they shall *be* a. of the. *Isa* 1:29
be thou a. O Zidon, the sea. 23:4
they shall see and *be* a. for. 26:11
they shall *be* greatly a. that. 42:17
know, that they may *be* a. 44:9
fellows shall *be* a. shall *be* a. 11
incensed against him shall *be* a. 45:24
rejoice, but ye shall *be* a. 65:13
your joy, and they shall *be* a. 66:5
shalt *be* a. of Egypt, as a. *Jer* 2:36
forehead. refusedst to *be* a. 3:3
they shall *be* a. of your. 12:13
all that forsake thee shall *be* a. 17:13
shall stumble and *be* a. 20:11
Moab shall *be* a. of Chemosh. 48:13
that bare you shall *be* a. 50:12
thy ways, and *be* a. *Ezek* 16:61
shew Israel, they may *be* a. 43:10
and if they *be* a. of all that. 11
they shall *be* a. because. *Hos* 4:19
and Israel shall *be* a. of his. 10:6
be ye a. O ye husbandmen. *Joel* 1:11
people shall never *be* a. 2:26, 27
her expectation shall *be* a. *Zech* 9:5
the prophets every one *be* a. 13:4
shall *be* a. of me and. *Mark* 8:38
         Luke 9:26
should *be* a. in this same. *2 Cor* 9:4
in nothing I shall *be* a. *Phil* 1:20
him, that he may *be* a. *2 Thes* 3:14
on the contrary part may *be* a. *Tit* 2:8
be a. that falsely accuse. *1 Pet* 3:16

not be, or *be not,* ashamed
should she *not be* a.? *Num* 12:14
in thee, let me *not be* a. *Ps* 25:2
me *not be* a. O Lord. 31:17; 119:116
shall *not be* a. in the evil time. 37:19
then shall I *not be* a. when. *Ps* 119:6
of thy testimonies, and *not be* a. 46
heart be sound, that I *be not* a. 80
they shall *not be* a. but shall. 127:5
Lord, Jacob shall *not be* a. *Isa* 29:22
ye shall *not be* a. world. 45:17
they shall *not be* a. that wait. 49:23
flint, I know I shall *not be* a. 50:7
fear not, for thou shalt *not be* a. 54:4
shalt thou *not be* a. *Zeph* 3:11
him shall *not be* a. *Rom* 9:33; 10:11
boast, I should *not be* a. *2 Cor* 10:8
be not therefore a. of. *2 Tim* 1:8
workman that needeth *not be* a. 2:15
Christian, let him *not be* a. *1 Pet* 4:16
not be a. before him. *1 John* 2:28

Ashdod
brought the ark to a. *1 Sam* 5:1
Lord was heavy on them of A. 6
wall of A. and built cities about A.
         2 Chr 26:6
had married wives of A. *Neh* 13:23
spake half in the speech of A. 24
came and fought against A. *Isa* 20:1
I made remnant of A. *Jer* 25:20
the inhabitant from A. *Amos* 1:8
publish in the palaces at A. and 3:9
they shall drive out A. *Zeph* 2:4
a bastard shall dwell in A. *Zech* 9:6

Asher
Leah called his name A. *Gen* 30:13
Zilpah, Leah's maid, Gad, A. 35:26
the children of A. 46:17; *Num* 1:13
   26:44; *1 Chr* 7:30, 40; 12:36
out of A. his bread shall. *Gen* 49:20
A. was Pagiel. *Num* 1:13; 2:27; 7:72
the name of the daughter of A. 26:46
to curse; Gad and A. *Deut* 27:13
A. he said, let A. be blessed. 33:24
A. continued on the sea. *Judg* 5:17
Gideon sent messengers to A. 6:35
men out of A. pursued the. 7:23
son of Hushai was in A. *1 Ki* 4:16
A. expert in war 40,000. *1 Chr* 12:36
divers of A. humbled. *2 Chr* 30:11
a portion for A. *Ezek* 48:2
one gate of A. 34

tribe of Asher
the *tribe of* A. 41,500. *Num* 1:41
the *tribe of* A. shall encamp. 2:27
over the host of *tribe of* A. 10:26
of the *tribe of* A. to spy the. 13:13
prince of the *tribe of* A. to. 34:27
lot for the *tribe of* A. *Josh* 19:24
inheritance of the *tribe of* A. 31
had cities out of the *tribe of* A. 21:6
   30; *1 Chr* 6:62, 74
of Phanuel of *tribe of* A. *Luke* 2:36
the *tribe of* A. were sealed. *Rev* 7:6

ashes
*The remains of fuel after it has
been burned,* 2 Pet 2:6. *They
were used in mourning to show that
joy had perished,* Esth 4:1; Isa 61:3.

which am but dust and a. *Gen* 18:27
priest shall take up the a. *Lev* 6:10
and carry forth the a. without. 11
clean shall gather the a. *Num* 19:9
Tamar put a. on her. *2 Sam* 13:19
altar shall be rent, and a. *1 Ki* 13:3
disguised himself with a. 20:38*
put on sackcloth with a. *Esth* 4:1
and many lay in sackcloth and a. 3
Job sat down among the a. *Job* 2:8
remembrances are like to a. 13:12
I am become like dust and a. 30:19
and repent in dust and a. 42:6
have eaten a. like bread. *Ps* 102:9
the hoar-frost like a. 147:16
he feedeth on a. *Isa* 44:20
to spread sackcloth and a. 58:5
to give them beauty for a. the. 61:3
wallow thyself in a. *Jer* 6:26
hath covered me with a. *Lam* 3:16
I will bring thee to a. on. *Ezek* 28:18
to seek in sackcloth and a. *Dan* 9:3
sackcloth, and sat in a. *Jonah* 3:6
wicked shall be a. under. *Mal* 4:3
have repented long ago in sackcloth
   and a. *Mat* 11:21; *Luke* 10:13
a. of an heifer sanctifieth. *Heb* 9:13
cities of Sodom into a. *2 Pet* 2:6

Ashtaroth

Og, who dwelt at A. *Deut* 1:4
  Josh 9:10; 12:4
Israel served A. *Judg* 2:13; 10:6
strange gods and A. *1 Sam* 7:3, 4
because we have served A. 12:10
armour in the house of A. 31:10
have worshipped A. *1 Ki* 11:33
Gershom was given A. *1 Chr* 6:71

Ashur, *or* Assur

A. went forth and built. *Gen* 10:11
Shem, Elam and A. 22; *1 Chr* 1:17
till A. shall carry thee. *Num* 24:22
from Chittim and afflict A. 24
Hezron's wife bare him A. *1 Chr* 2:24
A. had two wives, Helah and. 4:5
Esar-haddon king of A. *Ezra* 4:2
A. also is joined with them. *Ps* 83:8
A. and Chilmad were. *Ezek* 27:23
A. is there, and all her. 32:22
A. shall not save us, we. *Hos* 14:3

Asia

A. disputing with Stephen. *Acts* 6:9
to preach the word in A. 16:6
all they that dwelt in A. heard. 19:10
A. and the world worshippeth. 27
certain of the chief of A. sent. 31
he would not spend time in A. 20:16
first day that I came into A. 18
meaning to sail by coasts of A. 27:2
churches of A. salute. *1 Cor* 16:19
which came to us in A. *2 Cor* 1:8
they which are in A. *2 Tim* 1:15
strangers scattered in A. *1 Pet* 1:1

see **churches**

aside

said, thou shalt set a. *2 Ki* 4:4
he took him a. from the. *Mark* 7:33
he riseth and laid a. his. *John* 13:4
let us lay a. every weight. *Heb* 12:1

see **go, gone, turn, went, lay**

ask

[1] *To enquire,* Gen 32:29; Mark
9:32. [2] *To require, or demand,*
Gen 34:12; Dan 2:10. [3] *To seek
counsel,* Isa 30:2; Hag 2:11.
[4] *To pray,* John 15:7; Jas 1:6.
[5] *To expect,* Luke 12:48.

wherefore dost thou a.? *Gen* 32:29
a. me never so much dowry. 34:12
for a. now of the days. *Deut* 4:32
shall a. diligently, and if it be. 13:14
a. thy father, and he will shew. 32:7
children a. their fathers. *Josh* 4:6, 21
a. counsel, we pray thee. *Judg* 18:5
added this evil to a. *1 Sam* 12:19
why dost thou a. of me? 28:16
from me the thing I a. *2 Sam* 14:18
a. what I shall. *1 Ki* 3:5; *2 Chr* 1:7
Jeroboam cometh to a. *1 Ki* 14:5
Elijah said a. what I shall. *2 Ki* 2:9
Judah gathered to a. *2 Chr* 20:4
a. the beasts, and they. *Job* 12:7
a. thee a sign of Lord, a. it. *Isa* 7:11
I will not a. nor will I tempt. 12
the Lord. a. me of things. 45:11
they a. of me the ordinances of. 58:2
a. for the old paths, and. *Jer* 6:16
who shall go aside, to a. what. 15:5
a. ye now among the heathen. 18:13
a. and see whether a man doth. 30:6
I will a. thee a thing, hide. 38:14
a. him that fleeth, and her. 48:19
they shall a. the way to Zion. 50:5
the young children a. bread. *Lam* 4:4
a. a petition of any. *Dan* 6:7, 12
my people a. counsel at. *Hos* 4:12
a. now the priests. *Hag* 2:11
a. ye of the Lord rain. *Zech* 10:1
need of, before ye a. him. *Mat* 6:8
a. and it shall be. 7:7; *Luke* 11:9
his son a. bread. *Mat* 7:9; *Luke* 11:11
good things to them that a. *Mat* 7:11
her whatsoever she would a. 14:7
touching any thing they shall a. 18:19
what ye a. 20:22; *Mark* 10:38
whatsoever ye a. in prayer. *Mat* 21:22
nor durst any man a. him more.
 22:46; *Mark* 12:34; *Luke* 20:40
a. what thou wilt. *Mark* 6:22, 23
afraid to a. him. 9:32; *Luke* 9:45

---

taketh thy goods, a. them. *Luke* 6:30
Holy Spirit to them that a. 11:13
of him they will a. more. 12:48
Jews sent priests to a. *John* 1:19
he is of age, a. him. 9:21, 23
thou wilt a. of God, he will. 11:22
to him that he should a. 13:24*
whatsoever ye a. in. 14:13; 15:16
if ye a. any thing in my name I. 14:14
if ye abide in me, a. what ye. 15:7
that they were desirous to a. 16:19
and in that day ye shall a. me. 23
a. and ye shall receive, that your. 24
that any man should a. thee. 30
a. them which heard me what. 18:21
I a. therefore for what. *Acts* 10:29
them a. their husbands. *1 Cor* 14:35
above all that we can a. *Eph* 3:20
lack wisdom, let him a. *Jas* 1:5
but let him a. in faith, nothing. 6
yet ye have not, because ye a. 4:2
a. and receive not, because ye a. 3
whatsoever we a. we. *1 John* 3:22
if we a. any thing according to. 5:14
he heareth us, whatsoever we a. 15
is not unto death, he shall a. 16

see **counsel**

asked

Jacob a. him and said. *Gen* 32:29
the man a. us straitly of our. 43:7
him the city which he a. *Josh* 19:50
he a. water, she gave. *Judg* 5:25
I a. him not whence he was. 13:6
petition thou hast a. *1 Sam* 1:17
hath given me my petition I a. 27
a. this thing and not a. *1 Ki* 3:11
thou hast a. a hard thing. *2 Ki* 2:10
a. their names to certify. *Ezra* 5:10
have ye not a. them that. *Job* 21:29
he a. life of thee, thou. *Ps* 21:4
the people a. and he. 105:40
and have not a. at my. *Isa* 30:2
when I a. of them, could. 41:28
I am sought of them that a. 65:1
there is no king that a. *Dan* 2:10
I came and a. him the truth of. 7:16
he a. his disciples. *Mat* 16:13
 Mark 8:27; *Luke* 9:18
Sadducees a. him. *Mat* 22:23, 35
 Mark 9:11; 10:2; 12:18
when come near he a. *Luke* 18:40
thou wouldest have a. *John* 4:10
hitherto have ye a. nothing. 16:24
to them that a. not. *Rom* 10:20

Askelon, *or* Ashkelon

Judah took Gaza and A. *Judg* 1:18
Samson went down to A. and. 14:19
for A. one, for Gath one. *1 Sam* 6:17
not in the streets of A. *2 Sam* 1:20
I made A. and Azzah to. *Jer* 25:20
A. is cut off with remnant of. 47:5
hath given it a charge against A. 7
that holds sceptre from A. *Amos* 1:8
Gaza shall be forsaken, A. *Zeph* 2:4
in the houses of A. shall they lie. 7
A. shall see it, and fear; king shall
 perish from Gaza, and A. *Zech* 9:5

askest

why a. thou thus after. *Judg* 13:18
a. drink of me, a woman. *John* 4:9
why a. thou me, ask them. 18:21

asketh

thy son a. thee. *Ex* 13:14; *Deut* 6:20
prince a. and the judge a. *Mi* 7:3
give to him that a. thee. *Mat* 5:42
 Luke 6:30
that a. receiveth.*Mat* 7:8; *Luke* 11:10
of you a. me, whither? *John* 16:5
to every one that a. you. *1 Pet* 3:15

asking

wickedness in a. a king. *1 Sam* 12:19
Saul died for a. counsel. *1 Chr* 10:13
tempted God by a. meat. *Ps* 78:18
hearing them, and a. *Luke* 2:46
they continued a. he lifted. *John* 8:7
a. no question for. *1 Cor* 10:25, 27

asleep

[1] *To take rest in sleep,* Jonah
1:5; Mat 26:40. [2] *To die,* Acts
7:60; 2 Pet 3:4.

for Sisera was fast a. *Judg* 4:21
lips of those that are a. *S of S* 7:9

Jonah lay, and was fast a. *Jon'ah* 1:5
but he was a. *Mat* 8:24; *Mark* 4:38
disciples a. *Mat* 26:40; *Mark* 14:40
had said this, he fell a. *Acts* 7:60
but some are fallen a. *1 Cor* 15:6
which are fallen a. in Christ. 18
them that are a. *1 Thes* 4:13
shall not prevent them that are a. 15
since the fathers fell a. *2 Pet* 3:4

Asnappar

whom the noble A. brought. *Ezra* 4:10

asp, -s

is the cruel venom of a. *Deut* 32:33
his meat is the gall of a. *Job* 20:14
suck the poison of a. the viper's. 16
play on the hole of the a. *Isa* 11:8
the poison of a. is under. *Rom* 3:13

ass

up early, and saddled his a. *Gen* 22:3
abide you here with the a. and I. 5
Issachar is a strong a. 49:14
every firstling of an a. *Ex* 13:13
if thou meet thine enemy's a. 23:4
that thine ox and thine a. may. 12
taken one a. from them. *Num* 16:15
the a. saw the angel. 22:23; 25:27
opened the mouth of the a. 22:28
a. said to Balaam, am not I thine a.?
 30
plow with an ox and a. *Deut* 22:10
lighte off her a. Caleb. *Josh* 15:18
 Judg 1:14; *1 Sam* 25:23
the jaw-bone of an a. *Judg* 15:16
had not torn the a. *1 Ki* 13:28
until an a. head sold for. *2 Ki* 6:25
they drive away the a. of. *Job* 24:3
a bridle for the a. and a. *Pr* 26:3
ox his owner, and the a. his. *Isa* 1:3
forth the feet of the ox and a. 32:20
with the burial of an a. *Jer* 22:19
riding on an a. and on a colt the foal
 of an a. *Zech* 9:9; *Mat* 21:5
be the plague of the a. *Zech* 14:15
ye shall find an a. tied. *Mat* 21:2
not each loose his a. on. *Luke* 13:15
which of you shall have an a. 14:5
he found a young a. sat. *John* 12:14
the dumb a. speaking. *2 Pet* 2:16

see **saddle**

wild **ass**

doth the *wild* a. bray when? *Job* 6:5
sent out the *wild* a. free? 39:5
a *wild* a. used to the. *Jer* 2:24
they are gone, a *wild* a. alone. *Hos* 8:9

assault, -ed

perish all that would a. *Esth* 8:11
when there was an a. *Acts* 14:5
they a. the house of Jason, and. 17:5

assay, -ed, -ing

hath God a. to go and. *Deut* 4:34
David a. to go, for he. *1 Sam* 17:39
if we a. to commune with. *Job* 4:2
Saul a. to join himself to. *Acts* 9:26
they a. to go to Bithynia, but. 16:7
the Egyptians a. to do. *Heb* 11:29

assemble

the assembly shall a. *Num* 10:3
a. me the men of Judah. *2 Sam* 20:4
he shall a. the outcasts. *Isa* 11:12
a. yourselves, and come. draw.45:20
all ye a. yourselves and hear. 48:14
a. yourselves, and let us go. *Jer* 4:5
why do we sit still? a. 8:14
I will a. you out of the. *Ezek* 11:17
a. yourselves, gather to my. 39:17
they a. themselves for corn. *Hos* 7:14
a. the elders. gather the. *Joel* 2:16
a. yourselves and come, all. 3:11
a. yourselves on the. *Amos* 3:9
I will surely a. O Jacob. *Mi* 2:12
saith the Lord I will a. her. 4:6
I will a. the kingdoms to. *Zeph* 3:8

assembled

women which a. at the. *Ex* 38:8*
with the women that a. *1 Sam* 2:22*
David a. the children of. *1 Chr* 15:4
a. much people to keep. *2 Chr* 30:13
then a. to me every one. *Ezra* 9:4
had prayed. there a. to him. 10:1
the children of Israel a. *Neh* 9:1
lo the kings were a. they. *Ps* 48:4

let the people be a. who. *Isa* 43:9
a. themselves by troops in. *Jer* 5:7
these men a. and found. *Dan* 6:11
when they a. they gave. *Mat* 28:12
the disciples a. for fear. *John* 20:19
being a. commanded them. *Acts* 1:4
shaken where they were a. 4:31
a whole year they a. with. 11:26
it seemed good to us a. with. 15:25

assemblies
the a. of violent men. *Ps* 86:14*
by the masters of a. *Eccl* 12:11
the calling of a. I cannot. *Isa* 1:13
God will create on her a. a. 4:5
my laws in all mine a. *Ezek* 44:24*
smell in your solemn a. *Amos* 5:21

assembling
forsake not the a. *Heb* 10:25

assembly
to their a. mine honour be. *Gen* 49:6
the whole a. shall kill it. *Ex* 12:6
to kill this whole a. with. 16:3
hid from the eyes of the a. *Lev* 4:13
trumpets for calling the a. *Num* 10:2
Aaron went from presence of a. 20:6
of the midst of the fire, in the day of
your a. *Deut* 9:10; 10:4; 18:16
Jabesh-Gilead to the a. *Judg* 21:8
all this a. shall know. *1 Sam* 17:47
whole a. took counsel. *2 Chr* 30:23
I set a great a. against. *Neh* 5:7
the a. of the wicked have. *Ps* 22:16
God is to be feared in the a. 89:7*
praise him in the a. of the. 107:32
I will praise him in the a. of. 111:1
evil in the midst of the a. *Pr* 5:14
I will pour it on the a. of. *Jer* 6:11
for they be an a. of treacherous. 9:2
in the a. of the mockers. 15:17
the places of the a. *Lam* 2:6
shall not be in the a. of. *Ezek* 13:9*
against Aholibah with an a. 23:24
the a. was confused, and. *Acts* 19:32
determined in a lawful a. 39
thus spoken, he dismissed the a. 41
to the general a. of the. *Heb* 12:23
if there come to your a. *Jas* 2:2

solemn assembly
on the eighth day it is a *solemn a.*
Lev 23:36; *Num* 29:35; *Neh* 8:18
seventh day a *solemn a. Deut* 16:8
proclaim a *solemn a.* 2 *Ki* 10:20
eighth day . . . a *solemn a. 2 Chr* 7:9
call a *solemn a. Joel* 1:14; 2:15
are sorrowful for the *solemn a.*
Zeph 3:18

assent, -ed
to the king with one a. 2 *Chr* 18:12
Jews also a. that these. *Acts* 24:9

asses
had he-a. and she-a. *Gen* 12:16
much cattle, camels. and a. 30:43
as he fed the a. of Zibeon. 36:24
bread in exchange for a. 47:17
ye that ride on white a. *Judg* 5:10
he will take your a. to. *1 Sam* 8:16
the a. of Kish, Saul's. 9:3
thy a. that were lost, they. 20; 10:2
the a. be for the king's. 2 *Sam* 16:2
and over the a. was. *1 Chr* 27:30
feeble of them upon a. 2 *Chr* 28:15
a. that went up. *Ezra* 2:67; *Neh* 7:69
and a thousand she-a. *Job* 42:12
he saw a chariot of a. and. *Isa* 21:7
flesh is as the flesh of a. *Ezek* 23:20

wild asses
as *wild a.* in the desert. *Job* 24:5
the *wild a.* quench their. *Ps* 104:11
shall be a joy of *wild a. Isa* 32:14
wild a. snuffed up the wind. *Jer* 14:6
dwelling, was with *w. a. Dan* 5:21

young asses
their riches on *young a. Isa* 30:6
young a. that ear the ground shall. 24

assigned
priests had a portion a. *Gen* 47:22
they a. Bezer a city of. *Josh* 20:8
he a. Uriah to a place. 2 *Sam* 11:16

assist
that ye a. her in. *Rom* 16:2

associate
a. yourselves and ye shall. *Isa* 8:9*

---

as soon
a. as I am gone out of the. *Ex* 9:29
a. as the commandment. 2 *Chr* 31:5
a. as they hear of me. *Ps* 18:44
a. as Zion travailed, she. *Isa* 66:8
a. as the voice of thy. *Luke* 1:44
a. as it was sprung up, it. 8:6
a. as he said, I am he. *John* 18:6
came I a. as I was. *Acts* 10:29
a. as it was day there was no. 12:18
a. as I had eaten it, my. *Rev* 10:10
for to devour the child a. as it. 12:4

ass's colt
binding his a. *colt* to the. *Gen* 49:11
born like a wild a. *colt.* *Job* 11:12
sitting on an a. *colt.* *John* 12:15

assurance
have none a. of thy life. *Deut* 28:66
effect of righteousness, a. *Isa* 32:17*
whereof he hath given a. *Acts* 17:31
to all riches of the full a. of. *Col* 2:2
gospel came in much a. 1 *Thes* 1:5
to the full a. of hope to. *Heb* 6:11*
let us draw near in full a. 10:22*

assure
shall a. our hearts. 1 *John* 3:19

assured
fifth, and it shall be a. *Lev* 27:19
I will give you a. peace in. *Jer* 14:13
things thou hast been a. 2 *Tim* 3:14

assuredly
know a. thou shalt go. 1 *Sam* 28:1
a. Solomon thy son. 1 *Ki* 1:13, 17, 30
plant them in this land a. *Jer* 32:41
if thou a. go forth to the. 38:17
they have a. drunken, and. 49:12
house of Israel know a. *Acts* 2:36
a. gathering that the Lord. 16:10

asswage, -ed
(*Old spelling of* assuage)
and the waters were a. *Gen* 8:1
of my lips should a. your. *Job* 16:5
I speak, yet my grief is not a. 6

Assyria
goeth toward the east of A. *Gen* 2:14
sons dwelt as thou goest to A. 25:18
carried captive to A. 2 *Ki* 15:29
17:6; 18:11
bee that is in the land of A. *Isa* 7:18
remnant of his people from A. 11:11
for his people left from A. 16
an highway out of Egypt to A. 19:23
be the third with Egypt and A. 24
blessed be A. the work of my. 25
who were ready to perish in A. 27:13
to do in the way of A. ? *Jer* 2:18
Egypt, as wast ashamed of A. 36
whoredoms with men of A. *Ezek* 23:7
they go to A. *Hos* 7:11
they are gone up to A. 8:9
shall eat unclean things in A. 9:3
it shall be carried to A. for a. 10:6
as a dove out of land of A. 11:11
shall waste the land of A. *Mi* 5:6
he shall come to thee from A. 7:12
and he will destroy A. *Zeph* 2:13
gather them out of A. *Zech* 10:10
the pride of A. shall be brought. 11

see king, kings

Assyrian
O A. the rod of mine anger. *Isa* 10:5
people, be not afraid of the A. 24
that I will break the A. in my. 14:25
this people was not till the A. 23:13
the A. shall be beaten down. 30:31
then shall the A. fall with the. 31:8
the A. oppressed them without. 52:4
the A. was a cedar in. *Ezek* 31:3
went Ephraim to the A. *Hos* 5:13
but the A. shall be his king. 11:5
be the peace when A. come. *Mi* 5:5
shall he deliver us from the A. 6

Assyrians
smote in the camp of A. 185.000 men.
2 *Ki* 19:35; *Isa* 37:36
given the hand to the A. *Lam* 5:6
the whore with the A. *Ezek* 16:28
she doted on the A. her. 23:5, 12
delivered her into the hand of the A. 9
I will bring all the A. against. 23
a covenant with the A. *Hos* 12:1

---

astonied
(*Old form of* astonished)
the hair, and sat down a. *Ezra* 9:3
upright men shall be a. at. *Job* 17:8
come after him shall be a. 18:20
that they may be a. one. *Ezek* 4:17
Nebuchadnezzar was a. *Dan* 3:24
Daniel was a. for one hour. 4:19
was changed, his lords a. 5:9*

astonished
your enemies shall be a. *Lev* 26:32
passeth by shall be a. 1 *Ki* 9:8
Jer 18:16; 19:8; 49:17; 50:13
heaven tremble and are a. *Job* 26:11
as many were a. at thee. *Isa* 52:14
be a. O ye heavens, at this. *Jer* 2:12
heart of the priests shall be a. 4:9
shouldest thou be as a man a. 14:9
I remained a. among them. *Ezek* 3:15
at every moment, and be a. 26:16
know thee shall be a. at thee. 28:19
Daniel was a. at the vision. *Dan* 8:27
the people were a. *Mat* 7:28; 22:33
Mark 1:22; 6:2; 11:18; *Luke* 4:32
they were a. with great. *Mark* 5:42
beyond measure a. 7:37; 10:26
the disciples were a. at his. 10:24
a. at his understanding. *Luke* 2:47
a. at the draught of fishes. 5:9
her parents were a. but he. 8:56
certain women also made us a. 24:22
Saul trembling and a. said. *Acts* 9:6*
which believed, were a. 10:45
and saw Peter, they were a. 12:16
he saw, believed, being a. 13:12

astonishment
shall smite thee with a. *Deut* 28:28
thou shalt become an a. and a. 37
this house shall be an a. 2 *Chr* 7:21
he hath delivered them to a. 29:8
to drink the wine of a. *Ps* 60:3*
I am black, a. hath taken. *Jer* 8:21
I will make them an a. 25:9, 18
land shall be a desolation and a. 11
them to be a curse and an a. 29:18
an execration and an a. 42:18; 44:12
therefore is your land an a. 44:22
shall become heaps and an a. 51:37
they shall drink water by measure,
and with a. *Ezek* 4:16; 12:19
it shall be an a. to the nations. 5:15
filled with the cup of a. 23:33
smite every horse with a. *Zech* 12:4

astray, *see* **went, go, gone**

astrologers
[1] *Those we now call astrologers.*
[2] *Enchanters of any sort.*
a. the star-gazers, stand. *Isa* 47:13
ten times better than a. *Dan* 1:20
secret cannot the a. shew to. 2:27
in the magicians and the a. 4:7
cried aloud, to bring in the a. 5:7

asunder, *see* **cleave, cut, divide,
put**

as well
as well the stranger, as. *Lev* 24:16
one law, *as well* for the stranger. 22
heart faint, *as well* a. *Deut* 20:8
devours one *as well* as. 2 *Sam* 11:25
they cast lots, *as well.* 1 *Chr* 25:8
to give *as well* to the. 2 *Chr* 31:15
understanding *as well* as. *Job* 12:3
as well the singers as the. *Ps* 87:7
the Holy Ghost *as well.* *Acts* 10:47
about a sister *as well* as. 1 *Cor* 9:5
gospel preached *as well* as. *Heb* 4:2

Asyncritus
salute A. Phlegon. *Rom* 16:14

Atad
to the threshing-floor of A. *Gen* 50:10
saw mourning in floor of A. 11

ate
a. the sacrifices of the. *Ps* 106:28
I a. no pleasant bread. *Dan* 10:3
took the little book, and a. *Rev* 10:10

Athaliah
mother was. 2 *Ki* 8:26; 2 *Chr* 22:2
A. arose. 2 *Ki* 11:1; 2 *Chr* 22:10
hid from a. 2 *Ki* 11:2; 2 *Chr* 22:11
they slew A. 2 *Ki* 11:20; 2 *Chr* 23:21
Shehariah and A. 1 *Chr* 8:26

sons of *A.* that wicked. *2 Chr 24:7*
Jeshaiah son of *A.* with. *Ezra 8:7*

Athenians
A. spent their time in. *Acts 17:21*

Athens
and brought Paul to *A.* *Acts 17:15*
while Paul waited for them at *A.* 16
ye men of *A.* I perceive ye are. 22
Paul departed from *A.* and. 18:1
good to be left at *A.* *1 Thes 3:1*

athirst
Samson was sore *a.* and. *Judg 15:18*
when *a.* go to the vessels. *Ruth 2:9*
when saw we thee *a.?* *Mat 25:44*
give to him that is *a.* of. *Rev 21:6*
bride say, let him that is *a.* 22:17

atonement
*Reconciliation, at-one-ment; chiefly
used of Christ's atoning death,
Rom 5:11.*

eat things wherewith *a.* *Ex 29:33*
offer a bullock every day for *a.* 36
seven days thou shalt make *a.* for. 37
once in year shall make *a.* 30:10
to make an *a.* for your. 15; *Lev 17:11*
thou shalt take the *a.* money. *Ex 30:16*
I shall make an *a.* for sin. 32:30
accepted for him to make *a.* *Lev 1:4*
priest shall make an *a.* for them. 4:20
26, 31, 35; 5:6; 6:7; 12:8; 14:18
Num 15:25
hath commanded to make *a. Lev 8:34*
make *a.* for thyself and. 9:7; 16:24
given it you to make *a.* for. 10:17
make an *a.* for her, and she. 12:7
make an *a.* for the house. it. 14:53
shall be presented to make *a.* 16:10
Aaron shall make an *a.* for. 11
he shall make an *a.* for the holy. 16
no man there, when he maketh *a.* 17
he shall go and make *a.* for the. 18
was brought in to make *a.* 27
he shall make *a.* for the holy. 33
everlasting statute to make *a.* 34
there shall be a day of *a.* 23:27
it is a day of *a.* to make *a.* 28
in the day of *a.* make the. 25:9
given Levites to make *a.* *Num 8:19*
made *a.* for the Levites. 21
go quickly, make *a.* for wrath. 16:46
because he made an *a.* 25:13
sin-offering to make an *a.* 28:22, 30
goats to make an *a.* for you. 29:5
ear-rings to make an *a.* for. 31:50
shall I make the *a.?* *2 Sam 21:3*
sons appointed to make *a.* *1 Chr 6:49*
killed them to make *a.* *2 Chr 29:24*
for offering to make an *a.* *Neh 10:33*
we have now received *a.* *Rom 5:11*

attain
*(To reach by growth, or by con-
tinued effort)*
it is high, I cannot *a.* unto. *Ps 139:6*
of understanding shall *a.* *Pr 1:5*
as his hand shall *a.* to it. *Ezek 46:7*
ere they *a.* to innocency? *Hos 8:5*
they might *a.* to Phenice. *Acts 27:12*
a. to the resurrection. *Phil 3:11*

attained
have not *a.* to the days of. *Gen 47:9*
he *a.* not to the first. *2 Sam 23:19*
23; *1 Chr 11:21, 25*
the Gentiles have *a.* to. *Rom 9:30*
Israel hath not *a.* to the law of. 31
though I had already *a.* *Phil 3:12*
whereto we have already *a.* let. 16
whereto thou hast *a.* *1 Tim 4:6*

Attalia
they went down into *A.* *Acts 14:25*

attend
he appointed to *a.* her. *Esth 4:5*
a. to my cry. *Ps 17:1; 61:1; 142:6*
a. to me, hear me, I mourn. 55:2
and *a.* to the voice of. 86:6
hear and *a.* to know. *Pr 4:1*
my son, *a.* to my words. 20; 7:24
my son, *a.* to my wisdom, and. 5:1
may *a.* on the Lord. *1 Cor 7:35*

attendance
the *a.* of his ministers. *1 Ki 10:5*
2 Chr 9:4

till I come, give *a.* to. *1 Tim 4:13*
which no man gave *a.* at. *Heb 7:13*

attended
I *a.* to you, none of you. *Job 32:12*
he hath *a.* to the voice of. *Ps 66:19*
she *a.* to the things. *Acts 16:14*

attending
ministers *a.* continually. *Rom 13:6*

attent
(Old form of attentive)
let thine ears be *a.* to. *2 Chr 6:40*
mine ears shall be *a.* at the. 7:15

attentive
ear now be *a. Neh 1:6, 11; Ps 130:2*
the people were *a.* 8:3; *Luke 19:48*

attentively
hear *a.* the noise of his. *Job 37:2*

attire, -ed
mitre shall Aaron be *a.* *Lev 8:7*
him a woman with *a.* of an. *Pr 7:10*
can a bride forget her *a.?* *Jer 2:32*
exceeding in dyed *a.* on. *Ezek 23:15*

audience
*(Used as hearing, not a company of
hearers)*
spake to Ephron in *a.* of. *Gen 23:13*
covenant, and read in *a.* *Ex 24:7*
maid speak in thy *a.* *1 Sam 25:24*
in the *a.* of our God. *1 Chr 28:8*
the book of Moses in the *a. Neh 13:1*
all his sayings in the *a.* *Luke 7:1*
in *a.* of the people he said to. 20:45
ye that fear God, give *a.* *Acts 13:16*
then all the multitude gave *a.* 15:12
they gave him *a.* to this. 22:22

augment
ye are risen to *a.* the. *Num 32:14*

Augustus
a decree from Caesar *A.* *Luke 2:1*
had appealed to *A.* *Acts 25:21, 25*
Julius, a centurion of *A.* band. 27:1

aunt
to his wife, she is thy *a.* *Lev 18:14*

austere
because thou art an *a.* *Luke 19:21*

author
God is not the *a.* of. *1 Cor 14:33*
became the *a.* of eternal. *Heb 5:9*
Jesus, the *a.* and finisher of. 12:2

authority
[1] *Power, rule, or dignity,* Mat
7:29; 20:25; Luke 19:17. [2]
A warrant or order, Mat 21:23; Acts
9:14.

Mordecai wrote with *a.* *Esth 9:29*
when righteous are in *a.* *Pr 29:2*
taught them as one having *a.*
Mat 7:29; Mark 1:22
a man under *a. Mat 8:9; Luke 7:8*
exercise *a. Mat 20:25; Mark 10:42*
by what *a.* doest thou these things?
Mat 21:23; Mark 11:28
with *a.* commandeth he even the unclean. *Mark 1:27; Luke 4:36*
his house. and gave *a.* to. *Mark 13:34*
gave them power and *a.* *Luke 9:1*
been faithful. have thou *a.* 19:17
might deliver him to *a.* of. 20:20
that exercise *a.* are called. 22:25
hath given him *a.* to. *John 5:27*
eunuch of great *a.* under. *Acts 8:27*
hath *a.* to bind. 9:14; 26:10, 12
have put down all *a.* *1 Cor 15:24*
somewhat more of our *a. 2 Cor 10:8*
for kings and all in *a.* *1 Tim 2:2*
I suffer not a woman to usurp *a.* 12
and rebuke with all *a.* *Tit 2:15*
angels and *a.* made. *1 Pet 3:22*
him power and great *a.* *Rev 13:2*

availeth
yet all this *a.* me nothing. *Esth 5:13*
circumcision *a.* not. *Gal 5:6*; 6:15
a righteous man *a.* much. *Jas 5:16*

Aven
the young men of *A. Ezek 30:17*
the high places of *A.* the. *Hos 10:8*
cut off the inhabitant of *A. Amos 1:5*

avenge
thou shalt not *a.* nor. *Lev 19:18*
that shall *a.* the quarrel of. 26:25

a. Israel of the Midianites. *Num 31:2*
he will *a.* the blood of. *Deut 32:43*
the Lord judge and *a.* *1 Sam 24:12*
of Ahab, that I may *a.* *2 Ki 9:7*
Jews *a.* themselves on. *Esth 8:13*
a. me of mine enemies. *Isa 1:24*
vengeance that he may *a. Jer 46:10*
a. the blood of Jezreel. *Hos 1:4*
saying, *a.* me of mine. *Luke 18:3*
shall not God *a.* his own elect. 7
I tell you that he will *a.* them. 8
a. not yourselves, but. *Rom 12:19*
how long dost thou not *a.?* *Rev 6:10*

avenged
should be *a.* seven-fold. *Gen 4:24*
stayed till people had *a.* *Josh 10:13*
done this, yet I will be *a. Judg 15:7*
may be *a.* on Philistines for. 16:28
food, that I may be *a.* *1 Sam 14:24*
hundred foreskins, to be *a.* 18:25
or that my Lord hath *a.* 25:31
the Lord hath *a.* my. *2 Sam 4:8*
how the Lord hath *a.* him of. 18:19
the Lord hath *a.* thee this day. 31
my soul be *a.* on such a nation.
Jer 5:9, 29; 9:9
Moses *a.* him that was. *Acts 7:24*
rejoice, for God hath *a. Rev 18:20*
hath *a.* blood of his servants. 19:2

avenger
cities for refuge from the *a.*
Num 35:12; Josh 20:3
lest the *a.* of blood pursue. *Deut 19:6*
him into the hand of the *a.* 12
if the *a.* of blood pursue. *Josh 20:5*
not die by the hand of the *a.* till. 9
still the enemy and *a.* *Ps 8:2*
by reason of the enemy and *a.* 44:16
the Lord is the *a.* *1 Thes 4:6*

avengeth
God that *a. 2 Sam 22:48; Ps 18:47*

avenging
praise the Lord for the *a. Judg 5:2*
withholden thee from *a. 1 Sam 25:26*
thou who kept me from *a.* 33

averse
by securely, as men *a.* *Mi 2:8*

avoid
*(To shun, turn away from, escape
from)*
a. it, pass not by it. *Pr 4:15*
cause divisions, and *a.* *Rom 16:17*
to *a.* fornication. let. *1 Cor 7:2*
unlearned questions *a.* *2 Tim 2:23*
a. foolish questions and. *Tit 3:9*

avoided, -ing
David *a.* out of his. *1 Sam 18:11*
a. this, that no man. *2 Cor 8:20*
a. profane and vain. *1 Tim 6:20*

avouched
*(Acknowledged deliberately and
openly)*
this day *a.* the Lord to. *Deut 26:17*
the Lord hath *a.* thee to be his. 18

awake
[1] *To come out of natural sleep,*
Luke 9:32. [2] *To rouse out of
spiritual sleep,* Rom 13:11; Eph
5:14. [3] *To raise from the dead,*
Job 14:12; John 11:11.

a. a. Deborah *a.* a. utter. *Judg 5:12*
surely now he would *a.* *Job 8:6*
no more, they shall not *a.* 14:12
a. for me to the. *Ps 7:6; 35:23*
be satisfied when I *a.* with. 17:15
a. why sleepest thou, O Lord? 44:23
a. my glory, I myself will *a.* 57:8
108:2
they prepare, *a.* to help me. 59:4
O Lord God, *a.* to visit all the. 5
when shall I *a.* I will seek. *Pr 23:35*
a. my love. *S of S 2:7; 3:5; 8:4*
a. O north wind, and come. 4:16
a. and sing ye that dwell. *Isa 26:19*
a. a. put on strength, O arm of the
Lord, *a.* as in the. 51:9; 52:1
a. a. stand up, O Jerusalem. 51:17
perpetual sleep, and not *a. Jer 51:57*
sleep in the dust shall *a. Dan 12:2*
a. ye drunkards, weep. *Joel 1:5*
shall they not *a.* that. *Hab 2:7*

him that saith to the wood *a. Hab* 2:19
a. O sword, against my. *Zech* 13:7
asleep, and they *a.* him. *Mark* 4:38
when they were *a.* they. *Luke* 9:32
I go that I may *a.* him. *John* 11:11
it is high time to *a.* out. *Rom* 13:11
a. to righteousness, and. *1 Cor* 15:34
a. thou that sleepest, and. *Eph* 5:14

awaked
Jacob *a.* out of his sleep.. *Gen* 28:16
Samson *a.* and went. *Judg* 16:14
nor knew it, neither *a. 1 Sam* 26:12
and must be *a. 1 Ki* 18:27
him, the child is not *a. 2 Ki* 4:31
I *a.* for the Lord sustained. *Ps* 3:5
then the Lord *a.* as one out. 78:65
upon this I *a.* and beheld. *Jer* 31:26

awakest
when thou *a.* shalt despise. *Ps* 73:20
when thou *a.* it shall talk. *Pr* 6:22

awaketh, -ing
as a dream when one *a.* so. *Ps* 73:20
a. and his soul is empty. *a. Isa* 29:8
keeper of the prison *a. Acts* 16:27

aware
I was *a.* my soul made. *S of S* 6:12
Babylon, and thou art not *a. Jer* 50:24
over them, are not *a. Luke* 11:44

away
Abraham drove them *a. Gen* 15:11
not go very far *a. Ex* 8:28
the Lord said to him, *a.* get. 19:24*
have me *a.* for I am. *2 Chr* 35:23
assemblies I cannot, *a. Isa* 1:13
a. with this man, release. *Luke* 23:18
a. with him, *a.* with him. *John* 19:15
  Acts 21:36
a. with such a fellow. *Acts* 22:22

awe
stand in *a.* and sin not. *Ps* 4:4
of the world stand in *a.* of him. 33:8
my heart standeth in *a.* of. 119:161

awl
bore his ear with an *a. Ex* 21:6
thou shalt take an *a. Deut* 15:17

awoke
Noah *a.* from his wine. *Gen* 9:24
fat kine, so Pharaoh *a.* 41:4, 7, 21
Samson *a.* out of his. *Judg* 16:20
Solomon *a.* and behold it. *1 Ki* 3:15
disciples came an *a.* him. *Mat* 8:25
  Luke 8:24

ax
[1] *Literally, the ax similar to that
in modern use.* [2] *Figuratively,
any instrument used in inflicting
judgement,* Isa 10:15; Mat 3:10.

a stroke with the *ax. Deut* 19:5
the trees by forcing an *ax.* 20:19
Abimelech took an *ax* in. *Judg* 9:48
down to sharpen his *ax. 1 Sam* 13:20
neither hammer nor *ax. 1 Ki* 6:7
the *ax*-head fell into. *2 Ki* 6:5
shall the *ax* boast itself. *Isa* 10:15
cuts a tree with the *ax. Jer* 10:3
thou art my battle-*ax* and. 51:20
ax is laid to root of trees. *Mat* 3:10
  Luke 3:9

axes
had a file for the *a. 1 Sam* 13:21
under saws and *a.* of iron, and made
  them. *2 Sam* 12:31; *1 Chr* 20:3
famous as he lifted up *a. Ps* 74:5
down the carved work with *a.* 6
come against her with *a. Jer* 46:22
with *a.* he shall break. *Ezek* 26:9

axle-trees
the *a.-t.* of the wheel join. *1 Ki* 7:32
a.-t. naves, and felloes, were. 33

Azariah
A. was one of Solomon's. *1 Ki* 4:2
A. the son of Nathan was over. 5
Judah made *A.* king. *2 Ki* 14:21
A. son of Ethan. *1 Chr* 2:8
Jehu begat *A.* 38
Amaziah his son, *A.* his son. 3:12
Ahimaaz begat *A.* 6:9
Johanan begat *A.* 10
Hilkiah begat *A.* 13
Zephaniah begat *A.* 36
of God came on *A. 2 Chr* 15:1

A. son of Jehoshaphat. *2 Chr* 21:2
A. son of Jehoram. 22:6
A. son of Jehoram, and *A.* 23:1
A. the priest went in. 26:17, 20
the son of *A.* the son. *Ezra* 7:1, 3
A. the son of Maaseiah. *Neh* 3:23
Nehemiah *A.* came up with. 7:7
A. caused the people to. 8:7
those that sealed were *A.* 10:2
A. and all the proud men. *Jer* 43:2
of Judah was Daniel, *A. Dan* 1:6
A. the name of Abed-nego. 7
made the thing known to *A.* 2:17

Azekah
stones on them to *A. Josh* 10:11
Babylon fought against *A. Jer* 34:7

B

Baal
to high places of *B. Num* 22:41
Israel served *B.* and. *Judg* 2:13
throw down the altar of *B.* 6:25
will ye plead for *B.* ? will ye ? 31
Ahab served *B.* and. *1 Ki* 16:31
but if *B.* be God, then follow. 18:21
name of *B.* saying, O *B.* hear. 26
take the prophets of *B.* let none. 40
seven thousand in Israel . . . not
  bowed to *B.* 19:18; *Rom* 11:4
sacrifice to do to *B. 2 Ki* 10:19
a solemn assembly for *B.* 20
thus Jehu destroyed *B.* out of. 28
brake down the house of *B.* 11:18
host of heaven, served *B.* 17:16
reared up altars for *B.* 21:3
all the vessels made for *B.* 23:4
them that burnt incense to *B.* 5
prophets prophesied by *B. Jer* 2:8
burn incense to *B.* ? 7:9; 11:13, 17
  32:29
my people to swear by *B.* 12:16
built the high places of *B.* . . fire for
  burnt-offerings to *B.* 19:5
they prophesied in *B.* and. 23:13
have forgotten my name for *B.* 27
which they prepared for *B. Hos* 2:8
when Ephraim offended in *B.* 13:1
cut off the remnant of *B. Zeph* 1:4

Baal-berith
of Israel made *B. Judg* 8:33

Baal-hamon
had a vineyard at *B. S of S* 8:11

Baali
shalt call me no more *B. Hos* 2:16

Baalim
Israel served *B. Judg* 2:11; 3:7
  10:6, 10
Israel went a whoring after *B.* 8:33
of Israel put away *B. 1 Sam* 7:4
thou hast followed *B. 1 Ki* 18:18
sought not unto *B. 2 Chr* 17:3
things did they bestow on *B.* 24:7
also molten images for *B.* 28:2
reared up altars for *B.* 33:3
brake down the altars of *B.* 34:4
I have not gone after *B. Jer* 2:23
have walked after *B.* which. 9:14
visit on her the days of *B. Hos* 2:13
take away the names of *B.* 17

Baalis
B. king of Ammonites hath. *Jer* 40:14

Baal-meon
Beth-jeshimoth, *B. Ezek* 25:9

Baal-peor
Israel joined himself to *B.* and the.
  Num 25:3; *Ps* 106:28; *Hos* 9:10
men that were joined unto *B.*
  Num 25:5
Lord did because of *B. Deut* 4:3

Baal-perazim
that place *B. 2 Sam* 5:20; *1 Chr* 14:11

Baal-shalisha
came a man from *B. 2 Ki* 4:42

Baal-tamar
themselves in array at *B. Judg* 20:33

Baal-zebub
enquire of *B.* the God. *2 Ki* 1:2, 16

Baal-zephon
over against *B. Ex* 14:2; *Num* 33:7

Baanah
Rechab and *B.* his. *2 Sam* 4:6
Heleb the son of *B.* one of. 23:29
B. the son of Hushai. *1 Ki* 4:16
B. came to. *Ezra* 2:2; *Neh* 7:7
Harim, *B.* sealed the. *Neh* 10:27

Baasha
war between Asa and *B. 1 Ki* 15:16,32
thy league with *B.* 19; *2 Chr* 16:3
B. son of Ahijah conspired. *1 Ki* 15:27
Lord came to Jehu against *B.* 16:1
B. slept with his fathers and was. 6
slew all the house of *B.* 11, 12
like the house of *B.* 21:22; *2 Ki* 9:9
Asa made for fear of *B. Jer* 41:9

babbler
will bite, and a *b.* is. *Eccl* 10:11*
what will this *b.* say ? *Acts* 17:18

babbling, -s
contentions ? who hath *b.* ? *Pr* 23:29*
profane and vain *b.* *1 Tim* 6:20
shun profane and vain *b. 2 Tim* 2:16

babe
[1] *An infant or child,* Ex 2:6;
Luke 2:12. [2] *Such as are weak
in faith and knowledge,* 1 Cor 3:1;
Heb 5:13.

child, and behold the *b. Ex* 2:6
heard Mary, the *b. Luke* 1:41
the *b.* leaped in my womb for joy. 44
find *b.* wrapped in swaddling. 2:12
came and found the *b.* lying in. 16
the word, for he is a *b. Heb* 5:13

Babel
of his kingdom was *B. Gen* 10:10
is the name of it called *B.* 11:9

babes
the mouth of *b. Ps* 8:2; *Mat* 21:16
of their substance to their *b. Ps* 17:14
their princes and *b.* shall. *Isa* 3:4
hast revealed them to *b. Mat* 11:25
  Luke 10:21
foolish, a teacher of *b. Rom* 2:20
carnal, even as unto *b. 1 Cor* 3:1
as new-born *b.* desire the. *1 Pet* 2:2

Babylon
the men of *B.* made. *2 Ki* 17:30
that were in *B.* 25:28; *Jer* 52:32
of the princes of *B. 2 Chr* 32:31
vessels in his temple at *B.* 36:7
take out of temple of *B. Ezra* 5:14
treasures were laid up in *B.* 6:1
mention of Rahab and *B. Ps* 87:4
by the rivers of *B.* were. 137:1
burden of *B.* which Isaiah. *Isa* 13:1
B. shall be as when God. 19
B. is fallen. 21:9; *Jer* 51:8
  Rev 14:8; 18:2
will do his pleasure on *B. Isa* 48:14
go ye forth of *B.* flee from the. 20
carry them captive into *B. Jer* 20:4
of Judah that went into *B.* 28:4
be accomplished at *B.* 29:10
raised us up prophets in *B.* 15
to come with me into *B.* 40:4
the Lord spake against *B.* 50:1
remove out of the midst of *B.* 8
one that goeth by *B.* shall hiss. 13
how is *B.* become a desolation ? 23
together the archers against *B.* 29
disquiet the inhabitants of *B.* 34
counsel of the Lord against *B.* 45
flee out of the midst of *B.* 51:6
violence done to me be upon *B.* 35
the sea is come up upon *B.* she is. 42
and earth shall sing for *B.* 48
at *B.* shall fall the slain of all. 49
though *B.* should mount up. 53
because the Lord hath spoiled *B.* 55
broad walls of *B.* shall be. 58
the evil that shall come on *B.* 62
thus shall *B.* sink, and shall not. 64
him in the midst of *B. Ezek* 17:16
is not this great *B.* that I ? *Dan* 4:30
till the carrying into *B. Mat* 1:17
carry you away beyond *B. Acts* 7:43
the church at *B.* saluteth. *1 Pet* 5:13
great *B.* came in. *Rev* 16:19
B. the great, the mother of. 17:5*
alas, alas, that great city *B.* 18:10
thus shall that great city *B.* be. 21
see **daughter, province, wise men**

from Babylon
country *from B.* 2 Ki 20:14; Isa 39:3
began he to go up *from B.* Ezra 7:9
went up with me *from B.* 8:1
I will cut off *from B.* the. Isa 14:22
off the sower *from B.* Jer 50:16
sound of a cry cometh *from B.* 51:54
which are come *from B.* Zech 6:10

king of Babylon
serve the *king of B.* 2 Ki 25:24
     Jer 27:17; 40:9
the hand of the *king of B.* the.
     Ezra 5:12; Jer 21:7; 22:25
proverb against *king of B.* Isa 14:4
fight against the *king of B.* Jer 21:4
serve the *king of B.* 70 years. 25:11
I will punish the *king of B.*
will not serve *king of B.* 27:8, 13
the yoke of the *king of B.* 28:11
whom the *king of B.* roasted. 29:22
behold the eyes of *king of B.* 34:3
king of B. shall certainly come. 36:29
king of B. gave charge. 39:11
be not afraid of the *king of B.* 42:11
king of B. hath taken counsel. 49:30
the *king of B.* hath broken. 50:17
sword of the *king of B.* Ezek 21:19
king of B. caused his army. 29:18
give Egypt unto the *king of B.* 19
the arms of *king of B.* 30:24, 25
sword of the *king of B.* shall. 32:11

to or unto Babylon
shall be carried to *B.* 2 Ki 20:17
     24:15; 25:7, 13; 1 Chr 9:1
2 Chr 36:6, 7, 20; Ezra 5:12; Isa
     39:6; Jer 27:20; 28:3; 29:1, 4
     40:1, 7
and carried him *to B.* 2 Chr 33:11
all these he brought *to B.* 36:18
sake I have sent *to B.* Isa 43:14
thou shalt come *to B.* Jer 20:6
thou shalt go *to B.* 34:3
I will render *unto B.* 51:24
when comest *to B.* 61
I will bring him *to B.* Ezek 17:20
of Zion shall go *to B.* Mi 4:10
they were carried *to B.* Mat 1:11

Babylonians
manner of the *B.* of. Ezek 23:15
the *B.* came to her into the bed. 17

Babylonish
saw a goodly *B.* garment. Josh 7:21

Baca
through the valley of *B.* Ps 84:6

back
after he had sent her *b.* Ex 18:2
astray, thou shalt bring it *b.* 23:4
I will get me *b.* Num 22:34
Lord hath kept thee *b.* 24:11
drew not his hand *b.* till. Josh 8:26
damsel that came *b.* Ruth 2:6
return, and take *b.* thy. 2 Sam 15:20
not of bringing the king *b.* ? 19:10
but camest *b.* and hast. 1 Ki 13:22
and carry him *b.* to Amon. 22:26
when Judah looked *b.* 2 Chr 13:14
soldiers that Amaziah sent *b.* 25:13
he holdeth *b.* the face of. Job 26:9
fled apace, and look not *b.* Jer 46:5
slideth *b.* as a backsliding. Hos 4:16
they cry, none shall look *b.* Nah 2:8
that is in field return *b.* Mat 24:18
angel rolled *b.* the stone from. 28:2
the ship, and returned *b.* Luke 8:37
to plough, and looking *b.* 9:62
let him likewise not return *b.* 17:31

see draw, go, bring, keep, kept,
     turn, went

back, *substantive*
he turned his *b.* to go. 1 Sam 10:9
behind thy *b.* 1 Ki 14:9; Ezek 23:35
make them turn their *b.* Ps 21:12
the plowers plowed on my *b.* 129:3
b. of him. Pr 10:13; 19:29; 26:3
cast my sins behind thy *b.* Isa 38:17
I gave my *b.* to the smiters. 50:6
they have turned their *b.* Jer 2:27
I will shew them the *b.* and. 18:17
have turned to me the *b.* 32:33
how hath Moab turned the *b.* 48:39
which had on the *b.* of it. Dan 7:6
bow down their *b.* alway. Rom 11:10

backbiters
b. haters of God. Rom 1:30

backbiteth
he that *b.* not with his. Ps 15:3*

backbiting
countenance, a *b.* tongue. Pr 25:23
be debates, strifes, *b.* 2 Cor 12:20

back-bone
take off hard by the *b.-b.* Lev 3:9

back-parts
thou shalt see my *b.-p.* Ex 33:23

backs
thy law behind their *b.* Neh 9:26
with their *b.* towards. Ezek 8:16
their whole body and *b.* full. 10:12

see turned

backside
Moses led the flock to the *b.* Ex 3:1
shall hang over the *b.* 26:12
on the *b.* sealed with seven. Rev 5:1

backslider
b. in heart be filled. Pr 14:14

backsliding, -s
and thy *b.* shall reprove. Jer 2:19
hast thou seen what *b.* Israel? 3:6
whereby *b.* Israel committed. 8
the *b.* Israel hath justified. 11
return thou *b.* Israel, saith the. 12
b. children, saith the Lord. 14, 22
their transgressions and *b.* 5:6
slidden back by a perpetual *b.* 8:5
for our *b.* are many, we sinned. 14:7
about, O *b.* daughter. 31:22; 49:4
slideth back, as a *b.* Hos 4:16*
my people are bent to *b.* 11:7
I will heal their *b.* I will love. 14:4

backward
b. and their faces were *b.* Gen 9:23
that his rider shall fall *b.* 49:17
fell from off the seat *b.* 1 Sam 4:18
let the shadow return *b.* 2 Ki 20:10
     Isa 38:8
b. but I cannot perceive. Job 23:8
let them be driven *b.* that. Ps 40:14
them be turned *b.* that desire. 70:2
and are gone away *b.* Isa 1:4
that they might go and fall *b.* 28:13
that turneth wise men *b.* and. 44:25
judgement is turned away *b.* 59:14
but they went *b.* and not. Jer 7:24
thou art gone *b.* therefore I. 15:6
sigheth and turneth *b.* Lam 1:8
they went *b.* and fell to. John 18:6

bad
speak to thee *b.* or good. Gen 24:50
to Jacob good or *b.* 31:24, 29
good for a *b.* or a *b.* for. Lev 27:10
value it, whether it be good or *b.* 12
house, whether it be good or *b.* 14
search whether it be good or *b.* 33
dwell in, if good or *b.* Num 13:19
to do either good or *b.* of my. 24:13
neither good nor *b.* 2 Sam 13:22
lord the king to discern good or *b.*
     14:17
may discern good and *b.* 1 Ki 3:9*
the rebellious and *b.* city. Ezra 4:12
be eaten, they were so *b.* Jer 24:2
good but cast the *b.* away. Mat 13:48
good and *b.* and the wedding was.
     22:10
done, whether good or *b.* 2 Cor 5:10

bade, -est
according as thou *b.* me. Gen 27:19
the man did as Joseph *b.* 43:17
till morning, as Moses *b.* Ex 16:24
all the congregation *b.* Num 14:10
to them as the Lord *b.* Josh 11:9
that her mother-in-law *b.* Ruth 3:6
some *b.* me kill thee. 1 Sam 24:10
David *b.* them teach. 2 Sam 1:18
for thy servant Joab he *b.* me. 14:19
third day as the king *b.* 2 Chr 10:12
Esther *b.* them return. Esth 4:15
how he *b.* them not. Mat 16:12
b. thee and him. Luke 14:9, 10
man made a supper and *b.* 16
and the Spirit *b.* me go. Acts 11:12
but *b.* them farewell, saying. 18:21
b. that he should be. 22:24

badgers'-skins
     (*Revised Version*, seal-skins)
take of them. *b.-skins.* Ex 25:5
for the tent above of *b.-skins.* 26:14
rams' skins dyed red, *b.-skins.* 35:7
found skins of rams, and *b.-skins.* 23
made a covering of *b.-skins.* 36:19
a covering of *b.-skins.* Num 4:10
shod thee with *b.-skins.* Ezek 16:10

badness
the land of Egypt for *b.* Gen 41:19

bag
thy *b.* divers weights. Deut 25:13
and put them in a *b.* 1 Sam 17:40
is sealed up in a *b.* Job 14:17
he hath taken a *b.* of. Pr 7:20
all the weights of the *b.* Isa 46:6
lavish gold out of the *b.* 46:6
the *b.* of deceitful weights. Mi 6:11
to put in a *b.* with holes. Hag 1:6
a thief, and had the *b.* John 12:6
because Judas had the *b.* 13:29

bags
two talents in two *b.* 2 Ki 5:23
they put up in a *b.* and told. 12:10
provide yourselves *b.* Luke 12:33*

Bahurim
weeping behind her to *B.* 2 Sam 3:16
when David came to *B.* Shimei. 16:5
came to a man's house in *B.* 17:18
a Benjamite of *B.* 19:16; 1 Ki 2:8

Bajith
up to *B.* and to Dibon to. Isa 15:2

bake
Lot did *b.* unleavened. Gen 19:3
b. that which you will *b.* Ex 16:23
take flour and *b.* twelve. Lev 24:5
ten women shall *b.* your. 26:26
woman at Endor did *b.* 1 Sam 28:24
took flour and did *b.* 2 Sam 13:8
shalt *b.* it with man's. Ezek 4:12
the place where they shall *b.* 46:20

baked
they *b.* unleavened cakes. Ex 12:39
and *b.* it in pans, and. Num 11:8*
and for that which is *b.* 1 Chr 23:29

bake-meats
manner of *b.-meats* for. Gen 40:17

baken
meat-offering *b.* in. Lev 2:4; 7:9
it shall not be *b.* with leaven. 6:17
two wave-loaves shall be *b.* 23:17
behold, a cake was *b.* 1 Ki 19:6

baker
the butler and *b.* had. Gen 40:1
head of the chief butler and *b.* 20
he hanged the *b.* as Joseph.
ward both me and the chief *b.* 41:10
as an oven heated by the. Hos 7:4
their *b.* sleepeth all the night. 6

bakers
against the chief of the *b.* Gen 40:2
your daughters to be *b.* 1 Sam 8:13
Jeremiah bread out of *b.* Jer 37:21

baketh
he *b.* bread, yea, he. Isa 44:15

Balaam
sent messengers to *B.* Num 22:5
God came to *B.* and said, what. 9
they said, *B.* refuseth to come. 14
the ass crushed *B.* foot against. 25
Lord opened the eyes of *B.* 31
B. went with the princes of Balak. 35
God met *B.* and said. 23:4, 16
Balak did as *B.* had said, and. 30
B. lifted up his eyes and saw. 24:2
B. rose up and returned to his. 25
B. the son of Beor hath said. 3, 15
B. the son of Beor. 31:8; Josh 13:22
the counsel of *B.* to. Num 31:16
they hired *B.* Deut 23:4; Neh 13:2
would not hearken to *B.* Deut 23:5
Balak sent and called *B.* Josh 24:9
remember what *B.* Mi 6:5
way of *B.* the son of Bosor. 2 Pet 2:15
after the error of *B.* Jude 11
hold the doctrine of *B.* Rev 2:14

Balak
B. was king of the. Num 22:4
saith *B.* let nothing hinder thee. 16

B. did as Balaam had. *Num* 23:2, 30
B. king of Moab hath brought me. 7
rise up B. and hear. 18
B. anger kindled. 24:10
if B. would give me his house. 13
then B. arose and warred. *Josh* 24:9
any thing better than B. ? *Judg* 11:25
remember what B. king of. *Mi* 6:5
B. to cast a stumbling. *Rev* 2:14

balance
be weighed in an even b. *Job* 31:6
laid in the b. are altogether. *Ps* 62:9
a false b. is. *Pr* 11:1; 20:23
a just weight and b. are the. 16:11
weighed the hills in a b. ? *Isa* 40:12
as the small dust of the b. 15
gold, and weigh silver in the b. 46:6

balances
just b. a just. *Lev* 19:36; *Ezek* 45:10
calamity laid in the b. *Job* 6:2
him the money in the b. *Jer* 32:10
b. to weigh, and divide. *Ezek* 5:1
thou art weighed in the b. *Dan* 5:27
the b. of deceit are in. *Hos* 12:7
and falsifying the b. by. *Amos* 8:5
them pure with wicked b. ? *Mi* 6:11
on him had a pair of b. *Rev* 6:5

balancings
dost thou know the b. ? *Job* 37:16

bald
is b. yet is he clean. *Lev* 13:40, 41
b. head, go up thou b. *2 Ki* 2:23
nor make themselves b. *Jer* 16:6
every head shall be b. and. 48:37
themselves utterly b. *Ezek* 27:31
every head was made b. and. 29:18
make thee b. and poll thee. *Mi* 1:16

bald-locust
ye may eat the b.-locust. *Lev* 11:22

baldness
Frequently a sign of mourning,
Isa. 15:2; Jer 47:5.

they shall not make b. *Lev* 21:5
nor make any b. between. *Deut* 14:1
of well set hair, b. *Isa* 3:24
on all their heads shall be b. 15:2
did call to mourning and to b. 22:12
b. is come upon Gaza. *Jer* 47:5
and b. upon all. *Ezek* 7:18; *Amos* 8:10
enlarge thy b. as the eagle. *Mi* 1:16

ball
turn and toss thee like a b. *Isa* 22:18

balm
Ishmaelites bearing b. *Gen* 37:25
take in your vessels a little b. 43:11
is there no b. in Gilead ? *Jer* 8:22
go up to Gilead, and take b. 46:11
howl for her, take b. for her. 51:8
honey, and oil, and b.. *Ezek* 27:17

Bamah
thereof is called B. *Ezek* 20:29

band, -s
[1] *Material chains,* Luke 8:29;
Acts 16:26. [2] *Moral or spiritual*
bonds, as government and laws,
Ps 2:3; *or faith and love,* Col 2:19.

a b. round that it should. *Ex* 39:23
I have broken the b. of. *Lev* 26:13
his b. loosed from off. *Juda* 15:14
put Jehoahaz in b. *2 Ki* 23:33
darkness a swaddling b. *Job* 38:9
Pleiades, or loose the b. of ? 31
or who hath loosed the b. of ? 39:5
bind the unicorn with his b. ? 10
let us break their b. asunder. *Ps* 2:3
for there are no b. in their. 73:4
he brake their b. in sunder. 107:14
heart snares, hands as b. *Eccl* 7:26
be not mockers, lest b. *Isa* 28:22
loose thyself from the b. of thy. 52:2
this the fast, to loose the b. 58:6
thy yoke, burst thy b. *Jer* 2:20
they shall put b. on thee. *Ezek* 3:25
and behold I will lay b. upon. 4:8
when I have broken the b. 34:27
a b. of iron and brass. *Dan* 4:15, 23
drew them with b. of love. *Hos* 11:4
two staves, beauty and b. *Zech* 11:7
asunder mine other staff, even b. 14
he brake b. and was. *Luke* 8:29

and every one's b. were. *Acts* 16:26
loosed Paul from his b. 22:30
which all the body by b. *Col* 2:19
see **bonds**

band, -s
(Company of soldiers)
the camels into two b. *Gen* 32:7
and now I am become two b. 10
went with him a b. *1 Sam* 10:26*
two men, captains of b. *2 Sam* 4:2
so the b. of Syria came. *2 Ki* 6:23
b. of the Moabites invaded. 13:20
burying a man, they spied a b. 21
against him b. of Chaldeans, b. 24:2
them were b. of soldiers. *1 Chr* 7:4
made them captains of the b. 12:18
helped David against the b. of. 21
require of the king a b. *Ezra* 8:22
made out three b. and fell. *Job* 1:17
the b. of the wicked. *Ps* 119:61
go forth all of them by b. *Pr* 30:27
I will scatter all his b. *Ezek* 12:14
all his b. Togarmah his b. 38:6
rain upon him and upon his b. 22
of Israel thou and thy b. 39:4
him whole b. *Mat* 27:27; *Mark* 15:16
having received a b. *John* 18:3
the b. and captain and officers. 12
the b. called the Italian b. *Acts* 10:1
to the chief captain of the b. 21:31
a centurion of Augustus' b. 27:1

banded
certain of the Jews b. *Acts* 23:12

banished
not fetch home his b. *2 Sam* 14:13
doth devise means that his b. 14

banishment
it be to death or to b. *Ezra* 7:26
burdens and causes of b. *Lam* 2:14

bank
[1] *The side, or brink of a river,*
Gen 41:17. [2] *A mound, or heap of*
earth raised to cover besiegers, while
they batter the walls of a city, or
shoot at those who defend them,
2 Sam 20:15. [3] *A place where*
there is a great sum of money taken
in, and let out to use, Luke 19:23.

behold I stood on the b. *Gen* 41:17
by the b. of the river Arnon.
Deut 4:48; *Josh* 12:2*; 13:9, 16*
cast up a b. against. *2 Sam* 20:15
Elisha stood by the b. *2 Ki* 2:13
shall not cast a b. 19:32 ; *Isa* 37:33
at the b. of the river. *Ezek* 47:7
the b. of the river, the other on that
side of the b. *Dan* 12:5
my money into the b. ? *Luke* 19:23

banks
overfloweth all his b. *Josh* 3:15; 4:18
had overflowed his b. *1 Chr* 12:15
shall go over all his b. *Isa* 8:7
man's voice between the b. *Dan* 8:16

banner
hast given a b. to them. *Ps* 60:4
to banquet, and his b. *S of S* 2:4
lift ye up a b. on the high. *Isa* 13:2

banners
our God we set up our b. *Ps* 20:5
terrible as an army with b. *S of S* 6:4

banquet
Haman come to the b. *Esth* 5:4, 5, 8
to Esther at the b. of wine. 6; 7:2
companions make a b of ? *Job* 41:6*
the b. of them that. *Amos* 6:7

banquet-house
came into the b.-house. *Dan* 5:10

banqueting, -s
me into the b.-house. *S of S* 2:4
in lusts, revellings, b. *1 Pet* 4:3

baptism
[1] *The outward ordinance, or*
sacrament, wherein the washing
with water represents the cleansing
of the souls. Luke 7:29; Acts 18:25;
1 Pet 3:21. [2] *Inward spiritual*
washing, signified by the outward
sign. Mat 3:11. [3] *The sufferings*
of Christ, Mat 20:22; Luke 12:50.

Pharisees come to his b. *Mat* 3:7
be baptized with the b. 20:22*
Mark 10:38
the b. of John, whence was it, from ?
Mat 21:25; *Mark* 11:30; *Luke* 20:4
and preach the b. *Mark* 1:4; *Luke* 3:3
baptized with the b. of. *Luke* 7:29
I have a b. to be baptized. 12:50
beginning from the b. of. *Acts* 1:22
word, after the b. which John. 10:37
preached the b. of repentance. 13:24
Apollos knowing only the b 18:25
they said unto John's b. 19:3
John baptized with the b. of. 4
buried with him by b. *Rom* 6:4
one Lord, one faith, one b. *Eph* 4:5
buried with him in b. ye. *Col* 2:12
of doctrine of b. and laying. *Heb* 6:2
figure whereunto, even b. *1 Pet* 3:21

Baptist
in those days came John B. *Mat* 3:1
there hath not risen a greater than
John the B. 11:11; *Luke* 7:28
the days of John the B. *Mat* 11:12
this is John the B. he is risen. 14:2
said, give me John the B. head. *Mat* 14:8
art John the B. 16:14; *Mark* 8:28
he spake of John the B. *Mat* 17:13
John the B. was risen. *Mark* 6:14
charger the head of John the B. 25
John the B. hath sent us. *Luke* 7:20
John the B. came neither eating. 33
answering said, John the B. 9:19

baptize
I b. you with water, he shall b.
Mat 3:11; *Mark* 1:8; *Luke* 3:16
John 1:26
John did b. in the. *Mark* 1:4
that sent me to b. said. *John* 1:33
Christ sent me not to b. *1 Cor* 1:17

baptized
b. of him in. *Mat* 3:6; *Mark* 1:5
cometh Jesus to John to be b.
Mat 3:13
I have need to be b. of thee. 14
Jesus, when he was b. went up. 16
Jesus was b. of John. *Mark* 1:9
I am b. withal, shall ye be b. 10:39
he that believeth and is b. 16:16
that came to be b. *Luke* 3:7
publicans to be b. 12; 7:29
Jesus being b. and praying. 3:21
lawyers, being not b. of him. 7:30
tarried with them and b. *John* 3:22
and they came and were b. 23
Jesus made and b. more. 4:1
though Jesus himself b. not, but. 2
place where John at first b. 10:40
b. with water, but ye shall be b.
Acts 1:5; 11:16
repent, be b. every one of you. 2:38
gladly received his word were b. 41
they were b. both men and. 8:12
believed also, and when he was b. 13
only they were b. in the name of. 16
what doth hinder me to be b. ? 36
Philip and eunuch, and he b. him. 38
sight, and arose and was b. 9:18
that these should not be b. 10:47
Peter commanded them to be b. 48
Lydia when she was b. and. 16:15
jailer was b. and all his. 33
Corinth, believed, and were b. 18:8
to what then were ye b. ? 19:3
when they heard this they were b. 5
arise, and be b. and wash. 22:16
b. into Jesus, were b. *Rom* 6:3
were ye b. in the name ? *1 Cor* 1:13
thank God that I b. none of you. 14
b. household of Stephanas, not b. 16
and were all b. to Moses in. 10:2
by one Spirit are we all b. 12:13
what shall they do who are b. for the
dead, why are they b. ? 15:29
have been b. into Christ. *Gal* 3:27

baptizest
why b. thou, if thou be ? *John* 1:25

baptizeth
the same is he who b. *John* 1:33
behold, the same b. all men. 3:26

baptizing
teach all nations, b. them. *Mat* 28:19

Jordan, where John was b. *John* 1:28
am I come b. with water. 31
and John was also b. in Enon. 3:23

bar
them shut the doors, and b. *Neh* 7:3

bar, *substantive*
the middle b. in midst of. *Ex* 26:28
made the middle b. to shoot. 36:33
shall put it upon a b. *Num* 4:10*, 12*
of the city, posts, b. *Judg* 16:3
I will break also the b. *Amos* 1:5

Barabbas
release B. *Mat* 27:17, 21
 Mark 15:11; *Luke* 23:18
not this man but B. now B. was a.
 John 18:40

Barachias
of Zacharias, son of B. *Mat* 23:35

Barak
Deborah called B. the son. *Judg* 4:6
Deborah went with B. 9
B. pursued after. 16
then sang Deborah and B. son. 5:1
arise B. and lead thy captivity. 12
would fail me to tell of B. *Heb* 11:32

barbarian
a b. and he a b. to me. *1 Cor* 14:11
neither Greek nor Jew, b. *Col* 3:11

barbarians
the b. saw the venomous. *Acts* 28:4
both to the Greeks and b. *Rom* 1:14

barbarous
b. people shewed no. *Acts* 28:2

barbed
fill his skin with b. irons? *Job* 41:7

barber
son of man, take thee a b. *Ezek* 5:1

bare
b. the ark. *Gen* 7:17; *Deut* 31:9, 25
 Josh 3:15; 4:10; 8:33; *2 Sam* 6:13
 1 Chr 15:15, 26, 27
torn of beasts, I b. the. *Gen* 31:39
how I b. you on eagles'. *Ex* 19:4
thy God b. thee as a. *Deut* 1:31
sent the people that b. *Judg* 3:18
the young man that b. his armour.
 1 Sam 14:1, 6; *2 Sam* 18:15
that b. burdens. *1 Ki* 5:15; *Neh* 4:17
of Judah that b. shield. *1 Chr* 12:24
 2 Chr 14:8
he b. the sin of many. *Isa* 53:12
he b. them all the days of old. 63:9
the stuff I b. upon my. *Ezek* 12:7
saying, himself b. our. *Mat* 8:17
and they that b. him. *Luke* 7:14
made wine, and they b. it. *John* 2:8
had the bag, and b. what was. 12:6
his own self b. our sins. *1 Pet* 2:24

bare
was 60 years, when she b. *Gen* 25:26
then all the cattle b. speckled. 31:8
at Chezib, when she b. him. 38:5
ye know that my wife b. me. 44:27
Jochebed b. to Amram. *Ex* 6:20
wife was barren, and b. *Judg* 13:2
child Uriah's wife b. *2 Sam* 12:15
his mother b. him after. *1 Ki* 1:6
Jabez, because I b. him. *1 Chr* 4:9
bitterness to her that b. *Pr* 17:25
she that b. thee shall rejoice. 23:25
choice one of her that b. *S of S* 6:9
brought thee forth that b. thee. 8:5
look unto Sarah that b. you. *Isa* 51:2
their mother that b. them. *Jer* 16:3
wherein my mother b. me. 20:14
and thy mother that b. thee. 22:26
b. you shall be ashamed. 50:12
the womb that b. thee. *Luke* 11:27
are the wombs that never b. 23:29

bare *fruit*
sprang up, and b. *fruit*. an *Luke* 8:8
b. twelve manner of *fruits*. *Rev* 22:2

bare *rule*
officers that b. *rule* over the people.
 1 Ki 9:23; *2 Chr* 8:10
their servants b. *rule*. *Neh* 5:15

bare *witness*, and record
b. false *witness*. *Mark* 14:56, 57
all b. him *witness*, and. *Luke* 4:22
b. *witness* of him. *John* 1:15, 32, 34

John b. *witness* to truth. *John* 5:33
that was with him b. *record*. 12:17
he that saw it b. *record*, and. 19:35
hearts, b. them *witness*. *Acts* 15:8
who b. *record* of the word. *Rev* 1:2

bare, *adjective*
be rent and his head b. *Lev* 13:45*
whether it be b. within or without. 55
strip ye, make ye b. and. *Isa* 32:11
b. the leg, uncover the thigh. 47:2
the Lord hath made b. his. 52:10
are thy heels naked b. *Jer* 13:22
I have made Esau b. I have. 49:10
thou wast naked and b. *Ezek* 16:7
when thou wast naked, and b. 22
leave the naked and b. 39; 23:29
hath made it clean and b. *Joel* 1:7
shall be, but b. grain. *1 Cor* 15:37

barefoot
he went b. and the. *2 Sam* 15:30
so, walking naked and b. *Isa* 20:2, 3
Egyptians prisoners, naked and b. 4

barest
because thou b. the ark. *1 Ki* 2:26
never b. rule over them. *Isa* 63:19
he to whom thou b. *John* 3:26

Bar-jesus
whose name was B. *Acts* 13:6

Bar-jona
blessed art thou, Simon B. *Mat* 16:17

bark
dumb dogs, they cannot b. *Isa* 56:10

barked
laid my vine waste, and b. *Joel* 1:7

barley
b. was smitten, for b. *Ex* 9:31
an homer of b. seed. *Lev* 27:16
part of an ephah of b. *Num* 5:15
a land of wheat, and b. *Deut* 8:8
cake of b. bread tumbled. *Judg* 7:13
beginning of b. harvest. *Ruth* 1:22
gleaned about an ephah of b. 2:17
she kept fast to the end of b. 23
Boaz winnoweth b. to-night. 3:2
he measured six measures of b. 15
is near, he hath b. *2 Sam* 14:30
Barzillai brought beds, b. and. 17:28
Saul's sons were hanged in b. 21:9
b. also and straw for the. *1 Ki* 4:28
of God 20 loaves of b. *2 Ki* 4:42
of b. for a shekel. 7:1, 16, 18
of ground full of b. *1 Chr* 11:13
20,000 measures of b. *2 Chr* 2:10
wheat, and b. the oil, and wine. 15
gave 10,000 measures of b. 27:5
cockle grow instead of b. *Job* 31:40
wheat, and appointed b. *Isa* 28:25
treasures of wheat and b. *Jer* 41:8
take to thee wheat, and b. *Ezek* 4:9
thou shalt eat it as b. cakes, and. 12
pollute me for handfuls of b. 13:19
an ephah of an homer of b. 45:13
an homer of b. and half. *Hos* 3:2
howl for wheat and b. *Joel* 1:11
which hath five b. loaves. *John* 6:9
fragments of the five b. loaves. 13
voice say, 3 measures of b. *Rev* 6:6

barn
(*A storehouse for grain*)
thee out of the b. floor? *2 Ki* 6:27
thy seed into the b. *Job* 39:12*
is seed yet in b. vine. *Hag* 2:19
the wheat into my b. *Mat* 13:30
no store-house nor b. *Luke* 12:24

Barnabas
apostles was surnamed B. *Acts* 4:36
B. should go as far as. 11:22
departed B. to Tarsus to seek. 25
by the hands of B. and Saul. 30
B. and Saul returned from. 12:25
at Antioch were teachers, as B. 13:1
Holy Ghost said, separate me B. 2
they called B. Jupiter; Paul. 14:12
Paul and B. had no small. 15:2
the multitude gave audience to B. 12
B. determined to take with. 37
or I only and B. have. *1 Cor* 9:6
again to Jerusalem with B. *Gal* 2:1
gave to me and B. the right hands. 9

B. carried away with their. *Gal* 2:13
Marcus, sister's son to B. *Col* 4:10

see Saul, Paul

barns
so shall thy b. be filled. *Pr* 3:10
the b. are broken down. *Joel* 1:17
not, nor gather into b. *Mat* 6:26
I will pull down my b. *Luke* 12:18

barrel, -s
(*American Revision*, jar, jars)
handful of meal in a b. *1 Ki* 17:12
the b. of meal shall not waste. 14
fill four b. with water, and. 18:33

barren
but Sarai was b. she had. *Gen* 11:30
Rebekah was b. 25:21
Rachel was b. 29:31
cast young nor be b. *Ex* 23:26
not be male or female b. *Deut* 7:14
was b. and bare not. *Judg* 13:2, 3
so that the b. hath born. *1 Sam* 2:5
naught, and the ground b. *2 Ki* 2:19
from thence death, or b. land. 21
he evil entreateth the b. *Job* 24:21
I have made the b. land his. 39:6
he maketh the b. woman. *Ps* 113:9
the grave and b. womb. *Pr* 30:16
b. among them. *S of S* 4:2*; 6:6*
sing, O b. thou that didst. *Isa* 54:1
drive him into a land b. *Joel* 2:20
because Elisabeth was b. *Luke* 1:7
with her, who was called b. 36
shall say, blessed are the b. 23:29
is written, rejoice thou b. *Gal* 4:27
that ye be neither b. nor. *2 Pet* 1:8*

barrenness
a fruitful land into b. *Ps* 107:34*

bars
b. of shittim-wood for the boards.
 Ex 26:26; 36:31
of the sons of Merari, shall be the
 boards and b. *Num* 3:36; 4:31
fenced with gates and b. *Deut* 3:5
 1 Ki 4:13; *2 Chr* 8:5; 14:7
a town that hath b. *1 Sam* 23:7
set up locks thereof and b. *Neh* 3:3
 6, 13, 14, 15
shall go down to the b. *Job* 17:16
set b. and doors for the sea. 38:10
his bones are like b. of iron. 40:18
cut b. of iron. *Ps* 107:16; *Isa* 45:2
hath strengthened the b. *Ps* 147:13
contentions are like the b. *Pr* 18:19
have neither gates nor b. *Jer* 49:31
they have Babylon, her b. 51:30
and broken her b. *Lam* 2:9
neither gates nor b. *Ezek* 38:11
the earth with her b. was. *Jonah* 2:6
fire shall devour thy b. *Nah* 3:13

Barsabas
Joseph called B. *Acts* 1:23
Judas B. 15:22

Bartholomew
Mat 10:3; *Mark* 3:18; *Luke* 6:14
 Acts 1:13

Bartimaeus
B. sat by the way-side. *Mark* 10:46

Baruch
B. son of Zabbai earnestly. *Neh* 3:20
B. sealed the covenant. 10:6
Maaseiah son of B. dwelt at. 11:5
the evidence to B. *Jer* 32:12, 16
Jeremiah called B. and B. 36:4
read B. in the book in the house. 10
B. took the roll in his hand and. 14
king commanded to take B. the. 26
B. setteth thee on against us. 43:3
Johanan took Jeremiah and B. 6
word that Jeremiah spake to B. 45:1

Barzillai
B. of Rogelim brought. *2 Sam* 17:27
B. was a very aged man. 19:32
the king kissed B. and blessed. 39
brought up for Adriel son of B. 21:8
kindness to the sons of B. *1 Ki* 2:7
of B. which took a wife of the daughters of B. *Ezra* 2:61; *Neh* 7:63

base, -s
b. four cubits the length of one b.
 1 Ki 7:27
the b. Solomon made. *2 Ki* 25:13, 16

set the altar upon his *b.*   *Ezra 3:3*
set there upon her own *b.* *Zech 5:11*

base, *adjective*
(*Used mainly in the obsolete sense
of humble, lowly*)
and will be *b.* in mine.   *2 Sam 6:22*
they were children of *b.*   *Job 30:8*
and the *b.* against the.   *Isa 3:5*
kingdom might be *b.*   *Ezek 17:14*
and they shall be there a *b.*   29:14
I have made you *b.*   *Mal 2:9*
b. things of this world.   *1 Cor 1:28*
who in presence am *b.*   *2 Cor 10:1*

baser
lewd fellows of the *b.*   *Acts 17:5**

basest
Pathros shall be the *b.*   *Ezek 29:15*
up over it the *b.* of men. *Dan 4:17**

Bashan
up by the way of B.   *Num 21:33*
               Deut 3:1
Og king of B. *Num 32:33; Deut 1:4*
  3:1, 3, 11; 4:47; 29:7; *Josh 9:10*
  12:4; 13:30; *1 Ki 4:19; Neh 9:22*
      Ps 135:11; 136:20
kingdom of Og in B.   *Deut 3:4, 10*
        Josh 13:12, 30, 31
Golan in B.   *Deut 4:43; Josh 20:8*
                21:27
rams of the breed of B. *Deut 32:14*
Dan shall leap from B.   33:22
he had Gilead and B.   *Josh 17:1*
even Gilead and B.   *2 Ki 10:33*
of Gershon, Golan in B.   *1 Chr 6:71*
strong bulls of B. have.   *Ps 22:12*
hill of God is as the hill of B.   68:15
I will bring again from B.   22
B. and Carmel shake off.   *Isa 33:9*
lift up thy voice in B.   *Jer 22:20*
shall feed on Carmel and B.   50:19
all of them fatlings of B. *Ezek 39:18*
this word, ye kine of B.   *Amos 4:1*
let them feed in B. as in.   *Mi 7:14*
B. languished, Carmel.   *Nah 1:4*

      see **oaks**

Bashemath
Esau took to wife B. the. *Gen 26:34*
B. Ishmael's daughter, sister of. 36:3

basket
*These were of different sizes,
shapes, and construction, and had
different names.* [1] Sal, *made of
twigs, specially for bread,* Gen
40:17. [2] Salsillôth, *a similar basket used for gathering grapes,*
Jer 6:9. [3] Tene, *in which the
first-fruits were offered,* Deut 26:4.
[4] Dud, *to carry fruit,* Jer 24:1;
and clay to the brickyard, Ps 81:6
(pote, *in Authorized Version*), *or for
holding bulky articles,* 2 Ki 10:6.
*In the New Testament there were
three names used. One meant the
small wallet carried by travellers and
another the large sort in which Saul
escaped from Damascus,* Acts 9:25.
in the *b.* all manner of.   *Gen 40:17*
b. of the unleavened.   *Ex 29:23*
    Lev 8:2, 26; Num 6:15, 17
the bread in the *b.* of.   *Lev 8:31*
priest shall take the *b.*   *Deut 26:4*
blessed shall be thy *b.* and thy. 28:5
cursed shall be thy *b.* and thy.   17
put the flesh in a *b.*   *Judg 6:19*
b. had very good figs, the other *b.*
                Jer 24:2
a *b.* of summer fruit.   *Amos 8:1, 2*
wall in a *b.*   *Acts 9:25; 2 Cor 11:33*

baskets
I had three white *b.*   *Gen 40:16*
Joseph said, the three *b.* are.   18
put their heads in *b.*   *2 Ki 10:7*
grape-gatherer into the *b.*   *Jer 6:9*
behold, two *b.* of figs were set. 24:1
took up twelve *b.* full.   *Mat 14:20*
   Mark 6:43; Luke 9:17; John 6:13
seven *b.* full. *Mat 15:37; Mark 8:8*
five loaves, and how many *b.* ye took
  up? *Mat 16:9, 10; Mark 8:19, 20*

bason
    (*Revised Version,* basin)
blood that is in the *b.*   *Ex 12:22*

by weight for every *b.*   *1 Chr 28:17*
he poureth water into a *b. John 13:5*

basons
    (*Revised Version,* basins)
put half of the blood in *b.*   *Ex 24:6*
brought beds and *b.*   *2 Sam 17:28*
lavers and the shovels and the *b.*
    1 Ki 7:40, 45; *2 Chr* 4:8, 11
b. and fire-pans the.   *Jer 52:19*

bastard, -s
a *b.* shall not enter into. *Deut 23:2*
b. shall dwell in Ashdod. *Zech 9:6*
chastisement, then are *b. Heb 12:8*

bat, -s
lapwing and *b.* are.   *Lev 11:19*
               Deut 14:18
his idols to the moles and *b. Isa 2:20*

bath
(*A measure used among the
Hebrews which contained about
nine gallons. It was equal to the
Ephah*)
vineyard shall yield one *b. Isa 5:10*
just ephah, a just *b.*   *Ezek 45:10*
the ephah and *b.* shall be of one. 11
offer the tenth part of a *b.*   14

bathe
shall *b.* himself in water. *Lev 15:5*
  8, 11, 13, 21, 22, 27; 16:26, 28
      17:15; *Num* 19:7, 8, 19
them not, nor *b.* his flesh. *Lev 17:16*

bathed
my sword shall be *b.* in.   *Isa 34:5**

baths
sea contained 2000 *b.*   *1 Ki 7:26*
one laver containing 40 *b.* every. 38
servants 20,000 *b.* of.   *2 Chr 2:10*
sea received and held 3000 *b.*   4:5
b. of wine, 100 *b.* of oil.   *Ezra 7:22*
homer of ten *b.* for ten *b. Ezek 45:14*

Bath-sheba
is not this B. daughter. *2 Sam 11:3*
David comforted B. his wife.   12:24
B. went to the king into.   *1 Ki 1:15*
then the king said, call me B.   28
B. bowed.   31
Adonijah came to B. the.   2:13

battered
people with Joab *b.*   *2 Sam 20:15*

battering
set *b.* rams against it.   *Ezek 4:2*
to appoint *b.* rams against.   21:22

battle
[1] *A general fight,* Deut 20:3.
[2] *Victory,* Eccl 9:11.
they joined *b.* Gen 14:8; *1 Sam 4:2*
                1 Ki 20:29
before the Lord to *b.*   *Num 32:27*
contend with Sihon in *b.*   *Deut 2:24*
approach this day to *b.*   20:3
return, lest he die in the *b.*   5, 6, 7
all other they took in *b.*   *Josh 11:19*
yet again go out to *b.?*   *Judg 20:28*
they turned, but the *b.* overtook.   41
after Philistines in *b.*   *1 Sam 14:22*
the host shouted from the *b.*   17:20
art come down to see the *b.*   28
b. is the Lord's.   47; *2 Chr 20:15*
shall descend into the *b.*   *1 Sam 26:10*
thou shalt go out with me to *b.* 28:1
in the *b.* he be an adversary.   29:4
go forth to *b.* 2 Sam 11:1; *1 Chr 19:10*
front of the hottest *b.*   *2 Sam 11:15*
we anointed is dead in *b.*   19:10
if thy people go out to *b.*   *1 Ki 8:44*
went out into midst of the *b.*   20:39
go with me to *b.?*   22:4; *2 Ki 3:7*
they cried to God in the *b. 1 Chr 5:20*
men of war fit for the *b.*   12:8
David came upon them, and set *b.* in.
    19:17; *2 Chr* 13:3; 14:10
do it, be strong for *b.*   *2 Chr 25:8*
as a king ready to the *b.*   *Job 15:24*
he smelleth the *b.* afar off.   39:25
remember the *b.* do no more.   41:8
me with strength to *b.*   *Ps 18:39*
glory, the Lord mighty in *b.*   24:8
delivered my soul from the *b.* 55:18
shield, the sword, and the *b.*   76:3

made him to stand in the *b. Ps 89:43*
not to the swift, nor *b.*   *Eccl 9:11*
every *b.* of the warrior.   *Isa 9:5**
mustereth the host of the *b.*   13:4
thy slain men are not dead in *b.* 22:2
and thorns against me in *b.*   27:4
that turn the *b.* to the gate.   28:6
on him the strength of the *b.* 42:25
horse rusheth into the *b.*   *Jer 8:6*
men be slain by sword in *b.*   18:21
and shield, draw near to *b.*   46:3
her, and rise up to the *b.*   49:14
a sound of *b.* is in the land.   50:22
in array, like a man to *b.* against. 42
but none goeth to the *b. Ezek 7:14*
to stand in the *b.* in the day.   13:5
save them by bow nor by *b. Hos 1:7*
I will break the bow and *b.*   2:18
b. in Gibeah; did not overtake. 10:9
a strong people set in *b.*   *Joel 2:5*
rise up against Edom in *b.*   *Ob 1*
his goodly horse in the *b. Zech 10:3*
down their enemies in the *b.*   5
nations against Jerusalem to *b.* 14:2
prepare himself to the *b.? 1 Cor 14:8*
like horses prepared to *b.*   *Rev 9:7*
of many horses running to *b.*   9
the *b.* of the great day. 16:14; 20:8

      day of battle
pass in the day of *b.*   *1 Sam 13:22*
against the day of *b.*   *Job 38:23*
back in the day of *b.*   *Ps 78:9*
my head in the day of *b.*   140:7
prepared against the day of *b.*
                Pr 21:31
Beth-arbel in day of *b. Hos 10:14*
shouting in the day of *b. Amos 1:14*
fought in the day of *b.*   *Zech 14:3*

battle-ax, *see* **ax**

      battle-bow
and the *b.-bow* shall be.   *Zech 9:10*
of him came forth the *b.-bow.* 10:4

battlement, -s
thou shalt make a *b.* for. *Deut 22:8*
take away her *b.* they.   *Jer 5:10**

battles
before us and fight our *b. 1 Sam 8:20*
valiant, and fight the Lord's *b.* 18:17
my lord fighteth the *b.* of the. 25:28
spoils won in *b.* dedicate. *1 Chr 26:27*
God, to fight our *b.*   *2 Chr 32:8*
and in *b.* of shakings.   *Isa 30:32*

bay
grizzled and *b.* horses.   *Zech 6:3*
and the *b.* went forth and sought. 7

bay-tree
like a green *b.-tree.*   *Ps 37:35**

bdellium
in Havilah there is *b.*   *Gen 2:12*
manna as the colour of *b. Num 11:7*

be
that man should *be* alone. *Gen 2:18*
whether thou *be* my very son. 27:21
there they *be* as the.   *Deut 10:5*
if the Lord *be* with us.   *Judg 6:13*
thine enemies *be* as.   *2 Sam 18:32*
they that *be* with us are more than
  they that *be.*   *2 Ki 6:16*
God *be* with. *2 Chr 36:23; Ezra 1:3*
be ye far from thence.   *Ezra 6:6*
if I *be* wicked, woe to me; if I *be.*
               Job 10:15
and *be* it indeed that I have.   19:4
see if there *be* any.   *Ps 139:24*
be a wall, if she *be* a.   *S of S 8:9*
be your fear, let him *be.*   *Isa 8:13*
former things what they *be.*   41:22
none know where you *be. Jer 36:19*
it *be* ere thou *be* quiet?   47:6
thy way till the end *be. Dan 12:13*
how long will it *be* ere?   *Hos 8:5*
if thou *be* the Son of God. *Mat 4:3, 6*
                27:40
and many there *be* that go.   7:13
the things that *be* of God, but those
  that *be.*   16:23; *Mark 8:33*
be to thee as an heathen. *Mat 18:17*
put away, except it *be.*   19:9
if the son of peace *be.*   *Luke 10:6*
how can these things *be? John 3:9*
there *be* any Holy Ghost. *Acts 19:2*

except it *be* for this one　*Acts* 24:21
those things which *be* not.　*Rom* 4:17
if God *be* for us, who can *be*?　8:31
that he might *be* Lord of the.　14:9
that God may *be* all in.　*1 Cor* 15:28
him *be* anathema maran-atha. 16:22
if there *be* first a willing. *2 Cor* 8:12
they which *be* of faith are.　*Gal* 3:9
I beseech you, *be* as I am, for. 4:12
judgement, whosoever he *be*.　5:10
let this mind *be* in you.　*Phil* 2:5
but if ye *be* without.　*Heb* 12:8
if so *be* ye have tasted.　*1 Pet* 2:3
if the will of God *be* so.　3:17
whatsoever craft he *be*.　*Rev* 18:22
let him *be* unjust still; he which is
　filthy, let him *be* filthy.　22:11

if it be

if it be your mind that I.　*Gen* 23:8
she said, *if it be* so, why?　25:22
if it be a son kill him, *if it be* a.
　　　　　　　　　　Ex 1:16
if it be, give me thy.　*2 Ki* 10:15
if it be marvellous in the. *Zech* 8:6
if it be thou, bid me.　*Mat* 14:28
if it be of God, ye.　*Acts* 5:39
but *if it be* a question of.　18:15
in vain? *if it be* in vain.　*Gal* 3:4

may be, see **may**; *peace* **be**, see
peace

not **be**. **be** *not*

let it *not be* grievous in. *Gen* 21:12
if the woman will *not be*.　24:5
the seed should *not be* his.　38:9
my father, and the lad *be not*. 44:30
ye should *not be* their.　*Lev* 26:13
let her *not be* as one.　*Num* 12:12
that he *be not* as Korah and. 16:40
neither will I *be* with.　*Josh* 7:12
man will *not be* in rest.　*Ruth* 3:18
be not like your fathers. *2 Chr* 30:7
　　　　　　　　　　Zech 1:4
be not thou far away.　*Ps* 22:19
　　　　　35:22; 38:21; 71:12
be ye *not* mockers, lest. *Isa* 28:22
I will *not be* to the.　*Zech* 8:11
for it *cannot be* that a. *Luke* 13:33
he *cannot be* my disciple. 14:26, 33
if thou *be not* that Christ. *John* 1:25
be not wise in your own. *Rom* 12:16
if I *be not* an apostle.　*1 Cor* 9:2
be not children in.　14:20
be not unequally yoked. *2 Cor* 6:14
should *not be* the servant. *Gal* 1:10
be not therefore partakers. *Eph* 5:7
be ye *not* unwise, but.　17
works, that they *be not*.　*Tit* 3:14
thy benefit should *not be*. *Philem* 14
on earth, should *not be* a. *Heb* 8:4
not be that outward.　*1 Pet* 3:3

let there **be**

let there be light.　*Gen* 1:3
let there be a firmament.　6
let there be no strife between.　13:8
let there be now an oath.　26:28
let there be more work laid. *Ex* 5:9
let there be search made. *Ezra* 5:17

shall **be**, or *shalt* **be**

they *shall be* one flesh.　*Gen* 2:24
to thee *shall be* his desire.　4:7
a servant *shall he be* to his.　9:25
Shem, and Canaan *shall be*.　26
and thou *shall be* a blessing.　12:2
so *shall* thy seed *be*. 15:5; *Rom* 4:18
Sarah *shall be* a mother. *Gen* 17:16
and he *shall be* blessed.　27:33
then *shall* Lord *be* my God.　28:21
Israel *shall be*. 35:10; *1 Ki* 18:31
God *shall be* with you. *Gen* 48:21
shall the gathering of the people *be*.
　　　　　　　　　　49:10
shalt be to him instead.　*Ex* 4:16
ye *shall be* a peculiar.　19:5
the dead *shall be* his own.　21:36
shall his habitation *be*. *Lev* 13:46
shall be holy to me, ye *shall be*.
　　　　　　　　　　20:26
shall be head, and thou *shalt be*.
　　　　　　　　　Deut 28:44
I see what their end *shall be*. 32:20
Philistine *shall be* as.　*1 Sam* 17:11
shall thy judgement *be*. *1 Ki* 20:40
the Lord *shall be*.　*2 Chr* 19:11

3

in fulness he *shall be* in.　*Job* 20:22
yea, the Almighty *shall be*.　22:25
happy *shalt* thou *be*, it *shall be*.
　　　　　　　　　　Ps 128:2
my prayer also *shall be* in.　141:5
is that which *shall be*.　*Eccl* 1:9
man cannot tell what *shall be*. 10:14
falleth, there it *shall be*.　11:3
the holy seed *shall be*.　*Isa* 6:13
the glory of the Lord *shall be*.　58:8
when *shall* it once *be*.　*Jer* 13:27
thou *shalt be* as my mouth.　15:19
and there *shall* he *be* till I.　32:5
it *shall be* to me a name of.　33:9
neither *shall be* so.　*Ezek* 16:16
wicked *shall be* on him.　18:20
shalt be a terror, and never *shalt be*.
　　　　　　　　　　27:36
what *shall be* in the latter. *Dan* 2:28
the end *shall be*.　8:19; 11:27
known that which *shall be*. *Hos* 5:9
God of hosts *shall be*.　*Amos* 5:14
save you, and *shall be* a. *Zech* 8:13
shall be as David, house of David
　shall be as.　12:8
shall be a delightsome.　*Mal* 3:12
no, nor ever *shall be*.　*Mat* 24:21
　　　　　　　　　　Mark 13:19
shall I *be* with you.　*Mark* 9:19
　　　　　　　　　　Luke 9:41
with you, and *shall be* in. *John* 14:17
lots for it, whose it *shall be*.　19:24
that it *shall be* even as. *Acts* 27:25
that body that *shall be*. *1 Cor* 15:37
appear what we *shall be*. *1 John* 3:2
and wast, and *shall be*.　*Rev* 16:5
man as his work *shall be*.　22:12

shall not, or *shalt not* **be**

saying, this *shall not be*.　*Gen* 15:4
thou *shalt not be* to him.　*Ex* 22:25
shalt not be beneath.　*Deut* 28:13
see me not, it *shall not be* so.
　　　　　　　　　　2 Ki 2:10
morning, but I *shall not be*. *Job* 7:21
it *shall not be*.　*Ps* 37:10; *Jer* 48:30
　　　　　Dan 11:29; *Amos* 7:3, 6
thou *shalt not be* for.　*Hos* 3:3
this *shall not be* so. *Mat* 16:22
shall not be so among you.　20:26
　　　　Mark 10:43; *Luke* 22:26

to **be**

to be a God to thee and.　*Gen* 17:7
hearkened not to her *to be*.　39:10
out *to be* your God. *Lev* 22:33; 25:38
desire *to be* with them.　*Pr* 24:1
that which is *to be* hath.　*Eccl* 3:15
spent all, he began *to be*. *Luke* 15:14
good for a man so *to be*. *1 Cor* 7:26
which he seeth me *to be*. *2 Cor* 12:6
having a desire *to be*.　*Phil* 1:23
things ought not so *to be*.　*Jas* 3:10
persons ought ye *to be*.　*2 Pet* 3:11

will **be**

will be a wild man, his hand *will be*
　against every man.　*Gen* 16:12
I *will be* their God. 17:8; *Ex* 29:45
　　Jer 24:7; 32:38; *2 Cor* 6:16
I *will be* with thee.　*Gen* 26:3; 31:3
if God *will be* with me.　*Gen* 28:20
if ye *will be* as we be.　34:15
all places they *will be*.　*Neh* 4:12
he *will be* our guide.　*Ps* 48:14
I *will be* your God. *Jer* 7:23; 30:22
I *will be* to them as a. *Ezek* 11:16
that ye say, we *will be* as.　20:32
O death, I *will be* thy plagues. O
　grave, I *will be* thy.　*Hos* 13:14
I *will be* as the dew unto Israel. 14:5
the Lord *will be* the hope. *Joel* 3:16
will be to her a wall of fire round
　about, I *will be* the.　*Zech* 2:5
there *will* your heart be.　*Mat* 6:21
I *will be* a Father to you. *2 Cor* 6:18
such *will* we *be* also indeed.　11:3
they that *will be* rich fall. *1 Tim* 6:9
I *will be* to him a Father.　*Heb* 1:5
I *will be* to them a God, they.　8:10
whosoever *will be* a friend. *Jas* 4:4
I *will be* his God, and.　*Rev* 21:7

beacon

be left as a *b*. on the.　*Isa* 30:17

beam

with the pin of the *b*.　*Judg* 16:14
his spear was like a weaver's *b*.
　1 Sam 17:7; *1 Chr* 11:23; 20:5
and take thence a *b*.　*2 Ki* 6:2
as one was felling a *b*. ax-head.　5
the *b*. out of the timber.　*Hab* 2:11
not the *b*.　*Mat* 7:3; *Luke* 6:41, 42
behold, a *b*. is in thine own. *Mat* 7:4
first cast out the *b*.　5; *Luke* 6:42

beams

overlaid the *b*. the posts. *2 Chr* 3:7
give timber to make *b*.　*Neh* 2:8
who layeth the *b*. in the.　*Ps* 104:3
b. of our house are cedar. *S of S* 1:17

beans

Barzillai brought *b*.　*2 Sam* 17:28
take unto thee wheat, *b*.　*Ezek* 4:9

bear

[1] *To carry*, *Jer* 17:21; *Mat* 27:32.
[2] *To bring forth, produce, or
yield*, *Gen* 18:13; *Jas* 3:12.　[3]
To uphold, or support, *Ps* 91:12.

is greater than I can *b*.　*Gen* 4:13
land not able to *b*. them. 13:6; 36:7
let me *b*. the blame.　43:9; 44:32
Issachar bowed to *b*.　49:15
they shall *b*. the burden. *Ex* 18:22
b. the ark. 25:27; 27:7, 30:4; 37:5
　Deut 10:8; *Josh* 3:8, 13, 14; 4:16
　　　　　　　　　　2 Sam 15:24
Aaron shall *b*. their names. *Ex* 28:12
shalt not *b*. any grudge.　*Lev* 19:18
not able to *b*. all this people.
　　　　　Num 11:14; *Deut* 1:9
how long shall I *b*. with? *Num* 14:27
children shall *b*.　33; *Ezek* 23:35
God bare as a man *b*.　*Deut* 1:31
let me *b*. the king.　*2 Sam* 18:19
puttest on me, I will *b*.　*2 Ki* 18:14
b. up pillars of the earth.　*Ps* 75:3*
how I do *b*. in my bosom the. 89:50
they shall *b*. thee up.　91:12
　　　　　　Mat 4:6; *Luke* 4:11
scornest, thou shalt *b*. it.　*Pr* 9:12
a wounded spirit who can *b*.? 18:14
for four which it cannot *b*.　30:21
feasts, I am weary to *b*.　*Isa* 1:14
I have made and I will *b*. you. 46:4
b. him upon the shoulder.　7
be clean that *b*. vessels of.　52:11
truly this grief, I must *b*. *Jer* 10:19
b. no burden sabbath-day. 17:21, 27
I did *b*. the reproach of my.　31:19
so the Lord could no longer *b*. 44:22
good to *b*. yoke in youth. *Lam* 3:27
their sight shalt thou *b*. *Ezek* 12:6
the prince shall *b*. upon his.　12
b. punishment of iniquity.　14:10
b. thine own shame for. 16:52, 54
b. shame with. 32:30; 36:7; 44:13
nor *b*. shame of the heathen.
　　　　　Ezek 34:29; 36:15
land is not able to *b*.　*Amos* 7:10
b. reproach of my people.　*Mi* 6:16
I will *b*. indignation of the.　7:9
one *b*. holy flesh in skirt. *Hag* 2:12
do these *b*. ephah?　*Zech* 5:10
he shall *b*. glory.　6:13
shoes I am not worthy to *b*. *Mat* 3:11
found Simon, compelled him to *b*.
　27:32; *Mark* 15:21; *Luke* 23:26
avenge elect, though he *b*.　18:7
ye cannot *b*. them now. *John* 16:12
is chosen to *b*. my name. *Acts* 9:15
a yoke, we were able to *b*.　15:10
reason I should *b*. with you.　18:14
b. infirmities of the weak. *Rom* 15:1
were not able to *b*.　*1 Cor* 3:2
to escape, that ye may *b*.　10:13
shall *b*. the image of heavenly. 15:49
ye could *b*. with me.　*2 Cor* 11:1
ye might well *b*. with him.　4
b. one another's burdens.　*Gal* 6:2
for every man shall *b*. his own.　5
b. in my body marks of Lord.　17
fig-tree *b*. olive-berries?　*Jas* 3:12
not *b*. them that are evil.　*Rev* 2:2

bear *fruit, see* **fruit**

bear *iniquity*

Aaron may *b*. iniq.　*Ex* 28:38
and his sons, *b*. not iniq.　43

he shall *b.* his *iniq.* *Lev* 5:1, 17
  7:18; 17:16; 19:8; 20:17
hath given to you to *b. iniq.* 10:17
the goat *b.* upon him all *iniq.* 16:22
they shall *b.* their *iniq.* 20:19
  Num 18:23; *Ezek* 44:10, 12
or suffer them to *b. iniq. Lev* 22:16
this woman *b.* her *iniq.* *Num* 5:31
ye shall *b.* your *iniq.* 14:34
Aaron and his sons *b. iniq.* 18:1
he heard, he shall *b.* her *iniq.* 30:15
my servant shall *b. iniq. Isa* 53:11
number of days, thou shalt *b. iniq.*
  Ezek 4:4; 5:6
not son *b. iniq.* of father ? 18:19
the son not *b.* the *iniq.* of. 20

bear *judgement*
Aaron shall *b. judg.* of. *Ex* 28:30
that troubleth *b.* his *judg. Gal* 5:10

bear *record, see* **record**

bear *rule*
man *b. rule* in his house. *Esth* 1:22
hand of diligent *b. rule.* *Pr* 12:24
the priests *b. rule* by. *Jer* 5:31
strong rods for them that *b. rule.*
  Ezek 19:11
of brass shall *b. rule.* *Dan* 2:39

bear *sin*
they shall *b.* their sin. *Lev* 20:20
lest they *b. sin* for it, and die. 22:9
curseth his God, shall *b. sin.* 24:15
that man shall *b.* his *sin. Num* 9:13
come nigh, lest they *b. sin.* 18:22
shall *b.* no *sin* when ye heaved. 32
ye *b. sin* of your idols. *Ezek* 23:49
Christ was once offered to *b. sin.*
  Heb 9:28

bear *witness*
shalt not *b.* false *wit.* *Ex* 20:16
  Deut 5:20; *Mat* 19:18; *Rom* 13:9
set two men to *b. wit.* *1 Ki* 21:10
do not *b.* false *wit.* *Mark* 10:19
  Luke 18:20
ye *b. wit.* that ye allow. *Luke* 11:48*
same came to *b. wit.* of. *John* 1:7
was sent to *b. wit.* of that light. 8
yourselves *b.* me *wit.* that. 3:28
if I *b. wit.* of myself. 5:31
works I do *b. wit.* of me. 36; 10:25
b. wit. of myself, and the. 8:18
ye shall also *b. wit.* 15:27
if I have spoken evil, *b. wit.* 18:23
that I should *b. wit.* 37
priest doth *b.* me *wit.* *Acts* 22:5
thou must *b. wit.* at Rome. 23:11
have seen and *b. wit.* *1 John* 1:2
three that *b. wit.* in earth. 5:8

bear
Sarah that is old *b* ? *Gen* 17:17
shall I of a surety *b.* a child. 18:13
but if she *b.* a maid child. *Lev* 12:5
her children she shall *b. Deut* 28:57
conceive and *b.* a son. *Judg* 13:3
not my son that I did *b.* *1 Ki* 3:21
every one *b.* twins. *S of S* 4:2, 6:6
a virgin shall *b.* a son, and. *Isa* 7:14
sing, O barren, that didst not *b.* 54:1
b. sons and daughters. *Jer* 29:6
Elisabeth shall *b.* a son. *Luke* 1:13
women marry,*b.* children. *I Tim* 5:14

bear, -s
came a lion and a *b.* *1 Sam* 17:34
servant slew the lion and the *b.* 36
chafed, as a *b.* robbed. *2 Sam* 17:8
came forth two she-*b.* *2 Ki* 2:24
b. robbed of her whelps. *Pr* 17:12
a roaring lion, and ranging *b.* 28:15
cow and *b.* feed their. *Isa* 11:7
we roar like *b.* mourn like. 59:11
to me as a *b.* in wait. *Lam* 3:10
beast, a second like to a *b. Dan* 7:5
them as a *b.* bereaved. *Hos* 13:8
as a man did flee from *b. Amos* 5:19
his feet as the feet of a *b. Rev* 13:2

beard, -s
a man hath plague on. *Lev* 13:29
shall shave hair off head and *b.* 14:9
mar the corners of *b.* 19:27; 21:5
I caught him by his *b.* *1 Sam* 17:35
David let spittle fall on his *b.* 21:13
tarry at Jericho till *b.* grow, then.
  2 Sam 10:5; *1 Chr* 19:5

Mephibosheth trimmed not *b.*
  2 Sam 19:24
Joab took Amasa by the *b.* 20:9
plucked off hair of my *b.* *Ezra* 9:3
down on *b,* Aaron's *b.* *Ps* 133:2
shall also consume the *b.* *Isa* 7:20
on heads baldness, every *b.* cut. 15:2
fourscore men their *b.* *Jer* 41:5
head bald, every *b.* clipt. 48:37
a razor to pass on *b.* *Ezek* 5:1

bearers
set 70,000 to be *b.* of. *2 Chr* 2:18
also they were over the *b.* 34:13
strength of the *b.* is. *Neh* 4:10

bearest
art barren, and *b.* not. *Judg* 13:3
favour thou *b.* thy people. *Ps* 106:4
b. record of thyself, thy. *John* 8:13
b. not the root. *Rom* 11:18
rejoice thou that *b.* not. *Gal* 4:27

beareth
he that *b.* the carcase. *Lev* 11:28
and he that *b.* these things. 15:10
as a father *b.* child. *Num* 11:12
first-born she *b.* succeed. *Deut* 25:6
there be a root that *b.* gall. 29:18
it is not sown, nor *b.* 23
as an eagle *b.* her young. 32:11
evil entreateth that *b.* not. *Job* 24:21
every one *b.* twins. *S of S* 6:6
not afraid, the tree *b.* fruit. *Joel* 2:22
which also *b.* fruit. *Mat* 13:23
every branch that *b.* not. *John* 15:2
b. not the sword in vain. *Rom* 13:4
charity *b.* all things. *1 Cor* 13:7
which *b.* thorns is rejected. *Heb* 6:8

beareth *rule*
when the wicked *b.* rule. *Pr* 29:2

beareth *witness*
b. wit. to my face. *Job* 16:8
b. false *wit.* is a maul. *Pr* 25:18
another that *b. wit.* of me. *John* 5:32
and the Father *b. wit.* of me. 8:18
the Spirit *b. wit.* with. *Rom* 8:16
the Spirit that *b. wit.* *1 John* 5:6

bearing
every herb *b.* seed. *Gen* 1:29
the Lord restrained me from *b.* 16:2
called his name Judah, left *b.* 29:35
Ishmaelites *b.* spicery. 37:25
forward, *b.* tabernacle. *Num* 10:17
Kohathites set forward, *b.* 21
the priest *b.* the ark. *Josh* 3:3, 14
  2 Sam 15:24
one *b.* a shield went. *1 Sam* 17:7
goeth *b.* precious seed. *Ps* 126:6
meet you a man *b.* a pitcher of water.
  Mark 14:13; *Luke* 22:10
he *b.* his cross, went. *John* 19:17
conscience *b.* witness. *Rom* 2:15
my conscience *b.* me witness. 9:1
b. in the body dying of. *2 Cor* 4:10
God also *b.* them witness. *Heb* 2:4
let us go forth *b.* his reproach. 13:13
be saved in child-*b.* *1 Tim* 2:15

beast
(*Used for cattle, wild beasts or any
living thing apart from man*)
let earth bring forth *b.* *Gen* 1:24
God made *b.* of the earth. 25
serpent more subtil than any *b.* 3:1
evil *b.* hath devoured him. 37:20, 33
every firstling of a *b.* *Ex* 13:12
put his *b.* in another's field. 22:5
deliver to his neighbour any *b.* 10
whoso lieth with *b.* be put to. 19
  Lev 18:23; 20:15, 16; *Deut* 27:21
the *b.* of the field multiply. *Ex* 23:29
b. that may be eaten, and *b.* that
  may not. *Lev* 11:47
if it be *b.* men bring offering. 27:9
the likeness of any *b.* *Deut* 4:17
smote as well men as *b. Judg* 20:48
nor any *b.* save I. I rode. *Neh* 2:12
so ignorant, I was as a *b. Ps* 73:22
he giveth to the *b.* his food. 147:9
man regards life of *b.* *Pr* 12:10
no pre-eminence above *b. Eccl* 3:19
the *b.* shall honour me. *Isa* 40:20
as a *b.* that goeth into valley. 63:14
dead or torn, fowl or *b. Ezek* 44:31
let a *b.* heart be given. *Dan* 4:16

I beheld till the *b.* was. *Dan* 7:11
the truth of the fourth *b.* 19
set him on his own *b.* *Luke* 10:34
Paul shook off the *b.* *Acts* 28:5
a *b.* touch the mountain. *Heb* 12:20
first *b.* like a lion, second *b. Rev* 4:7
I heard the second *b.* say. 6:3
b. that ascendeth out of the pit. 11:7
I saw a *b.* rise up out of. 13:1
I beheld a *b.* out of earth. 11
got the victory over the *b.* 15:2
spirits out of mouth of *b.* 16:13
thou sawest the *b.* that. 17:8, 11
I saw *b.* and kings of the. 19:19
where *b.* and false prophet. 20:10

every **beast**
to *every b.* green herb. *Gen* 1:30
God formed *every b.* 2:19
gave names to *every b.* 20
art cursed above *every b.* 3:14
of *every* clean *b.* take to. 7:2, 8
and *every b.* after his kind. 14
every b. went out of the ark. 8:19
of *every* clean *b.* he offered. 20
of you shall be on *every b.* 9:2
your blood I require of *every b.* 5
to *every b.* of the earth. 10
shall not *every b.* be ours ? 34:23
the carcases of *every b.* which
  divideth. *Lev* 11:26; *Deut* 14:6
every b. of the forest is. *Ps* 50:10
they give drink to *every b.* 104:11
my flock meat to *every b. Ezek* 34:8
son of man, speak to *every b.* 39:17

beast, joined with *man*
will destroy both *man* and *b. Gen* 6:7
became lice in *man* and *b.* *Ex* 8:17
with blains on *man* and *b.* 9:9, 10
hail on *man* and *b.* 19, 22, 25
a dog move against *man* or *b.* 11:7
smite first-born in Egypt. *man* and *b.*
  12:12; 13:15; *Ps* 135:8
first-born of *man* and *b.* is mine.
  Ex 13:2; *Num* 8:17
man or *b.* it shall not live. *Ex* 19:13
thing of *man* or *b.* *Lev* 27:28
first-born of *man* and *b.* *Num* 3:13
prey taken, both of *man* and *b.* 31:26
thou preservest *man* and *b. Ps.* 36:6
fury on *man* and *b.* *Jer* 7:20; 21:6
  36:29; *Ezek* 14:13, 17, 19, 21
  25:13; 29:8; *Zeph* 1:3
I have made *man* and *b.* *Jer* 27:5
sow with seed of *man* and *b.* 31:27
it is desolate without *man* or *b.*
  32:43, 33:10, 12 ; 36:29; 51:62
they shall depart *man* and *b.* 50:3
will multiply *man* and *b. Ezek* 36:11
let not *man* nor *b.* taste. *Jonah* 3:7

unclean **beast**
soul touch *unclean b. Lev* 5:2; 7:21
if it be *unclean b.* 27:11, 27

wild **beast**
there passed by a *wild b.* and trod
  down. *2 Ki* 14:9; *2 Chr* 25:18
wild b. may break them. *Job* 39:15
the *wild b.* of the field. *Ps* 80:13
wild b. shall tear them. *Hos* 13:8

beasts
that which was torn of *b. Gen* 31:39
  Ex. 22:31; *Lev* 7:24; 17:15; 22:8
Esau took all his *b.* *Gen* 36:6
lade your *b.* and go. 45:17
the first-born of *b.* shall die. *Ex* 11:5
b. ye shall eat. *Lev* 11:2; *Deut* 14:4
chew cud among *b.* *Lev* 11:3
  Deut 14:6
for *b.* increase be meat. *Lev* 25:7
I will rid evil *b.* out of land. 26:6
congregation and *b.* drink. *Num* 20:8
of all *b.* give to the Levites. 31:30
I will send *b.* on them. *Deut* 32:24
Solomon spake of *b.* *1 Ki* 4:33
find grass, that we lose not *b.* 18:5
drink ye, cattle and *b.* *2 Ki* 3:17
help him with *b.* *Ezra* 1:4
ask the *b.* and they shall. *Job* 12:7
wherefore are we counted as *b.* 18:3
then the *b.* go into dens. 37:8
man is like the *b.* that. *Ps* 49:12, 20
wherein the *b.* of forest. 104:20
the sea, both small and great *b.* 25

beasts

b. and all cattle, praise. *Ps* 148:10
wisdom hath killed her b. *Pr* 9:2
a lion strongest among b. 30:30
themselves are b. *Eccl* 3:18
befalleth men, befalleth b. 19
burden of b. of the south. *Isa* 30:6
b. thereof for a burnt-offering. 40:16
their idols were on b. and. 46:1
swift b. to my holy mountain. 66:20
the b. are fled. *Jer* 9:10
the b. are consumed. 12:4
I send famine and evil b. pestilence.
 Ezek. 5:17; 14:15
I will fill the b. of whole. 32:4
I will destroy all the b. 13; 34:25, 28
let the b. get away. *Dan* 4:14
let his portion be with the b. 15
four great b. are four kings. 7:17
that no b. might stand before. 8:4
how do the b. groan! *Joel* 1:18
peace-offerings of fat b. *Amos* 5:22
spoil of b. *Hab* 2:17
place for b. to lie down. *Zeph* 2:15
the plague of all the b. *Zech* 14:15
have ye offered slain b.? *Acts* 7:42
provide b. to set Paul on. 23:24
an image made like to b. *Rom* 1:23
if I have fought with b. *1 Cor* 15:32
for every kind of b. is tamed. *Jas* 3:7
these as natural brute b. *2 Pet* 2:12
what they know as brute b. *Jude* 10
four b. full of eyes. *Rev* 4:6
the four b. had each six wings. 8
when b. give glory and honour. 9
midst of throne and four b. a. 5:6
the four b. said Amen. 14
one of four b. saying. 6:1; 15:7
angels about throne and four b. 7:11
song before throne and four b. 14:3
the elders and b. fell down to. 19:4

beasts *of the earth*

meat to all b. *of earth. Deut* 28:26
of Philistines to b. *of earth.*
 1 Sam 17:46
afraid of the b. *of earth. Job* 5:22
teacheth more than b. *of earth.* 35:11
saints to the b. *of earth. Ps* 79:2
be left to the b. *of earth. Isa* 18:6
the people meat for b. *of the earth.*
 Jer 7:33; 16:4; 19:7; 34:20
appoint b. *of earth* to devour. 15:3
all four-footed b. *of the earth.*
 Acts 10:12; 11:6
kill with the b. *of earth. Rev* 6:8

beasts *of the field*

poor leave, b. *of field* eat. *Ex* 23:11
lest b. *of field* increase. *Deut* 7:22
thy flesh to b. *of field. 1 Sam* 17:44
b. *of the field* by night. *2 Sam* 21:10
b. *of the field* at peace. *Job* 5:23
where b. *of the field* play. 40:20
b. *of field* under his feet. *Ps* 8:7
b. *of field* come to devour. *Isa* 56:9
assemble all b. *of field. Jer* 12:9
b. *of the field* have I given him
 27:6; 28:14; *Dan* 2:38
I have given thee for meat to b. *of*
 the field. Ezek 29:5; 34:5; 39:4
his branches b *of the field.* 31:6
b. *of field* on his branches. 13
b. *of the field* shall shake. 38:20
b. *of field* had shadow. *Dan* 4:12
dwelling with b. *of field.* 25, 32
covenant with b. *of field. Hos* 2:18
land shall mourn with b. *of field.* 4:3
b. *of field* cry also to. *Joel* 1:20
be not afraid, ye b. *of field.* 2:22

wild beasts

I will also send wild b. *Lev* 26:22
Philistines to wild b. *1 Sam* 17:46
wild b. of the field are. *Ps* 50:11
wild b. of the desert lie. *Isa* 13:21
wild b. of the islands cry. 22
wild b. of desert shall meet with *wild*
 b. of the island. 34:14; *Jer* 50:39
Christ was with wild b. *Mark* 1:13
sheet, with wild b. *Acts* 10:12; 11:6

beat

[1] *To strike, pound, or bruise,*
Num 11:8; 2 Ki 3:25; Mat 21:35.
[2] *To get the better of, or over-*
come, 2 Ki 13:25.

shalt b. spices very small. *Ex* 30:36
they b. the gold into thin. 39:3
people b. manna in a. *Num* 11:8
lest he exceed and b. him. *Deut* 25:3
b. down tower of Penuel. *Judg* 8:17
Abimelech b. down the city. 9:45
sons of Belial b. at the door. 19:22
b. that she had gleaned. *Ruth* 2:17
I b. them small. *2 Sam* 22:43
 Ps 18:42
Israelites b. down the. *2 Ki* 3:25
Joash did b. Ben-hadad. 13:25
altars did the king b. down. 23:12
I will b. down his foes. *Ps* 89:23
b. him with the rod. *Pr* 23:14
b. their swords. *Isa* 2:4; *Mi* 4:3
what mean ye, to b. my people?
 Isa 3:15*
Lord shall b. off from channel. 27:12
thresh mountains, b. small. 41:15
b. plowshares into swords. *Joel* 3:10
sun b. on head of Jonah. *Jonah* 4:8
b. in pieces many people. *Mi* 4:13
and b. on that house. *Mat* 7:25, 27
 Luke 6:48, 49
his servants, and b. one. *Mat* 21:35
 Mark 12:3; *Luke* 20:10, 11
waves b. into the ship. *Mark* 4:37
b. the men-servants. *Luke* 12:45
commanded to beat them. *Acts* 16:22
Greeks took Sosthenes and b. 18:17
imprisoned and b. in every. 22:19

beaten

officers of Israel were b. *Ex* 5:14, 16
cherubims of b. work. 25:18; 37:17
 22; *Num* 8:4
two cherubims b. out of one. *Ex* 37:7
offer corn b. out of full. *Lev* 2:14
man be worthy to be b. *Deut* 25:2
made as if were b. *Josh* 8:15
Abner was b. and men. *2 Sam* 2:17
b. images to powder. *2 Chr* 34:7
they have b. me. *Pr* 23:35
fitches are b. with staff. *Isa* 28:27
the Assyrian shall be b. 30:31*
their mighty ones are b. *Jer* 46:5
graven images b. to pieces. *Mi* 1:7
synagogue ye shall be b. *Mark* 13:9
and did not shall be b. *Luke* 12:47
called the apostles and b. *Acts* 5:40
b. us openly uncondemned. 16:37
thrice, was I b. with. *2 Cor* 11:25

beaten *gold*

candlestick was b. *gold. Num* 8:4
targets of b. *gold. 1 Ki* 10:16
shields of b. *gold.* 17; *2 Chr* 9:16
shekels of b. *gold. 2 Chr* 9:15

beaten *oil*

pure *oil* b. for the light. *Ex* 27:20
 Lev 24:2
an hin of b. *oil. Ex* 29:40; *Num* 28:5

beatest

when thou b. olive tree. *Deut* 24:20
b. him with rod, shall not. *Pr* 23:13

beateth

as one that b. the air. *1 Cor* 9:26

beating

b. down one another. *1 Sam* 14:16*
b. some, and killing. *Mark* 12:5

beauties

in b. of holiness, from. *Ps* 110:3*

beautiful

Rachel was b. *Gen* 29:17
the captives a b. woman. *Deut* 21:11
of a b. countenance. *1 Sam* 16:12
Abigail of a b. countenance. 25:3
Bath-sheba was very b. *2 Sam* 11:2
Esther was fair and b. *Esth* 2:7
b. for situation is mount. *Ps* 48:2
hath made every thing b. *Eccl* 3:11
thou art b. O my love. *S of S* 6:4
how b. thy feet, O princess. 7:1
the branch of Lord be b. *Isa* 4:2
Zion, put on thy b. garments. 52:1
b. feet of them that. 7; *Rom* 10:15
our holy and b. house is. *Isa* 64:11
where is thy b. flock? *Jer* 13:20
how is staff broken, and b. 48:17
a b. crown upon thine. *Ezek* 16:12
thou wast exceeding b. 13
the Sabeans put on b. crowns. 23:42

sepulchres, appear b. *Mat* 23:27
at the gate called b. *Acts* 3:2, 10

beautify

king's heart to b. Lord's. *Ezra* 7:27
he will b. the meek with. *Ps* 149:4
b. place of my sanctuary. *Isa* 60:13

beauty

[1] *Literally, outward comeliness,*
or handsomeness, 2 Sam 14:25.
[2] *Figuratively, for* (a) *a chief person,*
or city, 2 Sam 1:19; Isa 13:19; Lam
2:1; (b) *Splendour, glory, or dignity,*
Lam 1:6; (c) *Joy and gladness,* Isa
61:3.

for Aaron, for glory and b. *Ex* 28:2
the b. of Israel is slain. *2 Sam* 1:19*
so praised as Absalom for b. 14:25
worship the Lord in b. of holiness.
 1 Chr 16:29; *Ps* 29:2; 96:9
praise b. of holiness. *2 Chr* 20:21
to shew her b. *Esth* 1:11
array with glory and b. *Job* 40:10*
to behold the b. of the. *Ps* 27:4
makest his b. to consume. 39:11
shall greatly desire thy b. 45:11
their b. shall consume in. 49:14
perfection of b. God shined. 50:2
let the b. of the Lord be on. 90:17*
strength and b. in his sanctuary. 96:6
lust not after b. in thy. *Pr* 6:25
b. of old men is grey head. 20:29
favour is deceitful, b. is vain. 31:30
burning instead of b. *Isa* 3:24
Babylon the b. of the. 13:19
glorious b. is a fading. 28:1, 4
Lord will be for a diadem of b. 5
shalt see the King in his b. 33:17
according to the b. of a man. 44:13
no b. that we should desire. 53:2
them that mourn b. for ashes. 61:3*
Zion all b. is departed. *Lam* 1:6*
cast down from heaven b. of. 2:1
city men call the perfection of b. 15
the b. of his ornament. *Ezek* 7:20
went among heathen for b. 16:14
thou didst trust in thine own b. 15
thou hast made thy b. abhorred. 25
said, I am of perfect b. 27:3; 28:12
builders have perfected thy b.
 27:4, 11
swords against b. of thy. 28:7
heart lifted up because of thy b. 17
no tree was like Assyrian in b. 31:8
whom dost thou pass in b? 32:19
b. shall be as the olive-. *Hos* 14:6
great his goodness, and b. *Zech* 9:17
two staves, one I called b. 11:7, 10

became

man b. a living soul. *Gen* 2:7
Lot's wife b. a pillar of salt. 19:26
Issachar b. a servant. 49:15
it b. a serpent. *Ex* 4:3
b. a rod in his hand. 4
coupled it, it b. one tabernacle. 36:13
Nabal's heart b. as a. *1 Sam* 25:37
thing b. a sin. *1 Ki* 12:30; 13:34
the stone b. a great. *Dan* 2:35
to the Jews I b. a Jew. *1 Cor* 9:20
such an High Priest b. us. *Heb* 7:26
whilst ye b. companions of. 10:33
the sea b. as blood of. *Rev* 16:3

becamest

thou, Lord, b. their God. *1 Chr* 17:22
thou b. mine. *Ezek* 16:8

because

b. thou hast done this. *Gen* 3:14
b. even b. they despised. *Lev* 26:43
b. he did this, b. he had. *2 Sam* 12:6
b. I called, and ye refused. *Pr* 1:24
b. even b. they seduced. *Ezek* 13:10
shall be offended b. of. *Mat* 26:31*
water, b. ye belong to. *Mark* 9:41
ye seek me, not b. ye saw, but b. ye
 did eat and were filled. *John* 6:26
even b. ye cannot hear my. 8:43
fleeth, b. he is an hireling. 10:13
b. I live, ye shall live also. 14:19
life b. of righteousness. *Rom* 8:10
b. of these cometh wrath. *Eph* 5:6
b. he could swear by no. *Heb* 6:13
b. we love brethren. *1 John* 3:14
we love him b. he first loved. 4:19

beckoned
Zacharias b. speechless. *Luke* 1:22*
b. to their partners in other. 5:7
Peter b. that he should. *John* 13:24
Alexander b. with his. *Acts* 19:33
Paul stood on stairs, and b. 21:40
Paul, after the governor had b. 24:10

beckoning
Peter b. unto them. *Acts* 12:17
Paul stood up, b. with his. 13:16

become
man is b. as one of us. *Gen* 3:22
what will b. of his dreams. 37:20
the Lord my strength, is b. my.
　　　Ex 15:2; *Ps* 118:14; *Isa* 12:2
this Moses that brought us up, what
　　is b. *Ex* 32:1, 23; *Acts* 7:40
thou art b. the people. *Deut* 27:9
Lord is b. thine enemy. *1 Sam* 28:16
what would b. of the city. *Jonah* 4:5
is b. head of corner. *Mat* 21:42*
　　Mark 12:10*; *Luke* 20:17*
　　　　　　　　Acts 4:11*
power to b. the sons of. *John* 1:12
all things are b. new. *2 Cor* 5:17
b. the kingdoms of Lord. *Rev* 11:15

becometh
(*Sometimes used as meaning
　worthy of, or worthily*)
holiness b. thy house. *Ps* 93:5
he b. poor that dealeth. *Pr* 10:4
excellent speech b. not a fool. 17:7
man void of understanding b. 18
born in his kingdom b. *Eccl* 4:14*
thus it b. us to fulfil all. *Mat* 3:15
deceitfulness of riches choketh word,
　he b. 13:22; *Mark* 4:19
b. a tree. *Mat* 13:32; *Mark* 4:32
our sister as b. saints. *Rom* 16:2
not be named, as b. saints. *Eph* 5:3
be as b. the gospel. *Phil* 1:27
b. women professing. *1 Tim* 2:10
behaviour as b. holiness. *Tit* 2:3*

bed
(*Usually only a thick quilt or thin
mattrass. Sometimes the rich had
couches made of valuable materials.
Bedsteads such as we use were rare*)
bowed on b. *Gen* 47:31; *1 Ki* 1:47
thy father's b. *Gen* 49:4; *1 Chr* 5:1
he die not, keepeth his b. *Ex* 21:18
b. whereon he lieth. *Lev* 15:4, 24
took image laid it in b. *1 Sam* 19:13
who lay on a b. at noon. *2 Sam* 4:5
David arose from his b. 11:2
not come from that b. *2 Ki* 1:4; 6:16
let us set there for him a b. 4:10
my b. shall comfort me. *Job* 7:13
made my b. in the darkness. 17:13
in slumberings upon the b. 33:15
your heart on your b. *Ps* 4:4
he deviseth mischief on his b. 36:4
all his b. in his sickness. 41:3
I remember thee upon my b. 63:6
nor go up into my b. till. 132:3
if I make my b. in hell, thou. 139:8
my b. with tapestry. *Pr* 7:16, 17
why should he take thy b. ? 22:27
the slothful on his b. 26:14
also our b. is green. *S of S* 1:16
by night on my b. I sought. 3:1
behold, his b. which is Solomon's. 7*
the b. is shorter than. *Isa* 28:20
mountain hast thou set thy b. 57:7
out in the corner of a b. *Amos* 3:12
take up thy b. and walk. *Mat* 9:6
　　Mark 2:9, 11; *John* 5:11, 12
a candle under a b. *Mark* 4:21
　　　　　　　　Luke 8:16
children with me in b. *Luke* 11:7
two men in one b. one taken. 17:34
I will cast her into a b. *Rev* 2:22

bed of love
Babylonians in b. of love. *Ezek* 23:17

bed of spices
are as a b. of spices. *S of S* 5:13
is gone to the b. of spices. 6:2

bed undefiled
honourable and b. unde. *Heb* 13:4

Bedan
the Lord sent B. and. *1 Sam* 12:11
the sons of Ulam, B. *1 Chr* 7:17

bed-chamber
frogs came into thy b.-c. *Ex* 8:3
lay in his b.-c. they. *2 Sam* 4:7
telleth the words in b.-c. *2 Ki* 6:12
hid him in b.-c. 11:2; *2 Chr* 22:11
curse not ... in thy b.-c. *Eccl* 10:20

beds
sing aloud on their b. *Ps* 149:5
they shall rest in their b. *Isa* 57:2
they howled upon their b. *Hos* 7:14
lie on b. of ivory. *Amos* 6:4
them that work evil on b. *Mi* 2:1

bedstead
(*Rarely used, and only here named
in the Bible*)
his b. was a b. of iron. *Deut* 3:11

bee, bees
chased you as b. in Seir. *Deut* 1:44
a swarm of b. in carcase. *Judg* 14:8
compassed me like b. *Ps* 118:12
hiss for the b. in Assyria. *Isa* 7:18

Beelzebub
have called the master B. *Mat* 10:25
cast out devils, but by B. prince of.
　12:24; *Mark* 3:22; *Luke* 11:15
if I by B. cast. *Mat* 12:27
　　　　　　Luke 11:18, 19

been
pleasant hast thou b. *2 Sam* 1:26
if that had b. too little. 12:8
then had I b. at rest. *Job* 3:13
thou hast b. my help. *Ps* 27:9; 63:7
unless the Lord had b. my. 94:17*
thy peace b. as a river. *Isa* 48:18
these, where had they b. ? 49:21
we had b. in days of our. *Mat* 23:30
we trusted it had b. he. *Luke* 24:21
they had b. with Jesus. *Acts* 4:13
we had b. as Sodom. *Rom* 9:29
widow, having b. wife of. *1 Tim* 5:9
it had b. better not to. *2 Pet* 2:21
if they hath b. of us. *1 John* 2:19

hath been
God of my father hath b. *Gen* 31:5
thy God hath b. with. *Deut* 2:7
wherein this sin hath b. *1 Sam* 14:38
Israel hath b. without. *2 Chr* 15:3
which hath b. is now, that which is to
　be hath already b. *Eccl* 3:15
this hath b. thy manner. *Jer* 22:21
hath this b. in your days? *Joel* 1:2
hath b. dead four days. *John* 11:39
hath b. his counsellor? *Rom* 11:34

have been
servants as they have b. *1 Sam* 4:9
have b. with thee. *1 Chr* 17:8
our fathers have we b. *Ezra* 9:7
have b. as if I had not b. *Job* 10:19
thy tender mercies have b. *Ps* 25:6
have b. young, and now old. 37:25
my tears have b. my meat. 42:3
have b. as Sodom, have b. *Isa* 1:9
so have we b. in thy sight, O. 26:17
have b. with child, have b. in. 18
all those things have b. saith. 66:2*
have I b. a wilderness ? *Jer* 2:31
the prophets that have b. 28:8
I have b. a rebuker of. *Hos* 5:2*
have b. partial in the law. *Mal* 2:9*
they have b. with me. *Mark* 8:2
have b. since the world. *Luke* 1:70
have I b. so long time? *John* 14:9
because ye have b. with me. 15:27
what manner I have b. *Acts* 20:18
have I b. in the deep. *2 Cor* 11:25
righteousness should have b. by.
　　　　　　　　Gal 3:21

not been
as hath not b. in Egypt. *Ex* 9:18
hast not b. as my servant. *1 Ki* 14:8
untimely birth I had not b. *Job* 3:16
b. as though I had not b. 10:19
if it had not b. the Lord. *Ps* 124:1, 2
better is he that hath not b. *Eccl* 4:3
as though they had not b. *Ob* 16
good he had not b. born. *Mat* 26:24
have not b. faithful. *Luke* 16:11, 12

Beer-sheba
in wilderness of B. *Gen* 21:14
Abraham planted a grove in B. 33
to B. Abraham dwelt at B. 22:19

the name of the city is B. *Gen* 26:33
Jacob went out from B. 28:10
his journey and came to B. 46:1
in their inheritance B. *Josh* 19:2
for his life and came to B. *1 Ki* 19:3
Beth-el, and pass not to B. *Amos* 5:5
the manner of B. liveth. 8:14

beetle
(*Revised Version,* cricket)
ye may eat, the b. *Lev* 11:22

beeves
(*The plural of beef, used as a generic
term for bulls, cows, or oxen*)
offer of the b. *Lev* 22:19
offers a freewill offering in b. 21
tribute to the Lord of b. *Num* 31:28
Lord's tribute of b. threescore and. 38

befall
(*To happen or occur to, to come
upon*)
lest mischief b. him. *Gen* 42:4
if mischief b. him then. 38; 44:29
that I may tell you what shall b.
　49:1; *Deut* 31:29; *Dan* 10:14
troubles shall b. them. *Deut* 31:17
shall no evil b. thee. *Ps* 91:10
things that shall b. me. *Acts* 20:22

befallen
such things have b. me. *Lev* 10:17
travail that hath b. us. *Num* 20:14
many troubles are b. *Deut* 31:21
why is all this b. us ? *Judg* 6:13
something had b. him. *1 Sam* 20:26
every thing that had b. *Esth* 6:13
was b. to the possessed. *Mat* 8:33

befalleth
which b. sons of men, b. beasts, even
one thing b. them. *Eccl* 3:19

befell
worse than all that b. *2 Sam* 19:7
told how it b. to him. *Mark* 5:16
b. me by the lying in. *Acts* 20:19

before
[1] *In sight of,* Gen. 43:14. [2]
Rather than, 2 Sam 6:21. [3] *Free
to one's view and choice,* Gen 20:15.
[4] *First,* (a) *In order of time,* Isa
43:13 (*Revised Version frequently
changes to* beforehand); (b) *In
order of place,* Josh 8:10; *Luke*
22:47.
behold my land is b. *Gen* 20:15
b. I had done speaking. 24:45
countenance was not as b. 31:2
Lord give you mercy b. the. 43:14
he set Ephraim b. Manasseh. 48:20
Aaron laid it up b. the. *Ex* 16:34
days that were b. shall be. *Num* 6:12
flowed over banks as b. *Josh* 4:18
was no day like that b. it. 10:14
such as b. knew nothing. *Judg* 3:2
said, I will go as b. 16:20
chose me b. thy father, and b. his.
　　　　　　　　2 Sam 6:21
saw battle was against him b. 10:9
　　　　　　　　1 Chr 19:10
hand became as it was b. *1 Ki* 13:6
the battle was b. and. *2 Chr* 13:14
Manasseh his trespass b. 33:19
my sighing cometh b. I eat. *Job* 3:24
b. I go, whence I shall not. 10:21
Job twice as much as he had b. 42:10
I am cut off from b. *Ps* 31:22
spare me b. I go hence. 39:13
thou preparedst room b. it. 80:9
b. I was afflicted I went. 119:67
hast beset me behind and b. 139:5
thou die b. thy time ? *Eccl* 7:17
Syrians b. and Philistines. *Isa* 9:12
and behold, b. the morning. 17:14
the day was, I am he. 43:13*
that b. they call I will. 65:24
I formed thee b. I came. *Jer* 1:5
ministered b. their idols. *Ezek* 44:12
a widow that had a priest b. 22
doings, are b. my face. *Hos* 7:2
every cow at that b. her *Amos* 4:3
me, and was afraid b. *Mal* 2:5*
send Elijah b. the coming. 4:5
b. they came together. *Mat* 1:18
knoweth what things ye need b. 6:8

come to torment us b.? *Mat 8:29*
behold, I have told you b. 24:25
not see death b. he had. *Luke 2:26*
for b. they were at enmity. 23:12
of man where he was b. *John 6:62*
law judge man b. it hear? 7:51
I tell you b. it come. 13:19; 14:29
he seeing this b. spake. *Acts 2:31*
do thy counsel determined b. 4:28
to witnesses chosen b. of God. 10:41
who have begun b. to. *2 Cor 8:10**
of which I tell you b. *Gal 5:21**
to things that are b. *Phil 3:13*
whereof ye heard b. in. *Col 1:5*
that we had suffered b. *1 Thes 2:2*
with you, we told you b. 3:4
was b. a blasphemer. *1 Tim 1:13*
the command going b. *Heb 7:18**
after that he had said b. 10:15*
of words spoken b. *2 Pet 3:2*
seeing ye know these things b. 17
to worship b. thy feet. *Rev 3:9*
full of eyes b. and behind. 4:6

come before
shall *come* b. the judges. *Ex 22:9*
come b. his presence. *Ps 100:2*
shall I *come* b. the Lord? *Mi 6:6*
come b. winter. *2 Tim 4:21*

before the people
bowed b. *the people.* *Gen 23:12*
of fire from b. *the people.* *Ex 13:22*
said, go on b. *the people.* 17:5
b. *thy people* I will do marvels. 34:10
went b. *the people* to Ai. *Josh 8:10*
came in b. *the people.* *1 Sam 18:13*
set them b. *the people.* *Mark 8:6*
his words, b. *the people.* *Luke 20:26*
b. many *peoples.* *Rev 10:11**

before whom
Lord b. *whom* I walk. *Gen 24:40*
God b. *whom* my fathers. 48:15
As the Lord liveth, b. *whom* I stand.
1 Ki 17:1; 18:15; 2 Ki 3:14; 5:16
b. *whom* thou hast begun. *Esth 6:13*
b. *whom* were three horns. *Dan 7:8*
and b. *whom* three fell. 20
the king b. *whom* I. *Acts 26:26*
**see further, all, ark, God, him,
Lord, me, mount, stand, stood,
thee, them, as, went, you.**

beforehand
take no thought b. *Mark 13:11*
make up b. your bounty. *2 Cor 9:5*
some men's sins open b. *1 Tim 5:24**
works of some are manifest b. 25*
testified b. sufferings of. *1 Pet 1:11*

beforetime
he hated him not b. *Josh 20:5*
b. in Israel, when a man went to
enquire; he now called a prophet
was b. called a seer. *1 Sam 9:9*
nor afflict them as b. *2 Sam 7:10**
Israel dwelt in tents as b. *2 Ki 13:5*
I had not been b. sad. *Neh 2:1*
who hath declared b. *Isa 41:26*
Simon which b. used. *Acts 8:9*

beg
be vagabonds and b. *Ps 109:10*
shall the sluggard b. *Pr 20:4*
I cannot dig, to b. I am. *Luke 16:3*

began
b. men to call on the. *Gen 4:26*
b. to commit whoredom. *Num 25:1*
they b. to smite Israel. *Judg 20:31*
Lord b. to cut Israel. *2 Ki 10:32*
when they b. to sing. *2 Chr 20:22*
in the third month they b. 31:7
young Josiah b. to seek God. 34:3
then they b. at the ancient. *Ezek 9:6*
then Jesus b. to preach. *Mat 4:17*
been since the world b. *Luke 1:70*
this man b. to build. 14:30
the hour when he b. to. *John 4:52*
since the world b. 9:32; *Acts 3:21*
*Rom 16:25**
in Christ before the world b.
2 Tim 1:9; Tit 1:2**
salvation at first b. to be. *Heb 2:3**

begat
hearken to him that b. *Pr 23:22*
concerning fathers that b. *Jer 16:3*

and he that b. her. *Dan 11:6*
and mother that b. him. *Zech 13:3*
of his own will b. he us. *Jas 1:18*
that loveth him that b. *1 John 5:1*

beget
twelve princes shall he b. *Gen 17:20*
thou shalt b. children. *Deut 4:25*
thou shalt b. sons, but shalt. 28:41
sons which thou shalt b. shall they.
2 Ki 20:18; Isa 39:7
if a man b. 100 children. *Eccl 6:3*
take wives, and b. sons. *Jer 29:6*
if he b. a son that is. *Ezek 18:10*
he b. a son that seeth all. 14

begettest
issue which thou b. thine. *Gen 48:6*
his father, what b. thou? *Isa 45:10*

begetteth
he that b. a fool, doeth it. *Pr 17:21*
that b. a wise child shall. 23:24
he b. a son, and nothing. *Eccl 5:14*

beggar
he lifteth the b. from. *1 Sam 2:8**
a b. named Lazarus. *Luke 16:20*
b. died, and was carried by. 22

beggarly
turn ye again to b. elements. *Gal 4:9*

begged
b. the body of Jesus. *Mat 27:58*
Luke 23:52
is not this he that b.? *John 9:8*

begging
have not seen his seed b. *Ps 37:25*
Bartimaeus sat b. *Mark 10:46*
Luke 18:35

begin
this they b. to do, and. *Gen 11:6*
day I b. to put dread. *Deut 2:25*
day will I b. to magnify. *Josh 3:7*
when I b. I will also. *1 Sam 3:12*
did I then b. to inquire of? 22:15
Mattaniah to b. *Neh 11:17*
I b. to bring evil on the. *Jer 25:29*
and b. at my sanctuary. *Ezek 9:6*
and b. not to say. *Luke 3:8*
then shall he b. to say. 13:26
all that behold it, b. to mock. 14:29
these things b. to come to. 21:28
do we b. again to? *2 Cor 3:1*
that judgement b. at the house of God,
and if it first b. at us. *1 Pet 4:17*

beginnest
thou b. to put sickle. *Deut 16:9*

beginning, noun
[1] *That which is the first,* Ex 12:2.
[2] *The creation,* Gen 1:1.
Reuben, thou art the b. of. *Gen 49:3*
this month shall be the b. *Ex 12:2*
is the b. of his strength. *Deut 21:17*
though thy b. was small. *Job 8:7*
the latter more than b. 42:12
fear of Lord b. *Ps 111:10; Pr 9:10*
fear of the Lord is the b. of. *Pr 1:7*
b. of strife, as when one. 17:14
is the end than the b. *Eccl 7:8*
b. of words of his mouth is. 10:13
since b. of the world. *Isa 64:4**
is the b. of sin to the. *Mi 1:13*
these are b. of sorrows. *Mat 24:8*
Mark 13:8
tribulation, not since the b.
Mat 24:21
the b. of the gospel. *Mark 1:1*
this b. of miracles did. *John 2:11*
who is the b. the first born. *Col 1:18*
if we hold the b. of our. *Heb 3:14*
having neither b. of days. nor. 7:3
end is worse than the b. *2 Pet 2:20*
I am the b. *Rev 1:8*; 21:6; 22:13*
these things saith the b. 3:14

at the beginning
kindness than *at the* b. *Ruth 3:10*
waste as *at* b. *1 Chr 17:9**
an inheritance *at the* b. *Pr 20:21*
counsellors as *at the* b. *Isa 1:26*
at the b. of supplications. *Dan 9:23*
made them, *at* b. made. *Mat 19:4*
things I said not *at the* b. *John 16:4*
them as on us *at the* b. *Acts 11:15*

from the beginning
from the b. of year. *Deut 11:12*
from the b. of revenges. 32:42
is true *from the* b. *Ps 119:160**
I was set up *from the* b. *Pr 8:23*
work God maketh *from* b. *Eccl 3:11*
a people terrible *from* b. *Isa 18:2, 7*
not been told *from the* b.? 40:21
who hath declared *from* b.? 41:26
declaring the end *from the* b. 46:10
not spoken in secret *from* b. 48:16
high throne *from* b. *Jer 17:12*
us, which *from* b. were. *Luke 1:2*
Jesus knew *from the* b. *John 6:64*
saith, I said to you *from* b. 8:25
was a murderer *from* b. and. 44
been with me *from the* b. 15:27
which *from* b. of the world. *Eph 3:9**
hath *from* b. chosen. *2 Thes 2:13*
continue as *from the* b. *2 Pet 3:4*
which ye have heard *from* b.
1 John 2:7; 3:11
have known him that is *from* b. 2:13
for the devil sinneth *from the* b. 3:8
which we had *from the* b. *2 John 5*

in the beginning
in the b. God created. *Gen 1:1*
possessed me *in the* b. of. *Pr 8:22*
in b. was the Word. *John 1:1*
the same was *in the* b. with God. 2
ye know that *in the* b. *Phil 4:15*
thou Lord *in the* b. hast. *Heb 1:10*

beginning, verb
b. to sink he cried, Lord. *Mat 14:30*
give their hire, b. from the. 20:8
among all nations, b. at. *Luke 24:47*
went out, b. at the eldest. *John 8:9*
b. from baptism of John. *Acts 1:22*

beginnings
in b. of months. *Num 10:10; 28:11*
I will do better than at b. *Ezek 36:11*

begotten
have I b. them? *Num 11:12*
children b. of them. *Deut 23:8*
Gideon had 70 sons, b. *Judg 8:30*
or who hath b. drops of? *Job 38:28*
Son, this day have I b. thee. *Ps 2:7*
Acts 13:33; Heb 1:5; 5:5
say, who hath b. these? *Isa 49:21*
have b. strange children. *Hos 5:7*
glory as of the only b. of. *John 1:14*
only b. Son, he hath declared. 18
loved, that he gave his only b. 3:16
not believed in the only b. Son. 18
I have b. you through. *1 Cor 4:15*
Onesimus, I have b. *Philem 10*
bringeth in first b. *Heb 1:6*
by faith offered up only b. 11:17
who hath b. us again to. *1 Pet 1:3*
sent his only b. Son. *1 John 4:9*
that begat, loveth him that is b. 5:1
he that is b. of God keepeth. 18
Jesus who is the first b. *Rev 1:5*

beguile
lest any b. you with words. *Col 2:4**
let no man b. you of your. 18*

beguiled, -ing
said, serpent b. me. *Gen 3:13*
wherefore hast thou b. me? 29:25
b. you in the matter. *Num 25:18*
wherefore have ye b. us? *Josh 9:22*
fear lest as the serpent b. *2 Cor 11:3*
cease from sin, b. *2 Pet 2:14**

begun
the plague is b. *Num 16:46*
the plague was b. 47
b. to shew greatness. *Deut 3:24*
thou hast b. to fall. *Esth 6:13*
undertook to do as they had b. 9:23
he had b. to reckon. *Mat 18:24*
as he had b. so he would. *2 Cor 8:6*
expedient for you who have b. 10
are ye so foolish, having b.? *Gal 3:3*
which hath b. a good work. *Phil 1:6*
have b. to wax wanton. *1 Tim 5:11*

behalf
a statute on b. of Israel. *Ex 27:21*
Abner sent David on b. *2 Sam 3:12*
strong in b. of them. *2 Chr 16:9*

behave　　　　38　　　　being

yet to speak on God's b. *Job 36:2*
a prince for his own b. *Dan 11:18**
glad on your b. *Rom 16:19**
thank my God on your b. *1 Cor 1:4**
thanks given on your b. *2 Cor 1:11*
occasion to glory on our b. *5:12*
it is given in b. of Christ. *Phil 1:29*
glorify God on this b. *1 Pet 4:16*

behave
lest adversaries b. *Deut 32:27**
let us b. ourselves. *1 Chr 19:13**
I will b. wisely in perfect. *Ps 101:2*
the child shall b. himself. *Isa 3:5*
charity doth not b. itself. *1 Cor 13:5*
how thou oughtest to b. *1 Tim 3:15*

behaved
David b. wisely. *1 Sam 18:5*
14, 15, 30
b. as though he had been. *Ps 35:14*
I have b. myself as a child. *131:2**
b. themselves ill in doings. *Mi 3:4**
how unblameably we b. *1 Thes 2:10*
b. not ourselves disorderly.
2 Thes 3:7

behaveth
think he b. uncomely to. *1 Cor 7:36*

behaviour
David changed his b. *1 Sam 21:13*
bishop must be of good b. *1 Tim 3:2**
women in b. becometh. *Tit 2:3**

beheaded
hands over the heifer b. *Deut 21:6**
smote Ish-bosheth, and b. him.
2 Sam 4:7
b. John. *Mat 14:10; Mark 6:16, 27*
Luke 9:9
souls of them that were b. *Rev 20:4*

beheld
he b. serpent of brass. *Num 21:9*
hath not b. iniquity in Jacob. *23:21*
destroying, the Lord b. *1 Chr 21:15*
if I b. the sun when it. *Job 31:26*
I b. transgressors. *Ps 119:158*
I b. but there was no man. *142:4**
b. among the simple ones. *Pr 7:7*
then I b. the work of God. *Eccl 8:17*
I b. and there was no man. *Isa 41:28*
Jer 4:25
I b. the earth without form. *4:23*
Mary Magdalene and Mary b.
Mark 15:47; Luke 23:55
I b. Satan as lightning. *Luke 10:18*
he b. the city, and wept over. *19:41*
and we b. his glory. *John 1:14*
while they b. Jesus was. *Acts 1:9**
I passed by and b. your. *17:23*
I b. and in midst of the. *Rev 5:6*
and their enemies b. them. *11:12*

behemoth
(Probably the hippopotamus)
behold now b. which I. *Job 40:15*

behind
[1] *Backwards,* Judg 20:40. [2]
After, 2 Sam 3:16. [3] *Remaining,*
Lev 25:51. [4] *Past,* Phil. 3:13.

shall not an hoof be left b. *Ex 10:26*
be yet many years b. *Lev 25:51**
Benjamites looked b. *Judg 20:40*
those left b. stayed. *1 Sam 30:9*
husband went weeping b. *2 Sam 3:16*
cast me by back. *1 Ki 14:9*
Ezek 23:35
rulers were b. Judah. *Neh 4:16*
cast thy law b. their backs. *9:26*
he standeth b. our wall. *S of S 2:9*
cast all my sins b. thy. *Isa 38:17*
she came in the press b. *Mark 5:27*
the child Jesus tarried b. *Luke 2:43*
so that ye come b. in. *1 Cor 1:7*
I was not b. *2 Cor 11:5; 12:11*
forgetting those things b. *Phil 3:13*
what is b. of afflictions. *Col 1:24**

see further, **before, him, we, thee,
them, us**

behold
*(An interjection, calling attention
to what is to follow. Literally, lo,
look)*
b. I am with thee, and. *Gen 28:15*
looked, and b. they were sad. *40:6*
b. thy father is sick. *48:1*

Israel said, b. I die. *Gen 48:21*
b. the bush burned with. *Ex 3:2*
b. I will rain bread from. *16:4*
b. I send an angel before. *23:20*
b. we are in Kadesh. *Num 20:16*
b. king ye have chosen. *1 Sam 12:13*
answered, b. thy servant. *2 Sam 9:6*
b. child shall be born to. *1 Ki 13:2*
b. they spied band of. *2 Ki 13:21*
b. I will bring evil upon this. *22:16*
2 Chr 34:24
b. I say, how they. *2 Chr 20:11*
b. all that he hath is in. *Job 1:12*
b. the fear of the Lord. *28:28*
b. in this thou art not just. *33:12*
b. God is mighty, despiseth. *36:5, 26*
b. I am vile, what shall I ? *40:4*
b. eye of the Lord is on. *Ps 33:18*
b. I was shapen in iniquity. *51:5*
b. these are the ungodly. *73:12*
b. he smote the rock, waters. *78:20*
if I make my bed in hell, b. *139:8*
b. thou art fair, my love b.
S of S 1:15, 16; 4:1
b. a virgin. *Isa 7:14; Mat 1:23*
b. I and the children. *Isa 8:18*
Heb 2:13
look to the earth, and b. *Isa 8:22*
b. God is my salvation, I will. *12:2*
hungry man dreameth, and b. *29:8*
say to Judah, b. your God. *40:9*
first shall say to Zion, b. b. *41:27*
b. my servant whom I uphold. *42:1*
b. I will do a new thing. *43:19*
lest thou shouldest say b. I. *48:7*
looked for peace b. *Jer 8:15; 14:19*
b. I am in your hands. *26:14*
b. I am for you, and. *Ezek 36:9*
b. I will bring my servant. *Zech 3:8*
b. the man whose name is. *6:12*
b. thy King cometh. *9:9; Mat 21:5*
John 12:15
b. I will send my messenger. *Mal 3:1*
4:5; Mat 11:10; Mark 1:2
and b. beam in thine own. *Mat 7:4*
b. he is in the desert, b. he. *24:26*
is risen b. the place. *Mark 16:6*
b. I send the promise. *Luke 24:49*
b. the Lamb of God. *John 1:29, 36*
b. an Israelite indeed. *47*
Pilate saith b. the man. *19:5*
Saul of Tarsus, for b. he. *Acts 9:11*
as dying, and b. we live. *2 Cor 6:9*
b. what manner of love. *1 John 3:1*
b. I stand at the door. *Rev 3:20*
b. I come as a thief, blessed. *16:15*
b. I come quickly. *22:7, 12*

behold *it is*
b. it is between Kadesh. *Gen 16:14*
the land, b. it is large enough. *34:21*
b. it is a stiff-necked. *Ex 32:9*
but now b. it is dry. *Josh 9:12*
seen the land, b. it is. *Judg 18:9*
that doth speak, b. it is I. *Isa 52:6*
b. the day, b. it is come. *Ezek 7:10*
b. it is come, and it is done. *39:8*

now **behold,** *or* **behold** *now*
now b. the king walketh. *1 Sam 12:2*
now b. thou trustest on. *2 Ki 18:21*
also now b. my witness. *Job 16:19*
now b. I loose thee this. *Jer 40:4*
now b. ye have heard. *Mat 26:65*
now b. the hand of the. *Acts 13:11*
now b. I go bound in the. *20:22*
b. now is the time, b. now. *2 Cor 6:2*

behold *it was,* **behold** *there was,*
see was

behold, *verb*
[1] *To look on a thing with our
eyes,* Num. 24:17. [2] *To think
over a thing in our minds,* Lam 1:12;
Rom 11:22.

b. this heap, b. this. *Gen 31:51*
Moses said, b. the blood. *Ex 24:8*
of the Lord shall he b. *Num 12:8*
see him, from the hills I b. *23:9*
but not now, shall b. him. *24:17*
b. it with thine eyes. *Deut 3:27*
b. the king whom ye. *1 Sam 12:13*
mine eyes shall b. and. *Job 19:27*
nor shall his place any more b. *20:9*
but I cannot b. him. *23:9*
hideth his face, who can b. ? *34:29*

his work, which men b. *Job 36:24**
his eyes b. his eye-lids. *Ps 11:4*
countenance doth b. the upright. *7*
let thine eyes b. the things. *17:2*
will b. thy face in righteousness. *15*
b. the beauty of the Lord. *27:4*
mark the perfect man, b. *37:37*
come, b. the works of the Lord. *46:8*
awake to help me, and b. *59:4*
ruleth for ever, his eyes b. *66:7*
look down from heaven, b. *80:14*
with thine eyes shalt thou b. *91:8*
from heaven did the Lord b. *102:19*
he humbleth himself to b. *113:6*
open mine eyes, that I may b. *119:18*
thine eyes shall b. *Pr 23:33*
pleasant thing it is to b. *Eccl 11:7*
he will not b. majesty of. *Isa 26:10*
I said, I shall b. man no more. *38:11*
or evil, that we may b. it. *41:23*
b. from thy habitation. *63:15*
I said, b. me, b. me, to a. *65:1*
thine eyes shall b. thy. *Jer 20:4*
neither b. the good I will do. *29:32*
his eyes shall b. his. *32:4; 34:3*
but a few, as thine eyes do b. *42:2*
b. and see if any sorrow. *Lam 1:12*
hear all people, and b. my. *18*
the Lord look down and b. *3:50*
O Lord, consider and b. *5:1*
b. the wicked. *Ezek 8:9*
kings that they may b. *28:17*
ashes in sight of all that b. *18*
man, b. with thine eyes. *40:4; 44:5*
open thine eyes, and b. *Dan 9:18*
light, and I shall b. *Mi 7:9*
enemy, mine eyes shall b. her. *10*
cause me to b. grievances ? *Hab 1:3*
art of purer eyes than to b. evil. *13*
their angels alway b. *Mat 18:10*
all that b. it mock him. *Luke 14:29*
for these things which ye b. *21:6*
b. my hands and my feet. *24:39*
with me, to b. my glory. *John 17:24*
as he drew near to b. it. *Acts 7:31*
Moses trembled, and durst not b. *32*
Israel could not b. face. *2 Cor 3:7*
your good works they b. *1 Pet 2:12*
they b. your chaste conversation. *3:2*
they b. the beast that. *Rev 17:8*

beholdest
thou b. all mischief to. *Ps 10:14*
why b. thou the mote ? *Mat 7:3*
Luke 6:41
b. not the beam that is. *Luke 6:42*

beholdeth
b. not way of vineyards. *Job 24:18**
the Lord b. all the sons. *Ps 33:13*
he b. himself and goeth. *Jas 1:24*

beholding
turn mine eyes from b. *Ps 119:37*
Lord in every place, b. evil. *Pr 15:3**
saving the b. of them. *Eccl 5:11*
women b. *Mat 27:55; Luke 23:49*
Jesus b. him, loved him. *Mark 10:21*
people stood b. and. *Luke 23:35*
b. things done, smote their. *48*
b. man which was healed. *Acts 4:14*
Paul earnestly b. the council. *23:1**
with open face b. as in. *2 Cor 3:18*
in spirit, joying, and b. *Col 2:5*
a man b. his natural face. *Jas 1:23*

behoved
(Was necessary or proper for)
it b. Christ to suffer.. *Luke 24:46*
b. him to be made like. *Heb 2:17*

being
I b. in the way, the. *Gen 24:27**
the owner thereof not b. *Ex 22:14*
shall not defile himself, b. *Lev 21:4*
vow b. in her father's. *Num 30:3, 13*
our enemies b. judges. *Deut 32:31*
freed from b. bondmen. *Josh 9:23*
rejected thee from b. king.
1 Sam 15:23, 26
Maachah his mother, he removed
from b. *1 Ki 15:13; 2 Chr 15:16*
in b. like the house. *1 Ki 16:7*
who is there that b. as ? *Neh 6:11*
man b. in honour, abideth. *Ps 49:12*
cut them off from b. a nation. *83:4*
b. an Hebrew or. *Jer 34:9*
her husband b. a just. *Mat 1:19*

woman *b*. a daughter.   *Luke* 13:16
in hell he lift up his eyes *b*.   16:23
b. children of the resurrection. 20:36
b. in agony, he prayed.   22:44
conveyed—multitude *b*. *John* 5:13
that thou, *b*. a man, makest. 10:33
all the members *b*.   *1 Cor* 12:12
Jesus Christ *b*. the chief. *Eph* 2:20
who *b*. in the form of God. *Phil* 2:6
as *b*. yourselves also.   *Heb* 13:3
she *b*. with child, cried. *Rev* 12:2

being
praise my God while I have my *b*.
        Ps 104:33; 146:2
in him move, and have *b*. *Acts* 17:28

bekah
a *b*. for each, that is half a. *Ex* 38:26

Bel
B. boweth down, Nebo.   *Isa* 46:1
Babylon is taken, *B*. is. *Jer* 50:2
I will punish *B*. in Babylon. 51:44

belch
behold, they *b*. out.   *Ps* 59:7

Belial
certain children of *B*. *Deut* 13:13
certain sons of *B*. beset. *Judg* 19:22
the man, the children of *B*. 20:13
a daughter of *B*.   *1 Sam* 1:16
sons of Eli were sons of *B*.   2:12
children of *B*. said, how shall? 10:27
he is such a son of *B*.   25:17
lord regard this man of *B*.   25
then answered the men of *B*. 30:22
out, thou man of *B*. *2 Sam* 16:7
to be there a man of *B*. Sheba. 20:1
the sons of *B*. shall be as.   23:6
set two sons of *B*. *1 Ki* 21:10, 13
Jeroboam children of *B*. *2 Chr* 13:7
hath Christ with *B*. ? *2 Cor* 6:15

belied
they have *b*. the Lord.   *Jer* 5:12

belief
sanctification of Spirit, and *b*. of.
            2 Thes 2:13

believe
[1] *To give credit to any thing*,
Gen 45:26, Acts 8:13. [2] *To be
fully* persuaded, John 1:12; 3:15,
16; 6:69; Rom 9:33; 10:4. [3]
To put confidence in, 2 Chr 20:20.
that they may *b*. Lord hath. *Ex* 4:5
that they may hear and *b*.   19:9
how long ere they *b*. ? *Num* 14:11
b. in the Lord God, *b*. *2 Chr* 20:20
ye may know and *b*. me. *Isa* 43:10
b. ye that I am able ? *Mat* 9:28
whoso offend one of these little ones
  which *b*. in me. 18:6; *Mark* 9:42
repented not that ye might *b*.
               Mat 21:32
let him come down, we will *b*. 27:42
repent and *b*. the gospel. *Mark* 1:15
be not afraid, *b*. 5:36; *Luke* 8:50
thou canst *b*. all things. *Mark* 9:23*
Lord, I *b*. help mine. 24; *John* 9:38
shall *b*. those things. *Mark* 11:23
b. ye receive, and ye shall.   24
descend, that we may *b*.   15:32
shall follow them which *b*. 16:17
taketh word, lest they *b*. *Luke* 8:12
no root, which for a while *b*.   13
slow of heart to *b*.   24:25
men through him might *b*. *John* 1:7
of God, even to them that *b*. 12
how shall ye *b*. if I tell you ? 3:12
woman, *b*. me, hour cometh. 4:21
now we *b*. not because of.   42
ye *b*. which receive honour ? 5:44
if not writings, how shall ye *b*.? 47
work of God, that ye *b*. on. 6:29
we *b*. and are sure that thou art. 69
neither did his brethren *b*. in. 7:5
Spirit, which they that *b*.   39
dost thou *b*. on Son of God ? 9:35
who is he, Lord, that I might *b*.? 36
b. works, that ye may *b*. 10:38*
not there, to intent ye may *b*. 11:15
I *b*. that thou art the Christ.   27
said I not, if thou wouldst *b*.   40
they may *b*. that thou hast sent. 42
let him alone, all men will *b*.   48

while ye have light, *b*. in. *John* 12:36
it come to pass, ye may *b*. 13:19
not troubled, ye *b*. in God, *b*. 14:1
b. I am in the Father, or *b*.   11
when it come to pass ye might *b*. 29
by this we *b*. thou camest. 16:30
Jesus answered, do ye now *b*. ? 31
I pray for them which shall *b*. 17:20
that world may *b*. thou hast.   21
he saith true, that ye might *b*. 19:35
written that ye might *b*.   20:31
b. Jesus Christ is Son. *Acts* 8:37*
by him all that *b*. are.   13:39
a work you shall in no wise *b*. 41
by me should hear and *b*.   15:7
b. through grace we shall be.   11
b. on the Lord Jesus, and. 16:31
b. on him that should come. 19:4
many Jews there are which *b*. 21:20
touching the Gentiles which *b*. 25
I *b*. God that it shall be as. 27:25
righteousness on all that *b*.
            Rom 3:22
father of all them that *b*.   4:11
it shall be imputed, if we *b*.   24
if dead, we *b*. that we shall live. 6:8
b. in thy heart that God raised. 10:9
how shall they *b*. in him ?   14
save them that *b*.   *1 Cor* 1:21
be divisions, and I partly *b*. 11:18
that *b*. but prophesying serveth them
     which *b*.   14:22
we also *b*. and therefore. *2 Cor* 4:13
promise given to them that *b*.
            Gal 3:22
of power to us who *b*. *Eph* 1:19
it is given not only to *b*. *Phil* 1:29
ensamples to all that *b*. *1 Thes* 1:7
we behaved among you that *b*. 2:10
which worketh in you that *b*.   13
if we *b*. that Jesus died and. 4:14
admired in all those that *b*.
            2 Thes 1:10
delusion that they should *b*. 2:11
pattern to them that *b*. *1 Tim* 1:16
thanksgiving of them that *b*. 4:3
Saviour, especially those that *b*. 10
them that *b*. to saving. *Heb* 10:39*
that cometh to God must *b*. 11:6
the devils also *b*. and. *Jas* 2:19
who by him do *b*. in. *1 Pet* 1:21
to you which *b*. he is precious. 2:7
commandment that we should *b*.
            1 John 3:23
to you that *b*. that ye may *b*. 5:13*

believe *not*, or *not* **believe**
behold, they will *not b*. me. *Ex* 4:1
come to pass, if they will *not b*. 8, 9
yet in this ye did *not b*. *Deut* 1:32
their fathers did *not b*. *2 Ki* 17:14
yet would I *not b*. that he. *Job* 9:16
speaketh fair, *b*. him *not*. *Pr* 26:25
if ye will *not b*. ye shall not. *Isa* 7:9
b. *not* them.   *Jer* 12:6
which ye will *not b*. *Hab* 1:5
why did ye *not b*. him ? *Mat* 21:25
            Mark 11:31
b. it *not*. *Mat* 24:23, 26; *Mark* 13:21
if I tell you will *not b*. *Luke* 22:67
earthly things, ye *b*. *not*. *John* 3:12
except ye see ye will *not b*. 4:48
whom he hath sent, ye *not*. 5:38
b. *not* his writings how shall ye *b*.
  my words ?   47
also have seen me and *b*. *not*. 6:36
there some of you which *b*. *not*. 64
ye *b*. *not* I am he, ye shall die. 8:24
I tell you truth, ye *b*. me *not*.   45
why do ye *not b*. me ?   46
ye *b*. *not*, because ye are not. 10:26
do not the works, *b*. me *not*.   37
though ye *b*. *not* me, believe.   38
they could *not b*. because. 12:39
if any hear words, and *b*. *not*.   47
reprove of sin, they *b*. *not*. 16:9
into his side, I will *not b*. 20:25
what if some did *not b*. ? *Rom* 3:3*
from them that do *not b*. 15:31*
if any that *b*. *not* bid. *1 Cor* 10:27
a sign to them that *b*. *not*. 14:22
blinded minds that *b*. *not*. *2 Cor* 4:4
if we *b*. *not*, he abideth. *2 Tim* 2:13*
b. *not* every spirit. *1 John* 4:1

believed
b. in the Lord. *Gen* 15:6; *Rom* 4:3
          Gal 3:6; *Jas* 2:23
Aaron spake, people *b*.   *Ex* 4:31
b. the Lord and Moses.   14:31
and Achish *b*. David. *1 Sam* 27:12
had fainted, unless I had *b*. *Ps* 27:13
then *b*. they his words, they. 106:12
I *b*., therefore have I spoken. 116:10
            2 Cor 4:13
teach me, for I have *b*. *Ps* 119:66
who hath *b*. our report ? *Isa* 53:1
     John 12:38; *Rom* 10:16
hurt on him, because he *b*. *Dan* 6:23*
people of Nineveh *b*. God. *Jonah* 3:5
as thou hast *b*. so be it. *Mat* 8:13
publicans and harlots *b*. him. 21:32
and told it, neither *b*. *Mark* 16:13
are most surely *b*. *Luke* 1:1
blessed is she that *b*. for there. 45
his glory, and disciples *b*. *John* 2:11
they *b*. the scripture.   22
the man *b*. the word.   4:50
the father himself *b*. and.   53
ye *b*. Moses, ye would have *b*. 5:46
have any rulers or Pharisees *b*. ? 7:48
said Jesus to Jews that *b*.   8:31
had seen things Jesus did, *b*. 11:45
the Jews went away and *b*. 12:11
loveth you, because you *b*. 16:27
they have *b*. thou didst send. 17:8
that other disciple saw and *b*. 20:8
hast *b*. have not seen and *b*.   29
all that *b*. were together. *Acts* 2:44
many of them which heard *b*. 4:4
multitude of them that *b*. were. 32
but when they *b*. Philip.   8:12
then Simon himself *b*. also.   13
they of circumcision who *b*. 10:45
gave them gift as us who *b*. 11:17
great number *b*. and turned.   21
deputy *b*. being astonished. 13:12
were ordained to eternal life *b*. 48
of both Jews and Greeks *b*. 14:1
commended them to Lord they 23
some of them *b*. and.   17:4*
certain men clave to him and *b*. 34
Crispus chief ruler *b*. on Lord. 18:8
helped them which had *b*.   27
the Holy Ghost since ye *b*. ? 19:2
beat in synagogue them that *b*. 22:19
the centurion *b*. the master. 27:11*
some *b*., and some *b*. not. 28:24
against hope *b*. in hope. *Rom* 4:18
salvation nearer than when we *b*.
            13:11
ministers by whom ye *b*. *1 Cor* 3:5
unless ye have *b*. in vain. 15:2
so we preach, and so ye *b*.   11
even we have *b*. in Jesus. *Gal* 2:16
in whom after ye *b*. *Eph* 1:13
our testimony was *b*. *2 Thes* 1:10
b. on in the world.   *1 Tim* 3:16
I know whom I have *b*. *2 Tim* 1:12
they which have *b*. in God. *Tit* 3:8
which have *b*. do enter. *Heb* 4:3
have *b*. the love of God. *1 John* 4:16

many **believed**
at the passover *many b*. *John* 2:23
many of the Samaritans *b*. on. 4:39
many of the Jews *b*.   11:45
the chief rulers also *many b*. 12:42
many of Corinthians *b*. *Acts* 18:8
many that *b*. came and. 19:18

believed *not*, or *not* **believed**
heart fainted, he *b*. *not*. *Gen* 45:26
because he *b*. me *not*. *Num* 20:12
rebelled, and *b*. him *not*. *Deut* 9:23
I *b*. *not* words. *1 Ki* 10:7; *2 Chr* 9:6
I laughed, they *b*. it *not*. *Job* 29:24
because they *b*. *not* in God. *Ps* 78:22
sinned, and *b*. *not* for his.   32
despised the land, *b*. *not*. 106:24
but Gedaliah *b*. them *not*. *Jer* 40:14
world would *not* have *b*. *Lam* 4:12
came, and ye *b*. him *not*. *Mat* 21:32
they heard he was alive *b*. *not*.
            Mark 16:11
because they *b*. *not*.   14
why then *b*. him *not* ? *Luke* 20:5
while they *b*. *not* for joy. 24:41
because he hath *b*. *not*. *John* 3:18
Jesus knew who *b*. *not*.   6:64

I told you and ye *b. not. John* 10:25
many miracles, yet they *b. not.* 12:37
afraid, and *b. not* that.   *Acts* 9:26
Jews which *b. not* moved.   17:5
were hardened and *b. not.*   19:9*
in whom they have *not b. Rom* 10:14
times past have *not b.* God. 11:30*
even so have these *not b.*   31
damned who *b.* not.   *2 Thes* 2:12
into rest, that *b. not.   Heb* 3:18*
not with them that *b. not.*   11:31*
destroyed them that *b. not. Jude* 5

believers
b. were the more added.   *Acts* 5:14
be thou an example of *b. 1 Tim* 4:12

believest
dumb because thou *b. not. Luke* 1:20
I saw thee, *b.* thou ?   *John* 1:50
in me shall never die, *b.* ?   11:26
b. thou not ?   11:42
thou *b.* with thine heart. *Acts* 8:37*
b. thou ? I know thou *b.*   26:27
b. that there is one God. *Jas* 2:19

believeth
he *b.* not that he shall.   *Job* 15:22
simple *b.* every word.   *Pr* 14:15
that *b.* not make haste.   *Isa* 28:16
possible to him that *b.   Mark* 9:23
he that *b.* and is baptized . . .he that *b.*
  not shall be damned.   16:16
b. in him not perish. *John* 3:15, 16
he that *b.* on him is not condemned,
  that *b.* not is condemned.   18
that *b.* hath everlasting.   36; 6:47
b. on him that sent me hath.   5:24
he that *b.* shall never thirst.   6:35
he that *b.* seeth the Son and he   40
he that *b.* on me, out of his.   7:38
he that *b.* though he were.   11:25
whosoever liveth and *b.* in me.   26
he that *b.* on me, *b.* not on.   12:44
whoso *b.* on me, should not.   46
he that *b.* on me, the works.   14:12
whoso *b.* in him receive. *Acts* 10:43
God to every one that *b. Rom* 1:16
the justifier of him that *b.*   3:26*
him that worketh not, but *b.*   4:5
whoso *b.* shall not be.   9:33; 10:11
end of law to every one that *b.*   10:4
for with the heart man *b.*   10
for one *b.* that he may eat.   14:2*
hath a wife that *b.* not. *1 Cor* 7:12
love *b.* all things, hopeth all.   13:7
come in one that *b.* not.   14:24
part hath he that *b.* ?   *2 Cor* 6:15
if any man that *b.* have. *1 Tim* 5:16
he that *b.* shall not be.   *1 Pet* 2:6
whoso *b.* Jesus is Christ. *1 John* 5:1
overcometh, but he that *b.*   5
that *b.* on the Son; he that *b.* not God,
  because he *b.* not the record.   10

believing
ask in prayer, *b.* receive. *Mat* 21:22
be not faithless but *b.   John* 20:27
that *b.* ye might have life.   31
rejoiced, *b.* in God.   *Acts* 16:34
b. all things which are written. 24:14
all joy and peace in *b.   Rom* 15:13
they that have *b.* masters. *1 Tim* 6:2
yet *b.* ye rejoice with.   *1 Pet* 1:8

bell, -s
b. of gold.   *Ex* 28:33; 39:25
a golden *b.* and pomegranate. 28:34
                    39, 26
upon *b.* of horses.   *Zech* 14:20

bellow, see bulls

bellies
are alway liars, slow *b.*   *Tit* 1:12

bellows
b. are burnt, lead.   *Jer* 6:29

belly
[1] *The part of the body which
contains the bowels,* Mat 15:17.
[2] *The womb,* Jer 1:5.
b. shalt thou go, and.   *Gen* 3:14
goeth upon the *b.*   *Lev* 11:42
thigh to rot, thy *b.*   *Num* 5:21†
and woman through the *b.*   25:8†
and thrust it in his *b.   Judg* 3:21†
over against the *b.*   *1 Ki* 7:20
give up ghost out of the *b. Job* 3:11†

fill his *b.* with the east wind. *Job* 15:2
vanity, and their *b.* prepareth.   35
shall cast out of his *b.*   20:15
not feel quietness in his *b.*   20*
about to fill his *b.* God shall.   23
behold my *b.* is as wine.   32:19†
whose *b.* thou fillest.   *Ps* 17:14
my God from my mother's *b.* 22:10
soul bowed down, *b.*   44:25†
the *b.* of the wicked.   *Pr* 13:25
innermost parts of the *b.*   18:8†
                    26:22†
a man's *b.* shall be satisfied.   18:20
inward parts of the *b.*   20:27†
stripes inward parts of *b.*   30†
his *b.* is as bright ivory. *S of S* 5:14*
b. is like an heap of wheat.   7:2†
borne by me from the *b.   Isa* 46:3
I formed thee in the *b.* I.   *Jer* 1:5
he hath filled his *b.* with.   51:34*
man, cause thy *b.* to eat. *Ezek* 3:3
this image's *b.* of brass.   *Dan* 2:32
Jonah was in *b.* of the fish.
                Jonah 1:17; *Mat* 12:40
out of the *b.* of hell cried. *Jonah* 2:2
I heard, my *b.* trembled. *Hab* 3:16†
entereth mouth goeth into the *b.*
                Mat 15:17; *Mark* 7:19
fain have filled his *b.   Luke* 15:16
out of his *b.* shall flow. *John* 7:38†
our Lord but their own *b. Rom* 16:18
meats for the *b.* and *b. 1 Cor* 6:13
whose God is their *b.   Phil* 3:19
shall make thy *b.* bitter. *Rev* 10:9
as soon as I had eaten it, my *b.* 10

belong
interpretations *b.* to God. *Gen* 40:8
return to whom it did *b. Lev* 27:24
secret things *b.* to God, revealed *b.*
                    Deut 29:29
shields of earth *b.* to God. *Ps* 47:9
to our God *b.* the issues.   68:20
these things *b.* to wise.   *Pr* 24:23
to the Lord *b.* mercies.   *Dan* 9:9
my name, because ye *b. Mark* 9:41
the things which *b.* to.   *Luke* 19:42
careth for things that *b. 1 Cor* 7:32

belonged, -est
to whom *b.* thou ?   *1 Sam* 30:13
mighty men, which *b.* to.   *1 Ki* 1:8
as he knew he *b.* to.   *Luke* 23:7

belongeth
to me *b.* vengeance.   *Deut* 32:35
                Ps 94:1; *Heb* 10:30
b. to Benjamin   *Judg* 19:14; 20:4
arise, for this matter *b.   Ezra* 10:4
salvation *b.* unto the Lord.   *Ps* 3:8
have I heard, power *b.*   62:11
also unto thee, *b.* mercy.   12
righteousness *b.* to thee.   *Dan* 9:7
to us *b.* confusion of face.   8
strong meat *b.* to them.   *Heb* 5:14

belonging
of sanctuary *b.* to them.   *Num* 7:9
part of a field *b.* to Boaz.   *Ruth* 2:3
meddleth with strife *b.*   *Pr* 26:17
he went into a desert *b.   Luke* 9:10

beloved
two wives, the one *b.   Deut* 21:15
b. of the Lord shall dwell.   33:12
Solomon, of his God. *Neh* 13:26
that thy *b.* may.   *Ps* 60:5; 108:6
for so he giveth his *b.* sleep.   127:2
and only *b.* in the sight of.   *Pr* 4:3
drink abundantly, O *b.   S of S* 5:1
is thy *b.* more than another *b.* ?   9
whither is thy *b.* gone ?   6:1
who cometh leaning on her *b.* ?   8:5
art greatly *b.   Dan* 9:23; 10:11, 19
go yet, love a woman *b.*   *Hos* 3:1
I will slay the *b.*   9:16
men with *b.* Barnabas.   *Acts* 15:25
to all that are in Rome, *b.   Rom* 1:7
I will call *b.* which was not *b.*   9:25
they are *b.* for Father's sake. 11:28
salute to Persis who.   16:12
accepted in the *b.*   *Eph* 1:6
a *b.* brother and.   6:21; *Col* 4:7
elect of God, holy and *b.*   *Col* 3:12
Onesimus, a faithful and *b.*   4:9
Luke the *b.* physician and.   14
knowing *b.* your election. *1 Thes* 1:4

because they are *b.*   *1 Tim* 6:2
a servant, a brother *b.*   *Philem* 16
b. we are persuaded.   *Heb* 6:9
b. be not ignorant of this. *2 Pet* 3:8
even as our *b.* brother Paul.   15
b. now are we sons of.   *1 John* 3:2
b. condemn us not.   21
b. believe not every spirit, but.   4:1
b. let us love one another.   7
b. if God so loved us, we.   11
b. follow not evil, but.   *3 John* 11
but ye *b.* building up.   *Jude* 20
compassed the *b.* city.   *Rev* 20:9

dearly beloved, see dearly

my beloved
my *b.* is a cluster of.   *S of S* 1:14
behold thou art fair, my *b.*   16
as the apple-tree, so is my *b.*   2:3
it is the voice of my *b.*   2:8; 5:2
my *b.* is like a roe or a.   2:9
my *b.* is mine, I am his.   16; 6:3
turn my *b.* and be thou like.   2:17
let my *b.* come into his garden. 4:16
I rose up to open to my *b.*   5:5
I opened to my *b.*   6
my *b.* is white and ruddy.   10
this is my *b.*   16
my *b.* is gone.   6:2
I am my *b.* and my *b.* mine.   3; 7:10
I have laid up for thee, my *b.* 7:13
a song of my *b.* touching.   *Isa* 5:1
what hath my *b.* to do?   *Jer* 11:15
my *b.* Son.   *Mat* 3:17; 17:5
            Mark 1:11; 9:7; *Luke* 3:22
            9:35*; *2 Pet* 1:17
behold my *b.* in whom my. *Mat* 12:18
I will send my *b.* son.   *Luke* 20:13
greet Amplias my *b.*   *Rom* 16:8
as my *b.* sons I warn.   *1 Cor* 4:14
Timothy my *b.* son.   17; *2 Tim* 1:2
do not err, my *b.* brethren. *Jas* 1:16

Belshazzar
O *B.* hast not humbled.   *Dan* 5:22
in the first year of *B.*   7:1
in third year of *B.*   8:1

Belteshazzar
to Daniel the name of *B.   Dan* 1:7
name was *B.*   2:26; 4:8, 9, 19
            5:12; 10:1

bemoan, -ed, -ing
they *b.* Job, comforted.   *Job* 42:11
who shall *b.* thee ?   *Jer* 15:5
neither go to lament, nor *b.*   16:5
weep not for the dead, nor *b.* 22:10
I have heard Ephraim *b.*   31:18
all ye that are about him *b.*   48:17
is laid waste, who will *b.* ?   *Nah* 3:7

Benaiah
did *B.*   *2 Sam* 23:22; *1 Chr* 11:24
call me Zadok and *B.*   *1 Ki* 1:32
the king put *B.* in Joab's room. 2:35
B. the son of Jehoiada was.   4:4
Jesimiel and *B.* sons.   *1 Chr* 4:36
B. the Pirathonite, a mighty.   11:31
second degree *B.* 15:18,20; 16:5, 6
captain for third month, *B.*   27:5
for the eleventh month, *B.*   14
Mahath and *B.* were.   *2 Chr* 31:13
B. son of Parosh.   *Ezra* 10:25
B. son of Pahath-moab.   30
B. the son of Bani.   35
B. son of Nebo.   43
I saw Pelatiah son of *B. Ezek* 11:1
when I prophesied, the son of *B.* 13

Ben-ammi
called his name *B.*   *Gen* 19:38

benches
thy *b.* of ivory.   *Ezek* 27:6

bend
the wicked *b.* their bow.   *Ps* 11:2
who *b.* their bows to shoot.   64:3*
b. their tongue like a bow. *Jer* 9:3
Lydians, handle and *b.* bow.   46:9
all ye that *b.* the bow.   50:14, 29
against him, let the archer *b.*   51:3
this vine did *b.* roots.   *Ezek* 17:7

bendeth, -ing
when he *b.* his bow.   *Ps* 58:7*
that afflicted thee shall *b. Isa* 60:14
against him that *b.* let.   *Jer* 51:3*

beneath

in the earth *b.*   *Ex* 20:4; *Deut* 5:8
he brake the tables *b.* mount.
     Ex 32:19
on the earth *b.* there.   *Deut* 4:39
be above only, and not be *b.*   28:13
the deep that coucheth *b.*   33:13
roots shall be dried up *b. Job* 18:16
that ye depart from hell *b. Pr* 15:24
hell from *b.* is moved.   *Isa* 14:9
your eyes, look on the earth *b.* 51:6
foundations can be searched *b.*
     Jer 31:37
ye are from *b.* I am.   *John* 8:23

benefactors

that exercise authority are called *b.*
     Luke 22:25

benefit

good wherewith I *b.* them. *Jer* 18:10

benefit, -s

[1] *The gifts and favours of God*
to men, 2 Chr 32:25; Ps 68:19;
103:2.
not according to *b.*   *2 Chr* 32:25
Lord loadeth us with *b.*   *Ps* 68:19*
the Lord, forget not all his *b.* 103:2
shall I render for his *b.* ?   116:12
might have second *b.*   *2 Cor* 1:15
partakers of the *b.*   *1 Tim* 6:2
b. should not be of.   *Philem* 14*

benevolence

husband render due *b.*   *1 Cor* 7:3*

Ben-hadad

to B.   *1 Ki* 15:18; *2 Chr.* 16:2
thus saith B. thy silver.   *1 Ki* 20:2
B. was drinking himself drunk.   16
B. escaped on an horse, with.   20
thy servant B. saith, I pray thee. 32
B. went up and besieged. *2 Ki* 6:24
B. was sick.   8:7
thy son B. hath sent me.   9
Israel into the hand of B.   13:3
took again out of the hand of B. 25
palaces of B.   *Jer* 49:27; *Amos* 1:4

Benjamin

his father called him B.   *Gen* 35:18
Rachel, Joseph and B.   24; 46:19
not, and ye will take B.   42:36
away your brother and B.   43:14
and when Joseph saw B.   16, 29
B. mess was five times so.   34
cup was found in B. sack.   44:12
he fell on his brother B. neck. 45:14
sons of B.   46:21; *Num* 26:38, 41
1 Chr 7:6; 8:1, 40; 9:7; *Neh* 11:7
B. shall ravin as a wolf. *Gen* 49:27
prince of B. was Abidan. *Num* 1:11
stand to bless, Joseph, B. *Deut* 27:12
of B. Moses said, the.   33:12
after thee, B. among thy. *Judg* 5:14
Gibeah, which belongs to B.   19:14
out to battle against B.   20:20
the Lord smote B. before Israel. 35
all day of B. were 25,000 men.   46
give his daughter to B.   21:1, 18
women are destroyed out of B.   16
there ran a man of B.   *1 Sam* 4:12
there was a man of B. whose.   9:1
sepulchre, in the border of B.   10:2
in Gibeah of B. 13:2; 14:16; 15:16
by number twelve of B. *2 Sam* 2:15
also spake in the ears of B.   3:19
were a thousand men of B.   19:17
Saul buried they in B.   21:14
son of Elah officer in B.   *1 Ki* 4:18
Bilhan, Jeush and B.   *1 Chr* 7:10
Levi and B. counted he not.   21:6
over B. was Jaasiel the son.   27:21
of B. Eliada a mighty. *2 Chr* 17:17
all in Jerusalem and B.   34:32
after him repaired B. and. *Neh* 3:23
there is little B. with.   *Ps* 68:27
before B. and Manasseh, stir. 80:2
was in the gate of B.   *Jer* 37:13
sitting in the gate of B.   38:7
B. shall have a portion. *Ezek* 48:23
one gate of B.   32
Beth-aven, after thee, O B. *Hos* 5:8
possess Ephraim, B. shall.   *Ob* 19
inhabited from B. gate. *Zech* 14:10

see **children**

Benjamin with *Judah*

to fight *Judah* and B.   *Judg* 10:9
speak to house of *Judah* and B.
     1 Ki 12:23; *2 Chr* 11:3
came of B. and *Judah. 1 Chr* 12:16
having *Judah* and B.   *2 Chr* 11:12
Asa, and all *Judah* and B.   15:2
idols out of *Judah* and B.   8
captains through *Judah* and B. 25:5
altars out of *Judah* and B.   31:1
was gathered of *Judah* and B. 34:9
fathers of *Judah* and B.   *Ezra* 1:5
the adversaries of *Judah* and B. 4:1
children of *Judah* and B.   *Neh* 11:4
after them went *Judah*, B.   12:34
border of *Judah* and B. *Ezek* 48:22

land of Benjamin

go into the *land of* B.   *Judg* 21:21
man out of the *land of* B. *1 Sam* 9:16
idols out of *land of* B.   *2 Chr* 15:8
from *land of* B. bringing. *Jer* 17:26
witnesses in the *land of* B.   32:44
in the *land of* B. shall flocks. 33:13
went to go into the *land of* B. 37:12

tribe of Benjamin

tribe of B. numbered.   *Num* 1:37
captain of the *tribe of* B. 2:22; 10:24
of the *tribe of* B. to spy the.   13:9
of the *tribe of* B. to divide.   34:21
the lot of the *tribe of* B. *Josh* 18:11
the cities of the *tribe of* B.   21
of the tribe of *Judah* and the *tribe of*
B.   21:4, 17; *1 Chr* 6:60, 65
men through all the *tribe of* B.
     Judg 20:12
families of the *tribe of* B. *1 Sam* 9:21
come near, the *tribe of* B.   10:20
man of the *tribe of* B.   *Acts* 13:21
the *tribe of* B.   *Rom* 11:1; *Phil* 3:5
of the *tribe of* B. were.   *Rev* 7:8

Benjamite

Ehud a B.   *Judg* 3:15
Kish a B.   *1 Sam* 9:1
and said, am not I a B. ?   21
Shimei a B.   *2 Sam* 16:11; 19:16
     1 Ki 2:8
Sheba a B.   *2 Sam* 20:1
Mordecai a B.   *Esth* 2:5

Benjamites

men of the place were B. *Judg* 19:16
destroyed of the B. 25,100.   20:35
thus they inclosed the B. round. 43
Saul, hear now, ye B. *1 Sam* 22:7
was Abiezer a B.   *1 Chr* 27:12

Benoni

she called his name B.   *Gen* 35:18

bent

b. his bow. *Ps* 7:12; *Lam* 2:4; 3:12
have *b.* their bow to cast. *Ps* 37:14
sharp, and their bows *b.*   *Isa* 5:28
fled from the swords and *b.* 21:15
people *b.* to backsliding.   *Hos* 11:7
when I have *b.* Judah.   *Zech* 9:13

Beor

son of B. reigned.   *Gen* 36:32
     1 Chr 1:43
Balaam the son of B.   *Num* 22:5
24:3, 15; 31:8; *Deut* 23:4
Josh 13:22; 24:9; *Mi* 6:5

Berachah

B. came to David.   *1 Chr* 12:3
called the valley of B.   *2 Chr* 20:26

Berea

and Silas by night to B. *Acts* 17:10
heard that Paul preached at B.   13
Sopater of B. accompanied.   20:4

bereave

I labour and *b.* my soul.   *Eccl* 4:8*
I will *b.* them.   *Jer* 15:7; 18:21
evil beasts shall *b.* thee. *Ezek* 5:17
no more *b.* them of men.   36:12, 14
bring up children, will I *b. Hos* 9:12

bereaved

have *b.* of my children.   *Gen* 42:36
b. of my children, I am *b.*   43:14
land hast *b.* thy nations. *Ezek* 36:13
meet them as a bear *b.*   *Hos* 13:8

bereaveth

abroad the sword *b.*   *Lam* 1:20

Berith

the house of their God B. *Judg* 9:46

Bernice

B. came unto.   *Acts* 25:13, 23
the governor and B.   26:30

berries

two or three *b.* in bough.   *Isa* 17:6
fig-tree bear olive *b.* ?   *Jas* 3:12*

beryl

his body was like the *b.*   *Dan* 10:6
eighth foundation was *b. Rev* 21:20

beseech

(*Beg, pray, intreat*)
I *b.* thee shew me thy.   *Ex* 33:18
heal, O Lord, I *b.* thee. *Num* 12:13
return, we *b.* thee.   *Ps* 80:14
Lord, I *b.* thee deliver me.   116:4
save I *b.* O Lord, I *b.* thee. 118:25
accept, I *b.* thee, offerings. 119:108
obey, I *b.* thee, voice of. *Jer* 38:20
O Lord God, forgive I *b.* *Amos* 7:2
we *b.* thee, O Lord, we *b. Jonah* 1:14
O Lord, take, I *b.* thee my.   4:3
b. God, that he will be.   *Mal* 1:9
I *b.* thee, torment me.   *Luke* 8:28
saying, master, I *b.* thee look. 9:38
wherefore I *b.* thee to hear. *Acts* 26:3
I *b.* you by the mercies. *Rom* 12:1
I *b.* you, be followers.   *1 Cor* 4:16
I *b.* you, confirm your.   *2 Cor* 2:8
as though God did *b.* you by. 5:20
we *b.* you receive not.   6:1
I Paul *b.* you by the meekness. 10:1
I *b.* you, be as I am.   *Gal* 4:12
prisoner of the Lord *b.*   *Eph* 4:1
yet for love's sake I *b.*   *Philem* 9
I *b.* thee for my son Onesimus. 10
but I *b.* you the rather.   *Heb* 13:19
I *b.* you as strangers.   *1 Pet* 2:11
now I *b.* thee, lady, not.   *2 John* 5

see **brethren**

beseeching

came a centurion *b.* him.   *Mat* 8:5
     Luke 7:3
there came a leper *b.*   *Mark* 1:40

beset

sons of Belial *b. Judg* 19:22; 20:5
bulls of Bashan have *b.*   *Ps* 22:12
thou hast *b.* me behind and.   139:5
their own doings have *b.*   *Hos* 7:2
sin which doth so easily *b. Heb* 12:1

beside, besides

hast thou here any *b.*   *Gen* 19:12
a famine *b.* the first famine.   26:1
b. the other in her life.   *Lev* 18:18
b. sabbaths, *b.* gifts, *b.* vows *b.* your
offerings, which ye give.   23:38
man has lain with thee *b. Num* 5:20
law of Nazarite, *b.* that his.   6:21
there is nothing *b.* manna.   11:6
offer *b.* burnt-offering. 28:23; 29:6
b. the covenant he made. *Deut* 29:1
in building an altar, *b. Josh* 22:19, 29
if it be dry on earth *b.*   *Judg* 6:37
b. her Jephthah had no.   11:34
I will go out and stand *b. 1 Sam* 19:3
b. that which Solomon.   *1 Ki* 10:13
not a prophet *b.* 22:7; *2 Chr* 18:6
b. his sin, wherewith he. *2 Ki* 21:16
he leadeth me *b.* still.   *Ps* 23:2
feed thy kids *b.* the tents. *S of S* 1:8
blessed ye that sow *b.* all. *Isa* 32:20
I will gather others to him *b.*   56:8
b. this, between us and. *Luke* 16:26
b. all this, to-day is the third. 24:21
to me thine ownself *b.*   *Philem* 19

beside

friends said, he is *b.*   *Mark* 3:21
Paul, thou art *b.* thyself. *Acts* 26:24
we be *b.* ourselves.   *2 Cor* 5:13

besiege

he shall *b.* thee in gates. *Deut* 28:52
if enemies *b. 1 Ki* 8:37; *2 Chr* 6:28
go, O Elam, *b.* O Media. *Isa* 21:2

besieged

dried up all rivers of *b.* places.
   2 Ki 19:24*; *Isa* 37:25*
great king and *b.* it.   *Eccl* 9:14
daughter of Zion is as a *b. Isa* 1:8
he that is *b.* shall die by. *Ezek* 6:12

besom
(*A broom*)
it with *b.* of destruction.   *Isa* 14:23

Besor
men came to the brook *B.*
        1 Sam 30:9

besought
(*Begged, prayed, intreated*)
when he *b.* we would not. *Gen* 42:21
b. the Lord.   *Ex* 32:11; *Deut* 3:23
David *b.* God for.   *2 Sam* 12:16
and the man of God *b.*   *1 Ki* 13:6
fell on his knees and *b.*   *2 Ki* 1:13
Jehoahaz *b.* the Lord.   13:4
Manasseh *b.* the Lord. *2 Chr* 33:12
we fasted and *b.* our God. *Ezra* 8:23
b. him with tears to put. *Esth* 8:3
not Hezekiah fear, and *b. Jer* 26:19
so the devils *b.* him.   *Mat* 8:31
  Mark 5:10, 12; *Luke* 8:31, 32
b. him to depart.   *Mat* 8:34
        Luke 8:37
Jairus *b.* him greatly.   *Mark* 5:23
        Luke 8:41
Samaritans *b.* that he.   *John* 4:40
nobleman of Capernaum *b.*   47
b. Pilate that he might take. 19:38
Gentiles *b.* that these.   *Acts* 13:42
Lydia *b.* us, saying, if ye.   16:15
magistrates *b.* them, and.   39
b. him not to go to Jerusalem. 21:12
for this thing I *b.* Lord. *2 Cor* 12:8

best
take of the *b.* fruits in.   *Gen* 43:11
in *b.* of land make father.   47:6, 11
of *b.* of his own field.   *Ex* 22:5
heave-offering of the *b. Num* 18:29
marry to whom they think *b.*   36:6
dwell where it likes him *b.*
        Deut 23:16
he will take the *b.* of.   *1 Sam* 8:14
Saul spared the *b.* of sheep. 15:9, 15
seemeth you *b.* I will.   *2 Sam* 18:4
look out the *b.* of your.   *2 Ki* 10:3
every man at *b.* state is.   *Ps* 39:5
of thy mouth like *b.* wine. *S of S* 7:9
b. of them is as a brier.   *Mi* 7:4
bring forth the *b.* robe. *Luke* 15:22
covet earnestly the *b.*   *1 Cor* 12:31

bestead
pass through it hardly *b. Isa* 8:21†

bestir
hearest the sound *b.*   *2 Sam* 5:24

bestow
that he may *b.* a blessing. *Ex* 32:29
b. money for what.   *Deut* 14:26
they did *b.* on Baalim.   *2 Chr* 24:7
thou shalt have occasion to *b.* out of
  the king's treasure-.   *Ezra* 7:20
no room where to *b.* my. *Luke* 12:17
and there will I *b.* all my fruits. 18
on these we *b.* more.   *1 Cor* 12:23
though I *b.* all my goods to.   13:3

bestowed
Gehazi *b.* them in house. *2 Ki* 5:24
Lord *b.* on Solomon.   *1 Chr* 29:25
all the Lord hath *b.* on us. *Isa* 63:7
reap that whereon ye *b. John* 4:38
greet Mary, who *b.* much. *Rom* 16:6
his grace *b.* on me not. *1 Cor* 15:10
for the gift *b.* on us.   *2 Cor* 1:11
do you to wit of the grace *b.*   8:1
lest I have *b.* on you.   *Gal* 4:11
love Father *b.* on us.   *1 John* 3:1

Bethabara
these things done in *B.*   *John* 1:28

Bethany
Jesus went into *B. Mat* 21:17; 26:6
  Mark 11:1, 11; 14:3; *Luke* 19:29
        John 12:1
when come from *B.*   *Mark* 11:12
out as far as to *B.*   *Luke* 24:50
sick, named Lazarus of *B. John* 11:1

Beth-aven
Ai, which is beside *B.*   *Josh* 7:2
battle passed over to *B. 1 Sam* 14:23
Gilgal, nor go ye up to *B.*   *Hos* 4:15
cry aloud at *B.* after thee.   5:8
because of the calves of *B.*   10:5

Beth-diblathaim
judgement is come upon *B. Jer* 48:22

Beth-el
the place *B.*   *Gen* 28:19; 35:15
I am God of *B.* where thou.   31:13
go up to *B.*   35:1, 3
so Jacob came to *B.*   6
Joseph goeth from *B.*   *Josh* 16:2
Joseph went up against *B. Judg* 1:22
between Ramah and *B.*   4:5
is on the north side of *B.*   21:19
from year to year to *B. 1 Sam* 7:16
men going up to God to *B.*   10:3
were with Saul in mount *B.*   13:2
them which were in *B.*   30:27
the one calf in *B. 1 Ki* 12:29, 33
a man of God to *B.*   13:1
against the altar in *B.*   4, 32
dwelt an old prophet in *B.*   13:11
Lord hath sent me to *B.*   *2 Ki* 2:2
went up from thence unto *B.*   23
not from the calves in *B.*   10:29
priests came and dwelt in *B.*   17:28
and carried the ashes to *B.*   23:4
the altar at *B.* Josiah brake.   15
against the altar of *B.*   17
all that he had done in *B.*   19
men of *B.*   *Ezra* 2:28; *Neh* 7:32
Israel was ashamed of *B. Jer* 48:13
so shall *B.* do to you.   *Hos* 10:15
he found him in *B.* there he.   12:4
visit the altars of *B.*   *Amos* 3:14
come to *B.* and transgress.   4:4
seek not *B.* for *B.* shall come.   5:5
be none to quench it in *B.*   6
not again any more at *B.*   7:13

Beth-elite
Hiel the *B.* did build.   *1 Ki* 16:34

Bether
on the mountains of *B. S of S* 2:17

Bethesda
pool called in Hebrew *B. John* 5:2

Beth-ezel
in the mourning of *B.*   *Mi* 1:11

Beth-gamul
judgement is come upon *B. Jer* 48:23

Beth-haccerem
set up a sign of fire in *B.*   *Jer* 6:1

Beth-horon
going down to *B.* the.   *Josh* 10:11
gave Levites *B.*   21:22; *1 Chr* 6:68
company turned to *B. 1 Sam* 13:18
Solomon built *B.*   *1 Ki* 9:17
        2 Chr 8:5
daughter Sherah built *B. 1 Chr* 7:24

bethink
if they shall *b.* in the land whither
  were.   *1 Ki* 8:47; *2 Chr* 6:37

Bethlehem
Rachel died in way to *B.*
        Gen 35:19; 48:7
Idalah and *B.* cities of. *Josh* 19:15
after him Ibzan of *B.*   *Judg* 12:8
went till they came to *B. Ruth* 1:19
Boaz came from *B.*   2:4
be famous in *B.*   4:11
Samuel came to *B.*   *1 Sam* 16:4
asked leave to run to *B.*   20:6, 28
would give me water of the well of
  B.   *2 Sam* 23:15; *1 Chr* 11:17
Salma father of *B.*   *1 Chr* 2:51, 54
first-born of Ephratah, of *B.*   4:4
Rehoboam built *B.*   *2 Chr* 11:6
children of *B. Ezra* 2:21; *Neh* 7:26
dwelt in habitation by *B. Jer* 41:17
Jesus was born in *B.*   *Mat* 2:1, 5
B. in land of Judah, art not.   6
slew children in *B.*   16
went up from Galilee to *B. Luke* 2:4
let us now go to *B.* and see.   15
Christ cometh out of *B.*   *John* 7:42

Beth-lehem-ephratah
thou *B.-Ephratah*, though.   *Mi* 5:2

Beth-lehemite
Jesse the *B. 1 Sam* 16:1, 18; 17:58
Elhanan the *B.* slew.   *2 Sam* 21:19

Beth-lehem-judah
a Levite of *B.* went.   *Judg* 17:7, 8, 9
Levite took concubine out of *B.* 19:1
passing from *B.* I went to *B.*   18
Elimelech of *B.* went.   *Ruth* 1:1
son of Ephrathite of *B. 1 Sam* 17:12

Beth-peor
in valley over-against *B. Deut* 3:29
Moses spake over-against *B.*   4:46
buried Moses over-against *B.*   34:6

Bethphage
come to *B.*   *Mat* 21:1; *Mark* 11:1
        Luke 19:29

Bethsaida
woe unto *B. Mat* 11:21; *Luke* 10:13
disciples to go to *B.*   *Mark* 6:45
cometh to *B.* they bring blind.   8:22
he went into a desert place belonging
  to *B.*   *Luke* 9:10
Philip was of *B.*   *John* 1:44; 12:21

Beth-shan
fastened body to wall of *B.*
        1 Sam 31:10

Beth-shemesh
border of Judah went to *B.*
        Josh 15:10
Issachar's coast reacheth *B.*   19:22
Beth-anath and *B.* cities of.   38
Judah gave to Levites *B.*   21:16
inhabitants of *B.*   *Judg* 1:33
goeth up by way of *B. 1 Sam* 6:9
kine took straight way to *B.*   12
he smote the men of *B.*   19
son of Dekar was in *B.*   *1 Ki* 4:9
looked one another in the face at *B.*
  2 Ki 14:11; *2 Chr* 25:21
Philistines had taken *B. 2 Chr* 28:18
break the images of *B.*   *Jer* 43:13

Bethuel
Milcah bare to Nahor, *B. Gen* 22:22
B. begat Rebekah. 23; 24:15; 25:20
I am the daughter of *B.*   24:24, 47
go to the house of *B.*   28:2

betimes
[1] *Early*, Gen 26:31. [2] *Season-ably, in due and proper time*, Pr 13:24. [3] *Diligently*, Job 8:5.
rose up *b.* and.   *Gen* 26:31
God sent by messengers rising *b.*
        2 Chr 36:15
thou wouldest seek God *b. Job* 8:5
as wild asses go they, rising *b.* 24:5
loveth, chasteneth him *b. Pr* 13:24

betray
if ye be come to *b.* me. *1 Chr* 12:17
and shall *b.* one another. *Mat* 24:10
he sought opportunity to *b.* him.
  26:16; *Mark* 14:11; *Luke* 22:6
one of you shall *b.* me.   *Mat* 26:21
    Mark 14:18; *John* 13:21
he is at hand and doth *b. Mat* 26:46
brother shall *b.* brother. *Mark* 13:12
Jesus knew who should *b.* him.
        John 6:64; 13:11
put into heart of Judas to *b.*   13:2

betrayed
Judas who *b.* him.   *Mat* 10:4
        Mark 3:19
Son of man *b.* into hands of men.
  Mat 17:22; 20:18; 26:2, 45
        Mark 14:41
woe to man by whom Son of man is
  b.   *Mat* 26:24; *Mark* 14:21
        Luke 22:22
he that *b.*   *Mat* 26:48; *Mark* 14:44
I have sinned, in that I *b. Mat* 27:4
and ye shall be *b.*   *Luke* 21:16
Judas which *b.* him.   *John* 18:2
night he was *b.* he took. *1 Cor* 11:23

betrayers
of whom ye have been *b. Acts* 7:52

betrayest, -eth
let us go, lo, he that *b. Mark* 14:42
the hand of him that *b. Luke* 22:21
b. thou the Son of man with?   48
which is he that *b.* ?   *John* 21:20

betroth
(*In Bible times a betrothal was considered as binding as a marriage, and there were formal ceremonies to celebrate it*)
shall *b.* a wife, another *Deut* 28:30
I will *b.* thee to me for.   *Hos* 2:19
b. thee to me in faithfulness.   20

betrothed

please not master who *b*.   *Ex* 21:8*
man entice a maid not *b*.   22:16
Deut 22:28
lieth with a woman *b*.   *Lev* 19:20
who hath *b*. a wife, and.   *Deut* 20:7
if a man find a virgin *b*. and.   22:23
b. damsel cried there was none.   27

better

[1] *More valuable, or preferable,*
Eccl. 9:4, 16, 18. [2] *More acceptable,* 1 Sam 15:22. [3] *More able,* Dan 1:20. [4] *More advantageous,* Phil 1:23. [5] *More holy,* 1 Cor 8:8. [6] *More safe,* Ps 118:8. [7] *More comfortable,* Pr 15:16, 17. [8] *More precious,* Pr 8:11.

b. I give her to thee.   *Gen* 29:19
b. for us to have served.   *Ex* 14:12
were it not *b*. for us to ?   *Num* 14:3
gleanings of Ephraim *b*.   *Judg* 8:2
nor art thou any thing *b*.   11:25
am not I *b*. to thee ?   *1 Sam* 1:8
nothing *b*. than to go to.   27:1
name of king Solomon *b*.   *1 Ki* 1:47
fell upon two men *b*. than he.   2:32
Elijah said, I am not *b*. than.   19:4
I will give thee for it a *b*.   21:2
rivers of Damascus *b*.   *2 Ki* 5:12
hast slain. brethren *b*.   *2 Chr* 21:13
shall please the Lord *b*.   *Ps* 69:31
nothing *b*. for a man than.   *Eccl* 2:24
nothing *b*. than to rejoice in.   3:22
b. is he than both they, which.   4:3
two are *b*. than one.   9
what is man the *b*. ?   6:11
that the former days were *b*.   7:10
bite, and a babbler is no *b*.   10:11*
give a name *b*. than of.   *Isa* 56:5
they that be slain are *b*.   *Lam* 4:9
will settle you, and do *b*.   *Ezek* 36:11
in all matters he found *b*.   *Dan* 1:20
then was it *b*. than now.   *Hos* 2:7
be they *b*. than these ?   *Amos* 6:2
art thou *b*. than populous ?   *Nah* 3:8
the fowls of the air, are you not much *b*. ?   *Mat* 6:26; *Luke* 12:24
how much is a man *b*.?   *Mat* 12:12
were *b*. that a millstone were about.
Mat 18:6; *Mark* 9:42; *Luke* 17:2
are we *b*. than they ? no.   *Rom* 3:9
giveth her not, doth *b*.   *1 Cor* 7:38
for neither if we eat are we *b*.   8:8
b. for me to die, than to.   9:15
you come together not for *b*.   11:17
let each esteem other *b*.   *Phil* 2:3
being made so much *b*.   *Heb* 1:4
beloved, we are persuaded *b*.   6:9
contradiction less is blessed of *b*.   7:7
bringing in of a *b*. hope did.   19
Jesus was made a surety of a *b*.   22
he is the Mediator of a *b*. covenant,
established on *b*. promises.   8:6
heavenly things with *b*.   9:23
in heaven a *b*. and enduring.   10:34
they desire a *b*. country, an.   11:16
they might obtain a *b*.   35
God having provided *b*. thing.   40
speaketh *b*. things than Abel.   12:24
b. for them not to have.   *2 Pet* 2:21

better *is*

b. is little with fear of.   *Pr* 15:16
b. is a dinner of herbs where.   17
b. is a little with righteousness. 16:8
how much *b*. is it to get wisdom. 16:16
b. is a dry morsel and.   17:1
b. is the poor.   19:1; 28:6
b. is a neighbour that is near. 27:10
b. is an handful with.   *Eccl* 4:6
b. is a poor wise child than.   13
b. is the sight of the eyes than. 6:9
b. is the end of a thing than.   7:8
b. is thy love than wine. *S of S* 4:10

is better, or *is it* better

whether is *b*. for you.   *Judg* 9:2
is it *b*. to be a priest for one ? 18:19
thy daughter is *b*. to.   *Ruth* 4:15
obey is *b*. than sacrifice. *1 Sam* 15:22
given to a neighbour that is *b*.   28
counsel of Hushai is *b*. *2 Sam* 17:14
estate to another that is *b*. *Esth* 1:19
righteous man hath is *b*.   *Ps* 37:16

---

loving-kindness is *b*. than.   *Ps* 63:3
a day in thy courts is *b*. than. 84:10
the law of thy mouth is *b*.   119:72
merchandise of wisdom is *b*. *Pr* 3:14
wisdom is *b*. than rubies.   8:11
my fruit is *b*. than gold.   19
is *b*. than he that honoureth.   12:9
slow to anger is *b*. than.   16:32
and a poor man is *b*. than a.   19:22
open rebuke is *b*. than secret.   27:5
untimely birth is *b*. than.   *Eccl* 6:3
a good name is *b*. than precious. 7:1
sorrow is *b*. than laughter, by sadness of countenance heart is *b*.   3
patient in spirit is *b*. than proud.   8
living dog is *b*. than a dead lion. 9:4
wisdom is *b*. than strength.   16
wisdom is *b*. than weapons.   18
thy love is *b*. than wine. *S of S* 1:2
he saith, the old is *b*.   *Luke* 5:39
to be with Christ, is far *b*. *Phil* 1:23

it is better, or better *it is*

it is *b*. I give her to thee. *Gen* 29:19
it is *b*. to succour us. *2 Sam* 18:3
it is *b*. to trust in the Lord than.
Ps 118:8, 9
b. it is to be of humble.   *Pr* 16:19
it is *b*. to dwell in a.   21:9; 25:24
it is *b*. to dwell in wilderness. 21:19
b. it is that it be said to thee.   25:7
b. it is that thou shouldest. *Eccl* 5:5
it is *b*. to go to house of.   7:2
it is *b*. to hear rebuke of wise.   5
it is *b*. for me to die. *Jonah* 4:3, 8
it is *b*. to enter into life halt or.
Mat 18:8, 9; *Mark* 9:43, 45, 47
for it is *b*. to marry than. *1 Cor* 7:9
it is *b*. that ye suffer for. *1 Pet* 3:17

bettered

was nothing *b*. but.   *Mark* 5:26

between

I will put enmity *b*. thy.   *Gen* 3:15
the covenant *b*. God and.   9:16
a burning lamp passeth *b*.   15:17
nor a lawgiver from *b*. his.   49:10
a division *b*. my people.   *Ex* 8:23
and a memorial *b*. thine eyes.
13:9, 16; *Deut* 6:8; 11:18
they come, and I judge *b*. *Ex* 18:16
vail shall divide *b*. holy.   26:33
while flesh was *b*.   *Num* 11:33
b. blood and blood, *b*. plea, *b*.
Deut 17:8
he shall dwell *b*. his shoulders. 33:12
Deborah dwelt *b*. Ramah. *Judg* 4:5
there was peace *b*.   *1 Sam* 7:14
b. good and evil.   *2 Sam* 19:35
1 Ki 3:9
how long halt ye *b*. two ? *1 Ki* 18:21
the lot parteth *b*.   *Pr* 18:18
passed *b*. parts of.   *Jer* 34:18, 19
b. cattle and cattle, *b*. rams.
Ezek 34:17
her adulteries from *b*.   *Hos* 2:2
the priests weep *b*.   *Joel* 2:17
break brotherhood *b*.   *Zech* 11:14
slew *b*. the temple and.   *Mat* 23:35
b. John's disciples and.   *John* 3:25
no difference *b*. Jew and. *Rom* 10:12
difference *b*. wife and a. *1 Cor* 7:34
one Mediator *b*. God.   *1 Tim* 2:5

betwixt

the cloud that cometh *b*. *Job* 36:32*
lie all night *b*. my.   *S of S* 1:13
I am in a strait *b*. two.   *Phil* 1:23

Beulah

call thy land *B*. for Lord.   *Isa* 62:4

bewail

b. the burning the Lord.   *Lev* 10:6
and *b*. her father and.   *Deut* 21:13
I may go and *b*.   *Judg* 11:37, 38
I will *b*. with weeping of.   *Isa* 16:9
that I shall *b*. many.   *2 Cor* 12:21
shall *b*. her.   *Rev* 18:9

bewailed, -eth

daughter of Zion that *b*.   *Jer* 4:31*
and all wept and *b*. her. *Luke* 8:52
of women also who *b*.   23:27

beware

(*To take care : to be on one's guard*)
b. that thou bring not my. *Gen* 24:6
b. of him and obey.   *Ex* 23:21

---

b. lest thou forget. *Deut* 6:12; 8:11
b. there be not a wicked.   15:9
b. I pray thee.   *Judg* 13:4, 13
b. that none touch.   *2 Sam* 18:12
b. that thou pass not.   *2 Ki* 6:9
b. lest he take thee away. *Job* 36:18
scorner, and simple *b*.   *Pr* 19:25*
b. lest Hezekiah persuade. *Isa* 36:18
b. of false prophets.   *Mat* 7:15
b. of men.   10:17
b. of the leaven of the.   16:6, 11
Mark 8:15; *Luke* 12:1
b. of the scribes.   *Mark* 12:38
Luke 20:46
take heed and *b*.   *Luke* 12:15*
b. lest that come which. *Acts* 13:40
b. of dogs, *b*. of evil workers, *b*. of.
Phil 3:2
b. lest any man spoil.   *Col* 2:8
b. lest ye also.   *2 Pet* 3:17

bewitched

Simon *b*. the people.   *Acts* 8:9*, 11
Galatians, who hath *b*. ?   *Gal* 3:1

bewray

(*American Revision,* betray)
hide the outcasts, *b*. not.   *Isa* 16:3

bewrayeth

of his right hand *b*.   *Pr* 27:16*
heareth cursing, and *b*. it.   29:24*
of them, speech *b*. thee. *Mat* 26:73*

beyond

Balaam said, I cannot go *b*. word.
Num 22:18; 24:13
nor is it *b*. the sea.   *Deut* 30:13
arrows *b*. thee. *1 Sam* 20:22; 36:37
b. the river. *2 Sam* 10:16; *1 Ki* 14:15
1 Chr 19:16; *Ezra* 4:17, 20
6:6, 8; 7:21, 25; *Neh* 2:7, 9
Isa 7:20; 18:1; *Zeph* 3:10
b. the sea.   *2 Chr* 20:2; *Jer* 25:22
amazed *b*. measure.   *Mark* 6:51
7:37
and *b*. their power.   *2 Cor* 8:3
for we stretch not *b*.   10:14
b. measure I persecuted.   *Gal* 1:13
that no man go *b*. and.   *1 Thes* 4:6

beyond *Jordan, see* **Jordan**

Bezaleel

I have called by name *B*. of tribe of.
Ex 31:2; 35:30; *1 Chr* 2:20
then wrought *B*.   *Ex* 36:1
B. made the ark.   37:1
B. made all Lord commanded. 38:22
the brazen altar *B*. made. *2 Chr* 1:5
sons of Pahath-moab, *B*. *Ezra* 10:30

Bezek

slew in *B*. 10,000 men.   *Judg* 1:4, 5
numbered Israel in *B*.   *1 Sam* 11:8

Bichri

Sheba the son of *B*.   *2 Sam* 20:1
man followed Sheba son of *B*.   2
now shall the son of *B*. do.   6
cut off head of Sheba son of *B*.   22

bid

[1] *To invite,* Mat 22:9; Luke 14:12. [2] *To command,* Mat 14:28. [3] *To wish,* 2 John 10.

the day I *b*. you shout.   *Josh* 6:10
b. the servant pass on.   *1 Sam* 9:27
how long ere *b*. people. *2 Sam* 2:26
not riding except I *b*.   *2 Ki* 4:24
if the prophet had *b*. thee do.   5:13
all that thou shalt *b*. us.   10:5
the preaching that I *b*. *Jonah* 3:2
for the Lord hath *b*.   *Zeph* 1:7
b. me come to thee.   *Mat* 14:28
as many as ye shall find *b*.   22:9
what they *b*. you observe.   23:3
let me first *b*. them.   *Luke* 9:61
b. her therefore that she.   10:40
lest they also *b*. thee again.   14:12
if any that believe not *b*. *1 Cor* 10:27
receive him not, nor *b*.   *2 John* 10*

bidden

they eat that be *b*.   *1 Sam* 9:13
curse, for Lord hath *b*. *2 Sam* 16:11
Joseph did as angel had *b*.   *Mat* 1:24
sent to call them that were *b*.   22:3
tell them *b*. I have prepared my.   4
they who were *b*. were not.   8

biddeth

the Pharisee who had *b*. *Luke* 7:39
a parable to those who were *b*. 14:7
when thou art *b*. lest a more honourable man be *b*. 8
when thou art *b*. go and sit in. 10
none of those *b*. shall taste. 24

biddeth, bidding

goeth at thy *b*. *1 Sam* 22:14
he that *b*. him God. *2 John* 11*

bide

if they *b*. not in unbelief. *Rom* 11:23

Bidkar

Jehu said to B. his. *2 Ki* 9:25

bier

David followed the *b*. *2 Sam* 3:31
came and touched the *b*. *Luke* 7:14

Bigthan

B. sought to lay hand on. *Esth* 2:21
that Mordecai had told B. 6:2

Bildad

B. the Shuhite. *Job* 2:11; 8:1
18:1; 25:1; 42:9

Bilhah

Laban gave to Rachel B. *Gen* 29:29
behold my maid B. go in. 30:3, 4
B. conceived. 5, 7
Reuben lay with B. 35:22
sons of B. 35:25; 37:2; 46:25
1 Chr 7:13
his sons dwelt at B. *1 Chr* 4:29

bill

take thy *b*. and write 50. *Luke* 16:6*
take thy *b*. 7*

see divorce

billows

thy *b*. gone over me. *Ps* 42:7
Jonah 2:3

bind

[1] *To tie up, or fasten together*,
Gen 37:7; *Deut* 14:25. [2] *To
keep fast, or sure*, *Pr* 3:3; 6:21.
[3] *To engage by vow, or promise*,
Num 30:2. [4] *To restrain*, *Job*
28:11.

they shall *b*. the breast-. *Ex* 28:28
swear an oath to *b*. his. *Num*. 30:2
shalt *b*. them for a sign. *Deut* 6:8
shalt *b*. up the money. 14:25
thou shalt *b*. this line. *Josh* 2:18
to *b*. Samson are we. *Judg* 15:10
we are come down to *b*. thee. 12
no, but we will *b*. thee fast. 13
that we may *b*. Samson. 16:5
I will *b*. it as a crown. *Job* 31:36
canst *b*. sweet influences? 38:31
canst thou *b*. the unicorn? 39:10
hide them, and *b*. their. 40:13
wilt thou *b*. Leviathan? 41:5
to *b*. his princes at his. *Ps* 105:22
b. the sacrifice with cords. 118:27
to *b*. their kings with. 149:8
b. them about thy neck. *Pr* 3:3
b. them continually. 6:21
b. them on thy fingers, write. 7:3
b. up the testimony. *Isa* 8:16
and *b*. them on thee as a. 49:18
he hath sent me to *b*. up the. 61:1
I will *b*. up what was. *Ezek* 34:16
commanded most mighty men to *b*.
Dan 3:20
smitten us, and will *b*. us. *Hos* 6:1
when they *b*. themselves. 10:10
b. the chariot to the swift. *Mi* 1:13
first *b*. the strong man, then will.
Mat 12:29; *Mark* 3:27
b. the tares in bundles. *Mat* 13:30
whatsover thou shalt *b*. 16:19; 18:18
b. him hand and foot. 22:13
b. heavy burdens. 23:4
no man could *b*. him. *Mark* 5:3
authority to *b*. a¹¹ that. *Acts* 9:14
gird thyself, *b*. ᵗ thy sandals. 12:8
so shall the Jews *b*. 21:11

bindeth

maketh sore and *b*. up. *Job* 5:18
b. up the waters in his. 26:8
he *b*. the floods. 28:11
ıt *b*. me about as the collar. 30:18
they cry not when he *b*. them. 36:13
nor he that *b*. sheaves. *Ps* 129:7

the broken in heart, *b*. up. *Ps* 147:3
as he that *b*. a stone. *Pr* 26:8
the Lord *b*. up the breach. *Isa* 30:26

binding

we were *b*. sheaves in. *Gen* 37:7
b. his foal to the vine. 49:11
every *b*. oath. *Num* 30:13
b. and delivering into. *Acts* 22:4

bird

(*A fowl, small or large*)
every *b*. of every sort. *Gen* 7:14
cleanse the house with living *b*.
Lev 14:52
play with him as with a *b*.? *Job* 41:5
flee as a *b*. to your. *Ps* 11:1
our soul is escaped as a *b*. 124:7
net spread in sight of *b*. *Pr* 1:17
and as a *b*. from the hand. 6:5
as a *b*. hasteth to the snare. 7:23
as the *b*. by wandering. 26:2*
as a *b*. that wandereth from. 27:8
b. of the air shall tell. *Eccl* 10:20
rise up at the voice of the *b*. 12:4
as a wandering *b*. *Isa* 16:2
calling a ravenous *b*. 46:11
heritage is as speckled *b*. *Jer* 12:9
chased me like a *b*. *Lam* 3:52
shall fly away like a *b*. *Hos* 9:11
they shall tremble as a *b*. 11:11
can a *b*. fall where no gin? *Amos* 3:5
of unclean and hateful *b*. *Rev* 18:2

birds

the *b*. divided he not. *Gen* 15:10
the *b*. did eat them. 40:19
the *b*. shall eat thy flesh. 19
command to take two *b*. *Lev* 14:4
of all clean *b*. eat. *Deut* 14:11
suffered not *b*. to rest. *2 Sam* 21:10
where *b*. make their nests. *Ps* 104:17
as *b*. that are caught. *Eccl* 9:12
time of singing of *b*. is. *S of S* 2:12
as *b*. flying, so will Lord. *Isa* 31:5
all the *b*. of the heaven. *Jer* 4:25
as a cage full of *b*. so are. 5:27
beasts are consumed and *b*. 12:4
the *b*. round about are against. 9
give thee to ravenous *b*. *Ezek* 39:4
nails were grown like a. *Dan* 4:33
b. of the air. *Mat* 8:20; *Luke* 9:58
b. lodge in the branches. *Mat* 13:32
into an image like to *b*. *Rom* 1:23
of fishes, another of *b*. *1 Cor* 15:39
every kind of beasts and *b*. *Jas* 3:7

birth

Is [1] *Natural*, *Ex* 28:10. [2]
*Supernatural, as was the birth of
Christ*, *Mat* 1:18; *Luke* 1:14. [3]
Figurative, *2 Ki* 19:3; *Tit* 3:5; *Gal*
4:19.

children come to *b*. *2 Ki* 19:3
Isa 37:3
as an hidden untimely *b*. *Job* 3:16
pass like the untimely *b*. *Ps* 58:8
an untimely *b*. is better. *Eccl* 6:3
day of death better than day of *b*. 7:1
shall I bring to the *b*.? *Isa* 66:9
thy *b*. and nativity. *Ezek* 16:3
glory of Ephraim fly from *b*. *Hos* 9:11
the *b*. of Jesus Christ. *Mat* 1:18
shall rejoice at his *b*. *Luke* 1:14
a man blind from his *b*. *John* 9:1
of whom I travail in *b*. *Gal* 4:19
cried, travailing in *b*. *Rev* 12:2

birthday

third day, Pharaoh's *b*. *Gen* 40:20
Herod's *b*. *Mat* 14:6; *Mark* 6:21

birthright

sell me this day thy *b*. *Gen* 25:31
he sware, and sold his *b*. 33
thus Esau despised his *b*. 34
took my *b*., now my blessing. 27:36
first-born according to *b*. 43:33
Reuben's *b*. given to sons. *1 Chr* 5:1
for one morsel sold *b*. *Heb* 12:16

bishop, -s

saints at Philippi, with *b*. *Phil*. 1:1
if man desire office of *b*. *1 Tim* 3:1
a *b*. must be blameless. 2; *Tit* 1:7
returned to *b*. of your souls.
1 Pet 2:25

bishopric

his *b*. let another take. *Acts* 1:20*

bit, -s

mouth must be held in with *b*.
Ps 32:9
put *b*. in horses' mouths. *Jas* 3:3

bit

fiery serpents, *b*. people. *Num* 21:6
and a serpent *b*. him. *Amos* 5:19

bite

serpent shall *b*. him. *Eccl* 10:8
the serpent will *b*. without. 11
serpents, they shall *b*. you. *Jer* 8:17
command serpent, and he shall *b*.
Amos 9:3
prophets that *b*. with teeth. *Mi* 3:5
they rise up that shall *b*.? *Hab* 2:7
if ye *b*. and devour one. *Gal* 5:15

biteth

Dan an adder, that *b*. *Gen* 49:17
at the last it *b*. like. *Pr* 23:32

Bithynia

assayed to go into B. *Acts* 16:7
scattered throughout B. *1 Pet* 1:1

bitten

every one that is *b*. *Num* 21:8
if a serpent had *b*. any man. 9

bitter

Esau cried with a *b*. cry. *Gen* 27:34
made their lives *b*. *Ex* 1:14
with *b*. herbs eat it. 12:8; *Num* 9:11
waters of Marah were *b*. *Ex* 15:23
devoured with *b*. destruction.
Deut 32:24
grapes of gall, their clusters are *b*. 32
saw affliction of Israel it was *b*.
2 Ki 14:26
cried with a *b*. cry. *Esth* 4:1
is life given to *b*. in soul? *Job* 3:20
thou writest *b*. things against. 13:26
even to-day is my complaint *b*. 23:2*
their arrows, *b*. words. *Ps* 64:3
end is *b*. as wormwood. *Pr* 5:4
hungry soul *b*. thing is sweet. 27:7
I find more *b*. than death. *Eccl* 7:26
that put *b*. for sweet, sweet for *b*.
Isa 5:20
strong drink shall be *b*. to. 24:9
it is an evil thing and *b*. *Jer* 2:19
thy wickedness, because it is *b*. 4:18
most *b*. lamentation as for a. 6:26
voice heard in Ramah, *b*. 31:15
weep with *b*. wailing. *Ezek* 27:31
end thereof, as a *b*. day. *Amos* 8:10
Chaldeans, that *b*. and. *Hab* 1:6
love your wives, be not *b*. *Col* 3:19
if ye have *b*. envying. *Jas* 3:14
of waters because made *b*. *Rev* 8:11
eat it, it shall make thy belly *b*. 10:9
soon as I had eaten, belly was *b*. 10

bitter *water*

the *b*. *water* that causeth. *Num* 5:18
send sweet *water* and *b*.? *Jas* 3:11

bitterly

curse *b*. the inhabitants. *Judg* 5:23
Almighty hath dealt *b*. *Ruth* 1:20
look from me, I will weep *b*. *Isa* 22:4
of peace shall weep *b*. 33:7
pilots of Tyre shall cry *b*. *Ezek* 27:30
Ephraim provoked him *b*. *Hos* 12:14
mighty man shall cry *b*. *Zeph* 1:14
Peter wept *b*. *Mat* 26:75
Luke 22:62

bittern

(*Revised Version*, porcupine)
a possession for the *b*. *Isa* 14:23
34:11
the *b*. shall lodge in the. *Zeph* 2:14

bitterness

Hannah was in *b*. of. *1 Sam* 1:10
surely the *b*. of death is past. 15:32
the sword will be *b*. *2 Sam* 2:26
I will complain in *b*. *Job* 7:11
but filleth me with *b*. 9:18
I will speak in *b*. of my soul. 10:1
another dieth in the *b*. of. 21:25
heart knoweth his own *b*. *Pr* 14:10
a foolish son is *b*. 17:25
go softly all my years in *b*. *Isa* 38:15
behold, for peace I had great *b*. 17
are afflicted, she is in *b*. *Lam* 1:4

he hath filled me with *b.*   *Lam* 3:15
took me, I went in *b.*   *Ezek* 3:14
with *b.* sigh before their eyes.   21:6
shall weep for thee with *b.*   27:31
be in *b.* as one that is in *b.*
     Zech 12:10
thou art in the gall of *b.*   *Acts* 8:23
whose mouth is full of *b.*   *Rom* 3:14
let all *b.* be put away.   *Eph* 4:31
any root of *b.* springing.   *Heb* 12:15

black
there is no *b.* hair in it.   *Lev* 13:31
and there is *b.* hair grown.   37
the heaven was *b.*   *1 Ki* 18:45
my skin is *b.* upon me.   *Job* 30:30
in the evening, in the *b.*   *Pr* 7:9*
I am *b.* but comely, O.   *S of S* 1:5*
look not upon me, I am *b.*   6*
his locks are bushy and *b.*   5:11
the heavens like *b.*   *Jer* 4:28
my people am I hurt, I am *b.*   8:21
gates thereof languish, are *b.*   14:2
skin was *b.* like an oven.   *Lam* 5:10
in second chariot *b.*   *Zech* 6:2
b. horses go forth into north.   6
make one hair white or *b. Mat* 5:36
I beheld, lo a *b.* horse.   *Rev* 6:5
sun became *b.* as sackcloth.   12

blacker
visage is *b.* than a coal.   *Lam* 4:8

blackish
b. by reason of the ice.   *Job* 6:16

blackness
let *b.* of the day terrify it.   *Job* 3:5
I clothe heavens with *b.*   *Isa* 50:3
all faces gather *b.*   *Joel* 2:6*
     Nah 2:10
are not come to *b.*   *Heb* 12:18
to whom is reserved *b.* of.   *Jude* 13

blade
also went in after the *b.*   *Judg* 3:22
arm fall from shoulder-*b. Job* 31:22
b. was sprung up.   *Mat* 13:26
     Mark 4:28

blains
a boil breaking forth with *b.*
     Ex 9:9, 10

blame
let me bear *b.*   *Gen* 43:9; 44:32
no man should *b.* us.   *2 Cor* 8:20
holy and without *b.*   *Eph* 1:4*

blamed
the ministry be not *b.*   *2 Cor* 6:3
because he was to be *b. Gal* 2:11*

blameless
ye shall be *b.*   *Gen* 44:10
we will be *b.* of this.   *Josh* 2:17
now shall I be more *b. Judg* 15:3
profane sabbath, are *b. Mat* 12:5
ordinances of the Lord *b. Luke* 1:6
ye may be *b.* in the day. *1 Cor* 1:8
b. and harmless.   *Phil* 2:15
touching righteousness of law *b.* 3:6
spirit, soul, and body, *b. 1 Thes* 5:23
bishop must be *b.*   *1 Tim* 3:2
     Tit 1:7
office of a deacon, found *b.*
     1 Tim 3:10
in charge, that they may be *b.*   5:7
if any be *b.* the husband of. *Tit* 1:6
without spot and *b.*   *2 Pet* 3:14

blaspheme
(*In old Jewish law, to revile or
curse God, or the king, who was
God's representative. It means
intentional indignity offered to God
or sacred things*)
enemies of Lord to *b.*   *2 Sam* 12:14
b. God and the king. *1 Ki* 21:10, 13
shall the enemy *b.* thy ? *Ps* 74:10
wherewith they *b. Mark* 3:28
that shall *b.* against Holy Ghost. 29
I compelled them to *b.*   *Acts* 26:11
may learn not to *b.*   *1 Tim* 1:20
do not they *b.* that worthy ? *Jas* 2:7
to *b.* his name and.   *Rev* 13:6

blasphemed
Israelitish woman's son *b. Lev* 24:11
servants of king of Assyria have *b.*
me.   *2 Ki* 19:6, 22; *Isa* 37:6, 23
foolish have *b.* thy name. *Ps* 74:18

my name continually is *b. Isa* 52:5
have burnt incense, and *b.*   65:7
your fathers have *b.* me. *Ezek* 20:27
opposed themselves and *b. Acts* 18:6
the name of God is *b.*   *Rom* 2:24
God and doctrine be not *b. 1 Tim* 6:1
that word of God be not *b. Tit* 2:5
scorched with heat, and *b. Rev* 16:9
b. the God of heaven because.   11
men *b.* God because of plague.   21

blasphemer, -s
nor *b.* of your goddess.   *Acts* 19:37
who was before a *b.*   *1 Tim* 1:13
last days men shall be *b. 2 Tim* 3:2

blasphemest, -eth
whoso *b.* the Lord, be.   *Lev* 24:16
the voice of him that *b.*   *Ps* 44:16
scribes said, this man *b.*   *Mat* 9:3
Father sanctified, thou *b. John* 10:36

blasphemies
I have heard all thy *b. Ezek* 35:12
out of heart proceed *b. Mat* 15:19
doth this man speak *b.* ? *Mark* 2:7
and *b.* wherewith they shall.   3:28
who speaketh *b.* ?   *Luke* 5:21
given him speaking *b.*   *Rev* 13:5

blaspheming
contradicting and *b.*   *Acts* 13:45

blasphemous
heard him speak *b.* words. *Acts* 6:11
ceaseth not to speak *b.* words.   13

blasphemously
many things *b.* spake.   *Luke* 22:65

blasphemy
this day of *b.*   *2 Ki* 19:3; *Isa* 37:3
all manner of *b.* forgiven, *b.* against
Holy Ghost not be.   *Mat* 12:31
he hath spoken *b.* now ye have
heard his *b.*   26:65; *Mark* 14:64
out of heart proceed *b. Mark* 7:22
stone thee not, but for *b. John* 10:33
ye also put off malice, *b.*   *Col* 3:8
I know the *b.* of them that. *Rev* 2:9
upon his heads the name of *b.* 13:1
and he opened his mouth in *b.*   6

blast
[1] *A violent gust of wind,* Job 4:9.
[2] *To wither or blight,* Gen 41:6.
with *b.* of thy nostrils.   *Ex* 15:8
when they make a long *b. Josh* 6:5
at rebuke of Lord, at *b.* of breath of.
     2 Sam 22:16; *Ps* 18:15
a *b.* on Sennacherib.   *2 Ki* 19:7*
     Isa 37:7*
by *b.* of God they perish. *Job* 4:9*
when the *b.* of the terrible. *Isa* 25:4

blasted
seven thin ears *b.* with the east
wind.   *Gen* 41:6, 23, 27
as corn *b.*   *2 Ki* 19:26; *Isa* 37:27

blasting
Lord shall smite with *b. Deut* 28:22
if there be *b. 1 Ki* 8:37; *2 Chr* 6:28
have smitten you with *b. Amos* 4:9
smote you with *b.*   *Hag* 2:17

Blastus
having made *B.* friend. *Acts* 12:20

blaze
he began to *b.* abroad. *Mark* 1:45*

bleating, -s
abodest to hear *b.* of.   *Judg* 5:16
what meaneth this *b.* ? *1 Sam* 15:14

blemish
lamb without *b.*   *Ex* 12:5 ; *Lev* 9:3
     14:10 ; 23:12; *Num* 6:14
two rams without *b.*
    Ex 29:1; *Lev* 5:15, 18
    6:6; 9:2; *Ezek* 46:4
male without *b.*   *Lev* 1:3, 10; 4:23
     22:19
male or female without *b.*   3:1, 6
bullock without *b.*   4:3; *Deut* 17:1
     Ezek 45:18
bring kid, a female without *b.*
     Lev 4:28
hath *b.* not approach.   21:17, 18,
     21, 23
but whatsoever hath a *b.* shall not be
acceptable.   22:20; *Deut* 15:21

in offering no *b.*   *Lev* 22:21
if a man cause *b.* in neighbour 24:19
as he hath caused a *b.* in a man. 20
a red heifer without *b.*   *Num* 19:2
bullock, ram, lambs without *b.* 29:2
no *b.* in Absalom.   *2 Sam* 14:25
in whom was no *b.*   *Dan* 1:4
holy and without *b.*   *Eph* 5:27
as of a lamb without *b. 1 Pet* 1:19

blemishes
b. in them, they shall.   *Lev* 22:25
spots they are and *b.*   *2 Pet* 2:13

bless
I. *God blesses.* [1] *By giving
riches and prosperity,* Gen 30:27;
39:5. [2] *By giving spiritual and
temporal good things,* Ps 29:11;
Eph 1:3. [3] *By consecrating or
hallowing,* Gen 2:3; Ex 20:11. II.
Men bless God. [1] *When they
praise him for his goodness,* Ps
104:1. [2] *When they thank him
for his benefits to them,* Ps 103:1.
III. *Men bless other men.* [1]
*When they utter a solemn bene-
diction, as a father praying for his
son, and naming him heir and
successor,* Gen 27:23. [2] *When
they pray to God for his blessing on
other men,* Num 6:23, 24; 2 Sam
6:18.

bless, *God being agent*
I will *b.* thee.   *Gen* 12:2; 26:3, 24
I will *b.* them that bless thee. 12:3
I will *b.* her and give.   17:16
blessing I will *b.* thee.   22:17
     Heb 6:14
God Almighty *b.* thee, and. *Gen* 28:3
let thee go, except thou *b.*   32:26
b. the lads, and let my name. 48:16
the Almighty who shall *b.*   49:25
come to thee, and *b.* thee. *Ex* 20:24
he shall *b.* thy bread and.   23:25
the Lord *b.* thee.   *Num* 6:24
name on Israel, I will *b.* them.   27
saw it pleased the Lord to *b.* 24:1
b. you as he hath.   *Deut* 1:11
he will *b.* thee, *b.* the fruit.   7:13
the Lord *b.* thee.   14:29; 23:20
     24:19
no poor, for Lord shall *b.* thee. 15:4
the Lord thy God shall *b.*   10
Lord thy God shall *b.* thee. 18; 30:16
the Lord shall *b.* thee.   16:15
look down and *b.* thy people. 26:15
he shall *b.* thee in the land.   28:8
b. all the work of thine hand.   12
b. Lord, his substance.   33:11
the Lord *b.* thee.   *Ruth* 2:4
     Jer 31:23
let it please thee to *b.* the house of
thy.   *2 Sam* 7:29; *1 Chr* 17:27
O that thou wouldest *b. 1 Chr* 4:10
thou, Lord, wilt *b.* righteous. *Ps* 5:12
save thy people, *b.* thine.   28:9
the Lord will *b.* his people.   29:11
God, our God, shall *b.* us. 67:1, 6, 7
the Lord will *b.* us, *b.* the house of
Israel, *b.* the house of.   115:12
b. them that fear the Lord.   13
Lord shall *b.* thee out of Zion. 128:5
abundantly *b.* her provision. 132:15
Lord *b.* thee out of Zion.   134:3
the Lord of hosts shall *b. Isa* 19:25
this day will I *b.* you.   *Hag* 2:19
sent him to *b.* you.   *Acts* 3:26

bless, *God being the object*
then thou shalt *b.* the.   *Deut* 8:10
b. ye the Lord.   *Judg* 5:9; *Ps* 103:21
     134:1
David said, now *b.* Lord. *1 Chr* 29:20
stand up and *b.* the Lord. *Neh* 9:5
I will *b.* the Lord.   *Ps* 16:7
in congregations will I *b.* Lord. 26:12
I will *b.* the Lord at all times. 34:1
thus will I *b.* thee while I live. 63:4
O *b.* our God.   66:8
b. ye God in congregations. 68:26
sing to the Lord, *b.* his name. 96:2
be thankful, *b.* his name.   100:4
     103:1
b. the Lord.   103:1, 2, 22; 104:1, 35
b. the Lord, ye his angels. 103:20

b. the Lord, ye his hosts. *Ps* 103:21
b. the Lord all his works. 22
we will *b.* the Lord. 115:18
lift your hands, *b.* the Lord. 134:2
b. the Lord, O Israel, *b.* the Lord, O house of Aaron. 135:19
O, ye that fear the Lord, *b.* the. 20
I will *b.* thy name for ever. 145:1
every day will I *b.* thee. 2
O Lord, thy saints shall *b.* thee. 10
let all flesh is his holy name. 21
therewith *b.* we God. *Jas* 3:9

bless, *man agent and object*
my soul may *b.* thee. *Gen* 27:4, 25
b. me, even me my father. 34, 38
them to me, and I will *b.* 48:9
in thee shall Israel *b.* saying. 20
take flocks and begone, *b. Ex* 12:32
on this wise *b.* Israel. *Num* 6:23
received commandment to *b.* 23:20
neither curse them, nor *b.* 25
Lord separated Levi to *b.*
Deut 10:8; 21:5
in his own raiment, and *b.* 24:13
shall stand on Gerizim to *b.* 27:12
heareth words of curse, he *b.* 29:19
commanded they should *b.*
Josh 8:33
he doth *b.* the sacrifice. *1 Sam* 9:13
David returned to *b.* his household.
2 Sam 6:20; *1 Chr* 16:43
sent Joram to *b.* David. *2 Sam* 8:10
that ye may *b.* the inheritance. 21:3
came to *b.* David. *1 Ki* 1:47
and to *b.* in his name. *1 Chr* 23:13
they *b.* with their mouths. *Ps* 62:4
let them curse, but *b.* thou. 109:28
we *b.* you in name of the. 129:8
generation that curseth father, and doth not *b.* mother. *Pr* 30:11
shall *b.* himself in God. *Isa* 65:16
nations shall *b.* themselves. *Jer* 4:2
b. them that curse you. *Mat* 5:44
Luke 6:28
b. them which persecute you, *b.* and curse not. *Rom* 12:14
being reviled we *b.* *1 Cor* 4:12
else when shalt thou *b.* 14:16

bless
cup of blessing we *b.* *1 Cor* 10:16

blessed, *man agent and object*
Melchisedek *b.* Abram, and said *b.*
Gen 14:19
they *b.* Rebekah, and said. 24:60
Isaac *b.* Jacob and said. 27:23, 27
and *b.* be he that blesseth thee. 29
I have *b.* him, and he shall be *b.* 33
blessing wherewith his father *b.* 41
Isaac called Jacob, *b.* him. 28:1
as he *b.* him he gave. 6; *Heb* 11:20
daughters will call me *b. Gen* 30:13*
sons and daughters, and *b.* 31:55
Jacob *b.* Pharaoh. 47:7, 10
he *b.* Joseph. 48:15
Jacob *b.* Manasseh and. 48:20
Heb 11:21
Jacob *b.* his sons, every one he *b.*
Gen 49:28
Moses *b.* them. *Ex* 39:43
Deut 33:1
Aaron lifted up hand and *b. Lev* 9:22
Moses and Aaron *b.* people. 23
whom thou blessest is *b. Num* 22:6
thou hast *b.* them. 23:11; 24:10
b. he that enlargeth Gad. *Deut* 33:20
let Asher be *b.* with children. 24
Joshua *b.* Caleb, and. *Josh* 14:13
Joshua *b.* them. 22:6, 7
therefore Balaam *b.* you still. 24:10
b. above women Jael. *Judg* 5:24
b. be he that did take. *Ruth* 2:19
Eli *b.* Elkanah and. *1 Sam* 2:20
b. be thy advice, and *b.* be. 25:33
Saul said, *b.* be thou my son. 26:25
David *b.* the people. *2 Sam* 6:18
1 Chr 16:2
he would not go, but *b.* him.
2 Sam 13:25
king kissed Barzillai, and *b.* 19:39
king Solomon shall be *b. 1 Ki* 2:45
Solomon *b.* congregation. 8:14, 55
congregation *b.* Solomon. 66
2 Chr 6:3

and Levites *b.* people. *2 Chr* 30:27
people *b.* all that offered. *Neh* 11:2
the ear heard me, it *b. Job* 29:11
if his loins have not *b.* me. 31:20
while he lived *b.* his soul. *Ps* 49:18
men *b.* in him, nations call him *b.*
72:17*
b. he that cometh in name of the Lord, we have *b.* you. 118:26
her children call her *b. Pr* 31:28
b.,O land, when thy king. *Eccl* 10:17*
daughters saw her, and *b. S of S* 6:9
incense, as if he *b.* idol. *Isa* 66:3
my mother. bare me be *b. Jer* 20:14
all nations shall call you *b. Mal* 3:12*
b. be the kingdom of. *Mark* 11:10
all generations call me *b. Luke* 1:48
Simeon *b.* them, and said. 2:34
more *b.* to give than to. *Acts* 20:35
looking for that *b.* hope. *Tit* 2:13
met Abraham and *b.* him. *Heb* 7:1, 6
the less is *b.* of the better. 7

blessed, *God the agent*
God *b.* them. *Gen* 1:22, 28; 5:2
b. the seventh day. 2:3; *Ex* 20:11
b. Noah and his sons. *Gen* 9:1
in thee all families be *b.* 12:3; 18:18
22:18; 26:4; 28:14; *Acts* 3:25
Gal 3:8
I have *b.* Ishmael. *Gen* 17:20
Lord *b.* Abraham. 24:1
he said, come in, *b.* of the. 31
God *b.* Isaac. 25:11; 26:12
thou art the *b.* of the Lord. 26:29
smell of a field Lord hath *b.* 27:27
that the Lord hath *b.* me. 30:27
the Lord hath *b.* thee since. 30
b. Jacob there. 32:29; 35:9; 48:3
that the Lord *b.* Egyptian's. 39:5
for the people are *b.* *Num* 22:12
he hath *b.* and I cannot. 23:20
thy God hath *b.* thee. *Deut* 2:7
12:7; 15:14; 16:10
shalt be *b.* above all people. 7:14
when the Lord hath *b.* 14:24
b. shalt thou be in the city, *b.* 28:3
b. sha!l be fruit of thy body. 4
b. thy basket. 5
of Joseph he said, *b.* of Lord. 33:13
as the Lord hath *b.* me. *Josh* 17:14
Samson grew, the Lord *b. Judg* 13:24
b. be thou of Lord. 17:2; *Ruth* 3:10
1 Sam 15:13
b. be he of the Lord. *Ruth* 2:20
b. be thou of the Lord. 3:10
b. be ye. *1 Sam* 23:21; *2 Sam* 6:11
the Lord *b.* Obed-edom. *2 Sam* 6:11
12; *1 Chr* 13:14; 26:5
house of thy servant be *b. 2 Sam* 7:29
O Lord, and it shall be *b. 1 Chr* 17:27
the Lord hath *b.* *2 Chr* 31:10
thou hast *b.* the work. *Job* 1:10
Lord *b.* latter end of Job. 42:12
hast made him most *b.* *Ps* 21:6
b. is the nation whose God is. 33:12
such as be *b.* of him. 37:22
lendeth, and his seed is *b.* 26
and he shall be *b.* 41:2
therefore God hath *b.* thee. 45:2
b. is the people that know. 89:15
the upright shall be *b.* 112:2
you are *b.* of the Lord. 115:15
b. are the undefiled. 119:1
b. is every one that feareth. 128:1
thus the man be *b.* that feareth. 4
he hath *b.* thy children. 147:13
let thy fountain be *b.* *Pr* 5:18
the memory of the just is *b.* 10:7
just man's children are *b.* 20:7
end thereof shall not be *b.* 21
he that hath bountiful eye be *b.* 22:9
b. be Egypt my people. *Isa* 19:25
for I called him and *b.* him. 51:2
seed the Lord hath *b.* 61:9; 65:23
b. are the poor in spirit. *Mat* 5:3
b. are the meek. 4
b. are the merciful. 7
b. are the pure in heart. 8
b. are the peace-makers. 9
b. are they which are persecuted. 10
b. are your eyes. 13:16; *Luke* 10:23
he *b.* and brake. *Mat* 14:19; 26:26
Mark 6:41; 14:22; *Luke* 9:16
24:30

Jesus said, *b.* art thou. *Mat* 16:17
b. that servant. 24:46; *Luke* 12:43
come ye *b.* of my Father. *Mat* 25:34
them up in his arms, *b. Mark* 10:16
art thou Christ, Son of the *b.* ? 14:61
b. among women. *Luke* 1:28, 42
b. is she that believed. 45
b. be ye poor. 6:20
b. is the womb that bare. 11:27
b. are those servants whom Lord shall find watching. 12:37, 38
thou shalt be *b.* 14:14
b. be the King that cometh. 19:38
b. are the barren that never. 23:29
he *b.* them. 24:50
while he *b.* them. 51
b. with faithful Abraham. *Gal* 3:9
b. us with spiritual. *Eph* 1:3
this man shall be *b.* *Jas* 1:25
b. are the dead. *Rev* 14:13

blessed, *God the object*
he said, *b.* be the Lord. *Gen* 9:26
24:27; *Ex* 18:10; *Ruth* 4:14
1 Sam 25:32, 39; *2 Sam* 18:28
1 Ki 1:48; 5:7; 8:15, 56; 10:9
1 Chr 16:36; *2 Chr* 2:12; 6:4; 9:8
Ezra 7:27; *Ps* 28:6; 31:21; 41:13
68:19; 72:18; 89:52; 106:48;
124:6; 135:21; 144:1; *Zech* 11:5
Luke 1:68
b. be most high God. *Luke* 14:20
children of Israel *b.* God. *Josh* 22:33
and *b.* be my rock. *2 Sam* 22:47
Ps 18:46
David *b.* the Lord, *b.* *1 Chr* 29:10
all the congregation *b.* Lord. 20
there they *b.* Lord. *2 Chr* 20:26
they saw the heaps, they *b.* 31:8
and Ezra *b.* the Lord. *Neh* 8:6
b. be thy glorious. 9:5; *Ps* 72:19
b. be the name of Lord. *Job* 1:21
Ps 113:2
b. be God. *Ps* 66:20; 68:35
2 Cor 1:3
b. art thou, O Lord, teach. *Ps* 119:12
b. be the glory of. *Ezek* 3:12
Daniel *b.* God of. *Dan* 2:19, 20
Nebuchadnezzar *b.* most High. 4:34
him in his arms and *b.* *Luke* 2:28
b. is the King of Israel. *John* 12:13
than Creator, who is *b.* *Rom* 1:25
Christ, who is over all, God *b.* 9:5
is *b.* for evermore. *2 Cor* 11:31
b. be the Father. *Eph* 1:3; *1 Pet* 1:3
Gospel of the *b.* God. *1 Tim* 1:11
the *b.* and only Potentate. 6:15

blessed *are they*
b. are they that put trust. *Ps* 2:12
b. are they that dwell. 84:4
b. are they that keep judgement.
106:3
b. are they that keep. 119:2
for *b.* are they that wait. *Ps* 8:32
b. are they that wait. *Isa* 30:18
b. are they that mourn. *Mat* 5:4
b. are they who hunger. 6
b. are they who are persecuted. 10
b. are they that hear. *Luke* 11:28
b. are they that believed. *John* 20:29
b. are they whose iniquities. *Rom* 4:7
b. are they who are called. *Rev* 19:9
b. are they that do his. 22:14

blessed *are ye*
b. are ye that sow. *Isa* 32:20
b. are ye when men. *Mat* 5:11
b. are ye that hunger, be filled; *b.*
are ye that weep. *Luke* 6:21
b. are ye when men hate you. 22

blessed *is he*
b. is he that blesseth. *Num* 24:9
b. is he whose sin is. *Ps* 32:1
b. is he that considereth poor. 41:1
b. is he that waiteth. *Dan* 12:12
and *b.* is he whosoever shall not be.
Mat 11:6; *Luke* 7:23
b. is he that cometh in name.
Mat 21:9; 23:39; *Mark* 11:9
Luke 13:35
b. is he that shall eat. *Luke* 14:15
b. is he that readeth. *Rev* 1:3
b. is he that watcheth. 16:15
b. is he that hath part in. 20:6
b. is he that keepeth sayings. 22:7

blessed *is the man*
b. is the man that walketh not in.
Ps 1:1
b. is the man to whom Lord imputeth
not iniquity. 32:2; *Rom* 4:8
b. is the man that trusteth in him.
Ps 34:8; 84:12; *Jer* 17:7
b. is the man that maketh the Lord.
Ps 40:4
b. is the man whom thou choosest.
65:4
b. is the man whose strength. 84:5
b. is the man thou chastenest. 94:12
b. is the man that feareth Lord.
112:1
b. is the man that heareth. *Pr* 8:34
b. is the man that doth this. *Isa* 56:2
b. is the man that endureth. *Jas* 1:12

blessedness
as David describeth *b.* *Rom* 4:6
cometh this *b.* on the ? 9
where is then the *b.* ? *Gal* 4:15*

blessest
I wot that he thou *b.* *Num* 22:6
thou *b.* O Lord, and it. *1 Chr* 17:27
thou *b.* the springing. *Ps.* 65:10

blesseth
blessed is he that *b.* thee. *Gen* 27:29
Num 24:9
thy God *b.* thee as he. *Deut* 15:6
b. covetous whom the. *Ps* 10:3*
he *b.* them so that they are. 107:38
but he *b.* the habitation. *Pr* 3:33
he that *b.* his friend. 27:14
he *b.* himself in the earth. *Isa* 65:16

blessing
[1] *The favour, kindness, and
goodness of God, making what his
people do succeed and prosper,* Ps
3:8. [2] *All good things which
God bestows upon his people,
whether spiritual or temporal,*
Deut 28:2; Ps 24:5; Isa 44:3;
Eph 1:3. [3] *The means of con-
veying a blessing to others,* Isa
19:24. [4] *Wishing, praying for,
and endeavouring the good of our
enemies,* 1 Pet 3:9. [5] *A gift, or
present,* Gen 33:11; 1 Ki 5:15.
bless thee, thou shalt be a *b.*
Gen 12:2
in *b.* I will bless. 22:17; *Heb* 6:14
a curse on me, not a *b.* *Gen* 27:12
brother hath taken thy *b.* 35
hast thou but one *b.* ? 38
God give thee *b.* of Abraham. 28:4
take, I pray thee, my *b.* 33:11*
the *b.* of the Lord was on all. 39:5
every one according to his *b.* 49:28
bestow on you a *b.* *Ex* 32:29
command my *b.* on you. *Lev* 25:21
set before you *b.* *Deut* 11:26 ; 30:19
a *b.* if ye obey the. 11:27
put the *b.* on Gerizim. 29
to the *b.* of the Lord. 12:15; 16:17
Lord turned curse into *b.* 23:5
command a *b.* on store-houses. 28:8
is the *b.* wherewith Moses. 33:1, 7
let the *b.* come upon. 33:16
Naphtali full with the *b.* 23
give me a *b.* *Josh* 15:19; *Judg* 1:15
b. thy handmaid hath. *1 Sam* 25:27*
with thy *b.* let my house. *2 Sam* 7:29
I pray thee take a *b.* *2 Ki* 5:15*
exalted above all *b.* and. *Neh* 9:5
God turned the curse into a *b.* 13:2
b. of him that was ready. *Job* 29:13
thy *b.* is upon thy people. *Ps* 3:8
he shall receive the *b.* 24:5
as he delighted not in *b.* 109:17
b. of the Lord be upon you. 129:8
Lord commanded the *b.* 133:3
b. of Lord maketh rich. *Pr* 10:22
by the *b.* of the upright the. 11:11
a *b.* on the head of him. 26
a good *b.* shall come on. 24:25
a *b.* in midst of land. *Isa* 19:24
and I will pour my *b.* on thy. 44:3
destroy it not, a *b.* is in it. 65:8
I will make them a *b.* there shall be
showers of *b.* *Ezek* 34:26
may cause the *b.* to rest. 44:30

if he will leave a *b.* *Joel* 2:14
I will save, ye shall be a *b.* *Zech* 8:13
and pour you out a *b.* *Mal* 3:10
in the temple *b.* God. *Luke* 24:53
in the fulness of the *b.* *Rom* 15:29
the cup of *b.* which. *1 Cor* 10:16
the *b.* of Abraham. *Gal* 3:14
for the earth receiveth *b.* *Heb* 6:7
he would have inherited the *b.* 12:17
of same mouth proceed *b.* *Jas* 3:10
but contrariwise *b.*, that ye should
inherit a *b.* *1 Pet* 3:9
to receive honour glory, *b. Rev* 5:12
b. to him that sitteth on the. 13
b. and glory to our God. 7:12

blessings
Almighty bless thee with *b.* of
heaven, *b.* of deep, *b.* *Gen* 49:25
b. of father prevailed above *b.* of. 26
all these *b.* shall come. *Deut* 28:2
afterwards he read the *b. Josh* 8:34
thou preventest him with *b.* *Ps* 21:3
b. are upon head of just. *Pr* 10:6
faithful man abound with *b.* 28:20
and will curse your *b.* *Mal* 2:2
blessed us with spiritual *b.* *Eph* 1:3

blew, *verb*
priests passed on and *b.* *Josh* 6:8
Ehud *b.* a trumpet. *Judg* 3:27
Spirit come on Gideon, he *b.* 6:34
they *b.* the trumpets. 7:19, 20, 22
Saul *b.* saying, let. *1 Sam* 13:3
Joab *b.* a trumpet. *2 Sam* 2:28
18:16; 20:22
Sheba *b.* a trumpet and said. 20:1
b. the trumpet, people said, God.
1 Ki 1:39; *2 Ki* 9:13; 11:14
winds *b.*, beat on house. *Mat* 7:25, 27
a great wind that *b.* *John* 6:18
when the south-wind *b.* *Acts* 27:13
28:13*

blind
[1] *Those deprived of natural
sight,* John 9:1; Acts 13:11. [2]
*The morally blind, whose judgement
is so corrupted by taking of bribes
that they cannot, or will not discern
between right and wrong,* Ex 23:8;
Deut. 16:19. [3] *The spiritually
blind, whether through ignorance or
self-will,* Mat 15:14; Deut 27:18.
who maketh the seeing *b.* *Ex* 4:11
stumbling-block before *b. Lev* 19:14
a *b.* or lame man not offer. 21:18
not offer the *b.* to the Lord. 22:22
Deut 15:21
that maketh the *b.* to. *Deut* 27:18
grope at noon-day, as *b.* 28:29
take away the *b.* and. *2 Sam* 5:6
the lame and *b.*, the *b.* and the lame
shall not come into house. 8
I was eyes to the *b.* *Job* 29:15
Lord openeth eyes of *b.* *Ps* 146:8
eyes of *b.* shall see. *Isa* 29:18; 35:5
a light to open the *b.* eyes. 42:7
bring *b.* by a way they knew not. 16
hear ye deaf, look, ye *b.* 18
who is *b.* but my servant ? *b.* as he
that is perfect, and *b.* ? 19
bring forth the *b.* people. 43:8
his watchmen are *b.* 56:10
grope for the wall like the *b.* 59:10
gather with them the *b.* *Jer* 31:8
they wandered as *b.* *Lam* 4:14
shall walk like *b.* men. *Zeph* 1:17
offer the *b.* for sacrifice. *Mal* 1:8
two *b.* men followed him. *Mat* 9:27
20:30
b. receive their sight. 11:5; 12:22
Luke 7:22
b. leaders of the *b.* if the *b.* lead the
b. both. *Mat* 15:14; *Luke* 6:39
woe to you, ye *b.* guides. *Mat* 23:16
ye fools and *b.* 17, 19
b. Pharisee, cleanse first within. 26
he took the *b.* by hand. *Mark* 8:23
b. Bartimaeus sat by the way. 10:46
recovery of sight to *b.* *Luke* 4:18
to many that were *b.* he gave. 7:21
thou makest a feast, call *b.* 14:13
lay a great mulitude of *b.* *John* 5:3
he saw a man *b.* from his birth. 9:1
they which see might be made *b.* 39

are we *b.* also ? *John* 9:40
if ye were *b.* 41
can a devil open eyes of *b.* ? 10:21
thou shalt be *b.* not. *Acts* 13:11
thou art a guide to the *b. Rom* 2:19
he that lacketh these is *b.* *2 Pet* 1:9
not that thou art *b.* *Rev* 3:17

blind, *verb*
a gift doth *b.* the eyes. *Deut* 16:19
received I a bribe to *b.* *1 Sam* 12:3

blinded, -eth
take no gift, a gift *b.* *Ex* 23:8
he hath *b.* their eyes. *John* 12:40
obtained, the rest are *b.* *Rom* 11:7
their minds were *b.* *2 Cor* 3:14
god of this world hath *b.* his eyes.
because darkness hath *b.* his eyes.
4:4
1 John 2:11

blindfolded
when they had *b.* him. *Luke* 22:64

blindness
smote the men with *b.* *Gen* 19:11
shall smite thee with *b.* *Deut* 28:28
Elisha prayed, smite this people with
b., smote them with *b.* *2 Ki* 6:18
smite every horse with *b. Zech* 12:4
b. in part has happened. *Rom* 11:25
because of *b.* of heart. *Eph* 4:18

block, *see* **stumbling**

blood
The word is used [1] *literally as
in* Ex 29:12; Acts 17:26. [2] *Figuratively, for murder,* Hab 2:12;
Mat 27:24; *and for the blood of
Christ, the blood of the covenant,
where the idea is the death of
Christ on the cross,* Rom 3:25; 5:9;
Eph 1:7.
thy brother's *b.* crieth. *Gen* 4:10
the life which is the *b.* 9:4
your *b.* of your lives, I will require. 5
killed kid and dipped coat in *b.* 37:31
water shall become *b.* on. *Ex* 4:9
waters shall be turned into *b.* 7:17
b. shall be for a token, when I see *b.*
12:13
shalt not offer the *b.* with leaven.
23:18; 34:25
thou shalt take of the *b.* 29:21
b. of it was not brought. *Lev* 10:18
and if issue in flesh shall be *b.* 15:19
b. imputed unto that man. 17:4
for it is the *b.* that maketh. 11
not stand against the *b.* of thy. 19:16
and drink the *b.* of. *Num* 23:24
not cleansed but by the *b.* 35:33
matter between *b.* and *b.*
Deut 17:8; *2 Chr* 19:10
the *b.* shall be forgiven. *Deut* 21:8
battlement, that bring not *b.* 22:8
avenge the *b.* of his servants. 32:43
and their *b.* be laid upon. *Judg* 9:24
let not my *b.* fall. *1 Sam* 26:20
David said, thy *b.* be. *2 Sam* 1:16
from the *b.* of the slain, from. 22
I and kingdom guiltless the *b.* 3:28
hath returned upon thee the *b.* 16:8
Amasa wallowed in *b.* 20:12
b. of the men ? 23:17; *1 Chr* 11:19
the *b.* of war on his girdle. *1 Ki* 2:5
b. on thy head. 37; *Ezek* 33:4
the *b.* gushed out upon. *1 Ki* 18:28
saw the waters red as *b.* *2 Ki* 3:22
said, this is *b.* the kings are. 23
I have seen *b.* of Naboth, *b.* of. 9:26
O earth, cover not my *b.* *Job* 16:18
the eagles' young suck up *b.* 39:30
what profit is in my *b.* ? *Ps* 30:9
or will I drink *b.* of goats ? 50:13
righteous wash his feet in *b.* 58:10
foot may be dipped in the *b.* 68:23
precious shall their *b.* be in. 72:14
doth violence to *b.* of any. *Pr* 28:17
hands are full of *b.* *Isa* 1:15
the Lord shall purge the *b.* of. 4:4
noise, and garments rolled in *b.* 9:5
the waters of Dimon full of *b.* 15:9
his ear from hearing of *b.* 33:15
shall be melted with their *b.* 34:3
is found the *b.* of the poor. *Jer* 2:34
pour out their *b.* by the. 18:21*
he that keepeth sword from *b.* 48:10

b. be on the inhabitants. *Jer* 51:35
polluted themselves with *b.*
    Lam 4:14
pestilence and *b.* pass. *Ezek* 5:17
the land is full of *b.*   9:9
pour out my fury upon it in *b.* 14:19
to thee when thou wast in thy *b.* 16:6
I will give thee *b.* in fury and. 38
beget son that is shedder of *b.* 18:10
he shall die, his *b.* shall be upon. 13
mother is like a vine in thy *b.* 19:10
thy *b.* in midst of land. 21:32; 22:12
the city sheddeth *b.* in the.   22:3
and *b.* is in their hands. 23:37, 45
I have set her *b.* on the rock. 24:8
I will send *b.* into her streets. 28:23
I water with thy *b.* the land.   32:6
I will prepare thee to *b.* thou hast
  not hated *b.* even *b.* shall.   35:6
offer my bread, fat and *b.* 44:7, 15
I will avenge the *b.*   *Hos* 1:4
b. fire, and pillars of smoke.
   Joel 2:30; *Acts* 2:19
moon turned into *b.*   *Joel* 2:31
   Acts 2:20
I will cleanse their *b.* *Joel* 3:21
their *b.* shall be poured. *Zeph* 1:17
issue of *b.* twelve years. *Mat* 9:20
  Mark 5:25; *Luke* 8:43
b. hath not revealed. *Mat* 16:17
not partakers in the *b.* of.   23:30
b. of righteous Abel. 35; *Luke* 11:51
b. of the new testament. *Mat* 26:28
  Mark 14:24
because it is price of *b.* *Mat* 27:6
called the field of *b.*   8; *Acts* 1:19
innocent of the *b.* of this. *Mat* 27:24
whose *b.* Pilate had.   *Luke* 13:1
the new testament in my *b.* 22:20
   1 Cor 11:25
sweat was as great drops of *b.*
   Luke 22:44
which were born not of *b. John* 1:13
my flesh drinketh my *b.*   6:54, 56
my flesh is meat, my *b.* is drink. 55
forthwith came thereout *b.*   19:34
ye bring this man's *b.* *Acts* 5:28
they abstain from *b.* 15:20, 29; 21:25
and hath made of one *b.* all. 17:26
your *b.* be on your own heads. 18:6
I am pure from the *b.* of all. 20:26
guilty of body and *b.* of. *1 Cor* 11:27
flesh and *b.* cannot inherit.   15:50
not against flesh and *b.* *Eph* 6:12
peace through *b.* of cross. *Col* 1:20
partakers of flesh and *b.* *Heb* 2:14
not without *b.* which he offered. 9:7
by *b.* of goats, but by his own *b.* 12
b. of bulls and goats sanctifieth. 13
this is the *b.* of the testament. 20
without shedding of *b.* there is. 22
into holiest by *b.* of Jesus.   10:19
passover, and sprinkling of *b.* 11:28
ye have not yet resisted unto *b.* 12:4
b. of sprinkling that speaketh. 24
whose *b.* is brought into.   13:11
sprinkling of *b.* of Jesus. *1 Pet* 1:2
b. of Jesus Christ cleanseth us.
   1 John 1:7
he that came by water and *b.* 5:6
three in earth, Spirit, water, *b.* 8
hast redeemed us by thy *b. Rev* 5:9
dost thou not avenge our *b.* ? 6:10
and the moon became as *b.*   12
white in the *b.* of the Lamb. 7:14
third part of sea became *b.* 8:8; 16:3
power to turn the waters into *b.* 11:6
overcame him by *b.* of Lamb. 12:11
b. came out of the wine-press. 14:20
thou hast given them *b.* to drink. 16:6
in her was found the *b.* of.   18:24
avenged the *b.* of his servants. 19:2
clothed with vesture dipped in *b.* 13

see **avenger, revenger**

   blood *be upon*
curseth his father, his *b. be upon.*
   Lev 20:9
sodomy, their *b. be upon* them. 13
wizard, their *b. be upon* them. 27
b. shed, and *be upon. Deut* 19:10
abominations, his *b. be upon.*
   Ezek 18:13
warning, his *b.* shall *be upon.* 33:5*

   blood with *bullock*
take *b.* of *bullock.*   *Ex* 29:12
   Lev 4:5; 16:14, 18
pour *b.* of *bullock* at.   *Lev* 4:7
he did with *b.* of the *bullock.* 16:15
delight not in *b.* of *bullocks. Isa* 1:11

   blood *of Christ*
communion of the *b. of Christ* ?
   1 Cor 10:16
made nigh by *b.* of *Christ. Eph* 2:13
shall *b.* of *Christ* purge ? *Heb* 9:14
b. of Christ as of a lamb. *1 Pet* 1:19
b. of Christ cleanseth us. *1 John* 1:7

   blood *of the covenant*
behold the *b. of the covenant.*
   Ex 24:8
by the *b. of* thy *covenant. Zech* 9:11
hath counted *b. of covenant* unholy.
   Heb 10:29
b. of the everlasting *covenant.* 13:20

   blood, with *eat*
eat neither fat nor *b.*   *Lev* 3:17
ye shall *eat* no manner of *b.* 7:26
  27; 17:14; *Deut* 12:16, 23; 15:23
eateth b. that soul be cut off.
   Lev 7:27, 17:10
people did *eat* with *b.* 1 Sam 14:32
ye eat with *b.* and.   *Ezek* 33:25

   for **blood**
not pollute land, *for b. Num* 35:33
died *for* the *b.* of Asahel. *2 Sam* 3:27
for the *b.* of the sons. *2 Chr* 24:25
he maketh inquisition *for b. Ps* 9:12
let us lay wait *for b.* *Pr* 1:11, 18
wicked are to lie in wait *for b.* 12:6
they all lie in wait *for b.* *Mi* 7:2

   his **blood**
if we conceal *his b.* *Gen* 37:26
behold *his b.* is required.   42:22
his b. shall be upon his. *Josh* 2:19
I not require *his b.* ? *2 Sam* 4:11
Lord shall return *his b.* *1 Ki* 2:32
die in his iniquity, but *his b.* will I
  require. *Ezek* 3:18, 20; 33:4, 6, 8
shall he leave *his b.* on. *Hos* 12:14
take away *his b.*   *Zech* 9:7
his b. be on us.   *Mat* 27:25
purchased with *his b.* *Acts* 20:28
through faith in *his b.* *Rom* 3:25
being now justified by *his b.* 5:9
redemption through *his b. Eph* 1:7
   Col 1:14
by *his* own *b.* he entered. *Heb* 9:12
he might sanctify with *his b.* 13:12
from our sins in *his b.* *Rev* 1:5

   innocent **blood**
innoc. b. be not shed. *Deut* 19:10
put away guilt of *innoc. b.* 13; 21:9
lay not *innoc. b.* to people's 21:8
sin against *innocent b.* 1 Sam 19:5
take away *innoc. b.*   1 *Ki* 2:31
shed *innoc. b.* 2 *Ki* 21:16; 24:4
they condemn *innoc. b.* *Ps* 94:21
shed *innoc b.*, *b.* of sons and. 106:38
hands that shed *innoc. b.* *Pr* 6:17
haste to shed *innoc. b.* *Isa* 59:7
shed not *innoc. b.* *Jer* 7:6; 22:3
eyes and heart shed *innoc. b.* 22:17
ye shall surely bring *innoc. b.* 26:15
they have shed *innoc. b. Joel* 3:19
lay not on us *innoc. b. Jonah* 1:14
I have betrayed *innoc. b. Mat* 27:4

   shed **blood**
sheddeth man's *b.* his *b.* be *shed.*
   Gen 9:6
Reuben said, *shed* no *b.*   37:22
there shall no *b.* be *shed. Ex.* 22:2
be risen upon him, *b.* be *shed.* 3*
hath *shed b.* that man. *Lev* 17:4
cleansed of *b. shed* but by *b.*
   Num 35:33
have not *shed* this *b.* *Deut* 21:7
coming to *shed b.* 1 *Sam* 25:26*
slew and *shed b.* of war. 1 *Ki* 2:5
thou hast *shed b.* much *b.*
   1 *Chr* 22:8; 28:3
their *b. shed* like water. *Ps* 79:3
revenging *b.* of thy servants *shed.* 10
make haste to *shed b.* *Pr* 1:16
   Rom 3:15
prophets have *shed* the *b. Lam* 4:13

as women that *shed b.* *Ezek* 16:38
   23:45
guilty in thy *b.* thou hast *shed.* 22:4
to their power to *shed b.*   6
women that *shed b.*   23:45
ye *shed b.* shall ye possess ? 33:25
thou hast *shed b.* of children. 35:5*
fury on them for *b.* they *shed.* 36:18
all the righteous *b. shed. Mat* 23:25
my *b.* which is *shed.* *Mark* 14:24
   Luke 22:20
b. of the prophets *shed. Luke* 11:50
b. of Stephen was *shed. Acts* 22:20
they have *shed* the *b.* *Rev* 16:6

   sprinkle **blood**
ram's *b.* and *sprinkle* it. *Ex* 29:16
sprinkle b. on altar. 20; *Lev* 1:5
  11; 3:2, 8, 13; 7:2; 17:6
   Num 18:17
sprinkle b. seven times. *Lev* 4:6, 17
   16:14, 19
sprinkle b. of sin-offering on. 5:9
the priests that *sprinkle* the *b.* 7:14
sprinkle of the *b.* before. *Num* 19:4
sprinkle on it the *b.* 2 *Ki* 16:15
an altar to *sprinkle b.* *Ezek* 43:18

   blood *sprinkled*
half of *b.* Moses *sprinkled* on.
   Ex 24:6; *Lev* 8:19, 24
Moses took *b.* and *sprinkled* on.
   Ex 24:8
when there is *sprinkled b. Lev* 6:27
took *b.* and *sprinkled* on Aaron. 8:30
Aaron's sons *b.* he *sprinkled.* 9:12, 18
Athaliah's *b. sprinkled* on. 2 *Ki* 9:33
Ahaz *sprinkled* the *b.* of his. 16:13
sprinkled b. of bullocks. 2 *Chr* 29:22
   30:16
the priests *sprinkled* the *b.* 35:11
their *b.* shall be *sprinkled. Isa* 63:3
he *sprinkled* with *b.* the. *Heb* 9:21

   with **blood**
make atonement *with b.* *Ex* 30:10
cleanse the house *with b. Lev* 14:52
ye not eat any thing *with b.* 19:26
head bring down *with b.* 1 *Ki* 2:9
land was polluted *with b. Ps* 106:38
filled *with b.* made fat *with b.*
   Isa 34:6
their land shall be soaked *with b.* 7
be drunken *with* their own *b.* 49:26
your hands are defiled *with b.* 59:3
filled this place *with b.* *Jer* 19:4
be made drunk *with* their *b.* 46:10
polluted themselves *with b.*
   Lam 4:14
plead against him *with b. Ezek* 38:22
a city polluted *with b.* *Hos* 6:8
they build up Zion *with b.* *Mi* 3:10
buildeth a town *with b.* *Hab* 2:12
I conferred not *with b.* *Gal* 1:16
all things purged *with b. Heb* 9:22
and fire, mingled *with b.* *Rev* 8:7
saw woman drunken *with b.*   17:6

   bloodguiltiness
deliver me from *b.*   *Ps* 51:14

   bloodthirsty
the *b.* hate the upright. *Pr* 29:10

   bloody
a *b.* husband art thou. *Ex* 4:25, 26
come out, thou *b.* man. 2 *Sam* 16:7
famine is for Saul, and his *b.* 21:1
Lord will abhor *b.* man. *Ps* 5:6
gather not my life with *b.* men. 26:9
b. men not live out half their. 55:23
deliver me, save me from *b.* 59:2
depart from me ye *b.* men. 139:19
land is full of *b.* crimes. *Ezek* 7:23
wilt thou judge the *b.* city ? 22:2
woe to the *b.* city. 24:6, 9; *Nah* 3:1
lay sick of a *b.* flux. *Acts* 28:8*

   bloomed
Aaron's rod *b.* blossoms. *Num* 17:8

   blossom
her *b.* shot forth. *Gen* 40:10
their *b.* shall go as dust. *Isa* 5:24

   blossom, -ed
[1] *To put forth flowers,* Num 17:5;
Hab 3:17. [2] *To increase and
prosper,* Isa 27:6.
the man's rod shall *b.* *Num* 17:5*

Israel shall *b.* and bud.   *Isa* 27:6
desert shall rejoice and *b.*   35:1
b. abundantly and rejoice.   2
the rod hath *b.* pride.   *Ezek* 7:10
fig-tree shall not *b.* nor.   *Hab* 3:17

blot
(*Spot, stain, disgrace*)
if any *b.* hath cleaved.   *Job* 31:7
the wicked, getteth a *b.*   *Pr* 9:7

blot out
(*Cancel, expunge, efface*)
not, *b.* me out of thy book. *Ex* 32:32
whosoever sinned, will I *b. out.*   33
shall *b.* them out with.   *Num* 5:23
me alone that I *b. out.*   *Deut* 9:14
b. out the remembrance of.   25:19
Lord shall *b. out* his name.   29:20
he would *b. out* Israel.   *2 Ki* 14:27
have mercy, O God, *b. out. Ps* 51:1
hide my sins and *b. out* all.   9
nor *b. out* their sin from. *Jer* 18:23
I will not *b.* his name *out. Rev* 3:5

blotted
let not their sin be *b.* out.   *Neh* 4:5
let them be *b.* out of.   *Ps* 69:28
let their name be *b.* out.   109:13
not the sin of his mother be *b.*   14
b. out as a thick cloud.   *Isa* 44:22
your sins may be *b.* out.   *Acts* 3:19

blotteth, -ing
I am he that *b.* out thy.   *Isa* 43:25
b. out the hand-writing.   *Col* 2:14

blow
consumed by the *b.* of thy. *Ps* 39:10
broken with grievous *b. Jer* 14:17*

blow, *verb*
didst *b.* with thy wind.   *Ex* 15:10
when ye *b.* an alarm.   *Num* 10:5, 6
then ye shall *b.* an alarm.   9*
when I *b.*, then ye.   *Judg* 7:18
caused an cast-wind to *b. Ps* 78:26
caused his wind to *b.*   147:18
come, thou south, *b.*   *S of S* 4:16
he shall also *b.* upon them. *Isa* 40:24
I *b.* against these. *Ezek* 21:31; 22:21
b. ye the cornet in Gibeah. *Hos* 5:8
b. the trumpet in Zion.   *Joel* 2:15
ye brought it, I did *b.*   *Hag* 1:9
ye see south-wind *b.*   *Luke* 12:55
that wind should not *b.*   *Rev* 7:1

see **trumpet**

bloweth
Spirit of the Lord *b.* on it. *Isa* 40:7
I have created smith that *b.*   54:16
wind *b.* where it listeth.   *John* 3:8

blown
fire not *b.* shall consume. *Job* 20:26

blue
b. purple.   *Ex* 25:4; 26:1, 31, 36
  27:16
robe of the ephod of *b.* 28:31; 39:22
cut gold to work it in the *b.*   39:3
the fringes ribband of *b. Num* 15:38
cunning to work in *b.*   *2 Chr* 2:7, 14
b. hangings, pavement of *b. Esth* 1:6*
Mordecai went in apparel of *b.* 8:15
b. and purple is their.   *Jer* 10:9
Assyrians clothed with *b. Ezek* 23:6
b. and purple from the isles.   27:7
in *b.* clothes and broidered.   24

see **purple, cloth, lace, loops**

blueness
b. of a wound cleanseth. *Pr* 20:30*

blunt
if iron be *b.* and he do.   *Eccl* 10:10

blush
I *b.* to lift my face to thee. *Ezra* 9:6
neither could they *b. Jer* 6:15; 8:12

Boanerges
surnamed them *B.*   *Mark* 3:17

boar
b. out of the wood.   *Ps* 80:13

board, -s
overlay *b.* with gold. *Ex* 26:29; 36:34
hollow with *b.* make.   27:8
under every *b.* were two.   36:30
under Merari shall be *b. Num* 3:36
will enclose her with *b. S of S* 8:9
the rest, some on *b.*   *Acts* 27:44*

4

boast, *substantive*
my soul shall make her *b. Ps* 34:2
Jew, and makest thy *b.*   *Rom* 2:17*
thou that makest thy *b.*   23*

boast, *verb*
not *b.* as he that putteth. *1 Ki* 20:11
heart lifteth thee to *b.* *2 Chr* 25:19
in God we *b.* all the day.   *Ps* 44:8
b. themselves in their riches. 49:6
the workers of iniquity *b.*   94:4
confounded be they that *b.* of. 97:7
b. not thyself of.   *Pr* 27:1
shall the ax *b.* itself.   *Isa* 10:15
in their glory shall you *b.*   61:6
b. not against branches, if thou *b.*
  Rom 11:18*
for which I *b.* to them.   *2 Cor* 9:2*
for though I should *b.*   10:8*
we will not *b.* of things.   13*
to *b.* in another man's line.   16*
receive me that I may *b.*   11:16*
not of works lest any *b. Eph* 2:9*

boasted
with mouth ye have *b. Ezek* 35:13*
if I have *b.* any thing.   *2 Cor* 7:14*

boasters
proud, *b.* inventors of.   *Rom* 1:30
covetous, *b.* proud.   *2 Tim* 3:2

boastest, -eth
the wicked *b.* of his.   *Ps* 10:3
why *b.* thou in mischief ?   52:1
gone his way, then he *b. Pr* 20:14
whoso *b.* of a false gift.   25:14
a little member, and *b.*   *Jas* 3:5

boasting, *participle*
rose Theudas, *b.* himself. *Acts* 5:36*
not *b.* of things without. *2 Cor* 10:15*

boasting, *substantive*
where is *b.* then ?   *Rom* 3:27*
b. before Titus is.   *2 Cor* 7:14*
shew ye the proof of our *b.*   8:24*
lest our *b.* of you should be. 9:3*
should be ashamed in confident *b.* 4*
shall stop me of this *b.*   11:10*
were foolishly in confidence of *b.* 17*
but now ye rejoice in *b.*   *Jas* 4:16

boat, -s
people saw there was no *b.*, and that
Jesus went not into *b. John* 6:22
came other *b.* from Tiberias.   23
work to come by the *b. Acts* 27:16
when they had let down the *b.*   30
soldiers cut off the ropes of *b.*   32

Boaz
left pillar called *B.*   *1 Ki* 7:21
  2 Chr 3:17

Boaz
kinsman, his name was *B. Ruth* 2:1
with whom I wrought, is *B.*   3:2
is not *B.* of our kindred ?   3:2
when *B.* had eaten.   7
then went *B.* up to the gate.   4:1
so *B.* took Ruth.   13
B. begat Obed.   21; *1 Chr* 2:12
  Mat 1:5
Obed the son of *B.*   *Luke* 3:32

Bochim
came from Gilgal to *B.*   *Judg* 2:1
called the name of place *B.*   5

bodies
ought left, but our *b.*   *Gen* 47:18
took to of Saul's sons. *1 Sam* 31:12
  1 Chr 10:12
dominion over our *b.*   *Neh* 9:37
b. are like unto *b.* of.   *Job* 13:12*
two wings covered *b. Ezek* 1:11
on whose *b.* fire had.   *Dan* 3:27
yielded their *b.* that they might. 28
many *b.* of saints which. *Mat* 27:52
b. should not remain on. *John* 19:31
to dishonour their own *b. Rom* 1:24
shall quicken your mortal *b.*   8:11
that ye present your *b. a.*   12:1
b. are members of.   *1 Cor* 6:15
are celestial *b.* and *b.*   15:40
their wives as their own *b. Eph* 5:28
b. washed with pure.   *Heb* 10:22
the *b.* of beasts, whose.   13:11

dead bodies
were *dead b.* fallen.   *2 Chr* 20:24
they found with *dead b.*   25

dead b. of thy servants.   *Ps* 79:2
fill the places with the *dead b.* 110:6
valley of *dead b.* shall be. *Jer* 31:40
fill them with *dead b.* of men.   33:5
dead b. shall be for meat.   34:20
wherein Ishmael cast *dead b.* 41:9
shall be many *dead b.*   *Amos* 8:3
dead b. shall lie in.   *Rev* 11:8
nations see their *dead b.*, nor suffer
their *dead b.* to be put in.   9

bodily
descended in *b.* shape.   *Luke* 3:22
his *b.* presence is weak. *2 Cor* 10:10
fulness of the Godhead *b.*   *Col* 2:9
b. exercise profiteth little. *1 Tim* 4:8

body
[1] *The physical part of man as
distinct from the spiritual,* 1 Sam
31:4; Mat 6:22. [2] *Used figuratively for the Church,* 1 Cor 12:27;
Eph 3:6.

as the *b.* of heaven in.   *Ex* 24:10*
took the *b.* of Saul.   *1 Sam* 31:12
  1 Chr 10:12
sake of my own *b.*   *Job* 19:17†
my skin worms destroy this *b.*   26
drawn and cometh out of *b.*   20:25
when thy flesh and *b.*   *Pr* 5:11
consume both soul and *b. Isa* 10:18
and thou hast laid thy *b.*   51:23*
their whole *b.* full.   *Ezek* 10:12
in spirit in midst of *b.*   *Dan* 7:15
whole *b.* be cast into. *Mat* 5:29, 30
light of *b.* is eye. 6:22; *Luke* 11:34
b. full of light.   *Mat* 6:22
  Luke 11:34, 36
b. shall be full of darkness. *Mat* 6:23
no thought for *b.*   25; *Luke* 12:22
b. more than raiment.   *Mat* 6:25
  Luke 12:23
them which kill *b.*   *Mat* 10:28
  Luke 12:4
disciples came and took *b. Mat* 14:12
poured this ointment on my *b.* 26:12
Jesus said, take, eat, this is my *b.*
  26:26; *Mark* 14:22; *Luke* 22:19
  1 Cor 11:24
Joseph begged the *b.* of Jesus. *Mat*
27:58; *Mark* 15:43; *Luke* 23:52
in *b.* that she was healed. *Mark* 5:29
is come to anoint my *b.*   14:8
a linen cloth cast about his *b.*   51
gave *b.* to Joseph. 15:45; *Mat* 27:58
where the *b.* is, thither. *Luke* 17:37
found not *b.* of Lord Jesus.   24:3
the *b.* of Jesus had lain. *John* 20:12
the *b.* of sin destroyed.   *Rom* 6:6
dead to the law by *b.* of Christ. 7:4
deliver me from *b.* of this ?   24
Christ in you, the *b.* is dead.   8:10
the Spirit mortify deeds of *b.*   13
adoption, redemption of *b.*   23
b. is not for fornication, but the Lord,
and the Lord for *b.*   *1 Cor* 6:13
every sin is without the *b.*   18
b. is the temple of Holy Ghost.   19
hath no power of her own *b.*   7:4
I keep under my *b.*   9:27
communion of the *b.* of Christ. 10:16
guilty of the *b.* and blood of. 11:27
not discerning the Lord's *b.*   29
for the *b.* is not one member. 12:14
is it therefore not of *b.* ?   15, 16
whole *b.* were an eye where. 12:17
where were the *b.* ?   19
yet but one *b.*   20
now ye are the *b.* of Christ.   27
though I give my *b.* to be.   13:3
with what *b.* do dead come ? 15:35
thou sowest not that *b.* that.   37
but God giveth it a *b.* as.   38
natural *b.* raised spiritual *b.*   44
to be absent from *b.*   *2 Cor* 5:8
fellow-heirs of the same *b. Eph* 3:6
for edifying of *b.* of Christ.   4:12
from whom whole *b.* fitly joined. 16
he is the Saviour of the *b.*   5:23
shall change our vile *b.*   *Phil* 3:21
he is the head of the *b.*   *Col* 1:18
in putting off the *b.* of the sins. 2:11
a shadow, but the *b.* is of Christ. 17
from which the *b.* by joints.   19
shew of wisdom in neglecting *b.*   23

pray your soul and *b.*   *1 Thes* 5:23
b. hast thou prepared me. *Heb* 10:5
through offering of the *b.* of Jesus. 10
not things needful to *b.*   *Jas* 2:16
as *b.* without the Spirit is dead. 26
and is able to bridle the whole *b.* 3:2
we turn about their whole *b.*   3
the tongue defileth the whole *b.*   6
disputed about *b.* of Moses *Jude* 9

dead body
not go into any *dead b.*   *Lev* 21:11
  Num 6:6
defiled by a *dead b.*   *Num* 9:6, 7
unclean by *dead b.*   10; *Hag* 2:13
toucheth *dead b.*   *Num* 19:11, 16
restored a *dead b.* to life. *2 Ki* 8:5*
with my *dead b.* shall.   *Isa* 26:19*
cast his *dead b.* into.   *Jer* 26:23
nis *dead b.* shall be cast out. 36:30

fruit of the body
blessed the *fruit of thy b. Deut* 28:4
plenteous in *fruit of thy b.* 11; 30:9
cursed shall be *fruit of thy b.* 28:18
shalt eat the *fruit of thy b.*   53
fruit of thy b. will I set. *Ps* 132:11
fruit of my b. for sin of my. *Mi* 6:7

his body
his b. not remain.   *Deut* 21:23
had 70 sons of *his b.*   *Judg* 8:30
fastened *his b.* to wall. *1 Sam* 31:10
his b. wet with dew. *Dan* 4:33; 5:21
till beast was slain, and *his b.* 7:11
his b. also was like the beryl. 10:6
how *his b.* was laid. *Luke* 23:55
when they found not *his b.*   24:23
the temple of *his b.*   *John* 2:21
his b. were brought.   *Acts* 19:12
he considered not *his b. Rom* 4:19
sinneth against *his b.*   *1 Cor* 6:18
the power of *his own b.*   7:4
the things done in *his b. 2 Cor* 5:10
which is *his b.* fulness.   *Eph* 1:23
like to *his* glorious *b.*   *Phil* 3:21
for *his b.* sake.   *Col* 1:24
bare our sins in *his b.* *1 Pet* 2:24

in body
ruddy in *b.* than rubies.   *Lam* 4:7
let not sin reign in *b. Rom* 6:12
I verily as absent in *b.* *1 Cor* 5:3
glorify God in your *b.*   6:20
that she may be holy in *b.*   7:34
members every one in the *b.* 12:18
be no schism in the *b.*   25
bearing in the *b.* the dying of our
  Lord that life in our *b. 2 Cor* 4:10
whilst we are at home in *b.*   5:6
in *b.* or out of the.   12:2
I bear in *b.* marks of Lord. *Gal* 6:17
Christ magnified in my *b. Phil* 1:20
reconciled in *b.* of his.   *Col* 1:22
yourselves also in the *b. Heb* 13:3

one body
many members in *one b. Rom* 12:4
are *one b.* in Christ. 5; *1 Cor* 10:17
joined to harlot, is *one b. 1 Cor* 6:16
as the *b.* is one.   12:12
baptized into *one b.* whether.   13
many members, yet but *one b.* 20
both to God in *one b. Eph* 2:16
there is *one b.* and one Spirit. 4:4
ye are called in *one b.* *Col* 3:15

boil
it shall be a *b.* with blains. *Ex* 9:9
it became a *b.* breaking forth. 10
could not stand because of the *b.* 11
b. the flesh at the door. *Lev* 8:31
flesh also in which was a *b.* 13:18
took figs and laid on the *b. 2 Ki* 20:7
  Isa 38:21
smote Job with sore *b.*   *Job* 2:7
he maketh the deep to *b.*   41:31
fire causeth waters to *b. Isa* 64:2
and make it *b.* well. *Ezek* 24:5
place where priests shall *b.* 46:20, 24

boiled
yoke of oxen and *b.* them. *1 Ki* 19:21
so we *b.* my son.   *2 Ki* 6:29
my bowels *b.,* rested not. *Job* 30:27

boiling
made with *b.* places. *Ezek* 46:23

boisterous
when he saw wind *b.* *Mat* 14:30*

---

bold
righteous are *b.* as a lion. *Pr* 28:1
and Barnabas waxed *b.* *Acts* 13:46
Esaias is very *b.* and. *Rom* 10:20
being absent, am *b.* *2 Cor* 10:1*
b. wherewith I think to be *b.* 2*,
wherein any is *b.* I am *b.*   11:21
much more *b.* to speak. *Phil* 1:14
we were *b.* in our God. *1 Thes* 2:2
though I might be much *b. Philem* 8

boldly
Levi came on the city *b. Gen* 34:25*
came, and went in *b.* *Mark* 15:43
he speaketh *b.* and. *John* 7:26*
how he preached *b.*   *Acts* 9:27
he spake *b.* in name of the Lord. 29
time abode they, speaking *b.* 14:3
Apollos began to speak *b.* 18:26
spake *b.* for the space of.   19:8
have written the more *b. Rom* 15:15
I may open my mouth *b.* *Eph* 6:19
that I may speak *b.* as I ought. 20
let us come *b.* to.   *Heb* 4:16
that we may *b.* say.   13:6*

boldness
the *b.* of his face shall. *Eccl* 8:1*
when they saw the *b.* of. *Acts* 4:13
that with all *b.* they may speak. 29
spake the word of God with *b.* 31
great is my *b.* of speech. *2 Cor* 7:4
in whom we have *b.*   *Eph* 3:12
but that with all *b.*   *Phil* 1:20
they purchase great *b.* *1 Tim* 3:13
having *b.* to enter.   *Heb* 10:19
that we may have *b.* *1 John* 4:17

bolled
(Gone to seed)
barley in the ear, and flax *b. Ex* 9:31

bolster
goats' hair for his *b. 1 Sam* 19:13, 16
spear at *b.*   26:7, 11, 12
water at *b.*   16

bolt, -ed
b. the door.   *2 Sam* 13:17
he *b.* the door.   18

bond
bind his soul with a *b.* *Num* 30:2
vow and bind herself by a *b.*   3
father hear her vow and her *b.*   4
I will bring you into *b. Ezek* 20:37
be loosed from his *b.* *Luke* 13:16
in the *b.* of iniquity. *Acts* 8:23
baptized into one body, or free.
  1 Cor 12:13
unity of the Spirit, in *b.* *Eph* 4:3
put on charity, the *b.* of. *Col* 3:14

see free
bondage
[1] *Slavery, Ex* 2:23; *Ezra* 9:8, 9.
[2] *Subjection to sin,* Gal 4:3.
[3] *Subjection to the ceremonial law,* Gal 2:4.

lives bitter with hard *b.*   *Ex* 1:14
Israel sighed by reason of the *b.*
  cried to God by reason of *b.* 2:23
I will rid you out of their *b.*   6:6
not to Moses for cruel *b.*
ye came out of the house of *b.* 13:3
Lord brought us out of *b.* 14; 20:2
  Deut 5:6; 6:12; 8:14; 13:5, 10
  Josh 24:17; *Judg* 6:8
laid upon us hard *b.* *Deut* 26:6
bring into *b.* our sons and daughters,
  some are brought into *b. Neh* 5:5
because the *b.* was heavy.   18
a captain to return to *b.*   9:17
rest from thy hard *b.* *Isa* 14:3
not received spirit of *b. Rom* 8:15
delivered from *b.* of.   21
Sinai, which gendereth to *b. Gal* 4:24
be not entangled with yoke of *b.* 5:1
all their life subject to *b. Heb* 2:15

in, into, or under bondage
the Egyptians keep in *b.*   *Ex* 6:5
a little reviving in our *b. Ezra* 9:8
God hath not forsaken us in *b.* 9
we were never in *b.* *John* 8:33
should bring them into *b. Acts* 7:6
nation to whom they be in *b.*   7
or sister not under *b.* *1 Cor* 7:15
a man bring you into *b. 2 Cor* 11:20

---

bring us into *b.*   *Gal* 2:4
were in *b.* under the elements. 4:3
ye desire again to be in *b.*   9
to Jerusalem, which is in *b.*   25
is he brought into *b.* *2 Pet* 2:19

bondmaid, -s
whoso lieth with a *b.*   *Lev* 19:20
b. shall be heathen, buy ye *b.* 25:44
one by a *b.* the other by. *Gal* 4:22*

bondman
abide instead of lad a *b. Gen* 44:33
thou wast a *b.* the Lord redeemed.
  Deut 15:15; 16:12; 24:18, 22
every *b.* hid themselves. *Rev* 6:15

bondmen
he may take us for *b.* *Gen* 43:18
we will be my lord's *b.*   44:9
shall not be sold as *b.* *Lev* 25:42
b. of the heathen, of them buy *b.* 44
they shall be your *b.* for ever. 46
that ye should not be their *b.* 26:13
we were Pharaoh's *b.* *Deut* 6:21
you out of house of *b.*   7:8*
there ye shall be sold for *b.* 28:68
of you freed from *b.* *Josh* 9:23
Solomon made no *b.* *1 Ki* 9:22
to take my two sons to be *b. 2 Ki* 4:1
children of Judah for *b. 2 Chr* 28:10
we were *b.* yet God hath. *Ezra* 9:9
if we had been sold for *b. Esth* 7:4
out of the house of *b. Jer* 34:13*

bonds
not any of her vows or *b. Num* 30:5
b. wherewith she bound her.   7
he established all her *b.*   14
he looseth *b.* of kings. *Job* 12:18
thou hast loosed my *b. Ps* 116:16
the yoke, and burst the *b. Jer* 5:5*
make thee *b.* and yokes. 27:2*
his yoke, and burst thy *b.* 30:8*
I will burst *b.* in sunder. *Nah* 1:13
b. with afflictions abide. *Acts* 20:23
worthy of death or *b.* 23:29; 26:31
a certain man left in *b.* by. 25:14*
such as I am, except these *b.* 26:29
I am an ambassador in *b. Eph* 6:20*
in *b.* ye are partakers of. *Phil* 1:7
b. in Christ are manifest.   13
waxing confident by my *b.*   14
supposing to add affliction to *b.* 16
for which I am in *b.*   *Col* 4:3
remember my *b.*   18
I suffer trouble, even to *b. 2 Tim* 2:9
I have begotten in my *b. Philem* 10
ministered to me in the *b.*   13
had compassion in my *b. Heb* 10:34
of *b.* and imprisonment. 11:36
remember them that are in *b.* 13:3

bondservant
him to serve as a *b.* *Lev* 25:39

bondservice
levy a tribute of *b.*   *1 Ki* 9:21

bondwoman
cast out this *b.* and her son, son of
  b. shall not. *Gen* 21:10; *Gal* 4:30
not grievous because of *b. Gen* 21:12
son of the *b.* will I make.   13
son of the *b.* was born. *Gal* 4:23*
we are not children of the *b.* 31*

bondwomen, see bondmen

bone
this is *b.* of my bones. *Gen* 2:23
surely thou art my *b.*   29:14
break a *b. Ex* 12:46; *Num* 9:12
toucheth a *b.* of a man. *Num* 19:16
that I am your *b.*   *Judg* 9:2
are thy *b.* *2 Sam* 5:1; *1 Chr* 11:1
art thou not of my *b.* ? *2 Sam* 19:13
touch *his b.* and flesh. *Job* 2:5
my *b.* cleaveth to my skin. 19:20
arm be broken from the *b.* 31:22
soft tongue breaketh *b.* *Pr* 25:15
bones came together, *b.* to his *b.*
  Ezek 37:7
when any seeth a man's *b.* 37:8
a *b.* shall not be broken. *John* 19:36

bones
(Sometimes used as meaning the whole body)
Moses took the *b.* of. *Ex* 13:19
the *b.* of Joseph.   *Josh* 24:32

divided his concubine with her *b*.
         Judg 19:29*
took the *b*. of Saul, *b*. 2 *Sam* 21:12
b. of Saul and Jonathan buried. 14
men's *b*. shall be burnt. *1 Ki* 13:2
touched the *b*. of Elisha. *2 Ki* 13:21
filled the places with *b*. of.   23:14
and took the *b*. out of the.   16
he burnt men's *b*. upon altars. 20
he burnt the *b*. of the. *2 Chr* 34:5
hast fenced me with *b*. *Job* 10:11
b. thou hast broken may. *Ps* 51:8
God scattereth the *b*. of him. 53:5
our *b*. are scattered at grave's. 141:7
It shall be marrow to thy *b*. *Pr* 3:8
envy the rottenness of *b*. 14:30
a good report maketh the *b*. 15:30
pleasant words health to *b*. 16:24
a broken spirit drieth the *b*. 17:22
nor how the *b*. do grow. *Eccl* 11:5
Lord shall make fat thy *b*. *Isa* 58:11
your *b*. shall flourish. 66:14
bring the *b*. of the kings, *b*. of priests,
  b. of prophets, and *b*. *Jer* 8:1
I will scatter your *b*. *Ezek* 6:5
fill it with the choice *b*. 24:4
burn *b*. 5, 10
valley full of *b*. 37:1
can these *b*. live ? 3
prophesy upon these *b*, O ye dry *b*. 4
these *b*. are house of Israel, our *b*. 11
because he burnt *b*. of. *Amos* 2:1
burneth him, to bring out *b*. 6:10
they gnaw not the *b*. till. *Zeph* 3:3*
full of dead men's *b*. *Mat* 23:27
spirit hath not flesh and *b*.
      Luke 24:39

his bones
lay my *b*. beside his *b*. *1 Ki* 13:31
man move *his b*. so they let *his b*.
      2 Ki 23:18
his b. are full of sin of. *Job* 20:11
his b. are moistened with. 21:24
the multitude of *his b*. 33:19
and *his b*. that were not seen. 21
his b. as brass, *his b*. as iron. 40:18*
he keepeth all *his b*. *Ps* 34:20
let it come like oil into *his b*. 109:18
as rottenness in *his b*. *Pr* 12:4
hath broken *his b*. *Jer* 50:17
of his flesh and of *his b*. *Eph* 5:30
gave command concerning *his b*.
      Heb 11:22

my bones
carry up *my b. Gen* 50:25; *Ex* 13:19
ye are *my b*. and my. *2 Sam* 19:12
my b. beside his *b*. *1 Ki* 13:31
made all *my b*. to shake. *Job* 4:14
my b. are pierced in me. 30:17
my skin is black, *my b*. burnt. 30
O Lord, heal me, *my b*. are. *Ps* 6:2
all *my b*. are out of joint. 22:14
I may tell *my b*. 17
my b. are consumed. 31:10
my b. waxed old. 32:3
my b. shall say. Lord who ? 35:10
neither there rest in *my b*. 38:3
as with a sword in *my b*. 42:10
days consumed, *my b*. are. 102:3
by reason of groaning *my b*. 5
so will he break all *my b*. *Isa* 38:13
as a fire shut up in *my b*. *Jer* 20:9
is broken, all *my b*. shake. 23:9
he sent fire into *my b*. *Lam* 1:13
he hath broken *my b*. 3:4
rottenness entered *my b. Hab* 3:16

their bones
Israel shall break *their b. Num* 24:8
their b. and buried. *1 Sam* 31:13
buried *their b*. under. *1 Chr* 10:12
skin cleaveth to *their b*. *Lam* 4:8
shall be on *their b*. *Ezek* 32:27
lions brake all *their b*. *Dan* 6:24
skin and flesh from *their b*. *Mi* 3:2
they break *their b*. and chop. 3

bonnets
(Revised Version, headtires)
thou shalt make *b*. *Ex* 28:40
put the *b*. on them. 29:9; *Lev* 8:13
they made goodly *b*. *Ex* 39:28
Lord will take away *b*. *Isa* 3:20
they shall have linen *b*. *Ezek* 44:18

book
*(A record written in some perma-
nent form. Ancient books were
written on clay tablets, as in
Assyria; on sheets of papyrus
fastened together and (usually)
rolled on one or two sticks; or of
parchment in like form. Rarely
sheets were fastened together
somewhat like our books. The
word book is sometimes used
merely meaning record of any sort)*
a memorial in a *b*. *Ex* 17:14
blot me out of thy *b*. 32:32
sinned, will I blot out of my *b*. 33
write these curses in a *b. Num* 5:23
it is said in the *b*. of the wars. 21:14
a copy of his law in a *b. Deut* 17:18
made end of writing law in *b*. 31:24
in the book of Jasher. *Josh* 10:13
      2 Sam 1:18
seven parts in a *b*. *Josh* 18:9
Samuel wrote it in a *b. 1 Sam* 10:25
written in the *b*. of acts. *1 Ki* 11:41
Hilkiah gave the *b*. to. *2 Ki* 22:8
Hilkiah delivered me a *b*. 10
     2 Chr 34:15, 18
all the words of the *b*. *2 Ki* 22:16
the words written in *b*. 23:24
written in *b*. of kings. *1 Chr* 9:1
written in the *b*. of Samuel. 29:29*
acts of Solomon in *b*. *2 Chr* 9:29*
acts of Rehoboam in *b*. 12:15*
acts of Jehoshaphat in *b*. 20:34*
Shaphan carried *b*. to king. 34:16
words of the *b*. that is found. 21
curses that are written in the *b*. 24
search may be made in *b. Ezra* 4:15
Ezra opened the *b*. *Neh* 8:5
commanded to bring the *b. Esth* 6:1
Purim, and it was written in *b*. 9:32
they were printed in *b*. *Job* 19:23
adversary had written a *b*. 31:35*
in thy *b*. *Ps* 40:7; *Heb* 10:7
tears, are they not in thy *b*. ? *Ps* 56:8
let them be blotted out of *b*. 69:23
in thy *b*. all my members. 139:16
as the words of a *b*. *Isa* 29:11
b. is delivered to him that. 12
deaf shall hear words of the *b*. 18
now go and note it in a *b*. 30:8
seek ye out of *b*. of the Lord. 34:16
write the words in a *b*. *Jer* 30:2
that subscribed the *b*. of. 32:12*
take a roll of a *b*. 36:2
read in the *b*. 8
written the words in a *b*. 45:1
so Jeremiah wrote in a *b*. all. 51:60
and lo, a roll of a *b*. *Ezek* 2:9
one found written in *b. Dan* 12:1
O Daniel, seal the *b*. 4
b. of the vision of Nahum. *Nah* 1:1
a *b*. of remembrance. *Mal* 3:16
the *b*. of the generation. *Mat* 1:1
as it is written in the *b. Luke* 3:4
delivered to Jesus the *b*. of prophet
  Esaias, and he opened the *b*. 4:17
he closed the *b*. and gave it to. 20
in *b*. of Psalms. 20:42; *Acts* 1:20
it is written in the *b*. *Acts* 7:42
he sprinkled the *b*. *Heb* 9:19
what thou seest, write in *b. Rev* 1:11
a *b*. written within. 5:1
who is worthy to open the *b*. ? 2
no man was able to open the *b*. 3
he had in his hand a little *b*. 10:2
go and take the little *b*. 8
give me the little *b*. 9
I took the little *b*. 10
another *b*. was opened. the *b*. 20:12
if any take away from words of *b*.
      22:19*

see covenant

book *of the law*
plague not in *b*. of *law. Deut* 28:61
curses in this *b*. of the *law*. 29:21
statutes in this *b*. of the *law*. 30:10
take this *b*. of the *law*. 31:26
this *b*. of the *law*. *Josh* 1:8
in *b*. of the *law*. 8:31; *2 Ki* 14:6
have found in *b*. of the *law*. *2 Ki* 22:8
read in the *b*. of the *law*. *Neh* 8:8
are written in *b*. of the *law*. *Gal* 3:10

book *of life*
are written in *b*. of *life*. *Phil* 4:3
his name out of *b*. of *life*. *Rev* 3:5
not written in *b*. of *life*. 13:8; 17:8
b. opened, which is *b*. of *life*. 20:12
was not found in the *b*. of *life*. 15
written in Lamb's *b*. of *life*. 21:27
his part out of the *b*. of *life*. 22:19

book *of Moses*
is written in *b*. of *Moses*. *2 Chr* 25:4
as it is written in *b*. of *Moses*. 35:12
priests, as written in *b*. of *Moses*.
      Ezra 6:18
day they read in the *b*. of *Moses*.
      Neh 13:1
ye not read in the *b*. of *Moses* ?
      Mark 12:26

this **book**
this is the *b*. of generation. *Gen* 5:1
do all written in *this b. Deut* 28:58
      2 Chr 34:21
curses written in *this b*.
    Deut 29:20, 27
words of *this b*., not hearkened to
  the words of *this b*. *2 Ki* 22:13
perform words written in *this b*. 23:3
all that is written in *this b. Jer* 25:13
an end of reading *this b*. 51:63
are not written in *this b. John* 20:30
the prophecy of *this b*. *Rev* 22:7
keep the sayings of *this b*. 9
seal not prophecy of *this b*. 10
prophecy of *this b*. if any add, add to
  him plagues written in *this b*. 18
his part from things in *this b*. 19

books
of making many *b*. *Eccl* 12:12
the *b*. were opened. *Dan* 7:10
      Rev 20:12
I understood by *b*. the. *Dan* 9:2
could not contain the *b. John* 21:25
many brought their *b*. *Acts* 19:19
bring the *b*. especially. *2 Tim* 4:13
dead judged out of *b*. *Rev* 20:12

booth
as *b*. the keeper maketh. *Job* 27:18
Jonah made him a *b*. *Jonah* 4:5

booths
and Jacob made *b*. for. *Gen* 33:17
ye shall dwell in *b*. *Lev* 23:42
children of Israel dwell in *b. Neh* 8:14
Israel should dwell in *b*.   *Neh* 8:14
made *b*. 16

booty, -ies
b. the rest of the prey. *Num* 31:32
their camels shall be a *b. Jer* 49:32
thou shalt be for *b*. *Hab* 2:7
goods shall become a *b. Zeph* 1:13

border
Zebulun his *b*. shall. *Gen* 49:13
or touch the *b*. of the. *Ex* 19:12
it a *b*. of a handbreath, make a
  golden crown to the *b*. 25:25
Israel through his *b*. *Num* 21:23
ye shall point out your *b*. 34:8
slayer shall come without *b*. 35:26
Lord shall enlarge thy *b. Deut* 12:20
Lord made Jordan a *b*. *Josh* 22:25
buried Joshua in the *b*. of his inheritance in. 24:30; *Judg* 2:9
he went to recover his *b*. *2 Sam* 8:3*
Solomon reigned over kingdoms
  unto *b*. of. *1 Ki* 4:21; *2 Chr* 9:26
were able stood in *b*. *2 Ki* 3:21
brought them to the *b*. *Ps* 78:54
he will establish the *b*. *Pr* 15:25
into the height of his *b*. *Isa* 37:24
children come again to *b. Jer* 31:17
judge you in *b*. of. *Ezek* 11:10, 11
this shall be the *b*. whereby. 47:13
remove them from their *b. Joel* 3:6
might enlarge their *b*. *Amos* 1:13
their *b*. greater than your *b*. 6:2
have brought thee even to *b. Ob* 7
themselves against their *b. Zeph* 2:8
shall call them the *b*. of. *Mal* 1:4
Lord will be magnified from *b*. of. 5
if it were but the *b*. *Mark* 6:56
behind, and touched *b*. *Luke* 8:44

see east, south
border, *verb*
Hamath shall *b*. thereby. *Zech* 9:2

borders

the trees in all the *b.*   *Gen* 23:17
till they come to the *b.*   *Ex* 16:35
out nations, and enlarge *b.*   34:24
fringes in *b.* on fringe of *b.* a ribband.
         Num 15:38
until we passed *b.*   20:17; 21:22
they had *b.* and *b.* were. *1 Ki* 7:28†
Ahaz cut off the *b.* of.   *2 Ki* 16:17
I will enter lodgings of his *b.* 19:23*
thou hast set the *b.* of the. *Ps* 74:17
he maketh peace in thy *b.*   147:14
we will make the *b.* of. *S of S* 1:11*
I will make thy *b.* of.   *Isa* 54:12
for all thy sins, in thy *b.* *Jer* 15:13
shall be holy in the *b.*   *Ezek* 45:1
he treadeth within our *b.*   *Mi* 5:6
in the *b.* of Zabulon.   *Mat* 4:13
enlarge the *b.* of their garments. 23:5

bore, -ed

master shall *b.* his ear.   *Ex* 21:6
Jehoiada took chest *b.*   *2 Ki* 12:9
canst thou *b.* his jaw?   *Job* 41:2*

born again

except a man be *b. a.*   *John* 3:3, 5
ye must be *b. a.*   7
being *b. a.* not of.   *1 Pet* 1:23

see **first-born**

born, for *brought forth*

a child *b.* to him.   *Gen* 17:17; 21:5
I have *b.* him a son.   21:7
Rebekah came, who was *b.* 24:15
because I have *b.* him three. 29:34
because I have *b.* him six. 30:20
children which they have *b.?* 31:43
every son *b.* ye shall cast. *Ex* 1:22
law of her that hath *b.*   *Lev* 12:7
stranger shall be as one *b.* 19:34*
Israelites *b.* shall dwell in. 23:42
law for him that is *b.*   *Num* 15:29
b. in the wilderness.   *Josh* 5:5
as well stranger, as he *b.* 8:33*
the child that shall be *b.* *Judg* 13:8
city after name of Dan *b.* to. 18:29
daughter-in-law hath *b.*   *Ruth* 4:15
so that the barren hath *b.* *1 Sam* 2:5
fear not, thou hast *b.* a son. 4:20
child *b.* to thee shall.   *2 Sam* 12:14
a child shall be *b.* to.   *1 Ki* 13:2
the men of Gath *b.* in.   *1 Chr* 7:21
behold a son shall be *b.* 22:9
day perish wherein I was *b. Job* 3:3
yet man is *b.* to trouble as. 5:7
though man be *b.* like a wild. 11:12
thou the first man *b.?* 15:7
because thou wast then *b.?* 38:21
to people that shall be *b.* *Ps* 22:31
go astray as soon as they be *b.* 58:3
even children that should be *b.* 78:6
this man was *b.* there. 87:4, 6
that man *b.*   5
a brother is *b.* for.   *Pr* 17:17
a time to be *b.*   *Eccl* 3:2
b. in his kingdom.   4:14
for unto us a child is *b.* *Isa* 9:6
shall a nation be *b.* at once? 66:8
she that hath *b.* seven. *Jer* 15:9
woe is me, that thou hast *b.* 10
sons and daughters *b.* in this. 16:3
cursed be day wherein I was *b.* 20:14
where ye were not *b.* there. 22:26
in day thou wast *b. Ezek* 16:4
thy person in day thou wast *b.* 5
sons whom thou hast *b.* to me. 20
in the day that she was *b. Hos* 2:3
where is he that is *b.* king? *Mat* 2:2
where Christ should be *b.* 4
eunuchs which were so *b.* 19:12
had not been *b.* 26:24; *Mark* 14:21
holy thing that shall be *b. Luke* 1:35
to you is *b.* this day in city. 2:11
can a man be *b.* when? *John* 3:4
except a man be *b.* of water. 5
that *b.* of flesh is flesh, that *b.* of. 6
so is every one that is *b.* of. 8
they said to him, we be not *b.* 8:41
did sin, that he was *b.* blind? 9:2
wast altogether *b.* in sins, and? 34
for joy that a man is *b.* 16:21
to this end was I *b.* 18:37
tongue wherein we were *b. Acts* 2:8
in which time Moses was *b.* 7:20

Jew named Aquila *b.* in. *Acts* 18:2*
a Jew named Apollos *b.* at. 24*
I am a Jew *b.* in Tarsus. 22:3
I was free *b.* 28
children being not yet *b. Rom* 9:11
seen of me, as of one *b. 1 Cor* 15:8
of bond-woman, *b.*   *Gal* 4:23, 29
by faith Moses when *b. Heb* 11:23
as new *b.* babes desire. *1 Pet* 2:2
righteousness, is *b.* of. *1 John* 2:29*
the child as soon as *b.* *Rev* 12:4

born of *God*

b. not of blood, but *of God.*
           John 1:13
b. of God doth not commit sin, because *b. of God.*   *1 John* 3:9
one that loveth is *b. of God.* 4:7
Jesus is Christ is *b. of God.* 5:1
is *b. of God* overcometh. 4
is *b. of God* sinneth not. 18

born in *the house*

servants *b.* in his *house. Gen* 14:14
one *b.* in my *house* is my heir. 15:3
b. in the *house* circumcised. 17:12
           13, 23, 27
b. in the priest's *house. Lev* 22:11
servants *b.* in my *house. Eccl* 2:7

born in *the land*

stranger or *b.* in the *land. Ex* 12:19
the stranger as *b.* in the *land.* 48
b. in the *land* that blasphemeth.
           Lev 24:16*
stranger and *b.* in *land. Num* 9:14
whether is *b.* in *land.* 15:30*

born of *a woman, or women*

man that is *b. of a woman. Job* 14:1
that is *b. of a woman* that he? 15:14
he be clean *b. of a woman?* 25:4
them that are *b. of a woman.*
     Mat 11:11; *Luke* 7:28

borne

ark may be *b.* with them. *Ex* 25:14
that the table may be *b.* with. 28
which the house was *b. Judg* 16:29
I have *b.* chastisement. *Job* 34:31
enemy, then I could have *b. Ps* 55:12
for thy sake I have *b.* 69:7
surely he hath *b.* griefs. *Isa* 53:4
ye shall be *b.* upon her sides. 66:12
they must be *b.* because. *Jer* 10:5
because he hath *b.* it. *Lam* 3:28*
fathers sinned, and we have *b.* 5:7
hast *b.* thy lewdness. *Ezek* 16:58
b. their shame. 32:24; 36:6; 39:26
have *b.* the tabernacle of. *Amos* 5:26
which have *b.* burden. *Mat* 20:12
burdens, grievous to be *b.* 23:4
           Luke 11:46
sick of palsy, was *b.* of. *Mark* 2:3
hast *b.* him hence tell. *John* 20:15
he was *b.* of the soldiers. *Acts* 21:35
as we have *b.* image of. *1 Cor* 15:49
has *b.* and hast patience. *Rev* 2:3

see **witness**

borrow

every woman shall *b.* of. *Ex* 3:22*
           11:2*
if a man *b.* ought. 22:14
thou shalt not *b. Deut* 15:6; 28:12
go *b.* vessels abroad, *b.* *2 Ki* 4:3
him that would *b.* of thee. *Mat* 5:42

borrowed

they *b.* of Egyptians. *Ex* 12:35*
alas, master, for it was *b. 2 Ki* 6:5
we have *b.* money for. *Neh* 5:4

borrower

and the *b.* is servant to. *Pr* 22:7
with the lender, so with *b. Isa* 24:2

borroweth

wicked *b.* and payeth not. *Ps* 37:21

bosom

given my maid into thy *b. Gen* 16:5
put now thy hand into thy *b. Ex* 4:6
carry them in thy *b.* *Num* 11:12
the wife of thy *b.* entice. *Deut* 13:6
evil toward the wife of his *b.* 28:54
evil toward husband of her *b.* 56
child and laid it in her *b. Ruth* 4:16
lay in his *b.* *2 Sam* 12:3
thy master's wives into thy *b.* 8
let her lie in thy *b.* *1 Ki* 1:2

took my son, and laid it in her *b.* and
   laid dead child in my *b. 1 Ki* 3:20
Elijah took him out of her *b.* 17:19
hiding iniquity in my *b. Job* 31:33
prayer returned into my *b. Ps* 35:13
right hand out of thy *b.* 74:11
render seven-fold into their *b.* 79:12
bear in my *b.* the reproach. 89:50
he that bindeth sheaves, his *b.* 129:7
wilt thou embrace the *b.? Pr* 5:20
can a man take fire in his *b.?* 6:27
man taketh gift out of the *b.* 17:23
hideth his hand in *b.* 19:24*; 26:15*
a reward in the *b.* pacifieth. 21:14
anger resteth in the *b.* of. *Eccl* 7:9
carry the lambs in his *b. Isa* 40:11
even recompense into their *b.* 65:6
measure former work into their *b.* 7
iniquity of fathers into *b. Jer* 32:18
poured into mother's *b. Lam* 2:12
from her that lieth in thy *b. Mi* 7:5
good measure into your *b. Luke* 6:38
angels into Abraham's *b.* 16:22
Abraham, and Lazarus in his *b.* 23
in the *b.* of the Father. *John* 1:18
leaning on Jesus' *b.* a disciple. 13:23

Bosor, *see* **Balaam**

bosses

thick *b.* of his bucklers. *Job* 15:26

botch

(*Revised Version,* boil)
the Lord will smite thee with the *b.*
         Deut 28:27, 35

both

were *b.* naked.   *Gen* 2:25
the eyes of *b.* opened. 3:7
b. the daughters of Lot with. 19:36
b. of them made a covenant. 21:27
so they went *b.* of them. 22:8
deprived of you *b.* in one day? 27:45
they may judge betwixt us *b.* 31:37
cause of *b.* shall come. *Ex* 22:9
oath of the Lord be between *b.* 11
b. of them surely be put to death.
     Lev 20:11, 12; *Deut* 22:22
and Miriam, *b.* came. *Num* 12:5
Phinehas thrust *b.* through. 25:8
shall stand before Lord. *Deut* 19:17
they shall die *b.* of them. *1 Sam* 2:34
went out *b.* of them. 9:26
as we have sworn *b.* of us. 20:42
that might lay hand on *b. Job* 9:33
b. are abomination. *Pr* 17:15; 20:10
the Lord hath made even *b.* 20:12
knoweth the ruin of them *b.?* 24:22
better than *b.* is he that. *Eccl* 4:3
they shall *b.* burn together. *Isa* 1:31
land shall be forsaken of *b.* 7:16
and they are fallen *b.* *Jer* 46:12
b. twain shall come forth. *Ezek* 21:19
then I saw that they *b.* 23:13
do evil with *b.* hands. *Mi* 7:3
of peace between *b.* *Zech* 6:13
b. shall fall. *Mat* 15:14; *Luke* 6:39
frankly forgave them *b. Luke* 7:42
but Pharisees confess *b. Acts* 23:8
peace, who hath made *b. Eph* 2:14
he might reconcile *b.* unto God. 16
in *b.* I stir up your. *2 Pet* 3:1
b. were cast alive into. *Rev* 19:20

bottle

(*Ancient Eastern bottles were
generally the skins of the smaller
animals. Clay bottles made by the
potters were less common, but are
meant in some verses, as Jer* 19:1.
*Glass bottles were known in Egypt
and so probably to the Hebrews, but
were largely tear-bottles, in which
mourners collected their tears,
afterwards putting them into the
tombs. This custom is referred to in
Ps* 56:8)

took a *b.* of water. *Gen* 21:14
water was spent in the *b.* 15
she filled the *b.* 19
she opened a *b.* of milk. *Judg* 4:19
Hannah took a *b.* of. *1 Sam* 1:24
meet another carrying a *b.* 10:3
Jesse took a *b.* of wine. 16:20
fruits, a *b.* of wine. *2 Sam* 16:1
thou my tears into thy *b. Ps* 56:8

I am become like a *b.*   *Ps* 119:83
every *b.* shall be filled.   *Jer* 13:12
get a potter's earthen *b.*   19:1
break the *b.*   10
puttest thy *b.* to him.   *Hab* 2:15*

bottles
(Revised Version, wine-skins,
  except where marked *)
Gibeonites took wine *b.*   *Josh* 9:4
b. of wine which we filled.   13
Abigail took two *b.* of. *1 Sam* 25:18
ready to burst like new *b. Job* 32:19
or who can stay the *b.* of ?   38:37
empty his vessels, break *b. Jer* 48:12
sick with *b.* of wine.   *Hos* 7:5*
into old *b.* else *b.* break. *Mat* 9:17
  Mark 2:22; *Luke* 5:37, 38

bottom
they sank into the *b.* as.   *Ex* 15:5
pour blood beside *b.* of altar. 29:12
Lev 4:7, 18, 25, 30; 5:9; 8:15; 9:9
covereth the *b.* of the sea. *Job* 36:30
the *b.* thereof of gold. *S of S* 3:10
they came at the *b.* of.   *Dan* 6:24
hid from my sight in *b.*   *Amos* 9:3
I went down to the *b.* of. *Jonah* 2:6
myrtle-trees in the *b.*   *Zech* 1:8
top to *b.*   *Mat* 27:51; *Mark* 15:38

bottomless pit
(Revised Version, abyss)
given the key of the *b. pit. Rev* 9:1
he opened the *b. pit.*   2
a king, the angel of the *b. pit.* 11
that ascendeth out of *b. pit.* 11:7
beast shall ascend out of *b. pit.* 17:8
angel having key of the *b. pit.* 20:1
and cast him into the *b.*   3

bough
Joseph is a fruitful *b.* even a *b.* by a
  well.   *Gen* 49:22
Abimelech cut down a *b. Judg* 9:48
cut down every man his *b.*   49
the Lord shall lop the *b.*   *Isa* 10:33
berries in top of uttermost *b.* 17:6
strong cities be as a forsaken *b.* 9*

boughs
b. of goodly trees, *b.*   *Lev* 23:40*
shalt not go over *b.*   *Deut* 24:20
mule went under the *b. 2 Sam* 18:9
and brought forth *b.* like. *Job* 14:9
b. were like cedar-trees. *Ps* 80:10
she sent out her *b.*   11
I will take hold of the *b. S of S* 7:8
when the *b.* thereof are. *Isa* 27:11
it shall bring forth *b.*   *Ezek* 17:23
was among the thick *b.*   31:3, 14
made their nests in the. 6; *Dan* 4:12

bought
man-child born in house *b.* with his.
  Gen 17:12, 13, 23, 27; *Ex* 12:44
Jacob *b.* a field.   *Gen* 33:19
  Josh 24:32
Potiphar *b.* Joseph of the. *Gen* 39:1
money for the corn they *b.*   47:14
Joseph *b.* all land of Egypt. 20, 23
Abraham *b.* 49:30; 50:13; *Acts* 7:16
in hand of him that *b.* it. *Lev* 25:28
established for ever to him that *b.* 30
reckon with him that *b.* him. 50
the money that he was *b.* for. 51
sanctify a field which he *b.* 27:22
return to him of whom it was *b.* 24
father that *b.* thee ?   *Deut* 32:6
I have *b.* all that was.   *Ruth* 4:9
little ewe-lamb he had *b. 2 Sam* 12:3
David *b.* threshing-floor and. 24:24
Omri *b.* the hill Samaria. *1 Ki* 16:24
continued in work, nor *b. Neh* 5:16
I *b.* the field of Hanameel. *Jer* 32:9
fields shall be *b.* in this land. 43
I *b.* her to me for 15 pieces. *Hos* 3:2
all that he had, and *b.*   *Mat* 13:46
cast out them that sold and *b.* in.
  21:12; *Mark* 11:15; *Luke* 19:45
took counsel, and *b.* field. *Mat* 27:7
Joseph *b.* fine linen.   *Mark* 15:46
had *b.* sweet spices to come. 16:1
I have *b.* a piece of.   *Luke* 14:18
I have *b.* five yoke of oxen. 19
did eat, they drank, they *b.* 17:28
are *b.* with a price, *1 Cor* 6:20; 7:23
denying the Lord that *b.* *2 Pet* 2:1

---

bound, actively
b. Isaac his son, and laid. *Gen* 22:9
the midwife *b.* on his hand. 38:28
took Simeon and *b.* him.   42:24
he *b.* the ephod with.   *Lev* 8:7
she had *b.* her soul.   *Num* 30:4, 5
  6, 7, 8, 9, 10, 11
she *b.* a scarlet line in. *Josh* 2:21
they *b.* Samson with.   *Judg* 15:13
b. with withs.   16:8
b. with ropes.   12
b. with fetters.   21
he *b.* two talents of silver. *2 Ki* 5:23
he shut up Hoshea and *b.*   17:4
they *b.* Zedekiah with.   25:7
b. Manasseh.   *2 Chr* 33:11
b. Jehoiakim.   36:6
who hath *b.* the waters in. *Pr* 30:4
have *b.* and strengthened. *Hos* 7:15
Herod *b.* John.   *Mat* 14:3
  Mark 6:17
b. Jesus.   *Mat* 27:2; *Mark* 15:1
  John 18:12
daughter whom Satan *b. Luke* 13:16
Agabus *b.* his own.   *Acts* 21:11
as they *b.* Paul he said. 22:25*, 29
b. themselves under curse. 23:12
  14, 21
b. Satan a thousand years. *Rev* 20:2

bound, passively
king's prisoners are *b.*   *Gen* 39:20
prison where Joseph was *b.* 40:3
butler and baker which were *b.* 5
one of your brethren be *b.* 42:19
no cover *b.* on it.   *Num* 19:15
mightest be *b. Judg* 16:6, 10, 13
soul of my lord *b.*   *1 Sam* 25:29
thy hands were not *b.* *2 Sam* 3:34
if they be *b.* in fetters.   *Job* 36:8
being *b.* in affliction.   *Ps* 107:10
foolishness is *b.* in heart. *Pr* 22:15
b. by the archers, all are *b. Isa* 22:3
of prison to them that are *b.* 61:1
of my transgressions is *b. Lam* 1:14
b. in their coats.   *Dan* 3:21
fell down *b.*   23
did not we cast three men *b.* ? 24
be *b.* in heaven. *Mat* 16:19; 18:18
lay *b.* with them that.   *Mark* 15:7
b. hand and foot. face *b. John* 11:44
b. to Caiaphas.   18:24
bring them *b.*   *Acts* 9:2, 21; 22:5
Peter *b.* with chains.   12:6
behold I go *b.* in the Spirit. 20:22
I am ready not to be *b.* only. 21:13
left Paul *b.*   24:27
b. by law of husband.   *Rom* 7:2
  1 Cor 7:39
art thou *b.* unto a wife ? *1 Cor* 7:27
b. to thank God.   *2 Thes* 1:3; 2:13
the word of God is not *b. 2 Tim* 2:9
that are in bonds, as *b.*   *Heb* 13:3
loose the angels *b.*   *Rev* 9:14

bound with chains
which are *b.* with chains. *Ps* 68:6*
Zedekiah *b.* with chains.
  Jer 39:7; 52:11
Jeremiah *b.* with chains.   40:1
great men *b.* with chains. *Nah* 3:10
been often *b.* with chains. *Mark* 5:4
was kept *b.* with chains. *Luke* 8:29
Paul to be *b.* with two chains.
  Acts 21:33
I am *b.* with this chain.   28:20

bound up
his life is *b.* up in the. *Gen* 44:30
not been closed neither *b.* up. *Isa* 1:6
plead, that thou be *b.* up. *Jer* 30:13
it shall not be *b.* up.   *Ezek* 30:21
nor have ye *b.* up that.   34:4
the wind hath *b.* her up. *Hos* 4:19*
iniquity of Ephraim is *b.* up. 13:12
he *b.* up his wounds.   *Luke* 10:34

bound, substantive
to utmost *b.* of the.   *Gen* 49:26
take it to the *b.* thereof. *Job* 38:20
to waters set a *b.*   *Ps* 104:9
sand for the *b.* of the sea. *Hos* 5:10*
them that remove the *b.*

bounds
thou shalt set *b.* to the.   *Ex* 19:12
set *b.* about the mount.   23
I will set thy *b.* from the.   23:31

---

he set the *b.* of the.   *Deut* 32:8
hast appointed his *b.*   *Job* 14:5
compassed the waters with *b.* 26:10*
I have removed the *b.*   *Isa* 10:13
hast determined the *b.*   *Acts* 17:26

bountiful
he that hath a *b.* eye.   *Pr* 22:9
churl be said to be *b.*   *Isa* 32:5

bountifully
he hath dealt *b.* with me. *Ps* 13:6
the Lord hath dealt *b.*   116:7
deal *b.* with thy servant. 119:17
thou shalt deal *b.* with me. 142:7
soweth *b.* shall reap *b.* *2 Cor* 9:6

bountifulness
enriched to all *b.*   *2 Cor* 9:11*

bounty
gave of his royal *b.*   *1 Ki* 10:13
and make up your *b.* that the same
  might be ready as *b.* *2 Cor.* 9:5

bow, noun
[1] An instrument for shooting
  arrows, Gen. 27:3; 2 Ki 9:24. [2]
The rainbow, Gen 9:13, 14. [3]
Faith and patience, Gen 49:24.

set my *b.* in the cloud. *Gen* 9:13
the *b.* shall be seen.   14, 16
take, thy quiver and thy *b.* 27:3
I took of the Amorite with *b.* 48:22
his *b.* abode in strength.   49:24
with thy sword nor *b.* *Josh* 24:12
gave David his sword, *b. 1 Sam* 18:4
Judah use of the *b.*   *2 Sam* 1:18
b. of the *b.* Jonathan turned not. 22
a certain man drew a *b.* and smote
  the king. *1 Ki* 22:34; *2 Chr* 18:33
Jehu drew a *b.* with his full. 9:24
take *b.* and arrows, he took *b.* 13:15
put thy hand upon the *b.*   16
able to shoot with *b.*   *1 Chr* 5:18
armed with *b.* and shooting *b.* 12:2
my *b.* was renewed.   *Job* 29:20
I will not trust in my *b.* *Ps* 44:6
he breaketh the *b.* and.   46:9
there brake arrows of the *b.* 76:3
aside like a deceitful *b.*   78:57
gave them as stubble to *b. Isa* 41:2
escape to nations that draw *b.* 66:19
they shall lay hold on *b.* *Jer* 6:23
behold, I will break the *b.* 49:35
they shall hold the *b.*   50:42
he hath bent his *b.*   *Lam* 2:4
as appearance of the *b. Ezek* 1:28
I will smite thy *b.*   39:3
I will break *b.* of Israel. *Hos* 1:5
I will not save them by *b.*   7
I will break the *b.*   2:18
they are like a deceitful *b.* 7:16
he that handleth *b.*   *Amos* 2:15
thy *b.* was made naked. *Hab* 3:9
when I filled the *b.*   *Zech* 9:13
sat on the horse had a *b.* *Rev* 6:2

see bend, bent, battle-bow

bow, verb
nor serve, nor *b.* yourselves to their
  gods.   *Josh* 23:7; *2 Ki* 17:35
I *b.* myself in house of. *2 Ki* 5:18
they *b.* themselves.   *Job* 39:3
go down to dust, shall *b. Ps* 22:29
dwell in wilderness shall *b.* 72:9
b. thy heavens, O Lord.   144:5
and *b.* thine ear, to my. *Pr* 5:1*
evil *b.* before the good.   14:19
the strong men shall *b.* *Eccl* 12:3
and *b.* myself before ?   *Mi* 6:6
the perpetual hills did *b.* *Hab* 3:6

bow down
b. down, mother's sons *b.* down.
  Gen 27:29
shall thy brethren *b.* down ? 37:10
father's children shall *b.* down. 49:8
servants shall *b.* down to. *Ex* 11:8
shalt not *b.* down. 20:5; *Deut* 5:9
thou shalt not *b.* down to. *Ex* 23:24
up image to *b.* down to it. *Lev* 26:1
other gods to *b.* down.   *Judg* 2:19
I *b.* down in house of.   *2 Ki* 5:18
b. down thine ear. 19:16*; *Ps* 86:1
and let others *b.* down. *Job* 31:10
b. down thine ear. *Ps* 31:2; *Pr* 22:17

let us worship and b. down. Ps 95:6
without me they b. down. Isa 10:4
they stoop, they b. down. 46:2
and queens shall b. down. 49:23
have said, b. down. 51:23
is it to b. down his head ? 58:5
despised thee shall b. down. 60:14
ye shall all b. down to. 65:12
eyes darkened. b. down. Rom 11:10

bow knee
before him b. the knee. Gen 41:43
every knee shall b. Isa 45:23
Rom 14:11
I b. my knees unto Father. Eph 3:14
every knee shall b. Phil 2:10

bowed
and their children b. Gen 33:6
Leah with children b., Rachel b. 7
Joseph's brethren b. 43:26
Issachar b. his shoulder. 49:15
served other gods, and b. to them.
Josh 23:16; Judg 2:12, 17
he b. where he b. he fell. Judg 5:27
fell on her face and b. Ruth 2:10
Phinehas' wife b. 1 Sam 4:19
David b. himself. 20:41
Abigail b. 25:23, 41
David b. the heart of. 2 Sam 19:14
he b. heavens. 22:10; Ps 18:9
Bath-sheba b. 1 Ki 1:16, 31
not b. to Baal. 19:18; Rom 11:4
sons of the prophets b. 2 Ki 2:15
b. herself to ground. 4:37
b. themselves upon the. 2 Chr 7:3
the king and all present b. 29:29
b. to Haman. Esth 3:2
Mordecai b. not. 5
b. the knee before him. Mat 27:29*
spirit of infirmity, was b. Luke 13:11

bowed down
Abraham b. down. Gen 23:12
Joseph's brethren b. down. 42:6
43:28
did eat, and b. down to. Num 25:2
of the people b. down on. Judg 7:6
he his gods, and b. down. 2 Chr 25:14
I b. down heavily. Ps 35:14
I am b. down greatly. 38:6
our soul is b. down. 44:25
my soul is b. down. 57:6
raiseth those b. down. 145:14
146:8
haughtiness of men shall be b. down.
Isa 2:11
loftiness of man be b. down. 17
I was b. down at the hearing. 21:3*
were afraid and b. down. Luke 24:5

bowed head
man b. his head. Gen 24:26, 48
they b. their heads. 43:28
then they b. their heads and.
Ex 4:31; 12:27; Neh 8:6
Moses b. his head to earth. Ex 34:8
Balaam b. his head. Num 22:31
b. down their heads. 1 Chr 29:20
Jehoshaphat b. his head. 2 Chr 20:18
sang praises and b. heads. 29:30
Jesus b. his head and. John 19:30

bowed himself
Abraham b. himself. Gen 18:2; 23:7,
12
Lot b. himself. 19:1
Jacob b. himself. 33:3; 47:31
Joseph b. himself. 48:12
Samson b. himself. Judg 16:30
David stooped and b. himself.
1 Sam 24:8*
Saul b. himself. 28:14*
Mephibosheth b. himself.
2 Sam 9:8*
Joab b. himself. 14:22*
Absalom b. himself. 33
Cushi b. himself to Joab. 18:21
Araunah b. himself before king.
24:20; 1 Chr 21:21
Nathan b. himself. 1 Ki 1:23
the king b. himself on bed. 47
Adonijah came and b. himself. 53*
Solomon rose and b. himself. 2:19

bowels
(Used often in Scripture for the seat of pity or kindness)

out of thine own b. shall. Gen 15:4
people shall be from thy b. 25:23
for his b. did yearn. 43:30
water shall go into thy b. Num 5:22
which proceed of thy b. 2 Sam 7:12
son which came forth of my b. 16:11
Joab shed out Amasa's b. 20:10
for her b. yearned. 1 Ki 3:26
by disease of thy b. 2 Chr 21:15
the Lord smote him in his b. 18
his b. fell out. 19
that came of his own b. slew. 32:21
meat in his b. is turned. Job 20:14
my b. boiled, and rested not. 30:27
in the midst of my b. Ps 22:14
took me out of my mother's b. 71:6
let it come into his b. 109:18*
my b. were moved. S of S 5:4
my b. shall sound. Isa 16:11
the offspring of thy b. 48:19
from the b. of my mother. 49:1
is the sounding of thy b. ? 63:15
my b. my b. I am pained. Jer 4:19
therefore my b. are troubled. 31:20
O Lord, my b. are. Lam 1:20; 2:11
fill thy b. with this roll. Ezek 3:3
satisfy their souls, nor fill b. 7:19
Judas burst, and all his b. Acts 1:18
straitened in your b. 2 Cor 6:12*
long after you in b. of. Phil 1:8*
in Christ if there be any b. 2:1*
put on b. of mercies. Col 3:12*
the b. of the saints are. Philem 7*
receive him that is my own b. 12
yea, brother, refresh my b. 20*
and shutteth up his b. 1 John 3:17*

boweth
b. on his knees to drink. Judg 7:5
the mean man b. Isa 2:9

bowing
Eliezer b. himself to. Gen 24:52
set their eyes, b. down. Ps 17:11*
as a b. wall shall ye be. 62:3*
did spit upon him, b. Mark 15:19

bowl
each b. weighing seventy. Num 7:85
wringed the dew, a b. Judg 6:38
the golden b. be broken. Eccl 12:6
candlestick of gold with b. Zech 4:2
olive trees one on right side of b. 3

bowls
make b. to cover. Ex 25:29; 37:16
dishes and b. Num 4:7
b. and snuffers of pure. 1 Ki 7:50
1 Chr 28:17
that drink wine in b. Amos 6:6
shall be filled like b. Zech 9:15
pots in Lord's house like b. 14:20

bowmen
from the noise of the b. Jer 4:29

bows
b. are broken. 1 Sam 2:4
were armed with b. 1 Chr 12:2
army that drew b. 2 Chr 14:8
Uzziah prepared for them b. 26:14
I set the people with b. Neh 4:13
the other half held spears and b. 16
their b. shall be broken. Ps 37:15
with arrows and b. Isa 7:24
their b. shall dash young men. 13:18
every one of their b. Jer 51:56
they shall burn the b. Ezek 39:9

bowshot
him as it were a b. Gen 21:16

box
.(Revised Version, vial or cruse)
take this b. of oil. 2 Ki 9:1, 3
alabaster b. Mat 26:7; Mark 14:3
brake b. and poured. Mark 14:3
Luke 7:37

box-tree
the desert the pine and b. Isa 41:19
of Lebanon shall come, the b. 60:13

boy, -s
the b. grew, and Esau. Gen 25:27
they have given a b. Joel 3:3
streets shall be full of b. Zech 8:5

Bozrah
Jobab of B. reigned. Gen 36:33
Lord hath a sacrifice in B. Isa 34:6

with dyed garments from B. Isa 63:1
judgement is come from B. Jer 48:24
B. shall become desolation. 49:13
shall spread his wings over B. 22
shall devour palaces of B. Amos 1:12
together as sheep of B. Mi 2:12

bracelet, -s
when he saw b. Gen 24:30
thy signet, thy b. 38:18*, 25
were willing, brought b. Ex 35:22*
Num 31:50
the b. on his arm. 2 Sam 1:10
take away the chains, b. Isa 3:19
and I put b. Ezek 16:11

brake
the hail b. every tree. Ex 9:25
the people b. off the ear-rings. 32:3
cast tables and b. 19; Deut 9:17
they b. pitchers. Judg 7:19, 20
a piece of a millstone to b. 9:53
b. the withs as a thread. 16:9
b. new ropes. 12
Eli fell and his neck b. 1 Sam 4:18
mighty men b. through. 2 Sam 23:16
1 Chr 11:18
strong wind b. in pieces. 1 Ki 19:11
Baal's images b. they. 2 Ki 11:18
b. images, b. brazen serpent. 18:4
Josiah b. the images. 23:14
2 Chr 34:4
Arabians came and b. 2 Chr 21:17
shut up the sea when it b. ? 38:8
and b. up for it my decreed. 10*
there b. he the arrows. Ps 76:3
moreover, he b. the whole. 105:16
smote their vines, b. trees. 33
and the plague b. in. 106:29
out of darkness he b. their. 107:14
took the yoke and b. it. Jer 28:10
my covenant they b. through. 31:32
whose covenant he b. Ezek 17:16
spirit troubled and sleep b. Dan 2:1
smote the image and b. feet. 34, 45
the lions b. all their bones. 6:24
fourth beast devoured and b. 7:7
goat smote ram, and b. his. 8:7
blessed and b. Mat 14:19; 15:36
26:26; Mark 6:41; 8:6; 14:22
Luke 9:16; 22:19; 24:30
1 Cor 11:24
I b. the five loaves. Mark 8:19
she b. the box and poured. 14:3
their net b. Luke 5:6
he b. the bands. 8:29
soldiers b. the legs. of. John 19:32
saw that he was dead, b. not legs. 33

brake down
b. down image of Baal. 2 Ki 10:27
2 Chr 23:17
people went and b. down. 2 Ki 11:18
king of Israel b. down wall. 14:13
2 Chr 25:23; 36:19; Jer 39:8
52:14
he b. down the houses of. 2 Ki 23:7
he b. down high places. 8
b. down altars. 12, 15
Asa b. down images. 2 Chr 14:3
Uzziah b. down the wall of. 26:6
they b. down the altars. 34:4

brakest
the first table thou b. Ex 34:1
Deut 10:2
thou b. heads of. Ps 74:13, 14
leaned on thee, thou b. Ezek 29:7

bramble, -s
said all the trees to b. Judg 9:14
b. said, let fire come out of b. 15
nettles and b. shall come. Isa 34:13*
nor of a b.-bush gather. Luke 6:44

branch
knop and flower in one b. Ex 25:33
37:17
cut down a b. with. Num 13:23
his b. shooteth forth. Job 8:16*
and the tender b. thereof. 14:7
and his b. shall not be green. 15:32
above shall his b. be cut off. 18:16
dew lay all night upon my b. 29:19
the b. thou madest strong. Ps 80:15
righteous flourish as a b. Pr 11:28*
in that day shall b. of the. Isa 4:2
the Lord will cut off b. and. 9:14*

and a b. shall grow out. Isa 11:1
cast out like an abominable b. 14:19
cities be as an uppermost b. 17:9*
nor any work which b. or. 19:15*
the b. of terrible ones shall. 25:5*
the b. of my planting. 60:21
to David a righteous b. Jer 23:5
b. of righteousness grow. 33:15
they put the b. to their. Ezek 8:17
the vine tree more than b. ? 15:2
eagle took the highest b. 17:3*, 22*
out of a b. of her roots. Dan 11:7*
forth my servant the b. Zech 3:8
the man whose name is the b. 6:12
them neither root nor b. Mal 4:1
when b. is yet tender. Mat 24:32
    Mark 13:28
every b. that beareth not, and every
  b. that beareth. John 15:2
as the b. cannot bear fruit itself. 4
he is cast forth as a b. 6

branches

in vine were three b. Gen 40:10
the three b. are three days. 12
a bough, whose b. run over. 49:22
six b. come out of candlestick, three
  b. Ex 25:32; 37:18, 21
take b. of palm trees. Lev 23:40
    Neh 8:15
flame shall dry up his b. Job 15:30
she sent out her b. to. Ps 80:11*
fowls which sing among b. 104:12
Moab's b. are stretched. Isa 16:8
in the utmost fruitful b. 17:6
take away and cut down b. 18:5*
there shall he consume the b. 27:10
and the b. are broken. Jer 11:16
spreading vine whose b. Ezek 17:6
she was fruitful and full of b. 19:10
fire is gone out of a rod of her b. 14
not like the Assyrian's b. 31:8
of Israel, ye shall shoot b. 36:8
hew down trees, cut off b. Dan 4:14
consume Ephraim's b. Hos 11:6*
his b. shall spread. 14:6
my vine waste, b. Joel 1:7
have marred their vine b. Nah 2:2
be these two olive b. ? Zech 4:12
birds lodge in the b. Mat 13:32
    Luke 13:19
others cut down b. Mat 21:8
    Mark 11:8; John 12:13
shooteth out b. Mark 4:32
I am the vine, ye are b. John 15:5
root be holy, so the b. Rom 11:16
if the b. be broken off. 17, 19
boast not against the b. 18
God spared not the natural b. 21

brand, -s

he had set b. on fire. Judg 15:5
is not this a b. plucked. ? Zech 3:2

brandish

shall I b. my sword ? Ezek 32:10

brasen

(American Revision, brazen)
make b. rings. Ex 27:4
b. grate. 35:16; 38:4
their b. sockets twenty. 38:10
sodden in a b. pot. Lev 6:28
b. censers. Num 16:39
b. bars. 1 Ki 4:13
b. wheels. 7:30
made b. shields. 14:27
b. oxen. 2 Ki 16:17
brake the b. serpent. 18:4
b. sea Chaldees. 25:13; Jer 52:17
made a b. scaffold. 2 Chr 6:13
made thee this day b. Jer 1:18
make thee a fenced b. wall. 15:20
the b. bulls. 52:20
b. vessels. Mark 7:4

brass

(Modern brass, the alloy of copper
and zinc, is not meant by the name
in the Bible, as zinc was not then
known. The word is generally used
of a simple metal, and means copper. In other places it is properly
bronze, the alloy of copper and tin.
The word is very often used
figuratively to represent great
strength, or great hardness)

take gold, silver, b. Ex 25:3; 35:5
taches of b. 26:11; 36:18
cast five sockets of b. 26:37; 27:10
    17, 18; 36:38; 38:11, 17, 19
overlay altar with b. 27:2, 6; 38:2
net work of b. 27:4
pins of the court of b. 19
laver of b., foot of b. 30:18
work in gold, silver, b. 31:4; 35:32
rings of b. 38:5
overlaid the staves with b. 6
the b. of the offering was. 29
brasen altar, and grate of b. 39:39
made a serpent of b....a pole, when
  he beheld serpent of b. Num 21:9
hills thou mayest dig b. Deut 8:9
heaven over thy head be b. 28:23
bound with fetters of b. Judg 16:21
Goliath had an helmet of b.
    1 Sam 17:5, 38
and he had greaves of b. 6
David took much b. 2 Sam 8:8
    1 Chr 18:8
Hiram was worker in b. 1 Ki 7:14
cast pillars of b. 7:15; 2 Ki 25:13
chapiters of b. 1 Ki 7:16; 2 Ki 25:17
    Jer 52:22
bases of b. 1 Ki 7:27
plates of b. 30
lavers of b. 38; 2 Chr 4:16
pots and shovels of bright b.
    1 Ki 7:45
weight of the b. was not found.
    47; 2 Chr 4:18
Zedekiah with fetters of b. 2 Ki 25:7
carried b. to Babylon. 13; Jer 52:17
sound with cymbals of b. 1 Chr 15:19.
b. in abundance. 22:3; 29:7
prepared the b. for things of b.
    2 Chr 12:10
Rehoboam made shields of b.
    2 Chr 12:10
is my flesh b. ? Job 6:12
bones are as strong pieces of b. 40:18
Leviathan esteemeth b. as. 41:27
hath broken gates of b. Ps 107:16
in pieces the gates of b. Isa 45:2
for wood I bring b. for b. 60:17
that the b. of it may. Ezek 24:11
belly and thighs were of b. Dan 2:32
another third kingdom of b. 39
whose nails were of b. 7:19
his feet in colour polished b. 10:6
horn iron, and hoofs b. Mi 4:13
were mountains of b. Zech 6:1
provide neither gold nor b. Mat 10:9
sounding b. or cymbal. 1 Cor 13:1
feet like to fine b. Rev 1:15; 2:18
should not worship idols of b. 9:20

iron and brass

instructor in b. and iron. Gen 4:22
your heaven iron, your earth b.
    Lev 26:19
b. and iron which may. Num 31:22
shoes be iron and b. as. Deut 33:25
return with b. and iron. Josh 22:8
prepared b. and iron. 1 Chr 22:14, 16
to work in b. and iron. 2 Chr 2:7, 14
wrought in iron and b. to. 24:12
iron out of the earth, and b. Job 28:2
an iron sinew, and brow b. Isa 48:4
for b. gold, for iron silver. 60:17
they are b. and iron. Jer 6:28
    Ezek 22:18
they gather iron and b. Ezek 22:20
was iron, clay, b. Dan 2:35, 45
a band of iron and b. in. 4:15, 23
gods of silver, b. and iron. 5:4

vessels of brass

make all vessels of b. Ex 27:3
made vessels of b. 38:3
all vessels of b. Josh 6:19
vessels of b. and iron they put. 24
brought vessels of b. 2 Sam 8:10
    1 Chr 18:10
vessels of b. took they. 2 Ki 25:14
    Jer 52:18
the b. of all these vessels was without weight. 2 Ki 25:16; Jer 52:20
traded in vessels of b. Ezek 27:13
    Rev 18:12

bravery

will take away their b. Isa 3:18†

brawler, -s

(Revised Version, contentious)
a bishop must be no b. 1 Tim 3:3
to be no b. Tit 3:2

brawling

with b. woman in. Pr 25:24

bray, -ed

doth the wild ass b. Job 6:5
among the bushes they b. 30:7
though thou shouldest b. Prov. 27:22

breach

(A gap; a rupture; a breaking. Used
    literally and figuratively)
the midwife said, this b. Gen 38:29
b. for b. eye for eye. Lev 24:20
ye shall know my b. Num 14:34*
the Lord hath made a b. Judg 21:15
broken forth as the b. 2 Sam 5:20
Lord made a b. on Uzzah. 6:8*
    1 Chr 13:11*
any b. shall be found. 2 Ki 12:5
Lord our God made a b. 1 Chr 15:13
and there was no b. Neh 6:1
he breaketh me with b. upon b.
    Job 16:14
Moses stood in the b. Ps 106:23
but perverseness is a b. Pr 15:4
us make a b. therein. Isa 7:6
iniquity shall be to you as b. 30:13
the day the Lord bindeth up b. 26*
called repairer of the b. 58:12
people broken with a b. Jer 14:17
thy b. is great like sea. Lam 2:13
a city wherein is a b. Ezek 26:10

breaches

Asher abode in his b. Judg 5:17*
repaired b. of the city. 1 Ki 11:27
let them repair the b. 2 Ki 12:5
priests had not repaired the b. 6
masons to repair b. of. 12; 22:5
b. began to be stopped. Neh 4:7
heal the b. thereof. Ps 60:2
ye have seen the b. Isa 22:9
shall go out at the b. Amos 4:3
smite the great house with b. 6:11
I will close up the b. thereof. 9:11

bread

[1] The eatable made of grain,
Gen 3:19; 49:20. [2] All things
necessary for this life, Mat 6:11.
[3] Manna wherewith God fed the
children of Israel in the wilderness,
Neh 9:15; John 6:31.
(The word is used figuratively in
many ways. The best known is its
use for Christ in the term bread of
life)
king of Salem brought b. Gen 14:18
I will fetch a morsel of b. 18:5
Abraham took b. and gave to. 21:14
then Jacob gave Esau b. 25:34
savoury meat and b. to. 27:17
in land of Egypt was b. 41:54
people cried to Pharaoh for b. 55
set on b. 43:31
b. for his father. 45:23
his father's house with b. 47:12
give us b. 19
buy us and our land for b. 19
out of Asher his b. shall. 49:20
I will rain b. from heaven. Ex 16:4
in the morning b. to the full. 8, 12
giveth on the sixth day the b. 29
they may see the b. 32
he shall bless thy b. and. 23:25
and the b. in the basket. 29:32
if ought of the b. remain unto. 34
he set the b. in order. 40:23
he took a cake of oiled b. Lev 8:26
what remaineth of ye shall. 32
b. of their God. 21:6, 8, 17, 21, 22
nor from stranger offer b. 22:25
ye shall offer with the b. 23:18
women shall bake your b. 26:26
the continual b. shall be. Num 4:7
the people of the land are b. 14:9
b. nor water, our soul ... b. 21:5
my b. for my sacrifices. 28:2
man doth not live by b. only.
    Deut 8:3; Mat 4:4; Luke 4:4
met you not with b. and. Deut 23:4

ye have not eaten *b*. nor. *Deut* 29:6
all *b*. of their provision. *Josh* 9:5
this our *b*. we took hot for. 12
a cake of barley *b*. *Judg* 7:13
give *b*. to thy army. 8:6, 15
comfort thy heart with *b*. 19:5
and there is *b*. and wine. 19
visited his people giving *b*. *Ruth* 1:6
hired themselves for *b*. *1 Sam* 2:5
crouch to him for a morsel of *b*. 36
for the *b*. is spent in our. 9:7
took an ass laden with *b*. 16:20
but there is hallowed *b*. 21:4
b. is common. 5*
hallowed *b*. to put hot *b*. in day. 6
thou hast given him *b*. 22:13
shall I take my *b*. and my. 25:11
let me set a morsel of *b*. 28:22
Egyptian and gave him *b*. 30:11
fail one that lacketh *b*. *2 Sam* 3:29
if I taste *b*. or ought else till. 35
to every one a cake of *b*. 6:19
back and hast eaten *b*. *1 Ki* 13:22
after he had eaten *b*. and. 23
ravens brought *b*. and. 17:6
bring me, a morsel of *b*. 11
fed them with *b*. and. 18:4, 13
brought the man of God *b*. *2 Ki* 4:42
take you to a land of *b*. 18:32
Isa 36:17
Zabulon brought *b*. *1 Chr* 12:40
have not eaten the *b*. *Neh* 5:14
and gavest them *b*. from. 9:15
they met not Israel with *b*. 13:2
wandereth abroad for *b*. *Job* 15:23
thou hast withholden *b*. from. 22:7
offspring shall not be satisfied with *b*. 27:14
the earth, out of it cometh *b*. 28:5
his life abhorreth *b*. and. 33:20
nor his seed begging *b*. *Ps* 37:25
can he give *b*.? 78:20
feedest them with *b*. of tears. 80:5
eaten ashes like *b*. 102:9
and *b*. which strengtheneth. 104:15
satisfied them with the *b*. 105:40
let them seek their *b*. 109:10
will satisfy her poor with *b*. 132:15
b. eaten secret is pleasant. *Pr* 9:17
better than he that honoureth himself
and lacketh *b*. 12:9
land be satisfied with *b*. 11; 28:19
thou shalt be satisfied with *b*. 20:13
b. of deceit is sweet to a man. 17
he giveth of his *b*. to the poor. 22:9
eateth not the *b*. of idleness. 31:27
is not to swift. nor *b*. to. *Eccl* 9:11
cast thy *b*. upon the waters. 11:1
away the whole stay of *b*. *Isa* 3:1
for in my house is neither *b*. nor. 7
they prevented with their *b*. 21:14
the *b*. of adversity. 30:20
his *b*. shall be given him. 33:16
he baketh *b*. on coals. 44:15, 19
should not die, nor his *b*. fail. 51:14
money for that which is not *b*.? 55:2
seed to the sower, and *b*. to eater. 10
is it not to deal thy *b*. to? 58:7
nor have hunger of *b*. *Jer* 42:14
people sigh, they seek *b*. *Lam* 1:11
young children ask *b*. no man. 4:4
to be satisfied with *b*. 5:6
we gat our *b*. with peril of our. 9
thou shalt prepare thy *b*. *Ezek* 4:15
that they may want *b*. and water. 17
pride, fulness of *b*. 16:49
given his *b*. to the hungry. 18:7, 16
strangers when ye offer my *b*. 44:7
lovers that give me *b*. *Hos* 2:5
sacrifices shall be as the *b*. of. 9:4
given you want of *b*. *Amos* 4:6
not a famine of *b*. but of. 8:11
if one do.touch *b*. or. *Hag* 2:12
ye offer polluted *b*. *Mal* 1:7
these stones be made *b*. *Mat* 4:3
Luke 4:3
our daily *b*. *Mat* 6:11; *Luke* 11:11
if son ask *b*. will he give? *Mat* 7:9
take children's *b*. 15:26; *Mark* 7:27
whence have so much *b*.? *Mat* 15:33
Mark 8:4
had forgotten to take *b*. *Mat* 16:5
Mark 8:14
I spake not concerning *b*. *Mat* 16:11

not beware of leaven of *b*. *Mat* 16:12
Jesus took *b*. and blessed it. 26:26
Mark 14:22
came neither eating *b*. *Luke* 7:33
nothing for journey, neither *b*. 9:3
servants of my father's have *b*. 15:17
took *b*. gave thanks. 22:19; 24:30
known of them in breaking *b*. 24:35
two hundred penny-worth of *b*.
John 6:5
Moses gave you not that *b*. ... Father
giveth you the true *b*. *John* 6:32
the *b*. of God is he. 33
Lord, give us this *b*. 34
I am the *b*. of life. 35, 48
I am *b*. which came down. 41, 50, 58
he that eateth of this *b*. shall. 58
he that eateth *b*. with me. 13:18
fire and fish laid thereon and *b*. 21:9
Jesus then taketh *b*. and giveth. 13
continued in breaking of *b*. *Acts* 2:42
and breaking *b*. from house. 46
the disciples came to break *b*. 20:7
when he had broken *b*. and eaten. 11
he took *b*. and gave thanks. 27:35
b. we break, is it not? *1 Cor* 10:16
we being many are one *b*. 17
Lord Jesus, the same night in which
he was betrayed, took *b*. 11:23
minister *b*. to your food. *2 Cor* 9:10

see affliction

bread corn
b. corn is bruised. *Isa* 28:28

bread, with *eat*
sweat of thy face eat *b*. *Gen* 3:19
Lord will give me *b*. to eat. 28:20
called his brethren to eat *b*. 31:54
brethren sat down to eat *b*. 37:25
he had, save *b*. he did eat. 39:6
heard they should eat *b*. there. 43:25
Egyptians might not eat *b*. with. 32
him that he may eat *b*. *Ex* 2:20
and when we did eat *b*. 16:3
b. Lord hath given you to eat. 15
came to eat *b*. with. 18:12
did not eat *b*. forty days. 34:28
Deut 9:9, 18
there eat it, with the *b*. *Lev* 8:31
he shall eat the *b*. of his God. 21:22
ye shall neither eat *b*. nor. 23:14
ye shall eat your *b*. to the full. 26:5
when ye eat the *b*. of. *Num* 15:19
thou shalt eat *b*. without. *Deut* 8:9
I will not eat thy *b*. *Judg* 13:16
come thou, and eat *b*. *Ruth* 2:14
eat *b*. at my table. *2 Sam* 9:7, 10
neither did he eat *b*. with. 12:17
set *b*. and he did eat. 20
didst rise and eat *b*. 21
b. and summer fruit to eat. 16:2
nor will I eat *b*. *1 Ki* 13:8, 16
charged me, saying, eat no *b*. 9
come home with me and eat *b*. 15
arise, eat *b*. let thy heart. 21:7
constrained Elisha to eat *b*. *2 Ki* 4:8
b. and water, they may eat. 6:22
did eat of the unleavened *b*. 23:9
did eat *b*. before. 25:29; *Jer* 52:33
and did eat *b*. with Job. *Job* 42:11
eat up my people, as they eat *b*.
Ps 14:4; 53:4
who did eat of my *b*. hath. 41:9
that I forget to eat my *b*. 102:4
vain to sit up late, to eat the *b*. 127:2
they eat *b*. of wickedness. *Pr* 4:17
come, eat of my *b*. and drink of. 9:5
eat not the *b*. of him that hath. 23:6
if enemy hunger, give *b*. to eat. 25:21
go thy way, eat thy *b*. with. *Eccl* 9:7
we will eat our *b*. and wear. *Isa* 4:1
eat up thy harvest and thy *b*.
Jer 5:17
there they did eat *b*. together. 41:1
they eat their defiled *b*. *Ezek* 4:13
they shall eat *b*. by weight and. 16
eat *b*. with quaking. 12:18
eat *b*. with care. 19
and eat not *b*. of men. 24:17, 22
prince sit in it to eat *b*. before. 44:3
into Judah, there eat *b*. *Amos* 7:12
they that eat thy *b*. have. *Ob* 7
wash not when they eat *b*. *Mat* 15:2
not so much as eat *b*. *Mark* 3:20

b. they have nothing to eat. *Mark* 6:36
saw disciples eat *b*. with. 7:2, 5
Pharisee's house to eat *b*. *Luke* 14:1
is he that shall eat *b*. 15
b. that these may eat? *John* 6:5
place where they did eat *b*. 23
gave them *b*. from heaven to eat. 31
if any man eat of this *b*. he shall. 51
as often as ye eat this *b*. *1 Cor* 11:26
whosoever shall eat this *b*. and. 27
we eat any man's *b*.? *2 Thes* 3:8
quietness they work and eat *b*. 12

leavened **bread**
(*Bread leavened with yeast*)
who eateth *leav*. *b*. that. *Ex* 12:15
no *leav*. *b*. be eaten. 13:3
no *leav*. *b*. be seen. 7; *Deut* 16:3, 4
not offer blood with *leav*. *b*. *Ex* 23:18
shall offer *leav*. *b*. *Lev* 7:13

loaf, or *loaves of* **bread**
(*In the East, flat cakes like the
large, thin, American pilot bread*)
one *loaf* of *b*. with ram. *Ex* 29:23
give *loaf* of *b*. to people. *Judg* 8:5
three *loaves* of *b*. *1 Sam* 10:3
and give thee two *loaves* of *b*. 4
give me five *loaves* of *b*. 21:3
two hundred *loaves* of *b*. *2 Sam* 16:1
one of Israel a *loaf* of *b*. *1 Chr* 16:3

no **bread**
there was *no b*. in the. *Gen* 47:13
there is *no b*. and our. *Num* 21:5
there is *no* common *b*. *1 Sam* 21:4
for there was *no b*. there, but. 6
Saul had eaten *no b*. all the. 28:20
the Egyptian had eaten *no b*. 30:12
eat *no b*. nor. *1 Ki* 13:9; 17:22
away, and would eat *no b*. 21:4
that thou eatest *no b*.? 5
there was *no b*. for the. *2 Ki* 25:3
Jer 52:6
came, he did eat *no b*. *Ezra* 10:6
there is *no* more *b*. in. *Jer* 38:9
I ate *no* pleasant *b*. nor. *Dan* 10:3
it is because we have taken *no b*.
Mat 16:7, 8; *Mark* 8:16, 17
take *no* scrip, *no b*. no. *Mark* 6:8

piece, or *pieces of* **bread**
I may eat a *piece* of *b*. *1 Sam* 2:36
brought to a *piece* of *b*. *Pr* 6:26
for a *piece* of *b*. that man. 28:21
Jeremiah daily *piece* of *b*. *Jer* 37:21
ye pollute me for *pieces* of *b*.
Ezek 13:19

shewbread, *see* **shew**
staff of **bread**
broken *staff* of your *b*. *Lev* 26:26
brake whole *staff* of *b*. *Ps* 105:16
I will break *staff* of *b*. *Ezek* 4:16
5:16; 14:13

unleavened **bread**
(*Bread without yeast, used figuratively for purity*)
Lot did bake *unleav*. *b*. *Gen* 19:3
eat passover with *unleav*. *b*.
Ex 12:18; *Num* 9:11
seven days eat *unleav*. *b*. *Ex* 12:15
13:6, 7; 23:15; 34:18; *Lev* 23:6
Num 28:17; *Deut* 16:3
on fourteenth day eat *unleav*. *b*.
Ex 12:18
your habitations eat *unleav*. *b*. 20
take *unleav*. *b*. to hallow. 29:2
shall eat with *unleav*. *b*. *Lev* 6:16
wafers of *unleav*. *b*. *Num* 6:15
six days eat *unleav*. *b*. *Deut* 16:8
did bake *unleav*. *b*. *1 Sam* 28:24
did eat *unleav*. *b*. *2 Ki* 23:9
passover of *unleav*. *b*. *Ezek* 45:21
first day of *unleav*. *b*. *Mark* 14:12
came days of *unleav*. *b*. *Luke* 22:7
Acts 12:3
after days of *unleav*. *b*. *Acts* 20:6
with the *unleav*. *b*. *1 Cor* 5:8

see **basket, feast**

breadth
ark, and *b*. fifty cubits. *Gen* 6:15
through the land in the *b*. of. 13:17
b. of the court fifty cubits. *Ex* 27:18
a span the *b*. thereof. 28:6; 39:9
five cubits the *b*. thereof. 38:1

so much as a foot *b.*   *Deut* 2:5*
stones at an hair's *b.*   *Judg* 20:16
the *b.* of the Lord's house.   *1 Ki* 6:2
                 2 Chr 3:3
b. of the porch was thirty.   *1 Ki* 7:6
the *b.* of the altar was.   *2 Chr* 4:1
b. of the Lord's house.   *Ezra* 6:3
and the *b.* of the waters.   *Job* 37:10
hast thou perceived the *b.* ?   38:18
wings shall fill the *b.*   *Isa* 8:8
the *b.* of the building.   *Ezek* 40:5
b. of the entry.   11
the *b.* of the gate.   13, 20, 48
b. of the porch.   49
the *b.* of the tabernacle.   41:1
b. of the door.   2, 3
b. of side chambers.   5
b. of house was upward.   7
the *b.* of place left.   11
b. of face of the house.   14
the *b.* of the holy portion.   45:1
the *b.* of the image.   *Dan* 3:1
march through *b.* of land.   *Hab* 1:6
Jerusalem, to see the *b.*   *Zech* 2:2
I see a flying roll, the *b.*   5:2
what is the *b.* and length.   *Eph* 3:18
they went up on the *b.*   *Rev* 20:9
length is as large as the *b.*   21:16

break

to Hebron at *b.* of day.   *2 Sam* 2:32
he talked till *b.* of day.   *Acts* 20:11

break

they came near to *b.*   *Gen* 19:9
thou shalt *b.* his yoke from.   27:40*
nor *b.* a bone. *Ex* 12:46; *Num* 9:12
shalt *b.* his neck.   *Ex* 13:13; 34:20
but ye shall *b.* their images.   34:13
vessel unclean ye shall *b.* *Lev* 11:33
I will *b.* the pride of your.   26:19
shall *b.* their bones.   *Num* 24:8
if a man vow, he shall not *b.*   30:2
ye shall *b.* their pillars.   *Deut* 12:3
b. away every man.   *1 Sam* 25:10
b. thy league with.   *1 Ki* 15:19
                 2 Chr 16:3
should we again *b.* thy.   *Ezra* 9:14
wilt thou *b.* a leaf ?   *Job* 13:25*
forgetteth wild beast may *b.* 39:15*
let us *b.* their bands.   *Ps* 2:3
shalt *b.* them with a rod of iron.   9
b. thou the arm of wicked.   10:15
b. their teeth, O God.   58:6
if they *b.* my statutes.   89:31
an oil which shall not *b.*   141:5*
day *b.* and shadows flee away.
          S of S 2:17*; 4:6*
I will *b.* the Assyrians.   *Isa* 14:25
b. the clods.   28:24
not *b.* it with a wheel.   28
b. it as a potter's vessel.   30:14
as a lion so will he *b.* all.   38:13
reed will he not *b.* 42:3; *Mat* 12:20
is not this the fast, ye *b.* ? *Isa* 58:6
shall iron *b.* the northern ? *Jer* 15:12
b. bottle, so will I *b.*   19:10, 11
will *b.* yoke of king. 28:4, 11; 30:8
he shall *b.* the images.   43:13
I will send wanderers and *b.* 48:12
saith Lord, I will *b.* bow of.   49:35
b. the staff of bread.   *Ezek* 4:16
            5:16; 14:13
as women that *b.* wedlock.   16:38
thou shalt *b.* sherds thereof. 23:34*
they took hold thou didst *b.*   29:7
I shall *b.* the yokes of Egypt. 30:18
I will *b.* Pharaoh's arms.   22, 24
I will *b.* the bow of Israel. *Hos* 1:5
I will *b.* the bow.   2:18
shall plow, Jacob shall *b.*   10:11
march and not *b.*   *Joel* 2:7
b. the bar of Damascus.   *Amos* 1:5
flay their skin, and *b.*   *Mi* 3:3
now will I *b.* his yoke.   *Nah* 1:13
that I might *b.* the.   *Zech* 11:14
b. one of these least.   *Mat* 5:19
else the bottles *b.* and the.   9:17*
came together to *b.*   *Acts* 20:7
mean ye to weep and to *b.* ? 21:13
bread we *b.* is it ?   *1 Cor* 10:16

break covenant

but that I may *b.* my cov. *Lev* 26:15
I will not *b.* my cov.   44
people will *b.* cov.   *Deut* 31:16, 20

I will never *b.* my cov.   *Judg* 2:1
my cov. will I not *b.*   *Ps* 89:34
remember, *b.* not thy cov. *Jer* 14:21
if you can *b.* my cov.   33:20
shall he *b.* cov.?   *Ezek* 17:15
that I might *b.* my cov. *Zech* 11:10

break down

b. down their images.   *Ex* 23:24
                Deut 7:5
shall *b. down* house.   *Lev* 14:45
I will *b. down* tower.   *Judg* 8:9
if a fox go up, *b. down.*   *Neh* 4:3
now they *b. down* the.   *Ps* 74:6
a time to *b. down* and.   *Eccl* 3:3
I will *b. down* the wall.   *Isa* 5:5
over them to *b. down.*   *Jer* 31:28
I have built will I *b. down.*   45:4
so will I *b. down* wall.   *Ezek* 13:14
b. down thy high places.   16:39
b. down the towers of Tyrus.   26:4
they shall *b. down* thy walls.   12
he shall *b. down* their.   *Hos* 10:2

break forth

lest Lord *b. forth.*   *Ex* 19:22, 24
they *b. forth* into singing. *Isa* 14:7
       44:23; 49:13; 54:1
b. forth into joy.   52:9
for thou shalt *b. forth* on the. 54:3
hills shall *b. forth* before.   55:12
then shall thy light *b. forth.*   58:8
north an evil shall *b. forth. Jer* 1:14
b. forth and cry.   *Gal* 4:27

break off

thou shalt *b.* his yoke *off. Gen* 27:40
b. off golden ear-rings. *Ex* 32:2, 24
O king, *b. off* thy sins by. *Dan* 4:27

break out

if fire *b. out.*   *Ex* 22:6
if leprosy *b. out.*   *Lev* 13:12
if the plague again *b. out.*   14:43
b. out the great teeth of.   *Ps* 58:6
wilderness waters *b. out.*   *Isa* 35:6
b. out, and blood.   *Hos* 4:2
lest he *b. out* like fire.   *Amos* 5:6

break in pieces

Chaldeans *b. in pieces.*   *2 Ki* 25:13
will ye *b.* me *in pieces* ? *Job* 19:2
shall *b. in pieces* mighty.   34:24
he shall *b. in pieces* the.   *Ps* 72:4
they *b. in pieces* thy people.   94:5
I will *b. in pieces* the gates. *Isa* 45:2
thee will I *b. in pieces.*   *Jer* 51:20
b. in pieces horse and rider.   21
with thee *b. in pieces* man.   21
b. in pieces and bruise. *Dan* 2:40, 44
fourth beast shall *b. in pieces.* 7:23

break through

lest they *b. through* to.   *Ex* 19:21
not priests and people *b. through.* 24
to *b. through* to the king. *2 Ki* 3:26
thieves *b. through.*   *Mat* 6:19
thieves *b.* not *through.*   20

break up

b. up fallow ground.   *Jer* 4:3
             Hos 10:12

breaker

b. is come up.   *Mi* 2:13
if a *b.* of law.   *Rom* 2:25

breakers

covenant *b.*   *Rom* 1:31

breakest

thou *b.* ships of Tarshish.   *Ps* 48:7

breaketh

let me go, for the day *b. Gen* 32:26
for he *b.* me with tempest. *Job* 9:17
he *b.* down, and it cannot.   12:14
he *b.* me with breach upon.   16:14
the blood *b.* out from.   28:4
b. the cedars.   *Ps* 29:5
he *b.* the bow.   46:9
my soul *b.* for the longing.   119:20
a soft tongue *b.* the bone. *Pr* 25:15
whoso *b.* an hedge, a.   *Eccl* 10:8
which is crushed *b. out.*   *Isa* 59:5
as one *b.* a potter's vessel. *Jer* 19:11
my word like hammer that *b.* ? 23:29
ask bread, no man *b.*   *Lam* 4:4
forasmuch as iron *b.* in. *Dan* 2:40*

breaking

wrestled a man till *b.* of. *Gen* 32:24
shall be a boil *b.* forth. *Ex.* 9:9, 10

---

if a thief be found *b.* up.   *Ex* 22:2
on enemies, like *b.*   *1 Chr* 14:11
upon me as a wide *b.*   *Job* 30:14
by reason of *b.* they.   41:25
that there be no *b.*   *Ps* 144:14
b. down walls, and of.   *Isa* 22:5
whose *b.* cometh suddenly.   30:13
shall break it as the *b.* of.   14
despised the oath in *b.* *Ezek* 16:59
                17:18
sigh, son of man, with *b.*   21:6
long in place of *b.*   *Hos* 13:13
known of them in *b.* of. *Luke* 24:35
continued in *b.* of bread. *Acts* 2:42
in the temple, *b.* bread from.   46
through *b.* the law.   *Rom* 2:23*

breast

take the *b.* of the ram.   *Ex* 29:26
shall sanctify *b.* of wave.   27
fat with *b., b.* be waved.   *Lev* 7:30
but the *b.* shall be Aaron's.   31
the wave-*b.* and heave-shoulder. 34
Moses took the *b.* and waved. 8:29
the wave-*b.* shall ye eat.   10:14
to the priest, with wave-*b. Num* 6:20
as wave-*b.* and right.   18:18
pluck fatherless from *b.*   *Job* 24:9
thou shall suck the *b.* of. *Isa* 60:16
sea monsters draw out *b. Lam* 4:3
head of gold, his *b.*   *Dan* 2:32
publican smote upon *b. Luke* 18:13
on Jesus' *b.* saith. *John* 13:25; 21:20

breastplate

[1] *A piece of embroidery about
ten inches square, of very rich work,
which the high-priest wore upon
his breast, and which was set with
four rows of precious stones, upon
every one of which was engraven
the name of one of the tribes of
Israel. It was double, or made of
two pieces folded one upon the
other, like a kind of bag, in which
were put the Urim and Thummim,*
Lev 8:8. [2] *A piece of defensive
armour,* Rev 9:9. *In which sense,
faith and love are called breastplates,* 1 Thes 5:8.

stones to be set in *b. Ex* 25:7; 35:9
make a *b.* and.   28:4, 15; 39:8
make upon the *b.* chains.   28:22
rings on ends of *b.* 28:23, 26; 39:16
bind *b.* by the rings.   28:28; 39:21
bear the names of Israel in *b.* 28:29
b. of judgement Urim. 30; *Lev* 8:8
put on righteousness as *b. Isa* 59:17
having on the *b.* of.   *Eph* 6:14
putting on the *b.* of.   *1 Thes* 5:8
b. as it were *b.* of iron.   *Rev.* 9:9
having *b.* of fire, of jacinth.   17

breasts

bless with blessings of *b. Gen* 49:25
put fat on the *b.*   *Lev* 9:20
b. Aaron waved.   8
the *b.* that I should suck. *Job* 3:12
his *b.* full of milk, and.   21:24
I was on mother's *b.*   *Ps* 22:9
let her *b.* satisfy thee.   *Pr* 5:19
all night betwixt my *b. S of S* 1:13
two *b.* like two young roes. 4:5; 7:3
thy *b.* are like two clusters.   7:7
thy *b.* shall be as clusters.   8
my brother that sucked the *b.*   8:1
a little sister, and she hath no *b.* 8
I am a wall and my *b.* like towers. 10
weaned from the *b.*   *Isa* 28:9
be satisfied with the *b.* of her. 66:11
thy *b.* are fashioned.   *Ezek* 16:7
there were their *b.* pressed.   23:3
and they bruised the *b.*   8
thou shall pluck off thine own *b.* 34
away adulteries from her *b. Hos* 2:2
miscarrying womb and dry *b.*   9:14
those that suck the *b.*   *Joel* 2:16
doves tabering on their *b. Nah* 2:7
the people smote their *b. Luke* 23:48
having their *b.* girded.   *Rev* 15:6

breath

(*Used figuratively many times for
the life of man, or the anger of God*)
his nostrils or the life.   *Gen* 2:7
flesh wherein is the *b.* of life.   6:17

breathe

and two wherein is b. of. Gen 7:15
all in whose nostrils was b. of.   22
foundations discovered, at blast of
b. of his. 2 Sam 22:16; Ps 18:15
and there was no b.   1 Ki 17:17
by the b. of his nostrils.   Job 4:9*
not suffer to take my b.   9:18
in whose hand is the b. of.   12:10
by the b. of his mouth.   15:30
my b. is corrupt, my days.   17:1*
my b. is strange to my wife.   19:17
all the while my b. is in me.   27:3
the b. of the Almighty hath.   33:4
gather to himself Spirit and b. 34:14
by b. of God frost is given.   37:10
his b. kindleth coals.   41:21
all of them made by b. of. Ps 33:6
takest away their b. they.   104:29
nor is there any b. in their. 135:17
his b. goeth forth.   146:4
every thing that hath b. praise. 150:6
they have all one b.   Eccl 3:19
cease from man, whose b. Isa 2:22
with b. of his lips will he slay. 11:4
his b. as an overflowing.   30:28
b. of the Lord like a stream.   33
your b. as fire shall devour.   33:11
giveth to the people upon it. 42:5
no b. in them. Jer 10:14; 51:17
the b. of our nostrils.   Lam 4:20
I will cause b. to enter.   Ezek 37:5
cover you with skin and put b.   6
there was no b. in them.   8
and say, come, O b.   9
and the b. came into them.   10
God in whose hand b. is. Dan 5:23
no strength, neither is there b. 10:17
there is no b. at all in.   Hab 2:19
giveth to all life and b. Acts 17:25

breathe

was not any left to b. Josh 11:11, 14
such as b. out cruelty.   Ps 27:12
come, O breath, and b.   Ezek 37:9

breathed

b. into man's nostrils the breath of
life.   Gen 2:7
destroyed all that b.   Josh 10:40
to Jeroboam any that b.   1 Ki 15:29
he b. on them and saith. John 20:22

breatheth, -ing

save alive nothing that b. Deut 20:16
not thine ear at my b.   Lam 3:56
Saul yet b. out.   Acts 9:1

bred

some left, and it b.   Ex 16:20

breeches

make them linen b. Ex 28:42; 39:28
priest shall put on linen b. Lev 6:10
he shall have the linen b.   16:4
they shall have linen b. Ezek 44:18

breed

they may b. abundantly.   Gen 8:17
rams of b. of Bashan.   Deut 32:14

breeding

as Sodom, even b. of.   Zeph 2:9*

brethren

[1] The sons of one father and
mother, or of either of them, Gen
42:13. [2] Those neighbours or
kinsmen who are closely banded
together, Gen 13:8; 19:7. [3]
Those who have made profession
of the same faith and religion,
Acts 6:3, etc.

be no strife, we be b.   Gen 13:8
Lot said, I pray you b. do not. 19:7
led me to my master's b.   24:27
said to her father and to her b. 34:11
Dinah's b. took each man his.   25
Joseph's ten b. went down.   42:3
b. came and bowed.   6
we are twelve b.   13, 32
Joseph's b. are come.   45:16
are b. of cruelty.   49:5
Joseph's b. saw their father. 50:15
possession among the b. Num 27:4
possession among our father's b. 7
no b. give it to his father's b. 10
if his father have no b. ye shall. 11
if b. dwell together.   Deut 25:5
brought out father and b. Josh 6:23

brethren

an inheritance among the b.Josh 17:4
went to his mother's b.   Judg 9:1
his mother's b. spake of him to. 3
answered, we are b.   2 Ki 10:13
there came of Saul's b. 1 Chr 12:2
sons of Shemaiah, whose b.   26:7
Elihu, one of the b. of David. 27:18
he had b. the sons.   2 Chr 21:2
when Jehu found the b.   22:8
pleasant for b. to dwell. Ps 133:1
soweth discord among b.   Pr 6:19
part of the inheritance among b. 17:2
all the b. of the poor do hate. 19:7
Jesus saw two b.   Mat 4:18
saw other two b.   21
hath forsaken houses, b.   19:29
indication against two b.   20:24
with us seven b. 22:25; Mark 12:20
your Master, and b.   Mark 23:8
no man hath left b. for my sake.
                  Mark 10:29; Luke 18:29
receive hundred-fold, b. Mark 10:30
and hate not children, b. Luke 14:26
for I have five b. that he.   16:28
betrayed by parents and b.   21:16
went abroad among b.   John 21:23
b. I wot that through.   Acts 3:17
wherefore b. look among.   6:3
sirs, ye are b.   7:26
which when the b. knew.   9:30
certain b. from Joppa.   10:23
moreover these six b.   11:12
determined to send relief to b. 29
these things to James and to b. 12:17
minds evil-affected against b. 14:2
men from Judea taught the b. 15:1
caused great joy to all the b.   3
and Silas chief among the b.   22
apostles and elders and b. send
greeting to b. of the Gentiles. 23
exhorted the b. 15:32; 1 Thes 5:14
let go in peace from the b. Acts 15:33
being recommended by the b.   40
well reported of by the b.   16:2
when they had seen the b.   40
drew Jason and certain b.   17:6
b. immediately sent Paul.   10, 14
Paul took his leave of the b. 18:18
the b. wrote exhorting to.   27
now b. I commend you to.   20:32
to Ptolemais and saluted b.   21:7
come to Jerusalem, b. received. 17
also I received letters to the b. 22:5
I wist not b. that he was.   23:5
where we found b. and were. 28:14
when the b. heard of us.   15
nor any of the b. that came.   21
you ignorant b.   Rom 1:13; 11:25
           1 Cor 10:1; 12:1; 1 Thes 4:13
know ye not b. that the law. Rom 7:1
b. we are debtors, not to.   8:12
first-born among many b.   29
b. my prayer to God for Israel. 10:1
I beseech you therefore b.   12:1
    15:30; 16:17; 1 Cor 1:10; 16:15
                Gal 4:12; Heb 13:22
salute the b. Rom 16:14; Col 4:15
ye see your calling b.   1 Cor 1:26
and I b. when I came to you.   2:1
I b. could not speak to you.   3:1
these things b. I have in a.   4:6
but this I say b.   7:29; 15:50
when ye sin so against the b. 8:12
and as the b. of the Lord.   9:5
now I praise you b.   11:2
how is it b. when ye?   14:26
seen of above 500 b. at once.   15:6
beloved b. be steadfast. 58; Jas 2:5
I look for him with the b. 1 Cor 16:11
I desired him to come with b.   12
the b. greet you.   20; Phil 4:21
yet have I sent the b.   2 Cor 9:3
I thought it necessary to exhort b. 5
the b. which came from.   11:9
in perils among false b.   26
finally b. farewell.   13:11
all b. that are with me.   Gal 1:2
because of false b.   2:4
peace to the b.   Eph. 6:23
many of the b.   Phil 1:14
to saints and faithful b.   Col 1:2
we beseech you b.   1 Thes 4:1, 10
                5:12; 2 Thes 2:1
ye do it toward all b.   1 Thes 4:10

b. pray for us. 1 Thes 5:25; 2 Thes 3:1
greet b. with holy kiss. 1 Thes 5:26
this epistle be read to the holy b. 27
put b. in remembrance.   1 Tim 4:6
intreat younger men as b.   5:1
despise them because they are b. 6:2
ashamed to call them b.   Heb 2:11
holy b. partakers, consider.   3:1
unfeigned love of b.   1 Pet 1:22
be of one mind, love as b.   3:8
because we love b.   1 John 3:14
lay down our lives for the b.   16
rejoiced greatly when b.   3 John 3
whatsoever thou dost to the b.   5
neither doth he receive the b.   10

his brethren

Ham told his two b.   Gen 9:22
a servant of servants to his b. 25
in presence of his b.   16:12; 25:18
his b. have I given to him.   27:37
feeding the flock with his b. 37:2
dreamed a dream and told his b. 5
his b. envied him.   11
Reuben returned to his b.   30
lest he die also as his b. did. 38:11
let the lad go up with his b. 44:33
nourished his father and his b. 47:12
separate from his b.   49:26
                          Deut 33:16
Joseph died, his b. and.   Ex 1:6
Moses went out to his b.... spied an
Egyptian smiting one of his b. 2:11
high-priest among his b.   Lev 21:10
one of his b. may redeem.   25:48
brought to his b.   Num 25:6
give his inheritance to his b. 27:9
no part with his b.   Deut 10:9
be not lifted up above his b. 17:20
he shall minister as all his b. 18:7
lest his b. heart faint as.   20:8
stealing any of his b.   24:7
nor did he acknowledge his b. 33:9
blessed and acceptable to his b. 24
Abimelech slew his b.   Judg 9:5
Gaal came with his b.   26
which he did in slaying his 70 b. 56
Jephthah fled from his b.   `11:3
be not cut off from his b. Ruth 4:10
anointed him in midst of his b.
                          1 Sam 16:13
when his b. and father's.   22:1
rise up from among his b. 2 Ki 9:2
honourable than his b.   1 Chr 4:9
Judah prevailed above his b.   5:2
Ephraim mourned, his b. came. 7:22
with his b. and sons were.   25:9
Jehoram slew all his b.   2 Chr 21:4
was accepted of his b.   Esth 10:3
fruitful among his b.   Hos 13:15
remnant of his b. shall.   Mi 5:3
his mother and his b.   Mat 12:46
                Mark 3:31; Luke 8:19
neither did his b. believe. John 7:5
was known to his b.   Acts 7:13
into Moses' heart to visit his b. 23
for he supposed his b. would.   25
to judge between his b.   1 Cor 6:5
made like to his b.   Heb 2:17

men and brethren

men and b. this scripture. Acts 1:16
men and b. let me freely.   2:29
to Peter and rest, men and b.   37
he said, men, b. and fathers. 7:2
men and b. if ye have any.   13:15
men and b. children of stock of. 26
be it known to you, men and b. 38
men and b. ye know God.   15:7
answered, men and b. hearken. 13
men, b. and fathers, hear my. 22:1
men and b. I have lived in all. 23:1
men and b. I am a Pharisee.   6
men and b. I have committed. 28:17

my brethren

my b. whence be ye?   Gen 29:4
set it here before my b. and. 31:37
I seek my b. tell me where.   37:16
my b. and father's.   46:31; 47:1
return to my b. in Egypt.   Ex 4:18
alive father and my b.   Josh 2:13
my b. made the heart of.   14:8
they were my b.   Judg 8:19
my b. I pray you, do not.   19:23
away, and see my b.   1 Sam 20:29

brethren

ye shall not do so, *my b.* 1 Sam 30:23
ye are *my b.* my bones. 2 Sam 19:12
said, hear me, *my b.* 1 Chr 28:2
Hanani, one of *my b.* Neh 1:2
I nor *my b.* nor guard put off. 4:23
I and *my b.* might exact. 5:10
and *my b.* have not eaten bread. 14
my b. dealt deceitfully. Job 6:15
he hath put *my b.* far from. 19:13
thy name unto *my b.* Ps 22:22
Heb 2:12
I am a stranger unto *my b.* Ps 69:8
for *my b.* and companions. 122:8
who are *my b.*? Mat 12:48
Mark 3:33
mother and *my b.* Mat 12:49
Mark 3:34
the least of these *my b.* Mat 25:40
go tell *my b.* that they go. 28:10
my b. are these which. Luke 8:21
go to *my b.* and say. John 20:17
from Christ for *my b.* Rom 9:3
take *my b.* the prophets. Jas 5:10
above all things, *my b.* swear not. 12

our brethren

before *our b.* discern. Gen 31:32
when *our b.* died before. Num 20:3
our b. have discouraged. Deut 1:28
have *our b.* stolen? 2 Sam 19:41
send abroad to *our b.* 1 Chr. 13:2
flesh is as flesh of *our b.* Neh 5:5
ability have redeemed *our b.* 8
us go again visit *our b.* Acts 15:36
or *our b.* be inquired of. 2 Cor 8:23
the accuser of *our b.* Rev 12:10

their brethren

minister with *their b.* Num 8:26
no inheritance among *their b.*
Deut 18:2
a prophet from among *their b.* 18
to the voice of *their b.* Judg 20:13
when *their b.* come to us. 21:22
from following *their b.* 2 Sam 2:26
bread among *their b.* 2 Ki 23:9
dwelt with *their b.* 1 Chr 8:32; 9:38
all *their b.* were at their. 12:32
drinking, for *their b.* had. 39
brought them to *their b.* 2 Chr. 28:15
cry against *their b.* Neh 5:1
to distribute to *their b.* 13:13
inheritance among *their b.* Job 42:15
slew them not among *their b.*
Jer 41:8
tithes of people, of *their b.* Heb 7:5
their b. should be killed. Rev 6:11

thy brethren

be lord over *thy b.* Gen 27:29
set it before *thy b.* 31:37
I and *thy b.* come to bow? 37:10
do not *thy b.* feed the flock? 13
whether it be well with *thy b.* 14
one portion above *thy b.* 48:22
he whom *thy b.* shall. 49:8
if a poor man of *thy b.* Deut 15:7
from among *thy b.* shalt thou. 17:15
will raise a prophet of *thy b.* 18:15
not oppress the poor of *thy b.* 24:14
thou shalt bring *thy b.* Josh 2:18
among daughters of *thy b.* Judg 14:3
thy b. run to camp to *thy b.*
1 Sam 17:17
look how *thy b.* fare. 18
return, take *thy b.* 2 Sam 15:20
hast slain *thy b.* 2 Chr 21:13
thy b. dealt treacherously. Jer 12:6
thy b. even *thy b.* Ezek 11:15
mother and *thy b.* stand. Mat 12:47
Mark 3:32; Luke 8:20
call not *thy b.* Luke 14:12
strengthen *thy b.* 22:32
not, I am of *thy b.* Rev 19:10; 22:9

your brethren

one of *your b.* be. Gen 42:19
leave one of *your b.* here. 33
carry *your b.* from before. Lev 10:4
let *your b.* bewail the burning. 6
over *your b.* ye shall not. 25:46
I have taken *your b.* the. Num 18:6
shall *your b* go to war and? 32:6
causes between *your b.* Deut 1:16
over armed before *your b.* 3:18
Josh 1:14
rest to *your b.* Deut 3:20; Josh 1:15

ye have not left *your b.* Josh 22:3
hath given rest to *your b.* 4
divide the spoil with *your b.* 8
fight against *your b.* 1 Ki 12:24
2 Chr 11:4
come to you of *your b.* and wrath
come upon *your b.* 2 Chr 19:10
captives of *your b.* 28:11
be ye not like *your b.* which. 30:7
if ye turn, *your b.* shall. 9
and fight for *your b.* Neh 4:14
will you even seil *your b.*? 5:8
your b. that hated you. Isa 66:5
bring *your b.* for an. 20
I have cast out all *your b.* Jer 7:15
say to *your b.* Ammi. Hos 2:1
if ye salute *your b.* only. Mat 5:47
a prophet of *your b.* Acts 3:22; 7:37
defraud and that *your b.* 1 Cor 6:8
accomplished in *your b.* 1 Pet 5:9

bribe, -s

Samuel's sons took a. 1 Sam 8:3
whose hand received any b.? 12:3*
right hand is full of b. Ps 26:10
shaketh his hands from b. Isa 33:15
they take a b. and turn. Amos 5:12

bribery

consume tabernacles of b. Job 15:34

brick

us make b. they had b. Gen 11:3
made their lives bitter in b. Ex 1:14
more give straw to make b. 5:7, 16
incense on altars of b. Isa 65:3

brickkiln

them pass through b. 2 Sam 12:31
stones in the clay in b. Jer 43:9*
make strong the b. Nah 3:14

bricks

the tale of b. you shall lay. Ex 5:8
yet shall ye deliver tale of b. 18, 19
the b. are fallen down. Isa 9:10

bride

them on thee, as b. doth. Isa 49:18
as b. adorneth herself. 61:10
as bridegroom rejoiceth over b. 62:5
a b. forget her attire? Jer 2:32
cease the voice of b. 7:34; 16:9
in this place voice of the b. 33:11
and let the b. go out. Joel 2:16
he that hath the b. is the. John 3:29
voice of the b. heard. Rev 18:23
prepared as a b. adorned. 21:2
I will shew thee the b. the. 9
the Spirit and the b. say. 22:17

bridechamber

children of the b. mourn? Mat 9:15
children of b. fast? Mark 2:19
Luke 5:34

bridegroom

as a b. coming out of. Ps 19:5
as a b. decketh himself. Isa 61:10
as b. rejoiceth over bride. 62:5
children mourn while b.? Mat 9:15
Mark 2:19; Luke 5:34
went forth to meet b. Mat 25:1
while the b. tarried. 5
cry made, b. cometh. 6, 10
governor of feast called b. John 2:9
hath the bride is the b. but friend of
b. rejoiceth because of b. 3:29

see bride

bridle

(*Used both literally; and figuratively for restraint*)
put my b. in thy lips. 2 Ki 19:28
Isa 37:29
have let loose the b. Job 30:11
to him with his double b.? 41:13
mouth must be held with a b. Ps 32:9
keep my mouth with a b. 39:1
a b. for the ass, a rod. Pr 26:3
there shall be a b. Isa 30:28
any seem religious and b. Jas 1:26
able also to b. the whole body. 3:2
blood came out of wine-press even
unto horse b. Rev 14:20

briefly

it is b. comprehended. Rom 13:9*
Sylvanus I have written b. 1 Pet 5:12

brier

instead of the b. come up. Isa 55:13
no more a pricking b. Ezek 28:24
best of them is as a b. Mi 7:4

briers

will tear your flesh with b. Judg 8:7
took the elders of the city and b. 16
there shall come up b. and. Isa 5:6
it shall even be for b. 7:23
land shall become b. and thorns. 24
not come thither the fear of b. 25
wickedness shall devour b. 9:18
devour his b. and thorns. 10:17
would set b. and thorns. 27:4
on the land shall come up b. 32:13
though b. and thorns be. Ezek 2:6
that which beareth b. and. Heb 6:8*

brigandine

(*Revised Version*, coat of mail)
put on the b. Jer 46:4
that lifteth up himself in his b. 51:3

bright

have a b. spot. Lev 13:2, 24, 38
if the b. spot be white in the skin. 4
if b. spot stay in his place. 23, 28*
vessels Hiram made were of b.
1 Ki 7:45*; 2 Chr 4:16
scattered his b. cloud. Job 37:11*
now men see not the b. light. 21
belly is as b. ivory. S of S 5:14*
make b. the arrows. Jer 51:11*
the fire was b. Ezek 1:13
the sword is made b. 21:15*
king of Babylon made arrows b. 21*
b. iron and cassia were in. 27:19
b. lights I will make dark. 32:8
horseman lifteth up b. Nah 3:3*
Lord make b. clouds. Zech 10:1*
behold a b. cloud. Mat 17:5
as when the b. shining. Luke 11:36
man stood before me in b. Acts 10:30
the b. and morning star. Rev 22:16

brightness

through b. before him were coals of
fire. 2 Sam 22:13; Ps 18:12
the moon walking in b. Job 31:26
we wait for b. but walk. Isa 59:9
kings shall come to the b. 60:3
nor for b. shall the moon give. 19
righteousness go forth as b. 62:1
a fire and a b. about it. Ezek 1:4, 27
so was the appearance of b. 28
as the appearance of b. as. 8:2
the court was full of b. 10:4
strangers shall defile thy b. 28:7
corrupted by reason of thy b. 17
great image, whose b. Dan 2:31
my honour and b. returned. 4:36
wise shall shine as the b. 12:3
be very dark and no b. Amos 5:20
his b. was as the light. Hab 3:4
from heaven above b. Acts 26:13
destroy with the b. 2 Thes 2:8
being the brightness of his. Heb 1:3

brim

feet of priest dipped in b. Josh 3:15*
b. like b. of a cup. 1 Ki 7:26
2 Chr 4:5
a molten sea from b. to b. 2 Chr 4:2
filled them up to the b. John 2:7

brimstone

(Sulphur)
rained b. Gen 19:24; Luke 17:29
the whole land is b. Deut 29:23
b. shall be scattered on. Job 18:15
upon wicked he shall rain fire and b.
Ps 11:6; Ezek 38:22
like a stream of b. Isa 30:33
and the dust turned into b. 34:9
issued fire and b. Rev 9:17
third part of men killed by b. 18
tormented with fire and b. 14:10
of fire, burning with b. 19:20; 20:10
shall have their part in lake which
burneth with fire and b. 21:8

bring

I do b. a flood of waters. Gen 6:17
two of every sort shalt thou b. 19
when I b. a cloud over earth. 9:14
Abraham did b. them. 18:16
the Lord may b. on Abraham. 19

b. to me that I may eat. Gen 27:4, 25
b. me venison. 5
I shall b. a curse on me. 5
b. your youngest brother. 42:20, 34
if I b. him not. 37; 43:9; 44:32
b. these men home. 43:16
take wagons and b. your. 45:19
b. them I pray to me. 48:9
else to-morrow I will b. Ex 10:4
yet will I b. one plague more. 11:1
the Lord shall b. thee. 13:5, 11
that thou mayest b. causes. 18:19
his master shall b. him to. 21:6
if it be torn in pieces, b. it. 22:13
thou shalt surely b. it back. 23:4
first of first-fruits shalt b. 19; 34:26
I will send an Angel to b. thee. 23:20
of a willing heart, let him b. 35:5
the people b. much more. 36:5
not able to b. a lamb. Lev 5:7, 11
12:8
he shall b. them to the priest. 5:8, 12
shall b. fire and incense. 16:12
that Israel may b. their. 17:5
shalt b. the Levites. Num 8:9, 10
Lord delight in us, he will b. 14:8
Lord was not able to b. 16
Deut 9:28
Caleb, him will I b. Num 14:24
b. before the Lord every man. 16:17
shall not b. this congregation. 20:12
give this land, and b. us not. 32:5
too hard for you, b. it to. Deut 1:17
when the Lord shall b. thee. 7:1
then thou shalt b. her home. 21:12
then thou shalt b. it unto. 22:2
b. it to us. 30:12, 13
hear, Lord, and b. Judah. 33:7
child be weaned, then I will b. him.
1 Sam 1:22
Saul, what shall we b. the man ? 9:7
b. the portion I gave thee. 23
b. the men, that we may. 11:12
why shouldest thou b. me ? 20:8
hand with thee, to b. 2 Sam 3:12
except thou b. Michal. 13
saith aught to thee, b. me. 14:10
are ye last to b. the king ? 19:11
and the king said, b. me. 1 Ki 3:24
the wicked, b. his way. 8:32
b. him back with thee. 13:18
b. me a morsel of bread. 17:11
he said, go ye b. him. 20:33
b. me a new cruse. 2 Ki 2:20
b. yet a vessel. 4:6
b. meal and cast it. 41
I will b. you to the man. 6:19
b. an offering and come. 1 Chr 16:29
of them to me, that I may b. 21:2
since people began to b. 2 Chr 31:10
did not our God b. ? Neh 13:18
did I say b. unto me. Job 6:22
wilt thou b. me into ? 10:9
who can b. a clean thing ? 14:14
b. him to the king of terrors. 18:14
I know thou wilt b. me to. 30:23
to b. back his soul. 33:30
b. me to thy holy hill. Ps 43:3
b. me into strong city ? 60:9; 108:10
the mountains shall b. peace. 72:3
he shall b. on them. 94:23
scornful men b. Pr 29:8
who shall b. him ? Eccl 3:22
know that God will b. 11:9
God shall b. every work. 12:14
I would b. thee into my. S of S 8:2
Lord shall b. on thee. Isa 7:17
the people shall b. them. 14:2
for I will b. more upon Dimon. 15:9
shall he b. to the ground. 25:12
tell ye and b. them near. 45:21
I b. near my righteousness. 46:13
them will I b. to my holy. 56:7
that thou b. the poor to thy. 58:7
for brass b. gold, for iron b. 60:17
b. their fear upon them. 66:4
I will take you and b. Jer 3:14
not in anger, lest thou b. 10:24
I will b. on them all the. 11:8
b. upon them, day of evil. 17:18
I will b. them from north. 31:8
I will b. on them all the good. 32:42
I will b. it health and. 33:6
them that shall b. sacrifice of. 11

behold, I will b. a fear upon. Jer 49:5
I, even I, will b. a sword. Ezek 6:3
I will b. you out of. 11:9
that I would not b. them. 20:15
I will b. on the necks of. 21:29
I will b. them against thee. 23:22
b. them to land. 34:13; 36:24; 37:21
that I would b. thee against. 38:17
I will allure and b. her. Hos 2:14
b. and let us drink. Amos 4:1
b. your sacrifices. 4
yet will I b. an heir to. Mi 1:15
I will b. them, and. Zech 8:8
b. all the tithes into the. Mal 3:10
be thou there till I b. Mat 2:13
therefore if thou b. thy. 5:23
b. him hither to. 17:17; Mark 9:19
ass and a colt, loose them and b.
Mat 21:2; Mark 11:2; Luke 19:30
and they b. to him. Mark 7:32
for I b. you good tidings. Luke 2:10
choked with tares, b. no fruit. 8:14
when they b. you into the. 12:11
them also I must b. John 10:16
and b. all things to your. 14:26
what accusation b. you ? 18:29
b. of the fish which ye have. 21:10
ye intend to b. this. Acts 5:28
that they should b. them. 7:6
b. them bound to Jerusalem. 9:2, 21
went to Damascus to b. them. 22:5
commanded to b. Paul into. 23:10
b. this young man to the chief. 17
I will b. to nothing. 1 Cor 1:19
b. to nought things that are. 28
shall b. you into remembrance. 4:17
keep under my body, b. it. 9:27
that ye may b. me on my. 16:6
ye suffer, if a man b. 2 Cor 11:20
schoolmaster to b. us. Gal 3:24
will God b. with him. 1 Thes 4:14
take Mark and b. him. 2 Tim 4:11
he might b. us to God. 1 Pet 3:18
if any come and b. not. 2 John 10
whom if thou b. forward. 3 John 6
kings do b. their glory. Rev 21:24
b. the glory of nations into it. 26

see home, hither

bring again
I b. thy son again ? Gen 24:5
thou b. not my son again. 6, 8
I will b. thee again. 28:15; 48:21
and b. word again. 37:14
I will b. him to thee again. 42:37
b. it back to him again. Ex 21:34
b. Aaron's rod again. Num 17:10
lodge this night, b. word again. 22:8
b. us word again what. Deut 1:22
in any case b. them again. 22:1
b. thee into Egypt again. 28:68
if ye b. me home again. Judg 11:9
and went to b. her again. 19:3
can I b. him again ? 2 Sam 12:23
b. young man Absalom again. 14:21
the Lord shall b. me again. 15:8
he will b. me again and shew me. 25
forgive and b. again. 1 Ki 8:34
2 Chr 6:25
b. kingdom again to Rehoboam.
1 Ki 12:21; 2 Chr 11:1
let us b. again the ark. 1 Chr 13:3
what word I shall b. again. 21:2
sent prophets to b. them again.
2 Chr 24:19
mightest b. them again. Neh 9:29
Lord said, I will b. again, I will b.
again my people. Ps 68:22
not b. it to his mouth again. Pr 19:24
grieveth him to b. it again. 26:15
I will b. again the shadow. Isa 38:8
b. it again to mind. 46:8
to b. Jacob again to him. 49:5
when the Lord shall b. again. 52:8
will b. them again. Jer 12:15; 50:19
then will I b. thee again. Jer 15:19
I will b. them again to their land.
16:15; 24:6; 32:37
I will b. them again into their. 23:3
in two years I will b. again the. 28:3
b. again to this place Jeconiah. 4, 6
I will b. again captivity. 30:3, 18
31:23; Ezek 39:25; Amos 9:14
b. again captivity of Moab. Jer 48:47

b. again captivity of Ammon. Jer 49:6
when I b. again their captivity, I will
b. again. Ezek 16:53
b. again the captivity of Egypt. 29:14
that time I b. you again. Zeph 3:20
I will b. them again. Zech. 10:6
I will b. them again out of. 10
b. me word again. Mat 2:8

see **captivity**
bring down
b. down my grey hairs. Gen 42:38
44:29, 31
b. your brother down. 43:7; 44:21
haste and b. down my father. 45:13
he shall b. them down. Deut 9:3
b. them down to the water. Judg 7:4
b. me down, I will b. thee down.
1 Sam 30:15
haughty, to b. down. 2 Sam 22:28
Solomon b. him down. 1 Ki 1:33
his hoary head b. thou down. 2:9
b. down high looks. Ps 18:27
shalt b. them down to pit. 55:23
b. down noise of strangers. Isa 25:5
he shall b. down their pride. 11
the high fort shall he b. down. 12
I will b. down their strength. 63:6
I b. down from thence. Jer 49:16
Ob 4
I will b. them down like. Jer 51:40
I shall b. thee down. Ezek 26:20
they shall b. thee down to pit. 28:8
I will b. them down. Hos 7:12
b. them down to valley. Joel 3:2
b. down thy strength. Amos 3:11
thence will b. them down. 9:2
who shall b. me down ? Ob 3
that he b. him down. Acts 23:15
desire thou wouldst b. down. 20
that is to b. Christ down. Rom 10:6

see **evil**
bring forth
let earth b. forth. Gen 1:11, 24
waters b. forth. 20
in sorrow thou shalt b. forth. 3:16
and thistles shall it b. forth. 18
b. forth every living thing. 8:17
b. forth abundantly in the. 9:7
Judah said b. her forth. 38:24
thou mayest b. forth. Ex 3:10
that I should b. forth Israel ? 11
may b. forth my armies. 7:4
the river shall b. forth frogs. 8:3
magicians did so to b. forth lice. 18
b. forth him that hath cursed.
Lev 24:14, 23
it shall b. forth fruit for. 25:21
ye shall eat and b. forth. 26:10
shalt b. forth water. Num 20:8
b. forth all tithe of. Deut 14:28
b. forth that man or woman. 17:5
b. forth the tokens of. 22:15
b. forth the men. Josh 2:3
till I come and b. forth. Judg 6:18
b. forth the man that came. 19:22
b. forth vestments for. 2 Ki 10:22
is no strength to b. forth. 19:3
Isa 37:3
b. forth all the vessels. 2 Ki 23:4
those did Cyrus b. forth. Ezra 1:8
it will bud and b. forth. Job 14:9
mischief, and b. forth vanity. 15:35
thou b. forth Mazzaroth ? 38:32
wild goats b. forth ? 39:1, 2, 3
surely the mountains b. forth. 40:20
b. forth thy righteousness. Ps 37:6
they shall still b. forth fruit. 92:14
that he may b. forth food. 104:14
that our sheep may b. forth. 144:13
what a day may b. forth ? Pr 27:1
that it b. forth grapes. Isa 5:2, 4
I travail not, nor b. forth. 23:4
conceive chaff, and b. forth. 33:11
b. forth your strong reasons. 41:21
let them b. forth and shew. 22
he shall b. forth judgement. 42:1
b. forth judgement unto truth. 3
b. forth blind people. 43:8
let them b. forth witnesses. 9
open, and b. forth salvation. 45:8
earth, and maketh it b. forth. 55:10
mischief, and b. forth iniquity. 59:4

and I will *b. forth* a seed. *Isa* 65:9
not labour in vain, nor *b. forth.*   23
earth be made to *b. forth* in ? 66:8
and not cause *to b. forth* ?   9
grow, they *b. forth* fruit.   *Jer* 12:2
b. forth out of mouth what.   51:44
b. forth thy stuff.   *Ezek* 12:4
and it shall *b. forth* boughs.   17:23
to *b.* them *forth* of the land.   20:6
I will *b.* them *forth* out of.   38
therefore will I *b. forth* a fire. 28:18
I will *b.* thee *forth* thine army. 38:4
shall *b. forth* new fruit.   47:12
Ephraim shall *b. forth.*   *Hos* 9:13
though thy *b. forth*, yet will I.   16
labour to *b. forth*, O Zion. *Mi* 4:10
he will *b.* me *forth* to the light.   7:9
before the decree *b. forth. Zeph* 2:2
I will *b. forth* my servant. *Zech* 3:8
shall *b. forth* the head-stone.   4:7
b. forth a curse, and it shall.   5:4
virgin shall *b. forth* a son.
                        Mat 1:21, 23
b. forth fruit meet.   3:8; *Luke* 3:8
cannot *b. forth* evil fruit. *Mat* 7:18
                        Luke 6:43
b. forth fruit, some 30. *Mark* 4:20
b. forth a son, and shall. *Luke* 1:31
word, keep it, and *b. forth* fruit. 8:15
b. forth the best robe. *Luke* 15:22
may *b. forth* more fruit. *John* 15:2
that you should *b. forth* fruit.   16
I *b.* him *forth* to you.   19:4
Easter to *b.* him *forth.*   *Acts* 12:4
that we should *b. forth.*   *Rom* 7:4
the motions of sin to *b. forth.*   5

bring in
I will *b.* you *into* the land. *Ex* 6:8
shall *b. in* and plant them.   15:17
prepare that they *b. in.*   16:5
Angel shall *b.* thee *in.*   23:23
them will I *b. in.*   *Num* 14:31
proclamation to *b. in* to the Court of
    collection Moses laid. *2 Chr* 24:9
ye shall not *b. in* the captives. 28:13
b. in no burden on the.   *Jer* 17:24
b. me *in* before the king. *Dan* 2:24
king cried to *b. in* astrologers.   5:7
b. in everlasting righteousness. 9:24
sown much and *b. in* little. *Hag* 1:6
means to *b.* him *in.*   *Luke* 5:18
b. in hither the poor, the.   14:21
b. in damnable heresies. *2 Pet* 2:1

bring out
b. them *out* to us. *Gen* 19:5, 8, 12
make mention, and *b.* me *out.* 40:14
God will visit and *b.* you *out.* 50:24
I will *b.* you *out* from.   *Ex* 6:6
charge to *b.* Israel *out* of. 13, 26, 27
           7:5; 12:51; *Jer* 31:32
mishief did he *b.* them *out. Ex* 32:12
lay hold and *b.* him *out. Deut* 21:19
b. out the damsel.   22:21
b. both *out* to the gate.   24
shall *b. out* the pledge.   24:11
b. out thence Rahab.   *Josh* 6:22
b. out those five kings.   10:22
b. out thy son that.   *Judg* 6:30
them I will *b. out.*   19:24
O *b.* thou me *out* of.   *Ps* 25:17
b. my soul out of prison.   142:7
O Lord, *b.* my soul *out.*   143:11
to *b. out* the prisoners. *Isa* 42:7
shall *b. out* the bones.   *Jer* 8:1
b. out all thy wives and.   38:23
I will *b.* you *forth out. Ezek* 11:7
b. you *out* from people. 20:34; 34:13
accept you, when I *b.* you *out.* 20:41
b. it *out* piece by piece.   24:6
burneth him to *b. out.* *Amos* 5:10
sought to *b.* them *out.* *Acts* 17:5

bring to pass
will shortly *b.* it *to pass. Gen* 41:32
to *b. to pass* as at this day. 50:20
he shall *b.* it *to pass.*   *Ps* 37:5
and *b. to pass* his act. *Isa* 28:21
I will also *b.* it *to pass.*   46:11

bring up
will also *b.* thee *up* again. *Gen* 46:4
and to *b.* them *up* out.   *Ex* 3:8
I have said, I will *b.* you *up* out. 17
see, thou sayest to me, *b. up.* 33:12

men that *b. up* evil.   *Num* 14:37
b. up Aaron and his son.   20:25
b. up an evil name.   *Deut* 22:14
did not the Lord *b.* us *up* ? *Judg* 6:13
b. him *up* in the bed.   *1 Sam* 19:15
whom shall I *b. up*, *b. up* ?   28:11
men did David *b. up.*   *2 Sam* 2:3
to *b. up* from thence the ark.   6:2
  1 Ki 8:1, 4; *1 Chr* 13:6; 15:3, 12
              14, 25; *2 Chr* 5:2, 5
since I did *b. up* Israel. *1 Chr* 17:5
did Sheshbazzar *b. up.*   *Ezra* 1:11
shall *b. up* tithes.   *Neh* 10:38
b. not forth children, nor nourish *up*
  young men, nor *b. up.*   *Isa* 23:4
then will I *b.* them *up.*   *Jer* 27:22
shall *b. up* a company. *Ezek* 16:40
I will *b. up* a company.   23:46
when I shall *b. up* the.   26:19
will *b.* thee *up* out of the midst. 29:4
a company shall *b.* thee *up.*   32:3
I will *b.* up flesh on you.   37:6
though they *b. up* children. *Hos* 9:12
I will *b. up* sackcloth.   *Amos* 8:10
to *b. up* Christ.   *Rom* 10:7
b. them *up* in nurture of.   *Eph* 6:4

bringers
the *b. up* of children.   *2 Ki* 10:5

bringest
and *b.* me into judgement. *Job* 14:3
O Jerusalem that *b.* good. *Isa* 40:9
thou *b.* strange things. *Acts* 17:20

bringeth
who *b.* you out from.   *Ex* 6:7
I am the Lord that *b.* you. *Lev* 11:45
b. it not to door of tabernacle. 17:4, 9
the Lord *b.* thee into.   *Deut* 8:7
b. down to the grave, and *b.* up.
                          1 Sam 2:6
Lord maketh poor, he *b.* low.   7
that *b.* down the people. *2 Sam* 22:48
and that *b.* me forth from.   49
into whose hand God *b.*   *Job* 12:6
he *b.* to light the shadow.   22
wrath is the punishments.   19:29
the thing that is laid *b.* he.   28:11
that *b.* forth his fruit.   *Ps* 1:3
b. back the captivity.   14:7; 53:6
Lord *b.* the counsel of the.   33:10
the man whom *b.* wicked.   37:7
he *b.* out them that are bound. 68:6
b. them out.   107:28
he *b.* them to their desired.   30
b, wind out of treasuries.   135:7
  Jer 10:13; 51:16
the mouth of the just *b.* *Pr* 10:31
moving his lips he *b.* evil.   16:30
a man's gift *b.* him.   18:16
son that causeth shame, and *b.* 19:26
a wise king *b.* the wheel.   20:26
much more when he *b.* it.   21:27
a child left, *b.* his mother. 29:15
he that delicately *b.* up servant. 21
the fear of man *b.* a snare.   25
b. forth butter, *b.* blood, *b.* 30:33
like ships, she *b.* her food. 31:14
water the wood that *b.* *Eccl* 2:6
Lord *b.* on them waters. *Isa* 8:7
b. down them that dwell on high, *b.*
    to dust.   26:5
b. the princes to nothing.   40:23
that *b.* out their host.   26
which *b.* forth the chariot.   43:17
the smith that *b.* forth.   54:16
for as the earth *b.* forth.   61:11
anguish of her that *b.*   *Jer* 4:31
which *b.* iniquity.   *Ezek* 29:16
Israel *b.* forth fruit.   *Hos* 10:1
which ground *b.* forth. *Hag* 1:11
that *b.* not forth good fruit is hewn
    down. *Mat* 3:10; 7:19; *Luke* 3:9
every good tree, *b.* forth. *Mat* 7:17
good man *b.* forth good things, evil
    man *b.* forth. 12:35; *Luke* 6:45
b. forth some an hundred. *Mat* 13:23
who *b.* out of his treasures.   52
Jesus *b.* them up into.   17:1
the earth *b.* forth fruit. *Mark* 4:28
good tree *b.* not forth.   *Luke* 6:43
if it die, *b.* forth. *John* 12:24; 15:5
gospel *b.* forth fruit.   *Col* 1:6
grace of God *b.* salvation. *Tit* 2:11
b. in the first-begotten.   *Heb* 1:6

the earth *b.* forth herbs.   *Heb* 6:7
lust *b.* forth sin, sin *b.*   *Jas* 1:15

see tidings

bringing
much observed for *b.*   *Ex* 12:42
people were restrained from *b.* 36:6
an offering *b.* iniquity.   *Num* 5:15
by *b.* up a slander upon.   14:36
of *b.* the king back. *2 Sam* 19:10, 43
navy *b.* gold and silver. *1 Ki* 10:22
                        2 Chr 9:21
I am *b.* such evil on.   *2 Ki* 21:12
on the sabbath *b.* in.   *Neh* 13:15
rejoicing, *b.* his sheaves. *Ps* 126:6
b. burnt-offerings, *b.*   *Jer* 17:26
made myself known in *b. Ezek* 20:9
his word by *b.* upon us.   *Dan* 9:12
to a nation *b.* forth.   *Mat* 21:43
b. one sick of the palsy. *Mark* 2:3
b. the spices which.   *Luke* 24:1
multitude *b.* sick folks.   *Acts* 5:16
b. me into captivity to.   *Rom* 7:23
and *b.* into captivity.   *2 Cor* 10:5
b. many sons unto glory. *Heb* 2:10
the *b.* in of a better hope.   7:19
b. in the flood on the.   *2 Pet* 2:5

brink
by the kine on the *b.*   *Gen* 41:3
ark in flags by river's *b.*   *Ex* 2:3
shalt stand by the river's *b.*   7:15
from Aroer by the *b.* of. *Deut* 2:36
when ye are come to *b.* of. *Josh* 3:8
caused me return to the *b. Ezek* 47:6

broad
make censers, *b.* plates. *Num* 16:38
make *b.* plates for the.   39*
repaired, and they fortified Jerusalem to the *b.* wall. *Neh* 3:8; 12:38
out of strait into *b.* place. *Job* 36:16
thy commandment is exceeding *b.*
                          Ps 119:96
in the *b.* ways I will seek. *S of S* 3:2
Lord will be place of *b.*   *Isa* 33:21
know and seek in the *b.*   *Jer* 5:1
the *b.* walls of Babylon.   51:58
chariots shall justle in *b.* *Nah* 2:4
b. is the way that leadeth. *Mat* 7:13
make *b.* their phylacteries.   23:5

broader
the measure is *b.* than.   *Job* 11:9

broidered
make a robe, a *b.* coat. *Ex* 28:4*
clothed thee with *b.*   *Ezek* 16:10
raiment was of silk and *b.*   13
tookest thy *b.* garments and.   18
princes put off *b.* garments.   26:16
linen with *b.* work from.   27:7
occupied in thy fairs with *b.*   16
merchants in blue clothes and *b.* 24
women adorn, not with *b. 1 Tim* 2:9

broiled
gave him a piece of *b.*   *Luke* 24:42

broken
b. my covenant. *Gen* 17:14; *Ps* 55:20
              Isa 24:5; 33:8; *Jer* 11:10
vessel wherein sodden, shall be *b.*
                            Lev 6:28
vessel that he touched be *b.* 15:12
man that is *b.* footed, or *b.* 21:19
that hath his stones *b.* let.   20
blind, *b.* or maimed.   22:22, 24
and I have *b.* the bands.   26:13
when I have *b.* the staff of.   26
because he hath *b.*   *Num* 15:31
were the horse-hoofs *b. Judg* 5:22
the withs, as a thread is *b.*   16:9
bows of the mighty are *b. 1 Sam* 2:4
a bow of steel is *b.*   *2 Sam* 22:35
                          Ps 18:34
the ships were *b.*   *1 Ki* 22:48
God hath *b.* in upon.   *1 Chr* 14:11
b. thy works, ships *b.* *2 Chr* 20:37
also he built wall that was *b.* 32:5
teeth of young lions are *b. Job* 4:10
my skin is *b.* and become.   7:5
I was at ease, but he hath *b.* 16:12
arms of fatherless have been *b.* 22:9
and wickedness shall be *b.*   24:20
and let mine arm be *b.* from. 31:22
the high arm shall be *b.*   38:15

thou hast *b.* the teeth of. *Ps* 3:7
forgotten, I am like *b.* vessel. 31:12
Lord is nigh them of *b.* 34:18; 51:17
keepeth his bones, not one is *b.* 34:2G
their bows shall be *b.* 37:15
arms shall be *b.* 17
I am feeble and sore *b.* 38:8
though thou hast *b.* us in the. 44:19
that the bones thou hast *b.* 51:8
sacrifices of God are a *b.* spirit. 17
the earth to tremble, hast *b.* 60:2
reproach hath *b.* my heart. 69:20
he hath *b.* the gates of brass. 107:16
he might even slay the *b.* 109:16
the snare is *b.* and we are. 124:7
he healeth the *b.* in heart. 147:3
suddenly shall he be *b.* *Pr* 6:15
sorrow of heart spirit is *b.* 15:13
a *b.* spirit drieth the bones. 17:22
is like a *b.* tooth and a foot. 25:19
cord is not quickly *b.* *Eccl* 4:12
golden bowl be *b.* or pitcher *b.* 12:6
nor latchet of shoes be *b.* *Isa* 5:27
sixty-five years Ephraim be *b.* 7:8
many shall fall and be *b.* 8:15
for thou hast *b.* the yoke. 9:4
the Lord hath *b.* the staff. 14:5
rod of him that smote thee is *b.* 29
shall be *b.* in the purposes. 19:10
all graven images he hath *b.* 21:9
might fall backward and be *b.* 28:13
he hath *b.* the covenant. 33:8
nor the cords thereof be *b.* 20
trustest in staff of this *b.* reed. 36:6
hewed out *b.* cisterns that. *Jer* 2:13
the children have *b.* crown. 16
of old I have *b.* thy yoke. 20
these have *b.* thy yoke. 5:5
all my cords are *b.* 10:20
the branches of it are *b.* 11:16
daughter of my people is *b.* 14:17
Coniah a despised *b.* idol ? 22:28
mine heart is *b.* because. 23:9
I have *b.* the yoke of the. 28:2
Hananiah, thou hast *b.* 13
may also my covenant be *b.* 33:21
how is the strong staff *b.* ? 48:17
the arm of Moab is *b.* 25
I have *b.* Moab like a vessel. 38
this Nebuchadnezzar hath *b.* 50:17
hammer of whole earth cut and *b.* 23
every one of their bows is *b.* 51:56
walls of Babylon be utterly *b.* 58
he hath destroyed and *b.* *Lam* 2:9
he hath *b.* my bones. 3:4
he hath *b.* my teeth. 16
altars, and images be *b.* *Ezek* 6:4, 6
because I am *b.* with their. 9
my covenant that he hath *b.* 17:19
her strong rods were *b.* 19:12
aha, she is *b.* that was the. 26:2
the east-wind hath *b.* 27:26
time when thou shalt be *b.* 34
I have *b.* the arm of Pharaoh. 30:21
strong and that which was *b.* 22
his boughs are *b.* by all. 31:12
be *b.* in the midst of the. 32:28
nor bound up that which was *b.* 34:4
bind up that which was *b.* 16
when I have *b.* the bands. 27
and they have *b.* my covenant. 44:7
kingdom partly strong, and partly *b.*
Dan 2:42
the great horn was *b.* 8:8
now that being *b.* whereas four. 22
shall be *b.* without hand. 25
his kingdom shall be *b.* 11:4
with flood be overthrown and *b.* 22
Ephraim is oppressed and *b.*
Hos 5:11
ship was like to be *b.* *Jonah* 1:4
and it was *b.* in that day. *Zech* 11:11
shall not heal that which is *b.* 16
took up of the *b.* meat. *Mat* 15:37
Mark 8:8
on this stone, shall be *b.* *Mat* 21:44
Luke 20:18
suffered house to be *b.* *Luke* 12:39
not only *b.* the sabbath. *John* 5:18
that law of Moses not be *b.* 7:23
and scripture cannot be *b.* 10:35
besought Pilate their legs be *b.* 19:31
a bone of him shall not be *b.* 36
so many, yet was not net *b.* 21:11

had *b.* bread and talked. *Acts* 20:11
gave thanks, when he had *b.* 27:35
but the hinder part was *b.* 41*
my body *b.* for you. *1 Cor* 11:24
as vessels shall they be *b.* *Rev* 2:27

broken *down*
oven or ranges *b. d.* *Lev* 11:35
aitar that was *b. d.* *1 Ki* 18:30
watch, that it be not *b. d.* *2 Ki* 11:6*
Hezekiah had *b. d.* *2 Chr* 33:3
Josiah had *b. d.* the altars. 34:7
wall of Jerusalem is *b. d.* *Neh* 1:3
viewed walls which were *b. d.* 2:13
why hast thou *b. d.* ? *Ps* 80:12
thou hast *b. d.* all his hedges. 89:40
the stone wall was *b. d.* *Pr* 24:31
like a city *b. d.* 25:28
b. d. the principal plants. *Isa* 16:8
the houses have ye *b. d.* 22:10
city of confusion is *b. d.* 24:10
the earth is utterly *b. d.* 19
cities were *b. d.* *Jer* 4:26
Moab *b. d.* 48:20, 39
foundations shall be *b. d.* *Ezek* 30:4
the barns are *b. d.* *Joel* 1:17
Christ hath *b. d.* middle. *Eph* 2:14

broken *forth*
how hast thou *b. forth* ? *Gen* 38:29
the Lord hath *b. forth.* *2 Sam* 5:20

broken *in*
God hath *b. in.* *1 Chr* 14:11

broken *off*
my purposes are *b. off.* *Job* 17:11
boughs are withered, they shall be
b. off. *Isa* 27:11
branches be *b. off.* *Rom* 11:17, 19
unbelief they were *b. off.* 20

broken *out*
leprosy *b. out* of the. *Lev* 13:20, 25

broken *in,* or *to pieces*
adversaries *b. in pieces.* *2 Sam* 2:10
rock, were *b. in pieces.* *2 Chr* 25:12
hast *b.* Rahab *in pieces.* *Ps* 89:10
ye shall be *b. in pieces.* *Isa* 8:9
potter's vessel *b. in pieces.* 30:14
Merodach is *b. in pieces.* *Jer* 50:2*
silver, gold, *b. to pieces.* *Dan* 2:35
of Samaria in *pieces.* *Hos* 8:6
and fetters been *b. in p.* *Mark* 5:4

broken *up*
the great deep *b. up.* *Gen* 7:11
city Jerusalem was *b. up.* *2 Ki* 25:4
Jer 39:2; 52:7
sons of Athaliah *b. up.* *2 Chr.* 24:7
the depths are *b. up.* *Pr* 3:20
of Chaldeans was *b. up.* *Jer* 37:11
they have *b. up* and. *Mi* 2:13
suffered house be *b. up* *Mat* 24:43
they had *b.* roof *up.* *Mark* 2:4
congregation was *b. up.* *Acts* 13:43

brokenhearted
to bind up the *b.* *Isa* 61:1
to heal *b.,* to preach. *Luke* 4:18

brood
as a hen gathers her *b.* *Luke* 13:34

brook
sent them over the *b.* *Gen* 32:23*
take willows of the *b.* *Lev* 23:40
came to *b.* Eshcol and. *Num* 13:23*
called, *b.* Eshcol because of. 24*
b. Zered, went over *b. Deut* 2:13, 14
and cast the dust thereof into *b.* 9:21
smooth stones out of *b. 1 Sam* 17:40
David came to the *b.* Besor. 30:9
king passed over the *b.* *2 Sam* 15:23
they be gone over the *b.* 17:20
day thou passest over the *b.* *1 Ki* 2:37
idol burnt by the *b.* Kidron. 15:13
2 Chr 15:16
hide thyself by *b.* Cherith. *1 Ki* 17:3, 5
he drank of the *b.* 6
brought them to the *b.* Kishon. 18:40
burnt the grove at the *b.* *2 Ki* 23:6
dust into *b.* Kidron. 12; *2 Chr* 30:14
find them at end of the *b. 2 Chr* 20:16
Levites carried it to the *b.* 29:16
people stopped the *b.* 32:4
went up by the *b.* and. *Neh* 2:15
dealt deceitfully as a *b.* *Job* 6:15
the willows of the *b.* compass. 40:22

as to Jabin at *b.* Kison. *Ps* 83:9*
he shall drink of the *b.* in. 110:7
wisdom as a flowing *b.* *Pr* 18:4
carry away to the *b.* *Isa* 15:7
fields to *b.* Kidron be holy. *Jer* 31:40
with his disciples over *b.* *John* 18:1

brooks
in Red sea and *b.* of. *Num* 21:14
at the stream of the *b.* that. 15*
to a land of *b.* of water. *Deut* 8:7
of the *b.* of Gaash. *2 Sam* 23:30
1 Chr 11:32
go unto all *b.* of water. *1 Ki* 18:5
and as the stream of *b.* *Job* 6:15
he shall not see the *b.* of. 20:17*
gold as stones of the *b.* 22:24
hart panteth after water *b.* *Ps* 42:1
b. of defence shall be. *Isa* 19:6*
paper reeds by the *b.,* by the *b.,*
every thing sown by the *b.* 7*
they that cast angle into the *b.* 8

broth
Gideon put the *b.* in a. *Judg* 6:19
angel said, pour out the *b.* 20
b. of abominable things. *Isa* 65:4

brother
(*For uses see* **brethren**)
hand of every man's *b.* *Gen* 9:5
Rebekah had a *b.* 24:29
gave also to her *b.* and mother. 53
told Rachel he was father's *b.* 29:12
to tell ye had yet a *b.,* have ye
another *b.* ? 43:6, 7; 44:19
her husband's *b.* shall. *Deut* 25:5
blood laid on their *b.* *Judg* 9:24
repented them for their *b.* 21:6
eating in their elder *b.* *Job* 1:13, 18
I am a *b.* to dragons. 30:29
and a *b.* is born for. *Pr* 17:17
he that is slothful is *þ.* to him. 18:9
a *b.* offended is harder to be. 19
friend that sticketh closer than *b.* 24
better neighbour near than *b.* 27:10
he hath neither child nor *b. Eccl* 4:8
trust not in any *b.* for *b.* will. *Jer* 9:4
for *b.* they may. *Ezek* 44:25
not Esau Jacob's *b.* ? *Mal* 1:2
b. shall deliver up the *b. Mat* 10:21
Mark 13:12
if a man's *b.* die and. *Luke* 12:19
Luke 20:28
Mary, whose *b.* Lazarus. *John* 11:2
comfort them concerning their *b.* 19
b. Saul, receive. *Acts* 9:17; 22:13
he killed James the *b.* of. 12:2
thou seest, *b.* how many. 21:20
and Quartus a *b.* *Rom* 16:23
if any man called a *b.* *1 Cor* 5:11
b. goeth to law with *b.* 6:6
if any *b.* hath a wife. 7:12
a *b.* or sister is not under. 15
thy knowledge shall weak *b.* 8:11
have sent with him the *b.* *2 Cor* 8:18
withdraw from every *b.* *2 Thes* 3:6
but admonish him as a *b.* 15
are refreshed by thee, *b.* *Philem* 7
but above a servant, a *b.* 16
his **brother**
and after that came *his b. Gen* 25:26
should give seed to *his b.* 38:9
his is dead. 42:38; 44:20
slay every man *his b.* *Ex* 32:27
for his father or *his b.* *Lev* 21:2
not make unclean for *his b. Num* 6:7
not exact of neighbour or *his b.*
Deut 15:2
thought to have done to *his b.* 19:19
succeed in name of *his b.* 25:6
shall be evil towards *his b.* 28:54
fear of Abimelech *his b. Judg* 9:21
for blood of Asahel *his b. 2 Sam* 3:27
but Solomon *his b.* *1 Ki* 1:10
usury every one of his *b.* *Neh* 5:7
none can redeem *his b.* *Ps* 49:7
shall take hold of *his b.* *Isa* 3:6
no man shall spare *his b.* 9:19
fight every one against *his b.* 19:2
every one said to *his b.* 41:6
no more every man *his b. Jer* 31:34
Heb 8:11
none serve of a Jew *his b. Jer* 34:9
let ye go every man *his b.* 14
liberty every one to *his b.* 17

because he spoiled *his b. Ezek* 18:18
speak every one to *his b.* 33:30
Jacob took *his b. Hos* 12:3
he did pursue *his b. Amos* 1:11
hunt every man *his b. Mi* 7:2
by the sword of *his b. Hag* 2:22
mercy every man to *his b. Zech* 7:9
none imagine evil against *his b.* 10
treacherously against *his b. ?*
Mal 2:10
shall say to *his b.,* Raca ! *Mat* 5:22
also to you, if ye from your hearts
forgive not every one *his b.* 18:35
raise seed to *his b.* 22:24
Mark 12:19; *Luke* 20:28
left his wife unto *his b. Mat* 22:25
he findeth his b. *John* 1:41
occasion to fall in *his b.* way.
Rom 14:13
no man defraud *his b. 1 Thes* 4:6
evil of *his b.* and judgeth *his b.*
Jas 4:11
and hateth *his b. 1 John* 2:9, 11
he that loveth *his b.* 10
he that loveth not *his b.* 3:10, 14
who was of that wicked one, and
slew *his b.* because *his b.* 3:12
hateth *his b.* is a. 3:15; 4:20
loveth God. love *his b.* 4:21
if any see *his b.* sin a. 5:16

my brother

am I *my b.* keeper ? *Gen* 4:9
said, he is *my b.* 20:5, 13; *1 Ki* 20:32
then I slay *my b.* Jacob. *Gen* 27:41
because thou art *my b.* 29:15
battle against Benjamin *my b.*
Judg 20:23, 28
for thee, *my b. 2 Sam* 1:26
nay *my b.* do not force me. 13:12
saying, alas *my b. 1 Ki* 13:30
as he had been *my b. Ps* 35:14
thou wert as *my b. S of S* 8:1
lament, saying, ah *my b. Jer* 22:18
is *my b.* and sister. *Mat* 12:50
Mark 3:35
how oft shall *my b.* sin ? *Mat* 18:21
speak to *my b. Luke* 12:13
if hadst been here, *my b. John* 11:21
if meat make *my b.* to. *1 Cor* 8:13
I found not Titus *my b. 2 Cor* 2:13

our brother

profit if we slay *our b. ? Gen* 37:26
for he is *our b.* 27; *Judg* 9:3
guilty concerning *our b. Gen* 42:21
if thou wilt send *our b.* 43:4
sent with them *our b. 2 Cor* 8:22
and Timothy *our b. Philem* 1

thy brother

where is Abel *thy b. ? Gen* 4:9
voice of *thy b.* blood. 10
and shalt serve *thy b.* 27:40
thy b. wife raise up seed to *thy b.*
38:8
is not Aaron *thy b. ? Ex* 4:14
take to thee Aaron *thy b.* 28:1
shalt not hate *thy b. Lev* 19:17
fear thy God that *thy b.* 25:36
Aaron *thy b.* Num 27:13; *Deut* 32:50
if *thy b.* entice thee. *Deut* 13:6
open thy hand wide to *thy b.* 15:11
if *thy b.* an Hebrew be sold. 12
bring them again to *thy b.* 22:1
with all lost things of *thy b.* 3
not abhor Edomite, he is *thy b.* 23:7
not lend upon usury to *thy b.* 19
up my face to *thy b. 2 Sam* 2:22
hold thy peace, he is *thy b.* 13:20
said, *thy b.* Benhadad. *1 Ki* 20:33
a pledge from *thy b. Job* 22:6
speakest against *thy b. Ps* 50:20
nor go into *thy b.* house. *Pr* 27:10
thy violence against *thy b. Ob* 10
looked on the day of *thy b.* 12
rememberest that *thy b. Mat* 5:23
first be reconciled to *thy b.* 24
mote in *thy b.* eye. 7:3, 5
Luke 6:41, 42
if *thy b.* trespass, hast gained *thy b.*
Mat 18:15; *Luke* 17:3
thy b. shall rise again. *John* 11:23
judge *thy b. ?* why dost thou set at
nought *thy b. ? Rom* 14:10

your brother

bring *your b.* so will I deliver you
your b. Gen 42:34
not see my face, except *your b.* 43:3
take *your b.* arise, and go. 13
I am Joseph *your b.* 45:4
king, because he is *your b. Judg* 9:18
John, who also am *your b. Rev* 1:9

brotherhood

might break *b.* between. *Zech* 11:14
love the *b.* fear God. *1 Pet* 2:17

brotherly

remembered not the *b. Amos* 1:9
affectioned, with *b.* love. *Rom* 12:10
as touching *b.* love. *1 Thes* 4:9
let *b.* love continue. *Heb* 13:1
to godliness *b.* kindness, and to *b.*
kindness charity. *2 Pet* 1:7

brought

hast *b.* on me and my. *Gen* 20:9
the Lord thy God *b.* it to. 27:20
that torn of beasts I *b.* not. 31:39
they *b.* him the present. 43:26
beast in field not *b. Ex* 9:19
b. east-wind, east-wind *b.* 10:13
hard causes they *b.* to Moses. 18:26
how I bare you and *b.* you. 19:4
man that *b.* us out of Egypt. 32:1, 23
that thou hast *b.* so great a sin. 21
had purple and scarlet *b.* 35:23
b. to Aaron the priest. *Lev* 13:2, 9
till he have *b.* an offering. 23:14
they *b.* the blasphemer. 24:11
he shall be *b.* to door. *Num* 6:13
because *b.* not the offering. 9:13
wherefore hath the Lord *b. ?* 14:3
and he hath *b.* thee near. 16:10
Moses *b.* their cause. 27:5
have therefore *b.* an oblation. 31:50
till we have *b.* them. 32:17
the Lord thy God *b. Deut* 5:15
I have *b.* the first-fruits. 26:10
I have *b.* away the hallowed. 13
in morning ye shall be *b. Josh* 7:14
they took and *b.* them. 23
they *b.* them to the valley. 24
Lord *b.* the sea upon them. 24:7
I have *b.* you unto land. *Judg* 2:1
the Philistines *b.* money. 16:18
who *b.* thee hither ? 18:3
she *b.* Samuel to the. *1 Sam* 1:24
they slew a bullock and *b.* 25
despised him, and *b.* him no. 10:27
wherefore then have ye *b. ?* 21:14
what Abigail had *b.* him. 25:35
found and *b.* an Egyptian to. 30:11
crown and bracelet, *b. 2 Sam* 1:10
who am I ? what is my house, that
thou hast *b. ?* 7:18; *1 Chr* 17:16
Lord *b.* evil. *1 Ki* 9:9; *2 Chr* 7:22
they *b.* every man his present.
1 Ki 10:25; *2 Chr* 9:24
hast thou also *b.* evil ? *1 Ki* 17:20
the king died, and was *b.* to. 22:37
not receiving what he *b. 2 Ki* 5:20
Hoshea *b.* no presents to. 17:4
carry thither the priest ye *b.* 27
he *b.* the shadow ten degrees. 20:11
craftsmen the king *b.* captive. 24:16
with jeopardy of lives *b. 1 Chr* 11:19
the Lord *b.* fear of him. 14:17
children of Israel *b. 2 Chr* 13:18
b. to Jehoshaphat presents. 17:5
b. Ahaziah to Jehu, and. 22:9
the king of Syria *b.* Israel. 28:5
b. captives to Jericho to. 32:23
many *b.* gifts to the Lord. 32:23
they *b.* us a man of. *Ezra* 8:18
God had *b.* counsel. *Neh* 4:15
people *b.* them and made. 8:16
thou art just in all that is *b.* 9:33
Judah *b.* tithe of corn and. 13:12
the royal apparel be *b. Esth* 6:8
of slain in Shushan *b.* 9:11
a thing was secretly *b. Job* 4:12
yet shall he be *b.* to the. 21:32
be *b.* to confusion. *Ps* 35:4, 26
with joy shall they be *b.* 45:15
they are *b.* to shame. 71:24
a man is *b.* to a piece. *Pr* 6:26
b. me to banqueting-. *S of S* 2:4
Ar is *b.* to silence, Kir of Moab *b.* to
silence. *Isa* 15:1

b. Chaldeans to ruin. *Isa* 23:13
terrible one is *b.* to nought. 29:20
hast not *b.* small cattle. 43:23, 24
have called him, I have *b.* 48:15
b. as a lamb to the slaughter. 53:7
arm *b.* salvation. 59:16; 63:5
that their kings may be *b.* 60:11
they that *b.* it shall drink. 62:9
as an ox that is *b. Jer* 11:19
I have *b.* on them a spoiler. 15:8
as I have *b.* all this evil. 32:42
now Lord hath *b.* it and done. 40:3
concerning the evil I *b. Ezek* 14:22
left she her whoredoms *b.* 23:8
thou shalt not be *b.* together. 29:5
might shew them, art thou *b.* 40:4
b. me through the waters to. 47:3, 4
nor instruments of music *b. Dan* 6:18
b. him near before ancient of. 7:13
Lord watched evil, and *b.* it. 9:14
given up, and they that *b.* her. 11:6
when ye *b.* it home. *Hag* 1:9
ye *b.* what was torn. *Mal* 1:13
shall be *b.* before kings. *Mat* 10:18
Mark 13:9; *Luke* 21:12
kingdom *b.* to desolation. *Mat* 12:25
Luke 11:17
b. John Baptist's head. *Mat* 14:11
I *b.* him to thy disciples. 17:16
one was *b.* that owed him. 18:24
b. to him little children. 19:13
Mark 10:13
a candle *b.* to be put. *Mark* 4:21
king commanded head to be *b.* 6:27
disciples rebuked those that *b.* 10:13
b. him to Jerusalem. *Luke* 2:22
a woman *b.* an alabaster box. 7:37
b. him to an inn and. 10:34
why have any not *b.* him ? *John* 7:45
prison to have them *b. Acts* 5:21
Barnabas *b.* him to the. 9:27
and being *b.* on their way. 15:3
who *b.* her masters gain. 16:16
b. them to the magistrates. 20
from his body were *b.* 19:12
b. their books, and burned them. 19
Demetrius *b.* no small gain. 24
ye *b.* hither these men, no robbers. 37
and they *b.* the young man. 20:12
they all *b.* us on our way. 21:5
commanded Paul to be *b.* 25:6
thou must be *b.* before Caesar. 27:24
to be *b.* on my way. *Rom* 15:24
I will not be *b.* under. *1 Cor* 6:12
of you to be *b.* on. *2 Cor* 1:16
b. life and immortality. *2 Tim* 1:10
grace that is to be *b.* to. *1 Pet* 1:13
of the same is he *b.* in. *2 Pet* 2:19

brought *again*

Abram *b. again* his. *Gen* 14:16
the money that was *b. again.* 43:12
Moses and Aaron *b. again. Ex* 10:8
the Lord *b. again* the waters. 15:19
b. us word *again* and. *Deut* 1:25
b. him word *again. Josh* 14:7
hath *b.* me home *again. Ruth* 1:21
Philistines *b. again* ark. *1 Sam* 6:21
b. again Abner. *2 Sam* 3:26
came and *b.* the king word *again.*
2 Ki 22:9, 20; *1 Ki* 20:9; *2 Chr* 34:28
b. Manasseh *again.* *2 Chr* 33:13
b. I *again* the vessels of. *Neh* 13:9
vessels shall be *b. again. Jer* 27:16
ye have not *b. again. Ezek* 34:4
when I have *b. again.* 39:27
repented and *b. again. Mat* 27:3
of peace that *b. again. Heb* 13:20

brought *back*

Abram *b. back* all. *Gen* 14:16
b. back word to them. *Num* 13:26
prophet whom he had *b. back.*
1 Ki 13:23
Jehoshaphat *b.* them *back.*
2 Chr 19:4
hast *b. back* captivity of. *Ps* 85:1
come into land *b. back. Ezek* 38:8

brought *down*

Joseph was *b. down* into. *Gen* 39:1
he *b. down* the people. *Judg* 7:5
Philistines *b. down* Samson. 16:21
he had *b.* him *down. 1 Sam* 30:16
they *b.* Adonijah *down. 1 Ki* 1:53
Elijah *b.* the child *down.* 17:23

b. them *down* to brook. *1 Ki* 18:40
are *b. down* and fallen. *Ps* 20:8
he *b. down* their heart. 107:12
mean man shall be *b. down. Isa* 5:15
thy pomp is *b. down* to. 14:11
thou shalt be *b. down* to hell. 15
shalt be *b. down* and speak. 29:4
your sake I have *b. down.* 43:14
he hath *b.* them *down. Lam* 2:2
the Lord have *b. down. Ezek* 17:24
shall be *b. down* with. 31:18
of Assyria be *b. down. Zech* 10:11
Capernaum be *b. down. Mat* 11:23
brethren *b.* him *down. Acts* 9:30

brought *forth*
earth *b. forth* grass and. *Gen* 1:12
waters *b. forth* abundantly. 21
king of Salem *b. forth.* 14:18
Lord *b. forth* Abram abroad. 15:5
angels *b.* Lot *forth,* and. 19:16
the servant *b. forth* jewels. 24:53
when *b. forth,* she sent to. 38:25
earth *b. forth* by handfuls. 41:47
when thou hast *b. Ex* 3:12
for ye have *b.* us *forth.* 16:3
Lord who *b.* them *forth* out of Egypt.
29:46; *Lev* 25:38; 26:13, 45
Aaron's rod *b. forth. Num* 17:8
sent an angel, and *b.* us *forth.* 20:16
God *b.* him *forth* out of. 24:8
who *b.* thee *forth. Deut* 6:12; 8:14
who *b. forth* water out of. 8:15
people *b. forth* have corrupted. 9:12
the Lord *b.* us *forth* with a. 26:8
made when he *b.* them *forth.* 29:25
for precious fruits *b. forth.* 33:14
b. forth those five kings. *Josh* 10:23
she *b. forth* butter in. *Judg* 5:25
b. you *forth* out of house of. 6:8
Moses, who *b. forth. 1 Sam* 12:8
b. me *forth* into large. *2 Sam* 22:20
Ps 18:19
forsook the Lord who *b. forth* their
fathers. *1 Ki* 9:9; *2 Chr* 7:22
b. forth vestments. *2 Ki* 10:22
b. forth the king's son. 11:12
hast *b.* me *forth* out. *Job* 10:18
wicked shall be *b. forth.* 21:30
mischief, and *b. forth. Ps* 7:14
before mountains were *b. forth.* 90:2
their land *b. forth* frogs. 105:30
he *b. forth* his people with. 43
I was *b. forth. Pr* 8:24
before the hills was I *b. forth.* 25
mother *b.* thee *forth,* she *b. forth.*
S of S 8:5
for grapes, and it *b. forth. Isa* 5:2
b. forth wind. 26:18
what hast thou *b. forth.* 45:10
among sons, she hath *b. forth.* 51:18
she travailed, she *b. forth.* 66:7
as Zion travailed, she *b. forth.* 8
thou hast *b.* me *forth. Jer* 2:27
commanded in day I *b. forth.* 11:4
34:13
Pashur *b. forth* Jeremiah. 20:3
hast *b. forth* thy people. 32:21
Lord *b. forth* the weapons. 50:25
the Lord hath *b. forth* our. 51:10
I *b. forth* my stuff by. *Ezek* 12:7
a remnant shall be *b. forth.* 14:22
in whose sight *b.* them *forth.* 20:22
travaileth hath *b. forth. Mi* 5:3
olive-tree hath not *b. forth. Hag* 2:19
till she had *b. forth* her. *Mat* 1:25
good ground, and *b. forth* fruit.
13:8; *Mark* 4:8
Elisabeth's time came, she *b. forth.*
Luke 1:57
she *b. forth* her first-born son. 2:7
ground of a rich man *b. forth.* 12:16
that, he *b. forth* Jesus. *John* 19:13
prison doors, *b.* them *forth. Acts* 5:19
Herod would have *b.* him *forth.* 12:6
the man to be *b. forth.* 25:17
and the earth *b. forth. Jas* 5:18
she *b. forth* a man-child. *Rev* 12:5
persecuted woman which *b. forth.* 13

brought *in*
hath *b.* in an Hebrew. *Gen* 39:14
Joseph *b.* in Jacob his father. 47:7
blood was not *b. in. Lev* 10:18
goat, whose blood was *b. in.* 16:27

not till Miriam was *b. in. Num* 12:15
for righteousness Lord *b.* me in.
Deut 9:4
when the Lord hath *b.* thee *in.* 11:29
Joab *b. in* a great spoil. *2 Sam* 3:22
b. in the ark of the Lord.
1 Ki 8:6
no burden *b. in* on the. *Neh* 13:19
by his power he *b. in. Ps* 78:26
then was Daniel *b. in. Dan* 5:13
John's head was *b. in. Mat* 14:11
b. in with Jesus into. *Acts* 7:45
false brethren *b. in* to. *Gal* 2:4

brought *into*
not *b.* us *into* a land. *Num* 16:14
Lord hath *b.* thee *into. Deut* 6:10
31:20
b. ark *into* Dagon's. *1 Sam* 5:2
b. them *into* the parlour. 9:22
b. thy servant *into* a. 20:8
sin-money not *b. into. 2 Ki* 12:16
hast *b.* me *into. Ps* 22:15
king hath *b.* me *into* his. *S of S* 1:4
I *b.* you *into* a plentiful. *Jer* 2:7
hath *b.* me *into* darkness. *Lam* 3:2
have *b.* me *into* the waters. *Ezek* 27:26
b. into my sanctuary. 44:7
led him and *b.* him *into. Acts* 9:8
b. Greeks *into* the temple. 21:28
we *b.* nothing *into.* *1 Tim* 6:7
whose blood is *b. into. Heb* 13:11

brought *low*
hast *b.* me very *low. Judg* 11:35
Lord *b.* Judah *low. 2 Chr* 28:19
they are *b. low. Job* 14:21
wicked are gone and *b. low.* 24:24
prevent us, we are *b. low. Ps* 79:8
and were *b. low* for. 106:43
are *b. low,* through. 107:39
I was *b. low,* and he helped. 116:6
for I am *b.* very *low.* 142:6
of music shall be *b. low. Eccl* 12:4
lifted up, shall be *b. low. Isa* 2:12
of terrible ones be *b. low.* 25:5
mountain and hill *b. low. Luke* 3:5
Isa 40:4

brought *out*
that *b.* thee *out* of Ur. *Gen* 15:7
they *b.* him hastily *out.* 41:14
and he *b.* Simeon *out.* 43:23
by strength of hand Lord *b.* you *out.*
Ex 13:3, 9, 14, 16; *Deut* 6:21
which *b.* out. *Ex* 20:2; *Lev* 19:36
Num 15:41; *Deut* 5:6; *Ps* 81:10
b. them *out* of Egypt. *Lev* 23:43
1 Ki 8:21
Lord *b.* thee *out* thence. *Deut* 5:15
b. them *out* to slay them. 9:28
young men *b. out* Rahab. *Josh* 6:23
afterward I *b.* you *out.* 24:5
servant *b.* her *out. 2 Sam* 13:18
he *b. out* the grove. *2 Ki* 23:6
he *b. out* the people. *1 Chr* 20:3
b. out the king's son. *2 Chr* 23:11
priests *b. out* all uncleanness. 29:16
he *b.* streams also *out. Ps* 78:16
b. a vine *out* of Egypt. 80:8
he *b.* them *out* of darkness. 107:14
and *b. out* Israel from. 136:11
in the day I *b.* them *out. Jer* 7:22
father *b. out* of Jewry. *Dan* 5:13
the Lord *b.* Israel *out. Hos* 12:13
Moses, which *b.* us *out. Acts* 7:40
how the Lord *b.* him *out.* 12:17
with an high arm *b.* them *out.* 13:17
b. out, and said, what must? 16:30
besought them, and *b.* them *out.* 39

brought *to pass*
I have *b.* it *to pass. 2 Ki* 19:25
Isa 37:26
and shall be *b. to pass. Ezek* 21:7
shall be *b. to pass. 1 Cor* 15:54

brought *up*
hast thou *b.* us *up?*
Ex 17:3
Num 21:5
Moses that *b.* us *up. Ex* 32:1, 23
gods which *b.* thee *up.* 4, 8
1 Ki 12:28
and people thou hast *b.* up. *Ex* 33:1
b. up an evil report. *Num* 13:32
thing that thou hast *b.* us *up?* 16:13
have ye *b. up* congregation of? 20:4

with thee, which *b. up. Deut* 20:1
because he *b. up* an evil. 22:19
he it is that *b.* us *up. Josh* 24:17
bones of Joseph *b. up.* 24:32
I *b.* you up from Egypt. *Judg* 6:8
1 Sam 10:18
b. Samson *up. Judg* 15:13
the lords *b. up* to her. 16:8
b. him *up* and buried. 31
all flesh-hook *b. up* the. *1 Sam* 2:14
day I *b.* them *up.* 8:8; *2 Sam* 7:6
1 Chr 17:5
that *b.* your fathers *up. 1 Sam* 12:6
David went and *b.* up. *2 Sam* 6:12
15; *1 Ki* 8:4; *1 Chr* 15:28; *2 Chr* 1:4
b. up for Adriel. *2 Sam* 21:8
b. up the bones of Saul. 13
that *b. up* Ahab's. *2 Ki* 10:1, 6
against Lord who *b.* them *up.* 17:7
the Lord who *b.* you *up.* 36
b. up Zedekiah to king. 25:6
Jer 39:5
Solomon *b. up* daughter. *2 Chr* 8:11
with young men *b. up.* 10:8, 10
all these vessels *b. up. Ezra* 1:11
king of Assur *b.* us *up* hither. 4:2
God that *b.* thee *up. Neh* 9:18
Mordecai *b. up* Esther. *Esth* 2:7
like as when she was *b. up.* 20
from youth he was *b. up. Job* 31:18
thou hast *b. up* my soul. *Ps* 30:3
me *b. up* out of an horrible pit. 40:2
as one *b. up* with him. *Pr* 8:30
I nourished and *b. up. Isa* 1:2
who hath *b. up* these? 49:21
to guide of sons she *b. up.* 51:18
he that *b.* them *up?* 63:11; *Jer* 2:6
in the day I *b.* them *up. Jer* 11:7
Lord that *b. up* Israel. 16:14; 23:7
b. up Israel from the north. 15; 23:8
those I *b. up* hath my. *Lam* 2:22
that were *b. up* in scarlet. 4:5
b. up one of her whelps. *Ezek* 19:3
when I have *b.* you *up* out. 37:13
I *b.* you *up. Amos* 2:10; 3:1; 9:7
Mi 6:4
yet hast *b. up* my. *Jonah* 2:6
she shall be *b. up. Nah* 2:7
where she had been *b. up. Luke* 4:16
been *b. up* with Herod. *Acts* 13:1
yet *b. up* in this city at feet. 22:3
widow, if she have *b. up. 1 Tim* 5:10

broughtest
thy people thou *b.* out. *Ex* 32:7
thou *b.* up this people. *Num* 14:13
lest land whence thou *b.* out. *Deut* 9:28
thine inheritance thou *b.* out. 29
1 Ki 8:51
he that *b.* in Israel. *2 Sam* 5:2
1 Chr 11:2
b. our fathers out of. *1 Ki* 8:53
b. him forth out of Ur. *Neh* 9:7
thou *b.* forth water for them. 15
b. them into the land. 23
thou *b.* us into the net. *Ps* 66:11
but thou *b.* us out into a. 12

brow
iron sinew, thy *b.* brass. *Isa* 48:4
led him to the *b.* of hill. *Luke* 4:29

brown
(*Revised Version,* black)
b. cattle among the sheep. *Gen* 30:32
35:40
every one that is not *b.* shall be. 30:33

bruise, *noun*
saith the Lord, thy *b.* is. *Jer* 30:12*
is no healing of thy *b* *Nah* 3:19*

bruise
b. thy head, thou shalt *b. Gen* 3:15
nor will he *b.* it with. *Isa* 28:28*
it pleased the Lord to *b.* him. 53:10
iron shall it break and *b. Dan* 2:40*
of peace shall *b.* Satan. *Rom* 16:20

bruised
not offer to Lord what is *b. Lev* 22:24
trusteth on staff of this *b. 2 Ki* 18:21
b. reed shall he not break. *Isa* 42:3
Mat 12:20
he was *b.* for our iniquities. *Isa* 53:5
there they *b.* the teats. *Ezek* 23:3
b. the breasts of her virginity. 8
liberty them that are *b. Luke* 4:18

bruises
soundness, but wounds, *b.* *Isa* 1:6
bruising
b. thy teats by Egyptians. *Ezek* 23:21
the spirit *b.* him, hardly. *Luke* 9:39
bruit
behold, the noise of the *b. Jer* 10:22*
all that hear *b.* of thee. *Nah* 3:19†
brute, see beasts
brutish
fool and the *b.* person.   *Ps* 49:10
a *b.* man knoweth not.   92:6
understand, ye *b.* among.   94:8
he that hateth reproof is *b. Pr* 12:1
I am more *b.* than any man.   30:2
counsel of the wise counsellors of
  Pharaoh is become *b. Isa* 19:11
they are altogether *b.   Jer* 10:8
every man is *b.*   14; 51:17
pastors are become *b.*   10:21
deliver into hand of *b. Ezek* 21:31
bucket, -s
pour water out of his *b. Num* 24:7
nations are as a drop of a *b.*
                              Isa 40:15
buckler
A shield, 1 *Chr* 5:18. *God is
often called the buckler, or shield of
his people,* Ps 18:2; Pr 2:7. *Faith
is called the Christian's shield,*
Eph 6:16.
b. to all that trust in. *2 Sam* 22:31
                              Ps 18:30
men able to bear *b.*   *1 Chr* 5:18
Gadites that could handle *b.*   12:8*
Lord is my God, my *b.*   *Ps* 18:2
take hold of shield and *b.*   35:2
truth shall be thy shield and *b.* 91:4
he is a *b.* to them that.   *Pr* 2:7
order ye the *b.* and shield. *Jer* 46:3
set against the *b.* shield. *Ezek* 23:24
shall lift up the *b.* against.   26:8
bucklers
Jehoiada delivered spears, *b.*
                           2 Chr 23:9
upon thick bosses of *b.   Job* 15:26
hang a thousand *b.   S of S* 4:4
great company with *b. Ezek* 38:4
set on fire shields, *b.* and.   39:9

cause *b.* of the tender. *Job* 38:27
afore harvest, when *b.* is. *Isa* 18:5*
as earth bringeth forth her *b.* 61:11
thee to multiply as *b.   Ezek* 16:7
b. shall yield no meal.   *Hos* 8:7*
bud, verb
scent of water it will *b.   Job* 14:9
horn of David to *b.   Ps* 132:17
if pomegranates *b.* forth. *S of S* 7:12
Israel shall blossom and *b. Isa* 27:6
earth to bring forth and *b.*   55:10
cause horn of Israel to *b. Ezek* 29:21
budded
vine was as though it *b. Gen* 40:10
the house of Levi *b.   Num* 17:8
whether pomegranates *b. S of S* 6:11
blossomed, pride hath *b. Ezek* 7:10
was Aaron's rod that *b.   Heb* 9:4
buds
rod brought forth *b.   Num* 17:8
buffet
messenger of Satan to *b. 2 Cor* 12:7
buffeted
and *b.* him. *Mat* 26:67; *Mark* 14:65
to present hour we are *b. 1 Cor* 4:11
if when ye be *b.* for.   *1 Pet* 2:20
build referred to *God*
up a priest, and will *b. 1 Sam* 2:35
  2 *Sam* 7:27; 1 *Ki* 11:38
that the Lord will *b.   1 Chr* 17:10
hast told that thou wilt *b.* him. 25
shall destroy, and not *b. Ps* 28:5
do good to Zion, *b.* the walls. 51:18
for God will *b.* the cities.   69:35
and *b.* up thy throne to.   89:4
when Lord shall *b.* up Zion. 102:16
except Lord *b.* house.   127:1
Lord doth *b.* up Jerusalem. 147:2
concerning a nation to *b. Jer* 18:9
b. and not pull down. 24:6; 31:28

again I will *b.* thee.   *Jer* 31:4
I will *b.* Judah and Israel.   33:7
abide in this land I will *b.*   42:10
I the Lord *b.* ruined.   *Ezek* 36:36
I *b.* it as in days of old. *Amos* 9:11
on this rock will I *b.*   *Mat* 16:18
able to *b.* it in three days.   26:61
                            Mark 14:58
I will *b.* again tabernacle. *Acts* 15:16
build *altars*
shalt not *b.* an *altar* of. *Ex* 20:25
b. me here seven *altars. Num* 23:1
                                  29
thou shalt *b.* an *altar. Deut* 27:5
thou shalt *b. altar* of Lord of. 6
we rebel and *b.* an *altar. Josh* 22:29
   see **began**
build joined with *house*
not *b.* his brother's *house. Deut* 25:9
shalt *b.* an *house,* not dwell. 28:30
                             Zeph 1:13
two did *b.* the *house* of. *Ruth* 4:11
shalt *b.* me an *house ? 2 Sam* 7:5
spake I, why *b.* ye not me an *h.* ? 7
he shall *b.* an *house.* 7:13; *1 Ki* 5:5
  8:19; *1 Chr* 17:12; 22:10
b. thee an *h.* in Jerusalem. *1 Ki* 2:36
David could not *b.* an *house.* 5:3
I purpose to *b.* an *house* to Lord. 5
                             2 Chr 2:1
no city to *b.* an *house.*   *1 Ki* 8:16
                             2 Chr 6:5
heart of David my father to *b. house.*
  1 Ki 8:17; *1 Chr* 28:2; *2 Chr* 6:7
shall *b.* an *house.*   *1 Chr* 17:12
                             2 Chr 6:9
shalt not *b.* an *house* because.
                             1 Chr 22:8
my son, *b.* the *house* of Lord. 11
Solomon shall *b.* my *house.*   28:6
behold, I *b.* an *house.   2 Chr* 2:4
the *house* I *b.* is great.   5
who is able to *b.* him an *house ?* that
  I should *b.* an *house.*   6
charged me to *b.* an *house.*   36:23
                             Ezra 1:2
go to *b.* the *house* of Lord. *Ezra* 1:3
commanded you to *b. house* ? 5:3, 9
let the governor *b.* this *house.* 6:7
except the Lord *b. house.   Ps* 127:1
afterwards *b.* thy *house.   Pr* 24:27
they shall *b. houses* and. *Isa* 65:21
where is the *house* that ye *b.*? 66:1
I will *b.* me a wide *house. Jer* 22:14
b. houses and dwell in.   29:5, 28
neither shall ye *b. house* nor. 35:7
not near, let us *b. houses. Ezek* 11:3
safely, and shall *b. houses.*   28:26
bring wood, *b. house.   Hag* 1:8
to *b.* it an *house* in the. *Zech* 5:11
what *house* will ye *b.* ?   *Acts* 7:49
build
let us *b.* us a city and a. *Gen* 11:4
and they left off to *b.* the city. 8
we will *b.* sheep-folds. *Num* 32:16
b. cities for your little ones.   24
thou shalt *b.* bulwarks. *Deut* 20:20
Solomon desired to *b.* in Jerusalem.
  1 Ki 9:19; *2 Chr* 8:6
then did *b.* Millo.   *1 Ki* 9:24
Solomon did *b.* an high place. 11:7
Hiel the Bethelite *b.* Jericho. 16:34
b. ye the sanctuary.   *1 Chr* 22:19
an heart to *b.* the palace.   29:19
let us *b.* these cities. *2 Chr* 14:7
let us *b.* with you.   *Ezra* 4:2
let us *b.* the wall.   *Neh* 2:17
let us rise and *b.*   18
we his servants will rise and *b.* 20
which they *b.* if a fox go up.   4:3
so that we are not able to *b.*   10
and a time to *b.* up.   *Eccl* 3:3
we will *b.* upon her.   *S of S* 8:9
are fallen, but we will *b.* *Isa* 9:10
he shall *b.* my city   45:13
b. the old waste places. 58:12; 61:4
sons of strangers shall *b.* up. 60:10
they shall not *b.* and another. 65:22
set thee over nations to *b. Jer* 1:10
b. a fort against it. *Ezek* 4:2; 21:22
restore and *b.* Jerusalem. *Dan* 9:25
b. it as in the days of old. *Amos* 9:11
Israel shall *b.* the waste cities. 14

they *b.* up Zion with blood. *Mi* 3:10
he shall *b.* the temple. *Zech* 6:12, 13
that are far off shall *b.*   15
Tyrus did *b.* herself a strong. 9:3
they shall *b.* but I.   *Mal* 1:4
ye *b.* tombs of prophets. *Mat* 23:29
                            Luke 11:47, 48
down my barns and *b.   Luke* 12:18
which of you intending to *b.* ? 14:28
this man began to *b.* and not. 30
able to *b.* you up.   *Acts* 20:32
I *b.* on another man's   *Rom* 15:20
b. on this foundation.   *1 Cor* 3:12
if I *b.* again the things. *Gal* 2:18
builded
Cain *b.* a city.   *Gen* 4:17
Noah *b.* an altar to the Lord. 8:20
Asher *b.* Nineveh, Rehoboth. 10:11
the tower children of men *b.*   11:5
Abram *b.* an altar.   12:7; 13:18
Isaac *b.* an altar.   26:25
Moses *b.* an altar under.   *Ex* 24:4
ye have *b.* an altar.   *Josh* 22:16
less this house I have *b. 1 Ki* 8:27,43
wherewith Baasha had *b.*   15:22
Solomon had *b.* for.   *2 Ki* 23:13
house to be *b.* must be. *1 Chr* 22:5
adversaries heard that they *b.*
                             Ezra 4:1
that if this city be *b.*   13, 16
that this city be not *b.*   4:21
house of great God which is *b.* 5:8
we build the house that was *b.* 11
let the house of God be *b.* 15; 6:3
elders of the Jews *b.*   6:14
his sword girded, and so *b. Neh* 4:18
away an house he *b.* not. *Job* 20:19
Jerusalem is *b.* a city.   *Ps* 122:3
Wisdom hath *b.* her house. *Pr* 9:1
through wisdom is house *b.*   24:3
I *b.* me houses, I.   *Eccl* 2:4
like tower of David *b.   S of S* 4:4
the city shall be *b.*   *Jer* 30:18
he hath *b.* against me.   *Lam* 3:5
waste shall be *b.   Ezek* 36:10, 33
sold, they plant, they *b. Luke* 17:28
in whom ye are *b.* together. *Eph* 2:22
he who *b.* the house hath. *Heb* 3:3
for every house is *b.* by some.   4
builder, -s
Solomon's and Hiram's *b. 1 Ki* 5:18
laid money out to the *b. 2 Ki* 12:11
carpenters and *b.* 22:6; *2 Chr* 34:11
when *b.* laid foundation. *Ezra* 3:10
to anger before the *b.*   *Neh* 4:5
stone which *b.* refused. *Ps* 118:22
  Mat 21:42; *Mark* 12:10
                   Luke 20:17; *Acts* 4:11
thy *b.* have perfected. *Ezek* 27:4
as a wise master-*b.* I. *1 Cor* 3:10
city whose *b.* and maker. *Heb* 11:10
the stone which the *b.*   *1 Pet* 2:7
buildest
goodly cities thou *b.* not. *Deut* 6:10
thou *b.* a new house.   22:8
for which cause thou *b.*   *Neh* 6:6
in that thou *b.* thine.   *Ezek* 16:31
thou that destroyest the temple and
  b. it in. *Mat* 27:40; *Mark* 15:29
buildeth
cursed be the man that *b. Josh* 6:26
b. his house as a moth. *Job* 27:18
every wise woman *b.* her. *Pr* 14:1
woe to him that *b.* by.   *Jer* 22:13
Israel *b.* temples.   *Hos* 8:14
it is he that *b.* his stories. *Amos* 9:6
woe to him that *b.* a.   *Hab* 2:12
foundation, another *b.*   *1 Cor* 3:10
building
not against Lord in *b.   Josh* 22:19
till he made an end of *b.   1 Ki* 3:1
no tool of iron heard while *b.* 6:7
so was Solomon seven years in *b.* 38
Solomon was *b.* his own house. 7:1
wherewith Baasha was *b. 2 Chr* 16:6
b. rebellious and bad city. *Ezra* 4:12
by *b.* forts to cut off. *Ezek* 17:17
temple was forty-six years in *b.*
                             John 2:20
b. up yourselves on holy. *Jude* 20
building, *substantive*
Solomon finished *b.* house. *1 Ki* 9:1

he left off *b.* of Ramah. *1 Ki* 15:21
  2 Chr 16:5
made ready for the *b.* *1 Chr* 28:2
instructed for the *b.* *2 Chr* 3:3
of men that made this *b.* *Ezra* 5:4
what ye shall do for the *b.* of.   6:8
by slothfulness the *b.* *Eccl* 10:18*
measured the breadth of the *b.*
  Ezek 40:5; 41:15
there was a row of *b.* round. 46:23
God's husbandry, God's *b.* *1 Cor* 3:9
we have a *b.* of God. *2 Cor* 5:1
in whom all the *b.* *Eph* 2:21
tabernacle not of this *b.* *Heb* 9:11*
b. of wall was of jasper. *Rev* 21:18

buildings
to shew him *b.* of temple. *Mat* 24:1
see what *b.* are here. *Mark* 13:1, 2

built
it shall not be *b.* again. *Deut* 13:16
the cities that Ahab *b.* *1 Ki* 22:39
every side, so they *b.* *2 Chr* 14:7
have *b.* thee a sanctuary.   20:8
Uzziah *b.* towers in. 26:9, 10
Jotham *b.* in the forests.   27:4
who *b.* desolate places. *Job* 3:14
breaketh down, cannot be *b.* 12:14
to Almighty, shalt be *b.* up. 22:23
he *b.* his sanctuary. *Ps* 78:69
I have said, mercy shall be *b.* 89:2
b. a tower in the midst. *Isa* 5:2
saith to Judah, ye shall be *b.* 44:26
Jerusalem, thou shalt be *b.*   28
shall they be *b.* in midst. *Jer* 12:16
be *b.* O virgin of Israel. 31:4
provocation from day they *b.* 32:31
which I have *b.* will I break. 45:4
thou hast *b.* to thee. *Ezek* 16:24
hast *b.* thy high place at.   25
thou shalt be *b.* no more. 26:14
great Babylon I have *b.* ? *Dan* 4:30
the street shall be *b.* again. 9:25
that temple be *b.* *Zech* 8:9
b. a tower. *Mat* 21:33; *Mark* 12:1
the centurion hath *b.* us. *Luke* 7:5
abide which he hath *b.* *1 Cor* 3:14
b. on the foundation of. *Eph* 2:20
rooted and *b.* up in him. *Col* 2:7
he that *b.* all things is God. *Heb* 3:4

built *altar*
Moses *b.* an *altar.* *Ex* 17:15; 24:4
Aaron *b.* an *altar.* 32:5
Joshua *b.* an *altar.* *Josh* 8:30
half tribe *b.* an *altar.* 22:10
Gideon *b.* an *altar.* *Judg* 6:24
people *b.* an *altar.* 21:4
Samuel *b.* an *altar.* *1 Sam* 7:17
Saul *b.* an *altar.* 14:35
David *b.* an *altar.* *2 Sam* 24:25
offered on the *altar* he *b.* *1 Ki* 9:25
with stones Elisha *b. altar* in. 18:32
Urijah *b.* an *altar.* *2 Ki* 16:11

built *altars*
Balak *b.* seven *altars.* *Num* 23:14
he *b. altars* in house of. *2 Ki* 21:4
b. altars for all the host. 5; *2 Chr* 33:5
away *altars* he had *b.* *2 Chr* 33:15

built *city*
let city of Sihon be *b.* *Num* 21:27
Joshua *b.* the *city.* *Josh* 19:50
Danites *b. city.* *Judg* 18:28
Omri *b. city.* *1 Ki* 16:24
David *b. city* round. *1 Chr* 11:8
no *city* it shall never be *b.* *Isa* 25:2
city shall be *b.* to Lord. *Jer* 31:38
hill whereon *city* was *b.* *Luke* 4:29

built *cities*
b. for Pharaoh treasure-*cities.*
  Ex 1:11
cities which ye *b.* not. *Josh* 24:13
cities which Asa *b.* *1 Ki* 15:23
cities Huram restored, Solomon *b.*
  2 Chr 8:2
Rehoboam *b. cities* for defence. 11:5
Asa *b.* fenced *cities* in Judah. 14:6
Jehoshaphat *b.* castles and c. 17:12
Uzziah *b. cities* about. 26:6
Jotham *b. cities* in mountains. 27:4
saith to *cities* of Judah, ye shall be *b.*
  Isa 44:26

built *high places*
Judah *b. high p.* images. *1 Ki* 14:23

Israel *b. high p.* in cities. *2 Ki* 17:9
Manasseh *b.* up again *high p.* 21:3
  2 Chr 33:3
b. high p. of Tophet. *Jer* 7:31
b. high p. of Baal. 19:5; 32:35

built *house,* or *houses*
hast *b.* goodly *houses.* *Deut* 8:12
man hath *b.* a new *house* ? 20:5
there was no *house* *b.* to. *1 Ki* 3:2
Solomon *b. houses.* 6:9, 14
I have *b.* thee an *house.* 8:13
and have *b.* an *house* for the. 20
toward *house* I have *b.* 8:44, 48
  2 Chr 6:34, 38
sure *house,* as I *b.* for David.
  1 Ki 11:38
ye not *b.* me an *house* ? *1 Chr* 17:6
less this *house* I have *b.* ? *2 Chr* 6:18
ye have *b. houses* of. *Amos* 5:11
Lord's *house* should be *b.* *Hag* 1:2
my *house* shall he *b.* in. *Zech* 1:16
b. his *house* on a rock. *Mat* 7:24
  Luke 6:48
b. his house on sand. *Mat* 7:26
  Luke 6:49
Solomon *b.* him an *house. Acts* 7:47
are *b.* up a spiritual *h.* *1 Pet* 2:5

built *wall,* or *walls*
Solomon *b. walls* of. *1 Ki* 6:15
on *walls* of Ophel he *b.* *2 Chr* 27:3
Hezekiah *b.* up the *wall.* 32:5
Manasseh *b.* a *wall* without. 33:14
so *b.* we the *wall.* *Neh* 4:6
when *wall* was *b.* 7:1
one *b.* up the *wall.* *Ezek* 13:10
street be *b.* again and *wall. Dan* 9:25
day thy *walls* are to be *b.* *Mi* 7:11

Bul
in month *B.* house was. *1 Ki* 6:38

bull
[1] *The beast so called, or repre-*
sentations of it, Job 21:10; Jer
52:20. [2] *Wicked, violent, and*
furious enemies, Ps 22:12.
their *b.* gendereth and. *Job* 21:10
thy sons lie as wild *b.* *Isa* 51:20*

bullock
(*Generally used for a young bull*)
in the basket with *b.* *Ex* 29:3
kill *b.* before Lord. 11; *Lev* 1:5
  9:18*
bring the *b.* to the door. *Lev* 4:4
b. a meat-offering. *Num* 15:9; 29:37
sacrifice to Lord any *b. Deut* 17:1*
glory is like firstling of a *b.* 33:17
young *b.* the second *b. Judg* 6:25, 26
choose one *b.* *1 Ki* 18:23, 25
Elijah cut *b.* in pieces. 33
I will take no *b.* out. *Ps* 50:9
better than a *b.* that hath. 69:31
lion eat straw like *b.* *Isa* 65:25*
as *b.* unaccustomed to. *Jer* 31:18*

bullock with *sin-offering*
a *b.* for a *sin-offering.* *Ex* 29:36
offer *b.* of the *sin-offering. Lev* 16:6
prepare a *b.* for a *sin-offering.*
  Ezek 45:22

see **blood**

young **bullock**
bring a *young b.* *Lev* 4:3
  Ezek 43:19
shall offer a *young b.* *Lev* 4:14
  Num 15:24
holy place with a *young b. Lev* 16:3
one *young b.* one. *Num* 7:15, 21, 27
 33, 39, 45, 51, 57, 63, 69, 75, 81
himself with *young b.* *2 Chr* 13:9
take a *young b.* and. *Ezek* 45:18
day of new moon a *young b.* 46:6

bullocks
fourth day ten *b.* two. *Num* 29:23
offered thousand *b.* for. *1 Chr* 29:21
the dedication 100 *b.* *Ezra* 6:17
shall they offer *b.* on thy. *Ps* 51:19
I will offer unto thee *b.* 66:15
delight not in the blood of *b. Isa* 1:11
the *b.* with the bulls shall. 34:7
hired men like fatted *b. Jer* 46:21*
slay all her *b.* let them go. 50:27
the blood of goats, of *b. Ezek* 39:18
they sacrifice *b.* in Gilgal. *Hos* 12:11

see **seven**

---

bulls
Jacob took ten *b.* as. *Gen* 32:15
b. have compassed me, strong *b.*
  Ps 22:12
will I eat flesh of *b.* or drink. 50:13
rebuke multitude of the *b.* 68:30
bullocks with the *b.* *Isa* 34:7
ye bellow as *b.* *Jer* 50:11*
twelve brasen *b.* under the. 52:20
if the blood of *b.* and. *Heb* 9:13
not possible blood of *b.* take. 10:4

bulrush, -es
took for him an ark of *b.* *Ex* 2:3
ambassadors in vessels of *b.*
  Isa 18:2*
bow down his head like a *b.* ? 58:5*

bulwarks
thou shalt build *b.* *Deut* 20:20
engines on the *b.* *2 Chr* 26:15
mark well her *b.* consider. *Ps* 48:13
king came and built *b.* *Eccl* 9:14
appoint for walls and *b.* *Isa* 26:1

bunch, -es
take a *b.* of hyssop and. *Ex* 12:22
with 100 *b.* of raisins. *2 Sam* 16:1
Zebulun brought *b.* of. *1 Chr* 12:40
treasures upon *b.* of. *Isa* 30:6†

bundle, -s
every man's *b.* of money. *Gen* 42:35
bound in *b.* of life. *1 Sam* 25:29
a *b.* of myrrh my well-. *S of S* 1:13
bind the tares in *b.* *Mat* 13:30
Paul had gathered a *b.* of. *Acts* 28:3

burden
A weight or load of the capacity of
the bearer to carry, 2 Ki 5:17;
Jer 17:27. *This may be used*
literally or figuratively of taxes,
grief or illness, Ps 55:22; Hos 8:10;
Gal 6:2.
bear the *b.* with thee.
  Num 11:17
the ass lying under *b.* *Ex* 23:5
appoint each to his *b.* *Num* 4:19
layest the *b.* of all this people. 11:11
I myself bear your *b.* ? *Deut* 1:12
then thou shalt be a *b.* *2 Sam* 15:33
should thy servant be a *b.* ? 19:35
servant two mules' *b.* of. *2 Ki* 5:17
forty camels' *b.* to Elisha. 8:9
it shall not be a *b.* *2 Chr* 35:3
no *b.* be brought in. *Neh* 13:19
I am a *b.* to myself. *Job* 7:20
iniquities as a *b.* they are. *Ps* 38:4
cast thy *b.* on the Lord. 55:22
removed his shoulder from *b.* 81:6
grasshopper shall be a *b. Eccl* 12:5
broken the yoke of his *b. Isa* 9:4
his *b.* shall be taken from. 10:27
b. depart from off their. 14:25
name of the Lord, the *b.* 30:27*
your carriages are a *b.* to. 46:1
no *b.* on sabbath. *Jer* 17:21, 22, 27
reproach of it was a *b.* *Zeph* 3:18
and my *b.* is light. *Mat* 11:30
which have borne the *b.* and. 20:12
lay on you no greater *b. Acts* 15:28
the ship was to unlade *b.* 21:3
put upon you none other *b. Rev* 2:24

burden
(*Meaning here a prophecy of doom*)
Lord laid this *b.* upon. *2 Ki* 9:25
the *b.* of Babylon. *Isa* 13:1
king Ahaz died, was this *b.* 14:28
the *b.* of Moab. 15:1
the *b.* of Damascus. 17:1
the *b.* of Egypt. 19:1
the *b.* of the desert of the sea. 21:1
the *b.* of Dumah. 11
the *b.* upon Arabia. 13
the *b.* of the valley of vision. 22:1
the *b.* that was upon it shall. 25
the *b.* of Tyre. 23:1
b. of the beasts of south. 30:6
what is *b.* of the Lord ? what *b.* ?
  Jer 23:33
the *b.* of the Lord shall ye. 36
but since ye say, the *b.* of. 38
this *b.* concerneth the. *Ezek* 12:10
sorrow a little for the *b.* *Hos* 8:10

burden (continued)

the *b.* of Nineveh. *Nah* 1:1
b. which Habakkuk the. *Hab* 1:1
b. of the word of the Lord. *Zech* 9:1
b. of the word of the Lord for. 12:1
b. of the word of the Lord to. *Mal* 1:1
every man bear his own *b.* *Gal* 6:5

burden, -ed

all that *b.* themselves. *Zech* 12:3
we groan being *b.* *2 Cor* 5:4
not that others be eased, you *b.* 8:13
but be it so, I did not *b.* you. 12:16

burdens

couching between two *b.* *Gen* 49:14
to afflict them with their *b.* *Ex* 1:11
Moses looked on their *b.* 2:11
get you to your *b.* 5:4
you make them rest from *b.* 5
bring you from the *b.* of. 6:6, 7
appoint to them all their *b.* *Num* 4:27
strength of bearers of *b.* *Neh* 4:10
they that bare *b.* with other. 17
all manner of *b.* brought in. 13:15
the fast, to undo heavy *b.* *Isa* 58:6*
prophets have seen for thee false *b.*
Lam 2:14
ye take from the poor *b.* *Amos* 5:11*
bind heavy *b. Mat* 23:4; *Luke* 11:46
bear ye one another's *b.* *Gal* 6:2

burdensome

Jerusalem a *b.* stone. *Zech* 12:3
kept myself from being *b. 2 Cor* 11:9
it be that I was not *b.* 12:13
third time I come, I will not be *b.* 14
we might have been *b. 1 Thes* 2:6†

burial

also that he have no *b.* *Eccl* 6:3
joined with them in *b.* *Isa* 14:20
buried with the *b.* of an. *Jer* 22:19
she did it for my *b.* *Mat* 26:12
carried Stephen to his *b.* *Acts* 8:2

buried

there was Abraham *b.* *Gen* 25:10
b. Abraham and Sarah, Isaac and
Rebekah, there I. Leah. 49:31
there they *b.* people. *Num* 11:34
Miriam died, and was *b.* there. 20:1
Egyptians *b.* all first-born. 33:4
died, and there he was *b. Deut* 10:6
the bones of Joseph *b. Josh* 24:32
die, and there will be *b. Ruth* 1:17
took head and *b.* it. *2 Sam* 4:12
Saul and Jonathan they *b.* 21:14
where man of God is *b. 1 Ki* 13:31
and so I saw the wicked *b. Eccl* 8:10
not be gathered nor *b.* *Jer* 8:2
16:6; 20:6; 25:33
shall not be lamented nor *b.* 16:4
be *b.* with the burial of an ass. 22:19
sign, till buriers have *b. Ezek* 39:15
took the body and *b.* it. *Mat* 14:12
rich man died and was *b. Luke* 16:22
David is dead and *b.* *Acts* 2:29
feet of them which *b.* thy. 5:9
carrying her forth, *b.* her by. 10
b. with him by baptism. *Rom* 6:4
that he was *b.* and rose. *1 Cor* 15:4
b. with him in baptism. *Col* 2:12

buried *him*

he *b. him* in a valley. *Deut* 34:6
blessed be ye that *b.* Saul. *2 Sam* 2:5
they *b. him,* all Israel. *1 Ki* 14:18
they *b.* Jehoram in. *2 Chr* 21:20
b. Jehoiada in city of David. 24:16
they *b. him* not in the sepulchres. 25
men carried and *b. him. Acts* 5:6

buried *in*

and thou shalt be *b. in* a. *Gen* 15:15
David was *b. in* the city. *1 Ki* 2:10
Joab *b. in* his own house. 34
Manasseh was *b. in. 2 Ki* 21:18
Amon was *b. in* sepulchre, in. 26
that remain be *b. in. Job* 27:15

buried *with his fathers*

Rehoboam *b. with his f. 1 Ki* 14:31
Asa *b. with his f.* 15:24
Jehoshaphat *b. with his f.* 22:50
Joram *b. with his f. 2 Ki* 8:24
Joash *b. with his f.* 12:21
Amaziah *b. with his f.* 14:20
Azariah *b. with his f.* 15:7
Jotham *b. with his f.* 38
Ahaz *b. with his f.* 16:20

buriers

set up a sign till *b.* have. *Ezek* 39:15

burn

(To consume, or destroy with fire,
Josh 11:13. *Used also figuratively*
for intense indignation, passion, or
zeal)

let not thine anger *b.* *Gen* 44:18
bring pure olive-oil to cause the lamp
to *b.* alway. *Ex* 27:20; *Lev* 24:2
take caul, kidneys and fat and *b.*
Ex 29:13, 18, 25; *Lev* 1:9, 15
2:2, 9, 16; 3:5, 11, 16; 5:12; 6:15
9:17; *Num* 5:26
fat and *b.* upon. *Lev* 4:19, 26, 31
7:31; 16:25; 17:6; *Num* 18:17
one shall *b.* the heifer. *Num* 19:5
Hazor did, Joshua *b.* *Josh* 11:13
let them not fail to *b. 1 Sam* 2:16
save only to *b.* sacrifice. *2 Chr* 2:6
and they *b.* to the Lord. 13:11
they shall both *b.* together. *Isa* 1:31
it shall *b.* and devour. 10:17
go through them, and *b.* 27:4
Lebanon is not sufficient to *b.* 40:16
shall it be for a man to *b.* 44:15
my fury shall *b.* and not. *Jer* 7:20
so shall they *b.* odours for. 34:5
that the king would not *b.* 36:25
b. also the bones under it. *Ezek* 24:5
of it may be hot and may *b.* 11
they shall set on fire and *b.* 39:9
he shall *b.* bullock in the. 43:21
I will *b.* her chariots. *Nah* 2:13
day cometh that shall *b.* *Mal* 4:1
tares in bundles to *b.* *Mat* 13:30
but chaff he will *b.* with. *Luke* 3:17
did not heart *b.* within us? 24:32
better to marry than to *b. 1 Cor* 7:9
offended, and I *b.* not? *2 Cor* 11:29

burn, joined with *fire*

remaineth till morning *b.* with *fire.*
Ex 12:10; 29:34; *Lev* 8:32
b. that wherein the plague is with
fire. *Lev* 13:57
b. with *fire* their skins, flesh. 16:27
mountain did *b.* with *fire. Deut* 5:23
b. their images with *fire.* 7:5, 25
b. groves with *fire.* 12:3
fire shall *b.* to lowest hell. 32:22
Jer 17:4
b. their chariots with *fire. Josh* 11:6
tower to *b.* it with *fire. Judg* 9:52
we will *b.* thine house with *fire.* 14:15
b. thee with *fire.* 15:6
thy jealousy *b.* like *fire? Ps* 79:5
thy wrath *b.* like *fire?* 89:46
the *fire* shall *b.* them. *Isa* 47:14
forth like *fire* and *b. Jer* 4:4; 21:12
b. sons and daughters in *fire.* 7:31
19:5
shall *b.* city with *fire.* 21:10; 32:29
34:2, 22; 37:8, 10; 38:18
b. with *fire* a third part. *Ezek* 5:2
they *b.* thine houses with *fire.* 16:41
23:47
b. up the chaff with unquenchable
fire. Mat 3:12; *Luke* 3:17
flesh and *b.* her with *fire. Rev* 17:16

burn *incense*

an altar to *b. inc.* on. *Ex* 30:1
b. thereon sweet *inc.* 7, 8
by the altar to *b. inc. 1 Ki* 13:1
Israel did *b. inc.* to it. *2 Ki* 18:4
and his sons to *b. inc. 1 Chr* 23:13
house to *b.* sweet *inc. 2 Chr* 2:4
b. every morning sweet *inc.* 13:11
into temple to *b. inc.* 26:16, 19
made high places to *b. inc.* 28:25
Lord hath chosen you to *b. inc.* 29:11
and *b. inc.* on it. 32:12
steal and *b. inc.* to Baal? *Jer* 7:9
11:13
b. inc. to the queen of heaven. 44:17
they *b. inc.* upon the hills. *Hos* 4:13
therefore they *b. inc.* *Hab* 1:16
his lot was to *b. inc. Luke* 1:9

burned

bush *b.* with fire. *Ex* 3:2
the mountain *b.* with fire. *Deut* 4:11
I came down, and mount *b.* 9:15
b. them with fire. *Josh* 7:25

b. Ziklag with fire. *1 Sam* 30:1
men *b.* their images. *2 Sam* 5:21*
shall be utterly *b.* with fire. 23:7
b. the grove at the brook. *2 Ki* 23:6
b. the chariots with fire. 11
she *b.* the high place. 15
bones out of sepulchres and *b.* 16
gods were *b.* with fire. *1 Chr* 14:12
Amaziah *b.* incense to. *2 Chr* 25:14
forsaken me, and *b.* incense. 34:25
gates thereof *b.* with. *Neh* 1:3; 2:17
wroth, anger *b.* in him. *Esth* 1:12
God hath *b.* up the sheep. *Job* 1:16
and my bones are *b.* with heat. 30:30
I was musing, fire *b.* *Ps* 39:3*
b. up all the synagogues. 74:8
it is *b.* with fire, it is cut. 80:16
my skin black, bones are *b.* 102:3
flame *b.* up the wicked. 106:18
his clothes not be *b. Pr* 6:27
on coals and his feet not be *b.?* 28*
your cities are *b.* with fire. *Isa* 1:7
it *b.* him, yet he laid it not. 42:25
walkest through fire not be *b.* 43:2
and beautiful house *b.* with. 64:11
which have *b.* incense on the. 65:7
his cities are *b.* *Jer* 2:15
the bellows are *b.* 6:29
b. up that none can pass. 9:10, 12
my people have *b.* incense to. 18:15
in roll Jehoiakim hath *b.* 36:28
city shall not be *b.* with fire. 38:17
cause this city to be *b.* with fire. 23
that their wives had *b.* incense. 44:15
daughters be *b.* with fire. 49:2
reeds they have *b.* with fire. 51:32
high gates shall be *b.* with fire. 58
he *b.* against Jacob like. *Lam* 2:3
and all faces shall be *b. Ezek* 20:47
and let the bones be *b.* 24:10
wherein she *b.* incense. *Hos* 2:13
they sacrificed and *b.* incense. 11:2
the flame hath *b.* all the. *Joel* 1:19
because he *b.* the bones. *Amos* 2:1
hires thereof be *b.* with. *Mi* 1:7
and the earth is *b.* at. *Nah* 1:5
king sent and *b.* up their. *Mat* 22:7
are gathered and *b.* *John* 15:6
their books and *b.* *Acts* 19:19
b. in their lust one. *Rom* 1:27
if any man's work be *b. 1 Cor* 3:15
I give my body to be *b.* 13:3
whose end is to be *b.* *Heb* 6:8
not come to the mount that *b.* 12:18
those beasts are *b.* 13:11
works therein be *b.* up. *2 Pet* 3:10
his feet like brass, as if *b. Rev* 1:15
she be utterly *b.* with fire. 18:8

burneth

he that *b.* them shall wash clothes.
Lev 16:28; *Num* 19:8
breaketh the bow and *b.* *Ps* 46:9
as the fire *b.* wood, and as. 83:14
a fire *b.* up his enemies. 97:3
for wickedness *b.* as fire. *Isa* 9:18
he *b.* part thereof in fire. 44:16
thereof as a lamp that *b.* 62:1
as when the melting fire *b.* 64:2
are a smoke and fire that *b.* 65:5
he that *b.* incense, as if he. 66:3
cause to cease that *b.* *Jer* 48:35
behind them a flame *b.* *Joel* 2:3
part in lake which *b.* with. *Rev* 21:8

burning

b. lamp passed between. *Gen* 15:17
fire of altar shall be *b.* in it. *Lev* 6:9*
12, 13
appoint over you the *b.* ague. 26:16*
be devoured with *b.* heat. 32:24
of his mouth go *b.* lamps. *Job* 41:19
let *b.* coals fall upon. *Ps* 140:10
there is as a *b.* fire. *Pr* 16:27
as coals are to *b.* coals. 26:21*
b. lips and a wicked heart are. 23
of Lord cometh far, *b.* *Isa* 30:27
land shall become *b.* pitch. 34:9
was in my heart as *b.* fire. *Jer* 20:9
was like *b.* coals. *Ezek* 1:13
into midst of *b.* furnace. *Dan* 3:6, 11
able to deliver us from *b.* furnace. 17
and to cast them into the *b.* fiery
furnace. 3:20; 21, 23

burning

Nebuchadnezzar came near the *b.*
Dan 3:26
his wheels were as *b.* fire. 7:9
and *b.* coals went forth at. *Hab* 3:5*
be girded, and lights *b. Luke* 12:35
he was a *b.* and shining. *John* 5:35
were seven lamps *b.* before. *Rev* 4:5
as it were a great mountain *b.* 8:8
there fell a great star *b.* 10
were cast alive into a lake *b.* 19:20

burning, *substantive*

b. for *b.* wound for. *Ex* 21:25
bewail the *b.* which Lord. *Lev* 10:6
if spot stay, it is rising of *b.* 13:28
the Lord shall smite thee with an
extreme *b.* *Deut* 28:22*
is brimstone, salt, and *b.* 29:23
made a very great *b.* 2 *Chr* 16:14
people made no *b.* like the *b.* 21:19
there shall be *b.* instead. *Isa* 3:24*
purged Jerusalem by spirit of *b.* 4:4
but this shall be with *b.* and. 9:5
kindle *b.* like *b.* of fire. 10:16
people shall be as the *b.* of. 33:12
plucked out of the *b.* *Amos* 4:11
they see the smoke of *b. Rev* 18:9

burnings

dwell with everlasting *b.? Isa* 33:14
with *b.* of thy fathers. *Jer* 34:5

burnished

they sparkled like *b.* brass. *Ezek* 1:7

burnt

her forth, let her be *b.* *Gen* 38:24
see why bush is not *b.* *Ex* 3:3
for they shall not be *b.* *Lev* 2:12
meat-offering be wholly *b.* 6:22, 23
8:21
sought goat, and it was *b.* 10:16
took the brazen censers, wherewith
they that were *b.* *Num* 16:39
shall be *b.* with hunger. *Deut* 32:24
before they *b.* fat. 1 *Sam* 2:15
men's bones shall be *b.* 1 *Ki* 13:2
Asa *b.* her idol. 15:13; 2 *Chr* 15:16
b. the house of Lord. 2 *Ki* 25:9
2 *Chr* 36:19
I will make thee a *b.* *Jer* 51:25

burnt, joined with *fire*

he *b.* the calf in the *fire. Ex* 32:20
Deut 9:21
sin-offering be *b.* in the *fire.*
Lev 6:30
of flesh of sacrifice on third day be *b.*
with *fire.* 7:17; 19:6
man take a wife and her mother
they shall be *b.* with *fire.* 20:14
daughter of priest profane by playing
whore ... be burnt with *fire.* 21:9
fire of the Lord be. *Num* 11:1, 3
daughters *b.* in the *fire. Deut* 12:31
b. Jericho with *fire.* *Josh* 6:24
he that is taken with the accursed
thing shall be *b.* with *fire.* 7:15
b. their chariots with *fire.* 11:9
took Hazor and *b.* it with *fire.* 11
b. her and father with *fire. Judg* 15:6
as flax that was *b.* with *fire.* 14
Laish and *b.* it with *fire.* 18:27
had *b.* Gezer with *fire.* 1 *Ki* 9:16
Zimri *b.* king's house with *fire.* 16:18
fire from heaven *b.* 2 *Ki* 1:14
b. their children with *fire.* 17:31
man's house *b.* he with *fire.* 25:9
b. his children in the *fire.* 2 *Chr* 28:3

burnt *incense*

b. sweet *inc.* thereon. *Ex* 40:27
only Solomon *b. inc.* 1 *Ki* 3:3
Solomon *b. inc.* upon the. 9:25
Jeroboam offered and *b. inc.* 12:33
people *b. inc.* 22:43; 2 *Ki* 12:3
14:4; 15:4, 35
Ahaz *b. inc.* in high. 2 *Ki* 16:4
2 *Chr* 28:3, 4
and have not *b. inc.* 2 *Chr* 29:7

burnt-offering

is lamb for a *b.-off. ? Gen* 22:7
God will provide a lamb for a *b.-off.* 8
he offered him for a *b.-off.* 13
Jethro took a *b.-off.* *Ex* 18:12
the ram is a *b.-off.* 29:18
hand on head of *b.-off.* *Lev* 1:4

slay sin-offering in place of *b.-off.*
Lev 4:29, 33; 6:25; 7:2; 14:13
this is law of the *b.-off.* 6:9; 7:37
priest have skin of *b.-off.* 7:8
ram for a *b.-off.* 9:2; 16:3, 5; 23:18
calf and a lamb for a *b.-off.* 9:3; 12:6
23:12
one lamb of first year for a *b.-off.*
Num 7:15, 21, 27, 33, 39, 51, 57
63, 69, 75, 81; *Ezek* 45:15
stand by thy *b.-off.* *Num* 23:3, 15
this is the *b.-off.* 28:10
for a *b.-off.* of a sweet savour. 13
this is the *b.-off.* of every month. 14
meat-offering and daily *b.-off.* 29:6
altar not for a *b.-off.* *Josh* 22:26
a *b.-off.* at our hands. *Judg* 13:23
was offering up a *b.-off.* 1 *Sam* 7:10
offered a *b.-off.* 13:12
offered him for a *b.-off.* 2 *Ki* 3:27
fire consumed the *b.-off.* 2 *Chr* 7:1
the *b.-off.* should be made. 29:24
b.-off. hast thou not. *Ps* 40:6
delightest not in *b.-off.* 51:16
with *b.-off.* and whole *b.-off.* 19
nor beasts for a *b.-off.* *Isa* 40:16
for I hate robbery for *b.-off.* 61:8*
shall slay the *b.-off.* *Ezek* 44:11
prepare the *b.-off.* for Israel. 45:17
priest prepare prince's *b.-off.* 46:2
thou shalt daily prepare a *b.-off.* 13

continual burnt-offering

a continual *b.-off.* *Ex* 29:42
Num 28:3, 6, 10, 15, 24, 31; 29:11
16, 19, 22; *Ezra* 3:5; *Neh* 10:33
Ezek 46:15

offer burnt-offering

offer him there for a *b.-off. Gen* 22:2
and *offer* thy *b.-off.* *Lev* 9:7
of months *offer b.-off.* *Num* 28:11
offer these besides *b.-off.* 23
offer it up for a *b.-off.* *Judg* 11:31
if thou *offer* a *b.-off.: offer.* 13:16
offered kine for *b.-off.* 1 *Sam* 6:14
Samuel *offered* a sucking lamb for a
b.-off.: 7:9
offer neither *b.-off.* 2 *Ki* 5:17
commanded to *offer b.-off.*
2 *Chr* 29:27
offer up a *b.-off.* *Job* 42:8
b.-off. prince shall *offer. Ezek* 46:4

burnt-offerings

Noah offered *b.-off.* *Gen* 8:20
give sacrifices and *b.-off. Ex* 10:25
sacrifice thereon thy *b.-off.* 20:24
trumpets over *b.-off.* *Num* 10:10
bring your *b.-off.* *Deut* 12:6, 11
14, 27
of the Lord with *b.-off. Josh* 22:27
great delight in *b.-off.* 1 *Sam* 15:22
Solomon offered *b.-off.* 1 *Ki* 3:15
of the court, he offered *b.-off.* 8:64
they offered *b.-off.* to. 1 *Chr* 29:21
I build house for *b.-off.* 2 *Chr* 2:4
altar not able to receive *b.-off.* 7:7
have not offered *b.-off.* in. 29:7
could not slay all the *b.-off.* 34
Levites brought *b.-off.* 30:15
busied in offering *b.-off.* 35:14
offered daily *b.-off.* *Ezra* 3:4
they have need for *b.-off.* 6:9
offered *b.-off.* according. *Job* 1:5
not reprove thee for *b.-off. Ps* 50:8
into thy house with *b.-off.* 66:13
full of the *b.-off.* of. *Isa* 1:11
small cattle of thy *b.-off.* 43:23
their *b.-off.* shall be accepted. 56:7
your *b.-off.* are not. *Jer* 6:20
put your *b.-off.* to your. 7:21
spake not concerning *b.-off.* 22
from south, bringing *b.-off.* 17:26
burn their sons for *b.-off.* 19:5
part to give *b.-off.* *Ezek* 45:17
knowledge more than *b.-off. Hos* 6:6
before him with *b.-off. ?* *Mi* 6:6
is more than *b.-off.* *Mark* 12:33
in *b.-off.* for sin thou. *Heb* 10:6

offer burnt-offerings

down to *offer b.-off.* 1 *Sam* 10:8
nor *offer b.-off.* of that which cost
me. 2 *Sam* 24:24; 1 *Chr* 21:24
b.-off. did Solomon *offer.* 1 *Ki* 3:4

year did Solomon *offer b.-off.*
1 *Ki* 9:25
builded altar to *offer b.-off. Ezra* 3:2
want man to *offer b.-off. Jer* 33:18
make it to *offer b.-off. Ezek* 43:18
ye *offer* me *b.-off.* *Amos* 5:22

burnt-sacrifice

strange incense, nor *b.-s.* *Ex* 30:9
burn all to be a *b.-s.* *Lev* 1:9; 3:5
lo, he stood by his *b.-s.* *Num* 23:6
put whole *b.-s.* on. *Deut* 33:10
here be oxen for *b.-s.* 2 *Sam* 24:22
fire consumed the *b.-s.* 1 *Ki* 18:38
altar burn king's *b.-s.* 2 *Ki* 16:15
accept thy *b.-s.* *Ps.* 20:3

burnt-sacrifices

b.-s. in the sabbaths. 1 *Chr* 23:31
and evening *b.-s.* 2 *Chr* 13:11
I will offer to thee *b.-s.* *Ps* 66:15

burnt *up*

the foxes *b. up* shocks. *Judg* 15:5
fire came down, and *b. up.* 2 *Ki* 1:14
third part of trees was *b. up,* and all
green grass was *b. up.* *Rev* 8:7

burst

to *b.* like new bottles. *Job* 32:19
presses shall *b.* with new. *Pr* 3:10
I have *b.* thy bands. *Jer* 2:20; 5:5
30:8; *Nah* 1:13
new wine *b.* bottles. *Mark* 2:22
Luke 5:37
he *b.* asunder in midst. *Acts* 1:18

bursting

not be found in the *b.* *Isa* 30:14*

bury

that I may *b.* my dead. *Gen* 23:4
choice of our sepulchres *b.* 6, 11, 15
b. me not in Egypt. 47:29; 49:29
let me go and *b.* my father. 50:5
go up and *b.* thy father. 6
shalt in any wise *b.* *Deut* 21:23
fall upon Joab and *b.* 1 *Ki* 2:31
Joab was gone up to *b.* the. 11:15
came to mourn and *b.* 13:29
when I am dead, *b.* me in the. 31
Israel shall mourn and *b.* him. 14:13
be none to *b.* Jezebel. 2 *Ki* 9:10
see now this cursed woman, *b.* 34
they went to *b.* her, but. 35
there was none to *b.* them. *Ps* 79:3
shall *b.* in Tophet. *Jer* 7:32; 19:11
they shall have none to *b.* 14:16
there shall they *b.* Gog. *Ezek* 39:11
people of the land shall *b.* them. 13
Memphis shall *b.* them. *Hos* 9:6
me to go *b.* my father. *Mat* 8:21
Luke 9:59
let dead *b.* their dead. *Mat* 8:22
Luke 9:60
potter's field to *b.* *Mat* 27:7
manner of Jews is to *b.* *John* 19:40

burying

a possession of a *b.* place. *Gen* 23:4
9; 49:30; 50:13
buried Samson in *b.* *Judg* 16:31
as they were *b.* a man. 2 *Ki* 13:21
months shall Israel be *b. Ezek* 39:12
anoint my body to *b.* *Mark* 14:8
against day of my *b.* *John* 12:7

bush, -es

in fire in the *b.* *Ex* 3:2; *Acts* 7:30
out of the midst of the *b.* *Ex* 3:4
of him that dwelt in *b.* *Deut* 33:16
cut up mallows by the *b.* *Job* 30:4
among the *b.* they brayed. 7
come and rest upon all *b. Isa* 7:19*
how in *b.* God spake. *Mark* 12:26*
nor of a bramble *b.* *Luke* 6:44
dead are raised, Moses shewed at
the *b.* 20:37
angel which appeared in *b. Acts* 7:35

bushel

put it under a *b.* but on. *Mat* 5:15
Mark 4:21; *Luke* 11:33

bushy

his locks are *b.* and. *S of S* 5:11

business

into house to do his *b.* *Gen* 39:11
nor charged with any *b. Deut* 24:5
if ye utter not our *b.* *Josh* 2:14
if thou utter this our *b.* we will. 20

no b. with any man. *Judg* 18:7*, 28*
hide thyself when b. *1 Sam* 20:19
let no man know of the b. 21:2
because king's b. required haste. 8
Levites wait on their b. *2 Chr* 13:10*
in the b. of the ambassadors. 32:31
every man in his b. *Neh* 13:30*
that have charge of b. *Esth* 3:9*
do b. in great waters. *Ps* 107:23
man diligent in his b.? *Pr* 22:29
through multitude of b. *Eccl* 5:3
and did the king's b. *Dan* 8:27
about my Father's b.? *Luke* 2:49*
we may appoint over b. *Acts* 6:3
not slothful in b. *Rom* 12:11*
assist her in what b. 16:2*
study to do your own b. *1 Thes* 4:11

busy, -ied
servant was b. here and. *1 Ki* 20:40
the sons of Aaron b. in. *2 Chr* 35:14

busybody, -ies
but some of you are b. *2 Thes* 3:11
1 Tim 5:13
none of you suffer as a b. *1 Pet* 4:15

but
b. a step between me. *1 Sam* 20:3
kill us, we shall b. die. *2 Ki* 7:4
b. speak not; eyes b. *Ps* 115:5
ears b. hear not; noses b. 6
have hands b. handle not; feet b. 7
b. of that day and hour. *Mat* 24:36
b. as the days of Noe were. 37
said, if I may touch b. *Mark* 5:28
know not the speech, b. *1 Cor* 4:19
b. ye are washed. 6:11
yet not I, b. the Lord. 7:10
b. the same Spirit. 12:4
b. the same Lord. 5
b. it is the same God which. 6
hath not grieved me b. *2 Cor* 2:5
our light affliction, which is b. 4:17

butler
b. of the king of Egypt. *Gen* 40:1
chief b. told dream to Joseph. 9
he restored his b. to his. 21
the chief b. said, I remember. 41:9

butter
(*While butter was not unknown the
word usually means curdled milk*)
Abraham took b. and. *Gen* 18:8
b. of kine, milk of. *Deut* 32:14
she brought forth b. *Judg* 5:25
Barzillai brought b. *2 Sam* 17:29
brooks of honey and b. *Job* 20:17
I washed my steps with b. 29:6
words smoother than b. *Ps* 55:21
of milk bringeth forth b. *Pr* 30:33
b. and honey shall he. *Isa* 7:15, 22

buttocks
cut to b. *2 Sam* 10:4; *1 Chr* 19:4
with b. uncovered to he. *Isa* 20:4

buy
you down to Egypt and b. *Gen* 42:2
land of Canaan to b. food. 7; 43:20
b. us and our land for bread. 47:19
if thou b. an Hebrew. *Ex* 21:2
if priests b. any soul. *Lev* 22:11
after the jubilee b. of thy. 25:15
of them shall ye b. bondmen. 44, 45
ye shall b. meat of them. *Deut* 2:6
be sold, and no man shall b. 28:68
b. it before inhabitants. *Ruth* 4:4
thou must b. it also of Ruth. 5
b. the threshing-floor. *2 Sam* 24:21
24; *1 Chr* 21:24
masons o. timber. *2 Ki* 12:12; 22:6
we would not b. it on. *Neh* 10:31
come, b. and eat, b. wine. *Isa* 55:1
b. thee my field that is in. *Jer* 32:7
men shall b. fields for money. 44
b. victuals. *Mat* 14:15; *Mark* 6:36
go to them that sell, and b. *Mat* 25:9
while they went to b. the. 10
shall we go and b.? *Mark* 6:37
except we b. meat for. *Luke* 9:13
sell his garment and b. one. 22:36
disciples were gone to b. *John* 4:8
whence shall we b. bread? 6:5
b. those things that we have. 13:29
they that b. as though. *1 Cor* 7:30
and we will b. and sell. *Jas* 4:13

I counsel thee to b. of me. *Rev* 3:18
no man b. or sell, save he. 13:17

buy corn
came to Joseph to b. corn. *Gen* 41:57
brethren went to b. corn. 42:3
our lands to b. corn. *Neh* 5:3

buy poor
that we may b. the poor. *Amos* 8:6

buy truth
b. the truth and sell it not. *Pr* 23:23

buyer
it is naught, saith the b. *Pr* 20:14
as with the b. so with. *Isa* 24:2
let not the b. rejoice. *Ezek* 7:12

buyest
if thou sell ought, or b. *Lev* 25:14
day thou b. field of. *Ruth* 4:5

buyeth
considereth a field, b. it. *Pr* 31:16
selleth all he hath, and b. *Mat* 13:44
man b. her merchandise. *Rev* 18:11

Buz
Milcah bare to Nahor B. *Gen* 22:21
Jahdo, the son of B. *1 Chr* 5:14
made Dedan and B. to. *Jer* 25:23

Buzi
Ezekiel the priest, son of B. *Ezek* 1:3

Buzite
Elihu son of the B. *Job* 32:2, 6

by and by
b. and b. he is offended. *Mat* 13:21
give me b. and b. in a. *Mark* 6:25
say to him b. and b. *Luke* 17:7
but the end is not b. and b. 21:9

by-ways
walked through b. *Judg* 5:6

by-word
thou shalt become a b. *Deut* 28:37
Israel shall be a b. *1 Ki* 9:7
house a proverb and a b. *2 Chr* 7:20
he hath made me a b. *Job* 17:6
I their song, yea, their b. 30:9
thou makest us a b. *Ps* 44:14

C

cab
(*A measure of about 2 quarts*)
fourth part of a c. of. *2 Ki* 6:25

cabins
(*Revised Version, cells*)
Jeremiah entered the c. *Jer* 37:16

Cabul
called them land of C. *1 Ki* 9:13

Caesar (Cesar)
to give tribute to C.? *Mat* 22:17
Mark 12:14; *Luke* 20:22
to C. the things that are *Cesar's*. to.
Mat 22:21; *Mark* 12:17
decree from C. Augustus. *Luke* 2:1
the fifteenth year of Tiberius C. 3:1
forbidding to give tribute to C. 23:2
thou art not *Cesar's* friend
speaketh against C. *John* 19:12
we have no king but C. 15
in days of Claudius C. *Acts* 11:28
do contrary to decrees of C. 17:7
nor against C. have I offended. 25:8
I appeal unto C. 11
till I send him to C. 21
if he had not appealed to C. 26:32
must be brought before C. 27:24
constrained to appeal to C. 28:19
they that are of C.'s *Phil* 4:22

cage
as a c. is full of birds. *Jer* 5:27
Babylon is c. of unclean. *Rev* 18:2*

Caiaphas
high-priest who was C. *Mat* 26:3
they led Jesus away to C. 57
C. said, ye know nothing. *John* 11:49
C. was he that gave counsel. 18:14
led Jesus from C. to the hall. 28

see **Annas**

Cain
C. and Gibeah cities. *Josh* 15:57

Cain
but C. was a tiller of. *Gen* 4:2
to C. and his offering he. 5

the Lord set a mark on C. *Gen* 4:15
seed instead of Abel whom C. 25
excellent sacrifice than C. *Heb* 11:4
not as C. who was of. *1 John* 3:12
gone in the way of C. *Jude* 11

Cainan
was the son of C. *Luke* 3:36, 37

cake, -s
they baked unleavened c. *Ex* 12:39
thanksgiving, unleavened c. *Lev* 7:12
take fine flour, bake twelve c. 24:5
offer up a c. of the first. *Num* 15:20
and lo, a c. tumbled. *Judg* 7:13
dealt to every one c. *2 Sam* 6:19
make me a couple of c. 13:6
I have not a c. *1 Ki* 17:12
make me a little c. first. 13
there was a c. baken on coals. 19:6
to make c. to the. *Jer* 7:18; 44:19
shalt eat it as barley c. *Ezek* 4:12
Ephraim is a c. not turned. *Hos* 7:8

see **figs, unleavened**

calamity, -ies
the day of their c. *Deut* 32:35
in day of c. *2 Sam* 22:19; *Ps* 18:18
and my c. laid in. *Job* 6:2
they set forward my c. 30:13
my refuge until these c. *Ps* 57:1
prayer also be in their c. 141:5*
I will laugh at your c. *Pr* 1:26
therefore his c. shall come. 6:15
he that is glad at c. shall. 17:5
a foolish son is the c. 19:13
their c. shall rise suddenly. 24:22
brother's house in day of c. 27:10
shew the back in day of c. *Jer* 18:17
the day of their c. was come. 46:21
the c. of Moab is near to. 48:16
for I will bring the c. 49:8
I will bring their c. from all. 32
blood of Israel in their c. *Ezek* 35:5
in the day of their c. *Ob* 13

calamus
of sweet c. 250 shekels. *Ex* 30:23
spikenard, saffron, c. *S of S* 4:14
c. was in the market of. *Ezek* 27:19

caldron
struck it into the pan, c. *1 Sam* 2:14
as out of a seething c. *Job* 41:20*
this city is the c. *Ezek* 11:3, 7
this city shall not be your c. 11
chop them as flesh within c. *Mi* 3:3

caldrons
sold they in pots and c. *2 Chr* 35:13
c. also and spoons. *Jer* 52:18, 19

Caleb
the tribe of Judah, C. *Num* 13:6
and C. stilled the people. 30
my servant C. having another spirit.
14:24, 30; 32:12; *Deut* 1:36
and C. lived. *Num* 14:38; 26:65
of the tribe of Judah, C. 34:19
Joshua gave C. Hebron. *Josh* 14:13
C. drove thence three sons of. 15:14
C. said, he that smiteth. 16
C. gave her the springs. *Judg* 1:15
Nabal was of house of C. *1 Sam* 25:3
C. begat children. *1 Chr* 2:18, 42, 50
4:15

Caleb
on the south of C. we. *1 Sam* 30:14

Caleb-ephratah
Hezron was dead in C. *1 Chr* 2:24

calf
Abraham fetched a c. *Gen* 18:7
he made it a molten c. *Ex* 32:4
Moses burnt c. and strawed. 20
take thee a young c. *Lev* 9:2
take a c. and a lamb for. 3
and made a molten c. *Deut* 9:16
Neh 9:18; *Ps* 106:19
and casteth not her c. *Job* 21:10
them to skip like a c. *Ps* 29:6
the c. and the young lion. *Isa* 11:6
there shall the c. feed. 27:10
when they cut the c. *Jer* 34:18
were like the sole of a c. *Ezek* 1:7
thy c. O Samaria, hath. *Hos* 8:5
c. of Samaria shall be broken. 6
hither the fatted c. *Luke* 15:23

hath killed fatted c. *Luke* 15:27, 30
and they made a c. in.   *Acts* 7:41
second beast was like a c. *Rev* 4:7

calkers
of Gebal were thy c.   *Ezek* 27:9
c. shall fall into midst.   27

call
to see what he would c.   *Gen* 2:19
c. to thee a nurse of the.   *Ex* 2:7
where is he ? c. him that he.   20
Moses sent to c. Dathan. *Num* 16:12
if the men c. thee, rise up.   22:20
God is in all things we c. *Deut* 4:7
I c. to witness.   26; 30:19; 31:28
c. for Samson that he.   *Judg* 16:25
they sent to c. peaceably.   21:13
thou didst c. me.   *1 Sam* 3:6, 8
c. Jesse to the sacrifice, and.   16:3
king sent to c. Ahimelech.   22:11
then said Absalom, c.   *2 Sam* 17:5
c. Bath-sheba.   *1 Ki* 1:28
c. Zadok and Nathan.   32
hearken to them in all they c.   8:52
art come to me to c. my sin? 17:18
c. ye on name of your.   18:24, 25
Elisha said, c. this.   *2 Ki* 4:12
c. unto me all the prophets.   10:19
c. now if there be any.   *Job* 5:1
c. thou, I will answer. 13:22; 14:15
hear when I c. O God of.   *Ps* 4:1
the Lord will hear when I c.   3
who eat up my people, and c.   14:4
let king hear us when we c.   20:9
they c. their lands after their. 49:11
I c. to remembrance my song. 77:6
plenteous in mercy to all that c. 86:5
Samuel among them that c.   99:6
in the day when I c. answer. 102:2
Lord is nigh all them that c. 145:18
unto you, O men, I c.   *Pr* 8:4
to c. passengers who go right. 9:15
children arise, c. her blessed. 31:28
to them that c. evil good. *Isa* 5:20
in that day did the Lord c.   22:12
I the Lord which c. thee.   45:3
they c. themselves of holy.   48:2
when I c. to them they stand.   1
c. ye upon him while he is.   55:6
wilt thou c. this a fast ?   58:5
c. the sabbath a delight, holy.   13
c. his servants by another.   65:15
it shall come, that before they c. 24
consider and c. for the.   *Jer* 9:17
c. unto me, and I will.   33:3
is this city that men c. ? *Lam* 2:15
the Lord said, c. his.   *Hos* 1:4
God said unto him, c. her name.   6
c. his name Lo-ammi, for ye are.   9
they c. to Egypt, they go.   7:11
sanctify a fast, c.   *Joel* 1:14; 2:15
O sleeper, arise, c.   *Jonah* 1:6
ye shall c. every man.   *Zech* 3:10
now we c. proud happy.   *Mal* 3:15
not come to c. righteous.   *Mat* 9:13
     Mark 2:17; *Luke* 5:32
c. the labourers and give. *Mat* 20:8
sent his servants to c. them.   22:3
how then did David in spirit c. ? 43
c. no man your father upon.   23:9
why c. ye me Lord and ? *Luke* 6:46
when thou makest a feast c.   14:13
go c. thy husband and.   *John* 4:16
ye c. me Master and Lord.   13:13
to bind all that c. on.   *Acts* 9:14
to c. over them which had.   19:13
after the way they c. heresy.   24:14
Lord is rich to all that c. *Rom* 10:12
I c. God for a record.   *2 Cor* 1:23
when I c. to remembrance. *2 Tim* 1:5
follow peace with them that c.   2:22
not ashamed to c. them.   *Heb* 2:11
but c. to remembrance.   10:32
let him c. the elders of.   *Jas* 5:14
if ye c. on the Father.   *1 Pet* 1:17

call *on the name of the Lord*
c. upon name of the L.   *Gen* 4:26
I will c. on the name of the L.
     1 Ki 18:24; *Ps* 116:17
he will c. on name of L.   *2 Ki* 5:11
c. upon his name.   *Ps* 105:1; *Isa* 12:4
whosoever shall c. on name of L.
     Joel 2:32; *Acts* 2:21; *Rom* 10:13

all c. upon *name of L.*   *Zeph* 3:9
c. on *the name of the L.*   *1 Cor* 1:2

not **call**
not c. her name Sarai.   *Gen* 17:15
didst *not* c. us to go.   *Judg* 12:1
c. me *not* Naomi, c. me.   *Ruth* 1:20
and they c. *not* upon.   *Ps* 14:4
yet he will *not* c. back.   *Isa* 31:2
upon families that c. *not*.   *Jer* 10:25
c. *not* thy friends.   *Luke* 14:12
I c. you *not* servants.   *John* 15:15
c. *not* thou common. *Acts* 10:15; 11:9
God hath shewed me *not* to c. 10:28

shall or shalt **call**
and thou *shalt* c. his.   *Gen* 17:19
elders of this city *shall* c. *Deut* 25:8
thou *shalt* c. them to mind.   30:1
they *shall* c. the people.   33:19
thou *shalt* c. and I will.   *Job* 14:15
he *shall* c. to the heavens. *Ps* 50:4
all nations *shall* c. him.   72:17
shall c. his name Immanuel (or
     Emmanuel). *Isa* 7:14; *Mat* 1:23
they *shall* c. the nobles to. *Isa* 34:12
from rising of sun *shall* he c. 41:25
another *shall* c. himself by.   44:5
and who, as I, *shall* c. and.   7
thou *shalt* c. a nation that.   55:5
then *shalt* thou c. and Lord.   58:9
they *shall* c. thee the city of. 60:14
shalt c. thy walls salvation.   18
men *shall* c. you ministers of. 61:6
shalt c. them the holy people. 62:12
they *shall* c. Jerusalem.   *Jer* 3:17
shalt c. me, my father.   19
reprobate silver *shall* men c.   6:30
shalt c. to them, but they will. 7:27
shalt c. me no more.   *Hos* 2:16
whom the Lord *shall* c.   *Joel* 2:32
shall c. the husbandmen. *Amos* 5:16
shall c. on my name.   *Zech* 13:9
they *shall* c. them the.   *Mal* 1:4
all nations *shall* c. you blessed. 3:12
shalt c. his name Jesus. *Mat* 1:21
how much more *shall* c. them ? 10:25
shalt c. his name John. *Luke* 1:13
all generations *shall* c. me.   48
many as the Lord *shall* c. *Acts* 2:39
how then *shall* they c. on. *Rom* 10:14

will **call**
we *will* c. the damsel.   *Gen* 24:57
daughters *will* c. me blessed. 30:13
I *will* c. unto Lord.   *1 Sam* 12:17
will c. on the.   *2 Sam* 22:4; *Ps* 18:3
will hypocrite c. on God ? *Job* 27:10
I *will* c. upon God.   *Ps* 55:16; 86:7
quicken us, and we *will* c.   80:18
therefore *will* I c. on him.   116:2
that I *will* c. my servant. *Isa* 22:20
I *will* c. all families of.   *Jer* 1:15
I *will* c. for sword. 25:29; *Ezek* 38:21
will c. to remembrance. *Ezek* 21:23
I *will* c. for the corn.   36:29
season I *will* c. for.   *Acts* 24:25
I *will* c. them my people. *Rom* 9:25

call *upon me*
c. *upon me* in day of.   *Ps* 50:15
he shall c. *upon me*, and.   91:15
shall c. *upon me*, but.   *Pr* 1:28
shall ye c. *upon me* and. *Jer* 29:12

called
the name of it c. Babel.   *Gen* 11:9
angel of God c. to Hagar.   21:17
angel c. to Abraham out.   22:11
name shall not be c. Jacob.   35:10
c. him Ben-oni, but his father c.   18
she c. to the men of her.   39:14
King of Egypt c. for the.   *Ex* 1:18
Pharaoh c. for Moses.   8:8, 25
     9:27; 10:16, 24; 12:31
Moses c. Oshea son of.   *Num* 13:16
Moses c. all Israel.   *Deut* 5:1; 29:2
not exact it, because it is c.   15:2
shall see thou art c. by.   28:10
have ye c. us to take ?   *Judg* 14:15
cast away the jaw-bone, and c. 15:17
Samson was sore athirst, and c.   18
Samson c. to the Lord.   16:28
c. a prophet, c. a seer.   *1 Sam* 9:9
whose name is c. by.   *2 Sam* 6:2
take the city, and it be c.   12:28

watchman c. to porter. *2 Sam* 18:26
the king c. the Gibeonites.   21:2
Adonijah c. all.   *1 Ki* 1:9; 19:25
Ahab c. Obadiah.   18:3
c. on the name of Baal.   26
c. to her husband and.   *2 Ki* 4:22
they came and c. to porter.   7:10
and Jabez c. on the.   *1 Chr* 4:10
ark of God, whose name is c.   13:6
David c. on the Lord.   21:26
except she were c.   *Esth* 2:14
who is not c. I have not been c. 4:11
people have not c. upon G. *Ps* 53:4
the kingdoms that have not c. 79:6
of shepherds is c. forth.   *Isa* 31:4
but thou hast not c. on me.   43:22
O Jacob, ye that are c. by.   48:1
hearken, O Jacob, and Israel my c. 12
that they might be c. trees of. 61:3
shall no more be c.   *Jer* 7:32
wilt bring day thou hast c. *Lam* 1:21
thou hast c. as a solemn day.   2:22
thereof is c. Bamah.   *Ezek* 20:29
now let Daniel be c. and. *Dan* 5:12
Jesus, who is c. Christ.   *Mat* 1:16
first Simon, who is c. Peter.   10:2
is not his mother c. Mary ?   13:55
Jesus c. a little child unto.   18:2
many be c. few chosen. 20:16; 22:14
Jesus stood still, and c.   20:32
be not ye c. Rabbi.   23:8, 10
one of the twelve c. Judas.   26:14
release Jesus, c. Christ ? 27:17, 22
commanded him to be c. *Mark* 10:49
Peter c. to mind the word.   14:72
of thy kindred is c.   *Luke* 1:61
signs how he would have him c. 62
no more worthy to be c. thy. 15:19, 21
commanded servants to be c. 19:15
to the place that is c. Calvary. 23:33
before that Philip c. thee. *John* 1:48
Messiah cometh, who is c.   4:25
a man c. Jesus made clay.   9:11
into the street c. Straight. *Acts* 9:11
disciples were c. Christians.   11:26
who c. for Barnabas and Saul. 13:7
then Saul, c. Paul, filled with.   9
on whom my name is c.   15:17
to be c. in question for.   19:40
I am c. in question.   23:6; 24:21
Paul the prisoner c. and.   23:18
Paul c. to be an. *Rom* 1:1; *1 Cor* 1:1
among whom are ye also c. *Rom* 1:6
c. to be saints.   7; *1 Cor* 1:2
thou art c. a Jew.   *Rom* 2:17
who are the c.   8:28
by whom ye were c.   *1 Cor* 1:9
to them which are c.   24
not many mighty are c.   26
if any man c. a brother be.   5:11
is any man c. being circumcised ? 18
any c. in uncircumcision ?   7:18
art thou c. being a servant ?   21
let every man wherein he is c.   24
removed from him that c. *Gal* 1:6
brethren, ye have been c.   5:13
c. uncircumcision by that c. *Eph* 2:11
vocation wherewith ye are c.   4:1
even as ye are c. in one hope.   4
to the which ye are c.   *Col* 3:15
Jesus, which is c. Justus.   4:11
above all that is c. God. *2 Thes* 2:4
whereto thou art c.   *1 Tim* 6:12
of science, falsely so c.   20
exhort daily while it is c. *Heb* 3:13
the tabernacle which is c. the.   9:2
they that are c. might receive.   15
God is not ashamed to be c. 11:16
Moses refused to be c. son of.   24
name by which ye are c.   *Jas* 2:7
of him who hath c. you.   *1 Pet* 2:9
for hereunto were ye c.   21
knowing ye are thereunto c.   3:9
that hath c. us to glory.   *2 Pet* 1:3
that we should be c. the. *1 John* 3:1
in Jesus Christ. and c.   *Jude* 1
name of the star is c.   *Rev* 8:11
spiritually is c. Sodom and.   11:8
that old serpent c. the Devil.   12:9
that are with him, are c.   17:14
blessed that are c. to the.   19:9

called, joined with *God or Lord*
c. light day, darkness he c. *Gen* 1:5

God c. firmament, Heaven. Gen 1:8
c. dry-land Earth, waters c. Seas. 10
and c. their name Adam. 5:2
God c. to him out of the. Ex 3:4
the Lord c. to him out of the. 19:3
the Lord c. Moses up to the top. 20
see, the Lord hath c. my. 35:30
Lord c. Aaron and. Num 12:5
Lord c. Samuel. 1 Sam 3:4, 6, 8, 10
c. these three kings. 2 Ki 3:10, 13
the Lord hath c. for a famine. 8:1
Lord hath c. the earth. Ps 50:1
Lord raised, and c. him. Isa 41:2
the Lord have c. thee. 42:6
the Lord hath c. me. 49:1
the Lord hath c. thee as a. 54:6
Lord c. thy name a green. Jer 11:16
hath not c. thy name Pashur. 20:3
Lord God c. to contend. Amos 7:4
that the Lord had c. us. Acts 16:10
but God hath c. us. 1 Cor 7:15
as the Lord hath c. every one. 17
it pleased God, who c. Gal 1:15
c. you to his kingdom. 1 Thes 2:12
for God hath not c. us to. 4:7
whereunto God c. you. 2 Thes 2:14
who hath c. us. 2 Tim 1:9
but he that is c. of God. Heb 5:4
c. of God an high-priest after. 10
God of all grace, who c. 1 Pet 5:10

he called
he c. that place Beer-sheba.
Gen 21:31
he c. their names as his. 26:18
thy name is Jacob, he c. his. 35:10
the Lord c. to Moses. Ex 24:16
he c. him Jerubbaal. Judg 6:32
he saw me and c. to me. 2 Sam 1:7
then he c. his servant that. 13:17
Solomon his brother he c. not.
1 Ki 1:10; 19:26
he c. them land of Cabul. 9:13
he c. to Gehazi, so he c. 2 Ki 4:36
brake brazen serpent, he c. 18:4
he c. for a famine. Ps 105:16
then c. he Johanan and. Jer 42:8
he hath c. an assembly. Lam 1:15
he c. to the man. Ezek 9:3
he c. the twelve. Mat 10:1
he c. the multitude. 15:10
straightway he c. them. Mark 1:20
Jesus saw her, he c. Luke 13:12
if he c. them gods. John 10:35
he had c. the saints. Acts 9:41
then c. he them in. 10:23
then he c. for a light. 16:29
whom he c. together. 19:25
he c. unto him two centurions. 23:23
he also c. whom he. Rom 8:30
even us whom he hath c. not. 9:24
as he which hath c. you. 1 Pet 1:15

see called the name

I called, or, I have called
I c. thee to curse. Num 24:10
when I c. you, ye. Judg 12:2
Eli said, I c. not. 1 Sam 3:5, 6
I have c. thee. 28:15
in my distress I c. 2 Sam 22:7
Ps 18:6; 118:5
I c. the priests. Neh 5:12
if I had c. and he had. Job 9:16
I c. my servant, and he gave. 19:16
I have c. on thee, for. Ps 17:6
not be ashamed, for I have c. 31:17
Lord, I have c. daily upon. 88:9
then c. I upon the Lord. 116:4
because I have c. Pr 1:24
I c. him, but he gave. S of S 5:6
I have c. my mighty ones. Isa 13:3
I have c. thee from the. 41:9
I c. thee by thy name. 43:1; 45:4
yea, I have c. him. 48:15
when I c. was there none ? 50:2
for I c. him alone. 51:2
I c. ye did not answer. 65:12
Jer 7:13
because when I c. none did. Isa 66:4
because I have c. to them. Jer 35:17
I c. for my lovers. Lam 1:19
I c. on thy name out of. 3:55
drewest near in the day I c. 57
I c. my Son out of Egypt. Hos 11:1
Mat 2:15

I c. for a drought upon. Hag 1:11
one I c. Beauty, the other I c.
Zech 11:7
not servants, I have c. John 15:15
work whereto I have c. Acts 13:2
for this cause have I c. for. 28:20

called by my name
people who are c. by my n. 2 Chr 7:14
one that is c. by my n. Isa 43:7
nation that was not c. by my n. 65:1
house c. by my n. Jer 7:10, 11, 14
30; 32:34; 34:15
evil on the city c. by my n. 25:29
heathen which are c. by my n.
Amos 9:12

called by thy name
house is c. by thy n. 1 Ki 8:43
2 Chr 6:33
let us be c. by thy n. to. Isa 4:1
c. thee by thy n. 43:1; 45:4
they were not c. by thy n. 63:19
Lord, we are c. by thy n. Jer 14:9
for I am c. by thy n. 15:16
city which is c. by thy n. Dan 9:18
city and people are c. by thy n. 19

called his name
he c. his n. Israel. Gen 35:10
she c. his n. Benoni. 18
mother c. his n. Jabez. 1 Chr 4:9
she c. his n. Peresh. 7:16
and he c. his n. Beriah. 23
and he c. his n. Jesus. Mat 1:25
and his name is c. the. Rev 19:13

called the name
c. the n. of place. Gen. 28:19; 35:15
Israel c. the n. manna. Ex 16:31
c. the n. of the place Massah. 17:7
Moses c. the n. of the altar. 15
Samson c. the n. Judg 15:19
c. the n. of that place. 2 Sam 5:20
c. the n. thereof Jachin. 1 Ki 7:21
2 Chr 3:17
he c. the n. of the first. Job 42:12

sent and called
she sent and c. Jacob. Gen 27:42
Jacob sent and c. Rachel. 31:4
then Pharaoh sent and c. 41:14
Balak sent and c. Balaam. Josh 24:9
she sent and c. Barak. Judg 4:6
she sent and c. the lords. 16:18
he sent and c. his name. 2 Sam 12:25
king sent and c. for. 1 Ki 2:36, 42
sent and c. Jeroboam. 12:3
2 Chr 10:3
Haman sent and c. for. Esth 5:10
sent to Ephesus, and c. Acts 20:17

shall be called
shall be c. woman. Gen 2:23
thy name shall be c. Abraham. 17:5
in Isaac shall thy seed be c. 21:12
Rom 9:7; Heb 11:18
shall be c. no more Jacob. Gen 32:28
thy issue shall be c. after. 48:6
his name shall be c. in. Deut 25:10
wise in heart shall be c. Pr 16:21
deviseth evil, shall be c. a. 24:8
Jerusalem shall be c. Isa 4:3
name shall be c. Wonderful. 9:6
one shall be c. the city of. 19:18
vile person shall no more be c. 32:5
shall be c. way of holiness. 35:8
the whole earth shall be c. 54:5
shall be c. house of prayer. 56:7
Mat 21:13
shall no more be c. Tophet.
Jer 7:32; 19:6
shall be c. Lord our. 23:6; 33:16
Jerusalem shall be c. a. Zech 8:3
be fulfilled, shall be c. a. Mat 2:23
peace-makers shall be c. 5:9
he shall be c. the least in. 19
and he shall be c. the. Luke 1:32
that holy thing shall be c. the. 35
mother said he shall be c. John. 60
every male shall be c. holy. 2:23
she be married, shall be c. Rom 7:3
they shall be c. the children. 9:26

shalt be called
thou shalt be c. the city of. Isa 1:26
thou shalt be c. no more tender. 47:1
thou shalt no more be c. lady of. 5
thou shalt be c. the repairer. 58:12

shalt be c. by a new name. Isa 62:2
thou shalt be c. Hephzi-bah. 4
thou shalt be c. sought for. 12
thou shalt be c. Prophet. Luke 1:76
thou shalt be c. Cephas. John 1:42

they called
they c. Lot, and said. Gen 19:5
they c. the people to. Num 25:2
they c. for Samson. Judg 16:25
they c. these days Purim. Esth 9:26
they c. upon the Lord. Ps 99:6
they have c. a multitude. Jer 12:6
because they c. thee an. 30:17
as they c. to them, so. Hos 11:2
they c. them to the most High. 7
if they have c. master. Mat 10:25
they c. him Zacharias. Luke 1:59
they c. parents of him. John 9:18
then again they c. the man. 24
they c. them, and. Acts 4:18
when they had c. the apostles. 5:40
they c. Barnabas, Jupiter. 14:12

was called
which was c. the land of. Deut 3:13
place was c. the valley. 2 Chr 20:26
was c. after their name. Ezra 2:61
Neh 7:63
wast c. a transgressor. Isa 48:8
whose name was c. Dan 10:1
priest, who was c. Caiaphas. Mat 26:3
was c. the field of blood. 27:8
her who was c. barren. Luke 1:36
his name was c. Jesus. 2:21
Jesus was c. and his. John 2:2
Simeon, that was c. Niger. Acts 13:1
and when he was c. forth. 24:2
knew the island was c. Melita. 28:1
calling wherein he was c. 1 Cor 7:20
Abraham when he was c. Heb 11:8
was c. the friend of God. Jas 2:23
that set on him was c. Rev 19:11

calledst, callest
that thou c. us not when. Judg 8:1
here am I, for thou c. 1 Sam 3:5
thou c. in trouble, and I. Ps 81:7
c. to remembrance. Ezek 3:21
why c. thou me good ? Mat 19:7
Mark 10:18; Luke 18:19

calleth
do according to all that the stranger
c. to. 1 Ki 8:43; 2 Chr 6:33
who c. on God, and he. Job 12:4
deep c. unto deep at. Ps 42:7
c. them all by their names. 147:4
Isa 40:26
fool's mouth c. for strokes. Pr 18:6
he c. to me out of Seir. Isa 21:11
none c. for justice. 59:4
there is none that c. on thy. 64:7
there is none that c. to. Hos 5:8
c. for waters of the sea. Amos 5:8
9:6
c. for Elias. Mat 27:47; Mark 15:35
c. to him whom he would. Mark 3:13
c. to him the twelve. 6:7
Jesus c. his disciples. 6:7
arise, he c. thee. 10:49
if David therefore c. him Lord. 12:37
Luke 20:44
he c. together his friends. Luke 15:6
she c. her friends and her. 9
when he c. the Lord. 20:37
and he c. his own sheep. John 10:3
master is come and c. for. 11:28
c. things which be not. as. Rom 4:17
might stand. of him that c. 9:11
no man by the Spirit c. 1 Cor 12:3
cometh not of him that c. Gal 5:8
faithful is he that c. 1 Thes 5:24
Jezebel, that c. herself a. Rev 2:20

calling
[1] Any lawful employment, or way
of living, 1 Cor 7:20. [2] The
calling of the gospel of Christ,
Phil 3:14; Heb 3:1.
use trumpets for c. of. Num 10:2
the c. of assemblies. Isa 1:13
in c. to remembrance. Ezek
the c. of God without. Rom 11:29
see your c. brethren. 1 Cor 1:26
let every man abide in same c. 7:20
what is the hope of his c. Eph 1:18

called in one hope of your c. Eph 4:4
for the prize of the high c. Phil 3:14
you worthy of this c. 2 Thes 1:11
called us with an holy c. 2 Tim 1:9
partakers of the heavenly c. Heb 3:1
your c. and election sure. 2 Pet 1:10

calling, participle
c. the generations from. Isa 41:4
c. a ravenous bird from the. 46:11
c. to their fellows. Mat 11:16
Luke 7:32
Peter, c. to remembrance.
Mark 11:21
stoned Stephen c. upon. Acts 7:59
wash away thy sins, c. on. 22:16
obeyed Abraham, c. 1 Pet 3:6

calm
maketh the storm a c. Ps 107:29
that the sea may be c. Jonah 1:11
so shall the sea be c. to you. 12
there was a great c. Mat 8:26
Mark 4:39; Luke 8:24

Calneh
Babel and C. in land of. Gen 10:10
pass ye unto C. from. Amos 6:2

Calno
not C. as Carchemish? Isa 10:9

Calvary
come to place called C. Luke 23:33

calve, -ed, -eth
their cow c. and casteth. Job 21:10
mark when the hinds do c. ? 39:1
Lord maketh hinds to c. Ps 29:9
the hind c. in the field. Jer 14:5

calves
and bring their c. home. 1 Sam 6:7
king made two c. of gold. 1 Ki 12:28
sacrificing to the c. that he. 32
not from the golden c. 2 Ki 10:29
ordained priests, for c. 2 Chr 11:15
there are with you golden c. 13:8
rebuke bulls with the c. Ps 68:30
fear, because of the c. of. Hos 10:5
men that sacrifice kiss the c. 13:2
so will we render the c. of. 14:2
and eat c. out of the midst. Amos 6:4
shall I come with c. ? Mi 6:6
grow up as c. of the stall. Mal 4:2
by blood of goats and c. Heb 9:12
took blood of c. and sprinkled. 19

came
of whom c. Gen 10:14; 1 Chr 1:12
c. two angels to Sodom. Gen 19:1
God c. to Abimelech. 20:3
brother c. with subtilty. 27:35
God c. to Laban the Syrian. 31:24
c. to thy brother Esau. he. 32:6
laid up garment until his lord c. 39:16
c. to the land whither. Num 13:27
red heifer. upon which never c. 19:2
God c. to Balaam at. 22:9, 20
Spirit of God c. on him. 24:2
Judg 3:10; 1 Sam 10:10
we c. to Kadesh-barnea. Deut 1:19
the Lord c. from Sinai. 33:2
as she c. to him she moved.
Josh 15:18; Judg 1:14
kings c. and fought. Judg 5:19
cake of bread c. to a tent. 7:13
they robbed all that c. along. 9:25
upon them c. curse of Jotham. 57
c. not within border of Moab. 11:18
the man that c. to me. 13:10
Manoah arose and c. to the. 11
bring forth the man that c. 19:22
all that c. to hand. 20:48
Moabitish damsel that c. Ruth 2:6
priest's servant, c. 1 Sam 2:13, 15
to all Israelites that c. thither. 14
there c. a man of God to Eli. 27
and the word of Samuel c. 4:1
they c. no more into coast. 7:13
told Samuel before Saul c. 9:15
saw asses no where, c. to. 10:14
but Samuel c. not to Gilgal. 13:8
there c. a lion and a bear. 17:34
men of Judah c. and. 2 Sam 2:4
thou knowest Abner, that c. 3:25
the way tidings c. to David. 13:30
behold, king's sons c. and wept. 36
when any c. to king. 15:2

Absalom and Ahithophel c.
2 Sam 16:15
saw every one that c. by him. 20:12
Jonathan son of Abiathar c. 1 Ki 1:42
c. of all people to hear wisdom. 4:34
there c. no more such spices. 10:10
there c. no such almug-trees. 12
Jeroboam and all the people c.
12:12; 2 Chr 10:12
not by way he c. to. 1 Ki 13:10
he c. thither to a cave. 19:9
king of Israel c. heavy to. 20:43
it fell on a day that he c. 2 Ki 4:11
when she c. to the man of God. 27
Naaman c. and stood before. 5:15
the bands of Syria c. 6:23
but ere messenger c. to him. 32
Hazael departed from Elisha, c. 8:14
wherefore c. this mad fellow ? 9:11
Jehu arose, departed, and c. 10:12
all worshippers of Baal c. 21
of the priests c. and dwelt. 17:28
by the way that he c. shall. 19:33
command of the Lord c. this. 24:3
these c. in the days of. 1 Chr 4:41
Judah prevailed, of him c. 5:2
Ephraim's brethren c. to. 7:22
are they that c. to David. 12:1
there c. to David to help him. 22
Levites left all and c. 2 Chr 11:14
guard c. and fetched the. 12:11
fear of Lord c. upon them. 14:14
the band of men that c. with. 22:1
wrath c. on Judah and. 24:18
not hear, for it c. of God. 25:20
humbled themselves and c. 30:11
as soon as commandment c. 31:5
which c. with Zerubbabel. Ezra 2:2
cease till matter c. to Darius. 5:5
when seventh month c. Neh 7:73
Vashti brought in, she c. Esth 1:17
then thus c. every maiden to. 2:13
Mordecai c. even before. 4:2
whither the king's decree c. 8:17
rest, yet trouble c. Job 3:26
of him ready to perish c. 29:13
evil c. darkness c. 30:26
my cry c. before me. Ps 18:6
when my foes c. upon me. 27:2
wrath of God c. upon them. 78:31
until time that his word c. 105:19
spake, and there c. divers sorts. 31
he spake, and locusts c. and. 34
to go as he c. Eccl 5:15, 16
year that Tartan c. Isa 20:1
and his ambassadors c. to. 30:4
ends of earth, drew near and c. 41:5
nor c. it into my mind. Jer 7:31
19:5; 32:35
looked for peace. no good c. 8:15
incense you burnt, c. it not ? 44:21
nor c. abominable flesh. Ezek 4:14
c. to Lebanon, and took the. 17:3
afore he that escaped c. 33:22
the bones c. together. 37:7
breath c. into them, they lived. 10
glory of God of Israel c. 43:2
all this c. on the king. Dan 4:28
one like Son of Man c. 7:13
till the ancient of days c. 22
to whom house of Israel c. Amos 6:1
for word c. to the king. Jonah 3:6
God c. from Teman, and. Hab 3:3
and lo it c. to little. Hag 1:9
when one c. to the press-fat. 2:16
c. a great wrath from. Zech 7:12
in all the nations that c. 14:16
c. wise men from the east. Mat 2:1
till it c. and stood over where. 9
those days c. John the Baptist. 3:1
descended, and floods c. 7:25, 27
he passed over and c. into. 9:1
a woman c. behind, touched. 20
the blind men c. to Jesus. 28
Son of Man c. not to be. 20:28
c. to the first and said. 21:28
he c. to the second, and said. 30
John c. to you in the way of. 32
went to buy, bridegroom c. 25:10
in prison, and ye c. to me. 36
forthwith he c. to Jesus. 26:49
though false witnesses c. yet. 60
his disciples c. by night. 28:13
what he did, c. to him. Mark 3:8

how long is it since this c.? Mark 9:21
one of the scribes c. 12:28
c. a certain poor widow. 42
there c. a cloud and. Luke 9:34
there c. a voice out of the cloud. 35
when he c. to himself. 15:17
he arose and c. to his father. 20
same c. to bear witness. John 1:7
he c. to his own, and his own. 11
but grace and truth c. by Jesus. 17
same c. to Jesus by night. 3:2
7:50; 19:39
and they c. and were baptized. 3:23
upon this c. his disciples. 4:27
gods to whom word of God c. 10:35
the voice c. not because. 12:30
at even c. Jesus, and stood. 20:19
preached, till he c. to. Acts 8:40
c. hither for that intent. 9:21
as many as c. with Peter. 10:45
the vessel descended, and it c. 11:5
when he c. and had seen. 23
and many that believed c. 19:18
nor brethren that c. spake. 28:21
judgement c. free gift c. Rom 5:18
when the commandment c. sin. 7:9
concerning the flesh, Christ c. 9:5
man c. death, by man c. 1 Cor 15:21
for before that certain c. Gal 2:12
before faith c. we were kept. 3:23
and c. and preached peace. Eph 2:17
that Christ c. to save. 1 Tim 1:15
persecutions which c. 2 Tim 3:11
there c. such a voice. 2 Pet 1:17
this voice which c. from heaven. 18
prophecy c. not in old time. 21
this is he that c. by. 1 John 5:6
when brethren c. and. 3 John 3
and great Babylon c. Rev 16:19
see Spirit of the **Lord**

came again
angel c. again to the. Judg 13:9
spirit c. again. 15:19; 1 Sam 30:12
and Benjamin c. again. Judg 21:14
soul of the child c. again. 1 Ki 17:22
angel of the Lord c. again. 9
his flesh c. again like. 2 Ki 5:14
lepers c. again, and entered. 7:8
these c. again to. Ezra 2:1; Neh 7:6
Mordecai c. again. Esth 6:12
c. again and touched. Dan 10:18
the angel c. again. Zech 4:1
her spirit c. again. Luke 8:55
and early he c. again. John 8:2

came down
Lord c. down to see. Gen 11:5
when the fowls c. down. 15:11
O sir, we c. down at first. 43:20
the Lord c. down upon. Ex 19:20
when Moses c. down. 34:29
and Aaron c. down. Lev 9:22
Lord c. down in a cloud. Num 11:25
12:5
then Amalekites c. down. 14:45
out of Machir c. down. Judg. 5:14
and c. down. 2 Sam 22:10; Ps 18:9
c. down fire from heaven. 2 Ki 1:10
12, 14
men of Gath c. down. 1 Chr 7:21
of praying, fire c. down. 2 Chr 7:1, 3
therefore she c. down. Lam 1:9
an holy one c. down. Dan 4:13
evil c. down from Lord. Mi 1:12
c. down from mountain. Mat 17:9
Mark 9:9
c. down a certain priest. Luke 10:31
he made haste and c. down. 19:6
he that c. down from. John 3:13
I c. down from heaven, not. 6:38
bread which c. down. 41, 51, 58
men which c. down. Acts 15:1
c. down from Judea a. 21:10
fire c. down from God. Rev 20:9

came forth
to me when I c. forth. Ex 13:8
why c. we forth out of Egypt ?
Num 11:20
Aaron and Miriam, c. forth. 12:5
water when ye c. forth. Deut 23:4
hot on day we c. forth. Neh 9:12
out of eater c. forth meat, and out of
strong c. forth. Judg 14:14

Shimei *c. forth* and.   *2 Sam* 16:5
son which *c. forth* of my bowels.   11
c. forth a spirit, and.   *1 Ki* 22:21
c. forth little children.   *2 Ki* 2:23
c. forth two she-bears and tare.   24
fathers *c. forth.*   21:15; *Jer* 7:25
c. forth of his bowels.   *2 Chr* 32:21
therefore *c. I forth* to.   *Pr* 7:15
as he *c. forth* naked.   *Eccl* 5:15
wherefore *c. I forth.*   *Jer* 20:18
they *c. forth* of the.   *Dan* 3:26
c. forth fingers and wrote.   5:5
a fiery stream *c. forth.*   7:10
out of one of them *c. forth.*   8:9
the command *c. forth* and I.   9:23
out of him *c. forth* corner. *Zech* 10:4
for therefore *c. I forth. Mark* 1:38
that was dead *c. forth. John* 11:44
I *c. forth* from the Father.   16:28
Jesus *c. forth* wearing the.   19:5

I came

I c. this day to the well. *Gen* 24:42
little thou hadst before *I c.*   30:30
which were born before *I c.*   48:5
when *I c.* from Padan, Rachel.   7
I c. to speak to Pharaoh *Ex* 5:23
when *I c.* to her found. *Deut* 22:14
I c. into Gibeah.   *Judg* 20:4
believed me not till *I c.*   *1 Ki* 10:7
     2 Chr 9:6
afterwards *I c.* to the.   *Neh* 6:10
I c. to the king and.   13:6
I c. to Jerusalem and understood. 7
wherefore, when *I c.*   *Isa* 50:2
then *I c.* to them of the. *Ezek* 3:15
when *I c.* to destroy the city.   43:3
I c. not to send peace. *Mat* 10:34
I c. not to call the righteous.
   Mark 2:17; *Luke* 5:32
I know whence *I c.*   *John* 8:14
I c. from God, nor *c. I* of.   42
but for this cause *I c.*   12:27
for *I c.* not to judge the world.   47
for this cause *c. I* into the.   18:37
therefore *c. I* as soon as. *Acts* 10:29
the first day *I c.* into Asia.   20:18
being led by the hand, *I c.*   22:11
then *c. I* with an army.   23:27
I c. to bring alms to my.   24:17
when *I c.* to you *I c.* not. *1 Cor* 2:1
to spare you *I c.* not.   *2 Cor* 1:23
lest when *I c.* I should have.   2:3
when *I c.* to Troas to preach.   12
afterwards *I c.* into.   *Gal* 1:21

came *in*

sons of God, *c. in* to.   *Gen* 6:4
where are the men that *c. in.*   19:5
Judah *c. in* unto her.   38:18
he *c. in* to lie with me.   39:14
if he *c. in* by himself.   *Ex* 21:3
went out, and none *c. in. Josh* 6:1
went out and *c. in. 1 Sam* 18:13, 16
she *c. in* to him.   *2 Sam* 11:4
as she *c. in* at the door. *1 Ki* 14:6
no peace to him that *c. in. 2 Chr* 15:5
     Zech 8:10
c. in unto the king no more. *Esth* 2:14
and they *c. in* and.   *Jer* 32:23
now Jeremiah *c. in* and went.   37:4
way of the gate he *c. in. Ezek* 46:9
c. in the magicians.   *Dan* 4:7; 5:8
but at the last Daniel *c. in.*   4:8
my prayer *c. in.*   *Jonah* 2:7
when the king *c. in* to. *Mat* 22:11
the angel *c. in* to Mary. *Luke* 1:28
this woman since I *c. in.*   7:45
wife not knowing *c. in. Acts* 5:7
the young men *c. in* and found.   10
who *c. in* privily to spy. *Gal* 2:4

came *near*

they pressed, and *c. near. Gen* 19:9
the one *c.* not *near* the. *Ex* 14:20
when they *c. near* to the altar. 40:32
captains *c. near* to Moses.
     Num 31:48
the chief of Joseph *c. near.*   36:1
ye *c. near* to me. *Deut* 1:22; 5:23
c. near and put feet on. *Josh* 10:24
c. near before Eleazar.   17:4; 21:1
Elijah *c. near* and said. *1 Ki* 18:36
Gehazi *c. near* to thrust. *2 Ki* 4:27
Zedekiah *c. near* and. *2 Chr* 18:23

---

even to greatest *c. near.* *Jer* 42:1
Chaldeans *c. near* and. *Dan* 3:8
Nebuchadnezzar *c. near* to.   26
he *c. near* to Damascus. *Acts* 9:3

came *nigh*

as soon as he *c. nigh.* *Ex* 32:19
the children of Israel *c. nigh.* 34:32
when any *c. nigh* to do. *2 Sam* 15:5
Jesus *c. nigh* to the sea. *Mat* 15:29
when they *c. nigh* to. *Mark* 11:1
when he *c. nigh* to gate. *Luke* 7:12

came *over*

Israel *c. over* this Jordan. *Josh* 4:22
the Levite *c. over.*   *Judg* 19:10
they *c. over* to the other. *Mark* 5:1

came *out*

behold Rebekah *c. out.* *Gen* 24:15
first *c. out* red, all over like.   25:25
midwife said, this *c. out* first. 38:28
all the souls which *c. out* of.   46:26
day in which ye *c. out. Ex* 13:3, 4
a fire *c. out.*   *Lev* 9:24; *Num* 16:35
they three *c. out.*   *Num* 12:4
Dathan and Abiram *c. out.*   16:27
smote rock, and water *c. out.* 20:11
Egypt whence ye *c. out. Deut* 11:10
all that *c. out* were.   *Josh* 5:4, 5
all that *c. out* of Egypt.   6
Jael *c. out* to meet him. *Judg* 4:22
I am he that *c. out.*   *1 Sam* 4:16
three days since I *c. out.*   21:5
spear *c. out* behind.   *2 Sam* 2:23
Michal *c. out* to meet David.   6:20
men prevailed and *c. out.*   11:23
and all the people *c. out.*   18:4
covenant with Israel when they *c.
out ot.*   *1 Ki* 8:9; *2 Chr* 5:10
princes of provinces *c. out. 1 Ki* 20:19
when they *c. out.*   *2 Chr* 20:10
naked *c. I out* of my.   *Job* 1:21
why did I not give up the ghost,
when I *c. out* of the belly ?   3:11
that which *c. out* of my. *Jer* 17:16
whirlwind *c. out* of the. *Ezek* 1:4
c. out as a whirlwind. *Hab* 3:14
c. out two women.   *Zech* 5:9
the whole city *c. out* to. *Mat* 8:34
return to house whence I *c. out.*
     12:44; *Luke* 11:24
as they *c. out* they found. *Mat* 27:32
and *c. out* of the graves after.   53
unclean spirit *c. out. Mark* 1:26
     9:26
c. out he saw much people.   6:34
a voice *c. out* of the cloud.   9:7
when he *c. out* he could. *Luke* 1:22
and he *c. out* of him.   4:35
therefore *c. out* his father.   15:28
believed I *c. out* from. *John* 16:27
have known that I *c. out.*   17:8
forthwith *c. out* blood and.   19:34
unclean spirits *c. out. Acts* 8:7
and the spirit *c. out.*   16:18
c. word of God out. *1 Cor* 14:36
not all that *c. out* of. *Heb* 3:16
c. out of great tribulation. *Rev* 7:14
angel *c. out* of the temple. 14:15, 17
angel *c. out* from the altar.   18
seven angels *c. out* of temple. 15:6
a voice *c. out* of the throne.   19:5

came *to pass*

it *c. to pass,* even the self-same day
   it *c. to pass.*   *Ex* 12:41, 51
it *c. to pass. Deut* 2:16; *1 Sam* 13:22
   2 Ki 15:12; *Esth* 2:8; *Acts* 27:44
it *c. to pass* when Israel. *Josh* 17:13
all *c. to pass.*   21:45
for it *c. to pass.*   *Judg* 13:20
     1 Ki 11:34, 15
but it *c. to pass. Judg* 15:1; *2 Ki* 3:5
   Neh 2:1; 4:1, 7; 6:1; 7:1
     Jer 35:11
it *c. to pass* when the. *1 Sam* 1:20
and all those signs *c. to pass.* 10:9
it *c. to pass* when the evil.   16:23
it *c. to pass* after. *2 Sam* 2:1; 8:1
   10:1; *1 Ki* 6:24; *2 Chr* 20:1
it *c. to pass* on morrow. *2 Ki* 8:15
   1 Chr 10:8; *Jer* 20:3; *Acts* 4:5
and they *c. to pass.*   *Isa* 48:3
before it *c. to pass* I shewed.   5
even as it *c. to pass.*   *1 Thes* 3:4

---

then came

then c. Amalek and.   *Ex* 17:8
then c. the daughters. *Num* 27:1
then c. David to.   *1 Sam* 21:1
then c. all the tribes. *2 Sam* 5:1
then they c. to Gilead.   24:6
then c. Eliakim.   *2 Ki* 18:37
     Isa 36:22
then c. Solomon.   *2 Chr* 1:13
then c. Shemaiah the prophet.   12:5
then c. Sheshbazzar. *Ezra* 5:16
then Hanani *c.*   *Neh* 1:2
then I *c.* to the governors.   2:9
for good, *then* evil *c.* *Job* 30:26
then c. Jeremiah from. *Jer* 19:14
then c. all the princes.   38:27
then c. certain of elders. *Ezek* 14:1
then they c. the same day.   23:39
then c. to him the. *Mat* 9:14
then c. to Jesus scribes and.   15:1
then c. his disciples.   12; 17:19
then c. she, and worshipped.   15:25
     Mark 7:25
then c. Peter to him. *Mat* 18:21
then c. mother of Zebedee's. 20:20
then c. they, and laid hands. 26:50
then c. also publicans. *Luke* 3:12
then c. day of unleavened.   22:7
then c. the officers to. *John* 7:45
then c. a voice from heaven.   12:28
then c. Jesus, the doors.   20:26

they came, or came *they*

they c. to Haran and. *Gen* 11:31
into the land of Canaan, *they c.* 12:5
they c. to the place which God. 22:9
till *they c.* to a land. *Ex* 16:35
same day *c. they* into the   19:1
they c. he lay on bed. *2 Sam* 4:7
and Nathan, *they c.*   *1 Ki* 1:32
so *they c.* to me, when I fled.   2:7
they c. and told it in city.   13:25
I will not leave, so *they c. 2 Ki* 2:4
when *they c.* to Jordan.   6:4
whence *c. they?*   20:14; *Isa* 39:3
out of all Judah *they c. 2 Chr* 20:4
on eighth day *c. they* to.   29:17
some when *they c.* offered. *Ezra* 2:68
from that time *c. they. Neh* 13:21
they c. thither and were. *Job* 6:20
they c. upon me as a wide.   30:14
they c. round about me. *Ps* 88:17
they c. to the pits.   *Jer* 14:3
c. they even to Tahpanhes.   43:7
messenger was sent, lo *they c.*
     Ezek 23:40
they c. and stood before. *Dan* 2:2
or ever *they c.* at the bottom.   6:24
before *they c.* together. *Mat* 1:18
they c. into the land of.   14:34
they c. and told they Lord all.
   18:31; *Luke* 14:21
after a while *c. they. Mat* 26:73
they c. to him from. *Mark* 1:45
whom he would, and *they c.*   3:13
they c. with haste.   *Luke* 2:16
they c. saying, that they.   24:23
and *they c.* not for Jesus'. *John* 12:9
they c. unto a certain. *Acts* 8:36
they c. to the iron gate.   12:10
they c. with one accord and.   20
they c. thither also and stirred. 17:13
they c. to the chief priests.   23:14
who when *they c.* to Caesarea.   33
and whence *c. they ? Rev* 7:13

word of the Lord came

word of Lord c. to Abram.
     Gen 15:1, 4
word of Lord c. to Samuel.
     1 Sam 15:10
c. the *word of Lord* to Gad.
     2 Sam 24:11
word of Lord c. to Solomon. *1 Ki* 6:11
word of Lord c. to Jehu.   16:1, 7
the *word of Lord c.* unto Elijah.
   17:2, 8; 18:1; 19:9; 21:17, 28
whom *word of Lord c.* saying. 18:31
word of Lord c. to Isaiah.
     2 Ki 20:4; *Isa* 38:4
word of Lord c. to Nathan.
     1 Chr 17:3
word of Lord c. to David.   22:8
word of Lord c. to Shemaiah.
   2 Chr 11:2; 12:7; *1 Ki* 12:22

word of Lord c. to Jeremiah. *Jer* 1:2
 4; 2:1; 14:1; 29:30; 33:1, 19
        Dan 9:2
word of Lord c. expressly to Ezekiel.
      Ezek 1:3; 3:16
word of Lord c. to Hosea. *Hos* 1:1
word of Lord c. to Joel. *Joel* 1:1
word of Lord c. to Jonah. *Jonah* 1:1
         3:1
word of Lord c. to Micah. *Mi* 1:1
word of Lord c. to Zephaniah.
       Zeph 1:1
word of Lord c. by Haggai. *Hag* 1:1
word of Lord c. to Zechariah.
       Zech 1:1
c. word of Lord of hosts. 7:4; 8:1

camel
(Camels were the usual riding animals in the East, as they were stronger than horses, and had much more endurance. As so much of the Bible world was either desert, or dry at certain seasons of the year, the peculiar adaptation of the camel to deserts was of unusual importance. Very frequently a man's wealth was estimated in camels. They were bred for work or for swift riding, and their hair was used for clothing)

saw Isaac, lighted off c. *Gen* 24:64
shall not eat, the c. *Lev* 11:14
       Deut 14:7
slay infant, ox, and c. *1 Sam* 15:3
the plague of the c. and. *Zech* 14:15
easier for a c. to go. *Mat* 19:24
   Mark 10:25; *Luke* 18:25
at a gnat and swallow a c. *Mat* 23:24

camels
Abram had sheep, oxen, c. *Gen* 12:16
will draw water for thy c. 24:19, 44
had much cattle, asses, c. 30:43
Rachel put them in the c. 31:34
Ishmaelites came with their c. 37:25
hand of Lord on c. and. *Ex* 9:3
they and their c. *Judg* 6:5; 7:12
ornaments on c. necks. 8:21, 26
David took away c. and. *1 Sam* 27:9
men who rode on c. and fled. 30:17
to Jerusalem with c. *1 Ki* 10:2
       2 Chr 9:1
Hazael took forty c. *2 Ki* 8:9
took away of c. 50,000. *1 Chr* 5:21
Zebulun brought bread on c. 11:40
over the c. also was Obil. 27:30
c. were 435. *Ezra* 2:67; *Neh* 7:69
by post on mules, c. *Esth* 8:10*, 14*
also was three thousand c. *Job* 1:3
the Chaldeans fell on the c. 17
chariot of asses and of c. *Isa* 21:7
carry treasures on bunches of c. 30:6
multitude of c. cover thee. 60:6
take to themselves their c. *Jer* 49:29
their c. shall be a booty. 32
Rabbah a stable for c. *Ezek* 25:5
raiment of c. hair. *Mat* 3:4
       Mark 1:6

camest
Hagar, whence c. thou ? *Gen* 16:8
the land from whence thou c. 24:5
eaten of all before thou c. 27:33
in it thou c. from Egypt. *Ex* 23:15
       34:18
wherefore c. thou not ? *Num* 22:37
to land of Ammon c. not. *Deut* 2:37
day thou c. thou c. in haste. 16:3
thou c. not within the. *1 Sam* 13:11
why c. thou down hither ? 17:28
c. thou not from thy ? *2 Sam* 11:10
whereas thou c. but yesterday. 15:20
by the way thou c. *1 Ki* 13:9, 17
art thou the man of God that c. ? 14
turn thee back by the way by which
 thou c. *2 Ki* 19:28; *Isa* 37:29
thou c. down also on. *Neh* 9:13
c. down the mountains. *Isa* 64:3
before thou c. forth, I. *Ezek* 32:2*
and thou c. forth with. *Ezek* 32:2*
friend, how c. thou in ? *Mat* 22:12
said, Rabbi, when c. ? *John* 6:25
we believe that thou c. forth. 16:30
to thee in way, as thou c. *Acts* 9:17

Camon
Jair died, was buried in C. *Judg* 10:5

camp
of Lord went before c. *Ex* 14:19
quails came up and covered c. 16:13
there is a noise of war in c. 32:17
go through c. and slay every. 27
proclaimed through the c. 36:6
man killeth goat in c. ? *Lev* 17:3
strove together in the c. 24:10
every one by his own c. *Num* 1:52
on the east-side shall the c. of. 2:3
when c. setteth forward. 4:5
as the c. is to set forward. 15
them in utmost parts of the c. 11:1
and Medad prophesied in the c. 26
shall not come within c. *Deut* 23:10
Lord walked in midst of thy c. 14
make c. of Israel a curse. *Josh* 6:18
to the outside of the c. *Judg* 7:17
began to move him in the c. 13:25
there came none to the c. 21:8
they brought them to the c. 12
this great shout in the c. ? *1 Sam* 4:6
and run to thee to thy. 17:17
made Omri king in c. *1 Ki* 16:16
such a place shall be my c. *2 Ki* 6:8
they left the c. as it was. 7:7
when these lepers came to c. *2 Ki*
angel of Lord smote c. of Assyrians.
    19:35; *Isa* 37:36
came with Arabians to c. *2 Chr* 22:1
fall in the midst of their c. *Ps* 78:28
envied Moses also in the c. 106:16
lay siege, set the c. also. *Ezek* 4:2
for his c. is very great. *Joel* 2:11
compassed c. of saints. *Rev* 20:9

into the **camp**
he shall come into c. *Lev* 14:8
      16:26, 28
Moses gat him into c. *Num* 11:30
he shall come into c. *Deut* 23:11
God is come into c. *1 Sam* 4:7

out of the **camp**
forth people out of the c. *Ex* 19:17
your brethren out of c. *Lev* 10:4
priest shall go forth out of the c. 14:3
killeth a goat out of the c. 17:3
him that had cursed out of c. 24:23
put every leper out of c. *Num* 5:2
Miriam be shut out of the c. 12:14
Moses departed not out of c. 14:44
shall go abroad out of c. *Deut* 23:10
spoilers came out of c. *1 Sam* 13:17
out of c. from Saul. *2 Sam* 1:2
out of c. of Israel am I escaped. 3

round about the **camp**
quails fell, spread them round about
 c. *Num* 11:31, 32
stood every man in place round
 about c. *Judg* 7:21

without the **camp**
burn without the c. *Ex* 29:14
   Lev 8:17; 9:11; 16:27
sought Lord, went without c. *Ex* 33:7
ashes without the c. *Lev* 6:11
plague shall dwell without c. 13:46
leper be without the c. *Num* 5:3
stoned without the c. 15:35
bring red heifer without c. 19:3
do ye abide without the c. 31:19
place also without c. *Deut* 23:12
left kindred without the c. *Josh* 6:23
beasts burnt without c. *Heb* 13:11
let us go forth to him without c. 13

camp
I will c. against thee. *Isa* 29:3
bend the bow c. against. *Jer* 50:29
which c. in the hedges in. *Nah* 3:17

camped
there Israel c. before the. *Ex* 19:2

camphire
beloved is as cluster of c. *S of S* 1:14
plants are an orchard of c. 4:13

camps
that they defile not their c. *Num* 5:3
trumpets for journeying of c. 10:2
made stink of your c. *Amos* 4:10

can
c. we find such a one as ? *Gen* 41:38
I c. no more go out. *Deut* 31:2

he is dead, c. I bring ? *2 Sam* 12:23
c. I discern, c. I hear voice ? 19:35
c. that which is unsavoury ? *Job* 6:6
c. rush grow without mire ? c. 8:11
c. a man be profitable to God ? 22:2
c. he judge through dark cloud ? 13
c. any understand spreading ? 36:29
c. God furnish a table ? *Ps* 78:19
c. he give bread also ? c. he ? 20
who c. be compared ? c. be ? 89:6
c. a man take fire in his ? *Pr* 6:27
c. one go on hot coals and ? 28
yet c. he not answer. *Isa* 46:7
c. a woman forget her ? 49:15
c. a maid forget her ? *Jer* 2:32
c. any hide himself in secret ? 23:24
c. two walk together ? *Amos* 3:3
c. a bird fall in a snare where ? 5
who c. but prophesy ? 8
who c. be saved ? *Mat* 19:25
  Mark 10:26; *Luke* 18:26
make it as sure as you c. *Mat* 27:65
c. children of bridechamber fast ?
      Mark 2:19
this kind c. come forth but. 9:29
c. ye drink of the cup ? 10:38
c. the blind lead blind ? *Luke* 6:39
c. any good come out ? *John* 1:46
hard saying, who c. hear it ? 6:60
c. a devil open the eyes of ? 10:21
no more c. ye except ye. 15:4
c. any man forbid water ? *Acts* 10:47
to law, nor indeed c. *Rom* 8:7
not works, c. faith save ? *Jas* 2:14
c. the fig-tree bear olive- ? 3:12

how **can**
how c. I alone bear ? *Deut* 1:12
how c. I go, if Saul ? *1 Sam* 16:2
how c. I endure to see ? *Esth* 8:6
how c. a man be justified ? *Job* 25:4
how c. man understand ? *Pr* 20:24
how c. one be warm ? *Eccl* 4:11
how c. it be quiet seeing ? *Jer* 47:7
how c. ye being evil ? *Mat* 12:34
how c. a man be born ? *John* 3:4
how c. these things be ? 9
how c. this man give us ? 6:52
how c. we know the way ? 14:5
how c. I except some ? *Acts* 8:31

Cana
was a marriage in C. *John* 2:1
beginning of miracles in C. 11
so Jesus came again into C. 4:46
Thomas and Nathanael of C. 21:2

Canaan
Ham is the father of C. *Gen* 9:18
Ham the father of C. saw the. 22
cursed be C. 25
C. shall be his servant. 26, 27
C. begat Sidon. 10:15; 1 *Chr* 1:13
wife of daughters of C. *Gen* 28:1

Canaan
the inhabitants of C. *Ex* 15:15
not known all wars of C. *Judg* 3:1
sold them to Jabin king of C. 4:2
God subdued Jabin king of C. 23, 24
then fought the kings of C. 5:19
sacrificed to the idols of C. *Ps* 106:38
smote the kingdoms of C. 135:11
Egypt speak language of C. *Isa* 19:18
O C. I will even destroy. *Zeph* 2:5
a woman of C. cried. *Mat* 15:22

land of **Canaan**
go into the land of C. *Gen* 12:5
dwelt ten years in land of C. 16:3
give thee land of C. 17:8; *Lev* 25:38
  Num 34:2; *Deut* 32:49
   1 Chr 16:18; *Ps* 105:11
Jacob dwelt in land of C. *Gen* 37:1
famine was in the land of C. 42:5
they said, from land of C. 7
sons of one man in land of C. 13
get ye up unto land of C. 45:17
carried him into land of C. 50:13
come into the land of C. *Lev* 14:34
      Num 34:2
after doings of land of C. *Lev* 18:3
sent to spy land of C. *Num* 13:17
over armed into land of C. 32:32
fruit of land of C. *Josh* 5:12
altar over against land of C. 22:11
led him through the land of C. 24:3

nativity is of *land of C.* *Ezek* 16:3
dearth over all *land of C.* *Acts* 7:11
seven nations in *land of C.* 13:19
Canaanite, -s
C. was then in land. *Gen* 12:6; 13:7
the Amorites, *C.,* Girgashites. 15:21
Ex. 3:8, 17; 23:23; *Deut* 7:1
20:17; *Josh* 3:10; 12:8; *Judg* 3:5
Neh 9:8
shalt not take a wife of *C. Gen* 24:3
make me to stink amongst *C.* 34:30
daughter of a certain *C.* 38:2
drive out the *C.* *Ex* 23:28; 33:2
34:11
Lord delivered up the *C. Num* 21:3
Neh 9:24
C. would dwell in land. *Josh* 17:12
Judg 1:27
shalt drive out the *C.* *Josh* 17:18
up against the *C.* first ? *Judg* 1:1
to fight against the *C.* 9, 10
did Ephraim drive out *C.* 29
Naphtali dwelt among the *C.* 33
Pharaoh had slain the *C. 1 Ki* 9:16
to abominations of *C.* *Ezra* 9:1
shall possess that of *C.* *Ob* 20
no more *C.* in house of. *Zech* 14:21
Simon the *C. Mat* 10:4; *Mark* 3:18
Canaanitess
to Judah of Shua the *C.* *1 Chr* 2:3
Candace
eunuch of great authority under *C.*
Acts 8:27
candle
(Revised Version, lamp in every
case. The candle, cs we know it,
was not used in the East, the refer-
ence being to small earthen lamps
in which a wick floating in the oil
gave a feeble light. They were of
different sizes and shapes. The
word candlestick, however, re-
mains in the Revisions in nearly
every instance, a few being trans-
lated lampstand, Mat 5:15)
his *c.* shall be put out. *Job* 18:6
how oft is *c.* of wicked put ? 21:17
his *c.* shined upon my head. 29:3
thou wilt light my *c.* God. *Ps* 18:28
spirit of man is *c.* of. *Pr* 20:27
c. of wicked shall be put out. 24:20
her *c.* goeth not out by night. 31:18
from them light of *c.* *Jer* 25:10
light a *c.* and put it under. *Mat* 5:15
Mark 4:21; *Luke* 8:16; 11:33
bright shining of a *c.* *Luke* 11:36
doth not she light a *c.* and. 15:8
light of a *c.* shine no. *Rev* 18:23
and they need no *c.* nor light. 22:5
candles
search Jerusalem with *c. Zeph* 1:12
candlestick
c. of pure gold. *Ex* 25:31; 37:17
Num 8:4
six branches out of the *c. Ex* 25:33
37:19
in *c.* four bowls. 25:34; 37:20
thou shalt set the *c.* over. 26:35
put the *c.* in the tent. 40:24
order the lamps on the *c. Lev* 24:4
charge shall be ark and *c. Num* 3:31
take a cloth and cover the *c.* 4:9
light over against the *c.* 8:2
a bed, a table, a *c.* *2 Ki* 4:10
by weight for every *c.* *1 Chr* 28:15
set they in order the *c. 2 Chr* 13:11
wrote over against the *c.* *Dan* 5:5
I looked, and behold a *c.* *Zech* 4:2
two olive-trees on right side of *c.* 11
a *c.* and it giveth light. *Mat* 5:15*
Luke 8:16; 11:33
is a candle brought not to be set on a
c. ? *Mark* 4:21*
first, wherein was the *c.* *Heb* 9:2
I come and remove thy *c. Rev* 2:5
candlesticks
made *c.* of pure gold. *1 Ki* 7:49
2 Chr 4:7
weight for the *c.* of gold. *1 Chr* 28:15
he took away the *c.* *Jer* 52:19
two *c.* standing before the. *Rev* 11:4
see seven

cane
brought me no sweet *c.* *Isa* 43:24
sweet *c.* from a far. *Jer* 6:20
canker, -ed
will eat as doth a *c.* *2 Tim* 2:17*
your gold and silver is *c.* *Jas* 5:3*
cankerworm
c. eaten, and what *c.* left. *Joel* 1:4
2:25
like *c.* make thyself as *c.* *Nah* 3:15
the *c.* spoileth, and fleeth away. 16
cannot
calling of assemblies I *c.* *Isa* 1:13
read this, he saith, I *c.* for. 29:11
waves *c.* prevail, *c.* pass. *Jer* 5:22
c. I do with you as this potter ? 18:6
secret king demanded, *c. Dan* 2:27
c. ye discern the signs ? *Mat* 16:3
c. be that a prophet. *Luke* 13:33
pass from hence to you *c.* 16:26
of which we *c.* now speak. *Heo* 9:5
canst
c. not see my face and. *Ex* 33:20
itch, whereof thou *c.* *Deut* 28:27
if thou *c.* answer me, set. *Job* 33:5
Lord, if thou wilt, thou *c.* *Mark* 9:22
if thou *c.* do any thing. *Mark* 9:22
chief captain said, *c.* ? *Acts* 21:37
Capernaum
Nazareth, dwelt in *C.* *Mat* 4:13
Jesus was entered into *C.* 8:5
thou *C.* which art exalted. 11:23
Luke 10:15
they were come to *C.* *Mat* 17:24
they went into *C.* *Mark* 1:21; 2:1
have heard done in *C.* *Luke* 4:23
not many days in *C.* *John* 2:12
whose son was sick at *C.* 4:46
over the sea towards *C.* 6:17
people came to *C.* seeking. 24
things said he, as he taught in *C.* 59
Caphtor
remnant of country of *C.* *Jer* 47:4
the Philistines from *C.* *Amos* 9:7
Cappadocia
the dwellers in *C.* we hear. *Acts* 2:9
strangers scattered throughout *C.*
1 Pet 1:1
captain
A name applied, [1] To the king,
or prince of a people, 1 Sam 9:16.
[2] *To a general, or commander in*
an army, Gen 26:26; 2 Sam 5:8.
[3] *To the head of a family, or tribe,*
Num 2:3. [4] *To such as have the*
command of a company, Deut 1:15.
[5] *Christ Jesus is called the Cap-*
tain of salvation, Heb 2:10.
Joseph to Potiphar, *c.* *Gen* 37:36
c. of the guard charged Joseph. 40:4
Nahshon, *c.* of children of. *Num* 2:3
Nethaneel, *c.* of the children of. 5
make a *c.* and return. 14:4
Neh 9:17
as *c.* of the host of the. *Josh* 5:14
the *c.* of the Lord's host. 15
c. of Jabin's host. *Judg* 4:2, 7
1 Sam 12:9
come and be our *c.* *Judg* 11:6
him head and *c.* over them. 11
anoint him *c.* over. *1 Sam* 9:16; 10:1
commanded him to be *c.* 13:14
these ten cheeses to the *c.* 17:18
and David became a *c.* *2 Sam* 5:2
shalt feed, and be a *c.* *2 Sam* 5:2
be chief and *c.* 8; *1 Chr* 11:6
if thou be not *c.* of host. *2 Sam* 19:13
Abishai was therefore their *c.* 23:19
Israel made Omri, *c.* *1 Ki* 16:16
the king sent a *c.* with. *2 Ki* 1:9
sent to him another *c.* 11, 13
thou be spoken for to *c.* ? 4:13
Naaman, *c.* of the host of. 5:1
I have an errand to thee, O *c.* 9:5
Pekah, a *c.* of his, conspired. 15:25
turn away face of one *c.* 18:24
Isa 36:9
tell Hezekiah *c.* of my. *2 Ki* 20:5
Nebuzar-adan, *c.* of guard. 25:8
Jer 52:12

for he was their *c.* *1 Chr* 11:21
killed Shophach *c.* of. 19:18
2 Sam 10:18
the third *c.* Benaiah. *1 Chr* 27:5
fourth *c.* Asahel. 7
the fifth *c.* Shamhuth. 8
the sixth *c.* Ira. 9
God himself is our *c.* *2 Chr* 13:12
Lord doth take away *c.* *Isa* 3:3
a *c.* of the ward Irijah. *Jer* 37:13
c. of the guard took Jeremiah. 40:2
c. gave victuals and a reward. 5
call together, appoint a *c.* 51:27
band and the *c.* took. *John* 18:12
the *c.* with officers went. *Acts* 5:26
c. of their salvation. *Heb* 2:10
captains
chosen *c.* also are drowned. *Ex* 15:4
Moses was wroth with *c. Num* 31:14
I made wise men *c.* over. *Deut* 1:15
shall make *c.* of the army. 20:9
he will appoint *c.* *1 Sam* 8:12
son of Jesse make you all *c.* 22:7
king gave all *c.* charge. *2 Sam* 18:5
sat in the seat chief among *c.* 23:8
what Joab did to the *c.* *1 Ki* 2:5
they were his princes, and *c.* 9:22
take kings away, and put *c.* 20:24
when *c.* perceived that he was not
king of Israel. 22:23; *2 Chr* 18:32
Jehoiada commanded *c.* *2 Ki* 11:15
having for *c.* Pelatiah. *1 Chr* 4:42
now three of the 30 *c.* went. 11:15
of Naphtali a thousand *c.* 12:34
smote Edomites and *c.* *2 Chr* 21:9
Lord brought on them the *c.* 33:11
the king had sent *c.* of. *Neh* 2:9
the thunder of the *c.* *Job* 39:25
hast taught them to be *c. Jer* 13:21*
will I break in pieces *c.* 51:23
I will make drunk her *c.* 57
c. to open the mouth in. *Ezek* 21:22
c. and rulers all. 23:6, 12, 23
the *c.* saw these men. *Dan* 3:27
the *c.* have consulted to. 6:7
thy *c.* as the great. *Nah* 3:17
made supper to his *c.* *Mark* 6:21
communed with the *c.* *Luke* 22:4
may eat the flesh of *c.* *Rev* 19:18
captive
his brother was taken *c.* *Gen* 14:14
their wives took they *c.* 34:29
unto first-born of the *c.* *Ex* 12:29
hast taken them *c.* *Deut* 21:10
away *c.* a little maid. *2 Ki* 5:2
smite those thou hast taken *c.* 6:22
I am desolate, a *c.* and. *Isa* 49:21
or shall the lawful *c.* be ? 24
the *c.* exile hasteneth, that. 51:14
loose thyself, O *c.* daughter. 52:2
go *c.* with first that go *c.* *Amos* 6:7
who are taken *c.* by will. *2 Tim* 2:26

carry or *carried* **captive**, or
captives
carried away daughters as *c.*
Gen 31:26
shall *carry* thee away *c. Num* 24:22
they *carry* them away *c.* *1 Ki* 8:46
2 Chr 6:36
if bethink in land whither they were
carried c. 1 Ki 8:47; *2 Chr* 6:37
carried them *c.* to. *2 Ki* 15:29
carried people of Damascus *c.* 16:9
king of Assyria *carried c. 1 Chr* 5:6
other 10,000 did Judah *carry c.*
2 Chr 25:12
carried a great multitude *c.* 28:5
carried c. of their brethren. 8
that *carried* them *c.* *Ps* 106:46
that *carried* us *c.* required. 137:3
Lord's flock is *carried c. Jer* 13:17
Judah shall be *carried* away *c.* 19
carry them *c.* to Babylon. 20:4
them that are *carried c.* 24:5
took not when he *carried c.* 27:20
to all that are *carried c.* 29:4
bring you into place whence I caused
you to be *carried* away *c.* 14
which were *carried c.* 40:1; 52:27
that were not *carried c.* 40:7
Ishmael *carried* away *c.* 41:10
shall *carry* the Egyptians *c.* 43:12
Nebuchadnezzar *carried c.* 52:29

carried

carried away c. of the Jews. *Jer* 52:30
whither they be carried c. *Ezek* 6:9
and shall also carry c. *Dan* 11:8
because they carried c. *Amos* 1:6
that strangers carried c. *Ob* 11

carrying captive

carrying away of Jerusalem c.
                                    Jer 1:3

lead, or led captive

lead thy captivity c. thou. *Judg* 5:12
enemies who led them c. *1 Ki* 8:48
before them that lead c. *2 Chr* 30:9
hast led captivity c. *Ps* 58:18
                                    Eph 4:8
whither they led him c. *Jer* 22:12
Israel shall be led c. out. *Amos* 7:11
led c. her maids shall lead. *Nah* 2:7
shall be led away c. *Luke* 21:24
lead c. silly women. *2 Tim* 3:6

captives

all women of Midian c. *Num* 31:9
they brought the c. 12
purify your c. 19
seest among the c. a. *Deut* 21:11
arrows drunk with blood of c. 32:42
two wives were taken c. *1 Sam* 30:5
from Jerusalem 10,000 c. *2 Ki* 24:14
me, and deliver the c. *2 Chr* 28:11
ye shall not bring in the c. hither. 13
take them c. whose c. *Isa* 14:2
lead away the Ethiopians c. 20:4
he shall let go my c. not for. 45:13
c. of the mighty shall be. 49:25
proclaim liberty to the c. 61:1
                                    Luke 4:18
daughters are taken c. *Jer* 48:46
all that took them c. held. 50:33
I was among the c. by. *Ezek* 1:1
bring again captivity of thy c. 16:53
found a man of the c. *Dan* 2:25

captivity

(*The servitudes spoken of in Judges, and those under the Greeks and the Romans, are sometimes spoken of as Captivities. More exactly, however, the word is used of the carrying away of the people of Israel and of Judah into Babylonia and Assyria, when the kingdom of Israel was finally destroyed, and the kingdom of Judah lost its independence, Jerusalem and the Temple being destroyed.*
The word is also frequently used in the Bible in its ordinary sense of bondage or servitude without reference to any historical event)

his daughters into c. *Num* 21:29
put raiment of c. from. *Deut* 21:13
Lord will turn thy c. and have. 30:3
till the day of the c. *Judg* 18:30
carried into c. to Babylon. *2 Ki* 24:15
thirty-seventh year of the c. 25:27
                                    Jer 52:31
in their steads until c. *1 Chr* 5:22
Jehozadak went into c. when. 6:15
pray to thee in land of c. *2 Chr* 6:37
return to thee in land of their c. 38
sons and our wives are in c. 29:9
have been delivered to c. *Ezra* 9:7
Jews which were left of c. *Neh* 1:2
them for a prey in land of c. 4:4
carried away with the c. *Esth* 2:6
Lord turned the c. of Job. *Job* 42:10
bringeth back the c. *Ps* 14:7; 85:1
delivereth his strength into c. 78:61
when Lord turned again c. 126:1
turn again our c. O Lord. 4
my people are gone into c. *Isa* 5:13
thee away with a mighty c. 22:17
themselves are gone into c. 46:2
for the c. to the c. *Jer* 15:2; 43:11
I will turn away your c. 29:14
                                    30:3; 32:44; 33:7, 11, 26
hear ye, all ye of c. 29:20
a curse by all the c. of Judah. 22
this c. is long. 28
send to all them of the c. saying. 31
from the land of c. 30:10; 46:27
nor hath he gone into c. 48:11
Judah is gone into c. *Lam* 1:3
her children are gone into c. 5

to turn away thy c. *Lam* 2:14
no more carry thee into c. 4:22
fifth year of Jehoiachin's c. *Ezek* 1:2
get to them of the c. 3:11
I came to them of the c. 15; 11:24
I spake to them of the c. 11:25
as stuff for c. 12:7
bring again their c. the c. of Sodom,
    c. of Samaria. 16:53
when thou went into c. 25:3
in the twelfth year of the c. 33:21
house of Israel went into c. 39:23
five and twentieth year of c. 40:1
Daniel which is of the c. *Dan* 6:13
shall fall by c. and by spoil. 11:33
when I return the c. of. *Hos* 6:11
the c. of this host, the c. *Ob* 20
they are gone into c. *Mi* 1:16
she [No] went into c. *Nah* 3:10
shall gather c. as sand. *Hab* 1:9
shall turn away c. *Zeph* 2:7; 3:20
take of them of the c. *Zech* 6:10
and bringing me into c. *Rom* 7:23
bringing into c. every. *2 Cor* 10:5

see captive

bring captivity

bring up with them of c. *Ezra* 1:11
God bringeth back c. *Ps* 53:6
I will bring again the c. *Jer* 30:18
I shall bring again their c. 31:23
yet will I bring again the c. 48:47
I will bring again the c. of Ammon.
                                    49:6
I will bring again the c. of Elam. 39
I will bring again the c. of Egypt.
                                    Ezek 29:14
now will I bring again the c. 39:25
when I bring again the c. *Joel* 3:1
I will bring again the c. of my
    people. *Amos* 9:14

children of captivity

heard that children of c. *Ezra* 4:1
the rest of children of c. 6:16
the children of c. kept passover. 19
killed passover for children of c. 20
proclamation to children of c. 10:7
the children of c. did so. 16
of children of c. of Judah. *Dan* 5:13

go into captivity

daughters shall go into c. *Deut* 28:41
thine house shall go into c. *Jer* 20:6
thy lovers shall go into c. 22:12
one of them shall go into c. 30:16
furnish thyself to go into c. 46:19
Chemosh shall go into c. 48:7
their kings go into c. 49:3
as they that go into c. *Ezek* 12:4
these cities shall go into c. 30:17
her daughters shall go into c. 18
Syria shall go into c. unto. *Amos* 1:5
their king shall go into c. 15
Gilgal shall surely go into c. 5:5
will I cause you to go into c. 27
Israel shall surely go into c. 7:17
and though they go into c. 9:4
half of city shall go into c. *Zech* 14:2
leadeth into c. go into c. *Rev* 13:10

out of captivity

these went up out of c. *Ezra* 2:1
                                    Neh 7:6
up out of c. *Ezra* 3:8; *Neh* 8:17
children of Israel which were come
    again out of c. did eat. *Ezra* 6:21
were come out of c. offered. 8:35

carbuncle, -s

(*A precious stone of a red colour. Probably the red garnet*)

first row shall be a . *Ex* 28:17
                                    39:10
I will make thy gates of c. *Isa* 54:12
topaz and c. were thy. *Ezek* 28:13

carcase

touch c. of unclean thing. *Lev* 5:2
c. ye shall not touch. 11:8
                                    Deut 14:8
c. shall be meat unto. *Deut* 28:26
should take his c. down. *Josh* 8:29
see the c. of the lion, honey in c.
                                    Judg 14:8
thy c. shall not come to. *1 Ki* 13:22
c. cast in way, a lion stood by c. 24
the c. of Jezebel. *2 Ki* 9:37

cast out as a c. trodden. *Isa* 14:19
where the c. is, there. *Mat* 24:28

carcases

fowls came down on c. *Gen* 15:11
c. in abomination. *Lev* 11:11, 26
cast your c. on c. of your idols. 26:30
your c. shall fall in. *Num* 14:29
I will give the c. of. *1 Sam* 17:46
their c. were torn in midst. *Isa* 5:25
stink shall come up out of c. 34:3
look on c. of them that have. 66:24
c. of this people shall be meat for the.
                                    Jer 7:33; 16:4; 19:7
filled mine inheritance with c. 16:18
I will lay the c. of Israel. *Ezek* 6:5
my name no more defile by c. 43:7
put c. of their kings far from me. 9
there is a great number of c. *Nah* 3:3
grieved with them whose c. *Heb* 3:17

Carchemish

up to fight against C. *2 Chr* 35:20
is not Calno as C. ? *Isa* 10:9
river Euphrates in C. *Jer* 46:2

care

(*Formerly used in the sense of anxiety, especially the wearing, painful sense of anxiety. This is a common meaning of the word in the Bible, and in almost all such cases the Revised Version replaces it by a more modern term*)

father hath left the c. *1 Sam* 10:2
careful for us with all this c.
                                    2 Ki 4:13
nation that dwelleth without c.
                                    Jer 49:31
bread by weight with c. *Ezek* 4:16*
c. of this world chokes. *Mat* 13:22
he took c. of him. *Luke* 10:34
take c. of him. 35
doth God c. for oxen ? *1 Cor* 9:9*
should have the same c. one. 12:25
but that our c. for you. *2 Cor* 7:12
put the same earnest c. in. 8:16
besides c. of all churches. 11:28*
shall he take c. of church. *1 Tim* 3:5
casting your c. on him. *1 Pet* 5:7*

care, -ed

we flee, they will not c. *2 Sam* 18:3
no man c. for my soul. *Ps* 142:4
dost thou not c. that my? *Luke* 10:40
he said, not that he c. *John* 12:6
and Gallio c. for none. *Acts* 18:17
being a servant, c. not. *1 Cor* 7:21
who will naturally c. for. *Phil* 2:20

careful

behold thou hast been c. *2 Ki* 4:13
shall not be c. in year. *Jer* 17:8
O Nebuchadnezzar, we are not c.
                                    Dan 3:16*
Martha, thou art c. *Luke* 10:41
c. for nothing, but by. *Phil* 4:6
wherein ye were c. but lacked. 10*
c. to maintain good works. *Tit* 3:8

carefully

(*Revised Version, diligently*)
thou c. hearken unto. *Deut* 15:5
of Maroth waiteth c. *Mi* 1:12
I sent him the more c. *Phil* 2:28
though he sought it c. *Heb* 12:17

carefulness

drink water with trembling and c.
                                    Ezek 12:18
they shall eat their bread with c. 19
have you without c. *1 Cor* 7:32*
c. it wrought in you. *2 Cor* 7:11*

careless

saw how they dwelt c. *Judg* 18:7*
hear my voice, ye c. *Isa* 32:9
shall be troubled ye c. women. 10
ye c. ones : strip you, and. 11
make c. Ethiopians afraid. *Ezek* 30:9

carelessly

now thou that dwellest c. *Isa* 47:8
among them that dwell c. *Ezek* 39:6*
rejoicing city that dwelt c. *Zeph* 2:15

cares

c. of this world choke. *Mark* 4:19
they are choked with c. *Luke* 8:14
be overcharged with the c. 21:34

carest, -eth, -ing

which the Lord c. for.   Deut 11:12
lest thy father leave c.   1 Sam 9:5
thou art true, nor c.   Mat 22:16
c. thou not that we perish ?
               Mark 4:38
art true, and c. for no man.   12:14
because an hireling c.   John 10:13
unmarried c. for things.   1 Cor 7:32
married c. for things of.   33, 34
on him, for he c. for you.   1 Pet 5:7

Carmel

C. and Ziph in the.   Josh 15:55
Saul came to C.   1 Sam 15:12
Nabal's possessions were in C. 25:2
all the while they were in C.   7
were come to Abigail to C.   40
all Israel to mount C.   1 Ki 18:19
Elijah went up to top of C.   42
Elisha went to mount C.   2 Ki 2:25
of Shunem came to mount C.   4:25
into forest of his C. 19:23; Isa 37:24
vine-dressers in C.   2 Chr 26:10
thine head is like C.   S of S 7:5
the excellency of C.   Isa 35:2
and as C. by the sea.   Jer 46:18
the top of C. shall wither. Amos 1:2
they hide in the top of C.   9:3
solitarily in the midst of C. Mi 7:14

see Bashan

Carmelite

wife of Nabal the C.   1 Sam 30:5
          2 Sam 2:2; 3:3
Hezrai the C.   2 Sam 23:35

Carmi

C. son of Reuben.   Gen 46:9
Achan the son of C.   Josh 7:1, 18
           1 Chr 2:7
sons of Judah, Hezron, C. 1 Chr 4:1

carnal

(*Belonging to the flesh in distinction from the spirit. It does not necessarily infer sin, although when definitely contrasted with spirit it sometimes is so intended. It comes from the Latin carnis, flesh*)

spiritual, but I am c.   Rom 7:14
the c. mind is enmity against.   8:7*
duty to minister to them in c. 15:27
as unto c. even to babes.   1 Cor 3:1
for ye are yet c.   3
are ye not c.?   4*
thing if we reap c. things ?   9:11
of our warfare not c.   2 Cor 10:4*
not after the law of a c.   Heb 7:16
which stood in c. ordinances.   9:10

carnally

shalt not lie c. with thy.   Lev 18:20
lieth c. with a bond-maid.   19:20
a man lie with her c.   Num 5:13
for to be c. minded is.   Rom 8:6*

carpenter, -s

sent c. to David.   2 Sam 5:11
          1 Chr 14:1
they laid it out to c.   2 Ki 12:11
hired c. to repair.   2 Chr 24:12
          Ezra 3:7
c. encouraged goldsmith.   Isa 41:7
c. stretcheth out his rule.   44:13
c. and smiths he carried away.
      Jer 24:1*; 29:2*
Lord shewed me four c. Zech 1:20*
is not this the c. son ?   Mat 13:55
is not this the c. the son ?   Mark 6:3

Carpus

cloke that I left with C.   2 Tim 4:13

carriage, -s

(*This word means things carried, or burdens, not vehicles, and is so put in Revisions*)

the Danites, and the c. Judg 18:21*
left c. with keeper in c. 1 Sam 17:22
he hath laid up his c. at.   Isa 10:28
your c. were heavy laden.   46:1
we took up our c. went. Acts 21:15

carried

sons of Israel c. Jacob.   Gen 46:5
          50:13

c. them in their coats.   Lev 10:5
they c. the stones over.   Josh 4:8
he c. them up to top of.   Judg 16:3
let ark of God be c.   1 Sam 5:8
David c. the ark aside.   2 Sam 6:10
          1 Chr 13:13
Abiathar c. ark of God. 2 Sam 15:29
he c. him into a loft.   1 Ki 17:19
they c. Naboth forth and.   21:13
and c. thence silver and.   2 Ki 7:8
c. him in a chariot.   9:28; 23:30
laid up in store shall be c. to Babylon.
         20:17; Isa 39:6
c. the ashes of the vessels. 2 Ki 23:4
he c. out thence all the.   24:13
bound Zedekiah and c. him.   25:7
c. the chest to his.   2 Chr 24:11
and c. all the feeble of them. 28:15
who took and c. Manasseh.   33:11
Shaphan c. the book to.   34:16
Necho took and c. Jehoahaz.   36:4
of the froward is c.   Job 5:13
I should have been c. from.   10:19
the mountains be c. into.   Ps 46:2
remnant which are c. from. Isa 46:3
thy daughters shall be c. on.   49:22
borne our griefs, c. our.   53:4
he bare and c. them all.   63:9
c. into Babylon.   Jer 27:22; 28:3
         52:11, 17
he c. twigs into a.   Ezek 17:4
and c. me out in the Spirit.   37:1
which he c. into land.   Dan 1:2
be also c. into Assyria.   Hos 10:6
make a covenant, and oil is c. 12:1
and ye have c. into your.   Joel 3:5
was a dead man c. out.   Luke 7:12
and beggar was c. by angels. 16:22
parted from them, and c. up.   24:51
lame from his mother's womb was c.
         Acts 3:2
young men c. Ananias out.   5:6
our fathers were c. over into.   7:16
devout men c. Stephen to.   8:2
commanded him to be c.   21:34
c. about with every wind. Eph 4:14
be not c. about with.   Heb 13:9
clouds that are c. with.   2 Pet 2:17
clouds without water, c.   Jude 12

see captive

carried *away*

Jacob c. away all his.   Gen 31:18
hath c. away my daughters.   26
but c. them away.   1 Sam 30:2, 18
c. Israel away.   2 Ki 17:6, 23
heathen whom Lord c. away.   11
one whom they had c. away.   28
c. away all Jerusalem.   24:14
c. away Jehoiachin to Babylon.   15
so Judah was c. away.   25:21
Tilgath-pilneser c. away. 1 Chr 5:26
when the Lord c. away Judah. 6:15
who were c. away for their.   9:1
Shishak c. away the.   2 Chr 12:9
c. away much spoil.   14:13
         21:17
they c. away sheep and camels. 14:15
these that had been c. away. Ezra 2:1
         Neh 7:6
that had been c. away. Ezra 9:4; 10:6
congregation of those c. away.   10:8
upon camels, c. them away. Job 1:17
to be c. away captive.   Jer 29:4
and winds c. them away.   Dan 2:35
No was c. away into.   Nah 3:10
time they were c. away.   Mat 1:11
c. Jesus away and.   Mark 15:1
were Gentiles c. away.   1 Cor 12:2
Barnabas was c. away.   Gal 2:13
cause her to be c. away.   Rev 12:15
c. me away in Spirit.   17:3; 21:10

carriest, -eth, -ing

one c. three kids, c.   1 Sam 10:3
chaff that storm c. away. Job 21:18
east-wind c. rich man away.   27:21
Ephraim c. bows.   Ps 78:9
thou c. them away as with.   90:5
c. into Babylon, from the c.
         Mat 1:17
they c. her and buried.   Acts 5:10
mystery of beast that c.   Rev 17:7

carry

Ishmaelites going to c.   Gen 37:25
go ye, c. corn for the famine. 42:19
c. the man a present.   43:11
the money brought, c.   12
as much as they can c.   44:1
wagons Joseph sent to c. him. 45:27
         46:5
c. up my bones.   50:25; Ex 13:19
presence go not, c. us not. Ex 33:15
c. your brethren out of.   Lev 10:4
c. them in thy bosom.   Num 11:12
thou art not able to c. it. Deut 14:24
c. the twelve stones over. Josh 4:3
c. these ten cheeses.   1 Sam 17:18
Jonathan said, go c. them.   20:40
a ferry-boat to c. over. 2 Sam 19:18
Spirit of the Lord shall c. 1 Ki 18:12
his father said, c. him.   2 Ki 4:19
c. Jehu to an inner chamber.   9:2
c. thither one of the priests.   17:27
sent to Philistines to c. 1 Chr 10:9
none ought to c. the ark but.   15:2
the Levites shall no more c.   23:26
thou shalt c. the wood.   2 Chr 2:16
c. him to Babylon.   36:6; Jer 39:7
c. vessels into temple.   Ezra 5:15
c. the silver and gold freely.   7:15
bird of the air shall c.   Eccl 10:20
her own feet shall c. her.   Isa 23:7
they will c. their riches on.   30:6
c. the lambs in his bosom.   40:11
even to hoary hairs will I c. you. 46:4
they c. him and set him in.   7
will I take them and c.   Jer 20:5
should c. Jeremiah home.   39:14
in thee are men c. tales. Ezek 22:9
and began to c. about.   Mark 6:55
not suffer any to c. a vessel.   11:16
c. neither purse, nor.   Luke 10:4
not lawful for thee to c. John 5:10
and c. thee whither thou.   21:18

carry *away*

Assyria did c. away.   2 Ki 18:11
did Nebuzar-adan c. away.   25:11
than they could c. away. 2 Chr 20:25
heart c. thee away ?   Job 15:12
dieth he shall c. nothing away.
         Ps 49:17
which he may c. away.   Eccl 5:15
c. the prey away safe.   Isa 5:29
laid up, shall they c. away.   15:7
the Lord will c. thee away.   22:17
wind c. them away.   41:16; 57:13
no more c. thee away.   Lam 4:22
come to c. away silver ? Ezek 38:13
and I will c. you away.   Acts 7:43

see captive

carry *back*

c. back the ark of God. 2 Sam 15:25
c. Micaiah back.   1 Ki 22:26
         2 Chr 18:25

carry *forth*

shalt not c. forth aught.   Ex 12:46
thus with us to c. us forth.   14:11
bullock shall he c. forth. Lev 4:12, 21
c. forth ashes without camp.   6:11
       14:45; 16:27
c. forth filthiness out.   2 Chr 29:5
nor c. forth a burden on.   Jer 17:22
c. it forth in twilight.   Ezek 12:6

carry *out*

shalt c. me out of Egypt. Gen 47:30
shall c. much seed out. Deut 28:38
then c. him out and.   1 Ki 21:10
c. me out of the host.   22:34
         2 Chr 18:33
c. it out abroad into.   2 Chr 29:16
and c. out thereby.   Ezek 12:5
and shall c. thee out.   Acts 5:9
we can c. nothing out.   1 Tim 6:7

cart

new c. and tie kine to c. 1 Sam 6:7
set ark on a new c.   2 Sam 6:3
and Ahio drave the c.   1 Chr 13:7
corn with wheel of c.   Isa 28:28
as a c. is pressed that is. Amos 2:13

cart rope

draw sin as with a c. rope. Isa 5:18

cart wheel

nor is c. wheel turned.   Isa 28:27

carved, -ing, -ings
c. of timber. *Ex* 31:5; 35:33
fetched the c. image. *Judg* 18:18*
of house within was c. *1 Ki* 6:18
he c. all the walls of house. 29, 32
he set a c. image in. *2 Chr* 33:7*
Amon sacrificed to c. images. 22*
purged Judah from c. images. 34:3*
he cut down the c. images. 4
they break down the c. *Ps* 74:6
decked bed with c. work. *Pr* 7:16*

case, -s
that they were in evil c. *Ex* 5:19
is the c. of the slayer. *Deut* 19:4
thou shalt in any c. bring. 22:1
in any c. thou shalt deliver. 24:13
happy people in such a c. *Ps* 144:15
ye shall in no c. enter. *Mat* 5:20*
if the c. of the man be so. 19:10
been long time in that c. *John* 5:6
under bondage in such c. *1 Cor* 7:15

casement
I looked through my c. *Pr* 7:6*

Casiphia
chief at the place C. *Ezra* 8:17

cassia
(*A sweet spice, called in Hebrew
Kiddah, Ex* 30:21. *This aromatic is
said to be the bark of a tree very
like cinnamon, and grows in the
Indies without cultivation*)
take of c. 500 shekels. *Ex* 30:24
smell of aloes and c. *Ps* 45:8
c. and calamus were. *Ezek* 27:19

cast
about a stone's c. *Luke* 22:41

cast
[1] *To fling, or throw,* Dan 3:6.
[2] *To miscarry,* Gen 31:38, Ex
23:26. [3] *To melt, make, or
frame,* Ex 25:12.
c. the child under a. *Gen* 21:15
she-goats have not c. their. 31:38
let us slay him, and c. him. 37:20
his master's wife c. her eyes. 39:7
every son ye shall c. *Ex* 1:22
said, c. it, and he c. the rod. 4:3
Zipporah c. the foreskin at. 25
took locusts and c. them. 10:19
Pharaoh's chariots he c. 15:4
c. the tree into the waters. 25
not eat flesh torn of beasts, c. 22:31
shall nothing c. their young. 23:26
c. four rings of. 25:12; 37:3, 13
38:5
Moses c. tables out of his. 32:19
I c. into the fire, there came. 24
talents of the silver were c. 38:27
priest c. cedar wood. *Num* 19:6
c. any thing on him without. 35:22
seeing him not, and c. it. 23
the Lord c. them into. *Deut* 29:28
c. king of Ai at the gate. *Josh* 8:29
c. them into the cave wherein. 10:27
c. every one ear-rings. *Judg* 8:25
c. piece of millstone. 9:53
2 Sam 11:21
c. the javelin. *1 Sam* 18:11; 20:33
Shimei c. stones at. *2 Sam* 16:6
threw stones and c. dust. 13
c. Absalom into a great pit. 18:17
Joab's man c. a cloth upon. 20:12
in plain of Jordan c. *1 Ki* 7:46
2 Chr 4:17
thou hast c. me behind. *1 Ki* 14:9
Elijah c. mantle upon Elisha. 19:19
lest the Spirit c. him. *2 Ki* 2:16
went to spring and c. salt in. 21
every good piece of land c. 3:25
then bring meal, and he c. it. 4:41
he c. in the stick. 6:6
c. him in portion of field. 9:25, 26
c. the man into the. 13:21
neither c. he them from. 23
c. their gods into. 19:18; *Isa* 37:19
nor c. a bank. *2 Ki* 19:32; *Isa* 37:33
c. thy law behind their. *Neh* 9:26
they c. Pur, that is. *Esth* 3:7
Haman had c. Pur, that is. 9:24
for he is c. into a net. *Job* 18:8
God shall c. the fury of his. 20:23
God shall c. upon him, and. 27:22

hath c. me into the mire. *Job* 30:19
c. abroad the rage of thy. 40:11
I was c. upon thee from. *Ps* 22:10
they c. iniquity on me. 55:3
c. thy burden on the Lord. 22
they have c. fire into sanctuary. 74:7
chariot and horse are c. into. 76:6
he c. on them the fierceness. 78:49
let him be c. into the fire. 140:10
c. in thy lot among us. *Pr* 1:14
the lot is c. into the lap. 16:33
c. thy bread on the. *Eccl* 11:1
a man shall c. his idols. *Isa* 2:20
the face of the covering c. 25:7
thou hast c. all my sins. 38:17
are c. into a land which. *Jer* 22:28
c. Urijah's body into the. 26:23
c. it into the fire that was. 36:23
c. Jeremiah into dungeon. 38:6, 9
took thence old c. clouts and. 11
put now these old c. clouts under. 12
Ishmael slew, and c. them. 41:7
cut off my life, and c. *Lam* 1:53
they shall c. their silver. *Ezek* 7:19
although I have c. them far. 11:16
the vine-tree is c. into the. 15:4
because thou hast c. me. 23:35
I will c. thee to the ground. 28:17
be c. into the midst of a. *Dan* 3:6
to c. them into the fiery furnace. 20
these were c. into the midst of. 21
did not we c. three men bound? 24
be c. into the den of lions. 6:7, 16
c. them into the den of lions. 24
for thou hadst c. me. *Jonah* 2:3
then I said, I am c. out of. 4
I will make her c. off. *Mi* 4:7
wilt c. all their sins into. 7:19
will c. abominable filth on. *Nah* 3:6
c. it into the ephah, c. the. *Zech* 5:8
c. it to the potter, c. them. 11:13
nor vine c. her fruit. *Mal* 3:11
down, c. into the fire. *Mat* 3:10
7:19; *Luke* 3:9
John was c. into prison. *Mat* 4:12
deliver thee to judge, be c. 5:25
and c. it from thee. 29, 30; 18:8, 9
to-morrow is c. into oven. 6:30
Luke 12:28
nor c. your pearls before. *Mat* 7:6
children's bread, and c. it to. 15:26
Mark 7:27
c. an hook, and take up. *Mat* 17:27
c. him into prison, till he pay. 18:30
be thou c. into the sea. 21:21
c. him into outer. 22:13; 25:30
the thieves c. the same in. 27:44
oft-times it hath c. him. *Mark* 9:22
he were c. into sea. 42; *Luke* 17:2
two eyes, feet, c. *Mark* 9:45, 47
c. their garments on him. 11:7
Luke 19:35
at him they c. stones. *Mark* 12:4
c. money into the. 41; *Luke* 21:4
widow hath c. more. *Mark* 12:43, 44
power to c. into hell. *Luke* 12:5
thy enemies shall c. a trench. 19:43
for murder c. into prison. 23:19, 25
for John was not yet c. *John* 3:24
let him first c. a stone at her. 8:7
Peter did c. himself into sea. 21:7
c. thy garment about. *Acts* 12:8
c. Paul and Silas into prison. 16:23
we must be c. on a certain. 27:26
who could swim c. themselves. 43
not that I may c. snare. *1 Cor* 7:35
devil should c. some of. *Rev* 2:10
who taught Balak to c. 14
I will c. her into a bed, and. 22
the elders c. their crowns. 4:10
hail and fire were c. on the. 8:7
a mountain burning was c. into. 8
dragon saw that he was c. 12:13
like a mill-stone and c. it. 18:21
these both were c. alive into. 19:20
the devil was c. into lake. 20:10
death and hell were c. into. 14
not found in the book of life, c. 15

cast away
I will not c. them *away. Lev* 26:44*
c. away the jaw-bone. *Judg* 15:17
of the mighty is c. *away. 2 Sam* 1:21
Syrians had c. away in. *2 Ki* 7:15

Ahaz did c. away. *2 Chr* 29:19
have c. them *away* for. *Job* 8:4*
behold God will not c. *away* a. 20
let us c. away their cords. *Ps* 2:3
c. me not away from thy. 51:11
time to c. away stones. *Eccl* 3:5, 6
have c. away the law. *Isa* 5:24*
shall c. them away as a. 30:22
every man shall c. away his. 31:7
thee, and not c. thee away. 41:9
cut off hair, and c. it away. *Jer* 7:29
I c. away the seed of Jacob. 33:26
c. away from you all. *Ezek* 18:31
c. away abominations of his. 20:7
they did not c. away the. 8
my God will c. them away. *Hos* 9:17
but c. the bad away. *Mat* 13:48
or be c. away. *Luke* 9:25
hath God c. away his. *Rom* 11:1
God hath not c. away his people. 2
c. not away your confidence.
Heb 10:35

cast down
Aaron c. down his rod. *Ex* 7:10
they c. down. 12
c. down great stones. *Josh* 10:11
altar of Baal was c. down. *Judg* 6:28
Elijah c. himself down. *1 Ki* 18:42
to help and c. down. *2 Chr* 25:8
and c. them down from the top. 12
they were c. down in. *Neh* 6:16
own counsel c. him down. *Job* 18:7
when men are c. down. 22:29
countenance c. not down. 29:24
shall not one be c. down? 41:9
disappoint him, c. him down.
Ps 17:13
they are c. down and shall. 36:12
bent their bow to c. down. 37:14
shall not be utterly c. down. 24
art thou c. down? 42:5, 11; 43:5
O my God, my soul is c. down. 42:6
in anger c. down the people. 56:7
consult to c. him down from. 62:4
thou hast c. his throne down. 89:44
me up, and c. me down. 102:10
for she hath c. down. *Pr* 7:26
the Lord shall c. down. 6:32
they shall be c. down. *Jer* 6:15; 8:12
c. down to the earth the. *Lam* 2:1
I will c. down your slain. *Ezek* 6:4
thy mother was c. down to. 19:12
c. the Assyrian down to hell. 31:16
for Egypt, and c. her down. 32:18
the thrones were c. down. *Dan* 7:9*
the he-goat c. down the ram. 8:7
c. down some of the host. 10
sanctuary was c. down. 11
c. down truth to the ground. 12
he shall c. down many. 11:12
c. thyself down. *Mat* 4:6; *Luke* 4:9
c. them *down* at Jesus' feet.
Mat 15:30
he c. down the pieces of silver. 27:5
might c. Jesus down. *Luke* 4:29
we are c. down. *2 Cor* 4:9
comforteth those are c. down. 7:6
but c. the angels down. *2 Pet* 2:4
of brethren is c. down. *Rev* 12:10

cast forth
c. forth household stuff. *Neh* 13:8
c. forth lightning. *Ps* 144:6
Jehoiakim c. forth. *Jer* 22:19
I will c. thee forth. *Ezek* 32:4
shall c. forth his roots. *Hos* 14:5
mariners c. forth the. *Jonah* 1:5
c. me forth into the sea. 12
took Jonah and c. him forth. 15
would c. forth devil. *Mark* 7:26
c. forth as a branch. *John* 15:6

cast lots
Aaron shall c. lots. *Lev* 16:8
Joshua c. lots. *Josh* 18:10
c. lots between me. *1 Sam* 14:42
c. lots as well small as. *1 Chr* 26:13
they c. lots upon my vesture. *Ps* 22:18
Mat 27:35; *John* 19:24
hath c. the lot for them. *Isa* 34:17
c. lots for my people. *Joel* 3:3
c. lots upon Jerusalem. *Ob* 11
come and let us c. lots. *Jonah* 1:7
and they c. lots for her. *Nah* 3:10

cast off

I will c. off this city. *2 Ki 23:27*
he will c. thee off for. *1 Chr 28:9*
Jeroboam had c. them off.
2 Chr 11:14
shall c. off his flower. *Job 15:33*
dost thou c. me off ? *Ps 43:2*
thou hast c. off. 44:9; 60:1, 10
89:38; 108:11
O Lord, c. us not off for ever. 44:23
c. me not off in the time of. 71:9
hast thou c. us off for ever ? 74:1
will the Lord c. off for ever ? 77:7
not c. off his people. 94:14
Lam 3:31
I will c. Hananiah off. *Jer 28:16*
c. off seed of Israel. 31:37; 33:24
hath c. off his altar. *Lam 2:7*
Israel hath c. off the thing. *Hos 8:3*
calf, O Samaria, hath c. thee off. 5
Edom did c. off all pity. *Amos 1:11*
I had not c. them off. *Zech 10:6*
they cried and c. off. *Acts 22:23*
let us c. off works of. *Rom 13:12*
c. off their first faith. *1 Tim 5:12**

cast out

c. out this bondwoman. *Gen 21:10*
I will c. out the nations. *Ex 34:24*
nations are defiled which I c. out.
Lev 18:24; 20:23; Deut 7:1
I c. the two tables out. *Deut 9:17*
Moses smite, and c. out. *Josh 13:12*
c. out Sheba's head to. *2 Sam 20:22*
house will I c. out. *1 Ki 9:7*
2 Chr 7:20
Amorites, whom the Lord c. out.
1 Ki 21:26; 2 Ki 16:3
the captains c. them out. *2 Ki 10:25*
till he had c. them out. 17:20; 24:20
have ye not c. out priests ? *2 Chr 13:9*
to come to c. us out of. 20:11
they were of you c. out. *Neh 1:9*
God shall c. them out of. *Job 20:15*
bow themselves, they c. out. 39:3
c. them out in their. *Ps 5:10*
I did c. them out as dirt. 18:42
afflict people and c. them out. 44:2
over Edom will I c. out. 60:8; 108:9
c. out the heathen. 78:55; 80:8
c. out scorner, contention go out.
Pr 22:10
art c. out of thy grave. *Isa 14:19*
as a wandering bird c. out of. 16:2
earth shall c. out the dead. 26:19
their slain also be c. out. 34:3
bring poor that are c. out. 58:7
brethren that c. you out for. 66:5
c. you out of my sight, as I have c.
out. *Jer 7:15*
our dwellings have c. us out. 9:19
c. them out of my sight. 15:1
23:39; 52:3
will I c. you out of this land. 16:13
I will c. thee out, and thy. 22:26
his dead body shall be c. out. 36:30
Nebuchadnezzar hath c. me out.
51:34
but thou wast c. out in. *Ezek 16:5*
will c. thee as profane out. 28:16
land shall be c. out. *Amos 8:8*
my people have ye c. out *Mi 2:9*
Lord hath c. out thine. *Zeph 3:15*
to c. out the horns of. *Zech 1:21*
the Lord will c. her out. 9:4
unsavoury to be c. out. *Mat 5:13*
Luke 14:35
first c. out the beam. *Mat 7:5*
Luke 6:42
in thy name c. out devils ? *Mat 7:22*
of the kingdom be c. out. 8:12
and he c. out the spirits with. 16
if thou c. us out, suffer us to. 31
when the devil was c. out. 9:33
against spirits to c. them out. 10:1
raise the dead, c. out devils. 8
not c. out devils. 12:24; *Luke 11:18*
if Satan c. out Satan. *Mat 12:26*
the Spirit of God c. out devils. 28
into belly, and is c. out. 15:17
could not we c. him out ? 17:19
Mark 9:28
c. out all that sold. *Mat 21:12*
Mark 11:15; Luke 19:45

c. him out of vineyard. *Mat 21:39*
Mark 12:8; Luke 20:15
and c. out many devils. *Mark 1:34*
39; 6:13
power to heal and c. out devils. 3:15
how can Satan c. out Satan ? 23
out of whom he had c. seven. 16:9
in my name shall they c. out. 17
c. out your name as evil. *Luke 6:22*
if I with finger of God c. out. 11:20
I c. out devils, and do cures. 13:32
wounded him also and c. him out.
20:12
I will in no wise c. out. *John 6:37*
and they c. him out. 9:34
prince of this world be c. out. 12:31
c. out their young. *Acts 7:19*
Moses was c. out Pharaoh's. 21
they c. Stephen out of the city. 58
third day we c. out the. 27:19
c. four anchors out. 29
c. out wheat into the sea. 38
c. out the bondwoman. *Gal 4:30*
great dragon was c. out. *Rev 12:9*
serpent c. out of his mouth. 15, 16

Lord cast out

which the Lord c. out. *1 Ki 14:24*
2 Ki 16:3; 2 Chr 28:3; 33:2
Lord c. out before. *2 Ki 17:8; 21:2*
the Lord will c. her out. *Zech 9:4*

cast up

they c. up a bank. *2 Sam 20:15*
c. ye up, prepare. *Isa 57:14; 62:10*
sea, whose waters c. up. 57:20
in a way not c. up. *Jer 18:15*
c. her up as heaps. 50:26
c. up dust. *Lam 2:10; Ezek 27:30*
king of north shall c. up. *Dan 11:15*

castaway

I myself should be a c. *1 Cor 9:27**

castest, -eth

yea, thou c. off fear and. *Job 15:14*
thy cow calveth and c. not. 21:10
seeing thou c. my words. *Ps 50:17*
thou c. them down into. 73:18
why c. thou off my soul ? 88:14
the Lord c. the wicked down. 147:6
he c. forth his ice like morsels. 17
he c. away the substance. *Pr 10:3*
slothfulness c. into a deep. 19:15
c. down the strength of the. 21:22
as a madman c. fire-brands. 26:18
as a fountain so she c. *Jer 6:7*
c. out devils. *Mat 9:34; Mark 3:22*
Luke 11:15
but perfect love c. fear. *1 John 4:18*
c. them out of church. *3 John 10*
fig-tree c. untimely figs. *Rev 6:13*

casting

he smote Moab, c. *2 Sam 8:2*
all of them had one c. *1 Ki 7:37*
weeping and c. himself. *Ezra 10:1*
ye see my c. down and. *Job 6:21*
by c. down dwelling place. *Ps 74:7*
profaned his crown by c. it. 89:39
thy c. down shall be in. *Mi 6:14*
c. a net into the sea. *Mat 4:18*
parted his garments, c. lots. 27:35
Mark 15:24
saw one c. out devils. *Mark 9:38*
Luke 9:49
he saw the rich men c. *Luke 21:1*
also a poor widow c. in two mites. 2
if c. away of them be. *Rom 11:15*
c. down imaginations. *2 Cor 10:5*
c. all your care upon him. *1 Pet 5:7*

castle

David took c. of Zion. *1 Chr 11:5**
David dwelt in c. the city of. 7*
are like bars of a c. *Pr 18:19*
Paul to be carried into c. *Acts 21:34*
37; 22:24; 23:10
into the c. and told Paul. 23:16

castles

of Ishmael's sons by their c.
Gen 25:16*
burnt their goodly c. *Num 31:10*
these the priests' c. in. *1 Chr 6:54**
over treasures, and in c. 27:25
Jehoshaphat built c. in. *2 Chr 17:12*
Jotham in the forest built c. 27:4

castor, see sign

catch

fire break out and c. *Ex 22:6*
c. you every man his. *Judg 21:21*
men did hastily c. it. *1 Ki 20:33*
we shall c. them alive. *2 Ki 7:12*
wait to c. poor, he doth c. *Ps 10:9*
let his net that he hath hid c. 35:8
let the extortioner c. all. 109:11
set a trap, they c. men. *Jer 5:26*
learned to c. the prey. *Ezek 19:3, 6*
c. them in their net and. *Hab 1:15*
send Herodians to c. *Mark 12:13*
thou shalt c. men. *Luke 5:10*
seeking to c. something. 11:54

catcheth, -ing

who c. any beast or. *Lev 17:13*
the devil c. away. *Mat 13:19*
wolf c. and scattereth. *John 10:12*

caterpiller, -s

if there be any c. *1 Ki 8:37*
2 Chr 6:28
gave their increase to c. *Ps 78:46*
he spake, and c. came. 105:34
spoil like gathering of c. *Isa 33:4*
thee with men as with c. *Jer 51:14*
horses come up as the rough c. 27
worm left, hath c. eaten. *Joel 1:4*
restore the years the c. hath. 2:25

cattle

*(This word is sometimes used for
sheep, etc., and is then translated
in the Revised Version by flock
or flocks)*
God made the c. after. *Gen 1:25*
thou art cursed above all c. 3:14
died, both of fowl and c. 7:21
God remembered Noah, and c. 8:1
establish covenant with fowls, c. 9:10
Abram was very rich in c. 13:2
put them not to Laban's c. 30:40
God hath taken away the c. 31:9
these c. are my c. all. 43
his sons were with the c. 34:5
trade hath been to feed c. 46:32
make them rulers over my c. 47:6
gave bread in exchange for c. 17
sever between c. of Israel and c.
Ex 9:4
made his servants and c. flee. 20
smote all first-born of c. 12:29
bring your offering of c. *Lev 1:2*
take c. of the Levites. *Num 3:41*
if I and my c. drink, I will. 20:19
land for c. thy servants have c. 32:4
c. we took for a. *Deut 2:35; 3:7*
c. shall ye take for a prey. *Josh 8:2*
only c. Israel took. 11:14
slew oxen and c. *1 Ki 1:9, 19, 25*
the c. also concerning the. *Job 36:33*
c. upon a thousand hills. *Ps 50:10*
causeth grass to grow for c. 104:14
beasts and all c. praise. 148:10
of great and small c. *Eccl 2:7*
for treading of lesser c. *Isa 7:25*
hast not brought small c. 43:23
idols were upon beasts and c. 46:1
hear the voice of the c. *Jer 9:10*
between c. and c. *Ezek 34:17, 20, 22*
drought upon land and c. *Hag 1:11*
multitude of men and c. *Zech 2:4*
men taught me to keep c. 13:5
servant feeding c. will. *Luke 17:7*
children drank, and his c. *John 4:12*

much cattle

and had much c. *Gen 30:43*
of Egypt with much c. *Ex 12:38*
I know ye have much c. *Deut 3:19*
return with very much c. *Josh 22:8*
Uzziah had much c. *2 Chr 26:10*
wherein is much c. *Jonah 4:11*

our cattle

our c. also shall go. *Ex 10:26*
our children, and our c. 17:3
that we and our c. *Num 20:4*
build sheepfolds for our c. 32:16
all our c. shall be there. 26
with suburbs for our c. *Josh 21:2*
over our bodies and our c. *Neh 9:37*
first-born of our sons and our c.
10:36

their cattle

shall not their c. and. *Gen 34:23*

took spoil of *their c.*　Num 31:9
for *their c.*　35:3; Josh 14:4
Midianites came up with *their c.*
　　　　　　　　　　　Judg 6:5
brought away *their c.*　1 Sam 23:5
because *their c.* were.　1 Chr 5:9
down to take away *their c.*　7:21
he gave up *their c.* also.　Ps 78:48
he suffered not *their c.* to.　107:38
camels a booty, *their c.*　Jer 49:32

thy **cattle**
knowest how *thy c.* was.　Gen 30:29
thee six years for *thy c.*　31:41
of the Lord is on *thy c.*　Ex 9:3
send now and gather *thy c.*　19
servant nor *thy c.* do any.　20:10
　　　　　　　　　　　Deut 5:14
firstling among *thy c.* is.　Ex 34:19
let not *thy c.* gender.　Lev 19:19
the land meat for *thy c.*　25:7
grass in fields for *thy c.* Deut 11:15
be the fruit of *thy c.* 28:4, 11; 30:9
shall eat the fruit of *thy c.*　28:51
day shall *thy c.* feed.　Isa 30:23

your **cattle**
give *your c.* ; and I will give you for
　your c.　Gen 47:16
will destroy *your c.*　Lev 26:22
your c. shall abide in.　Deut 3:19
　　　　　　　　　　　Josh 1:14
be barren among *your c.* Deut 7:14
drink, both ye and *your c.* 2 Ki 3:17

caught
behind him a ram c. by.　Gen 22:13
she c. him by garment.　39:12
put forth his hand, and c.　Ex 4:4
the men of war had c.　Num 31:32
c. Adoni-bezek, and cut.　Judg 1:6
c. a young man of the men.　8:14
Samson went and c. 300.　15:4
took wives whom they c.　21:23
I c. him by his beard. 1 Sam 17:35
and they c. every one.　2 Sam 2:16
Absalom's head c. hold of.　18:9
and Adonijah c. hold.　1 Ki 1:50
Joab c. hold on the horns of.　2:28
Ahijah c. the new garment.　11:30
the Shunammite c. Elisha. 2 Ki 4:27
they c. Ahaziah and.　2 Chr 22:9
so she c. him, and kissed.　Pr 7:13
thou art found and also c. Jer 50:24
Jesus c. Peter, and said. Mat 14:31
the husbandmen c. him.　21:39
they c. the servant and.　Mark 12:3
oftentimes it c. him.　Luke 8:29
that night c. nothing.　John 21:3
came upon Stephen and c. Acts 6:12
Spirit of the Lord c. away.　8:39
they c. Paul and Silas.　16:19
for these causes the Jews c.　26:21
when the ship was c. we let.　27:15
I know a man c. up to.　2 Cor 12:2
how he was c. up into paradise.　4
being crafty, I c. you with guile.　16
we shall be c. up.　1 Thes 4:17
her child was c. up to God. Rev 12:5

caul, -s
the c. above liver.　Ex 29:13, 22
　Lev 3:4, 10, 15; 4:9; 7:4; 8:16,
　　　　　　　　　　25; 9:10, 19
will take away their c.　Isa 3:18
will rend the c. of their.　Hos 13:8

cause
[1] *A ground, reason, or motive,*
1 Sam 17:29. [2] *A suit, action, or*
controversy, Ex 22:9; Isa 1:23.
[3] *Sake, or account,* 2 Cor 7:12.

c. of both shall come.　Ex 22:9
nor speak in a c. to decline.　23:2
countenance a poor man in his c.　3
wrest judgement of poor in his c.　6
for which c. thou and all. Num 16:11
Moses brought their c. before.　27:5
the c. that is too hard.　Deut 1:17
manslayer shall declare his c.
　　　　　　　　　　　Josh 20:4
said, is there not a c. ?　1 Sam 17:29
Lord hath pleaded the c. of.　25:39
there is no c. this evil. 2 Sam 13:16
that hath any suit or c.　15:4
maintain their c.　1 Ki 8:45, 49, 59
　　　　　　　　　　2 Chr 6:35, 39

was the c. that he lift.　1 Ki 11:27
for the c. was from the Lord.　12:15
　　　　　　　　　　　2 Chr 10:15
he be a c. of trespass.　1 Chr 21:3
what c. shall come.　2 Chr 19:10
for which c. this city.　Ezra 4:15
for which c. thou buildest.　Neh 6:6
God will I commit my c.　Job 5:8
I have ordered my c.　13:18
I would order my c. before.　23:4
the c. which I knew not.　29:16
if I did despise the c. of my.　31:13
hast maintained my c.　Ps 9:4
awake to my c. my God.　35:23
that favour my righteous c.　27
Lord will maintain the c.　140:12
first in his own c.　Pr 18:17
debate thy c. with thy.　25:9
righteous considereth the c.　29:7
for the dumb in the c.　31:8
what is the c. that.　Eccl 7:10
nor doth c. of the widow.　Isa 1:23
produce your c. saith the.　41:21
God that pleadeth the c. of.　51:22
judge not the c. of the.　Jer 5:28
thee have I revealed my c.　11:20
unto thee have I opened my c. 20:12
he judged the c. of the.　22:16
to subvert in a c. the.　Lam 3:36
Lord, judge my c.　59
know for whose c.　Jonah 1:7, 8
wife, saving for the c.　Mat 5:32
put away his wife for every c.　19:3
declared for what c.　Luke 8:47
found no c. of death in him.　23:22
what the c. wherefore ?　Acts 10:21
though they found no c. of.　13:28
Festus declared Paul's c. to.　25:14
was no c. of death in me.　28:18
which c. we faint not.　2 Cor 4:16
it is for your c.　5:13
I did it not for his c. that had.　7:12
for the same c. also do.　Phil 2:18
for which c. I suffer.　2 Tim 1:12
for which c. he is not.　Heb 2:11

plead **cause**
the Lord *plead* my c.　1 Sam 24:15
　　Ps 35:1; 43:1; 119:154
plead thine own c.　Ps 74:22
Lord will *plead* their c.　Pr 22:23
he shall *plead* their c.　23:11
open thy mouth, *plead* the c.　31:9
none to *plead* thy c.　Jer 30:13
thoroughly *plead* their c.　50:34
behold, I will *plead* thy c.　51:36
until he *plead* my c.　Mi 7:9

for this **cause**
for this c. have I raised.　Ex 9:16
for this c. Hezekiah.　2 Chr 32:20
for this c. the king.　Dan 2:12
for this c. shall a man.　Mat 19:5
　　　　　Mark 10:7; Eph 5:31
but *for this* c. came I.　John 12:27
and *for this* c. came I.　18:37
for this c. God gave.　Rom 1:26
for this c. pay ye tribute.　13:6
for this c. I will confess to.　15:9
for this c. many are.　1 Cor 11:30
for this c. I bow my knees. Eph 3:14
for this c. thank God.　1 Thes 2:13
for this c. God shall.　2 Thes 2:11
howbeit, *for this* c. I.　1 Tim 1:16
for this c. he is the.　Heb 9:15
for this c. was the gospel. 1 Pet 4:6

without **cause**
slay David *without* a c.? 1 Sam 19:5
destroy him *without* c.　Job 2:3
my wounds *without* c.　9:17
I delivered him that *without* c. is.
　　　　　　　　　　　Ps 7:4
that transgress *without* c.　25:3
without c. they hid for me a net,
　digged a pit *without* c.　35:7
that hate me *without* c.　19; 69:4
　　　　　　　　　　　John 15:25
against me *without* c.　Ps 109:3
perversely with me *without* c. 119:78
persecuted me *without* c.　161
for the innocent *without* c.　Pr 1:11
strive not with a man *without* c. 3:30
who hath wounds *without* c. ? 23:29
against neighbour *without* c.　24:28
oppressed them *without* c. Isa 52:4

me sore *without* c.　Lam 3:52
have not done *without* c. Ezek 14:23
with his brother *without* c. Mat 5:22

cause
I will c. it to rain upon the. Gen 7:4
he cried, c. every man to go.　45:1
c. frogs to come up on land.　Ex 8:5
and shall c. him to be.　21:19
thy daughter, to c. her.　Lev 19:29
and c. sorrow of heart.　26:16
is holy, the Lord will c.　Num 16:5
he shall c. Israel to inherit it.
　　　　Deut 1:38; 3:28; 31:7
choose to c. his name to.　12:11
thou shalt not c. the land.　24:4
whither shall I c. my ? 2 Sam 13:13
oath laid on him to c.　1 Ki 8:31
I will c. him to fall by sword.　2 Ki 19:7
　　　　　　　　　　　Isa 37:7
outlandish women c. to.　Neh 13:26
c. to perish all the Jews. Esth 3:13
　　　　　　　　　　　8:11
c. Haman make haste to do.　5:5
c. me to understand.　Job 6:24
c. every man to find.　34:11
wilt c. thine ear to hear.　Ps 10:17
c. his face to shine.　67:1; 80:3
　　　　　　　　　　　7, 19
thou didst c. judgement to.　76:8
c. me to hear, c. me to.　143:8
unless they c. some to fall.　Pr 4:16
suffer not thy mouth to c.　Eccl 5:6
hearken to thy voice, c. S of S 8:13
who lead thee c.　Isa 3:12; 9:16
he shall c. them of Jacob.　27:6
this is the rest ye may c.　28:12
the Lord c. his glorious voice. 30:30
nor c. his voice to be heard.　42:2
I will c. thee to ride upon.　58:14
Lord will c. righteousness.　61:11
bring to birth, and not c. ?　66:9
not c. mine anger to fall.　Jer 3:12
I will c. you to dwell in this.　7:3, 7
Lord before he c. darkness.　13:16
I will c. the enemy to.　15:11
think to c. my people.　23:27
Israel, when I went to c.　31:2
I will c. them to walk by rivers.　9
c. their captivity to.　32:44; 33:26
though he c. grief.　Lam 3:32
I will c. you to pass.　Ezek 20:37
that it might c. fury to come.　24:8
I will c. them to lie down.　34:15
I will c. men to walk on you.　36:12
he shall c. craft to prosper. Dan 8:25
c. thy face to shine on.　9:17
thither c. thy mighty.　Joel 3:11
c. the seat of violence to. Amos 6:3
I will c. sun to go down at.　8:9
c. me to behold grievance ? Hab 1:3
c. them to be put to death. Mat 10:21
　　　　Mark 13:12; Luke 21:16
mark them who c.　Rom 16:17
c. that it be read in.　Col 4:16

cause *to cease, see* **cease**

caused
God c. a deep sleep to.　Gen 2:21
God c. me to wander from.　20:13
Lord c. the sea to go.　Ex 14:21
c. Israel to commit.　Num 31:16
is the land, I have c.　Deut 34:4
c. thee to rest from.　2 Sam 7:11
c. a seat to be set for.　1 Ki 2:19
he c. all present in.　2 Chr 34:32
God hath c. his name.　Ezra 6:12
Levites c. people to.　Neh 8:7, 8
Haman c. gallows to be.　Esth 5:14
if I have c. eyes of.　Job 31:16
hast c. men to ride.　Ps 66:12
and c. them to pass through. 78:13
he c. an east-wind to blow in.　26
word on which thou hast c.　119:49
with fair speech she c.　Pr 7:21
they have c. Egypt to err. Isa 19:14
I have not c. thee to serve.　43:23
Spirit of the Lord c. him.　63:14
I have c. my people Israel. Jer 12:14
I have c. to cleave to me.　13:11
Shemaiah c. you to trust in.　29:31
therefore thou hast c. all this. 32:23
c. the servants to return. 34:11, 16
her little ones have c. a cry.　48:4
I have c. thee to multiply. Ezek 16:7

till I have c. my fury to. *Ezek* 24:13
Nebuchadnezzar c. his army. 29:18
c. terror in land. 32:23, 24, 25, 26
Gabriel being c. to fly. *Dan* 9:21
spirit of whoredoms c. *Hos* 4:12
their lies c. them to err. *Amos* 2:4
I c. rain on one city, I c. not. 4:7
I have c. thine iniquity. *Zech* 3:4
ye have c. many to. *Mal* 2:8
have c. this man should. *John* 11:37
they c. great joy to all. *Acts* 15:3
but if any have c. grief. *2 Cor* 2:5
c. all to receive a mark. *Rev* 13:16

causeless
thou hast shed blood c. *1 Sam* 25:31
curse c. shall not come. *Pr* 26:2

causes
that thou mayest bring c. *Ex* 18:19
hard c. they brought to Moses. 26
hear the c. between. *Deut* 1:16
c. whereby backsliding. *Jer* 3:8
but have seen for thee c. *Lam* 2:14
thou hast pleaded the c. of. 3:58
for these c. the Jews. *Acts* 26:21

causest
thou c. me to ride. *Job* 30:22
blessed is man thou c. *Ps* 65:4

causeth
water that c. curse. *Num* 5:18, 19
22, 24, 27
c. them to wander in. *Job* 12:24
Ps 107:40
spirit of understanding c. *Job* 20:3
he c. it to come hither. 37:13
c. the grass to grow. *Ps* 104:14
c. vapours to ascend. 135:7
Jer 10:13; 51:16
c. his wind to blow. *Ps* 147:18
son that c. shame. *Pr* 10:5; 17:2
19:26
servant shall rule over a son c. 17:2
instruction that c. to err. 19:27
whoso c. righteous to go. 28:10
fire c. the waters to boil. *Isa* 64:2
any thing that c. sweat. *Ezek* 44:18
put away wife c. her to. *Mat* 5:32
thanks be to God, who c. *2 Cor* 2:14*
c. through us thanksgiving. 9:11
c. the earth to worship. *Rev* 13:12

causeway
lot came forth by c. of. *1 Chr* 26:16
at Parbar westward, four at c. 18

causing
c. the lips of those. *S of S* 7:9*
a bridle in the jaws c. *Isa* 30:28
in c. you to return to. *Jer* 29:10
shepherds c. their flocks. 33:12

cave, -s
Lot dwelt in a c. he and. *Gen* 19:30
field and c. made sure. 23:17, 20
buried Sarah in the c. 19
me with my father in c. 49:29
kings fled and hid in c. *Josh* 10:16
17
Midianites Israel made c. *Judg* 6:2
hide in c. in rocks. *1 Sam* 13:6
David escaped to the c. of. 22:1
into my hand in the c. 24:10
came to David to c. *2 Sam* 23:13
hid by fifty in a c. *1 Ki* 18:4, 13
Elijah came to a c. and. 19:9
they shall go into c. *Isa* 2:19
die that be in the c. *Ezek* 33:27
grave, it was a c. a. *John* 11:38
wandered in dens and c. *Heb* 11:38*

cease
day and night shall not c. *Gen* 8:22
the thunder shall. *Ex* 9:29
from age of fifty shall c. *Num* 8:25
elders prophesied, did not c. 11:25
I will make to c. murmurings. 17:5
the poor shall never c. *Deut* 15:11
remembrance of them to c. *Josh* 22:25
so make our children c. 22:25
be avenged, after I will c. *Judg* 15:7
go to battle, or shall I c.? 20:28
c. not to cry to Lord. *1 Sam* 7:8
Baasha heard it, let his work c.
2 Chr 16:5
made them to c. by force. *Ezra* 4:23
why should the work c.? *Neh* 6:3

there the wicked c. from. *Job* 3:17
my days few, c. then. 10:20
branch thereof will not c. 14:7
c. from anger, forsake. *Ps* 37:8
he maketh wars to c. to the. 46:9
hast made his glory to c. 89:44
c. to hear instruction. *Pr* 19:27
honour for a man to c. from. 20:3*
yea strife and reproach shall c. 22:10
labour to be rich, c. from. 23:4
the grinders c. because. *Eccl* 12:3
c. to do evil. *Isa* 1:16
c. ye from man. 2:22
and indignation shall c. 10:25*
their vintage shouting to c. 16:10
the fortress also shall c. from. 17:3
thereof have I made to c. 21:2
when thou shalt c. to spoil. 33:1
and let them not c. *Jer* 14:17
leaf green, nor shall c. from. 17:8
then seed of Israel shall c. 31:36
not apple of thine eye c. *Lam* 2:18
idols may be broken and c. *Ezek* 6:6
pomp of the strong to c. 7:24
I will make this proverb c. 12:23
I make thy lewdness to c. 23:27
the multitude of Egypt to c. 30:10
of her strength shall c. 18; 33:28
c. by whom shall Jacob. *Amos* 7:5
c. will not c. to pervert. *Acts* 13:10
be tongues, they shall c. *1 Cor* 13:8
I c. not to give thanks. *Eph* 1:16
we do not c. to pray for. *Col* 1:9
eyes that cannot c. from. *2 Pet* 2:14

cause to cease
cause these men to c. *Ezra* 4:21
they could not cause them to c. 5:5
slay and cause work to c. *Neh* 4:11
cause thine anger to c. *Ps* 85:4
lot causeth contentions to c. *Pr* 18:18
cause arrogancy of proud to c.
Isa 13:11
cause holy One of Israel to c. 30:11
cause mirth to c. from. *Jer* 7:34
cause to c. man. 36:29; *Hos* 2:11
I will cause to c. in. *Jer* 48:35
cause thee to c. from. *Ezek* 16:41
will I cause lewdness to c. 23:48
cause noise of thy songs to c. 26:13
I will cause their images to c. 30:13
cause them to c. from. 34:10
I will cause to c. evil beasts. 25
cause the oblation to c. *Dan* 9:27
cause reproach offered by him to c.
11:18
will cause to c. kingdom. *Hos* 1:4

ceased
it c. to be with Sarai. *Gen* 18:11
thunders and hail c. *Ex* 9:33
saw that the thunders c. 34
the manna c. on the. *Josh* 5:12
they c. not from their. *Judg* 2:19
inhabitants of villages c. they c. 5:7
they that were hungry c. *1 Sam* 2:5
in the name of David and c. 25:9
then c. the work of. *Ezra* 4:24
so these three men c. to. *Job* 32:1
did tear me and c. not. *Ps* 35:15
sore ran in the night and c. 77:2*
oppressor c. golden city c. *Isa* 14:4
the elders have c. from. *Lam* 5:14
the joy of our heart is c. 15
took up Jonah, sea c. *Jonah* 1:15
the wind c. *Mat* 14:32; *Mark* 4:39
6:51
woman hath not c. to. *Luke* 7:45
praying in a place, when he c. 11:1
they c. not to teach and. *Acts* 5:42
after the uproar was c. Paul. 20:1
by space of three years I c. not. 31
would not be persuaded we c. 21:14
then is offence of cross c. *Gal* 5:11*
he also hath c. from his. *Heb* 4:10
then they would not have c. 10:2
suffered in flesh, hath c. *1 Pet* 4:1

ceaseth
help, Lord, for godly man c. *Ps* 12:1
precious, and it c. for ever. 49:8*
is no tale-bearer strife c. *Pr* 26:20
the spoiler c. *Isa* 16:4
of tabrets c. joy of harp c. 24:8
the way-faring man c. 33:8
eye trickleth down c. not. *Lam* 3:49

c. from raising after he. *Hos* 7:4
this man c. not to speak. *Acts* 6:13

ceasing
I should sin in c. to. *1 Sam* 12:23
was made without c. *Acts* 12:5*
without c. I make. *Rom* 1:9
1 Thes 1:3
we thank God without c. *1 Thes* 2:13
pray without c. in every. 5:17
without c. I have. *2 Tim* 1:3

cedar
(An evergreen tree of great value to building in Bible times. It was much used in building the Temple. The cedars of Lebanon are the most famous; of them only a few remain)
I dwell in an house of c. *2 Sam* 7:2
build ye not me an house of c.? 7
he spake from the c. to. *1 Ki* 4:33
all thy desire concerning c. 5:8
thistle sent to the c. *2 Ki* 14:9
2 Chr 25:18
moveth his tail like a c. *Job* 40:17
shall grow like a c. *Ps* 92:12
beams of house are c. *S of S* 1:17
inclose her with boards of c. 8:9
in the wilderness the c. *Isa* 41:19
it is cieled with c. *Jer* 22:14
thou closest thyself in c. 15
eagle took highest branch of c.
Ezek 17:3
of the highest branch of the c. 22
bear fruit and be a goodly c. 23
chests made of c. among. 27:24
the Assyrian was a c. in. 31:3
he shall uncover the c. *Zeph* 2:14
howl, fir-tree, for the c. *Zech* 11:2

cedar trees
Israel's tabernacles are c. *Num* 24:6
Hiram sent c. to David. *2 Sam* 5:11
they hew me c. out of. *1 Ki* 5:6
so Hiram gave Solomon c. 10; 9:11
cut down the tall c. *2 Ki* 19:23
David prepared c. in. *1 Chr* 22:4
c. made he as sycomore. *2 Chr* 1:15
9:27
send me c. and fir-trees. 2:8
gave money to bring c. *Ezra* 3:7

cedar wood
c. and hyssop. *Lev* 14:4, 6, 49, 51, 52
priest shall take c. and. *Num* 19:6
they brought much c. *1 Chr* 22:4

cedars
c. made he to be as. *1 Ki* 10:27
I dwell in an house of c. *1 Chr* 17:1
didst send David c. to. *2 Chr* 2:3
voice of Lord breaketh c. *Ps* 29:5
boughs were like goodly c. 80:10
praise him also c. and. 148:9
excellent as the c. *S of S* 5:15
the sycomores into c. *Isa* 9:10
I will cut down the tall c. 37:24
he heweth him down c. 44:14
cut down thy choice c. *Jer* 22:7
Lebanon, that makest nest in c. 23
c. in garden of God. *Ezek* 31:8
height as height of c. *Amos* 2:9
fire may devour thy c. *Zech* 11:1

cedars of Lebanon
fire devour c. of Leb. *Judg* 9:15
the c. of Leb. which. *Ps* 104:16
upon all the c. of Leb. *Isa* 2:13
c. of Leb. rejoice at thee. 14:8
c. from Leb. to make. *Ezek* 27:5

Cedron
disciples over brook C. *John* 18:1*

celebrate
from even to even shall c. *Lev* 23:32
a statute, ye shall c. it in. 41
death cannot c. the. *Isa* 38:18

celestial
c. bodies, glory of c. is. *1 Cor* 15:40

cellars
over the c. of oil was. *1 Chr* 27:28

Cenchrea
shorn his head in C. *Acts* 18:18
a servant of church at C. *Rom* 16:1

censer, -s

took either of them c.   Lev 10:1
he shall take a c. full of.   16:12
upon it vessels, even c.   Num 4:14*
this do, take ye c.   16:6
every man his c.   17
Eleazar took the brasen c.   39
made c. of pure gold.   1 Ki 7:50*
                                          2 Chr 4:22*
Uzziah had a c. in his.   2 Chr 26:19
with every man his c.   Ezek 8:11
had the golden c. and the ark of the
   covenant.   Heb 9:4
came, having a golden c.   Rev 8:3
the angel took the c. and filled.   5

centurion, -s

(Officer in the Roman army over a
   century, or 100 men)
there came unto him a c.   Mat 8:5
c. said, Lord, I am not worthy.   8
when the c. saw earthquake.   27:54
certain c.'s servant, who was dear
   unto him.   Luke 7:2
now when the c. saw what.   23:47
Cornelius was a c. of.   Acts 10:1
Cornelius the c. a just man.   22
who immediately took soldiers and
   c. and ran down.   21:32
when the c. heard that.   22:26
Paul called one of the c. to.   23:17
called to him two c. saying.   23
and he commanded a c. to.   24:23
delivered Paul to Julius a c.   27:1
c. believed the master more.   11
c. wiliing to save Paul, kept.   43
c. delivered the prisoners to.   28:16

Cephas

thou shalt be called C.   John 1:42
I am of C.   1 Cor 1:12
whether Paul, or Apollos, or C.   3:22
brethren of the Lord, and C.   9:5
that he was seen of C.   15:5
James, C. and John, who seemed to
   be pillars.   Gal 2:9

ceremonies

passover according to all the c.
   thereof.   Num 9:3*

certain

gather a c. rate every day. Ex 16:4
Korah rose with c. of.   Num 16:2
c. men the children of Belial.
                                  Deut 13:13
wicked man be beaten by a c.   25:2
after a c. rate every day, offering
   according.   2 Chr 8:13
Hanani came, he and c.   Neh 1:2
I mourned c. days, and fasted.   4
a c. portion should be for the singers.
                                       11:23
I smote c. of them, and.   13.25
came c. from Shechem.   Jer 41:5
captain carried away c. of.   52:15
fainted and was sick c.   Dan 8:27
king of north shall come after c.
   years.   11:13
likened to c. king. Mat 18:28; 22:2
and her sons desiring a c.   20:20
came a c. poor widow.   Mark 12:42
                                  Luke 21:2
arose c. and bare false witness
   against him.   Mark 14:57
when he was in a c.   Luke 5:12
told him by c. thy mother.   8:20
went into a c. village.   10:38; 17:12
a c. woman lifted up voice.   11:27
a c. Pharisee besought him to.   37
this parable to c. who trusted.   18:9
who for a c. sedition and.   23:19
c. women also made us.   24:22
c. of them with us went to the.   24
angel went down at a c.   John 5:4
Saul was c. days with.   Acts 9:19
prayed Peter to tarry c. days. 10:48
Herod the king to vex c.   12:1
c. which went from us have.   15:24
as c. of your own poets.   17:28
contribution for c. saints. Rom 15:26
for before that c. came.   Gal 2:12
one in a c. place testified.   Heb 2:6
he spake in a c. place of the seventh
   day.   4:4
he limiteth a c. day, saying.   7

a c. fearful looking for. Heb 10:27
there are c. men crept in.   Jude 4

certain

it be truth and thing c.   Deut 13:14
                                       17:4
for c. thou shalt die.   1 Ki 2:37, 42
know for c. if ye put.   Jer 26:15
the dream is c. and.   Dan 2:45
I have no c. thing to write unto my
   lord.   Acts 25:26
no c. dwelling-place.   1 Cor 4:11
c. we can carry nothing.   1 Tim 6:7

certainly

I will c. return to thee.   Gen 18:10
we saw c. that the Lord was with
   thee.   26:28
could we c. know he would.   43:7*
such a man as I can c.?   44:15
will c. requite us all the.   50:15*
c. I will be with thee.   Ex 3:12
if theft be c. found in his.   22:4
he hath c. trespassed.   Lev 5:19
congregation shall c. stone.   24:16
because it was c. told.   Josh 9:24
if ye can c. declare the.   Judg 14:12
thy father c. knoweth.   1 Sam 20:3
if I knew c. evil were.   9*
c. heard that Saul with.   23:10
Lord will c. make my lord.   25:28
even so will I c. do.   1 Ki 1:30
thou mayest c. recover.   2 Ki 8:10
thou c. return in peace.   2 Chr 18:27
for riches c. make.   Pr 23:5
lo, c. in vain made he it.   Jer 8:8
do we not c. know every.   13:12
ye shall c. drink.   25:28
king of Babylon shall c.   36:29
dost thou c. know that Baal ? 40:14
know c. I have admonished.   42:19
c. ye shall die by sword and.   22
c. do what thing goeth out.   44:17
c. this is the day that.   Lam 2:16
one shall c. come.   Dan 11:10*, 13*
saying, c. this was a righteous man.
                               Luke 23:47

certainty

know for c. Lord will.   Josh 23:13
come ye again with c.   1 Sam 23:23
make known the c. of.   Pr 22:21
I know of c. ye would.   Dan 2:8
thou mightest know the c. Luke 1:4
could not know the c.   Acts 21:34
would have known the c.   22:30

certify, -ied

word from you to c.   2 Sam 15:28
we sent and c. the king.   Ezra 4:14
we c. the king, that if this city.   16
their names also to c. thee.   5:10
we c. you not to impose toll.   7:24
Esther c. king thereof.   Esth 2:22*
I c. you gospel I preached. Gal 1:11*

Cesar, see Caesar

Cesarea (Caesarea)

came into coasts of C.   Mat 16:13
into the towns of C.   Mark 8:27
till he came to C.   Acts 8:40
brought Paul down to C.   9:30
morrow after entered into C.   10:24
sent three men from C.   11:11
Herod went from Judea to C. 12:19
when he had landed at C.   18:22
with us also certain of the disciples
   of C.   21:16
200 soldiers to go to C.   23:23
3 days he ascended from C.   25:1
Paul should be kept at C.   4

chafed

they be c. in their minds. 2 Sam 17:8

chaff

(The refuse of winnowed grain)
as c. that the storm carrieth away.
                                Job 21:18
like the c. which the wind.   Ps 1:4
let them be as c. before wind. 35:5
as flame consumeth the c. Isa 5:24*
nations shall be chased as c.   17:13
terrible ones shall be as c.   29:5
ye shall conceive c. and.   33:11
and make the hills as c.   41:15
is the c. to the wheat ?   Jer 23:28*
became like the c. of.   Dan 2:35

as the c. which is driven.   Hos 13:3
before day pass as c.   Zeph 2:2
burn up the c. with fire.   Mat 3:12
                               Luke 3:17

chain

gold c. about his neck.   Gen 41:42
                                Dan 5:7, 16, 29
them about as a c.   Ps 73:6
ravished my heart with one c. of thy
   neck.   S of S 4:9
hath made my c. heavy.   Lam 3:7
make a c. for land is full of crimes.
                                Ezek 7:23
bracelets, and a c. on thy.   16:11
I am bound with this c.   Acts 28:20
not ashamed of my c.   2 Tim 1:16
an angel and a great c.   Rev 20:1

chains

fasten the wreathen c.   Ex 28:14, 24
made on breast-plate c.   39:15
for atonement, c. and.   Num 31:50*
besides the c. about.   Judg 8:26
by the c. of gold before.   1 Ki 6:21
bind their kings with c.   Ps 149:8
instruction shall be c.   Pr 1:9
thy neck comely with c. S of S 1:10*
Lord will take away c.   Isa 3:19*
and casteth silver c.   40:19
shall come after thee in c.   45:14
loose thee this day from c. Jer 40:4
brought him with c. into. Ezek 19:4*
they put in ward in c.   9
bind him, no not with c.   Mark 5:3
the c. had been oft plucked by him. 4
Peter's c. fell off.   Acts 12:7
delivered them into c. of.   2 Pet 2:4
reserved in everlasting c.   Jude 6*

see bound

chainwork

wreaths of c. for.   1 Ki 7:17

chalcedony

third foundation was a c. Rev 21:19

Chalcol

Solomon was wiser than C.
                              1 Ki 4:31
of Zerah, Heman, C.   1 Chr 2:6

Chaldea

C. shall be a spoil.   Jer 50:10
render to inhabitants of C.   51:24
blood be upon inhabitants of C. 35
thy fornication to C.   Ezek 16:29
messengers to them into C.   23:16

Chaldean

hand of Nebuchadnezzar the C.
                              Ezra 5:12
asked such things at any C. Dan 2:10

Chaldeans

C. made out three bands.   Job 1:17
land of C. the Assyrian.   Isa 13:13
I have brought down the C.   43:14
throne, O daughter of the C.   47:1
darkness, O daughter of the C.   5
his arm shall be on the C.   48:14
flee from the C.   20
ye fight against the C.   Jer 21:4
he that falleth to the C.   9; 38:2
punish land of C.   25:12; 50:1, 45
though ye fight with the C.   32:5
is given into hand of the C. 24, 43
the C. shall come and set fire.
come to fight with the C.   33:5
the C. shall come again and.   37:8
surely the C. shall depart.   9
though ye had smitten army of C. 10
I fall not away to the C.   14
of Jews that are fallen to C. 38:19
bring out thy children to the C. 23
C. burnt king's house, and.   39:8
fear not to serve the C.   40:9
at Mizpah, to serve the C.   10
Ishmael slew the C. that were. 41:3
thee on to deliver us to C.   43:3
a sword is upon the C.   50:35
Lord hath purposed against C.   45
shall fall in the land of C.   51:4
army of C. pursued Zedekiah. 52:8
to the land of the C.   Ezek 12:13
she saw the images of the C. 23:14
teach tongue of the C.   Dan 1:4
king commanded to call the C. 2:2
at that time certain C. accused. 3:8

then came in the C. and the. *Dan 4:7*
king cried aloud to bring in C. 5:7
thy father made master of C. 11
Darius made king over the C. 9:1
lo, I raise up the C. that. *Hab 1:6*
came out of land of C. *Acts 7:4*

Chaldees
him bands of the C. *2 Ki 24:2*
the C. were against the city. 25:4
the army of the C. brake. 10
for they were afraid of the C. 26
brought king of C. *2 Chr 36:17*
Babylon the beauty of C. *Isa 13:19*
see Ur

chalk-stones
stones of the altar c. *Isa 27:9*

challengeth
any lost thing another c. *Ex 22:9*

chamber
(*An apartment, or room in a house, not confined, as now generally understood, to bed-chamber, 2 Sam 13:10; Ps 104:3; Ezek 42:13*)
Joseph entered into his c. *Gen 43:30*
in to my wife into the c. *Judg 15:1*
in wait abiding in the c. 16:9, 12
bring meat into the c. *2 Sam 13:10*
Elisha turned into the c. *2 Ki 4:11*
for Tobiah a great c. *Neh 13:5*
cast household stuff out of the c. 8
bridegroom cometh out of his c.
Ps 19:5
into the c. of her that. *S of S 3:4*
read the book in the c. *Jer 36:10*
laid up the roll in c. of. 20
c. whose prospect. *Ezek 40:45, 46*
being open in his c. to. *Dan 6:10*
bridegroom go forth of c. *Joel 2:16*
bed-chamber, see bed ; guard-chamber, see guard

guest-chamber
where is the *guest-c.?* *Mark 14:14*
Luke 22:11

inner **chamber**
and came into *inner* c. *1 Ki 20:30*
into *inner* c. to hide. 22:25
2 Chr 18:24
carry Jehu into *inner* c. *2 Ki 9:2*

little **chamber**
let us make a *little* c. *2 Ki 4:10*
little c. was one reed. *Ezek 40:7**
gate from roof of one *little* c. 13*

side chamber, -s
breadth of every *side-c.* *Ezek 41:5*
the *side-c.* were three, one. 6
thickness of wall for *side-c.* 9

upper chamber
lattice in his *upper-c.* *2 Ki 1:2*
altars in top of the *upper-c.* 23:12
laid Dorcas in an *upper-c.* *Acts 9:37*
Peter, when come into *upper-c.* 39
many lights in *upper-c.* where. 20:8

chambering
walk not in c. and. *Rom 13:13*

chamberlain, -s
chamber of the c. *2 Ki 23:11*
seven c. that served. *Esth 1:10*
but what Hegai the king's c. 2:15
two of king's c. were wroth. 21
Blastus the king's c. *Acts 12:20*
Erastus, c. of the city. *Rom 16:23*

chambers
wall of house he built c. *1 Ki 6:5*
chief porters over the c. *1 Chr 9:26*
23:28
to prepare c. *2 Chr 31:11*
ye weigh them in the c. *Ezra 8:29*
and they cleansed the c. *Neh 13:9*
which maketh the c. of. *Job 9:9*
layeth beams of his c. *Ps 104:3*
watereth the hills from his c. 13
brought forth frogs in c. 105:30
to hell going down to c. *Pr 7:27*
by knowledge c. shall be. 24:4
hath brought me into c. *S of S 1:4*
enter thou into thy c. *Isa 26:20*
woe to him that buildeth c. *Jer 22:13*
a wide house, and large c. 14
Rechabites into one of c. 35:2
every man in the c. *Ezek 8:12*

entereth into their privy c. *Ezek 21:14*
they be holy c. where priests. 42:13
he is in the secret c. *Mat 24:26*

upper-**chambers**
overlaid the *upper-c.* *2 Chr 3:9*
the *upper-c.* were shorter. *Ezek 42:5*

chameleon
ferret, and the c. and. *Lev 11:30*

chamois
eat, wild ox and the c. *Deut 14:5*

champaign
who dwell in the c. *Deut 11:30**

champion
there went out a c. *1 Sam 17:4*
when Philistines saw c. was dead. 51

chance
if a bird's nest c. to. *Deut 22:6*
it may c. of wheat. *1 Cor 15:37*

chance
it was a c. that. *1 Sam 6:9*
as I happened by c. *2 Sam 1:6*
time and c. happeneth. *Eccl 9:11*
by c. a priest came. *Luke 10:31*

chancellor
Rehum c. wrote letter. *Ezra 4:8, 9*
king sent answer to Rehum the c. 17

chanceth
uncleanness that c. him. *Deut 23:10*

change, -s
both it and the c. *Lev 27:33*
will give you thirty c. *Judg 14:12*
shall give me thirty c. of. 13
days will I wait till my c. *Job 14:14*
with them given to c. *Pr 24:21*
clothe thee with c. of. *Zech 3:4**
necessity a c. of the law. *Heb 7:12*

change, verb
be clean and c. your. *Gen 35:2*
he shall not c. it. *Lev 27:10*
nor c. it, if he c. 33
they c. the night into day. *Job 17:12*
as a vesture shalt thou c. *Ps 102:26*
but we will c. them. *Isa 9:10*
gaddest thou to c. thy way? *Jer 2:36*
can Ethiopian c. his skin? 13:23
think to c. times and laws. *Dan 7:25*
I will c. their glory into. *Hos 4:7*
then shall his mind c. *Hab 1:11*
I am the Lord, I c. not. *Mal 3:6*
shall c. the customs. *Acts 6:14*
their women did c. the. *Rom 1:26*
present, and c. my voice. *Gal 4:20*
who shall c. our vile body. *Phil 3:21*

changeable
Lord take away the c. *Isa 3:22**

changed, -eth
father c. my wages. *Gen 31:7, 41*
Joseph c. his raiment, and. 41:14
raw flesh turn and be c. *Lev 13:16*
if plague have not c. his colour. 55
he c. his behaviour. *1 Sam 21:13*
David c. his apparel. *2 Sam 12:20*
king of Babylon c. his. *2 Ki 24:17*
c. prison-garments. 25:29; *Jer 52:33*
disease is my garment c. *Job 30:18**
sweareth to his hurt, c. not. *Ps 15:4*
as vesture shall be c. 102:26
Heb 1:12
thus they c. their glory. *Ps 106:20*
boldness of face shall be c. *Eccl 8:1*
c. the ordinance, broken. *Isa 24:5*
c. their gods, people have c. *Jer 2:11*
and his scent is not c. 48:11
is the most fine gold c.! *Lam 4:1*
hath c. my judgements. *Ezek 5:6**
till the time be c. *Dan 2:9*
he c. the times and seasons. 21
form of his visage was c. 3:19
nor were their coats c. nor. 27
let his heart be c. from man's. 4:16
sign writing that it be not c. 6:8
no decree may be c. 15
purpose might not be c. 17
he hath c. the portion of. *Mi 2:4*
the barbarians c. their. *Acts 28:6*
c. the glory of the. *Rom 1:23*
c. the truth of God into a lie. 25
we shall all be c. *1 Cor 15:51, 52*
c. into same image from. *2 Cor 3:18*
for priesthood being c. a. *Heb 7:12*

changers
tables of money-c. *Mat 21:12*
Mark 11:15; John 2:14, 15

changes
he gave c. to Benjamin five c.
Gen 45:22
took with him ten c. *2 Ki 5:5*
give them, I pray thee, two c. 22
bound two c. of garments. 23
c. and war are against. *Job 10:17*
because they have no c. *Ps 55:19*

changest, -ed, *countenance*
thou c. his *countenance.* *Job 14:20*
king's *countenance* was c. *Dan 5:6, 9*
nor let thy *countenance* be c. 10
my *countenance* c. in me. 7:28

changing
in Israel concerning c. *Ruth 4:7*

channel, -s
c. of the sea appeared. *2 Sam 22:16*
Ps 18:15
come up over all his c. *Isa 8:7*
Lord shall beat off from c. 27:12*

chant
they c. to the sound of. *Amos 6:5**

chapel
it is the king's c. *Amos 7:13**

chapiter, -s
(*American Revision, capital*)
overlaid their c. with gold.
Ex 36:38; 38:28
overlaying of their c. 38:17, 19
made two c. of brass. *1 Ki 7:16*
2 Chr 4:12, 13
c. upon it was brass. *2 Ki 25:17*
Jer 52:22

chapmen
besides what c. and. *2 Chr 9:14**

chapt
because ground is c. *Jer 14:4*

Charashim
father of the valley of C. *1 Chr 4:14*

charge
[1] *To command,* Ex 1:22. [2] *To adjure, or bind by a solemn oath,* 1 Sam 14:27. [3] *To load, or burden,* Deut 24:5; 1 Tim 5:16. [4] *An office, or duty,* Num 8:26.
Abraham kept my c. *Gen 26:5*
Isaac gave Jacob a c. saying. 28:6
Moses and Aaron a c. *Ex 6:13*
this is the c. of their. *Num 4:31*
the Levites, touching their c. 8:26
Israel kept c. of the Lord. 9:19, 23
gave Joshua a c. 27:23; *Deut 31:23*
blood to people's c. *Deut 21:8*
Reubenites have kept c. *Josh 22:3*
the king gave c. *2 Sam 18:5*
ruler over all the c. *1 Ki 11:28*
the lord to have the c. *2 Ki 7:17*
because the c. was. *1 Chr 9:27*
Levites had the c. of. *2 Chr 30:17*
I gave Hanani c. over. *Neh 7:2*
of those that had c. of. *Esth 3:9*
who hath given him a c. *Job 34:13*
laid to my c. things I. *Ps 35:11*
king of Babylon gave c. *Jer 39:11*
Lord hath given it a c. 47:7
cause them that have c. *Ezek 9:1*
ye have not kept the c. of. 44:8
priests that kept the c. of. 15
priests kept my c. who. 48:11
lay not this sin to their c. *Acts 7:60*
an eunuch, who had c. of. 8:27
received such a c. thrust. 16:24
nothing laid to his c. worthy. 23:29
shall lay any thing to c. *Rom 8:33*
gospel of Christ without c.
1 Cor 9:18
c. I commit to thee. *1 Tim 1:18*
not be laid to their c. *2 Tim 4:16*

see keep

give charge
and *give* Joshua a c. *Num 27:19*
I may *give* him a c. *Deut 31:14*
go, and I will *give* c. *2 Sam 14:8*
give thee wisdom and c. *1 Chr 22:12*
give his angels c. *Ps 91:11*
Mat 4:6; Luke 4:10

charge (continued)

will I *give* him a *c.*   *Isa* 10:6
these things *give* in *c.*   *1 Tim* 5:7
I *give* thee *c.* in sight of God.   6:13

charge

go down, *c.* the people.   *Ex* 19:21
priest shall *c.* her.   *Num* 5:19
but *c.* Joshua and.   *Deut* 3:28
to *c.* ourselves yearly.   *Neh* 10:32
c. Esther that she go in.   *Esth* 4:8
I *c.* you, O ye daughters.   *S of S* 2:7
     3:5; 5:8; 8:4
that thou dost so *c.* us ?   5:9
I *c.* thee come out and.   *Mark* 9:25
I *c.* you that this.   *1 Thes* 5:27
c. that they teach no.   *1 Tim* 1:3
I *c.* thee before God and.   5:21
     2 Tim 4:1
c. them that are rich in.   *1 Tim* 6:17

chargeable

lest we be *c.* to thee.   *2 Sam* 13:25*
governors were *c.* to.   *Neh* 5:15
with you, I was *c.*   *2 Cor* 11:9*
we would not be *c.*   *1 Thes* 2:9*
we might not be *c.* to.   *2 Thes* 3:8*

charged

Abimelech *c.* his people.   *Gen* 26:11
Isaac called Jacob, and *c.*   28:1
captain of the guard *c.*   40:4
Jacob *c.* his sons, and.   49:29
Pharaoh *c.* all his people.   *Ex* 1:22
I *c.* your judges.   *Deut* 1:16
nor shall he be *c.* with.   24:5
Moses *c.* the people the.   27:11
when Saul *c.* people.   *1 Sam* 14:27
the king *c.* thee.   *2 Sam* 18:12
David *c.* Solomon his son.   *1 Ki* 2:1
the commandment that I have *c.* 43
so was it *c.* me by.   13:9
Lord *c.* me to build.   *2 Chr* 36:23
     Ezra 1:2
c. they not be opened.   *Neh* 13:19
as Mordecai *c.* her.   *Esth* 2:10, 20
Job sinned not, nor *c.*   *Job* 1:22
and his angels he *c.* with folly. 4:18
c. Baruch before them.   *Jer* 32:13
Jonadab in all that he *c.* us.   35:8
Jesus straitly *c.* them.   *Mat* 9:30
     Mark 5:43; *Luke* 9:21
Jesus *c.* them not make him known.
     Mat 12:16 *Mark* 3:12
c. not to tell.   *Mark* 7:36; 8:30
     9:9; *Luke* 5:14; 8:56
many *c.* him that he.   *Mark* 10:48
we *c.* every one of.   *1 Thes* 2:11
let not church be *c.*   *1 Tim* 5:16

chargedst

thou *c.* us, saying.   *Ex* 19:23

charger, -s

(A sort of dish or platter)
offering was one silver *c. Num* 7:13
   19, 25, 31, 37, 43, 49, 61, 67, 73, 79
dedication of altar, twelve *c.*   7:84
each *c.* of silver weighing 130.   85
number one thousand *c.*   *Ezra* 1:9
John Baptist's head in a *c. Mat* 14:8
     Mark 6:25

charges

the Levites to their *c.*   *2 Chr* 8:14
from 20 years old in their *c.*   31:17
he set priests in their *c.*   35:2
them take, and be at *c. Acts* 21:24
warfare at his own *c.?*   *1 Cor* 9:7

chargest

thou *c.* me to day.   *2 Sam* 3:8

charging

c. the jailor to keep.   *Acts* 16:23
c. that they strive.   *2 Tim* 2:14

chariot

(Among the ancients a two-wheeled vehicle for war, racing, or pleasure)
to ride in the second *c.*   *Gen* 41:43
Lord took off *c.* wheels.   *Ex* 14:25
like work of a *c.* wheel.   *1 Ki* 7:33
prepare thy *c.* and get.   18:44
number thee *c.* for *c.* and.   20:25
caused him to come into the *c.*   33
blood ran into the midst of *c.* 22:35
washed the *c.* in pool of.   38
appeared a *c.* of fire and.   *2 Ki* 2:11
father, the *c.* of Israel.   12; 13:14
lighted from the *c.* to meet.   5:21

Jehu rode in a *c.*   *2 Ki* 9:16
smite him in the *c.*   27
carried him in a *c.* to.   28; 23:30
gold for pattern of *c.*   *1 Chr* 28:18
took him out of the *c.*   *2 Chr* 35:24
he burneth the *c.* in.   *Ps* 46:9
c. and horse are cast into.   76:6
made a *c.* of the wood. *S of S* 3:9*
a *c.* with horsemen, a *c. Isa* 21:7*
here cometh a *c.* of men.   9*
who bringeth forth the *c.*   43:17
break in pieces the *c.*   *Jer* 51:21
bind the *c.* to the swift.   *Mi* 1:13
first *c.* red horses, second *c.*
     Zech 6:2
I will cut off the *c.* from.   9:10
go join thyself to his *c. Acts* 8:29
commanded *c.* to stand still.   38

his chariot

Joseph made ready his *c. Gen* 46:29
Pharaoh made ready his *c. Ex* 14:6
Sisera lighted off his *c. Judg* 4:15
why is his *c.* so long in ?   5:28
made speed to his *c.*   *1 Ki* 12:18
     2 Chr 10:18
said to the driver of his *c. 1 Ki* 22:34
Ahab was stayed up in his *c.*   35
Naaman came with his *c. 2 Ki* 5:9
turned again from his *c.*   26
his *c.* was made ready, went out each
   in his *c.*   9:21
and he sunk down in his *c.*   24
made him to ride in his *c.*   10:16
who maketh clouds his *c. Ps* 104:3
his *c.* shall be as a.   *Jer* 4:13
sitting in his *c.* read.   *Acts* 8:28

chariot-cities

horsemen placed in *c.-cities.*
     2 Chr 1:14
all the *c.-cities.*   8:6
bestowed in the *c.-cities* and.   9:25

chariot-horses

houghed all *c.-horses.*   *2 Sam* 8:4
     1 Chr 18:4
therefore two *c.-horses. 2 Ki* 7:14

chariot-man

he said to the *c.-man. 2 Chr* 18:33

chariots

went up with Joseph *c.*   *Gen* 50:9
took 600 *c.* and all the *c. Ex* 14:7
I will get honour upon his *c.*   17
the waters covered all the *c.*   28
Pharaoh's *c.* and host.   15:4
horse of Pharaoh went in with *c.* 19
have *c.* of iron.   *Josh* 17:16, 18
     Judg 1:19; 4:3
Sisera and all his *c.*   *Judg* 4:15
why tarry the wheels of his *c.?* 5:28
appoint them for his *c.*   *1 Sam* 8:11
fight against Israel, 30,000 *c.*   13:5
c. and horsemen followed. *2 Sam* 1:6
David slew the men of 700 *c.* 10:18
Solomon had 1400 *c.*   *1 Ki* 10:26
Zimri captain of half his *c.*   16:9
when the captains of the *c.*   22:32
left but ten *c.* and.   *2 Ki* 13:7
thy trust on Egypt for *c.*   18:24
     Isa 36:9
the *c.* of God are 20,000.   *Ps* 68:17
my soul like the *c.* of. *S of S* 6:12
nor is any end of their *c.*   *Isa* 2:7
c. of thy glory be the shame.   22:18
woe to them that trust in *c.*   31:1
by the multitude of my *c.*   37:24
Lord will come with fire and *c.* 66:15
     Jer 4:13; *Dan* 11:40
at rushing of his *c.*   *Jer* 47:3
come against these with *c. Ezek* 23:24
shake at the noise of the *c.*   26:10
like the noise of the *c.*   *Joel* 2:5
off horses, and destroy *c. Mi* 5:10
c. shall be with flaming.   *Nah* 2:3
c. shall rage in streets and.   4
I am against, and will burn her *c.* 13
I will overthrow the *c. Hag* 2:22
as the sound of *c.*   *Rev* 9:9

chariots with horses

the *horses* and *c.* of.   *Ex* 14:9, 23
did to their *horses* and *c. Deut* 11:4
when thou seest *horses* and *c.* 20:1
hough their *horses,* burn *c. Josh* 11:6
houghed *horses,* burnt their *c.*   9

prepared *horses* and *c.*   *2 Sam* 15:1
Samaria with *c.* and *horses.*
     1 Ki 20:1
was full of *c.* and *horses. 2 Ki* 6:17
to hear a noise of *horses* and *c.*   7:6
are with you *c.* and *horses.*   10:2
in *c.* and some in *horses.*   *Ps* 20:7
to *horses* in Pharaoh's *c. S of S* 1:9
on *horses* and in *c.*   *Isa* 66:20
enter princes riding in *c.* and on
   horses.   *Jer* 17:25; 22:4
ye *horses,* and rage, ye *c.*   46:9
upon their *horses* and their *c.* 50:37
with *horses* and with *c. Ezek* 26:7
my table with *horses* and *c.*   39:20
prancing *horses* and jumping *c.*
     Nah 3:2
ride on thy *horses* and *c. Hab* 3:8
buys their *horses* and *c. Rev* 18:13

charitably

now walkest not *c.*   *Rom* 14:15*

charity

[1] *Christian love or benevolence.*
[2] *More generally, love, good will.*
[3] *Good will to the poor, hence almsgiving. The word is used in the New Testament only, and in the Revised Version is always translated love, since the word charity has now come to have to most readers only the third meaning given above.*

but *c.* edifieth.   *1 Cor* 8:1
and have not *c.*   13:1, 2, 3
c. suffereth long, and is kind, *c.*   4
c., but the greatest of these is *c.*   13
follow after *c.* and desire.   14:1
all things be done with *c.*   16:14
above all put on *c.*   *Col* 3:14
of your faith and *c.*   *1 Thes* 3:6
c. towards each other.   *2 Thes* 1:3
end of commandment is *c. 1 Tim* 1:5
continue in faith and *c.*   2:15
be an example in *c.* in spirit.   4:12
follow faith, *c.* peace.   *2 Tim* 2:22
my doctrine, life, faith, *c.*   3:10
sound in faith, in *c.*   *Tit* 2:2
fervent *c.* for *c.* shall.   *1 Pet* 4:8
one another with a kiss of *c.*   5:14
to brotherly-kindness, *c. 2 Pet* 1:7
borne witness of thy *c.*   *3 John* 6
spots in your feasts of *c.*   *Jude* 12
I know thy works, and *c. Rev* 2:19

charmed

serpents which will not be *c. Jer* 8:17

charmer, -s

found among you a *c.*   *Deut* 18:11
not hearken to voice of *c.*   *Ps* 58:5

Charran

Abraham dwelt in *C.*   *Acts* 7:2, 4

chase

shall *c.* your enemies.   *Lev* 26:7
five of you shall *c.* an.   8
sound of a shaking leaf shall *c.*   36
should one *c.* 1000.   *Deut* 32:30
     Josh 23:10
let angel of Lord *c.*   *Ps* 35:5*

chased, -eth, -ing

the Amorites *c.* you as.   *Deut* 1:44
Abimelech *c.* him.   *Judg* 9:40
inclosed Benjamites and *c.*   20:43
Israel returned from *c. 1 Sam* 17:53
therefore I *c.* him.   *Neh* 13:28
he shall be *c.* out of.   *Job* 18:18
he shall be *c.* away as a vision. 20:8
and he that *c.* away.   *Pr* 19:26
it shall be as the *c.* roe.   *Isa* 13:14
they shall be *c.* as the chaff.   17:13
mine enemies *c.* me sore.   *Lam* 3:52

chaste

you as a *c.* virgin.   *2 Cor* 11:2
young women be *c.* obedient. *Tit* 2:5
your *c.* conversation.   *1 Pet* 3:2

chasten

(To correct or punish)
I will *c.* him with rod.   *2 Sam* 7:14
nor *c.* me in displeasure.   *Ps* 6:1
     38:1
c. thy son while there is.   *Pr* 19:18
thou didst *c.* thyself.   *Dan* 10:12*
as I love I rebuke and *c. Rev* 3:19

chastened
they have c. him. *Deut* 21:18
he is c. also with pain. *Job* 33:19
I wept, and c. my soul. *Ps* 69:10
all day been plagued, and c. 73:14
Lord hath c. me sore. 118:18
we are c. that we be. *1 Cor* 11:32
dying, yet live, as c. and. *2 Cor* 6:9
they for a few days c. *Heb* 12:10

chastenest, -eth, -ing
c. his son, so Lord c. *Deut* 8:5
despise not thou the c. of Almighty.
Job 5:17; *Pr* 3:11; *Heb* 12:5
is the man whom thou c. *Ps* 94:12
he that loveth him c. *Pr* 13:24
a prayer when thy c. *Isa* 26:16
whom Lord loveth he c. *Heb* 12:6
endure c. what son father c. not ? 7
no c. for present seems to be. 11

chastise
I will c. you seven. *Lev* 26:28
take the man and c. *Deut* 22:18
I will c. you with. *1 Ki* 12:11, 14
2 Chr 10:11, 14
I will c. them as their. *Hos* 7:12
my desire that I should c. 10:10
I will c. him, and. *Luke* 23:16, 22

chastised, -eth
c. you with whips. *1 Ki* 12:11, 14
2 Chr 10:11, 14
he that c. heathen. *Ps* 94:10
hast c. me, and I was c. *Jer* 31:18

chastisement
who have not seen the c. *Deut* 11:2
I have borne c. I will not. *Job* 34:31
c. of our peace was. *Isa* 53:5
have wounded with the c. *Jer* 30:14
if without c. then are. *Heb* 12:8

chatter
so did I c. *Isa* 38:14

Chebar
by river of C. *Ezek* 1:1, 3; 3:15
23; 10:15, 20

check
I have heard the c. of. *Job* 20:3*

checker work
Hiram made nets of c.-w *1 Ki* 7:17

cheek
smote Micaiah on the c. *1 Ki* 22:24
2 Chr 18:23
smitten me on the c. *Job* 16:10
he giveth his c. to him. *Lam* 3:30
Judge with a rod on the c. *Mi* 5:1
smiteth one c. offer also. *Luke* 6:29

right cheek
smite thee on thy *right* c. *Mat* 5:39

cheek-bone
all mine enemies on c.-bone. *Ps* 3:7

checks
to priest the two c. *Deut* 18:3
thy c. are comely with. *S of S* 1:10
his c. are as a bed of spices. 5:13
I gave my c. to them. *Isa* 50:6
and her tears are on her c. *Lam* 1:2

cheek-teeth
come up, hath c.-teeth. *Joel* 1:6

cheer
shall c. up his wife he. *Deut* 24:5
let thy heart c. thee in. *Eccl* 11:9
son, be of good c. thy. *Mat* 9:2
be of good c. it is I. 14:27
Mark 6:50
be of good c. *John* 16:33
be of good c. Paul. *Acts* 23:11
I exhort you to be of good c. 27:22
wherefore, sirs, be of good c. 25
then were they all of good c. 36

cheereth
leave my wine, which c. *Judg* 9:13

cheerful
merry heart maketh a c. *Pr* 15:13
house of Judah joy and c. *Zech* 8:19
corn shall make young men c. 9:17*
for God loveth a c. *2 Cor* 9:7

cheerfully
I do the more c. answer. *Acts* 24:10

cheerfulness
sheweth mercy with c. *Rom* 12:8

cheese, -s
carry these ten c. to. *1 Sam* 17:18
sheep and c. to David. *2 Sam* 17:29
curdled me like c.? *Job* 10:10

Chemarims
cut off the name of C. *Zeph* 1:4

Chemosh
undone, O people of C. *Num* 21:29
possess what C. giveth ? *Judg* 11:24
an high place for C. *1 Ki* 11:7, 33
and C. shall go forth. *Jer* 48:7
Moab shall be ashamed of C. 13
woe to thee, O Moab, people of C. 46

Chenaniah
C. chief of Levites. *1 Cor* 15:22, 27

Cherethims
behold, I will cut off C. *Ezek* 25:16

Cherethites
invasion on south of C. *1 Sam* 30:14
Benaiah was over C. *2 Sam* 8:18
20:23; *1 Chr* 18:17
unto the nation of the C. *Zeph* 2:5

cherish
let her c. him, and lie. *1 Ki* 1:2

cherished
damsel was fair, and c. *1 Ki* 1:4

cherisheth
c. his own flesh, as the. *Eph* 5:29
gentle, even as a nurse c. *1 Thes* 2:7

Cherith
hide thyself by brook C. *1 Ki* 17:3

cherub
[1] *One of an order of angels,*
usually below the seraphim. Plural
properly cherubim, in Authorized
Version cherubims. [2] *A winged*
figure used in connection with the
mercy seat of the Jewish ark of
the covenant, Ex 25:18–22; 37:7–9.
[3] *A mysterious composite figure*
described in Ezek 1 and 10.
one c. on one end, and the other c.
Ex 25:19; 37:8
he rode upon a c. *2 Sam* 22:11
Ps 18:10
other c. was ten cubits. *1 Ki* 6:25
the height of one c. ten cubits. 26
glory of God was gone from the c. to.
Ezek 9:3; 10:4
and one c. stretched forth his. 10:7
first face was the face of a c. 14
thou art the anointed c. 28:14
will destroy thee, O covering c. 16
between a c. and a c. every c. 41:18

cherubims
at the east of the garden c. *Gen* 3:24
thou shalt make two c. *Ex* 25:18
tabernacle of cunning. 26:1, 31
he made two c. of beaten. 37:7
within oracle two c. *1 Ki* 6:23
both the c. were of one measure. 25
overlaid the c. with gold. 28
c. covered the ark. 8:7; *2 Chr* 5:8
Heb 9:5
most holy place two c. *2 Chr* 3:10
sound of the c. wings. *Ezek* 10:5
when c. went, the wheels went. 16
c. lift up their wings and. 19; 11:22

between **the cherubims**
thee from *between* the c. *Ex* 25:22
from *between* the two c. *Num* 7:89
dwelleth *between* the c. *1 Sam* 4:4
2 *Sam* 6:2; *2 Ki* 19:15; *Isa* 37:16
dwelleth *between* the c. shine.
Ps 80:1
he sitteth *between* the c. 99:1
of fire from *between* the c. *Ezek* 10:2
between c. to fire was *between* c. 7

chesnut-tree, -s
took him rods of c.-*tree*. *Gen* 30:37*
the c.-*trees* were not. *Ezek* 31:8*

chest, -s
Jehoiada took c. and. *2 Ki* 12:9
they made c. *2 Chr* 24:8
and emptied the c. 11
in c. of rich apparel. *Ezek* 27:24

chew
of them that c. cud. *Lev* 11:4
Deut 14:7

chewed
ere the flesh was c. *Num* 11:33

cheweth
because he c. cud. *Lev* 11:4, 5, 6
Deut 14:6
swine c. not cud. *Lev* 11:7; *Deut* 14:8

chickens
a hen gathereth her c. *Mat* 23:37

chide
people did c., why c. ye ? *Ex* 17:2*
men of Ephraim did c. *Judg* 8:1
he will not always c. *Ps* 103:9

chiding
Meribah, because of c. *Ex* 17:7*

chief
[1] *The head of a family, tribe,*
army, etc., Num 3:30; Deut 1:15;
1 Sam 14:38; 2 Sam 5:8. *In such*
cases the Revised Version com-
monly changes the word to princes,
or captains, or heads. [2] *The*
best, or most valuable, 1 Sam 15:21.
[3] *The dearest, or most familiar,*
Pr 16:28.
the c. butler told his. *Gen* 40:9
he restored the c. butler to. 21
but hanged the c. baker as. 22
c. over c. of Levites. *Num* 3:32
the c. of your tribes. *Deut* 1:15
the people took the c. *1 Sam* 15:21
brother of Joab c. *2 Sam* 23:18
these were the c. of. *1 Ki* 9:23
of Judah came the c. *1 Chr* 5:2
first shall be c. and captain, Joab
went first and was c. 11:6
sons of David were c. about. 18:17
his father made him c. 26:10
the rulers have been c. *Ezra* 9:2
c. of the province that. *Neh* 11:3
taketh away heart of c. *Job* 12:24
chose out their way, and sat c. 29:25
behemoth is the c. of the. 40:19
smote c. of their strength. *Ps* 78:51
105:36
Jerusalem above my c. joy. 137:6
Wisdom crieth in c. place. *Pr* 1:21
a whisperer separateth c. friends.
16:28
orchard with all the c. *S of S* 4:14
stirreth up the c. ones. *Isa* 14:9
hast taught them as c. *Jer* 13:21
sing and shout among the c. 31:7*
her adversaries are the c. *Lam* 1:5
c. of children of Ammon. *Dan* 11:41
which are named c. *Amos* 6:1
anoint themselves with c.
whosoever will be c. *Mat* 20:27
c. seats in the synagogues. 23:6
Mark 12:39
supper to his c. estates. *Mark* 6:21
out devils through c. *Luke* 11:15
house of one of c. Pharisees. 14:1
they chose c. rooms. 7; 20:46
and he that is c. as he that. 22:26
among c. rulers many. *John* 12:42
Paul was the c. speaker. *Acts* 14:12
and of c. women not a few. 17:4
c. of Asia. 19:31*
the c. corner-stone. *Eph* 2:20
1 Pet 2:6
sinners, of whom I c. *1 Tim* 1:15
when c. Shepherd shall. *1 Pet* 5:4

chief *captain*
shall be c. and captain. *2 Sam* 5:8
came to the c. captain. *Acts* 21:31
when they saw the c. captain. 32
this young man to c. captain. 23:17
c. captain Lysias came upon. 24:7
c. captain shall come. 22

chief *captains*
Tachmonite sat c. among captains.
2 Sam 23:8
c. of all the *captains*. *1 Chr* 27:3
c. of Solomon's *captains*. *2 Chr* 8:9
Agrippa entered with c. captains.
Acts 25:23
rich men and c. captains. *Rev* 6:15

chief *fathers*
thou and c. *fathers* of. *Num* 31:26
c. *fathers* of Levites. *1 Chr* 9:34
the c. *fathers* of priests and. 24:31
2700 c. *fathers* made rulers. 26:32

chief (continued)

of c. *fathers* of mighty. *2 Chr 26:12*
c. of the *fathers* of Judah. *Ezra 1:5*
c. of the *fathers* gave. *Neh 7:70, 71*

chief house
c. of *house* of Gershonites.
Num 3:24
c. of *house* of Kohathites. 30
c. of the *house* of the Merarites. 35
Zimri was of a c. *house*. 25:14
Cozbi, of a c. *house* in Midian. 15
out of each c. *house* a. *Josh 22:14*

chief man, or men
being a c. *man* *Lev 21:4*
all of them c. *men*. *1 Chr 7:3*
more c. *men* of Eleazar than. 24:4
names of *men* that were c. *Ezra 5:10*
I gathered together c. *men*. 7:28
thee from the c. *men*. *Isa 41:9*
Jews stirred up c. *men*. *Acts 13:50*
Judas and Silas, c. *men*. 15:22
possessions of the c. *man*. 28:7

chief priest
Seraiah the c. *priest* *2 Ki 25:18*
Benaiah a c. *priest*. *1 Chr 27:5*
anointed Zadok to be c. *priest*. 29:22
Amariah c. *priest* is. *2 Chr 19:11*
and Azariah the c. *priest*. 26:20

chief priests
twelve of c. *priests*. *Ezra 8:24*
made the c. *priests* and all. 10:5
these were c. *priests* in. *Neh 12:7*
many things of c. *priests*. *Mat 16:21*
multitude from the c. *priests*. 26:47
c. *priests* sought to. 59
Mark 14:1, 55; Luke 9:22; 22:2
was accused of c. *priests*. *Mat 27:12*
Mark 15:3
c. *priests* mocking. *Mat 27:41*
Mark 15:31
voices of them and c. *priests*.
Luke 23:23
c. *priests* sent officers to. *John 7:32*
18:3
c. *priests* answered, we have. 19:15
authority from c. *priests*. *Acts 9:14*
26:10
commanded the c. *priests*. 22:30

chief prince, or princes
of Asher, c. *princes*. *1 Chr 7:40*
Gog c. *prince* of. *Ezek 38:2, 3; 39:1*
Michael one of c. *princes*. *Dan 10:13*

chief singer, or singers
were c. of the *singers*. *Neh 12:46*
to the c. *singer* on my. *Hab 3:19*

chiefest
fat with c. offerings. *1 Sam 2:29*
made them sit in c. place. 9:22
Doeg an Edomite, c. of herd-. 21:7
Hezekiah buried in c. *2 Chr 32:33*
my beloved is the c. *S of S 5:10*
who will be c. shall. *Mark 10:44*
not a whit behind c. *2 Cor 11:5*
12:11

chiefly
c. because to them were. *Rom 3:2*
c. of they that are of. *Phil 4:22*
c. them that walk after. *2 Pet 2:10*

child
[1] *One young in years*, 1 Sam
1:22. [2] *One weak in knowledge*,
Isa 10:19; 1 Cor 13:11. [3] *Such
as are humble and docile*, Mat
18:3, 4.

(*The words child, children are
frequently used for any descendant
or descendants however remote, as
the children of Israel. Such expressions as children of light,
children of darkness, mean those
who follow the light, or try to hide in
the darkness. " Children of God "
in the Old Testament is used
sometimes for angels, sometimes for
good men. In the New Testament
the term is more often used of those
who have believed and accepted
Christ*)

see **son, sons**
Hagar cast the c. under. *Gen 21:15*
let me not see the death of c. 16
the c. is not, and I, whither ? 37:30

do not sin against the c.? *Gen 42:22*
called the c. mother. *Ex 2:8*
not afflict any fatherless c. 22:22
was his only c. *Judg 11:34*
teach us what we shall do to c. 13:8
brought the c. to Eli. *1 Sam 1:25*
the Lord had called the c. 3:8
c. that is born to thee. *2 Sam 12:14*
Lord struck the c. that Uriah's. 15
David besought God for the c. 16
David perceived that c. was dead. 19
divide the living c. in. *1 Ki 3:25*
what shall become of the c. 14:3
the soul of the c. came into. 17:22
he told him, the c. is. *2 Ki 4:31*
the c. sneezed, and c. opened. 35
correction from the c. *Pr 23:13*
he hath neither c. nor. *Eccl 4:8*
with second c. that shall stand. 15
c. shall behave himself. *Isa 3:5*
for before the c. shall know. 7:16
the c. shall know to cry, my. 8:4
weaned c. shall put his hand. 11:8
the c. shall die an hundred. 65:20
bringeth forth her first c. *Jer 4:31*
is he a pleasant c.? 31:20
cut off man, woman, and c. 44:7
father shall deliver c. to. *Mat 10:21*
the c. was cured from. 17:18
twofold more the c. of hell. 23:15
came to circumcise c. *Luke 1:59*
what manner of c. shall this ? 66
thou c. shalt be called Prophet. 76
the c. grew, and waxed. 80; 2:40
parents brought in c. Jesus. 2:27
my son, he is my only c. 9:38
Jesus healed c. and delivered. 42
come down ere my c. die. *John 4:49*
as she is delivered of c. 16:21
against thy holy c. Jesus. *Acts 4:27*
signs may be done by name of c. 30*
Saul said, thou c. of the devil. 13:10
to devour her c. as soon. *Rev 12:4*
her c. was caught up to God. 5

a child
bear a c. who am I ? *Gen 18:13*
father, and a c. of his old age. 44:20
saw he was a goodly c. *Ex 2:2*
Heb 11:23
Samuel, a c. girded. *1 Sam 2:18*
wast delivered of a c. *1 Ki 3:17*
a c. shall be born to house of. 13:2
shall be fresher than a c. *Job 33:25*
as a c. as a weaned c. *Ps 131:2*
even a c. is known. *Pr 20:11*
train up a c. in the way he. 22:6
bound in the heart of a c. 15
a c. left to himself bringeth. 29:15
bringeth up his servant from a c. 21
better is a wise c. than. *Eccl 4:13*
to thee, when thy king is a c. 10:16
for unto us a c. is born. *Isa 9:6*
trees shall be few, that a c. 10:19
cannot speak, I am a c. *Jer 1:6, 7*
tidings, saying, a man c. is. 20:15
when Israel was a c. *Hos 11:1*
he said of a c. *Mark 9:21*
took a c. and set. 36; *Luke 9:47*
a c. I spake as a c. understood as a
c. I thought as a c. *1 Cor 13:11*
heir as long as he is a c. *Gal 4:1*
from a c. hast known. *2 Tim 3:15*
Sarah delivered of a c. *Heb 11:11*
brought forth a man c. *Rev 12:5*

little child
am a *little* c. I know not. *1 Ki 3:7*
fled into Egypt, being a *little* c. 11:17
the flesh of a *little* c. *2 Ki 5:14*
a *little* c. shall lead them. *Isa 11:6*
Jesus called a *little* c. to. *Mat 18:2*
shall receive one such *little* c. 5
not receive the kingdom of God as a
little c. *Mark 10:15; Luke 18:17*

no child
but Sarai had no c. *Gen 11:30*
priest's daughter have no c.
Lev 22:13
die, and have no c. *Deut 25:5*
Michal had no c. unto. *2 Sam 6:23*
verily she hath no c. *2 Ki 4:14*
they had no c. because. *Luke 1:7*
promised when he had no c. *Acts 7:5*

children

sucking **child**
father beareth sucking c. *Num 11:12*
sucking c. shall play on. *Isa 11:8*
woman forget her sucking c.? 49:15
tongue of sucking c. *Lam 4:4*

this **child**
take this c. and nurse. *Ex 2:9*
told concerning this c. *Luke 2:17*
this c. is set for fall and rising. 34
whoso shall receive this c. 9:48

with **child**
Hagar, thou art with c. *Gen 16:11*
daughters of Lot were with c. 19:36
Tamar thy daughter is with c. 38:24
whose these are, am I with c. 25
hurt a woman with c. *Ex 21:22*
Phinehas' wife was with c.
1 Sam 4:19
Bath-sheba said, I am with c.
2 Sam 11:5
rip up women with c. *2 Ki 8:12*
15:16
of her that is with c. *Eccl 11:5*
like a woman with c. *Isa 26:17*
we have been with c. we have. 18
that didst not travail with c. 54:1
man doth travail with c. *Jer 30:6*
from north woman with c. 31:8
the women with c. *Hos 13:16*
ripped up the women with c.
Amos 1:13
she was found with c. of. *Mat 1:18*
a virgin shall be with c. 23
woe to them that are with c. 24:19
Mark 13:17; Luke 21:23
Mary, being great with c. *Luke 2:5*
upon a woman with c. *1 Thes 5:3*
she being with c. cried. *Rev 12:2*

young **child**
and the c. was young. *1 Sam 1:24*
search diligently for the young c.
Mat 2:8
take young c. and his mother. 13
took the young c. and his mother. 14

childbearing
she shall be saved in c. *1 Tim 2:15*

childhood
before you from my c. *1 Sam 12:2*
c. and youth are vanity. *Eccl 11:10*

childish
I put away c. things. *1 Cor 13:11*

childless
give me, seeing I go c.? *Gen 15:2*
their sin, shall die c. *Lev 20:20*
thy sword hath made women c. so
shall thy mother be c. *1 Sam 15:33*
write you this man c. *Jer 22:30*
her to wife, and died c. *Luke 20:30*

children
(*Revised Version frequently
changes this word to sons*)
in sorrow bring forth c. *Gen 3:16*
it may be I may obtain c. 16:2
the c. struggled together. 25:22
give me c. or I die. 30:1
the c. which God hath given. 33:5
thy father's c. shall bow down. 49:8
600,000 men, besides c. *Ex 12:37*
iniquity of the fathers upon c. 20:5
34:7; *Num 14:18; Deut 5:9*
the wife and her c. shall. *Ex 21:4*
saw the c. of Anak. *Num 13:28*
the c. of Korah died not. 26:11
Ar to the c. of Lot. *Deut 2:9, 19*
can stand before the c. of Anak ? 9:2
the c. of Belial are gone. 13:13*
ye are the c. of the Lord. 14:1
have born him c. both beloved. 21:15
the c. begotten of them shall. 23:8
fathers shall not be put to death for
c. nor c. for. 24:16; *2 Chr 25:4*
c. in whom there is no faith.
Deut 32:20
let Asher be blessed with c. 33:24
c. of Reuben, Gad and Manasseh,
built there an. *Josh 22:9, 10, 11*
take 10,000 men of c. of. *Judg 4:6*
each one resembled the c. of. 8:18
a riddle to c. of people. 14:16
deliver us the c. of Belial. 20:13*

she that hath many c.   *1 Sam* 2:5
c. of Belial said, how shall ?   10:27†
neither shall c. of wickedness afflict
   them.   *2 Sam* 7:10; *1 Chr* 17:9
two men, c. of Belial.   *1 Ki* 21:13*
bears came and tare 42 c. *2 Ki* 2:24
Elisha called one of the c.   9:1
salute the c. of the king.   10:13
but the c. of murderers he slew not.
   14:6; *2 Chr* 25:4
do as Lord commanded c. *2 Ki* 17:34
c. are come to birth. 19:3; *Isa* 37:3
Seled died without c.   *1 Chr* 2:30
and Jether died without c.   32
Shimei's brethren had not many c.
   4:27
c. of Jacob his.   16:13; *Ps* 105:6
gathered to Jeroboam c. *2 Chr* 13:7*
Lord is not with the c. of.   25:7
smote c. of Seir 10,000.   11
are c. of the province.   *Ezra* 2:1
   Neh 7:6
by whom they had c.   *Ezra* 10:44
c. multipliedst thou as.   *Neh* 9:23
I intreated for the c. sake. *Job* 19:17
were c. of fools, yea c.   30:8
he is a king over all the c.   41:34
they are full of c. and.   *Ps* 17:14
come, ye c. hearken to me.   34:11
an alien to my mother's c.   69:8
he shall save the c. of needy.   72:4
the c. which should be born.   78:6
and all of you are c. of the   82:6
have holpen the c. of Lot.   83:8
the c. of thy servants shall.   102:28
to be a joyful mother of c.   113:9
lo c. are an heritage of Lord. 127:3
as arrows in the hand, so are c.   4
remember, O Lord, c. of.   137:7
let old men and c. praise.   148:12
let the c. of Zion be joyful.   149:2
hear, ye c. instruction.   *Pr* 4:1
   5:7; 7:24; 8:32
and the glory of c. are.   17:6
her c. arise up and call her.   31:28
if a man beget 100 c.   *Eccl* 6:3
mother's c. were angry. *S of S* 1:6
I have brought up c.   *Isa* 1:2
ah sinful nation, c. that are.   4
they please themselves in c.   2:6
I will give c. to be their princes. 3:4
as for my people, c. are their.   12
c. whom Lord hath. 8:18; *Heb* 2:13
their eye not spare c.   *Isa* 13:18
mighty men of c. of Kedar.   21:17
I travail not, nor bring forth c. 23:4
woe to the rebellious c. saith.   30:1
lying c. c. that will not hear Lord. 9
father to the c. make known. 38:19
neither know the loss of c.   47:8
come in one day the loss of c.   9
the c. which thou shalt have. 49:20
for more are c. of the desolate than c.
   54:1; *Gal* 4:27
are ye not c. of transgression ?
   Isa 57:4
slaying the c. in the valleys.   5
they are my people, c. that.   63:8
she brought forth c.   66:8
turn, O backsliding c. *Jer* 3:14, 22
how shall I put thee among c.?   19
they are sottish c.   4:22
I will pour it out upon the c.   6:11
the c. gather wood.   7:18
for death entered to cut off c.   9:21
I will bereave them of c.   15:7
weeping for her c. 31:15; *Mat* 2:18
c. teeth are set on edge. *Jer* 31:29
   Ezek 18:2
shall the women eat c.?   *Lam* 2:20
young men to grind, c. fell.   5:13
for they are impudent c. *Ezek* 2:4
the c. rebelled against me.   20:21
the c. still are talking.   33:30
strangers shall beget c.   47:22
c. in whom was no blemish. *Dan* 1:4
fairer and fatter than all c.   15
as for these four c. God gave.   17
Michael shall stand for the c.   12:1
take unto thee c. of.   *Hos* 1:2
not have mercy on her c. they be c.
   2:4
the battle against the c. of.   10:9
dashed in pieces upon her c.   14

then the c. shall tremble. *Hos* 11:10
in place of breaking forth of c. 13:13
gather c. and those that.   *Joel* 2:16
be glad then ye c. of Zion.   23
are ye not as c. of the ?   *Amos* 9:7
poll thee for delicate c.   *Mi* 1:16
I will punish the king's c. *Zeph* 1:8
turn the heart of fathers to the c. and
   heart of c.   *Mal* 4:6; *Luke* 1:17
Herod slew all the c. in.   *Mat* 2:16
of these stones to raise up c.   3:9
   Luke 3:8
that ye may be c. of your. *Mat* 5:45
but the c. of the kingdom.   8:12
can c. of bride-chamber mourn ?
   9:15; *Mark* 2:19; *Luke* 5:34
c. shall rise against.   *Mat* 10:21
   Mark 13:12
wisdom justified of her c. *Mat* 11:19*
   Luke 7:35
good seed are the c. of kingdom,
   tares are the c. of.   *Mat* 13:38
not meet to take c. bread.   *Mark* 7:27
then are the c. free.   *Mat* 17:26
forsaken wife or c. for my.   19:29
   Mark 10:29
mother of Zebedee's c.   *Mat* 20:20
priests and scribes saw c.   21:15
c. of them that killed.   23:31
let the c. first be filled. *Mark* 7:27
dogs eat of the c. crumbs.   28
receive one of such c.   9:37, 41
be the c. of the Highest. *Luke* 6:35
c. of this world wiser than c.   16:8
a wife, and died without c.   20:29
the c. of this world marry.   34
if ye were Abraham's c. *John* 8:39
c. have ye any meat ?   21:5
ye are c. of the prophets. *Acts* 3:25
if c. then heirs, heirs of. *Rom* 8:17
seed of Abraham are they all c. 9:7
for c. being not yet born, nor.   11
be not c. in understanding; howbeit
   in malice be c.   *1 Cor* 14:20
c. ought not to lay up for the parents,
   but parents for c.   *2 Cor* 12:14
of faith, the same are c.   *Gal* 3:7
so we, when we were c. were.   4:3
in bondage with her c.   25
are not c. of bond-woman.   31
us to adoption of c.   *Eph* 1:5
the spirit that worketh in c.   2:2
were by nature c. of wrath.   3
no more c., tossed to and fro.   4:14
followers of God as dear c.   5:1
wrath cometh on c. of.   6; *Col* 3:6
c. obey your parents.   *Eph* 6:1
   Col 3:20
if any widow have c.   *1 Tim* 5:4
if she hath brought up c.   10
younger women marry, bear c.   14
the c. are partakers of.   *Heb* 2:14
speaketh to you as to c.   12:5
as obedient c. not.   *1 Pet* 1:14
of adultery, cursed c.   *2 Pet* 2:14
c. of God manifest, c. of. *1 John* 3:10
to the elect lady and her c. *2 John* 1
c. of thy elect sister greet thee.   13
I will kill her c. with.   *Rev* 2:23

see **Ammon, captivity**

children *of Benjamin*
of the c. of B. by their.   *Num* 1:36
c. of B. did not drive.   *Judg* 1:21
c. of B. would not hearken.   20:13
c. of B. gathered.   *2 Sam* 2:25
dwelt of c. of B.   *1 Chr* 9:3
   Neh 11:4
there came of c. of B. *1 Chr* 12:16
O ye c. of Benjamin.   *Jer* 6:1

children's **children**
thou and thy c. h.   *Gen* 45:10
iniquity of fathers on ch. c. *Ex* 34:7
beget c. and ch. c.   *Deut* 4:25
both their c. and ch. c.   *2 Ki* 17:41
righteousness unto ch. c. *Ps* 103:17
shalt see thy ch. c. and.   128:6
inheritance to his ch. c.   *Pr* 13:22
ch. c. are crown of old men, glory of
   c.   17:6
with your ch. c. will I plead. *Jer* 2:9
their ch. c. for ever.   *Ezek* 37:25

fatherless children
any to favour c.   *Ps* 109:12
leave thy *father*. c. I.   *Jer* 49:11

children *of God*
be called the c. of G.   *Mat* 5:9
the c. of G. being c. of. *Luke* 20:36
together in one c. of G. *John* 11:52
that we are the c. of G.   *Rom* 8:16
glorious liberty of c. of G.   21
c. of the flesh, not c. of G.   9:8
be called c. of living G.   26
ye are all c. of G. by.   *Gal* 3:26
c. of G. manifest, c. of. *1 John* 3:10
know that we love c. of G.   5:2

his **children**
Abraham will command *his* c.
   Gen 18:19
loved Joseph more than *his* c. 37:3
his days, he and *his* c. *Deut* 17:20
their spot is not spot of *his* c. 32:5
nor knew *his* own c.   33:9
his wife and *his* c.   *1 Sam* 30:22
it grew up with *his* c.   *2 Sam* 12:3
give him a light, and *his* c. *2 Ki* 8:19
burnt *his* c. in fire after. *2 Chr* 28:3
caused *his* c. to pass through. 33:6
his c. are far from safety. *Job* 5:4
even the eyes of *his* c.   17:5
his c. shall seek to please.   20:10
layeth up his iniquity for *his* c. 21:19
if *his* c. be multiplied, it is.   27:14
if *his* c. forsake my law.   *Ps* 89:30
as a father pitieth *his* c.   103:13
let *his* c. be fatherless.   109:9
let *his* c. be vagabonds.   10
his c. shall have a place. *Pr* 14:26
the just man, *his* c. are.   20:7
slaughter for *his* c. for.   *Isa* 14:21
when he seeth *his* c. in.   29:23
Ephraim bring forth *his* c. *Hos* 9:13
his c. and cattle drank.   *John* 4:12
charged you as father doth *his* c.
   1 Thes 2:11
having *his* c. in subjection. *1 Tim* 3:4

children *of Israel*
an oath of the c. of Isr. *Gen* 50:25
c. of Isr. were fruitful.   *Ex* 1:7
grieved because of c. of Isr.   12
c. of Isr. sighed.   2:23
God looked on c. of Isr.   25
Lord had visited c. of Isr.   4:31
heard groaning of the c. of Isr. 6:5
bring c. of Isr. out. 13, 26, 27; 12:51
nothing die of all that is c. of Isr. 9:4
c. of Isr. journeyed about.   12:37
there I will meet with c. of Isr. 29:43
sign between me and c. of Isr. 31:17
whosoever he be, c. of Isr. *Lev* 17:13
for to me the c. of Isr.   25:55
Lord appeared before c. of Isr.
   Num 14:10
c. of Isr. could not stand. *Josh* 7:12
numbered c. of Isr.   *1 Sam* 11:8
were not of c. of Isr.   *2 Sam* 21:2
them instead of c. of Isr. *2 Ki* 17:24
had not the c. of Isr. done. *Neh* 8:17
his acts to c. of Isr.   *Ps* 103:7
even of the c. of Isr., a.   148:14
one by one, O ye c. of Isr. *Isa* 27:12
when c. of Isr. went.   *Ezek* 44:15
   48:11
thus, O ye c. of Isr.?   *Amos* 2:11
liketh you, O ye c. of Isr.   4:5
many of the c. of Isr.   *Luke* 1:16
visit brethren c. of Isr.   *Acts* 7:23
Moses which said to the c. of Isr. 37
bear my name before c. of Isr. 9:15
word God sent to c. of Isr.   10:36
number of c. of Isr. be.   *Rom* 9:27
c. of Isr. could not behold face of.
   2 Cor 3:7
of departing of c. of Isr. *Heb* 11:22
block before c. of Isr.   *Rev* 2:14
of all tribes of c. of Isr.   7:4
of twelve tribes of c. of Isr.   21:12

children *of Judah*
of the c. of Judah by.   *Num* 1:26
c. of Judah came to.   *Josh* 14:6
bade teach c. of Judah. *2 Sam* 1:18
c. of Judah prevailed. *2 Chr* 13:18
other 10,000 did c. of Judah. 25:12
to keep under c. of Judah.   28:10

the evil of c. of Judah. *Jer* 32:32
they and the c. of Judah going. 50:4
Israel and c. of Judah were. 33
against tne c. of Judah. *Joel* 3:19

children *of light*
c. of this world wiser than c. *of light.*
    Luke 16:8
may be the c. *of light.* *John* 12:36
walk as c. *of light.* *Eph* 5:8
ye are all c. *of light.* *1 Thes* 5:5

little children
little c. stood in door. *Num* 16:27
came forth little c. and. *2 Ki* 2:23
one day to destroy little c. *Esth* 3:13
slay utterly maids, little c. *Ezek* 9:6
and become as little c. *Mat* 18:3
were brought to him little c. 19:13
suffer little c. to come. 14
    Mark 10:14; *Luke* 18:16
little c. yet a little while. *John* 13:33
my little c. of whom. *Gal* 4:19
my little c. I write. *1 John* 2:1, 12, 13
are of God, little c. and have. 4:4
little c. keep from idols. 5:21

children *of men*
tower which c. *of men.* *Gen* 11:5
if they be c. *of men.* *1 Sam* 26:19
with stripes of c. *of men.* *2 Sam* 7:14
hearts of c. *of men.* *1 Ki* 8:39
    2 Chr 6:30
eye-lids try the c. *of men.* *Ps* 11:4
fail from among c. *of men.* 12:1
down upon c. *of men.* 14:2; 53:2
c. *of men* put their trust. 36:7
thou art fairer than c. *of men.* 45:2
sayest, return ye c. *of men.* 90:3
works to c. *of men.* 107:8, 15, 21, 31
earth given to c. *of men.* 115:16
then hearts of c. *of men.* *Pr* 15:11
nor grieve c. *of men.* *Lam* 3:33
wherever c. *of men* dwell. *Dan* 2:38

men-children
saved men-c. alive. *Ex* 1:17, 18
all the men-c. shall appear. 34:23
the *male* c. of Manasseh. *Josh* 17:2

men, women, and children
destroyed m. w. and c. *Deut* 3:6
gather m. w. and c. to hear. 31:12
smote Nob, m. w. and c. and.
    1 Sam 22:19
congregation of m. w. and c.
    Ezra 10:1
to Gedaliah m. w. and c. *Jer* 40:7
about 5000 m. beside w. and c.
    Mat 14:21; 15:38

my children
my wives and my c. for. *Gen* 30:26
these c. are my c. these cattle. 31:43
me ye have bereaved of my c. 42:36
if I be bereaved of my c. I. 43:14
the first-born of my c. *Ex* 13:15
love my master, wife, and my c. 21:5
for my wives and my c. *1 Ki* 20:7
that I were as when my c. *Job* 29:5
seeing I have lost my c. *Isa* 49:21
my c. are gone forth of. *Jer* 10:20
my c. are desolate. *Lam* 1:16
thou hast slain my c.? *Ezek* 16:21
trouble me not, my c. *Luke* 11:7
I speak as to my c. *2 Cor* 6:13
joy to hear that my c. walk. *3 John* 4

no children
Abram's wife bare him no c.
    Gen 16:1
Rachel saw that she bare no c. 30:1
died, and had no c. *Num* 3:4
but Hannah had no c. *1 Sam* 1:2
man die having no c. *Mat* 22:24
    Mark 12:19
seven left no c. *Luke* 20:31

our children
riches are ours and our c. *Gen* 31:16
to kill us, and our c. *Ex* 17:3
our wives and our c. be. *Num* 14:3
belong to us and to our c.
    Deut 29:29
your c. speak to our c. *Josh* 22:24
your c. make our c. cease from. 25
brethren, our c. as their c. *Neh* 5:5
blood be on us and our c. *Mat* 27:25

children *of promise*
c. of prom. are counted. *Rom* 9:8
Isaac was, are c. of prom. *Gal* 4:28

strange children
deliver me from strange c. *Ps* 144:7†
    11†
have begotten strange c. *Hos* 5:7

their children
to daughters or their c. *Gen* 31:43
they may teach their c. *Deut* 4:10
might be well with their c. 5:29
that their c. may learn to. 31:13
and their c. them Joshua. *Josh* 5:7
of their c. did Solomon. *1 Ki* 9:21
wilt dash their c. and. *2 Ki* 8:12
burnt their c. in the fire to. 17:31
their c. served images as did. 41
with wives and their c. *2 Chr* 20:13
he slew not their c. but did. 25:4
their c. thou multipliedst. *Neh* 9:23
their c. spake half in the. 13:24
their c. dance. *Job* 21:11
yieldeth food for their c. 24:5
not hide them from their c. *Ps* 78:4
and declare them to their c. 6
let thy glory appear to their c. 90:16
their c. shall sit on thy. 132:12
their c. shall be dashed. *Isa* 13:16
whilst their c. remember. *Jer* 17:2
therefore deliver up their c. 18:21
their c. also shall be as. 30:20
iniquity into bosom of their c. 32:18
for good of them and of their c. 39
shall not look back to their c. 47:3
have sodden their c. *Lam* 4:10
I said to their c. in. *Ezek* 20:18
when they had slain their c. 23:39
they and their c. shall. 37:25
cast them and their c. *Dan* 6:24
though bring up their c. *Hos* 9:12
c. tell their c. and their. *Joel* 1:3
from their c. have ye taken. *Mi* 2:9
yea, their c. shall see it. *Zech* 10:7
they shall live with their c. 9
fulfilled to us their c. *Acts* 13:33
deacons rule their c. *1 Tim* 3:12
to love husbands and their c. *Tit* 2:4

thy children
first-born among thy c. *Ex* 13:13
well with thy c. *Deut* 4:40; 12:25, 28
teach them diligently to thy c. 6:7
thou and thy c. shall obey. 30:2
be thine and thy c. for. *Josh* 14:9
are here all thy c.? *1 Sam* 16:11
if thy c. take heed to. *1 Ki* 2:4
that thy c. heed. 8:25; *2 Chr* 6:16
wives also and thy c. *1 Ki* 20:3
live thou and thy c. *2 Ki* 4:7
thy c. of fourth generation. 10:30
smite thy people and c. *2 Chr* 21:14
if thy c. have sinned. *Job* 8:4
instead of fathers shall be thy c.
    Ps 45:16
against generation of thy c. 73:15
thy c. like olive-plants. 128:3
if thy c. will keep my. 132:12
he hath blessed thy c. 147:13
thy c. shall make haste. *Isa* 49:17
and I will save thy c. 25
thy c. shall be taught of Lord, great
    shall be peace of thy c. 54:13
thy c. have forsaken me. *Jer* 5:7
there is hope that thy c. shall. 31:17
they shall bring out thy c. to. 38:23
by blood of thy c. thou. *Ezek* 16:36
I will also forget thy c. *Hos* 4:6
would I have gathered thy c.
    Mat 23:37; *Luke* 13:34
shall lay thy c. within. *Luke* 19:44
found of thy c. walking. *2 John* 4

your children
when your c. shall say. *Ex* 12:26
wives be widows, and your c. 22:24
as inheritance for your c. *Lev* 25:46
beasts shall rob you of your c. 26:22
your c. shall wander. *Num* 14:33
your c. shall go in thither. *Deut* 1:39
I speak not with your c. who. 11:2
ye shall teach them your c. 19
days of your c. be multiplied. 21
generation to come of your c. 29:22
ye shall command your c. 32:46

when your c. ask. *Josh* 4:6, 21
then ye shall let your c. know. 22
if your c. turn from. *1 Ki* 9:6
an inheritance to your c. *1 Chr* 28:8
    Ezra 9:12
your c. shall find. *2 Chr* 30:9
increase you and your c. *Ps* 115:14
have I smitten your c. *Jer* 2:20
good gifts to your c. *Mat* 7:11
    Luke 11:13
by whom do your c. cast? *Mat* 12:27
weep for yourselves and your c.
    Luke 23:28
for the promise is unto you and to
    your c. *Acts* 2:39
else were your c. unclean. *1 Cor* 7:14
provoke not your c. to. *Eph* 6:4
    Col 3:21

young children
young c. despised me. *Job* 19:18
the young c. ask bread. *Lam* 4:4
her young c. were dashed. *Nah* 3:10
brought young c. to him. *Mark* 10:13
cast out their young c. *Acts* 7:19

Chilion, *see* **Mahlon**

Chilmad
Ashur and C. were. *Ezek* 27:23

Chimham
thy servant C. *2 Sam* 19:37, 38, 40
dwelt in habitation of C. *Jer* 41:17

chimney
be as smoke out of the c. *Hos* 13:3

Chios
next day over-against C. *Acts* 20:15

Chisleu
in the month C. *Neh* 1:1
ninth month C. *Zech* 7:1

Chittim
ships shall come from C. *Num* 24:24
from the land of C. *Isa* 23:1
pass over to C. 12
pass over the isles of C. *Jer* 2:10
ivory brought out of isles C.
    Ezek 27:6
ships of C. shall come. *Dan* 11:30

Chiun
have born Moloch and C. *Amos* 5:26

Chloe
which are of house of C. *1 Cor* 1:11

chode
Jacob was wroth, and. *Gen* 31:36
people c. with Moses. *Num* 20:3*

choice
in c. of our sepulchres. *Gen* 23:6
ass's colt to the c. vine. 49:11
bring all your c. vows. *Deut* 12:11
Saul a c. young man. *1 Sam* 9:2
c. of Israel. *2 Sam* 10:9; *1 Chr* 19:10
cut down c. fir-trees. *2 Ki* 19:23
    Isa 37:24
found 300,000 c. men. *2 Chr* 25:5
for me daily six c. sheep. *Neh* 5:18
knowledge rather than c. gold.
    Pr 8:10
revenue is better than c. silver. 19
tongue of just is as c. silver. 10:20
she is the c. one of her. *S of S* 6:9
they shall cut down thy c. *Jer* 22:7
set on a pot, fill it with c. *Ezek* 24:4
take the c. of the flock and burn. 5
God made c. among us. *Acts* 15:7

choicest
vineyard with the c. vine. *Isa* 5:2
thy c. valley shall be full of. 22:7

choke
deceitfulness of riches c. the word.
    Mat 13:22; *Mark* 4:19

choked
thorns c. them. *Mat* 13:7
    Mark 4:7; *Luke* 8:7
were c. in the sea. *Mark* 5:13
    Luke 8:33†
go forth and are c. with. *Luke* 8:14

choler
an he-goat moved with c. *Dan* 8:7
south shall be moved with c. 11:11

choose, *as an act of God*
Lord doth c. shall be holy. *Num* 16:7
man's rod whom I shall c. 17:5

Lord did not c. you.   *Deut 7:7*
place Lord shall c.   12:5, 11, 14, 18
  26; 14:23, 24, 25; 15:20; 16:2, 6
  7, 15, 16; 17:8, 10; 18:6; 26:2
  31:11; *Josh 9:27*
king, whom Lord shall c. *Deut 17:15*
did I c. him out of.   *1 Sam 2:28*
Lord and his people c. *2 Sam 16:18*
in Gibeah whom Lord did c.   21:6
city which Lord did c.   *1 Ki 14:21*
God who didst c. Abram. *Neh 9:7*
teach in way he shall c. *Ps 25:12*
he shall c. our inheritance. 47:4
the Lord will yet c. Israel. *Isa 14:1*
he shall c. thee.   49:7
I also will c. their delusions. 66:4
yet c. Jerusalem. *Zech 1:17; 2:12*

choose
c. us out men, and go.   *Ex 17:9*
dwell in place he shall c. *Deut 23:16*
therefore c. life, that thou. 30:19
c. this day whom you. *Josh 24:15*
c. you a man for you. *1 Sam 17:8*
let me c. 12,000 men. *1 Sam 17:1*
c. one of them. 24:12; *1 Chr 21:10*
c. one bullock.   *1 Ki 18:23, 25*
c. out my words to reason. *Job 9:14*
let us c. to us judgement. 34:4
thou refuse, or whether thou c. 33
and did not c. the fear. *Pr 1:29*
the oppressor, and c. none. 3:31
refuse evil, and c. good. *Isa 7:15, 16*
to the eunuchs that c. things. 56:4
and did c. that wherein I. 65:12
c. a place, c. it at the. *Ezek 21:19**
yet what I shall c.   *Phil 1:22*

choosest, -eth, -ing
so that my soul c.   *Job 7:15*
and thou c. the tongue of. 15:5
blessed is the man whom thou c.
      Ps 65:4
he c. a tree that will not. *Isa 40:20*
abomination is he that c. you. 41:24
c. rather to suffer. *Heb 11:25*

chop
break bones and c. them. *Mi 3:3*

Chorazin
woe unto thee, C.   *Mat 11:21*
     Luke 10:13

chose
wives of all which they c. *Gen 6:2*
then Lot c. him all the plain. 13:11
Moses c. able men, and. *Ex 18:25*
he c. their seed. *Deut 4:37; 10:15*
c. 30,000 mighty men. *Josh 8:3*
they c. new gods.   *Judg 5:8*
the Lord who c. me. *2 Sam 6:21*
I c. no city out of all Israel to build.
    1 Ki 8:16; 2 Chr 6:5
the Lord c. me before. *1 Chr 28:4*
I c. out their way.   *Job 29:25*
and c. not the tribe of. *Ps 78:67*
but c. the tribe of Judah. 68
he c. David also his servant. 70
and c. that in which I. *Isa 66:4*
day when I c. Israel. *Ezek 20:5*
of his disciples he c. *Luke 6:13*
when he marked how they c. 14:7
c. Stephen a man full of. *Acts 6:5*
God of this people Israel c. 13:17
Paul c. Silas and departed. 15:40

chosen
his c. captains are drowned. *Ex 15:4*
him whom he hath c. *Num 16:5*
ye have c. you the Lord. *Josh 24:22*
cry to gods ye have c. *Judg 10:14*
king ye have c. *1 Sam 8:18; 12:13*
I know that thou hast c. the. 20:30
hast c. a great people. *1 Ki 3:8*
the city thou hast c. 8:44, 48
    2 Chr 6:34, 38
children of Jacob his c. *1 Chr 16:13*
this hast thou c.   *Job 36:21*
people he hath c. for. *Ps 33:12*
made a covenant with my c. 89:3
I have exalted one c. 19
ye children of Jacob his c. 105:6
forth his c. with gladness. 43
see the good of thy c. 106:5
had not Moses his c. stood. 23
understanding to be c. *Pr 16:16*
good name rather to be c. 22:1

drink to my people, my c. *Isa 43:20*
your name a curse to my c. 65:15
they have c. their own ways. 66:3
death shall be c. rather. *Jer 8:3*
who is a c. man. 49:19; 50:44
called, but few c. *Mat 20:16; 22:14*
elect's sake whom he hath c.
    Mark 13:20
and Mary hath c. the. *Luke 10:42*
of these two thou hast c. *Acts 1:24*
for he is a c. vessel to me. 9:15
salute Rufus, c. in the. *Rom 16:13*
c. of the churches to. *2 Cor 8:19*
please him who hath c. *2 Tim 2:4*
ye are a c. generation. *1 Pet 2:9*
they are called,.   *Rev 17:14*

chosen of God
Christ, the c. of God. *Luke 23:35*
witnesses c. before of God.
    Acts 10:41
living stone, c. of God. *1 Pet 2:4*

God hath chosen
God hath c. to put. *Deut 12:21*
    16:11
God hath c. to minister unto. 21:5
Solomon whom God hath c.
    1 Chr 29:1
God of our fathers hath c. *Acts 22:14*
God hath c. foolish things, God hath
  c. weak things. *1 Cor 1:27*
things despised God hath c. and. 28
God from the beginning hath c.
    2 Thes 2:13
hath not God c. the poor? *Jas 2:5*

I have chosen
David's sake and Jerusalem's sake
  I have c. *1 Ki 11:13; 2 Ki 21:7*
    23:27; *2 Chr 6:6*
the city which I have c. *1 Ki 11:32*
them to place I have c. *Neh 1:9*
I have c. way of. *Ps 119:30, 173*
Jacob whom I have c. *Isa 41:8*
I have c. thee, and not cast. 9
servant whom I have c. 43:10
    Mat 12:18
Israel whom I have c. *Isa 44:1*
Jesurun whom I have c. 2
I have c. thee in the furnace. 48:10
this the fast I have c.? 58:5, 6
I have c. thee, saith. *Hag 2:23*
I know whom I have c. *John 13:18*
not c. me, but I have c. 15:16
I have c. you out of the world. 19

Lord hath chosen
Lord hath c. thee. *Deut 7:6; 14:2*
the Lord hath c. him out of. 18:5
whom Lord hath c. like. *1 Sam 10:24*
neither hath the Lord c. this. 16:8
the Lord hath not c. these. 10
them the Lord hath c. *1 Chr 15:2*
Lord hath c. Judah ruler. 28:4
Lord hath c. Solomon to sit. 5, 10
Lord hath c. you to. *2 Chr 29:11*
Aaron whom he had c. *Ps 105:26*
Lord hath c. Zion.   132:13
Lord hath c. Jacob. 135:4
families Lord hath c. *Jer 33:24*
Lord that hath c. Jerusalem.
    Zech 3:2
according as he hath c. *Eph 1:4*

chosen men
seven hundred c. men. *Judg 20:16*
Judah 180,000 c. men. *1 Ki 12:21*
    2 Chr 11:1
array with 400,000 c. men. Jeroboam
  800,000 c. men. *2 Chr 13:3*
smote down the c. men of Israel.
    Ps 78:31*
to send c. men of. *Acts 15:22*, 25*

Christ
*The anointed one. The Greek
name Christos from the word
anointed. The Hebrew word was
Messiah. The expected king and
deliverer of the Jews, who expected
a strong and glorious earthly king,
to deliver them from oppressors
and form again a great independent
kingdom of the Jews. He was to
be a descendant of David, and bring
the whole world under his sway.*

*There are many passages in the
Old Testament which refer to this
great deliverer under various names.
Among these references are verses
in Ps 22, 45, 55; Isa 9, 11, 53;
Dan 2, 9; etc.*
*The Jews were looking for this
deliverer down the ages from the
time of the Captivity, and more
definitely at about the time of the
coming of Jesus. When he was
announced as being the Christ, or
the Messiah, the rulers among the
Jews refused to accept him largely
because he and the method of his
coming were so utterly different
from their ideas of what the
Messiah was to be. There are,
however, very many verses in the
Old Testament which were believed by the Jews themselves to
refer to the Messiah and his
coming which speak of his suffering and lowliness, etc. But their
minds were shut against such ideas
as these.*
*In modern usage the name is
used as a synonym for Jesus, or
added to that name to refer to
Jesus, the Christ of the Jews, and
the Saviour of mankind.*

see **Messiah, Jesus**
demanded where C. *Mat 2:4*
thou art C. the Son of the. 16:16
is your Master, even C. 23:8, 10
I am C. and shall deceive. 24:5
    Mark 13:6; Luke 21:8
thou C. who smote thee. *Mat 26:68*
because ye belong to C. *Mark 9:41*
C. descend now from. 15:32
not die, before he had seen C.
    Luke 2:26
they knew that he was C. 4:41
if he be C. the chosen of God. 23:35
saying, if thou be C. save. 39
ought not C. have suffered? 24:26
thus it behoved C. to suffer. 46
which is called C. *John 4:25*
when C. cometh no man. 7:27, 28
when C. cometh, will he do? 31
shall C. come out of Galilee? 41
C. cometh of seed of David.
any did confess that he was C. 9:22
we have heard that C. abideth. 12:34
he would raise up C. to. *Acts 2:30**
made that Jesus both Lord and C. 36
God had before shewed that C. 3:18
Philip went and preached C. to. 8:5
straightway he preached C. 9:20*
alleging that C. must needs. 17:3
that C. should suffer. 26:23
in due time C. died for. *Rom 5:6*
like as C. was raised up from. 6:4
knowing that C. being raised.
dead to law by the body of C. 7:4
if any have not the Spirit of C. 8:9
if C. be in you, the body is dead. 10
he that raised up C. from dead. 11
wish myself accursed from C. 9:3
of whom C. came, who is over. 5
that is, to bring C. down. 6
that is, to bring up C. 7
for to this end C. died. 14:9
destroy not him for whom C. died. 15
that in these things serveth C. 18
for even C. pleased not himself. 15:3
as C. also received us. 7
of things which C. hath not. 18
I strived to preach, not where C. 20
the first-fruits of Achaia to C. 16:5
we preach C. crucified. *1 Cor 1:23*
C. the power of God. 24
ye are C. and C. is God's. 3:23
C. our passover is sacrificed. 5:7
brother perish, for whom C. 8:11
but under the law to C. 9:21
and that rock was C. 10:4
nor let us tempt C. as some. 9*
how C. died for our sins. 15:3
if C. be preached that he rose. 12
dead rise not, then is not C. 16

and if C. be not raised. *1 Cor* 15:17
every man in his own order, C. 23
trust have we through C. *2 Cor* 3:4
though we have known C. 5:16
what concord hath C. with? 6:15
you as a chaste virgin to C. 11:2
I live, yet not I, but C. *Gal* 2:20
then C. died in vain. 21
C. hath redeemed us from. 3:13
our schoolmaster, to bring us to C. 24
if ye be C. then are Abraham's. 29
heir of God through C. 4:7*
of whom I travail, till C. be. 19
the liberty wherewith C. hath. 5:1
if ye be circumcised, C. shall. 2
C. is become of no effect unto. 4
that are C. have crucified flesh. 24
ye were without C. *Eph* 2:12
C. may dwell in your hearts. 3:17
which is the head, even C. 4:15
ye have not so learned C. 20
as C. also loved us, and hath. 5:2
arise from the dead, and C. shall. 14
head of the wife, as C. is the head. 23
as the church is subject to C. 24
love your wives, as C. also. 25
but I speak concerning C. and. 32
in singleness of heart as to C. 6:5
some indeed preach C. *Phil* 1:15
the one preach C. of contention. 16
C. is preached, and I therein. 18
so now C. shall be magnified in. 20
but dung, that I may win C. 3:8
I can do all through C. who. 4:13*
world, and not after C. *Col* 2:8
where C. sitteth on the right. 3:1
when C. who is our life shall. 4
bond nor free, but C. is all. 11
even as C. forgave you, 13*
for ye serve the Lord C. 24
but C. as a son. *Heb* 3:6
so also C. glorified not himself. 5:5
C. being come an high-priest. 9:11
C. not entered into holy place. 24
C. was once offered to bear the. 28
because C. also suffered. *1 Pet* 2:21
C. hath once suffered for sins. 3:18
C. suffered for us in the flesh. 4:1
of our Lord and his C. *Rev* 11:15
now is come power of his C. 12:10

against Christ
gathered *against* his C. *Acts* 4:26*
sin against brethren ye sin *against* C.
1 Cor 8:12
wax wanton *against* C. *1 Tim* 5:11

by Christ
consolation aboundeth *by* C.
2 Cor 1:5
seek to be justified *by* C. *Gal* 2:17
glory in church *by* C. Jesus. *Eph* 3:21

for Christ
for C. sent me not to. *1 Cor* 1:17
fools *for* C. sake, ye are wise in.
4:10
are ambassadors *for* C. *2 Cor* 5:20
pleasure in distresses *for* C. 12:10
as God *for* C. sake hath. *Eph* 4:32
those I counted loss *for* C. *Phil* 3:7
patient waiting *for* C. *2 Thes* 3:5

Jesus with Christ
Jesus, who is called C. *Mat* 1:16
27:17, 22
truth came by Jesus C. *John* 1:17
know thee, and Jesus C. 17:3
baptized in name of Jesus C.
Acts 2:38
in the name of Jesus C. rise up. 3:6
shall send Jesus C. who was. 20
by the name of Jesus C. doth. 4:10
ceased not to preach Jesus C. 5:42
Philip preaching things concerning
Jesus C. they were baptized. 8:12
I believe that Jesus C. is the. 37*
Jesus C. maketh thee whole. 9:34
preaching peace by Jesus C. 10:36
in name of Jesus C. come out. 16:18
Jesus I preach to you is C. 17:3
to the Jews that Jesus was C. 18:5
the scriptures that Jesus was C. 28
should believe on C. Jesus. 19:4*
Paul a servant of Jesus C. *Rom* 1:1
Phil 1:1

concerning Son Jesus C. *Rom* 1:3*
the called of Jesus C. 6
through Jesus C. for you all. 8
secrets of men by Jesus C. 2:16
which is by faith of Jesus C. 3:22
through redemption in Jesus C. 24
which is by one man Jesus C. 5:15
reign in life by one Jesus C. 17
were baptized into Jesus C. 6:3
to them that are in C. Jesus. 8:1
Spirit of life in C. Jesus hath. 2
my helpers in C. Jesus. 16:3
Paul apostle of Jesus C. *1 Cor* 1:1
2 Cor 1:1; *Eph* 1:1
call on the name of Jesus C.*1 Cor* 1:2
grace given you by Jesus C. 4
but of him are ye in C. Jesus. 30
save Jesus C. crucified. 2:2
for in C. Jesus have I begotten. 4:15
knowledge of God in Jesus C.
2 Cor 4:6
us to himself by Jesus C. 5:18
how that Jesus C. is in you. 13:5
by the faith of Jesus C. *Gal* 2:16
the Gentiles through Jesus C. 3:14
for ye are all one in C. Jesus. 28
an angel, even as C. Jesus. 4:14
heavenly places in C. Jesus.*Eph* 2:6
Jesus C. the chief corner stone. 20
I long after you in Jesus C. *Phil* 1:8
which was also in C. Jesus. 2:5
Jesus C. is Lord, to glory of. 2:11
all the things which are Jesus C. 21
loss for excellency of C. Jesus. 3:8
I am apprehended of C. Jesus. 12
riches in glory by C. Jesus. 4:19
have received C. Jesus so. *Col* 2:6
C. Jesus came to save. *1 Tim* 1:15
one mediator, man C. Jesus. 2:5
before C. Jesus who witnessed. 6:13
grace given us in C. Jesus. *2 Tim* 1:9
love, which is in C. Jesus. 13
prisoner of Jesus C. *Philem* 1, 9, 23
Jesus C. same yesterday. *Heb* 13:8
blood of Jesus C. *1 John* 1:7*
an advocate, Jesus C. the. 2:1
by water and blood, Jesus C. 5:6
even in his Son Jesus C. 20

Lord Jesus Christ
believed on the L. J. C. *Acts* 11:17
through the grace of L. J. C. 15:11
believe on the L. J. C. 16:31*
faith toward our L. J. C. 20:21
peace with God through L. J. C.
Rom 5:1
joy in God, through our L. J. C. 11
eternal life through our L. J. C. 6:23
love of God in C. our L. 8:39
put ye on L. J. C. and make. 13:14
grace of L. J. C. be with. 16:20, 24*
2 Cor 13:14; *Gal* 6:18
2 Thes 3:18; *Rev* 22:21
for coming of L. J. C. *1 Cor* 1:7
but to us one L. J. C. by whom. 8:6
victory through our L. J. C. 15:57
any man love not the L. J. C. 16:22
and peace from L. J. C. *2 Cor* 1:2
Gal 1:3; *Eph* 1:2; *Col* 1:2*
know grace of our L. J. C. *2 Cor* 8:9
in cross of our L. J. C. *Gal* 6:14
Father of our L. J. C. *Eph* 1:3
God of our L. J. C. give you. 17
of hope in our L. J. C. *1 Thes* 1:3
joy in presence of our L. J. C. 2:19
at coming of our L. J. C. 3:13
unto coming of our L. J. C. 5:23
by coming of L. J. C. *2 Thes* 2:1
now our L. J. C. hath given us. 16
charge before L. J. C. *1 Tim* 5:21
2 Tim 4:1
the L. J. C. be with thy. *2 Tim* 4:22
into kingdom of L. J. C. *2 Pet* 1:11
in knowledge of L. J. C. 3:18

in Christ
concerning the faith in C. *Acts* 24:24
I say the truth in C. *Rom* 9:1
many are one body in C. 12:5
of note, who also were in C. 16:7
salute Urbane, our helper in C. 9
salute Apelles approved in C. 10
even as unto babes in C. *1 Cor* 3:1
fools, but ye are wise in C. 4:10
10,000 instructors in C. not. 15

fallen asleep in C. *1 Cor* 15:18
in this life only hope in C. 19
even so in C. shall all be made. 22
stablisheth us in C. *2 Cor* 1:21
causeth us to triumph in C. 2:14
speak we in C. 17
vail is done away in C. 3:14
if any man be in C. he is. 5:17
that God was in C. reconciling. 19
we pray you in C. stead. 20
I knew a man in C. above. 12:2
we speak before God, in C. 19
to churches of Judea in C. *Gal* 1:22
confirmed before of God in C. 3:17*
as have been baptized into C. 27
spiritual blessings in C. *Eph* 1:3
gather in one all things in C. 10
his glory, who first trusted in C. 12
which he wrought in C. 20
partakers of his promise in C. 3:6
bonds in C. are manifest. *Phil* 1:13
if there be any consolation in C. 2:1
stedfastness of faith in C. *Col* 2:5
dead in C. shall rise. *1 Thes* 4:16
I speak the truth in C. *1 Tim* 2:7
good conversation in C. *1 Pet* 3:16

is Christ
say, lo, here is C. *Mat* 24:23
Mark 13:21
C. is the son of David. *Mark* 12:35
Luke 20:41
Saviour who is C. the. *Luke* 2:11
he himself is C. a king. 23:2
others said, this is the C. *John* 7:41
proving this is very C. *Acts* 9:22
Jesus whom I preach you is C. 17:3
it is C. that died, yea. *Rom* 8:34
is C. divided? *1 Cor* 1:13
being free, is C.'s servant. 7:22
the head of every man is C. 11:3
many are one body, so is C. 12:12
dead rise not, then is C. 15:13, 16
but now is C. risen from dead. 20
trust that he is C. *2 Cor* 10:7
is therefore C. the? *Gal* 2:17
to thy seed, which is C. 3:16
for me to live is C. *Phil* 1:21
which is C. in you the hope. *Col* 1:27

of Christ
in prison works of C. *Mat* 11:2
what think you of C.? 22:42
have not the Spirit of C. *Rom* 8:9
separate us from love of C.? 35
before judgement seat of C. 14:10*
lest cross of C. be made. *1 Cor* 1:17
we have the mind of C. 2:16
bodies are members of C. 6:15
cup, communion of blood of C. bread,
communion of body of C. 10:16
followers of me, as I am of C. 11:1
the head of C. is God. 3
now ye are the body of C. 12:27
as the sufferings of C. *2 Cor* 1:5
forgave it in the person of C. 2:10
a sweet savour of C. 15
ye are the epistles of C. 3:3
light of glorious gospel of C. 4:4
love of C. constraineth us. 5:14
they are the glory of C. 8:23
meekness and gentleness of C. 10:1
thought to the obedience of C. 5
as the truth of C. is in me. 11:10
power of C. may rest on me. 12:9
Rev 12:10
ye seek a proof of C. *2 Cor* 13:3
not be servant of C. *Gal* 1:10
be justified by the faith of C. 2:16
persecution for the cross of C. 6:12
nigh by the blood of C. *Eph* 2:13
knowledge in mystery of C. 3:4
preach unsearchable riches of C. 8
know the love of C. which. 19
the measure of the gift of C. 4:7
inheritance in the kingdom of C. 5:5
as servants of C. doing. 6:6
offence till day of C. *Phil* 1:10
it is given in behalf of C. 29
rejoice in the day of C. 2:16
for work of C. he was nigh to. 30
enemies of the cross of C. 3:18
fill up afflictions of C. *Col* 1:24
mystery of Father, and of C. 2:2
shadow, but the body is of C. 17

let the word of C. dwell in. *Col 3:16*
to speak the mystery of C. 4:3
nameth the name of C. *2 Tim 2:19**
we are partakers of C. if. *Heb 3:14*
how much more blood of C. 9:14
reproach of C. greater. 11:26
what time Spirit of C. *1 Pet 1:11*
redeemed with blood of C. 19
partakers of C. sufferings. 4:13
reproached for name of C. 14
priests of God and of C. *Rev 20:6*

that Christ
if be not that C. nor Elias. *John 1:25*
we are sure thou art that C. 6:69*

the Christ
tell no man he was the C. *Mat 16:20*
tell whether thou be the C. 26:63
thou art the C. *Mark 8:29*
art thou the C. the Son of? 14:61
whether he were the C. *Luke 3:15*
thou art the C. of God. 9:20
art thou the C.? tell us. 22:67
confessed, I am not the C. *John 1:20*
the Messias, which is the C. 41
I said, I am not the C. but. 3:28
is not this the C.? 4:29
this is indeed the C. 42; 7:26
others said, this is the C. but. 7:41
if thou be the C. tell us. 10:24
I believe thou art the C. 11:27
believe that Jesus is the C. 20:31
denieth that Jesus is the C.
1 John 2:22
whoso believeth Jesus is the C. 5:1

with Christ
if we be dead with C. *Rom 6:8*
then joint-heirs with C. 8:17
crucified with C. I live, *Gal 2:20*
quickened us together with C.
Eph 2:5
to depart and be with C. *Phil 1:23*
if ye be dead with C. *Col 2:2)*
if ye be risen with C. seek. 3:1
and your life is hid with C. 3
and they reigned with C. a. *Rev 20:4*

christian, -s
disciples first called c. *Acts 11:26*
almost persuadest me to be c. 26:28
any man suffer as a c. not. *1 Pet 4:16*

christs
there shall arise false c. *Mat 24:24*
Mark 13:22

chronicles
acts of Jeroboam are in c. *1 Ki 14:19*
put in the account of c. *1 Chr 27:24*
book of the records of c. *Esth 6:1*
see book

chrysolite
(*A semi-precious stone of a yellow
or green colour*)
seventh foundation c. *Rev 21:20*

chrysoprasus
(*A light green chalcedony*)
tenth foundation of city was a c.
Rev 21:20

church
[1] *The body of Christians in
general.* [2] *A body of Christians
with the same general creed and
under the same ecclesiastical
authority.* [3] *Any body of worshippers of God, as the Jewish
church,* Acts 7:38.
rock I will build my c. *Mat 16:18*
tell it to c. if he neglect to hear c.
18:17
Lord added to c. daily. *Acts 2:47*
fear came on all the c. and as. 5:11
great persecution against c. 8:1
assembled themselves with c. 11:26
ordained elders in every c. 14:23
gathered the c. together. 27
brought on way by the c. 15:3
it pleased elders with whole c. 22
gone up and saluted the c. 18:22
greet the c. that is in. *Rom 16:5*
every where, in every c. *1 Cor 4:17*
prophesieth edifieth the c. 14:4
except interpret that the c. may. 5
if the c. be come together. 23
salute you, with c. that is. 16:19

head over all to the c. *Eph 1:22*
might be known by the c. the. 3:10
as the c. is subject to Christ. 5:24
Christ loved the c. and gave. 25
present to himself a glorious c. 27
even as the Lord the c. 29
speak concerning Christ and c. 32
persecuting the c. *Phil 3:6*
no c. communicated with me. 4:15
head of the body the c. *Col 1:18*
body's sake, which is the c. 24
salute the c. which is in. 4:15
let not the c. be charged. *1 Tim 5:16*
Paul a prisoner, to c. in. *Philem 2*
to c. of the first-born in. *Heb 12:23*
the c. at Babylon. *1 Pet 5:13*
witness of thy charity before c.
3 John 6
I wrote unto c. but Diotrephes. 9

in the church
is he that was in the c. *Acts 7:38*
prophets in the c. at Antioch. 13:1
least esteemed in the c. *1 Cor 6:4*
ye come together in the c. 11:18
God hath set some in the c. 12:28
yet in the c. I had rather. 14:19
let him keep silence in the c. 28
for women to speak in the c. 35
to him be glory in the c. *Eph 3:21*
it to be read in the c. *Col 4:16*

of the church
made havock of the c. *Acts 8:3*
tidings came to ears of the c. 11:22
Herod vexed certain of the c. 12:1
prayer was made of the c. unto. 5
they were received of the c. 15:4
called the elders of the c. 20:17
a servant of the c. *Rom 16:1*
mine host and of the whole c. 23
excel to edifying of the c. *1 Cor 14:12*
Christ is head of the c. *Eph 5:23*
in midst of the c. I will. *Heb 2:12*
call for elders of the c. *Jas 5:14*
casteth them out of the c. *3 John 10*
angel of the c. of Ephesus. *Rev 2:1*
of the c. in Smyrna. 8
of the c. in Pergamos. 12
of the c. in Thyatira. 18
of the c. of Sardis. 3:1
of the c. in Philadelphia. 7
of the c. of the Laodiceans. 14

church of God
feed the c. of God. *Acts 20:28*
to the c. of God which. *1 Cor 1:2*
none offence to c. of God. 10:32
or despise ye the c. of God. 11:22
I persecuted c. of God. 15:9
Gal 1:13
care of the c. of God ? *1 Tim 3:5*

churches
then had the c. rest. *Acts 9:31*
through Syria confirming the c. 15:41
so were the c. established. 16:5
who are neither robbers of c. 19:37*
to whom all c. of. *Rom 16:4*
salute one another, the c. of. 16
so ordain I in all c. *1 Cor 7:17*
neither c. of Christ. 11:16
author of peace as in all c. 14:33
women keep silence in the c. 34
as I have given order to c. 16:1
c. of Asia salute you. 19
the grace bestowed on c. *2 Cor 8:1*
who was chosen of the c. to. 19
are the messengers of the c. 23
I robbed other c. taking. 11:8
upon me daily care of all c. 28
wherein ye were inferior to c.? 12:13
unknown by face to c. of. *Gal 1:22*
followers of c. of God. *1 Thes 2:14*
glory in you in the c. *2 Thes 1:4*
John to the seven c. in. *Rev 1:4*
send it to the seven c. which. 11
angels of the seven c. and seven
candlesticks are the seven c. 20
hear what Spirit saith unto c. 2:7
11, 17, 29; 3:6, 13, 22
c. know I am he which. 2:23
testify these things in the c. 22:16

churl
nor shall the c. be said. *Isa 32:5*
instruments also of the c. are. 7

churlish
man Nabal was c. and. *1 Sam 25:3*

churning
surely the c. of milk. *Pr 30:33*

Chushan-rishathaim
Israel into the hand of C. *Judg 3:8*

Chuza
Joanna wife of C. *Luke 8:3*

cieled (ceiled)
he c the greater house. *2 Chr 3:5*
it is c. with cedar and. *Jer 22:14*
to dwell in your c. houses. *Hag 1:4*

cieling (ceiling)
built walls of house with c. *1 Ki 6:15*

Cilicia
they of C. disputed with. *Acts 6:9*
which are of Gentiles in C. 15:23
through C. confirming the. 41
of Tarsus, a city in C. 21:39; 22:3
23:34
sailed over the sea of C. 27:5
into the regions of C. *Gal 1:21*

cinnamon
take of sweet c. haif so. *Ex 30:23*
my bed with aloes and c. *Pr 7:17*
an orchard of calamus and c.
S of S 4:14
her merchandise of c. *Rev 18:13*

circle
he that sitteth on the c. *Isa 40:22*

circuit, -s
from year to year in c. *1 Sam 7:16*
he walked in the c. of. *Job 22:14†*
c. and his c. from ends. *Ps 19:6*
again according to his c. *Eccl 1:6*

circumcise
ye shall c. the flesh of. *Gen 17:11*
c. therefore fore-skin. *Deut 10:16*
the Lord thy God will c. 30:6
c. again children of Israel. *Josh 5:2*
this is cause why Joshua did c. 4
c. yourselves to the Lord. *Jer 4:4*
day they came to c. *Luke 1:59*
ye on the sabbath-day c. *John 7:22*
it was needful to c. them. *Acts 15:5*
that they ought not to c. 21:21

circumcised
every man-child be c. *Gen 17:10*
whose flesh is not c. that soul. 14
and Abraham c. the flesh of their. 23
in that day Abraham was c. 26
that every male of you be c. 34:15
every male was c. 24; *Ex 12:48*
Joshua c. children of. *Josh 5:3*
because they had not c. them. 7
will punish all c. with. *Jer 9:25*
except ye be c. ye. *Acts 15:1, 24*
Paul c. Timothy because. 16:3
that believe, though not c. *Rom 4:11*
c. let him not become uncircumcised,
in uncircumcision not be c.
1 Cor 7:18
neither Titus be c. *Gal 2:3*
if c. Christ profit you nothing. 5:2
constrain you to be c. lest. 6:12
that they are c. kept not the law. 13
c. the eighth day. *Phil 3:5*
in whom also ye are c. *Col 2:11*

circumcising
when they had done c. *Josh 5:8*
accomplished for to c. child. *Luke 2:21*

circumcision
(*Literally, the cutting off of the
prepuce, a religious rite of the
Jews. Metaphorically, the purifying spiritually. Since all male
Jews must by law be circumcised,
the word is often used to mean the
Jews in distinction from Gentiles.
In this case also it is used metaphorically*)
Moses gave unto you c. *John 7:22*
if man on sabbath-day receive c. 23
c. profiteth, if thou keep law; if break
law, c. is made. *Rom 2:25*
nor is that c. which is outward. 28
and c. is that of the heart. 29
who shall justify the c. 3:30
blessedness then on c. only ? 4:9
when he was in c.? not in c. 10

c. is the keeping of the. *1 Cor 7:19*
they should go unto the c. *Gal 2:9*
in Jesus Christ neither c. *5:6; 6:15*
brethren, if I yet preach c. *5:11*
that which is called c. *Eph 2:11*
we are the c. which. *Phil 3:3*
c. without hands, by c. of. *Col 2:11*
neither c. nor uncircumcision. *3:11*

of circumcision
bloody husband, because of c.
Ex 4:26
Abraham covenant of c. *Acts 7:8*
they of c. which believed. *10:45*
they of the c. contended with. *11:2*
what profit is there of c.? *Rom 3:1*
he received the sign of c. a. *4:11*
father of c. to them not of c. *12*
Jesus Christ a minister of c. *15:8*
as the gospel of c. was. *Gal 2:7*
Peter to apostleship of the c. *8*
who are of c. salute you. *Col 4:11*
especially they of the c. *Tit 1:10*

circumspect
I have said to you, be c. *Ex 23:13**

circumspectly
see that ye walk c. not as. *Eph 5:15**

cistern
(*An artificial reservoir, built of rock or brick, excavated in the rock to hold rain water. Many of the houses had their own private cisterns, provided with a bucket and windlass (Eccl. 12:6) and filled as are ours by water conducted to them from the roof*)
drink ye waters of his c. *2 Ki 18:31*
waters out of thine own c. *Pr 5:15*
wheel broken at the c. *Eccl 12:6*
drink waters of own c. *Isa 36:16*

cisterns
hewed out c. broken c. *Jer 2:13*

cities
destroyed the c. of the. *Gen 19:29*
terror of God upon the c. *35:5*
laid up food in the c. *41:48*
people removed to the c. *47:21*
the c. of the Levites. *Lev 25:32*
what c. they be that. *Num 13:19*
every one shall give of his c. *35:8*
nor camest thou to c. *Deut 2:37*
c. thereof gave I to Reubenites. *3:12*
abide in your c. which I have. *19*
to give thee great and goodly c. *6:10*
flee to one of these c. *19:5*
Israel came to their c. *Josh 9:17*
not to enter into their c. *10:19*
as for the c. that stood still in. *11:13*
described it by c. into seven. *18:9*
buried in one of the c. *Judg 12:7*
set fire on all the c. they. *20:48*
they repaired the c. *21:23*
Israelites forsook the c. *1 Sam 31:7*
for the c. of our God. *2 Sam 10:12*
1 Chr 19:13
from Tyre to see the c. *1 Ki 9:12*
what c. are these that thou? *13*
the c. my father took I will. *20:34*
Jair had 23 c. in the. *1 Chr 2:22*
these were their c. to the. *4:31*
so did he in the c. of. *2 Chr 34:6*
Israelites were in their c. *Ezra 3:1*
Neh 7:73
nine parts dwell in other c. *Neh 11:1*
dwelleth in desolate c. *Job 15:28*
thou hast destroyed c. *Ps 9:6*
answered, till c. be wasted. *Isa 6:11*
nor fill face of world with c. *14:21*
in that day shall five c. in. *19:18*
he hath despised the c. he. *33:8*
thy holy c. are a wilderness. *64:10*
his c. are burnt. *Jer 2:15*
according to thy c. *28; 11:13*
c. of south be shut up. *19:8*
that man be as the c. which. *20:16*
turn again to these thy c. *31:21*
all the c. thereof shall be. *49:13*
I will kindle fire in his c. *50:32*
like the c. that are not. *Ezek 26:19*
and these c. shall go into. *30:17*
thy c. shall not return. *35:9*
I will send fire upon his c. *Hos 8:14*
sword shall abide on his c. *11:6*

two or three c. wandered. *Amos 4:8*
I will cut off the c. of. *Mi 5:11*
so will I destroy thy c. *14*
their c. are destroyed. *Zeph 3:6*
my c. by prosperity shall. *Zech 1:17*
not have gone over c. *Mat 10:23*
teach and preach in their c. *11:1*
persecuted them even to strange c.
Acts 26:11
turning c. of Sodom and. *2 Pet 2:6*
and c. about them in like. *Jude 7*
the c. of the nations. *Rev 16:19*

all cities
took all these c. and dwelt in c.
Num 21:25; Deut 2:34; 3:4
Josh 10:39
they burnt all their c. *Num 31:10*
Judg 20:48
all c. of Levites 48 c. *Num 35:7*
thus do to all c. *Deut 20:15*
all the c. of the kings. *Josh 11:12*
all c. of Aaron were 13 c. *21:19*
all c. of Gershonites were 13 c. *33*
all c. of Merari by lot 12 c. *40*
all c. of Levites were 48 c. *41*
women came out of all c. *1 Sam 18:6*
thus did he to all c. *2 Sam 12:31*
they came to all the c. of. *1 Ki 22:39*
Asa smote all the c. *2 Chr 14:14*
tithes in all the c. of. *Neh 10:37*
all the c. thereof were. *Jer 4:26*
in all c. thereof an habitation. *33:12*
save thee in all thy c. *Hos 13:10*
preached in all c. till he. *Acts 8:40*

defenced cities
against the defenced c. *Isa 36:1*
lay waste the defenced c. *37:26*
let us go into defenced c. *Jer 4:5*
8:14
these defenced c. remained. *34:7*

fenced cities
dwell in the fenced c. *Num 32:17*
all these c. were fenced. *Deut 3:5*
c. fenced to heaven. *9:1; Josh 14:12*
entered into fenced c. *Josh 10:20*
lest he get him fenced c. *2 Sam 20:6*
Shishak took fenced c. *2 Chr 12:4*
Asa built fenced c. in Judah. *14:6*
forces in the fenced c. *17:2*
through all fenced c. of. *19:5*
gave his sons fenced c. in. *21:3*
impoverish thy fenced c. *Jer 5:17*
take the most fenced c. *Dan 11:15*
Judah multiplied fenced c. *Hos 8:14*
alarm against fenced c. *Zeph 1:16*

cities of Judah
to any of c. of Judah. *2 Sam 2:1*
incense in c. of Judah. *2 Ki 23:5*
gave the c. of Judah. *1 Chr 6:57*
to teach in c. of Judah. *2 Chr 17:7*
business in c. of Judah. *13*
set judges in c. of Judah. *19:5*
Levites out of all c. of Judah. *23:2*
Israel in the c. of Judah. *31:6*
in c. of Judah each dwelt. *Neh 11:3*
Zion, build c. of Judah. *Ps 69:35*
say to the c. of Judah. *Isa 40:9*
and that saith to c. of Judah. *44:26*
north against c. of Judah. *Jer 1:15*
against the c. of Judah. *4:16*
do in the c. of Judah. *7:17*
c. of Judah desolate. *9:11; 10:22*
34:22
shall c. of Judah go and cry. *11:12*
witness in the c. of Judah. *32:44*
even in the c. of Judah. *33:10*
in c. of Judah shall flocks pass. *13*
anger kindled in c. of Judah. *44:6*
incense burnt in c. of Judah. *21*
maids in the c. of Judah. *Lam 5:11*
mercy on the c. of Judah. *Zech 1:12*

cities of refuge
six c. for refuge. *Num 35:6, 13, 14*
appoint c. of refuge. *11; Josh 20:2*
of Kohath of c. of refuge. *1 Chr 6:67*

six cities
six c. for refuge. *Num 35:6, 13, 15*
mountains of Judah six c. *Josh 15:59*

cities with suburbs
the suburbs of their c. *Lev 25:34*

to Levites suburbs for c. *Num 35:2*
Levites c. and suburbs. *Josh 21:3*
c. of Levites 48 with suburbs. *41*

cities with villages
c. and country villages. *1 Sam 6:18*
houses in c. and villages. *1 Chr 27:25*
all the c. and villages teaching and
preaching. *Mat 9:35; Luke 13:22*
entered into villages or c. *Mark 6:56*

cities with waste
make your c. waste. *Lev 26:31, 33*
waste c. desolations. *Isa 61:4*
c. shall be laid waste. *Jer 4:7*
dwellings your c. shall be waste.
Ezek 6:6
laid waste their c. *19:7*
I will lay thy c. waste. *35:4*
waste c. are become fenced. *36:35*
so shall waste c. be filled. *38*
shall build thy waste c. *Amos 9:14*

your cities
your c. are burnt with fire. *Isa 1:7*
and dwell in your c. *Jer 40:10*
cleanness of teeth in your c.
Amos 4:6

citizen, -s
joined himself to a c. *Luke 15:15*
his c. hated him, and sent. *19:14*
I am of Tarsus, a c. of. *Acts 21:39*
but fellow-c. with saints. *Eph 2:19*

city
(*In Hebrew usage, a collection of permanent human habitations, whether many or few, especially if surrounded by a wall. The word was also used, as now, metaphorically for the people of the city*)
Cain builded a c. and. *Gen 4:17*
let us build us a c. and a. *11:4*
Lord came down to see c. and. *5*
and they left off to build c. *8*
fifty righteous within the c. *18:26*
destroy all c. for lack of five? *28*
daughters of the c. come to. *24:13*
all that went out of gate of c. *34:24*
came upon the c. boldly. *25*
flame is gone out from c. *Num 21:28*
there was not one c. *Deut 2:36*
not one c. we took not from. *3:4*
smite inhabitants of that c. *13:15*
c. next to slain man take. *21:3, 6*
very far from c. Adam. *Josh 3:16*
ye shall compass c. and go. *6:3, 7*
burnt the c. with fire. 24; *Deut 13:16*
Josh 8:8, 19; Judg 1:8; 18:27
an ambush for c. behind it. *Josh 8:2*
they left the c. open, and. *17*
smoke of the c. ascended up. *20*
was not a c. made peace. *11:19*
c. of Arba, which c. is. *15:13*
they gave Joshua the c. which. *19:50*
at the entry of the gate of c. *20:4*
feared men of the c. *Judg 6:27*
Gideon slew men of the c. *8:17*
and beat down the c. and. *9:45*
all they of the c. fled, and. *51*
flame of the c. ascended. *20:40*
all the c. was moved. *Ruth 1:19*
for all the c. of my people. *3:11*
this man went out of c. *1 Sam 1:3*
when man told it, all c. cried. *4:13*
deadly destruction through c. *5:11*
go ye every man to his c. *8:22*
1 Ki 22:36; Ezra 2:1; Neh 7:6
buried him in Ramah, his c.
1 Sam 28:3
two men in one c. one. *2 Sam 12:1*
of what c. art thou? *15:2*
I may die in mine own c. *19:37*
seekest to destroy a c. and. *20:19*
so that the c. rang again. *1 Ki 1:45*
for Jerusalem's sake, c. *11:32, 36*
neither is this the c. *2 Ki 6:19*
and the c. was in quiet. *11:20*
c. Jerusalem was. *24:10; 25:2*
was destroyed the c. for. *2 Chr 15:6*
judges in the land c. by c. *19:5*
posts passed from c. to c. *30:10*
that they might take the c. *32:18*
building the rebellious c. *Ezra 4:12*
sad, when c. lieth waste. *Neh 2:3, 5*

Judah was second over c. *Neh* 11:9
but the c. Shushan. *Esth* 3:15
c. of Shushan rejoiced. 8:15
c. of the great King. *Ps* 48:2
              Mat 5:35
go round about the c. *Ps* 59:6, 14
they of c. shall flourish. 72:16
they found no c. to dwell in. 107:4
Jerusalem is builded as a c. 122:3
except Lord keep the c. 127:1
Wisdom crieth at entry of c. *Pr* 8:3
wealth is his strong c. 10:15; 18:11
c. rejoiceth, shouting when. 11:10
by blessing of upright the c. 11
than he that taketh a c. 16:32
is like a c. broken down. 25:28
scornful men bring a c. into. 29:8
there was a little c. *Eccl* 9:14
poor wise man delivered the c. 15
c. of righteousness, faithful c.
           Isa 1:26, 21
cry, O c. whole Palestina. 14:31
taken away from being a c. 17:1
shall fight, c. against c. 19:2
the c. of confusion is. 24:10
of a c. an heap, to be no c. 25:2
Zion, c. of our solemnities. 33:20
they shall call these the c. of. 60:14
thou shalt be called a c. 62:12
I will take you one of a c. *Jer* 3:14
whole c. shall flee from noise. 4:29
even make this c. as Tophet. 19:12
to bring evil on the c. called. 25:29
come to the c. and the c. is. 32:24
the c. was broken up. 39:2; 52:7
I will destroy the c. and the. 46:8
c. of praise not left, c. of joy. 49:25
how doth c. sit solitary! *Lam* 1:1
c. that men called perfection? 2:15
pourtray on it the c. even. *Ezek* 4:1
make a chain, for the c. is. 7:23
them that have charge over c. 9:1
go through midst of c. Jerusalem. 4
land full of blood, the c. is full. 9
scatter coals of fire over c. 10:2
what c. is like Tyrus? 27:32
the c. is smitten. 33:21
name of the c. shall be. 48:35
the c. called by thy. *Dan* 9:18, 19
Gilead a c. of them. *Hos* 6:8
I caused to rain on one c. *Amos* 4:7
c. that went out by thousand. 5:3
Lord's voice crieth to c. *Mi* 6:9
him that stablisheth c. by. *Hab* 2:12
to polluted, oppressing c. *Zeph* 3:1
Jerusalem called a c. of. *Zech* 8:3
streets of the c. shall be full. 5
c. shall be taken, residue of people
  shall not be cut off from c. 14:2
a c. that is set on a hill. *Mat* 5:14
Jerusalem, is c. of great King. 35
the whole c. came out to. 8:34
into whatsoever c. ye shall. 10:11
than for that c. 15; *Mark* 6:11
          Luke 10:12
all the c. was moved. *Mat* 21:10
sent and burnt up their c. 22:7
persecute them from c. to c. 23:34
all c. was gathered. *Mark* 1:33
told it in c. 5:14; *Luke* 8:34
every one to his own c. *Luke* 2:3
much people of the c. was. 7:12
he beheld the c. and wept. 19:41
of Arimathaea, a c. of the. 23:51
many of that c. believed. *John* 4:39
great joy in that c. *Acts* 8:8
almost the whole c. to hear. 13:44
we were abiding in that c. 16:12
set all the c. in an uproar. 17:5
the whole c. was filled. 19:29
all the c. was moved, and. 21:30
he looked for a c. that. *Heb* 11:10
hath prepared for them a c. 16
ye are come to the c. of the. 12:22
we have no continuing c. 13:14
go into such a c. buy and. *Jas* 4:13
compassed the beloved c. *Rev* 20:9
wall of the c. had twelve. 21:14
c. was pure gold, like to. 18
c. had no need of the sun nor. 23

bloody **city**
thou judge the *bloody* c.? *Ezek* 22:2
woe to *bloody* c. 24:6, 9; *Nah* 3:1

defenced **city**
of a *defenced* c. a ruin. *Isa* 25:2
the *defenced* c. shall be. 27:10
thee this day a *defenced* c. *Jer* 1:18

city of David
the c. of D. 2 *Sam* 5:9; *1 Chr* 11:7
the ark into the c. of D. 2 *Sam* 6:10
ark into the c. of D. 12, 16
David buried in c. of D. *1 Ki* 2:10
brought her into the c. 3:1
ark out of c. of D. 8:1; *2 Chr* 5:2
Solomon buried in c. of D.
    1 Ki 11:43; *2 Chr* 9:31
Rehoboam buried in c. of D.
    1 Ki 14:31; *2 Chr* 12:16
buried Abijam in c. of D. *1 Ki* 15:8
           2 *Chr* 14:1
Jehoshaphat buried in c. of D.
    1 Ki 22:50; *2 Chr* 21:1
Joram buried in c. of D. *2 Ki* 8:24
          2 *Chr* 21:20
Ahaziah buried in c. of D. 2 *Ki* 9:28
Jehoash buried in c. of D. 12:21
          2 *Chr* 24:25
Amaziah buried in c. of D. 2 *Ki* 14:20
Azariah buried in c. of D. 15:7
Jothan buried in c. of D. 38
          2 *Chr* 27:9
Ahaz buried in c. of D. 2 *Ki* 16:20
buried Jehoiada in c. of D. 2 *Chr* 24:16
breaches of the c. of D. *Isa* 22:9
the c. where D. dwelt. 29:1
Joseph went into c. of D. *Luke* 2:4
to you is born in c. of D. a. 11

elders with **city**
elders of his c. shall. *Deut* 19:12
the *elders* of that c. next to. 21:6
say to the *elders* of his c. our. 20
spread cloth before *elders* of c. 22:17
elders of his c. shall call him. 25:8
cause to *elders* of c. *Josh* 20:4
Gideon took *elders* of c. *Judg* 8:16
ten men of *elders* of c. *Ruth* 4:2
them *elders* of every c. *Ezra* 10:14

every **city**
smote men of *every* c. *Judg* 20:48
smite *every* fenced c. 2 *Ki* 3:19
in *every* c. Rehoboam. 2 *Chr* 11:12
in *every* c. of Judah he. 28:25
of sons of Aaron in *every* c. 31:19
every c. shall be forsaken. *Jer* 4:29
spoiler come upon *every* c. 48:8
every c. divided against. *Mat* 12:25
two and two into *every* c. *Luke* 10:1
hath in *every* c. them. *Acts* 15:21
visit our brethren in *every* c. 36
witnesseth in *every* c. that. 20:23
ordain elders in *every* c. *Tit* 1:5

fenced **city**
with you a *fenced* c. 2 *Ki* 10:2
watchmen to the *fenced* c. 17:9
dispersed of all his children unto
  every fenced c. 2 *Chr* 11:23

city of God
make glad the c. of G. *Ps* 46:4
to be praised in c. of our G. 48:1
c. of G. God will establish it. 8
spoken of thee, O c. of G. 87:3
to the c. of the living G. *Heb* 12:22
the name of c. of my G. *Rev* 3:12

great **city**
Resen, same is a *great* c. *Gen* 10:12
Gibeon was a *great* c. *Josh* 10:2
c. was large and *great*. *Neh* 7:4
done thus to this *great* c.? *Jer* 22:8
Nineveh, that *great* c. *Jonah* 1:2; 3:2
was an exceeding *great* c. 3:3
spare Nineveh that *great* c.? 4:11
bodies in streets of *great* c. *Rev* 11:8
that *great* c. 14:8; 18:10, 16, 19, 21
the *great* c. was divided. 16:19
the woman is that *great* c. 17:18
he shewed me that *great* c. 21:10

holy **city**
in Jerusalem the *holy* c. *Neh* 11:1
the Levites of the *holy* c. were. 18
themselves of the *holy* c. *Isa* 48:2
beautiful garments, O *holy* c. 52:1
determined on thy *holy* c. *Dan* 9:24
taketh him up into *holy* c. *Mat* 4:5
went into the *holy* c. and. 27:53

holy c. shall they tread. *Rev* 11:2
I John saw the *holy* c. coming. 21:2
his part out of the *holy* c. 22:19

in, or *into the* **city**
hast *in the* c. bring. *Gen* 19:12
all that is *in the* c. *Deut* 20:14
blessed shalt thou be *in the* c. 28:3
cursed shalt thou be *in the* c. 16
people went *into the* c. *Josh* 6:20
destroyed all that was *in the* c. 21
they entered *into the* c. and. 8:19
the entrance *into the* c. *Judg* 1:24
Gideon put the ephod *in his* c. 8:27
man came *into the* c. *1 Sam* 4:13
carry ark *into the* c. 2 *Sam* 15:25
return *into the* c. and your. 27
and told it *in the* c. *1 Ki* 13:25
dieth of Jeroboam *in the* c. 14:11
when thy feet enter *into the* c. 12
that dieth of Baasha *in the* c. 16:4
came *into the* c. into an. 20:30
in the c. dogs eat. 21:24
we will enter *into the* c. 2 *Ki* 7:4
catch them, get *into the* c. 12
brought water *into the* c. 20:20
famine prevailed *in the* c. 25:3
he hath shewed me marvellous
  kindness *in a* strong c. *Ps* 31:21
violence and strife *in the* c. 55:9
in the c. Wisdom. *Pr* 1:21
mighty men *in the* c. *Eccl* 7:19
wicked were forgotten *in* c. 8:10
in the c. is left desolation. *Isa* 24:12
if I enter *into the* c. *Jer* 14:18
is no more bread *in the* c. 38:9
famine was sore *in the* c. 52:6
gave up the ghost *in the* c. *Lam* 1:19
in the c. famine shall. *Ezek* 7:15
went forth and slew *in the* c. 9:7
I will not enter *into the* c. *Hos* 11:9
run to and fro *in the* c. *Joel* 2:9
trumpet be blown *in the* c. shall
  there be evil *in a* c. *Amos* 3:6
an harlot *in the* c. thy sons. 7:17
began to enter *into the* c. *Jonah* 3:4
and came *into* his own c. *Mat* 9:1
into any c. of the Samaritans. 10:5
and *into* whatsoever c. ye. 11
go *into the* c. to such a man. 26:18
some of watch came *into the* c. 28:11
saith, go *into the* c. *Mark* 14:13
          Acts 9:6
taxed, every one *into* his c. *Luke* 2:3
a woman *in the* c. which. 7:37
there was *in a* c. a judge. 18:2
there was a widow *in that* c. 3
when ye are entered *into the* c. 22:10
tarry ye *in the* c. of. 24:49
were gone *into the* c. *John* 4:8
I was *in the* c. of Joppa. *Acts* 11:5
rose up and came *into the* c. 14:20
Trophimus with him *in the* c. 21:29
in synagogues nor *in the* c. 24:12
perils *in the* c. *in* sea. 2 *Cor* 11:26
through gates *into the* c. *Rev* 22:14

city of the Lord
wicked doers from c. of *L*. *Ps* 101:8
call thee c. of the *L*. *Isa* 60:14

out of the **city**
were gone out of the c. *Gen* 44:4
as I am gone *out of the* c. *Ex* 9:29
Moses went *out of the* c. 33
them forth *out of the* c. *Lev* 14:45
side issued *out of the* c. *Josh* 8:22
man come *out of the* c. *Judg* 1:24
succour us *out of the* c. 2 *Sam* 18:3
a wise woman *out of the* c. 20:16
Naboth *out of the* c. *1 Ki* 21:13
come *out of the* c. 2 *Ki* 7:12
let none escape *out of the* c. 9:15
much spoil *out of the* c. *1 Chr* 20:2
cast idols *out of the* c. 2 *Chr* 33:15
groan from *out of the* c. *Job* 24:12
went *out of the* c. *Jer* 39:4; 52:7
the goings *out of the* c. *Ezek* 48:30
go forth *out of the* c. *Mi* 4:10
left them, and went *out of the* c.
          Mat 21:17
even was come, went *out of the* c.
          Mark 11:19
thrust him *out of the* c. *Luke* 4:29
when ye go *out of* that c. 9:5

went *out of c.* and came. *John* 4:30
cast Stephen *out of the c. Acts* 7:58
Paul, drew him *out of the c.* 14:19
sabbath we went *out of the c.* 16:13
till we were *out of the c.* 21:5

city *of refuge*
restore him to *c. of refuge.*
Num 35:25
without border of *c. of refuge.* 26, 27
remained in the *c. of refuge.* 28
fled to the *c. of refuge.* 32
Hebron to be a *c. of refuge.*
Josh 21:13, 21, 27, 32, 38
of Aaron, Hebron a *c. of refuge.*
1 Chr 6:57

this city
Lord will destroy *this c. Gen* 19:14
behold now, *this c.* is near to. 20
I will not overthrow *this c.* 21
he that buildeth *this c. Josh* 6:26
us turn in unto *this c. Judg* 9:11
there is in *this c. a. 1 Sam* 9:6
the situation of *this c. 2 Ki* 2:19
this c. shall not. 18:30; *Isa* 36:15
not come into *this c. 2 Ki* 19:32, 33
Isa 37:34
I will defend *this c. 2 Ki* 19:34
20:6; *Isa* 37:35; 38:6
cast off *this c.* Jerusalem. *2 Ki* 23:27
pray to thee toward *this c. 2 Chr* 6:34
if *this c.* be builded. *Ezra* 4:13, 16
this c. is a rebellious city. 15
bring evil upon *this c.? Neh* 13:18
this is the *c.* to be visited. *Jer* 6:6
Jerusalem, and *this c.* shall. 17:25
I will make *this c.* desolate. 19:8
break this people and *this c.* 11
I will bring upon *this c.* and. 15
the strength of *this c.* 20:5
he that abideth in *this c.* shall. 21:9
I set my face against *this c.* 10
Lord done thus unto *this c.?* 22:8
I will make *this c.* a curse. 26:6
innocent blood on *this c.* 15
should *this c.* be laid waste ? 27:17
this c. to Chaldeans. 32:3, 28; 34:2
this c. hath been to me as a. 32:31
have hid my face from *this c.* 33:5
cause them to return to *this c.* 34:22
this c. shall not be burnt. 38:17
thou shalt cause *this c.* to be. 23
my words on *this c.* for evil. 39:16
wicked counsel in *this c. Ezek* 11:2
this c. is the caldron, and we. 3, 7
this c. shall not be your caldron. 11
persecute you in *this c. Mat* 10:23
much people in *this c. Acts* 18:10
I was brought up in *this c.* 22:3

without the city
men set him *without the c. Gen* 19:16
unclean place *without the c.*
Lev 14:40, 41
measure from *without c. Num* 35:5
fountains *without the c. 2 Chr* 32:3
trodden *without the c. Rev* 14:20

clad
Jeroboam *c.* himself with. *1 Ki* 11:29
for clothing was *c.* with. *Isa* 59:17

clamorous
a foolish woman is *c.* *Pr* 9:13

clamour
all anger and *c.* be put. *Eph* 4:31

clap
men shall *c.* hands at. *Job* 27:23
c. your hands, all ye. *Ps* 47:1
let floods *c.* their hands, let. 98:8
trees of the field shall *c. Isa* 55:12
all that pass by *c.* their. *Lam* 2:15
fruit of thee shall *c. Nah* 3:19

clapped
c. their hands, and said. *2 Ki* 11:12
thou hast *c.* thine hands. *Ezek* 25:6

clappeth
he *c.* his hands among us. *Job* 34:37

clave
(*Cut, split*)
Abraham *c.* the wood. *Gen* 22:3
the ground *c.* asunder. *Num* 16:31
God *c.* an hollow place. *Judg* 15:19
they *c.* wood of cart. *1 Sam* 6:14
c. the rocks in. *Ps* 78:15; *Isa* 48:21

clave
(*Held to, clung to*)
his soul *c.* to Dinah. *Gen* 34:3
but Ruth *c.* to her. *Ruth* 1:14
men of Judah *c.* to. *2 Sam* 20:2
he smote till his hand *c.* to. 23:10
Solomon *c.* to these in. *1 Ki* 11:2
for Hezekiah *c.* to Lord. *2 Ki* 18:6
they *c.* to their brethren. *Neh* 10:29
certain men *c.* to Paul. *Acts* 17:34

claws
cleaveth cleft in two *c. Deut* 14:6*
nails grown like birds' *c. Dan* 4:33
he shall tear their *c. Zech* 11:16*

clay
dwell in houses of *c.* *Job* 4:19
thou hast made me as the *c.* 10:9
bodies are like to bodies of *c.* 13:12
prepare raiment as the *c.* 27:16
am formed out of the *c.* 33:6
it is turned as *c.* to the seal. 38:14
brought me out of miry *c. Ps* 40:2
esteemed as potter's *c. Isa* 29:16
as the potter treadeth the *c.* 41:25
shall the *c.* say to him ? 45:9
we are *c.* thou our potter 64:8
vessel that he made of *c. Jer* 18:4
as *c.* is in the potter's hand. 6
stones, hide them in the *c.* 43:9*
part of iron, part *c. Dan* 2:33, 34, 42
c. broken in pieces. 35, 45
feet and toes part of potter's *c.* 41
go into *c.* and tread the. *Nah* 3:14
ladeth himself with *c. Hab* 2:6*
made *c* of spittle, anointed eyes of
blind man with *c. John* 9:6
he put *c.* on mine eyes, I see. 15
potter power over the *c.? Rom* 9:21

clean
not make *c.* riddance in. *Lev* 23:22
passed *c.* over Jordan. *Josh* 3:17
4:1, 11
is his mercy *c.* gone for ? *Ps* 77:8
earth is *c.* dissolved, is. *Isa* 24:19
he hath made it *c.* bare. *Joel* 1:7
arm shall be *c.* dried up. *Zech* 11:17
c. escaped from them. *2 Pet* 2:18

clean. *adjective*
[1] *Free from filth or dirt.* [2]
Ceremonially pure, Lev 10:10;
Acts 10:15. [3] *Metaphorically,
innocent, delivered from the power
of sin,* Acts 18:6; Ps 51:10; 1 John
1:9.
of every *c.* beast thou. *Gen* 7:2
of every *c.* beast and *c.* fowl. 8:20
Jacob said, be *c.* and change. 35:2
bullock unto *c.* place. *Lev* 4:12; 6:11
the flesh, all that be *c.* shall. 7:19
put difference between *c.* 10:10
11:47; 20:25; *Ezek* 22:26; 44:23
eat in *c.* place. *Lev* 10:14; *Num* 19:9
that ye may be *c.* from. *Lev* 16:30
not eat of holy things till he be *c.* 22:4
on seventh day be *c. Num* 19:12
a *c.* person shall take hyssop. 18
unclean and *c.* may eat. *Deut* 12:15
15:22
not *c.* surely he is not *c. 1 Sam* 20:26
again, and thou be *c. 2 Ki* 5:10, 14
I wash in them and be *c.?* 12
wash and be *c.* 13
I am *c.* in thine eyes. *Job* 11:4
who can bring a *c.* thing out ? 14:4
man that he should be *c.?* 15:14
heavens are not *c.* in his sight. 15
how can he be *c.* that is ? 25:4
I am *c.* without transgression. 33:9
the ways of a man are *c. Pr* 16:2
things come alike to the *c. Eccl* 9:2
wash ye, make you *c. Isa* 1:16
so that there is no place *c.* 28:8
and young asses shall eat *c.* 30:24*
be ye *c.* that bear the vessels. 52:11
bring an offering in a *c.* vessel. 66:20
wilt thou not be made *c.? Jer* 13:27
then will I sprinkle *c. Ezek* 36:25
thou canst make me *c. Mat* 8:2
Mark 1:40; *Luke* 5:12
I will, be thou *c.* *Mat* 8:3
Mark 1:41; *Luke* 5:13

make *c.* the outside. *Mat* 23:25
Luke 11:39
all things are *c.* unto you. *Luke* 11:41
ye are not all *c.* *John* 13:11
now ye are *c.* through word I. 15:3
own heads, I am *c.* *Acts* 18:6
in fine linen, *c.* *Rev* 19:8*, 14*

clean hands
make my *hands* ever so *c. Job* 9:30
he that hath *c.* hands shall. 17:9
he that hath *c. hands* and a pure
heart. *Ps* 24:4

clean heart
create in me a *c. heart. Ps* 51:10
and such as are of a *c. heart.* 73:1*
I have made my *heart c.? Pr* 20:9

is clean
he *is c.* *Lev* 13:13, 17, 37, 39
yet *is* he *c.* 40, 41
spit on him that is *c.* 15:8
man that *is c. Num* 9:13; 19:9
fear of the Lord is *c. Ps* 19:9
no oxen are, the crib *is c. Pr* 14:4
wash his feet, but is *c. John* 13:10

pronounce clean
pronounce him *c.* *Lev* 13:6; 14:7

shall be clean
is water *shall be c. Lev* 11:36
she *shall be c.* 12:8; 15:28
it *shall be c.* 13:58; 14:53
Num 31:23
in water, he *shall be c. Lev* 14:9, 20
15:13; 17:15; 22:7; *Num* 19:12, 19
and ye *shall be c.* *Num* 31:24
Ezek 36:25
hyssop, and I *shall* be *c. Ps* 51:7

cleanness
to *c.* of my hands hath Lord.
2 Sam 22:21; *Ps* 18:20
to my *c.* in his sight. *2 Sam* 22:25
Ps 18:24
I have also given you *c. Amos* 4:6

cleanse
shalt *c.* altar. *Ex* 29:36; *Lev* 16:19
to *c.* house, two birds. *Lev* 14:49, 52
take the Levites and *c.* *Num* 8:6
c. house of Lord. *2 Chr* 29:15, 16
Levites should *c.* themselves.
Neh 13:22
c. thou me from secret. *Ps* 19:12*
wash me throughly, and *c.* 51:2
a young man *c.* his way ? 119:9
wind not to fan nor to *c. Jer* 4:11
c. them from iniquity. 33:8
Ezek 37:23
from idols will I *c.* you. *Ezek* 36:25
they may *c.* the land. 39:12, 16
thus shalt thou *c.* and purge it. 43:20
a young bullock, and *c.* the. 45:18
I will *c.* their blood. *Joel* 3:21
heal the sick, *c.* lepers. *Mat* 10:8
c. first that which is within. 23:26
let us *c.* ourselves from. *2 Cor* 7:1
might *c.* it with washing. *Eph* 5:26
c. your hands, ye sinners. *Jas* 4:8
to *c.* us from all. *1 John* 1:9

cleansed
so shall it be *c.* *Lev* 11:32
she shall be *c.* from the issue. 12:7
him that is to be *c.* 14:4, 14, 17
18, 19, 25, 28, 31
the land cannot be *c. Num* 35:33
from which we are not *c. Josh* 22:17
we have *c.* all house of. *2 Chr* 29:18
many had not *c.* themselves. 30:18
though he be not *c.* 19
Josiah *c.* Judah and Jerusalem. 34:5
they *c.* the chambers. *Neh* 13:9
thus I *c.* them from strangers. 30
what profit, if I be *c.? Job* 35:3*
I have *c.* my heart in vain. *Ps* 73:13
the land that is not *c. Ezek* 22:24
after he is *c.* reckon to him. 44:26
then shall sanctuary be *c. Dan* 8:14
c. their blood I have not *c. Joel* 3:21
his leprosy was *c.* *Mat* 8:3
the lepers are *c.* 11:5; *Luke* 7:22
leprosy departed, and he was *c.*
Mark 1:42
was *c.* save Naaman. *Luke* 4:27
the lepers *c.,* the deaf hear. 7:22
as lepers went they were *c.* 17:14

were there not ten c.? *Luke* 17:17
what God hath c. *Acts* 10:15; 11:9

cleanseth
wind passeth and c. them. *Job* 37:21
blueness of a wound c. *Pr* 20:30
blood of Jesus Christ c. *1 John* 1:7

cleansing
of the priest for his c. *Lev* 13:7
shave head in day of his c. *Num* 6:9
go and offer for thy c. *Mark* 1:44
   Luke 5:14

clear
thou shalt be c. from. *Gen* 24:8, 41
hdw shall we c. ourselves? 44:16
no means c. the guilty. *Ex* 34:7
as tender grass, by c. *2 Sam* 23:4
mightest be c. when. *Ps* 51:4
c. as the sun, terrible as. *S of S* 6:10
dwelling-place like a c. *Isa* 18:4
darken earth in a c. day. *Amos* 8:9
light shall not be c. nor. *Zech* 14:6*
approved yourselves to be c.
   2 Cor 7:11*
c. as crystal. *Rev* 21:11; 22:1*
city was pure gold, like to c. 21:18*

clearer
thine age shall be c. *Job* 11:17

clearing
and by no means c. *Num* 14:18
what c. of yourselves. *2 Cor* 7:11

clearly
my lips shall utter knowledge c.
   Job 33:3
see c. to pull out the. *Mat* 7:5
   Luke 6:42
and saw every man c. *Mark* 8:25
things from creation c. *Rom* 1:20

clearness
body of heaven in his c. *Ex* 24:10

cleave
man shall c. to his wife. *Gen* 2:24
  Mat 19:5; *Mark* 10:7
he shall c. it with the. *Lev* 1:17
ye that did c. to Lord. *Deut* 4:4
to him shalt thou c. 10:20; 11:22
  13:4; 30:20; *Josh* 22:5
shall c. nought of cursed. *Deut* 13:17
but c. to Lord your God. *Josh* 23:8
leprosy of Naaman shall c. *2 Ki* 5:27
and the clods c. fast. *Job* 38:38
thou didst c. the fountain. *Ps* 74:15
hate the work, it shall not c. 101:3
my bones c. to my skin. 102:5
let my tongue c. to roof of. 137:6
they shall c. to house of. *Isa* 14:1
so have I caused to c. *Jer* 13:11
I make thy tongue c. to. *Ezek* 3:26
but they shall not c. one. *Dan* 2:43
many shall c. to them with. 11:34
thou didst c. the earth. *Hab* 3:9
the mount shall c. in. *Zech* 14:4
with purpose of heart c. *Acts* 11:23
abhor evil, c. to that. *Rom* 12:9

cleaved
Jehoram c. to Jeroboam's. *2 Ki* 3:3
their tongue c. to roof of. *Job* 29:10
and if any blot have c. to my. 31:7

cleaveth
my bone c. to my skin. *Job* 19:20
my tongue c. to jaws. *Ps* 22:15
an evil disease, say they, c. 41:8
our belly c. to earth. 44:25
my soul c. to the dust. 119:25
as the girdle c. to loins of. *Jer* 13:11
tongue of sucking child c. *Lam* 4:4
their skin c. to their bones. 8
dust of your city which c. *Luke* 10:11

cleaveth
beast that c. the cleft. *Deut* 14:6*
he c. my reins asunder. *Job* 16:13
when one cutteth and c. *Ps* 141:7
that c. wood shall be. *Eccl* 10:9

cleft
that cleaveth the c. *Deut* 14:6*
the valleys shall be c. as. *Mi* 1:4

clefts
thou art in c. of the. *S of S* 2:14
into the c. of the rocks. *Isa* 2:21*
thou that dwellest in c. *Jer* 49:16
   Ob 3
smite little house with c. *Amos* 6:11

clemency
hear us of thy c. a few. *Acts* 24:4

Cleopas
whose name was C. *Luke* 24:18
Mary the wife of C. *John* 19:25

clerk
when town c. had. *Acts* 19:35

cliff, -s
come up by the c. of. *2 Chr* 20:16*
to dwell in the c. of the. *Job* 30:6*

clift, -s
will put thee in the c. *Ex* 33:22*
in valleys under c. of. *Isa* 57:5*

climb, -ed, -eth
Jonathan c. up upon. *1 Sam* 14:13
they shall c. up upon. *Jer* 4:29
they shall c. the wall. *Joel* 2:7
they shall c. up upon the houses. 9
they c. up to heaven. *Amos* 9:2
Zaccheus c. up into a. *Luke* 19:4
c. up some other way. *John* 10:1

clipped
head be bald, beard be c. *Jer* 48:37

clods
flesh is clothed with c. *Job* 7:5
the c. of the valley shall. 21:33
and the c. cleave fast. 38:38
doth plowman break c.? *Isa* 28:24
Jacob shall break his c. *Hos* 10:11
seed is rotten under c. *Joel* 1:17

cloke
clad with zeal as a c. *Isa* 59:17†
let him have thy c. also. *Mat* 5:40
him that taketh thy c. *Luke* 6:29
now they have no c. *John* 15:22*
nor used we a c. of. *1 Thes* 2:5
the c. I left at Troas. *2 Tim* 4:13
not using liberty for a c. *1 Pet* 2:16

close
and it be kept c. from. *Num* 5:13
afraid out of c. places. *2 Sam* 22:46
   Ps 18:45
David yet kept himself c. *1 Chr* 12:1
and kept c. from fowls. *Job* 28:21
shut up together as with a c. 41:15
famine follow c. after you. *Jer* 42:16
and I saw him come c. *Dan* 8:7
and c. up the breaches. *Amos* 9:11
kept it c. and told no man. *Luke* 9:36
they sailed c. by Crete. *Acts* 27:13

closed
Lord c. up the flesh. *Gen* 2:21
the Lord had fast c. up all. 20:18
earth c. upon them. *Num* 16:33
fat c. upon the blade. *Judg* 3:22
they have not been c. *Isa* 1:6
Lord hath c. your eyes. 29:10
for the words are c. up. *Dan* 12:9
the depth c. me round. *Jonah* 2:5
eyes have c. *Mat* 13:15; *Acts* 28:27
he c. book, and gave it. *Luke* 4:20

closer
friend that sticketh c. *Pr* 18:24

closest
thou reign, because c. *Jer* 22:15*

closet, -s
bride go out of her c. *Joel* 2:16
enter into thy c. *Mat* 6:6*
ye have spoken in c. *Luke* 12:3*

cloth
spread on them a c. *Num* 4:8
put them in a c. of blue. 12
shall spread the c. *Deut* 22:17*
covered image with a c. *1 Sam* 19:13
sword of Goliath, wrapt in a c. 21:9
and cast a c. on him. *2 Sam* 20:12*
Hazael took a thick c. *2 Ki* 8:15*
away as a menstruous c. *Isa* 30:22*
putteth a piece of new c. *Mat* 9:16
   Mark 2:21
he wrapped it in a linen c. *Mat* 27:59
having a linen c. *Mark* 14:51

clothe
bring his sons and c. *Ex* 40:14
raiment to c. Mordecai. *Esth* 4:4
c. will c. her priests. *Ps* 132:16
his enemies will I c. with. 18
drowsiness shall c. a. *Pr* 23:21
I will c. him with thy robe. *Isa* 22:21

thou shalt surely c. thee. *Isa* 49:18
I c. the heavens with blackness. 50:3
shall c. themselves with. *Ezek* 26:16
ye eat the fat, and c. you. 34:3
ye c. you, but there is. *Hag* 1:6
I will c. thee with. *Zech* 3:4
if God so c. grass of field, much more
 c. you? *Mat* 6:30; *Luke* 12:28

clothed
coats of skins and c. *Gen* 3:21
Moses c. Aaron with robe. *Lev* 8:7
weep over Saul who c. *2 Sam* 1:24
David and Israel c. with. *1 Chr* 21:16
priests be c. with. *2 Chr* 6:41
king of Israel and Judah c. 18:9
spoil c. all that were naked. 28:15
none enter king's gate c. *Esth* 4:2
flesh is c. with worms. *Job* 7:5
c. me with skin and flesh. 10:11
put on righteousness and it c. 29:14
hast thou c. his neck. 39:19
be c. with shame. *Ps* 35:26; 109:29
the pastures are c. with. 65:13
c. with majesty, Lord is c. 93:1
thou art c. with honour and. 104:1
as he c. himself with cursing. 109:18
let thy priests be c. with. 132:9
her household are c. with. *Pr* 31:21
c. me with garments of. *Isa* 61:10
I c. thee also with. *Ezek* 16:10
c. Daniel with scarlet. *Dan* 5:29
all such as are c. with. *Zeph* 1:8
Joshua was c. with filthy. *Zech* 3:3
man c. in soft raiment. *Mat* 11:8
   Luke 7:25
naked and ye c. me. *Mat* 25:36
naked and ye c. me not. 43
John was c. with camel's. *Mark* 1:6
sitting and c. 5:15; *Luke* 8:35
c. Jesus with purple. *Mark* 15:17
certain rich man c. in. *Luke* 16:19
desiring to be c. upon. *2 Cor* 5:2
if so be that being c. we shall not. 3
and be c. with humility. *1 Pet* 5:5*
that thou mayest be c. *Rev* 3:18
I saw another mighty angel c. 10:1
two witnesses shall prophesy c. 11:3
appeared a woman c. with. 12:1
he was c. with a vesture 19:13

clothed with linen
one man c. with linen. *Ezek* 9:2
be c. with linen garments. 44:17
certain man c. with linen. *Dan* 10:5
said to man c. in linen. 12:6
c. in pure and white linen. *Rev* 15:6
   18:16; 19:14

shall be clothed
that hate thee shall be c. *Job* 8:22
the prince shall be c. *Ezek* 7:27
read this writing, shall be c. *Dan* 5:7
wherewithal shall we be c.?
   Mat 6:31
overcometh shall be c. *Rev* 3:5; 4:4

clothes
he washed his c. in the. *Gen* 49:11
troughs bound up in their c. *Ex* 12:34
the c. of service. 35:19; 39:1, 41
nor rend your c. *Lev* 10:6; 21:10
c. are not waxen old. *Deut* 29:5
   Neh 9:21
Saul stript off his c. *1 Sam* 19:24
covered David with c. *1 Ki* 1:1
took hold of his own c. *2 Ki* 2:12
thou didst rend thy c. *2 Chr* 34:27
none of us put off our c. *Neh* 4:23
and my own c. shall abhor. *Job* 9:31
take fire, and his c. not? *Pr* 6:27
strip thee also of c. *Ezek* 16:39
   23:26
return back to take his c. *Mat* 24:18
if I touch but his c. *Mark* 5:28
put his own c. on him. 15:20
him in swaddling. *Luke* 2:7, 12
a man that ware no c. neither. 8:27
went they spread their c. 19:36
the linen c. laid. 24:12; *John* 20:5
bound with grave c. *John* 11:44
and wound it in linen c. 19:40
napkin not lying with linen c. 20:7*
laid down their c. *Acts* 7:58
cried out and cast off their c. 22:23

rent clothes

Reuben rent his c.   Gen 37:29
Jacob rent his c.   34
Joseph's brethren rent their c. 44:13
and Caleb rent their c.   Num 14:6
Joshua rent his c.   Josh 7:6
Jephthah rent his c.   Judg 11:35
rend your c. gird you.   2 Sam 3:31
Ahab rent his c.   1 Ki 21:27
king of Israel rent c. 2 Ki 5:8; 6:30
Athaliah rent her c.   11:14
       2 Chr 23:13
Hezekiah heard he rent his c.
      2 Ki 19:1; Isa 37:1
Mordecai perceived, he rent his c.
      Esth 4:1
high priest rent his c.   Mat 26:65
      Mark 14:63
and Paul rent their c.   Acts 14:14
magistrates rent off their c.   16:22

clothes rent

leper's c. shall be rent.   Lev 13:45
to Shiloh with c. rent.   1 Sam 4:12
from Saul with c. rent.   2 Sam 1:2
servants stood with c. rent.   13:31
to Hezekiah with c. rent. 2 Ki 18:37
      Isa 36:22
men having their c. rent.   Jer 41:5

wash clothes

wash their c.   Ex 19:10; Num 8:7
wash his c.   Lev 11:25, 40; 13:6
14:8, 9, 47; 15:5, 8, 11, 22; 16:26
      28; Num 19:10, 19
priest shall wash c. Num 19:7, 8, 19
ye shall wash your c. on.   31:24

washed clothes

people washed their c.   Ex 19:14
Levites washed their c.   Num 8:21
washed not his c.   2 Sam 19:24

clothest

though thou c. thyself.   Jer 4:30

clothing

stripped naked of their c.   Job 22:6
naked to lodge without c.   24:7
to go naked without c.   10
any perish for want of c.   31:19
as for me, my c. was.   Ps 35:13
king's daughter, her c. is.   45:13
lambs are for thy c.   Pr 27:26
virtuous woman's c. is silk.   31:22
strength and honour are her c.   25
thou hast c. be thou our.   Isa 3:6
house is neither bread nor c.   7
shall be for durable c.   23:18
garments of vengeance for c.   59:17
and purple is their c.   Jer 10:9
in sheep's c.   Mat 7:15
that wear soft c.   11:8
scribes that go in long c. Mark 12:38
man stood before me in bright c.
      Acts 10:30
him that weareth gay c.   Jas 2:3

cloud

In addition to the common meaning this word is used frequently of, [1] A great number, Heb 12:1. [2] A fog, or mist, Hos 6:4. [3] The sky, Ps 36:5; 68:34; Pr 8:28.

(At the Exodus God gave the Israelites a pillar of cloud to direct them in their march. This attended them through the wilderness. It was clear and bright during the night, in order to give them light when it grew dark; and in the day time it was thick and gloomy, the better to defend them from the excessive heats of the Arabian deserts. It also gave the signal for marching and for halting)

set my bow in the c. for.   Gen 9:13
bow shall be seen in c.   14, 16
it was c. and darkness.   Ex 14:20
glory of Lord appeared in c.   16:10
I come unto thee in a thick c.   19:9
Moses went up, and a c.   24:15
c. covered it six days, seventh day
    God called out of c.   16
Moses went into midst of c.   18
Lord descended in the c.   34:5
      Num 11:25

c. covered the tent of the. Ex 40:34
the c. of Lord was on the.   38
I will appear in the c.   Lev 16:2
when the c. tarried long. Num 9:19
the c. of the Lord was upon.   10:34
the c. filled house of Lord. 1 Ki 8:10
     2 Chr 5:13; Ezek 10:4
ariseth a little c. like.   1 Ki 18:44
day be darkness, let a c.   Job 3:5
he judge through dark c.?   22:13
welfare passeth away as a c.   30:15
when I made the c. the.   38:9
day-time led them with c. Ps 78:14
spread a c. for a covering.   105:39
his favour is as a c.   Pr 16:15
create on her assemblies a. Isa 4:5
like a c. of dew in heat of.   18:4
Lord rideth upon a swift c.   19:1
blotted out as a thick c. transgressions, and as c. thy sins.   44:22
are these that flee as a c.?   60:8
daughter of Zion with c.   Lam 2:1
covered thyself with a c.   3:44
a great c. and a fire.   Ezek 1:4
appearance of bow in the c.   28
a thick c. of incense.   8:11
the house was filled with the c. 10:4
as for her, a c. shall cover.   30:18
I will cover sun with a c.   32:7
shalt be like a c. to.   38:9, 16
a bright c. overshadowed them and a
   voice out of c. said.   Mat. 17:5
     Mark 9:7; Luke 9:34, 35
when ye see a c. rise.   Luke 12:54
Son of Man coming in a c.   21:27
a c. received him out of.   Acts 1:9
fathers were under the c. 1 Cor 10:1
all baptized to Moses in the c.   2
angel clothed with a c.   Rev 10:1
ascended to heaven in a c.   11:12
c. and upon c. one sat. 14:14, 15, 16

cloud abode

because the c. abode.   Ex 40:35
where c. abode there.   Num 9:17
as long as c. abode they.   18

morning cloud

is as a morning c.   Hos 6:4
shall be as the morning c.   11:3

pillar of cloud

by day in a p. of c.   Ex 13:21
took not away the p. of c.   22
on Egyptians through p. of c. 14:24
down in p. of c. and.   Num 12:5
in p. of c. and p. of c.   Deut 31:15
p. of c. departed not.   Neh 9:19

cloud taken up

the c. was taken up.   Ex 40:36
      Num 9:17
if the c. were not taken up. Ex 40:37
c. was taken up from tabernacle.
      Num 9:17; 10:11

white cloud

a white c. and on c. one. Rev 14:14

cloud of witnesses

with so great a c. of w.   Heb 12:1

clouds

with darkness, c. and.   Deut 4:11
heavens dropped, c. also. Judg 5:4
about him thick c. of. 2 Sam 22:12
as a morning without c.   23:4
heaven was black with c. 1 Ki 18:45
though head reach to c.   Job 20:6
thick c. are a covering that.   22:14
bindeth up waters in thick c.   26:8
understand spreadings of c.? 36:29
the balancings of the c.?   37:16
who can number the c. in ?   38:37
faithfulness reacheth to c. Ps 36:5
thy truth reacheth to the c.   57:10
      108:4
and his strength is in the c.   68:34
c. poured out water.   77:17
commanded the c. from.   78:23
c. and darkness are round.   97:2
maketh the c. his chariot.   104:3
covers heaven with c.   147:8
c. dropped down the dew. Pr 3:20
when he established the c.   8:28
is like a c. and wind without.   25:14
regardeth the c. shall not. Eccl 11:4
nor c. return after the rain.   12:2

I will command the c.   Isa 5:6
ascend above height of the c. 14:14
shall come up as c. and.   Jer 4:13
with the c. of heaven.   Dan 7:13
c. and darkness. Joel 2:2; Zeph 1:15
c. are the dust of his feet.   Nah 1:3
Lord shall make bright c. Zech 10:1
Son of Man coming in c.   Mat 24:30
   26:64; Mark 13:26; 14:62
up with them in c.   1 Thes 4:17
they are c. carried.   2 Pet 2:17
c. they are without water.   Jude 12
behold he cometh with c.   Rev 1:7

cloudy

the c. pillar descended.   Ex 33:9
people saw the c. pillar.   10
in day by c. pillar.   Neh 9:12
spake in the c. pillar.   Ps 99:7
day of the Lord, a c. day. Ezek 30:3
been scattered in the c. day.   34:12

clouted

old shoes and c. on.   Josh 9:5†

clouts

took old cast c. and rags. Jer 38:11
put these old cast c. under.   12

cloven

whatsoever is c.-footed.   Lev 11:3
though the swine be c.-footed.   7
not c.-footed are unclean to you. 26
      Deut 14:7
to them c. tongues.   Acts 2:3*

cluster

a branch with one c.   Num 13:23
my beloved is as a c.   S of S 1:14
wine found in the c. so.   Isa 65:8
woe is me, there is no c.   Mi 7:1

clusters

the c. thereof brought.   Gen 40:10
grapes their c. bitter.   Deut 32:32
Abigail brought 100 c. 1 Sam 25:18
gave the Egyptian two c.   30:12
breasts like two c. of. S of S 7:7, 8
gather the c. of the vine. Rev 14:18

coal

so shall quench my c.   2 Sam 14:7
seraphim having a live c.   Isa 6:6
there shall not be a c. to.   47:14
visage is blacker than c.   Lam 4:8

coals

censer full of burning c. Lev 16:12
a cake baken on the c.   1 Ki 19:6
his breath kindleth c.   Job 41:21
there went fire, c. were.   Ps 18:8
hail-stones and c. of fire.   12
arrows of mighty with c.   120:4
let burning c. fall on them.   140:10
can one go on hot c.?   Pr 6:28
heap c. of fire.   25:22; Rom 12:20
as c. are to burning c. and. Pr 26:21
c. thereof are c. of fire.   S of S 8:6
the smith worketh in c.   Isa 44:12
have baked bread upon the c.   19
smith that bloweth the c.   54:16
appearance like burning c. Ezek 1:13
fill thine hand with c. of fire.   10:2
set it empty on the c.   24:11
burning c. went forth at.   Hab 3:5
had made a fire of c.   John 18:18
they saw a fire of c. and fish.   21:9

coast

(Not as now sea-coast but border, whether by the sea or not. It is usually rendered in the Revisions by border, or side)

the locusts into thy c.   Ex 10:4
ships shall come from c. Num 24:24
uttermost sea shall c. be. Deut 11:24
if the Lord enlarge thy c.   19:8
going down of sun your c. Josh 1:4
Judah shall abide in their c.   18:5
not Israel to pass his c. Judg 11:20
up by way of his own c. 1 Sam 6:9
no more into the c. of Israel.   7:13
to seek any more in any c.   27:1
made an invasion on the c.   30:14
Jeroboam restored c. of. 2 Ki 14:25
me, and enlarge my c.   1 Chr 4:10
the c. shall be for the.   Zeph 2:7

sea coast
remnant of the *sea c.* *Ezek* 25:16
woe to inhabitants of *sea c.* *Zeph* 2:5
the *sea c.* shall be dwellings for. 6
in Capernaum upon *sea c.* *Mat* 4:13
multitude from *sea c.* *Luke* 6:17

south coast
uttermost part of *south c.* *Josh* 15:1
this shall be your *south c.* 4
this was the *south c.* 18:19

coasts
locusts rested in all the *c.* *Ex* 10:14
not one locust in all the *c.* of. 19
to pass through *c.* of. *Deut* 2:4
no leavened bread seen in thy *c.* 16:4
thou shalt divide the *c.* 19:3
shall abide in their *c.* on. *Josh* 18:5
five men from their *c.* *Judg* 18:2*
sent concubine into all the *c.* 19:29
the *c.* thereof did Israel. *1 Sam* 7:14
send messengers into all *c.* 11:3, 7
destroyed from *c.* of. *2 Sam* 21:5
destroyed through all *c. 1 Chr* 21:12
to him out of all *c.* *2 Chr* 11:13
lice in all their *c.* *Ps* 105:31
and brake trees of their *c.* 33
whirlwind raised from *c.* *Jer* 25:32
take a man of their *c.* *Ezek* 33:2
to do with me, all *c.* *Joel* 3:4*
slew children in all *c.* *Mat* 2:16
depart out of their *c.* 8:34; *Mark* 5:17
Jesus departed into *c.* of Tyre.
        Mat 15:21*
departing from *c.* of. *Mark* 7:31
and Barnabas out of *c.* *Acts* 13:50

coat
Jacob made Joseph a *c.* *Gen* 37:3
sent *c.* of many colours, and said,
  know whether it be thy son's *c.* 32
Aaron a robe and a broidered *c.*
        Ex 28:4
shalt put upon Aaron the *c.* 29:5
he put upon him the *c.* *Lev* 8:7
put on the holy linen *c.* 16:4
made Samuel a little *c. 1 Sam* 2:19*
armed with a *c.* of mail. 17:5, 38
met David with *c.* rent. *2 Sam* 15:32
as collar of my *c.* *Job* 30:18
I have put off my *c.* *S of S* 5:3
and take away thy *c.* *Mat* 5:40
forbid not to take thy *c.* *Luke* 6:29
c. was without seam. *John* 19:23
Peter girt his fisher's *c.* unto. 21:7

coats
God made *c.* of skins. *Gen* 3:21
for Aaron's sons make *c.* *Ex* 28:40
and put *c.* on them. 29:8; 40:14
Moses put *c.* upon. *Lev* 8:13
they carried them in their *c.* 10:5
were bound in their *c.* *Dan* 3:21*
nor were their *c.* changed, nor. 27*
neither provide two *c.* *Mat* 10:10
and put not on two *c.* *Mark* 6:9
he that hath two *c.* *Luke* 3:11
shewing the *c.* which. *Acts* 9:39

cock
night before *c.* crow. *Mat* 26:34, 75
  Mark 14:30, 72; *Luke* 22:34, 61
c. crew. *Mat* 26:74; *Luke* 22:60
        John 18:27
master cometh at *c.* crow.
        Mark 13:35
porch, and the *c.* crew. 14:68, 72
the *c.* shall not crow till thou hast
  denied me thrice. *John* 13:38

cockatrice, -s
  (*A basilisk, or adder*)
his hand on the *c.* den. *Isa* 11:8
root shall come forth a *c.* 14:29
they hatch *c.* eggs. 59:5
I will send serpents, *c.* *Jer* 8:17

cockle
and let *c.* grow instead. *Job* 31:40

coffer
jewels of gold in a *c.* *1 Sam* 6:8
they laid ark and *c.* with mice. 11
Levites took down the *c.* with. 15

coffin
Joseph was put in *c.* in. *Gen* 50:26

cogitations
my *c.* much troubled me. *Dan* 7:28*

cold
c. and heat, day and. *Gen* 8:22
no covering in the *c.* *Job* 24:7
and *c.* cometh out of north. 37:9
stand before his *c.?* *Ps* 147:17
not plow by reason of *c.* *Pr* 20:4*
as the *c.* of snow in time. 25:13
taketh away a garment in *c.* 20
as *c.* waters to a thirsty soul. 25
shall *c.* flowing waters ? *Jer* 18:14
camp in hedges in *c.* day. *Nah* 3:17
a cup of *c.* water. *Mat* 10:42
love of many shall wax *c.* 24:12
a fire, for it was *c.* *John* 18:18
received us, because of *c.* *Acts* 28:2
in fastings often, in *c.* *2 Cor* 11:27
neither *c.* nor hot. *Rev* 3:15, 16

collar, -s
from Midian, beside *c.* *Judg* 8:26*
disease bindeth me as *c.* *Job* 30:18

collection
bring out of Judah *c. 2 Chr* 24:6*, 9*
concerning the *c.* for. *1 Cor* 16:1

college
dwelt in *c. 2 Ki* 22:14*; *2 Chr* 34:22*

collops
because he maketh *c.* of. *Job* 15:27†

colony
city of Macedonia, and *c.* *Acts* 16:12

Colosse
saints and brethren at *C.* *Col* 1:2

colour
have not changed his *c.* *Lev* 13:55
the *c.* as the *c.* of. *Num* 11:7*
when wine giveth his *c.* *Pr* 23:31
as the *c.* of amber. *Ezek* 1:4†
sparkled like *c.* of. 7†; *Dan* 10:6
wheels like unto *c.* of a. *Ezek* 1:16†
        10:9
firmament was as the *c.* of. 1:22†
under *c.* as though they. *Acts* 27:30
in purple and scarlet *c.* *Rev* 17:4*

coloured
woman sit on scarlet *c.* *Rev* 17:3

colours
coat of many *c.* for. *Gen* 37:3
Sisera a prey of divers *c.* *Judg* 5:30
a garment of divers *c.* *2 Sam* 13:18
stones of divers *c.* *1 Chr* 29:2
lay thy stones with fair *c.* *Isa* 54:11
deckedst high places with *c.*
        Ezek 16:16
an eagle with divers *c.* came. 17:3

colt, -s
camels with their *c.* forty. *Gen* 32:15
binding his ass' *c.* to the. 49:11
sons that rode on 30 ass *c.*
        Judg 10:4
nephews rode on 70 ass *c.* 12:14
born like a wild ass's *c.* *Job* 11:12
riding upon a *c.* *Zech* 9:9; *Mat* 21:5
        John 12:15
find ass tied. *c.* with her. *Mat* 21:2
  Mark 11:2; *Luke* 19:30
brought ass and *c.* and. *Mat* 21:7
        Mark 11:7
what do ye, loosing the *c.?*
    Mark 11:5; *Luke* 19:33
cast garments on *c.* *Luke* 19:35

come
[1] *To draw nigh, or approach,*
Ex 34:3. [2] *To proceed from,*
Chr 29:14. [3] *To attain to,*
Acts 26:7. [4] *To touch,* *Ezek*
44:25. [5] *To arise,* *Num* 24:7.
two of every sort shall *c.* *Gen* 6:20
c. thou, and all thy house. 7:1
c. let us make our father. 19:32
wherefore *c.* ye to me ? 26:27
c. let us make a covenant. 31:44
c. let us slay him, and cast. 37:10
whence *c.* ye ? 42:7; *Josh* 9:8
bring your father and *c.* *Gen* 45:19
from Judah till Shiloh *c.* 49:10
lo, I *c.* to thee in a. *Ex* 19:9
I record name I will *c.* and. 20:24
people to whom thou shalt *c.* 23:27
c. thou with us, we will. *Num* 10:29
c. I pray thee, curse this. 22:6, 11
out of Jacob shall *c.* he. 24:19
if a Levite *c.* and *c.* *Deut* 18:6

all these blessings shall *c.* *Deut* 28:2
all these curses *c.* on thee. 15, 45
no razor *c.* on his head. *Judg* 13:5
        1 Sam 1:11
shall *c.* on thy two sons. *1 Sam* 2:34
people will not eat till he *c.* 9:13
tarry, till I *c.* to thee. 10:8
but I *c.* to thee in the name. 17:45
then *c.* thou, for there is. 20:21
shall ark of Lord *c.* to ? *2 Sam* 6:9
I will *c.* on him while he is. 17:2
c. thou over with me and I. 19:33
and the oath *c.* before. *1 Ki* 8:31
if any thing would *c.* from. 20:33
feed this fellow until I *c.* in. 22:27
let him *c.* now to me. *2 Ki* 5:8
till I *c.* and take. 18:32; *Isa* 36:17
riches and honour *c.* *1 Chr* 29:12
all things *c.* of thee, and of. 14
ark of Lord hath *c.* *2 Chr* 8:11
Vashti refused to *c.* at. *Esth* 1:12
how endure to see evil *c.* to ? 8:6
let no joyful voice *c.* *Job* 3:7
that I may speak, let *c.* on. 13:13
will I wait till my change *c.* 14:14
his sons *c.* to honour, and he. 21
caused it to *c.* for correction. 37:13
hitherto shalt thou *c.* but. 38:11
lo, I *c.* *Ps* 40:7; *Heb* 10:7, 9
when shall I *c.* and appear ? *Ps* 42:2
our God shall *c.* and not. 50:3
unto thee shall all flesh *c.* 65:2
stir up thy strength, and *c.* 80:2
all nations shall *c.* and. 86:9
when wilt thou *c.* unto me ? 101:2
loved cursing, so let it *c.* 109:17
mercies *c.* unto me. 119:41, 77
shall thy poverty *c.* *Pr* 6:11; 24:34
fear of the wicked shall *c.* 10:24
curse causeless shall not *c.* 26:2
all things *c.* alike to all. *Eccl* 9:2
up, my love, and *c.* *S of S* 2:10, 13
c. with me from Lebanon. 4:8
and *c.* thou south, blow upon. 16
of Holy One of Israel. *Isa* 5:19
c. from a far country. 13:5
the day of the Lord, it shall *c.* 6
inquire ye ; return, *c.* 21:12
c. my people, enter into. 26:20
cause them that *c.* of Jacob. 27:6
c. with vengeance, he will *c.* 35:4
the Lord will *c.* with a. 40:10
raised up one, and he shall *c.* 41:25
things coming, and shall *c.* 44:7
assemble yourselves, and *c.* 45:20
even to him shall men *c.* 24
the redeemed shall *c.* with. 51:11
c. ye to the waters, *c.* ye, buy, *c.* 55:1
c. unto me, hear, and your. 3
and the Redeemer shall *c.* 59:20
Gentiles shall *c.* to thy light. 60:3, 5
behold, Lord will *c.* with fire. 66:15
say they, we will *c.* *Jer* 2:31
behold, we *c.* to thee, for thou. 3:22
mourning women, that they *c.* 9:17
wherefore *c.* these things ? 13:22
word of the Lord ? let it *c.* 17:15
him till time of his land *c.* 27:7
they shall *c.* with weeping. 31:9
princes hear, and *c.* to thee. 38:25
good to *c.* If ill to *c.* forbear. 40:4
as Carmel, so shall he *c.* 46:18
trusted, saying, who shall *c.?* 49:4
none *c.* to solemn feasts. *Lam* 1:4
let all their wickedness *c.* 22
abominations whither they *c.*
        Ezek 12:16
save souls alive that *c.?* 13:18
that sword may *c.* 21:19, 20 ; 32:11
shall be no more, till he *c.* 21:27
he seeth the sword *c.* on. 33:3, 6
they *c.* to thee as the people. 34
lo it will *c.* then shall know. 33
they are at hand to *c.* 36:8
c. let us return to Lord. *Hos* 6:1
and he shall *c.* to us, as the. 3
to seek the Lord till he *c.* 10:12
as a destruction shall it *c.* *Joel* 1:15
before terrible day of Lord *c.* 2:31
c. let us cast lots. *Jonah* 1:7
to thee shall it *c.* kingdom. *Mi* 4:8
because it will surely *c.* *Hab* 2:3
anger of Lord *c.* on you. *Zeph* 2:2
what *c.* these to do ? *Zech* 1:21

7

God shall *c.* and all the. *Zech* 14:5
Lord ye seek shall *c.* *Mal* 3:1
lest I *c.* and smite the earth. 4:6
for out of thee shall *c.* *Mat* 2:6
first be reconciled, then *c.* 5:24
thy kingdom *c.* thy. 6:10; *Luke* 11:2
false prophets *c.* to you in. *Mat* 7:15
Jesus saith to him, I will *c.* 8:7
not worthy thou shouldest *c.* 8
and to another, *c.* and. 9; *Luke* 7:8
many shall *c.* from east. *Mat* 8:11
he that should *c.?* 11:3; *Luke* 7:19
　　　　　　　　　　　　　　　20
c. all ye that labour and. *Mat* 11:28
if any man will *c.* after me. 16:24
Elias must first *c.?* 17:10, 11
sell, and *c.* 19:21; *Luke* 18:22
all things are ready, *c.* *Mat* 22:4
preached, then shall end *c.* 24:14
what hour your Lord doth *c.* 42
c. ye blessed of my Father. 25:34
art thou *c.* to destroy us ?
　　　　　　　Mark 1:24 *Luke* 4:34
whosoever will *c.* after me let him
deny. *Mark* 8:34; *Luke* 9:23; 14:27
suffer the little children to *c.* unto
me. *Mark* 10:14; *Luke* 18:16
c. take up the cross. *Mark* 10:21
this is the heir, *c.* let us kill.
　　　　　　　　　　　Luke 20:14
he himself would *c.* *Luke* 10:1
three years I *c.* seeking fruit. 13:7
there are six days, in them *c.* 14
kingdom of God should *c.* 17:20
occupy till I *c.* 19:13
he shall *c.* and destroy. 20:16
till kingdom of God shall *c.* 22:18
c. and see. *John* 1:39
baptizeth, and all men *c.* to him. 3:26
lest a worse thing *c.* to thee. 5:14
ye will not *c.* to me, that ye. 40
Father giveth me shall *c.* 6:37
c. to me, except Father. 44, 65
thither ye cannot *c.* 7:34
let him *c.* to me and drink. 37
ye cannot tell whence I *c.* and. 8:14
you before it *c.* that when it *c.* 13:19
comfortless, I will *c.* 14:18
and we will *c.* unto him. 23
these are in the world, I *c.* 17:11, 13
if I will he tarry till I *c.?* 21:22, 23
this Jesus shall so *c.* *Acts* 1:11
and notable day of Lord *c.* 2:20
when times of refreshing *c.* 3:19
c. down and now *c.* I will send. 7:34
pray that none of these *c.* 8:24
that he would not delay to *c.* 9:38
lest that *c.* on you that is. 13:40
c. over into Macedonia. 16:9
believe on him that should *c.* 19:4
forbid no acquaintance to *c.* 24:23
our twelve tribes hope to *c.* 26:7*
and Moses did say should *c.* 22
let us do evil, that good *c.* *Rom* 3:8
at this time, will I *c.* 9:9
judge nothing till Lord *c.* *1 Cor* 4:5
the Lord's death till he *c.* 11:26
rest will I set in order when I *c.* 34
with what body do they *c.?* 15:35
no gatherings when I *c.* 16:2
if Timothy *c.* see he be with you. 10
I desired him to *c.* to you. 12
I was minded to *c.* to. *2 Cor* 1:15
for I fear, lest when I *c.* I. 12:20
if righteousness *c.* by law. *Gal* 2:21
blessing of Abraham *c.* on. 3:14
till the seed should *c.* to whom. 19
when he shall *c.* to be. *2 Thes* 1:10
day shall not *c.* except there *c.* 2:3*
and of that to *c.* *1 Tim* 4:8
till I *c.* give attendance to. 13
perilous times shall *c.* *2 Tim* 3:1
time will *c.* they will not endure. 4:3
be diligent to *c.* to me. *Tit* 3:12
let us *c.* boldly to the. *Heb* 4:16
he is able to save them that *c.* 7:25
he that shall *c.* will *c.* and. 10:37
whence *c.* wars, *c.* they ? *Jas* 4:1
weep for miseries that shall *c.* 5:1
but that all should *c.* *2 Pet* 3:9
day of Lord will *c.* as a thief in the
night. 10; *Rev* 3:3; 16:15
antichrist shall *c.* *1 John* 2:18
if I *c.* I will remember. *3 John* 10

repent, or else I will *c.* *Rev* 2:5
hold fast till I *c.* 25
I *c.* quickly, hold. 3:11; 22:7, 20
four beasts, saying, *c.* 6:1, 3, 5, 7
in one hour is judgement *c.* 18:10
and let him that is athirst *c.* 22:17

come *again*
so that I *c. again* to my. *Gen* 28:21
that waters may *c. again.* *Ex* 14:26
if the plague *c. again.* *Lev* 14:43
when I *c. again* in peace. *Judg* 8:9
let man of God *c. again* to us. 13:8
to Gath, and was *c. again. 1 Ki* 2:41
and then *c. again.* 12:5; *2 Chr* 10:5
this child's soul *c. again. 1 Ki* 17:21
Israel *c. again. Ezra* 6:21; *Neh* 8:17
he shall *c. again.* *Ps* 126:6
say not go and *c. again.* *Pr* 3:28
Chaldeans shall *c. again.* *Jer* 37:8
when I *c. again* I will. *Luke* 10:35
I will *c. again* and. *John* 14:3
I go away and *c. again.* 28
that I would not *c. again. 2 Cor* 2:1
lest, when I *c. again,* God. 12:21
I write, that if I *c. again.* I. 13:2

come *down*
c. down to me, tarry not. *Gen* 45:9
I am *c. down* to deliver. *Ex* 3:8
the Lord will *c. down* on. 19:11
I will *c. down* and talk. *Num* 11:17
from heaven it *c. down.* *Deut* 28:24
saying, *c. down* against. *Judg* 7:24
they said, we are *c. down.* 15:12
c. down and fetch ark. *1 Sam* 6:21
will Saul *c. down* ? he will *c. down.*
　　　　　　　　　　　　　　　23:11
c. down, according to the. 20
thou shalt not *c. down.* *2 Ki* 1:4
　　　　　　　　　　　　　　　6:16
thou man of God, *c. down.* 1:9
let fire *c. down.* 10, 11, 12
work, I cannot *c. down.* *Neh* 6:3
his dealing shall *c. down.* *Ps* 7:16
he shall *c. down* like rain. 72:6
the heavens, and *c. down.* 144:5
my sword, it shall *c. down. Isa* 34:5
c. down, sit in the dust. 47
that thou wouldest *c. down.* 64:1
your principalities shall *c. down.*
　　　　　　　　　　　　　　　Jer 13:18
who shall *c. down* against us ? 21:13
c. down from thy glory. 48:18
of the sea shall *c. down. Ezek* 26:16
all pilots shall *c. down* from. 27:29
of her power shall *c. down.* 30:6
cause mighty to *c. down.* *Joel* 3:11
not *c. down* to take. *Mat* 24:17
c. down from cross. 27:40, 42
　　　　　　　　　　　　Mark 15:30
fire to *c. down* ? *Luke* 9:54
Zacchaeus, haste and *c. down.* 19:5
Sir, *c. down* ere child. *John* 4:49
the gods are *c. down.* *Acts* 14:11
devil is *c. down* to you. *Rev* 12:12
maketh fire *c. down* from. 13:13
angel *c. down* having key. 20:1

come *forth*
he that shall *c. forth* out. *Gen* 15:4
Hebrews *c. forth* out. *1 Sam* 14:11
thus saith king, *c. forth. 1 Ki* 2:30
slay them, let none *c. forth.*
　　　　　　　　　　　　2 Ki 10:25
I shall *c. forth* as gold. *Job* 23:10
let my sentence *c. forth.* *Ps* 17:2
and I cannot *c. forth.* 88:8
feareth God shall *c. forth. Eccl* 7:18
shall *c. forth* a rod out of. *Isa* 11:1
art *c. forth* out of waters. 48:1
my fury *c. forth* like fire. *Jer* 4:4*
Pharaoh's army was *c. forth.* 37:5, 7
let mighty men *c. forth.* 46:9*
a fire shall *c. forth* out of. 48:45
twain shall *c. forth. Ezek* 21:19
servants of most high God, *c. forth.*
　　　　　　　　　　　　Dan 3:26
O Daniel, I am *c. forth* to. 9:22
a fountain shall *c. forth.* *Joel* 3:18
out of thee shall *c. forth.* *Mi* 5:2
c. forth and flee from land. *Zech* 2:6
angels shall *c. forth.* *Mat* 13:49
c. forth from the heart. 15:18
this kind *c. forth* by. *Mark* 9:29

and will *c. forth* and. *Luke* 12:37
shall *c. forth,* they that. *John* 5:29
cried, Lazarus, *c. forth.* 11:43
shall *c. forth* and serve. *Acts* 7:7

come *hither*
fourth generation *c. hither.*
　　　　　　　　　　　　Gen 15:16
Samson is *c. hither.* *Judg* 16:2
c. thou *hither* and eat. *Ruth* 2:14
inquired if the man should *c. hither.*
　　　　　　　　　　　　1 Sam 10:22
not sit down till he *c. hither.* 16:11
c. hither that I may. *2 Sam* 14:32
say to Joab, *c. hither* that I. 20:16
man of God is *c. hither.* *2 Ki* 8:7
said to thee, *c.* up *hither.* *Pr* 25:7
c. forth and *c. hither.* *Dan* 3:26
thou *c. hither* to torment ? *Mat* 8:29
neither *c. hither* to draw. *John* 4:15
call thy husband and *c. hither.* 16
turned world are *c. hither. Acts* 17:6
c. up h. *Rev* 4:1; 11:12; 17:1; 21:9

I am **come,** or *am I* **come**
I thy father-in-law am *c.* *Ex* 18:6
lo *I am c.* to thee. *Num* 22:38
I am c. into country. *Deut* 26:3
I am c. to sacrifice. *1 Sam* 16:2, 5
now that *I am c.* to. *2 Sam* 14:15
wherefore *am I c.* from ? 32
I am c. first to meet my. 19:20
I am c. into deep waters. *Ps* 69:2
I communed, lo, *I am c.* *Eccl* 1:16
I am c. into my garden. *S of S* 5:1
I am c. to shew. *Dan* 9:23; 10:14
I am c. for thy words. 10:12
think not *I am c.* to. *Mat* 5:17
I am not *c.* to call righteous. 9:13
think not that *I am c.* to. 10:34
I am c. to set a man at. 35
suppose ye that *I am c. Luke* 12:51
am *I c.* baptizing with. *John* 1:31
I am c. in my Father's name. 5:43
I am not *c.* of myself. 7:28
for judgement *I am c.* into. 9:39
I am c. that they might have. 10:10
I am c. a light into world. 12:46
I am c. into the world. 16:28

come *in,* or *into.*
shalt *c. into* the ark, and. *Gen* 6:18
not a man in earth to *c. in.* 19:31
said, *c. in* thou blessed of. 24:31
destroyer to *c. in.* *Ex* 12:23
when they *c. in* unto the. 28:43*
afterward shall *c. into* the camp.
　　　　Lev 16:26, 28; *Num* 19:7; 31:24
at his word shall *c. in.* *Num* 27:21
no more go out and *c. in. Deut* 31:2
to go out and *c. in.* *Josh* 14:11
I will *c. in* after thee. *1 Ki* 1:14
not how to go out or *c. in.* 3:7
he said, *c. in* thou wife of. 14:6
suffer any to go out or *c. in.* 15:17
when *c. in* shut door. *2 Ki* 4:4
took each his men to *c. in.* 11:9
go out and *c. in* before. *2 Chr* 1:10
let none go out or *c. in* to Asa. 16:1
none *c. into* the house of Lord. 23:6
till I *c. into* Judah. *Neh* 2:7
Esther let no man *c. in. Esth* 5:12
king said, let Haman *c. in.* 6:5
King of glory shall *c. in. Ps* 24:7, 9
for the waters are *c. in.* 69:1
offering and *c. into* his courts. 96:8
so let it *c. into* his bowels. 109:18
let my beloved *c. into. S of S* 4:16
Lord shall *c. into* Egypt. *Isa* 19:1
the Assyrian shall *c. into.* 23
shut up, that no man *c. in.* 24:10
when the enemy shall *c. in.* 59:19
the kings of Judah *c. in. Jer* 17:19
and let Jerusalem *c. in.* 51:50
strangers are *c. into* the. 51
things that *c. into* mind. *Ezek* 11:5
shall things *c. into* thy mind. 38:10
Assyrian shall *c. into* land. *Mi* 5:5
ye *c. into* an house. *Mat* 10:12*
Son of man shall *c. in* glory. 16:27
many shall *c. in* my name. 24:5
　　　　　　Mark 13:6; *Luke* 21:8
Son of man *c. in* his glory. *Mat* 25:31
which *c. in* may see. *Luke* 11:33*
c. in second watch, or *c. in.* 12:38

will *c. in* a day when he. *Luke* 12:46
and compel them to *c. in.*   14:23
lest they *c. into* this place.   16:28
c. in my Father's name, if another *c.*
   in his own name.   *John* 5:43
should *c. into* world.   6:14; 11:27
Lydia, saying, *c. into.*   *Acts* 16:15
of Gentiles be *c. in.*   *Rom* 11:25
there is *c. in* those that.   *1 Cor* 14:23
if there *c. in* one that.   24
there is *c. in* also a poor man. *Jas* 2:2
I will *c. in* to him, and.   *Rev* 3:20

come, *passive*

the end of all flesh *is c.*   *Gen* 6:13
for therefore are ye *c. to.*   18:5
the cry which *is c.* to me.   21
therefore *is* this distress *c.*   42:21
cry of children of Israel *is c. Ex* 3:9
fear not, for God *is c.* to.   20:20
there is a people *c. out. Num* 22:11
when all Israel *is c.* to. *Deut* 31:11
host of Lord am I *c.*   *Josh* 5:14
Samson *is c.* hither.   *Judg* 16:2
said, God *is c.* into.   *1 Sam* 4:7
because their cry *is c.* to me.   9:16
anguish *is c.* upon me.   *2 Sam* 1:9
speech of all Israel *is c.* to.   19:11
the creditor *is c.* to.   *2 Ki* 4:1
when this letter *is c.* to thee.   5:6
man of God *is c.* hither.   8:7
and after all that *is c.*   *Ezra* 9:13
thing I feared *is c.*   *Job* 3:25; 4:5
all this *is c.* upon us.   *Ps* 44:17
salvation of Israel were *c.*   53:6
and trembling are *c.*   55:5
I am *c.* into deep waters.   69:2
yea the set time *is c.*   102:13
he *is c.* to Aiath.   *Isa* 10:28
my salvation *is* near to *c.*   56:1
light *is c.* and glory of Lord.   60:1
year of my redeemed *is c.*   63:4
sinned, therefore this *is c. Jer* 40:3
baldness *is c.* on Gaza.   47:5
woe to them, their day *is c.*   50:27
thy day *is c.* the time that.   31
on many waters, thy end *is c.* 51:13
our end *is c.*   *Lam* 4:18
remember, O Lord, what *is c.*   5:1
end, the end *is c.*   *Ezek* 7:2, 6
an only evil, behold, *is c.*   5
the morning *is c.* upon thee.   7
the day, behold, it *is c.*   10; 39:8
king of Babylon *is c.* to.   17:12
prince whose day *is c.*   21:25, 29
all this evil *is c.* on us.   *Dan* 9:13
the end *is c.* on my.   *Amos* 8:2
he *is c.* to gate of my.   *Mi* 1:9
to flee from wrath to *c.? Mat* 3:7
the kingdom of God *is c.*   12:28
when he *is c.* he findeth it.   44
Son of man *is c.* to save lost. 18:11
because the harvest *is c. Mark* 4:29
she *is c.* aforehand to anoint.   14:8
it is enough, the hour *is c.*   41
the Son of man *is c. Luke* 7:34
thy brother *is c.* father hath. 15:27
this day *is* salvation to *c.* to. 19:9
the Son of man *is c.* to seek.   10
that light *is c.* into the. *John* 3:19
when he *is c.* he will tell.   4:25
the Master *is c.* and calleth. 11:28
hour *is c.* Son of man. 12:23; 17:1
when the Comforter *is c.*   15:26
when he *is c.* he will reprove. 16:8
when the Spirit of truth *is c.*   13
sorrow because hour *is c.*   22
salvation *is c.* unto the. *Rom* 11:11
for your obedience *is c.*   16:19
is perfect *is c.* then.   *1 Cor* 13:10
but after that faith *is c.*   *Gal* 3:25
which gospel *is c.* to you.   *Col* 1:6
Jesus Christ *is c. in. 1 John* 4:2
confesseth not that Jesus Christ *is c.*
   in flesh is not of God. 3; *2 John* 7
know Son of God *is c. 1 John* 5:20
great day of wrath *is c.*   *Rev* 6:17
and thy wrath *is c.* and.   11:18
is c. salvation and strength. 12:10
hour of his judgement *is c.*   14:7
great riches *is c.* to nought. 18:17
for marriage of Lamb *is c.*   19:7

come *near*

Abram was *c. near* to.   *Gen* 12:11

will *c. in* a day when he. *Luke* 12:46

Abimelech had not *c. near. Gen* 20:4
let him *c. near* and keep. *Ex* 12:48
c. near before the Lord.   16:9
c. near to the altar.   28:43; 30:20
cause him to *c. near. Num* 16:5
that no stranger *c. near* to.   40
c. near, put feet on.   *Josh* 10:24
caused tribes to *c. near. 1 Sam* 10:20
lest they *c. near* unto thee. *Ps* 32:9*
let my cry *c. near* before.   119:169
let us *c. near* together.   *Isa* 41:1
c. ye near unto me, hear ye. 48:16
adversary ? let him *c. near* me. 50:8
nor hath *c. near* to a.   *Ezek* 18:6
which *c. near* to the Lord to. 40:46
they shall *c. near* to me.   44:15
they shall *c. near* to my table.   16
of violence to *c. near. Amos* 6:3
and I will *c. near* to you.   *Mal* 3:5
when he was *c. near. Luke* 19:41
we, or he *c. near,* are.   *Acts* 23:15

come *nigh*

afraid to *c. nigh* him.   *Ex* 34:30
sanctified in all that *c. nigh* me.
              Lev 10:3
hath blemish *c. nigh.*   21:21, 23
a stranger not *c. nigh. Num* 18:4
you are *c. nigh* to battle. *Deut* 20:2
kingdom of God *c. nigh* unto you.
           Luke 10:9, 11

come *not*

be ready, *c. not* at your.   *Ex* 19:15
but they shall *c. nigh.*   24:2
ye shall *not c.* into land. *Num* 14:30
we will *not c.* up.   16:12, 14
unclean shall *not c.*   *Deut* 23:10
c. not near unto the ark. *Josh* 3:4
that ye *c. not* among.   23:7
hath *not c.* a razor on. *Judg* 16:17
would *not c.* he sent the second time,
   he would *not c.*   *2 Sam* 14:29
carcase *not c.* to.   *1 Ki* 13:22
king of Assyria shall *not c.* into.
   2 Ki 19:32, 33; *Isa* 37:33, 34
I *c. not* against thee.   *2 Chr* 35:21
whosoever would *not c. Ezra* 10:8
Moabite *not c.* into.   *Neh* 13:1*
not c. into the number.   *Job* 3:6
an hypocrite shall *not c.*   13:16
floods they shall *not c.*   *Ps* 32:6
let them *not c.* into thy.   69:27
it shall *not c.* nigh thee.   91:7
I will *not c.* into tabernacle. 132:3
c. not nigh the door.   *Pr* 5:8
days that have *not c.*   *Isa* 7:17
there shall *not c.* the fear of.   25
scourge shall *not c.* to me.   28:15
the gathering shall *not c.*   32:10
terror, it shall *not c.* near thee. 54:14
by thyself, *c. not* near me.   65:5
king of Babylon shall *not c. Jer* 37:19
like things shall *not c. Ezek* 16:16
they shall *not c.* near to me. 44:13
c. not ye unto Gilgal.   *Hos* 4:15
their soul shall *not c.* into.   9:4
family of Egypt *c. not. Zech* 14:18*
and they would *not c.*   *Mat* 22:3
could *not c.* nigh for.   *Mark* 2:4
          Luke 8:19
married a wife, I *cannot c.*
         Luke 14:20
and shall *not c.* into.   *John* 5:24
ye will *not c.* to me that ye.   40
thither ye *cannot c.*   7:34, 36
think ye that he will *not c.?* 11:56
if I had *not c.* they had.   15:22
not away, Comforter will *not c.* 16:7
as though I would *not c. 1 Cor* 4:18

come *out*

afterwards shall *c. out. Gen* 15:14
kings. *c. out* of thee.   17:6; 35:11
daughters of city *c. out.*   24:13
till he *c. out* and have.   *Lev* 16:17
shall eat till it *c. out. Num* 11:20
c. out ye three unto.   12:4
lest I *c. out* against thee.   20:18
people *c. out* of Egypt.   22:5, 11
year after Israel were *c. out.* 33:38
c. out one way, and.   *Deut* 28:7
let fire *c. out* of the.   *Judg* 9:15
increase army and *c. out.*   29
let not arrogancy *c. out. 1 Sam* 2:3
to-morrow we will *c. out.*   11:3, 10

---

king of Israel *c. out ?*   *1 Sam* 24:14
c. out, c. out, thou.   *2 Sam* 16:7*
480th year after Israel were *c. out.*
          1 Ki 6:1
there are men *c. out.*   20:17
he will *c. out* to me.   *2 Ki* 5:11
agreement and *c. out.*   18:31
         Isa 36:16
behold, he is *c. out* to fight. *2 Ki* 19:9
salvation were *c. out.*   *Ps* 14:7
princes shall *c. out* of.   68:31
the just shall *c. out.*   *Pr* 12:13
their stink shall *c. out. Isa* 34:3
there is one *c. out.*   *Nah* 1:11*
by no means *c. out* till.   *Mat* 5:26
are ye *c. out* as against a thief? 26:55
   Mark 14:48; *Luke* 22:52
hold thy peace, and *c. out* of him.
   Mark 1:25; *Luke* 4:35
c. out, unclean spirit.   *Mark* 5:8
         Luke 8:29
any good thing *c. out* of ? *John* 1:46
Christ *c. out* of Galilee ?   7:41
name of Jesus to *c. out. Acts* 16:18
there shall *c. out* of.   *Rom* 11:26
wherefore *c. out* from.   *2 Cor* 6:17
though they *c. out* of loins. *Heb* 7:5
saw spirits *c. out* of.   *Rev* 16:13
c. out of her, my people.   18:4

come *to pass*

it shall *c. to pass* if they. *Ex* 4:8, 9
word shall *c. to pass* or. *Num* 11:23
c. to pass the man's rod I.   17:5
c. to pass if ye hearken. *Deut* 7:12
         11:13; 28:1
sign or wonder *c. to pass.*   13:2
all are *c. to pass,* no.   *Josh* 23:14
let thy words *c. to pass. Judg* 13:12
when thy sayings *c. to pass.*   17
why is this *c. to pass in ?*   21:3
shall surely *c. to pass. 1 Ki* 13:32
nor shall it *c. to pass.*   *Isa* 7:7
so shall it *c. to pass.*   14:24
former things are *c. to pass.*   42:9
it shall *c. to pass* if ye.   *Jer* 17:24
hast spoken is *c. to pass.*   32:24
I speak shall *c. to pass. Ezek* 12:25
it shall *c. to pass,* I will do it. 24:14
to thee what shall *c. to p. Dan* 2:29
c. to pass that I will break. *Hos* 1:5
c. to pass that whosoever. *Joel* 2:32
c. to pass I will cause sun. *Amos* 8:9
this shall *c. to pass.*   *Zech* 6:15
therefore it is *c. to pass,* that. 7:13
things must *c. to pass.*   *Mat* 24:6
saith shall *c. to pass.*   *Mark* 11:23
ye shall see these *c. to pass.* 13:29
         Luke 21:31
thing which is *c. to pass. Luke* 2:15
sign when things shall *c. to pass.*
         21:7, 28
wondering at what was *c. to pass.*
         24:12
not known things which *c. to pass.* 18
when it is *c. to pass. John* 13:19
         14:29
c. to pass that every.   *Acts* 3:23
must shortly *c. to pass. Rev* 1:1
         22:6

come *short*

sinned and *c. short* of.   *Rom* 3:23
seem to *c. short* of it.   *Heb* 4:1

come *joined with time*

answer in *time* to *c.*   *Gen* 30:33
son asketh thee in *time* to *c.*
   Ex 13:14; *Deut* 6:20; *Josh* 4:6, 21
in *time* to *c.* your.   *Josh* 22:24, 28
time was *c.* after.   *1 Sam* 1:20
time to favour Zion, set *time* is *c.*
         Ps 102:13
rejoice in *time* to *c.*   *Pr* 31:25
time of singing of birds is *c.*
         S of S 2:12
her *time* is near to *c.*   *Isa* 13:22
that it may be for *time* to *c.*   30:8
hearken and hear for *time* to *c.* 42:23
time is *c.* the day of.   *Ezek* 7:7
time is not *c.* the Lord's.   *Hag* 1:2
time was *c.* he should.   *Luke* 9:51
fulness of *time* was *c.*   *Gal* 4:4
foundation against *time* to *c.*
         1 Tim 6:19
time is *c.* that judgement. *1 Pet* 4:17

come together

we should c. together. *Job* 9:32
his troops c. together against. 19:12
shall c. together out of. *Jer* 3:18
and Judah shall c. together. 50:4
were c. together. *Acts* 1:6; 28:17
many that were c. together. 10:27
wherefore they were c. together.
　　　　　　　　　　　　　19:32
multitude must c. together. 21:22
c. together again, that. *1 Cor* 7:5*
c. together, not for better. 11:17
c. together in church. 18, 20, 33
　　　　　　　　　　　　14:26
c. not together to condemnation.
　　　　　　　　　　　　11:34
if church be c. together. 14:23

come up

trumpet sound shall c. up. *Ex* 19:13
thou shalt c. up, thou and. 24
c. up to me into the mount. 24:12
I will c. up into midst of. 33:5
and c. up in the morning to. 34:2
no man shall c. up with thee. 3
us c. up out of Egypt ? *Num* 20:5
c. up out of Jordan. *Josh* 4:16, 17, 18
c. up to me, and help me to. 10:4
c. up to us quickly, save us. 6
c. up with me into my lot. *Judg* 1:3
why are ye c. up against ? 15:10
saying, c. up this once. 16:18
if they say, c. up to us. *1 Sam* 14:10
this man that is c. up ? 17:25
then ye shall c. up. *1 Ki* 1:35
king of Syria will c. up. 20:12
c. up and save me. *2 Ki* 16:7
am I now c. up without Lord. 18:25
　　　　　　　　　　　Isa 36:10
they c. up by the cliff. *2 Chr* 20:16
shall c. up no more. *Job* 7:9
be said, c. up hither. *Pr* 25:7
there shall c. up briers. *Isa* 5:6
and he shall c. up over all his. 8:7
laid down no fellow is c. up. 14:8
they shall c. up with. 60:7
death is c. up into our. *Jer* 9:21
c. up like a lion. 49:19; 50:44
behold, he shall c. up and fly. 49:22
cause the horses to c. up as. 51:27
sea is c. up upon Babylon. 42
and c. up upon my neck. *Lam* 1:14
cause fury to c. up to. *Ezek* 24:8
and cause you to c. up out. 37:12
thou shalt c. up against my. 38:16
c. up out of the land. *Hos* 1:11*
the thistle shall c. up on. 10:8
wind of Lord shall c. up. 13:15
and ill savour shall c. up. *Joel* 2:20
draw near, let them c up. 3:9
let heathen c. up to valley of.
of your camps to c. up. *Amos* 4:10
saviours shall c. up on. *Obad* 21
wickedness is c. up before me.
　　　　　　　　　　　Jonah 1:2
made a gourd to c. up over. 4:6
the breaker c. up before. *Mi* 2:13
dasheth in pieces is c. up. *Nah* 2:1
whoso will not c. up. *Zech* 14:17
desired Philip to c. up. *Acts* 8:31
were c. up out of the water.
Cornelius, thy alms are c. up. 10:4*
c. up hither, and I. *Rev* 4:1; 11:12

yet come

ye are not as yet c. *Deut* 24:3
my hour is not yet c. *John* 2:4
my time is not yet c. 7:6, 8
his hour was not yet c. 30; 8:20
Jesus was not yet c. 11:30
the other is not yet c. *Rev* 17:10

comeliness

he hath no form nor c. nor. *Isa* 53:2
perfect through my c. *Ezek* 16:14*
Persia and Lud set forth thy c. 27:10
my c. was turned in me. *Dan* 10:8
have more abundant c. *1 Cor* 12:23

comely

David, a c. person. *1 Sam* 16:18
not conceal c. proportion. *Job* 41:12†
praise is c. for the. *Ps* 33:1; 147:1
yea, four are c. in going. *Pr* 30:29*
it is c. for one to eat. *Eccl.* 5:18
I am black but c. *S of S* 1:5
thy cheeks are c. with rows. 10

and thy countenance is c. *S of S* 2:14
thy speech is c. 4:3
thou art c. O my love, as. 6:4
shall be excellent and c. *Isa* 4:2
daughter of Zion to a c. *Jer* 6:2
speak for that which is c. *1 Cor* 7:35*
is it c. that a woman pray ? 11:13*
our c. parts have no need. 12:24

comers

can never make the c. *Heb* 10:1*

comest

from Sidon as thou c. *Gen* 10:19*
Egypt, as thou c. unto Zoar. 13:10*
when thou c. to my kindred. 24:41
thou c. nigh children of. *Deut* 2:19
when thou c. nigh to city. 20:10*
blessed when thou c. in. 28:6
cursed when thou c. in. 19
Micah ... whence c. thou ? *Judg* 17:9
old man ... whence c. thou ? 19:17
c. thou peaceably ? *1 Sam* 16:4
　　　　　　　　　　　1 Ki 2:13
I a dog, that thou c. to. *1 Sam* 17:43
thou c. to me with a sword. 45
bring Michal when c. *2 Sam* 3:13
when thou c. anoint. *1 Ki* 19:15
whence c. thou, Gehazi ? *2 Ki* 5:25
whence c. thou ? Satan. *Job* 1:7; 2:2
when thou c. to Babylon. *Jer* 51:61
occupation ? whence c.? *Jonah* 1:8
and c. thou to me ? *Mat* 3:14
remember me when c. *Luke* 23:42

cometh

behold this dreamer c. *Gen* 37:19
on which such water c. is. *Lev* 11:34
beside what c. of sale. *Deut* 18:8
cover that which c. from. 23:13
when ark c. among us. *1 Sam* 4:3
all that man of God saith c. 9:6
wherefore c. not the son of ? 20:27
he c. not to the king's table. 29
for when she c. in will. *1 Ki* 14:5
but he c. not again. *2 Ki* 9:18, 20
king as he c. in. 11:8; *2 Chr* 23:7
for death, and it c. not. *Job* 3:21
whence c. wisdom ? 28:20
but joy c. in the morning. *Ps* 30:5
from him cometh my salvation. 62:1
promotion c. not from the east. 75:6
before Lord, for he c. to. 96:13
blessed is he that c. in name. 118:26
from whence c. my help. 121:1
will mock when your fear c. *Pr* 1:26
when your destruction c. 27
when pride c. then c. shame. 11:2
when the wicked c. then c. 18:3
he c. in with vanity. *Eccl* 6:4
all that c. is vanity. 11:8
he c. leaping upon. *S of S* 2:8
the day of the Lord c. *Isa* 13:9
whose breaking c. suddenly. 30:13
the name of the Lord c. from. 27
behold, thy salvation c. 62:11
is this that c. from Edom ? 63:1
shall not see when good c. *Jer* 17:6
and shall not see when heat c. 8
when he c. he shall smite. 43:11
saith, and it c. to pass. *Lam* 3:37
c. to a prophet to. *Ezek* 14:4, 7
that which c. in your mind. 20:32
because it c. behold it c. 21:7
when this c. ye shall know I. 24:24
come to these as people c. 33:31
when this c. to pass, then shall. 33
thing live whither rivers c. 47:9
that c. against him. *Dan* 11:16
blessed is he that c. to. 12:12
the thief c. in, and the. *Hos* 7:1*
day of the Lord c. *Joel* 2:1
　　　　Zech 14:1; *1 Thes* 5:2
from Assyrians when he c. *Mi* 5:6
the day c. that shall burn as an oven;
　　the day that c. *Mal* 4:1
he that c. after me is. *Mat* 3:11
　　　　　Mark 1:7; *Luke* 3:16
more than these c. of evil. *Mat* 5:37
come, and he c. 8:9; *Luke* 7:8
then c. the wicked one. *Mat* 13:19
king c. unto thee. 21:5; *John* 12:15
he that c. in name of Lord. *Mat* 21:9
　　　Mark 11:9; *Luke* 13:35; 19:38
lord of those servants c. *Mat* 25:19

he c. to them walking. *Mark* 6:48
be ashamed when he c. in. 8:38
Elias c. first, and restoreth. 9:12
while he yet spake, c. Judas. 14:43
whoso c. to me. *Luke* 5:47
the Lord when he c. 12:37
Son of man c. at an hour. 40
his lord, when he c. shall find. 43
there will be heat, and it c. 55
kingdom of God c. not. 17:20
Son of man c. shall he find ? 18:8
canst not tell whence it c. *John* 3:8
nor c. to the light. 20
he that doeth the truth, c. to the. 21
the hour c. 4:21, 23; 16:32
he that c. to me shall. 6:35, 37
learned of the Father c. to me. 45
when Christ c. no man. 7:27, 31
Christ c. of the seed of. 42
the night c. when no man can. 9:4
c. unto the Father but by me. 14:6
the time c. that whosoever. 16:2
time c. I shall no more speak. 25
the hour c. that ye shall be. 32
who when he c. shall. *Acts* 10:32
c. this blessedness upon ? *Rom* 4:9*
so then, faith c. by hearing. 10:17
then c. the end, when. *1 Cor* 15:24
besides that which c. *2 Cor* 11:28*
c. wrath of God. *Eph* 5:6; *Col* 3:6
day of Lord so c. as a *1 Thes* 5:2
he that c. to God must. *Heb* 11:6
the Lord c. with 10,000 of. *Jude* 14
he c. with clouds. *Rev* 1:7
when he c. he must continue a. 17:10

cometh down

as the rain c. down. *Isa* 55:10
is he which c. down. *John* 6:33, 50
and perfect gift c. down. *Jas* 1:17
Jerusalem which c. down. *Rev* 3:12

cometh forth

when virgin c. forth. *Gen* 24:43
also behold he c. forth. *Ex* 4:14
Pharaoh, lo, he c. forth to. 8:20
c. forth of the doors. *Judg* 11:31
whosoever c. not forth. *1 Sam* 11:7
affliction c. not forth. *Job* 5:6
he c. forth like a flower. 14:2
this also c. forth from. *Isa* 28:29
words c. forth from. *Ezek* 33:30
behold, the Lord c. forth. *Mi* 1:3

cometh nigh

the stranger that c. nigh shall be.
　　　　Num 1:51; 3:10, 38; 18:7

cometh out

be heard when he c. out. *Ex* 28:35
when he c. out. *Num* 12:12
toward young that c. out. *Deut* 28:57
a stranger that c. out of. *1 Ki* 8:41
drawn, and c. out of. *Job* 20:25
fair weather c. out of the. 37:22
who is this that c. out ? *S of S* 3:6
the Lord c. out of his. *Isa* 26:21
and that which c. out of it. 42:5
it c. out of the north. *Jer* 46:20
it with dung that c. out. *Ezek* 4:12
that which c. out of the mouth.
　　　　Mat 15:11*; *Mark* 7:20
for as lightning c. out of. 24:27

cometh up

old man c. up covered. *1 Sam* 28:14
who is this that c. up ? *S of S* 8:5
and he that c. up out. *Isa* 24:18
who is this that c. up ? *Jer* 46:7*
out of north there c. up a. 50:3
when he c. up to people. *Hab* 3:16
up the fish first c. up. *Mat* 17:27

comfort, substantive

then should I yet have c. *Job* 6:10†
that I may take c. a little. 10:20
this is my c. in my. *Ps* 119:50
kindness be for my c. 76
should I receive c. ? *Isa* 57:6*
thou art a c. to them. *Ezek* 16:54
daughter, be of good c. *Mat* 9:22*
　　　　　　　　　　　Mark 8:48
be of good c. rise. *Mark* 10:49*
walking in the c. of the. *Acts* 9:31
through patience and c. *Rom* 15:4
to exhortation and c. *1 Cor* 14:3*
even the God of all c. *2 Cor* 1:3
by the c. wherewith we are. 4

I am filled with c.   *2 Cor* 7:4
comforted in your c.   13
be perfect, be of good c.   13:11
if there be any c. of love.   *Phil* 2:1*
that I may also be of good c.   19
have been a c. to me.   *Col* 4:11

comfort, *verb*
this same shall c. us.   *Gen* 5:29
c. ye your hearts.   18:5
as touching thee doth c.   27:42
and daughters rose up to c.   37:35
c. thy heart with a.   *Judg* 19:5, 8
David sent to c. him.   *2 Sam* 10:2
  1 Chr 19:2
brethren came to c. him.   *1 Chr* 7:22
came to Hanun to c. him.   19:2
to mourn with and c.   *Job* 2:11
I say, my bed shall c. me.   7:13
I will forget, I will c. myself.   9:27*
how then c. ye me in vain.   21:34
rod and thy staff, they c.   *Ps* 23:4
thou shalt increase and c.   71:21
when wilt thou c. me?   119:82
c. me with apples.   *S of S* 2:5
labour not to c. me.   *Isa* 22:4
c. ye, ye my people.   40:1
Lord shall c. Zion, he will c.   51:3
by whom shall I c. thee?   19
he hath sent me to c.   61:2
so will I c. you.   66:13
when I would c. myself.   *Jer* 8:18
neither shall men tear to c.   16:7
for I will c. them.   31:13
hath none to c. her.   *Lam* 1:2, 17
there is none to c. me.   21
that I may c. thee?   2:13
they shall c. you when.   *Ezek* 14:23
Lord shall yet c. Zion.   *Zech* 1:17
told false dreams, they c. in.   10:2
to c. them concerning.   *John* 11:19*
we may be able to c.   *2 Cor* 1:4
rather to forgive and c. him.   2:7
and that he might c.   *Eph* 6:22
know your estate, c.   *Col* 4:8
to c. you concerning.   *1 Thes* 3:2
wherefore c. one another.   4:18
wherefore c. yourselves.   5:11*
c. the feeble-minded.   14*
our Lord Jesus c.   *2 Thes* 2:17

comfortable
word of my Lord be c. *2 Sam* 14:17
the angel with c. words.   *Zech* 1:13

comfortably
go forth and speak c.   *2 Sam* 19:7
he spake c. to all.   *2 Chr* 30:22
over people, and spake c.   32:6
speak c. to Jerusalem.   *Isa* 40:2
allure her, and speak c.   *Hos* 2:14

comforted
Isaac was c. after his.   *Gen* 24:67
Jacob refused to be c.   37:35
Judah was c. and went.   38:12
Joseph c. his brethren.   50:21
that thou hast c. me.   *Ruth* 2:13
David c. Bath-sheba. *2 Sam* 12:24
c. concerning Ammon.   13:39
all his brethren c. him.   *Job* 42:11
my soul refused to be c.   *Ps* 77:2
Lord, hast holpen and c.   86:17
judgements, have c. myself. 119:52
hath c. his people.   *Isa* 19:10 , 5L:9
afflicted, tossed, and not c.   54:11
ye shall be c. in Jerusalem.   66:13
refused to be c. for child. *Jer* 31:15
to rest, I will be c.   *Ezek* 5:13
ye shall be c. concerning.   14:22
all that drink water be c.   31:16
see them, and shall be c.   32:31
would not be c. because.   *Mat* 2:18
for they shall be c.   5:4
now he is c. and thou.   *Luke* 16:25
the Jews which c. her.   *John* 11:31
seen brethren, c. them.   *Acts* 16:40
were not a little c.   20:12
that I may be c. with.   *Rom* 1:12
and all may be c.   *1 Cor* 14:31
wherewith we are c. of.   *2 Cor* 1:4
God c. us by coming of Titus.   7:6
wherewith he was c. in you.   7
therefore we were c. in your.   13
their hearts might be c.   *Col* 2:2
how he exhorted and c. *1 Thes* 2:11*
we comfort c. over you in all.   3:7

comfortedst
is turned away, thou c.   *Isa* 12:1*

comforter, -s
hath sent c. *2 Sam* 10:3; *1 Chr* 19:3
miserable c. are ye all.   *Job* 16:2
I looked for c. but.   *Ps* 69:20
and they had no c.   *Eccl* 4:1
she had no c.   *Lam* 1:9
c. that should relieve is far.   16
whence shall I seek c.?   *Nah* 3:7
another C. to abide.   *John* 14:16
the C. which is Holy Ghost.   26
when the C. is come.   15:26
if I go not C. will not come.   16:7

comforteth
I dwelt, as one that c.   *Job* 29:25
I, even I, am he that c.   *Isa* 51:12
as one whom his mother c.   66:13
who c. us in all our.   *2 Cor* 1:4
God that c. those that are cast. 7:6

comfortless
I will not leave you c. *John* 14:18*

comforts
thy c. delight my soul.   *Ps* 94:19
and restore c. to him.   *Isa* 57:18

coming
blessed thee since my c. *Gen* 30:30*
nothing hinder from c.   *Num* 22:16
chariot so long in c.?   *Judg* 5:28
tremble at his c.   *1 Sam* 16:4*
c. in with me, since day of c.   29:6
going out and thy c. in.   *2 Sam* 3:25
invaded the land at c.   *2 Ki* 13:20
going out and c. in. 19:27; *Isa* 37:28
he seeth that his day is c. *Ps* 37:13
preserve going out and c. in. 121:8
to meet thee at c.   *Isa* 14:9
the things that are c.   44:7
observe time of their c.   *Jer* 8:7
saw an holy one c. down. *Dan* 4:23
days of c. out of Egypt.   *Mi* 7:15
may abide day of his c.?   *Mal* 3:2
before the c. of the great day. 4:5
they see Son of man c. *Mat*·16:28
shall be the sign of thy c.?   24:3
so shall the c. of the Son. 27, 37, 39
see the Son of man c.   30; 26:64
my Lord delayeth c.   *Mat* 24:48
  Luke 12:45
at my c. received own.   *Mat* 25:27
  Luke 19:23
for there were many c.   *Mark* 6:31
as he was yet c. the.   *Luke* 9:42
lest by her continual c. she.   18:5
while I am c. another   *John* 5:7
the hour is c.   25, 28
seeth the wolf c.   10:12
shewed before of the c.   *Acts* 7:52
with them c. in and going.   9:28*
as Peter was c. in Cornelius. 10:25
had preached before his c.   13:24
waiting for the c. of.   *1 Cor* 1:7*
they that are Christ's at his c. 15:23
glad of c. of Stephanas and.   16:17
comforted us by the c.   *2 Cor* 7:6
not by his c. only, but by.   7
more abundant by my c.   *Phil* 1:26*
rejoicing at our Lord's c. *1 Thes* 2:19
hearts unblameable at the c.   3:13
we who remain to the c.   4:15
preserved blameless to the c.   5:23
beseech you by c. of.   *2 Thes* 2:1
destroy with brightness of his c.   8
even him whose c. is after the.   9
patient, brethren, to the c.   *Jas* 5:7
for the c. of the Lord.   8
to whom c. as unto a.   *1 Pet* 2:4
make known power and c. *2 Pet* 1:16
where is promise of his c.?   3:4
looking and hasting to the c. of.   12
not be ashamed before him at his c.   *1 John* 2:28
beheld another beast c.   *Rev* 13:11
Jerusalem c. down from God. 21:2

comings
goings out and c. in.   *Ezek* 43:11

command
Abraham will c. his.   *Gen* 18:19
sacrifice as God shall c.   *Ex* 8:27
and God c. thee so.   18:23

hear what Lord will c.   *Num* 9:8
thing which the Lord doth c.   36:6
the Lord shall c. the.   *Deut* 28:8
ye shall c. your children.   32:46
so did Moses c. Joshua. *Josh* 11:15
eagle mount up at thy c.? *Job* 39:27
the Lord will c. his.   *Ps* 42:8
art my king, O God, c.   44:4
work of my hands, c. me. *Isa* 45:11
c. them to say to their.   *Jer* 27:4
heathen didst c. they.   *Lam* 1:10
c. these stones be made.   *Mat* 4:3
  Luke 4:3
why did Moses c. to?   *Mat* 19:7
c. therefore that sepulchre.   27:64
what did Moses c. you? *Mark* 10:3
he would not c. them.   *Luke* 8:31
wilt thou we c. fire to come?   9:54
did not we straitly c. you? *Acts* 5:28
and to c. them to keep.   15:5
and will do things we c. *2 Thes* 3:4
we c. you, brethren, in name.   6
that are such we c. and exhort.   12
these c. and teach.   *1 Tim* 4:11

I command
speak all that I c. thee.   *Ex* 7:2
  Jer 1:7, 17
observe what I c. thee.   *Ex* 34:11
  Deut 12:28
I will c. my blessing.   *Lev* 25:21
not add to the word I c.   *Deut* 4:2
I c. thee this day. 7:11; 8:11; 10:13
  11:8, 27; 13:18; 30:8
I c. thee to do this.   24:18, 22
I c. thee this day to love.   30:16
I will c. the clouds.   *Isa* 5:6
do all which I c. you.   *Jer* 11:4
I will c. saith the Lord.   34:22
thence will I c. serpent.   *Amos* 9:3
thence I c. the sword.   4
I will c. and I will sift the.   9
friends, if ye do what I c. *John* 15:14
these things I c. you, that ye.   17
I c. thee in the name.   *Acts* 16:18
I c. yet not I, but Lord.   *1 Cor* 7:10

commanded
now thou art c. this do.   *Gen* 45:19
to him as he c. them.   50:12
not as king of Egypt c.   *Ex* 1:17
for so I am c.   *Lev* 10:13
I c. you all things.   *Deut* 1:18
  3:18, 21
Israel did as Joshua c.   *Josh* 4:8
see I have c. you.   8:8
obeyed my voice in all I c.   22:2
all that I c. her.   *Judg* 13:14
hath c. me to be there. *1 Sam* 20:29
the king c. me a business.   21:2
have not I c. you?   *2 Sam* 13:28
performed all the king c.   21:14
that Jehoiada priest c.   *2 Ki* 11:9
to all that king Ahaz c.   16:16
is it not I c. people to? *1 Chr* 21:17
David man of God c.   *2 Chr* 8:14
Asa c. Judah to seek Lord.   14:4
Manasseh c. Judah.   33:16
I c. that the gates.   *Neh* 13:19
I c. Levites to cleanse.   22
for the king had so c.   *Esth* 3:2
according to all that Haman c.   12
according as Esther c. him.   4:17
according to all Mordecai c.   8:9
hast thou c. morning?   *Job* 38:12
my molten image hath c. *Isa* 48:5
our father c. us. *Jer* 35:6, 10, 14, 16
  18
so as I was c.   *Ezek* 12:7; 37:7
to you it is c. O people.   *Dan* 3:4
he c. that they should heat.   19
king c. and they brought Daniel. 6:16
king c. and they brought those.   24
c. the prophets, saying.   *Amos* 2:12
c. it to be given her.   *Mat* 14:9
  Mark 6:27
c. multitude to sit down. *Mat* 14:19
  15:35; *Mark* 6:39
his lord c. him to be sold. *Mat* 18:25
and did as Jesus c. them.   21:6*
observe all things I have c.   28:20
he c. them to tell no.   *Luke* 9:21
c. them to be baptized. *Acts* 10:48
Festus c. Paul to be brought. 25:6
c. to be under.   *1 Cor* 14:34*

with hands as we *c*.   *1 Thes* 4:11
we *c*. you that if any.   *2 Thes* 3:10
endure that which was *c. Heb* 12:20
it was *c*. them not to.   *Rev* 9:4

God commanded

God I *c*. man to eat.   *Gen* 2:16
according to all that God *c*.   6:22
into ark as *God* had *c*.   7:9, 16
   21:4; *Deut* 20:17; *Josh* 10:40
God *c*. thee to keep.   *Deut* 5:15
do as the Lord your *God c*.   32
in ways the Lord your *God c*.   33
God *c*. to teach you.   6:1, 20; 13:5
this day Lord thy *God c*.   26:16
hath not Lord *God c*. to go? *Judg* 4:6
did as *God c*. him.   *1 Chr* 14:16
God *c*. me, make haste. *2 Chr* 35:21
c. by the *God* of heaven. *Ezra* 7:23
God hath *c*. thy strength. *Ps* 68:28
for *God c*. saying.   *Mat* 15:4
things that are *c*. of *God. Acts* 10:33
God who *c*. light to.   *2 Cor* 4:6

Lord or God commanded

tree I *c*. not to eat.   *Gen* 3:11, 17
according to all *Lord c*.   7:5
did as the *Lord c*. them.   *Ex* 7:6
   10:20; 12:28, 50; *Num* 17:11
this is the thing *Lord c*.   *Ex* 16:16
   32; 35:4; *Num* 30:1
Lord *c*. Moses.   *Ex* 16:34; 34:4
   39:1, 5, 7, etc.; 40:19, etc.
   Lev 8:9; 9:10
as I *c*. in the time.   *Ex* 23:15
in the day he *c*. the.   *Lev* 7:38
did as *Lord c*. him.   8:4
   Num 20:27; 27:11
strange fire which he *c*. not.
   Lev 10:1
Lord *c*. my lord to.   *Num* 36:2
the *Lord c*. us to do all. *Deut* 6:24
aside out of the way *Lord c*.   9:16
there they be as *Lord c*.   10:5
gods, which I have not *c*.   17:3
   18:20; *Jer* 19:5; 23:32; 29:23
have not I *c*. thee ?   *Josh* 1:9
my covenant I *c*.   7:11; *Judg* 2:20
lot, as I have *c*. thee.   *Judg* 13:6
Lord *c*. him to be.   *1 Sam* 13:14
c. to feed my people.   *2 Sam* 7:7
   1 Chr 17:6
since I *c*. judges.   *2 Sam* 7:11
   1 Chr 17:10
went up, as *Lord c*. *2 Sam* 24:19
c. him concerning this. *1 Ki* 11:10
I have *c*. the ravens to feed.   17:4
I have *c*. a widow woman.   17:9
the word which he *c*. to. *1 Chr* 16:15
   Ps 105:8
in the law, which he *c*. *1 Chr* 16:40
Lord *c*. the angel.   21:27
Lord *God* of Israel *c*. him.   24:19
to judgement thou has *c*.   *Ps* 7:6
he *c*. and it stood fast.   33:9
whom the *Lord c*. them.   106:34
c. his covenant for ever.   111:9
thou hast *c*. us to keep thy.   119:4
testimonies thou hast *c*. are.   138
there the *Lord c*. the blessing. 133:3
for the Lord *c*. and they.   148:5
I have *c*. my sanctified.   *Isa* 13:3
for my mouth it hath *c*.   34:16
heavens and their host I *c*.   45:12
but this thing *c*. I them.   *Jer* 7:23
c. them not.   31; 19:5; 32:35
words of covenant which I *c*.   11:8
by Euphrates, as *Lord c*.   13:5
hallow the sabbath, as I *c*.   17:22
all that I have *c*. thee.   50:21
Lord hath *c*. concerning. *Lam* 1:17
his word he had *c*. in days.   2:17
I have done as thou hast *c*. me.
   Ezek 9:11
in morning as I was *c*. 24:18; 37:10
my words which I *c*.   *Zech* 1:6
law which I *c*. in Horeb.   *Mal* 4:4
is done as thou hast *c*. *Luke* 14:22
he *c*. us to preach to.   *Acts* 10:42
so hath the *Lord c*.   13:46, 47

Moses commanded

took as Moses had *c*.   *Num* 16:47
aside from way I *c*.   *Deut* 31:29
Moses *c*. us a law.   33:4

according to all *Moses c*.   *Josh* 1:7
kept all that *Moses c*. you.   22:2
Moses *c*. according to.   *1 Chr* 15:15
offer the gift that *Moses c. Mat* 8:4
offer those things which *Moses c*.
   Mark 1:44; *Luke* 5:14
Moses in law *c*. that.   *John* 8:5

commandedst

which thou *c*. thy.   *Neh* 1:7, 8
thou *c*. them precepts.   9:14
done nothing that thou *c. Jer* 32:23

commander

him for a leader and *c*.   *Isa* 55:4

commandest

all that thou *c*. us we.   *Josh* 1:16
hearken in all that thou *c*.   18
nothing of all thou *c*.   *Jer* 32:23
c. me to be smitten?   *Acts* 23:3

commandeth

will do as my lord *c*.   *Num* 32:25
God, who *c*. the sun.   *Job* 9:7
he *c*. that they return from.   36:10
and *c*. it not to shine.   32
they may do whatever he *c*.   37:12
he *c*. and raiseth the.   *Ps* 107:25
when *Lord c*. it not ?   *Lam* 3:37
Lord *c*. and he will.   *Amos* 6:11
he *c*. the unclean spirits. *Mark* 1:27
   Luke 4:36
he *c*. the winds.   *Luke* 8:25
c. all men to repent.   *Acts* 17:30

commanding

Jacob made an end of *c. Gen* 49:33
Jesus made an end of *c*.   *Mat* 11:1
c. his accusers to come. *Acts* 24:8
c. to abstain from meats. *1 Tim* 4:3

commandment

he gave them in *c*. all.   *Ex* 34:32
broken his *c*. that soul. *Num* 15:31
I have received *c*. to bless.   23:20
ye rebelled against my *c*.   27:14
this *c*. I command.   *Deut* 30:11
thou not kept the *c*. I ?   *1 Ki* 2:43
king's *c*. was, answer him not.
   2 Ki 18:36; *Isa* 36:21
brethren were at their *c*. *1 Chr* 12:32
people will be wholly at thy *c*. 28:31
according to the *c*. of.   *2 Chr* 8:13
shall come between law and *c*. 9:10
one heart to do the *c*. of.   30:12
and as soon as the *c*. came.   31:5
I sent them with *c*. to.   *Ezra* 8:17
those that tremble at the *c*.   10:3
it was the king's *c*.   *Neh* 11:23
to come at king's *c*.   *Esth* 1:12
Esther did the *c*. of Mordecai.   2:20
transgressest thou king's *c*. ?   3:3
when king's *c*. drew nigh to be.   9:1
nor gone back from *c*.   *Job* 23:12
thy *c*. is exceeding broad. *Ps* 119:96
he sendeth forth his *c*.   147:15
the *c*. is a lamp.   *Pr* 6:23
waters should not pass his *c*.   8:29
he that feareth the *c*. shall.   13:13
he that keepeth the *c*.   19:16
whoso keepeth *c*. shall.   *Eccl* 8:5
their father Jonadab's *c. Jer* 35:14
because the king's *c*.   *Dan* 3:22
the *c*. came forth, and I am.   9:23
willingly walked after *c*.   *Hos* 5:11
O ye priests, this *c*. is for. *Mal* 2:1
that I have sent this *c*. to.   4
why transgress the *c*. of ? *Mat* 15:3
thus have ye made the *c*. of.   6
which is the great *c*. in law? 22:36
first and great *c*.   38; *Mark* 12:30
aside the *c*. of God.   *Mark* 7:8
full well ye reject the *c*. of.   9
is no other *c*. greater than.   12:31
transgressed I thy *c*.   *Luke* 15:29
rested according to the *c*.   23:56
this *c*. have I received. *John* 10:18
he gave me a *c*. what.   12:49
I know that his *c*. is life.   50
as the Father gave me *c*.   14:31
my *c*. that ye love one.   15:12
   1 John 3:23
we gave no such *c*.   *Acts* 15:24
receiving a *c* to Silas.   17:15
and gave *c*. to his accusers.   23:30
at Festus' *c*. Paul was.   25:23

sin taking occasion by *c. Rom* 7:8, 11
when the *c*. came, sin revived.   9
c. which was ordained to life.   10
and the *c*. is holy, and just.   12
that sin by *c*. might become.   13
if there be any other *c*. it is.   13:9
according to the *c*. of the.   16:26
by permission, not of *c*.   *1 Cor* 7:6
I speak not by *c*. but by. *2 Cor* 8:8
the first *c*. with promise.   *Eph* 6:2
by the *c*. of God our.   *1 Tim* 1:1
   Tit 1:3
the end of the *c*. is charity. *1 Tim* 1:5
not after law of a carnal *c. Heb* 7:16
there is a disannulling of *c*.   18
Joseph gave *c*. concerning.   11:22
not afraid of the king's *c*.   23
to turn from holy *c*.   *2 Pet* 2:21
mindful of *c*. of us the apostles. 3:2
but an old *c*.   *1 John* 2:7
this is his *c*. that we should.   3:23
this *c*. have we from him.   4:21
we have received a *c*.   *2 John* 4
this is the *c*. that as ye have.   6

give or given commandment

which I will *give* thee in *c. Ex* 25:22
Lord had *given* him in *c. Deut* 1:3
give c. to cease till *c*.   *Ezra* 4:21
hast *given c*. to save me.   *Ps* 71:3
hath *given c*. against.   *Isa* 23:11
hath *given c*. concerning. *Nah* 1:14
given c. if any knew.   *John* 11:57

keep commandment, see keep

commandment *of the Lord*
journeyed according to the *c*. *of Lord*.
   Ex 17:1; *Num* 9:18, 20; 10:13
numbered at *c*. of *Lord. Num* 3:39
go beyond *c*. of *Lord* to.   24:13
went up to Hor at *c*. of *Lord*. 33:38
charge of *c*. of *Lord* your. *Josh* 22:3
not rebel against the *c*. of *Lord*.
   1 Sam 12:14
but rebel against *c*. of *Lord*.   15
hast not kept the *c*. of *Lord*.   13:13
I have performed the *c*. of *Lord*. 15:13
have transgressed the *c*. of *Lord*. 24
despised *c*. of *Lord*.   *2 Sam* 12:9
at the *c*. of *Lord* came.   *2 Ki* 24:3
for so was *c*. of *Lord. 2 Chr* 29:25
the *c*. of *Lord* is pure.   *Ps* 19:8
I have no *c*. of *Lord*.   *1 Cor* 7:25

new commandment

a *new* I give unto.   *John* 13:34
I write no *new c*. unto. *1 John* 2:7
a *new c*. I write unto you.   8
though I wrote a *new c*.   *2 John* 5

rebelled against the commandment

ye *rebelled ag*. my *c*.   *Num* 27:14
ye *rebelled ag*. *c*. of the Lord your
   God.   *Deut* 1:26, 43
rebelled ag. *c*. of Lord and.   9:23
I have *rebelled ag*. his *c*. *Lam* 1:18

commandments

Abraham kept my *c*.   *Gen* 26:5
thou wilt give ear to his *c. Ex* 15:26
wrote on tables the ten *c*.   34:28
   Deut 4:13; 10:4
somewhat against any of the *c*.
   Lev 4:13, 27
commit sin forbidden by *c*.   5:17
these are the *c*. of Lord.   27:34
remember all the *c*. of. *Num* 15:39
in not keeping *c*.   *Deut* 8:11
shall hearken to *c*.   11:13; 28:13
   Judg 3:4
if ye obey the *c*. of. *Deut* 11:27
if ye will not obey the *c*. of.   28
hath not performed *c*. *1 Sam* 15:11
because he kept my *c*.   *1 Ki* 11:34
David who kept my *c*.   14:8
in that ye have forsaken *c*.   18:18
and they left all *c*. of. *2 Ki* 17:16
Judah kept not the *c*. of.   19
but kept his *c*. which he.   18:6
if ye forsake my *c*. *2 Chr* 7:19
why transgress ye the *c*. of ? 24:20
we have forsaken thy *c*. *Ezra* 9:10
should we again break thy *c*.   14
if they keep not my *c*.   *Ps* 89:31
all his *c*. are sure.   111:7*
delighteth greatly in his *c*.   112:1

commandments

me not wander from thy *c.*	*Ps* 119:10
I am a stranger, hide not thy *c.*	19
make me to go in path of thy *c.*	35
I will delight in thy *c.*	47
I have believed thy *c.*	66
that I may learn thy *c.*	73
all thy *c.* are faithful.	86
thou through thy *c.* hast made.	98
I love thy *c.*	127
I longed for thy *c.*	131
thy *c.* are my delights.	143
all thy *c.* are truth.	151
I have done thy *c.*	166
all thy *c.* are righteousness.	172
not forget thy *c.*	176
if thou wilt hide my *c.*	*Pr* 2:1
keep my words and lay up *c.*	7:1
wise in heart will receive *c.*	10:8
hadst hearkened to my *c.*	*Isa* 48:18
break one of these least *c.*	*Mat* 5:19
for doctrines the *c.* of men.	15:9*
	Mark 7:7*
on these two *c.* hang all.	*Mat* 22:40
thou knowest the *c.*	*Mark* 10:19
	Luke 18:20
the first of all the *c.* is.	*Mark* 12:29
walking in all the *c.* of.	*Luke* 1:6
he that hath my *c.* and.	*John* 14:21
c. as I have kept Father's *c.*	15:10
keeping the *c.* of God.	*1 Cor* 7:19
things I write you, are the *c.*	14:37
after the *c.* and.	*Col* 2:22*
for ye know what *c.*	*1 Thes* 4:2*
that keepeth not his *c.*	*1 John* 2:4
he that keepeth his *c.* dwelleth.	3:24
that we walk after his *c.*	*2 John* 6

do commandments

do all my *c.* and be.	*Num* 15:40
observe to do all *c.*	*Deut* 6:25
	15:5; 28:1, 15; 30:8
constant to do my *c.*	*1 Chr* 28:7
remember his *c.* to do.	*Ps* 103:18*
they that do his *c.*	111:10†
blessed that do his *c.*	*Rev* 22:14*

not do commandments

ye will not do these *c.*	*Lev* 26:14
so that ye will not do all my *c.*	15

keep **commandments,** *see* **keep**

commend

[1] *To praise,* 2 Cor 3:1; 5:12.
[2] *To commit, or give in charge,*
Luke 23:46. [3] *To make one more
acceptable,* 1 Cor 8:8.

into thy hands I *c.* my.	*Luke* 23:46
brethren, I *c.* you to God.	*Acts* 20:32
our unrighteousness *c.*	*Rom* 3:5
I *c.* unto you Phebe our sister.	16:1
do we begin again to *c.?*	*2 Cor* 3:1
for we *c.* not ourselves.	5:12
ourselves with some that *c.*	10:12

commendation

need we, epistles of *c.?*	*2 Cor* 3:1

commended

the princes *c.* Sarai.	*Gen* 12:15*
a man shall be *c.*	*Pr* 12:8
then I *c.* mirth.	*Eccl* 8:15
Lord *c.* the unjust.	*Luke* 16:8
c. them to the Lord.	*Acts* 14:23
I ought to have been *c.*	*2 Cor* 12:11

commendeth

but God *c.* his love.	*Rom* 5:8
but meat *c.* us not to.	*1 Cor* 8:8
not he that *c.* himself is approved.	
	2 Cor 10:18

commending

c. ourselves to every.	*2 Cor* 4:2

commission, -s

delivered the king's *c.*	*Ezra* 8:36
as I went with *c.* from.	*Acts* 26:12

commit

thou shalt not *c.* adultery.	*Ex* 20:14
	Deut 5:18; *Mat* 5:27; 19:18
	Rom 13:9
if sin, and *c.* any of.	*Lev* 5:17
not *c.* any of these.	18:26, 30
who shall *c.* any of these.	29
if man or woman *c.* any.	*Num* 5:6
c. no more any such.	*Deut* 19:20
caused Jerusalem to *c.*	*2 Chr* 21:11
unto God would I *c.* my.	*Job* 5:8
into thine hand I *c.* my.	*Ps* 31:5

c. thy way unto the Lord.	*Ps* 37:5
c. thy works unto the.	*Pr* 16:3
an abomination to kings to *c.*	12
I will *c.* thy government.	*Isa* 22:21
c. Jeremiah to court of.	*Jer* 37:21
why *c.* ye this great evil ?	44:7
c. abominations they *c.*	*Ezek* 8:17
and thou shalt not *c.* this.	16:43
in the midst of thee they *c.*	22:9
priests murder, they *c.*	*Hos* 6:9
for they *c.* falsehood, and.	7:1
and did *c.* things worthy.	*Luke* 12:48
who will *c.* to your trust ?	16:11
Jesus did not *c.* himself.	*John* 2:24
they which *c.* such things.	*Rom* 1:32
against them which *c.* such.	2:2
abhorrest idols, dost thou *c.?*	22
neither *c.* fornication.	*1 Cor* 10:8
this charge I *c.* to thee.	*1 Tim* 1:18
the same *c.* thou to.	*2 Tim* 2:2
respect to persons ye *c.*	*Jas* 2:9
c. the keeping of souls.	*1 Pet* 4:19
born of God doth not *c.*	*1 John* 3:9
Israel to *c.* fornication.	*Rev* 2:14
my servants to *c.* fornication.	20

see **adultery**

commit *iniquity*

if he *c.* iniquity I will.	*2 Sam* 7:14
he should *c.* iniquity.	*Job* 34:10
themselves to *c.* iniquity.	*Jer* 9:5
and *c.* iniquity.	*Ezek* 3:20; 33:13

commit *trespass*

if a soul *c.* a trespass.	*Lev* 5:15
go aside and *c.* a trespass.	*Num* 5:12
caused Israel to *c.* trespass.	31:16
Achan *c.* a trespass.	*Josh* 22:20

commit *whoredom* or *whoredoms*

will cut off that *c. whor.*	*Lev* 20:5
to *c. whor.* with the.	5:12
and thou didst *c. whor.*	*Ezek* 16:17
none followeth to *c. whor.*	34
c. ye *whor.* after their ?	20:30
will they *c. whor.* with her.	23:43
they shall *c. whor.* and.	*Hos* 4:10
daughters shall *c. whor.*	13, 14

committed

c. all that he hath to.	*Gen* 39:8
the keeper *c.* to Joseph all.	22
for sin he hath *c.*	*Lev* 4:35
customs which were *c.*	18:30
they *c.* these things, and.	20:23
if aught be *c.* by.	*Num* 15:24*
man or woman that *c.*	*Deut* 17:5
if a man have *c.* a sin worthy.	21:22
they have *c.* folly and.	*Judg* 20:6
sinned, we have *c.*	*1 Ki* 8:47
provoked him with sins, they *c.*	14:22
brasen shields *c.* he. 27; *2 Chr* 12:10
died for his transgression he *c.*	
	1 Chr 10:13
people have *c.* two evils.	*Jer* 2:13
and horrible thing is *c.* in.	5:30
our sin that we have *c.*	16:10
which they have *c.* to	44:3, 9
hast *c.* fornication with.	*Ezek* 16:26
nor hath Samaria *c.* half.	51
from all sins he hath *c.* 18:21, 22, 28
for evils ye have *c.*	20:43
they *c.* whoredoms in Egypt.	23:3
thus she *c.* whoredoms with.	7
none of the sins he *c.* shall.	33:16
for the land hath *c.* great.	*Hos* 1:2
they have *c.* whoredom.	4:18
who had *c.* murder in.	*Mark* 15:7
to whom men have *c.*	*Luke* 12:48
Father hath *c.* judgement.	*John* 5:22
c. them to prison.	*Acts* 8:3
if I have *c.* any thing.	25:11
had found he had *c.* nothing.	25
they *c.* themselves to sea.	27:40*
though I have *c.* nothing.	28:17
to them were *c.* oracles.	*Rom* 3:2
gospel is *c.* to me.	*1 Cor* 9:17
	Tit 1:3
fornication as some of them *c.*	10:8
hath *c.* to us the word.	*2 Cor* 5:19
lasciviousness which they *c.*	12:21
gospel of uncircumcision *c.*	*Gal* 2:7
	1 Tim 1:11
keep what is *c.* to thee.	*1 Tim* 6:20
to keep that which I *c.*	*2 Tim* 1:12
if he have *c.* sins, they.	*Jas* 5:15

c. himself to him that.	*1 Pet* 2:23
deeds which they have *c.*	*Jude* 15
kings *c.* fornication.	*Rev* 17:2
	18:3, 9

see **abominations**

committed *iniquity*

we have *c. iniq.* we.	*Ps* 106:6
for *iniq.* he hath *c.*	*Ezek* 33:13, 18
we have *c. iniq.* and.	*Dan* 9:5

committed *trespass*

for his *tres.* he *c.* two.	*Lev* 5:7
Israel *c.* a *tres.* in the.	*Josh* 7:1
what *tres.* is this ye have *c.?*	22:16
not *c.* this *tres.* against Lord.	31
they have *c. tres.,* I will.	*Ezek* 15:8
in that they *c.* a *tres.*	20:27

committest, -eth, -ing

poor *c.* himself to thee.	*Ps* 10:14
abomination that Israel *c.*	*Ezek* 8:6
in statutes of life without *c.*	33:15
killing, stealing, and *c.*	*Hos* 4:2
O Ephraim, thou *c.* whoredom.	5:3
whosoever *c.* sin is the.	*John* 8:34
he that *c.* fornication.	*1 Cor* 6:18
c. sin transgresseth.	*1 John* 3:4
he that *c.* sin is of the devil.	8

commodious

the haven was not *c.* to. *Acts* 27:12

common

[1] *That which is ordinary,* or
usual ; as a common death, Num
16:29. [2] *That which is ceremonially unclean,* Acts 11:9. [3]
*Had in common ; to use together
as belonging to all,* Acts 2:44.

if these men die the *c.*	*Num* 16:29
there is no *c.* bread.	*1 Sam* 21:4
bread is in a manner *c.*	5
an evil, and it is *c.*	*Eccl* 6:1*
shall eat them as *c.* things.	*Jer* 31:5*
men of *c.* sort were.	*Ezek* 23:42
took Jesus into the *c.*	*Mat* 27:27*
had all things *c.*	*Acts* 2:44; 4:32
put apostles in the *c.* prison.	5:18*
never eaten anything *c.* 10:14; 11:8
God cleansed call not *c.* 10:15; 11:9
should not call any thing *c.*	10:28
no temptation but *c.*	*1 Cor* 10:13*
my own son, after *c.* faith.	*Tit* 1:4
to write to you of the *c.*	*Jude* 3

common *people*

if any of *c. people* sin.	*Lev* 4:27
body into graves of *c. people.*	
	Jer 26:23
and the *c. people* heard.	*Mark* 12:37

commonwealth

being aliens from *c.* of. *Eph* 2:12

commonly, *see* **reported**

commotion, -s

a great *c.* out of north.	*Jer* 10:22
when ye hear of *c.* be.	*Luke* 21:9*

commune

I will meet and *c.* with.	*Ex* 25:22
c. with David secretly.	*1 Sam* 18:22
and I will *c.* with my father.	19:3
if we essay to *c.* with thee ?	*Job* 4:2
c. with your own heart on.	*Ps* 4:4
they *c.* of laying snares.	64:5
in the night I *c.* with mine.	77:6

communed

Abraham *c.* with them.	*Gen* 23:8
Hamor *c.* with Jacob.	34:6, 8
Joseph *c.* with them.	42:24
Abimelech *c.* with them.	*Judg* 9:1
Samuel *c.* with Saul.	*1 Sam* 9:25
David *c.* with Abigail.	25:39
queen of Sheba *c.* with Solomon of.	
	1 Ki 10:2; *2 Chr* 9:1
they *c.* with Huldah.	*2 Ki* 22:14
I *c.* with mine own heart.	*Eccl* 1:16
and king *c.* with them.	*Dan* 1:19
the angel that *c.* with.	*Zech* 1:14
they *c.* what they might.	*Luke* 6:11
Judas *c.* to betray Jesus.	22:4
while they *c.* Jesus himself.	24:15
Felix sent and *c.*	*Acts* 24:26

communicate

let him that is taught *c.* to.	*Gal* 6:6
that ye did *c.* with my.	*Phil* 4:14*

do good, be willing to c. *1 Tim* 6:18
to do good and to c. *Heb* 13:16

communicated
I c. to them that gospel. *Gal* 2:2*
no church c. with me. *Phil* 4:15

communication, -s
Abner had c. with. *2 Sam* 3:17
the man and his c. *2 Ki* 9:11*
let your c. be yea. *Mat* 5:37
what manner of c. are? *Luke* 24:17
evil c. corrupt good. *1 Cor* 15:33*
no corrupt c. proceed. *Eph* 4:29
       Col 3:8
that c. of thy faith may. *Philem* 6*

communing
Lord left c. with. *Gen* 18:33
had made an end of c. on. *Ex* 31:18

communion
*This word signifies fellowship,
concord, or agreement,* 2 Cor 6:14.
*Communion is likewise taken for a
sacrament, or sacred sign of our
spiritual fellowship with Christ,*
1 Cor 10:16.

blood of Christ, c. of body of Christ.
      1 Cor 10:16
what c. hath light with ? *2 Cor* 6:14
c. of the Holy Ghost be. 13:14

compact
Jerusalem is a city c. *Ps* 122:3

compacted
body fitly joined and c. *Eph* 4:16*

companied
these men which have c. *Acts* 1:21

companies
men into three c. *Judg* 7:16
three c. blew the trumpets. 20
against Shechem in four c. 9:34
divided them into three c. 43
put people in three c. *1 Sam* 11:11
spoilers came out in three c. 13:17
Syrians had gone out by c. *2 Ki* 5:2*
two great c. of them. *Neh* 12:31, 40
the c. of Sheba waited. *Job* 6:19
O ye travelling c. of. *Isa* 21:13†
when thou criest, let thy c. 57:13*
make all sit down by c. *Mark* 6:39

companion
slay every man his c. *Ex* 32:27
wife given to c. *Judg* 14:20; 15:6
Hushai was king's c. *1 Chr* 27:33*
brother to dragons, a c. *Job* 30:29
I am a c. to all them. *Ps* 119:63
but a c. of fools shall. *Pr* 13:20
but a c. of riotous men. 28:7
the same is the c. of a destroyer. 24
yet she is thy c. wife. *Mal* 2:14
and c. in labour. *Phil* 2:25*
I John, your brother and c. *Rev* 1:9*

companions
with her c. and bewailed. *Judg* 11:38
they brought thirty c. to. 14:11
answer thee and thy c. *Job* 35:4
shall the c. make a banquet. 41:6*
her c. shall be brought. *Ps* 45:14
for my c. sake, I will say. 122:8
aside by flocks of thy c. *S of S* 1:7
c. hearken to thy voice. 8:13
princes are rebellious and c. *Isa* 1:23
Judah and Israel his c. *Ezek* 37:16
the thing known to his c. *Dan* 2:17
having caught Paul's c. *Acts* 19:29
ye became c. of them. *Heb* 10:33*

company
if Esau come to the one c. *Gen* 32:8
lodged that night in the c. 21
a c. of nations shall be of. 35:11
Korah and his c. *Num* 16:6
be thou and all thy c. 16*
he be not as Korah and c. 40
now shall this c. lick up. 22:4*
strove in c. of Korah. 26:9; 27:3
another c. come along. *Judg* 9:37
thou comest with such a c.? 18:23
thou shalt meet a c. of. *1 Sam* 10:5*
they saw the c. of prophets. 19:20
bring me down to this c.? 30:15
he and all his c. came. *2 Ki* 5:15
c. of Jehu, said, I see a c. 9:17
came with a small c. *2 Chr* 24:24

made desolate all my c. *Job* 16:7
goeth in c. with workers of. 34:8
to house of God in c. *Ps* 55:14*
rebuke the c. of spearmen. 68:30*
earth covered c. of Abiram. 106:17
fire was kindled in their c. 18
that keepeth c. with. *Pr* 29:3
to a c. of horses in. *S of S* 1:9*
as it were the c. of two. 6:13*
bring up a c. against. *Ezek* 16:40*
I will bring up a c. on them. 23:46*
Ashur is there and all her c. 32:22
thou and all thy c. 38:7
c. of priests murder in. *Hos* 6:9
supposing him in the c. *Luke* 2:44
he came down the c. of. 6:17
separate you from their c. 22
sit down by fifties in a c. 9:14*
a man of the c. cried out. 38
a woman of our c. made. 24:22
they went to their own c. *Acts* 4:23
unlawful for Jew to keep c. 10:28*
to send chosen men of their c. 15:22
Jews gathered a c. and set. 17:5*
we of Paul's c. departed. 21:8
filled with your c. *Rom* 15:24
not to keep c. with a. *1 Cor* 5:11
and have no c. with. *2 Thes* 3:14
to an innumerable c. of. *Heb* 12:22*
c. in ships and sailors. *Rev* 18:17*

great company
with Joseph a great c. *Gen* 50:9
Sheba came with great c. *2 Chr* 9:1*
no might against this great c. 20:12
great was the c. of those. *Ps* 68:11*
a great c. shall return. *Jer* 31:8
Pharaoh with great c. *Ezek* 17:17
saw a great c. come to. *John* 6:5
great c. of priests. *Acts* 6:7

comparable
precious sons of Zion c. to. *Lam* 4:2

compare, -ed, -ing
who in heaven can be c.? *Ps* 89:6
all the things thou canst desire are
  not to be c. unto her. *Pr* 3:15; 8:11
I have c. thee, O my. *S of S* 1:9
what likeness will ye c.? *Isa* 40:18
to whom will ye c. me? 46:5
are not worthy to be c. *Rom* 8:18
c. spiritual things. *1 Cor* 2:13†
c. ourselves with some. c. themselves amongst. *2 Cor* 10:12

comparison
have I done in c. of? *Judg* 8:2, 3
it not in your eyes in c.? *Hag* 2:3
or with what c. shall it ? *Mark* 4:30*

compass, substantive
put the net under the c. *Ex* 27:5*
a grate of net-work under c. 38:4*
but fetch a c. behind. *2 Sam* 5:23*
they fetched a c. of. *2 Ki* 3:9*
when he set a c. on the. *Pr* 8:27*
marketh image out with c. *Isa* 44:13
thence we fetched a c. *Acts* 28:13*

compass, verb
they journeyed to c. the. *Num* 21:4
ye shall c. the city. *Josh* 6:3
the seventh day c. the city. 4
c. the king round about. *2 Ki* 11:8
       2 Chr 23:7
his archers c. me round. *Job* 16:13
willows of the brook c. 40:22
with favour wilt thou c. *Ps* 5:12
congregation of the people c. 7:7
deadly enemies who c. me. 17:9
so will I c. thine altar, O Lord. 26:6
shalt c. me about with songs. 32:7
trusteth in Lord, mercy shall c. 10
iniquity of my heels shall c. 49:5
the head of those that c. 140:9
the righteous shall c. me. 142:7
that c. yourselves about. *Isa* 50:11*
a woman shall c. a man. *Jer* 31:22
the wicked doth c. about. *Hab* 1:4
woe to you, ye c. sea. *Mat* 23:15
thine enemies shall c. *Luke* 19:43

compassed
the men of Sodom c. *Gen* 19:4
and we c. mount Seir. *Deut* 2:1
ark of the Lord c. city. *Josh* 6:11
then they c. land of. *Judg* 11:18
they c. Samson, and laid. 16:2

Saul and his men c. *1 Sam* 23:26
waves of death c. me. *2 Sam* 22:5
     Ps 18:4; 116:3
host c. city with horses. *2 Ki* 6:15*
smote Edomites which c. *2 Chr* 21:9
God hath c. me with his. *Job* 19:6
he hath c. the waters. 26:10*
they have now c. us in. *Ps* 17:11
many bulls c. me. 22:12
for dogs c. me. 16
he hath c. me with. *Lam* 3:5
ye see Jerusalem c. *Luke* 21:20
that he himself also is c. *Heb* 5:2

compassed about
men c. Absalom about. *2 Sam* 18:15
sorrows of hell c. me about. 22:6
       Ps 18:5
night and c. city about. *2 Ki* 6:14
Edomites which c. him about. 8:21
c. about Jehoshaphat. *2 Chr* 18:31
evils have c. me about. *Ps* 40:12
they c. me about together. 88:17
    109:3; 118:11, 12
all nations c. me about. 118:10
floods c. me about thy. *Jonah* 2:3
Jericho fell. c. about 7. *Heb* 11:30
c. about with such a cloud of. 12:1
c. camp of saints about. *Rev* 20:9

compassest, -eth
c. Havilah. *Gen* 2:11
c. the land of Ethiopia. 13
c. them about as a chain. *Ps* 73:6
thou c. my path and my. 139:3*
Ephraim c. me about. *Hos* 11:12

compassion
(*Literally, suffering with another ;
hence having pity or sympathy for
another*)

give them c. before. *1 Ki* 8:50
children shall find c. *2 Chr* 30:9
Jesus moved with c. *Mat* 9:36
    14:14; *Mark* 6:34
lord of servant moved with c.
       Mat 18:27
Jesus moved with c. *Mark* 1:41
be of one mind, having c. *1 Pet* 3:8
shutteth up bowels of c. *1 John* 3:17

full of compassion
(*Revised Version,* merciful)
being full of c. forgave. *Ps* 78:38
thou art a God full of c. 86:15
   111:4; 112:4; 145:8

have or had compassion
and she had c. on him. *Ex* 2:6
Lord may have c. on. *Deut* 13:17
Lord thy God will have c. on. 30:3
be ye, for ye have c. *1 Sam* 23:21
that they may have c. *1 Ki* 8:50
was gracious and had c. *2 Ki* 13:23
because he had c. on. *2 Chr* 36:15
Chaldees had no c. on young. 17
she should not have c. *Isa* 49:15
return and have c. on. *Jer* 12:15
will he have c. *Lam* 3:32; *Mi* 7:19
I have c. *Mat* 15:32; *Mark* 8:2
also have had c. on them. *Mat* 18:33*
so Jesus had c. on them. 20:34
Lord hath had c. on. *Mark* 5:19*
if thou canst, have c. on us. 9:22
saw her, he had c. on. *Luke* 7:13
Samaritan saw him, had c. 10:33
father had c. and ran and. 15:20
have c. on whom I have c. *Rom* 9:15
can have c. on ignorant. *Heb* 5:2*
had c. of me in my bonds. 10:34
of some have c. making. *Jude* 22*

compassions
not consumed, because his c.
       Lam 3:22
shew mercy and c. every. *Zech* 7:9

compel
not c. him to serve as a. *Lev* 25:39
c. thee to go a mile. *Mat* 5:41
they c. one Simon to. *Mark* 15:21
go into highways, c. *Luke* 14:23

compelled, -est
servants with woman c. *1 Sam* 28:23
Jehoram c. Judah. *2 Chr* 21:11
Simon, him they c. to. *Mat* 27:32
I c. them to blaspheme. *Acts* 26:11*
glorying, ye have c. me. *2 Cor* 12:11

complain

nor Titus a Greek was *c.* *Gal* 2:3
why *c.* thou the Gentiles to ? 14

complain, -ed, -ing
people *c.* it displeased. *Num* 11:1
brethren came to us to *c.* *Judg* 21:22
I will *c.* in bitterness of. *Job* 7:11
furrows likewise thereof *c.* 31:38*
I *c.* and my spirit was. *Ps* 77:3
that there be no *c.* in. 144:14
doth a living man *c.?* *Lam* 3:39

complainers
these are murmurers, *c.* *Jude* 16

complaint, -s
of abundance of my *c.* *1 Sam* 1:16
couch shall ease my *c.* *Job* 7:13
if I say, I will forget my *c.* 9:27
I will leave my *c.* on myself. 10:1
as for me, is my *c.* to man ? 21:4
even to-day is my *c.* bitter. 23:2
I mourn in my *c.* *Ps* 55:2
I poured out my *c.* before. 142:2
laid *c.* against Paul. *Acts* 25:7

complete
seven sabbaths shall be *c.* *Lev* 23:15
ye are *c.* in him who is. *Col* 2:10
that ye may stand *c.* in all. 4:12

composition
nor make any after *c.* *Ex* 30:32, 37

compound, -eth
an ointment *c.* after art. *Ex* 30:25
whosoever *c.* any thing like it. 33

comprehend
things which we cannot *c.* *Job* 37:5
able to *c.* with saints. *Eph* 3:18*

comprehended
hath *c.* the dust of the. *Isa* 40:12
the darkness *c.* it not. *John* 1:5*
is briefly *c.* in this saying. *Rom* 13:9*

conceal, -ed, -eth
if we slay brother and *c.* *Gen* 37:26
neither shalt thou *c.* him. *Deut* 13:8
I have not *c.* the words. *Job* 6:10*
the Almighty will I not *c.* 27:11
I will not *c.* his parts nor. 41:12*
not *c.* thy loving-kindness. *Ps* 40:10
of a faithful spirit *c.* the. *Pr* 11:13
a prudent man *c.* knowledge. 12:23
it is the glory of God to *c.* 25:2
publish and *c.* not. *Jer* 50:2

conceit, -s
as an high wall in *c.* *Pr* 18:11*
lest he be wise in his own *c.* 26:5
seest a man wise in his own *c.?* 12
sluggard is wiser in his own *c.* 16
rich man is wise in his own *c.* 28:11
ye be wise in own *c.* *Rom* 11:25
be not wise in your own *c.* 12:16

conceive, -ing
they should *c.* when. *Gen* 30:38
shall be free, and *c.* seed. *Num* 5:28
c. and bear a son. *Judg* 13:3, 5, 7
                                    Luke 1:31
they *c.* mischief. *Job* 15:35; *Isa* 59:4
in sin did my mother *c.* me. *Ps* 51:5
a virgin shall *c.* and bear. *Isa* 7:14
shall *c.* chaff. 33:11
c. words of falsehood. 59:13
received strength to *c.* *Heb* 11:11

conceived
Eve *c.* and bare Cain. *Gen* 4:1
Cain's wife *c.* and bare Enoch. 17
Hagar *c.* 16:4
Sarah *c.* and bare Isaac. 21:2
Rebekah his wife *c.* 25:21
Leah *c.* 29:32, 33
Bilhah *c.* 30:5
Rachel *c.* and bare a son. 23
the flocks *c.* 39; 31:10
Shuah *c.* 38:3, 4, 5
Tamar *c.* 18
Jochebed *c.* and bare. *Ex* 2:2
have *c.* seed, and born. *Lev* 12:2
have I *c.* all this people ? *Num* 11:12
c. and bare son, Samuel. *1 Sam* 1:20
                                    2:21
Bath-sheba *c.* and sent. *2 Sam* 11:5
Shunammite *c.* *2 Ki* 4:17
prophetess *c.* *Isa* 8:3
there is a man child *c.* *Job* 3:3
c. mischief, brought forth. *Ps* 7:14

chamber of her that *c.* *S of S* 3:4
and hath *c.* a purpose. *Jer* 49:30
Gomer which *c.* and. *Hos* 1:3
she that *c.* them hath done. 2:5
that which is *c.* in her is of the Holy
  Ghost. *Mat* 1:20
Elisabeth hath *c.* a son. *Luke* 1:36
named before he was *c.* 2:21
hast thou *c.* this thing ? *Acts* 5:4
when Rebekah had *c.* *Rom* 9:10
when lust hath *c.* it. *Jas* 1:15

conception
multiply sorrow and *c.* *Gen* 3:16
the Lord gave her *c.* *Ruth* 4:13
shall flee from birth and *c.* *Hos* 9:11

concern, -eth
perfect that which *c.* me *Ps* 138:8
this burden *c.* the prince. *Ezek* 12:10
things which *c.* Lord Jesus Christ.
                                    Acts 28:31
glory in things which *c.* *2 Cor* 11:30

concerning
accepted thee *c.* this. *Gen* 19:21
c. which I did swear to. *Ex* 6:8
                                    Num 14:30
atonement for him *c.* *Lev* 4:26; 5:6
found what was lost, lieth *c.* it. 6:3
hath spoken good *c.* *Num* 10:29
commanded him *c.* this. *1 Ki* 11:10
I asked them *c.* the Jews. *Neh* 1:2
repent thee *c.* servants. *Ps* 90:13
                                    135:14
dost not inquire wisely *c.* *Eccl* 7:10
therefore have I cried *c.* this. 30:7
ask me *c.* my sons, and *c.* 45:11
saith Lord *c.* sons, *c.* daughters, *c.*
  mothers, *c.* fathers. *Jer* 16:3
c. pillars, *c.* sea, *c.* bases, *c.* vessels.
                                    27:19
comforted *c.* the evil, even *c.* all that
  I have brought. *Ezek* 14:22
the Lord *c.* Ammonites. 21:28
c. which I have lifted up. 47:14
desire mercies of God *c.* *Dan* 2:18
might not be changed *c.* Daniel. 6:17
I speak it not to you *c.* *Mat* 16:11
saw, told also *c.* swine. *Mark* 5:16
expounded the things *c.* *Luke* 24:27
as *c.* that he raised. *Acts* 13:34
as *c.* this sect, we know. 28:22
as *c.* flesh Christ came. *Rom* 9:5
as *c.* the gospel, are enemies. 11:28
and simple *c.* evil. 16:19
I speak as *c.* reproach. *2 Cor* 11:21
but I speak *c.* Christ. *Eph* 5:32
c. giving and receiving. *Phil* 4:15
professing have erred *c.* *1 Tim* 6:21
who *c.* the truth have. *2 Tim* 2:18
reprobates *c.* the faith. 3:8
think it not strange *c.* *1 Pet* 4:12
see him, me, thee, them, us, you

concision
(*A cutting off, hence,* a faction)
beware of the *c.* *Phil* 3:2

conclude
we *c.* a man is justified. *Rom* 3:28*

concluded
the Gentiles. we have *c.* *Acts* 21:25*
for God hath *c.* them. *Rom* 11:32*
the scripture hath *c.* *Gal* 3:22*

conclusion
let us hear the *c.* of. *Eccl* 12:13

concord
what *c.* hath Christ ? *2 Cor* 6:15

concourse
crieth in chief place of *c.* *Pr* 1:21
give account of this *c.* *Acts* 19:40

concubine
(*A secondary wife under the
system of polygamy practised by
the Jews and named in the Bible.
Concubines were frequently purchased slaves. They were more
easily put away than a wife, but
their rights were carefully guarded
under Jewish law*)
his *c.* played the whore. *Judg* 19:2
he laid hold on his *c.* and. 29
Gibeah, I and my *c.* to. 20:4
in to my father's *c.?* *2 Sam* 3:7
Rizpah the *c.* of Saul had. 21:11

concubines
to sons of *c.* Abraham. *Gen* 25:6
David took more *c.* *2 Sam* 5:13
Absalom went in to father's *c.* 16:22
thy life, and lives of thy *c.* 19:5
king put his *c.* in ward and. 20:3
had three hundred *c.* *1 Ki* 11:3
Rehoboam took threescore *c.*
                                    2 Chr 11:21
Shaashgaz who kept *c.* *Esth* 2:14
60 queens and 80 *c.* and. *S of S* 6:8
yea, the queens and the *c.* 9
king and his *c.* drank. *Dan* 5:3, 23

concupiscence
wrought all manner of *c.* *Rom* 7:8*
mortify members, evil *c.* *Col* 3:5*
not in the lust of *c.* *1 Thes* 4:5*

condemn
whom the judges shall *c.* *Ex* 22:9
judge them, and *c.* the. *Deut* 25:1
my mouth shall *c.* me. *Job* 9:20
I will say to God do not *c.* 10:2
and wilt thou *c.* him ? 34:17
wilt thou *c.* me, that thou ? 40:8
not leave him, , or *c.* *Ps* 37:33
they *c.* the innocent blood. 94:21
save him from those that *c.* 109:31
wicked devices will he *c.* *Pr* 12:2
is he that shall *c.* me ? *Isa* 50:9
shall rise against thee shall *c.* 54:17
shall *c.* it. *Mat* 12:41; *Luke* 11:32
rise up in judgement and *c.* it.
                                    Mat 12:42; *Luke* 11:31
c. him to death. *Mat* 20:18
                                    Mark 10:33
c. not, and ye shall not. *Luke* 6:37
God sent not Son to *c.* *John* 3:17
neither do I *c.* thee, go and. 8:11
I speak not this to *c.* *2 Cor* 7:3
if our heart *c.* us, God. *1 John* 3:20
if our heart *c.* us not, then. 21

condemnation
[1] *Declaring guilty, or pronouncing the sentence,* John 8:10.
[2] *Censuring other men's persons,
purposes, words, or actions, either
rashly, unjustly, or uncharitably,*
Luke 6:37.
thou art in the same *c.* *Luke* 23:40
this is the *c.* that light. *John* 3:19*
believeth not come into *c.* 5:24*
judgement was by one to *c.* *Rom* 5:16
judgement came on all men to *c.* 18
there is no *c.* to them who are. 8:1
come not together to *c.* *1 Cor* 11:34*
if the ministration of *c.* *2 Cor* 3:9
lest he fall into the *c.* *1 Tim* 3:6
shall receive greater *c.* *Jas* 3:1*
lest ye fall into *c.* 5:12
of old ordained to this *c.* *Jude* 4

condemned
and *c.* the land in. *2 Chr* 36:3*
answer, yet had *c.* Job. *Job* 32:3
judged, let him be *c.* *Ps* 109:7
drink the wine of *c.* in. *Amos* 2:8*
would not have *c.* the. *Mat* 12:7
by thy words thou shalt be *c.* 37
when he saw that he was *c.* 27:3
they all *c.* him to be. *Mark* 14:64
delivered him to be *c.* *Luke* 24:20
believeth on him is not *c.* but he that
  believeth not is *c.* *John* 3:18*
hath no man *c.* thee ? 8:10
c. sin in the flesh. *Rom* 8:3
we should not be *c.* *1 Cor* 11:32
speech that cannot be *c.* *Tit* 2:8
sinneth, being *c.* of himself. 3:11
by which he *c.* the world. *Heb* 11:7
ye have *c.* and killed just. *Jas* 5:6
not one another, lest ye be *c.* 9*
God *c.* them with. *2 Pet* 2:6

condemnest, eth, -ing
judge thy servants *c.* *1 Ki* 8:32
thine own mouth *c.* thee. *Job* 15:6
he that *c.* the just, is. *Pr* 17:15
fulfilled them in *c.* him. *Acts* 13:27
judgest another thou *c.* *Rom* 2:1
who is he that *c.?* 8:34
that *c.* not himself in that. 14:22

condescend
not high things, but *c.* *Rom* 12:16

condition, -s
on this c. I will make. *1 Sam 11:2*
sendeth and desireth c. *Luke 14:32*

conduct, -ed
came to c. king. *2 Sam 19:15, 31*
all the people of Judah c. *40**
they that c. Paul. *Acts 17:15*
c. him forth in peace. *1 Cor 16:11**

conduit
came and stood by c. *2 Ki 18:17*
Isa 36:2
he made a pool and a c. *2 Ki 20:20*
meet Ahaz at end of the c. *Isa 7:3*

coney, -ies
(*A variety of rabbit*)
and the c. because he is unclean to.
Lev 11:5; Deut 14:7
rocks are a refuge for c. *Ps 104:18*
c. are but a feeble folk. *Pr 30:26*

confection
shalt make a c. after. *Ex 30:35**

confectionaries
your daughters to be c. *1 Sam 8:13†*

confederacy
a c. to whom people say a c.
Isa 8:12*
all men of thy c. brought. *Ob 7*

confederate
and these were c. *Gen 14:13*
they are c. against thee. *Ps 83:5**
it was told, Syria is c. *Isa 7:2*

conference
for they in c. added. *Gal 2:6**

conferred
Adonijah c. with Joab. *1 Ki 1:7*
they c. among themselves. *Acts 4:15*
Festus, when he had c. *25:12*
immediately I c. not with. *Gal 1:16*

confess
[1] *Publicly to own and acknowledge as his own*, Luke 12:8.
[2] *To profess Christ, and to obey his commandments*, Mat 10:32.
[3] *To own our sins and offences, either in private or public*, Josh 7:19; Ps 32:5; Mat 3:6; Jas 5:16; 1 John 1:9.
he shall c. that he hath. *Lev 5:5*
Aaron shall c. over live goat. *16:21*
if they shall c. their iniquity. *26:40*
they shall c. their sins. *Num 5:7*
Israel c. thy name and. *1 Ki 8:33*
2 Chr 6:24
c. thy name and turn. *1 Ki 8:35*
2 Chr 6:26
and c. the sins of the. *Neh 1:6*
I will c. that thy hand. *Job 40:14*
I will c. my transgressions. *Ps 32:5*
shall c. me before men, him will I c.
before. *Mat 10:32; Luke 12:8*
if any man did c. that. *John 9:22*
rulers did not c. him. *12:42*
but Pharisees c. both. *Acts 23:8*
this I c. that after the way. *24:14*
shalt c. with thy mouth. *Rom 10:9*
every tongue shall c. to God. *14:11*
I will c. to thee among the. *15:9**
every tongue shall c. *Phil 2:11*
c. your faults one to. *Jas 5:16*
if we c. our sins. *1 John 1:9*
whoso shall c. that Jesus. *4:15*
who c. not that Jesus. *2 John 7*
but I will c. his name. *Rev 3:5*

confessed, -eth, -ing
when Ezra had c. *Ezra 10:1*
c. their sins, a fourth part c. *Neh 9:2*
but whoso c. and forsaketh. *Pr 28:13*
while c. my sin and the. *Dan 9:20*
baptized c. their sins. *Mat 3:6*
John c. I am not Christ. *John 1:20*
many came and c. and. *Acts 19:18*
these c. that they were. *Heb 11:13*
every spirit that c. Christ. *1 John 4:2*
every spirit that c. not that. *3*

confession
and make c. to him. *Josh 7:19*
offerings and making c. *2 Chr 30:22*
now therefore make c. *Ezra 10:11*
to my God and made c. *Dan 9:4*

with the mouth c. is. *Rom 10:10*
Pilate witnessed good c. *1 Tim 6:13*

confidence
[1] *Boldness*, Acts 28:31. [2] *Trust*, Job 4:6. [3] *That wherein one trusts*, Jer 48:13.
put their c. in Gaal. *Judg 9:26*
great king of Assyria, what c. is this
wherein ? *2 Ki 18:19; Isa 36:4*
is not this thy fear, thy c.? *Job 4:6*
his c. shall be rooted out. *18:14*
thou art my c. *31:24*
who art the c. of all. *Ps 65:5*
trust in Lord than to put c. *118:8*
to trust in Lord than to put c. in. *9*
for Lord shall be thy c. *Pr 3:26*
in fear of Lord is strong c. *14:26*
the strength of the c. thereof. *21:22*
c. in an unfaithful man is. *25:19*
in quietness and c. shall. *Isa 30:15*
ashamed of Beth-el their c. *Jer 48:13*
they shall dwell with c. *Ezek 28:26*
no more the c. of house of. *29:16*
put ye not c. in a guide. *Mi 7:5*
of God with all c. *Acts 28:31*
in this c. I was minded. *2 Cor 1:15*
having c. in you all. *2:3*
I rejoice that I have c. *7:16*
the great c. I have in you. *8:22*
that c. wherewith I think to. *10:2*
foolishly in this c. of boast. *11:17*
I have c. in you through. *Gal 5:10*
in whom access with c. *Eph 3:12*
having this c. I shall. *Phil 1:25*
and have no c. in flesh. *3:3*
though I might have c. in flesh. *4*
we have c. in Lord. *2 Thes 3:4*
c. in thy obedience. *Philem 21*
if we hold fast the c. *Heb 3:6*
hold beginning of our c. stedfast. *14*
cast not away your c. *10:35*
appear, we may have c. *1 John 2:28*
then have c. toward God. *3:21*
and this is the c. that we. *5:14*

confidences
Lord hath rejected thy c. *Jer 2:37*

confident
in this will I be c. *Ps 27:3*
the fool rageth and is c. *Pr 14:16*
art c. thou thyself art a. *Rom 2:19*
we are always c. *2 Cor 5:6*
we are c. willing rather to be. *8*
ashamed in this same c. *9:4*
c. of this very thing. *Phil 1:6*
many of the brethren waxing c. *14*

confidently
another c. affirmed. *Luke 22:59*

confirm
[1] *To strengthen, settle, or establish*, 1 Chr 14:2; Acts 14:22. [2] *To give new assurance of the truth and certainty of any thing*, 1 Ki 1:14; 2 Cor 2:8. [3] *To ratify, or make sure*, Ruth 4:7.
the manner for to c. all. *Ruth 4:7*
come in after and c. thy. *1 Ki 1:14*
to c. the kingdom. *2 Ki 15:19*
wrote to c. second letter. *Esth 9:29*
to c. these days of Purim in. *31*
didst c. thine inheritance. *Ps 68:9*
weak hands and c. feeble. *Isa 35:3*
hope that they would c. *Ezek 13:6*
he shall c. the covenant. *Dan 9:27*
even I stood to c. and to. *11:1*
to c. the promises made. *Rom 15:8*
who shall also c. you. *1 Cor 1:8*
ye would c. your love. *2 Cor 2:8*

confirmation
in defence and c. of the. *Phil 1:7*
an oath of c. is to them. *Heb 6:16*

confirmed
c. to thyself thy people. *2 Sam 7:24*
soon as kingdom was c. *2 Ki 14:5*
Lord had c. him king. *1 Chr 14:2*
hath c. the same. *16:17; Ps 105:10*
Esther c. these matters. *Esth 9:32*
hath c. his words which. *Dan 9:12*
exhorted brethren and c. *Acts 15:32*
testimony of Christ was c. *1 Cor 1:6*
yet if it be c. no man. *Gal 3:15*
the covenant that was c. *17*

was c. to us by them. *Heb 2:3*
immutability of counsel, he c. *6:17*

confirmeth, -ing
bonds on her, he c. *Num 30:14*
cursed be he that c. not. *Deut 27:26*
that c. the word of. *Isa 44:26*
preached, c. word with. *Mark 16:20*
c. souls of the disciples. *Acts 14:22*
through Syria and Cilicia c. *15:41*

confiscation
let judgement be executed to c.
Ezra 7:26

conflict
having the same c. *Phil 1:30*
ye knew what great c. *Col 2:1**

conformable
him, being made c. *Phil 3:10**

conformed
predestinate to be c. *Rom 8:29*
be not c. to this world. *12:2**

confound
[1] *To throw into confusion*, Gen 11:7. [2] *To confute*, Acts 9:22. [3] *To discomfit*, Job 6:20. [4] *To be amazed, astonished*, Acts 2:6.
let us go down and c. *Gen 11:7, 9*
be not dismayed, lest I c. *Jer 1:17**
c. the wise, to c. things. *1 Cor 1:27**

confounded
the inhabitants were c. *2 Ki 19:26*
Isa 37:27
they were c. because. *Job 6:20*
let them be c. that seek. *Ps 35:4**
not those that seek thee be c. *69:6**
let them be c. that are. *71:13**
for they are c. that seek. *24*
let them be c. and troubled. *83:17**
c. be all they that serve. *97:7**
let them all be c. turned. *129:5**
shall be c. for gardens. *Isa 1:29*
weave net-works shall be c. *19:9**
were dismayed and c. *37:27*
greatly c. because we have. *Jer 9:19*
is c. by graven image. *10:14*; 51:17*
let them be c. that persecute. *17:18**
daughter of Egypt c. *46:24**
Moab is c. *48:20**
Hamath is c. *49:23*
Babylon taken, Bel c. *50:2**
mother shall be sore c. *12**
her whole land shall be c. *51:47**
we are c. because we have. *51**
be thou c. and. *Ezek 16:52*, 54, 63*
nations shall see and be c. *Mi 7:16**
riders on horses be c. *Zech 10:5*
came together and were c. *Acts 2:6*
Saul c. the Jews who dwelt. *9:22*

ashamed and confounded
asha. and c. that seek. *Ps 40:14*
70:2
moon be c. and sun asha. *Isa 24:23*
thee shall be asha. and c. *41:11*
idol-makers be asha. and c. *45:16*
not be asha., neither be thou c. *54:4*
little ones asha. and c. *Jer 14:3*
hath been asha. and c. *15:9*
shalt thou be asha. and c. *22:22*
I was asha. yea, even c. *31:19*
be asha. and c. for your. *Ezek 36:32*
seers be asha. and diviners c. *Mi 3:7*

not confounded
trusted, and were not c. *Ps 22:5**
not ashamed nor c. *Isa 45:17*
therefore shall I not be c. *50:7*
believeth on him not be c. *1 Pet 2:6**

confused
battle of warrior with c. *Isa 9:5*
for the assembly was c. *Acts 19:32*

confusion
lie down thereto, it is c. *Lev 18:23*
put to death, have wrought c. *20:12*
chosen David to thine own c. and
unto the c. *1 Sam 20:30**
been delivered to c. of. *Ezra 9:7*
I am full of c. therefore. *Job 10:15**
let them be brought to c. *Ps 35:4**
c. is continually before me. *44:15**
let them be put to c. that. *70:2**
let me never be put to c. *71:1**
cover themselves with own c. *109:29**

the city of *c*. is broken.   *Isa* 24:10
in the shadow of Egypt your *c*. 30:3
stretch out upon it line of *c*.   34:11
images are wind and *c*.   41:29
makers of idols go to *c*.   45:16
for *c*. they shall rejoice in.   61:7*
lie in shame and our *c*.   *Jer* 3:25
provoke themselves to *c*.   7:19
their everlasting *c*. shall.   20:11*
us belongeth *c*. of face.   *Dan* 9:7, 8
city was filled with *c*.   *Acts* 19:29
God is not author of *c*. *1 Cor* 14:33
and strife is, there is *c*.   *Jas* 3:16

congealed
the depths were *c*. in.   *Ex* 15:8

congratulate
of his welfare and *c*.   *1 Chr* 18:10*

congregation
(Generally this means assembly or meeting)
a sin-offering for the *c*.   *Lev* 4:21
you to bear iniquity of *c*.   10:17
make an atonement for the *c*. 16:33
the renowned of the *c*.   *Num* 1:16
but when *c*. is to be gathered.   10:7
shall I bear with this evil *c*.? 14:27
one ordinance shall be for *c*.   15:15
separate yourselves from *c*.   16:21
get you from among this *c*.   45
Aaron ran into the midst of *c*.   47
that soul cut off from the *c*.   19:20
Lord set a man over the *c*.   27:16
manslayer die not, till he stand
   before *c*.   35:12; *Josh* 20:6
drawers of water for *c*.   *Josh* 9:27
the *c*. was gathered as.   *Judg* 20:1
came not up with the *c*.   21:5
called Jeroboam to *c*.   *1 Ki* 12:20
Hezekiah did give to *c*. *2 Chr* 30:24
separated from the *c*.   *Ezra* 10:8
should not come into the *c*. *Neh* 13:1
for the *c*. of hypocrites.   *Job* 15:34
I stood up and cried in the *c*. 30:28
nor sinners in the *c*. of.   *Ps* 1:5
in the midst of the *c*. will I. 22:22
I have hated the *c*. of evil.   26:5
speak righteousness, O *c*.?   58:1
remember thy *c*. thou hast.   74:2
forget not the *c*. of thy poor.   19*
when I receive the *c*. I will.   75:2*
God standeth in the *c*. of.   82:1
thy faithfulness also in *c*.   89:5
let them exalt him also in *c*. 107:32
Lord in the assembly and *c*. 111:1
in all evil in midst of *c*.   *Pr* 5:14
men shall remain in the *c*.   21:16
sit upon the mount of *c*.   *Isa* 14:13
and know, O *c*. what is.   *Jer* 6:18
their *c*. shall be established.   30:20
not enter into thy *c*.   *Lam* 1:10
chastise them as their *c*.   *Hos* 7:12
sanctify the *c*.   *Joel* 2:16
now when the *c*. was.   *Acts* 13:43*

all the congregation
gather *all the c*. together.   *Lev* 8:3
atonement for *all the c*.   16:17
all the c. stone him.   24:14, 16
   Num 15:35
all the c. bade stone.   *Num* 14:10
seeing *all the c*. are holy.   16:3
wilt thou be wroth with *all c*.?'   22
in sight of *all the c*.   20:27; 25:6
Eleazar and *all the c*.   27:19, 22
read not before *all the c*. *Josh* 8:35
all the c. murmured.   9:18
wrath fell on *all the c*.   22:20
king blessed *all the c*. *1 Ki* 8:14, 55
all the c. blessed.   *1 Chr* 29:20
all the c. made a.   *2 Chr* 23:3
all the c. worshipped and.   29:28
all the c. said, amen.   *Neh* 5:13
all the c. that were come.   8:17

elders of the congregation
elders of the c. shall.   *Lev* 4:15
elders of c. said, how? *Judg* 21:16

great congregation
a feast, all Israel with him, a *great c*.
  1 Ki 8:65; *2 Chr* 7:8; 30:13
out of Israel a *great c*.   *Ezra* 10:1
be of thee in the *great c*. *Ps* 22:25
thanks in the great *c*.   35:18

---

righteousness in the *great c*. *Ps* 40:9
not concealed truth from *great c*. 10

congregation *of Israel*
c. of Israel shall kill it.   *Ex* 12:6
cut off from the *c. of Israel*.   19
all the *c. of Israel* shall keep.   47
if whole *c. of Israel* sin.   *Lev* 4:13
separated you from *c. of Israel*.
  Num 16:9
Solomon and *c. of Israel*. *2 Chr* 5:6
commandment of *c. of Israel*.   24:6

congregation *of the Lord*
why lift yourselves above the *c. of*
   the Lord?   *Num* 16:3
c. of Lord not as sheep that.   27:17
plague among *c. of the Lord*.   31:16
  Josh 22:17
not enter into the *c. of the Lord*.
  Deut 23:1, 2, 3
in sight of *c. of Lord*.   *1 Chr* 28:8
a cord by lot in *c. of Lord*.   *Mi* 2:5

tabernacle of the congregation
brought before *tab. of c*.   *Ex* 29:10
I will sanctify *tab. of c*.   44
anoint *tab. of c*.   30:26
called it the *tab. of c*. went out to the
   tab. of c.   33:7
kill it before *tab. of c*.   *Lev* 3:8, 13
bring it to *tab. of c*.   4:5
not go out from door of *tab. of c*. 10:7
no wine when ye go into *tab. of c*. 9
so do for *tab. of c*.   16:16
atonement for *tab. of c*.   33
work of *tab. of c. Num* 4:3, 23, 25
  30, 35, 39, 43
bring Levites before *tab. of c*.   8:9
come out ye three to *tab. of c*. 12:4
appeared in the *tab. of c*.   14:10
lay up in *tab. of c*.   17:4
keep charge of *tab. of c*.   18:4
weeping before door of *tab. of c*. 25:6
yourselves in *tab. of c. Deut* 31:14
set up *tab of c*. there.   *Josh* 18:1
brought up *tab. of c*.   *1 Ki* 8:4
  2 Chr 5:5
was *tab. of c*. of God.   *2 Chr* 1:3

see **door**

tent of the congregation
tent of the c. finished.   *Ex* 39:32
set up *tent of the c*.   40:2
table in *tent of the c*.   22
candlestick in *tent of the c*.   24
golden altar in the *tent of the c*. 26
cloud covered the *tent of the c*. 35
not able to enter into *tent of the c*. 35

whole congregation
the *whole c*. of Israel.   *Ex* 16:2
the charge of *whole c*.   *Num* 3:7
be wroth with *whole c*.   *Josh* 22:18
whole c. sent to speak. *Judg* 21:13
king blessed the *whole c*. *2 Chr* 6:3
the *whole c*.   *Ezra* 2:64; *Neh* 7:66
shewed before *whole c*.   *Pr* 26:26

congregations
in the *c*. will I bless.   *Ps* 26:12
bless ye God in the *c*. even.   68:26
enemies roar in midst of thy *c*. 74:4

Coniah
though *C*. were the signet. *Jer* 22:24
man *C*. despised, broken idol?   28
Zedekiah reigned instead of *C*. 37:1

conquer
conquering and to *c*.   *Rev* 6:2

conquerors
we are more than *c*.   *Rom* 8:37

conscience
*(That faculty within us which de-
cides as to the moral quality of our
thoughts, words, and acts. It
gives consciousness of the good of
one's conduct or motives, or causes
feelings of remorse at evil-doing.
A conscience can be educated, or
trained to recognize good and evil,
but its action is involuntary. A good
conscience is one which has no
feeling of reproach against oneself,
does not accuse oneself of wilful
wrong,* Acts 24:16)
convicted by their own *c*.   *John* 8:9

I have lived in all good *c*. *Acts* 23:1
to have a *c*. void of offence.   24:16
their *c*. also bearing.   *Rom* 2:15
my *c*. bearing me witness in.   9:1
subject also for *c*. sake.   13:5
with *c*. of the idol to this hour eat it,
   and their *c*. being weak. *1 Cor* 8:7
shall not *c*. of him which is weak? 10
when ye wound their weak *c*.   12
no question for *c*. sake.   10:25, 27
eat not, for *c*. sake.   28
c. I say, not thine own, but.   29
testimony of our *c*.   *2 Cor* 1:12
commending to every man's *c*.   4:2
pure heart, and a good *c*. *1 Tim* 1:5
holding faith and a good *c*.   19
mystery of faith in a pure *c*.   3:9
having their *c*. seared.   4:2
God, whom I serve with *c*. *2 Tim* 1:3
even their mind and *c*. is.   *Tit* 1:15
as pertaining to the *c*.   *Heb* 9:9
purge *c*. from dead works to.   14
should have had no more *c*. of. 10:2
hearts sprinkled from an evil *c*.   22
we trust we have a good *c*.   13:18
if a man for *c*. toward.   *1 Pet* 2:19
having a good *c*. as they.   3:16
but the answer of a good *c*.   21

consciences
made manifest in your *c*. *2 Cor* 5:11

consecrate
*To devote any thing to God's
worship and service ; to hallow, or
sanctify whether persons,* Ex 13:2,
12, 15; 19:6; Num 1:49; 3:12
1 Sam 1:11, 22; *or things,* Lev 27:28.
c. Aaron.   *Ex* 28:3*
anoint and *c*. Aaron's sons.   41
c. Aaron and sons.   29:9; 30:30*
seven days shalt thou *c*. 35; *Lev* 8:33
Moses said, *c*. yourselves. *Ex* 32:29
shall *c*. to Lord the days. *Num* 6:12*
to *c*. his service this.   *1 Chr* 29:5
to *c*. himself with a.   *1 Chr* 13:9
they shall *c*. themselves. *Ezek* 43:26*
I will *c*. their gain to.   *Mi* 4:13*

consecrated
sons of Aaron, whom he *c*. *Num* 3:3
vessels are *c*. to the.   *Josh* 6:19
Micah *c*. one of sons. *Judg* 17:5, 12
Jeroboam *c*. him.   *1 Ki* 13:33
ye have *c*. yourselves. *2 Chr* 29:31
c. things were 600 oxen.   33
holy things which were *c*.   31:6
feasts of Lord that were *c*. *Ezra* 3:5
the Son, for evermore. *Heb* 7:28*
living way which he hath *c*.   10:20*

consecration, -s
of ram, for it is ram of *c*. *Ex* 29:22
if aught of the flesh of the *c*.   34
this is the law of the *c*.   *Lev* 7:37
c. for a sweet savour to the.   8:28
with bread that is in basket of *c*.   31
till the days of your *c*. be.   33
because the *c*. of his God. *Num* 6:7*
hath defiled the head of his *c*.   9

consent, -ed, -ing
but in this will we *c*.   *Gen* 34:15
only let us *c*. to them.   23
shalt not *c*. to him.   *Deut* 13:8
but would not *c*.   *Judg* 11:17
hearken not to him, nor *c*. *1 Ki* 20:8
the priests *c*. to receive.   *2 Ki* 12:8
sawest a thief, thou *c*.   *Ps* 50:18
if sinners entice thee, *c*. not. *Pr* 1:10
so he *c*. to them, and.   *Dan* 1:14*
the same had not *c*.   *Luke* 23:51
and Saul was *c*. to. *Acts* 8:1; 22:20
tarry longer with them, *c*. not. 18:20
if I do that which I would not, I *c*.
   unto the law.   *Rom* 7:16
if any man *c*. not to.   *1 Tim* 6:3

consent, *substantive*
came out with one *c*.   *1 Sam* 11:7*
together with one *c*.   *Ps* 83:5
of the priests murder by *c*. *Hos* 6:9
to serve him with one *c*.   *Zeph* 3:9
all with one *c*. began to. *Luke* 14:18
except it be with *c*. for.   *1 Cor* 7:5

consider
[1] *To meditate upon,* 2 Tim 2:7.
[2] *To view, or observe,* Lev 13:13.

[3] *To determine,* Judg 18:14.
[4] *To pity, comfort, or relieve,*
Ps 41:1. [5] *To remember,* 1 Sam
12:24.
then the priest shall *c.*   Lev 13:13
know this day and *c.*   Deut 4:39
that they were wise to *c.*   32:29
now therefore *c.* what.   Judg 18:14
c. how great things.   1 Sam 12:24
therefore know and *c.* what.   25:17
will he not then *c.* it ?   Job 11:11
when I *c.* I am afraid of him.   23:15
and would not *c.* of his ways.   34:27
stand still and *c.* the works.   37:14
c. my meditation.   Ps. 5:1
when I *c.* the heavens.   8:3
c. my trouble.   9:13
c. and hear.   13:3; 45:10
c. my enemies.   25:19
shalt diligently *c.* his place.   37:1u
c. her palaces, that ye may.   48:13
now *c.* this, ye that forget.   50:22
for they shall wisely *c.*   64:9
I will *c.* thy testimonies.   119:95
c. mine affliction, and deliver.   153
c. how I love thy precepts.   159
go to the ant, *c.* her ways.   Pr 6:6
with a ruler, *c.* diligently.   23:1
pondereth the heart *c.* it ?   24:12
for f.ey *c.* not that they.   Eccl 5:1
c. the work of God, who.   7:13
but in day of adversity *c.*   14
my people doth not *c.*   Isa 1:3
neither *c.* the operation of.   5:12
narrowly look upon thee and *c.* 14:16
and I will *c.* in my dwelling-.   18:4
may see, and know, and *c.*   41:20
remember ye not, nor *c.*   43:18
had not heard shall they *c.*   52:15
c. and see if there be.   Jer 2:10
latter days ye shall *c.* 23:20; 30:24
O Lord, *c.* to whom.   Lam 2:20
O Lord, *c.* and behold our.   5:1
it may be they will *c.*   Ezek 12:3
understand, and *c.* the vision.
    Dan 9:23
they *c.* not in their hearts.   Hos 7:2
c. your ways.   Hag 1:5, 7
pray you, *c.* from this day. 2:15, 18
c. the lilies.   Mat 6:28; Luke 12:27
c. the ravens, for they.   Luke 12:24
nor *c.* it is expedient.   John 11:50
the elders came to *c.*   Acts 15:6
c. and the Lord give.   2 Tim 2:7
brethren, *c.* the Apostle.   Heb 3:1
now *c.* how great this man.   7:4
c. one another to provoke.   10:24
c. him that endured.   12:3

considered, -est
when I *c.* in morning.   1 Ki 3:21
I have *c.* things which thou.   5:8
c. my servant Job ?   Job 1:8; 2:3
glad, for thou hast *c.* my.   Ps 31:7
then I saw and *c.* it well.   Pr 24:32
I *c.* all the oppressions.   Eccl 4:1
again I *c.* all travail.   4
for all this I *c.* in my heart.   9:1
c. not what this people.   Jer 33:24
c. the horns, and behold.   Dan 7:8
c. not the beam that is.   Mat 7:3
they *c.* not the miracle.   Mark 6:52
when Peter had *c.* the.   Acts 12:12
he *c.* not his own body.   Rom 4:19

considereth, -ing
hearts alike, he *c.* all.   Ps 33:15
blessed is he that *c.* the poor.   41:1
righteous man *c.* house.   Pr 21:12
and *c.* not that poverty shall.   28:22
the righteous *c.* the cause of.   29:7
c. a field, and buyeth it.   31:16
none *c.* in his heart to say.   Isa 44:19
none *c.* that the righteous is.   57:1
c. and doth not.   Ezek 18:14, 28
as I was *c.* behold.   Dan 8:5
c. thyself, lest thou.   Gal 6:1
c. the end of their.   Heb 13:7

consist, -eth
a man's life *c.* not in.   Luke 12:15
by him all things *c.*   Col 1:17

consolation
(*Comfort or relief in distress or
depression*)
men give them cup of *c.*   Jer 16:7

waiting for the *c.* of.   Luke 2:25
for ye have received your *c.*   6:24
interpreted, the son of *c.* Acts 4:36*
they rejoiced for the *c.*   15:31
God of *c.* grant you to.   Rom 15:5
so our *c.* also aboundeth.   2 Cor 1:5
we be afflicted, it is for your *c.*   6
so shall ye be partakers of the *c.* 7
but by the *c.* wherewith he was. 7:7
if there be any *c.* in Christ. Phil 2:1*
given us everlasting *c.* 2 Thes 2:16
have great joy and *c.*   Philem 7
might have a strong *c.*   Heb 6:18*

consolations
are the *c.* of God small ?   Job 15:11
and let this be your *c.*   21:2
with the breasts of her *c.* Isa 66:11

consorted
(*Companied with*)
some of them *c.* with.   Acts 17:4

conspiracy
and Absalom's *c.* was.   2 Sam 15:12
his servants made a *c.*   2 Ki 12:20
made a *c.* against Amaziah.   14:19
    2 Chr 25:27
Shallum and his *c.*   2 Ki 15:15
Hoshea made a *c.* against.   30
the king of Assyria found *c.*   17:4
a *c.* is found among the.   Jer 11:9
is a *c.* of her prophets.   Ezek 22:25
forty who had made this *c.* Acts 23:13

conspirators
Ahithophel is among *c.* 2 Sam 15:31

conspired
they *c.* against Joseph.   Gen 37:18
that all of you have *c.* 1 Sam 22:8
why have ye *c.* against me ?   13
Baasha son of Ahijah *c.* 1 Ki 15:27
Zimri *c.* against Elah.   16:9, 16
Jehu son of Nimshi *c.* 2 Ki 9:14
I *c.* against my master.   10:9
Shallum *c.* against Zachariah. 15:10
Pekah *c.* against Pekahiah.   25
servants of Amon *c.*   21:23
slew all that *c.*   24; 2 Chr 33:25
they *c.* against Jehoiada. 2 Chr 24:21
the servants of Joash *c.*   25, 26
c. all of them together.   Neh 4:8
Amos hath *c.* against.   Amos 7:10

constant, -ly
if he be *c.* to do my.   1 Chr 28:7
that heareth, speaketh *c.* Pr 21:28*
Rhoda *c.* affirmed that. Acts 12:15*
these things thou affirm *c.* Tit 3:8*

constellations
the *c.* thereof shall not.   Isa 13:10

constrain
c. you to be circumcised. Gal 6:12*

constrained, -eth
woman of Shunem *c.*   2 Ki 4:8
spirit within me *c.* me.   Job 32:18
Jesus *c.* his disciples.   Mat 14:22
    Mark 6:45
they *c.* him, saying.   Luke 24:29
Lydia *c.* us to come.   Acts 16:15
I was *c.* to appeal to Caesar.   28:19
for love of Christ *c.* us.   2 Cor 5:14

constraint
oversight, not by *c.* but.   1 Pet 5:2

consult
only *c.* to cast him down.   Ps 62:4

consultation
chief priests held a *c.*   Mark 15:1

consulted
Rehoboam *c.* with.   1 Ki 12:6, 8
David *c.* with captains.   1 Chr 13:1
Jehoshaphat *c.* with.   2 Chr 20:21
I *c.* with myself, and.   Neh 5:7
they have *c.* against thy.   Ps 83:3
for they have *c.* together with.   5
king of Babylon *c.* with. Ezek 21:21
presidents and captains *c.* Dan 6:7
Balak king of Moab *c.*   Mi 6:5
hast *c.* shame to thy.   Hab 2:10
c. that they might take.   Mat 26:4
chief priests *c.* to put.   John 12:10

consulter
not found among you a *c.* Deut 18:11

consulteth
c. whether he be able.   Luke 14:31

consume
[1] *To destroy,* Ex 32:10. [2] *To
spend, or squa:der away,* Jas 4:3.
[3] *To burn up,* Luke 9:54.
famine shall *c.* the land.   Gen 41:30
lest I *c.* thee in the way. Ex 33:3, 5
that shall *c.* the eyes.   Lev 26:16
this great fire will *c.* us.   Deut 5:25
thou shalt *c.* all people.   7:16
for locust shall *c.* it.   28:38, 42*
kindled in mine anger shall *c.* 32:22*
will *c.* you after he hath. Josh 24:20
shall be to *c.* thine eyes. 1 Sam 2:33
let fire *c.* thee and.   2 Ki 1:10, 12
fire shall *c.* the tabernacles. Job 15:34
a fire not blown shall *c.* him. 20:26*
drought and heat *c.* the.   24:19
c. into smoke shall they *c.* Ps 37:20
makest his beauty to *c.*   39:11
their beauty shall *c.* in.   49:14
their days did he *c.* in.   78:33
it shall also *c.* the beard.   Isa 7:20
and shall *c.* the glory of his.   10:18
there shall the calf *c.* the.   27:10
fire shall *c.* the palaces. Jer 49:27*
and *c.* away for their.   Ezek 4:17*
hail-stones in my fury to *c.* it. 13:13
is drawn, it is furbished to *c.* 21:28*
I will *c.* thy filthiness out.   22:15
kindle the fire, *c.* the flesh.   24:10*
desolate, are given us to *c.*   35:12*
c. all these kingdoms.   Dan 2:44
and the sword shall *c.*   Hos 11:6
I will *c.* all things from.   Zeph 1:2
c. man and beast, I will *c.* fowls. 3
remain in his house and *c.* Zech 5:4
their flesh, eyes, shall *c.* away. 14:12
whom the Lord shall *c.* 2 Thes 2:8*
ye ask that ye may *c.*   Jas 4:3*

consume them
that I may *c.* them.   Ex 32:10, 12
c. them in moment.   Num 16:21, 45
thou mayest not *c.* them. Deut 7:22
didst not utterly *c.* them. Neh 9:31
c. them in wrath, *c.* Ps 59:13
I will surely *c.* them.   Jer 8:13
but I will *c.* them by the.   14:12
fury on them to *c.* them. Ezek 20:13
and *c.* them, as Elias did. Luke 9:54

consumed
lest thou be *c.* in the.   Gen 19:15
mountain, lest thou be *c.*   17
in day the drought *c.* me.   31:40
bush burned, was not *c.*   Ex 3:2
sentest thy wrath, which *c.*   15:7
if the corn or the field be *c.*   22:6
and *c.* upon the altar.   Lev 9:24
c. them in uttermost.   Num 11:1*
one of whom flesh is half *c.*   12:12
depart lest ye be *c.* in all.   16:26
there came out fire and *c.* the.   35*
a fire is gone out, it hath *c.* 21:28*
I *c.* not the children of Israel. 25:11
generation . . . done evil was *c.* 32:13
men of war were *c.*   Deut 2:16
rose fire out of rock and *c.* Judg 6:21
the man that *c.* us.   2 Sam 21:5
fire of Lord fell and *c.*   1 Ki 18:38
    2 Chr 7:1
fire *c.* him and fifty.   2 Ki 1:10, 12
children of Israel *c.* not.   2 Chr 8:8
gates are *c.* with fire.   Neh 2:3, 13
fire of God hath *c.* sheep.   Job 1:16
by breath of his nostrils *c.*   4:9
snow and ice are *c.* out.   6:17
as the cloud is *c.* and.   7:9
though my reins be *c.*   19:27
his flesh is *c.* away.   33:21
mine eyes *c.*   Ps 6:7; 31:9
my bones *c.*   31:10*; 102:3
I am *c.* by the blow of.   39:10
be confounded and *c.* that.   71:13
are utterly *c.* with terrors.   73:19
fire *c.* their young men.   78:63*
for we are *c.* by thine anger.   90:7
let the sinners be *c.* out of.   104:35
they had almost *c.* me upon. 119:87
my zeal hath *c.* me.   139
flesh and thy body are *c.*   Pr 5:11
the oppressors are *c.*   Isa 16:4
scorner is *c.* and all that.   29:20
thou hast *c.* us.   64:7
hast *c.* them, but they.   Jer 5:3

the lead is *c*.   *Jer* 6:29
the beasts are *c*.   12:4
that my days should be *c*.   20:18
till all the roll was *c*.   36:23
we have been *c*. by sword.   44:18
hath mine enemy *c*.   *Lam* 2:22
Lord's mercies we are not *c*.   3:22
her rods broken, fire *c*.   *Ezek* 19:12
   22:31
that the scum of it may be *c*.   24:11
wherefore I have *c*. them.   43:8
sons of Jacob are not *c*.   *Mal* 3:6
take heed ye be not *c*.   *Gal* 5:15

shall be consumed
in wilderness *shall be c*. *Num* 14:35
shall die, *shall* we be *c*.?   17:13*
ye *shall be c*. both you. *1 Sam* 12:25
forsake Lord *shall be c*.   *Isa* 1:28
shall be c. together : they that eat
swine's flesh *shall be c*.   66:17
famine *shall* prophets *be c. Jer* 14:15
shall be c. by sword. 16:4; 44:12, 27
famine *shall they be c*. *Ezek* 5:12
it shall fall, ye *shall be c*. in.   13:14
they *shall be* no more *c*.   34:29
nor *shall* the fruit *be c*.   47:12*
by his hand *shall be c*. *Dan* 11:16*

consumed with *till*, or *until*
to destroy, *until* they were *c*.
   Deut 2:15; *Josh* 5:6
until he have *c*. thee. *Deut* 28:21
slaying them *till* they were *c*.
   Josh 10:20
fight *until* they be *c*. *1 Sam* 15:18
I turned not again *until* I had *c*. them.
   2 Sam 22:38; *Ps* 18:37
Syrians *until* thou have *c*. *1 Ki* 22:11
   2 Ki 13:17, 19; *2 Chr* 18:10
angry *till* thou hadst *c*. us. *Ezra* 9:14
a sword after them *till* I have *c*.
   Jer 9:16; 24:10; 27:8; 49:37

consumeth, -ing
thy God is a *c*. fire.   *Deut* 4:24*
   Heb 12:29
before thee as a *c*. fire. *Deut* 9:3*
he *c*. as a garment. *Job* 13:28
remnant of them the fire *c*.   22:20
for it is a fire that *c*. to.   31:12
as the flame *c*. chaff. *Isa* 5:24*

consummation
desolate, even until *c*. *Dan* 9:27

consumption
(*Wasting*)
appoint over you terror, *c. Lev* 26:16
Lord smite thee with a *c. Deut* 28:22
the *c*. decreed shall. *Isa* 10:22
Lord God of hosts make a *c*.   23*
I have heard from Lord God of hosts
a *c*.   28:22*

contain
of heavens cannot *c*. thee. *1 Ki* 8:27
   2 Chr 2:6; 6:18
bath may *c*. tenth part. *Ezek* 45:11
the world could not *c*. *John* 21:25
but if they cannot *c*. *1 Cor* 7:9*

contained, -eth, -ing
drink of sister's cup, it *c. Ezek* 23:32
six water pots of 0 or 0. *John* 2.0
do by nature things *c*. *Rom* 2:14
having abolished law *c*. *Eph* 2:15
it is *c*. in scripture. *1 Pet* 2:6

contemn, -ed, -eth
(*To scorn or despise*)
do the wicked *c*. God ? *Ps* 10:13
a vile person is *c*.   15:4
they *c*. the counsel of the.   107:11
for love, it would be *c*. *S of S* 8:7
glory of Moab shall be *c*. *Isa* 16:14
it *c*. the rod of my son. *Ezek* 21:10
and what if the sword *c*. even ?   13

contempt
thus shall arise much *c*. *Esth* 1:18
he poureth *c*. on princes. *Job* 12:21
   Ps 107:40
did *c*. of families terrify ? *Job* 31:34
remove reproach and *c*. *Ps* 119:22
are exceedingly filled with *c*.   123:3
our soul is filled with the *c*.   4
then cometh *c*. *Pr* 18:3
to bring into *c*. all the. *Isa* 23:9
awake to everlasting *c*. *Dan* 12:2

---

contemptible
ye say, table of Lord is *c*. *Mal* 1:7
even his meat is *c*.   12
I also made you *c*.   2:9
is weak, his speech *c*. *2 Cor* 10:10

contemptuously
which speak *c*. against. *Ps* 31:18

contend
To strive, either bodily or in
debate or discussion, to dispute,
Job 9:3; 40:2; Jer 18:19; Acts 11:2.
c. with Moabites. *Deut* 2:9, 24
if *c*. he cannot answer. *Job* 9:3
accept his person, and *c*.   13:8
such as keep the law *c*. *Pr* 28:4
nor may he *c*. with him. *Eccl* 6:10
c. with them that *c*. with. *Isa* 49:25
that justifieth me, who will *c*.?   50:8
I will not *c*. for ever.   57:16
then how canst thou *c*.? *Jer* 12:5
to voice of them that *c*. with. 18:19
Lord God called to *c*. *Amos* 7:4
hear ye, arise, *c*. thou. *Mi* 6:1
should earnestly *c*. for faith. *Jude* 3

contended
then *c*. I with rulers. *Neh* 13:11, 17
I *c*. with them, and cursed.   25
servants when they *c*. *Job* 31:13
not find them that *c*. *Isa* 41:12
they of circumcision *c*. *Acts* 11:2

contendest
shew me wherefore thou *c. Job* 10:2

contendeth
shall he that *c*. with ? *Job* 40:2
if a wise man *c*. with. *Pr* 29:9

contending
c. with devil, he disputed. *Jude* 9

content
his brethren were *c*. *Gen* 37:27
Moses was *c*. to dwell. *Ex* 2:21
heard that, he was *c*. *Lev* 10:20
to God we had been *c*. *Josh* 7:7
Levite was *c*. to dwell. *Judg* 17:11
be *c*. I pray thee, and.   19:6
Naaman said, be *c*. *2 Ki* 5:23
one said, be *c*. and go with.   6:3
now therefore be *c*. *Job* 6:28
nor will he rest *c*. though. *Pr* 6:35
Pilate willing to *c*. *Mark* 15:15
nor accuse falsely, be *c*. *Luke* 3:14
in every state to be *c*. *Phil* 4:11
and raiment, let us be *c*. *1 Tim* 6:8
be *c*. with such things. *Heb* 13:5
and not *c*. with prating. *3 John* 10

contention
only by pride cometh *c*. *Pr* 13:10
leave off *c*. before it be.   17:14
a fool's lips enter into *c*.   18:6
cast out the scorner, and *c*.   22:10
hast borne me a man of *c*. *Jer* 15:10
that raise up strife and *c*. *Hab* 1:3
the *c*. was so sharp. *Acts* 15:39
preach Christ of *c*. *Phil* 1:16*
gospel of God with much *c*.
   1 Thes 2:2

contentions
let causeth *c*. to cease. *Pr* 18:18
and their *c*. are like the bars.   19
c. of a wife are a. 19:13; 27:15
who hath woe ? who hath *c*.?   23:29
that there are *c*. among. *1 Cor* 1:11
avoid *c*. and strivings. *Tit* 3:9

contentious
than with a *c*. and angry. *Pr* 21:19
as wood to fire, so is a *c*.   26:21
a continual dropping and a *c*. 27:15
but to them that are *c*. *Rom* 2:8
if any man seem to be *c*. *1 Cor* 11:16

contentment
but godliness with *c*. *1 Tim* 6:6

continual
this shall be a *c*. burnt-. *Ex* 29:42
and the *c*. bread shall. *Num* 4:7
house for *c*. shew-bread. *2 Chr* 2:4
merry heart hath a *c*. feast. *Pr* 15:15
smote the people with *c*. *Isa* 14:6
for in going up *c*. weeping. *Jer* 48:5
there was a *c*. diet given him. 52:34
   2 Ki 25:30
sever out men of *c*. *Ezek* 39:14

---

lest by her *c*. coming she. *Luke* 18:5
that I have *c*. sorrow.   *Rom* 9:2*

continually
imagination of heart evil *c. Gen* 6:5
before the Lord *c*.   *Ex* 28:30
lambs of first year, day by day *c*.
   29:38
to cause lamps to burn *c. Lev* 24:2
David's enemy *c*. *1 Sam* 18:29
eat bread at my table *c*. *2 Sam* 9:7
Jehoiakim eat bread *c*. *2 Ki* 25:29
   Jer 52:33
seek his face *c*. *1 Chr* 16:11
between Jeroboam and Rehoboam *c*.
   2 Chr 12:15
his sons, thus did Job *c*. *Job* 1:5
his praise shall be *c*. *Ps* 34:1; 71:6
say *c*. the Lord be magnified. 35:27
   40:16; 70:4
and my sorrow is *c*. before.   38:17
loving-kindness and truth *c*.   40:11
they *c*. say, Where is thy God ? 42:3
my confusion is *c*. before me. 44:15
burnt-offerings to have been *c*.   50:8
goodness of God endureth *c*.   52:1
whereunto I *c*. resort.   71:3
my praise shall be *c*.   6
I will hope *c*. and praise thee.   14
I am *c*. with thee.   73:23
tumult increaseth *c*.   74:23
be before the Lord *c*.   109:15
so shall I keep thy law *c*.   119:44
my soul is *c*. in my hand.   109
have respect to thy statutes *c*.   117
c. are they gathered for war. 140:2
he deviseth mischief *c*. *Pr* 6:14
bind them on thy heart.   21
I stand *c*. upon watch-. *Isa* 21:8
walls are *c*. before me.   49:16
and hast feared *c*. every day. 51:13
my name *c*. every day is.   52:5
Lord shall guide thee *c*.   58:11
thy gates shall be open *c*.   60:11
provoketh me to anger *c*.   65:3
before me *c*. is grief and. *Jer* 6:7
a meat-offering *c*. to. *Ezek* 46:14
God whom thou servest *c*.
   Dan 6:16, 20
committed whoredom *c*. *Hos* 4:18
and wait on thy God *c*.   12:6
so shall the heathen drink *c*. *Ob* 16
thy wickedness passed *c*.? *Nah* 3:19
shall they not spare *c*.? *Hab* 1:17
were *c*. in the temple. *Luke* 24:53
we will give ourselves *c*. *Acts* 6:4*
that waited on Cornelius *c*.   10:7
attending *c*. upon this. *Rom* 13:6
abideth a priest *c*. *Heb* 7:3
sacrifices offered year by year *c*.
   10:1
offer the sacrifice of praise *c*. 13:15

continuance
great plagues of long *c. Deut* 28:59
my members which in *c. Ps* 139:16
in those is *c*. and we. *Isa* 64:5*
by patient *c*. in well doing. *Rom* 2:7*

continue
if he *c*. a day or two. *Ex* 21:21
c. in blood of purifying. *Lev* 12:4, 5
c. following the Lord. *1 Sam* 12:14
thy kingdom shall not *c*.   13:14
that it may *c*. for ever. *2 Sam* 7:29
Lord may *c*. his word. *1 Ki* 2:4*
nor shall his substance *c. Job* 15:29
doth not mine eye *c*. in their ? 17:2
O *c*. thy loving-kindness. *Ps* 36:10
that their houses shall *c*.   49:11
children of thy servants *c*.   102:28
they *c*. according to thine. 119:91
that *c*. till night, till wine. *Isa* 5:11
that the evidences may *c. Jer* 32:14
c. more years than the. *Dan* 11:8*
because they *c*. with me. *Mat* 15:32
if ye *c*. in my word. *John* 8:31
so have I loved you, *c*.   15:9
persuaded to *c*. in. *Acts* 13:43
and exhorting them to *c*.   14:22
obtained help of God, I *c*.   26:22
shall we *c*. in sin that ? *Rom* 6:1
goodness, if thou *c*. in.   11:22
truth of gospel might *c*. *Gal* 2:5
I know that I shall *c*. *Phil* 1:25

continued (continued)

if ye *c.* in the faith. *Col 1:23*
c. in prayer, and watch. *4:2*
if they *c.* in faith. *1 Tim 2:15*
take heed to thy doctrine, *c.* *4:16*
c. in the things which. *2 Tim 3:14*
priests not suffered to *c.* *Heb 7:23*
let brotherly love *c.* *13:1*
and *c.* there a year. *Jas 4:13*
the fathers, all things *c.* *2 Pet 3:4*
ye shall *c.* in the Son. *1 John 2:24*
power was given him to *c.* *Rev 13:5*
when he cometh, he must *c.* *17:10*

continued

served them, and *c.* a. *Gen 40:4*
as she *c.* praying. *1 Sam 1:12*
c. till burnt-offering was. *2 Chr 29:28*
also I *c.* in the work of. *Neh 5:16*
his name shall be *c.* as. *Ps 72:17*
Daniel *c.* to first year. *Dan 1:21*
c. all night in prayer. *Luke 6:12*
ye are they that *c.* with me. *22:28*
all *c.* with one accord. *Acts 1:14*
they *c.* stedfastly in the. *2:42*
Simon himself *c.* with Philip. *8:13*
but Peter *c.* knocking. *12:16*
Paul preached *c.* his. *20:7*
because they *c.* not in. *Heb 8:9*
would no doubt have *c.* *1 John 2:19*

continueth, -ing

as a shadow, and *c.* *Job 14:2*
a *c.* whirlwind, it shall. *Jer 30:23*
c. daily with one accord. *Acts 2:46*
rejoicing in hope, *c.* *Rom 12:12*
cursed that *c.* not in all. *Gal 3:10*
she that is a widow *c.* *1 Tim 5:5*
this man, because he *c.* *Heb 7:24**
here we have no *c.* city. *13:14**
into perfect law, and *c.* *Jas 1:25*

contradicting

filled with envy, *c.* and. *Acts 13:45*

contradiction

without *c.* the less is. *Heb 7:7*
him that endured such *c.* *12:3**

contrariwise

c. ye ought rather to. *2 Cor 2:7*
c. when they saw the gospel. *Gal 2:7*
not rendering railing. *1 Pet 3:9*

contrary

if ye walk *c.* *Lev 26:21, 23, 27, 40*
then will I walk *c.* to you. *24, 28, 41*
it was turned to the *c.* *Esth 9:1*
the *c.* is in thee, therefore thou art *c.*
 Ezek 16:34
for the wind was *c.* *Mat 14:24*
these all do *c.* to the. *Acts 17:7*
men to worship *c.* to the law. *18:13*
me to be smitten *c.* to the law. *23:3*
to do many things *c.* to the. *26:9*
grafted *c.* to nature into. *Rom 11:24*
c. to the doctrine ye have. *16:17*
and these are *c.* the one. *Gal 5:17*
hand-writing which was *c.* *Col 2:14*
not God, and are *c.* to. *1 Thes 2:15*
if any thing that is *c.* *1 Tim 1:10*
that he of the *c.* part. *Tit 2:8*

contribution

to make *c.* for the poor. *Rom 15:26*

contrite

saveth such as be of *c.* *Ps 34:18*
a *c.* heart, O God, thou. *51:17*
c. and humble spirit, to revive heart
 of *c.* ones. *Isa 57:15*
that is of a *c.* spirit and. *66:2*

controversy

being matters of *c.* *Deut 17:8*
men between whom the *c.* *19:17*
shall every *c.* be tried. *21:5*
if there be a *c.* between men. *25:1*
any that had a *c.* came. *2 Sam 15:2*
set the Levites for *c.* *2 Chr 19:8*
recompences for the *c.* of. *Isa 34:8*
the Lord hath a *c.* *Jer 25:31*
in *c.* they shall stand. *Ezek 44:24*
the Lord hath a *c.* with. *Hos 4:1*
Lord hath a *c.* with Judah. *12:2*
Lord hath *c.* with his people. *Mi 6:2*
without *c.* great is the. *1 Tim 3:16*

convenient

[1] *Needful, Pr 30:8.* [2] *Fitting,
Rom 1:28.* [3] *Befitting, Eph 5:4;
Philem 8.*

---

feed me with food *c.* *Pr 30:8**
seemeth good and *c.* *Jer 40:4, 5*
when a *c.* day was. *Mark 6:21*
when I have a *c.* season. *Acts 24:25*
things which are not *c.* *Rom 1:28**
he shall have *c.* time. *1 Cor 16:12**
jesting, which are not *c.* *Eph 5:4**
to enjoin that which is *c.* *Philem 8**

conveniently

how he might *c.* betray. *Mark 14:11*

conversant

and strangers were *c.* *Josh 8:35*
as long as we were *c.* *1 Sam 25:15*

conversation

(*Behaviour, or manner of life. It
does not in the Bible mean dis-
course with another. The Revised
Versions change the word in all
cases*)

slay such as be of upright *c.* *Ps 37:14*
to him that ordereth his *c.* *50:23*
we have had our *c.* *2 Cor 1:12*
ye have heard of my *c.* *Gal 1:13*
whom also we all had our *c.* *Eph 2:3*
put off concerning former *c.* *4:22*
only let your *c.* be as. *Phil 1:27*
for our *c.* is in heaven. *3:20*
example of believers in *c.* *1 Tim 4:12*
let your *c.* be without. *Heb 13:5*
considering the end of their *c.* *7*
shew out of a good *c.* *Jas 3:13*
holy in all manner of *c.* *1 Pet 1:15*
corruptible things from vain *c.* *18*
having your *c.* honest among. *2:12*
they also may be won by the *c.* *3:1*
behold your chaste *c.* *2*
falsely accuse your good *c.* *16*
Lot vexed with filthy *c.* *2 Pet 2:7*
ought ye to be, in all holy *c.* *3:11*

conversion

(*Literally, a turning, the word is
used to mean, theologically, the
spiritual or moral change which
accompanies the turning of a sinner
from his sins to God, Ps 51:13*)

the *c.* of the Gentiles. *Acts 15:3*

convert, -ed

(*The Revised Versions usually use
the literal form, turn again*)

and sinners shall be *c.* *Ps 51:13*
they understand, and *c.* *Isa 6:10*
abundance of sea shall be *c.* *60:5**
should be *c.* and I should heal them.
 Mat 13:15; Mark 4:12
ye be *c.* and become as. *Mat 18:3*
when *c.* strengthen thy. *Luke 22:32*
be *c.* and I heal them. *John 12:40*
 Acts 28:27
repent and be *c.* that sins. *Acts 3:19*
err from truth, and one *c.* *Jas 5:19*

converteth, -ing

law of Lord is perfect, *c.* *Ps 19:7**
that he who *c.* a sinner. *Jas 5:20*

converts

her *c.* shall be redeemed. *Isa 1:27*

convey, -ed

I will *c.* them by sea. *1 Ki 5:9**
that they may *c.* me over. *Neh 2:7*
Jesus had *c.* himself. *John 5:13*

convicted

c. by their own conscience. *John 8:9*

convince, -ed, -eth

none of you *c.* Job. *Job 32:12*
which of you *c.* me of? *John 8:46**
for he mightily *c.* the. *Acts 18:28**
he is *c.* of all, he is. *1 Cor 14:24**
that he may be able to *c.* *Tit 1:9**
and are *c.* of the law. *Jas 2:9**
to *c.* all that are ungodly. *Jude 15**

convocation, -s

(*An assembly of persons called
together for a purpose*)

shall be an holy *c.* *Ex 12:16*
 Lev 23:7, 24, 35; Num 28:18; 29:1
proclaim to be holy *c.* *Lev 23:2*
 4, 21, 37
seventh day as an holy *c.* *23:3, 8*
 Num 28:25
tenth day an holy *c.* *Lev 23:27*
 Num 29:7

---

eighth day shall be holy *c.* *Lev 23:36*
first-fruits have holy *c.* *Num 28:26*
day seventh month holy *c.* *29:12*

cook, -s

take daughters to be *c.* *1 Sam 8:13*
Samuel said to *c.* bring portion. *9:23*
c. took up the shoulder and set. *24*

cool

walking in garden in the *c.* *Gen 3:8*
dip tip of finger and *c.* *Luke 16:24*

copied

men of Hezekiah *c.* out. *Pr 25:1*

coping

stones from foundation to *c.* *1 Ki 7:9*

copper

two vessels of fine *c.* *Ezra 8:27*

coppersmith

Alexander the *c.* did. *2 Tim 4:14*

copulation

if any man's seed of *c.* *Lev 15:16*
skin whereon is seed of *c.* shall. *17*
shall lie with seed of *c.* *18*

copy

write him a *c.* of law. *Deut 17:18*
he wrote on stones a *c.* *Josh 8:32*
c. of a letter sent. *Ezra 4:11; 5:6*
c. of Artaxerxes' letter was. *4:23*
c. of the letter Artaxerxes gave. *7:11*
c. of a writing for. *Esth 3:14; 8:13*
Mordecai gave Hatach a *c.* *4:8*

cor

(*A measure, either dry or liquid.
About 11 bushels or 90 gallons*)

part of a bath out of *c.* *Ezek 45:14*

coral

no mention made of *c.* *Job 28:18*
was thy merchant in *c.* *Ezek 27:16*

corban

it is *c.* that is to say. *Mark 7:11*

cord

let spies down by a *c.* *Josh 2:15*
he hath loosed my *c.* *Job 30:11*
out leviathan's tongue with *c.* ? *41:1*
a threefold *c.* is not. *Eccl 4:12*
or ever the silver *c.* be loosed. *12:6*
spare not, lengthen *c.* *Isa 54:2*
a *c.* by lot in congregation. *Mi 2:5*

cords

of the court and their *c.* *Ex 35:18*
Samson with new *c.* *Judg 15:13**
if they be holden in *c.* *Job 36:8*
cast away their *c.* from us. *Ps 2:3*
bind the sacrifice with *c.* *118:27*
he hath cut asunder the *c.* *129:4*
have hid a snare and *c.* *140:5*
shall be holden with *c.* *Pr 5:22*
that draw iniquity with *c.* *Isa 5:18*
nor shall any of the *c.* thereof. *33:20*
all my *c.* broken. *Jer 10:20*
let down Jeremiah with *c.* *38:6*
drew up Jeremiah with *c.* *13*
in chests bound with *c.* *Ezek 27:24*
I drew them with the *c.* *Hos 11:4*
a scourge of small *c.* *John 2:15*

coriander

manna was like *c.* seed. *Ex 16:31*
 Num 11:7

Corinth

things, Paul came to *C.* *Acts 18:1*
while Apollos was at *C.* *19:1*
unto church of God at *C.* to them.
 1 Cor 1:2; 2 Cor 1:1
I came not as yet to *C.* *2 Cor 1:23*
Erastus abode at *C.* *2 Tim 4:20*

Corinthians

many of the *C.* hearing. *Acts 18:8*
O ye *C.* our mouth is. *2 Cor 6:11*

cormorant

have in abomination *c.* and great.
 Lev 11:7; Deut 14:17
but the *c.* shall possess. *Isa 34:11**
 Zeph 2:14*

corn

(*Always, in the Bible, grain of
various sorts, not Indian corn as
would be understood in the United
States by the term. The American
Revision changes the word in the
Old Testament to grain*)

came to Joseph to buy c. *Gen 41:57*
there was c. in Egypt.   42:2
     Acts 7:12
carry c. for the famine. *Gen 42:19*
so that the stacks of c.   *Ex 22:6*
burn part of beaten c.   *Lev 2:16*
neither bread nor parched c.   23:14
as though it were the c. *Num 18:27*
to put the sickle to c.   *Deut 16:9*
not muzzle ox when he treadeth out
     c.   25:4; *1 Cor 9:9; 1 Tim* 5:18
did eat of the old c.   *Josh 5:11, 12*
he reached her parched c. *Ruth 2:14*
lie down at end of heap of c.   3:7
an ephah of parched c.   *1 Sam 17:17*
five measures of parched c.   25:18
brought parched c.   *2 Sam 17:28*
as blasted. *2 Ki 19:26; Isa 37:27*
we take up c. for them.   *Neh 5:2*
as a shock of c. cometh.   *Job 5:26*
they reap every one his c.   24:6
young ones grow up with c.   39:4
preparest them c.   *Ps 65:9*
valleys are covered with c.   13
there shall be a handful of c.   72:16
had given them of the c.   78:24
that withholdeth c.   *Pr 11:26*
harvest-man gathereth c. *Isa 17:5*
I will no more give thy c.   62:8
I will call for the c.   *Ezek 36:29*
I will take away my c.   *Hos 2:9*
loveth to tread out the c.   10:11
they shall revive as the c.   14:7
for the c. is wasted.   *Joel 1:10*
barns are broken down, for c.   17
that we may sell c.   *Amos 8:5*
I will sift Israel like as c.   9:9
after that the full c.   *Mark 4:28*
except a c. of wheat. *John 12:24**

ears of corn
seven ears of c. came up. *Gen 41:5*
offer green ears of c.   *Lev 2:14*
let me glean ears of c.   *Ruth 2:2*
brought full ears of c.   *2 Ki 4:42*
off as tops of the ears of c. *Job 24:24*
to pluck ears of c.   *Mat 12:1*
     Mark 2:23; Luke 6:1

corn fields
c. fields on the sabbath. *Mark 2:23*
     Mat 12:1; Luke 6:1

corn floor
and the c. of my floor.   *Isa 21:10*
reward on every c. floor.   *Hos 9:1*

standing corn
that the standing c. be.   *Ex 22:6*
come into standing c.   *Deut 23:25*
foxes go into standing c. burn up
     standing c.   *Judg 15:5*

corn and wine
plenty of c. and wine.   *Gen 27:28*
with c. and wine have I.   37
bless thy c. and wine.   *Deut 7:13*
gather in thy c. and wine.   11:14
not eat tithe of c. and wine.   12:17
     14:23
hast gathered in c. and wine.   16:13
first-fruit of c. and wine and.   18:4
not leave thee c. and wine or.   28:51
upon a land of c. and wine.   33:28
to a land of c. and wine. *2 Ki 18:32*
     Isa 36:17
brought first-fruits of c. and wine.
     2 Chr 31:5
for increase of c. and wine.   32:28
restore part of c. wine.   *Neh 5:11*
of c. of new wine.   10:39; 13:5, 12
in time their c. and wine.   *Ps 4:7*
where is c. and wine ?   *Lam 2:12*
I gave her c. wine, and oil. *Hos 2:8*
earth shall hear c. and wine.   22
assemble for c. and wine.   7:14
will send you c. and wine. *Joel 2:19*
drought on c. and new wine.
     Hag 1:11
c. shall make young men cheerful,
     and new wine maids. *Zech 9:17*

Cornelius
man in Cesarea, called C. *Acts 10:1*
the angel which spake to C.   7
C. met Peter, and fell down.   25
C. thy prayer is heard.   31

corner
shave off the c. of their.   *Lev 21:5*
altars in every c. of.   *2 Chr 28:24*
through street near c.   *Pr 7:8*
lieth in wait at every c.   12
better to dwell in c. of.   21:9; 25:24
not be removed into a c.   *Isa 30:20*
flame shall devour the c.   *Jer 48:45*
take of thee a stone for a c.   51:26
in every c. of court.   *Ezek 46:21*
in Samaria in the c. of.   *Amos 3:12*
came forth the c. and.   *Zech 10:4**
stone builders rejected is become
     head of c. *Mat 21:42; Ps 118:22*
     Mark 12:10; Luke 20:17
     Acts 4:11; 1 Pet 2:7
was not done in a c.   *Acts 26:26*

corner-gate
Ephraim to the c.-gate.   *2 Ki 14:13*
towers at c.-gate.   *2 Chr 26:9*
built from tower to gate of c.
     Jer 31:38
inhabited to the c.-gate. *Zech 14:10*

corner-stone
or who laid the c.-stone ?   *Job 38:6*
head-stone of the c.   *Ps 118:22*
daughters be as c.-stones.   144:12
a precious c.-stone.   *Isa 28:16*
     1 Pet 2:6
Christ chief c.-stone.   *Eph 2:20*

corners
rings in four c. of ark.   *Ex 25:12**
     26; 27:4; 37:13
horns upon the four c.   27:2; 38:2
not reap the c. of field.   *Lev 19:9*
     23:22
ye shall not round c. of heads.   27
shall smite c. of Moab. *Num 24:17*
will scatter them into c. *Deut 32:26**
thou didst divide into c. *Neh 9:22**
wind smote the four c.   *Job 1:19*
dispersed of Judah from c. *Isa 11:12*
punish circumcised with ... in utter-
     most c. *Jer 9:25, 26; 25:23; 49:32*
end is come upon four c. *Ezek 7:2*
put blood upon four c.   45:19
pray in c. of the streets.   *Mat 6:5*
sheet knit at c.   *Acts 10:11; 11:5*
angels standing on four c.   *Rev 7:1*

cornet
ark with sound of c.   *1 Chr 15:28*
with sound of the c. make. *Ps 98:6*
hear the sound of c.   *Dan 3:5, 15*
every man shall hear sound of c. 10
blow ye the c. in Gibeah.   *Hos 5:8*

cornets
played before Lord on c. *2 Sam 6:5**
shouting with c.   *2 Chr 15:14*

corpse, -s
they were all dead c.   *2 Ki 19:35*
     Isa 37:36
no end of c. stumble on c. *Nah 3:3*
disciples took John's c. *Mark 6:29*

correct
when thou dost c. man.   *Ps 39:11*
heathen, shall not he c.?   94:10
c. thy son, and he shall.   *Pr 29:17*
own wickedness shall c.   *Jer 2:19*
c. me, but with judgement.   10:24
c. thee in measure.   30:11; 46:28

corrected, -eth
is man whom God c.   *Job 5:17*
whom Lord loveth, he c.   *Pr 3:12**
a servant will not be c.   29:19
of our flesh which c.   *Heb 12:9**

correction
whether for c. or mercy. *Job 37:13*
neither be weary of his c. *Pr 3:11**
he goeth as a fool to the c.   7:22
c. is grievous to him that.   15:10
but the rod of c. shall.   22:15
withhold not c. from child.   23:13
children received no c.   *Jer 2:30*
have refused to receive c.   5:3
a nation that receiveth not c. 7:28*
hast established them for c. *Hab 1:12*
obeyed not, received not c. *Zeph 3:2*
scripture is profitable for c.
     2 Tim 3:16

corrupt
[1] To consume, *Mat* 6:19. [2]
To defile, or pollute, *Ex* 32:7.
[3] To mar, or spoil, 1 *Cor* 15:33.
[4] To pervert or lead astray,
2 *Cor* 11:3. [5] To break, or make
void, *Mal* 2:8. [6] Vicious and
unsound, 1 *Tim* 6:5; 2 *Tim* 3:8.

earth also was c.   *Gen 6:11, 12*
my breath is c. my days. *Job 17:1**
they are c.   *Ps 14:1; 53:1; 73:8*
my wounds stink and are c.   38:5
troubled fountain and c.   *Pr 25:26*
not according to your c. *Ezek 20:44*
she was more c. in her.   23:11
lying and c. words.   *Dan 2:9*
that sacrificeth a c. thing. *Mal 1:14**
a c. tree bringeth forth. *Mat 7:17*
nor can a c. tree.   18; *Luke 6:43*
tree c. and his fruit c.   *Mat 12:33*
the old man which is c.   *Eph 4:22*
let no c. communication proceed. 29
disputings of men of c.   *1 Tim 6:5*
men of c. minds.   *2 Tim 3:8*

corrupt, verb
lest ye c. yourselves. *Deut 4:16, 25*
after my death ye will c.   31:29
do wickedly shall he c. *Dan 11:32**
behold I will c. your.   *Mal 2:3**
moth and rust doth c.   *Mat 6:19**
neither moth nor rust doth c.   20*
evil communications c. *1 Cor 15:33*
which c. the word of God. *2 Cor 2:17*
in those things they c.   *Jude 10**
great whore did c. earth. *Rev 19:2*

corrupted, -eth
for all flesh had c. his way. *Gen 6:12*
the land was c. by.   *Ex 8:24*
for thy people have c. themselves.
     32:7; *Deut 9:12*; 32:5
c. themselves more.   *Judg 2:19*
thou wast c. more.   *Ezek 16:47*
thou hast c. thy wisdom.   28:11
have deeply c. themselves. *Hos 9:9*
rose early and c. all.   *Zeph 3:7*
ye have c. covenant of.   *Mal 2:8*
nor moth c.   *Luke 12:33*
have c. no man.   *2 Cor 7:2*
lest your minds be c. from.   11:3
your riches are c.   *Jas 5:1, 2*

corrupters
children that are c.   *Isa 1:4*
brass and iron, all c.   *Jer 6:28*

corruptible
image made like to c.   *Rom 1:23*
they do it to obtain c.   *1 Cor 9:25*
for this c. must put on.   15:53
not redeemed with c.   *1 Pet 1:18*
born again, not of c. seed.   23
let it be in that which is not c.   3:4

corrupting
daughter of women c. *Dan 11:17*

corruption
(Frequently used as a synonym of
death; laying stress on the decay
of the body after it is in the grave)
their c. is in them.   *Lev 22:25*
right hand of mount of c. *2 Ki 23:13*
I have said to c. thou.   *Job 17:14*
nor wilt thou suffer thine holy One to
     see c. *Ps 16:10; Acts 2:27; 13:35*
live for ever, and not see c. *Ps 49:9*
delivered it from pit of c. *Isa 38:17*
was turned in me to c.   *Dan 10:8*
up my life from c.   *Jonah 2:6**
nor his flesh did see c.   *Acts 2:31*
no more to return to c.   13:34
laid to his fathers and saw c.   36
raised again saw no c.   37
from the bondage of c. *Rom 8:21*
it is sown in c.; raised. *1 Cor 15:42*
neither doth c. inherit.   50
shall of flesh reap c.   *Gal 6:8*
escaped the c. that.   *2 Pet 1:4*
utterly perish in own c.   2:12*
themselves are servants of c.   19

corruptly
people did yet c.   *2 Chr 27:2*
we have dealt very c.   *Neh 1:7*

cost
eaten at all of king's c.? *2 Sam 19:42*

of that which c. nothing. *2 Sam 24:24*
offerings without c. *1 Chr 21:24*
and counteth c. *Luke 14:28*

costliness
ships made rich by her c. *Rev 18:19*

costly
they brought c. stones. *1 Ki 5:17*
all these were of c. stones. *7:9*
foundation was of c. stones. *10*
and above were c. stones. *11*
of spikenard, very c. *John 12:3**
not with c. array. *1 Tim 2:9*

cotes
Hezekiah made c. *2 Chr 32:28**

cottage, -s
of Zion is left as a c. *Isa 1:8**
earth shall be removed like c. *24:20**
sea-coast shall be c. *Zeph 2:6*

couch, -es
and went up to my c. *Gen 49:4*
I say, my c. shall ease. *Job 7:13*
all night I water my c. *Ps 6:6*
in Damascus in a c. *Amos 3:12*
stretch themselves upon c. *6:4*
through tiling with his c. *Luke 5:19*
arise, take up thy c. *24*
laid sick folk on c. *Acts 5:15*

couch
when they c. in dens. *Job 38:40*

couched
Judah c. as a lion. *Gen 49:9*
he c. he lay down as. *Num 24:9*

coucheth
and for deep that c. *Deut 33:13*

couching
Issachar c. down. *Gen 49:14*
make Ammonites a c. *Ezek 25:5*

could
o1d, so that he c. not see. *Gen 27:1*
forth lice, but c. not. *Ex 8:18*
he c. not see. *1 Sam 3:2*
Ahijah c. not see. *1 Ki 14:4*
to king of Edom, c. not. *2 Ki 3:26*
but David c. not go. *1 Chr 21:30*
c. not withstand them. *2 Chr 13:7*
but he c. not be found. *Ps 37:36*
what c. have been done? *Isa 5:4*
my mind c. not be. *Jer 15:1*
bring it to land, c. not. *Jonah 1:13*
Herodias would have killed him, but
she c. not. *Mark 6:19*
cast him out, c. not. *9:18; Luke 9:40*
she hath done what she c. *Mark 14:8*
the world c. not contain. *John 21:25*
from which ye c. not be. *Acts 13:39*

couldest
evil things as thou c. *Jer 3:5**
yet c. not be satisfied. *Ezek 16:28*

coulter -s
to sharpen each his c. *1 Sam 13:20*
they had a file for their c. *21*

council, -s
shall be in danger of c. *Mat 5:22*
deliver you to c. *10:17; Mark 13:9*
c. sought false witness. *Mat 26:59*
Mark 14:55
elders, scribes and whole c.
Mark 15:1
elders led Jesus into c. *Luke 22:66*
chief priests gathered c. *John 11:47*
Acts 5:21
them to go out of the c. *Acts 4:15*
and set them before the c. *5:27*
then stood up one in the c. *34*
departed from the c. rejoicing. *41*
and brought him to the c. *6:12*
all in the c. looking on him. *15*
commanded all their c. to. *22:30*
ye with the c. signify to the. *23:15*
while I stood before the c. *24:20*

counsel
[1] *Advice,* Pr 20:18; Dan 4:27.
[2] *God's purpose,* Acts 4:28. [3]
The most secret resolutions, 1 Cor
4:5.
I will give thee c. *Ex 18:19*
Eleazar, who shall ask c. for.
Num 27:21*
caused Israel through c. of Balaam,
to commit trespass. *31:16*

are a nation void of c. *Deut 32:28*
asked not c. at mouth. *Josh 9:14*
give here advice and c. *Judg 20:7*
turn c. of Ahithophel. *2 Sam 15:31*
all the c. of Ahithophel. *16:23*
Lord defeated the good c. of. *17:14*
shall surely ask c. at Abel. *20:18*
let me give thee c. *1 Ki 1:12*
forsook c. of old men. *12:8, 13*
2 Chr 10:8, 13
king of Syria took c. *2 Ki 6:8*
c. and strength for war. *18:20*
Isa 36:5
Saul died for asking c. *1 Chr 10:13*
Ahaziah walked after c. *2 Chr 22:5*
art thou made of king's c.? *25:16*
the king had taken c. to. *30:2*
the assembly took c. to keep. *23*
according to c. of my. *Ezra 10:3*
according to the c. of the princes. *8*
God brought their c. to. *Neh 4:15*
the c. of the froward. *Job 5:13*
should shine upon the c. of. *10:3*
and strength he hath c. and. *12:13*
the c. of the wicked is. *21:16; 22:18*
who is this that darkeneth c.? *38:2*
who is he that hideth c.? *42:3*
walketh not in the c. *Ps 1:1*
you have shamed the c. of. *14:6*
who hath given me c. *16:7*
and fulfil all thy c. *20:4*
while they took c. together. *31:13*
Lord brings the c. of the. *33:10*
we took sweet c. together. *55:14*
hide me from the secret c. *64:2*
princes of Judah and their c. *68:27*
shalt guide me with thy c. *73:24*
they have taken crafty c. *83:3*
they waited not for his c. *106:13*
provoked him with their c. *43*
the c. of the Most High. *107:11*
c. is mine, sound wisdom. *Pr 8:14*
where no c. is, the people. *11:14**
he that hearkeneth unto c. *12:15*
without c. purposes are. *15:22*
hear c. and receive. *19:20*
c. in the heart of man is. *20:5*
every purpose established by c. *18*
there is no wisdom nor c. *21:30*
for by wise c. thou shalt. *24:6**
of a friend by hearty c. *27:9*
let c. of the Holy One. *Isa 5:19*
they have taken evil c. *7:5*
spirit of c. and might shall. *11:2*
I will destroy the c. of Egypt. *19:3*
c. of counsellors of Pharaoh. *11*
taken this c. against Tyre? *23:8**
Lord, who is wonderful in c. *28:29*
that seek deep to hide c. *29:15*
with whom took he c.? *14*
and performeth the c. *44:26*
nor shall c. perish. *Jer 18:18*
thou knowest all their c. *23*
I will make void c. of Judah. *19:7*
mighty God, great in c. *32:19*
if I give thee c. wilt not. *38:15*
is c. perished from prudent? *49:7*
king of Babylon hath taken c. *30*
and c. shall perish. *Ezek 7:26*
and that give wicked c. *11:2*
Daniel answered with c. *Dan 2:14*
my people ask c. at their. *Hos 4:12*
neither understand his c. *Mi 4:12*
the c. of peace shall be. *Zech 6:13*
the Pharisees held a c. *Mat 12:14*
they took c. and bought. *27:7*
when they had taken c. *28:12*
took c. against Jesus. *Mark 3:6*
John 11:53
not consented to the c. *Luke 23:51*
Caiaphas gave c. *John 18:14*
what thy c. determined. *Acts 4:28*
when they heard, they took c. *5:33**
if this c. be of men, it will. *38*
the Jews took c. to kill him. *9:23**
soldiers' c. was to kill the. *27:42*
worketh after the c. of. *Eph 1:11*
the immutability of his c. *Heb 6:17*

counsel of God or Lord
ask c. we pray of God. *Judg 18:5*
Israel asked c. of God. *20:18*
Saul asked c. of God. *1 Sam 14:37*
c. of the Lord standeth. *Ps 33:11*

c. of the Lord of hosts. *Isa 19:17**
stood in c. of the Lord? *Jer 23:18**
hear c. of the Lord. *49:20; 50:45*
rejected the c. of God. *Luke 7:30*
by determinate c. of God. *Acts 2:23*
declare to you all c. of God. *20:27*

my counsel
not hearkened to my c. *2 Chr 25:16*
kept silence at my c. *Job 29:21*
set at nought all my c. *Pr 1:25*
they would none of my c. *30*
man c. shall stand and. *Isa 46:10*
man that executeth my c. *11*
they had stood in my c. *Jer 23:22*
my c. be acceptable to. *Dan 4:27*

own counsel
his own c. shall cast him. *Job 18:7*
ashamed of his own c. *Hos 10:6*

take counsel
let us take c. together. *Neh 6:7*
rulers take c. against. *Ps 2:2*
how long shall I take c.? *13:2*
take c. together. *71:10*
take c. and it shall. *Isa 8:10*
take c. execute judgement. *16:3*
woe to children that take c. *30:1*
let them take c. together. *45:21*

counsel, -ed
which Ahithophel. *2 Sam 16:23*
c. that all Israel be gathered. *17:11*
thus Ahithophel c. thus I c. *15, 21*
how hast thou c. him? *Job 26:3*
c. thee to keep the king's. *Eccl 8:2*
I c. thee to buy of me. *Rev 3:18*

counsellor
David's c. *2 Sam 15:12; 1 Chr 27:33*
Zechariah his son, a wise c.
1 Chr 26:14
David's uncle, was a c. *27:32*
Athaliah was his c. *2 Chr 22:3*
Lord taketh away the c. *Isa 3:3*
shall be called Wonderful, C. *9:6*
or being his c. hath taught? *40:13*
there was no man, no c. *41:28*
is thy c. perished? *Mi 4:9*
out of thee a wicked c. *Nah 1:11**
Joseph an honourable c. *Mark 15:43*
Luke 23:50
who hath been his c.? *Rom 11:34*

counsellors
they were his c. after. *2 Chr 22:4*
they hired c. against them. *Ezra 4:5*
sent of king, and his seven c. *7:14*
mercy to me before king and c. *28*
gold, which king and c. had. *8:25*
rest with kings and c. *Job 3:14*
leadeth c. away spoiled. *12:17*
thy testimonies my c. *Ps 119:24*
in multitude of c. *Pr 11:14; 24:6*
deceit in heart, but to the c. *12:20*
in the multitude of c. they. *15:22*
I will restore thy c. *Isa 1:26*
counsel of wise c. of Pharaoh. *19:11*
said to his c. did not we? *Dan 3:24*
king's c. being gathered, saw. *27*
my c. and my lords sought. *4:36*
all the c. and the captains. *6:7*

counsels
turned round by his c. *Job 37:12**
them fall by their own c. *Ps 5:10*
walked in their own c. *81:12*
shall attain to wise c. *Pr 1:5*
c. of the wicked are deceit. *12:5*
written excellent things in c.? *22:20*
thy c. of old are. *Isa 25:1*
wearied in multitude of c. *47:13*
walked in the c. of their. *Jer 7:24*
because of their own c. *Hos 11:6*
walk in c. of house of. *Mi 6:16*
will make manifest c. of. *1 Cor 4:5*

count
shall make your c. *Ex 12:4*
c. from the morrow after. *Lev 23:15*
let him c. the years. *25:27, 52*
who can c. the dust? *Num 23:10*
c. not me daughter of. *1 Sam 1:16*
and my maids c. me. *Job 19:15*
doth not he see my ways, c.? *31:4**
the Lord shall c. when. *Ps 87:6*
if I c. them, they are more. *139:18*
I c. them mine enemies. *22†*

shall I *c*. them pure. *Mi* 6:11*
neither *c*. I my life dear. *Acts* 20:24*
I *c*. all things loss, and do *c*. them.
  Phil 3:8
I *c*. not myself to have. 13
God would *c*. you. *2 Thes* 1:11
c. him not as an enemy. 3:15
c. their masters worthy. *1 Tim* 6:1
if thou *c*. me a partner. *Philem* 17
c. it joy when ye fall. *Jas* 1:2
behold, we *c*. them happy. 5:11*
as they that *c*. it pleasure. *2 Pet* 2:13
as some men *c*. slackness. 3:9
let him *c*. the number. *Rev* 13:18

counted
believed, and he *c*. it for. *Gen* 15:6
 Ps 106:31; *Rom* 4:3; *Gal* 3:6
the sheep that shall be *c*. *Gen* 30:33
are we not *c*. strangers? 31:15
cannot be numbered or *c*. *1 Ki* 3:8
Levi and Benjamin *c*. *1 Chr* 21:6
for they were *c*. faithful. *Neh* 13:13
wherefore we are *c*. as. *Job* 18:3
darts are *c*. as stubble. 41:29
we are *c*. as sheep for. *Ps* 44:22
I am *c*. with them that go. 88:4
a fool, when he holdeth his peace is
 c. wise. *Pr* 17:28
rising early, it shall be *c*. 27:14
horses' hoofs shall be *c*. *Isa* 5:28
and the fruitful field be *c*. 32:15
where is he that *c*. towers? 33:18*
the nations are *c*. as. 40:15
all nations are *c*. to him. 17
but they were *c*. as a. *Hos* 8:12
c. him as a prophet. *Mat* 14:5
  Mark 11:32
be *c*. worthy to escape. *Luke* 21:36
that they were *c*. worthy. *Acts* 5:41
burned their books, and *c*. 19:19
uncircumcision be *c*. for. *Rom* 2:26
him that believeth, his faith is *c*. 4:5
children of promise are *c*. 9:8
gain, those I *c*. loss for. *Phil* 3:7
c. worthy of kingdom of. *2 Thes* 1:5
for that he *c*. me faithful. *1 Tim* 1:12
let elders be *c*. worthy of. 5:17
this man was *c*. worthy. *Heb* 3:3
he whose descent is not *c*. 7:6
hath *c*. blood of the covenant. 10:29

see **accounted**
countenance
wroth, and his *c*. fell. *Gen* 4:5
Jacob beheld the *c*. of Laban. 31:2
I see your father's *c*. that it. 5
nor shalt thou *c*. a poor. *Ex* 23:3*
the Lord lift up his *c*. *Num* 6:26
bring a nation of fierce *c*. *Deut* 28:50
c. was like *c*. of an angel. *Judg* 13:6
Hannah, her *c*. was no. *1 Sam* 1:18
look not on his *c*. or the. 16:7
David was of beautiful *c*. 12; 17:42
Abigail of beautiful *c*. 25:3
Tamar of a fair *c*. *2 Sam* 14:27
settled his *c*. stedfastly. *2 Ki* 8:11
why is thy *c*. sad? *Neh* 2:2
why should not my *c*. be sad? 3
thou changest his *c*. and. *Job* 14:20
and the light of my *c*. 29:24
lift thou up the light of thy *c*. *Ps* 4:6
wicked, through pride of *c*. 10:4
his *c*. doth behold upright. 11:7
made him glad with thy *c*. 21:6*
praise him for help of his *c*. 42:5
who is the health of my *c*. 11; 43:5
light of thy *c*. did save them. 44:3
perish at rebuke of thy *c*. 80:16
in the light of thy *c*. 89:15
our secret sins in light of thy *c*. 90:8
heart maketh cheerful *c*. *Pr* 15:13
in the light of the king's *c*. 16:15
so doth the angry *c*. a. 25:23
so a man sharpeneth the *c*. 27:17
by sadness of *c*. the. *Eccl* 7:3
see thy *c*. thy *c*. is. *S of S* 2:14
his *c*. is as Lebanon. 5:15*
the shew of their *c*. doth. *Isa* 3:9
troubled in their *c*. *Ezek* 27:35
king's *c*. was changed. *Dan* 5:6
king of fierce *c*. shall stand. 8:23
hypocrites, of a sad *c*. *Mat* 6:16
c. like lightning. 28:3*; *Luke* 9:29
full of joy with thy *c*. *Acts* 2:28

Moses for glory of his *c*. *2 Cor* 3:7
and his *c*. was as. *Rev* 1:16

see **changed**
countenances
let our *c*. be looked. *Dan* 1:13
their *c*. appeared fairer and. 15

countervail
enemy could not *c*. king's. *Esth* 7:4*

counteth, -ing
c. me as one of his enemies.
 Job 19:11; 33:10
c. one by one, to find. *Eccl* 7:27*
down first, *c*. the cost. *Luke* 14:28

countries
will I give these *c*. *Gen* 26:3, 4
all *c*. came into Egypt to. 41:57
who among all *c*. *2 Ki* 18:35
and glory throughout *c*. *1 Chr* 22:5
fear of God on all those *c*.
 2 Chr 20:29
because of people of *c*. *Ezra* 3:3
who have ruled over all *c*. 4:20
wound heads over many *c*. *Ps* 110:6
give ear all ye of far *c*. *Isa* 8:9
gather remnant of my flock out of all
 c. and. *Jer* 23:3, 8; 32:37
prophesied against many *c*. 28:8
Jerusalem in midst of *c*. *Ezek* 5:5
changed my statutes more than *c*. 6
be scattered through the *c*. 6:8
scattered among the *c*. yet I will be
 as a little sanctuary in *c*. 11:16
assemble you out of *c*. 17; 20:34, 41
thee a mocking to all *c*. 22:4
cause thee to perish out of *c*. 25:7
disperse them through *c*. 29:12
  36:19
these two *c*. shall be mine. 35:10
he shall enter into *c*. *Dan* 11:40
many *c*. shall be overthrown. 41
stretch forth his hand upon *c*. 42
remember me in far *c*. *Zech* 10:9
not them that are in *c*. *Luke* 21:21

country
smoke of the *c*. went up. *Gen* 19:28
but thou shalt go to my *c*. 24:4
must not be so done in our *c*. 29:26
that I may go to my *c*. 30:25
Shechem the prince of the *c*. 34:2
the lord of the *c*. said unto us. 42:33
all born in the *c*. shall. *Num* 15:13*
the *c*. which the Lord smote. 32:4
I am come into the *c*. *Deut* 26:3
men to search out the *c*. *Josh* 2:2, 3
go up and view the *c*. 7:2
possessed that *c*. *Judg* 11:21
and the destroyer of our *c*. 16:24
came into the *c*. of Moab. *Ruth* 1:2
returned out of *c*. of Moab. 6
cities and *c*. villages. *1 Sam* 6:18
all thy *c*. wept with. *2 Sam* 15:23
bones of Saul buried they in *c*. 21:14
Syrians filled the *c*. *1 Ki* 20:27
and the *c*. was filled. *2 Ki* 3:20
your *c*. is desolate, your. *Isa* 1:7
toss thee like a ball in large *c*. 22:18
nor see his native *c*. *Jer* 22:10
bring them from the north *c*. 31:8
is come upon the plain *c*. 48:21
to come from the north *c*. 50:9
them forth out of the *c*. *Ezek* 20:38
glory of *c*. Beth-jeshimoth. 47:22*
be to you as born in the *c*. 47:22*
when I was yet in my *c*. *Jonah* 4:2
abroad his fame in *c*. *Mat* 9:31
not send them out of *c*. *Mark* 5:10
told it in city, and *c*. 14; *Luke* 8:34
to a citizen of that *c*. *Luke* 15:15
c. was nourished by king's *c*.
  Acts 12:20
they drew near to some *c*. 27:27
promise as in strange *c*. *Heb* 11:9*
that they seek a *c*. 14
had been mindful of that *c*. 15
now they desire a better *c*. 16

far **country**
be come from far *c*. *Josh* 9:6, 9
out of far *c*. *1 Ki* 8:41; *2 Chr* 6:32
they are come from a far *c*.
 2 Ki 20:14; *Isa* 39:3
good news from a far *c*. *Pr* 25:25
from a far *c*. to destroy. *Isa* 13:5

my counsel from far *c*. *Isa* 46:11
watchers come from far *c*. *Jer* 4:16
them that dwell in a far *c*. 8:19*
went into a far *c*. *Mat* 21:33
  Mark 12:1
man travelling into far *c*. *Mat* 25:14
his journey into far *c*. *Luke* 15:13

own **country**
one of your *own c*. *Lev* 16:29*
  17:15*; 24:22*
went to her *own c*. *1 Ki* 10:13
that I may go to my *own c*. 11:21
every man to his *own c*. 22:36
go every one to his *own c*. *Jer* 51:9
departed into their *own c*. *Mat* 2:12
save in his *own c*. 13:57
 Mark 6:4; *Luke* 4:24
and came into his *own c*. *Mark* 6:1
prophet hath no honour in *own c*.
  John 4:44

thy **country**
get thee out of *thy c*. *Gen* 12:1
  Acts 7:3
return unto *thy c*. and. *Gen* 32:9
us pass through *thy c*. *Num* 20:17
what is *thy c*.? *Jonah* 1:8
do here in *thy c*. *Luke* 4:23

countrymen
in perils by mine own *c*. *2 Cor* 11:26
like things of your *c*. *1 Thes* 2:14

couple
make me a *c*. of cakes. *2 Sam* 13:6
Ziba met David with a *c*. 16:1
chariot with a *c*. of. *Isa* 21:7, 9

couple, *verb*
c. curtains with taches. *Ex* 26:6, 9
make taches to *c*. tent. 11; 36:18
made shoulder-pieces to *c*. 39:4*

coupled, -eth
curtains be *c*. *Ex* 26:3; 36:10, 13, 16
in edge of the curtain which *c*. 26:10
two boards shall be *c*. 24; 36:29
by the two edges was it *c*. 39:4*
chaste conversation *c*. *1 Pet* 3:2

coupling, -s
loops from selvedge in *c*. *Ex* 26:4
  36:11
in *c*. of second. 26:4; 36:11, 12
that is outmost in *c*. 26:10; 36:17
over-against other *c*. 28:27; 39:20
stone and timber for *c*. *2 Sam* 34:11

courage
remain any more *c*. *Josh* 2:11*
he took *c*. and put. *2 Chr* 15:8
shall stir up his *c*. *Dan* 11:25
Paul thanked God, took *c*. *Acts* 28:15

good **courage**
be ye of *good c*. and. *Num* 13:20
strong, and of *good c*. *Deut* 31:6
 7, 23; *Josh* 1:6, 9, 18; 10:25
  1 Chr 22:13; 28:20
be of *good c*. let us. *2 Sam* 10:12
1 Chr 19:13; *Ezra* 10:4; *Isa* 41:6
be of *good c*. and he shall strengthen
 thine heart. *Ps* 27:14; 31:24

courageous
be thou strong and very *c*. *Josh* 1:7
  23:6; *2 Chr* 32:7
fear not, be *c*. and be. *2 Sam* 13:28
that is *c*. among mighty. *Amos* 2:16

courageously
deal *c*. and Lord shall. *2 Chr* 19:11

course
[1] *A prescribed track for a race.
Used figuratively for the work
given one to do in life*, Acts 13:25;
2 Tim 4:7. [2] *Order or turn*,
2 Chr 5:11. [3] *Progress and success*, 2 Thes 3:1. [4] *A voyage*,
Acts 21:7.
chief fathers of every *c*. *1 Chr* 27:1
priests did not wait by *c*. *2 Chr* 5:11
they sung together by *c*. *Ezra* 3:11
of earth are out of *c*. *Ps* 82:5*
every one turned to his *c*. *Jer* 8:6
their *c*. is evil, and their. 23:10
Zacharias was of the *c*. *Luke* 1:5
executed in the order of his *c*. 8
as John fulfilled his *c*. *Acts* 13:25
came with straight *c*. 16:11; 21:1

might finish my c. with joy. *Acts* 20:24
we had finished our c. 21:7*
three, and that by c. *1 Cor* 14:27
the Lord have free c. *2 Thes* 3:1*
I have finished my c. *2 Tim* 4:7
tongue setteth on fire c. of. *Jas* 3:6*

water-course, *see* water

courses
stars in their c. fought. *Judg* 5:20
divided Levites into c. *1 Chr* 23:6
Solomon appointed c. *2 Chr* 8:14
Jehoiada dismissed not the c. 23:8
Hezekiah appointed the c. 31:2
Levites stood in their c. 35:10
set the Levites in their c. *Ezra* 6:18

court
In the Bible, [1] *Usually the uncovered area enclosed within the
walls of the tabernacle or temple ;
or* [2] *a similar area surrounded by
the rooms of the house, that being
the general way of building in the
East,* 2 Sam 17:18; Esth 6:4, 5.
(*The great courts belonging to the
temple were three ; the first called
the court of the Gentiles, because
the Gentiles were allowed to enter
so far, and no farther. The second
called the court of Israel, because
all the Israelites, if purified, had the
right of admission. The third
court was that of the Priests, where
the altar of burnt-offerings stood,
and where the Priests and Levites
exercised their ministry*)
c. of tabernacle: shall be hangings
for c. *Ex* 27:9; 35:17; 38:9; 39:40
breadth of the c. 27:12, 13
length of the c. 18
pins of the c. 19; 35:18; 38:20, 31
thou shalt set up the c. 40:8
in c. of tabernacle eat. *Lev* 6:16, 26
had a well in his c. *2 Sam* 17:18
Isaiah gone into middle c. *2 Ki* 20:4*
stood before the new c. *2 Chr* 20:5
stoned Zechariah in c. of. 24:21
out the uncleanness into c. 29:16
Esther stood in inner c. *Esth* 5:1
king said, who is in the c.? 6:4
behold Haman standeth in c. 5
and a c. for owls. *Isa* 34:13
Jeremiah stood in the c. *Jer* 19:14
stand in the c. of the Lord's. 26:2
prophet was shut in c. of. 32:2
33:1; 39:15
into the dungeon in the c. 38:6
me to the door of c. *Ezek* 8:7, 16
the cloud filled the inner c. 10:3
into outward c. 40:17; 42:1; 46:21
he brought me to the inner c. 40:28
Spirit brought me into inner c. 43:5
blood upon gate of inner c. 45:19
in every corner of c. was a c. 46:21
and it is the king's c. *Amos* 7:13*
c. without the temple. *Rev* 11:2

courteous
love, be pitiful, be c. *1 Pet* 3:8*

courteously
Julius c. entreated Paul. *Acts* 27:3*
and lodged us 3 days c. 28:7

courts
altars for all host of heaven in two c.
2 Ki 21:5; *2 Chr* 33:5
altars in the two c. *2 Ki* 23:12
office was to wait in c. *1 Chr* 23:28
Solomon shall build my c. 28:6
David gave Solomon pattern of c. 12
people shall be in the c. *2 Chr* 23:5
that he dwell in thy c. *Ps* 65:4
my soul fainteth for the c. 84:2
shall flourish in the c. of. 92:13
offering and come into c. 96:8
enter into his c. with praise. 100:4
pay my vows in the c. 116:19
ye that stand in the c. of. 135:2
this to tread my c.? *Isa* 1:12
they shall drink in the c. *Ezek* 9:7
fill the c. with slain. 9:7
my house, and keep my c. *Zech* 3:7
live delicately in king's c. *Luke* 7:25

cousin
thy c. Elisabeth hath. *Luke* 1:36*

cousins
her neighbours and c. *Luke* 1:58*

covenant
*The most common uses of the word
in the Bible are for the covenant
between God and his people.* [1]
*The covenant between God and
man, of continued life and favour
on condition of obedience,* Gen
2:16. [2] *That between God and
Noah, that there should not be
another flood,* Gen 9:12-16. [3]
*With Abraham and his descendants
as individuals and as a nation,
frequently mentioned throughout
the history. This was the Old
Covenant, the Old Dispensation.
The New Covenant is the spiritual
covenant of God in Christ with his
followers, frequently mentioned in
the New Testament.*
token of c. *Gen* 9:12; 13:17; 17:11
behold, my c. is with thee. 17:4
c. be in your flesh for everlasting c.
13
he hath broken my c. 14
sabbath for a perpetual c. *Ex* 31:16
he wrote the words of the c. 34:28
but ye break my c. *Lev* 26:15
I give to him my c. *Num* 25:12
c. of everlasting priesthood 13
declared unto you his c. *Deut* 4:13
lest ye forget the c. of the. 23
Lord will not forget the c. 31
gone to receive tables of c. 9:9
Lord gave me tables of the c. 11
the two tables of the c. were. 15
these are the words of the c. 29:1
thou shouldest enter into c. 12
according to curses of the c. 21
because ye have forsaken the c. 25
provoke me, and break c. 31:20
I will never break my c. *Judg* 2:1
thy servant into c. of. *1 Sam* 20:8
Israel have forsaken c. *1 Ki* 19:10

I will send thee away with c. 20:34
because of his c. with. *2 Ki* 13:23
to perform words of c. and people
stood to c. 23:3; *2 Chr* 34:31
be always of c. *1 Chr* 16:15
they entered into c. *2 Chr* 15:12
they have defiled the c. *Neh* 13:29
he will shew them his c. *Ps* 25:14
neither dealt falsely in c. 44:17
that thou shouldest take my c. 50:16
he hath broken c. 55:20
have respect to the c. 74:20
were we they stedfast in c. 78:37
mercy keep and c. shall. 89:28
my c. will I not break. 34
thou hast made void the c. 39
will ever be mindful of his c. 111:5
commanded his c. for ever. 9
and forgetteth the c. of. *Pr* 2:17
your c. with death shall. *Isa* 28:18
he hath broken the c. he. 33:8
and give thee for a c. 42:6; 49:8
nor the c. of my peace be. 54:10
eunuchs that take hold of c. 56:4, 6
as for me, this is my c. *Jer* 11:2, 6
hear words of this c. 11:2, 6
man that obeyeth not words of c. 3
break not thy c. with us. 14:21
they have forsaken the c. of. 22:9
which my c. they brake. 31:32
break my c. of day and c. 33:20
then may c. be broken with. 21
if my c. be not with day. 25
had entered into c. heard. 34:10
not performed words of this c. 18
join to Lord in perpetual c. 50:5
and entered into a c. with. *Ezek* 16:8
in breaking the c. 59; 17:18
for daughters, not by thy c. 16:61
or shall he break the c.? 17:15
oath he despised, whose c. 16
my c. he hath broken, it. 19
bring you into bond of c. 20:37
they have broken my c. 44:7
confirm c. with many. *Dan* 9:27
yea also the prince of the c. 11:22
shall be against the holy c. 28

indignation against holy c. *Dan* 11:30
such as do wickedly against c. 32
falsely in making c. *Hos* 10:4
I might break my c. *Zech* 11:10
my c. might be with. *Mal* 2:4, 5
ye have corrupted c. of Levi. 8
by profaning the c. of our. 10
and the wife of thy c. 14
even messenger of the c. 3:1
ye are children of c. *Acts* 3:25
and he gave him the c. of. 7:8
c. breakers. *Rom* 1:31
this is my c. when I take. 11:27
though it be a man's c. *Gal* 3:15
that the c. was confirmed. 17
Mediator of a better c. *Heb* 8:6
if first c. had been faultless. 7
they continued in my c. 9
then verily the first c. 9:1
and tables of the c. 4

see ark, blood, break

book of the covenant
took the *book of the c.* *Ex* 24:7
Josiah read all the words of the book
of the c. *2 Ki* 23:2; *2 Chr* 34:30
it is written in *book of c. 2 Ki* 23:21

establish covenant
will I *establish* my c. *Gen* 6:18; 9:9
I will *establish* my c. between. 17:7
establish c. with Isaac and. 19, 21
I have *established* my c. *Ex* 6:4
establish my c. with you. *Lev* 26:9
he may *establish* his c. *Deut* 8:18
establish to thee an everlasting c.
Ezek 16:60
I will *establish* my c. with thee. 62

everlasting covenant
remember everlast. c. *Gen* 9:16
in your flesh for an *everlast.* c. 17:13
c. with Isaac for an *everlast.* c. 19
Israel by an *everlast.* c. *Lev* 24:8
with me an *everlast.* c. *2 Sam* 23:5
confirmed the same to Israel for
everlast. c. *1 Chr* 16:17; *Ps* 105:10
broken the *everlast.* c. *Isa* 24:5
make *everlast.* c. with you. 55:3
61:8; *Jer* 32:40
an *everlast.* c. with them. *Ezek* 37:26
blood of the *everlast.* c. *Heb* 13:20

keep, keeping, keepeth, or
kept covenant
thou shalt *keep* my c. *Gen* 17:9
my c. which ye shall *keep.* 10
my voice and *keep* my c. *Ex* 19:5
who *keepeth* c. *Deut* 7:9, 12
1 Ki 8:23; *2 Chr* 6:14; *Neh* 1:5
9:32
keep the words of this c. *Deut* 29:9
observed thy word, *kept* c. 33:9
not *kept* my c. *1 Ki* 11:11; *Ps* 78:10
to such as *keep* c. *Ps* 25:10; 103:18
children will *keep* my c. and. 132:12
by *keeping* of his c. *Ezek* 17:14
keeping c. and mercy to. *Dan* 9:4

made covenant
day the Lord *made* a c. *Gen* 15:18
and Abimelech *made* a c. 21:27, 32
I have *made* a c. with. *Ex* 34:27
Lord our God *made* a c. *Deut* 5:2
made not this c. with. 3; *Heb* 8:9
besides the c. he *made.* *Deut* 29:1
break my c. I have *made.* 31:16
Joshua *made* a c. with. *Josh* 24:25
David *made* c. *1 Sam* 18:3; 23:18
Jonathan *made* a c. with. 20:16
Lord *made* a c. with. *1 Ki* 8:9
2 Chr 6:11
c. of Lord which he *made. 1 Ki* 8:21
made a c. with Ben-hadad. 20:34
Jehoiada *made* a c. *2 Ki* 11:4
made c. between the Lord and. 17
Israel rejected his c. he *made.* 17:15
whom the Lord had *made* a c. 35
the c. *made* with you ye shall. 38
Josiah *made* a c. 23:3; *2 Chr* 34:31
David *made* a c. with. *1 Chr* 11:3
mindful even of the c. *made.*
16:16; *Neh* 9:8; *Ps* 105:9
of c. he had *made* with David.
2 Chr 21:7
all congregation *made* a c. 23:3
I *made* a c. with mine. *Job* 31:1

that have *made* a c. with. *Ps* 50:5
have *made* a c. with my. 89:3
ye have *made* a c. with. *Isa* 28:15
enlarged thy bed, and *made* c. 57:8
broke the c. I *made*. *Jer* 11:10
not according to c. I *made*. 31:32
Zedekiah had *made* a c. 34:8, 15
saith the Lord, I *made* a c. 13
ye had *made* a c. before me. 15
words of the c. ye had *made*. 18
and *made* a c. with him. *Ezek* 17:13

make covenant

I will *make* my c. *Gen* 17:2
let us *make* a c. 26:28; 31:44
Ezra 10:3
shalt *make* no c. *Ex* 23:32; *Deut* 7:2
I *make* a c. before all thy. *Ex* 34:10
lest thou *make* a c. with. 12, 15
do I *make* this c. *Deut* 29:14
make a c. with us. *1 Sam* 11:1
on this condition will I *make* a c. 2
my heart to *make* a c. *2 Chr* 29:10
and we *make* a sure c. *Neh* 9:38
will he *make* a c.? *Job* 41:4
this shall be the c. that I will *make*.
Jer 31:33; *Heb* 8:10; 10:16
make with them a c. of peace.
Ezek 34:25; 37:26
I will *make* a c. for them. *Hos* 2:18
and they do *make* a c. with. 12:1

new covenant

new c. with Israel. *Jer* 31:31
Heb 8:8
a *new* c. he hath made. *Heb* 8:13
Jesus the Mediator of *new* c. 12:24

remember covenant

I will *remember* my c. *Gen* 9:15
Lev 26:42; *Ezek* 16:60
I have *rem*. my c. *Ex* 6:5, 6
for their sakes *rem*. c. *Lev* 26:45
hath *rem*. c. for ever. *Ps* 105:8
106:45
rem. not brotherly c. *Amos* 1:9
and to *rem*. his holy c. *Luke* 1:72

covenant of salt

the *salt* of thy God. *Lev* 2:13
it is a c. of *salt* for. *Num* 18:19
to David and sons by c. of *salt*.
2 Chr 13:5

transgressed covenant

hath wrought wickedness in *trans*.
his c. *Deut* 17:2
have also *trans*. my c. *Josh* 7:11
he *trans*. c. of Lord. 15; *Judg* 2:20
2 Ki 18:12
ye *trans*. c. of the Lord. *Josh* 23:16
men that *trans*. my c. *Jer* 34:18
men have *trans*. the c. *Hos* 6:7
because they have *trans*. my c. 8:1

covenanted

according as I have c. *2 Chr* 7:18
the word that I c. with. *Hag* 2:5
they c. with him for. *Mat* 26:15*
were glad, and c. to. *Luke* 22:5

covenants

pertaineth the glory and c. *Rom* 9:4
these are the two c. *Gal* 4:24
strangers from the c. of. *Eph* 2:12

cover

[1] To *hide*, Pr 12:16. [2] To *clothe*, 1 Sam 28:14. [3] To *protect and defend*, Ps 91:4. [4] To *pardon, or forgive*, Ps. 32:1; Rom 4:7. [5] To *vail*, 1 Cor 11:6.

the locusts shall c. the. *Ex* 10:5
shall dig a pit and not c. it. 21:33
linen breeches to c. 28:42
I will c. thee with my hand. 33:22
thou shalt c. the ark with. 40:3*
cloud of incense may c. *Lev* 16:13
pour out the blood, and c. 17:13
behold they c. the face. *Num* 22:5
and c. that which. *Deut* 23:13
the Lord shall c. him all day. 33:12
Saul went in to c. his. *1 Sam* 24:3
c. not their iniquity. *Neh* 4:5
c. not thou my blood. *Job* 16:18
down in dust, worms shall c. 21:26
abundance of waters c. thee. 22:11
38:34
the shady trees c. him with. 40:22

he shall c. thee with his. *Ps* 91:4
they turn not again to c. 104:9
c. themselves with their. 109:29
surely darkness shall c. me. 139:11*
mischief of their lips c. them. 140:9
as the waters c. the sea. *Isa* 11:9
Hab 2:14
the worms c. thee. *Isa* 14:11
the Lord will surely c. thee. 22:17*
the earth shall no more c. 26:21
that c. with a covering. 30:1†
that thou c. him. 58:7
neither c. themselves. 59:6
darkness shall c. the earth. 60:2
multitude of camels shall c. 6
and will c. the earth. *Jer* 46:8
horror shall c. them. *Ezek* 7:18
thou shalt c. thy face. 12:6
he shall c. his face that. 12
poured it not on ground to c. 24:7
c. not thy lips, and eat not. 17
ye shall not c. your lips. 22
their dust shall c. thee. 26:10
great waters shall c. thee. 19
a cloud shall c. her and. 30:18
I will c. the heaven, I will c. 32:7
I will c. you with skin. 37:6
like a cloud to c. land. 38:9, 16
recover my flax given to c. *Hos* 2:9
say to the mountains, c. us. 10:8
Luke 23:30
shame shall c. thee. *Ob* 10
yea, they shall all c. their. *Mi* 3:7
and shame shall c. her that. 7:10
violence of Lebanon c. *Hab* 2:17
to spit on him and c. *Mark* 14:65
a man ought not to c. *1 Cor* 11:7*
for charity shall c. the. *1 Pet* 4:8

covered

mountains were c. *Gen* 7:19, 20
they c. the nakedness of. 9:23
took a vail and c. herself. 24:65
Tamar c. her with a vail. 38:14
frogs came up and c. land. *Ex* 8:6
the waters c. the chariots. 14:28
the depths c. them, they. 15:5
the sea c. them. 10; *Josh* 24:7
came and c. the camp. *Ex* 16:13
a cloud c. the mount. 24:15, 16
c. with their wings over. 37:9
the vail c. the ark of the. 40:21*
a cloud c. the tent of the. 34
if the leprosy have c. *Lev* 13:13
when holy things are c. *Num* 4:20*
cloud c. the tabernacle. 9:15, 16
16:42
waxen fat, thou art c. *Deut* 32:15*
Jael c. him with a. *Judg* 4:18, 19
Michal c. the pillow. *1 Sam* 19:13
an old man cometh up c. 28:14
c. king David with clothes. *1 Ki* 1:1
cherubims c. ark. 8:7; *1 Chr* 28:18
2 Chr 5:8
rent his clothes and c. *2 Ki* 19:1
Isa 37:1
nor c. he the darkness. *Job* 23:17
if I c. my transgressions. 31:33
shame of face hath c. me. *Ps* 44:15
though thou hast c. us with. 19
the valleys also are c. over. 65:13
as the wings of a dove c. 68:13
let them be c. with reproach. 71:13
glory to cease, thou hast c. 89:45
the earth c. the company of. 106:17
thou hast c. me in my. 139:13
like a potsherd c. with. *Pr* 26:23*
whose hatred is c. by deceit. 26
his name shall be c. with. *Eccl* 6:4
he c. his face, he c. his feet. *Isa* 6:2
and the seers hath he c. 29:10
I have c. thee in the shadow. 51:16
he c. me with the robe of. 61:10
she is c. with multitude. *Jer* 51:42
c. the daughter of Zion. *Lam* 2:1
he hath me with ashes. 3:16
thou hast c. with anger. 43
thou shalt c. thyself with a cloud. 44
two wings c. bodies. *Ezek* 1:11, 23
I spread my skirt, and c. thy. 16:8
girded thee with linen, I c. thee. 10
and hath c. the naked. 16
that her blood should not be c. 24:8
blue and purple c. thee. 27:7*

I c. the deep for him. *Ezek* 31:15
flesh came up, and skin c. 37:8
the king of Nineveh c. *Jonah* 3:6
let man and beast be c. 8
God came, his glory c. *Hab* 3:3
the ship was c. with. *Mat* 8:24
there is nothing c. that shall not be
revealed. 10:26; *Luke* 12:2
if the woman be not c. *1 Cor* 11:6

covered face

Tamar had c. her face. *Gen* 38:15
the locusts c. the face of. *Ex* 10:15
David c. his face and. *2 Sam* 19:4
they c. Haman's face. *Esth* 7:8
shame hath c. my face. *Ps* 69:7
nettles had c. the face. *Pr* 24:31
with twain he c. his face. *Isa* 6:2
shame hath c. our face. *Jer* 51:51

head covered

man had his head c. *2 Sam* 15:30
mourning, his head c. *Esth* 6:12
hast c. my head in the. *Ps* 140:7
confounded, and c. their heads.
Jer 14:3, 4
praying, having his head c. *1 Cor* 11:4

covered sin, or sins

whose *sin* is c. *Ps* 32:1; *Rom* 4:7
thou hast c. all their *sins*. *Ps* 85:2

coveredst

thou c. it with the deep. *Ps* 104:6
garments and c. them. *Ezek* 16:18

coverest

wherewith thou c. thyself.
Deut 22:12
who c. thyself with light. *Ps* 104:2

covereth

take all the fat that c. *Ex* 29:13, 22
Lev 3:3, 9, 14; 4:8; 7:3; 9:19
a people which c. the. *Num* 22:11
surely he c. his feet in. *Judg* 3:24
c. the faces of the judges. *Job* 9:24
because he c. his face. 15:27
he c. the bottom of the sea. 36:30
with clouds he c. light. 32
violence c. them as a. *Ps* 73:6
as the garment which c. him. 109:19
c. the heavens with clouds. 147:8
violence c. the mouth. *Pr* 10:6, 11
love c. all sins. 12
a prudent man c. shame. 12:16
he that c. a transgression. 17:9
he that c. his sins shall not. 28:13
our confusion c. us. *Jer* 3:25
anointed cherub that c. *Ezek* 28:14
one c. violence with his. *Mal* 2:16
he lighted candle c. it. *Luke* 8:16

covering

Noah removed the c. *Gen* 8:13
behold, he is to thee a c. 20:16
that is his c. raiment. *Ex* 22:27
leper shall put a c. on. *Lev* 13:45
vessel which hath no c. *Num* 19:15
woman spread a c. *2 Sam* 17:19
thick clouds are a c. *Job* 22:14
that the naked have no c. 24:7
destruction hath no c. 26:6
seen any poor without c. 31:19
a cloud for c. and fire. *Ps* 105:39
the c. of it of purple. *S of S* 3:10
he discovered c. of Judah. *Isa* 22:8
destroy the face of the c. 25:7
the c. narrower than he can. 28:20
that cover with a c. but not. 30:1
ye shall defile the c. of thy. 22
and make sackcloth their c. 50:3
stones was thy c. *Ezek* 28:13
hair is given her for a c. *1 Cor* 11:15

see badgers' skins

covering

c. the mercy seat with. *Ex* 25:20
take down the c. vail. *Num* 4:5*
c. the c. cherub. *Ezek* 28:16
c. the altar with tears. *Mal* 2:13

coverings

decked my bed with c. *Pr* 7:16*
she maketh herself c. of. 31:22*

covers

and make c. thereof. *Ex* 25:29*
he made his c. 37:16
put thereon c. to cover. *Num* 4:7*

covert

[1] *A covered, protected place,*
1 Sam 25:20. [2] *A thicket for wild beasts,* Job 38:40.

Abigail came down by c. *1 Sam* 25:20
the c. for the sabbath. *2 Ki* 16:18*
lions abide in the c. *Job* 38:40
behemoth lieth in the c. 40:21
will trust in the c. of. *Ps* 61:4
a tabernacle for a c. *Isa* 4:6
be thou a c. to them from. 16:4
a man shall be a c. from. 32:2
he hath forsaken his c. *Jer* 25:38

covet

(*To wish for with eagerness; usually used in the sense of a fault, though not always*)

thou shalt not c. thy. *Ex* 20:17
Deut 5:21; *Rom* 7:7; 13:9
they c. fields and take. *Mi* 2:2
but c. earnestly the. *1 Cor* 12:31*
c. to prophesy, and forbid. 14:39*

coveted

then I c. them, took. *Josh* 7:21
c. no man's silver or. *Acts* 20:33
which while some c. *1 Tim* 6:10*

coveteth

he c. greedily all the. *Pr* 21:26
woe to him that c. an. *Hab* 2:9*

covetous

the wicked blesseth c. *Ps* 10:3
Pharisees who were c. *Luke* 16:14*
not altogether with c. *1 Cor* 5:10
if any brother be c. with such. 11
nor c. shall inherit. 6:10; *Eph* 5:5
a bishop must not be c. *1 Tim* 3:3*
men shall be c. boasters. *2 Tim* 3:2*
with c. practices. *2 Pet* 2:14*

covetousness

able men, men hating c. *Ex* 18:21*
incline not my heart to c. *Ps* 119:36
he that hateth c. shall. *Pr* 28:16
for the iniquity of his c. *Isa* 57:17
is given to c. *Jer* 6:13; 8:10
but for thy c. 22:17
and the measure of thy c. 51:13
their heart goeth after their c.
Ezek 33:31*
him that coveteth an evil c. *Hab* 2:9*
of heart proceedeth c. *Mark* 7:22
heed, and beware of c. *Luke* 12:15
being filled with all c. *Rom* 1:29
of bounty, and not of c. *2 Cor* 9:5*
but c. let it not be named. *Eph* 5:3
mortify your members and c. *Col* 3:5
nor used we a cloke of c. *1 Thes* 2:5
let your conversation be without c.
Heb 13:5*
through c. shall they make. *2 Pet* 2:3

cow

whether c. or ewe. *Lev* 22:28
firstling of a c. thou. *Num* 18:17*
their c. calveth, and. *Job* 21:10
nourisheth a young c. *Isa* 7:21
and the c. and the bear shall. 11:7
I have given thee c. *Ezek* 4:15
every c. at that which. *Amos* 4:3*

Cozbi

name of woman was C. *Num* 25:15
beguiled you in matter of C. 18

crackling

as c. of thorns under a pot. *Eccl* 7:6

cracknels

thee ten loaves and c. *1 Ki* 14:3†

craft

policy shall cause c. to. *Dan* 8:25
take him by c. and put. *Mark* 14:1
he was of the same c. *Acts* 18:3*
ye know that by this c. 19:25*
so that not only this our c. 27*
of whatsoever c. he be. *Rev* 18:22

craftiness

the wise in their c. *Job* 5:13
1 Cor 3:19
he perceived their c. *Luke* 20:23
not walking in c. nor. *2 Cor* 4:2
no more carried by c. *Eph* 4:14

craftsman

the work of the c. *Deut* 27:15
no c. shall be found any. *Rev* 18:22

craftsmen

carried away all c. *2 Ki* 24:14, 16
for they were c. *1 Chr* 4:14
the valley of c. *Neh* 11:35
all of it the work of c. *Hos* 13:2
no small gain to c. *Acts* 19:24
if the c. have a matter. 38

crafty

disappointed devices of c. *Job* 5:12
choosest the tongue of the c. 15:5
have taken c. counsel. *Ps* 83:3
being c. I caught. *2 Cor* 12:16

crag

the eagle abideth on c. *Job* 39:28†

crane

like a c. or swallow. *Isa* 38:14
c. and swallow observe time. *Jer* 8:7

crashing

there shall be a great c. *Zeph* 1:10

craved

Joseph went, and c. *Mark* 15:43*

craveth

his mouth c. it. *Pr* 16:26

create

To bring into being, usually understood as meaning to make out of nothing, Gen 1:1.

c. in me a clean heart. *Ps* 51:10
c. on every dwelling-place. *Isa* 4:5
and c. darkness, I c. evil. 45:7
I c. the fruit of the lips. 57:19
behold, I c. new heavens. 65:17
rejoice for ever in that which I c. 18

created

in the beginning God c. *Gen* 1:1
God c. great whales and. 21
c. man in his own image, male and
female c. he them. 27; 5:2
he had rested from all he c. 2:3
I will destroy man whom I c. 6:7
since day God c. man. *Deut* 4:32
and south thou hast c. *Ps* 89:12
people which shall be c. 102:18
forth thy Spirit, they are c. 104:30
commanded, and they were c. 148:5
behold who hath c. *Isa* 40:26
holy One of Israel hath c. it. 41:20
he that c. the heavens. 42:5
Lord that c. thee, O Jacob. 43:1
have c. him for my glory. 7
I the Lord have c. it. 45:8
I have made the earth, and c. 12
he hath established it, c. it. 18
they are c. now, and not. 48:7
I have c. the smith, I have c. 54:16
for the Lord hath c. a. *Jer* 31:22
judge thee where thou wast c.
Ezek 21:30
in the day that thou wast c. 28:13
perfect from day that thou wast c. 15
hath not one God c. us ? *Mal* 2:10
creation which God c. *Mark* 13:19
neither was the man c. *1 Cor* 11:9
we are his workmanship, c. *Eph* 2:10
hid in God, who c. all things. 3:9
the new man, after God is c. 4:24
by him were all things c., all things
were c. by him. *Col* 1:16
after image of him that c. him. 3:10
from meats which God c. *1 Tim* 4:3
thou hast c. all things, and for thy
pleasure they were c. *Rev* 4:11
who c. heaven and the things. 10:6

createth

he that c. the wind. *Amos* 4:13

creation

from the c. God made. *Mark* 10:6
was not from beginning of c. 13:19
things of him from c. *Rom* 1:20
we know that the whole c. 8:22
continue as from the c. *2 Pet* 3:4
beginning of the c. of God. *Rev* 3:14

creator

remember thy c. in the. *Eccl* 12:1
the Lord, the c. of the. *Isa* 40:28
Lord, the c. of Israel. 43:15
creature more than the c. *Rom* 1:25
in well-doing as to a faithful c.
1 Pet 4:19

creature

bring forth moving c. *Gen* 1:20
is the law of every c. *Lev* 11:46
the gospel to every c. *Mark* 16:15*
Col 1:23
expectation of c. waiteth. *Rom* 8:19
for c. was made subject to. 20*
the c. shall be delivered. 21*
nor any c. shall be able to. 39
in Christ, he is a new c. *2 Cor* 5:17
but a new c. *Gal* 6:15
first-born of every c. *Col* 1:15*
for every c. of God. *1 Tim* 4:4
nor is there any c. that. *Heb* 4:13
every c. in heaven heard. *Rev* 5:13*

living creature

created every *living* c. *Gen* 1:21
earth bring forth the *living* c. 24
Adam called every *living* c. 2:19
covenant with every *living* c. 9:10
between me and *living* c. 12, 15
law of every *living* c. *Lev* 11:46
spirit of *living* c. *Ezek* 1:20, 21
10:17
the *living* c. that I saw. 10:15, 20

creatures

houses full of doleful c. *Isa* 13:21
a kind of first-fruits of c. *Jas* 1:18
a third part of the c. in. *Rev* 8:9

living creatures

likeness of four *living* c. *Ezek* 1:5
up and down among the *living* c. 13
living c. ran, and returned. 14
living c., one wheel by *living* c. 15
when the *living* c. went, the. 19
noise of wings of *living* c. 3:13

creditor

every c. that lendeth. *Deut* 15:2
c. is come to take my. *2 Ki* 4:1
there was a certain c. *Luke* 7:41*

creditors

which of my c. is it ? *Isa* 50:1

creek

discovered a certain c. *Acts* 27:39*

creep

unclean among all that c. *Lev* 11:31
beasts of the forest do c. *Ps* 104:20
this sort are they who c. *2 Tim* 3:6

creepeth

every thing that c. *Gen* 1:25, 26
to every thing that c. upon. 30
every thing that c. went. 7:8, 14
died of every thing that c. 21
bring forth every thing that c. 8:17
whatsoever c. on the earth. 19*
c. on the earth shall be an abomination. *Lev* 11:41*, 43, 44; 20:25*
likeness of any thing that c. on.
Deut 4:18

creeping

dominion over every c. *Gen* 1:26
every c. thing after his kind. 7:14
touch carcase of c. things. *Lev* 5:2
these may ye eat, of c. thing. 11:21
whosoever toucheth c. thing. 22:5
every c. thing that. *Deut* 14:19
spake of beasts, c. things. *1 Ki* 4:33
in the sea are c. things. *Ps* 104:25
all cattle, c. things praise. 148:10
form of c. things. *Ezek* 8:10
all c. things shall shake. 38:20
a covenant with the c. *Hos* 2:18
maketh men as c. things. *Hab* 1:14
Peter saw c. things. *Acts* 10:12
11:6
an image like c. things. *Rom* 1:23

crept

for there are certain men c. *Jude* 4

Crescens

C. is departed to Galatia. *2 Tim* 4:10

Crete

we sailed under C. *Acts* 27:7
Phenice, an haven of C. 12
close by C. 13
and not have loosed from C. 21
cause left I thee in C. *Tit* 1:5

Cretes

C., we do hear them speak. *Acts* 2:11

Cretians

the C. are always liars. *Tit* 1:12

crew

immediately the cock c. *Mat* 26:74
 Mark 14:68; *Luke* 22:60
second time cock c. *Mark* 14:72
 John 18:27

crib

will unicorn abide by c.? *Job* 39:9
where no oxen are, the c. is. *Pr* 14:4
ass knoweth his master's c. *Isa* 1:3

cried

Esau c. with a great. *Gen* 27:34
lifted up my voice and c. 39:15
and they c. before him. 41:43
people c. to Pharaoh for. 55
he c. cause every man to go. 45:1
the officers came and c. *Ex* 5:15
the people c. to Moses. *Num* 11:2
damsel, because she c. *Deut* 22:24
the damsel c. and there was. 27
Sisera's mother c. *Judg* 5:28
and all the host ran and c. 7:21
and ye c. to me, and I. 10:12
he stood and c. unto the. *1 Sam* 17:8
Jonathan c. after the lad. 20:37, 38
then c. a wise woman. *2 Sam* 20:16
I c. to my God, and he did. 22:7
he c. against the altar. *1 Ki* 13:2, 4
and they c. aloud. 18:28
Elisha saw it, and c. *2 Ki* 2:12
he c. alas, master, for it was. 6:5
the woman c. to the king. 8:5
and Athaliah c., Treason. 11:14
they c. to God in battle. *1 Chr* 5:20
Isaiah prayed and c. *2 Chr* 32:20
when they c. to thee. *Neh* 9:27, 28
delivered the poor that c. *Job* 29:12
they c. after them. 30:5
in my distress I c. unto. *Ps* 18:6
they c. but there was none. 41
they c. to thee and. 22:5
but when he c. unto him. 24
O Lord my God, I c. to thee. 30:2
I c. to thee, O Lord, and. 8
my supplications when I c. 31:22
this poor man c. and the. 34:6
I c. with him with. 66:17; 77:1
O Lord, I have c. day and. 88:1
unto thee have I c. O Lord. 13
I c. with my whole heart. 119:145
out of the depths have I c. 130:1
in the day when I c. thou. 138:3
moved at voice of him that c. *Isa* 6:4
therefore I c. concerning this. 30:7
upon destruction is c. *Jer* 4:20
fell on my face and c. *Ezek* 9:8
it was c. to them in my. 10:13
c. with a lamentable voice. *Dan* 6:20
they have not c. to me. *Hos* 7:14
the mariners c. every. *Jonah* 1:5
c. by reason of mine affliction; out of
 the belly of hell c. I. 2:2
as he c. and they would not hear, so
 they c. and I would. *Zech* 7:13
Peter c. saying, Lord. *Mat* 14:30
they c. the more, saying. 20:31
 Mark 10:48; *Luke* 18:39
the spirit c. and rent. *Mark* 9:26
Jesus c. if any man thirst. *John* 7:37
some c. one thing. *Acts* 19:32; 21:34
might know wherefore they c. 22:24
when he c. seven thunders. *Rev* 10:3
and she being with child, c. 12:2
c. with a loud cry to him. 14:18
he c. mightily with a strong. 18:2
c. when they saw the smoke. 18
they c. weeping and wailing. 19

cried to the Lord

Moses c. to Lord. *Ex* 8:12; 15:25
 17:4; *Num* 12:13
Israel c. to the Lord. *Ex* 14:10
 Judg 3:9, 15; 4:3; 6:7; 10:10
when we c. to the Lord. *Num* 20:16
 Deut 26:7
when they c. to the Lord. *Josh* 24:7
Samuel c. to Lord. *1 Sam* 7:9; 15:11
Elijah c. to the Lord. *1 Ki* 17:20, 21
Isaiah c. to the Lord. *2 Ki* 20:11
they c. to the Lord. *2 Chr* 13:14
 Ps 107:6, 13; *Jonah* 1:14
Asa c. to the Lord. *2 Chr* 14:11
I c. to Lord. *Ps* 3:4; 120:1; 142:1
their heart c. to the Lord. *Lam* 2:18

cried with a loud voice

woman c. with a loud voice.
 1 Sam 28:12
David c. with loud voice. *2 Sam* 19:4
Rabshakeh c. with a loud voice.
 2 Ki 18:28; *Isa* 36:13
Levites c. with loud voice. *Neh* 9:4
Ezekiel c. with a loud voice.
 Ezek 11:13
Jesus c. with loud voice. *Mat* 27:46
 50; *Mark* 15:34, 37; *Luke* 23:46
 John 11:43
evil spirit c. with a loud voice.
 Mark 1:26
Stephen's enemies c. with a loud
 voice. *Acts* 7:57
Stephen c. with a loud voice. 60
Paul c. with a loud voice. 16:28
they c. with loud voice. *Rev* 6:10
angel c. with a loud voice. 7:2; 10:3
 19:17
before Lamb c. with a loud voice.
 7:10

cried out

all the city c. out. *1 Sam* 4:13
Ekronites c. out. 5:10
Jehoshaphat c. out. *1 Ki* 22:32
 2 Chr 18:31
c. out, there is death. *2 Ki* 4:40
I c. out, I cried violence. *Jer* 20:8
the spirits c. out. *Mat* 8:29
 Luke 4:33
disciples c. out for fear. *Mat* 14:26
 Mark 6:49
blind men c. out, have. *Mat* 20:30
they c. out the more. 23
 Mark 15:13; *Luke* 23:18
 John 19:6
with unclean spirit c. out. *Mark* 1:23
father of the child c. out. 9:24
 Luke 9:38
they c. out, saying. *Acts* 19:28, 34
as they c. out, and threw. 22:23
Paul c. out in the council. 23:6

cries

the c. of them that reaped. *Jas* 5:4

criest, -eth

of thy brother's blood c. *Gen* 4:10
wherefore c. thou to me? *Ex* 14:15
when he c. unto me. 22:27
who art thou that c. to? *1 Sam* 26:14
soul of wounded c. out. *Job* 24:12
deliver needy when he c. *Ps* 72:12
my heart and flesh c. out for. 84:2
wisdom c. *Pr* 1:20; 8:3; 9:3
yea, if thou c. after. 2:3
like as a woman that c. *Isa* 26:17
the voice of him that c. in. 40:3
when thou c. let companies. 57:13
my heritage c. out. *Jer* 12:8
c. thou for thine affliction? 30:15
Lord's voice c. to city. *Mi* 6:9
send her away, she c. *Mat* 15:23
he suddenly c. out. *Luke* 9:39
Esaias also c. concerning. *Rom* 9:27
hire of the labourers c. *Jas* 5:4

crime, -s

this is an heinous c. *Job* 31:11
land is full of bloody c. *Ezek* 7:23
to answer concerning c. *Acts* 25:16*
and not to signify the c. 27

crimson

(A deep red colour tinged with
blue, derived from kermes, the
dried bodies of certain insects
allied to the cochineal insects.
Three Hebrew words are used, the
most frequent being cochineal)

a man cunning to work in c.
 2 Chr 2:7, 14
the vail of blue, c. and. 3:14
your sins be red like c. *Isa* 1:18
clothest thyself with c. *Jer* 4:30*

cripple

being a c. from his. *Acts* 14:8

crisping-pins

take away mantles and c. *Isa* 3:22*

Crispus

C. chief ruler of the. *Acts* 18:8
that I baptized none of you, but C.
 1 Cor 1:14

crookbackt

a man that is c. shall. *Lev* 21:20

crooked

and c. generation. *Deut* 32:5
hand formed c. serpent. *Job* 26:13*
turn aside to their c. ways. *Ps* 125:5
whose ways are c. and. *Pr* 2:15
what is c. cannot. *Eccl* 1:15; 7:13
punish Leviathan, that c. *Isa* 27:1
c. be made straight. 40:4; 42:16
 Luke 3:5
make c. places straight. *Isa* 45:2*
they have made them c. paths. 59:8
he hath made my paths c. *Lam* 3:9
in midst of a c. nation. *Phil* 2:15

crop

shall pluck away his c. *Lev* 1:16
I will c. off from top. *Ezek* 17:22

cropped

he c. off the top of his. *Ezek* 17:4

cross

[1] An instrument of punishment
used by the Romans generally for
the punishment of slaves. Specifically, the cross on which our Lord
died, as recorded in the Gospels.
[2] Trials or misfortunes, especially
when considered as tests of
Christian patience or virtue, Mat
16:24.

he that taketh not his c. *Mat* 10:38
 Luke 14:27
take up his c. and follow. *Mat* 16:24
 Mark 8:34; 10:21; *Luke* 9:23
compelled to bear his c. *Mat* 27:32
 Mark 15:21; *Luke* 23:26
be Son of God, come down from c.
 Mat 27:40, 42; *Mark* 15:30, 32
he bearing his c. went. *John* 19:17
a title, and put it on the c. 19
there stood by the c. of Jesus. 25
should not remain on the c. on. 31
lest c. of Christ be. *1 Cor* 1:17
preaching of the c. is to them. 18
then is offence of the c. *Gal* 5:11
persecution for the c. of Christ. 6:12
glory, save in the c. 14
reconcile both by the c. *Eph* 2:16
obedient unto death of the c.
 Phil 2:8
enemies of the c. of Christ. 3:18
peace through blood of c. *Col* 1:20
nailing it to his c. 2:14
before him, endured the c. *Heb* 12:2

crossway

thou have stood in c. *Ob* 14

crouch

shall come and c. to. *1 Sam* 2:36*

croucheth

he c. humbleth himself. *Ps* 10:10

crow, crowing, see cock

crown

A garland or fillet for the head,
used as a mark of distinction.
Hence [1] the special head-dress of
a sovereign, 2 Ki 11:12. [2] The
wreath given to a victor in a Greek
game, 1 Cor 9:25. [3] Any honour
or dignity, Lam 5:16; Phil 4:1;
Rev 4:4.

shalt make a golden c. *Ex* 25:25
put the holy c. upon the mitre. 29:6
rings to it under the c. 30:4; 37:27
the plate of the c. of gold. 39:30
he put the holy c. *Lev* 8:9
c. of the anointing oil is. 21:12
put the c. upon Joash. *2 Ki* 11:12
 2 Chr 23:11
bring Vashti with the c. *Esth* 1:11
I would bind it as a c. *Job* 31:36
thou hast profaned his c. *Ps* 89:39
upon himself shall his c. 132:18
a c. of glory shall she. *Pr* 4:9
a virtuous woman is a c. 12:4
the c. of the wise is their. 14:24
hoary head is a c. of glory. 16:31
children's children are c. of. 17:6
doth the c. endure to every? 27:24
king Solomon with c. *S of S* 3:11
woe to the c. of pride. *Isa* 28:1

Lord of hosts shall be for a c. *Isa* 28:5
thou shalt also be a c. of glory. 62:3
the c. of your glory shall. *Jer* 13:18
take off the c. *Ezek* 21:26
as stones of a c. lifted. *Zech* 9:16
Jesus wearing a c. of. *John* 19:5
to obtain a corruptible c. *1 Cor* 9:25
my joy and c. *Phil* 4:1
what is our hope, or c. *1 Thes* 2:19
is laid up for me a c. *2 Tim* 4:8
shall receive the c. of life. *Jas* 1:12
receive a c. of glory. *1 Pet* 5:4
I will give a c. of life. *Rev* 2:10
that no man take thy c. 3:11
a c. given to him, went forth. 6:2

crown of gold
make upon it a c. of gold. *Ex* 25:11
24; 30:3; 37:2, 11, 12, 26
out with great c. of gold. *Esth* 8:15
c. of pure gold on his head. *Ps* 21:3

crown with head
on c. of Joseph's head. *Gen* 49:26
arm with c. of head. *Deut* 33:20
took c. upon his head. *2 Sam* 1:10
took king's c. from his head. 12:30
1 Chr 20:2
even to c. of his head. *2 Sam* 14:25
Job 2:7
set royal c. on her head. *Esth* 2:17
the c. royal upon his head. 6:8
taken c. from my head. *Job* 19:9
smite with scab c. of head. *Isa* 3:17
broken the c. of thy head. *Jer* 2:16
the c. of the head of the. 48:45
c. is fallen from our head. *Lam* 5:16
c. on thine head. *Ezek* 16:12
c. of thorns, and put it on his head.
Mat 27:29; *Mark* 15:17; *John* 19:2
upon her head a c. of. *Rev* 12:1
having on his head a golden c. 14:14

crowned
thou hast c. him with glory. *Ps* 8:5
the prudent are c. with. *Pr* 14:18
wherewith his mother c. *S of S* 3:11
thy c. are as the locusts. *Nah* 3:17
he is not c. except he. *2 Tim* 2:5
we see Jesus c. with. *Heb* 2:9

crownedst
thou c. him with glory. *Heb* 2:7

crownest
c. year with thy goodness. *Ps* 65:11

crowneth
who c. thee with loving-. *Ps* 103:4

crowning
against Tyre the c. city. *Isa* 23:8

crowns
c. on their heads. *Ezek* 23:42
take gold, and make c. *Zech* 6:11
the c. shall be to Helem. 14
elders had c. of gold. *Rev* 4:4
and they cast their c. before. 10
on locusts' heads were c. 9:7
red dragon having seven c. 12:3*
upon his horns ten c. 13:1*
on his head were many c. 19:12*

crucified
is betrayed to be c. *Mat* 26:2
Luke 24:7
said, let him be c. *Mat* 27:22, 23
delivered him to be c. 26; *John* 19:16
c. him and parted his garments.
Mat 27:35; *John* 19:23
two thieves c. with. *Mat* 27:38, 44
Mark 15:32; *Luke* 23:33
John 19:18
I know ye seek Jesus which was c.
Mat 28:5; *Mark* 16:6
where Jesus was c. *John* 19:20, 41
by wicked hands have c. *Acts* 2:23
Jesus, whom ye c. Lord. 36; 4:10
our old man is c. with. *Rom* 6:6
was Paul c. for you? *1 Cor* 1:13
we preach Christ c. unto the. 23
save Jesus Christ and him c. 2:2
would not have c. Lord of glory. 8
for though he was c. *2 Cor* 13:4
I am c. with Christ. *Gal* 2:20
Christ hath been set forth, c. 3:1
they that are Christ's have c. 5:24
by whom the world is c. to me. 6:14
also our Lord was c. *Rev* 11:8

crucify
To put to death on a cross (Latin crux, gen. crucis, a cross)
him to Gentiles to c. *Mat* 20:19
of them ye shall kill, and c. 23:34
led him away to c. him. 27:31
Mark 15:20
cried out again, c. *Mark* 15:13, 14
with him they c. two thieves. 27
cried, c. him, c. him. *Luke* 23:21
John 19:6, 15
they c. to themselves. *Heb* 6:6

cruel
their wrath, for it was c. *Gen* 49:7
hearkened not for c bondage. *Ex* 6:9
wine as the c. venom. *Deut* 32:33
thou art become a c. to me. *Job* 30:21
hate me with c. hatred. *Ps* 25:19
deliver me out of hand of c. 71:4
thou give thy years to c. *Pr* 5:9
but he that is c. troubleth. 11:17
mercies of wicked are c. 12:10
a c. messenger shall be sent. 17:11
wrath is c. 27:4
jealousy is c. *S of S* 8:6
day of Lord cometh, c. *Isa* 13:9
Egyptians will I give over to c. 19:4
they are c. and. *Jer* 6:23; 50:42
with chastisement of a c. 30:14
of my people is become c. *Lam* 4:3
trial of c. mockings. *Heb* 11:36

cruelly
because he c. oppressed. *Ezek* 18:18

cruelty
instruments of c. are. *Gen* 49:5*
c. done to the sons of. *Judg* 9:24*
such as breathe out c. *Ps* 27:12
full of habitations of c. 74:20*
force and c. have ye. *Ezek* 34:4*

crumbs
dogs eat of the c. which fall from.
Mat 15:27; *Mark* 7:28
to be fed with c. which. *Luke* 16:21

cruse
take spear and c. of. *1 Sam* 26:11
took the spear and c. 12, 16
take with thee a c. *1 Ki* 14:3
I have but a little oil in a c. 17:12
nor c. of oil fail, till the Lord. 14, 16
Elijah had a c. of water. 19:6
bring me a new c. *2 Ki* 2:20

crush
forgetteth her foot may c. *Job* 39:15
assembly against me to c. *Lam* 1:15
to c. under his feet the. 3:34
kine of Bashan which c. *Amos* 4:1

crushed
not offer that which is c. *Lev* 22:24
the ass c. Balaam's. *Num* 22:25
oppressed and c. alway. *Deut* 28:33
in dust, which are c. *Job* 4:19
children far from safety, are c. 5:4
that which is c. breaketh. *Isa* 59:5
Nebuchadnezzar hath c. *Jer* 51:34

cry
according to the c. *Gen* 18:21
their c. came up. *Ex* 2:23; 3:9
I have heard their c. 3:7
Israel fled at the c. of. *Num* 16:34
c. of the city went up. *1 Sam* 5:12
because their c. is come up. 9:16
and my c. did enter. *2 Sam* 22:7
hearken unto the c. and to the
prayer. *1 Ki* 8:28; *2 Chr* 6:19
angry when I heard their c. *Neh* 5:6
thou heardest their c. by the. 9:9
with loud and bitter c. *Esth* 4:1
of their fastings and their c. 9:31
O earth, let my c. have. *Job* 16:18
cause the c. of the poor to come, he
heareth the c. of the. 34:28
hearken to voice of my c. *Ps* 5:2
forgetteth not the c. of. 9:12
O Lord, attend unto my c. 17:1
my c. came before him. 18:6
his ears are open to their c. 34:15
O Lord, give ear to my c. 39:12
unto me, and heard my c. 40:1
incline thine ear unto my c. 88:2
O Lord, and let my c. come. 102:1
when he heard their c. 106:44

let my c. come near. *Ps* 119:169
attend to my c. 142:6
stoppeth his ears at c. of. *Pr* 21:13
more than the c. of him. *Eccl* 9:17
righteousness, behold a c. *Isa* 5:7
they shall raise up a c. of. 15:5
the c. is gone round about the. 8
gracious at voice of thy c. 30:19
Chaldeans, whose c. is in. 43:14
nor lift up c. nor. *Jer* 7:16; 11:14
voice of the c. of my people. 8:19
the c. of Jerusalem is gone up. 14:2
let a c. be heard from. 18:22
c. of the shepherds shall be. 25:36
thy c. hath filled the land. 46:12
her little ones have caused a c. 48:4
the enemies have heard a c. of. 5
the earth is moved at the c. 49:21
the c. is heard at taking of. 50:46
a sound of a c. cometh. 51:54
not thine ear at my c. *Lam* 3:56
suburbs shake at c. of. *Ezek* 27:28
there shall be a c. from. *Zeph* 1:10
at midnight a c. made. *Mat* 25:6

great cry
c. of Sodom is great. *Gen* 18:20
19:13
with a great and bitter c. 27:34
a great c. through Egypt. *Ex* 11:6
was a great c. in Egypt. 12:30
was great c. of the people. *Neh* 5:1
there arose a great c. *Acts* 23:9

hear cry
will surely hear their c. *Ex* 22:23
will God hear his c.? *Job* 27:9
hear my c. O God. *Ps* 61:1
he also will hear their c. 145:19
let them hear the c. *Jer* 20:16

not hear cry
I will not hear their c. *Jer* 14:12

cry, verb
idle, therefore they c. *Ex* 5:8
and they c. unto me. 22:23
is it voice of them that c. 32:18
cover his upper lip, and c. *Lev* 13:45
go c. to the gods ye. *Judg* 10:14
right have I yet to c. *2 Sam* 19:28
she went to c. for her. *2 Ki* 8:3
and c. in our affliction. *2 Chr* 20:9
I c. unto thee. *Job* 30:20
c. in his destruction. 24
make oppressed to c. they c. 35:9
they c. but none giveth answer. 12
they c. not when he. 36:13
when his young ones c. to. 38:41
I c. in the day time. *Ps* 22:2
hear, O Lord, when I c. 27:7; 28:2
to thee will I c. O Lord. 28:1, 2
the righteous c. and the. 34:17
when I c. then shall mine. 56:9
I will c. to God most high. 57:2
from end of earth will I c. 61:2
O Lord, for I c. to thee. 86:3
he shall c. unto me. 89:26
Lord, I c. unto thee. 141:1
food to young ravens which c. 147:9
doth not wisdom c. and. *Pr* 8:1
he also shall c. but shall. 21:13
child have knowledge to c. *Isa* 8:4
wild beasts of island shall c. 13:22
c. O city, thou Palestina. 14:31
Heshbon shall c. and Elealeh. 15:4
their valiant ones shall c. 33:7
and the satyr shall c. to. 34:14
c. to Jerusalem, her warfare. 40:2
c. and he said, what shall I c.? 6
he shall not c. nor cause. 42:2
he shall c. yea, prevail. 13
now will I c. like a travailing. 14
one shall c. to him, yet can. 46:7
thou shalt c. and he shall say. 58:9
ye shall c. for sorrow of. 65:14
c. in ears of Jerusalem. *Jer* 2:2
wilt thou not from this time c.? 3:4
blow trumpet in land, c. gather. 4:5
though they c. to me. 11:11
c. to the gods to whom they. 12
not hear when they c. 14; *Ezek* 8:18
go up to Lebanon, and c. *Jer* 22:20
howl, ye shepherds, and c. 25:34
48:20; *Ezek* 21:12

watchmen on Ephraim shall c.
    Jer 31:6
when I c. and shout he. *Lam* 3:8
c. for all abominations. *Ezek* 9:4
forbear to c. make no.   24:17*
shake, when the wounded c. 26:15
they shall c. bitterly for. 27:30
Israel shall c. unto me. *Hos* 8:2
O Lord, to thee will I c. *Joel* 1:19
the beasts of the field c.   20
let man and beast c. *Jonah* 3:8
bite with their teeth, and c. *Mi* 3:5
stand, stand, shall they c. *Nah* 2:8
mighty men shall c. *Zeph* 1:14
angel said unto me, c. *Zech* 1:14
shall not strive, nor c. *Mat* 12:19
God avenge elect, who c. *Luke* 18:7
the Spirit, whereby we c. *Rom* 8:15
break forth and c. thou. *Gal* 4:27

cry against
c. to the Lord *against.* *Deut* 15:9
    24:15
to c. alarm *against* you. *2 Chr* 13:12
if my land c. *against* me. *Job* 31:38
to Nineveh, c. *against* it. *Jonah* 1:2

cry aloud
Elijah said, c. *aloud.* *1 Ki* 18:27
I c. *aloud,* but there is no. *Job* 19:7
will I pray and c. *aloud.* *Ps* 55:17
they shall c. *aloud* from. *Isa* 24:14
into singing, and c. *aloud.* 54:1
c. *aloud,* spare not. 58:1
in Ramah, c. *aloud* at. *Hos* 5:8
why dost thou c. *aloud* ? *Mi* 4:9

cry to the Lord
c. unto *the Lord* for us. *1 Sam* 7:8
they c. *to the Lord* in. *Ps* 107:19, 28
they shall c. *to the Lord.* *Isa* 19:20
fast, and c. *to the Lord.* *Joel* 1:14
shall c. *to the Lord,* but. *Mi* 3:4

cry out
ye shall c. *out* that day. *1 Sam* 8:18
I c. *out* of wrong, but. *Job* 19:7
they c. *out* by reason of. 35:9
c. *out* and shout. *Isa* 12:6
soldiers of Moab shall c. *out.* 15:4
my heart shall c. *out* for Moab. 5
wonder, c. *out* and cry. 29:9*
I will howl, and c. *out* for. *Jer* 48:31
arise, c. *out* in the night. *Lam* 2:19
will a young lion c. *out* ? *Amos* 3:4
I c. *out* to thee, but. *Hab* 1:2
for the stone shall c. *out* of. 2:11
he began to c. *out* and. *Mark* 10:47
stones would c. *out.* *Luke* 19:40

crying
Eli heard noise of the c. *1 Sam* 4:14
ashes, and went on c. *2 Sam* 13:19
nor regardeth he the c. *Job* 39:7
thy soul spare for his c. *Pr* 19:18
leech hath two daughters c. 30:15
it is day of trouble and c. *Isa* 22:5
there is a c. for wine. 24:11
voice of c. shall be no more. 65:19
a voice of c. shall be. *Jer* 48:3
forth head-stone with c. *Zech* 4:7
altar of the Lord with c. *Mal* 2:13
voice of one c. in wilderness. *Mat* 3:3
    Mark 1:3; *Luke* 3:4; *John* 1:23
and saw children c. in. *Mat* 21:15
devils c. thou art Christ. *Luke* 4:41
for unclean spirits c. *Acts* 8:7
ran in among the people, c. 14:14
laid hands on him, c. out. 21:28
the multitude followed, c. away. 36
Spirit into your hearts, c. *Gal* 4:6
prayers with strong c. *Heb* 5:7
no more death nor c. *Rev* 21:4

crystal
the gold and the c. *Job* 28:17*
as colour of terrible c. *Ezek* 1:22
a sea of glass like unto c. *Rev* 4:6
light of city was clear as c. 21:11
river of water of life, clear as c. 22:1

cubit
(*The distance from the elbow
bending inwards to the extremity
of the middle finger, or about 18
inches. Standards varied, however, in different places, and no
measures can be defined with*

*exactness. Different periods also
had different standards*)
in a c. shalt thou finish. *Gen* 6:16
breadth of it, after c. *Deut* 3:11
compassing it, ten in a c. *1 Ki* 7:24
ten in a c. compassing. *2 Chr* 4:3
the c. is a c. and an. *Ezek* 43:13
add one c. to stature. *Mat* 6:27
    Luke 12:25

cubits
of ark 300 c. breadth 50 c. *Gen* 6:15
fifteen c. upward did the. 7:20
two c. and a half the. *Ex* 25:10
Goliath's height six c. *1 Sam* 17:4
length of the house 60 c. *1 Ki* 6:2
each of cherubims ten c. 23
and every laver was four c. 7:38
brake down the walls of Jerusalem,
    400 c. *2 Ki* 14:13; *2 Chr* 25:23
height 60 c. breadth 60 c. *Ezra* 6:3
gallows be fifty c. high. *Esth* 5:14
    7:9
from gate to gate 100 c. *Ezek* 40:23
the court 100 c. 47
breadth of the door was ten c. 41:2
thickness of the wall five c. 9
and the altar twelve c. long. 43:16
the settle 14 c. 17
height of image 60 c. *Dan* 3:1
length of flying roll 20 c. *Zech* 5:2
land as it were 200 c. *John* 21:8
the wall of the city 144 c. *Rev* 21:17

cuckow
c. have in abomination. *Lev* 11:16*
    Deut 14:15*

cucumbers
we remember the c. and. *Num* 11:5
a lodge in a garden of c. *Isa* 1:8

cud, *see* **chew** and **cheweth**

cumbered
Martha was c. about. *Luke* 10:40

cumbereth
cut it down, why c. it ? *Luke* 13:7

cumbrance
can I alone bear your c.? *Deut* 1:12

cummin
doth he not scatter c. *Isa* 28:25
cart-wheel turned upon the c. but
    the c. is beaten out with a. 27
ye pay tithes of c. *Mat* 23:23

cunning
(*American Revision changes to
skilful or expert*)
Esau was a c. hunter. *Gen* 25:27
cherubims of c. work. *Ex* 26:1; 36:8
make breast-plate of c. work. 28:15
to devise a c. works in gold. 31:4
Aholiab a c. workman and. 38:23
made breast-plate of c. work. 39:8
man who is a c. player. *1 Sam* 16:16
seen a son of Jesse that is c. 18
all that were c. in songs. *1 Chr* 25:7
man c. to work in gold. *2 Chr* 2:7
I have sent a c. man of Huram. 13
let right hand forget her c. *Ps* 137:5
work of a c. workman. *S of S* 7:1
take away the c. artificer. *Isa* 3:3
seeketh to him a c. workman. 40:20
send for c. women that. *Jer* 9:17
they are all the work of c. 10:9
well favoured, c. in. *Dan* 1:4
about by c. craftiness. *Eph* 4:14

cunningly
not followed c. devised. *2 Pet* 1:16

cup
This word is used, [1] *literally, for
a material cup from which one
drinks ; and* [2] *figuratively, for the
contents of a cup.* 1 Cor 11:27; *or* [3]
*for sufferings which one undergoes
as one drinks a cup of nauseous
medicine to the dregs.* Isa 51:17;
Mat 26:39; *or* [4] *for the blessings
which God gives to us, as a
pleasant and refreshing drink,*
Ps 23:5.

and Pharaoh's c. was in. *Gen* 40:11
put my c. my silver c. in the. 42:2
it drank of its own c. *2 Sam* 12:3
wrought like brim of a c. *1 Ki* 7:26
    2 Chr 4:5

be the portion of their c. *Ps* 11:6
Lord is the portion of my c. 16:5
my c. runneth over. 23:5
waters of a full c. are wrung. 73:10
in the hand of Lord there is a c. 75:8
I will take the c. of salvation. 116:13
giveth his colour in the c. *Pr* 23:31
drunk at the hand of the Lord the c.
    the dregs of the c. of. *Isa* 51:17
taken out of thy hand c. of. 22
nor shall men give them c. *Jer* 16:7
take the wine-c. of his fury. 25:15
then took I the c. at the Lord's. 17
if they refuse to take the c. 28
Babylon hath been a golden c. 51:7
c. also shall pass through. *Lam* 4:21
I will give her c. into. *Ezek* 23:31
thou shalt drink of thy sister's c. 32
c. of Lord's right hand. *Hab* 2:16
Jerusalem c. of trembling. *Zech* 12:2
c. of cold water only. *Mat* 10:42
    Mark 9:41
are ye able to drink of the c.?
    Mat 20:22; *Mark* 10:38
ye shall drink indeed of my c.
    Mat 20:23; *Mark* 10:39
make clean outside of c. *Mat* 23:25
cleanse first what is within c. 26
took the c. and gave thanks. 26:27
    Mark 14:23; *Luke* 22:17, 20
    1 Cor 11:25
let this c. pass from. *Mat* 26:39
    Mark 14:36; *Luke* 22:42
this c. may not pass away. *Mat* 26:42
c. is the new testament. *Luke* 22:20
    1 Cor 11:25
c. which my Father hath. *John* 18:11
the c. of blessing we. *1 Cor* 10:16
the c. of Lord and c. of devils. 21
as often as ye drink of this c. 11:26
and drink this c. of the Lord. 27
without mixture into c. *Rev* 14:10
to give unto her the c. 16:19
the woman having a golden c. 17:4
in the c. she filled, fill to her. 18:6

cup-bearer, -s
queen of Sheba saw cup-*bearers.*
    1 Ki 10:5; *2 Chr* 9:4
was the king's cup-*bearer.* *Neh* 1:11

cups
pure gold for the c. *1 Chr* 28:17
on Eliakim vessels of c. *Isa* 22:24
sets pots full of wine and c. *Jer* 35:5
took away spoons and c. 52:19
washing of c. and pots. *Mark* 7:4, 8

curdled
hast not thou c. me ? *Job* 10:10

cure, -ed
I will c. them, and will. *Jer* 33:6
of Egypt, shalt not be c. 46:11
yet could he not c. you. *Hos* 5:13
they could not c. him. *Mat* 17:16
the child was c. from that. 18
in that hour he c. many. *Luke* 7:21
gave them power to c. diseases. 9:1
said to him that was c. *John* 5:10

cures
cast out devils, do c. *Luke* 13:32

curious
c. girdle. *Ex* 28:8*, 27*, 28*; 29:5*
    39:5*; *Lev* 8:7*
and to devise c. works. *Ex* 35:32*
used c. arts brought. *Acts* 19:19

curiously
and c. wrought in the. *Ps* 139:15

current
c. money with the. *Gen* 23:16

curse
[1] *To call on divine power to send
some injury upon the one cursed.
This was often pronounced as by a
mouthpiece of God to man, and
sometimes as a statement of what
would happen, uttered without
ill-feeling,* Gen 9:25; 49:7; Josh
6:26. [2] *Profanity or blasphemy,*
Ex 22:28; Ps 11:26; Mat 26:74.
I shall bring a c. on me. *Gen* 27:12
upon me be thy c. my son. 13

the bitter water that causeth the *c.*
 Num 5:18, 19, 22, 24, 27
the woman shall be a *c.* 27
I set before you a blessing and *c.*
 Deut 11:26; 30:1
a *c.* if you will not obey the. 11:28
and shalt put the *c.* upon. 29
c. into a blessing. 23:5; *Neh* 13:2
heareth words of this *c. Deut* 29:29
make camp of Israel a *c. Josh* 6:18
on them came the *c.* of. *Judg* 9:57
me with a grievous *c.* *1 Ki* 2:8
they should become a *c.* *2 Ki* 22:19
they entered into a *c.* *Neh* 10:29
to sin by wishing a *c.* *Job* 31:30
the *c.* of Lord is in the. *Pr* 3:33
so the *c.* causeless shall not. 26:2
it shall be counted a *c.* to. 27:14
eyes shall have many a *c.* 28:27
hath the *c.* devoured. *Isa* 24:6
come down on people of my *c.* 34:5
I have given Jacob to the *c.* 43:28
shall leave your name for a *c.* 65:15
them to be a taunt and *c.* *Jer* 24:9
 25:18; 29:18*; 42:18; 44:8, 12
I will make this city a *c.* 26:6
therefore is your land a *c.* 44:22
that Bozrah shall become a *c.* 49:13
give them sorrow, thy *c. Lam* 3:65
therefore the *c.* is poured. *Dan* 9:11
this is the *c.* that goeth. *Zech* 5:3
that as we were a *c.* among. 8:13
I will send a *c.* upon you. *Mal* 2:2
ye are cursed with a *c.* 3:9
and smite the earth with a *c.* 4:6
themselves under *c. Acts* 23:12, 14
of law, are under the *c. Gal* 3:10
from the *c.* being made a *c.* 13
shall be no more *c.* but. *Rev* 22:3

curse, *verb*

Lord said, I will not *c.* *Gen* 8:21
and I will *c.* him that curseth. 12:3
thou shalt not *c.* ruler. *Ex* 22:28
thou shalt not *c.* the deaf. *Lev* 19:14
I pray thee, *c.* me this. *Num* 22:6, 17
now, *c.* me them. 11; 23:7, 13
thou shalt not *c.* the people. 22:12
how shall I *c.* whom God? 23:8
to *c.* mine enemies. 11; 24:10
neither *c.* them at all. 23:25
hired Balaam to *c.* thee. *Deut* 23:4
 Neh 13:2
stand on mount Ebal to *c. Deut* 27:13
called Balaam to *c.* *Josh* 24:9
c. ye Meroz, said the angel, *c.* ye
 bitterly. *Judg* 5:23
should this dead dog *c.? 2 Sam* 16:9
let him *c.* because Lord hath said
 unto him, *c.* David. 10, 11
and he will *c.* thee. *Job* 1:11*; 2:5*
said his wife to him, *c.* God. 2:9*
let them *c.* it that *c.* the day. 3:8
bless with mouth but *c.* *Ps* 62:4
let them *c.* but bless thou. 109:28
people shall *c.* him. *Pr* 11:26
him shall the people *c.* 24:24
servant to master, lest he *c.* 30:10
hear thy servant *c.* thee. *Eccl* 7:21
c. not the king in thought, *c.* 10:20
c. their king and God. *Isa* 8:21
every one of them doth *c. Jer* 15:10
I will *c.* your blessings, I. *Mal* 2:2
bless them that *c.* you. *Mat* 5:44
 Luke 6:28
he began to *c.* and to. *Mat* 26:74
 Mark 14:71
bless and *c.* not. *Rom* 12:14
therewith *c.* we men. *Jas* 3:9

cursed

the serpent *c.* *Gen* 3:14
c. is the ground. 17
now art thou [Cain] *c.* 4:11
ground which Lord hath *c.* 5:29
Noah said, *c.* be Canaan. 9:25
c. be every one. 27:29; *Num* 24:9
c. be their anger, for it. *Gen* 49:7
he hath *c.* his father or. *Lev* 20:9
name of the Lord and *c.* 24:11
bring forth him that *c.* 14, 23
whom thou cursest is *c.* *Num* 22:6
c. be he. *Deut* 27:15, 16, 17, 18
 19, 20, 21, 22, 23, 24, 25, 26
c. shalt thou be in the city, *c.* 28:16

c. shall be thy basket. *Deut* 28:17
c. shall be the fruit of thy body. 18
c. when thou comest in, when. 19
c. be man that buildeth. *Josh* 6:26
ye Gibeonites are *c.* none of. 9:23
eat and drink, and *c.* *Judg* 9:27
c. be he that giveth a wife to. 21:18
c. that eateth food. *1 Sam* 14:24, 28
and the Philistine *c.* David. 17:43
but if men, *c.* be they before. 26:19
came forth, and *c.* still. *2 Sam* 16:5
 7, 13
for this, because he *c.* the. 19:21
Shimei who *c.* me with. *1 Ki* 2:8
and *c.* them in the name. *2 Ki* 2:24
go see now this *c.* woman. 9:34
I contended with them, and *c.*
 Neh 13:25
my sons have sinned and *c. Job* 1:5
Job opened his mouth and *c.* 3:1
taking root, suddenly I *c.* 5:3
their portion is *c.* in earth. 24:18
they that be *c.* of him. *Ps* 37:22
rebuked the proud that are *c.* 119:21
likewise hast *c.* others. *Eccl* 7:22
c. be the man obeyeth not. *Jer* 11:3
c. be the man that trusteth. 17:5
c. be the day wherein I was. 20:14
c. be the man who brought. 15
c. be he that doeth Lord's work deceitfully, *c.* that keepeth. 48:10
but *c.* be the deceiver. *Mal* 1:14
yea, I have *c.* your blessings. 2:2
ye are *c.* with a curse, for. 3:9
depart from me, ye *c.* *Mat* 25:41
knoweth not law, are *c.* *John* 7:49
c. is every one that. *Gal* 3:10
c. is every one that hangeth. 13
c. children, who have. *2 Pet* 2:14*

cursed *thing*

be a *c.* thing, for it is a *c.* thing.
 Deut 7:26*
cleave nought of the *c.* thing. 13:17*

cursedst

from thee, which thou *c. Judg* 17:2
the fig-tree thou *c.* is. *Mark* 11:21

curses

shall write these *c.* in. *Num* 5:23
all these *c.* shall. *Deut* 28:15, 45
all the *c.* that are written. 29:20, 27
 2 Chr 34:24
all *c.* of the covenant in. *Deut* 29:21
thy God will put these *c.* on. 30:7

curseth

c. his father or mother shall be put.
 Ex 21:17; *Lev* 20:9; *Pr* 20:20
whosoever *c.* his God. *Lev* 24:15
generation that *c.* father. *Pr* 30:11
he that *c.* father or mother, let.
 Mat 15:4*; *Mark* 7:10*

cursing

woman with oath of *c.* *Num* 5:21
shall send upon thee a *c. Deut* 28:20
set before you blessing and *c.* 30:19
me good for his *c.* *2 Sam* 16:12
his mouth is full of *c.* *Ps* 10:7
 Rom 3:14
and for *c.* and lying. 59:12
as he loved *c.* so let it. 109:17
as he clothed himself with *c.* 18
he beareth *c.* and. *Pr* 29:24*
beareth thorns is nigh to *c. Heb* 6:8
same mouth blessing and *c. Jas* 3:10

cursings

read the blessings and *c. Josh* 8:34

curtain, -s

tabernacle with ten *c.* *Ex* 26:1, 2
 36:9
bear the *c.* of tabernacle. *Num* 4:25
ark dwelleth within *c.* *2 Sam* 7:2
 1 Chr 17:1
stretchest out the heavens like a *c.*
 Ps 104:2; *Isa* 40:22
but I am comely as the *c. S of S* 1:5
let them stretch forth *c.* *Isa* 54:2
tents spoiled, and my *c.* *Jer* 4:20
and set up my *c.* 10:20
take to themselves their *c.* 49:29
c. of the land of Midian. *Hab* 3:7

Cush

sons of Ham, *C. Gen* 10:6; *1 Chr* 1:8

the sons of *C.* Seba, and. *Gen* 10:7
 1 Chr 1:9
remnant left from *C.* *Isa* 11:11

Cushan

I saw the tents of *C.* in. *Hab* 3:7

Cushi

C. tell the king what. *2 Sam* 18:21
Ahimaaz ran, and overran *C.* 23
all princes sent son of *C. Jer* 36:14
to Zephaniah son of *C.* *Zeph* 1:1

custody

c. of sons of Merari. *Num* 3:36*
fair virgins to the *c.* *Esth* 2:3, 8
to the *c.* of Shaashgaz the king's. 14

custom

[1] *Manner, or way,* Luke 4:16.
[2] *A duty paid to the king or
prince upon the importation or
exportation of goods,* Rom 13:7.
for the *c.* of women is. *Gen* 31:35
and it was a *c.* in Israel. *Judg* 11:39
the priests' *c.* with. *1 Sam* 2:13
according to the *c.* *Ezra* 3:4*
 Jer 32:11
not pay toll, tribute, and *c. Ezra* 4:13
been mighty kings, and *c.* was. 20
not be lawful to impose *c.* on. 7:24
sitting at the receipt of *c. Mat* 9:9*
 Mark 2:14*; *Luke* 5:27*
kings of earth take *c.? Mat* 17:25*
according to the *c.* of. *Luke* 1:9
to do for him after *c.* of law. 2:27
went to Jerusalem after the *c.* 42
as Jesus' *c.* was, he went. 4:16
ye have a *c.* that I should. *John* 18:39
render *c.* to whom *c.* is. *Rom* 13:7
we have no such *c.* nor. *1 Cor* 11:16

customs

commit none of these *c.* *Lev* 18:30
c. of the people are vain. *Jer* 10:3
shall change the *c.* Moses. *Acts* 6:14
teach *c.* which are not lawful. 16:21
ought not to walk after *c.* 21:21
thee to be expert in all *c.* 26:3
committed nothing against *c.* 28:17

cut

and *c.* it in wires to work. *Ex* 39:3
shall *c.* the burnt-. *Lev* 1:6, 12
c. ram into pieces. 8:20; *Ex* 29:17
not offer to Lord what is *c. Lev* 22:24
ye shall not *c.* yourselves. *Deut* 14:1
my concubine and *c.* *Judg* 20:6
c. bullock in pieces. *1 Ki* 18:23, 33
c. themselves after their manner. 28
he *c.* in pieces all the vessels of.
 2 Ki 24:13; *2 Chr* 28:24
people, he *c.* them with. *1 Chr* 20:3
servants can skill to *c. 2 Chr* 2:8, 10
let them be as *c.* in pieces. *Ps* 58:7
c. bars of iron. 107:16; *Isa* 45:2
art thou not it that hath *c.? Isa* 51:9
nor lament, nor *c.* *Jer* 16:6
when they *c.* the calf in. 34:18
he *c.* the roll with the. 36:23
clothes rent, and having *c.* 41:5
how long wilt thou *c.* thyself? 47:5
born thy navel was not *c. Ezek* 16:4
ye will not, ye shall be *c. Dan* 2:5
speak against God shall be *c.* 3:29
and *c.* them in the head. *Amos* 9:1*
all that burden themselves with it
 shall be *c.* *Zech* 12:3*
when they heard that, they were *c.* to
 the heart. *Acts* 5:33; 7:54

cut *asunder*

he hath *c.* asunder cords. *Ps* 129:4
hammer of earth *c.* asunder.
 Jer 50:23
staff Beauty, and *c.* it asunder.
 Zech 11:10
then I *c.* asunder my other staff. 14
shall *c.* him asunder. *Mat* 24:51
 Luke 12:46

cut *down*

but ye shall *c.* down. *Ex* 34:13
will *c.* down your images. *Lev* 26:30
c. down from thence. *Num* 13:23, 24
and *c.* down groves. *Deut* 7:5*
 2 Ki 18:4; 23:14
thou shalt not *c.* them down.
 Deut 20:19

not for meat c. *down*. *Deut* 20:20
and c. *down* the grove. *Judg* 6:25
I will c. *down* cedars. 2 *Ki* 19:23
    Isa 37:24
Asa c. *down* her idol. 2 *Chr* 15:16
Josiah c. *down* all the idols. 34:7*
greenness, not c. *down*. *Job* 8:12
cometh like a flower, is c. *down*. 14:2
hope of a tree if it be c. *down*. 7
the wicked were c. *down*. 22:16*
our substance is not c. *down*. 20
shall soon be c. *down*. *Ps* 37:2
is burnt, and is c. *down*. 80:16
in the evening it is c. *down*. 90:6
sycamores are c. *down*. *Isa* 9:10
how art thou c. *down!* 14:12
nail be removed and c. *down*. 22:25*
shall c. *down* thy choice. *Jer* 22:7
peaceable habitation c. *down*. 25:37*
also thou shalt be c. *down*. 48:2*
your images be c. *down*. *Ezek* 6:6*
yet shall they be c. *down*. *Nah* 1:12
merchant-people are c. *down*.
    Zeph 1:11*
others c. *down* branches. *Mat* 21:8
    Mark 11:8
c. it *down*; why cumbereth it the
ground ? *Luke* 13:7
after that thou shalt c. it *down*. 9

cut off

neither all flesh be c. *off*. *Gen* 9:11
uncircumcised child be c. *off*. 17:14
and c. *off* fore-skin of son. *Ex* 4:25
soul shall be c. *off* from. 12:15, 19
   31:14; *Num* 15:30, 31; 19:13
and I will c. them *off*. *Ex* 23:23
be c. *off* from people. 30:33, 38
 Lev 7:20, 21, 25, 27; 17:4, 9
  19:8; 23:29; *Num* 9:13
will c. him *off* from his people.
 Lev 17:10; 18:29; 20:3, 6, 18
    Num 19:20
whosoever eateth blood be c. *off*.
    Lev 17:14
shall be c. *off* in sight of. 20:17
that soul shall be c. *off* from. 22:3
c. ye not *off* the tribe. *Num* 4:18
that soul shall utterly be c. *off*. 15:31
when God shall c. *off*. *Deut* 12:29
hath c. *off* nations. 19:1; *Josh* 23:4
hath privy member c. *off*. *Deut* 23:1
thou shalt c. *off* her hand. 25:12
waters of Jordan shall be c. *off*.
    Josh 3:13, 16; 4:7
and shall c. *off* our name. 7:9
at that time Joshua c. *off*. 11:21
and c. *off* his thumbs. *Judg* 1:6.
there is one tribe c. *off* from. 21:6
name of dead be not c. *off*. *Ruth* 4:10
days come that I will c. *off*.
    1 *Sam* 2:31
man whom I shall not c. *off*. 33
palms of Dagon's hands c. *off*. 5:4
David ran and c. *off*. 17:51
not c. *off* kindness from my. 20:15
David c. *off* the skirt of. 24:4, 5
for in that I c. *off* the. 11
thou wilt not c. *off* my seed. 21
knowest how Saul hath c. *off*. 28:9
and they c. *off* Saul's head. 31:9
slew them and c. *off*. 2 *Sam* 4:12
and c. *off* their garments in the.
    10:4; 1 *Chr* 19:4
c. *off* head of Sheba. 2 *Sam* 20:22
then will I c. *off* Israel. 1 *Ki* 9:7
till he had c. *off* every male. 11:16
to c. *off* Jeroboam's. 13:34; 14:14
I will c. *off* from Jeroboam. 14:10
when Jezebel c. *off* prophets. 18:4
I will c. *off* from Ahab him. 21:21
    2 *Ki* 9:8
Ahaz c. *off* borders. 2 *Ki* 16:17
Hezekiah c. *off* the gold from. 18:16
have c. *off* all thine. 1 *Chr* 17:8
Lord anointed to c. *off*. 2 *Chr* 22:7
angel to c. *off* all mighty men. 32:21
were the righteous c. *off* ? *Job* 4:7
loose his hand, and c. me *off*. 6:9
whose hope shall be c. *off*. 8:14*
if he c. *off*, then who can ? 11:10*
shall his branch be c. *off*. 18:16
of his months is c. *off*. 21:21
because I was not c. *off*. 23:17

they are c. *off* as tops of. *Job* 24:24
when people are c. *off* in their. 36:20
the Lord shall c. *off* all. *Ps* 12:3
I am c. *off* from before. 31:22
to c. *off* remembrance of. 34:16
for evil doers shall be c. *off*. 37:9
cursed of him, shall be c. *off*. 22
seed of wicked shall be c. *off*. 28
when the wicked are c. *off*. 34
end of wicked shall be c. *off*. 38
he shall reward, c. them *off*. 54:5
horns of wicked will I c. *off*. 75:10
he shall c. *off* the spirit. 76:12
come, and let us c. them *off*. 83:4
and they are c. *off* from thy. 88:5
terrors have c. me *off*. 16
he shæll c. them *off* in their. 94:23
neighbour will I c. *off*. 101:5*
that I may c. *off* all wicked doers. 8
let his posterity be c. *off*. 109:13
that the Lord may c. *off* the. 15
and of thy mercy c. *off*. 143:12
wicked shall be c. *off* from. *Pr* 2:22
expectation not be c. *off*. 23:18
    24:14
Lord will c. *off* from Israel. *Isa* 9:14
to destroy and c. *off* nations. 10:7
adversaries of Judah be c. *off*. 11:13
I will c. *off* from Babylon. 14:22
and every beard c. *off*. 15:2
burden upon it shall be c. *off*. 22:25
watch for iniquity are c. *off*. 29:20*
he will c. me *off* with. 38:12*
refrain, that I c. thee not *off*. 48:9
name should not have been c. *off*. 19
he was c. *off* out of the land. 53:8
a sign that shall not be c. *off*. 55:13
as if he c. *off* a dog's neck. 66:3*
truth is perished and c. *off*. *Jer* 7:28
c. *off* thine hair, O Jerusalem. 29
to c. *off* the children without. 9:21
let us c. him *off* from land. 11:19
to c. *off* from you man and. 44:7
that ye might c. yourselves *off*. 8
and to c. *off* all Judah. 11
to c. *off* from Tyrus. 47:4
Ashkelon is c. *off*. 5*
come, let us c. it *off* from. 48:2
horn of Moab is c. *off*, his arm. 25
men of war be c. *off*. 49:26*; 50:30*
c. *off* the sower from. 50:16
flee out, and be not c. *off*. 51:6
against this place to c. it *off*. 62
c. *off* in his anger the. *Lam* 2:2
they have c. *off* my life in. 3:53
and I will c. him *off*. *Ezek* 14:8
c. *off* man and beast. 13, 17, 19, 21
    25:13; 29:8
shall he not c. *off* fruit ? 17:9
building forts to c. *off* many. 17
c. *off* the righteous and. 21:3, 4
behold, I will c. thee *off*. 25:7
I will c. *off* the Cherethims. 16
and I will c. *off* the multitude. 30:15
terrible nations will c. *off*. 31:12
I will c. *off* from Seir him. 35:7
hope is lost, we are c. *off*. 37:11
hew down the tree, c. *off*. *Dan* 4:14
Messiah shall be c. *off*. 9:26
made idols, that they be c. *off*.
    Hos 8:4
her king is c. *off* as the. 10:7, 15
the new wine is c. *off*. *Joel* 1:5, 9
is not the meat c. *off* ? 16
I will c. *off* the inhabitant. *Amos* 1:5
I will c. *off* the inhabitant from
  Ashdod. 8
I will c. *off* the judge from. 2:3
horns of altar shall be c. *off*. 3:14
by night, art thou c. *off*. *Ob* 5
every one of Esau may be c. *off*. 9
and thou shalt be c. *off* for ever. 10
nor stand to c. *off* those of his. 14
thine enemies shall be c. *off*. *Mi* 5:9
witchcrafts be c. *off*. 11
graven images I c. *off*. 13; *Nah* 1:14
wicked is utterly c. *off*. *Nah* 1:15
and I will c. *off* thy prey. 2:13
the sword shall c. thee *off*. 3:15
the flock shall be c. *off*. *Hab* 3:17
I will c. *off* man from. *Zeph* 1:3
c. *off* remnant of Baal. 4
that bear silver c. *off*. 11
I have c. *off* the nations. 3:6

should not be c. *off*. *Zeph* 3:7
stealeth, and every one that sweareth, shall be c. *off*. *Zech* 5:3
I will c. *off* pride of Philistines. 9:6
I will c. *off* chariot from. 10
three shepherds also I c. *off*. 11:8
is to be c. *off*, let it be c. *off*. 9
I will c. *off* the names of. 13:2
two parts in land shall be c. *off*. 8
of people shall not be c. *of*. 14:2
Lord will c. *off* the. *Mal* 2:12
right hand offend thee, c. it *off*.
  Mat 5:30; 18:8; *Mark* 9:43, 45
and c. *off* his ear. *Mark* 14:47*
  Luke 22:50*; *John* 18:10, 26
soldiers c. *off* the ropes. *Acts* 27:32
thou shalt also be c. *off*. *Rom* 11:22
I may c. *off* occasion. 2 *Cor* 11:12
I would they were c. *off*. *Gal* 5:12

cut out

froward tongue be c. *out*. *Pr* 10:31
stone c. *out* without. *Dan* 2:34, 45
for if thou wert c. *out*. *Rom* 11:24

cut short

began to c. Israel *short*. 2 *Ki* 10:32
will finish and c. it *short*. *Rom* 9:28

cut up

who c. *up* mallows by. *Job* 30:4*
as thorns c. *up* shall. *Isa* 33:12

cuttest, -eth

when thou c. *down*. *Deut* 24:19*
he c. *out* rivers among. *Job* 28:10
he breaketh bow, and c. *Ps* 46:9
as when one c. and cleaveth. 141:7
message by fool, c. *off*. *Pr* 26:6
one c. a tree out of the. *Jer* 10:3
build chambers and c. him. 22:14

cutting

c. of stones to set. *Ex* 31:5; 35:33
I said in the c. *off* of my. *Isa* 38:10*
consulted shame by c. *Hab* 2:10
crying and c. himself. *Mark* 5:5

cuttings

not any c. for dead. *Lev* 19:28; 21:5
all hands shall be c. and. *Jer* 48:37

cymbal

brass, or a tinkling c. 1 *Cor* 13:1

cymbals

played on cornets and c. 2 *Sam* 6:5
    1 *Chr* 13:8
harps and c. 1 *Chr* 15:16; 16:42
Asaph made a sound with c. 16:5
in the house of Lord with c. 25:6
lift up their voice with c. 2 *Chr* 5:13
Levites in house of Lord with c. 29:25
sons of Asaph with c. *Ezra* 3:10
    Neh 12:27
upon loud-sounding c. *Ps* 150:5

cypress

he taketh the c. and oak. *Isa* 44:14*

Cyprus

Joses was of country of C. *Acts* 4:36
as far as Phenice and C. 11:19
some of them were men of C. 20
from Seleucia they sailed to C. 13:4
Barnabas sailed to C. 15:39
when we had discovered C. 21:3
with him Mnason of C. 16
launched, sailed under C. 27:4

Cyrene

found a man of C. *Mat* 27:32
parts of Lybia about C. *Acts* 2:10
were men of Cyprus and C. 11:20
Lucius of C. was in church. 13:1

Cyrenian

compel Simon a C. to. *Mark* 15:21

Cyrenians

the synagogue of the C. *Acts* 6:9

Cyrenius

made when C. was. *Luke* 2:2

Cyrus

first year of C. the Lord stirred up
  spirit of C. 2 *Chr* 36:22; *Ezra* 1:1
saith C. king of Persia. 2 *Chr* 36:23
    Ezra 1:2
C. brought forth. *Ezra* 1:7, 8; 5:14
grant they had of C. 3:7
will build as C. the king hath. 4:3
C. made a decree to build. 5:13, 17
that saith of C. he is. *Isa* 44:28

saith Lord to anointed, to C. *Isa* 45:1
to the first year of C.   *Dan* 1:21
Daniel prospered in reign of C. 6:28
third year of C. a thing was.   10:1

D

Dabbasheth
toward sea reached to D. *Josh* 19:11
Daberath
and then goeth out to D. *Josh* 19:12
out of Issachar, D.   *1 Chr* 6:72
dagger
Ehud made him a d.   *Judg* 3:16*
took the d. from right thigh.   21*
that he could not draw the d.   22*
Dagon
to offer a sacrifice to D. *Judg* 16:23
ark unto the house of D. *1 Sam* 5:2
D. was fallen.   3
the head of D. was cut off.   4
is sore on us, and on D. our.   7
head in temple of D.   *1 Chr* 10:10
daily
as much as gathered d.   *Ex* 16:5
d. meat-offering.   *Num* 4:16*
                Ezek 46:13
after this manner offer d. *Num* 28:24
beside the d. burnt-offering. 29:6*
                Ezra 3:4
when she pressed him d. *Judg* 16:16
allowance was a d. rate. *2 Ki* 25:30
was prepared for me d.   *Neh* 5:18*
spake d. hearkened not.   *Esth* 3:4
sorrow in my heart d.   *Ps* 13:2*
while they say d. to me.   42:10*
be merciful. he fighting d.   56:1*
mine enemies would d. swallow. 2*
I will sing, that I may d.   61:8
the Lord who d. loadeth us. 68:19
he shall live and d. shall be. 72:15*
man reproacheth thee d.   74:22*
I cry to thee d.   86:3*
I called d. upon thee.   88:9
came round about me d.   17*
I was d. his delight.   *Pr* 8:30
that heareth me, watching d.   34
yet they seek me d. and.   *Isa* 58:2
d. rising up early and.   *Jer* 7:25
I am in derision d.   20:7*, 8*
Noph have distresses d. *Ezek* 30:16*
king appointed them a d.   *Dan* 1:5
and by him the d. sacrifice was.
        8:11*; 11:31*; 12:11*
Ephraim d. increaseth.   *Hos* 12:1*
give us this day our d. bread.
        Mat 6:11; *Luke* 11:3
sat d. with you teaching. *Mat* 26:55
Mark 14:49; *Luke* 19:47; 22:53
take up his cross d.   *Luke* 9:23
continuing d. with one.   *Acts* 2:46
Lord added to the church d.   47
widows were neglected in d.   6:1
churches increased in number d.
                16:5
searched the scriptures d.   17:11
I die d.   *1 Cor* 15:31
but exhort d.   *Heb* 3:13
who needeth not d. to.   7:27
and destitute of d. food.   *Jas* 2:15
dainty, -ies
shall yield royal d.   *Gen* 49:20
soul abhorreth d. meat.   *Job* 33:20
let me not eat of their d.   *Ps* 141:4
be not desirous of his d.   *Pr* 23:3
neither desire thou his d. meats.   6
all things which were d.   *Rev* 18:14
dale
which is the king's d.   *Gen* 14:17*
a pillar in the king's d. *2 Sam* 18:18
Dalmatia
Titus is departed to D. *2 Tim* 4:10
dam
seven days with his d. on eighth give
it me.   *Ex* 22:30; *Lev* 22:27
shalt not take the d.   *Deut* 22:6
in any wise let the d. go.   7
damage
d. grow to the hurt of.   *Ezra* 4:22
not countervail king's d.   *Esth* 7:4

and drinketh d.   *Pr* 26:6
king should have no d.   *Dan* 6:2
with hurt and much d.   *Acts* 27:10*
that ye might receive d.   *2 Cor* 7:9*
Damaris
and a woman named D.   *Acts* 17:34
Damascus
steward is Eliezer of D.   *Gen* 15:2
David put garrisons in Syria of D.
        2 Sam 8:6; *1 Chr* 18:6
Rezon went to D. reigned in D.
                1 Ki 11:24
on way to wilderness of D.   19:15
make streets for thee in D.   20:34
Pharpar, rivers of D.?   *2 Ki* 5:12
Elisha came to D.   8:7
Jeroboam recovered D.   14:28
king of Assyria went against D. 16:9
Ahaz saw an altar at D.   10
Syrians of D. came to.   *1 Chr* 18:5
the spoil to king of D. *2 Chr* 24:23
multitude of captives to D.   28:5
Ahaz sacrificed to gods of D.   23
Lebanon, looketh toward D.
                S of S 7:4
of Syria is D. head of D.   *Isa* 7:8
riches of D. shall be taken.   8:4
is not Samaria as D.?   10:9
the burden of D.   17:1; *Jer* 49:23
kingdom cease from D.   *Isa* 17:3
D. is waxed feeble.   *Jer* 49:24
I will kindle a fire in wall of D.   27
D. thy merchant in.   *Ezek* 27:18
three transgressions of D. *Amos* 1:3
I will break also the bar of D.   5
that dwell in D. in a couch.   3:12
go into captivity beyond D.   5:27
and D. shall be the rest.   *Zech* 9:1
desired letters to D.   *Acts* 9:2
there was a disciple at D.   10
was Saul with the disciples at D. 19
confounded Jews who dwelt at D. 22
how he preached boldly at D.   27
come nigh to D.   22:6; 26:12
arise, and go into D.   22:10
in D. governor desirous. *2 Cor* 11:32
I returned again unto D.   *Gal* 1:17
damnable
shall bring in d. heresies. *2 Pet* 2:1*
damnation
(*In Revised Versions this word is
rendered judgement or condemnation in every case except those
starred. A similar change also in
the other forms of the word*)
receive the greater d.   *Mat* 23:14*
        Mark 12:40; *Luke* 20:47
can ye escape of hell ? *Mat* 23:33
is in danger of eternal d. *Mark* 3:29*
to the resurrection of d.   *John* 5:29
good may come, whose d. *Rom* 3:8
shall receive to themselves d.   13:2
eateth and drinketh d.   *1 Cor* 11:29
having d. because they.   *1 Tim* 5:12
not, and their d.   *2 Pet* 2:3*
damned
believeth not shall be d. *Mark* 16:16
he that doubteth is d.   *Rom* 14:23
all might be d. who.   *2 Thes* 2:12
damsel
the d. abide few days.   *Gen* 24:55
loved d. and spake kindly to d. 34:3
but give me the d. to wife.   12
forth tokens of the d.   *Deut* 22:15
tokens be not found for the d.   20
they shall bring out the d. and.   21
the d. because she cried not.   24
there is in the d. no sin worthy.   26
shall give the d.'s father fifty.   29
to every man a d.   *Judg* 5:30
the d.'s father retained him.   19:4
Boaz said, whose d. is ?   *Ruth* 2:5
it is Moabitish d. that came back. 6
and the d. was very fair.   *1 Ki* 1:4
brought in a charger, and given to d.
        Mat 14:11; *Mark* 6:28
a d. came to Peter.   *Mat* 26:69*
                John 18:17*
the d. is not dead.   *Mark* 5:39
father and mother of the d. and entereth in where d. was lying.   40

a d. came to hearken.   *Acts* 12:13*
a certain d. possessed with. 16:16*
damsels
Rebekah arose and her d. *Gen* 24:61
Abigail rode with five d. *1 Sam* 25:42
amongst them were the d. *Ps* 68:25
Dan, *a person*
called she his name D.   *Gen* 30:6
son of Bilhah, D.   35:25
sons of D.   46:23; *Num* 26:42
D. shall judge his people. *Gen* 49:16
D. shall be a serpent by.   17
of D. Ahiezer the son.   *Num* 1:12
standard of the camp of D.   2:25
all numbered in the camp of D.   31
of D. he said, D. is.   *Deut* 33:22
after the name of D.   *Josh* 19:47
                Judg 18:29
and why did D. remain ? *Judg* 5:17
moved him in camp of D.   13:25
a portion for D.   *Ezek* 48:1
one gate of D.   32
see **children**
tribe of **Dan**
Aholiab of the *tribe of* D.   *Ex* 31:6
        35:34; 38:23
Dibri, of *tribe of* D.   *Lev* 24:11
of *tribe of* D. 62,700.   *Num* 1:39
of *tribe of* D. to spy the land. 13:12
of *tribe of* D. to divide the.   34:22
for the *tribe of* D.   *Josh* 19:40, 48
out of the *tribe of* D.   21:5, 23
priests to *tribe of* D.   *Judg* 18:30
Dan, *a place*
pursued them unto D.   *Gen* 14:14
Moses all Gilead unto D. *Deut* 34:1
they called Leshem, D.   *Josh* 19:47
                Judg 18:29
from D. to Beer-sheba.   *Judg* 20:1
1 Sam 3:20; *2 Sam* 3:10; 17:11
24:2, 15; *1 Ki* 4:25; *1 Chr* 21:2
                2 Chr 30:5
other calf put he in D.   *1 Ki* 12:29
                2 Ki 10:29
smote D.   *1 Ki* 15:20; *2 Chr* 16:4
voice declareth from D.   *Jer* 4:15
of horses heard from D.   8:16
D. and Javan occupied. *Ezek* 27:19
thy God, O D. liveth.   *Amos* 8:14
dance
praise in the d.   *Ps* 149:3; 150:4
virgins shall rejoice in d. *Jer* 31:13
d. is turned into mourning. *Lam* 5:15
dance, *verb*
of Shiloh come to d.   *Judg* 21:21
their children d.   *Job* 21:11
mourn, a time to d.   *Eccl* 3:4
satyrs shall d. there.   *Isa* 13:21
danced
to their number that d.   *Judg* 21:23
and David d. before.   *2 Sam* 6:14
and ye have not d.   *Mat* 11:17
                Luke 7:32
daughter of Herodias d.   *Mat* 14:6
                Mark 6:22
dances
went after her with d.   *Ex* 15:20
to meet him with d.   *Judg* 11:34
not sing of him in d.   *1 Sam* 21:11
                29:5
shalt go forth in the d.   *Jer* 31:4
dancing
he saw the calf and d.   *Ex* 32:19
came out singing and d. *1 Sam* 18:6
on all earth, eating and d.   30:16*
she saw king David d.   *2 Sam* 6:16
                1 Chr 15:29
my mourning into d.   *Ps* 30:11
he heard music and d.   *Luke* 15:25
dandled
and ye shall be d. upon.   *Isa* 66:12
danger
shall be in d. of.   *Mat* 5:21, 22
be in d. of the council, in d.   22
but is in d. of eternal.   *Mark* 3:29*
this our craft is in d.   *Acts* 19:27
in d. to be called in question.   40
dangerous
when sailing was now d.   *Acts* 27:9
Daniel
David had D. of.   *1 Chr* 3:1

of Ithamar, *D.*   *Ezra* 8:2
D. sealed.   *Neh* 10:6
though Noah, *D.*   *Ezek* 14:14, 20
thou art wiser than *D.*   28:3
D. of Judah.   *Dan* 1:6
to *D.* the name of Belteshazzar. 7
D. had understanding in.   17
none was found like *D.*   19
sought *D.* to be slain.   2:13
then *D.* went in.   16
the secret was revealed to *D.* 19
Nebuchadnezzar worshipped *D.* 46
then king made *D.* a great man. 48
D. sat in the gate.   49
at last *D.* came in.   4:8
then *D.* was astonied for.   19
of doubts found in *D.*   5:12
they clothed *D.* with scarlet and. 29
of whom *D.* was first.   6:2
not find occasion against *D.*   5
these men found *D.* praying.   11
D. regardeth not thee, O king,   13
king set his heart on *D.*   14
that they should take up *D.*   23
men tremble before God of *D.*   26
who hath delivered *D.* from.   27
so this *D.* prospered in reign.   28
D. had a dream, and visions.   7:1
as for me *D.*   28
a vision, even unto me *D.*   8:1
he said, fear not, *D.*   10:12
he said, go thy way, *D.*   12:9
of desolation, spoken of by *D.*
   Mat 24:15; *Mark* 13:14

I Daniel
I *D.* was grieved.   *Dan* 7:15
when I, even I *D.* had seen.   8:15
I *D.* fainted.   27
I *D.* understood by books.   9:2
I *D.* was mourning three.   10:2
I *D.* alone saw the vision.   7
I *D.* looked.   12:5

O Daniel
O *D.* servant of the.   *Dan* 6:20
O *D.* I am now come to.   9:22
O *D.* a man greatly beloved.   10:11
O *D.* shut up the words and.   12:4

dare
none is so fierce that *d.* *Job* 41:10
good man some would *d.* *Rom* 5:7
for I will not *d.* to speak of.   15:18
d. any of you go to law ? *1 Cor* 6:1
d. not make ourselves. *2 Cor* 10:12*

Darius
till the reign of *D.* *Ezra* 4:5, 24
till the matter came to *D.*   5:5
D. the king made a decree. 6:1, 12
finished in sixth year of *D.*   15
priests to the reign of *D.* *Neh* 12:22
D. the Median took. *Dan* 5:31
king *D.* signed the writing.   6:9
king *D.* wrote to all people.   25
in the first year of *D.*   9:1; 11:1
in second year of *D.* *Hag* 1:1, 15
   2:10; *Zech* 1:7
in fourth year of *D.* *Zech* 7:1

dark
went down, and it was *d. Gen* 15:17
if plague be *d.* *Lev* 13:6, 21, 26
   28, 56
and not in *d.* speeches. *Num* 12:8
when it was *d.* the men. *Josh* 2:5
d. waters. *2 Sam* 22:12; *Ps* 18:11
Jerusalem began to be *d. Neh* 13:19
stars of the twilight be *d.* *Job* 3:9
they grope in the *d.*   12:25
the light shall be *d.* in his.   18:6
judge through the *d.* cloud ? 22:13
in the *d.* they dig through. 24:16
let their way be *d.* and. *Ps* 35:6
I will open my *d.* saying. 49:4
d. places of the earth are. 74:20
I will utter *d.* sayings of old. 78:2
thy wonders be known in *d.?* 88:12
sent darkness and made it *d.* 105:28
words of wise and their *d.* *Pr* 1:6
in the black and *d.* night. 7:9
their works are in the *d. Isa* 29:15
not spoken in a *d.* place. 45:19
feet stumble upon the *d. Jer* 13:16
he hath set me in *d.* places. *Lam* 3:6
house of Israel do in the *d. Ezek* 8:12

make the stars thereof *d. Ezek* 32:7
bright lights of heaven I make *d.* 8
in the cloudy and *d.* day.   34:12
king understanding *d.* *Dan* 8:23
sun and moon shall be *d.* *Joel* 2:10
that maketh day *d.* *Amos* 5:8, 20
it shall be *d.* unto you, the day shall
   be *d.* *Mi* 3:6*
light not be clear, nor *d. Zech* 14:6*
light, having no part *d.* *Luke* 11:36
and it was now *d.* *John* 6:17
early, when it was yet *d.* 20:1
light that shineth in a *d.* *2 Pet* 1:19

darken
I will *d.* the earth. *Amos* 8:9

darkened
so that the land was *d.* *Ex* 10:15
let eyes be *d. Ps* 69:23; *Rom* 11:10
or the stars be not *d.* *Eccl* 12:2
look out of the windows be *d.* 3
the light is *d.* in the. *Isa* 5:30
the land is *d.*   9:19*
the sun *d.*   13:10; *Joel* 3:15
all joy is *d.* the mirth of. *Isa* 24:11
Tehaphnehes day be *d. Ezek* 30:18*
eye shall be utterly *d. Zech* 11:17
then shall the sun be *d.* *Mat* 24:29
   Mark 13:24
and the sun was *d.* *Luke* 23:45*
their foolish heart was *d. Rom* 1:21
the understanding *d.* *Eph* 4:18
third part of them was *d. Rev* 8:12
the sun and the air were *d.* 9:2

darkeneth
who is this that *d.?* *Job* 38:2

darkish
bright spots in skin be *d. Lev* 13:39

darkly
see through a glass *d.* *1 Cor* 13:12

darkness
*Literally, the absence of natural
light,* Mat 27:45.
Figuratively, [1] *The place of
misery,* Mat 22:13. [2] *Ignorance,*
John 3:19. [3] *Secret,* Mat 10:27.
[4] *The land of darkness of the
grave,* Job 10:21, 22. [5] *The
children of darkness are the
wicked, in opposition to the good
who are called children of light,*
2 Cor 6:14.

d. was upon face of deep. *Gen* 1:2
the light day, and the *d.* night. 5
to divide the light from the *d.* 18
an horror of great *d.* fell upon. 15:12
there be *d.* over Egypt. *Ex* 10:21
there was a thick *d.* in all.   22
it was a cloud and *d.* to. 14:20
Moses drew near to thick *d.* 20:21
burnt with thick *d.* *Deut* 4:11
Lord spake out of thick *d.* 5:22
d. between you and the. *Josh* 24:7
d. was under his feet. *2 Sam* 22:10
   Ps 18:9
made *d.* pavilions. *2 Sam* 22:12
will enlighten my *d.* 29; *Ps* 18:28
d. and the shadow of. *Job* 3:5
as for that night, let *d.* seize. 6
meet with *d.* in the day time. 5:14
a land of *d.* as itself. 10:22†
and he hath set *d.* in my. 19:8
all *d.* shall be hid in his. 20:26
or *d.* that thou canst not see. 22:11
not cut off before *d.* neither hath he
   covered the *d.* 23:17
an end to *d.* the stones of. 28:3
no *d.* where workers of. 34:22
our speech by reason of *d.* 37:19
when I made thick *d.* a. 38:9
and as for *d.* where is the ? 19
d. his secret place. *Ps* 18:11
mine acquaintance into *d.* 88:18
clouds and *d.* round about. 97:2
makest *d.* and it is night. 104:20
he sent *d.* and made it dark. 105:28
if I say, surely the *d.* shall. 139:11
yea, the *d.* hideth not from thee. 12
to walk in ways of *d.* *Pr* 2:13
the way of wicked is as *d.* 4:19
name be covered with *d.* *Eccl* 6:4
look to the land, behold *d. Isa* 5:30
and behold trouble and *d.* 8:22

give thee treasures of *d.* *Isa* 45:3
get thee into *d.* O daughter of. 47:5
d. shall cover the earth, and gross *d.*
   the people, but. 60:2
d. and make gross *d.* *Jer* 13:16
I will set *d.* upon thy. *Ezek* 32:8
d. of clouds and of thick *d. Joel* 2:2
sun shall be turned into *d.* 31
   Acts 2:20
maketh the morning *d.* *Amos* 4:13
d. shall pursue his enemies. *Nah* 1:8
whole body full of *d.* *Mat* 6:23
   Luke 11:34
cast out into outer *d.* *Mat* 8:12
   22:13; 25:30
from sixth hour was *d.* 27:45
   Mark 15:33
hour and power of *d.* *Luke* 22:53
there was *d.* over all earth. 23:44
on him a mist and a *d.* *Acts* 13:11
fellowship with works of *d. Eph* 5:11
against the rulers of the *d.* 6:12
us from power of *d.* *Col* 1:13
not of night nor of *d.* *1 Thes* 5:5
to blackness and *d.* *Heb* 12:18
delivered them into *d.* *2 Pet* 2:4
to whom the mist of *d.* is. 17
because that *d.* hath. *1 John* 2:11
in chains under *d.* *Jude* 6
is reserved blackness of *d.* 13
kingdom was full of *d.* *Rev* 16:10

darkness with *day*
let that *day* be *d.* let not. *Job* 3:4
he knoweth that *day* of *d.* 15:23
remember the *days* of *d. Eccl* 11:8
thy *d.* be as noon-*day.* *Isa* 58:10
a *day* of *d.* and gloominess.
   Joel 2:2; *Zeph* 1:15
day of the Lord be *d.?* *Amos* 5:20

in darkness
grope as the blind *in d. Deut* 28:29
wicked be silent *in d.* *1 Sam* 2:9
Lord said that he would dwell *in*
   thick *d.* *1 Ki* 8:12; *2 Chr* 6:1
made my bed *in* the *d.* *Job* 17:13
they walk on *in d.* *Ps* 82:5
thou hast laid me *in d.* 88:6
pestilence that walketh *in d.* 91:6
such as sit *in d.* and shadow. 107:10
made me to dwell *in d.* 143:3
lamp be put out *in d.* *Pr* 20:20
the fool walketh *in d.* *Eccl* 2:14
he eateth *in d.* 5:17
he departeth *in d.* 6:4
bring them that sit *in d.* *Isa* 42:7
to them that are *in d.* 49:9
wait for light, we walk *in d.* 59:9
as slippery ways *in d.* *Jer* 23:12
knoweth what is in the *d. Dan* 2:22
me shall not walk *in d.* *John* 8:12
that walketh *in d.* knoweth not. 12:35
should not abide *in d.* 46
brethren, are not *in d.* *1 Thes* 5:4
and walk *in d.* we lie. *1 John* 1:6
hateth his brother, is *in d.* 2:9
he that hateth his brother, is *in d.*
   and walketh *in d.* 11

land of darkness
even to the *land of d.* *Job* 10:21
a *land of d.* as *d.* itself. 22
have I been a *land of d.?* *Jer* 2:31

darkness with *light*
divided *light* from the *d.* *Gen* 1:4
lights to divide *light* from *d.* 18
a land where *light* is as *d. Job* 10:22
light is short because of *d.* 17:12
driven from *light* into *d.* 18:18
his *light* I walked through *d.* 29:3
for *light,* there came *d.* 30:26
there ariseth *light* in *d.* *Ps* 112:4
d. and *light* are both alike. 139:12
far as *light* excelleth *d. Eccl* 2:13
d. for light, and *light* for *d. Isa* 5:20
walked in *d.* have seen great *light,*
   upon them *light.* 9:2; *Mat* 4:16
make *d.* *light* before. *Isa* 42:16
I form *light* and create *d.* 45:7
walketh in *d.* and hath no *light.* 50:10
light, he make gross *d.* *Jer* 13:16
d. but not *light.* *Lam* 3:2
Lord is *d.* and not *light. Amos* 5:18
in *d.* Lord shall be a *light.* *Mi* 7:8

darkness

light in thee be *d.* how great is that
 d.! *Mat* 6:23
tell in *d.* speak in *light.* 10:27
  Luke 12:3
light to them that sit in *d.*
 Luke 1:79; *Rom* 2:19
light which is in thee be not *d.*
  Luke 11:35
light shineth in *d. d.* *John* 1:5
men loved *d.* rather than *light.* 3:19
while ye have *light,* lest *d.* 12:35
them from *d.* to *light.* *Acts* 26:18
works of *d.* put on *light.* *Rom* 13:12
to *light* hidden things of *d. 1 Cor* 4:5
light to shine out of *d.* *2 Cor* 4:6
communion hath *light* with *d.?* 6:14
d. into marvellous *light. 1 Pet* 2:9
God is *light,* and in him is no *d.*
  1 John 1:5
d. is past, and true *light* now. 2:8

out of darkness

the voice *out of* the *d.* *Deut* 5:22
deep things *out of d.* *Job* 12:22
he shall return *out of d.* 15:22
he shall not depart *out of d.* 30
brought them *out of d.* *Ps* 107:14
of blind shall see *out of d. Isa* 29:18

darling

deliver my *d.* from power. *Ps* 22:20
rescue my *d.* from the lions. 35:17

dart, -s

Joab took three *d.* in. *2 Sam* 18:14
Hezekiah made *d.* and. *2 Chr* 32:5*
the spear nor the *d.* *Job* 41:26
d. are counted as stubble. 29*
till a *d.* strike through. *Pr* 7:23*
to quench the fiery *d.* *Eph* 6:16
thrust through with a *d. Heb* 12:20*

dash

thou wilt *d.* their children. *2 Ki* 8:12
lest *d.* them in pieces like. *Ps* 2:9
bear thee up, lest thou *d.* thy foot.
 91:12; *Mat* 4:6; *Luke* 4:11
their bows shall *d.* the. *Isa* 13:18
I will *d.* them one. *Jer* 13:14

dashed

hand, hath *d.* in pieces. *Ex* 15:6
children also shall be *d.* *Isa* 13:16
 Hos 13:16; *Nah* 3:10
the mother was *d.* upon. *Hos* 10:14

dasheth

that *d.* thy little ones. *Ps* 137:9

Dathan, *see* **Abiram**

daub, -ed, -ing

she *d.* the ark with slime. *Ex* 2:3
others *d.* it with. *Ezek* 13:10
say to them which *d.* it. 11
where is *d.* wherewith ye *d.* it ? 12
break down wall ye have *d.* 14
her prophets have *d.* them. 22:28

daughter

[1] *A female child, without particular meaning as to exact relationship.*
Gen 34:1; Ex 2:21; Ruth 3:18.
[2] *The inhabitants of a city or country,* Isa 16:2; Mat 21;5.
[3] *In a figurative use, as daughters of music, or singing birds, which may mean the power of making music,* Eccl 12:4.

d. of my father, not *d.* *Gen* 20:12
whose *d.* art thou ? 24:23, 47
take my master's brother's *d.* 48
Dinah, *d.* of Leah. 34:1
folly in lying with Jacob's *d.* 7
Shechem longeth for your *d.* 8
then will we take our *d.* and. 17
he had delight in Jacob's *d.* 19
but if it be a *d.* then. *Ex* 1:16
whether he gored a son or a *d.* 21:31
days are fulfilled for a *d. Lev* 12:6
nor take her daughter's *d.* 18:17
the *d.* of any priest, if she. 21:9
if the priest's *d.* be married. 22:12
if the priest's *d.* be a widow. 13
if he have no *d.* give. *Num* 27:9
every *d.* that possesseth an. 36:8
lieth with sister, *d.* of his father or *d.*
 of his mother. *Deut* 27:22
eye be evil towards her *d.* 28:56
Jephthah's *d.* came out. *Judg* 11:34

to lament Jephthah's *d. Judg* 11:40
not thine handmaid a *d. 1 Sam* 1:16†
when Saul's *d.* should have. 18:19
lamb was unto him as *d. 2 Sam* 12:3
Solomon tooh Pharaoh's *d. 1 Ki* 3:1
with the *d.* of Pharaoh. 11:1
the *d.* of Ahab was. *2 Ki* 8:18
Jezebel, for she is a king's *d.* 9:34
and the *d.* of Caleb. *1 Chr* 2:49
uncle's *d.* for his own *d.* *Esth* 2:7
O *d.* and consider, and. *Ps* 45:10
king's *d.* is all glorious within. 13
with shoes, O prince's *d. S of S* 7:1
about, backsliding *d. Jer* 31:22; 49:4
O *d.* dwelling in Egypt. 46:19
d. that dost inhabit Dibon. 48:18
deliver son nor *d. Ezek* 14:16; 18:20
is the mother, so is her *d.* 16:44
thou art thy mother's *d.* that. 45
for son or *d.* they may defile. 44:25
king's *d.* of the south. *Dan* 11:6
shall give him the *d.* of women. 17
again, and bare a *d.* *Hos* 1:6
O *d.* of troops. *Mi* 5:1
d. riseth up against her mother. 7:6
 Mat 10:35; *Luke* 12:53
d. of my dispersed shall. *Zeph* 3:10
hath married the *d.* of. *Mal* 2:11
d. be of good comfort. *Mat* 9:22
 Mark 5:34; *Luke* 8:48
he that loveth son or *d. Mat* 10:37
the *d.* of Herodias danced. 14:6
her *d.* was made whole from. 15:28
forth devil out of her *d. Mark* 7:26
he had one only *d.* *Luke* 8:42
not this woman, being *d.* 13:16
Pharaoh's *d.* took him. *Acts* 7:21
to be son of Pharaoh's *d. Heb* 11:24

daughter *of Babylon*

O *d.* of *Babylon,* who art. *Ps* 137:8
O *d.* of *Babylon,* sit on. *Isa* 47:1
against thee *d.* of *Babylon. Jer* 50:42
d. of *Babylon* is like a. 51:33
O *Zion,* that dwellest with the *d.* of
 Babylon. *Zech* 2:7

daughter *of the Chaldeans*

throne, O *d.* of *Chaldeans. Isa* 47:1
darkness, O *d.* of *Chaldeans.* 5

daughter *of Edom*

be glad, O *d.* of *Edom.* *Lam* 4:21
visit thine iniquity, O *d.* of *Edom.* 22

daughter *of Egypt*

O virgin, *d.* of *Egypt.* *Jer* 46:11
d. of *Egypt* shall be confounded. 24

daughter *of Gallim*

voice, O *d.* of *Gallim.* *Isa* 10:30

his daughter

Rachel *his d.* cometh. *Gen* 29:6
if a man sell *his d.* *Ex* 21:7
for his son or *his d.* *Lev* 21:2
to pass to *his d.* *Num* 27:8
between the father and *his d.* 30:16
nor *his d.* shalt thou. *Deut* 7:3
that maketh *his d.* to pass through
 fire. 18:10; *2 Ki* 23:10
not any of us give *his d. Judg* 21:1
and give him *his d.* *1 Sam* 17:25

daughter *of Jerusalem*

the *d.* of *Jerusalem* hath shaken.
 2 Ki 19:21; *Isa* 37:22
I liken to thee, O *d.* of *Jerusalem.*
  Lam 2:13
wag head at *d.* of *Jerusalem.* 15
come to *d.* of *Jerusalem.* *Mi* 4:8
rejoice, O *d.* of *Jerusalem.*
  Zeph 3:14
shout, O *d.* of *Jerusalem. Zech* 9:9

daughter *of Judah*

trodden *d.* of *Judah.* *Lam* 1:15
strong holds of *d.* of *Judah.* 2:2
increased in *d.* of *Judah* mourning. 5

daughter-in-law

she was *his d.-in-law.* *Gen* 38:16
Tamar thy *d.-in-law* hath.
uncover thy *d.-in-law. Lev* 18:15
a man lie with his *d.-in-law.* 20:12
and Ruth her *d.-in-law. Ruth* 1:22
d.-in-law which loveth thee. 4:15
d.-in-law Phinehas' wife. *1 Sam* 4:19
defiled his *d.-in-law. Ezek* 22:11

d.-in-law riseth up against the.
 Mi 7:6; *Mat* 10:35; *Luke* 12:53

my daughter

gave *my d.* to this man. *Deut* 22:16
the tokens of *my d.'s* virginity. 17
him will I give *my d.* *Josh* 15:16
  Judg 1:12
alas, *my d.* thou hast. *Judg* 11:35
behold, here is *my d.* a. 19:24
said unto her, go, *my d. Ruth* 2:2
blessed be thou of Lord, *my d.* 3:10
who art thou, *my d.?* 16
sit still, *my d.* till thou know. 18
a ruler, saying, *my d.* *Mat* 9:18
my d. is grievously vexed. 15:22
my little d. lieth at death. *Mark* 5:23

daughter *of my people*

spoiling of *d.* of *my p.* *Isa* 22:4
wind toward *d.* of *my p.* *Jer* 4:11
healed hurt of *d.* of *my p.* 6:14; 8:11
O, *d.* of *my people,* gird thee. 6:26
voice of cry of *d.* of *my p.* 8:19
for hurt of *d.* of *my p.* am I. 21
why is not health of *d.* of *my p.?* 22
weep for slain of *d.* of *my p.* 9:1
how shall I do for *d.* of *my p.?* 7
virgin *d.* of *my p.* is broken. 14:17
destruction of *d.* of *my p. Lam* 2:11
  3:48
d. of *my p.* is become cruel. 4:3
the iniquity of the *d.* of *my p.* 6
meat in destruction of *d.* of *my p.* 10

daughter *of Tarshish*

a river, O *d.* of *Tarshish. Isa* 23:10

thy daughter

7 years for *thy* younger *d. Gen* 29:18
nor thy son, nor *thy d.* *Ex* 20:10
  Deut 5:14
nakedness of *thy* daughter's *d.*
  Lev 18:10
do not prostitute *thy d.* to. 19:29
thy d. shalt thou not. *Deut* 7:3
rejoice and *thy d.* 12:18; 16:11, 14
if thy son or *thy d.* entice. 13:6
I found not *thy d.* a maid. 22:17
give *thy d.* to my son. *2 Ki* 14:9
  2 Chr 25:18
said, *thy d.* is dead. *Mark* 5:35
  Luke 8:49
devil is gone out of *thy d. Mark* 7:29
d. of *Tyre* shall be there. *Ps* 45:12

daughter *of Zidon*

virgin, *d.* of *Zidon.* *Isa* 23:12

daughter *of Zion*

d. of *Z.* hath despised thee.
 2 Ki 19:21; *Isa* 37:22
the gates of the *d.* of *Z.* *Ps* 9:14
d. of *Z.* left as a cottage. *Isa* 1:8
washed away filth of *d.* of *Z.* 4:4
against mount of *d.* of *Z.* 10:32; 16:1
loose thyself, *d.* of *Z.* 52:2
say to the *d.* of *Z.* thy. 62:11
voice of the *d.* of *Z.* *Jer* 4:31
I have likened *d.* of *Z.* to a. 6:2
of war against thee, *d.* of *Z.* 23
from the *d.* of *Z.* beauty. *Lam* 1:6
Lord covereth the *d.* of *Z.* 2:1
slew in tabernacle of *d.* of *Z.* 4
to destroy wall of *d.* of *Z.* 8
the elders of *d.* of *Z.* sit on the. 10
shall I equal to thee, *d.* of *Z.?* 13
O wall of the *d.* of *Z.* let tears. 18
accomplished, O *d.* of *Z.* 4:22
beginning of sin to *d.* of *Z. Mi* 1:13
strong hold of the *d.* of *Z.* 4:8
labour to bring forth, O *d.* of *Z.* 10
arise and thresh, O *d.* of *Z.* 13
sing, O *d.* of *Z.* shout. *Zeph* 3:14
rejoice, O *d.* of *Z. Zech* 2:10; 9:9
tell ye the *d.* of *Z.* thy. *Mat* 21:5
fear not, *d.* of *Z.* thy. *John* 12:15

daughter *of Zur*

Cozbi the *d.* of *Zur.* *Num* 25:15

daughters

and when *d.* were born. *Gen* 6:1
sons of God saw the *d.* of men. 2
sons of God came in unto *d.* 4
to them which married his *d.* 19:14
both *d.* of Lot with child by. 36

a wife of d. of Canaan. Gen 24:3, 37
                28:1, 6
the d. of the city came.   24:13
because of the d. of Heth.   27:46
happy am I, for the d. will.   30:13
thou hast carried away my d. 31:26
these d. are my   43
if thou afflict my d.   50
Dinah went out to see d.   34:1
give your d. to us, and take our d. 9
we give our d. to you, take d.   16
priest of Midian had seven d. Ex 2:16
deal with her after manner of d. 21:9
their d. go a whoring after.   34:16
the flesh of your d. shall. Lev 26:29
d. of Zelophehad. Num 26:33; 27:1
                Josh 17:3
d. of Zelophehad speak. Num 27:7
so did the d. of Zelophehad. 36:10
no whore of the d. of. Deut 23:17
they took their d. to be. Judg 3:6
we will not give them of our d. 21:7
not give them wives of our d. 18
turn again, my d. Ruth 1:11, 12
nay, my d. it grieveth me.   13
take your d. to be. 1 Sam 8:13
were king's d. virgins. 2 Sam 13:18
Shallum, he and his d. Neh 3:12
d. are brought into bondage. 5:5
one of the d. of Barzillai to wife. 7:63
                Ezra 2:61
not give our d. to people. Neh 10:30
women so fair as d. of. Job 42:15
king's d. among thy. Ps 45:9
that our d. may be as. 144:12
d. have done virtuously. Pr 31:29
so is my love among d. S of S 2:2
the d. saw her and blessed. 6:9
ye careless d. give ear. Isa 32:9
thy d. shall be nursed at. 60:4
teach your d. wailing. Jer 9:20
give your d. to husbands, that. 29:6
her d. shall be burnt with. 49:2
cry, ye d. of Rabbah, gird ye. 3
because of all the d. of. Lam 3:51
set thy face against d. Ezek 13:17
and her d. Sodom, and her d. 16:46
idleness was in her and in her d. 49
bring back the captivity of her d. 53
when thy sister Sodom and d. 55
I will give them unto thee for d. 61
two women, the d. of one. 23:2
her d. shall be slain. 26:6, 8
d. shall go into captivity. 30:18
the d. of the nations shall. 32:16
your d. shall commit. Hos 4:13
I will not punish your d. when. 14
his wife was of the d. of. Luke 1:5
the same man had four d. Acts 21:9
whose d. ye are as long. 1 Pet 3:6*

daughters of Israel
be no whore of d. of Isr. Deut 23:17
d. of Isr. went yearly. Judg 11:40
ye d. of Isr. weep. 2 Sam 1:24

daughters of Jerusalem
comely, O d. of Jerus. S of S 1:5
charge you, O d. of Jerus. 2:7
           3:5; 5:8; 8:4
love for the d. of Jerus. 3:10
my beloved, O d. of Jerus. 5:16
d. of Jerus. weep not. Luke 23:28

daughters of Judah
let d. of Judah be glad. Ps 48:11
the d. of Judah rejoiced. 97:8

daughters-in-law
arose with her d.-in-law. Ruth 1:6, 7
Naomi said to her two d.-in-law. 8

daughters of Moab
whoredom with d. of M. Num 25:1
so the d. of M. shall be at. Isa 16:2

daughters of music
the d. of music shall be. Eccl 12:4

daughters of the Philistines
woman of d. of the Phil. Judg 14:1
seen a woman of d. of Phil. 2
lest d. of Phil. rejoice. 2 Sam 1:20
delivered thee to d. of Phil.
               Ezek 16:27
the d. of Phil. which despise. 57

daughters of Shiloh
d. of Shiloh come out, catch a wife
of d. of Shiloh. Judg 21:21

daughters joined with sons
he begat sons and d. Gen 5:4
       7:10, 13, 16; 11:11
thy sons and d. bring out. 19:12
to kiss my sons and d. 31:28
he kissed his sons and d. and. 55
all his sons and d. rose to. 37:35
them on your sons and d. Ex 3:22
with our sons and with our d. 10:9
she have born him sons or d. 21:4
ear-rings of your sons and d. 32:2
take of their d. to thy sons. 34:16
thou, thy sons and d. shall eat in the.
     Lev 10:14; Num 18:11, 19
given his sons and d. Num 21:29
Zelophehad had no sons, but d.
       26:33; Josh 17:3
ye and your sons and d. rejoice.
               Deut 12:12
sons and d. they have burnt in fire.
  31; 2 Ki 17:17; Jer 7:31; 32:35
thy sons and d. given to. Deut 28:32
beget sons and d. but shalt not. 41
the flesh of thy sons and d. 53
provoking of his sons and d. 32:19
Achan, his sons and d. Josh 7:24
d. of Manasseh had inheritance
  among sons. 17:6
gave their d. to their sons. Judg 3:6
took in thirty d. for his sons. 12:9
Peninnah, her sons and d. portions.
               1 Sam 1:4
Hannah bare three sons and two d.
               2:21
their sons and d. were taken. 30:3
grieved, every man for sons and d. 6
lacking, neither sons nor d. 19
were yet sons and d. born to David.
    2 Sam 5:13; 1 Chr 14:3
saved lives of thy sons and d.
            2 Sam 19:5
Sheshan had no sons but d.
            1 Chr 2:34
Shimei had sixteen sons six d. 4:27
died, and had no sons but d. 23:22
Heman fourteen sons and three d.
              25:5
had 28 sons and 60 d. 2 Chr 11:21
Abijah begat 22 sons and d. 13:21
wives and begat sons and d. 24:3
200,000 women, sons and d. 28:8
our sons, d. and wives are in. 29:9
genealogy of their sons and d. 31:18
of their d. for their sons. Ezra 9:2
give not your d. to their sons. 12
              Neh 13:25
fight for your sons and d. Neh 4:14
our sons and our d. are many 5:2
bondage our sons and our d. 5
their sons and d. clave to. 10:28
born to Job 7 sons and 3 d. Job 1:2
              42:13
a day when sons and d. 1:13, 18
their sons and d. to devils. Ps 106:37
shed blood of their sons and d. 38
my sons from far, and my d. from.
              Isa 43:6
sons in their arms, and thy d. 49:22
a name better than of s. and d. 56:5
devoured sons and d. Jer 3:24
eat that which thy sons and d. 5:17
sons and their d. shall die. 11:22
none to bury their sons and d. 14:16
have sons and d. in this place. 16:2
concerning the sons and d. 3
eat the flesh of sons and d. 19:9
wives and beget sons and d. 29:6
we, our sons and our d. drink. 35:8
sons and thy d. taken captives. 48:46
deliver neither sons nor d.
           Ezek 14:16, 18
brought forth, sons and d. 22
sons and d. and sacrificed. 16:20
mine, and bare sons and d. 23:4
her sons and d. and slew her. 10, 25
they shall slay their sons and d. 47
your sons and d. fall by sword.
        24:21; Amos 7:17
take from them their sons and d.
            Ezek 24:25
sons and d. prophesy. Joel 2:28
              Acts 2:17
will sell your sons and d. Joel 3:8
shall be my sons and d. 2 Cor 6:18

daughters of Syria
reproach of d. of Syria. Ezek 16:57

two daughters
I have two d. let me. Gen 19:8
take thy wife and thy two d. 15
in a cave, he and his two d. 30
Laban had two d. Leah and. 29:16
fourteen years for thy two d. 31:41
went out with her two d. Ruth 1:7
Hannah conceived and bare two d.
            1 Sam 2:21
two d. were Merab and Michal. 14:49
the horseleech hath two d. Pr 30:15

daughters of the uncircumcised
lest d. of the uncirc. 2 Sam 1:20

daughters of Zion
go forth, O ye d. of Z. S of S 3:11
because the d. of Z. Isa 3:16
smite head of the d. of Z. 17
washed away filth of d. of Z. 4:4

David
Jesse begat D. Ruth 4:22; Mat 1:6
              Luke 3:31
Spirit of Lord came upon D.
           1 Sam 16:13
send me D. thy son. 19
D. came to Saul. 21
D. played. 23; 18:10; 19:9
D. was youngest. 17:14
D. returned from Saul. 15
D. heard the words of Goliath. 23
Eliab's anger kindled against D. 28
Saul armed D. 38
when Goliath saw D. 42
the Philistines cursed D. 43
D. prevailed over Philistine. 50
as D. returned from slaughter. 57
soul of Jonathan knit to D. 18:1
Jonathan and D. made a covenant. 3
D. went out whithersoever Saul. 5
D. hath slain ten thousands. 7; 29:5
Saul eyed D. from that day. 18:9
D. behaved himself wisely in all. 14
all Israel and Judah loved D. 16
on this manner spake D. 24
knew the Lord was with D. 28
and Saul became D.'s enemy. 29
spake to his servants to kill D. 19:1
against innocent blood to slay D.? 5
sought to smite D. but D. 10, 18
D. is at Naioth. 19
where are Samuel and D.? 22
D. asked leave of me to. 20:6, 28
and Jonathan caused D. to. 17
D. hid himself. 24
D.'s place was empty. 25, 27
for he was grieved for D. 34
wept one with another till D. 41
afraid at the meeting of D. 21:1
D. arose, and fled to Achish. 10
is not this D. the king? 11; 29:3
D. departed and escaped to. 22:1
and D. went thence to Mizpeh. 3
D. departed and came into forest. 5
who is so faithful as D.? 14
their hand also is with D. 17
D. inquired of the Lord. 23:2, 4
    30:8; 2 Sam 2:1; 3:19, 22; 21:1
D. and his men went to. 1 Sam 23:5
D. knew that Saul practised. 9
D. was in the wilderness of Ziph. 15
D. and his men were in. 24
Saul returned from pursuing D. 28
D. is in wilderness of En-gedi. 24:1
D.'s heart smote him. 5
D. stayed his servants. 7
this thy voice, my son D.? 16; 26:17
D. sware unto Saul. 24:22
D. went to Paran. 25:1
D. sent out ten young men. 5
do God to the enemies of D. 5
doth not D. hide himself in? 26:1
and D. beheld the place where. 5
D. took the spear and the cruse. 12
Saul knew D.'s voice. 17
return, my son D. 21
D. said, I shall perish by the. 27:1
D. was fled to Gath. 4
D. invaded Geshurites. 8
so did D. and so will be. 11
it to thy neighbour, to D. 28:17
is not this D.? 29:3

then Achish called *D.*   *1 Sam* 29:6
when *D.* and his men were.   30:1
and *D.*'s two wives were taken.   5
D. pursued.   10
D. smote them from the twilight.   17
D. recovered all.   18, 19
D. took the flocks.   20
D. took hold on clothes. *2 Sam* 1:11
D. called one of the young men.   15
D. lamented over Saul.   17
D. sent messengers to men.   2:5
house of Judah followed *D.*   10
house of *D.* waxed stronger.   3:1
unto *D.* were sons born in Hebron. 2
except as Lord hath sworn to *D.*   9
ye sought for *D.* in times past.   17
D. said, I and my kingdom are.   28
came all tribes of Israel to *D.*   5:1
thinking, *D.* cannot come in.   6
D. took the strong-hold of Zion.   7
D. grew great.   10
D. perceived the Lord had.   12
D. heard of it, and went down.   17
D. burnt their images.   21
D. went to bring up the ark.   6:2
D. all Israel played before the.   5
and *D.* was afraid of the Lord.   9
D. danced.   14
so *D.* brought up the ark.   15
what can *D.* say more to thee ?
    7:20; *1 Chr* 17:18
D. smote the Philistines. *2 Sam* 8:1
D. smote Hadadezer.   3
Lord preserved *D.*   6, 14
D. took shields of gold. 7; *1 Chr* 18:7
D. gat him a name.   *2 Sam* 8:13
D. reigned over.   15; *1 Chr* 18:14
D. reigned; executed.   *2 Sam* 8:15
D. sent to comfort. 10:2; *1 Chr* 19:2
thinkest thou *D.* doth honour thy ?
    2 Sam 10:3; *1 Chr* 19:3
D. slew men of 700.   *2 Sam* 10:18
D. sent and enquired after.   11:3
D. sent for Uriah.   6
D. wrote a letter to Joab.   14
the thing *D.* had done displeased. 27
D.'s anger was kindled.   12:5
D. said, I have sinned against.   13
D. besought God for child, *D.*   16
D. perceived child was dead.   19
and *D.* comforted Bath-sheba.   24
D. fought against Rabbah and.   29
king's crown was set on *D.*   30
D. sent to Tamar.   13:7
tidings came to *D.*   30
D. went up by the ascent of.   15:30
Shimei cast stones at *D.*   16:6
said unto him, curse *D.*   10
I will arise and pursue after *D.* 17:1
send quickly and tell *D.*   16
then *D.* arose.   22
D. was come to Mahanaim.   27
honey for *D.*   29
D. numbered the people that.   18:1
D. sat between the two gates.   24
we have also more right in *D.* 19:43
we have no part in *D.*   20:1
and *D.* came to his house.   3
he that is for *D.* let him go.   11
Ishbi-benob thought to have slain *D.*
    21:16
mercy unto *D.*   22:51; *Ps* 18:50
the last words of *D.*   *2 Sam* 23:1
mighty men *D.* had.   8; *1 Chr* 11:10
D. longed and said.   *2 Sam* 23:15
D.'s heart smote him.   24:10
D. built there an altar unto.   25
and *D.* our Lord.   *1 Ki* 1:11
D. slept with his fathers.   2:10
slew them, my father *D.* not.   32
knowest what thou didst to *D.*   44
thou wilt walk as thy father *D.* 3:14
who hath given *D.* a wise son.   5:7
D. to be over my people.   8:16
I am risen up in the room of *D.*   20
as I promised to *D.*   9:5
as I built for *D.*   11:38
for this afflict the seed of *D.*   39
portion have we in *D.*? see to thine
    own house, *D.* 12:16; *2 Chr* 10:16
turned kingdom to *D.*   *1 Chr* 10:14
D. made a covenant with them. 11:3
thine are we, *D.* then *D.*   12:18
they helped *D.* against the.   21

the fame of *D.* went out. *1 Chr* 14:17
D. was clothed with a robe.   15:27
set the ark in tent *D.* had.   16:1
and *D.* returned to bless his.   43
Ornan saw *D.* bowed to *D.*   21:21
so when *D.* was old and full.   23:1
D. blessed Lord before the.   29:10
great mercy unto *D.*   *2 Chr* 1:8
began to seek after God of *D.*   34:3
of sons of *D.* Hattush.   *Ezra* 8:2
against sepulchres of *D.*   *Neh* 3:16
with musical instruments of *D.* 12:36
prayers of *D.* the son of.   *Ps* 72:20
I will not lie unto *D.*   89:35
swarest to *D.*   49
Lord, remember *D.*   132:1
hath sworn to *D.*   11
there will I make horn of *D.* to   17
is like the tower of *D.*   *S of S* 4:4
on the throne of *D.* and.   *Isa* 9:7
woe to Ariel, city where *D.*   29:1
the sure mercies of *D.*   55:3
    Acts 13:34
sitting on throne of *D.*   *Jer* 17:25
I will raise to *D.* a righteous.   23:5
branch to grow up unto *D.*   33:15
D. shall never want a man to.   17
none to sit on throne of *D.*   36:30
of music like *D.*   *Amos* 6:5
will I raise up the tabernacle of *D.*
    9:11; *Acts* 15:16
feeble be as *D.* and *D.*   *Zech* 12:8
son of *D.* have mercy.   *Mat* 9:27
    15:22; 20:30, 31; *Mark* 10:47, 48
    Luke 18:38, 39
D. did when he was an hungered ?
    Mat 12:3; *Mark* 2:25; *Luke* 6:3
is not this the son of *D.*?   *Mat* 12:23
Hosanna to the son of *D.*   21:9, 15
Christ is the son of *D.*   22:42
    Mark 12:35
if *D.* then call him Lord. *Mat* 22:45
    Mark 12:37; *Luke* 20:41, 44
the kingdom of our father *D.*
    Mark 11:10
Christ cometh of the seed of *D.*
    John 7:42
speak of patriarch *D.*   *Acts* 2:29
for *D.* is not ascended into the.   34
he raised up to them *D.* to.   13:22
for *D.* fell on sleep.   36
made of the seed of *D.*   *Rom* 1:3
    2 Tim 2:8
even as *D.* also describeth. *Rom* 4:6
certain day, saying, in *D.* *Heb* 4:7
time would fail me to tell of *D.* 11:32
hath the key of *D.*   *Rev* 3:7
root of *D.*   5:5; 22:16

see city, father

days of David
famine in the *days of D.* *2 Sam* 21:1
days of D. drew nigh.   *1 Ki* 2:1
number was in *days of D.* *1 Chr* 7:2
in the *days of D.* were.   *Neh* 12:46
drave out *days of D.* *Acts* 7:45

hand of David
require it at *h. of D.*   *1 Sam* 20:16
thee into *h. of D.*   *2 Sam* 3:8
by *h. of* my servant *D.* I will.   18
fell by *h. of D.*   21:22; *1 Chr* 20:8

house of David
covenant with *h. of D.* I *Sam* 20:16
the *h. of* Saul and *D.* *2 Sam* 3:1, 6
let *h. of* thy servant *D.*   7:26
Israel rebelled against the *h. of D.*
    1 Ki 12:19; *2 Chr* 10:19
none followed *h. of D.*   *1 Ki* 12:20
shall kingdom return to *h. of D.* 26
a child be born to the *h. of D.* 13:2
rent kingdom from *h. of D.*   14:8
    2 Ki 17:21
not destroy the *h. of D.* *2 Chr* 21:7
thrones of the *h. of D.*   *Ps* 122:5
it was told the *h. of D.*   *Isa* 7:2
hear, O *h. of D.*   13; *Jer* 21:12
key of *h. of D.* I will lay. *Isa* 22:22
that the glory of *h. of D.* *Zech* 12:7
feeble as *D.* and the *h. of D.*   8
I will pour on *h. of D.* the spirit. 10
the family of the *h. of D.* shall.   12
a fountain opened to *h. of D.*   13:1
was Joseph, of *h. of D.* *Luke* 1:27

horn of salvation in *h. of D.* *Luke* 1:69
was of *h.* and lineage *of D.*   2:4

David joined with king
is not this *D.* the king ? *1 Sam* 21:11
they anointed *D.* king.   *2 Sam* 2:4
time that *D.* was *king* in Hebron. 11
and *king D.* himself followed.   3:31
king D. made a league... anointed
    D. king. 5:3; *1 Chr* 11:3; 12:31, 38
which *king D.* did dedicate to Lord.
    2 Sam 8:11; *1 Chr* 26:26
against *king*, even *D.* *2 Sam* 20:21
than throne of *king D.*   *1 Ki* 1:37
servants came to bless *king D.*   47
D. the *king* rejoiced.   *1 Chr* 29:9
to *D.* the *king* a wise son. *2 Chr* 2:12
ordained by *D. king* of.   29:27
    Ezra 3:10
serve Lord and *D.* their *king.Jer* 30:9
seek Lord and *D.* their *king. Hos* 3:5
D. the *king* and *D.* the *king. Mat* 1:6
raised up *D.* to be *king. Acts* 13:22

servant **David**
by hand of my *servant D.* *2 Sam* 3:18
go and tell my *servant D.*   7:5, 8
let the house of thy *servant D.*
    established.   26; *1 Chr* 17:24
shewed thy *servant D.*   *1 Ki* 3:6
kept with thy *servant D.* that.   8:24
keep with thy *servant D.*   25, 26
    2 Chr 6:16
done for *D.* his *servant.*   *1 Ki* 8:66
D. my *servant*'s sake, and for Jeru-
    salem's. 11:13, 32, 34; *Ps* 132:10
    Isa 37:35
D. my *servant* may have a light.
    1 Ki 11:36
keep my statutes, as my *servant D.*
    38; 14:8
mercies of *D.* thy *servant. 2 Chr* 6:42
chose *D.* also his *servant.*   *Ps* 78:70
sworn unto *D.* my *servant.*   89:3
I have found *D.* my *servant.*   20
who delivered *D.* his *servant.* 144:10
broken with *D.* my *servant. Jer* 33:21
multiply seed of *D.* my *servant.* 22
away the seed of *D.* my *servant.* 26
my *servant D.* shall feed them.
    Ezek 34:23
my *servant D.* shall be a prince. 24
D. my *servant* shall be king. 37:24
servant D. shall be their prince. 25
house of his *servant D.* *Luke* 1:69
mouth of thy *servant D.* *Acts* 4:25

dawn, -ing
they rose about the *d.*   *Josh* 6:15
woman in the *d.* of day. *Judg* 19:26
neither let it see the *d.* of. *Job* 3:9
full of tossings to the *d.* of.   7:4
I prevented the *d.* of.   *Ps* 119:147
as it began to *d.* towards. *Mat* 28:1
till day *d.* and day-star. *2 Pet* 1:19

day
The word *day* is used of [1] one
period of the earth's revolution,
or twenty-four hours, Gen 7:24;
Job 3:6. *This period the Hebrews*
reckoned as beginning at sunset,
Lev 23:32. [2] *The period between*
dawn and dark, variable in different
latitudes and at different seasons,
Gen 8:22; Ps 19:2; 2 Pet 1:19.
[3] *Any period of action or state of*
being, without definite reference
to time, Job 19:25; Zech 4:10;
Hos 1:11; Eccl. 7:14; Ezek 30:9.
In the day that *usually has merely*
the meaning of when, and is some-
times so translated, 1 Ki 2:8; Isa
30:26. " *In thy days* " *means* " *in*
thy lifetime," 1 Ki 11:12.
God called the light a.   Gen 1:5
let me go, for *d.* breaketh.   32:26
if he continue a *d.* or two.   *Ex* 21:21
journeyed not, till the *d.* it.   40:37
every thing upon his *d.*   *Lev* 23:37
the *d.* I smote first-born.   *Num* 3:13
offer his offering on his *d.*   7:11
each *d.* for a year shall bear.   14:34
husband disallow her on *d.* 30:8, 12
d. thou stoodest before.   *Deut* 4:10
no manner of similitude on *d.*   15

from *d.* thou didst depart. *Deut* 9:7
have been rebellious from *d.* 24
at his *d.* thou shalt give him. 24:15
till *d.* I bid you shout. *Josh* 6:10
on *d.* we came forth to go to. 9:12
sun hasted not down about a *d.* 10:13
was no *d.* like that before or. 14
when it is *d.* we shall kill. *Judg* 16:2*
from the *d.* that Israel came out. 30
what *d.* thou buyest the. *Ruth* 4:5
Lord told Samuel a *d.* *1 Sam* 9:15
behold the *d.* of which the. 24:4
smite him, or his *d.* shall. 26:10
while it was yet *d.* *2 Sam* 3:35
Jer 15:9
d. he forced his sister. *2 Sam* 13:32
from *d.* king departed, till *d.* 19:24
on *d.* thou goest out. *1 Ki* 2:37, 42
till *d.* the Lord sendeth rain. 17:14
it fell on a *d.* that Elisha passed.
2 Ki 4:8, 11, 18
they make an end in a *d.?* *Neh* 4:2
and labour in the *d.* 3
d. of feasting. *Esth* 9:17, 18, 19
feasted, every one his *d.* *Job* 1:4
a *d.* when sons of God. 6, 13; 2:1
let *d.* perish wherein I was. 3:3
till he accomplish his *d.* 14:6
be astonied at his *d.* 18:20
he shall stand at latter *d.* 19:25
the wicked is reserved to *d.* 21:30
d. unto *d.* uttereth speech. *Ps* 19:2
seeth that his *d.* is coming. 37:13
nor remembered *d.* when he. 78:42
a *d.* in thy courts is better. 84:10
seven times a *d.* do I. 119:164
and more to perfect *d.* *Pr* 4:18
he will come home at the *d.* 7:20*
knowest not what a *d.* may. 27:1
till *d.* break, and. *S of S* 2:17; 4:6
from *d.* that Ephraim. *Isa* 7:17
before the *d.* was, I am he. 43:13
a *d.* for a man to afflict his soul ? this
a fast, an acceptable *d.* to ? 58:5
d. of vengeance of God. 61:2; 63:4
prepare them for the *d.* *Jer* 12:3
there shall they be till *d.* 27:22
d. they built it, even to this *d.* 32:31
d. I spake, even to this *d.* 36:2
till *d.* Jerusalem was taken. 38:28
because of the *d.* that cometh. 47:4
woe, for their *d.* is come. 50:27
appointed thee each *d.* *Ezek* 4:6
behold the *d.* behold it is. 7:10
wicked prince, whose *d.* 21:25, 29
from *d.* thou wast created. 28:15
howl ye, woe worth the *d.!* 30:2
for the *d.* is near. 3
at Tehaphnehes the *d.* shall. 18
petition three times a *d.* *Dan* 6:10
13
will ye do in solemn *d.?* *Hos* 9:5
a *d.* of darkness and. *Joel* 2:2
him that maketh *d.* dark. *Amos* 5:8
the end thereof as a bitter *d.* 8:10
and *d.* shall be dark. *Mi* 3:6
the *d.* of thy watchmen. 7:4
before decree, the *d.* pass. *Zeph* 2:2
till the *d.* that I rise up to. 3:8
who hath despised *d.?* *Zech* 4:10
who may abide the *d.?* *Mal* 3:2
d. cometh that shall burn. 4:1
till the *d.* Noe entered. *Mat* 24:38
Luke 17:27
come in a *d.* when he looketh not.
Mat 24:50; *Luke* 12:46
neither know the *d.* nor. *Mat* 25:13
great while before *d.* *Mark* 1:35
dumb till *d.* these things. *Luke* 1:20
child grew till *d.* of his shewing. 80
trespass seven times in a *d.* 17:4
Son of man be in his *d.* 24
raise it again at last *d.* *John* 6:39
raise him up at last *d.* 40, 44, 54
Abraham rejoiced to see my *d.* 8:56
work of him while it is *d.* 9:4
until the *d.* in which he. *Acts* 1:2
on a set *d.* Herod sat upon. 12:21
when it was *d.* 16:35; 23:12; 27:39
he hath appointed a *d.* 17:31
anchors, and wished for *d.* 27
wrath against the *d.* of. *Rom* 2:5
d. is at hand, let us therefore. 13:12
regardeth a *d.* regardeth it. 14:6

for the *d.* shall declare it. *1 Cor* 3:13
behold, now is the *d.* of. *2 Cor* 6:2
ye are sealed to the *d.* *Eph* 4:30
will perform it until *d.* *Phil* 1:6
ye are all children of *d.* *1 Thes* 5:5
let us who are of *d.* be sober. 8
he limiteth a certain *d.* *Heb* 4:7
afterward spoken of another *d.?* 8
the more as ye see the *d.* 10:25
till the *d.* dawn, and the. *2 Pet* 1:19
hasting to coming of the *d.* 3:12
in the Spirit on the Lord's *d.* *Rev.* 1:10
for an hour and a *d.* 9:15

see **atonement, battle, calamity,
darkness, evil, holy, last**

all the **day**
on thee do I wait *all the d.* *Ps* 25:5
forth thy salvation *all the d.* 71:15
shall they rejoice *all the d.* 89:16
reproach me *all the d.* 102:8
law is my meditation *all the d.* 119:97
plowman plow *all d.* *Isa* 28:24*
spread out hands *all the d.* 65:2
a fire that burneth *all the d.* 5
and faint *all the d.* *Lam* 1:13
turneth hand against me *all d.* 3:3
derision to my people *all the d.* 14
their device against me *all the d.* 62
here *all the d.* idle ? *Mat* 20:6

all the **day long**
longing for them *all the d. long.*
Deut 28:32
shall cover him *all the d. long.* 33:12
roaring *all the d. long.* *Ps* 32:3
thy praise *all the d. long.* 35:28
I go mourning *all the d. long.* 38:6
imagine deceits *all the d. long.* 12
God we boast *all the d. long.* 44:8
thy sake are killed *all the d. long.* 22
righteousness *all the d. long.* 71:24
for *all the d. long* have I. 73:14
greedily *all the d. long.* *Pr* 21:26
in fear of Lord *all the d. long.* 23:17
all d. long I stretched. *Rom* 10:21

by **day**, and *day by day*
spake to Joseph *d. by d.* *Gen* 39:10
went before them *by d.* *Ex* 13:21
not away pillar of cloud *by d.* 22
two lambs of the first year *d. by d.*
29:38; *Num* 28:3
cloud was upon the tabernacle *by d.*
fire by. *Ex* 40:38; *Num* 9:16*
cloud was on them *by d.* *Num* 10:34
14:14; *Deut* 1:23; *Neh* 9:19
he could not do it *by d.* *Judg* 6:27
nor birds rest *by d.* *2 Sam* 21:10
d. by d. there came to. *1 Chr* 12:22
of the sickness. *d. by d.* *2 Chr* 21:15
thus they did *d. by d.* and. 24:11
priests praised Lord *d. by d.* 30:21
let it be given *d. by d.* *Ezra* 6:9
d. by d. he read in law. *Neh* 8:18
nor arrow that flieth *by d.* *Ps* 91:5
sun shall not smite thee *by d.* 121:6
sun to rule *by d.* for his. 136:8
no more thy light *by d.* *Isa* 60:19
the sun for a light *by d.* *Jer* 31:35
and remove *by d. in.* *Ezek* 12:3
I brought forth my stuff *by d.* 7
give us *d. by d.* our. *Luke* 11:3
man renewed *by d.* *2 Cor* 4:16
gates not be shut *by d.* *Rev* 21:25

day *of death*
I know not *d.* of my death. *Gen* 27:2
be a Nazarite to *d.* of his death.
Judg 13:7
see Saul till *d.* of death. *1 Sam* 15:35
no child till *d.* of death. *2 Sam* 6:23
shut up to *d.* of their death. 20:3
Uzziah was a leper to the *d.* of his
death. *2 Ki* 15:5; *2 Chr* 26:21
d. of death better than *d.* *Eccl* 7:1
power in the *d.* of death. 8:8
prison till *d.* of death. *Jer* 52:11
portion, till *d.* of his death. 34

every **day**
a certain rate *every d.* *Ex* 16:4
offer a bullock *every d.* 29:36
sought David *every d.* *1 Sam* 23:14
David mourned for his son *every d.*
2 Sam 13:37
daily rate for *every d.* *2 Ki* 25:30

minister, as *every d.* *1 Chr* 16:37
a certain rate *every d.* *2 Chr* 8:13
duty *every d.* required. 14; *Ezra* 3:4
singers, due for *every d.* *Neh* 11:23
and the porters *every d.* his. 12:47
Mordecai walked *every d.* *Esth* 2:11
angry with wicked *every d.* *Ps* 7:11
every d. they wrest my words. 56:5
every d. will I bless thee. 145:2
feared continually *every d.* *Isa* 51:13
and my name *every d.* is. 52:5
prepare *every d.* a goat. *Ezek* 43:25
sumptuously *every d.* *Luke* 16:19
esteemed *every d.* alike. *Rom* 14:5

feast **day**
trumpet on solemn *feast-d.* *Ps* 81:3
they said, not on the *feast-d.*
Mat 26:5*; *Mark* 14:2*
feast-d. many believed. *John* 2:23*

first **day**
and morning were *first d.* *Gen* 1:5
on *first d.* of the month mountains.
8:5, 13; *Ex* 40:2, 17; *Lev* 23:24
the *first d.* put away leaven, whoso
eateth from *first d.* *Ex* 12:15
in the *first d.* an holy convocation. 16
Lev 23:7, 35; *Num* 28:18; 29:1
first d. shall be sabbath. *Lev* 23:39
shall take on *first d.* boughs of. 40
spake to Moses on *first d.* *Num* 1:1
assembled congregation on *first d.* 18
on the *first d.* Aaron went. 33:38
flesh sacrificed *first d.* not. *Deut* 16:4
on *first d.* to sanctify. *2 Chr* 29:17
from the *first d.* began. *Ezra* 3:6
on the *first d.* began he to go up . . . on
first d. came he to Jerusalem. 7:9
sat down on *first d.* of the. 10:16
by *first d.* of first month they. 17
brought law on *first d.* of. *Neh* 8:2
from *first* unto last *d.* he read. 18
in *first d.* word of Lord. *Ezek* 26:1
29:17; 31:1; 32:1; *Hag* 1:1
in *first d.* of the month. *Ezek* 45:18
from *first d.* thou didst. *Dan* 10:12
first d. of unleavened bread.
Mat 26:17; *Mark* 14:12
first d. I came into Asia. *Acts* 20:18
fellowship from *first d.* *Phil* 1:5

see **week**
second **day**
and morning *second d.* *Gen* 1:8
went out the *second d.* *Ex* 2:13
on *second d.* Nethaneel. *Num* 7:18
on *second d.* offer twelve. 29:17
second d. they compassed. *Josh* 6:14
took Lachish on *second d.* 10:32
Benjamin *second d.* *Judg* 20:24
eat no meat *second d.* *1 Sam* 20:34
began to build *second d.* *2 Chr* 3:2
on the *second d.* were. *Neh* 8:13
to Esther the *second d.* *Esth* 7:2
second d. after he had. *Jer* 41:4
second d. thou shalt offer a kid.
Ezek 43:22

third **day**
and morning *third d.* *Gen* 1:13
on *third d.* Abraham saw. 22:4
it was told Laban on *third d.* 31:22
on *third d.* when they were. 34:25
ready against the *third d.* for the
third d. Lord will. *Ex* 19:11, 15
remainder of flesh of sacrifice on
third d. shall be. *Lev* 7:17; 19:6
purify himself on *third d.*
Num 19:12; 31:19
sprinkle unclean on *third d.* 19:19
on *third d.* eleven bullocks. 29:20
to cities on *third d.* *Josh* 9:17
Benjamin the *third d.* *Judg* 20:30
to Rehoboam *third d.* *1 Ki* 12:12
2 Chr 10:12
on the *third d.* go up. *2 Ki* 20:5, 8
house finished on *third d.* *Ezra* 6:15
on *third d.* Esther put on. *Esth* 5:1
in *third d.* he will raise. *Hos* 6:2
and be raised again the *third d.*
Mat 16:21; 17:23; *Luke* 9:22
the *third d.* rise again. *Mat* 20:19
Mark 9:31; 10:34; *Luke* 18:33
24:7, 46
sepulchre be made sure till the *third
d.* *Mat* 27:64

the *third d.* I shall be.   *Luke* 13:32
to-day is the *third d.* since.   24:21
on *third d.* there was a.   *John* 2:1
the *third d.* we cast out. *Acts* 27:19
he rose again the *third d.* *1 Cor* 15:4

fourth day
and morning *fourth d.*   *Gen* 1:19
fourth d. ten bullocks.   *Num* 29:23
on the *fourth d.* they assembled.
    2 Chr 20:26
on *fourth d.* was silver.   *Ezra* 8:33
Zechariah on *fourth d.*   *Zech* 7:1

fifth day
and morning *fifth d.*   *Gen* 1:23
fifth d. nine bullocks. *Num* 29:26
in the *fifth d.* of.   *Ezek* 1:1, 2; 8:1
in the *fifth d.* one came.   33:21

sixth day
and morning *sixth d.*   *Gen* 1:31
on *sixth d.* gather twice. *Ex* 16:5, 22
giveth you on the *sixth d.* bread. 29
on the *sixth d.* Eliasaph. *Num* 7:42
on *sixth d.* eight bullocks.   29:29

seventh day
seventh d. God ended his. *Gen* 2:2
God blessed *seventh d.* 3; *Ex* 20:11
leaven from first *d.* to *seventh d.*
    Ex 12:15
on *seventh d.* an holy convocation.
    16; *Lev* 23:8; *Num* 28:25
in the *seventh d.* shall be. *Ex* 13:6
but the *seventh d.* is the sabbath.
    16:26; 20:10; *Lev* 23:3; *Deut* 5:14
went some on *seventh d.* *Ex* 16:27
out of his place on *seventh d.*   29
seventh d. he called Moses.   24:16
seventh d. God rested.   31:17
    Heb 4:4
seventh d. thou shalt rest. *Ex* 34:21
seventh d. there shall be holy *d.* 35:2
priest shall look on him *seventh d.*
    Lev 13:5, 6, 27, 32, 34, 51; 14:39
the *seventh d.* he shall shave. 14:9
    Num 6:9
seventh d. he shall be clean.
    Num 19:12
on the *seventh d.* purify. 19; 31:19
wash your clothes on *seventh d.*
    31:24
on *seventh d.* a solemn. *Deut* 16:8
seventh d. compass. *Josh* 6:4, 15
seventh d. they said to. *Judg* 14:15
on the *seventh d.* he told her.   17
seventh d. child died.   *2 Sam* 12:18
in *seventh d.* battle was. *1 Ki* 20:29
seventh d. came Nebuzar-adan.
    2 Ki 25:8
seventh d. when Ahasuerus was.
    Esth 1:10
seventh d. word came. *Ezek* 30:20
and so do the *seventh d.*   45:20
spake of *seventh d.* on this wise,
God did rest *seventh d.* *Heb* 4:4

eighth day
on the *eighth d.* thou.   *Ex* 22:30
on the *eighth d.* Moses.   *Lev* 9:1
on *eighth d.* flesh of fore-skin. 12:3
eighth d. take two he-lambs. 14:10
two turtles on *eighth d.* 23; 15:14
    Num 6:10
the *eighth d.* it shall be. *Lev* 22:27
on the *eighth d.* shall be an. 23:36
on the *eighth d.* a sabbath.   39
eighth d. a solemn assembly.
    Num 29:35; *2 Chr* 7:9; *Neh* 8:18
on *eighth d.* priests. *Ezek* 43:27
eighth d. came to circumcise child.
    Luke 1:59; *Acts* 7:8; *Phil* 3:5

ninth day
your souls in *ninth d.*   *Lev* 23:32
on *ninth d.* famine was. *2 Ki* 25:3
    Jer 52:6
the *ninth d.* the city.   *Jer* 39:2

tenth day
tenth d. of this month.   *Ex* 12:3
tenth d. of month ye shall afflict.
    Lev 16:29; 23:27; *Num* 29:7
on *tenth d.* the trumpet of. *Lev* 25:9
of Jordan on *tenth d.*   *Josh* 4:19
tenth d. Nebuchadnezzar came.
    2 Ki 25:1; *Jer* 52:4; *Ezek* 24:1
tenth d. burnt house of. *Jer* 52:12

on *tenth d.* elders came. *Ezek* 20:1
on *tenth d.* hand of Lord was.   40:1

eleventh day
eleventh d. Pagiel offered. *Num* 7:72

twelfth day
on *twelfth d.* Ahira.   *Num* 7:78
departed on *twelfth d.* to. *Ezra* 8:31
on *twelfth d.* word came. *Ezek* 29:1

thirteenth day
scribes were called on *thirteenth d.*
    Esth 3:12
destroy all Jews on *thirteenth d.*
    13; 8:12; 9:1
thirteenth d. of Adar they.   9:17
Jews assembled on *thirteenth d.* 18

fourteenth day
lamb till *fourteenth d.*   *Ex* 12:6
on *fourteenth d.* ye shall eat.   18
fourteenth d. is the Lord's. *Lev* 23:5
    Num 9:3, 5; 28:16; *Josh* 5:10
    2 Chr 30:15; 35:1; *Ezra* 6:19
on *fourteenth d.* at even. *Num* 9:11
gathered on *fourteenth d. Esth* 9:15
fourteenth d. of same rested.   17
this is *fourteenth d.* ye. *Acts* 27:33

fifteenth day
of Sinai on *fifteenth d.*   *Ex* 16:1
on *fifteenth d.* is feast. *Lev* 23:6
    Num 28:17
fifteenth d. of seventh month.
    Lev 23:34, 39; *Num* 29:12
    Ezek 45:25
Ramases on *fifteenth d.* *Num* 33:3
feast on *fifteenth d.* 1 *Ki* 12:32, 33
fifteenth d. rested. *Esth* 9:18, 21
on *fifteenth d.* word. *Ezek* 32:17

sixteenth day
in *sixteenth d.* they.   *2 Chr* 29:17

seventeenth day
on *seventeenth d.* were. *Gen* 7:11
ark rested on *seventeenth d.*   8:4

twentieth day
on *twentieth d.* cloud. *Num* 10:11
on *twentieth d.* people. *Ezra* 10:9

twenty-first day
bread till *twenty-first d.* *Ex* 12:18
twenty-first d. came word. *Hag* 2:1

twenty-third day
twenty-third day Solomon sent.
    2 Chr 7:10
on *twenty-third d.* written. *Esth* 8:9

twenty-fourth day
twenty-fourth d. Israel.   *Neh* 9:1
twenty-fourth d. I was by. *Dan* 10:4
in *twenty-fourth d.* Lord. *Hag* 1:15
in *twenty-fourth d.* 2:10, 20
consider from *twenty-fourth d.*   18
on *twenty-fourth d.* came word to
Zechariah.   *Zech* 1:7

twenty-fifth day
finished in *twenty-fifth d.* *Neh* 6:15
on *twenty-fifth d.* Evil-merodach.
    Jer 52:31

twenty-seventh day
on *twenty-seventh d.* was. *Gen* 8:14
on *twenty-seventh d.* Evil-merodach.
    2 Ki 25:27

good day
we come in a *good d.*   *1 Sam* 25:8
gladness and a *good d.*   *Esth* 8:17
    9:19
from mourning into a *good d.*   9:22

great day
alas, that *d.* is great.   *Jer* 30:7
for *great* shall be the *d.* *Hos* 1:11
d. of the Lord is *great.*   *Joel* 2:11
before the *great* and terrible *d.* of the
    Lord come.   31; *Acts* 2:20
the *great d.* of the Lord. *Zeph* 1:14
before coming of *great d.* *Mal* 4:5
that *great d.* of the feast. *John* 7:37
the *judgement* of *great d.* *Jude* 6
great d. of his wrath is. *Rev* 6:17
gather to battle of the *great d.* 16:14

in the day
in the *d.* the Lord made. *Gen* 2:4
in the *d.* thou eatest thereof.   17
in the *d.* ye eat. your eyes.   3:5
in the *d.* drought consumed.   31:40
answered me *in the d.* of.   35:3

in the *d.* when I visit.   *Ex* 32:34
in the *d.* of his trespass.   *Lev* 6:5
offer *in the d.* when he is. 20; 7:36
in the *d.* he presented.   7:35
law of leper *in the d.* 14:2; *Num* 6:9
in the *d.* of first-fruits. *Num* 28:26
if her father disallow *in the d.* 30:5
husband held his peace *in the d.* 7
in the *d.* Lord delivered. *Josh* 10:12
as strong as I was *in the d.*   14:11
put hot bread *in the d.* 1 *Sam* 21:6
in the *d.* the Lord had. *2 Sam* 22:1
cursed me *in the d.* that.   1 *Ki* 2:8
in the *day* wherein they. *Neh* 13:15
in the *d.* the enemies. *Esth* 9:1
goods flow away *in the d.* *Job* 20:28
as *in the d.* of temptation. *Ps* 95:8
    Heb 3:8
hide not thy face *in the d.* of trouble,
in the *d.* when I call.   *Ps* 102:2
people be willing *in the d.*   110:3
strike through kings *in the d.*   5
remember Edom *in the d.* of. 137:7
in the *d.* when I cried, thou. 138:3
not spare *in the d.* of.   *Pr* 6:34
riches profit not *in the d.* of.   11:4
faint *in the d.* of adversity.   24:10
in the *d.* of prosperity be joyful, in
    the *d.* of adversity. *Eccl* 7:14
power *in the d.* of death.   8:8
in the *d.* when the keepers.   12:3
crowned him *in the d.* of his es-
    pousals, and *in the d. S of S* 3:11
in the *d.* when she shall be.   8:8
broken yoke as *in the d.*   *Isa* 9:4
what will ye do *in the d.* of ?   10:3
in the *d.* he came out of Egypt. 11:16
    Hos 2:15
remove *in the d.* of his. *Isa* 13:13
in the *d.* shalt thou make thy plant
    grow, *in the d.* of grief.   17:11
in the *d.* of great slaughter. 30:25
in the *d.* that the Lord bindeth.   26
in the *d.* of your fast you.   58:3
my refuge *in the d.* of.   *Jer* 16:19
my hope *in the d.* of evil.   17:17
back and not face *in the d.*   18:17
dead body be cast out *in the d.* 36:30
afflicted me *in the d.* of. *Lam* 1:12
not his footstool *in the d.* of.   2:1
thou drewest near *in the d.*   3:57
not deliver them *in the d. Ezek* 7:19
thy nativity *in the d.* thou. 16:4, 5
Sodom not mentioned *in the d.*   56
fall *in the d.* of thy ruin.   27:27
great pain came as *in the d.* of. 30:9
every man for life *in the d.*   32:10
in the *d.* he turneth from wickedness,
    not able to live *in the d.*   33:12
lest I set her as *in the d.* *Hos* 2:3
shalt thou fall *in the d.*   4:5
with a tempest *in the d.* *Amos* 1:14
darken earth *in the* clear *d.*   8:9
in the d. thou stoodest.   *Ob* 11
nor rejoiced *in the d.* of their.   12
did remain *in the d.* of distress. 14
in the *d.* that I shall do. *Mal* 4:3
in the *d.* when Son is. *Luke* 17:30
if any walk *in the d.* *John* 11:9
in d. when God shall. *Rom* 2:16
walk honestly as *in the d.*   13:13
be blameless *in the d.* 1 *Cor* 1:8
in the d. of salvation I. *2 Cor* 6:2
rejoice *in the d.* of Christ. *Phil* 2:16
in the *d.* when I took them. *Heb* 8:9
glorify God *in the d.* of. 1 *Pet* 2:12

day of judgement
tolerable for Sodom in *d.* of *judg.*
    Mat 10:15; 11:24; *Mark* 6:11*
and Sidon in *d.* of *judg.* *Mat* 11:22
give account in *d.* of *judg.*   12:36
the unjust to *d.* of *judg.* *2 Pet* 2:9
reserved against *d.* of *judg.*   3:7
boldness in *d.* of *judg.* 1 *John* 4:17

day of the Lord
d. of the *L.* shall be on. *Isa* 2:12
d. of the *L.* is at hand.   13:6
    Joel 1:15; *Zeph* 1:7
d. of the *L.* cometh. *Isa* 13:9
Joel 2:1; *Zech* 14:1
d. of the *L.'s* vengeance. *Isa* 34:8
this is the *d.* of the *L.* *Jer* 46:10
in *d.* of the *L.'s* anger. *Lam* 2:22

in battle in *d. of the L.*   Ezek 13:5
the *d. of the L.* is near.   30:3
Joel 3:14; Ob 15
desire the *d. of the L.*   Amos 5:18
in *d. of the L.'s* sacrifice.   Zeph 1:8
deliver them in *d. of L.'s* wrath.   18
before the *d. of the L.'s* anger.   2:2
hid in *d. of the L.'s* anger.   3
coming of the *d. of the L.*   Mal 4:5
saved in *d. of the L.*   1 Cor 5:5
ours in the *d. of the L.*   2 Cor 1:14
d. of the L. cometh as a thief.
1 Thes 5:2; 2 Pet 3:10

one day

of you both in *one d.?*   Gen 27:45
not kill it and her young both in
one d.   Lev 22:28
ye shall not eat *one d.*   Num 11:19
in *one d.* they shall die. *1 Sam 2:34*
I shall *one d.* perish by the.   27:1
provision for *one d.* was. *1 Ki 4:22*
of Syrians 100,000 in *one d.*   20:29
in Judah 120,000 in *one d. 2 Chr 28:6*
is this work of *one d.*   Ezra 10:13
kill in *one d.*   Esth 3:13; 8:12
branch and rush in *one d.*   Isa 9:14
his thorns and briers in *one d.* 10:17
two things shall come in *one d.* 47:9
earth bring forth in *one d.?*   66:8
iniquity of land in *one d.*   Zech 3:9
it shall be *one d.* which.   14:7
abode with brethren *one d.* Acts 21:7
after *one d.* the south wind.   28:13
one esteemeth *one d.*   Rom 14:5
fell in *one d.* 23,000.   1 Cor 10:8
one d. is with the Lord as. *2 Pet 3:8*
her plagues come in *one d.* Rev 18:8

day joined with *night*

to divide *d.* from *night.*   Gen 1:14
rule over *d.* and over the *night.*   18
cold and heat, *d.* and *night.*   8:22
whether stolen by *d.* or *night.* 31:39
east-wind *d.* and *night.*   Ex 10:13
light to go by *d.* and *night.*   13:21
abide at door *d.* and *night. Lev 8:35*
that *d.* and all *night.*   Num 11:32
shalt fear *d.* and *night. Deut 28:66*
thou shalt meditate therein *d.* and
night.   Josh 1:8; Ps 1:2
that *d.* and that *night. 1 Sam 19:24*
toward this house *night* and *d.*
1 Ki 8:29; 2 Chr 6:20
I pray before thee *d.* and *night.*
Neh 1:6
watch against them *d.* and *night.* 4:9
eat nor drink *night* or *d.* Esth 4:16
they change *night* into *d. Job 17:12*
till the *d.* and *night* come.   26:10*
d. and *night* thy hand was. *Ps 32:4*
tears my meat *d.* and *night.*   42:3
d. and *night* they go about it.   55:10
the *d.* is thine, the *night* also. 74:16
I have cried *d.* and *night.*   88:1
the *night* shineth as the *d.* 139:12
neither *d.* nor *night* seeth. Eccl 8:16
smoke by *d.*, fire by *night. Isa 4:5*
Lord will keep it *d.* and *night.* 27:3
not be quenched *d.* nor *night.* 34:10
sickness from *d.* to *night.*   38:12
from *d.* to *night* wilt thou make. 13
not be shut *d.* nor *night.*   60:11
hold their peace *d.* nor *night.* 62:6
might weep *d.* and *night.*   Jer 9:1
eyes run down tears *d.* and *night.*
14:17; Lam 2:18
other gods *d.* and *night.*   Jer 16:13
should not be *d.* nor *night.*   33:20
not *d.* nor *night.*   Zech 14:7
and rise *night* and *d.*   Mark 4:27
d. and *night* he was in.   5
this *d.* even this *night*, before. 14:30
and prayers *night* and *d. Luke 2:37*
elect, which cry *d.* and *night.* 18:7
watched gates *night* and *d.* Acts 9:24
warn every one *night* and *d.* 20:31
serving God *d.* and *night.*   26:7
suffered shipwreck, a *night* and a *d.*
2 Cor 11:25
I have been.
labouring *d.* and *night. 1 Thes 2:9*
night and *d.* praying. 3:10; 1 Tim 5:5
with labour *night* and *d. 2 Thes 3:8*
remembrance of thee in my prayers
night and *d.*   2 Tim 1:3

9

rest not *d.* and *night.*   Rev 4:8
and serve him *d.* and *night.*   7:15
d. shone not for a third part of it
and the *night.*   8:12
accused them *d.* and *night.*   12:10
have no rest *d.* nor *night.*   14:11
tormented *d.* and *night* for ever.
20:10

sabbath-day

seventh *d.* is the *sabbath. Ex 16:26*
20:10
remember the *sabbath-d.* to. 20:8
Deut 5:12
Lord blessed the *sabbath-d. Ex* 20:11
doth any work on *sabbath-d.* 31:15
kindle no fire on *sabbath-d.*   35:3
sticks on *sabbath-d.*   Num 15:32
offer on *sabbath-d.* two lambs. 28:9
to keep the *sabbath-d.*   Deut 5:15
sell victuals on *sabbath-d. Neh* 10:31
burdens brought on *sabbath-d.* 13:15
and profane the *sabbath-d.*   17
no burden brought in *sabbath-d.* 19
keep gates to sanctify *sabbath-d.* 22
no burden on *sabbath-d.*   Jer 17:21
nor carry burden on *sabbath-d.* 22
shall offer in *sabbath-d.*   Ezek 46:4
the *sabbath-d.* through the corn.
Mat 12:1; Mark 2:23
Son of man is Lord of *sabbath-d.*
Mat 12:8
a pit on *sabbath-d.*   11; Luke 14:5
flight be not on *sabbath-d. Mat* 24:20
why do they on *sabbath-d.* that ?
Mark 2:24
would heal on *sabbath-d.*   3:2
Luke 6:7
into synagogue on the *sabbath-d.*
Mark 6:2; Luke 4:16; Acts 13:14
from bond on *sabbath-d. Luke* 13:16
to eat bread on *sabbath-d.*   14:1
and rested the *sabbath-d.*   23:56
it is *sabbath-d.* it is not. John 5:10
done these things on *sabbath-d.* 7:22
ye on *sabbath-d.* circumcise. 7:23
it was the *sabbath-d.* when.   9:14
remain on cross on *sabbath-d.* 19:31
read every *sabbath-d.*   Acts 13:27
15:21
next *sabbath-d.* came almost. 13:44

same day

the *same d.* were the.   Gen 7:11
the self-*same d.* entered Noah.   13
in that *same d.* the Lord.   15:18
same d. I brought.   Ex 12:17, 51
flesh eaten that *same d. Lev 7:15, 16*
19:6; 22:30
no parched corn till *same d.* 23:14
do no work in that *same d.*   28
not be afflicted in that *same d.* 29
his head that *same d.*   Num 6:11
to Moses that *same d. Deut 32:48*
same d. king hallowed. *1 Ki 8:64*
a sign the *same d.* saying.   13:3
defiled my sanctuary, *same d.*
Ezek 23:38, 39
same d. king of Babylon set himself
against Jerusalem *same d.* 24:2
same d. will I punish.   Zeph 1:9
and come the *same d.*   Zech 6:10
the *same d.* Lot went.   Luke 17:29
same d. Pilate and Herod.   23:12
and on the *same d.* was.   John 5:9
same d. at evening, Jesus.   20:19
unto the *same d.* that he. Acts 1:22
same d. were added to church. 2:41

since the day

since the *d.* they were.   Ex 10:6
since the *d.* that God.   Deut 4:32
since the *d.* that I brought them.
1 Sam 8:8; 1 Ki 8:16; 1 Chr 17:5
since the *day* that she left. 2 Ki 8:6
since the *d.* your fathers.   Jer 7:25
as in you, since the *d.*   Col 1:6
since the *d.* we heard it, do not.   9

that day

I will sever in *that d.* land. Ex 8:22
east-wind on land all *that d.* 10:13
that d. thou seest my face, thou. 28
shalt shew thy son in *that d.* 13:8
Lord saved Israel *that d.*   14:30
fell of the people *that d.*   32:28
that d. shall the priest. Lev 16:30

not keep passover *that d. Num* 9:6
held his peace *that d.*   30:14
your children in *that d.*   Deut 1:39
in any wise bury him *that d.* 21:23
hide my face in *that d.*   31:18
that d. they compassed.   Josh 6:15
heardest in *that d.* how.   14:12
fasted *that d.* Judg 20:26; 1 Sam 7:6
cry out in *that d.* and Lord will not
hear you in *that d.*   1 Sam 8:18
did eat with Samuel *that d.*   9:24
signs came to pass *that d.*   10:9
sent thunder and rain *that d.* 12:18
Lord saved Israel *that d.*   14:23
he answered him not *that d.*   37
of Lord on David from *that d.* 16:13
Saul eyed David from *that d.* 18:9
afraid of Lord *that d.*   2 Sam 6:9
abode in Jerusalem *that d.*   11:12
cut off Jeroboam *that d. 1 Ki* 14:14
thou shalt see on *that d. 2 Chr 18:24*
to *that d.* Israel had not.   Neh 8:17
ready against *that d. Esth 3:14; 8:13*
let *that d.* be darkness.   Job 3:4
in *that very d.* his.   Ps 146:4
shall be exalted *that d. Isa 2:11, 17*
he remain at Nob *that d.*   10:32
Egyptians know Lord *that d.* 19:21
in *that d.* the Lord shall.   24:21
in *that d.* shall this song be.   26:1
in *that d.* shall the deaf hear. 29:18
they shall know in *that d.*   52:6
accomplished in *that d.*   Jer 39:16
I will deliver thee in *that d.*   17
in *that d.* Israel shall be. Ezek 29:21
in *that d.* there shall be a.   38:19
know I am Lord from *that d.* 39:22
name of city from *that d.*   48:35
in *that d.* will I make.   Hos 2:18
in *that d.* mountains shall. Joel 3:18
flee away naked in *that d.* Amos 2:16
songs be howlings in *that d.*   8:3
shall I not in *that d.* destroy ? Ob 8
that d. is a day of wrath. Zeph 1:15
joined to Lord in *that d.* Zech 2:11
God shall save them in *that d.* 9:16
my covenant broken in *that d.* 11:11
the feeble at *that d.* shall be. 12:8
that d. shall be great mourning. 11
that d. shall there be a fountain. 13:1
his feet shall stand *that d.*   14:4
in *that d.* shall there be one Lord. 9
that d. when I make up.   Mal 3:17
many will say in *that d.*   Mat 7:22
of *that d.* knoweth no man.   24:36
Mark 13:32
that d. I drink it new.   Mat 26:29
Mark 14:25
rejoice ye in *that d.*   Luke 6:23
more tolerable in *that d.*   10:12
and so *that d.* come on you. 21:34
that d. was the preparation. 23:54
abode with him *that d.*   John 1:39
from *that d.* they took.   11:53
at *that d.* ye shall know I.   14:20
in *that d.* ye shall ask me.   16:23
that d. ye shall ask in my name. 26
that d. should overtake. *1 Thes 5:4*
testimony was believed in *that d.*
2 Thes 1:10
that d. shall not come, except. 2:3
to him against *that d.*   2 Tim 1:12
find mercy of Lord in *that d.*   18
Lord shall give me at *that d.*   4:8

this day

driven me out *this d.*   Gen 4:14
send me good speed *this d.* 24:12
sell me *this d.* thy birthright. 25:31
swear *this d.* and he sware.   33
I remember my faults *this d.* 41:9
fed me all my life to *this d.* 48:15
this d. shall be for a.   Ex 12:14
therefore observe *this d.* in.   17
remember *this d.* in which. 13:3, 4
this d. as the stars of.   Deut 1:10
this d. will I begin to put dread. 2:25
alive every one *this d.*   4:4; 5:3
I command thee *this d.*   4:40; 6:6
7:11; 8:1, 11; 10:13; 30:2, 8
this d. that God doth talk.   5:24
it is at *this d.* 6:24; 8:18; Ezra 9:7
testify against you *this d. Deut 8:19*
I command you *this d.* 11:8, 13, 27
28; 13:18; 15:5; 19:9; 27:1, 4

set before you this d. Deut 11:32
all things ye do here this d. 12:8
avouched this d. the Lord. 26:17
this d. thou art become people. 27:9
you ears to hear to this d. 29:4
ye stand this d. all of you. 10
whose heart turneth away this d. 18
before thee this d. life. 30:15, 19
I commanded thee this d. to. 16
yet alive with you this d. 31:27
knoweth his sepulchre to this d. 34:6
this d. will I begin to. Josh 3:7
twelve stones there unto this d. 4:9
Lord shall trouble thee this d. 7:25
now I am this d. eighty-five. 14:10
I am as strong this d. as when. 11
to turn away this d. from. 22:16
not cleansed till this d. 17
save us not this d. 22
cleave to Lord as unto this d. 23:8
choose you this d. whom ye. 24:15
Luz is name unto this d. Judg 1:26
us only, we pray thee, this d. 10:15
Israel came up out of Egypt to this d.
19:30; 1 Sam 8:8; 2 Sam 7:6
2 Ki 21:15; 1 Chr 17:5; Jer 7:25
are witnesses this d. Ruth 4:9, 10
have this d. rejected. 1 Sam 10:19
man be put to death this d. 11:13
hath wrought with God this d. 14:45
rent kingdom from thee this d. 15:28
I defy armies of Israel this d. 17:10
thou shalt this d. be my. 18:21
it were sanctified this d. in. 21:5
lie in wait as at this d. 22:8, 13
Lord which sent thee this d. 25:32
who kept me this d. from. 33
precious in thine eyes this d. 26:21
thy life was much set by this d. 24
ordinance for Israel to this d. 30:25
I am this d. weak. 2 Sam 3:39
sojourners unto this d. 4:3
his commands as at this d. 1 Ki 8:61
this d. is a day of good. 2 Ki 7:9
this d. do after former. 17:34, 41
there it is unto this d. 2 Chr 5:9
come not against thee this d. 35:21
we are servants this d. Neh 9:36
thou art my Son, this d. have I.
Ps 2:7; Acts 13:33; Heb 1:5
this is the d. which the Lord. 118:24
they continue this d. 119:91
this d. have I paid vows. Pr 7:14
made known to thee this d. 22:19
praise thee, as I do this d. Isa 38:19
to-morrow shall be as this d. 56:12
a curse, as at this d. Jer 25:18
44:22
for to this d. they drink none. 35:14
days of Josiah even to this d. 36:2
not humbled even unto this d. 44:10
certainly this is the d. Lam 2:16
this is the d. whereof. Ezek 39:8
of faces, as at this d. Dan 9:7
consider from this d. Hag 2:15, 18
from this d. will I bless you. 19
this d. our daily bread. Mat 6:11
have remained to this d. 11:23
field of blood to this d. 27:8
suffered many things this d. 19
reported among Jews to this d. 28:15
to you is born this d. Luke 2:11
this d. is this scripture. 4:21
this d. is salvation come to. 19:9
hadst known, in this thy d. 42
cock not crow this d. before. 22:34
his sepulchre is with us to this d.
Acts 2:29
as ye are all this d. 22:3
before God till this d. 23:1
in question by you this d. 24:21
unto this d. witnessing to. 26:22
I would all that hear me this d. 29
not hear unto this d. Rom 11:8
till this d. remaineth. 2 Cor 3:14, 15

to-day
heard I of it but to-d. Gen 21:26
pass through all thy flock to-d. 30:32
look ye so sadly to-d.? 40:7
are come so soon to-d.? Ex 2:18
salvation he will shew to-d. 14:13
bake that which you will to-d. 16:23*
consecrate yourselves to-d. 32:29

for to-d. the Lord will. Lev 9:4
command thee this to-d. Deut 15:15
he may establish thee to-d. 29:13
Lord smitten us to-d.? 1 Sam 4:3
to-d. Lord wrought salvation. 11:13
the Lord had delivered thee to-d.
into mine hand. 24:10; 26:23
glorious was king to-d.! 2 Sam 6:20
to-d. shall house of Israel. 16:3
shew myself to him to-d. 1 Ki 18:15
enquire at word of Lord to-d. 22:5
2 Chr 18:4
thou go to him to-d.? 2 Ki 4:23
son that we may eat him to-d. 6:28
to-d. is my complaint. Job 23:2
to-d. if ye will hear his voice.
Ps 95:7; Heb 3:7, 15; 4:7
to-d. do I declare. Zech 9:12
grass of field, which to-d. is, and.
Mat 6:30; Luke 12:28
son, go work to-d. in. Mat 21:28
seen strange things to-d. Luke 5:26
behold, I do cures to-d. and. 13:32
I must walk to-d. and the day. 33
for to-d. I must abide at thy. 19:5
to-d. shalt thou be with me. 23:43
besides all this, to-d. is the. 24:21
while it is called to-d. Heb 3:13
thou art my Son, to-d. have I. 5:5
Christ, same yesterday, to-d. 13:8
ye that say, to-d. or. Jas 4:13

day to day
why art thou lean from day to d.?
2 Sam 13:4
shew from day to d. his salvation.
1 Chr 16:23; Ps 96:2
cast the lot from day to d. Esth 3:7
vexed righteous soul from day to d.
2 Pet 2:8

day of trouble
is a d. of trouble. 2 Ki 19:3
Isa 37:3
hear thee in d. of trouble. Ps 20:1
call upon me in d. of trouble. 50:15
my refuge in d. of trouble. 59:16
in the d. of trouble I sought. 77:2
in d. of trouble I will call on. 86:7
it is a d. of trouble, and. Isa 22:5
in the d. of trouble they. Jer 51:2
time is come, d. of trouble. Ezek 7:7
strong hold in d. of trouble. Nah 1:7
might rest in d. of trouble. Hab 3:16
that day is a d. of trouble. Zeph 1:15

days
after 150 d. waters were. Gen 8:3
d. of mourning for my father. 27:41
the d. of my pilgrimage are. 47:9
when the d. of his mourning. 50:4
after the number of the d. ye. Num 14:34
ask now of the d. past. Deut 4:32
I stayed in the mount forty d. 10:10
camest not within d. 1 Sam 13:11
and the d. were not expired. 18:26
been with me these d. 29:3
the d. David reigned. 1 Ki 2:11
house built to Lord till those d. 3:2
d. that Jeroboam reigned. 14:20
war all their d. 30
between Asa and Baasha all their d.
15:16, 32
into the hand of Ben-hadad all their
d. 2 Ki 13:3
to those d. Israel did burn. 18:4
from d. of the judges. 23:22
David old and full of d. 1 Chr 23:1
d. are on earth as. 29:15; Job 8:9
died full of d. riches. 1 Chr 29:28
Jehoiada was old and full of d.
2 Chr 24:15
d. Esar-haddon brought us. Ezra 4:2
since d. of our fathers have we. 9:7
and mourned certain d. Neh 1:4
since d. of Jeshua, son of. 8:17
as the d. whereon the. Esth 9:22
they called these d. Purim. 26
these d. should be remembered. 28
let it not be joined to the d. Job 3:6
are not his d. also like the d.? 7:1
in length of d. understanding. 12:12
they spend their d. in wealth. 21:13
the d. of affliction have taken. 30:16
the d. of affliction prevented me. 27
I said, d. should speak, and. 32:7

he shall return to the d. of. Job 33:25
they shall spend their d. in. 36:11
Job died, old and full of d. 42:17
gavest me length of d. Ps 21:4
the Lord knoweth the d. of. 37:18
work thou didst in their d. 44:1
not live out half their d. 55:23
I have considered the d. of old. 77:5
did he consume in vanity. 78:33
his throne as d. of heaven. 89:29
the d. of his youth hast thou. 45
all our d. are passed away in. 90:9
of our years threescore and. 10
so teach us to number our d. 12
and be glad all our d. 14
give him rest from the d. 94:13
how many are the d. of thy? 119:84
I remember the d. of old. 143:5
length of d. shall they add. Pr 3:2
length of d. is in her right hand. 16
not much remember d. of. Eccl 5:20
the cause that the former d. 7:10
shall abide with him the d. 8:15
him remember d. of darkness. 11:8
while the evil d. come not. 12:1
antiquity is of ancient d. Isa 23:7
according to d. of one king. 15
the d. of thy mourning shall. 60:20
no more thence an infant of d. 65:20
as the d. of a tree are the d. 22
forgotten me d. without. Jer 2:32
with him that is full of d. 6:11
after those d. I will put my. 31:33
from the d. of Josiah even to. 36:2
our d. are fulfilled, our. Lam 4:18
to number of the d. Ezek 4:4; 5:9
d. are at hand, and effect. 12:23
not remembered d. of youth. 16:22
43
unto 2300 d. sanctuary. Dan 8:14*
abomination set up, 1290 d. 12:11
blessed that waiteth to 1335 d. 12
I will visit on her the d. Hos 2:13
d. of visitation, d. of recompence. 9:7
sinned from d. of Gibeah. 10:9
according to d. of thy coming. 7:15
since those d. were. Hag 2:16*
ye that hear in these d. Zech 8:9
before these d. there was no. 10
I will not be as in former d. 11
so have I thought in these d. 15
from d. of our fathers even. Mal 3:7
from d. of John the. Mat 11:12
except those d. should be shortened.
24:22; Mark 13:20
as d. of Noe, so shall the coming.
Mat 24:37
after those d. Elisabeth. Luke 1:24
these be the d. of vengeance. 21:22
likewise foretold of these d.
Acts 3:24
for before these d. rose up. 5:36
in these d. came prophets. 11:27
the d. of unleavened bread. 12:3
sailed after d. of unleavened. 20:6
which before these d. madest. 21:38
ye observed d. and. Gal 4:10
because the d. are evil. Eph 5:16
neither beginning of d. nor. Heb 7:3
to remembrance former d. 10:32
would see good d. let. 1 Pet 3:10
shall prophesy 1260 d. in. Rev 11:3
should feed her there 1260 d. 12:6

see David, last, old, journey

all the days
dust shalt thou eat all the d.
Gen 3:14
all the d. Adam lived 930 years. 5:5
all the d. of Seth 912 years. 8
all the d. of Enos 905 years. 11
all the d. of Cainan 910 years. 14
all the d. of Enoch 365 years. 23
all the d. of Methuselah 969. 27
all the d. of Noah 950 years. 9:29
all the d. wherein plague. Lev 13:46
all the d. of her issue. 15:25, 26
all the d. of his separation. Num 6:4
5, 6, 8
from thy heart all the d. Deut 4:9
to fear me all the d. 10; 1 Ki 8:40
to possess it all the d. ye. 4:40
served Lord all the d. of Joshua and
all the d. Josh 24:31; Judg 2:7

delivered them all the d.   Judg 2:18
him to Lord all d. of.   1 Sam 1:11
against Philistines all the d.   7:13
Samuel judged Israel all the d.   15
dwelt safely all the d.   1 Ki 4:25
Rezon was adversary all the d. 11:25
oppressed Israel all the d. 2 Ki 13:22
nor in all the d. of kings of.   23:22
all the d. of Jehoiada. 2 Chr 24:2, 14
their purposes all the d.   Ezra 4:5
all the d. of my appointed. Job 14:14
mercy shall follow me all the d.
                                    Ps 23:6
in the house of Lord all the d. 27:4
all the d. of afflicted are.   Pr 15:15
not evil, all the d. of her life. 31:12
in holiness all the d.   Luke 1:75

see his **life**, thy **life**

days come

bring d. that have not come. Isa 7:17
behold the d. come.   Jer 23:5, 7
            30:3; 31:27, 31, 38
d. come that he will.   Amos 4:2
d. shall come when bridegroom.
    Mat 9:15; Mark 2:20; Luke 5:35
d. come when ye shall. Luke 17:22
d. come thy enemies shall.   19:43
d. come in which there shall.   21:6
d. come when I will make. Heb 8:8

few days

abide with us a few d.   Gen 24:55
tarry a few d. till thy.   27:44
seemed to him but a few d.   29:20
few and evil are the d. of.   47:9
cloud was a few d. on.   Num 9:20
born of woman is of few d. Job 14:1
let his d. be few.   Ps 109:8
within few d. he shall be. Dan 11:20
for a few d. chastened.   Heb 12:10

his days

his d. shall be 120 years.   Gen 6:3
in his d. was earth divided.   10:25
                                1 Chr 1:19
her away all his d.   Deut 22:19, 29
Asa was perfect all his d.
    1 Ki 15:14; 2 Chr 15:17
in his d. did Hiel build.   1 Ki 16:34
not bring the evil in his d.   21:29
in his d. Edom revolted.   2 Ki 8:20
                                2 Chr 21:8
Jehoash did right all his d. 2 Ki 12:2
he departed not all his d.   15:18
quietness to Israel in his d.
                                1 Chr 22:9
all his d. departed.   2 Chr 34:33
his d. are determined.   Job 14:5
travaileth with pain all his d. 15:20
know him not see his d.?   24:1
in his d. shall righteous.   Ps 72:7
as for man, his d. are as.   103:15
his d. are as a shadow.   144:4
covetousness prolong his d. Pr 28:16
all his d. are sorrows.   Eccl 2:23
all his d. also he eateth in.   5:17
though his d. be prolonged.   8:12
wicked shall not prolong his d.   13
that hath not filled his d. Isa 65:20
leave them in midst of his d.
                                Jer 17:11
that shall not prosper in his d. 22:30
in his d. Judah shall be saved. 23:6

in the days

Reuben went in the d.   Gen 30:14
in the d. of Shamgar, in the d.
                                Judg 5:6
quietness 40 years in the d.   8:28
old man in the d. of.   1 Sam 17:12
famine in the d. of.   2 Sam 21:1
put to death in the d. of harvest, in
    the first d. in beginning of.   9
silver was nothing accounted of in
    the d. of. 1 Ki 10:21; 2 Chr 9:20
remained in the d. of Asa.
                                1 Ki 22:46
in the d. of Hezekiah.   1 Chr 4:41
enquired not at it in the d. of. 13:3
sought God in the d. of. 2 Chr 26:5
came not on them in the d.   32:26
in the d. when God.   Job 29:2
as I was in the d. of my youth.   4
in the d. of famine.   Ps 37:19
should I fear in the d. of evil? 49:5

in the d. to come shall.   Eccl 2:16
thy heart cheer thee in the d.   11:9
remember thy Creator in the d. 12:1
Micah prophesied in the d. Jer 26:18
Jerusalem remembered in the d.
                                    Lam 1:7
my covenant in the d.   Ezek 16:60
or hands be strong in the d.   22:14
in the d. of these kings. Dan 2:44
in the d. of thy father, light.   5:11
shall sing as in the d.   Hos 2:15
deeply corrupted as in the d.   9:9
to dwell, as in the d. of the.   12:9
hath this been in the d.?   Joel 1:2
Jesus was born in the d.   Mat 2:1
if we had been in the d. of.   23:30
for as in the d. that were.   24:38
the house of God in the d. Mark 2:26*
dealt with me in the d.   Luke 1:25
many widows were in the d.   4:25
as in the d. of Noe.   17:26
in the d. of Lot.   28
rose up Judas in the d. of. Acts 5:37
came to pass in the d. of.   11:28
who in the d. of his flesh. Heb 5:7
waited in the d. of Noah. 1 Pet 3:20
in the d. of the voice.   Rev 10:7
that it rain not in the d. of.   11:6

in those days

giants in earth in those d. Gen 6:4
judge in those d. Deut 17:9; 19:17
priest that shall be in those d. 26:3
in those d. there was no king in.
        Judg 17:6; 18:1; 21:25
ark of God there in those d. 20:27
word precious in those d. 1 Sam 3:1
counselled in those d. 2 Sam 16:23
in those d. was Hezekiah sick unto.
    2 Ki 20:1; 2 Chr 32:24; Isa 38:1
in those d. shall Judah. Jer 33:16
in those d. Israel shall go up. 50:4
in those d. iniquity shall.   50:20
in those d. will I pour out my Spirit.
            Joel 2:29; Acts 2:18
give suck in those d.   Mat 24:19
            Mark 13:17; Luke 21:23
Mary arose in those d.   Luke 1:39
one of those d. as he taught. 20:1
made a calf in those d.   Acts 7:41
not denied faith in those d. Rev 2:13
in those d. shall men seek.   9:6

latter days

to thy people in latter d. Num 24:14
latter d. if thou turn.   Deut 4:30
evil befall you in latter d.   31:29
latter d. consider. Jer 23:20; 30:24
captivity of Moab in latter d. 48:47
captivity of Elam in latter d. 49:39
people in the latter d. Ezek 38:16
what shall be in latter d. Dan 2:28
befall thy people in latter d. 10:14
fear Lord in latter d.   Hos 3:5

many days

mourned for son many d. Gen 37:34
brethren these many d.   Josh 22:3
at Jerusalem many d.   1 Ki 2:38
her house, did eat many d.   17:15
Ephraim mourned many d. 1 Chr 7:22
what man loveth many d.? Ps 34:12
how many are the d. of ?   Eccl 6:3
d. of his years be many.   11:1
shalt find it after many d.
        Isa 24:22; Ezek 38:8
many d. and years shall ye. Isa 32:10
continue many d. Jer 32:14; 35:7
remained there many d.   37:16
the vision is for many d. Ezek 12:27
                                Dan 8:26; 10:14
captivity spoil many d. Dan 11:33
abide for me many d.   Hos 3:3
Israel shall abide many d.   4
not many d. after.   Luke 15:13
continued not many d.   John 2:12
Holy Ghost, not many d. Acts 1:5
he was seen many d. of.   13:31
this did she many d.   16:18
nor sun nor stars in many d. 27:20

my days

me my wife, for my d.   Gen 29:21
and truth be in my d.   2 Ki 20:19
my d. are swifter than a.   Job 7:6
for my d. are vanity.   16

now my d. are swifter than. Job 9:25
are not my d. few ? cease then. 10:20
my d. are extinct, graves are. 17:1
my d. are past, my purposes.   11
shall multiply my d. as sand. 29:18
and measure of my d.   Ps 39:4
hast made my d. as an hand-breadth.
                                    5
for my d. are consumed like. 102:3
my d. are like a shadow that.   11
he shortened my d.   23
take not away in midst of my d. 24
in cutting off of my d.   Isa 38:10
peace and truth in my d.   39:8
my d. shall be consumed. Jer 20:18

now-a-**days**

many servants now-a-d. break.
                                1 Sam 25:10

prolong, -ed, -eth, **days**

ye shall not prolong your d.
                                Deut 4:26; 30:18
thou mayest prolong d. 4:40; 22:7
that thy d. be prolonged. 5:16; 6:2
prolong your d. in land. 5:33; 11:9
end that he may prolong d.   17:20
ye shall prolong your d. in.   32:47
fear of Lord prolongeth d. Pr 10:27
covetousness, prolong his d. 28:16
sinner's d. be prolonged.   Eccl 8:12
neither wicked prolong his d.   13
d. shall not be prolonged. Isa 13:22
seed, he shall prolong his d. 53:10
d. are prolonged, vision. Ezek 12:22

sabbath-**days**

how on the sabbath-d.   Mat 12:5
is it lawful to heal on sabbath-d.? 10
to do well on the sabbath-d.   12
do good on sabbath-d.   Mark 3:4
                                    Luke 6:9
taught them on sabbath-d. Luke 4:31
not lawful to do on sabbath-d.   6:2
three sabbath-d. reasoned. Acts 17:2
in respect of sabbath-d.   Col 2:16

thy days

honour thy father and thy mother,
    that thy d. may be.   Ex 20:12
the number of thy d. I will.   23:26
prosperity all thy d.   Deut 23:6
thy d. may be lengthened.   25:15
and the length of thy d.   30:20
thy d. approach that thou.   31:14
and as thy d. so shall thy.   33:25
evil not found all thy d. 1 Sam 25:28
and when thy d. be.   2 Sam 7:12
any like thee all thy d.   1 Ki 3:13
then I will lengthen thy d.   14
in thy d. I will not do it.   11:12
I will add to thy d. 15 years.
                2 Ki 20:6; Isa 38:5
when thy d. be expired. 1 Chr 17:11
thy d. as the days of man. Job 10:5
morning since thy d.?   38:12
the number of thy d. is great.   21
for by me thy d. shall be. Pr 9:11
thou hast caused thy d. Ezek 22:4

two days

sixth day bread of two d.   Ex 16:29
whether it were two d. Num 9:22
not eat one, nor two d. nor. 11:19
David had abode two d. 2 Sam 1:1
work of one day or two d. Ezra 10:13
would keep these two d. Esth 9:27
after two d. will he revive. Hos 6:2
after two d. is the feast. Mat 26:2
                                Mark 14:1
he abode there two d.   John 4:40
now after two d. he departed.   43
he abode two d. still in the.   11:6

three days

branches are three d.   Gen 40:12
within three d. shall Pharaoh. 13, 19
three baskets are three d.   18
into ward three d.   42:17
let us go three d. journey to sacri-
    fice. Ex 3:18; 5:3; 8:27; 15:22
darkness in Egypt three d.   10:22
rose any from place for three d. 23
three d. ye shall pass.   Josh 1:11
hide yourselves three d.   2:16, 22
abode with him three d. Judg 19:4
asses lost three d. ago. 1 Sam 9:20
kept from us these three d.   21:5

had eaten no bread *three d.*
         1 Sam 30:12
master left me, because *three d.* 13
assembled men of Judah in *three d.*
         2 Sam 20:4
there be *three d.*' pestilence. 24:13
         1 Chr 21:12
depart for *three d.*   *1 Ki* 12:5
         2 Chr 10:5
sought him *three d.*   *2 Ki* 2:17
were *three d.* gathering. *2 Chr* 20:25
abode in tents *three d.*   *Ezra* 8:15
would not come in *three d.* 10:8, 9
eat nor drink *three d.*   *Esth* 4:16
Jonah was in belly of fish *three d.*
     Jonah 1:17; *Mat* 12:40
they continue with me now *three d.*
     Mat 15:32; *Mark* 8:2
build it in *three d. Mat* 26:61; 27:40
     Mark 14:58; 15:29; *John* 2:19
after *three d.* I will rise again.
     Mat 27:63; *Mark* 8:31
after *three d.* found him. *Luke* 2:46
three d. without sight.   *Acts* 9:9
Publius lodged us *three d.*   28:7
their dead bodies *three d. Rev* 11:9
after *three d.* and an half.   11

four days
lament *four d.*   *Judg* 11:40
lain in grave *four d.*   *John* 11:17
he hath been dead *four d.*   39
four d. ago I was fasting. *Acts* 10:30

five days
nor *five d.* nor ten d.   *Num* 11:19
came to Troas in *five d. Acts* 20:6
after *five d.* Ananias the high. 24:1

six days
six d. ye shall gather it.   *Ex* 16:26
six d. shalt thou labour and do all.
    20:9; 23:12; 34:21; *Deut* 5:13
six d. Lord made heaven.
     Ex 20:11; 31:17
cloud covered Sinai *six d.*   24:16
six d. may work be done.   31:15
     35:2; *Lev* 23:3
six d. shalt thou eat.   *Deut* 16:8
thus shalt thou do *six d.*   *Josh* 6:3
so they did *six d.*   14
gate shut *six* working *d. Ezek* 46:1
six d. in which men.   *Luke* 13:14
Jesus *six d.* before.   *John* 12:1

seven days
yet *seven d.* I will cause. *Gen* 7:4
stayed yet other *seven d.* 8:10, 12
Joseph mourned *seven d.*   50:10
seven d. eat unleavened.   *Ex* 12:15
   13:6, 7; 23:15; 34:18; *Lev* 23:6
     Num 28:17; *Deut* 16:3
seven d. no leaven be found.
     Ex 12:19; *Deut* 16:4
seven d. with the dam.   *Ex* 22:30
     Lev 22:27
priest shall put them on *seven d.*
     Ex 29:30
seven d. shalt thou consecrate.
     Lev 8:33
seven d. shalt make an atonement.
     Ex 29:37
shall be unclean *seven d. Lev* 12:2
then priest shall shut him up *seven d.*
    13:5, 21, 26, 33, 50, 54
abroad out of tent *seven d.*   14:8
shall be put apart *seven d.*   15:19
offering by fire to Lord *seven d.* 23:8
keep a feast to the Lord *seven d.*
    23:39, 40, 41; *Num* 29:12
be ashamed *seven d.? Num* 12:14
shall be unclean *seven d.*   19:14
of tabernacles *seven d. Deut* 16:13
it to me within *seven d. Judg* 14:8
wept before him *seven d.*   17
seven d. shalt thou tarry till I come.
     1 Sam 10:8
give us *seven d.*' respite.   11:3
he tarried *seven d.* according. 13:8
fasted *seven d.* 31:13; *1 Chr* 10:12
feast before Lord *seven d. 1 Ki* 8:65
Zimri did reign *seven d.* in. 16:15
of altar *seven d.*   *2 Chr* 7:9
kept the feast of unleavened bread
   seven d. 30:21; 35:17; *Ezra* 6:22
to keep other *seven d. 2 Chr* 30:23
a feast *seven d.*   *Esth* 1:5

as the light of *seven d. Isa* 30:26
astonished *seven d.*   *Ezek* 3:15
seven d. shall they purge.   43:26
were compassed *seven d. Heb* 11:30

eight days
he that is *eight d.* old shall be circumcised.   *Gen* 17:12; 21:4
sanctify house in *eight d. 2 Chr* 29:17
when *eight d.* were accomplished.
     Luke 2:21
after *eight d.* Jesus.   *John* 20:26

ten days
not eat *ten d.* nor.   *Num* 11:19
ten d. after Lord smote. *1 Sam* 25:38
once in *ten d.* store of.   *Neh* 5:18
after *ten d.* word of Lord. *Jer* 42:7
prove thy servants *ten d. Dan* 1:12
at the end of *ten d.* their.   15
tarried more than *ten d. Acts* 25:6
have tribulation *ten d.*   *Rev* 2:10

eleven days
eleven d.' journey.   *Deut* 1:2

twelve days
there are but *twelve d. Acts* 24:11

fourteen days
held a feast *fourteen d.*   *1 Ki* 8:65

fifteen days
abode with Peter *fifteen d. Gal* 1:18

twenty days
not eat flesh *twenty d. Num* 11:19

twenty-one days
withstood me *twenty-one d.*
     Dan 10:13

thirty days
for Aaron *thirty d.*   *Num* 20:29
wept for Moses *thirty d. Deut* 34:8
to king these *thirty d.*   *Esth* 4:11
petition for *thirty d.*   *Dan* 6:7, 12

thirty-three days
purifying *thirty-three d.*   *Lev* 12:4

forty days
to rain on earth *forty d.*   *Gen* 7:4
forty d. were fulfilled for.   50:3
in mount *forty d.* and *forty* nights.
   Ex 24:18; 34:28; *Deut* 9:9; 10:10
returned after *forty d. Num* 13:25
     14:34
before the Lord *forty d. Deut* 9:25
strength of meat *forty d. 1 Ki* 19:8
iniquity of Judah *forty d. Ezek* 4:6
forty d. and Nineveh be. *Jonah* 3:4
fasted *forty d.* and forty.   *Mat* 4:2
Jesus was *forty d.* in the wilderness.
     Mark 1:13; *Luke* 4:2
seen of them *forty d.*   *Acts* 1:3

fifty-two days
wall was finished in *fifty-two d.*
     Neh 6:15

your days
that *your d.* may be.   *Deut* 11:21
to cease in *your d.* mirth. *Jer* 16:9
all *your d.* ye shall dwell in.   35:7
your d. will I say word. *Ezek* 12:25
hath this been in *your d.? Joel* 1:2
work a work in *your d.*   *Hab* 1:5
     Acts 13:41

daysman
neither is there any *d.*   *Job* 9:33

dayspring
caused the *d.* to know.   *Job* 38:12
d. from on high visited. *Luke* 1:78

daystar
and the *d.* arise in.   *2 Pet* 1:19

daytime
meet with darkness in *d. Job* 5:14
through houses marked in *d.* 24:16
I cry in the *d.* but thou.   *Ps* 22:2
command loving-kindness in *d.* 42:8
in *d.* also he led them.   78:14
tabernacle for shadow in *d. Isa* 4:6
I stand on watch-tower in *d.* 21:8
in *d.* he was teaching in. *Luke* 21:37
it pleasure to riot in *d. 2 Pet* 2:13

deacon, -s
saints with bishops and *d. Phil* 1:1
d. must be grave.   *1 Tim* 3:8
let them use the office of a *d.* 10, 13
d. be the husband of one wife. 12

dead
[1] *Deprived of natural life*, Ruth
1:8 ; Job 1:19. [2] *Without warmth
or fervour, or energy in the spiritual
life*, Eph 2:1 ; 1 Tim 5:6. [3]
Entirely without life, Isa 8:19;
Mat 22:32.

thou art but a *d.* man.   *Gen* 20:3
Abraham stood up from his *d.* 23:3
the men are *d.* which.   *Ex* 4:19
not one of Israelites' cattle *d.* 9:7
house where was not one *d.* 12:30
Egyptians said, we be all *d.* men. 33
Israel saw Egyptians *d.* on. 14:30
the *d.* beast shall be his. 21:34, 36
and the *d.* ox also they shall.   35
thing unclean by the *d. Lev* 22:4
whosoever is defiled by *d. Num* 5:2
let her not be as one *d.*   12:12
he stood between the *d.* and. 16:48
wife of the *d.* not marry. *Deut* 25:5
lord was fallen down *d. Judg* 3:25
he came in, Sisera lay *d.*   4:22
the *d.* which Samson slew. 16:30
as ye heard dealt with *d. Ruth* 1:8
to raise up name of the *d.*   4:5
and Phinehas are *d.*   *1 Sam* 4:17
father-in-law and husband were *d.* 19
thou pursue ? after a *d.* dog. 24:14
Saul and his sons were *d.*   31:7
     1 Chr 10:7
on such a *d.* dog as I. *2 Sam* 9:8
all the king's sons are *d.*   13:33
why should this *d.* dog curse. 16:9
my father's house were but *d.* 19:28
the living is my son, and the *d.* is
   thy son.   *1 Ki* 3:22, 23
when I am *d.* bury me in.   13:31
Naboth is not alive but *d.*   21:15
on young men, they are *d. Job* 1:19
d. things are formed from.   26:5
forgotten as a *d.* man.   *Ps* 31:12
and horse are cast into *d.*   76:6
free among the *d.* like slain. 88:5
wilt thou shew wonders to *d.?* 10
ate the sacrifices of the *d.* 106:28
the *d.* praise not the Lord. 115:17
those that have been long *d.* 143:3
and her paths unto the *d. Pr* 2:18
he knoweth not that the *d.* 9:18
remain in congregation of *d.* 21:16
the *d.* which are already *d. Eccl* 4:2
and after that they go to the *d.* 9:3
living dog is better than *d.* lion. 4
the *d.* know not any thing.   5
d. flies cause the ointment. 10:1
for the living to the *d.*   *Isa* 8:19
it stirreth up the *d.* for thee. 14:9
not slain with sword, nor *d.* 22:2
they are *d.*, they shall not live. 26:14
d. men shall live, with my *d.* 19
desolate places as *d.* men. 59:10
they that be *d.* of old.   *Lam* 3:6
come at no *d.* person. *Ezek* 44:25
are *d.* that sought the.   *Mat* 2:20
and let the *d.* bury their *d.* 8:22
give place, for the maid is not *d.*
   9:24; *Mark* 5:39; *Luke* 8:52
heal sick, raise the *d.*   *Mat* 10:8
deaf hear, *d.* are raised.   11:5
     Luke 7:22
touching resurrection of the *d.*
    Mat 22:31; *Mark* 12:26
not the God of the *d.* but. *Mat* 22:32
    Mark 12:27; *Luke* 20:38
full of *d.* men's bones. *Mat* 23:27
the keepers became as *d.*   28:4
one *d.* many said, he is *d. Mark* 9:26
if he were already *d.*   15:44
a *d.* man carried out. *Luke* 7:12
departed, leaving him half *d.* 10:30
why seek ye living among *d.?* 24:5
the Father raiseth up *d. John* 5:21
when the *d.* shall hear voice of. 25
did eat manna, and are *d.* 6:49, 58
believeth, though he were *d.* 11:25
patriarch David is both *d. Acts* 2:29
came in and found her *d.*   5:10
ordained of God to be the Judge of
   quick and *d.*   10:42; *2 Tim* 4:1
supposing he had been *d. Acts* 14:19
down, and was taken up *d.* 20:9
that God should raise the *d.* 26:8

swollen, or fallen down *d. Acts* 28:6
God who quickeneth *d. Rom* 4:17
considered not his body now *d.*   19
thro' offence of one many be *d.* 5:15
we that are *d.* to sin, live.   6:2
if we be *d.* with Christ.   8
reckon ye yourselves to be *d.* to.   11
if husband be *d.* 7:2, 3; *1 Cor* 7:39
are become *d.* to the law. *Rom* 7:4
                       Gal 2:19
lord both of *d.* and living. *Rom* 14:9
if so be that *d.* rise not. *1 Cor* 15:15
how are the *d.* raised ?   35
and the *d.* shall be raised.   52
trust in God who raiseth *d. 2 Cor* 1:9
one died for all, then all *d.*   5:14
were *d.* in trespasses and sins.
            Eph 2:1, 5; *Col* 2:13
if ye be *d.* with Christ.   *Col* 2:20
                    2 Tim 2:11
ye are *d.* and your life hid. *Col* 3:3
and the *d.* in Christ.   *1 Thes* 4:16
repentance from *d.* works. *Heb* 6:1
conscience from *d.* works.   9:14
is of force after men are *d.*   17
and by it he being *d.* yet.   11:4
of one, and him as good as *d.*   12
women received their *d.* raised.   35
we being *d.* to sin should. *1 Pet* 2:24
ready to judge the quick and *d.*   4:5
gospel preached to them that are *d.* 6
twice *d.* plucked up by the. *Jude* 12
first-begotten of the *d.*   *Rev* 1:5
saw him, fell at his feet as *d.*   17
name that thou livest, and art *d.* 3:1
blessed are the *d.* who die.   14:13
sea became as blood of *d.*   16:3
rest of the *d.* lived not again. 20:5
saw the *d.* stand before God.   12
sea gave up *d.* which were in it. 13

see body, bury, carcase, resurrection

for the dead
not make cuttings *for d. Lev* 19:28
none be defiled *for the d.*   21:1
not make baldness *for d. Deut* 14:1
not given ought thereof *for d.* 26:14
that mourned *for the d. 2 Sam* 14:2
to comfort them *for the d. Jer* 16:7
weep ye not *for the d.* nor.   22:10
no mourning *for the d. Ezek* 24:17
baptized *for the d.* why baptized *for
the d.?*   *1 Cor* 15:29

from the dead
he is risen *from the d.*   *Mat* 14:2
rising *from the d.* mean ? *Mark* 9:10
if one went *from the d. Luke* 16:30
though one rose *from the d.*   31
rise *from the d.* third day.   24:46
                  John 20:9
after he rose *from d.*   *Acts* 10:41
first that should rise *from d.* 26:23
that are alive *from the d. Rom* 6:13
bring Christ again *from the d.* 10:7
be, but life *from the d.?*   11:15
              1 Cor 15:12
arise *from the d.* Christ.   *Eph* 5:14
first-born *from the d.*   *Col* 1:18
able to raise him *from d. Heb* 11:19
brought again *from the d.*   13:20

see raised, risen

is dead
his brother *is d. Gen* 42:38; 44:20
name of brother that *is d. Deut* 25:6
Moses my servant *is d.*   *Josh* 1:2
they forced, that she *is d. Judg* 20:5
Saul *is d.*   *2 Sam* 2:7; 4:10
Uriah *is d.*   11:21, 24
the child *is d.*   12:18, 19
Amnon only *is d.*   13:32
a widow, my husband *is d.*   14:5
                    2 Ki 4:1
because king's son *is d. 2 Sam* 18:20
Absalom *is d.*   19:10
Naboth *is d.*   *1 Ki* 21:14
priests eat not that *is d. Ezek* 44:31
my daughter *is d.*   *Mat* 9:18
       Mark 5:35; *Luke* 8:49
that many said, he is *d. Mark* 9:26
Abraham *is d.* and.   *John* 8:52, 53
Lazarus *is d.*   11:14

he that *is d.* is freed.   *Rom* 6:7
if Christ be in you, body *is d.* 8:10
law, Christ *is d.* in vain.   *Gal* 2:21
liveth in pleasure, *is d. 1 Tim* 5:6
hath not works *is d. Jas* 2:17, 20*
body without spirit *is d.* so.   26

was dead
when the judge *was d.*   *Judg* 2:19
men saw Abimelech *was d.*   9:55
their champion *was d. 1 Sam* 17:51
David heard Nabal *was d.*   25:39
saw Saul *was d.* 31:5; *1 Chr* 10:5
son heard Abner *was d. 2 Sam* 4:1
Bath-sheba heard husband *was d.*
                     11:26
David perceived child *was d.* 12:19
Amnon, seeing he *was d.*   13:39
my child suck, it *was d. 1 Ki* 3:21
Hadad heard that Joab *was d.* 11:21
Jezebel heard Naboth *was d.* 21:15
when Ahab *was d.* Moab. *2 Ki* 3:5
child *was d.* and laid on his.   4:32
Athaliah saw her son *was d.*   11:1
                 2 Chr 22:10
but when Herod *was d.*   *Mat* 2:19
he that *was d.* sat up.   *Luke* 7:15
to scorn, knowing she *was d.*   8:53
my son *was d.* and is alive.   15:24
for this thy brother *was d.* and is. 32
sister of him that *was d. John* 11:39
and he that *was d.* came forth.   44
saw that Jesus *was d.* brake.   19:33
Jesus which *was d.*   *Acts* 25:19
without the law sin *was d. Rom* 7:8
he that liveth, and was *d. Rev* 1:18

deadly
was a *d.* destruction.   *1 Sam* 5:11
deliver me from *d.* enemies. *Ps* 17:9
groanings of a *d.* wounded man.
                 Ezek 30:24
drink *d.* thing, it shall. *Mark* 16:18
unruly evil, full of *d.*   *Jas* 3:8
d. wound was healed. *Rev* 13:3, 12

deadness
neither yet the *d.* of.   *Rom* 4:19

deaf
or who maketh the *d.?*   *Ex* 4:11
shalt not curse the *d.*   *Lev* 19:14
but I as a *d.* man heard. *Ps* 38:13
they are like the *d.* adder.   58:4
in that day shall *d.* hear. *Isa* 29:18
the ears of the *d.* shall be.   35:5
hear, ye *d.* look, ye blind.   42:18
who is *d.* as my messenger ?   19
bring forth blind, and the *d.*   43:8
their ears shall be *d.*   *Mi* 7:16
the *d.* hear. *Mat* 11:5; *Luke* 7:22
brought one that was *d. Mark* 7:32
he maketh the *d.* to hear.   37
thou dumb and *d.* spirit.   9:25

deal, verb
now will we *d.* worse.   *Gen* 19:9
now if you will *d.* truly.   24:49
return, and I will *d.* well with. 32:9
should he *d.* with our sister ? 34:31
come on, let us *d.* wisely. *Ex* 1:10
d. with her after the manner. 21:9
in like manner *d.* with thy. 21:11
not steal, nor *d.* falsely. *Lev* 19:11
if thou *d.* thus with me. *Num* 11:15
thus shall ye *d.* with.   *Deut* 7:5
as thou didst *d.* with David my
father, even so *d.*   *2 Chr* 2:3
lest I *d.* with you after. *Job* 42:8
I said to fools, *d.* not.   *Ps* 75:4
d. subtilly with his.   105:25
d. bountifully with.   119:17; 142:7
d. with thy servant.   119:124
but they that *d.* truly.   *Pr* 12:22
he will *d.* unjustly.   *Isa* 25:10
my servant shall *d.* prudently. 52:13
is it not to *d.* thy bread to ? 58:7
d. thus with them in.   *Jer* 18:23
if so be that the Lord *d.* with. 21:2
will I also *d.* in fury.   *Ezek* 8:18
I will *d.* with thee as thou. 16:59
hands be strong in days I *d.* 22:14
and they shall *d.* furiously. 23:25
he shall surely *d.* with him. 31:11
and as thou seest *d.*   *Dan* 1:13
and shall *d.* against them and. 11:7

see treacherously

deal
a tenth *d.* of flour.   *Ex* 29:40*
   Lev 14:21*; *Num* 15:4*; 29:1*
a several tenth *d.*   *Num* 28:13*
                     29:15*
so much more a great *d. Mark* 7:36
cried a great *d.* Son of David. 10:48

dealer
the treacherous *d.* dealeth. *Isa* 21:2

dealers
treacherous *d.* have dealt. *Isa* 24:16

dealest
wherefore *d.* thou thus ?   *Ex* 5:15
thee that spoilest and *d.*   *Isa* 33:1

dealeth
thus and thus *d.* Micah. *Judg* 18:4
told me he *d.* subtilly. *1 Sam* 23:22
he becometh poor that *d.*   *Pr* 10:4
every prudent man *d.*   13:16*
that is soon angry *d.* foolishly. 14:17
scorner is his name, who *d.* 21:24*
treacherous dealer *d.*   *Isa* 21:2
from the prophet even to the priest
every one *d.*   *Jer* 6:13; 8:10
God *d.* with you as sons. *Heb* 12:7

dealing, -s
I hear of your evil *d.*   *1 Sam* 2:23
his violent *d.* shall come. *Ps* 7:16
the Jews have no *d.* with. *John* 4:9

deals
(Revised Version, parts of an ephah)
take three tenth *d.* of fine flour.
        Lev 14:10; *Num* 15:9
two tenth *d.* for a meat. *Lev* 23:13
                Num 28:9
two wave-loaves of two tenth *d.*
                Lev 23:17
two tenth *d.* in one cake.   24:5
for a ram two tenth *d.* of flour.
  Num 15:6; 28:20, 28; 29:3, 9, 14
three tenth *d.* 28:20, 28; 29:3, 9, 14

dealt
when Sarai *d.* hardly.   *Gen* 16:6
God hath *d.* graciously with. 33:11
wherefore *d.* ye so ill with me ? 43:6
therefore God *d.* well.   *Ex* 1:20
wherefore hast thou *d.* thus ? 14:11
wherein they *d.* proudly.   18:11
seeing he hath *d.* deceitfully. 21:8
if ye have *d.* well with Jerubbaal.
                Judg 9:16
if ye have *d.* truly, rejoice in.   19
have *d.* with the dead. *Ruth* 1:8
the Almighty hath *d.* bitterly.   20
hast *d.* well with me. *1 Sam* 24:18
Lord shall have *d.* well.   25:31
d. among the people.   *2 Sam* 6:19
                 1 Chr 16:3
they *d.* faithfully. *2 Ki* 12:15; 22:7
Manasseh *d.* with familiar.   21:6
                2 Chr 33:6
so *d.* David with cities. *1 Chr* 20:3
amiss, and *d.* wickedly. *2 Chr* 6:37
Rehoboam *d.* wisely.   11:23
have *d.* very corruptly. *Neh* 1:7
knewest they *d.* proudly. 9:10; 16:29
have *d.* deceitfully.   *Job* 6:15
Lord hath *d.* bountifully. *Ps* 13:6
                   116:7
nor have we *d.* falsely in.   44:17
and *d.* unfaithfully like.   78:57
he hath not *d.* with us.   103:10
hast *d.* well with servant. 119:65
they *d.* perversely with me.   78*
he hath not *d.* so with.   147:20
dealers have *d.* very. *Isa* 24:16
  Jer 3:20; 5:11; 12:6; *Lam* 1:2
they *d.* by oppression. *Ezek* 22:7
Edom hath *d.* against Judah. 25:12
because Philistines have *d.*   15
have *d.* treacherously. *Hos* 5:7
d. treacherously against me.   6:7
of your God that hath *d. Joel* 2:26
Lord thought, so hath he *d. Zech* 1:6
Judah hath *d.* treacherously and.
                  Mal 2:11
thou hast *d.* treacherously.   14
thus hath Lord *d.* with. *Luke* 1:25*
hast thou thus *d.* with us ?   2:48
the same *d.* subtilly with. *Acts* 7:19
multitude of Jews have *d.* 25:24*
according as God hath *d. Rom* 12:3

dear

Ephraim my *d.* son, is he ? *Jer* 31:20
servant, who was *d.* to. *Luke* 7:2
neither count I my life *d. Acts* 20:24
followers of God as *d.* *Eph* 5:1*
of Epaphras our *d.* fellow. *Col* 1:7*
into kingdom of his *d.* Son. 13*
because ye were *d.* unto. *1 Thes* 2:8*

dearly *beloved*

(*In the Revised Versions the word
dearly is omitted in all but the first
of these references*)

given *d. beloved* of my soul to.
Jer 12:7
d. beloved, avenge not. *Rom* 12:19
my *d. beloved.* *1 Cor* 10:14
Phil 4:1; *2 Tim* 1:2
d. beloved. *2 Cor* 7:1; 12:19
1 Pet 2:11
Philemon our *d. beloved. Philem* 1

dearth

d. began to come, *d.* *Gen* 41:54*
there was a *d.* in land. *2 Ki* 4:38
if there be a *d.* in land. *2 Chr* 6:28*
buy corn because of the *d. Neh* 5:3
to Jeremiah concerning a. *Jer* 14:1*
there came a *d.* over. *Acts* 7:11*
there should be a great *d.* 11:28*

death

[1] *Total and final cessation of all
vital functions,* Gen 25:11. [2]
*Cessation of spiritual life, spoken
of as spiritual death,* Rom 7:24;
1 John 3:14. [3] *Used figuratively
for what would cause death,*
2 Ki 4:40. [4] *Gates of death, the
brink of the grave,* Ps 9:13.

let me not see the *d.* of. *Gen* 21:16
comforted after mother's *d.* 24:67
after the *d.* of Abraham, God. 25:11
and bless thee before my *d.* 27:7
bless thee before his *d.* 10:17
take from me this *d.* only. *Ex* 10:17
men die common *d.* of. *Num* 16:29
let me die *d.* of righteous. 23:10
slayer shall abide in it unto *d.* of.
35:25, 28, 32; *Josh* 20:6
life of murderer guilty *d. Num* 35:31
set before you life and good, *d.* and
evil. *Deut* 30:15; *Jer* 21:8
rebel after my *d.!* *Deut* 31:27
I know after my *d.* ye will. 29
blessed Israel before his *d.* 33:1
jeoparded lives to the *d. Judg* 5:18
that his soul was vexed unto *d.* 16:16
dead which he slew at his *d.* 30
if ought but *d.* part thee. *Ruth* 1:17
all thou hast done since *d.* of. 2:11
about time of her *d.* *1 Sam* 4:20
surely the bitterness of *d.* 15:32
but a step between me and *d.* 20:3
I have occasioned *d.* of thy. 22:22
in their *d.* were not. *2 Sam* 1:23
in *d.* or life, there will thy. 15:21
when waves of *d.* compassed me.
22:5; *Ps* 18:4; 116:3
the snares of *d.* prevented me.
2 Sam 22:6; *Ps* 18:5
Egypt till *d.* of Solomon. *1 Ki* 11:40
shall not be any more *d.* *2 Ki* 2:21
man of God, there is *d.* in pot. 4:40
so David prepared before his *d.*
1 Chr 22:5
counsellors after *d.* of. *2 Chr* 22:4
did Hezekiah honour at his *d.* 32:33
whether it be unto *d.* or to. *Ezra* 7:26
which long for *d.* but it. *Job* 3:21
so that my soul chooseth *d.* 7:15
first-born of *d.* shall devour. 18:13
remain of him be buried in *d.* 27:15
destruction and *d.* say, we. 28:22
thou wilt bring me to *d.* 30:23
in *d.* is no remembrance. *Ps* 6:5
prepared instruments of *d.* 7:13
lest I sleep the sleep of *d.* 13:3
brought me into dust of *d.* 22:15
be our guide, even unto *d.* 48:14
grave, *d.* shall feed on them. 49:14
terrors of *d.* are fallen upon me. 55:4
let *d.* seize on them, and let. 15
there are no bands in their *d.* 73:4
man liveth, shall not see *d.?* 89:48

loose those appointed to *d. Ps* 102:20
precious in sight of Lord is *d.* 116:15
not given me over unto *d.* 118:18
her house inclineth to *d.* *Pr* 2:18
her feet go down to *d.*; her steps. 5:5
going down to chambers of. 7:27
all they that hate me love *d.* 8:36
evil, pursueth it to his own *d.* 11:19
ways thereof there is no *d.* 12:28
to depart from the snares of *d.*
13:14; 14:27
righteous hath hope in his *d.* 14:32
as messengers of *d.* 16:14
d. and life are in the power. 18:21
of them that seek *d.* 21:6
them that are drawn to *d.* 24:11
who casteth arrows and *d.* 26:18
I find more bitter than *d. Eccl* 7:26
for love is strong as *d.* *S of S* 8:6
he will swallow up *d.* in. *Isa* 25:8
for *d.* cannot celebrate thee. 38:18
and with the rich in his *d.* 53:9
he poured out his soul unto *d.* 12
d. shall be chosen rather. *Jer* 8:3
d. is come up to our windows. 9:21
such as are for *d.* to *d.* 15:2; 43:11
at home there is as *d.* *Lam* 1:20
no pleasure in the *d.* of the wicked.
Ezek 18:32; 33:11
are all delivered unto *d.* 31:14
O *d.* I will be thy plagues. *Hos* 13:14
to be angry even unto *d.* *Jonah* 4:9
who is as *d.* and cannot. *Hab* 2:5
there till *d.* of Herod. *Mat* 2:15
brother deliver brother to *d.* 10:21
Mark 3:12
curseth father or mother, let him die
the *d.* *Mat* 15:4; *Mark* 7:10
shall not taste of *d.* till. *Mat* 16:28
Mark 9:1; *Luke* 9:27
shall condemn him to *d.* *Mat* 20:18
Mark 10:33
soul is sorrowful to *d.* *Mat* 26:38
Mark 14:34
said, he is guilty of *d.* *Mat* 26:66
Mark 14:64
lieth at the point of *d.* *Mark* 5:23
should not see *d.* before. *Luke* 2:26
with thee both to prison and *d.* 22:33
I have found no cause of *d.* 23:22
heal his son, at point of *d. John* 4:47
if a man keep my saying, he shall
never see *d.* 8:51, 52
this sickness is not unto *d.* 11:4
howbeit, Jesus spake of his *d.* 13
signifying what *d.* 12:33; 18:32
by what *d.* he should glorify. 21:19
having loosed pains of *d. Acts* 2:24
Saul consenting to his *d.* 8:1; 22:20
found no cause of *d.* in him. 13:28
persecuted this way unto *d.* 22:4
was no cause of *d.* in me. 28:18
we were reconciled to God by the *d.*
of his Son. *Rom* 5:10; *Col* 1:22
and *d.* by sin, and so *d.* *Rom* 5:12
d. reigned from Adam to. 14, 17
as sin hath reigned to *d.* even. 21
so many of us as were baptized into
Christ, baptized into his *d.?* 6:3
buried with him by baptism into *d.* 4
planted in likeness of his *d.* 5
dieth no more, *d.* hath no more. 9
servants, whether of sin unto *d.* 16
for end of those things is *d.* 21
for the wages of sin is *d.* but. 23
sins did work to bring *d.* 7:5
commandment of life to be to *d.* 10
which is good made *d.* to me ? 13
me from the body of this *d.?* 24
free from law of sin and *d.* 8:2
to be carnally minded is *d.* but. 6
nor *d.* nor life shall separate us. 38
world, life, or *d.* all are. *1 Cor* 3:22
as it were appointed to *d.* 4:9
ye do shew the Lord's *d.* 11:26
for since by man came *d.* by. 15:21
last enemy be destroyed is *d.* 26
d. is swallowed up in victory. 54
O *d.*, where is thy sting ? 55
sting of *d.* is sin. 56
we had the sentence of *d. 2 Cor* 1:9
delivered us from so great *d.* 10
we are the savour of *d.* unto *d.* 2:16
if the ministration of *d.* was. 3:7

always delivered to *d.* *2 Cor* 4:11
so then *d.* worketh in us. 12
sorrow of world worketh *d.* 7:10
whether by life or by *d.* *Phil* 1:20
obedient unto *d.* even *d.* of. 2:8
Epaphroditus was nigh to *d.* 27
work of Christ was nigh to *d.* 30
made conformable unto his *d.* 3:10
who hath abolished *d.* *2 Tim* 1:10
Jesus, for suffering of *d.* crowned,
that he should taste *d.* *Heb* 2:9
through *d.* might destroy him that
had power of *d.* 14
them who through fear of *d.* 15
to continue, by reason of *d.* 7:23
that by means of *d.* for the. 9:15
there must of necessity be *d.* 16
that he should not see *d.* 11:5
finished bringeth forth *d.* *Jas* 1:15
his brother abideth in *d. 1 John* 3:14
there is a sin unto *d.* 5:16
a sin not unto *d.* 17
keys of hell and of *d.* *Rev* 1:18
be faithful unto *d.* I will give. 2:10
shall not be hurt of second *d.* 11
name that sat on him was *d.* 6:8
men shall seek *d.* and *d.* shall. 9:6
loved not their lives to *d.* 12:11
as it were wounded to *d.* 13:3
plagues come in one day, *d.* 18:8
on such the second *d.* hath no. 20:6
and *d.* and hell delivered up. 13
d. and hell cast into lake, this is the
second *d.* 14
and there shall be no more *d.* 21:4

see day
from death

deliver our lives *from d.* *Josh* 2:13
shall redeem them *from d.* *Job* 5:20
deliver their soul from *d.* *Ps* 33:19
delivered my soul *from d.* 56:13
116:8
to God belong issues *from d.* 68:20
spared not their soul *from d.* 78:50
delivereth *from d.* *Pr* 10:2; 11:4
will redeem thee *from d.* *Hos* 13:14
is passed *from d.* to life. *John* 5:24
1 John 3:14
able to save him *from d.* *Heb* 5:7
shall save a soul *from d.* *Jas* 5:20

gates *of* death

have *gates of d.* been ? *Job* 38:17
me up from *gates of d.?* *Ps* 9:13
draw near to the *gates of d.* 107:18

put *to* death

man, shall be *put to d.* *Gen* 26:11
his owner also be *put to d. Ex* 21:29
on sabbath, shall be *put to d.* 35:2
shall not be *put to d.* *Lev* 19:20
both of them shall be *put to d.* 20:11
killeth *put to d.* 24:21; *Num* 35:30
stranger that cometh nigh be *put to d.*
Num 1:51; 3:10, 38; 18:7
dreamer be *put to d.* *Deut* 13:5
first upon him to *put to d.* 9; 17:7
of one witness not be *put to d.* 17:6
be *put to d.* and thou hang. 21:22
not be *put to d.* for children, nor
children *put to d.* 24:16; *2 Ki* 14:6
rebel be *put to d.* *Josh* 1:18
for Baal be *put to d.* *Judg* 6:31
we may *put them to d.* 20:13
1 Sam 11:12
not a man be *put to d.* *1 Sam* 11:13
2 Sam 19:22
measured he to *put to d. 2 Sam* 8:2
shall not Shimei be *put to d.?* 19:21
were *put to d.* in the days. 21:9
I will not *put thee to d.* *1 Ki* 2:8
Adonijah shall be *put to d.* 24
not at this time *put thee to d.* 26
seek Lord be *put to d. 2 Chr* 15:13
into house, shall be *put to d.* 23:7
law of his to *put him to d. Esth* 4:11
their men be *put to d.* *Jer* 18:21
that if ye put me to *d.* 26:15
all Judah *put* him at all *to d.?* 19
sought to *put* Urijah to *d.* 21
let this man be *put to d.* 38:4 (?)
thou not surely *put* me to *d.?* (?)
I will not *put thee to d.* 16, 25
that they might *put us to d.* 43:3
and *put them to d.* in Riblah 52:27

cause them to be *put to d. Mat* 10:21
 Mark 13:12; *Luke* 21:16
would *put* him *to d.* he. *Mat* 14:5
sought false witness to *put* him *to d.*
 26:59; 27:1; *Mark* 14:55
by craft and *put to d.* *Mark* 14:1
scourge and *put to d.* *Luke* 18:33
malefactors led to be *put to d.* 23:32
counsel to *put to d. John* 11:53
put Lazarus also *to d.* 12:10
for us to *put* any man *to d.* 18:31
keepers to be *put to d.* *Acts* 12:19
when they were *put to d.* I. 26:10
put to d. in flesh, but. *1 Pet* 3:18

see **surely**

shadow of **death**
let the *shad. of d.* stain it. *Job* 3:5
darkness and *shad. of d.* 10:21, 22
bringeth to light *shad. of d.* 12:22
on eyelids is *shad. of d.* 16:16
morning is even as *shad. of d.* 24:17
out darkness and *shad. of d.* 28:3
is no *shad. of d.* where. 34:22
seen doors of the *shad. of d.?* 38:17
valley of *shad. of d.* *Ps* 23:4
covered us with *shad. of d.* 44:19
in darkness, and *shad. of d.* 107:10
of darkness and *shad. of d.* 14
in land of the *shad. of d.* *Isa* 9:2
land of *shad. of d.* *Jer* 2:6
light, he turn it into *shad. of d.* 13:16
turneth *shad. of d.* into. *Amos* 5:8
in region and *shad. of d.* *Mat* 4:16
light to them in *shad. of d. Luke* 1:79

ways of **death** ′
the end *ways of d. Pr* 14:12; 16:25

with **death**
made a covenant *with d.* *Isa* 28:15
your covenant *with d.* shall. 18
kill her children *with d.* *Rev* 2:23
power was given to kill *with d.* 6:8

worthy of **death**
that is *worthy of d.* *Deut* 17:6*
he was not *worthy of d.* 19:6
committed a sin *worthy of d.* 21:22
in damsel no sin *worthy of d.* 22:26
thou art *worthy of d.* *1 Ki* 2:26
lo, nothing *worthy of d. Luke* 23:15
his charge *worthy of d.* *Acts* 23:29
any thing *worthy of d.* 25:11
committed nothing *worthy of d.* 25
doth nothing *worthy of d.* 26:31
such things *worthy of d.* *Rom* 1:32

deaths
shall die of grevious *d.* *Jer* 16:4
shalt die *d.* of them that. *Ezek* 28:8
thou shalt die the *d.* of the. 10
in prisons frequent, in *d. 2 Cor* 11:23

debase
and didst *d.* thyself. *Isa* 57:9

debate, *verb*
d. thy cause with thy. *Pr* 25:9
in measure, thou wilt *d.* *Isa* 27:8*

debate, -s
ye fast for strife and *d.* *Isa* 58:4*
full of envy, murder, *d.* *Rom* 1:29*
I fear lest there be *d.* wrath.
 2 Cor 12:20*

Deborah
but *D.* Rebekah's nurse. *Gen* 35:8
D. a prophetess judged. *Judg* 4:4
D. arose a mother in Israel. 5:7
awake *D.* 12
the princes were with *D.* 15

debt
*That which is due by one man to
another, Neh* 10:31. *Sins are by
resemblance called* debts, *Mat* 6:12.
every one that was in *d. 1 Sam* 22:2
sell the oil, pay thy *d.* *2 Ki* 4:7
the exaction of every *d.* *Neh* 10:31
and forgave him the *d.* *Mat* 18:27
cast into prison till he pay *d.* 30
I forgave thee all that *d.* 32
reckoned of grace but *d.* *Rom* 4:4

debtor
restored to the *d.* his. *Ezek* 18:7
by gold of temple is a *d. Mat* 23:16
I am *d.* to the Greeks. *Rom* 1:14
he is a *d.* to do the whole. *Gal* 5:3

debtors
as we forgive our *d.* *Mat* 6:12
creditor had two *d.* *Luke* 7:41
called every one of his lord's *d.* 16:5
we are *d.* not to flesh. *Rom* 8:12
and their *d.* they are 15:27

debts
that are sureties for *d.* *Pr* 22:26
forgive us our *d.* as we. *Mat* 6:12

Decapolis
followed him from *D.* *Mat* 4:25
he began to publish in *D. Mark* 5:20
through midst of coasts of *D.* 7:31

decay
be poor and fallen in *d. Lev* 25:35*

decayed
of bearers of burdens *d.* *Neh* 4:10
I will raise up the *d.* *Isa* 44:26*

decayeth
and as the flood *d.* and. *Jer* 14:11†
slothfulness building *d. Eccl* 10:18*
that which *d.* is ready to. *Heb* 8:13*

decease
and spake of his *d.* at. *Luke* 9:31
after my *d.* to have in. *2 Pet* 1:15

deceased
they are *d.* they shall. *Isa* 26:14
when he had married, *d. Mat* 22:25

deceit
their belly prepareth *d.* *Job* 15:35
nor my tongue utter *d.* 27:4
if my foot hath hasted to *d.* 31:5
full of cursing, *d.* and. *Ps* 10:7
words are iniquity and *d.* 36:3
thy tongue frameth *d.* 50:19
d. and guile depart not. 55:11*
redeem their soul from *d.* 72:14*
he that worketh *d.* shall not. 101:7
them that err, their *d.* is. 119:118
counsels of the wicked are *d. Pr* 12:5
a false witness sheweth forth *d.* 17
d. is in the heart of them that. 20
but the folly of fools is *d.* 14:8
bread of *d.* is sweet to a. 20:17
he that hateth, layeth up *d.* 26:24
whose hatred is covered by *d.* 26
neither was any *d.* in his. *Isa* 53:9
so are houses full of *d.* *Jer* 5:27
hold fast *d.* they refuse to. 8:5
through *d.* they refuse to know. 9:6
tongue, it speaketh *d.* 8
they prophesy the *d.* of their. 14:14
they are prophets of *d.* 23:26
compasseth me with *d.* *Hos* 11:12
the balances of *d.* are in. 12:7
falsifying balances by *d. Amos* 8:5
fill masters' houses with *d. Zeph* 1:9
heart of men proceed, *d. Mark* 7:22
of murder, debate, *d.* *Rom* 1:29
tongues they have used *d.* 3:13
through philosophy and vain *d.*
 Col 2:8
exhortation was not of *d. 1 Thes* 2:3*

deceitful
abhor bloody and *d.* man. *Ps* 5:6
they devise *d.* matters. 35:20
deliver me from the *d.* and. 43:1
O thou *d.* tongue. 52:4
bloody and *d.* men shall not. 55:23
turned aside like a *d.* bow. 78:57
the mouth of the *d.* are. 109:2
deliver my soul from a *d.* 120:2
wicked worketh a *d.* work. *Pr* 11:18
but a *d.* witness speaketh 14:25
for they a *d.* meat. 23:3
kisses of an enemy are *d.* 27:6*
the poor and the *d.* man. 29:13*
favour is *d.* and beauty is. 31:30
heart is *d.* above all. *Jer* 17:9
are like a *d.* bow. *Hos* 7:16
and with bag of *d.* weights. *Mi* 6:11
and their tongue is *d.* in. 12
nor shall a *d.* tongue be. *Zeph* 3:13
apostles, *d.* workers. *2 Cor* 11:13
corrupt according to *d.* *Eph* 4:22

deceitfully
Hamor and Shechem *d. Gen* 34:13
let not Pharaoh deal *d.* *Ex* 8:29
seeing he hath dealt *d.* with. 21:8
which he hath *d.* gotten. *Lev* 6:4
brethren have dealt *d.* *Job* 6:15

will ye talk *d.* for him ? *Job* 13:7
up his soul nor sworn *d.* *Ps* 24:4
a sharp razor, working *d.* 52:2
doeth the work of Lord *d. Jer* 48:10
made, he shall work *d.* *Dan* 11:23
handling word of God *d.* *2 Cor* 4:2

deceitfulness
and the *d.* of riches choke the word.
 Mat 13:22; *Mark* 4:19
hardened through *d.* of sin. *Heb* 3:13

deceits
and imagine *d.* all day. *Ps* 38:12
smooth things, prophesy *d. Isa* 30:10

deceive
Abner came to *d.* thee. *2 Sam* 3:25
I say, do not *d.* me ? *2 Ki* 4:28
let not Hezekiah *d.* you. 18:29
 2 Chr 32:15; *Isa* 36:14
let not thy God *d.* thee. *2 Ki* 19:10
 Isa 37:10
be not a witness, and *d.* *Pr* 24:28
they will *d.* every one. *Jer* 9:5
that be in midst of you *d.* 29:8
saith the Lord *d.* not yourselves. 37:9
neither wear garment to *d. Zech* 13:4
take heed that no man *d.* you.
 Mat 24:4; *Mark* 13:5
I am Christ; and shall *d.* many.
 Mat 24:5, 11; *Mark* 13:6
if possible they shall *d. Mat* 24:24
by fair speech *d.* the. *Rom* 16:18
let no man *d.* himself. *1 Cor* 3:18
they lie in wait to *d.* *Eph* 4:14
let no man *d.* you. 5:6; *2 Thes* 2:3
 1 John 3:7
we have no sin, we *d.* *1 John* 1:8
that he should *d.* the. *Rev* 20:3
go to *d.* nations in four quarters. 8

deceivableness
and with all *d.* of. *2 Thes* 2:10

deceived
father hath *d.* me and. *Gen* 31:7
or if a soul sin, or hath *d. Lev* 6:2*
your heart be not *d.* *Deut* 11:16
why hast thou *d.* me ? *1 Sam* 19:17
 28:12
O king, my servant *d.* *2 Sam* 19:26
the *d.* and the deceiver. *Job* 12:16
let not him that is *d.* trust. 15:31
if mine heart have been *d.* 31:9
princes of Noph are *d.* *Isa* 19:13
a *d.* heart hath turned him. 44:20
thou hast greatly *d.* *Jer* 4:10
thou hast *d.* me, and I was *d.* 20:7
thy terribleness hath *d.* thee. 49:16
my lovers, but they *d.* *Lam* 1:19
if prophet be *d.* I have *d. Ezek* 14:9
of thine heart hath *d.* *Ob* 3
men at peace with thee have *d.* 7
heed that ye be not *d.* *Luke* 21:8
answered, are ye also *d.? John* 7:47
by commandment *d.* me. *Rom* 7:11
be not *d. 1 Cor* 6:9; 15:33; *Gal* 6:7
d. but woman being *d.* *1 Tim* 2:14
deceiving and being *d.* *2 Tim* 3:13
we were foolish, *d.* *Tit* 3:3
all nations were *d.* *Rev* 18:23
he *d.* them that had received. 19:20
devil that *d.* them was cast. 20:10

deceiver
seem to my father as a *d. Gen* 27:12
the deceived and the *d.* *Job* 12:16
cursed be *d.* who hath. *Mal* 1:14
remember that that *d.* *Mat* 27:63
not Jesus this is a *d.* *2 John* 7

deceivers
and good report, as *d.* *2 Cor* 6:8
many *d.* especially of. *Tit* 1:10
for many *d.* are entered. *2 John* 7

deceiveth
so is the man that *d.* his. *Pr* 26:19
nay, but he *d.* the people. *John* 7:12
when nothing, *d.* himself. *Gal* 6:3
d. his own heart. *Jas* 1:26
called the devil, which *d.* *Rev* 12:9
and *d.* them that dwell on. 13:14

deceiving
men wax worse, *d.* *2 Tim* 3:13
not hearers only, *d.* your. *Jas* 1:22

deceivings
sporting with their own *d. 2 Pet* 2:13
decently
let all things be done *d. 1 Cor* 14:40
decided
thyself hast *d.* it. *1 Ki* 20:40
decision
in valley of *d.* for day. *Joel* 3:14
deck
d. thyself now with. *Job* 40:10
they *d.* it with silver. *Jer* 10:4
decked
d. my bed with covering. *Pr* 7:16*
I *d.* thee also with. *Ezek* 16:11
thou wast thus *d.* with gold. 13
and she *d.* herself with. *Hos* 2:13
was arrayed and *d.* with. *Rev* 17:4
that great city that was *d.* 18:16
deckedst
didst take garments and *d.*
 Ezek 16:16*
didst wash and *d.* thyself. 23:40
deckest, -eth
as a bridegroom *d.* *Isa* 61:10
though thou *d.* thee with. *Jer* 4:30
declaration
d. of the greatness of. *Esth* 10:2*
and hear my *d.* with. *Job* 13:17
to set forth in order a *d.* *Luke* 1:1*
and to the *d.* of your. *2 Cor* 8:19*
declare
none that could *d.* it. *Gen* 41:24
Moab began Moses to *d.* *Deut* 1:5
d. his cause in ears of. *Josh* 20:4
if ye can *d.* it me within. *Judg* 14:12
words of the prophets *d.* good.
 1 Ki 22:13; *2 Chr* 18:12
d. his glory among the heathen.
 1 Chr 16:24; *Ps* 96:3
to shew copy and *d.* it. *Esth* 4:8
fishes of the sea shall *d.* *Job* 12:8
d. his way to his face ? 21:31
then did he see it, and *d.* it. 28:27
I would *d.* to him the. 31:37
foundations of earth, *d.* if thou. 38:4
breadth of earth, *d.* if thou. 18
will demand of thee, *d.* 40:7; 42:4
d. among the people his. *Ps* 9:11
the heavens *d.* the glory. 19:1
come and *d.* righteousness. 22:31
 50:6; 97:6
shall it *d.* thy truth ? 30:9
if I would *d.* and speak of. 40:5
what hast thou to do to *d.*? 50:16
all men shall fear and *d.* 64:9
trust in Lord that I may *d.* 73:28*
is near, wondrous works *d.* 75:1*
should arise and *d.* them. 78:6*
to *d.* the name of the Lord. 102:21
and *d.* his works with. 107:22
but live and *d.* the works. 118:17
one generation shall *d.* thy. 145:4
in my heart even to *d.* *Eccl* 9:1*
d. their sin as Sodom. *Isa* 3:9
d. his doings among people. 12:4
set a watchman, let him *d.* 21:6
or let them *d.* to us things. 41:22
and new things do I *d.* 42:9
and let them *d.* his praise. 9:2*
who among them can *d.* this ? 43:9
d. thou that thou mayest be. 26*
I shall call, and shall *d.* it ? 44:7
I the Lord *d.* things that are. 45:19
all this, and will not ye *d.* 48:6
who shall *d.* his generation ? 53:8*
 Acts 8:33
they shall *d.* my glory. *Isa* 66:19
d. this in house of Jacob. *Jer* 5:20
hath spoken, that he may *d.* 9:12
d. it in isles afar off, and say. 31:10
if I *d.* it to thee, wilt thou ? 38:15
d. unto us what thou hast said. 25
what God shall say, *d.* to us. 42:20
d. in Zion the vengeance of. 50:28
let us *d.* in Zion work of. 51:10
may *d.* all their. *Ezek* 12:16; 23:36
d. all that thou seest to the. 40:4
O Belteshazzar, *d.* the. *Dan* 4:18
to *d.* to Jacob his. *Mi* 3:8
even to-day do I *d.* that. *Zech* 9:12
d. unto us this parable. *Mat* 13:36*
d. unto us this parable. 15:15

d. unto you glad. *Acts* 13:32*
though a man *d.* it to you. 41
ignorantly worship, him *d.* 17:23*
not shunned to *d.* to you the. 20:27
set forth to *d.* his righteousness.
 Rom 3:25*, 26*
the day shall *d.* it. *1 Cor* 3:13
in this that I *d.* to you. 11:17*
I *d.* unto you the gospel. 15:1*
state shall Tychicus *d.* *Col* 4:7*
that say such things *d.* *Heb* 11:14*
which we have seen *d.* *1 John* 1:3
then is message which we *d.* 5*
I will declare
I have seen I will *d.* *Job* 15:17
I will *d.* the decree. *Ps* 2:7*
I will *d.* thy name to brethren.
 22:22; *Heb* 2:12
I will *d.* mine iniquity. *Ps* 38:18
I will *d.* what he hath done. 66:16
but I will *d.* for ever, I will. 75:9
I will *d.* thy greatness. 145:6
I will *d.* thy righteousness. *Isa* 57:12
I will *d.* it, I will keep. *Jer* 42:4
thy name, will *d.* it. *John* 17:26*
declare ye
a voice of singing *d. ye.* *Isa* 48:20
d. ye in Judah, and. *Jer* 4:5
d. ye in Egypt, and publish. 46:14
d. ye among the nations. 50:2
d. ye it not at Gath. *Mi* 1:10*
declared
that my name may be *d.* *Ex* 9:16
Moses *d.* to children of. *Lev* 23:44
they *d.* their pedigrees. *Num* 1:18
because it was not *d.* 15:34
and he *d.* to you his. *Deut* 4:13
for thou hast *d.* this. *2 Sam* 19:6
words that were *d.* to. *Neh* 8:12
plentifully *d.* thing as it. *Job* 26:3
I have *d.* thy faithfulness. *Ps* 40:10
hitherto have I *d.* thy works. 71:17
hast *d.* thy strength among. 77:14*
loving-kindness be *d.* in the. 88:11
with my lips have I *d.* all. 119:13
I have *d.* my ways, and thou. 26
a grievous vision is *d.* *Isa* 21:2
heard of God have I *d.* unto you. 10
who hath *d.* from. 41:26; 45:21*
I have *d.* and have saved. 43:12
 44:8; 48:5
I have *d.* former things from. 48:3
them hath *d.* these things ? 14
Micaiah *d.* all the words. *Jer* 36:13
I have this day *d.* it to you. 42:21
she *d.* to him before all. *Luke* 8:47
he hath *d.* him. *John* 1:18
I have *d.* to them thy name. 17:26*
he *d.* to them how he had. *Acts* 9:27
when he had *d.* all these. 10:8*
d. how Lord had brought him. 12:17
d. all things that God had. 15:4*
Simeon had *d.* how God at. 14*
Festus *d.* Paul's cause to. 25:14
d. to be the Son of God. *Rom* 1:4
that my name might be *d.* 9:17*
for it hath been *d.* to. *1 Cor* 1:11*
d. to be the epistle of. *2 Cor* 3:3*
who also *d.* to us your. *Col* 1:8
of God be finished as he *d. Rev* 10:7
declareth, -ing
there is none that *d.* *Isa* 41:26
d. the end from beginning. 46:10
a voice *d.* from Dan. *Jer* 4:15
my people, their staff *d.* *Hos* 4:12
he that *d.* to man what. *Amos* 4:13
d. the conversion of the. *Acts* 15:3
d. what miracles God hath. 12*
d. to you the testimony. *1 Cor* 2:1*
decline
(*To turn aside, deviate, or stray*)
speak in a cause, to. *Ex* 23:2
not *d.* from sentence. *Deut* 17:11
d. from thy testimonies. *Ps* 119:157
neither *d.* from words of. *Pr* 4:5
heart *d.* to her ways, go not. 7:25
declined, -eth
d. neither to right hand. *2 Chr* 34:2
way have I kept and not *d. Job* 23:11
nor have our steps *d.* *Ps* 44:18
days are like shadow that *d.* 102:11

like the shadow when it *d. Ps* 109:23
yet have I not *d.* from thy. 119:51
decrease
and suffer not cattle to *d. Ps* 107:38
increase, but I must *d.* *John* 3:30
decreased
waters *d.* continually until. *Gen* 8:5
decree, *substantive*
[1] *An authoritative order,* 2 Chr
30:5; Ezra 6:1. [2] *An eternal
purpose of God,* Ps 2:7; Dan 4:24.
so they established a *d. 2 Chr* 30:5
king Cyrus made a *d. Ezra* 5:13, 17
Darius made a *d.* 6:1, 12
Artaxerxes do make a *d.* 7:21
the *d.* was given to Shushan.
 Esth 3:15; 9:14
d. of Esther confirmed. 9:32
made a *d.* for the rain. *Job* 28:26
I will declare the *d.* the. *Ps* 2:7
he hath made a *d.* which. 148:6
he gave to sea his *d.* *Pr* 8:29
sea by a perpetual *d.* *Jer* 5:22
there is but one *d.* for. *Dan* 2:9
this matter is by the *d.* of the. 4:17
this is the *d.* of the most High. 24
now, O king, establish the *d.* 6:8
regardeth not thee, nor *d.* 13
I make a *d.* that in every. 26
proclaimed by the *d* of. *Jonah* 3:7
in that day shall the *d.* be. *Mi* 7:11
before the *d.* bring forth. *Zeph* 2:2
there went out a *d.* *Luke* 2:1
decree, *verb*
thou shalt also *d.* a. *Job* 22:28
kings reign, and princes *d.* *Pr* 8:15
woe to them that *d.* *Isa* 10:1
decreed
remembered what was *d.* *Esth* 2:1
as they had *d.* for themselves. 9:31
brake up for it my *d.* *Job* 38:10
consumption *d.* overflow. *Isa* 10:22
hath so *d.* in his heart. *1 Cor* 7:37
decrees
that decree unrighteous *d.* *Isa* 10:1
they delivered them the *d. Acts* 16:4
do contrary to the *d.* of Caesar. 17:7
Dedan
Sheba, D. *Gen* 10:7; *1 Chr* 1:9
Jokshan, Sheba, and D. *1 Chr* 1:32
made D. and Tema, and. *Jer* 25:23
deep, O inhabitants of D. 49:8
they of D. shall fall by. *Ezek* 25:13
D. was thy merchant in. 27:20
Dedanim
travelling companies of D. *Isa* 21:13
dedicate
die and another man *d.* *Deut* 20:5
which also David did *d. 2 Sam* 8:11
out of spoils did they *d.* to. 27
I build an house to *d.* *2 Chr* 2:4
dedicated
a new house and not *d.* *Deut* 20:5
I had wholly *d.* the silver. *Judg* 17:3
things which David had *d. 1 Ki* 7:51
 1 Chr 18:11; *2 Chr* 5:1
the king and Israel *d.* *1 Ki* 8:63
 2 Chr 7:5
had *d.* and things himself had *d.*
 1 Ki 15:15; *2 Chr* 15:18
all the money of the *d.* *2 Ki* 12:4*
hallowed things that kings of Judah
had *d.* 12:18
over treasures of *d. 1 Chr* 26:20, 26
captains of hosts had *d.* 26
that Samuel, Saul, and Joab *d.* 28
pattern of the treasuries of the *d.*
 things 28:12
the *d.* things did they bestow.
 2 Chr 24:7
and brought in the *d.* things. 31:12
every *d.* thing in Israel. *Ezek* 44:29*
nor first testament *d.* *Heb* 9:18
dedicating
princes offered for *d.* *Num* 7:10
each prince on his day for *d.* 11
dedication
this was the *d.* of. *Num* 7:84, 88
for they kept the *d.* of. *2 Chr* 7:9

kept the d. with joy.   *Ezra 6:16*
offered at d. of house of God.   17
at the d. of the wall.   *Neh 12:27*
come to d. of image.   *Dan 3:2, 3*
at Jerusalem feast of d. *John 10:22*

deed

what d. is this ye have ? *Gen 44:15*
in very d. for this cause.   *Ex 9:16*
was no such d. done.   *Judg 19:30*
in very d. except thou. *1 Sam 25:34*
Saul was come in very d.   26:4*
by this d. given great. *2 Sam 12:14*
for this d. of queen shall. *Esth 1:17*
had not consented to d. *Luke 23:51*
a prophet mighty in d.   24:19
be examined of the good d. *Acts 4:9*
obedient by word and d. *Rom 15:18*
that hath done this d. *1 Cor 5:2*
him that hath done this d.   3
ye do in word or d. do. *Col 3:17*
shall be blessed in his d. *Jas 1:25*
love in d. and in truth. *1 John 3:18*

deeds

hast done d. that ought not. *Gen 20:9*
make known his d.   *1 Chr 16:8*
  Ps 105:1
his d. first and last. *2 Chr 35:27*
come upon us for evil d. *Ezra 9:13*
also reported his good d. *Neh 6:19*
wipe not out my good d.   13:14
them according to their d. *Ps 28:4*
according to their d. *Isa 59:18*
they overpass the d. of. *Jer 5:28*
them according to their d.   25:14
that ye allow the d. of. *Luke 11:48*
the due reward of our d.   23:41
because their d. were. *John 3:19*
to the light, lest his d. should.   20
that his d. may be made.   21
ye do the d. of your father.   8:41
mighty in word and in d. *Acts 7:22*
Dorcas was full of alms-d.   9:36
confessed, and shewed their d. 19:18
very worthy d. are done.   24:2*
man according to his d. *Rom 2:6*
by the d. of the law shall no.   3:20
is justified by faith without d.   28*
if ye mortify the d. of the.   8:13
in signs and mighty d. *2 Cor 12:12*
put off old man with his d. *Col 3:9*
soul with their unlawful d. *2 Pet 2:8*
is partaker of his evil d. *2 John 11*
I will remember his d. *3 John 10*
them of their ungodly d. *Jude 15*
thou hatest the d. of the. *Rev 2:6*
except they repent of their d.   22
repented of their d.   16:11

deemed

the shipmen d. that. *Acts 27:27*

deep

[1] *Extending a great way below
the surface,* Ezek 32:24. [2] *The
sea,* Job 41:31. [3] *Used for any
great danger or profound or incomprehensible matter,* Ps 69:15;
Isa 33:19; Dan 2:22.

darkness was upon the face of the d.
  Gen 1:2
the fountains of the d. were.   7:11
fountains also of the d. were.   8:2
thee with blessings of the d. 49:25
the d. that coucheth. *Deut 33:13*
face of the d. is frozen. *Job 38:30*
the d. to boil like a pot.   41:31
would think the d. to be hoary.   32
judgements are a great d. *Ps 36:6*
d. calleth unto d. at noise of.   42:7
neither let the d. swallow.   69:15
coveredst it with the d. as.   104:6
these see wonders in the d. 107:24
strengthens fountains of d. *Pr 8:28*
saith to the d. be dry. *Isa 44:27*
dried waters of great d.?   51:10
led them through the d.   63:13
when I bring up the d. *Ezek 26:19*
the d. set him on high with.   31:4
I covered the d. for him.   15
devoured great d. and. *Amos 7:4*
hast cast me into the d. *Jonah 2:3*
the d. uttered his voice. *Hab 3:10*
launch out into the d. and. *Luke 5:4*
command them to go into d.   8:31*

---

shall descend into d.?   *Rom 10:7**
night and day in the d. *2 Cor 11:25*

deep, *adjective*

he discovereth d. things. *Job 12:22*
thought and heart is d.   *Ps 64:6*
I sink in d. mire, I am come into d.
  waters.   69:2
delivered out of the d. waters.   14
didst cause it to take d. root.   80:9
thy thoughts are very d.   92:5
in his hand are the d. places.   95:4
in the seas and all d. places. 135:6
them be cast into d. pits.   140:10
mouth are as d. waters.   *Pr 18:4*
counsel is like d. waters.   20:5
of strange women is a d. pit. 22:14
for a whore is a d. ditch.   23:27
exceeding d. who can ? *Eccl 7:24*
woe to them that seek d. *Isa 29:15*
made Tophet and large.   30:33
turn back, dwell d.   *Jer 49:8*
drink thy sister's cup d. *Ezek 23:32*
will I make their waters d.   32:14*
and to have drunk d. waters. 34:18*
he revealeth the d. and. *Dan 2:22*
digged d. laid foundation. *Luke 6:48*
to draw, and well is d. *John 4:11*
Spirit searcheth d. *1 Cor 2:10*
d. poverty abounded to. *2 Cor 8:2*

deep *sleep*

God caused a d. *sleep.* *Gen 2:21*
a d. *sleep* fell on Abram.   15:12
a d. *sleep* was fallen. *1 Sam 26:12*
d. *sleep* falleth. *Job 4:13; 33:15*
casteth into d. *sleep.* *Pr 19:15*
on you spirit of d. *sleep.* *Isa 29:10*
I was in a d. *sleep.* *Dan 8:18; 10:9*
fallen into d. *sleep.* *Acts 20:9*

deeper

plague in sight be d. than skin.
  Lev 13:3; 25:30
bright spot in sight be not d.   13:4
  31, 32, 34
it is d. than hell.   *Job 11:8*
a people of d. speech. *Isa 33:19*

deeply

of Israel d. revolted. *Isa 31:6*
they have d. corrupted. *Hos 9:9*
Jesus sighed d. in his. *Mark 8:12*

deepness

they had no d. of earth. *Mat 13:5*

deeps

thou threwest into d. *Neh 9:11*
hast laid me in the d. *Ps 88:6*
praise Lord, dragons and all d. 148:7
all the d. of the river. *Zech 10:11*

deer

shall eat the fallow d. *Deut 14:5**
Solomon had fallow d. *1 Ki 4:23*

defamed

being d. we intreat. *1 Cor 4:13*

defaming

for I heard d. of many. *Jer 20:10*

defeat

d. the counsel of Ahithophel.
  2 Sam 15:34; 17:14

defence

their d. is departed. *Num 14:9*
Rehoboam built cities for d.
  2 Chr 11:5
Almighty shall be thy d. *Job 22:25**
my d. is of God who. *Ps 7:10**
be thou an house of d. to.   31:2
for God is my d.   59:9*, 17*
thou hast been my d. and.   16*
God is my d. I shall not.   62:2*, 6*
for the Lord is our d.   89:18*
Lord is my d. and God.   94:22*
is a d. money is a d. *Eccl 7:12*
all glory shall be a d. *Isa 4:5*
the brooks of d. shall be.   19:6*
his place of d. shall be the.   33:16
the d. shall be prepared. *Nah 2:5**
would have made his d. *Acts 19:33*
hear my d. which I make.   22:1
in my bonds and in d. *Phil 1:7*
I am set for the d. of the gospel. 17

defenced

(*Fortified by a wall*)
of a d. city a ruin. *Isa 25:2*

---

against all d. cities of Judah. *Isa 36:1*
to lay waste d. cities into.   37:26
let us go into the d. cities. *Jer 4:5*
for these d. cities remained.   34:7

see city, cities

defend

Tolah arose to d. Israel. *Judg 10:1**
I will d. city. *2 Ki 19:34; 20:6*
  Isa 37:35; 38:6
name of God of Jacob d. *Ps 20:1**
d. me from them that rise up. 59:1*
d. the poor and fatherless.   82:3*
so will Lord of hosts d. *Isa 31:5**
Lord of hosts shall d. *Zech 9:15*
d. inhabitants of Jerusalem.   12:8

defended

Shammah stood and d. *2 Sam 23:12*
he d. them and. *Acts 7:24*

defendest

for joy, because thou d. *Ps 5:11*

defending

d. Jerusalem he will. *Isa 31:5*

defer

thou vowest a vow, d. *Eccl 5:4*
name's sake will I d. *Isa 48:9*
d. not for thine own sake. *Dan 9:19*

deferred

the young man d. not. *Gen 34:19*
hope d. maketh heart sick. *Pr 13:12*
when Felix heard he d. *Acts 24:22*

deferreth

discretion of a man d. *Pr 19:11**

defied

whom Lord hath not d.? *Num 23:8*
he hath d. the armies. *1 Sam 17:36*
the God whom thou hast d.   45
when he d. Israel, Jonathan slew
  him. *2 Sam 21:21; 1 Chr 20:7*
d. the Philistines. *2 Sam 23:9*

defile

[1] *To make foul,* 1 Cor 8:7; Tit
1:15. [2] *To make ceremonially
unclean,* Lev 11:44; Mark 7:2.

nor d. yourselves. *Lev 11:44; 18:24*
when they d. my tabernacle. 15:31
to d. thyself with thy.   18:20
neither lie with any beast to d.   23
spue not you out when ye d.   28
to d. my sanctuary.   20:3
he shall not d. himself.   21:4
nor d. himself for his father or.   11
he shall not eat to d. himself. 22:8
they d. not their camps. *Num 5:3*
d. not the land which ye.   35:34
high places did king d. *2 Ki 23:13*
how shall I d. them ? *S of S 5:3*
shall d. the covering of. *Isa 30:22*
called by my name to d. *Jer 32:34*
robbers enter into it and d. it.
  *Ezek 7:22**
d. the house, fill courts with.   9:7
d. not yourselves with idols. 20:7, 18
idols against herself to d.   22:3
they shall d. thy brightness.   28:7
ye d. every one his.   33:26
nor shall they d. themselves. 37:23
name shall Israel no more d.   43:7
at no dead person to d.   44:25
would not d. himself. *Dan 1:8*
and they d. the man. *Mat 15:18*
  Mark 7:15, 23
if any man d. temple. *1 Cor 3:17**
law is for them that d. *1 Tim 1:10**
these filthy dreamers d. *Jude 8*

defiled

with Dinah, and d. her. *Gen 34:2**
Jacob heard that he had d. Dinah. 5
because he had d. Dinah.   13, 27
a man shall be d. with. *Lev 5:3*
that he should be d. thereby. 11:43
plague is in him be d.   13:46*
the law of him that is d.   15:32*
all these things nations are d. 18:24
the land is d. I visit.   25, 27
seek after wizards to be d.   19:31
shall none be d. for the dead. 21:1
a virgin, for her may he be d.   3
put out whosoever is d. *Num 5:2**
and if she be d.   13, 27
if she be not d.   14, 28

and he hath *d.* the head of. *Num* 6:9
because his separation was *d.* 12
men who were *d.* by dead. 9:6*, 7*
d. the sanctuary of Lord. 19:20
that thy land be not *d.* *Deut* 21:23
fruit of thy vineyard be *d.* 22:9*
may not take her after *d.* 24:4
Josiah *d.* high places. *2 Ki* 23:8
d. Topheth. 10
forasmuch as he *d.* his. *1 Chr* 5:1
because they have *d.* *Neh* 13:29
I have *d.* my horn. *Job* 16:15*
d. dwelling-place of. *Ps* 74:7*; 79:1
thus were they *d.* with. 106:39
the earth is *d.* under. *Isa* 24:5*
your hands are *d.* with blood. 59:3
but when ye entered, ye *d.* *Jer* 2:7
lightness of whoredom she *d.* 3:9*
because they have *d.* land. 16:18*
of the kings of Judah be *d.* 19:13
Israel eat *d.* bread. *Ezek* 4:13*
surely because thou hast *d.* 5:11
their holy places shall be *d.* 7:24*
neither *d.* neighbour's wife. 18:6, 15
hath even *d.* his neighbour's. 11
wherein ye have been *d.* 20:43*
and hast *d.* thyself. 22:4; 23:7
another hath lewdly *d.* his. 22:11
I saw that she was *d.* 23:13
the Babylonians *d.* her. 17
they have *d.* my sanctuary. 38
thou hast *d.* thy sanctuaries. 28:18*
they *d.* it by their own way. 36:17
they have *d.* my holy name. 43
and Israel is *d.* *Hos* 5:3; 6:10
nations say, let her be *d.* *Mi* 4:11
disciples eat bread with *d.* *Mark* 7:2
not in, lest they be *d.* *John* 18:28
conscience being weak is *d.* *1 Cor* 8:7
to *d.* is nothing pure, mind and conscience *d.* *Tit* 1:15
and therefore many be *d.* *Heb* 12:15
a few who have not *d.* *Rev* 3:4
these are they who are not *d.* 14:4

defiledst
to father's bed, then *d.* it. *Gen* 49:4

defileth
that *d.* sabbath. *Ex* 31:14*
d. the tabernacle. *Num* 19:13
not pollute land, blood *d.* 35:33
goeth into the mouth *d.* *Mat* 15:11
eat with unwashen hands *d.* not. 20
out of man that *d.* *Mark* 7:20
so is tongue, that it *d.* the. *Jas* 3:6
enter any thing that *d.* *Rev* 21:27*

defraud
not *d.* thy neighbour. *Lev* 19:13*
do not bear false witness, *d.* not.
Mark 10:19
nay you do wrong, and *d.* *1 Cor* 6:8
d. not, except it be with. 7:5
no man *d.* his brother. *1 Thes* 4:6*

defrauded
whom have I *d.*? *1 Sam* 12:3
thou hast not *d.* nor oppressed. 4
rather suffer yourselves to be *d.*
1 Cor 6:7
wronged no man, have *d.* *2 Cor* 7:2*

defy
curse me Jacob, *d.* *Num* 23:7
how shall I *d.* whom Lord hath? 8
I *d.* the armies of. *1 Sam* 17:10
is come up, surely to *d.* Israel. 25
that he should *d.* the armies. 26

degenerate
turned into the *d.* plant. *Jer* 2:21

degree, -s
Songs of degrees : *This title is given to fifteen Psalms, from 120 to 134, inclusive. The Hebrew text calls each, A song of ascents. There is a great diversity of views as to the meaning of this title, but the most probable is that they were pilgrim songs, sung by the people as they went up to Jerusalem.*
or backward ten *d.* *2 Ki* 20:9*, 10*
11*; *Isa* 38:8*
brethren of second *d.* *1 Chr* 15:18
state of a man of high *d.* 17:17
low *d.* vanity, high *d.* a lie. *Ps* 62:9
exalted them of low *d.* *Luke* 1:52

to themselves a good *d.* *1 Tim* 3:13*
let brother of low *d.* *Jas* 1:9

delay, -ed, -eth
thou shalt not *d.* to offer. *Ex* 22:29
the people saw that Moses *d.* 32:1
d. not to keep thy. *Ps* 119:60
my lord *d.* his coming. *Mat* 24:48*
Luke 12:45
that he would not *d.* *Acts* 9:38
without any *d.* I sat on. 25:17

delectable
their *d.* things not profit. *Isa* 44:9

delicacies
merchants rich through *d.* *Rev* 18:3*

delicate
the *d.* man or. *Deut* 28:54, 56
more called tender and *d.* *Isa* 47:1
Zion to comely *d.* woman. *Jer* 6:2
bald for thy *d.* children. *Mi* 1:16*

delicately
Agag came to him *d.* *1 Sam* 15:32†
he that *d.* bringeth up his. *Pr* 29:21
they that did feed *d.* are. *Lam* 4:5
they that live *d.* are in. *Luke* 7:25

delicateness
foot on ground for *d.* *Deut* 28:56

delicates
filled his belly with *d.* *Jer* 51:34†

deliciously
glorified herself and lived *d.*
Rev 18:7*, 9*

delight, substantive
Shechem had *d.* in. *Gen* 34:19
Lord had a *d.* in thy. *Deut* 10:15
if thou have no *d.* in her. 21:14
great *d.* in offerings ? *1 Sam* 15:22
behold, the king hath *d.* in. 18:22
I have no *d.* in thee. *2 Sam* 15:26
shalt thou have *d.* in. *Job* 22:26
but his *d.* is in the law. *Ps* 1:2
excellent, in whom is my *d.* 16:3
testimonies also are my *d.* 119:24
for thy law is my *d.* 77, 174
I was daily his *d.* *Pr* 8:30
a just weight is the Lord's *d.* 11:1
upright in their way are his *d.* 20
they that deal truly are his *d.* 12:22
prayer of the upright is his *d.* 15:8
righteous lips are *d.* of kings. 16:13
fool hath no *d.* in understanding. 18:2
d. is not seemly for a fool. 19:10*
that rebuke him shall be *d.* 24:25
he shall give *d.* unto thy soul. 29:17
under his shadow with *d.* *S of S* 2:3
take *d.* in approaching to. *Isa* 58:2
if thou call the sabbath a *d.* 13
they have no *d.* in word. *Jer* 6:10

delight, verb
if the Lord *d.* in us, then. *Num* 14:8
why should the king *d.*? *2 Sam* 24:3
will he *d.* himself in ? *Job* 27:10
that he *d.* himself with God. 34:9
d. thyself also in the Lord. *Ps* 37:4
meek shall *d.* in abundance of. 11
I *d.* to do thy will, O my God. 40:8
they *d.* in lies. 62:4
the people that *d.* in war. 68:30
thy comforts *d.* my soul. 94:19
d. myself in thy statutes. 119:16, 35
d. in thy commandments. 47
d. in thy law 70
how long will scorners *d.*? *Pr* 1:22
and *d.* in frowardness of. 2:14
I *d.* not in the blood of. *Isa* 1:11
they shall not *d.* in it. 13:17
and let your soul *d.* itself 55:2
they seek me, and *d.* to know. 58:2
then shalt thou *d.* thyself in. 14
in these things I *d.* *Jer* 9:24
covenant whom ye *d.* in. *Mal* 3:1
I *d.* in the law of God. *Rom* 7:22

delighted
Jonathan *d.* much in. *1 Sam* 19:2
because he *d.* in me. *2 Sam* 22:20
Ps 18:19
the Lord who *d.* in thee. *1 Ki* 10:9
2 Chr 9:8
and *d.* themselves in thy. *Neh* 9:25
no more, except king *d.* *Esth* 2:14
deliver him, seeing he *d.* *Ps* 22:8
as he *d.* not in blessing. 109:17

choose that wherein I *d.* not.
Isa 65:12; 66:4
be *d.* with the abundance of. 66:11

delightest
not sacrifice, thou *d.* not. *Ps* 51:16

delighteth
king *d.* to honour. *Esth* 6:6, 7, 9, 11
ordered by Lord, and he *d. Ps* 37:23
that *d.* greatly in his. 112:1
he *d.* not in the strength. 147:10
as father son in whom he *d. Pr* 3:12
in whom my soul *d.* *Isa* 42:1
Hephzi-bah, for the Lord *d.* 62:4
and their soul *d.* in their. 66:3
not anger, *d.* in mercy. *Mi* 7:18
when ye say, God *d.* in. *Mal* 2:17

delights
in scarlet with other *d.* *2 Sam* 1:24*
unless law had been my *d. Ps* 119:92
thy commandments are my *d.* 143
my *d.* with the sons of. *Pr* 8:31
men-singers, and *d.* of. *Eccl* 2:8
art thou, O love, for *d.* *S of S* 7:6

delightsome
ye shall be a *d.* land. *Mal* 3:12

Delilah
in valley of Sorek, *D.* *Judg* 16:4
D. therefore took new ropes. 12

deliver
[1] *Restore, or give,* Gen 37:22; 40:13. [2] *Save, rescue,* Ps 7:2; 2 Cor 1:10.
thou shalt *d.* Pharaoh's. *Gen* 40:13*
yet shall ye *d.* the tale. *Ex* 5:18
if a man shall *d.* unto. 22:7, 10
d. it by that the sun goes down. 26*
I will *d.* the inhabitants of. 23:31
if thou wilt indeed *d.* *Num* 21:2
the congregation shall *d.* the. 35:25
he shall *d.* their kings. *Deut* 7:24
thou shalt not *d.* to his. 23:15
to *d.* her husband out of the. 25:11
any that can *d.* out. 32:39; *Isa* 43:13
that ye will *d.* our lives. *Josh* 2:13
for your God will *d.* it into. 8:7
they shall not *d.* the slayer. 20:5
and the Midianites. *Judg* 7:7
if thou shalt without fail *d.* 11:30
Samson shall begin to *d.* 13:5*
the coasts did Israel *d.* *1 Sam* 7:14
which cannot profit nor *d.* 12:21
I will *d.* the Philistines. 23:4
2 Sam 5:19
I will *d.* thine enemy. *1 Sam* 24:4
the Lord will *d.* Israel to. 28:19
king will hear to *d.* his. *2 Sam* 14:16
d. thy servant to Ahab. *1 Ki* 18:9
I will *d.* this multitude. 20:13, 28
go up, for the Lord shall *d.* it.
22:6, 12, 15; *2 Chr* 18:5, 11
he will *d.* the Moabites. *2 Ki* 3:18
d. it for breaches of house. 12:7
Lord *d.* Jerusalem. 18:35; *Isa* 36:20
let them *d.* it into hand. *2 Ki* 2:5
who could not *d.* their. *2 Chr* 25:15
now hear me and *d.* the. 28:11*
gods of nations able to *d.*? 32:13
that your God be able to *d.* 14, 17
those *d.* thou before the. *Ezra* 7:19
there is none can *d.* out. *Job* 10:7
he shall *d.* the island of. 22:30
he will *d.* his soul from. 33:28*
d. my soul. *Ps* 6:4; 17:13; 22:20
116:4; 120:2
while there is none to *d.* 7:2; 50:22
nor shall he *d.* any by his. 33:17
to *d.* their soul from death. 19
not *d.* my feet from falling ? 56:13
for he shall *d.* the needy. 72:12
d. not soul of thy turtle-dove. 74:19
d. poor and needy out of. 82:4
shall he *d.* his soul from ? 89:48
crown of glory shall she *d.* to. *Pr* 4:9
do this now, and *d.* thyself. 6:3
thou shalt *d.* his soul from. 23:14
wickedness *d.* those. *Eccl* 8:8
safe, and none shall *d.* it. *Isa* 5:29
which men *d.* to one. 29:11
defending also he will *d.* it. 31:5
he cannot *d.* his soul. 44:20
they stoop, they could not *d.* 46:2
they shall not *d.* themselves. 47:14

have I no power to *d.?* *Isa* 50:2
residue of them will I *d.* *Jer* 15:9
therefore *d.* up their children. 18:21
I will *d.* all strength of city. 20:5*
afterwards I will *d.* Zedekiah. 21:7
d. the spoiled out of the hand. 22:3
d. such as are for death. 43:11
d. every man his soul. 51:6*, 45*
I will *d.* my people. *Ezek* 13:21, 23
should *d.* but own souls. 14:14, 20
shall *d.* neither sons nor. 16, 18, 20
taketh warning shall *d.* soul. 33:5
I will *d.* my flock from. 34:10
no other god can *d.* *Dan* 3:29
nor was there any that could *d.* 8:4
none that could *d.* the ram. 7
none shall *d.* her out of. *Hos* 2:10
neither shall mighty *d.* *Amos* 2:14
swift of foot shall not *d.* himself. 15
I will *d.* the city. 6:8
in pieces and none *d.* *Mi* 5:8
take hold, but shalt not *d.* 6:14*
d. thyself, O Zion, that. *Zech* 2:7*
I will *d.* every one into his. 11:6
brother shall *d.* brother. *Mat* 10:21
manner of Romans to *d.* *Acts* 25:16*
d. such one to Satan. *1 Cor* 5:5
from death, and doth *d.* *2 Cor* 1:10
Lord knoweth how to *d.* *2 Pet* 2:9

deliver him
rid him, to *d.* *him* to. *Gen* 37:22*
d. him into my hand. 42:37
but God will *d.* *him.* *Ex* 21:13
that he might *d.* *him.* *Deut* 2:30
I will *d.* him and his people. 3:2
d. him into the hand of. 19:12
in any case shalt *d.* *him.* 24:13*
draw Sisera and *d.* *him.* *Judg* 4:7
our part be to *d.* *him.* *1 Sam* 23:20
d. him that smote his. *2 Sam* 14:7
d. him and I will depart. 20:21
d. him from going down. *Job* 33:24
d. him, let him *d.* *him.* *Ps* 22:8*
Lord will *d.* him in time of. 41:1
thou wilt not *d.* him to will of. 2
for there is none to *d.* *him.* 71:11
therefore will I *d.* *him.* 91:14
I will be with him, will *d.* *him.* 15
if thou *d.* him, thou must. *Pr* 19:19
d. him that is spoiled. *Jer* 21:12
righteousness of righteous shall not
d. him. *Ezek* 33:12
on Daniel to *d.* *him.* *Dan* 6:14*
a shadow to *d.* *him* from. *Jonah* 4:6
d. him to Gentiles to crucify.
Mat 20:19; *Mark* 10:33
Luke 20:20; *Acts* 21:11
give, and I will *d.* *him.* *Mat* 26:15
let him *d.* *him* now. 27:43

deliver me
d. me, I pray thee, from. *Gen* 32:11
he will *d.* me out of. *1 Sam* 17:37
will men of Keilah to *d.* ? 23:11, 12
and *d.* me out of thy hand. 24:15
let him *d.* me out of all. 26:24
nor *d.* me into the hands. 30:15
d. me my wife Michal. *2 Sam* 3:14
d. me silver and gold. *1 Ki* 20:5
d. me from enemies. *Job* 6:23
Ps 31:15; 59:1
me from them and *d.* me. *Ps* 7:1
keep my soul, and *d.* me. 25:20
d. me not over to the will. 27:12
d. me in thy righteousness. 31:1
71:2
d. me speedily. 31:2
d. me from my transgressions. 39:8
be pleased to *d.* me. 40:13
d. me from the deceitful and. 43:1
d. me from blood-guiltiness. 51:14
d. me from workers of. 59:2
d. me out of the mire. 69:14
and redeem it, *d.* me. 18*
make haste to *d.* me. 70:1
d. me, O my God, out of. 71:4*
mercy is good *d.* thou me. 109:21
d. me from oppression. 119:134*
mine affliction, and *d.* me. 153
plead my cause, and *d.* me. 154*
d. me according to thy word. 170
d. me, O Lord, from the evil. 140:1
d. me from my persecutors. 142:6
d. me from mine enemies. 143:9

d. me out of great waters. *Ps* 144:7
d. me from the hand of strange. 11
d. me, for thou art my. *Isa* 44:17
the Jews, lest they *d.* me. *Jer* 38:19
no man may *d.* me. *Acts* 25:11*
who shall *d.* me from ? *Rom* 7:24
the Lord shall *d.* me. *2 Tim* 4:18

deliver thee
people which Lord *d.* thee. *Deut* 7:16
midst of thy camp to *d.* thee. 23:14
that we may *d.* thee. *Judg* 15:12, 13
the Lord will *d.* thee. *1 Sam* 17:46
they will *d.* thee up. 23:12
will *d.* thee two. *2 Ki* 18:23*
will *d.* thee and city. 20:6; *Isa* 38:6
d. thee in six troubles. *Job* 5:19
great ransom cannot *d.* thee. 36:18*
I will *d.* thee, and thou. *Ps* 50:15
he shall *d.* thee from snare. 91:3
to *d.* thee from the way. *Pr* 2:12
to *d.* thee from the strange. 16
let thy companies *d.* thee. *Isa* 57:13
to *d.* thee. *Jer* 1:8, 19; 15:20, 21
they shall not *d.* thee. 38:20
I will *d.* thee in that day. 39:17
I will surely *d.* thee. 18
d. thee into the hand. *Ezek* 21:31
I will *d.* thee to them. 23:28
I will *d.* thee to men of east. 25:4
thou servest will *d.* thee. *Dan* 6:16
is thy God able to *d.* thee ? 20
how shall I *d.* thee, Israel ?
Hos 11:8
judge *d.* thee to the. *Mat* 5:25
Luke 12:58

deliver them
come down to *d.* them. *Ex* 3:8
Acts 7:34
thy God shall *d.* them. *Deut* 7:2, 23
to-morrow will I *d.* them. *Josh* 11:6
and if the Lord *d.* them. *Judg* 11:9
to-morrow will I *d.* them. 20:28
wilt thou *d.* them. *1 Sam* 14:37
2 Sam 5:19; *1 Chr* 14:10
d. them to the enemy. *1 Ki* 8:46
2 Ki 21:14
d. them into hand of. *2 Ki* 3:10, 13
will *d.* them into thy. *1 Chr* 14:10
and *d.* them over. *2 Chr* 6:36
that he might *d.* them. *Neh* 9:28
times didst *d.* them. *Job* 5:19
neither any to *d.* them. *Ps* 22:4
trusted, thou didst *d.* them. 37:40*
many times did he *d.* them. 106:43
of upright shall *d.* them. *Pr* 11:6
mouth of upright shall *d.* them. 12:6
forbear to *d.* them that. 24:11
a Saviour to *d.* them. *Isa* 19:20
I will *d.* them to. *Jer* 24:9*; 29:18
d. them into hand of. 29:21; 46:26
gold shall not *d.* them. *Ezek* 7:19
Zeph 1:18
will I seek and *d.* them. *Ezek* 34:12
carried away to *d.* them. *Amos* 1:6
I will not *d.* them. *Zech* 11:6
God would *d.* them. *Acts* 7:25
d. them who through fear. *Heb* 2:15

deliver us
to *d.* us into hand of. *Deut* 1:27
Josh 7:7
d. us only, we pray. *Judg* 10:15
d. us the men, the children. 20:13
who shall *d.* us out of ? *1 Sam* 4:8
d. us out of hand of enemies. 12:10
the Lord will *d.* us. *2 Ki* 18:30, 32
Isa 36:15, 18
d. us from the heathen. *1 Chr* 16:35
our God shall *d.* us. *2 Chr* 32:11
d. us, and purge away. *Ps* 79:9
to *d.* us into the hand. *Jer* 43:3
none that doth *d.* us out. *Lam* 5:8
to *d.* us, and will *d.* us. *Dan* 3:17
thus shall he *d.* us from. *Mi* 5:6
but *d.* us from evil. *Mat* 6:13
Luke 11:4
that he will yet *d.* us. *2 Cor* 1:10
that he might *d.* us from. *Gal* 1:4

deliver you
I *d.* you your brother. *Gen* 42:34
they shall *d.* you your. *Lev* 26:26

did not I *d.* you from ? *Judg* 10:11*
forsaken me, I will *d.* you no. 13*
let them *d.* you in the time of. 14*
he will *d.* you from. *1 Sam* 7:3
he shall *d.* you from. *2 Ki* 17:39
shall not be able to *d.* you. 18:29
Isa 36:14
be able to *d.* you out. *2 Chr* 32:14
I will carry, and will *d.* you. *Isa* 46:4
I will *d.* you into hands. *Ezek* 11:9
God that shall *d.* you ? *Dan* 3:15
for they will *d.* you up. *Mat* 10:17
Mark 13:9
but when they *d.* you up. *Mat* 10:19
24:9; *Mark* 13:11

deliverance
your lives by a great *d.* *Gen* 45:7
hast given this great *d.* *Judg* 15:18
Lord had given *d.* to. *2 Ki* 5:1*
arrow of the Lord's *d.* of *d.* 13:17*
saved them by great *d.* *1 Chr* 11:14*
grant them some *d.* *2 Chr* 12:7
given us such a *d.* as. *Ezra* 9:13*
d. arise to the Jews. *Esth* 4:14
great *d.* giveth he to. *Ps* 18:50
with songs of *d.* 32:7
wrought any *d.* in earth. *Isa* 26:18
in Jerusalem shall be *d.* *Joel* 2:32*
upon mount Zion shall be *d.* *Ob* 17
sent me to preach *d.* to. *Luke* 4:18*
tortured, not accepting *d.* *Heb* 11:35

deliverances
my King, command *d.* *Ps* 44:4

delivered
into your hand are they *d.* *Gen* 9:2
God who *d.* thine enemies. 14:20
d. ere the midwives come. *Ex* 1:19
neither hast thou *d.* thy. 5:23
smote the Egyptians, and *d.* 12:27
who hath *d.* people from. 18:10
the Lord our God *d.* all. *Deut* 2:36
God *d.* into our hands the. 3:3
Lord *d.* unto me two tables. 9:10
and Moses *d.* the law unto. 31:9
Lord *d.* their enemies. *Josh* 21:44
he *d.* the Canaanites into. *Judg* 1:4
after him Shamgar *d.* Israel. 3:31*
they that are *d.* from the. 5:11*
when Lord hath *d.* Zebah and. 8:7
God *d.* Sihon into hand. 11:21
our god hath *d.* Samson. 16:23, 24
was near to be *d.* *1 Sam* 4:19
I smote him and *d.* it. 17:35
who *d.* the company that. 30:23
of Saul's sons be *d.* *2 Sam* 21:6
and I was *d.* of child. *1 Ki* 3:17
I was *d.* this woman was *d.* 18
and shalt thou be *d.?* *2 Ki* 19:11
Isa 37:11
d. that parcel and slew. *1 Chr* 11:14*
on that day David *d.* 16:7*
Jehoiada *d.* to the. *2 Chr* 23:9
d. money that was brought. 34:9
Hilkiah *d.* book to Shaphan. 15
the vessels were *d.* to. *Ezra* 5:14
d. the king's commissions. 8:36
it is *d.* by the pureness. *Job* 22:30
so should I be *d.* for ever. 23:7
I *d.* the poor that cried. 29:12
a mighty man is not *d.* by. 33:16
he hath *d.* my soul in peace. 55:18*
d. my soul from death. 56:13; 86:13
116:8
beloved may be *d.* 60:5; 108:6
let me be *d.* from them. 69:14
and *d.* his strength into. 78:61
the righteous is *d.* out of. *Pr* 11:8
knowledge shall the just be *d.* 9
seed of righteous shall be *d.* 21
whoso walketh wisely be *d.* 28:26
by wisdom he *d.* city. *Eccl* 9:15
to be *d.* from the king. *Isa* 20:6
the book is *d.* to him that is. 29:12
and have they *d.* Samaria ? 36:19
thou hast *d.* it from the pit of. 38:17
shall the lawful captive be *d.?* 49:24
prey of the terrible shall be *d.* 25
before pain came, she was *d.* 66:7
we are *d.* to do all. *Jer* 7:10
d. the soul of the poor. 20:13
when I had *d.* the evidence. 32:16

but thou hast *d.* thy soul.
    Ezek 3:19, 21; 33:9
they only shall be *d.*   14:16, 18
break covenant and be *d.?* 17:15*
for they are all *d.* unto.   31:14
she is *d.* to the sword.   32:20
and *d.* his servants.   *Dan* 3:28
who *d.* Daniel from the power. 6:27
thy people shall be *d.*   12:1
name of Lord shall be *d.* *Joel* 2:32
that escapeth not be *d.* *Amos* 9:1*
there shalt thou be *d.* *Mi* 4:10*
that he may be *d.* from. *Hab* 2:9
they that tempt God *d.* *Mal* 3:15†
all things are *d.* unto me of my.
    Mat 11:27; *Luke* 10:22
commanded body be *d.* *Mat* 27:58*
tradition which ye have *d. Mark* 7:13
Son of man shall be *d.* to. 10:33
Barabbas, and *d.* Jesus.   15:15
    Luke 23:25
time that she be *d. Luke* 1:57; 2:6
that is *d.* unto me, and to. 4:6
there was *d.* unto him the book. 17
Son of man shall be *d.* into. 9:44
diligence that thou be *d.* 12:58*
for he shall be *d.* unto. 18:32
as soon as she is *d.* of. *John* 16:21
that I should not be *d.* 18:36
being *d.* by the counsel. *Acts* 2:23
came to Antioch and *d.* 15:30
and they *d.* the epistle to. 23:33
they *d.* Paul to one Julius. 27:1
yet was I *d.* prisoner. 28:17
was *d.* for our offences. *Rom* 4:25
now we are *d.* from the law. 7:6*
creature itself shall be *d.* 8:21
I may be *d.* from them. 15:31
are alway *d.* to death. *2 Cor* 4:11
we may be *d.* from. *2 Thes* 3:2
I have *d.* to Satan. *1 Tim* 1:20
d. out of mouth of lion. *2 Tim* 4:17
by faith Sarah was *d.* *Heb* 11:11
and *d.* just Lot. *2 Pet* 2:7
from the commandment *d.* 21
the faith which was once *d. Jude* 3
and pained to be *d.* *Rev* 12:2
before woman ready to be *d.* 4

see **hand, hands**

delivered him
Reuben *d. him.* *Gen* 37:21
was *d. him* to keep. *Lev* 6:2*, 4
Lord our God *d. him. Deut* 2:33
Lord *d. him* to the lion. *1 Ki* 13:26
Elijah *d. him* unto his mother. 17:23
d. him that is mine. *Ps* 7:4
the Lord *d. him* to the. *Mat* 18:34
d. him to Pilate. 27:2; *Mark* 15:1
for envy they had *d. him. Mat* 27:18
    Mark 15:10
d. him to be crucified. *Mat* 27:26
    John 19:16
and Jesus *d. him* to. *Luke* 7:15*
healed child and *d. him.* 9:42
d. him to be condemned. 24:20
not have *d. him* to thee. *John* 18:30
God *d. him* out of his. *Acts* 7:10
d. him to four quaternions. 12:4

delivered me
God *d. me* from sword. *Ex* 18:4
I saw ye *d. me* not. *Judg* 12:3*
the Lord that *d. me.* *1 Sam* 17:37
d. me from strong. *2 Sam* 22:18
he *d. me* because. 20; *Ps* 18:19
hast *d. me* from violent man.
    2 Sam 22:49; *Ps* 18:48
Hilkiah *d. me* a book. *2 Ki* 22:10
God hath *d. me* to the. *Job* 16:11
d. me from strong enemies. *Ps* 18:17
hast *d. me* from the strivings. 43
the Lord heard and *d. me.* 34:4
d. me out of all trouble. 54:7
he that *d. me* to thee. *John* 19:11
of them all Lord *d. me.* *2 Tim* 4:17

delivered thee
Lord *d. thee* to-day. *1 Sam* 24:10
I *d. thee* out of hand of. *2 Sam* 12:7
in trouble, and I *d. thee.* *Ps* 81:7
I *d. thee* to will of them. *Ezek* 16:27
chief priests *d. thee.* *John* 18:35

delivered them
how the Lord *d. them.* *Ex* 18:8
tables of stone, *d. them. Deut* 5:22*
deliverer, who *d. them. Judg* 3:9*
gods of nations *d. them.* *2 Ki* 19:12
    Isa 37:12
hath *d. them* to trouble. *2 Chr* 29:8
when he *d. them.* *Ps* 78:42*
d. them out of their. 107:6
d. them from destructions. 20
d. them to the slaughter. *Isa* 34:2
d. them to cause them. *Ezek* 16:21
and *d.* to *them* his goods. *Mat* 25:14
even as they *d. them* to. *Luke* 1:2
he *d. them* ten pounds, and. 19:13*
they *d. them* the decrees. *Acts* 16:4
as I *d. them* to you. *1 Cor* 11:2
and *d. them* into chains. *2 Pet* 2:4*

delivered up
Lord *d. up* Canaanites. *Num* 21:3
Lord *d. up* Amorites. *Josh* 10:12
d. up the men that. *2 Sam* 18:28
because they *d. up* the. *Amos* 1:9
nor shouldest have *d. up.* *Ob* 14
his Son whom ye *d. up.* *Acts* 3:13
but *d. him up* for us. *Rom* 8:32
have *d. up* kingdom. *1 Cor* 15:24
death and hell *d. up.* *Rev* 20:13*

delivered us
an Egyptian *d. us* from. *Ex* 2:19
customs Moses *d. us. Acts* 6:14
d. us from so great a. *2 Cor* 1:10
hath *d. us* from power of. *Col* 1:13
Jesus, who *d. us* from. *1 Thes* 1:10

deliveredst, -est
thou *d.* them to enemies. *Neh* 9:27
who *d.* poor from him. *Ps* 35:10
what thou *d.* will I give. *Mi* 6:14*
Lord, thou *d.* unto me. *Mat* 25:20
thou *d.* unto me two talents. 22

deliverer
a *d.* to Israel. *Judg* 3:9*, 15*
there was no *d.* 18:28
Lord is my rock and *d.* *2 Sam* 22:2
my help and my *d. Ps* 40:17; 70:5
my high tower, and my *d.* 144:2
did God send to be a *d. Acts* 7:35
out of Sion the *d.* *Rom* 11:26

delivereth
he *d.* the poor in his. *Job* 36:15
he *d.* me from mine. *Ps* 18:48*
and *d.* them. 34:7
the Lord *d.* them out of. 17*, 19
he *d.* them out of the hand. 97:10
who *d.* David from. 144:10*
righteousness *d.* *Pr* 10:2; 11:4
a true witness *d.* souls. 14:25
and she *d.* girdles. 31:24
for a prey, and none *d. Isa* 42:22
God *d.* and rescueth. *Dan* 6:27

delivering
d. you up to synagogues. *Luke* 21:12
d. into prisons both. *Acts* 22:4
d. thee from the people. 26:17

delivery
near the time of her *d.* *Isa* 26:17

delusion
send them strong *d.* *2 Thes* 2:11*

delusions
I also will choose their *d. Isa* 66:4

demand
the *d.* by the word of. *Dan* 4:17

demand, -ed, verb
d. why have ye not? *Ex* 5:14
David *d.* of Uriah. *2 Sam* 11:7*
I will *d.* of thee, answer. *Job* 38:3
    40:7; 42:4
secret which the king *d. Dan* 2:27
d. where Christ should. *Mat* 2:4*
the soldiers *d.* of him. *Luke* 3:14*
and when he was *d.* of the. 17:20*
the chief captain *d.* *Acts* 21:33*

Demas
Luke and *D.* greet you. *Col* 4:14
    Philem 24
D. hath forsaken me. *2 Tim* 4:10

Demetrius
D. a silversmith, who. *Acts* 19:24
if *D.* have a matter against. 38
D. hath good report of. *3 John* 12

demonstration
but in *d.* of the Spirit. *1 Cor* 2:4

den, -s
of Israel made them *d.* *Judg* 6:2
then beasts go into *d.* *Job* 37:8*
they couch in their *d.* 38:40
in wait as a lion in his *d. Ps* 10:9
lay themselves down in *d.* 104:22
from the lion's *d.* *S of S* 4:8
hand on cockatrice' *d.* *Isa* 11:8*
the towers shall be for *d.* 32:14
house become a *d.* of? *Jer* 7:11
Jerusalem a *d.* of dragons. 9:11*
cities of Judah a *d.* of. 10:22*
cast into *d.* of lions. *Dan* 6:7, 12
they cast him into the *d.* 16
king arose went in haste to the *d.* 19
take Daniel up out of the *d.* 23
cast them into the *d.* of lions. 24
lion cry out of his *d.?* *Amos* 3:4
the lion filled his *d.* with. *Nah* 2:12
house of prayer, but ye have made
  it a *d.* *Mat* 21:13; *Mark* 11:17
in deserts and in *d.* *Heb* 11:38*
and freeman hid in *d.* *Rev* 6:15*

denied
Sarah *d.* saying, I. *Gen* 18:15
and I *d.* him not. *1 Ki* 20:7
I should have *d.* God. *Job* 31:28*
Peter *d.* before them all, saying, I.
  Mat 26:70, 72; *Mark* 14:70
  Luke 22:57; *John* 18:25, 27
when all *d.* that they. *Luke* 8:45
who denies shall be *d.* before. 12:9
and *d.* not, I am not. *John* 1:20
till thou hast *d.* me thrice. 13:38
d. in presence of Pilate. *Acts* 3:13
but ye *d.* the holy One and the. 14
he hath *d.* the faith. *1 Tim* 5:8
and not *d.* my faith. *Rev* 2:13
and hast not *d.* my name. 3:8

denieth, -ing
he that *d.* me before. *Luke* 12:9
form of godliness, but *d.* *2 Tim* 3:5
that *d.* ungodliness and. *Tit* 2:12
even *d.* the Lord that. *2 Pet* 2:1
is a liar, that *d.* Jesus. *1 John* 2:22
who *d.* the Son. 23
d. the only Lord God. *Jude* 4

denounce
I *d.* this day. *Deut* 30:18

deny
lest ye *d.* your God. *Josh* 24:27
d. me not. *1 Ki* 2:16; *Pr* 30:7
then it shall *d.* him. *Job* 8:18
lest I be full and *d.* thee. *Pr* 30:9
d. me, him will I *d.* *Mat* 10:33
let him *d.* himself. 16:24
    Mark 8:34; *Luke* 9:23
cock crow thou shalt *d.* me thrice.
  Mat 26:34, 75; *Mark* 14:30, 72
yet will I not *d.* thee. *Mat* 26:35
    Mark 14:31
d. there is any resurrection.
    Luke 20:27
d. him, he will *d.* us. *2 Tim* 2:12
abideth faithful, cannot *d.* 13
but in works they *d.* him. *Tit* 1:16

depart
if thou *d.* to the right. *Gen* 13:9
Moses let father-in-law *d. Ex* 18:27
d. thou and the people thou. 33:1
I will *d.* to mine own. *Num* 10:30
from day thou didst *d. Deut* 9:7
Joshua let people *d.* to. *Josh* 24:28
Levite rose up to *d. Judg* 19:5, 7, 8, 9
abide not in hold. *1 Sam* 23:13
be up and have light, *d.* 29:10
and his men rose up to *d.* 11
lead them away and *d.* 30:22
I will let thee *d.* *2 Sam* 11:12
make speed to *d.* lest. 15:14
d. for three days. *1 Ki* 12:5
increase of house shall *d. Job* 20:28
envy of Ephraim shall *d. Isa* 11:13
d. ye, *d.* ye, out. 52:11; 54:10
for the mountains shall *d. Isa* 54:10
they shall *d.* man and. *Jer* 50:3

arise ye, and *d.* this is.   *Mi* 2:10
sceptre of Egypt shall *d. Zech* 10:11
besought him that he *d.* out of their
   coasts.   *Mat* 8:34; *Mark* 5:17
when ye *d.* out of that house or city.
   Mat 10:14; *Mark* 6:11; *Luke* 9:4
thy servant *d.* in peace.   *Luke* 2:29
d. hence, Herod will kill thee. 13:31
which are in midst *d.* out.   21:21
they said, *d.* hence and.   *John* 7:3
when Jesus knew he should *d.* 13:1
but if I *d.* I will send him.   16:7
d. and go in peace.   *Acts* 16:36
desired them to *a.* out of city.   39
them ready to *d.* on morrow.   20:7
d. for I will send thee to the. 22:21
that he himself would *d.*   25:4
more part advised to *d.*   27:12
if she *d.* let her remain. *1 Cor* 7:11
if the unbelieving *d.* let him *d.* 15
a desire to *d.* and to be.   *Phil* 1:23
say to them, in peace.   *Jas* 2:16

depart *from*

frogs shall *d. from* thee.   *Ex* 8:11
swarms of flies may *d. from.*   29
so that her fruit *d. from.*   21:22
then shall he *d. from.*   *Lev* 25:41
d. from the tents of.   *Num* 16:26
lest they *d. from* thy.   *Deut* 4:9
fearful, let him *d. from.*   *Judg* 7:3
d. from the Amalekites. *1 Sam* 15:6
sword never *d. from.*   *2 Sam* 12:10
and I will *d. from* the city.   20:21
d. from me. *1 Ki* 15:19; *2 Chr* 16:3
moved them to *d. from. 2 Chr* 18:31
to God, *d. from* us. *Job* 21:14; 22:17
and to *d. from* evil is.   28:28
d. from me, ye workers.   *Ps* 6:8
   Mat 7:23; *Luke* 13:27
d. from evil, and do good. *Ps* 34:14
   37:27
froward heart shall *d. from.*   101:4
d. from me, ye evil doers. 119:115
d. from me therefore.   139:19
and *d. from* evil.   *Pr* 3:7
to *d. from* the snares. 13:14; 14:27
to fools to *d. from* evil.   13:19
that he may *d. from* hell.   15:24
fear of Lord men *d. from* evil. 16:6
of upright is to *d. from* evil.   17
his burden *d. from* off.   *Isa* 14:25
lest my soul *d. from* thee. *Jer* 6:8*
that *d. from* me shall be.   17:13
if those ordinances *d. from.* 31:36
Chaldeans shall surely *d. from.* 37:9
jealousy shall *d. from. Ezek* 16:42
to them when I *d. from. Hos* 9:12
d. from me, ye cursed. *Mat* 25:41
abide, till ye *d. from. Mark* 6:10
besought him to *d. from.*   8:37
not *d. from* Jerusalem.   *Acts* 1:4
all the Jews to *d. from* Rome. 18:2
let not wife *d. from* her. *1 Cor* 7:10
that it might *d. from. 2 Cor* 12:8
shall *d. from* the faith. *1 Tim* 4:1*
d. from iniquity.   *2 Tim* 2:19

not depart

sceptre shall *not d.*   *Gen* 49:10
book of law shall *not d.*   *Josh* 1:8
d. not hence, till I come. *Judg* 6:18
my mercy shall *not d. 2 Sam* 7:15
his statutes, I did *not d.* from. 22:23
they might *not d. 2 Chr* 35:15
how long wilt thou *not d.? Job* 7:19*
shall *not d.* out of darkness. 15:30
deceit and guile *d. not.*   *Ps* 55:11
let them *not d.*   *Pr* 3:21; 4:21
hear me, and *d. not* from.   5:7
evil shall *not d.* from his.   17:13
when old he will *not d.* from it. 22:6
will *not* his foolishness *d.*   27:22
kindness shall *not d.*   *Isa* 54:10
Spirit, and words, shall *not d.* 59:21
they shall *not d.* from.   *Jer* 32:40
for they shall *not d.*   37:9
they need *not d.* give.   *Mat* 14:16
that should *not d.* from. *Luke* 4:42
thou shalt *not d.* thence, till. 12:59

departed

so Abraham *d.* as.   *Gen* 12:4
they took Lot and *d.*   14:12
Hagar *d.*   21:14

Eliezer *d.*   *Gen* 24:10
Isaac *d.*   26:17
Laban *d.*   31:55
they are *d.* hence, to Dothan. 37:17
laded their asses and *d.*   42:26
brethren away, and they *d.*   45:24
was kindled, and he *d.*   *Num* 12:9
elders of Moab and Midian *d.* 22:7
spies away, and they *d.*   *Josh* 2:21
d. every man to his.   *Judg* 9:55
   2 Sam 6:19
then the five men *d. Judg* 18:7, 21
the Levite *d.*   19:10
Israel *d.* thence.   21:24
Israel go, and they *d.? 1 Sam* 6:6
David *d.*   20:42; 22:1, 5
so Nathan *d.*   *2 Sam* 12:15
from day the king *d.*   19:24
and the people *d.*   *1 Ki* 12:5
   2 Chr 10:5
wife arose and *d.* to.   *1 Ki* 14:17
Elijah *d.* and.   19:19; *2 Ki* 1:4
the messengers *d.* and.   *1 Ki* 20:9
prophet *d.* and waited for.   38
Naaman *d.*   *2 Ki* 5:5
so Sennacherib *d.* 19:36; *Isa* 37:37
all people *d.* every.   *1 Chr* 16:43
wherefore Joab *d.* and.   21:4
Jehoram *d.* without.   *2 Chr* 21:20
Egypt glad when they *d. Ps* 105:38
mine age is *d.* and.   *Isa* 38:12
Ishmael *d.* to go over.   *Jer* 41:10
all her beauty is *d.*   *Lam* 1:6
king, wise men *d.*   *Mat* 2:9, 12
arose, and *d.* into Egypt.   14
Jesus *d.* 4:12; 9:27; 11:1; 12:9
   13:53; 14:13; 15:21, 29; 16:4
   19:15; *Mark* 1:35; 6:46
   8:13; *Luke* 4:42; *John* 4:3, 43
   6:15; 12:36
Judas *d.*   *Mat* 27:5
Zacharias *d.* to his house. *Luke* 1:23
he *d.* to his own house.   5:25
messengers of John were *d.*   7:24
out of whom the devils were *d.* 8:35
thieves wounded him and *d.* 10:30
when the Samaritan *d.*   35
the man *d.* and told.   *John* 5:15
when the angel *d.*   *Acts* 10:7
Barnabas *d.*   11:25
Peter *d.*   12:17
they *d.* to Seleucia.   13:4
Paul *d.*   14:20; 18:7, 23
   20:1, 11
Paul and Barnabas *d.* asunder. 15:39
Paul and Silas *d.*   16:40
d. and went. 21:5, 8; 28:10, 11
these words, the Jews *d.*   28:29
forsaken me, is *d.* to. *2 Tim* 4:10
perhaps he therefore *d. Philem* 15*
and the heaven *d.* as.   *Rev* 6:14

departed *from*

arose and *d. from. Gen* 26:31
my sleep *d. from* mine.   31:40*
were *d. from. Ex* 19:2; *Num* 33:15
all Israel *d. from* presence. *Ex* 35:20
plague be *d. from* them. *Lev* 13:58
they *d. from* the mount. *Num* 10:33*
the cloud *d. from* off.   12:10
defence is *d. from* them.   14:9
they *d. from* Rameses.   33:3
d. from Succoth.   6
d. from Pi-hahiroth.   8
d. from Dophkah.   13
All their departures set down to
   verse 49
we *d. from* Horeb.   *Deut* 1:19
not that Lord *d. from. Judg* 16:20
glory is *d. from. 1 Sam* 4:21, 22
when thou art *d. from* me.   10:2
Kenites *d. from* among the.   15:6
Spirit *d. from* Saul. 16:14; 18:12
the evil spirit *d. from* him.   23
God is *d. from* me.   28:15
seeing the Lord is *d. from* thee. 16
as thou art *d. from* me. *1 Ki* 20:36
they *d. from* him to.   *2 Ki* 3:27
so he *d. from* Elisha.   5:19; 8:14
Sennacherib *d. from.* 19:8; *Isa* 37:8
they were *d. from* him. *2 Chr* 24:25
then we *d. from* the river. *Ezra* 8:31
wickedly *d. from* my God. *Ps* 18:21

Ephraim *d.* from Judah.   *Isa* 7:17
smiths were *d.* from.   *Jer* 29:2
Chaldeans heard they *d.* from. 37:5*
which hath *d.* from us.   *Ezek* 6:9
glory of the Lord *d.* from.   10:18
the kingdom is *d.* from.   *Dan* 4:31
glory of Samaria *d.* from. *Hos* 10:5
Jesus *d.* from thence.   *Mat* 15:29
he *d.* from Galilee.   19:1
as they *d.* from Jericho.   20:29
Jesus *d.* from the temple.   24:1
they *d.* quickly from the.   28:8
leprosy *d.* from him.   *Mark* 1:42
   Luke 5:13
angel *d.* from Mary.   *Luke* 1:38
the devil *d.* from him for.   4:13
as they *d.* from him.   9:33
d. from the presence.   *Acts* 5:41
forthwith angel *d.* from him. 12:10
they had *d.* from Perga.   13:14*
John *d.* from them from.   15:38
Paul *d.* from them. 17:33; 18:1
   19:9; *Phil* 4:15
diseases *d.* from them.   *Acts* 19:12
after are *d.* from thee, and all things
   dainty are *d.* from.   *Rev* 18:14*

departed *not from*

not *d.* from my God.   *2 Sam* 22:22
   Ps 18:21
he *d.* not therefrom. *2 Ki* 3:3; 13:2
Jehu *d.* not from sins of. 10:29, 31
   13:6, 11; 14:24; 15:9, 18; 17:22
Hezekiah *d.* not from.   18:6
d. not from commandment of.
   2 Chr 8:15
Jehoshaphat *d.* not from the. 20:32*
d. not from following Lord.   34:33
cloud *d.* not from them.   *Neh* 9:19
I have not *d.* from thy. *Ps* 119:102
Anna *d.* not from temple. *Luke* 2:37

departed *out*

old when he *d.* out of.   *Gen* 12:4
when she is *d.* out of.   *Deut* 24:2
angel of the Lord *d.* out. *Judg* 6:21
Levite *d.* out of Beth-lehem. 17:8
David and men *d.* out. *1 Sam* 23:13
Uriah *d.* out of king's. *2 Sam* 11:8
ye are *d.* out of the way. *Mal* 2:8*
devil, and he *d.* out of. *Mat* 17:18

departed *not out*

Joshua *d.* not out of.   *Ex* 33:11
and Moses *d.* not out. *Num* 14:44

departeth

him away, and he *d.*   *Job* 27:21
a wise man feareth, and *d.*   14:16
in with vanity, and *d.*   *Eccl* 6:4
he that *d.* from evil.   *Isa* 59:15
wife treacherously *d.*   *Jer* 3:20
cursed be man whose heart *d.* 17:5
bloody city, prey *d.* not.   *Nah* 3:1
hardly *d.* from him.   *Luke* 9:39

departing

as her soul was in *d.*   *Gen* 35:18
after their *d.* out of land.   *Ex* 16:1
in lying and *d.* away.   *Isa* 59:13
we have sinned, by *d. Dan* 9:5*, 11
committed whoredom *d.*   *Hos* 1:2
the people saw them *d. Mark* 6:33
d. from coast of Tyre and.   7:31
John *d.* from them.   *Acts* 13:13
after my *d.* shall wolves.   20:29
an evil heart, in *d.*   *Heb* 3:12
Joseph made mention of *d.*   11:22

departure

isles shall be troubled at thy *d.*
   Ezek 26:18
time of my *d.* is at hand. *2 Tim* 4:6

deposed

was *d.* from kingly.   *Dan* 5:20

deprived

why should I be *d.? Gen* 27:45*
because God hath *d.* her. *Job* 39:17
I am *d.* of the residue of. *Isa* 38:10

depth

d. saith it is not in me. *Job* 28:14*
walked in search of the *d.?* 38:16*
he layeth up the *d.*   *Ps* 33:7*
compass on face of the *d. Pr* 8:27*
and the earth for *d.*   25:3
ask it either in the *d.*   *Isa* 7:11

the *d.* closed me round. *Jonah* 2:5
drowned in the *d.* of the. *Mat* 18:6
because it had no *d.* of. *Mark* 4:5
nor *d.* separate us from. *Rom* 8:39
O the *d.* of the riches both. 11:33
what is breadth and *d.* *Eph* 3:18

depths
the *d.* have covered them. *Ex* 15:5
the *d.* were congealed in the. 8*
the *d.* that spring out of. *Deut* 8:7
my people from the *d.* *Ps* 68:22
shall bring me up from the *d.* 71:20
waters were afraid, the *d.* 77:16
drink as out of great *d.* 78:15
he led them through *d.* as. 106:9
they go down again to *d.* 107:26
out of the *d.* have I cried. 130:1
by his knowledge the *d.* *Pr* 3:20
when there no *d.* I was. 8:24
guests are in *d.* of hell. 9:18
that hath made the *d.* of. *Isa* 51:10
broken in *d.* of waters. *Ezek* 27:34
cast their sins into *d.* of. *Mi* 7:19
have not known the *d.* *Rev* 2:24

deputed
there is no man *d.* of. *2 Sam* 15:3

deputies
written to *d.* and rulers. *Esth* 8:9*
and the *d.* and officers. 9:3*
there are *d.* let them. *Acts* 19:38*

deputy
no king in Edom, a *d.* *1 Ki* 22:47
Bar-jesus which was with the *d.*
Acts 13:7*
seeking to turn away the *d.* 8*
and when Gallio was the *d.* 18:12*

deride
shall *d.* every strong hold. *Hab* 1:10

derided
these things, and *d.* *Luke* 16:14
rulers also with people *d.* 23:35

derision
than I, have me in *d.* *Job* 30:1
Lord shall have them in *d.* *Ps* 2:4
a *d.* to them that are. 44:13; 79:4
all the heathen in *d.* 59:8
proud had me greatly in *d.* 119:51
I am in *d.* daily. *Jer* 20:7
was made a *d.* daily. 8
Moab also shall be in *d.* 48:26, 39
for was not Israel a *d.*? 27
I was a *d.* to my people. *Lam* 3:14
drink and be glad in *d.* *Ezek* 23:32
to cities which became a *d.* 36:4
this shall be their *d.* *Hos* 7:16

descend
the border shall *d.* *Num* 34:11
he shall *d.* into battle. *1 Sam* 26:10
his glory shall not *d.* *Ps* 49:17
with them that *d.* *Ezek* 26:20; 31:16
let Christ *d.* now. *Mark* 15:32
vessel *d.* as a great sheet. *Acts* 11:5
or who shall *d.* into ? *Rom* 10:7
Lord shall *d.* from. *1 Thes* 4:16

descended
because the Lord *d.* on. *Ex* 19:18
the cloudy pillar *d.* 33:9
d. in a cloud. 34:5
brook that *d.* out of. *Deut* 9:21
so the two men *d.* *Josh* 2:23
as dew that *d.* on. *Ps* 133:3
up to heaven, or *d.*? *Pr* 30:4
the rain *d.* and. *Mat* 7:25, 27
for angel of the Lord *d.* 28:2
the Holy Ghost *d.* in a. *Luke* 3:22
Ananias high-priest *d.* *Acts* 24:1
he that *d.* is the same. *Eph* 4:10

descendeth
this wisdom *d.* not from. *Jas* 3:15

descending
and angels ascending and *d.*
Gen 28:12; *John* 1:51
saw the Spirit of God *d.* *Mat* 3:16
Mark 1:10
I saw the Spirit *d.* from. *John* 1:32
whom thou shalt see the Spirit *d.* 33
a vessel *d.* as it had. *Acts* 10:11
that great city *d.* out of. *Rev* 21:10

descent
when come nigh at *d.* *Luke* 19:37

father, mother, and *d.* *Heb* 7:3*
but he whose *d.* is not counted. 6*

describe, -ed, -eth
go through land *d.* it. *Josh* 18:4, 6, 8
charged them that went to *d.* 8
and they *d.* it by cities into seven. 9
he *d.* to him the princes. *Judg* 8:14
even as David also *d.* *Rom* 4:6
for Moses *d.* righteousness. 10:5*

description
and ye shall bring the *d.* *Josh* 18:6

descry
of Joseph sent to *d.* *Judg* 1:23*

desert
(*In the Bible this word means
a deserted place, wilderness, not
desert in the modern usage of the
term. Revised Versions frequently
translate by* wilderness)
flock to backside of the *d.* *Ex* 3:1
three days' journey into *d.* 5:3
they were come to the *d.* 19:2
I will set thy bounds from *d.* 23:31
Israel came into *d.* of Zin. *Num* 20:1
against me in the *d.* of Zin. 27:14
removed from the *d.* of Sinai. 33:16
built towers in the *d.* *2 Chr* 26:10
as wild asses in the *d.* go. *Job* 24:5
grieve him in the *d.*? *Ps* 78:40
like pelican, an owl of *d.* 102:6
and tempted God in the *d.* 106:14
wild beasts of *d.* shall lie. *Isa* 13:21
34:14; *Jer* 50:39
so it cometh from the *d.* *Isa* 21:1
the *d.* shall rejoice. 35:1
streams in the *d.* 6
make straight in *d.* a high. 40:3
I will set in *d.* the fir-tree. 41:19
make rivers in the *d.* 43:19, 20
will make her *d.* like garden. 51:3
be like heath in the *d.* *Jer* 17:6
people that dwell in *d.* shall. 25:24
be a dry land and a *d.* 50:12
waters go down into *d.* *Ezek* 47:8*
behold, he is in the *d.* *Mat* 24:26
did eat manna in the *d.* *John* 6:31
to Gaza, which is *d.* *Acts* 8:26

desert
render them their *d.* *Ps* 28:4

desert *land*
found him in a *d. land.* *Deut* 32:10

desert *place*
departed into a *d. place.* *Mat* 14:13
Mark 6:32; *Luke* 4:42
this is a *d. place.* *Mat* 14:15
Mark 6:35; *Luke* 9:12
come ye into a *d. place. Mark* 6:31
aside into a *d. place.* *Luke* 9:10

deserts
he led them through *d.* *Isa* 48:21
that led us through *d.* *Jer* 2:6
prophets like foxes in *d.* *Ezek* 13:4
John was in the *d.* till. *Luke* 1:80
they wandered in *d.* *Heb* 11:38

deserts
according to their *d.* *Ezek* 7:27

deserve
less than our iniquities *d. Ezra* 9:13

deserveth
less than thy iniquity *d.* *Job* 11:6

deserving
done according to *d.* of. *Judg* 9:16

desirable
all of them *d.* young men. *Ezek* 23:6

desire
[1] *Longing, coveting,* 2 Sam 23:5;
Pr 11:23; 2 Cor 7:7. [2] *An expressed wish, or petition,* Ps 10:17;
1 Ki 2:20.
thy *d.* shall be to thy. *Gen* 3:16
to thee shall be his *d.* 4:7
and come with all the *d.* *Deut* 18:6
and hast a *d.* to her. 21:11
on whom is the *d.* of Israel ?
1 Sam 9:20*
according to all the *d.* of. 23:20
my salvation, all my *d.* *2 Sam* 23:5
I will do all thy *d.* *1 Ki* 5:8
thou shalt accomplish my *d.* 9

to all Solomon's *d.* *1 Ki* 5:10; 9:11
and all his *d.* 9:1
gave to the queen of Sheba all her *d.*
10:13; *2 Chr* 9:12
sought him with their whole *d.*
2 Chr 15:15
thou wilt have a *d.* to work. *Job* 14:15
withheld poor from their *d.* 31:16
my *d.* is that Almighty would. 35*
d. is that Job may be tried. 34:36*
boasteth of his heart's *d.* *Ps* 10:3
thou hast heard the *d.* of. 17
hast given his heart's *d.* 21:2
Lord, all my *d.* is before. 38:9
eye hath seen his *d.* 54:7; 92:11
God shall let me see my *d.* 59:10
he gave them their own *d.* 78:29*
mine ears shall hear my *d.* of. 92:11
till he see his *d.* on his. 112:8
d. of the wicked shall perish. 10
therefore shall I see my *d.* 118:7
thou satisfiest the *d.* of. 145:16
he will fulfil the *d.* of them. 19
the *d.* of righteous shall. *Pr* 10:24
the *d.* of the righteous is. 11:23
but when *d.* cometh. 13:12
the *d.* accomplished is sweet. 19
d. of a man is his kindness. 19:22*
the *d.* of the slothful. 21:25
than wandering of *d.* *Eccl* 6:9
d. shall fail, because man. 12:5*
my beloved's, his *d.* is. *S of S* 7:10
d. of our soul is to thy. *Isa* 26:8
snuffeth up wind at *d.* *Jer* 2:24
land to which you have a *d.* 44:14
I will take from thee *d.* *Ezek* 24:16
profane *d.* of your eyes. 21, 25
neither shall he regard *d.* *Dan* 11:37
it is my *d.* I should. *Hos* 10:10
uttereth his mischievous *d.* *Mi* 7:3
enlargeth his *d.* as hell. *Hab* 2:5
the *d.* of all nations. *Hag* 2:7*
which *d.* have I desired. *Luke* 22:15
my heart's *d.* to God. *Rom* 10:1
having a great *d.* to come. 15:23
told us your earnest *d.* *2 Cor* 7:7
what fear, what vehement *d.* 11
in a strait, having a *d.* to. *Phil* 1:23
your face with great *d.* *1 Thes* 2:17

desire, *verb*
for that ye did *d.* *Ex* 10:11
neither shall any man *d.* 34:24
nor shalt thou *d.* thy. *Deut* 5:21
thou shalt not *d.* the silver. 7:25*
I would *d.* a request of. *Judg* 8:24
I *d.* one small petition. *1 Ki* 2:20
did I *d.* a son of my lord ? *2 Ki* 4:28
thy servants who to. *Neh* 1:11*
surely I *d.* to reason. *Job* 13:3
for we *d.* not knowledge of. 21:14
speak, for I *d.* to justify thee. 33:32
d. not the night when. 36:20
offering thou didst not *d.* *Ps* 40:6
so shall the king greatly *d.* 45:11
put to confusion that *d.* my. 70:2
there is none on earth I *d.* 73:25
all thou canst *d.* are not. *Pr* 3:15
neither *d.* thou his dainty. 23:6
against evil men, nor *d.* to be. 24:1
no beauty that we should *d.* *Isa* 53:2
land whereunto they *d.* *Jer* 22:27
die in the place whither ye *d.* 42:22
I would *d.* mercies of the. *Dan* 2:18
woe to you that *d.* day. *Amos* 5:18
if any man *d.* to be first. *Mark* 9:35
for us whatsoever we shall *d.* 10:35
what things soever ye *d.* 11:24
began to *d.* him to do as. 15:8
when ye shall *d.* to see. *Luke* 17:22
the scribes which *d.* to walk. 20:46
Jews have agreed to *d.* *Acts* 23:20
we *d.* to hear of thee. 28:22
follow after charity, and *d.* *1 Cor* 14:1
from them which *d.* *2 Cor* 11:12
though I would *d.* to glory. 12:6
whereunto ye *d.* again to. *Gal* 4:9
I *d.* to be present with you now. 20
tell me, ye that *d.* to be under ? 21
as many as *d.* to make fair. 6:12
but *d.* to have you circumcised. 13
wherefore I *d.* that ye. *Eph* 3:13
d. a gift, but I *d.* fruit. *Phil* 4:17
to *d.* that ye might be filled. *Col* 1:9

if a man *d*. the office of a. *1 Tim* 3:1
we *d*. every one of you.   *Heb* 6:11
they *d*. a better country.   11:16
ye kill, ye *d*. to have.   *Jas* 4:2*
which things angels *d*. to. *1 Pet* 1:12
as new-born babes *d*. sincere.   2:2
men shall *d*. to die, and.   *Rev* 9:6

desired
and a tree to be *d*. to.   *Gen* 3:6
the king whom ye *d*.   *1 Sam* 12:13
desire which Solomon *d*. *1 Ki* 9:19
              2 Chr 8:6
and Rehoboam *d*. many. *2 Chr* 11:23
whatsoever she *d*. was.   *Esth* 2:13
save of that which he *d*. *Job* 20:20*
more to be *d*. are they.   *Ps* 19:10
one thing I *d*. of the Lord.   27:4
bringeth them to *d*. haven.   107:30
he hath *d*. Zion for his.   132:13
will I dwell, for I have *d*.   14
all that may be *d*. not.   *Pr* 8:11
there is a treasure to be *d*.   21:20*
what my eyes *d*. I kept.   *Eccl* 2:10
of the oaks ye have *d*.   *Isa* 1:29
with my soul have I *d*.   26:9
nor have I *d*. woeful day. *Jer* 17:16
Daniel went and *d*. of.   *Dan* 2:16
known unto me what we *d*.   23
for I *d*. mercy and not.   *Hos* 6:6
no cluster, my soul *d*. fruit. *Mi* 7:1
O nation not *d*.   *Zeph* 2:1*
righteous men have *d*. to. *Mat* 13:17
the Pharisees *d*. he would.   16:1
prisoner whom they *d*. *Mark* 15:6
              Luke 23:25
one of the Pharisees *d*. *Luke* 7:36
Herod *d*. to see him.   9:9*
many kings have *d*. to.   10:24
I have *d*. to eat passover.   22:15
Satan hath *d*. to have you to.   31
released him whom they *d*.   23:25
d. a murderer to be.   *Acts* 3:14
and *d*. to find a tabernacle.   7:46
the eunuch *d*. Philip to come.   8:31
Paul *d*. of the high priest.   9:2
Tyre and Sidon *d*. peace.   12:20
Sergius Paulus *d*. to hear.   13:7*
afterward they *d*. a king.   21
yet *d*. they Pilate that he.   28
and *d*. them to depart out of.   16:39
d. favour against Paul that.   25:3
I greatly *d*. him to.   *1 Cor* 16:12
we *d*. Titus to finish in. *2 Cor* 8:6*
I *d*. Titus, and with him.   12:18*
we have petitions we *d*. *1 John* 5:15

desiredst
according to all thou *d*. *Deut* 18:16
thee, because thou *d*.   *Mat* 18:32

desires
he shall give thee the *d*.   *Ps* 37:4
grant not, O Lord, the *d*.   140:8
fulfilling the *d*. of the.   *Eph* 2:3

desirest
thou *d*. truth in the.   *Ps* 51:6
thou *d*. not sacrifice.   16*

desireth
whatsoever thy soul *d*. *Deut* 14:26
take as much as soul *d*. *1 Sam* 2:16
king *d*. not any dowry.   18:25
what thy soul *d*. *1 Ki* 11:37
over all that thy heart *d*. *2 Sam* 3:21
as a servant earnestly *d*.   *Job* 7:2
what his soul *d*. even that.   23:13
what man is he that *d*. life. *Ps* 34:12
the hill which God *d*. to.   68:16
the wicked *d*. the net.   *Pr* 12:12
the soul of the sluggard *d*.   13:4
soul of the wicked *d*. evil.   21:10
nothing of all that he *d*.   *Eccl* 6:2
old wine straightway *d*. *Luke* 5:39
he sendeth and *d*. conditions. 14:32
office of a bishop, *d*.   *1 Tim* 3:1

desiring
his brethren *d*. to. *Mat* 12:46*, 47*
worshipping and *d*. a.   20:20
brethren stand without *d*. *Luke* 8:20
d. to be fed with the crumbs. 16:21
d. to have judgement. *Acts* 25:15*
d. to be clothed upon.   *2 Cor* 5:2
d. greatly to see us.   *1 Thes* 3:6
d. to be teachers.   *1 Tim* 1:7
greatly *d*. to see thee.   *2 Tim* 1:4

desirous
be not *d*. of his dainties.   *Pr* 23:3
Herod was *d*. to see him. *Luke* 23:8
Jesus knew they were *d*. *John* 16:19
with a garrison *d*. to. *2 Cor* 11:32*
let us not be *d*. of vain.   *Gal* 5:26*
so being affectionately *d*. *1 Thes* 2:8

desolate
[1] *Deserted, hence gloomy*, *Jer*
6:8; 12:10. [2] *Laid waste*, *Isa* 1:7.
[3] *Left alone ; forsaken*, *Ps* 34:22.
Tamar remained *d*.   *2 Sam* 13:20
he dwelleth in *d*. cities.   *Job* 15:28
made *d*. all my company.   16:7
wilderness in former time *d*.   30:3
to satisfy the *d*. and waste.   38:27
mercy on me, for I am *d*. *Ps* 25:16
let them be *d*. for a reward. 40:15
let their habitation be *d*.   69:25
my heart within me is *d*.   143:4
your country is *d*. your.   *Isa* 1:7
she being *d*. shall sit upon.   3:26
shall rest all of them in *d*.   7:19
beast shall cry in their *d*.   13:22*
they that dwell therein are *d*. 24:6*
to inherit the *d*. heritages.   49:8
have lost my children, am *d*.   21*
more are the children of the *d*. 54:1
              Gal 4:27
make the *d*. cities to be.   *Isa* 54:3
be ye very *d*. saith.   *Jer* 2:12
lest I make thee *d*. a land not. 6:8
make cities of Judah *d*. 9:11; 10:22
           33:10; 44:6
have made his habitation *d*. 10:25
made it *d*. and being *d*. it.   12:11
I will make this city *d*.   19:8*
it is *d*. without.   32:43; 33:12
their habitations *d*.   49:20; 50:45
all her gates are *d*.   *Lam* 1:4
he hath made me *d*.   13; 3:11
my children are *d*. the.   1:16
did feed delicately are *d*.   4:5
mountain of Zion which is *d*.   5:18
altars may be made *d*.   *Ezek* 6:6
he knew their *d*. palaces.   19:7
that I might make them *d*.   20:26
I will make Edom *d*. from.   25:13
when I make thee a *d*. city.   26:19
midst of countries that are *d*. 29:12
I will make Pathros *d*. and.   30:14
I will make thee most *d*.   35:3, 7
they are *d*. they are given us.   12
I will make them *d*.   14
rejoice, because it was *d*.   15
because they have made you *d*. 36:3
saith Lord to hills and *d*. wastes. 4
the *d*. cities are become fenced. 35
I plant that that was *d*.   36
on sanctuary that is *d*.   *Dan* 9:17
for abominations shall make it *d*. 27
that maketh *d*.   11:31; 12:11
Samaria shall become *d*. *Hos* 13:16*
the garners are laid *d*.   *Joel* 1:17
flocks of sheep are made *d*.   18
the idols thereof will I lay *d*. *Mi* 1:7
in making thee *d*. because of. 6:13
their towers are *d*.   *Zeph* 3:6
house is left to you *d*.   *Mat* 23:38
              Luke 13:35
let his habitation be *d*.   *Acts* 1:20
a widow indeed and *d*.   *1 Tim* 5:5
hate whore, and make *d*. *Rev* 17:16
in one hour is she made *d*.   18:19

land desolate
seed that *land* be not *d*. *Gen* 47:19
lest *land* become *d*.   *Ex* 23:29
land enjoy her sabbaths lieth *d*.
     Lev 26:34, 35, 43; *2 Chr* 36:21
until the *land* be utterly *d*. *Isa* 6:11
cometh to lay the *land d*.   13:9
land any more be termed *d*.   62:4
gone forth to make *land d*. *Jer* 4:7
the whole *land* shall be *d*.   27
for the *land* shall be *d*.   7:34
d. the whole *land* is made *d*.   12:11
to make their *land d*. and.   18:16*
for their *land* is *d*. because.   25:38
land whereof ye say it is *d*.   32:43
nation which shall make *land d*. 50:3
the *land d*. yea more *d*. *Ezek* 6:14
her *land* may be *d*. from.   12:19
cities laid waste, *land* be *d*.   20

land shall be *d*. *Ezek* 14:16; *Mi* 7:13
I will make the *land d*.   *Ezek* 15:8
land was *d*. and the fulness.   19:7
the *land* of Egypt shall be *d*.   29:9
      10, 12; 30:7; 32:15
I will lay the *land d*.   33:28
when I have laid the *land* most *d*. 29
d. land tilled, whereas it lay *d*. 36:34
the *land* that was *d*. is like.   35
to a *land* barren and *d*. *Joel* 2:20
land was *d*. for they laid pleasant
    land d.   *Zech* 7:14

desolate places
which built *d. places* for. *Job* 3:14*
bread out of *d. places*. *Ps* 109:10
thy waste and *d. places*. *Isa* 49:19
we are in *d. places* as dead. 59:10*
high *places* shall be *d*. *Ezek* 6:6
set thee in *places d*. of old.   26:20
thine hand upon the *d. places*. 38:12
high *places* of Isaac be *d*. *Amos* 7:9
return, and build *d. places*. *Mal* 1:4

shall be, or shalt be desolate
your highways *shall be d*. *Lev* 26:22
your land *shall be d*.   33
hypocrites *shall be d*. *Job* 15:34*
hate righteous *shall be d*. *Ps* 34:21*
none that trust in him *shall be d*. 22*
many houses *shall be d*. *Isa* 5:9
waters of Nimrim *shall be d*. 15:6
             Jer 48:34
defenced city *shall be d*. *Isa* 27:10*
this city *shall be d*.   *Jer* 26:9
place which ye say *shall be d*. 33:10
Noph *shall be d*. without.   46:19*
cities thereof *shall be d*.   48:9
Rabbah *shall be a d*. heap.   49:2
Babylon *shall be* wholly *d*.   50:13
thou *shalt be d*. for ever.   51:26
your altars *shall be d*. *Ezek* 6:4
cities of Egypt *shall be d*.   29:12
mountains of Israel *shall be d*. 33:28
mount Seir, thou *shalt be d*. 35:4, 15
Ephraim *shall be d*. in day. *Hos* 5:9

desolate wilderness
portion a *d. wilderness*. *Jer* 12:10
behind it is a *d. wilderness*. *Joel* 2:3
and Edom a *d. wilderness*.   3:19

desolation
your sanctuaries to *d*.   *Lev* 26:31
and I will bring the land into *d*. 32
made Ai a *d*. unto this day. *Josh* 8:28
that they become a *d*.   *2 Ki* 22:19
who gave them to *d*.   *2 Chr* 30:7
in *d*. they rolled.   *Job* 30:14*
d. in a moment.   *Ps* 73:19
your fear cometh as *d*.   *Pr* 1:27*
be not afraid of *d*. of wicked.   3:25
in that day shall be *d*.   *Isa* 17:9
in the city is left *d*. the gate.   24:12
and *d*. shall come upon thee.   47:11
two things come unto thee, *d*. 51:19
a wilderness, Jerusalem a *d*. 64:10
house shall become a *d*.   *Jer* 22:5
this whole land shall be a *d*.   25:11
make Jerusalem and Judah a *d*. 18
I will make cities of Judah a *d*. 34:22
this day they are a *d*.   44:2
is your land a *d*. and a curse.   22
Bozrah a *d*.   49:13*
Edom a *d*.   17*
Hazor a *d*.   33
how is Babylon become a *d*.! 50:23
to make Babylon a *d*.   51:29
her cities are a *d*. a dry land.   43*
snare is come on us, *d*. *Lam* 3:47*
prince be clothed with *d*. *Ezek* 7:27
filled with the cup of *d*.   23:33
the transgression of *d*.   *Dan* 8:13
increaseth lies and *d*.   *Hos* 12:1
and Edom shall be a *d*.   *Joel* 3:19
I should make thee a *d*.   *Mi* 6:16
houses shall become a *d*. *Zeph* 1:13
day of wrath, wasteness, and *d*. 15
Ashkelon shall be a *d*.   2:4
Moab a perpetual *d*.   9
he will make Nineveh a *d*.   13
d. shall be in thresholds.   14
how is Nineveh become a *d*.!   15
every kingdom divided against itself
   is brought to *d*.   *Mat* 12:25
              Luke 11:17

see abomination of d.   *Mat* 24:15
                 Mark 13:14
then know that the d.   *Luke* 21:20

desolations
and to repair d. thereof.   *Ezra* 9:9*
what d. he hath made.   *Ps* 46:8
lift up thy feet to perpetual d. 74:3*
shall raise up the former d. the d. of
   many generations.   *Isa* 61:4
these nations perpetual d. *Jer* 25:9
land of Chaldeans perpetual d.   12
mount Seir perpetual d. *Ezek* 35:9
seventy years in d. of.   *Dan* 9:2
thine eyes, and behold our d.   18
to the end of the war d.   26

despair
and Saul shall d. of me. *1 Sam* 27:1
cause my heart to d.   *Eccl* 2:20
perplexed, but not in d. *2 Cor* 4:8

despaired
insomuch that we d.   *2 Cor* 1:8

desperate
reprove speeches of one d. *Job* 6:26
of grief and of d. sorrow. *Isa* 17:11

desperately
deceitful, and d. wicked. *Jer* 17:9

despise
if ye shall d. my statutes. *Lev* 26:15*
that d. me shall be.   *1 Sam* 2:30
why then did ye d. us ? *2 Sam* 19:43
they d. their husbands. *Esth* 1:17*
d. not thou the chastening of the.
       Job 5:17; *Pr* 3:11; *Heb* 12:5
I were perfect, I would d. *Job* 9:21
thou shouldest d. the work of. 10:3
if I did d. the cause of my.   31:13
heart, thou wilt not d. *Ps* 51:17
thou shalt d. their image.   73:20
he will not d. their prayer. 102:17
but fools d. wisdom.   *Pr* 1:7
d. not chastening of Lord.   3:11
               Heb 12:5
men do not d. a thief. if. *Pr* 6:30
a fool will d. the wisdom of. 23:9
and d. not thy mother when.   22
because ye d. this word. *Isa* 30:12
thy lovers will d. thee. *Jer* 4:30
say still to them that d. me. 23:17
all that honoured her, d. *Lam* 1:8
Philistines which d. thee. *Ezek* 16:57*
judgement on all that d.   28:26*
I hate, I d. your feast. *Amos* 5:21
O priests, that d. my.   *Mal* 1:6
one, and d. the other. *Mat* 6:24
             Luke 16:13
that ye d. not one of these. *Mat* 18:10
not him that eateth, d. *Rom* 14:3*
or d. ye the church of. *1 Cor* 11:22
let no man therefore d. him. 16:11
d. not prophesyings. *1 Thes* 5:20
let none d. thy youth. *1 Tim* 4:12
let them not d. them.   6:2
let no man d. thee.   *Tit* 2:15
them that d. government. *2 Pet* 2:10
d. dominion, and speak evil. *Jude* 8*

despised
Hagar's mistress was d. *Gen* 16:4
she had conceived, I was d.   5
thus Esau d. his birthright. 25:34
they d. my judgements. *Lev* 26:43*
ye have d. the Lord. *Num* 11:20*
know the land ye have d. 14:31*
because ye d. word of Lord. 15:31
the people thou hast d.? *Judg* 9:38
d. him and brought. *1 Sam* 10:27
she d. him in her heart. *2 Sam* 6:16
           1 Chr 15:29
why hast thou d. commandment ?
            2 Sam 12:9
because thou hast d. me.   10
daughter of Zion hath d. thee.
       2 Ki 19:21; *Isa* 37:22
but they mocked and d. *2 Chr* 36:16
laughed us to scorn and d. *Neh* 2:19
hear, for we are d. and turn. 4:4
he is a lamp d. of him. *Job* 12:5*
yea, young children d. me. 19:18
I am d. of the people.   *Ps* 22:6
            Isa 53:3
he hath not d. the affliction. *Ps* 22:24
because God hath d. them. 53:5*
yea, they d. the pleasant. 106:24

I am small and d. yet do. *Ps* 119:141
they d. all my reproof.   *Pr* 1:30
hath my heart d. reproof ?   5:12
of a perverse heart shall be d. 12:8
he that is d. and hath a servant. 9*
poor man's wisdom is d. *Eccl* 9:16
yea I should not be d. *S of S* 8:1
d. the word of holy One. *Isa* 5:24
he hath d. the cities, he.   33:8
he is d. and rejected of men, he was
   d. and we esteemed him not. 53:3
all they that d. thee shall bow. 60:14
Coniah a d. broken idol. *Jer* 22:28
thus they have d. my people. 33:24
I will make thee small and d. 49:15
he hath d. in indignation. *Lam* 2:6
hast d. oath.   *Ezek* 16:59; 17:16
               18, 19
they d. my judgements.   20:13*
because they d. my judgements. 16*
but had d. my statutes.   24*
thou hast d. mine holy things. 22:8
because they d. the law. *Amos* 2:4*
thou art greatly d.   *Ob* 2
who hath d. day of ? *Zech* 4:10
have we d. thy name ? *Mal* 1:6
righteous, and d. others. *Luke* 18:9*
of Diana should be d. *Acts* 19:27*
things which are d. hath. *1 Cor* 1:28
ye are honourable, we are d. 4:10*
my temptation ye d. not. *Gal* 4:14
d. Moses' law, died. *Heb* 10:28*
but ye have d. the poor. *Jas* 2:6*

despisers
behold, ye d. and.   *Acts* 13:41
incontinent, fierce, d. of. *2 Tim* 3:3*

despisest
or d. thou the riches of ? *Rom* 2:4

despiseth
God is mighty, and d. not. *Job* 36:5
for the Lord d. not.   *Ps* 69:33
void of wisdom d.   *Pr* 11:12
whoso d. the word shall be. 13:13
perverse in his ways d. him. 14:2
that d. his neighbour sinneth.   21
fool d. his father's instruction. 15:5
but a foolish man d. his mother. 20
he that refuseth instruction d. 32
he that d. his ways shall. 19:16*
eye that d. to obey his mother. 30:17
he that d. the gain of. *Isa* 33:15
saith Lord to him whom man d. 49:7
d. you, d. me; d. me, d. him that.
            Luke 10:16*
d. d. not man but God. *1 Thes* 4:8*

despising
the cross, d. the shame. *Heb* 12:2

despite
thy d. against the land *Ezek* 25:6
hath done d. to the Spirit. *Heb* 10:29

despiteful
vengeance with a d. *Ezek* 25:15
with d. minds to cast it out. 36:5
haters of God, d. proud. *Rom* 1:30*

despitefully
pray for them that d.   *Mat* 5:44
            Luke 6:28
assault was made to use them d.
           Acts 14:5*

destitute
who hath not left d. my. *Gen* 24:27
regard prayer of the d. *Ps* 102:17
leave not my soul d.   141:8
folly is joy to him that is d. *Pr* 15:21*
he d. of that whereof. *Ezek* 32:15
of corrupt minds, d. of. *1 Tim* 6:5*
being d. afflicted.   *Heb* 11:37
or sister be naked and d. *Jas* 2:15*

destroy
This is used [1] of demolishing
buildings or cities, Gen 18:28;
Jer 6:5; [2] of putting an end to
anything, 1 Ki 16:12; Jer 51:20;
[3] of killing a person or persons,
Deut 9:14, 25; [4] of nullifying,
Isa 19:3.

wilt thou d. righteous ? *Gen* 18:23
wilt thou d. and not spare ?   24
wilt thou d. all city for ?   28
we will d. this place.   19:13
d. this city.   14

my hand shall d. them. *Ex* 15:9
ye shall d. their altars.   34:13
            Deut 7:5
I will send beasts to d. *Lev* 26:22
d. the children of Sheth. *Num* 24:17
and ye shall d. all his people. 32:15
shall d. their pictures and. 33:52
lest anger of Lord d. thee.
            Deut 6:15
Lord shall d. them with a. 7:23*
thou shalt d. their name.   24
he shall d. them, and.   9:3
let me alone, that I may d.   14
Lord had said he would d.   25
trees that are not for meat d. 20:20
the Lord thy God he will d. 31:3
d. the young man and virgin. 32:25
thrust out enemy, and say, d. 33:27
except ye d. accursed. *Josh* 7:12
depart, lest I d. you. *1 Sam* 15:6
we will d. the heir also. 2 *Sam* 14:7
not suffer revengers to d. any more,
   lest they d. my son.   11
that would d. me and my son. 16
I should swallow or d.   20:20
I might d. them that hate me. 22:41
            Ps 18:40
thus did Zimri d. the. *1 Ki* 16:12
he might d. worshippers. 2 *Ki* 10:19
against this land, and d. it. 18:25
            Isa 36:10
d. kings that had put to. *Ezra* 6:12
if he d. him from his place. *Job* 8:18
yet thou dost d. me.   10:8
after my skin worms d. this. 19:26
thou shalt d. them.   *Ps* 5:6
d. them, O God. let them fall. 10*
their fruit shalt thou d.   21:10
he shall d. them, and not.   28:5
God shall likewise d. thee. 52:5
d. O Lord, and divide their. 55:9
that would d. me are mighty. 69:4
let us d. them together.   74:8
and d. all them that afflict. 143:12
shoot out thine arrows and d. 144:6*
all the wicked will he d. 145:20
prosperity of fools shall d. *Pr* 1:32
of transgressors shall d.   11:3
Lord will d. house of proud. 15:25
robberies of wicked shall d. 21:7
why should God d. work ? *Eccl* 5:6
why shouldest thou d. thyself ? 7:16
and they d. the way of. *Isa* 3:12
nor d. in holy mountain. 11:9; 65:25
he shall d. the sinners thereof. 13:9
he will d. in this mountain. 25:7
go ye upon her walls and d. *Jer* 5:10
let us go by night and d. her. 6:5
let us d. the tree with the. 11:19
I will pluck up and d. that. 12:17
spare nor have mercy, but d. 13:14
my hand against thee and d. 15:6
and d. them with double. 17:18
woe to pastors that d. sheep. 23:1
king of Babylon shall d. 36:29
he shall d. thy strong holds. 48:18
thieves by night will d. 49:9
spare ye not, d. ye utterly all. 51:3
persecute and d. them. *Lam* 3:66
thou d. all the residue ? *Ezek* 9:8
d. the remnant of sea-coast. 25:16
and they shall d. the walls. 26:4
shall d. thy pleasant houses. 12
hew tree down and d. it. *Dan* 4:23
d. wonderfully, and d. mighty. 8:24
by peace shall he d. many. 25
people shall d. the city and. 9:26
that feed on his meat shall d. 11:26
shall I not d. the wise men ? *Ob* 8
it is polluted, it shall d. *Mi* 2:10
north. and d. Assyria. *Zeph* 2:13
they might d. him.   *Mat* 12:14
        Mark 3:6; 11:18
d. those wicked men. *Mat* 21:41
should ask Barabbas, and d. 27:20
will d. the husbandmen. *Mark* 12:9
          Luke 20:16
d. this temple.   *John* 2:19
Jesus of Nazareth shall d. *Acts* 6:14
God shall d. both it and. *1 Cor* 6:13
shall d. with brightness. *2 Thes* 2:8
d. him that had power of. *Heb* 2:14
that he might d. works. *1 John* 3:8
d. them which d. earth. *Rev* 11:18

destroy

I will, or *will I* **destroy**
I will d. man whom I. *Gen 6:7*
I will d. them with the earth. 13
every living substance *will I d.* 7:4
and *I will d.* all people. *Ex 23:27**
the same soul *will I d.* *Lev 23:30*
I will d. your high places. 26:39
       Ezek 6:3
I will early *d.* all wicked. *Ps 101:8*
name of Lord *will I d.* 118:10, 11, 12
and *I will d.* the counsel. *Isa 19:3*
I will cry, *I will d.* and. 42:14*
I will d. my people. *Jer 15:7*
I will d. the city, and the. 46:8
I will d. from thence the king. 49:38
battle-ax, with thee *will I d.* 51:20
I the Lord *will d.* that. *Ezek 14:9*
I will d. thee, and thou shalt know.
    25:7; 28:16; *Zeph 2:5*
I will d. the idols. *Ezek 30:13*
I will d. also all the beasts. 32:13
but *I will d.* the fat and. 34:16
I will d. her vines and. *Hos 2:12*
and *I will d.* thy mother. 4:5
I will d. sinful kingdom. *Amos 9:8*
I will d. thy chariots. *Mi 5:10*
so *will I d.* thy cities. 14
I will d. the strength of. *Hag 2:22*
I will d. this temple. *Mark 14:58*
I will d. the wisdom of. *1 Cor 1:19*

not **destroy**
find forty-five I will *not d. Gen 18:28*
will *not d.* it for twenty's sake. 31
not d. Sodom for ten's sake. 32
not forsake thee, nor *d. Deut 4:31*
d. not thy people and. 9:26
the Lord would *not d.* thee. 10:10
thou shalt *not d.* the trees. 20:19
wilt *not d.* my name. *1 Sam 24:21*
David said to Abishai, *d. not.* 26:9
would *not d.* Judah for. *2 Ki 8:19*
would *not d.* them, nor cast. 13:23
therefore I will *not d.* *2 Chr 12:7*
that the Lord would *not d.* him. 12
Lord would *not d.* the house. 21:7
forbear that he *d.* thee *not.* 35:21
they did *not d.* nations. *Ps 106:34*
d. it *not,* for a blessing is in it; that I
 may *not d.* them all. *Isa 65:8*
that I should *not d.* it. *Ezek 22:30*
d. not the wise men of. *Dan 2:24*
he shall *not d.* fruits of. *Mal 3:11*
d. not him with thy meat. *Rom 14:15*
for meat is *not* the work of God. 20

to **destroy**
flood of waters to *d.* all. *Gen 6:17*
any more a flood to *d.* 9:11, 15
the Lord hath sent us to *d.* it. 19:13
intreat for thee to *d.* frogs. *Ex 8:9*
plague shall not be on you to *d.* 12:13
to deliver us into hand of Amorites
 to *d.* us. *Deut 1:27; Josh 7:7*
hand of Lord to *d.* them. *Deut 2:15*
them that hate him to *d.* them. 7:10
was wroth against you to *d.* 9:19
Lord will rejoice over you to *d.* 28:63
to *d.* all the inhabitants. *Josh 9:24*
to *d.* land where Reubenites. 22:33
Midianites entered to *d.* *Judg. 6:5*
Saul seeketh to *d.* city. *1 Sam 23:10*
came in one of people to *d.* 26:15
not afraid to *d.* Lord's. *2 Sam 1:14*
suffer revengers of blood to *d.* 14:11
thou seekest to *d.* a. 20:19
his hand on Jerusalem to *d.* 24:16
house of Jeroboam to *d.* *1 Ki 13:34*
them against Judah to *d.* *2 Ki 24:2*
angel to Jerusalem to *d.* *1 Chr 21:15*
determined to *d.* thee. *2 Chr 25:16*
Haman sought to *d.* Jews. *Esth 3:6*
    13; 4:7, 8; 9:24
thou movedst me to *d.* *Job 2:3*
it would please God to *d.* me. 6:9
seek after my soul to *d.* it.
    Ps 40:14; 63:9
wicked have waited to *d.* me. 119:95
it is in his heart to *d.* and. *Isa 10:7*
they come from far to *d.* 13:5
hath given commandment to *d.* 23:11
deviseth wicked devices to *d.* 32:7
oppressor were ready to *d.* 51:13
I have created waster to *d.* 54:16

I have set thee *to d.*
    Jer 1:10
    18:7; 31:28
appoint beasts of earth to *d.* 15:3
device against Babylon to *d.* it. 51:11
Lord hath purposed to *d.* *Lam 2:8*
I will send *to d.* you. *Ezek 5:16*
and *to d.* souls, to get gain. 22:27
a despiteful heart *to d.* it. 25:15
nations shall be brought to *d.* 30:11
vision I saw when I came *to d.* 43:3
to d. all wise men of. *Dan 2:12, 24*
and *to d.* his dominion. 7:26
go forth with great fury to *d.* 11:44
not return to *d.* Ephraim. *Hos 11:9*
that I will seek to *d.* all. *Zech 12:9*
seek young child *to d.* *Mat 2:13*
think not that I am come to *d.* law, I
 am not come *to d.* but to. 5:17
fear him who is able to *d.* 10:28
I am able to *d.* the temple. 26:61
art thou come to *d.* us ? *Mark 1:24*
     Luke 4:34
sabbath to save life or to *d. Luke 6:9*
Son of man is not come to *d.* 9:56
chief of people sought to *d.* 19:47
thief cometh not but to *d. John 10:10*
able to save and to *d.* *Jas 4:12*

destroyed
before Lord *d.* Sodom. *Gen 13:10*
when God *d.* the cities of. 19:29
knowest not Egypt is *d.?* *Ex 10:7*
the Lord *d.* them. *Deut 2:21; 4:3*
   11:4; *2 Ki 21:9; 2 Chr 33:9*
destruction, till they be *d. Deut 7:23*
able to stand till thou have *d.* 24
was angry with you to have *d.* 9:8
after that they be *d.* from. 12:30
until thou be *d.* 28:20, 24, 45, 51, 61
yoke on thy neck till he have *d.* 48
and I *d.* them from. *Josh 24:8*
Benjamin *d.* of Israel. *Judg* 20:21, 25
children of Israel *d.* 35, 42
that we should be *d.* *2 Sam 21:5*
the angel that *d.* 24:16; *1 Chr 21:15*
Asa *d.* her idol and. *1 Ki 15:13*
thus Jehu *d.* Baal. *2 Ki 10:28*
Athaliah arose and *d.* all the. 11:1
they have *d.* them. 19:18; *Isa 37:19*
people whom God *d.* *1 Chr 5:25*
were *d.* before Lord. *2 Chr 14:13*
nation was *d.* of nation. 15:6
which kings of Judah had *d.* 15:16
for which cause was city *d. Ezra 4:15*
written, that they may be *d. Esth 3:9*
he hath *d.* me on every. *Job 19:10*
thou hast *d.* the wicked. *Ps 9:5*
thou hast *d.* cities. 6
all them that go a whoring. 73:27
frogs among them, which *d.* 78:45
d. their vines with hail, and. 47
Babylon, who art to be *d.* 137:8
there is that is *d.* for. *Pr 13:23*
because thou hast *d.* land. *Isa 14:20*
hast thou visited and *d.* 26:14
many pastors have *d.* *Jer 12:10*
Moab is *d.* 48:4
Babylon is suddenly *d.* 51:8
hath *d.* out of Babylon. 55
Lord hath *d.* his strong. *Lam 2:5*
he hath *d.* his places of the. 6
he hath *d.* and broken her bars. 9
Tyrus, like the *d.* in the. *Ezek 27:32*
beast was slain, his body *d. Dan 7:11*
O Israel, thou hast *d.* *Hos 13:9*
yet *d.* I the Amorite, I *d. Amos 2:9*
sent his armies and *d.* *Mat 22:7*
the flood came, and *d.* *Luke 17:27*
it rained fire from heaven and *d.* 29
is not this he that *d.?* *Acts 9:21*
when he had *d.* seven nations. 13:19
magnificence should be *d.* 19:27*
body of sin might be *d.* *Rom 6:6*
d. of serpents. *1 Cor 10:9*
d. of the destroyer. 10
preacheth faith which he *d. Gal 1:23*
build again things which I *d.* 2:18
lent that *d.* first-born. *Heb 11:28*
as brute beasts made to be *d.*
    2 Pet 2:12
the Lord afterward *d.* them. *Jude 5*
third part of ships were *d.* *Rev 8:9*

are **destroyed**
the women *are d.* out. *Judg 21:16*

they *are d.* from morning. *Job 4:20*
overturneth them so they *are d.* 34:25
are led of them *are d.* *Isa 9:16*
for all thy lovers *are d.* *Jer 22:20*
my people *are d.* for lack. *Hos 4:6*
their cities *are d.* *Zeph 3:6*

not **destroyed**
but they *d.* them *not.* *2 Chr 20:10*
      Ps 78:38
kingdom which shall *not* be *d.*
      Dan 7:14
cast down, but *not d.* *2 Cor 4:9*

shall be **destroyed**
and I *shall be d.* I and. *Gen 34:30*
father's house *shall be d. Esth 4:14*
transgressors *shall be d.* *Ps 37:38*
i* is that they *shall be d.* 92:7
despiseth word *shall be d. Pr 13:13*
companion of fools *shall be d.* 20*
hardeneth his neck *shall be d.* 29:1
the yoke *shall be d.* *Isa 10:27*
the plain *shall be d.* *Jer 48:8*
all her helpers *shall be d. Ezek 30:8*
a kingdom which *shall* never be *d.*
    Dan 2:44; 6:26
within few days he *shall be d.* 11:20
sin of Israel *shall be d.* *Hos 10:8*
will not hear *shall be d.* *Acts 3:23*
last enemy that *shall be d.* is death.
     1 Cor 15:26

utterly **destroyed**
sacrificeth to any god, save unto the
 Lord, shall be *utterly d. Ex 22:20*
utterly d. the Canaanites. *Num 21:3*
we *utterly d.* Sihon. *Deut 2:34*
we *utterly d.* cities of Og. 3:6
     Josh 2:10
if ye corrupt yourselves ye shall be
 utterly d. *Deut 4:26*
Jericho *utterly d.* *Josh 6:21*
Ai *utterly d.* 8:26; 10:1
Hebron *utterly d.* 10:37
he *utterly d.* all that breathed. 40
Joshua *utterly d.* them. 11:12, 21
and Simeon *utterly d.* *Judg 1:17*
Saul *utterly d.* people. *1 Sam 15:8*
he would not *utterly d.* the best. 9
and rest we have *utterly d.* 15
I have *utterly d.* Amalekites. 20
should have been *utterly d.* 21*
[of Gedor] *utterly d.* *1 Chr 4:41*
Hezekiah *utterly d.* the images.
     2 Chr 31:1
nations my father *utterly d.* 32:14
hath *utterly d.* all nations. *Isa 34:2*

destroyer
will not suffer *d.* to come. *Ex 12:23*
hath delivered the *d.* of. *Judg 16:24*
in prosperity the *d.* shall. *Job 15:21*
kept me from paths of *d.* *Ps 17:4*
is the companion of a *d.* *Pr 28:24*
the *d.* of the Gentiles. *Jer 4:7*
were destroyed of the *d. 1 Cor 10:10*

destroyers
life draweth near to *d.* *Job 33:22*
thy *d.* shall go forth. *Isa 49:17*
and I will prepare *d.* *Jer 22:7*
ye rejoiced, O *d.* of my. 50:11*

destroyest, -eth
as nations the Lord *d.* *Deut 8:20*
he *d.* the perfect and the. *Job 9:22*
increaseth the nations, and *d.* 12:23
and thou *d.* the hope of man. 14:19
he that doth it, *d.* his. *Pr 6:32*
hypocrite with his mouth *d.* 11:9
thy ways to that which *d.* kings. 31:3
and a gift *d.* heart. *Eccl 7:7*
sinner *d.* much good. 9:18
which *d.* all the earth. *Jer 51:25*
thou that *d.* the temple. *Mat 27:40*
     Mark 15:29

destroying
angel of the Lord *d.* *1 Chr 21:12*
as he was *d.* the Lord repented. 15
a strong one, as a *d.* *Isa 28:2*
sword devoured like a *d.* *Jer 2:30*
against Babylon a *d.* wind. 51:1
against them, O *d.* mountain. 25
withdrawn his hand from *d. Lam 2:8*
every man with *d.* weapon. *Ezek 9:1*
mine eye spared them from *d.* 20:17

see **utterly**

10

destruction

destroy them with a mighty d.
              Deut 7:23*
devoured with bitter d.   32:24
Lord was against the city with a
   great d.   1 Sam 5:9*
for there was a deadly d.   11*
I appointed to utter d.   1 Ki 20:42
his counsellors to his d.   2 Chr 22:4
d. of Ahaziah was of God, by.   7
heart was lifted up to his d.   26:16*
how endure to see the d.?   Esth 8:6
smote their enemies with d.   9:5
neither be afraid of d.   Job 5:21
at d. and famine thou shalt laugh. 22
and d. shall be ready.   18:12*
how oft cometh their d.?   21:17*
his eyes shall see his d. and.   20
wicked is reserved to day of d.   30*
hell is naked before him, d.   26:6*
d. and death say, we have.   28:22
against me ways of their d.   30:12
though they cry in his d.   24*
is not d. to the wicked ?   31:3
a fire that consumeth to d.   12
for d. from God was a terror.   23*
if I rejoiced at the d. of him.   29
let d. come upon him, his net catch
   himself, into that very d. Ps 35:8
them down to the pit of d.   55:23
castedst them down into d.   73:18
faithfulness be declared in d.? 88:11
thou turnest man to d. and.   90:3
nor for the d. that wasteth.   91:6
redeemeth thy life from d.   103:4
when your d. cometh.   Pr 1:27*
mouth of foolish is near d.   10:14
the d. of poor is their poverty.   15
d. shall be to workers of. 29; 21:15
openeth his lips shall have d.   13:3
want of people is the d. of.   14:28
hell and d. are before Lord. 15:11*
pride goeth before d.   16:18
that exalteth gate seeketh d. 17:19
a fool's mouth is his d.   18:7
before d. the heart of man is.   12
for their heart studieth d.   24:2*
hell and d. are never full.   27:20*
as are appointed to d.   31:8
d. of transgressors and.   Isa 1:28
anger shall cease in their d.   10:25
it shall come as a d. from.   13:6
Babylon with the besom of d. 14:23
shall raise up a cry of d.   15:5
shall be called city of d.   19:18
the gate is smitten with d.   24:12
the land of thy d. shall be.   49:19
desolation and d. are come. 51:19
wasting and d. are in their.   59:7
d. shall no more be heard.   60:18
from north a great d.   Jer 4:6; 6:1
d. upon d. is cried, for the land. 4:20
destroy them with double d.   17:18
d. cometh, it cometh out.   46:20
Horonaim, spoiling and d.   48:3
enemies have heard a cry of d.   5
a sound of great d. is in.   50:22
great d. from land of.   51:54
d. of the daughter. Lam 2:11; 3:48
desolation and d. is come.   3:47
in the d. of the daughter of.   4:10
send famine for their d.   Ezek 5:16
d. cometh, and they shall.   7:25
when I bring thy d. among.   32:9
d. to them, because they.   Hos 7:13
they are gone, because of d.   9:6
I will be thy d. repentance hid. 13:14
as a d. from Almighty.   Joel 1:15
rejoiced in day of their d.   Ob 12
destroy you with a sore d.   Mi 2:10
be no more utter d.   Zech 14:11*
is way that leadeth to d.   Mat 7:13
d. and misery are in.   Rom 3:16
vessels of wrath fitted to d.   9:22
deliver to Satan for d.   1 Cor 5:5
given us not for your d.   2 Cor 10:8
                 13:10
walk whose end is d.   Phil 3:19*
then sudden d. cometh. 1 Thes 5:3
punished with everlasting d.
               2 Thes 1:9
which drown men in d.   1 Tim 6:9
upon themselves swift d.   2 Pet 2:1
unstable wrest to their own d. 3:16

destructions

O enemy, d. are come.   Ps 9:6*
rescue my soul from their d.   35:17
delivereth them from their d. 107:20

detain, -ed

let us d. thee till we.   Judg 13:15
though thou d. me, I will not.   16
Doeg was that day d.   1 Sam 21:7

determinate

delivered by d. counsel.   Acts 2:23

determination

d. is to gather nations.   Zeph 3:8

determine

shall pay as the judges d. Ex 21:22

determined

sure that evil is d. by.   1 Sam 20:7
if I knew that evil were d.   9
Jonathan knew that it was d.   33
for evil is d. against our.   25:17
Absalom hath been d.   2 Sam 13:32
Solomon d. to build a.   2 Chr 2:1
I know that God hath d.   25:16
that there was evil d.   Esth 7:7
seeing his days are d.   Job 14:5
a consumption d.   Isa 10:23; 28:22
of Lord which hath d.   19:17*
seventy weeks are d.   Dan 9:24*
to end of war desolations are d.   26
and that d. shall be poured upon. 27
that is d. shall be done.   11:36
of man goeth as was d. Luke 22:22
when Pilate was d. to.   Acts 3:13
to do what thy counsel d.   4:28*
the disciples d. to send.   11:29
d. that Paul and Barnabas.   15:2*
and Barnabas to take with.   37*
and hath d. the times before. 17:26
be d. in a lawful assembly.   19:39
for Paul had d. to sail by.   20:16
I have d. to send Paul.   25:25
it was d. that we should sail.   27:1
I d. not to know any thing. 1 Cor 2:2
but I d. this with myself.   2 Cor 2:1
Nicopolis, for I have d.   Tit 3:12

detest

but thou shalt utterly d.   Deut 7:26

detestable

defiled my land with d.   Jer 16:18
defiled sanctuary with d. Ezek 5:11
made images of their d. things. 7:20
shall take away all d. things. 11:18
heart walketh after their d. things. 21
any more defile with their d.   37:23

device

to find out every d.   2 Chr 2:14
to put away his d. that.   Esth 8:3
his wicked d. should return.   9:25
imagined a mischievous d. Ps 21:11
further not his wicked d.   140:8
there is no work nor d.   Eccl 9:10
I devise a d. against you. Jer 18:11
for his d. is against Babylon. 51:11
and their d. against me.   Lam 3:62*
stone graven by man's d. Acts 17:29

devices

he disappointeth the d.   Job 5:12
d. which ye wrongfully.   21:27
let them be taken in d.   Ps 10:2
he maketh the d. of people. 33:10*
man who bringeth wicked d.   37:7
filled with their own d.   Pr 1:31
but a man of wicked d. will.   12:2
there are many d. in a man's. 19:21
he deviseth wicked d. to.   Isa 32:7
they had devised d.   Jer 11:19
we will walk after our own d. 18:12
come and let us devise d.   18
he shall forecast his d.   Dan 11:24
for they shall forecast d.   25
are not ignorant of his d. 2 Cor 2:11

devil

[1] Satan, (i.e. adversary), the
supreme evil spirit, referred to in
the N.T. under the name of
devil, Mat 4:1; Luke 8:12; John
8:44; Rev 12:9. The word devil
is not used of Satan in the Old
Testament. Abaddon in Hebrew,
Apollyon in Greek, that is, destroyer, Rev 9:11.—Angel of the
bottomless pit, Rev. 9:11.—Prince
of this world, John 12:31.—Prince
of darkness, Eph 6:12.—A roaring
Lion, and an Adversary, 1 Pet 5:8.
—Beelzebub, Mat 12:24.—Accuser,
Rev 12:10.—Dragon, Rev 12:7.—
Lucifer, Isa 14:12.—Serpent, Rev
20:2.—Satan, Job 2:6.—The god
of this world, 2 Cor 4:4.
[2] Inferior evil spirits. In this
sense the American Revision translates the word demon.

led to be tempted of the d. Mat 4:1
d. taketh him up to holy city.   5
the d. taketh him up to an high.   8
d. leaveth him.   11
man possessed with a d. 9:32; 12:22
say he hath a d.   11:18; Luke 7:33
that sowed them is d.   Mat 13:39
daughter is vexed with a d.   15:22
Jesus rebuked the d.   17:18
fire, prepared for the d.   25:41
possessed with the d.   Mark 5:15
                 16, 18
the d. is gone out of.   7:29, 30
forty days tempted of d.   Luke 4:2
the d. said to him, all this power. 3, 6
the d. taking him up.   5
when the d. had ended all the.   13
had a spirit of an unclean d.   33
and when the d. had thrown him. 35
then cometh the d. and taketh. 8:12
was driven of the d. into the.   29
as he was coming the d.   9:42
casting out a d. when the d. 11:14
and one of you is a d.   John 6:70
said, thou hast a d.   7:20; 8:48
ye are of your father the d.   8:44
I have not a d.   49
we know that thou hast a d.   52
many said, he hath a d.   10:20
not words of him that hath a d.   21
the d. having put into heart.   13:2
that were oppressed of d. Acts 10:38
thou child of the d.   13:10
neither give place to d.   Eph 4:27
to stand against wiles of d.   6:11
into condemnation of d.   1 Tim 3:6
into reproach, and snare of d.   7
out of the snare of the d. 2 Tim 2:26
power of death, that is d. Heb 2:14
resist the d. and he will.   Jas 4:7
your adversary the d.   1 Pet 5:8
sin is of the d. that he might destroy
   the works of the d.   1 John 3:8
in this the children of the d. are   10
when contending with the d. Jude 9
the d. shall cast some.   Rev 2:10
the old serpent called the d.   12:9
for the d. is come down to you. 12
that old serpent, which is d.   20:2
d. that deceived them was cast. 10

devilish

this wisdom is earthy, d.   Jas 3:15

devils

more offer sacrifices to d. Lev 17:7*
they sacrificed to d.   Deut 32:17*
he ordained him priests for the d.
               2 Chr 11:15*
sons and daughters to d. Ps 106:37*
those possessed with d.   Mat 4:24
8:16, 28, 33; Mark 1:32; Luke 8:36
the d. besought him.   Mat 8:31
                Mark 5:12
saw one casting out d. in thy name.
        Mark 9:38; Luke 9:49
my name shall cast out d. Mark 16:17
and d. also came out of. Luke 4:41
out of whom went seven d.   8:2
he that was possessed of d.   36
and authority over all d.   9:1
even the d. are subject to us. 10:17
that fox, behold, I cast out d. 13:32
sacrifice to d. . . . ye should have
   fellowship with d.   1 Cor 10:20
cup of Lord and cup of d; of Lord's
   table and of table of d.   21
heed to doctrines of d.   1 Tim 4:1
the d. also believe and.   Jas 2:19
should not worship d.   Rev 9:20
spirits of d. working miracles. 16:14
is become habitation of d.   18:2
         see cast

devise

d. cunning works in gold. *Ex* 31:4
 35:35
to d. curious works in gold. 35:32
yet doth he d. means. *2 Sam* 14:14
to confusion, that d. my. *Ps* 35:4
but they d. deceitful matters. 20
against me do they d. my hurt. 41:7
d. not evil against. *Pr* 3:29
they not err that d. evil ? mercy and
 truth to them that d. good. 14:22
shutteth his eyes to d. 16:30
behold, I d. a device. *Jer* 18:11
come and let us d. devices. 18
men that d. mischief. *Ezek* 11:2
woe to them that d. *Mi* 2:1
against this family do I d. an evil. 3

devised

that consumed us d. *2 Sam* 21:5
month which he had d. of. *1 Ki* 12:33
devise that he had d. *Esth* 8:3
be written to reverse letters d. 5
d. to take away my life. *Ps* 31:13
not that they had d. *Jer* 11:19
in Heshbon they have d. evil. 48:2
Lord hath both d. and done. 51:12
 Lam 2:17
not followed cunningly d. *2 Pet* 1:16

deviseth

he d. mischief on his bed. *Ps* 36:4
thy tongue d. mischief like. 52:2
d. mischief continually. *Pr* 6:14
an heart that d. wicked. 18
man's heart d. his way. 16:9
d. to do evil shall be called. 24:8
he d. wicked devices to. *Isa* 32:7
but the liberal d. liberal things. 8

devote

thing that a man shall d. *Lev* 27:28

devoted

to Lord, as a field d. *Lev* 27:21
no d. thing sold, every d. thing. 28
every thing d. in Israel. *Num* 18:14
thy servant, who is d. *Ps* 119:38*

devotions

by and beheld your d. *Acts* 17:23*

devour

[1] *To eat up, or swallow greedily,
either literally or figuratively,*
Gen 37:20; Mat 23:14. [2] *To
waste, or spend riotously,* Luke
15:30.

in morning he shall d. *Gen* 49:27
and sword d. flesh. *Deut* 32:42
shall sword d. for ever ? *2 Sam* 2:26
command locusts to d. *2 Chr* 7:13
firstborn of death shall d. *Job* 18:13
wild beasts of field doth d. *Ps* 80:13
jaw-teeth as knives to d. *Pr* 30:14
your land strangers d. it. *Isa* 1:7
they shall d. Israel with. 9:12
for wickedness shall d. briers. 18
not of a mean man, shall d. 31:8
I will destroy d. at. 42:14*
all ye beasts of the field come to d.
 56:9; *Jer* 12:9; 15:3
that d. Israel shall offend. *Jer* 2:3
sword of the Lord shall d. 12:12
 46:10, 14
and all that d. thee shall. 30:16
flame shall d. corner of Moab. 48:45
and pestilence shall d. *Ezek* 7:15
neither shall beasts of land d. 34:28
therefore shalt thou d. men. 36:14
arise, d. much flesh. *Dan* 7:5
d. whole earth. 23
now shall a month d. them. *Hos* 5:7
sword shall d. his branches. 11:6
there will I d. them like a lion. 13:8
fire shall d. the palaces. *Amos* 1:4
 7, 10, 12
kindle in them, and d. them. *Ob* 18
sword shall d. young. *Nah* 2:13
rejoicing was as to d. *Hab* 3:14
they shall d. and subdue. *Zech* 9:15
they shall d. all the people. *Mat* 23:14
 Mark 12:40; *Luke* 20:47
suffer, if a man d. you. *2 Cor* 11:20
but if ye bite and d. one. *Gal* 5:15
shall d. adversaries. *Heb* 10:27

seeking whom he may d. *1 Pet* 5:8
to d. her child as soon. *Rev* 12:4

fire devour
let *fire* d. the cedars. *Judg* 9:15
let *fire* d. the men of Shechem. 20
and *fire* shall d. them. *Ps* 21:9
shall come, a *fire* shall d. 50:3
fire of thine enemies shall d.
 Isa 26:11
your breath as *fire* shall d. 33:11
another *fire* shall d. *Ezek* 15:7
for them through *fire* to d. 23:37
break out like *fire* and d. *Amos* 5:6
the *fire* shall d. thy bars. *Nah* 3:13
there shall the *fire* d. thee. 15
fire may d. thy cedars. *Zech* 11:1

it shall devour
it shall d. the strength. *Job* 18:13
it shall burn and d. his. *Isa* 10:17
my words fire, it shall d. *Jer* 5:14
a fire and it shall d. the palaces of
 Jerusalem. 17:27; *Amos* 2:5
it shall d. all things. *Jer* 21:14
 50:32
it shall d. every tree. *Ezek* 20:47
it shall d. and I will bring. 28:18
it shall d. palaces of Judah. *Hos* 8:14
it shall d. palaces of Rabbah.
 Amos 1:14
it shall d. palaces of Kirioth. 2:2

devoured
and quite d. our money. *Gen* 31:15
some evil beast hath d. 37:20, 33
seven thin ears d. seven. 41:7, 24
fire from Lord and d. *Lev* 10:2
time the fire d. 250 men. *Num* 26:10
my face, they shall be d. *Deut* 31:17
they shall be d. with burning. 32:24
d. more than sword d. *2 Sam* 18:8
and fire out of his mouth d. 22:9
 Ps 18:8
sorts of flies which d. *Ps* 78:45
for they have d. Jacob. 79:7
the locusts d. the fruit of. 105:35
if ye rebel, ye shall be d. *Isa* 1:20
therefore hath the curse d. 24:6
sword hath d. prophets. *Jer* 2:30
for shame hath d. the labour. 3:24
they are come, and have d. 8:16
have eaten up Jacob, and d. 10:25
that devour thee shall be d. 30:16
all that found them have d. 50:7
king of Assyria hath d. him. 17
Nebuchadrezzar hath d. me. 51:34
it hath d. foundations. *Lam* 4:11
when the fire hath d. it. *Ezek* 15:5
sacrificed thy sons to be d. 16:20
to catch prey, d. men. 19:3, 6
fire is gone out, which hath d. 14
a roaring lion, they have d. 22:25
and thy residue shall be d. 23:25
give to the beasts to be d. 33:27
 39:4
d. and brake in pieces. *Dan* 7:7, 19
and have d. their judges. *Hos* 7:7
strangers have d. his strength. 9
fire hath d. pastures. *Joel* 1:19, 20
palmer-worm d. them. *Amos* 4:9
and it d. the great deep. 7:4
they shall be d. as stubble. *Nah* 1:10
land shall be d. by fire. *Zeph* 1:18
all the earth shall be d. with. 3:8
Tyrus shall be d. with fire. *Zech* 9:4
fowls came and d. them. *Mat* 13:4
 Mark 4:4; *Luke* 8:5
thy son who hath d. *Luke* 15:30
fire came down and d. *Rev* 20:9

devourer
I will rebuke the d. for. *Mal* 3:11

devourest
thou land d. up men. *Ezek* 36:13

devoureth
sword d. one as well. *2 Sam* 11:25
mouth of the wicked d. *Pr* 19:28
a snare to the man who d. 20:25
as fire d. stubble, and. *Isa* 5:24
 Joel 2:5
a flaming fire which d. *Lam* 2:3
the fire d. both the ends. *Ezek* 15:4
a fire d. before them. *Joel* 2:3
wicked d. man that is. *Hab* 1:13
fire d. their enemies. *Rev* 11:5

devouring

appearance like d. fire. *Ex* 24:17
thou lovest all d. words. *Ps* 52:4
visited with d. fire. *Isa* 29:6; 30:30
his tongue is as a d. fire. 30:27
shall dwell with the d. fire ? 33:14

devout

Simeon was just and d. *Luke* 2:25
at Jerusalem Jews, d. *Acts* 2:5
d. men carried Stephen to his. 8:2
Cornelius was a d. man. 10:2
a d. soldier. 7
Jews stirred up d. women. 13:50
of the d. Greeks a multitude. 17:4
Paul disputed with Jews and d. 17
Ananias a d. man. 22:12

dew

This was formerly thought to fall
like a light rain during the night,
and the references to it in the Bible
are usually worded according to this
idea, as are many of our customary
phrases with reference to it as the
falling of the dew. In warm
countries, and in places where it
rains but seldom, the night-dews
supply in some sort the want of
rain. And therefore the bestowing
of it is a blessing from God, Deut
33:13; and the withholding of it a
curse, 2 Sam 1:21.

God give thee of d. of. *Gen* 27:28, 39
in the morning d. lay. *Ex* 16:13
and when the d. that lay was. 14
when d. fell on camp. *Num* 11:9
speech shall distil as d. *Deut* 32:2
blessed is Joseph's land for d. 33:13
his heaven shall drop down d. 28
if d. be on fleece only. *Judg* 6:37
on ground let there be d. 39
there was d. 40
let there be no d. nor. *2 Sam* 1:21
we will light on him as d. 17:12
there shall not be d. nor. *1 Ki* 17:1
the d. lay all night on. *Job* 29:19
hath begotten drops of d.? 38:28
hast the d. of thy youth. *Ps* 110:3
as d. of Hermon, and as d. 133:3
clouds drop down the d. *Pr* 3:20
but his favour is as d. 19:12
my head is filled with d. *S of S* 5:2
like a cloud of d. in heat. *Isa* 18:4
for thy d. is as the d. of. 26:19
wet with d. of heaven. *Dan* 4:15, 23
shall wet thee with d. of heaven. 25
his body was wet with d. 33; 5:21
goodness is as early d. *Hos* 6:4
 13:3
I will be as d. to Israel. 14:5
Jacob shall be as the d. *Mi* 5:7
over you stayed from d. *Hag* 1:10
heavens shall give their d. *Zech* 8:12

diadem

was as a robe and a d. *Job* 29:14
and for a d. of beauty. *Isa* 28:5
and a royal d. in the hand. 62:3
remove the d. take off. *Ezek* 21:26*

dial

gone down in d. of Ahaz. *2 Ki* 20:11
 Isa 38:8

diamond

second row a d. *Ex* 28:18; 39:11
is written with point of d. *Jer* 17:1
the d. the beryl. *Ezek* 28:13

Diana

silver shrines for D. *Acts* 19:24
temple of great goddess D. 27
great is D. of Ephesians. 28, 34
worshipper of the goddess D. 35

Dibon

perished even to D. *Num* 21:30
children of Gad built D. 32:34
Moses gave D. to Reuben. *Josh* 13:17
Judah dwelt at D. *Neh* 11:25
gone up to D. the high. *Isa* 15:2
that dost inhabit D. *Jer* 48:18
judgement is come upon D. 22

Dibon-gad

pitched in D. *Num* 33:45
removed from D. 46

did

mischief that Hadad d. *1 Ki 11:25*
d. right according to all David d.
2 Ki 18:3
I knew not what I d. *Neh 2:16*
to know how Esther d. *Esth 2:11*
not read what David d.? *Mat 12:3*
saw wonderful things he d. *21:15*
what great things he d. *Mark 3:8*
saw miracles which he d. *John 2:23*
6:2, 14
me all things that ever I d. *4:29, 39*
what d. he to thee ? *9:26*
works which none other man d. *15:24*
through ignorance ye d. it, as d.
Acts 3:17
I also d. in Jerusalem. *26:10*
and this they d. not as. *2 Cor 8:5*
who d. no sin, nor was. *1 Pet 2:22*

did joined with as
Lord d. to Sarah as he. *Gen 21:1*
the man d. as Joseph bade. *43:17*
his sons d. to him as he. *50:12*
d. as Lord commanded. *Ex 7:6*
10, 20; 12:28, 50; 39:32; Lev 8:4
16:34; 24:23; Num 1:54; 2:34
20:7; 27:22; 31:31
as he d. with the bullock. *Lev 4:20*
16:15
Balak d. as Balaam. *Num 23:2, 30*
as Israel d. to the land. *Deut 2:12*
as he d. to children of Esau. *22*
as we d. unto Sihon. *3:6*
flowed, as they d. before. *Josh 4:18*
as the Lord your God d. to. *23*
d. to king of Makkedah, as he d.
10:28
Joshua d. to them as Lord. *11:9*
Gideon d. as Lord had. *Judg 6:27*
as they d. to me, so I have. *15:11*
as what the king d. *2 Sam 3:36*
and David d. so as the Lord. *5:25*
elders d. as Jezebel had. *1 Ki 21:11*
Ahab d. according as d. the. *26*
Jehoram, as d. the. *2 Ki 8:18*
as d. their fathers, so do they. *41*
David d. as God. *1 Chr 14:16*
d. as it is written in law. *2 Chr 25:4*
seek me as a nation that d. *Isa 58:2*
gave thanks as he d. *Dan 6:10*
Joseph d. as the angel. *Mat 1:24*
d. as Jesus commanded. *21:6; 26:19*
so watch d. as they were. *28:15*
them, even as Elias d. *Luke 9:54*
ignorance ye did it, as. *Acts 3:17*
Holy Ghost, as your fathers d. *7:51*
gave them like gift, as he d. *11:17*
from works, as God d. *Heb 4:10*

did joined with evil
requite us the evil we d. *Gen 50:15*
for they d. to thee evil. *17*
d. evil in sight of. *Judg 2:11*
3:7, 12; 4:1; 6:1; 10:6; 13:1
1 Ki 14:22; 15:26, 34; 16:7, 30
2 Ki 8:27; 13:2, 11; 14:24; 15:9
18, 24, 28; 17:2; 2 Chr 22:4
Solomon d. evil in sight. *1 Ki 11:6*
Manasseh d. evil. *2 Ki 21:2*
2 Chr 33:2
Jehoahaz d. evil. *2 Ki 23:32*
Jehoiakim d. evil. *37*
Jehoiachim d. evil *24:9*
Zedekiah d. evil. *19*
Rehoboam d. evil. *2 Chr 12:14*
Amon d. evil. *33:22*
they had rest, they d. evil. *Neh 9:28*
the evil that Eliashib d. *13:7*
but d. evil before mine eyes.
Isa 65:12; 66:4
Alexander d. me much evil.
2 Tim 4:14

did not
midwives d. not as king. *Ex 1:17*
Ahaz d. not what was right.
2 Ki 16:2; 2 Chr 28:1
d. not your fathers thus, and d. not
our God bring this ? *Neh 13:18*
but they d. them not. *Jer 11:8*
of the evil, and d. it not. *Jonah 3:10*
d. not many mighty. *Mat 13:58*
d. it not to these, d. it not to. *25:45*

me, this d. not Abraham. *John 8:40*
I d. it not for his cause. *2 Cor 7:12**

did so
as God commanded so d. he.
Gen 6:22
Jacob d. so and fulfilled. *29:28*
youngest brother, they d. so. *42:20*
Lord commanded so d. *Ex 7:6, 10*
12:28, 50; 39:32; 40:16; Num 1:54
magicians d. so. *Ex 7:22; 8:7, 18*
Lord d. so. *8:24*
Moses d. so. *17:6*
Joshua d. so. *10*
Aaron d. so. *Num 8:3*
so d. the daughters of. *36:10*
city, so they d. six days. *Josh 6:14*
so d. Moses command, and so d.
11:15
they d. not so. *Judg 2:17*
God d. so that night. *6:40*
as he d. so year by year. *1 Sam 1:7*
so they d. in Shiloh to all. *2:14*
so d. David, and so will be. *27:11*
so d. he in Beth-el. *1 Ki 12:32*
Jeroboam's wife d. so, and. *14:4*
so they d. *Ezra 6:13*
but so d. not I. *Neh 5:15*
Isaiah d. so, walking naked. *Isa 20:2*
Jeremiah d. so. *Jer 38:12*
and I d. so. *Ezek 12:7*
Jesus arose, and so d. *Mat 9:19*
his hand, and he d. so. *Luke 6:10*
so d. their fathers to false. *26*
followed Jesus and so d. *John 18:15*
sons of Sceva who d. so. *Acts 19:14*

thus did
fill their sacks, thus d. *Gen 42:25*
thus d. he to both of. *Ex 36:29*
thus d. Moses, according as. *40:16*
thus d. your fathers. *Num 32:8*
thus d. he to all cities. *2 Sam 12:31*
thus d. Urijah the priest. *2 Ki 16:16*
thus they d. day by day. *2 Chr 24:11*
thus d. Hezekiah throughout. *31:20*
d. not your fathers thus. *Neh 13:18*
sanctified them, thus d. *Job 1:5*

didst
d. this in integrity of. *Gen 20:6*
do as thou d. to Sihon. *Num 21:34*
Deut 3:2
as thou d. to Jericho. *Josh 8:2*
thou d. it secretly. *2 Sam 12:12*
than other that thou d. to. *13:16*
that thou d. to David. *1 Ki 2:44*
d. well that it was in thy. *8:18*
2 Chr 6:8
thy wonders that thou d. *Neh 9:17*
dumb, because thou d. it. *Ps 39:9*
told us what work thou d. *44:1*
when d. terrible things. *Isa 64:3*
thou kill me as thou d.? *Acts 7:28**

Didymus
Thomas, who is called D. *John 11:16*
20:24; 21:2

die
see dead and death
every thing in earth shall d.
Gen 6:17
overdrive them, flock will d. *33:13*
let him d. *44:9*
his father would d. *22*
now let me d. *46:30*
that Israel must d. *47:29*
fish in the river shall d. *Ex 7:18*
nothing shall d. that is the. *9:4*
thou seest my face shall d. *10:28*
firstborn in land of Egypt shall d.
11:5
that they bear not iniquity and d.
28:43; Lev 22:9
beast which ye may eat d. *Lev 11:39*
sin, they shall d. childless. *20:20*
holy thing, lest they d. *Num 4:15*
things covered, lest they d. *20*
if any man d. very suddenly. *6:9*
and there they shall d. *14:35*
if these d. the common death. *16:29*
near tabernacle d. *17:13; 18:22*
neither they, nor you also d. *18:3**
Aaron, shall d. on mount Hor. *20:26*
let me d. death of righteous. *23:10*
speak, saying, if a man d. *27:8*

shalt stone them that they d.
Deut 17:5; 22:21, 24
that men shall d. *17:12*
prophet shall d. *18:20*
both shall d. *22:22*
the man only shall d. *25*
if the latter husband d. *24:3*
that thief shall d. *7*
one d. and have no children. *25:5*
Mark 12:19
to Moses, thy days approach that
thou d. *Deut 31:14*
land of Canaan, and d. *32:50*
me d. with Philistines. *Judg 16:30*
increase of house shall d. *1 Sam 2:33*
in one day they shall d. both. *34*
said, shall Jonathan d.? *14:45*
nor if half of us d. *2 Sam 18:3*
enter city, child shall d. *1 Ki 14:12*
shalt d. and not live. *2 Ki 20:1*
Isa 38:1
fathers not d. for children, man
shall d. *2 Chr 25:4; Jer 31:30*
wife said, curse God and d. *Job 2:9*
excellency goeth away, they d. *4:21*
wisdom shall d. with you. *12:2*
though the stock thereof d. *14:8*
if a man d. shall he live again ? *14*
in a moment shall they d. *34:20*
if obey not, they shall d. *36:12*
they d. in youth, their life is. *14*
seeth that wise men d. *Ps 49:10*
away their breath, they d. *104:29*
fools d. for want of. *Pr 10:21*
shouldest thou d. before ? *Eccl 7:17*
living know they shall d. but. *9:5*
country, there thou shalt. *Isa 22:18*
that dwell therein shall d. *51:6*
be afraid of a man that shall d. *12*
for child shall d. a hundred. *65:20*
young men shall d. by sword, their
sons and daughters. *Jer 11:22*
shall d. of grievous deaths. *16:4*
both great and small shall d. *6*
this year thou shalt d. *28:16*
but thou shalt d. in peace. *34:5*
the soul that sinneth, it shall d.
Ezek 18:4, 20
thou shalt d. deaths of them. *28:8*
thou shalt d. the deaths of the. *10*
that wicked man shall d. in. *33:8*
they in the caves shall d. *27*
Moab shall d. with. *Amos 2:2*
men in one house they shall d. *6:9*
Jeroboam shall d. by sword. *7:11*
shalt d. in a polluted land. *17*
sinners of my people shall d. *9:10*
that that dieth, let it d. *Zech 11:9*
two parts shall be cut off and d. *13:8*
he that curseth father or mother, let
him d. *Mat 15:4; Mark 7:10*
man d. having no seed. *Mat 22:24*
Luke 20:28
nor can they d. any. *Luke 20:36*
down ere my child d. *John 4:49*
one man d. for people. *11:50; 18:14*
prophesied that Jesus should d. *11:51*
corn of wheat d. but if it d. *12:24*
righteous man will one d. *Rom 5:7*
for as in Adam all d. *1 Cor 15:22*
sowest not quickened except it d. *36*
here men that d. receive. *Heb 7:8*
blessed are dead that d. *Rev 14:13*

he die
for he said, lest he d. as. *Gen 38:11*
lad is not with us, he will d. *44:31*
a man, so that he d. *Ex 21:12*
take him from altar, that he d. *14*
smite his servant, and he d. *20*
found and smitten that he d. *22:2*
smite him so that he d. *Num 35:16*
20, 21, 23; Deut 13:10; 19:5, 11
21:21
wherewith he may d. *Num 35:17*
18:23; Deut 19:12
return, lest he d. in battle.
Deut 20:5, 6, 7
bring thy son that he d. *Judg 6:30*
from him that he d. *2 Sam 11:15*
if wickedness be in him, he shall d.
1 Ki 1:52
of David drew nigh that he d. *2:1*
Elijah requested that he might d. *19:4*

stone him that he may d. 1 Ki 21:10
when shall he d. and ? Ps 41:5
he shall d. without instruction. Pr 5:23
he that hateth reproof d. 15:10
he that despiseth ways shall d. 19:16
he shall d. whither they. Jer 22:12
out of dungeon before he d. 38:10
wicked, he shall d. in his. Ezek 3:19
20; 18:18, 24, 26; 33:9, 13, 18
not see it, though he shall d. 12:13
in Babylon he shall d. 17:16
what death he should d. John 12:33
18:32

I die
evil take me, and I d. Gen 19:19
I said, lest I d. for her. 26:9
soul may bless thee before I d. 27:4
give me children, or else I d. 30:1
go and see him before I d. 45:28
said to Joseph, behold, I d. 48:21
lo, I die there bury me. 50:5
Joseph said to his brethren, I d. 24
I must d. in this land. Deut 4:22
now shall I d. for thirst. Judg 15:18
where thou diest will I d. Ruth 1:17
but taste, and I must d. 1 Sam 14:43
that I may d. in mine. 2 Sam 19:37
nay, but I will d. here. 1 Ki 2:30
till I d. I will not remove. Job 27:5
then I said, I shall d. in my. 29:18
deny me them not before I d. Pr 30:7
to return, lest I d. there. Jer 37:20
though I should d. with. Mat 26:35
Mark 14:31
by your rejoicing, I d. 1 Cor 15:31

not die
may live and not d. Gen 42:2; 43:8
47:19
be verified, ye shall not d. 42:20
and he d. not, but. Ex 21:18
sound heard, that he d. not. 28:35
that they d. not. 30:20, 21
charge of the Lord that ye d. not.
Lev 8:35
they d. not. 15:31; Num 4:19; 17:10
at all times, that he d. not. Lev 16:2
cloud cover mercy-seat, he d. not. 13
the manslayer d. not. Num 35:12
Josh 20:9
this fire, that I d. not. Deut 18:16
let Reuben live and not d. 33:6
fear not, thou shalt not d. Judg 6:23
1 Sam 20:2; 2 Sam 12:13; 19:23
Jer 38:24
for us, that we d. not. 1 Sam 12:19
kindness of Lord that I d. not. 20:14
ye may live and not d. 2 Ki 18:32
fathers shall not d. for. 2 Chr 25:4
I shall not d. but live. Ps 118:17
with rod, he shall not d. Pr 23:13
Ezek 18:17, 21, 28; 33:15
John 21:23
that he should not d. Isa 51:14
their worm shall not d. nor. 66:24
d. not by our hand. Jer 11:21
Zedekiah, thou shalt not d. by. 34:4
souls that should not d. Ezek 13:19
we shall not d. Lord. Hab 1:12
eat thereof, and not d. John 6:50
that disciple should not d. 21:23

surely die
shalt surely d. Gen 2:17; 20:7
1 Sam 14:44; 22:16; 1 Ki 2:37, 42
Jer 26:8; Ezek 3:18; 33:8, 14
ye shall not surely d. Gen 3:4
they shall surely d. Num 26:65
we shall surely d. Judg 13:22
my son, he shall surely d.
1 Sam 14:39; 20:31; 2 Sam 12:5
2 Ki 8:10; Ezek 18:13
child born to thee shall surely d.
2 Sam 12:14
shalt not come down, but shalt surely
d. 2 Ki 1:4, 6, 16

to die
I am at the point to d. Gen 25:32
to d. in the wilderness. Ex 14:11
Num 21:5
any, to cause him to d. Num 35:30
his day shall come to d. 1 Sam 26:10
ye are worthy to d. because. 16
my life, to cause me to d. 28:9

to give yourselves to d. 2 Chr 32:11
that are appointed to d. Ps 79:11
afflicted and ready to d. 88:15
to be born, a time to d. Eccl 3:2
is worthy to d. Jer 26:11
not worthy to d. 16
he is like to d. for hunger. 38:9
return to Jonathan's house to d. 26
better for me to d. Jonah 4:3, 8
wished in himself to d. 8
servant ready to d. Luke 7:2
by our law he ought to d. John 19:7
I am ready also to d. Acts 21:13
I refuse not to d.: but if. 25:11
Romans to deliver any to d. 16
would even dare to d. Rom 5:7
better for me to d. than. 1 Cor 9:15
are in our hearts to d. 2 Cor 7:3
live is Christ, and to d. is. Phil 1:21
to men once to d. Heb 9:27
that are ready to d. Rev 3:2
desire to d. and death shall. 9:6

we die
why should we d.? Gen 47:15
than that we should d. Ex 14:12
let not God speak, lest we d. 20:19
Deut 5:25
we d. we perish, we all. Num 17:12
we and out cattle should d. 20:4
pray, that we d. not. 1 Sam 12:19
for we must needs d. 2 Sam 14:14
we may eat it and d. 1 Ki 17:12
sit we here till we d.? 2 Ki 7:3, 4
if they kill us, we shall but d. 4
to-morrow we shall d. Isa 22:13
1 Cor 15:32
let us go that we may d. John 11:16
whether we d. we d. Rom 14:8

ye die
neither touch it, lest ye d. Gen 3:3
rend clothes, lest ye d. Lev 10:6*
go out from door, lest ye d. 7
nor pollute, lest ye d. Num 18:32
but ye shall d. like men. Ps 82:7
not be purged till ye d. Isa 22:14
there shall ye d. Jer 22:26; 42:16
for why will ye d.? 27:13
Ezek 18:31; 33:11
know that ye shall d. Jer 42:22
ye shall d. in sins. John 8:21, 24
after the flesh ye shall d. Rom 8:13

died
all flesh d. Gen 7:21, 22
and Haran d. 11:28
Terah d. 32
Sarah d. 23:2
Abraham d. 25:8
Ishmael d. 17
Deborah the nurse d. 35:8
Rachel d. 18, 19; 48:7
Isaac d. 35:29
Belah d. 36:33
Jobab d. 34
Husham d. 35
Hadad d. 36; 1 Chr 1:51
Samlah d. Gen 36:37
Saul d. 38
Baal-hanan son of Achbor d. 39
Judah's wife d. 38:12
Er and Onan d. in Canaan. 46:12
Jacob d. 50:16
Joseph d. 26; Ex 1:6
the king of Egypt d. Ex 2:23
the fish d. 7:21
the frogs d. 8:13
the cattle of Egypt d. 9:6
would to God we had d. in Egypt. 16:3
Num 14:2; 20:3; 26:10
Nadab and Abihu d. Lev 10:2; 16:1
Num 3:4; 26:61; 1 Chr 24:2
searchers of the land d. Num 14:37
Aaron d. 20:28; 33:38, 39
Deut 10:6; 32:50
they that d. beside them that d. about
matter of Korah. Num 16:49
Miriam d. 20:1
much people of Israel d. 21:6
those that d. in plague were. 25:9
the children of Korah d. not. 26:11
Zelophehad our father, d. in the wilderness, but d. in his own sin. 27:3
Moses d. Deut 34:5
he was 120 years when he d. 7

even all men of war d. Josh 5:4
which d. with hailstones. 10:11
Joshua the son of Nun d. 24:29
Judg 2:8
Eleazar the son of Aaron d.
Josh 24:33; 1 Chr 23:22
Adonibezek d. Judg 1:7
Othniel d. 3:11
Gibeon d. 8:32
men of tower of Shechem d. 9:49
Tola d. 10:2
Jair d. 5
judged Israel six years, then d. 12:7
Ibzan d. 10
Elon d. 12
Abdon d. 15
Elimelech d. Ruth 1:3
Mahlon, Chilion d. 5
that d. not were smitten. 1 Sam 5:12
Samuel d. 25:1
Nabal's heart d. within him. 37
Saul was dead, armour-bearer . . .
and d. 31:5, 6; 1 Sam 10:5, 13
Asahel d. 2 Sam 2:23
d. Abner as a fool. 3:33
he before Lord. 6:7; 1 Chr 13:10
king of Ammon d. 2 Sam 10:1
1 Chr 19:1
Shobach d. 2 Sam 10:18
Uriah the Hittite d. 11:17
on seventh day child d. 12:18
Ahithophel hanged himself d. 17:23
would God I had d. for thee. 18:33
and all we had d. this day. 19:6
d. of people, even from Dan. 24:15
this woman's child d. 1 Ki 3:19
came to threshold child d. 14:17
Zimri d. 16:18
Tibni d. 22
Ahab d. 22:35, 37
till noon and then d. 2 Ki 4:20
fled to Megiddo and d. there. 9:27
Elisha d. 13:14, 20
Hazael king of Syria d. 24
came to Egypt and d. there. 23:34
but Seled d. without. 1 Chr 2:30
and Jether d. 32
Asa d. 2 Chr 16:13
Jehoiada full of days d. 24:15
when he d. he said. 22
why d. I not from womb? Job 3:11
so Job d. being old and. 42:17
year that king Uzziah d. Isa 6:1
year that king Ahaz d. 14:28
Hananiah d. Jer 28:17
Pelatiah d. Ezek 11:13
at even my wife d. 24:18
he offended in Baal, he d. Hos 13:1
last of all the woman d. Mat 22:27
Mark 12:22; Luke 20:32
d. rich man also d. Luke 16:22
my brother not d. John 11:21, 32
this man should not have d. 37
Dorcas was sick and d. Acts 9:37
in due time Christ d. Rom 5:6, 8
sin revived and I d. 7:9
it is Christ that d. 8:34
to this end Christ both d. rose. 14:9
destroy not him with thy meat for
whom Christ d. 15; 1 Cor 8:11
how that Christ d. 1 Cor 15:3
if one d. for all, then. 2 Cor 5:14
should live to him who d. for. 15
we believe that Jesus d. 1 Thes 4:14
who d. for us that we should. 5:10
despised Moses' law d. Heb 10:28
these d. in faith, not having. 11:13
by faith Joseph when he d. 22
third part of creatures d. Rev 8:9
many men d. of waters that. 11
every living soul d. in the sea. 16:3

and he, so he, that he died
Adam 930 years and he d. Gen 5:5
Noah's days 950 years, and he d. 9:29
into his temple, so he d. Judg 4:21
Eli's neck brake and he d. for he.
1 Sam 4:18
Jonathan that he d. not. 14:45
Lord smote Nabal that he d. 25:38
Abimelech that he d. 2 Sam 11:21
stoned Adoram that he d.
1 Ki 12:18; 2 Chr 10:18

so he *d.* according to the. *2 Ki 1:17*
him in the gate *and he d.* 7:17, 20
cloth on his face, *so that he d.* 8:15
Jeroboam *and he d.* *2 Chr 13:20*
bowels fell out, *so he d.* 21:19
and he d. without. *Luke 20:29, 30*
Jacob *d.* in Egypt, *he and. Acts 7:15*
in *that he* he *d.* unto. *Rom 6:10*
that he d. for all. *2 Cor 5:15*

diest
where thou *d.* will I die. *Ruth 1:17*

diet
for his *d.* there was a continual *d.*
given him. *Jer 52:34**

dieth
fat of beast that *d.* of. *Lev 7:24*
d. of itself not eat. 22:8; *Deut 14:21*
when a man *d.* in a tent. *Num 19:14*
died Abner as a fool *d.?* *2 Sam 3:33*
him that *d.* in the city. *1 Ki 14:11*
d. in field fowls of air. 16:4; 21:24
man *d.* and wasteth. *Job 14:10*
one *d.* in his full strength. 21:23
another *d.* in the bitterness. 25
when he *d.* he shall carry. *Ps 49:17*
when a wicked man *d.* *Pr 11:7*
how *d.* the wise man ? *Eccl 2:16*
as the one *d.* so *d.* the other. 3:19
their fish stinketh and *d.* *Isa 50:2*
he that eateth of their eggs *d.* 59:5
nor eaten that which *d.* *Ezek 4:14*
committeth iniquity, and *d.* 18:26
in the death of him that *d.* 31
that that *d.* let it die. *Zech 11:9*
worm *d.* not. *Mark 9:44, 46, 48*
raised from dead *d.* no. *Rom 6:9*
and no man *d.* to himself. 14:7

differ
who maketh thee *to d.?* *1 Cor 4:7*

difference
Lord put a *d.* between. *Ex 11:7*
put a *d.* between holy. *Lev 10:10*
to make a *d.* between unclean. 11:47
d. between clean beasts and. 20:25*
no *d.* they shewed no *d. Ezek 22:26**
shall teach my people the *d.* 44:23
and put no *d.* between. *Acts 15:9**
for there is no *d.* *Rom 3:22**
is no *d.* between Jew and. 10:12*
is *d.* between a wife and. *1 Cor 7:34*
compassion making a *d.* *Jude 22**

differences
d. of administration. *1 Cor 12:5**

differeth
star *d.* from another in. *1 Cor 15:41*
heir when a child *d.* *Gal 4:1*

differing
gifts *d.* according to the grace.
Rom 12:6

dig
if a man *d.* a pit, and not. *Ex 21:33*
of whose hills mayest *d.* *Deut 8:9*
shalt have a paddle, and *d.* 23:13
d. for it more than for. *Job 3:21*
ye *d.* a pit for your friend. 6:27*
thou shalt *d.* about thee. 11:18*
in the dark they *d.* 24:16
son of man, *d.* now in. *Ezek 8:8*
d. thou through the wall. 8:8
though they *d.* in hell. *Amos 9:2*
let it alone, till I shall *d. Luke 13:8*
cannot *d.* to beg I am ashamed. 16:3

digged
a witness that I have *d.* *Gen 21:30*
wells his father's servants had *d.*
26:15, 18
Isaac's servants *d.* in. 19, 21, 22, 25
told Isaac of well they had *d.* 32
in their self-will they *d.* 49:6*
my grave which I had *d.* 50:5
Egyptians *d.* for water to. *Ex 7:24*
princes *d.* the well, nobles *d.* it.
Num 21:18*
wells *d.* thou. *Deut 6:11*; Neh 9:25**
I have *d.* and drunk strange waters,
and dried. *2 Ki 19:24; Isa 37:25*
Uzziah *d.* many wells. *2 Chr 26:10**
made a pit and *d.* it. *Ps 7:15; 57:6*
without cause they *d.* a pit. 94:13
till pit be *d.* for the wicked. 94:13
proud have *d.* pits for me. 119:85

shall not be pruned nor *d.* *Isa 5:6**
all hills be *d.* with the mattock. 7:25
to the pit whence ye are *d.* 51:1
I went to Euphrates and *d. Jer 13:7*
have *d.* a pit for my soul. 18:20, 22
when I had *d.* in the wall. *Ezek 8:8*
hedged it, and *d.* a. *Mat 21:33*
d. in the earth, and hid. 25:18
who *d.* and laid the. *Luke 6:48*
Lord, they have *d.* down. *Rom 11:3*

diggedst
wells digged which thou *d.* not.
Deut 6:11*

diggeth
an ungodly man *d.* up. *Pr 16:27**
whoso *d.* pit fall. 26:27; *Eccl 10:8*

dignity
thou art excellency of *d.* *Gen 49:3*
what *d.* hath been done ? *Esth 6:3*
folly is set in great *d.* *Eccl 10:6*
d. shall proceed of. *Hab 1:7*

dignities
speak evil of *d.* *2 Pet 2:10; Jude 8*

diligence
keep thy heart with all *d.* *Pr 4:23*
give *d.* that thou mayest. *Luke 12:58*
that ruleth with *d.* *Rom 12:8*
abound in faith and *d.* *2 Cor 8:7**
do thy *d.* to come. *2 Tim 4:9, 21*
one of you shew same *d. Heb 6:11*
giving all *d.* to add to. *2 Pet 1:5*
brethren, give *d.* to make your. 10
when I gave all *d.* to write. *Jude 3*

diligent
judges shall make *d.* *Deut 19:18*
take *d.* heed to do the. *Josh 22:5*
accomplish a *d.* search. *Ps 64:6*
and spirit made *d.* search. 77:6
but the hand of the *d.* *Pr 10:4*
the hand of the *d.* bear rule. 12:24
but the substance of a *d.* man. 27
but the soul of the *d.* shall. 13:4
the thoughts of *d.* tend. 21:5
seest thou a man *d.* in his ? 22:29
be thou *d.* to know state of. 27:23
proved *d.* but now much more *d.*
2 Cor 8:22*
be *d.* to come unto me. *Tit 3:12*
be *d.* that ye be found. *2 Pet 3:14*

diligently
if thou wilt *d.* hearken to. *Ex 15:26*
Deut 11:13; 28:1; Jer 17:24
Moses *d.* sought the goat. *Lev 10:16*
heed and keep soul *d.* *Deut 4:9*
thou shalt teach them *d.* to. 6:7
d. keep commandments. 17; 11:22
make search, and ask *d.* 13:14
heed that thou observe *d.* 24:8
now the men did *d.* *1 Ki 20:33*
let it be *d.* done for. *Ezra 7:23**
hear *d.* my speech. *Job 13:17; 21:2*
shalt *d.* consider his place. *Ps 37:10*
us to keep thy precepts *d.* 119:4
I came forth *d.* to. *Pr 7:15*
he that *d.* seeketh good. 11:27
consider *d.* what is before thee. 23:1
he hearkened *d.* with. *Isa 21:7*
hearken *d.* to me, and eat. 55:2
consider *d.* see if there. *Jer 2:10*
if they will *d.* learn the ways. 12:16
if ye will *d.* obey the. *Zech 6:15*
he inquired *d.* when. *Mat 2:7**
Herod said, go and search *d.* 8
which he had *d.* inquired. 16*
sweep house and seek *d. Luke 15:8*
taught *d.* the things of. *Acts 18:25*
if she have *d.* followed. *1 Tim 5:10*
in Rome he sought me *d. 2 Tim 1:17*
bring Zenas and Apollos on their
journey *d.* *Tit 3:13*
rewarder of them that *d. Heb 11:6*
looking *d.* lest any man fail. 12:15*
the prophets searched *d.* *1 Pet 1:10*

dim
Isaac was old, his eyes *d. Gen 27:1*
the eyes of Israel were *d.* 48:10
Moses' eye was not *d.* *Deut 34:7*
Eli's eyes began to wax *d.*
1 Sam 3:2; 4:15*
mine eye also is *d.* by. *Job 17:7*
eyes of them that see not be *d.*
Isa 32:3

how is gold become *d.!* *Lam 4:1*
for these things our eyes are *d.* 5:17

diminish, -ed
you shall not *d.* ought. *Ex 5:8*
not ought of your work be *d.* 11, 19
duty of marriage not *d.* 21:10
to the years thou *d.* *Lev 25:16*
nor shall you *d.* *Deut 4:2; 12:32*
gotten by vanity be *d.* *Pr 13:11*
men of Kedar shall be *d. Isa 21:17**
speak, *d.* not a word. *Jer 26:2*
may be increased and not *d.* 29:6
will I also *d.* thee. *Ezek 5:11*
behold, I have *d.* thine. 16:27
I will *d.* them, they shall. 29:15

diminishing
d. of them be riches. *Rom 11:12**

dimness
behold trouble darkness *d. Isa 8:22**
d. shall not be such as was. 9:1*

Dimon
waters of *D.* shall be full of blood, for
I will bring more upon *D. Isa 15:9*

Dinah
bare daughter called *D.* *Gen 30:21*
Jacob heard he had defiled *D.* 34:5

dine, -d
these men shall *d.* *Gen 43:16*
Pharisee besought him to *d.*
Luke 11:37
come and *d.* *John 21:12**
so when they had *d.* Jesus. 15*

dinner
better is a *d.* of herbs. *Pr 15:7*
I have prepared my *d.* *Mat 22:4*
first washed before *d.* *Luke 11:38*
when makest a *d.* or supper. 14:12

Dionysius
among which was *D.* *Acts 17:34*

Diotrephes
D. who loveth to have pre-eminence.
3 John 9

dip
d. it in the blood that is. *Ex 12:22*
priest shall *d.* finger. *Lev 4:6; 17:14*
16
d. the cedar wood and. 14:6, 51
clean person should *d.* *Num 19:18*
let Asher *d.* his foot in. *Deut 33:24*
Boaz said to Ruth, *d.* *Ruth 2:14*
Lazarus that he may *d. Luke 16:24*

dipped, -eth
d. the coat in blood. *Gen 37:31*
Aaron *d.* his finger in the. *Lev 9:9*
the priests' feet were *d.* *Josh 3:15*
he *d.* end of rod in an. *1 Sam 14:27*
Naaman *d.* in Jordan. *2 Ki 5:14*
Hazael took a cloth and *d.* it. 8:15
that thy foot be *d.* in. *Ps 68:23*
he that *d.* his hand with me in the.
Mat 26:23; Mark 14:20
I give a sop, when I have *d.*; *d.* the
sop, gave it to Judas. *John 13:26*
with a vesture *d.* in blood. *Rev 19:13*

direct
he sent Judah to *d.* his. *Gen 46:28**
in the morning will I *d.* *Ps 5:3**
he shall *d.* thy paths. *Pr 3:6*
righteousness of perfect shall *d.* 11:5
wisdom is profitable to *d. Eccl 10:10*
raised him up, I will *d.* *Isa 45:13**
I will *d.* their way in truth. 61:8*
man that walketh to *d.* *Jer 10:23*
Lord Jesus Christ *d.* *1 Thes 3:11*
Lord *d.* your hearts into. *2 Thes 3:5*

directed
he hath not *d.* his words. *Job 32:14*
that my ways were *d.* to. *Ps 119:5**
who hath *d.* the Spirit ? *Isa 40:13*

directeth
he *d.* it under the heaven. *Job 37:3**
ways, but the Lord *d.* his. *Pr 16:9*
as for upright he *d.* his way. 21:29*

direction
princes judged it by *d. Num 21:18**

directly
sprinkle blood *d.* before. *Num 19:4**
even the way *d.* before. *Ezek 42:12*

dirt

fat closed, and d. came.   Judg 3:22
cast them out as d. in.   Ps 18:42*
waters cast up mire and d. Isa 57:20

disallow, -ed

because her father d.   Num 30:5
but if her husband d. her.   8
he d. her not.   11
d. indeed of men, but.   1 Pet 2:4*
stone which the builders d. is.   7*

disannul

wilt thou also d. my ?   Job 40:8†
purposed who shall d. it ? Isa 14:27†
covenant law cannot d.   Gal 3:17

disannulled

with death shall be d.   Isa 28:18†

disannulleth

covenant no man d. or.   Gal 3:15*

disannulling

there is a d. of the.   Heb 7:18

disappoint

arise, O Lord, d.   Ps 17:13*

disappointed

without counsel purposes d. Pr 15:22

disappointeth

he d. devices of crafty.   Job 5:12*

discern

[1] To see and identify by noting differences, Gen 31:32. [2] To see by the eye or the understanding, 2 Sam 14:17; Heb 5:14.

d. thou what is thine.   Gen 31:32
d. I pray thee, whose are.   38:25
so is my lord to d.   2 Sam 14:17
can I d. between good and ?   19:35
I may d. between good.   1 Ki 3:9
hast asked understanding to d.   11
people could not d. the.   Ezra 3:13
but I could not d. the.   Job 4:16
my taste d. perverse things ?   6:30
d. between unclean and. Ezek 44:23
d. between right hand.   Jonah 4:11
d. between the righteous.   Mal 3:18
d. the face of the sky.   Mat 16:3
     Luke 12:56
senses exercised to d.   Heb 5:14

discerned, -eth

d. him not, his hands.   Gen 27:23
king of Israel d. him.   1 Ki 20:41
I d. among the youth a.   Pr 7:7
a wise man d. time and.   Eccl 8:5
they are spiritually d.   1 Cor 2:14

discerner

word is a d. of thoughts.   Heb 4:12

discerning

unworthily, not d.   1 Cor 11:29
another is given d. of spirits. 12:10

discharge, -d

will cause them to be d.   1 Ki 5:9*
there is no d. in that war. Eccl 8:8

disciple

Literally, a scholar, a learner ; especially one who believes in the doctrine of his teacher and follows him. In the New Testament the followers of John the Baptist were called his disciples, Mark 2:18; John 3:25. Also the followers of Moses, in distinction from the followers of Jesus, Mark 2:18; John 9:28. But most often the word is used with reference to the believers in Christ, both those who believed during his life, and those who later joined the early Church, Matt 27:57; John 19:38; Acts 9:36. The twelve Apostles, also, are frequently called by this name, Mat. 10:1; John 20:2.

d. not above master.   Mat 10:24
     Luke 6:40
it is enough for the d.   Mat 10:25
give a cup of cold water to a d.   42
of Arimathaea was Jesus' d.   27:57
thou art his d. we are.   John 9:28
so did another d. that d. was. 18:15
then went out that other d. that. 16
the d. standing by, whom.   19:26

to that d. behold thy mother, and from
that hour that d. took. John 19:27
being a d. but secretly, for fear. 38
other d. Jesus loved. 20:2; 21:7, 20
went forth, and that other d.   20:3
the other d. did outrun Peter.   4
went in also that other d. and.   8
saying, that that d. should.   21:23
this is the d. that testifieth these. 24
there was a certain d. at. Acts 9:10
believed not that he was a d.   26
at Joppa a d. named Tabitha.   36
a certain d. was there.   16:1
an old d. with whom we.   21:16

my disciple

not life, cannot be my d. Luke 14:26
bear his cross, cannot be my d.   27
forsaketh not all, cannot be my d. 33

disciples

then came the d. of John. Mat 9:14
unto him his twelve d.   10:1
an end of commanding his d.   11:1
when the d. saw him walking. 14:26
when the d. heard it they.   19:13
the d. rebuked them.   19:13
     Mark 10:13
Jesus took the twelve d. Mat 20:17
Jesus sent two d. saying, go.   21:1
sent unto him their d.   22:16
bread, and gave it to the d.   26:26
not deny thee, likewise said the d. 35
then all the d. forsook him.   56
do d. of John and of Pharisees fast,
thy d.?   Mark 2:18; Luke 5:33
now d. had forgotten to. Mark 8:14
the d. began to rejoice. Luke 19:37
between John's d. and.   John 3:25
that Jesus baptized more d.   4:1
but we are Moses' d.   9:28
he began to wash the d'. feet. 13:5
also one of this man's d.?   18:17
Mary told d. that she had.   20:18
out slaughter against d.   Acts 9:1
Saul essayed to join himself to d. 26
the d. were called Christians. 11:26
and finding certain d.   19:1
Paul would have entered, d.   30
first day of week d. came.   20:7
to draw away d. after them.   30

his disciples

his d. came and awoke.   Mat 8:25
and followed, and so did his d. 9:19
and tell his d. he is risen.   28:7
say ye, his d. came by night and. 13
in house his d. asked.   Mark 10:10
murmured against his d. Luke 5:30
he lifted up his eyes on his d.   6:20
teach us, as John taught his d. 11:1
his glory, and his d.   John 2:11
Jesus baptized not, but his d.   4:2
upon this came his d. and.   27
and there he sat with his d.   6:3
but his d. were gone away alone. 22
will ye be his d.   9:27
said his d. Lord if he sleep.   11:12
he went with his d. over brook. 18:1
often resorted thither with his d. 2
again, his d. were within.   20:26

of his disciples

John sent two of his d.   Mat 11:2
   Mark 11:1; 14:13; Luke 19:29
some of his d. eat with.   Mark 7:2
time many of his d.   John 6:66
priest asked Jesus of his d.   18:19
art not thou also one of his d.?   25
none of his d. durst ask him. 21:12

to his disciples

gave the loaves to his d. Mat 14:19
all things to his d.   Mark 4:34
turned to his d. and.   Luke 10:23
shewed himself to his d. John 21:14

my disciples

seal law among my d.   Isa 8:16
keep the passover at thy house
with my d.   Mat 26:18
     Mark 14:14; Luke 22:11
then are ye my d. John 8:31; 13:35
so shall ye be my d.   15:8

thy disciples

we fast, thy d. fast not.   Mat 9:14
     Mark 2:18

thy d. do that which is not. Mat 12:2
why do thy d. trangress the ?   15:2
I brought him to thy d. they.   17:16
why walk not thy d.?   Mark 7:5
to thy d. to cast him out.   9:18
     Luke 9:40
Master, rebuke thy d.   Luke 19:39
thy d. may see works.   John 7:3

discipline

also their ears to d.   Job 36:10*

disclose

earth also shall d. her.   Isa 26:21

discomfited

Joshua d. Amalek and.   Ex 17:13
smote and d. them.   Num 14:45
d. them before Israel.   Josh 10:10
the Lord d. Sisera and.   Judg 4:15
Gideon pursued them, and d.   8:12
Philistines, and d. them. 1 Sam 7:10
and d. them. 2 Sam 22:15; Ps 18:14
young men shall be d.   Isa 31:8*

discomfiture

was a very great d.   1 Sam 14:20

discontented

every one that was d.   1 Sam 22:2

discontinue

and thou shalt d. from.   Jer 17:4

discord

mischief, he soweth d.   Pr 6:14
and him that soweth d.   19

discover

[1] An old meaning, reveal, uncover. [2] To manifest, especially unintentionally, Pr 18:2. [3] To detect for the first time, Acts 27:39.

a man shall not d. his.   Deut 22:30
we will d. ourselves.   1 Sam 14:8
who can d. the face ?   Job 41:13
that his heart may d.   Pr 18:2
and d. not a secret to another. 25:9
the Lord will d. their.   Isa 3:17
I will d. thy skirts.   Jer 13:26
     Nah 3:5
of Edom, he will d. thy.   Lam 4:22
I will d. thy nakedness. Ezek 16:37
in thee have they d. their. Hos 2:10
I will d. the foundations.   Mi 1:6

discovered

thy nakedness be not d.   Ex 20:26
he hath d. her fountain.   Lev 20:18
both d. themselves.   1 Sam 14:11
Saul heard David was d.   22:6
foundations of world were d. at the
rebuking. 2 Sam 22:16; Ps 18:15
he d. covering of Judah.   Isa 22:8
for thou hast d. thyself to.   57:8
iniquity of thy skirts d.   Jer 13:22
have not d. thine iniquity. Lam 2:14
foundation thereof be d. Ezek 13:14
thy nakedness d. through.   16:36
before thy wickedness was d.   57
your transgressions are d.   21:24
in thee have they d. their.   22:10
these d. nakedness, they.   23:10
she d. her whoredoms, d. her.   18
of whoredoms shall be d.   29
iniquity of Ephraim was d. Hos 7:1
when we had d. Cyprus. Acts 21:3*
but they d. a certain creek. 27:39*

discovereth

he d. deep things out of. Job 12:22
voice of Lord d. forest.   Ps 29:9

discovering

by d. the foundation to.   Hab 3:13

discourage

why d. ye hearts of people ?
     Num 32:7

discouraged

soul of people much d.   Num 21:4
they d. the heart of children.   32:9
it, fear not, nor be d.   Deut 1:21
our brethren have d. our heart. 28
shall not fail nor be d.   Isa 42:4
children, lest they be d.   Col 3:21

discreet

look out a man d. and.   Gen 41:33
there is none so d. and wise as. 39
teach young women to be d. Tit 2:5*

discreetly

saw that he answered d. Mark 12:34

discretion

guide his affairs with d.   *Ps* 112:5*
young man knowledge and d. *Pr* 1:4
d. shall preserve thee.   2:11
keep sound wisdom and d.   3:21
thou mayest regard d. and keep. 5:2
fair woman who is without d. 11:22
d. of a man deferreth his.   19:11
doth instruct him to d.   *Isa* 28:26*
out heavens by his d.   *Jer* 10:12*

disdained

Goliath saw David, he d. him.
  1 Sam 17:42
would d. to set with dogs. *Job* 30:1

disease

*The ancient Hebrews, who were
very little versed in the study of
natural philosophy, and not much
accustomed to consult physicians
when they were sick, imputed their
diseases generally to evil spirits, or
to the hand of God, generally in
punishment for some sin; and
king Asa is blamed for placing his
confidence in physicians, when he
had a very painful fit of the gout
in his feet, instead of to God,
2 Chr. 16:12.
In the New Testament, the cause
of many diseases is attributed to the
devil, Luke 13:16. And the various
forms of insanity and allied troubles
were spoken of as being possessed
of a devil. There seems to have
been also something beyond ordinary insanity included among these,
but there is no means of telling
either what it was, or what proportion of the cases might be considered as coming under it.
The diseases of Egypt, from which
God promised to defend his people,
Ex 15:26; and which he threatens,
in case of their disobedience, to in-
flict upon them, Deut 28:60; are
either the plagues with which God
afflicted Egypt before the departure
of the Israelites, or the diseases
which were most common in the
country, such as blindness, ulcers in
the legs, consumptions, and the
leprosy, called Elephantiasis, which
was peculiar to this country (Pliny).*

if I shall recover of d.   *2 Ki* 1:2
shall I recover of this d.? 8:8, 9
Asa diseased till his d. was exceeding great, yet in his d. *2 Chr* 16:12
great sickness by d. of thy.   21:15
smote him with an incurable d. 18
my d. is my garment.   *Job* 30:18
filled with a loathsome d. *Ps* 38:7*
an evil d. say they, cleaveth. 41:8
vanity, and it is an evil d. *Eccl.* 6:2
healing all manner of d. *Mat* 4:23
  9:35; 10:1
whole of whatsoever d. *John* 5:4

diseased

Asa was d. in his feet.   *1 Ki* 15:23
  2 Chr 16:12
d. have not strengthened. *Ezek* 34:4
pushed the d. with your horns. 21
d. with an issue of blood. *Mat* 9:20
they brought all that were d. 14:35
  Mark 1:32
did on them that were d. *John* 6:2

diseases

put none of these d. on you.
  Ex 15:26; *Deut* 7:15
thee all the d. of Egypt. *Deut* 28:60
out, he died of sore d. *2 Chr* 21:19
him in great d. his servants. 24:25
Lord, who healeth all thy d. *Ps* 103:3
people that were taken with divers d.
 Mat 4:24; *Mark* 1:34; *Luke* 4:40
over devils. and cure d. *Luke* 9:1
d. departed from them. *Acts* 19:12
others which had d. in island. 28:9

disfigure

hypocrites, for they d.   *Mat* 6:16

disgrace

do not d. the throne.   *Jer* 14:21

disguise, -d

and Saul d. himself.   *1 Sam* 28:8
Jeroboam said, arise, and d.
  1 Ki 14:2
sons of the prophets d.   20:38
Ahab king of Israel said, I will d. myself, and he d. 22:30; *2 Chr* 18:29
Josiah d. himself to. *2 Chr* 35:22

disguiseth

waiteth and d. his face. *Job* 24:15

dish, -es

make d. thereof. *Ex* 25:29; 37:16
thereon d. and spoons. *Num* 4:7
forth butter in a lordly d. *Judg* 5:25
as a man wipeth a d. *2 Ki* 21:13
dippeth with me in the d. *Mat* 26:23
  Mark 14:20

dishonest, *see* gain

dishonesty

hidden things of d.   *2 Cor* 4:2

dishonour

for us to see king's d. *Ezra* 4:14
clothed with shame and d. *Ps* 35:26
  71:13
known my shame and my d. 69:19
wound and d. shall he get. *Pr* 6:33
to honour, another to d. *Rom* 9:21
sown in d. it is raised. *1 Cor* 15:43
by honour and d. by.   *2 Cor* 6:8
to honour, some to d. *2 Tim* 2:20

dishonour, -est, -eth, *verb*

for the son d. father.   *Mi* 7:6
my Father, and ye d. me. *John* 8:49
to d. their own bodies. *Rom* 1:24
of the law, d. thou God?   2:23
man d. his head.   *1 Cor* 11:4
woman d. her head.   5

disinherit

will d. them, and make. *Num* 14:12

dismayed

nor forsake thee, fear not, nor be d.
Deut 31:8; *Josh* 1:9; 8:1; 10:25
1 Chr 22:13; 28:20; *2 Chr* 20:15
  17; 32:7
they were d.   *1 Sam* 17:11
  2 Ki 19:26; *Isa* 37:27
I was bowed down, d. at. *Isa* 21:3
fear not, be not d. 41:10; *Jer* 1:17
  10:2; 23:4; 30:10; 46:27
  Ezek 2:6; 3:9
may be d. and behold it. *Isa* 41:23
wise men are d.   *Jer* 8:9; 10:2
be d. but let not me be d. 17:18
seen them d. turned back? 46:5
Misgab is d.   48:1*
cause Elam to be d.   49:37
men of Babylon shall be d. 50:36
O Teman, shall be d.   *Ob* 9

dismaying

Moab shall be a d. to. *Jer* 48:39†

dismissed

Jehoiada the priest d. not. *2 Chr* 23:8
d. they came to Antioch. *Acts* 15:30
spoken, he d. assembly.   19:41

disobedience

by one man's d. many. *Rom* 5:19
to revenge all d.   *2 Cor* 10:6
worketh in children of d. *Eph* 2:2
wrath of God on children of d. 5:6
  Col 3:6
d. received a just.   *Heb* 2:2

disobedient

who was d. to the word. *1 Ki* 13:26
were d. and rebelled. *Neh* 9:26
turn d. to the wisdom of. *Luke* 1:17
not d. to the heavenly. *Acts* 26:19
boasters d. to parents. *Rom* 1:30
  2 Tim 3:2
forth my hands to a d. *Rom* 10:21
made for lawless and d. *1 Tim* 1:9*
being abominable and d. *Tit* 1:16
we also were sometimes d. 3:3
which be d. stone which. *1 Pet* 2:7*
who stumble at word, being d. 8
spirits in prison, which sometime
  were d.   3:20

disobeyed

hast d. mouth of Lord. *1 Ki* 13:21

disorderly

warn them that are d. *1 Thes* 5:14

---

brother who walks d. *2 Thes* 3:6
we behaved not ourselves d. 7
some who walk among you d. 11

dispatch

d. them with swords. *Ezek* 23:47

dispensation

a d. of the gospel is. *1 Cor* 9:17*
in d. of fulness of times. *Eph* 1:10
ye have heard of the d. of grace. 3:2
a minister according to d. *Col* 1:25

disperse

Saul said, d.   *1 Sam* 14:34
lips of wise d. knowledge. *Pr* 15:7
scatter them and d. *Ezek* 12:15
  20:23; 29:12; 30:23, 26
and I will d. thee in countries. 22:15

dispersed

Rehoboam d. of all his. *2 Chr* 11:23
certain people d. among. *Esth* 3:8
he hath d. he hath given. *Ps* 112:9
  2 Cor 9:9
let thy fountains be d. *Pr* 5:16
together d. of Judah. *Isa* 11:12
d. through countries. *Ezek* 36:19
daughter of my d. shall. *Zeph* 3:10
to d. among Gentiles? *John* 7:35*
as obeyed him were d. *Acts* 5:37*

dispersions

days of your d. are. *Jer* 25:34*

displayed

banner that it may be d. *Ps* 60:4

displease

let it not d. my lord. *Gen* 31:35*
if it d. thee, I will get. *Num* 22:34
that thou d. not lords. *1 Sam* 29:7
to Joab, let not this d. *2 Sam* 11:25
Lord see it, and it d. him. *Pr* 24:18

displeased

he did d. the Lord. *Gen* 38:10*
on head of Ephraim, it d. 48:17
complained, it d. Lord. *Num* 11:1*
was kindled, Moses also was d. 10
but the thing d. Samuel. *1 Sam* 8:6
very wroth, and the saying d. 18:8
David was d. because the Lord had.
  2 Sam 6:8; *1 Chr* 13:11
David had done d. Lord. *2 Sam* 11:27
his father had not d. him. *1 Ki* 1:6
king of Israel went to his house d.
  20:43; 21:4
God was d. with this. *1 Chr* 21:7
been d. O turn thyself to. *Ps* 60:1
d. him that there was. *Isa* 59:15
the king was sore d. *Dan* 6:14
it d. Jonah exceedingly. *Jonah* 4:1
was the Lord d. against? *Hab* 3:8
Lord hath been sore d. *Zech* 1:2
I am very sore d. with heathen; for I
  was but a little d. they helped. 15
scribes saw, were d. *Mat* 21:15*
Jesus saw it, he was much d.
  Mark 10:14*
began to be much d. with James. 41*
d. was highly d. with. *Acts* 12:20

displeasure

afraid of the hot d. of. *Deut* 9:19
though I do them a d. *Judg* 15:3*
vex them in his sore d. *Ps* 2:5
neither chasten me in hot d. 6:1
  38:1

disposed

who hath d. whole world? *Job* 34:13
thou know when God d.? 37:15*
when he was d. to pass. *Acts* 18:27*
and ye be d. to go. *1 Cor* 10:27

disposing

the whole d. thereof is. *Pr* 16:33

disposition

received law by d. of. *Acts* 7:53*

dispossess, -ed

children of Machir d. *Num* 32:39
ye shall d. the inhabitants of. 33:53
how can I d. them? *Deut* 7:17
Lord God hath d. the. *Judg* 11:23

disputation

had no small d.   *Acts* 15:2*

disputations

but not to doubtful d. *Rom* 14:1

dispute

there righteous might d. *Job* 23:7*

disputed
was it that ye d.? Mark 9:33*
for they had d. who should be. 34
Saul d. against Grecians. Acts 9:29
Paul d. in synagogue with. 17:17*
Michael d. about body of. Jude 9

disputer
where is d. of world? 1 Cor 1:20

disputing
them of Asia d. with. Acts 6:9
had been much d. Peter rose. 15:7
d. and persuading things. 19:8*, 9*
they neither found me d. 24:12

disputings
things without murmurings and d.
Phil 2:14†
perverse d. of men of. 1 Tim 6:5*

disquiet
and d. inhabitants of. Jer 50:34

disquieted
why hast thou d. me? 1 Sam 28:15
surely they are d. in vain. Ps 39:6
O my soul, why art thou d. within?
42:5, 11; 43:5
three things earth is d. Pr 30:21*

disquietness
roared by reason of d. Ps 38:8

dissembled
also stolen and d. also. Josh 7:11
for ye d. in your hearts. Jer 42:20*
other Jews d. likewise. Gal 2:13

dissemblers
nor will I go in with d. Ps 26:4

dissembleth
he that hateth d. with. Pr 26:24

dissension
Barnabas had no small d. Acts 15:2
arose a d. between Pharisees. 23:7
when there arose a great d. 10

dissimulation
let love be without d. Rom 12:9*
Barnabas carried away with their d.
Gal 2:13

dissolve
that thou canst d. doubts. Dan 5:16

dissolved
and all inhabitants are d. Ps 75:3
whole Palestina are d. Isa 14:31*
earth is clean d. the earth. 24:19
the host of heaven be d. 34:4
and the palace shall be d. Nah 2:6
this tabernacle were d. 2 Cor 5:1
all these things shall be d. 2 Pet 3:11
heavens being on fire shall be d. 12

dissolvest
and thou d. my substance. Job 30:22

dissolving
d. of doubts found in. Dan 5:12

distaff
her hands hold the d. Pr 31:19

distant
had two tenons equally d. Ex 36:22*

distil
speech shall d. as dew. Deut 32:2
the clouds d. on man. Job 36:28*

distinction
except they give a d. 1 Cor 14:7

distinctly
in book of the law of God d. Neh 8:8

distracted
suffer thy terrors, I am d. Ps 88:15

distraction
attend on Lord without d. 1 Cor 7:35

distress
me in day of my d. Gen 35:3
therefore is this d. come. 42:21
me now, when in d. Judg 11:7
one in d. came to David. 1 Sam 22:2
in my d. I called on. 2 Sam 22:7
Ps 18:6; 118:5; 120:1
my soul out of all d. 1 Ki 1:29*
his d. Ahaz trespassed. 2 Chr 28:22
I said, ye see the d. Neh 2:17*
and we are in great d. 9:37
enlarged me when I was in d. Ps 4:1
I will mock when d. Pr 1:27
strength to the needy in d. Isa 25:4

O Lord, for I am in d. Lam 1:20
proudly in day of d. Ob 12
delivered up those in day of d. 14
a day of trouble and d. Zeph 1:15
I will bring d. upon men. 17
there shall be great d. Luke 21:23
on the earth d. of nations. 25
d. separate us from love. Rom 8:35*
good for the present d. 1 Cor 7:26
over you in your d. 1 Thes 3:7

distress, -ed, verb
was greatly afraid and d. Gen 32:7
Moab was d. Num 22:3
d. not the Moabites. Deut 2:9*
Ammonites, d. them not. 19*
enemies shall d. 28:53†, 55†, 57†
Israel d. Judg 2:15; 10:9
for people were d. did. 1 Sam 13:6
men of Israel were d. 14:24
Saul was d. 28:15
David was greatly d. for. 30:6
I am d. for thee. 2 Sam 1:26
king of Assyria d. Ahaz. 2 Chr 28:20
yet I will d. Ariel. Isa 29:2
that d. her shall be as a dream. 7
I will d. the inhabitants. Jer 10:18
on every side, yet not d. 2 Cor 4:8*

distresses
bring thou me out of my d. Ps 25:17
delivered them out of their d. 107:6
saved them out of their d. 13, 19
bringeth them out of their d. 28
Noph shall have d. Ezek 30:16*
approving ourselves in d. 2 Cor 6:4
I take pleasure in d. for. 12:10

distribute
which Moses did d. for. Josh 13:32
Kore to d. oblations. 2 Chr 31:14
office was to d. to. Neh 13:13
sell all thou hast, and d. Luke 18:22
rich to be ready to d. 1 Tim 6:18

distributed
Eleazar and Joshua d. for. Josh 14:1
David d. them, according to their.
1 Chr 24:3*; 2 Chr 23:18
Jesus gave thanks and d. John 6:11
but as God hath d. 1 Cor 7:17
the rule God hath d. to. 2 Cor 10:13

distributeth, -ing
God d. sorrows in his. Job 21:17
d. to the necessities of. Rom 12:13*

distribution
d. was made to every one. Acts 4:35
for your liberal d. to. 2 Cor 9:13

ditch
shalt thou plunge me in d. Job 9:31
he is fallen into the d. Ps 7:15
a whore is a deep d. Pr 23:27
ye made a d. between. Isa 22:11*
both shall fall into d. Mat 15:14*
Luke 6:39*

ditches
this valley full of d. 2 Ki 3:16*

divers, diverse
cattle gender with d. Lev 19:19
not sow vineyard with d. Deut 22:9*
not wear garment of d. sorts. 11*
not have in thy bag d. 25:13
in thy house d. measures. 14
of d. colours, a prey of d. Judg 5:30
Tamar had a garment of d. colours.
2 Sam 13:18, 19
glistering stones of d. 1 Chr 29:2
they laid Asa in the bed filled with
odours and d. kinds. 2 Chr 16:14
Jehoram slew d. of the princes. 21:4
d. of Asher humbled. 30:11
the vessels being d. one. Esth 1:7
their laws are d. from all. 3:8
he sent d. sorts of flies. Ps 78:45*
there came d. sorts of flies. 105:31*
d. weights and d. measures. Pr 20:10
d. weights are an abomination to. 23
there are also d. vanities. Eccl 5:7
deckest high places with d. colours.
Ezek 16:16
great eagle had d. colours. 17:3
beasts came up, d. one. Dan 7:19
a fourth beast d. from all. 7, 19
d. from all kingdoms. 23
d. from the first. 24

brought to Jesus sick people with d.
Mat 4:24; Mark 1:34; Luke 4:40
pestilences, and earthquakes in d.
Mat 24:7; Mark 13:8; Luke 21:11
for d. of them came. Mark 8:3*
when d. were hardened. Acts 19:9*
to another d. kinds. 1 Cor 12:10
women led away with d. 2 Tim 3:6
deceived, serving d. lusts. Tit 3:3
who in d. manners spake. Heb 1:1
witness with signs and d. 2:4*
stood in d. washings. 9:10
d. and strange doctrines. 13:9
fall into d. temptations. Jas 1:2*

diversities
d. of gifts. 1 Cor 12:4
d. of operations. 6
God hath set in church d. 28*

divide
and let the firmament d. Gen 1:6
be lights, to d. day from. 14, 18
and at night he shall d. 49:27
hand over sea and d. it. Ex 14:16
d. the money, d. the dead ox. 21:35
veil shall d. between holy. 26:33
but not d. it asunder. Lev 1:17; 5:8
not eat of them that d. hoof. 11:4, 7
Deut 14:7
and d. the prey into. Num 31:27
d. land by lot. 33:54*; 34:17, 18, 29
d. the coasts of thy land. Deut 19:3
d. for an inheritance. Josh 1:6*
13:6*, 7; 18:5
d. the spoil of your enemies. 22:8
thou and Ziba d. land. 2 Sam 19:29
d. living child in two. 1 Ki 3:25, 26
thou didst d. the sea. Neh 9:11
Ps 74:13
and thou didst d. them into. Neh 9:22*
innocent shall d. silver. Job 27:17
and d. their tongues. Ps 55:9
than to d. the spoil. Pr 16:19
as men rejoice when they d. Isa 9:3
he shall d. the spoil with. 53:12
take the balances and d. Ezek 5:1
d. land by lot. 45:1; 47:21, 22
the land which ye shall d. 48:29
he shall d. the land. Dan 11:39
that he d. inheritance. Luke 12:13
take this, and d. it among. 22:17

I will divide
I will d. them in Jacob. Gen 49:7
enemy said, I will d. Ex 15:9
I will d. Shechem. Ps 60:6; 108:7
will I d. him a portion. Isa 53:12

divided
God d. the light. Gen 1:4
God d. the waters. 7
these the isles of Gentiles d. 10:5
in his days was the earth d. 25
1 Chr 1:19
by these were nations d. Gen 10:32
Abram d. himself against. 14:15
Abram d. them, the birds d. 15:10
Jacob d. the people that was. 32:7
d. children to Leah and. 33:1
and waters were d. Ex 14:21
to these land shall be d. Num 26:53
lot shall possession of land be d. 56
which Moses d. from men. 31:42
which Lord hath d. Deut 4:19
when the most High d. to. 32:8*
they d. the land. Josh 14:5; 18:10
19:51*; 23:4
have they not d. the prey. Judg 5:30
d. the 300 men into three. 7:16
Abimelech d. them into three. 9:43
Levite d. her with her bones. 19:29
death they were not d. 2 Sam 1:23
were people of Israel d. 1 Ki 16:21
Ahab and Obadiah d. the land. 18:6
waters were d. hither. 2 Ki 2:8
David d. them into. 1 Chr 23:6
chief men, thus were they d. 24:4, 5
they d. other offerings. 2 Chr 35:13*
hath d. a water-course? Job 38:25*
that tarried at home d. Ps 68:12
he d. the sea and caused. 78:13*
d. them an inheritance by line. 55*
Acts 13:19
which d. the Red Sea. Ps 136:13
is prey of great spoil d. Isa 33:23
his hand hath d. it to them. 34:17

the Lord that *d.* the sea. *Isa* 51:15*
anger of the Lord hath *d. Lam* 4:16
nor shall they be *d.* into. *Ezek* 37:22
kingdom shall be *d.* but. *Dan* 2:41
thy kingdom is *d.* and given.   5:28
his kingdom shall be *d.* toward. 11:4
their heart is *d.* now. *Hos* 10:2
thy land shall be *d.* by line. *Amos* 7:17
he hath *d.* our fields. *Mi* 2:4
thy spoil shall be *d.* in. *Zech* 14:1
kingdom or house *d. Mat* 12:25
Mark 3:24, 25; *Luke* 11:17
he is *d.* against himself. *Mat* 12:26
Mark 3:26; *Luke* 11:18
the two fishes *d.* he. *Mark* 6:41
five in one house *d. Luke* 12:52
the father shall be *d.* against.   53
he *d.* unto them his living. 15:12
multitude of the city was *d.*
Acts 14:4; 23:7
is Christ *d.*? *1 Cor* 1:13
the great city was *d. Rev* 16:19

divider
who made me a *d.* over ? *Luke* 12:14

divideth
cheweth cud, but *d. Lev* 11:4, 5, 6
carcases of every beast which *d.* 26
swine, because it *d. Deut* 14:8
d. the sea with his. *Job* 26:12*
voice of the Lord *d. Ps* 29:7
which *d.* the sea when. *Jer* 31:35*
as a shepherd *d.* his. *Mat* 25:32
his armour, and *d. Luke* 11:22

dividing
an end of *d.* the land. *Josh* 19:49*
so they made an end of *d.* the. 51
led them, *d.* the water. *Isa* 63:12
times, and a *d.* of time. *Dan* 7:25
d. to every man. *1 Cor* 12:11
a workman rightly *d. 2 Tim* 2:15
piercing to *d.* asunder. *Heb* 4:12

divination
A foreseeing or foretelling of future events or discovery of hidden knowledge. In eastern nations, and especially in Bible times, this was done by interpreting dreams or other signs, or by some peculiarities in the sacrifices, whether offered to God or to an idol. There were several sorts of divinations, namely, by water, fire, earth, air ; by the flight of birds, and their singing ; by lots, by dreams, by the staff, or wand, by the entrails of victims, and by cups. The custom has been universal in all ages and all nations, civilized or savage. In the Bible, the word is used of false systems of ascertaining the Divine will.
with the rewards of *d. Num* 22:7
neither is there any *d.* 23:23
or that useth *d. Deut* 18:10
2 Ki 17:17
prophesy visions and *d. Jer* 14:14
nor flattering *d.* in. *Ezek* 12:24
seen vanity, and lying *d.* 13:6
have ye not spoken a lying *d.*? 7
of Babylon stood to use *d.* 21:21
at his right hand was the *d.* of. 22
as a false *d.* in their sight. 23
possessed with spirit of *d. Acts* 16:16

divinations
see no more divine *d. Ezek* 13:23

divine
such a man as I can *d. Gen* 44:15
d. to me by familiar. *1 Sam* 28:8
on prophets that *d.* lies. *Ezek* 13:9
no more vanity, or *d.* divinations. 23
whiles they *d.* a lie unto thee. 21:29
you, that ye shall not *d. Mi* 3:6
and the prophets thereof *d.* 11

divine, adjective
a *d.* sentence is in the. *Pr* 16:10
had ordinances of *d. Heb* 9:1
as his *d.* power hath. *2 Pet* 1:3
be partakers of the *d.* nature. 4

diviner, -s
nations hearkened to *d. Deut* 18:14
Philistines called for *d. 1 Sam* 6:2
turneth, that maketh *d. Isa* 44:25

hearken not to your *d. Jer* 27:9
let not your prophets and *d.* 29:8
and the *d.* confounded. *Mi* 3:7
the *d.* have seen a lie. *Zech* 10:2

divineth
it whereby indeed he *d.*? *Gen* 44:5

divining
and *d.* lies to them. *Ezek* 28:28

division
will put a *d.* between. *Ex* 8:23
according to the *d.* of. *2 Chr* 35:5*
nay, but rather *d. Luke* 12:51
a *d.* among the people, because of.
John 7:43; 9:16; 10:19

divisions
gave the land to Israel, according to
their *d. Josh* 11:23; 12:7; 18:10
2 Chr 35:5, 12
for *d.* of Reuben, there were great
thoughts of heart. *Judg* 5:15*, 16*
these are *d.* of the sons of. 26:1*
the *d.* of porters. 26:1*, 12*, 19*
the priests in their *d. Neh* 11:36*
them which cause *d. Rom* 16:17
that there be no *d. 1 Cor* 1:10
is among you strife and *d.* 3:3
I hear there be *d.* among you 11:18

divorce
*The legal dissolution of marriage.
Moses tolerated divorces, Deut 24:1-4.
The school of Shammah, who lived a little before our Saviour, taught, that a man could not lawfully be divorced from his wife, unless he had found his guilty of some action which was really infamous, and contrary to the rules of virtue. But the school of Hillel, who was Shammah's disciple, taught, on the contrary, that the least reasons were sufficient to authorize a man to put away his wife ; for example, if she did not cook his food well, or if he found any woman whom he liked better.
The Pharisees attempted to trap our Lord into some statement by which they could take issue, but he declined to interpret Moses' words, though he declared that he regarded all lesser causes than fornication as standing on too weak ground.*
and given a bill of *d. Jer* 3:8

divorced
high priest not take a *d.* woman.
Lev 21:14
daughter be a widow or *d.* 22:13
vow of her that is *d. Num* 30:9
marry her that is *d. Mat* 5:32

divorcement
write her a bill of *d. Deut* 24:1, 3
is bill of your mother's *d.? Isa* 50:1
suffered to write bill of *d. Mark* 10:4
see writing

do
do to her as it pleaseth. *Gen* 16:6
Judge of all earth *do* right ? 18:25
God hath said to thee, *do.* 31:16
I will surely *do* thee good. 32:12
what he is about to *do.* 41:25, 28
teach you what ye shall *do. Ex* 4:15
if thou wilt *do* that which is. 15:26
Deut 6:18; 12:25; 13:18; 21:9
the work that they must *do.*
Ex 18:20
Lord hath spoken we will *do.* 19:8
six days *do* all thy work. 20:9; 23:12
Deut 5:13
shalt thou *do* to Aaron. *Ex* 29:35
ye shall *do* my judgements. *Lev* 18:4
19:37; 20:22; *Ezek* 36:27
which if a man *do. Lev* 18:5
Neh 9:29; *Ezek* 20:11, 13, 21
ye shall *do* my statutes. *Lev* 25:18
20:8; 22:31; *Deut* 17:19; 26:16
that shalt thou *do. Num* 22:20
what this people shall *do* to. 24:14
servants will *do* as my lord. 32:25

keep commandments to *do* them.
Deut 7:11; 11:22
do according to sentence. 17:10, 11
do to him as he thought to *do.* 19:19
shalt thou *do* to all the cities. 20:15
all the words of this law to *do.* 27:26
may hear it and *do* it. 30:12, 13
the Lord shall *do* to them as. 31:4
do ye thus requite the Lord. 32:6
thus shalt thou *do* six days. *Josh* 6:3
what wilt thou *do* to thy ? 7:9
thus shall the Lord *do* to. 10:25
what have ye to *do* with God ? 22:24
d. all that is written in book of law of.
23:6; *1 Chr* 16:40; *2 Chr* 34:21
as I *do* so shall ye *do. Judg* 7:17
what was I able to *do* in ? 8:3
do to us whatsover seemeth. 10:15
what ye have to *do.* 18:14
then said the priest, what *do* ye ? 18
tell thee what thou shalt *do. Ruth* 3:4
shew thee what thou shalt *do.*
1 Sam 16:3
till I know what God will *do.* 22:3
thou shalt *do* great things. 26:25
now then *do* it. *2 Sam* 3:18
I were judge, I would *do.* 15:4
here I am, let him *do* to me. 26
do it to thee. 24:12; *1 Chr* 21:10
do therefore according. *1 Ki* 2:6
do as he hath said. 31
then hear, and *do,* and judge. 8:32
forgive, and *do.* 39; *2 Chr* 6:23
do that is right. *1 Ki* 11:33, 38; 14:8
do it the second time. 18:34
what hast thou to *do* ? *2 Ki* 9:18, 19
to this day they *do* after the. 17:34
the Lord will *do* as he. 20:9*
Nathan said, *do* all that. *1 Chr* 17:2
and *do* as thou hast said. 23
do away the iniquity of. 21:8
king, to *do* judgement. *2 Chr* 9:8
take heed what ye *do.* 19:6
now take heed and *do* it. 7
thus shall ye *do* in the fear of. 9
nor know we what to *do.* 20:12
if thou wilt go, *do* it, be strong. 25:8
seek your God, as ye *do. Ezra* 4:2
to seek law of Lord, and *do.* 7:10
that *do* after the will of your. 18
hath put in my heart to *do. Neh* 2:12
they should *do* according to. 5:12
that they might *do* with them. 9:24
what shall I *do* to thee ? *Job* 7:20
as heaven, what canst thou *do* ? 11:8
only *do* not two things unto. 13:20
I delight to *do* thy will. *Ps* 40:8
what hast thou to *do* to ? 50:16
do unto them as unto the. 83:9
but *do* thou for me. 109:21*
as thou usest to *do* to those. 119:132
teach me to *do* thy will. 143:10
power of thy hand to *do. Pr* 3:27
do it with thy might. *Eccl* 9:10
what will ye *do* in day of ? *Isa* 10:3
that he may *do* his work. 28:21
I the Lord *do* all these things. 45:7
hast thou to *do* in way of Egypt ?
what hast thou to *do* ? *Jer* 2:18
what wilt thou *do* ? 4:30
and what will ye *do* in the end ? 5:31
seest thou not what they *do* ? 7:17
obey my voice, and *do* them. 11:4
what hath my beloved to *do* in ? 15
how wilt thou *do* in swelling ? 12:5
do thou it for thy name's sake. 14:7
do to him, even as he shall. 39:12
shew thing that we may *do.* 42:3
as she hath done, *do.* 50:15, 29
do unto them as thou. *Lam* 1:22
seest thou what they *do* ? *Ezek* 8:6
no eye pitied thee, to *do* any. 16:5
man be just, and *do* that which is.
18:5, 21; 33:14, 19
shall *do* as I have done. 24:22, 24
I will be enquired of to *do* it. 36:37
hearken and *do,* defer. *Dan* 9:19
do according to will. 11:3, 16, 36
thus shall he *do* in the most. 39
what will ye *do* in solemn ? *Hos* 9:5
what then should a king *do* ? 10:3
what have ye to *do* with ? *Amos* 3:7
the Lord will *do* nothing. *Amos* 3:7
I *do* well to be angry. *Jonah* 4:9

but to *do* justly, and to.   *Mi* 6:8
what come these to *do* ? *Zech* 1:21
are the things that ye shall *do*. 8:16
but whosover shall *do*.   *Mat* 5:19
brethren only, what *do* ye more ? 47
what have we to *do* with thee ?
     8:29; *Mark* 1:24; *Luke* 4:34
whosoever shall *do* the will of my
    Father.   *Mat* 12:50; *Mark* 3:35
lawful to *do* what I will. *Mat* 20:15
do to you ?   20:32; *Mark* 10:36
by what authority I *do* these things.
       Mat 21:24; *Mark* 11:29
neither tell by what authority I *do*.
  Mat 21:27; *Mark* 11:33; *Luke* 20:8
what will he *do* to those ? *Mat* 21:40
       Mark 12:9; *Luke* 20:15
all their works they *do*.   *Mat* 23:5
have nothing to *do* with.   27:19
such like things, ye *do*. *Mark* 7:8, 13
ye suffer him no more to *do*. 12
gave thee authority to *do* ? 11:28
have heard done, *do* in.   *Luke* 4:23
do that which is not lawful to *do* ? 6:2
commened what they might *do*. 11
as ye would that men *do*, *do* ye. 31
hear the word of God and *do* it. 8:21
I am resolved what to *do*.   16:4
that which was duty to *do*.   17:10
not find what they might *do*. 19:48
if they *do* these things in a. 23:31
they know not what they *do*. 34
whatsoever he saith, *do* it. *John* 2:5
my meat is to *do* the will of. 4:34
of mine own self *do* nothing. 5:30
the works that I *do* bear.   36
himself knew what he would *do*. 6:6
what shall we *do* ?   28; *Acts* 2:37
       16:30
if thou *do* these things, shew. *John* 7:4
if any man will *do* his will.
I *do* always those things.   8:29
ye would *do* the works of.   39
if not of God, he could *do*.   9:33
the works that I *do* in my. 10:25
Pharisees said, what *do* we ? 11:47
what I *do* thou knowest not. 13:7
that ye should *do* as I have done. 15
happy are ye if ye *do* them. 17
works that I *do* shall he *do*. 14:12
any thing in my name, I will *do* it. 14
my friends, if ye *do*.   15:14
these things will they *do*. 21; 16:3
the work thou gavest me to *do*. 17:4
what shall this man *do* ? 21:21
all that Jesus began to *do*. *Acts* 1:1
to *do* whatsoever thy counsel. 4:28
what wilt thou have me to *do* ? 9:6
thee what thou oughtest to *do*. 10:6
sirs, why *do* ye these things ? 14:15
brethren, see how they *do*. 15:36
do thyself no harm, for we. 16:28
these *do* contrary to decrees of. 17:7
not only *do* the same.   *Rom* 1:32
do by nature things contained. 2:14
I *do* I allow not, what I would that *do*
   not, what I hate *do* I.   7:15
if I *do* that which I would not. 16
it is no more I that *do* it. 17, 20
let him *do* it with simplicity. 12:8
let him *do* what he will. *1 Cor* 7:36
whatsoever ye *do*, *do* all to. 10:31
work of Lord as I also *do*. 16:10
not only to *do*, but also. *2 Cor* 8:10
that ye should *do* that. 13:7
which I was forward to *do*. *Gal* 2:10
as *do* the Jews, to live as *do*. 3:14
written in book of the law to *do*. 3:10
they which *do* such things. 5:21
masters, *do* the same.   *Eph* 6:9
know my affairs, and how I *do*. 21
both to will and to *do*.   *Phil* 2:13
ye have heard and seen, *do*.   4:9
whatsoever ye *do* in word or deed,
   do all in the name of.   *Col* 3:17
whatsoever ye *do*, *do* it heartily. 23
in love, even as we *do*. *1 Thes* 3:12
indeed ye *do* it towards. 4:10
let us not sleep as others. 5:6
edify one another, as also ye *do*. 11
who also will *do* it. 24
ye both *do* and will *do*. *2 Thes* 3:4
do the work of an evangelist.
       2 Tim 4:5

do thy diligence to come.
       2 Tim 4:9, 21
thou wilt *do* more than. *Philem* 21
with whom we have to *do*. *Heb* 4:13
lo, I come to *do* thy will.   10:7, 9
not fear what man shall *do*. 13:6
in every work, to *do*.   *1 Pet* 4:11*
him *do* it as of ability.   *2 Pet* 1:10
if ye *do* these. 21
wrest, as they *do* also other. 3:16
we lie, *do* not the truth. *1 John* 1:6
do those things that are. 3:22
and repent, and *do* the.   *Rev* 2:5

can or **canst do**
what can I *do* to these ? *Gen* 31:43
none can *do* according. *Deut* 3:24
what thy servant can *do*. *1 Sam* 28:2
speeches wherewith he can *do* no.
       Job 15:3
what can the Almighty *do* ? 22:17
I know that thou canst *do*. 42:2
what can the righteous *do* ? *Ps* 11:3
not fear what flesh can *do*. 56:4, 11
not fear what man can *do* to. 118:6
what can man *do* that ? *Eccl* 2:12
that can *do* any thing.   *Jer* 38:5
if thou canst *do*.   *Mark* 9:22
no more they can *do*.   *Luke* 12:4
for no man can *do* these. *John* 3:2
the Son can *do* nothing. 5:19, 30
without me ye can *do* nothing. 15:5
we can *do* nothing.   *2 Cor* 13:8
I can *do* all things through. *Phil* 4:13

do with **evil**
a multitude to *do* evil.   *Ex* 23:2
if a soul swear to *do* evil. *Lev* 5:4
shall *do* evil in sight.   *Deut* 4:25
because ye will *do* evil in. 31:29
please my father to *do* thee evil.
       1 Sam 20:13
despised Lord to *do* evil. *2 Sam* 12:9
know the evil thou wilt *do*. *2 Ki* 8:12
sold themselves to *do* evil in. 17:17
seduced them to *do* more evil. 21:9
against them that *do* evil. *Ps* 34:16
in any wise to *do* evil. 37:8
who rejoice to *do* evil.   *Pr* 2:14
he that deviseth to *do* evil. 24:8
not that they *do* evil.   *Eccl* 5:1
of men fully set to *do* evil. 8:11
though a sinner *do* evil an. 12
you clean, cease to *do* evil. *Isa* 1:16
do good or evil, that we may. 41:23
people are wise to *do* evil. *Jer* 4:22
for they cannot *do* evil. 10:5
accustomed to *do* evil. 13:23
if it *do* evil in my sight. 18:10
that I would *do* this evil. *Ezek* 6:10
that they may *do* evil.   *Mi* 7:3
not *do* good, nor *do* evil. *Zeph* 1:12
to *do* good or *do* evil ? *Mark* 3:4
       Luke 6:9
let us *do* evil that good. *Rom* 3:8
but if thou *do* that which is evil. 13:4
God that ye *do* no evil. *2 Cor* 13:7
against them that *do* evil. *1 Pet* 3:12

do joined with **good**
do ye to them as is good. *Gen* 19:8
what good shall my life *do* ? 27:46
pronouncing to *do* good.   *Lev* 5:4
we will *do* thee good. *Num* 10:29
to *do* either good or bad of. 24:13
is good for us to *do*.   *Deut* 1:14
prove thee, to *do* thee good. 8:16
rejoiced over you to *do* good. 28:63
and he will *do* thee good, and. 30:5
Lord will *do* me good. *Judg* 17:13
do with them what seemeth good to.
       19:24
do what seemeth thee good.
    1 Sam 1:23; 14:36, 40
     2 Sam 19:27, 37
Lord, let him *do* what seemeth him
   good.   *1 Sam* 3:18; *2 Sam* 10:12
do that which is good.   *2 Ki* 10:5
Lord *do* what is good.   *1 Chr* 19:13
king *do* that which is good. 21:23
is not good that ye *do*. *Neh* 5:9
do good. *Ps* 34:14; 37:3, 27; 51:18
   125:4; *Mat* 5:44; *Luke* 6:9, 35
to be wise and to *do* good. *Ps* 36:3
she will *do* him good.   *Pr* 31:12
for a man to *do* good.   *Eccl* 3:12

yea *do* good or do evil.   *Isa* 41:23
but to *do* good they have. *Jer* 4:22
nor is it in them to *do* good. 10:5
then may ye *do* good that. 13:23
with me as seemeth good. 26:14
behold the good I will *do*. 29:32
from them to *do* them good. 32:40
over them to *do* them good. 41
shall hear all the good I *do*. 33:9
not my words *do* good to.   *Mi* 2:7
Lord will not *do* good.   *Zeph* 1:12
is it lawful to *do* good on sabbath-
   days, or ?   *Mark* 3:4; *Luke* 6:9
ye may *do* them good. *Mark* 14:7
do good to them that *do* good to you.
       Luke 6:33
good that I would, I *do*. *Rom* 7:19
when I would *do* good evil is. 21
do what is good, and thou. 13:3
let us *do* good to all.   *Gal* 6:10
rich, that they *do* good. *1 Tim* 6:18
to *do* good and communicate.
       Heb 13:16
that knoweth to *do* good.   *Jas* 4:17
eschew evil, and *do* good. *1 Pet* 3:11

have I to do
what *have I to do* ?   *2 Sam* 16:10
       19:22
have I to do with thee ? *1 Ki* 17:18
  2 Ki 3:13; *2 Chr* 35:21; *Mark* 5:7
    Luke 8:28; *John* 2:4
what *have I to do* any ? *Hos* 14:8
have I to do to judge ? *1 Cor* 5:12

I shall, or **I will do**; or **will I**,
shall I do
what *shall I do* now to ? *Gen* 27:37
I *will do* as thou hast said. 47:30
I *will do* in the midst. *Ex* 3:20
shalt see what I *will do*. 6:1
shall I do to this people ? 17:4
I *will do* marvels, for it is a terrible
   thing that I *will do*. 34:10
I *will surely do* it to. *Num* 14:35
I *will do* whatsoever thou. 22:17
I *shall do* to you as I thought. 33:56
sayest to me I *will do*.   *Ruth* 3:5
I *will do* to thee all that thou. 11
then *will I do* the part of a. 13
behold, I *will do* a.   *1 Sam* 3:11
saying, what *shall I do* for ? 10:2
thy soul desireth, I *will do* it. 20:4
known to me what I *shall do*. 28:15
but I *will do* this thing. *2 Sam* 12:12
seemeth best I *will do*. 18:4; 19:38
what *shall I do* for you ? 21:3
that *will I do* for you. 4
I *will do* all thy desire for. *1 Ki* 5:8
didst send for I *will do*. 20:9
what I *shall do* for thee.   *2 Ki* 2:9
Elisha said, what *shall I do* ? 4:2
I *will do* to-morrow as. *Esth* 5:8
what *shall I do* to thee ? *Job* 7:20
what then *shall I do* when ? 31:14
I *will do* no more. 34:32
I *will do* so to him as he. *Pr* 24:29
I will tell what I *will do*. *Isa* 5:5
these things *will I do*. 42:16
I *will do* a new thing. 43:19
I *will do* all my pleasure. 46:10
purposed it, I *will* also *do* it. 11
for mine own sake *will I do* it. 48:11
therefore *will I do* unto. *Jer* 7:14
how *shall I do* for daughter ? 9:7
therefore in this place. 19:12
provoke me not, and I *will do*. 25:6
the good that I *will do* for. 29:32
I *will do* judgement on. 51:47
I *will do* in thee what I. *Ezek* 5:9
I *will do* unto them after. 7:27
I have spoken, and *will do* it. 12:25
       24:14; 36:36
I *will* even *do* according to. 35:11
I *will do* better to you than. 36:11
what *shall I do* unto thee ? *Hos* 6:4
thus will I *do* unto thee. *Amos* 4:12
good *thing shall I do* ? *Mat* 19:16
what *shall I do* with Jesus ? 27:22
what *shall I do*, because. *Luke* 12:17
what *shall I do* ? 16:3; 20:13
       Acts 22:10
ask, that *will I do*.   *John* 14:13
ask in my name I *will do* it. 14
what I *do*, that I *will do*. *2 Cor* 11:12

without thy mind *would I do* nothing.
Philem 14
see **judgement**
must **do**
work that they *must do.* *Ex 18:20*
all the Lord speaketh, that I *must do.*
Num 23:26
thou *must do* it again. *Pr 19:19*
must I do to be saved ? *Acts 16:30*
do joined with *no,* or *not*
not do it for forty's sake. *Gen 18:29*
I will *not do* it if I find thirty. 30
I *cannot do* any thing till. 19:22
deferred *not* to do the thing. 34:19
shalt *not do* any work. *Ex 20:10*
Lev 23:31
if he *do not* these three. *Ex 21:11*
shalt *not do* after their works. 23:24
afflict your souls and *do no* work.
Lev 16:29; 23:3, 28; Deut 15:19
Jer 17:24
doings ye shall *not do.* *Lev 18:3*
do no unrighteousness. 19:15, 35
do no servile work. 23:7, 8, 21
25, 35, 36; *Num 28:18, 25, 26*
will *not do* my commandments.
Lev 26:14, 15
fifty years shall *do no.* *Num 8:26*
said, and shall he *not do* it ? 23:19
ye shall *not do* any work. 29:7
Deut 5:14; 16:8
shall *not do* after all the. *Deut 12:8*
do no more such wickedness. 13:11
fear and *do no* more. 17:13
could *not do* it by day. *Judg 6:27*
I pray you, *do not* this folly. 19:23
to this man *do not* so vile a. 24
will *not do* the part of a. *Ruth 3:13*
no more *do* thee harm. *1 Sam 26:21*
days I will *not do* it. *1 Ki 11:12*
lepers said we *do not.* *2 Ki 7:9*
charged they should *not do.* 17:15
not hear them, *nor do* them. 18:12
whoso will *not do* law. *Ezra 7:26*
only *do not* two things. *Job 13:20*
God will *not do* wickedly. 34:12
remember the battle, *do no.* 41:8
they *do no* iniquity. *Ps 119:3*
cannot I do with you as this potter ?
Jer 18:6
do no wrong, *do no* violence. 22:3
be a true witness, if we *do not.* 42:5
I will *not do* any more. *Ezek 5:9*
may be taught *not* to do after. 23:48
but they will *not do* them. 33:31
but they *do* them *not.* 32
Lord, will *not do* iniquity. *Zeph 3:5*
remnant of Israel shall *not do.* 13
do not even publicans ? *Mat 5:46, 47*
take heed ye *do not* your. 6:1
doest alms *do not* sound a trumpet. 2
which is *not* lawful to *do* on. 12:2
thou shalt *do no* murder. 19:18
friend, I *do* thee *no* wrong. 20:13
do not after their works, they say
and *do not.* 23:3
could there *do no* mighty. *Mark 6:5*
and *do not* the things. *Luke 6:46*
I came down *not* to do. *John 6:38*
if I *do not* the works of. 10:37
would, that *do* I *not.* *Rom 7:15, 19*
for what law could *not do.* 8:3
ye *cannot do* the things. *Gal 5:17*
lie, and *do not* the truth. *1 John 1:6*
see thou *do* it *not.* *Rev 19:10; 22:9*
observe with **do**
ye shall *observe* to do as. *Deut 5:32*
8:1; 11:32; 12:1; 24:8; *2 Ki 17:37*
observe to do. *Deut 6:3; 12:32*
28:13, 15, 58; 31:12; 32:46
if *we observe* to do these. 6:25
to *observe* to do all these. 15:5
thou shalt *observe* and do. 16:12
shalt *observe* to do as they. 17:10
mayest *observe* to do. *Josh 1:7*
if they will *observe* to do. *2 Ki 21:8*
oath to *observe* and do. *Neh 10:29*
observe and do them. *Ezek 37:24*
bid, that *observe* and do. *Mat 23:3*
will we **do,** we will **do**
said *we will do.* *Ex 19:8; 24:3, 7*
goodness *will we do* to. *Num 10:32*
we will hear it and do it. *Deut 5:27*

thou commandest us *we will do.*
Josh 1:16
thing which *we will do.* *Judg 20:9*
we will do all that thou. *2 Ki 10:5*
we will every one *do.* *Jer 18:12*
declare unto us, *we will do* it. 42:20
we will certainly *do.* 44:17
shall *we do,* *we shall do*
teach us what *we shall do.* *Judg 13:8*
how *shall we do* unto him ? 12
how *shall we do* for wives ? 21:7, 16
shall we do with ark ? *1 Sam 5:8*
what *shall we do* to the ark ? 6:2
counsel what *shall do.* *2 Sam 16:20*
shall we do after this saying ? 17:6
master, how *shall we do* ? *2 Ki 6:15*
shall we do for the 100 ? *2 Chr 25:9*
shall we do to the queen ? *Esth 1:15*
through God *we shall do.* *Ps 60:12*
108:13
what *shall we do* for our ? *S of S 8:8*
what *shall we do* to thee ? *Jonah 1:11*
what *shall we do* ? *Luke 3:10, 12, 14*
shall we do that we ? *John 6:28*
brethren, what *shall we do* ?
Acts 2:37
shall we do to these men ? 4:16
do joined with *so*
so do as thou hast said. *Gen 18:5*
do not so wickedly. 19:7; *Judg 19:23*
forbid that I should *do so.* *Gen 44:17*
it is *not* meet *so* to do. *Ex 8:26*
so shall he *do.* *Lev 4:20; 16:16*
Num 9:14; 15:14
so Lord hath commanded to *do.*
Lev 8:34
so will I *do.* *Num 14:28; 32:31*
Isa 65:8; Ezek 35:15
so shall he *do* to every one.
Num 15:12
was I ever wont to *do so* ? 22:30
if ye will *not do so* ye have. 32:23
so shall the Lord *do* to. *Deut 3:21*
shall *not do so* to the Lord. 12:4, 31
nations serve gods ? *so I do.* 30
hath *not* suffered thee *so* to do. 18:14
and *so* shalt thou *do* with. 22:3
all that *do so* are abomination. 5
as I *do, so* shall ye *do.* *Judg 7:17*
if we *do not so* according. 11:10
so used the young men to *do.* 14:10
this man *do not so* vile a. 19:24
Lord *do so* to me. *Ruth 1:17*
1 Sam 14:44
God *do so* to thee. *1 Sam 3:17*
so do they also *to* thee. 8:8
Lord *do so* and much more. 20:13
so and more also *do* God. 25:22
shall *not do so,* my brethren. 30:23
so do God to Abner, even *so* I *do* to.
2 Sam 3:9
do so to me, and more. 3:35; 19:13
1 Ki 2:23; 20:10; 2 Ki 6:31
so shall thy servant *do.* *2 Sam 9:11*
so will I certainly *do.* *1 Ki 1:30*
so will thy servant *do.* 2:38
so let the gods *do* to me. 19:2
forth and *do so.* 22:22; *2 Chr 18:21*
did their fathers, *so do.* *2 Ki 17:41*
said they would *do so.* *1 Chr 13:4*
hast said, *so* must we *do.* *Ezra 10:12*
said, *so* will we *do* as. *Neh 5:12*
I should be afraid, and *do so.* 6:13
if ye *do so* again I will. 13:21
do even *so* to Mordecai. *Esth 6:10*
is he durst presume to *do so* ? 7:5
man mocketh, *do ye so* ? *Job 13:9*
so do stripes the inward. *Pr 20:30*
say not, I will *do so* to him as. 24:29
I *so do* to Jerusalem. *Isa 10:11*
the Lord *do so,* the Lord. *Jer 28:6*
so thou shalt *do* seventh. *Ezek 45:20*
so shall he *do.* *Dan 11:30*
so shall Beth-el *do* to. *Hos 10:15*
do not even publicans *so* ? *Mat 5:47*
do to you, *do* ye even *so* to. 7:12
so shall my heavenly Father *do.*
18:35
commandment, *so* I *do.* *John 14:31*
as fathers did, *so do* ye. *Acts 7:51*
order, even *so do* ye. *1 Cor 16:1*
Christ forgave you, *so do.* *Col 3:13*
which is in faith, *so do.* *1 Tim 1:4*

so do ye, as they that. *Jas 2:12*
do joined with *this*
and *this* they begin to *do.* *Gen 11:6*
I *do this* great wickedness. 39:9
let Pharaoh *do this,* let him. 41:34
Joseph said, *this do* and. 42:18
it must be, *do this.* 43:11; 45:17, 19
I will *do this* to you. *Lev 26:15*
this do, take you censers. *Num 16:6*
this we will *do* to the. *Josh 9:20*
I pray, *do* not *this* folly. *Judg 19:23*
do not thou *this* folly. *2 Sam 13:12*
far from me that I *do this.* 23:17
zeal of Lord shall *do this.* *2 Ki 19:31*
Isa 37:32
this do and ye shall. *2 Chr 19:10*
fail not to *do this.* *Ezra 4:22*
do this now, my son. *Pr 6:3*
praise thee, as I *do this.* *Isa 38:19*
they should *do this.* *Jer 32:35*
I would *do this* evil. *Ezek 6:10*
I *do* not *this* for your. 36:22, 32
because I shall *do this.* *Amos 4:12*
in day that I shall *do this.* *Mal 4:3*
to my servant, *do this,* and he doeth
it. *Mat 8:9; Luke 7:8*
I am able to *do this* ? *Mat 9:28*
ye shall not only *do this.* 21:21
why *do* ye *this* ? *Mark 11:3*
whom he should *do this.* *Luke 7:4*
he said to him, *this do,* and. 10:28
he said, *this* will I *do.* 12:18
this do in remembrance. 22:19
1 Cor 11:24, 25
do therefore *this.* *Acts 21:23*
if I *do this* thing. *1 Cor 9:17*
and *this* I *do* for the gospel's. 23
and *this* will we *do.* *Heb 6:3*
I beseech you rather to *do this.* 13:19
we will *do this* or that. *Jas 4:15*
see **this, thing**
do well
learn to *do well.* *Isa 1:17*
I *do well* to be angry. *Jonah 4:9*
do well to Jerusalem. *Zech 8:15*
is lawful to *do well* on. *Mat 12:12*
sleep, he shall *do well.* *John 11:12*
yourselves, ye *do well.* *Acts 15:29*
royal law, ye *do well.* *Jas 2:8*
praise of them that *do well.*
1 Pet 2:14
but if when ye *do well* and. 20
daughters as long as ye *do well.* 3:6
whereto ye *do well.* *2 Pet 1:19*
thou bring, shalt *do well.* *3 John 6*

doctor
(*Used in its old meaning of teacher,
or learned man. Latin, doctor
from docere, to teach*)
stood up Gamaliel, a *d.* *Acts 5:34*

doctors
Jesus sitting in midst of the *d.*
Luke 2:46
there were Pharisees and *d.* 5:17

doctrine
(*Used in old meaning of teaching,
instruction (see doctor). In the
New Testament the Revised Version almost universally translates it
teaching*)
make to understand *d.* *Isa 28:9**
murmured shall learn *d.* 29:24†
the stock is a *d.* of vanities. *Jer 10:8*
people astonished at his *d.* *Mat 7:28*
22:33; *Mark 1:22; 11:18*
Luke 4:32
beware of the *d.* of the. *Mat 16:12*
saying, what new *d.* ? *Mark 1:27*
and said to them in *d.* 4:2; 12:38
he shall know of the *d.* *John 7:17*
priest then asked Jesus of *d.* 18:19
continued in apostles' *d.* *Acts 2:42*
filled Jerusalem with your *d.* 5:28
astonished at *d.* of Lord. 13:12
know what this new *d.* is ? 17:19
obeyed that form of *d.* *Rom 6:17*
contrary to the *d.* which ye. 16:17
except I speak by *d.* *1 Cor 14:6*
every one of you hath a *d.* 26
with every wind of *d.* *Eph 4:14*
they teach no other *d.* *1 Tim 1:3*
attendance to reading, to *d.* 4:13

heed to thyself, and to thy *d.*
    1 Tim 4:16
labour in the word and *d.*   5:17
the name of God and his *d.* be.   6:1
and to *d.* which is according to.   3
is profitable for *d.*   *2 Tim 3:16*
with all long suffering and *d.*   4:2
in *d.* shewing incorruptness. *Tit 2:7*
that they may adorn the *d.* of.   10
leaving principles of *d.*   *Heb 6:1**
of the *d.* of baptisms, and of.   2
whoso abideth not in the *d.*; he that
   abideth in *d.* of Christ.   *2 John 9*
hast them that hold *d.* of.   *Rev 2:14*
that hold *d.* of the Nicolaitans.   15

good doctrine
I give you *good d.*   *Pr 4:2*
in the words of *good d.*   *1 Tim 4:6*

my doctrine
my d. shall drop as rain.   *Deut 32:2*
my d. is pure, and I am.   *Job 11:4*
my d. is not mine.   *John 7:16*
hast fully known *my d.*   *2 Tim 3:10*

sound doctrine
is contrary to *sound d.*   *1 Tim 1:10*
will not endure *sound d.*   *2 Tim 4:3*
by *sound d.* to exhort.   *Tit 1:9*
things which become *sound d.*   2:1

this doctrine
and bring not *this d.*   *2 John 10*
many as have not *this d.*   *Rev 2:24*

doctrines
for *d.* the commandments of men.
    Mat 15:9; Mark 7:7
after commandments and *d.* *Col 2:22*
heed to *d.* of devils.   *1 Tim 4:1*
about with strange *d.*   *Heb 13:9*

Doeg
and his name was *D.*   *1 Sam 21:7*
D. turned and slew priests.   22:18
I knew it that day *D.* was there.   22

doer
he was the *d.* of it.   *Gen 39:22*
Lord reward *d.* of evil.   *2 Sam 3:39*
rewardeth the proud *d.*   *Ps 31:23*
a wicked *d.* giveth heed.   *Pr 17:4*
an hypocrite and evil *d.*   *Isa 9:17*
suffer trouble as an evil *d.* *2 Tim 2:9*
a hearer, not a *d.* of word. *Jas 1:23*
not a forgetful hearer, but a *d.*   25
thou art not a *d.* of the law.   4:11
none suffer as an evil *d.* *1 Pet 4:15*

doers
let them give it to the *d.* *2 Ki 22:5**
cut off all wicked *d.*   *Ps 101:8**
but the *d.* of the law.   *Rom 2:13*
be ye *d.* of the word.   *Jas 1:22*
    see evil

doest
if *d.* well, and if thou *d.* not. *Gen 4:7*
with thee in all that thou *d.*   21:22
that thou *d.* is not good.   *Ex 18:17*
when thou *d.* that which. *Deut 12:28*
bless thee in all that thou *d.*   15:18
to know all that thou *d.* *2 Sam 3:25*
prosper in all thou *d.*   *1 Ki 2:3*
what *d.* thou here, Elijah ?   19:9, 13
and see what thou *d.*   20:22
say, what *d.* thou ?   *Job 9:12*
    Eccl 8:4; Dan 4:35
if thou sinnest, what *d.?*   *Job 35:6*
when thou *d.* well to.   *Ps 49:18*
the God that *d.* wonders.   77:14
thou art great, and *d.*   86:10
thou art good, and *d.* good. 119:68
when thou *d.* evil.   *Jer 11:15*
aside to ask how thou *d.?*   15:5*
house said, what *d.* thou ? *Ezek 12:9*
weak heart, seeing thou *d.*   16:30
these are to us, that thou *d.*   24:19
d. thou well to be angry ?
    Jonah 4:4, 9
thou *d.* thine alms.   *Mat 6:2, 3*
what authority *d.* thou these things ?
   21:23; *Mark 11:28; Luke 20:2*
sign seeing that thou *d.?*   *John 2:18*
these miracles that thou *d.*   3:2
disciples may see works thou *d.* 7:3
that thou *d.* do quickly.   13:27
take heed what thou *d.* *Acts 22:26*

thou that judgest, *d.*   *Rom 2:1, 3*
believest on God, thou *d.*   *Jas 2:19*
d. faithfully what thou *d.*   *3 John 5*

doeth
seen all that Laban *d.* to. *Gen 31:12*
whosoever *d.* work therein shall be
   cut off.   *Ex 31:14, 15; Lev 23:30*
these that a man *d.*   *Lev 6:3*
shall live when God *d.!*   *Num 24:23*
to God who *d.* great.   *Job 5:9*
   9:10; 37:5; *Ps 72:18; 136:4*
soul desireth, that he *d.*   *Job 23:13*
whatsoever he *d.* prosper.   *Ps 1:3*
there is none that *d.* good.   14:1, 3
    53:1, 3; *Rom 3:12*
he that *d.* these things shall. *Ps 15:5*
blessed is he that *d.*   106:3
right hand of Lord *d.*   118:15, 16
he that *d.* it, destroyeth.   *Pr 6:32*
merciful man *d.* good to.   11:17
a merry heart *d.* good like.   17:22
I said of mirth, what *d.* it ? *Eccl 2:2*
God *d.* shall be for ever, and God *d.*
   it that men should fear.   3:14
there is not a man *d.* good.   7:20
he *d.* whatsoever pleaseth him. 8:3
blessed is the man that *d.* *Isa 56:2*
shall he escape that *d.?* *Ezek 17:15*
that *d.* the like to any one of. 18:10
that *d.* not any of those duties.   11
d. that which is lawful and.   27
d. according to will in.   *Dan 4:35*
God is righteous in all he *d.*   9:14
saith Lord that *d.* this.   *Amos 9:12*
cut off man that *d.* this.   *Mal 2:12*
know what thy right *d.*   *Mat 6:3*
he that *d.* will of my Father.   7:21
whoso heareth sayings, and *d.*   24
heareth and *d.* not.   26; *Luke 6:49*
and he *d.* it.   *Mat 8:9; Luke 7:8*
every one that *d.* evil.   *John 3:20*
but he that *d.* truth cometh.   21
things soever he *d.* these *d.*   5:19
hear him and know what he *d.*   7:51
but if any man *d.* his will.   9:31
knoweth not what his lord *d.*   15:15
will think he *d.* God service.   16:2
every soul that *d.* evil.   *Rom 2:9*
the man that *d.* these things shall
   live by them.   10:5; *Gal 3:12*
wrath upon him that *d.*   *Rom 13:4*
every sin a man *d.* is.   *1 Cor 6:18*
that he keep his virgin, *d.* well. 7:37
giveth her in marriage *d.* well.   38
d. he it by works of law ?   *Gal 3:5*
good thing any man *d.*   *Eph 6:8*
forth fruit, as it *d.* also.   *Col 1:6*
but he that *d.* wrong, shall.   3:25
exhorted as a father *d.* *1 Thes 2:11*
to do good, and *d.* it not.   *Jas 4:17*
he that *d.* will of God.   *1 John 2:17*
that *d.* righteousness is born. 29; 3:7
remember his deeds which he *d.*
    3 John 10
but he that *d.* evil hath not.   11
and he *d.* great wonders.   *Rev 13:13*

dog
*Frequently mentioned in the
Scripture. It was used by the
Hebrews as a watch for their
houses, Isa 56:10, and for guarding
their flocks, Job 30:1. There were
numerous troops of wild, masterless
dogs which devoured dead bodies
and other offal, 1 Ki 14:11, and
became so fierce and such objects
of dislike that fierce and cruel
enemies were poetically called
dogs, Ps 22:16, etc. The dog
being an unclean animal the name
was used as a term of reproach, or
of humility of speaking of oneself,
1 Sam 24:14; 2 Sam 16:9.*

against Israel shall not a *d.* *Ex 11:7*
not bring price of a *d.*   *Deut 23:18*
that lappeth as a *d.*   *Judg 7:5*
Philistine said to David, Am I a *d.?*
    1 Sam 17:43
thou pursue ? after a *d.?*   24:14
Abner said, Am I a *dog's* ? *2 Sam 3:8*
look upon such dead *d.* as I am. 9:8
this dead *d.* curse my lord ?   16:9
is thy servant a *d.?*   *2 Ki 8:13*

darling from power of *d.*   *Ps 22:20*
they make a noise like a *d.* 59:6, 14
as *d.* returneth to his vomit, so a
   fool.   *Pr 26:11; 2 Pet 2:22*
like one that taketh a *d.*   *Pr 26:17*
a living *d.* is better than.   *Eccl 9:4*
as if he cut off a *dog's.*   *Isa 66:3*

dogs
torn of beasts, ye shall cast it to *d.*
   Ex 22:31; Mat 15:26; Mark 7:27
shall the *d.* eat.   *1 Ki 14:11; 16:4*
    21:24
place where *d.* licked the blood of
   Naboth, shall *d.* lick thy.   21:19
d. eat Jezebel.   23; *2 Ki 9:10, 36*
d. licked up Ahab's.   *1 Ki 22:38*
to have set with *d.* of.   *Job 30:1*
for *d.* have compassed me.   *Ps 22:16*
and the tongue of thy *d.* in.   68:23
they are all dumb *d.*   *Isa 56:10*
greedy *d.*   11
to slay, the *d.* to tear.   *Jer 15:3*
give not holy unto *d.*   *Mat 7:6*
d. eat of crumbs. 15:27; *Mark 7:28*
d. came and licked.   *Luke 16:21*
beware of *d.* beware of.   *Phil 3:2*
for without are *d.* and.   *Rev 22:15*

doing
done foolishly in so *d.*   *Gen 31:28*
ye have done evil in so *d.*   44:5
in praises, *d.* wonders.   *Ex 15:11*
without *d.* any thing.   *Num 20:19*
ye sinned in *d.* wickedly. *Deut 9:18*
he sinned in *d.* evil.   *1 Ki 16:19*
    2 Ki 21:16
d. that which was right. *1 Ki 22:43*
    2 Chr 20:32
arise, and be *d.*   *1 Chr 22:16*
I am *d.* a great work.   *Neh 6:3*
in so *d.* my Maker.   *Job 32:22*
wisely consider of his *d.*   *Ps 64:9*
he is terrible in *d.* toward.   66:5
the Lord's *d.* marvellous in our.
   118:23; *Mat 21:42; Mark 12:11*
keepeth his hand from *d.*   *Isa 56:2*
from *d.* thy pleasure on my.   58:13
his Lord shall find so *d.*   *Mat 24:46*
    Luke 12:43
who went about *d.* good. *Acts 10:38*
they have found any evil *d.* in. 24:20
for in so *d.* thou shalt.   *Rom 12:20*
therefore perform the *d.* *2 Cor 8:11*
servants of Christ, *d.* will.   *Eph 6:6*
in *d.* this shalt save.   *1 Tim 4:16*
d. nothing by partiality.   5:21

well-doing
patient continuance in *well-d.*
    Rom 2:7
not be weary in *well-d.*   *Gal 6:9*
    2 Thes 3:13
with *well-d.* ye may.   *1 Pet 2:15*
better that ye suffer for *well-d.* 3:17
their souls to him for *well-d.*   4:19

doings
after *d.* of Egypt, and after *d.* of
   Canaan, shall ye not.   *Lev 18:3*
of wickedness of thy *d.* *Deut 28:20*
not from their own *d.*   *Judg 2:19*
and evil in his *d.*   *1 Sam 25:3*
walked not after the *d.* *2 Chr 17:4*
among the people his *d.*   *Ps 9:11*
    Isa 12:4
I will talk of thy *d.*   *Ps 77:12*
child is known by his *d.*   *Pr 20:11*
put away evil of your *d.*   *Isa 1:16*
because their tongue and *d.*   3:8
shall eat the fruit of their *d.*   10
because of the evil of your *d.*
   Jer 4:4; 21:12; 26:3; 44:22
thy *d.* have procured these.   4:18
amend your *d.* 7:3, 5; 26:13; 35:15
thou shewedst me their *d.*   11:18
according to fruit of *d.* 17:10; 21:14
make your ways and *d.* good. 18:11
upon you evil of your *d.*   23:2
from evil of their *d.*   22; 25:5
    Zech 1:4
according to fruit of his *d.* *Jer 32:19*
see their way and *d.*   *Ezek 14:22*
shall ye remember your *d.*   20:43
nor according to your corrupt *d.*   44
in all your *d.* your sins do.   21:24
according to thy *d.* shall.   24:14

defiled it by their own way and d. Ezek 36:17
and according to their d. I. 19
remember your d. that were. 31
and reward their d. Hos 4:9
they will not frame their d. to. 5:4
now their own d. have set. 7:2
for the wickedness of their d. 9:15
according to his d. will he. 12:2
Jacob, are these his d.? Mi 2:7
themselves ill in their d. 3:4
desolate for fruit of their d. 7:13
corrupted all their d. Zeph 3:7
not be ashamed for all thy d.? 11
according to our d. so. Zech 1:6

doleful
houses full of d. creatures. Isa 13:21
day shall lament with a d. Mi 2:4

dominion
[1] Supreme power or sovereignty, Neh 9:28; Rom 6:9. [2] Persons or territory ruled over, Ps 114:2.
have d. over fish. Gen 1:26, 28
when thou shalt have d. 27:40*
shalt thou indeed have d.? 37:8
he that shall have d. Num 24:19
he made him have d. Judg 5:13*
time Philistines had d. over. 14:4*
Solomon had d. over all. 1 Ki 4:24
build in land of his d. 9:19; 2 Chr 8:6
nothing in his house or in all his d. 2 Ki 20:13; Isa 39:2
men of Chozeba had d. 1 Chr 4:22
as he went to stablish his d. 18:3
Edomites from under Judah's d. 2 Chr 21:8*
so that they had the d. Neh 9:28
also they have d. over our. 37*
d. and fear are with him. Job 25:2
canst thou set d. thereof? 38:33
to have d. over the works. Ps 8:6
let them not have d. over. 19:13
the upright shall have d. 49:14
he shall have d. also from. 72:8
bless Lord in places of his d. 103:22
his sanctuary, Israel his d. 114:2
let not iniquity have d. 119:133
thy d. endureth through. 145:13
other lords had d. over. Isa 26:13
his d. is from generation. Dan 4:3
thy d. reacheth to the end. 22
whose d. is an everlasting d. 34; 7:14
d. of my kingdom men tremble before God of Daniel, his d. 6:26
beast had four heads, and d. 7:6
the rest of the beasts had their d. 12
there was given him d. and. 14
they shall take away his d. 26
d. shall be given to saints of. 27
mighty king rule with great d. 11:3, 5
not according to his d. which he. 4
shall come even first d. Mi 4:8
d. shall be from sea to. Zech 9:10
of Gentiles exercise d. Mat 20:25*
death hath no more d. Rom 6:9
sin shall not have d. over you. 14
law hath d. over a man as long. 7:1
not that we have d. 2 Cor 1:24*
all power, might, and d. Eph 1:21
to whom be praise and d. 1 Pet 4:11
　　　5:11; Rev 1:6
to the only wise God be d. Jude 25

dominions
and all d. shall serve. Dan 7:27
they be thrones, or d. or. Col 1:16

done
what younger son had d. Gen 9:24
they have d. according to the. 18:21
told Isaac all that he had d. 24:66
have d. to thee nothing but. 26:29
not be d. in our country. 29:26
folly, which ought not to be d. 34:7
ye have d. evil in so doing. 44:5
what deed is this ye have d.? 15
have ye d. this thing? Ex 1:18
stood to wit what would be d. 2:4
no manner of work shall be d., save that which man must eat. 12:16
this is d. because of that the. 13:8
Jethro heard all that God had d. 18:1
goodness which Lord had d. 9
this judgement shall it be d. 21:31

six days work be d. Ex 31:15; 35:2
　　　Lev 23:3
they had d. it as Lord commanded, even so had they d. it. Ex 39:43
things forbidden to be d. Lev 5:17
commanded to be d. 8:5; Deut 26:14
wherein any work is d. Lev 11:32
have the men of land d. 18:27
eye for eye, so shall it be d. 24:20
confess sin they have d. Num 5:7
wherein we have d. foolishly. 12:11
not declared what should be d. 15:34
Balak saw all that Israel had d. 22:2
name of father be d. away? 27:4*
all that had d. evil in sight. 32:13
is thy God that hath d. Deut 10:21
so shall it be d. to that man. 25:9
wherefore hath the Lord d. thus to? 29:24; 1 Ki 9:8; 2 Chr 7:21
as he had d. also to. Josh 10:32, 39
he had d. to Lachish. 35
he had d. to Eglon. 37
if we had not rather d. it. 22:24
had known all that he had d. 24:31
not works he had d. Judg 2:10
because they had d. evil in. 3:12
d. truly and sincerely, and have d. to Jerubbaal according to. 9:16
cruelty d. to the seventy sons of. 24
there was no such deed d. 19:30
her all the man had d. Ruth 3:16
what is there d. my son? 1 Sam 4:16*
so shall it be d. to his oxen. 11:7
what shall be d. to the man? 17:26
so shall it be d. to the man that. 27
when Lord shall have d. 25:30
Lord hath d. as he spake. 28:17
　　　Ezek 12:28
thing David had d. 2 Sam 11:27
no such thing ought to be d. 13:12
have they d.? 24:17; 1 Chr 21:17
goodness Lord hath d. 1 Ki 8:66
above all their fathers had d. 14:22
told Jezebel all Elijah had d. 19:1
according to all his father had d. 22:53; 2 Ki 15:3, 9, 34; 23:32
what is to be d. for thee? 2 Ki 4:13
great things Elisha hath d. 8:4
d. that which he spake by servant. 10:10; Isa 38:15; Jer 40:3
heard what kings of Assyria have d. 2 Ki 19:11; 2 Chr 32:13; Isa 37:11
they have d. evil. 2 Ki 21:15
　　　2 Chr 29:6
all acts that he had d. in. 2 Ki 23:19
because he had d. good. 2 Chr 24:16
rejoiced, for the thing was d. 29:36
not according to benefit d. to. 32:25
to inquire of wonder that was d. 31
a decree, let it be d. Ezra 6:12
when these things were d. the. 9:1
are no such things d. Neh 6:8
we have d. wickedly. 9:33; Ps 106:6
　　　Dan 9:5, 15
Vashti, and what she had d. Esth 2:1
Mordecai perceived all was d. 4:1
what shall be d. to the man? 6:6
thus shall it be d. to the man. 9
him what he hath d.? Job 21:31
whether it be d. against a. 34:29
he spake and it was d. Ps 33:9
he hath d. great things. 71:19
　　　106:21; 126:2, 3
what shall be d. to thee? 120:3
strive not if he have d. Pr 3:30
sleep not, except they have d. 4:16
d. is that which shall be d. Eccl 1:9
have seen the works are d. 14; 4:1, 3
that which hath been already d. 2:12
who hath wrought and d. it? Isa 41:4
sing, for the Lord hath d. 44:23
lest my idol hath d. them. 48:5
backsliding Israel hath d. Jer 3:6
thus shall it be d. unto them. 5:13
ye have d. all these works. 7:13
children of Judah have d. evil. 30
had d. right in my sight. 34:15
have d. all that Jonadab. 35:10, 18
these men have d. evil to. 38:9
have d. we and our fathers. 44:17
and say, what is d. 48:19
vengeance as she hath d. 50:15, 29
the violence d. to me. 51:35
Lord hath d. that which. Lam 2:17

thus have they d. in. Ezek 23:39
it is come, it is d. saith. 39:8
of all that they have d. 43:11
and for all that shall be d. 44:14
is determined shall be d. Dan 11:36
priests have d. violence. Zeph 3:4
thy will be d. Mat 6:10; 26:42
　　　Luke 11:2; 22:42
believed, so be it d. Mat 8:13
mighty works d. in you had been d. 11:21; Luke 10:13
they ask, it shall be d. for. Mat 18:19
fellow-servants saw what was d. 31
cast into sea, it shall be d. 21:21
these ought ye to have d. 23:23
　　　Luke 11:42
well d. good and. Mat 25:21, 23
as ye have d. it to one of least of these my brethren, ye have d. 40
things that were d. 27:54; 28:11
out to see what was d. Mark 5:14
　　　Luke 8:35
tell what great things the Lord hath d. for. Mark 5:19, 20; Luke 8:39
what was d. in her. Mark 5:33
told him what they had d. 6:30
have d. to him whatsoever. 9:13
not pass till these things be d. 13:30
him to do, as he had ever d. 15:8
he that is mighty hath d. Luke 1:49
for the evils Herod had d. 3:19
to tell no man what was d. 8:56
told him all that they had d. 9:10
Lord, it is d. as thou. 14:22
ye, when ye shall have d. all, we have d. that which was our duty. 17:10
what shall be d. in the dry? 23:31
centurion saw what was d. 47
third day since these were d. 24:21
d. good to resurrection of life; have d. evil, to damnation. John 5:29
what ye will, and it shall be d. 15:7
these things were d. that the. 19:36
many signs were d. by. Acts 2:43
of the good deed d. to the. 4:9
a notable miracle hath been d. 16
God for that which was d. 21
determined before to be d. 28
wife, not knowing what was d. 5:7
not it was true which was d. 12:9
all that God had d. 14:27; 15:4
the will of the Lord be d. 21:14
captain demanded what he had d. 33
neither having d. good. Rom 9:11
nor that it should be d. 1 Cor 9:15
in part shall be d. away. 13:10
all things be d. to edifying. 14:26
be d. decently. 40
be d. with charity. 16:14
glory was to be d. away. 2 Cor 3:7
which veil is d. away in Christ. 14
receive the things d. in his body, according to that he hath d. 5:10
things which are d. of. Eph 5:12
and having d. all to stand. 6:13
nothing be d. through. Phil 2:3
ye have well d. that ye did. 4:14
known all things that are d. Col 4:9
righteousness we have d. Tit 3:5
d. despite to the Spirit. Heb 10:29
saying, it is d. Rev 16:17; 21:6
which must shortly be d. 22:6

have I done
in innocency have I d. Gen 20:5
and here also have I d. 40:15
what have I d.? Num 22:28
　　　1 Ki 19:20; Mi 6:3
thus and thus have I d. Josh 7:20
what have I now d.? Judg 8:2
　　　1 Sam 17:29
what have I d.? 1 Sam 20:1; 26:18
　　　29:8; Jer 8:6
transgressions have I d. Ezek 39:24
Jews have I d. no wrong. Acts 25:10

he hath done, or, hath he done
he hath d. evil to this. Ex 5:23
for harm he hath d. Lev 5:16
as he hath d. so Lord. 8:34
atonement for sin he hath d. 19:21
as he hath d. so shall it be. 24:19
you, after he hath d. Josh 24:20
to him as he hath d. to. Judg 15:10
then he hath d. us this. 1 Sam 6:9

how great things he hath d.
      1 Sam 12:24
what hath he d.? 20:32
marvellous works that he hath d.
    1 Chr 16:12; Ps 78:4; 98:1; 105:5
declare what he hath d. Ps 66:16
God hath d. whatsoever he. 115:3
to him as he hath d. to me. Pr 24:29
to Lord for he hath d. Isa 12:5
righteousness he hath d. Ezek 3:20
      18:24
he hath d. these things. 17:18
he hath d. all these abominations.
      18:13
father's sins which he hath d. 14
righteousness that he hath d. 22
to all that he hath d. 24:24
he hath d. that which is. 33:16
because he hath d. great. Joel 2:20
what evil hath he d.? Mat 27:23
    Mark 15:14; Luke 23:22
he hath d. all things. Mark 7:37
much evil hath he d. to. Acts 9:13
receive according to that he hath d.
      2 Cor 5:10
for wrong he hath d. Col 3:25

I have done

nor smite every thing as I have d.
      Gen 8:21
kindness I have d. thee. 21:23
I have d. as thou badest me. 27:19
till I have d. that which I. 28:15
my service I have d. thee. 30:26
signs which I have d. Ex 10:2
have seen what I have d. Josh 24:7
as I have d. so God hath. Judg 1:7
they did to me, so have I d. 15:11
behold now I have d. 2 Sam 14:21
I have sinned in that I have d., I have
  d. very. 24:10; 1 Chr 21:8
and I have d. wickedly. 2 Sam 24:17
I have d. according to. 1 Ki 3:12
heard, how I have d. it? 2 Ki 19:25
that I have d. for house. Neh 13:14
if I have d. iniquity. Job 34:32
O Lord, if I have d. this. Ps 7:3
I have d. judgement and. 119:121
I have d. no wickedness. Pr 30:20
as I have d. to Samaria. Isa 10:11
strength of my hand I have d. 13
ye far off what I have d. 33:13
not heard how I have d. it? 37:26
repent of evil I have d. to. Jer 42:10
I have d. as thou hast. Ezek 9:11
as I have d. so shall it be. 12:11
know that I have not d. without
  cause, all that I have d. in. 14:23
ye shall do as I have d. 24:22
thee, have I d. no hurt. Dan 6:22
weep, as I have d. these. Zech 7:3
I have d. one work. John 7:21
he had washed their feet, he said,
  know ye what I have d. to? 13:12
should do as I have d. to you. 15

hast thou done

said, what hast thou d.? Gen 4:10
  31:26; Num 23:11; 1 Sam 13:11
  2 Sam 3:24; John 18:35
what hast thou d. to us? Gen 20:9
     Judg 15:11
to heart hast thou d. 2 Sam 7:21
wherefore hast thou d. so? 16:10
why hast thou d. so? 1 Ki 1:6
O Lord, hast thou d. 1 Chr 17:19
these things hast thou d. Ps 50:21
why hast thou d. this? Jonah 1:10

thou hast done

is this that thou hast d.? Gen 3:13
  12:18; 26:10; 29:25; Judg 15:11
     2 Sam 12:21
because thou hast d. this. Gen 3:14
  22:16; 2 Chr 25:16
thou hast d. deeds which. Gen 20:9
that which thou hast d. to. 27:45
thou hast now d. foolishly. 31:28
    1 Sam 13:13; 2 Chr 16:9
tell me what thou hast d. Josh 7:19
     1 Sam 14:43
me all thou hast d. Ruth 2:11
thou hast d. to me this. 1 Sam 24:19
not good that thou hast d. 26:16
but thou hast d. evil. 1 Ki 14:9
thou hast d. well in. 2 Ki 10:30

thou hast d. against altar. 2 Ki 23:17
for thou hast d. right. Neh 9:33
works which thou hast d. Ps 40:5
thee, because thou hast d. it. Ps 52:9
know that thou hast d. it. 109:27
if thou hast d. foolishly. Pr 30:32
exalt thee, for thou hast d. Isa 25:1
know what thou hast d. Jer 2:23
thou hast spoken and d. evil. 3:5
glad that thou hast d. it. Lam 1:21
do unto them as thou hast d. 2:20
consider to whom thou hast d. 2:20
Sodom hath not done as thou hast d.
     Ezek 16:48
abominations which thou hast d. 51
deal with thee as thou hast d. 59
pacified for all that thou hast d. 63
as thou hast d. it shall be. Ob 15
O Lord, thou hast d. as. Jonah 1:14
thou hast d. well that. Acts 10:33

not done

that ought not to be d. Gen 20:9
which thing ought not to be d. 34:7
such as have not been d. Ex 34:10
things which ought not to be d.
     Lev 4:2, 13
I have not d. them of. Num 16:28
Lord hath not d. all. Deut 32:27
wouldest thou not have d.? 2 Ki 5:13
they had not d. it of. 2 Chr 30:5
from work, that it be not d. Neh 6:9
Israel had not d. so. 8:17
Vashti had not d. wrong. Esth 1:16
that I have not d. Isa 5:4
things that are not yet d. 46:10
neither shall that be d. Jer 3:16
in thee that I have not d. Ezek 5:9
for under heaven hath not been d. as
  hath been done upon. Dan 9:12
that which fathers have not d. 11:24
and Lord hath not d. it. Amos 3:6
if I had not d. among. John 15:24
scarce restrained they had not d.
     Acts 14:18
this thing not d. in a corner. 26:26

done with this

wot not who hath d. this. Gen 21:26
what is this that God hath d.? 42:28
deed is this that ye have d.? 44:15
have ye d. this thing. Ex 1:18
this is d. because of that which. 13:8
why have we d. this? Josh 9:24
afraid, and have d. this? Josh 9:24
as ye have d. this day. Judg 2:2
why have ye d. this? Judg 2:2
who hath d. this thing? 6:29; 15:6
she said, let this thing be d. 11:37
ye have d. this, yet will. 15:7
wickedness is this that is d. 20:12
d. all this wickedness. 1 Sam 12:20
hath the Lord d. this thing. 28:18
ye have d. this thing. 2 Sam 2:6
man that hath d. this thing. 12:5
hath Joab d. this thing? 14:20
now, I have d. this thing. 21
is this d. by my lord? 1 Ki 1:27
forasmuch as this is d. of. 11:4
return, for this thing is d. 2 Chr 11:4
O Lord, if I have d. this. Ps 7:3
declare that he hath d. this. 22:31
I have sinned, and d. this evil. 51:4
hand of Lord hath d. this. Isa 41:20
this they have d. unto. Ezek 23:38
this have ye d. again. Mal 2:13
now all this was d. Mat 1:22; 21:4
     26:56
an enemy hath d. this. 13:28
this which is d. to fig-tree. 21:21
this that this woman hath d. 26:13
     Mark 14:9
that had d. this thing. Mark 5:32
when they had d. this. Luke 5:6
but this man hath d. nothing. 23:41
miracles than these this man hath d.
     John 7:31
heard he had d. this miracle. 12:18
what power have ye d. this? Acts 4:7
this was d. thrice. 10:16; 11:10
so when this was d. others. 28:9
not mourned that he hath d. this.
     1 Cor 5:2

door

Besides its common uses as the

entrance to a house or building, this
word is used metaphorically as the
entrance to any thing: as our
Saviour says, I am the door, the
entrance into the kingdom, John
10:1. The door of faith is the
opportunity of belief offered to the
Gentiles, Acts 14:27. Elsewhere
also it means opportunity, 2 Cor
2:12; Rev 3:8.

sin lieth at the d. Gen 4:7
came near to break the d. 19:9
Lord will pass over d. Ex 12:23
master shall bring him to d. 21:6
it through his ear to d. Deut 15:17
put her from me, bolt d. 2 Sam 13:17
and he bolted the d. after her. 18
called, she stood in d. 2 Ki 4:15
then open the d. and flee. 9:3
those who kept d. Esth 2:21* 6:2*
laid wait at neighbour's d. Job 31:9
that I went not out of the d.? 34
keep d. of my lips. Ps 141:3
as d. turneth upon. Pr 26:14
hand by hole of d. S of S 5:4
if she be a d. we will inclose. 8:9
brought me to the d. Ezek 8:3, 7
digged in the wall, behold a d. 8
every one stood at the d. 10:19
behold, at the d. of the gate. 11:1
the breadth of the d. was. 41:2*
people shall worship at the d. 46:3
valley of Achor for a d. of. Hos 2:15
smite the lintel of the d. Amos 9:1*
he rolled a great stone to the d. of.
  Mat 27:60; Mark 15:46
angel rolled stone from d. Mat 28:2*
city was gathered at d. Mark 1:33
not so much as about the d. 2:2
shall roll the stone from d.? 16:3
entereth not by the d. John 10:1
that entereth in by the d. 2
I am the d. 7, 9
but Peter stood at the d. 18:16
damsel that kept the d. to Peter. 17
feet of them are at the d. Acts 5:9
as Peter knocked at the d. 12:13
when they had opened the d. 14:27
opened the d. of faith to. 14:27
a great d. and effectual. 1 Cor 16:9
a d. was opened to me. 2 Cor 2:12
God would open a d. of. Col 4:3
judge standeth before d. Jas 5:9
set before thee an open d. Rev 3:8
at d. and knock, if any open. 20
I looked, and a d. was open. 4:1

door with house

smote them at d. of the house.
     Gen 19:11
communed at d. of the house. 43:19
out at d. of his house. Ex 12:22
shall go to d. of house. Lev 14:38
d. of her father's house. Deut 22:21
fell down at d. of the man's house.
     Judg 19:26, 27
slept at d. of king's house.
     2 Sam 11:9
Naaman stood at d. of house.
     2 Ki 5:9
unto the d. of the house. Neh 3:20
repaired from d. of the house. 21
not nigh d. of her house. Pr 5:8
sitteth at the d. of her house. 9:14
to d. of Lord's h. Ezek 8:14; 47:1

door with shut

Lot shut the d. Gen 19:6
angels shut the d. 10
when come in shalt shut d. 2 Ki 4:4
she shut d. upon her. 5
she shut d. on him. 21
he went in and shut the d. 33
shut the d. and hold him at d. 6:32
when thou hast shut thy d. Mat 6:6
the d. was shut. 25:10
the d. is now shut. Luke 11:7
and hath shut to the d. 13:25
open d. no man can shut. Rev 3:8

door with tabernacle

bring to d. of tabernacle. Ex 29:4
40:12; Lev 4:4; 8:3, 4; 12:6
     Num 6:10

kill bullock by *d. of tabernacle.*
  Ex 29:11, 32; 40:29; Lev 1:5
  Num 27:2
burnt offering at *d. of tabernacle.*
  Ex 29:42; 33:9, 10; 38:8; 40:28
  Lev 1:3; 3:2; 4:7, 18
before the *d. of the tabernacle.*
  Ex 40:6; Num 25:6
at the *d. of the tabernacle. Lev 8:31*
  35; 14:11; 16:7; 17:6; Num 6:18
  10:3; Josh 19:51
not go out of *d. of the tabernacle.*
  Lev 8:33
go out from *d. of tabernacle.* 10:7
unto *d. of tabernacle.* 14:23; 15:14
  29; 19:21; Num 16:18, 19, 50; 20:6
not to *d. of tabernacle. Lev 17:4, 9*
stood in the *d. of the tabernacle.*
  Num 12:5; 16:18
pillar of cloud over *d. of tabernacle.*
  Deut 31:15
porter of *d. of tabernacle. 1 Chr 9:21*

door joined with *tent*
Abraham sat in *tent d.* *Gen 18:1*
he ran to meet them from *tent d.* 2
Sarah heard it in the *tent d.* 10
every man at *tent d.* *Ex 33:8*
worshipped, every man in *tent d.* 10
weeping, every man in the *d.* of his
  tent. *Num 11:10*
Abiram in *d.* of their *tents.* 16:27
stand in *d.* of the *tent. Judg 4:20*

doorkeeper
be a *d.* in house of God. *Ps 84:10*
of Maaseiah *keeper of d. Jer 35:4*

doorkeepers
which *keepers of the d.* *2 Ki 22:4*
the *keepers of the d.* to bring. 23:4
of guard took chief priest and three
  keepers of the. 25:18; *Jer 52:24*
Berechiah, Elkanah, *d.* *1 Chr 15:23*
Obed-edom and Jehiah *d.* 24
keepers of the d. sought. *Esth 6:2**

door-post
bring him to the *d.-post.* *Ex 21:6*
measured *post* of the *d. Ezek 41:3**

door-posts
blood on upper *d.-posts.* *Ex 12:7**
write them on *d.-posts. Deut 11:20*
the *posts* of the *d.* moved. *Isa 6:4*
he measured the *d.-posts.*
  *Ezek 41:16**

doors
shall go out of the *d.* *Josh 2:19*
the *d.* of the parlour. *Judg 3:24*
opened not *d.* of the parlour. 25
what cometh forth of the *d.* 11:31
Samson took the *d.* of the gate. 16:3
her lord rose up, opened the *d.* 19:27
Samuel opened the *d.* *1 Sam 3:15*
David scrabbled on the *d.* of. 21:13
cut off gold from the *d.* *2 Ki 18:16*
Levites be porters of *d.* *2 Chr 23:4*
Hezekiah opened the *d.* of. 29:3
set up the *d.* of it. *Neh 3:1, 3; 7:1*
but I opened my *d.* to. *Job 31:32*
when I set bars and *d.* 38:10
hast thou seen the *d.* of the ? 17*
who can open the *d.* of his ? 41:14
up, ye everlasting *d.* *Ps 24:7, 9*
though he had opened *d.* of. 78:23
crieth at coming in at *d.* *Pr 8:3*
waiting at the posts of my *d.* 34
behind *d.* hast thou set up. *Isa 57:8*
still talking in the *d.* *Ezek 33:30*
keep the *d.* of thy mouth. *Mi 7:5*
open thy *d.* O Lebanon. *Zech 11:1*
know it is near, at the *d. Mat 24:33*
  Mark 13:29
angel opened prison *d.* *Acts 5:19*
keepers standing before the *d.* 23
immediately all the *d.* were. 16:26
awaking and seeing prison *d.* 27

shut doors
Ehud *shut* the *d.* of. *Judg 3:23*
Ahaz *shut* up the *d.* of. *2 Chr 28:24*
our fathers have *shut* the *d.* 29:7
and let us *shut* the *d.* of. *Neh 6:10*
shut the *d.* and bar them. 7:3
because *shut* not up *d.* of. *Job 3:10*
or who *shut* up sea with *d.*? 38:8
the *d.* shall be *shut* in. *Eccl 12:4*

enter, and *shut* thy *d.* *Isa 26:20*
that would *shut* the *d.*? *Mal 1:10*
when *d.* were *shut.* *John 20:19, 26*
forthwith *d.* were *shut.* *Acts 21:30*

Dor
drive out inhabitants of D. *Judg 1:27*
Abinadab in region of D. *1 Ki 4:11*

Dorcas
by interpretation is D. *Acts 9:36*
shewing coats and garments D. 39

dote
and they shall *d.* *Jer 50:36*

doted
Aholah *d.* on her lovers. *Ezek 23:5*
whoredoms with all on whom she *d.* 7
Assyrians, on whom she *d.* 9, 12
as soon as she saw them, she *d.* 16
for she *d.* upon their paramours. 20

Dothan
to D. he found them in D. *Gen 37:17*
behold Elisha is in D. *2 Ki 6:13*

doting
d. about questions and. *1 Tim 6:4*

double
and take *d.* money in. *Gen 43:12*
and they took *d.* money. 15
theft be found, restore *d.* *Ex 22:4*
if found, let him pay *d.* 7
he shall pay *d.* 9
made breast-plate *d.* a span. 39:9
been worth a *d.* hired. *Deut 15:18*
by giving him a *d.* portion. 21:17
let a *d.* portion of thy. *2 Ki 2:9*
they were not of a *d.* *1 Chr 12:33*
that they are *d.* to that. *Job 11:6**
to him with his *d.* bridle ? 41:13
with a *d.* heart do speak. *Ps 12:2*
she hath received *d.* for. *Isa 40:2*
for shame ye shall have *d.* in their
  land they shall possess the *d.* 61:7
recompense their sin *d.* *Jer 16:18*
destroy them with *d.* 17:18
I will render *d.* to thee. *Zech 9:12*
deacons grave, not *d.* *1 Tim 3:8*
counted worthy of *d.* honour. 5:17
d. unto her, *d.* according to works,
  cup fill to her *d.* *Rev 18:6*

double, *verb*
shalt *d.* sixth curtain. *Ex 26:9*
and *d.* unto her *d.* *Rev 18:6*

double-minded
d.-minded man is unstable. *Jas 1:8*
your hearts, ye *d.*-minded. 4:8

doubled
the dream was *d.* to. *Gen 41:32*
four-square, being *d.* *Ex 28:16*
was breadth thereof, being *d.* 39:9
let the sword be *d.* the. *Ezek 21:14*

doubt
Joseph is without *d.* *Gen 37:33*
life shall hang in *d.* *Deut 28:66*
no *d.* but ye are the people. *Job 12:2*
no *d.* kingdom of God. *Luke 11:20*
were in *d.* saying. *Acts 2:12**
no *d.* this man is a murderer. 28:4
for our sakes, no *d.* *1 Cor 9:10*
voice I stand in *d.* of you. *Gal 4:20**
no *d.* have continued. *1 John 2:19*

doubt, *verb*
wherefore didst thou *d.*? *Mat 14:31*
if ye have faith, and *d.* not. 21:21
not *d.* in his heart, but. *Mark 11:23*
thou make us to *d.*? *John 10:24*

doubted
worshipped him, some *d. Mat 28:17*
they *d.* whereunto. *Acts 5:24**
now while Peter *d.* in. 10:17*
because I *d.* of such manner. 25:20*

doubteth
d. is damned if he eat. *Rom 14:23*

doubtful
neither be of *d.* mind. *Luke 12:29*
not to *d.* disputations. *Rom 14:1*

doubting
looked, *d.* of whom he. *John 13:22*
with them, nothing *d.* *Acts 10:20*
  11:12*
pray without wrath and *d. 1 Tim 2:8**

doubtless
d. ye shall not come. *Num 14:30*
I will *d.* deliver the. *2 Sam 5:19*
he shall *d.* come again. *Ps 126:6*
d. thou art our Father. *Isa 63:16*
if not to others, yet *d.* *1 Cor 9:2*
is not expedient for me *d. 2 Cor 12:1*
yea *d.* I count all things. *Phil 3:8*

doubts
dissolving of *d.* was. *Dan 5:12*
heard that thou canst dissolve *d.* 16

dough
people took their *d.* before it was
  leavened. *Ex 12:34*
unleavened cakes of the *d.* 39
offer a cake of the first of your *d.*
  Num 15:20, 21
bring firstfruits of our *d.* *Neh 10:37*
women knead their *d.* to. *Jer 7:18*
priests first of your *d.* *Ezek 44:30*
he hath kneaded the *d.* *Hos 7:4*

dove
[1] *Any one of numerous birds of
the pigeon family, although commonly the name is applied to the
smaller varieties. This bird is
very common in Palestine. It was
considered clean and was used in
sacrifices. Because of this they
were sold in the temple courts,*
Lev 12:6, 8; Luke 2:24; Mark
11:15. [2] *The dove is the symbol
of gentleness and innocence,* Mat
10:16. *It is defenceless, faithful to
its mate and home-loving. This
last is the secret of the success
of the training of carrier-pigeons,*
[3] *The dove is used as a symbol of
the Holy Spirit,* Mat 3:16.
The expression dove's dung, in
2 Ki 6:25, *may mean what it ap-
parently does ; or it may mean a
common plant which had some
nutritive quality, and which rose
to famine prices at the siege of
Jerusalem.*
Noah sent forth a *d. Gen 8:8, 10, 12*
the *d.* found no rest for the. 8:9
the *d.* came in to him in the. 11
take a turtle-*d.* 15:9; *Lev 12:6*
oh that I had wings like a *d. Ps 55:6*
ye shall be as wings of a *d.* 68:13
not the soul of thy turtle-*d.* 74:19
thou hast *d.* eyes. *S of S 1:15; 4:1*
O my *d.* let me see thy. 2:14
open to me, my sister, my *d.* 5:2
my *d.* my undefiled is but one. 6:9
I did mourn as a *d.* *Isa 38:14*
dwell in rock, be like *d.* *Jer 48:28*
Ephraim is like a silly *d.* *Hos 7:11*
shall tremble as a *d.* out. 11:11
God descending like a *d.* *Mat 3:16*
  Mark 1:10; Luke 3:22; John 1:32

doves
fourth part of a cab of *d.* *2 Ki 6:25*
eyes are as eyes of *d.* *S of S 5:12*
we mourn sore like *d.* *Isa 59:11*
that flee as the *d.* to their. 60:8
shall be like the *d.* of. *Ezek 7:16*
lead her as with voice of *d. Nah 2:7*
serpents, harmless as *d.* *Mat 10:16*
of them that sold *d.* 21:12
  Mark 11:15
temple those that sold *d. John 2:14*
said unto them that sold *d.* 16

turtle-doves
shall take two turtle-*d.* *Lev 14:22*
sacrifice of two turtle-*d. Luke 2:24*

down
when the sun is *d.* *Lev 22:7*
  Deut 23:11
sun was *d.* commanded to take king
  of Ai's carcase *d.* *Josh 8:29*
taste aught till sun be *d. 2 Sam 3:35*
walking up and *d.* *Job 1:7; 2:2*
let them wander up and *d. Ps 59:15*
I am tossed up and *d.* as. 109:23
hast walked up and *d.* *Ezek 28:14*
shall walk up and *d.* *Zech 10:12*
we were driven up and *d. Acts 27:27*
clothed with a garment *d. Rev 1:13*

down-sitting

thou knowest my d.-s. *Ps* 139:2

downward

again take root d. *2 Ki* 19:30
Isa 37:31
of beast that goeth d. *Eccl* 3:21
appearance of his loins d. *Ezek* 1:27
8:2

dowry

(The money or estate a woman brings to her husband on marriage)
endued me with good d. *Gen* 30:20
ask me never so much d. and. 34:12
pay according to the d. *Ex* 22:17
king desireth not any d. *1 Sam* 18:25

drag

gather them in their d. *Hab* 1:15
they burn incense to their d. 16

dragging

in little ship, d. the net. *John* 21:8

dragon

[1] *The Hebrew word tan, translated in Authorized Version dragon, is always used in the plural, and is applied to some creatures inhabiting the desert. It probably refers to wild beasts and not to any of the serpent family to which a dragon belongs. The Revised Version translates it in every case by the word jackals. [2] The Hebrew word tannin seems to refer to any great monster of land or sea, usually some kind of serpent or reptile, but not invariably. In the New Testament it is found only in the Revelation, applied metaphorically to Satan, Rev 12:3, etc. Either word is frequently used metaphorically.*
d. shalt thou trample. *Ps* 91:13*
he shall slay the d. that. *Isa* 27:1†
Rahab, and wounded the d. 51:9†
hath swallowed me up like a d.
Jer 51:34†
Pharaoh, the great d. *Ezek* 29:3
behold, a great red d. *Rev* 12:3
the d. stood. 4
d. fought. 7
d. was cast out. 9, 13
flood which the d. cast out. 16
the d. was wroth with the woman. 17
the d. gave him his power. 13:2
they worshipped the d. 4
he spake as a d. 11
frogs came out of mouth of d. 16:13
he laid hold on the d. 20:2

dragons

wine is the poison of d. *Deut* 32:33
I am a brother to d. *Job* 30:29*
broken us in place of d. *Ps* 44:19*
thou breakest the heads of d. 74:13
praise Lord from earth, ye d. 148:7
d. in pleasant palaces. *Isa* 13:22*
an habitation for d. 34:13*; 35:7*
the d. and owls shall honour. 43:20*
Jerusalem a den of d. *Jer* 9:11*
cities of Judah a den of d. 10:22*
snuffed up the wind like d. 14:6*
Hazor a dwelling for d. 49:33*
Babylon a dwelling for d. 51:37*
make a wailing like the d. *Mi* 1:8*
his heritage waste for d. *Mal* 1:3*

dragon well

even before the d.-well. *Neh* 2:13

drams

(The Persian daric worth about five dollars, or a little more than an English pound. Daric always in Revisions)
gold ten thousand d. *1 Chr* 29:7
gave 61,000 d. of gold. *Ezra* 2:69
of gold, of a thousand d. 8:27
a thousand d. of gold. *Neh* 7:70
twenty thousand d. of gold. 71, 72

drank

Noah d. of the wine. *Gen* 9:21
I d. and she made camels drink.
24:46
brought him wine, and he d. 27:25
the congregation d. *Num* 20:11

11

and d. wine of their. *Deut* 32:28
nor d. water three days. *1 Sam* 30:12
his own meat, and d. *2 Sam* 12:3
his house, and d. water. *1 Ki* 13:19
flesh, and he d. of the brook. 17:6
of the wine which he d. *Dan* 1:5
not defile himself with wine he d. 8
Belshazzar d. wine before the. 5:1
wives and his concubines d. in. 3
d. wine, and praised the gods. 4
and they all d. of it. *Mark* 14:23
they eat, they d. *Luke* 17:27, 28
our father Jacob who d. *John* 4:12
d. of that spiritual rock. *1 Cor* 10:4

draught

is cast out in the d. *Mat* 15:17
Mark 7:19
let down your nets for a d. *Luke* 5:4
for he was astonished at the d. 9

draught house

made Baal's house a d.-h. *2 Ki* 10:27

drave

(The old form of drove. The American Revision replaces it with the modern form)
chariot wheels, they d. *Ex* 14:25
they d. not out the. *Josh* 16:10
and d. them out. 24:12; *Judg* 6:9
Lord d. out before us all. *Josh* 24:18
Judah d. out inhabitants. *Judg* 1:19
which they d. before. *1 Sam* 30:20
Uzzah and Ahio d. the new cart.
2 Sam 6:3; *1 Chr* 13:7
that time Rezin d. Jews. *2 Ki* 16:6
Jeroboam d. Israel from. 18:21
whom God d. out. *Acts* 7:45*
Gallio d. them from. 18:16
see **drove**

draw

and I will also d. for. *Gen* 24:44
said, I will d. my sword. *Ex* 15:9
d. toward mount Tabor. *Judg* 4:6
will d. to thee Sisera. 7
Abimelech said, d. thy sword. 9:54
1 Sam 31:4; *1 Chr* 10:4
d. them from the city. *Judg* 20:32
d. that city into river. *2 Sam* 17:13
every man shall d. after. *Job* 21:33
d. me not away with the. 24:2
d. me, we will run after. *S of S* 1:4
woe to those who d. iniquity. *Isa* 5:18
to the nations that d. the bow. 66:19
I will d. my sword out. *Ezek* 21:3
strangers shall d. their swords. 28:7
they shall d. their swords. 30:11
d. her, and all her multitudes. 32:20
hast nothing to d. with. *John* 4:11
thirst not, nor come hither to d. 15
except Father which sent me d. 6:44
be lifted up from earth, d. all. 12:32
now they were not able to d. 21:6
to d. away disciples. *Acts* 20:30
d. you before judgement seats.
Jas 2:6*

draw back

faith, but if any d. back. *Heb* 10:38*
are not of them who d. back to. 39*

draw near

let us d. near to one. *Judg* 19:13
let us d. near to God. *1 Sam* 14:36
Saul said, d. ye near hither. 38
good for me to d. near. *Ps* 73:28
they d. near to the gates. 107:18
this people d. near with their lips.
Isa 29:13
d. near, ye that are escaped. 45:20
d. near hither, ye sons of. 57:3
will cause him to d. near. *Jer* 30:21
order buckler, and d. near to. 46:3
charge over city to d. near. *Ezek* 9:1
hast caused thy days to d. near. 22:4
let all men of war d. near. *Joel* 3:9
d. near with a true heart. *Heb* 10:22

draw nigh

d. not nigh hither, put off. *Ex* 3:5
d. nigh to my soul. *Ps* 69:18
d. nigh that follow mischief. 119:150
nor years d. nigh. *Eccl* 12:1
counsel of Holy One d. nigh. *Isa* 5:19
by the which we d. nigh. *Heb* 7:19
d. nigh to God, will d. nigh. *Jas* 4:8

draw out

d. out and take you a. *Ex* 12:21
I will d. out a sword. *Lev* 26:33
could not d. dagger out. *Judg* 3:22
thou d. out leviathan ? *Job* 41:1
d. out also the spear. *Ps* 35:3
wilt thou d. out thine anger ? 85:5
of understanding will d. out. *Pr* 20:5
against whom do ye d. out ? *Isa* 57:4
if thou d. out thy soul to the. 58:10
least of the flock d. them out.
Jer 49:20*; 50:45*
even sea monsters d. out. *Lam* 4:3
I will d. out a sword after them.
Ezek 5:2, 12; 12:14
one came to d. out fifty. *Hag* 2:16
d. out now, and bear to. *John* 2:8

draw up

trusteth that he can d. up. *Job* 40:23*

draw water

women go out to d. water.
Gen 24:11, 43
daughters come out to d. water. 13
ran again to well to d. water. 20
maidens going to d. water.
1 Sam 9:11
with joy shall ye d. water. *Isa* 12:3
d. thee waters for siege. *Nah* 3:14
of Samaria to d. water. *John* 4:7

drawer

from hewer of wood to d. *Deut* 29:11

drawers

be d. of water to. *Josh* 9:21, 27
d. of water for house of my God. 23

draweth

wife of the one d. near. *Deut* 25:11
now the day d. towards. *Judg* 19:9
he d. also the mighty. *Job* 24:22
yea his soul d. near to grave. 33:22
catch the poor when he d. *Ps* 10:9
my life d. nigh unto the grave. 88:3
that d. near the time of. *Isa* 26:17
time is come, day d. *Ezek* 7:12
this people d. nigh with. *Mat* 15:8
I am Christ, the time d. *Luke* 21:8
for your redemption d. nigh. 28
the coming of Lord d. nigh. *Jas* 5:8

drawing

delivered in places of d. *Judg* 5:11
they see Jesus d. nigh. *John* 6:19

drawn

angel, and his sword d. *Num* 22:23
31; *Josh* 5:13; *1 Chr* 21:16
heifer, which hath not d. *Deut* 21:3
but shalt be d. away, and. 30:17
till we have d. them. *Josh* 8:6
they were d. away. 16; *Judg* 20:31
which young men have d. *Ruth* 2:9
it is d. and cometh out. *Job* 20:25
wicked have d. out sword. *Ps* 37:14
softer than oil, yet d. swords. 55:21
deliver them that are d. *Pr* 24:11*
fled from the d. swords. *Isa* 21:15
that are d. from the breasts. 22:19
d. and cast forth beyond. *Jer* 22:19
with lovingkindness have I d. 31:3
d. back his right hand. *Lam* 2:3
I Lord have d. sword. *Ezek* 21:5, 28
all were d. up again to. *Acts* 11:10
when he is d. away of. *Jas* 1:14

dread

the d. of you shall be on. *Gen* 9:2
fear and d. shall fall upon. *Ex* 15:16
this day will I begin to put the d.
Deut 2:25; 11:25
shall not his d. fall ? *Job* 13:11
let not thy d. make me afraid. 21*
let him be your d. *Isa* 8:13

dread, verb

I said to you, d. not. *Deut* 1:29
be strong, d. not. *1 Chr* 22:13*

dreadful

how d. is this place ! *Gen* 28:17
a d. sound in his ears. *Job* 15:21
their rings, they were d. *Ezek* 1:18
fourth beast, d. and. *Dan* 7:7*, 19*
O Lord, the great and d. God. 9:4
the Chaldeans are terrible and d.
Hab 1:7
my name is d. among. *Mal* 1:14*
coming of great and d. day. 4:5*

dream

The Eastern people, and in particular the Jews, had a very great regard for dreams; they observed them, and applied to those who professed to explain them. We see the antiquity of this custom among the Egyptians, in the history of Pharaoh's butler and baker, and in Pharaoh himself, Gen 40:5, 8; 41:15. Nebuchadnezzar is an instance of the same among the Chaldeans, Dan 2:1, 2, 3, etc. As the belief in dreams was generally connected with consultation of idol-priests, or those pretending to deal in magic, the Israelites were warned against dealing with these. But God revealed his will frequently in dreams, and there were those who could explain them, Gen 20:3; 28:12; 37:4; Num 12:6; Deut 13:1.

to Abimelech in a d.   Gen 20:3, 6
Jacob saw in a d. the rams.   31:10
angel of God spake to Jacob in d. 11
God came to Laban in a d.   24
Joseph dreamed a d.   37:5, 9, 10
butler and baker dreamed a d. 40:5
and behold, it was a d.   41:7
                    1 Ki 3:15
to each according to d.   Gen 41:12
the d. of Pharaoh is one.   25, 26
for that the d. was doubled.   32
will speak to him in a d. Num 12:6
a man that told a d. to.   Judg 7:13
Gideon heard telling of the d.   15
Lord appeared in a d.   1 Ki 3:5
shall fly away as a d.   Job 20:8
in a d. he openeth the ears. 33:15
as a d. when one awaketh. Ps 73:20
for a d. cometh through.   Eccl 5:3
against Ariel be as a d.   Isa 29:7
hath a d. let him tell a d. Jer 23:28
was troubled to know d.   Dan 2:3
tell thy servants the d.   4
if ye shew the d.   6
this is the d. and we will tell.   36
my lord, the d. be to them.   4:19
Daniel had a d. he wrote the d. 7:1
the angel appeared to Joseph in a d.
          Mat 1:20; 2:13, 19
being warned of God in a d. 2:12, 22
suffered many things in a d. 27:19

dream, verb

we were like them that d. Ps 126:1
your old men d. dreams. Joel 2:28
                  Acts 2:17

dreamed

Jacob d.   Gen 28:12
Joseph d. a dream.   37:5
the officers d.   40:5
Pharaoh d.   41:1, 15
Joseph remembered the dreams
  which he d.   42:9
I have d. I have d.   Jer 23:25
dreams which you cause to be d. 29:8
Nebuchadnezzar d. dreams. Dan 2:1
the king said, I have d. a dream. 5

dreamer

behold, this d. cometh. Gen 37:19
if a d. of dreams arise. Deut 13:1
thou shalt not hearken to that d. 3
that prophet or d. of dreams.   5

dreamers

not to diviners nor d.   Jer 27:9
those filthy d. defile flesh. Jude 8

dreameth

man d. a thirsty man d. Isa 29:8

dreams

hated Joseph for his d. Gen 37:8
see what will become of his d. 20
and he interpreted our d.   41:12
Joseph remembered the d. he. 42:9
Lord answered him not by d.
                1 Sam 28:6, 15
thou scarest me with d. Job 7:14
in multitude of d. are.   Eccl 5:7
forget my name with d. Jer 23:27
them that prophesy false d.   32
Daniel had understanding in d.
         Dan 1:17; 5:12

diviners have told false d. Zech 10:2

dregs

d. thereof the wicked.   Ps 75:8
hast drunken the d. Isa 51:17*, 22*

dress

[1] To till or prune, as land, trees, etc., Gen 2:15. [2] To prepare for food, Gen 18:7.

man into the garden to d. Gen 2:15
a young man, he hasted to d. 18:7
plant vineyards, and d. Deut 28:39
to d. of his own for the. 2 Sam 12:4
let Tamar d. the meat in.   13:5
go to Amnon's house, d. him meat. 7
that I may d. it for me. 1 Ki 17:12
I will d. the other bullock. 18:23
d. it first, for ye are many.   25

dressed

took calf which he had d. Gen 18:8
d. in the fryingpan be.   Lev 7:9
took five sheep ready d. 1 Sam 25:18
poor man's lamb and d. 2 Sam 12:4
Mephibosheth had not d. his. 19:24
they d. it, and called on. 1 Ki 18:26
herbs for them by whom it is d.
                  Heb 6:7*

dresser

then said he to the d.   Luke 13:7

dresseth

when he d. the lamps.   Ex 30:7

drew

Rebekah d. water.   Gen 24:20, 45
they d. and lifted up Joseph. 37:28
Zarah d. back his hand.   38:29
because I d. him out of.   Ex 2:10
Jethro's daughters came and d. 16
an Egyptian d. water enough. 19
for Joshua d. not his hand. Josh 8:26
fell 120,000 men that d. Judg 8:10
but the youth d. not his sword. 20
chief of Israel 400,000 that d. 20:2
numbered 26,000 that d. sword. 15
all these d. the sword.   25, 35
liers in wait d. themselves along. 37
of Benjamin 25,000 that d. sword. 46
buy it for them, so he d. Ruth 4:8
to Mizpeh, and d. water. 1 Sam 7:6
David d. Goliath's sword.   17:51
he took me, he d. me out of many
  waters   2 Sam 22:17; Ps 18:16
three mighty men d. water out of well
  of.   2 Sam 23:16; 1 Chr 11:18
in Israel 800,000 that d. 2 Sam 24:9
certain man d. a bow.   1 Ki 22:34
                  2 Chr 18:33
Moab took 700 that d.   2 Ki 3:26
Jehu d. a bow with his full.   9:24
they sent and d. forth. 1 Chr 19:16
eleven hundred thousand men that d.
  sword, Judah 470,000 that d. 21:5
d. out staves of the ark. 2 Chr 5:9
                  1 Ki 8:8
of Benjamin that d. bows. 2 Chr 14:8
they d. up Jeremiah.   Jer 38:13
I d. them with cords.   Hos 11:4
full, they d. to shore.   Mat 13:48
                  Mark 6:53*
Peter d. his sword.   Mat 26:51
    Mark 14:47; John 18:10
and the sabbath d. on. Luke 23:54
servants which d. water. John 2:9
and d. the net to land full. 21:11
and d. away much people. Acts 5:37
stoned Paul and d. him out. 14:19
and d. Paul and Silas into. 16:19
the jailor d. his sword, and.   27
they d. Jason and certain.   17:6
d. Alexander out of the.   19:33
they took Paul and d. him out. 21:30
his tail d. the third part. Rev 12:4

drew near, or nigh

Abraham d. near and. Gen 18:23
time d. nigh that Israel.   47:29
when Pharaoh d. nigh.   Ex 14:10
Moses d. near to thick.   20:21
the congregation d. near. Lev 9:5
people d. nigh before Ai. Josh 8:11
the Philistines d. near. 1 Sam 7:10
Saul d. near to Samuel.   9:18
Goliath d. near morning and. 17:16
                  41, 48
David d. near to Goliath the. 40

Joab d. nigh against. 2 Sam 10:13
Ahimaaz came and d. near. 18:25
Esther d. near and.   Esth 5:2
the king's decree d. near to be. 9:1
she d. not near to God. Zeph 3:2
and when they d. nigh. Mat 21:1
when the time of fruit d. near. 34
d. near the publicans. Luke 15:1
elder son came, as he d. nigh. 25
feast of unleavened bread d. nigh.
                  22:1
and Judas d. near to Jesus.   47
Jesus himself d. near.   24:15
they d. nigh to the village where. 28
time of promise d. nigh. Acts 7:17
as he d. near to behold it.   31
as they d. nigh to the city. 10:9
deemed that they d. near. 27:27

drewest

thou d. near in the day. Lam 3:57

dried

until waters were d. up. Gen 8:7, 13
twenty-seventh day was earth d. 14
green ears of corn d. by. Lev 2:14
nor eat moist grapes or d. Num 6:3
our soul is d. away.   11:6
heard how Lord d. up. Josh 2:10
your God d. up Jordan, as Lord did
  Red sea, which he d. up.   4:23
heard Lord had d. up Jordan. 5:1
bind with withs never d. Judg 16:7
Jeroboam's hand d. up. 1 Ki 13:4
brook d. because there had. 17:7
with the sole of my feet have I d. all
  the rivers. 2 Ki 19:24; Isa 37:25
his roots shall be d. up. Job 18:16
they are d. up, they are.   28:4
my strength is d. up.   Ps 22:15
my throat is d. mine eyes. 69:3
the Red sea, and it was d. 106:9
and their multitude d. up. Isa 5:13
river shall be wasted and d. up. 19:5
of defence be emptied and d. up. 6
art thou not it which hath d.? 51:10
places of wilderness d. up. Jer 23:10
and they shall be d. up.   50:38
know that I have d. up. Ezek 17:24
the east wind d. up her fruit. 19:12
our bones are d. and hope is. 37:11
their root is d. up.   Hos 9:16
his fountain shall be d. up. 13:15
the new wine is d. up.   Joel 1:10
the vine is d. up.   12
rivers of water are d. up.   20
arm shall be clean d. up. Zech 11:17
fountain of blood was d. Mark 5:29
they saw the fig tree d.   11:20
water of Euphrates was d. up.
                  Rev 16:12

driedst

the flood, thou d. up.   Ps 74:15

drieth

flood decayeth and d. up. Job 14:11
but a broken spirit d.   Pr 17:22
makes sea dry, and d.   Nah 1:4

drink, noun

bottle, and gave lad d. Gen 21:19
I will give thy camels d. 24:14, 46
all d. that may be drunk. Lev 11:34
give the congregation d. Num 20:8
she gave Sisera d. and. Judg 4:19
gave meat and d. to.   Ezra 3:7
them d. in vessels of gold. Esth 1:7
he gave them d. as out. Ps 78:15
I have mingled my d. with. 102:9
gave d. to every beast of. 104:11
he will cause the d. of. Isa 32:6
to give d. to my people. 43:20
my lovers that give me d. Hos 2:5
their d. is sour, they have. 4:18
giveth his neighbour d. Hab 2:15
ye are not filled with d. Hag 1:6
I was thirsty, and ye gave me d.
                  Mat 25:35
when gave thee d.?   37
thirsty, and ye gave me no d. 42
a Jew, askest d. of me. John 4:9
my blood is d. indeed.   6:55
enemy thirst, give him d. Rom 12:20
of God not meat and d.   14:17
drink same spiritual d. 1 Cor 10:4
man judge in meat or in d. Col 2:16

drink, verb
*The word drink is frequently used
of taking in through the senses, or
through the mind, the pleasures or
the sorrows sent upon man. To
eat and drink meant to enjoy themselves in any manner, Eccl 5:18.
To drink blood was to be satiated
with slaughter, Ezek 39:18. As
cup is used figuratively for the
blessings and punishments of God,
so to drink of the cup was to receive these, Ps 75:8.*

let me d.   Gen 24:14, 17, 45
d. my lord.   18, 46
rods when flocks came to d.   30:38
what shall we d.?   Ex 15:24
Moses made Israel d. of it.   32:20
not d. wine nor strong d.   Lev 10:9
neither shall he d.   Num 6:3
down on knees to d.   Judg 7:5
go to the vessels and d.   Ruth 2:9
drew water, but David would not d.
  2 Sam 23:16, 17; 1 Chr 11:18, 19
that thou shalt d.   1 Ki 17:4
and Haman sat down to d.   Esth 3:15
he shall d. the wrath of.   Job 21:20
make them d. of the river.   Ps 36:8
made us to d. the wine of.   60:3
they gave me vinegar to d.   69:21
wicked of earth shall d.   75:8
they could not d.   78:44
thou gavest them tears to d.   80:5
he shall d. of the brook.   110:7
for they d. the wine of.   Pr 4:17
lest they d. and forget law.   31:5
let him d. and forget his poverty.   7
d. yea d. abundantly.   S of S 5:1
bitter to them that d. it.   Isa 24:9
thou shalt no more d. it.   51:22
shall d. it in the courts.   62:9
my servants shall d. but ye.   65:13
cup of consolation to d.   Jer 16:7
make them d. water of gall.   23:15
nations, to whom I send thee, to d.
                                   25:15
and they shall d. and be moved.   16
cup and made all nations to d.   17
d. ye, and be drunken, and spue.   27
saith Lord, ye shall certainly d. 35:14
to this day they d. none.   35:14
they whose judgement was not to d.
cup, shall surely d. of it.   49:12
d. by measure, from time to time
  shalt thou d.   Ezek 4:11
shalt d. of sister's cup deep.   23:32
they d. that which ye have.   34:19
that concubines might d.   Dan 5:2
bring, and let us d.   Amos 4:1
so shall all the heathen d., yea, they
  shall d. and shall.   Ob 16
d. thou, let thy foreskin.   Hab 2:16
ye d. but ye are not filled.   Hag 1:6
and they shall d. and.   Zech 9:15
whoso shall give to d.   Mat 10:42
able to d. of cup that I shall d. of and
  be baptized? 20:22; Mark 10:38
d. indeed of my cup.   Mat 20:23
                                 Mark 10:39
gave the cup, saying d.   Mat 26:27
not d. henceforth till that day when I
  d.   29; Mark 14:25; Luke 22:18
if cup may not pass except I d.
                                 Mat 26:42
gave him vinegar to d.   27:34
filled a sponge with vinegar, and gave
  him to d.   48; Mark 15:36
d. any deadly thing.   Mark 16:18
to thee, give me to d.   John 4:10
let him come to me and d.   7:37
cup given me, shall I not d.?   18:11
all d. same spiritual drink.   1 Cor 10:4
cannot d. the cup of the Lord.   21
oft as ye d. in remembrance.   11:25
have been all made to d. into.   12:13

strong drink
do not drink strong d.   Lev 10:9
himself from strong d.   Num 6:3
money for strong d.   Deut 14:26
nor have ye drunk strong d.   29:6
not drink strong d.   Judg 13:4, 7, 14
wine nor strong d.   1 Sam 1:15
wine is a mocker, strong d.   Pr 20:1

---

for princes to drink strong d.   Pr 31:4
give strong d. to him that is.   6
may follow strong d. woe.   Isa 5:11
of strength to mingle strong d.   22
strong d. shall be bitter to.   24:9
erred through strong d. and are out
  of way through strong d.   28:7
stagger, but not with strong d.   29:9
fill ourselves with strong d.   56:12
of wine and strong d.   Mi 2:11
drink wine nor strong d.   Luke 1:15

drink water, or waters
water of thy pitcher to d. Gen 24:43
shall lothe to d. water.   Ex 7:18, 21
digged about river for water to d. 24
could not d. of the waters.   15:23
no water for the people to d.   17:1
water out of it, that they may d.   6
cause to d. bitter water.   Num 5:24
                                   26:27
neither any water to d. 20:5; 33:14
nor will we d. of water. 20:17; 21:22
buy water for money, that ye may d.
                                 Deut 2:6, 28
give me a little water to d.   Judg 4:19
bowed upon knees to d. water.   7:6
the Egyptian to d. water.   1 Sam 30:11
to d. of the water of well of Beth-
  lehem. 2 Sam 23:15; 1 Chr 11:17
eat bread, nor d. water. 1 Ki 13:8, 9
water in a vessel that I may d.   17:10
filled with water that ye may d.
                                 2 Ki 3:17
d. every one waters of his.   18:31
                                 Isa 36:16
given water to weary to d.   Job 22:7
d. waters out of thine own.   Pr 5:15
if enemy be thirsty, give water to d.
                                   25:21
to d. the waters of Sihor.   Jer 2:18
water of gall to d.   8:14; 9:15
d. water by measure. Ezek 4:11, 16
d. thy water with trembling.   12:18
they shall d. their water with.   19
all trees that d. water.   31:14, 16
pulse to eat, water to d.   Dan 1:12
wandered to d. water but.   Amos 4:8
not feed nor d. water.   Jonah 3:7
a cup of water to d.   Mark 9:41
give me water to d.   John 4:7
d. no longer water, but.   1 Tim 5:23

drink with wine
our father d. wine.   Gen 19:32, 34
made their father d. wine.   33, 35
nor d. wine when ye go.   Lev 10:9
Nazarite d. no vinegar of wine.
                                 Num 6:3
after that Nazarite may d. wine.   20
plant vineyards, but shalt not d. of
  wine.   Deut 28:39; Amos 5:11
Manoah's wife might d. no wine.
                                 Judg 13:4, 7, 14
wine, that such as be faint may d.
                                 2 Sam 16:2
hast made us d. wine of.   Ps 60:3
for they d. the wine of.   Pr 4:17
and d. of the wine which I.   31:4
not for kings, to d. wine.   31:4
go and d. thy wine   Eccl 9:7
thee to d. spiced wine.   S of S 8:2
are mighty to d. wine.   Isa 5:22
shall not d. wine with a song.   24:9
of stranger not d. thy wine.   62:8
give Rechabites wine to d. Jer 35:2
will d. no wine, ye shall d. no wine. 6
shall any priest d. wine. Ezek 44:21
took away wine that they should d.
                                 Dan 1:16
sold a girl for wine to d.   Joel 3:3
they d. the wine of the.   Amos 2:8
gave the Nazarites wine to d.   12
that d. wine in bowls.   6:6
plant vineyards, and d. wine.   9:14
but shall not d. wine.   Mi 6:15
                                 Zeph 1:13
gave him to d. wine.   Mark 15:23
John shall d. neither wine. Luke 1:15
to eat flesh or d. wine.   Rom 14:21
all nations of the wine.   Rev 14:8
same shall d. of the wine of the. 10

drinkers
and howl, all ye d. of wine. Joel 1:5

---

drinketh
in which my lord d.?   Gen 44:5
land d. water of rain.   Deut 11:11
the poison whereof d. up.   Job 6:4
who d. iniquity like water!   15:16
like Job who d. up scorning.   34:7
behold, he d. up a river.   40:23*
sendeth by a fool, d.   Pr 26:6
he d. but he awaketh.   Isa 29:8
the smith, he d. no water.   44:12
he d. with publicans?   Mark 2:16
whosoever d. of this water shall.
                                 John 4:13
whosoever d. of water that I.   14
whoso d. of my blood.   6:54
that d. my blood dwelleth in me. 56
he that d. unworthily d. 1 Cor 11:29
earth which d. in rain.   Heb 6:7

drinking
camels till they have done d.
                                 Gen 24:19
as camels had done d. man took. 22
till Boaz have done eating and d.
                                 Ruth 3:3
eating and d. and.   1 Sam 30:16
multitude, eating and d.   1 Ki 4:20
d. vessels of gold. 10:21; 2 Chr 9:20
Elah was d.   1 Ki 16:9
Ben-hadad was d.   20:12, 16
three days eating and d. 1 Chr 12:39
d. was according to the law. Esth 1:8
and daughters were d. Job 1:13, 18
eating flesh, and d. wine. Isa 22:13
John came neither eating nor d.
                      Mat 11:18; Luke 7:33
Son of man came eating and d.
                      Mat 11:19; Luke 7:34
were eating and d. till.   Mat 24:38
eating and d. such things. Luke 10:7

drink offering
Jacob poured a d.-off.   Gen 35:14
and fourth part of an hin of wine for
  d.-off.   Ex 29:40; Num 15:5
do according to the d.-off. Ex 29:41
nor shall ye pour d.-off.   30:9
d.-off. shall be of wine.   Lev 23:13
priest shall offer also his d.-off.
                                 Num 6:17
for a d.-off. a third part.   15:7
bring for a d.-off. half an hin.   10
his d.-off. according to the.   24
besides the continual d.-off.   28:10
                              15, 24; 29:16
hast thou poured a d.-off.   Isa 57:6
that furnish the d.-off.   65:11*
the d.-off. is cut off from.   Joel 1:9
the d.-off. is withholden.   13
return and leave a d.-off.   2:14

drink offerings
for a burnt-offering with d.-off.
       Lev 23:18, 37; Num 6:15; 28:31
   29:11, 18, 19, 21, 24, 30, 33, 37, 39
their d.-off. shall be.   Num 28:14
drank the wine of their d.-off.
                                 Deut 32:38
offered with their d.-off. 1 Chr 29:21
                                 2 Chr 29:35
buy meat-offerings and d.-off.
                                 Ezra 7:17
their d.-off. of blood.   Ps 16:4
pour out d.-off. to other gods.
                      Jer 7:18; 19:13; 32:29
pour out d.-off.   44:17, 18, 19, 25
poured out their d.-off. Ezek 20:28
princes part to give d.-off.   45:17

drinks
only in meats, and d.   Heb 9:10

drive
strong hand shall he d.   Ex 6:1
send hornets, which shall d.   23:28
I will not d. them out before thee. 29
by little and little I will d. them. 30
and thou shall d. them out.   31
I will d. out the Canaanite.   33:2
behold I d. out before thee.   34:11
I may d. them out of the. Num 22:6
I may be able to overcome and d. 11
then shall ye d. out all.   33:52
but if ye will not d. out the.   55
to d. out nations greater and.
                      Deut 4:38; 9:4, 5; Josh 3:10
so shalt thou d. them out. Deut 9:3

driven (cont.)

then will the Lord d. out. Deut 11:23
Lord thy God doth d. them. 18:12
them will I d. out from. Josh 13:6
then I shall be able to d. them. 14:12
children of Judah could not d. 15:63
of Manasseh could not d. out. 17:12
did not utterly d. them out. 13
    Judg 1:28
shalt d. out Canaanites. Josh 17:18
Lord shall d. them out of. 23:5
the Lord will no more d. out. 13
    Judg 2:3, 21
not d. inhabitants of. Judg 1:19
did not d. out Jebusites. 21
other tribes, 27, 29, 30, 31, 33
whom Lord our God shall d. 11:24*
d. go forward, slack not. 2 Ki 4:24
who didst d. out the. 2 Chr 20:7
make afraid, and d. Job 18:11*
they d. away the ass of. 24:3
how thou didst d. out. Ps 44:2
smoke is driven away, so d. 68:2
rod of correction shall d. it. Pr 22:15
and I will d. thee from. Isa 22:19*
be a curse, whither I shall d. Jer 24:9
that I should d. you out. 27:10, 15
because Lord did d. them. 46:15
Gentiles, whither I will d. Ezek 4:13
and they shall d. thee. Dan 4:25, 32
I will d. them out of my. Hos 9:15
I will d. the northern. Joel 2:20
shalt d. out Ashdod. Zeph 2:4
ship was caught, we let her d.
    Acts 27:15

driven
thou hast d. me out this. Gen 4:14
were d. from Pharaoh's. Ex 10:11
the beast be d. away. 22:10
have d. out enemies. Num 32:21
thou shouldest be d. to. Deut 4:19*
whither Lord hath d. thee. 30:1
if any of them be d. out to. 4*
the Lord hath d. out. Josh 23:9
they have d. me out. 1 Sam 26:19
wisdom d. quite from me? Job 6:13
wilt thou break a leaf d. to? 13:25
he shall be d. from light into. 18:18
d. forth from among men. 30:5
let them be d. backward. Ps 40:14
as smoke is d. away, so drive. 68:2
Jordan was d. back. 114:3, 5*
wicked is d. away in his. Pr 14:32*
shall be d. to darkness. Isa 8:22
sown by brooks be d. away. 19:7
he gave them as d. stubble. 41:2
places whither I have d. Jer 8:3
    23:3, 8; 29:14, 18; 32:37
from lands whither he had d. 16:15
ye have d. them away. 23:2
shall be d. on and fall therein. 12
out of all places whither they were d.
    40:12; 43:5
of nations whither I have d. 46:28
ye shall be d. out every man. 49:5
the lions have d. him away. 50:17
I have d. him out for his. Ezek 31:11
again which was d. away. 34:4, 16
and he was d. from men. Dan 4:33
    5:21
countries whither thou hast d. 9:7
as the chaff that is d. Hos 13:3
I will gather her that was d. Mi 4:6
    Zeph 3:19
he was d. of the devil. Luke 8:29
strake sail, and were d. Acts 27:17
we were d. up and down in. 27
is like a wave of the sea. Jas 1:6
ships though great are d. of. 3:4

driver
Ahab said to d. of his. 1 Ki 22:34
nor regardeth crying of d. Job 39:7

driveth
is like Jehu, for he d. 2 Ki 9:20
like chaff which wind d. Ps 1:4
the north wind d. away. Pr 25:23*
the spirit d. him into. Mark 1:12

driving
those nations without d. Judg 2:23
d. is like the d. of Jehu. 2 Ki 9:20
by d. out nations before. 1 Chr 17:21

dromedaries
(Originally this word was applied

to any fleet camel bred especially
for riding. See camel)
barley and straw for d. 1 Ki 4:28*
letters by riders on d. Esth 8:10*
d. of Midian and Ephah. Isa 60:6

dromedary
thou art a swift d. Jer 2:23

drop
nations are as the d. of. Isa 40:15

drop, verb
my doctrine shall d. as. Deut 32:2
heavens shall d. down dew. 33:28
    Pr 3:20
which clouds do d. and. Job 36:28*
and thy paths d. fatness. Ps 65:11
they d. on the pastures of the. 12
lips of a strange woman d. Pr 5:3
thy lips, my spouse, d. S of S 4:11
d. down, ye heavens. Isa 45:8
d. thy word toward. Ezek 20:46
d. thy word toward holy places. 21:2
mountains shall d. down new wine.
    Joel 3:18; Amos 9:13
d. not thy word against. Amos 7:16

dropped
d. the clouds also d. water. Judg 5:4
into wood, honey d. 1 Sam 14:26
till water d. on them. 2 Sam 21:10
and my speech d. upon. Job 29:22
the heavens also d. at. Ps 68:8
my hands d. with myrrh. S of S 5:5

droppeth
idleness the house d. Eccl 10:18*

dropping
contentions of a wife are a continual
d. Pr 19:13; 27:15
d. sweet smelling myrrh. S of S 5:13

drops
he maketh small the d. Job 36:27
who hath begotten the d.? 38:28
my locks with the d. S of S 5:2
sweat was as great d. Luke 22:44

dropsy
a man before him, who had d.
    Luke 14:2

dross
take away the d. from. Pr 25:4
potsherd covered with silver d. 26:23
silver is become d. wine. Isa 1:22
I will purely purge away thy d. 25
house of Israel is to me become d.
    Ezek 22:18, 19

drought
in the day d. consumed. Gen 31:40
fiery serpents and d. Deut 8:15*
d. and heat consume. Job 24:19
moisture is turned into d. Ps 32:4
Lord satisfy thy soul in d. Isa 58:11*
us through a land of d. Jer 2:6
not be careful in year of d. 17:8
a d. is upon her waters. 50:38
thee in land of great d. Hos 13:5
and I called for a d. Hag 1:11

drove, -s
every d. by themselves, and put a
space betwixt d. and d. Gen 32:16
commanded all that followed d. 19
meanest thou by all this d.? 33:8*

drove, verb
so God d. out the man. Gen 3:24
fowls came, Abram d. them. 15:11
shepherds came and d. Ex 2:17
they d. out the Amorites. Num 21:32
Caleb d. thence the. Josh 15:14
who d. away the. 1 Chr 8:13*
and d. asunder the nations. Hab 3:6
he d. them all out of. John 2:15*

drown
love, nor can floods d. it. S of S 8:7
foolish lusts, that d. 1 Tim 6:9

drowned
chosen captains are d. Ex 15:4*
it shall be d. as by flood. Amos 9:5*
better he were d. in. Mat 18:6*
Egyptians assaying to do, were d.
    Heb 11:29*

drowsiness
d. shall clothe a man. Pr 23:21

drunk
all drink that may be d. Lev 11:34
not eaten bread, nor d. Deut 29:6
I will make mine arrows d. 32:42
when Samson had d. Judg 15:19
Boaz had eaten and d. Ruth 3:7
Hannah rose up after they d.
    1 Sam 1:9
I have d. neither wine nor. 15
David made Uriah d. 2 Sam 11:13
hast eaten bread and d. 1 Ki 13:22
Elah was in Tirzah, drinking himself
d. 16:9
Ben-hadad drinking himself d. 20:16
they had eaten and d. 2 Ki 6:23
digged and d. strange waters. 19:24
    Isa 37:25
I have d. my wine with. S of S 5:1
which hast d. the cup of. Isa 51:17
will make them d. in my fury. 63:6
sword shall be made d. Jer 46:10
I will make d. her princes. 51:57
and to have d. of the. Ezek 34:18
they d. wine, and praised. Dan 5:4
and thy concubines have d. 23
as ye have d. upon my. Ob 16
man having d. old wine. Luke 5:39
we have eaten and d. in. 13:26
when men have well d. John 2:10
be not d. with wine. Eph 5:18
made d. with the wine of. Rev 17:2
for all nations have d. of wine. 18:3

drunkard
son is a glutton and d. Deut 21:20
for d. and glutton shall. Pr 23:21
thorn goeth up into hand of d. 26:9
reel to and fro like a d. Isa 24:20
with a fornicator or d. eat. 1 Cor 5:11

drunkards
I was the song of the d. Ps 69:12
woe to pride, to the d. Isa 28:1, 3
awake, ye d. and weep. Joel 1:5
they are drunken as d. Nah 1:10
nor d. shall inherit the. 1 Cor 6:10

drunken
Noah was d. and he. Gen 9:21
Hannah had been d. 1 Sam 1:13
how long wilt thou be d.? 14
merry, for he was very d. 25:36
to stagger like a d. man. Job 12:25
    Ps 107:27
as a d. man staggereth. Isa 19:14
they are d. but not. 29:9; 51:21
be d. with their own blood. 49:26
thou hast d. the dregs of cup. 51:17
I am like a d. man. Jer 23:9
be d. and spue, and fall. 25:27
make ye him d. for he. 48:26
they have assuredly d. and. 49:12
cup that made all earth d. 51:7
I will make them d. that they. 39
he hath made me d. Lam 3:15*
O Edom, thou shalt be d. 4:21
    Nah 3:11
have d. water for money. Lam 5:4
drink blood till ye be d. Ezek 39:19
and while they are d. Nah 1:10
and makest him d. also. Hab 2:15
fellow-servants, to eat and drink
with d. Mat 24:49; Luke 12:45
till I have eaten and d. Luke 17:8
for these are not d. as. Acts 2:15
and another is d. 1 Cor 11:21
they that be d. are d. 1 Thes 5:7
I saw the woman d. with. Rev 17:6

drunkenness
to add d. to thirst. Deut 29:19*
strength, and not for d. Eccl 10:17
of Jerusalem with d. Jer 13:13
shalt be filled with d. Ezek 23:33
be overcharged with d. Luke 21:34
not in rioting and d. Rom 13:13
of flesh are murders, d. Gal 5:21

Drusilla
came with his wife D. Acts 24:24

dry
mingled with oil and d. Lev 7:10
it is a d. scald, a leprosy. 13:30
was d. and mouldy. Josh 9:5, 12
it be d. on all earth. Judg 6:37
it now be d. only on the fleece. 39

dry

wilt thou pursue the *d.?* *Job* 13:25
they ran in *d.* places. *Ps* 105:41
better is a *d.* morsel and. *Pr* 17:1
as the heat in a *d.* place. *Isa* 25:5
as rivers of water in a *d.* 32:2
that saith to the deep, be *d.* 44:27
neither let eunuch say, I am a *d.* 56:3
a *d.* wind, not to fan, nor. *Jer* 4:11*
dry up, and make springs *d.* 51:36
made the *d.* tree flourish. *Ezek* 17:24
it shall devour every *d.* tree. 20:47
I will make the rivers *d.* 30:12
the bones were very *d.* 37:2
O ye *d.* bones. 4
Lord give them *d.* breasts. *Hos* 9:14
spring shall become *d.* 13:15
the sea, and maketh it *d.* *Nah* 1:4
devoured as stubble fully *d.* 10
will make Nineveh *d.* *Zeph* 2:13
he walketh through *d.* places.
Mat 12:43; *Luke* 11:24
green tree what shall be done in *d.?*
Luke 23:31

dry ground

face of the *ground* was *d.* *Gen* 8:13
shall go on *d.* *ground.* *Ex* 14:16, 22
ark stood on *d. ground,* Israel passed
on *d. ground.* *Josh* 3:17
Elijah and Elisha went on *d. ground.*
2 Ki 2:8
springs into *d. ground.* *Ps* 107:33*
turneth *d. ground* into water. 35
floods upon the *d. ground.* *Isa* 44:3
root out of a *d. ground.* 53:2
a *d.* and thirsty *ground. Ezek* 19:13
see land

dry, verb

waters and they *d.* up. *Job* 12:15
the flame shall *d.* up his. 15:30
d. up herbs, I will. *Isa* 42:15
I will *d.* up thy rivers. 44:27
I *d.* up the sea. 50:2
Lord, I will *d.* up her sea. *Jer* 51:36
deeps of river shall *d.* up. *Zech* 10:11

dryshod

river, and men go *d.-shod. Isa* 11:15

due

thy *d.* and thy son's *d. Lev* 10:13, 14
this shall be priest's *d.* *Deut* 18:3
sought him not after *d. 1 Chr* 15:13*
the glory of *d.* to his name. 16:29
Ps 29:2; 96:8
portion for singers, *d.* for. *Neh* 11:23
withhold not to whom it is *d. Pr* 3:27
he pay all that was *d.* *Mat* 18:34
receive the *d.* reward. *Luke* 23:41
to whom tribute is *d.* *Rom* 13:7

due benevolence

render to wife *d.* ben. *1 Cor* 7:3

due season

you rain in *d. season.* *Lev* 26:4
Deut 11:14
to me in their *d. season.* *Num* 28:2
give them their meat in *d. season.*
Ps 104:27; 145:15
word spoken in *d. season. Pr* 15:23
princes eat in *d. season. Eccl* 10:17
to give them meat in *d. season.*
Mat 24:45; *Luke* 12:42
in *d. season* we shall reap. *Gal* 6:9

due time

foot shall slide in *d. time. Deut* 32:35
in *d. time* Christ died. *Rom* 5:6
one born out of *d. time. 1 Cor* 15:8
ransom, testified in *d. time. 1 Tim* 2:6
in *d. time* manifested. *Tit* 1:3
exalt you in *d. time.* *1 Pet* 5:6

dues

to all their *d.* tribute. *Rom* 13:7

duke

d. Alvah, *d.* Jetheth. *Gen* 36:40†
1 Chr 1:51†

dukes

d. of sons of Esau. *Gen* 36:15†, 19†
the *d.* of the Horites. 21†, 29†
then the *d.* of Edom. *Ex* 15:15†
which were *d.* of Sihon. *Josh* 13:21*

dulcimer

flute, *d.* all kinds. *Dan* 3:5, 10, 15

---

dull

heart is waxed gross, and ears are *d.*
Mat 13:15; *Acts* 28:27
utter, seeing ye are *d.* *Heb* 5:11

Dumah

sons of Ishmael, *D.* Massa.
Gen 25:14; *1 Chr* 1:30

Dumah

D. was in Judah's. *Josh* 15:52
the burden of *D.* he. *Isa* 21:11

dumb

[1] *Unable to speak for want of
physical power,* Ex 4:11. [2] *Unable to speak to, and teach others,
for lack of grace and knowledge,*
Isa 56:10. [3] *Unable to speak
for oneself, either through ignorance
or fear of those in whose presence
one is,* Ps 39:9; Pr 31:8; Dan 10:15.
who maketh the *d.* or deaf ? *Ex* 4:11
I was as a *d.* man. *Ps* 38:13
I was *d.* with silence. 39:2, 9
open thy mouth for *d.* *Pr* 31:8
and the tongue of the *d.* *Isa* 35:6
a sheep before shearers is *d.* 53:7
are blind, all *d.* dogs. 56:10
be *d.* and shalt not be. *Ezek* 3:26
speak, and be no more *d.* 24:27
and I was no more *d.* 33:22
face to ground, became *d. Dan* 10:15
to make him *d.* idols. *Hab* 2:18
woe to him that saith to *d.* stone. 19
brought to him a *d.* man. *Mat* 9:32
devil was cast out, the *d.* spake. 33
Luke 11:14
one blind and *d.* and he. *Mat* 12:22
those that were blind, 15:30
wondered, when they saw the *d.*
speak, the blind. 31; *Mark* 7:37
son who hath a *d.* spirit. *Mark* 9:17
thou *d.* spirit, I charge thee. 25
be *d.* until the day thou. *Luke* 1:20
like a lamb *d.* before. *Acts* 8:32
carried away to *d.* idols. *1 Cor* 12:2
the *d.* ass speaking with. *2 Pet* 2:16

dung

By dung is represented any thing
that is nauseous or loathsome,
Jer 8:2; 9:22; Job 20:7; Phil 3:8.
flesh, skin, and *d.* burn. *Ex* 29:14
Lev 4:11; 8:17; 16:27; *Num* 19:5
a man taketh away *d.* *1 Ki* 14:10
of a cab of doves' *d.* *2 Ki* 6:25
of Jezebel shall be as *d.* 9:37
eat their own *d.* 18:27; *Isa* 36:12
for ever like his own *d. Job* 20:7
they became as *d.* *Ps* 83:10
they shall be for *d.* on. *Jer* 8:2
they shall be as *d.* 16:4
they shall be *d.* 25:33
bake it with *d.* that. *Ezek* 4:12
given thee cow's *d.* for man's *d.* 15
flesh shall be as the *d.* *Zeph* 1:17
spread *d.* on your faces, even the *d.*
of your solemn feasts. *Mal* 2:3
count all things but *d.* *Phil* 3:8†

dove's dung, see on dove

dung, verb

I dig about it, and *d.* it. *Luke* 13:8

dungeon

should put me into *d.* *Gen* 40:15
Joseph hastily out of *d.* 41:14
firstborn of captive in *d.* *Ex* 12:29
was entered into the *d.* *Jer* 37:16
cast him into *d.* no water in *d.* 38:6, 9
take up Jeremiah out of the *d.* 10
down by cords into the *d.* to. 13
drew up Jeremiah out of *d.* 13
cut off my life in the *d.* *Lam* 3:53
I called on thy name, out of *d.* 55

dung gate

valley gate to *d.-gate.* *Neh* 3:13
the *d.-gate* repaired Malchiah. 14
company went toward *d.-gate.* 12:31

dunghill

lifteth up beggar from *d. 1 Sam* 2:8
Ps 113:7
his house be made a *d.* *Ezra* 6:11
straw is trodden for *d.* *Isa* 25:10
your houses be made a *d. Dan* 2:5
their houses shall be made a *d.* 3:29

---

unsavoury salt not fit for land or *d.*
Luke 14:35

dunghills

up in scarlet, embrace *d.* *Lam* 4:5

Dura

set image up in plain of *D. Dan* 3:1

durable

yea, *d.* riches and. *Pr* 8:18
merchandise shall be for *d. Isa* 23:18

dureth

not root in himself, *d.* *Mat* 13:21

durst

he that *d.* presume in. *Esth* 7:5
afraid, I *d.* not shew. *Job* 32:6
nor *d.* ask any more. *Mat* 22:46
Mark 12:34; *Luke* 20:40
none of disciples *d.* ask. *John* 21:12
and of the rest *d.* no man. *Acts* 5:13
Moses trembled and *d.* not. 7:32
he *d.* not bring a railing. *Jude* 9

dust

*The Hebrews, when they mourned,
put dust or ashes upon their heads,*
Josh 7:6; Isa 47:1; Lam 3:29.
*The Dust denotes likewise the
grave and death,* Gen 3:19; Job
7:21; Ps 22:15. *The Dust represents also a multitude,* Gen 13:16;
Num 23:10; Ps 78:27.
d. shalt thou eat all days. *Gen* 3:14
thou art, and unto *d.* shalt. 19
if a man can number the *d.* 13:16
speak to Lord, who am but *d.* 18:27
say to Aaron, smite the *d.* *Ex* 8:16
Aaron smote *d.* of the earth. 17
become small *d.* in all the land. 9:9
shall pour out the *d.* *Lev* 14:41*
pour out blood, cover it with *d.* 17:13
can count the *d.* of Jacob ? 23:10
I cast the *d.* into brook. *Deut* 9:21
2 Ki 23:12
make rain of thy land *d. Deut* 28:24
and the elders put *d.* on. *Josh* 7:6
Shimei cursed David, and cast *d.*
2 Sam 16:13
fire of Lord consumed *d. 1 Ki* 18:38
if the *d.* of Samaria shall. 20:10
Josiah made *d.* of the. *2 Chr* 34:4
they sprinkled *d.* upon. *Job* 2:12
with worms and clods of *d.* 7:5
wilt bring me into *d.* again ? 10:9
as for the earth, it hath *d.* of. 28:6
man shall turn again to *d.* 34:15
d. groweth into hardness. 38:38
repent in *d.* and ashes. 42:6
brought me into the *d.* *Ps* 22:15
shall *d.* praise thee, shall it ? 30:9
his enemies shall lick the *d.* 72:9
flesh also upon them as *d.* 78:27
thy servants favour the *d.* 102:14
remembereth that we are *d.* 103:14
then shall *d.* return. *Eccl* 12:7
their *d.* shall be made fat. *Isa* 34:7
the *d.* thereof shall be turned. 9
who hath comprehended *d.?* 40:12
lick up the *d.* of thy feet. 49:23
shake thyself from the *d.* 52:2
d. shall be the serpent's meat. 65:25
cast *d.* on their heads,
Ezek 27:30
to cover it with *d.* *Ezek* 24:7
I will also scrape her *d.* from. 26:4
their *d.* shall cover thee. 10
that pant after the *d.* of. *Amos* 2:7
shall lick the *d.* like. *Mi* 7:17
and the clouds are the *d.* *Nah* 1:3
for they shall heap *d.* *Hab* 1:10
shake off the *d.* of your. *Mat* 10:14
Mark 6:11; *Luke* 9:5
d. of your city we do. *Luke* 10:11
they shook off the *d.* *Acts* 13:51
as they threw *d.* into the air. 22:23
cast *d.* on their heads. *Rev* 18:19

as the dust

and make thy seed as the *d.* of the.
Gen 13:16; 28:14; *2 Chr* 1:9
calf small as the *d.* *Deut* 9:21
I beat them as small as *d.*
2 Sam 22:43; *Ps* 18:42
lay up gold as the *d.* *Job* 22:24
heap up silver as the *d.* 27:16
blossom shall go up as *d. Isa* 5:24

nations *as the* small *d.* of. *Isa* 40:15
he gave them *as the d.* to his. 41:2
blood be poured out *as d. Zeph* 1:17
Tyrus heaped up silver *as the d.*
Zech 9:3

in the dust
foundation is *in the d.* *Job* 4:19
now shall I sleep *in the d.* 7:21
defiled my horn *in the d.* 16:15
rest together is *in the d.* 17:16
lie down with him *in the d.* 20:11
shall lie down alike *in the d.* 21:16
warmeth them *in the d.* 39:14
hide them *in the d.* together. 40:13
lay mine honour *in the d. Ps* 7:5
hide thee *in the d.* for fear. *Isa* 2:10
sing, ye that dwell *in the d.* 26:19
come down and sit *in the d.* 47:1
putteth his mouth *in the d. Lam* 3:29
many that sleep *in the d. Dan* 12:2
roll thyself *in the d. Mi* 1:10
nobles shall dwell *in the d. Nah* 3:18

like the dust
make them *like the d.* *2 Ki* 13:7
thy strangers be *like d.* *Isa* 29:5

of the dust
Lord formed man *of the d. Gen* 2:7
priest take *of the d.* *Num* 5:17
of serpents *of the d. Deut* 32:24
raiseth poor out *of the d. 1 Sam* 2:8
Ps 113:7
exalted thee out *of the d.* *1 Ki* 16:2
affliction cometh not *of the d. Job* 5:6
things that grow out *of the d.* 14:19
nor highest part *of the d. Pr* 8:26
all are *of the d.* *Eccl* 3:20
speech shall be out *of the d. Isa* 29:4

to the dust
all that go down *to the d. Ps* 22:29
soul is bowed down *to the d.* 44:25
die and return *to their d.* 104:29
my soul cleaveth *to the d.* 119:25
d. and all turn *to the d.* again. *Eccl* 3:20
bring fortress *to the d. Isa* 25:12
the lofty city *to the d.* 26:5

duties
son that doth not those *d. Ezek* 18:11

duty
her *d.* of marriage shall. *Ex* 21:10
perform *d.* of husband's. *Deut* 25:5
will not perform the *d.* of my. 7
d. of every day required. *2 Chr* 8:14
Ezra 3:4
this is whole *d.* of man. *Eccl* 12:13
which was our *d.* to do. *Luke* 17:10
their *d.* is to minister. *Rom* 15:27*

dwarf
a *d.* shall not come nigh. *Lev* 21:20

dwell
(*To abide as a resident ; live ; re-
side. To continue a long time*)
Japhet shall *d.* in tents. *Gen* 9:27
he shall *d.* in the presence 16:12
for he feared to *d.* in Zoar. 19:30
d. where it pleaseth thee. 20:15
Canaanites, amongst whom I *d.* 24:3
land before you, *d.* and trade. 34:10
we will *d.* with you, and. 16
go up to Beth-el, and *d.* there. 35:1
Moses was content to *d.* *Ex* 2:21
d. amongst them. 25:8; 29:46
I will *d.* amongst children of. 29:45
unclean shall *d.* alone. *Lev* 13:46
d. in booths. 23:42, 43; *Neh* 8:14
camps, in the midst whereof I *d.*
Num 5:3
lo, the people shall *d.* alone. 23:9
our little ones shall *d.* in. 32:17
give to the Levites, cities to *d.* in.
35:2, 3; *Josh* 14:4; 21:2
Lord *d.* among children. *Num* 35:34
to cause his name to *d.* there.
Deut 12:11; *Ezra* 6:12
servant escaped shall *d. Deut* 23:16
he shall *d.* between his. 33:12
ye *d.* among us. *Josh* 9:7, 22
he shall *d.* in that city. 20:6
cities ye built not, and ye *d.* 24:13
Gaal should not *d.* in. *Judg* 9:41
Micah said to Levite, *d.* with. 17:10
that I may *d.* there, why should thy
servant *d.* in the ? *1 Sam* 27:5

d. among children of. *1 Ki* 6:13
would *d.* in thick darkness. 8:12
2 Chr 6:1
to Zarephath, and *d.* there. *1 Ki* 17:9
I *d.* among own people. *2 Ki* 4:13
let them go and *d.* there. 17:27
let a cloud *d.* upon it. *Job* 3:5
let not wickedness *d.* in thy. 11:14
shall *d.* in his tabernacle. 18:15
to *d.* in the clifts of the. 30:6
neither evil *d.* with thee. *Ps* 5:4*
who shall *d.* in thy holy hill ? 15:1
his soul shall *d.* at ease. 25:13
depart from evil, and *d.* 37:27
that he may *d.* in thy courts. 65:4
they that *d.* in uttermost parts. 8
hill which God desireth to *d.* in, yea
the Lord will *d.* in it. 68:16
Lord might *d.* among them. 18
build Judah that they may *d.* 69:35
they that *d.* in the wilderness. 72:9
and made Israel to *d.* in. 78:55
d. in tents of wickedness. 84:10
faithful, that they may *d.* with. 101:6
they found no city to *d.* in. 107:4
he maketh the hungry to *d.* 36
that I *d.* in tents of Kedar. 120:5
will I *d.* for I have desired it. 132:14
if I *d.* in uttermost parts of. 139:9
upright shall *d.* in thy. 140:13
made me to *d.* in darkness. 143:3
hearkeneth to me shall *d.* *Pr* 1:33
I wisdom *d.* with prudence. 8:12
it is better to *d.* in wilderness. 21:19
I *d.* in midst of a people. *Isa* 6:5
the wolf shall *d.* with the. 11:6
owls shall *d.* there, satyrs. 13:21
let mine outcasts *d.* with thee. 16:4
merchandise for them that *d.* 23:18
that *d.* therein are desolate. 24:6
bringeth down them that *d.* on. 26:5
awake and sing, ye that *d.* 19
people *d.* in Zion at Jerusalem. 30:19
then judgement shall *d.* in. 32:16
people *d.* in peaceful habitation. 18
who shall *d.* with devouring fire ?
who *d.* with everlasting ? 33:14
he shall *d.* on high. 16
the people that *d.* therein. 24
owl and the raven shall *d.* 34:11
them out as a tent to *d.* in. 40:22
give place that I may *d.* 49:20
restorer of paths to *d.* in. 58:12
and my servants shall *d.* there. 65:9
Shemaiah shall not have a man to *d.*
Jer 29:32
shall *d.* in Judah husbandmen. 31:24
all your days ye shall *d.* in. 35:7
and *d.* with him among. 40:5
d. at Mizpah to serve Chaldeans. 10
into Egypt, and there *d.* 42:14
a desire to return to *d.* there. 44:14
flee ye, *d.* deep, O inhabitants. 49:8
nor a son of man *d.* 18*, 33*; 50:40*
which *d.* alone. 43:19
that *d.* in midst of them. 51:1
dost *d.* among scorpions. *Ezek* 2:6
and her daughters *d.* at left. 16:46
where I will *d.* in midst of Israel for.
43:7, 9; *Zech* 2:10, 11
I will make thee to *d.* in. *Hos* 12:9
they that *d.* under his shadow. 14:7
but Judah shall *d.* for ever. *Joel* 3:20
be taken out that *d.* in. *Amos* 3:12*
thou shalt *d.* in the field. *Mi* 4:10
the flock which *d.* solitarily. 7:14
thy nobles *d.* in dust. *Nah* 3:18*
to *d.* in cieled houses ? *Hag* 1:4
old men and women shall *d.* in.
Zech 8:4
a bastard shall *d.* in Ashdod. 9:6
and men shall *d.* in it. 14:11
enter in and *d.* there. *Mat* 12:45
as a snare shall it come on all that *d.*
Luke 21:35; *Acts* 17:26
into land wherein ye *d.* *Acts* 7:4
Paul was suffered to *d.* by. 28:16
Spirit of God *d.* in you. *Rom* 8:9, 11
and she be pleased to *d.* *1 Cor* 7:12
God hath said, I will *d.* *2 Cor* 6:16
Christ may *d.* in your. *Eph* 3:17
in him should all fulness *d. Col* 1:19
word of Christ *d.* in you richly. 3:16

likewise, ye husbands, *d.* *1 Pet* 3:7
know we that we *d.* in. *1 John* 4:13
on the throne shall *d.* *Rev* 7:15*
heavens, and ye that *d.* in. 12:12
against them that *d.* in heaven. 13:6
men, and he will *d.* with them. 21:3

dwell with earth
will God *d.* on *earth* ? *1 Ki* 8:27
2 Chr 6:18
languages, that *d.* in all the *earth.*
Dan 4:1; 6:25
try them that *d.* on *earth. Rev* 3:10
avenge on them that *d.* on *earth.* 6:10
they that *d.* on the *earth.* 11:10
all that *d.* on the *earth* shall. 13:8
deceiveth them that *d.* on *earth.* 14
preach to them that *d.* on *earth.* 14:6
they that *d.* on the *earth.* 17:8

dwell with house
build an *house,* and not *d.* therein.
Deut 28:30; *Amos* 5:11
I *d.* in a *house* of cedar. *2 Sam* 7:2
1 Chr 17:1
shall build me an *house* to *d.* in.
2 Sam 7:5; *1 Chr* 17:1
build *house* in Jerusalem and *d.*
1 Ki 2:36
this woman *d.* in one *house.* 3:17
surely built thee *house* to *d.* in. 8:13
not *d.* in *house* of David. *2 Chr* 8:11
that *d.* in *houses* of clay. *Job* 4:19
they that *d.* in my *house.* 19:15
will *d.* in the *house* of the. *Ps* 23:6
that I may *d.* in the *house* of. 27:4
blessed that *d.* in thy *house.* 84:4
worketh deceit, shall not *d.* in my
house. 101:7
better *d.* in the corner of a *house.*
Pr 21:9; 25:24
d. in thy *house* go to. *Jer* 20:6
build ye *houses, d.* in them. 29:5, 28
not to build *houses* for us to *d.* 35:9

dwell with Jerusalem
d. in *Jerusalem* for ever. *1 Chr* 23:25
of ten to *d.* in *Jerusalem. Neh* 11:1
offered to *d.* at *Jerusalem.* 2
Jerusalem shall *d.* safely. *Jer* 33:16
for fear we *d.* at *Jerusalem.* 35:11
d. in midst of *Jerusalem. Zech* 8:3
d. in the midst of *Jerusalem.* 8
all ye that *d.* at *Jerusalem. Acts* 2:14
all them that *d.* in *Jerusalem.* 4:16
they that *d.* at *Jerusalem.* 13:27

dwell with land
Canaanites in whose *land* I *d.*
Gen 24:37
d. in the *land* which I shall. 26:2
let them *d.* in the *land.* 34:21
and thou shalt *d.* in *land.* 45:10
may *d.* in the *land* of Goshen. 46:34
in *land* of Goshen ye *d.* 47:6
land of Goshen, in which my people
d. *Ex* 8:22
they shall not *d.* in thy *land.* 23:33
ye shall *d.* in the *land.* *Lev* 25:18
shall eat and *d.* in your *land.* 26:5
what the *land* is they *d.* *Num* 13:19
defile not *land* wherein I *d.* 35:34
d. in the *land* which the Lord giveth.
Deut 12:10
d. in the *land* Lord sware. 30:20
but the Canaanites would *d.* in that
land. *Josh* 17:12; *Judg* 1:27
the gods in whose *land* ye *d.*
Josh 24:15; *Judg* 6:10
fear not, *d.* in *land.* *2 Ki* 25:24
Jer 25:5; 40:9
so shalt thou *d.* in the *land. Ps* 37:3
rebellious *d.* in a dry *land.* 68:6
glory may *d.* in our *land.* 85:9
upright shall *d.* in *land.* *Pr* 2:21
d. in *land* of shadow. *Isa* 9:2
d. in their own *land. Jer* 23:8; 27:11
that *d.* in the *land* of Egypt. 24:8
44:1, 8, 13, 26
ye shall *d.* in the *land.* 35:15
Ezek 36:28; 37:25
we will not *d.* in this *land. Jer* 42:13
to *d.* in the *land* of Judah. 43:4, 5*
land desolate, none shall *d.* 50:3
then *d.* in their *land.* *Ezek* 28:25
people that *d.* in midst of *land.* 38:12
not *d.* in Lord's *land.* *Hos* 9:3

violence of *land*, and all that *d.*
   Hab 2:8, 17
riddance of all that *d.* in the *land.*
   Zeph 1:18

dwell with *place*
place thou hast made to *d. Ex* 15:17
made them to *d.* in this *place.*
   1 Sam 12:8
may *d.* in a *place* of. *2 Sam* 7:10
place where we *d.* is. *2 Ki* 6:1
make us a *place* where we may *d.* 2
shall *d.* in their *place.* *1 Chr* 17:9
d. in high and holy *place. Isa* 57:15
I will cause you to *d.* in this *place.*
   Jer 7:3, 7

dwell *safely*
hearkeneth to me shall *d. safely.*
   Pr 1:33
Israel shall *d. safely.* *Jer* 23:6
   Ezek 28:26; 34:25, 28; 38:8
cause them to *d. safely.* *Jer* 32:37
at rest that *d. safely.* *Ezek* 38:11

dwell *in safety*
and ye shall *d.* in the land *in safety.*
   Lev 25:18, 19; *Deut* 12:10
of Lord *d. in safety.* *Deut* 33:12
Israel shall *d. in safety* alone. 28
makest me to *d. in safety.* *Ps* 4:8

dwell *therein*
enemies which *d. therein. Lev* 27:32
land I sware to make you *d. therein.*
   Num 14:30
shall *d. therein.* 33:53; *Deut* 11:31
world and they that *d. therein.*
   Ps 24:1
righteous shall *d. therein.* 37:29
love his name shall *d. therein.* 69:36
for wickedness of them that *d. there-*
in. 107:34; *Jer* 12:4
that *d. therein* are desolate.
   Isa 24:6; *Amos* 9:5
people that *d. therein* are. *Isa* 33:24
to generation shall *d. therein.* 34:17
they that *d. therein* shall die. 51:6
not a man *d. therein.* *Jer* 4:29
the city, all that *d. therein.* 8:16
wickedness of them that *d. therein.*
   12:4
land and them that *d. therein.* 47:2
desolate without any to *d. therein.*
   48:9
and the owls shall *d. therein.* 50:39
violence of them that *d. therein.*
   Ezek 12:19
smite them that *d. therein.* 32:15
they and children *d. therein.* 37:25
desolate, because of them that *d.*
therein. *Mi* 7:13
world is burnt, and all that *d. therein.*
   Nah 1:5
his habitation, let no man *d. therein.*
   Acts 1:20

dwell *together*
d. together, their substance . . . they
could not *d. together. Gen* 13:6
more than might *d. together.* 36:7
if brethren *d. together. Deut* 25:5
for brethren to *d. together. Ps* 133:1

dwelled
the Perizzite *d.* then in. *Gen* 13:7
Abram *d.* in the land of Canaan, Lot
d. in the cities of the plain. 12
Abraham *d.* between Kadesh. 20:1
d. there about ten years. *Ruth* 1:4
delivered you, ye *d.* *1 Sam* 12:11

dwellers
ye *d.* on earth, see ye. *Isa* 18:3
it was known to the *d.* *Acts* 1:19
the *d.* in Mesopotamia. 2:9

dwellest
succeedest them and *d. Deut* 12:29
God of Israel, which *d.* between.
   2 Ki 19:15*; *Ps* 80:1*; *Isa* 37:16*
O thou that *d.* in the. *Ps* 123:1*
thou that *d.* in gardens. *S of S* 8:13
O my people that *d.* in. *Isa* 10:24
hear now this, thou that *d.* 47:8
thou that *d.* in the clefts. *Jer* 49:16
   Ob 3
that *d.* upon many waters. *Jer* 51:13
of Edom, that *d.* in land. *Lam* 4:21

thou that *d.* in the land. *Ezek* 7:7
d. in the midst of rebellious. 12:2
that *d.* with the daughter. *Zech* 2:7
Master, where *d.* thou ? *John* 1:38
works, and where thou *d. Rev* 2:13

dwelleth
stranger that *d.* with you. *Lev* 19:34*
brother that *d.* by thee be. 25:39, 47
God *d.* as a lion. *Deut* 33:20
Rahab *d.* in Israel. *Josh* 6:25
wherein Lord's tabernacle *d.* 22:19
covenant of Lord, who *d.* *1 Sam* 4:4*
   2 Sam 6:2*; *1 Chr* 13:6*
ark *d.* within curtains. *2 Sam* 7:2
he *d.* in desolate cities. *Job* 15:28
where is way where light *d.?* 38:19
she *d.* and abideth on rock. 39:28
to the Lord who *d.* in Zion. *Ps* 9:11
place where thine honour *d.* 26:8
d. in secret place of most High. 91:1
Lord our God who *d.* on high ? 113:5
blessed be the Lord who *d.* 135:21
seeing he *d.* securely. *Pr* 3:29
Lord, who *d.* in mount. *Isa* 8:18
Lord is exalted, for he *d.* on. 33:5
desolation, and no man *d. Jer* 44:2
wealthy nation that *d.* without. 49:31
she *d.* among the heathen. *Lam* 1:3
younger sister *d.* at right. *Ezek* 16:46
where king *d.* that made him. 17:16
and the light *d.* with him. *Dan* 2:22
land shall mourn, every one that *d.*
therein. *Hos* 4:3; *Amos* 8:8
the Lord *d.* in Zion. *Joel* 3:21
sweareth by it and him that *d.*
   Mat 23:21
drinketh my blood, *d.* in. *John* 6:56
the Father than *d.* in me. 14:10
the Spirit, for he *d.* in you. 17
d. not in temples made with hands.
   Acts 7:48; 17:24
more I, but sin that *d. Rom* 7:17, 20
I know that in my flesh *d.* no. 18
by his Spirit that *d.* in you. 8:11
that Spirit of God *d.* in. *1 Cor* 3:16
d. fulness of Godhead. *Col* 2:9
Holy Ghost which *d.* in. *2 Tim* 1:14
spirit that *d.* in us lusteth. *Jas* 4:5
a new earth wherein *d.* *2 Pet* 3:13
how *d.* the love of God ? *1 John* 3:17
keepeth his commandments, *d.* 24
love one another, God *d.* in. 4:12
Jesus is Son of God, God *d.* in. 15
he that *d.* in love, *d.* in God. 16
truth's sake which *d.* in us. *2 John* 2
among you, where Satan *d. Rev* 2:13

dwelling, *substantive*
d. shall be the fatness. *Gen* 27:39
at beginning of their *d.* *2 Ki* 17:25
built a place for thy *d.* *2 Chr* 6:2
in grave from their *d.* *Ps* 49:14
any plague come nigh thy *d.* 91:10
there is oil in the *d.* of. *Pr* 21:20
lay not wait against the *d.* 24:15
Hazor shall be a *d.* for. *Jer* 49:33
gods, whose *d.* is not. *Dan* 2:11
thy *d.* be with beasts. 4:25, 32; 5:21
where is the *d.* of lions ? *Nah* 2:11
his *d.* among the tombs. *Mark* 5:3

dwelling
Jacob a plain man, *d.* in. *Gen* 25:27
any man sell a *d.* house. *Lev* 25:29
strong is thy *d.* place. *Num* 24:21
hear in heaven thy *d.* place. *1 Ki* 8:30
   39, 43, 49; *2 Chr* 6:21, 30, 39
their prayer came up to his holy *d.*
   2 Chr 30:27
Lord hath compassion of. 36:15
the *d.* place of the wicked. *Job* 8:22
are *d.* places of wicked ? 21:28
d. places to all generations. *Ps* 49:11
pluck thee out of thy *d.* 52:5
by casting down the *d.* place. 74:7
Salem his tabernacle, his *d.* 76:2
have laid waste his *d.* place. 79:7
Lord, thou hast been our *d.* 90:1
Lord will create on every *d. Isa* 4:5
I will consider in my *d.* place. 18:4
I will have mercy on his *d. Jer* 30:18
O thou daughter *d.* in Egypt. 46:19
have burnt their *d.* places. 51:30
Babylon shall become a *d.* place. 37
all your *d.* places the cities. *Ezek* 6:6

save them out of all *d.* *Ezek* 37:23
all of them *d.* without walls. 38:11
Lord your God *d.* in Zion. *Joel* 3:17
to possess the *d.* places. *Hab* 1:6
their *d.* should not be cut. *Zeph* 3:7
were *d.* at Jerusalem. *Acts* 2:5
known to the Greeks, *d.* at. 19:17
have no certain *d.* place. *1 Cor* 4:11
d. in the light no man. *1 Tim* 6:16
d. in tabernacles with. *Heb* 11:9
Lot, that righteous man, *d.* *2 Pet* 2:8

dwellings
of Israel had light in *d.* *Ex* 10:23
perpetual statute throughout your *d.*
   Lev 3:17; 23:14; *Num* 35:29
no blood in any of your *d. Lev* 7:26
do no work in all your *d.* 23:3, 31
have any remaining in *d. Job* 18:19*
surely such are the *d.* of the. 21
made the barren land his *d.* 39:6
wickedness is in their *d.* *Ps* 55:15
more than all the *d.* of Jacob. 87:2
people dwell in sure *d.* *Isa* 32:18
our *d.* have cast us out. *Jer* 9:19
men of east make their *d. Ezek* 25:4
sea coast shall be *d.* *Zeph* 2:6*

dwelt
and they *d.* there. *Gen* 11:2, 31
   26:17; *2 Ki* 16:6; *1 Chr* 4:43
   2 Chr 28:18
d. among children of. *Gen* 23:10*
of Egypt wherein ye *d.* *Lev* 18:3
wherein they *d.* *Num* 31:10
   2 Ki 17:29
d. an old prophet. *1 Ki* 13:11, 25
and I *d.* as a king in. *Job* 29:25
Zion wherein thou hast *d. Ps* 74:2
Ariel, city where David *d. Isa* 29:1*
a land where no man *d.* *Jer* 2:6
Jeremiah *d.* among people. 39:14
d. by the river of Chebar. *Ezek* 3:15
under shadow of great. 31:6, 17
lands wherein your fathers *d.* 37:25
which beasts of field *d.* *Dan* 4:21
rejoicing city that *d.* *Zeph* 2:15
fear came on all that *d.* *Luke* 1:65
Word was made flesh and *d.*
   John 1:14
came and saw where he *d.* 39
they *d.* as strangers. *Acts* 13:17*
good report of all that *d.* 22:12
Paul *d.* two years in his own. 28:30
tormented them that *d.* *Rev* 11:10

dwelt *at*
and Abraham *d. at* Beer-sheba.
   Gen 22:19
Amorites which *d. at* Heshbon.
   Num 21:34; *Deut* 3:2
Abimelech *d. at* Arumah. *Judg* 9:41
Ben-hadad *d. at* Damascus.
   1 Ki 15:18; *2 Chr* 16:2
Sennacherib *d. at* Nineveh.
   2 Ki 19:36; *Isa* 37:37
of the scribes which *d. at. 1 Chr* 2:55
of Levites *d. at* Jerusalem. 9:34
Saul confounded Jews that *d. at.*
   Acts 9:22
Peter came to saints who *d. at.* 32

dwelt *in*
we have *d. in* Egypt. *Num* 20:15
Israel *d. in* the land of the. 21:31
d. in their stead. *Deut* 2:12, 21, 22
   23; *1 Chr* 5:22
good will of him that *d. in. Deut* 33:16
way of them that *d. in. Judg* 8:11
Jerubbaal went and *d. in* his. 29
and Samuel *d. in.* *1 Sam* 19:18
Philistines came and *d. in* them.
   31:7; *1 Chr* 10:7
I have not *d. in* any house since I
brought. *2 Sam* 7:6; *1 Chr* 17:5
that *d. in* house of Ziba. *2 Sam* 9:12
Absalom *d.* two full years in. 14:28
Shimei *d. in* Jerusalem. *1 Ki* 2:28
Jeroboam fled from Solomon, *d. in*
Egypt. 12:2
Israel *d. in* their tents. *2 Ki* 13:5
Ahaziah *d. in* a. 15:5; *2 Chr* 26:21
Huldah the prophetess *d. in* Jerusa-
lem. *2 Ki* 22:14; *2 Chr* 34:22
and *d. in* their rooms. *1 Chr* 4:41
Hagarites fell, and they *d. in.* 5:10
chief men *d. in* Jerusalem. 8:28

and David d. in the castle. *1 Chr 11:7*
2 Sam 5:9
priests, Levites, and Nethinims, d.
in. *Ezra 2:70; Neh 3:26; 11:21*
Nethinims and all Israel d. in their.
Neh 7:73
honourable men d. in it. *Job 22:8*
my soul had almost d. in. *Ps 94:17*
nor shall it be d. in from generation.
Isa 13:20; Jer 50:39
but we have d. in tents. *Jer 35:10*
they d. in the habitation. *41:17*
Israel d. in their own. *Ezek 36:17*
when d. safely in their land. *39:26*
fowls of the heaven d. in. *Dan 4:12*
Joseph d. in a city called. *Mat 2:23*
Jesus d. in Capernaum. *4:13*
sinners above all d. in. *Luke 13:4*
Abraham d. in Charran. *Acts 7:2, 4*
all they who d. in Asia heard. *19:10*
faith which d. first in thy grandmother
Lois. *2 Tim 1:5*

dwelt therein
gave Gilead to Machir, he d. therein.
Num 32:40
Enims d. therein. *Deut 2:10*
giants d. therein in old time. *20*
Damascus and d. therein. *1 Ki 11:24*
built Shechem, and d. therein. *12:25*
there d. men of Tyre also therein.
Neh 13:16
thy congregation hath d. therein.
Ps 68:10

dwelt with
and Ruth d. with her. *Ruth 2:23*
and mother d. with. *1 Sam 22:4*
there they d. with king. *1 Chr 4:23*
d. with their brethren. *8:32; 9:38*
my soul hath long d. with. *Ps 120:6*
Jeremiah d. with him. *Jer 40:6*

dyed
rams' skins d. red. *Ex 25:5; 26:14*
35:7; 36:19; 39:34
cometh with d. garments. *Isa 63:1*
exceeding in d. attire. *Ezek 23:15*

dying
be consumed with d.? *Num 17:13**
the first, d. left no seed. *Mark 12:20*
Jairus' daughter lay a d. *Luke 8:42*
bearing in body the d. of. *2 Cor 4:10*
as d. and behold we live. *6:9*
by faith, Jacob when d. *Heb 11:21*

E

each
Abram laid e. piece. *Gen 15:10*
Simeon and Levi took e. *34:25*
e. man his dream. *40:5*
e. changes of raiment. *45:22*
asked e. other of their. *Ex 18:7*
of e. there be a like weight. *30:34*
e. one was for house of. *Num 1:44*
they brought for e. one an ox. *7:3*
thou also and Aaron e. of you. *16:17*
of e. chief house a prince, e. one.
Josh 22:14
e. one resembled children. *Judg 8:18*
we reserved not to e. man. *21:22*
they may find rest e. of you. *Ruth 1:9*
e. man his month in year. *1 Ki 4:7*
and the kings e. sat on. *22:10*
exacted of e. man fifty. *2 Ki 15:20*
and peace kissed e. other. *Ps 85:10*
they made e. one for. *Isa 2:20*
stood the seraphims, e. one. *6:2*
where e. lay, shall be grass. *35:7*
e. one walking in uprightness. *57:2*
appointed thee e. day for. *Ezek 4:6*
doth not e. on sabbath. *Luke 13:15*
cloven tongues sat upon e. *Acts 2:3*
let e. esteem other better. *Phil 2:3*
charity toward e. other. *2 Thes 1:3*
four beasts had e. of them. *Rev 4:8*

eagle
At least eight distinct kinds of
eagles and vultures have been observed in Palestine. The Hebrew
word nesher is used almost entirely
in the Bible for eagle, and it is
impossible to determine exactly
which is intended. Most probably
it is the general term for any eagle,

as it merely means a tearer with
the beak.
Most frequently in the Bible the
reference is to some characteristic
of the eagle, and is made as a vivid
expression of some quality in that
which is compared to it. Among
these are its swiftness of flight,
Deut 28:49; Pr 23:5; its strength
of wing, Pr 30:19; Ezek 17:3; its
eating of carrion, Mat 24:28 (this is
true only of the vultures); the building of its nest high on the mountain cliff, Jer 49:16; the baldness
of one variety, Mi 1:16. There is
also reference to the ancient belief
that at the end of a certain period
the eagle moults and by some unknown means renews its youth,
Ps 103:5; probably derived from
the extreme length of the eagle's
vigorous life. The custom of
carrying its young from the inac-
cessible cliffs on its broad wings is
also made a symbol for the deliverance of the Israelites, Ex 19:4.
have e. in abomination. *Lev 11:13*
Deut 14:12
a nation as swift as e. *Deut 28:49*
as an e. stirreth up her nest. *32:11*
as the e. that hasteth. *Job 9:26*
doth the e. mount up at thy? *39:27*
riches fly away as an e. *Pr 23:5*
the way of an e. in the air. *30:19*
fly as an e. over Moab. *Jer 48:40*
make thy nest high as e. *49:16*
four also had the face of an e.
Ezek 1:10; 10:14
a great e. with great wings. *17:3, 7*
grown like e. feathers. *Dan 4:33*
like a lion, and had e. wings. *7:4*
as an e. against the house. *Hos 8:1*
though thou exalt thyself as e. *Ob 4*
enlarge thy baldness as e. *Mi 1:16*
Chaldeans shall fly as e. *Hab 1:8*
beast was like a flying e. *Rev 4:7*
were given wings of great e. *12:14*

eagles
I bare you on e'. wings. *Ex 19:4*
were swifter than e. *2 Sam 1:23*
thy youth is renewed like e. *Ps 103:5*
and the young e. shall. *Pr 30:17*
mount up with wings as e. *Isa 40:31*
horses are swifter than e. *Jer 4:13*
persecutors swifter than e. *Lam 4:19*
there will be gathered. *Mat 24:28*
Luke 17:37

ear
(The use of the word ear in the
Bible is used most often as attention, hearing, etc., rather than of
the actual physical ear. To have
the ears heavy is to pay no attention; to open the ear is to pay
attention: uncircumcised ears are
those which are deaf to the word
of God. To tell something in the
ear, is to speak in secret)
master shall bore his e. *Ex 21:6*
Deut 15:17
hath told Samuel in e. *1 Sam 9:15**
bow down thine e. *1 Ki 19:16*
Ps 31:2; 86:1
let thine e. be attentive. *Neh 1:6, 11*
mine e. received a little. *Job 4:12*
doth not the e. try? *12:11; 34:3*
mine e. hath heard and. *13:1*
when the e. heard me. *29:11*
to me men gave e. waited. *21*
behold, I gave e. to. *32:11**
he openeth also their e. *36:10*
of thee by hearing of the e. *42:5*
wilt cause thine e. to hear. *Ps 10:17*
bow down thine e. to me. *31:2*
deaf adder, that stoppeth her e. *58:4*
unto God, and he gave e. *77:1*
he that planted the e. *94:9*
because he hath inclined e. *116:2*
and bow thine e. to my. *Pr 5:1*
nor inclined my e. to them. *13*
the e. that heareth the. *15:31*
and a liar giveth e. to a. *17:4*
e. of the wise seeketh. *18:15*

hearing e. the seeing eye. *Pr 20:12*
bow thine e. hear the words. *22:17*
a wise reprover on obedient e. *25:12*
that turneth away his e. from. *28:9*
nor is the e. filled. *Eccl 1:8*
thine e. was not opened. *Isa 48:8*
he wakeneth my e. to hear. *50:4*
Lord hath opened mine e. *5*
nor is his e. heavy that it. *59:1*
not heard, nor perceived by e. *64:4*
behold, their e. is. *Jer 6:10*
not, nor inclined e. *7:24, 26; 11:8*
17:23; 25:4; 34:14; 44:5
let your e. receive the word. *9:20*
ye have not inclined your e. *35:15*
hide not thine e. at my. *Lam 3:56*
from lion a piece of an e. *Amos 3:12*
what ye hear in the e. *Mat 10:27*
smote off his e. *26:51; Mark 14:47*
ye have spoken in e. *Luke 12:3*
and he touched his e. *22:51*
servant, whose e. Peter. *John 18:26*
not seen, nor e. heard. *1 Cor 2:9*
if e. shall say, because I am. *12:16*
he that hath an e. let. *Rev 2:7, 11*
17, 29; 3:6, 13, 22; 13:9

give ear
if wilt give e. to his. *Ex 15:26*
Lord would not hearken nor give e.
Deut 1:45; 2 Chr 24:19; Neh 9:30
give e. O heavens. *Deut 32:1*
O ye kings, give e. O. *Judg 5:3*
give e. to me, ye that. *Job 34:2*
give e. to my words. *Ps 5:1; 54:2*
give e. unto my prayer. *17:1; 55:1*
86:6
give e. to my cry. *39:12; 141:1*
give e. all ye inhabitants. *49:1*
give e. O my people. *78:1*
give e. shepherd. *80:1*
hear my prayer, give e. *84:8*
give e. to my supplications. *143:1*
give e. O earth, for the. *Isa 1:2*
give e. to law of our God. *10*
give e. all ye of far countries. *8:9*
give ye e. and hear my voice. *28:23*
careless daughters, give e. to. *32:9*
who among you will give e.? *42:23*
hearken and give e. to me. *51:4*
give e. be not proud. *Jer 13:15*
and give ye e. O house of. *Hos 5:1*
give e. all ye inhabitants. *Joel 1:2*

incline ear
incline thine e. to me. *Ps 17:6*
71:2; 88:2; Isa 37:17; Dan 9:18
consider, and incline thine e. *Ps45:10*
I will incline mine e. to a. *49:4*
thou incline thine e. to. *Pr 2:2*
my son, incline thine e. *4:20*
incline your e. and come. *Isa 55:3*

right ear
upon tip of right e. of. *Ex 29:20*
Lev 8:23, 24; 14:14, 17, 25, 28
one cut off his right e. *Luke 22:50*
John 18:10

ear, grain
for barley was in the e. *Ex 9:31*
e. the full corn in the e. *Mark 4:28*

ear, verb
(An old word for plow or till)
king will set them to e. *1 Sam 8:12**
oxen that e. the ground. *Isa 30:24**

eared
rough valley neither e. *Deut 21:4**

earing
neither e. nor harvest. *Gen 45:6**
in e. time and harvest. *Ex 34:21**

early
ye shall rise e. and go. *Gen 19:2*
fearful, let him depart e. *Judg 7:3*
to-morrow get you e. on your. *19:9*
man of God was risen e. *2 Ki 6:15*
help her, and that right e. *Ps 46:5*
myself will awake e. *57:8; 108:2*
my God, e. will I seek thee. *63:1†*
and enquired e. after God. *78:34*
O satisfy us e. with thy. *90:14*
I will e. destroy all the. *101:8*
they shall seek me e. *Pr 1:28**
those that seek me e. shall. *8:17**
let us get up e. to the. *S of S 7:12*
will I seek thee e. *Isa 26:9†*

in affliction seek me e.   Hos 5:15*
and as the e. dew it.   6:4; 13:3
women who were e. at.   Luke 24:22
Jesus to hall, it was e.   John 18:28
cometh Mary Magdalene e.   20:1
receive the e. and latter.   Jas 5:7
see **arose, rise, risen, rising, rose, morning**

earnest
(*The word used as a noun means a pledge : as an adjective or adverb, eager, sincere, serious, etc.*)
e. expectation of the.   Rom 8:19
hath given the e. of the Spirit.
   2 Cor 1:22; 5:5
he told us your e. desire.   7:7*
put same e. care into Titus.   8:16
the e. of our inheritance.   Eph 1:14
e. expectation and hope.   Phil 1:20
ought to give the more e.   Heb 2:1

earnestly
did I not e. send to?   Num 22:37
David e. asked leave of me.
   1 Sam 20:6, 28
Baruch e. repaired the.   Neh 3:20
as a servant e. desireth.   Job 7:2
for I e. protested to.   Jer 11:7
I do e. remember him still.   31:20
do evil with both hands e.   Mi 7:3*
agony prayed more e.   Luke 22:44
but a certain maid e. looked.   56*
why look ye so e. on us?   Acts 3:12*
Paul e. beholding council.   23:1*
but covet e. best gifts.   1 Cor 12:31
in this we groan, e.   2 Cor 5:2*
Elias prayed e. that.   Jas 5:17*
that ye should e. contend.   Jude 3

earneth
he that e. wages, e. to.   Hag 1:6

earring
the man took a golden e.   Gen 24:22*
when Laban saw e. and.   30
I put the e. upon her face.   47*
gave Job an e. of gold.   Job 42:11*
as an e. of gold.   Pr 25:12

earrings
gave to Jacob all their e.   Gen 35:4*
break off the golden e.   Ex 32:2*
brought e. for their offerings.   35:22
we have brought e. to.   Num 31:50
give every man the e.   Judg 8:24
Lord will take away e.   Isa 3:20*
I put e. in thine ears.   Ezek 16:12
decked herself with her e.   Hos 2:13

ears
a word in my lord's e.   Gen 44:18
in the e. of Pharaoh.   50:4
tell it in e. of thy son.   Ex 10:2
rehearse it in e. of Joshua.   17:14
for ye have wept in e.   Num 11:18
Moses spake in the e.   Deut 31:30
declare cause in the e. of.   Josh 20:4
in the e. of the men of.   Judg 9:2, 3
the e. of every one that heareth shall.
   1 Sam 3:11; 2 Ki 21:12; Jer 19:3
rehearseth them in e. of.   1 Sam 8:21
according to all we have heard with
  our e.   2 Sam 7:22; 1 Chr 17:20
cry did enter into his e.   2 Sam 22:7
sound is in his e. in.   Job 15:21
the fame thereof with our e.   28:22
he openeth the e. of men.   33:16
cry came even into his e.   Ps 18:6
and his e. are opened to.   34:15
we have heard with our e.   44:1
e. but hear not.   115:6; 135:17
whoso stoppeth his e. at.   Pr 21:13
speak not in the e. of a fool.   23:9
that taketh a dog by e.   26:17
after the hearing of his e.   Isa 11:3
the e. of them that hear.   32:3
that stoppeth his e. from.   33:15
e. of deaf shall be unstopped.   35:5
opening the e. but he heareth not.
   42:20
blind and deaf that have e.   43:8
go, and cry in the e. of.   Jer 2:2
people, which have e. and.   5:21
Zephaniah read in the e. of.   29:29
sit down and read it in our e.   36:15
Jehudi read it in the e. of.   21

come to governor's e.   Mat 28:14
put his fingers into his e.   Mark 7:33
straightway his e. were opened.   35
having e. hear ye not?   8:18
in heart and e. resist.   Acts 7:51
tidings came to the e. of.   11:22
strange things to our e.   17:20
hath given e. that they.   Rom 11:8
having itching e.   2 Tim 4:3
are entered into e. of Lord.   Jas 5:4
and his e. are open to.   1 Pet 3:12

ears to hear
not given you e. to hear.   Deut 29:4
they have e. to hear.   Ezek 12:2
he that hath e. to hear.   Mat 11:15
   13:9, 43; Mark 4:9, 23; 7:16
   Luke 8:8; 14:35

mine ears
spoken in mine e. I will.   Num 14:28
thou spakest of in mine e.   Judg 17:2
of sheep in mine e.?   1 Sam 15:14
tumult come into mine e.
   2 Ki 19:28; Isa 37:29
and mine e. attent to.   2 Chr 7:15
mine e. hast thou opened.   Ps 40:6
mine e. hear my desire of.   92:11
in mine e. said the Lord.   Isa 5:9
it was revealed in mine e.   22:14
cry in mine e. with loud.   Ezek 8:18
cried also in mine e. with loud.   9:1
thy salutation sounded in mine e.
   Luke 1:44

ears of the people
speak now in e. of the people.
   Ex 11:2
spake in e. of the people.   Deut 32:44
proclaim in the e. of the people.
   Judg 7:3
tidings in the e. of the people.
   1 Sam 11:4
talk not in the e. of the people.
   2 Ki 18:26; Isa 36:11
e. of the people were attentive.
   Neh 8:3
read in e. of the people.   Jer 28:7
   36:6, 10, 13, 14

their ears
these things in their e.   Gen 20:8
earrings which were in their e.   35:4
brake off earrings in their e.
   Ex 32:3
these words in their e.   Deut 31:28
read in their e.   2 Ki 23:2
   2 Chr 34:30; Jer 36:15
he openeth their e. in.   Job 36:15
make heart fat, their e. heavy, lest
  they hear with their e.   Isa 6:10
   Mat 13:15; Acts 28:27
their e. shall be deaf.   Mi 7:16
but they stopped their e.   Zech 7:11
   Acts 7:57
away their e. from truth.   2 Tim 4:4

thine ears
let thine e. be attent.   2 Chr 6:40
wilt cause thine e. to.   Ps 10:17
let thine e. be attentive to.   130:2
apply thine e. to words.   Pr 23:12
thine e. hear a word.   Isa 30:21
children say again in thine e.   49:20
that I speak in thine e.   Jer 28:7
and hear with thine e.   Ezek 3:10
   40:4; 44:5
earrings in thine e. and.   16:12
away thy nose and thine e.   23:25
thee to hear with thine e.   24:26

your ears
which I speak in your e.   Deut 5:1
declaration with your e.   Job 13:17
incline your e. to words.   Ps 78:1
have heard with your e.   Jer 26:11
sent me to speak in your e.   15
but blessed are your e.   Mat 13:16
scripture is fulfilled in your e.
   Luke 4:21
sayings sink down in your e.   9:44

ears
e. of corn came up.   Gen 41:5, 22
a meat offering green e.   Lev 2:14
not eat green e. till ye bring.   23:14
mayest pluck the e.   Deut 23:25
go and glean e. of corn.   Ruth 2:2
man of God full e. of.   2 Ki 4:42

wicked cut off as tops of e.   Job 24:24
as when one reapeth e.   Isa 17:5
an hungered, and began to pluck e.
   Mat 12:1; Mark 2:23; Luke 6:1
   see **seven**

earth
[1] The globe or planet which we inhabit, Gen 1:10; Ps 24:1. [2] The world in distinction from heaven or hell, John 3:31; Col 3:1, 2. [3] The people on the globe, Gen 11:1, Ps 96:1. [4] Certain parts of the earth—countries, Ezra 1:2; Rom 9:28. [5] The ground, in distinction from the water of the globe, Gen 4:11; Num 6:30. A man of the earth is taken as meaning a mortal, earthly-minded man, Ps 10:18.
e. was without form.   Gen 1:2
and God called the dry land e.   10
let e. bring forth grass.   11, 24
e. brought forth grass and herb.   12
be fruitful, replenish e. and. 28; 9:1
the e. also was corrupt before.   6:11
ark was lifted up above e.   7:17
in second month was the e.   8:14
while e. remaineth, seedtime.   22
covenant between me and e.   9:13
in his days was the e. divided.
   10:25; 1 Chr 1:19
nations of e. shall be blessed in.
   Gen 18:18; 22:18; 26:4; 28:14
give thee of fatness of the e.   27:28
in plenteous years e. brought.   41:47
the Lord in midst of the e.   Ex 8:22
know that e. is the Lord's.   9:29
   Deut 10:14; Ps 24:1; 1 Cor 10:26
one cannot be able to see e.   Ex 10:5
e. swallowed them.   15:12
an altar of e. thou shalt.   20:24
if e. open her mouth.   Num 16:30*
the e. opened. 32; 26:10; Ps 106:17
lest the e. swallow us up.   Num 16:34
above all nations of e.   Deut 28:1
e. under thee shall be iron.   23
O e. the words of my mouth.   32:1
ride on high places of e.   13
a fire shall consume the e.   22
for the pillars of the e.   1 Sam 2:8
so that the e. rang again.   4:5
trembled, and the e. quaked.   14:15
a man came out with e. upon his
  head.   2 Sam 1:2; 15:32
then e. shook and.   22:8; Ps 18:7
so that the e. rent.   1 Ki 1:40
two mules' burden of e.   2 Ki 5:17
and let the e. rejoice.   1 Chr 16:31
   Ps 96:11
because God cometh to judge the e.
   1 Chr 16:33; Ps 96:13; 98:9
of God of heaven and e.   Ezra 5:11
thou hast made the e.   Neh 9:6
   Isa 45:12
offspring as grass of e.   Job 5:25
which shaketh the e.   9:6
the e. is given into the hand of.   24
thereof is longer than the e.   11:9
waters and they overturn e.   12:15
to whom alone the e. was.   15:19*
O e. cover not thou my.   16:18
shall the e. be forsaken?   18:4
and the e. shall rise up.   20:27
as for mighty man, he had e.   22:8
the poor of the e. hide.   24:4
he hangeth the e. upon nothing. 26:7
to dwell in caves of the e.   30:6
they were viler than the e.   8*
him a charge over the e.?   34:13
when he quieteth the e. by.   37:17
I laid the foundations of e.   38:4
perceived breadth of the e.?   Ps 2:8
uttermost parts of the e.   8
be instructed, ye judges of e.   10
that the man of the e. may.   10:18
silver tried in a furnace of e.   12:6
his seed shall inherit the e.   25:13
e. is full of the goodness of.   33:5
looketh on all inhabitants of e.   14
those that wait upon the Lord shall
  inherit the e.   37:9*, 11*, 22*
not fear though e. be removed.   46:2
uttered his voice, e. melted.   6

for the shields of the *e*.   *Ps* 47:9
the joy of the whole *e*. is.   48:2
hast made *e*. to tremble.   60:2*
into lower parts of the *e*.   63:9
in uttermost parts of the *e*.   65:8
thou visitest tne *e*. and waterest.   9
then shall *e*. yield her increase. 67:5
    Ezek 34:27
the *e*. shook, the heavens.   *Ps* 68:8
sing unto God, ye kingdoms of *e*. 32
up from depths of the *e*.   71:20
as showers that water the *e*.   72:6
tongue walketh through *e*.   73:9
the *e*. and all the inhabitants are
  dissolved.   75:3; *Isa* 24:19
wicked of *e*. shall wring.   *Ps* 75:8
the *e*. feared.   76:8
God arose to save meek of *e*.   9
the *e*. trembled.   77:18; 97:4
like *e*. which he hath.   78:69
O God, judge the *e*. thou.   82:8
ever thou hadst formed the *e*. 90:2
Lord reigneth, let *e*. rejoice.   97:1
Lord reigneth, let the *e*. be.   99:1
thou laid foundation of the *e*. 102:25
   104:5; *Pr* 8:29; *Isa* 48:13
the *e*. is satisfied with fruit. *Ps* 104:13
the *e*. is full of thy riches.   24
tremble, O *e*. at presence.   114:7
e. hath he given to the.   115:16
the *e*. O Lord, is full of.   119:64
thou hast established the *e*.   90
prepareth rain for the *e*.   147:8
his glory is above the *e*.   148:13
Lord hath founded the *e*.   *Pr* 3:19
    Isa 24:1
from everlasting, or ever *e*. *Pr* 8:23
had not made the *e*. nor fields. 26
e. for depth and heart of.   25:3
the *e*. that is not filled.   30:16
for three things the *e*. is.   21
the *e*. abideth for ever.   *Eccl* 1:4
the profit of the *e*. is for all.   5:9
the fruit of the *e*. shall be. *Isa* 4:2*
that smiteth the *e*. with rod.   11:4
e. shall be full of the knowledge. 9
the *e*. shall remove out of.   13:13
man that made the *e*. to ?   14:16
the *e*. mourneth and.   24:4; 33:9
the *e*. is defiled under the.   24:5
e. is utterly broken down, *e*.   19
e. shall reel.   20
e. shall cast out the dead.   26:19
the *e*. also shall disclose.   21
let the *e*. hear, and all.   34:1
sitteth on circle of the *e*.   40:22
the Creator of ends of the *e*.
that spread abroad the *e*.   44:24
let the *e*. open.   45:8
I have made the *e*.   12
be ye saved, all the ends of the *e*. 22
and be joyful, O *e*.   49:13
look on the *e*. the *e*. shall.   51:6
saith the Lord, the *e*. is my.   66:1
shall the *e*. be made to bring ?   8*
I beheld the *e*. it was.   *Jer* 4:23
for this shall the *e*. mourn.   28
hear, O *e*. I will bring evil.
at his wrath the *e*. shall.   10:10
O *e*. *e*. *e*. hear word of Lord, write.
   22:29; *Mi* 1:2
go up and cover the *e*.   *Jer* 46:8
the *e*. is moved at.   49:21; 50:46
made the *e*. by his power.   51:15
give it to wicked of the *e*. *Ezek* 7:21
the Lord hath forsaken the.   9:9
and the *e*. shined with his.   43:2
the *e*. shall hear the corn. *Hos* 2:22
e. shall quake before.   *Joel* 2:10
darken *e*. in clear day.   *Amos* 8:9
the *e*. with her bars.   *Jonah* 2:6
strong foundations of *e*.   *Mi* 6:2
move out like worms of *e*.   7:17
the *e*. is burnt up at.   *Nah* 1:5
e. filled with knowledge. *Hab* 2:14
the *e*. was full of his praise.   3:3
didst cleave the *e*. with rivers.   9
the *e*. is stayed from.   *Hag* 1:10
sent to walk to and fro through the *e*.
   Zech 1:10; 6:7
eyes of Lord run through *e*.   4:10
smite the *e*. with a curse.   *Mal* 4:6
for they shall inherit *e*.   *Mat* 5:5
swear not by the *e*. it is God's.   35

had not much *e*.   *Mat* 13:5
    Mark 4:5
for the *e*. bringeth forth. *Mark* 4:28
he that is of the *e*. is earthly, and
  speaketh of the *e*.   *John* 3:31
first man is of the *e*.   *1 Cor* 15:47
vessels of wood and of *e*. *2 Tim* 2:20
the *e*. which drinketh in. *Heb* 6:7*
voice then shook the *e*. but.   12:26
for precious fruit of *e*.   *Jas* 5:7
the *e*. brought forth her fruit.   18
the *e*. and works therein. *2 Pet* 3:10
hurt not the *e*. nor sea.   *Rev* 7:3
trees before the God of the *e*.   11:4
have power to smite the *e*. with.   6
the *e*. opened and swallowed. 12:16
causeth the *e*. to worship.   13:12
and the *e*. was lightened.   18:1
whore, which did corrupt *e*.   19:2
from whose face *e*. fled away. 20:11
see **beasts, dust, ends, face,**
  heaven, kings, people, whole

all the **earth**

dominion over *all the e*.   *Gen* 1:26
seed alive on face of *all the e*.   7:3
confound language of *all the e*. 11:9
not Judge of *all the e*. do ?   18:25
us after manner of *all the e*.   19:31
none like me in *all the e*.   *Ex* 9:14
my name declared through *all the e*.
    16; *Rom* 9:17
treasure; for *all the e*. is. *Ex* 19:5
not been done in *all the e*.   34:10
all the e. shall be filled. *Num* 14:21
the Lord of *all the e*.   *Josh* 3:11
    Zech 6:5
going way of *all the e*. *Josh* 23:14
    1 Ki 2:2
be dry on *all the e*. *Judg* 6:37*
all the e. may know. *1 Sam* 17:46
all the e. sought to. *1 Ki* 10:24
no God in *all the e*. but. *2 Ki* 5:15
judgements are in *all the e*.
   1 Chr 16:14; *Ps* 105:7
sing to the Lord, *all the e*.
   1 Chr 16:23; *Ps* 96:1
fear before him, *all the e*. *1 Chr* 16:30
   Ps 33:8; 96:9
thy name in *all the e*.   *Ps* 8:1, 9
make princes in *all the e*.   45:16
great king over *all the e*.   47:2
    Zech 14:9
let thy glory be above *all the e*.
   Ps 57:5, 11; 108:5
all the e. shall worship thee.   66:4
most high over *all the e*. 83:18; 97:9
make a joyful noise, *all the e*.   98:4
I gathered *all the e*.   *Isa* 10:14
excellent things, known in *all e*. 12:5
of his people, from *all the e*.   25:8
city a curse to *all the e*.   *Jer* 26:6
an honour before *all the e*.   33:9
golden cup that made *all the e*. 51:7
O mountain, destroyest *all the e*. 25
shall fall the slain of *all the e*.   49*
bear rule over *all the e*. *Dan* 2:39
let *all the e*. keep silence. *Hab* 2:20
all the e. be devoured. *Zeph* 3:8
all the e. sitteth still. *Zech* 1:11
darkness over *all the e*. *Luke* 23:44*
sound went into *all the e*. *Rom* 10:18
of God sent into *all the e*. *Rev* 5:6

from the **earth**

up a mist *from the e*.   *Gen* 2:6
cursed *from the e*.   4:11*
were destroyed *from the e*.   7:23
waters were abated *from the e*. 8:11
thou shalt be cut off *from the e*.
   Ex 9:15; *Josh* 7:9; *Ps* 109:15
   Pr 2:22; *Nah* 2:13
Saul arose *from the e*. *1 Sam* 28:23
shall I not take you away *from the*
  e.?   *2 Sam* 4:11
to raise him *from the e*.   12:17
David arose *from the e*.   20
shall perish *from the e*. *Job* 18:17
their fruit *from the e*. *Ps* 21:10
remembrance of them *from the e*.
    34:16
praise Lord *from the e*.   148:7
to devour poor *from the e*. *Pr* 30:14
shall perish *from the e*. *Jer* 10:11
were lifted up *from e*. *Ezek* 1:19, 21

it was lifted up *from the e*. *Dan* 7:4
up a snare *from the e*. *Amos* 3:5*
I be lifted up *from the e*. *John* 12:32
life is taken *from the e*. *Acts* 8:33
Saul arose *from the e*.   9:8
with such a fellow *from the e*. 22:22
to take peace *from the e*. *Rev* 6:4
were redeemed *from the e*.   14:3

in the **earth**

let fowl multiply *in the e*. *Gen* 1:22
a vagabond *in the e*.   4:12, 14
of man was great *in the e*.   6:5
Nimrod a mighty one *in the e*.   10:8
not a man *in the e*. to come.   19:31
you a posterity *in the e*.   45:7
that is *in the e*. beneath.   *Ex* 20:4
they are hid *in the e*. *Judg* 18:10
any thing that is *in the e*. *Judg* 18:10
like to name of the great men *in the*
  e.   *2 Sam* 7:9; *1 Chr* 17:8
what nation *in e*. like Israel ?
   2 Sam 7:23; *1 Chr* 17:21
all things that are *in the e*.
    2 Sam 14:20
all that is *in the e*. is. *1 Chr* 29:11
no God like thee *in the e*. *2 Chr* 6:14
to and fro *in the e*. *Job* 1:7; 2:2
none like him *in the e*.   1:8; 2:3
root thereof wax old *in the e*.   14:8
portion is cursed *in the e*.   24:18
leaveth her eggs *in the e*.   39:14
saints that are *in the e*.   *Ps* 16:3
what desolations *in the e*.   46:8
I will be exalted *in the e*.   10
God that judgeth *in the e*.   58:11
redeemed of corn *in the e*.   72:16
I am a stranger *in the e*.   119:19
speaker be established *in e*. 140:11
be recompensed *in the e*. *Pr* 11:31
judgements are *in the e*. *Isa* 26:9
not wrought deliverance *in the e*. 18
not take root *in the e*.   40:24
have set judgement *in the e*.   42:4
Jerusalem a praise *in the e*.   62:7
who blesseth himself *in the e*. and he
  that sweareth *in the e*.   65:16
thee, be written *in the e*. *Jer* 17:13
created a new thing *in the e*. 31:22
sow her unto me *in the e*. *Hos* 2:23
shew wonders *in the e*. *Joel* 2:30
off righteousness *in the e*. *Amos* 5:7
digged *in the e*. and hid. *Mat* 25:18
and hid thy talent *in the e*.   25
when it is sown *in the e*. less than
  all seeds *in the e*. *Mark* 4:31
three that bear witness *in the e*.
    1 John 5:8

on, or, upon the **earth**

had made man *on the e*. *Gen* 6:6
God looked *upon the e*. behold. 12
cause it to rain *upon the e*.   7:4
rain was *upon the e*. forty. 12, 17
and multiply *upon the e*.   8:17
sun was risen *upon the e*.   19:23
a ladder set *upon the e*.   28:12
day they were *upon the e*. *Ex* 10:6
things that creep *upon the e*.
   Lev 11:29, 42, 44
live *upon the e*. *Deut* 4:10; 12:1, 19
upon the e. he shewed thee his. 4:36
shall pour it *upon the e*. 12:16, 24
David lay *upon the e*. *2 Sam* 12:16
nor remainder *upon the e*.   14:7
but will God indeed dwell on the *e*.?
   1 Ki 8:27; *2 Chr* 6:18
sends rain *upon the e*. *1 Ki* 17:14
our days on *e*. as a. *1 Chr* 29:15
    Job 8:9
time to man *upon e*.?   *Job* 7:1
stand at latter day *upon the e*. 19:25
since man was placed on the *e*. 20:4
the snow, be thou on the *e*.   37:6
on *e*. there is not his like.   41:33
tread down my life on the *e*. *Ps* 7:5
he shall be blessed *upon the e*. 41:2
way may be known *upon the e*. 67:2
there is none *upon e*. I.   73:25
seed be mighty *upon the e*.   112:2
four things little *upon the e*. *Pr* 30:24
not a just man *upon the e*. *Eccl* 7:20
princes walking *upon the e*.   10:7
evil shall be done *upon e*.   11:2
empty themselves *upon the e*.   18:1
flowers appear *on the e*. *S of S* 2:12

determined *upon the e.* Isa 28:22
lift your eyes, look *upon the e.* 51:6
for truth *upon the e.* Jer 9:3*
liver is poured *upon the e.* Lam 2:11
not a man *on the e.* can. Dan 2:10
fall in snare *upon the e.* Amos 3:5
least grain fall *upon the e.* 9:9
not up treasures *upon e.* Mat 6:19
Son of man hath power *on e.* to. 9:6
Mark 2:10; Luke 5:24
come to send peace *on e.*
Mat. 10:34
thou shalt bind *on e.* 16:19; 18:18
two of you shall agree *on e.* 18:19
no man your father *upon the e.* 23:9
blood shed *upon the e.* 35
so as no fuller *on e.* can. Mark 9:3
glory to God, *on e.* Luke 2:14
that built a house *upon the e.* 6:49
come to send fire *on the e.* 12:49
come to give peace *on e.?* 51
shall he find faith *on e.?* 18:8
for things coming *on the e.* 21:26*
glorified thee *on the e.* John 17:4
short work will Lord make *on the e.*
Rom 9:28
not on things *on the e.* Col 3:2
mortify members *upon the e.* 5
if he were *on e.* he. Heb 8:4
they were strangers *on the e.* 11:13
refused him that spake *on e.* 12:25
lived in pleasure *on the e.* Jas 5:5
it rained not *on the e.* for. 17
that dwell *upon the e.* Rev 3:10
priests, we shall reign *on e.* 5:10
on them that dwell *on the e.* 6:10
wind should not blow *on the e.* 7:1
hail, and fire, cast *upon the e.* 8:7
which standeth *upon the e.* 10:8
dwell *on the e.* 11:10; 13:8, 14
14:6; 17:8
thrust in his sickle *on e.* 14:16
first poured out vial *upon the e.* 16:2
blood of all slain *upon the e.* 18:24

out of the **earth**
ascending *out of the e.* 1 Sam 28:13
springing *out of the e.* 2 Sam 23:4
and *out of the e.* shall. Job 8:19
iron is taken *out of the e.* 28:2
as for the *e. out of* it cometh. 5
shall spring *out of the e.* Ps 85:11
bring food *out of the e.* 104:14
be consumed *out of the e.* 35
kings, arise *out of the e.* Dan 7:17
break battle *out of the e.* Hos 2:18
man perished *out of the e.* Mi 7:2
coming up *out of the e.* Rev 13:11

to, or, *unto the* **earth**
bowing himself *to the e.* Gen 24:52
bow down to thee, *to the e.* 37:10
bowed *to the e.* 42:6; 43:26
bowed with his face *to the e.* 48:12
Joshua fell on his face *to the e.*
Josh 5:14; 7:6
Dagon fallen on his face *to the e.*
1 Sam 5:3*
Goliath fell on face *to the e.* 17:49
David stooped face *to the e.* 24:8
she bowed herself *to the e.* 25:41
1 Ki 1:31
me smite him, *to the e.* 1 Sam 26:8
not my blood fall *to the e.* 20
to David he fell *to the e.* 2 Sam 1:2
not one hair shall fall *to the e.*
14:11; 1 Ki 1:52
fall *to the e.* nothing. 2 Ki 10:10
bodies fallen *to the e.* 2 Chr 20:24
or speak *to the e.* Job 12:8
bowing down *to the e.* Ps 17:11
belly cleaveth *unto the e.* 44:25
he shall call *to the e.* that. 50:4
he returneth *to the e.* 146:4
beast that goeth *to the e.* Eccl 3:21
then shall dust return *to the e.* 12:7
they shall look *unto the e.* Isa 8:22
bring down strength *to the e.* 63:6
of contention *to the e.* Jer 15:10
and former rain *to the e.* Hos 6:3
their faces *to the e.* Luke 24:5
Saul fell *to the e.* and. Acts 9:4
great sheet, let down *to the e.* 10:11
we were all fallen *to the e.* 26:14
of heaven fell *to the e.* Rev 6:13

did not cast them *to the e.* Rev 12:4
saw he was cast *unto the e.* 13

earthen
the *e.* vessel wherein it. Lev 6:28
the *e.* vessel whereinto. 11:33
of birds killed in *e.* vessel. 14:5, 50
holy water in *e.* vessel. Num 5:17
brought beds, and *e.* 2 Sam 17:28
and get a potter's *e.* bottle. Jer 19:1
put evidences in an *e.* vessel. 32:14
esteemed as *e.* pitchers. Lam 4:2
treasure in *e.* vessels. 2 Cor 4:7

earthly
if I have told you *e.* John 3:12
he that is of the earth is *e.* 31
if our *e.* house of. 2 Cor 5:1
walk, who mind *e.* things. Phil 3:19
this wisdom is *e.,* sensual. Jas 3:15

earthquake
*The scripture speaks of several
earthquakes. One of the most remarkable occurred in the twenty-
seventh year of Uzziah, king of
Judah,* Zech 14:5.
*Another very memorable earth-
quake, was that at the time of our
Saviour's crucifixion,* Mat 27:51.
*Great alterations and changes are
expressed in scripture by a shaking
of the earth,* Heb 12:26. *The delivering of the Israelites out of
Egypt is called a moving, or shaking,
of the earth,* Ps 68:8. *And an
extraordinary and unexpected alteration in the state of affairs, civil
or ecclesiastical, is represented by
a great earthquake,* Rev 6:12 and
16:18.
an *e.* Lord was not in a. 1 Ki 19:11
after the *e.* a fire, Lord was not. 12
visited of the Lord with *e.* Isa 29:6
saw two years before *e.* Amos 1:1
ye fled from before the *e.* Zech 14:5
when centurion saw the *e.* Mat 27:54
there was a great *e.,* the angel. 28:2
Acts 16:26; Rev 6:12; 11:13
thunderings and an *e.* Rev 8:5; 11:19
a great *e.* so mighty an *e.* 16:18

earthquakes
and *e.* in divers places. Mat 24:7
Mark 13:8; Luke 21:11

earthy
first man is of earth, *e.* 1 Cor 15:47
e. such are they also that are *e.* 48
have borne the image of the *e.* 49

ease
nations shalt find no *e.* Deut 28:65
trod the Benjamites down with *e.*
Judg 20:43*
in thought of him at *e.* Job 12:5
I was at *e.* 16:12
dieth, being wholly at *e.* 21:23
his soul shall dwell at *e.* Ps 25:13
with scorning of those at *e.* 123:4
ye women that are at *e.* Isa 32:9
tremble, ye women that are at *e.* 11
Jacob shall return, be in rest, at *e.*
Jer 46:27
Moab hath been at *e.* from. 48:11
of a multitude being at *e.* Ezek 23:42
woe to them that are at *e.* Amos 6:1
with heathen at *e.* Zech 1:15
take thine *e.* eat, drink. Luke 12:19

ease, *verb*
when thou *e.* thyself. Deut 23:13*
e. thou somewhat the. 2 Chr 10:4, 9
my couch *e.* my complaint. Job 7:13
ah, I will *e.* me of mine. Isa 1:24

eased
I forbear, what am I *e.?* Job 16:6
that other men be *e.* and. 2 Cor 8:13

easier
so shall it be *e.* for. Ex 18:22
e. to say, thy sins be forgiven, or to.
Mat 9:5; Mark 2:9; Luke 5:23
e. for a camel to go. Mat 19:24
Mark 10:25; Luke 18:25
it is *e.* for heaven and. Luke 16:17

easily
charity is not *e.* provoked. 1 Cor 13:5
sin which doth so *e.* beset. Heb 12:1

east
*(The Hebrews express the east,
west, north, and south, by words
which signify, before, behind, left,
and right, according to the position
of a man with his face turned towards the east. The term Kedem
(before or east), as generally used,
refers to the lands directly east of
Palestine : Arabia, Mesopotamia,
and Babylon. Another term, Miz-
rach, used of far east, has no definite
signification)*
God placed at the *e.* of. Gen 3:24
removed to a mountain on *e.* 12:8
Lot chose plain, journeyed *e.* 13:11
abroad to the west and *e.* 28:14
into land of people of the *e.* 29:1
that encamp toward *e.* Num 3:38
Balak hath brought me out of *e.* 23:7
the children of the *e.* came. Judg 6:3
33; 7:12; 8:10; 1 Ki 4:30
three looking toward *e.* 1 Ki 7:25
2 Chr 4:4
porters towards the *e.* 1 Chr 9:24
to flight them toward the *e.* 12:15
greatest of all men of *e.* Job 1:3
cometh not from *e.* nor. Ps 75:6
as far as *e.* is from west. 103:12
gathered them from the *e.* 107:3
be replenished from *e.* Isa 2:6
spoil them of *e.* 11:14; Jer 49:28
righteous man from the *e.* Isa 41:2
thy seed from the *e.* 43:5; Zech 8:7
ravenous bird from the *e.* Isa 46:11
their faces towards *e.* Ezek 8:16
deliver thee to men of *e.* 25:4, 10
to gate which looketh toward *e.*
40:6, 22; 43:1; 44:1; 46:1, 12
of God came from way of *e.* 43:2
waters issue out toward the *e.* 47:8
toward the *e.* ten thousand. 48:10
suburbs of city toward the *e.* 17
waxed great toward *e.* Dan 8:9
tidings out of the *e.* shall. 11:44
drive him toward *e.* sea. Joel 2:20
wander from north to *e.* Amos 8:12
mount cleave toward *e.* Zech 14:4
came wise men from *e.* Mat 2:1
we have seen star in the *e.* 2, 9
come from *e.* and. 8:11; Luke 13:29
lightning cometh out of *e.* Mat 24:27
angel ascending from *e.* Rev 7:2*
the way of kings of *e.* 16:12*
on the *e.* three gates, on the. 21:13

east border
point out *e.* border. Num 34:10
in *e.* border of Jericho. Josh 4:19
e. border was the salt sea. 15:5
west border to *e.* border. Ezek 45:7
oblation toward *e.* border. 48:21

Easter
*(The Passover. The name Easter
was given later to the Christian
celebration of this season)*
intending after *E.* to. Acts 12:4

east gate
the keeper of the *e.* gate. Neh 3:29
by entry of the *e.* gate. Jer 19:2*
stood at door of *e.* gate. Ezek 10:19
Spirit brought me unto *e.* gate. 11:1

east side
of court on the *e.-side.* Ex 27:13
and on the *e.-side* shall. Num 2:3
Ai, on *e.-side* of Beth-el. Josh 7:2
of inheritance on the *e.-side.* 16:5
came by *e.-side* of land. Judg 11:18
mountain on the *e.-side.* Ezek 11:23
he measured the *e.-side* with. 42:16
from the *e.-side* even unto the. 48:2
3, 4, 5, 6, 7, 8, 23, 24, 25, 26, 27
Jonah sat on the *e.-side.* Jonah 4:5

eastward
lift up thine eyes *e.* and. Gen 13:14
Deut 3:27
open the window *e.* and. 2 Ki 13:17
e. were six Levites. 1 Chr 26:17
with line went forth *e.* Ezek 47:3

east wind
blasted with the *e.* wind. Gen 41:6
23, 27

Lord brought an *e.-wind.* *Ex* 10:13
14:21
fill his belly with *e.-wind.* *Job* 15:2
e.-wind carrieth him away. 27:21
which scattereth *e.-wind.* 38:24
ships with an *e.-wind.* *Ps* 48:7
caused an *e.-wind* to blow. 78:26
wind in day of *e.-wind.* *Isa* 27:8
scatter them as with an *e.-wind.*
Jer 18:17
wither when the *e.-wind.* *Ezek* 17:10
and the *e.-wind* drieth up. 19:12
the *e.-wind* hath broken. 27:26
followeth after *e.-wind.* *Hos* 12:1
he be fruitful, an *e.-wind.* 13:15
a vehement *e.-wind.* *Jonah* 4:8
faces sup up as the *e.-wind.* *Hab* 1:9

easy

knowledge is *e.* to him. *Pr* 14:6
my yoke is *e.* my burden. *Mat* 11:30
except ye utter words *e.* *1 Cor* 14:9
wisdom from above is *e.* *Jas* 3:17

eat

*The word is used in Scripture as
we use it and its synonyms devour,
consume, etc., both literally and
figuratively.* [1] *To chew and
swallow food,* Gen 27:4. [2] *To
waste, consume,* Eccl 5:11. [3]
To oppress and destroy, Ps 14:4.
[4] *To have close union with Christ,
symbolized by eating his flesh,*
John 6:56. [5] *To read closely and
attentively, as we say devour a
book,* Jer 15:16.

*Eating with a person, in the East,
is regarded almost as making a
covenant of friendship which must
not be broken ; hence the scandal
to the Jews of Jesus' eating with
publicans and sinners,* Mat 9:11;
*and the special sin of the betrayal
by Judas, who had so often eaten
with his Master.*

of every tree freely *e.* *Gen* 2:16
in the day ye *e.* your eyes. 3:5
Eve took and did *e.* 6
and I did *e.* 12, 13
dust shalt thou *e.* all days. 14
in sorrow shalt thou *e.* of it all. 17
by angels, they did *e.* 18:8; 19:3
bring it to me, that I may *e.* 27:4
and they did *e.* there upon. 31:46
the birds did *e.* them out. 40:17
Egyptians did *e.* by themselves.
43:32
locusts shall *e.* every. *Ex* 10:5
the locusts may *e.* every herb. 12
with bitter herbs they shall *e.* it. 12:8
save that which every man *e.* 16
shall no stranger *e.* 43, 48; *Lev* 22:13
circumcised, then shall he *e.*
Ex 12:44
e. that to-day, for to-day is. 16:25
children of Israel did *e.* manna forty.
35; *John* 6:31, 49, 58
poor of thy people may *e.* *Ex* 23:11
Aaron and sons shall *e.* 29:32
Lev 6:16; 8:31
thou *e.* of his sacrifice. *Ex* 34:15
males shall *e.* it. *Lev* 6:18, 29; 7:6
Num 18:10
priest that offereth it *e.* it. *Lev* 6:26
all that be clean *e.* 7:19; *Num* 18:11
shall in no wise *e.* of it. *Lev* 7:24
e. of it without leaven. 10:12
yet these ye may *e.* 11:21, 22
Deut 14:20
Aaron and his sons shall *e.* *Lev* 24:9
what shall we *e.* the seventh. 25:20
your enemies shall *e.* it. 26:16
remember fish we did *e.* *Num* 11:5
give us flesh, that we may *e.* 13
shall not lie down till he *e.* 23:24
the people eat of their. 25:2
buy meat of them that ye may *e.*
Deut 2:6
e. in gates. 12:15, 21; 15:22; 26:12
unclean and clean may *e.* 12:15, 22
15:22
e. before Lord. 12:18; 14:26; 15:20
I will *e.* flesh, thou mayest *e.* 12:20
give it to stranger that he *e.* 14:21

and another man *e.* of it. *Deut* 20:6*
then thou mayest *e.* grapes. 23:24
gather grapes, worms shall *e.* 28:39
e. fruit of own body. 53; *Lam* 2:20
which did *e.* the fat of. *Deut* 32:38
did *e.* of the old corn. *Josh* 5:11
vineyards ye planted not ye *e.* 24:13
they tarried, and did *e.* *Judg* 19:8
Hannah did *e.* and was. *1 Sam* 1:18
and afterwards they *e.* 9:13
and *e.* and sin not against. 14:34
Jonathan did *e.* no meat. 20:34
and *e.* that thou mayest have. 28:22
he shall *e.* at my table. *2 Sam* 9:1
1 Ki 2:7
of Jeroboam shall dogs *e.* *1 Ki* 14:11
16:4; 21:23; *2 Ki* 9:10, 36
that we may *e.* and die. *1 Ki* 17:12
angel said, arise and *e.* 19:5
Acts 10:13; 11:7
they shall *e.* and leave. *2 Ki* 4:43
they did *e.* and left thereof. 44
give thy son that we may *e.* him to-
day, and we will *e.* my son. 6:28
we boiled my son, and did *e.* 29
ye *e.* every man of. 18:31; *Isa* 36:16
yet did they *e.* passover. *2 Chr* 30:18
children of Israel did *e.* *Ezra* 6:21
take corn, that we may *e.* *Neh* 5:2
so they shall *e.* and. 9:25; *Ps* 78:29
sighing cometh before I *e.* *Job* 3:24
let me sow, and let another *e.* 31:8
the meek shall *e.* and. *Ps* 22:26
they that be fat on earth shall *e.* 29
will I *e.* the flesh of bulls. 50:13
man did *e.* angels' food. 78:25
shalt *e.* the labour of thine. 128:2
e. the fruit of own way. *Pr* 1:31
Isa 3:10
soul of transgressors shall *e.* *Pr* 13:2
they that love it shall *e.* 18:21
my son, *e.* thou honey. 24:13
whoso keepeth fig-tree shall *e.* 27:18
and young eagles shall *e.* it. 30:17
for who can *e.* or hasten ? *Eccl* 2:25
they are increased that *e.* 5:11
sleep is sweet, whether he *e.* 12
princes *e.* in the morning. 10:16
blessed, when thy princes *e.* in. 17
his garden and *e.* his. *S of S* 4:16
we will *e.* our own bread. *Isa* 4:1
butter and honey shall he *e.* 7:15
and honey shall every one *e.* 22
e. on the left hand. 9:20
lion shall *e.* straw. 11:7; 65:25
oxen and asses shall *e.* 30:24
plant vineyards, and *e.* fruit thereof.
37:30; 65:21; *Jer* 29:5, 28
the worm shall *e.* them. *Isa* 51:8
come ye, buy and *e.* yea. 55:1
hearken to me, and *e.* that which. 2
they that gathered it shall *e.* 62:9
a people which *e.* swine's. 65:4
my servants shall *e.* but ye shall. 13
shall not plant and another *e.* 22
words were found, and I did *e.* them.
Jer 15:16
shall *e.* every one the flesh of. 19:9
open thy mouth and *e.* *Ezek* 2:8
e. that thou findest, *e.* this roll. 3:1
e. by weight. 4:10
fathers shall *e.* sons. 5:10
thou didst *e.* fine flour, and. 16:13
and in thee they *e.* upon the. 22:9
ye *e.* the fat, and clothe you. 34:3
Nebuchadnezzar did *e.* *Dan* 4:33
for they shall *e.* and not. *Hos* 4:10
Mi 6:14; *Hag* 1:6
shall *e.* unclean things. *Hos* 9:3
all that *e.* thereof shall be. 4
that *e.* the lambs out of. *Amos* 6:4
who also *e.* the flesh. *Mi* 3:3
let the rest *e.* every one. *Zech* 11:9
but he shall *e.* the flesh of the. 16
how David did *e.* the. *Mat* 12:4
did all *e.* and were filled. 14:20
15:37; *Mark* 6:42; 8:8; *Luke* 9:17
yet the dogs *e.* of the. *Mat* 15:27
Mark 7:28
that did *e.* were 4,000. *Mat* 15:38
as they did *e.* he said. 26:21
Mark 14:18, 22
brake it, and said, take *e.* *Mat* 26:26
Mark 14:22; *1 Cor* 11:24

when they saw him *e.* *Mark* 2:16
they that did *e.* were above. 6:44
no man *e.* fruit of thee. 11:14
that thou mayest *e.* passover ? 14:12
14; *Luke* 22:8, 11; *John* 18:28
and did *e.* rubbing them. *Luke* 6:1
him that he would *e.* with. 7:36
e. such things as are set. 10:8
let us *e.* and be merry. 15:23
took it, and did *e.* before. 24:43
prayed him, Master, *e.* *John* 4:31
because ye did *e.* of loaves. 6:26
that a man may *e.* thereof. 50
except ye *e.* the flesh of Son. 53
they did *e.* their meat. *Acts* 2:46
wentest in and didst *e.* with. 11:3
we will *e.* nothing till we. 23:14*
one believeth he may *e.* *Rom* 14:2
doubteth is damned if he *e.* 23
some *e.* it as a thing. *1 Cor* 8:7
we *e.* are we better ; if we *e.* not. 8
I will *e.* no flesh while the. 13
all *e.* the same spiritual meat. 10:3
who *e.* of the sacrifices. 18
whatsoever is sold, that *e.* 25
e. asking no question for. 27
if any man hunger, let him *e.* 11:34
not, neither should he *e.* *2 Thes* 3:10
their word will *e.* as. *2 Tim* 2:17
and shall *e.* your flesh. *Jas* 5:3
shall *e.* her flesh, and. *Rev* 17:16
that ye may *e.* flesh of kings. 19:18

see blood, bread

eat *with* drink

they did *e.* and drink. *Gen* 24:54
26:30; *Ex* 24:11; *Judg* 9:27; 19:4
sat down to *e.* and drink. *Ex* 32:6
1 Cor 10:7
nor *e.* bread, nor drink. *Ex* 34:28
Deut 9:9, 18
did *e.* bread and drink. *1 Sam* 30:11
house to *e.* and drink ? *2 Sam* 11:11
did *e.* of his meat and drink. 12:3
taste what I *e.* or drink ? 19:35
they *e.* and drink before. *1 Ki* 1:25
neither will I *e.* bread nor drink
water. 13:8, 9, 17, 22
will I *e.* bread nor drink. 16
get thee up, and *e.* and drink. 18:41
they may *e.* and drink. *2 Ki* 6:22
one tent did *e.* and drink. 7:8
e. own dung, drink. 18:27; *Isa* 36:12
and did *e.* and drink before Lord.
1 Chr 29:22
them to *e.* and drink. *2 Chr* 28:15
e. no bread nor drink. *Ezra* 10:6
e. the fat and drink. *Neh* 8:10
nor *e.* nor drink three. *Esth* 4:16
sisters to *e.* and drink. *Job* 1:4
so is he, *e.* and drink. *Pr* 23:7
better than that he *e.* and drink.
Eccl 2:24; 3:13; 5:18; 8:15
e., yea, drink abundantly. *S of S* 5:1
e. drink, ye princes. *Isa* 21:5
let us *e.* and drink, to-morrow we
shall die. 22:13; *1 Cor* 15:32
not father *e.* and drink ? *Jer* 22:15
e. thy fruit and drink. *Ezek* 25:4
may *e.* flesh and drink blood. 39:17
pulse to *e.* and water to drink.
Dan 1:12
e. and when ye did drink. *Zech* 7:6
what shall *e.* or drink. *Mat* 6:25, 31
Luke 12:29
to *e.* and drink with drunken.
Mat 24:49; *Luke* 12:45
why do ye *e.* and d.? *Luke* 5:30
but thy disciples *e.* and d. 33
take thine ease, *e.* drink. 12:19
afterward thou shalt *e.* and drink.
17:8
e. to *e.* they drank, they. 27, 28
e. and drink at my table. 22:30
Saul three days did neither *e.* nor
drink. *Acts* 9:9
e. nor drink till they. 23:12, 21
e. flesh nor drink wine. *Rom* 14:21
power to *e.* and drink ? *1 Cor* 9:4
ye *e.* or drink, or whatever. 10:31
not houses to *e.* and drink in ? 11:22
as ye *e.* this bread and drink. 26
shall *e.* and drink unworthily. 27
and so let him *e.* and drink. 28

he did eat

Eve gave, and he did e. | Gen 3:6
loved Esau, because he did e. | 25:28
near to Isaac, and he did e. | 27:25
not aught, save bread he did e. | 39:6
Egyptian bread, and he did e. | 1 Sam 30:11
he did e. continually. | 2 Sam 9:13
bread before him, he did e. | 12:20
John did e. locusts and. | Mark 1:6
those days he did e. | Luke 4:2
for before he did e. | Gal 2:12

eat not

tree of knowledge of good and evil, shalt not e. | Gen 2:17; 3:1, 3
commanded thee not to e. | 3:11, 17
blood thereof shall ye not e. | 9:4
Lev 19:26; Deut 12:16, 23, 24, 25 | 15:23
I will not e. till I have. | Gen 24:33
children of Israel e. not. | 32:32
Egyptians might not e. with. | 43:32
e. not of it raw, nor. | Ex 12:9
a foreigner shall not e. | 45; 29:33
these shall ye not e. | Lev 11:4
| Deut 14:3, 7
a leper not e. of. | Lev 22:4, 6, 10, 12
that torn he shall not e. to. | 8
ye shall not e. one day. | Num 11:19
ye shall not e. of any thing that. | Deut 14:21; Ezek 44:31
ox slain, thou shalt not e. | Deut 28:31
and e. not any unclean. | Judg 13:4
| 7, 14
she wept and did not e. | 1 Sam 1:7
for the people will not e. till. | 9:13
and said, I will not e. | 28:23
and they could not e. | 2 Ki 4:8
with thy eyes, but not e. | 7:2, 19
not e. of most holy things. | Ezra 2:63
| Neh 7:65
and let me not e. of. | Ps 141:4
e not bread of him that. | Pr 23:6
e. not bread of men. | Ezek 24:17
except they wash, e. not. | Mark 7:3, 4
I will not e. thereof. | Luke 22:16
such an one not to e. | 1 Cor 5:11
neither if we e. not are we. | 8:8
e. not, for his sake that. | 10:28

shall ye eat

thus shall ye e. it. | Ex 12:11
seven days shall ye e. | 15, 20
nor shall ye e. flesh torn. | 22:31
wave-breast shall ye e. | Lev 10:14
cheweth the cud, that shall ye e. | 11:3; Deut 14:6
these shall ye e. of all that. | Lev 11:9
in fifth year shall ye e. | 19:25
flesh of daughters shall ye e. | 26:29
fins and scales shall ye e. | Deut 14:9

ye shall eat

and ye shall e. the fat. | Gen 45:18
ye shall e. it in haste. | Ex 12:11
first month at even ye shall e. | 18
at even ye shall e. flesh. | 16:12
ye shall e. no fat. | Lev 7:23, 24
ye shall e. no blood. | 26; 17:14
ye shall e. it in holy place. | 10:13
ye shall e. neither bread nor. | 23:14
ye shall e. the increase. | 25:12
ye shall e. your fill. | 19
ye shall e. of old store. | 22; 26:10
ye shall e. and not be. | 26:26
ye shall e. flesh of your sons. | 29
Lord will give flesh, and ye shall e. | Num 11:18
and ye shall e. in every place. | 18:31
ye shall e. before Lord. | Deut 12:7
of all clean birds ye shall e. | 14:11
go up, for ye shall e. | 1 Sam 9:19
a sign, ye shall e. this year such. | 2 Ki 19:29; Isa 37:30
obedient ye shall e. good. | Isa 1:19
ye shall e. the riches of the. | 61:6
and ye shall e. fat till. | Ezek 39:19
ye shall e. in plenty. | Joel 2:26
thought what ye shall e. | Luke 12:22

to eat

in evening flesh ye shall e. | Ex 16:8
who shall give us flesh to e.? | Num 11:4, 18
soul longeth to e. flesh. | Deut 12:20
have like portions to e. | 18:8

to the high place to e. | 1 Sam 9:13
king sat him down to e. meat. | 20:24
to cause David to e. | 2 Sam 3:35
master's son have food to e. | 9:10
but he refused to e. | 13:9
fruit for the young men to e. | 16:2
for people with him to e. | 17:29
poured out for men to e. | 2 Ki 4:40
have had enough to e. | 2 Chr 31:10
land thou gavest, to e. the. | Neh 9:36
manna on them to e. | Ps 78:24
when thou sittest to e. | Pr 23:1
not good to e. much honey. | 25:27
given him power to e. | Eccl 5:19
God giveth him not power to e. | 6:2
shall be for them to e. | Isa 23:18
cause them to e. flesh. | Jer 19:9
he caused me to e. roll. | Ezek 3:2
son of man, cause thy belly to e. | 3
make thee to e. grass. | Dan 4:25, 32
there is no cluster to e. | Mi 7:1
as eagle that hasteth to e. | Hab 1:8*
pluck ears of corn and to e. | Mat 12:1
not lawful for him to e. | 4
| Mark 2:26; Luke 6:4
give ye them to e. | Mat 14:16
| Mark 6:37; Luke 9:13
to e. with unwashen. | Mat 15:20
multitude have nothing to e. | 32
| Mark 8:1, 2
prepare to e. passover. | Mat 26:17
should be given her to e. | Mark 5:43
no leisure so much as to e. | 6:31
to e. this passover. | Luke 22:15
I have meat to e. that ye. | John 4:32
any brought him aught to e.? | 33
this man give us his flesh to e.? | 6:52
broken it, he began to e. | Acts 27:35
emboldened to e. things. | 1 Cor 8:10
ye come, this is not to e. | 11:20
when ye come together to e. | 33
have no right to e. | Heb 13:10
will I give to e. of tree of. | Rev 2:7
to e. things sacrificed unto. | 14, 20
I will give to e. of hidden manna. | 17

eat up

lean did e. up the. | Gen 41:4, 20
land of enemies e. you up. | Lev 26:38
he shall e. up nations. | Num 24:8
nation thou knowest not shall e. up. | Deut 28:33
on me to e. up my flesh. | Ps 27:2
did e. up all the herbs. | 105:35
moth e. them up. | Isa 50:9; 51:8
shall e. up thine harvest, e. up thy flocks, e. up thy vines. | Jer 5:17
wind shall e. up thy pastures. | 22:22*
e. up the sin of my people. | Hos 4:8*
and did e. up a part. | Amos 7:4
it shall e. thee up like. | Nah 3:15*
said, take it, and e. it up. | Rev 10:9

eaten

hast thou e. of tree? | Gen 3:11
that which young men have e. | 14:24
rams of thy flock have I not e. | 31:38
had e. them up, it could not be known that they had e. them. | 41:21
in one house shall it be e. | Ex 12:46
no leavened bread be e. | 13:3, 7
his flesh shall not be e. | 21:28
a field or vineyard to be e. | 22:5
it shall be e. because. | 29:34
be e. in the holy place. | Lev 6:16
| 26; 7:6
burnt, it shall not be e. | 6:23; 7:19
no sin-offering shall be e. | 6:30
be e. the same day it. | 7:15, 16
if sacrifice of peace-offering be e. | 18
ye not e. the sin offering? | 10:17
ye should indeed have e. it in. | 18
if I had e. the sin-offering. | 19
shall not be e. | 11:13. 41; Deut 14:19
be e. the same day. | Lev 19:6; 22:30
be e. at all on the third day. | 19:7
unleavened bread be e. | Num 28:17
| Ezek 45:21
when thou shalt have e. and be full. | Deut 6:11; 8:10, 12
roe-buck and the hart is e. | 12:22
vineyard, hath not e. of it. | 20:6*
I have not e. thereof. | 26:14
ye have not e. bread nor. | 29:6
when they shall have e. and. | 31:20

had e. of the old corn. | Josh 5:12
when Boaz had e. and. | Ruth 3:7
if people had e. freely. | 1 Sam 14:30
for he had e. no bread all. | 28:20
had e. his spirit came again. | 30:12
have we e. at all of? | 2 Sam 19:42
camest back, and hast e. | 1 Ki 13:22
the lion had not e. the carcase. | 28
have not e. the bread. | Neh 5:14
unsavoury to be e. without salt. | Job 6:6
have e. my morsel alone. | 31:17
if I have e. the fruits thereof. | 39
zeal of thine house hath e. me up. | Ps 69:9; John 2:17
I have e. ashes like bread. | Ps 102:9
and bread e. in secret. | Pr 9:17
morsel that thou hast e. shalt. | 23:8
I have e. my honey-comb. | S of S 5:1
have e. up the vineyard. | Isa 3:14
they have e. up Jacob. | Jer 10:25
figs could not be e. | 24:2, 3, 8; 29:17
e. sour grapes. | 31:29; Ezek 18:2
I have not e. that. | Ezek 4:14
not e. upon mountains. | 18:6, 15
even hath e. upon mountains. | 11
ye have e. fruit of lies. | Hos 10:13
locust hath left, canker-worm e. | Joel 1:4; 2:25
and they that had e. | Mat 14:21
| Mark 8:9
we have e. and drunk. | Luke 13:26
e. afterward thou shalt e. | 17:8
to them that had e. | John 6:13
became hungry, and would have e. | Acts 10:10
Lord, I have never e. any. | 14
he was e. of worms, and. | 12:23
broken bread and e. departed. | 20:11
when they had e. enough. | 27:38
as soon as I had e. it. | Rev 10:10

eater

out of the e. came meat. | Judg 14:14
may give bread to the e. | Isa 55:10
fall into mouth of the e. | Nah 3:12

eaters

be not among riotious e. | Pr 23:20

eatest

in the day thou e. thou. | Gen 2:17
said Elkanah, why e.? | 1 Sam 1:8
spirit so sad that thou e.? | 1 Ki 21:5

eateth

e. leavened bread be. | Ex 12:15, 19
the soul that e. | Lev 7:18, 20, 25, 27
| 17:10, 15
every one that e. shall bear. | 19:8
a land that e. up the. | Num 13:32
cursed be the man that e. | 1 Sam 14:24, 28
harvest the hungry e. up. | Job 5:5
and another never e. with. | 21:25*
behemoth which I made, he e. | 40:15
similitude of ox that e. | Ps 106:20
righteous e. to satisfying. | Pr 13:25
she e. and wipeth her mouth. | 30:20
and she e. not the bread. | 31:27
fool foldeth hands and e. | Eccl 4:5
all his days also he e. in. | 5:17
but a stranger e. it, this is. | 6:2
yet in his hand he e. it up. | Isa 28:4
behold, he e. but awaketh. | 29:8
with part thereof he e. flesh. | 44:16
he that e. of their eggs dieth. | 59:5
man that e. sour grape. | Jer 31:30
why e. your master with publicans? | Mat 9:11; Mark 2:16; Luke 15:2
one of you who e. with me, shall betray me. | Mark 14:18; John 13:18
whoso e. my flesh hath. | John 6:54
so he that e. me, even he. | 57
he that e. of this bread, shall. | 58
another who is weak e. | Rom 14:2
e. despise him that e. not. | 3
he that e., e. to Lord; he that e. not, to Lord he e. not. | 6
evil for that man who e. with. | 20
because he e. not of faith. | 23
planteth vineyard, and e. not of fruit thereof? and e. not of. | 1 Cor 9:7
e. unworthily, e. damnation. | 11:29

eating

a lamb according to number of souls to e. | Ex 12:4; 16:16, 18, 21

Samson took thereof, and went on *e.*
                   Judg 14:9
not against Lord in *e.* *1 Sam* 14:34
spread abroad on all earth *e.* 30:16
guests made an end of *e. 1 Ki* 1:41
they were *e.* of pottage. *2 Ki* 4:40
upon him while he is *e.* *Job* 20:23
e. swine's flesh, and the. *Isa* 66:17
they made an end of *e.* *Amos* 7:2
were *e.* Jesus took bread. *Mat* 26:26
concerning *e.* of things. *1 Cor* 8:4
in *e.* every one taketh his.   11:21
    see **drinking**

Ebal
put curse upon mount *E. Deut* 11:29
these stones in mount *E.*   27:4
stand upon mount *E.* to curse. 13
built an altar in mount *E. Josh* 8:30
half of them over-against *E.*   33

Ebed
words of Gaal son of *E. Judg* 9:30
E. the son of Jonathan. *Ezra* 8:6

Ebed-melech
E. spake to the king. *Jer* 38:8
speak to *E.* the Ethiopian. 39:16

Eben-ezer
Israel pitched beside *E. 1 Sam* 4:1
Philistines brought ark from *E.* 5:1
Samuel called name of stone *E.* 7:12

Eber
Shem father of the children of *E.*
                 Gen 10:21
unto *E.* were born two sons.   25
                1 Chr 1:19
ships shall afflict *E.* *Num* 24:24

Ed
called the altar *E.* *Josh* 22:34

Eden
put man into garden of *E. Gen* 2:15
forth from the garden of *E.*   3:23
make her wilderness like *E.*
       Isa 51:3; *Ezek* 36:35
been in *E.* the garden. *Ezek* 28:13
so that all the trees of *E.*   31:9
the trees of *E.* be comforted. 16
brought down with trees of *E.* 18
land is as the garden of *E. Joel* 2:3
holds sceptre from *E.* *Amos* 1:5

edge
Etham in *e.* of wilderness. *Ex* 13:20
                 Num 33:6
make fifty loops in the *e. Ex* 26:10
and he do not whet the *e. Eccl* 10:10
    see **teeth**
    edge *of the sword*
slew Hamor with the *e.* of sword.
                Gen 34:26
Amalek with *e.* of sword. *Ex* 17:13
Sihon with *e.* of sword. *Num* 21:24
all with *e.* of sword. *Josh* 6:21
smote Ai with *e.* of sword. 8:24
Sisera with *e.* of sword. *Judg* 4:15
Jabesh-gilead with *e. of sword.* 21:10
servants slain with *e. of sword.*
                Job 1:15, 17
turned the *e.* of the sword. *Ps* 89:43
them with *e. of sword.* *Jer* 21:7
fall by the *e. of sword. Luke* 21:24
escaped the *e. of sword. Heb* 11:34

edged
and a two-*e.* sword in. *Ps* 149:6
sharp as a two-*e.* sword. *Pr* 5:4
sharper than two-*e.* *Heb* 4:12
out of mouth went two-*e. Rev* 1:16

edges
joined at the two *e. Ex* 28:7*; 39:4*
dagger had two *e.* *Judg* 3:16
sharp sword with two *e.* *Rev* 2:12

edification
*(Literally, a building up, con-
structing; hence* edify *meant to
organize, establish: also to instruct
and improve, especially morally)*
his neighbour to *e.* *Rom* 15:2
prohesieth speaketh to *e. 1 Cor* 14:3
Lord hath given us for *e. 2 Cor* 10:8*
which Lord hath given to *e.* 13:10*

edified
churches had rest, were *e. Acts* 9:31
but the other is not *e. 1 Cor* 14:17

---

edifieth
but charity *e.* *1 Cor* 8:1
speaks in an unknown tongue *e.* him-
    self; he that prophesieth *e.* 14:4

edify
wherewith one may *e.* *Rom* 14:19
things lawful, but *e.* not. *1 Cor* 10:23
e. one another, even. *1 Thes* 5:11*

edifying
that church may receive *e. 1 Cor* 14:5
that ye may excel to the *e.*   12
let all things be done to *e.*   26
do all things for your *e. 2 Cor* 12:19
for the *e.* of the body. *Eph* 4:12*
increase of the body to the *e.* 16*
which is good to use of *e.*   29
questions rather than *e. 1 Tim* 1:4*

Edom
his name called *E.* *Gen* 25:30
Esau is *E.*   36:1
dukes of *E.* amazed. *Ex* 15:15
Moses sent messengers to the king
    of *E.* *Num* 20:14; *Judg* 11:17
E. refused to give Israel. *Num* 20:21
E. shall be a possession.   24:18
against Moab and *E.* *1 Sam* 14:47
David put garrisons in *E.*
      2 Sam 8:14; *1 Chr* 18:13
Hadad of king's seed in *E.*
               1 Ki 11:14
he had cut off every male in *E.* 16
there was then no king in *E.* 22:47
water by the way of *E.* *2 Ki* 3:20
in his days *E.* revolted from. 8:20
thou hast indeed smitten *E.* 14:10
sought after gods of *E. 2 Chr* 25:20
over *E.* will I cast out my shoe.
            Ps 60:8; 108:9
lead me into *E.?* 60:9; 108:10
the tabernacles of *E.* are.   83:6
remember the children of *E.* 137:7
shall lay their hand on *E. Isa* 11:14
who cometh from *E.?*   63:1
E. I will punish. *Jer* 9:26; 25:21
and yokes to king of *E.*   27:3
concerning *E.* saith Lord. 49:7; *Ob* 1
E. shall be a desolation. *Jer* 49:17
counsel he hath taken against *E.* 20
because *E.* hath dealt. *Ezek* 25:12
lay my vengeance upon *E.*   14
there is *E.* her kings and. 32:29
E. shall escape out of. *Dan* 11:41
E. shall be a wilderness. *Joel* 3:19
deliver them up to *E.* *Amos* 1:6, 9
burnt bones of the king of *E.* 2:1
possess the remnant of *E.* 9:12
destroy wise men out of *E.* *Ob* 8
whereas *E.* saith, we are. *Mal* 1:4
    see **daughter**

Edomite, -s
Esau father of *E.* *Gen* 36:9, 43
shalt not abhor an *E.* *Deut* 23:7
stirred up Hadad the *E. 1 Ki* 11:14
Joram smote the *E.* *2 Ki* 8:21
                2 Chr 21:9
E. became David's. *1 Chr* 18:13
the *E.* revolted from. *2 Chr* 21:10
lo, thou hast smitten the *E.* 25:19
the *E.* had come and smitten. 28:17
    see **Doeg**

effect
make her vow of no *e.* *Num* 30:8
spake to her to that *e. 2 Chr* 34:22
of people of none *e.* *Ps* 33:10
the *e.* of righteousness. *Isa* 32:17
his lies shall not so *e.* it. *Jer* 48:30*
days are at hand, and *e. Ezek* 12:23
commandment of none *e. Mat* 15:6*
word of God of none *e. Mark* 7:13*
faith of God without *e.?* *Rom* 3:3
promise of none *e.* 4:14; *Gal* 3:17
word hath taken none *e. Rom* 9:6*
of Christ be of none *e.* *1 Cor* 1:17*
Christ become of no *e.* to. *Gal* 5:4*

effected
Solomon prosperously *e. 2 Chr* 7:11

effectual
for a great door and *e.* *1 Cor* 16:9
e. in enduring the same. *2 Cor* 1:6*
e. working of his power. *Eph* 3:7
according to the *e.* working. 4:16*

---

thy faith may become *e.* *Philem* 6
the *e.* prayer of righteous. *Jas* 5:16*

effectually
that wrought *e.* in Peter. *Gal* 2:8
the word *e.* worketh in. *1 Thes* 2:13

effeminate
nor *e.* shall inherit the. *1 Cor* 6:9

egg
any taste in white of an *e.? Job* 6:6
if he ask an *e.* will offer. *Luke* 11:12

eggs
young ones or *e.* the dam sitting on
    the young or *e.* shall. *Deut* 22:6
ostrich leaveth her *e.* *Job* 39:14
one gathereth *e.* that are. *Isa* 10:14
cockatrice' *e.* he that eateth *e.* 59:5
as partridge sitteth on *e. Jer* 17:11

Egiah
Ithream, by *E.* David's wife.
                2 Sam 3:5

Eglaim
howling is gone unto *E.* *Isa* 15:8

Eglon
Israel served *E.* the king. *Judg* 3:14
brought presents to *E.* and *E.* 17

Egypt
from the river of *E.* to. *Gen* 15:18
God hath made me lord of all *E.* 45:9
I will smite *E.* *Ex* 3:20; *Jer* 9:26
               46:25
I may lay my hand on *E.* *Ex* 7:4
stretched hand over waters of *E.* 8:6
between cattle of Israel and *E.* 9:4
knowest thou not that *E.* is? 10:7
thou camest out of *E.* 23:15; 34:18
thou hast forgiven this people from
    E. *Num* 14:19
is a people come out of *E.* 22:5
shewed great signs upon *E.*
               Deut 6:22
none of the diseases of *E.* on. 7:15
what he did unto army of *E.* 11:4
smite thee with botch of *E.* 28:27
on thee all diseases of *E.*   60
rolled away reproach of *E. Josh* 5:9
and I plagued *E.*   24:5
I am a young man of *E. 1 Sam* 30:13
excelled wisdom of Egypt. *1 Ki* 4:30
thou trustest on *E. 2 Ki* 18:21, 24
              Isa 36:9, 9
E. was glad when. *Ps* 105:38
who smote firstborn of *E.* 135:8
wonders into midst of thee, O *E.* 9
to him that smote *E.* in. 136:10
bed with fine linen of *E.* *Pr* 7:16
after the manner of *E.* *Isa* 10:24
              Amos 4:10
recover remnant from *E. Isa* 11:11
burden of *E.* the idols of *E.* 19:1
the spirit of *E.* shall fail in.
in that day shall *E.* be like. 16
shall Israel be third with *E.* 24
blessed be ye *E.* my people. 25
be ashamed of *E.* their glory. 20:5
as at report concerning *E.* so. 23:5
beat off from stream of *E.* 27:12
trust in the shadow of *E.* your. 30:3
I gave *E.* for thy ransom. 43:3
the labour of *E.* shall come. 45:14
what to do in way of *E.? Jer* 2:18
shalt be ashamed of *E.* as. 36
of Lord which came against *E.* 46:2
E. is like a fair heifer, but. 20
defile not yourselves with the idols
    of *E.* *Ezek* 20:7
nor left she her idols from *E.* 23:8
thou shalt not remember *E.* 27
with broidered work from *E.* 27:7
prophesy against *E.* and all *E.* 29:2
bring again the captivity of *E.* 14
they also that uphold *E.* shall. 30:6
pain come as in day of *E.* 9
fury on Sin, strength of *E.* 15
shall spoil the pomp of *E.* 32:12
lament for ever, even for *E.* 16
wail for the multitude of *E.* 18
precious things of *E.* *Dan* 11:43
gone, *E.* shall gather them. *Hos* 9:6
E. shall be a desolation. *Joel* 3:19
as by the flood of *E. Amos* 8:8; 9:5
Ethiopia and *E.* were her. *Nah* 3:9
the sceptre of *E.* shall. *Zech* 10:11

if family of *E.* go not up. *Zech* 14:18
him governor over *E.* *Acts* 7:10
by faith he forsook *E.* *Heb* 11:27
is called Sodom and *E.* *Rev* 11:8

see daughter

in Egypt

tell of all my glory *in E.* *Gen* 45:13
me not, I pray thee *in E.* 47:29
affliction of my people *in E.* *Ex* 3:7
which is done to you *in E.* 16
hail, such as hath not been *in E.* 9:18
I wrought *in E.* 10:2; *Josh* 24:7
a great cry *in E.* *Ex* 12:30
no graves *in E.* 14:11
it was well with us *in E.* *Num* 11:18
and we have dwelt *in E.* a. 20:15
all that he did for you *in E.*
Deut 1:30; 4:34
all that he did *in E.* *Josh* 9:9
wrought his signs *in E.* *Ps* 78:43
smote all the firstborn *in E.* 51
not thy wonders *in E.* 106:7
had done great things *in E.* 21
famine shall follow after you *in E.*
Jer 42:16
declare ye *in E.* and publish. 46:14
whoredoms *in E.* *Ezek* 23:3
I have set a fire *in E.* 30:8, 16
will I execute judgements *in E.* 19
an angel appeared *in E.* *Mat* 2:19
dwellers *in E.* we do hear. *Acts* 2:10
than the treasures *in E.* *Heb* 11:26

into Egypt

countries came *into E.* *Gen* 41:57
I will go down with thee *into E.* 46:4
that came with Jacob *into E.* 26
better to return *into E.* *Num* 14:3, 4
Lord shall come *into E.* *Isa* 19:1
walk to go down *into E.* 30:2
fled and went *into E.* *Jer* 26:21
faces to go *into E.* 41:17; 42:15
go ye not *into E.* 42:19; 43:2
ambassadors *into E.* *Ezek* 17:15
carry captives *into E.* *Dan* 11:8
and oil is carried *into E.* *Hos* 12:1
flee *into E.* *Mat* 2:13
he departed *into E.* 14
sold Joseph *into E.* *Acts* 7:9
come, I will send thee *into E.* 34
hearts turned back again *into E.* 39

see king

land of Egypt

Sodom like *land of E.* *Gen* 13:10
Ishmael's wife out of *land of E.* 21:21
never saw in all the *land of E.* 41:19
plenty through *land of E.* 29, 30, 53
set over *land of E.* 41; 45:8, 26
in the *land of E.* was bread. 41:54
good of the *land of E.* 45:18, 20
the *land of E.* is before thee. 47:6
money failed in the *land of E.* 15
Joseph bought all the *land of E.* 20
made it a law over *land of E.* 26
all elders of *land of E.* 50:7
blood in all *land of E.* *Ex* 7:19
frogs, lice, flies covered *land of E.*
8:6, 16, 24
blains, hail, locusts in *land of E.*
9:9, 22; 10:14
darkness over *land of E.* 10:21, 22
Moses was great in *land of E.* 11:3
Lord smote firstborn in *land of E.*
12:29; 13:15
would God we had died in *land of E.*
16:3; *Num* 14:2
you out of *land of E.* *Ex* 16:6
20:2; 29:46
strangers in *land of E.* 22:21; 23:9
Lev 19:34; *Deut* 10:19; *Acts* 13:17
gods which brought thee out of *land
of E. Ex* 32:4; *1 Ki* 12:28; *Neh* 9:18
after doings of *land of E.* *Lev* 18:3
Lord thy God, who brought you out
of *land of E.* 19:36; 26:13
Num 15:41; *Deut* 5:6; 13:5, 10
20:1; *Judg* 2:12; *1 Sam* 12:6
from day thou didst depart out of
land of E. Deut 9:7; *Judg* 19:30
Isa 11:16; *Jer* 7:22; 11:7; 34:13
Mi 7:15
goest is not *land of E. Deut* 11:10
camest out of the *land of E.* in. 16:3

things in the *land of E.* *Ps* 78:12
out through the *land of E.* 81:5
shall in *land of E.* speak. *Isa* 19:18
altar for witness in *land of E.* 19, 20
outcasts in the *land of E.* 27:13
will go into *land of E.* *Jer* 42:14
sword overtake you in *land of E.* 16
they came into the *land of E.* 43:7
array himself with *land of E.* 12
return out of the *land of E.* 44:28
to them in *land of E.* *Ezek* 20:5
the harlot in the *land of E.* 23:19
whoredom from the *land of E.* 27
the *land of E.* desolate. 29:9, 12
land of E. utterly waste. 10
given him the *land of E.* for. 20
no more prince of *land of E.* 30:13
land of E. not escape. *Dan* 11:42
derision in *land of E.* *Hos* 7:16
thy God from *land of E.* 12:9; 13:4
them out of *land of E.* *Zech* 10:10
lead them out of *land of E. Heb* 8:9
people out of *land of E.* *Jude* 5

out of Egypt

Abraham *out of E.* *Gen* 13:1
carry me *out of E.* 47:30
bring Israel *out of E.* *Ex* 3:11
they were thrust *out of E.* 12:39
with a strong hand hath the Lord
brought thee *out of E.* 13:9, 16
came we forth *out of E.? Num* 11:20
is a people come *out of E.* 22:11
of men that came *out of E.* 32:11
thou camest *out of E.* *Deut* 16:6
when ye came *out of E.* *Josh* 2:10
till all that came *out of E.* 5:6
I made you go *out of E.* *Judg* 2:1
1 Sam 10:18
Israel came *out of E.* *1 Sam* 15:6
hast redeemed *out of E. 1 Chr* 17:21
came with him *out of E. 2 Chr* 12:3
princes come *out of ye.* *Ps* 68:31
brought a vine *out of E.* 80:8
when Israel went *out of E.* 114:1
a highway *out of E.* *Isa* 19:23
set forth Urijah *out of E.* *Jer* 26:23
army was come *out of E.* 37:5
called my son *out of E.* *Hos* 11:1
Mat 2:15
tremble as a bird *out of E.* *Hos* 11:11
Lord brought Israel *out of E.* 12:13
when ye came *out of E.* *Hag* 2:5
not all that came *out of E. Heb* 3:16

to Egypt

the Edomites came *to E. 1 Ki* 11:18
Jehoahaz came *to E.* *2 Ki* 23:34
2 Chr 36:4
Judah be a terror *to E.* *Isa* 19:17
Lord shall be known *to E.* 21
woe to them that go *to E.* for. 31:1
they call *to E.* they go. *Hos* 7:11

see return

Egyptian

handmaid an *E.* *Gen* 16:1, 3; 21:9
an *E.* bought Joseph of. 39:1
Lord blessed the *E.* house for. 5
Hebrews are not as *E.* *Ex* 1:19
Moses spied an *E.* smiting. 2:11
slew *E.* and hid him. 12; *Acts* 7:24
an *E.* delivered us out of the. *Ex* 2:19
whose father was an *E.* *Lev* 24:10
shalt not abhor an *E.* *Deut* 23:7
they found an *E.* *1 Sam* 30:11
Benaiah slew an *E.*, and the *E.* had a.
2 Sam 23:21; *1 Chr* 11:23
had servant an *E.* Jarha. *1 Chr* 2:34
Lord destroy tongue of *E. Isa* 11:15
and the *E.* shall come into. 19:23
art not thou that *E.* who? *Acts* 21:38

Egyptians

Pharaoh said to the *E.* *Gen* 41:55
abomination to *E.* 43:32; 46:34
the *E.* mourned for Jacob. 50:3
ye shall spoil the *E. Ex* 3:22; 12:36
sacrifice abomination of *E.?* 8:26
difference between *E.* and. 11:7
they borrowed of the *E.* 12:35
but the *E.* pursued them. 14:9, 10
E. whom ye have seen to-day. 13
E. said, let us flee from Israel...
fighteth for them against *E.* 25
the Lord overthrew *E.* in the. 27

seen what I did to the *E.* *Ex* 19:4
should the *E.* speak and say? 32:12
then the *E.* shall hear it. *Num* 14:13
E. vexed us and our fathers. 20:15
E. evil entreated and. *Deut* 26:6
darkness between you and the *E.*
Josh 24:7
deliver you from the *E.?* *Judg* 10:11
gods that smote the *E.* *1 Sam* 4:8
why harden your hearts, as *E.?* 6:6
to abominations of *E.* *Ezra* 9:1
set the *E.* against the. *Isa* 19:2
the *E.* will I give into hand of a. 4
the *E.* shall know the Lord in. 21
the *E.* shall serve with the. 23
king of Assyria lead away *E.* 20:4
the *E.* shall help in vain and. 30:7
now *E.* are men and not God. 31:3
houses of gods of the *E.* *Jer* 43:13
given the hand to the *E.* *Lam* 5:6
fornication with *E.* *Ezek* 16:26
in bruising thy teats by *E.* 23:21
and I will scatter the *E.* 29:12
30:23, 26
I will gather the *E.* from. 29:13
learned in wisdom of *E.* *Acts* 7:22
which *E.* assaying to do. *Heb* 11:29

Ehud

raised up *E.* the son of. *Judg* 3:15
E. made him a dagger. 16
E. went forth. 23
and *E.* escaped while they. 26
Israel again did evil, when *E.* 4:1
sons of Bilham, *E.* *1 Chr* 7:10
the sons of *E.* 8:6

eight

is *e.* days old shall be circumcised.
Gen 17:12; 21:4; *Luke* 2:21
these *e.* Milcah did bear. *Gen* 22:23
they shall be *e.* boards. *Ex* 26:25
Moses gave *e.* oxen to. *Num* 7:8
on the sixth day *e.* bullocks. 29:29
Israel served Chushan-rishathaim
e. years. *Judg* 3:8
Abdon judged Israel *e.* years. 12:14
the Ephrathite had *e.* *1 Sam* 17:12
was of stones of *e.* cubits. *1 Ki* 7:10
Jehoram reigned *e.* *2 Ki* 8:17
Josiah was *e.* years old when he.
22:1; *2 Chr* 34:1
e. among sons of Ithamar.
1 Chr 24:4
sanctified house of Lord in *e.* days.
2 Chr 29:17
to seven, and also to *e.* *Eccl* 11:2
Ishmael escaped with *e.* *Jer* 41:15
going up had *e.* steps. *Ezek* 40:31
34, 37
e. tables, whereon slew sacrifices. 41
e. principal men. *Mi* 5:5
about an *e.* days after. *Luke* 9:28
after *e.* days disciples. *John* 20:26
had kept his bed *e.* years. *Acts* 9:33
wherein *e.* souls were. *1 Pet* 3:20

eight hundred

begat Seth *e. hun.* years. *Gen* 5:4
he begat Enoch *e. hun.* years. 19
Adino slew *e. hun.* *2 Sam* 23:8
array an *e. hun.* thousand. *2 Chr* 13:3

eighteen

served Eglon *e.* years. *Judg* 3:14
oppressed Israel *e.* years. 10:8
two pillars of brass *e.* *1 Ki* 7:15
2 Ki 25:17; *Jer* 52:21
sons and brethren *e.* *1 Chr* 26:9
Rehoboam took *e.* *2 Chr* 11:21
those *e.* on whom tower. *Luke* 13:4
Satan hath bound these *e.* years. 16

eighteen thousand

of Israel *e. thous.* *Judg* 20:25
there fell of Benjamin *e. thous.* 44
of Manasseh, *e. thous. 1 Chr* 12:31
slew of Edomites *e. thous.* 18:12
princes gave of brass *e. thous.* 29:7
city round was *e. thous. Ezek* 48:35

eighteenth

in *e.* year of Jeroboam. *1 Ki* 15:1
2 Chr 13:1
Jehoram reigned the *e.* *2 Ki* 3:1
in the *e.* year of king Josiah.
23:23; *2 Chr* 34:8; 35:19
the *e.* lot came forth. *1 Chr* 24:15

the e. to Hanani, he.   1 Chr 25:25
e. year of Nebuchadnezzar.
                         Jer 32:1; 52:29

eighth
and ye shall sow the e.   Lev 25:22
in Bul, which is e.   1 Ki 6:38
ordained a feast in the e.   12:32
the e. lot came forth to. 1 Chr 24:10
the e. to Jeshaiah.   25:15
Peulthaia the e.   26:5
the e. captain for the e.   27:11
in e. month word came.   Zech 1:1
but saved Noah the e.   2 Pet 2:5*
is not, even he is the e.   Rev 17:11
the e. foundation was a beryl. 21:20
           see day, days

either
Jacob e. good or bad. Gen 31:24, 29
Nadab and Abihu took e. his censer.
                               Lev 10:1
other gods, e. sun or.   Deut 17:3
nation shall not leave thee e. 28:51
e. he is talking, or.   1 Ki 18:27
prosper, e. this or that.   Eccl 11:6
ask a sign e. in depth or.   Isa 7:11
for e. he will hate the one, and.
                  Mat 6:24; Luke 16:13
e. make the tree good.   Mat 12:33
e. how canst thou say to. Luke 6:42
e. what woman having ten.   15:8
crucified, on e. side one. John 19:18
except I speak to you e. 1 Cor 14:6
e. can a vine bear figs?   Jas 3:12
of e. side the river there. Rev 22:2

Ekron
as the ark came to E.   1 Sam 5:10
restored to Israel from E.   7:14
Baal-zebub the god of E.   2 Ki 1:2
                              3, 6, 16
mine hand against the E.   Amos 1:8
E. shall be rooted up.   Zeph 2:4
E. very sorrowful.   Zech 9:5
E. a Jebusite.   7

Ekronites
the land of the E. not.   Josh 13:3
ark came to Ekron, E.   1 Sam 5:10

Elah
duke E.   Gen 36:41
Shimei son of E.   1 Ki 4:18
E. son of Baasha began.   16:8
Hoshea son of E. 2 Ki 15:30; 17:1
                               18:1, 9
Caleb, E. the sons of. 1 Chr 4:15
E. the son of Uzzi, the son of.   9:8

Elah
pitched by valley of E.   1 Sam 17:2
slew Goliath in valley of E.   21:9

Elam
of Shem, E. and Ashur.   Gen 10:22
of Chedorlaomer king of E.   14:1
Hananiah and E. of.   1 Chr 8:24
E. fifth son of Meshelemiah.   26:3
the children of E.   Ezra 2:7, 31
                       8:7; Neh 7:12, 34
one of sons of E. answered. Ezra 10:2
chief of the people, E.   Neh 10:14
Jehohanan and E. and Ezer.   12:42
recover people from E.   Isa 11:11
go up, O E.   21:2
and E. bare the quiver.   22:6
made the kings of E. to.   Jer 25:25
of Lord that came against E. 49:34
upon E. will I bring the four.   36
bring again the captivity of E.   39
there is E. and all her.   Ezek 32:24
Shushan in province of E.   Dan 8:2

Elamites
the E. wrote a letter to.   Ezra 4:9
Parthians, E. we hear them. Acts 2:9

Elath
Azariah built E.   2 Ki 14:22
that time Rezin recovered E.   16:6

El-bethel
altar, and called it E.   Gen 35:7

Eldad
name of the one was E. Num 11:26
E. and Medad do prophesy.   27

elder
*The original government of the
Hebrews was patriarchal, where the*

head of the family exercised the
supreme rule over all of his descendants ; his married sons doing
the same with their children and
other descendants, but still remaining subordinate to the supreme
head. At the father's death his
firstborn succeeded him in supreme
headship. Naturally only men of
mature age came into these posi-
tions, hence the designation elder.
In that way Jacob was the head of
all who went to Egypt with him,
although his sons had families of
their own. From this came [1] the
great influence of the older people
of the nation ; [2] the division of the
Israelites into tribes, with a head,
chief, or prince over each as a whole ;
[3] the general use, in other
nations as well as the Hebrews, of
the term elder as an official title for
those who as representatives of the
people made all their decisions.
   The earliest mention of elders as
a political body is at the time of the
Exodus. The seventy elders mentioned in Exodus and Numbers
were a sort of governing body, a
parliament, and the origin of the
tribunal of seventy elders called
the Sanhedrin or Council. There
were also, after the founding of
towns and cities, those who were
put at the head of affairs who
could not always derive their
authority from their position in the
tribe. These were also called
elders, and they served as judges,
to decide both civil and criminal
causes.
   The Sanhedrin was a supreme
council, serving as a court of appeal, and having a general oversight over the inferior courts, and
the general affairs of the nation.
In the New Testament Church the
elders or presbyters were the same
as the bishops. It was an office
derived from the Jewish usage of
elders or rulers of synagogues.
Shem the brother of Japhet the e.
                            Gen 10:21*
e. serve younger. 25:23; Rom 9:12
my e. daughter Merab. 1 Sam 18:17
kingdom, he is mine e.   1 Ki 2:22
aged men, much e. than.   Job 15:10
Elihu waited, they were e.   32:4
thy e. sister is Samaria. Ezek 16:46
names were Aholah the e.   23:4
his e. son was in field.   Luke 15:25
intreat the e. women.   1 Tim 5:2
younger, submit to the e. 1 Pet 5:5

elder for *ruler*
rebuke not an e. but.   1 Tim 5:1
against an e. receive not.   19
exhort, who am also an e. 1 Pet 5:1
the e. to the elect lady.   2 John 1
e. unto well-beloved.   3 John 1

elders
e. of his house went.   Gen 50:7
the e. of congregation.   Lev 4:15
of Spirit to seventy e.   Num 11:25
go to the gate to the e.   Deut 25:7
stand before the Lord your e. 29:10
gather to me all e. of your.   31:28
ask thy father and e. and.   32:7
Israel served Lord all days of Joshua
and e.   Josh 24:31; Judg 2:7
described to him the e. Judg 8:14
e. of the town trembled. 1 Sam 16:4
sent of the spoil to the e. of.   30:26
all the e. said to him.   1 Ki 20:8
the e. did as Jezebel had.   21:11
Elisha sat in house, e.   2 Ki 6:32
Jehu wrote letters and sent to e. 10:1
Hezekiah sent e. of priests to Isaiah
the prophet.   19:2; Isa 37:2
eye of God upon the e.   Ezra 5:5
the e. of the Jews builded.   6:14
counsel of the princes and e.   10:8
him in assembly of e.   Ps 107:32
husband known among e.   Pr 31:23

my priests and e. gave.   Lam 1:19
e. of Zion sit upon the ground. 2:10
favoured not e.   4:16; 5:12
e. have ceased from gate.   5:14
and the e. of Judah.   Ezek 8:1
sanctify a fast, gather e.   Joel 1:14
                               2:16
the tradition of the e.?   Mat 15:2
suffer many things of the e.   16:21
                               27:12
the e. sought false witness.   26:59
priests and e. persuaded the. 27:20
chief priests mocking with e.   41
they were assembled with e. 28:12
the tradition of the e.   Mark 7:3
be rejected of e.   8:31; Luke 9:22
great multitude from e. Mark 14:43
priests held consultation with e. 15:1
unto the captains and e. Luke 22:52
their rulers and e. were.   Acts 4:5
they reported all that e. had.   23
stirred up the people and e.   6:12
sent it to e. by Barnabas.   11:30
when they ordained e. in.   14:23
of the church and of the e.   15:4
apostles and e. came together.   6
the apostles, e. and brethren.   23
decrees ordained of the e.   16:4
he sent and called the e. of.   20:17
all the estate of the e. bear.   22:5
Ananias descended with e.   23:1
about whom the e. of Jews.   25:15
let e. that rule well be. 1 Tim 5:17
thou shouldest ordain e.   Tit 1:5
by faith the e. obtained.   Heb 11:2
let him call for the e.   Jas 5:14
e. which are among you.   1 Pet 5:1
upon seats I saw 24 e.   Rev 4:4
the 24 e. fall before him.   10
                    5:8, 14; 11:16; 19:4
one of e. saith unto me, weep. 5:5
in midst of the e. a Lamb.   6
voice of many angels about e.   11
all angels stood about e.   7:11
one of e. answered saying to me. 13
new song before throne and e. 14:3

elders with *city*
e. of his city shall fetch. Deut 19:12
e. of that city shall take and. 21:3
e. of that city wash their hands.   6
their son to e. of his city.   19
of virginity to e. of the city. 22:15
the e. of his city shall call.   25:8
declare his cause to e.   Josh 20:4
took the e. of the city.   Judg 8:16
ten men of e. of city.   Ruth 4:2
them e. of every city.   Ezra 10:14

elders of *Israel*
gather e. of Israel together. Ex 3:16
called for all the e. of Israel. 12:21
take with thee of e. of Israel. 17:5
e. of Israel came to eat with. 18:12
seventy of the e. of Israel. 24:1, 9
                            Num 11:16
e. of Israel commanded. Deut 21:1
this law to the e. of Israel.   31:9
e. of Israel put dust on.   Josh 7:6
so all the e. of Israel came to king.
           2 Sam 5:3; 1 Ki 8:3; 2 Chr 5:4
pleased all e. of Israel. 2 Sam 17:4
Ahithophel counsel e. of Israel. 15
e. of Israel came to king. 1 Chr 11:3
David and e. of Israel fell.   21:16
came the e. of Israel.   Ezek 14:1
e. of Israel came to inquire.   20:1
rulers of people, e. of Israel. Acts 4:8

elders with *people*
called for e. of the people. Ex 19:7
to be e. of the people.   Num 11:16
70 men of the e. of the people.   24
buy it before e. of people.   Ruth 4:4
before e. of my people. 1 Sam 15:30
the e. of the people came.
                  Mat 21:23; Luke 22:66
a multitude from e. of the people.
                            Mat 26:47
e. of the people took counsel.   27:1
stirred up people and e.   Acts 6:12

eldest
Abraham said to his e.   Gen 24:2
Isaac called Esau his e. son.   27:1
searched, and began at the e. 44:12
Israel's e. son.   Num 1:20; 26:5

three *e.* sons of Jesse followed.
1 Sam 17:13, 14
Eliab his *e.* brother heard. 28
he took his *e.* son and. *2 Ki* 3:27
of men had slain the *e.* *2 Chr* 22:1
drinking in their *e.* *Job* 1:13, 18
one by one, beginning at *e. John* 8:9

Elealeh
of Reuben built *E.* *Num* 32:37
Heshbon shall cry, and *E. Isa* 15:4
water thee with my tears, O *E.* 16:9
cry of Hesbon even to *E. Jer* 48:34

Eleazar
Aaron's son *E.* *Ex* 6:25; 28:1
Num 3:2; 26:60; *1 Chr* 6:3; 24:1
Ezra 8:33
Moses was angry with *E. Lev* 10:16
E. ministered in priest's. *Num* 3:4
E. son of Aaron shall be chief. 32
to the office of *E.* pertaineth. 4:16
E. the priest took the. 16:39
put his garments upon *E.* 20:26
Moses and *E.* came down. 28
numbered by Moses and *E.* 26:63
he set Joshua before *E.* 27:22
brought spoil to Moses and *E.* 31:12
take sum of prey thou and *E.* 26
Moses gave tribute unto *E.* 41
E. and Joshua divide land. 34:17
came near before *E.* *Josh* 17:4
E. died. 24:33
sanctified *E.* to keep. *1 Sam* 7:1
after him *E.* son of Dodo.
2 Sam 23:9; *1 Chr* 11:12
son of *F.* was ruler. *1 Chr* 9:20
sons of Mahli, *E.* 23:21; 24:28
E. died, and had no sons. 23:22
more chief men of sons of *E.* 24:4
governors were of sons of *E.* 5
Shemaiah and *E.* were. *Neh* 12:42
Eliud begat *E.* and *E.* *Mat* 1:15

elect
Or Chosen, is used, [1] *Of Christ,
Isa* 42:1. [2] *Of good angels,*
1 *Tim* 5:21. [3] *Of the Israelites,
who were God's chosen and
peculiar people, Isa* 65:9, 22. [4]
*Of those in whom Divine grace has
achieved its supreme triumph, and
who have passed from death unto
life, and from the power of sin to the
glad and eager service of God and
our Lord Jesus Christ.*

behold mine *e.* in whom. *Isa* 42:1*
Israel mine *e.* I have called. 45:4*
mine elect shall inherit it. 65:9*
mine *e.* shall long enjoy work. 22*
but for the *e.'s* sake those days shall.
Mat 24:22; *Mark* 13:20
possible deceive very *e. Mat* 24:24
Mark 13:22
and they shall gather his *e.* from.
Mat 24:31; *Mark* 13:27
not God avenge his *e.? Luke* 18:7
any thing to charge of God's *e.?*
Rom 8:33
put on as the *e.* of God. *Col* 3:12
charge thee before the *e. 1 Tim* 5:21
endure all things for *e.'s. 2 Tim* 2:10
according to faith of God's *e. Tit* 1:1
e. according to foreknowledge.
1 Pet 1:2
Sion a chief corner-stone, *e.* 2:6
the elder to the *e.* lady. *2 John* 1
the children of thy *e.* sister. 13

elected
church at Babylon *e.* *1 Pet* 5:13

election
to *e.* might stand. *Rom* 9:11
a remnant according to *e.* of 11:5
the *e.* hath obtained it, the rest. 7
but as touching the *e.* they. 28
brethren, your *e.* of God. *1 Thes* 1:4
your calling and *e.* sure. *2 Pet* 1:10

El-elohe-Israel
called altar *E.-Israel.* *Gen* 33:20

elements
in bondage under *e.* of. *Gal* 4:3*
again to weak and beggarly *e.* 9*
the *e.* shall melt. *2 Pet* 3:10, 12
elephant, see ivory

12

eleven
Jacob took his *e.* sons. *Gen* 32:22
sun, moon, and *e.* stars made. 37:9
curtains of goats' hair, *e.* *Ex* 26:7
the *e.* curtains shall be all of. 8
e. curtains he made. 36:14
e. of one size. 15
on third day *e.* bullocks. *Num* 29:20
are *e.* days' journey. *Deut* 1:2
e. cities with villages. *Josh* 15:51
give thee *e.* hundred pieces of silver.
Judg 16:5
I took the *e.* hundred shekels. 17:2
restored *e.* hundred shekels to. 3
Jehoiakim reigned *e.* years in.
2 Ki 23:36; *2 Chr* 36:5
Zedekiah *e.* years. *2 Ki* 24:18
2 Chr 36:11; *Jer* 52:1
then the *e.* disciples. *Mat* 28:16
he appeared to the *e.* *Mark* 16:14
all these things to the *e. Luke* 24:9
found the *e.* gathered together. 33
was numbered with the *e. Acts* 1:26
Peter standing up with *e.* 2:14

eleventh
in the *e.* year was house. *1 Ki* 6:38
in *e.* year of Joram. *2 Ki* 9:29
Jerusalem was besieged to the *e.*
2 Ki 25:2; *Jer* 52:5
the *e.* lot came forth. *1 Chr* 24:12
the *e.* to Azareel, he, his. 25:18
e. captain for the *e.* month. 27:14
Jeremiah prophesied in *e.* *Jer* 1:3
in the *e.* year the city was. 39:2
word of the Lord came to Ezekiel in
e. year. *Ezek* 26:1; 30:20; 31:1
and about the *e.* hour. *Mat* 20:6
that were hired about the *e.* hour. 9
e. foundation of city was. *Rev* 21:20

Elhanan
E. slew brother of Goliath.
2 Sam 21:19; *1 Chr* 20:5
E. the son of Dodo. *2 Sam* 23:24
1 Chr 11:26

Eli
brought the child to *E. 1 Sam* 1:25
minister to Lord before *E.* 2:11; 3:1
now the sons of *E.* were sons. 2:12
came a man of God to *E.* and. 27
Samuel ran to *E.* and. 3:5; 6:8
in that day perform against *E.* 3:12
iniquity of *E.'s* house shall. 14
came in hastily and told *E.* 4:14
he spake concerning *E.* *1 Ki* 2:27

Eli, Eli, *lama sabachthani*
E. E. lama sab. *Mat* 27:46
Eloi, Eloi, lama sab. *Mark* 15:34

Eliab
of tribe of Zebulun, *E.* *Num* 1:9
2:7; 7:24, 29; 10:16
Abiram son of *E.* 16:1, 12; 26:9
sons of Pallu, *E.* 26:8
he did to sons of *E. Deut* 11:6
looked on *E.* *1 Sam* 16:6
E. heard, and his anger. 17:28
begat his firstborn *E.* *1 Chr* 2:13
E. the son of Nahath, the. 6:27
E. captain of the Gadites. 12:9
E. porter. 15:18, 20
E. with a psaltery. 16:5
took the daughter of *E. 2 Chr* 11:18

Eliada
E. a son of David. *2 Sam* 5:16
1 Chr 3:8
of Benjamin, *E.* *2 Chr* 17:17

Eliakim
came out *E.* the son of Hilkiah.
2 Ki 18:18; *Isa* 36:3
Hezekiah sent *E.* to Isaiah.
2 Ki 19:2; *Isa* 37:2
made *E.* son of Josiah king.
2 Ki 23:34; *2 Chr* 36:4
E. and Maaseiah the. *Neh* 12:41
will call my servant *E.* *Isa* 22:20
Abiud begat *E.* and *E.* *Mat* 1:13
Jonan, the son of *E.* *Luke* 3:30

Eliam
the daughter of *E.* *2 Sam* 11:3
E. the son of Ahithophel the. 23:34

Elias, *see* **Elijah**

Eliashib
E. and Pelaiah sons of. *1 Chr* 3:24

eleventh lot came forth to *E.*
1 Chr 24:12
Johanan the son of *E.* *Ezra* 10:6
Neh 12:23
E. a singer. *Ezra* 10:24
E. the son of Zattu. 27
son of Bani. 36
E. the high priest. *Neh* 3:1
Joiakim begat *E.* and *E.* 12:10
E. was allied to Tobiah. 13:4
the evil *E.* did. 7
of sons of Joiada, son of *E.* 28

Eliezer
steward of my house is *E. Gen* 15:2
name of Moses' son was *E.*
Ex 18:4; *1 Chr* 23:15
sons of Becher, *E.* and. *1 Chr* 7:8
Benaiah and *E.* the priests. 15:24
son of *E.* was Rehabiah the. 23:17
ruler of Reubenites was *E.* 27:16
E. prophesied against. *2 Chr* 20:37
then sent I for *E.* and. *Ezra* 8:16
E. had taken strange. 10:18, 23, 31
Jose, the son of *E.* *Luke* 3:29

Elihoreph
E. and Ahiah, sons of. *1 Ki* 4:3

Elihu
of Jeroham, son of *E.* *1 Sam* 1:1
E. fell to David out. *1 Chr* 12:20
E. and Semachiah strong men. 26:7
of Judah, *E.* one of the. 27:18
wrath of *E.* the Buzite. *Job* 32:2
E. had waited. 4
E. answered. 6; 34:1; 35:1

Elijah, or Elias
E. the Tishbite said to. *1 Ki* 17:1
did according to saying of *E.* 15
Lord heard the voice of *E.* 22
E. took the child, and brought. 23
E. went to shew himself. 18:2
art thou that my lord *E.?* 7
E. is here. 8
Ahab went to meet *E.* 16
E. mocked them. 27
E. slew all the prophets of Baal. 40
hand of the Lord was on *E.* 46
Ahab told Jezebel all that *E.* 19:1
what doest thou here, *E.?* 9, 13
and ran after *E.* 20, 21
Ahab said to *E.* hast thou ? 21:20
it is *E.* the Tishbite. *2 Ki* 1:8
third captain fell before *E.* 13
according to the word *E.* had. 17
when Lord would take up *E.* 2:1
E. took his mantle, and wrapt it. 8
E. went up by a whirlwind. 11
where is Lord God of *E.?* 14
spirit of *E.* doth rest on Elisha. 15
poured water on the hands of *E.* 3:11
which he spake by *E.* 9:36; 10:10, 17
a writing from *E.* *2 Chr* 21:12
Maaseiah and *E.* sons of. *Ezra* 10:21
behold, I will send you *E. Mal* 4:5
this is *Elias* which was. *Mat* 11:14
some say, *Elias.* 16:14; *Mark* 6:15
Luke 9:8, 19
there appeared *Elias.* *Mat* 17:3
Mark 9:4; *Luke* 9:30
three tabernacles, one for *Elias.*
Mat 17:4; *Mark* 9:5; *Luke* 9:33
that *Elias* must first come.
Mat 17:10; *Mark* 9:11
Elias shall come and restore things.
Mat 17:11; *Mark* 9:12
Elias is come already. *Mat* 17:12
Mark 9:13
this man calleth for *Elias.*
Mat 27:47; *Mark* 15:35
let us see whether *Elias* will.
Mat 27:49; *Mark* 15:36
in the power of *Elias.* *Luke* 1:17
widows in the days of *Elias.* 4:25
fire to consume them as *Elias.* 9:54
art thou *Elias* ? *John* 1:21
if thou be not *Elias,* why ? 25
scripture saith of *Elias.* *Rom* 11:2
Elias was a man subject. *Jas* 5:17

Elim
came to *E.* *Ex* 15:27; *Num* 33:9
took their journey from *E.*
Ex 16:1; *Num* 33:10

Elimelech
name of man was E. *Ruth* 1:2
E. died. 3
Boaz a kinsman of family of E. 2:1
I have bought all that was E.'s 4:9

Eliphalet
Eliada and E. David's son.
2 Sam 5:16; *1 Chr* 3:6, 8

Eliphaz
Adah bare to Esau, E. *Gen* 36:4, 10
1 Chr 1:35
the sons of E. *Gen* 36:11, 12, 15
1 Chr 1:36
E. came from his place. *Job* 2:11
E. the Temanite. 4:1; 15:1; 22:1
E. did as Lord commanded. 42:9

Elisabeth
Zacharias' wife E. *Luke* 1:5
E. was barren. 7
E. conceived. 24, 36
Mary saluted E. 40
E.'s full time came that she. 57

Elisha, Eliseus
thou shalt anoint E. *1 Ki* 19:16
escaped from Jehu, shall E. slay. 17
Elijah departed, and found E. 19
at Jericho came to E. *2 Ki* 2:5
E. saw it, and cried, my father. 12
spirit of Elijah doth rest on E. 15
is E. the son of Shaphat. 3:11
cried a certain woman unto E. 4:1
E. passed to Shunem, where was. 8
bare a son at that season that E. 17
when E. was come, behold. 32
came and stood at door of E. 5:9
E. telleth the words that. 6:12
E. prayed to the Lord . . . according
to the word of E. 18
E. said, Lord, open eyes of. 20
if the head of E. stand on him. 31
the great things that E. hath. 8:4
the woman whose son E. restored. 5
what said E. to thee ? 14
E. was fallen sick. 13:14
E. put his hands upon king's. 16
E. said, shoot. 17
cast man into sepulchre of E. 21
lepers in Israel in days of *Eliseus.*
Luke 4:27

Elishah
blue and purple from E. *Ezek* 27:7

Elishama
E. the son of Ammihud. *Num* 1:10
2:18; 7:48, 53; 10:22; *1 Chr* 7:26
E. David's son. *2 Sam* 5:16
1 Chr 3:6, 8; 14:7
and Jekamiah begat E. *1 Chr* 2:41
he sent with them E. *2 Chr* 17:8
E. scribe. *Jer* 36:12
E. of the seed royal. 41:1

Elisheba
Aaron took him E. *Ex.* 6:23

Elishua
E. David's. *2 Sam* 5:15; *1 Chr* 14:5

Eliud
Achim begat E. *Mat* 1:14
E. begat Eleazar. 15

Elkanah
sons of Korah; Assir, and E. *Ex* 6:24
his name was E. *1 Sam* 1:1
E. went up to offer sacrifice. 21
E. went to his house. 2:11
Eli blessed E. 20
the son of E. *1 Chr* 6:23, 27, 34
35; 9:16
the sons of E. 6:25, 26
E. the Korhite. 12:6
E. was doorkeeper for ark. 15:23
E. that was next to king. *2 Chr* 28:7

Elmodam
Cosam, the son of E. *Luke* 3:28

Elnathan
Nehushta daughter of E. *2 Ki* 24:8
I sent for E. and Jarib, *Ezra* 8:16
Jehoiakim sent E. into. *Jer* 26:22
E. the son of Achbor. 36:12
E. had made intercession to. 25

Elon
Bashemath daughter of E.
Gen 26:34

Esau took Adah daughter of E.
Gen 36:2
sons of Zebulun, Sered and E. 46:14
E. judged Israel. *Judg* 12:11
E. died. 12

eloquent
O my Lord, I am not e. *Ex* 4:10
doth take away e. orator. *Isa* 3:3*
named Apollos, an e. *Acts* 18:24*

else
give me children or e. I. *Gen* 30:1
doing any thing e. go. *Num* 20:19
the Lord he is God, there is none e.
Deut 4:35, 39; *1 Ki* 8:60; *Isa* 45:5
6, 14, 18, 21, 22; 46:9; *Joel* 2:27
e. if ye in any wise go. *Josh* 23:12
nothing e. save sword. *Judg* 7:14
if I taste aught e. till. *2 Sam* 3:35
or e. three days sword. *1 Chr* 21:12
whoso e. cometh in. *2 Chr* 23:7
nothing e. but sorrow of. *Neh* 2:2
not sacrifice, e. would I. *Ps* 51:16
who e. can hasten here ? *Eccl* 2:25
I am, none e. besides. *Isa* 47:8, 10
or e. believe me for. *John* 14:11
time in nothing e. but. *Acts* 17:21
accusing, or e. excusing. *Rom* 2:15
e. were your children. *1 Cor* 7:14
e. when thou shalt bless. 14:16
repent, or e. I will. *Rev* 2:5, 16

Elul
25th day of the month E. *Neh* 6:15

Elymas
but E. the sorcerer. *Acts* 13:8

embalm
physicians to e. his. *Gen* 50:2

embalmed
the physicians e. Israel. *Gen* 50:2
days of those that are e. 3
they e. Joseph, put him in a. 26

emboldened
conscience of weak be e. *1 Cor* 8:10

emboldeneth
what e. thee that thou ? *Job* 16:3*

embrace
about this season thou shalt e.
2 Ki 4:16
they e. the rock for want. *Job* 24:8
when thou dost e. her. *Pr* 4:8
why wilt thou e. bosom of ? 5:20
a time to e. and refrain. *Eccl* 3:5
right hand doth e. *S of S* 2:6; 8:3
brought up in scarlet e. *Lam* 4:5

embraced
Laban e. Jacob. *Gen* 29:13
Esau ran and e. Jacob. 33:4
Jacob kissed and e. Joseph's. 48:10
Paul e. disciples and. *Acts* 20:1*
having seen and e. *Heb* 11:13*

embracing
and a time to refrain e. *Eccl* 3:5
Paul e. Eutychus said. *Acts* 20:10

embroider
thou shalt e. the coat. *Ex* 28:39*

embroiderer
manner of work of e. *Ex* 35:35
with him Aholiab, an e. in. 38:23

emerald, -s
second row an e. *Ex* 28:18; 39:11
in thy fairs with e. *Ezek* 27:16
precious stone thy covering, e. 28:13
in sight like unto e. *Rev* 4:3
fourth foundation was an e. 21:19

emerods
Lord will smite with e. *Deut* 28:27
smote Ashdod with e. *1 Sam* 5:6*
men of the city had e. 9*
that died not were smitten with e. 12*
five golden e. and five. 6:4*, 17*
make images of your e. 5*, 11*

Emims
came and smote the E. *Gen* 14:5
the E. dwelt therein. *Deut* 2:10

eminent
built to thee an e. *Ezek* 16:24, 31
shall throw down thine e. place. 39
an high mountain and e. 17:22

Emmanuel
Or Immanuel, *is a* Hebrew *word,
meaning* God *with us. A child
whose birth is prophesied in
Isa* 7:14 *as a sign from God.
In its final fulfilment it has always
been held to refer to the Messiah,
Mat* 1:23, *and the name is applied
to Christ by early Christian writers,
and by modern writers down to our
own day.*
shall call his name Em. *Isa* 7:14
Mat 1:23
fill breadth of thy land, O Em.
Isa 8:8

Emmaus
that same day to E. *Luke* 24:13

Emmor
bought of sons of E. *Acts* 7:16

empire
published throughout all his e.
Esth 1:20*

employ
tree is man's life, to e. *Deut* 20:19*

employed
these singers e. day and. *1 Chr* 9:33
and Jahaziah e. about. *Ezra* 10:15*

employment
out men of continual e. *Ezek* 39:14

emptied
hasted and e. her. *Gen* 24:20
came to pass as they e. sacks.
42:35
high priest's officer e. *2 Chr* 24:11
be he shaken out and e. *Neh* 5:13
brooks of defence shall be e. *Isa* 19:6*
land shall be utterly e. and. 24:3
Moab not been e. from. *Jer* 48:11
emptiers have e. them. *Nah* 2:2

emptiers
e. have emptied them out. *Nah* 2:2

emptiness
upon it the stones of e. *Isa* 34:11

empty
hadst sent me away e. *Gen* 31:42
the pit was e. there was no. 37:24
the seven e. ears blasted. 41:27
go, ye shall not go e. *Ex* 3:21
Egypt, none shall appear before me e.
23:15; 34:20; *Deut* 16:16
not let him go away e. *Deut* 15:13
in every man's hand e. *Judg* 7:16
brought me home e. *Ruth* 1:21
not e. to thy mother-in-law. 3:17
send not ark away e. *1 Sam* 6:3
thy seat will be e. 20:18, 25, 27
sword of Saul returned not e.
2 Sam 1:22
borrow thee e. vessels. *2 Ki* 4:3
hast sent widows away e. *Job* 22:9
stretcheth north over e. place. 26:7
Lord maketh earth e. *Isa* 24:1
awaketh, and his soul is e. 29:8
make e. soul of the hungry. 32:6
returned with their vessels e.
Jer 14:3
king of Babylon made me e. 51:34
then set it e. upon the. *Ezek* 24:11
Israel is an e. vine. *Hos* 10:1*
Nineveh is e. and void. *Nah* 2:10
is come, he findeth it e. *Mat* 12:44
and sent him away e. *Mark* 12:3
Luke 20:10, 11
rich he hath sent e. away. *Luke* 1:53

empty, *verb*
command that they e. *Lev* 14:36
clouds e. themselves. *Eccl* 11:3
wanderers shall e. his. *Jer* 48:12
fanners fan her and e. her. 51:2
they therefore e. their net.
Hab 1:17
which e. the golden oil. *Zech* 4:12

emulation
if I may provoke to e. *Rom* 11:14*

emulations
works of the flesh are e. *Gal* 5:20*

enabled
Christ Jesus who hath e. *1 Tim* 1:12

encamp

e. before Pi-hahiroth. | *Ex* 14:2
the Levites shall e. | *Num* 1:50
as they e. so set forward. | 2:17
but those that e. before the. | 3:38
knowest how we are to e. | 10:31
e. against Rabbah. | *2 Sam* 12:28
his troops come and e. | *Job* 19:12
host should e. against me. | *Ps* 27:3
I will e. about mine house. *Zech* 9:8

encamped

e. in Etham. | *Ex* 13:20
e. by the waters. | 15:27
where Moses e. at mount. | 18:5
from Elim they e. by. | *Num* 33:10
from Red Sea, and e. in the. | 11
people came up and e. in Gilgal. | *Josh* 4:19; 5:10
kings of the Amorites e. | 10:5
Midianites e. against. | *Judg* 6:4
Abimelech e. against Thebez. | 9:50
children of Ammon e. in Gilead, |
Israel e. at Mizpeh. | 10:17
Nahash e. against. | *1 Sam* 11:1
Philistines e. in Michmash. | 13:16
the servants are e. in. | *2 Sam* 11:11
e. against Gibbethon. *1 Ki* 16:15, 16
the Philistines e. in. | *1 Chr* 11:15
Sennacherib e. against. | *2 Chr* 32:1

encampeth

angel of the Lord e. | *Ps* 34:7
scattered bones of him that e. | 53:5

encamping

Egyptians overtook them e. *Ex* 14:9

enchanter

shall not be found an e. *Deut* 18:10

enchanters

not to dreamers nor e. | *Jer* 27:9*

enchantments

magicians did so with e. | *Ex* 7:11, 22; 8:7, 18
nor shall ye use e. nor. | *Lev* 19:26
there is no e. against. | *Num* 23:23
Balaam went not to seek for e. 24:1
used divination and e. | *2 Ki* 17:17
Manasseh used e. 21:6; *2 Chr* 33:6
serpent will bite without e. | *Eccl* 10:11*
for abundance of thine e. | *Isa* 47:9
stand now with thine e. and. | 12

encline, enclose, see incline, inclose

certain philosophers e. | *Acts* 17:18

encourage

e. him, he shall cause to inherit it. | *Deut* 1:38; 3:28
say to Joab, and e. | *2 Sam* 11:25
they e. themselves in an. | *Ps* 64:5

encouraged

David e. himself in. | *1 Sam* 30:6*
priests and Levites be e. *2 Chr* 31:4*
Josiah e. them to the service. | 35:2
the carpenter e. goldsmith. *Isa* 41:7

end

[1] *A limit or boundary*, Job 37:3; 38:18. [2] *Termination, issue, or result*, 1 Sam 14:27. [3] *Death or destruction*, Gen 6:13; Amos 8:2; Mat 24:6. [4] *Purpose, aim*, Rom 10:4; 1 Tim 1:5.

the e. of all flesh is. | *Gen* 6:13
e. of Egypt to the other e. | 47:21
feast of in-gathering in the e. of year. | *Ex* 23:16; 34:22
one cherub on the one e. the other cherub on other e. of. | 25:19
scatter from one e. of. *Deut* 28:64
I will see what their e. shall. | 32:20
angel put forth the e. | *Judg* 6:21
the day groweth to an e. | 19:9
Jonathan put forth e. of. *1 Sam* 14:27
Baal was full from one e. *2 Ki* 10:21
with blood from one e. | 21:16
after the e. of two years. *2 Chr* 21:19
uncleanness from one e. to. *Ezra* 9:11
what is my e. that I? | *Job* 6:11
shall vain words have e.? | 16:3
day and night come to an e. | 26:10
he setteth an e. to darkness. | 28:3
of wicked come to an e. | *Ps* 7:9

destructions come to perpetual e. | *Ps* 9:6
going forth is from the e. of. | 19:6
for the e. of that man is. | 37:37
the e. of the wicked shall be. | 38†
make me to know mine e. | 39:4
from the e. of the earth will. | 61:2
I understood their e. | 73:17*
and thy years have no e. | 102:27
seen an e. of all perfection. | 119:96
her e. is bitter. | *Pr* 5:4*
but the e. thereof are. | 14:12
there is an e. | 23:18
not what to do in the e. | 25:8
yet there is no e. of all. | *Eccl* 4:8
there is no e. of all people. | 16
the e. of all men. | 7:2
better the e. of a thing. | 8
e. of his talk is mischievous. | 10:13
many books there is no e. | 12:12
nor is there any e. of their treasures, |
nor any e. of their. | *Isa* 2:7
his government shall be no e. | 9:7
come from the e. of heaven. | 13:5*
the extortioner is at an e. | 16:4
after e. of 70 years Tyre. | 23:15, 17
sing praise from e. of earth. | 42:10
confounded world without e. | 45:17
declaring the e. from the. | 46:10
will you do in the e.? | *Jer* 5:31
sword of Lord shall devour from one e. to the other e. | 12:12; 25:33
at his e. he shall be a fool. | 17:11
to give you an expected e. | 29:11
there is hope in thine e. | 31:17
till there be an e. of them. | 44:27
his city is taken at one e. | 51:31
our e. is near, our e. is. | *Lam* 4:18
an e. the e. is come. *Ezek* 7:2, 3, 6
iniquity have an e. 21:25, 29; 35:5
hitherto is the e. of. | *Dan* 7:28
time of e. shall be vision. | 8:17
time appointed the e. | 19*; 11:27
e. with a flood, and to e. | 9:26
in the e. of years they shall. | 11:6
purge them even to time of e. | 35
at time of the e. king of south. | 40
yet he shall come to his e. | 45
seal book to time of the e. | 12:4
shall be the e. of these things? | 8*
words are closed, till time of the e. 9
go thou thy way till the e. be. | 13
great houses have an e. | *Amos* 3:15
to what e. is it for you? | 5:18
the e. is come upon my people. | 8:2
I will make the e. thereof. |
for there is none e. | *Nah* 2:9
there is none e. of their corpses. 3:3
the harvest is the e. of. *Mat* 13:39
shall be the sign of the e.? | 24:3
gospel be preached, then shall e. | 14
gather from one e. of heaven to. | 31
went in and sat to see the e. | 26:58
in the e. of the sabbath came. | 28:1
cannot stand, hath an e. *Mark* 3:26
kingdom shall be no e. | *Luke* 1:33
a parable to them, to this e. | 18:1
things concerning me have e. | 22:37
a king, to this e. was. *John* 18:37
for the e. of those. | *Rom* 6:21
fruit to holiness, e. everlasting. | 22
Christ is the e. of the law. | 10:4
to this e. Christ both died. | 14:9
for to this e. also. | *2 Cor* 2:9
e. shall be according to their. | 11:15
glory world without e. | *Eph* 3:21
many walk, whose e. is. | *Phil* 3:19
e. of commandment is. | *1 Tim* 1:5
whose e. is to be burned. | *Heb* 6:8
oath is to them an e. of all. | 16
having neither beginning nor e. | 7:3
but now once in the e. hath. | 9:26
considering the e. of their. | 13:7
and ye have seen e. of. | *Jas* 5:11
receiving e. of your faith. | *1 Pet* 1:9
what shall be the e. of them? | 4:17
I am Alpha and Omega, the beginning and the e. | *Rev* 21:6; 22:13

at the end

at the e. of forty days. | *Gen* 8:6
at the e. of two years Pharaoh. 41:1
at the e. of 430 years. | *Ex* 12:41
of consecration at an e. | *Lev* 8:33

at the e. of 40 days. | *Deut* 9:11
at the e. of three years. | 14:28
at the e. of every seventh year a release. | 15:1
at the e. of every seventh year read this law. | 31:10
at the e. of three days. | *Josh* 9:16
at the e. of two months. *Judg* 11:39
Boaz lay down at e. of. | *Ruth* 3:17
at the e. of every year. *2 Sam* 14:26
came to Jerusalem at the e. | 24:8
at the e. of 3 years two. *1 Ki* 2:39
at the e. of 7 years the. | *2 Ki* 8:3
at the e. of three years they. | 18:10
find them at the e. of brook. |
at the e. of year host of Syria. 24:23
stagger, and are at wits' e. *Ps* 107:27
go to meet Ahaz at the e. | *Isa* 7:3
at the e. of seven years let go. |
at the e. of seven days. *Jer* 34:14
at the e. they might stand. *Dan* 1:5
at the e. of 12 months he. | 4:29
stand in the lot at the e. of. | 12:13
at the e. it shall speak. | *Hab* 2:3
in the e. of this world. | *Mat* 13:40

but the end

seems right to a man, but the e. are ways of death. *Pr* 14:12; 16:25
but the e. thereof shall not. | 20:21
but the e. is not yet. | *Mat* 24:6
| *Mark* 13:7; *Luke* 21:9
but the e. of all things. | *1 Pet* 4:7

last end

let my last e. be like. | *Num* 23:10
shall not see our last e. | *Jer* 12:4
remembereth not her last e. *Lam* 1:9
what shall be in last e. | *Dan* 8:19

latter end

his latter e. shall be. | *Num* 24:20
good at thy latter e. | *Deut* 8:16
would consider their latter e. 32:29
kindness in the latter e. | *Ruth* 3:10
bitterness in latter e. | *2 Sam* 2:26
yet thy latter e. should. | *Job* 8:7
Lord blessed the latter e. of. 42:12
be wise in thy latter e. | *Pr* 19:20
and know the latter e. | *Isa* 41:22
remember the latter e. of it. | 47:7
the latter e. is worse. | *2 Pet* 2:20

made an end

as Isaac had made an e. | *Gen* 27:30
Jacob made an e. of. | 49:33
made an e. of reconciling. *Lev* 16:20
made an e. of covering. | *Num* 4:15
had made an e. of speaking. | 16:31
| *Deut* 20:9
made an e. of tithing. | *Deut* 26:12
Moses had made an e. | 31:24
made an e. of speaking. | 32:45
Judg 15:17; *1 Sam* 18:1; 24:16
2 Sam 13:36; *1 Ki* 1:41; 3:1
| *Jer* 26:8; 43:1; 51:63
made an e. of slaying. | *Josh* 8:24
| 10:20
made an e. of dividing. | 19:49, 51
had made an e. to offer. | *Judg* 3:18
| *1 Sam* 13:10
he had made an e. of. *1 Sam* 10:13
made an e. of telling. | *2 Sam* 11:19
Hiram made an e. of. | *1 Ki* 7:40
Solomon made an e. of praying. | 8:54; *2 Chr* 7:1
made an e. of offering. *2 Ki* 10:25
| *1 Chr* 16:2; *2 Chr* 29:29
made an e. of the. | *2 Chr* 20:23
till they had made an e. | 24:10
made an e. with all that. *Ezra* 10:17
he had made an e. of speaking. inner house. | *Ezek* 42:15
thou hast made an e. of. | 43:23
made an e. of eating. | *Amos* 7:2
made an e. of commanding. *Mat* 11:1

make an end

I will also make an e. | *1 Sam* 3:12
will they make an e. in a? *Neh* 4:2
long ere you make an e.? *Job* 18:2
thou shalt make an e. to. *Isa* 33:1
thou make an e. of me. | 38:12, 13
nor did I make an e. of. *Ezek* 20:17
to make an e. of sins. | *Dan* 9:24
he will make an utter e. *Nah* 1:8, 9

make a full end
desolate, yet will I not *make a full e.*
   Jer 4:27; 5:18; 30:11; 46:28
destroy, but *make* not *a full e.* 5:10
thou *make a full e.?*   *Ezek* 11:13

to the end
to the e. thou mayest know that I.
   Ex 8:22; *Ezek* 20:26
to the e. Israel may.   *Lev* 17:5
to the e. that he should. *Deut* 17:16
to the e. that he may prolong. 20
their words *to the e.* of.   *Ps* 19:4
to the e. my glory may sing. 30:12
thy statutes even *to the e.* 119:112
from beginning *to the e.* *Eccl* 3:11
to the e. man should find. 7:14
utter it even *to the e.*   *Isa* 48:20
be my salvation *to the e.* 49:6
will he keep it *to the e.?* *Jer* 3:5
to the e. that none of. *Ezek* 31:14
sight thereof *to the e.*   *Dan* 4:11
dominion reacheth *to the e.* of. 7:14
how long shall be *to the e.?* 12:6
to the e. that every one.   *Ob* 9
endureth *to the e.* shall be saved.
   Mat 10:22; 24:13; *Mark* 13:13
cast out, *to the e.* they. *Acts* 7:19
to the e. you may be. *Rom* 1:11
to the e. the promise might. 4:16
acknowledge *to the e.* *2 Cor* 1:13
look *to the e.* of that. 3:13
to the e. he may establish.
   1 Thes 3:13
sober, and hope *to the e.* *1 Pet* 1:13

unto the end
beginning *unto the e.* *Deut* 11:12
the east border was *unto the e.*
   Josh 15:5
to glean *unto the e.* of. *Ruth* 2:23
may be tried *unto the e.* *Job* 34:36
wars to cease *unto the e.* *Ps* 46:9
I shall keep it *unto the e.* 119:33
proclaimed *unto the e.* of. *Isa* 62:11
it came *unto the e.* of.   *Jer* 1:3
dominion even *unto the e.* *Dan* 6:26
destroy his dominion *unto the e.* 7:26
and *unto the e.* of the war. 9:26
alway, even *unto the e.* *Mat* 28:20
loved them *unto the e.* *John* 13:1
confirm you *unto the e.* *1 Cor* 1:8
fast confidence *unto the e.* *Heb* 3:6
beginning stedfast *unto the e.* 14
assurance of hope *unto the e.* 6:11
my works *unto the e.*   *Rev* 2:26

endamage
so thou shalt *e.* the.   *Ezra* 4:13†

endanger
make me *e.* my head to. *Dan* 1:10

endangered
cleaveth wood shall be *e.* *Eccl* 10:9

endeavour
I will *e.* that you may. *2 Pet* 1:15*

endeavoured
we *e.* to go into Macedonia.
   Acts 16:10*
we *e.* to see your face. *1 Thes* 2:17

endeavouring
e. to keep the unity of. *Eph* 4:3*

endeavours
to wickedness of their *e.* *Ps* 28:4*

ended
seventh day God *e.* work. *Gen* 2:2
years of plenteousness *e.* 41:53
words till they were *e.* *Deut* 31:30
mourning for Moses were *e.* 34:8
so they *e.* the matter. *2 Sam* 20:18
the words of Job are *e.* *Job* 31:40
prayers of David are *e.* *Ps* 72:20
days of thy mourning *e.* *Isa* 60:20
is past, summer is *e.*   *Jer* 8:20
when Jesus had *e.* these. *Mat* 7:28
when forty days were *e.* *Luke* 4:2
when the devil had *e.* all. 13
supper being *e.* the devil. *John* 13:2

endeth
noise of them that rejoice *e.* *Isa* 24:8

ending
I am the beginning and *e.* *Rev* 1:8

endless
heed to *e.* genealogies. *1 Tim* 1:4
after power of an *e.* life. *Heb* 7:16

En-dor
Manasseh had *E.*   *Josh* 17:11
a woman at *E.* hath a. *1 Sam* 28:7
Jabin, which perished at *E.* *Ps* 83:10

endow
he shall surely *e.* her. *Ex* 22:16*

ends
push the people to *e.* *Deut* 33:17
shall judge the *e.* of the. *1 Sam* 2:10
the *e.* of staves were seen. *1 Ki* 8:8
   2 Chr 5:9
for he looketh to the *e.* *Job* 28:24
directeth his lightning to *e.* 37:3
it might take hold of the *e.* 38:13
and his circuit to the *e.* *Ps* 19:6
all the *e.* of the world shall. 22:27
thy praise to *e.* of the earth. 48:10
God ruleth in Jacob to the *e.* 59:13
confidence of all the *e.* of. 65:5
all the *e.* of the earth shall fear. 67:7
the *e.* of earth have seen the. 98:3
vapours to ascend from the *e.* of the
  earth. 135:7; *Jer* 10:13; 51:16
eyes of a fool are in *e.* *Pr* 17:24
established all *e.* of the earth? 30:4
creator of the *e.* of earth. *Isa* 40:28
e. of the earth were afraid. 41:5
taken from *e.* of the earth. 9
daughters from *e.* of the earth. 43:6
to me and be saved, all the *e.* 45:22
all *e.* shall see the salvation. 52:10
Gentiles come from *e.* *Jer* 16:19
a noise shall come to the *e.* 25:31
fire devoureth both the *e.* *Ezek* 15:4
shall he be great to *e.* *Mi* 5:4
dominion to *e.* of earth. *Zech* 9:10
salvation to *e.* of earth. *Acts* 13:47*
words to *e.* of the world. *Rom* 10:18
on whom *e.* of the world. *1 Cor* 10:11

endued
God hath *e.* me with. *Gen* 30:20*
a wise son, *e.* with. *2 Chr* 2:12
have sent a cunning man, *e.* with. 13
till ye be *e.* with. *Luke* 24:49*
and *e.* with knowledge ? *Jas* 3:13*

endure
[1] *To last, Ps* 72:12; 1 *Pet* 1:25.
[2] *To suffer patiently, Mat* 24:13.
[3] *To sustain or bear up under,*
Gen 33:14. [4] *To tolerate,* *Esth*
8:6.
as children be able to *e. Gen* 33:14*
thou shalt be able to *e.* *Ex* 18:23
for how can I *e.* to see evil. *Esth* 8:6
fast, but it shall not *e.* *Job* 8:15
I could not *e.* 31:23*
the Lord shall *e.* for ever. *Ps* 9:7*
   102:12, 26; 104:31
weeping may *e.* for a night. 30:5
as long as sun and moon *e.* 72:5
his name shall *e.* for ever. 17
seed will I make to *e.* 89:29, 36
doth the crown *e.* to ? *Pr* 27:24
can thy heart *e.* or ? *Ezek* 22:14
that shall *e.* to the end. *Mat* 24:13
   Mark 13:13
no root, and so *e.* but. *Mark* 4:17
tribulations that ye *e.* *2 Thes* 1:4
therefore *e.* hardness. *2 Tim* 2:3*
therefore I *e.* all things for. 10
will not *e.* sound doctrine. 4:3
watch in all things, *e.* afflictions. 5
if ye *e.* chastening.   *Heb* 12:7
they could not *e.* what was. 20
count them happy who *e.* *Jas* 5:11
for conscience *e.* grief. *1 Pet* 2:19

endured
time should have *e.* for. *Ps* 81:15
if God *e.* with much. *Rom* 9:22
persecutions I *e.* *2 Tim* 3:11
after he had patiently *e.* *Heb* 6:15
ye *e.* a great fight of afflictions. 10:32
for Moses *e.* as seeing him. 11:27
he *e.* the cross, 12:2
he *e.* such contradiction. 3

endureth
for his anger *e.* but a. *Ps* 30:5
goodness of God *e.* continually. 52:1
peace so long as moon *e.* 72:7
truth *e.* to all generations. 100:5
dominion *e.* throughout all. 145:13
he that *e.* to the end. *Mat* 10:22

---

meat which *e.* unto life. *John* 6:27
hopeth all things, *e.* all. *1 Cor* 13:7
blessed is man that *e.*   *Jas* 1:12

endureth *for ever*
his mercy *e. for ever. 1 Chr* 16:34, 41
  2 Chr 5:13; 7:3, 6; 20:21
Ezra 3:11; *Ps* 106:1; 107:1
118:1, 2, 3, 4; 136:1, 2, 3, etc.
   138:8; *Jer* 33:11
his righteousness *e. for ever.*
   Ps 111:3; 112:3, 9
his praise *e. for ever.* 111:10
his truth *e. for ever.* 117:2
thy judgements *e. for ever.* 119:160
name, O Lord, *e. for ever.* 135:13
word of Lord *e. for ever.* 1 *Pet* 1:25

enduring
fear of Lord is clean, *e.* *Ps* 19:9
is effectual in *e.* the. *2 Cor* 1:6
in heaven a better and *e. Heb* 10:34

Eneas, Aeneas
E. had kept his bed eight. *Acts* 9:33
E. Jesus maketh thee whole. 34

En-eglaim
from En-gedi to *E.* *Ezek* 47:10

enemies
(*The Revised Version frequently*
substitutes the words adversaries,
adversary, *which have slightly*
different meanings, but not so
different as to make it worth while
to star each reference so changed)
avenged of the king's *e. 1 Sam* 18:25
when Lord hath cut off *e.* 20:15
Lord require it of David's *e.* 16
so and more do God to *e.* 25:22
a present of the spoil of *e.* 30:26
to *e.* to blaspheme. *2 Sam* 12:14
the *e.* of my lord be as. 18:32
Lord fought against *e.* *2 Chr* 20:29
e. of the Jews hoped to. *Esth* 9:1
me from my deadly *e.*   *Ps* 17:9
the *e.* of the Lord shall be. 37:20
sharp in heart of king's *e.* 45:5
speak with the *e.* in gate. 127:5
beloved into hands of *e.* *Jer* 12:7
the *e.* have heard a cry of. 48:5
her friends become her *e. Lam* 1:2
her *e.* prosper. 5
a man's *e.* are the men of. *Mi* 7:6
if when we were *e.* *Rom* 5:10
concerning gospel, they are *e.* 11:28
till he hath put all *e.* *1 Cor* 15:25
are the *e.* of the cross. *Phil* 3:18
were *e.* in your mind. *Col* 1:21

his enemies
possess the gate of *his e. Gen* 22:17
eat up nations *his e.* *Num* 24:8*
he hath driven out *his e.* 32:21
help to him from *his e. Deut* 33:7
him rest from *his e.* *2 Sam* 7:1
hath avenged him of *his e.* 18:19
him out of hand of *his e.* 22:1
him rest from all *his e. 1 Chr* 22:9
counteth me as one of *his e.*
   Job 19:11
as for all *his e.* he.   *Ps* 10:5
not deliver him to will of *his e.* 41:2
let *his e.* be scattered. 68:1
God shall wound head of *his e.* 21
his e. shall lick the dust. 72:9
he smote all *his e.* in the hinder. 78:66
made all *his e.* to rejoice. 89:42
a fire burneth up *his e.* 97:3
see his desire upon *his e.* 112:8
his e. will I clothe with. 132:18
he maketh *his e.* to be at. *Pr* 16:7
Lord shall join *his e.* *Isa* 9:11
shall prevail against *his e.* 42:13
repay, recompence to *his e.* 59:18
rendereth recompence to *his e.* 66:6
indignation known towards *his e.* 14
Pharaoh into hand of *his e. Jer* 44:30
reserveth wrath for *his e.* *Nah* 1:2
darkness shall pursue *his e.* 8
till *his e.* be made his footstool.
   Heb 10:13

mine enemies
curse *mine e.* *Num* 23:11; 24:10
vengeance to *mine e. Deut* 32:41
enlarged over *mine e.* *1 Sam* 2:1

I be avenged on *mine e. 1 Sam* 14:24
Lord hath broken forth upon *mine e.*
   2 Sam 5:20; *1 Chr* 14:11
be saved from *mine e. 2 Sam* 22:4
   Ps 18:3
have pursued *mine e. 2 Sam* 22:38
   Ps 18:3
hast given me the necks of *mine e.*
   2 Sam 22:41; *Ps* 18:40
me forth from *mine e. 2 Sam* 22:49
to betray to *mine e. 1 Chr* 12:17*
hast smitten all *mine e. Ps* 3:7
lead me, because of *mine e.* 5:8
eye waxeth old because of *mine e.*
   6:7
let all *mine e.* be ashamed. 10
because of rage of *mine e.* 7:6
when *mine e.* are turned. 9:3
delivereth me from *mine e.* 18:48
table in presence of *mine e.* 23:5
let not *mine e.* triumph. 25:2; 35:19
consider *mine e.* for they. 25:19
mine e. came upon me. 27:2
head be lifted above *mine e.* 6
plain path, because of *mine e.* 11
deliver me not to will of *mine e.* 27
a reproach among all *mine e.* 31:11
deliver me from *mine e.* 15
but *mine e.* are lively. 38:19
mine e. speak evil of me. 41:5
mine e. reproach. *42:10; 102:8
shall reward evil to *mine e.* 54:5
mine eye hath seen his desire upon
   mine e. 7; 59:10
mine e. would swallow me up. 56:2
then shall *mine e.* turn back. 9
deliver me from *mine e.* 59:1; 143:9
they being *mine e.* wrongfully. 69:4
deliver me because of *mine e.* 18
mine e. speak against me. 71:10
see my desire on *mine e.* 92:11
made me wiser than *mine e.* 119:98
because *mine e.* have forgotten. 139
many are *mine e.* yet do I not. 157
forth thy hand against *mine e.* 138:7
I count them *mine e.* 139:22
of thy mercy cut off *mine e.* 143:12
avenge me of *mine e. Isa* 1:24
all *mine e.* have heard. *Lam* 1:21
mine e. chased me sore like. 3:52
mine e. bring hither. *Luke* 19:27

our enemies
they join also to *our e. Ex* 1:10
our e. themselves being. *Deut* 32:31
out of hand of *our e. 1 Sam* 4:3
deliver us out of hand of *our e.* 12:10
   2 Sam 19:9; *Ps* 44:7
of the reproach of *our e. Neh* 5:9
when rest of *our e.* heard. 6:1, 16
will we push down *our e. Ps* 44:5
tread down *our e.* 60:12; 108:13
and *our e.* laugh among. 80:6
redeemed us from *our e.* 136:24
our e. have opened their. *Lam* 3:46
be saved from *our e. Luke* 1:71
delivered out of hands of *our e.* 74

their enemies
naked amongst *their e. Ex* 32:25
faintness in land of *their e. Lev* 26:36
when they be in land of *their e.* 44
backs before *their e. Josh* 7:8, 12
stood not a man of all *their e*; Lord
   delivered *their e.* into. 21:44
rest from *their e.* 23:1; *Esth* 9:16
sold into hand of *their e. Judg* 2:14
out of hand of *their e.* 18; 8:34
into the hand of *their e. 2 Ki* 21:14
   2 Chr 6:36; 25:20; *Neh* 9:27
sea overwhelmed *their e. Ps* 78:53
soon have subdued *their e.* 81:14
stronger than *their e.* 105:24
the waters covered *their e.* 106:11
their e. oppressed them. 42
to sword before *their e. Jer* 15:9
by sword before *their e.* 19:7; 20:4
their e. shall straiten them. 9
of Judah give into hands of *their e.*
   20:5; 21:7; 34:20, 21; *Ezek* 39:23
out of *their e.* lands. *Ezek* 39:27
captivity before *their e. Amos* 9:4
which tread down *their e. Zech* 10:5
fire devoureth *their e. Rev* 11:5
ascended, and *their e.* beheld. 12

thine enemies
who delivered *thine e. Gen* 14:20
hand be in neck of *thine e.* 49:8
be an enemy to *thine e. Ex* 23:22
I will make *thine e.* to turn. 27
rise, Lord, let *thine e. Num* 10:35
cast out all *thine e. Deut* 6:19
goest against *thine e.* 20:1; 21:10
thine e. distress thee. 28:53, 55, 57
thine e. be found liars to. 33:29
not stand before *thine e. Josh* 7:13
so let all *thine e.* perish. *Judg* 5:31
vengeance for thee of *thine e.* 11:36
thine e. be as Nabal. *1 Sam* 25:26
the souls of *thine e.* shall. 29
cut off all *thine e. 2 Sam* 7:9
   1 Chr 17:8
in that lovest *thine e. 2 Sam* 19:6
three months before *thine e.* 24:13
nor hast asked life of *thine e.*
   1 Ki 3:11; *2 Chr* 1:11
while sword of *thine e. 1 Chr* 21:12
strength because of *thine e. Ps* 8:2
hand find out all *thine e.* 21:8
power shall *thine e.* submit. 66:3
foot dipped in blood of *thine e.* 68:23
thine e. roar. 74:4
forget not the voice of *thine e.* 23
thine e. make a tumult. 83:2
thou hast scattered *thine e.* 89:10
wherewith *thine e.* have. 51
lo, *thine e.* O Lord, *thine e.* 92:9
make *thine e.* thy footstool. 110:1
   Mat 22:44; *Mark* 12:36
   Luke 20:43; *Heb* 1:13
rule in midst of *thine e. Ps* 110:2
thine e. take thy name in. 139:20
the fire of *thine e.* shall. *Isa* 26:11
corn to be meat for *thine e.* 62:8
thee pass with *thine e. Jer* 15:14
thine e. have opened. *Lam* 2:16
interpretation to *thine e. Dan* 4:19
redeem thee from *thine e. Mi* 4:10
all *thine e.* shall be cut off. 5:9
gate be set open to *thine e. Nah* 3:13
thine e. cast a trench. *Luke* 19:43

your enemies
ye shall chase *your e. Lev* 26:7
your e. shall fall before you. 8
sow in vain, for *your e.* shall. 16
ye shall be slain before *your e.* 17
no power to stand before *your e.* 37
be saved from *your e. Num* 10:9
be not smitten before *your e.* 14:42
   Deut 1:42
rest from all *your e. Deut* 12:10
to battle against *your e.* 20:3
goeth to fight against *your e.* 4
ye shall be sold to *your e.* 28:68
Lord do to all *your e. Josh* 10:25
divide the spoil of *your e.* 22:8
delivered you out of hand of *your e.*
   1 Sam 12:11; *2 Ki* 17:39
but I say, love *your e. Mat* 5:44
   Luke 6:27, 35

enemy
hand dashed in pieces *e. Ex* 15:6
the *e.* said, I will pursue. 9
then I will be an *e.* to. 23:22
go to war against the *e. Num* 10:9
and was not his *e.* nor. 35:23
I feared wrath of the *e. Deut* 32:27
the beginning of revenges upon *e.* 42
he shall thrust out the *e.* 33:27
hath delivered an *e. Judg* 16:23, 24
thou shalt see an *e. 1 Sam* 2:32*
Saul became David's *e.* 18:29
if a man find his *e.* will he ? 24:19
thy people be smitten down before *e.*
   1 Ki 8:33; *2 Chr* 6:24
thou deliver them to *e. 1 Ki* 8:46
make thee fall before *e. 2 Chr* 25:8
e. could not countervail. *Esth* 7:4
the *e.* is this wicked Haman. 6
deliver me from *e.'s* hand ? *Job* 6:23
he counteth me for his *e.* 33:10
let the *e.* persecute my. *Ps* 7:5
thou mightest still the *e.* 8:2
e. destructions are come to. 9:6
mourning because of *e.?* 42:9; 43:2
us turn back from the *e.* 44:10
because of voice of the *e.* 55:3
not an *e.* that reproached me. 12

a strong tower from the *e. Ps* 61:3
my life from fear of *e.* 64:1
even all that the *e.* hath. 74:3
shall *e.* blaspheme thy name ? 10
e. hath reproached, O Lord. 18
when he delivered from *e.* 78:42
his glory into the *e.'s* hand. 61
e. shall not exact upon him. 89:22
for the *e.* hath persecuted. 143:3
kisses of an *e.* are. *Pr* 27:6
when the *e.* shall come in. *Isa* 59:19
he was turned to be their *e.* 63:10
the sword of the *e.* is. *Jer* 6:25
I will cause the *e.* to entreat. 15:11
them with east wind before *e.* 18:17
thee with wound of an *e.* 30:14
into captivity before *e. Lam* 1:5
for *e.* hath magnified himself. 9
children are desolate, because *e.* 16
drawn back his hand before *e.* 2:3
he hath bent his bow like an *e.* 4
the Lord was an *e.* he hath. 5
that *e.* should have entered. 4:12
because the *e.* had said. *Ezek* 36:2
the *e.* shall pursue him. *Hos* 8:3
people is risen up as an *e. Mi* 2:8
seek strength because of *e. Nah* 3:11
his *e.* came, sowed tares. *Mat* 13:25
said, an *e.* hath done this. 28
the *e.* that sowed them is. 39
tread over power of *e. Luke* 10:19
child of devil, thou *e.* of. *Acts* 13:10
last *e.* to be destroyed. *1 Cor* 15:26
am I become your *e.? Gal* 4:16
count him not as an *e. 2 Thes* 3:15
a friend of world is the *e. Jas* 4:4

hand of the enemy
into the *hand of the e. Lev* 26:25
   Neh 9:27
delivered us from the *hand of the e.*
   Ezra 8:31
not shut me up into *hand of the e.*
   Ps 31:8
his glory into the *hand of e.* 78:61
redeemed from the *hand of the e.*
   106:10; 107:2
fell into *hand of the e. Lam* 1:7
given into the *hand of the e.* 2:7

mine enemy
sent away *mine e.? 1 Sam* 19:17
delivered me from *my e.*
   2 Sam 22:18; *Ps* 18:17
found me, O *mine e.? 1 Ki* 21:20
mine e. sharpeneth his. *Job* 16:9
let *mine e.* be as wicked. 27:7
delivered him that is *mine e. Ps* 7:4
how long shall *mine e.* be ? 13:2
lest *mine e.* say, I have prevailed. 4
because *mine e.* doth not. 41:11
I swaddled hath *mine e. Lam* 2:22
rejoice not, O *mine e. Mi* 7:8
then she that is *mine e.* shall. 10

thine enemy
if thou meet *thine e. Ex* 23:4
thine e. shall distress. *Deut* 28:57
deliver thee from *e. 1 Sam* 24:4; 26:8
Lord is become *thine e.* 28:16
of Ish-bosheth *thine e. 2 Sam* 4:8
thou me for *thine e.? Job* 13:24
rejoice not when *thine e. Pr* 24:17
if *thine e.* hunger. 25:21; *Rom* 12:20
hath caused *thine e.* to. *Lam* 2:17
Lord hath cast out *thine e. Zeph* 3:15
thou shalt hate *thine e. Mat* 5:43

enflame, see inflame

engaged
who is this that *e.* his ? *Jer* 30:21*

En-gedi
wilderness of Judah, *E. Josh* 15:62
David dwelt in the holds at *E.*
   1 Sam 23:29; 24:1
Hazazon-tamar, is *E. 2 Chr* 20:2
in the vineyards of *E. S of S* 1:14
fishers stand from *E. Ezek* 47:10

engine, -s
Uzziah made *e. 2 Chr* 26:15
set *e.* of war against. *Ezek* 26:9

engrafted
with meekness *e.* word. *Jas* 1:21*

engrave
like a signet shalt *e. Ex* 28:11
I will *e.* the graving. *Zech* 3:9

engraven
ministration of death e. 2 Cor 3:7

engraver
with the work of an e. Ex 28:11
all manner of work of the e. 35:35
Aholiab, of tribe of Dan, an e. 38:23

engravings
like e. of a signet. Ex 28:11, 21, 36
39:14, 30

enjoin
to e. thee that which is. Philem 8

enjoined
Purim as Esther had e. Esth 9:31
who hath e. him his ways ? Job 36:23
blood of testament God e. Heb 9:20*

enjoy
land e. her sabbaths. Lev 26:34, 43
that Israel may e. Num 36:8*
beget sons, not e. them. Deut 28:41
return to land and e. it. Josh 1:15*
e. pleasure, behold this. Eccl 2:1
make soul e. good. 24; 3:13; 5:18
elect shall long e. work. Isa 65:22
thee we e. great quietness. Acts 24:2
giveth us all things to e. 1 Tim 6:17
than e. the pleasures of. Heb 11:25

enjoyed
till the land e. her. 2 Chr 36:21

enlarge
God shall e. Japhet. Gen 9:27
cast out nations and e. Ex 34:24
when Lord shall e. thy. Deut 12:20
if the Lord e. thy coast as. 19:8
bless me, and e. coast. 1 Chr 4:10
thou shalt e. my heart. Ps 119:32
e. the place of thy tent. Isa 54:2
might e. their border. Amos 1:13
make bald, e. thy. Mi 1:16
and e. the borders of. Mat 23:5

enlarged
my mouth is e. over. 1 Sam 2:1
thou hast e. my steps. 2 Sam 22:37
Ps 18:36
thou hast e. me when I. Ps 4:1*
troubles of my heart are e. 25:17
hell hath e. herself. Isa 5:14
thou hast e. thy bed, and. 57:8
thine heart shall fear and be e. 60:5
our heart is e. 2 Cor 6:11
recompence in same, be ye also e. 13
we shall be e. by you. 10:15*

enlargement
then e. shall arise from. Esth 4:14*

enlargeth
blessed be he that e. Deut 33:20
he e. the nations, and. Job 12:23*
who e. his desire as hell. Hab 2:5

enlarging
and there was an e. Ezek 41:7*

enlighten
Lord will e. my darkness. Ps 18:28*

enlightened
Jonathan's eyes were e. 1 Sam 14:27
29
to be e. with the light of. Job 33:30
his lightnings e. the world. Ps 97:4*
understanding being e. Eph 1:18
for those who were e. Heb 6:4

enlightening
Lord is pure, e. the eyes. Ps 19:8

enmity
I will put e. between thee. Gen 3:15
or in e. smite him. Num 35:21
thrust him suddenly without e. 22
before they were at e. Luke 23:12
carnal mind is e. against. Rom 8:7
abolished in his flesh e. Eph 2:15
cross, having slain the e. 16
friendship of world is e. Jas 4:4

Enoch
Cain's wife bare E. Gen 4:17
Jared begat E. 5:18
E. walked with God. 22, 24
which was the son of E. Luke 3:37
by faith E. was translated. Heb 11:5
E. also prophesied of these. Jude 14

Enon
John was baptizing in E. John 3:23

Enos
Seth called son's name E. Gen 4:26
which was son of E. Luke 3:38

enough
straw and provender e. Gen 24:25
I have e. my brother. 33:9
my blessing, because I have e. 11
it is large e. for them. 34:21
it is e. Joseph is yet alive. 45:28
entreat Lord, for it is e. Ex 9:28
bring much more than e. for. 36:5
dwelt long e. in this mount. Deut 1:6
compassed this mountain long e. 2:3
the hill is not e. for us. Josh 17:16
it is e.: stay now thine hand.
2 Sam 24:16; 1 Ki 19:4; 1 Chr 21:15
Mark 14:41; Luke 22:38
we have had e. to eat. 2 Chr 31:10
have goats' milk e. for. Pr 27:27
he that followeth after vain persons
shall have poverty e. 28:19
four things say not, it is e. 30:15
the fire that saith not, it is e. 16
which can never have e. Isa 56:11
destroy till they have e. Jer 49:9
eat, and not have e. Hos 4:10
not have stolen till they had e. Ob 5
the lion did tear e. for. Nah 2:12
but ye have not e. Hag 1:6
not be room e. to receive it. Mal 3:10
it is e. for the disciple. Mat 10:25
lest there be not e. for us. 25:9
servants have bread e. Luke 15:17
they had eaten e. Acts 27:38

enquire
call damsel, and e. at her. Gen 24:57
Rebekah went to e. of Lord. 25:22
the people come to e. of. Ex 18:15
and that thou e. not. Deut 12:30
then shalt thou e. and. 13:14
come unto the judge and e. 17:9
man doth come and e. of. Judg 4:20
when a man went to e of. 1 Sam 9:9
did I then begin to e. of God ? 22:15
woman, that I may e. of her. 28:7
Jehoshaphat said, e. I pray thee, at.
1 Ki 22:5; 2 Chr 18:4
we may e. of. 1 Ki 22:7; 2 Chr 18:6
go, e. of Baal-zebub. 2 Ki 1:2
not here a prophet to e.? 3:11
meet the man, and e. of the. 8:8
altar shall be for me to e. 16:15
go ye, e. of Lord. 22:13; 2 Chr 34:21
which sent you to e. 2 Ki 22:18
2 Chr 34:26
a familiar spirit, to e. 1 Chr 10:13
Tou sent to David to e. of. 18:10*
David could not go to e. of. 21:30
to e. concerning Judah. Ezra 7:14
for e. I pray thee of the. Job 8:8
beauty of Lord and to e. in. Ps 27:4
thou dost not e. wisely. Eccl 7:10
if ye will e. e. ye. Isa 21:12
e. I pray thee, of Lord. Jer 21:2
of Judah that sent you to e. 37:7
cometh to prophet to e. Ezek 14:7
elders of Israel came to e. 20:1
saith Lord, are ye come to e.? 3
e. who in it is worthy. Mat 10:11*
to e. among themselves.
Luke 22:23*; John 16:19
e. for Saul. Acts 9:11
if ye e. concerning other. 19:39*
as though ye would e. 23:15*, 20
any do e. of Titus my. 2 Cor 8:23

enquired
heard of it, and e. Deut 17:4
children of Israel e. of. Judg 20:27
they e. of the Lord. 1 Sam 10:22
and he e. of the Lord. 22:10, 13
David e. of Lord. 23:2, 4; 30:8
2 Sam 2:1; 5:19, 23; 21:1*
1 Chr 14:10, 14
Saul e. Lord answered. 1 Sam 28:6
David sent and e. 2 Sam 11:3
as if a man had e. at the. 16:23
Saul e. not of the Lord. 1 Chr 10:14
for we e. not at the ark in. 13:3*
they returned and e. Ps 78:34*
should I be e. of at all ? Ezek 14:3
saith the Lord, I will not be e. 20:3
shall I be e. of by you ? as I live, saith
Lord God, I will not be e. of. 31

I will yet for this be e. of. Ezek 36:37
matters the king e. of. Dan 1:20
those that have not e. for. Zeph 1:6
Herod e. of wise men. Mat 2:7*, 16*
then e. he the hour he. John 4:52
or our brethren be e. of. 2 Cor 8:23
of salvation prophets e. 1 Pet 1:10*

enquirest
e. after mine iniquity and. Job 10:6

enquiry
after vows to make e. Pr 20:25
the men had made e. Acts 10:17

enrich
the king will e. him. 1 Sam 17:25
thou didst e. the kings. Ezek 27:33

enriched
in every thing ye are e. 1 Cor 1:5
being e. in every thing. 2 Cor 9:11

enrichest
thou greatly e. it with. Ps 65:9

En-rogel
Ahimaaz stayed by E. 2 Sam 17:17
slew sheep and oxen by E. 1 Ki 1:9

enrolled
*This word is used in the Revisions
in two places ; in place of taxed in
Luke 2:1; and in place of written in
Heb 12:23. The word was also
put into the margin of the old
version, previous to the revision.*
all the world should be e. Luke 2:1
church of firstborn e. in. Heb 12:23

ensample
as ye have us for an e. Phil 3:17
to make ourselves an e. 2 Thes 3:9
an e. to those that. 2 Pet 2:6*

ensamples
happened to them for e. 1 Cor 10:11*
so that ye were e. to all. 1 Thes 1:7
but being e. to the flock. 1 Pet 5:3

ensign
he will lift up an e. to. Isa 5:26
which shall stand for an e. 11:10
shall set up an e. for nations. 12
when he lifteth up an e. 18:3
left as an e. on an hill. 30:17
princes shall be afraid of e. 31:9
of a crown lifted as e. Zech 9:16

ensigns
they set up their e. for. Ps 74:4

ensnared
reign not, lest people be e. Job 34:30

ensue
seek peace, and e. it. 1 Pet 3:11*

entangle
(*Frequently used as meaning per-
plex, bewilder, or insnare*)
how they might e. him. Mat 22:15*

entangled
Pharaoh will say, they are e. Ex 14:3
be not e. again with yoke. Gal 5:1
are again e. therein and. 2 Pet 2:20

entangleth
e. himself with affairs of. 2 Tim 2:4

enter
not slothful to e. to. Judg 18:9
prince shall e. by the porch.
Ezek 44:3; 46:2, 8
also set his face to e. Dan 11:17
he shall e. peaceably on fattest. 24
some must e. therein. Heb 4:6

enter *in or into*
near to e. into Egypt. Gen 12:11
Moses not able to e. into. Ex 40:35
all that e. in to perform. Num 4:23
water that causeth curse shall e.
into the woman, and. 5:24, 27
children shall e. into. Deut 23:8
shouldest e. into covenant. 29:12
not to e. into their cities. Josh 10:19
cry did e. into his ears. 2 Sam 22:7
thy feet e. into city. 1 Ki 14:12
disguise myself and e into. 22:30
if we e. into the city. 2 Ki 7:4
third part of you that e. in. 11:5
will e. into lodgings of borders, and.
19:23; Isa 37:24
unclean should e. in. 2 Chr 23:19
e. into his sanctuary. 30:8

house that I shall *e. into.*   *Neh* 2:8
none might *e. into* king's.   *Esth* 4:2
will he *e.* with thee *into?*   *Job* 22:4
he should *e. into* judgement.   34:23
sword *e. into* their heart.   *Ps* 37:15
e. into the king's palace.   45:15
e. into his gates with.   100:4
gate *into* which righteous shall *e.*
  118:20
a fool's lips *e. into.*   *Pr* 18:6
e. into the rock, and.   *Isa* 2:10
Lord will *e. into* judgement.   3:14
righteous nation may *e. in.*   26:2
my people, *e.* thou *into* thy.   20
he shall *e. into* peace.   57:2
that *e. in* at these gates.   *Jer* 7:2
  17:20; 22:2
e. into defenced cities.   8:14
if I *e. into* the city, behold.   14:18
e. into gates kings.   17:25; 22:4
who shall *e. into* habitations? 21:13
departed to go to *e. into.*   41:17
set your faces to *e. into.*   42:15
caused arrows to *e. into. Lam* 3:13
robbers shall *e. into* it.   *Ezek* 7:22
nor shall they *e. into* land of.   13:9
shall *e. into* thy gates, as men *e. into*
  a city wherein is.   26:10
cause breath to *e. into* you.   37:5
the priests *e. therein,* then.   42:14
gate be shut, no man *e. in* by.   44:2
they shall *e. into* my sanctuary.   16
when they *e. in* at the gates of.   17
shall *e. into* the fortress. *Dan* 11:7
he shall *e. into* the countries.   40
shall *e.* also *into* glorious land.   41
like a thief they shall *e. in. Joel* 2:9
nor *e. into* Gilgal.   *Amos* 5:5
Jonah began to *e. into. Jonah* 3:4
flying roll shall *e. into.*   *Zech* 5:4
in no case *e. into* kingdom. *Mat* 5:20
prayest, *e. into* thy closet.   6:6
e. in at strait gate. 7:13; *Luke* 13:24
not every one shall *e. in. Mat* 7:21
into what city ye shall *e.*   10:11
  Luke 10:8, 10
e. into a strong man's house.
  Mat 12:29; *Mark* 3:27
e. in and dwell there.   *Mat* 12:45
  Luke 11:26
better for thee to *e. into* life halt.
  Mat 18:8; *Mark* 9:43, 45, 47
wilt *e. into* life, keep.   *Mat* 19:17
a rich man shall hardly *e. into.*   23
than for rich man to *e. into* kingdom.
  24; *Mark* 10:25; *Luke* 18:25
e. into joy of thy Lord. *Mat* 25:21
no more openly *e. into. Mark* 1:45
may *e. into* the swine.   5:12
  Luke 8:32
what house ye *e. into. Mark* 6:10
  Luke 9:4; 10:5
and *e.* no more *into. Mark* 9:25
lest ye *e. into* temptation.   14:38
  Luke 22:46
they which *e. in* may see. *Luke* 8:16
many will seek to *e. in* and.   13:24
and to *e. into* his glory?   24:26
can he *e. into* his?   *John* 3:4
cannot *e. into* kingdom of God.   5
by me, if any man *e. in* he.   10:9
tribulation *e. into* the.   *Acts* 14:22
grievous wolves shall *e. in.*   20:29
do *e. into* rest, if they *e. into* rest.
  Heb 4:3, 5
labour therefore to *e. into* rest.   11
boldness to *e. into* holiest by. 10:19
man was able to *e. into. Rev* 15:8
in no wise *e. into* it any.   21:27
may *e. in* through the gates.   22:14

enter not

e. not into judgement.   *Ps* 143:2
e. not into the path.   *Pr* 4:14
e. not into the fields of the.   23:10
e. not into house of.   *Jer* 16:5
city of Samaritans *e. not. Mat* 10:5
that ye *e. not* into temptation. 26:41
  Luke 22:40

not enter

Aaron shall *not e.* into. *Num* 20:24
not e. into congregation. *Deut* 23:1
  2, 3
priests could *not e.* into. *2 Chr* 7:2

---

not e. into my rest.   *Ps* 95:11
and equity *cannot e.*   *Isa* 59:14
they should *not e.* into.   *Lam* 1:10
shall *not e.* into the land. *Ezek* 20:38
nor uncircumcised *e.* into.   44:9
I will *not e.* into city.   *Hos* 11:9
not e. into kingdom of.   *Mat* 18:3
he shall *not e.* therein.   *Mark* 10:15
  Luke 18:17
shall *not e.* into rest. *Heb* 3:11, 18
we see they could *not e.*   19

see kingdom of God

entered

self-same day *e.* Noah. *Gen* 7:13
the angels turned in, and *e.*   19:3
sun was risen when Lot *e.* into.   23
Joseph *e.* into his chamber.   43:30
as Moses *e.* into the.   *Ex* 33:9
bring men that are *e.* into. *Josh* 2:3
and they *e.* into the land. *Judg* 6:5
e. into an hold of god Berith.   9:46
e. into another tent.   *2 Ki* 7:8
as Jehu *e. in* at the gate.   9:31
when king *e.* into the. *2 Chr* 12:11
e. into a covenant to seek.   15:12
Jotham *e.* not into the temple. 27:2
they *e.* into a curse. *Neh* 10:29
hast thou *e.* into springs? *Job* 38:16
hast thou *e.* into treasures of?   22
but when ye *e.* ye defiled. *Jer* 2:7
death is *e.* into our windows.   9:21
the people which had *e.* into. 34:10
when Jeremiah was *e.* into. 37:16
heathen *e.* her sanctuary. *Lam* 1:10
enemy should have *e.* gates.   4:12
spirit *e.* into me. *Ezek* 2:2; 3:24
I sware and *e.* into a covenant. 16:8
they *e.* unto the heathen.   36:20
the God of Israel hath *e.*   44:2
in day that foreigners *e.*   *Ob* 11
shouldest not have *e.* into gate. 13
e. into my bones, I.   *Hab* 3:16
when Jesus was *e.* into.   *Mat* 8:5
he *e.* into a ship and passed.   9:1
how he *e.* into house of God.   12:4
day Noah *e.* into the ark.   24:38
  Luke 17:27
the unclean spirits went out and *e.*
  Mark 5:13; *Luke* 8:33
whithersoever he *e. Mark* 6:56
Mary *e.* into house.   *Luke* 1:40
I *e.* thine house, thou gavest.   7:44
feared as they *e.* into cloud.   9:34
woe to lawyers, ye *e.* not in. 11:52
then *e.* Satan into Judas.   22:3
  John 13:27
when ye are *e.* the city. *Luke* 22:10
are *e.* into their labours. *John* 4:38
a garden, into the which he *e.* 18:1
Pilate *e.* into the judgement-hall. 33
Ananias *e.* and putting. *Acts* 9:17
nothing unclean hath *e.* into.   11:8
e. into castle and told Paul. 23:16
Agrippa was *e.* into place of. 25:23
to whom Paul *e. in,* and.   28:8
sin *e.* into the world.   *Rom* 5:12
the law *e.*   20
neither have *e.* into heart. *1 Cor* 2:9
e. not in because of.   *Heb* 4:6
for he that is *e.* into his rest.   10
forerunner is for us *e.* even.   6:20
e. in once into holy place. 9:12, 24
are *e.* into the ears of.   *Jas* 5:4
many deceivers are *e.*   *2 John* 7
Spirit of life from God *e. Rev* 11:11

entereth

number every one that *e.* into the.
  Num 4:30, 35, 39, 43
to every one that *e.*   *2 Chr* 31:16
when wisdom *e.* into.   *Pr* 2:10
reproof *e.* more into a wise. 17:10
sword *e.* into their.   *Ezek* 21:14
he that *e. in* by the way of.   46:9
whatsoever *e. in* at the mouth.
  Mat 15:17*; *Mark* 7:18
and *e. in* where the.   *Mark* 5:40
follow him where he *e. Luke* 22:10
e. not by the door into. *John* 10:1
he that *e. in* by the door.   2
which *e.* into that within. *Heb* 6:19
as the high priest *e.* every.   9:25

entering

cast it at the *e.* of gate. *Josh* 8:29

---

shall stand at the *e.* of gate.
  Josh 20:4
Gaal stood in the *e.* *Judg* 9:35
Abimelech stood in the *e.*   44
men of Dan stood by the *e.* 18:16
the priest stood in the *e.* of gate. 17
by *e.* into a town that. *1 Sam* 23:7
battle in array at *e.* in. *2 Sam* 10:8
for the *e.* of the oracle. *1 Ki* 6:31
Elijah stood in the *e.* in.   19:13
four leprous men at *e.*   *2 Ki* 7:3
lay heads in two heaps at *e.* 10:8
that were in the *e.* of the gate. 23:8
kings sat at *e.* of gate. *2 Chr* 18:9*
there is no house, no *e.*   *Isa* 23:1
thrones at the *e.* of. *Jer* 1:15; 17:27
mark well the *e.* in of. *Ezek* 44:5
nor suffer ye them that are *e.* to.
  Mat 23:13; *Luke* 11:52
lusts of other things *e. Mark* 4:19
nothing without *e.* into him. 7:15*
e. into the sepulchre they saw. 16:5
at your *e.* ye shall.   *Luke* 19:30
Saul *e.* into every house. *Acts* 8:3
what manner of *e.* in. *1 Thes* 1:9
a promise left us of *e.*   *Heb* 4:1

enterprise

hands cannot perform *e.* *Job* 5:12

entertain

be not forgetful to *e.* *Heb* 13:2*

entertained

some have *e.* angels. *Heb* 13:2

entice

To persuade, or allure, Judg 14:15;
16:5; 2 Chr 18:19. *In the Bible
usually in the bad sense.*

if a man *e.* a maid not. *Ex* 22:16
if wife *e.* thee secretly. *Deut* 13:6
e. husband, that he may. *Judg* 14:15
lords said to Delilah, *e.* him. 16:5
who shall *e.* Ahab? *2 Chr* 18:19
I will *e.* him.   20
thou shalt *e.* him and prevail. 21
if sinners *e.* thee.   *Pr* 1:10

enticed

if heart been secretly *e. Job* 31:27
peradventure he will be *e. Jer* 20:10†
when drawn away and *e. Jas* 1:14

enticeth

a violent man *e.* his. *Pr* 16:29

enticing

was not with *e.* words. *1 Cor* 2:4*
man beguile you with *e.* *Col* 2:4*

entire

that ye be perfect and *e.* *Jas* 1:4

entrance

us the *e.* into the city. *Judg* 1:24
shewed them the *e.* they smote it. 25
ran before Ahab to *e.* of. *1 Ki* 18:46
the two kings sat in the *e.* 22:10
kept the *e.* of king's. *2 Chr* 12:10*
the *e.* of thy words. *Ps* 119:130*
yourselves know our *e.* *1 Thes* 2:1
so an *e.* shall be.   *2 Pet* 1:11

entreat

*In the Bible, frequently, to treat,
deal with, use (obsolete elsewhere),*
Jer 15:11.

cause the enemy to *e.* *Jer* 15:11*
e. them evil 400 years. *Acts* 7:6

see intreat

entreated

he *e.* Abraham for. *Gen* 12:16†
so evil *e.* this people? *Ex* 5:22†
and Egyptians evil *e.* us. *Deut* 26:6†
and *e.* them spitefully. *Mat* 22:6
  Luke 18:32
e. him shamefully. *Luke* 20:11*
same evil *e.* our fathers. *Acts* 7:19
Julius courteously *e.* Paul. 27:3*
we were shamefully *e.* *1 Thes* 2:2

entreateth

he evil *e.* the barren. *Job* 24:21*

entries

the chambers of *e.* *Ezek* 40:38*

entry

king's *e.* without turned. *2 Ki* 16:18
fathers were keepers of *e. 1 Chr* 9:19

doors of *e.* of house.   *2 Chr* 4:22
crieth at the gates, at *e.*   *Pr* 8:3
Jeremiah into third *e.*   *Jer* 38:14
hide the stones at the *e.* of.   43:9
image of jealousy in the *e. Ezek* 8:5

envied
the Philistines *e.* Isaac.   *Gen* 26:14
Rachel *e.* her sister, and.   30:1
Joseph's brethren *e.* him.   37:11
they *e.* Moses also in.   *Ps* 106:16
for this man is *e.* of.   *Eccl* 4:4
trees in garden of God *e. Ezek* 31:9

envies
aside all malice, guile, *e. 1 Pet* 2:1

enviest
Moses said, *e.* thou ?   *Num* 11:29*

envieth
charity suffereth, and *e. 1 Cor* 13:4

envious
nor be *e.* against workers. *Ps* 37:1
for I was *e.* at the foolish.   73:3
be not thou *e.* against.   *Pr* 24:1
fret not, neither be thou *e.*   19

environ
Canaanites hear and *e. Josh* 7:9*

envy
*(Discontent at the excellence or
good fortune of another. Frequently in the Bible with the
distinct idea of malice or spite.
The Revisions often replace it by
jealousy)*
wrath killeth, and *e.*   *Job* 5:2
e. is rottenness of bones. *Pr* 14:30
who is able to stand before *e.?* 27:4
love, hatred, and *e.* is.   *Eccl* 9:6
the *e.* also of Ephraim.   *Isa* 11:13
and be ashamed for their *e.* 26:11
do according to thine *e. Ezek* 35:11
for *e.* they delivered him. *Mat* 27:18
                Mark 15:10
patriarchs moved with *e.* *Acts* 7:9
Jews filled with *e.* spake.   13:45
believed not, moved with *e.*   17:5
full of *e.* murder, debate. *Rom* 1:29
preach Christ, even of *e.* *Phil* 1:15
whereof cometh *e.* strife. *1 Tim* 6:4
living in malice and *e.*   *Tit* 3:3
dwelleth in us lusteth to *e. Jas* 4:5

envy, *verb*
e. thou not oppressor.   *Pr* 3:31
let not thine heart *e.* sinners. 23:17
Ephraim not *e.* Judah.   *Isa* 11:13

envying
not in strife and *e.*   *Rom* 13:13*
there is among you *e.*   *1 Cor* 3:3*
provoking one another, *e. Gal* 5:26
but if ye have bitter *e.*   *Jas* 3:14*
where *e.* is, there is confusion. 16*

envyings
there be debates, *e.*   *2 Cor* 12:20*
works of the flesh are *e. Gal* 5:21

Epaphras
as ye learned of *E.* our.   *Col* 1:7
E. saluteth you.   4:12; *Philem* 23

Epaphroditus
to send to you *E.*   *Phil* 2:25
received of *E.*   4:18

Epenetus
salute my well-beloved *E. Rom* 16:5

ephah
*(A Hebrew measure of the same
capacity as the bath, containing ten
homers. About a bushel, dry
measure, or nine gallons liquid
measure)*
see **bath,** *and* **homer**
homer is tenth part of *e.*   *Ex* 16:36
tenth part of an *e. Lev* 5:11; 6:20
have a just *e.*   19:36; *Ezek* 45:10
tenth part of an *e.* of.   *Num* 5:15
unleavened cakes of an *e. Judg* 6:19
and it was about an *e.*   *Ruth* 2:17
take now an *e.* of this.   *1 Sam* 17:17
seed of an homer shall yield an *e.*
                Isa 5:10
the *e.* and baths shall. *Ezek* 45:11
an hin of oil to an *e.*   46:5, 7, 11
making the *e.* small.   *Amos* 8:5

he said, this is an *e.*   *Zech* 5:6
cast it into midst of the *e.*   8

Ephah
E. the son of Midian.   *Gen* 25:4
                1 Chr 1:33
E. Caleb's concubine.   *1 Chr* 2:46
sons of Jahdai, Pelet, *E.*   47
the dromedaries of *E.*   *Isa* 60:6

Ephes-dammim
Philistines pitched in *E. 1 Sam* 17:1

Ephesians
great is Diana of *E.* *Acts* 19:28, 34
the city of the *E.* is a worshipper. 35

Ephesus
Paul came to *E.*   *Acts* 18:19
sailed from *E.*   21
Jew named Apollos came to *E.* 24
to Jews and Greeks at *E.*   19:17
not alone at *E.* but through Asia. 26
ye men of *E.*   35
Paul determined to sail by *E.* 20:16
fought with beasts at *E. 1 Cor* 15:32
I will tarry at *E.*   16:8
thee to abide still at *E.*   *1 Tim* 1:3
ministered to me at *E.* *2 Tim* 1:18
Tychicus have I sent to *E.*   4:12
send it to *E.*   *Rev* 1:11
to the angel at *E.*   2:1

ephod
*The upper garment worn by the
Jewish priests. There were two
sorts of ephods, one of plain linen
for the priests, and another embroidered for the high priest. That
for the high priest was of gold, blue,
purple, crimson, and twisted linen.
The shoulder pieces were held
together by two onyx stones,
each engraved with the names of
six tribes of Israel, Ex* 28:4, 5, 6, etc.
*The Ephod worn by ordinary priests
was of linen only, neither so rich,
nor so much adorned.*
to be set in. *e.*   *Ex* 25:7; 35:9, 27
they shall make an *e.* and.   28:4, 6
curious girdle of *e.*   8*, 27, 28
       39:5*, 20; *Lev* 8:7
on shoulders of *e.*   *Ex* 28:12, 25
after the work of the *e.*   15; 39:8
robe of the *e.* of blue. 28:31; 39:22
he made the *e.* of gold, blue. 39:2
he put the *e.* upon him.   *Lev* 8:7
and Gideon made an *e. Judg* 8:27
man Micah made an *e.* and.   17:5
there is in these houses an *e.* 18:14
girded with a linen *e.*   *1 Sam* 2:18
choose him to wear an *e.*   28
the Lord's priest wearing an *e.* 14:3
sword is wrapt in cloth behind *e.* 21:9
85 persons that did wear *e.*   22:18
Abimelech fled with an *e.* in. 23:6
bring hither the *e.*   9; 30:7
danced before Lord, girded with
linen *e. 2 Sam* 6:14; *1 Chr* 15:27
shall abide without an *e.* *Hos* 3:4

Ephphatha
he saith to him, *E.* that. *Mark* 7:34

Ephraim, *a place*
had sheep-shearers beside *E.*
                2 Sam 13:23
Abijah took *E.* and.   *2 Chr* 13:19
into a city called *E.*   *John* 11:54

mount Ephraim
if *mount E.* be too.   *Josh* 17:15
Shechem in *mount E.*   20:7; 21:21
Joshua in *mount E.*   *Judg* 2:9
messengers through *mount E.* 7:24
Micah of *mount E.*   17:1
Levite came to *mount E.*   8
Danites passed unto *mount E.* 18:13
sojourning on side of *mount E.* 19:1
Elkanah of *mount E.*   *1 Sam* 1:1
Saul passed through *mount E.* 9:4
Sheba of *mount E.*   *2 Sam* 20:21
two men be come from *mount E.*
                2 Ki 5:22
affliction from *mount E.*   *Jer* 4:15
watchman upon *mount E.*   31:6
Israel be satisfied on *mount E.* 50:19

Ephraim, *a person,* or *people*
of Joseph's second son *E. Gen* 41:52

Israel laid right hand on *E. Gen* 48:14
saying, God make thee as *E,* and he
   set *E.* before Manasseh.   20
prince of *E.* was.   *Num* 1:10; 7:48
on west side standard of *E.*   2:18
standard of the camp of *E.*   10:22
the sons of *E.*   26:35; *1 Chr* 7:20
the ten thousands of *E. Deut* 33:17
cities for the children of *E.*
            Josh 16:9; 17:9
nor did *E.* drive out the.   *Judg* 1:29
out of *E.* was there a root.   5:14
gleaning of the grapes of *E.*   8:2
fought with *E.* smote *E.*   12:4
Ish-bosheth king over *E. 2 Sam* 2:9
E. their father mourned. *1 Chr* 7:22
dwelt of the children of *E.*   9:3
strangers out of *E.* fell. *2 Chr* 15:9
set garrisons in cities of *E.*   17:2
separated the army out of *E.* 25:10
Zichri a mighty man of *E.*   28:7
of *E.* had not cleansed.   30:18
all Israel brake images in *E.*   31:1
children of *E.* being armed. *Ps* 78:9
before *E.* stir up thy strength. 80:2
Syria is confederate with *E. Isa* 7:2
E. hath taken evil counsel.   5
sixty-five years shall *E.*   8
the head of *E.* is Samaria.   9
from the day that *E.* departed. 17
E. that say in the pride and.   9:9
Manasseh shall eat *E.* and *E.*   21
E. shall depart; *E.* not envy Judah,
   Judah not vex *E.*   11:13
fortress also shall cease from *E.* 17:3
woe to the drunkards of *E.*   28:1
drunkards of *E.* be trodden under. 3
cast out whole seed of *E. Jer* 7:15
I have heard *E.* bemoaning.   31:18
the stick of *E.*   *Ezek* 37:16
stick of Joseph in hand of *E.*   19
a portion for *E.*   48:5
E.-E. thou committest.   *Hos* 5:3
Israel and *E.* shall fall in iniquity. 5
E. shall be desolate.   9
I will be unto *E.* as a moth.   12
when *E.* saw his sickness, *E.*   13
E. as a lion.   14
O. *E.* what shall I do to thee ?   6:4
there is the whoredom of *E.*   10
the iniquity of *E.*   7:1
E. hath mixed himself among.   8
E. hired lovers.   8:9
E. made altars to sin.   11
E. shall eat unclean things.   9:3
watchmen of *E.* was with my God. 8
E. their glory shall fly away.   11
E. shall bring forth children to.   13
E. shall receive shame.   10:6
I will make *E.* to ride.   11
I taught *E.* to go.   11:3
how shall I give thee up, *E.?*   8
I will not return to destroy *E.*   9
E. compasseth me about with.   12
E. feedeth on wind.   12:1
E. said, I am rich.   8
E. provoked him to anger.   14
when *E.* spake trembling, *E.*   13:1
iniquity of *E.* is bound up.   12
E. say, what have I to do ?   14:8
shall possess the fields of *E. Ob* 19
cut off chariot from *E.*   *Zech* 9:10
have filled the bow with *E.*   13
they of *E.* be like a mighty.   10:7

see **gate**

Ephraim *is*
E. is the strength.   *Ps* 60:7; 108:8
E. is my firstborn.   *Jer* 31:9
is *E.* my dear son ?   20
E. is joined to idols.   *Hos* 4:17
E. is oppressed.   5:11
E. is a cake not turned.   7:8
E. is like a silly dove.   11
E. is smitten.   9:16
E. is as an heifer that is.   10:11

Ephraim *with* **tribe**
of the *tribe* of *E.* 40,500. *Num* 1:33
of the *tribe* of *E.* to spy.   13:8
of *tribe* of *E.* to divide.   34:24
inheritance of *tribe* of *E. Josh* 16:8
Kohathites had cities out of the *tribe*
of *E.*   21:5, 20; *1 Chr* 6:66
chose not the *tribe* of *E. Ps* 78:67

Ephraimite, -s
art thou an *E.*? *Judg* 12:5
fell at that time of *E.* 42,000. 6

Ephratah
do thou worthily in *E.* *Ruth* 4:11
Hur, firstborn of *E.* *1 Chr* 2:50; 4:4
lo, we heard of it at *E.* *Ps* 132:6
thou, Beth-lehem *E.* *Mi* 5:2

Ephrath
little way to come to *E.* *Gen* 35:16
Rachel buried in way to *E.* 19; 48:7
Caleb took to him *E.* *1 Chr* 2:19

Ephrathite, -s
Mahlon, Chilion, *E.* of. *Ruth* 1:2
Elkanah was an *E.* *1 Sam* 1:1
Jesse an *E.* 17:12
Jeroboam *E.* of Zereda. *1 Ki* 11:26

Ephron
intreat for me to *E.* the. *Gen* 23:8
to *E.* weighed silver to *E.* 16
buried in the field of *E.* 25:9
bought with field of *E.* 49:30; 50:13

Epicureans
certain of *E.* encountered. *Acts* 17:18

epistle
(*A letter. In the New Testament,*
usually, a letter of an Apostle to
a church or an individual)
delivered the *e.* *Acts* 15:30; 23:33
Tertius who wrote this *e.* *Rom* 16:22
I wrote to you in an *e.* *1 Cor* 5:9
e. written in our hearts. *2 Cor* 3:2
declared to be the *e.* of Christ. 3
I perceive the same *e.* made. 7:8
when this *e.* is read, likewise read
the *e.* from. *Col* 4:16
this *e.* be read to all. *1 Thes* 5:27
by word or our *e.* *2 Thes* 2:15
any obey not our word by this *e.* 3:14
which is the token in every *e.* 17
this second *e.* I now. *2 Pet* 3:1

epistles
we *e.* of commendation. *2 Cor* 3:1
as also in all his *e.* *2 Pet* 3:16

equal
behold things that are *e.* *Ps* 17:2*
it was thou, a man, mine *e.* 55:13
legs of the lame are not *e.* *Pr* 26:7*
whom shall I *e.*? *Isa* 40:25; 46:5
what shall I *e.* to thee. *Lam* 2:13
way of Lord not *e.* hear, is not my
way *e.*? *Ezek* 13:25, 29; 33:17, 20
Israel, are not my ways *e.*? 18:29
for them, their way is not *e.* 33:17
hast made them *e.* to us. *Mat* 20:12
for they are *e.* to angels. *Luke* 20:36
himself *e.* with God. *John* 5:18
not robbery to be *e.* *Phil* 2:6*
your servants what is *e.* *Col* 4:1
and height of city are *e.* *Rev* 21:16

equal, verb
gold and crystal cannot *e.* *Job* 28:17
the topaz of Ethiopia not *e.* it. 19

equality
an *e.* that there be an *e.* *2 Cor* 8:14

equally
two tenons *e.* distant. *Ex* 36:22

equals
above many my *e.* *Gal* 1:14*

equity
judge the people with *e.* *Ps* 98:9
thou dost establish *e.* 99:4
instruction of wisdom and *e.* *Pr* 1:3
understand judgement and *e.* 2:9
nor to strike princes for *e.* 17:26*
man whose labour is in *e.* *Eccl* 2:21*
with *e.* for meek of the. *Isa* 11:4
truth is fallen in street, and *e.* 59:14*
hear this, ye that pervert *e.* *Mi* 3:9
with me in peace and *e.* *Mal* 2:6*

Er
called his name *E.* *Gen* 38:3
took a wife for *E.* 6
E. was wicked. 7; *1 Chr* 2:3
E. father of Lecah. *1 Chr* 4:21
Elmodam, the son of *E.* *Luke* 3:28

Erastus
sent Timotheus and *E.* *Acts* 19:22
E. abode at Corinth. *2 Tim* 4:20

ere
delivered *e.* midwives. *Ex* 1:19
long *e.* they believe me? *Num* 14:11
how long *e.* you make? *Job* 18:2
long *e.* thou be quiet? *Jer* 47:6
how long *e.* they attain? *Hos* 8:5
come down *e.* my child. *John* 4:49

erected
Jacob *e.* there an altar. *Gen* 33:20

err
(*To go astray ; to fall into error*)
made Judah to *e.* *2 Chr* 33:9
a people that do *e.* in. *Ps* 95:10
which do *e.* from thy. 119:21*
hast trodden them that *e.* 118
not *e.* that devise evil? *Pr* 14:22
instruction that causeth to *e.* 19:27
they which lead thee cause thee to *e.*
Isa 3:12; 9:16
have caused Egypt to *e.* 19:14*
they *e.* in vision, they. 28:7
a bridle causing them to *e.* 30:28
the wayfaring men shall not *e.* 35:8
why hast thou made us to *e.*? 63:17
prophets in Baal, and caused people
Israel to *e.* *Jer* 23:13; *Mi* 3:5
of whoredom caused them to *e.*
Hos 4:12
lies caused them to *e.* *Amos* 2:4
ye do *e.* not knowing the scriptures.
Mat 22:29; *Mark* 12:24, 27
always *e.* in their hearts. *Heb* 3:10
do not *e.* my brethren. *Jas* 1:16*
if any of you do *e.* from truth. 5:19

errand
eat till I have told *e.* *Gen* 24:33
I have a secret *e.* unto. *Judg* 3:19
I have an *e.* to thee, O. *2 Ki* 9:5

erred
ignorance wherein he *e.* *Lev* 5:18
ye have *e.* and not. *Num* 15:22
I have *e.* exceedingly. *1 Sam* 26:21
understand wherein I have *e.*
Job 6:24
be it indeed that I have *e.* 19:4
yet I *e.* not from. *Ps* 119:110*
e. through wine and . . . priest and the
prophet have *e.* *Isa* 28:7*
they also that *e.* in spirit. 29:24
coveted they have *e.* *1 Tim* 6:10*
some professing have *e.* 21
concerning truth have *e.* *2 Tim* 2:18

erreth
he that refuseth reproof *e.* *Pr* 10:17
do for every one that *e.* *Ezek* 45:20

error
[1] *A mistake or oversight,* *Eccl*
5:6. [2] *False doctrine, which is*
not agreeable to the word of God,
1 John 4:6. [3] *Sins of all sorts,*
Ps 19:12; Heb 9:7.
smote Uzzah for his *e.* *2 Sam* 6:7
if erred mine *e.* remaineth. *Job* 19:4
neither say that it was an *e.* *Eccl* 5:6
evil which I have seen as an *e.* 10:5
and to utter *e.* against. *Isa* 32:6
neither was there any *e.* found.
Dan 6:4
last *e.* shall be worse. *Mat* 27:64
recompence of their *e.* *Rom* 1:27
converteth sinner from *e.* *Jas* 5:20
from them who live in *e.* *2 Pet* 2:18
ye being led away with the *e.* 3:17
know we the spirit of *e.* *1 John* 4:6
have ran greedily after *e.* *Jude* 11

errors
who can understand his *e.*? *Ps* 19:12
vanity, the work of *e.* *Jer* 10:15*
51:18*
he offered for *e.* of people. *Heb* 9:7

Esaias, *see* Isaiah

Esarhaddon
E. reigned in his stead. *2 Ki* 19:37
Isa 37:38
since the days of *E.* king. *Ezra* 4:2

Esau
they called his name *E.* *Gen* 25:25

E. was a hunter. *Gen* 25:27
E. came from field. 29
thus *E.* dispised his birthright. 34
E. my brother is a hairy man. 27:11
whether thou be my son *E.* 21, 24
E. hated Jacob because of the. 41
these words of *E.* were told to. 42
then went *E.* to Ishmael. 28:9
Jacob sent messengers to *E.* 32:3
deliver me from hand of *E.* 11
a present sent unto my lord *E.* 18
E. ran to meet him. 33:4
E. said, I have enough, my. 9
thou fleddest from *E.* thy. 35:1
these are generations of *E.* 36:1
E. the father of the Edomites. 43
given mount Seir to *E.* *Deut* 2:5, 12
Josh 24:4
did to the children of *E.* *Deut* 2:22
unto Isaac, Jacob, and *E.* *Josh* 24:4
1 Chr 1:34
calamity of *E.* on him. *Jer* 49:8
I have made *E.* bare. 10
are things of *E.* searched out! *Ob* 6
house of *E.* shall be for stubble. 18
to judge the mount of *E.* 21
was not *E.* Jacob's? *Mal* 1:2
and I hated *E.* 3; *Rom* 9:13
blessed Jacob and *E.* *Heb* 11:20
be any profane person, as *E.* 12:16

escape
e. for thy life, *e.* to. *Gen* 19:17
O let me *e.* 20
haste thee, *e.* thither. 22
company which is left shall *e.* 32:8
none of them remain or *e.* *Josh* 8:22
e. into the land of the. *1 Sam* 27:1
for we shall not else *e.* *2 Sam* 15:14
get him fenced cities and *e.* 20:6
let none of them *e.* *1 Ki* 18:40
2 Ki 9:15
if any I have brought *e.* *2 Ki* 10:24
that *e.* out of Zion. 19:31; *Isa* 37:32
leave us a remnant to *e.* *Ezra* 9:8
think not thou shalt *e.* *Esth* 4:13
wicked shall not *e.* *Job* 11:20
shall they *e.* by iniquity? *Ps* 56:7
me, and cause me to *e.* 71:2*
wicked fall, whilst I *e.* 141:10
speaketh lies shall not *e.* *Pr* 19:5
pleaseth God shall *e.* *Eccl* 7:26
help, how shall we *e.*? *Isa* 20:6
I will send those that *e.* to. 66:19
shall not be able to *e.* *Jer* 11:11
nor principal of flock to *e.* 25:35
Zedekiah shall not *e.* 32:4; 34:3
38:18, 23
that go into Egypt *e.* 42:17; 44:14
return but such as shall *e.* 44:14
yet a small number that *e.* 28
swift flee, nor mighty man *e.* 46:6
spoiler shall come, no city *e.* 48:8
of them that flee and *e.* 50:28
let none thereof *e.* recompense. 29
some that shall *e.* the. *Ezek* 6:8
and they that *e.* of you shall. 9
they that *e.* shall *e.* and be. 7:16
e. that doth such things? 17:15
all these things, shall not *e.* 18
but these shall *e.* out. *Dan* 11:41*
land of Egypt shall not *e.* 42
and nothing shall *e.* them. *Joel* 2:3
off those by that did *e.* *Ob* 14
can ye *e.* damnation of? *Mat* 23:33
accounted worthy to *e.* *Luke* 21:36
kill prisoners, lest any *e.* *Acts* 27:42
that thou shalt *e.* the? *Rom* 2:3
also make a way to *e.* *1 Cor* 10:13
and they shall not *e.* *1 Thes* 5:3
shall we *e.* if we neglect? *Heb* 2:3
much more shall not we *e.* 12:25

escape
I would hasten my *e.* *Ps* 55:8*

escaped
came one that had *e.* *Gen* 14:13
the locust eat what is *e.* *Ex* 10:5
given his sons that *e.* *Num* 21:29*
not deliver servant *e.* *Deut* 23:15
and Ehud *e.* while. *Judg* 3:26
there *e.* not a man. 29; *1 Sam* 30:17
for them that be *e.* *Judg* 21:17
Jonathan taken, but people *e.*
1 Sam 14:41

David fled and e. *1 Sam* 19:10,12,18
of camp of Israel I e. *2 Sam* 1:3
and Baanah his brother e. 4:6
Ben-hadad the king e. *1 Ki* 20:20
remnant that is e. of Judah take root.
    2 Ki 19:30; *Isa* 37:31
smote rest that were e. *1 Chr* 4:43
is the host of Syria e. *2 Chr* 16:7
will return to you that are e. 30:6
for we remain yet e. *Ezra* 9:15
concerning Jews that had e. *Neh* 1:2
I only am e. *Job* 1:15, 16, 17, 19
am e. skin of my teeth. 19:20
is e. as a bird, the snare is broken
    and we are e. *Ps* 124:7
comely for them that are e. *Isa* 4:2
remnant and such as are e. 10:20
draw near, ye that are e. 45:20
son of Nethaniah e. *Jer* 41:15
ye that have e. remember. 51:50
that none in that day e. *Lam* 2:22
opened to him that is e. *Ezek* 24:27
one that had e. came. 33:21, 22
he e. out of their hands. *John* 10:39
to pass, they all e. safe. *Acts* 27:44
though he e. the sea, yet. 28:4
I was let down and e. *2 Cor* 11:33
through faith e. edge of. *Heb* 11:34
if they e. not who refused. 12:25
e. the corruption that. *2 Pet* 1:4
those that were clean e. 2:18*
after they have e. the pollutions. 20

escapeth
him that e. the sword of Hazael shall
    Jehu slay; him that e. *1 Ki* 19:17
lions upon him that e. of. *Isa* 15:9
ask her that e. and ? *Jer* 48:19
he that e. in that day. *Ezek* 24:26
he that e. of them shall. *Amos* 9:1

escaping
be no remnant nor e. *Ezra* 9:14

eschew
e. evil and do good. *1 Pet* 3:11*

eschewed
feared God and e. *Job* 1:1†, 8†; 2:3†

Esek
called name of well E. *Gen* 26:20

Eshcol
Amorite, brother of E. *Gen* 14:13
E. let them take their portion. 24
was called the brook E. *Num* 13:24
up unto the valley of E. 32:9

Esli
Naum, the son of E. *Luke* 3:25

especially *and* **specially**
s. the day thou stoodest. *Deut* 4:10
a reproach e. among. *Ps* 31:11*
and s. before thee. *Acts* 25:26
e. because I know thee expert. 26:3
e. to them of household. *Gal* 6:10
the Saviour, s. of those. *1 Tim* 4:10
provide, s. for them of his. 5:8
e. they who labour in word. 17
the cloke bring, but e. *2 Tim* 4:13
deceivers, s. they of the. *Tit* 1:10
brother beloved, s. to. *Philem* 16

espied
he e. his money in his. *Gen* 42:27
a land that I had e. for. *Ezek* 20:6
    see **spy, spied**

espousals
him in day of his e. *S of S* 3:11
the love of thine e. *Jer* 2:2

espoused
*Espousing, or betrothing, was done
either by a formal contract in
presence of witnesses; or without
writing, by the man's giving a piece
of silver to the bride before witnesses, and saying to her, Receive
this piece of silver as a pledge that
at such a time you shall become my
spouse. After the marriage was thus
contracted, the young people had
the liberty of seeing each other,
which was not allowed them before.
The union of believers with Christ
is expressed under the figure of a
marriage,* Isa 54:5; 2 Cor 11:2.
wife Michal whom I e. *2 Sam* 3:14
his mother Mary was e. *Mat* 1:18

to a virgin e. to a man. *Luke* 1:27
to be taxed with Mary his e. 2:5
for I have e. you to one. *2 Cor* 11:2

espy
Moses sent me to e. *Josh* 14:7*
stand by way, and e. *Jer* 48:19

Esrom
E. begat Aram. *Mat* 1:3; *Luke* 3:33

establish *and* **stablish**
*Stablish is an obsolete form of
establish, which word is most frequently substituted for it in the
Revisions. Such passages are not
here marked.* [1] *To settle,* 1 Ki
9:5. [2] *To confirm,* Num 30:13.
[3] *To perform, or make good,*
Ps 119:38. [4] *To ordain, or appoint,* Hab 1:12.
thee will I e. my covenant. *Gen* 6:18
    9:9; 17:7; *Lev* 26:9; *Ezek* 16:62
e. my covenant with. *Gen* 17:19, 21
her husband may e. it. *Num* 30:13
may e. his covenant he. *Deut* 8:18
the Lord shall e. thee an. 28:9
that he may e. thee to-day. 29:13
only Lord e. his word. *1 Sam* 1:23
    2 Sam 7:25*
I will e. his kingdom. *2 Sam* 7:12
    13; *1 Chr* 17:11; 22:10; 28:7
I will e. throne of thy. *1 Ki* 9:5
to set up his son, and to e. 15:4
and I will s. his throne. *1 Chr* 17:12
as he went to s. his dominion. 18:3
then will I s. throne. *2 Chr* 7:18
God loved Israel to e. them. 9:8
to s. among them days. *Esth* 9:21
yea he doth e. them for. *Job* 36:7*
but e. the just. *Ps* 7:9*
God will e. it. 48:8
the Highest himself shall e. 87:5
thy faithfulness shalt thou e. 89:2
thy seed will I e. for ever. 4
e. thou work of our hands, e. 90:17
thou dost e. equity, thou. 99:4
s. thy word to thy servant. 119:38
he will e. the border of. *Pr* 15:25
to e. it with judgement. *Isa* 9:7
give thee for a covenant to e. 49:8*
till he e. and make Jerusalem. 62:7
Lord that formed it, to e. it. *Jer* 33:2
I will e. an everlasting. *Ezek* 16:60
consulted to e. a royal. *Dan* 6:7
O king, e. the decree, and sign. 8
shall exalt themselves to e. 11:14
love the good, and e. *Amos* 5:15
yea, we e. the law. *Rom* 3:31
going about to e. their own. 10:3
to him that is of power to s. 16:25
Timothy our brother to e. *1 Thes* 3:2
to the end he may s. your hearts. 13
s. you in every good. *2 Thes* 2:17
the Lord shall s. you, and keep. 3:3
first, that he may e. *Heb* 10:9
also patient, s. your hearts. *Jas* 5:8
God of all grace s. *1 Pet* 5:10

established, stablished
covenant which I have e. *Gen* 9:17
because the thing is e. 41:32
have also e. my covenant. *Ex* 6:4
in sanctuary thy hands have e. 15:17
made thee, and e. thee ? *Deut* 32:6
Samuel was e. prophet. *1 Sam* 3:20
now would Lord have e. thy. 13:13
not be e. nor thy kingdom. 20:31
perceived Lord had e. *2 Sam* 5:12
let house of thy servant David be e.
    for ever. 7:26; *1 Chr* 17:24
his kingdom was e. *1 Ki* 2:12
Lord liveth, which hath e. me. 24
kingdom was e. in the hand. 46
let the thing be e. *1 Chr* 17:23, 24
let thy promise be e. *2 Chr* 1:9
when Rehoboam had e. the. 12:1
the Lord s. the kingdom in his. 17:5
when the kingdom was e. to. 25:3
so they e. a decree to keep. 30:5
their seed is e. in their. *Job* 21:8
he hath e. it upon floods. *Ps* 24:2
set my feet on a rock, and e. 40:2
he e. a testimony in Jacob. 78:5
earth he hath e. for. 69; 119:90
the world is e. 93:1

thy throne is e. of old. *Ps* 93:2
his heart is e. he shall not. 112:8
let not an evil speaker be e. 140:11
he hath s. the waters for. 148:6
by understanding, hath e. *Pr* 3:19
and let all thy ways be e. 4:26
when he e. the clouds above. 8:28*
man shall not be e. by. 12:3
of counsellors tney are e. 15:22
for the throne is e. 16:12
purpose is e. by counsel. 20:18
by understanding an is house e. 24:3
e. all the ends of the earth. 30:4
believe, ye shall not be e. *Isa* 7:9
in mercy shall the throne be e. 16:5
God made earth, he hath e. it. 45:18
he e. the world. *Jer* 10:12; 51:15
I was e. in my kingdom. *Dan* 4:36
O mighty God, thou e. *Hab* 1:12
in the mouth of two witnesses every
    word be e. *Mat* 18:16
so were the churches e. *Acts* 16:5
to end you may be e. *Rom* 1:11
built up in him, and s. *Col* 2:7
which was e. upon better. *Heb* 8:6*
it is good that the heart be e. 13:9
though ye be e. in the. *2 Pet* 1:12

    shall be established
house *shall be e.* for. *Lev* 25:30*
    2 Sam 7:16
of two or three witnesses *shall* mat-
    ter *be e. Deut* 19:15; *2 Cor* 13:1
kingdom *shall be e. 1 Sam* 24:20
thy kingdom, and thy throne, *shall* be
    e. for. *2 Sam* 7:16*; *1 Ki* 2:45
and his throne *shall be e.* for ever-
    more. *1 Chr* 17:14; *Ps* 89:37
believe in God, so *shall* ye *be e.*
    2 Chr 20:20
decree, and it *shall be e. Job* 22:28
my hand *shall be e. Ps* 89:21
world *shall be e.* before thee. 96:10
and their seed *shall be e.* 102:28
of truth *shall be e.* for. *Pr* 12:19
thy thoughts *shall be e.* 16:3
his throne *shall be e.* 25:5; 29:14
of Lord's house *shall be e. Isa* 2:2
in mercy *shall* throne *be e.* 16:5
in righteousness *shall be e. Jer* 30:20
congregation *shall be e. Mi* 4:1
house, and it *shall be e. Zech* 5:11*

establisheth
he e. all her vows. *Num* 30:14
the king by judgement, e. *Pr* 29:4
no decree the king e. *Dan* 6:15
woe to him that e. city. *Hab* 2:12
he which e. us with you. *2 Cor* 1:21

establishment
after e. Sennacherib. *2 Chr* 32:1*

estate, state
[1] *Condition of life,* Gen 43:7.
[2] *Social standing,* 1 Chr. 17:17.
[3] *Pomp,* Esth 1:19.
man asked us of our s. *Gen* 43:7*
to the e. of a man of. *1 Chr* 17:17*
set house of God in his s. *2 Chr* 24:13
according to the s. of. *Esth* 1:7*
let the king give her royal e. to. 19
gifts according to the s. of. 2:18
every man at best s. *Ps* 39:5
remembered us in our low e. 136:23
diligent to know s. of thy. *Pr* 27:23
by a man of knowledge s. 28:2
lo, I am come to great e. *Eccl* 1:16
concerning the e. of sons of. 3:18*
from thy s. shall he pull. *Isa* 22:19
return to her former e. *Ezek* 16:55
stand up in his e. *Dan* 11:7*, 21*
then shall stand up in his. 20*
but in his e. shall he honour. 38*
other spirits enter, the last s. of that
    man. *Mat* 12:45; *Luke* 11:26
hath regarded low e. of. *Luke* 1:48
all the e. of the elders. *Acts* 22:5
condescend to men of low e.
    Rom 12:16*
when I know your s. *Phil* 2:19
will naturally care for your s. 20
in whatsover s. I am to be. 4:11
all my s. shall Tychicus. *Col* 4:7
sent, that he might know your e. 8
angels which kept not first e. *Jude* 6*

estates

you after your old e.   *Ezek* 36:11
supper to his chief e.   *Mark* 6:21*

esteem

will he e. thy riches ?   *Job* 36:19*
I e. all thy precepts to.   *Ps* 119:128
we did e. him smitten of.   *Isa* 53:4
each e. other better than.   *Phil* 2:3
to e. them highly for.   *1 Thes* 5:13

esteemed

e. rock of his salvation.   *Deut* 32:15
me shall be lightly e.   *1 Sam* 2:30
a poor man and lightly e.   18:23
I have e. the words of.   *Job* 23:12*
e. a man of understanding. *Pr* 17:28
turning shall be e. as the. *Isa* 29:16*
fruitful field shall be e. as a.   17*
despised, and we e. him not.   53:3
how are they e. as !   *Lam* 4:2
highly e. among men. *Luke* 16:15*
to judge who are least e. *1 Cor* 6:4*

esteemeth

he e. iron as straw.   *Job* 41:27*
one e. one day above another;
   another e. every day. *Rom* 14:5
to him that e. any thing to.   14*

esteeming

e. reproach of Christ.   *Heb* 11:26*

Esther

brought up Hadassah, E.   *Esth* 2:7
the king loved E.   17
king made feast, even E.'s feast. 18
told it to E.   22
E.'s maids came, she sent.   4:4
told to Mordecai E.'s words.   12
Mordecai did all that E. had.   17
king held out to E. golden. 5:2; 8:4
what wilt thou, queen E.?   5:3
E. let no man come in with.   12
what is thy petition, queen E.?   7:2
to make request for life to E.   7
and E. spake yet again.   8:3
I have given E. the house.   7
E. the queen wrote with.   9:29
decree of E. confirmed these.   32

estimate

priest shall e. it good or bad, as the
   priest shall e. it. *Lev* 27:14

estimation

bring a ram with thy e.   *Lev* 5:15
shall be for Lord, by thy e.   27:2
thy e. shall be of the male from. 3, 5
*This word frequently occurs in this
chapter*
old, according to thy e. *Num* 18:16

estimations

all thy e. according to. *Lev* 27:25

estranged

mine acquaintance are e. *Job* 19:13
the wicked are e. from.   *Ps* 58:3
were not e. from their lust.   78:30
because they have e. this. *Jer* 19:4
they are all e. from me. *Ezek* 14:5

Etam

Samson dwelt in top of E. *Judg* 15:8
men went to top of the rock E.   11

eternal

e. God is thy refuge.   *Deut* 33:27
thee an e. excellency.   *Isa* 60:15
is in danger of e.   *Mark* 3:29
even his e. power and. *Rom* 1:20*
worketh an e. weight of. *2 Cor* 4:17
things which are not seen are e.   18
an house e. in the heavens.   5:1
according to e. purpose. *Eph* 3:11
unto the King e. be. *1 Tim* 1:17
salvation with e. glory. *2 Tim* 2:10
the author of e. salvation. *Heb* 5:9
doctrine of baptisms, and e.   6:2
having obtained e. redemption. 9:12
who through the e. Spirit offered. 14
the promise of e. inheritance.   15
us unto his e. glory. *1 Pet* 5:10
suffering the vengeance of e. *Jude* 7

eternal life

that I may have e. *life ? Mat* 19:16
righteous shall go into *life* e.   25:46
shall I do, that I may inherit e. *life* ?
   Mark 10:17; *Luke* 10:25; 18:18
in world to come e. *life. Mark* 10:30

in him should have e. *life. John* 3:15
gathereth fruit unto *life* e.   4:36
in them ye have e. *life.*   5:39
drinketh my blood hath e. *life.* 6:54
hast words of e. *life.*   68
give unto my sheep e. *life.*   10:28
his life, keep it to e. *life.*   12:25
he should give e. *life* to as.   17:2
this is *life* e. that they might.   3
were ordained to e. *life. Acts* 13:48
who seek glory, e. *life.*   *Rom* 2:7
might grace reign to e. *life.*   5:21
but the gift of God is e. *life.*   6:23
lay hold on e. *life. 1 Tim* 6:12, 19*
in hope of e. *life.*   *Tit* 1:2
according to hope of e. *life.*   3:7
e. *life* which was with. *1 John* 1:2
promise he promised, e. *life.*   2:25
no murderer hath e. *life.*   3:15
God hath given to us e. *life.*   5:11
may know that ye have e. *life.*   13
is the true God, and e. *life.*   20
mercy of Lord unto e. *life. Jude* 21

eternity

One that inhabiteth e.   *Isa* 57:15

Etham

encamped in E. *Ex* 13:20; *Num* 33:6
three days' journey in E. *Num* 33:8

Ethan

Solomon was wiser than E.
   1 Ki 4:31
Zerah, Zimri, and E.   *1 Chr* 2:6

Ethanim

Israel assembled in the month E.
   1 Ki 8:2

Ethiopia

heard say of Tirhakah king of E.
   2 Ki 19:9; *Isa* 37:9
Ahasuerus reigned from India to E.
   Esth 1:1; 8:9
the topaz of E. not equal. *Job* 28:9
E. stretch out hands to. *Ps* 68:31
Philistia and Tyre with E.   87:4
is beyond the rivers of E. *Isa* 18:1
   Zeph 3:10
bare-foot for sign on E. *Isa* 20:3
they shall be ashamed of E.   5
gave Egypt for thy ransom, E. 43:3
the merchandise of E. shall. 45:14
great pain in E.   *Ezek* 30:4
E. shall fall.   5; 38:5
E. and Egypt were the. *Nah* 3:9
a man of E. eunuch of. *Acts* 8:27

Ethiopian

because of E. woman.   *Num* 12:1
Zerah the E. came out. *2 Chr* 14:9
can E. change his skin ? *Jer* 13:23
Ebed-melech the E.   38:7, 10, 12
   39:16

Ethiopians

Lord smote E. the E. *2 Chr* 14:12
the E. and Lubims a huge ?   16:8
stirred Arabians near E.   21:16
shall lead the E. captives. *Isa* 20:4
E. that handle the shield. *Jer* 46:9
make careless E. afraid. *Ezek* 30:9
the Lybians and E. shall. *Dan* 11:43
ye not as children of E.? *Amos* 9:7
ye E. shall be slain. *Zeph* 2:12
under Candace of E.   *Acts* 8:27

Eubulus

E. greeteth thee.   *2 Tim* 4:21

Eunice

faith which dwelt in E. *2 Tim* 1:5

eunuch

*Originally an impotent man.
Since those put in charge of the
harems of Eastern monarchs were
as a general rule of this class, the
name became practically synonymous with chamberlain, with no
indication of his condition, although
probably its use in scripture was
strict. Eunuchs were not allowed
by Jewish law to enter the house of
God, Deut 23:1; but they were present at the court, 1 Chr 28:1, marg.
A eunuch was over the treasure of
queen Candace of Ethiopia, and he
was admitted to baptism, Acts 8:27,
37.*
neither let the e. say.   *Isa* 56:3

an e. had come to.   *Acts* 8:27
e. said, of whom speaks ?   34
e. said, what doth hinder me ?   36
Spirit caught Philip, e. saw.   39

eunuchs

looked out two or three e. *2 Ki* 9:32
and they shall be e. in palace. 20:18
   Isa 39:7
Ahab called for one of e. *2 Chr* 18:8
saith the Lord to the e.   *Isa* 56:4
after that the e. were.   *Jer* 29:2
e. which passed between the. 34:19
when Ebed-melech one of e.   38:7
e. whom he had brought.   41:16
spake to master of his e. *Dan* 1:3
to whom the prince of the e.   7
Daniel requested of prince of e.   8
into favour with prince of e.   9
then prince of the e. brought.   18
e. who were so born, made e. of men.
   Mat 19:12

Euodias

I beseech E. and.   *Phil* 4:2

Euphrates

the fourth river is E.   *Gen* 2:14
unto great river, the river E. 15:18
go to great river E.   *Deut* 1:7
   Josh 1:4
yours from the river E. *Deut* 11:24
smote Hadadezer at the river E.
   2 Sam 8:3; *1 Chr* 18:3
Necho went up to E.   *2 Ki* 23:29
   2 Chr 35:20
took from Egypt to E.   *2 Ki* 24:7
inhabited from river E. *1 Chr* 5:9
arise, go to E.   *Jer* 13:4
so I hid it by E.   5
I went to E.   7
came against Pharaoh by E. 46:2
stumble and fall by river E.   6
hath a sacrifice by E.   10
cast it into midst of E.   51:63
bound in the river E.   *Rev* 9:14
angel poured out vial on E.   16:12

euroclydon

*(A tempestuous north-east wind of
the Mediterranean, very dangerous
to the sort of shipping used in the
time of the Apostles. In the
Revisions the name is given as
Euraquilo)*
arose tempestuous wind, called e.
   Acts 27:14

Eutychus

a young man named E.   *Acts* 20:9

evangelist

house of Philip the e.   *Acts* 21:8
do the work of an e.   *2 Tim* 4:5

evangelists

some apostles, some e.   *Eph* 4:11

Eve

called his wife's name E. *Gen* 3:20
Adam knew E. his wife.   4:1
as serpent beguiled E. *2 Cor* 11:3
first formed, then E. *1 Tim* 2:13

even

(The close of the day)
two angels to Sodom at e. *Gen* 19:1
fourteenth day of month at e.
   Ex 12:18
Moses said, at e. then shall. 16:6
at e. eat flesh.   12
at e. the quails came.   13
stand from morning to e.   18:14
Aaron lighteth lamps at e.   30:8
unclean until e. *Lev* 11:24, 25, 27, 28
   31, 39, 40; 14:46; 15:5, 6, 7, etc.
   17:15; 22:6; *Num* 19:7, 8, 10, 21
   22
fourteenth day of first month, at e.
   Lev 23:5; *Num* 9:3; *Deut* 16:6
day of second month at e. *Num* 9:11
when cloud abode from e. to.   21
shall be clean at e.   19:19
would God it were e. *Deut* 28:67
wept before Lord till e. *Judg* 20:23
and fasted till e.   26; *2 Sam* 1:12
the people abode till e.   21:2
gleaned in field until e.   *Ruth* 2:17
unto third day at e.   *1 Sam* 20:5
Ahab died at e.   *1 Ki* 22:35
   2 Chr 18:34

praise Lord every morning and *e.*
　　　　　　　　1 Chr 23:30
shalt go forth at *e.* in.　　*Ezek* 12:4
in the *e.* I digged through the wall. 7
and at *e.* my wife died.　　　24:18
when the *e.* was come.　*Mat* 8:16
20:8; 26:20; 27:57; *Mark* 4:35
　　　　　6:47; 11:19; 15:42
at *e.* they brought to.　*Mark* 1:32
at *e.* at midnight, or cockcrow. 13:35
when *e.* was come.　　*John* 6:16

even

mine eyes *e.* seeing it.　*1 Ki* 1:48
known to thee, *e.* to.　*Pr* 22:19
flock of sheep that are *e. S of S* 4:2
e. saying to Jerusalem.　*Isa* 44:28
e. to them will I give a name. 56:5
if a man do, he shall *e. Ezek* 20:11
if sword contemn *e.* the rod. 21:13
e. we ourselves groan.　*Rom* 8:23
not *e.* nature itself ?　*1 Cor* 11:14
kingdom to God, *e.* the.　　15:24
e. the Father of our Lord. *2 Cor* 1:3
a measure to reach *e.* to you. 10:13
obedient to death, *e.*　*Phil* 2:8

even, *adjective*

that net may be *e.* to.　*Ex* 27:5
weighed in an *e.* balance.　*Job* 31:6
my foot standeth in *e.*　*Ps* 26:12
shall lay thee *e.* with.　*Luke* 19:44

evening

came in to him in the *e. Gen* 8:11
came out of field in *e.*　　30:16
of Israel kill it in *e.*　　*Ex* 12:6
but when *e.* cometh.　*Deut* 23:11
hanging on trees until *e. Josh* 10:26
day draweth towards *e. Judg* 19:9
cursed that eateth till *e. 1 Sam* 14:24
David smote them to the *e.*　30:17
in the *e.* she went.　　*Esth* 2:14
they return at *e.* they.　*Ps* 59:6
at *e.* let them return and.　　14
in the *e.* it is cut down.　　90:6
forth to his labour until *e.*　104:23
went way to her house in *e. Pr* 7:9
in the *e.* withhold not.　*Eccl* 11:6
the shadows of the *e.*　　*Jer* 6:4
of Lord was on me in *e. Ezek* 33:22
gate shall not be shut till *e.*　46:2
in Ashkelon lie down in *e. Zeph* 2:7
when *e.* was come.　　*Mat* 14:23
when it is *e.* ye say, it.　　16:2
in the *e.* he cometh.　*Mark* 14:17
abide with us, for it is *e. Luke* 24:29
same day at *e.* came.　*John* 20:19

evening with *morning*

the *e.* and *morning* were first day.
　　　Gen 1:5, 8, 13, 19, 23, 31
Moses from *morning* to *e. Ex* 18:13
shall order it from *e.* to *morning.*
　　　　　27:21; *Lev* 24:3
Philistine drew near *morning* and *e.*
　　　　　　1 Sam 17:16
bread *morning* and *e.*　*1 Ki* 17:6
offerings *morning* and *e. 1 Chr* 16:40
2 Chr 2:4; 13:11; 31:3; *Ezra* 3:3
are destroyed from *morning* to *e.*
　　　　　　　　Job 4:20
e. and *morning,* and at.　*Ps* 55:17
outgoings of *morning* and *e.*　65:8
vision of *e.* and *morning* is. *Dan* 8:26
persuading them from *morning* to *e.*
　　　　　　　Acts 28:23

evening, *adjective*

prophesied till *e.*　　*1 Ki* 18:29
at time of offering of the *e.*　36
on great altar burn *e.*　*2 Ki* 16:15
astonished until the *e.*　*Ezra* 9:4
at *e.* sacrifice I arose from my.　5
let my prayer be as the *e. Ps* 141:2
the time of *e.* oblation.　*Dan* 9:21
more fierce than the *e.*　*Hab* 1:8
her judges are *e.* wolves. *Zeph* 3:3
at *e.* time shall be light. *Zech* 14:7

evenings

a wolf of the *e.* shall.　　*Jer* 5:6

event

one *e.* happeneth to. *Eccl* 2:14; 9:3
one *e.* to the righteous and.　9:2

eventide, *or* **eveningtide**
went out to meditate at *e. Gen* 24:63

Joshua fell on his face till *e. Josh* 7:6
of Ai he hanged on tree till *e.*　8:29
in an *e.* David walked.　*2 Sam* 11:2
behold, at *e.* trouble.　　*Isa* 17:14
now the *e.* was come.　*Mark* 11:11
him in hold, for it was *e.*　*Acts* 4:3

ever

fire shall *e.* be burning.　*Lev* 6:13
hast ridden on, *e.* since. *Num* 22:30
did *e.* people hear voice ? *Deut* 4:33
to love God, and to walk *e.*　19:9
e. fight against Israel ? *Judg* 11:25
Hiram was *e.* a lover.　　*1 Ki* 5:1
who *e.* perished, being ?　*Job* 4:7
that trust, let them *e.*　*Ps* 5:11
tender mercies have been *e.*　25:6
mine eyes are *e.* towards Lord.　15
he is *e.* merciful, and.　　37:26*
and my sin is *e.* before me.　51:3
or *e.* thou hadst formed earth. 90:2
　　　　　　　　Pr 8:23
will *e.* be mindful of his. *Ps* 111:5
commandments are *e.* with.　119:98
or *e.* I was aware, my. *S of S* 6:12†
because he will not *e.* be. *Isa* 28:28
not one of the stakes shall *e.*　33:20
e. they came at bottom.　*Dan* 6:24†
hath not been *e.* the like.　*Joel* 2:2
was not, no, nor *e.* shall. *Mat* 24:21
him to do as he had *e. Mark* 15:8*
son, thou art *e.* with.　*Luke* 15:31
told me all things *e.* I. *John* 4:29, 39
but the Son abideth *e.*　　8:35
all that *e.* came before me.　10:8
I *e.* taught in the synagogue. 18:20
we, or *e.* he come, are. *Acts* 23:15
for no man *e.* yet hated.　*Eph* 5:29
so shall we *e.* be with. *1 Thes* 4:17
but *e.* follow that which is.　5:15
e. learning, and never.　*2 Tim* 3:7
because he continueth *e. Heb* 7:24
e. liveth to make intercession.　25
be glory, now and *e.*　　*Jude* 25

see **endureth**

for ever

(*Many believe that the words for
ever or everlasting are not to be
taken as synonymous with eternal,
as being without end, but to be
understood merely as meaning a
very long time, to be left indeter-
minate. There seems to be a
considerable amount of argument
in favour of this in many cases, but
it is not safe to conclude that it
always should be so limited*)
give it and thy seed *for e. Gen* 13:15
me bear blame *for e.*　43:9; 44:32
this is my name *for e.*　*Ex* 3:15
feast by an ordinance *for e.* 12:14, 17
to thee, and to thy sons *for e.*　24
see them again no more *for e.* 14:13
people may believe thee *for e.* 19:9
and he shall serve him *for e.*　21:6
between me and Israel *for e.* 31:17
and they shall inherit it *for e.* 32:13
land not be sold *for e. Lev* 25:23*
the house be established *for e.*　30*
shall be your bondmen *for e.*　46
for an ordinance *for e.*　*Num* 10:8
　　　　　　15:15; 18:8
covenant of salt *for e.*　　18:19
Amalek shall perish *for e.*　24:20
afflict Eber, he shall perish *for e.* 24
earth which God giveth thee *for e.*
　　　　　　　Deut 4:40
be well with them *for e.* 5:29; 12:28
it shall be an heap *for e.*　13:16
shall be thy servant *for e.*　15:17
him and his sons *for e.*　　18:5
not seek their peace *for e.*　23:6
upon thee for a sign *for e.*　28:46
revealed belong to us *for e.*　29:29
stones be a memorial *for e. Josh* 4:7
fear the Lord your God *for e.*　24
Ai, made it an heap *for e.*　8:28
land be thine inheritance *for e.* 14:9
before the Lord and abide *for e.*
　　　　　　　1 Sam 1:22
house walk before me *for e.*　2:30
not be an old man in house *for e.* 32
walk before mine Anointed *for e.* 35

I will judge his house *for e.*
　　　　　　　1 Sam 3:13
of Eli's house not purged *for e.*　14
not cut off thy kindness *for e.* 20:15
between thee and me *for e.*　23, 42
shall be my servant *for e.*　27:12
keeper of mine head *for e.*　28:2
sword devour *for e.?*　*2 Sam* 2:26
and my kingdom guiltless *for e.* 3:28
confirmed Israel to thee *for e.*　7:24
let thy name be magnified *for e.*　26
his house may continue *for e.*　29
for thee to abide in *for e. 1 Ki* 8:13
to put my name there *for e.*　9:3
the Lord loved Israel *for e.*　10:9
David's seed, but not *for e.*　11:39
will be thy servants *for e.*　12:7
　　　　　　　　2 Chr 10:7
leprosy cleave to thee *for e.*
　　　　　　　2 Ki 5:27
make thine own *for e. 1 Chr* 17:22
he and sons *for e.* to burn.　23:13
he will cast thee off *for e.*　28:9
God of Israel, keep this *for e.* 29:18
name may be there *for e. 2 Chr* 7:16
to give a light to sons *for e.*　21:7
which he hath sanctified *for e.* 30:8
Jerusalem my name be *for e.*　33:4
congregation of God *for e. Neh* 13:1
they perish *for e.* without. *Job* 4:20
prevaileth *for e.* against.　　14:20
iron pen in the rock *for e.*　19:24
yet he shall perish *for e.*　20:7
should I be delivered *for e.*　23:7
he doth establish them *for e.*　36:7
Lord shall endure *for e.*　*Ps* 9:7
of poor shall not perish *for e.*　18
thou shalt preserve them *for e.* 12:7
thou forget me, O Lord, *for e.?* 13:1
fear of Lord enduring *for e.*　19:9
made him most blessed *for e.* 21:6
in house of the Lord *for e.*　23:6
and lift them up *for e.*　　28:9
the Lord sitteth king *for e.*　29:10
thanks to thee *for e.* 30:12; 79:13
counsel of Lord standeth *for e.* 33:11
their inheritance shall be *for e.* 37:18
his saints are preserved *for e.*　28
righteous shall dwell in land *for e.* 29
me before thy face *for e.*　41:12
and we praise thy name *for e.* 44:8
O Lord, cast us not off *for e.*　23
God hath blessed thee *for e.*　45:2
redemption of their soul ceaseth *for
e.*　　　　　　　　49:8
their houses continue *for e.*　11
God shall destroy thee *for e.*　52:5
I will praise thee *for e.*　　9
abide in thy tabernacle *for e.* 61:4
he shall abide before God *for e.*　7
sing praise unto thy name *for e.*　8
he ruleth by his power *for e.*　66:7
Lord will dwell in it *for e.*　68:16
his name shall endure *for e.*　72:17
blessed be his glorious name *for e.* 19
my strength and portion *for e.* 73:26
hast thou cast us off *for e.?*　74:1
enemy blaspheme name *for e.?*　10
forget not thy poor *for e.*　19
I will declare *for e.* I will.　75:9
will Lord cast off *for e.?*　77:7
is mercy clean gone *for e.?*　9
wilt thou be angry *for e.?*　79:5
should have endured *for e.*　81:15
confounded and troubled *for e.* 83:17
thou be angry with us *for e.?*　85:5
sing of mercies of Lord *for e.*　89:1
mercy shall be built up *for e.*　2
his seed will I make to endure *for e.*
　　　　　　　　29, 36
wilt thou hide thyself *for e.?*　46
they should be destroyed *for e.* 92:7
holiness becometh house *for e.* 93:5
neither keep his anger *for e.*　103:9
remembered his covenant *for e.*
　　　　　　　　105:8
thou art a priest *for e.* after. 110:4
　　　　Heb 5:6; 6:20; 7:17, 21
commanded his covenant *for e.*
　　　　　　　　Ps 111:9
he shall not be moved *for e.* 112:6
for e. O Lord, thy word is.　119:89
from henceforth even *for e.*　125:2
131:3; *Isa* 9:7

this is my rest *for e.*   *Ps* 132:14
Lord who keepeth truth *for e.* 146:6
the Lord shall reign *for e.*   10
for riches are not *for e.*   *Pr* 27:24
wise more than fool *for e. Eccl* 2:16
God doth, it shall be *for e.*   3:14
have they more a portion *for e.* 9:6
trust ye in Lord *for e.*   *Isa* 26:4
and assurance *for e.*   32:17
smoke shall go up *for e.*   34:10
shall possess it *for e.* from.   17
word of our God stand *for e.* 40:8
I shall be a lady *for e.*   47:7
my salvation shall be *for e.* 51:6
my righteousness shall be *for e.* 8
will not contend *for e.* nor.   57:16
words shall not depart *for e.* 59:21
people shall inherit land *for e.* 60:21
nor remember iniquity *for e.* 64:9
be glad and rejoice *for e.* 65:18
he reserve anger *for e.?*   *Jer* 3:5
I will not keep anger *for e.* 12
a fire which shall burn *for e.* 17:4
and this city shall remain *for e.* 31:40
not be plucked up *for e.* 32:39
heart that they may fear *for e.* 32:39
ye shall drink no wine *for e.* 35:6
Jonadab shall not want a man to
   stand before me *for e.* 19
dragons and a desolation *for e.* 49:33
more inhabited *for e.* 50:39; 51:26
   62
will not cast off *for e.*   *Lam* 3:31
thou remainest *for e.* thy.   5:19
dost thou forget us *for e.?*   20
their children dwell *for e.* and David
   be their prince *for e. Ezek* 37:25
in midst of Israel *for e.*   43:7, 9
kingdom shall stand *for e. Dan* 2:44
honoured him that liveth *for e.* 4:34
living God and stedfast *for e.* 6:26
saints possess kingdom *for e.* 7:18
sware by him that liveth *for e.* 12:7
betroth thee unto me *for e. Hos* 2:19
Judah shall dwell *for e.*   *Joel* 3:20
off pity kept wrath *for e. Amos* 1:11
Edom, shalt be cut off *for e. Ob* 10
with bars about me *for e. Jonah* 2:6
taken away my glory *for e. Mi* 2:9
Lord shall reign over them *for e.* 4:7
retaineth not anger *for e.*   7:18
Lord hath indignation *for e. Mal* 1:4
is power and glory *for e. Mat* 6:13
no fruit grow on thee *for e.*   21:19
   Mark 11:14
reign over Jacob *for e.*   *Luke* 1:33
to Abraham and seed *for e.*   55
abideth not in house *for e. John* 8:35
that Christ abideth *for e.*   12:34
may abide with you *for e.*   14:16
Creator, who is blessed *for e.*
   Rom 1:25
is over all, God blessed *for e.* 9:5
to whom be glory *for e.* 11:36; 16:27
righteousness remaineth *for e.*
   2 Cor 9:9
receive him *for e.*   *Philem* 15
for *e.* sat down on the. *Heb* 10:12
perfected *for e.* them that are.   14
the same to-day and *for e.*   13:8
word of God, liveth *for e.* *1 Pet* 1:23
word of Lord endureth *for e.*   25
to whom mist of darkness is reserved *for e. 2 Pet* 2:17; *Jude* 13
shall be with us *for e.*   *2 John* 2

     live for ever

tree of life, and *live for e. Gen* 3:22
hand and say, I *live for e. Deut* 32:40
king David *live for e.*   *1 Ki* 1:31
let the king *live for e.*   *Neh* 2:3
hearts shall *live for e.*   *Ps* 22:26
that he should still *live for e.* 49:9
O king, *live for e.*   *Dan* 2:4; 3:9
   5:10; 6:6, 21
do they *live for e.?*   *Zech* 1:5
if any man eat of this bread he shall
   live for e.   *John* 6:51, 58

     for ever and ever

Lord reign *for e.* and *e.*   *Ex* 15:18
blessed be God *for e.* and *e.* people.
   1 Chr 16:36*; 29:10; *Dan* 2:20
bless your God *for e.* and *e. Neh* 9:5

out their name *for e* and *e.*   *Ps* 9:5
Lord is King *for e.* and *e.*   10:16
him length of days *for e.* and *e.* 21:4
thy throne is *for e.* and *e.*   45:6
people praise thee *for e.* and *e.* 17
God is our God *for e.* and *e.* 48:14
in mercy of God *for e.* and *e.* 52:8
they stand fast *for e.* and *e.* 111:8
I keep thy law *for e.* and *e.* 119:44
bless thy name *for e.* and *e.* 145:1
praise thy name *for e.* and *e.* 2, 21
stablished them *for e.* and *e.* 148:6
time to come, *for e.* and *e. Isa* 30:8
pass through it *for e.* and *e.* 34:10
land I gave *for e.* and *e.*   *Jer* 7:7*
you and fathers *for e.* and *e.* 25:5*
the kingdom *for e.* and *e. Dan* 7:18
shine as stars *for e.* and *e.* 12:3
walk in the name of God *for e.* and *e.*
   Mi 4:5
whom be glory *for e.* and *e. Gal* 1:5
   Phil 4:20; *1 Tim* 1:17
   2 Tim 4:18; *Heb* 13:21
throne, O God, is *for e.* and *e.*
   Heb 1:8
to him who liveth *for e.* and *e.*
   Rev 4:9, 10; 5:14; 10:6; 15:7
be to the Lamb *for e.* and *e.* 5:13
power be unto God *for e.* and *e.* 7:12
Christ shall reign *for e.* and *e.* 11:15
ascendeth *for e.* and *e.* 14:11; 19:3
tormented day and night *for e.* and *e.*
   20:10
shall reign *for e.* and *e.* 22:15

     statute for **ever**

be a *statute for e.*   *Ex* 27:21; 28:43
   30:21; *Lev* 6:18; 10:9; 17:7
   23:14, 21, 31, 41; 24:3
   Num 18:23
a *statute for e. Ex* 29:28; *Lev* 7:34
   36; 10:15; 16:31; *Num* 18:11, 19
a *statute for e.* unto Lord. *Lev* 6:22
stranger for *statute for e. Num* 19:10

     everlasting

(See note on **for ever**. The
Revisions very frequently substitute the word eternal for everlasting)
land of Canaan for an *e.* possession.
   Gen 17:8; 48:4
the *e.* God.   21:33; *Isa* 40:28
   Rom 16:26
utmost bound of *e.* hills. *Gen* 49:26
an *e.* priesthood.   *Ex* 40:15
   Num 25:13
be an *e.* statute.   *Lev* 16:34
e. arms.   *Deut* 33:27
lift up, ye *e.* doors.   *Ps* 24:7, 9
mercy *e.*   100:5
righteous in *e.* remembrance. 112:6
is an *e.* righteousness. 119:142, 144
and lead me in way *e.*   139:24
kingdom is an *e.* kingdom. 145:13
   Dan 4:3; 7:27; *2 Pet* 1:11
righteous is an *e.* foundation.
   Pr 10:25
be called, the *e.* Father.   *Isa* 9:6
Jehovah is *e.* strength.   26:4
dwell with *e.* burnings?   33:14
they shall come with *e.* joy.   35:10
   51:11; 61:7
with an *e.* salvation.   45:17
with *e.* kindness.   54:8
for an *e.* sign.   55:13
an *e.* name.   56:5; 63:12
unto thee an *e.* light.   60:19, 20
God is an *e.* King.   *Jer* 10:10
e. confusion.   20:11
an *e.* reproach upon you.   23:40
I have loved thee with *e.* love. 31:3
dominion is an *e.* dominion. *Dan* 4:34
   7:14
e. mountains were.   *Hab* 3:6
cast into *e.* fire.   *Mat* 18:8, 25, 41
go away into *e.* punishment. 25:46
you into *e.* habitations.   *Luke* 16:9
with *e.* destruction.   *2 Thes* 1:9
hath given us *e.* consolation.   2:16
be honour and power *e. 1 Tim* 6:16
angels reserved in *e.* chains. *Jude* 6
having the *e.* gospel to.   *Rev* 14:6
   see **covenant**

     from **everlasting**

blessed be God *from e.*   *Ps* 41:13
   106:48
even *from e.* to everlasting.   90:2
thou art *from e.*   93:2
mercy of Lord is *from e.*   103:17
I was set up *from e.*   *Pr* 8:23
thy name is *from e.*   *Isa* 63:16
forth have been *from e.*   *Mi* 5:2
art thou not *from e.?*   *Hab* 1:12

     everlasting *life*

awake, some to *e. life.*   *Dan* 12:2
shall inherit *e. life.*   *Mat* 19:29
world to come *e. life.*   *Luke* 18:30
believeth have *e. life. John* 3:16, 36
a well springing up to *e. life.* 4:14
heareth my words hath *e. life.* 5:24
meat which endureth to *e. life.* 6:27
who seeth Son may have *e. life.* 40
believeth on me hath *e. life.* 47
his commandment is *life e.*   12:50
unworthy of *e. life.*   *Acts* 13:46
ye have the end *e. life.*   *Rom* 6:22
of Spirit reap *life e.*   *Gal* 6:8
believe on him to *life e. 1 Tim* 1:16

     evermore

oppressed and spoiled *e. Deut* 28:29
mercy unto David *e.*   *2 Sam* 22:51
observe to do for *e.*   *2 Ki* 17:37
throne shall be established for *e.*
   1 Chr 17:14
right hand pleasures for *e. Ps* 16:11
mercy to David and seed for *e.* 18:50
do good, and dwell for *e.*   37:27
doth his promise fail for *e.?*   77:8
and glorify thy name for *e.*   86:12
mercy I keep for him for *e.*   89:28
blessed be the Lord for *e.*   52
thou, Lord, most high for *e.*   92:8
seek his face *e.*   105:4
him for righteousness for *e.* 106:31
blessed be name of Lord for *e.* 113:2
we will bless the Lord for *e.* 115:18
going out and coming in *e.*   121:8
shall sit upon throne for *e.*   132:12
the blessing, life for *e.*   133:3
will set my sanctuary in the midst of
   them for *e.*   *Ezek* 37:26, 28
e. give us this bread.   *John* 6:34
of Lord blessed for *e.*   *2 Cor* 11:31
rejoice *e.* pray.   *1 Thes* 5:16
who is consecrated for *e. Heb* 7:28
was dead, I am alive for *e. Rev* 1:18

     every

e. imagination of his heart. *Gen* 6:5
e. man-child be circumcised. 17:10
nor shalt gather *e.*   *Lev* 19:10
put out of camp *e.* leper. *Num* 5:2
Samuel told him *e.* whit. *1 Sam* 3:18
refrained from *e.* evil. *Ps* 119:101
I hate *e.* false way.   104, 128
understand *e.* good path.   *Pr* 2:9
she lieth in wait at *e.* corner.   7:12
the simple believeth *e.* word. 14:15
eyes of Lord in *e.* place.   15:3
but *e.* fool will be meddling.   20:3
e. word of God is pure.   30:5
e. knee shall bow, *e.*   *Isa* 45:23
   Rom 14:11
e. purpose of Lord shall. *Jer* 51:29
and effect of *e.* vision. *Ezek* 12:23
magnify himself above *e. Dan* 11:36
land mourn, *e.* family.   *Zech* 12:12
e. place incense offered.   *Mal* 1:11
by *e.* word that.   *Mat* 4:4
put away his wife for *e.*   19:3
came to him from *e.*   *Mark* 1:45
fame of him went into *e. Luke* 4:37
for *e.* tree is known by his.   6:44
and fear came upon *e.*   *Acts* 2:43
Moses hath in *e.* city them.   15:21
teach *e.* where in *e.*   *1 Cor* 4:17
bringing into captivity *e. 2 Cor* 10:5
far above *e.* name named. *Eph* 1:21
   Phil 2:9
e. joint supplieth, in measure of *e.*
   Eph 4:16
salute *e.* saint in Christ. *Phil* 4:21
e. creature of God is.   *1 Tim* 4:4
prepared unto *e.* good. *2 Tim* 2:21
let us lay aside *e.* weight. *Heb* 12:1
e. good and perfect gift.   *Jas* 1:17
submit to *e.* ordinance. *1 Pet* 2:13

believe not *e.* spirit, but. *1 John* 4:1
see **beast, city, day, man, morning, side, thing, way**

every one

that *e.* one that findeth.	*Gen* 4:14
cursed be *e.* one that curseth.	27:29
are holy, *e.* one of them.	*Num* 16:3
ye are alive *e.* one of you.	*Deut* 4:4
hearken, *e.* one of you.	*1 Ki* 22:28
eat ye *e.* one of his fig.	*2 Ki* 18:31
Lord pardon *e.* one.	*2 Chr* 30:18
of *e.* one that willingly.	*Ezra* 3:5
were assembled to me *e.* one.	9:4
e. one that is proud.	*Job* 40:11
look on *e.* one that is proud.	
in temple *e.* one doth.	*Ps* 29:9
for this shall *e.* one that is.	32:6
e. one that sweareth by him.	63:11
till *e.* one submit himself.	68:30
thy power to *e.* one that is.	71:18
is *e.* one that trusteth.	115:8; 135:18
e. one of thy judgements	119:160
blessed is *e.* one that feareth.	128:1
he saith to *e.* one that.	*Eccl* 10:3
e. one beareth twins.	*S of S* 4:2; 6:6
honey shall *e.* one eat.	*Isa* 7:22
for *e.* one is an hypocrite.	9:17
vultures be gathered, *e.* one.	34:15
even *e.* one that is called by.	43:7
ho, *e.* one that thirsteth.	55:1
e. one that goeth out.	*Jer* 5:6
e. one neighed after neighbour's.	8
e. one is given to covetousness.	6:13
derision daily, *e.* one mocketh.	20:7
turn ye now *e.* one from.	25:5
mourning, *e.* one for.	*Ezek* 7:16
opened thy feet to *e.* one.	16:25
behold *e.* one were in thee to.	22:6
e. one that be found.	*Dan* 12:1
they shall march *e.* one.	*Joel* 2:7
e. one that stealeth shall.	*Zech* 5:3
e. one that asketh.	*Mat* 7:8
	Luke 11:10
to me, *e.* one of you.	*Mark* 7:14
to *e.* one which hath.	*Luke* 19:26
so is *e.* one that is born of.	*John* 3:8
e. one that is of truth.	18:37
and be baptized, *e.* one of.	*Acts* 2:38
not far from *e.* one of us.	17:27
I ceased not to warn *e.* one.	20:31
e. one give account of.	*Rom* 14:12
Lord hath called *e.* one.	*1 Cor* 7:17
cursed is *e.* one that.	*Gal* 3:10
e. one that nameth the.	*2 Tim* 2:19
e. one that loveth is.	*1 John* 4:7
white robes given to *e.* one.	*Rev* 6:11

every where

to our brethren *e. where.*	*1 Chr* 13:2
and preached *e. where.*	*Mark* 16:20
preaching gospel *e. where.*	*Luke* 9:6
	Acts 8:4
all men *e. where* to.	17:30
it is *e. where* spoken against.	28:22
as I teach *e. where* in.	*1 Cor* 4:17
e. where, and in all.	*Phil* 4:12
that men pray *e. where.*	*1 Tim* 2:8

evidence

I subscribed the *e.*	*Jer* 32:10*
so I took the *e.*	11*
I gave the *e.* to Baruch.	12*
e. both which is sealed, *e.* open.	14*
when I delivered the *e.* of the.	16*
faith is the *e.* of things.	*Heb* 11:1*

evidences

take these *e.*	*Jer* 32:14*
fields for money subscribe *e.*	44*

evident

it is *e.* to you if I lie.	*Job* 6:28*
no man justified by law is *e.*	*Gal* 3:11
an *e.* token of perdition.	*Phil* 1:28
it is *e.* our Lord sprang.	*Heb* 7:14
and it is yet far more *e.* for.	15

evidently

saw in a vision *e.* an.	*Acts* 10:3*
Christ hath been *e.* set.	*Gal* 3:1*

evil

[1] *Sin, moral evil,* 1 Ki 16:25; Eccl 9:3. [2] *Injurious or mischievous beasts or men,* Gen 37:20. [3] *Calamity,* Pr 22:3; Job 2:10. *The evil eye, according to ancient superstition, was one which could*

harm by merely looking at a person or his possessions. In the Bible, however, it more generally means the eye of envy, or of grudging benevolence, Pr 23:6; Mat 20:15.

lest some *e.* take me.	*Gen* 19:19
ye have done *e.* in so doing.	44:5
lest I see the *e.* that shall come.	34
ye thought *e.* against me.	50:20
he hath done *e.* to people.	*Ex* 5:23
look to it, for *e.* is before you.	10:10
the Lord repented of the *e.*	32:14
	2 Sam 24:16; *1 Chr* 21:15
commit no more such *e. Deut* 19:20	
shall separate him to *e.* out.	29:21
set before thee death and *e.*	30:15
and *e.* will befall you in.	31:29
if it seem *e.* to you to. *Josh* 24:15	
hand of Lord against them for *e.*	
	Judg 2:15
e. of the men of Shechem.	9:57
but they knew not that *e.* was.	20:34
that *e.* is determined. *1 Sam* 20:7	
if I knew certainly that *e.* were.	9
e. nor transgression in.	24:11
whereas I have rewarded thee *e.*	17
for *e.* is determined against.	25:17
they that seek *e.* to my lord.	26
e. hath not been found in thee.	28
what *e.* is in my hand?	26:18
I have not found *e.* in thee.	29:6
shall reward doer of *e. 2 Sam* 3:39	
I will raise up *e.* against thee.	12:11
will be worse than all the *e.*	19:7
but hast done *e.* above. *1 Ki* 14:9	
Omri wrought *e.* in eyes of.	16:25
and the Lord hath spoken *e.* concern-	
ing thee.	22:23; *2 Chr* 18:22
I am bringing such *e.* on. *2 Ki* 21:2	
eyes shall not see all *e.* on.	22:20
have sinned and done *e. 1 Chr* 21:17	
if when *e.* cometh on us. *2 Chr* 20:9	
there was *e.* determined. *Esth* 7:7	
how can I endure to see *e.?*	8:6
feared God, eschewed *e. Job* 1:1, 8	
	2:3
in seven there shall no *e.*	5:19
lift up myself when *e.* found.	31:29
comforted him over all the *e.*	42:11
neither *e.* dwell with thee.	*Ps* 5:4
if I have rewarded *e.* to him.	7:4
nor doth *e.* to his neighbour.	15:3
they intended *e.* against thee.	21:11
I will fear no *e.* thou art with.	23:4
e. shall slay wicked.	34:21
mischief, he abhorreth not *e.*	36:4
to shame that wish me *e.*	40:14
mine enemies speak *e.* of me.	41:5
should I fear in days of *e.?*	49:5
thou givest thy mouth to *e.*	50:19
reward *e.* unto mine enemies.	54:5
thoughts are against me for *e.*	56:5
years wherein we have seen *e.*	90:15
no *e.* befall thee.	91:10; *Jer* 23:17
that love the Lord, hate *e. Ps* 97:10	
and of them that speak *e.*	109:20
e. shall hunt violent man to.	140:11
for their feet run to *e.*	*Pr* 1:16
	Isa 59:7
be quiet from fear of *e. Pr* 1:33	
devise not *e.* against neighbour.	3:29
I was almost in all *e.* in midst.	5:14
he that pursueth *e.* pursueth.	11:19
heart of them that imagine *e.*	12:20
no *e.* happen to the just.	21
e. pursueth sinners.	13:21
the *e.* bow before the good.	14:19
that devise *e.*	22
even wicked for day of *e.*	16:4
ungodly man diggeth up *e.* fire.	27
moving his lips he bringeth *e.*	30
shall not be visited with *e.*	19:23
king scattereth away all *e.*	20:8
say not thou, I will recompense *e.*	22
soul of wicked desireth *e.*	21:10
prudent man foreseeth *e.*	22:3
	27:12
if thou hast thought *e.* lay.	30:32
is vanity, and a great *e. Eccl* 2:21	
there is a sore *e.* which I.	5:13, 16
an *e.* which I have seen.	6:1; 10:5
this is an *e.* among things. . .the heart	
of sons of men is full of *e.*	9:3
knowest not what *e.* shall be.	11:2

for they have rewarded *e.*	*Isa* 3:9
punish world for their *e.*	13:11
shutteth eyes from seeing *e.*	33:15
I make peace and create *e.*	45:7
shall *e.* come upon thee.	47:11
keepeth his hand from any *e.*	56:2
is taken away from the *e.*	57:1
out of north *e.* break. *Jer* 1:14; 6:1	
e. shall come upon them.	2:3
forth like fire, because of *e.* of.	
	4:4; 23:2; 26:3; 44:22
neither shall *e.* come upon us.	5:12
children of Judah have done *e.*	7:30
when thou dost *e.* then thou.	11:15
pronounced *e.* against thee for *e.*	17
thee well in time of *e.*	15:11
my hope in the day of *e.*	17:17
bring on them the day of *e.*	18
nation turn from *e.* I will repent of *e.*	
	18:8; 26:3, 13, 19; 42:10
I frame *e.* against you.	18:11
I will bring all *e.* that I.	19:15
my face against city for *e.*	21:10
e. shall go forth from.	25:32
prophesied of war and of *e.*	28:8
of peace and not of *e.*	29:11
children of Judah have done *e.* 32:20	
because of all the *e.* of the.	32
on Judah and Jerusalem all the *e.*	
I have.	35:17; 36:31
these men have done *e.* in.	38:9
against you for *e.* and cut off.	44:11
and were well, and saw no *e.*	17
I will watch over them for *e.* and.	27
words stand against you for *e.*	29
Heshbon they have devised *e.*	48:2
will render to Babylon all *e.*	51:24
wrote all *e.* that should come.	60
an *e.* an only *e.* behold.	*Ezek* 7:5
comforted concerning the *e.*	14:22
hath watched upon *e.*	*Dan* 9:14
repenteth him of the *e.*	*Joel* 2:13
there be *e.* in a city?	*Amos* 3:6
who say, *e.* shall not overtake.	9:10
God repented of *e. Jonah* 3:10; 4:2	
but *e.* came down from.	*Mi* 1:12
this family do I devise *e.*	3
no *e.* can come.	3:11
that imagineth *e.* against. *Nah* 1:11	
purer eyes than to behold *e. Hab* 1:13	
delivered from the power of *e.*	2:9
not see *e.* any more.	*Zeph* 3:15
none imagine *e.*	*Zech* 7:10; 8:17
and sick, is it not *e.?*	*Mal* 1:8
every one that doeth *e.* is.	2:17
shall say all manner of *e. Mat* 5:11	
more than these, cometh of *e.*	37*
that ye resist not *e.*	39*
sufficient for day is *e.* thereof.	6:34
wherefore think ye *e.* in your?	9:4
what *e.* hath he done?	27:23
	Mark 15:14; *Luke* 23:22
lightly speak *e.* of me. *Mark* 9:39	
evil man bringeth forth *e. Luke* 6:45	
every one that doeth *e.*	*John* 3:20
they that have done *e.* to.	5:29
e. bear witness of the.	18:23
how much *e.* he hath.	*Acts* 9:13
we find no *e.* in this man.	23:9
soul of man that doeth *e.*	*Rom* 2:9
the *e.* which I would not.	7:19
abhor that which is *e.*	12:9
recompense to no man *e.* for *e.*	17
not overcome of *e.* overcome *e.*	21
wrath on him doeth *e.*	13:4
is *e.* for that man who eateth.	14:20
simple concerning *e.*	16:19
charity thinketh no *e.*	*1 Cor* 13:5
none render *e.* for *e.* to. *1 Thes* 5:15	
abstain from all appearance of *e.*	22
money is root of all *e.*	*1 Tim* 6:10*
in mind to speak *e.* of no.	*Tit* 3:2
tongue is an unruly *e.*	*Jas* 3:8
not rendering *e.* for *e.* or. *1 Pet* 3:9	
he that doeth *e.* hath not. *3 John* 11	

evil, *adjective*

thoughts were only *e. Gen* 6:5; 8:21	
e. beast devoured him.	37:20, 33
did see they were in *e.* case. *Ex* 5:19	
people heard these *e.* tidings.	33:4
bear this *e.* congregation. *Num* 14:27	
bring us in unto this *e.* place.	20:5

not one of e. generation. *Deut* 1:35
bring up an e. name. 22:14, 19
his eye shall be e. toward. 28:54
eye shall be e. toward her. 56
hear of your e. dealings. *1 Sam* 2:23
neither adversary nor e. *1 Ki* 5:4
that is come on us for e. *Ezra* 9:13
an e. disease cleaveth. *Ps* 41:8
encourage themselves in an e. 64:5
trouble by sending e. angels. 78:49
shall not be afraid of e. tidings. 112:7
let not an e. speaker be. 140:11
to keep thee from e. *Pr* 6:24
riches perish by e. travel. *Eccl* 5:14
vanity, and it is an e. disease. 6:2
as fishes taken in an e. net. 9:12
have taken e. counsel. *Isa* 7:5
instruments of churl are e. 32:7
remain of this e. family. *Jer* 8:3
against all mine e. neighbours. 12:14
this e. people refuse to hear. 13:10
their course is e. their force. 23:10
e. figs, very e. so e. 24:3, 8; 29:17
they have heard e. tidings. 49:23
send on them e. arrows. *Ezek* 5:16
send on you famine and e. beasts. 6:11
alas, for e. abominations of. 6:11
I will cause the e. beasts to. 34:25
shalt think an e. thought. 38:10
that coveteth an e. *Hab* 2:9
his sun to rise on e. *Mat* 5:45
if ye being e. 7:11; *Luke* 11:13
not bring forth e. fruit. *Mat* 7:18
how can ye being e. speak? 12:34
an e. generation seeketh a sign. 39
             Luke 11:29
out of heart proceed e. thoughts,
murders. *Mat* 15:19; *Mark* 7:21
if that e. servant shall say. *Mat* 24:48
cast out your name as e. *Luke* 6:22
kind to unthankful and to the e. 35
for their deeds were e. *John* 3:19
have found any e. doing. *Acts* 24:20
e. communications. *1 Cor* 15:33
might deliver us from e. *Gal* 1:4
let e. speaking be put. *Eph* 4:31
beware of e. workers. *Phil* 3:2
mortify e. concupiscence. *Col* 3:5
whereof cometh e. *1 Tim* 6:4
the Cretians are e. beasts. *Tit* 1:12
hearts sprinkled from e. *Heb* 10:22
become judges of e. *Jas* 2:4
all such rejoicing is e. 4:16
all malice and e. *1 Pet* 2:1
not bear them who are e. *Rev* 2:2

evil, *adverb*

why so e. entreated? *Ex* 5:22†
Egyptians e. entreated. *Deut* 26:6†
because it went e. *1 Chr* 7:23
he e. entreateth barren. *Job* 24:21*
if I have spoken e. *John* 18:23
entreat them e. 400 years. *Acts* 7:6
same e. entreated our fathers. 19
their minds e. affected. 14:2
but spake e. of that way. 19:9
shall not speak e. of ruler. 23:5
good be e. spoken of. *Rom* 14:16
why am I e. spoken of? *1 Cor* 10:30
e. one of another, he that speaks e. of
brother, speaks e. of. *Jas* 4:11
whereas they speak e. *1 Pet* 3:16
for well-doing than for e. 17
think it strange, speaking e. 4:4
their part he is e. spoken of. 14
way of truth be e. *2 Pet* 2:2
are not afraid to speak e. 10; *Jude* 8
as natural brute beasts, speak e.
           2 Pet 2:12; *Jude* 10

bring, brought evil

shall *bring* on you all e. *Josh* 23:15
overtake and *bring* e. *2 Sam* 15:14
that Lord might *bring* e. 17:14
I will *bring* e. on house. *1 Ki* 14:10
hast thou also *brought* e. on? 17:20
I will *bring* e. upon thee. 21:21
not *bring* e. in his days, but. 29
behold, I will *bring* e. upon this.
      2 Ki 22:16; *2 Chr* 34:24
all the e. I will *bring*. *2 Chr* 34:28
I will *bring* e. and not. *Isa* 31:2
I will *bring* e. from north. *Jer* 4:6
will *bring* e. upon this people. 6:19
I will *bring* e. upon them. 11:11

I will *bring* e. upon men of. *Jer* 11:23
will *bring* e. on this place. 19:3, 15
I will *bring* e. even year of. 23:12
I begin to *bring* e. on city. 25:29
will *bring* on Judah e. 35:17; 36:31
bring my words on city for e. 39:16
will *bring* e. upon all flesh. 45:5
        see **did, do**

evil joined with **good**

tree of knowledge of *good* and e.
          Gen 2:9, 17
gods knowing *good* and e. 3:5, 22
ye rewarded e. for *good*? 44:4
no knowledge between *good* and e.
          Deut 1:39
requited me e. for *good*. *1 Sam* 25:21
between *good* and e.? *2 Sam* 19:35
not prophesy *good* concerning me,
but e. *1 Ki* 22:8, 18
never *good* to me, but e. *2 Chr* 18:7
not prophesy *good* to me, but e. 17
receive *good*, and not e.? *Job* 2:10
looked for *good*, then e. came. 30:26
rewarded me e. for *good*. *Ps* 35:12
          109:5
that render e. for *good* are. 38:20
lovest e. more than *good*. 52:3
beholding e. and the *good*. *Pr* 15:3
whoso rewardeth e. for *good*. 17:13
will do him *good* and not e. 31:12
call e. *good*, and *good* e. *Isa* 5:20
to refuse e. choose *good*. 7:15, 16
e. be recompensed for *good*?
          Jer 18:20
whether it be *good* or e. we. 42:6
proceedeth not e. and *good*.
          Lam 3:38
seek *good* and not e. *Amos* 5:14
eyes on them for e. not for *good*. 9:4
who hate *good*, and love e. *Mi* 3:2
when I would do *good*, e. present.
          Rom 7:21
neither having done *good* or e. 9:11
to discern *good* and e. *Heb* 5:14
is e. but what is *good*. *3 John* 11
        see **great**

from evil

redeemed me *from* all e. *Gen* 48:16
kept his servant *from* e. *1 Sam* 25:39
wouldest keep me *from* e. *1 Chr* 4:10
and to depart *from* e. is. *Job* 28:28
keep thy tongue *from* e. 14; 37:27; *Pr* 3:7
depart *from* e. 14; 37:27; *Pr* 3:7
preserve thee *from* all e. 121:7
remove thy foot *from* e. *Pr* 4:27
to fools to depart *from* e. 13:19
and departeth *from* e. 14:16
of Lord men depart *from* e. 16:6
of upright is to depart *from* e. 17
that departeth *from* e. *Isa* 59:15
they proceed *from* e. to evil. *Jer* 9:3
have turned them *from* their e. way,
Babylon not rise *from* e. 51:64
deliver us *from* e. *Mat* 6:13*
          Luke 11:14
keep them *from* e. *John* 17:15*
stablish you, keep you *from* e.
          2 Thes 3:3*
refrain his tongue *from* e. *1 Pet* 3:10

put away evil

put the e. *away* from. *Deut* 13:5
so thou shalt *put* the e. *away*. 17:7
19:19; 21:21; 22:21, 24; 24:7
put ye *away* e. from Israel. 17:12
22:21; *Judg* 20:13
put away e. *from* flesh. *Eccl* 11:10
put away e. of your doings. *Isa* 1:16

evil in the sight of the Lord

had done e. in the sight of the Lord.
      Num 32:13; *Judg* 3:12
Israel did e. in the sight of the Lord.
    Judg 2:11; 3:7, 12; 4:1; 6:1
10:6; 13:1; *1 Ki* 11:6; 14:22
15:26, 34; 16:7, 30; 22:52
2 Ki 8:18, 27; 13:2, 11; 14:24
15:9, 18, 24, 28; 17:2; 21:2, 20
2 Chr 22:4; 33:2, 22; 36:5, 9, 12
thou didst e. in the sight of the Lord.
          1 Sam 15:19
in doing e. in the sight of the Lord.
          1 Ki 16:19

sold to work e. in the sight of the
Lord. *1 Ki* 21:20
he wrought e. in the sight of the
Lord. *2 Ki* 3:2
sold themselves to do e. in the sight
of the Lord. 17:17
to sin, doing e. in the sight of the
Lord. 21:16; 23:32, 37; 24:9, 19
Er was e. in the sight of the Lord.
          1 Chr 2:3
wrought much e. in the sight of Lord.
          2 Chr 33:6

this evil

and repent of this e. *Ex* 32:12
done us this great e. *1 Sam* 6:9
we have added this e. to. 12:19
this e. in sending. *2 Sam* 13:16*
brought on them all this e. *1 Ki* 9:9
this e. is of the Lord. *2 Ki* 6:33
therefore he brought this e. on them.
          2 Chr 7:22
God bring all this e. on? *Neh* 13:18
to you to do all this great e.? 27
friends heard of this e. *Job* 2:11
done this e. in thy sight. *Ps* 51:4
pronounced all this e. *Jer* 16:10
hast caused all this e. on. 32:23
like as I have brought all this e. 42
God hath pronounced this e. 45:2
why commit ye this great e.? 44:7
therefore this e. is happened. 23
it is written, all this e. is. *Dan* 9:13
for whose cause this e. *Jonah* 1:7, 8

evil day or days

few and e. have the days. *Gen* 47:9
days of the afflicted are e. *Pr* 15:15
while the e. days come not. *Eccl* 12:1
put far away the e. day. *Amos* 6:3
because days are e. *Eph* 5:16
be able to withstand in e. day. 6:13
day of evil, *see* evil, *substantive*

evil doer, or doers

neither help the e. doers. *Job* 8:20
hated the congregation of e. doers.
          Ps 26:5
fret not because of e. doers. 37:1
e. doers shall be cut off. 9
up for me against e. doers? 94:16
depart from me, ye e. doers. 119:115
nation, a seed of e. doers. *Isa* 1:4
an hypocrite, an e. doer. 9:17
the seed of e. doers shall. 14:20
arise against house of e. doers. 31:2
soul of poor from e. doers. *Jer* 20:13
strengthen hands of e. doers. 23:14
trouble as an e. doer. *2 Tim* 2:9*
against you as e. doers. *1 Pet* 2:12
for the punishment of e. doers. 14
evil of you as of e. doers. 3:16
suffer as thief or an e. doer. 4:15
        see doings, eye

evil heart

of man's e. heart is e. *Gen* 8:21
the imagination of e. heart. *Jer* 3:17
walked in imagination of e. heart.
          7:24
every one in imagination of his e.
heart. 11:8
every one after his e. heart. 16:12
do imagination of his e. heart. 18:12
be in any an e. heart. *Heb* 3:12

evil man or men

of pride of e. men. *Job* 35:12
arm of the e. man. *Ps* 10:15
deliver me from the e. man. 140:1
from way of the e. man. *Pr* 2:12
go not in the way of e. men. 4:14
wicked desireth net of e. men. 12:12
e. man seeketh only rebellion. 17:11
not envious against e. men. 24:1
fret not because of e. men. 19
be no reward to the e. man. 20
e. men understand not. 28:5
in transgression of an e. man. 29:6
e. man out of the evil treasure.
      Mat 12:35; *Luke* 6:45
e. men shall wax worse. *2 Tim* 3:13
        see report

evil spirit or spirits

e. sp. between Abimelech. *Judg* 9:23
an e. sp. from Lord. *1 Sam* 16:14, 15
when e. sp. from God is upon. 16

and the *e. sp.* departed from.
　　　　　　　　　　　1 Sam 16:23
e. sp. from God came. 18:10; 19:9
cured many of *e. sp.* *Luke* 7:21
a woman healed of *e. sp.* 8:2
and the *e. sp.* went out. *Acts* 19:12
over them which had *e. sp.* 13
e. sp. said, Jesus I know. 15
man in whom the *e. sp.* was. 16

evil thing
what *e. thing* is this ? *Neh* 13:17
not heart to any *e. thing.* *Ps* 141:4
stand not in an *e. thing.* *Eccl* 8:3
shall feel no *e. thing.* 5
thing, whether good or *e.* 12:14
know that it is an *e. thing. Jer* 2:19
having no *e. thing* to say. *Tit* 2:8

evil things
bring on you *e. things. Josh* 23:15
poureth out *e. things.* *Pr* 15:28
hast done *e. things.* *Jer* 3:5
man bringeth *e. things. Mat* 12:35
all these *e. things* come. *Mark* 7:23
Lazarus *e. things.* *Luke* 16:25
inventors of *e. things.* *Rom* 1:30
not lust after *e. things.* *1 Cor* 10:6

evil time
be ashamed in *e. time.* *Ps* 37:19
men snared in an *e. time. Eccl* 9:12
for it is an *e. time.* *Amos* 5:13
haughtily, for *time* is *e.* *Mi* 2:3

evil way
returned not from *e. way. 1 Ki* 13:33
feet from every *e. way. Ps* 119:101
fear of Lord to hate *e. way. Pr* 8:13
to go astray in *e. way.* 28:10
every one from him *e. way. Jer* 18:11
　　　　　25:5; 26:3; 35:15; 36:3, 7
turned them from *e. way.* 23:22
every one from *e. way.* *Jonah* 3:8
they turned from *e. way.* 10

evil ways
turn from your *e. ways. 2 Ki* 17:13
　　　　　　　　　　　Ezek 33:11
your own *e. ways.* *Ezek* 36:31
now from your *e. ways.* *Zech* 1:4

evil work or works
not seen *e. work* that is. *Eccl* 4:3
sentence against an *e. work* is. 8:11
the *works* thereof are *e. John* 7:7
terror to good *works* but *e. Rom* 13:3
me from every *e. work. 2 Tim* 4:18
and every *e. work.* *Jas* 3:16
his own *works* were *e. 1 John* 3:12

Evil-merodach
E. king of Babylon did lift up the.
　　　　　2 Ki 25:27; *Jer* 52:31

evils
e. and troubles befall them, they say,
　are not these *e.?* *Deut* 31:17
for all the *e.* which they have. 18
when many *e.* and troubles are. 21
innumerable *e.* compassed. *Ps* 40:12
people committed two *e.* *Jer* 2:13
lothe themselves for *e.* *Ezek* 6:9
lothe yourselves for all your *e.* 20:43
all the *e.* which Herod. *Luke* 3:19

ewe or ewes
Abraham set seven *e.* *Gen* 21:28
mean these seven *e.* lambs ? 29
e. and she goats have not. 31:38
two hundred *e.* and twenty. 32:14
take one *e.* lamb of. *Lev* 14:10
whether cow or *e.* ye. 22:28
save one *e.* lamb. *2 Sam* 12:3
him from following the *e. Ps* 78:71

exact
not *e.* it of neighbour. *Deut* 15:2
of a foreigner thou mayest *e.* 3
you *e.* usury every one of. *Neh* 5:7
I likewise might *e.* of them. 10*
hundredth part of money ye *e.* 11
enemy shall not *e.* upon. *Ps* 89:22
in your fasts ye *e.* all. *Isa* 58:3
e. no more than what. *Luke* 3:13*

exacted
Menahem *e.* the money. *2 Ki* 15:20
Jehoiakim *e.* the silver and. 23:35

exacteth
e. of thee less than. *Job* 11:6

exaction
we should leave the *e.* *Neh* 10:31

exactions
take away your *e.* *Ezek* 45:9

exactors
will also make thine *e.* *Isa* 60:17

exalt
my father's God, I will *e.* *Ex* 15:2
he shall *e.* the horn of. *1 Sam* 2:10
shalt thou not *e.* them. *Job* 17:4
and let us *e.* his name. *Ps* 34:3
he shall *e.* thee to inherit. 37:34
let not rebellious *e.* themselves. 66:7
but my horn shall thou *e.* 92:10
e. ye the Lord our God. 99:5, 9
let them *e.* him in the. 107:32
my God, I will *e.* thee. 118:28
lest wicked *e.* themselves. 140:8
e. her, and she shall. *Pr* 4:8
e. the voice unto them. *Isa* 13:2
I will *e.* my throne above. 14:13
thou art my God, I will *e.* 25:1
e. him that is low. *Ezek* 21:26
nor shall it *e.* itself any. 29:15
that none of the trees *e.* 31:14
robbers of people shall *e. Dan* 11:14
the king shall *e.* himself. 36
none at all would *e.* him. *Hos* 11:7
though thou *e.* thyself as. *Ob* 4*
whoso shall *e.* himself. *Mat* 23:12
if a man *e.* himself. *2 Cor* 11:20
that he may *e.* in due. *1 Pet* 5:6

exalted
his kingdom shall be *e.* *Num* 24:7
mine horn is *e.* in Lord. *1 Sam* 2:1
Lord had *e.* his kingdom. *2 Sam* 5:12
e. be the God of the rock of my.
　　　　　　　　　22:47; *Ps* 18:46
then Adonijah *e.* himself. *1 Ki* 1:5
I *e.* thee from people. 14:7; 16:2
against whom hast thou *e.* thy voice ?
　　　　　　　2 Ki 19:22; *Isa* 37:23
and thou art *e.* as. *1 Chr* 29:11
is *e.* above all blessings. *Neh* 9:5
who mourn may be *e.* *Job* 5:11
they are *e.* for a little while. 24:24
them for ever, they are *e.* 36:7
walk when vilest men are *e. Ps* 12:8
long shall my enemy be *e.?* 13:2
be thou *e.* Lord, in thine. 21:13
I will be *e.* among the heathen, I will
　be *e.* in the earth. 46:10
he is greatly *e.* 47:9
be thou *e.* O God, above. 57:5, 11
horns of righteous shall be *e.* 75:10
righteousness shall they be *e.* 89:16
in thy favour our horn shall be *e.* 17
I have *e.* one chosen out. 19
in my name shall his horn be *e.* 24
thou, Lord, art *e.* far above. 97:9
be thou *e.* O God, above. 108:5
horn shall be *e.* with honour. 112:9
right hand of the Lord is *e.* 118:16
of the upright city is *e.* *Pr* 11:11
mountain of Lord's house shall be *e.*
　　　　　　　Isa 2:2; *Mi* 4:1
be *e.* in that day. *Isa* 2:11, 17; 5:16
mention that his name is *e.* 12:4
will be *e.* that he may have. 30:18
the Lord is *e.* 33:5
now will I be *e.* 10
every valley shall be *e.* 40:4
my highways shall be *e.* 49:11
behold my servant shall be *e.* 52:13
Lord have *e.* the low. *Ezek* 17:24
and her stature was *e.* 19:11; 31:5
he *e.* himself in Israel. *Hos* 13:1
and their heart was *e.* 6
Capernaum *e.* to heaven. *Mat* 11:23
　　　　　　　　　　　Luke 10:15
e. himself abased, humble himself *e.*
　　　Mat 23:12; *Luke* 14:11; 18:14
e. them of low degree. *Luke* 1:52
right hand of God *e.* *Acts* 2:33
hath God *e.* with his right. 5:31
God of Israel *e.* people. 13:17
that you might be *e.* *2 Cor* 11:7
lest I should be *e.* 12:7
God hath highly *e.* him. *Phil* 2:9
brother rejoice that he is *e. Jas* 1:9

exaltest
as yet *e.* thou thyself. *Ex* 9:17

exalteth
God *e.* by his power. *Job* 36:22*
he *e.* horn of his people. *Ps* 148:14
hasty of spirit *e.* folly. *Pr* 14:29
righteousness *e.* a nation. 34
he that *e.* his gate seeketh. 17:19
he that *e.* himself shall. *Luke* 14:11
　　　　　　　　　　　　18:14
every thing that *e.* itself. *2 Cor* 10:5
who *e.* himself above all. *2 Thes* 2:4

examination
that, after *e.* had, I. *Acts* 25:26

examine
sat down to *e.* matter. *Ezra* 10:16
e. me, O Lord, prove me. *Ps* 26:2
answer to them that *e.* *1 Cor* 9:3
let a man *e.* himself. 11:28
e. yourselves, prove. *2 Cor* 13:5

examined
I have *e.* him before you. *Luke* 23:14
if we this day be *e.* of. *Acts* 4:9
Herod *e.* keepers. 12:19
brought, that he should be *e.* 22:24
who should have *e.* him. 29
when they had *e.* me would. 28:18

examining
by *e.* of whom thou. *Acts* 24:8

example
not make her a publick *e. Mat* 1:19
have given you an *e.* *John* 13:15
but be thou an *e.* of. *1 Tim* 4:12
man fall after same *e.* *Heb* 4:11
serve unto the *e.* of heavenly. 8:5
take prophets for an *e.* *Jas* 5:10
for us, leaving us an *e.* *1 Pet* 2:21
set forth for an *e.*, suffering. *Jude* 7

examples
these things were our *e. 1 Cor* 10:6
see ensample, -s

exceed
not *e.:* lest, if he should *e.*, thy brother
　seem vile to thee. *Deut* 25:3
except righteousness *e.* *Mat* 5:20
of righteousness doth *e.* *2 Cor* 3:9

exceeded
wept, till David *e.* *1 Sam* 20:41
Solomon *e.* all kings of. *1 Ki* 10:23
transgressions that they *e. Job* 36:9*

exceedest
thou *e.* the fame that I. *2 Chr* 9:6

exceedeth
thy wisdom *e.* the fame. *1 Ki* 10:7

exceeding
and thy *e.* great reward. *Gen* 15:1
I will make thee *e.* fruitful. 17:6
Esau cried with an *e.* bitter. 27:34
Israel waxed *e.* mighty. *Ex* 1:7
voice of trumpet *e.* loud. 19:16
land we passed through *e. Num* 14:7
talk no more so *e.* *1 Sam* 2:3
David took *e.* much brass.
　　　　　　　　　　　2 Sam 8:8
rich man had *e.* many flocks. 12:2
gave Solomon wisdom *e. 1 Ki* 4:29
vessels unweighed, were *e.* 7:47
he brought *e.* much spoil. *1 Chr* 20:2
house must be *e.* magnifical. 22:5
made cities *e.* strong. *2 Chr* 11:12
there was *e.* much spoil. 14:14
until his disease waxed *e.* 16:12
Hezekiah had *e.* much riches. 32:27
thou hast made him *e.* *Ps* 21:6
I go unto God, my *e.* joy. 43:4
thy commandment is *e.* 119:96
four things which are *e.* *Pr* 30:24
that which is *e.* deep. *Eccl* 7:24
pride of Moab, he is *e.* *Jer* 48:29
iniquity of Israel *e.* great. *Ezek* 9:9
didst eat oil, and wast *e.* 16:13
e. in dyed attire upon heads. 23:15
upon feet an *e.* great army. 37:10
fish of the great sea, *e.* many. 47:10
the furnace was *e.* hot. *Dan* 3:22
then was the king *e.* glad. 6:23
fourth beast *e.* dreadful. 7:19
a little horn, which waxed *e.* 8:9
Nineveh was an *e.* great. *Jonah* 3:3
so Jonah was *e.* glad of 4:6
they rejoiced with *e.* great. *Mat* 2:10
Herod was *e.* wroth. 16
taketh him up into *e.* high. 4:8

rejoice and be e. glad. *Mat 5:12*
two possessed with devils, e. 8:28
kill him; they were e. sorry. 17:23
they were e. sorrowful. 26:22
soul e. sorrowful. 38; *Mark 14:34*
the king was e. sorry. *Mark 6:26*
raiment became e. white as. 9:3
Herod saw Jesus, was e. *Luke 23:8*
Moses born, and was e. *Acts 7:20*
that sin become e. sinful. *Rom 7:13*
worketh for us an e. *2 Cor 4:17*
I am e. joyful in all our. 7:4
who long after you, for e. 9:14
what is the e. greatness. *Eph 1:19*
might shew the e. riches of. 2:7
able to do e. abundantly. 3:20
grace of our Lord e. *1 Tim 1:14*
be glad also with e. joy. *1 Pet 4:13*
given to us e. great and *2 Pet 1:4*
faultless with e. joy. *Jude 24*
plague thereof was e. *Rev 16:21*

exceedingly

the waters prevailed e. *Gen 7:19*
men of Sodom were sinners e. 13:13
I will multiply thy seed e. 16:10
covenant and multiply thee e. 17:2
I will multiply Ishmael e. 20
Isaac trembled very e. and. 27:33
Jacob increased e. 30:43; 47:27
the fool and erred e. *1 Sam 26:21*
Amnon hated her e. *2 Sam 13:15*
the elders were e. afraid. *2 Ki 10:4*
magnified Solomon e. *1 Chr 29:25*
2 Chr 1:1
Jehoshaphat great e. *2 Chr 17:12*
Uzziah strengthened himself e. 26:8
heard, it grieved them e. *Neh 2:10*
queen was e. grieved. *Esth 4:4*
rejoice e. when they can. *Job 3:22*
let the righteous to. rejoice. *Ps 68:3*
lusted e. in the wilderness. 106:14
testimonies, I love them e. 119:167
for we are e. filled with. 123:3, 4
earth is moved e. *Isa 24:19*
a fourth beast strong e. *Dan 7:7*
men were e. afraid. *Jonah 1:10*
then men feared the Lord e. 16
but it displeased Jonah e. 4:1
they were e. amazed. *Mat 19:25*
they feared e. and. *Mark 4:41*
cried out the more e. crucify. 15:14
these men do e. trouble. *Acts 16:20*
being e. mad against them. 26:11
and we being e. tossed. 27:18
and e. the more joyed. *2 Cor 7:13*
being more e. zealous of. *Gal 1:14*
night and day praying e. *1 Thes 3:10*
your faith groweth e. *2 Thes 1:3*
I e. fear and quake. *Heb 12:21*

excel

thou shalt not e. *Gen 49:4**
on the Sheminith to e. *1 Chr 15:21**
angels, that e. in. *Ps 103:20**
graven images did e. *Isa 10:10*
seek that ye may e. *1 Cor 14:12**

excelled

Solomon's wisdom e. *1 Ki 4:30*

excellency

the e. of dignity, and e. *Gen 49:3†*
in the greatness of thine e. *Ex 15:7*
who rideth in his e. *Deut 33:26*
who is the sword of thy e. 29
doth not their e. go? *Job 4:21**
his e. make you afraid? 13:11
though his e. mount up. 20:6
thundereth with voice of his e. 37:4
thyself with majesty and e. 40:10
the e. of Jacob. *Ps 47:4†*
to cast him down from his e. 62:4†
his e. is over Israel. 68:34
the e. of knowledge is. *Eccl 7:12*
beauty of Chaldees' e. *Isa 13:19**
e. of Carmel, Sharon; the e. 35:2
make thee an eternal e. 60:15
my sanctuary, the e. *Ezek 24:21**
I abhor the e. of Jacob. *Amos 6:8*
Lord hath sworn by the e. of Jacob. 8:7
Lord hath turned away e. of Jacob,
as the e. of Israel. *Nah 2:2*
not with e. of speech. *1 Cor 2:1*
e. of the power be of. *2 Cor 4:7**
all things loss for the e. *Phil 3:8*

13

excellent

Ahasuerus shewed e. *Esth 1:4*
Almighty is e. in power. *Job 37:23*
how e. is thy name in! *Ps 8:1, 9*
and to the e. in whom is all. 16:3
e. is thy lovingkindness! 36:7*
thou art more e. than the. 76:4
me, it shall be an e. oil. 141:5*
his name alone is e. 148:13*
according to e. greatness. 150:2
for I will speak of e. things. *Pr 8:6*
righteous is more e. than. 17:7
e. speech becometh not a fool. 17:7
man of understanding is of an e. 27*
written to thee e. things? 22:20
his countenance e. as. *S of S 5:15*
fruit of earth shall be e. *Isa 4:2*
sing to Lord, he hath done e. 12:5
the Lord of hosts is e. in. 28:29
come to e. ornaments. *Ezek 16:7*
whose brightness was e. *Dan 2:31*
an e. majesty was added. 4:36
e. spirit found in Daniel. 5:12; 6:3
I heard that e. wisdom is. 5:14
to thee, e. Theophilus. *Luke 1:3*
to e. governor Felix. *Acts 23:26*
approvest things more e. *Rom 2:18*
Phil 1:10
shew you a more e. way. *1 Cor 12:31*
obtained a more e. name. *Heb 1:4*
he obtained a more e. ministry. 8:6
Abel offered a more e. sacrifice. 11:4
a voice from the e. *2 Pet 1:17†*

excellest

virtuously, but thou e. all. *Pr 21:29*

excelleth

wisdom e. folly, as light e. *Eccl 2:13*
by reason of glory that e. *2 Cor 3:10*

except

e. the God of my father. *Gen 31:42*
not let thee go, e. thou bless. 32:26
e. youngest brother. 42:15; 43:3, 5
e. we had lingered, we. 43:10
e. the land of the priests only. 47:26
e. thou make thyself a. *Num 16:13*
e. their Rock had. *Deut 32:30*
e. you destroy accursed. *Josh 7:12*
e. thou hadst hasted. *1 Sam 25:34*
e. as the Lord hath. *2 Sam 3:9*
e. thou first bring Michal. 13
e. thou take away the blind. 5:6
slack not thy riding, e. I. *2 Ki 4:24*
e. the king delighted in. *Esth 2:14*
e. king hold out golden. 4:11
e. Lord build the house, e. Lord keep
the city, the watchman. *Ps 127:1*
sleep not, e. they have. *Pr 4:16*
e. the Lord had left a. *Isa 1:9*
Rom 9:29
none other can shew it, e. *Dan 2:11*
nor worship any god, e. their. 3:28
e. we find it concerning the law. 6:5
two walk together, e.? *Amos 3:3*
e. your righteousness. *Mat 5:20*
e. he first bind the strong man.
12:29; *Mark 3:27*
e. ye be converted. *Mat 18:3*
put away his wife, e. for. 19:9
e. those days be shortened should no
flesh be saved. 24:22; *Mark 13:20*
cup may not pass, e. I drink.
Mat 26:42
Pharisees, e. they wash. *Mark 7:3*
e. we go and buy meat. *Luke 9:13*
e. ye repent, ye shall all. 13:3, 5
these miracles, e. God. *John 3:2*
e. a man be born again, he cannot. 3
e. a man be born of water and. 5
nothing, e. it be given from. 27
e. ye see signs and wonders. 4:48
e. the Father who hath sent. 6:44
e. ye eat the flesh of the Son. 53
e. it were given unto him of. 65
e. a corn of wheat fall. 12:24
cannot bear fruit, e. ye abide. 15:4
no power, e. it were given. 19:11
e. I shall see the prints of. 20:25
all scattered, e. apostles. *Acts 8:1*
how can I, e. some man? 31
e. ye be circumcised, ye. 15:1
e. it be for this one voice. 24:21
such as I am, e. these bonds. 26:29
e. these abide in ship, ye. 27:31

not known lust, e. the law. *Rom 7:7*
preach, e. they be sent? 10:15
not one another e. it. *1 Cor 7:5*
speaketh with tongues, e. he. 14:5
e. I shall speak to you either. 6
e. they give a distinction in the. 7
e. ye utter words easy to be. 9
sowest is not quickened, e. 15:36
e. it be that I was not. *2 Cor 12:13*
Christ is in you, e. ye be? 13:5
e. there come a falling. *2 Thes 2:3*
he is not crowned, e. *2 Tim 2:5*
remove thy candlestick, e. *Rev 2:5*
e. they repent their deeds. 22

excepted

he is e. who did put all. *1 Cor 15:27*

excess

full of extortion and e. *Mat 23:25*
with wine, wherein is e. *Eph 5:18**
walked in lusts, e. of. *1 Pet 4:3*
run not with them to same e. 4

exchange

bread in e. for horses. *Gen 47:17*
then it and the e. thereof. *Lev 27:10*
and the e. of it shall not. *Job 28:17*
what shall a man give in e. for his
soul? *Mat 16:26; Mark 8:37*

exchange

not sell of it, nor e. *Ezek 48:14*

exchangers

to put my money to e. *Mat 25:27*

exclude

they would e. you, that. *Gal 4:17*

excluded

is boasting? it is e. *Rom 3:27*

excommunicated

*Excommunication is an ecclesias-
tical censure, whereby the person
against whom it is pronounced is,
for the time, cast out of the communion of the church.
The word is not used in the Bible,
but the act is referred to in various
ways, all easily recognizable. An
example in the Jewish church is in
John 9:34.*

excuse

began to make e. *Luke 14:18*
that they are without e. *Rom 1:20*

excuse

that we e. ourselves? *2 Cor 12:19*

excused

pray thee have me e. *Luke 14:18, 19*

excusing

thoughts accusing or else e.
Rom 2:15

execration

and ye shall be an e. *Jer 42:18*
they shall be an e. and a. 44:12

execute

e. judgement on gods of. *Ex 12:12*
the priest shall e. upon. *Num 5:30*
that they may e. the service. 8:11
doth e. the judgement of. *Deut 10:18*
if thou e. my judgements. *1 Ki 6:12*
when wilt thou e.? *Ps 119:84*
to e. vengeance upon. 149:7
to e. upon them the judgement. 9
take counsel, e. judgement. *Isa 16:3*
e. judgement between man. *Jer 7:5*
e. judgement in the morning. 21:12
e. judgement and. 22:3
branch e. judgement. 23:5; 33:15
I will e. judgements. *Ezek 5:8, 10*
when I shall e. judgements in. 15
will e. judgements among you. 11:9
they shall e. judgements. 16:41
and I will e. judgements. 25:11
and I will e. great vengeance. 17
fire in Zoan, e. judgements. 30:14
thus e. judgements in Egypt. 19
remove violence, e. judgement. 45:9
not e. fierceness of mine. *Hos 11:9*
and I will e. vengeance. *Mi 5:15*
plead my cause, e. judgement. 7:9
e. true judgement and. *Zech 7:9*
e. the judgement of truth and. 8:16
authority to e. judgement. *John 5:27*
minister of God to e. *Rom 13:4*
to e. judgement on all. *Jude 15*

executed

on their gods Lord e. | Num 33:4
he e. justice of Lord. | Deut 33:21
David e. judgement. | 2 Sam 8:15
 | 1 Chr 18:14
that e. priest's office. | 1 Chr 6:10
Eleazar and Ithamar e. the. | 24:2
they e. judgement. | 2 Chr 24:24
judgement be e. speedily. | Ezra 7:26
Phinehas, e. judgement. | Ps 106:30
sentence is not e. | Eccl 8:11
not return till he have e. | Jer 33:20
neither e. judgements. | Ezek 11:12
 | 20:24
hath e. true judgement. | 18:8, 17
for they had e. judgement. | 23:10
shall have e. judgements. | 28:22, 26
heathen see judgement I have e. | 39:21
Zacharias e. priest's office. | Luke 1:8

executedst

nor e. his fierce wrath. | 1 Sam 28:18

executest

thou e. judgement and. | Ps 99:4

executeth

known by judgement he e. | Ps 9:16
the Lord e. righteousness. | 103:6
the Lord e. judgement for. | 146:7
man that e. my counsel. | Isa 46:11
if any e. judgement. | Jer 5:1
is strong that e. his word. | Joel 2:11

executing

thou hast done well in e. | 2 Ki 10:30
cast them off from e. | 2 Chr 11:14
when Jehu was e. judgement. | 22:8

execution

drew near to be put in e. | Esth 9:1

executioner

king sent an e. and. | Mark 6:27*

exempted

proclamation, none was e. | 1 Ki 15:22

exercise

bodily e. profiteth little. | 1 Tim 4:8

exercise

nor do I e. myself. | Ps 131:1
Lord which e. loving. | Jer 9:24
Gentiles e. dominion over them, and
they that are great e. | Mat 20:25*
 | Mark 10:42*; Luke 22:25*
herein do I e. myself. | Acts 24:16
and e. thyself rather. | 1 Tim 4:7

exercised

be e. therewith. | Eccl 1:13; 3:10
of land have e. robbery. | Ezek 22:29
senses e. to discern. | Heb 5:14
to them which are e. thereby. | 12:11
an heart e. with. | 2 Pet 2:14

exerciseth

he e. all the power of. | Rev 13:12

exhort

did he testify and e. | Acts 2:40
and now I e. you to be of. | 27:22
it necessary to e. | 2 Cor 9:5*
beseech you and e. you. | 1 Thes 4:1
now we e. you, warn them. | 5:14
we command and e. | 2 Thes 3:12
I e. that first of all. | 1 Tim 2:1
these things teach and e. | 6:2
e. with all long suffering. | 2 Tim 4:2
may be able to e. and. | Tit 1:9
young men likewise e. to be. | 2:6
e. servants to be obedient to. | 9
speak, e. rebuke with authority. | 15
e. one another daily. | Heb 3:13
elders among you, I e. | 1 Pet 5:1
for me to write and e. | Jude 3

exhortation

other things in his e. | Luke 3:18
have any word of e. say. | Acts 13:15
when Paul had given them e. | 20:2
let him wait on e. | Rom 12:8
speaketh unto men to e. | 1 Cor 14:3*
he accepted the e. | 2 Cor 8:17
for our e. was not of. | 1 Thes 2:3
give attendance to e. | 1 Tim 4:13
ye have forgotten the e. | Heb 12:5
suffer the word of e. | 13:22

exhorted

Barnabas e. them to. | Acts 11:23

they e. the brethren with. | Acts 15:32
as you know how we e. | 1 Thes 2:11

exhorting

e. them to continue in. | Acts 14:22
wrote, e. disciples to. | 18:27*
but e. one another, and. | Heb 10:25
I have written briefly, e. | 1 Pet 5:12

exile

stranger and also an e. | 2 Sam 15:19
the captive e. hasteneth. | Isa 51:14

exorcists

(This word comes from the Greek
exorkizein, and means one who
drives off an evil spirit by adjura-
tion)
of vagabond Jews, e. | Acts 19:13

expectation

the e. of the poor shall. | Ps 9:18
wait thou on God, for my e. | 62:5
e. of wicked shall. | Pr 10:28; 11:7
but the e. of the wicked is. | 11:23
e. not be cut off. | 23:18*; 24:14*
be ashamed of their e. | Isa 20:5
behold, such is our e. | 6
Ekron; for her e. shall. | Zech 9:5
people were in e., John. | Luke 3:15
delivered me from the e. of. | Acts 12:11
for the e. of creature. | Rom 8:19
to my earnest e. and. | Phil 1:20

expected

to give you an e. end. | Jer 29:11*

expecting

e. to receive something. | Acts 3:5
e. till his enemies be. | Heb 10:13

expedient

that it is e. for us. | John 11:50
I tell you, it is e. for you that. | 16:7
it was e. that one man die. | 18:14
all things not e. | 1 Cor 6:12; 10:23
this is e. for you who. | 2 Cor 8:10
not e. for me doubtless to. | 12:1

expel

God shall e. them. | Josh 23:5*
did not ye hate me, e.? | Judg 11:7*

expelled

Israel e. not Geshurites. | Josh 13:13*
e. thence sons of Anak. | Judg 1:20*
his banished be not e. | 2 Sam 14:14*
they e. them out of. | Acts 13:50*

expences

e. be given out of king's. | Ezra 6:4
decree that e. forthwith be given. | 8

experience

by e. the Lord hath. | Gen 30:27*
my heart had great e. | Eccl 1:16
worketh e. and e. hope. | Rom 5:4*

experiment

whiles by the e. of. | 2 Cor 9:13

expert

of Zebulun fifty thousand e. in war.
 | 1 Chr 12:33*
of Danites 28,600. e. | 35*
of Asher 40,000. e. | 36*
swords, being e. in war. | S of S 3:8
arrows as of an e. man. | Jer 50:9
I know thee to be e. in. | Acts 26:3

expired

the days were not e. | 1 Sam 18:26
after the year was e. | 2 Sam 11:1*
 | 1 Chr 20:1*
come to pass days be e. | 1 Chr 17:11*
when year e. Nebuchadnezzar sent.
 | 2 Chr 36:10*
when these days were e. | Esth 1:5*
when these days are e. | Ezek 43:27*
when forty years were e. | Acts 7:30*
when 1000 years are e. | Rev 20:7*

exploits

his land he shall do e. | Dan 11:28*
people shall be strong and do e. | 32

expound

not in three days e. | Judg 14:14*

expounded

garments to them who e. the riddle.
 | Judg 14:19
alone, he e. all things. | Mark 4:34
he e. to them in all. | Luke 24:27*
but Peter e. it by order. | Acts 11:4

Aquila and Priscilla e. | Acts 18:26
Paul e. and testified the. | 28:23

express

being the e. image of. | Heb 1:3*

expressed

men which are e. by. | Num 1:17
of Manasseh 18,000, e. | 1 Chr 12:31
who were e. by name. | 16:41
men e. took captives. | 2 Chr 28:15
men e. to give portions to. | 31:19
Nethinims were e. by. | Ezra 8:20

expressly

if I e. say to the lad. | 1 Sam 20:21
the word came e. to. | Ezek 1:3
the Spirit speaketh e. | 1 Tim 4:1

extend

none to e. mercy to him. | Ps 109:12
behold, I will e. peace. | Isa 66:12

extended

e. mercy to me. | Ezra 7:28
e. mercy to us. | 9:9

extendeth

my goodness e. not to. | Ps 16:2*

extinct

my days are e. the graves. | Job 17:1
they are e. are quenched. | Isa 43:17

extol

I will e. thee, O Lord. | Ps 30:1
e. him that rideth upon. | 68:4*
I will e. thee, my God. | 145:1
Nebuchadnezzar e. King. | Dan 4:37

extolled

and he was e. with. | Ps 66:17
my servant shall be e. | Isa 52:13*

extortion

greedily gained by e. | Ezek 22:12*
they are full of e. | Mat 23:25

extortioner

let the e. catch all. | Ps 109:11
the e. is at an end. | Isa 16:4
any man be drunkard, e. | 1 Cor 5:11

extortioners

not as other men are, e. | Luke 18:11
not altogether with e. | 1 Cor 5:10
nor e. inherit kingdom of God. | 6:10

extreme

shall smite thee with e. | Deut 28:22*

extremity

knoweth it not in great e. | Job 35:15*

eye

This is used [1] literally, in many
places. [2] Figuratively, for dis-
cernment, judgement, that by
which the mind apprehends.
e. for e. | Ex 21:24; Lev 24:20
 | Deut 19:21; Mat 5:38
man smite e. of servant, or e.
 | Ex 21:26
hath a blemish in his e. | Lev 21:20
his e. shall be evil. | Deut 28:54
her e. shall be evil towards. | 56
he kept him as apple of his e. | 32:10
his e. was not dim, nor. | 34:7
the e. of their God was. | Ezra 5:5
e. that hath seen me. | Job 7:8
given up ghost, and no e. had. | 10:18
the e. which saw him, see. | 20:9
e. of adulterer waiteth for twilight
saying, no e. shall see me. | 24:15
a path which vulture's e. | 28:7
and his e. seeth every precious. | 10
when the e. saw me. | 29:11
e. of the Lord is on them. | Ps 33:18
neither wink with the e. | 35:19
aha, aha, our e. hath seen it. | 21
he that formed the e. shall? | 94:9
that winketh with the e. | Pr 10:10
the seeing e. hearing ear. | 20:12
he that hath a bountiful e. shall. | 22:9
the e. that mocketh at. | 30:17
the e. is not satisfied. | Eccl 1:8
neither is his e. satisfied. | 4:8
their e. shall not spare. | Isa 13:18
for they shall see e. to e. | 52:8
neither hath the e. seen what he hath
prepared. | 64:4; 1 Cor 2:9
that were pleasant to the e. | Lam 2:4
let not your e. spare. | Ezek 9:5
none e. pitied, to do any of. | 16:5

defiled, and let our *e.*   *Mi* 4:11
light of the body is the *e.* *Mat* 6:22
            Luke 11:34
mote in thy brother's *e.* and not beam
  in own *e. Mat* 7:3; *Luke* 6:41, 42
e. offend thee, pluck it out. *Mat* 18:9
easier for camel to go through *e.* of.
  19:24; *Mark* 10:25; *Luke* 18:25
because I am not the *e. 1 Cor* 12:16
if the whole body were an *e.*   17
e. cannot say.   21
in twinkling of an *e.* at last. 15:52
he cometh, and every *e.* *Rev* 1:7

evil eye

bread of him that hath an *evil e.*
              Pr 23:6
to be rich hath an *evil e.*   28:22
but if thine *e.* be *evil.*   *Mat* 6:23
            Luke 11:34
is thine *e. evil* because ? *Mat* 20:15
heart proceedeth *evil e. Mark* 7:22

mine eye

kill thee, but *mine e.* *1 Sam* 24:10
mine e. no more see good. *Job* 7:7
mine e. hath seen all this.   13:1
mine e. poureth out tears.   16:20
doth *mine e.* continue in ?   17:2
mine e. also is dim by.
but now *mine e.* seeth thee. 42:5
mine e. consumed. *Ps* 6:7; 31:9
I will guide thee with *mine e.* 32:8
mine e. hath seen his desire. 54:7
mine e. mourneth by reason. 88:9
mine e. shall see my desire. 92:11
mine e. mine e. runneth down.
        Lam 1:16; 3:48
mine e. trickleth down and. 3:49
mine e. affecteth my heart.   51
shall *mine e.* spare. *Ezek* 5:11
     7:4, 9; 8:18; 9:10
mine e. spared them.   20:17

right eye

sword shall be on arm, and his *right*
  e.: his *right e.* utterly. *Zech* 11:17
if *right e.* offend thee. *Mat* 5:29

thine eye

thine e. shall not pity. *Deut* 7:16
    13:8; 19:13, 21; 25:12
and *thine e.* be evil against. 15:9
apple of *thine e.* cease. *Lam* 2:18
if *thine e.* be single. *Mat* 6:22
            Luke 11:34
beam in *thine* own *e.*   *Mat* 7:3
            Luke 6:41
if *thine e.* offend thee. *Mat* 18:9
            Mark 9:47

see **apple**

eyebrows

shave all his hair off *e.* *Lev* 14:9

eyed

and Saul *e.* David.   *1 Sam* 18:9

tender **eyed**

Leah was *tender* **eyed.** *Gen* 29:17

eyelids

on mine *e.* is shadow of. *Job* 16:16
eyes are like *e.* of morning. 41:18
e. try the children of men. *Ps* 11:4
or slumber to mine *e.*   132:4
let thine *e.* look straight. *Pr* 4:25
to thine eyes, slumber to *e.* 6:4
let her take thee with her *e.* 25
their *e.* are lifted up.   30:13
that our *e.* may gush out. *Jer* 9:18

eyes

for food pleasant to *e.* *Gen* 3:6
e. of them both were opened.   7
mistress was despised in her *e.* 16:4
conceived, I was despised in her *e.* 5
is to thee a covering of *e.* 20:16
God opened Hagar's *e.*   21:19
Jacob laid rods before *e.* of. 30:41
master's wife cast her *e.* on. 39:7
good in the *e.* of Pharaoh. 41:37
the *e.* of Israel were dim. 48:10
to be abhorred in the *e.* of. *Ex* 5:21
glory of Lord like fire in *e.* 24:17
and the thing be hid from the *e.* of.
             Lev 4:13
burning ague consume the *e.* 26:16
be hid from the *e.* of her. *Num* 5:13
thou mayest be to us *e.*   10:31
wilt thou put out the *e.* of ? 16:14

sanctify me in *e.* of Israel. *Num* 20:12
Lord opened *e.* of Balaam. 22:31
man whose *e.* are open. 24:3, 15
a gift doth blind the *e.* *Deut* 16:19
Lord give thee failing of *e.* 28:65
Lord hath not given you *e.* to. 29:4
be avenged for my two *e. Judg* 16:28
uncovered himself in *e. 2 Sam* 6:20
that the *e.* of my lord the king. 24:3
e. of all Israel upon thee. *1 Ki* 1:20
Lord opened the *e.* of the. *2 Ki* 6:17
Lord, open the *e.* of these men. 20
put out *e.* of Zedekiah.   25:7
      Jer 39:7; 52:11
was right in the *e.* of. *1 Chr* 13:4
hast thou *e.* of flesh ? *Job* 10:4
the *e.* of the wicked shall fail. 11:20
even the *e.* of his children. 17:5
seeing it is hid from the *e.* 29:15
I was *e.* to the blind.   29:15
caused *e.* of the widow to fail. 31:16
and her *e.* behold afar off. 39:29
in whose *e.* a vile person. *Ps* 15:4
pure, enlightening *e.*   19:8
e. have they, but. 115:5; 135:16
as the *e.* of servants, the. 123:2
the *e.* of all wait upon thee. 145:15
Lord openeth the *e.* of blind. 146:8
as smoke to the *e.* so is. *Pr* 10:26
light of the *e.* rejoiceth. 15:30
as a precious stone in *e.* of. 17:8
the *e.* of a fool are in ends.   24
who hath redness of *e.*? 23:29
e. of man are never satisfied. 27:20
the wise man's *e.* are. *Eccl* 2:14
better the sight of *e.* than. 6:9
pleasant for the *e.* to behold. 11:7
thou hast dove's *e. S of S* 1:15; 4:1
to provoke the *e.* of his. *Isa* 3:8
daughters walk with wanton *e.* 16
e. of the lofty be humbled. 5:15
the *e.* of the blind shall see. 29:18
the *e.* of them that see. 32:3
the *e.* of the blind shall be. 35:5
to open the blind to bring. 42:7
bring forth blind that have *e.* 43:8
Lord made bare his arm in *e.* 52:10
we grope as if we had no *e.* 59:10
which have *e.* and see not. *Jer* 5:21
          Ezek 12:2
their rings were full of *e. Ezek* 1:18
the wheels were full of *e.* 10:12
as she saw them with her *e.* 23:16
known in *e.* of many nations. 38:23
in horn were *e.* like the. *Dan* 7:8
even of that horn that had *e.* 20
of purer *e.* than to behold. *Hab* 1:13
upon one stone seven *e.* *Zech* 3:9
if it be marvellous in the *e.* 8:6
when the *e.* of man shall be. 9:1
rather than having two *e.* to be cast.
      Mat 18:9; *Mark* 9:47
having *e.* see ye not ? *Mark* 8:18
e. of all were fastened. *Luke* 4:20
blessed are the *e.* which see. 10:23
anointed the *e.* of blind. *John* 9:6
any opened *e.* of one born blind. 32
can a devil open *e.* of blind ? 10:21
this man, which opened *e.*? 11:37
Dorcas opened her *e.* *Acts* 9:40
hath given them *e.* they. *Rom* 11:8
before whose *e.* Christ. *Gal* 3:1
e. of your understanding. *Eph* 1:18
things are open to *e.* of. 4:13
having *e.* full of adultery. *2 Pet* 2:14
the lust of the *e.* and. *1 John* 2:16
of throne beasts full of *e.* *Rev* 4:6
each six wings, full of *e.* within. 8
a Lamb having seven *e.* 5:6

his **eyes**

old, and *his e.* were dim. *Gen* 27:1
his e. red with wine.   49:12
having *his e.* open. *Num* 24:4, 16
find no favour in *his e. Deut* 24:1
Philistines put out *his e. Judg* 16:21
Eli, *his e.* began to. *1 Sam* 3:2; 4:15
he tasted, and *his e.* were. 14:27
Ahijah not see, *his e.* were. *1 Ki* 14:4
put *his e.* on *his e.* *2 Ki* 4:34
the child opened *his e.*   35
I pray thee, open *his e.*   6:17
slew sons of Zedekiah before *his e.*
  25:7; *Jer* 39:6; 52:10

king do what is good in *his e.*
           1 Chr 21:23
and I be pleasing in *his e. Esth* 8:5
enemy sharpeneth *his e.* *Job* 16:9
his e. shall see his destruction. 21:20
resteth, yet *his e.* are on. 24:23
the rich man openeth *his e.* 27:19
his e. are on the ways of. 34:21
he withdraweth not *his e.* 36:7
he taketh it with *his e.* 40:24*
his e. are like the eyelids. 41:18
his e. are privily set. *Ps* 10:8
his e. behold children of men. 11:4
no fear of God before *his e.* 36:1
ruleth by power, *his e.* behold. 66:7
he winketh with *his e.* *Pr* 6:13
he shutteth *his e.* to. 16:30
scattereth away evil with *his e.* 20:8
findeth no favour in *his e.* 21:10
he that hideth *his e.* shall. 28:27
sleepeth with *his e.* *Eccl* 8:16
his e. are as eyes of. *S of S* 5:12
in *his e.* as one that found. 8:10
after the sight of *his e.* *Isa* 11:3
his e. shall have respect to. 17:7
and shutteth *his e.* from. 33:15
his e. shall behold *his e. Jer* 32:4
see not the ground with *his e.*
           Ezek 12:12
away abomination of *his e.* 20:7
horn between *his e.* *Dan* 8:5, 21
his e. were as lamps of fire. 10:6
he had spit on *his e.* *Mark* 8:23
he put his hands again on *his e.* 25
made clay, opened *his e. John* 9:14
or who hath opened *his e.* 21
Peter fastening *his e.* *Acts* 3:4
and when *his e.* were opened. 9:8
there fell from *his e.* as it had. 18
then Saul set *his e.* on him. 13:9
because darkness hath blinded *his e.*
          1 John 2:11
his e. as a flame of fire. *Rev* 1:14
        2:18; 19:12

lift or *lifted up* **eyes**

Lot *lifted up* his *e.* and. *Gen* 13:10
lift up now thine *e.* and. 14; 31:12
  Deut 3:27; *2 Ki* 19:22; *Isa* 49:18
  60:4; *Jer* 3:2; *Ezek* 8:5; *Zech* 5:5
Abraham *lift up* his *e.*
       Gen 18:2; 22:4, 13
Isaac *lifted up* his *e.* 24:63
Rebekah *lifted up* her *e.* 64
Jacob *lifted up* his *e.* 31:10; 33:1
Joseph *lifted up* his *e.* 43:29
lifted up their *e.* the Egyptians.
          Ex 14:10
Balaam *lifted up* his *e.* *Num* 24:2
lest thou *lift up* thine *e. Deut* 4:19
Joshua *lifted up* his *e.* *Josh* 5:13
old man *lifted up* his *e. Judg* 19:17
lifted up their *e.* and. *1 Sam* 6:13
young man that kept the watch *lifted*
  up *e.*   *2 Sam* 13:34; 18:24
David *lifted up* his *e.* and. *1 Chr* 21:16
lift up their *e.* and. *Job* 2:12
lift up mine *e.* to hills. *Ps* 121:1
unto thee *lift up* I mine *e.* 123:1
hast thou *lifted up* thy *e.*? *Isa* 37:23
lift up your *e.* 51:6; *Ezek* 33:25
          John 4:35
lifted up e. to idols. *Ezek* 18:6, 15
hath *lifted up* his *e.* to idols. 12
thou shalt not *lift up* thine *e.* 23:27
Nebuchadnezzar *lift. up e. Dan* 4:34
then I *lifted up* mine *e.* 8:3; 10:5
  Zech 1:18; 2:1; 5:1, 5, 9; 6:1
had *lifted up* their *e.* they. *Mat* 17:8
Jesus *lifted up* his *e.* *Luke* 6:20
     John 6:5; 11:41; 17:1
in hell he *lift up* his *e.* *Luke* 16:23
not *lift up* so much as his *e.* 18:13

eyes of the Lord

grace in *e.* of the Lord. *Gen* 6:8
the *e.* of the Lord are. *Deut* 11:12
right in the *e.* of the Lord. 12:28
set by in *e.* of the Lord. *1 Sam* 26:24
favour in *e.* of the Lord. *2 Sam* 15:25
David did right in the *e.* of the Lord.
  1 Ki 15:5, 11; 22:43; *2 Chr* 14:2
e. of the Lord run to and fro through.
      2 Chr 16:9; *Zech* 4:10

e. of the Lord are upon the righteous.
Ps 34:15; 1 Pet 3:12
of man before e. of the Lord. Pr 5:21
the e. of the Lord are in. 15:3
e. of the Lord preserve. 22:12
glorious in e. of the Lord. Isa 49:5
the e. of the Lord are on the.
Amos 9:8

mine eyes
departed from mine e. Gen 31:40
that I may set mine e. upon. 44:21
bribe to blind mine e. 1 Sam 12:3
see how mine e. have been. 14:29
life much set by in mine e. 26:24
one to sit, mine e. seeing. 1 Ki 1:48
hallowed house, mine e. and mine
heart shall be. 9:3; 2 Chr 7:16
mine e. had seen it. 1 Ki 10:7
2 Chr 9:6
in my ways, to do right in mine e.
1 Ki 11:33; 14:8; 2 Ki 10:30
now mine e. be open. 2 Chr 7:15
hid not sorrow from mine e. Job 3:10
an image was before mine e. 4:16
mine e. shall behold. 19:27
made a covenant with mine e. 31:1
mine heart walked after mine e. 7
lighten mine e. lest I sleep. Ps 13:3
mine e. are toward the Lord. 25:15
lovingkindness before mine e. 26:3
as for the light of mine e. it. 38:10
mine e. fail, whilst I wait. 69:3
thou holdest mine e. waking. 77:4
no evil thing before mine e. 101:3
mine e. shall be on the faithful. 6
delivered mine e. from tears. 116:8
open mine e. 119:18
turn away mine e. 37
mine e. fail for thy word. 82
mine e. fail for thy salvation. 123
of waters run down mine e. 136
mine e. prevent night watches. 148
heart not haughty, nor mine e. 131:1
I will not give sleep to mine e. 132:4
but mine e. are unto thee. 141:8
mine e. desired, I kept not. Eccl 2:10
hide mine e. from you. Isa 1:15
away evil doings from mine e. 16
mine e. have seen the King. 6:5
mine e. fail with looking. 38:14
evil before mine e. 65:12; 66:4
they are hid from mine e. 65:16
O that mine e. were a. Jer 9:1
mine e. shall weep sore. 13:17
let mine e. run down with. 14:17
mine e. are on their ways, nor is their
iniquity hid from mine e. 16:17
I will set mine e. upon them. 24:6
mine e. do fail with. Lam 2:11
be hid from mine e. Hos 13:14
I will set mine e. on. Amos 9:4
mine e. shall behold her. Mi 7:10
marvellous in mine e. Zech 8:6
now have I seen with mine e. 9:8
I will open mine e. on the. 12:4
mine e. seen salvation. Luke 2:30
anointed mine e. John 9:11, 15
yet he hath opened mine e. 30
I had fastened mine e. Acts 11:6

our eyes
manna before our e. Num 11:6
signs before our e. Deut 6:22
nor have our e. seen it. 21:7
O God, our e. are upon thee.
2 Chr 20:12
God may lighten our e. Ezra 9:8
it is marvellous in our e. Ps 118:23
Mat 21:42; Mark 12:11
so our e. wait upon the Lord.
Ps 123:2
that our e. may run down. Jer 9:18
our e. as yet failed for. Lam 4:17
for these things our e. are. 5:17
meat cut off before our e. Joel 1:16
our e. may be opened. Mat 20:33
have seen with our e. 1 John 1:1

own eyes
not after you own e. Num 15:39
man whatsoever is right in own e.
Deut 12:8; Judg 17:6; 21:25
cast down in their own e. Neh 6:16
righteous in his own e. Job 32:1

flattereth himself in his own e.
Ps 36:2
not wise in thine own e. Pr 3:7
of a fool right in his own e. 12:15
of man are clean in his own e. 16:2
way of man right in his own e. 21:2
generation pure in their own e. 30:12
to them wise in own e. Isa 5:21
plucked out your own e. Gal 4:15

their eyes
Simeon before their e. Gen 42:24
Egyptians before their e. Ex 8:26
any ways hide their e. Lev 20:4
speak to rock before their e.
Num 20:8
me at the water before their e. 27:14
the Lord opened their e. 2 Ki 6:20
was laid before their e. Ezra 3:12
their husbands in their e. Esth 1:17
offspring before their e. Job 21:8
have set their e. bowing. Ps 17:11
let their e. be darkened. 69:23
their e. stand out with fatness. 73:7
lighteneth both their e. Pr 29:13
O how lofty are their e. 30:13
beholding them with their e.
Eccl 5:11
their e. lest they see with their e.
Isa 6:10; Mat 13:15; Acts 28:27
to pieces before their e. Isa 13:16
for he hath shut their e. 44:18
their e. did fail, because. Jer 14:6
and with their e. Ezek 6:9
away abominations of their e. 20:8
their e. after father's idols. 24
bitterness sigh before their e. 21:6
and have hid their e. from. 22:26
from them desire of their e. 24:25
sanctified in you before their e. 36:23
in thy hand before their e. 37:20
sanctified in thee before their e.
38:16
their e. shall consume. Zech 14:12
then touched he their e. Mat 9:29
their e. were opened. 30
their e. they have closed. 13:15
Jesus touched their e., their e. 20:34
for their e. were heavy. 26:43
Mark 14:40
but their e. were holden. Luke 24:16
their e. were opened. 31
he hath blinded their e. John 12:40
to open their e. Acts 26:18
fear of God before their e. Rom 3:18
let their e. be darkened. 11:10
and God shall wipe away all tears
from their e. Rev 7:17; 21:4

thine eyes
found favour in thine e. Gen 30:27
put his hand on thine e. 46:4
shall we die before thine e.? 47:19
memorial between thine e. Ex 13:9
frontlets between thine e. 16
Deut 6:8
thine e. have seen all. Deut 3:21
lift up thine e. behold with thine e. 27
forget things thine e. have. 4:9
temptations thine e. saw. 7:19; 29:3
terrible things thine e. seen. 10:21
ox be slain before thine e. 28:31
thine e. shall look, and. 32
mad for sight of thine e. 34, 67
thee to see it with thine e. 34:4
let thine e. be on field. Ruth 2:9
have I found grace in thine e.? 10
to consume thine e. 1 Sam 2:33
I have found grace in thine e. 20:3
I have found favour in thine e. 29
thine e. have seen how the. 24:10
men find favour in thine e. 25:8
soul was precious in thine e. 26:21
found grace in thine e. 27:5
take thy wives before thine e.
2 Sam 12:11
what is good in thine e. 19:27
thine e. are on the haughty. 22:28
that thine e. may be open toward.
1 Ki 8:29, 52; 2 Chr 6:20, 40
is pleasant in thine e. 1 Ki 20:6
shalt see it with thine e. 2 Ki 7:2
open, Lord, thine e. and see.
19:16; Isa 37:17
thine e. shall not see. 2 Ki 22:20

a small thing in thine e. 1 Chr 17:17
nor thine e. see all evil. 2 Chr 34:28
ear be attentive, thine e. Neh 1:6
thine e. are upon me. Job 7:8
I am clean in thine e. 11:4
dost thou open thine e. upon? 14:3
what do thine e. wink at? 15:12
cut off from before thine e. Ps 31:22
in order before thine e. 50:21
only with thine e. shalt thou. 91:8
thine e. did see my substance.
139:16
not depart from thine e.
Pr 3:21, 4:21
let thine e. look right on. 4:25
give not sleep to thine e. nor. 6:4
open thine e. and thou. 20:13
wilt thou set thine e. on? 23:5
let thine e. observe my ways. 33
thine e. shall behold strange. 33
of prince thine e. have seen. 25:7
walk in sight of thine e. Eccl 11:9
my heart with thine e. S of S 4:9
turn away thine e. from me. 6:5
thine e. like the fishpools in. 7:4
thine e. shall see teachers. Isa 30:20
thine e. shall see the king in. 33:17
thine e. see Jerusalem a quiet. 20
not thine e. upon truth? Jer 5:3
thine e. shall behold it. 20:4
thine e. are not but for thy. 22:17
and thine e. from tears. 31:16
thine e. are open on all. 32:19
thine e. shall behold king of. 34:3
we are but few, as thine e. do. 42:2
whom paintedst thine e. Ezek 23:40
from thee desire of thine e. 24:16
behold with thine e. 40:4; 44:5
open thine e. and behold. Dan 9:18
are hid from thine e. Luke 19:42
were thine e. opened? John 9:10, 26
he hath opened thine e.? 17
thine e. with eyesalve. Rev 3:18

your eyes
in day ye eat your e. Gen 3:5
to them as is good in your e. 19:8
let me find grace in your e. 34:11
your e. see and the eyes of my. 45:12
I have found grace in your e. 50:4
pricks in your e. thorns in sides.
Num 33:55; Josh 23:13
he did before your e. Deut 1:30
4:34; 29:2
your e. have seen what the Lord.
4:3; 11:7; Josh 24:7
tables before your e. Deut 9:17
as frontlets between your e. 11:18
any baldness between your e. 14:1
Lord do before your e. 1 Sam 12:16
hissing, as ye see with your e.
2 Chr 29:8
Lord hath closed your e. Isa 29:10
lift up your e. 40:26; Jer 13:20
a den of robbers in your e. Jer 7:11
out of this place in your e. 16:9
slay them before your e. 29:21
the desire of your e. Ezek 24:21
captivity before your e. Zeph 3:20
in your e. in comparison. Hag 2:3
your e. shall see, Lord. Mal 1:5
but blessed are your e. Mat 13:16

right eyes
out all your right e. 1 Sam 11:2

eyesalve
anoint thine eyes with e. Rev 3:18

eyeservice
not with e. as menpleasers.
Eph 6:6; Col 3:22

eyesight
according to my cleanness in his e.
2 Sam 22:25; Ps 18:24

eyewitnesses
from beginning were e. Luke 1:2
were e. of his majesty. 2 Pet 1:16

Ezekiel
E. is unto you a sign. Ezek 24:24

Ezel
remain by the stone E. 1 Sam 20:19

Ezra
sons of E. Jether and. 1 Chr 4:17

Artaxerxes king to E.   *Ezra* 7:12
thou, E. after the wisdom of.   25
when E. had prayed and.   10:1
E. brought the law.   *Neh* 8:2
and E. blessed the Lord.   6
priests, Seraiah, Jeremiah, E.   12:1
of E. Meshullam was priest.   13
were in days of E. the priest.   26
and E. the scribe before them.   36

F

fables
nor give heed to *f*. and.   *1 Tim* 1:4
refuse profane and old wives' *f*. 4:7
shall be turned unto *f*.   *2 Tim* 4:4
not giving heed to Jewish *f*. *Tit* 1:14
cunningly devised *f*.   *2 Pet* 1:16

face
[1] *The literal meaning, the face,
the front part of the head,* Gen 3:19.
[2] *Presence,* Lev 19:32. [3] *Before the face of means in the sight
of,* Ps 41:12.
in sweat of thy *f*. shalt.   *Gen* 3:19
I flee from the *f*. of mistress.   16:8
put the earring upon her *f*. 24:47*
fleddest from the *f*. of Esau. 35:1, 7
Esau went from *f*. of his.   36:6
sent to Joseph to direct his *f*. 46:28*
bowed with his *f*. to the earth. 48:12
Moses fled from the *f*.   *Ex* 2:15
let us flee from the *f*. of.   14:25
the skin of *f*. shone.   34:29, 30, 35
he put a vail on his *f*.   33
hair fallen towards his *f*. *Lev* 13:41
honour the *f*. of old man.   19:32
father had spit in her *f*. *Num* 12:14
slay red heifer before his *f*.   19:3
shall not be afraid of *f*. *Deut* 1:17
them that hate him to *f*.   7:10
Lord destroyeth before your *f*. 8:20
wicked man be beaten before *f*. 25:2
and spit in his *f*. and say.   9
ass taken before thy *f*.   28:31
give them up before your *f*.   31:5
liest thou upon thy *f*.?   *Josh* 7:10
Dagon was fallen on his *f*.
  1 Sam 5:3, 4
David stooped with his *f*. to.   24:8
Abigail bowed on her *f*. and.   25:41
Saul stooped with his *f*. to.   28:14
should I hold up my *f*.? *2 Sam* 2:22
Absalom bowed on his *f*. to.   14:33
bowed himself before the king on his
  f.   24:20; *1 Chr* 21:21
Nathan bowed with his *f*. *1 Ki* 1:23
Bath-sheba bowed with her *f*.   31
king turned *f*. about. 8:14; *2 Chr* 6:3
put *f*. between knees.   *1 Ki* 18:42
wrapped his *f*. in his mantle. 19:13
himself with ashes on his *f*. 20:38*
Ahab turned away his *f*. and. 21:4
lay my staff upon *f*. of. *2 Ki* 4:29
Gehazi laid staff on the *f*. of.   31
Hazael spread it on his *f*. so.   8:15
Jezebel painted her *f*. and.   9:30*
Jehu lifted his *f*. to the window. 32
Joash wept over his *f*. and.   13:14
wilt thou turn away *f*. of one. 18:24
  Isa 36:9
Hezekiah turned *f*. to wall. *2 Ki* 20:2
  Isa 38:2
turn not away the *f*. of thine.
  2 Chr 6:42; *Ps* 132:10
Lord will not turn away his *f*. from.
  2 Chr 30:9
he returned with shame of *f*. 32:21
Josiah would not turn his *f*.   35:22
I blush to lift up my *f*.   *Ezra* 9:6
to confusion of *f*.   7; *Dan* 9:8
will curse thee to thy *f*. Job 1:11; 2:5
a spirit passed before my *f*.   4:15
then shalt thou lift up thy *f*. 11:15
leanness beareth witness to *f*. 16:8
my *f*. is foul with weeping.   16
declare his way to his *f*.?   21:31
and thou shalt lift up thy *f*. 22:26
and disguiseth his *f*.   24:15
he holdeth back the *f*. of.   26:9
spare not to spit in my *f*.   30:10

who can discover the *f*. of ? *Job* 41:13
who can open doors of his *f*.?   14
way straight before my *f*.   *Ps* 5:8
behold thy *f*. in righteousness. 17:15
arrows against the *f*. of them. 21:12
thou settest me before thy *f*. 41:12
look upon the *f*. of thine.   84:9
and truth go before thy *f*.   89:14
beat down his foes before his *f*. 23
with an impudent *f*. said.   *Pr* 7:13
wicked man hardeneth his *f*. 21:29
the boldness of his *f*.   *Eccl* 8:1
covert from *f*. of the spoiler. *Isa* 16:4
destroy the *f*. of the covering. 25:7
he hath made plain the *f*.   28:25
neither his *f*. now wax pale. 29:22
bow down to thee with their *f*. 49:23
me continually to my *f*.   65:3
back, and not *f*.   *Jer* 2:27; 32:33
though thou rentest thy *f*.   4:30*
I discover thy skirts upon thy *f*. that.
  13:26; *Nah* 3:5
the back, and not the *f*.   *Jer* 18:17
from hand of them whose *f*. 22:25
remove it from before my *f*. 32:31
the right of man before *f*. *Lam* 3:35
the *f*. of a man, the *f*. of a lion, *f*. of an
ox, the *f*. of an eagle. *Ezek* 1:10
I made thy *f*. strong against.   3:8
my *f*. will I also turn from.   7:22
f. of a man, *f*. of a lion, *f*. of an eagle.
  10:14; 41:19
stumblingblock before their *f*. 14:3
fury shall come up in my *f*. 38:18*
a deep sleep on *f*. *Dan* 8:18; 10:9
f. as appearance of lightning. 10:6
turn his *f*. unto the isles.   11:18
pride of Israel testifieth to his *f*.
  Hos 5:5; 7:10
they are before my *f*.   7:2
before their *f*. people be. *Joel* 2:6*
drive him with his *f*. toward.   20*
come before thy *f*.   *Nah* 2:1
anoint head, wash thy *f*. *Mat* 6:17
I send my messenger before thy *f*.
  11:10; *Mark* 1:2; *Luke* 7:27
angels behold *f*. of my. *Mat* 18:10
then did they spit in his *f*.   26:67
hast prepared before *f*. *Luke* 2:31
messengers before his *f*. 9:52; 10:1
his *f*. was as though he would. 9:53
they struck him on the *f*.   22:64
his *f*. was bound about. *John* 11:44
foresaw Lord always before my *f*.
  Acts 2:25
God drave out before the *f*.   7:45
so falling down on his *f*. *1 Cor* 14:25
not stedfastly behold *f*.   *2 Cor* 3:7
as Moses, who put vail over *f*.   13
but we all with open *f*. beholding. 18
glory of God, in *f*. of Jesus.   4:6
if a man smite you on the *f*.   11:20
I was unknown by *f*. to.   *Gal* 1:22
I withstood him to the *f*.   2:11
natural *f*. in a glass.   *Jas* 1:23
third beast had a *f*. as a.   *Rev* 4:7
his *f*. was as it were the sun. 10:1
were nourished from the *f*. 12:14
from whose *f*. the earth and. 20:11
see seek, set, shine, sky, waters,
wilderness, world

face with cover, or covered
she covered her *f*.   *Gen* 38:15
locusts cover *f*. of the earth.
  Ex 10:5, 15
they cover *f*. of the earth. *Num* 22:5
the king covered his *f*. *2 Sam* 19:4
they covered Haman's *f*. *Esth* 7:8
covereth his *f*. with.   *Job* 15:27
neither hath he covered darkness
  from my *f*.   23:17
shame of my *f*. hath covered me.
  Ps 44:15
sake shame hath covered my *f*. 69:7
nettles had covered *f*.   *Pr* 24:31
with twain he covered his *f*. *Isa* 6:2
thou shalt cover thy *f*. *Ezek* 12:6
the prince shall cover his *f*.   12
spit on him, and cover his *f*.
  Mark 14:65

face of the country
scattered over *f*. of the country.
  2 Sam 18:8

face of the deep
darkness upon *f*. of the deep.
  Gen 1:2
f. of the deep is frozen. *Job* 38:30
compass on *f*. of the depth. *Pr* 8:27

face of the earth
herb upon *f*. of the earth. *Gen* 1:29
driven me from *f*. of the earth. 4:14
to multiply on *f*. of the earth.   6:1
seed alive on *f*. of all the earth. 7:3
destroy from off *f*. of the earth.   4
Deut 6:15; *1 Ki* 13:34; *Amos* 9:8
waters on *f*. of the whole earth.
  Gen 8:9
scattered on *f*. of the earth.   11:4
famine over *f*. of the earth. 41:56
consume them from *f*. of the earth.
  Ex 32:12
all people unto *f*. of the earth. 33:16
meek above all men on *f*. of the
  earth.   *Num* 12:3
above all people on *f*. of the earth.
  Deut 7:6
cut off every one from *f*. of the earth.
  1 Sam 20:15
renewest the *f*. of the earth.
  Ps 104:30
kingdoms on the *f*. of the earth.
  Isa 23:17
dung on the *f*. of the earth.
  Jer 8:2; 16:4
cast thee from *f*. of the earth. 28:16
men on the *f*. of the earth shake.
  Ezek 38:20
he goat came on the *f*. of the earth.
  Dan 8:5
poureth them on *f*. of the earth.
  Amos 5:8; 9:6
curse goeth over the *f*. of the earth.
  Zech 5:3
discern *f*. of the earth. *Luke* 12:56
dwell on *f*. of the whole earth. 21:35
dwell on *f*. of the earth. *Acts* 17:26

face to face
I have seen God *f*. to *f*. *Gen* 32:30
Lord spake to Moses *f*. to *f*.
  Ex 33:11
Lord, art seen *f*. to *f*. *Num* 14:14
talked with you *f*. to *f*. *Deut* 5:4
whom Lord knew *f*. to *f*.   34:10
seen an angel *f*. to *f*.   *Judg* 6:22
in water *f*. answereth to *f*. *Pr* 27:19
plead with you *f*. to *f*. *Ezek* 20:35
have accusers *f*. to *f*. *Acts* 25:16
a glass, then *f*. to *f*.   *1 Cor* 13:12
to you, speak *f*. to *f*.   *2 John* 12
see thee and speak *f*. to *f*. *3 John* 14

fell on face or faces
Joseph fell on father's *f*. *Gen* 50:1
brethren fell down before his *f*. 18
people saw, fell on their *f*. *Lev* 9:24
Moses and Aaron fell on *f*. *Num* 14:5
  16:22, 45
Moses fell on *f*.   16:4
Balaam fell flat on his *f*.   22:31
Joshua fell on *f*.   *Josh* 5:14; 7:6
and his wife fell on *f*. *Judg* 13:20
then she fell on her *f*. *Ruth* 2:10
Goliath fell on *f*.   *1 Sam* 17:49
David fell on his *f*.   20:41
Abigail fell on *f*.   25:23
Mephibosheth fell on *f*. *2 Sam* 9:6
woman of Tekoah fell on *f*.   14:4
Joab fell on *f*.   22
Ahimaaz fell on his *f*.   18:28
Obadiah fell on *f*.   *1 Ki* 18:7
people fell on their *f*.   39
and elders fell on *f*. *1 Chr* 21:16
I saw it I fell upon *f*. *Ezek* 1:28
  3:23; 9:8; 11:13; 43:3; 44:4
  Dan 8:17
Nebuchadnezzar fell upon his *f*.
  Dan 2:46
disciples fell on *f*.   *Mat* 17:6
Jesus fell on his *f*.   26:39
leper fell on *f*.   *Luke* 5:12
Samaritan fell on his *f*.   17:16
four and twenty elders fell on their
  f.   *Rev* 11:16

face of the field
dung on *f*. of the field.   *2 Ki* 9:37

face *of the gate*
from *f. of the gate.*   *Ezek* 40:15
  face *of the ground*
mist watered the *f. of the ground.*
               Gen 2:6
was on the *f. of the ground.*   7:23
abated from *f. of the ground.*   8:8
the *f. of the ground* was dry.   13
  hide, hideth, or *hid* **face**
from thy *f.* shall I *be hid. Gen* 4:14
and Moses *hid* his *f.*   *Ex* 3:6
hide my *f.* from them.   *Deut* 31:17
              18; 32:20
wherefore *hidest* thou thy *f.* and?
     Job 13:24; *Ps* 44:24; 88:14
when he *hideth* his *f.*   *Job* 34:29
he *hideth* his *f.* he will.   *Ps* 10:11
how long wilt thou *hide* thy *f.?* 13:1
neither hath he *hid* his *f.*   22:24
hide not thy *f.*   27:9; 69:17; 102:2
               143:7
thou didst *hide* thy *f.* 30:7; 104:29
hide thy *f.* from my sins.   51:9
hideth his *f.* from the.   *Isa* 8:17
I *hid* not my *f.* from shame.   50:6
a little wrath I *hid* my *f.*   54:8
your sins have *hid* his *f.*   59:2
thou hast *hid* thy *f.* from us.   64:7
ways not *hid* from my *f.*   *Jer* 16:17
hid my *f.* from this city.   33:5
therefore *hid* I my *f. Ezek* 39:23, 24
nor will I *hide* my *f.* any more.   29
will even *hide* his *f.*   *Mi* 3:4
hide us from the *f. of.*   *Rev* 6:16
  face *of the house*
breadth of *f. of the house.*
            Ezek 41:14
  face *of the Lord*
cry great before *f. of the Lord.*
             Gen 19:13
blood fall before *f. of Lord.*
           1 Sam 26:20
entreat *f. of the* Lord.   *1 Ki* 13:6*
f. of the Lord is against them.
         Ps 34:16; *1 Pet* 3:12
heart before *f. of the Lord. Lam* 2:19
go before *f. of the Lord. Luke* 1:76
  face *of the porch*
f. of the porch were.   *Ezek* 40:15*
thick planks on *f. of the p.*   41:25
  face joined with *see, saw, seen*
afterward will *see* his *f. Gen* 32:20
therefore have I *seen* thy *f.* 33:10
not *see f.* except.   43:3, 5; 44:23
may not *see* man's *f.*   44:26
me die, I have *seen* thy *f.*   46:30
not thought to *see* thy *f.*   48:11
Pharaoh said, *see* my *f.*   *Ex* 10:28
I will *see* thy *f.* again no more.   29
thou canst not *see* my *f.*   33:20
my *f.* shall not be *seen.*   23
children of Israel *saw f.* of.   34:35
not *see* my *f.* except.   *2 Sam* 3:13
let him not *see* my *f.*   14:24
dwelt and *saw* not king's *f.*   28
now let me *see* the king's *f.*   32
let us *look* one another in *f.*
     2 Ki 14:8; *2 Chr* 25:17
looked one another in *f. 2 Ki* 14:11
princes who *saw* king's *f. Esth* 1:14
he shall *see* his *f.* with.   *Job* 33:26
saw his *f.* as it had been *f. Acts* 6:15
shall *see* my *f.* no more.   20:25, 38
as have not *seen* my *f.*   *Col* 2:1
endeavoured to *see* your *f.*
           1 Thes 2:17
that we might *see* your *f.*   3:10
and they shall *see* his *f. Rev* 22:4
  seek face
seek his *f.* continually. *1 Chr* 16:11
            Ps 105:4
people pray and *seek* my *f.*
           2 Chr 7:14
generation that *seek* thy *f. Ps* 24:6
seek ye my *f.* my heart said, thy *f.*
   Lord will I *seek.*   27:8
diligently to *seek* thy *f.*   *Pr* 7:15
return, till they *seek* my *f. Hos* 5:15
  set face
Jacob *set* his *f.* toward. *Gen* 31:21
I will *set* my *f.* against that soul.
         Lev 17:10; 20:6

set my *f.* against that man.
     Lev 20:3, 5; *Ezek* 14:8
set my *f.* against you.   *Lev* 26:17
            Jer 44:11
Balaam *set* his *f.* toward. *Num* 24:1
Hazael *set* his *f.* to.   *2 Ki* 12:17
I have *set* my *f.* like a.   *Isa* 50:7
set my *f.* against this city. *Jer* 21:10
set thy *f.* against.   *Ezek* 4:3
thou shalt set thy *f.* towards.   7
set thy *f.* towards mountains.   6:2
set thy *f.* against daughters.   13:17
I will *set* my *f.* against them.   15:7
set thy *f.* toward south.   20:46
set thy *f.* toward Jerusalem.   21:2
go whithersoever thy *f.* is *set.*   16
set thy *f.* against Ammonites.   25:2
set thy *f.* against Zidon.   28:21
set thy *f.* against Pharaoh.   29:2
set thy *f.* against mount Seir.   35:2
set thy *f.* against Gog.   38:2
I *set* my *f.* unto Lord.   *Dan* 9:3
I *set* my *f.* toward ground and. 10:15
he shall *set* his *f.* to enter.   11:17
stedfastly *set* his *f.* to.   *Luke* 9:51
  face *shine*
his *f.* to *shine* upon thee. *Num* 6:25
make thy *f.* to *shine* on thy.
         Ps 31:16; 119:135
cause his *f.* to *shine* on us.   67:1
cause thy *f.* to *shine.*   80:3, 7, 19
oil to make his *f.* to *shine.*   104:15
wisdom maketh *f.* to *shine. Eccl* 8:1
cause thy *f.* to *shine* on.   *Dan* 9:17
his *f.* did *shine* as sun.   *Mat* 17:2
  face *of the sky*
ye can discern the *f. of the sky.*
     Mat 16:3; *Luke* 12:56
  face *of the waters*
moved on *f. of the waters. Gen* 1:2
ark went upon *f. of the waters.* 7:18
  face *of the wilderness*
on *f. of the wilderness.*   *Ex* 16:14
  face *of the world*
commandment on *f. of world.*
           Job 37:12
nor fill *f. of the world. Isa* 14:21
Israel shall fill *f. of the world.* 27:6

  faces
their *f.* were backward. *Gen* 9:23
set f. of the flocks toward.   30:40
bowed with *f.* to the earth.   42:6
Moses laid before their *f. Ex* 19:7
fear may be before your *f.*   20:20
and their *f.* shall look one.   25:20
mercy seatward were *f.* of.   37:9
turned their *f.* and said. *Judg* 18:23
thou hast shamed the *f. 2 Sam* 19:5
all Israel set their *f.* on.   *1 Ki* 2:15
whose *f.* were like the *f. 1 Chr* 12:8
their *f.* were inward.   *2 Chr* 3:13
fathers have turned away *f.*   29:6
worshipped with their *f.*   *Neh* 8:6
covereth *f.* of the judges. *Job* 9:24
and bind their *f.* in secret.   40:13
and *f.* were not ashamed. *Ps* 34:5
fill their *f.* with shame.   83:16
ye grind the *f.* of the poor. *Isa* 3:15
amazed, their *f.* shall be as.   13:8
wipe away tears from off all *f.* 25:8
hid as it were our *f.* from him. 53:3
be not afraid of their *f.*   *Jer* 1:8
be not dismayed at their *f.*   17
their *f.* harder than a rock.   5:3
to confusion of their own *f.*   7:19
all *f.* are turned into paleness. 30:6
set their *f.* to enter Egypt.   42:15
             17; 44:12
with their *f.* thitherward.   50:5
shame hath covered our *f.*   51:51
the *f.* of elders were not. *Lam* 5:12
every one four *f. Ezek* 1:6, 10, 11, 15
face strong against their *f.*   3:8
shame shall be on their *f.*   7:18
men, with *f.* toward the east.   8:16
turn away your *f.* from.   14:6
all *f.* shall be burnt therein.   20:47
every cherub had two *f.*   41:18
he see your *f.* worse.   *Dan* 1:10
but unto us confusion of *f.* as.   9:7
be much pained, all *f.*   *Joel* 2:6
f. of them all gather.   *Nah* 2:10

their *f.* shall sup up as.   *Hab* 1:9
spread dung on your *f.*   *Mal* 2:3
hypocrites disfigure their *f. Mat* 6:16
bowed down their *f.* to. *Luke* 24:5
before throne on their *f.*   *Rev* 7:11
f. of the locusts were as *f.*   9:7
        fade
strangers *f.* away.   *2 Sam* 22:46
            Ps 18:45
we all *f.* as a leaf.   *Isa* 64:6
them, and leaf shall *f.*   *Jer* 8:13
whose leaf shall not *f.*   *Ezek* 47:12
rich man shall *f.* away.   *Jas* 1:11
        fadeth
an oak, whose leaf *f.*   *Isa* 1:30
mourneth and *f.,* the world *f.*   24:4
grass withereth, the flower *f.* 40:7, 8
inheritance that *f.* not.   *1 Pet* 1:4
a crown of glory that *f.* not.   5:4
        fading
glorious beauty a *f.* flower. *Isa* 28:1
beauty shall be a *f.* flower.   4
        fail
will without *f.* drive out. *Josh* 3:10
f. deliver Ammon.   *Judg* 11:30*
shalt without *f.* recover. *1 Sam* 30:8
day by day without *f.*   *Ezra* 6:9
        fail, *verb*
your cattle, if money *f.*   *Gen* 47:16
eyes shall *f.* with longing. *Deut* 28:32
he will not *f.* thee nor forsake thee.
     31:6, 8; *Josh* 1:5; *1 Chr* 28:20
not *f.* to burn fat.   *1 Sam* 2:16
let no man's heart *f.* him.   17:32
I should not *f.* to sit with.   20:5
not *f.* from house of.   *2 Sam* 3:29
not *f.* thee a man on.   *1 Ki* 2:4
     8:25; 9:5; *2 Chr* 6:16
neither cruse of oil *f. 1 Ki* 17:14, 16
take heed that ye *f.* not. *Ezra* 4:22*
let nothing *f.* of all.   *Esth* 6:10
not *f.* to keep these days.   9:27, 28
eyes of the wicked *f.*   *Job* 11:20
as waters *f.* from the sea.   14:11
even eyes of children shall *f.*   17:5
caused eyes of widow to *f.*   31:16
for the faithful *f.* from.   *Ps* 12:1
mine eyes *f.* while I wait.   69:3
doth his promise *f.* for ?   77:8
nor my faithfulness to *f.*   89:33
mine eyes *f.* for thy word.   119:82
mine eyes *f.* for thy salvation.   123
rod of his anger shall *f.*   *Pr* 22:8
desire *f.* because man.   *Eccl* 12:5
spirit of Egypt shall *f.*   *Isa* 19:3*
waters shall *f.*   5
glory of Kedar *f.*   21:16
and they all shall *f.* together.   31:3
cause drink of the thirsty to *f.* 32:6
troubled, for vintage shall *f.*   10
no one of these shall *f.* nor.   34:16*
mine eyes *f.* with.   38:14
he shall not *f.* nor be.   42:4
that his bread should not *f.*   51:14
for the spirit should *f.*   57:16
spring whose waters *f.* not.   58:11
their eyes did *f.* because. *Jer* 14:6
unto me as waters that *f.?*   15:18
I caused wine to *f.* from.   48:33*
           Hos 9:2
eyes do *f.* with tears.   *Lam* 2:11
his compassions *f.* not.   3:22
poor of the land to *f.*   *Amos* 8:4
labour of olive shall *f.*   *Hab* 3:17
that when ye *f.* they.   *Luke* 16:9
than one tittle of the law to *f.*   17*
prayed that thy faith *f.* not.   22:32
prophecies, they shall *f. 1 Cor* 13:8*
thy years shall not *f.*   *Heb* 1:12
the time would *f.* me to tell.   11:32
looking lest any man *f.* of.   12:15*
       failed
their heart *f.* them.   *Gen* 42:28
and when money *f.* in the.   47:15*
waters *f.* were cut off. *Josh* 3:16*
f. not any good thing which Lord.
     21:45; 23:14; *1 Ki* 8:56
my kinsfolk have *f.* and. *Job* 19:14
refuge *f.* me, no man.   *Ps* 142:4
my soul *f.* when he.   *S of S* 5:6
their might *f.* they.   *Jer* 51:30
our eyes as yet *f.* for.   *Lam* 4:17

faileth
should we die ? money f. Gen 47:15
bull gendereth and f. not. Job 21:10
my strength f. me. Ps 31:10; 38:10
my heart f. me. 40:12; 73:26
forsake me not when strength f. 71:9
knees are weak, my flesh f. 109:24
O Lord, my spirit f. 143:7
his wisdom f. him. Eccl 10:3
the grass f. there is. Isa 15:6
strong in power, not one f. 40:26*
seek water, their tongue f. 41:17
hungry and his strength f. 44:12
truth f. and he that. 59:15*
and every vision f. Ezek 12:22
judgement to light, f. not. Zeph 3:5
treasure in the heavens that f. not.
Luk: 12:33
charity never f. but. 1 Cor 13:8

failing
Lord shall give thee f. Deut 28:65
men's hearts f. them. Luke 21:26

fain
he would f. flee. Job 27:22
f. have filled his belly. Luke 15:16

faint
field, and he was f. Gen 25:29, 30
smote thee when thou wast f.
Deut 25:18
f. yet pursuing. Judg 8:4
bread to people, for they be f. 5
people were very f. 1 Sam 14:28, 31
so f. they could not go. 30:10, 21
wine, that such as be f. 2 Sam 16:2
David fought and waxed f. 21:15
the whole heart is f. Isa 1:5
therefore shall all hands be f. 13:7*
awaketh, and behold he is f. 29:8
he giveth power to the f. 40:29
he drinketh no water, and is f. 44:12
my heart is f. Jer 8:18
are many, my heart is f. Lam 1:22
for this our heart is f. our. 5:17

faint, verb
let not your hearts f. Deut 20:3
lest his brethren's heart f. 8*
inhabitants of land f. Josh 2:9*
all the inhabitants of country f. 24*
if thou f. in the day of. Pr 24:10
even the youths shall f. Isa 40:30
Amos 8:13
not be weary, walk, not f. Isa 40:31
lest your hearts f. Jer 51:46
he hath made me f. all. Lam 1:13
young children f. 2:19
every spirit shall f. Ezek 21:7
their heart may f. and. 15*
send fasting, lest they f. Mat 15:32
them fasting, they will f. Mark 8:3
ought to pray, not to f. Luke 18:1
received mercy we f. not. 2 Cor 4:1
for which cause we f. not. 16
shall reap, if we f. not. Gal 6:9
that ye f. not at my. Eph 3:13
lest ye be wearied and f. Heb 12:3
nor f. when thou art rebuked. 5

fainted
Jacob's heart f. for he. Gen 45:26
all the land of Canaan f. by. 47:13
I had f. unless I had. Ps 27:13
hungry and thirsty, soul f. 107:5
thy sons f. they lie at. Isa 51:20
I f. in my sighing. Jer 45:3*
trees of the field f. for. Ezek 31:15
I Daniel f. and was sick. Dan 8:27
soul f. I remembered. Jonah 2:7
that he f. and wished in. 4:8
compassion on them, because they f.
Mat 9:36*
laboured and hast not f. Rev 2:3*

faintest
come upon thee, and thou f. Job 4:5

fainteth
my soul f. for courts. Ps 84:2
my soul f. for thy salvation. 119:81
a standardbearer f. Isa 10:18
Creator of ends of earth f. not. 40:28

fainthearted
who is fearful and f. let. Deut 20:8
fear not, nor be f. for. Isa 7:4
Hamath and Arpad f. Jer 49:23*

faintness
I will send a f. into. Lev 26:36

fair
daughters of men were f. Gen 6:2
Sarah was f. 12:11, 14
Rebekah was f. 24:16; 26:7
David was of f. countenance.
1 Sam 17:42
Tamar was f. 2 Sam 13:1; 14:27
Abishag a f. damsel. 1 Ki 1:4
Vashti the queen was f. Esth 1:11
let f. virgins be sought for. 2:2
gather the f. young virgins. 3
Esther was f. and beautiful. 7
f. weather cometh out. Job 37:22*
no women found so f. as. 42:15
with f. speech she. Pr 7:21
so is a f. woman without. 11:22
when he speaketh f. believe. 26:25
thou art f. S of S 1:15, 16; 4:1, 7
rise up, my love, my f. one. 2:10, 13
how f. is thy love, my sister ! 4:10
f. as the moon. 6:10
how f. art thou, O love. 7:6
many houses great and f. Isa 5:9
thy stones with f. colours. 54:11
in vain make thyself f. Jer 4:30
and olive tree f. and of fruit. 11:16
though they speak f. words. 12:6
Egypt is like a very f. heifer. 46:20
also taken thy f. jewels. Ezek 16:17
shall take thy f. jewels. 39; 23:26
a cedar in Lebanon with f. 31:3
thus was he f. in his greatness. 7
I have made him f. by multitude. 9
leaves were f. fruit. Dan 4:12, 21
passed over her f. neck. Hos 10:11
f. virgins shall faint for. Amos 8:13
set a f. mitre upon his. Zech 3:5†
it will be f. weather, for. Mat 16:2
Moses was born, exceeding f.
Acts 7:20
by f. speeches deceive. Rom 16:18
a desire to make a f. shew. Gal 6:12

fair havens
place called f. havens. Acts 27:8

fairer
is not younger sister f.? Judg 15:2
thou art f. than the. Ps 45:2
countenances appeared f. Dan 1:15

fairest
f. among women. S of S 1:8; 5:9
6:1

fairs
(Revisions, wares)
traded in f. Ezek 27:12, 14, 16, 19, 22
thy riches and thy f. shall. 27

faith
Faith is a dependence on the veracity of another; firm belief or trust in a person, thing, doctrine, or statement. And one is said to keep faith when he performs a promise made to another.
I. Historical faith is a belief in the truthfulness and accuracy of the Scriptural narrative and teachings, Jas 2:17, 24.
II. Saving faith is the acceptance by the intellect, affection, and will of God's favour extended to man through Christ. This faith produces a sincere obedience in the life and conversation. The firm foundation of faith is the essential supreme perfection of God; his unerring knowledge, immutable truth, infinite goodness, and almighty power. By this faith, we are said to be justified, Rom 5:1. Not formally, as if it were our righteousness before God. It is called the faith through which we are saved, Eph 2:8. Faith is, as it were, a condition on our part whereby we come to be partakers of the blessings of the new covenant. It is a faith which worketh by love, Gal 5:6. It is not an idle, inactive grace, but shews itself by producing in us love to God and our neighbour.
Faith, in scripture, is also taken for

the truth and faithfulness of God, Rom 3:3. Faith is also used for the doctrine of the gospel, which is the object of faith, Acts 24:24; Gal 1:23.
children in whom is no f. Deut 32:20
O ye of little f. Mat 6:30; 8:26
14:31; 16:8; Luke 12:28
so great f. no, not in Israel.
Mat 8:10; Luke 7:9
f. as a grain of mustard seed.
Mat 17:20
if ye have f. ye shall not. 21:21
judgement, mercy, and f. 23:23
how is it ye have no f.? Mark 4:40
have f. in God. 11:22
Lord, increase our f. Luke 17:5
if ye had f. ye might say to. 6
shall he find f.? 18:8
f. which is by him. Acts 3:16
Stephen, a man full of f. 6:5, 8
of priests obedient to the f. 7
Barnabas a good man, full of f. 11:24
to turn the deputy from the f. 13:8
perceiving that he had f. 14:9
them to continue in the f. 22
he had opened door of f. 27
churches established in the f. 16:5
f. toward our Lord Jesus. 20:21
Felix heard Paul concerning the f.
24:24
grace for obedience to f. Rom 1:5
revealed from f. to f. 17
unbelief make f. without effect. 3:3*
is excluded by law of f. 27
f. counted for righteousness. 4:5, 9
a seal of righteousness of f. 11
also walk in steps of that f. 12
through the righteousness of f. 13
if they of law be heirs, f. is. 14
it is of f. .... which is of f. of. 16
righteousness, which is of f. 9:30
10:6
that is the word of f. which. 10:8
f. cometh by hearing, hearing. 17*
God hath dealt measure of f. 12:3
according to proportion of f. 6
hast thou f.? have it to. 14:22
of f. what is not of f. is sin. 23
to nations for obedience of f. 16:26
to another f. by the. 1 Cor 12:9
though I have all f. and have. 13:2
now abideth f. hope, charity. 13
having same Spirit of f. 2 Cor 4:13
now preached f. which. Gal 1:23
or by the hearing of f. 3:2, 5
that they which are of f. 7, 9
law is not of f. but the man. 12
before f. came. 23
after that f. is come. 25
but f. which worketh by love. 5:6
fruit of Spirit is love, joy, f. 22*
who are of household of f. 6:10
one Lord, one f. one. Eph 4:5
all come in the unity of the f. 13
taking the shield of f. 6:16
peace to brethren, with f. from. 23
furtherance and joy of f. Phil 1:25
striving together for the f. of the. 27
remembering work of f. 1 Thes 1:3
putting on breastplate of f. 5:8
glory for patience and f. 2 Thes 1:4
would fulfil the work of f. 11
for all men have not f. 3:2
f. unfeigned. 1 Tim 1:5
grace of Lord abundant with f. 14
f. and a good conscience; some put
away, concerning f. have. 19
holding the mystery of f. in a. 3:9
some shall depart from the f. 4:1
nourished up in words of f. 6
he hath denied the f. 5:8
they have cast off their first f. 12†
erred from the f. 6:10, 21
and follow after f. 11
fight the good fight of f. 12
the unfeigned f. that is. 2 Tim 1:5
overthrow the f. of some. 2:18
follow f. 22
reprobate concerning the f. 3:8
hast fully known my f., charity. 3:10
finished my course, kept f. 4:7
according to the f. of. Tit 1:1
mine own son, after common f. 4

hearing of thy f. toward. *Philem* 5
not being mixed with f. *Heb* 4:2
not laying again foundation of f. 6:1
heart in full assurance of f. 10:22
hold fast profession of our f. 23*
f. is substance of things hoped. 11:1
without f. it is impossible to. 6
the author and finisher of our f. 12:2
whose f. follow, considering 13:7
have not f. with respect. *Jas* 2:1
a man say he hath f. can f. save ? 14
f. without works is dead. 17, 20, 26
a man say, thou hast f. and. 2:18
how f. wrought with his works, and
  by works was f. made. 22
the prayer of f. shall save. 5:15
obtained like precious f. *2 Pet* 1:1
the world, even our f. *1 John* 5:4
earnestly contend for f. *Jude* 3
building up on your most holy f. 20
and hast not denied my f. *Rev* 2:13
I know thy works, and f. and. 19
the patience and the f. of. 13:10
they that keep f. of Jesus. 14:12

by faith
just shall live by his f. *Hab* 2:4
  Rom 1:17; *Gal* 3:11; *Heb* 10:38
purifying hearts by f. *Acts* 15:9
who are sanctified by f. 26:18
comforted by mutual f. *Rom* 1:12
the righteousness of God by f. 3:22
justified by f. 28; 5:1; *Gal* 2:16
                                    3:24
justify circumcision by f. *Rom* 3:30
by whom we have access by f. 5:2
they sought it not by f. 9:32
standest by f. 11:20; *2 Cor* 1:24
for we walk by f. not. *2 Cor* 5:7
I live by the f. of the Son. *Gal* 2:20
the promise by f. 3:22
ye are children of God by f. 26
for hope of righteousness by f. 5:5
whom have access by f. *Eph* 3:12
Christ dwell in your hearts by f. 17
righteousness of God by f. *Phil* 3:9
by f. Abel. *Heb* 11:4
by f. Enoch. 5
by f. Noah. 7
by f. Abraham. 8, 9, 17
by f. Isaac blessed Jacob. 20
by f. Jacob. 21
by f. Joseph made mention. 22
by f. Moses. 23, 24, 27
by f. passed through Red sea. 29
by f. walls of Jericho fell down. 30
by f. Rahab. 31
by works a man is justified, not by f.
  only. *Jas* 2:24

in faith
being not weak in f. *Rom* 4:19
staggered not, was strong in f. 20
him that is weak in the f. 14:1
stand fast in f. *1 Cor* 16:13
as ye abound in f. *2 Cor* 8:7
examine whether ye be in the f. 13:5
if ye continue in the f. *Col* 1:23
and stablished in the f. 2:7
Timothy my own son in f. *1 Tim* 1:2
godly edifying which is in f. 4
a teacher of the Gentiles in f. 2:7
saved, if they continue in f. 15
purchase great boldness in f. 3:13
an example of believers in f. 4:12
hold fast form in f. *2 Tim* 1:13
be found in the f. *Tit* 1:13; 2:2
greet them that love us in f. 3:15
these all died in f. *Heb* 11:13
but let him ask in f. *Jas* 1:6
poor of this world, rich in f. 2:5
resist, stedfast in the f. *1 Pet* 5:9

their faith
Jesus seeing their f. *Mat* 9:2
  Mark 2:5; *Luke* 5:20

through faith
through f. in his name. *Acts* 3:16
a propitiation through f. *Rom* 3:25
uncircumcision through f. 30
make void law through f.? 31
justify heathen through f. *Gal* 3:8
promise of Spirit through f. 14
grace saved through f. *Eph* 2:8
righteousness which is through f.
                                    Phil 3:9

risen through the f. of. *Col* 2:12
to salvation through f. *2 Tim* 3:15
who through f. inherit. *Heb* 6:12
through f. we understand. 11:3
through f. Sara received. 11
through f. he kept passover. 28
through f. subdued kingdoms. 33
a good report through f. 39
power of God through f. *1 Pet* 1:5

thy faith
thy f. made thee whole. *Mat* 9:22
  Mark 5:34; 10:52; *Luke* 8:48
                                    17:19
O woman, great is thy f. *Mat* 15:28
thy f. hath saved. *Luke* 7:50; 18:42
prayed that thy f. fail not. 22:32
communication of thy f. *Philem* 6
shew me thy f. without. *Jas* 2:18

your faith
according to your f. be. *Mat* 9:29
where is your f.? *Luke* 8:25
your f. is spoken of. *Rom* 1:8
your f. should not stand. *1 Cor* 2:5
your f. is also vain. 15:14, 17
dominion over your f. *2 Cor* 1:24
having hope when your f. is. 10:15
after I heard of your f. *Eph* 1:15
on service of your f. *Phil* 2:17
since we heard of your f. *Col* 1:4
stedfastness of your f. in Christ. 2:5
your f. toward God. *1 Thes* 1:8
comfort you concerning your f. 3:2
I sent to know your f. 5
Timothy brought tidings of your f. 6
comforted over you by your f. 7
perfect what is lacking in your f. 10
that your f. groweth. *2 Thes* 1:3
trying of your f. worketh. *Jas* 1:3
the trial of your f. being. *1 Pet* 1:7
end of your f. even salvation. 9
that your f. and hope might be. 21
add to your f. virtue, to. *2 Pet* 1:5

faithful
Moses is f. in mine house.
                    Num 12:7; *Heb* 3:2, 5
the f. God who keepeth. *Deut* 7:9
raise me up a f. priest. *1 Sam* 2:35
who is so f. as David ? 22:14
one of them f. in Israel. *2 Sam* 20:19
Hananiah was a f. man. *Neh* 7:2
for they were counted f. 9:8
for the f. fail from among. *Ps* 12:1
for Lord preserveth the f. 31:23
as a f. witness in heaven. 89:37
eyes shall be on the f. of. 101:6
all thy commandments are f. 119:86
testimonies righteous and very f. 138
a f. spirit concealeth. *Pr* 11:13
a f. ambassador is health. 13:17
a f. witness will not lie, but. 14:5
a f. man who can find ? 20:6
as snow in harvest, so is a f. 25:13
f. are the wounds of a friend. 27:6
a f. man shall abound with. 28:20
how is the f. city become ! *Isa* 1:21
afterwards be called f. city. 26
I took unto me f. witnesses. 8:2
because of the Lord that is f. 49:7
Lord be a f. witness. *Jer* 42:5
forasmuch as he was f. *Dan* 6:4
but Judah is f. with. *Hos* 11:12
who then is a f. and ? *Mat* 24:45
well done, thou good and f. 25:21
f. in a few things. 23; *Luke* 19:17
who then is that f. and ? *Luke* 12:42
is f. in the least is f. also. 16:10
not been f. in unrighteous. 11
have not been f. in what is. 12
judged me f. to Lord. *Acts* 16:15
God is f. by whom. *1 Cor* 1:9; 10:13
in stewards, that a man be f. 4:2
sent you Timothy f. in Lord. 17
mercy of Lord to be f. 7:25†
blessed with f. Abraham. *Gal* 3:9
to the saints and f. in. *Eph* 1:1
Tychicus a f. minister. 6:21
saints and f. brethren. *Col* 1:2
Epaphras, for you f. minister. 7; 4:7
Onesimus, a f. brother. 4:9
f. is he that calleth you. *1 Thes* 5:24
the Lord is f. who shall. *2 Thes* 3:3
that he counted me f. *1 Tim* 1:12

is a f. saying. *1 Tim* 1:15; 4:9; *Tit* 3:8
must be sober, and f. *1 Tim* 3:11
service because they are f. 6:2*
same commit to f. men. *2 Tim* 2:2
it is a f. saying. 11
yet he abideth f. 13
blameless, having f. *Tit* 1:6*
holding fast the f. word. 9
might be a f. high priest. *Heb* 2:17
f. to him that appointed him. 3:2
is f. that promised. 10:23; 11:11
souls, as unto a f. *1 Pet* 4:19
by Silvanus a f. brother. 5:12
he is f. to forgive us. *1 John* 1:9
Christ the f. witness. *Rev* 1:5; 3:14
be f. unto death, I will give. 2:10
wherein Antipas was f. martyr. 13
with him, are called, and f. 17:14
that sat upon him was called f. 19:11
words are true and f. 21:5; 22:6

faithfully
for they dealt f. *2 Ki* 12:15; 22:7
do in fear of Lord f. *2 Chr* 19:9
they brought in offerings f. 31:12
the men did the work f. 34:12
the king that f. judgeth. *Pr* 29:14
him speak my word f. *Jer* 23:28
doest f. whatsoever thou. *3 John* 5

faithfulness
render to every man f. *1 Sam* 26:23
there is no f. in their mouth. *Ps* 5:9
thy f. reacheth unto clouds. 36:5
I have declared thy f. and. 40:10
or shall thy f. be declared ? 88:11
I will make known thy f. 89:1
thy f. shalt thou establish. 2
thy f. also in the congregation. 5
who is like to thee, or to thy f.? 8
but my f. and my mercy shall. 24
nor will I suffer my f. to fail. 33
good to shew forth thy f. 92:2
thou in f. hast afflicted me. 119:75
thy f. is unto all generations. 90
in thy f. answer me. 143:1
and f. the girdle of his. *Isa* 11:5
thy counsels of old are f. 25:1
great is thy f. *Lam* 3:23
betroth thee unto me in f. *Hos* 2:20

faithless
O f. generation. *Mat* 17:17
  Mark 9:19; *Luke* 9:41
be not f. but believing. *John* 20:27

fall, *substantive*
haughty spirit before a f. *Pr* 16:18
righteous shall see their f. 29:16
moved at noise of their f. *Jer* 49:21
isles shake at sound of their f.
                                    Ezek 26:15
isles tremble in day of thy f. 18
to shake at sound of his f. 31:16
for his life in day of thy f. 32:10
and great was the f. of it. *Mat* 7:27
child is set for the f. *Luke* 2:34
through their f. salvation. *Rom* 11:11
if the f. of them be riches of. 12

fall, *verb*
a deep sleep to f. upon. *Gen* 2:21
occasion against us, and f. 43:18
see that ye f. not out by way. 45:24
so that rider f. backward. 49:17
fear and dread shall f. *Ex* 15:16
dig a pit, ox or ass f. therein. 21:33
on whatsoever any f. *Lev* 11:32
if their carcase f. on any. 37, 38
lest land f. to whoredom. 19:29
they shall f. before you. 26:7, 8
shall f. when none pursueth. 36
shall f. one upon another. 37*
let them f. by the camp. *Num* 11:31
your carcases shall f. in. 14:29, 32
is the land that shall f. to. 34:2
if any man f. from. *Deut* 22:8
rise thou, and f. upon us. *Judg* 8:21
swear ye will not f. upon me. 15:12
and f. into the hand of the. 18
let f. some handfuls of. *Ruth* 2:16*
know how matter will f. 3:18
none of his words f. *1 Sam* 3:19
not one hair of his head f. to. 14:45
  2 Sam 14:11; *1 Ki* 1:52; *Acts* 27:34
to make David f. *1 Sam* 18:25
would not f. on the priests. 22:17

turn thou, and *f.* on priests.
1 Sam 22:18
therefore let not my blood *f.* 26:20
near and *f.* on him. *2 Sam* 1:15
1 Ki 2:29, 31
let us *f.* into the hand of God, not *f.*
2 Sam 24:14; *1 Chr* 21:13
shall persuade Ahab to go up and *f.*
1 Ki 22:20; *2 Chr* 18:19
let us *f.* unto the host. *2 Ki* 7:4
shall *f.* nothing of word of. 10:10
meddle, that thou shouldst *f.?* 14:10
f. to his master Saul. *1 Chr* 12:19
till thy bowels *f.* out. *2 Chr* 21:15
God shall make thee *f.* 25:8*
that thou shouldest *f.* and Judah. 19
thou hast begun to *f.* shall not prevail,
but shalt surely *f.* *Esth* 6:13
not his dread *f.* upon you ? *Job* 13:11
let thine arm *f.* from my. 31:22
let them *f.* by their own. *Ps* 5:10
mine enemies shall *f.* and. 9:3*
that the poor may *f.* by. 10:10
into that destruction let him *f.* 35:8
f. shall not be utterly cast. 37:24
arrows, whereby people *f.* 45:5
make their tongue to *f.* 64:8*
and he let it *f.* in midst of. 78:28
but ye shall *f.* like one of the. 82:7
a thousand shall *f.* at thy side. 91:7
thrust at me that I might *f.* 118:13
burning coals *f.* upon them. 140:10
let wicked *f.* into their own. 141:10
Lord upholdeth all that *f.* 145:14
unless they cause some to *f. Pr* 4:16
a prating fool shall *f.* 10:8, 10
the wicked shall *f.* by his. 11:5
where no counsel is people *f.* 14
trusteth in his riches shall *f.* 28
of the Lord shall *f.* therein. 22:14
wicked shall *f.* into mischief. 24:16*
whoso diggeth a pit shall *f.* therein.
26:27; *Eccl* 10:8
causeth to go astray shall *f. Pr* 28:10
that hardeneth his heart shall *f.* 14
he that is perverse shall *f.* at. 18
if they *f.* one will lift. *Eccl* 4:10
if the tree *f.* toward the south. 11:3
shall stumble and *f.* *Isa* 8:15
they shall *f.* under the slain. 10:4
and Lebanon shall *f.* by a. 34
nail fastened in sure place *f.* 22:25
fleeth from fear *f.* into pit. 24:18
the earth shall *f.* and not rise. 20
that they might go and *f.* 28:13
as a breach ready to *f.* 30:13
of slaughter, when towers *f.* 25
young men shall utterly *f.* 40:30
therefore mischiefs shall *f.* 47:11
whoso gather against shall *f.* 54:15
anger to *f.* on you. *Jer* 3:12*
f. amongst them that *f.* 6:15; 8:12
the fathers and sons shall *f.* 6:21*
shall they *f.* and not arise ? 8:4
the carcases of men shall *f.* 9:22
I have caused him to *f.* 15:8
shall be driven out and *f.* 23:12
a whirlwind *f.* on head. 19*; 30:23*
be drunken, and spue, and *f.* 25:27
ye shall *f.* like a pleasant vessel. 34
it is false; I *f.* not away to. 37:14
shall all *f.* in the land of. 44:12*
they shall stumble and *f.* 46:6
made many to *f.* yea one. 16*
fleeth shall *f.* into the pit. 48:44
her young men *f.* in. 49:26; 50:30
most proud stumble and *f.* 50:32
the slain shall *f.* in land. 51:4, 47, 49
wall of Babylon shall *f.* 51:44
Babylon caused slain of Israel to *f.* 49
made my strength to *f. Lam* 1:14*
the slain shall *f.* in the. *Ezek* 6:7
that it shall *f.* and ye, O great hail-
stones, shall *f.* and a. 13:11
foundation discovered, it shall *f.* 14
let no lot *f.* on it. 24:6
all thy company shall *f.* 27:27, 34
thou shalt *f.* upon. 29:5; 39:5
when slain shall *f.* in Egypt. 30:4
they that uphold Egypt shall *f.* 6
I will cause the sword to *f.* out. 22
I cause multitude to *f.* 32:12
not *f.* thereby in the day. 33:12
in all thy rivers shall they *f.* 35:8

steep places shall *f.*, every wall
shall *f.* *Ezek* 38:20
arrows to *f.* 39:3
shalt *f.* on the mountains. 4
they caused Israel to *f.* 44:12
this land shall *f.* to you for. 47:14
robbers of thy people shall *f.*
Dan 11:14
but he shall stumble and *f.* 19
when they shall *f.* 34
some *f.* to try them. 35
shalt thou *f.* in the day, the prophet
also shall *f.* with thee. *Hos* 4:5*
that doth not understand shall *f.* 14*
and Ephraim *f.* Judah shall *f.* 5:5*
shall say to the hills, *f.* on us. 10:8
transgressors shall *f.* therein. 14:9
can a bird *f.* in a snare ? *Amos* 3:5
the horns of the altar shall *f.* 14
even they shall *f.* and never. 8:14
shall not the least grain *f.* to. 9:9
rejoice not, when I *f.* *Mi* 7:8
they shall *f.* into mouth. *Nah* 3:12
not one sparrow *f.* to. *Mat* 10:29
if it *f.* into a pit on sabbath. 12:11
both shall *f.* into the ditch. 15:14
Luke 6:39
crumbs which *f.* from. *Mat* 15:27
whoso *f.* on this stone be broken, on
whom it *f.* it. 21:44; *Luke* 20:18
and the stars shall *f.* from heaven.
Mat 24:29; *Mark* 13:25
Satan as lightning *f.* *Luke* 10:18
to say to mountains, *f.* on us. 23:30
except a corn *f.* into. *John* 12:24
fearing lest they should *f.* into.
Acts 27:17*
soldiers cut ropes and let her *f.* 32
shall not an hair *f.* from head. 34*
stumbled that they should *f.*
Rom 11:11
put an occasion to *f.* in his. 14:13
take heed lest he *f.* *1 Cor* 10:12
he *f.* into condemnation. *1 Tim* 3:6
a good report, lest he *f.* into. 7
they that be rich *f.* 6:9
lest any *f.* after the. *Heb* 4:11
fearful to *f.* into hands of. 10:31
when ye *f.* into temptation. *Jas* 1:2
lest ye *f.* into condemnation. 5:12
things ye shall never *f.* *2 Pet* 1:10*
beware lest ye *f.* from your. 3:17
mountains and rocks, *f.* on. *Rev* 6:16
I saw a star *f.* from heaven. 9:1

fall away
of temptation *f. away.* *Luke* 8:13
if they *f. away* to renew. *Heb* 6:6

fall down
brother's ass *f. down.* *Deut* 22:4
of city shall *f. down* flat. *Josh* 6:5
David let his spittle *f. down.*
1 Sam 21:13
all kings shall *f. down.* *Ps* 72:11
that is holpen shall *f. down. Isa* 31:3
their host shall *f. down* as. 34:4
f. down to stock of a tree ? 44:19
Sabeans shall *f. down* unto. 45:14
they *f. down*, they worship. 46:6
of Pharaoh *f. down.* *Ezek* 30:25
ye *f. down* and worship. *Dan* 3:5, 10
if ye *f. down* and worship image. 15
many shall *f. down* slain. 11:26
these things will I give thee, if thou
wilt *f. down. Mat* 4:9; *Luke* 4:7
twenty-four elders *f. down. Rev* 4:10

fall, joined with *sword*
f. on us with pestilence or *sword.*
Ex 5:3
this land to *f.* by *sword. Num* 14:3
ye shall *f.* by the *sword.* 43
Sennacherib *f.* by *sword. 2 Ki* 19:7
they shall *f.* by the *sword.*
Ps 63:10*; *Ezek* 6:11
thy men shall *f.* by *sword. Isa* 3:25
every one shall *f.* by *sword.* 13:15
Assyrian *f.* with the *sword.* 31:8
I will cause him to *f.* by the *sword* in.
37:7; *Jer* 19:7
friends *f.* by *sword. Jer* 20:4
thou shalt not *f.* by *sword.* 39:18
third part *f.* by *sword. Ezek* 5:12
that is near *f.* by the *sword.* 6:12
ye shall *f.* by the *sword.* 11:10

fugitives shall *f.* by *sword.*
Ezek 17:21
remnant shall *f.* by the *sword.* 23:25
and daughters *f.* by *sword.* 24:21
of Dedan shall *f.* by *sword.* 25:13
men in league *f.* by the *sword.* 30:5
tower of Syene, *f.* by the *sword.* 6
young men shall *f.* by the *sword.* 17
I will cause the *sword* to *f.* 22
in wastes shall *f.* by *sword.* 33:27
understand *f.* by *sword. Dan* 11:33
princes *f.* by the *sword.* *Hos* 7:16
Samaria shall *f.* by the *sword.* 13:16
when they *f.* on *sword.* *Joel* 2:8
sons and daughters *f.* by *sword.*
Amos 7:17
f. by edge of the *sword. Luke* 21:24

fallen
why is thy countenance *f.?* *Gen* 4:6
that hath his hair *f.* off. *Lev* 13:41
if thy brother be *f.* in decay. 25:35*
all Ai were *f.* on edge of. *Josh* 8:24
lord was *f.* down dead. *Judg* 3:25
inheritance had not *f.* unto. 18:1
the woman was *f.* at the. 19:27
Dagon was *f.* *1 Sam* 5:3
a deep sleep *f.* 26:12
found Saul and his sons *f.* 31:8
1 Chr 10:8
not live after he was *f. 2 Sam* 1:10
mourned, because they were *f.* 12
there is a great man *f.* this. 3:38
now Elisha was *f.* sick. *2 Ki* 13:14
dead bodies *f.* to earth. *2 Chr* 20:24
our fathers have *f.* by sword. 29:9
Haman was *f.* on bed. *Esth* 7:4
brought down and *f.* *Ps* 20:8
there are workers of iniquity *f.* 36:12
how art thou *f.* from! *Isa* 14:12
nor inhabitants of world *f.* 26:18
f. by the sword. *Ezek* 32:22, 23, 24
hast *f.* by thine iniquity. *Hos* 14:1
of you have an ox *f.?* *Luke* 14:5
the Holy Ghost was *f.* *Acts* 8:16
Eutychus being *f.* into a. 20:9*
when we were all *f.* I heard. 26:14
lest they should have *f.* 27:29*
when Paul should have *f.* 28:6
f. out to the furtherance. *Phil* 1:12
from whence thou art *f.* *Rev* 2:5

are fallen
are *f.* and dead. *2 Sam* 1:4
how are the mighty *f.!* 19, 25, 27
are *f.* under feet. 22:39; *Ps* 18:38
the lines are *f.* to me. *Ps* 16:6
terrors of death are *f.* upon. 55:4
midst whereof they are *f.* 57:6
reproaches of them are *f.* 69:9
the bricks are *f.* down. *Isa* 9:10
the Jews that are *f.* to. *Jer* 38:19
mighty men, they are *f.* 46:12
Babylon's foundations are *f.* 50:15
my virgins are *f.* by. *Lam* 2:21
his branches are *f.* his. *Ezek* 31:12
not lie with mighty that are *f.* 32:27
all their kings are *f.* *Hos* 7:7
some are *f.* asleep. *1 Cor* 15:6, 18
ye are *f.* from grace. *Gal* 5:4
seven kings, five are *f.* *Rev* 17:10

is fallen
man whose hair is *f.* *Lev* 13:40
our lot is *f.* on this. *Num* 32:19
your terror is *f.* upon us. *Josh* 2:9
fire of God is *f.* from. *Job* 1:16
and is *f.* into the ditch. *Ps* 7:15
and Judah is *f.* *Isa* 3:8
for thy harvest is *f.* 16:9
Babylon is *f.* is *f.* 21:9
Rev 14:8; 18:2
truth is *f.* in the streets. *Isa* 59:14
the spoiler is *f.* on thy. *Jer* 48:32
Babylon is suddenly *f.* 51:8
crown is *f.* from our. *Lam* 5:16
lo, when the wall is *f.* *Ezek* 13:12
virgin of Israel is *f.* *Amos* 5:2
raise up tabernacle that is *f.* 9:11
for the cedar is *f.* *Zech* 11:2
tabernacle of David which is *f.*
Acts 15:16

fallest
f. away to Chaldeans. *Jer* 37:13

falleth
when there *f.* out any. *Ex* 1:10

falling (col 1)

vessel whereinto any f. Lev 11:33
whereupon their carcase f. 35
inheritance where lot f. Num 33:54
not fail one that f. on. 2 Sam 3:29
as a man f. before wicked men. 34
will light on him as dew f. 17:12
when deep sleep f. on men. Job 4:13
33:15
wicked messenger f. Pr 13:17
perverse tongue f. into. 17:20
a just man f. seven times. 24:16
rejoice not when thine enemy f. 17
to him alone when he f. Eccl 4:10
of men are snared when it f. 9:12
where tree f. there shall it be. 11:3
leaf f. off from vine. Isa 34:4*
and f. down thereto. 44:15, 17
he that f. to Chaldeans. Jer 21:9
whoso f. not down. Dan 3:6, 11
oft-times he f. into fire. Mat 17:15
a house divided f. Luke 11:17
give me the portion that f. 15:12
own master standeth or f. Rom 14:4
the flower thereof f. Jas 1:11
1 Pet 1:24

falling
f. into a trance. Num 24:4, 16
upholden him that was f. Job 4:4
the mountain f. cometh to. 14:18
deliver feet from f. Ps 56:13; 116:8
a righteous man f. Pr 25:26*
and as a f. fig from. Isa 34:4*
came trembling and f. Luke 8:47
great drops of blood f. down. 22:44
and Judas f. headlong. Acts 1:18
and f. into a place where. 27:41*
and so f. down, he. 1 Cor 14:25
except there come a f. 2 Thes 2:3
able to keep you from f. Jude 24*

fallow
break up your f. ground. Jer 4:3
Hos 10:12

see deer
false
shalt not raise a f. report. Ex 23:1
keep thee far from a f. matter. 7
it is f. tell us now. 2 Ki 9:12
my words shall not be f. Job 36:4
hate every f. way. Ps 119:104, 128
done to thee, thou f. tongue ? 120:3*
a f. balance is an. Pr 11:1
wicked doer giveth heed to f. 17:4*
and f. balance is not good. 20:23
whoso boasteth of a f. gift. 25:14
they prophesy a f. vision. Jer 14:14*
them that prophesy f. 23:32*
it is f. I fall not away. 37:14
have seen f. burdens. Lam 2:14*
them as a f. divination. Ezek 21:23*
love no f. oath. Zech 8:17
diviners have told f. dreams. 10:2
swift witness against f. Mal 3:5
there arise f. Christs and f. prophets.
Mat 24:24; Mark 13:22
taken by f. accusation. Luke 19:8*
for such are f. apostles. 2 Cor 11:13
in perils among f. brethren. 26
because of f. brethren. Gal 2:4
without affection. f. 2 Tim 3:3
they be not f. accusers. Tit 2:3*
f. teachers among you. 2 Pet 2:1

see prophet
false prophets
beware of f. prophets. Mat 7:15
many f. prophets rise. 24:11, 24
f. prophets shall rise. Mark 13:22
fathers to f. prophets. Luke 6:26
f. prophets among people. 2 Pet 2:1
f. prophets are gone out. 1 John 4:1

false witness
shalt not bear f. witness against thy.
Ex 20:16; Deut 5:20; Mat 19:18
if a f. witness rise up. Deut 19:16*
if witness be a f. witness. 18
a f. witness that speaketh. Pr 6:19
f. witness sheweth forth. 12:17; 14:5
f. witness not be unpunished. 19:5, 9
a f. witness shall perish. 21:28
man that beareth f. witness. 25:18
heart proceed f. witness. Mat 15:19
elders sought f. witness. 26:59
bare f. witness against him.
Mark 14:56, 57

false witnesses (col 2)

f. witnesses are risen up. Ps 27:12
f. witnesses did rise. 35:11*
f. witnesses came, at last came two
f. witnesses. Mat 26:60
set up f. witnesses. Acts 6:13
f. witnesses of God. 1 Cor 15:15

falsehood
wrought f. against my. 2 Sam 18:13*
in answers remaineth f. Job 21:34
he hath brought forth f. Ps 7:14
them down, deceit is f. 119:118
is a right hand of f. 144:8, 11
under f. have we hid. Isa 28:15
are ye not a seed of f.? 57:4
words of f. 59:13
his molten image is f.
Jer 10:14; 51:17
forgotten me, and trusted in f. 13:25
they commit f. and thief. Hos 7:1
walking in spirit and f. Mi 2:11

falsely
thou wilt not deal f. Gen 21:23
was lost, sweareth f. Lev 6:3
which he hath sworn f. 5
neither deal f. nor lie. 19:11
shall not swear by my name f. 12
witness have testified f. Deut 19:18
nor have we dealt f. Ps 44:17
they swear f. Jer 5:2
prophets prophesy f. 31; 29:9
every one dealeth f. 6:13; 8:10
steal, murder, and swear f.? 7:9
thou speakest f. of Ishmael. 40:16
speakest f. the Lord hath. 43:2
swearing f. in making. Hos 10:4
house that sweareth f. Zech 5:4
say evil against you f. Mat 5:11
nor accuse any f. Luke 3:14*
oppositions of science, f. 1 Tim 6:20
f. accuse conversation. 1 Pet 3:16

falsifying
and f. the balances. Amos 8:5*

fame
f. heard in Pharaoh's. Gen 45:16
nations heard of thee. Num 14:15
Joshua's f. was noised. Josh 6:27
we heard the f. of God. 9:9
his f. was in all nations. 1 Ki 4:31
queen heard f. of. 10:1; 2 Chr 9:1
wisdom exceedeth f. 1 Ki 10:7
2 Chr 9:6
the f. of David went to. 1 Chr 14:17
house must be of f. and of. 22:5
Mordecai's f. went. Esth 9:4
heard f. with our ears. Job 28:22*
isles that have not heard my f.
Isa 66:19
have heard the f. our hands. Jer 6:24
and I will get them f. Zeph 3:19*
the f. of Jesus went. Mat 4:24*
Mark 1:28*; Luke 4:14, 37*; 5:15*
f. thereof went abroad. Mat 9:26
departed, spread abroad his f. 31
Herod heard of f. of Jesus. 14:1*

familiar
f. friends have forgotten. Job 19:14
my f. friend hath lifted up. Ps 41:9

familiar spirit
woman of a f. spirit. Lev 20:27
a f. spirit to enquire of her; a f. spirit
at Endor. 1 Sam 28:7
divine to me by the f. spirit. 8
of one that had f. spirit. 1 Chr 10:13
Manasseh dealt with a f. spirit.
2 Chr 33:6
of one that hath a f. spirit. Isa 29:4

familiar spirits
that have f. spirits. Lev 19:31
that turneth after f. spirits. 20:6
consulter with f. spirits. Deut 18:11
put away those that had f. spirits.
1 Sam 28:3
cut off those that have f. spirits. 9
Manasseh dealt with f. spirits.
2 Ki 21:6
workers with f. spirits Josiah. 23:24
say, seek f. spirits. Isa 8:19
to them that have f. spirits. 19:3

familiars
all my f. watched for. Jer 20:10*

families (col 3)

isles of Gentiles divided after f.
Gen 10:5
were the f. of the Canaanites. 18
the sons of Ham after their f. 20
f. of Shem. 31
all f. of earth blessed. 12:3; 28:14
dukes of Esau according to f. 36:40
nourished brethren with f. 47:12
these be f. of Reuben. Ex 6:14
Num 26:7; Josh 13:15, 23
these are the f. of Simeon. Ex 6:15
Num 26:12, 14; Josh 19:1, 8
f. of Gershon. Ex 6:17; Num 3:18
21; 4:22, 24, 38, 40, 41; Josh 21:33
f. of Levi. Ex 6:19, 25; Num 4:46
26:57, 58; Josh 21:27; 1 Chr 6:19
lamb according to your f. Ex 12:21
of the f. of strangers. Lev 25:45
of Israel after their f. Num 1:2
sons of Kohath by their f. 3:19
27, 29, 30; 4:37; Josh 21:4, 10
sons of Merari, by f. Num 3:20, 33, 35
4:33, 42, 44, 45; Josh 21:34, 40
1 Chr 6:63
cut not off tribe of f. of. Num 4:18
heard them weep through f. 11:10
the f. of Gad. 26:15, 18
Josh 13:24, 28
the f. of Judah. Num 26:20, 22
Josh 15:1, 12, 20
sons of Issachar after f. Num 26:23
25; Josh 19:17, 23; 21:6
1 Chr 6:62; 7:5
f. of Zebulun. Num 26:26, 27
Josh 19:10, 16
Joseph after f. Num 26:28; 36:1
the f. of Manasseh. 26:34; 36:12
Josh 13:29; 17:2
Ephraim after f. Num 26:35, 37
Josh 16:5, 8; 21:5, 20; 1 Chr 6:66
of Benjamin after f. Num 26:38, 41
Josh 18:11, 20, 21; 1 Sam 10:21
sons of Dan after their f. Num 26:42
Josh 19:40, 48
sons of Asher after f. Num 26:44
Josh 19:24, 31
sons of Naphtali after f. Num 26:48
50; Josh 19:32
of Zelophehad of Manasseh's f.
Num 27:1
divide land by lot among f. 33:54
chief fathers of f. of Gilead. 36:1
come according to f. Josh 7:14
half children of Machir, by f. 13:31
tribe of Dan according to f. 19:40, 48
least of f. of Benjamin. 1 Sam 9:21
f. of Kirjath-jearim. 1 Chr 2:53
f. of scribes which dwelt at Jabez. 55
these are f. of Zorathites. 4:2
f. of them that wrought fine. 21
mentioned princes in their f. 38
according to divisions of the f.
2 Chr 35:5*, 12*
set people after their f. Neh 4:13
contempt of f. terrify me ? Job 31:34
God setteth solitary in f. Ps 68:6
maketh him f. like a flock. 107:41
I will call all the f. of. Jer 1:15
hear, all ye f. of the house. 2:4
fury on the f. that call not on. 10:25
I will take all f. of the north. 25:9
I will be God of all the f. of. 31:1
the two f. which Lord hath. 33:24
we will be as the f. of. Ezek 20:32
you have I known of all f. Amos 3:2
that selleth f. through. Nah 3:4
all the f. that remain. Zech 12:14
will not come up of the f. 14:17

family
my face against his f. Lev 20:5
return every man to his f. 25:10, 41
himself to stock of stranger's f.
his uncle or any of his f. may. 49
of Gershon was the f. Num 3:21
of Kohath was the f. of. 27
f. of Hanochites, f. of Palluites. 26:5
family mentioned often to the
59th verse
name done away from f.? 27:4
inheritance to next of his f. 11
marry to f. of father's. 36:6, 8, 12
lest a f. turn away. Deut 29:18

the f. which the Lord.   Josh 7:14
took the f. of the Zarhites.   17
go man and all his f.   Judg 1:25
my f. is poor in Manasseh.   6:15
communed with the f. of his.   9:1
Manoah a man of f. of the.   13:2
a Levite of the f. of Judah.   17:7
Danites sent of their f. five.   18:2
be a priest to a f. in Israel.   19
departed every man to his f.   21:24
a kinsman of the f. of.   Ruth 2:1
f. least of Benjamin.   1 Sam 9:21
f. of Matri was taken.   10:21
my life, or my father's f.   18:18
yearly sacrifice for all f.   20:6, 29
whole f. is risen against.   2 Sam 14:7
a man of the f. of Saul.   16:5
neither did f. multiply.   1 Chr 4:27
to f. of Kohath cities.   6:61, 70
ark remained with f. of.   13:14
of Purim kept by every f.   Esth 9:28
a city, and two of a f.   Jer 3:14
chosen by residue of this evil f.   8:3
against f. I brought out.   Amos 3:1
every f. mourn.   Zech 12:12, 13, 14
if the f. of Egypt go not up.   14:18
whole f. in heaven and.   Eph 3:15

famine
Famines of more or less intensity frequently occurred in Palestine because of its dependence upon the rain, and in Egypt because of its dependence on a proper overflow of the Nile. Not until modern times has it been possible to store rain, or to regulate the flow of rivers, to any appreciable extent. Famine also came naturally when locusts or other insects destroyed the crops. The worst famine named in the Bible is that in Egypt and the surrounding countries in the time of Joseph, Gen 41.

for the f. was grievous.   Gen 12:10
a f. in land, besides first f.   26:1
empty ears seven years of f.   41:27
the f. shall consume the land.   30
not be known by reason of f.   31
to Joseph two sons before the f.   50
the f. was over all the face of.   56
land fainted by reason of f.   47:13
there was a f.   Ruth 1:1
a f. in days of David.   2 Sam 21:1
shall seven years of f. come?   24:13
if there be in land f.   1 Ki 8:37
    2 Chr 20:9
a sore f. in Samaria.   1 Ki 18:2
    2 Ki 6:25
then f. is in the city.   2 Ki 7:4
the Lord hath called for a f.   8:1
the f. prevailed in Jerusalem.   25:3
you to die by f.   2 Chr 32:11
in f. he shall redeem thee.   Job 5:20
at destruction and f. thou.   22
for want and f. were solitary.   30:3
keep them alive in f.   Ps 33:19
in the days of f. they shall be.   37:19
he called for a f. on land.   105:16
I will kill thy root with f.   Isa 14:30
destruction, f. and sword.   51:19
see sword, nor f. Jer 5:12; 14:13, 15
sword and f. shall prophets.   14:15
people cast out, because of f.   16
behold them that are sick with f.   18
as are for the f. to the f.   15:2
deliver up their children to f.   18:21
from f. to Nebuchadnezzar.   21:7
send the f. among.   24:10; 29:17
nation will I punish with the f.   27:8
persecute with sword and f.   29:18
to Chaldeans because of f.   32:24
a liberty for you to the f.   34:17
f. shall follow close after.   42:16
the f. was sore in the city.   52:6
was black, because of f.   Lam 5:10
part consumed with f.   Ezek 5:12
send on them evil arrows of f.   16
so will I send on you f.   17; 14:13
f. within, f. and pestilence.   7:15
leave a few men from f.   12:16
and I will lay no f. upon you.   36:29
receive no more reproach of f.   30
a f. not of bread, but of.   Amos 8:11

great f. was through the.   Luke 4:25
there arose a mighty f.   15:14
shall f. separate us from?   Rom 8:35
in one day, death, f.   Rev 18:8

by the famine
sons and daughters die by the f.
    Jer 11:22
consume them by the f.   14:12, 16
shall be consumed by f.   16:4
    44:12, 18, 27
abideth in city die by the f.   21:9
why will ye die by the f.?   27:13
to king of Babylon by the f.   32:36
remaineth in city die by f.   38:2
    Ezek 6:12
die by f. and pestilence.   Jer 42:17
know that ye shall die by the f.   22
punished Jerusalem by the f.   44:13
they shall fall by the f.   Ezek 6:11

famines
there shall be f. pestilences, and.
    Mat 24:7; Mark 13:8; Luke 21:11

famish *and* famished
all land of Egypt was f.   Gen 41:55
suffer righteous to f.   Pr 10:3
honourable men are f.   Isa 5:13
he will f. all gods of the.   Zeph 2:11

famous
princes f. in.   Num 16:2*; 26:9*
thou f. in Beth-lehem.   Ruth 4:11
his name may be f. in Israel.   14
were f. men.   1 Chr 5:24; 12:30
a man was f. as he had.   Ps 74:5*
thanks to him who slew f.   136:18
and she became f.   Ezek 23:10*
daughters of the f. nations.   32:18

fan, *substantive*
winnowed with the f.   Isa 30:24
I will fan them with a f.   Jer 15:7
whose f. is in his hand.   Mat 3:12
    Luke 3:17

fan, *verb*
shalt f. them, wind shall.   Isa 41:16†
a dry wind not to f. nor.   Jer 4:11†
I will f. them with a fan.   15:7
fanners that shall f. her.   51:2†

far
that be f. from thee to.   Gen 18:25
you shall not go very f.   Ex 8:28
keep thee f. from false matter.   23:7
if the place be too f.   Deut 12:21
    14:24
stranger come from a f. land.   29:22
waters stood very f.   Josh 3:16
go not very f. from the city.   8:4
we are f. from you, when ye.   9:22
father adventured life f.   Judg 9:17
f. from the Zidonians.   18:7, 28
by Jebus, day was f. spent.   19:11
f. be it from thee.   1 Sam 20:9
they carry them away f.   1 Ki 8:46
his name spread f.   2 Chr 26:15
now therefore be ye f.   Ezra 6:6
separated one f. from.   Neh 4:19
all Jews both nigh and f.   Esth 9:20
children are f. from safety.   Job 5:4
put iniquity f. away.   11:14; 22:23
f. be it from God to do.   34:10
judgements are f. out of.   Ps 10:5
why art thou so f. from?   22:1
they that are f. from thee.   73:27
thou art exalted f. above all.   97:9
as f. as the east is from the west, so
    f. hath he removed.   103:12
let blessing be f. from him.   109:17
that follow mischief are f.   119:150
salvation is f. from wicked.   155
perverse lips put f. from.   Pr 4:24
remove thy way f. from her.   5:8
Lord is f. from wicked.   15:29
his friends go f. from him.   19:7
his soul shall be f. from them.   22:5
rod of correction shall drive it f.   15
price is f. above rubies.   31:10
as f. as light excelleth.   Eccl 2:13
Lord have removed men f.   Isa 6:12
shall turn the rivers f. away.   19:6
removed the nations f.   26:15
hear ye that are f. from.   46:12
swallowed the bee f. away.   49:19
shalt be f. from oppression.   54:14
therefore is judgement f. from.   59:9

thou art f. from their.   Jer 12:2
all the kings of the north f.   25:26
to remove you f. from land.   27:10
upon all cities of Moab f. or.   48:24
thus f. is judgement of Moab.   47
thus f. are words of Jeremiah.   51:64
my soul f. from peace.   Lam 3:17
have I set if f. from.   Ezek 7:20
said, get ye f. from Lord.   11:15
the fourth king f. richer.   Dan 11:2
ye might remove them f.   Joel 3:6
that put f. away evil day.   Amos 6:3
in that day decree be f.   Mi 7:11
be it f. from thee, Lord.   Mat 16:22
when day was now f.   Mark 6:35
not f. from the kingdom of.   12:34
is as a man taking f. journey.   13:34
was not f. from house.   Luke 7:6
Jesus said, suffer ye thus f.   22:51
abide with us, for day is f.   24:29
led them out as f. as to.   50
were not f. from land.   John 21:8
travelled as f. as Phenice. Acts 11:19
Barnabas go as f. as Antioch.   22
he be not f. from every one.   17:27
I will send thee f. hence to.   22:21
came to meet us as f. as.   28:15
the night is f. spent, the. Rom 13:12
a f. more exceeding.   2 Cor 4:17
we are come as f. as to you.   10:14
f. above all principality.   Eph 1:21
that ascended up f. above all.   4:10
Christ, which is f. better. Phil 1:23
it is yet f. more evident. Heb 7:15*

see country, countries

far *from me*
saith, be it f. from me.   1 Sam 2:30
    22:15; 2 Sam 20:20; 23:17
withdraw hand f. from me. Job 13:21
my brethren f. from me.   19:13
of wicked f. from me.   21:16; 22:18
they flee f. from me.   30:10
not f. from me, for trouble. Ps 22:11
    19; 35:22; 38:21; 71:12
hide not thy face f. from me.   27:9
mine acquaintance f. from me.   88:8
lover and friend f. from me.   18
remove f. from me vanity.   Pr 30:8
but it was f. from me.   Eccl 7:23
their heart f. from me.   Isa 29:13
they are gone f. from me.   2:5
comforter is f. from me.   Lam 1:16
of kings f. from me.   Ezek 43:9
Levites gone f. from me.   44:10
heart is f. from me.   Mat 15:8
    Mark 7:6

from far
against thee from f.   Deut 28:49
    Jer 5:15
fetch my knowledge from f. Job 36:3
up an ensign from f.   Isa 5:26
which shall come from f.   10:3
bound which are fled from f.   22:3
name of Lord cometh from f. 30:27
bring my sons from f.   43:6; 60:9
hearken, ye people, from f.   49:1
these shall come from f.   12
sons shall come from f.   60:4
I will save thee from f.   Jer 30:10
for men to come from f. Ezek 23:40
horsemen shall come from f.
    Hab 1:8
divers of them came from f.
    Mark 8:3

far off
gone, and not yet f. off.   Gen 44:4
shall pitch f. off about.   Num 2:2
gods of people f. off.   Deut 13:7
do to all the cities f. off.   20:15
neither is commandment f. off. 30:11
king tarried in a place f. off.
    2 Sam 15:17
captives to a land f. off. 2 Chr 6:36
lo, I would wander f. off.   Ps 55:7
than a brother f. off.   Pr 27:10
f. off who can find out? Eccl 7:24
they shall flee f. off.   Isa 17:13
hear, ye that are f. off.   33:13
shall behold land that is f. off. 14
righteousness not be f. off.   46:13
send thy messengers f. off.   57:9
peace to him that is f.   19
look for salvation, it is f. off. 59:11

he that is *f. off* shall die. *Ezek* 6:12
that I should go *f. off.* 8:6
although I cast them *f. off.* 11:16
prophesieth of times *f. off.* 12:27
those that be *f. off* from thee. 22:5
to Israel near and *f. off.* *Dan* 9:7
I will remove *f. off* the. *Joel* 2:20
sell them to Sabeans *f. off.* 3:8
her that was cast *f. off.* *Mi* 4:7
f. off shall come and. *Zech* 6:15
ye who were *f. off* made. *Eph* 2:13

fare
look how thy brethren *f.* *1 Sam* 17:18

fare
so he paid the *f.* thereof. *Jonah* 1:3

fared
the rich man *f.* *Luke* 16:19

farewell
first go bid them *f.* at. *Luke* 9:61
yourselves, ye do well, *f.* *Acts* 15:29
Paul bade them *f.* saying. 18:21
they had to say against him, *f.* 23:30
finally, brethren, *f.* be. *2 Cor* 13:11

farm
their ways, one to his *f.* *Mat* 22:5

farther
f. though a wise man. *Eccl* 8:17
f. and fell on his face. *Mat* 26:39
had gone a little *f.* thence. *Mark* 1:19
see **further**

farthing, -s
paid the uttermost *f.* *Mat* 5:26
two sparrows sold for a *f.?* 10:29†
in two mites, a *f.* *Mark* 12:42
sparrows sold for two *f.?* *Luke* 12:6†

fashion
this is the *f.* thou shalt. *Gen* 6:15*
f. of the tabernacle. *Ex* 26:30
bowls made he after the *f.* 37:19*
according to all the *f.* *1 Ki* 6:38
Ahaz sent the *f.* of. *2 Ki* 16:10
shew them form and *f.* *Ezek* 43:11
never saw it on this *f.* *Mark* 2:12
f. of his countenance. *Luke* 9:29
tabernacle according to *f.* *Acts* 7:44*
f. of this world passeth. *1 Cor* 7:31
found in *f.* as a man. *Phil* 2:8
grace of *f.* of it perisheth. *Jas* 1:11

fashion
one *f.* us in the womb? *Job* 31:15

fashioned
Aaron *f.* the calf. *Ex* 32:4
thine hands have *f.* me. *Job* 10:8
Ps 119:73
in continuance were *f.* *Ps* 139:16
respect to him that *f.* it. *Isa* 22:11
thy breasts are *f.* thine. *Ezek* 16:7
that it may be *f.* like. *Phil* 3:21*

fashioneth
he *f.* their hearts alike. *Ps* 33:15
the smith *f.* it with the. *Isa* 44:12
clay say to him that *f.* it? 45:9

fashioning
not *f.* yourselves to. *1 Pet* 1:14

fashions
were according to *f.* *Ezek* 42:11

fast, adverb
the Lord had *f.* closed. *Gen* 20:18
Sisera was *f.* asleep and. *Judg* 4:21
but we will bind thee *f.* 15:13
if they bind me *f.* with. 16:11*
here *f.* by my maidens. *Ruth* 2:8
Boaz said to me, keep *f.* by. 21
this work goeth *f.* on. *Ezra* 5:8*
clods cleave *f.* together. *Job* 38:38
he commanded, it stood *f.* *Ps* 33:9
his strength setteth. 65:6
f. hold of instruction. *Pr* 4:13
of Moab hasteth *f.* *Jer* 48:16
took captives held them *f.* 50:33
in ship, and was *f.* asleep. *Jonah* 1:5
who made their feet *f.* *Acts* 16:24
forepart stuck *f.* remained. 27:41*

fast
Fasting has, in all ages, and among all nations, been much in use in times of mourning, sorrow, and afflictions. It is in some sort in-spired by nature, which, in these circumstances, denies itself nourishment, and takes off the edge of hunger. There is no example of fasting, properly so called, to be seen before Moses; yet it is presumable that the patriarchs fasted, since we see that there were very great mournings among them, such as that of Abraham for Sarah, Gen 23:2; and that of Jacob for his son Joseph, Gen 37:34.
Moses enjoins no particular fast, excepting that upon the day of atonement, which was generally and strictly observed, Lev 23:27, 29. Since the time of Moses, examples of fasting have been very common among the Jews. Joshua and the elders of Israel remained prostrate before the ark from morning until evening, without eating, after the Israelites were defeated by the men of Ai, Josh 7:6. The eleven tribes which had taken arms against that of Benjamin, seeing they could not hold out against the inhabitants of Gibeah, fell down before the ark upon their faces, and so continued till the evening without eating, Judg 20:26. The Israelites perceiving themselves to be pressed by the Philistines, assembled before the Lord at Mizpeh, and fasted in his presence till the evening, 1 Sam 7:6. And David fasted while the first child he had by Bath-sheba, the wife of Uriah, was sick, 2 Sam 12:16.
Moses fasted forty days on mount Horeb, Ex 34:28. Elijah passed as many days without eating any thing, 1 Ki 19:8. And our Saviour fasted in the wilderness forty days and forty nights, Mat 4:2. These fasts were out of the common rules of nature.
It does not appear by our Saviour's own practice, or any commands that he gave to his disciples, that he instituted any particular fasts, or enjoined any to be kept out of pure devotion. It is however inferred from such statements as those in Luke 5:33–35, that he expected his followers would do so. The one condition he made was that it be sincere, Mat. 6:16.
proclaim a *f.*, set Naboth. *1 Ki* 21:9
they proclaimed a *f.* and set. 12
Jehoshaphat proclaimed a *f.*
2 Chr 20:3
Ezra proclaimed a *f.* at. *Ezra* 8:21
in the day of your *f.* you. *Isa* 58:3
such *f.* I have chosen? call this *f.?* 5
is not this *f.* that I have chosen? 6
they proclaimed a *f.* *Jer* 36:9
sanctify a *f.* *Joel* 1:14; 2:15
Nineveh proclaimed a *f.* *Jonah* 3:5
f. of the fourth month, of. *Zech* 8:19
f. was now already past. *Acts* 27:9

fast, verb
thou didst *f.* and weep. *2 Sam* 12:21
is dead, wherefore should I *f.?* 23
I and my maidens *f.* *Esth* 4:16
ye *f.* for strife, not *f.* as. *Isa* 58:4
when they *f.* I will not. *Jer* 14:12
did ye at all *f.* unto me? *Zech* 7:5
f. be not as hypocrites of a sad . . .
appear to men to *f.* *Mat* 6:16
thou appear not to men to *f.* 18
why do we *f.* disciples *f.* not? 9:14
Mark 2:18
then shall they *f.* *Mat* 9:15
Mark 2:20; *Luke* 5:35
disciples of John used to *f.*
Mark 2:18
f. while bridegroom with them? they
cannot *f.* 19; *Luke* 5:33
of John *f.* often? *Luke* 5:33
I *f.* twice in the week. 18:12

fasted
the people *f.* that day. *Judg* 20:26

drew water, and *f.* *1 Sam* 7:6
buried them, and *f.* seven days. 31:13
1 Chr 10:12
and *f.* for Saul. *2 Sam* 1:12
David *f.* 12:16
while the child was alive I *f.* 22
Ahab *f.* *1 Ki* 21:27
so we *f.* *Ezra* 8:23
Nehemiah *f.* and prayed. *Neh* 1:4
why have we *f.* say they? *Isa* 58:3
when ye *f.* in fifth and. *Zech* 7:5
Jesus *f.* forty days and. *Mat* 4:2
ministered to Lord and *f.* *Acts* 13:2
when they had *f.* they laid hands. 3

fasten
shalt *f.* the chains. *Ex* 28:14*, 25*
to *f.* the plate on high. 39:31
I will *f.* him as a nail. *Isa* 22:23
they *f.* it with nails. *Jer* 10:4

fastened
ends of chains they *f.* *Ex* 39:18*
Moses *f.* his sockets, set up. 40:18*
Jael *f.* the nail into. *Judg* 4:21*
Delilah *f.* it with a pin, and. 16:14
f. Saul's body to wall. *1 Sam* 31:10
with a sword *f.* upon. *2 Sam* 20:8
beams should not be *f.* *1 Ki* 6:6*
f. his head in temple. *1 Chr* 10:10
six steps were *f.* to. *2 Chr* 9:18
hangings *f.* with cords of. *Esth* 1:6
are the foundations *f.* *Job* 38:6
as nails *f.* by masters. *Eccl* 12:11
nail *f.* in the sure place. *Isa* 22:25
f. it with nails that it should. 41:7
within were hooks *f.* *Ezek* 40:43
the eyes of all were *f.* on. *Luke* 4:20
when I had *f.* mine eyes. *Acts* 11:6
a viper out of heat and *f.* on. 28:3

fastening
Peter *f.* his eyes upon him. *Acts* 3:4

fastest
thou *f.* anoint thy head. *Mat* 6:17

fasting
were assembled with *f.* *Neh* 9:1
decree came, was *f.* *Esth* 4:3
humbled my soul with *f.* *Ps* 35:13
and chastened soul with *f.* 69:10
knees are weak through *f.* 109:24
words of Lord on the *f.* *Jer* 36:6
king passed the night *f.* *Dan* 6:18
himself to seek by prayer and *f.* 9:3
turn ye with *f.* weeping. *Joel* 2:12
not send them away *f.* *Mat* 15:32
goeth not out but by *f.* 17:21
Mark 9:29
if I send them away *f.* *Mark* 8:3
four days ago I was *f.* *Acts* 10:30
ordained elders, and prayed *f.* 14:23
fourteenth day ye continued *f.* 27:33
may give yourselves to *f.* *1 Cor* 7:5

fastings
the matters of the *f.* *Esth* 9:31
Anna served God with *f.* *Luke* 2:37
approving ourselves in *f.* *2 Cor* 6:5
in *f.* often, in cold and. 11:27

fat
The Mosaic law declared that to the Lord belongs all the fat of sacrificial animals, Lev 3:16, 17. Neither it nor the blood was eaten, but was burned as an offering to God, Ex 29:13, 22; Lev 4:8, 9. The ground of this law was that the fat was the richest part of the animal, and therefore belonged to God.
The word is used figuratively to mean the best part of a thing, or the richest productions, Neh 9:25; Ps 63:5; Isa 25:6; Rom 11:17.
Abel also brought of *f.* *Gen* 4:4
the *f.* of sacrifice remain. *Ex* 23:18
take *f.* that covereth the inwards, and *f.* upon kidneys. 29:13, 22
Lev 3:3, 4, 9, 10, 14, 15; 4:8; 7:3, 4
head and *f.* in order. *Lev* 1:8, 12
sweet savour, the *f.* is Lord's. 3:16
he shall take off the *f.* of. 4:8, 31, 35
burn his *f.* 26; 6:12; 7:3, 31; 17:6
Num 18:17
f. of beast dieth of itself. *Lev* 7:24
the *f.* with breast, it shall he. 30

he that offereth *f.* shall have. *Lev* 7:33
Moses burnt head and *f.* of.   8:20
one wafer and put them on *f.*   26
but the *f.* he burnt.   9:10, 20
fire from Lord consumed *f.*   24
the *f.* of sin offering shall.   16:25
f. of lambs with *f.* of   *Deut* 32:14
and the *f.* closed upon.   *Judg* 3:22
before they burnt *f.*   *1 Sam* 2:15
let them not fail to burn the *f.*   16
to hearken is better than *f.* of. 15:22
from *f.* of mighty.   *2 Sam* 1:22
altar too little to receive *f. 1 Ki* 8:64
offered *f.* of.   *2 Chr* 7:7; 29:35
priests busied in offering *f.*   35:14
he maketh collops of *f.*   *Job* 15:27
inclosed in their own *f.*   *Ps* 17:10
enemies of Lord as the *f.* of. 37:20
full of *f.* of fed beasts.   *Isa* 1:11
made *f.* with the *f.* of kidneys. 34:6
nor hast filled me with *f.* of.   43:24
when ye offer the *f.* and. *Ezek* 44:7
stand to offer to me the *f.*   15

fat, *adjective*

came seven kine *f.*   *Gen* 41:2
did eat up seven *f.* kine.   4, 20
out of Asher bread shall be *f.* 49:20
land is, whether *f.* or. *Num* 13:20
waxen *f.* then they turn. *Deut* 31:20
f. and kicked, thou waxen *f.* 32:15
Eglon was a very *f.* man. *Judg* 3:17
to make yourselves *f.*   *1 Sam* 2:29
the woman had a *f.* calf.   28:24
Adonijah slew *f.* cattle.   *1 Ki* 1:9
                                  19, 25
provision for one day ten *f.*   4:23
they found *f.* pasture.   *1 Chr* 4:40
a *f.* land became *f.*   *Neh* 9:25
not served thee in large and *f.*   35
that be *f.* on earth shall. *Ps* 22:29
shall be *f.* and flourishing.   92:14*
their heart as *f.* as grease.   119:70
soul shall be made *f.*   *Pr* 11:25
soul of diligent be made *f.*   13:4
a good report maketh bones *f.* 15:30
in Lord shall be made *f.*   28:25
waste places of *f.* ones.   *Isa* 5:17
make heart of this people *f.*   6:10
Lord shall send among his *f.*   10:16
make a feast of *f.* things.   25:6
on the head of *f.* valleys.   28:1
on the head of *f.* valley.   4
and bread shall be *f.* and.   30:23
sword of Lord is made *f.*   34:6
and their dust shall be made *f.*   7
Lord shall make *f.* thy.   58:11*
they are waxen *f.* they. *Jer* 5:28
grown *f.* as the heifer at.   50:11*
in a *f.* pasture shall feed. *Ezek* 34:14
but I will destroy the *f.* and.   16
I will judge between the *f.*   20
one lamb out of *f.* pastures. 45:15†
offering of *f.* beasts.   *Amos* 5:22
by them their portion is *f. Hab* 1:16

eat fat

and ye shall *eat* the *f.* *Gen* 45:18
a statute that ye *eat* no *f.*
                   Lev 3:17; 7:23
whoso *eateth f.* of the beast.   7:25
which did *eat* the *f.*   *Deut* 32:38
eat the *f.* and drink sweet. *Neh* 8:10
ye *eat f.* and clothe you. *Ezek* 34:3
eat f. till ye be full and.   39:19
eat the flesh of the *f.* *Zech* 11:16

father

*In addition to its common use,
this word is also used* [1] *in the
sense of seniors,* Acts 7:2; 22:1;
*and of parents in general, or an-
cestors,* Dan 5:2; Jer 27:7; Mat
23:30, 32. [2] *The founder of a
trade or profession, and the head
of the inhabitants of a town,*
Gen 4:20–22; 1 Chr 2:51; 4:14, 18.
[3] *God, either as the Creator of the
human race or as the loving guardian of his spiritual children, or in
his relation to Jesus Christ,* Mal
2:10; Rom 8:15; Mark 14:36.
Jabal was *f.* of such as. *Gen* 4:20
Jubal was the *f.* of all such as.   21
and Ham is the *f.* of.   9:18
f. of nations. 17:4, 5; *Rom* 4:17, 18

have ye a *f.*?   *Gen* 44:19
and we said, we have a *f.*   20
God made me *f.* to Pharaoh.   45:8
whose *f.* was an Egyptian. *Lev* 24:10
as a nursing *f.* beareth. *Num* 11:12
statutes between *f.* and.   30:16
f. shall bring forth.   *Deut* 22:15
man give damsel's *f.* fifty.   29
of house of mother's *f.*   *Judg* 9:1
with me, and be to me a *f.*   17:10
go with us, and be to us a *f.*   18:19
the *f.* of the damsel saw him. 19:3
damsel's *f.* retained him, he.   4
Kish was the *f.* of Saul. *1 Sam* 9:3
                                   14:51
Salem the *f.* of.   *1 Chr* 2:51
of Hemath the *f.* of house of.   55
Joab the *f.* of the valley of.   4:14
at Gibeon dwelt *f.* of.   8:29; 9:35
Esther had neither *f.* nor. *Esth* 2:7
I was a *f.* to the poor.   *Job* 29:16
up with me, as with a *f.*   31:18
hath the rain a *f.*?   38:28
f. of fatherless, and judge. *Ps* 68:5
as a *f.* pitieth his children.   103:13
correcteth, even as a *f.*   *Pr* 3:12
hear the instruction of a *f.*   4:1
son maketh a glad *f.*   10:1; 15:20
f. of a fool hath no joy.   17:21
f. of the righteous rejoice.   28:24
called, the everlasting *f. Isa* 9:6
Eliakim shall be a *f.* to.   22:21
the *f.* to child shall make.   38:19
for I am a *f.* to Israel.   *Jer* 31:9
as the soul of the *f.* so. *Ezek* 18:4
son bear the iniquity of *f.*?   19
son shall not bear iniquity of *f.* 20
in thee they set light by *f.*   22:7
for *f.* or mother they may.   44:25
the son dishonoureth *f.*   *Mi* 7:6
if I then be a *f.* where?   *Mal* 1:6
have we not all one *f.*?   2:10
f. deliver up the child.   *Mat* 10:21
                             Mark 13:12
he that loveth *f.* or.   *Mat* 10:37
I thank thee, O *F.* Lord of.   11:25
so *F.* it seemed good. 26; *Luke* 10:21
                             John 11:41
knoweth Son, but the *F.* *Mat* 11:27
that curseth *f.* let him die.   15:4
                             Mark 7:10
leave *f.* and mother, and. *Mat* 19:5
that hath forsaken *f.* mother, or.
                         29; *Mark* 10:29
baptizing in name of *F. Mat* 28:19
taketh *f.* of damsel.   *Mark* 5:40
                             Luke 8:51
the *f.* of the child cried. *Mark* 9:24
knoweth no man, but the *F.* 13:32
Abba, *F.*, all things are.   14:36
Simon *f.* of Alexander.   15:21
no man knows who *F.* is. *Luke* 10:22
ask bread of any that is a *f.*   11:11
f. shall be divided against the son,
    the son against the *f.*   12:53
f. I have sinned against.   15:21
f. said, bring forth best robe.   22
I pray thee, *f.* send to my.   16:27
F. if thou be willing, remove. 22:42
F. forgive them, they know.   23:34
F. into thy hands I commend.   46
of the only begotten of *F. John* 1:14
Son which is in bosom of the *F.*   18
the *F.* loveth the Son. 3:35; 5:20
nor at Jerusalem worship *F.*   4:21
shall worship the *F.* in spirit.   23
the *f.* knew that it was at the.   53
but what he seeth *F.* do.   5:19
for as the *F.* raiseth up dead.   21
F. judgeth no man, but hath.   22
they honour the *F.*: he that honoureth
    not Son, honoureth not *F.*   23
for as the *F.* hath life in himself. 26
seek not mine own, but will of *F.* 30
works which *F.* hath given me bear
    witness that the *F.* hath sent. 36
F. which sent me, hath borne.   37
  8:16; 12:49; 14:24; *1 John* 4:14
think not that I accuse you to the *F.*
                             John 5:45
him hath God the *F.* sealed.   6:27
all that the *F.* giveth me shall.   37
and this is the *F.*'s will, that.   39
is not this Jesus, whose *f.* and?   42

no man can come, except *F.*
                             John 6:44
that hath learned of the *F.*   45
any hath seen *F.* he hath seen *F.* 46
F. hath sent me, and I live by *F.* 57
not alone, but I and the *F.*   8:16
the *F.* that sent me beareth.   18
understood not he spake of *F.*   27
F. hath not left me alone.   29
we have one *F.* even God.   41
devil is a liar, and the *f.* of it. 44
F. knoweth me, so know I *F.* 10:15
say ye of him whom the *F.*   36
believe that the *F.* is in me.   38
F. save me from this hour.   12:27
F. glorify thy name; then came.   28
even as the *F.* said unto me.   50
he should depart unto *F.*   13:1
knowing that the *F.* had given all. 3
I am the way, truth, and life, no man
    cometh to the *F.* but by me. 14:6
Lord, shew us the *F.* and.   8
hath seen me, hath seen the *F.*   9
I am in the *F.* and *F.* in. 11; 17:21
that the *F.* may be glorified.   14:13
I will pray the *F.* for you. 16; 16:26
Comforter whom the *F.* will. 14:26
I love the *F.*: as the *F.* gave me. 31
as the *F.* hath loved me, so.   15:9
whatsoever ye shall ask of the *F.* in
    my name, he may.   16; 16:23
from the *F.* the Spirit who pro-
    ceedeth from the *F.*   15:26
they have not known the *F.*   16:3
all things that the *F.* hath are.   15
because I go the the *F.*   16, 17
shew you plainly of the *F.*   25
the *F.* loveth you, because ye.   27
forth from the *F.* and go to the *F.* 28
not alone, because the *F.* is.   32
F. the hour is come.   17:1
O *F.* glorify thou me with.   5
Holy *F.* keep those whom thou.   11
F. I will that they also, whom.   24
O righteous *F.* the world hath.   25
for promise of the *F.*   *Acts* 1:4
the *F.* hath put in his own power.   7
received of the *F.* the promise. 2:33
he might be *f.* of all.   *Rom* 4:11
and the *f.* of circumcision to them. 12
faith of Abraham, the *f.* of.   16
raised from the dead by the *F.*   6:4
whereby we cry, Abba, *F.*   8:15
are beloved for *F.*'s sake.   11:28
glorify God the *F.* of our.   15:6
            2 Cor 1:3; 11:31; *Eph* 1:3
                                1 Pet 1:3
but one God, the *F.*   *1 Cor* 8:6
up kingdom to God the *F.*   15:24
F. of mercies, the God.   *2 Cor* 1:3
I will be a *F.* unto you.   6:18
Paul an apostle by Jesus Christ and
    God the *F.*   *Gal* 1:1
peace from God the *F.* 3; *2 Tim* 1:2
                                Tit 1:4
will of God and our *F.*   *Gal* 1:4
until time appointed of the *F.*   4:2
Spirit into your hearts, crying, *F.* 6
our Lord Jesus, the *F.*   *Eph* 1:17
access by one Spirit to the *F.* 2:18
for this cause I bow unto *F.*   3:14
one God and *F.* of all.   4:6
giving thanks to the *F.*   5:20
                    Col 1:3, 12; 3:17
faith from God the *F.*   *Eph* 6:23
to the glory of the *F.*   *Phil* 2:11
as a son with the *f.* he hath.   22
it pleased *F.* that in him. *Col* 1:19
of the mystery of the *F.*   2:2
church which is in God *F. 1 Thes* 1:1
we charged you, as a *f.* doth. 2:11
entreat him as a *f.*   *1 Tim* 5:1
will be to him a *F.*   *Heb* 1:5
Melchisedec without *f.*   7:3
whom the *F.* chasteneth not?   12:7
be in subjection to *F.* of spirits. 9
good gift cometh from *F.* *Jas* 1:17
religion before God and *F.*   27
therewith bless God, even *F.*   3:9
foreknowledge of God *F. 1 Pet* 1:2
if ye call on the *F.* who.   17
received from God the *F. 2 Pet* 1:17
life, which was with *F.* *1 John* 1:2
our fellowship is with the *F.*   3

have an Advocate with the *F.*
        1 John 2:1
because ye have known the *F.* 13
the love of *F.* is not in him. 15
pride of life is not of the *F.* 16
he is antichrist that denieth *F.* 22
denieth the Son, hath not *F.*: he that
  acknowledgeth Son hath *F.* 23
continue in Son and in the *F.* 24
what manner of love *F.* hath. 3:1
three bear record, *F.* the Word. 5:7
the *F.* and from Lord Jesus Christ
  the Son of the *F.* *2 John* 3
a commandment from the *F.* 4
he that abideth in Christ hath *F.* 9
sanctified by God the *F.* *Jude* 1

see **Abraham**

her father

in and lay with her *F.* *Gen* 19:33
Rachel came with her *f.'s*. 29:9
her *f.'s* brother, told her *f.* 12
images that were her *f.'s*. 31:19
Tamar dwelt in her *f.'s*. 38:11
if her *f.* utterly refuse. *Ex* 22:17
she profaneth her *f.* *Lev* 21:9
returned to her *f.'s* house as in youth,
  shall eat of her *f.'s* meat. 22:13
her *f.* had but spit in. *Num* 12:14
woman vow a vow in her *f.'s*. 30:3
and her *f.* hear her, and shall hold. 4
if her *f.* disallow her in the day. 5
her youth, in her *f.'s* house. 16
wife to one of tribe of her *f.* 36:8
bewail her *f.* and mother a month.
        Deut 21:13
to door of her *f.'s* house, to play
  whore in her *f.'s* house. 22:21
brought Rahab and her *f. Josh.* 6:23
he saved her *f.'s* household. 25
to ask of her *f.* a field. 15:18
        Judg 1:14
months returned to her *f. Judg* 11:39
but her *f.* would not suffer. 15:1
Philistines burnt her and her *f.* 6
brought him into her *f.'s*. 19:3
when her *f.* and *mother*. *Esth* 2:7

his father

shall a man leave his *f.* and mother.
  Gen 2:24; *Mark* 10:7; *Eph* 5:31
saw nakedness of his *f.* *Gen* 9:23
Haran died before his *f.* 11:28
blessing wherewith his *f.* 27:41
Jacob obeyed his *f.* and. 28:7
Jacob sware by fear of his *f.* 31:53
in the land wherein his *f.* 37:1
Joseph brought to his *f.* their. 2
told the dream to his *f.* his *f.* 10
brethren envied, but his *f.* 11
rid him, to deliver him to his *f.* 22
the lad cannot leave his *f.* 44:22
sacrifices to the God of his *f.* 46:1
went up to meet Israel his *f.* 29
Joseph nourished his *f.* and. 47:12
made a mourning for his *f.* 50:10
Amram took his *f.'s* sister. *Ex* 6:20
he that smiteth his *f.* shall. 21:15
curseth his *f.* shall die. 17; *Lev* 20:9
fear every man his mother and his *f.*
        Lev 19:3
man that lieth with his *f.'s*. 20:11
if a man take his *f.'s* daughter. 17
of Aaron be defiled for his *f.* 21:2
priest not defile himself for his *f.* 11
Nazarite not unclean for his *f.*
        Num 6:7
inheritance to his *f.'s*. 27:10
if his *f.* have no brethren. 11
will not obey his *f.* *Deut* 21:18
his *f.* bring him to the elders. 19
man shall not take his *f.* 22:30
he that setteth light by his *f.* 27:16
lieth with daughter of his *f.* 33:9
said to his *f.* I have not seen. 33:9
Gideon feared his *f.'s. Judg* 6:27
buried in sepulchre of his *f.* 8:32
wickedness he did to his *f.* 9:56
his *f.* knew not that it was of. 14:4
Jonathan told not his *f.* 1 *Sam* 14:1
heard not when his *f.* charged. 27
spake good of David to his *f.* 19:4
it was determined of his *f.* 20:33
because his *f.* had done shame. 34
in sepulchre of his *f.* *2 Sam* 2:32

I will be his *f.* and he. *2 Sam* 7:14
as his *f.* shewed kindness. 10:2
        1 Chr 19:2
Absalom went in unto his *f.'s*.
        2 Sam 16:22
Ahithophel buried in sepulchre of his
  f. 17:23
Saul buried in sepulchre of his *f.*
        21:14
his *f.* was a man of Tyre. *1 Ki* 7:14
        2 Chr 2:14
his *f.* had dedicated. *1 Ki* 7:51
  15:15; *2 Chr* 15:18
as heart of David his *f.* *1 Ki* 11:4
Solomon went not fully after Lord,
  as did David his *f.* 6; 15:11
not as did David his *f.* *1 Ki* 11:33
      2 Ki 14:3; 16:2
walked in all sins of his *f. 1 Ki* 15:3
Nadab did evil and walked in way of
  his *f.* 26; 22:43, 52; *2 Ki* 21:21
did evil, not like his *f.* *2 Ki* 3:2
together after Ahab his *f.* 9:25
cities taken out of hand of his *f.*
        13:25
son of Joash, slew servants who had
  slain his *f.* 14:5; *2 Chr* 25:3
king instead of his *f.* *2 Ki* 14:21
  23:30, 34
Reuben defiled his *f.'s*. *1 Chr* 5:1
I will be his *f.* he shall. 17:13; 28:6
not firstborn, yet his *f.* 26:10
appeared to David his *f. 2 Chr* 3:1
to order of David his *f.* 8:14
walked in first ways of his *f.* 17:3
Jehoshaphat sought God of his *f.* 4
walked in way of Asa his *f.* 20:32
counsellors after death of his *f.* 22:4
in ways of David his *f.* 34:2, 3
heareth instruction of his *f. Pr* 13:1
fool despiseth his *f.'s* instruction.
        15:5
foolish son is a grief to his *f.* 17:25
foolish son calamity of his *f.* 19:13
he that wasteth his *f.*, is a son. 26
whoso curseth his *f.* his lamp. 20:20
of riotous men shameth his *f.* 28:7
whoso robbeth his *f.* or mother. 24
wisdom, rejoiceth his *f.* 29:3
ravens pick out eye that mocketh his
  f. 30:17
to him that saith to his *f. Isa* 45:10
a son that seeth his *f.'s. Ezek* 18:14
not die for iniquity of his *f.* 17
as for his *f.* because he cruelly. 18
bring golden vessels his *f. Dan* 5:2
a man and his *f.* go in to. *Amos* 2:7
his *f.* and mother shall. *Zech* 13:3
a son honours his *f. a.* *Mal* 1:6
at variance against his *f. Mat* 10:35
whoso shall say to his *f.* it. 15:5
        Mark 7:11
and honour not his *f.* or. *Mat* 15:6
of man come in glory of his *F.* 16:27
      Mark 8:38; *Luke* 9:26
did the will of his *f.?* *Mat* 21:31
he asked his *f.* how ? *Mark* 9:21
him the throne of his *f.* *Luke* 1:32
called him after name of his *f.* 59
they made signs unto his *f.* 62
his *f.* Zacharias was filled with. 67
Jesus delivered him to his *f.* 9:42
to me, and hate not his *f.* 14:26
younger of them said to his *f.* 15:12
arose and came to his *f.* he *f.* saw. 20
therefore came his *f.* and. 28
said, God was his *F.* *John* 5:18
but his *f.* was a Greek. *Acts* 16:1
have his *f.'s* wife. *1 Cor* 5:1
was yet in loins of his *f.* *Heb* 7:10
priests to God and his *F.* *Rev* 1:6
his *F.'s* name written in. 14:1

see **house**

my father

yesternight with my *f.* *Gen* 19:34
she is daughter of my *f.* not. 20:12
my *f.* peradventure will feel. 27:12
bless me, even me also, O my *f.* 34
the God of my *f.* 31:5, 42; 32:9
        Ex 18:4
came to thy servant my *f.*
      Gen 44:24, 27, 30

surety for the lad to my *f. Gen* 44:32
doth my *f.* yet live ? 45:3
haste to go up to my *f.* 9
tell my *f.* 13
my *f.* and brethren are come. 47:1
not so, my *f.* for this is. 48:18
ready to perish my *f.* *Deut* 26:5
will save alive my *f.* *Josh* 2:13
my *f.* fought for you. *Judg* 9:17
my *f.* if thou hast opened. 11:36
not told it my *f.* nor my. 14:16
lest my *f.* leave caring. *1 Sam* 9:5
my *f.* troubled the land. 14:29
and what is my *f.'s* family ? 18:18
Saul my *f.* seeketh to kill. 19:2
I will commune with my *f.* of thee. 3
my *f.* will do nothing, but he. 20:2
as he hath been with my *f.* 13
let my *f.* and my mother be. 22:3
hand of Saul my *f.* shall not. 28:17
the kingdom of my *f.* *2 Sam* 16:3
buried by grave of my *f.* 19:37
ark of Lord before David my *f.* in all
  wherein my *f.* was. *1 Ki* 2:26
my *f.* David not knowing. 32
that thou didst to David my *f.* 44
thou hast shewed to David my *f.* 3:6
thy servant king instead of my *f.* 7
David my *f.* could not build. 5:3
Lord spake to David my *f.* saying. 5
in the heart of David my *f.* to. 8:17
kept with thy servant David my *f.* 24
let my word be verified to my *f.* 26
        2 Chr 6:16
shall be thicker than my *f.'s.* loins.
  1 Ki 12:10; *2 Chr* 10:10
my *f.* did lade you with. *1 Ki* 12:11
        2 Chr 10:11
my *f.* chastised you. *1 Ki* 12:14
        2 Chr 10:14
league between my *f.* *1 Ki* 15:19
        2 Chr 16:3
kiss my *f.* and mother. *1 Ki* 19:20
cities my *f.* took I will. 20:34
saw it, cried, my *f.* my *f. 2 Ki* 2:12
my *f.* shall I smite them ? 6:21
my *f.* my *f.* the chariot of. 13:14
chose me before house of my *f.* and
  among sons of my *f.* *1 Chr* 28:4
didst deal with my *f.* *2 Chr* 2:3
of my *f.'s* sepulchres. *Neh* 2:3
send me to city of my *f.'s*. 5
corruption, thou art my *f. Job* 17:14
my *f.* and my mother. *Ps* 27:10
cry unto me, thou art my *F.* 89:26
for I was my *f.'s* son. *Pr* 4:3
knowledge to cry, my *f.* *Isa* 8:4
stock, thou art my *f.* *Jer* 2:27
not cry unto me, my *f.?* 3:4, 19
who brought tidings to my *f.* 20:15
whom my *f.* brought out. *Dan* 5:13
doeth the will of my *F.* *Mat* 7:21
        12:50
go and bury my *f.* 8:21; *Luke* 9:59
I confess before my *F.* *Mat* 10:32
him will I deny before my *F.* 33
are delivered to me of my *F.* 11:27
        Luke 10:22
plant my heavenly *F.* *Mat* 15:13
my *F.* who is in heaven. 16:17
angels behold face of my *F.* 18:10
it shall be done of my *F.* 19
so shall my heavenly *F.* also. 35
whom prepared of my *F.* 20:23
no man but my *F.* only. 24:36
come ye blessed of my *F.* 25:34
new with you in my *F.'s*. 26:29
O my *F.* if it be possible, let. 39
my *F.* if this cup may not pass. 42
thinkest I cannot pray to my *F.?* 53
must be about my *F.'s. Luke* 2:49
many hired servants of my *f.* 15:17
arise, and go to my *f.* and say, *f.* 18
send him to my *f.'s* house. 16:27
as my *F.* hath appointed. 22:29
I send the promise of my *F.* 24:49
my *F.* worketh hitherto. *John* 5:17
but the will of my *F.* 30
I am come in my *F.'s* name. 43
my *F.* giveth you true bread. 6:32
except it be given of my *F.* 65
neither know me, nor my *F.* 8:19
my *F.* hath taught me, I speak. 28
which I have seen with my *F.* 38

but I honour *my* F. and ye.
     John 8:49
it is *my* F. that honoureth me. 54
therefore doth *my* F. love. 10:17
commandment received of *my* F. 18
works I do in *my* F.'s name bear. 25
my F. who gave them, none is able
 to pluck them out of *my* F.'s. 29
I and *my* F. are one.   30
works I shewed from *my* F. 32
if I do not works of *my* F. 37
me, him will *my* F. honour. 12:26
should have known *my* F. 14:7
because I go to *my* F. 12; 16:10
know that I am in *my* F. 14:20
loveth me, be loved of *my* F. 21, 23
my F. is greater than I.   28
I am the vi~e, *my* F. is the. 15:1
herein is *my* F. glorified.   8
kept *my* F.'s commandments. 10
all that I heard of *my* F. I have. 15
hateth me, hateth *my* F. 23, 24
the cup *my* F. hath given. 18:11
for I am not yet ascended to *my* F.
 I ascend to *my* F. and. 20:17
as *my* F. hath sent me.   21
as I received of *my* F. *Rev* 2:27
confess his name before *my* F. 3:5

our **father**

our f. is old.   *Gen* 19:31
make *our* f. drink wine.   32
away all that was *our* f.'s. 31:1, 16
youngest is this day with *our* f.
     42:13, 32
thy servant *our* f. is in. 43:28
bring *our* f. with sorrow. 44:31
our f. died in wilderness. *Num* 27:3
why should the name of *our* f.? 4
God of Israel *our* F. *1 Chr* 29:10
thou art *our* F., Abraham. *Isa* 63:16
O Lord, thou art *our* F.   64:8
our f. commanded us. *Jer* 35:6
obeyed the voice of *our* f. 8, 10
our F. which art in heaven.
   Mat 6:9; *Luke* 11:2
kingdom of *our* f. David. *Mark* 11:10
sware to *our* f. Abraham. *Luke* 1:73
we have Abraham to *our* f. 3:8
art thou greater than *our* f.?
   John 4:12; 8:53
of glory appeared to *our* f. *Acts* 7:2
and peace from God *our* F. *Rom* 1:7
 1 Cor 1:3; *2 Cor* 1:2; *2 Thes* 1:2
  1 Tim 1:2; *Philem* 3
even by *our* f. Isaac. *Rom* 9:10
will of God, and *our* F. *Gal* 1:4
peace from God *our* F. *Eph* 1:2
 Phil 1:2; *Col* 1:2; *1 Thes* 1:1
unto God *our* F. be. *Phil* 4:20
sight of God and *our* F. *1 Thes* 1:3
now God *our* F. direct our. 3:11
you in holiness before *our* F. 13
Paul unto church in God *our* F.
    2 Thes 1:1
now God, even *our* F. comfort. 2:16

their **father**

nakedness of *their* f. and saw not
 nakedness of *their* f. *Gen* 9:23
made *their* f. drink wine. 19:33
daughters with child by *their* f. 36
went to feed *their* f.'s flock. 37:12
to water *their* f.'s flock. *Ex* 2:16
anoint them as thou didst *their* f.
     40:15
to the tribe of *their* f. *Num* 36:6
after Dan *their* f. *Josh* 19:47
    Judg 18:29
to voice of *their* f. *1 Sam* 2:25
one said, who is *their* f.? 10:12
prophet's sons told *their* f.*1 Ki* 13:11
Ephraim *their* f. *1 Chr* 7:22
died before *their* f. 25:3, 6
their f. gave them gifts. *2 Chr* 21:3
their f. gave inheritance. *Job* 42:15
a generation that curseth *their* f.
    Pr 30:11
consolation for *their* f. *Jer* 16:7
Jonadab's sons obeyed *their* f.'s.
    35:14, 16
their f.'s nakedness. *Ezek* 22:10
ship with Zebedee *their* f. *Mat* 4:21
they left ship and *their* f. and. 22

shine in kingdom of *their* f.
    Mat 13:43

thy **father**

thee from *thy* f.'s house. *Gen* 12:1
I heard *thy* f. speak to Esau. 27:6
thou shalt bring it to *thy* f. 10
remain a widow at *thy* f.'s. 38:11
I am the God of *thy* f., fear. 46:3
by the God of *thy* f. 49:25
the blessings of *thy* f. have. 26
thy f. commanded before he. 50:16
forgive servants of God of *thy* f. 17
honour *thy* f. and mother. *Ex* 20:12
 Deut 5:16; *Mat* 15:4; 19:19
brethren of tribe of *thy* f. *Num* 18:2
God of *thy* f. promised. *Deut* 6:3
is not he *thy* f.?   32:6
ask *thy* f. and he will shew thee. 7
hast left *thy* f. and. *Ruth* 2:11
is my sin before *thy* f.? *1 Sam* 20:1
if *thy* f. miss me, then say. 6
chose me before *thy* f. *2 Sam* 6:21
David doth honour *thy* f. that he sent
 comforters to ? 10:3; *1 Chr* 19:3
served in *thy* f.'s presence.
    2 Sam 16:19
do it for David *thy* f.'s. *1 Ki* 11:12
thy f. made yoke grievous. 12:4, 10
    2 Chr 10:4
a league between my father and *thy*
 f.   *1 Ki* 15:19
cities my father took from *thy* f.
    20:34
thee to prophets of *thy* f. *2 Ki* 3:13
Lord, the God of David *thy* f. 20:5
 2 Chr 21:12; *Isa* 38:5
know thou the God of *thy* f.
    1 Chr 28:9
walk before me as *thy* f. *2 Chr* 7:17
aged men elder than *thy* f. *Job* 15:10
instruction of *thy* f. *Pr* 1:8; 23:22
keep *thy* f.'s commandment. 6:20
thy f. and mother be glad. 23:25
thine own and *thy* f.'s. friend. 27:10
thy first f. hath sinned. *Isa* 43:27
thee with heritage of *thy* f. 58:14
house of *thy* f. dealt. *Jer* 12:6
did not *thy* f. eat, drink, and ? 22:15
of *thy* f. was an Amorite. *Ezek* 16:3
thy f. the king, *thy* f. *Dan* 5:11
God gave *thy* f. a kingdom. 18
thy F. which seeth. *Mat* 6:4, 6, 18
shut *thy* door, pray to *thy* F. 6
honour *thy* f. and mother. *Mark* 7:10
 10:19; *Luke* 18:20; *Eph* 6:2
thy f. and I sought. *Luke* 2:48
thy f. hath killed the fatted. 15:27
said they, where is *thy* f.? *John* 8:19

your **father**

power I served *your* f. *Gen* 31:6
your f. hath deceived me. 7
is *your* f. alive ?   43:7
you up in peace to *your* f. 44:17
you wagons, bring *your* f. 45:19
hearken unto Israel *your* f. 49:2
obeyed Jonadab *your* f. *Jer* 35:18
your f. an Amorite. *Ezek* 16:45
may glorify *your* F. who. *Mat* 5:16
may be children of *your* F. 45
be ye perfect, as *your* F. in. 48
have no reward of *your* F. 6:1
your F. knoweth what things ye.
   8, 32; *Luke* 12:30
forgive, *your* heavenly F. *Mat* 6:14
if ye forgive not, neither will *your* f.
   15; *Mark* 11:25, 26
sparrow fall without *your* F.
    Mat 10:29
it is not the will of *your* F. 18:14
call no man *your* f. upon earth, one is
 your F. which is in heaven. 23:9
your F. also is merciful. *Luke* 6:36
it is *your* F.'s pleasure to. 12:32
have seen with *your* f. *John* 8:38
ye do the deeds of *your* f. then. 41
if God were *your* F. ye would. 42
ye are of *your* f. the devil, the lusts
 of *your* f. ye will do. 44
I ascend to my Father and *your* F.
    20:17

father-in-law

thy f.-*in-law* goeth to Timnath.
    Gen 38:13

she went to her f.-*in-law*. *Gen* 38:25
flock of Jethro his f.-*in-law*.
    Ex 3:1; 4:18
Moses' f.-*in-law*. 18:1, 8, 14, 17
   Judg 1:16*; 4:11*
let his f.-*in-law* depart. *Ex* 18:27
Raguel, Moses' f.-*in-law*.
    Num 10:29
f.-*in-law* retained him. *Judg* 19:4
rose to depart, his f.-*in-law* urged. 7
f.-*in-law* was dead. *1 Sam* 4:19, 21
Annas was f.-*in-law* to. *John* 18:13

fatherless

not afflict any f. child. *Ex* 22:22
be widows, and children f. 24
execute the judgement of the f. and.
 Deut 10:18; *Ps* 82:3; *Isa* 1:17
ye overwhelm the f. and *Job* 6:27
the arms of the f. have been. 22:9
they drive away the ass of f. 24:3
pluck the f. from the breast. 9
delivered the poor and the f. 29:12
eaten alone, and f. have not. 31:17
lifted up my hand against the f. 21
art the helper of the f. *Ps* 10:14
to judge the f. and the oppressed. 18
a father of the f. a judge of. 68:5
let his children be f.   109:9
nor any favour his f. children. 12
not into fields of the f. *Pr* 23:10
judge not the f. *Isa* 1:23; *Jer* 5:28
not have mercy on their f. *Isa* 9:17
that they may rob the f. 10:2
leave thy f. children. *Jer* 49:11
we are orphans and f. *Lam* 5:3
have they vexed the f. *Ezek* 22:7
in thee f. findeth mercy. *Hos* 14:3
those that oppress the f. *Mal* 3:5
pure religion to visit f. and. *Jas* 1:27

fatherless with *stranger*

the *stranger*, the f., the widow come.
 Deut 14:29; 24:19, 20, 21; 26:12, 13
stranger and f. rejoice. 16:11, 14
judgement of *stranger* nor f. 24:17
judgement of *stranger* and f. 27:19
they slay *stranger*, murder the f.
    Ps 94:6
preserveth *strangers* and f. 146:9
oppressed not *stranger*, f. and.
 Jer 7:6; 22:3; *Zech* 7:10

fathers

heads of their f.' houses. *Ex* 6:14, 25
 Josh 14:1; 19:51; 21:1
   1 Chr 8:10, 13, 28
thy father, nor thy f. *Ex* 10:6
iniquity of the f. upon the. 20:5
 34:7; *Num* 14:18; *Deut* 5:9
f. shall not be put to death ... for f.
   Deut 24:16; *2 Ki* 14:6
whose f. I would have. *Job* 30:1
and riches inheritance of f. *Pr* 19:14
kings be thy nursing f. *Isa* 49:23
f. and sons shall fall. *Jer* 6:21; 13:14
children gather wood, f. 7:18
f. eaten sour grapes. 31:29
   Ezek 18:2
iniquity of the f. on. *Jer* 32:18
the f. shall not look back to. 47:3
f. shall eat the sons in. *Ezek* 5:10
the f. to children, and children to f.
   Mal 4:6; *Luke* 1:17
not of Moses, but of the f. *John* 7:22
and f. hearken. *Acts* 7:2; 22:1
promise made unto the f. 13:32
of the law of the f. 22:3
whose are the f. of whom. *Rom* 9:5
yet have not many f. *1 Cor* 4:15
f. provoke not children. *Eph* 6:4
   Col 3:21
in times past to the f. *Heb* 1:1
we had f. of our flesh who. 12:9
since the f. fell asleep. *2 Pet* 3:4
I write unto you f. *1 John* 2:13, 14
 see **buried, chief**

his **fathers**

removed his idols *his* f. *1 Ki* 15:12
the things *his* f. had. *2 Ki* 12:18
did what was evil as *his* f. 15:9
forsook Lord God of *his* f. 21:22
   2 Chr 21:10
according to all *his* f. had done.
   2 Ki 23:32, 37; 24:9

like burning of his f.   2 Chr 21:19
Ahaz provoked God of his f.   28:25
heart to seek God of his f.   30:19
himself before God of his f.   33:12
to generation of his f.   Ps 49:19
let the iniquity of his f. be.   109:14
do what his f. have not.   Dan 11:24
regard the God of his f.   37
and a god whom his f. knew not. 38
David was laid to his f.   Acts 13:36

my **fathers**
to the years of my f.   Gen 47:9
I will lie with my f.   30
the name of my f. be named.   48:16
bury me with my f. in the.   49:29
he is my f.' God, I will.   Ex 15:2
no better than my f.   1 Ki 19:4
inheritance of my f. to thee.   21:3, 4
have gods delivered them my f.?
2 Ki 19:12; 2 Chr 32:14; Isa 37:12
not what I and my f.   2 Chr 32:13
sojourner as all my f.   Ps 39:12
praise thee, O God of my f. Dan 2:23
worship I God of my f.   Acts 24:14
of traditions of my f.   Gal 1:14

our **fathers**
now both we and also our f.
Gen 46:34; 47:3
how our f. went down.   Num 20:15
not covenant with our f.   Deut 5:3
land which he sware to our f.   6:23
26:3, 15
cried to the God of our f.   26:7
pattern of altar our f.   Josh 22:28
brought our f. out of Egypt.   24:17
miracles which our f. told of ?
Judg 6:13
with us, as with our f.   1 Ki 8:57
which he commanded our f.   58
because our f. have not. 2 Ki 22:13
the God of our f. look.   1 Chr 12:17
sojourners, as were all our f. 29:15
Lord God of our f. keep in thoughts
of thy people.   18; 2 Chr 20:6
thou gavest our f.   2 Chr 6:31
Neh 9:36
for our f. have trespassed. 2 Chr 29:6
our f. have fallen by the sword.   9
our f. have not kept word of. 34:21
our f. provoked God.   Ezra 5:12
blessed be the God of our f.   7:27
since the days of our f. in a.   9:7
affliction of our f. in Egypt. Neh 9:9
our f. dealt proudly, and.   16
our f. trusted in thee.   Ps 22:4
our f. have told us.   41:1; 78:3
we have sinned with our f.   106:6
our f. understood not thy wonders. 7
where our f. praised thee. Isa 64:11
devoured labour of our f.   Jer 3:24
we and our f. have not obeyed.   25
our f. have inherited lies.   16:19
have done, we and our f.   44:17
our f. have sinned, and.   Lam 5:7
confusion of face to our f.   Dan 9:8
our sins and iniquities of our f.   16
sworn to our f. from.   Mi 7:20
the covenant of our f.   Mal 2:10
had been in days of our f. Mat 23:30
as he spake to our f.   Luke 1:55
mercy promised to our f.   72
our f. worshipped in.   John 4:20
our f. did eat manna in the.   6:31
God of our f. hath glorified his Son.
Acts 3:13
covenant God made with our f.   25
God of our f. raised up Jesus.   5:30
our f. found no sustenance.   7:11
Jacob died, and our f.   15
and evil entreated our f. and.   19
spake in Sinai and with our f.   38
to whom our f. would not obey.   39
our f. had the tabernacle of.   44
God of Israel chose our f.   13:17
a yoke which our f. nor we.   15:10
promise made to our f.   26:6
spake Holy Ghost to our f.   28:25
our f. were under cloud. 1 Cor 10:1

slept with **fathers**
David slept with his f.   1 Ki 2:10
11:21
Solomon slept with his f.   2:43
2 Chr 9:31

Jeroboam *slept with* f.   1 Ki 14:20
2 Ki 14:29
Rehoboam *slept with* f.   1 Ki 14:31
2 Chr 12:16
Abijam *slept with* his f.   1 Ki 15:8
2 Chr 14:1
Asa *slept with* his f.   1 Ki 15:24
2 Chr 16:13
so Baasha *slept with* f.   1 Ki 16:6
Omri *slept with* f.   28
Ahab *slept with* f.   22:40
Jehoshaphat *slept with* f.   50
2 Chr 21:1
Joram *slept with* his f.   2 Ki 8:24
Jehu *slept with* his f.   10:35
Jehoahaz *slept with* his f.   13:9
Joash *slept with* his f.   13; 14:16
that the king *slept with* his f. 14:22
2 Chr 26:2
Azariah *slept with* his f.   2 Ki 15:7
Menahem *slept with* his f.   22
Jotham *slept with* f. 38; 2 Chr 27:9
Ahaz *slept with* his f.   2 Ki 16:20
2 Chr 28:27
Hezekiah *slept with* f.   2 Ki 20:21
2 Chr 32:33
Manasseh *slept with* f.   2 Ki 21:18
2 Chr 33:20
Jehoiakim *slept with* f.   2 Ki 24:6
Uzziah *slept with* f. 2 Chr 26:23

their **fathers**
God of their f. hath.   Ex 4:5
heads of their f. 6:14, 25; Josh 14:1
19:51; 21:1; 1 Chr 5:24; 7:2, 7
8:6; 9:9, 13
in iniquity of their f.   Lev 26:39
confess iniquity of their f.   40
land thou swarest to give to their f.
Num 11:12; 14:23; Deut 10:11
31:20; Josh 1:6; 5:6; 21:43, 44
Jer 32:22
the covenant of their f. Deut 29:25
children ask their f.   Josh 4:6, 21
head of house of their f.   Judg 2:10
forsook the Lord God of their f.   12
turned out of way their f. walked. 17
corrupted more than their f.   19
covenant I commanded their f.   20
keep way of Lord, as their f.   22
which he commanded their f.   3:4
again to land thou gavest to their f.
1 Ki 8:34, 48; 2 Chr 6:25, 38
their f. out of Egypt.   1 Ki 9:9
of land he gave to their f.   14:15
2 Ki 21:8; Jer 16:15; 24:10
above all that their f.   1 Ki 14:22
since day their f. came.   2 Ki 21:15
house of their f. increased greatly.
1 Chr 4:38
against God of their f.   5:25
blessed the God of their f.   29:20
forsook God of their f.   2 Chr 7:22
24:24; 28:6
sacrifice to God of their f.   11:16
relied on Lord God of their f.   13:18
to seek God of their f. 14:4; 15:12
them to the God of their f.   19:4
hearts to God of their f.   20:33
trespassed against God of their f.
30:7
confession to God of their f.   22
covenant of God of their f.   34:32
following the God of their f.   33
God of their f. sent by his.   36:15
confessed sins of their f.   Neh 9:2
into land promisedst to their f.   23
to the search of their f.   Job 8:8
men have told from their f.   15:18
as their f. a stubborn.   Ps 78:8
things did he in sight of their f.   12
dealt unfaithfully like their f.   57
of children are like their f.   Pr 17:6
for iniquity of their f.   Isa 14:21
did worse than their f.   Jer 7:26
after Baalim, which their f.   9:14
whom they nor their f. have. 16; 19:4
covenant I made with their f.
11:10; 31:32; Heb 8:9
as their f. have forgotten.   23:27
against Lord, hope of their f. Jer 50:7
they and their f. have.   Ezek 2:3
eat sons, and sons eat their f.   5:10

know abominations of their f.
Ezek 20:4
eyes were after their f.' idols.   24
which their f. walked.   Amos 2:4
heart of children to their f. Mal 4:6
like manner did their f.   Luke 6:23
for so did their f. to the false.   26

thy **fathers**
go to thy f. in peace.   Gen 15:15
thy f.' children shall bow.   49:8
land which he sware to thy f.
Ex 13:5, 11; Deut 6:10, 18; 7:12
13; 8:18; 9:5; 13:17; 19:8; 28:11
29:13; 30:20
it, as God of thy f. said. Deut 1:21
nor forget covenant of thy f.   4:31
because he loved thy f.   37; 10:15
with manna which thou knewest not,
neither did thy f.   8:3, 16
thy f. went into Egypt.   10:22
the God of thy f. giveth thee.   12:1
gods thou nor thy f.   13:6; 28:64
land he promised thy f.   19:8; 27:3
nation thou nor thy f. have.   28:36
multiply thee above thy f.   30:5
rejoice over thee, as over thy f.   9
sleep with thy f. 31:16; 2 Sam 7:12
to sepulchre of thy f.   1 Ki 13:22
what thy f. laid up.   2 Ki 20:17
I will gather thee to thy f.   22:20
2 Chr 34:28
go to be with thy f.   1 Chr 17:11
book of records of thy f.   Ezra 4:15
instead of thy f. shall be.   Ps 45:16
not land-mark thy f. set.   Pr 22:28
with burnings of thy f.   Jer 34:5
I am God of thy f. the.   Acts 7:32

your **fathers**
you to land of your f.   Gen 48:21
God of your f. sent me.   Ex 3:13
Deut 1:11; 4:1; Josh 18:3
2 Chr 28:9; 29:5
did your f.   Num 32:8; Neh 13:18
risen up in your f.' stead. Num 32:14
land Lord sware to your f. Deut 1:8
35; 7:8; 8:1; 11:9, 21; Judg 2:1
sacrificed to gods whom your f.
Deut 32:17
your f. dwelt on other.   Josh 24:2
I brought your f. out of Egypt.   6
put away gods your f. served.   14
the gods which your f. served.   15
did to you and your f. 1 Sam 12:7
your f. cried, Lord brought your f. 8
Lord against you as against your f. 15
I commanded your f.   2 Ki 17:13
fight not against God of your f.
2 Chr 13:12
not like your f. and brethren. 30:7, 8
Zech 1:4
of land appointed for your f.
2 Chr 33:8
offering to God of your f. Ezra 8:28
confession to God of your f.   10:11
when your f. tempted me.   Ps 95:9
Heb 3:9
and iniquities of your f.   Isa 65:7
what iniquity have your f.? Jer 2:5
to land I have given to your f.   3:18
dwell in land I gave to your f.   7:7
14; 23:39; 25:5; 35:15
Ezek 20:42; 36:28; 47:14
I spake not to your f. in.   Jer 7:22
since the day your f. came.   22
I commanded your f.   11:4; 17:22
earnestly protested unto your f. 11:7
your f. have forsaken me.   16:11
done worse than your f.   12
ye nor your f.   13
made covenant with your f.   34:13
but your f. hearkened not unto.   14
not, neither they nor your f.   44:3
forgotten wickedness of your f.? 9
I set before you and your f.   10
the incense ye, your f. and.   21
not in statutes of your f. Ezek 20:18
in this your f. have blasphemed.   27
polluted after manner of your f.? 30
like as I pleaded with your f.
in land wherein your f. dwelt. 37:25
I saw your f. as the first. Hos 9:10
been in days of your f.? Joel 1:2
displeased with your f.   Zech 1:2

be not as your f.   Zech 1:4
your f. where are they?   5
my words take hoid of your f.?   6
when your f. provoked me to.   8:14
from days of your f.   Mal 3:7
the measure of your f.   Mat 23:32
prophets, and your f.   Luke 11:47
ye allow the deeds of your f.   48
your f. did eat manna.   John 6:49
not as your f. did eat manna.   58
ye resist Holy Ghost as your f. did.
                              Acts 7:51
who of prophets have not your f.? 52
by tradition from your f. 1 Pet 1:18

fathoms
twenty f. again fifteen f. Acts 27:28

fatling
calf, young lion, and f.   Isa 11:6

fatlings
Agag and best of the f. 1 Sam 15:9
sacrificed oxen and f.   2 Sam 6:13
offer burnt sacrifices of f. Ps 66:15
all of them f. of Bashan. Ezek 39:18
my oxen and my f. are.   Mat 22:4

fatness
God give thee of f. of.   Gen 27:28
thy dwelling shall be the f. of.   39
thick and covered with f. Deut 32:15
should I leave my f.?   Judg 9:9
his face with his f.   Job 15:27
thy table should be full of f.   36:16
be satisfied with the f.   Ps 36:8
as with marrow and f.   63:5
all thy paths drop f.   65:11
eyes stand out with f.   73:7
my flesh faileth of f.   109:24
f. of his flesh wax lean. Isa 17:4
sword of Lord is made fat with f.
                              34:6
dust shall be made ...t with f.   7
let your soul delight its... n f. 55:2
the soul of priests with f. Jer 31:14
with them partakest of f. Rom 11:17

fats
(Revisions, vats)
the f. shall overflow with. Joel 2:24
press is full, the f. overflow.   3:13

fatted
oxen, harts, f. fowl.   1 Ki 4:23
hired men are like f.   Jer 46:21*
see calf
fatter, see countenances

fattest
wrath of God slew the f. Ps 78:31
shall enter on f. places. Dan 11:24

fault, -s
I remember my f. this.   Gen 41:9
f. is in thine own people. Ex 5:16
be beaten according to f. Deut 25:2*
I have found no f. in.   1 Sam 29:3
me this day with f.   2 Sam 3:8
cleanse me from secret f. Ps 19:12
and prepare without my f.   59:4
find no occasion or f.   Dan 6:4
if thy brother trespass, tell him his f.
                              Mat 18:15
they found f.   Mark 7:2
I find no f. in this man. Luke 23:4
   14; John 18:38*: 19:4, 6*
why doth he yet find f.?   Rom 9:19
now there is utterly a f. 1 Cor 6:7*
man be overtaken in a f.   Gal 6:1*
finding f. with them, he. Heb 8:8
confess your f. one to.   Jas 5:16*
be buffeted for your f. 1 Pet 2:20*
without f. before throne. Rev 14:5*

faultless
first covenant had been f. Heb 8:7
is able to present you f. Jude 24

faulty
doth speak as one which is f.
                          2 Sam 14:13*
shall they be found f.   Hos 10:2*

favour
gave Joseph f. in sight of. Gen 39:21
f. in sight of the Egyptians, not go
empty.   Ex 3:21; 11:3; 12:36
which shall not shew f. Deut 28:50
O Naphtali, satisfied with f.   33:23
that they might have no f. Josh 11:20

Samuel was in f. with.   1 Sam 2:26
granted me life and f.   Job 10:12†
with f. wilt compass him.   Ps 5:12
his f. is life, weeping may.   30:5
thy f. thou hast made mountain to. 7
thou hadst a f. unto them.   44:3
even rich shall entreat thy f. 45:12
in thy f. horn shall be exalted. 89:17
remember me with the f.   Ps 106:4
a good man sheweth f. and. 112:5*
I entreated thy f. with my.   119:58
seeketh good procureth f. Pr 11:27
good understanding giveth f. 13:15
among the righteous there is f. 14:9*
king's f. is toward a wise.   35
his f. is as a cloud of the.   16:15
many will entreat the f. of.   19:6
the king's f. is as dew upon.   12
his neighbour findeth no f.   21:10
loving f. rather to be chosen. 22:1
may seek the ruler's f.   29:26
f. is deceitful, beauty is vain. 31:30†
race not to swift, nor f.   Eccl 9:11
f. be shewed to wicked.   Isa 26:10
them will shew them no f.   27:11
but in my f. have I had.   60:10
I will not shew you f.   Jer 16:13
had brought Daniel into f. Dan 1:9†
Jesus increased in f.   Luke 2:52
having f. with all people. Acts 2:47
God gave Moses f. in sight of. 7:10
high priest desired f. against. 25:3

find, or found favour
have found f. in thy sight. Gen 18:3
   30:27; Num 11:15; 1 Sam 20:29
   Neh 2:5; Esth 5:8; 7:3; 8:5
have I not found f.?   Num 11:11
to pass she find no f.   Deut 24:1
let me find f. in thy sight. Ruth 2:13
David hath found f. in. 1 Sam 16:22
let the young men find f. in.   25:8
shall find f. in eyes of. 2 Sam 15:25
Hadad found f. in sight. 1 Ki 11:19
so shalt thou find f. in.   Pr 3:4
shall find more f. than he.   28:23
as one that found f.   S of S 8:10*
hast found f. with God.   Luke 1:30
David found f. before.   Acts 7:46

obtain, or obtained favour
Esther obtained f.   Esth 2:15, 17†
                                5:2
findeth me, shall obtain f. Pr 8:35
a good man obtaineth f. of.   12:2
findeth a wife, obtaineth f.   18:22

favour, verb
the lords f. thee not.   1 Sam 29:6
glad, that f. my righteous. Ps 35:27
the set time to f. her is.   102:13*
thy servants f. dust thereof.   14*
let any to f. his fatherless. 109:12*

favourable
be f. unto them for our. Judg 21:22*
and God will be f. unto.   Job 33:26
cast off, be f. no more?   Ps 77:7
thou hast been f. to thy land. 85:1

favoured
beautiful and well f.   Gen 29:17
Joseph was well f.   39:6
well f. kine.   41:2, 4, 18
of river ill f. kine.   3, 4, 19, 21, 27
they f. not the elders.   Lam 4:16
children well f. and.   Dan 1:4
whoredoms of well f. harlot. Nah 3:4
thou art highly f. Lord.   Luke 1:28

evil favouredness
bullock wherein any evil f. Deut 17:1

favourest
I know that thou f. me.   Ps 41:11*

favoureth
he that f. Joab, let him. 2 Sam 20:11

fear
(The fear of God means that
reverence for God which leads to
obedience because of one's realiza-
tion of his power, as well as of his
love to man)
the f. of you shall be.   Gen 9:2
except the f. of Isaac had.   31:42
Jacob sware by the f. of his.   53
f. and dread fall upon.   Ex 15:16*
I will send my f. before thee. 23:27*

I will put the f. of thee. Deut 2:25
Lord shall lay the f. of you.   11:25
Lord brought f. of him.   1 Chr 14:17
f. was on them because.   Ezra 3:3
them that put me in f.   Neh 6:14, 19
the f. of the Jews.   Esth 8:17; 9:2
f. of Mordecai fell on.   9:3
this thy f. thy confidence? Job 4:6
f. came upon me and trembling. 14
forsaketh f. of the Almighty. 6:14
let not his f. terrify me.   9:34*
yea, thou castest off f. and.   15:4
houses safe from f. nor.   21:9
snares round about, sudden f. 22:10
dominion and f. are with him. 25:2
he mocketh at f. and is not.   39:22
f. will I worship.   Ps 5:7
put them in f. O Lord.   9:20
there were they in great f.   14:5
a f. to mine acquaintance.   31:11
f. was on every side.   13*
f. took hold upon them.   48:6*
in f. where no f. was.   53:5
preserve my life from f. of.   64:1
to thy f. so is thy wrath.   90:11
f. of them fell upon them.   105:38
who is devoted to thy f.   119:38
mock when your f. cometh. Pr 1:26
your f. cometh as desolation.   27
shall be quiet from f. of evil. 33
be not afraid of sudden f. nor. 10:24
the f. of the wicked shall.   10:24
the f. of a king is as roaring. 20:2*
f. of man bringeth a snare.   29:25
his sword because of f.   S of S 3:8
not come the f. of briers. Isa 7:25
neither f. ye their f. nor.   8:12
the Lord, let him be your f. and. 13
give thee rest from thy f.   14:3*
of pleasure turned unto f.   21:4*
f. and the pit, and the snare. 24:17
that fleeth from f.   18; Jer 48:44
f. toward me is taught.   Isa 29:13
our heart from thy f.   63:17
evil thing, that my f. is not. Jer 2:19
sword and f. on every. 6:25*; 20:10
have heard a voice of f. not.   30:5
will put my f. in their hearts. 32:40
f. and the pit shall be upon. 48:43
I will bring a f. upon thee.   49:5
hath seized on Damascus.   24*
cry to them, f. is on every side. 29*
f. and a snare is come.   Lam 3:47
a f. in land of Egypt.   Ezek 30:13
if master, where is my f.? Mal 1:6
Zacharias saw him, f.   Luke 1:12
f. came on all. 5:5, 11; 19:17; Acts 2:43
                5:5, 11; 19:17; Rev 11:11
f. to whom f. is due.   Rom 13:7
in weakness and in f.   1 Cor 2:3
what f.! what desire!   2 Cor 7:11
not given us spirit of f.   2 Tim 1:7
them who through f. of.   Heb 2:15
God with reverence, godly f. 12:28*
your sojourning here in f. 1 Pet 1:17
answer with meekness and f.   3:15
no f. in love, love casteth out f.
                          1 John 4:18

for fear
for the f. wherewith.   Deut 28:67
not rather done it for f. Josh 22:24*
dwelt for f. of Abimelech. Judg 9:21
fled that day for f. of. 1 Sam 21:10
he got away for f. of Saul.   23:26
he reprove thee for f. of? Job 22:4
over to strong hold for f. Isa 31:9*
f. of the army of.   Jer 35:11
army broken up for f.   37:11
Asa had made for f. of Baasha. 41:9
for f. was round about.   46:5*
for f. of the oppressing.   50:16
for the f. wherewith he.   Mal 2:5
disciples cried out for f. Mat 14:26
for f. of him keepers did shake. 28:4
hearts failing for f.   Luke 21:26
no man spake openly for f. John 7:13
but secretly for f. of the Jews. 19:38
disciples assembled for f. of Jews.
                              20:19
off for f. of torment.   Rev 18:10, 15

fear of God
surely f. of God is not.   Gen 20:11
ruling in the f. of God. 2 Sam 23:3
the f. of God was on.   2 Chr 20:29

to walk in f. of God ?   Neh 5:9
because of the f. of God.   15
is no f. of God before his   Ps 36:1
no f. of God before their.   Rom 3:18
holiness in the f. of God.   2 Cor 7:1
to another in f. of God.   Eph 5:21

fear of the Lord
f. of Lord fell on people.
   1 Sam 11:7*; 2 Chr 17:10
f. of the Lord came.   2 Chr 14:14
let the f. of the Lord be upon.   19:7
thus do, in the f. of the Lord.   9
the f. of Lord is wisdom. Job 28:28
the f. of Lord is clean.   Ps 19:9
will teach you f. of the Lord. 34:11
f. of the Lord is beginning of 111:10
f. of Lord beginning of knowledge.
   Pr 1:7; 9:10
did not choose f. of the Lord.   1:29
understand the f. of the Lord.   2:5
f. of the Lord is to hate evil.   8:13
the f. of the Lord prolongeth days. 10:27
in the f. of the Lord is strong. 14:26
the f. of the Lord is fountain of.   27
better little with f. of the Lord. 15:16
f. of the Lord is instruction of.   33
by f. of the Lord men depart. 16:6
the f. of the Lord tendeth.   19:23
by the f. of the Lord are riches. 22:4
f. of the Lord all day long.   23:17
in dust for f. of the Lord. Isa 2:10
into caves for f. of the Lord.   19
clefts of rocks for f. of the Lord. 21
knowledge, and of the f. of the Lord.
   11:2
understanding in f. of the Lord   3
f. of the Lord is his treasure. 33:6
walking in f. of the Lord. Acts 9:31

with **fear**
serve Lord with f.   Ps 2:11
they departed with f.   Mat 28:8
were all filled with f.   Luke 5:26
were taken with great f.   8:37
how with f. ye received. 2 Cor 7:15
to masters with f. and.   Eph 6:5
work out salvation with f. Phil 2:12
Noah moved with f.   Heb 11:7
subject to masters with f. 1 Pet 2:18
conversation coupled with f.   3:2
and others save with f.   Jude 23

without **fear**
labour is in vain without f. Job 39:16
like, who is made without f.   41:33
serve him without f.   Luke 1:74
be with you without f. 1 Cor 16:10
to speak word without f.   Phil 1:14
feeding themselves without f.
   Jude 12

fear, *verb*
shall f. every man his.   Lev 19:3
neither f. ye the people. Num 14:9
they may learn to f. me. Deut 4:10
O that they would f. me.   5:29
f. this glorious name.   28:58
thou shalt f. day and night.   66
of heart wherewith thou shalt f.
if thou f. to go down.   Judg 7:10
that they may f. thee.   1 Ki 8:40
   2 Chr 6:31
may know thy name to f. 1 Ki 8:43
   2 Chr 6:33
neither f. other gods.   2 Ki 17:38
but Lord your God ye shall f.   39
f. before him all earth. 1 Chr 16:30*
   Ps 96:9
servants who desire to f. Neh 1:11
did I f. a great multitude? Job 31:34
I will f. no evil.   Ps 23:4
whom shall I f.?   27:1
laid up for them that f.   31:19
and f. and shall trust in Lord. 40:3
wherefore should I f. in days? 49:5
righteous also shall see, and f. 52:6
given a banner to them that f. 60:4
heritage of those that f.   61:5
shall f. and declare the work. 64:9
shall f. thee as long as the sun. 72:5
unite my heart to f. thy name. 86:11
heathen shall f. thy name. 102:15
my reproach which I f.   119:39
a companion of them that f.   63
they that f. thee will be glad.   74
those that f. thee turn unto me.   79

men should f. before him. Eccl 3:14
neither f. ye their fear.   Isa 8:12
like to women, afraid and f.   19:16
city of terrible nations shall f. 25:3
the workmen shall f. and be. 44:11
f. the name of the Lord.   59:19
thine heart shall f. and be.   60:5*
who would not f. thee ?   Jer 10:7
and they shall f. no more.   32:39
them one heart that may f.   32:39
they shall f. and tremble for.   33:9
your heart faint, and ye f. for. 51:46
I f. my lord the king.   Dan 1:10
that men f. before God of.   6:26
inhabitants of Samaria f. Hos 10:5*
move as worms, and f.   Mi 7:17
surely thou wilt f. me.   Zeph 3:7
the people did f. before.   Hag 1:12
Ashkelon shall see it and f. Zech 9:5
to you that f. my name.   Mal 4:2
say, of men, we f. the.   Mat 21:26
forewarn you whom ye shall f.
   Luke 12:5
of bondage again to f.   Rom 8:15
be not highminded, but f.   11:20
I f. lest as the serpent. 2 Cor 11:3
I f. lest I shall not find you.   12:20
rebuke that others may f. 1 Tim 5:20
let us f. lest promise.   Heb 4:1
I exceedingly f. and quake.   12:21
f. none of those things.   Rev 2:10
reward to them that f. thy.   11:18

fear God
and live, for I f. God.   Gen 42:18
men, such as f. God.   Ex 18:21
but thou shalt f. thy God. Lev 19:14
   32 ; 25:17, 36, 43
Job f. God for nought ?   Job 1:9
hear, all ye that f. God.   Ps 66:16
but f. thou God.   Eccl 5:7
be well with them that f. God. 8:12
f. God and keep his.   12:13
shall f. God of Israel.   Isa 29:23*
dost not f. God ?   Luke 23:40
f. God give audience.   Acts 13:16
f. God, honour king.   1 Pet 2:17
f. God, and give glory to. Rev 14:7

hear and **fear**
Israel shall hear and f. Deut 13:11
   21:21
the people shall hear and f.   17:13
those shall hear and f.   19:20

fear him
for I f. him.   Gen 32:11
after God, and f. him.   Deut 13:4
him shall ye f. him shall. 2 Ki 17:36
men therefore f. him.   Job 37:24
and f. him, seed of.   Ps 22:23*
vows before them that f. him 25
Lord with them that f. him. 25:14
of Lord on them that f. him. 33:18
angel encampeth about them that f.
him.   34:7
no want to them that f. him.   9
ends of earth shall f. him.   67:7
is nigh them that f. him.   85:9
mercy to them that f. him. 103:11
Lord pitieth them that f. him.   13
mercy of the Lord is upon them that
f. him.   17 ; Luke 1:50
meat to them that f. him. Ps. 111:5
desire of them that f. him. 145:19
pleasure in them that f. him. 147:11
f. him who is able to.   Mat 10:28
   Luke 12:5
praise God, ye that f. him. Rev 19:5

fear the Lord
that thou mightest f. the Lord.
   Deut 6:2
thou shalt f. Lord thy.   13; 10:20
   2 Ki 17:39
to f. the Lord our God. Deut 6:24
f. the Lord, walk in his ways. 10:12
learn to f. the Lord.   14:23; 17:19
   31:12, 13
that ye might f. the Lord. Josh 4:24
now therefore f. the Lord.   24:14
if ye will f. the Lord. 1 Sam 12:14
only f. the Lord and serve him. 24
I thy servant f. the Lord. 1 Ki 18:12
   2 Ki 4:1

taught them f. Lord.   2 Ki 17:28
honoureth them that f. the Lord.
   Ps 15:4
ye that f. the Lord, praise.   22:23
let all the earth f. the Lord.   33:8
O f. the Lord, ye his saints.   34:9
ye that f. the Lord trust.   115:11
will bless them that f. the Lord. 13
that f. the Lord, say, his.   118:4
that f. the Lord, bless the. 135:20
f. the Lord, depart from.   Pr 3:7
my son, f. thou the Lord.   24:21
say, let us f. the Lord.   Jer 5:24
did he not f. the Lord, and? 26:19
shall Israel f. the Lord.   Hos 3:5
and I f. the Lord, the.   Jonah 1:9

fear not
f. not, Abram, I am thy.   Gen 15:1
f. not, God hath heard voice. 21:17
f. not, I am with thee.   26:24
midwife said to Rachel, f. not. 35:17
said, peace be to you, f. not. 43:23
f. not to go down into Egypt. 46:3
Joseph said, f. not, for am I ? 50:19
f. not, I will nourish you and your. 21
f. not, stand and see.   Ex 14:13
Moses said, f. not, God is. 20:20
Lord is with us, f. them not.
   Num 14:9
Lord said to Moses, f. him not. 21:34
possess the land, f. not. Deut 1:21
f. not Og.   3:2, 22
f. not your enemies.   20:3
f. not the Canaanites.   31:6
   Josh 10:8, 25
Lord will go before thee, f. not.
   Deut 31:8; Josh 8:1; 1 Chr 28:20
turn in to me, f. not.   Judg 4:18
f. not gods of the Amorites.   6:10
peace be to thee, f. not   23
now, my daughter, f. not. Ruth 3:11
women that stood by said, f. not.
   1 Sam 4:20
Samuel said to people, f. not. 12:20
abide thou with me, f. not.   22:23
said unto David, f. not.   23:17
to Mephibosheth, f. not. 2 Sam 9:7
servants, kill Amnon, f. not.   13:28
Elijah said to widow, f. not.
   1 Ki 17:13
f. not: for they that be. 2 Ki 6:16
unto this day, they f. not.   17:34
f. not to serve.   25:24; Jer 40:9
will be with you, f. not. 2 Chr 20:17
therefore they f. not God. Ps 55:19
do they shoot, and f. not.   64:4
f. not the tails of firebrands. Isa 7:4
are of a fearful heart, f. not.   35:4
f. thou not, I am with. 41:10; 43:5
thy God will hold thy right hand, saying to thee, f. not.   41:13
f. not, thou worm Jacob.   14
f. not, I have redeemed thee. 43:1
f. not, O Jacob, and Jeshurun I have.
   44:2; Jer 30:10; 46:27, 28
f. ye not, nor be afraid.   Isa 44:8
f. not the reproach of men.   51:7
f. not, thou shalt not be.   54:4
f. ye not me ?   Jer 5:22
thou saidst, f. not.   Lam 3:57
f. not, nor be dismayed.   Ezek 3:9
f. not, Daniel.   Dan 10:12, 19
f. not, O land, be glad.   Joel 2:21
said to Jerusalem, f. not. Zeph 3:16
Spirit remaineth, f. not.   Hag 2:5
shall be a blessing, f. not. Zech 8:13
do well to Judah, f. ye not.   15
against them that f. not me. Mal 3:5
f. not to take to thee Mary. Mat 1:20
f. them not, there is nothing.   10:26
f. not them which kill the body.   28
f. not, ye are of.   31; Luke 12:7
angel said to women, f. not. Mat 28:5
f. not, Zacharias.   Luke 1:13
f. not, Mary.   30
to the shepherds, f. not.   2:10
Simon, f. not.   5:10
Jairus, f. not.   8:50
f. not, little flock.   12:32
though I f. not God, nor.   18:4
f. not, daughter of Sion. John 12:15
f. not, Paul, thou must. Acts 27:24
f. not, I am the first and. Rev 1:17

not fear
I know ye will *not* yet *f.*   *Ex* 9:30
not f. other gods.   *2 Ki* 17:35, 37
I speak, and *not f.* him.   *Job* 9:35
far away, thou shalt *not f.*   11:15
my heart shall *not f.*   *Ps* 27:3
we will *not f.* though earth be.   46:2
I will *not f.* what.   56:4; 118:6
oppression, shalt *not f.*   *Isa* 54:14
who would *not f.* thee?   *Jer* 10:7
roared, who will *not f.*?   *Amos* 3:8
dost *not* thou *f.* God?   *Luke* 23:40
not f. what man shall do.   *Heb* 13:6
who shall *not f.* thee?   *Rev* 15:4

feared
Lot *f.* to dwell in Zoar.   *Gen* 19:30
Isaac *f.* to say of Rebekah.   26:7
Moses *f.* and said, this.   *Ex* 2:14
he that *f.* the word of Lord.   9:20
Amalek smote thee, *f.*   *Deut* 25:18
gods whom your fathers *f.*   32:17*
were it not that I *f.* the wrath.   27
f. Joshua as they did.   *Josh* 4:14
Gideon *f.*   *Judg* 6:27
Jether *f.* to slay them.   8:20
Samuel *f.* to shew Eli.   *1 Sam* 3:15
honey dropped, for people *f.*   14:26
because I *f.* the people.   15:24
answer, he *f.* Abner.   *2 Sam* 3:11
the Syrians *f.* to help.   10:19
David's servants *f.* to tell.   12:18
Adonijah *f.* because of.   *1 Ki* 1:50
Israel heard judgement, and *f.* 3:28
f. other gods.   *2 Ki* 17:7
they *f.* not the Lord.   25
to be *f.* above all gods.   *1 Chr* 16:25
   Ps 96:4
Jehoshaphat *f.* and.   *2 Chr* 20:3
even thou, art to be *f.*   *Ps* 76:7
the earth *f.*   8
presents to him that ought to be *f.* 11
safely, so that they *f.* not.   78:53
that thou mayest be *f.*   130:4
the isles saw it and *f.*   *Isa* 41:5
and hast *f.* continually.   51:13
whom hast thou *f.* that thou.   57:11
sister Judah *f.* not.   *Jer* 3:8
the sword which ye *f.* shall.   42:16
humbled, nor have they *f.*   44:10
ye have *f.* the sword.   *Ezek* 11:8
all people and nations *f.*   *Dan* 5:19
fear wherewith he *f.* me.   *Mal* 2:5
Herod *f.* the multitude.   *Mat* 14:5
   21:46
and they *f.* exceedingly.   *Mark* 4:41
Herod *f.* John, knowing he.   6:20
and chief priests *f.* Jesus.   11:18
of men, they *f.* people.   32; 12:12
   Luke 20:19; 22:2; *Acts* 5:26
and they *f.* as they.   *Luke* 9:34
and they *f.* to ask him.   45
a city a judge which *f.* not.   18:2
I *f.* thee because thou art.   19:21
because they *f.* the Jews. *John* 9:22
the magistrates *f.* when. *Acts* 16:38
Christ was heard in that he *f.*
   Heb 5:7

feared God
but the midwives *f.* God.   *Ex* 1:17
because they *f.* God, he made.   21
was faithful, and *f.* God.   *Neh* 7:2
Job was one that *f.* God.   *Job* 1:1
Cornelius *f.* God with his. *Acts* 10:2

feared greatly
the Canaanites *f.* greatly. *Josh* 10:2
all people greatly *f.* the. *1 Sam* 12:18
Obadiah *f.* Lord greatly.   *1 Ki* 18:3
the thing I greatly *f.* is.   *Job* 3:25
God is greatly to be *f.*   *Ps* 89:7
they with him *f.* greatly. *Mat* 27:54

feared the Lord
the people *f.* the Lord.   *Ex* 14:31
so they *f.* the Lord. *2 Ki* 17:32, 33, 41
we *f.* not the Lord.   *Hos* 10:3
the men *f.* the Lord.   *Jonah* 1:16
that *f.* Lord spake one to another . . .
that *f.* the Lord.   *Mal* 3:16

fearest
I know that thou *f.* God. *Gen* 22:12
have not I held my peace even of old,
   and thou *f.* me not?   *Isa* 57:11
hand of them thou *f.*   *Jer* 22:25

feareth
behold, Adonijah *f.* king.   *1 Ki* 1:51
Job, one that *f.* God.   *Job* 1:8; 2:3
what man *f.* the Lord?   *Ps* 25:12
blessed is man that *f.* Lord.   112:1
blessed is every one that *f.*   128:1
shall the man be blessed that *f.* 4
that *f.* commandment.   *Pr* 13:13
walketh in his uprightness *f.* 14:2
a wise man *f.* and departeth.   16
happy is man that *f.* always.   28:14
woman that *f.* Lord shall be.   31:30
that *f.* God shall come.   *Eccl* 7:18
because the wicked *f.* not.   8:13
as he that *f.* an oath.   9:2
among you *f.* the Lord?   *Isa* 50:10
Cornelius, one that *f.*   *Acts* 10:22
he that *f.* him, is accepted.   35
whosoever among you *f.* God. 13:26
he that *f.* is not perfect. *1 John* 4:18

fearful
who is like thee, *f.* in?   *Ex* 15:11
what man is *f.* let him.   *Deut* 20:8
   Judg 7:3
mayest fear this *f.* name. *Deut* 28:58
say to them of a *f.* heart.   *Isa* 35:4
why are ye *f.* O ye of?   *Mat* 8:26
why are ye so *f.*?   *Mark* 4:40
f. sights in divers.   *Luke* 21:11*
a certain *f.* looking for.   *Heb* 10:27
f. to fall into the hands of.   31
f. have their part in the.   *Rev* 21:8

fearfully
f. and wonderfully made.   *Ps* 139:14

fearfulness
f. and trembling are.   *Ps* 55:5
heart panteth, *f.* affrighted. *Isa* 21:4*
f. hath surprised hypocrites. 33:14*

fearing
children cease from *f.*   *Josh* 22:25
the woman *f.* and.   *Mark* 5:33
the chief captain *f.* lest.   *Acts* 23:10
f. lest they fall into the.   27:17, 29
f. them which were of.   *Gal* 2:12
in singleness of heart *f.*   *Col* 3:22
forsook Egypt, not *f.*   *Heb* 11:27

fears
delivered me from all my *f. Ps* 34:4
and when *f.* shall be in.   *Eccl* 12:5*
will bring their *f.* upon.   *Isa* 66:4
were fightings, within *f.*   *2 Cor* 7:5

feast
The Hebrews had a great number
of feasts. The first, and most
ancient of all, was the sabbath, or
the seventh day of the week,
instituted to preserve the memory
of the world's creation, Gen 2:3.
The Passover celebration began
on the evening of the fourteenth
day of the first month in the
ecclesiastical year, which was the
seventh of the civil year. It lasted
seven days, but the first and last
days only were days of rest, Ex
12:14, etc.
The feast of Pentecost was celebrated on the fiftieth day after the
Passover, or seven complete weeks
after the consecration of the harvest
season by the offering of the sheaf
of the first ripe barley, Ex 23:16;
Lev 23:15–22; Num 28.
The feast of Trumpets was celebrated on the first day of the civil
year, in the month Tisri, answering
to our September. This day was
kept solemn; all manual labour was
forbidden to be done upon it; and
particular sacrifices were offered,
Lev 23:24, 25.
The new moons, or first days of
every month, were also celebrated
as minor feasts.
The feast of Tabernacles, the
feast of ingathering or real harvest
festival, was kept for a week in the
month Tisri, beginning five days
after the day of atonement.
Besides these feasts mentioned by
Moses, we find the feasts of lots,
or Purim, which celebrated the

escape of the Jews from Haman;
the feast of Dedication, or rather
of the restoration of the temple
after it had been profaned by Anti-
ochus Epiphanes, which is thought
to be the feast mentioned in the
gospel, John 10:22, was celebrated
in the winter. Josephus says it
was called the feast of lights.
The Day of Atonement, which
was not a feast but a fast, was
kept upon the tenth day of the
month Tisri, or September. The
Hebrews call it Kippur, that is,
pardon or expiation, because it was
instituted for the expiation of all the
sins, irreverences, and pollutions of
all the Israelites, from the high
priest to the lowest of the people,
committed by them throughout the
whole year.

Lot made a *f.*   *Gen* 19:3
Abraham made a *f.*   21:8
Isaac made a *f.*   26:30
Laban made a *f.*   29:22
Pharaoh made a *f.* to servants. 40:20
they may hold a *f.*   *Ex* 5:1; 10:9
keep it a *f.*   12:14; *Lev* 23:39, 41
the seventh day shall be a *f. Ex* 13:6
three times thou shalt keep a *f.* 23:14
the *f.* of harvest, the firstfruits. 16
Aaron said, to-morrow is a *f.* 32:5
fifteenth day is the *f.*   *Num* 28:17
ye shall keep a *f.* to the Lord. 29:12
shalt rejoice in thy *f.*   *Deut* 16:14
Samson made there a *f. Judg* 14:10
within the seven days of the *f.* 12
wept before him while *f.* lasted. 17
Nabal held a *f.* in his.   *1 Sam* 25:36
David made Abner a *f. 2 Sam* 3:20
Solomon made a *f.*   *1 Ki* 3:15; 8:65
all Israel assembled at the *f.*   8:2
a *f.* like to the *f.* in Judah.   12:32
he ordained a *f.* to the children. 33
f. in the seventh month.   *2 Chr* 5:3
   Neh 8:14
Solomon kept the *f.* seven. *2 Chr* 7:8
   9; 30:22; *Neh* 8:18; *Ezek* 45:25
Ahasuerus made *f. Esth* 1:3, 5; 2:18
Vashti made a *f.*   1:9
the Jews had a *f.*   8:17
heart hath continual *f.*   *Pr* 15:15
f. is made for laughter.   *Eccl* 10:19
make to all people a *f.*   *Isa* 25:6
seven days of the *f.*   *Ezek* 45:23
Belshazzar made a great *f. Dan* 5:1
at that *f.* the governor was wont to
   release.   *Mat* 27:15; *Mark* 15:6
up after custom of the *f. Luke* 2:42
Levi made him a great *f.*   5:29
but when thou makest a *f.* call. 14:13
release one unto them at *f.*   23:17
bear to governor of the *f. John* 2:8
when the ruler of the *f.* tasted. 9
things he did at Jerusalem at the *f.*,
   for they also went to the *f.*   4:45
after this a *f.* of the Jews.   5:1
the passover, a *f.* of the Jews. 6:4
to this *f.* I go not up yet to *f.* 7:8
then went he also up to the *f.* 10
the Jews sought him at the *f.* 11
about midst of the *f.* Jesus.   14
that great day of the *f.*   37
at Jerusalem the *f.* of.   10:22
that he will not come to *f.*?   11:56
much people were come to *f.* 12:12
Greeks among them that came *f.* 20
we have need of against the *f.* 13:29
I must keep this *f.*   *Acts* 18:21
let us keep the *f.* not.   *1 Cor* 5:8
believe not bid you to a *f.*   10:27
sporting while they *f.*   *2 Pet* 2:13
spots, when they *f.* with you. *Jude* 12*

feasted
his sons went and *f.*   *Job* 1:4

feast *of the passover*
nor sacrifice of *f.* of passover be left.
   Ex 34:25
two days *f.* of passover.   *Mat* 26:2
   Mark 14:1
year at *f.* of passover.   *Luke* 2:41
before the *f.* of passover when Jesus
knew his hour was come. *John* 13:1

feast

solemn **feast**
days keep a *solemn f.* *Deut* 16:15
trumpet on *solemn f.* day. *Ps* 81:3
noise as in *solemn f.* day. *Lam* 2:7*

feast *of tabernacles*
fifteenth day *f. of taber.* *Lev* 23:34
shalt observe *f. of taber. Deut* 16:13
three times appear in *f. of taber.*
   16; 31:10; *2 Chr* 8:13
kept *f. of taber.* as it.   *Ezra* 3:4
go up to keep *f. of taber. Zech* 14:16
not to keep *f. of taber.*   18, 19
Jews' *f. of taber.* was at. *John* 7:2

feast *of unleavened bread*
observe *f. of unl. br.*   *Ex* 12:17
   23:15; 34:18
fifteenth day is *f. of unl. br.*
   Lev 23:6
appear in *f. of unl. br. Deut* 16:16
   2 Chr 8:13
to keep *f. of unl. br.*   *2 Chr* 30:13
children of Israel kept *f. of unl. br.* 21
f. of unl. br. seven days.   35:17
   Ezra 6:22; *Ezek* 45:21
first day of *f. of unl. br. Mat* 26:17
after two days was *f. of unl. br.*
   Mark 14:1; *Luke* 22:1

feast *of weeks*
shalt observe *f. of weeks. Ex* 34:22
   Deut 16:10
appear in *f. of weeks. Deut* 16:16
burnt offerings in *f. of weeks.*
   2 Chr 8:13

feast day, -s
will also cause her *f. of days. Hos* 2:11
will ye do in *day of the f. of?* 9:5
I despise your *f. days. Amos* 5:21
said, not on the *f. day.*   *Mat* 26:5
   Mark 14:2
in the *f. day* many.   *John* 2:23

feasting
made it a day of *f.*   *Esth* 9:17, 18
should make them days of *f.* 22
days of their *f.* were gone. *Job* 1:5
than to go to house of *f.* *Eccl* 7:2
not go into house of *f.*   *Jer* 16:8

feasts
these are my *f. Lev* 23:2, 4, 37, 44
hypocritical mockers in *f. Ps* 35:16
pipe, and wine in their *f.* *Isa* 5:12
I will make their *f.*   *Jer* 51:39
part to give offerings in *f. Ezek* 45:17
in *f.* the meat offering shall. 46:11
I will turn your *f.* into. *Amos* 8:10
joy, gladness, cheerful *f. Zech* 8:19
love uppermost rooms at *f. Mat* 23:6
   Mark 12:39; *Luke* 20:46
spots in your *f.* of charity. *Jude* 12

appointed **feasts**
your *appointed f.* my soul. *Isa* 1:14

set **feasts**
things do in your *set f. Num* 29:39
to offer on the *set f.*   *1 Chr* 23:31
   Ezra 3:5
king's portion for *set f. 2 Chr* 31:3
for offering in the *set f. Neh* 10:33

solemn **feasts**
offering in your *solemn f. Num* 15:3
house for offering on *solemn f.*
   2 Chr 2:4
offering on *solemn f.* three. 8:13
none come to *solemn f.* *Lam* 1:4*
caused the *solemn f.* to be. 2:6*
Jerusalem in *solemn f. Ezek* 36:38
come before Lord in *solemn f.* 46:9
to cease her *solemn f.* *Hos* 2:11*
dwell as in days of *solemn f.* 12:9
Judah, keep thy *solemn f. Nah* 1:15
even dung of your *solemn f. Mal* 2:3

feathered, *see* fowl

feathers
away crop with his *f.*   *Lev* 1:16*
goodly wings to peacock? or wings
  and *f.* to the ostrich? *Job* 39:13
f. covered with yellow. *Ps* 68:13*
shall cover thee with his *f.* 91:4*
long-winged, full of *f. Ezek* 17:3, 7
were grown like eagle's *f. Dan* 4:33

fed
Jacob *f.* Laban's flock. *Gen* 30:36
he *f.* the asses of Zibeon. 36:24

the seven kine *f.* in a. *Gen* 41:2, 18
he *f.* them with bread for. 47:17
the God who *f.* me all my. 48:15
bread wherewith I have *f. Ex* 16:32
he *f.* thee with manna. *Deut* 8:3
who *f.* thee in the wilderness. 16
concubines in ward, *f.* *2 Sam* 20:3*
f. them with bread. *1 Ki* 18:4, 13
over the herds that *f.* *1 Chr* 27:29
in Lord, thou shalt be *f.* *Ps* 37:3*
f. them, according to.   78:72
he should have *f.* them with. 81:16
full of fat of *f.* beasts.   *Isa* 1:11
I had *f.* them to the full. *Jer* 5:7
were as *f.* horses in the morning. 8
honey wherewith I *f.* *Ezek* 16:19
and kill them that are *f.*   34:3
shepherds *f.* themselves, *f.* not. 8
all flesh was *f.* with it. *Dan* 4:12
they *f.* Nebuchadnezzar with. 5:21
two staves, and I *f.* flock. *Zech* 11:7
thee hungered, and *f.?* *Mat* 25:37
that *f.* the swine fled.   *Mark* 5:14
   Luke 8:34
desiring to be *f.* with. *Luke* 16:21
I have *f.* you with milk. *1 Cor* 3:2

feeble
when cattle were *f.* he. *Gen* 30:42
Amalekites smote all *f. Deut* 25:18
many children, waxen *f. 1 Sam* 2:5
Ish-bosheth's hands were *f.*
   2 Sam 4:1
carried all the *f.* of. *2 Chr* 28:15
what do these *f.* Jews? *Neh* 4:2
hast strengthened the *f.* *Job* 4:4
I am *f.* and sore broken. *Ps* 38:8*
not one *f.* person amongst. 105:37
the conies are but a *f.* folk. *Pr* 30:26
remnant very small and *f. Isa* 16:14*
confirm *f.* knees.   35:3
fame, our hands wax *f. Jer* 6:24
Damascus is waxed *f.* and. 49:24
of Babylon's hands waxed *f.* 50:43
all hands shall be *f.* *Ezek* 7:17
   21:7
he that is *f.* be as David. *Zech* 12:8
which seem to be *f.* *1 Cor* 12:22
comfort the *f.*-minded. *1 Thes* 5:14
hands and *f.* knees. *Heb* 12:12*

feebler
so the *f.* were Laban's. *Gen* 30:42

feebleness
not look back for *f.*   *Jer* 47:3

feed
brethren went to *f.*   *Gen* 37:12
where they *f.* their flocks. 16
trade hath been to *f.* cattle. 46:32*
shall *f.* in another man's. *Ex* 22:5
neither let flocks *f.* before. 34:3
thou shalt *f.* my people. *2 Sam* 5:2†
I commanded to *f.* Israel. 7:7†
   1 Chr 17:6†
commanded ravens to *f. 1 Ki* 17:4
take away flocks and *f.* *Job* 24:2
the worms shall *f.* sweetly on. 20
f. them, and lift them up. *Ps* 28:9†
in grave, death *f.* on them. 49:14*
he brought David to *f.* Jacob. 78:71
lips of the righteous *f.* *Pr* 10:21
like two rows which *f.* *S of S* 4:5
my beloved is gone to *f.* in. 6:2
f. after their manner. *Isa* 5:17
the cow and the bear shall *f.* 11:7
firstborn of poor shall *f.* 14:30
there shall the calf *f.* and. 27:10
cattle *f.* in large pastures. 30:23
f. his flock as a shepherd. 40:11
they shall *f.* in the ways. 49:9
strangers shall stand and *f.* 61:5
wolf and the lamb shall *f.* 65:25
pastors who shall *f.* you. *Jer* 3:15
f. every one in his place. 6:3
pastors that *f.* my people. 23:2
shepherds which shall *f.* them. 4
Israel shall *f.* on Carmel. 50:19
they that *f.* delicately. *Lam* 4:5
woe to shepherds that *f. Ezek* 34:2
eat the fat, but ye *f.* not flock. 3
neither shall shepherds *f.*   10
my servant David shall *f.* them. 23
that *f.* of his meat. *Dan* 11:26*
now the Lord will *f.* them. *Hos* 4:16
the flour and winepress not *f.* 9:2

let them not *f.* nor drink. *Jonah* 3:7
f. in strength of the Lord. *Mi* 5:4
they shall *f.* thereupon. *Zeph* 2:7
they shall *f.* none make afraid. 3:13
I will not *f.* you.   *Zech* 11:9
the shepherd shall not *f.* that. 16
sent him to fields to *f. Luke* 15:15
take heed to *f.* church of. *Acts* 20:28
all my goods to *f.* poor. *1 Cor* 13:3
for the Lamb shall *f.* *Rev* 7:17*
that they should *f.* her there. 12:6*

feed, *imperatively*
f. me with that red. *Gen* 25:30
water the sheep, go and *f.* 29:7
f. him with bread and water.
   1 Ki 22:27; *2 Chr* 18:26
f. me with food convenient. *Pr* 30:8
f. thy kids beside the. *S of S* 1:8
f. thy people with thy rod. *Mi* 7:14
saith Lord, the flock. *Zech* 11:4
f. my lambs.   *John* 21:15
f. my sheep.   16*, 17
if enemy hunger, *f.* him. *Rom* 12:20
the flock of God.   *1 Pet* 5:2*

I will **feed**
I will again *f.* and keep. *Gen* 30:31
I will *f.* thee with me. *2 Sam* 19:33
I will *f.* them that oppress. *Isa* 49:26
I will *f.* thee with heritage of. 58:14
I will *f.* them with wormwood.
   Jer 9:15; 23:15
I will *f.* them upon the mountains.
   Ezek 34:13
I will *f.* them in a good pasture. 14
I will *f.* my flock, and cause. 15
I will *f.* the fat and the strong. 16
I will *f.* the flock of. *Zech* 11:7

feedest
f. them with bread of tears. *Ps* 80:5
me where thou *f.* flock. *S of S* 1:7

feedeth
mouth of fools *f.* on. *Pr* 15:14
my beloved *f.* among lilies.
   S of S 2:16; 6:3
he *f.* on ashes, a deceived. *Isa* 44:20
Ephraim *f.* on wind. *Hos* 12:1
your heavenly Father *f. Mat* 6:26
ravens sow not, yet God *f.* them.
   Luke 12:24
who *f.* a flock, and. *1 Cor* 9:7

feeding
Joseph was *f.* his flock. *Gen* 37:2
plowing, the asses *f.* by. 14:14
to cease from *f.* flock. *Ezek* 34:10
where is the *f.* place? *Nah* 2:11
an herd of swine *f.* *Mat* 8:30
   Mark 5:11; *Luke* 8:32
a servant *f.* cattle. *Luke* 17:7*
f. themselves without fear. *Jude* 12*

feel
peradventure will *f.* me. *Gen* 27:12
come near, that I may *f.* thee. 21
suffer me that I may *f. Judg* 16:26
he shall not *f.* quietness. *Job* 20:20*
before pots can *f.* thorns. *Ps* 58:9
commandment *f.* no evil. *Eccl* 8:5*
if haply they might *f.* *Acts* 17:27

feeling
being past *f.* have given. *Eph* 4:19
touched with the *f.* of. *Heb* 4:15

feet
lawgiver from between his *f.*
   Gen 49:10
Jacob gathered up *f.* in the bed. 33
thy shoes from off thy *f.* *Ex* 3:5
   Acts 7:33
passover with shoes on *f. Ex* 12:11
have legs above their *f. Lev* 11:21
will pass through on *f. Deut* 2:28
cometh from between her *f.* 28:57
they sat down at thy *f.* every. 33:3
the *f.* of the priests were. *Josh* 3:15
old shoes, and clouted upon *f.* 9:5
put your *f.* on the necks of. 10:24
land whereon thy *f.* have. 14:9
he covereth his *f.* in. *Judg* 3:24
Sisera fled away on his *f.* 4:15, 17
at her *f.* bowed, at her *f.* fell. 5:27
go in, uncover his *f.* and. *Ruth* 3:4
behold a woman lay at his *f.* 8
he will keep the *f.* of *1 Sam* 2:9

Jonathan climbed on hands and *f.*
　　　　　1 Sam 14:13
Saul went in to cover his *f.*　24:3
rode with five damsels at *f.*　25:42
thy *f.* put into fetters. *2 Sam* 3:34
Jonathan's son lame of *f.* 4:4; 9:3, 13
cut off their hands and their *f.* 4:12
Mephibosheth had neither dressed
　his *f.*　19:24
he maketh my *f.* like hinds' *f.* 22:34
　　Ps 18:33; *Hab* 3:19
my *f.* did not slip.　*2 Sam* 22:37
　　　　　Ps 18:36
of war in shoes on his *f.*　*1 Ki* 2:5
Ahijah heard sound of her *f.*　14:6
when thy *f.* enter the city, the.　12
Asa was diseased in his *f.*　15:23
　　　　2 Chr 16:12
came, caught him by *f.*　*2 Ki* 4:27
not sound of his master's *f.?*　6:32
no more of her than the *f.*　9:35
man revived, stood upon his *f.* 13:21
nor make the *f.* of Israel.　21:8
David king stood on his *f. 1 Chr* 28:2
not old, their *f.* swelled.　*Neh* 9:21
ready to slip with his *f.*　*Job* 12:5
puttest my *f.* in stocks, thou settest
　a print upon heels of my *f.*　13:27
cast into a net by his own *f.*　18:8
and drive him to his *f.*　11
blind, *f.* was I to the lame.　29:15
youth rise, push away my *f.*　30:12
he putteth my *f.* in the stocks.　33:11
my hands and my *f.*　*Ps* 22:16
for he shall pluck my *f.* out.　25:15
hast set my *f.* in large room.　31:8
he set my *f.* on rock, and.　40:2
deliver my *f.* from falling ?　56:13
suffereth not our *f.* to be.　66:9
my *f.* were almost gone.　73:2
lift up thy *f.* unto perpetual.　74:3
f. they hurt with fetters.　105:18
f. have they, but they walk not. 115:7
hast delivered my *f.* from.　116:8
my *f.* unto thy testimonies. 119:59
I refrained my *f.* from every.　101
thy word is a lamp to my *f.*　105
f. shall stand within thy gates. 122:2
their *f.* run to evil.　*Pr* 1:16; 6:18
　　　　　Isa 59:7
ponder the path of thy *f.*　*Pr* 4:26
her *f.* go down to death.　5:5
wicked man speaketh with his *f.* 6:13
on coals and his *f.* not be burnt ? 28
her *f.* abide not in her house.　7:11
hasteth with his *f.* sinneth.　19:2
cutteth off the *f.* and drinketh. 26:6
spreadeth a net for his *f.*　29:5*
beautiful are thy *f.* with. *S of S* 7:1
a tinkling with their *f.*　*Isa* 3:16
away ornaments about their *f.*　18
with twain covered his *f.*, with.　6:2
Lord shall shave hair of the *f.*　7:20
own *f.* shall carry her afar.　23:7
f. of the poor shall tread.　26:6
send forth the *f.* of the ox.　32:20
he had not gone with his *f.*　41:3
shall lick up dust of thy *f.*　49:23
f. of him that bringeth tidings. 52:7
　　　　　Nah 1:15
place of my *f.* glorious.　*Isa* 60:13
before your *f.* stumble.　*Jer* 13:16
not refrained with my *f.*　14:10
and hid snares for my *f.*　18:22
thy *f.* are sunk in the mire.　38:22
spread a net for my *f.*　*Lam* 1:13
their *f.* were straight *h.*　*Ezek* 1:7
son of man, stand upon thy *f.*　2:1
Spirit set me upon my *f.*　2; 3:24
hast opened thy *f.* to.　16:25
put on thy shoes upon thy *f.*　24:17
your heads, shoes on your *f.*　23
thou hast stamped with *f.*　25:6
troubledst waters with thy *f.*　32:2
foul residue with your *f.*　34:18
trodden and fouled with *f.*　19
and stood upon their *f.*　37:10
f. part of iron.　*Dan* 2:33, 42
stone smote image upon his *f.*　34
thou sawest the *f.* and toes.　41
stamped residue with *f.* of it. 7:7, 19
his *f.* like polished brass.　10:6
　　　　Rev 1:15; 2:18
clouds are dust of his *f.*　*Nah* 1:3

his *f.* shall stand upon.　*Zech* 14:4
depart, shake off the dust of your *f.*
Mat 10:14; *Mark* 6:11; *Luke* 9:5
lame and blind at Jesus' *f. Mat* 15:30
rather than having two *f.* to.　18:8
they held him by the *f.* and.　28:9
to guide our *f.* into way. *Luke* 1:79
she kissed his *f.* and.　7:38
woman not ceased to kiss my *f.*　45
man sitting at the *f.* of Jesus.　8:35
Jairus fell down at Jesus' *f.*　41
Mary, who sat at Jesus' *f.*　10:39
ring on hand, shoes on his *f.*　15:22
behold my hands and my *f.*　24:39
shewed them his hands and *f.*　40
wiped his *f.* with.　*John* 11:2; 12:3
Mary anointed the *f.* of Jesus. 12:3
angel at head, the other at *f.* 20:12
immediately his *f.* received strength.
　　　　　Acts 3:7
laid them down at apostles' *f.* 4:35;
　　　　　37; 5:2
f. of them who have buried.　5:9
their clothes at young man's *f.* 7:58
shoes of his *f.* I am not.　13:25
they shook off the dust of their *f.* 51
Lystra a man impotent in his *f.* 14:8
stand upright on thy *f.* he.　10
who made their *f.* fast in.　16:24
Agabus bound hands and *f.*　21:11
brought up at *f.* of Gamaliel.　22:3
rise, and stand upon thy *f.*　26:16
f. are swift to shed.　*Rom* 3:15
the *f.* of them that preach.　10:15
nor head to the *f. I.*　*1 Cor* 12:21
your *f.* shod with the.　*Eph* 6:15
straight paths for *f.*　*Heb* 12:13
and worship before thy *f.*　*Rev* 3:9
mighty angel, his *f.* as pillars. 10:1
witnesses stood upon their *f.* 11:11
his *f.* were as *f.* of a bear.　13:2
to worship before his *f.*　22:8

at his feet
cast foreskin *at his f.*　*Ex* 4:25
ten thousand *at his f.*　*Judg* 4:10
she lay *at his f.* until.　*Ruth* 3:14
Abigail fell *at his f.* 　*1 Sam* 25:24
of Shunem fell *at his f.*　*2 Ki* 4:37
Esther fell down *at his f.*　*Esth* 8:3
coals went forth *at his f.*　*Hab* 3:5
servant fell *at his f.*　*Mat* 18:29
Jairus fell *at his f.*　*Mark* 5:22
Syrophenician woman fell *at his f.*
　　　　　7:25
stood *at his f.* behind.　*Luke* 7:38
Mary fell down *at his f. John* 11:32
Sapphira fell *at his f.*　*Acts* 5:10
Cornelius met him, fell *at his f.*
　　　　　10:25
I fell *at his f.* as dead.　*Rev* 1:17
fell *at his f.* to worship him.　19:10

feet joined with **sole** or **soles**
soles of your *f.* tread.　*Deut* 11:24
as soles of priests' *f. Josh* 3:13; 4:18
them under soles of his *f.*　*1 Ki* 5:3
sole of my *f.* dried.　*2 Ki* 19:24
　　　　　Isa 37:25
bow at the soles of thy *f.*　*Isa* 60:14
the sole of their *f.* was.　*Ezek* 1:7
the place of soles of my *f.*　43:3
be ashes under soles of *f.*　*Mal* 4:3

under feet
under his *f.* as it were.　*Ex* 24:10
darkness *under* his *f.*　*2 Sam* 22:10
　　　　　Ps 18:9
fallen *under* my *f.*　*2 Sam* 22:39
put all things *under* his *f.*　*Ps* 8:6
　　1 Cor 15:27; *Eph* 1:22
subdue nations *under* our *f. Ps* 47:3
dragon shalt trample *under f.* 91:13
carcase trodden *under f. Isa* 14:19
drunkards trodden *under f.*　28:3
to crush *under* his *f.* all. *Lam* 3:34
trample them *under* their *f. Mat* 7:6
bruise Satan *under* your *f.*
　　　　　Rom 16:20
all enemies *under* his *f. 1 Cor* 15:25
in subjection *under* his *f.*　*Heb* 2:8
sun, moon *under* her *f.*　*Rev* 12:1

feet with **wash**, or **washed**
fetched, *wash* your *f.*　*Gen* 18:4
tarry all night, *wash* your *f.*　19:2
gave water to *wash* his *f.*　24:32

and they *washed* their *f. Gen* 43:24
Aaron and his sons shall *wash* hands
　and *f.*　*Ex* 30:19, 21; 40:31
and concubine *washed f. Judg* 19:21
to *wash* the *f.* of.　*1 Sam* 25:41
thy house, *wash* thy *f. 2 Sam* 11:8
wash his *f.* in blood of.　*Ps* 58:10
have *washed* my *f.* how. *S of S* 5:3
began to *wash* his *f.*　*Luke* 7:38
hath *washed* my *f.* with tears.　44
to *wash* disciples' *f.*　*John* 13:5
Lord dost thou *wash* my *f.?*　6
thou shalt never *wash* my *f.*　8
needeth not save to *wash* his *f.*　10
after he had *washed* their *f.*　12
if I have *washed* your *f.*　14
have *washed* saints' *f.*　*1 Tim* 5:10

feign
f. thyself to be a mourner.
　　　　　2 Sam 14:2
f. herself to be another.　*1 Ki* 14:5
should *f.* themselves.　*Luke* 20:20

feigned
David *f.* himself mad. *1 Sam* 21:13
prayer that goeth not out of *f.* lips.
　　　　　Ps 17:1
with *f.* words make.　*2 Pet* 2:3

feignedly
turned to me but *f.*　*Jer* 3:10

feignest
f. thou to be another ?　*1 Ki* 14:6
but thou *f.* them out of.　*Neh* 6:8

Felix
bring Paul safe to F.　*Acts* 23:24
Lysias to excellent governor F.　26
accepted always, most noble F. 24:3
when F. came with his wife.　24
Paul reasoned of judgement, F.　25
certain man left in bonds by F. 25:14

fell
and his countenance *f.*　*Gen* 4:5
of Sodom and Gomorrah *f.*　14:10
a deep sleep *f.* on Abram.　15:12
Esau ran, and *f.* on his.　33:4
Joseph's brethren *f.* before.　44:14
Joseph *f.* on Benjamin's neck. 45:14
Jacob *f.* on Joseph's neck.　46:29
f. of the people 3000.　*Ex* 32:28
goat on which the Lord's lot *f.*
　　　　　Lev 16:9, 10
mixt multitude *f.* lusting. *Num* 11:4
dew *f.* on the camp, the manna.　9
Moses and Aaron *f.* 14:5; 16:22, 45
　　　　　20:6
that *f.* that day, 12,000.　*Josh* 8:25
Joshua came and *f.* upon.　11:7
and wrath *f.* on all the.　22:20
Sisera's host *f.* on edge. *Judg* 4:16
Sisera *f.*　5:27
of bread smote tent that it *f.*　7:13
for there *f.* 120,000 men.　8:10
there *f.* of Ephraimites 42,000. 12:6
the house *f.* on the lords.　16:30
there *f.* of Benjamin 18,000.　20:44
f. of Israel 30,000.　*1 Sam* 4:10
Eli *f.* from his seat backward.　18
fear of the Lord *f.* on people.　11:7
Philistines *f.* before Jonathan. 14:13
Doeg turned, and *f.* upon.　22:18
Abigail *f.* at David's feet.　25:24
Saul *f.* straightway along on. 28:20
no fault in him since he *f.*　29:3
three days agone I *f.* sick.　30:13
Saul took a sword and *f.*　31:4
armourbearer.　5; *1 Chr* 10:4, 5
Mephibosheth *f.* and.　*2 Sam* 4:4
f. some of the people of.　11:17
Amnon *f.* sick for his sister.　13:2
Joab's sword *f.* out as he.　20:8
they *f.* all seven together.　21:9
f. by hand of David. 22; *1 Chr* 20:8
Benaiah *f.* on Adonijah.　*1 Ki* 2:25
who *f.* upon two men better than. 32
Benaiah *f.* on Joab.　34
Benaiah *f.* on Shimei.　46
Abijah son of Jeroboam *f.*　14:1
the son of the woman *f.* sick. 17:17
fire of Lord *f.* and consumed. 18:38
a wall *f.* on 27,000 men.　20:30
third captain *f.* on knees. *2 Ki* 1:13
mantle of Elijah that *f.* from.　2:13
it *f.* on a day Elisha passed. 4:8, 11

it f. on a day the child went. *2 Ki 4*:18
Shunammite f. at his feet. 37
the axe head f. into water. 6:5
man of God said, where f. it ? 6
so it f. out to him, the. 7:20*
the fugitives that f. away. 25:11
f. some of Manasseh. *1 Chr 12*:19
there f. of Israel 70,000. 21:14
because there f. wrath for. 2 *Chr 15*:9
for they f. to David.
the fear of Lord f. on all. 17:10
inhabitants of Jerusalem f. 20:18
bowels f. out by reason of. 21:19
the soldiers of Israel f. on. 25:13
I f. on my knees and. *Ezra 9*:5
fear of Jews f. on. *Esth 8*:17; 9:2
the fear of Mordecai f. upon. 9:3
Sabeans f. on the asses. *Job 1*:15
Chaldeans f. on camels, and. 17
the house f. on young men, and. 19
to eat my flesh, they f. *Ps 27*:2
their priests f. by sword. 78:64
the fear of Israel f. on. 105:38
that f. away, f. to. *Jer 39*:9; 52:15
one f. upon another. 46:16
her people f. into hand. *Lam 1*:7
and children f. under wood. 5:13*
hand of the Lord f. *Ezek 8*:1; 11:5
so f. they all by the sword. 39:23
f. a voice from heaven. *Dan 4*:31
came up, before whom three f. 7:20
a great quaking f. upon them. 10:7
and the lot f. on Jonah. *Jonah 1*:7
the house f. not. *Mat 7*:25
house, and it f. 27; *Luke 6*:49
seed f. by way side. *Mat 13*:4
Mark 4:4; *Luke 8*:5
f. upon stony places. *Mat 13*:5
Mark 4:5; *Luke 8*:6
some f. among thorns. *Mat 13*:7
Mark 4:7; *Luke 8*:7
other f. into good. *Mat 13*:8
Mark 4:8; *Luke 8*:8
Jairus f. at his feet. *Mark 5*:22
Syrophenician woman came, f. 7:25
he f. on the ground and. 9:20
Jesus f. on the ground. 14:35
fear f. upon Zacharias. *Luke 1*:12
as they sailed, Jesus f. asleep. 8:23
a certain man f. among. 10:30, 36
upon whom tower in Siloam f. 13:4
his father f. on his neck. 15:20
crumbs which f. from rich. 16:21
went backward and f. to. *John 18*:6
Judas by transgression f. *Acts 1*:25
gave forth lots, and the lot f. 26
he had said this, he f. asleep. 7:60
Saul f. to the earth and. 9:4
there f. from his eyes as it had. 18
Peter became hungry, f. into. 10:10
Holy Ghost f. on them. 44; 11:15
chains f. from Peter's hands. 12:7
there f. on him a mist and. 13:11
David f. on sleep and saw. 36
and fear f. on all the Jews. 19:17
Paul went down, f. on. 20:10
they all f. on Paul's neck. 37
I f. unto the ground, and. 22:7
them which f. severity. *Rom 11*:22
reproaches of them f. on me. 15:3
and f. in one day. *1 Cor 10*:8
whose carcases f. in the. *Heb 3*:17
since fathers f. asleep. *2 Pet 3*:4
when I saw him I f. at. *Rev 1*:17
the stars of heaven f. unto. 6:13
there f. a great star from. 8:10
and great fear f. on them who. 11:11
the tenth part of the city f. by. 13
and there f. a noisome air. 16:2
and cities of nations f. 19
there f. upon men, great hail out. 21
I f. at his feet to worship him. 19:10

see **face, faces**

fell down
ass saw angel, she f. down.
Num 22:27*
and I f. down before. *Deut 9*:18, 25
shouted, wall f. down. *Josh 6*:20
there he f. down dead. *Judg 5*:27
concubine f. down at door. 19:26
Philistines f. down. *1 Sam 17*:52
Israel f. down in Gilboa. 31:1
1 Chr 10:1

so they f. down together. *2 Sam 2*:16
Asahel f. down there, and. 23
Ahimaaz f. down. 18:28*
Shimei f. down. 19:18
and Ahaziah f. down. *2 Ki 1*:2
f. down many slain. *1 Chr 5*:22
there f. down of Israel. *2 Chr 13*:17
Esther f. down at. *Esth 8*:3
Job f. down on ground. *Job 1*:20
f. down there was none. *Ps 107*:12
all nations f. down and. *Dan 3*:7
these three f. down bound in. 23
wise men f. down and. *Mat 2*:11
servant therefore f. down, saying.
18:26, 29
unclean spirits f. down. *Mark 3*:11
with issue of blood f. down. 5:33
Simon Peter f. down at. *Luke 5*:8
which had devils f. down. 8:28
Jairus f. down. 41
the Samaritan f. down. 17:16
Mary f. down at feet. *John 11*:32
Ananias f. down. *Acts 5*:5
Sapphira f. down. 10
Cornelius f. down at his feet. 10:25
keeper f. down before Paul. 16:29
image which f. down from. 19:35
Eutychus f. down from third. 20:9
walls of Jericho f. down. *Heb 11*:30
elders f. down before the Lamb.
Rev 5:8, 14; 19:4
John f. down to worship. 22:8

fell
shall f. every good tree. *2 Ki 3*:19

felled
and they f. all good trees. *2 Ki 3*:25

feller
no f. is come up against. *Isa 14*:8

fellest
before wicked men, so f. *2 Sam 3*:34

felling
as one was f. a beam. *2 Ki 6*:5

felloes
their f. and their spokes. *1 Ki 7*:33

fellow
this one f. came in to. *Gen 19*:9
smitest thou thy f.? *Ex 2*:13
told a dream to his f. *Judg 7*:13
Lord set every man's sword against
his f. through. 22; *1 Sam 14*:20
brought this f. to play the madman;
shall this f. come. *1 Sam 21*:15
in vain have I kept all this f. 25:21
make this f. return. 29:4
caught every one his f. *2 Sam 2*:16
put this f. in prison. *1 Ki 22*:27
2 Chr 18:26
wherefore came this mad f. to ?
2 Ki 9:11
one will lift up his f. *Eccl 4*:10
the satyr shall cry to his f. *Isa 34*:14
said every one to his f. *Jonah 1*:7
awake, O sword, against the man
that is my f., saith Lord. *Zech 13*:7
f. doth not cast out. *Mat 12*:24*
this f. said, I am able to. 26:61*
this f. was also with Jesus. 71*
Luke 22:59*
found this f. perverting. *Luke 23*:2*
as for this f. we know. *John 9*:29*
Didymus said to f. disciples. 11:16
this f. persuadeth men. *Acts 18*:13*
away with such a f. from. 22:22
this man a pestilent f. 24:5

fellow-citizens
but f.-citizens with saints. *Eph 2*:19

fellow-heirs
Gentiles be f.-heirs. *Eph 3*:6

fellow-helper
Titus my f.-helper. *2 Cor 8*:23

fellow-helpers
we might be f.-helpers. *3 John 8*

fellow-labourer
Timotheus our f.-labourer.
1 Thes 3:2
Philemon our f.-labour. *Philem 1*

fellow-labourers
other my f.-labourers. *Phil 4*:3
Lucas, my f.-labourers. *Philem 24*

fellow-prisoner
Aristarchus my f.-prisoner. *Col 4*:10
Epaphras my f.-prisoner. *Philem 23*

fellow-prisoners
Andronicus and Junia f.-prisoners.
Rom 16:7

fellows
virginity, I and my f. *Judg 11*:37*
lest angry f. run on thee. 18:25
as one of the vain f. *2 Sam 6*:20
with oil of gladness above f.
Ps 45:7; *Heb 1*:9
his f. shall be ashamed. *Isa 44*:11
tribes of Israel his f. *Ezek 37*:19*
sought Daniel and his f. *Dan 2*:13*
that Daniel and his f. not. 18*
was more stout than his f. 7:20
thou and thy f. that set. *Zech 3*:8
children calling to their f. *Mat 11*:16
Jews took lewd f. of. *Acts 17*:5

fellow-servant, or *servants*
found one of his f.-serv. *Mat 18*:28
his f.-serv. fell at his feet. 29
so when his f.-serv. saw what. 31
have had compassion on f.-serv. 33
begin to smite his f.-serv. 24:49
of Epaphras our f.-serv. *Col 1*:7
Tychicus, who is a f.-serv. in. 4:7
till their f.-serv. should. *Rev 6*:11
it not, I am thy f.-serv. 19:10; 22:9

fellowship
him to keep, or in f. *Lev 6*:2
of iniquity they f. with ? *Ps 94*:20
apostles' doctrine and f. *Acts 2*:42
called to the f. of his Son. *1 Cor 1*:9
not that ye should have f. 10:20*
what f. hath righteousness with ?
2 Cor 6:14
take on us the f. of ministering. 8:4
gave to me right hand of f. *Gal 2*:9
make men see what is f. *Eph 3*:9*
have no f. with works of. 5:11
for your f. in the gospel. *Phil 1*:5
if there be any f. of the spirit. 2:1
that I may know the f. of. 3:10
also may have f. with us, and our f.
is with Father, and. *1 John 1*:3
if we say that we have f. with. 6
if we walk in light, we have f. 7

fellow-soldier
Epaphroditus my f.-soldier.
Phil 2:25
Paul to Archippus our f.-soldier.
Philem 2

fellow-workers
only are my f.-workers. *Col 4*:11

felt
and Isaac f. him. *Gen 27*:22
darkness that may be f. *Ex 10*:21
beaten me, and I f. it not. *Pr 23*:35
she f. she was healed. *Mark 5*:29
shook off the beast and f. *Acts 28*:5*

female
male and f. created. *Gen 1*:27; 5:2
they shall be male and f. 6:19
sevens, the male and his f. 7:2, 3
went in two and two, male and f. 9
went in, went in male and f. 16
whether it be male or f. *Lev 3*:1
offering be of flock, male or f. 6
a f. without blemish. 4:28, 32; 5:6
that hath born a male or f. 12:7
if it be a f. thy estimation shall. 27:4
thy estimation for the f. ten. 5, 7
for the f. from a month old. 6
both male and f. shall. *Num 5*:3
the likeness of male or f. *Deut 4*:16
not be a male or f. barren. 7:14
made them male and f. *Mat 19*:4
Mark 10:6
in Christ neither male nor f.
Gal 3:28

fence
wall and a tottering f. *Ps 62*:3

fenced, *verb*
f. me with bones and. *Job 10*:11
he hath f. up my way that. 19:8
hath a vineyard, f. it. *Isa 5*:2

fenced
till thy high and f. walls. *Deut 28*:52
must be f. with iron. *2 Sam 23*:7
ye shall smite every f. *2 Ki 3*:19

there are with you a *f.* city. *2 Ki* 10:2
tower to the *f.* city. 17:9; 18:8
day of Lord on every *f.* *Isa* 2:15
make thee a *f.* brasen. *Jer* 15:20
ruined cities become *f.* *Ezek* 36:35

fenced *cities*
(*American Revision uses here
the word* fortified)
ones dwell in *f.* cities. *Num* 32:17
all these *cities* were *f.* *Deut* 3:5
to possess *cities* great and *f.* 9:1
rest entered into *f.* cities. *Josh* 10:20
the *cities* were great and *f.* 14:12
number of *f.* cities. *1 Sam* 6:18
lest he get *f.* cities. *2 Sam* 20:6
Sennacherib came against all the *f.*
cities of. *2 Ki* 18:13; *2 Chr* 12:4
lay waste *f.* cities. *2 Ki* 19:25
Solomon built *f.* cities. *2 Chr* 8:5
Shishak took the *f.* cities. 12:4
Asa built *f.* cities in Judah. 14:6
placed forces in *f.* cities. 17:2, 19
judges throughout all *f.* cities. 19:5
gave them *f.* cities in Judah. 21:3
put captains in *f.* cities. 33:14
impoverish *f.* cities. *Jer* 5:17
of north take *f.* cities. *Dan* 11:15
Judah multiplied *f.* cities. *Hos* 8:14
alarm against *f.* cities. *Zeph* 1:16

fens
in covert of reed and *f.* *Job* 40:21

ferret
f. chameleon and lizard. *Lev* 11:30*

ferry boat
there went a *f.* boat. *2 Sam* 19:18

fervent
Apollos, being *f.* in spirit. *Acts* 18:25
f. in spirit, serving Lord. *Rom* 12:11
he told us your *f.* mind. *2 Cor* 7:7*
f. prayer of a righteous. *Jas* 5:16*
above all things *f.* charity. *1 Pet* 4:8
elements melt with *f.* heat.
　　　　　　　2 Pet 3:10, 12

fervently
Epaphras labouring *f.* *Col* 4:12
love one another with a pure heart *f.*
　　　　　　　1 Pet 1:22

Festus
Porcius F. come into. *Acts* 24:27
F. willing to do Jews a pleasure. 25:9
came to Caesarea to salute F. 13
F. declared Paul's cause unto. 14
at F.' commandment Paul was. 23
not mad, most noble F. 26:25

fetch
I will *f.* a morsel of bread. *Gen* 18:5
go, *f.* me two good kids. 27:9, 13
then I will send and *f.* thee. 45
ark, sent maid to *f.* it. *Ex* 2:5
must we *f.* water out ? *Num* 20:10*
elders shall send and *f.* *Deut* 19:12
shalt not go to *f.* pledge. 24:10, 19
from thence will Lord *f.* thee. 30:4
of Gilead went to *f.* *Judg* 11:5
take men to *f.* victuals. 20:10
let us *f.* the ark. *1 Sam* 4:3
come ye down, and *f.* it up. 6:21
Samuel said, Send and *f.* him. 16:11
　　　　　　　20:31
let us come over and *f.* 26:22
f. a compass behind. *2 Sam* 5:23*
doth king not *f.* home his. 14:13
to *f.* about this form of speech. 20*
f. me, I pray thee, a. *1 Ki* 17:10
as she was going to *f.* it. 11
he is, that I may *f.* him. *2 Ki* 6:13
f. quickly Micaiah the. *2 Chr* 18:8
f. olive branches, pine. *Neh* 8:15
I will *f.* my knowledge. *Job* 36:3
say they, I will *f.* wine. *Isa* 56:12
king sent Jehudi to *f.* *Jer* 36:21
come and *f.* us out. *Acts* 16:37*

fetched
water, I pray you, be *f.* *Gen* 18:4
Abraham *f.* a calf tender and. 7
Jacob went and *f.* the kids. 27:14
they *f.* carved image. *Judg* 18:18
men came and *f.* up ark. *1 Sam* 7:1
they ran, and *f.* Saul thence. 10:23
they would have *f.* wheat. *2 Sam* 4:6
David sent and *f.* Mephibosheth. 9:5
David sent and *f.* Bath-sheba. 11:27*

Joab *f.* from Tekoah a. *2 Sam* 14:2
king Solomon *f.* Hiram. *1 Ki* 7:13
f. from Ophir gold, 420 talents. 9:28
f. a compass of seven. *2 Ki* 3:9
Jehoiada sent and *f.* rulers. 11:4
f. from Egypt a chariot. *2 Chr* 1:17
guard came and *f.* the. 12:11*
and they *f.* forth Urijah. *Jer* 26:23
and from thence *f.* a. *Acts* 28:13*

fetcheth
and his hand *f.* a stroke. *Deut* 19:5

fetters
bound Samson with *f.* *Judg* 16:21
hands were not bound, nor thy feet
put into *f.* *2 Sam* 3:34
put out eyes of Zedekiah, and bound
him with *f.* of brass. *2 Ki* 25:7
Manasseh was bound with *f.*
　　　　　　　2 Chr 33:11
Jehoiakim bound with *f.* to. 36:6
feet they hurt with *f.* *Ps* 105:18
their nobles with *f.* of iron. 149:8
being often bound with *f.* *Mark* 5:4
　　　　　　　Luke 8:29

fever
shall smite thee with a *f.* *Deut* 28:22
Peter's wife's mother sick of a *f.*
　　Mat 8:14; *Mark* 1:30; *Luke* 4:38
at 7th hour *f.* left him. *John* 4:52
of Publius sick of a *f.* *Acts* 28:8

few
damsel abide a *f.* days. *Gen* 24:55
tarry a *f.* days till thy. 27:44
I being *f.* in number, they. 34:30
f. and evil the days of my life. 47:9
I will make you *f.* *Lev* 26:22
　　　　　　Deut 4:27; 28:62
the cloud was a *f.* days. *Num* 9:20
see people whether they be *f.* 13:18
to *f.* shall give less. 26:54; 35:8
divided between many and *f.* 26:56
sojourned there with a *f.* *Deut* 26:5
live, let not his men be *f.* 33:6
to save by many or *f.* *1 Sam* 14:6
whom hast thou left *f.* sheep ? 17:28
but priests were too *f.* *2 Chr* 29:34
I and some *f.* men with. *Neh* 2:12
large, but the people were *f.* 7:4
are not my days *f.*? *Job* 10:20
man is of *f.* days and full. 14:1
when a *f.* years are come. 16:22
let his days be *f.* and let. *Ps* 109:8
therefore let words be *f.* *Eccl* 5:2
a little city, and *f.* men in it. 9:14
cease, because they are *f.* 12:3
trees of forest shall be *f.* *Isa* 10:19
inhabitants are burned, and *f.* 24:6
shalt also take a *f.* in. *Ezek* 5:3
I will leave a *f.* men from. 12:16
f. days be destroyed. *Dan* 11:20
strait is gate, and *f.* *Mat* 7:14
labourers are *f.* 9:37; *Luke* 10:2
seven, and a *f.* little fishes.
　　　　　Mat 15:34; *Mark* 8:7
f. are chosen. *Mat* 20:16; 22:14
faithful in a *f.* things. 25:21, 23
laid hands on a *f.* sick. *Mark* 6:5
be beaten with *f.* stripes. *Luke* 12:48
are there *f.* that be saved ? 13:23
hear us a *f.* words. *Acts* 24:4
as I wrote in *f.* words. *Eph* 3:3
for a *f.* days chastened. *Heb* 12:10
written unto you in *f.* words. 13:22
wherein *f.* that is, eight. *1 Pet* 3:20
a *f.* things against. *Rev* 2:14, 20
hast a *f.* names even in. 3:4

but a **few**
to him *but a few* days. *Gen* 29:20
but f. years to jubile. *Lev* 25:52
the men of Ai are *but f.* *Josh* 7:3
when ye were *but f.* *1 Chr* 16:19
　　　　　　　Ps 105:12
we are left *but a f.* of. *Jer* 42:2

not a **few**
vessels, borrow *not a f.* *2 Ki* 4:3
cut off nations *not a f.* *Isa* 10:7
and they shall *not be f.* *Jer* 30:19
chief women *not a f.* *Acts* 17:4
of men *not a f.* 12

fewer
to *f.* ye shall give less. *Num* 33:54

fewest
ye were *f.* of all people. *Deut* 7:7

fewness
according to *f.* of years. *Lev* 25:16

fidelity
servants shewing good *f.* *Tit* 2:10

field
the *f.* give I thee. *Gen* 23:11
the *f.* and cave were made sure. 20
of my son is as smell of a *f.* 27:27
called Rachel and Leah to *f.* 31:4
in *f.* which Abraham. 49:30; 50:13
a man shall cause a *f.* to. *Ex* 22:5
that the corn or *f.* be consumed. 6
shalt not sow thy *f.* with. *Lev* 19:19
six years shalt sow thy *f.* 25:3
seventh year shalt not sow thy *f.* 4
if he sanctify his *f.* from. 27:17, 18
redeem the *f.* or if he sold the *f.* 20
covet thy neighbour's *f.* *Deut* 5:21
ask of her father a *f.* *Josh* 15:18
　　　　　　　Judg 1:14
not to glean in another *f.* *Ruth* 2:2
what day thou buyest *f.* of. 4:5
Joab's *f.* is near mine. *2 Sam* 14:30
servants set my *f.* on fire ? 31
upper pool, in highway of fuller's *f.*
　　　2 Ki 18:17; *Isa* 7:3; 36:2
fled every one to his *f.* *Neh* 13:10
let the *f.* be joyful. *Ps* 96:12
I went by the *f.* of slothful. *Pr* 24:30
and goats the price of *f.* 27:26
considereth a *f.* and buyeth. 31:16
king himself is served by *f.* *Eccl* 5:9
woe to them that lay *f.* to *f.* *Isa* 5:8
joy is taken out of plentiful *f.* 16:10
herbs of every *f.* wither. *Jer* 12:4
Zion plowed like a *f.* 26:18; *Mi* 3:12
my *f.* in Anathoth. *Jer* 32:7, 8, 25
have we vineyard, nor *f.* 35:9
gladness is taken from plentiful *f.*
　　　　　　　48:33
the *f.* is wasted, the. *Joel* 1:10
good seed in his *f.* *Mat* 13:24, 31
the *f.* is the world, good seed. 38
of heaven is like to treasure hid in a
f.; he selleth all, buyeth that *f.* 44
with them the potter's *f.* 27:7, 10
f. was called *f.* of blood. 8; *Acts* 1:19
when come from the *f.* *Luke* 17:7
man purchased a *f.* with. *Acts* 1:18

fruitful **field**
glory of his *fruitful f.* *Isa* 10:18
Lebanon turned into *fruitful f.* 29:17
till wilderness be a *fruitful f.* and the
fruitful f. be counted a. 32:15
righteousness in the *fruitful f.* 16
the seed in a *fruitful f.* *Ezek* 17:5

in the **field**
when they were in the *f.* *Gen* 4:8
out to meditate in the *f.* 24:63
and behold a well in the *f.* 29:2
Joseph was wandering in the *f.* 37:15
gather all thou hast in the *f.* *Ex* 9:19
hail smote all that was in the *f.* 25
ye shall not find it in the *f.* 16:25
found slain, lying in the *f.* *Deut* 21:1
find a betrothed damsel in *f.* 22:25
blessed in city and in the *f.* 28:3
cursed in city and in the *f.* 16
angel came to woman in *f.* *Judg* 13:9
stone remaineth in *f.* of. *1 Sam* 6:18
stand beside my father in the *f.* 19:3
found an Egyptian in the *f.* 30:11
they two strove in the *f.* *2 Sam* 14:6
two were alone in the *f.* *1 Ki* 11:29
dieth of Jeroboam in the *f.* 14:11
dieth of Ahab in the *f.* fowls. 21:24
kings by themselves in *f.* *1 Chr* 19:9
over them that did work in *f.* 27:26
every one his corn in *f.* *Job* 24:6
marvellous things in *f.* of Zoan.
　　　　　　　Ps 78:12, 43
it fit for thyself in the *f.* *Pr* 24:27
the hind calved in the *f.* *Jer* 14:5
O my mountain in the *f.* 17:3
we have treasures in the *f.* 41:8
is in the *f.* shall die. *Ezek* 7:15
slay thy daughters in the *f.* 26:6, 8
shalt dwell in the *f.* and. *Mi* 4:10
every one grass in the *f.* *Zech* 10:1

nor vine cast her fruit *in the f.*
    Mal 3:11
let him who is *in f.* return to.
    Mat 24:18 ; *Mark* 13:16
    Luke 17:31
shall two be *in the f.*   *Mat* 24:40
    Luke 17:36
shepherds abiding *in f.*   *Luke* 2:8
grass which is to-day *in the f.* 12:28
his elder son was *in the f.* 15:25

into the **field**
and went *into the f.*   *Num* 22:23
people went *into the f.* *Judg* 9:42
cart came *into the f.* *1 Sam* 6:14
come let us go *into the f.* 20:11
men came out *into f.* *2 Sam* 11:23
removed Amasa *into the f.* 20:12
one went *into f.* and. *2 Ki* 4:39
let us go forth *into f.* *S of S* 7:11
go not forth *into f.* nor. *Jer* 6:25
if I go forth *into the f.* 14:18

of the **field**
plant and herb *of the f.* *Gen* 2:5
sons of Jacob came out *of the f.* 34:7
four parts, for seed *of the f.* 47:24
trees *of the f.* yield fruit. *Lev* 26:4
no devoted thing *of the f.* 27:28
for the tree *of the f.* is. *Deut* 20:19
marchedst out *of the f.* *Juda* 5:4
old man from work out *of f.* 19:16
on a part *of the f.* *Ruth* 2:3
Saul came out *of the f.* *1 Sam* 11:5
of the f. of Naboth. *2 Ki* 9:25
as dung upon the face *of the f.* 37
league with stones *of the f.* *Job* 5:23
as a flower *of the f.* *Ps* 103:15
charge you by the roes *of the f.*
    S of S 2:7; 3:5
were as grass *of the f.* *Isa* 37:27
as the flower *of the f.* 40:6
beast *of the f.* honour me. 43:20
trees *of the f.* shall clap. 55:12
as keepers *of the f.* are. *Jer* 4:17
of Lebanon from rock *of the f.* 18:14
want of fruits *of the f.* *Lam* 4:9
multiply as bud *of the f.* *Ezek* 16:7
all trees *of the f.* shall know. 17:24
tree *of the f.* shall yield fruit. 34:27
multiply increase of the f. 36:30
take no wood out *of the f.* 39:10
in tender grass *of the f.* *Dan* 4:15
hemlock in furrows *of f.* *Hos* 10:4
altars as heaps in furrows *of f.* 12:11
harvest *of the f.* is. *Joel* 1:11
even all the trees *of the f.* are. 12
flame hath burnt all trees *of f.* 19
Samaria as an heap *of f.* *Mi* 1:6
consider lilies *of the f.* *Mat* 6:28
if God so clothe grass *of the f.* 30
parable of the tares *of the f.* 13:36

see **beast, beasts**

open **field**
bird loose into *open f.* *Lev* 14:7
sacrifices which they offer in *open f.*
    17:5
carcases as dung upon the *open f.*
    Jer 9:22
cast out in the *open f.* *Ezek* 16:5
cast thee forth upon *open f.* 32:4
him that is in the *open f.* I. 33:27
thou shalt fall upon the *open f.* 39:5

fields
died out of houses and *f.* *Ex* 8:13
shall be counted as the *f.* *Lev* 25:31
which is not of the *f.* of. 27:22
us inheritance of *f.* *Num* 16:14
not pass through *f.* or. 20:17; 21:22
send grass into thy *f.* *Deut* 11:15
might eat increase of the *f.* 32:13
vine is as vine of the *f.* of. 32
f. and villages gave they. *Josh* 21:12
he will take your *f.* *1 Sam* 8:14
of Jesse give each of you *f.?* 22:7
wall to us when we were in *f.* 25:15
Anathoth, to thine own *f.* *1 Ki* 2:26
that dieth of Baasha in *f.* 16:4
let the *f.* rejoice, and. *1 Chr* 16:32
over storehouses in the *f.* 27:25
sendeth waters upon *f.* *Job* 5:10
sow the *f.* and plant. *Ps* 107:37
we found it in the *f.* of wood. 132:6
yet he had not made the *f.* *Pr* 8:26

into *f.* of the fatherless. *Pr.* 23:10
for *f.* of Heshbon. *Isa* 16:8
lament for pleasant *f.* 32:12
their *f.* turned to. *Jer* 6:12; 8:10
seen abominations in the *f.* 13:27
f. shall be possessed again. 32:15
f. bought. 43
men shall buy *f.* for money. 44
Nebuzar-adan gave them *f.* 39:10
captains of forces in the *f.* 40:7, 13
shall possess *f.* of Ephraim.
they covet *f.* and take. *Mi* 2:2
turning away, hath divided our *f.* 4
although *f.* yield no meat. *Hab* 3:17
went through the corn *f.* *Mark* 2:23
    Luke 6:1
your eyes, look on the *f.* *John* 4:35
which reaped down your *f.* *Jas* 5:4

open **fields**
living bird into *open f.* *Lev* 14:53
with sword in *open f.* *Num* 19:16
encamped in the *open f.* *2 Sam* 11:11
shalt fall upon *open f.* *Ezek* 29:5

fierce
be their anger, it was *f.* *Gen* 49:7
nation of *f.* countenance. *Deut* 28:50
the voice of *f.* lion and. *Job* 4:10
huntest me as a *f.* lion. 10:16
nor the *f.* lion passed by it. 28:8
none is so *f.* that dare stir. 41:10
a *f.* king shall rule over. *Isa* 19:4
shalt not see a *f.* people. 33:19
king of *f.* countenance. *Dan* 8:23
horses are more *f.* than. *Hab* 1:8
with devils, exceeding *f.* *Mat* 8:28
and they were more *f.* *Luke* 23:5
shall be incontinent, *f.* *2 Tim* 3:3
ships which are driven of *f.* winds.
    Jas 3:4*

see **anger, wrath**

fierceness
swalloweth ground with *f.* and.
    Job 39:24
land desolate for the *f.* *Jer* 25:38

fiercer
words of Judah *f.* than. *2 Sam* 19:43

fiery
the Lord sent *f.* serpents. *Num* 21:6
make thee a *f.* serpent, and set. 8
wherein were *f.* serpents. *Deut* 8:15
from his right hand a *f.* law. 33:2
make them as a *f.* oven. *Ps* 21:9
fruit a *f.* flying serpent. *Isa* 14:29
into midst of *f.* furnace. *Dan* 3:6, 11
    15, 21
God is able to deliver us from *f.* 17
three men into midst of *f.* furnace. 23
came near to mouth of *f.* furnace. 26
his throne was like the *f.* flame. 7:9
a *f.* stream issued and came. 10
able to quench *f.* darts. *Eph* 6:16
of judgement, and *f.* *Heb* 10:27*
not strange concerning *f.* *1 Pet* 4:12

fifteen
f. cubits upwards did. *Gen* 7:20
hangings to be *f.* cubits. *Ex* 27:14
    15; 38:14
shall be *f.* shekels. *Lev* 27:7
now Ziba had *f.* sons. *2 Sam* 9:10
Ziba and his *f.* sons went. 19:17
on forty-five pillars, *f.* *1 Ki* 7:3
Amaziah lived after Jehoash *f.* years.
    2 Ki 14:17
I will add to thy days *f.* years. 20:6
    2 Chr 25:25; *Isa* 38:5
f. shekels shall be. *Ezek* 45:12
bought her to me for *f.* *Hos* 3:2
Bethany was *f.* furlongs. *John* 11:18
and found it *f.* fathoms. *Acts* 27:28
I abode with Peter *f.* days. *Gal* 1:18

fifteenth
in *f.* year of Amaziah. *2 Ki* 14:23
f. to Bilgah. *1 Chr* 24:14
f. to Jerimoth. 25:22
to Jerusalem in *f.* year. *2 Chr* 15:10
in the *f.* year of reign. *Luke* 3:1

fifteenth day
came to Sin, on *f.* day. *Ex* 16:1
on *f.* day of the same month.
    Lev 23:6; *Num* 28:17; 33:3

f. day of this seventh month feast of.
    Lev 23:34, 39; *Num* 29:12
on *f.* day of the eighth month was
  Jeroboam's. *1 Ki* 12:32, 33
on *f.* day they rested. *Esth* 9:18, 21
f. day of twelfth year. *Ezek* 32:17
in *f.* day do like in feast 45:25

fifth
Leah bare Jacob the *f.* *Gen* 30:17
f. lot came out for Asher. *Josh* 19:24
smote Asahel under *f.* *2 Sam* 2:23*
Abner under the *f.* rib. 3:27*
Joab smote Amasa in the *f.* 20:10*
Sanballat sent *f.* time. *Neh* 6:5
when he had opened *f.* seal. *Rev* 6:9
the *f.* angel sounded, and I saw. 9:1
f. angel poured out his vial. 16:10
the *f.* a sardonyx. 21:20

see **day, part**

fifth month
Aaron died first day of *f.* month.
    Num 33:38
f. month came Nebuzar-adan.
    2 Ki 25:8; *Jer* 52:12
fifth captain for *f.* month. *1 Chr* 27:8
Ezra came in *f.* month. *Ezra* 7:8, 9
Jerusalem captive in the *f.* month.
    Jer 1:3
in *f.* month Hananiah spake. 28:1
in *f.* month the elders. *Ezek* 20:1
I weep in *f.* month ? *Zech* 7:3
fasted and mourned in *f.* month. 5
fast of fourth and of *f.* month. 8:19

fifth year
in *f.* year ye shall eat. *Lev* 19:25
f. year of king Rehoboam Shishak
  came. *1 Ki* 14:25; *2 Chr* 12:2
in the *f.* year of Joram. *2 Ki* 8:16
in *f.* year of Jehoiakim. *Jer* 36:9
f. year of Jehoiachin's. *Ezek* 1:2

fifties
place rulers of *f.* *Ex* 18:21, 25
    Deut 1:15
appoint captains over *f.* *1 Sam* 8:12
burnt two captains of *f.* *2 Ki* 1:14

fiftieth
ye shall hallow *f.* year. *Lev* 25:10
a jubile shall that *f.* year be to. 11
in *f.* year of Azariah. *2 Ki* 15:23

fifty
breadth of ark *f.* cubits. *Gen* 6:15
not spare the place for *f.?* 18:24, 26
f. loops shalt thou make. *Ex* 26:5
    10; 36:12, 17
make *f.* taches of gold. 26:6, 11
    36:13, 18
hangings of *f.* cubits. 27:12; 38:12
two hundred and *f.* shekels, of sweet
  calamus two hundred *f.* 30:23
7th sabbath, number *f.* *Lev* 23:16
males thy estimation *f.* shekels. 27:3
homer of barley seed valued at *f.* 16
from thirty years old even to *f.* years.
    Num 4:3, 23, 30, 35, 39
from age of *f.* shall serve no. 8:25
two hundred and *f.* princes of. 16:2
fire devoured two hundred *f.* 26:10
one portion of *f.* for Levites. 31:30
Moses took one portion of *f.* of. 47
give damsel's father *f.* *Deut* 22:29
a wedge of gold of *f.* *Josh* 7:21
Absalom had *f.* men to. *2 Sam* 15:1
Adonijah had *f.* men to. *1 Ki* 1:5
breadth of house of forest *f.* 7:2
hid them by *f.* in a cave. 18:4, 13
captain of *f.* with his *f.* *2 Ki* 1:9
    11, 13
fire consume thee and thy *f.* 10, 12
f. men of sons of the prophets. 2:7
they sent therefore *f.* men to. 17
left to Jehoahaz but *f.* 13:7
Menahem exacted of each *f.* 15:20
but Pekah slew *f.* men of. 25
weight of nails was *f.* *2 Chr* 3:9
Ebed went up with *f.* *Ezra* 8:6
Tirshatha gave *f.* basons. *Neh* 7:70
gallows *f.* cubits. *Esth* 5:14; 7:9
Lord will take captain of *f.* *Isa* 3:3
to face of captain of *f.* *Ezek* 40:15
length *f.* cubits. 21, 25, 29, 33, 36
    42:7

of north door f. cubits. *Ezek* 42:2
to draw out f. vessels. *Hag* 2:16
owed 500 pence, other f. *Luke* 7:41
sit down quickly, and write f. 16:6
art not yet f. years old. *John* 8:57

fifty-two
Azariah reigned f.-two. *2 Ki* 15:2
children of Nebo f.-two. *Ezra* 2:29
Neh 7:33
wall finished in f.-two days.*Neh* 6:15

fifty-six
of Netophah, f. and six. *Ezra* 2:22

fifty thousand
of people f. thousand. *1 Sam* 6:19
of camels f. thousand. *1 Chr* 5:21
of Zebulun f. thousand. 12:33
price of books f. thousand pieces of
silver. *Acts* 19:19

fifty-three thousand
of Naphtali numbered f.-three thousand. *Num* 1:43; 2:30; 26:47

fifty-four thousand
of Issachar f.-four thousand four
hundred. *Num* 1:29; 2:6

fifty-seven thousand
Zebulun f.-seven thousand four.
Num 1:31; 2:8

fifty-nine thousand
of Simeon numbered f.-nine thousand three hundred. *Num* 1:23

fig, -s
*The fig tree and its fruit are well
known; they were very common in
Palestine, and there is mention
often made of them in scripture.
Our first parents clothed themselves
with fig leaves, Gen 3:7. The prophet Isaiah gave orders to apply a
lump of figs to Hezekiah's boil;
and immediately after he was
cured, 2 Ki 20:7.
The cursing of the fig tree, in
Mat 21:19, is explained by the fact
that the fruit of this tree appears before the leaves, and a tree so full of
leaves indicated that ripe figs
should be there, even though it was
not yet the regular season. The
meaning is then, that when one
has the outward show of a good
character, without its fruits, he is
but a hypocrite, and of no value to
the kingdom of God.
To dwell under one's own vine, or
fig tree, represents in scripture a
time of happiness and prosperity,
safety and security, 1 Ki 4:25.*

sewed f. leaves together. *Gen* 3:7
of pomegranates and f. *Num* 13:23
no place of seed, or of f. or. 20:5
Abigail took cakes of f. *1 Sam* 25:18
gave Egyptian a cake of f. 30:12
said, take a lump of f. *2 Ki* 20:7
Isa 38:21
that were nigh brought f. *1 Chr* 12:40
sabbath some brought f. *Neh* 13:15
putteth forth green f. *S of S* 2:13
as a falling f. from. *Isa* 34:4*
there shall be no f. on. *Jer* 8:13
of f. one had very good f. 24:1, 2, 3
as the evil f. that cannot be eaten. 8
I will make them like vile f. 29:17
fig trees with first ripe f. *Nah* 3:12
men gather f. of thistles ? *Mat* 7:16
Luke 6:44
bear berries, or a vine f.? *Jas* 3:12
casteth her untimely f. *Rev* 6:13

fig tree
trees said to f. come, reign. *Judg* 9:10, 11
dwelt safely under his f. *1 Ki* 4:25
Mi 4:4
eat every one of his f. *2 Ki* 18:31
Isa 36:16
whoso keepeth f. shall eat. *Pr* 27:18
fathers as firstripe in the f. *Hos* 9:10
he hath barked my f. *Joel* 1:7
vine is dried, the f. languisheth. 12
the f. and vine do yield. 2:22
the f. shall not blossom. *Hab* 3:17
as yet the f. hath not. *Hag* 2:19

---

call every man under f. *Zech* 3:10
when he saw a f. in way. *Mat* 21:19
Mark 11:13
how soon is f. withered ! *Mat* 21:20
Mark 11:20, 21
a parable of the f. *Mat* 24:32
Mark 13:28
a man had a f. planted. *Luke* 13:6
I come, seeking fruit on this f. 7
behold the f. and all trees. 21:29
under the f. I saw. *John* 1:48, 50

fig trees
of wheat, vines, and f. *Deut* 8:8
smote their vines also and f.
Ps 105:33
eat up thy vines and f. *Jer* 5:17
destroy her vines and f. *Hos* 2:12
when your gardens and f. *Amos* 4:9
strong holds shall be like f. *Nah* 3:12

fight, substantive
as host was going forth to the f.
1 Sam 17:20
fight the good f. of faith. *1 Tim* 6:12
I have fought a good f. *2 Tim* 4:7
ye endured a great f. *Heb* 10:32*
strong, waxed valiant in f. 11:34*

fight, verb
we will go up and f. *Deut* 1:41
go not up, nor f., I am not among. 42
Sihon and his people came to f. 2:32*
art come against me to f. *Judg* 11:12
yourselves like men, f. *1 Sam* 4:9
me a man that we may f. 17:10
nigh when ye did f.? *2 Sam* 11:20
f. not small nor great. *1 Ki* 22:31
2 Chr 18:30
about Jehoshaphat to f. *2 Chr* 18:31
ye shall not need to f. in. 20:17
teacheth my fingers to f. *Ps* 144:1
men have forborn to f. *Jer* 51:30
shall f. because Lord is. *Zech* 10:5
Judah also shall f. at. 14:14
would my servants f. *John* 18:36
so I, not as one that. *1 Cor* 9:26
f. the good fight of faith. *1 Tim* 6:12
ye kill, ye f. and war.' *Jas* 4:2

see battles

fight against
join enemies, f. against us. *Ex* 1:10
to a city to f. against it. *Deut* 20:10
to enemies against whom ye f.
Josh 10:25
pitched to f. against Israel. 11:5
Danites went up to f. against. 19:47
first to f. against them ? *Judg* 1:1
that we may f. against Canaanites. 3
over Jordan to f. against Judah. 10:9
to f. against Ammon. 11:8, 9
against Israel, or f. against them ? 25
come to f. against me ? 12:3
set themselves to f. against. 20:20
f. against Amalekites. *1 Sam* 15:18
Philistines f. against Keilah. 23:1
not f. against enemies of king. 29:8
Judah with Benjamin to f. against
Israel. *1 Ki* 12:21; *2 Chr* 11:1
not f. against your brethren.
1 Ki 12:24; *2 Chr* 11:4
let us f. against them in plain.
1 Ki 20:23, 25
to f. against Jehoshaphat. 22:32
kings were come to f. against them.
2 Ki 3:21
he is come out to f. against. 19:9
O Israel, f. not against. *2 Chr* 13:12
Sennacherib to f. against. 32:2
Necho came to f. against. 35:20
and f. against Jerusalem. *Neh* 4:8
f. against them that f. against me.
Ps 35:1
be many that f. against me. 56:2
f. every one against his brother.
Isa 19:2
nations that f. against Ariel. 29:7
nations that f. against Zion. 8
f. against thee, not prevail. *Jer* 1:19
15:20
wherewith ye f. against king. 21:4
I myself will f. against you. 5
city is given to the Chaldeans that f.
against it. 32:24, 29; 34:22; 37:8
Chaldeans that f. against you. 37:10
Lord shall f. against. *Zech* 14:3

---

found to f. against God. *Acts* 5:39
let us not f. against God. 23:9
f. against them with sword.
Rev 2:16*

fight for
f. for you. *Ex* 14:14; *Deut* 1:30
3:22; 20:4
f. for your master's. *2 Ki* 10:3
f. for your brethren, sons. *Neh* 4:14
our God shall f. for us. 20
Lord shall come to f. for. *Isa* 31:4

fight with
go out, f. with Amalek. *Ex* 17:9
gathered to f. with Joshua. *Josh* 9:2
to f. with the Midianites. *Judg* 8:1
go out and f. with Abimelech. 9:38
may f. with children of Ammon. 11:6
gathered to f. with Israel.
1 Sam 13:5; 28:1
if he be able to f. with me. 17:9
servant will f. with this Philistine. 32
disguised himself to f. with him.
2 Chr 35:22
of shaking f. with it. *Isa* 30:32
ye f. with Chaldeans. *Jer* 32:5
came to f. with. 33:5
went to f. with Ishmael. 41:12
return to f. with prince of. *Dan* 10:20
south come and f. with him. 11:11

fighteth
Lord f. for them against. *Ex* 14:25
the Lord God, that f. for. *Josh* 23:10
my lord f. the battles. *1 Sam* 25:28

fighting
were f. Philistines. *1 Sam* 17:19
Uzziah had host of f. *2 Chr* 26:11
O God, he f. oppresseth. *Ps* 56:1

lightings
without were f. within. *2 Cor* 7:5
whence come wars and f.? *Jas* 4:1

figure
similitude of any f. *Deut* 4:16
maketh it after the f. of. *Isa* 44:13
who is the f. of him. *Rom* 5:14
I have in a f. transferred. *1 Cor* 4:6
which was a f. of the time. *Heb* 9:9
whence he received him in a f. 11:19
the like f. whereunto. *1 Pet* 3:21*

figures
carved with carved f. *1 Ki* 6:29
f. ye made to worship. *Acts* 7:43
holy places, f. of the true. *Heb* 9:24*

file
had a f. for mattocks. *1 Sam* 13:21

fill, substantive
shall eat f. in safety. *Lev* 25:19
mayest eat grapes thy f. *Deut* 23:24
let us take our f. of love. *Pr* 7:18

fill, verb
multiply, and f. waters. *Gen* 1:22
Joseph commanded to f. 42:25
44:1
locusts shall f. thy houses. *Ex* 10:6
Moses said, f. an homer. 16:32*
f. thine horn with oil. *1 Sam* 16:1
f. four barrels with water. *1 Ki* 18:33
till he f. thy mouth with. *Job* 8:21
a wise man f. belly with east. 15:2
when he is about to f. his. 20:23
f. my mouth with arguments. 23:4
f. appetite of young lions. 38:39*
canst thou f. his skin with ? 41:7
thy mouth and I will f. it. *Ps* 81:10
f. their faces with shame. 83:16
shall f. places with dead. 110:6
shall f. our houses with. *Pr* 1:13
I will f. their treasures. 8:21
wings shall f. breadth of. *Isa* 8:8
nor f. face of world with. 14:21
f. face of the world with fruit. 27:6
we will f. ourselves with. 56:12
I will f. inhabitants with. *Jer* 13:13
not I f. heaven and earth ? 23:24
it is to f. them with the dead. 33:5
surely I will f. thee with. 51:14
f. thy bowels with this roll. *Ezek* 3:3
not satisfy their souls nor f. 7:19
f. the courts with slain. 9:7
f. thine hand with coals of fire. 10:2
gather pieces, f. it with choice. 24:4
shall f. the land with slain. 30:11

_f._ beasts of whole earth. _Ezek_ 32:4*
I will _f._ the valleys with thy. 5
_f._ his mountains with slain. 35:8
_f._ masters' house with. _Zeph_ 1:9
I will _f._ this house with. _Hag_ 2:7
which is put in to _f._ it up. _Mat_ 9:16
have bread to _f._ such a ? 15:33
_f._ ye up then the measure of. 23:32
_f._ the water-pots with. _John_ 2:7
God of hope _f._ you with. _Rom_ 15:13
ascended, that he might _f._ all. _Eph_ 4:10
_f._ up what is behind of. _Col_ 1:24
Jews, to _f._ up their sins. _1 Thes_ 2:16
cup she hath filled, _f._ _Rev_ 18:6*

filled

earth is _f._ with violence. _Gen_ 6:13
Hagar went and _f._ the bottle. 21:19
Rebekah _f._ her pitcher. 24:16
Philistines had _f._ the wells. 26:15
children of Israel _f._ land. _Ex_ 1:7
_f._ the troughs to water flock. 2:16
I have _f._ with wisdom. 28:3; 35:35
I have _f._ him with Spirit. 31:3; 35:31
of Lord _f._ tabernacle. 40:34, 35
within thy gates and be _f._ _Deut_ 26:12
have eaten and _f._ themselves. 31:20
these bottles we _f._ were. _Josh_ 9:13
cloud _f._ house of Lord. _1 Ki_ 8:10
glory of Lord _f._ house. 1
2 Chr 5:14; 7:1, 2
he _f._ the trench also with. 18:35
but Syrians _f._ the country. 20:27
man his stone and _f._ it. _2 Ki_ 3:25
Manasseh _f._ Jerusalem. 21:16; 24:4
Josiah _f._ places with bones. 23:14
which have _f._ it from end. _Ezra_ 9:11
with princes who _f._ their. _Job_ 3:15
hast _f._ me with wrinkles. 16:8*
yet he _f._ their houses with. 22:18
are _f._ with loathsome. _Ps_ 38:7
let my mouth be _f._ with thy. 71:8
let the whole earth be _f._ 72:19
to take deep root, it _f._ the. 80:9
openest thine hand, _f._ with. 104:28*
exceedingly _f._ with contempt. 123:3
our soul is _f._ with scorning. 4
lest strangers be _f._ with. _Pr_ 5:10
lest thou be _f._ with honey. 25:16
earth that is not _f._ with. 30:16*
a fool when he is _f._ with meat. 22
nor the ear _f._ with hearing. _Eccl_ 1:8
his soul be not _f._ with good. 6:3
and yet the appetite is not _f._ 7
my head is _f._ with dew. _S of S_ 5:2
and his train _f._ temple. _Isa_ 6:1
are my loins _f._ with pain. 21:3
Lord hath _f._ Zion with. 33:5
sword of Lord is _f._ with blood. 34:6
nor _f._ me with the fat of thy. 43:24
old man that hath not _f._ 65:20
thou hast _f._ me with. _Jer_ 15:17
they _f._ mine inheritance. 16:18
_f._ this place with blood of. 19:4
Ishmael _f._ the pit with them. 41:9
and thy cry hath _f._ the land. 46:12
he hath _f._ his belly with. 51:34
hath _f._ me with bitterness. _Lam_ 3:15
he is _f._ full with reproach. 30
have _f._ the land with. _Ezek_ 8:17
and the cloud _f._ the inner. 10:3
have _f._ the streets with slain. 11:6
_f._ the midst of thee with. 28:16
waste cities be _f._ 36:38
glory of Lord _f._ the house. 43:5
44:4
the stone cut out _f._ the. _Dan_ 2:35
lion _f._ his holes with. _Nah_ 2:12
thou art _f._ with shame. _Hab_ 2:16
but are not _f._ with drink. _Hag_ 1:6
I have _f._ the bow with. _Zech_ 9:13
and _f._ a spunge with. _Mat_ 27:48
Mark 15:36; _John_ 19:29
new piece that _f._ it up. _Mark_ 2:21
let the children first be _f._ 7:27
he hath _f._ the hungry. _Luke_ 1:53
strong in spirit, _f._ with wisdom. 2:40
they came and _f._ both ships. 5:7
come, that my house be _f._ 14:23
_f._ his belly with husks. 15:16
they _f._ them up to brim. _John_ 2:7
they _f._ twelve baskets with. 6:13
sorrow hath _f._ your heart. 16:6
rushing mighty wind, _f._ _Acts_ 2:2

Peter, _f._ with Holy Ghost. _Acts_ 4:8
why hath Satan _f._ thine heart ? 5:3
_f._ Jerusalem with your doctrine. 28
mightest be _f._ with Holy Ghost. 9:17
Paul, _f._ with the Holy Ghost. 13:9
being _f._ with all unrighteousness.
Rom 1:29
are _f._ with all knowledge. 15:14
if first I be somewhat _f._ with. 24*
I am _f._ with comfort. _2 Cor_ 7:4
_f._ with the fulness of God. _Eph_ 3:19
not drunk with wine, be _f._ with. 5:18
_f._ with the fruits of _Phil_ 1:11
might be _f._ with knowledge. _Col_ 1:9
that I may be _f._ with joy. _2 Tim_ 1:4
in peace, be warmed and _f._ _Jas_ 2:16
angel _f._ the censer with. _Rev_ 8:5
for in them is _f._ up the wrath. 15:1*
cup which she hath _f._ fill. 18:6*

shall be **filled**

morning ye _shall be f._ _Ex_ 16:12
earth _shall be f._ with. _Num_ 14:21
valley _shall be f._ with. _2 Ki_ 3:17
shall be f. with own. _Pr_ 1:31
shall thy barns be _f._ with plenty. 3:10
wicked _shall be f._ with. 12:21
the backslider _shall be f._ 14:14
increase of lips _shall_ he be _f._ 18:20*
his mouth _shall be f._ with. 20:17
knowledge _shall_ chambers be _f._ 24:4
every bottle _shall be f._ _Jer_ 13:12
shalt be _f._ with drunkenness.
Ezek 23:33
ye _shall be f._ at my table. 39:20
earth _shall be f._ with. _Hab_ 2:14
shall be f. like bowls. _Zech_ 9:15
blessed they that hunger, they _shall_
be _f._ _Mat_ 5:6
John _shall be f._ with. _Luke_ 1:15
every valley _shall be f._ 3:5
ye that hunger, ye _shall be f._ 6:21

was **filled**

earth _was f._ with violence. _Gen_ 6:11
Hiram _was f._ with. _1 Ki_ 7:14
country _was f._ with water. _2 Ki_ 3:20
house _was f._ with a. _2 Chr_ 5:13
was f. with sweet odours. 16:14
our mouth _was f._ with. _Ps_ 126:2
house _was f._ with smoke. _Isa_ 6:4
land _was f._ with sin. _Jer_ 51:5
house _was f._ with cloud. _Ezek_ 10:4
Elisabeth _was f._ with Holy Ghost.
Luke 1:41
Zacharias _was f._ with Holy Ghost. 67
house _was f._ with odour. _John_ 12:3
city _was f._ with confusion. _Acts_ 19:29
temple _was f._ with smoke. _Rev_ 15:8

were **filled**

so were they _f._ they were _f._ _Hos_ 13:6
they _were f._ with wrath. _Luke_ 4:28
were f. with fear, saying. 5:26
they _were f._ with madness. 6:11
they _were f._ with water. 8:23
when they _were f._ he. _John_ 6:12
did eat of loaves, and _were f._ 26
they _were_ all _f._ with the Holy Ghost.
Acts 2:4; 4:31
they _were f._ with wonder. 3:10
and _were f._ with indignation. 5:17
the Jews _were f._ with envy. 13:45
disciples _were f._ with joy and. 52
fowls _were f._ with their. _Rev_ 19:21

see **eat**

filledst

houses, which thou _f._ not. _Deut_ 6:11
thou _f._ many people. _Ezek_ 27:33

fillest

belly thou _f._ with hid. _Ps_ 17:14

fillet

a _f._ of twelve cubits. _Jer_ 52:21*

filleth

he _f._ me with bitterness. _Job_ 9:18
the rain also _f._ pools. _Ps_ 84:6*
he _f._ hungry soul with. 107:9
the mower _f._ not his hand. 129:7
_f._ thee with finest of wheat. 147:14
fulness of him that _f._ all. _Eph_ 1:23

fillets

hooks of the pillars, and their _f._ be.
_Ex_ 27:10, 11; 38:10, 11, 12, 17, 19
chapiters and _f._ with gold. 36:38

filletted

_f._ with silver. _Ex_ 27:17; 38:17
overlaid chapiters and _f._ 38:28

filling

_f._ our hearts with food. _Acts_ 14:17

filth

Lord washed away _f._ of. _Isa_ 4:4
cast abominable _f._ upon. _Nah_ 3:6
made as the _f._ of world. _1 Cor_ 4:13
putting away _f._ of flesh. _1 Pet_ 3:21

filthiness

_f._ out of the holy place. _2 Chr_ 29:5
had separated from _f._ of. _Ezra_ 6:21
an unclean land with the _f._ 9:11
is not washed from their _f._ _Pr_ 30:12
are full of vomit and _f._ _Isa_ 28:8
her _f._ is in her skirts. _Lam_ 1:9
thy _f._ was poured out. _Ezek_ 16:36
and I will consume thy _f._ 22:15
that the _f._ of it may be. 24:11
in thy _f._ is lewdness, shalt not be
purged from thy _f._ 13
from all _f._ will I cleanse you. 36:25
cleanse ourselves from all _f._ of.
2 Cor 7:1*
nor let _f._ be once named. _Eph_ 5:4
wherefore lay apart all _f._ _Jas_ 1:21
of abomination and _f._ of. _Rev_ 17:4*

filthy

more abominable and _f._ _Job_ 15:16*
altogether become _f._ _Ps_ 14:3; 53:3
righteousness as _f._ rags. _Isa_ 64:6*
woe to her that is _f._ _Zeph_ 3:1*
Joshua clothed with _f._ _Zech_ 3:3
take away _f._ garments from him. 4
you also put off _f._ communication.
Col 3:8*
nor greedy of _f._ lucre. _1 Tim_ 3:3*, 8
not given to _f._ lucre. _Tit_ 1:7
teaching things for _f._ lucre's sake. 11
1 Pet 5:2
Lot vexed with _f._ _2 Pet_ 2:7*
these _f._ dreamers defile. _Jude_ 8
he that is _f._ let him be _f._ _Rev_ 22:11

finally

_f._ my brethren, farewell. _2 Cor_ 13:11
Eph 6:10; _Phil_ 3:1; 4:8
2 Thes 3:1; _1 Pet_ 3:8

find

wearied themselves to _f._ _Gen_ 19:11
speak to Esau, when you _f._ 32:19
sin shall _f._ you out. _Num_ 32:23
the revenger of blood _f._ him. 35:27
a man _f._ a damsel. _Deut_ 22:25, 28
sojourn where he could _f._ a place.
Judg 17:8, 9
Lord grant ye may _f._ rest. _Ruth_ 1:9
go, _f._ out arrows. _1 Sam_ 20:21, 36
if a man _f._ his enemy. 24:19
peradventure we may _f._ _1 Ki_ 18:5
to _f._ out every device. _2 Chr_ 2:14*
Assyria come and _f._ much. 32:4
I knew where I might _f._ _Job_ 23:3
every man to _f._ according to. 34:11
seek out his wickedness till thou _f._
_Ps_ 10:15
thou shalt _f._ knowledge. _Pr_ 2:5
words are like to those that _f._ 4:22
right to them that _f._ knowledge. 8:9
I _f._ out knowledge of inventions. 12
a man should _f._ nothing. _Eccl_ 7:14
counting one by one, to _f._ out the. 27
sought to _f._ acceptable. 12:10
if _f._ my beloved, tell him. _S of S_ 5:8
screech owl shall _f._ a. _Isa_ 34:14
in the day of fast you _f._ 58:3
that they may _f._ it so. _Jer_ 10:18*
like harts that _f._ no. _Lam_ 1:6
her prophets also _f._ no vision. 2:9
sought to _f._ occasion against Daniel,
but could _f._ none. _Dan_ 6:4
not _f._ except we _f._ it concerning. 5
and few there be that _f._ it. _Mat_ 7:14
and if so be that he _f._ it. 18:13
if haply he might _f._ any. _Mark_ 11:13
coming suddenly, _f._ you. 13:36
that they might _f._ an. _Luke_ 6:7
and _f._ them so, blessed are. 12:38
I come seeking fruit and _f._ 13:7
that which is lost, till he _f._ it. 15:4
seek dilgently till she _f._ it ? 8
go in and out and _f._ _John_ 10:9

f. a tabernacle for God. *Acts* 7:46
might feel after him and f. 17:27
we f. no evil in this man. 23:9
why doth he yet f. fault? *Rom* 9:19
and f. you unprepared. *2 Cor* 9:4
he may f. mercy of Lord. *2 Tim* 1:18
see **favour**

can or canst find
can we f. such a one as? *Gen* 41:38
straw where you can f. it. *Ex* 5:11
and gold thou canst f. *Ezra* 7:16
when they can f. the grave. *Job* 3:22
canst thou by searching f. out God?
canst thou f. out Almighty? 11:7
faithful man who can f.? *Pr* 20:6
who can f. virtuous woman? 31:10
no man can f. out work. *Eccl* 3:11
exceeding deep, who can f. it? 7:24
can f. a man that seeketh. *Jer* 5:1

cannot find
said, I cannot f. her. *Gen* 38:22
if he cannot f. thee, will slay me.
1 Ki 18:12
I cannot f. one wise man. *Job* 17:10
Almighty, we cannot f. him. 37:23
a man cannot f. out work. *Eccl* 8:17

find grace
may f. *grace* in thy sight. *Gen* 32:5
Ex 33:13
are to f. *grace* in sight. *Gen* 33:8
let me f. *grace*. 15
let me f. *grace* in your eyes. 34:11
f. *grace* in sight of my lord. 47:25
in whose sight I f. *grace*. *Ruth* 2:2
thy handmaid f. *grace*. *1 Sam* 1:18
f. *grace* in thy sight. *2 Sam* 16:4
we may f. *grace* to help. *Heb* 4:16

I find
if I f. in Sodom fifty. *Gen* 18:26
if I f. there forty-five. 28
if I f. thirty there. 30
till I f. out a place for. *Ps* 132:5
and I f. more bitter than. *Eccl* 7:26
when I should f. thee. *S of S* 8:1
sighing, and I f. no. *Jer* 45:3
Pilate said, I f. no fault. *Luke* 23:4
John 18:38; 19:4, 6
to perform good, I f. not. *Rom* 7:18*
I f. then a law, that when I. 21

not find, or find not
to-day ye shall not f. it. *Ex* 16:25
Saul shall not f. thee. *1 Sam* 23:17
sought, could not f. *2 Sam* 17:20
but they shall not f. me. *Pr* 1:28
Hos 5:6; *John* 7:34, 36
soul seeketh, but I f. not. *Eccl* 7:28
him, could not f. him. *S of S* 5:6
seek, but shalt not f. them. *Isa* 41:12
Hos 2:7
not f. any occasion. *Dan* 6:5
shall not f. her paths. *Hos* 2:6
seek the word, not f. it. *Amos* 8:12
not f. what way they. *Luke* 5:19
could not f. what they might. 19:48
that we shall not f. him. *John* 7:35
that which is good, I f. not. *Rom* 7:18
I shall not f. you such. *2 Cor* 12:20
death, and shall not f. *Rev* 9:6

shall, or shalt find
seek Lord thou shalt f. *Deut* 4:29
shalt f. no ease among these. 28:65
do as thou shalt f. *Judg* 9:33
ye shall f. him before. *1 Sam* 9:13
there shall f. two men by. 10:2
ye shall f. them at end. *2 Chr* 20:16
children shall f. compassion. 30:9
thou shalt f. in book of. *Ezra* 4:15
tried me, and shalt f. *Ps* 17:3
shalt f. out thine enemies. 21:8
shalt f. precious substance. *Pr* 1:13
that seek me early shall f. me. 8:17
Jer 29:13
matter wisely, shall f. good. *Pr* 16:20
understanding shall f. good. 19:8
for thou shalt f. it after. *Eccl* 11:1
in her month shall f. her. *Jer* 2:24
ye shall f. rest to your souls. 6:16
Mat 11:29
shall f. none iniquity in. *Hos* 12:8
seek and ye shall f. *Mat* 7:7
Luke 11:9

life for my sake shall f. it. *Mat* 10:39
thou shalt f. a piece of money. 17:27
ye shall f. an ass tied, and a colt.
21:2; *Mark* 11:2
as many as ye shall f. *Mat* 22:9
cometh, shall f. so doing. 24:46
Luke 12:37, 43
ye shall f. babe wrapt. *Luke* 2:12
shall he f. faith on earth? 18:8
cast the net on the right side, ye
shall f. *John* 21:6
shalt f. them no more. *Rev* 18:14

findest
with whomsover thou f. *Gen* 31:32
eat thou f. eat this roll. *Ezek* 3:1

findeth
every one that f. me. *Gen* 4:14
he f. occasions against. *Job* 33:10
as one that f. spoil. *Ps* 119:162
happy is man that f. *Pr* 3:13
whoso f. me, f. life. 8:35
scorner seeketh wisdom, f. it. 14:6
a froward heart, f. no good. 17:20
whoso f. a wife f. good. 18:22
his neighbour f. no favour. 21:10
that followeth after mercy f. life. 21
whatsoever thy hand f. *Eccl* 9:10
heathen. she f. no rest. *Lam* 1:3
in tree the fatherless f. *Hos* 14:3
and he that seeketh f. *Mat* 7:8
Luke 11:10
f. his life shall lose it. *Mat* 10:39
walketh, seeking rest, f. none. 12:43
f. it empty, swept. 44; *Luke* 11:25
he f. his disciples asleep. *Mat* 26:40
Mark 14:37
f. his own brother Simon. *John* 1:41
Jesus f. Philip. 43
Philip f. Nathanael. 45
afterward Jesus f. him in. 5:14

finding
any f. Cain kill him. *Gen* 4:15
who doeth things past f. *Job* 9:10
f. thine own pleasure. *Isa* 58:13
seeking rest, and f. *Luke* 11:24
f. nothing how they. *Acts* 4:21
Paul came f. certain. 19:1; 21:4
f. ship sailing over to. 21:2
his ways past f. out. *Rom* 11:33*
for f. fault with them. *Heb* 8:8

fine
for gold where they f. it. *Job* 28:1*

fine
and two vessels of f. *Ezra* 8:27
they that work in f. flax. *Isa* 19:9
feet lunto brass. *Rev* 1:15; 2:18

fine flour
offering of f. *flour*. *Lev* 2:1; 24:5
cakes of f. f. mingled with oil. 2:4,5,7
7:12; 14:10, 21; 23:13; *Num* 6:15
7:13, 19, 25, 31, 37, 43, 49, 55, 61
8:8
tenth part of an ephah of f. *flour*.
Lev 5:11; 6:20
measures of f. *flour* in. *1 Ki* 4:22
measure f. *flour* sold for shekel.
2 Ki 7:1, 16, 18
appointed to oversee f. *flour*.
1 Chr 9:29; 23:29
didst eat f. *flour*, honey. *Ezek* 16:13
I gave thee f. *flour*, and oil. 19
of oil to temper with f. *flour*. 46:14
merchandise of f. *flour*. *Rev* 18:13

fine gold
he overlaid with f. *gold*. *2 Chr* 3:5
most holy he overlaid with f. *gold*. 8
for jewels of f. *gold*. *Job* 28:17
or said to f. *gold*, thou. 31:24
desired than f. *gold*. *Ps* 19:10
thy commandments above f. *gold*.
119:127
of wisdom than f. *gold*. *Pr* 3:14
better than gold, than f. *gold*. 8:19
as an ornament of f. *gold*. 25:12
head is as most f. *gold*. *S of S* 5:11
pillars set on sockets of f. *gold*. 15
more precious than f. *gold*. *Isa* 13:12
most f. *gold* changed! *Lam* 4:1*
of Zion comparable to f. *gold*. 2
image's head f. *gold*. *Dan* 2:32
loins were girded with f. *gold*. 10:5*
Tyrus heaped f. *gold*. *Zech* 9:3

fine linen
in vestures of f. *linen*. *Gen* 41:42
offering ye shall take, f. *linen*.
Ex 25:4
ten curtains of f. twined *linen*. 26:1
the vail of f. *linen*. 31; 36:35
2 Chr 3:14
hanging of f. twined *linen*. *Ex* 26:36
27:9, 16, 18; 36:37; 38:9, 16, 18
take gold and f. *linen*. 28:5
the ephod of f. *linen*. 28:6; 39:2
girdle f. *linen*. 28:8; 39:5, 29
breastplate f. *linen*. 28:15; 39:8
the coat of f. *linen*, thou shalt make
mitre of f. *linen*. 28:39
bring an offering of f. *linen*. 35:6
with whom was found f. *linen*. 23
brought scarlet and f. *linen*. 25
with wisdom to work all manner of f.
linen. 35; 38:23, *2 Chr* 2:14
curtains of f. *linen* and. *Ex* 36:8
coats of f. *linen* for Aaron. 39:27
of f. *linen*, bonnets of f. *linen*. 28
that wrought f. *linen*. *1 Chr* 4:21
clothed with robe of f. *linen*. 15:27
with cords of f. *linen*. *Esth* 1:6
Mordecai with garment of f. *linen*.
8:15
my bed with f. *linen*. *Pr* 7:16*
she maketh f. *linen*. 31:24*
take away f. *linen*. *Isa* 3:23
girded thee with f. *linen*. *Ezek* 16:10
thy raiment was of f. *linen*. 13
f. *linen* from Egypt was. 27:7
occupied in thy fairs with f. *linen*. 16
Joseph bought f. *linen*. *Mark* 15:46*
in purple and f. *linen*. *Luke* 16:19
merchandise of f. *linen*. *Rev* 18:12
that city clothed in f. *linen* is. 16
to be arrayed in f. *linen*. 19:8
in heaven clothed in f. *linen*. 14

fine meal
measures of f. *meal*. *Gen* 18:6

finer
forth a vessel for the f. *Pr* 25:4†

finest
fed thee with the f. of. *Ps* 81:16
filleth thee with f. of wheat. 147:14

finger
The finger of God is used to mean
his power, his working. Pharaoh's
magicians discovered the finger of
God in the miracles which Moses
wrought, Ex 8:19. This legislator
gave the law written with the finger
of God to the Hebrews, Ex 31:18.

magicians said, this is f. of. *Ex* 8:19
blood on altar with thy f. 29:12
written with the f. of God. 31:18
Deut 9:10
priest dip his f. in blood. *Lev* 4:6
17, 25, 30, 34; 8:15; 9:9; 16:14, 19
his right f. in the oil, and sprinkle
of the oil with his f. 14:16, 27
take of blood with his f. *Num* 19:4
my little f. thicker. *1 Ki* 12:10
2 Chr 10:10
the putting forth of the f. *Isa* 58:9
if I with the f. of God. *Luke* 11:20
he dip tip of his f. in water. 16:24
and with his f. wrote. *John* 8:6
put my f. into the print. 20:25
reach hither thy f. and behold. 27

fingers
on every hand six f. *2 Sam* 21:20
1 Chr 20:6
heavens, work of thy f. *Ps* 8:3
who teacheth my f. to fight. 144:1
man teacheth with his f. *Pr* 6:13
bind them on thy f. write. 7:3
f. with sweetsmelling. *S of S* 5:5
which their own f. have made.
Isa 2:8; 17:8
hands defiled with blood, and f. 59:3
thickness of pillar four f. *Jer* 52:21
came forth f. of a man's. *Dan* 5:5
but will not move them with one of
their f. *Mat* 23:4; *Luke* 11:46
and he put his f. into. *Mark* 7:33

fining
f. pot is for silver. *Pr* 17:3†; 27:21

finish

in a cubit shalt thou *f.* Gen 6:16
to *f.* transgression. Dan 9:24
Zerubbabel's hands shall *f.* Zech 4:9
have sufficient to *f.* Luke 14:28*
laid foundation, is not able to *f.* 29
to build, was not able to *f.* 30
his will, and *f.* his work. John 4:34
Father hath given me to *f.* 5:36*
I might *f.* my course. Acts 20:24*
for he will *f.* the work. Rom 9:28
f. in you the same grace. 2 Cor 8:6*

finished

heavens and earth were *f.* Gen 2:1
thus was the work *f.* Ex 39:32; 40:33
till they were *f.* Deut 31:24
till every thing was *f.* Josh 4:10
till he have *f.* the thing. Ruth 3:18
Solomon built house and *f.* 1 Ki 6:9
14, 22, 38; 2 Chr 5:1; 7:11
Solomon *f.* all his house. 1 Ki 7:1
9:1, 25; 2 Chr 8:16
so was work of pillars *f.* 1 Ki 7:22
to number, but *f.* not. 1 Chr 27:24
not fail thee, till thou hast *f.* 28:20
they had *f.* repairing. 2 Chr 24:14
sang, till burnt offering was *f.* 29:28
they *f.* the heaps in the. 31:7
and yet it is not *f.* Ezra 5:16*
elders of Jews builded and *f.* 6:14, 15
so the wall was *f.* in. Neh 6:15
numbered thy kingdom and *f.* it.
Dan 5:26
all these things shall be *f.* 12:7
when Jesus had *f.* these. Mat 13:53
Jesus *f.* these sayings. 19:1; 26:1
I have *f.* the work thou. John 17:4*
it is *f.* and he bowed his head. 19:30
we had *f.* our course. Acts 21:7
I have *f.* my course. 2 Tim 4:7
were *f.* from foundation. Heb 4:3
sin, when it is *f.* bringeth. Jas 1:15*
mystery of God should be *f.*
Rev 10:7
witnesses have *f.* their testimony.
11:7
till the thousand years were *f.* 20:5

finisher

Jesus, author and *f.* of. Heb 12:2*

fins

hath *f.* and scales eat. Lev 11:9
Deut 14:9
all that hath not *f.* shall be an abomination. Lev 11:10, 12

fir

concerning timber of *f.* 1 Ki 5:8
covered floor with planks of *f.* 6:15
are cedar, rafters of *f.* S of S 1:17

fire

*Fire is often used as a symbol of
God,* Deut 4:24; Ps 18:12, 13, 14;
Ezek 1:4; Rev 1:14. *And it is
said that Jesus will appear in the
midst of fire at his second coming,*
2 Thes 1:8. *The wrath of God is
compared to fire,* Ps 18:8.
Our Saviour is compared to fire,
Mal 3:2. *The Holy Ghost is likewise compared to fire,* Mat 3:11.
*The angels themselves, as the
ministers of God, are compared to a
burning fire, speedy and irresistible
in the execution of his commands,*
Ps. 104:4.
*Fire from heaven fell frequently
on the victims sacrificed to the
Lord, as a mark of his presence
and approbation. It is thought that
God in this manner expressed his
acceptance of Abel's sacrifices,*
Gen 4:4. *When the Lord made a
covenant with Abraham, a fire,
like that of a furnace, passed
through the divided pieces of the
sacrifices, and consumed them,*
Gen 15:17. *Fire fell upon the
sacrifices which Moses offered
at the dedication of the tabernacle,* Lev 9:24; *and upon those of
Manoah, Samson's father,* Judg
13:19, 20; *upon Solomon's, at the
dedication of the temple,* 2 Chr

7:1; *and upon Elijah's, at mount
Carmel,* 1 Ki 18:38.
*The word of God is compared to
fire,* Jer 23:29.
Abraham took *f.* in his. Gen 22:6
behold the *f.* and the wood, but. 7
the bush burned with *f.* Ex 3:2
Lord sent hail and the *f.* along. 9:23
hail, and *f.* mingled with hail. 24
flesh in that night roast with *f.* 12:8, 9
upon mount Sinai in *f.* 19:18
if *f.* break out, and catch. 22:6
then I cast gold into *f.* and. 32:24
f. was on the tabernacle by night.
40:38; Num 9:16; Deut 1:33
the priest put *f.* on the altar, and lay
wood in order upon *f.* Lev 1:7
upon the wood in *f.* 8, 12, 17; 3:5
green ears of corn dried by *f.* 2:14
f. of the altar be burning. 6:9, 10
12, 13
came a *f.* out from before. 9:24
the sons of Aaron put *f.* in. 10:1
there went out *f.* from Lord. 2
shall put incense upon *f.* 16:13
pass through *f.* to Molech. 18:21
Deut 18:10; 2 Ki 17:17; 23:10
hair, and put it in the *f.* Num 6:18
Moses prayed, the *f.* was. 11:2
censers, and put *f.* therein. 16:7, 18
take the censers, and scatter *f.* 37
take a censer, and put *f.* therein. 46
holy things reserved from *f.* 18:9
for there is a *f.* gone out. 21:28
may abide *f.* go through *f.* 31:23
mountain burnt with *f.* Deut 4:11
9:15
earth he shewed his great *f.* 4:36
afraid by reason of the *f.* 5:5
nor let me see this great *f.* 18:16
burned Achan with *f.* Josh 7:25
there rose up *f.* out of. Judg 6:21
let *f.* come out of bramble. 9:15
tow when it toucheth the *f.* 16:9
lay it on wood, put no *f.* under.
1 Ki 18:23, 25
the God that answereth by *f.* 24
then *f.* of Lord fell. 38; 2 Chr 7:1, 3
after earthquake a *f.*, Lord was not in
f., after *f.* a still small. 1 Ki 19:12
then let *f.* come down. 2 Ki 1:10
and the *f.* of God came down. 12
a chariot and horses of *f.* 2:11
mountain, full of chariots of *f.* 6:17
Ahaz made son pass through *f.* 16:3
have cast their gods into *f.* 19:18
made son pass through *f.* 21:6
2 Chr 33:6
make son pass through *f.* 2 Ki 23:10
answered him from heaven by *f.*
1 Chr 21:26
roasted passover with *f.* 2 Chr 35:13
the gates are consumed with *f.*
Neh 2:3, 13
the *f.* of God is fallen. Job 1:16
the spark of his *f.* shall not. 18:5
is turned up as it were *f.* 28:5
and sparks of *f.* leap out. 41:19
while I was musing the *f.* Ps 39:3
he burneth chariot in the *f.* 46:9
we went through *f.* and. 66:12
as wax melteth before *f.* so. 68:2
cast *f.* into thy sanctuary. 74:7
with a light of *f.* 78:14; 105:39
as the *f.* burneth the wood. 83:14
a *f.* goeth before him and. 97:3
gave hail and flaming *f.* in. 105:32
they are quenched as *f.* 118:12
be cast into the *f.* into deep. 140:10
f. and hail, stormy wind. 148:8
can a man take *f.* in bosom. Pr 6:27
in his lips as a burning *f.* 16:27
where no wood is, the *f.* 26:20
as wood is to *f.* so is contentious. 21
the grave and the *f.* saith not. 30:16
burning and fuel of *f.* Isa 9:5
wickedness burneth as the *f.* 18
the people shall be as fuel of *f.* 19
a burning like burning of a *f.* 10:16
light of Israel shall be for a *f.* 17
not be found a sherd to take *f.* 30:14
the pile thereof is *f.* and wood. 33
whose *f.* is in Zion. 31:9
of Assyria cast gods into *f.* 37:19

walkest through *f.* not be. Isa 43:2
in the *f.* he warmeth himself, saith,
I have seen the *f.* 44:16
as stubble, the *f.* shall burn. 47:14
walk in light of your *f.* and. 50:11
when the melting *f.* burneth, the *f.*
causeth the waters to boil. 64:2
a *f.* that burneth all the day. 65:5
the Lord will come with *f.* 66:15
by *f.* will Lord plead with all. 16
worm not die, neither *f.* be. 24
fury come forth like *f.* Jer 4:4
my words in thy mouth *f.* 5:14
his word was as a *f.* shut up. 20:9
lest my fury go out like *f.* 21:12
cut down choice cedars, cast in *f.* 22:7
king of Babylon roasted in *f.* 29:22
sons to pass through *f.* to Molech.
32:35; Ezek 16:21; 20:26, 31
was a *f.* on the hearth. Jer 36:22
Jehudi cut roll, cast it into *f.* 23
but a *f.* shall come forth. 48:45
labour in vain and in the *f.* 51:58
against Jacob like flaming *f.* Lam 2:3
bent his bow, poured out fury like *f.* 4
I looked, behold, a *f.* Ezek 1:4
the *f.* was bright, out of the *f.* 13
take *f.* from between wheels. 10:6
cherub stretched forth hand to *f.* 7
blow against thee in *f.* 21:31; 22:21
thou shalt be for fuel to *f.* 21:32
to blow *f.* upon it. 22:20
I will even make pile for *f.* 24:9
her scum shall be in the *f.* 12
will I bring forth a *f.* from. 28:18
in *f.* of my jealousy have I spoken.
36:5; 38:19
bodies the *f.* had no power, nor the
smell of *f.* passed on. Dan 3:27
wheels like burning *f.* 7:9
his eyes as lamps of *f.* 10:6
burneth as a flaming *f.* Hos 7:6
blood, *f.* and pillars of smoke.
Joel 2:30; Acts 2:19
lest he break out like *f.* Amos 5:6
Lord God called to contend by *f.* 7:4
house of Jacob shall be a *f.* Ob 18
under him as wax before *f.* Mi 1:4
fury poured out like *f.* Nah 1:6
people shall labour in *f.* Hab 2:13
be unto her a wall of *f.* Zech 2:5
brand plucked out of *f.*? 3:2
hearth of *f.* and like torch of *f.* 12:6
the third part through the *f.* 13:9
he is like a refiner's *f.* Mal 3:2
bringeth not forth good fruit is cast
into *f.* Mat 3:10; 7:19; Luke 3:9
John 15:6
baptize with Holy Ghost, and *f.*
Mat 3:11; Luke 3:16
cast them into a furnace of *f.*
Mat 13:42, 50
ofttimes falleth into *f.* Mat 17:15
Mark 9:22
or two feet, be cast into everlasting *f.*
Mat 18:8; Mark 9:43, 46
me, into everlasting *f.* Mat 25:41
f. is not quenched. Mark 9:44, 45
Peter warmed himself at *f.* 14:54
command *f.* to come ? Luke 9:54
the same day it rained *f.* 17:29
behold him as he sat by *f.* 22:56
cloven tongues like as of *f.* Acts 2:3
when Paul laid sticks on the *f.* 28:3
he shook off the beast into *f.* 5
revealed by *f.* and the *f.* shall try
every man's work. 1 Cor 3:13
shall be saved, yet so as by *f.* 15
in flaming *f.* taking. 2 Thes 1:8
his ministers a flame of *f.* Heb 1:7
faith quenched violence of *f.* 11:34
to mount that burned with *f.* 12:18
how great matter a little *f.* Jas 3:5
and the tongue is a *f.*, a world of. 6
eat your flesh as it were *f.* 5:3
gold, though it be tried with *f.*
1 Pet 1:7
reserved unto *f.* against. 2 Pet 3:7
heavens being on *f.* be dissolved. 12
vengeance of eternal *f.* Jude 7
others save, pulling out of the *f.* 23
of me gold tried in the *f.* Rev 3:18
seven lamps of *f.* burning. 4:5
angel filled the censer with *f.* 8:5

there followed hail and f. | Rev 8:7
great mountain burning with f. | 8
of their mouths issued f. 9:17; 11:5
part of men killed by the f. | 9:18
he maketh f. come down. | 13:13
angel which had power over f. 14:18
sea of glass mingled with f. | 15:2
him to scorch men with f. | 16:8
and f. came down from God. 20:9
the devil was cast into lake of f. 10
hell cast into the lake of f. | 14
in book of life, cast into f. | 15
lake which burneth with f. | 21:8
see **brimstone, burn** or **burnt, coals, consume, consuming, devour, devoured, devouring, flame, hell, midst**

kindle, or kindled **fire**
he that *kindled* the f. | Ex 22:6
kindle no f. on sabbath day. | 35:3
a f. is *kindled* in my anger, and.
   Deut 32:22; Jer 15:14; 17:4
him coals of f. *kindled*. 2 Sam 22:13
so a f. was *kindled* against Jacob.
   Ps 78:21
f. *kindled* in their company. 106:18
kindle a burning like a f. Isa 10:16
behold, all ye that *kindle* a f. 50:11
fathers *kindled* a f. | Jer 7:18
hath *kindled* f. on green. | 11:16
then will I *kindle* a f. in gates. 17:27
I will *kindle* a f. in forest. | 21:14
I will *kindle* a f. in houses of. 43:12
I will *kindle* a f. in the wall. 49:27
I will *kindle* a f. in his cities. 50:32
Lord hath *kindled* a f. in. Lam 4:11
kindle a f. in the forest. Ezek 20:47
heap on wood, *kindle* a f. | 24:10
I will *kindle* a f. in wall of Rabbah.
   Amos 1:14
neither do ye *kindle* f. on my altar.
   Mal 1:10
f. on the earth; and what if it be
already *kindled* ? | Luke 12:49
when they had *kindled* a f. | 22:55
barbarians *kindled* a f. | Acts 28:2

made with **fire**
an offering *made* by f. unto Lord.
Ex 29:18, 25, 41; Lev 1:9, 13, 17
2:2, 9, 16; 3:3, 5, 9, 11, 14, 16
7:5, 25, 8:21, 28; 21:6, 22:27
23:8, 13, 18, 25, 27, 36, 37; 24:7
Num 15:3, 10, 13, 14; 18:17; 28:3
the offerings of Lord *made* by f.
Lev 2:3, 10; 4:35; 5:12; 6:17, 18
7:30, 35; 10:12, 15; 21:21; 24:9
   Deut 18:1; 1 Sam 2:28
sacrifices *made* by f. | Lev 10:13
   Num 28:2; Josh 13:14
bring sacrifice *made* by f. unto Lord.
Num 15:25; 28:6, 8, 13, 19, 24
   29:6, 13, 36

pillar of **fire**
Lord looked through *pillar of f.*
   Ex 14:24
his feet as *pillars of f.* | Rev 10:1
see, by **night**

send, or sent **fire**
from above he *sent* f. | Lam 1:13
and I will *send* a f. | Ezek 39:6
send a f. upon his cities. Hos 8:14
send a f. into house of. Amos 1:4
I will *send* a f. on the wall. | 7
I will *send* a f. on wall of Tyrus. 10
send f. on Teman. | 12
I will *send* a f. on Moab. | 2:2
send f. on Judah. | 5
I am come to *send* f. on. Luke 12:49

set **fire**
set on f. foundations of. Deut 32:22
set city of Ai on f. | Josh 8:8
hasted, and set the city on f. | 19
had set Jerusalem on f. | Judg 1:8
the people set the hold on f. | 9:49
had set the brands on f. and. | 15:5
set on f. all the cities of. | 20:48
set Joab's field on f. 2 Sam 14:30
have thy servants set field on f.? 31
set strong holds on f. | 2 Ki 8:12
them that are set on f. | Ps 57:4
women set them on f. | Isa 27:11
hath set him on f. round. | 42:25

set up a sign of f. in. | Jer 6:1
Chaldeans shall set on f. this. 32:29
when I have set a f. in. | Ezek 30:8
I will set f. in Zoan. | 14
set f. in Egypt. | 16
set on f. and burn weapons. | 39:9
tongue is a fire, setteth on f. . . . it
is set on f. of hell. | Jas 3:6

strange **fire**
Abihu offered *strange* f. | Lev 10:1
died when they offered *strange* f.
   Num 3:4; 26:61

firebrand, -s
took f. and put a f. in. | Judg 15:4
mad man who casteth f. | Pr 26:18
tails of these smoking f. | Isa 7:4
ye were as a f. plucked. Amos 4:11

firepans
make basons and f. | Ex 27:3
f. and all vessels of brass. | 38:3
f. carried he away. | 2 Ki 25:15
   Jer 52:19

fires
glorify ye the Lord in f. Isa 24:15*

firkins
waterpots containing two or three f.
   John 2:6

firm
priests stood f. on dry. | Josh 3:17
place where priests' feet stood f. 4:3
are f. in themselves. | Job 41:23
his heart is as f. as a stone. | 24
no bands in death, their strength is f.
   Ps 73:4
to make a f. decree. | Dan 6:7*
rejoicing of the hope f. | Heb 3:6

firmament
By the word firmament (Hebrew, rakiah), the Hebrews understood the heavens, which they thought to be like a solid arch between the upper and lower waters. They also believed that the stars are set in this arch, like so many precious stones in gold and silver, Gen 1:17.
let there be a f. in midst. | Gen 1:6
f. waters under and above f. | 7
God called the f. Heaven. | 8
let there be lights in the f. | 14, 15
God set them in f. of heaven. | 17
fowl that fly above open f. | 20
f. sheweth his handy work. Ps 19:1
praise him in f. of his power. 150:1
of f. was as crystal. | Ezek 1:22
a voice from the f. over their. | 25
above the f. was the likeness of. 26
in f. above the cherubims. | 10:1
shine as brightness of f. | Dan 12:3

fir tree
the two doors were of f. | 1 Ki 6:34
house he cieled with f. | 2 Chr 3:5
I will set in desert the f. | Isa 41:19
instead of the thorn the f. | 55:13
the f. the pine tree and box. 60:13
I am like a green f. | Hos 14:8
howl, f. | Zech 11:2

fir trees
so Hiram gave Solomon f.
   1 Ki 5:10; 9:11
I will cut down tall f. | 2 Ki 19:23
   Isa 37:24
   2 Chr 2:8
send me f.
the f. rejoice. | Isa 14:8
the stork the f. are her. Ps 104:17
ship boards of f. of Senir. Ezek 27:5
the f. were not like his boughs. 31:8
f. shall be terribly shaken. Nah 2:3

fir wood
on instruments of f. | 2 Sam 6:5

first
the f. came out red. | Gen 25:25
a famine beside the f. famine. 26:1
midwife said, this came out f. 38:28
not hearken to f. sign. | Ex 4:8
the f. of the firstfruits bring. 23:19
the f. row a sardius. 28:17; 39:10
two tables like to the f. | 34:1, 4
   Deut 10:1, 5
what is for sin offering f. | Lev 5:8
Judah, these shall f. set. | Num 2:9
and they f. took their journey. 10:13

time of the f. ripe grapes. Num 13:20
offer up a cake of the f. of your.
   15:20, 21; Ezek 44:30
whatsoever is f. ripe. | Num 18:13
Amalek was f. of nations. | 24:20
according to the f. time. Deut 10:10
I will give thee f. rain. | 11:14*
thine hand shall be f. upon. | 13:9
hands of witnesses be f. upon. 17:7
f. of the fleece of thy sheep. | 18:4
provided f. part for himself. 33:21
theirs was f. lot. | Josh 21:10
   1 Chr 24:7; 25:9
who shall go up f. | Judg 1:1; 20:18
Israel are smitten as in f. | 20:39
f. slaughter twenty. | 1 Sam 14:14
same was f. altar Saul built. | 35
thou f. bring Michal. | 2 Sam 3:13
I am come the f. this day to. 19:20
that advice should not be f. | 43
captain, howbeit he attained not unto
f. | 23:19, 23; 1 Chr 11:21, 25
thereof a little cake f. | 1 Ki 17:13
and dress it f. for ye are. | 18:25
men of princes went out f. | 20:17
now f. inhabitants that. | 1 Chr 9:2
smiteth the Jebusites f. | 11:6
day David delivered f. this. | 16:7
length by cubits after f. | 2 Chr 3:3
had seen glory of the f. | Ezra 3:12
sat f. in the kingdom. | Esth 1:14
art thou f. man born ? | Job 15:7
that is f. in his own cause. Ps 18:17
the f. shall say to Zion. | Isa 41:27
thy f. father hath sinned. | 43:27
ships of Tarshish f. to bring. | 60:9
bringeth forth her f. child. Jer 4:31
like the figs that are f. ripe. | 24:2
words that were in f. roll. | 36:28
f. king of Assyria devoured. | 50:17
Daniel was f. president. | Dan 6:2*
the f. beast was like a lion.
   7:4
   Rev 4:7
be diverse from the f. | Dan 7:24*
horn between eyes is f. king. | 8:21
return to my f. husband. | Hos 2:7
f. ripe in fig tree at f. time. | 9:10
go captive with the f. | Amos 6:7
to thee shall come f. | Mi 4:8*
like fig trees with f. ripe. Nah 3:12
that saw house in f. glory? Hag 2:3*
in the f. chariot red. | Zech 6:2
shall save tents of Judah f. | 12:7
f. be reconciled to thy. | Mat 5:24
seek ye f. the kingdom of. | 6:33
f. cast beam out of. 7:5; Luke 6:42
suffer me f. to go and bury. Mat 8:21
   Luke 9:59
f. bind the strong man. | Mat 12:29
   Mark 3:27
state worse than the f. | Mat 12:45
   Luke 11:26
gather ye together f. tares. Mat 13:30
Elias f. come. 17:10, 11; Mark 9:12
take up fish that f. | Mat 17:27
but when the f. came, they. 20:10
he came to the f. and said. | 21:28
they say unto him, the f. | 31
other servants more than f. | 36
f. when married. | 22:25
   Mark 12:20; Luke 20:29
this is f. commandment. Mat 22:38
   Mark 12:28, 29, 30
cleanse f. that which is. Mat 23:26
f. the blade, then ear. Mark 4:28
let the children f. be filled. | 7:27
desire to be f. he shall be last. 9:35
and the gospel must f. be. | 13:10
appeared f. to Mary. | 16:9
perfect understanding from the f.
   Luke 1:3
was f. made when Cyrenius. | 2:2
second sabbath after the f. he. | 6:1
f. say, Peace be to this house. 10:5
that he had not f. washed. | 11:38
sitteth not down f. and. | 14:28
f. must he suffer many. | 17:25
things must f. come to pass. | 21:9
f. findeth his brother. | John 1:41
whosoever f. stepped in, made. 5:4
without sin, let him f. cast. | 8:7
where John at f. baptized. | 10:40
led him away to Annas f. | 18:13

brake the legs of the *f.*   *John* 19:32
disciple came *f.* to the.   20:4, 8
to you *f.* God sent him.   *Acts* 3:26
Jacob sent out our fathers *f.*   7:12*
called Christians *f.* at.   11:26
past the *f.* and second ward.   12:10
when John had *f.* preached.   13:24
it should *f.* have been spoken.   46
f. unto them of Damascus.   26:20
Christ *f.* that should rise from.   23
cast themselves *f.* into sea.   27:43
f. I thank my God.   *Rom* 1:8
of the Jew *f.* and also of.   2:9, 10
who hath *f.* given to him ?   11:35
if *f.* I be somewhat filled.   15:24
f. apostles, secondarily. *1 Cor* 12:28
let the *f.* hold his peace.   14:30
for I delivered *f.* of all that.   15:3
the *f.* man Adam a living soul.   45
howbeit that was not *f.* which.   46
the *f.* man is of the earth.   47
f. gave their own selves. *2 Cor* 8:5
for if there be *f.* a willing mind.   12
who *f.* trusted in Christ.   *Eph* 1:12
descended *f.* into lower parts.   4:9
which is the *f.* commandment.   6:2
in Christ shall rise *f.*   *1 Thes* 4:16
come a falling away *f.*   *2 Thes* 2:3
that in me *f.* Christ.   *1 Tim* 1:16*
for Adam was *f.* formed.   2:13
let these also *f.* be proved.   3:10
learn *f.* to shew piety at home.   5:4
have cast off their *f.* faith.   12
faith dwelt *f.* in thy grandmother.
          2 Tim 1:5
husbandman be *f.* partaker of.   2:6
at my *f.* answer no man stood.   4:16
after *f.* and second.   *Tit* 3:10
to whom it was *f.* preached. *Heb* 4:6*
teach you which be the *f.*   5:12
f. being by interpretation, king.   7:2
offer *f.* for his own sins.   27
the *f.* covenant. 8:7, 13; 9:1, 15, 18
f. tabernacle, wherein.   9:2, 6, 8
he taketh away the *f.* that.   10:9
wisdom from above, is *f.*   *Jas* 3:17
if judgement *f.* begin at. *1 Pet* 4:17
knowing this *f.* that no prophecy.
          2 Pet 1:20; 3:3
because he *f.* loved us. *1 John* 4:19
who kept not their *f.* estate. *Jude* 6*
thou hast left thy *f.* love. *Rev* 2:4
repent, and do the *f.* works.   5
the power of the *f.* beast.   13:12
this is the *f.* resurrection.   20:5
f. heaven and *f.* earth were.   21:1
the *f.* foundation was jasper.   19

see **day, last**

at the first

made the altar *at the f.* *Gen* 13:4
city was called Luz *at the f.*   28:19
of money returned *at the f.*   43:18
down *at the f.* to buy food.   20
down before Lord as *at the f.*
          Deut 9:18, 25
come against us *at the f.* *Josh* 8:5
they flee before us as *at the f.*   6
of city Laish *at the f.*   *Judg* 18:29
smitten before us as *at the f.* 20:32
be overthrown *at the f.* *2 Sam* 17:9
send for to thy servant *at f.* *1 Ki* 20:9
ye did it not *at the f.*   *1 Chr* 15:13
which came up *at the f.*   *Isa* 1:26
thy judges as *at the f.*   9:1*
I set my name *at the f.* *Jer* 7:12
I will build them as *at the f.* 33:7
return captivity of land, as *at the f.* 11
which appeared *at the f.* *Dan* 8:1
understood not *at the f.* *John* 12:16
which *at the f.* came by night. 19:39
God *at the f.* did visit. *Acts* 15:14
at the f. among mine own.   26:4
gospel unto you, *at the f.* *Gal* 4:13*
at the f. began to be spoken by.
          Heb 2:3

first month

f. month, the *f.* day of the month.
          Gen 8:13
the *f. month* of year to. *Ex* 12:2
f. month eat unleavened bread. 18
          Lev 23:5
day of *f. month* set up. *Ex* 40:2, 17

f. month keep passover. *Num* 9:1
  28:16; *2 Chr* 35:1; *Ezra* 6:19
          Ezek 45:21
desert of Zin in *f. month.* *Num* 20:1
from Rameses in *f. month.*   33:3
of Jordan in *f. month.* *Josh* 4:19
over Jordan in *f. month.* *1 Chr* 12:15
captain that served *f. month.* 27:2, 3
f. month opened doors. *2 Chr* 29:3
first day of *f. month* to sanctify and
  sixteenth day of *f. month.*   17
f. month began he to go. *Ezra* 7:9
the *f. month* we departed.   8:31
end with them by *f. month.* 10:17
in *f. month* cast Pur, on thirteenth
  day of the *f. month.* *Esth* 3:7, 12
f. month take a young. *Ezek* 45:18
and latter rain in *f. month.* *Joel* 2:23

first year

*(In the giving of the age, as lamb
of the first year, the American Revision changes to* lamb a year old*)*

lambs male of the *f. year.* *Ex* 12:5
offer two lambs of *f. year* day by.
  29:38; *Lev* 23:19; *Num* 28:3, 9
take a kid of the *f. year.* *Lev* 9:3
bring a lamb of the *f. year.*   12
  Num 6:12; 7:15, 21, 27, 33, 39, 45
  51, 57, 63, 69, 75, 81; *Ezek* 46:13
take an ewe lamb of the *f. year.*
          Lev 14:10; *Num* 6:14
an he lamb of *f. year.* *Lev* 23:18
          Num 6:14
seven lambs of *f. year.* *Lev* 23:18
  Num 28:11, 19, 27; 29:2, 8, 36
peace offering five lambs of *f. year.*
  Num 7:17, 23, 29, 35, 41, 47, 53, 59
lambs of the *f. year* twelve.   87
the lambs of the *f. year* sixty. 88
a she goat of the *f. year.*   15:27
a burnt offering, fourteen lambs of
  f. year. 29:13, 17, 20, 23, 26, 29, 32
Hezekiah in *f. year* of *2 Chr* 29:3
in *f. year* of Cyrus.   36:22
       Ezra 1:1; 5:13; 6:3
f. year of Nebuchadnezzar. *Jer* 25:1
f. year of Evil-merodach.   52:31
to the *f. year* of Cyrus. *Dan* 1:21
in the *f. year* of Belshazzar. 7:1
in the *f. year* of Darius I, Daniel.
          9:1, 2; 11:1

first begotten

when he bringeth in the *f. b. Heb* 1:6
Jesus, who is *f. b.* of dead. *Rev* 1:5

firstborn

*The firstborn of both man and
beast was considered as belonging
to God. If of man, the child was
redeemed,* Ex 13:13, 15; 34:20.
*If of a clean beast it was sacrificed,
and if unclean either had the neck
broken or was replaced by a lamb,*
Ex 13:13, 15; 22:30; 34:20. *Later
the Levites were substituted for the
Israelites' firstborn,* Num 3:12, 41,
46; 8:13–19.
*To the firstborn son belonged the
birthright, which included the headship of the family or tribe, and a
double portion of his father's property.*

f. said to younger. *Gen* 19:31, 34
f. went in, lay with her father. 33
f. bare a son, called name Moab. 37
said, I am Esau, thy *f.* 27:19, 32
to give younger before *f.*   29:26
f. according to his birthright. 43:33
not so my father, this is *f.* 48:18
Israel is my son, even my *f. Ex* 4:22
I will slay thy son, even thy *f.* 23
all the *f.* in Egypt shall die.   12:12
and I will smite all the *f.* 12:12
Lord smote all the *f. in.* 29; 13:15
sanctify unto me all the *f.*   13:2
the *f.* of thy sons shalt thou. 22:29
f. of thy sons. 34:20; *Num* 18:15
instead of all the *f.* *Num* 3:12
    41, 45; 8:17, 18
the *f.* of Israel are mine, I hallowed
  to me all the *f.*   3:13
number the *f.* of the males of. 40
Moses numbered *f.* of Israel. 42

of *f.* of Israel took he money.
          Num 3:50
the Egyptians buried all their *f.* 33:4
if *f.* son be her's that. *Deut* 21:15
for the right of *f.* is his.   17
f. which she beareth, succeed. 25:6
lay foundation in his *f.* *Josh* 6:26
foundation in Abiram *f.* *1 Ki* 16:34
Reuben *f.* he was the *f.* *1 Chr* 5:1
though he was not the *f.* yet. 26:10
Jehoram, the *f.*   *2 Chr* 21:3
the *f.* to the house of. *Neh* 10:36
the *f.* of death shall.   *Job* 18:13
he smote all the *f. in. Ps* 78:51
    105:36; 135:8; 136:10
my *f.* higher than kings.   89:27
f. of the poor shall feed. *Isa* 14:30
Israel, Ephraim is my *f. Jer* 31:9
my *f.* for my transgression ? *Mi* 6:7
in bitterness for his *f. Zech* 12:10
Mary brought forth her *f.* son.
    Mat 1:25; *Luke* 2:7
f. among many brethren. *Rom* 8:29
the *f.* of every creature. *Col* 1:15
the beginning, *f.* from the dead. 18
lest he that destroyed *f. Heb* 11:28
ye are come to the church of *f.* 12:23

firstfruits

*The firstfruits were to be given as
an offering to Jehovah,* Lev 23:10,
17; Ex 23:19. *The term is used
figuratively also,* Rom 8:23; Jas
1:18.

to offer *f.* ripe *fruits.* *Ex* 22:29
f. of thy labour thou hast.   23:16
first of *f.* 23:19; 34:26; *Deut* 26:2
of *f.* of wheat harvest. *Ex* 34:22
oblation of the *f.* offer. *Lev* 2:12
the meat offering of *f.* green. 14
a sheaf of the *f.* of harvest. 23:10
they are the *f.* unto the Lord. 17
wave them with bread of the *f.* 20
f. of oil, wine, wheat. *Num* 18:12
in the day of *f.* when ye.   28:26
the *f.* of thy corn, wine. *Deut* 18:4
brought the *f.* of the land. 26:10
brought man of God *f.* *2 Ki* 4:42
brought in abundance *f. 2 Chr* 31:5
bring *f.* of our ground. *Neh* 10:35
should bring the *f.* of our dough. 37
over, chambers for *f.* 12:44; 13:31
honour Lord with the *f.* *Pr* 3:9
Israel was the *f.* of his. *Jer* 2:3
there will I require *f. Ezek* 20:40
the first of all the *f.*   44:30
nor exchange the *f.* of land. 48:14
have the *f.* of the Spirit. *Rom* 8:23
if the *f.* be holy.   11:16
who is the *f.* of Achaia.   16:5
       1 Cor 16:15
Christ the *f.* of them that slept.
       1 Cor 15:20, 23
f. of his creatures. *Jas* 1:18
being the *f.* unto God. *Rev* 14:4

firstling

*(The same as firstborn, but con-
fined to the firstborn of beasts)*
shalt set apart every *f.* of beast,
  males shall be. *Ex* 13:12; 34:19
every *f.* of an ass. 13:13; 34:20
the Lord's *f.* no man. *Lev* 27:26
f. of unclean beasts. *Num* 18:15
the *f.* of a cow, sheep, or goat. 17
all the *f.* males sanctify. *Deut* 15:19
Joseph's glory is like *f.* of. 33:17

firstlings

Abel brought *f.* of his flock. *Gen* 4:4
instead of all the *f.* *Num* 3:41
ye shall bring *f.* of your. *Deut* 12:6
not eat within thy gates the *f.* 17
eat the *f.* in place Lord shall. 14:23
f. of our herds bring to. *Neh* 10:36

fish

dominion over *f.* *Gen* 1:26, 28
f. in river shall die. *Ex* 7:18, 21
f. we did eat in Egypt. *Num* 11:5
all the *f.* of the sea be gathered ? 22
nor likeness of any *f. in. Deut* 4:18
of Tyre, which brought *f. Neh* 13:16
his head with *f.* spears ? *Job* 41:7
thou hast put the *f.* under. *Ps* 8:8
waters into blood, slew *f.* 105:29

sluices and ponds for *f.*   *Isa* 19:10*
their *f.* stinketh because there. 50:2
will cause the *f.* to stick. *Ezek* 29:4
and all the *f.* of thy rivers.   5
very great multitude of *f.*   47:9
their *f.* as the *f.* of the great sea. 10
a great *f.* to swallow Jonah, in belly
   of *f.* three days.   *Jonah* 1:17
to Lord out of the *f.'s* belly.   2:1
Lord spake to the *f.* and it.   10
if he ask a *f.* will he give ? *Mat* 7:10
take up *f.* that first cometh.   17:27
a piece of a broiled *f.*   *Luke* 24:42
they saw *f.* laid thereon. *John* 21:9
bring of *f.* ye have now caught.   10
Jesus taketh bread, and *f.*   13

fish, *verb*
fishers, they shall *f.*   *Jer* 16:16

fishermen
but the *f.* were gone out. *Luke* 5:2

fisher, -s
the *f.* also shall mourn. *Isa* 19:8
I will send for many *f.* *Jer* 16:16
that the *f.* shall stand. *Ezek* 47:10
for they were *f.*   *Mat* 4:18
   Mark 1:16
make you *f.* of men.   *Mat* 4:19
   Mark 1:17
Peter girt *f.'s* coat to him. *John* 21:7

fishes
you shall be on all *f.*   *Gen* 9:2
creeping things and *f.*   *1 Ki* 4:33
f. of the sea shall.   *Job* 12:8
the *f.* that are taken in. *Eccl* 9:12
the *f.* of the sea.   *Ezek* 38:20
f. of the sea shall be taken. *Hos* 4:3
makest men as *f.* of sea. *Hab* 1:14
consume the *f.* of the sea. *Zeph* 1:3
five loaves and two *f.*   *Mat* 14:17
   Mark 6:38; *Luke* 9:13; *John* 6:9
seven loaves and a few *f.* *Mat* 15:34
   Mark 8:7
a great multitude of *f.*   *Luke* 5:6
astonished at the draught of *f.*   9
not able to draw it for *f.* *John* 21:6
drew net to land full of great *f.*   11
of beasts, another of *f.* *1 Cor* 15:39

fish gate
on entering of *f. gate.*   *2 Chr* 33:14
f. gate did the sons of. *Neh* 3:3
after them from above *f. gate.* 12:39
noise of a cry from *f. gate.* *Zeph* 1:10

fishhooks
your posterity with *f.*   *Amos* 4:2

fishing
Peter saith unto them, I go a *f.*
   John 21:3

fishpools
thine eyes like the *f.* in. *S of S* 7:4

fist, -s
smite another with his *f.* *Ex* 21:18
gathered wind in his *f.?* *Pr* 30:4
with *f.* of wickedness. *Isa* 58:4

fit
him away by a *f.* man. *Lev* 16:21*
f. to go out to war and battle.
   1 Chr 7:11*; 12:8*
is it *f.* to say to a king ? *Job* 34:18
make it *f.* for thyself. *Pr* 24:27*
vine made *f.* for no. *Ezek* 15:5
f. for kingdom of God. *Luke* 9:62
it is not *f.* for the land nor. 14:35
not *f.* that he should live. *Acts* 22:22
submit as it is *f.* in Lord. *Col* 3:18

fitches
he not cast abroad the *f.* *Isa* 28:25
f. are not threshed, the *f.* are.   27
wheat, barley, millet, *f.* *Ezek* 4:9*

fitly
a word *f.* spoken is like. *Pr* 25:11
eyes washed with milk, *f. S of S* 5:12
in whom building *f.*   *Eph* 2:21
from whom the whole body *f.*   4:16

fitted
with gold *f.* upon carved. *1 Ki* 6:35
they shall withal be *f.* *Pr* 22:18*
vessels of wrath *f.* to. *Rom* 9:22

fitteth
the carpenter *f.* it. *Isa* 44:13*

five
Siddim, four kings with *f. Gen* 14:9
destroy all for lack of *f.?*   18:28
Benjamin's mess was *f.*   43:34
f. years in which no earing. 45:6, 11
to Benjamin he gave *f.* changes. 22
presented *f.* of his brethren.   47:2
thief restore *f.* oxen for. *Ex* 22:1
other *f.* curtains coupled.   26:3, 9
   36:10, 16
make *f.* bars for the boards.   26:26
   27; 36:31, 32
f. pillars.   26:37; 36:38
an altar *f.* cubits long, *f.*   27:1
height of hangings *f.*   18; 38:18
f. sockets of brass.   36:38
f. cubits breadth, *f.* the length. 38:1
f. of you chase an hundred. *Lev* 26:8
estimation be from *f.* years.   27:5
from a month old to *f.* years.   6
take *f.* shekels apiece. *Num* 3:47
   18:16
of peace offerings, *f.* rams, *f.* goats,
   f.   7:17, 23, 29, 35, 41, 47, 53
slew *f.* kings of Midian.   31:8
f. kings of Amorites. *Josh* 10:5
these *f.* kings fled and hid.   16
f. kings hid.   17
bring out the *f.* kings.   22
brought out these *f.* kings unto. 23
hanged them on *f.* trees.   26
f. lords of the Philistines. 13:3
   Judg 3:3
children of Dan sent *f.* *Judg* 18:2
f. golden emerods, *f.* *1 Sam* 6:4
when *f.* lords of Philistines had. 16
David chose *f.* smooth stones. 17:40
give me *f.* loaves of bread. 21:3
f. sheep, *f.* measures of corn. 25:18
Abigail rode on an ass with *f.*   42
Mephibosheth was *f.*   *2 Sam* 4:4
David took the *f.* sons of.   21:8
f. bases on the right, *f.* *1 Ki* 7:39
f. on right side, *f.* on. 49; *2 Chr* 4:7
cab of dove's dung sold *f. 2 Ki* 6:25
let some take *f.* of the horses. 7:13
have smitten *f.* or six times. 13:19
f. men in king's presence. 25:19
the sons of Zera, *f.*   *1 Chr* 2:6
Benaiah slew an Egyptian *f.*   11:23
four or *f.* in fruitful. *Isa* 17:6
f. cities in Egypt speak. 19:18
at the rebuke of *f.* shall ye. 30:17
but *f.* loaves and two. *Mat* 14:17
   Mark 6:38; *Luke* 9:13
f. loaves of the thousand.
   Mat 16:9; *Mark* 8:19
f. were wise, *f.* foolish. *Mat* 25:2
unto one he gave *f.* talents. 15, 16
are not *f.* sparrows sold ? *Luke* 12:6
f. in one house divided.   52
I have bought *f.* yoke of. 14:19
I have *f.* brethren   16:28
thy pound hath gained *f.* 19:18
be thou also over *f.* cities. 19
hast had *f.* husbands. *John* 4:18
pool Bethesda having *f.* porches 5:2
lad which had *f.* barley loaves. 6:9
fragments of *f.* barley loaves. 13
rather speak *f.* words. *1 Cor* 14:19
f. times received I forty stripes.
   2 Cor 11:24
seven kings, *f.* are fallen. *Rev* 17:10

fixed
my heart is *f.*   *Ps* 57:7; 108:1
his heart is *f.* trusting.   112:7
there is a gulf *f.*   *Luke* 16:26

flag, -s
she laid the ark in the *f.* *Ex* 2:3
when she saw the ark among *f.*   5
f. grow without water ? *Job* 8:11
the reeds and *f.* shall. *Isa* 19:6

flagon
each a *f.* of wine.   *2 Sam* 6:19*
   1 Chr 16:3*

flagons
stay me with *f.*   *S of S* 2:5*
to all the vessels of *f.* *Isa* 22:24
to other gods, love *f.* *Hos* 3:1*

flakes
the *f.* of his flesh joined. *Job* 41:23

flame
angel appeared in a *f.*   *Ex* 3:2
   Acts 7:30
a *f.* from the city of. *Num* 21:28
   Jer 48:45
f. went up, angel went in the *f.*
   Judg 13:20
make a great *f.* to rise.   20:38*
the *f.* of the city ascended up.   40*
the *f.* shall dry up his. *Job* 15:30
a *f.* goeth out of his mouth. 41:21
f. setteth mountains on. *Ps* 83:14
the *f.* burnt up the wicked. 106:18
which hath a vehement *f. S of S* 8:6
f. consumeth the chaff. *Isa* 5:24
Holy One shall be for a *f.*   10:17
with *f.* of devouring fire.   29:6
with *f.* of a devouring fire.   30:30
neither the *f.* kindle upon thee. 43:2
not deliver themselves from *f.* 47:14
flaming *f.* not quenched. *Ezek* 20:47
f. slew those men that. *Dan* 3:22
his throne was like fiery *f.*   7:9
body was given to burning *f.*   11*
shall fall by sword and by *f.* 11:33
the *f.* hath burnt all trees. *Joel* 1:19
and behind them a *f.* burneth. 2:3
like the noise of a *f.*   5
house of Joseph shall be a *f. Ob* 18
am tormented in this *f. Luke* 16:24
maketh his ministers a *f. Heb* 1:7
eyes as a *f. Rev* 1:14; 2:18; 19:12

flames
of Lord divideth the *f.*   *Ps* 29:7
their faces shall be as *f. Isa* 13:8
to render rebuke with *f.*   66:15

flaming
at Eden a *f.* sword. *Gen* 3:24
the *f.* flame shall not be quenched.
   Ezek 20:47
chariots with *f.* torches. *Nah* 2:3
   see fire

flanks
(*Revised Version*, loins)
the fat which is by the *f.* shall he.
   Lev 3:4, 10, 15; 4:9; 7:4
collops of fat on his *f.* *Job* 15:27

flash
as the appearance of a *f. Ezek* 1:14

flat
hath a *f.* nose shall not. *Lev* 21:18
Balaam bowed, fell *f.* *Num* 22:31
of city shall fall down *f.* *Josh* 6:5
people shouted, wall fell down *f.* 20

flatter
they *f.* with their tongue. *Ps* 5:9
they did *f.* him with their. 78:36

flattereth
f. himself in his own eyes. *Ps* 36:2
stranger who *f.* with. *Pr* 2:16; 7:5
meddle not with him that *f.* 20:19*
more favour than he that *f.* 28:23
a man that *f.* spreadeth a net. 29:5

flatteries
obtain the kingdom by *f. Dan* 11:21
do wickedly be corrupt by *f.*   32
shall cleave to them with *f.*   34

flattering
neither let me give *f.* titles to man.
   Job 32:21
for I know not to give *f.* titles.   22
with *f.* lips and double. *Ps* 12:2
the Lord shall cut off all *f.* lips.   3
with the *f.* of her lips. *Pr* 7:21
a *f.* mouth worketh ruin. 26:28
no more *f.* divination. *Ezek* 12:24
neither used we *f.* *1 Thes* 2:5

flattery
speaketh *f.* to his friends. *Job* 17:5*
from *f.* of strange woman. *Pr* 6:24

flax
and barley smitten, *f.* *Ex* 9:31
hid them with stalks of *f. Josh* 2:6
cords became as *f.* that. *Judg* 15:14
she seeks wool and *f.* *Pr* 31:13
they that work in fine *f.* *Isa* 19:9
the smoking *f.* shall he not quench.
   42:3; *Mat* 12:20
a man with a line of *f. Ezek* 40:3
lovers that give me *f.* *Hos* 2:5
I will recover my wool and my *f.*   9

flay
f. their skins from off them. Mi 3:3

flayed
the Levites f. them. 2 Chr 35:11

flea
is king come after a f.? 1 Sam 24:14
26:20

fled
kings of Sodom and Gomorrah f.
Gen 14:10
Hagar f. 16:6
Jacob f. 31:22; Hos 12:12
Moses f. from Pharaoh. Ex 2:15
4:3; Acts 7:29
king of Egypt that people f. Ex 14:5
Egyptians f. against the sea. 27
f. at the cry of them. Num 16:34
Israel f. by way of the. Josh 8:15
these five kings f. and hid. 10:16
Adoni-bezek f. Judg 1:6
Sisera f. away. 4:15
host ran and cried, and f. 7:21*, 22
Zalmunna f. 8:12
Jotham ran and f. 9:21
to the tower f. men and. 51
Jephthah f. 11:3
the Benjamites f. 20:45, 47
and I f. to-day out of. 1 Sam 4:16
heard that Philistines f. 14:22
men of Israel f. from Goliath. 17:24
David f. and escaped. 19:10
12, 18; 20:1; 21:10
Abiathar escaped and f. 22:20; 23:6
four hundred which rode and f. 30:17
Israel f. from Philistines. 31:1, 7
2 Sam 19:8
Beerothites f. to Gittaim. 2 Sam 4:3
and his nurse f. 4
the Syrians f. 10:14, 18
Absalom and king's sons f. 13:29
34:37, 38
all Israel f. every one to tent. 18:17
came to me when I f. 1 Ki 2:7
Joab f. to the tabernacle. 28, 29
Hadad f. 11:17
Rezon f. from his lord. 23
Jeroboam f. 40
the Syrians f. 20:20; 1 Chr 19:18
2 Ki 7:7
the people f. to their. 2 Ki 8:21
prophet opened door and f. 9:10
Joram f. 23
all the men of war f. by night. 25:4
Jer 52:7
the men of Israel f. 1 Chr 10:1
11:13; 2 Chr 14:12
Ethiopians and they f. 2 Chr 14:12
the Levites f. every one. Neh 13:10
they that did see me f. Ps 31:11
the sea saw it and f. 114:3
with bread him that f. Isa 21:14
all thy rulers are f. together. 22:3
noise of tumult the people f. 33:3
birds of the heavens were f. Jer 4:25
the fowl and beast are f. 9:10
Urijah heard and f. 26:21
Egyptians are f. 46:5
also her hired men are f. 21
I f. before to Tarshish. Jonah 4:2
flee as ye f. before the. Zech 14:5
they that kept them f. Mat 8:33
disciples forsook him and f. 26:56
Mark 14:50
they went out and f. Mark 16:8
the prisoners had been f. Acts 16:27*
f. for refuge to lay hold. Heb 6:18
the woman f. Rev 12:6
every island f. away. 16:20
earth and heaven f. away. 20:11

he fled
told him not that he f. Gen 31:20
so he f. 21
when he f. from his brother. 35:7
he left his garment and f. 39:12
13, 15, 18
to the city of his refuge, whither he
was f. Num 35:25; Josh 20:6
Abimelech chased Gaal, and he f.
Judg 9:40
they knew when he f. 1 Sam 22:17
Ahaziah fled, and he f. 2 Ki 9:27
he f. to Lachish. 14:19; 2 Chr 25:27

he f. from presence of. Jonah 1:10
he left linen cloth, and f. naked.
Mark 14:52

is fled
no satisfaction for him that is f.
Num 35:32
is f. before Philistines. 1 Sam 4:17
David is f. out of the. 2 Sam 19:9
Gibeah of Saul is f. Isa 10:29

they fled
they that remained f. Gen 14:10
they f. from before men of Ai.
Josh 7:4
as they f. Lord cast down. 10:11
Israel was smitten, they f. every
man to. 1 Sam 4:10; 2 Ki 14:12
champion dead they f. 1 Sam 17:51
slew Philistines, and they f. 19:8
Joab drew nigh, they f. 2 Sam 10:13
1 Chr 19:14
Moabites, they f. before them.
2 Ki 3:24
Israel saw that they f. 1 Chr 10:7
at thy rebuke they f. Ps 104:7
they f. from swords. Isa 21:15
they f. and went forth. Jer 39:4
when they f. away. Lam 4:15
they f. to save themselves. Dan 10:7
for they have f. from me. Hos 7:13*
what was done, they f. Luke 8:34
they f. out of that house. Acts 19:16

fleddest
thou f. from Esau. Gen 35:1
ailed thee, O sea, thou f.? Ps 114:5

flee
I f. from the face of. Gen 16:8
this city is near to f. unto. 19:20
arise, f. to Laban my. 27:43
us f. from face of Israel. Ex 14:25
a place whither he shall f. 21:13
f. when none pursueth. Lev 26:17, 36
hate thee f. before thee. Num 10:55
Ps 68:1
now f. thou to thy place. Num 24:11
that the manslayer may f. 35:6
11, 15; Deut 4:42; 19:3, 4, 5
Josh 20:3, 4, 9
and f. before thee. Deut 28:7, 25
first we f. before them. Josh 8:5, 6
had no power to f. this way or. 20
let us f. and draw them. Judg 20:32
but didst f. on spoil. 1 Sam 15:19
nurse made haste to f. 2 Sam 4:4
f. else we shall not escape. 15:14
men steal away when they f. 19:3
f. three months before ? 24:13
made speed to get to chariot, and f.
1 Ki 12:18; 2 Chr 10:18
then open door, and f. 2 Ki 9:3
such a man as I f.? Neh 6:11
f. from the iron weapon. Job 20:24
would fain f. out of hand. 27:22
abhor me, they f. far from. 30:10*
arrow cannot make him f. 41:28
f. as bird to your ? Ps 11:1
kings of armies f. apace. 68:12
I f. from thy presence ? 139:7
O Lord, I f. to thee to hide. 143:9
wicked f. when no man. Pr 28:1
he shall f. to the pit. 17
whom will ye f. for help ? Isa 10:3
f. every one into his own. 13:14
his fugitives shall f. unto Zoar. 15:5
they shall f. far off. 17:13
expectation whither we f. for. 20:6
no, for we will f. on horses. 30:16
at rebuke of five shall ye f. 17
f. ye from the Chaldeans. 48:20
the city shall f. for noise. Jer 4:29
to f. out of Jerusalem. 6:1
shepherds have no way to f. 25:35
f. save your lives, and be. 48:6
wings to Moab, that it may f. 9
Edom shall f. 49:8
Damascus turned to f. 24
f. dwell deep, inhabitants of. 30
f. every one to his own land. 50:16
voice of them that f. and escape. 28
f. out of midst of Babylon. 51:6
Zech 2:6
man did f. from a lion. Amos 5:19
Jonah rose up to f. to. Jonah 1:3

that look on, shall f. Nah 3:7
take young child and f. Mat 2:13
hath warned you f. from wrath ? 3:7
Luke 3:7
persecute you in city f. Mat 10:23
be in Judea f. to the mountains.
24:16; Mark 13:14; Luke 21:21
stranger not follow, but f. John 10:5
shipmen were about to f. Acts 27:30
f. fornication. 1 Cor 6:18
f. from idolatry. 10:14
O man of God, f. these. 1 Tim 6:11
f. also youthful lusts. 2 Tim 2:22
devil, he will f. from you. Jas 4:7
death shall f. from them. Rev 9:6
that the woman might f. into. 12:14

flee away
wherefore didst thou f. away ?
Gen 31:27
if f. away, they will not. 2 Sam 18:3
my days f. away. Job 9:25
f. away as a dream. 20:8
that see, shall f. away. Ps 64:8*
day break, and shadows f. away.
S of S 2:17; 4:6
sighing f. away. Isa 35:10; 51:11
let not swift f. away. Jer 46:6
courageous shall f. away. Amos 2:16
O thou seer, go, f. away into. 7:12
fleeth of them, shall not f. away. 9:1
Nineveh shall f. away. Nah 2:8
grasshoppers in hedges f. away. 3:17

fleece
first of f. of sheep give. Deut 18:4
a f. of wool in floor. Judg 6:37
Gideon wringed dew out of f. 38
let it be dry only upon the f. 39
not warmed with f. of. Job 31:20

fleeing
flee as f. from sword. Lev 26:36
that f. to one of these. Deut 4:42
for want and famine f. to. Job 30:3*

fleeth
smite him mortally, f. Deut 19:11
he f. as a shadow. Job 14:2
he who f. from noise of. Isa 24:18
ask him that f. and. Jer 48:19
he that f. from the fear, shall. 44
f. shall not flee away. Amos 9:1*
that is an hireling f. John 10:12, 13

flesh
[1] The muscles and other soft parts of the animal body, whether of man, beast, bird, or fish, Ex 12:8; Mat 26:41. [2] All beings possessed of flesh, man and the inferior animals, especially man; often in contrast with God, who is spirit, Gen 6:13. [3] Human nature considered as unregenerate and unsanctified, Rom 7:5. [4] The word is also used for one of near kindred, Gen 37:27; 2 Sam 19:12, 13.
To be one flesh, denotes an intimate communion, as if the two were but one person or one body, Gen 2:24. This phrase is used by the Apostle to shew the union between Christ and believers, Eph 5:30, 31. Flesh also signifies the human nature of Christ, Heb 10:20.
God closed up the f. Gen 2:21
to his wife, they shall be one f. 24
not strive with man, he is f. 6:3
ye shall circumcise the f. of. 17:11
whose f. is not circumcised. 14
Abraham circumcised f. of. 23
he is our brother and our f. 37:27
turned again as his other f. Ex 4:7
burn the f. 29:14; Lev 9:11; 16:27
Num 19:5
man's f. not be poured. Ex 30:32
what shall touch f thereof. Lev 6:27
as for f., all that be clean shall. 7:19
boil the f. at the door of. 8:31
be quick raw f. 13:10, 14, 15, 16, 24
if skin of their f. have bright. 38, 39
that toucheth the f. of him. 15:7
if her issue in her f. be blood. 19
make any cuttings in their f. 21:5

while f. was between. *Num* 11:33
whom f. is half consumed. 12:12
the f. of them shall be thine. 18:18
my sword shall devour f. *Deut* 32:42
take f. and unleavened cakes.
Judg 6:20
fire out of rock, and consumed f. 21
while f. was in seething. *1 Sam* 2:13
give f. to roast for the priest. 15
David dealt to each f. *2 Sam* 6:19
1 Chr 16:3
him bread and f. in morning, bread
and f. in evening. *1 Ki* 17:6
boiled f. with instruments of. 19:21
f. of the child waxed. *2 Ki* 4:34
with him is an arm of f. *2 Chr* 32:8
yet our f. is as the f. of. *Neh* 5:5
hast thou eyes of f.? *Job* 10:4
clothed me with skin and f. 11
I will not fear what f. can. *Ps* 56:4
he provide f. for his people? 78:20
rained f. also upon them as dust. 27
remembered they were but f. 39
the f. of thy saints given to. 79:2
sayings are health to their f. *Pr* 4:22
not among riotous eaters of f. 23:20
and their horses are f. 31:3
I will feed them with own f. 49:26
and the holy f. is passed. *Jer* 11:15
spoilers come, no f. have. 12:12
cursed be man that maketh f. 17:5
nor came abominable f. *Ezek* 4:14
city is caldron, and we be f. 11:3
slain in midst of it, they are the f. 7
nor ye be the f. in the midst. 11
give them a heart of f. 19; 36:26
great of f. and hast increased. 16:26
whose f. is as f. of asses. 23:20
consume the f., spice it well. 24:10
I will bring f. upon you. 37:6, 8
dwelling is not with f. *Dan* 2:11
arise, devour much f. 7:5
neither came f. nor wine. 10:3
sacrifice f. for sacrifices. *Hos* 8:13
f. from off their bones. *Mi* 3:2
their f. shall be poured. *Zeph* 1:17
if one bear holy f. in. *Hag* 2:12
f. shall consume away. *Zech* 14:12
f. and blood hath not. *Mat* 16:17
and they twain be one f. 19:5, 6
Mark 10:8; *1 Cor* 6:16; *Eph* 5:31
should no f. be saved. *Mat* 24:22
Mark 13:20
spirit willing, f. is weak. *Mat* 26:41
Mark 14:38
spirit hath not f. and. *Luke* 24:39
the Word was made f. *John* 1:14
the f. profiteth nothing. 6:63
of David according to f. *Acts* 2:30
Rom 1:3
shall no f. be justified. *Rom* 3:20
Abraham as pertaining to f. 4:1
with f. I serve the law of sin. 7:25
law was weak through f. God sent
own Son in likeness of sinful f. 8:3
and kinsmen according to f. 9:3
of whom as concerning the f.
make not provision for the f. 13:14
that no f. should glory. *1 Cor* 1:29
there is one f. of men, and. 15:39
f. and blood cannot inherit. 50
purpose according to f.? *2 Cor* 1:17
of Jesus manifest in our f. 4:11
our f. had no rest, but. 7:5
walked according to the f. 10:2
conferred not with f. and. *Gal* 1:16
by works of law no f. justified. 2:16
are ye made perfect by the f.? 3:3
not liberty for occasion to the f. 5:13
f. lusteth against the Spirit, Spirit
against f. 17
Christ's have crucified the f. 24
in lusts of our f. *Eph* 2:3
masters according to the f. 6:5
Col 3:22
wrestle not against f. and. *Eph* 6:12
children partakers of f. *Heb* 2:14
we had fathers of our f. who. 12:9
going after strange f. are. *Jude* 7
these filthy dreamers defile the f. 8
hating even garment spotted by f. 23
eat f. of captains, f. of. *Rev* 19:18
all the fowls filled with their f. 21
see **eat, eateth**

15

---

after the **flesh**
ye judge *after the* f. *John* 8:15
who walk not *after the* f. *Rom* 8:1, 4
are *after the* f. mind things of f. 5
debtors to flesh to live *after the* f. 12
if ye live *after the* f. ye shall die. 13
many wise men *after* f. *1 Cor* 1:26
behold Israel *after the* f. 10:18
no man *after the* f.: though we have
known Christ *after* f. *2 Cor* 5:16
we do not war *after the* f. 10:3
many glory *after the* f. I also. 11:18
Ishmael born *after the* f. *Gal* 4:23, 29
them that walk *after* f. *2 Pet* 2:10

all **flesh**
for *all* f. had corrupted. *Gen* 6:12
God said, the end of *all* f. is. 13
of *all* f. two of every sort bring into
the ark to keep. 19; 7:15
all f. died that moved upon. 7:21
bring forth of *all* f. both of. 8:17
nor *all* f. cut off any more. 9:11, 15
covenant between me and *all* f. 16:17
the life of *all* f. is blood. *Lev* 17:14
shave *all* their f. and. *Num* 8:7
God of spirits of *all* f. 16:22; 27:16
that openeth matrix of *all* f. 18:15
who of *all* f. heard word. *Deut* 5:26
all f. shall perish together. *Job* 34:15
to thee shall *all* f. come. *Ps* 65:2
who giveth food to *all* f. 136:25
let *all* f. bless his holy name. 145:21
all f. shall see it together. *Isa* 40:5
all f. is grass. 6; *1 Pet* 1:24
all f. shall know I am thy Saviour.
Isa 49:26; *Ezek* 21:5
by fire will Lord plead with *all* f.
Isa 66:16
all f. shall come to worship. 23
an abhorring to *all* f. 24
will plead with *all* f. *Jer* 25:31
I am Lord the God of *all* f. 32:27
I will bring evil on *all* f. 45:5
all f. shall see that I. *Ezek* 20:48
sword go forth against *all* f. 21:4
and *all* f. was fed of it. *Dan* 4:12
will pour out my Spirit on *all* f.
Joel 2:28; *Acts* 2:17
be silent, O *all* f. *Zech* 2:13
all f. shall see salvation. *Luke* 3:6
given him power over *all* f. *John* 17:2
all f. is not same flesh. *1 Cor* 15:39

his **flesh**
his f. shall not be eaten. *Ex* 21:28
seethe *his* f. in holy place. 29:31
burn all *his* f. with. *Lev* 4:11; 8:17
linen breeches on *his* f. 6:10; 16:4
a rising in the skin of *his* f. 13:2
look on plague in skin of *his* f. 3
spot be white in skin of *his* f. 4
old leprosy in skin of *his* f. 11, 13
also wash *his* f. in water. 14:9
15:16; 16:24, 28; *Num* 19:7
running issue out of *his* f. *Lev* 15:2
whether *his* f. run with his issue. 3
wash them not, nor bathe *his* f. 17:16
unclean, unless he wash *his* f. 22:6
Ahab put sackcloth on *his* f.
1 Ki 21:27
his f. came again, and. *2 Ki* 5:14
Joram had sackcloth on *his* f. 6:30
touch his bone and *his* f. *Job* 2:5
his f. upon him shall have. 14:22
O that we had of *his* f. 31:31
his f. is consumed away. 33:21
his f. be fresher than a child's. 25
flakes of *his* f. are joined. 41:23
cruel troubleth *his* f. *Pr* 11:17
foldeth hands, eateth *his* f. *Eccl* 4:5
fatness of *his* f. wax lean. *Isa* 17:4
man give us *his* f. to eat? *John* 6:52
his f. did see corruption. *Acts* 2:31
he that soweth to *his* f. *Gal* 6:8
abolished in *his* f. the. *Eph* 2:15
no man yet hated his own f. 5:29
members of his body, of *his* f. 30
reconciled in body of *his* f. *Col* 1:22
in days of *his* f. when. *Heb* 5:7
that is to say, *his* f. 10:20

in the **flesh**, or *in* **flesh**
Abraham was circumcised *in the* f.
Gen 17:24
Ishmael circumcised *in the* f. 25

---

uncircumcised *in the* f. *Ezek* 44:7
uncircumcised *in the* f. not enter. 9
fairer and fatter *in* f. *Dan* 1:15
circumcision outward *in the* f.
Rom 2:28
for when we were *in the* f. 7:5
for sin condemned sin *in the* f. 8:3
are *in the* f. cannot please God. 8
but ye are not *in the* f. but. 9
have trouble *in the* f. *1 Cor* 7:28
in the f. not war after f. *2 Cor* 10:3
given to me a thorn *in the* f. 12:7
which I now live *in the* f. *Gal* 2:20
to make a fair shew *in the* f. 6:12
Gentiles *in the* f. called the circumcision *in the* f. made. *Eph* 2:11
if I live *in the* f. this is. *Phil* 1:22
to abide *in the* f. more needful. 24
have no confidence *in the* f. 3:3
might have confidence *in the* f. 4
not seen my face *in the* f. *Col* 2:1
though I be absent *in the* f. 5
God manifest *in the* f. *1 Tim* 3:16
more to thee, both *in the* f. *Philem* 16
put to death *in the* f. *1 Pet* 3:18
Christ suffered for us *in the* f.: he
that hath suffered *in the* f. 4:1
no longer live *in the* f. 2
judged according to men *in the* f. 6
denieth Christ *in the* f. *1 John* 4:2, 3
not Christ is come *in the* f. *2 John* 7

my **flesh**
my bread and *my* f.? *1 Sam* 25:11
the hair of *my* f. stood. *Job* 4:15
or is *my* f. brass? 6:12
my f. is clothed with worms. 7:5
I take *my* f. in my teeth? 13:14
cleaveth to skin, and *my* f. 19:20
and not satisfied with *my* f.? 22
yet in *my* f. shall I see God. 26
trembling taketh hold of *my* f. 21:6
my f. shall rest in hope. *Ps* 16:9
Acts 2:26
no soundness in *my* f. *Ps* 38:3, 7
my f. longeth for thee in a dry. 63:1
my f. faileth, but God is my. 73:26
my heart and *my* f. crieth out. 84:2
my knees are weak, *my* f. 109:24
my f. trembleth for fear. 119:120
done to me, and to *my* f. *Jer* 51:35
my f. and my skin hath. *Lam* 3:4
bread I will give is *my* f. *John* 6:51
eateth *my* f. hath eternal. 54, 56
my f. is meat indeed. 55
in *my* f. dwelleth no. *Rom* 7:18
provoke them which are *my* f. 11:14
temptation which was in *my* f.
Gal 4:14
afflictions of Christ in *my* f. *Col* 1:24

see **bone**

of the **flesh**
carry forth aught *of the* f. *Ex* 12:46
if aught *of the* f. remain. 29:34
nor give *of the* f. *Deut* 28:55
sound heart is life *of the* f. *Pr* 14:30
study weariness *of the* f. *Eccl* 12:12
is born *of the* f. is flesh. *John* 1:13
is born *of the* f. is flesh. 3:6
do mind the things *of the* f. *Rom* 8:5
which are children *of the* f. 9:8
for destruction *of the* f. *1 Cor* 5:5
cleanse from all filthiness *of the* f.
2 Cor 7:1
through infirmity *of the* f. *Gal* 4:13
shall not fulfil the lust *of the* f. 5:16
now works *of the* f. are manifest. 19
soweth to flesh *of the* f. reap. 6:8
in lusts of our f. desires *of the* f.
Eph 2:3
putting off sins *of the* f. *Col* 2:11
to the satisfying *of the* f. 23
to the purging *of the* f. *Heb* 9:13
away the filth *of the* f. *1 Pet* 3:21
through lusts *of the* f. *2 Pet* 2:18
the lust *of the* f. the. *1 John* 2:16

thy **flesh**
birds shall eat *thy* f. *Gen* 40:19
give *thy* f. unto fowls. *1 Sam* 17:44
are thy bone and *thy* f. *2 Sam* 5:1
1 Chr 11:1
wash, *thy* f. shall come. *2 Ki* 5:10
when *thy* f. is consumed. *Pr* 5:11

not mouth to cause thy f. *Eccl 5:6*
put away evil from thy f. *11:10*
hide not thyself from thine own f.
    Isa 58:7
lay thy f. on mountains. *Ezek 32:5*

your flesh
make cuttings in your f. *Lev 19:28*
then I will tear your f. *Judg 8:7*
stony heart out of your f. *Ezek 36:26*
of the infirmity of your f. *Rom 6:19*
they may glory in your f. *Gal 6:13*
uncircumcision of your f. *Col 2:13*
rust shall eat your f. *Jas 5:3*

fleshhook
servant came with a f. *1 Sam 2:13*
all that the f. brought up. *14*

fleshhooks
shalt make his f. and. *Ex 27:3*
made vessels and the f. *38:3*
upon purple cloth the f. *Num 4:14*
pure gold for the f. *1 Chr 28:17*
also the pots and f. *2 Chr 4:16*

fleshly
simplicity, not f. wisdom. *2 Cor 1:12*
but in f. tables of the heart. *3:3*
puffed up by his f. mind. *Col 2:18*
abstain from f. lusts. *1 Pet 2:11*

flesh pots
we sat by the f. pots. *Ex 16:3*

flew
people f. upon spoil. *1 Sam 14:32*
f. one of the seraphims. *Isa 6:6*

flies
swarms of f. upon thee. *Ex 8:21*
he removed the swarms of f. *31*
he sent divers sorts of f. *Ps 78:45*
there came divers sorts of f. 105:31
dead f. cause ointment. *Eccl 10:1*

flieth
any winged fowl that f. *Deut 4:17*
every creeping thing that f. *14:19**
a nation swift as the eagle f. *28:49*
for arrow that f. by day. *Ps 91:5*
cankerworm spoileth and f. *Nah 3:16*

flight
go out with haste nor f. *Isa 52:12*
the f. shall perish from. *Amos 2:14*
pray f. be not in winter. *Mat 24:20*
    Mark 13:18
to f. armies of aliens. *Heb 11:34*

see put

flint
water out of rock of f. *Deut 8:15*
turning f. into a fountain. *Ps 114:8*
horses be counted like f. *Isa 5:28*
have I set my face like a f. *50:7*
harder than f. have I. *Ezek 3:9*

flinty
to suck oil out of the f. rock.
    Deut 32:13

floats
by sea in f. *1 Ki 5:9; 2 Chr 2:16*

flock
Abel brought firstlings of his f.
    Gen 4:4
Abraham set ewe lambs of f. *21:28*
go to f. and fetch two good. *27:9*
Jacob watered the f. of Laban. 29:10
again feed and keep thy f. *30:31*
I will pass through all thy f. *32*
Jacob fed rest of Laban's f. *36*
separate all the brown in the f. *40*
Rachel and Leah to his f. *31:4*
rams of thy f. have I not eaten. *38*
overdrive them, the f. will die. 33:13
Joseph was feeding the f. with. 37:2
brethren went to feed their f. 12, 13
I will send a kid from the f. *38:17*
water their father's f. *Ex 2:16*
Moses helped, watered f. *17, 19*
Moses led the f. to the desert. *3:1*
of your offering for f. *Lev 1:2*
bring a female from the f. *5:6*
ram without blemish out of f. *18*
  6:6; Ezra 10:19; Ezek 43:23, 25
concerning tithe of the f. *Lev 27:32*
savour of the herd or f. *Num 15:3*
kill of thy herd and f. *Deut 12:21*
him liberally out of thy f. *15:14*
all the firstling males of thy f. *19*

sacrifice to Lord of the f. *Deut 16:2*
lion took lamb out of f. *1 Sam 17:34*
spared to take of own f. *2 Sam 12:4*
gave to people of the f. *2 Chr 35:7*
to set with dogs of my f. *Job 30:1*
makest thy f. to rest at. *S of S 1:7*
go by the footsteps of the f. *8*
hair is as a f. of goats. *4:1; 6:5*
teeth are like f. of sheep. *4:2; 6:6*
feed his f. like a shepherd. *Isa 40:11*
them with shepherd of his f. *63:11*
Lord's f. is carried. *Jer 13:17*
where is the f., thy beautiful f.? *20*
ye have scattered my f. and. *23:2*
gather the remnant of my f. *3*
ye principal of the f. *25:34*
nor principal of the f. to escape. *35*
an howling of principal of the f. *36*
him as a shepherd doth his f. *31:10*
shall sing for the young of the f. *12*
least of f. draw them. *49:20; 50:45*
in pieces shepherd and his f. *51:23*
take the choice of the f. *Ezek 24:5*
eat the fat, ye feed not the f. *34:3**
my f. was scattered on the face. *6**
my f. became a prey, my f. meat. *8**
require my f. I will deliver my f. *10**
as a shepherd seeketh out his f. *12*
I will feed my f. *15**
as for you, O my f. *17*
therefore will I save my f. *22*
ye my f. the f. of my pasture. *31**
the holy f. as f. of Jerusalem. *36:38*
offer one lamb out of the f. *45:15*
eat lambs out of the f. *Amos 6:4*
Lord took me as I followed f. *7:15*
let not herd nor f. taste. *Jonah 3:7*
as the f. in the midst. *Mi 2:12*
O tower of the f. the strong. *4:8*
thy people, f. of thine heritage. *7:14*
the f. shall be cut off. *Hab 3:17*
save them as the f. of. *Zech 9:16*
they went their way as a f. *10:2**
Lord of hosts hath visited his f. *3*
will feed f. of slaughter. *11:4, 7*
poor of the f. that waited on. *7, 11*
woe to shepherd, that leaveth f. *17*
deceiver which hath in his f. a male.
    Mal 1:14
sheep of f. be scattered. *Mat 26:31*
keeping watch over their f. *Luke 2:8*
fear not little f. it is your. *12:32*
take heed to all the f. *Acts 20:28*
wolves enter, not sparing f. *29*
who feedeth a f. and. *1 Cor 9:7*
feed the f. of God. *1 Pet 5:2*
but being ensamples to the f. *3*

like a flock
their little ones like a f. *Job 21:11*
leddest thy people like a f. *Ps 77:20*
guided them in wilderness like a f.
    78:52
that leadest Joseph like a f. *80:1*
maketh him families like a f. *107:41*
them with men like a f. *Ezek 36:37*

flocks
f. of sheep lying by well, out of that
  they watered the f. *Gen 29:2*
thither were all the f. gathered. *3*
we cannot until the f. be gathered. *8*
Jacob set rods before the f. *30:38*
the f. conceived before the rods. *39*
faces of the f. towards the ringstraked, he put his own f. by. *40**
I have oxen, asses, f. and. *32:5*
he divided the f. and herds. *7*
whether it be well with f. *37:14*
tell me where they feed their f. *16*
have no pasture for their f. *47:4*
in exchange for horses and f. *16*
if his offering be of the f. *Lev 1:10*
ram without blemish out of f. *5:15*
took spoil of all their f. *Num 31:9*
take one portion of the f. *30*
our wives, our f. and cattle. *32:26*
also bless f. of thy sheep. *Deut 7:13*
blessed be the f. of thy sheep. *28:4*
cursed be the f. of thy sheep. *18*
not leave the f. of thy sheep. *51*
hear bleatings of the f. *Judg 5:16*
like two little f. of kids. *1 Ki 20:27*
seek pasture for their f. *1 Chr 4:39*
there was pasture for their f. *41*

and over the f. was Jaziz. *1 Chr 27:31*
Arabians brought him f. *2 Chr 17:11*
violently take away f. *Job 24:2*
pastures are clothed with f. *Ps 65:13*
their f. to hot thunderbolts. *78:48*
turn aside by the f. of. *S of S 1:7*
cities of Aroer shall be. *Isa 17:2*
palaces be a pasture of f. *32:14*
all the f. of Kedar shall be. *60:7*
strangers shall feed your f. *61:5*
Sharon shall be a fold for f. *65:10*
the shepherds with their f. *Jer 6:3*
all f. shall be scattered. *10:21*
Judah they that go forth with f. 31:24
shepherds causing f. to lie. *33:12*
the f. shall pass again under rod. *13*
tents and f. shall take away. *49:29*
as the he goats before the f. *50:8*
a couching place for f. *Ezek 25:5*
not the shepherds feed the f.? *34:2**
the waste cities filled with f. *36:38*
f. of sheep are desolate. *Joel 1:18*
as a young lion among f. *Mi 5:8*
sea coast be folds for f. *Zeph 2:6*
f. lie down in midst of Nineveh. *14**

flocks with herds
Lot also had f. and herds. *Gen 13:5*
given Abraham f. and herds. *24:35*
possession of f. and herds. *26:14*
Jacob divided f. and herds. *32:7*
the f. and herds with young. *33:13*
me, thou, thy f. and herds. *45:10*
brethren, their f. and herds. *47:1*
their f. and herds left they. *50:8*
go with f. and herds. *Ex 10:9*
let your f. and your herds be. *24*
take your f. and your herds. *12:32*
neither let f. nor herds feed. *34:3*
and herds be slain. *Num 11:22*
thy herds and f. multiply. *Deut 8:13*
firstling of herds and f. *12:6, 17*
    14:23; Neh 10:36
took all f. and herds. *1 Sam 30:20*
had exceeding many f. and herds.
    2 Sam 12:2
possessions of f. and herds.
    2 Chr 32:29
thy f. look to thy herds. *Pr 27:23*
devoured f. and herds. *Jer 3:24*
nation eat thy f. and herds. *5:17*
go with f. and herds to. *Hos 5:6*

flood
[1] *A great flow of water; inunda-*
tion. [2] *Figuratively, of dangers*
or sorrows or temptations which
come like a flood of water. [3]
Specifically, the great flood of
Noah's time.

I bring a f. of water on. *Gen 6:17*
when the f. of waters was. *7:6*
because of the waters of the f. *7*
after seven days f. was on earth. *10*
f. was forty days on earth. *17*
any more a f. to destroy. *9:11*
lived after the f. 350 years. *28*
to them were sons born after f. 10:1
nations divided in earth after f. *32*
your fathers on either side of f.
    Josh 24:2*, 3*, 14*, 15*
as the f. decayeth and. *Job 14:11**
foundation overthrown with f. 22:16*
f. breaketh out from the. *28:4**
Lord sitteth upon the f. *Ps 29:10*
went through the f. on foot. *66:6*
let not the water-f. overflow. *69:15*
cleave fountain and the f. *74:15*
them away as with a f. *90:5*
strong one, which as a f. *Isa 28:2**
enemy come in like a f. *59:19**
who cometh up as a f.? *Jer 46:7**
Egypt riseth up like a f. *8**
waters be an overflowing f. *47:2**
end shall be with a f. *Dan 9:26*
with arms of a f. shall be. *11:22*
it shall rise up wholly as a f.
    Amos 8:8*; 9:5*
be drowned as by the f. of. *9:5**
with an overrunning f. *Nah 1:8*
in days before the f. *Mat 24:38*
and knew not till the f. came. *39*
    Luke 17:27
when the f. arose the. *Luke 6:48*
bringing in the f. on world. *2 Pet 2:5*

floods

dragon poured out water as a *f.*
     Rev 12:15*
earth helped, swallowed up the *f. 16*

floods

the *f.* stood upright.   *Ex* 15:8
f. of ungodly made me afraid.
    2 *Sam* 22:5; *Ps* 18:4
not see rivers and *f.* *Job* 20:17*
bindeth *f.* from overflowing. 28:11*
established it upon the *f.* *Ps* 24:2
surely in *f.* of great waters. 32:6*
deep waters, where the *f.* 69:2
turned their *f.* into blood. 78:44*
f. have lifted up, O Lord, *f.* 93:3
let the *f.* clap their hands. 98:8
neither can *f.* drown love. *S of S* 8:7
f. upon the dry ground. *Isa* 44:3*
I restrained the *f.* *Ezek* 31:15*
f. compassed me about. *Jonah* 2:3
the *f.* came, winds. *Mat* 7:25, 27

floor, substantive

the threshing *f.* of Atad. *Gen* 50:10
inhabitants saw mourning in *f.* 11
priests take dust in *f.* *Num* 5:17
heave offering of threshing *f.* 15:20
as the corn of the threshing *f.* 18:27
as increase of threshing *f.* 30
furnish him out of thy *f. Deut* 15:14*
a fleece of wool in the *f. Judg* 6:37*
winnoweth in threshing *f. Ruth* 3:2
came to Nachon's threshing *f.*
   2 *Sam* 6:6; 1 *Chr* 13:9
altar in threshing *f.* of. 2 *Sam* 24:18
David said, to buy threshing *f.* 21
he overlaid the *f.* of. *1 Ki* 6:30
cedar from one side of the *f.* 7:7
out of the barn–*f.* or the. 2 *Ki* 6:27
answered in threshing *f. 1 Chr* 21:28
prepared in threshing *f.* of. 2 *Chr* 3:1
and the corn of my *f.* *Isa* 21:10
is like a threshing *f.* *Jer* 51:33
a reward on every corn *f.* *Hos* 9:1
the *f.* and winepress shall not. 2*
as chaff driven out of the *f.* 13:3*
them as sheaves into *f.* *Mi* 4:12*
he will throughly purge his *f.*
   Mat 3:12*; *Luke* 3:17*

floor, verb

timber to *f.* the houses. 2 *Chr* 34:11*

floors

rob the threshing *f.* *1 Sam* 23:1
of summer threshing *f.* *Dan* 2:35
f. shall be full of wheat. *Joel* 2:24

flour

of wheaten *f.* make them. *Ex* 29:2
his handful of the *f.* *Lev* 2:2; 6:15
tenth part of ephah of *f.* for a meat–.
  Num 28:5, 20, 28; 29:3, 9, 14
cakes of an ephah of *f.* *Judg* 6:19
      1 Sam 1:24
she took *f.* and kneaded it.
  1 Sam 28:24; 2 *Sam* 13:8*
brought *f.* parched corn. 2 *Sam* 17:28
    see **deal, fine**

flourish

in his days the righteous *f. Ps* 72:7
they of the city shall *f.* like. 16
the workers of iniquity *f.* 92:7
the righteous shall *f.* like the. 12
f. in the courts of our God. 13
himself shall his crown *f.* 132:18
the righteous shall *f.* *Pr* 11:28
tabernacle of upright shall *f.* 14:11
the almond tree shall *f.* *Eccl* 12:5*
let us see if vine *f.* *S of S* 7:12*
shalt make thy seed to *f. Isa* 17:11*
your bones shall *f.* like an. 66:14
made the dry tree to *f. Ezek* 17:24

flourished

to see whether vine *f. S of S* 6:11*
your care of me hath *f.* *Phil* 4:10*

flourisheth

in the morning it *f.* *Ps* 90:6
as a flower of field, so he *f.* 103:15

flourishing

in old age, fat and *f.* *Ps* 92:14*
I was at rest, and *f.* in. *Dan* 4:4

flow

his goods shall *f.* away. *Job* 20:28
wind blow, and waters *f. Ps* 147:18
spices thereof may *f.* out. *S of S* 4:16

---

all nations shall *f.* unto it. *Isa* 2:2
waters to *f.* out of the rock. 48:21
shalt see and *f.* together. 60:5*
mountains might *f.* down at. 64:1
f. to goodness of Lord. *Jer* 31:12
nations shall not *f.* together. 51:44
the hills shall *f.* with milk, the rivers
of Judah *f.* with waters. *Joel* 3:18
people shall *f.* to mountain. *Mi* 4:1
out of his belly *f.* living. *John* 7:38

flowed

Jordan *f.* over all banks. *Josh* 4:18
the mountains *f.* down. *Isa* 64:3
the waters *f.* over mine. *Lam* 3:54

floweth

land that *f.* with milk and honey.
 Lev 20:24; *Num* 13:27; 14:8
 16:13, 14; *Deut* 6:3; 11:9; 26:15
   27:3; 31:20; *Josh* 5:6

flowing

to a land *f.* with milk and honey.
 Ex 3:8, 17; 13:5; 33:3; *Jer* 11:5
  32:22; *Ezek* 20:6, 15
wellspring of wisdom as a *f. Pr* 18:4
glory of Gentiles like a *f. Isa* 66:12
or shall cold *f.* waters ? *Jer* 18:14
gloriest thou in thy *f.* valley ? 49:4

flower

increase shall die in *f.* 1 *Sam* 2:33
if she pass *f.* of her age. 1 *Cor* 7:36

flower

with knop and *f.* in one branch.
   Ex 25:33; 37:19
he cometh forth as a *f.* *Job* 14:2
he shall cast off his *f.* as. 15:33
as a *f.* of field, so he. *Ps* 103:15
sour grape is ripening in *f. Isa* 18:5
glorious beauty is a fading *f.* 28:1, 4
goodliness thereof is as *f.* of. 40:6
f. fadeth. 7, 8; *Neh* 1:4; *Jas* 1:10
    11; *1 Pet* 1:24

flowers

his *f.* shall be of same. *Ex* 25:31
     37:17
his knops and his *f.* 37:20
if her *f.* be upon him, he. *Lev* 15:24*
of her that is sick of her *f.* of. 33*
to the *f.* thereof was. *Num* 8:4
of house within carved with open *f.*
 1 *Ki* 6:18, 29, 32, 35; 7:26, 49
like brim of cup with *f.* 2 *Chr* 4:5
the *f.* lamps, and tongs made. 21
the *f.* appear on earth. *S of S* 2:12
cheeks as a bed of spices, sweet *f.*
     5:13*

flute

ye hear the *f.* *Dan* 3:5, 7, 10, 15

fluttereth

eagle *f.* over her young. *Deut* 32:11

flux

of Publius sick of a *f.* *Acts* 28:8

fly

Lord shall hiss for the *f.* in. *Isa* 7:18

fly, verb

and fowl that may *f.* *Gen* 1:20
rode upon a cherub, and did *f.*
  2 *Sam* 22:11; *Ps* 18:10
born to trouble as sparks *f. Job* 5:7
doth the hawk *f.* by thy ? 39:26*
he did *f.* upon the wings. *Ps* 18:10
for then would I *f.* away. 55:6
is soon cut off, we *f.* away. 90:10
riches *f.* away as an eagle. *Pr* 23:5
with twain he did *f.* *Isa* 6:2
shall *f.* upon the shoulders of. 11:14
who are these that *f.* as a cloud. 60:8
he shall *f.* as an eagle. *Jer* 48:40
hunt the souls to make them *f.*
    Ezek 13:20
Gabriel being caused to *f. Dan* 9:21
their glory shall *f.* away. *Hos* 9:11
they shall *f.* as the eagle. *Hab* 1:8
I saw another angel *f.* *Rev* 14:6
to all the fowls that *f.* in. 19:17
   see **flee, flieth**

flying

eat of every *f.* creeping. *Lev* 11:21*
but all other *f.* creeping things. 23*
all cattle and *f.* fowl. *Ps* 148:10
as the swallow by *f.* so. *Pr* 26:2

---

fruit shall be a fiery *f.* *Isa* 14:29
come viper and fiery *f.* serpent. 30:6
as birds *f.* so will the Lord. 31:5†
and behold, a *f.* roll. *Zech* 5:1, 2
fourth beast like a *f.* eagle. *Rev* 4:7
heard an angel *f.* through. 8:13

foal, –s

bulls, twenty asses, ten *f. Gen* 32:15
binding his *f.* to the vine. 49:11
f. of an ass. *Zech* 9:9; *Mat* 21:5

foam

of Samaria cut off as *f.* *Hos* 10:7

foameth

f. gnasheth with his teeth. *Mark* 9:18
     Luke 9:39

foaming

on ground wallowed *f.* *Mark* 9:20
raging waves of sea. *f.* *Jude* 13

fodder

or loweth the ox over his *f. Job* 6:5

foes

destroyed before thy *f. 1 Chr* 21:12
the Jews slew of their *f. Esth* 9:16
mine enemies and *f.* *Ps* 27:2
thou hast not made my *f.* to. 30:1
I will beat down his *f.* 89:23
a man's *f.* shall be they. *Mat* 10:36
make thy *f.* thy footstool. *Acts* 2:35

fold

as vesture shalt thou *f.* *Heb* 1:12*

fold

shepherds make their *f. Isa* 13:20*
Sharon shall be *f.* for flocks. 65:10
on mountains their *f.* be. *Ezek* 34:14
as flock in midst of their *f. Mi* 2:12*
flock be cut off from the *f. Hab* 3:17
hundred, some sixty, some thirty *f.*
 Mat 13:8, 23; *Mark* 4:8, 20
shall receive 100 *f.* *Mat* 19:29
other sheep which are not of this *f.*
there shall be one *f. John* 10:16*

folden

while they be *f.* together. *Nah* 1:10

foldeth

the fool *f.* his hands. *Eccl* 4:5

folding

leaves of one door were *f. 1 Ki* 6:34
a little *f.* of hands. *Pr* 6:10; 24:33

folds

build ye *f.* for. *Num* 32:24, 36
no he goats out of thy *f. Ps* 50:9
bring them again to their *f. Jer* 23:3
the sea coast shall be *f. Zeph* 2:6

folk

leave with thee some of *f. Gen* 33:15
conies are but a feeble *f.* *Pr* 30:26
the *f.* shall labour in fire. *Jer* 51:58*
hands upon few sick *f.* *Mark* 6:5
multitude of impotent *f. John* 5:3*
a multitude bringing sick *f. Acts* 5:16

follow

woman not willing to *f. Gen* 24:8
Joseph said, *f.* after the men. 44:4
out, and people that *f.* *Ex* 11:8
harden Pharaoh that he shall *f.* 14:4
the Egyptians shall *f.* them. 17*
a woman, and no mischief *f.* 21:22
and if any mischief *f.* then. 23
not *f.* a multitude to do evil. 23:2
what is altogether just *f. Deut* 16:20
if the thing *f.* not. 18:22
inclined to *f.* Abimelech. *Judg* 9:3
men, who *f.* my lord. 1 *Sam* 25:27
faint they could not *f.* David. 30:21
people that *f.* Absalom. 2 *Sam* 17:9
then I will *f.* thee. 1 *Ki* 19:20
I *f.* the thing that good is. *Ps* 38:20
virgins her companions that *f.* 45:14
upright in heart shall *f.* it. 94:15
they draw nigh that *f.* 119:150
that they *f.* strong drink. *Isa* 5:11
ye that *f.* after righteousness. 51:1
being a pastor to *f.* thee. *Jer* 17:16
the famine shall *f.* close. 42:16
prophets that *f.* own spirit. *Ezek* 13:3
shall *f.* after her lovers. *Hos* 2:7
if we *f.* on to know the Lord. 6:3
Master, I will *f.* thee. *Mat* 8:19
    Luke 9:57, 61
these signs *f.* them. *Mark* 16:17

follow (continued)

not after them, nor f. Luke 17:23
about him saw what would f. 22:49
a stranger will they not f. John 10:5
why cannot I f. thee now? 13:37
from Samuel, and that f. Acts 3:24
f. things that make for peace.
Rom 14:19
f. after charity. 1 Cor 14:1
but I f. after. Phil 3:12*
f. that which is good. 1 Thes 5:15
know how ye ought to f. 2 Thes 3:7*
ourselves an ensample to you to f. 9*
some men they f. after. 1 Tim 5:24
f. righteousness. 6:11; 2 Tim 2:22
f. peace with all men. Heb 12:14
whose faith f. considering end. 13:7*
the glory that should f. 1 Pet 1:11
that ye should f. his steps. 2:21
f. their pernicious ways. 2 Pet 2:2
f. not that which is evil. 3 John 11*
are they that f. Lamb. Rev 14:4
they may rest from their labours, and
their works do f. them. 13

follow him
if Lord be God, f. him. 1 Ki 18:21
suffered no man to f. him. Mark 5:37
out, and his disciples f. him. 6:1
f. him into the house. Luke 22:10
Mark 14:13
before, the sheep f. him. John 10:4

follow me
woman will not be willing to f. me.
Gen 24:5, 39
Ehud said, f. after me. Judg 3:24
bread, to the people that f. me. 8:5
handfuls for people that f. me.
1 Ki 20:10
f. me, I will bring you to. 2 Ki 6:19
and mercy shall f. me. Ps 23:6
Jesus saith, f. me, I. Mat 4:19*
8:22; 9:9; Mark 2:14; Luke 5:27
take up his cross, f. me. Mat 16:24
Mark 8:34; 10:21; Luke 9:23
sell that thou hast, f. me. Mat 19:21
Luke 18:22
he said, f. me. Luke 9:59
John 1:43; 21:22
sheep hear my voice and f. me.
John 10:27
if any serve me, let him f. me. 12:26
thou canst not f. me now. 13:36
garment about thee, f. me. Acts 12:8

followed
Rebekah and her damsels f. the.
Gen 24:61
so commanded he all that f. 32:19
they have wholly f. the Lord.
Num 32:12; Deut 1:36
the men that f. Baal-peor. Deut 4:3
ark of the covenant f. Josh 6:8
but I wholly f. Lord. 14:8, 9, 14
forsook the Lord, f. other. Judg 2:12
cut down bough. f. Abimelech 9:49
f. hard after Philistines. 1 Sam 14:22
Jesse's three sons f. Saul. 17:13, 14
Philistines f. Saul. 31:2; 2 Sam 1:6
1 Chr 10:2
house of Judah f. David. 2 Sam 2:10
king David himself f. the bier. 3:31
Ahithophel saw counsel was not f.
17:23
Israel f. Sheba the son of. 20:2
none f. house of David. 1 Ki 12:20
of people f. Tibni, half f. 16:21, 22
forsaken Lord, thou hast f. 18:18
and the army which f. them. 20:19
no water for cattle that f. 2 Ki 3:9
Elisha rose and f. her. 4:30
so Gehazi f. after Naaman. 5:21
Jehu f. after Ahaziah. 9:27
Jehoahaz f. sins of Jeroboam. 17:15
and they f. vanity. 17:15
players on instruments f. Ps 68:25
head looked, they f. it. Ezek 10:11
Lord took me as I f. Amos 7:15
women which f. Jesus. Mat 27:55
we left all and f. thee. Mark 10:28
Luke 18:28
they f. they were afraid. Mark 10:32
Peter f. afar off. Luke 22:54
religious proselytes f. Acts 13:43
the same f. Paul and us. 16:17

f. not after righteousness. Rom 9:30
who f. after law of righteousness. 31
drank that rock that f. 1 Cor 10:4
diligently f. every good. 1 Tim 5:10
not f. cunningly devised. 2 Pet 1:16
was Death, and hell f. Rev 6:8
there f. hail and fire mingled. 8:7
and there f. another angel. 14:8
and the third angel f. them. 9

followed him
elders of Israel f. him. Num 16:25
and light persons f. him. Judg 9:4
and all people f. him. 1 Sam 13:7
f. him a mess of meat. 2 Sam 11:8
they left their nets and f. him.
Mat 4:20; Mark 1:18
left the ship and f. him. Mat 4:22
f. him great multitudes. 25; 8:1
12:15; 19:2; 20:29; Mark 2:15
5:24; Luke 23:27; John 6:2
when entered, his disciples f. him.
Mat 8:23; Luke 22:39
two blind men f. him. Mat 9:27
but Peter f. him afar off. 26:58
Mark 14:54
f. him a young man. Mark 14:51
forsook all and f. him. Luke 5:11, 28
said unto the people that f. him. 7:9
Peter went out and f. him. Acts 12:9
armies f. him on white. Rev 19:14

followed me
Caleb hath f. me fully. Num 14:24
have not wholly f. me. 32:11
David who f. me with all. 1 Ki 14:8
of the guard which f. me. Neh 4:23
f. me, in the regeneration. Mat 19:28

followedst
thou f. not young men. Ruth 3:10

followers
I beseech you, be f. of me.
1 Cor 4:16*; 11:1*; Phil 3:17*
be ye f. of God as dear. Eph 5:1*
ye became f. of us and. 1 Thes 1:6*
became f. of the churches. 2:14*
f. of them who through. Heb 6:12*
f. of that which is good. 1 Pet 3:13*

followeth
that f. her be killed. 2 Ki 11:15
2 Chr 23:14
my soul f. hard after. Ps 63:8
but he that f. vain persons.
Pr 12:11; 28:19
that f. righteousness. 15:9; 21:21
one loveth gifts and f. Isa 1:23
none f. thee to commit. Ezek 16:34
Ephraim feeds on wind, f. Hos 12:1
not up his cross and f. Mat 10:38
because he f. not us. Mark 9:38
Luke 9:49
f. me shall not walk in. John 8:12

following
by reason of famine f. Gen 41:31
turn away thy son from f. Deut 7:4
thou be not snared by f. them. 12:30
from f. the Lord. Josh 22:16, 18, 23
29; 1 Sam 12:20; 2 Ki 17:21
2 Chr 25:27; 34:33
corrupted in f. other. Judg 2:19
to return from f. after. Ruth 1:16
if ye continue f. Lord. 1 Sam 12:14
went up from f. Philistines. 14:46
Saul is turned back from f. 15:11
Saul was returned from f. 24:1
Asahel turned not from f. Abner.
2 Sam 2:19, 30
bid people return from f. their. 26
I took thee from f. the sheep, to.
7:8; 1 Chr 17:7; Ps 78:71
and they f. Adonijah. 1 Ki 1:7
if you shall at all turn from f. 9:6
Ahab did abominably in f. 21:26
tell it to the generation f. Ps 48:13
in generation f. name be. 109:13
the word with signs f. Mark 16:20
to-morrow, and day f. Luke 13:33
Jesus turned, saw them f. John 1:38
the day f. 43
the day f. when the people. 6:22
seeth disciple Jesus loved f. 21:20
we came day f. unto. Acts 21:1, 18
night f. Lord stood by him. 23:11
gone astray, f. way of. 2 Pet 2:15

folly
Shechem had wrought f. Gen 34:7
f. by playing the whore. Deut 22:21
because Achan wrought f. Josh 7:15
I pray you, do not this f. Judg 19:23
committed lewdness and f. in. 20:6
according to f. that they wrought. 10
Nabal his name, and f. 1 Sam 25:25
do not thou this f. 2 Sam 13:12
angels he charged with f. Job 4:18
God layeth not f. to them. 24:12
lest I deal with you after f. 42:8
their way is their f. Ps 49:13
let them not turn again to f. 85:8
in the greatness of his f. Pr 5:23
but a fool layeth open his f. 13:16
but the f. of fools is deceitful. 14:8
the simple inherit f. 18
foolishness of fools is f. 24
hasty of spirit exalteth f. 29
f. is joy to him destitute of. 15:21
the instruction of fools is f. 16:22
rather than a fool in his f. 17:12
is f. and shame to him. 18:13
not a fool according to his f. 26:4
answer a fool according to his f. 5
so a fool returneth to his f. 11
my heart to know wisdom and f.
Eccl 1:17
in my heart to lay hold on f. 2:3
turned to behold f. 12
wisdom excelleth f. 13
to know wickedness of f. 7:25
so doth a little f. him that. 10:1
f. is set in great dignity. 6
every mouth speaketh f. Isa 9:17
seen f. in the prophets of. Jer 23:13
bear with me a little in my f.
2 Cor 11:1
their f. shall be made. 2 Tim 3:9

food
pleasant and that is good for f.
Gen 2:9
woman saw tree was good for f. 3:6
take thou to thee of all f. 6:21
gather all f. of those good. 41:35
came to buy f. 42:7, 10; 43:2, 4
20, 22; 44:25
take f. for the famine. 42:33*
commanded to fill sacks with f. 44:1
your f. and for f. for your. 47:24
her f. not be diminished. Ex 21:10
the f. of the offering. Lev 3:11, 16
all manner of trees for f. 19:23
eat holy things, it is his f. 22:7*
him f. and raiment. Deut 10:18
cursed that eateth f. 1 Sam 14:24, 28
that master's son have f. to eat.
2 Sam 9:10*
my desire, in giving f. for. 1 Ki 5:9
gave Hiram wheat for f. to his. 11
more than necessary f. Job 23:12
wilderness yieldeth f. for. 24:5†
provideth for raven f.? 38:41†
mountains bring him forth f. 40:20
man did eat angels' f. Ps 78:25*
he may bring forth f. out. 104:14
who giveth f. to all flesh. 136:25
Lord who giveth f. to the. 146:7
he giveth to the beast his f. 147:9
ant gathereth her f. in. Pr 6:8
much f. is in the tillage of. 13:23
goats' milk enough for thy f. 27:27
rain which leaveth no f. 28:3
feed me with f. convenient for. 30:8
she bringeth her f. from afar. 31:14†
I have diminished thine ordinary f.
Ezek 16:27
increase thereof shall be for f. 48:18
filling our hearts with f. Acts 14:17
minister bread for your f. 2 Cor 9:10
having f. and raiment. 1 Tim 6:8
and destitute of daily f. Jas 2:15

fool
I have played f. and. 1 Sam 26:21
f. hath said in heart. Ps 14:1; 53:1
likewise the f. and brutish. 49:10
neither doth a f. understand. 92:6
prating f. shall fall. Pr 10:8, 10
it is a sport to a f. to do mischief. 23
the f. shall be servant to. 11:29*
way of a f. right in own eyes. 12:15*
a f.'s wrath is presently known. 16

but *f.* layeth open his folly. *Pr* 13:16
the *f.* rageth and is confident. 14:16
f. despiseth father's instruction. 15:5
speech becometh not a *f.* 17:7
than a hundred stripes into a *f.* 10
a bear meet a man rather than *f.* 12
price in hand of a *f.* to get. 16
begetteth a *f.* doth it to sorrow. 21
f. when he holdeth his peace. 28
f. hath no delight in understanding.
18:2
a *f.'s* lips enter into contention. 6
but every *f.* will be meddling. 20:3
answer not a *f.* 26:4
answer a *f.* 5
so is he that giveth honour to a *f.* 8
the great God rewardeth the *f.* 10
as a dog so a *f.* returneth to his. 11
but a *f.'s* wrath is heavier. 27:3
though they bray a *f.* in a mortar. 22
f. uttereth all his mind. 29:11
f. walketh in darkness. *Eccl* 2:14
as it happeneth to the *f.* so. 15
of wise man more than of *f.* 16
whether he be wise or a *f.?* 19
the *f.* foldeth his hands. 4:5
a *f.'s* voice is known by. 5:3
hath wise more than the *f.?* 6:8
but a *f.'s* heart is at his left. 10:2
f. is full of words. 14
at his end he shall be a *f.* *Jer* 17:11
whosoever shall say, Thou *f.* shall be
in danger. *Mat* 5:22
f., this night thy soul. *Luke* 12:20*
let him become a *f.* *1 Cor* 3:18
thou *f.,* that thou sowest is. 15:36*
no man think me a *f.* *2 Cor* 11:16*
to glory, I shall not be a *f.* 12:6*
I am become a *f.* in glorying. 11*

as a fool

died Abner *as a f.* dieth ? *2 Sam* 3:33
as a f. to correction of. *Pr* 7:22
how dieth wise ? *as the f. Eccl* 2:16
yet *as a f.* receive me. *2 Cor* 11:16
I speak *as a f.* I am more. 23

for a fool

delight not seemly *for a f. Pr* 19:10
wisdom is too high *for a f.* 24:7
honour is not seemly *for a f.* 26:1
and a rod *for the f.'s* back. 3
for a f. when filled with meat. 30:22

is a fool

uttereth slander *is a f. Pr* 10:18
perverse in lips, and *is a f.* 19:1
in his own heart *is a f.* 28:26
he that *is a f.* walketh, saith to every
one that he *is a f. Eccl* 10:3
the prophet *is a f.,* the. *Hos* 9:7

of a fool

way *of a f.* is right in. *Pr* 12:15
the father *of a f.* hath no joy. 17:21
eyes *of a f.* in ends of the earth. 24
speak not in the ears *of a f.* 23:9
a message by hand *of a f.* 26:6
more hope *of a f.* than. 12; 29:20
so laughter *of the f. Eccl* 7:6
lips *of a f.* will swallow. 10:12

foolish

thus requite Lord, O *f.?* *Deut* 32:6
provoke them with a *f.* nation. 21
Rom 10:19
speakest as one of *f.* *Job* 2:10
for wrath killeth the *f.* man. 5:2
I have seen the *f.* taking root. 3
the *f.* shall not stand. *Ps* 5:5*
make me not reproach of the *f.* 39:8
for I was envious at the *f.* 73:3*
so *f.* was I and ignorant. 22*
f. people have blasphemed. 74:18
remember how the *f.* man. 22
forsake the *f.* and live. *Pr* 9:6*
a *f.* woman is clamorous. 13
f. son is heaviness of his. 10:1
mouth of *f.* is near destruction.
but the *f.* plucketh it down. 14:1
in the mouth of the *f.* is a rod. 3
go from presence of a *f.* man. 7
heart of the *f.* doeth not so. 15:7
f. man despiseth his mother. 20
a *f.* son is a grief to his father. 17:25
a *f.* son is the calamity of. 19:13
a *f.* man spendeth a treasure. 21:20

wise man contendeth with *f. Pr* 29:9
better is a wise child than a *f.* king.
Eccl 4:13
neither be thou *f.* 7:17
labour of the *f.* wearieth. 10:15
maketh knowledge *f.* *Isa* 44:25
for my people are *f.* *Jer* 4:22
surely these are poor, they are *f.* 5:4
hear now this, O *f.* people. 21
are altogether brutish and *f.* 10:8
seen vain and *f.* things. *Lam* 2:14
woe unto *f.* prophets. *Ezek* 13:3
instruments of a *f.* shepherd.
Zech 11:15
likened unto a *f.* man. *Mat* 7:26
five virgins were wise, five *f.* 25:2
f. heart was darkened. *Rom* 1:21*
an instructor of the *f.* 2:20
hath not God made *f.?* *1 Cor* 1:20
O *f.* Galatians, who ? *Gal* 3:1
are ye so *f.?* having begun. 3
filthiness, nor *f.* talking. *Eph* 5:4
be rich fall into *f.* lusts. *1 Tim* 6:9
but *f.* questions avoid. *2 Tim* 2:23
Tit 3:9
were sometimes *f.* deceived. *Tit* 3:3
put to silence ignorance of *f.* men.
1 Pet 2:15

foolishly

thou hast now done *f.* *Gen* 31:28
1 Sam 13:13; *2 Chr* 16:9
wherein we have done *f. Num* 12:11
I have done very *f.* *2 Sam* 24:10
1 Chr 21:8
not, nor charged God *f.* *Job* 1:22
said to fools, deal not *f.* *Ps* 75:4
soon angry dealeth *f.* *Pr* 14:17
if thou hast done *f.* in lifting. 30:32
I speak it as it were *f.* *2 Cor* 11:17
I speak *f.* I am bold also. 21

foolishness

of Ahithophel into *f.* *2 Sam* 15:31
stink because of my *f.* *Ps* 38:5
thou knowest my *f.* 69:5
of fools proclaimeth *f.* *Pr* 12:23
but the *f.* of fools is folly. 14:24
mouth of fools poureth out *f.* 15:2
mouth of fools feedeth on *f.* 14
the *f.* of man perverteth way. 19:3
f. is bound in heart of child. 22:15
the thought of *f.* is sin. 24:9
yet will not his *f.* depart. 27:22
know wickedness of *f. Eccl* 7:25
of the words of his mouth is *f.* 10:13
thefts, pride, *f.* come. *Mark* 7:22
preaching of cross to them that
perish *f.* *1 Cor* 1:18
pleased God by *f.* of preaching. 21
Christ crucified, to the Greeks *f.* 23
because the *f.* of God is wiser. 25
of Spirit of God are *f.* to him. 2:14
wisdom of world is *f.* with God. 3:19

fools

be as one of the *f.* in. *2 Sam* 13:13
he maketh the judges *f.* *Job* 12:17
they were children of *f.* 30:8
I said to *f.* deal not. *Ps* 75:4*
ye *f.* when will ye be wise ? 94:8
f. because of transgression. 107:17
but *f.* despise wisdom. *Pr* 1:7*
how long, *f.* hate knowledge ? 22
prosperity of *f.* destroy them. 32
shame be the promotion of *f.* 3:35
ye *f.* be ye of an understanding. 8:5
f. die for want of wisdom. 10:21*
heart of *f.* proclaimeth. 12:23
abomination to *f.* depart. 13:19
companion of *f.* be destroyed. 20
folly of *f.* is deceit. 14:8
f. make a mock at sin. 9*
foolishness of *f.* is folly. 24
what is in the midst of *f.* is. 33
mouth of *f.* poureth foolishness. 15:2
mouth of *f.* feedeth on foolishness. 14
instruction of *f.* is folly. 16:22
stripes are prepared for *f.* 19:29
a parable in mouth of *f.* 26:7, 9
than give sacrifice of *f.* *Eccl* 5:1
he hath no pleasure in *f.* 4
heart of *f.* is in house of. 7:4
than for man to hear the song of *f.* 5
anger resteth in the bosom of *f.* 9
of him that ruleth among *f.* 9:17

princes of Zoan are *f. Isa* 19:11*, 13
wayfaring men, though *f.* 35:8
ye *f.* and blind. *Mat* 23:17, 19
ye *f.* did not he that ? *Luke* 11:40*
O *f.* and slow of heart to. 24:25*
wise, they became *f.* *Rom* 1:22
we are *f.* for Christ's. *1 Cor* 4:10
for ye suffer *f.* gladly. *2 Cor* 11:19*
that ye walk not as *f.* *Eph* 5:15*

foot

thee no man lift up his *f. Gen* 41:44
six hundred thousand on *f. Ex* 12:37
give *f.* for *f.* 21:24; *Deut* 19:21
shalt make a laver of brass and his *f.*
30:18, 28; 31:9*; 35:16*; 38:8*
39:39*; 40:11*; *Lev* 8:11*
leprosy cover from head to *f.*
Lev 13:12
ass crushed Balaam's *f. Num* 22:25
nor did thy *f.* swell. *Deut* 8:4
and wateredst it with thy *f.* 11:10
loose his shoe from off his *f.* 25:9
shoe not waxen old upon thy *f.* 29:5
their *f.* shall slide in due. 32:35
let Asher dip his *f.* in oil. 33:24
every place your *f.* *Josh* 1:3
loose thy shoe from off thy *f.* 5:15
Barak was sent on *f.* to. *Judg* 5:15
Asahel was as light of *f.* as a roe.
2 Sam 2:18
every *f.* six toes. 21:20; *1 Chr* 20:6
trod Jezebel under *f.* *2 Ki* 9:33
any more remove the *f.* *2 Chr* 33:8
my *f.* hath held his steps. *Job* 23:11
even waters forgotten of the *f.* 28:4
or if my *f.* hath hasted to. 31:5
forgetteth that *f.* may crush. 39:15
in net they hid is their *f.* *Ps* 9:15
my *f.* standeth in even place. 26:12
let not the *f.* of pride come. 36:11
when my *f.* slippeth. 38:16
went through the flood on *f.* 66:6
thy *f.* be dipped in blood. 68:23
lest thou dash thy *f.* against a stone.
91:12; *Mat* 4:6; *Luke* 4:11
I said my *f.* slippeth, thy. *Ps* 94:18
not suffer thy *f.* to be moved. 121:3
refrain thy *f.* from their. *Pr* 1:15
safely, thy *f.* shall not stumble. 3:23
the Lord shall keep thy *f.* from. 26
remove thy *f.* from. 4:27
withdraw thy *f.* from thy. 25:17
is like *f.* out of joint. 19
keep thy *f.* when goest. *Eccl* 5:1
mountains tread under *f. Isa* 14:25
meted out trodden under *f.* 18:7*
off thy shoe from off thy *f.* 20:2
the *f.* shall tread it down. 26:6
called righteous man to his *f.* 41:2
if thou turn away thy *f.* from. 58:13
withhold thy *f.* from. *Jer* 2:25
trodden my portion under *f.* 12:10
hath trodden under *f.* *Lam* 1:15*
stamp with thy *f.* and. *Ezek* 6:11
no *f.* of man, no *f.* of beast. 29:11
neither shall the *f.* of man. 32:13
give host to be trodden under *f.*
Dan 8:13
that is swift of *f.* shall. *Amos* 2:15
salt trodden under *f.* of. *Mat* 5:13
the people followed him on *f.* 14:13
if thy *f.* offend thee. 18:8; *Mark* 9:45
bind him hand and *f.* *Mat* 22:13
many ran a *f.* thither. *Mark* 6:33
forth bound hand and *f. John* 11:44
so much as to set his *f.* on. *Acts* 7:5
minding himself to go a *f.* 20:13
if the *f.* say, because I. *1 Cor* 12:15
trodden under *f.* the Son. *Heb* 10:29
with a garment to the *f.* *Rev* 1:13
holy city shall tread under *f.* 11:2

sole of foot

no rest for *sole of* her *f. Gen* 8:9
a botch from *sole of f. Deut* 28:35
not set *sole of* her *f.* on ground. 56
nor the *sole of* thy *f.* have rest. 65
sole of your *f.* shall tread. *Josh* 1:3
Absalom, from *sole of f. 2 Sam* 14:25
with boils from *sole of f. Job* 2:7
from *sole of f.* to head. *Isa* 1:6
sole of f. like *sole of* a calf's *f.*
Ezek 1:7

foot

left foot
he set his *left f.* upon.   *Rev* 10:2
right foot
he set his *right f.* on sea.   *Rev* 10:2
foot breadth
not so much as *f.* breadth. *Deut* 2:5*
footed
whatsoever is cloven *f.*   *Lev* 11:3
though he be cloven *f.* is unclean.   7
a man that is broken *f.* shall.   21:19
all manner of four *f.* beasts.
                            Acts 10:12; 11:6
birds and four *f.* beasts. *Rom* 1:23
footmen
six hundred thousand *f. Num* 11:21
Saul said to the *f.   1 Sam* 22:17*
if thou hast run with *f.* and. *Jer* 12:5
footsteps
up my goings that my *f.   Ps* 17:5*
thy way is in sea. thy *f.* are. 77:19
they reproached the *f.* of.   89:51
go thy way by the *f.* of. *S of S* 1:8
footstool
an house for *f.* of our.   *1 Chr* 28:2
six steps to throne with *f.* of gold.
                            2 Chr 9:18
worship at his *f.   Ps* 99:5; 132:7
hand till I make thine enemies thy *f.*
110:1; *Mat* 22:44; *Mark* 12:36
Luke 20:43; *Acts* 2:35; *Heb* 1:13
earth is my *f.   Isa* 66:1; *Acts* 7:49
remembered not his *f.   Lam* 2:1
swear not by earth, his *f.   Mat* 5:35
enemies be made his *f.   Heb* 10:13
poor, sit here under my *f.   Jas* 2:3

for

all things we call on him *f. Deut* 4:7
all Joab had sent him *f. 2 Sam* 11:22
f. piece of bread that.   *Pr* 28:21
f. he maketh his sun to.   *Mat* 5:45
to be heard *f.* much speaking.   6:7
f. I was hungry, and ye.   25:35, 42
we received grace *f.   John* 1:16
f. f. this cause ye pay.   *Rom* 13:6
f. we know, if this house. *2 Cor* 5:1
f. we can do nothing against but *f.*
    the truth.   13:8
looking *f.* the coming of. *2 Pet* 3:12

forasmuch

f. as God hath shewed.   *Gen* 41:39
f. as he hath no inheritance with.
                            Deut 12:12
f. as the Lord hath taken. *Judg* 11:36
f. as we have sworn.   *1 Sam* 20:42
f. as my lord is come. *2 Sam* 19:30
f. as thou hast disobeyed. *I Ki* 13:21
f. as Reuben defiled.   *1 Chr* 5:1
f. as this people draw. *Isa* 29:13
f. as there is none like. *Jer* 10:6
f. among all wise men of nations. 7
f. as iron breaketh.   *Dan* 2:40
f. as he also is son of. *Luke* 19:9
f. then as God gave them. *Acts* 11:17
f. then as we are offspring.   17:29
f. as I know that thou hast.   24:10
f. as he is the image.   *1 Cor* 11:7
f. as ye are zealous of.   14:12*
f. as ye know your labour is. 15:58
f. as we know ye were. *1 Pet* 1:18
f. then as Christ suffered for us. 4:1

forbad

whatsoever Lord *f.* us. *Deut* 2:37
but John *f.* him, saying. *Mat* 3:14*
casting out devils in thy name, we *f.*
    him.   *Mark* 9:38; *Luke* 9:49
the ass *f.* the madness. *2 Pet* 2:16*

forbare

escaped, and Saul *f.   1 Sam* 23:13
then the prophet *f.* and. *2 Chr* 25:16
Ishmael *f.* and slew.   *Jer* 41:8

forbear

if see his ass, and would *f. Ex* 23:5
if thou shalt *f.* to vow. *Deut* 23:22
shall I go, or *f.?   1 Ki* 22:6
                            2 Chr 18:5, 14
f. why shouldest thou be smitten?
                            2 Chr 25:16
f. thee from meddling with   35:21
many years didst thou *f. Neh* 9:30*
and though I *f.* what?   *Job* 16:6
thou *f.* to deliver them. *Pr* 24:11*

---

seem ill to thee to come, *f. Jer* 40:4
whether they will hear or *f.*
                            Ezek 2:5, 7; 3:11
he that forbeareth, let him *f.*   3:27
f. to cry, make no mourning. 24:17*
give me my price, if *f. Zech* 11:12
have not we power to *f.? 1 Cor* 9:6
f. lest any should think. *2 Cor* 12:6
we could no longer *f.   1 Thes* 3:1

forbearance

thou the riches of his *f.?   Rom* 2:4
of sins, through the *f.* of God. 3:25

forbeareth

that *f.* keep passover.   *Num* 9:13
he that *f.* let him forbear. *Ezek* 3:27

forbearing

by long *f.* is prince.   *Pr* 25:15
I was weary with *f.   Jer* 20:9
f. one another in love.   *Eph* 4:2
                                Col 3:13
do the same things, *f.   Eph* 6:9

forbid

my lord Moses, *f.   Num* 11:28
Lord *f.* I should do.   *1 Sam* 24:6
f. I should stretch forth hand. 26:11
Naboth said, the Lord *f.   1 Ki* 21:3
my God *f.* it me.   *1 Chr* 11:19
Jesus said, *f.* him not.   *Mark* 9:39
                            Luke 9:50
suffer little children, and *f.* them not.
            Mark 10:14; *Luke* 18:16
f. not to take coat also. *Luke* 6:29*
can any *f.* water?   *Acts* 10:47
f. none acquaintance to come. 24:23
f. not to speak with.   *1 Cor* 14:39

God forbid

*(American Revision renders this
far be it from me)*
God *f. Gen* 44:7, 17; *Josh* 22:29
24:16; *1 Sam* 12:23; 14:45; 20:2
Job 27:5; *Luke* 20:16; *Rom* 3:4, 6
31; 6:2, 15; 7:7, 13; 9:14; 11:1
11; *1 Cor* 6:15; *Gal* 2:17; 3:21
                                    6:14

forbidden

commit any of things *f.   Lev* 5:17*
of what Lord hath *f.   Deut* 4:23
and were *f.* to preach. the. *Acts* 16:6

forbiddeth

f. them that would.   *3 John* 10

forbidding

f. to give tribute to.   *Luke* 23:2
preaching kingdom of God, no man *f.*
                            Acts 28:31
f. us to speak to the. *1 Thes* 2:16
f. to marry.   *1 Tim* 4:3

forborn

men of Babylon *f.* to.   *Jer* 51:30

force

wouldest take by *f.   Gen* 31:31
nor was his natural *f.   Deut* 34:7
if not, I will take it by *f. 1 Sam* 2:16
made them to cease by *f. Ezra* 4:23
by great *f.* of my disease. *Job* 30:18
and his *f.* is in the navel.   40:16
out their blood by *f.   Jer* 18:21*
and their *f.* is not right.   23:10
under shadow, because of *f.* 48:45*
with *f.* and cruelty have. *Ezek* 34:4
hast shed blood by *f.* of.   35:5*
shall not strengthen his *f. Amos* 2:14
violent take it by *f.   Mat* 11:12
would take him by *f.   John* 6:15
to take Paul by *f.   Acts* 23:10
for a testament is of *f.   Heb* 9:17

force, *verb*

if the man *f.* her and.   *Deut* 22:25
brother, do not *f.* me. *2 Sam* 13:12
will he *f.* the queen?   *Esth* 7:8

forced

Ammonites *f.* children.   *Judg* 1:34
my concubine have they *f.*   20:5
I *f.* myself therefore. *1 Sam* 13:12
Amnon *f.* Tamar and.   *2 Sam* 13:14
hated Amnon, because he *f.* his. 22
determined from day he *f.* his.   32
flattering of lips she *f.   Pr* 7:21

forces

placed *f.* in fenced.   *2 Chr* 17:2
will not esteem all the *f. Job* 36:19

---

the *f.* of the Gentiles.   *Isa* 60:5*
men may bring to thee the *f.*   11*
the captains of the *f.* that. *Jer* 40:7
13; 41:11, 13, 16; 42:1, 8; 43:4, 5
a multitude of great *f.   Dan* 11:10
in his estate honour God of *f.*   38*
carried away captive his *f.   Ob* 11

forcible

how *f.* right words.   *Job* 6:25

forcing

not destroy trees by *f. Deut* 20:19*
so the *f.* of wrath.   *Pr* 30:33

ford, -s

Jacob passed over the *f. Gen* 32:22
men pursued spies to *f.   Josh* 2:7
Israel took the *f.* of.   *Judg* 3:28
daughters of Moab at *f.   Isa* 16:2

forecast

shall *f.* devices.   *Dan* 11:24*, 25*

forefathers

the iniquities of their *f.   Jer* 11:10
whom I serve from my *f. 2 Tim* 1:3

forefront

six curtains in the *f.   Ex* 26:9
on the *f.* of the mitre it shall. 28:37
upon his *f.* did he put.   *Lev* 8:9*
f. of one rock was.   *1 Sam* 14:5*
set Uriah in the *f.* of. *2 Sam* 11:15
the brazen altar from *f. 2 Ki* 16:14
Jehoshaphat in the *f.   2 Chr* 20:27
f. of lower gate to *f.* of. *Ezek* 40:19
the *f.* of the house stood.   47:1

forehead

plate shall be on Aaron's *f. Ex* 28:38
he is *f.* bald: yet is he. *Lev* 13:41
a leprosy sprung up in bald *f.*   42
if rising be reddish in bald *f.*   43
smote the Philistine in *f.*, stone sunk
    in his *f.*   *1 Sam* 17:49
leprosy rose up in Uzziah's *f.*
                            2 Chr 26:19
behold he was leprous in his *f.*   20
thou hadst a whore's *f.   Jer* 3:3
have made thy *f.* strong. *Ezek* 3:8
harder than flint have made thy *f.*   9
put a jewel upon thy *f.* and. 16:12*
mark of beast in his *f.   Rev* 14:9
and upon her *f.* was a name. 17:5

foreheads

forehead strong against their *f.*
                            Ezek 3:8
set a mark on the *f.* of them.   9:4
sealed servants of God in their *f.*
                            Rev 7:3
not seal of God in their *f.*   9:4
all to receive mark in their *f.* 13:16
Father's name written in their *f.* 14:1
received the mark upon their *f.* 20:4
his name shall be in their *f.* 22:4

foreigner

f. and hired servant not. *Ex* 12:45*
of a *f.* thou mayest.   *Deut* 15:3

foreigners

in the day that *f.* entered. *Ob* 11
no more strangers and *f. Eph* 2:19*

foreknew

away people which he *f.   Rom* 11:2

foreknow

whom he did *f.* he also. *Rom* 8:29

foreknowledge

being delivered by the *f. Acts* 2:23
elect according to *f.* of. *1 Pet* 1:2

foremost

Jacob commanded the *f. Gen* 32:17
put handmaids and children *f.* 33:2
the running of the *f.* is. *2 Sam* 18:27

foreordained

who verily was *f.   1 Pet* 1:20*

forepart

two rings towards *f.* of. *Ex* 28:27
                                39:20
the oracle in the *f.   1 Ki* 6:20*
wall on *f.* of chambers. *Ezek* 42:7
the *f.* of ship stuck.   *Acts* 27:41*

forerunner

whither the *f.* is for us. *Heb* 6:20

foresaw

I *f.* the Lord always.   *Acts* 2:25*

foreseeing
the scripture f. God.   Gal 3:8
foreseeth
a prudent man f. the evil.   Pr 22:3*
   27:12*
foreship
cast anchors out of f.   Acts 27:30
foreskin
circumcise flesh of your f.   Gen 17:11
flesh of his f. is not circumcised. 14
circumcised flesh of their f. 23, 24, 25
Zipporah cut off the f.   Ex 4:25
the flesh of his f. shall.   Lev 12:3
circumcise therefore f.   Deut 10:16
let thy f. be uncovered.   Hab 2:16*
foreskins
circumcised Israel at hill of the f.
   Josh 5:3
but an hundred f. of.   1 Sam 18:25
David brought their f.   27
to me for an hundred f.   2 Sam 3:14
take away f. of your heart.   Jer 4:4
forest
David came into the f.   1 Sam 22:5
Solomon built house of f.   1 Ki 7:2
them in the house of the f.   10:17
   2 Chr 9:16
into the f. of his Carmel.   2 Ki 19:23
   Isa 37:24
Asaph, keeper of king's f.   Neh 2:8
every beast of the f. is.   Ps 50:10
wherein all beasts of the f.   104:20
kindle in thickets of f.   Isa 9:18
shall consume glory of his f.   10:18
the rest of the trees of his f.   19
in the f. of Arabia ye lodge.   21:13
didst look to armour of the f.   22:8
field be esteemed as a f.   29:17
   32:15
hail, coming down on the f.   32:19
cypress from among trees of f.   44:14
break forth into singing, O f.   23
all ye beasts of the f. come.   56:9
a lion out of f. shall slay.   Jer 5:6
one cutteth a tree out of f.   10:3
heritage is to me as a lion in f.   12:8
I will kindle a fire in the f.   21:14
become as high places of the f.
   26:18; Mi 3:12
they shall cut down her f.   Jer 46:23
vine tree among the trees of the f.
   Ezek 15:6
prophesy against the f. of the. 20:46
say unto the f. of the south.   47
I will make them a f.   Hos 2:12
will lion roar in the f.?   Amos 3:4
as lion among beasts of the f.   Mi 5:8
the f. of the vintage is.   Zech 11:2
forests
Jotham built castles in f.   2 Chr 27:4
voice of the Lord discovereth the f.
   Ps 29:9
cut down thickets of the f.   Isa 10:34
cut down any out of f.   Ezek 39:10
foretell
I f. you as if I were.   2 Cor 13:2*
foretold
I have f. you all things.   Mark 13:23
prophets have likewise f.   Acts 3:24*
forewarn
but I will f. you whom.   Luke 12:5*
forewarned
as we also have f. you.   1 Thes 4:6
forfeited
his substance should be f.   Ezra 10:8
forgat
remember Joseph, but f.   Gen 40:23
children of Israel f. Lord.   Judg 3:7
and when they f. Lord.   1 Sam 12:9
and they f. his works.   Ps 78:11
soon f. his works.   106:13
f. God their Saviour.   21
far from peace, I f.   Lam 3:17
after her lovers and f. me.   Hos 2:13
forgave
he f. their iniquity.   Ps 78:38
loosed him, and f. him.   Mat 18:27
I f. thee all that debt.   32
he frankly f. them.   Luke 7:42
he to whom he f. most.   43

if I f. any thing to whom I f. it for
your sakes f. I it in.   2 Cor 2:10
even as Christ f. you.   Col 3:13
forgavest
thou f. the iniquity of.   Ps 32:5
thou wast a God that f. them.   99:8
forged
the proud have f. a lie.   Ps 119:69
forgers
ye are f. of lies, are all.   Job 13:4
forget
till he f. that which thou.   Gen 27:45
for God hath made me f.   41:51
lest thou f. the things.   Deut 4:9
lest ye f. covenant of the Lord.   23
the Lord will not f. the covenant. 31
lest thou f. Lord. 6:12; 8:11, 14, 19
f. not how thou provokedst.   9:7
out Amalek, thou shalt not f.   25:19
if thou wilt not f. thine.   1 Sam 1:11
covenant I made ye shall not f.
   2 Ki 17:38
paths of all that f. God.   Job 8:13
if I say, I will f. my complaint. 9:27
thou shalt f. thy misery.   11:16
the womb shall f. him.   24:20
all the nations that f. God.   Ps 9:17
O Lord, f. not the humble.   10:12
how long wilt thou f. me ?   13:1
f. also thine own people.   45:10
consider this, ye that f. God.   50:22
lest my people f.: scatter.   59:11
f. not the congregation of thy. 74:19
f. not the voice of thine enemies. 23
might not f. the works of God. 78:7
so that I f. to eat my bread.   102:4
f. not all his benefits.   103:2
I will not f. thy word.   119:16
do I not f. thy statutes. 83, 109, 141
I will never f. thy precepts.   93
for I do not f. thy law.   153
I do not f. thy commandments.   176
if I f. thee let my hand f.   137:5
my son, f. not my law.   Pr 3:1
wisdom, get understanding, f.   4:5
lest they drink and f. the law. 31:5
let him drink and f. poverty.   7
f. her sucking child ? yea, they may f.
yet will I not f. thee.   Isa 49:15
shalt f. the shame of thy youth. 54:4
they that f. my holy mountain. 65:11
can maid f. ornaments ?   Jer 2:32
think to cause my people to f. 23:27
I, even I, will utterly f. you.   39
thou f. us for ever ?   Lam 5:20
forgotten law, I will also f.   Hos 4:6
never f. any of their works.   Amos 8:7
is not unrighteous to f.   Heb 6:10
good and communicate f. not. 13:16
forgetful
not f. to entertain.   Heb 13:2
he be not a f. hearer.   Jas 1:25
forgetfulness
righteousness in land of f.   Ps 88:12
forgettest
f. thou our affliction ?   Ps 44:24
and f. the Lord thy maker.   Isa 51:13
forgetteth
and f. that the foot.   Job 39:15
he f. not the cry of.   Ps 9:12
f. the covenant of her God.   Pr 2:17
f. what manner of man.   Jas 1:24
forgetting
f. those things behind.   Phil 3:13
forgive
f. I pray, the trespass, f. the trespass
of servants of God.   Gen 50:17
f. I pray thee, my sin.   Ex 10:17
if thou wilt f. their sin.   32:32
Lord shall f. her.   Num 30:5, 8, 12
he will not f. your sins.   Josh 24:19
I pray, f. the trespass.   1 Sam 25:28
when thou hearest, f.   1 Ki 8:30, 39
   2 Chr 6:21, 30
f. the sin of thy people.   1 Ki 8:34
f. the sin of thy servants.   36
   2 Chr 6:25, 27, 39
f. thy people have sinned.   1 Ki 8:50
then will I hear and f.   2 Chr 7:14
look on my pain, and f.   Ps 25:18
Lord, art good and ready to f.   86:5

man boweth, therefore f.   Isa 2:9
f. not their iniquity nor.   Jer 18:23
for I will f. their iniquity.   31:34
that I may f. their iniquity.   36:3
O Lord f. Lord hearken.   Dan 9:19
O Lord God, f. I beseech.   Amos 7:2
f. us, as we f. our debtors.
   Mat 6:12; Luke 11:4
f. men trespasses, Father will f.
   Mat 6:14
if ye f. not, nor will your Father f. 15
hath power to f. sin.   9:6
   Mark 2:10; Luke 5:24
how oft my brother sin, and I f. him ?
   Mat 18:21
if ye from your hearts f. not.   35
who can f. sins but God only ?
   Mark 2:7; Luke 5:21
f. that your Father may f. you.
   Mark 11:25
not f. your Father will not f.   26
f. and ye shall be.   Luke 6:37*
if thy brother repent, f. him. 17:3, 4
Father, f. them, they know.   23:34
ye ought rather to f.   2 Cor 2:7
to whom ye f. any thing, I f. also. 10
not burdensome, f. me this.   12:13
faithful and just to f.   1 John 1:9
forgiven
atonement, and it shall be f. them.
   Lev 4:20, 26, 31, 35; 5:10, 13, 16
   18; 6:7; 19:22; Num 15:25, 26
   28; Deut 21:8
thou hast f. from Egypt.   Num 14:19
blessed, whose transgression is f.
   Ps 32:1; Rom 4:7
hast f. the iniquity of thy.   Ps 85:2
the people shall be f.   Isa 33:24
cheer, thy sins be f.   Mat 9:2, 5
   Mark 2:5, 9; Luke 5:20, 23; 7:48
blasphemy be f.; against Holy Ghost
not be f.   Mat 12:31, 32
   Mark 3:28; Luke 12:10
their sins be f. them.   Mark 4:12
forgive, and ye shall be f.   Luke 6:37
sins are f. but to whom little is f. 7:47
of heart may be f. thee.   Acts 8:22
for Christ's sake hath f.   Eph 4:32
he quickened, having f.   Col 2:13
sins, they shall be f. him.   Jas 5:15
because your sins are f.   1 John 2:12
forgiveness
f. with thee that be.   Ps 130:4
hath never f. but is in.   Mark 3:29
God exalted to give f.   Acts 5:31*
him is preached unto you f.   13:38*
to God, that they receive f.   26:18*
in whom we have f. of.   Eph 1:7
   Col 1:14
forgivenesses
God belong mercies and f.   Dan 9:9
forgiveth
heals thy diseases, who f.   Ps 103:3
say, who is this f. sins ?   Luke 7:49
forgiving
f. iniquity, transgression.   Ex 34:7
   Num 14:18
forbearing, f. one another.
   Eph 4:32; Col 3:13
forgot
and hast f. a sheaf in.   Deut 24:19
forgotten
all the plenty shall be f.   Gen 41:30
nor have I f. them.   Deut 26:13
not be f. out of mouths.   31:21
hast f. God that formed thee.   32:18
familiar friends have f.   Job 19:14
flood breaks out, even waters f. 28:4
needy shall not alway be f.   Ps 9:18
said in his heart, God hath f.   10:11
I am f. as a dead man.   31:12
rock, why hast thou f. me ?   42:9
is come, yet have we not f.   44:17
if we have f. name of our God. 20
hath God f. to be gracious ?   77:9
I have not f. thy law.   119:61
because mine enemies have f.   139
days to come all be f.   Eccl 2:16
and the wicked were f. in the. 8:10
for the memory of them is f.   9:5
thou hast f. God of thy.   Isa 17:10
Tyre shall be f. seventy years. 23:15

thou harlot that hast been *f.* *Isa* 23:16
thou shalt not be *f.* of me.   44:21
my Lord hath *f.* me.   49:14
the former troubles are *f.*   65:16
my people have *f.* me.   *Jer* 2:32
     13:25; 18:15
have *f.* the Lord their God.   3:21
confusion never be *f.* 20:11; 23:40
as their fathers have *f.* my.   23:27
all thy lovers have *f.* thee.   30:14
f. wickedness of your fathers.   44:9
covenant that shall not be *f.*   50:5
they turned away, have *f.*   6
caused Sabbath to be *f.*   *Lam* 2:6
thou hast *f.* me.   *Ezek* 22:12
because thou hast *f.* me.   23:35
seeing thou hast *f.* the law. *Hos* 4:6
for Israel hath *f.* Maker.   8:14
exalted, therefore have *f.* me.   13:6
they had *f.* to take bread. *Mat* 16:5
     Mark 8:14
and not one of them is *f.* *Luke* 12:6
have *f.* the exhortation.   *Heb* 12:5
f. that he was purged.   *2 Pet* 1:9

forks

they had a file for *f.*   *1 Sam* 13:21

form

the earth was without *f.*   *Gen* 1:2*
what *f.* is he of ?   *1 Sam* 28:14
about this *f.* of speech. *2 Sam* 14:20*
I could not discern *f.*   *Job* 4:16*
his *f.* more than sons of. *Isa* 52:14
he hath no *f.* nor comeliness.   53:2
and, lo, it was without *f.* *Jer* 4:23*
appeared the *f.* of man's. *Ezek* 10:8
shew them the *f.* of the house. 43:11
and the *f.* of his visage. *Dan* 3:19
the *f.* of the fourth is like the.   25*
appeared in another *f.* *Mark* 16:12
hast *f.* of knowledge.   *Rom* 2:20
ye have obeyed that *f.* of.   6:17
who being in the *f.* of God. *Phil* 2:6
took upon him the *f.* of a servant.   7
hold fast *f.* of sound.   *2 Tim* 1:13
having *f.* of godliness.   3:5

formed

the Lord God *f.* man of.   *Gen* 2:7
out of the ground God *f.* every.   19
forgotten God that *f.* *Deut* 32:18*
I have *f.* it.   *2 Ki* 19:25; *Isa* 37:26
dead things are *f.* from. *Job* 26:5*
hand hath *f.* crooked serpent.   13*
I also am *f.* out of the clay.   33:6
or ever thou hadst *f.* earth. *Ps* 90:2
he that *f.* the eye.   94:9
sea is his, his hands *f.* the.   95:5
the great God that *f.* all. *Pr* 26:10*
he that *f.* them will shew. *Isa* 27:11
thus saith he that *f.* thee.   43:1
I have *f.* him, yea, I have.   7
before me there was no god *f.* nor. 10
this people have I *f.* for myself.   21
that made thee, and *f.* thee   44:2
who hath *f.* a god ?   10*
art my servant, I have *f.* thee.   21
thus saith he that *f.* thee.   24
I *f.* the light and create.   45:7
God that *f.* the earth, he *f.* it.   18
Lord that *f.* me from womb to. 49:5
no weapon *f.* against thee.   54:17
before I *f.* thee I knew.   *Jer* 1:5
Lord that *f.* it to establish it.   33:2
behold, he *f.* grasshoppers. *Amos* 7:1
shall the thing *f.* say to him that *f.* it ?
     Rom 9:20
in birth, till Christ be *f.* in. *Gal* 4:19
Adam was first *f.*, then. *1 Tim* 2:13

former

deliver cup after the *f.*   *Gen* 40:13
fought against the *f.* king of Moab.
     Num 21:26
her *f.* husband which. *Deut* 24:4
was the manner in *f.* time. *Ruth* 4:7
answered after the *f.*   *1 Sam* 17:30
the two captains of *f.*   *2 Ki* 1:14
do after the *f.* manner.   17:34, 40
the *f.* governors were.   *Neh* 5:15
inquire, I pray, of *f.* age.   *Job* 8:8
the wilderness in *f.* time.   30:3*
O remember not *f.* iniquities.
     Ps 79:8
where are thy *f.* loving- ?   89:49

no remembrance of *f.*   *Eccl* 1:11
f. days were better than these. 7:10
shew the *f.* things. *Isa* 41:22; 43:9
the *f.* things are come to pass. 42:9
remember ye not the *f.*   43:18
remember *f.* things of old.   46:9
I have declared *f.* things.   48:3
raise up the *f.* desolations.   61:4
I will measure their *f.* work. 65:7*
the *f.* troubles are forgotten.   16
f. shall not be remembered.   17
that giveth the *f.* and latter rain.
     Jer 5:24; *Hos* 6:3; *Joel* 2:23
is *f.* of all things. *Jer* 10:16; 51:19
the *f.* kings before thee.   34:5
write in it all the *f.* words.   36:28
thy daughter return to *f.* *Ezek* 16:55
multitude greater than *f.* *Dan* 11:13
but it shall not be as the *f.* or.   29
glory greater than of the *f.* *Hag* 2:9
the *f.* prophets have cried. *Zech* 1:4
     7:7, 12
not be to people as in *f.* days. 8:11
waters go half toward the *f.* 14:8*
pleasant to Lord as in *f.* *Mal* 3:4*
the *f.* treatise have I made. *Acts* 1:1
concerning *f.* conversation. *Eph* 4:22
not according to *f.* lusts. *1 Pet* 1:14
f. things are passed.   *Rev* 21:4*

formeth

lo, he that *f.* mountains. *Amos* 4:13
and *f.* the spirit of man. *Zech* 12:1

fornication

This word is taken [1] For the sin
of impurity, Mat 5:32; 1 Cor 7:2.
[2] For the sin of idolatry, which is
infidelity to and forsaking of the
true God for false gods, 2 Chr 21:11.
caused Jerusalem to commit *f.*
     2 Chr 21:11
Tyre shall commit *f.* with. *Isa* 23:17
hast multiplied thy *f.* *Ezek* 16:29
saving for cause of *f.* *Mat* 5:32; 19:9
we be not born of *f.*   *John* 8:41
that they abstain from *f.* *Acts* 15:20
     29; 21:25
being filled with all *f.*   *Rom* 1:29
f. among you, and such *f.* *1 Cor* 5:1
the body is not for *f.* but for. 6:13
flee *f.*   18
nevertheless, to avoid *f.*   7:2
not repented of their *f.* *2 Cor* 12:21
works of the flesh, *f.*   *Gal* 5:19
f. let it not be named.   *Eph* 5:3
mortify therefore *f.*   *Col* 3:5
will of God that ye abstain from *f.*
     1 Thes 4:3
cities giving themselves over to *f.*
     Jude 7
space to repent of her *f.* *Rev* 2:21
neither repented they of their *f.* 9:21
the wine of wrath of her *f.*   14:8
made drunk with wine of her *f.* 17:2
golden cup full of filthiness of *f.*   4
with wine of wrath of her *f.*   18:3
did corrupt earth with her *f.*   19:2

fornications

pouredst out thy *f.* on. *Ezek* 16:15
out of heart proceed *f.* thefts.
     Mat 15:19; *Mark* 7:22

see commit, committed

fornicator

called a brother be a *f.* *1 Cor* 5:11
lest there be any *f.* or. *Heb* 12:16

fornicators

you not to company with *f.* *1 Cor* 5:9
yet not altogether with the *f.* of. 10
nor shall *f.* inherit the kingdom. 6:9

forsake

this people will *f.* me. *Deut* 31:16
in that day I will *f.* them.   17
God forbid we should *f.* *Josh* 24:16
if ye *f.* the Lord and serve.   20
should I *f.* my sweetness? *Judg* 9:11*
I will *f.* remnant of.   *2 Ki* 21:14*
if thou *f.* him, cast thee. *1 Chr* 28:9
if ye turn away, and *f.* *2 Chr* 7:19
but if ye *f.* him, he will *f.* you. 15:2
wrath is against them that *f.* him.
     Ezra 8:22
father and mother *f.* me. *Ps* 27:10
cease from anger and *f.* wrath. 37:8

if his children *f.* my law. *Ps* 89:30
will he *f.* his inheritance.   94:14
because wicked *f.* law.   119:53
let not mercy and truth *f.* *Pr* 3:3
f. the foolish, and live.   9:6*
they that *f.* the law.   28:4
they that *f.* the Lord.   *Isa* 1:28
let wicked *f.* his way.   55:7
ye are they that *f.* Lord.   65:11
all that *f.* the Lord.   *Jer* 17:13
I will even *f.* you.   23:33*, 39*
f. her, and let us go every one. 51:9
wherefore dost thou *f.*?   *Lam* 5:20
that *f.* the holy covenant. *Dan* 11:30
f. their own mercy.   *Jonah* 2:8
teachest the Jews to *f.* *Acts* 21:21

forsake not

thou *f.* not the Levite. *Deut* 12:19
wickedness and *f.* it not. *Job* 20:13*
f. me not, O.   *Ps* 38:21; 71:9, 18
thy statutes, O *f.* me not.   119:8
f. not works of thine own.   138:8
f. not law of mother.   *Pr* 1:8; 6:20
good doctrine, *f.* ye not my.   4:2
f. her not, she shall preserve thee. 6
and father's friend *f.* not.   27:10

not forsake

he will *f.* thee.   *Deut* 4:31*
     31:6, 8; *1 Chr* 28:20
Levite, thou shalt not *f.* *Deut* 14:27
not fail nor *f.* thee.   *Josh* 1:5
     Heb 13:5
Lord will not *f.* his people.
     1 Sam 12:22; *1 Ki* 6:13
not leave us, nor *f.* us.   *1 Ki* 8:57
didst not consume, nor *f.* *Neh* 9:31
we will not *f.* the house of.   10:39
neither *f.* me, O God of.   *Ps* 27:9
God of Israel, will not *f.* *Isa* 41:17
will I do, and not *f.* them.   42:16
nor did they *f.* the idols. *Ezek* 20:8

forsaken

because he had *f.* the Lord.
     2 Chr 21:10; 24:24; 28:6
why is house of God *f.*? *Neh* 13:11
shall earth be *f.* for thee ? *Job* 18:4
not seen righteous *f.*   *Ps* 37:25
the land shall be *f.* of. *Isa* 7:16
the cities of Aroer are *f.*   17:2
shall be as a *f.* bough, and an.   9
the habitation shall be *f.*   27:10
because palaces shall be *f.*   32:14
hath called thee as a woman *f.* 54:6
shalt no more be termed *f.*   62:4
every city shall be *f.*   *Jer* 4:29
cold waters from another place be *f.*?
     18:14*
saith Lord to cities *f.*   *Ezek* 36:4
the virgin of Israel is *f.* *Amos* 5:2*
Gaza shall be *f.* and.   *Zeph* 2:4

have, hast, hath forsaken

whereby thou *hast f.* *Deut* 28:20
have f. the Lord. 29:25; *Judg* 10:10
now the Lord *hath f.* us. *Judg* 6:13*
yet ye *have f.* me.   10:13
works wherewith they *have f.* me.
     1 Sam 8:8
sinned, because we *have f.*   12:10
because they *have f.* me. *1 Ki* 11:33
ye *have f.* commandments of. 18:18
Israel *have f.* thy covenant. 19:10, 14
have f. me and burnt.   *2 Ki* 22:17
     2 Chr 34:25; *Jer* 16:11; 19:4
ye *have f.* me, I have.   *Jer* 12:5
charge of Lord ye *have f.*   13:11
ye *have f.* the Lord, he *hath f.* 24:20
have done evil, *have f.*   29:6
for we *have f.* thy commandments.
     Ezra 9:10
he *hath* oppressed and *f.* *Job* 20:19
my God, my God, why *hast* thou *f.*?
     Ps 22:1; *Mat* 27:46; *Mark* 15:34
saying, God *hath f.* him. *Ps* 71:11
they *have f.* the Lord.   *Isa* 1:4
the Lord *hath f.* me.   49:14
for a small moment *have* I *f.* 54:7
have f. me, burnt.   *Jer* 1:16
they *have f.* me, the fountain. 2:13
in that thou *hast f.* the Lord. 17, 19
thy children *have f.* me.   5:7
answer, like as ye *have f.* me.   19
saith, because they *have f.*   9:13
confounded, because ye *have f.*   19

I *have f.* my house.   *Jer* 12:7
thou *hast f.* me, saith Lord.   15:6*
have f. fountain of living.   17:13
because they *have f.* covenant. 22:9
he *hath f.* his covert as lion. 25:38
Lord *hath f.* earth. *Ezek* 8:12; 9:9
we *have f.* all and.   *Mat* 19:27*
every one that *hath f.* houses. 29*
Demas *hath f.* me.   *2 Tim* 4:10
which *have f.* right way. *2 Pet* 2:15

not forsaken
the Lord is our God, we have *not f.*
  2 Chr 13:10
yet God hath *not f.* us.   *Ezra* 9:9
thou hast *not f.* them.   *Ps* 9:10
sought out, a city *not f.* *Isa* 62:12
Israel hath *not* been *f.*   *Jer* 51:5
persecuted, but *not f.*   *2 Cor* 4:9

forsaketh
f. the fear of the Almighty. *Job* 6:14
for the Lord *f.* not his. *Ps* 37:28
from her *f.* the guide of. *Pr* 2:17
grievous to him that *f.* way. 15:10
confesseth and *f.* have mercy. 28:13
whoso *f.* not all that. *Luke* 14:33*

forsaking
until there be a great *f.* *Isa* 6:12
not *f.* the assembling of. *Heb* 10:25

forsook
he *f.* God that made. *Deut* 32:15
they *f.* the Lord God. *Judg* 2:12, 13
  10:6
f. their cities and fled. *1 Sam* 31:7
  1 Chr 10:7
because they *f.* the Lord. *1 Ki* 9:9
Rehoboam *f.* the counsel of old men.
  12:8, 13; *2 Chr* 10:8, 13
Amon *f.* the God of his. *2 Ki* 21:22
f. God of their fathers. *2 Chr* 7:22
Rehoboam *f.* law of Lord. 12:1
he *f.* tabernacle of Shiloh. *Ps* 78:60
but I *f.* not thy precepts. 119:87
f. not ordinance of God. *Isa* 58:2
hind calved in field and *f.* *Jer* 14:5
disciples *f.* him and fled.
  Mat 26:56*; *Mark* 14:50*
they *f.* their nets and. *Mark* 1:18*
they *f.* all and followed. *Luke* 5:11*
all men *f.* me.   *2 Tim* 4:16
by faith Moses *f.* Egypt. *Heb* 11:27

forsookest
God slow to anger, *f.* not. *Neh* 9:17
thou in thy mercies *f.* them not. 19

forswear
thou shalt *not f.* thyself. *Mat* 5:33

fort, -s
so David dwelt in the *f.* *2 Sam* 5:9*
they built *f.* against Jerusalem.
  2 Ki 25:1; *Jer* 52:4
high *f.* of walls bring. *Isa* 25:12
and I will raise *f.* against. 29:3*
the *f.* and towers shall be. 32:14*
and built a *f.* against it. *Ezek* 4:2
  21:22; 26:8
building *f.* to cut off.   17:17
for Jerusalem to build a *f.* 21:22
he shall make a *f.* against. 26:8
they that be in the *f.* shall die. 33:27*
shall turn toward the *f.* *Dan* 11:19

forth
that time *f.* servants. *Neh* 4:16
from that time *f.* came they. 13:21
name of the Lord, from this time *f.*
  Ps 113:2; 115:18; 121:8
out every man right *f.* *Jer* 49:5
from that time *f.* began. *Mat* 16:21
nor durst from that day *f.* 22:46
from that day *f.* took. *John* 11:53

forthwith
that *f.* expenses be. *Ezra* 6:8*
f. sprung up, because. *Mat* 13:5*
he *f.* came to Jesus, and. 26:49*
f. when they were. *Mark* 1:29*
charged him, and *f.* sent him. 43*
and *f.* Jesus gave unclean. 5:13*
and *f.* came thereout. *John* 19:34*
he received sight *f.* and. *Acts* 9:18*
and *f.* the angel departed. 12:10*
drew Paul out, and *f.* doors. 21:30*

fortieth
Aaron died there in *f.* *Num* 33:38

---

in *f.* year Moses spake. *Deut* 1:3
in *f.* year of reign of. *1 Chr* 26:31
Asa died in one and *f.* *2 Chr* 16:13

fortify
they *f.* the city against. *Judg* 9:31*
will these feeble Jews *f.*? *Neh* 4:2
houses broken down to *f.* *Isa* 22:10
she should *f.* height of. *Jer* 51:53
watch the way, *f.* thy. *Nah* 2:1
waters for siege, *f.* strong. 3:14*

fortified
Rehoboam *f.* the strong. *2 Chr* 11:11
Uzziah built towers and *f.* 26:9
they *f.* Jerusalem to broad. *Neh* 3:8
shall come from *f.* cities. *Mi* 7:12*

fortress, -es
the Lord is my rock and my *f.*
  2 Sam 22:2; *Ps* 18:2; 31:3; 71:3
  91:2; 144:2
the *f.* also shall cease. *Isa* 17:3
the *f.* of the high fort shall. 25:12
brambles come up in the *f.* 34:13
I have set thee for a *f.* *Jer* 6:27
wares, O inhabitant of the *f.* 10:17*
O Lord, my *f.* in day of. 16:19*
enter into the *f.* of king. *Dan* 11:7
and be stirred up even to his *f.* 10
all thy *f.* be spoiled. *Hos* 10:14
spoiled come against *f.* *Amos* 5:9
day come to thee from *f.* *Mi* 7:12*

Fortunatus
glad of the coming of F. *1 Cor* 16:17

forty
there shall be *f.* found; he said, I will
  not do it for *f.*'s sake. *Gen* 18:29
shalt make *f.* sockets. *Ex* 26:19
f. sockets of silver. 21; 36:24, 26
Abdon had *f.* sons and. *Judg* 12:14
Hazael went and took *f.* *2 Ki* 8:9
governors had taken *f.* *Neh* 5:15
more than *f.* made. *Acts* 23:13, 21
  see **days**

forty baths
one contained *f. baths.* *1 Ki* 7:38

forty cubits
house before it was *f. cubits* long.
  1 Ki 6:17
the length *f. cubits.* *Ezek* 41:2
courts joined of *f. cubits.* 46:22

forty kine
f. kine, ten bulls. *Gen* 32:15

forty stripes
f. stripes he may give. *Deut* 25:3
f. stripes save one. *2 Cor* 11:24

forty years
Isaac was *f. years.* *Gen* 25:20
Esau *f. years* when he took. 36:34
Israel did eat manna *f. years.*
  Ex 16:35; *Neh* 9:21
wander in wilderness *f. years.*
  Num 14:33; 32:13
your iniquities *f. years.* 34
thy walking these *f. years. Deut* 2:7
God led thee *f. years.* 8:2; 29:5
thy foot swell these *f. years.* 4
Israel walked *f. years* in. *Josh* 5:6
f. years old was I when. 14:7
the land had rest *f. years.*
  Judg 3:11; 5:31; 8:28
hand of Philistines *f. years.* 13:1
Eli judged *f. years.* *1 Sam* 4:18
Ish-bosheth *f. years* old. *2 Sam* 2:10
David reigned *f. years.* 5:4
  1 Ki 2:11
after *f. years* Absalom. *2 Sam* 15:7
Solomon reigned *f. years.* *1 Ki* 11:42
Jehoash reigned *f. years.* *2 Ki* 12:1
Joash reigned *f. years.* *2 Chr* 24:1
f. years was I grieved. *Ps* 95:10
it be inhabited *f. years. Ezek* 29:11
cities be desolate *f. years.* 12
at the end of *f. years* I will. 13
I led you *f. years* in the. *Amos* 2:10
ye offered sacrifices *f. years.* 5:25
  Acts 7:42
healed was above *f. years. Acts* 4:22
Moses was *f. years* old, he. 7:23
when *f. years* expired, there. 30
wonders in wilderness *f. years.* 36
the time of *f. years* suffered. 13:18
them Saul by space of *f. years.* 21

---

saw my works *f. years.* *Heb* 3:9
with whom he grieved *f. years* ? 17

forty-one years
Rehoboam *f.-one years* old when he.
  1 Ki 14:21; *2 Chr* 12:13
Asa reigned *f.-one years. 1 Ki* 15:10
Jeroboam reigned *f.-one years.*
  2 Ki 14:23

forty-two
cities add *f.-two* cities. *Num* 35:6
two bears tare *f.* and *two. 2 Ki* 2:24
them alive, *f.* and *two* men. 10:14
f.-two years old Ahaz. *2 Chr* 22:2
of Azmaveth *f.* and *two. Ezra* 2:24
Beth-azmaveth *f.* and *two. Neh* 7:28
holy city tread *f.-two.* *Rev* 11:2
to continue *f.-two* months. 13:5

forty-five
if I find *f.-five,* I will. *Gen* 18:28
me alive *f.-five* years. *Josh* 14:10
that lay on *f.-five* pillars. *1 Ki* 7:3

forty-six
f.-six years was temple. *John* 2:20

forty-eight
cities of Levites *f.-eight. Num* 35:7
  Josh 21:41

forty-nine
space be to thee *f.-nine* years.
  Lev 25:8

forty thousand
tribe of Ephraim were *f. thousand.*
  Num 1:33; 2:19; 26:18
about *f. thousand* prepared for war.
  Josh 4:13
shield or spear seen among *f. thou-*
  sand. *Judg* 5:8
David slew *f. thousand* horsemen.
  2 Sam 10:18; *1 Chr* 19:18
Solomon had *f. thousand. 1 Ki* 4:26
of Asher expert in war *f. thousand.*
  1 Chr 12:36

forty-one thousand
Asher were *f.* and *one thousand.*
  Num 1:41; 2:28

forty-two thousand
fell of Ephraimites *f.-two thousand.*
  Judg 12:6

forward
not inherit on yonder side or *f.*
  Num 32:19
backward and not *f.* *Jer* 7:24
upon eighth day and so *f. Ezek* 43:27
helped *f.* the affliction. *Zech* 1:15
also to be *f.* year ago. *2 Cor* 8:10*
but being more *f.* of own. 17*
same which I also was *f. Gal* 2:10*
whom if thou bring *f.* on. *3 John* 6
  see that **day, go, set, went**

forwardness
by occasion of the *f.* *2 Cor* 8:8*
for I know *f.* of your mind. 9:2*

fought
then came Amalek and *f.* *Ex* 17:8
so Joshua *f.* with Amalek. 10
then king Arad *f.* against Israel.
  Num 21:1
Sihon came and *f.* against Israel. 23
  Judg 11:20
Sihon *f.* against former. *Num* 21:26
Lord *f.* for Israel. *Josh* 10:14, 42
  23:3
all Israel *f.* against Libnah. 10:29
f. against Lachish. 31
Amorites on the other side *f.* 24:8
men of Jericho *f.* against you. 11
found Adoni-bezek and *f.* *Judg* 1:5
Judah had *f.* against Jerusalem. 8
kings came, then *f.* kings of. 5:19
f. from heaven, stars in courses *f.* 20
my father *f.* for you and. 9:17
Gaal went out and *f.* with. 39
the men of Gilead *f.* with. 12:4
Philistines *f. 1 Sam* 4:10; *1 Chr* 10:1
Saul *f.* against all his. *1 Sam* 14:47
David *f.* with Philistines. 19:8; 23:5
people stood still, nor *f. 2 Sam* 2:28
f. against Hadadezer. 8:10
  1 Chr 18:10
the Syrians *f.* against David.
  2 Sam 10:17; *1 Chr* 19:17

David f. against Rabbah and took.
   2 Sam 12:29
Joram f. Hazael. *2 Ki* 8:29; 9:15
Hazael f. against Gath.   12:17
Joash f. against Amaziah.   13:12
              14:15
Lord f. against enemies. *2 Chr* 20:29
f. against me without a. *Ps* 109:3
Tartan f. against Ashdod. *Isa* 20:1
turned their enemy and f.   63:10
f. against Jerusalem. *Jer* 34:1, 7
when he f. in day of. *Zech* 14:3
smite them that f. against.   12*
I have f. with beasts at. *1 Cor* 15:32
I have f. a good fight. *2 Tim* 4:7
Michael and his angels f. *Rev* 12:7*

foul. *adj.*

my face is f. with.   *Job* 16:16
it will be f. weather. *Mat* 16:3
he rebuked the f. spirit. *Mark* 9:25*
Babylon, the hold of every f. spirit.
             Rev 18:2*

foul, -ed

ye must f. the residue. *Ezek* 34:18
they drink that ye have f. with.   19

fouledst

troubledst waters and f. *Ezek* 32:2

found

for Adam not f. an help. *Gen* 2:20
dove f. no rest for sole of her. 8:9
Isaac's servants digged and. f. 26:19
Isaac's servants said we have f. 32
is it that thou f. it so ?   27:20
Reuben went and f. mandrakes in.
              30:14
tents, but f. not images.   31:33
what hast thou f. of all thy stuff ? 37
Anah that f. the mules in.   36:24
coat, said, this have we f.   37:32
kid, and thou hast not f. her. 38:23
money which we f. in our.   44:8
God hath f. out the iniquity of. 16
went three days and f. no. *Ex* 15:22
went to gather manna and f. 16:27
or if he have f. that.   *Lev* 6:3
f. a man that gathered. *Num* 15:32
f. him brought him to Moses.   33
with what thou hast f. *Deut* 22:3
came to her I f. her not a maid. 14, 17
f. her in field, and the.   22:27
he hath f. some uncleanness.   24:1
he f. him in a desert land.   32:10
pursuers sought, but f. them not.
            Josh 2:22
five kings are f. hid in a cave. 10:17
they f. Adoni-bezek in. *Judg* 1:5
not plowed with heifer, not f. 14:18
he f. a new jawbone of ass.   15:15
f. four hundred young virgins. 21:12
but they f. not asses. *1 Sam* 9:4
they f. young maidens going to. 11
asses, they are f. 9:20; 10:2, 16
Lord is witness ye have not f. 12:5
was no smith f. in Israel.   13:19
no sword nor spear f. in hand.   22
evil hath not been f. with.   25:28
I have f. no fault in him.   29:3
they f. an Egyptian in field.   30:11
f. Saul and his three sons.   31:8
thy servant f. in his heart to pray.
    2 Sam 7:27; *1 Chr* 17:25
nor was weight of brass f. *1 Ki* 7:47
prophet Ahijah f. Jeroboam. 11:29
he went and f. his carcase.   13:28
an oath that they f. thee not. 18:10
Elijah departed and f. Elisha. 19:19
a lion f. him and slew him.   20:36
f. me, O mine enemy ? have f. 21:20
sought Elijah, but f. not. *2 Ki* 2:17
f. no more of her than skull.   9:35
I f. the book of the law in.   22:8
sixty men that were f. in city. 25:19
they f. fat pasture and. *1 Chr* 4:40
whom precious stones were f. 29:8
there are good things f. *2 Chr* 19:3
by genealogy, but they were not f.
    Ezra 2:62; *Neh* 7:64
f. there none of sons of. *Ezra* 8:15
f. nothing to answer. *Neh* 5:8
they f. written in the law of.   8:14
nor is wisdom f. in land. *Job* 28:13
up myself when evil f. mine. 31:29
because they had f. no answer. 32:3

lest ye say, we have f. wisdom.
           Job 32:13
I have f. a ransom.   33:24
no women f. so fair as the.   42:15
looked for comforters, f. *Ps* 69:20
none of men of might f. their.   76:5
yea sparrow hath f. an house. 84:3
I have f. David my servant.   89:20
wandered and f. no city.   107:4
we f. it in the fields of wood. 132:6
seek thy face, and I have f. *Pr* 7:15
wisdom be when thou hast f. 24:14
hast thou f. honey ?   25:16
this have I f. saith the preacher.
          Eccl 7:27
man among a thousand have I f. but
   woman have I not f.   28
f. that God made man upright. 29
sought him, f. him not. *S of S* 3:1, 2
the watchmen f. me.   3; 5:7
f. him whom my soul loveth.   3:4
hand hath f. kingdoms. *Isa* 10:10
my hand hath f. the riches of.   14
all that are f. in thee are.   22:3
hast f. the life of thine hand. 57:10
f. of them that sought me not. 65:1
iniquity have your fathers f.? *Jer* 2:5
in thy skirts is f. the blood of.   34
among my people are f.   5:26
to the pits and f. no water.   14:3
words were f. and I did eat. 15:16
house I f. their wickedness. 23:11
ten men were f. that said.   41:8
all that f. them devoured.   50:7
this is the day we have f. *Lam* 2:16
for man, but I f. none. *Ezek* 22:30
excellent spirit was f. in Daniel.
          Dan 5:12
weighed, and art f. wanting.   27
nor any fault f. in Daniel.   6:4
these men f. Daniel praying.   11
I f. Israel like grapes. *Hos* 9:10
he f. him in Beth-el, and.   12:4
Ephraim said, I have f. me out. 8
from me is thy fruit f.   14:8
he f. a ship for Tarshish. *Jonah* 1:3
transgressions of Israel f. *Mi* 1:13
when ye have f. him. *Mat* 2:8
I have not f. so great faith.   8:10
          Luke 7:9
when a man hath f. he. *Mat* 13:44
when he had f. one pearl of.   46
and f. one of his fellow.   18:28
went on and f. others standing. 20:6
f. nothing thereon.   21:19
  Mark 11:13; *Luke* 13:6
gathered all as many as they f.
         Mat 22:10
he f. them asleep.   26:43
  Mark 14:40; *Luke* 22:45
sought witnesses, yet f. they none.
   Mat 26:60; *Mark* 14:55
f. a man of Cyrene. *Mat* 27:32
when they had f. him. *Mark* 1:37
ate with defiled hands, f. fault. 7:2
when she was come, f. devil gone. 30
they f. the colt tied by door. 11:4
f. the babe in a manger. *Luke* 2:16
after three days they f. him.   46
f. the place where it was.   4:17
returning f. the servant whole. 7:10
they f. man clothed and in.   8:35
when he hath f. the sheep. 15:5
for I have f. my sheep.   6
when she hath f. the piece.   9
are not any f. that returned. 17:18
they f. even as he had. 19:32; 22:13
f. this fellow perverting nation. 23:2
I have f. no fault in this man.   14
f. the stone rolled away.   24:2
they f. not the body of Lord Jesus. 3
when they f. not his body.   23
and they f. the eleven gathered. 33
we have found Messias. *John* 1:41
            45
Jesus f. in the temple those. 2:14
young men came in f. her. *Acts* 5:10
when the officers f. them not.   22
our fathers f. no sustenance. 7:11
that if he f. any of this way.   9:2
Peter f. many come together. 10:27
Herod sought Peter, f. him. 12:19
they f. a certain sorcerer.   13:6
I have f. David, a man after.   22

I f. an altar with this. *Acts* 17:23
f. this man a pestilent fellow.   24:5
if they have f. any evil doing.   20
I f. he hath done nothing.   25:25
came to Puteoli, where we f. 28:14
Abraham our father hath f. *Rom* 4:1
ordained to life, I f. to be to.   7:10
yea, we are f. false. *1 Cor* 15:15
because I f. not Titus. *2 Cor* 2:13
ourselves are f. sinners. *Gal* 2:17
being f. in fashion as a man. *Phil* 2:8
the office, f. blameless. *1 Tim* 3:10
Onesiphorus sought me, f. *2 Tim* 1:17
f. no place of repentance. *Heb* 12:17
your faith might be f. *1 Pet* 1:7
I f. of thy children. *2 John* 4
tried them, and hast f. *Rev* 2:2
I have not f. thy works perfect. 3:2
nor was their place f. any.   12:8
and mountains were not f.   16:20

be found

there shall be f. forty f. *Gen* 18:29
with whomsoever it be f.   44:9
no leaven be f. in houses. *Ex* 12:19
stealeth a man, if he be f. in. 21:16
if a thief be f. breaking up. 22:2, 7
if theft be certainly f. in his hand. 4
lie with her, they be f. *Deut* 22:28
him, he could not be f. *1 Sam* 10:21
on him where he be f. *2 Sam* 17:12
if wickedness be f. in. *1 Ki* 1:52
if thou seek him, he will be f. of
  thee. *1 Chr* 28:9; *2 Chr* 15:2
fly away and not be f. *Job* 20:8
but where shall wisdom be f.? 28:12
pray in time when thou mayest be f.
         Ps 32:6
till his iniquity be f. to be.   36:2
him, but he could not be f.   37:36
if he be f. he shall restore. *Pr* 6:31
be f. in way of righteousness. 16:31
reprove thee and thou be f. guilty. 30:6
curse thee, and thou be f. guilty.   10
not be f. a sherd to take. *Isa* 30:14
nor beast shall be f. there.   35:9
joy and gladness shall be f.   51:3
seek Lord while he may be f.   55:6
I will be f. of you. *Jer* 29:14
sins of Judah be sought for, not be f.
          50:20
shalt thou never be f. *Ezek* 26:21
and fall, and not be f. *Dan* 11:19
every one shall be f. written in. 12:1
now shall they be f. faulty. *Hos* 10:2
deceitful tongue be f. in. *Zeph* 3:13
place shall not be f. for. *Zech* 10:10
be f. to fight against God. *Acts* 5:39
that a steward be f. *1 Cor* 4:2
we shall not be f. naked. *2 Cor* 5:3
they may be f. even as we. 11:12
that I shall be f. such as ye. 12:20
be in him, not having my. *Phil* 3:9
that ye may be f. of him. *2 Pet* 3:14
city of Babylon be f. no. *Rev* 18:21
no craftsman shall be f. any.   22

see **favour**

found grace

Noah f. grace in eyes of. *Gen* 6:8
thy servant hath f. grace.   19:19
f. grace in thy sight.   33:10; 47:29
          50:4
Joseph f. grace in his sight.   39:4
hast also f. grace in. *Ex* 33:12, 17
if I have f. grace in thy sight.   13
  34:9; *Judg* 6:17; *1 Sam* 27:5
thy people have f. grace? *Ex* 33:16
if we have f. grace in thy sight.
         Num 32:5
why have I f. grace in ? *Ruth* 2:10
father knoweth I f. grace. *1 Sam* 20:3
thy servant knoweth I have f. grace.
         2 Sam 14:22
the people f. grace in. *Jer* 31:22

is found

with whom it is f. be my servant.
         Gen 44:10, 16
people that is f. shall. *Deut* 20:11
is f. some good thing. *1 Ki* 14:13
this book that is f. *2 Ki* 22:13
         2 Chr 34:21
is f. city hath been. *Ezra* 4:19
seeing root of matter is f. *Job* 19:28
in lips of him wisdom is f. *Pr* 10:13

every one that is f. shall.   *Isa* 13:15
as new wine is f. in cluster.   65:8
thief is ashamed when he is f.
                Jer 2:26
in thy skirts is f. the blood.   34
a conspiracy is f. among the.   11:9
excellent wisdom is f.   *Dan* 5:12, 14
from me is thy fruit f.   *Hos* 14:8
my son lost and is f.   *Luke* 15:24, 32
our boasting which I made is f. a
  truth.   *2 Cor* 7:14

was found

cup was f. in Benjamin's.   *Gen* 44:12
gathered money that was f.   47:14
with whom was f. purple.   *Ex* 35:23
with whom was f. shittim wood.   24
and Jonathan was f.   *1 Sam* 13:22
told the money that was f. *2 Ki* 12:10
shewed all that was f. in treasury.
         20:13; *Isa* 39:2
gathered the money that was f.
     2 Ki 22:9; *2 Chr* 34:17
read book which was f.   *2 Ki* 23:2
           2 Chr 34:30
sought him, he was f. *2 Chr* 15:4, 15
away substance that was f.   21:17
was f. at Achmetha a roll. *Ezra* 6:2
was f. in it a poor wise.   *Eccl* 9:15
was he f. among thieves ? *Jer* 48:27
perfect till iniquity was f. *Ezek* 28:15
none was f. like Daniel.   *Dan* 1:19
clay broken, no place was f.   2:35
like wisdom of the gods was f. 5:11
before him innocency was f.   6:22
she was f. with child of.   *Mat* 1:18
past, Jesus was f. alone. *Luke* 9:36
Philip was f. at Azotus.   *Acts* 8:40
I was f. of them that.   *Rom* 10:20
neither was guile f. in.   *1 Pet* 2:22
no man was f. worthy.   *Rev* 5:4
in their mouth was f. no guile. 14:5
in her was f. the blood of.   18:24
there was f. no place for them. 20:11

was not found

iniquity was not f. in his.   *Mal* 2:6
Enoch was not f. because. *Heb* 11:5
was not f. written in.   *Rev* 20:15

foundation

not been in Egypt since f.   *Ex* 9:18
he shall lay the f. in his. *Josh* 6:26
hewn stones to lay the f.   *1 Ki* 5:17
in fourth year was f. of house. 6:37
of costly stones even from f. 7:9, 10
he laid the f. of Jericho in.   16:34
work was prepared of f. *2 Chr* 8:16
they began to lay the f.   31:7
f. of temple not yet laid. *Ezra* 3:6
when the builders laid f. of. 10, 12
Sheshbazzar laid f. of house.   5:16
much less in them whose f. *Job* 4:19
whose f. was overflown.   22:16
his f. is in holy mountains. *Ps* 87:1
of old thou hast laid the f. 102:25
Rase it, even to the f. thereof. 137:7
righteous are everlasting f. *Pr* 10:25
I lay in Zion for a f.   *Isa* 28:16
to temple, thy f. shall be.   44:28
my hand hath laid the f. of.   48:13
f. thereof be discovered. *Ezek* 13:14
discovering the f. to neck. *Hab* 3:13
from day the f. was laid. *Hag* 2:18
Zerubbabel laid f.   *Zech* 4:9
prophets which were when f.   8:9
Lord, which layeth the f. of.   12:1
and laid the f. on a rock. *Luke* 6:48
like a man that without a f. built. 49
lest haply after he hath laid f. 14:29
build on another man's f. *Rom* 15:20
as a wise masterbuilder I laid the f.
           1 Cor 3:10
for other f. can no man lay than. 11
if any man build on this f. gold. 12
built on the f. of prophets. *Eph* 2:20
up in store a good f.   *1 Tim* 6:19
f. of God standeth sure. *2 Tim* 2:19
thou, Lord, hast laid the f. *Heb* 1:10
not laying the f. of repentance. 6:1
the first f. jasper.   *Rev* 21:19

foundation of the world
kept secret from the f. of the world.
           Mat 13:35
prepared from f. of the world. 25:34

blood shed from the f. of the world.
           Luke 11:50
lovedst me before f. of the world.
           John 17:24
chosen us in him before the f. of the
  world.   *Eph* 1:4
finished from f. of world.   *Heb* 4:3
oft suffered since f. of world.   9:26
foreordained before f. of the world.
           1 Pet 1:20
slain from f. of the world. *Rev* 13:8
not written from f. of the world. 17:8

foundations

and set on fire the f.   *Deut* 32:22
the f. of heaven moved. *2 Sam* 22:8
f. of the world were discovered. 16
         Ps 18:7, 15
set up walls and joined f. *Ezra* 4:12
let the f. thereof be strongly. 5:9
wast thou when I laid f.? *Job* 38:4
whereupon are the f. fastened. 6
if f. be destroyed, what ?   *Ps* 11:3
all the f. of the earth are out. 82:5
laid the f. of earth not to be. 104:5
when he appointed the f.   *Pr* 8:29
for f. of Kir-hareseth.   *Isa* 16:7*
the f. of the earth do shake.   24:18
have ye not understood from f. of
  earth ?   40:21
Lord that laid f. of earth.   51:13
that I may lay f. of the earth.   16
I will lay thy f. with sapphires. 54:11
thou shalt raise up the f. of.   58:12
f. of earth can be searched. *Jer* 31:37
her f. are fallen, her walls.   50:15*
not take of thee a stone for f. 51:26
and it hath devoured the f. *Lam* 4:11
Egypt's f. shall be broken. *Ezek* 30:4
the f. of the side chambers.   41:8
and I will discover the f.   *Mi* 1:6
and ye strong f. of earth.   6:2
f. of prison were shaken. *Acts* 16:26
for a city that hath f.   *Heb* 11:10
walls of city had twelve f. *Rev* 21:14
f. garnished with precious stones. 19

founded

for he hath f. it upon seas. *Ps* 24:2
fulness thereof, thou hast f. 89:11
to place which thou hast f.   104:8
testimonies thou hast f.   119:152
Lord by wisdom f. earth.   *Pr* 3:19
that Lord hath f. Zion.   *Isa* 14:32
people was not till Assyrian f. 23:13†
and he hath f. his troop. *Amos* 9:6
fell not, for it was f. on a rock.
           Mat 7:25
it was f. on a rock.   *Luke* 6:48

founder

mother gave them to f.   *Judg* 17:4
bellows are burnt, f.   *Jer* 6:29
work of the hands of the f.   10:9*
every f. confounded by. 14*; 51:17*

foundest

and f. his heart faithful.   *Neh* 9:8

fountain

*Is properly the source or spring-
head of waters. It is often used of a
well. Metaphorically, God is called
the fountain of living waters, Jer
2:13. Springs or fountains are
called living, when they never
cease, but are always sending forth
their waters. All spiritual graces
and refreshments communicated by
the Spirit, are also compared to a
fountain, Joel 3:18; Zech 13:1.*

found Hagar by a f.   *Gen* 16:7
f. wherein is water.   *Lev* 11:36
he discovered her f. the f. of. 20:18
f. of Jacob shall be on a. *Deut* 33:28
Israelites pitched by a f. *1 Sam* 29:1
for with thee is f. of life. *Ps* 36:9
bless the Lord from the f.   68:26
didst cleave the f. and the.   74:15
turned flint into a f. of water. 114:8
let thy f. be blessed.   *Pr* 5:18
law of the wise is a f. of life. 13:14
the fear of Lord is a f. of life. 14:27
is a troubled f. and corrupt. 25:26
pitcher be broken at f.   *Eccl* 12:6
a f. sealed.   *S of S* 4:12

a f. of gardens.   *S of S* 4:15
forsaken f. of living. *Jer* 2:13; 17:13
as a f. casteth out her waters. 6:7*
oh that mine eyes were a f. of.   9:1
a f. shall come forth of.   *Joel* 3:18
in that day a f. shall be. *Zech* 13:1
the f. of her blood.   *Mark* 5:29
doth a f. send forth sweet waters ?
           Jas 3:11
no f. can yield salt water and.   12
I will give of the f. of life. *Rev* 21:6

fountains

f. of the great deep.   *Gen* 7:11
the f. also of the deep were.   8:2
God bringeth thee into a land of f.
           Deut 8:7
go into land, to all f.   *1 Ki* 18:5
took counsel to stop waters of f.
           2 Chr 32:3
much people, who stopped all the f. 4
let thy f. be dispersed.   *Pr* 5:16*
there were no f. abounding.   8:24
when he strengthened the f.   28
I will open f. in midst.   *Isa* 41:18
and his f. shall be dried. *Hos* 13:15
he shall lead them to living f.
           Rev 7:17
star fell upon f. of waters.   8:10
worship him that made the f. 14:7
third angel poured vial upon f. 16:4

four

river became f. heads.   *Gen* 2:10
f. kings joined battle with five. 14:9
and f. parts shall be your.   47:24
he shall restore f. sheep.   *Ex* 22:1
shalt make for it f. rings.   25:26
shall be f. bowls made like.   34
of one curtain f. cubits.   26:2, 8
their pillars f. their sockets f.
        27:16; 38:19
in candlestick were f. bowls. 37:20
he cast f. rings for the f. ends. 38:5
f. rows of stones set in the. 39:10
fowls that creep going on all f.
           Lev 11:20
of beasts that go on all f.   27, 42
two wagons, f. oxen to.   *Num* 7:7
f. wagons, eight oxen to sons of. 8
fringes on the f. quarters. *Deut* 22:12
a custom to lament f.   *Judg* 11:40
these f. were born.   *2 Sam* 21:22
fill f. barrels with water. *1 Ki* 18:33
there were f. leprous men. *2 Ki* 7:3
saw his son's sons, even f. *Job* 42:16
f. things say not, it is.   *Pr* 30:15
be f. things which I know not.   18
f. things which it cannot bear. 21
there be f. things which are little. 24
f. things are comely in going. 30:29
f. or five in the utmost.   *Isa* 17:6
appoint over them f. kinds. *Jer* 15:3
Jehudi read three or f. leaves. 36:23
likeness of f. living creatures.
           Ezek 1:5
every one had f. faces.
           6, 15
they f. had one likeness. 1:16; 10:10
went upon their f. sides. 1:17; 10:11
every one had f. wings.   10:21
send my f. sore judgements. 14:21
and say, come from f. winds. 37:9
f. tables were on this side, f. 40:41
altar f. cubits; and f. horns. 43:15
these f. children, God.   *Dan* 1:17
lo, I see f. men loose, walking. 3:25
the f. winds of heaven strove. 7:2
f. great beasts came from sea.   3
these f. beasts are f. kings.   17
f. notable horns towards f.   8:8
whereas f. stood up, f. kingdoms. 22
kingdom divided towards f. winds.
           11:4
f. I will not turn away punishment.
     Amos 1:3, 6, 9, 11, 13; 2:1, 4, 6
I saw, and behold f. horns. *Zech* 1:18
the Lord shewed me f. carpenters. 20
there came f. chariots out.   6:1
and they shall gather elect from f.
  winds.   *Mat* 24:31; *Mark* 13:27
sick of palsy borne of f. *Mark* 2:3
are yet f. months, then. *John* 4:35
Lazarus had lain in grave f. 11:17
the soldiers made f. parts. 19:23

four

f. days ago I was fasting. *Acts* 10:30
Philip had f. daughters. 21:9
have f. men which have a vow. 23
cast f. anchors out of stern. 27:29
about throne were f. beasts. *Rev* 4:6
the f. beasts had each of them. 8
the f. beasts said, amen. 5:14
a voice in the midst of f. beasts. 6:6
f. angels, on f. corners, holding 7:1
a voice from the f. horns of. 9:13
loose the f. angels bound in. 14
sung new song before f. beasts. 14:3
one of f. beasts gave seven. 15:7
elders and the f. beasts fell. 19:4
see **corners, days, footed, twenty, hundred, thousand**

four *times*
they sent to me f. *times*. *Neh* 6:4

fourfold
shall restore lamb f. *2 Sam* 12:6
taken any thing, I restore f. *Luke* 19:8

fourscore
Moses was f. years old, Aaron f. and three, when they spake. *Ex* 7:7
land had rest f. years. *Judg* 3:30
Barzillai was f. old. *2 Sam* 19:32, 35
ass's head was sold for f. *2 Ki* 6:25
Jehu appointed f. men. 10:24
Eliel chief, his brethren f. *1 Chr* 15:9
with him f. priests. *2 Chr* 26:17
Zebadiah, and with him f. *Ezra* 8:8
if by strength they be f. *Ps* 90:10
threescore queens, f. *S of S* 6:8
came from Samaria, f. *Jer* 41:5
widow about f. and four. *Luke* 2:37
take thy bill, and write f. 16:7

fourscore *and five*
I am this day f. *and five* years old. *Josh* 14:10
Doeg slew f. *and five*. *1 Sam* 22:18

fourscore *and six*
Abram was f. *and six*. *Gen* 16:16
one hundred and **fourscore**
days of Isaac were *one hundred and* f. *Gen* 35:28
four hundred and **fourscore**
in *four hundred* f. years after Israel were come out of Egypt. *1 Ki* 6:1

fourscore *thousand*
f. *thousand* hewers in mountains. *1 Ki* 5:15; *2 Chr* 2:18

fourscore *and seven thousand*
Issachar reckoned in all f. *and seven thousand*. *1 Chr* 7:5

one hundred fourscore *and five thousand*
angel smote in camp *one hundred* f. *and five thousand*. *2 Ki* 19:35

foursquare
altar shall be f. *Ex* 27:1
the breastplate f. 28:16
he measured court f. *Ezek* 40:47
ye shall offer holy oblation f. 48:20
and the city lieth f. *Rev* 21:16

fourteen
I served f. years for. *Gen* 31:41
born to Jacob, all souls were f. 46:22
offer for burnt offering f. lambs of.
Num 29:13, 17, 20, 23, 26, 29, 32
tribe of Judah had in valley f. cities with their. *Josh* 15:36; 18:28
and Israel held a feast f. *1 Ki* 8:65
God gave to Heman f. *1 Chr* 25:5
waxed mighty, married f. wives. *2 Chr* 13:21
settle be f. cubits long. *Ezek* 43:17
to David f. from David to carrying to Babylon to Christ f. *Mat* 1:17
a man above f. years. *2 Cor* 12:2
then f. years after I went. *Gal* 2:1

fourteen *thousand*
Job had f. *thousand* sheep. *Job* 42:12
fourteen *thousand seven hundred*
died in plague were f. *thousand seven hundred*. *Num* 16:49

fourteenth
in the f. year came Chedorlaomer. *Gen* 14:5

in f. year of Hezekiah. *2 Ki* 18:13
the f. lot came forth to. *1 Chr* 24:13
f. lot came forth to Mattithiah. 25:21
in the f. year after city. *Ezek* 40:1
but when the f. night was come. *Acts* 27:27

see **day**
fourth
f. river is Euphrates. *Gen* 2:14
in f. generation they shall. 15:16
iniquity of fathers to the f. *Ex* 20:5
34:7; *Num* 14:18; *Deut* 5:9
and f. row a beryl. 28:20; 39:13
in f. year fruit shall be. *Lev* 19:24
f. lot came to Issachar. *Josh* 19:17
David's f. son, Adonijah. *2 Sam* 3:4
1 Chr 3:2
thy children of f. generation.
2 Ki 10:30; 15:12
f. had the face of eagle. *Ezek* 10:14
f. kingdom strong as. *Dan* 2:40
form of f. is like Son of God. 3:25
a f. beast dreadful and strong. 7:7
then I would know truth of f. 19
the f. beast shall be the f. 23
the f. shall be far richer. 11:2
in the f. chariot were. *Zech* 6:3
Jesus came in f. watch. *Mat* 14:25
f. beast was like a flying eagle.
Rev 4:7
when he had opened the f. seal. 6:7
the f. angel sounded, the sun. 8:12
the f. angel poured out his vial. 16:8
third, a chalcedony; f. an. 21:19

see **day, month, part**
fourth *year*
in the f. *year* of Solomon's reign he began. *1 Ki* 6:1, 37; *2 Chr* 3:2
Jehoshaphat began to reign in f. *year* of Ahab. *1 Ki* 22:41
in the f. *year* of Hezekiah Shalmaneser came up against. *2 Ki* 18:9
word came to Jeremiah in f. *year* of Jehoiakim. *Jer* 25:1
in the f. *year* of Zedekiah. 28:1
in the f. *year* of Jehoiakim this word came to. 36:1; 45:1; 46:2
commanded Seraiah in f. *year*. 51:59
in f. *year* of Darius. *Zech* 7:1

fowl
have dominion over f. *Gen* 1:26, 28
of ground God formed every f. 2:19
the f. of the heaven destroyed. 7:23
bring forth of all flesh, of f. 8:17
fear of you shall be on every f. 9:2
I establish my covenant with f. 10
no blood, whether of f. or. *Lev* 7:26
law of the beasts and f. 11:46
likeness of any winged f. *Deut* 4:17
there is a path which no f. *Job* 28:7*
dominion over f. of air. *Ps* 8:8
beasts and flying f. praise. 148:10
f. of heavens and beast. *Jer* 9:10
under it shall dwell all f. *Ezek* 17:23
speak to every feathered f. 39:17*
priest not eat any thing torn, f. 44:31
back of it four wings of a f. *Dan* 7:6

fowler
deliver thee from snare of f. *Ps* 91:3
a bird from hand of the f. *Pr* 6:5
prophet is a snare of a f. *Hos* 9:8

fowlers
escaped out of snare of f. *Ps* 124:7

fowls
take of f. also of air by. *Gen* 7:3
when the f. came down on. 15:11*
if the burnt sacrifice to Lord be of f.
Lev 1:14
these f. ye shall have in. 11:13
of all clean f. ye may. *Deut* 14:20
carcase be meat to all f. of. 28:26
thy flesh to the f. *1 Sam* 17:44, 46
spake of beasts and of f. *1 Ki* 4:33
that dieth in fields, f. eat. 14:11
16:4; 21:24
f. were prepared for me. *Neh* 5:18
ask the f. they shall tell. *Job* 12:7
know all f. of mountains. *Ps* 50:11
he rained f. like as the sand. 78:27
left to the f. of the mountains, and the f. summer upon. *Isa* 18:6*

let f. get from branches. *Dan* 4:14
f. sow not, neither reap. *Mat* 6:26*
the f. devoured the seed. 13:4*
Mark 4:4*; *Luke* 8:5*
that f. may lodge under it.
Mark 4:32*; *Luke* 13:19*
much better than f. *Luke* 12:24*
a sheet wherein were f. *Acts* 10:12
11:6
an angel cried to all the f. *Rev* 19:17*
and all the f. were filled with. 21*

fowls *of the heaven*
wiser than f. *of heaven*. *Job* 35:11
bodies of thy servants meat to f. *of the heaven*. *Ps* 79:2
by them the f. *of heaven*. 104:12
of people meat for f. *of the heaven*.
Jer 7:33; 16:4; 19:7; 34:20
will appoint f. *of the heaven*. 15:3
given Pharaoh for meat to f. *of heaven*. *Ezek* 29:5
f. *of heaven* made their nests in Assyria. 31:6
ruin all f. *of heaven* remain. 13
will cause all f. *of heaven* to. 32:4
the f. *of heaven* shall shake. 38:20
f. *of heaven* given to Nebuchadnezzar. *Dan* 2:38
covenant for them with f. *of heaven*.
Hos 2:18
languish with f. *of heaven*. 4:3
down as the f. *of heaven*. 7:12
consume f. *of the heaven*. *Zeph* 1:3
f. *of heaven* lodged in. *Luke* 13:19

fox
The Hebrew word Shual is used generally of any sort of fox or of jackal, which really belongs to the dog family. Most probably jackals are intended in Judg 15:4, as they were much more numerous, and remained in packs, which made them easier to capture. Although several species of foxes are found in Palestine, it is impossible to decide with certainty in any particular case which species is intended, if it is not the jackal.
a f. break down stone. *Neh* 4:3
go and tell that f. I cast. *Luke* 13:32

foxes
caught three hundred f. *Judg* 15:4
shall be a portion for f. *Ps* 63:10
take the f. the little f. *S of S* 2:15
Zion is desolate, f. walk. *Lam* 5:18
thy prophets are like f. *Ezek* 13:4
f. have holes. *Mat* 8:20; *Luke* 9:58

fragments
(Revisions substitute for this broken pieces)
up f. twelve baskets full. *Mat* 14:20
Mark 6:43; *Luke* 9:17; *John* 6:13
baskets full of f.? *Mark* 8:19, 20
gather up f. that remain. *John* 6:12

frail
I may know how f. I am. *Ps* 39:4

frame
he knoweth our f. *Ps* 103:14
which was as f. of a city. *Ezek* 40:2

frame, *verb*
could not f. to pronounce. *Judg* 12:6
behold, I f. evil against. *Jer* 18:11
will not f. their doings. *Hos* 5:4*

framed
thing f. say to him that f. it?
Isa 29:16†
building fitly f. groweth. *Eph* 2:21
worlds f. by word of God. *Heb* 11:3

frameth
evil, thy tongue f. deceit. *Ps* 50:19
f. mischief by a law. 94:20

frankincense
spices with pure f. *Ex* 30:34
put f. thereon. *Lev* 2:1, 15; 5:11
24:7; *Num* 5:15
oil with all the f. thereof. *Lev* 2:2
priest shall burn the oil with all f.
6:15
appointed to oversee f. *1 Chr* 9:29
where they laid the f. *Neh* 13:5
brought I the vessels and the f. 9

comes perfumed with ƒ.? *S of S* 3:6
I will get me to the hill of ƒ.   4:6
cinnamon, with all trees of ƒ.   14
presented to him gold, ƒ. *Mat* 2:11
no man buyeth ƒ. wine.   *Rev* 18:13

frankly
nothing to pay, he ƒ.   *Luke* 7:42*

fraud
his mouth is full of cursing and ƒ.
  Ps 10:7*
kept back by ƒ. crieth.   *Jas* 5:4

fray
(*American Revision substitutes for
this* frighten)
no man shall ƒ. them away.
  Deut 28:26; *Jer* 7:33
these are come to ƒ. them. *Zech* 1:21

freckled
a ƒ. spot that groweth.   *Lev* 13:39*

free
an Hebrew servant, in the seventh
year shall go out ƒ.   *Ex* 21:2
  Deut 15:12; *Jer* 34:9, 14
say, I will not go out ƒ.   *Ex* 21:5
then shall she go out ƒ.   11*
he shall let him go ƒ. for his.   26
he shall let him go ƒ. for tooth's.   27
not be put to death because not ƒ.
  Lev 19:20
ƒ. from this bitter water. *Num* 5:19
woman be not defiled, shall be ƒ.   28
thou sendest him out ƒ. *Deut* 15:13
hard when thou sendest him ƒ.   18
but he shall be ƒ. at home.   24:5
his father's house ƒ.   *1 Sam* 17:25
the singers, who remaining were ƒ.
  1 Chr 9:33
as many as were of ƒ. *2 Chr* 29:31*
the servant is ƒ. from.   *Job* 3:19
who sent out the wild ass ƒ.?   39:5
uphold me with thy ƒ.   *Ps* 51:12†
ƒ. among the dead, like slain. 88:5*
king loosed him, let him go ƒ. 105:20
to let the oppressed go ƒ.   *Isa* 58:6
man let his servant go ƒ.   *Jer* 34:9
caused them whom they let go ƒ. 11
honour not his father, he shall be ƒ.
  Mat 15:6
saith, then are the children ƒ. 17:26
it is Corban, he shall be ƒ. *Mark* 7:11
truth shall make you ƒ.   *John* 8:32
sayest thou, ye shall be made ƒ.? 33
make you ƒ. ye shall be ƒ. indeed. 36
but I was ƒ. born.   *Acts* 22:28*
offence, so is the ƒ. gift. *Rom* 5:15
but ƒ. gift is of many offences.   16
even so the ƒ. gift came upon.   18
being made ƒ. from sin.   6:18, 22
servants of sin ye were ƒ.   20
her husband be dead, she is ƒ.   7:3
Spirit of life made me ƒ.   8:2
mayest be made ƒ. use. *1 Cor* 7:21
not an apostle ? am I not ƒ.?   9:1
though I be ƒ. from all men.   19
whether bond or ƒ.   12:13
there is neither bond nor ƒ. *Gal* 3:28
  Col 3:11
Jerusalem above, is ƒ.   *Gal* 4:26
children of bondwoman, but of ƒ. 31
wherewith Christ hath made us ƒ. 5:1
receive of Lord, bond or ƒ. *Eph* 6:8
that word may have ƒ. *2 Thes* 3:1*
as ƒ. and not using your liberty.
  1 Pet 2:16
causeth all, ƒ. and bond. *Rev* 13:16
eat flesh of both bond and ƒ.   19:18

free *offerings*
brought ƒ. *offerings.*   *Ex* 36:3
and publish ƒ. *offerings.*   *Amos* 4:5

freed
shall none of you be ƒ. *Josh* 9:23*
that is dead is ƒ. from sin. *Rom* 6:7*

freedom
with a woman, not ƒ.   *Lev* 19:20
great sum obtained ƒ. *Acts* 22:28*

freely
of every tree ƒ. eat.   *Gen* 2:16
the fish we did eat ƒ.   *Num* 11:5
of people had eaten ƒ. *1 Sam* 14:30

of chief fathers offered ƒ. *Ezra* 2:68
which king hath offered ƒ. to.   7:15
I will ƒ. sacrifice unto thee. *Ps* 54:6
I will love them ƒ.   *Hos* 14:4
ƒ. ye have received ƒ. give. *Mat* 10:8
let me ƒ. speak.   *Acts* 2:29
before whom I speak ƒ.   26:26
justified ƒ. by his grace. *Rom* 3:24
will with him also ƒ. give us.   8:32
know things ƒ. given us. *1 Cor* 2:12
preached the gospel of God ƒ.
  2 Cor 11:7
give of fountain of life ƒ. *Rev* 21:6
whosoever will, let him take ƒ. 22:17

freeman
called, is the Lord's ƒ. *1 Cor* 7:22
every bondman and ƒ.   *Rev* 6:15

freewill
ƒ. to go up to Jerusalem. *Ezra* 7:13

freewill *offering*
who offereth ƒ. off. it.   *Lev* 22:21
bullock thou mayest offer ƒ. *off.* 23
make sacrifice in ƒ. *off.* *Num* 15:3
with a tribute of ƒ. *off. Deut* 16:10
a ƒ. *off.* shalt thou keep.   23
beasts besides ƒ. *off.*   *Ezra* 1:4
that willingly offered a ƒ. *off.*   3:5
silver thou canst find with ƒ. *off.* 7:16
silver and gold are a ƒ. *off.*   8:28

freewill *offerings*
offer oblation for ƒ. *off. Lev* 22:18
beside all your ƒ. *off.*   23:38
  Num 29:39
thither bring your ƒ. *off. Deut* 12:6
not eat within thy gates ƒ. *off.*   17
Kore was over ƒ. *off.* of. *2 Chr* 31:14
accept the ƒ. *off.* of my. *Ps* 119:108

freewoman
two sons, by bondmaid, and by a ƒ.
  Gal 4:22
but he of the ƒ. was by promise. 23
not be heir with son of the ƒ.   30
children of bondwoman, but of ƒ. 31

frequent
in prisons more ƒ.   *2 Cor* 11:23*

fresh
manna was as taste of ƒ. *Num* 11:8
my glory was ƒ. in me.   *Job* 29:20
anointed with ƒ. oil.   *Ps* 92:10
yield salt water and ƒ. *Jas* 3:12*

fresher
flesh shall be ƒ. than a. *Job* 33:35

fret
burn it in the fire, it is ƒ. *Lev* 13:55

fret, *verb*
provoked her to make her ƒ.
  1 Sam 1:6
ƒ. not thyself.   *Ps* 37:1, 7, 8
  Pr 24:19
be hungry, they shall ƒ. *Isa* 8:21

fretted
but thou hast ƒ. me in. *Ezek* 16:43†

fretteth
and his heart ƒ. against.   *Pr* 19:3

fretting
the plague is a ƒ. leprosy.
  Lev 13:51, 52; 14:44

fried
cakes mingled with oil of flour ƒ.
  Lev 7:12*
Levites to wait about that which is ƒ.
  1 Chr 23:29*

friend
*The friend of the king was a high
court official, probably the king's
confidential adviser,* Gen 26:26;
1 Ki 4:5.
*The friend of God is a title given
to Abraham because of his close
relations with God and his faithfulness,* 2 Chr. 20:7; Jas 2:23.
*The word friend was used as a
general salutation, whether to friend
or foe,* Mat 22:12; 26:50.
sent kid by hand of his ƒ. *Gen* 38:20
God spake to Moses as a man to ƒ.
  Ex 33:11
or if thy wife or ƒ. entice. *Deut* 13:6

companion whom he used as his ƒ.
  Judg 14:20
Amnon had a ƒ. his.   *2 Sam* 13:3
Hushai David's ƒ. came into city.
  15:37; 16:16
this thy kindness to thy ƒ.? why wentest thou not with thy ƒ.?   16:17
Zabud was principal officer, the
king's ƒ.   *1 Ki* 4:5
gavest to the seed of Abraham thy ƒ.
  2 Chr 20:7
pity be shewed from his ƒ. *Job* 6:14
and ye dig a pit for your ƒ.   27
as though he had been my ƒ.
  Ps 35:14
my familiar ƒ. hath lifted up.   41:9
lover and ƒ. hast thou put far. 88:18
be surety for thy ƒ.   *Pr* 6:1*
hand of thy ƒ.; make sure thy ƒ.   3*
ƒ. loveth at all times.   17:17
surety in the presence of his ƒ.   18
a ƒ. that sticketh closer.   18:24
every man is a ƒ. to him that.   19:6
the king shall be his ƒ.   22:11
faithful are the wounds of a ƒ.   27:6
so doth sweetness of man's ƒ.   9
thine own ƒ. and father's ƒ.   10
blesseth his ƒ. with a loud voice.   14
sharpeneth countenance of his ƒ.   17
this is my ƒ. O daughter. *S of S* 5:16
seed of Abraham my ƒ.   *Isa* 41:8
neighbour and his ƒ.   *Jer* 6:21
eat every one flesh of his ƒ.   19:9
beloved of her ƒ. yet an.   *Hos* 3:1
trust ye not in a ƒ. put.   *Mi* 7:5
behold, a ƒ. of publicans. *Mat* 11:19
  Luke 7:34
ƒ. I do thee no wrong.   *Mat* 20:13
ƒ. how camest thou hither ?   22:12
ƒ. wherefore art thou come ?   26:50
which of you have a ƒ. and go at midnight and say, ƒ. lend. *Luke* 11:5
for a ƒ. of mine in his journey.   6
not give him because he is his ƒ.   8
bade thee say, ƒ. go up higher. 14:10
the ƒ. of the bridegroom. *John* 3:29
our ƒ. Lazarus sleepeth.   11:11
this man go, art not Cesar's ƒ. 19:12
made Blastus their ƒ.   *Acts* 12:20
Abraham called ƒ. of God. *Jas* 2:23
will be a ƒ. of the world.   4:4

friendly
Levite went to speak ƒ. *Judg* 19:3*
thou hast spoken ƒ. to. *Ruth* 2:13*
must shew himself ƒ.   *Pr* 18:24*

friends
David sent spoil to his ƒ. *1 Sam* 30:26
shew kindness to Saul's ƒ. *2 Sam* 3:8
thine enemies, hatest thy ƒ.   19:6*
left him not one of his ƒ. *1 Ki* 16:11
sent and called for his ƒ. *Esth* 5:10
said his wife and all his ƒ.   14
Haman told his wife and ƒ.   6:13
when Job's three ƒ. heard. *Job* 2:11
my ƒ. scorn me, but mine eye. 16:20
speaketh flattery to his ƒ.   17:5
familiar ƒ. have forgotten me. 19:14
all my inward ƒ. abhorred me.   19
have pity on me, O ye ƒ.   21
Elihu's wrath kindled against ƒ. 32:3
Lord's wrath kindled against ƒ. 42:7
Lord turned when he prayed for ƒ. 10
my ƒ. stand aloof.   *Ps* 38:11
is hated, rich hath ƒ.   *Pr* 14:20
whisperer separateth chief ƒ. 16:28
a matter, separateth ƒ.   17:9
hath ƒ. shew himself friendly. 18:24
wealth maketh many ƒ. but.   19:4
how much more do his ƒ. go.   7
eat, O ƒ.; drink, yea. *S of S* 5:1
thee a terror to thy ƒ.   *Jer* 20:4
shalt be buried there, thou and ƒ. 6
thy ƒ. have set thee on.   38:22*
ƒ. have dealt treacherously. *Lam* 1:2
wounded in house of my ƒ. *Zech* 13:6
when his ƒ. heard of it. *Mark* 3:21
go home to thy ƒ.   5:19
centurion sent ƒ. to him. *Luke* 7:6
my ƒ. be not afraid of them.   12:4
a dinner, call not thy ƒ.   14:12
he calleth together her ƒ.   15:6
she calleth her ƒ. and neighbours. 9
make merry with my ƒ.   29

f. of the mammon. *Luke* 16:9
betrayed by parents and f. 21:16
and Herod were made f. 23:12
man lay down life for f. *John* 15:13
ye are my f. if ye do what I. 14
but I have called you f. 15
Cornelius called together his f.
Acts 10:24
certain which were his f. sent. 19:31
Julius gave liberty to go to f. 27:3
our f. salute thee, greet the f. by.
3 John 14

friendship
make no f. with angry. *Pr* 22:24
the f. of world is enmity. *Jas* 4:4

fringe, -s
them make f. put on f. *Num* 15:38
it shall be to you for a f. 39
make thee f. on the four quarters.
Deut 22:12

to and fro
raven, which went to and f. *Gen* 8:7
Elisha walked to and f. *2 Ki* 4:35
Satan said, from going to and f. in
earth. *Job* 1:7; 2:2
I am full of tossings to and f. 7:4
break a leaf driven to and f.? 13:25
reel to and f. and stagger. *Ps* 107:27
vanity tossed to and f. *Pr* 21:6
earth shall reel to and f. *Isa* 24:20
running to and f. of locusts. 33:4
and removing to and f. 49:21
Javan going to and f. *Ezek* 27:19
Lord sent to walk to and f. through.
Zech 1:10
walked to and f. through earth. 6:7
that they might walk to and f. so
they walked to and f. 6:7
no more children tossed to and f.
Eph 4:14
see run

frogs
smite thy borders with f. *Ex* 8:2
the magicians brought up f. 7
sent f. which destroyed. *Ps* 78:45
the land brought forth f. 105:30
unclean spirits like f. *Rev* 16:13

from
hand f. off you, and f. off. *1 Sam* 6:5
multitudes f. Decapolis, f. Jerusalem, f. Judea, f. beyond. *Mat* 4:25

front
Joab saw f. of battle. *2 Sam* 10:9
porch in the f. of house. *2 Chr* 3:4

frontiers
from cities on his f. *Ezek* 25:9

frontlets
*These are square pieces of hard
calf's skin, including four pieces of
parchment, upon which the Jews
wrote four passages of the law, and
bound them with strings on their
foreheads. The four passages which
they wrote are these: On the first
piece of parchment, Ex 13, from
verse 2 to 10. On the second,
Ex 13, from verse 11 to 16. On
the third, Deut 6, from verse 4 to 9.
And on the fourth, Deut 11, from
verse 13 to 21.*
it shall be for f. between. *Ex* 13:16
shall be a f. between thine eyes.
Deut 6:8; 11:18

frost
drought consumed by day, f. by night.
Gen 31:40
as small as the hoar f. *Ex* 16:14
by breath of God f. is. *Job* 37:10*
the f. of heaven, who hath? 38:29
destroyeth trees with f. *Ps* 78:47
he scattereth the hoar f. 147:16
body cast out to the f. *Jer* 36:30

froward
a very f. generation. *Deut* 32:20†
thyself pure, with the f. shew thyself
f. *2 Sam* 22:27*; *Ps* 18:26*
the counsel of the f. is. *Job* 5:13†
a f. heart shall depart. *Ps* 101:4
man that speaketh f. *Pr* 2:12†
ways are crooked, and they f. 15*
for the f. is abomination. 3:32*

put away a f. mouth. *Pr* 4:24†
wicked walketh with f. mouth. 6:12†
there is nothing f. or perverse. 8:8*
the evil way, and the f. mouth. 13†
the f. tongue be cut out. 10:31†
of a f. heart, are abomination. 11:20*
a f. man soweth strife. 16:28†
shutteth eyes to devise f. things. 30†
he that hath a f. heart. 17:20†
the way of a man is f. and. 21:8*
thorns and snares in way of f. 22:5†
subject to masters, to f. *1 Pet* 2:18

frowardly
went on f. in way of his. *Isa* 57:17†

frowardness
who delight in the f. of. *Pr* 2:14†
f. is in his heart, he deviseth. 6:14†
mouth of wicked speaketh f. 10:32†

frozen
the face of the deep is f. *Job* 38:30

fruit
every tree wherein is f. *Gen* 1:29
Cain brought of the f. of the. 4:3
hath withheld from thee f. of. 30:2
so that her f. depart. *Ex* 21:22
count f. uncircumcised. *Lev* 19:23
in fourth year f. shall be holy. 24
six years thou shalt gather f. 25:3
the tithe of the f. is the. 27:30
shewed them the f. *Num* 13:26
and this is the f. of it. 27
they took of the f. in. *Deut* 1:25
he will bless the f. of thy land. 7:13
lest f. of thy seed, f. of thy. 22:9
take of the first of all the f. 26:2
blessed shall be the f. of thy. 28:4
plenteous in f. of thy body. 11; 30:9
cursed shall be the f. of thy. 28:18
for thine olive shall cast his f. 40
thy trees and f. shall locust. 42
forsake my sweetness and f.?
Judg 9:11
summer f. for young. *2 Sam* 16:2
f. shalt thou destroy. *Ps* 21:10
f. thereof shall shake like. 72:16
earth is satisfied with f. of. 104:13
locusts devoured the f. 105:35
f. of the womb is his reward. 127:3
of f. of thy body will I set. 132:11
my f. better than fine gold. *Pr* 8:19
the f. of the wicked tendeth. 10:16
f. of the righteous is a tree. 11:30
a man is satisfied by the f. 12:14
satisfied with the f. of mouth. 18:20
with the f. of her hand she. 31:16
give her of the f. of her hands. 31
and his f. was sweet to. *S of S* 2:3
those that keep the f. thereof. 8:12
eat the f. of their doings. *Isa* 3:10
f. of the earth be excellent. 4:2
I will punish the f. of the. 10:12
no pity on the f. of womb. 13:18
his f. a fiery flying serpent. 14:29
fill face of the world with f. 27:6
the f. to take away his sin. 9
as the hasty f. before summer. 28:4*
I create the f. of the lips. 57:19
plant vineyards, eat f. of. 65:21
bring f. of their thoughts. *Jer* 6:19
my fury shall be on the f. of. 7:20
green olive tree, fair, and of goodly
f. 11:16
let us destroy the tree with f. 19
f. of his doings. 17:10; 21:14; 32:19
cut off the f. thereof. *Ezek* 17:9
the east wind dried up her f. 19:12
which hath devoured her f. 14
they shall eat thy f. and drink. 25:4
I will multiply the f. of tree. 36:30
nor f. thereof be consumed. 47:12
the leaves fair and f. *Dan* 4:12, 21
and said thus, scatter his f. 14:8
ye have eaten the f. of lies. *Hos* 10:13
from me is thy f. found. 14:8
destroyed his f. from. *Amos* 2:9
turned f. of righteousness. 6:12
a gatherer of sycamore f. 7:14*
behold a basket of summer f. 8:1, 2
f. of body for sin of my? *Mi* 6:7
desolate, for the f. of their. 7:13
neither f. be in the vines. *Hab* 3:17
earth is stayed from her f. *Hag* 1:10

the vine shall give her f. *Zech* 8:12
table is polluted, and f. *Mal* 1:12
nor shall your vine cast her f. 3:11
f. good, tree corrupt, f. corrupt, tree
is known by his f. *Mat* 12:33
let no f. grow on thee for. 21:19
when the time of f. drew near. 34
not drink of f. of the vine, till I drink
it new in. 26:29; *Mark* 14:25
might receive the f. of. *Mark* 12:2
blessed is the f. of thy. *Luke* 1:42
he sought f. thereon. 13:6
I come seeking f. on this fig tree. 7
should give him of the f. 20:10
gathereth f. to life. *John* 4:36
of the f. of his loins. *Acts* 2:30
that I might have some f. *Rom* 1:13
what f. had ye then in those? 6:21
ye have your f. unto holiness. 22
have sealed to them this f. 15:28
but the f. of Spirit is love. *Gal* 5:22
the f. of the Spirit is in. *Eph* 5:9
this is the f. of my labour. *Phil* 1:22
I desire f. that may abound to. 4:17
by him let us offer the f. *Heb* 13:15
f. of righteousness is. *Jas* 3:18
husbandman waiteth for f. 5:7
f. withereth, without f. *Jude* 12*
see eat

bear, or beareth fruit
shall bear f. upward. *2 Ki* 19:30
Isa 37:31
good soil, that it bear f. *Ezek* 17:8
in height of Israel it shall bear f. 23
they shall bear no f. *Hos* 9:16
the tree beareth her f. *Joel* 2:22
good ground, is he who beareth f.
Mat 13:23
fell on good ground, and bare f.
Luke 8:8
if it bear f. well, if not, cut. 13:9
branch that beareth not f. every
branch that beareth f. *John* 15:2
as the branch cannot bear f. of. 4
that ye bear much f. so shall. 8

**bring, bringeth, or brought forth
fruit**
it shall bring forth f. for. *Lev* 25:21
bring of the f. of land. *Num* 13:20
to bring the f. of all. *Neh* 10:35, 37
that bringeth forth f. *Ps* 1:3
they shall bring forth f. 92:14
f. was to bring silver. *S of S* 8:11
the wicked grow, they bring forth f.
Jer 12:2
they shall increase, and bring forth f.
Ezek 36:11
bring forth new f. for meat. 47:12
Israel bringeth forth f. to. *Hos* 10:1
bringeth not forth good f. *Mat* 3:10
7:19; *Luke* 3:9
good tree bringeth forth good f.
Mat 7:17
good tree cannot bring forth evil. 18
when blade brought forth f. 13:26
hear the word and bring forth f.
Mark 4:20
for the earth bringeth forth f. 28
bring no f. to perfection. *Luke* 8:14
they keep it and bring forth f. 15
die, it bringeth forth f. *John* 12:24
it may bring forth more f. 15:2
abideth, bringeth forth much f. 5
ordained that you bring forth f. 16
that we bring forth f. to. *Rom* 7:4
motions did work to bring forth f. 5
the gospel bringeth forth f. *Col* 1:6
prayed, earth brought forth f.
Jas 5:18
see firstfruit

yield, yieldeth, yielding fruit
fruit tree yielding f. *Gen* 1:11, 12
land shall yield her f. *Lev* 25:19
trees of field shall yield their f. 26:4
land yield not her f. *Deut* 11:17
root of the righteous yieldeth f.
Pr 12:12
cease from yielding f. *Jer* 17:8
tree of the field shall yield her f.
Ezek 34:27
yield your f. to my people. 36:8
choked it, it yielded no f. *Mark* 4:7
on good ground and did yield f. 8

yieldeth peaceable f. of. *Heb* 12:11
the tree yielded her f. *Rev* 22:2
fruitful
saying, Be f. and multiply. *Gen* 1:22
28; 8:17; 9:7; 35:11
I will make thee exceeding f. 17:6
I will make Ishmael f. 20
room for us, we shall be f. 26:22
bless thee, and make thee f. 28:3
make Jacob f. 48:4
Joseph is a f. bough, a f. 49:22
children of Israel were f. *Ex* 1:7
I will make you f. and. *Lev* 26:9
he turneth a f. land into. *Ps* 107:34
thy wife shall be as a f. vine. 128:3
mountains and f. trees, praise. 148:9
beloved hath vineyard in a f. hill.
Isa 5:1
four or five in the outmost f. 17:6
shall lament for the f. vine. 32:12
f. place was a wilderness. *Jer* 4:26
they shall be f. and increase. 23:3
was f. and full of. *Ezek* 19:10
though he be f. an east. *Hos* 13:15
gave us rain and f. *Acts* 14:17
being f. in every good. *Col* 1:10
see **field**
fruits
take of the best f. in land. *Gen* 43:11
to offer first of ripe f. *Ex* 22:29
six years gather in the f. 23:10
according to years of the f.
Lev 25:15*, 16*
till her f. come in. 22
neither the trees yield their f. 26:20
precious f. brought forth. *Deut* 33:14
thy sons shall bring in f. *2 Sam* 9:10
restore to her all the f. of. *2 Ki* 8:6
and eat the f. thereof. 19:29
if I have eaten the f. *Job* 31:39
fields, which may yield f. *Ps* 107:37
I planted trees of all kind of f.
Eccl 2:5
orchard with pleasant f. *S of S* 4:13
my beloved eat his pleasant f. 16
I went down to see the f. of. 6:11*
gates all manner of pleasant f. 7:13
and Carmel shake off f. *Isa* 33:9*
pine away for want of f. *Lam* 4:9
not destroy the f. of your. *Mal* 3:11
bring f. meet for repentance.
Mat 3:8; *Luke* 3:8
know them by their f. *Mat* 7:16, 20
that they receive the f. of it. 21:34
who shall render him the f. in. 41
given to a nation bringing f. 43
I have no room where to bestow my
f. *Luke* 12:17
there will I bestow all my f. 18*
increase the f. of your. *2 Cor* 9:10
filled with the f. of. *Phil* 1:11
husbandman first partaker of the f.
2 Tim 2:6
wisdom from above full of good f.
Jas 3:17
f. thy soul lusted after. *Rev* 18:14
of life bare twelve manner of f. 22:2
see **first**
summer fruits
hundred of summer f. *2 Sam* 16:1
summer f. and harvest. *Isa* 16:9
ye wine and summer f. *Jer* 40:10
wine and summer f. very much. 12
spoiler is fallen on summer f. 48:32
when they gathered the summer f.
Mi 7:1
fruit trees
and possessed f. trees. *Neh* 9:25
frustrate
hired counsellors to f. *Ezra* 4:5
I do not f. grace of God. *Gal* 2:21*
frustrateth
that f. the tokens of liars. *Isa* 44:25
fryingpan
be a meat offering in the f. *Lev* 2:7
all that is dressed in the f. 7:9
fuel
be with burning and f. of. *Isa* 9:5
people shall be as f. of the fire. 19
vine tree is cast into the fire for f.
Ezek 15:4, 6
thou shalt be for f. to the fire. 21:32

fugitive
a f. and a vagabond. *Gen* 4:12
I shall be a f. and a vagabond. 14
fugitives
Gileadites f. of Ephraim. *Judg* 12:4
and the f. that fell away. *2 Ki* 25:11
cry for Moab, his f. shall. *Isa* 15:5*
all his f. shall fall by. *Ezek* 17:21
fulfil
f. her week, and we will. *Gen* 29:27
f. your works. *Ex* 5:13
number of thy days I will f. 23:26
he might f. the word. *1 Ki* 2:27
if thou takest heed to f. *1 Chr* 22:13*
to f. threescore and. *2 Chr* 36:21
canst thou number months they f.?
Job 39:2
Lord grant thee, and f. all. *Ps* 20:4
the Lord f. all thy petitions. 5
he will f. the desire of them. 145:19
becometh us to f. all. *Mat* 3:15
not come to destroy, but to f. 5:17
David, who shall f. my. *Acts* 13:22*
if it f. the law. *Rom* 2:27
for the flesh, to f. the lusts. 13:14
ye shall not f. the lust. *Gal* 5:16
and so f. the law of Christ. 6:2
f. ye my joy, that ye be. *Phil* 2:2
given to me, to f. word. *Col* 1:25
heed ministry, that thou f. 4:17
f. good pleasure of his. *2 Thes* 1:11
if ye f. the royal law. *Jas* 2:8
put in their hearts to f. *Rev* 17:17*
fulfilled
to be delivered were f. *Gen* 25:24
my wife, for my days are f. 29:21
forty days were f. for so are f. 50:3
have ye not f. your task? *Ex* 5:14
seven days f. after Lord hath. 7:25
till purification be f. *Lev* 12:4, 6
of his separation are f. *Num* 6:13
when days be f. and. *2 Sam* 7:12
in that the king f. request. 14:22
hath with his hand f. it. *1 Ki* 8:15
hast f. it with hand. 24; *2 Chr* 6:15
the Lord hath f. that. *2 Chr* 6:4
word of Lord might be f. *Ezra* 1:1
thou hast f. judgement. *Job* 36:17*
and your wives have f. *Jer* 44:25
he hath f. his word he. *Lam* 2:17
our days are f. our end is. 4:18
when days of siege are f. *Ezek* 5:2
the same hour was thing f. *Dan* 4:33
till three whole weeks were f. 10:3
that it might be f. *Mat* 1:22; 2:15,
23; 8:17; 12:17; 13:35; 21:4
27:35; *John* 12:38; 15:25; 17:12
18:9, 32; 19:24, 28, 36
f. that which was spoken. *Mat* 2:17
27:9
pass from law till all be f. 5:18
in them is f. the prophecy. 13:14
not pass till these things be f. 24:34
the time is f. kingdom. *Mark* 1:15
sign when these things be f.? 13:4*
words which shall be f. *Luke* 1:20
when they had f. the days. 2:43
all things written may be f. 21:22
until times of Gentiles be f. 24
not eat till it be f. in kingdom. 22:16
all things must be f. 24:44
this my joy therefore is f. *John* 3:29†
they might have my joy f. in. 17:13†
God shewed, he hath f. *Acts* 3:18
after many days were f. Jews. 9:23
and Barnabas f. their ministry. 12:25
and as John f. his course. 13:25
have f. them in condemning. 27
had f. all that was written of. 29
God hath f. the same to us. 33
grace of God for work they f. 14:26
righteousness of law might be f. in.
Rom 8:4
loveth another hath f. the law. 13:8
when obedience is f. *2 Cor* 10:6
law is f. in one word. *Gal* 5:14
killing of brethren be f. *Rev* 6:11
plagues of seven angels f. 15:8*
till words of God be f. 17:17*
no more, till 1000 years be f. 20:3*
see **scripture**

fulfilling
fire, hail, stormy wind f. *Ps* 148:8
love is the f. of the law. *Rom* 13:10
f. the desires of the flesh. *Eph* 2:3*
full
of Amorites not yet f. *Gen* 15:16
Abraham an old man, and f. 25:8
Isaac old and f. of days. 35:29
at the end of two f. years. 41:1
thin ears devoured seven f. 7, 22
money in his sack f. weight. 43:21
be f. of swarms of flies. *Ex* 8:21
an homer f. of manna therein. 16:33
he should make f. restitution. 22:3
corn beaten out of f. ears. *Lev* 2:14
censer f. of coals, hands f. of. 16:12
land became f. of wickedness. 19:29
within a f. year redeem it. 25:29
if not redeemed in a f. year. 30
both f. of fine flour. *Num* 7:13, 19
25, 31, 37, 43, 49, 55, 61, 67, 73, 79
spoon of ten shekels f. of. 14, 20, 26
32, 38, 44, 50, 56, 62, 68, 74, 80, 86
Balak give house f. of. 22:18; 24:13
houses f. of good things, have eaten
and be f. *Deut* 6:11; 8:10, 12
will send grass, that thou mayest eat
and be f. 11:15
bewail her father a f. month. 21:13
Naphtali f. of the blessing. 33:23
Joshua was f. of Spirit of. 34:9
dew, a bowl f. of water. *Judg* 6:38
house was f. of men and. 16:27
I went out f. and Lord. *Ruth* 1:21
and a f. reward be given thee. 2:12
they that were f. hired. *1 Sam* 2:5
they gave them in f. tale. 18:27
in country of Philistines a f. 27:7
and with one f. line to. *2 Sam* 8:2
make valley f. of ditches. *2 Ki* 3:16
when vessels were f. she said. 4:6
mountain was f. of horses. 6:17
all the way was f. of garments. 7:15
house of Baal was f. from one. 10:21
grant it me for f. price. *1 Chr* 21:22
I will verily buy it for a f. price. 24
David old and f. of. 23:1; 29:28
was Haman f. of wrath. *Esth* 3:5
f. of indignation against. 5:9
come to grave in a f. age. *Job* 5:26
I am f. of tossings to and fro. 7:4
I am f. of confusion. 10:15
a man f. of talk be justified? 11:2
man is of few days f. of trouble. 14:1
bones are f. of sins of youth. 20:11
one dieth in his f. strength. 21:23
his breasts are f. of milk, his. 24
I am f. of matter, the Spirit. 32:18
on thy table should be f. 36:16
Job died, old and f. of days. 42:17
they are f. of children. *Ps* 17:14*
broken my heart, I am f. of. 69:20
waters of a f. cup are wrung. 73:10
dark places f. of habitations of. 74:20
sent meat to the f. 78:25
trees of Lord are f. of sap. 104:16*
happy that hath quiver f. of. 127:5
that our garners may be f. 144:13
an house f. of sacrifices. *Pr* 17:1
the f. soul loatheth honeycomb. 27:7
hell and destruction are never f. 20
lest I be f. and deny thee. 30:9
yet the sea is not f. *Eccl* 1:7
all things are f. of labour. 8
than both hands f. with travail. 4:6*
if the clouds be f. of rain. 11:3
I am f. of burnt offerings. *Isa* 1:11
your hands are f. of blood. 15
faithful city f. of judgement. 21
earth shall be f. of knowledge. 11:9
houses shall be f. of doleful. 13:21
waters of Dimon f. of blood. 15:9
thou art f. of stirs 22:2
valleys shall be f. of chariots. 7
a feast f. of marrow. 25:6
tables are f. of vomit and. 28:8
his lips are f. of indignation. 30:27
they are f. of the fury of. 51:20
a f. wind from those. *Jer* 4:12
when I had fed them to the f. 5:7
I am f. of the fury of the Lord. 6:11
within two f. years will I. 28:3, 11
the Rechabites pots f. of wine. 35:5

city sit solitary that was *f.* *Lam* 1:1
he is filled *f.* with reproach.   3:30
their wings were *f.* of.   *Ezek* 1:18
court was *f.* of the brightness.   10:4
the wheels were *f.* of eyes.   12
great eagle with wings *f.* of.   17:3
fruitful and *f.* of branches.   19:10
the sum, *f.* of wisdom and.   28:12
rivers shall be *f.* of thee.   32:6
in midst of valley which was *f.* 37:1
ye shall eat fat till ye be *f.* and. 39:19
then was Nebuchadnezzar *f.* of fury.
     Dan 3:19
transgressors are come to *f.*   8:23
Daniel mourned three *f.* weeks. 10:2
floors shall be *f.* of wheat. *Joel* 2:24
but truly I am *f.* of power. *Mi* 3:8
the rich men are *f.* of violence. 6:12
earth is *f.* of his praise. *Hab* 3:3
streets shall be *f.* of boys. *Zech* 8:5
thy body shall be *f.* of light.
     Mat 6:22; *Luke* 11:36
when it was *f.* they drew. *Mat* 13:48
twelve baskets *f.* 14:20; *Mark* 6:43
left seven baskets *f.*   *Mat* 15:37
but within are *f.* of extortion. 23:25
within *f.* of dead men's bones.   27
within ye are *f.* of hypocrisy.   28
f. well ye reject commandment of.
     Mark 7:9
filled a spunge *f.* of vinegar.   15:36
now Elizabeth's *f.* time. *Luke* 1:57
Jesus being *f.* of the Holy Ghost. 4:1
behold a man *f.* of leprosy fell. 5:12
woe unto you that are *f.*   6:25
Lazarus laid at his gate *f.* of. 16:20
among us, *f.* of grace. *John* 1:14
for my time is not yet *f.* come. 7:8
that your joy be *f.*   15:11; 16:24
was set a vessel *f.* of vinegar. 19:29
men are *f.* of new wine. *Acts* 2:13
shalt make me *f.* of joy.   28
look out men *f.* of Holy Ghost. 6:3
Stephen *f.* of faith and. 5, 8; 7:55
Moses was *f.* forty years old. 7:23
Dorcas *f.* of good works.   9:36
Barnabas *f.* of the Holy Ghost. 11:24
O *f.* of all subtilty and.   13:10
they were *f.* of wrath and.   19:28
being *f.* of envy, murder. *Rom* 1:29
ye also are *f.* of goodness.   15:14
now ye are *f.* now ye are. *1 Cor* 4:8
and was *f.* of heaviness. *Phil* 2:26*
I am instructed to be *f.* and.   4:12
I have all and abound, I am *f.*   18
f. proof of thy ministry. *2 Tim* 4:5
meat to them of *f.* age. *Heb* 5:14*
tongue an unruly evil, *f.* *Jas* 3:8
wisdom from above is pure, *f.*   17
with joy unspeakable, *f.* of. *1 Pet* 1:8
eyes *f.* of adultery. *2 Pet* 2:14
that your joy may be *f.* *1 John* 1:4
that we receive a *f.* reward. *2 John* 8
to face, that our joy may be *f.*   12
four beasts *f.* of eyes. *Rev* 4:6, 8
every one golden vials *f.* of.   5:8
seven golden vials *f.* of wrath. 15:7
kingdom was *f.* of darkness. 16:10*
I saw a woman *f.* of names of. 17:3
a golden cup *f.* of abominations.   4
seven vials *f.* of seven last.   21:9
see **assurance, compassion**

is full

set aside that which *is f.* *2 Ki* 4:4
his mouth *is f.* of cursing. *Ps* 10:7
     Rom 3:14
right hand *is f.* of bribes. *Ps* 26:10
of the Lord *is f.* of majesty.   29:4
earth *is f.* of goodness of the. 33:5
hand *is f.* of righteousness. 48:10
river of God, which *is f.* of.   65:9
wine is red, it *is f.* of mixture. 75:8
my soul *is f.* of troubles. 88:3
the earth *is f.* of thy riches. 104:24
earth *is f.* of thy mercy. 119:64
heart of sons of men *is f.* of. *Eccl* 9:3
a fool *is f.* of words. 10:14*
land *is f.* of silver, *is f.* of. *Isa* 2:7
their land also *is f.* of idols.   8
the whole earth *is f.* of his.   6:3
as a cage *is f.* of birds. *Jer* 5:27
with him that *is f.* of days.   6:11
the land *is f.* of adulterers.   23:10

land *is f.* of crimes, city *is f.* of.
     Ezek 7:23
land *is f.* of blood, city *is f.* of.   9:9
for the press *is f.* the fats. *Joel* 3:13
cart is pressed, that *is f.* of sheaves.
     Amos 2:13
it *is* all *f.* of lies and. *Nah* 3:1
body *is f.* of light, *is f.* of. *Luke* 11:34
inward part *is f.* of ravening.   39

to the **full**

and did eat bread *to the f.* *Ex* 16:3
when Lord shall give bread in morning *to the f.*   8
eat your bread *to the f.* *Lev* 26:5

fuller, -s

and stood in the highway of the *f.*'s
   field. *2 Ki* 18:17; *Isa* 7:3; 36:2
like a refiner's fire, and *f.*'s. *Mal* 3:2
so as no *f.* on earth can. *Mark* 9:3

fully

Caleb followed me *f.* *Num* 14:24
Boaz said, it hath *f.* been. *Ruth* 2:11
Solomon went not *f.* after. *1 Ki* 11:6
heart of men is *f.* set to. *Eccl* 8:11
devoured as stubble *f.* *Nah* 1:10*
day of Pentecost *f.* come. *Acts* 2:1
being *f.* persuaded, that. *Rom* 4:21
let every man be *f.* persuaded. 14:5
I have *f.* preached the gospel. 15:19
thou hast *f.* known my. *2 Tim* 3:10
by me preaching might be *f.*   4:17
thrust in sickle, grapes *f.* *Rev* 14:18

fulness

the *f.* of the winepress. *Num* 18:27
precious things of the earth, *f.*
     Deut 33:16
the sea roar and the *f.* thereof.
   1 Chr 16:32; *Ps* 96:11; 98:7
in *f.* of sufficiency shall. *Job* 20:22
in thy presence is *f.* of joy. *Ps* 16:11
earth is the Lord's and the *f.*   24:1
     1 Cor 10:26, 28
the world is mine, and *f.* thereof.
     Ps 50:12; 89:11
iniquity of Sodom, *f.* of. *Ezek* 16:49
of his *f.* have we received grace for.
     John 1:16
how much more their *f.*? *Rom* 11:12
till *f.* of Gentiles be come in.   25
come in the *f.* of the gospel. 15:29
when *f.* of time was come. *Gal* 4:4
that in the *f.* of times he. *Eph* 1:10
the *f.* of him that filleth all in all. 23
be filled with the *f.* of God.   3:19
come to stature of *f.* of Christ. 4:13
in him should all *f.* dwell. *Col* 1:19
in him dwelleth *f.* of Godhead.   2:9

furbish

f. the spears, put on the. *Jer* 46:4

furbished

a sword is sharpened and also *f.*
     Ezek 21:9, 10
given to be *f.*   11
sword *f.* to consume.   28

furious

(*Revisions substitute* wrathful)
with *f.* man thou shalt. *Pr* 22:24
a *f.* man aboundeth in.   29:22
execute judgement in *f.* rebukes.
     Ezek 5:15; 25:17
Nebuchadnezzar the king was very *f.*
     Dan 2:12
Lord revengeth, and is *f.* *Nah* 1:2

furiously

of Jehu, he driveth *f.* *2 Ki* 9:20
they shall deal *f.* with. *Ezek* 23:25*

furlongs

(*A furlong was about an eighth of*
     a mile)
from Jerusalem sixty *f.* *Luke* 24:13
rowed about five and twenty *f.*
     John 6:19
nigh Jerusalem about fifteen *f.* 11:18
out by space of 1600 *f.* *Rev* 14:20
the city with reed, 12,000 *f.*   21:16

furnace

[1] *An oven for smelting iron from
the ore,* Deut 4:20; 1 Ki 8:51. [2]
*A crucible for refining gold and
silver,* Pr 17:3; Ezek 22:20. [3]
A bake oven, Neh 3:11; Isa 31:9.

a smoking *f.* and a.   *Gen* 15:17
went up as the smoke of a *f.* 19:28
handfuls of ashes of the *f.* *Ex* 9:8
and they took ashes of the *f.*   10
ascended as the smoke of a *f.* 19:18
taken you out of the *f.* *Deut* 4:20
from the midst of the *f.* *1 Ki* 8:51
     Jer 11:4
pure words, as silver tried in a *f.* of
   earth. *Ps* 12:6
as the *f.* for gold. *Pr* 17:3; 27:21
his *f.* in Jerusalem. *Isa* 31:9
chosen thee in *f.* of affliction. 48:10
dross in midst of a *f.* *Ezek* 22:18
gather you as tin in midst of *f.*   20
silver melted in midst of the *f.*   22
be cast into midst of a burning fiery
   f. *Dan* 3:6, 11
cast them into a *f.* *Mat* 13:42, 50
brass, as if burned in a *f.* *Rev* 1:15
a smoke, as smoke of a great *f.* 9:2

furnaces

Hashub repaired tower of *f.*
     Neh 3:11
from the tower of the *f.* to. 12:38

furnish

shalt *f.* him liberally. *Deut* 15:14
can God *f.* a table in? *Ps* 78:19*
that *f.* the drink offering. *Isa* 65:11*
f. thyself to go into. *Jer* 46:19

furnished

Hiram *f.* Solomon with. *1 Ki* 9:11
she hath also *f.* her table. *Pr* 9:2
wedding *f.* with guests. *Mat* 22:10*
will shew you a room *f.* *Mark* 14:15
     Luke 22:12
throughly *f.* unto all. *2 Tim* 3:17

furniture

(*General meaning, fittings*)
put them in camels' *f.* *Gen* 31:34
tabernacle and his *f.* *Ex* 31:7; 39:33
table and his *f.*   8*
altar with all his *f.*   9*
the candlestick and his *f.*   35:14*
none end of all pleasant *f.* *Nah* 2:9

furrow

bind the unicorn in the *f.*? *Job* 39:10

furrows

or the *f.* thereof likewise. *Job* 31:38
thou settlest the *f.* *Ps* 65:10
plowed, made long their *f.*   129:3
might water it by *f.* of. *Ezek* 17:7*
it shall wither in the *f.* where. 10*
as hemlock in the *f.* *Hos* 10:4
bind themselves in their two *f.* 10*
their altars as heaps in the *f.* 12:11

further

angel went *f.* and stood. *Num* 22:26
officers shall speak *f.* to. *Deut* 20:8
inquired of the Lord *f.* *1 Sam* 10:22
shalt thou come, but no *f.* *Job* 38:11
yea, twice, will proceed no *f.*   40:5
f. by these, my son, be admonished.
     Eccl 12:12
f. need have we of witnesses?
   Mat 26:65; *Mark* 14:63; *Luke* 22:71
why troublest Master *f.*? *Mark* 5:35
as he would have gone *f.* *Luke* 24:28
that it spread no *f.* *Acts* 4:17
when they had *f.* threatened them. 21
Herod proceeded *f.* to take.   12:3
f. he brought Greeks also.   21:28
that I be not *f.* tedious.   24:4
they had gone a little *f.*   27:28*
they shall proceed no *f.* *2 Tim* 3:9
f. need another priest. *Heb* 7:11

further, verb

f. not his wicked device. *Ps* 140:8

furtherance

things which happened have fallen
   out unto *f.* of gospel. *Phil* 1:12*
shall abide with you for your *f.* 25*

furthered

f. the people and house of. *Ezra* 8:36

furthermore

the Lord said *f.* to Moses. *Ex* 4:6
Lord said *f.* to Ezekiel. *Ezek* 8:6

fury

(American Revision usually substitutes wrath)

tarry, till brother's f. Gen 27:44
walk contrary to you in f. Lev 26:28
God shall cast the f. of. Job 20:23*
f. is not in me, who. Isa 27:4
his f. is upon all their armies. 34:2
feared because of f. of the oppressor; where is the f. of the ? 51:13
which hast drunk cup of his f. 17
they are full of the f. of the Lord. 20
even the dregs of cup of my f. 22
repay f. to his adversaries. 59:18
I will trample them in my f. 63:3
arm brought salvation, my f. it. 5
I will make them drunk in my f. 6
to render his anger with f. 66:15†
lest my f. come forth like. Jer 4:4
I am full of the f. of the Lord. 6:11
I will fight against you in f. 21:5
lest f. go out like fire and burn. 12
a whirlwind is gone forth in f. 23:19
30:23
take the wine cup of this f. 25:15
city hath been a provocation of my f.
32:31
slain in mine anger and f. 33:5
great is the f. the Lord hath. 36:7
hath accomplished his f. Lam 4:11
cause my f. to rest on them...I have
accomplished my f. Ezek 5:13
when I execute judgements in f. 15
thus will I accomplish my f. 6:12
therefore will I deal in f. 8:18
with a stormy wind in my f. 13:13
I will give thee blood in f. 16:38
make my f. towards thee to rest. 42
she was plucked up in my f. 19:12
with f. poured out will I rule. 20:33
I will cause my f. to rest. 21:17
gather you in mine anger and f. 22:20
that it might cause f. to come. 24:8
till I have caused my f. to rest. 13
do in Edom according to my f. 25:14
in my jealousy and in my f. 36:6
f. shall come up in my face. 38:18
Nebuchadnezzar in his f. Dan 3:13
was Nebuchadnezzar full of f. 19
ran unto him in the f. of his. 8:6
let thy f. be turned away from. 9:16
shall go forth with great f. to. 11:44
will execute f. on heathen. Mi 5:15
jealous for her with great f. Zech 8:2
see **pour, poured**

G

Gaal
Zebul thrust out G. Judg 9:41

Gabbatha
pavement, in Hebrew, G. John 19:13

Gabriel
G. make this man understand.
Dan 8:16
while I was praying, the man G. 9:21
I am G. that stand in. Luke 1:19
the angel G. was sent from God. 26

Gad
she called his name G. Gen 30:11
sons of Zilpah, G. and Asher. 35:26
sons of G. 46:16; Num 1:24; 26:15
18; 1 Chr 12:14
G. troop shall overcome. Gen 49:19
prince of G. Num 1:14; 2:14; 7:42
children of G. had a multitude. 32:1
children of G. came and spake. 2
children of G. will pass over. 29
Moses gave to G. the kingdom of. 33
tribe of the children of G. have.
34:14; Josh 13:28; 18:7
mount Ebal to curse G. Deut 27:13
and of G. he said, Blessed be he that
enlargeth G. 33:20
the children of G. passed. Josh 4:12
the children of G. returned out. 22:9
went to land of G. 1 Sam 13:7
the midst of river of G. 2 Sam 24:5
to the prophet G. David's seer. 11
1 Chr 21:9, 18
David said unto G. I am in a. 14
according to the saying of G. 19

16

are in the book of G. 1 Chr 29:29
to command of G. 2 Chr 29:25
their king inherit G.? Jer 49:1
a portion for G. Ezek 48:27
one gate of G. 34
tribe of Gad
of tribe of G. 45,650. Num 1:25
then the tribe of G. shall set forward,
captain of G. shall. 2:14; 10:20
of tribe of G. to spy the land. 13:15
tribe of the children of G. have.
34:14; Josh 13:24
assigned Ramoth in Gilead out of the
tribe of G. Josh 20:8; 21:7
38; 1 Chr 6:63, 80
tribe of G. were sealed 12,000.
Rev 7:5

Gadarenes
into country of the G. Mark 5:1
Luke 8:26
country of G. besought. Luke 8:37

gaddest
why g. thou about to ? Jer 2:36

Gadite, -s
gave I unto the G. Deut 3:12, 16
the Reubenites and G. Josh 22:1
Bani G. one of David's. 2 Sam 23:36
Hazael smote the G. 2 Ki 10:33
of the G. there separated. 1 Chr 12:8
made rulers over the G. 26:32

gain
kings of Canaan took no g. Judg 5:19
is it g. to him to make ? Job 22:3
of every one greedy of g. Pr 1:19
the g. thereof is better than. 3:14
that is greedy of g. troubleth. 15:27
that by usury and unjust g. 28:8*
he that despiseth the g. of. Isa 33:15
every one for his g. from his. 56:11
hand at thy dishonest g. Ezek 22:13
like as wolves to get dishonest g. 27
divide the land for g. Dan 11:39
I will consecrate their g. Mi 4:13
her masters much g. Acts 16:16
brought no small g. to the. 19:24*
did I make a g. of you ? 2 Cor 12:17*
did Titus make a g. of you ? 18*
Christ, and to die is g. Phil 1:21
what things were g. to me. 3:7
supposing that g. is. 1 Tim 6:5
with contentment is great g. 6
there buy, sell and get g. Jas 4:13

gain, verb
I know that ye would g. Dan 2:8
g. the whole world, and ? Mat 16:26
Mark 8:36; Luke 9:25
to all, that I might g. the. 1 Cor 9:19
that I might g. the Jews. 20
that I might g. them that are. 21
g. the weak. 22

gained
what is the hope of the hypocrite,
though he hath g.? Job 27:8
thou hast greedily g. by. Ezek 22:12
if he hear, thou hast g. Mat 18:15
received two had also g. 25:17, 22
have g. besides them five talents. 20
much every man had g. Luke 19:15
thy pound hath g. ten pounds. 16
thy pound hath g. five pounds. 18
and to have g. this harm. Acts 27:21*

gains
hope of their g. was. Acts 16:19

gainsay
shall not be able to g. Luke 21:15

gainsayers
be able to convince the g. Tit 1:9

gainsaying
came I to you without g. Acts 10:29
forth my hands to a g. Rom 10:21
they have perished in the g. Jude 11

Gaius
having caught G. a man. Acts 19:29
G. of Derbe accompanied Paul. 20:4
G. mine host saluteth. Rom 16:23
none but Crispus and G. 1 Cor 1:14
unto the wellbeloved G. 3 John 1

Galatia
had gone through the region of G.
Acts 16:6; 18:23
order to churches of G. 1 Cor 16:1

is departed to G. 2 Tim 4:10
through Pontus, G. 1 Pet 1:1

Galatians
O foolish G. who hath ? Gal 3:1

galbanum
spices, onycha, and g. Ex 30:34

Galeed
Jacob called the heap G. Gen 31:47
was the name of it called G. 48

Galilean, -s
art a G. Mark 14:70; Luke 22:59
some told him of the G. Luke 13:1
these G. were sinners above all G.? 2
whether the man were a G.? 23:6
all these that speak, G.? Acts 2:7

Galilee
Kedesh in G. for a city. Josh 20:7
Kedesh in G. to. 21:32; 1 Chr 6:76
Hiram 20 cities in G. 1 Ki 9:11
took Ijon and G. 2 Ki 15:29
grievously afflict her in G. Isa 9:1
turned into parts of G. Mat 2:22
cometh Jesus from G. to John. 3:13
Mark 1:9
G. of the Gentiles. Mat 4:15
walking by sea of G. 18; Mark 1:16
there followed multitudes from G.
Mat 4:25; Mark 3:7
nigh unto the sea of G. Mat 15:29
Jesus of G. 21:11
I will go before you into G. 26:32
Mark 14:28
followed Jesus from G. Mat 27:55
Mark 15:41; Luke 23:49, 55
he goeth before you into G.
Mat 28:7; Mark 16:7
he preached throughout all G.
Mark 1:39
power of Spirit into G. Luke 4:14
he preached in synagogues of G. 44
beginning from G. to this place. 23:5
of G. he asked whether Galilean ? 6
to you when he was in G. 24:6
Christ come out of G.? John 7:41
art thou of G.? out of G. ariseth. 52
who was of Bethsaida in G. 12:21
ye men of G. Acts 1:11
Judas of G. rose up. 5:37
churches rest through all G. 9:31
know which began from G. 10:37
them that came from G. 13:31
see **Cana**

gall
[1] The bitter secretion from the
liver, bile, Job 16:13; 20:25. [2]
A poisonous, bitter herb, called in
the Hebrew, rosh, Deut 29:18.
[3] Used metaphorically for bitter
affliction, Jer 8:15.
be a root that beareth g. Deut 29:18
their grapes are grapes of g. 32:32
he poureth out my g. on. Job 16:13
his meat is the g. of asps. 20:14
sword cometh out of his g. 25
they gave me also g. for. Ps 69:21
hath given us water of g. Jer 8:14
give them water of g. 9:15; 23:15
hath compassed me with g. Lam 3:5
the wormwood and the g. 19
turned judgement into g. Amos 6:12
vinegar mingled with g. Mat 27:34
I perceive thou art in g. Acts 8:23

gallant
no galley, nor shall g. ship. Isa 33:21

galleries
king is held in the g. S of S 7:5*
measured the g. thereof. Ezek 41:15

gallery
the pavement was g. against g.
Ezek 42:3

galley
wherein shall go no g. Isa 33:21

Gallim
Michal to Phalti of G. 1 Sam 25:44
O daughter of G. Isa 10:30

Gallio
when G. was the deputy. Acts 18:12
and G. cared for none of those. 17

gallows

to hang Mordecai on g.　　*Esth* 6:4
hanged Haman on the g.　7:10; 8:7
sons be hanged on the g.　9:13, 25

Gamaliel

of Manasseh, G. son of.　*Num* 1:10
　2:20; 7:54, 59; 10:23
a Pharisee named G.　*Acts* 5:34
brought up at the feet of G.　22:3

Gammadims

and the G. were in the.　*Ezek* 27:11

gap

man that should stand in g. before.
　Ezek 22:30

gaped

have g. upon.　*Job* 16:10; *Ps* 22:13

gaps

not gone up into the g.　*Ezek* 13:5

garden

man and put him in g.　*Gen* 2:15
sent him forth from the g.　3:23
plain of Jordan was as the g.　13:10
and wateredst it as a g. *Deut* 11:10
I may have it for a g.　*1 Ki* 21:2
shooteth forth in his g.　*Job* 8:16
g. inclosed is my sister. *S of S* 4:12
g. let him come into his g.　16
I am come into my g. my sister. 5:1
is gone down into his g.　6:2, 11
Zion is as a lodge in a g.　*Isa* 1:8
ye shall be as a g. which hath.　30
desert like the g. of God.　51:3
shalt be like a watered g.　58:11
as the g. causeth things sown. 61:11
shall be as a watered g.　*Jer* 31:12
away his tabernacle, as it were of a g.
　Lam 2:6
in Eden the g. of God.　*Ezek* 28:13
cedars in g. of God could not.　31:8
all the trees in the g. of God.　9
land is become like the g. of. 36:35
land is as the g. of Eden.　*Joel* 2:3
took and cast into his g. *Luke* 13:19
Cedron, where was a g.　*John* 18:1
did not I see thee in the g.?　26
there was a g. and in the g.　19:41

gardener

he had been the g.　*John* 20:15

gardens

thy tents as g. by the.　*Num* 24:6
I made me g. and orchards. *Eccl* 2:5
a fountain of g. a well.　*S of S* 4:15
to feed in the g. and to gather.　6:2
thou that dwellest in the g.　8:13
be confounded for the g.　*Isa* 1:29
a people that sacrificeth in g.　65:3
purify themselves in the g.　66:17
g. and eat the fruit.　*Jer* 29:5, 28
sent blasting, when your g. *Amos* 4:9
they shall also make g. and　9:14

garlands

brought oxen and g.　*Acts* 14:13

garlick

we remember the g. we. *Num* 11:5

garment

and Japhet took a g.　*Gen* 9:23
came out red, like a hairy g.　25:25
by his g. he left his g.　39:12
he left his g. with me.　15, 18
she laid up his g. till her lord. 39:16
blood thereof on any g.　*Lev* 6:27
g. wherein is the plague.　13:47, 49
if plague be spread in the g. in.　51
plague of leprosy in a g.　59; 14:55
every g. whereon is the seed. 15:17
nor g. mingled.　19:9; *Deut* 22:11*
not put on a woman's g.　*Deut* 22:5
goodly Babylonish g.　*Josh* 7:21
Achan, the silver, and the g.　24
they spread a g. and.　*Judg* 8:25
Tamar had a g. of.　*2 Sam* 13:18
she rent her g. and went on.　19
clad himself with a new g. *1 Ki* 11:29
took every man his g.　*2 Ki* 9:13
I heard this I rent my g.　*Ezra* 9:3
having rent my g. and mantle I.　5
Mordecai went with a g.　*Esth* 8:15
consumeth, as a g. that.　*Job* 13:28
force of my disease is my g.　30:18
when I made the cloud the g.　38:9
clay to seal, they stand as a g.　14

---

discover the face of his g.? *Job* 41:13
sackcloth also my g.　　*Ps* 69:11
violence covereth them as g.　73:6
yea all of them shall wax old like a g.
　102:26; *Isa* 50:9; 51:6, *Heb* 1:11
with light, as with a g.　*Ps* 104:2
it with the deep as with a g.　6
himself with cursing as a g.　109:18
as the g. which covereth him.　19
g. that is surety.　*Pr* 20:16; 27:13
as he that taketh away a g. in. 25:20
bound the waters in a g.?　30:4
eat them up like a g.　*Isa* 51:8
to give g. of praise for spirit.　61:3
shepherd putteth on his g. *Jer* 43:12
the naked with a g.　*Ezek* 18:7, 16
whose g. was white as.　*Dan* 7:9
ye pull off robe with the g.　*Mi* 2:8
holy flesh in skirt of his g. *Hag* 2:12
shall wear a rough g.　*Zech* 13:4*
violence with his g.　*Mal* 2:16
new cloth to old g.　*Mat* 9:16
　Mark 2:21; *Luke* 5:36
touched the hem of his g. *Mat* 9:20
　21; 14:36; *Mark* 5:27; *Luke* 8:44
not on a wedding g.　*Mat* 22:11, 12
back again to take up his g.
　Mark 13:16
clothed with a long white g.　16:5
sell his g. and buy one. *Luke* 22:36
cast thy g. about thee.　*Acts* 12:8
hating even the g. spotted. *Jude* 23
of man clothed with a g. *Rev* 1:13

garments

and change your g.　*Gen* 35:2
Tamar put her widow's g.　38:14
washed his g. in wine, his.　49:11
may make Aaron's g. to.　*Ex* 28:3
sprinkled the blood on Aaron's g.
　29:21; *Lev* 8:30
them wisdom to make g.　*Ex* 31:10
put off his g. put on other g.
　Lev 6:11; 16:23, 24
borders of their g.　*Num* 15:38
strip Aaron of his g. put.　20:26
Moses stripped Aaron of g. put.　28
Gibeonites brought old g. *Josh* 9:5
you thirty changes of g. *Judg* 14:12
gave David his g.　*1 Sam* 18:4
cut off their g. in the middle.
　2 Sam 10:4; *1 Chr* 19:4
David tare his g.　*2 Sam* 13:31
to receive money and g.? *2 Ki* 5:26
all the way was full of g. and　7:15
Jehoiekim's g.　25:29; *Jer* 52:33
one hundred priests' g.　*Ezra* 2:69
gave 530 priests' g.　*Neh* 7:70
gave sixty-seven priests' g.　72
how thy g. are warm.　*Job* 37:17
they part my g. among.　*Ps* 22:18
all thy g. smell of myrrh.　45:8
went down to skirts of his. 133:2
let thy g. be always white. *Eccl* 9:8
smell of thy g. is like.　*S of S* 4:11
every battle is with g.　*Isa* 9:5
put on thy beautiful g.　52:1
their webs shall not become g.　59:6
he put on the g. of vengeance.　17
he hath clothed me with g.　61:10
that cometh with dyed g.　63:1
shall be sprinkled upon my g.　3
not afraid, nor rent g.　*Jer* 36:24
could not touch their g.　*Lam* 4:14
tookest thy broidered g. *Ezek* 16:18
there shall lay their g. they.　42:14
sanctify people with their g.　44:19
in their coats and other g. *Dan* 3:21
heart, and not your g.　*Joel* 2:13
clothed with filthy g.　*Zech* 3:3
take the filthy g. from him.　4
spread their g. in the way. *Mat* 21:8
　Mark 11:8
the borders of their g.　*Mat* 23:5
they parted his g. casting lots.
　27:35; *Mark* 15:24
casting away his g.　*Mark* 10:50
g. on the colt.　11:7; *Luke* 19:35
by them in shining g.　*Luke* 24:4*
he laid aside his g.　*John* 13:4
shewing coats and g.　*Acts* 9:39
and your g. are motheaten. *Jas* 5:2
have not defiled their g.　*Rev* 3:4
watcheth and keepeth his g.　16:15

---

holy garments

make holy g. for Aaron.　*Ex* 28:2, 4
put wisdom to make holy g.　31:10
holy g. he shall wash.　*Lev* 16:4, 32
lay their holy g.　*Ezek* 42:14

garner

gather his wheat into the g.
　Mat 3:12; *Luke* 3:17

garners

our g. may be full.　*Ps* 144:13
the g. are laid desolate.　*Joel* 1:17

garnish, -ed

he g. the house with.　*2 Chr* 3:6
by his Spirit he hath g.　*Job* 26:13
findeth it swept and g.　*Mat* 12:44
　Luke 11:25
you g. the sepulchres of. *Mat* 23:29
of the wall are g.　*Rev* 21:19*

garrison, -s

to hill where is g. of.　*1 Sam* 10:5
Jonathan smote the g. of the.　13:3
over to the Philistines' g.　14:1, 6
the g. and the spoilers, they also. 15
David put g. in Syria.　*2 Sam* 8:6
　1 Chr 18:6
David put g. in Edom.　*2 Sam* 8:14
　1 Chr 18:13
g. of Philistines in Beth-lehem.
　2 Sam 23:14; *1 Chr* 11:16
Jehoshaphat set g. in Judah.
　2 Chr 17:2
strong g. shall go down. *Ezek* 26:11
kept the city with a g.　*2 Cor* 11:32

gat

Moses g. him up into.　*Ex* 24:18
g. up from tabernacle.　*Num* 16:27
and g. them up to the top. *Judg* 9:51
and David g. him a.　*2 Sam* 8:13
covered him, but he g.　*1 Ki* 1:1
the pains of hell g. hold.　*Ps* 116:3
I g. men singers, and.　*Eccl* 2:8
we g. our bread with the.　*Lam* 5:9

gate

*The gates were the important part
of an ancient city. They gave the
only means of passing through the
wall and were usually closed at
night and were strengthened by
bars of brass or iron. The gate
was the place of public concourse,
partly because it was an open
space, not usually found elsewhere
in a city. Much of the legal
business of the city was done there,
Ruth 4:11.
The word gate is sometimes used
to mean power or dominion. God
promises Abraham, that his posterity should possess the gates of
their enemies, their towns, their
fortresses, Gen 22:17. They
should conquer them, they should
have dominion over them.
The gates of death are the brink,
or mouth of the grave, Ps 9:13.*
thy seed possess the g. of enemies.
　Gen 22:17; 24:60
Jacob said, this is the g. of.　28:17
go in and out from g. to g. *Ex* 32:27
bring him to the g.　*Deut* 21:19
bring them both out to the g.　22:24
brother's wife go up to g.　25:7
they shut the g.　*Josh* 2:7
took the doors of the g.　*Judg* 16:3
then went Boaz to the g.　*Ruth* 4:1
dead be not cut off from the g.　10
by the side of the g.　*1 Sam* 4:18
beside the way of the g. *2 Sam* 15:2
to the chamber over the g.　18:33
water by g.　23:15, 16; *1 Chr* 11:18
when Elijah came to g.　*1 Ki* 17:10
have the charge of the g. *2 Ki* 7:17
cast lots for every g.　*1 Chr* 26:13
porters at every g.　*2 Chr* 8:14
the g. should be shut.　*Neh* 13:19
before the king's g.　*Esth* 4:2; 6:12
when I went out to the g.　*Job* 29:7
this g. of the Lord, the.　*Ps* 118:20
the fish pools by the g.　*S of S* 7:4
howl, O g. cry, O city.　*Isa* 14:31
the g. is smitten with.　24:12

to turn the battle to the *g.*   *Isa* 28:6
at the entry of new *g.*   *Jer* 36:10
have ceased from the *g.*   *Lam* 5:14
to door of the inner *g.*   *Ezek* 8:3
at the door of the *g.* twenty-.   11:1
Lord come by way of the *g.*   43:4
this *g.* shall be shut, none.   44:2
enter by way of *g.*   3; 46:2, 8
blood on the posts of the *g.*   45:19
the *g.* of the inner court shall.   46:1
but the *g.* shall not be shut till.   2
open the *g.* one shall shut the *g.*   12
g. of Reuben, one *g.* of Judah. 48:31
the *g.* of my people.   *Ob* 13
he is come into the *g.*   *Mi* 1:9
from Lord to the *g.* of Jerusalem. 12
have passed through the *g.*   2:13
strait is wide is the *g.* and broad is.
  Mat 7:13, 14; *Luke* 13:24*
when he came nigh *g.*   *Luke* 7:12
a beggar Lazarus laid at his *g.* 16:20
Cornelius stood before *g.* *Acts* 10:17
they came to the iron *g.*   12:10
Rhoda opened not the *g.* for.   14
suffered without the *g.*   *Heb* 13:12
every several *g.* was of.   *Rev* 21:21
  see **entereth, entering**

gate
he that exalteth his *g.*   *Pr* 17:19

at the **gate**
of all that went in *at the g.* of city.
  Gen 23:10, 18
Jehu entered in *at the g.*   *2 Ki* 9:31
at the g. of Sur, and a third *at the g.*
  11:6; *2 Chr* 23:5
man's left hand *at the g.*   *2 Ki* 23:8
set a chest *at the g.* of.   *2 Chr* 24:8
I see Mordecai sitting *at the* king's
  g.   *Esth* 5:13
in array *at the g.*   *Isa* 22:7
they laid daily *at the g.*   *Acts* 3:2*
who sat for alms *at beautiful g.*   10
  see **fish gate**

high **gate**
through the *high g.*   *2 Chr* 23:20
Jotham built the *high g.* of.   27:3
in stocks in the *high g.*   *Jer* 20:2
  see **horse gate**

in the **gate**
and Lot sat *in the*   *Gen* 19:1
Moses stood *in the g.* of.   *Ex* 32:26
virginity to elders *in g.* *Deut* 22:15
wait for Samson *in the g.* *Judg* 16:2
people *in the g.* said, we. *Ruth* 4:11
near to Samuel *in the g.* *1 Sam* 9:18
Abner aside *in the g.*   *2 Sam* 3:27
king sat *in the g.* they told all. 19:8
a shekel *in the g.*   *2 Ki* 7:1, 18
the people trod on him *in the g.*   20
sat *in the* king's *g.*   *Esth* 2:19, 21
saw him *in the* king's *g.*   5:9
his children are crushed *in the g.*
  Job 5:4
when I saw my help *in the g.* 31:21
that sit *in the g.* speak. *Ps* 69:12
speak with the enemies *in g.* 127:5
the afflicted *in the g.*   *Pr* 22:22
openeth not his mouth *in the g.* 24:7
him that reproveth *in g.* *Isa* 29:21
stand *in the g.* of the Lord's. *Jer* 7:2
stand *in the g.* of children.   17:19
when he was *in the g.* of.   37:13
king then sitting *in the g.* of. 38:7
princes of Babylon sat *in the g.* 39:3
but Daniel sat *in the g.*   *Dan* 2:49
that rebuketh *in the g.*   *Amos* 5:10
turn aside the poor *in the g.*   12
establish judgement *in the g.*   15

old **gate**
old g. repaired Jehoiada. *Neh* 3:6
priests went above the *old g.* 12:39

prison **gate**
stood still in the *prison g.* *Neh* 12:39

sheep **gate**
went even unto *sheep g.* *Neh* 12:39

valley **gate**
towers at the *valley g.* *2 Chr* 26:9
out by *g.* of the *valley.* *Neh* 2:13
entered by the *g.* of the *valley.*   15
the *valley g.* repaired Hanun. 3:13

water **gate**
over against *water g.*   *Neh* 3:26
the street before the *water g.* 8:1
in the law before the *water g.*   3
in the street of the *water g.*   16
even to the *water g.* eastward. 12:37

gates
Levite within your *g.* *Deut* 12:12
son set up *g.* *Josh* 6:26; *1 Ki* 16:34
gods, then was war in *g.* *Judg* 5:8
the Lord shall go to the *g.*   5:11
appointed to praise in *g.* *2 Chr* 31:2
g. are burnt. *Neh* 1:3; 2:3, 13, 17
let not the *g.* of Jerusalem be.   7:3
and Levites purified the *g.*   12:30
my servants set I at the *g.*   13:19*
the Levites to keep the *g.*   22
thy praise in the *g.*   *Ps* 9:14
lift up your heads, O ye *g.*   24:7, 9
the Lord loveth the *g.* of Zion. 87:2
enter into his *g.* with.   100:4
for he hath broken the *g.* of. 107:16
open to me the *g.* of.   118:19
in openings of *g.*   *Pr* 1:21; 8:3
watching daily at my *g.*   8:34
the wicked at the *g.* of the.   14:19
husband is known in the *g.* 31:23
works praise her in the *g.*   31
our *g.* are all manner. *S of S* 7:13*
and her *g.* shall lament. *Isa* 3:26
they may go into the *g.* of the. 13:2
open ye the *g.* that righteous. 26:2
I shall go to the *g.* of the.   38:10
before him the two leaved *g.* 45:1*
I will break in pieces the *g.* of.   2*
go through, go through the *g.* 62:10
hear the word, all ye that enter in at
  the *g.*   *Jer* 7:2; 17:20; 22:2
Judah mourneth, and the *g.*   14:2
fan them with a fan in the *g.* of. 15:7
go and stand in all the *g.* of. 17:19
on the sabbath by the *g.*   21, 24
there enter into the *g.*   25; 22:4
I will kindle a fire in the *g.* of.   27
and cast forth beyond the *g.* 22:19
Zion's *g.* are desolate. *Lam* 1:4
her *g.* are sunk into the ground. 2:9
should have entered the *g.*   4:12
of sword against their *g.* *Ezek* 21:15
battering rams against the *g.*   22
she is broken that was the *g.* of. 26:2
at the east side three *g.* one. 48:32
foreigners entered his *g.*   *Ob* 11
the *g.* of the rivers shall. *Nah* 2:6
the *g.* of thy land shall be set.   3:13
truth and peace in your *g.* *Zech* 8:16
g. of hell shall not prevail. *Mat* 16:18
and they watched the *g.* *Acts* 9:24
priests brought oxen to the *g.* 14:13
the city had twelve *g.* at *g.* *Rev* 21:12
three *g.* on the north three *g.*   13
the twelve *g.* were twelve pearls. 21
the *g.* of it shall not be shut at.   25
  see **bars, death**

thy **gates**
thy stranger within *thy g.* *Ex* 20:10
  Deut 5:14
thou shalt write them on *thy g.*
  Deut 6:9; 11:20
eat flesh in *thy g.*   12:15, 21
mayest not eat within *thy g.* the. 17
thou and Levite in *thy g.*   18
the stranger that is in *thy g.* 14:21
Levite within *thy g.* thou shalt. 27
up the tithe within *thy g.*   28
the widow within *thy g.* shall. 29
poor man within any of *thy g.* 15:7
eat the firstling within *thy g.*   22
the passover within *thy g.*   16:5
Levite in *thy g.*   11, 14; 26:12
shalt thou make in all *thy g.* 16:18
that man or woman to *thy g.* 17:5
Levite come from any of *thy g.* 18:6
escaped dwell in one of *thy g.* 23:16
not oppress within *thy g.* 24:14
besiege thee in all *thy g.* 28:52
distress thee in all *thy g.*   55
gather the people within *thy g.* 31:12
stand within *thy g.* O.   *Ps* 122:2
I will make *thy g.* of. *Isa* 54:12
therefore *thy g.* shall be open. 60:11
thy walls salvation, and *thy g.*   18
enter *thy g.* as men. *Ezek* 26:10

Gath
ark be carried about to G. *1 Sam* 5:8
golden emerods, for G. one.   6:17
that David was fled to G.   27:4
tell it not in G. publish. *2 Sam* 1:20
giant in G. and fell by the hand of
  David and.   21:22; *1 Chr* 20:8
Shimei ran to G.   *1 Ki* 2:39
Shimei went to G. to seek.   40
and fought against G.   *2 Ki* 12:17
drove away inhabitants of G.
  1 Chr 8:13
David took G. from the.   18:1
brake down wall of G. *2 Chr* 26:6
then go down to G. of. *Amos* 6:2
declare ye it not at G.   *Mi* 1:10

gather
Jacob said, *g.* stones, and. *Gen* 31:46
let them *g.* all the food of.   41:35
let them go and *g.* straw. *Ex* 5:7
g. stubble.   12
g. thy cattle.   9:19*
shall *g.* a certain rate.   16:4
g. twice as much.   5
six days *g.* it.   26
sow thy land and *g.* 23:10; *Lev* 25:3
not *g.* the gleanings. *Lev* 19:9; 23:22
thou shalt not *g.* every grape of. 10
nor *g.* grapes of the vine. 25:5, 11
we shall not sow, nor *g.* in our. 20
trumpet, then princes *g.* *Num* 10:4
g. seventy men of the elders. 11:16
a man that is clean shall *g.*   19:9
rain that thou mayest *g.* *Deut* 11:14
thou shalt *g.* all the spoil of. 13:16
vineyard and not *g.* grapes. 28:30, 39
carry much seed out, and *g.* but. 38
g. thee from all nations.   30:3
  Ezek 36:24
into the field to *g.* herbs. *2 Ki* 4:39
g. thee to thy   22:20; *2 Chr* 34:28
Levites to *g.*   *1 Chr* 13:2
g. money to repair.   *2 Chr* 24:5
yet will I *g.* them from. *Neh* 1:9
some appointed to *g.* for the. 12:44
they *g.* the vintage of the. *Job* 24:6*
if he *g.* to himself his spirit. 34:14
will he bring seed, and *g.* it ? 39:12
g. not my soul with sinners. *Ps* 26:9
and knoweth not who shall *g.* 39:6
that thou givest them they *g.* 104:28
save us, and *g.* us from   106:47
shall *g.* for him that will. *Pr* 28:8
to sinner travail, to *g.* *Eccl* 2:26
gone down to *g.* lilies. *S of S* 6:2
there the owl *g.* under. *Isa* 34:15
he shall *g.* the lambs with. 40:11
fear not, I will *g.* thee from. 43:5
great mercies will I *g.* thee. 54:7
yet will I *g.* others to him. 56:8
cast up the highway, *g.* out. 62:10
I will *g.* all nations and. 66:18
g. to flee.   *Jer* 6:1*
the children *g.* wood.   7:18
none shall *g.* them.   9:22
g. up thy wares.   10:17
I will *g.* the remnant of my. 23:3
I will *g.* you from all the. 29:14
I will *g.* them from coasts of. 31:8
  32:37; *Ezek* 20:34, 41; 34:13
he that scattered Israel will *g.*
  Jer 31:10
g. ye wine, and summer. 40:10
and none shall *g.* up him that. 49:5
I will even *g.* you from. *Ezek* 11:17
I will *g.* all thy lovers against. 16:37
I will *g.* you into the midst of. 22:19
as they *g.* silver, so will I *g.* 20, 21
g. the pieces.   24:4
I will *g.* the Egyptians. 29:13
I will *g.* them on every. 37:21; 39:17
among nations, I will *g.* *Hos* 8:10
Egypt shall *g.* them up.   9:6
g. the elders and the. *Joel* 1:14
much pained, all faces shall *g.* 2:6*
g. the people, *g.* the children.   16
I will *g.* all nations, and bring. 3:2
will surely *g.* remnant. *Mi* 2:12
g. her that was driven out.   4:6
  Zeph 3:19
he shall *g.* them as sheaves into. 12
g. thyself in troops, O daughter. 5:1
the faces of them all *g.* *Nah* 2:10*

they shall *g*. captivity as. *Hab* 1:9
they catch them, and *g*. them in. 15
my determination is to *g*. *Zeph* 3:8
I will *g*. them that are sorrowful. 18
even in the time that I *g*. you. 20
I will hiss for them and *g*. *Zech* 10:8
I will *g*. them out of Assyria. 10
I will *g*. all nations against. 14:2
g. his wheat into his garner.
　　　　　Mat 3:12; *Luke* 3:17
they sow not, nor do they *g*. *Mat* 6:26
do men *g*. grapes ? 7:16; *Luke* 6:44
wilt that we go and *g*.? *Mat* 13:28
he said, nay, lest while ye *g*. up. 29
burn tares, but *g*. the wheat into. 30
shall *g*. out of his kingdom all. 41
and that *g*. where I have not. 25:26
as a hen doth *g*. her. *Luke* 13:34
g. up the fragments that. *John* 6:12
men *g*. them and cast them. 15:6
•*g*. the clusters of vine. *Rev* 14:18
g. them to the battle of that. 16:14
gather *together*
few they shall *g*. *tog*. *Gen* 34:30
g. yourselves *tog*. ye sons. 49:1, 2*
g. the elders of Israel *tog*. *Ex* 3:16
g. congregation of Israel *tog*.
　　　　　Lev 8:3*; *Num* 8:9*
g. thou the assembly *tog*. *Num* 20:8*
g. the people *tog*. 21:16; *Deut* 4:10*
　　　　　　　　　31:12*
g. the rest *tog*. and. 2 *Sam* 12:28
O God, and *g*. us *tog*. 1 *Chr* 16:35
David commanded to *g*. *tog*. 22:2
in my heart to *g*. *tog*. *Neh* 7:5
may *g*. *tog*. all the fair. *Esth* 2:3
g. *tog*. the Jews present in. 4:16
if he *g*. *tog*. who can ? *Job* 11:10*
g. my saints *tog*. unto me. *Ps* 50:5
they *g*. themselves *tog*. to. 56:6
they *g*. *together* against the. 94:21
they *g*. themselves *tog*. 104:22*
time to *g*. stones *tog*. *Eccl* 3:5
shall *g*. *tog*. the dispersed. *Isa* 11:12
these *g*. *tog*. and. 49:18; 60:4
they shall surely *g*. *tog*. but. 54:15
the trumpet, cry, *g*. *tog*. *Jer* 4:5*
g. ye *tog*. and come against. 49:14
king sent to *g*. *tog*. *Dan* 3:2
g. yourselves *tog*. round. *Joel* 3:11
g. *tog*. yea, *g*. *tog*. O. *Zeph* 2:1
g. *tog*. first the tares. *Mat* 13:30
they shall *g*. *tog*. his elect. 24:31
　　　　　　　　　Mark 13:27
he should *g*. *tog*. in one. *John* 11:52
　　　　　　　　　Eph 1:10*
g. *tog*. to the supper of. *Rev* 19:17
g. Gog and Magog *tog*. to. 20:8
gathered
Abraham died and was *g*. *Gen* 25:8
Ishmael was *g*. 17
Isaac was *g*. to people. 35:29
Jacob was *g*. to his people. 49:29, 33
and they *g*. some more. *Ex* 16:17
that *g*. much, he that *g*. little. 18
　　　　　　　　　2 *Cor* 8:15
they *g*. it every morning, *Ex* 16:21
hast *g*. in thy labours. 23:16
ye have *g*. in the fruits. *Lev* 23:39
the people *g*. quails. *Num* 11:32
g. sticks. 15:32
g. congregation against. 16:19*, 42*
Aaron *g*. the people. 20:24, 26
Moses *g*. to his people. 27:13
　　　　　31:2; *Deut* 32:50
kings *g*. their meat. *Judg* 1:7
that generation was *g*. to. 2:10
and Abiezer was *g*. after. 6:34
there were *g*. vain men to. 11:3
they *g*. all the lords of. 1 *Sam* 5:8
every one that was in distress *g*. 22:2
which cannot be *g*. up. 2 *Sam* 14:14
they *g*. all able to put. 2 *Ki* 3:21
Josiah be *g*. to grave in peace. 22:20
　　　　　　　　　2 *Chr* 34:28
all my servants were *g*. *Neh* 5:16
down, but shall not be *g*. *Job* 27:19
the mighty are *g*. against. *Ps* 59:3
and he *g*. them out of lands. 107:3
of the mountains are *g*. *Pr* 27:25
who hath *g*. the winds in his ? 30:4
I *g*. me also silver. *Eccl* 2:8
I have *g*. my myrrh with. *S of S* 5:1

he fenced it, and *g*. out. *Isa* 5:2
one gathereth eggs, have I *g*. 10:14
ye shall be *g*. one by one. 27:12
vultures be *g*. 34:15
his Spirit *g*. them. 16
though Israel be not *g*. yet. 49:5
besides those that are *g*. 56:8
but they that have *g*. it shall. 62:9*
and all nations shall be *g*. 3:17
they shall not be *g*. 8:2; 25:33
all people *g*. against Jeremiah. 26:9
all the Jews *g*. to thee should. 40:15
I shall have *g*. house. *Ezek* 28:25
be brought together nor *g*. 29:5
hast thou *g*. thy company to ? 38:13*
have *g*. them out of their. 39:27
but I have *g*. them to their own. 28
the people shall be *g*. *Hos* 10:10
I am as when they *g*. *Mi* 7:1
tares are *g*. and burnt. *Mat* 13:40
a net cast into the sea, and *g*. of. 47
before him shall be *g*. all. 25:32
and *g*. to him the whole band. 27:27
g. chief priests a council. *John* 11:47
g. a company, set city. *Acts* 17:5
when Paul had *g*. a bundle of. 28:3
the angel *g*. the vine of. *Rev* 14:19
gathered *together*
they *g*. them *tog*. upon. *Ex* 8:14
congregation to be *g*. *tog*. *Num* 10:7
fish of the sea be *g*. *tog*.? 11:22
congregation was *g*. *tog*. *Judg* 20:1*
　　　11; *Ezra* 3:1; *Neh* 8:1
Judah *g*. *tog*. to ask. 2 *Chr* 20:4
they *g*. themselves *tog*. *Job* 16:10
under nettles were they *g*. 30:7
abjects *g*. themselves *tog*. *Ps* 35:15
of the people are *g*. *tog*. 47:9
when people are *g*. *tog*. to. 102:22
are they *g*. *tog*. for war. 140:2
children of Judah be *g*. *tog*. *Hos* 1:11
nations are *g*. *tog*. against. *Mi* 4:11*
all people be *g*. *tog*. *Zech* 12:3
two or three are *g*. *tog*. *Mat* 18:20
I have *g*. thy children *tog*., as a hen.
　　　　　23:37; *Luke* 13:34
there will eagles be *g*. *tog*.
　　　　　Mat 24:28; *Luke* 17:37
all the city was *g*. *tog*. *Mark* 1:33
younger son *g*. all *tog*. *Luke* 15:13
they found the eleven *g*. *tog*. 24:33
rulers were *g*. *tog*. *Acts* 4:26
where many were *g*. *tog*. 12:12
had *g*. the church *tog*. 14:27
when ye are *g*. *tog*. and. 1 *Cor* 5:4
g. *tog*. into a place called. *Rev* 16:16
beast and his army *g*. *tog*. 19:19
gatherer, -s
thy hand as a grape *g*. *Jer* 6:9
grape *g*. come to thee. 49:9; *Ob* 5
I was a *g*. of sycamore. *Amos* 7:14*
gatherest
when thou *g*. the grapes. *Deut* 24:21
gathereth
that *g*. the ashes shall. *Num* 19:10
he *g*. the waters of sea. *Ps* 33:7
his heart *g*. iniquity to itself. 41:6
he *g*. the outcasts. 147:2; *Isa* 56:8
the ant *g*. her food in the. *Pr* 6:8
he that *g*. in summer is a wise. 10:5
but he that *g*. by labour shall. 13:11
one *g*. eggs that are left. *Isa* 10:14
as when the harvestman *g*. 17:5*
scattered, and no man *g*. *Nah* 3:18
but *g*. to him all nations. *Hab* 2:5
he that *g*. not scattereth. *Mat* 12:30
　　　　　　　　　Luke 11:23
as a hen *g*. her chickens. *Mat* 23:37
he that reapeth *g*. fruit. *John* 4:36
gathering
to him shall the *g*. of. *Gen* 49:10*
they that found him *g*. *Num* 15:33
was there *g*. sticks. 1 *Ki* 17:10
were three days in *g*. 2 *Chr* 20:25*
vintage shall fail, the *g*. *Isa* 32:10*
your spoil like the *g*. of the. 33:4
g. where thou hast not. *Mat* 25:24
g. that the Lord had. *Acts* 16:10*
and by our *g*. together. 2 *Thes* 2:1
gatherings
that there be no *g*. 1 *Cor* 16:2*

gave
Adam *g*. names to all. *Gen* 2:20
the woman *g*. me of the tree. 3:12
he *g*. him tithes. 14:20; *Heb* 7:2, 4
Abraham *g*. all that he. *Gen* 25:5
land which God *g*. 28:4; 35:12
Lord *g*. the people favour. *Ex* 11:3
　　　　　　　　　12:36
the cloud *g*. light by night to. 14:20
took of Spirit, and *g*. *Num* 11:25
I *g*. my daughter to. *Deut* 22:16
they *g*. him the city. *Josh* 19:50
the Lord *g*. to Israel all the. 21:43
the Lord *g*. them rest. 44
　　　　　2 *Chr* 15:15; 20:30
I drave them out, and *g*. *Judg* 6:9
Lord *g*. her conception. *Ruth* 4:13
God *g*. to Saul another. 1 *Sam* 10:9
I *g*. thee thy master's. 2 *Sam* 12:8
Lord *g*. Solomon. 1 *Ki* 4:29; 5:12
and the Lord *g*. Israel. 2 *Ki* 13:5
God *g*. to Heman. 1 *Chr* 25:5
and God *g*. Hezekiah. 2 *Chr* 32:24
read book, *g*. the sense. *Neh* 8:8
Lord *g*. and the Lord. *Job* 1:21
God *g*. Job twice as much as. 42:10
and the Highest *g*. his. *Ps* 18:13
the Lord *g*. the word, great. 68:11
g. me also gall, they *g*. me. 69:21
for he *g*. them their. 78:29; 106:15
return to God that *g*. it. *Eccl* 12:7
who *g*. Jacob for a spoil ? *Isa* 42:24
I *g*. Egypt for thy ransom. 43:3
I *g*. my back to the smiters. 50:6
my meat also which I *g*. *Ezek* 16:19
I *g*. them my statutes. 20:11
moreover also, I *g*. them my. 12
I *g*. them also statutes that were. 25
God *g*. these four children. *Dan* 1:17
Daniel prayed and *g*. thanks. 6:10
she did not know that I *g*. *Hos* 2:8
g. thee a king in mine anger. 13:11
ye *g*. the Nazarites wine. *Amos* 2:12
I *g*. my covenant to Levi. *Mal* 2:5
Jesus *g*. them power against unclean.
　　　　　Mat 10:1; *Mark* 6:7; *Luke* 9:1
he brake and *g*. loaves. *Mat* 14:19
　　　15:36; 26:16; *Mark* 6:41; 8:6
　　　14:22; *Luke* 9:16; 22:19
who *g*. thee authority ? *Mat* 21:23
　　　　　Mark 11:28; *Luke* 20:2
ye *g*. me meat, ye *g*. me. *Mat* 25:35
ye *g*. me no meat, and ye *g*. me. 42
husks, and no man *g*. *Luke* 15:16
to them *g*. he power to. *John* 1:12
God so loved world that he *g*. 3:16
he *g*. them bread from heaven. 6:31
my Father who *g*. them me. 10:29
Father *g*. me commandment. 31
to speak as Spirit *g*. them. *Acts* 2:4
and he *g*. them no inheritance. 7:5
God *g*. Joseph favour and. 10
Cornelius *g*. much alms to the. 10:2
as God *g*. them the like gift. 11:17
smote him, because he *g*. not. 12:23
afterward God *g*. them Saul. 13:21
he did good, and *g*. us rain. 14:17
to whom we *g*. no such. 15:24
when put to death, I *g*. my. 26:10
God *g*. them over to a. *Rom* 2:28
even as the Lord *g*. to. 1 *Cor* 3:5
Apollos watered, but God *g*. the. 6
but first *g*. their own. 2 *Cor* 8:5
who *g*. himself. *Gal* 1:4; *Tit* 2:14
who loved me, and *g*. *Gal* 2:20
but God *g*. it to Abraham by. 3:18
and *g*. him to be head. *Eph* 1:22
he led captivity captive and *g*. 4:8
and he *g*. some apostles; some. 11
Christ loved the church, and *g*. 5:25
commandment we *g*. 1 *Thes* 4:2
who *g*. himself a ransom. 1 *Tim* 2:6
corrected us, we *g*. them. *Heb* 12:9
and the heavens *g*. rain. *Jas* 5:18
love one another, as he *g*. us.
　　　　　　　　　1 *John* 3:23
believeth not the record God *g*. 5:10
Jesus Christ which God *g*. *Rev* 1:1
g. her space to repent of her. 2:21
the dragon *g*. him his power. 13:2, 4
gave up
Abraham *g*. up ghost. *Gen* 25:8
Isaac *g*. up the ghost. 35:29

Joab *g. up* the sum of. *2 Sam* 24:9
g. them *up* to desolation. *2 Chr* 30:7
he *g. up* their cattle. *Ps* 78:48
I *g.* them *up* to their own. 81:12*
my elders *g. up* ghost. *Lam* 1:19
a loud voice, and *g. up. Mark* 15:37
    39; *Luke* 23:46; *John* 19:30
Ananias *g. up* the ghost. *Acts* 5:5
God *g.* them *up* to worship. 7:42
God also *g.* them *up* to. *Rom* 1:24
for this cause God *g.* them *up* to. 26
the sea *g. up* the dead. *Rev* 20:13

gavest
the woman whom thou *g. Gen* 3:12
land which thou *g. 1 Ki* 8:34, 40, 48
    2 Chr 6:25, 31, 38; *Neh* 9:35
thou *g.* him the name of. *Neh* 9:7
thou *g.* them right judgements. 13
g. them bread from heaven. 15
g. also thy good Spirit, *g.* water. 20
g. them kingdoms and nations. 22
thou *g.* them saviours who saved. 27
g. the goodly wings to? *Job* 39:13*
life of thee; thou *g.* it him. *Ps* 21:4
thou *g.* him to be meat to. 74:14
thou *g.* me no water for. *Luke* 7:44
g. me no kiss, but this woman. 45
yet thou never *g.* me a kid, to. 15:29
finished work thou *g. John* 17:4
men whom thou *g.* me out of world,
    thine they were, and thou *g.* 6
the words which thou *g.* me. 8
those that thou *g.* me I have kept. 12
the glory which thou *g.* me. 22
of them whom thou *g.* me. 18:9

gay
that weareth *g.* clothing. *Jas* 2:3*

Gaza
Samson went to G. and. *Judg* 16:1
brought Samson down to G. 21
Pharaoh smote G. *Jer* 47:1
baldness is come upon G. 5
three transgressions of G. *Amos* 1:6
will send a fire on the wall of G. 7
G. shall be forsaken. *Zeph* 2:4
G. shall see it, king shall perish from
    G. *Zech* 9:5
from Jerusalem to G. *Acts* 8:26

gaze
through unto the Lord to *g. Ex* 19:21

gazing
I will set thee as a *g.*-stock. *Nah* 3:6
why stand ye *g.* up into? *Acts* 1:11
ye were made a *g.*-stock. *Heb* 10:33

Geba
G. with her suburbs. *Josh* 21:17
    1 Chr 6:60
king Asa built G. *1 Ki* 15:22
    2 Chr 16:6
Josiah defiled the high places from
    G. *2 Ki* 23:8
taken up lodging at G. *Isa* 10:29
be as a plain from G. *Zech* 14:10

Gebal
G. and Ammon are. *Ps* 83:7
the ancients of G. were. *Ezek* 27:9

Gebim
inhabitants of G. gather. *Isa* 10:31

Gedaliah
and G. sware to them. *2 Ki* 25:24
    Jer 40:9
Jeduthun, G. and Zeri. *1 Chr* 25:3
second lot came forth to G. 9
Jarib and G. had taken. *Ezra* 10:18
G. the son of Pashur. *Jer* 38:1
G. son of Ahikam believed not. 40:14
Ishmael smote G. with sword. 41:2
took all that were left with G. 43:6
son of Cushi, son of G. *Zeph* 1:1
    see **Ahikam**

Gehazi
Elisha said to G. *2 Ki* 4:12, 36
but G. came near to thrust. 27
G. followed after Naaman. 5:21
to him, Whence comest thou, G.? 25
the king talked with G. servant. 8:4

Gemariah
Jeremiah sent by G. *Jer* 29:3
G. made intercession to not. 36:25

gender
shalt not let cattle *g. Lev* 19:19
knowing that they do *g. 2 Tim* 2:23

gendereth
their bull *g.* and faileth not. *Job* 21:10
frost of heaven, who hath *g.*? 38:29
which *g.* to bondage. *Gal* 4:24

genealogies
Comes from the Greek word
Genealogia, which signifies a his-
tory of the descent of an individual
or family from an ancestor. The
Jews were very exact in their gene-
alogies, partly in order that family
honours and family property should
descend properly; partly to keep
the line wherein the Messiah was to
come.
Even the Babylonian Exile did not
prevent the keeping of these, as a
rule, for we find that some, who
claimed Jewish descent but could
not produce their genealogy, were
not allowed part in the Return as
were the others.
were reckoned by *g. 1 Chr* 9:1
Shemaiah concerning *g. 2 Chr* 12:15
to all reckoned by *g.* 31:9
fables and endless *g. 1 Tim* 1:4
avoid foolish questions, *g. Tit* 3:9

genealogy
and the *g.* is not to be. *1 Chr* 5:1
these sought their *g. Ezra* 2:62
    Neh 7:64
the *g.* of them that went. *Ezra* 8:1
I found a register of *g. Neh* 7:5

general
g. of the king's army. *1 Chr* 27:34*
to *g.* assembly and. *Heb* 12:23

generally
I counsel that Israel be *g.* gathered.
    2 Sam 17:11*
lamentation *g.* on house. *Jer* 48:38

generation
[1] A begetting or producing, or the
person or thing produced, Gen 2:4;
5:1. *[2] Each succession of persons*
from a common ancestor, Gen
50:23; Deut 23:2. *[3] An age or*
period, not meaning as now the
average lifetime of man, but the
average period of the activity of
any body of contemporaries, Ex
1:6; Num 32:13; Judg 2:10.
seen righteous in this *g. Gen* 7:1
Joseph died, and all that *g. Ex* 1:6
war with Amalek from *g.* to *g.* 17:16
till that *g.* was consumed.
    Num 32:13; *Deut* 2:14
not one of this evil *g. Deut* 1:35
enter even to his tenth *g.* 23:2
an Ammonite to tenth *g.* shall not. 3
Edomite and Egyptian in third *g.* 8
so that the *g.* to come shall. 29:22
perverse and crooked *g.* 32:5, 20
g. were gathered to their fathers. and
    there arose another *g. Judg* 2:10
remembered in every *g. Esth* 9:28
preserve them from this *g. Ps* 12:7
for God is in the *g.* of the. 14:5
to the Lord for a *g.* 22:30
this is the *g.* of them that. 24:6
that ye may tell it to the *g.* 48:13
he shall go to the *g.* of his. 49:19
shewed thy strength to this *g.* 71:18
I should offend against the *g.* 73:15
shewing to the *g.* to come the. 78:4
that the *g.* to come might know. 6
a stubborn and rebellious *g.* 8
forty years grieved with this *g.*
    95:10; *Heb* 3:10
this shall be written for *g.* 102:18
in *g.* following let their. 109:13
the *g.* of the upright shall be. 112:2
one *g.* shall praise thy works. 145:4
crown endure to every *g.*? *Pr* 27:24
there is a *g.* that curseth. 30:11
there is a *g.* that are pure in. 12
a *g.* lofty. 13
a *g.* whose teeth are swords. 14
g. passeth away, another *g. Eccl* 1:4

not dwelt in from *g.* to *g. Isa* 13:20
    Jer 50:39
from *g.* to *g.* it shall lie. *Isa* 34:10
from *g.* to *g.* they shall dwell. 17
salvation shall be from *g.* to *g.* 51:8
who declare his *g.*? 53:8; *Acts* 8:33
O *g.* see ye the word of. *Jer* 2:31
the Lord hath rejected *g.* 7:29
remains from *g.* to *g. Lam* 5:19
and his dominion is from *g.* to *g.*
    Dan 4:3, 34
children tell another *g. Joel* 1:3
shall dwell from *g.* to *g.* 3:20
the *g.* of Jesus Christ. *Mat* 1:1
O *g.* of vipers. 3:7*; 12:34*; 23:33*
    Luke 3:7*
whereto shall I liken this *g.*?
    Mat 11:16; *Luke* 7:31
evil and adulterous *g. Mat* 12:39
    16:4; *Mark* 8:12; *Luke* 11:29
shall rise in judgement with this *g.*
    Mat 12:41; *Luke* 11:32
queen of the south rise up with *g.*
    Mat 12:42; *Luke* 11:31
also to this wicked *g. Mat* 12:45
O perverse *g.* 17:17; *Mark* 9:19
    Luke 9:41
shall come on this *g. Mat* 23:36
this *g.* shall not pass. 24:34
    Mark 13:30; *Luke* 21:32
of me in this sinful *g. Mark* 8:38
on them from *g.* to *g. Luke* 1:50
Son of man be to this *g.* 11:30
prophets required of this *g.* 50, 51
children of this world in their *g.* 16:8
must be rejected of this *g.* 17:25
from this untoward *g. Acts* 2:40
he had served his own *g.* 13:36
ye are a chosen *g.* a. *1 Pet* 2:9*
    see **fourth**

generations
g. of the heavens and. *Gen* 2:4
the *g.* of Adam. 5:1
the *g.* of Noah. 6:9; 10:1
just man and perfect in his *g.* 6:9
I make for perpetual *g.* 9:12
these are the *g.* of Shem. 11:10
g. of Terah.
me and thy seed in their *g.* 17:7
thy seed after thee in their *g.* 9
every man child in your *g.* must. 12
g. of Ishmael. 25:12, 13; *1 Chr* 1:29
these the *g.* of Isaac. *Gen* 25:19
the *g.* of Esau. 36:1
g. of Jacob, Joseph. 37:2
memorial unto all *g. Ex* 3:15
of Levi according to their *g.* 6:16
to Lord throughout your *g.* 12:14
observe this day in your *g.* 17
observed by Israel in their *g.*
    16:32, 33
statute for ever to their *g.* 27:21
    30:21; *Lev* 3:17; 6:18; 7:36
    10:9; 17:7; 23:14, 21, 31, 41
throughout your *g. Ex* 29:42
burn incense throughout your *g.* 30:8
oil throughout your *g.* 31
a sign throughout your *g.* 31:13, 16
priesthood through their *g.* 40:15
of thy seed in their *g. Lev* 21:17
your *g.* may know that I. 23:43
for ever in *g.* 24:3; *Num* 10:8
    18:23
covenant to a thousand *g. Deut* 7:9
consider the years of many *g.* 32:7
between you and our *g. Josh* 22:27
when they should say to our *g.* 28
g. of Israel might teach. *Judg* 3:2
now these are the *g.* of. *Ruth* 4:18
word which he commanded to a
    thousand *g. 1 Chr* 16:15; *Ps* 105:8
sons' sons, even four *g. Job* 42:16
his heart to all *g. Ps* 33:11
to be remembered in all *g.* 45:17
places continue to all *g.* 49:11
the king's years as many *g.* 61:6
fear thee throughout all *g.* 72:5
shew forth thy praise to all *g.* 79:13
out thine anger to all *g.*? 85:5
known thy faithfulness to all *g.* 89:1
build up thy throne to all *g.* 4
our dwelling place in all *g.* 90:1
his truth endureth to all *g.* 100:5

remembrance unto all *g. Ps* 102:12
thy years are throughout all *g.* 24
him for righteousness to all *g.* 106:31
thy faithfulness is unto all *g.* 119:90
memorial throughout all *g.* 135:13
dominion throughout all *g.* 145:13
O Zion, shall reign to all *g. Isa* 41:4
calling the *g.* from the. *Isa* 41:4
O arm of the Lord as in the *g.* 51:9
up the foundations of many *g.* 58:12
make thee a joy of many *g.* 60:15
the desolations of many *g.* 61:4
to the years of many *g. Joel* 2:2
g. from Abraham to David are 14 *g.*
Mat 1:17
behold, all *g.* shall call. *Luke* 1:48
been hid from ages and *g. Col* 1:26

Gennesaret
land of *G. Mat* 14:34; *Mark* 6:53
Jesus stood by lake of *G. Luke* 5:1

Gentile
The Hebrews call the Gentiles by the general name of Goiim, which signifies the nations that have not received the faith, or law of God. All who are not Jews and circumcised, are comprised under the word Goiim. Those who were converted, and embraced Judaism, they called Proselytes.

The apostle Paul generally includes all Gentiles under the name of Greeks, Rom 1:16.

The old prophets declared in a very particular manner the calling of the Gentiles. Jacob foretold, that when Shiloh, or the Messiah should come, to him should the gathering of the people be ; that is, the Gentiles should yield obedience to Christ, and acknowledge him for their Lord and Saviour.

and also of the *g. Rom* 2:9*, 10*

Gentiles
(The Revisions very often substitute for this the word nations)
by these the isles of the *g. Gen* 10:5
dwelt in Harosheth of *g. Judg* 4:2
Jesse, to it shall the *g. Isa* 11:10
judgement to the *g.* 42:1; *Mat* 12:18
light to *g. Isa* 42:6; 49:6
Luke 2:32; *Acts* 13:47
will lift up mine hand to *g. Isa* 49:22
thy seed shall inherit the *g.* 54:3
and the *g.* shall come to thy. 60:3
the forces of the *g.* shall come. 5, 11
also suck the milk of the *g.* 16
ye shall eat the riches of the *g.* 61:6
seed shall be known among the *g.* 9
and the *g.* shall see thy. 62:2
the glory of the *g.* like a. 66:12
declare my glory among the *g.* 19
destroyer of the *g.* is on. *Jer* 4:7
any of the vanities of the *g.?* 14:22*
the *g.* shall come to thee from. 16:19
came to Jeremiah against *g.* 46:1
princes are among the *g. Ezek* 4:13
defiled bread among *g. Ezek* 4:13
shall they be among the *g. Hos* 8:8
proclaim ye this among *g. Joel* 3:9
Jacob shall be among the *g. Mi* 5:8
cast out the horns of *g. Zech* 1:21
be great among the *g. Mal* 1:11
Jordan, Galilee of the *g. Mat* 4:15
these things do the *g.* seek. 6:32
go not into the way of the *g.* 10:5
testimony against them and the *g.* 18
his name shall the *g.* trust. 12:21
deliver him to the *g.* to mock. 20:19
Mark 10:33; *Luke* 18:32
of *g.* exercise dominion. *Mat* 20:25
Luke 22:25
g., until the times of *g. Luke* 21:24
among *g.* and teach *g. John* 7:35
Pilate with *g.* were. *Acts* 4:27
into the possession of the *g.* 7:45
to bear my name before the *g.* 9:15
on the *g.* also was poured out. 10:45
heard that the *g.* received. 11:1
God to *g.* granted repentance ? 18
g. besought these words. 13:42
Barnabas said, lo, we turn to *g.* 46
when the *g.* heard this, they. 48

Jews stirred up the *g. Acts* 14:2*
assault made both of Jews and *g.* 5
opened the door of faith to the. 27
conversion of the *g.* great joy. 15:3
the *g.* by my mouth should hear. 7
God had wrought among the *g.* 12
how God at first did visit *g.* 14
all the *g.* on whom my name. 17
them, which from among the *g.* 19
greeting to the brethren of the *g.* 23
henceforth I will go to the *g.* 18:6
Paul into the hands of the *g.* 21:11
God wrought among the *g.* by. 19
teachest the Jews among *g.* to. 21
as touching the *g.* which believe. 25
send thee far hence to the *g.* 22:21
thee from the people and *g.* 26:17
shewing to the *g.* that they. 20
Christ should shew light to the *g.* 23
salvation of God is sent to *g.* 28:28
fruit, as among other *g. Rom* 1:13
when the *g.* which have not. 2:14
God is blasphemed among the *g.* 24
have proved both Jews and *g.* 3:9
also of the *g.?* yes, of the *g.* 29
Jews only, but also of the *g.* 9:24
g. which followed not after. 30
salvation is come to the *g.* 11:11
of them the riches of the *g.* 12
you *g.* as the apostle of the *g.* 13
till the fulness of the *g.* be come. 25
g. might glorify God . . . I will confess
to thee among the *g.* 15:9
he saith, rejoice, ye *g.* with his. 10
praise Lord, all ye *g.* and laud him. 11
reign over the *g.* in him shall *g.* 12
minister of Jesus Christ to the *g.*
that the offering up of the *g.* 16
to make the *g.* obedient by word. 18
for if the *g.* have been made. 27
but all the churches of the *g.* 16:4
as named among the *g. I Cor* 5:1
things which the *g.* sacrifice. 10:20
offence, neither to Jews nor *g.* 32
ye know ye were *g.* carried. 12:2
whether we be Jews or *g.* 13
I preach among the *g. Gal* 2:2
mighty in me towards the *g.* 8
he did eat with the *g.* 12
manner of *g.,* why compellest *g.?* 14
Jews, and not sinners of the *g.* 15
Abraham might come on the *g.* 3:14
ye being in time past *g.* in. *Eph* 2:11
of Jesus Christ for you *g.* 3:1
that *g.* should be fellowheirs of. 6
among the *g.* the unsearchable. 8
henceforth walk not as other *g.* 4:17
this mystery among the *g. Col* 1:27
to speak to the *g. 1 Thes* 2:16
lust of concupiscence, as the *g.* 4:5
a teacher of the *g. 1 Tim* 2:7
preached to the *g.* believed on. 3:16
apostle and teacher of *g. 2 Tim* 1:11
and that all the *g.* might hear. 4:17
honest among the *g. 1 Pet* 2:12
wrought the will of the *g.* 4:3
taking nothing of the *g. 3 John* 7
court is given to the *g. Rev* 11:2

gentle
we were *g.* among you. *1 Thes* 2:7
of the Lord must be *g. 2 Tim* 2:24
g. shewing all meekness. *Tit* 3:2
above is pure and *g. Jas* 3:17
only to the good and *g. 1 Pet* 2:18

gentleness
g. hath made me. *2 Sam* 22:36
Ps 18:35
I beseech you by the *g. 2 Cor* 10:1
the fruit of the Spirit is *g. Gal* 5:22*

gently
deal *g.* with the young. *2 Sam* 18:5
he will *g.* lead those with. *Isa* 4:11

Gera
Ehud the son of *G. Judg* 3:15
son of *G. 2 Sam* 16:5; 19:16, 18
1 Ki 2:8

gerahs
a shekel is twenty *g. Ex* 30:13
Lev 27:25; *Num* 3:47; 18:16
Ezek 45:12

Gerar
Abraham sojourned in *G. Gen* 20:1
Abimelech king of *G.* 2

Isaac dwelt in *G. Gen* 26:6
the herdmen of *G.* 20

Gergesenes
into the country of the *G. Mat* 8:28

Gerizim
blessing on mount *G. Deut* 11:29
these shall stand on mount *G.* 27:12
over against mount *G. Josh* 8:33
stood on top of mount *G. Judg* 9:7

Gershom, Gershon
sons of Levi, *G.* Kohath. *Gen* 46:11
Ex 6:16; *Num* 3:17; *I Chr* 6:1, 16
23:6
of Moses' son was *G. Ex* 2:22
of *G.* Libni, Shimei. 6:17; *Num* 3:18
of *G.* was the family of. *Num* 3:21
charge of the sons of *G.* 25
sum of the sons of *G.* 4:22, 38
service of the sons of *G.* 28
four oxen gave to sons of *G.* 7:7
the sons of *G.* bearing the. 10:17
children of *G.* had. *Josh* 21:6, 27
Jonathan the son of *G. Judg* 18:30
of the sons of Phinehas, *G. Ezra* 8:2

Geshur
fled and went to *G. 2 Sam* 13:37, 38
Joab went to *G.* 14:23
why I come from *G.* 32
thy servant vowed a vow at *G.* 15:8
Jair took *G.* and Aram. *1 Chr* 2:23

Geshurites
the *G.* dwell among the. *Josh* 13:13
his men invaded the *G. 1 Sam* 27:8

get
saying, *g.* me this damsel. *Gen* 34:4
and so *g.* them out of the. *Ex* 1:10
and I will *g.* me honour upon. 14:17
he be poor and cannot *g. Lev* 14:21
such as he is able to *g.* 22, 30, 31
whose hand is not able to *g.* 32
that his hand shall *g. Num* 6:21
now therefore I will *g.* me. 22:34
giveth thee power to *g. Deut* 8:18
strangers shall *g.* up above. 28:43
g. her for me to wife. *Judg* 14:2, 3
let me *g.* away and. *1 Sam* 20:29
David haste to *g.* 23:26
lest Sheba *g.* fenced. *2 Sam* 20:6
lord the king may *g. 1 Ki* 1:2
Rehoboam made speed to *g.* up to
his chariot. 12:18; *2 Chr* 10:18
catch them alive, and *g. 2 Ki* 7:12
through thy precepts I *g. Ps* 119:104
g. wisdom, *g. Pr* 4:5, 7
dishonour shall he *g.* 6:33
better it is to *g.* wisdom . . . to *g.*
understanding rather to be. 16:16
price in the hand of a fool to *g.* 17:16
thou learn his ways and *g.* 22:25
there is a time to *g.* and. *Eccl* 3:6
I will *g.* me to the mountains.
S of S 4:6
let us *g.* up early to vineyards. 7:12
I will *g.* me to great men. *Jer* 5:5
g. a potter's earthen bottle. 19:1
harness the horses, and *g.* up. 46:4
wings to Moab, that it may *g.* 48:9
hedged me about, I cannot *g.* out.
Lam 3:7
to destroy souls, to *g. Ezek* 22:27
let the beasts *g.* away. *Dan* 4:14
I will *g.* them praise. *Zeph* 3:19
to *g.* into ship. *Mat* 14:22
Mark 6:45
they may lodge and *g. Luke* 9:12
into sea, and *g.* to land. *Acts* 27:43
lest Satan should *g. 2 Cor* 2:11
buy, sell, and *g.* gain. *Jas* 4:13

get thee
g. thee out of. *Gen* 12:1; *Acts* 7:3
g. thee into the land. *Gen* 22:2
g. thee out from this land. 31:13
g. thee to Pharaoh in. *Ex* 7:15
g. thee from me, take heed. 10:28
g. thee out, and all people. 11:8
Moses, away, *g. thee* down and thou
shalt. 19:24; 32:7; *Deut* 9:12
g. thee up to mount. *Num* 27:12
Deut 33:49
g. thee up to the top. *Deut* 3:27
g. thee up to the place the. 17:8
g. thee up, wherefore ? *Josh* 7:10

g. thee up to the wood. *Josh* 17:15
arise, *g. thee* down unto. *Judg* 7:9
wash thyself, *g. thee*. *Ruth* 3:3
depart, *g. thee* into. *1 Sam* 22:5
g. thee in to king David. *1 Ki* 1:13
g. thee to Anathoth to thine. 2:26
g. thee to Shiloh, behold there. 14:2
arise therefore, *g. thee* to thine. 12
g. thee hence. 17:3
g. thee to Zarephath. 9
Elijah said, *g. thee* up, eat. 18:41
g. thee down, that the rain stop. 44
g. thee to the prophets of. *2 Ki* 3:13
so didst thou *g. thee* a. *Neh* 9:10
g. thee to this treasurer, *Isa* 22:15
thou shalt say unto it, *g. thee*. 30:22
O Zion, *g. thee* up into the. 40:9
sit thou silent, and *g. thee*. 47:5
g. thee a linen girdle, put. *Jer* 13:1
son of man, *g. thee* to the. *Ezek* 3:4
and go, *g. thee* to them of the. 11
Jesus saith to him, *g. thee*. *Mat* 4:10
Peter, *g. thee* behind me, Satan.
16:23; *Mark* 8:33; *Luke* 4:8
g. thee out, for Herod. *Luke* 13:31
arise, *g. thee* down, go. *Acts* 10:20
g. thee quickly out of. 22:18

get ye

Lot said, up, *g. ye* out. *Gen* 19:14
g. ye out of the way, turn. *Isa* 30:11
arise, *g. ye* up to the. *Jer* 49:31
said, *g. ye* far from. *Ezek* 11:15
come, *g. ye* down, for the. *Joel* 3:13
he said, *g. ye* hence, walk. *Zech* 6:7

get you

g. you possessions. *Gen* 34:10
g. you down thither and buy. 42:2
rise up, *g. you* up in peace. 44:17
the king said, *g. you* to. *Ex* 5:4
go you, *g. you* straw where you. 11
rise up, *g. you* forth from. 12:31
turn you, *g. you* into. *Num* 14:25
g. you up from tabernacle. 16:24
Balaam said, *g. you* into your. 22:13
g. you into your tents. *Deut* 5:30
Josh 22:4
g. you to the mountain. *Josh* 2:16
to-morrow *g. you* early. *Judg* 19:9
g. you up, for ye shall. *1 Sam* 9:13
g. you down from among the. 15:6
g. you up to Carmel, and go. 25:5
flee, *g. you* off, dwell. *Jer* 49:30

Gethsemane

to a place called G. *Mat* 26:36
Mark 14:32

getteth

whosoever *g.* up to the. *2 Sam* 5:8
happy is the man that *g.* *Pr* 3:13
reproveth a scorner *g.* shame, rebuketh a wicked man *g.* blot. 9:7
he that heareth reproof *g.* 15:32
the heart of the prudent *g.* 18:15
he that *g.* wisdom loveth his. 19:8
so he that *g.* riches. *Jer* 17:11
he that *g.* out of the pit shall. 48:44

getting

away the cattle of his *g. Gen* 31:18
with all thy *g.* get. *Pr* 4:7
g. of treasures by a lying. 21:6

ghost

(*American Revision renders this spirit*)
Jacob yielded up the *g. Gen* 49:33
I had given up the *g. Job* 10:18
shall be as the giving up of *g.* 11:20
yea, man giveth up the *g.* 14:10
she hath given up the *g. Jer* 15:9
cried, and yielded up *g. Mat* 27:50
down and yielded up *g. Acts* 5:10
see gave, give, holy

Giah

Ammah that lieth before G.
2 Sam 2:24

giant

The Hebrew Nephel may signify a monster, or a terrible man, who beats and bears down other men. The Scripture speaks of Giants who lived before the flood; they are called Nephilim, mighty men which were of old, men of renown. Gen 6:4. The words Emim and

Rephaim *are also used to denote these unusual men.*
The Anakims, or the sons of Anak, were the most famous giants of Palestine. They dwelt near Hebron. Their stature was so much above what was common, that the Israelites, who were sent to view the promised land, told the people at their return, that they had seen giants of the race of Anak in that country, who were of so monstrous a size, that the Israelites, in comparison, were but grasshoppers, Num 13:33.
sons of the *g.* *2 Sam* 21:16, 18
1 Chr 20:4
the son of the *g.* *1 Chr.* 20:6
born to the *g.* 8
runneth upon me like a *g. Job* 16:14

giants

(*The Revisions replace this word in all passages by the Hebrew word, using it as a proper name*)
were *g.* in the earth. *Gen* 6:4
the *g.* the sons of Anak. *Num* 13:33
Emims were counted *g. Deut* 2:11
remained of the remnant of *g.* 3:11*
Josh 12:4; 13:12
was called the land of *g. Deut* 3:13
the end of the valley of *g. Josh* 15:8
up to the land of the *g.* 17:15
came to the valley of the. 18:16

Gibeah

when they were by G. *Judg* 19:14
of mount Ephraim sojourned in G. 16
the thing we will do to G. 20:9
the children of Belial in G. 13
themselves in array against G. 30
went home to G. *1 Sam* 10:26; 15:34
in the uttermost part of G. 14:2
up to the Lord in G. *2 Sam* 21:6
Ramah is afraid, G. of Saul.
Isa 10:29
blow ye the cornet in G. *Hos* 5:8
themselves as in the days of G. 9:9
days of G. the battle of G. 10:9

Gibeon

feared, because G. was. *Josh* 10:2
help me, that we may smite G. 4
sun, stand thou still upon G. 4
by the pool of G. *2 Sam* 2:13
he had slain Asahel at G. 3:30
at the great stone in G. 20:8
in G. Lord appeared. *1 Ki* 3:5; 9:2
at G. dwelt father of G. *1 Chr* 8:29
9:35
burnt offering was at G. 21:29
as in the valley of G. *Isa* 28:21
the son of Azur in G. *Jer* 28:1
Ishmael by the waters in G. 41:12

Gibeonites

because Saul slew G. *2 Sam* 21:1
them into the hands of the G. 9

Gideon

G. threshed wheat by. *Judg* 6:11
G. built an altar there unto the. 24
Spirit of the Lord came upon G. 34
Jerubbaal, who is G. rose up. 7:1
nothing else, save sword of G. 14
sword of the Lord and of G. 18, 20
G. slew Zeba. 8:21
G. made an ephod thereof. 27
G. had 70 sons. 30
G. died in a good old age. 32
nor kindness to the house of G. 35
fail me to tell of G. *Heb* 11:32

Gideoni

prince of Benjamin, Abidan the son of G. *Num* 1:11; 2:22; 7:60, 65

gier eagle

abomination, the *g. e.* *Lev* 11:18*
Deut 14:17*

gift

so much dowry and *g. Gen* 34:12
take no *g.* a *g.* blindeth. *Ex* 23:8
Deut 16:19
the Levites as a *g. Num* 8:19; 18:6
office as a service of *g.* 18:7
the heave offering of their *g.* 11
given us any *g.?* *2 Sam* 19:42

Tyre shall be there with *g. Ps* 45:12
a *g.* is as a precious stone. *Pr* 17:18
a wicked man taketh a *g.* out. 23
a man's *g.* maketh room for. 18:16
a *g.* in secret pacifieth anger. 21:14
boasteth himself of a false *g.* 25:14
enjoy good, it is *g. Eccl* 3:13; 5:19
and a *g.* destroyeth the heart. 7:7
if a prince give a *g.* to. *Ezek* 46:16
if he give a *g.* to one of his. 17
if thou bring thy *g.* to. *Mat* 5:23
leave there thy *g.* before the. 24
and offer the *g.* that Moses. 8:4
it is a *g.* by me. 15:5; *Mark* 7:11
sweareth by the *g.* is. *Mat* 23:18, 19
if thou knewest the *g.* *John* 4:10
ye shall receive the *g.* *Acts* 2:38
thought the *g.* of God may be. 8:20
also was poured out the *g.* 10:45
God gave them the like *g.* as. 11:17
to you some spiritual *g. Rom* 1:11
is free *g.* of God and the *g.* by grace abounded. 5:15
so is the *g.* the free *g.* is of. 16
receive the *g.* of righteousness. 17
the free *g.* came on all men. 18
the *g.* of God is eternal life. 6:23
ye come behind in no *g.* *1 Cor* 1:7
man hath his proper *g.* of God. 7:7
though I have the *g.* of. 13:2
that for the *g.* bestowed. *2 Cor* 1:11
that we would receive the *g.* 8:4*
God for his unspeakable *g.* 9:15
it is the *g.* of God. *Eph* 2:8
a minister, according to the *g.* 3:7
the measure of the *g.* of Christ. 4:7
not because I desire a *g. Phil* 4:17
neglect not the *g.* that. *1 Tim* 4:14
stir up the *g.* that is in. *2 Tim* 1:6
tasted of the heavenly *g. Heb* 6:4
good *g.* and perfect *g. Jas* 1:17
man hath received the *g. 1 Pet* 4:10

gifts

Abraham gave *g.* to sons. *Gen* 25:6
shall hallow in their *g. Ex* 28:38
feasts, besides your *g. Lev* 23:38
out of all your *g.* offer. *Num* 18:29
David's servants, and brought *g.*
2 Sam 8:2, 6; *1 Chr* 18:2
Lord is no taking of *g.* *2 Chr* 19:7
Jehoshaphat gave great *g.* of. 21:3
Ammonites gave *g.* to Uzziah. 26:8
and many brought *g.* unto. 32:23
a feast and gave *g.* *Esth* 2:18
make them days of sending *g.* 9:22
hast received *g.* for men. *Ps* 68:18
though thou givest many *g. Pr* 6:35
he that hateth *g.* shall live. 15:27
is friend to him that giveth *g.* 19:6
that receiveth *g.* overthroweth. 29:4
every one loveth *g.* *Isa* 1:23
g. to whores, *g.* to lovers. *Ezek* 16:33
polluted them in their own *g.* 20:26
when ye offer your *g.* ye pollute. 31
holy name no more with your *g.* 39
in thee have they taken *g.* 22:12
dream, ye shall receive *g. Dan* 2:6
king gave Daniel many great *g.* 48
then Daniel said, let thy *g.* be. 5:17
they presented to him *g. Mat* 2:11
how to give good *g.* 7:11
Luke 11:13
rich casting their *g.* into. *Luke* 21:1
adorned with goodly stones and *g.* 5
g. of God are without. *Rom* 11:29
having *g.* differing according. 12:6
concerning spiritual *g.* *1 Cor* 12:1
there are diversities of *g.* but the. 4
to another the *g.* of healing. 9, 28, 30
but covet earnestly the best *g.* 12:31
charity, and desire spiritual *g.* 14:1
ye are zealous of spiritual *g.* 12
captive, gave *g.* to men. *Eph* 4:8
bearing witness with *g.* *Heb* 2:4
he may offer *g.* and sacrifices. 5:1
high priest ordained to offer *g.* 8:3
there are priests that offer *g.* 4
which were offered, both *g.* and. 9:9
God testifying of Abel's *g.* 11:4
dwell on earth shall send *g.Rev* 11:10

Gihon

the second river is G. *Gen* 2:13

Solomon down to G. *1 Ki* 1:33, 38
anointed him king in G. 45

Gilboa
all Israel pitched in G. *1 Sam* 28:4
Saul fell down slain in mount G. 31:1
8; *2 Sam* 21:12; *1 Chr* 10:1, 8
by chance on mount G. *2 Sam* 1:6
ye mountains of G. let there be. 21

Gilead
saw the land of G. was. *Num* 32:1
G. to Machir. 40; *Deut* 3:15
shewed him land of G. *Deut* 34:1
a man of war, had G. *Josh* 17:1
Phinehas into the land of G. *Judg* 10:18
the inhabitants of G. *Judg* 10:18
went with the elders of G. 11:11
Ish-bosheth king over G. *2 Sam* 2:9
Absalom pitched in land of G. 17:26
Tishbite, who was of G. *1 Ki* 17:1
G. is mine. *Ps* 60:7; 108:8
of goats from G. *S of S* 4:1; 6:5
is there no balm in G.? *Jer* 8:22
thou art G. to me. 22:6
go up into G. 46:11
shall be satisfied on mount G. 50:19
G. is the city of them. *Hos* 6:8
is there iniquity in G.? they 12:11
they have threshed G. *Amos* 1:3
up women with child of G. 13
Benjamin shall possess G. *Ob* 19
feed in Bashan and G. *Mi* 7:14
them into the land of G. *Zech* 10:10
see Ramoth

Gileadite, -s
G. judged Israel. *Judg* 10:3
Jephthah the G. 11:1
ye G. are fugitives of. 12:4
and the G. took the passages. 5
Barzillai the G. *2 Sam* 17:27
see Barzillai

Gilgal
up and encamped in G. *Josh* 4:19
Joshua unto the camp at G. 9:6
of G. sent to the camp at. 10:6
an angel came up from G. *Judg* 2:1
went in circuit to G. *1 Sam* 7:16
go down before me to G. 10:8
let us go to G. and renew. 11:14
Saul was in G. 13:7
Samuel came not to G. 15:33
hewed Agag in pieces in G. 15:33
come not ye to G. nor. *Hos* 4:15
their wickedness is in G. 9:15
they sacrifice bullocks in G. 12:11
G. multiply transgression. *Amos* 4:4
enter not into G. for G. shall. 5:5
him from Shittim to G. *Mi* 6:5

Gilonite
the G. *2 Sam* 15:12; 23:34

gin
the g. shall take him by. *Job* 18:9
for a g. to the inhabitants. *Isa* 8:14
fall into a snare where no g is? *Amos* 3:5

gins
they spread a net, they set g. for me. *Ps* 140:5
keep me from the g. of the. 141:9

gird
g. him with the curious. *Ex* 29:5, 9
Ehud did g. his dagger. *Judg* 3:16
g. ye on every man his. *1 Sam* 25:13
g. thy sword on thy thigh. *Ps* 45:3
g. yourselves, and ye shall. *Isa* 8:9
not g. with what. *Ezek* 44:18
g. yourselves, and lament. *Joel* 1:13
shall g. himself, and. *Luke* 12:37
g. thyself, and serve me, till. 17:8
another shall g. thee. *John* 21:18
g. thyself and bind on. *Acts* 12:8
see loins, sackcloth

girded
g. him with the girdle. *Lev* 8:7
when ye g. on every man. *Deut* 1:41
six hundred men g. *Judg* 18:11
Samuel g. with a linen. *1 Sam* 2:18
David danced, and g. *2 Sam* 6:14
Joab's garment was g. unto. 20:8
thou hast g. me with. 22:40; *Ps* 18:39
they g. sackcloth on. *1 Ki* 20:32

thou hast g. me with. *Ps* 30:11
setteth fast mountains, being g. 65:6
strength wherewith he hath g. 93:1
girdle wherewith he is g. 109:19
I g. thee, though thou. *Isa* 45:5
elders of Zion g. with. *Lam* 2:10
I g. thee about with fine. *Ezek* 16:10
images of the Chaldeans g. 23:15
lament like a virgin g. with. *Joel* 1:8
he took a towel and g. *John* 13:4
the towel wherewith he was g. 5
seven angels, breasts g. *Rev* 15:6
see loins, sword

girdedst
young thou g. thyself. *John* 21:18

girdeth
let not him that g. on. *1 Ki* 20:11
he g. their loins with. *Job* 12:18*
it is God that g. me. *Ps* 18:32
g. her loins with strength. *Pr* 31:17

girding
instead of a stomacher, a g. *Isa* 3:24
the Lord did call to g. with. 22:12

girdle
With the long loose robes which were commonly worn in the East a girdle was very necessary when a man wished to do any active work. When men were at ease the robes fell loosely around them, but the first thing in preparing for walking or for work was to tighten the girdle and tuck up the long skirts of the robe, 1 Ki 18:46.
The girdle was sometimes of leather, but more usually a long piece of soft cloth, or silk that could be easily wrapped around the body and tied tightly.
they shall make a g. *Ex* 28:4
g. of the ephod which is. 8*, 27*
28*; 29:5*; 39:5*, 20*; *Lev* 8:7*
make g. of needlework. *Ex* 28:39*
they made a g. of fine twined. 39:29
David his bow and g. *1 Sam* 18:4
have given thee a g. *2 Sam* 18:11
blood of war on his g. *1 Ki* 2:5
Elijah was girt with a g. *2 Ki* 1:8
loins of kings with a g. *Job* 12:18
for a g. wherewith he. *Ps* 109:19
instead of a g. there shall. *Isa* 3:24
nor shall the g. of their loins. 5:27
shall be the g. of his loins, and faithfulness the g. of his reins. 11:5
strengthen Eliakim with thy g. 22:21
get thee a linen g. put it. *Jer* 13:1
this people shall be as this g. 10
a leathern g. *Mat* 3:4; *Mark* 1:6
g. man that owneth this g. *Acts* 21:11
the paps with a golden g. *Rev* 1:13

girdles
make for Aaron's sons g. *Ex* 28:40
gird Aaron and sons with g. 29:9
gird Aaron's sons with g. *Lev* 8:13
she delivereth g. to the. *Pr* 31:24
of Chaldeans girded with g. *Ezek* 23:15
girded with golden g. *Rev* 15:6

Girgashite, -s
begat the G. *Gen* 10:16; *1 Chr* 1:14
land of the G. *Gen* 15:21; *Neh* 9:8
Lord hath cast out the G. *Deut* 7:1
without fail drive out G. *Judg* 3:10

girl, -s
have sold a g. for wine. *Joel* 3:3
city be full of boys and g. *Zech* 8:5

girt
they that stumbled are g. *1 Sam* 2:4
he was g. with a girdle. *2 Ki* 1:8
Peter g. his fisher's coat. *John* 21:7
stand, having your loins g. *Eph* 6:14
g. about the paps with a. *Rev* 1:13

Gittite, -s
Obed-edom the G. *2 Sam* 6:10, 11
Ittai the G. 15:19, 22; 18:2
Goliath the G. 21:19

Gittith
This is the title prefixed to Psalms 8. 81, and 84.
It probably means either a musical instrument in use in Gath, or a vintage song to the tune of which the psalm should be sung, or a march of the Gittite guard, 2 Sam 15:18.

give
g. me the persons, and. *Gen* 14:21
what wilt g. me, seeing ? 15:2
the field I g. thee, and the. 23:11
therefore God g. thee of dew. 27:28
all thou shalt g. me I will g. 28:22
better I g. her thee, than g. 29:19
g. me my wife. 21
g. me children or else I die. 30:1
g. me my wives and my. 26
will we g. our daughters. 34:16
thou must g. us also. *Ex* 10:25
her father utterly refuse to g. 22:17
on the eighth day thou shalt g. 30
then they shall g. every man. 30:12
this they shall g. every one half. 13
thou shalt g. the Levites. *Num* 3:9
Lord g. thee peace. 6:26
said, who shall g. us flesh ? 11:4, 18
if Balak would g. me. 22:18; 24:13
I g. to Phinehas my covenant. 25:12
g. thou the more inheritance, to few thou shalt g. 26:54; 33:54
ye shall g. to Levites suburbs. 35:2
thou shalt g. him. *Deut.* 15:10, 14
every man g. as he is able. 16:17
Ezek 46:5, 11
day thou shalt g. him. *Deut* 24:15
forty stripes he may g. him. 25:3
swear to me, and g. me. *Josh* 2:12
now therefore g. me this. 14:12
g. me a blessing, g. springs. 15:19
Judg 1:15
that fleeth, they shall g. *Josh* 20:4
to g. the Midianites into. *Judg* 7:2
answered, we will willingly g. 8:25
nay, but thou shalt g. *1 Sam* 2:16
wealth which God shall g. Israel. 32
they said g. us a king. 8:6
g. me a man that we may. 17:10
king will g. him his daughter. 25
David said, g. it me. 21:9
will the son of Jesse g. every ? 22:7
shall I then g. it to men whom. 25:11
would g. me drink of the water of the well. *2 Sam* 23:15; *1 Chr* 11:17
these did Araunah g. *2 Sam* 24:23
1 Chr 21:23
g. thy servant an. *1 Ki* 3:9
O my lord, g. her the living. 26, 27
g. every man according to. 8:39*
if thou wilt g. me half. 13:8
he said, g. me thy son, and. 17:19
I said, G. thy son, that. *2 Ki* 6:29
if it be, g. me thine hand. 10:15
saying, G. thy daughter to my. 14:9
g. to Lord, ye kindreds of the people.
1 Chr 16:28, 29; *Ps* 29:1, 2; 96:7, 8
Lord g. thee wisdom. *1 Chr* 22:12
g. me now wisdom. *2 Chr* 1:10
hand of God was to g. them. 30:12
and to g. us a nail in his. *Ezra* 9:8
to g. us a reviving, to g. us a wall. 9
g. them for a prey in land. *Neh* 4:4
all that a man hath will he g. *Job* 2:4
g. flattering titles to man. 32:21
ask of me, and I shall g. *Ps* 2:8
g. them according to. 28:4
he shall g. thee the desires. 37:4
none can g. to God a ransom. 49:7
not sacrifice, else would I g. 51:16
g. us help from. 60:11; 108:12
can he g. bread also? can he? 78:20
O turn, g. thy strength to. 86:16
shall g. his angels. 91:11; *Mat* 4:6
but I g. myself unto. *Ps* 109:4
g. me. 119:34, 73, 125, 144, 169
g. instruction to a wise. *Pr* 9:9
my son, g. me thine heart. 23:26
if enemy hunger, g. him. 25:21
Rom 12:20
the rod and reproof g. *Pr* 29:15
shall g. thee rest, shall g. delight. 17
g. me neither poverty nor. 30:8
two daughters, crying, g. 15
that he may g. to him. *Eccl* 2:26
g. a portion to seven. 11:2
man would g. substance. *S of S* 8:7
then he shall g. the rain. *Isa* 30:23
g. place to me, that I. 49:20

may g. seed to the sower. *Isa* 55:10
g. unto them beauty for ashes. 61:3
g. him no rest till he establish. 62:7
shall I g. thee a pleasant? *Jer* 3:19
to whom shall I speak and g.? 6:10*
to g. man according. 17:10; 32:19
g. heed to me, O Lord. 18:19
I think to g. you an expected. 29:11
bring them, and g. them wine. 35:2
tears run down, g. thyself. *Lam* 2:18
g. them sorrow of heart, thy. 3:65
mouth, eat that I g. thee. *Ezek* 2:8
with this roll that I g. thee. 3:3
and g. them warning. 17
thy children, which didst g. 16:36
to land, I lifted up mine hand to g. it
to them. 20:28, 42; 47:14
if wicked g. again that he. 33:15
prince g. a gift to his sons. 46:16, 17
and g. thy rewards to. *Dan* 5:17
I am come forth to g. 9:22*
with shame do love, g. ye. *Hos* 4:18
g. O Lord, what wilt thou g.? 9:14
thou saidst, g. me a king and. 13:10
shall I g. my firstborn? *Mi* 6:7
g. her fruit, the ground shall g. increase, and heavens g. *Zech* 8:12
g. me my price, if not. 11:12
g. to him that asketh thee. *Mat* 5:42
g. us this day our. 6:11; *Luke* 11:3
if he ask bread, will he g.? *Mat* 7:9
will he g. a serpent? 10; *Luke* 11:11
g. gifts unto your children, your
Father g. to them that ask him?
Mat 7:11; *Luke* 11:13
g. place. *Mat* 9:24
freely ye received, freely g. 10:8
shall g. to drink a cup. 42
he promised to g. her what. 14:7
g. ye them to eat. 16; *Mark* 6:37
Luke 9:13
what g. in exchange for his soul?
Mat 16:26; *Mark* 8:37
and g. to them for. *Mat* 17:27
command to g. a writing? 19:7
g. to the poor. 19:21; *Mark* 10:21
call the labourers, and g. *Mat* 20:8
is not mine to g. 20:23; *Mark* 10:40
g. us of your oil, for our. *Mat* 25:8
what will ye g. me? 26:15
I will that thou g. me. *Mark* 6:25
and he will g. the vineyard. 12:9
whomsoever I will, I g. it. *Luke* 4:6
g. and it shall be given . . . good
measure shall men g. 6:38
he will g. him as many as he. 11:8
g. alms of such things. 41; 12:33
he that bade thee say, g. this. 14:9
younger said, g. me the. 15:12
who shall g. you that which? 16:12
Jesus saith, G. me. *John* 4:7, 10
drinketh water I shall g. 14
the Son of man shall g. you. 6:27
said, Lord, evermore g. us. 34
how can this man g. us his? 52
g. God the praise, this man. 9:24
I g. to them eternal life. 10:28
thou wilt ask, God will g. 11:22
that he should g. something. 13:29
g. you another Comforter. 14:16
my peace I g. unto you not as world
giveth, g. I unto you. 27
shall ask, he may g. it. 15:16
whatsoever ye ask he will g. 16:23
that he should g. eternal life. 17:2
such as I have g. I thee. *Acts* 3:6
we will g. ourselves to prayer. 6:4*
he promised he would g. it for. 7:5
Simon said, G. me also. 8:19
it is more blessed to g. than. 20:35
with him also freely g. us. *Rom* 8:32
avenge not, but rather g. 12:19
ye may g. yourselves. *1 Cor* 7:5
g. none offence, neither. 10:32
let him g. not grudgingly. *2 Cor* 9:7
God may g. you the. *Eph* 1:17
that he may have to g. to him. 4:28
g. to your servants that. *Col* 4:1*
g. attendance to reading. *1 Tim* 4:13
meditate, g. thyself wholly to. 15
righteous Judge shall g. *2 Tim* 4:8
we ought to g. the more. *Heb* 2:1
g. life for them that sin. *1 John* 5:16
g. me the little book. *Rev.* 10:9

he had power to g. life. *Rev* 13:15
to g. her the cup of the wine. 16:19
torment and sorrow g. her. 18:7
to g. every man according. 22:12*

see **account, charge, ear, glory,
light, sware**

I will give
I will g. to thee and thy seed the
land. *Gen* 17:8; 48:4; *Deut* 34:4
I will g. thee a son also. *Gen* 17:16
I will surely g. the tenth to. 28:22
shall say to me I will g. 34:11, 12
and I will g. this people. *Ex* 3:21
with thee, and I will g. 33:14
I will g. you rain in due season.
Lev 26:4; *Deut* 11:14
I will g. peace in the land. *Lev* 26:6
I will g. him to the. *1 Sam* 1:11
I will g. her, that she may be. 18:21
I will g. thy wives to. *2 Sam* 12:11
not rend all, but I will g. *1 Ki* 11:13
I will g. ten tribes to thee. 31
come home, and I will g. thee. 13:7
I will g. thee for it a better. 21:2
I will g. thee the vineyard of. 7
I will g. him rest, I will g. *1 Chr* 22:9
I will g. the riches. *2 Chr* 1:12
O Lord, I will g. thanks. *Ps* 30:12
I will g. sing and g. 57:7*; 108:1*
to-morrow I will g. when. *Pr* 3:28
I will g. them children to. *Isa* 3:4
Zion, behold, and I will g. 41:27
I will g. thee for. 42:6; 49:8
I will g. thee the treasures. 45:3
I will g. thee for a light to the. 49:6
I will g. them an everlasting. 56:5
I will g. pastors according. *Jer* 3:15
I will g. them waters of gall. 9:15
I will g. you assured peace. 14:13
I will g. thy substance to the. 17:3
I will g. them an heart to. 24:7
I will g. them one heart. 32:39
Ezek 11:19
I will g. men that have. *Jer* 34:18
I will g. it into the hand. *Ezek* 7:21
and I will g. you the land of. 11:17
I will g. thee blood in fury. 16:38*
I will g. also g. thee into their. 39
I will g. them to thee for. 61
whose right it is, I will g. 21:27
I will g. them to be removed. 29:19
I will g. land of Egypt to. 29:19
I will g. thee the opening of the. 21
and I will g. you an heart. 36:26
I will g. her vineyards. *Hos* 2:15
unto me, and I will g. *Mat* 11:28
I will g. to thee the keys of. 16:19
is right, I will g. you. 20:4
I will g. to this last even as. 14
what thou wilt, I will g. *Mark* 6:22
for I will g. you a mouth. *Luke* 21:15
I will g. is my flesh, which I will g.
for the life of the world. *John* 6:51
I will g. you the sure. *Acts* 13:34
be faithful, I will g. thee. *Rev* 2:10
I will g. him a white stone and. 17
I will g. to every one according. 23
I will g. him the morning star. 28
and I will g. power to my two. 11:3
I will g. to him that is athirst. 21:6

will I give
will I g. this land. *Gen* 12:7; 13:15
24:7; 28:13; 35:12; *Ex* 32:13
33:1
Caleb, to him will I g. *Deut* 1:36
go in thither, to him will I g. 39
to him will I g. Achsah. *Josh* 15:16
Judg 1:12
will I g. to the man of. *1 Sam* 9:8
Merab, her will I g. thee. 18:17
to thee will I g. land. *1 Chr* 16:18
Ps 105:11
therefore will I g. thanks. *Ps* 18:49
there will I g. thee my. *S of S* 7:12
therefore will I g. men for. *Isa* 43:4
them will I g. in mine house. 56:5
so will I g. Zedekiah. *Jer* 34:8
thy life will I g. thee for a. 45:5
so will I g. inhabitants. *Jer* 34:8*
new heart also will I g. you. 36:26
and in this place will I g. *Hag* 2:9
all these things will I g. *Mat* 4:9

all this power will I g. *Luke* 4:6
overcometh will I g. *Rev* 2:7, 17, 26

Lord give
land which Lord will g. you. *Ex* 12:25
Lev 14:34; 23:10; 25:2; *Num* 15:2
the Lord shall g. you flesh. *Ex* 16:8
therefore the Lord will g. *Num* 11:18
Lord delight in us, he will g. 14:8
Lord refuseth to g. me leave. 22:13
Lord commanded to g. nine. 34:13
Lord commanded to g. the land. 36:2
land the Lord doth g. *Deut* 1:25
the Lord shall g. thee a. 28:65
Lord commanded Moses to g.
Josh 9:24
Lord commanded to g. us. 17:4
the Lord commanded to g. us cities.
21:2
which the Lord shall g. *Ruth* 4:12
the Lord his God did g. *1 Ki* 15:4
the Lord is able to g. *2 Chr* 25:9
the Lord will g. strength. *Ps* 29:11
the Lord will g. grace and. 84:11
the Lord shall g. that which. 85:12
the Lord himself shall g. *Isa* 7:14
the Lord shall g. thee rest. 14:3
though the Lord g. you bread. 30:20
Lord shall g. them showers.
Zech 10:1
Lord shall g. him the. *Luke* 1:32
Lord g. mercy to house. *2 Tim* 1:16

not give, or **give not**
said, thou shalt not g. *Gen* 30:31
I will not g. you straw. *Ex* 5:10
shall not g. more, poor nor g. 30:15
shalt not g. thy money. *Lev* 25:37
I will not g. you of. *Deut* 2:5; 9:19
thy daughter thou shalt not g. 7:3
he will not g. of the flesh of. 28:55
shall not any of us g. *Judg* 21:1
we have sworn we will not g. 7
we will not g. them. *1 Sam* 30:22
I will not g. inheritance. *1 Ki* 21:4
g. not your daughters. *Ezra* 9:12
Neh 10:30; 13:25
not g. sleep to mine. *Ps* 132:4
g. not sleep to thine eyes. *Pr* 6:4
g not thy strength unto. 31:3
constellations shall not g. *Isa* 13:10
my glory will I not g. 42:8; 48:11
I will no more g. thy corn. 62:8
let us not g. heed to any. *Jer* 18:18
not g. Jeremiah into the hand. 26:24
a cloud, the moon shall not g. her
light. *Ezek* 32:7; *Mat* 24:29
Mark 13:24
to whom not g. honour. *Dan* 11:21
g. not thine heritage to. *Joel* 2:17
g. not that which is holy. *Mat* 7:6
g. or shall we not g.? *Mark* 12:15
neither g. place to the. *Eph* 4:27
g. not those things they. *Jas* 2:16

give thanks
I will g. thanks. *2 Sam* 22:50
Ps 18:49
g. thanks to the Lord, call upon.
1 Chr 16:8; *Ps* 105:1; 106:1
107:1; 118:1, 29; 136:1, 3
God of our salvation, that we may g.
thanks. *1 Chr* 16:35; *Ps* 106:47
by name, to g. thanks. *1 Chr* 16:41
with a harp to g. thanks. 25:3
appointed Levites to g. thanks.
2 Chr 31:2
who shall g. thee thanks? *Ps* 6:5
g. thanks at the remembrance of his
holiness. 30:4; 97:12
Lord, I will g. thanks to thee. 30:12
I will g. thanks in the great. 35:18
do we g. thanks, do g. thanks. 75:1
people will g. thee thanks. 79:13
it is a good thing to g. thanks. 92:1
save us to g. thanks to thy. 106:47
I will rise to g. thanks. 119:62
the tribes go up to g. thanks. 122:4
g. thanks unto God of gods. 136:2
O g. thanks unto God of heaven. 26
righteous shall g. thanks to. 140:13
not only I g. thanks. *Rom* 16:4
for which I g. thanks. *1 Cor* 10:30
I cease not to g. thanks. *Eph* 1:16
we g. thanks to God and. *Col* 1:3

g. thanks to God always. *1 Thes* 1:2
in every thing *g. thanks.* 5:18
bound to *g. thanks.* *2 Thes* 2:13
g. thee *thanks,* Lord God. *Rev* 11:17

give up

the Lord walketh, to *g. up* thine
enemies. *Deut* 23:14; 31:5
he shall *g.* Israel *up.* *1 Ki* 14:16
did not I *g. up* the ghost ? *Job* 3:11
hold my tongue, I shall *g. up.* 13:19
I will say to north, *g. up.* *Isa* 43:6
how shall I *g.* thee *up* ? *Hos* 11:8
therefore will he *g.* them *up. Mi* 5:3
thou deliverest will I *g. up.* 6:14

given

Sarah should have *g.* *Gen* 21:7
because he hath *g.* his. *Lev* 20:3
they are *g.* as a gift for. *Num* 18:6
to the blessing *g. Deut* 12:15; 16:17
a full reward be *g.* thee. *Ruth* 2:12
thought I would have *g.* *2 Sam* 4:10
would have *g.* thee such and. 12:8*
I would have *g.* thee ten. 18:11
hath the king *g.* us any gift ? 19:42
the man of God had *g.* *1 Ki* 13:5
thine own have we *g.* *1 Chr* 29:14
let it be *g.* them day by. *Ezra* 6:9
the silver is *g.* to thee. *Esth* 3:11
let my life be *g.* me at my. 7:3
why is light *g.* to him? *Job* 3:20
why is light *g.* to a man whose ? 23
whom alone the earth was *g.* 15:19
bodies of thy servants *g.* *Ps* 79:2
he hath *g.* to the. 112:9; *2 Cor* 9:9
the earth hath he *g.* to the. *Ps* 115:16
that which he hath *g.* will. *Pr* 19:17
deliver those that are *g.* *Eccl* 8:8
are *g.* from one shepherd. 12:11
Child is born, to us Son is *g. Isa* 9:6
therefore hear, thou that art *g.* 47:8
g. to covetousness. *Jer* 6:13; 8:10
he said to all who had *g.* him. 44:20
we have *g.* the hand to. *Lam* 5:6
is this land *g.* *Ezek* 11:15; 33:24
they are desolate, they are *g.* 35:12
beasts, fowls hath he *g. Dan* 2:38
lion, and a man's heart was *g.* 7:4
she shall be *g.* up, and they. 11:6
it is *g.* to you to know the mysteries.
Mat 13:11; *Mark* 4:11; *Luke* 8:10
save they to whom it is *g. Mat* 19:11
be *g.* to a nation bringing. 21:43
are *g.* in marriage. 22:30
Mark 12:25; *Luke* 20:35
sold for much and *g.* *Mat* 26:9
Mark 14:5
all power is *g.* to me in. *Mat* 28:18
hear more shall be *g.* *Mark* 4:24
to whom much is *g.* of. *Luke* 12:48
nothing, except it be *g.* *John* 3:27
hath *g.* to the Son to have life. 5:26
of all he hath *g.* me, I should. 6:39
come to me, except it were *g.* 65
except it were *g.* thee from. 19:11
is none other name *g.* *Acts* 4:12
hoped that money should be *g.* 24:26
Holy Ghost which is *g.* *Rom* 5:5
who hath first *g.* to him. 11:35
because of the grace that is *g.* 15:15
freely *g.* us of God. *1 Cor* 2:12
that thanks may be *g.* *2 Cor* 1:11
law *g.* which could have *g. Gal* 3:21*
dispensation, which is *g.* *Eph* 3:2
unto me, the least, is this grace *g.* 8
who have *g.* themselves over. 4:19
Christ hath loved us, and *g.* 5:2
to you it is *g.* in behalf. *Phil* 1:29*
and hath *g.* him a name above. 2:9
if Jesus had *g.* them rest. *Heb* 4:8
Spirit which he hath *g. 1 John* 3:24
because he hath *g.* us of his. 4:13
white robes were *g.* to. *Rev* 6:11
power was *g.* to him to. 13:5
it was *g.* unto him to make war. 7

God or Lord ha... given

the Lord hath *g.* Abraham flocks.
Gen 24:35
and Rachel said, *God hath g.* 30:6
and Leah said, *God hath g.* me. 18
God hath g. me your father's. 31:9
G. hath graciously *g.* me. 33:5
God hath g. you treasure in. 43:23
the children *God hath g.* me. 48:9

the *Lord hath g.* you. *Ex* 16:15
for that the *Lord hath g.* you the. 29
land which the *Lord hath g.* them.
Num 32:7, 9; *Deut* 3:18; 28:52
Josh 2:9, 14; 23:13, 15; *Jer* 25:5
shout, for *Lord hath g.* *Josh* 6:16
land which the *Lord hath g.* 18:3
Lord hath g. me my. *1 Sam* 1:27
Lord hath g. it to a neighbour.
15:28; 28:17
with what the *Lord hath g.* 30:23
the kingdom *hath God g.* me.
2 Chr 36:23; *Ezra* 1:2
man to whom God *hath g. Eccl* 5:19
children *Lord hath g.* *Isa* 8:18
Heb 2:13
Lord hath g. a command. *Isa* 23:11
Lord hath g. me the tongue. 50:4
Lord hath g. knowledge. *Jer* 11:18
seeing the *Lord hath g.* it. 47:7
the *Lord had g.* thanks. *John* 6:23
whom *God hath g.* to. *Acts* 5:32
God hath g. thee all that. 27:24
God hath g. them spirit. *Rom* 11:8
the *Lord hath g.* us for edification.
2 Cor 10:8; 13:10
but *God* who *hath g.* us. *1 Thes* 4:8
the record *God hath g.* *1 John* 5:11

see rest

I have, or *have I* **given**

brethren *have I g.* him. *Gen* 27:37
I have g. thee that thou. *1 Ki* 3:13
therefore *I have g.* Jacob. *Isa* 43:28*
I have g. him for a witness. 55:4
things *I have g.* shall pass. *Jer* 8:13
I have g. it to whom it seemed. 27:5
I have g. thee cow's dung. *Ezek* 4:15
I have g. him land of Egypt. 29:20
I have g. you cleanness. *Amos* 4:6
be pulled out of land *I have g.* 9:15
I have g. you example. *John* 13:15
I have g. them the words. 17:8, 14
gavest me, *I have g.* them. 22
I have g. order to the. *1 Cor* 16:1

not given

and she was *not g.* unto. *Gen* 38:14
I have *not g.* ought. *Deut* 26:14
Lord hath *not g.* you an heart. 29:4
hath he *not g.* you rest ? *1 Chr* 22:18
Levites had *not* been *g.* *Neh* 13:10
thou hast *not g.* water to. *Job* 22:7
maidens were *not g.* *Ps* 78:63
but he hath *not g.* me over. 118:18
who hath *not g.* us as a prey. 124:6
Jerusalem *not* be *g.* into. *Isa* 37:10
thou shalt *not* be *g.* into. *Jer* 39:17
because thou hast *not g.* forth upon. *Ezek* 3:20
he that hath *not g.* forth upon. 18:8
to them it is *not g.* *Mat* 13:11
Holy Ghost was *not* yet *g. John* 7:39
bishop *not g.* to wine. *1 Tim* 3:3*
Tit 1:7*
not g. to much wine. *1 Tim* 3:8
God hath *not g.* us the. *2 Tim* 1:7
women likewise *not g.* to. *Tit* 2:3*

shall be given

shall inheritance be *g.* *Num* 26:54
thy sheep *shall* be *g.* to. *Deut* 28:31
thy sons *shall* be *g.* to another. 32
commandment *shall* be *g. Ezra* 4:21
it *shall* be *g.* to half of. *Esth* 5:3
to him *shall* be *g.* of gold. *Ps* 72:15
what *shall* be *g.* to thee ? 120:3
reward *shall* be *g.* him. *Isa* 3:11
bread *shall* be *g.* him, waters. 33:16
glory of Lebanon *shall* be *g.* 35:2
this city *shall* be *g.* into the hand of
king. *Jer* 21:10; 38:3, 18
marishes, they *shall* be *g. Ezek* 47:11
the saints *shall* be *g.* into. *Dan* 7:25
the kingdom *shall* be *g.* to the. 27
ask and it *shall* be *g.* you in that
same hour. *Mat* 7:7; *Luke* 11:9
shall be *g.* you in same. *Mat* 10:19
Mark 13:11
no sign *shall* be *g.* *Mat* 12:39
Mark 8:12; *Luke* 11:29
hath, to him *shall* be *g.* and more
abundance. *Mat* 13:12; 25:29
Mark 4:25; *Luke* 8:18
it *shall* be *g.* them for. *Mat* 20:23
kingdom of God *shall* be *g.* 21:43
give, and it *shall* be *g.* *Luke* 6:38

your prayers I *shall* be *g. Philem* 22
God, and it *shall* be *g.* him. *Jas* 1:5

thou hast, or *hast thou* **given**

thou hast g. no seed. *Gen* 15:3
which *thou hast g.* us. *Deut* 26:15
thou hast g. me south. *Josh* 15:19*
Judg 1:15*
why *hast thou g.* me ? *Josh* 17:14
thou hast g. this great. *Judg* 15:18
thou hast g. him bread. *1 Sam* 22:13
this deed *thou hast g.* *2 Sam* 12:14
thou hast g. me the shield of thy
salvation. 22:36; *Ps* 18:35
thou hast g. me the necks.
2 Sam 22:41; *Ps* 18:40
thou hast g. him a son to. *1 Ki* 3:6
land *thou hast g.* 8:36; *2 Chr* 6:27
are these *thou hast g.*? *1 Ki* 9:13
possession *thou hast g.* 2 *Chr* 20:11
thou hast g. us such. *Ezra* 9:13
thou hast g. him his heart's. *Ps* 21:2
thou hast g. us like sheep. 44:11
thou hast g. a banner to them. 60:4
thou hast g. me the heritage. 61:5
thou hast g. commandment to. 71:3
thou hast g. him power. *John* 17:2
that all things *thou hast g.* me. 7
but for them which *thou hast g.* 9
thy name those *thou hast g.* me. 11
thou hast g. them blood. *Rev* 16:6

giver

taker of usury, so with *g.* *Isa* 24:2
God loveth a cheerful *g.* *2 Cor* 9:7

givest

thou *g.* him nought, and. *Deut* 15:9
not be grieved when thou *g.* him. 10
if righteous, what *g.* thou ? *Job* 35:7
thou *g.* thy mouth to evil. *Ps* 50:19
thou *g.* them tears to drink. 80:5
thou *g.* them, they gather. 104:28
thou *g.* them their meat in. 145:15
rest content, though thou *g.* *Pr* 6:35
thou *g.* not warning, to. *Ezek* 3:18
but thou *g.* thy gifts to all. 16:33
that thou *g.* a reward, and none. 34
thou verily *g.* thanks. *1 Cor* 14:17

giveth

he *g.* you on sixth day. *Ex* 16:29
in land which Lord thy God *g.* thee.
20:12; *Deut* 4:40; 5:16; 25:15
every man that *g.* willingly. *Ex* 25:2*
all that any man *g.* *Lev* 27:9
the Lord our God *g.* thee. *Deut* 2:29
4:1, 21; 11:17, 31; 12:1, 10*
15:4, 7; 16:20; 17:14; 18:9; 19:1
2, 10, 14; 21:1, 23; 24:4; 26:1, 2
27:2, 3; 28:8; *Josh* 1:11, 15
he that *g.* thee power. *Deut* 8:18
God *g.* not this land for thy. 9:6
g. you rest from. 12:10; 25:19
if a prophet *g.* thee a sign or. 13:1
gates which Lord *g.* 16:5, 18; 17:2
who *g.* rain upon the earth. *Job* 5:10
he *g.* no account of any of his. 33:13
when he *g.* quietness. 34:29
who *g.* songs. 35:10
but *g.* right to the poor. 36:6
he *g.* meat. 31
great deliverance *g.* he. *Ps* 18:50
righteous sheweth mercy, *g.* 37:21
God of Israel is he that *g.* 68:35
of thy words *g.* light. 119:130
for so he *g.* his beloved. 127:2
who *g.* food to all flesh. 136:25
146:7; 147:9
g. salvation to kings. 144:10
he *g.* snow. 147:16
the Lord *g.* wisdom out. *Pr* 2:6
he *g.* grace to the lowly. 3:34
Jas 4:6; *1 Pet* 5:5
good understanding *g.* *Pr* 13:15
g. and spareth not. 21:26; 22:9
he that *g.* to the poor shall. 28:27
g. to a man that is good, but to the
sinner he *g.* travail. *Eccl* 2:26
yet God *g.* him not power to. 6:2
he *g.* power to the faint. *Isa* 40:29
g. breath. 42:5
g. rain. *Jer* 5:24
woe to him that *g.* him not. 22:13
g. the sun for a light. 31:35
he *g.* his cheek to him. *Lam* 3:30

he g. wisdom to the wise. Dan 2:21
and g. it to whomsoever. 4:17, 25, 32
woe to him that g. his. Hab 2:15
it g. light to all that are. Mat 5:15
God g. not the Spirit. John 3:34
but my Father g. you the true. 6:32
who cometh down and g. life. 33
all that the Father g. me shall. 37
the good shepherd g. his. 10:11
not as the world g. give I. 14:27
he g. to all life, breath. Acts 17:25
he that g. let him do it. Rom 12:8
he eateth to the Lord, for he g. 14:6
but God that g. the. 1 Cor 3:7
he that g. her in marriage. 7:38
God g. it a body as it hath. 15:38
but thanks be to God who g. us. 57
killeth, but the Spirit g. 2 Cor 3:6
g. us richly all things. 1 Tim 6:17
ask of God, that g. to. Jas 1:5
g. more grace, God g. grace to. 4:6
as of ability that God g. 1 Pet 4:11*
for the Lord God g. Rev 22:5

giving

loveth the stranger in g. Deut 10:18
by g. him a double portion of. 21:17
visited his people in g. Ruth 1:6
my desire, in g. food. 1 Ki 5:9
by g. him according to. 2 Chr 6:23
their hope be as the g. Job 11:20
were marrying and g. Mat 24:38
g. out that himself was. Acts 8:9
g. them the Holy Ghost, as he. 15:8
was strong in faith, g. Rom 4:20
g. of the law, and the service. 9:4
things g. sound. 1 Cor 14:7
at thy g. of thanks. 16
g. no offence in any thing. 2 Cor 6:3
concerning g. and. Phil 4:15
g. heed to seducing. 1 Tim 4:1
g. honour to the wife as. 1 Pet 3:7
g. all diligence, add to. 2 Pet 1:5
g. themselves over to. Jude 7
see thanks

glad

seeth thee, he will be g. Ex 4:14
the priest's heart was g. Judg 18:20
men of Jabesh were g. 1 Sam 11:9
Israel went to tents g. 1 Ki 8:66
2 Chr 7:10
Haman g. Esth 5:9
the city Shushan was g. 8:15
are g. when they can find. Job 3:22
see it and are g. 22:19; Ps 64:10
therefore my heart is g. Ps 16:9
thou hast made him g. with. 21:6
shall hear and be g. 34:2; 69:32
them be g. that favour my. 35:27
they have made thee g. 45:8
the streams shall make g. the. 46:4
let the nations be g. and sing. 67:4
make us g. 90:15
thou, Lord, hast made me g. 92:4
let the isles be g. 97:1
Zion heard, and was g. 8
wine that maketh g. the. 104:15
I will be g. in the Lord. 34*
Egypt was g. 105:38
then are they g. because. 107:30
they that fear thee will be g. 119:74
I was g. when they said unto. 122:1
whereof we are g. 126:3
a wise son maketh a g. father.
Pr 10:1; 15:20
but a good word maketh it g. 12:25
that is g. at calamities, not. 17:5
and thy mother shall be g. 23:25
let not thy heart be g. when. 24:17
wise, and make my heart g. 27:11
wilderness shall be g. Isa 35:1
Hezekiah was g. of them, and. 39:2
is born, making him very g. Jer 20:15
because ye were g. O ye. 50:11
they are g. that thou. Lam 1:21
was the king exceeding g. Dan 6:23
they make the king g. Hos 7:3
Jonah was g. because of. Jonah 4:6
shall see it and be g. Zech 10:7
were g. and promised money.
Mark 14:11; Luke 22:5
I am sent to shew thee these g.
tidings. Luke 1:19*
shewing the g. tidings of the. 8:1*

make merry and be g. Luke 15:32
saw my day and was g. John 8:56
I am g. for your sakes that I. 11:15
seen grace of G. he was g. Acts 11:23
heard this, they were g. 13:48
I am g. therefore on. Rom 16:19*
I am g. of the coming. 1 Cor 16:17*
then that maketh me g.? 2 Cor 2:2
we are g. when we are weak. 13:9*
glory revealed, ye may be g. also.
1 Pet 4:13*

glad joined with rejoice

be g. and let the earth rejoice.
1 Chr 16:31; Ps 96:11
I will be g. and rejoice. Ps 9:2
rejoice, Israel being g. 14:7; 53:6
I will be g. and rejoice in thy. 31:7
be g. and rejoice, ye righteous.
32:11; 68:3
that seek thee, be g. and rejoice.
40:16; 70:4
rejoice, daughters of Judah be g.
48:11*
that we may be g. and rejoice. 90:14
we will rejoice and be g. in it. 118:24
we will be g. and rejoice in thee.
S of S 1:4
we will rejoice and be g. in his salvation. Isa 25:9*
but be you g. and rejoice for. 65:18
rejoice ye with Jerusalem, and be g.
66:10
rejoice and be g. O Edom. Lam 4:21
O land, be g. and rejoice. Joel 2:21
g. ye children of Zion, and rejoice. 23
they rejoice and are g. Hab 1:15
be g. and rejoice, O. Zeph 3:14
rejoice and be g. great. Mat 5:12
rejoice, my tongue was g. Acts 2:26*
be g. and rejoice, the. Rev 19:7*

gladly

Herod heard John g. Mark 6:20
people heard Christ g. 12:37
that g. received the word. Acts 2:41
the brethren received us g. 21:17
ye suffer fools g. seeing. 2 Cor 11:19
most g. therefore will I rather. 12:9
I will very g. spend and be. 15

gladness

in the day of your g. ye. Num 10:10
not the Lord with g. of. Deut 28:47
brought up ark with g. 2 Sam 6:12*
strength and g. are in. 1 Chr 16:27
drink that day with great g. 29:22
sang praises with g. 2 Chr 29:30
of unleavened bread with g. 30:21
kept other seven days with g. 23
there was very great g. Neh 8:17
keep the dedication with g. 12:27
light, and g. and joy. Esth 8:16, 17
a day of feasting and g. 9:17, 18, 19
thou hast put g. in my heart. Ps 4:7
thou hast girded me with g. 30:11
thee with oil of g. 45:7; Heb 1:9
with g. and rejoicing shall. Ps 45:15
make me to hear joy and g. 51:8
and g. is sown for the upright. 97:11
serve the Lord with g.: come. 100:2
forth his chosen with g. 105:43*
that I may rejoice in the g. 106:5
the righteous shall be g. Pr 10:28
and in the day of the g. S of S 3:11
joy and g. is taken away. Isa 16:10
behold joy and g. 22:13
ye shall have a song and g. 30:29
obtain joy and g. 35:10; 51:11
joy and g. shall be found. 51:3
cease voice of mirth and g. Jer 7:34
16:9; 25:10
sing with g. for Jacob, shout. 31:7
heard a voice of joy and g. 33:11
joy and g. taken from the. 48:33
joy and g. from house. Joel 1:16
house of Judah joy and g. Zech 8:19
receive it with g. Mark 4:16*
shalt have joy and g. Luke 1:14
did eat their meat with g. Acts 2:46
opened not the gate for g. 12:14*
our hearts with food and g. 17
in the Lord with all g. Phil 2:29*

glass

see through a g. darkly. 1 Cor 13:12*

beholding as in a g. 2 Cor 3:18*
his natural face in a g. Jas 1:23*
there was a sea of g. like. Rev 4:6
I saw a sea of g. mingled. 15:2
pure gold, like clear g. 21:18, 21

glasses

Lord will take away g. Isa 3:23*
see looking

glean

thou shalt not g. vineyard.
Lev 19:10; Deut 24:21
go to field and g. ears. Ruth 2:2
they shall thoroughly g. Jer 6:9

gleaned

g. of them in highways. Judg 20:45
she came and g. after. Ruth 2:3

gleaning, -s

the g. of harvest. Lev 19:9; 23:22
is not the g. of grapes? Judg 8:2
yet g. grapes shall be left. Isa 17:6
the g. grapes when vintage is. 24:13
they not leave some g.? Jer 49:9
I am as the grape g. of the. Mi 7:1

glede

ye shall not eat the g. Deut 14:13

glistering

now I have prepared g. 1 Chr 29:2*
the g. sword cometh out. Job 20:25
raiment was white and g. Luke 9:29*

glitter, -ing

if I whet my g. sword. Deut 32:41
g. spear rattleth against. Job 39:23
furbished that it may g. Ezek 21:10*
to consume, because of the g. 28*
lifteth up the g. spear. Nah 3:3
shining of thy g. spear. Hab 3:11

gloominess

a day of darkness and g. Joel 2:2
Zeph 1:15

gloriest

wherefore g. thou in the? Jer 49:4

glorieth

let him that g. Jer 9:24
1 Cor 1:31; 2 Cor 10:17

glorified

all the people I will be g. Lev 10:3
hast increased nation, thou art g.
Isa 26:15
for the Lord hath g. himself. 44:23
O Israel, in whom I will be g. 49:3
of Israel he hath g. thee. 55:5; 60:9
my hands, that I may be g. 61:3
of the Lord that he might be g. 5
said. let the Lord be g. 66:5
I will be g. in midst. Ezek 28:22
in the day I shall be g. 39:13
hast thou not g. Dan 5:23
pleasure in it, and be g. Hag 1:8
marvelled, and g. God. Mat 9:8
Mark 2:12; Luke 5:26
they g. the God of Israel. Mat 15:31
synagogues, being g. of. Luke 4:15
fear on all, and they g. God. 7:16
made straight, and g. God. 13:13
the leper g. God. 17:15
the centurion g. God. 23:47
Holy Ghost was not yet given,
because Jesus not g. John 7:39
Son of God might be g. 11:4
but when Jesus was g. 12:16
the Son of man should be g. 23
I have both g. it, and will. 28
Son of man g. God is g. in. 13:31
if God be g. in him, God shall. 32
that the Father may be g. in. 14:13
herein is my Father g. that ye. 15:8
I have g. thee on earth. 17:4
and thine are mine, and I am g. 10
God of our fathers hath g. Acts 3:13
for all men g. God for what. 4:21
they held their peace, and g. 11:18
Gentiles heard this, they g. 13:48
they of Jerusalem g. the Lord. 21:20
they knew God, they g. Rom 1:21
with him, that we may be g. 8:17
whom he justified, them he also g. 30
and they g. God in me. Gal 1:24
come to be g. in saints. 2 Thes 1:10
the name of Jesus may be g. 12
word of the Lord may be g. 3:1
so Christ g. not himself. Heb 5:5

that God in all things may be g.
  through Jesus Christ. *1 Pet 4:11*
spoken of, but on your part he is g. 14
how much she hath g. *Rev 18:7*

glorifieth, -ing
whoso offereth praise g. *Ps 50:23*
shepherds returned, g. *Luke 2:20*
he departed to his own house, g. 5:25
the blind man followed him, g. 18:43

glorify
all ye seed of Jacob g. *Ps 22:23*
thee, and thou shalt g. me. 50:15
all nations shall come and g. 86:9
and I will g. thy name for ever. 12
wherefore g. ye the Lord. *Isa 24:15*
shall the strong people g. thee. 25:3
and I will g. the house of. 60:7
multiply, I will also g. *Jer 30:19*
g. your Father which is. *Mat 5:16*
g. thy name, I will g. it. *John 12:28*
God shall also g. him in. 13:32
he shall g. me; for he shall. 16:14
g. thy Son, that thy Son also may g. 17:1
now, O Father, g. me with thine. 5
what death he should g. God. 21:19
with one mind and mouth g. God. *Rom 15:6*
that the Gentiles might g. God. 9
g. God in body and. *1 Cor 6:20*
g. God for your professed. *2 Cor 9:13*
may g. God in the day. *1 Pet 2:12*
let him g. God on this behalf. 4:16
fear thee, and g. thy name. *Rev 15:4*

glorious
hand, O Lord, is become g. *Ex 15:6*
who is like thee, O Lord, g. in. 11
mayest fear this g. *Deut 28:58*
g. was king of Israel! *2 Sam 6:20*
thank and praise thy g. *1 Chr 29:13*
blessed be thy g. name. *Neh 9:5*
the king's daughter is all g. *Ps 45:13*
his honour, make his praise g. 66:2
and blessed be his g. name. 72:19
more g. than the mountains. 76:4
g. things are spoken of thee. 87:3
his work is honourable and g. 111:3*
I will speak of the g. honour. 145:5
to make known the g. majesty of. 12*
of the Lord shall be g. *Isa 4:2*
Jesse, and his rest shall be g. 11:10
he shall be for a g. throne. 22:23
whose g. beauty is a fading. 28:1
the g. beauty which is on head of. 4
Lord shall cause his g. voice. 30:30
the g. Lord will be to us a. 33:21*
yet shall I be g. in the eyes. 49:5*
make the place of my feet g. 60:13
who is this that is g. in his? 63:1
led them by Moses with his g. 12
people to make thyself a g. name. 14
a g. high throne from. *Jer 17:12*
made very g. in midst. *Ezek 27:25*
he shall stand in the g. *Dan 11:16*
he shall enter also into the g. 41
between the seas in the g. holy. 45
people rejoiced for g. *Luke 13:17*
into the g. liberty of the. *Rom 8:21*
engraven in stones was g. *2 Cor 3:7*
of the Spirit be rather g. 3:8
lest light of g. gospel should. 4:4
it to himself a g. church. *Eph 5:27*
like to his g. body. *Phil 3:21*
according to his g. power. *Col 1:11*
according to g. gospel. *1 Tim 1:11*
looking for g. appearing. *Tit 2:13*

gloriously
he hath triumphed g. *Ex 15:1*
reign before his ancients g. *Isa 24:23*

glory
hath he gotten all this g. *Gen 31:1*
for Aaron for g. *Ex 28:2, 40*
inherit the throne of g. *1 Sam 2:8*
g. is departed from Israel. 4:21. 22
for Lord must be of g. *1 Chr 22:5*
thine is greatness, power, and g. 29:11; *Mat 6:13*
Haman told of the g. of. *Esth 5:11*
the g. of his nostrils is. *Job 39:20*
and array thyself with g. and. 40:10*
King of g. shall come in. *Ps 24:7, 9*
who is this King of g.? the Lord. 10

the God of g. thundereth. *Ps 29:3*
when the g. of his house. 49:16
afterward receive me to g. 73:24
help us, O God, for the g. of. 79:9
that g. may dwell in our land. 85:9
for thou art the g. of their. 89:17
they changed their g. into. 100:20
speak of the g. of thy. 145:11
let the saints be joyful in g. 149:5
the wise shall inherit g. *Pr 3:35*
the g. of children are their. 17:6
the g. of young men is their. 20:29
search their own g. is not g. 25:27
men rejoice there is g. 28:12
hide thee in the dust, for the g. of his majesty. *Isa 2:10, 19, 21*
for upon all the g. shall be a. 4:5
their g. and pomp shall descend. 5:14
where will ye leave your g.? 10:3
I will punish the g. of his high. 12
and shall consume the g. of his. 18
Babylon the g. of kingdom. 13:19
all of them lie in g. each in. 14:18
the g. of Moab shall be. 16:14
they shall be as the g. of the. 17:3
g. of Jacob shall be made thin. 4
be ashamed of Egypt their g. 20:5
and all the g. of Kedar shall. 21:16
g. of his Father's house. 22:24
to stain the pride of all g. 23:9
we heard songs, even g. to. 24:16
the g. of Lebanon shall be. 35:2
in their g. ye shall boast. 61:6
with the abundance of her g. 66:11
the g. of the Gentiles as a. 12
have changed their g. *Jer 2:11*
might be to me for a g. 13:11
even the crown of your g. 18
g. of all lands. *Ezek 20:6, 15*
take from them joy of their g. 24:25
I will open the g. of the. 25:9
I shall set g. in the land of. 26:20
whom art thou thus like in g.? 31:18
hath given thee power and g. *Dan 2:37; 7:14*
the g. of my kingdom returned. 4:36
and increase with g. 11:39
I will change their g. *Hos 4:7*
as for Ephraim, their g. shall. 9:11
priests that rejoiced for the g. 10:5
come to Adullam the g. *Mi 1:15*
end of the store and g. *Nah 2:9*
filled with shame for g. *Hab 2:16*
this house in her first g.? *Hag 2:3*
I will fill this house with g. saith. 7
g. of this latter house greater. 9
will be the g. in midst. *Zech 2:5*
after the g. hath he sent me to. 8
temple, he shall bear the g. 6:13
their g. is spoiled, a voice of. 11:3
g. of the house of David, g. of. 12:7
kingdoms of world, and g. *Mat 4:8*
trumpet, that they may have g. 6:2
shall come in the g. of his Father. *Mat 16:27; Mark 8:38*
Son of man coming with power and great g. *Mat 24:30; Mark 13:26; Luke 21:27*
saying, G. to God in the highest. *Luke 2:14; 19:38*
light to Gentiles, and the g. 2:32
will I give thee, and the g. 4:6
who appeared in g. and spake. 9:31
with the g. which I had. *John 17:5*
the g. thou gavest me, I have. 22
the God of g. appeared. *Acts 7:2*
he gave not God the g. 12:23
could not see for the g. of. 22:11
strong in faith, giving g. *Rom 4:20*
raised from the dead by the g. 6:4
to be compared with the g. 8:18
to whom pertaineth the g. and. 9:4
had afore prepared unto g. 23
of him are all things, to whom be g. 11:36; *Gal 1:5; 2 Tim 4:18*
Heb 13:21; 1 Pet 5:11
to God only wise be g. *Rom 16:27; 1 Tim 1:17*
hath ordained to our g. *1 Cor 2:7*
have crucified the Lord of g. 8
but the woman is the g. of the. 11:7
woman have long hair, it is a g. 15
g. of celestial is one, the g. of. 15:40
one g. of the sun, another g. of. 41

dishonour, it is raised in g. *1 Cor 15:43*
for the g. of his countenance, which g. *2 Cor 3:7*
be g. the ministration of righteousness doth exceed in g. 9
had no g. by reason of the g. 10
we are all changed from g. to g. 18
us an eternal weight of g. 4:17
administered to us to the g. of. 8:19
they are messengers, and the g. 23
to the praise of the g. of. *Eph 1:6*
the Father of g. may give you. 17
what is the riches of the g. 18
for ye, which is your g. 3:13
to him be g. in the church by. 21
are by Christ to g. of. *Phil 1:11*
and whose g. is in their shame. 3:19
according to his riches in g. by. 4:19
now to God and our Father be g. 20
the g. of this mystery, which is Christ in you, the hope of g. *Col 1:27*
ye appear with him in g. 3:4
nor of men sought we g. *1 Thes 2:6*
called you to his kingdom and g. 12
for ye are our g. and joy. 20
punished from the g. of. *2 Thes 1:9*
to the obtaining of the g. of. 2:14
seen of angels, received up into g. *1 Tim 3:16*
in Christ, with eternal g. *2 Tim 2:10*
in bringing many sons to g. *Heb 2:10*
was counted worthy of more g. 3:3
over it the cherubims of g. 9:5
Lord Jesus, the Lord of g. *Jas 2:1*
joy unspeakable, full of g. *1 Pet 1:8*
it testified the g. that should. 11
raised him up, and gave him g. 21
all the g. of man, as the flower. 24
for what g. is it, if when ye be? 2:20
the Spirit of g. and of God. 4:14
a partaker of the g. that shall. 5:1
hath called us to eternal g. by. 10
that hath called us to g. *2 Pet 1:3*
voice to him from the excellent g. 17
g. both now and ever. 3:18; *Rev 1:6*
wise God our Saviour be g. *Jude 25*
worthy to receive g. *Rev 4:11; 5:12*
blessing and g. and wisdom. 7:12
affrighted, and gave g. to God. 11:13

see **crown, honour, vain**

give glory
my son, give g. to God. *Josh 7:19*
ye shall give g. to God. *1 Sam 6:5*
give to Lord g. *1 Chr 16:28, 29*
Ps 29:1, 2; 96:7, 8; Jer 13:16
will give grace and g. *Ps 84:11*
but to thy name give the g. 115:1
let them give g. unto the. *Isa 42:12*
not lay it to heart to give g. *Mal 2:2*
that returned to give g. *Luke 17:18*
when those beasts give g. *Rev 4:9*
fear God, and give g. to him. 14:7
and repented not to give g. 16:9

glory of God
declare the g. of God. *Ps 19:1*
the g. of God to conceal. *Pr 25:2*
g. of the God of Israel. *Ezek 8:4*
the g. of God was gone up from. 9:3
the g. of God was over them. 10:19; 11:22
the g. of God came from the. 43:2
is for the g. of God. *John 11:4*
thou shouldest see the g. of God. 40
up and saw the g. of God. *Acts 7:55*
come short of the g. of God. *Rom 3:23*
in hope of the g. of God. 5:2
received us to the g. of God. 15:7
do all to the g. of God. *1 Cor 10:31*
man is image and g. of God. 11:7
and amen, to g. of God. *2 Cor 1:20*
the knowledge of the g. of God. 4:6
many redound to g. of God. 15
by Christ to the g. of God. *Phil 1:11*
Jesus is Lord to the g. of God. 2:11
smoke from g. of God. *Rev 15:8*
Jerusalem, having g. of God. 21:11
no need of the sun, g. of God. 23

his glory
God hath shewed us his g. *Deut 5:24*
his g. like the firstling of. 33:17*
declare his g. among. *1 Chr 16:24*
Ps 96:3

glory

his *g.* is great in thy. *Ps* 21:5
doth every one speak of *his g.* 29:9
his g. shall not descend after. 49:17
earth be filled with *his g.* 72:19
delivered *his g.* into the. 78:61
thou hast made *his g.* to. 89:44*
and all the people see *his g.* 97:6
Zion, he shall appear in *his g.* 102:16
and *his g.* above the. 113:4; 148:13
it is *his g.* to pass over. *Pr* 19:11
provoke the eyes of *his g.* *Isa* 3:8
the whole earth is full of *his g.* 6:3
the king of Assyria and *his.* 8:7
under *his g.* he shall kindle. 10:16
shall fear *his g.* from rising. 59:19
and *his g.* shall be seen upon. 60:2
Ah lord, or, Ah *his g.* *Jer* 22:18
earth shined with *his g.* *Ezek* 43:2
and they took *his g.* *Dan* 5:20
God came, *his g.* covered. *Hab* 3:3
Solomon in all *his g.* *Mat* 6:29
Luke 12:27
shall sit in *his g.* *Mat* 19:28
Luke 9:26
awake, they saw *his g.* *Luke* 9:32
and to enter into *his g.* 24:26
we beheld *his g.* glory as. *John* 1:14
and manifested forth *his g.* 2:11
but he that seeketh *his g.* that. 7:18
Esaias, when he saw *his g.* 12:41
through my lie unto *his g.* *Rom* 3:7
make known riches of *his g.* 9:23
to the praise of *his g.* *Eph* 1:12, 14
according to riches of *his g.* 3:16
being brightness of *his g.* *Heb* 1:3
that when *his g.* shall be. *1 Pet* 4:13
before the presence of *his g.* *Jude* 24
was lightened with *his g.* *Rev* 18:1

my glory

tell my father of all *my g.* *Gen* 45:13
be sanctified by *my g.* *Ex* 29:43
while *my g.* passeth by. 33:22
which have seen *my g.* *Num* 14:22
he hath strip me of *my g.* *Job* 19:9
my g. was fresh in me, my. 29:20
thou art *my g.* and lifter. *Ps* 3:3
how long will ye turn *my g.*? 4:2
my g. rejoiceth. 16:9
my g. may sing. 30:12
awake up *my g.* 57:8
in God is *my g.* 62:7
sing and give praise with *my g.* 108:1
my g. will I not give to another.
Isa 42:8; 48:11
have created him for *my g.* 43:7
salvation for Israel, *my g.* 46:13
glorify the house of *my g.* 60:7
shall come and see *my g.* 66:18
my g. they shall declare *my g.* 19
I will set *my g.* among. *Ezek* 39:21
have ye taken away *my g.* *Mi* 2:9
I seek not *mine* own *g.* *John* 8:50
that they may behold *my g.* 17:24

glory of the Lord

ye shall see *g. of the Lord.* *Ex* 16:7
g. of Lord appeared. 10; *Lev* 9:23
Num 14:10; 16:19, 42; 20:6
the *g. of the Lord* abode. *Ex* 24:16
the *g. of the Lord* was like. 17
the *g. of the Lord* filled. 40:34, 35
the *g. of the Lord* shall. *Lev* 9:6
filled with *g. of the Lord.* *Num* 14:21
the *g. of the Lord* filled. *1 Ki* 8:11
2 Chr 5:14; 7:1, 2, 3; *Ezek* 43:5
44:4
g. of Lord shall endure. *Ps* 104:31
great is the *g. of the Lord.* 138:5
shall see *g. of the Lord.* *Isa* 35:2
g. of the Lord be revealed. 40:5
g. of the Lord shall be thy. 58:8
and the *g. of the Lord* is risen. 60:1
the likeness of *g. of Lord.* *Ezek* 1:28
blessed be the *g. of the Lord.* 3:12
and behold, the *g. of the Lord.* 23
the *g. of the Lord* went up. 10:4
g. of the Lord departed from. 18
the *g. of the Lord* stood upon. 11:23
g. of the Lord came into. 43:4
knowledge of *g. of Lord.* *Hab* 2:14
g. of the Lord shone. *Luke* 2:9
as in a glass, *g. of the Lord.*
2 Cor 3:18

thy glory

I beseech thee shew me *thy g.*
Ex 33:18
who hast set *thy g.* above. *Ps* 8:1
sword on thy thigh with *thy g.* 45:3
to see thy power and *thy g.* 63:2
let *thy g.* appear unto their. 90:16
kings of the earth *thy g.* 102:15
the chariots of *thy g.* *Isa* 22:18
thy God *thy g.* 60:19
kings shall see *thy g.* 62:2
from the habitation of *thy g.* 63:15
disgrace throne of *thy g.* *Jer* 14:21
come down from *thy g.* and. 48:18
shall be on *thy g.* *Hab* 2:16
thy left hand,in *thy g.* *Mark* 10:37

glory, verb

g. over me, when shall I. *Ex* 8:9
g. of this, and tarry at. *2 Ki* 14:10
g. ye in his holy name. *1 Chr* 16:10
Ps 105:3
give thanks, and *g.* *1 Chr* 16:35
swearth by him shall *g.* *Ps* 63:11
upright in heart shall *g.* 64:10
that I may *g.* with thine. 106:5
shalt *g.* in Holy One of. *Isa* 41:16
shall all the seed of Israel *g.* 45:25
and in him shall they *g.* *Jer* 4:2
let not the rich man *g.* 9:23
let him *g.* in this, that he. 24
he hath whereof to *g.* *Rom* 4:2
but we *g.* in tribulations also. 5:3*
whereof I may *g.* through. 15:17
that no flesh should *g.* *1 Cor* 1:29
he that glorieth, let him *g.* in the
Lord. 31; *2 Cor* 10:17
therefore, let no man *g.* *1 Cor* 3:21
why dost thou *g.* as if thou? 4:7
preach, I have nothing to *g.* of. 9:16
to *g.* on our behalf, to answer them
who *g.* *2 Cor* 5:12
wherein they *g.* they may be. 11:12
many *g.* after the flesh, I will. 18
if I must needs *g.* I will *g.* of. 30
expedient for me doubtless to *g.* 12:1
will I *g.* of myself I will not *g.* 5
for though I would desire to *g.* I. 6
therefore I will rather *g.* in. 9
circumcised, that they may *g.* in.
Gal 6:13
should *g.* save in the cross of. 14
that we ourselves *g.* in. *2 Thes* 1:4
envying in hearts, *g.* not. *Jas* 3:14

glorying

your *g.* is not good. *1 Cor* 5:6
man should make my *g.* void. 9:15
great is my boldness, great my *g.*
of you. *2 Cor* 7:4
I am become a fool in *g.* 12:11

glutton, -s

this our son, is a *g.* *Deut* 21:20*
drunkard and *g.* shall. *Pr* 23:21

gluttonous

they said, behold a man *g.*
Mat 11:19; *Luke* 7:34

gnash

he shall *g.* with his teeth. *Ps* 112:10
thine enemies hiss and *g.* *Lam* 2:16

gnashed

they *g.* upon me with. *Ps* 35:16
and they *g.* on him with. *Acts* 7:54

gnasheth

he *g.* on me with his teeth.
Job 16:9; *Ps* 37:12
he foameth and *g.* *Mark* 9:18*

gnashing

weeping and *g.* of teeth. *Mat* 8:12
13:42, 50; 22:13; 24:51; 25:30
Luke 13:28

gnat

who strain at a *g.* and. *Mat* 23:24

gnaw

her judges *g.* not bones. *Zeph* 3:3*

gnawed

they *g.* their tongues. *Rev* 16:10

go

on thy belly shalt thou go. *Gen* 3:14
whither wilt thou go? 16:8

prosper my way which I go.
Gen 24:42
after that Rebekah shall go. 55
that I may go to my master. 56
go with this man? she said, I will go.
58
Abimelech said to Isaac, go. 26:16
keep me in this way that I go. 28:20
send me away that I may go. 30:25
me go, for the day breaketh... said,
I will not let thee go. 32:26
and I, whither shall I go? 37:30
and we will arise, and go. 43:8
will not let you go. *Ex* 3:19; 4:21
he will let you go. 3:20; 11:1
go, ye shall not go empty. 3:21
go; if thou refuse to let him go, I.
4:23; 8:2, 21; 9:2; 10:4
he let him go, then she said. 4:26*
let my people go. 5:1; 7:16; 8:1
20; 9:1, 13; 10:3
nor will I let Israel go. 5:2
he refuseth to let the people go.
7:14; 8:32; 9:35; 10:27
let the people go. 8:8, 28; 9:28
let the men go. 10:7
who are they that shall go? 8
we will go with our young and. 9
light to go by day and night. 13:21
Neh 9:12, 19
we have let Israel go from. *Ex* 14:5
Lord said to Moses, go on. 17:5
shall go before thee. 23:23; 32:34
gods to go before us. 32:23
Acts 7:40
my presence shall go. *Ex* 33:14
have found grace in sight, go. 34:9
shall be, if thou go with. *Num* 10:32
go by the king's highway. 20:17, 19
to give me leave to go. 22:13
men call thee, rise up, and go. 20, 35
and now behold, I go unto. 24:14
shall make it go through fire. 31:23
shall your brethren go to war? 32:6
but we will go ready armed. 17
by what way ye should go. *Deut* 1:33
in land whither ye go. 4:5, 26
11:8, 11; 30:18
it may go well. 4:40; 5:16; 19:13
ye go after other gods. 11:28; 28:14
go and return to his house. 20:5, 6
7, 8
then thou shalt let her go. 21:14
in anywise let the dam go. 22:7
she may go and be another. 24:2
thy God, he it is that doth go. 31:6
for thou must go with this people.
the Lord, he it is that doth go. 8
the land whither they go to be. 16
know their imagination they go. 21*
sendest us we will go. *Josh* 1:16
the way by which ye must go. 3:4
but they let go the man. *Judg* 1:25
go with me, then I will go. 4:8
the Lord said to him, go in. 6:14
this shall go, the same shall. 7:4
to thee, that thou mayest go. 11:8
then my strength will go. 16:17
whether our way we go shall? 18:5
is your way wherein ye go. 6
be not slothful to go to possess. 9
when ye go. 10
hold thy peace, go with us. 19
to spring, they let her go. 19:25
again, why will ye go? *Ruth* 1:11
she was stedfastly minded to go. 18
let me go to field and glean, go. 2:2
let it go again to its. *1 Sam* 5:11
did they not let people go? 6:6
ark, send it away that it may go. 8
let us go thither, he can shew. 9:6
if we go what shall we bring the? 7
go up before me, to-morrow I will let
thee go. 19
when he turned his back to go. 10:9
for then should ye go. 12:21
how can I go? if Saul hear it. 16:2
thou art not able to go against. 17:33
Saul would let him go no more. 18:2
he said, let me go, why? 19:17
but let me go, that I may hide. 20:5
David went whither could he. 23:13
driven me out, saying, go. 26:19
a woman, that I may go and. 28:7

shall *go* to him, he. *2 Sam 12:23*
I cause my shame to *go* ? 13:13
Absalom said, let me *go* and. 15:7
seeing I *go* whither I may. 20
that thou *go* to battle in thy. 17:11
thy servant will *go* a little. 19:36
that is for David, let him *go*. 20:11
go the way of all the. *1 Ki 2:2*
let me depart, that I may *go*. 11:21
nothing, howbeit, let me *go* in. 22
shall kill me, and *go* to. 12:27*
nor turn to *go* by the way. 13:17
because thou hast let *go* a. 20:42
wilt thou *go* with me to battle? 22:4
2 Chr 18:3
wilt thou *go* with me ? *2 Ki 3:7*
wherefore wilt thou *go* to ? 4:23
water, that they may *go* and. 6:22
he that letteth him *go*, his life. 10:24
it will *go* into hand. 18:21; *Isa 36:6*
in thy name we *go*. *2 Chr 14:11**
let not the army of Israel *go*. 25:7
if thou wilt *go*, do it, be strong. 8
go to nothing and perish. *Job 6:18*
before I *go* whence I shall not return.
10:21; 16:22
it shall *go* ill with him that. 20:26*
ye not asked them that *go* by ? 21:29
righteousness will not let *go*. 27:6
in the way thou shalt *go*. *Ps 32:8*
before I *go* hence, and be. 39:13
God, why *go* I mourning ? 42:9; 43:2
he shall *go* to the generation. 49:19
they *go* from strength to. 84:7
righteousness shall *go* before. 85:13
mercy and truth shall *go*. 89:14
that they might *go* to a city. 107:7
we will *go* into his tabernacles. 132:7
whither shall I *go* from thy ? 139:7
none that *go* unto her. *Pr 2:19*
go and come again, to-morrow. 3:28
can one *go* on hot coals ? 6:28
to call passengers who *go* right. 9:15
go from the presence of a. 14:7
neither will the scorner *go*. 15:12
much more do his friends *go*. 19:7
child in the way he should *go*. 22:6
that *go* to seek mixed wine. 23:30
be three things which *go* well. 30:29
all *go* unto one place. *Eccl 3:20*
return to *go* as he came. 5:15, 16
hath seen no good, do not all *go*? 6:6
it is better to *go* to the house. 7:2
after that, they *go* to the dead. 9:3
not how to *go* to city. 10:15
and the mourners *go* about. 12:5
I would not let him *go*. *S of S 3:4*
mincing as they *go*. *Isa 3:16*
and who will *go* for us ? 6:8
he said, *go* and tell. 9; *Acts 28:26*
I would *go* through them. *Isa 27:4*
that they might *go* and fall. 28:13
he shall let *go* my captives. 45:13
the way thou shouldest *go*. 48:17
thy righteousness shall *go*. 58:8
go through, *go* through the. 62:10
thou shalt *go* to all that. *Jer 1:7*
I might leave my people, and *go*. 9:2
ye shall *go* and pray to me. 29:12
how long wilt thou *go* about? 31:22
go to Babylon. 34:3; *Mi 4:10*
good to *go*, there *go*. *Jer 40:4, 5*
reward, and let him *go*. 5
saying, let me *go*, and I will. 15
place whither ye desire to *go*. 42:22
the voice thereof shall walke. 46:22
they shall *go* and seek Lord. 50:4
they refused to let them *go*. 33
the Spirit was to *go*. *Ezek 1:12, 20*
that I should *go* far from my. 8:6
go through the midst of. 9:4, 5
high place whereto ye *go* ? 20:29
go thee one way or other. 21:16
they shall *go* with flocks. *Hos 5:6*
they call to Egypt, they *go* to. 7:11
when they shall *go* I will spread.
I taught Ephraim also to *go*. 11:3
who, if he *go* through. *Mi 5:8*
and sought to *go*. *Zech 6:7*
these that *go* toward the north. 8
inhabitants of one city shall *go*. 8:21
we will *go* with you, for we. 23
and shall *g.* with whirlwinds. 9:14
Joseph was afraid to *go*. *Mat 2:22*

compel thee to *go* a mile, *go* twain.
Mat 5:41; Luke 7:8
and I say to this man, *go*. *Mat 8:9*
he said to them, *go*, they went. 32
but *go* ye learn what that. 9:13
go rather to the lost sheep of. 10:6
he answered, I *go* sir, and. 21:30
but *go* rather to them that sell. 25:9
sit ye here, while I *go* and. 26:36
go, tell my brethren that they *go* to
Galilee. 28:10
go ye therefore and teach all. 19
go and see. *Mark 6:38*
and they let them *go*. 11:6
shall *go* before him in. *Luke 1:17*
he stedfastly set his face to *go*. 9:51
but *go* thou and preach the. 60
then said Jesus, *go* and do. 10:37
ground and must needs *go*. 14:18
I am ready to *go* with thee. 22:33
not answer me, nor let me *go*. 68
chastise him, and let him *go*. 23:22
to whom shall we *go* ? *John 6:68*
and then I *go* unto him that. 7:33
whence I came and whither I *go*. 8:14
I *go* my way, whither I *go* ye. 21
loose him, and let him *go*. 11:44
whither I *go* thou canst not. 13:36
I *go* to prepare a place for. 14:2
whither I *go* ye know, the way. 4
I *go* unto my Father. 12; 16:10
I *go* to the Father. 14:28; 16:17, 28
cried, if thou let this man *go*. 19:12
I *go* a fishing, they say, we also *go*.
21:3
that he might *go* to his. *Acts 1:25*
determined to let him *go*. 3:13
them, they let them *go*. 4:21
being let *go* they went to their. 23
not speak, and let them *go*. 5:40
should *go* as far as Antioch. 11:22
essayed to *go* into Bithynia. 16:7
saying, let those men *go*. 35
taken Jason, they let them *go*. 17:9
I *go* bound in the Spirit to. 20:22
Cesar, to Cesar shalt thou *go*. 25:12
would have let me *go*. 28:18
now I *go* to Jerusalem. *Rom 15:25*
dare you *go* to law ? *1 Cor 6:1*
bid, and ye be disposed to *go*. 10:27
that I *go* also, they shall *go*. 16:4
brethren that they *go*. *2 Cor 9:5*
I shall see how it will *go*. *Phil 2:23*
will *go* into such a city. *Jas 4:13*

see **free**

go aside
if any man's wife *go aside*. *Num 5:12*
shalt not *go aside* from. *Deut 28:14*
who shall *go aside* to ask ? *Jer 15:5*
commanded them to *go aside*.
Acts 4:15

go astray
brother's ox *go astray*. *Deut 22:1*
go astray as soon as they. *Ps 58:3*
folly he shall *go astray*. *Pr 5:23*
not to her ways, *go* not *astray*. 7:25
righteous to *go astray*. 28:10
caused them to *go astray*. *Jer 50:6*
may *go* no more *astray*. *Ezek 14:11*

go away
go very far *away*. *Ex 8:28*
let him *go away* empty. *Deut 15:13*
if he say, I will not *go away*. 16
Samuel turned about to *go away*.
1 Sam 15:27
will he let him *go away* ? 24:19
their excellency *go away* ? *Job 4:21**
his mouth shall he *go away*. 15:30
ye that escaped the sword, *go away*.
Jer 51:50
I will tear and *go away*. *Hos 5:14*
suffer us to *go away*. *Mat 8:31*
go away into everlasting. 25:46
will ye also *go away* ? *John 6:67*
how I said, I will *go away*. 14:28; 16:7

go back
caused the sea to *go back*. *Ex 14:21*
do in any wise *go back*. *Josh 23:12*
mouth, I cannot *go back*. *Judg 11:35*
go back again, what? *1 Ki 19:20*
shall the shadow *go back* ? *2 Ki 20:9*
so will not we *go back*. *Ps 80:18*

go back to Gedaliah. *Jer 40:5*
I will not *go back*, nor. *Ezek 24:14*

go down
let us *go down* and confound their.
Gen 11:7
I will *go down* now, and see. 18:21
the Lord said, *go* not *down*. 26:2
send him, we will not *go down*. 43:5
we cannot *go down*, then will we *go
down*. 44:26
fear not, Jacob, to *go down*. 46:3
Lord said, *go down*. *Ex 19:21*
and they *go down* quick. *Num 16:30*
nor shall sun *go down*. *Deut 24:15*
the sun hasted not to *go down* about
a whole day. *Josh 10:13*
if thou fear to *go down*. *Judg 7:10*
thou shalt *go down*. *1 Sam 10:8*
go down after Philistines by. 14:36
go down to Keilah, I will. 23:4
who will *go down* with me ? 26:6
let him not *go down* with us. 29:4
David said, *go down* to. *2 Sam 11:8*
why didst thou not *go down* ? 10
make thee *go* up and *down*. 15:20
go down to meet Ahab. *1 Ki 21:18*
go down with him, be. *2 Ki 1:15*
for the shadow to *go down*. 20:10*
to-morrow *go down*. *2 Chr 20:16*
in a moment *go down* to. *Job 21:13*
that *go down* to the dust. *Ps 22:29*
become like them that *go down*. 28:1
and let them *go down* quick. 55:15
they that *go down* to the sea. 107:23
neither any that *go down*. 115:17
I be like them that *go down*. 143:7
her feet *go down* to death. *Pr 5:5*
as those that *go down*. *Isa 14:19*
woe to them that walk to *go down*.
30:2; 31:1
they that *go down* into pit. 38:18
sun shall not *go down*, nor. 60:20
let them *go down* to. *Jer 50:27*
garrisons shall *go down*. *Ezek 26:11*
with them that *go down* to the pit.
20; 31:14; 32:18, 24, 25, 29, 30
these waters *go down* into. 47:8
then *go down* to Gath. *Amos 6:2*
I will cause the sun to *go down*. 8:9
the sun shall *go down*. *Mi 3:6*
is on housetop not *go down*.
Mark 13:15
which are able to *go down*. *Acts 25:5*
let not the sun *go down* on. *Eph 4:26*

go forth
go forth of the ark, thou. *Gen 8:16*
not *go forth* hence, except. 42:15
the priest shall *go forth*. *Lev 14:3*
all able to *go forth* to war.
Num 1:3; 2 Chr 25:5
have a place to *go forth*. *Deut 23:12*
forbare to *go forth*. *1 Sam 23:13*
when kings *go forth* to. *2 Sam 11:1*
I will surely *go forth* with you. 18:2
thou *go* not *forth*, there will. 19:7
and *go* not *forth* thence. *1 Ki 2:36*
said, I will *go forth*; *go forth*. 22:22
minds, let none *go forth*. *2 Ki 9:15*
Jerusalem shall *go forth* a remnant.
19:31; *Isa 37:32*
as wild asses *go* they *forth*. *Job 24:5*
own people to *go forth*. *Ps 78:52*
wilt not thou *go forth* with ? 108:11
go not *forth* hastily to. *Pr 25:8*
no king, yet so they *forth*. 30:27
go forth, O ye daughters. *S of S 3:11*
come, let us *go forth* into the. 7:11
out of Zion shall *go forth* the law.
Isa 2:3; Mi 4:2
the Lord shall *go forth*. *Isa 42:13*
go forth of Babylon. 48:20; *Jer 50:8*
say to prisoners, *go forth*. *Isa 49:9*
made thee waste shall *go forth*. 17
righteousness thereof *go forth*. 62:1
go not *forth* into the field. *Jer 6:25*
if I *go forth* into the field. 14:18
let them *go forth*. 15:1
whither shall we *go forth* ? 2
evil shall *go forth* from. 25:32
O Israel, thou shalt *go forth*. 31:4
measuring line shall yet *go forth*. 39
if thou wilt *go forth* to the king. 38:17
but if thou wilt not *go forth* to. 18, 21

he shall *go forth* from. *Jer* 43:12
go forth as they that *go forth*.
      Ezek 12:4
the prince shall *go forth*. 12
my sword shall *go forth*. 21:4
messengers shall *go forth*. 30:9
and he shall *go forth* by the. 46:8
shall *go forth* over against it. 9
shall *go forth* with great. *Dan* 11:44
let bridegroom *go forth*. *Joel* 2:16
judgement doth never *go forth*.
      Hab 1:4
four spirits which *go forth*. *Zech* 6:5
black horses *go forth* into the. 6
then shall the Lord *go forth*. 14:3
ye shall *go forth* and grow. *Mal* 4:2
behold, he is in the desert, *go* not
   forth. *Mat* 24:26
Paul have to *go forth*. *Acts* 16:3
let us *go forth* to him. *Heb* 13:13
devils which *go forth*. *Rev* 16:14

go forward
Israel that they *go forward*. *Ex* 14:15
they shall *go forward* in. *Num* 2:24
shall shadow *go forward*? 2 *Ki* 20:9
behold, I *go forward*, but. *Job* 23:8

go his way
and went to *go his way*. *Judg* 19:27

go their way
let these *go their way*. *John* 18:8

go thy way
thy wife, take her, *go thy way*.
      Gen 12:19
go thy way, the Lord. *1 Sam* 20:22
my staff, and *go thy way*. 2 *Ki* 4:29
go thy way, eat thy bread. *Eccl* 9:7
go thy way forth by. *S of S* 1:8
go thy way, for words. *Dan* 12:9
go thy way till the end be, for. 13
go thy way, be reconciled. *Mat* 5:24
that thine is, and *go thy way*. 20:14
this saying, *go thy way*. *Mark* 7:29
go thy way, sell whatsoever. 10:21
go thy way; thy faith hath made thee
   whole. 52; *Luke* 17:19
Jesus saith, *go thy way*. *John* 4:50
go thy way, for he is a. *Acts* 9:15
Felix answered, *go thy way*. 24:25

go your way, -s
up and *go* on your ways. *Gen* 19:2
afterward *go your way*. *Josh* 2:16
      Judg 19:5
daughters, *go your way*. *Ruth* 1:12
go your way, eat the fat. *Neh* 8:10
go your way, make it as. *Mat* 27:65
go your way into village. *Mark* 11:2
go your way, tell his disciples. 16:7
go your way, tell John. *Luke* 7:22
go your ways, I send you as. 10:3
receive you not, *go your ways*. 10
go your ways, pour out. *Rev* 16:1

go in, or into, or not *go in*
from Ur, to *go into* land of Canaan.
      Gen 11:31; 12:5
when *go into* tabernacle. *Ex* 30:20
go in and out from gate to. 32:27
wine, when ye *go into*. *Lev* 10:9
house, before the priest *go in*. 14:36
neither shall he *go in* to any. 21:11
only he shall not *go in* to the vail. 23
his sons shall *go in*. *Num* 4:19
but they shall not *go in* to see. 20
that shall the Levites *go in*. 8:15
which may *go* out, and *go in*. 27:17
that they should not *go into*. 32:9
thou also shalt not *go in* thither.
      Deut 1:37; 4:21
son of Nun he shall *go in*. 1:38
live, and *go in* and possess. 4:1
go in and possess. 6:18; 10:11
strong, and *go in* and possess. 11:8
not *go into* his house to fetch. 24:10
turned aside to *go in*. *Judg* 19:15
shalt *go in*, and uncover. *Ruth* 3:4
shall I then *go into*? 2 *Sam* 11:11
I will not *go in*, nor eat. 1 *Ki* 13:8
I may not return, nor *go in* with. 16
may *go in*, and dress it for. 17:12
look out Jehu, and *go in*. 2 *Ki* 9:2
go in and slay them, let none. 10:25
shalt *go into* an inner. 2 *Chr* 18:24
of the Levites shall *go in*. 23:6*

would *go into* the temple to save his
   life? I will not *go in*. *Neh* 6:11
turn was come to *go in*. *Esth* 2:15
her that she should *go in*. 4:8
and so will I *go in* unto the king. 16
then *go* thou *in* merrily unto. 5:14
nor will I *go in* with. *Ps* 26:4
open the gates, I will *go in*. 118:19
make me *go in* path of thy. 119:35
we will *go into* his tabernacle. 132:7
nor *go into* thy brother's *Pr* 27:10
they shall *go into* holes. *Isa* 2:19
and let us *go into* the. *Jer* 31:5
I cannot *go into* the house of. 36:5
but we will *go into* the land. 42:14
go ye not *into* Egypt. 19
when they *go in* shall *go in*.
      Ezek 46:10
go into clay, and tread. *Nah* 3:14
go into house of Josiah. *Zech* 6:10
take the young child, and *go into* the
   land of Israel. *Mat* 2:20
and many there be that *go in*. 7:13
go into the vineyard, and. 20:4, 7
go into village. 21:2; *Luke* 19:30
harlots *go into* kingdom. *Mat* 21:31
go ye *into* the highways. 22:9
go in, nor suffer others to *go in*. 23:13
go into the city, to such a man. 26:18
      Mark 14:13
that they may *go into*. *Mark* 6:36
nor *go into* the town, nor tell. 8:26
go into all the world, preach. 16:15
suffered no man to *go in*. *Luke* 8:51
angry, and would not *go in*. 15:28
he shall *go in* and out. *John* 10:9
see him *go into* heaven. *Acts* 1:11
shall *go into* perdition. *Rev* 17:8

see captivity

go in
Sarai said, I pray thee, *go in* unto.
      Gen 16:2
drink wine, and *go* thou *in*. 19:34
behold my maid Bilhah, *go in*. 30:3
go in unto thy brother's wife. 38:8
that thou shalt *go in*. *Deut* 21:13
if take a wife, and *go in* unto. 22:13
husband's brother shall *go in*. 25:5
marriages, and *go in*. *Josh* 23:12
I will *go in* to my wife. *Judg* 15:1
go in unto thy father's. 2 *Sam* 16:21
shall not *go in* to them. 17:21
went to her as they *go in*. *Ezek* 23:44
a man and his father *go in*. *Amos* 2:7

go in peace
go to thy fathers in *peace*. *Gen* 15:15
to Moses, *go in peace*. *Ex* 4:18
shall *go* to their place in *peace*. 18:23
to Danites, *go in peace*. *Judg* 18:6
to Hannah, *go in peace*. 1 *Sam* 1:17
to David, *go in peace*. 20:42
to Abigail, *go* up in *peace*. 25:35
Achish said to David, *go in peace*.
      29:7
to Absalom, *go in peace*. 2 *Sam* 15:9
let not his hoary head *go* down in
   peace. 1 *Ki* 2:6
to Naaman, *go in peace*. 2 *Ki* 5:19
go in peace, and be whole of thy.
      Mark 5:34
faith hath saved thee, *go in peace*.
      Luke 7:50; 8:48
they were let *go in peace*. *Acts* 15:33

let us go
say, *let us go* to Dothan. *Gen* 37:17
let us go three days'. *Ex* 3:18; 5:3
say, *let us go* sacrifice. 5:8, 17
would hardly *let us go*. 13:2, 6, 13
let us go after. *Deut* 13:2, 6, 13
he spake, *let us go*. 1 *Sam* 9:9, 10
let us go to Gilgal and renew. 11:14
let us go over to Philistines'. 14:1, 6
let us go to Jordan. 2 *Ki* 6:2
let us go into the house. *Ps* 122:1
let us go up to mountain. *Isa* 2:3
let us go into defenced. *Jer* 4:5
let us go by night and destroy. 6:5
let us go to Jerusalem for. 35:11
let us go again to our own. 40:16
let us go, every one to his own. 51:9
let us go to pray before. *Zech* 8:21
let us go into next towns. *Mark* 1:38
let us go, he that betrayeth. 14:42

let us go to Bethlehem. *Luke* 2:15
then saith he, *let us go*. *John* 11:7
let us go to him. 15
let us go that we may die. 16
even so I do; arise, *let us go*. 14:31
let us go again and. *Acts* 15:36
let us go on to perfection. *Heb* 6:1

I will go
I will *go* to the right, *I will go* to the.
      Gen 13:9
with this man? *I will go*. 24:58
let us *go*, *I will go*. 33:12; *Isa* 45:2
son is alive, *I will go* see. *Gen* 45:28
I will only *go* through. *Num* 20:19
thy burnt offering, and *I will go*. 23:3
I will go along by the. *Deut* 2:27
I will go likewise with. *Judg* 1:3
go with me, then *will I go*. 4:8
and she said, *I will* surely *go* with. 9
I will go out as at other. 16:20
thou goest, *I will go*. *Ruth* 1:16
he answered, *I will go*. 1 *Ki* 6:3
he said, *I will go*. 2 *Chr* 18:29
then *will I go* to the altar. *Ps* 43:4
I will go into thy house with. 66:13*
I will go in the strength of. 71:16*
of righteousness, *I will go* in. 118:19*
after them *I will go*. *Jer* 2:25
I will go to them that. *Ezek* 38:11
for she said, *I will go* after. *Hos* 2:5
I will go and return to my first. 7
I will go to my place, till they. 5:15
I will wail, *I will go*. *Mi* 1:8
seek the Lord; *I will go*. *Zech* 8:21
I will go before you into Galilee.
     Mat 26:32; *Mark* 14:28
I will arise and *go* to. *Luke* 15:18
henceforth *I will go* to. *Acts* 18:6

go near
go near, and hear all. *Deut* 5:27
David said, *go near*. 2 *Sam* 1:15
prince would I *go near*. *Job* 31:37
go near, join thyself to. *Acts* 8:29

go not, or not go
if thy presence *go* not. *Ex* 33:15
Hobab said, I will not *go*. *Num* 10:30
he said, thou shalt not *go*. 20:20
Balaam, shalt not *go*. 22:12
I cannot *go* beyond word. 18; 24:13
thou shalt *go* not over. *Deut* 3:27
ye shall not *go* after other gods.
   6:14; 1 *Ki* 11:10
if he say, I will not *go*. *Deut* 15:16
thou shalt not *go* again to. 24:19
but thou shalt not *go* thither to. 32:52
go not far from the city. *Josh* 8:4
if wilt not *go* with me, I will not *go*.
      Judg 4:8
not *go*, the same shall not *go*. 7:4
we will not any of us *go* to his. 20:8
go not empty to thy mother-in-law.
      Ruth 3:17
David said, I cannot *go* with these.
      1 *Sam* 17:39
I may not *go* fight against. 29:8
let not all *go*, howbeit he would not
   go. 2 *Sam* 13:25
not say to you, *go* not? 2 *Ki* 2:18
David could not *go*. 1 *Chr* 21:30
should not *go* to battle. 2 *Chr* 25:13
instruction, let her not *go*. *Pr* 4:13
and *go* not into the way of evil. 14
furious man thou shalt not *go*. 22:24
for ye shall not *go* out. *Isa* 52:12
because they cannot *go*. *Jer* 10:5
thou shalt not *go* into house. 16:8
go not after other gods. 25:6; 35:15
that the vessels left *go* not. 27:18
go not into Egypt. 42:19; 43:2
thou shalt not *go* unpunished. 49:12
steps, that we cannot *go*. *Lam* 4:18
priests shall not *go* out. *Ezek* 42:14
go not into the way of. *Mat* 10:5
go not from house to. *Luke* 10:7
see here or there; *go* not. 17:23; 21:8

go over
I pray thee let me *go over*. *Deut* 3:25
Joshua shall *go over* before. 28; 31:3
land whither ye *go over*. 4:14, 26
      31:13; 32:47
go over Jordan, ye shall *go over*. 4:22
thou shalt not *go over* the. 24:20

who shall *go over* sea for us?
   Deut 30:13
the Lord thy God will *go over*. 31:3
but thou shalt not *go over*. 34:4
therefore arise, *go over*. *Josh* 1:2
said, let me *go over*. *Judg* 12:5
come, let us *go over*. *1 Sam* 14:1, 6
faint, they could not *go over*. 30:10
me *go over* and take. *2 Sam* 16:9
Chimham, let him *go over*. 19:37
he shall come and *go over*. *Isa* 8:7
make men *go over* dryshod. 11:15
down, that we may *go over*. 51:23
Noah should no more *go over*. 54:9
Ishmael departed to *go over* to.
   Jer 41:10
let us *go over* to other. *Luke* 8:22

go out

from all that *go out* of. *Gen* 9:10
time that women *go out* to. 24:11
cause every man to *go out*. 45:1
children of Israel *go out*. *Ex* 6:11
behold, I *go out* from thee, I. 8:29
after that I will *go out*, and. 11:8
let the children of Israel *go out*. 10
none of you shall *go out* at the. 12:22
people shall *go out* and gather. 16:4
let no man *go out* of his place on. 29
seventh year he shall *go out*. 21:2
go out by himself; if married, his
   wife shall *go out* with him. 3
her master's, and he shall *go out*. 4
if the servant say, I will not *go out*. 5
a maidservant not *go out* as.
   then shall she *go out* free. 11
fire on altar never *go out*. *Lev* 6:13
shall not *go out* of tabernacle in. 8:33
ye shall not *go out* at the door. 10:7
then the priest shall *go out*. 14:38
seed of copulation *go out*. 15:16
shall *go out* to the altar. 16:18
he *go out* of the sanctuary. 21:12
jubile it shall *go out*. 25:28, 31, 33
it shall not *go out* in jubile. 30
he shall *go out*. 54
he shall not *go out* to war. *Deut* 24:5
thou shalt *go out* one way. 28:25
who shall *go out*, his blood. *Josh* 2:19
go out. I pray now, and. *Judg* 9:38
he said, I will *go out* as at. 16:20
shall I yet again *go out* to. 20:28
it is good thou *go out*. *Ruth* 2:22
I will *go out* and stand. *1 Sam* 19:3
come, let us *go out* into field. 28:1
Achish said, thou shalt *go out*. 28:1
then Lord shall *go out*. *2 Sam* 5:24
thou shalt *go no more out*. 21:17
not suffer any to *go out*, or come in
   to Asa. *1 Ki* 15:17; *2 Chr* 16:1
put ropes on heads, and *go out* to.
   1 Ki 20:31
at the time kings *go out*. *1 Ki* 20:1
go out and be a lying spirit, *go out*.
   2 Chr 18:21
fear not, to-morrow *go out*. 20:17
go out of sanctuary, for thou. 26:18
himself hasted also to *go out*. 20
lettest such words *go out*. *Job* 15:13
which didst not *go out* with. *Ps* 60:10
scorner, contention *go out*. *Pr* 22:10
be not hasty to *go out*. *Eccl* 8:3
depart ye, *go ye out*. *Isa* 52:11
ye shall not *go out* with haste.
ye shall *go out* with joy, and. 55:12
lest my fury *go out* like. *Jer* 21:12
my people, *go ye out* of the. 51:45
they shall *go out* from. *Ezek* 15:7
prince shall *go out* the same. 44:3
entereth by north, shall *go out*. 46:9
and ye shall *go out* at. *Amos* 5:3
living waters *go out* from. *Zech* 14:8
bridegroom cometh, *go ye out* to.
   Mat 25:6
ye *go out* of city, shake off. *Luke* 9:5
go out quickly into the streets. 14:21
go out into the highways and. 23
must ye needs *go out*. *1 Cor* 5:10
he was called to *go out*. *Heb* 11:8
shall *go no more out*. *Rev* 3:12
and shall *go out* to deceive. 20:8

go to

go to, let us make brick. *Gen* 11:3
go to, let us build. 4

go to, let us confound. *Gen* 11:7
go to now, I will prove. *Eccl* 2:1
go to, I will tell you what. *Isa* 5:5
go to now, ye that say. *Jas* 4:13
go to now, ye rich men, weep. 5:1

go up

arise, *go up* to Beth-el. *Gen* 35:1, 3
and let the lad *go up* with. 44:33
how shall I *go up* to? 34; 45:9
Pharaoh said, *go up* and. 50:6
frogs shall *go up* and. *Ex* 8:3
take heed ye *go not up* into. 19:12
nor shalt thou *go up* by steps. 20:26
neither shall people *go up*. 24:2
a great sin, I will *go up*. 32:30
depart and *go up*, thou and. 33:1
for I will not *go up* in the midst. 3
land, when thou shalt *go up*. 34:24
shalt not *go up* and down. *Lev* 19:16
let us *go up* at once and. *Num* 13:30
we be not able to *go up* against. 31
lo, we be here, and will *go up*. 14:40
go not up. *Deut* 1:41
but they presumed to *go up*. *Num* 14:42
his brother's wife *go up*. *Deut* 25:7
shall *go up* for us to heaven. 30:12
go up, let 3000 men *go up*. *Josh* 7:3
did not intend to *go up* against. 22:33
who shall *go up* for us to? *Judg* 1:1
said, Judah shall *go up*. 2; 20:18
an angel said, I made you *go up*. 2:1
that I may *go up* and down on. 11:37
arise, that we may *go up*. 18:9
we will *go up* by lot against. 20:9
which of us shall *go up* first to ? 18
shall I *go up* again ? 23
go up against him. 28
go not up till the child. *1 Sam* 1:22
if it *go up* by the way of his. 6:9
and to whom shall he *go up*? 20
shall find him before he *go up*. 9:13
Samuel came to *go up* to. 14, 19
say, Tarry; we will not *go up*. 14:9
come up unto us, we will *go up*. 10
shall I *go up* to any of cities of Judah?
   the Lord said, *go up*. *2 Sam* 2:1
shall I *go up* against the? 5:19
should I make thee *go up*? 15:20
I to live, that I should *go up*. 19:34
go up, rear an altar in floor. 24:18
   1 Chr 21:18
ye shall not *go up*. *1 Ki* 12:24
   2 Chr 11:4
if this people *go up* to. *1 Ki* 12:27
it is too much for you to *go up*. 28
go up, look towards the sea. 18:43
go up, for the Lord shall deliver. 22:6
   12; *2 Chr* 18:11, 14
may *go up* and fall at Ramoth.
   1 Ki 22:20; *2 Chr* 18:19
go up, meet messengers. *2 Ki* 1:3
go up thou bald head, *go up*. 2:23
wilt thou *go up* with me ? 3:7
which way shall we *go up*? 8
Hazael set his face to *go up* to. 12:17
Lord said, *go up* against the land.
   18:25; *Isa* 36:10
third day thou shalt *go up*. *2 Ki* 20:5
sign that I shall *go up* ? 8; *Isa* 38:22
go up to Hilkiah. *2 Ki* 22:4
shall I *go up*? *1 Chr* 14:10
go not up after them. 14
we *go up* to Ramoth ? *2 Chr* 18:5
let him *go up*. 36:23; *Ezra* 1:3
he began to *go up* from. *Ezra* 7:9
all which are minded to *go up*. 13
if a fox *go up* he shall. *Neh* 4:3
go up by the mountains. *Ps* 104:8
surely I will not *go up* into. 132:3
flock of sheep that *go up*. *S of S* 6:6
I will *go up* to the palm tree. 7:8
let us *go up* to mountain of Lord.
   Isa 2:3; *Mi* 4:2
let us *go up* against Judah. *Isa* 7:6
weeping shall they *go* it *up*. 15:5
go up, O Elam. 21:2
the smoke shall *go up*. 34:10
ravenous beast shall *go up*. 35:9
go up against this land, and. 36:10
go ye up upon her walls. *Jer* 5:10
arise, and let us *go up* at noon. 6:4
Nebuchadnezzar may *go up*. 21:2

go up to Lebanon, and cry. *Jer* 22:20
let us *go up* to Zion, to the. 31:6
he saith, I will *go up* and. 46:8
go up into Gilead, and take. 11
continual weeping shall *go up*. 48:5
go up to Kedar, and spoil men. 49:28
go up against the land of. 50:21
I will *go up* to land of *Ezek* 38:11
were seven steps to *go up*. 40:26
neither *go up* to Beth-aven. *Hos* 4:15
go up to the mountain. *Hag* 1:8
go up from year to year. *Zech* 14:16
we *go up* to Jerusalem. *Mat* 20:18
   Mark 10:33; *Luke* 18:31
friend, *go up* higher. *Luke* 14:10
go ye up to this feast, I *go not up*.
   John 7:8
go up to Jerusalem. *Acts* 15:2
that Paul should not *go up* to. 21:4
we besought him not to *go up* to. 12
wilt thou *go up* to Jerusalem ? 25:9

go a whoring

lest they *go a whoring*. *Ex* 34:15
and thy sons *go a whoring* after. 16
cut off all that *go a whoring*. *Lev* 20:5
I will cut off such as *go a whoring*. 6
ye use to *go a whoring*. *Num* 15:39
people will *go a whoring*. *Deut* 31:16
Judah *go a whoring*. *2 Chr* 21:13
destroyed all that *go a whoring*.
   Ps 73:27
eyes which *go a whoring*. *Ezek* 6:9

goad, -s

slew 600 men with an ox *g*. *Judg* 3:31
a file to sharpen the *g*. *1 Sam* 13:21
words of wise are as a *g*. *Eccl* 12:11

goat

take a heifer, a she *g*. *Gen* 15:9
if his offering be a *g*. *Lev* 3:12
lay his hand on the head of *g*. 4:24
eat no fat of ox, sheep, or of *g*. 7:23
he took the *g*. which was the. 9:15
Moses sought the *g*. of the. 10:16
Aaron shall bring the *g*. on. 16:9
the *g*. in the wilderness. 22
whosoever killeth a *g*. in the. 17:3
when a *g*. is brought forth. 22:27
he shall bring a *g*. *Num* 15:27
the firstling of a *g*. thou shalt. 18:17
one *g*. for a sin offering, to. 28:22
   29:22, 28, 31, 34, 38
eat the ox, sheep, and *g*. *Deut* 14:4
prepare every day a *g*. *Ezek* 45:23
g. had a notable horn. *Dan* 8:5
rough *g*. is the king of Grecia. 21

he goat

comely in going, an *he g*. *Pr* 30:31
down like rams with *he g*. *Jer* 51:40
behold, an *he g*. came. *Dan* 8:5
therefore the *he g*. waxed very. 8

live goat

bring *live g*. *Lev* 16:20
lay both hands on *live g*. 21

scapegoat

other lot for the *scapegoat*. *Lev* 16:8
to let him go for a *scapegoat*. 10
let go *scapegoat* shall wash. 26

wild goat

ye shall eat the *wild g*. *Deut* 14:5

goats

from thence two kids of *g*. *Gen* 27:9
she put the skins of the *g*. on. 16
and speckled among the *g*. 30:32
is not speckled among *g*. 33
he removed *g*. 35
thy she *g*. have not cast. 31:38
she *g*. and twenty he *g*. 32:14
brethren killed a kid of the *g*. 37:31
take it from sheep or *g*. *Ex* 12:5
offering be of sheep or *g*. *Lev* 1:10
knowledge, he shall bring his offering, a kid of the *g*. 4:23, 28; 5:6
take a kid of *g*. for a sin offering. 9:3
two kids of the *g*. 16:5
two *g*. and present them. 7
offer a male of sheep or *g*. 22:19
sacrifice one kid of the *g*. for a sin
   offering. 23:19; *Num* 7:16; 15:24
five he *g*. five lambs. *Num* 7:17, 23
   29, 35, 41, 47, 53, 59, 65, 71, 77, 83
kids of the *g*. for a sin offering. 7:87
he *g*. sixty, the lambs of first. 88

rams and he *g.* of breed. *Deut* 32:14
Nabal had a thousand *g. 1 Sam* 25:2
brought 7,700 he *g.* 2 *Chr* 17:11
they brought seven he *g.* for. 29:21
the dedication twelve he *g. Ezra* 6:17
of captivity offered 12 he *g.* 8:35
I will take no he *g.* out. *Ps* 50:9
or will I drink the blood of *g.*? 13
offer to thee bullocks with *g.* 66:15
the *g.* are the price of. *Pr* 27:26
thou shalt have *g.*' milk enough. 27
hair is as a flock of *g. S of S* 4:1; 6:5
not in the blood of he *g. Isa* 1:11
fat with the blood of *g.* 34:6
and be as the he *g.* before. *Jer* 50:8
occupied with thee in *g. Ezek* 27:21
between the rams and he *g.* 34:17
drink the blood of lambs and *g.* 39:18
second day offer a kid of the *g.* 43:22
a kid of the *g.* daily for a. 45:23
kindled, I punished the *g. Zech* 10:3
divideth sheep from *g. Mat* 25:32
shall set the *g.* on his left hand. 33
nor entered by blood of *g. Heb* 9:12
blood of bulls and *g.* sanctifieth. 13
blood of *g.* and sprinkled book. 19
not possible that the blood of *g.* 10:4

wild goats

David on rocks of *wild g. 1 Sam* 24:2
knowest thou when the *wild g.* bring.
Job 39:1
are a refuge for *wild g. Ps* 104:18

goats' hair

offering ye shall take *gs.*' *hair.*
Ex 25:4
shalt make curtains of *gs.*' *hair.* 26:7
willing, let him bring *gs.*' *hair.* 35:6
with whom we found *gs.*' *hair.* 23
and all the women spun *gs.*' *hair.* 26
made curtains of *gs.*' *hair* for. 36:14
purify all works of *gs.*' *hair* and
wood. *Num* 31:20
gs.' *hair* for bolster. *1 Sam* 19:13, 16

goatskins

in sheepskins and *g. Heb* 11:37

Gob

with Philistines at *G. 2 Sam* 21:18

goblet

thy navel is like a round *g. S of S* 7:2

god referred to man

made thee a *g.* to Pharaoh. *Ex* 7:1

god for idol

with that which is. *Deut* 32:21
if he be a *g.* let him plead. *Judg* 6:31
they made Baal-berith their *g.* 8:33
went into house of their *g.* 9:27
which Chemosh thy *g.* giveth. 11:24
Philistines' *g.* was Dagon. *16*:23, 24
sore on us, and our *g. 1 Sam* 5:7
Israel worshipped the *g. 1 Ki* 11:33
he is a *g.* either talking, or. 18:27
Baal-zebub the *g.* of Ekron.
2 Ki 1:2, 3, 6, 16
house of Nisroch his *g.*, his sons.
19:37; *2 Chr* 32:21; *Isa* 37:38
hasten after other *g. Ps* 16:4
formed a *g.* or molten? *Isa* 44:10
maketh a *g.* and worshippeth. 15, 17
and that pray to a *g.* that. 45:20
he maketh it a *g.*: they fall. 46:6
vessels into house of his *g. Dan* 11:8
according to the name of my *g.* 4:8
magnify self above every *g.* 11:36
the star of your *g.* ye made.
Amos 5:26; *Acts* 7:43
swear, and say, thy *g. O. Amos* 8:14
cried, every man to his *g. Jonah* 1:5
will walk in name of his *g. Mi* 4:5
this his power to his *g. Hab* 1:11
it is the voice of a *g. Acts* 12:22
the *g.* of this world hath blinded.
2 Cor 4:4

any god

that sacrifice to *any g. Ex* 22:20
nor is there *any g.* beside.
2 Sam 7:22; *1 Chr* 17:20
might not worship *any g. Dan* 3:28
ask a petition of *any g.* or. 6:7, 12
neither shall he regard *any g.* 11:37

17

other god

shalt worship no *other g. Ex* 34:14
because there is no *other g.* can
deliver. *Dan* 3:29
there is none *other g. 1 Cor* 8:4

strange god

there was no *strange g. Deut* 32:12
our hands to a *strange g. Ps* 44:20
no *strange g.* be in thee, nor worship
strange g. 81:9
there was no *strange g. Isa* 43:12
he do with a *strange g. Dan* 11:39

God

*The Creator and Father of all
things, supreme Ruler of the
world. The usual name given to
God by the Hebrews was that which
is rendered into English by the
word Jehovah. Where the older
version has the word GOD printed
in capitals the American Revision
has substituted the word Jehovah.
This word Jehovah was so reverenced by the ancient Hebrews that
it was not generally pronounced, its
place being taken, in speaking, by
Adonai, Lord, Elohim, or El-Shad-
dai, all of which are really expressions for the attributes of God.*

Lord, thou *G.* seest me. *Gen* 16:13
to be a *G.* to thee and thy. 17:7
I am the *G.* of Beth-el, where. 31:13
what is this that *G.* hath? 42:28
you that sent me hither, but *G.* 45:8
behold, I die, but *G.* shall be. 48:21
be to Aaron instead of *G. Ex* 4:16
to me, and be to you a *G.* 6:7
and *G.* shall be with thee. 18:19
what hath *G.* wrought? *Num* 23:23
alas, who shall live when *G.*? 24:23
what nation which hath *G.*? *Deut* 4:7
that he may be to thee a *G.* 29:13
G. do so and more also. *1 Sam* 3:17
14:44; 25:22; *2 Sam* 3:9, 35
19:13; *1 Ki* 2:23; *2 Ki* 6:31
know that there is a *G. 1 Sam* 17:46
till I know what *G.* will do for. 22:3
who is *G.* save the Lord?
2 Sam 22:32; *Ps* 18:31
if the Lord be *G. 1 Ki* 18:21
the *G.* the Lord, he is the *G.* 39
thou art the *G.* even. *2 Ki* 19:15
G., art not thou *G.* in? *2 Chr* 20:6
G. be with him, he is the *G. Ezra* 1:3
art a *G.* ready to pardon. *Neh* 9:17
sayest, how doth *G.* know?
Job 22:13; *Ps* 73:11
art not a *G.* that hast. *Ps* 5:4
the man that made not *G.* his. 52:7
art great, thou art *G.* alone. 86:10
Isa 37:16
behold, *G.* is my salvation. *Isa* 12:2
a *G.* besides me? yea, there is no *G.*
44:8
look unto me, I am *G.* there is. 45:22
I am *G.* there is none else. 46:9
I will be their *G.* they my people.
Jer 31:33; 32:38
a god, I sit in seat of *G. Ezek* 28:2
shalt be a man, and no *G.* 9
therefore it is not *G. Hos* 8:6
for I am *G.* and not man, the. 11:9
who is a *G.* like unto thee? *Mi* 7:18
Emmanuel, which is *G. Mat* 1:23
ye cannot serve *G.* and mammon.
6:24; *Luke* 16:13
good but one, that is *G. Mat* 19:17
Mark 10:18; *Luke* 18:19
there is one *G.* and. *Mark* 12:32
with *G.* and Word was *G. John* 1:1
can do miracles, except *G.* be. 3:2
we have one Father, even *G.* 8:41
forth, and came from *G.* 42
know thee, the only true *G.* 17:3
by wonders, which *G.* did. *Acts* 2:22
we ought to obey *G.* rather. 5:29
patriarchs sold Joseph, but *G.* 7:9
I perceive *G.* is no respecter. 10:34
let *G.* be true, and. *Rom* 3:4
if *G.* be for us, who can be? 8:31
now the *G.* of patience and. 15:5
to us there is but one *G. 1 Cor* 8:6
that *G.* may be all in all. 15:28

hath anointed us, is *G. 2 Cor* 1:21
G. of love and peace shall. 13:11
called *G.* so that he as *G. 2 Thes* 2:4
G. was manifest in the. *1 Tim* 3:16
profess that they know *G. Tit* 1:16
that built all things is *G. Heb* 3:4
ceased from his works, as *G.* 4:10
I will be to them a *G.*, they to. 8:10
G. is light, in him is no. *1 John* 1:5
no man hath seen *G.* at any. 4:12
and *G.* himself shall be. *Rev* 21:3
G. shall wipe away all tears. 4
I will be his *G.* and he shall be. 7

against God

wickedness, and sin *against G.*?
Gen 39:9
the people spake *against G.*
Num 21:5; *Ps* 78:19
transgressed *against G. 1 Chr* 5:25
spake *against* the *G.* of. *2 Chr* 32:19
thy spirit *against G. Job* 15:13
stretcheth out his hand *against G.* 25
multiplieth his words *against G.*
34:37
speak amiss *against G. Dan* 3:29
marvellous things *against G.* 11:36
rebelled *against* her *G. Hos* 13:16
found to fight *against G. Acts* 5:39
blasphemous words *against G.* 6:11
let us not fight *against G.* 23:9
mind is enmity *against G. Rom* 8:7
thou that repliest *against G.*? 9:20
in blasphemy *against G. Rev* 13:6

see almighty

before God

was corrupt *before G. Gen* 6:11
Moses' father *before G. Ex* 18:12
themselves *before G. Josh* 24:1
abode till even *before G. Judg* 21:2
Israel played *before G. 1 Chr* 13:8
and there Uzza died *before G.* 10
burnt sacrifices *before G.* 16:1
Manasseh humbled himself *before
G. 2 Chr* 33:12
heart was humbled *before G.* 34:27
deliver *before* the *G.* of. *Ezra* 7:19
restrainest prayer *before G.*
Job 15:4
shall I appear *before G.*? *Ps* 42:2
may walk *before G.* in light. 56:13
he shall abide *before G.* for. 61:7
let righteous rejoice *before G.* 68:3
in Zion appeareth *before G.* 84:7
him that is good *before G. Eccl* 2:26
to utter any thing *before G.* 5:2
he feareth not *before G.* 8:13
gave thanks *before* his *G. Dan* 6:10
making supplication *before G.* 11
that men tremble *before G.* 26
both righteous *before G. Luke* 1:6
of them is forgotten *before G.* 12:6
in deed and word *before G.* 24:19
found favour *before G. Acts* 7:46
come for a memorial *before G.* 10:4
we are all here present *before G.* 33*
all good conscience *before G.* 23:1
of law are just *before G. Rom* 2:13
may become guilty *before G.* 3:19
to glory, but not *before G.* 4:2
have it to thyself *before G.* 14:22
we speak *before G.* in. *2 Cor* 12:19
behold, *before G.* I lie not. *Gal* 1:20
your hearts *before G. 1 Thes* 3:13
and acceptable *before G. 1 Tim* 5:4
thee *before G.* 21:1; *2 Tim* 4:1
and undefiled *before G. Jas* 1:27
words perfect *before G. Rev* 3:2
the horns of the altar *before G.* 9:13
which accused them *before G.* 12:10
in remembrance *before G.* 16:19
and great, stand *before G.* 20:12*

see called, chosen, commanded

eternal God

eternal G. is thy refuge. *Deut* 33:27

everlasting God

called on name of *ever. G. Gen* 21:33
the *ever. G.* fainteth not. *Isa* 40:28
to commandment of *ever. G.*
Rom 16:26
**see father, fear, forbid, gave,
glorify**

high God

was priest of the most *high G.*
Gen 14:18; *Heb* 7:1
Abraham of most *high G. Gen* 14:19
blessed be the most *high G.* 20
up my hand to the most *high G.* 22
cry unto *G.* most *high. Ps* 57:2
G. was their rock, the *high G.* 78:35
provoked the most *high G.* 56
servants of most *high G. Dan* 3:26
shew the wonders the *high G.* 4:2
high G. gave Nebuchadnezzar. 5:18
that the most *high G.* ruled. 21
before the most *high G. Mi* 6:6
thou Son of the most *high G.*
Mark 5:7; *Luke* 8:28
servants of most *high G. Acts* 16:17

holy God

he is an *holy G.* he is. *Josh* 24:19
stand before this *holy G.*?1 *Sam* 6:20
the Lord our *G.* is *holy. Ps* 99:9
G. that is *holy* shall be. *Isa* 5:16

God of heaven

all earth hath the Lord *G. of heaven*
given. 2 *Chr* 36:23; *Ezra* 1:2
servants of the *G. of heaven. Ezra* 5:11
provoked *G. of heaven.* 12
offerings of the *G. of heaven.* 6:9, 10
law of the *G. of heaven.* 7:12, 21
commanded by the *G. of heaven.* 23
prayed before *G. of heaven. Neh* 1:4
so I prayed to the *G. of heaven.* 2:4
to the *G. of heaven. Ps* 136:26
desire mercies of *G. of heaven.*
Dan 2:18
Daniel blessed the *G. of heaven.* 19
the *G. of heaven* shall set up a. 44
Lord, the *G. of heaven. Jonah* 1:9
glory to *G. of heaven. Rev* 11:13
blasphemed the *G. of heaven.* 16:11

God of hosts

again, O *G. of hosts. Ps* 80:7, 19
we beseech thee, O *G. of hosts.* 14
name is the *G. of hosts. Amos* 5:27

see Lord God

God is

G. is with thee in all. *Gen* 21:22
see, *G. is* witness betwixt me. 31:50
fear not, for *G. is* come. *Ex* 20:20
G. is not a man, that. *Num* 23:19
G. is there in heaven ? *Deut* 3:24
the eternal *G. is* thy refuge. 33:27
our holy *G. is* a jealous God.
Josh 24:19; *Nah* 1:2
G. is come into the camp. 1 *Sam* 4:7
for *G. is* come. 10:7; 1 *Chr* 17:2
G. is departed from me. 1 *Sam* 28:15
G. is my strength and. 2 *Sam* 22:33
G. is gone forth before. 1 *Chr* 14:15
G. himself *is* with us. 2 *Chr* 13:12
I answer thee, *G. is.* *Job* 33:12
G. is mighty and despiseth. 36:5
behold, *G. is* great, and we know. 26
G. is angry with wicked. *Ps* 7:11
G. is not in all his thoughts. 10:4
for *G. is* in the generation of. 14:5
whose *G. is* Lord. 33:12; 144:15
G. is our refuge and. 46:1; 62:8
G. is in midst of her, she shall. 46:5
G. is gone up with a shout. 47:5
for *G. is* King. 7
G. is known in her palaces. 48:3
for *G. is* judge himself. 50:6; 75:7
behold, *G. is* my helper, Lord. 54:4
this I know, for *G. is* for me. 56:9
for *G. is* my defence. 59:9, 17
in *G. is* my salvation and glory.
62:7; *Isa* 12:2
of the fatherless *is G.* *Ps* 68:5
truly *G. is* good to Israel. 73:1
G. is strength of my heart, and. 26
G. is my King of old, working. 74:12
G. is greatly to be feared in. 89:7
gracious is the Lord, our *G. is.* 116:5
G. is the Lord that hath. 118:27
for *G. is* in heaven, and. *Eccl* 5:2
G. that *is* holy shall be. *Isa* 5:16
for *G. is* with us. 8:10
surely *G. is* in thee. 45:14
we have heard that *G. is. Zech* 8:23
G. is able of these stones to raise.
Mat 3:9; *Luke* 3:8
G. is not God of dead. *Mat* 22:32

to his seal that *G. is.* *John* 3:33
G. is a Spirit. 4:24
G. is glorified in him. 13:31
G. is no respecter of. *Acts* 10:34
for *G. is* my witness. *Rom* 1:9
for *G. is* able to graff them. 11:23
for *G. is* able to make him. 14:4*
G. is faithful, by whom. 1 *Cor* 1:9
G. is faithful who will not. 10:13
and report that *G. is* in you. 14:25
G. is not author of confusion, but. 33
as *G. is* true, our word. 2 *Cor* 1:18
G. is able to make all grace. 9:8
but *G. is* one. *Gal* 3:20
G. is not mocked. 6:7
but *G.* who is rich in. *Eph* 2:4
G. is my record, how. *Phil* 1:8
whose *g. is* their belly. 3:19
G. is witness. 1 *Thes* 2:5
G. is not unrighteous to. *Heb* 6:10
G. is not ashamed to be. 11:16
for our *G. is* a consuming fire. 12:29
for with such sacrifices *G. is.* 13:16
G. is light. 1 *John* 1:5
for *G. is* love. 4:8, 16
G. is greater than our heart. 3:20

God of Israel

and saw the *G. of Israel. Ex* 24:10
the *G. of Israel* hath. *Num* 16:9
to give glory to the *G. of Israel.*
Josh 7:19; 1 *Sam* 6:5
G. of Israel was their. *Josh* 13:33
ye committed against *G. of Israel.*
22:16
to do with the *G. of Israel* ? 24
heart to the *G. of Israel.* 24:23
G. of Israel dispossessed the.
Judg 11:23
given thee of *G. of Israel. Ruth* 2:12
the *G. of Israel* grant. 1 *Sam* 1:17
the ark of the *G. of Israel.* 5:11
Lord *G. of Israel,* no God like thee.
1 *Ki* 8:23; 2 *Chr* 6:14
thing toward *G. of Israel.* 1 *Ki* 14:13
called on *G. of Israel.* 1 *Chr* 4:10
of hosts is the *G. of Israel.* 17:24
not seek *G. of Israel* ? 2 *Chr* 15:13
offered to *G. of Israel. Ezra* 7:15
words of the *G. of Israel.* 9:4
blessed be the Lord *G. of Israel.*
Ps 41:13; 72:18; 106:48
Luke 1:68
I the *G. of Israel* will. *Isa* 41:17
call thee by name, *G. of Israel.* 45:3
themselves on the *G. of Israel.* 48:2
glory of the *G. of Israel. Ezek* 8:4
glorified the *G. of Israel. Mat* 15:31

living God

voice of the *living G. Deut* 5:26
hereby know *living G.* is. *Josh* 3:10
armies of *living G.* 1 *Sam* 17:26, 36
Assyria hath sent to reproach *living
G.* 2 *Ki* 19:4. 16; *Isa* 37:4, 17
soul thirsteth for God, the *living G.*
Ps 42:2
flesh crieth out for *living G.* 84 2
living G. an everlasting. *Jer* 10:10
the words of the *living G.* 23:36
living G. and stedfast. *Dan* 6:26
ye are sons of *living G. Hos* 1:10
art Christ, Son of *living G.*
Mat 16:16; *John* 6:69
I adjure thee by the *living G.* 26:63
vanities to *living G. Acts* 14:15
children of *living G. Rom* 9:26
Spirit of the *living G.* 2 *Cor* 3:3
the temple of the *living G.* 6:16
serve *living* and true *G.* 1 *Thes* 1:9
church of the *living G.* 1 *Tim* 3:15
trust in the *living G.* 4:10; 6:17
in departing from *living G. Heb* 3:12
conscience to serve *living G.* 9:14
to fall into hands of *living G.* 10:31
Zion, the city of *living G.* 12:22
the seal of the *living G. Rev* 7:2
For combinations of **Lord with God,**
see in divisions under **Lord**

merciful God

Lord, the Lord *G. merciful. Ex* 34:6
God is a *merciful G. Deut* 4:31
Lord your *G.* is *merciful* if ye turn.
2 *Chr* 30:9
gracious and *merciful G. Neh* 9:31

gracious is the Lord, our *G.* is *merciful.* *Ps* 116:5
thou art a *G. merciful. Jonah* 4:2

mighty God

by hands of *mighty G. Gen* 49:24
Lord is among you, a *mighty G.*
Deut 7:21; 10:17
our God, the *mighty G. Neh* 9:32
G. is *mighty,* and. *Job* 36:5
the *mighty G.* the Lord. *Ps* 50:1
how he vowed to *mighty G.* 132:2
I find an habitation for *mighty G.* 5
be called the *mighty G. Isa* 9:6
shall return to the *mighty G.* 10:21
mighty G. Lord of hosts. *Jer* 32:18
O *mighty G.* thou hast. *Hab* 1:12

my God

then shall Lord be *my G. Gen* 28:21
he is *my G.* my father's. *Ex* 15:2
my people, thy God *my G. Ruth* 1:16
I cried to *my G.* he heard.
2 *Sam* 22:7; *Ps* 18:6
and have not departed from *my G.*
2 *Sam* 22:22; *Ps* 18:21
by *my G.* I have leaped over a.
2 *Sam* 22:30; *Ps* 18:29
for God, even *my G.* 1 *Chr* 28:20
what *my G.* saith, that. 2 *Chr* 18:13
think upon me, *my G.* for good.
Neh 5:19; 13:31
remember me, *my G.* 13:14, 22
my G. my G. why hast thou forsaken
me ? *Ps* 22:1; *Mat* 27:46
thou art *my G.* from my. *Ps* 22:10
I said, Thou art *my G.* 31:14
O *my G.* be not far. 38:21; 71:12
thou art my *Father, my G.* 89:26
sing praise to *my G.* 104:33; 146:2
thou art *my G.* and I will. 118:28
I will extol thee, *my G.* O. 145:1
and take name of *my G. Pr* 30:9
but will ye weary *my G.? Isa* 7:13
is passed over from *my G.* 40:27
deliver me, for thou art *my G.* 44:17
soul shall be joyful in *my G.* 61:10
my G. hath sent his angel. *Dan* 6:22
they shall say, Thou art *my G.*
Hos 2:23; *Zech* 13:9
Israel shall cry to me, *my G. Hos* 8:2
my G. will cast them away. 9:17
I will wait, for *my G.* will. *Mi* 7:7
ascend to *my G.* and. *John* 20:17
and said, My Lord and *my G.* 28
I thank *my G. Rom* 1:8; 1 *Cor* 1:4
14:18; *Phil* 1:3; *Philem* 4
lest when I come, *my G.* 2 *Cor* 12:21
my G. shall supply all. *Phil* 4:19
on him the name of *my G. Rev* 3:12

no God

I am he, there is *no G. Deut* 32:39
there is *no G.* like thee. 1 *Ki* 8:23
2 *Chr* 6:14
there is *no G.* in Israel ? 2 *Ki* 1:16
now I know there is *no G.* in. 5:15
no g. of any nation. 2 *Chr* 32:15
said, There is *no G. Ps* 14:1; 53:1
before me there was *no G. Isa* 43:10
beside me there is *no G.* 44:6, 8
45:5, 14, 21
shalt be a man, and *no G. Ezek* 28:9
shalt know *no G.* but me. *Hos* 13:4

O God

heal her now, *O G. Num* 12:13
only this once, *O G. Judg* 16:28
hear me, *O G.* of my. *Ps* 4:1
redeem Israel, *O G.* out of. 25:22
from bloodguiltiness, *O G.* 51:14
thy vows are upon me, *O G.* 56:12
nor hath eye seen, *O G. Isa* 64:4
to do thy will, *O G. Heb* 10:7, 9

of God

for the cause was *of G.* 2 *Chr* 10:15
not hear, for it came *of G.* 25:20
my defence is *of G.* who. *Ps* 7:10
esteem him smitten *of G. Isa* 53:4
savourest not things *of G.*
Mat 16:23; *Mark* 8:33
of will of man, but *of G. John* 1:13
he which is *of G.* hath seen. 6:46
of doctrine whether it be *of G.* 7:17
of G. heareth: ye are not *of G.* 8:47
this man is not *of G.* 9:16

God

if he were not *of* G. John 9:33
praise of men more than *of* G. 12:43
if it be *of* G. ye cannot. Acts 5:39
is not of men, but *of* G. Rom 2:29
but *of* G. that sheweth mercy. 9:16
of G. powers ordained *of* G. 13:1
of G. is made unto us. 1 Cor 1:30
which ye have *of* G. ye are. 6:19
things are *of* G. 11:12; 2 Cor 5:18
as *of* G. in the sight *of* G. 2 Cor 2:17
our sufficiency is *of* G. 3:5
salvation, and that *of* G. Phil 1:28
righteousness which is *of* G. 3:9
he that was called *of* G. Heb 5:4
not righteousness, is not *of* G.
   1 John 3:10
spirits whether they are *of* G. 4:1
not that Christ is come, is not *of* G. 3
we are *of* G. 6
we know that we are *of* G. 5:19
he that doeth good is *of* G. 3 John 11
see **angel, ark, born, children,**
   chosen, church, counsel, fear,
   glory, grace, hand, house,
   kingdom, knowledge, love,
   man, people, power, servant,
   sight, son, sons, spirit, will,
   words, work, works, world,
   wrath

our God

go and sacrifice to our G. Ex 5:8
because our G. is not. Deut 31:17
ye greatness unto our G. 32:3
serve Lord, he is our G. Josh 24:18
have forsaken our G. Judg 10:10
any rock like our G. 1 Sam 2:2
people, and for the cities of our G.
   2 Sam 10:12; 1 Chr 19:13
who is a rock, save our G.?
   2 Sam 22:32; Ps 18:31
now therefore, our G. 1 Chr 29:13
for great is our G. 2 Chr 2:5
O Lord, thou art our G. 14:11
art not thou our G. who didst? 20:7
now, O our G. what? Ezra 9:10
hear, O our G. Neh 4:4
our G. shall fight for us.
work was wrought of our G. 6:16
our G. the great, mighty God. 9:32
our G. turned the curse into a. 13:2
song, even praise to our G. Ps 40:3
this God is our G. for ever. 48:14
our G. shall come and not. 50:3
and God, even our own G. 67:6
he that is our G. is the God. 68:20
so great a God as our G.? 77:13
he is our G. 95:7
our G. is in the heavens. 115:3
gracious is the Lord, our G. 116:5
lo, this is our G. we. Isa 25:9
to our G. for he will. 55:7
departing away from our G. 59:13
day of vengeance of our G. 61:2
our G. whom we serve. Dan 3:17
remaineth be for our G. Zech 9:7
by the Spirit of our G. 1 Cor 6:11
our G. is a consuming. Heb 12:29
hast made us to our G. Rev 5:10
salvation to our G. who sitteth. 7:10
honour, and power be to our G. 12
see **peace, said, saith, serve, sent,**
   speak, speed, spoken

their God

I will be their G. Gen 17:8
  Ex 29:45; Jer 24:7; 31:33; 32:38
  Ezek 11:20; 34:24; 37:23, 27
  Zech 8:8; 2 Cor 6:16; Rev 21:3
to their G. for offerings of the Lord,
  and bread of their G. Lev 21:6
might be their G. 26:45; Ezek 14:11
thou art become their G.
   2 Sam 7:24; 1 Chr 17:22
the eye of their G. was. Ezra 5:5
where is their G.? Ps 79:10
   115:2; Joel 2:17
people seek to their G.? Isa 8:19
and curse their king, and their G. 21
not the ordinance of their G. 58:2
judgement of their G. Jer 5:4, 5
people that know their G. Dan 11:32
gone a whoring from under their G.
   Hos 4:12
their doings to turn to their G. 5:4
in Lord of hosts their G. Zech 12:5

not ashamed to be called *their* G.
   Heb 11:16

thy God

fear *thy* G. Lev 19:14; 25:17, 36, 43
praise, and he is *thy* G. Deut 10:21
this day the Lord to be *thy* G. 26:17
my people, *thy* G. my. Ruth 1:16
let not *thy* G. deceive thee.
   2 Ki 19:10; Isa 37:10
peace to thee, for *thy* G. 1 Chr 12:18
because *thy* G. loved Israel made he
  thee king. 2 Chr 9:8
to law of *thy* G. in thy. Ezra 7:14
wisdom of *thy* G. laws of *thy* G. 25
this is *thy* G. that brought. Neh 9:18
to me, Where is *thy* G.? Ps 42:3, 10
God, *thy* G. hath anointed thee.
   45:7; Heb 1:9
I am God, even *thy* G. Ps 50:7
thy G. commanded strength. 68:28
praise the Lord, praise *thy* G. 147:12
dismayed, for I am *thy* G. Isa 41:10
full of the rebuke of *thy* G. 51:20
that saith to Zion, Thy G. 52:7
Lord be a light, and *thy* G. 60:19
shall *thy* G. rejoice over thee. 62:5
thy G. whom thou servest. Dan 6:16
is *thy* G. whom thou servest? 20
chasten thyself before *thy* G. 10:12
gone a whoring from *thy* G. Hos 4:6
to *thy* G. and wait on *thy* G. 12:6
prepare to meet *thy* G. Amos 4:12
arise, call upon *thy* G. Jonah 1:6
to walk humbly with *thy* G. Mi 6:8

to, or unto God

interpretations belong to G.?
   Gen 40:8
their cry came up unto G. Ex 2:23
for he is holy unto his G. Lev 21:7
sacrifice to devils, not to G.
   Deut 32:17; 1 Cor 10:20
none like unto the G. of. Deut 33:26
shall be a Nazarite unto G.
   Judg 13:5, 7; 16:17
three men going up to G. 1 Sam 10:3
matter pertaining to G. 1 Chr 26:32
man be profitable unto G.? Job 22:2
meet to be said unto G. I. 34:31
power belongeth unto G. Ps 62:11
to G. the Lord belong issues. 68:20
shall stretch her hands to G. 31
for me to draw near to G. 73:28
I cried to G. even to G. with. 77:1
spirit shall return unto G. Eccl 12:7
in approaching to G. Isa 58:2
our heart with hands to G. Lam 3:41
render unto G. the things. Mat 22:21
   Mark 12:17; Luke 20:25
from God, went to G. John 13:3
you more than unto G. Acts 4:19
not lied unto men, but unto G. 5:4
from power of Satan unto G. 26:18
turn to G. and do works meet. 20
he liveth unto G. Rom 6:10
but alive unto G. 11
yield yourselves unto G. as alive. 13
should bring forth fruit unto G. 7:4
a living sacrifice unto G. 12:1
give account of himself to G. 14:12
not unto men but unto G. 1 Cor 14:2
delivered up kingdom to G. 15:24
unto G. and our Father. Phil 4:20
them that come unto G. Heb 7:25
to G. must believe that he is. 11:6
ye are come to G. the Judge. 12:23
yourselves therefore to G. Jas 4:7
might bring us to G. 1 Pet 3:18
but live according to G. in the. 4:6
hast redeemed us to G. Rev 5:9
child was caught up unto G. 12:5
being the firstfruits unto G. 14:4

see **true**

with God

Enoch walked with G. Gen 5:22, 24
Noah walked with G. 6:9
thou hast power with G. 32:28
people to meet with G. Ex 19:17
hath wrought with G. 1 Sam 14:45
house be not so with G. 2 Sam 23:5
from meddling with G. 2 Chr 35:21
man be just with G.? Job 9:2
and I desire to reason with G. 13:3

might plead for a man with G.
   Job 16:21
a man be justified with G.? 25:4
portion of a wicked man with G.
   27:13
should delight himself with G. 34:9
enter into judgement with G. 23
with G. is terrible majesty. 37:22
is not stedfast with G. Ps 78:8
Judah yet ruleth with G. Hos 11:12
his strength had power with G. 12:3
but with G. all things are possible.
   Mat 19:26; Mark 10:27
   Luke 1:37; 18:27
found favour with G. Luke 1:30
increased in favour with G. 2:52
Word was with G. John 1:1
himself equal with G. 5:18; Phil 2:6
respect of persons with G. Rom 2:11
faith, we have peace with G. 5:1
there unrighteousness with G.? 9:14
labourers together with G. 1 Cor 3:9
this world is foolishness with G. 19
man therein abide with G. 7:24
righteous thing with G. 2 Thes 1:6
of world is enmity with G. Jas 4:4
this is acceptable with G. 1 Pet 2:20
would God, see **would**

your God

your G. hath given you. Gen 43:23
go ye, sacrifice to *your* G. Ex 8:25
of Egypt to be *your* G. Lev 11:45
   22:33; 25:38; Num 15:41
I will be *your* G. and ye. Lev 26:12
  Jer 7:23; 11:4; 30:22; Ezek 36:28
memorial before *your* G. Num 10:10
be holy to *your* G. 15:40
lest ye deny *your* G. Josh 24:27
day rejected *your* G. 1 Sam 10:19
your G. should deliver. 2 Chr 32:14
how much less shall *your* G.? 15
we seek *your* G. as ye do. Ezra 4:2
your G. will come with. Isa 35:4
ye my people, saith *your* G. 40:1
cities of Judah, behold *your* G. 9
between you and *your* G. 59:2
your G. saith the Lord. Ezek 34:31
of a truth it is, *your* G. Dan 2:47
I will not be *your* G. Hos 1:9
say that he is *your* G. John 8:54
to my God and *your* G. 20:17

goddess

after *g.* of Zidonians. 1 Ki 11:5
worshipped Ashtoreth, the *g.* 33
temple of great *g.* Diana. Acts 19:27
worshippers of the *g.* Diana. 35
nor yet blasphemers of your *g.* 37

godhead

think that *g.* is like to. Acts 17:29
eternal power and *g.* Rom 1:20*
dwelleth the fulness of *g.* Col 2:9

godliness

lead a quiet life in all *g.* 1 Tim 2:2
becometh women professing *g.* 10
great is the mystery of *g.* 3:16
exercise thyself rather unto *g.* 4:7
g. is profitable unto all things. 8
doctrine which is according to *g.* 6:3
men, supposing that gain is *g.* 5
g. with contentment is great gain. 6
follow after righteousness, *g.* 11
having a form of *g.* but. 2 Tim 3:5
the truth which is after *g.* Tit 1:1
that pertain to life and *g.* 2 Pet 1:3
add to patience *g.* to *g.* brotherly. 6, 7
of persons ought to be in all *g.* 3:11

godly

set apart him that is *g.* Ps 4:3
help, Lord, for the *g.* man. 12:1
every one that is *g.* pray. 32:6
he might seek a *g.* seed. Mal 2:15
in *g.* sincerity had our. 2 Cor 1:12
sorry after a *g.* manner. 7:9, 11
g. sorrow worketh repentance.
I am jealous over you with *g.* 11:2
will live *g.* in Christ. 2 Tim 3:12
that ye should live *g.* in. Tit 2:12
God with reverence and *g.* fear.
   Heb 12:28*
how to deliver the *g.* 2 Pet 2:9
forward after a *g.* sort. 3 John 6

gods

ye shall be as *g.* knowing. *Gen* 3:5
hast thou stolen my *g.*? 31:30
against all *g.* of Egypt. *Ex* 12:12
shalt not make with me *g.* of. 20:23
thou shalt not revile the *g.* 22:28
not bow down to their *g.* 23:24
covenant with them nor their *g.* 32
up, make us *g.* to go before us.
   32:1, 23; *Acts* 7:40
these be thy *g.* O Israel. *Ex* 32:4, 8
they have made them *g.* of gold. 31
go a whoring after their *g.* 34:15
the sacrifices of their *g.* *Num* 25:2
upon the Egyptians' *g.* also. 33:4
   Jer 43:12, 13; 46:25
images of their *g.* shall. *Deut* 7:25
Lord your God is God of *g.* 10:17
down the images of their *g.* 12:3
thou enquire not after their *g.* 30
their *g.* burnt their sons and daughters in the fire to their *g.* 31
entice thee to the *g.* of people. 13:7
they have done to their *g.* 20:18
say, where are their *g.*? 32:37
Lord God of *g.* knoweth. *Josh* 22:22
mention of the name of their *g.* 23:7
they chose new *g.* then. *Judg* 5:8
I said, fear not the *g.* of the. 6:10
go and cry to the *g.* which ye. 10:14
Micah had an house of *g.* 17:5
ye have taken away my *g.* 18:24
is gone back to her *g.* *Ruth* 1:15
are the *g.* that smote. *1 Sam* 4:8
hand from off you and your *g.* 6:5
cursed David by his *g.* 17:43
she said, I saw *g.* ascending. 28:13
from Egypt and their *g.* *2 Sam* 7:23
your heart after their *g.* *1 Ki* 11:2
incense and sacrificed to their *g.* 8
to go up, behold thy *g.* 12:28
the name of your *g.* 18:24, 25
let the *g.* do so to me. 19:2; 20:10
their *g.* are *g.* of the hills. 20:23
every nation made *g.* *2 Ki* 17:29
and served their own *g.* 33
g. delivered his land? 18:33; 19:12
   2 Chr 32:13, 14; *Isa* 36:18; 37:12
where are the *g.* of Hamath?
   2 Ki 18:34; *Isa* 36:19
g. into fire they were no *g.2 Ki* 19:18
went a whoring after *g.* *1 Chr* 5:25
armour in the house of their *g.* 10:10
their *g.* David burnt them. 14:12
Jeroboam made for *g.* *2 Chr* 13:8
be a priest to them that are no *g.* 9
g. of Seir to be his *g.* 25:14
Ahaz sacrificed to the *g.* of. 28:23
the *g.* of the nations have not. 32:17
vessels in house of his *g.* *Ezra* 1:7
he judgeth among the *g.* *Ps* 82:1
said, ye are *g.* 6; *John* 10:34
thanks unto the God of *g.* *Ps* 136:2
before *g.* will I sing praise. 138:1
fallen, and her *g.* broken. *Isa* 21:9
may know that ye are *g.* 41:23
molten images, ye are our *g.* 42:17
changed her *g.* are no *g.*? *Jer* 2:11
g. thou hast made? . . . number of
   thy cities are thy *g.* 28; 11:13
sworn by them that are no *g.* 5:7
the *g.* that have not made the. 10:11
cry to the *g.* to whom they. 11:12
make *g.* and they are no *g.*? 16:20
that burneth incense to his *g.* 48:35
can shew it, except the *g.* *Dan* 2:11
that your God is a God of *g.* 47
is the spirit of the holy *g.* 4:8
of holy *g.* is in thee. 9, 18; 5:14
the *g.* of gold and silver. 5:4, 23
like the wisdom of the *g.* 11
carry captives into Egypt *g.* 11:8
things against God of *g.* 36
say any more, ye are our *g. Hos* 14:3
out of the house of thy *g. Nah* 1:14
if he called them *g.* to. *John* 10:35
the *g.* are come down to. *Acts* 14:11
they be no *g.* which are made. 19:26
are called *g.* there be *g.* *1 Cor* 8:5
which by nature are no *g.* *Gal* 4:8

see serve

all gods

Lord is greater than all *g. Ex* 18:11

to be feared above all *g.*
   1 Chr 16:25; *Ps* 96:4
all *g.* of the people are idols.
   1 Chr 16:26; *Ps* 96:5
great is God above all *g.* *2 Chr* 2:5
   Ps 135:5
a great King above all *g.* *Ps* 95:3
worship him, all ye *g.* 97:7
exalted above all *g.* 9
he will famish all the *g. Zeph* 2:11

among the gods

among the *g.* who is like. *Ex* 15:11
who among the *g.* could deliver?
   2 Ki 18:35; *2 Chr* 32:14; *Isa* 36:20
among the *g.* there is. *Ps* 86:8

molten gods

no molten *g.* *Ex* 34:17; *Lev* 19:4

other gods

shalt have no other *g.* before me.
   Ex 20:3; *Deut* 5:7
of names of other *g.* *Ex* 23:13
ye shall not go after other *g.*
   Deut 6:14; 11:28; 28:14
thy son to serve other *g. Deut* 7:4
if thou walk after other *g.* 8:19
let us go after other *g.* 13:2, 6, 13
hath gone and served other *g.* 17:3
   29:26; *Josh* 23:16; *Judg* 10:13
   1 Sam 8:8; *Jer* 11:10
speak in name of other *g. Deut* 18:20
away, and worship other *g.* and serve
   them. *Deut* 30:17; *Jer* 22:9
they turned to other *g. Deut* 31:18
then will they turn to other *g.* 20
and followed other *g.* *Judg* 2:12
went a whoring after other *g.* 17
in following other *g.* to serve. 19
go serve other *g.* *1 Sam* 26:19
upon other *g.* *1 Ki* 9:9; *2 Chr* 7:22
his heart after other *g.* *1 Ki* 11:4
gone and made thee other *g.* 14:9
offer sacrifice to other *g.* *2 Ki* 5:17
sinned, and had feared other *g.* 17:7
ye shall not fear other *g.* 35, 37, 38
burnt incense to other *g.* 22:17
   2 Chr 34:25; *Jer* 1:16; 19:4
incense to other *g.* *2 Chr* 28:25
nor walk after other *g.* *Jer* 7:6
walk after other *g.* whom. 9; 13:10
and walked after other *g.* 16:11
burn no incense to other *g.* 44:5
burning incense to other *g.* in. 8, 15
look to other *g.* and love. *Hos* 3:1

see **serve**

strange gods

the *strange g. Gen* 35:2; *1 Sam* 7:3
they gave Jacob the *strange g.*
   Gen 35:4; *Josh* 24:23
jealousy with *strange g. Deut* 32:16
and serve *strange g.* *Josh* 24:20
away their *strange g.* *Judg* 10:16
away altar of *strange g.* *2 Chr* 14:3
away the *strange g.* and idol. 33:15
as ye served *strange g.* so. *Jer* 5:19
setter forth of *strange g.* *Acts* 17:18

God-ward

be thou for people to G. *Ex* 18:19
we through Christ to G. *2 Cor* 3:4
your faith to G. is. *1 Thes* 1:8

goest

in places whither *g. Gen* 28:15
whither *g.* thou? 32:17; *Judg* 19:17
   Zech 2:2; *John* 13:36; 16:5
is it not in that thou *g.*? *Ex* 33:16
inhabitants whither thou *g.* 34:12
thou *g.* before them by. *Num* 14:14
God shall bring thee into the land
   whither thou *g. Deut* 7:1; 11:29
the land whither thou *g.* is. 11:10
cut off nations whither thou *g.* 12:29
when thou *g.* to battle. 20:1; 21:10
thou settest thine hand to, whither
   thou *g.* 23:20; *Josh* 1:7
shalt thou be when thou *g. Deut* 28:6
cursed shalt thou be when thou *g.* 19
cleave to thee whither thou *g.* 21
plucked off land whither thou *g.* 63
die in mount whither thou *g.* 32:50
with thee whither thou *g. Josh* 1:9
thou *g.* to take a wife of. *Judg* 14:3
whither thou *g.* I will go. *Ruth* 1:16

wherefore *g.* thou also? *2 Sam* 15:19
thou *g.* over brook. *1 Ki* 2:37, 42
but thou *g.* not forth with. *Ps* 44:9
when thou *g.* steps shall. *Pr* 4:12
when thou *g.* it shall lead thee. 6:22
keep thy foot when thou *g. Eccl* 5:1
in grave whither thou *g.* 9:10
a prey whither thou *g.* *Jer* 45:5
I will follow thee whither *g.*
   Mat 8:19; *Luke* 9:57
when thou *g.* with thine. *Luke* 12:58
sought to stone thee, *g.* *John* 11:8
we know not whither thou *g.* 14:5

goeth

lo, he *g.* out unto the. *Ex* 7:15
deliver it by that the sun *g.* 22:26
shall bear them when he *g.* 28:29
on Aaron's heart when he *g.* 30
shall be heard when he *g.* in. 35
these ye may eat that *g. Lev* 11:21
he that *g.* into the house. 14:46
him whose seed *g.* from. 15:32; 22:4
the tabernacle when he *g.* in. 16:17
who *g.* to holy things having. 22:3
when it *g.* out in jubile. 27:21
when a wife *g.* aside. *Num* 5:29
the Lord which *g.* before. *Deut* 1:30
thy God is he that *g.* over. 9:3
as when a man *g.* into wood. 19:5
Lord your God is he that *g.* 20:4
when the host *g.* forth against. 23:9
pledge when the sun *g.* down. 24:13
as the sun when he *g.* *Judg* 5:31
as David, who *g.* at. *1 Sam* 22:14
as his part is that *g.* down to. 30:24
thy master *g.* to house of. *2 Ki* 5:18
be with the king as he *g.* out. 11:8
   2 Chr 23:7
this work *g.* fast on. *Ezra* 5:8
that *g.* down to grave. *Job* 7:9
lo, he *g.* by me, and I see. 9:11
when *g.* in company with. 34:8
hear the sound that *g.* out of. 37:2
g. on to meet the armed men. 39:21
prayer that *g.* not out of. *Ps* 17:1
when he *g.* abroad, he telleth. 41:6
such a one as *g.* on in his. 68:21
thy fierce wrath *g.* over me. 88:16
a fire *g.* before him, and. 97:3
man *g.* forth to his work. 104:23
he that *g.* forth and weepeth. 126:6
his breath *g.* forth; he. 146:4
so he that *g.* in to his. *Pr* 6:29
g. after her, as an ox *g.* to the. 7:22
when it *g.* well with righteous. 11:10
pride when *g.* before destruction. 16:18
g. about as a talebearer. 20:19
as a thorn *g.* up into hand of. 26:9
no wood is, there the fire *g.* out. 20
her candle *g.* not out by. 31:18
sun *g.* down, and hasteth. *Eccl* 1:5
man *g.* up, spirit of beast *g.* 3:21
because man *g.* to his long. 12:5
that *g.* down sweetly. *S of S* 7:9
from the time it *g.* forth. *Isa* 28:19
when one *g.* with a pipe to. 30:29
so shall my word be that *g.* 55:11
whoso *g.* therein shall not. 59:8
as a beast *g.* down into the. 63:14
every one that *g.* out. *Jer* 5:6
woe unto us, for the day *g.* 6:4
that *g.* out to Chaldeans. 21:9; 38:2
but weep sore for him that *g.* 22:10
whirlwind of the Lord *g.* 30:23
we will do what *g.* out of our. 44:17
every one that *g.* by it. 49:17; 50:13
have blown, but none *g.* *Ezek* 7:14
their heart *g.* after their. 33:31
in the day that he *g.* into the. 44:27
as the early dew, it *g.* *Hos* 6:4
thy judgements are as light that *g.* 5
this is the curse that *g.* *Zech* 5:3
he said, this is an ephah that *g.* 6
I say to this man go, and he *g.*
   Mat 8:9; *Luke* 7:8
then *g.* he and taketh. *Mat* 12:45
   Luke 11:26
for joy thereof *g.* and. *Mat* 13:44
not that which *g.* into mouth. 15:11
this kind *g.* not out but by. 17:21
Son of man *g.* as it is written. 26:24
   Mark 14:21; *Luke* 22:22
he *g.* before you into Galilee.
   Mat 28:7; *Mark* 16:7

not tell whither it *g.* *John* 3:8
thou hast a devil; who *g.?* 7:20
g. before them, the sheep. 10:4
she *g.* unto the grave to weep. 11:31
not whither he *g.* 12:35; *1 John* 2:11
brother *g.* to law with. *1 Cor* 6:6
who *g.* a warfare any time at. 9:7
beholdeth himself and *g.* *Jas* 1:24
Lamb whithersoever he *g.* *Rev* 14:4
and is of the seven, and *g.* 17:11
and out of his mouth *g.* a. 19:15

Gog
G. his son, Shimei his. *1 Chr* 5:5
set thy face against G. *Ezek* 38:2
I am against thee, O G. 3; 39:1
be sanctified in thee, O G. 38:16
when G. shall come against. 18
give to G. a place of graves. 39:11
G. and Magog, to gather. *Rev* 20:8

Golan, *see* **Bashan**

going
sun *g.* down, a deep. *Gen* 15:12
his hands steady, to *g.* *Ex* 17:12
thou meet thine enemy's ox *g.* 23:4
g. forth of border from. *Num* 34:4
sacrifice the passover at *g.* *Deut* 16:6
rejoice, Zebulun, in thy *g.* 33:18
and smote them in the *g.* *Josh* 7:5
as they were in the *g.* down. 10:11
at the *g.* down of the sun carcases. 27
I am *g.* the way of all the. 23:14
I am now *g.* to house of. *Judg* 19:18
up, let us be *g.* but none. 28
meet thee three men *g.* *1 Sam* 10:3
in *g.* turned not from. *2 Sam* 2:19
hearest a sound of *g.* in trees. 5:24
1 Chr 14:15
as she was *g.* to fetch. *1 Ki* 17:11
went a proclamation at *g.* 22:36
g. by the way, children. *2 Ki* 2:23
they smote Ahaziah at the *g.* 9:27
time of sun *g.* down, he. *2 Chr* 18:34
from *g.* to and fro in. *Job* 1:7; 2:2
deliver him from *g.* down to. 33:24
he will deliver his soul from *g.* 28
his *g.* forth is from end. *Ps* 19:6
calleth earth, from rising of sun to *g.*
down. 50:1; 113:3; *Mal* 1:11
sun knoweth his *g.* down. *Ps* 104:19
g. down to the chambers. *Pr* 7:27
man looketh well to his *g.* 14:15
yea, four are comely in *g.* 30:29
shall be darkened in his *g.* *Isa* 13:10
g. up to Luhith, continual weeping
shall *g.* up; in the *g.* *Jer* 48:5
g. and weeping they shall. 50:4
g. up had eight. *Ezek* 40:31, 34, 37
with every *g.* forth of the. 44:5
after his *g.* forth, one shut. 46:12
and laboured till *g.* down. *Dan* 6:14
g. forth of the commandment. 9:25
his *g.* forth is prepared. *Hos* 6:3
rise, let us be *g.* *Mat* 25:46
what king *g.* to war. *Luke* 14:31
g. through midst of. *John* 8:59
these *g.* before, tarried. *Acts* 20:5
g. about to establish. *Rom* 10:3
some men's sins *g.* *1 Tim* 5:24
disannulling of command *g.* before.
Heb 7:18
g. after strange flesh are. *Jude* 7
see **coming**

goings
and Moses wrote their *g.* *Num* 33:2
the *g.* out of their borders. 34:5
8, 9, 12; *Josh* 15:4, 7, 11; 16:3, 8
18:12, 14
man, he seeth all his *g.* *Job* 34:21
hold up my *g.* in thy paths. *Ps* 17:5
on a rock, established my *g.* 40:2
seen thy *g.* even the *g.* of. 68:24
purposed to overthrow my *g.* 140:4
and he pondereth all his *g.* *Pr* 5:21
man's *g.* are of the Lord. 20:24
is no judgement in their *g.* *Isa* 59:8
there *g.* out were. *Ezek* 42:11
shew them the *g.* out thereof. 43:11
whose *g.* forth have been. *Mi* 5:2

gold
Havilah, where there is *g.* *Gen* 2:11
the *g.* of that land is good. 12
chain of *g.* on Joseph's neck. 41:42

make you gods of *g.* *Ex* 20:23
cast four rings of *g.* for. 25:12, 26
26:29; 28:23, 26, 27; 37:3, 13
overlay them with *g.* 25:13, 28
26:29, 37; 30:5; 37:4, 15, 28
make fifty taches of *g.* 25:18; 37:7
hooks shall be of *g.* 26:6; 36:13
ephod of *g.* 28:6
girdle of *g.* 8
ouches of *g.* 11, 13; 39:6, 13, 16
breastplate of *g.* 15
chains of *g.* 28:24
thou shalt make bells of *g.* 33
who hath any *g.* let him. 32:24
have made them gods of *g.* 31
jewels of *g.* an offering of *g.* 35:22
the boards with *g.* bars with *g.* 36:34
their chapiters and fillets with *g.* 38:24
all the *g.* that was occupied. 38:24
they did beat the *g.* into thin. 39:3
thou shalt set the altar of *g.* 40:5
ten shekels of *g.* *Num* 7:14, 20
the altar twelve spoons of *g.* 84
of the spoons was 120. 86
captains' oblation, jewels of *g.* 31:50
a wedge of *g.* of 50. *Josh* 7:21
Achan and the wedge of *g.* 2
1700 shekels of *g.* *Judg* 8:26
and put the jewels of *g.* *1 Sam* 6:8
laid coffer and the mice of *g.* 11
the coffer with the jewels of *g.* 15
David took shields of *g.* *2 Sam* 8:7
1 Chr 18:7
altar, he overlaid with *g.* *1 Ki* 6:22
cherubims with *g.* 28; *2 Chr* 3:10
the altar and table of *g.* *1 Ki* 7:48
lamps and tongs of *g.* 49
hinges of *g.* 50
Tyre furnished Solomon with *g.* and.
9:11; 10:11; *2 Chr* 9:10
queen of Sheba came with *g.*
1 Ki 10:2; *2 Chr* 9:1
the weight of *g.* came in one year.
1 Ki 10:14; *2 Chr* 9:13
200 targets of beaten *g.* *1 Ki* 10:16
made three hundred shields of *g.* 17
the throne with the best *g.* 18
made two calves of *g.* 12:28
made ships to go for *g.* 22:48
Hezekiah cut off *g.* *2 Ki* 18:16
of *g.* by weight for *g.* *1 Chr* 28:14
and the *g.* was *g.* of. *2 Chr* 3:6
ten candlesticks of *g.* 4:7
basons of *g.* 8
censers, and spoons of pure *g.* 22
throne, with a footstool of *g.* 9:18
carried away the shields of *g.* 12:9
g. copper precious as *g.* *Ezra* 8:27
thousand drachms of *g.* *Neh* 7:70
chief of the fathers gave *g.* 71
people gave *g.* 72
lay up *g.* as dust, the *g.* *Job* 22:24*
I shall come forth like *g.* 23:10
earth, it hath the dust of *g.* 28:6
wisdom cannot be gotten for *g.* 15
it cannot be valued with the *g.* 16
the *g.* and the crystal cannot. 17
g. my hope, or said to fine *g.* 31:24
esteem thy riches? no, not *g.* 36:19*
gave Job an earring of *g.* 42:11
desired are they than *g.* *Ps* 19:10
stand the queen in *g.* of Ophir. 45:9
be given of the *g.* of Sheba. 72:15
as a jewel of *g.* in a. *Pr* 11:22
it is to get wisdom than *g.* 16:16
also a multitude of. 20:15
comely with chains of *g.* *S of S* 1:10*
his hands are as *g.* rings set. 5:14
of thy images of *g.* *Isa* 30:22
spreadeth it over with *g.* 40:19
for brass I will bring *g.* for. 60:17
thee with ornaments of *g.* *Jer* 4:30
g. become dim! fine *g.* *Lam* 4:1
Sheba occupied with *g.* *Ezek* 27:22
art head of *g.* *Dan* 2:38
Nebuchadnezzar made image of *g.*
3:1
hast praised the gods of *g.* 5:23
they put a chain of *g.* about. 29
a candlestick all of *g.* *Zech* 4:2
and I will try them as *g.* is. 13:9
they presented to him *g.* *Mat* 2:11
whoso shall swear by the *g.* of. 23:16

for whether is greater, the *g.* or the
temple? *Mat* 23:17
not adorned with *g.* or pearls.
1 Tim 2:9; *1 Pet* 3:3
round about with *g.* *Heb* 9:4
come a man with a *g.* ring. *Jas* 2:2
faith more precious than *g.* *1 Pet* 1:7
thee to buy of me *g.* tried. *Rev* 3:18
their heads crowns of *g.* 4:4; 9:7
woman was decked with *g.* 17:4
city that was decked with *g.* 18:16
see **beaten, crown, fine**

pure gold
overlay the ark with *pure g.* within.
Ex 25:11, 24; 30:3; 37:2, 11, 26
a mercy seat of *pure g.* 25:17; 37:6
dishes, spoons and covers of *pure g.*
25:29; 37:16, 23
make a candlestick of *pure g.* 25:31
37:17; *1 Ki* 7:49
snuffdishes *pure g.* *Ex* 25:38
1 Ki 7:50; *2 Chr* 4:22
two chains of *pure g.* at ends.
Ex 28:14, 22; 39:15
a plate of *pure g.* 28:36; 39:30
he overlaid with *pure g.* *1 Ki* 6:20
vessels of Lebanon of *pure g.* 10:21
2 Chr 9:20
pure g. for fleshhooks. *1 Chr* 28:17
porch within with *pure g.* *2 Chr* 3:4
the throne with *pure g.* 9:17
to be valued with *pure g.* *Job* 28:19
settest a crown of *pure g.* *Ps* 21:3
city was *pure g.* *Rev* 21:18
street of *pure g.* 21

gold with *silver*
Abram was rich in *silver* and *g.*
Gen 13:2; 24:35
my lord's house *silver* or *g.* 44:8
jewels of *silver* and *g.* *Ex* 3:22
11:2; 12:35
offering, take *silver* and *g.* 25:3
to work in *g. silver.* 31:4; 35:32
his house full of *silver* and *g.*
Num 22:18; 24:13
only *g.* and *silver* that may. 31:22
not desire *silver* and *g.* *Deut* 7:25
when thy *silver* and *g.* is. 8:13
greatly multiply *silver* and *g.* 17:17
seen their idols, *silver* and *g.* 29:17
silver and *g.* are consecrated to.
Josh 6:19, 24
your tents with *silver* and *g.* 22:8
silver and *g.* David dedicated.
2 Sam 8:11; *1 Ki* 7:51
will have no *silver* or *g.* *2 Sam* 21:4
house of Lord *silver* and *g.* he had.
1 Ki 15:15; *2 Chr* 15:18
Asa took all the *silver* and *g.*
1 Ki 15:18; *2 Chr* 16:2
I have sent a present of *silver* and *g.*
1 Ki 15:19; *2 Chr* 16:3
silver and *g.* is mine. *1 Ki* 20:3
deliver *silver* and *g.* 5
thence *silver* and *g.* *2 Ki* 7:8
Jehoash took the *silver* and *g.*
2 Ki 14:14; *2 Chr* 25:24
Ahaz took *silver* and *g.* *2 Ki* 16:8
Hezekiah shewed them *silver* and *g.*
20:13; *Isa* 39:2
Jehoiakim gave *silver* and *g.* exacted
silver and *g.* *2 Ki* 23:35
things of *g.* in *g.* of *silver* in *silver.*
25:15; *Jer* 52:19
good, of *g.* and *silver.* *1 Chr* 29:3
king made *silver* and *g.* *2 Chr* 1:15
place help with *silver* and *g.* *Ezra* 1:4
gave *silver* and *g.* 2:69
to carry *silver* and *g.* 7:15
weighed them *silver* and *g.* 8:25, 33
beds were of *g.* and *silver.* *Esth* 1:6
for *silver*, a place for *g.* *Job* 28:1
silver her feathers with *g.* *Ps* 68:13
them out with *silver* and *g.* 105:37
are *silver* and *g.* 115:4; 135:15
is better than *g.* and *silver.* 119:72
silver receive knowledge rather than
g. *Pr* 8:10
silver, furnace for *g.* 17:3; 27:21
favour rather than *silver* or *g.* 22:1
of *g.* in pictures of *silver.* 25:11
me also *silver* and *g.* *Eccl* 2:8

of *g.* with studs of *silver*. *S of S* 1:11
pillars of *silver*, bottom of *g.* 3:10
is full of *silver* and *g.* *Isa* 2:7
cast his idols of *silver* and *g.* 20; 31:7
shall not regard *silver* or *g.* 13:17
g. out of the bag, and weigh *silver*. 46:6
their *silver* and *g.* with them. 60:9
deck it with *silver* and *g.* *Jer* 10:4
away their *silver* and *g.* *silver* and *g.*
not able. *Ezek* 7:19; *Zeph* 1:18
wast thou decked with *g.* and *silver*. *Ezek* 16:13
silver and *g.* broken. *Dan* 2:35, 45
the gods of *silver* and *g.* 5:4, 23
he honour with *g.* and *silver*. 11:38
over treasures of *g.* and *silver*. 43
I multiplied her *silver* and *g.* *Hos* 2:8
of their *silver* and *g.* have they. 8:4
taken my *silver* and *g.* *Joel* 3:5
of *silver* and spoil of *g.* *Nah* 2:9
laid over with *silver* and *g.* *Hab* 2:19
silver is mine, and the *g.* *Hag* 2:8
then take *silver* and *g.* *Zech* 6:11
purge them as *g.* and *silver*. *Mal* 3:3
provide neither *g.* nor *silver*. *Mat* 10:9
Peter said, *silver* and *g.* *Acts* 3:6
Godhead like to *silver* and *g.* 17:29
coveted no man's *silver* or *g.* 20:33
this foundation *g.* *silver*. *1 Cor* 3:12
vessels of *silver* and *g.* *2 Tim* 2:20
your *g.* and *silver* cankered. *Jas* 5:3
were not redeemed with *silver* and *g.* *1 Pet* 1:18
of idols of *silver* and *g.* *Rev* 9:20

talent and *talents* of **gold**
of a *talent of* pure *g.* *Ex* 25:39
of a *talent of* pure *g.* made. 37:24
weight of crown a *talent of g.* *2 Sam* 12:30; *1 Chr* 20:2
Solomon 120 *talents of g.* *1 Ki* 9:14
from Ophir 420 *talents of g.* 28
she gave Solomon 120 *talents of g.* 10:10; *2 Chr* 9:9
came to Solomon 666 *talents of g.* *1 Ki* 10:14
put the land to a *talent of g.* *2 Ki* 23:33; *2 Chr* 36:3
100,000 *talents of g.* *1 Chr* 22:14
proper good 3000 *talents of g.* 29:4
fathers gave 5000 *talents of g.* 7
Ophir 450 *talents of g.* *2 Chr* 8:18
of *g.* vessels 100 *talents*. *Ezra* 8:26

vessels of **gold**
Toi sent to David *vessels of g.* *2 Sam* 8:10; *1 Chr* 18:10
Solomon's drinking *vessels* were of *g.* *1 Ki* 10:21; *2 Chr* 9:20
every man brought present, *vessels* of *g.* *1 Ki* 10:25; *2 Chr* 9:24
for house of Lord *vessels of g.* *2 Ki* 12:13
cut in pieces *vessels of g.* 24:13
of rest of money made they *vessels* of *g.* *2 Chr* 24:14
the *vessels of g.* and silver 5400. *Ezra* 1:11
vessels of g. Cyrus deliverd. 5:14
I weighed of *vessels of g.* 100. 8:26
drink in *vessels of g.* *Esth* 1:7
into Egypt *vessels of g.* *Dan* 11:8
not only *vessels of g.* *2 Tim* 2:20

golden
a *g.* crown to the border. *Ex* 25:25
a *g.* bell. 28:34
two *g.* rings, 30:4; 39:20
Aaron said, break off the *g.* 32:2
upon forefront he put *g.* *Lev* 8:9
one *g.* spoon of ten. *Num* 7:26
had *g.* earrings, because. *Judg* 8:24
the weight of *g.* earrings he. 26
g. emerods, five *g.* *1 Sam* 6:4, 17, 18
departed not from the *g.* *2 Ki* 10:29
for the *g.* basons he. *1 Chr* 28:17
there are with you *g.* *2 Chr* 13:8
and also let the *g.* vessels. *Ezra* 6:5
king shall hold out a *g.* sceptre. *Esth* 4:11; 5:2; 8:4
or the *g.* bowl be broken. *Eccl* 12:6
more precious than the *g.* *Isa* 13:12
how hath the *g.* city ceased! 14:4
Babylon hath been *g.* *Jer* 51:7

and worship *g.* image. *Dan* 3:5, 12
commanded to bring the *g.* 5:2
they brought the *g.* vessels taken. 3
g. pipes, empty the *g.* oil. *Zech* 4:12
g. censer and ark where was *g.* pot. *Heb* 9:4
turned, I saw seven *g.* *Rev* 1:12
girt about the paps with a *g.* 13
the mystery of the seven *g.* 20
who walketh in midst of the *g.* 2:1
g. vials. 5:8; 15:7
having a *g.* censer. 8:3
on his head a *g.* crown. 14:14
a *g.* cup full. 17:4
had a *g.* reed to measure the. 21:15
see **altar**

goldsmith, -s
Uzziel of the *g.* repaired. *Neh* 3:8
the *g.'s* son. 31
and merchants repaired and *g.* 32
the *g.* spreadeth it over. *Isa* 40:19
carpenter encouraged the *g.* 41:7
they hire a *g.* and he maketh. 46:6

Golgotha
come to a place called *G.* *Mat* 27:33
Mark 15:22; *John* 19:17

Goliath
G. of Gath a. *1 Sam* 17:4, 23
sword of *G.* the Philistine. 21:9
he gave him the sword of *G.* 22:10
slew the brother of *G.* *2 Sam* 21:19
1 Chr 20:5

Gomer
sons of Japheth, *G.* Magog. *Gen* 10:2; *1 Chr* 1:5
the sons of *G.* Ashkenaz, Riphath. *Gen* 10:3; *1 Chr* 1:6
G. and all his bands. *Ezek* 38:6
he took *G.* the daughter. *Hos* 1:3

Gomorrah
destroyed Sodom and *G.* *Gen* 13:10
goods of Sodom and *G.* 14:11
cry of Sodom and *G.* is. 18:20
the Lord rained on *G.* fire. 19:24
looked towards Sodom and *G.* 28
like the overthrow of Sodom and *G.*
Deut 29:23; *Isa* 1:9; 13:19
Jer 23:14; 49:18; 50:40
Amos 4:11; *Rom* 9:29
2 Pet 2:6; *Jude* 7
vine is of fields of *G.* *Deut* 32:32
the law, ye people of *G.* *Isa* 1:10
of Ammon shall be as *G.* *Zeph* 2:9
be more tolerable for *G.* *Mat* 10:15
Mark 6:11

gone
thou wouldest needs be *g.* *Gen* 31:30
daughter, and we will be *g.* 34:17
for your households, and be *g.* 42:33
flocks and herds, and be *g.* *Ex* 12:32
seeth their power is *g.* *Deut* 32:36
not Jonathan was *g.* *1 Sam* 14:3
number now, and see who is *g.* 17
I have *g.* the way which the. 15:20
as soon as the lad was *g.* 20:41
g. in to my father's? *2 Sam* 3:7
he is quite *g.* 24
Amnon said, Arise, be *g.* 13:15
that Shimei had *g.* from. *1 Ki* 2:41
when he was *g.* a lion met. 13:24
away dung till it be all *g.* 14:10
as soon as I am *g.* Spirit. 18:12
busy here and there, he was *g.* 20:40
messenger that was *g.* to call. 22:13
but have *g.* from tent to. *1 Chr* 17:5
I rise, and the night be *g.*? *Job* 7:4
destroyed me, and I am *g.* 19:10
exalted for a while, but are *g.* 24:24
are dried up and *g.* away. 28:4*
of mine eyes, it also is *g.* *Ps* 38:10
I had *g.* with the multitude to. 42:4
me, my feet were almost *g.* 73:2
is his mercy clean *g.* for ever? 77:8
passeth over it, and it is *g.* 103:16
I am *g.* like the shadow that. 109:23
good man is *g.* a long. *Pr* 7:19
when he is *g.* his way, then. 20:14
who had come and *g.* *Eccl* 8:10*
the rain is over and *g.* *S of S* 2:11
had withdrawn, and was *g.* 5:6
whither is thy beloved *g.* O? 6:1
therefore my people are *g.* *Isa* 5:13

the mirth of the land *g.* *Isa* 24:11
the way he had not *g.* 41:3
in me, that they are *g.* *Jer* 2:5
I have not *g.* after Baalim? 23
this people are revolted and *g.* 5:23
beasts are *g.* 9:10
thou art *g.* backward. 15:6
none that are *g.* into Egypt. 44:14
all remnant that are *g.* shall. 28
they have *g.* from mountain. 50:6
Judah is *g.* *Lam* 1:3
Zion's children are *g.* 5
g. without strength. 6
my virgins are *g.* 18
from heathen whither *g.* *Ezek* 37:21
the thing is *g.* from me. *Dan* 2:5, 8
lo, they are *g.* because of. *Hos* 9:6
will new moon be *g.* *Amos* 8:5
angels were *g.* from. *Luke* 2:15
as if he would have *g.* further. 24:28
for his disciples were *g.* *John* 4:8
behold, the world is *g.* after. 12:19
saw hope of gains was *g.* *Acts* 16:19
among whom I have *g.* 20:25
who is *g.* into heaven. *1 Pet* 3:22
have *g.* in the way of Cain. *Jude* 11

gone *about*
Saul is *g. about* and. *1 Sam* 15:12
feastings were *g. about*. *Job* 1:5
city is *g. about* the. *Isa* 15:8
hath *g. about* to profane. *Acts* 24:6*

gone *aside*
if thou hast not *g. aside*. *Num* 5:19
if hast *g. aside* to another. 20
they are all *g. aside*, they. *Ps* 14:3
they were *g. aside*, they. *Acts* 26:31

gone *astray*
I have *g. astray* like. *Ps* 119:176
like sheep have *g. astray*. *Isa* 53:6
one of them be *g. astray*, he seeketh
that which is *g. astray*. *Mat* 18:12
way, and are *g. astray*. *2 Pet* 2:15

gone *away*
Abner was *g. away*. *2 Sam* 3:22, 23
men of Israel were *g. away*. 29
the waters were *g. away*. *Job* 28:4
they are *g. away* backward. *Isa* 1:4
Levites which are *g. away* from.
Ezek 44:10
are *g. away* from mine. *Mal* 3:7*
disciples are *g. away*. *John* 6:22

gone *back*
sister-in-law is *g. back*. *Ruth* 1:15
nor have I *g. back*. *Job* 23:12
every one is *g. back*. *Ps* 53:3
he was not yet *g. back*, he. *Jer* 40:5

gone *down*
passed, and *g. down*. *1 Sam* 15:12
Adonijah is *g. down*. *1 Ki* 1:25
Ahab *g. down* to possess. 21:18
shadow had *g. down* in the dial of
Ahaz. *2 Ki* 20:11; *Isa* 38:8
my beloved is *g. down*. *S of S* 6:2
her sun is *g. down* while. *Jer* 15:9
his young men are *g. down*. 48:15
all people *g. down*. *Ezek* 31:12
the strong are *g. down*, slain. 32:21
Tubal *g. down*. 27
Zidonians *g. down*. 30
Jonah was *g. down* to. *Jonah* 1:5

gone *forth*
when Israel was *g. forth*. *Ex* 19:1
of Elisha was *g. forth*. *2 Ki* 6:15
God is *g. forth* before. *1 Chr* 14:15
my salvation is *g. forth*. *Isa* 51:5
g. forth to make thy land. *Jer* 4:7
my children are *g. forth* of me. 10:20
is profaneness *g. forth* into. 23:15
whirlwind of Lord is *g. forth*. 19
brethren that are not *g. forth*. 29:16
the morning is *g. forth*. *Ezek* 7:10
of the Lord and are *g. forth*. 36:20
g. forth to slay wise men. *Dan* 2:14
when I am *g. forth*, prince. 10:20
when he was *g. forth*. *Mark* 10:17

gone *out*
as soon as I am *g. out* I. *Ex* 9:29
there is wrath *g. out*. *Num* 16:40
certain men *g. out*. *Deut* 13:13
which is *g. out* of thy lips. 23:23
is not the Lord *g. out*? *Judg* 4:14

hand of Lord is *g. out.*   *Ruth* 1:13
when wine was *g. out.* *1 Sam* 25:37
the Syrians had *g. out.*   *2 Ki* 5:2
therefore they are *g. out.*   7:12
afore Isaiah was *g. out* into.   20:4
their line is *g. out.*   *Ps* 19:4
alter the thing that is *g. out.* 89:34
the word is *g. out* of my. *Isa* 45:23
scum is not *g. out* of it. *Ezek* 24:6
when unclean spirit is *g. out.*
    Mat 12:43; *Luke* 11:24
our lamps are *g. out.* *Mat* 25:8
that virtue had *g. out* of him.
    Mark 5:30; *Luke* 8:46
devil is *g. out* of daughter.
    Mark 7:29, 30; *Luke* 11:14
he was *g. out,* Jesus. *John* 13:31
are all *g. out* of way. *Rom* 3:12*
false prophets are *g. out.* *1 John* 4:1

gone *over*

be *g. over* the brook. *2 Sam* 17:20
iniquities are *g. over.*   *Ps* 38:4
and billows are *g. over* me.   42:7
then the stream had *g. over.* 124:4
the proud waters had *g. over.*   5
they are *g. over* passage. *Isa* 10:29
g. over the sea. 16:8; *Jer* 48:32
shall not have *g. over.* *Mat* 10:23

gone *up*

my son, thou art *g. up.* *Gen* 49:9
bed on which *g. up.* *2 Ki* 1:4, 6, 16
God is *g. up* with a shout. *Ps* 47:5
he is *g. up* to Bajith. *Isa* 15:2
than me, and art *g. up.*   57:8
she is *g. up* on every. *Jer* 3:6
cry of Jerusalem is *g. up.* 14:2
army, which are *g. up.* 34:21
Moab is spoiled, and *g. up.* 48:15
God of Israel was *g. up.* *Ezek* 9:3
ye have not *g. up* into the gaps. 13:5
are *g. up* to Assyria. *Hos* 8:9
his brethren were *g. up.* *John* 7:10
had *g. up* and saluted. *Acts* 18:22

gone *a whoring*

they have *g. a whoring.* *Lev* 17:7
thou hast *g. a whoring.* *Ezek* 23:30
g. a whoring from under. *Hos* 4:12
for thou hast *g. a whoring* from. 9:1

good, *substantive*

done to thee nothing but *g. Gen* 26:29
I will surely do thee *g.*   32:12
I will give you the *g.* of the. 45:18
for the *g.* of the land of Egypt. 20
God meant it unto *g.* to bring. 50:20
Lord hath spoken *g.* *Num* 10:29
after he hath done you *g. Josh* 24:20
behold, if there be *g. 1 Sam* 20:12
for thou hast rewarded me *g.* 24:17
Lord rewarded thee *g.*   19
according to all the *g.* he. 25:30
it had been *g.* for me. *2 Sam* 14:32
Lord will requite *g.* for his. 16:12
prophets declare *g.* to the king.
    1 Ki 22:13; *2 Chr* 18:12
of mine own proper *g. 1 Chr* 29:3*
because he had done *g. 2 Chr* 24:16
be strong, and eat the *g. Ezra* 9:12
who had spoken *g.* for. *Esth* 7:9
shall we receive *g.* at ? *Job* 2:10
know thou it for thy *g.*   5:27
mine eye shall no more see *g.* 7:7
flee away, they see no *g.* 9:25
wherewith he can do no *g.* 15:3
lo, their *g.* is not in their. 21:16*
be at peace: thereby *g.* shall. 22:21
he doeth not *g.* to the widow. 24:21
who will shew us any *g.* ? *Ps* 4:6
none doeth *g.,* no, not one. 14:1, 3
    53:1, 3; *Rom* 3:12
days, that he may see *g. Ps* 34:12
held my peace even from *g.* 39:2
hand, they are filled with *g.* 104:28
that I may see the *g.* of. 106:5*
of Lord I will seek thy *g.* 122:9
shall see the *g.* of Jerusalem. 128:5
withhold not *g.* from them. *Pr* 3:27
the merciful man doth *g.* to. 11:17
he that diligently seeketh *g.* 27
a man satisfied with *g.* by. 12:14
a man shall eat *g.* bv fruit. 13:2
but to the righteous *g.* shall be. 21
truth be to them that devise *g.* 14:22
matter wisely, shall find *g.* 16:20

a froward heart findeth no *g.*
    Pr 17:20
a merry heart doeth *g.* like a. 17:22
understanding shall find *g.* 19:8
soul enjoy *g. Eccl* 2:24; 3:13; 5:18
I know that there is no *g.* in. 3:12*
and bereave my soul of *g.?* 4:8
and what *g.* is there to the ? 5:11*
his soul be not filled with *g.* 6:3
yet hath he seen no *g.* all go. 6
not a man just, that doeth *g.* 7:20
one sinner destroyeth much *g.* 9:18
ye shall eat the *g.* of. *Isa* 1:19
bringeth good tidings of *g.* 52:7
we looked for peace, no *g.* came.
    Jer 8:15; 14:19
shall not see when *g.* cometh. 17:6
evil, I will repent of the *g.* 18:10
I stood before thee to speak *g.* 20
shall he behold the *g.* I will. 29:32
I will bring all the *g.* I have. 32:42
which shall hear all the *g.* that. 33:9
them away as I saw *g. Ezek* 16:50
I said, if ye think *g.* *Zech* 11:12
been *g.* for that man. *Mat* 26:24
that have done *g.* to the. *John* 5:29
who went about doing *g. Acts* 10:38
in that he did *g.* and gave us 14:17
every man that worketh *g. Rom* 2:10
thought it *g.* to be left. *1 Thes* 3:1
hath this world's *g.* and. *1 John* 3:17

for good

fear the Lord *for* our *g. Deut* 6:24
thee this day *for* thy *g.* 10:13
again rejoice over thee *for g.* 30:9
God on all of them *for g. Ezra* 8:22
think upon me, O my God, *for g.*
    Neh 5:19; 13:31
and know thou it *for* thy *g. Job* 5:27
shew me a token *for g.* *Ps* 86:17
surety for thy servant *for g.* 119:122
this people *for* their *g. Jer* 14:11
out of this place *for* their *g.* 24:5
set mine eyes on them *for g.* 6
me for ever, *for* the *g.* of. 32:39
waited carefully *for g.* *Mi* 1:12
things work together *for g. Rom* 8:28
minister of God to thee *for g.* 13:4
please his neighbour *for g.* 15:2

see **bad, evil**

good, *adjective*

Hagar sat her down a *g. Gen* 21:16
I pray thee, send me *g.* 24:12
Rebekah said, what *g.* shall ? 27:46
g. ears.   41:5
g. kine.   26
g. years.   35
our father is in *g.* health. 43:28
on his father's neck a *g.* 46:29
for *g.*-will of him that. *Deut* 33:16
sons, it is no *g.* report. *1 Sam* 2:24
I will teach you the *g.* and. 12:23
men were very *g.* to us, we. 25:15
I know that thou art *g.* in my. 29:9
see thy matters are *g. 2 Sam* 15:3
what the king thought *g.* 19:18
teach them the *g.* way. *1 Ki* 8:36
not failed one word of all his *g.* 56
speak *g.* words. 12:7; *2 Chr* 10:7
g. is the word of the Lord.
    2 Ki 20:19*; *Isa* 39:8
Lord be with the *g.* *2 Chr* 19:11
saying, the *g.* Lord pardon. 30:18
the *g.* hand of his God on him.
    Ezra 7:9; *Neh* 2:8
the *g.* hand of our God. *Ezra* 8:18
them true laws, *g.* *Neh* 9:13
gavest thy *g.* Spirit to instruct. 20
is it *g.* that thou shouldest ? *Job* 10:3
is it *g.* that he should search ? 13:9
their young ones are in *g.* 39:4
g. and upright is the Lord. *Ps* 25:8
steps of a *g.* man are ordered. 37:23
heart is inditing a *g.* matter. 45:1
Lord, art *g.,* ready. 86:5; 119:68
a man sheweth favour. 112:5*
thy judgements are *g.* 119:39
teach me *g.* judgement and. 66
understand every *g.* path. *Pr* 2:9
mayest walk in the way of *g.* men. 20
g. word maketh the heart. 12:25
evil bow before the *g.* and. 14:19
in due season, how *g.* is it! 15:23

g. report maketh bones fat. *Pr* 15:30
with *g.* advice make war. 20:18*
a *g.* name rather to be chosen. 22:1
they have a *g.* reward. *Eccl* 4:9
what *g.* is there to the owners ? 5:11
there is one event to the *g.* and. 9:2
they both shall be alike *g.* 11:6
where is the *g.* way. *Jer* 6:16
g. figs. 24:2
the good figs, very *g.* 3
like *g.* figs, so will I. 5
I will perform my *g.* word. 29:10
planted in a *g.* soil. *Ezek* 17:8
gather every *g.* piece, thigh. 24:4
I thought it *g.* to shew. *Dan* 4:2
the angel with *g.* words. *Zech* 1:13
receiveth it with *g.*-will. *Mal* 2:13
know how to give *g.* gifts.
    Mat 7:11; *Luke* 11:13
g. tree bringeth forth *g. Mat* 7:17, 18
daughter, be of *g.* 9:22; *Luke* 8:48
fell in *g.* ground. *Mat* 13:8, 23
    Mark 4:8, 20; *Luke* 8:8, 15
g. seed. *Mat* 13:24
g. Master, what *g.* thing. 19:16
why callest thou me *g.?* none *g.* 17
eye evil because I am *g.?* 20:15
well done, thou *g.* and. 25:21
peace on earth, *g.*-will. *Luke* 2:14*
g. measure, pressed down. 6:38
Mary hath chosen that *g.* 10:42
it is your Father's *g.* pleasure. 12:32
hast kept the *g.* wine. *John* 2:10
I am the *g.* Shepherd, the *g.* 10:11
ye know how that a *g.* *Acts* 15:7
is holy, and just, and *g.* *Rom* 7:12
what is that *g.* and perfect. 12:2
corrupt *g.* manners. *1 Cor* 15:33
g. remembrance of us. *1 Thes* 3:6*
of those that are *g.* *2 Tim* 3:3
must be a lover of *g.* men. *Tit* 1:8
that have tasted the *g.* *Heb* 6:5
every *g.* gift. *Jas* 1:17
sit in a *g.* place. 2:3
subject not only to *g.* *1 Pet* 2:18
will love life, and see *g.* days. 3:10

see **bad, cheer, conscience, courage, day, do, old** age

as good

of one, and him *as g.* *Heb* 11:12

good heed

take ye *g. heed.* *Deut* 2:4; 4:15
    Josh 23:11
preacher gave *g. heed.* *Eccl* 12:9

is good

gold of that land *is g.* *Gen* 2:12
thou hast spoken *is g.* *Deut* 1:14
do that which is *g.* in sight. 6:18
me in the host *is g.* *1 Sam* 29:6
said, the saying *is g.* *1 Ki* 2:38
word that I have heard *is g.* 42
and speak that which *is g.* 22:13
I have done that which *is g.*
    2 Ki 20:3; *Isa* 38:3
Lord *is g. 1 Chr* 16:34; *2 Chr* 5:13
   7:3; *Ezra* 3:11; *Ps* 100:5; 106:1
   107:1; 118:1, 29; 135:3; 136:1
    145:9; *Jer* 33:11; *Lam* 3:25
    Nah 1:7
which *is g.* in his sight. *1 Chr* 19:13
ourselves what *is g.* *Job* 34:4
see that the Lord *is g.* *Ps* 34:8
thy lovingkindness *is g.* 69:16
truly God *is g.* to Israel, to. 73:1
Lord shall give that which *is g.* 85:12
because thy mercy *is g.* 109:21
thy Spirit *is g.*; lead me into. 143:10
the righteous *is* only *g.* *Pr* 11:23
so *is g.* news from a far. 25:25
her merchandise *is g.* 31:18*
man that *is g.* in his sight, may give
to him that *is g. Eccl* 2:26*
who knoweth what *is g.* for ? 6:12
wisdom *is g.* with an. 7:11
as *is* the *g.* so is the sinner. 9:2
eat ye that which *is g.* *Isa* 55:2
this girdle which *is g.* *Jer* 13:10
shadow thereof *is g.* *Hos* 4:13
thee, O man, what *is g.* *Mi* 6:8
one that doeth evil *is g. Mal* 2:17
salt *is g.* but if the salt. *Mark* 9:50
    Luke 14:34

forth that which is g. *Luke* 6:45
none is g. save one, that. 18:19
then that which is g. *Rom* 7:13
but how to perform that is g. I. 18
cleave to that which is g. 12:9
you wise to that which is g. 16:19
that this is g. for the. *1 Cor* 7:26
but that is g. *Eph* 4:29
follow that which is g. *1 Thes* 5:15
3 John 11
hold fast that which is g. *1 Thes* 5:21
know that the law is g. *1 Tim* 1:8
is g. and acceptable in sight. 2:3
for every creature of God is g. 4:4
for that is g. and acceptable. 5:4
be followers of that which is g.
1 Pet 3:13

it is good
wait on thy name, for it is g.
Ps 52:9; 54:6
it is g. for me to draw near. 73:28
it is a g. thing to give thanks. 92:1
it is g. for me that I have. 119:71
it is g. to sing praises unto. 147:1
thou honey, because it is g. *Pr* 24:13
it is g. and comely for. *Eccl* 5:18
it is g. that thou shouldest. 7:18
it is g. that a man should. *Lam* 3:26
it is g. that a man bear the yoke. 27
it is g. for nothing but. *Mat* 5:13
it is g. for us to be here. 17:4
Mark 9:5; *Luke* 9:33
unto the law that it is g. *Rom* 7:16
it is g. neither to eat. 14:21
it is g. for a man not to touch a.
1 Cor 7:1, 8
I say, it is g. for a man so to be. 26
it is g. to be zealously. *Gal* 4:18

good land
come to bring them to g. land.
Ex 3:8; *Deut* 8:7
we searched is a g. land. *Num* 14:7
is a g. land which Lord. *Deut* 1:25
generation see that g. land. 35
over, and see the g. land. 3:25
not go unto that g. land. 4:21
over and possess that g. land. 22
go in and possess the g. land. 6:18
God bringeth thee into a g. land. 8:7
Lord thy God for the g. land. 10
giveth not this g. land for thy. 9:6
lest ye perish from off g. land. 11:17
until ye perish from this g. land.
Josh 23:13, 15
perish from off the g. land. 16
land, and it is very g. *Judg* 18:9
Israel out of this g. land. *1 Ki* 14:15
g. piece of land. *2 Ki* 3:19, 25
possess this g. land. *1 Chr* 28:8

good with make
the owner of pit shall make it g.
Ex 21:34; 22:14*
shall not make it g. 22:11*, 13, 15
shall make it g.; beast for. *Lev* 24:18
shall he not make it g.? *Num* 23:19
make your ways and your doings g.
Jer 18:11*

good man
Ahimaaz is a g. man. *2 Sam* 18:27
steps of a g. man are. *Ps* 37:23
a g. man sheweth favour. 112:5
the g. man is not at home. *Pr* 7:19
g. man obtaineth favour of. 12:2
a g. man satisfied. 12:14; 14:14
a g. man leaveth an. 13:22
the g. man is perished. *Mi* 7:2*
g. man out of good treasure.
Mat 12:35; *Luke* 6:45
against the g. man. *Mat* 20:11*
if the g. man of the house had known.
24:43*; *Luke* 12:39*
Joseph was a g. man. *Luke* 23:50
some said, he is a g. man. *John* 7:12
Barnabas was a g. man. *Acts* 11:24
for a g. man some would. *Rom* 5:7

not good
it is not g. that man. *Gen* 2:18
the counsel is not g. *2 Sam* 17:7
in a way that is not g. *Ps* 36:4
into way that is not g. *Pr* 16:29
punish the just is not g. 17:26
is not g. to accept the person. 18:5
without knowledge is not g. 19:2

and a false balance is not g. *Pr* 20:23
not g. to have respect. 24:23; 28:21
it is not g. to eat much honey. 25:27
in a way that is not g. *Isa* 65:2
did that which is not g. *Ezek* 18:18
statutes that were not g. 20:25
doings that were not g. 36:31
case be so, it is not g. *Mat* 19:10*
Paul thought not g. to. *Acts* 15:38
your glorying is not g. *1 Cor* 5:6

seem, seemed, seemeth good
as it seemeth g. to thee. *Josh* 9:25
Judg 10:15; *1 Sam* 14:36, 40
Ezra 7:18; *Esth* 3:11; *Jer* 26:14
40:4
do to them what seemeth g. unto.
Judg 19:24
do what seemeth g. *1 Sam* 1:23
3:18; 11:10; 24:4
Abner spake all seemed g. to.
2 Sam 3:19
the Lord do that seemeth him g.
10:12; 15:26
Chimham what seem g. 19:37, 38
and offer up what seemeth g. 24:22
if it seem g. to thee. *1 Ki* 31:2
Jer 40:4
if it seem g. to you, let. *1 Chr* 13:2
if it seem g. to the king. *Ezra* 5:17
Esth 5:4
as seemed g. to potter. *Jer* 18:4
so it seemed g. in sight.
Mat 11:26*; *Luke* 10:21*
it seemed g. to me. *Luke* 1:3
it seemed g. unto us. *Acts* 15:25
it seemed g. to the Holy Ghost. 28

good with thing
the thing that thou doest is not g.
Ex 18:17
rejoice in every g. thing. *Deut* 26:11
aught of any g. thing. *Josh* 21:45
the thing is not g. *1 Sam* 26:16
is found some g. thing. *1 Ki* 14:13
Hazael took of every g. thing of.
2 Ki 8:9
Lord not want any g. thing. *Ps* 34:10
I follow the thing that g. is. 38:20
no g. thing will he withhold. 84:11
it is a g. thing to give thanks. 92:1
a wife, findeth a g. thing. *Pr* 18:22
I will perform g. thing. *Jer* 33:14
cast off the thing that is g. *Hos* 8:3
what g. thing shall I do? *Mat* 19:16
can any g. thing come? *John* 1:46
flesh, dwelleth no g. thing. *Rom* 7:18
affected in a g. thing. *Gal* 4:18
his hands thing which is g. *Eph* 4:28
knowing that what g. thing any. 6:8
that g. thing committed. *2 Tim* 1:14
acknowledging every g. thing in you.
Philem 6
it is a g. thing the heart. *Heb* 13:9

good things
houses full of all g. things. *Deut* 6:11
failed of all the g. things. *Josh* 23:14
that as all g. things are come. 15
there were g. things. *2 Chr* 12:12
there are g. things found. 19:3
houses with g. things. *Job* 22:18
thy mouth with g. things. *Ps* 103:5
the upright shall have g. things.
Pr 28:10
have withholden g. things. *Jer* 5:25
give g. things to them? *Mat* 7:11
ye being evil speak g. things? 12:34
good man bringeth forth g. things. 35
the hungry with g. things. *Luke* 1:53
time receivedst thy g. things. 16:25
glad tidings of g. things. *Rom* 10:15
unto him in all g. things. *Gal* 6:6
be teachers of g. things. *Tit* 2:3
these things are g. and. 3:8
high priest of g. things. *Heb* 9:11
a shadow of g. things to come. 10:1

good tidings
have brought g. tidings. *2 Sam* 4:10
and cometh with g. tidings. 18:27
and bringest g. tidings. *1 Ki* 1:42
is a day of g. tidings. *2 Ki* 7:9
that bringest g. tidings. *Isa* 40:9
one that bringeth g. tidings. 41:27
him that bringeth g. tidings. 52:7

me to preach g. tidings. *Isa* 61:1
who bringeth g. tidings. *Nah* 1:15
I bring you g. tidings. *Luke* 2:10
brought us g. tidings of. *1 Thes* 3:6

was good
God saw that it was g. *Gen* 1:4, 10
12, 18, 21, 25
thing, behold it was very g. 31
woman saw that the tree was g. 3:6
saw the interpretation was g. 40:16
thing was g. in eyes of. 41:37
Issachar saw that rest was g. 49:15
spared all that was g. *1 Sam* 15:9
did that which was g. *2 Chr* 14:2
wrought that which was g. 31:20
hand of God which was g. *Neh* 2:18
see what was that g. for. *Eccl* 2:3

good understanding
woman of g. unders. *1 Sam* 25:3
g. unders. have all that. *Ps* 111:10
find favour and g. unders. *Pr* 3:4
g. unders. giveth favour. 13:15

good work
hands for this g. work. *Neh* 2:18
she hath wrought a g. work.
Mat 26:10; *Mark* 14:6
for a g. work we stone. *John* 10:33
abound to every g. work. *2 Cor* 9:8
hath begun a g. work. *Phil* 1:6
fruitful in every g. work. *Col.* 1:10
every g. word and work. *2 Thes* 2:17
bishop, desireth a g. work. *1 Tim* 3:1
followed every g. work. 5:10
unto every g. work. *2 Tim* 2:21
every g. work reprobate. *Tit* 1:16
to be ready to every g. work. 3:1
perfect in every g. work. *Heb* 13:21

good works
his works to thee have been very g.
1 Sam 19:4
may see your g. works. *Mat* 5:16
many g. works have I. *John* 10:32
Dorcas full of g. works. *Acts* 9:36
not a terror to g. works. *Rom* 13:3
Christ Jesus unto g. works. *Eph* 2:10
adorned with g. works. *1 Tim* 2:10
well reported of for g. works. 5:10
the g. works of some are. 25
that they be rich in g. works. 6:18
furnished to all g. works. *2 Tim* 3:17
a pattern of g. works. *Tit* 2:7
people, zealous of g. works. 14
to maintain g. works. 3:8, 14
unto love and g. works. *Heb* 10:24
may by your g. works. *1 Pet* 2:12

goodlier
not in Israel a g. person. *1 Sam* 9:2

goodliest
he will take your g. *1 Sam* 8:16
thy children, even the g. *1 Ki* 20:3

goodliness
the g. thereof as flower of. *Isa* 40:6

goodly
Rebekah took g. raiment. *Gen* 27:15
Joseph was a g. person and. 39:6*
hind let loose, giveth g. words. 49:21
when she saw he was g. *Ex* 2:2
they made g. bonnets of. 39:28
day of boughs, the g. *Lev* 23:40
how g. are thy tents. *Num* 24:5
they burnt all their g. castles. 31:10*
me see that g. mount. *Deut* 3:25
great and g. cities which thou. 6:10
lest when thou hast built g. 8:12
I saw a g. Babylonish. *Josh* 7:21
young man, and a g. *1 Sam* 9:2
David was ruddy and g. to. 16:12
Egyptian, a g. man. *2 Sam* 23:21
also was a very g. man. *1 Ki* 1:6
Babylon the g. vessels. *2 Chr* 36:10
and destroyed the g. vessels. 19
gavest thou g. wings? *Job* 39:13
yea, I have a g. heritage. *Ps* 16:6
boughs were like the g. 80:10*
how shall I give thee a g.? *Jer* 3:19
olive tree, fair, and of g. fruit. 11:16
that it might be a g. *Ezek* 17:8
shall bear fruit, and be a g. 23
have made g. images. *Hos* 10:1
temples my g. things. *Joel* 3:5
as his g. horse in battle. *Zech* 10:3
g. price that I was prized. 11:13

man seeking g. pearls. *Mat* 13:45
adorned with g. stones. *Luke* 21:5
if there come a man in g. *Jas* 2:2*
all things dainty and g. *Rev* 18:14*

goodness
Jethro rejoiced for all g. *Ex* 18:9
I will make all my g. pass. 33:19
the Lord God abundant in g. 34:6
what g. the Lord shall. *Num* 10:32
thou promisedst this g. *2 Sam* 7:28
    1 Chr 17:26
joyful for all the g. that the Lord had
  done. *1 Ki* 8:66; *2 Chr* 7:10
thy saints rejoice in g. *2 Chr* 6:41
Hezekiah his g. 32:32
Josiah and his g. 35:26
themselves in thy g. *Neh* 9:25
not served thee in thy great g. 35
my g. extendeth not to. *Ps* 16:2
him with blessings of g. 21:3
g. and mercy shall follow me. 23:6
remember thou me, for thy g. 25:7
I had believed to see the g. 27:13
O how great is thy g. thou. 31:19
the earth is full of the g. of. 33:5
the g. of God endureth. 52:1
shall be satisfied with the g. of. 65:4
crownest the year with thy g. 11
thou hast prepared of thy g. 68:10
praise the Lord for his g. 107:8, 15
    21, 31
and filleth the hungry soul with g. 9
my g. and my fortress, my. 144:2
utter the memory of thy g. 145:7
proclaim every one his g. *Pr* 20:6
g. toward house of Israel. *Isa* 63:7
I brought you to eat the g. *Jer* 2:7
shall flow together to the g. 31:12
satisfied with my g. saith Lord. 14
and tremble for all the g. 33:9
fear the Lord and his g. *Hos* 3:5
your g. is as a morning cloud. 6:4
according to g. of his land. 10:1
for how great is his g. *Zech* 9:17
riches of his g. not knowing that the g.
  of God leadeth thee. *Rom* 2:4
g. and severity of God, toward thee
  g. if thou continue in his g. 11:22
that you are full of g. 15:14
the fruit of the Spirit is g. *Gal* 5:22
    Eph 5:9
good pleasure of his g. *2 Thes* 1:11

goods
back all the g. and Lot. *Gen* 14:16
the persons, and take the g. 21
the g. of his master were in. 24:10
carried away all g. 31:18*; 46:6
to his neighbour's g. *Ex* 22:8, 11
earth swallowed them and their g
    Num 16:32
spoil of Midian and their g. 31:9
be for Levites' cattle and g. 35:3*
thee plenteous in g. *Deut* 28:11
smite thy wives, thy g. *2 Chr* 21:14*
let men help him with g. *Ezra* 1:4
strengthened their hands with g. 6
that of king's g. expenses be. 6:8
or to confiscation of g. 7:26
houses full of all g. *Neh* 9:25*
shall restore their g. *Job* 20:10*
shall no man look for his g. 21*
his g. shall flow away in the day. 28
when g. increase, they. *Eccl* 5:11
gotten cattle and g. *Ezek* 38:12
to take away cattle and g.? 13
their g. shall become a. *Zeph* 1:13*
man's house, and spoil his g.
    Mat 12:29; *Mark* 3:27
ruler over all his g. *Mat* 24:47
delivered to them his g. 25:14
that taketh away thy g. *Luke* 6:30
keepeth his palace, his g. are. 11:21
all my fruits and my g. 12:18
thou hast much g. laid up for. 19
give me the portion of thy g. that. 15:12*
him that he had wasted his g. 16:1
the half of my g. I give to. 19:8
sold their g. and parted. *Acts* 2:45
though I bestow all my g. *1 Cor* 13:3
the spoiling of your g. *Heb* 10:34*
rich, and increased with g. *Rev* 3:17*

gopher wood
an ark of g. wood. *Gen* 6:14

gore, -d
an ox g. man or woman. *Ex* 21:28
whether he have g. a son or a. 31

gorgeous
arrayed Jesus in a g. *Luke* 23:11

gorgeously
clothed most g. *Ezek* 23:12
are g. apparelled in. *Luke* 7:25

Goshen
dwell in G. *Gen* 45:10; 46:34
    47:4, 6, 27
that day the land of G. *Ex* 8:22
only in the land of G. was. 9:26
smote the country of G. *Josh* 10:41
Joshua took all the land of G. 11:16
inheritance of Judah, G. 15:51

gospel
*The English word gospel comes
from the Anglo-Saxon gödspel
which meant good tidings, through
gödspel, or god-story. The word
in the original (Greek) in the
New Testament is euaggelion, from
which, through the Latin evange-
lium, comes our word evangel, with
its derivatives. In the New Testament it is the Christ-message, not
the books which were written to
spread that message. Later it was
applied to the four books which
tell of the earthly life of Jesus—
Matthew, Mark, Luke, and John.*
of the g. of Jesus Christ. *Mark* 1:1
came, saying, repent and believe g. 15
lose his life for my sake and g.'s. 8:35
his house for my sake and g.'s. 10:29
the g. must be published. 13:10
by my mouth hear g. *Acts* 15:7
testify the g. of grace of God. 20:24
apostle, separated to g. *Rom* 1:1
whom I serve with my spirit in g. 9
for I am not ashamed of g. of. 16
secrets of men according to my g.
    2:16
have not all obeyed the g. 10:16
as concerning the g. they. 11:28
ministering the g. of God. 15:16
fulness of the blessing of the g. 29
stablish you according to g. 16:25
begotten you through g. *1 Cor* 4:15
lest we should hinder the g. 9:12
a dispensation of the g. 17*
g. I may make the g. of Christ without charge . . . my power in g. 18
this I do for the g.'s sake. 23
if our g. be hid, it is hid. *2 Cor* 4:3
lest light of glorious g. of Christ. 4
brother, whose praise is in g. 8:18
your professed subjection to g. 9:13
another Spirit or g. 11:4; *Gal* 1:6
and would pervert the g. *Gal* 1:7
I communicated to them the g. 2:2
that the truth of the g. might. 5
they saw the g. of uncircumcision. 7
according to the truth of the g. 14
of truth the g. of your. *Eph* 1:13
his promise in Christ by the g. 3:6
preparation of the g. of peace. 6:15
known the mystery of the g. 19
fellowship in the g. till now. *Phil* 1:5
and confirmation of the g. 7, 17
to the furtherance of the g. 12
becometh the g. striving together for
  the faith of the g. 27
served with me in the g. 2:22
laboured with me in the g. 4:3
that in the beginning of the g. 15
in word of truth of the g. *Col* 1:5
away from the hope of the g. 23
g. came not in word but. *1 Thes* 1:5
we were bold to speak the g. 2:2
allowed to be put in trust with g. 4
to have imparted not the g. only. 8
our fellow-labourer in the g. 3:2
on them that obey not the g.
    2 Thes 1:8; *1 Pet* 4:17
he called you by our g. *2 Thes* 2:14
g. of the blessed God. *1 Tim* 1:11
of the afflictions of the g. *2 Tim* 1:8
immortality to light through g. 10
raised according to my g. 2:8
to me in bonds of the g. *Philem* 13

gospel joined with *preach,*
  preached, preaching
Jesus went *preaching* g. *Mat* 4:23
    9:35; *Mark* 1:14
the poor have the g. *preached.*
    Mat 11:5*; *Luke* 7:22
this g. shall be *preached.*
    Mat 24:14; 26:13; *Mark* 14:9
go, *preach* the g. to. *Mark* 16:15
me to *preach* the g. *Luke* 4:18*
they departed, *preaching* the g. 9:6
taught, and *preaching* the g. 20:1
and *preached* the g. to. *Acts* 8:25
and there they *preached* the g. 14:7
when they had *preached* the g. 21
called us to *preach* the g. 16:10
preach the g. at Rome. *Rom* 1:15
feet of them that *preach* g. 10:15
I have fully *preached* the g. 15:19
I strived to *preach* the g. not. 20
baptize, but to *preach* g. *1 Cor* 1:17
that *preach* the g. should live. 9:14
I *preach* the g. have nothing to glory,
  woe to me if I *preach* not g. 16
that when I *preach* the g. I may. 18
the g. which I *preached.* 15:1
Troas to *preach* the g. *2 Cor* 2:12
as to you in *preaching* the g. 10:14
preached to you freely the g. 11:7
angel *preach* any other g. *Gal* 1:8, 9
the g. *preached* of me is not. 11
preached before the g. to. 3:8
of flesh I *preached* the g. 4:13
preached to you the g. *1 Thes* 2:9
to us was the g. *preached.* *Heb* 4:2*
that *preached* the g. to. *1 Pet* 1:12
which by g. is *preached* to you. 25
this cause was the g. *preached.* 4:6
g. to *preach* to them. *Rev* 14:6†

got
her and g. him out. *Gen* 39:12, 15
they g. not the land by. *Ps* 44:3
I g. me servants and. *Eccl* 2:7
I g. a girdle according. *Jer* 13:2*
take the girdle that thou hast g. 4*

gotten
she said, I have g. a. *Gen* 4:1
was our father's hath he g. all. 31:1
when I have g. me honour. *Ex* 14:18
he hath deceitfully g. *Lev* 6:4
what every man hath g. *Num* 31:50
of my hand hath g. this. *Deut* 8:17
moreover if he be g. *2 Sam* 17:13
wisdom cannot be g. *Job* 28:15
because my hand had g. 31:25
his holy arm hath g. *Ps* 98:1
wealth g. by vanity shall. *Pr* 13:11
an inheritance may be g. 20:21
have g. more wisdom. *Eccl* 1:16
the abundance g. they. *Isa* 15:7
because riches he hath g. *Jer* 48:36
thou hast g. riches. *Ezek* 28:4
thou hast g. thee renown. *Dan* 9:15
I saw them that had g. *Rev* 15:2*

gourd
[1] *Hebrew* Kikayon, *used only in*
Jonah 4:6. *It may mean the castor-
oil plant, or a genuine gourd.*
[2] *Wild gourd of 2 Ki* 4:39 *was a
poisonous gourd, supposed to be the
colocynth, which might be mistaken
for the wholesome globe cucumber.*
a g. Jonah glad of the g. *Jonah* 4:6
a worm smote the g. that it. 7
thou hast had pity on the g. for. 16

wild gourds
one gathered wild g. his. *2 Ki* 4:39

govern
dost thou now g. the. *1 Ki* 21:7
he that hateth right g.? *Job* 34:17
for thou shalt g. the nations. *Ps* 67:4

government, -s
and the g. shall be upon. *Isa* 9:6
of the increase of his g. there. 7
I will commit thy g. into his. 22:21
helps, g. diversities of. *1 Cor* 12:28
them that despise g. *2 Pet* 2:10*

governor
Joseph was g. *Gen* 42:6; 45:26*
Obadiah was g. over. *1 Ki* 18:3*
Solomon to be chief g. *1 Chr* 29:22*

the vessels to the *g.*   *Ezra* 5:14
not eaten bread of the *g.* *Neh* 5:14
I required not bread of the *g.* 18
he is the *g.* among the. *Ps* 22:28*
their *g.* shall proceed. *Jer* 30:21*
back also to Gedaliah the *g.* 40:5
smote Gedaliah the *g.* 41:2, 18
stirred up Zerubbabel *g.* *Hag* 1:14
the *g.* and to Joshua. 2:2, 21
and he shall be as a *g.* *Zech* 9:7*
offer it now to thy *g.* *Mal* 1:8
of thee shall come a *g.* *Mat* 2:6
him to Pontius Pilate the *g.* 27:2
if this come to the *g.'s* ears. 28:14
and bear to the *g.* of. *John* 2:8*
informed the *g.* against. *Acts* 24:1
g. under Aretas king. *2 Cor* 11:32
ships turned whither *g.* *Jas* 3:4*

governors

heart is towards the *g.* *Judg* 5:9
out of Machir came down *g.* 14
king's commissions to *g.* *Ezra* 8:36
letters be given me to *g.* *Neh* 2:7
the former *g.* were chargeable. 5:15
Daniel chief of the *g.* *Dan* 2:48
the *g.* of Judah shall. *Zech* 12:5*
I will make the *g.* of Judah. 6*
shall be brought before *g. Mat* 10:18
heir is under tutors and *g. Gal* 4:2*
submit yourselves to *g.* *1 Pet* 2:14

Gozan

placed Israel by the river of G.
  2 Ki 17:6; 18:11; *1 Chr* 5:26
my fathers have destroyed, as G.
  2 Ki 19:12; *Isa* 37:12

grace

[1] *The free mercy of God, or the
enjoyment of his favour,* Rom 11:6;
2 Tim 1:9. [2] *A Christian virtue,*
2 Cor 8:7.

for a little space *g.* hath. *Ezra* 9:8
Esther obtained *g.* in. *Esth* 2:17*
g. is poured into lips. *Ps* 45:2
Lord is a sun, he will give *g.* 84:11
shall be an ornament of *g. Pr* 1:9
so shall they be life and *g.* to. 3:22
but he giveth *g.* to. 34; *Jas* 4:6
head an ornament of *g.* *Pr* 4:9
for the *g.* of his lips the king. 22:11
shoutings, crying, *g. g.* *Zech* 4:7
I will pour the Spirit of *g.* 12:10
of Father, full of *g.* and. *John* 1:14
we have all received, *g.* for *g.* 16
but *g.* and truth came by Jesus. 17
and great *g.* was on. *Acts* 4:33
testimony to word of his *g.* 14:3
had believed through *g.* 18:27
you to the word of his *g.* 20:32
whom we received *g. Rom* 1:5
g. and peace to you from God. 7
  1 Cor 1:3; *2 Cor* 1:2; *Gal* 1:3
  Eph 1:2; *Phil* 1:2; *Col* 1:2
  1 Thes 1:1; *2 Thes* 1:2; *Philem* 3
justified freely by his *g. Rom* 3:24
reward is not reckoned of *g.* but. 4:4
faith, that it might be by *g.* 16
have access into this *g.* wherein. 5:2
who receive abundance of *g.* 17
where sin abounded *g.* did much. 20
even so might *g.* reign through. 21
shall we continue in sin, that *g.?* 6:1
not under law, but under *g.* 14
shall we sin, because under *g.?* 15
according to the election of *g.* 11:5
and if by *g.* then it is no more. 6
for I say, through the *g.* given. 12:3
gifts differing according to the *g.* 6
because of the *g.* given to. 15:15
I by *g.* be a partaker. *1 Cor* 10:30
his *g.* bestowed upon me was. 15:10
abundant *g.* might redound to.
  2 Cor 4:15
finish in you the same *g.* also. 8:6
see that ye abound in this *g.* 7
to travel with us with this *g.* 19
God is able to make all *g.* 9:8
said my *g.* is sufficient for thee. 12:9
him who called you to *g. Gal* 1:6
God, who called me by his *g.* 15
when James perceived the *g.* 2:9
the law, ye are fallen from *g.* 5:4
praise of the glory of his *g. Eph* 1:6
according to the riches of his *g.* 7

by *g.* ye are saved. *Eph* 2:5, 8
the exceeding riches of his *g.* 7
least of all saints is·this *g.* 3:8
every one of us is given *g.* 4:7
that it may minister *g.* to the. 29
g. be with all that love our. 6:24
ye are all partakers of my *g. Phil* 1:7
singing with *g.* in your. *Col* 3:16
let speech be alway with *g.* 4:6
g. be with you. 18; *2 Tim* 4:22
  Tit 3:15; *Heb* 13:25
us good hope through *g. 2 Thes* 2:16
g. mercy, and peace from. *1 Tim* 1:2
  2 Tim 1:2; *Tit* 1:4; *2 John* 3
g. of our Lord was. *1 Tim* 1:14
g. be with thee. Amen. 6:21
us according to his *g.* *2 Tim* 1:9
be strong in the *g.* that is in. 2:1
being justified by his *g.* *Tit* 3:7
boldly to the throne of *g. Heb* 4:16
done despite to the Spirit of *g.* 10:29
let us have *g.* to serve God. 12:28
heart be established with *g.* 13:9
the *g.* of the fashion of. *Jas* 1:11
he giveth more *g.* giveth *g.* to. 4:6
g. and peace. *1 Pet* 1:2; *2 Pet* 1:2
who prophesied of the *g. 1 Pet* 1:10
hope to the end for the *g.* 13
as being heirs of *g.* 3:7
God resisteth proud, giveth *g.* 5:5
the God of *g.* who hath called. 10
grow in *g.* and. *2 Pet* 3:18
turning the *g.* of God into. *Jude* 4
g. and peace from him. *Rev* 1:4

see **find, found**

grace *of God*

and the *g.* of God was. *Luke* 2:40
he had seen *g.* of God. *Acts* 11:23
to continue in the *g.* of G. 13:43
recommended to *g.* of G. 14:26
  15:40
gospel of the *g.* of God. 20:24
much more *g.* of God. *Rom* 5:15
the *g.* of God given you. *1 Cor* 1:4
according to *g.* of God which. 3:10
g. of God I am what I am, yet not I,
  but the *g.* of God which. 15:10
by the *g.* of God we had. *2 Cor* 1:12
ye receive not the *g.* of God in. 6:1
of the *g.* of God bestowed on. 8:1
for the exceeding *g.* of God in. 9:14
frustrate the *g.* of God. *Gal* 2:21
dispensation of *g.* of God. *Eph* 3:2
to gift of the *g.* of God given me. 7
day ye knew *g.* of God. *Col* 1:6
according to *g.* of God. *2 Thes* 1:12
g. of God that bringeth. *Tit* 2:11
that he by *g.* of God. *Heb* 2:9
any man fail of *g.* of God. 12:15
of the manifold *g.* of God. *1 Pet* 4:10
this is true *g.* of God. 5:12

grace *of our Lord Jesus*

through *g.* of Lord Jesus we shall.
  Acts 15:11
the *g.* of our Lord Jesus. *Rom* 16:20
  24; *1 Cor* 16:23; *Phil* 4:23
  1 Thes 5:28; *2 Thes* 3:18
know *g.* of our Lord Jesus. *2 Cor* 8:9
the *g.* of our Lord Jesus Christ, love
  of God, and communion. 13:14
g. of our Lord Jesus Christ be with
  your spirit. *Gal* 6:18; *Philem* 25
g. of Lord Jesus Christ be with you.
  Rev 22:21

gracious

he said, God be *g.* to. *Gen* 43:29
I will hear, for I am *g.* *Ex* 22:27
be *g.* to whom I will be *g.* 33:19
the Lord, the Lord God, *g.* 34:6
  2 Chr 30:9; *Ps* 103:8; 116:5
  145:8; *Joel* 2:13
his face shine, and be *g. Num* 6:25
whether God will be *g.? 2 Sam* 12:22
the Lord was *g.* unto them. 13:23
to pardon, *g.* merciful. *Neh* 9:17, 31
then he is *g.* to him. *Job* 33:24
hath God forgotten to be *g.? Ps* 77:9
thou, O Lord, art a God *g.* 86:15
  111:4; 112:4
a *g.* woman retaineth. *Pr* 11:16
wise man's mouth are *g. Eccl* 10:12
wait that he may be *g.* *Isa* 30:18
he will be very *g.* to thee. 19

be *g.* to us. *Isa* 33:2
how *g.* when pangs. *Jer* 22:23*
may be the Lord will be *g. Amos* 5:15
that thou art a *g.* God. *Jonah* 4:2
God that he will be *g.* to. *Mal* 1:9
wondered at *g.* words. *Luke* 4:22
tasted that the Lord is *g.* *1 Pet* 2:3

graciously

children which G. hath *g.* *Gen* 33:5
because God hath dealt *g.* with. 11
and grant me thy law *g.* *Ps* 119:29
iniquity, and receive us *g. Hos* 14:2*

graft, -ed

olive tree wert *g.* in. *Rom* 11:17
broken that I might be *g.* in. 19
g. in, for God is able to *g.* them. 23
and *g.* much more these be *g.* 24

grain

yet shall not least *g.* fall. *Amos* 9:9*
is like a *g.* of mustard. *Mat* 13:31
  Mark 4:31; *Luke* 13:19
faith as a *g.* of mustard seed, ye
  shall say unto this mountain.
  Mat 17:20; *Luke* 17:6
bare *g.* wheat, or some other *g.*
  1 Cor 15:37*

grandmother

dwelt first in thy *g.* Lois. *2 Tim* 1:5

grant

according to the *g.* they. *Ezra* 3:7

grant

ye shall *g.* a redemption. *Lev* 25:24
Lord *g.* you that you. *Ruth* 1:9
God of Israel *g.* thee. *1 Sam* 1:17
g. me place of this threshingfloor;
  thou shalt *g.* it me. *1 Chr* 21:22*
but I will *g.* them some. *2 Chr* 12:7
and *g.* him mercy in. *Neh* 1:11
it please the king to *g.* *Esth* 5:8
that God would *g.* the. *Job* 6:8
g. thee according to thine. *Ps* 20:4
us thy mercy, O Lord, *g.* us. 85:7
and *g.* me thy law graciously. 119:29
g. not, O Lord, the desires. 140:8
g. my two sons may sit. *Mat* 20:21*
  Mark 10:37
g. to us, that we being. *Luke* 1:74
g. that with boldness we. *Acts* 4:29
God *g.* you be likeminded.
  Rom 15:5
g. you to be strengthened. *Eph* 3:16
the Lord *g.* that he may. *2 Tim* 1:18
will I *g.* to sit with me. *Rev* 3:21*

granted

God *g.* him that which. *1 Chr* 4:10
knowledge is *g.* thee. *2 Chr* 1:12
and the king *g.* him all. *Ezra* 7:6
g. according to good hand. *Neh* 2:8
what is thy petition ? and it shall be *g.*
  Esth 5:6; 7:2; 9:12
let it be *g.* to the Jews in. 9:13
thou hast *g.* me life and. *Job* 10:12
of righteous shall be *g.* *Pr* 10:24
a murderer to be *g.* you. *Acts* 3:14
God also to the Gentiles *g.* 11:18
who *g.* signs to be done by. 14:3
to her was *g.* she should. *Rev* 19:8*

grape

*There was an abundance of vine-
yards in Palestine from the earliest
times. The vines were celebrated
both for luxuriant growth and for the
immense clusters of grapes which
they produced which were sometimes carried on a staff between two
men as in the case of the spies,
Num 13:23, 24, and as has been
done in some instances in modern
times.
From the abundance and excellence of the vines, it may readily be
understood how frequently this
plant is the subject of metaphor in
the Holy Scriptures.*

nor gather every *g.* of. *Lev* 19:10*
drink the blood of the *g. Deut* 32:14
shake off his unripe *g.* *Job* 15:33
vines with tender *g.* *S of S* 2:13*
us see whether the tender *g.* 7:12*
the sour *g.* is ripening in. *Isa* 18:5
have eaten a sour *g.* *Jer* 31:29

that eateth the sour *g.* | Jer 31:30
I am as the *g.*-gleanings. | Mi 7:1

grapegatherer
turn back thy hand as a *g.* | Jer 6:9
g. come, would they ? | 49:9; Ob 5

grapes
brought forth ripe *g.* | Gen 40:10
his clothes in blood of *g.* | 49:11
nor gather the *g.* of thy. | Lev 25:5
in jubile, nor gather *g.* of thy. | 11
shall he eat moist *g.* or. | Num 6:3
the time of the firstripe *g.* | 13:20
a branch with one cluster of *g.* | 23
then thou mayest eat *g.* | Deut 23:24
when thou gatherest the *g.* of. | 24:21
vineyard, not gather the *g.* | 28:30*, 39
their *g.* are *g.* of gall, their. | 32:32
is not gleaning of the *g.?* | Judg 8:2
they trode the *g.* and cursed. | 9:27
bringing in wine and *g.* | Neh 13:15
our vines have tender *g.* | S of S 2:15*
breasts are like to clusters of *g.* | 7:7
it should bring forth *g.* | Isa 5:2
forth *g.* brought it forth wild *g.?* | 4
yet gleaning *g.* shall be left. | 17:6
as gleaning *g.* when vintage. | 24:13
there shall be no *g.* on. | Jer 8:13
as they that tread the *g.* | 25:30
leave some gleaning *g.* | 49:9; Ob 5
fathers have eaten sour *g.* | Ezek 18:2
I found Israel like *g.* in the. | Hos 9:10
treader of *g.* shall overtake the. | Amos 9:13
men gather *g.* of thorns ? | Mat 7:16
bush gather they *g.* | Luke 6:44
thrust in sickle, her *g.* | Rev 14:18

grass
let earth bring forth *g.* | Gen 1:11
and the earth brought forth *g.* | 12
as the ox licketh up *g.* | Num 22:4
I will send *g.* in thy. | Deut 11:15
not sown, not any *g.* | 29:23
distil as showers upon the *g.* | 32:2
as the *g.* springeth out. | 2 Sam 23:4
peradventure find *g.* to. | 1 Ki 18:5
the *g.* of the field, as green herb, as
g. on. | 2 Ki 19:26; Isa 37:27
thine offspring is the *g.* of. | Job 5:25
wild ass bray when he hath *g.?* | 6:5
behold, behemoth eateth *g.* | 40:15
be cut down like the *g.* | Ps 37:2
down like rain upon mown *g.* | 72:6
they of city shall flourish like *g.* | 16
in the morning they are like *g.* | 90:5
when wicked spring as the *g.* | 92:7
smitten, and withered like *g.* | 102:4
a shadow; I am withered like *g.* | 11
as for man, his days are as *g.* | 103:15
he causeth *g.* to grow for. | 104:14
of an ox that eateth *g.* | 106:20
let them be as the *g.* upon. | 129:6
who maketh *g.* to grow upon. | 147:8
is as dew upon the *g.* | Pr 19:12
hay appeareth, the tender *g.* | 27:25
g. faileth, there is no. | Isa 15:6
of dragons, shall be *g.* | 35:7
cry, all flesh is *g.* | 40:6; 1 Pet 1:24
g. withereth, surely the people is *g.* | Isa 40:7, 8
spring up as among the *g.* | 44:4
man which shall be made as *g.* | 51:12
because there was no *g.* | Jer 14:5, 6
grown fat as the heifer at *g.* | 50:11
stump in tender *g.* | Dan 4:15, 23
make thee eat | 25, 32, 33; 5:21
made an end of eating *g.* | Amos 7:2
as showers upon the *g.* | Mi 5:7
shall give every one *g.* | Zech 10:1
if God so clothe the *g.* | Mat 6:30
| Luke 12:28
the multitude to sit down on *g.* | Mat 14:19; Mark 6:10
now there was much *g.* | John 6:10
as the flower of the *g.* he. | Jas 1:10
sun risen, but it withereth the *g.* | 11
and all green *g.* was. | Rev 8:7
they should not hurt the *g.* of. | 9:4

grasshopper, -s
(*Grasshoppers or locusts are frequently mentioned in the Bible as very destructive agents. They came over the land in huge numbers, eating every green leaf, and*

very *often leaving famine in their path*)
these ye may eat, the *g.* | Lev 11:22
in our own sight as *g.* | Num 13:33
as *g.* for multitude. | Judg 6:5*; 7:12*
make him afraid as a *g.?* | Job 39:20*
and the *g.* shall be a. | Eccl 12:5
thereof are as *g.* | Isa 40:22
they are more than *g.* | Jer 46:23*
behold, he formed *g.* in. | Amos 7:1*
captains are as great *g.* | Nah 3:17

grave, *substantive*
(*The Revisions very frequently substitute for grave the Hebrew word Sheol, which means the place of the dead*)
pillar upon her *g.* that is the pillar of
Rachel's *g.* unto this. | Gen 35:20
I will go down to *g.* to my. | 37:35
hairs with sorrow to *g.* | 42:38; 44:31
bury me in the *g.* which I. | 50:5
whosoever toucheth a *g.* | Num 19:16
that touched one dead, or a *g.* | 18
bringeth down to one the *g.* | 1 Sam 2:6
wept at Abner's *g.* | 2 Sam 3:32
and be buried by the *g.* of. | 19:37
his head go to the *g.* in. | 1 Ki 2:6
his head bring down to the *g.* | 9
laid his carcase in his own *g.* | 13:30
Jeroboam shall come to *g.* | 14:13
thou shalt be gathered into thy *g.* | 2 Ki 22:20; 2 Chr 34:28
when they can find the *g.* | Job 3:22
thou shalt come to thy *g.* in. | 5:26
so he that goeth to *g.* shall. | 7:9
been carried from womb to *g.* | 10:19
wouldest hide me in the *g.* | 14:13
if I wait, the *g.* is my house. | 17:13
they go down to the *g.* | 21:13
yet shall he be brought to the *g.* | 32
so doth the *g.* those that have. | 24:19
stretch out his hand to the *g.* | 30:24
soul draweth near to the *g.* | 33:22*
in the *g.* who shall give? | Ps 6:5
brought up my soul from the *g.* | 30:3
the wicked be silent in the *g.* | 31:17
laid in the *g.*: consume in the *g.* | 49:14
my soul from the power of *g.* | 15
life draweth nigh to the *g.* | 88:3
like slain that lie in the *g.* | 5
be declared in the *g.* | 11
his soul from hand of *g.?* | 89:48
scattered at the *g.'s* mouth. | 141:7
them alive as the *g.* | Pr 1:12
g. and barren womb, say not. | 30:16
no wisdom in *g.* whither. | Eccl 9:10
jealousy is cruel as the *g.* | S of S 8:6
pomp is brought down to *g.* | Isa 14:11
thou art cast out of thy *g.* like. | 19
go to the gates of the *g.* | 38:10
the *g.* cannot praise thee, death. | 18
he made his *g.* with wicked. | 53:9
might have been my *g.* | Jer 20:17
he went down to the *g.* | Ezek 31:15
company is round about her *g.* | 32:23
from the power of *g.*; I will redeem
from death: O *g.* I will. | Hos 13:14
I will make thy *g.* for. | Nah 1:14
he had lain in the *g.* | John 11:17*
saying, she goeth to the *g.* | 31*
again groaning, cometh to the *g.* | 38*
called Lazarus out of the *g.* | 43*
g. where is thy victory? | 1 Cor 15:55*

grave, *adjective*
deacons must be *g.* | 1 Tim 3:8
wives must be *g.* | 11
aged men be sober, *g.* | Tit 2:2

grave, *verb*
g. on the onyx stones. | Ex 28:9
a plate of pure gold, and *g.* on it. | 36
a man that can skill to *g.* | 2 Chr 2:7
sent a cunning man to *g.* any. | 14

graveclothes
came forth bound with *g.* | John 11:44

graved
on the borders *g.* | 1 Ki 7:36
and he *g.* cherubims on. | 2 Chr 3:7

gravel
mouth be filled with *g.* | Pr 20:17
of thy bowels like *g.* | Isa 48:19*
broken my teeth with *g.* | Lam 3:16

graven
was writing of God *g.* | Ex 32:16
g. as signets are *g.* with the. | 39:6
g. with an iron pen. | Job 19:24
I have *g.* thee on palms of. | Isa 49:16
g. upon the table of their. | Jer 17:1
maker thereof hath *g.* it. | Hab 2:18
Godhead is like gold *g.* | Acts 17:29

graven *image*
make unto thee any *g. image.*
| Ex 20:4; Lev 26:1; Deut 5:8
corrupt and make a *g. image.*
| Deut 4:16, 25
that maketh any *g. image.* | 27:15
son to make a *g. image.* | Judg 17:3
founder, who made a *g. image.* | 4
in these houses a *g. image.* | 18:14
the *g. image.* | 17
Dan set up the *g. image.* | 30, 31
Manasseh set up *g. image.* | 2 Ki 21:7
melteth a *g. image.* | Isa 40:19
workman to prepare a *g. image.* | 20
they that make a *g. image* are. | 44:9
who hath molten a *g. image?* | 10
thereof he maketh his *g. image.* | 17
the wood of their *g. image.* | 45:20
my *g. image* hath commanded. | 48:5
founder confounded by *g. image.*
| Jer 10:14; 51:17
cut off the *g.* and molten *image.*
| Nah 1:14
profiteth the *g. image?* | Hab 2:18

graven *images*
burn their *g. images* with fire.
| Deut 7:5, 25
hew down the *g. images* of. | 12:3
nations feared the Lord, and served
their *g. images.* | 2 Ki 17:41
set up *g. images* before. | 2 Chr 33:19
he had beaten the *g. images.* | 34:7
to jealousy with *g. images.* | Ps 78:58
they that serve *g. images.* | 97:7
whose *g. images* did excel. | Isa 10:10
fallen, and all the *g. images.* | 21:9
covering of thy *g. images.* | 30:22
I give my praise to *g. images.* | 42:8
ashamed that trust in *g. images.* | 17
anger with their *g. images.* | Jer 8:19
it is the land of *g. images.* | 50:38
judgement on *g. images.* | 51:47, 52
incense to *g. images.* | Hos 11:2
g. images shall be beaten. | Mi 1:7
thy *g. images* also will I cut. | 5:13

graves
were no *g.* in Egypt. | Ex 14:11
cast powder on the *g.* | 2 Ki 23:6
strowed it upon the *g.* | 2 Chr 34:4
days extinct, the *g.* are. | Job 17:1
remain among the *g.* | Isa 65:4
priests' bones out of their *g.* | Jer 8:1
and cast his dead body into *g.* | 26:23
his *g.* are about him. | Ezek 32:22
| 23, 25, 26
I will open your *g.* and cause you to
come up out of your *g.* | 37:12
opened your *g.* brought out of *g.* | 13
give Gog a place of *g.* in. | 39:11*
the *g.* were opened. | Mat 27:52*
bodies of saints came out of *g.* | 53*
for ye are as *g.* which. | Luke 11:44
all that are in the *g.* | John 5:28*
bodies to be put in *g.* | Rev 11:9*

graveth
that *g.* an habitation in. | Isa 22:16

graving
golden calf with a *g.* tool. | Ex 32:4
grave any manner of *g.* | 2 Chr 2:14
I will engrave *g.* thereof. | Zech 3:9

gravings
on mouth of laver were *g.* | 1 Ki 7:31

gravity
subjection with all *g.* | 1 Tim 3:4
in doctrine shewing *g.* | Tit 2:7

gray, *see* hairs *and* head

grayheaded
I am old and *g.* my. | 1 Sam 12:2
with us are the *g.* | Job 15:10
when I am old and *g.* | Ps 71:18

grease
heart is as fat as *g.* | Ps 119:70

great

[1] *Large in size,* 2 Chr 2:5. [2] *Considerable in degree of qualities or feelings,* Gen 39:9; Ps 14:5. [3] *Eminent or important,* Gen 24:35; 2 Chr 17:12.

and make thy name *g.*   *Gen* 12:2
my master is become *g.*   24:35
with *g.* wrestlings have I.   30:8
can I do this *g.* wickedness? 39:9
to save your lives by a *g.*   45:7
my son, he also shall be *g.* 48:19
unwalled towns a *g.* many. *Deut* 3:5
God is a *g.* God. 10:17; *2 Chr* 2:5
eyes have seen *g.* acts. *Deut* 11:7
neither let me see this *g.* fire 18:16
meaneth the heat of his *g.*? 29:24
wilt thou do unto thy *g.*? *Josh* 7:9
thou heardest cities were *g.* 14:12
there a *g.* altar by Jordan. 22:10
for he did those *g.* signs in. 24:17
divisions of Reuben *g.* *Judg* 5:15
your wickedness is *g.* 1 *Sam* 12:17
David went on, and grew *g.* and the
  Lord was with him. *2 Sam* 5:10
I have made thee a *g.* name. 7:9
thou art *g.* O Lord God, none is. 22
given *g.* occasion to enemies. 12:14
gentleness hath made me *g.* 22:36
  Ps 18:35
shall hear of thy *g.* name. 1 *Ki* 8:42
  2 Chr 6:32
the journey is too *g.* for. 1 *Ki* 19:7
Shunem, where a *g.* woman. 2 *Ki* 4:8
g. is the wrath of the Lord. 22:13
g. is the Lord, and.   1 *Chr* 16:25
 Ps 48:1; 96:4; 135:5; 145:3
Lord's hand, for very *g.* 1 *Chr* 21:13
thine hand it is to make *g.* 29:12
house I build is *g.* for *g.* *2 Chr* 2:5
I am to build shall be wonderful *g.* 9
Jehoshaphat waxed *g.* 17:12
our trespass is *g.* 28:13
g. wrath poured. 34:21
Lord who is *g.* and terrible. *Neh* 4:14
now therefore our God, the *g.* 9:32
his empire, for it is *g.* *Esth* 1:20
that thy seed shall be *g.* *Job* 5:25
is not thy wickedness *g.*? 22:5
by *g.* force of my disease. 30:18
yet he knoweth it not in *g.* 35:15
a *g.* ransom. 36:18
God is *g.,* and we know him not. 26
the number of thy days is *g.* 38:21
in him, because strength is *g.*? 39:11
were they in *g.* fear. *Ps* 14:5; 53:5
keeping of them there is *g.* 19:11
his glory is *g.* in thy salvation. 21:5
mine iniquity, for it is *g.* 25:11
O how *g.* is thy goodness! 31:19
art *g.* and doest wondrous. 86:10
how *g.* are thy works! 92:5
O God, how *g.* is the sum! 139:17
this wisdom seemed *g.* *Eccl* 9:13
houses even *g.* and fair. *Isa* 5:9
people that walked in darkness have
  seen *g.* light. 9:2; *Mat* 4:16
g. is the Holy One of. *Isa* 12:6
send them a Saviour and a *g.* 19:20*
divide him a portion with *g.* 53:12
and *g.* shall be the peace of. 54:13
are become *g.* and rich. *Jer* 5:27
art *g.* and thy name is *g.* in. 10:6
her womb to be always *g.* 20:17
the G., the mighty God is his. 32:18
g. in counsel, and mighty in. 19
I have sworn by my *g.* name. 44:26
they are new, *g.* is thy. *Lam* 3:23
increased and waxed *g.* *Ezek* 16:7
a *g.* eagle with *g.* wings. 17:3, 7
even make the pile for fire *g.* 24:9
to serve a *g.* service against. 29:18
the waters made him *g.* 31:4*
I will sanctify my *g.* name. 36:23
how *g.* his signs, how. *Dan* 4:3
ram pushing, and he became *g.* 8:4*
for their wickedness is *g.* *Joel* 3:13
go to Hamath the *g.* *Amos* 6:2
shall he be *g.* unto the ends. *Mi* 5:4
g. his goodness, how *g.* *Zech* 9:17
my name shall be *g.* *Mal* 1:11
exceeding glad, for *g.* is your reward. *Mat* 5:12; *Luke* 6:23, 35

shall be called *g.* in the. *Mat* 5:19
if light be darkness, how *g.* is! 6:23
one pearl of *g.* price. 13:46
g. is thy faith. 15:28
g. possessions. 19:22; *Mark* 10:22
they that are *g.* exercise. *Mat* 20:25
be *g.* among you. 26; *Mark* 10:43
Master, which is the *g.*? *Mat* 22:36
is the first and *g.* commandment. 38
g. in sight of Lord. *Luke* 1:15, 32
you, the same shall be *g.* 9:48
the harvest truly is *g.* but. 10:2*
us and your there is a *g.* gulf. 16:26
out that he was some *g.* *Acts* 8:9
g. is Diana of the. 19:28, 34
g. is my boldness, *g.* is. *2 Cor* 7:4
that he hath a *g.* zeal for. *Col* 4:13
g. is mystery of. 1 *Tim* 3:16
in *g.* house not only. 2 *Tim* 2:20
appearing of the *g.* God. *Tit* 2:13
now consider how *g.* this. *Heb* 7:4
how *g.* a matter a little. *Jas* 3:5*
another sign in heaven, *g.* *Rev* 15:1
g. Babylon came in. 16:19
Babylon the *g.* mother. 17:5; 18:2
unto supper of the *g.* God. 19:17
see city, company, congregation, cry, day, destruction

great evil

hath done us *g. evil.* 1 *Sam* 6:9
to do all this *g. evil.* *Neh* 13:27
vanity, and a *g. evil.* *Eccl* 2:21
pronounced this *g. evil.* *Jer* 16:10
thus might we procure *g. evil.* 26:19
I have brought this *g. evil.* 32:42
why commit this *g. evil*? 44:7
bringing upon us a *g. evil. Dan* 9:12
see exceeding, joy

great king or kings

thus saith the *g. king.* 2 *Ki* 18:19
 28; *Isa* 36:4, 13
which a *g. king* of Israel. *Ezra* 5:11
the Lord is a *g. King.* *Ps* 47:2
Zion, the city of the *g. King.* 48:2
the Lord is a *g. King* above. 95:3
to him that smote *g. kings.* 136:17
there came a *g. king.* *Eccl* 9:14
g. kings shall serve. *Jer* 25:14; 27:7
for I am a *g. King,* saith. *Mal* 1:14
is city of the *g. King.* *Mat* 5:35

great men

like name of *g.* men in earth.
  2 Sam 7:9; 1 *Chr* 17:8
sons were with *g.* men. 2 *Ki* 10:6
Jehu slew all Ahab's *g.* men. and. 11
son of one of *g.* men. *Neh* 11:14*
g. men are not always wise. *Job* 32:9
him before *g.* men. *Pr* 18:16
stand not in place of *g.* men. 25:6
get me unto the *g.* men. *Jer* 5:5
all houses of the *g.* men. 52:13
is sword of the *g.* men. *Ezek* 21:14
all her *g.* men were bound. *Nah* 3:10
g. men hid themselves. *Rev* 6:15*
merchants were the *g.* men. 18:23*

great multitude, multitudes

Gad had a *g. multitude.* *Num* 32:1
hast thou seen all this *g. multi-*
  tude? 1 *Ki* 20:13
I will deliver this *g. multitude.* 28
be ye a *g. multitude.* 2 *Chr* 13:8
there cometh a *g. multitude.* 20:2
by reason of this *g. multitude.* 15
carried a *g. multitude* captives. 28:5
did I fear a *g. multitude*? *Job* 31:34
all that *g. multitude.* *Isa* 16:14
by, even a *g. multitude.* *Jer* 44:15
very *g. multitude* of fish. *Ezek* 47:9
set forth a *g. multitude.* *Dan* 11:11
g. multitudes followed him.
 Mat 4:25; 8:1; 12:15*; 19:2
 20:29; *Mark* 3:7; *John* 6:2
when Jesus saw a *g. multitude.*
 Mat 8:18; 14:14; *Mark* 9:14
g. multitudes came. *Mat* 15:30
bread as to fill so *g. multitude.* 33
a *g. multitude* spread their. 21:8
with Judas a *g. multitude* with.
 26:47; *Mark* 14:43
inclosed a *g. multitude.* *Luke* 5:6
a *g. multitude* came together to. 15
in these lay a *g. multitude.* *John* 5:3
a *g. multitude* of Jews. *Acts* 14:1

Greeks a *g. multitude.* *Acts* 17:4
a *g. multitude* which no. *Rev* 7:9
the voice of a *g. multitude.* 19:6

great nation and nations

a *g. nation,* and will bless. *Gen* 12:2
 18:18; 46:3; *Ex* 32:10
Ishmael a *g. nation.* 17:20; 21:18
surely this *g. nation* is. *Deut* 4:6
he became there a *nation g.* 26:5
before you *g. nations.* *Josh* 23:9
who smote *g. nations.* *Ps* 135:10*
a *g. nation* shall be raised. *Jer* 6:22
Babylon an assembly of *g.* nations.
  50:9
from the north, a *g. nation.* 41
dwelt all *g. nations.* *Ezek* 31:6

great people

therein, a *people g.* *Deut* 2:10
Zamzummims, a *people g.* many. 21
a *people g.* and tall, children. 9:2
seeing I am a *g. people. Josh* 17:14
if thou be a *g. people.* 15
thou art a *g. people.* 17
g. people that cannot be. 1 *Ki* 3:8
judge this *g. people* ? 9; 2 *Chr* 1:10
son over this *g. people.* 1 *Ki* 5:7
mountains like as of *g. people.*
  Isa 13:4
g. people hath not been. *Joel* 2:2

great power

out of Egypt with *g. power. Ex* 32:11
 2 *Ki* 17:36; *Neh* 1:10
power of my lord be *g. Num* 14:17
people and hast *g. power. Josh* 17:17
against me with *g. power* ? *Job* 23:6
Lord, and of *g. power.* *Ps* 147:5
man and beast upon the ground, by
  my *g. power.* *Jer* 27:5; 32:17
wither even without *g. power.*
  Ezek 17:9*
slow to anger, *g.* in *power. Nah* 1:3
clouds with *g. power.* *Mark* 13:26
g. power gave the. *Acts* 4:33
saying, this man is the *g. power.* 8:10
to thee thy *g. power.* *Rev* 11:17
from heaven, having *g. power.* 18:1

great sea

shall have the *g. sea.* *Num* 34:6
wilderness unto *g. sea.* *Josh* 1:4
kings in the coasts of *g. sea.* 9:1
border was to the *g. sea.* 15:12
inheritance of Judah, to *g. sea.* 47
I have cut off to the *g. sea.* 23:4
as fish of the *g. sea.* *Ezek* 47:10
land toward north from *g. sea.* 15
winds strove upon *g. sea.* *Dan* 7:2
see sin

great slaughter

with a *g. s.* at Gibeon. *Josh* 10:10
end of slaying them with *g. s.* 20
Ammonites with *g. s.* *Judg* 11:33
smote Philistines with *g. s.* 15:8
Israel with *g. s.* 1 *Sam* 4:10, 17
smitten with *g. s.* 6:19
David slew Philistines with a *g. s.*
  19:8; 23:5
a *g. s.* that day. 1 *Sam* 18:7
slew Assyrians with *g. s.* 1 *Ki* 20:21
slew Israel with a *g. s.* 2 *Chr* 13:17
smote Ahaz with a *g. s.* 28:5
in day of *g. s.* when. *Isa* 30:25
Lord hath a *g. s.* in the land. 34:6

so great

hast brought so *g.* a sin. *Ex* 32:21
what nation so *g.* hath? *Deut* 4:7, 8
who is able to judge so *g.* a people?
 1 *Ki* 3:9; 2 *Chr* 1:10
who is so *g.* a God as ? *Ps* 77:13
so *g.* in his mercy to them. 103:11
I have not found so *g.* faith, no, not
  in Israel. *Mat* 8:10; *Luke* 7:9
bread as to fill so *g.* *Mat* 15:33
delivered us from so *g.* 2 *Cor* 1:10
we neglect so *g.* salvation? *Heb* 2:3
are compassed with so *g.* a. 12:1
ships though so *g.* yet. *Jas* 3:4
earthquake and so *g.* *Rev* 16:18
in one hour so *g.* riches come. 18:17

small and great

blindness *small* and *g.* *Gen* 19:11
hear *small* as well as *g.* *Deut* 1:17
divers weights. a *g.* and small. 25:13

measures, a *g. and small. Deut* 25:14
smote men *small and g. 1 Sam* 5:9
do nothing *g. or small.* 20:2
not any either *g. or small.* 30:2
lacking neither *small* nor *g.* 19
fight not with *small* nor *g.*
    1 Ki 22:31; *2 Chr* 18:30
small and g. went to house.
    2 Chr 23:2; *2 Chr* 34:30
people *small and g.*   *2 Ki* 25:26
lots, as well *small* as *g. 1 Chr* 26:13
he put to death, whether *small* or *g.*
    2 Chr 15:13
by courses, *g. and small.* 31:15
hand vessels, *g. and small.* 36:18
feast unto *g. and small. Esth* 1:5
husbands honour *g. and small.* 20
small and g. are there. *Job* 3:19
the *small* rain, and to *g.* rain. 37:6*
creeping, *small and g. Ps* 104:25
fear the Lord, *small and g.* 115:13
possessions of *g. and small. Eccl* 2:7
g. and small shall die. *Jer* 16:6
ephah *small, small and g. Amos* 8:5
witnessing to *small and g. Acts* 26:22
fear him, *small and g. Rev* 11:18
he caused *small and g.* to. 13:16
ye that fear him, *small and g.* 19:5
flesh of all men, *small and g.* 18
I saw dead, *small and g.* 20:12

great stone and stones
a *g. stone* was upon the. *Gen* 29:2
that set up *g. stones. Deut* 27:2
cast down *g. stones. Josh* 10:11
roll *g. stones* upon the mouth of. 18
Joshua took a *g. stone*, and. 24:26
there was a *g. stone. 1 Sam* 6:14
Levites put them on the *g. stone.* 15
to the *g. stone* of Abel, whereon. 18
transgressed, roll a *g. stone.* 14:33
were at *g. stone* in. *2 Sam* 20:8
they brought *g. stones* to. *1 Ki* 5:17
was of *g. stones.*   7:10; *Ezra* 5:8
to shoot *g. stones.*   *2 Chr* 26:15
three rows of *g. stones. Ezra* 6:4
take *g. stones* and hide. *Jer* 43:9
he rolled a *g. stone* to. *Mat* 27:60

great thing and things
thing as this *g. thing* is. *Deut* 4:32
God that hath done *g. things.* 10:21
and see this *g. thing. 1 Sam* 12:16
consider how *g. things* he hath. 24
shalt both do *g. thing.* and. 26:25*
hast done *g. things.*   *2 Sam* 7:21*
and to do for you *g. things* and. 23
bid thee do some *g. thing. 2 Ki* 5:13
tell me all the *g. things* Elisha. 8:4
he should do this *g. thing* ? 13
known these *g. things. 1 Chr* 17:19
to God who doeth *g. things.*
    Job 5:9; 9:10; 37:5
hast done *g. things,* who. *Ps* 71:19
God who had done *g. things.* 106:21
done *g. things* for them.   126:2, 3
g. and mighty *things.*   *Jer* 33:3
and seekest thou *g. things* ? 45:5
a mouth speaking *g. things.*
    Dan 7:8, 20; *Rev* 13:5
I have written *g. things. Hos* 8:12*
he hath done *g. things. Joel* 2:20
the Lord will do *g. things.* 21
heard what *g. things* he. *Mark* 3:8
tell them how *g. things* the Lord
  hath done.   5:19; *Luke* 8:39
hath done *g. things. Luke* 1:49
he published how *g. things.* 8:39
will shew how *g. things. Acts* 9:16*
a *g. thing* if we reap ? *1 Cor* 9:11
no *g. thing* if his ministers be.
    2 Cor 11:15
member boasteth *g. things. Jas* 3:5

very great
till he became *very g. Gen* 26:13
man Moses was *very g. Ex* 11:3
people with a *very g.* plague.
    Num 11:33
cities are walled and *very g.* 12:28
promote thee unto *very g.* 22:17
of young men was *very g. 1 Sam* 2:17
there was a *very g.* slaughter. 4:10
very g. trembling. 14:15
very g. discomfiture. 20
Nabal wa~ *s very g.* man, he. 25:2

laid a *very g.* heap.   *2 Sam* 18:17
for Barzillai was a *very g.* 19:32
came with a *very g.* train. *1 Ki* 10:2
very g. are his mercies. *1 Chr* 21:13
very g. burning for Asa. *2 Chr* 16:14
very g. host into their hand. 24:24
a *very g.* congregation. 30:13
    Ezra 10:1
up wall a *very g.* height. *2 Chr* 33:14
and there was a *very g. Neh* 8:17
Job a *very g.* household. *Job* 1:3
that his grief was *very g.* 2:13
God, thou art *very g. Ps* 104:1
there shall be a *very g.* multitude
  of fish.   *Ezek* 47:9
he goat waxed *very g. Dan* 8:8
up with a *very g.* army. 11:25
for his camp is *very g. Joel* 2:11
shall be a *very g.* valley. *Zech* 14:4
very g. multitude spread. *Mat* 21:8
multitude *very g.* having. *Mark* 8:1
rolled away, for it was *very g.* 16:4

was great
wickedness of man *was g. Gen* 6:5
their substance *was g.* so that. 13:6
to Gibeon, that *was g.* 13:6
there *was g.* indignation. *2 Ki* 3:27
where decree came *was g. Esth* 4:3
Mordecai *was g.* in the. 9:4; 10:3
because my wealth *was g. Job* 31:25
I *was g.* and increased. *Eccl* 2:9
she that *was g.* among. *Lam* 1:1
tree's height *was g. Dan* 4:10
it fell, and *g. was* the fall of it.
    Mat 7:27; *Luke* 6:49

great waters
in floods of *g. waters. Ps* 32:6
sea, thy path in *g. waters.* 77:19
do business in *g. waters.* 107:23
deliver me out of *g. waters.* 144:7
and by *g. waters* the seed. *Isa* 23:3
Ishmael by *g. waters. Jer* 41:12
do roar like *g. waters. Ps* 51:55*
their wings like *g. waters. Ezek* 1:24
of the seed by *g. waters,* set. 17:5*
in a good soil by *g. waters.* 8*
when *g. waters* shall cover. 26:19
brought thee into *g. waters.* 27:26
his root was by *g. waters.* 31:7*
floods, the *g. waters* were stayed. 15
all beasts beside *g. waters.* 32:13
through heap of *g. waters. Hab* 3:15

great while
of thy servant's house for a *g. while.*
    2 Sam 7:19; *1 Chr* 17:17
rising up a *g. while. Mark* 1:35
g. while ago repented. *Luke* 10:13
barbarians looked a *g. while.*
    Acts 28:6

great work and works
Israel saw that *g. work. Ex* 14:31
had seen all *g. works. Judg* 2:7
young, and *work* is *g. 1 Chr* 29:1
the *work* is *g.* and we. *Neh* 4:19
I am doing a *g. work.* I cannot. 6:3
the *works* of the Lord are *g.*
    Ps 111:2; *Rev* 15:3
I made *g. works,* I builded. *Eccl* 2:4

greater
God made the *g.* light to. *Gen* 1:16
my punishment is *g.* than I can. 4:13
there is none *g.* in this house. 39:9
only in throne will I be *g.* than. 41:40
younger brother shall be *g.* 48:19
know the Lord is *g.* than. *Ex* 18:11
make of thee *g.* nation. *Num* 14:12
    Deut 9:14
people is *g.* and taller. *Deut* 1:28
drive nations *g.* than thou. 4:38
    7:1; 9:1; 11:23
because Gibeon was *g. Josh* 10:2
there been a much *g. 1 Sam* 14:30
the hatred was *g.* than. *2 Sam* 13:15
this evil is *g.* than the other. 16*
make his throne *g. 1 Ki* 1:37, 47
David waxed *g.* and *g. 1 Chr* 11:9
the *g.* house he cieled. *2 Chr* 3:5
Mordecai waxed *g.* and *g. Esth* 9:4
answer, that God is *g. Job* 33:12
is *g.* than the punishment. *Lam* 4:6
g. abominations. *Ezek* 8:6, 13, 15
set forth a multitude *g. Dan* 11:13

or their border *g.* than.   *Amos* 6:2
glory of latter house *g.*   *Hag* 2:9
hath not risen a *g.* than John the
  Baptist.   *Mat* 11:11; *Luke* 7:28
in this place is one *g.*   *Mat* 12:6
g. than Jonas is.   41; *Luke* 11:32
behold a *g.* than Solomon is here.
    Mat 12:42; *Luke* 11:31
receiving *g.* damnation. *Mat* 23:14
    Mark 12:40; *Luke* 20:47
whether is *g.* the gold or ? *Mat* 23:17
for whether is *g.* the gift or the ? 19
sown, it becometh *g.*   *Mark* 4:32
is no other commandment *g.* 12:31
my barns, and build *g. Luke* 12:18
whether is *g.* he that sitteth ? 22:27
thou shalt see *g.* things.
    John 1:50; 5:20; 14:12
art thou *g.* than our father ? 4:12
I have a *g.* witness than that. 5:36
art thou *g.* than our father ? 8:53
Father is *g.* than all.   10:29; 14:28
the servant is not *g.*   13:16; 15:20
g. love hath no man than this. 15:13
delivered me to thee hath *g.* 19:11
to lay upon you no *g. Acts* 15:28
g. is he that prophesieth. *1 Cor* 14:5
of whom the *g.* part remain. 15:6
he could swear by no *g. Heb* 6:13
men verily swear by the *g.* 16
by a *g.* and more perfect. 9:11
reproach of Christ *g.* riches. 11:26
we shall receive *g. Jas* 3:1*
angels which are *g.* in. *2 Pet* 2:11
God is *g.* than our. *1 John* 3:20
g. is he that is in you, than he. 4:4
witness of God is *g.* this is the. 5:9
I have no *g.* joy than to. *3 John* 4

greatest
was over 100, *g.* over. *1 Chr* 12:14
hitherto the *g.* part had kept the. 29
this man was the *g.* of. *Job* 1:3
from least to *g.* given. *Jer* 6:13; 8:10
from least to the *g.* 31:34; *Heb* 8:11
people from least to the *g. Jer* 42:1
called people from least to *g.* 8
die, from the least to the *g.* 44:12
sackcloth, from the *g. Jonah* 3:5
when grown, it is the *g. Mat* 13:32
who is the *g.* in the kingdom ? 18:1
as this little child, same is *g.* 4
but he that is *g.* shall be. 23:11
disputed who should be *g.*
    Mark 9:34; *Luke* 9:46
strife who should be *g. Luke* 22:24
but he that is *g.* let him be as. 26
heed from least to the *g. Acts* 8:10
but the *g.* of these is. *1 Cor* 13:13

greatly
I will *g.* multiply thy. *Gen* 3:16
Lot pressed upon them *g.* and. 19:3
hath blessed my master *g.* 24:35
then Jacob was *g.* afraid and. 32:7
whole mount quaked *g. Ex* 19:18
of Lord was kindled *g. Num* 11:10
and the people mourned *g.* 14:39
Lord shall *g.* bless thee. *Deut* 15:4*
nor shall he *g.* multiply silver. 17:17
they were *g.* distressed. *Judg* 2:15
Israel was *g.* impoverished. 6:6*
anger was kindled *g. 1 Sam* 11:6
all men of Israel rejoiced *g.* 15
the people *g.* feared the Lord. 12:18
he loved him *g.* became his. 16:21
Philistine, they were *g.* 17:11
Philistines his heart trembled *g.* 28:5
David was *g.* distressed, for. 30:6
the men were *g.* ashamed.
    2 Sam 10:5; *1 Chr* 19:5
David's anger was *g.* kindled.
    2 Sam 12:5
David said, I have sinned *g.* 24:10
    1 Chr 21:8
kingdom was established *g. 1 Ki* 2:12
Solomon's words, he rejoiced *g.* 5:7
now Obadiah feared the Lord *g.* 18:3
fathers increased *g. 1 Chr* 4:38
great is the Lord, *g.* to be. 16:25*
    Ps 48:1; 96:4; 145:3
their anger was *g. 2 Chr* 25:10
Manasseh humbled himself *g.* 33:12
latter end should *g. Job* 8:7
in thy salvation how *g. Ps* 21:1

greatness (continued)

my heart g. rejoiceth, I will. *Ps* 28:7
bowed down g. go mourning. 38:6
so shall the king g. desire. 45:11
earth belong to God, he is g. 47:9
my defence, I shall not be g. 62:2
thou g. enrichest it with river. 65:9
my lips shall g. rejoice when. 71:23
wroth, and g. abhorred. 78:59
his people g. 105:24; 107:38
I will g. praise the Lord. 109:30
blessed that delighteth g. in. 112:1
I was g. afflicted, I said in. 116:10
proud have had me g. in. 119:51
of righteous shall g. *Pr* 23:24
be g. ashamed that. *Isa* 42:17†
I will g. rejoice in the Lord. 61:10
shall not that land be g.? *Jer* 3:1
surely thou hast g. deceived. 4:10
we are g. confounded, have. 9:19
persecutors shall be g. 20:11†
my sabbaths they g. *Ezek* 20:13
because that Edom hath g. 25:12
was king Belshazzar g. *Dan* 5:9
thou art g. beloved. 9:23; 10:11, 19
made thee small, thou art g. *Ob* 2
day of Lord hasteth g. *Zeph* 1:14
g. O daughter of Zion. *Zech* 9:9
governor marvelled g. *Mat* 27:14
Jairus besought him g. *Mark* 5:23
them that wept and wailed g. 38
beheld, they were amazed g. 9:15
the living, ye therefore do g. 12:27
rejoiceth g. because of. *John* 3:29
people ran to porch, g. *Acts* 3:11
disciples multiplied in Jerusalem g.
6:7
I g. desired Apollos. *1 Cor* 16:12
how g. I long after you all. *Phil* 1:8
I rejoiced in the Lord g. that. 4:10
desiring g. to see us, as. *1 Thes* 3:6
g. desiring to see thee. *2 Tim* 1:4
for he hath g. withstood our. 4:15
ye g. rejoice though now. *1 Pet* 1:6
I rejoiced g. that I found. *2 John* 4
I rejoiced g. when the. *3 John* 3
see **feared**

greatness
in g. of thy excellency. *Ex.* 15:7
by g. of thine arm they shall be. 16
pardon according to g. *Num* 14:19
to shew thy servant thy g. *Deut* 3:24
shewed us his glory and g. 5:24
hast redeemed through thy g. 9:26
who have not seen his g. 11:2
ascribe ye g. unto our God. 32:3
hast done all this g. *1 Chr* 17:19
to make thee a name of g. and. 21
O Lord is the g., the power. 29:11
half of g. of thy wisdom. *2 Chr* 9:6
and the g. of the burdens. 24:27
spare me according to g. *Neh* 13:22
the declaration of the g. *Esth* 10:2
by g. of thy power. *Ps* 66:3
thou shalt increase my g. 71:21
according to the g. of thy. 79:11
his g. is unsearchable. 145:3
I declare thy. 6
according to his excellent g. 150:2
in the g. of his folly he. *Pr* 5:23
calleth by name, by g. *Isa* 40:26
thou art wearied in the g. 57:10*
travelling in the g. of his. 63:1
for g. of iniquity thy. *Jer* 13:22
art thou like in thy g.? *Ezek* 31:2
thus was he fair in his g. 7
thy g. is grown and. *Dan* 4:22
the g. of the kingdom shall. 7:27
what is exceeding g. of. *Eph* 1:19

greaves
Goliath had g. of brass. *1 Sam* 17:6

Grecia
rough goat is king of G. *Dan* 8:21
when I am gone, prince of G. 10:20
stir up all against realm of G. 11:2

Grecians
Judah sold to the G. *Joel* 3:6
a murmuring of the G. *Acts* 6:1
and disputed against the G. 9:29
spoke to the G. preaching. 11:20

Greece
against thy sons, O G. *Zech* 9:13
Paul came to G. and abode. *Acts* 20:2

greedily
he coveteth g. all day. *Pr* 21:26
hast g. gained of thy. *Ezek* 22:12
they ran g. after the error. *Jude* 11*

greediness
all uncleanness with g. *Eph* 4:19

greedy
as a lion that is g. of. *Ps* 17:12
every one that is g. of. *Pr* 1:19
he that is g. of gain troubleth. 15:27
they are g. dogs, can. *Isa* 56:11
not g. of filthy lucre. *1 Tim* 3:3, 8

Greek
superscription written in G.
Luke 23:38; *John* 19:20
canst thou speak G.? *Acts* 21:37
G. tongue hath his name. *Rev* 9:11

Greek
the woman was a G. *Mark* 7:26
Timotheus was a G. *Acts* 16:1, 3
Jew first, and also to G. *Rom* 1:16
no difference between Jew and G.
10:12; *Gal* 3:28; *Col* 3:11
was with me, being a G. *Gal* 2:3
see **appellatives**

Greeks
certain G. came to. *John* 12:20
a multitude of G. believed.
Acts 14:1; 17:4, 12
persuaded the Jews and the G. 18:4
then the G. took Sosthenes. 17
Jews and G. heard the word. 19:10
this was known to all the G. 20:21
testifying to Jews and G. 20:21
he brought the G. also into. 21:28
both to G. and Barbarians. *Rom* 1:14
G. seek after wisdom. *1 Cor* 1:22
preach Christ crucified, to the G. 23
unto called, Jews and G., Christ. 24

green
have given every g. herb. *Gen* 1:30
as the g. herb have I given you. 9:3
Jacob took rods of g. poplar. 30:37*
remained not any g. *Ex* 10:15
for thy firstfruits g. ears. *Lev* 2:14*
eat no g. ears, till ye have. 23:14*
bind me with seven g. *Judg* 16:7
brought to her seven g. withs. 8
inhabitants were as g. herbs.
2 Ki 19:26; *Isa* 37:27
where were white, g., blue. *Esth* 1:6
he is g. before the sun. *Job* 8:16
and his branch shall not be g. 15:32
searcheth after every g. thing. 39:8
maketh me lie down in g. *Ps* 23:2
they shall wither as the g. herb. 37:2
wicked spreading like a g. bay. 35
fair, also our bed is g. *S of S* 1:16
fig tree putteth forth her g. 2:13
grass faileth, there is no g. *Isa* 15:6
called thy name, a g. *Jer* 11:16
her roots, leaf shall be g. 17:8
I am like a g. fir tree. *Hos* 14:8
companies on g. grass. *Mark* 6:39
hail and fire, and all g. *Rev* 8:7
commanded not to hurt any g. 9:4

green *tree*
under every g. *tree.* *Deut* 12:2
images under every g. *tree.*
1 Ki 14:23; *2 Ki* 17:10
Ahaz sacrificed under every g. *tree.*
2 Ki 16:4; *2 Chr* 28:4
I am like a g. olive *tree.* *Ps* 52:8
under every g. *tree.* *Isa* 57:5
under every g. *tree* thou. *Jer* 2:20
under every g. *tree,* there played. 3:6
thy ways under every g. *tree.* 13
be under every g. *tree.* *Ezek* 6:13
I have dried up the g. *tree.* 17:24
it shall devour every g. *tree.* 20:47
things in a g. *tree.* *Luke* 23:31

green *trees*
groves by g. *trees.* *Jer* 17:2

greenish
if the plague be g. in. *Lev* 13:49
be with hollow strakes g. or. 14:37

greenness
it is yet in his g. and. *Job* 8:12

greet
(*The Revisions change this word
to salute when used in the New
Testament*)
go to Nabal and g. *1 Sam* 25:5
g. Priscilla and Aquila. *Rom* 16:3
g. church. 5
g. Mary who bestowed labour. 6
g. Amplias. 8
g. the household of Narcissus. 11
all the brethren g. you. *1 Cor* 16:20
Phil 4:21
g. ye one another. *1 Cor* 16:20
2 Cor 13:12; *1 Pet* 5:14
and Demas g. you. *Col* 4:14
g. the brethren with an. *1 Thes* 5:26
g. them that love us in. *Tit* 3:15
of thy elect sister g. thee. *2 John* 13
peace be to thee, g. the. *3 John* 14

greeteth
Eubulus g. thee. *2 Tim* 4:21*

greeting, -s
g. in markets. *Mat* 23:7*
Luke 11:43*; 20:46*
and brethren, send g. *Acts* 15:23
Lysias to Felix sendeth g. 23:26
tribes scattered abroad, g. *Jas* 1:1

grew
every herb before it g. *Gen* 2:5*
he overthrew that which g. 19:25
Isaac g. 21:8; 26:13
Ishmael g. and dwelt in. 21:20
the boys g. 25:27
Israel g. and multiplied. 47:27*
afflicted, more they g. *Ex* 1:12*
Moses g. 2:10
his wife's sons g. up. *Judg* 11:2
Samson g. and the Lord. 13:24
the child Samuel g. *1 Sam* 2:21, 26
David went on and g. *2 Sam* 5:10
lamb g. up together with him. 12:3
it g. and became a. *Ezek* 17:6
tree g. and was strong. *Dan* 4:11
and the thorns g. up. *Mark* 4:7
bettered, but rather g. worse. 5:26
child g. and waxed. *Luke* 1:80; 2:40
it g. and waxed a great tree. 13:19
people g. and multiplied. *Acts* 7:17
word of God g. and multiplied. 12:24
so mightily g. the word of. 19:20

greyhound
for comely in going, a g. *Pr* 30:31

grief, -s
a g. unto Isaac and. *Gen* 26:35
out of abundance of g. *1 Sam* 1:16*
be no g. to thee, or offence. 25:31
shall know his own g. *2 Chr* 6:29*
they saw that his g. was. *Job* 2:13
oh that my g. were throughly. 6:2*
lips should assuage your g. 16:5
speak, my g. is not assuaged. 6
my eye is consumed because of g.
Ps 6:7; 31:9
my life is spent with g. my. 31:10*
they talk to g. of those thou. 69:26*
a foolish son is a g. to. *Pr* 17:25
much wisdom is much g. *Eccl* 1:18
are sorrows, and his travail g. 2:23
be a heap in day of g. *Isa* 17:11
and acquainted with g. 53:3
he hath borne our g. and carried. 4
bruise him, he put him to g. 10
before me continually is g. *Jer* 6:7*
truly this is a g. and I must. 10:19
for the Lord hath added g. 45:3*
though he cause g. he will. *Lam* 3:32
a gourd, a shadow to deliver him
from g. *Jonah* 4:6*
if any caused g. he hath. *2 Cor* 2:5*
with joy and not with g. *Heb* 13:17
toward God endure g. *1 Pet* 2:19

grievance
cause me to behold g.? *Hab* 1:3*

grieve
man shall be to g. *1 Sam* 2:33
that it may not g. me. *1 Chr* 4:10*
how oft did they g.? *Ps* 78:40
doth not willingly g. *Lam* 3:33
g. not the Holy Spirit of. *Eph* 4:30

grieved

the earth, and it g. him. Gen 6:6
sons heard and were g. and. 34:7
now be not g. that ye sold me. 45:5
archers have sorely g. him. 49:23
and they were g. because. Ex 1:12
shall not be g. when. Deut 15:10
soul was g. for misery. Judg 10:16
why is thy heart g.? 1 Sam 1:8
it g. Samuel, and he cried. 15:11*
Jonathan knew this lest he be g. 20:3
arose, for he was g. for David. 34
soul of all the people was g. 30:6
heard how king was g. 2 Sam 19:2
it g. them exceedingly. Neh 2:10
it g. me sore, and I cast forth. 13:8
was queen exceedingly g. Esth 4:4
commune, wilt thou be g.? Job 4:2
was not my soul g. for the? 30:25
thus my heart was g., I. Ps 73:21
forty years was I g. with. 95:10
wicked shall see it, and be g. 112:10
transgressors and was g. 119:158
am not I g. with those that? 139:21
called thee as a woman g. Isa 54:6
therefore thou wast not g. 57:10*
them, they have not g. Jer 5:3
I Daniel was g. in spirit. Dan 7:15
therefore he shall be g. and. 11:30
not g. for the affliction. Amos 6:6
being g. for the hardness. Mark 3:5
he went away g. for he had. 10:22
Peter was g. because. John 21:17
being g. that they taught. Acts 4:2
Paul being g. said to spirit. 16:18*
if thy brother be g. Rom 14:15
that ye should be g. 2 Cor 2:4*
caused grief, he hath not g. me. 5
wherefore I was g. with. Heb 3:10*
but with whom was he g. forty? 17*

grieveth

for it g. me much for. Ruth 1:13
it g. him to bring it. Pr 26:15

grieving

shall be no more a g. Ezek 28:24

grievous

for the famine was g. Gen 12:10*
because their sin is very g. 18:20
the thing was very g. in. 21:11
God said, let it not be g. in thy. 12
famine shall be very g. 41:31
this is a g. mourning to the. 50:11
came a g. swarm of flies. Ex 8:24
a g. murrain. 9:3
to rain a very g. hail. 18, 24
locusts were very g. before. 10:14
Shimei cursed me with a g. 1 Ki 2:8
g. service lighter. 12:4; 2 Chr 10:4
his ways always g. Ps 10:5*
speak g. things against. 31:18*
but g. words stir up anger. Pr 15:1
correction is g. unto him that. 10
wrought under sun is g. Eccl 2:17
his life shall be g. unto. Isa 15:4*
g. vision is declared unto me. 21:2
they are all g. revolters. Jer 6:28
my hurt, my wound is g. 10:19
people broken with a g. blow. 14:17
they shall die of g. deaths. 16:4
a g. whirlwind shall fall on. 23:19*
thy wound is g. 30:12; Nah 3:19
bind heavy burdens and g.
Mat 23:4; Luke 11:46
shall g. wolves enter in. Acts 20:29
Jews laid many g. complaints. 25:7
to me indeed is not g. but. Phil 3:1*
seemeth joyous, but g. Heb 12:11
commandments are not g. 1 John 5:3
a g. sore on men that. Rev 16:2

grievously

afterward did more g. Isa 9:1*
it shall fall g. upon head. Jer 23:19*
Jerusalem hath g. sinned. Lam 1:8
turned, for I have g. rebelled. 20
land sinneth by trespassing g.
Ezek 14:13*
g. tormented. Mat 8:6
daughter g. vexed. 15:22

grievousness

that write g. which they. Isa 10:1*
they fled from the g. of war. 21:15

grind

Samson did g. in the. Judg 16:21
then let my wife g. unto. Job 31:10
what mean ye to g. the? Isa 3:15
take millstones and g. meal. 47:2
took the young men to g. Lam 5:13*
it will g. him to powder.
Mat 21:44*; Luke 20:18*

grinders

the g. cease, because. Eccl 12:3

grinding

when sound of the g. is. Eccl 12:4
two women g. at the mill.
Mat 24:41; Luke 17:35

grisled

were speckled and g. Gen 31:10, 12
in fourth chariot were g. Zech 6:3
the g. go forth toward the south. 6

groan

men g. from out of city. Job 24:12
her land wounded shall g. Jer 51:52
Pharaoh shall g. before. Ezek 30:24
how do the beasts g.! Joel 1:18
we ourselves g. within. Rom 8:23
in this we g. desiring to. 2 Cor 5:2
we in this tabernacle do g. being. 4

groaned

he g. in the spirit. John 11:33

groaneth

the whole creation g. Rom 8:22

groaning, -s

God heard their g. and. Ex 2:24
the g. of Israel. 6:5; Acts 7:34
Lord because of their g. Judg 2:18
is heavier than my g. Job 23:2
I am weary with my g. all. Ps 6:6
my g. is not hid from thee. 38:9
by reason of my g. my bones. 102:5
to hear the g. of the prisoner. to. 20
with the g. of a deadly. Ezek 30:24
Jesus g. in himself. John 11:38
for us with g. that. Rom 8:26

grope, -eth

shalt g. at noonday as the blind g.
Deut 28:29
they g. in noonday as. Job 5:14
they g. in the dark without. 12:25
g. for the wall like the blind, we g.
Isa 59:10

gross

g. darkness shall cover. Isa 60:2
for light, make it g. Jer 13:16
people's heart is waxed g.
Mat 13:15; Acts 28:27

ground

he g. the calf to powder. Ex 32:20
Deut 9:21
the people g. the manna. Num 11:8

ground corn

spread g. corn on the. 2 Sam 17:19*

ground

not a man to till the g. Gen 2:5
formed man of the dust of the g. 7
out of the g. the Lord formed. 19
he said, cursed is the g. for. 3:17
but Cain a tiller of g. 4:2
blood crieth to me from the g. 10
because of the g. the Lord. 5:29
I will not again curse the g. 8:21
bowed himself toward the g. 18:2*
with his face toward g. 19:1*
where thou standest is holy g.
Ex 3:5; Acts 7:33
g. whereon they are shall. Ex 8:21
the g. clave asunder. Num 16:31
be the fruit of thy g. Deut 28:4, 11
fastened the nail into g. Judg 4:21
set them to ear his g. 1 Sam 8:12
his spear stuck in the g. at. 26:7
was a piece of g. full. 2 Sam 23:11
he stood in midst of the g. and. 12*
water is naught, and g. 2 Ki 2:19*
cast him into the plat of g. 9:26
where was a parcel of g. 1 Chr 11:13
did cast them in clay g. 2 Chr 4:17
the firstfruits of our g. Neh 10:35
bring the tithes of our g. to. 37
trouble spring out of the g. Job 5:6
the stock thereof die in the g. 14:8
snare is laid for him in the g. 18:10
the desolate and waste g. 38:27

he swallows the g. with. Job 39:24
devoured fruit of their g. Ps 105:35
watersprings into dry g. 107:33
he turneth dry g. into water. 35*
break clods of his g.? Isa 28:24
shalt speak out of the g. 29:4
seed that thou shalt sow the g. 30:23
oxen and young asses that ear g. 24
and the parched g. shall. 35:7*
laid thy body as the g. 51:23
break up your fallow g. Jer 4:3
Hos 10:12
poured on fruit of the g. Jer 7:20
because the g. is chapt, there. 14:4
gates are sunk into the g. Lam 2:2
face, thou see not g. Ezek 12:6, 12
cieled from the g. up to the. 41:16
and touched not the g. Dan 8:5
face was towards g. 18; 10:9, 15
with them for things of g. Hos 2:18
and the g. shall give her. Zech 8:12
not destroy fruits of your g. Mal 3:11
but other fell into good g. Mat 13:8
Luke 8:8
he that received seed into good g.
Mat 13:23; Luke 8:15
cast seed into the g. Mark 4:26*
the g. of a certain rich. Luke 12:16
why cumbereth it the g.? 13:7
I have bought a piece of g. 14:18*
lay these even with the g. 19:44
near the parcel of g. John 4:5
corn of wheat fall into g. 12:24*

see dry, face

on or upon the ground

he spilled it on the g. Gen 38:9
fell before him on the g. 44:14
cast the rod on the g. he cast it on
the g. Ex 4:3
and fire ran along upon the g. 9:23*
on dry g. through the sea. 14:16, 22
as the hoar frost on the g. 16:14
pour blood upon the g. Deut 15:23
nest chance to be on the g. 22:6
would not set her foot upon g. 28:56
upon all the g. let there. Judg 6:39
there was dew upon all the g. 40
was honey upon the g. 1 Sam 14:25
slew oxen and calves on the g. 32
son of Jesse liveth on the g. 20:31
water spilt on the g. 2 Sam 14:14
him as dew falleth on the g. 17:12
said, Smite upon the g. 2 Ki 13:18
Job fell upon the g. and. Job 1:20
down with him upon the g. 2:13
out my gall upon the g. 16:13
shall sit on the g. Isa 3:26
of Babylon, sit on the g. 47:1
be dung upon the g. Jer 25:33
man and beast upon the g. 27:5*
of Zion sit on the g. Lam 2:10
young and old lie on the g. in. 21
poured it not upon the g. Ezek 24:7
princes shall sit upon the g. 26:16
the multitude to sit on the g.
Mat 15:35; Mark 8:6
some fell on stony g. Mark 4:5. 16*
fell on good g. 8, 20; Luke 8:8, 15
and he fell on the g. Mark 9:20
forward, and fell on g. and. 14:35
he wrote on the g. John 8:6, 8
he spat on the g. 9:6

to or unto the ground

till thou return unto the g. Gen 3:19
Jacob bowed himself to the g. 33:3
his wife fell to the g. Judg 13:20
Benjamin destroyed to the g. 20:21
and destroyed to the g. of Israel. 35
bowed and fell to the g. Ruth 2:10
his words fall to the g. 1 Sam 3:19
fallen on his face to the g. 5:4
not one hair fall to the g. 14:45
and fell on his face to the g. 20:41
Abigail bowed to the g. before. 25:23
with his face to the g. 28:14
I smite thee to the g.? 2 Sam 2:22
casting him down to the g. 8:2
fell on her face to the g. 14:4
Joab fell to the g. 22
Absalom bowed to the g. 33
not thou smite him to the g. 18:11
out Amasa's bowels to the g. 20:10
Nathan bowed to the g. 1 Ki 1:23

ground (continued)

prophets bowed *to the g.* 2 Ki 2:15
she bowed herself *to the g.* 4:37
Ornan bowed *to the g.* 1 Chr 21:21
Israel bowed with their faces *to g.*
2 Chr 7:3
bowed with his face *to the g.* 20:18
with their faces *to the g.* Neh 8:6
casting down the dwelling place of
thy name *to the g.* Ps 74:7
crown, by casting it *to the g.* 89:39
cast his throne down *to the g.* 44
smitten my life down *to the g.* 143:3
the wicked down *to the g.* 4:37
thou cut down *to the g.*! Isa 14:12
images he hath broken *to the g.* 21:9
bring *to the g.* even to dust. 25:12
city he layeth even *to the g.* 26:5
languish, are black *to the g.* Jer 14:2
strong holds of Judah *to g.* Lam 2:2
hang their heads *to the g.* 10
down the wall *to the g.* Ezek 13:14
mother was cast down *to the g.* 19:12
garrison shall go down *to g.* 26:11
I will cast thee *to the g.* 28:17
cast the ram down *to the g.* Dan 8:7
some of hosts and stars *to the g.* 10
and cast down the truth *to the g.* 12
altar shall fall *to the g.* Amos 3:14
bring me down *to the g.?* Ob 3
shall not fall *to the g.* Mat 10:29
blood falling *to the g.* Luke 22:44
went backward, and fell *to the g.*
John 18:6
I fell *to the g.* and heard. Acts 22:7

ground

is the pillar and *g.* of. 1 Tim 3:15

grounded

in every place where *g.* Isa 30:32*
ye being rooted and *g.* Eph 3:17
continue in the faith, *g.* Col 1:23

grove

[1] *A tamarisk tree*, Gen 21:33
(R.V.). [2] *The Asherah* (R.V.) *is
in all other places, for singular,*
Asherim, *for plural.*
Abraham planted a *g.* Gen 21:33
shalt not plant a *g.* Deut 16:21
and cut down the *g.* Judg 6:25
g. was cut down that was by. 28
she had made an idol in a *g.*
1 Ki 15:13; 2 Chr 15:16
Ahab made a *g.* and. 1 Ki 16:33
there remained the *g.* 2 Ki 13:6
Israel made a *g.* and served. 17:16
up altars, and made a *g.* 21:3
the vessels made for the *g.* 23:4
he brought out the *g.* from house. 6
burnt the high place and the *g.* 15

groves

ye shall cut down their *g.* Ex 34:13
Deut 7:5
ye shall burn their *g.* Deut 12:3
forgat Lord and served *g.*
Judg 3:7; 2 Chr 24:18
out of this good land, because they
have made their *g.* 1 Ki 14:15
built them *g.* on. 23; 2 Ki 17:10
the prophets of the *g.* 1 Ki 18:19
Hezekiah cut down *g.* 2 Ki 18:4
cut down the *g.* 23:14; 2 Chr 34:3, 4
and cut down the *g.* 2 Chr 14:3
Jehoshaphat took away the *g.* 17:6
thou hast taken away the *g.* 19:3
all Israel cut down the *g.* 31:1
Manasseh made *g.* 33:3
where he set up *g.* 19
to purge Judah from the *g.* 34:3
broken down the altars and *g.* 7
nor shall he respect the *g.* Isa 17:8
the *g.* and the images shall. 27:9
remember altars and *g.* Jer 17:2
I will pluck up thy *g.* Mi 5:14

grow

God made every tree to *g.* Gen 2:9
them *g.* into a multitude. 48:16
let locks of his hair *g.* Num 6:5
hair of head began to *g.* Judg 16:22
he make it not to *g.* 2 Sam 23:5
eat such things as *g.* 2 Ki 19:29
why should damage *g.?* Ezra 4:22
can the rush *g.* up? Job 8:11
out of the earth shall others *g.* 19*

---

washest away things that *g.*
Job 14:19*
thistles *g.* instead of wheat. 31:40
they *g.* up with corn, they go. 39:4
he shall *g.* like a cedar. Ps 92:12
causeth grass to *g.* 104:14; 147:8
nor how the bones *g.* in. Eccl 11:5
and a branch shall *g.* Isa 11:1*
shalt thou make thy plant *g.* 17:11*
he shall *g.* up before him. 53:2
they *g.* yea, they bring. Jer 12:2
Branch to *g.* up unto David. 33:15
suffer their locks to *g.* Ezek 44:20
by the river shall *g.* all trees. 47:12
shall *g.* as the lily, cast. Hos 14:5*
shall revive as the corn, and *g.* as. 7*
nor madest it *g.* which. Jonah 4:10
the Branch, he shall *g.* up. Zech 6:12
ye shall *g.* up as calves. Mal 4:2*
consider the lilies how they *g.*
Mat 6:28; Luke 12:27
let both *g.* together until. Mat 13:30
let no fruit *g.* on thee. 21:19
seed should *g.* up, he. Mark 4:27
whereunto this would *g.* Acts 5:24
may *g.* up into him in all. Eph 4:15
of word, that ye may *g.* 1 Pet 2:2
g. in grace and in. 2 Pet 3:18

groweth

shall eat every tree that *g.* Ex 10:15
freckled spot that *g.* in. Lev 13:39*
which *g.* of its own accord. 25:5, 11
nor any grass *g.* therein. Deut 29:23
behold, the day *g.* to. Judg 19:9
the dust *g.* into hardness. Job 38:38*
like grass which *g.* up. Ps 90:5, 6
which withereth afore it *g.* up. 129:6
eat this year such as *g.* Isa 37:30
when it is sown, it *g.* Mark 4:32
g. unto an holy temple. Eph 2:21
because your faith *g.* 2 Thes 1:3

grown

till Shelah be *g.* Gen 38:11
Shelah was *g.* 14
when Moses was *g.* he. Ex 2:11
for they were not *g.* up. 9:32
thou art *g.* thick. Deut 32:15
for them till they were *g.* Ruth 1:13
tarry until your beards be *g.*
2 Sam 10:5; 1 Chr 19:5
with young men *g.* 1 Ki 12:8, 10
when the child was *g.* up. 2 Ki 4:18
as corn blasted before it be *g.* 19:26
Isa 37:27
our trespass is *g.* up to. Ezra 9:6
sons may be as plants *g.* Ps 144:12
and lo, it was all *g.* over. Pr 24:31
because ye are *g.* fat as. Jer 50:11*
fashioned, thy hair is *g.* Ezek 16:7
art *g.* strong, thy greatness is *g.*
Dan 4:22
his hairs were *g.* like eagles'. 33
when *g.* it is the greatest. Mat 13:32

growth

g. lo, it was latter *g.* Amos 7:1

grudge

nor bear any *g.* against. Lev 19:18
let them *g.* if they be. Ps 59:15*
g. not one against. Jas 5:9*

grudging

to another without *g.* 1 Pet 4:9*

grudgingly

let him give, not *g.* or. 2 Cor 9:7

guard

a captain of the *g.* Gen 37:36; 39:1
servant to a captain of the *g.* 41:12
David set him over his *g.*
2 Sam 23:23; 1 Chr 11:25
shields to captain of *g.* 1 Ki 14:27
2 Chr 12:10
g. bare them and brought them.
1 Ki 14:28; 2 Chr 12:11
part at gate behind *g.* 2 Ki 11:6
captain of *g.* came to Jerusalem.
25:8; Jer 52:12
captain of *g.* brake down walls.
2 Ki 25:10; Jer 52:14
rest of people captain of *g.* 2 Ki 25:11
the captain of the *g.* left of poor. 12
in that they may be a *g.* Neh 4:22
nor I nor men of the *g.* put off. 23
captain of *g.* concerning. Jer 39:11

---

when the captain of *g.* had. Jer 40:1
captain of the *g.* gave him. &
the captain of the *g.* took. 52:30
and be a *g.* to them. Ezek 38:7
answered captain of *g.* Dan 2:14
prisoners to captain of *g.* Acts 28:16

guard chamber

guard bare them to *g. chamber.*
1 Ki 14:28; 2 Chr 12:11

guest

he was gone to be *g.* Luke 19:7*

guestchamber

where is the *g.?* Mark 14:14
Luke 22:11

guests

Adonijah and all the *g.* 1 Ki 1:41
all *g.* with Adonijah were afraid. 49
her *g.* are in the depths. Pr 9:18
hath prepared and bid *g.* Zeph 1:7
was furnished with *g.* Mat 22:10
the king came in to see the *g.* 11

guide, -s

he will be our *g.* even. Ps 48:14
it was thou, a man, my *g.* 55:13
who forsaketh the *g.* of. Pr 2:17
which having no *g.*, overseer. 6:7
my father, thou art the *g.* Jer 3:4
put ye not confidence in *g.* Mi 7:5
to you, ye blind *g.* Mat 23:16, 24
who was *g.* to them. Acts 1:16
confident thou art a *g.* of. Rom 2:19

guide, verb

canst thou *g.* Arcturus? Job 38:32
the meek will he *g.* in. Ps 25:9
lead me and *g.* me. 31:3
I will teach and *g.* thee with. 32:8*
thou shalt *g.* me with thy. 73:24
he will *g.* his affairs with. 112:5*
of the upright shall *g.* Pr 11:3
be wise, and *g.* thine heart in. 23:19
of water shall he *g.* them. Isa 49:10
is none to *g.* her among. 51:18
the Lord shall *g.* thee. 58:11
to *g.* our feet into the way. Luke 1:79
he will *g.* you into all. John 16:13
except some man *g.* me? Acts 8:31
bear children, *g.* house. 1 Tim 5:14*

guided, -ing

Israel *g.* his hands. Gen 48:14
thou hast *g.* them in thy. Ex 15:13
the Lord *g.* them on. 2 Chr 32:22
I have *g.* her from my. Job 31:18
g. them in the wilderness. Ps 78:52
nast *g.* them by the skilfulness. 72

guile

if a man slay with *g.* Ex 21:14
in whose spirit there is no *g.* Ps 32:2
keep lips from speaking *g.* 34:13
1 Pet 3:10
deceit and *g.* depart not. Ps 55:11
indeed, in whom is no *g.* John 1:47
I caught you with *g.* 2 Cor 12:16
exhortation was not of *g.* 1 Thes 2:3
aside all malice and *g.* 1 Pet 2:1
who did no sin, neither was *g.* 22
mouth was found no *g.* Rev 14:5*

guilt

g. of innocent. Deut 19:13; 21:9

guiltiness

have brought *g.* on us. Gen 26:10
me from blood-*g.* O God. Ps 51:14

guiltless

Lord will not hold him *g.* Ex 20:7
Deut 5:11
then shall the man be *g.* Num 5:31
shall return and be *g.* 32:22
on him, and he will be *g.* Josh 2:19
anointed and be *g.* 1 Sam 26:9
my kingdom are *g.* 2 Sam 3:28
king and his throne be *g.* 14:9
hold him not *g.* for thou. 1 Ki 2:9
not have condemned the *g.* Mat 12:7

guilty

verily *g.* concerning. Gen 42:21
will by no means clear *g.* Ex 34:7
Num 14:18
not be done are *g.* Lev 4:13; 22:27
he shall be unclean and *g.* 5:2
knoweth of it, he shall be *g.* 3, 4
he shall be *g.*, he shall confess. 5

gulf

he wist it not, yet is he *g*. *Lev* 5:17
because he sinned and is *g*. he. 6:4
the slayer shall not be *g*. *Num* 35:27
no satisfaction for a murderer *g*. 31
that you should be *g*. *Judg* 21:22
being *g*. offered a ram. *Ezra* 10:19
and thou be found *g*. *Pr* 30:10
become *g*. in blood. *Ezek* 22:4
hold themselves not *g*. *Zech* 11:5
by the gift on it, he is *g*. *Mat* 23:18*
they said, he is *g*. of death. 26:66*
Mark 14:64*
world may become *g*. *Rom* 3:19*
shall be *g*. of the body. *1 Cor* 11:27
in one point, he is *g*. *Jas* 2:10

gulf
us and you is a great *g*. *Luke* 16:26

Gur
smote Ahaziah at the going up to G.
2 Ki 9:27

gush, -ed
till the blood *g*. out. *1 Ki* 18:28
rock, the waters *g*. out. *Ps* 78:20
opened rock, waters *g*. out. 105:41
clave the rock, and the waters *g*. out.
Isa 48:21
and our eyelids *g*. out. *Jer* 9:18
and his bowels *g*. out. *Acts* 1:18

gutter, -s
Jacob set rods in the *g*. *Gen* 30:38
before the eyes of the cattle in *g*. 41
who getteth up to the *g*. *2 Sam* 5:8*

H

ha
the trumpets, ha, ha. *Job* 39:25

habergeon
hole of an *h*. *Ex* 28:32*; 39:23*
spear, the dart, the *h*. *Job* 41:26*

habergeons
h. and bows (Uzziah). *2 Chr* 26:14*
servants held bows and *h*. *Neh* 4:16*

habitable
rejoicing in the *h*. part. *Pr* 8:31

habitation
I will prepare him an *h*. *Ex* 15:2*
camp shall his *h*. be. *Lev* 13:46
even to his *h*. shall ye. *Deut* 12:5
why kick at offering, commanded in
my *h*.? *1 Sam* 2:29
thou shalt see an enemy in my *h*. 32
me both it, and his *h*. *2 Sam* 15:25
built an house of *h*. for. *2 Chr* 6:2
and have turned from the *h*. 29:6
God of Israel whose *h*. is. *Ezra* 7:15
but suddenly I cursed *h*. *Job* 5:3
thou shalt visit thy *h*. and shalt. 24
make *h*. of thy righteousness. 8:6
be scattered upon his *h*. 18:15
I have loved the *h*. of thy. *Ps* 26:8
from the place of his *h*. he. 33:14
let their *h*. be desolate. 69:25
thou my strong *h*. whereunto. 71:3
and judgement the *h*. 89:14; 97:2
made the most High thy *h*. 91:9
fowls of heaven have their *h*. 104:12
might go to a city of *h*. 107:7, 36
find an *h*. for the mighty God. 132:5
for Lord hath desired it for his *h*. 13
but he blesseth the *h*. of. *Pr* 3:33
and that graveth an *h*. *Isa* 22:16
and the *h*. shall be forsaken. 27:10
shall dwell in a peaceable *h*. 32:18
see Jerusalem a quiet *h*. 33:20
it shall be an *h*. of dragons. 34:13
in the *h*. of dragons shall be. 35:7
and behold from the *h*. of. 63:15
thine *h*. is in midst of. *Jer* 9:6
have made his *h*. desolate. 10:25
mightily roar upon his *h*. 25:30
thee, O *h*. of justice. 31:23; 50:7
cities thereof be an *h*. of. 33:12
they dwelt in the *h*. of. 41:17
against *h*. of strong. 49:19; 50:44
Israel again to his *h*. 50:19
surely he shall make their *h*. 45
Egypt to return to their *h*. *Ezek* 29:14
whose *h*. is high, that saith. *Ob* 3
moon stood still in their *h*. *Hab* 3:11

18

---

it is written, let his *h*. be. *Acts* 1:20
the bounds of their *h*. 17:26
for an *h*. of God through. *Eph* 2:22
which left their own *h*. *Jude* 6
Babylon is become the *h*. *Rev* 18:2

holy habitation
guided them to thy *holy h*. *Ex* 15:13
down from thy *holy h*. *Deut* 26:15
is God in his *holy h*. *Ps* 68:5
his voice from *holy h*. *Jer* 25:30
up out of his *holy h*. *Zech* 2:13

habitations
cruelty are in their *h*. *Gen* 49:5*
in all your *h*. eat unleaven. *Ex* 12:20
kindle no fire through your *h*. 35:3
ye be come into the *h*. *Num* 15:2
places of earth full of *h*. *Ps* 74:20
fall round about their *h*. 78:28
forth curtains of thy *h*. *Isa* 54:2
for *h*. of the wilderness. *Jer* 9:10
who shall enter into our *h*.? 21:13
and the peaceable *h*. are cut. 25:37
surely he shall make their *h*. 49:20
swallowed up the *h*. of. *Lam* 2:2
in all their *h*. make land. *Ezek* 6:14
the *h*. of the shepherds. *Amos* 1:2
you into everlasting. *Luke* 16:9*

Hachilah
hid in hill of *H*. *1 Sam* 23:19; 26:1
Saul pitched in the hill of *H*. 26:3

had
ruled over all that he *h*. *Gen* 24:2
he knew not aught he *h*. save. 39:6
he that gathered much *h*. *Ex* 16:18
the Lord *h*. a delight in. *Deut* 10:15
Rahab and all that she *h*. *Josh* 6:25
Achan and all that he *h*. 7:24
of them shall I be *h*. in. *2 Sam* 6:22
did this thing, and *h*. no pity. 12:6
mighty men whom David *h*. 23:8
she said, *h*. Zimri peace. *2 Ki* 9:31
house and all he *h*. *1 Chr* 13:14
as for me, I *h*. in my heart to. 28:2
and pattern of all that he *h*. by. 12
in safety, neither *h*. I rest. *Job* 3:26
if men said not, oh that we *h*. 31:31
him twice as much as he *h*. 42:10
I said, O that I *h*. wings. *Ps* 55:6
I *h*. rather be a doorkeeper. 84:10
to be *h*. in reverence of all. 89:7
proud have *h*. me greatly. 119:51
as were oppressed, they *h*. *Eccl* 4:1
behold, for peace I *h*. *Isa* 38:17
in my favour have I *h*. mercy. 60:10
and they *h*. no light. *Jer* 4:23
then *h*. we plenty of victuals. 44:17
pleasant things she *h*. in. *Lam* 1:7
she came down wonderfully: *h*. no. 9
yet *h*. he no wages for. *Ezek* 29:18
but I *h*. pity for mine holy. 36:21
by his strength Jacob *h*. *Hos* 12:3
yea he *h*. power over the angel. 4
against which thou hast *h*. *Zech* 1:12
yet *h*. he the residue of. *Mal* 2:15
he sold all that he *h*. *Mat* 13:46
seven, for they all *h*. her? 22:28
did cast in all she *h*. *Mark* 12:44
thou hast *h*. five husbands. *John* 4:18
of whatsoever disease he *h*. 5:4
Judas *h*. the bag, and bare. 12:6
if I *h*. not come, they *h*. not *h*. 15:22
the glory I *h*. with thee before. 17:5
all that believed he. all. *Acts* 2:44
shorn his head, for he *h*. 18:18
that after examination *h*., I. 25:26
faith he *h*. yet being. *Rom* 4:11, 12
what fruit *h*. ye in those things? 6:21
wives be as though they *h*. none.
1 Cor 7:29
but we *h*. the sentence of. *2 Cor* 1:9
of entering in we *h*. *1 Thes* 1:9
and blessed him that *h*. *Heb* 7:6
old commandment which ye *h*. from.
1 John 2:7
that which we *h*. from. *2 John* 5

Hadadezer, Hadarezer
David smote *H*. *2 Sam* 8:3; 9:10
1 Chr 18:3
came to succour *H*. *2 Sam* 8:5
shields of gold on servants of *H*. 7
cities of *H*. 8

H. had wars with Toi. *2 Sam* 8:10
the spoil of *H*. 12
H. sent and brought out the. 10:16
Rezon fled from *H*. *1 Ki* 11:23

Hadadrimmon
the mourning of *H*. in. *Zech* 12:11

Hadassah
H. his uncle's daughter. *Esth* 2:7

Hadoram
begat *H*. *Gen* 10:27; *1 Chr* 1:21
Tou sent *H*. his son. *1 Chr* 18:10
Rehoboam sent *H*. *2 Chr* 10:18

Hadrach
word of Lord in land of *H*. *Zech* 9:1

hadst
for it was little thou *h*. *Gen* 30:30
because thou *h*. a favour. *Ps* 44:3
thou *h*. a whore's forehead. *Jer* 3:3
neither *h*. pleasure therein. *Heb* 10:8

haft
and the *h*. also went in. *Judg* 3:22

Hagar
H. an Egyptian. *Gen* 16:1, 3, 8
H. bare Abram a son. 15, 16; 25:12
Sarah saw son of *H*. the. 21:9
Abraham gave *H*. bread. 14
called to *H*., What aileth thee, *H*.? 17
see Agar

Hagarenes
the *H*. are confederate. *Ps* 83:6

Hagarites
made war with *H*. *1 Chr* 5:10, 19
H. were delivered into their. 20

Haggai
son of Gad, *H*. Shuni. *Gen* 46:16
H. prophesied to the Jews. *Ezra* 5:1
prophesying of *H*. the prophet. 6:14
word of the Lord by *H*. *Hag* 1:1, 3
2:1, 10, 20

Haggith
Adonijah the son of *H*. *2 Sam* 3:4
1 Ki 1:5, 11; 2:13; *1 Chr* 3:2

hail
rain a very grievous *h*. *Ex* 9:18
Lord sent thunder and *h*., fire. 23
of Israel were, was there no *h*. 26
nor shall there be any more *h*. 29
h. ceased. 33
remaineth from the *h*. 10:5, 12, 15
the treasures of the *h*.? *Job* 38:22
their vines with *h*. *Ps* 78:47
gave up their cattle also to the *h*. 48
he gave them *h*. for rain. 105:32
fire, *h*. snow and vapour. 148:8
which as a tempest of *h*. *Isa* 28:2
the *h*. shall sweep away the. 17
I smote you with *h*. in all. *Hag* 2:17
there followed *h*. and fire. *Rev* 8:7
and there was great *h*. 11:19
fell on men a great *h*. out of. 16:21

hail, verb
dwell when it shall *h*. *Isa* 32:19

hail
Judas said, *H*. master. *Mat* 26:49
H. King of the Jews. 27:29
Mark 15:18; *John* 19:3
to Mary, and said, *H*. *Luke* 1:28

hailstones
which died with *h*. *Josh* 10:11
clouds passed, *h*. and. *Ps* 18:12, 13
shew indignation with *h*. *Isa* 30:30
and ye, O great *h*. shall. *Ezek* 13:11
there shall be great *h*. in my. 13
I will rain great *h*. fire, and. 38:22

hair
when the *h*. in the plague. *Lev* 13:3
if in plague a yellow *h*. 30
no black *h*. in it. 37
there is black *h*. grown. 37
shave off *h*. 14:8, 9
the *h*. of his separation. *Num* 6:19*
sling stones *h*.'s breadth. *Judg* 20:16
not one *h*. of thy son. *2 Sam* 14:11
because the *h*. was heavy on. 26
there shall not an *h*. of. *1 Ki* 1:52
I plucked off their *h*. *Neh* 13:25
spirit passed, *h*. of my. *Job* 4:15
thy *h*. is as a flock. *S of S* 4:1; 6:5

and instead of well set *h*. *Isa 3:24*
shave the head and *h*. of feet. *7:20*
to them that plucked off *h*. *50:6*
cut off thy *h*. O. *Jer 7:29*
and divide the *h*. *Ezek 5:1*
thy *h*. is grown. *16:7*
John had raiment of camel's *h*.
Mat 3:4; Mark 1:6
canst not make one *h*. *Mat 5:36*
his feet with her *h*. *John 11:2; 12:3*
if a man have long *h*. *1 Cor 11:14*
a woman have long *h*. it is a. *15*
not with broidered *h*. or. *1 Tim 2:9*
not of plaiting the *h*. *1 Pet 3:3*
black as sackcloth of *h*. *Rev 6:12*
had *h*. as the *h*. of women. *9:8*
see goats, head

hairs
ye shall bring down my *h*.
Gen 42:38; 44:29, 31
if there be no white *h*. *Deut 32:25*
also with man of gray *h*. *Deut 32:25*
are more than the *h*. of my head.
Ps 40:12; 69:4
and even to hoar *h*. will. *Isa 46:4*
h. were grown like eagles'. *Dan 4:33*
gray *h*. are here and there. *Hos 7:9*
the very *h*. of your head are all
numbered. *Mat 10:30; Luke 12:7*
did wipe them with *h*. *Luke 7:38, 44*
head and *h*. were white. *Rev 1:14*

hairy
red, all over like an *h*. *Gen 25:25*
Esau is an *h*. man. *27:11*
his hands were *h*. *23*
Elijah was an *h*. man. *2 Ki 1:8*
the *h*. scalp of such an one. *Ps 68:21*

hale
lest adversary *h*. thee. *Luke 12:58†*

half
Moses took *h*. the blood, *h*. *Ex 24:6*
of sweet cinnamon *h*. so much. *30:23*
h. of it in morning, and *h*. *Lev 6:20*
of whom the flesh is *h*. *Num 12:12*
take it of their *h*. and give it. *31:29*
h. of them over against. *Josh 8:33*
within as it were an *h*. *1 Sam 14:14*
Hanun shaved off one *h*. *2 Sam 10:4*
nor if *h*. of us die, will they. *18:3*
h. the people of Israel. *19:40*
h. of the child to one, *h*. *1 Ki 3:25*
h. was not told. *10:7; 2 Chr 9:6*
give me *h*. thine house. *1 Ki 13:8*
h. of people followed Tibni, *h*. *16:21*
the ruler of the *h*. part. *Neh 3:9, 12*
h. part of Bethzur. *16*
h. of Keilah. *17, 18*
children spake *h*. in speech. *13:24*
to the *h*. of the kingdom. *Esth 5:3*
7:2; Mark 6:23
bloody men shall not live *h*. *Ps 55:23*
Samaria committed *h*. *Ezek 16:51*
be for time, times, and an *h*.
Dan 12:7; Rev 12:14
I bought her for an *h*. *Hos 3:2*
h. of the city shall go. *Zech 14:2*
h. of mount toward the south. *4*
h. toward the sea. *8*
leaving him *h*. dead. *Luke 10:30*
behold, the *h*. of my goods. *19:8*
silence about space of *h*. *Rev 8:1*
bodies three days and an *h*. *11:9, 11*
see shekel, tribe

haling
Saul *h*. men and women. *Acts 8:3†*

hall
Jesus into common *h*. *Mat 27:27**
led him away to the *h*. *Mark 15:16**
fire in midst of the *h*. *Luke 22:55**
see judgement

hallow
children of Israel shall *h*. *Ex 28:38*
h. them to minister to me in. *29:1*
things which they *h*. to. *Lev 22:2, 3*
hallowed. I am the Lord which *h*. *32*
h. the fiftieth year, proclaim. *25:10*
and he shall *h*. his head. *Num 6:11*
same day did king *h*. court.
1 Ki 8:64; 2 Chr 7:7
h. ye sabbath. *Jer 17:22, 24, 27*
and *h*. my sabbaths. *Ezek 20:20*
keep laws and *h*. my sabbaths. *44:24*

hallowed
the sabbath day and *h*. it. *Ex 20:11*
Aaron shall be *h*. and his. *29:21*
she shall touch no *h*. *Lev 12:4*
he hath profaned the *h*. *19:8**
I will be *h*. among children. *22:32*
h. me all the firstborn. *Num 3:13*
and every man's *h*. things. *5:10*
censers, for they are *h*. *16:37*, 38**
of all the *h*. things I have. *18:8*
the *h*. part thereof out of it. *29*
have brought away *h*. *Deut 26:13*
common, but there is *h*. *1 Sam 21:4**
the priest gave him *h*. bread. *6**
I have *h*. this house. *1 Ki 9:3, 7*
Jehoash took all the *h*. *2 Ki 12:18*
polluted the house of Lord which he
had *h*. *2 Chr 36:14*
h. be thy name. *Mat 6:9; Luke 11:2*

halt
(*Lame, limping*)
is better to enter into life *h*.
Mat 18:8*; Mark 9:45
bring in hither the *h*. *Luke 14:21**
of *h*. waiting for moving. *John 5:3*

halt
how long *h*. ye between? *1 Ki 18:21†*
ready to *h*., my sorrow is. *Ps 38:17†*

halted
Jacob passed, he *h*. *Gen 32:31*
I will make her that *h*. *Mi 4:7*

halteth
will assemble her that *h*. *Mi 4:6†*
I will save her that *h*. *Zeph 3:19†*

halting
familiars watched for my *h*.
Jer 20:10†

Ham
Noah begat Shem, *H*. *Gen 5:32*
6:10; 9:18; 10:1; 1 Chr 1:4
selfsame day *H*. *Gen 7:13*
H. is the father of Canaan. *9:18*
sons of *H*. *10:6; 20; 1 Chr 1:8*
smote the Zuzims in *H*. *Gen 14:5*
they of *H*. had dwelt. *1 Chr 4:40*
in the tabernacles of *H*. *Ps 78:51*
sojourned in the land of *H*. *105:23*
wonders in land of *H*. *27; 106:22*

Haman
king promoted *H*. *Esth 3:1*
king's servants reverenced *H*. *2*
H. full of wrath. *5*
wherefore *H*. sought to destroy. *6*
cast the lot before *H*. *7*
and the king and *H*. sat down. *15*
H. promised to pay. *4:7*
H. came to banquet. *5:4, 5, 8; 7:1*
went *H*. forth that day joyful. *5:9*
H. told them of the glory of his. *11*
the thing pleased *H*. *14*
H. standeth in the court. *6:5*
H. thought in his heart. *6*
then *H*. took the apparel. *11*
H. hasted to his house mourning. *12*
H. told Zeresh his wife. *13*
this wicked *H*. *7:6*
H. made request. *7*
H. was fallen on the bed. *8*
so they hanged *H*. *10*
gave Esther the house of *H*. *8:1*
slew the sons of *H*. *9:10*
they hanged *H*.'s ten sons. *14*

Hamath
as men come to *H*. *Num 13:21*
Hor to the entrance of *H*. *34:8*
Josh 13:5; Judg 3:3; 1 Ki 8:65
2 Ki 14:25; 2 Chr 7:8
king of *H*. *2 Sam 8:9; 1 Chr 18:9*
Jeroboam recovered *H*. *2 Ki 14:28*
Assyria brought men from *H*. *17:24*
the men of *H*. made Ashima. *30*
the gods of *H*.? *18:34; Isa 36:19*
where is the king of *H*.? *2 Ki 19:13*
Isa 37:13
put in bands in the land of *H*.
2 Ki 23:33; 25:21
smote Hadarezer to *H*. *1 Chr 18:3*
built store cities in *H*. *2 Chr 8:4*
is not *H*. as Arpad? *Isa 10:9*
recover his people from *H*. *11:11*
to *H*. where he gave. *Jer 39:5; 52:9*
Damascus, *H*. is confounded. *49:23*

on the north, *H*. *Ezek 47:16, 17*
till a man come over against *H*. *20*
H. also shall border. *Zech 9:2*

Hammedatha
the son of *H*. *Esth 8:5; 9:10, 24*

hammer
then Jael took an *h*. in. *Judg 4:21*
with *h*. she smote Sisera. *5:26*
neither *h*. nor axe heard. *1 Ki 6:7*
smootheth with the *h*. *Isa 41:7*
like a *h*. that breaketh. *Jer 23:29*
how is the *h*. of whole earth. *50:23*

hammers
the carved work with *h*. *Ps 74:6*
fashioneth it with *h*. *Isa 44:12*
fasten it with nails and *h*. *Jer 10:4*

Hamon-Gog
call it the valley of *H*. *Ezek 39:11*
have buried it in the valley of *H*. *15*

Hamor
field of the children of *H*. Shechem's
father. *Gen 33:19; Josh 24:32*
H. went out to commune.
Gen 34:6, 8
to *H*. and Shechem hearkened all. *24*
they slew *H*. and Shechem. *26*
serve the men of *H*. *Judg 9:28*

Hanameel
H. thine uncle's son. *Jer 32:7, 8*
bought the field of *H*. my uncle's. *9*
evidence to Baruch in sight of *H*. *12*

Hananeel
tower of *H*. *Neh 3:1; 12:39*
Jer 31:38; Zech 14:10

Hanani
to Jehu son of *H*. the. *1 Ki 16:1*
H. son of Heman. *1 Chr 25:4*
18th lot to *H*. *25*
at that time *H*. the seer. *2 Chr 16:7*
Jehu son of *H*. went to meet. *19:2*
in book of Jehu son of *H*. *20:34*
of the sons of Imman, *H*. *Ezra 10:20*
H. one of my brethren. *Neh 1:2*
I gave my brother *H*. charge. *7:2*
H. with the musical. *12:36*

Hananiah
Meshullam and *H*. and. *1 Chr 3:19*
the sons of *H*. *21*
H. Benjamite. *8:24*
H. son of Heman. *25:4*
sixteenth lot to *H*. *23*
Uzziah had an host under *H*.
2 Chr 26:11
sons of Bebai; *H*. Zabbai. *Ezra 10:28*
H. the son of an. *Neh 3:8*
I gave *H*. ruler of palace. *7:2*
H. sealed. *10:23*
chief fathers: *H*. *12:12, 41*
H. son of Azur the prophet. *Jer 28:1*
H. spake in the presence of all. *11*
after that *H*. had broken. *12*
H. died that year in the seventh. *17*
Zedekiah son of *H*. sat in. *36:12*
Irijah the son of *H*. took. *37:13*
of Judah, Daniel, *H*. *Dan 1:6*
he gave to *H*. the name of. *7*
Melzar was set over Daniel, *H*. *11*
was found none like Daniel, *H*. *19*
made the thing known to *H*. *2:17*

hand
The word hand is sometimes used
for power, as in 1 Sam 5:6, 7.
This is especially the case where
the expression right hand is used.
To pour water on any one's hands,
meant to serve him, 2 Ki 3:11.
To wash one's hands, denoted that
the person was innocent of crime,
Deut 21:6, 7; Mat 27:24.
To kiss one's hand, is an act of
adoration, Job 31:27.
To lift up one's hand, is a way of
taking an oath, in use with all
nations, Gen 14:22. It was likewise a posture used in praying for
a blessing, Lev 9:22. To lift up
the hand against one, is to rebel
against him, 2 Sam 20:21.
To give one's hand, means to
swear friendship, to promise security, to make alliance, 2 Ki 10:15.

The right hand *denotes power-strength. The scripture generally imputes to God's right hand all the effects of his omnipotence,* Ex 15:6; Ps 17:7; 20:6; 44:3.

Often, to' *be at one's right hand signifies to defend, to protect, to support,* Ps 16:8; 109:31.

Laying on of hands is understood in different ways both in the Old and New Testaments. [1] *It is often taken for ordination and consecration of priests and ministers, as well among the Jews as the Christians,* Num 8:10; Acts 6:6; 13:3; 1 Tim 4:14. [2] *It is sometimes also made use of to signify the establishment of judges and magistrates,* Gen 48:14; Num 27:18.

into your *h.* are they.	*Gen* 9:2
all that he had in Joseph's *h.*	39:6
man in whose *h.* the cup.	44:17
with a strong *h.* shall he.	*Ex* 6:1
by strength of *h.* Lord brought.	13:3
Israel went out with an high *h.*	14:8
	Num 33:3
stretch out thine *h.* over.	*Ex* 14:16
there shall not a *h.* touch it.	19:13
h. for *h.,* foot for. 21:24; *Deut* 19:21	
testimony in Moses' *h.*	*Ex* 34:29
on this *h.* and that *h.*	38:15
remain in the *h.* of him.	*Lev* 25:28
afterwards the *h.* of all.	*Deut* 13:9
thou shalt cut off her *h.*	25:12
on our head if any *h.*	*Josh* 2:19
h. of the house of Joseph. *Judg* 1:35	
Lord shall sell Sisera into *h.*	4:9
now fall into the *h.* of the.	15:18
smote all that came to *h.* of. 20:48*	
of whose *h.* have I?	*1 Sam* 12:3
nor spear found in the *h.* of.	13:22
was no sword in the *h.* of.	17:50
when the business was in *h.*	20:19
their *h.* also is with David.	22:17
and eat it at her *h.*	*2 Sam* 13:5, 6
is not the *h.* of Joab with?	14:19
h. six fingers. 21:20; *1 Chr* 20:6	
let me not fall into *h.* of men.	
2 Sam 24:14; *1 Chr* 21:13	
kingdom established in *h.* *1 Ki* 2:46	
and the king's *h.* was restored.	13:6
a cloud like a man's *h.*	18:44
Lord shall deliver it into the king's *h.*	
22:6, 12, 15; *2 Chr* 28:5	
lord on whose *h.* the.	*2 Ki* 7:2, 17
went out from under the *h.*	13:5
hath Lord left you in *h.*	*2 Chr* 12:5
according to good *h.* of his. *Ezra* 7:9	
the *h.* of princes hath been.	9:2
earth is given into *h.* of.	*Job* 9:24
into whose *h.* God bringeth.	12:6
in whose *h.* is the soul of every.	10
every *h.* of the wicked shall.	20:22
their good is not in their *h.*	21:16
mighty taken away without *h.*	34:20
he sealeth up the *h.* of every.	37:7
hast not shut me into *h.*	*Ps* 31:8
let not the *h.* of the wicked.	36:11
deliver me out of *h.* of wicked.	
71:4; 82:4; 97:10	
servants look to the *h.*	123:2
as arrows are in the *h.* of.	127:4
two-edged sword be in their *h.* 149:6	
thou art come into *h.*	*Pr* 6:3
with a slack *h.* but the *h.* of. *Pr* 10:4	
though *h.* join in *h.,* the wicked shall	
not be unpunished.	11:21; 16:5
the *h.* of the diligent shall.	12:24
why a price in *h.* of a fool?	17:16
as a thorn goeth up into the *h.* 26:9	
the staff in their *h.* is.	*Isa* 10:5
shake the *h.* that they may go. 13:2	
this is the *h.* that is stretched. 14:26	
I will give over into the *h.*	19:4
down to the earth with the *h.*	28:2
dearly beloved into *h.* of.	*Jer* 12:7
vessel was marred in the *h.*	18:4
as clay in the potter's *h.* so are.	6
with an outstretched *h.* I will.	21:5
h. of Ahikam was with Jeremiah, not	
to give him into *h.* of people. 26:24	
she hath given her *h.*	50:15*

we have given the *h.* to.	*Lam* 5:6
princes are hanged up by their *h.* 12	
an *h.* was sent me, and lo. *Ezek* 2:9	
forth the form of an *h.*	8:3; 10:8
nor did she strengthen *h.* of.	16:49
shall be taken with the *h.*	21:24
no god in the *h.* of him that.	28:9
require my flock at their *h.*	34:10
stick which is in the *h.* of.	37:19
in man's *h.* a measuring reed.	40:5
forth fingers of a man's *h.*	*Dan* 5:5
God in whose *h.* thy breath is.	23
he shall be broken without *h.*	8:25
behold, an *h.* touched me.	10:10
and daughters into *h.*	*Joel* 3:8
in the power of their *h.*	*Mi* 2:1
shall see plummet in *h.*	*Zech* 4:10
he touched her *h.*	*Mat* 8:15
bind him *h.* and foot.	22:13
a man who had a withered *h.*	
Mark 3:1, 3; *Luke* 6:8	
is betrayed into *h.*	*Mark* 14:41
as many have taken in *h.*	*Luke* 1:1
being delivered out of the *h.*	74
the *h.* of him that betrayeth.	22:21
escaped out of their *h.*	*John* 10:39
dead came forth, bound *h.*	11:44
beckoning to them with *h.* *Acts* 12:17	
because I am not the *h.* *1 Cor* 12:15	
eye cannot say to the *h.* I have.	21
ordained by angels in the *h.* *Gal* 3:19	
take little book open in *h.*	*Rev* 10:8
having a golden cup in her *h.*	17:4
blood of his servants at her *h.*	19:2

at hand, or at the hand
at the *h.* of every beast, *at the h.* of	
man, *at the h.* of man's.	*Gen* 9:5
days of mourning for my father are	
at *h.*	27:41
field Jacob bought *at h.* of.	33:19
year of release is *at h.*	*Deut* 15:9
day of their calamity is *at h.*	32:35
I have here *at h.* fourth. *1 Sam* 9:8	
Lord require it *at h.* of.	20:16
avenge blood *at h.* the. of.	*2 Ki* 9:7
was *at the* king's *h.* in.	*Neh* 11:24
day of Lord is *at h.*	*Isa* 13:6
Joel 1:15; *Zeph* 1:7	
am I a God *at h.* and?	*Jer* 23:23
the days are *at h.* and.	*Ezek* 12:23
I require at watchman's *h.*	33:6
fruit, for they are *at h.* to.	36:8
cometh, it is nigh *at h.*	*Joel* 2:1
kingdom of heaven is *at h.*	
Mat 3:2; 4:17; 10:7	
my time is *at h.*	26:18
the hour is *at h.*	45
he is *at h.* that doth. 46; *Mark* 14:42	
kingdom of God is *at h.* *Mark* 1:15	
Luke 21:31	
summer is now nigh *at h.* *Luke* 21:30	
and the Jews' passover was *at h.*	
John 2:13; 11:55	
feast of tabernacles was *at h.*	7:2
sepulchre was nigh *at h.*	19:42
spent, the day is *at h.*	*Rom* 13:12
be known, Lord is *at h.*	*Phil* 4:5
the day of Christ is *at h.* *2 Thes* 2:2*	
my departure is *at h.*	*2 Tim* 4:6*
end of all things is *at h.*	*1 Pet* 4:7
for time is *at h.*	*Rev* 1:3; 22:10

by the hand
send *by h.* of him whom.	*Ex* 4:13
of tabernacle counted *by h.*	38:21
Lord commanded *by h.*	*Lev* 8:36
10:11; 26:46; *Num* 4:37, 45, 49	
9:23; 10:13; 15:23; 16:40; 27:23	
36:13; *Josh* 14:2; 20:2; 21:2, 8	
22:9; *Judg* 3:4; *1 Ki* 8:53, 56	
2 Chr 33:8; 35:6; *Neh* 9:14	
send him away *by the h.* *Lev* 16:21	
by the h. of avenger of. *Josh* 20:9	
lad that held *by the h.* *Judg* 16:26	
David fall *by the h. of. 1 Sam* 18:25	
one day perish *by the h.* of.	27:1
by the h. of my servant. *2 Sam* 3:18	
comfort him *by h.* of servants. 10:2	
letter, sent it *by h.* of Uriah.	11:14
sent *by the h.* of Nathan the.	12:25
these fell *by the h.* of David.	21:22
1 Chr 20:8	
Solomon sent *by the h.*	*1 Ki* 2:25

by the h. of his servant.	*1 Ki* 14:18
by the h. of Jehu came.	16:7
spake *by the h.* of Jonah. *2 Ki* 14:25	
by the h. of Jeroboam.	27
spake *by h.* of Ahijah. *2 Chr* 10:15	
not pour out wrath *by the h.*	12:7
out vessels *by the h.* of.	*Ezra* 1:8
weighed *by the h.* of.	8:33
sendeth a message *by h.*	*Pr* 26:6
taketh her *by the h.*	*Isa* 51:18
send yokes *by the h.* of.	*Jer* 27:3
in the day I took them *by the h.* 31:32	
Heb 8:9	
on Edom *by h.* of Israel. *Ezek* 25:14	
lay the land waste *by h.* of.	30:12
took her *by the h.*	*Mat* 9:25
Mark 1:31; 5:41; *Luke* 8:54	
took the blind man *by h.* *Mark* 8:23	
that was possessed *by the h.*	9:27
to be a deliverer *by h.*	*Acts* 7:35
they led him *by the h.*	9:8
some to lead him *by the h.*	13:11
the salutation *by the h.*	*Col* 4:18

see Chaldeans, enemy

hand joined with **enemies.**	
may save us out of the *h.* of our *e.*	
1 Sam 4:3; 12:10; *2 Sam* 3:18	
deliver you out of *h.* of *e.*	
1 Sam 12:11; *2 Ki* 17:39	
saved us out of the *h.* of our *e.*	
2 Sam 19:9	
into the *h.* of their *e.*	*2 Ki* 21:14
2 Chr 25:20; *Neh* 9:27	
them in *h.* of their *e.*	*Neh* 9:28
me from *h.* of mine *e.*	*Ps* 31:15
this city into *h.* of their *e.*	20:5
21:7; 34:20, 21; *Ezek* 39:23	
give Pharaoh into *h.* of his *e.* 44:30	
thee from the *h.* of thy *e.*	*Mi* 4:10
out of the *h.* of our *e.*	*Luke* 1:74

from the hand
deliver me *from h.* of my. *Gen* 32:11	
redeemed you *from the h. Deut* 7:8	
delivered us *from h.* of. *Judg* 8:22	
my reproach *from h.* of. *1 Sam* 25:39	
saveth the poor *from the h.* *Job* 5:15	
redeem me *from the h.* of the. 6:23	
deliver his soul *from the h.* *Ps* 89:48	
from the h. of him that hated, and	
redeemed them *from h.*	106:10
me *from h.* of strange.	144:7, 11
thyself as a roe *from h.* of.	*Pr* 6:5
poor *from h.* of evil.	*Jer* 20:13
from h. of him that was.	31:11
be saved *from the h.*	*Luke* 1:71

hand of God
h. of God was heavy.	*1 Sam* 5:11
h. of God was to give. *2 Chr* 30:12	
according to the good *h.* of God.	
Ezra 7:9; *Neh* 2:8	
by good *h.* of God upon us.	8:18
h. of God is upon all them for.	22
the *h.* of God is upon us.	31
told them of *h.* of God.	*Neh* 2:18
good at the *h.* of God?	*Job* 2:10
pity on me, *h.* of God hath.	19:21
teach you by the *h.* of God.	27:11
it was from the *h.* of God. *Eccl* 2:24	
works are in the *h.* of God.	9:1
diadem in *h.* of thy God.	*Isa* 62:3
heaven, and sat on right *h.* of God.	
Mark 16:19; *Rom* 8:34; *Col* 3:1	
Heb 10:12; *1 Pet* 3:22	
by the right *h.* of.	*Acts* 2:33
standing on right *h.* of *G.* 7:55, 56	
under the *h.* of God.	*1 Pet* 5:6

his hand
lest he put forth *his h.*	*Gen* 3:22
his h. will be against every.	16:12
men laid hold on *his h.*	19:16
of his master were in *his h.*	24:10
that which came to *his h.*	32:13*
that he did prosper in *his h.*	39:3
Pharaoh took ring off *his h.*	41:42
his h., and caught it and it became	
a rod in *his h.*	*Ex* 4:4
when he took it out, *his h.* was.	6
took the rod of God in *his h.*	20
out *his h.* over the waters.	8:6, 17
Moses stretched forth *his h.*	10:22
held up *his h.* let down *his h.*	17:11
God delivered him into *his h.*	21:13

if found in *his h.*   *Ex* 21:16
he die under *his h.*   20
theft be certainly found in *his h.* 22:4
he hath put *his h.* to goods.   8, 11
on the nobles he laid not *his h.* 24:11
testimony were in *his h.* 32:15; 34:4
shall put *his h.* on head.   *Lev* 1:4
priest shall have in *his h. Num* 5:18
beside that that *his h.* shall.   6:21*
all his land out of *his h.*   21:26
his sword drawn in *his h.* 22:23, 31
       1 Chr 21:16
took a javelin in *his h. Num* 25:7
his h. fetcheth a stroke. *Deut* 19:5
man with his sword drawn in *his h.*
       Josh 5:13
Joshua drew not *his h.* back.   8:26
deliver the slayer up into *his h.* 20:5
end of the staff in *his h. Judg* 6:21
into *his h.* hath God delivered. 7:14
his h. is not removed.   *1 Sam* 6:3
it is not *his h.* that smote us.   9
no man put *his h.* to his.   14:26
Jonathan put *his h.* to his.   27
he shall play with *his h.*   16:16
harp and played with *his h.* 23; 18:10
staff and his sling in *his h.*   17:40
head of the Philistine in *his h.*   57
he put his life in *his h.* and.   19:5
strengthened *his h.* in God.   23:16
Uzzah put *his h.* to ark. *2 Sam* 6:6
       1 Chr 13:10
and hath with *his h.*   *1 Ki* 8:15
whole kingdom out of *his h.*   11:34
his h. which he put forth.   13:4
strike *his h.* over place. *2 Ki* 5:11
he gave *his h.* took him up.   10:15
every man with his weapons in *his h.*
   11:8, 11; *2 Chr* 23:7
was confirmed in *his h.*   *2 Ki* 14:5
his h. might be with him to.   15:19
man lean, it will go into *his h.* 18:21
save us out of *his h.*   19:19
understand by *his h.*   *1 Chr* 28:19
had a censer in *his h. 2 Chr* 26:19
he gave them all into *his h.*   36:17
with open letter in *his h. Neh* 6:5
he would let loose *his h.*   *Job* 6:9
darkness is ready at *his h.*   15:23
he stretcheth out *his h.* against. 25
his h. hath formed the.   26:13
would rain flee out of *his h.*   27:22
he putteth forth *his h.* upon.   28:9
upholdeth him with *his h. Ps* 37:24
will not leave him in *his h.*   33
they remembered not *his h.*   78:42
I will set *his h.* also in sea.   89:25
in *his h.* are the deep places. 95:4
sheep of *his h.* To-day, if ye will. 7
therefore he lifted up *his h.* 106:26
the mower filleth not *his h. Pr* 19:24
a slothful man hideth *his h.* 19:24
       26:15
and nothing is in his *h. Eccl* 5:14
he may carry away in *his h.*   5
beloved put in *his h. S of S* 5:4
his h. is stretched out still. *Isa* 5:25
   9:12, 17, 21; 10:4; 14:27
shall shake *his h.* against. *Isa* 10:32
Lord shall set *his h.* again.   11:11
shake *his h.* over the river.   15
thy government into *his h.*   22:21
while it is yet in *his h.* he.   28:4
Lord shall stretch out *his h.*   31:3
Lord, save us from *his h.*   37:20
waters in hollow of *his h.*   40:12
shall subscribe with *his h.* to. 44:5
in the shadow of *his h.* hath. 49:2
of Lord shall prosper in *his h.* 53:10
keepeth *his h.* from doing.   56:2
consumed them by *his h. Jer* 27:8
my transgression bound by *his h.*
       Lam 1:14
he hath not withdrawn *his h.*   2:8
he turneth *his h.* against me.   3:3
with his censer in *his h. Ezek* 8:11
his destroying weapon in *his h.* 9:1
lo, he had given *his h.*   17:18
the sword to fall out of *his h.* 30:22
I will put my sword in *his h.*   24
according as *his h.* shall.   46:7
none can stay *his h.* or. *Dan* 4:35
could deliver out of *his h.*   8:4, 7
cause craft to prosper in *his h.* 25

multitude be given into *his h.*
       Dan 11:11
but these shall escape out of *his h.* 41
he stretched out *his h.*   *Hos* 7:5
balances of deceit are in *his h.* 12:7
horns coming out of *his h. Hab* 3:4
hiss, and wag *his h.*   *Zeph* 2:15
man with staff in *his h.*   *Zech* 8:4
his h. rise up against hand.   14:13
whose fan is in *his h.*   *Mat* 3:12
*   *Luke* 3:17
he that dippeth *his h.*   *Mat* 26:23
and *his h.* was restored whole.
   Mark 3:5; *Luke* 6:10
beseech him to put *his h. Mark* 7:32
man having put *his h.* to. *Luke* 9:62
a ring on *his h.,* and shoes.   15:22
all things into *his h.*   *John* 3:35
him with the palm of *his h.*   18:22
how God by *his h.*   *Acts* 7:25
a viper fastened on *his h.*   28:3
bang on *his h.*   4
pair of balances in *his h.*   *Rev* 6:5
and he had in *his h.* a little.   10:2
in his forehead, or in *his h.*   14:9
crown, and in *his h.* sharp sickle. 14
with a great chain in *his h.*   20:1

hand of the Lord, or Lord's **hand**
the *h. of the Lord* is upon.   *Ex* 9:3
had died by *h. of the Lord.*   16:3
is Lord's *h.* waxed ?   *Num* 11:23
h. of the Lord was against them to
destroy.   *Deut* 2:15
know that *h. of Lord* is. *Josh* 4:24
Israel out of *h. of the Lord.*   22:31
the *h. of the Lord* was against them
for evil.   *Judg* 2:15
h. of the Lord is gone.   *Ruth* 1:13
h. of Lord was heavy.   *1 Sam* 5:6
h. of Lord was against the city.   9
the *h. of the Lord* was against the
Philistines.   7:13
then shall *h. of the Lord* be.   12:15
let us now fall into *h. of the Lord.*
   2 Sam 24:14; *1 Chr* 21:13
h. of the Lord was on.   *1 Ki* 18:46
h. of the Lord came upon. *2 Ki* 3:15
according to *h. of Lord.*   *Ezra* 7:6
h. of Lord hath wrought this.
   Job 12:9; *Isa* 40:20
in *h. of the Lord* there.   *Ps* 75:8
heart is in *h. of the Lord. Pr* 21:1
shaking of the *h. of Lord. Isa* 19:16
mountain shall *h. of the Lord.* 25:10
received of the *Lord's h.*   40:2
hast drunk at *h. of Lord* cup. 51:17
Lord's h. is not shortened.   59:1
a crown of glory in *h. of Lord.* 62:3
h. of Lord shall be known.   66:14
the cup at the *Lord's h. Jer* 25:17
been a golden cup in *Lord's h.* 51:7
h. of the Lord was there. *Ezek* 1:3
the *h. of the L.* was upon me. 3:14
   22; 8:1; 37:1
h. of the Lord was on me.   33:22
selfsame day the *h. of Lord.* 40:1
and the *h. of the Lord* was with him.
   Luke 1:66; *Acts* 11:21
behold, the *h. of the Lord* is.
       Acts 13:11

see lay, or laid

left **hand**
if thou wilt take *left h.* I. *Gen* 13:9
Hobah which is on *left h.* of.   14:15
to the right *h.* or to the *left.*   24:49
his right hand toward Israel's *left h.*
and Manasseh in his *left h.* 48:13
Israel laid his *left h.* upon.   14
wall on right *h.* and *left. Ex* 14:22
oil into his own *left h. Lev* 14:15, 27
we will not turn to the right *h.* nor to
the *left.*   *Num* 20:17; *Deut* 2:27
   5:32; 17:11, 20; 28:14
either to right *h.* or *left. Num* 22:26
from it to right *h.* or to *left. Josh* 1:7
   23:6; *1 Sam* 6:12; *Pr* 4:27
Ehud put forth *left h. Judg* 3:21
held lamps in their *left h.*   7:20
hold of other pillar with *left h.* 16:29
he turned not to *left h. 2 Sam* 2:19
none can turn to right *h.* or to *left.*
       14:19
were on right *h.* and *left.*   16:6

host of heaven on his *left h.*
   1 Ki 22:19; *2 Chr* 18:18
Josiah turned not to the right *h.* or
left.   *2 Ki* 22:2
which were on a man's *left h.*   23:8
Merari stood on *left h.*   *1 Chr* 6:44
use both right *h.* and *left* in.   12:2
name of that on *left h.*   *2 Chr* 3:17
and he put five on the *left h.*   4:6
on the right, five on the *left h.*   7
on pulpit, on his *left h.*   *Neh* 8:4
on *left h.* he doth work.   *Job* 23:9
and in her *left h.* riches.   *Pr* 3:16
fool's heart is at his *left h. Eccl* 10:2
his *left h.* is under my head.
   S of S 2:6; 8:3
he shall eat on *left h.* and. *Isa* 9:20
when ye turn to the *left h.*   30:21
forth on the right *h.* and *left.*   54:3
dwell at thy *left h.*   *Ezek* 16:46
on the right *h.* or on the *left.* 21:16
smite thy bow out of thy *left h.* 39:3
he held up his *left h.* to. *Dan* 12:7
between right *h.* and *left. Jonah* 4:11
all people on right *h.* and *left.*
       Zech 12:6
let not *left h.* know what. *Mat* 6:3
one on right *h.* other on *left.*   20:21
       Mark 10:37
to sit on right *h.* and *left* not mine.
   Mat 20:23; *Mark* 10:40
right *h.,* goats on *left.*   *Mat* 25:33
shall say to them on *left h.*   41
crucified on right *h.* other on *left.*
   27:38; *Mark* 15:27; *Luke* 23:33
Cyprus on the *left h.*   *Acts* 21:3
righteousness on right *h.* and *left.*
       2 Cor 6:7

see **lift** *hand* or *hands*

mighty **hand**
go, no not with *mighty h.*   *Ex* 3:19
forth with *mighty h.*   32:11
servant thy *mighty h. Deut* 3:24
him a nation by a *mighty h.*   4:34
God brought thee out of Egypt
through a *mighty h.*   5:15; 6:21
   7:8, 19; 9:26; 11:2
   26:8; 34:12
come for thy *mighty h.*   *2 Chr* 6:32
a *mighty h.* will I rule. *Ezek* 20:33
bring you out with a *mighty h.*   34
you out of Egypt with *mighty h.*
       Dan 9:15
under *mighty h.* of God. *1 Pet* 5:6

mine and *my* **hand**
I have lifted up *mine h. Gen* 14:22
lambs shalt thou take of *my h.* 21:30
it is in power of *my h.* to do.   31:29
I bear loss, of *my h.* didst thou.   39
receive my present at *my h.*   33:10
deliver him into *my h.* I will.   42:37
I will be surety, of *my h.* shalt. 43:9
with rod that is in *mine h. Ex* 7:17
my h. shall destroy them.   15:9
rod in *mine h.*   17:9
will cover thee with *mine h.*   33:22
I will take away *mine h.* and thou. 23
this people into *my h.*   *Num* 21:2
there were a sword in *mine h.* 22:29
might of *my h.* hath.   *Deut* 8:17
the two tables in *mine h.*   10:3
neither any that can deliver out of
my h.   32:39; *Isa* 43:13
I lift up *my h.* to heaven. *Deut* 32:40
and if *mine h.* take hold on.   41
save Israel by *my h. Judg* 6:36, 37
lest vaunt, saying, *mine own h.* 7:2
delivered Zeba into *mine h.*   8:7
this people were under *my h.* 9:29
Lord delivered them into *my h.* 12:3
silver unto Lord from *my h.* 17:3
not found aught in *my h. 1 Sam* 12:5
this day into *mine h.*   17:46
let not *mine h.* be upon him. 18:17
common bread under *mine h.* 21:4
delivered him into *mine h.*   23:7
stretch *mine h.* against Lord's. 24:6
see the skirt in *my h.,* no transgression in *mine h.*   11
mine h. shall not be upon.   12, 13
into *mine h.* to day.   24:10; 26:23
what evil is in *mine h.?*   26:18
I have put my life in *my h.*   28:21

my h. shall be with. 2 Sam 3:12
deliver Philistines into mine h.?
   5:19; 1 Chr 14:10
forth mine h. against Absalom.
   2 Sam 18:12
that my h. may be. 1 Ki 13:6
leaneth on my h. in. 2 Ki 5:18
Samaria out of my h.? 18:34
out of mine h., that Lord should deliver Jerusalem out of mine h.? 35
of land into my h. 1 Chr 22:18
you out of my h.? 2 Chr 32:15, 17
put my life into mine h.? Job 13:14
bow was renewed in my h. 29:20
rejoiced because mine h. had. 31:25
or my mouth hath kissed my h. 27
neither shall my h. be heavy. 33:7*
turned my h. against. Ps 81:14
with whom my h. shall be. 89:21
soul is continually in my h. 119:109
stretched out my h. Pr 1:24
I will turn my h. upon. Isa 1:25
as my h. hath found the. 10:10
by the strength of my h. I have. 13
my h. hath found a nest the. 14
Samaria out of my h.? 36:19
deliver Jerusalem out of my h. 20
mine h. also hath laid. 48:13
is my h. shortened at all? 50:2
this ye have of my h. 11
in the shadow of mine h. 51:16
mine h. made. 66:2; Acts 7:50
I will stretch out my h. Jer 6:12
   15:6; 51:25
cause them to know mine h. 16:21
so are ye in mine h. O house. 18:6
wine cup of this fury at my h. 25:15
will I stretch out my h. Ezek 6:14
digged through wall with my h. 12:7
mine h., shall be upon prophets. 13:9
mine h., saying I am the Lord. 20:5, 6
   23, 28, 42; 36:7; 44:12; 47:14
withdrew my h. and wrought. 20:22
I have smitten mine h. at thy. 22:13
they shall be one in mine h. 37:19
deliver her out of mine h. Hos 2:10
I will turn mine h. Amos 1:8
into hell, thence shall mine h. 9:2
I will shake mine h. Zech 2:9
I will turn mine h. upon the. 13:7
pluck them out of my h. John 10:28
pluck them out of my Father's h. 29
except I shall thrust my. 20:25
salutation of me Paul with mine own
   h. 1 Cor 16:21; 2 Thes 3:17
I have written with my h. Gal 6:11
   Philem 19

our hand
let not our h. be on him. Gen 37:27
have brought it again in our h. 43:21
say, Our h. is high. Deut 32:27
Samson into our h. Judg 16:23
Lord hath delivered them into our h.
   1 Sam 14:10; 30:23
thou die not by our h. Jer 11:21
made ready to our h. 2 Cor 10:16

out of hand, or out of the hand
I took out of the h. of. Gen 48:22
Egyptian delivered us out of h. of.
   Ex 2:19
out of h. of Egyptians. 3:8; 14:30
offering out of woman's h. Num 5:25
kill me, I pray thee, out of h. 11:15
deliver him out of h. of the. 35:25
out of the h. of Israel. Josh 9:26
judges which delivered them out of
   the h. Judg 2:16
delivered you out of the h. 6:9
out of the h. of the Philistines. 13:5
out of h. of these gods? 1 Sam 4:8
me out of h. of this Philistine. 17:37
I delivered thee out of h. of Saul.
   2 Sam 12:7; 22:1
spear out of the Egyptian's h. 23:21
kingdom out of h. of. 1 Ki 11:12, 31
we take it not out of h. of. 22:3
took again out of h. of. 2 Ki 13:25
out of h. of the king of Assyria. 20:6
   Isa 38:6
deliver me out of h. of. Ps 71:4
rid them out of the h. of. 82:14
he delivereth them out of h. 97:10
out of h. of the wicked. Jer 15:21

spoiled out of h. of. Jer 21:12; 22:3
not escape out of h. 32:4; 38:18, 23
deliver us out of their h. Lam 5:8
out of their h. I will not. Zech 11:6
escaped out of their h. John 10:39
out of the h. of Herod. Acts 12:11
ascended before God out of angel's
   h. Rev 8:4; 10:10

right hand
right h. on Ephraim's. Gen 48:14, 18
thy right h. O Lord, is. Ex 15:6
the thumb of their right h. 29:20
   Lev 8:23, 24; 14:14, 17, 25, 28
from his right h. went. Deut 33:2
right h. to workman's. Judg 5:26
Amasa with right h. 2 Sam 20:9
on Solomon's right h. 1 Ki 2:19
on right h. of mount. 2 Ki 23:13
himself on the right h. Job 23:9
upon my right h. rise the. 30:12
that thine own right h. can. 40:14
he is at my right h. I. Ps 16:8
at thy right h. are pleasures for. 11
savest by thy right h. them. 17:7
thy right h. hath holden me. 18:35
saving strength of his right h. 20:6
thy right h. shall find out. 21:8
their right h. is full of bribes. 26:10
but thy right h. and thy arm. 44:3
thy right h. shall teach thee. 45:4
on thy right h. did stand queen. 9
thy right h. is full of. 48:10
save with thy right h. and. 60:5
my soul followeth, thy right h. 63:8
holden me by my right h. 73:23
withdrawest thy right h.? 74:11
remember years of the right h. 77:10
mountain which his right h. 78:54
the vineyard which thy right h. 80:15
upon the man of thy right h. 17
thy hand, high is thy right h. 89:13
I will also set his right h. in the. 25
thou hast set up the right h. of his. 42
shall fall at thy right h. 91:7
his right h. hath gotten him. 98:1
save with thy right h. and. 108:6
let Satan stand at his right h. 109:6
he shall stand at the right h. of. 31
sit thou at my right h. until I. 110:1
   Luke 20:42; Acts 2:34; Heb 1:13
the Lord at thy right h. Ps 110:5
the right h. of the Lord. 118:15
right h. of the Lord is exalted. 16
thy shade upon thy right h. 121:5
I forget, let my right h. forget. 137:5
and thy right h. shall save. 138:7
even there thy right h. shall. 139:10
looked on my right h., no man. 142:4
right h. is a right h. of falsehood.
   144:8, 11
of days is in her right h. Pr 3:16
the ointment of his right h. 27:16
heart is at his right h. Eccl 10:2
and his right h. doth. S of S 2:6
his right h. should embrace me. 8:3
thee with right h. of. Isa 41:10
Lord thy God will hold thy right h. 13
is there not a lie in my right h.? 44:20
to Cyrus whose right h. I have. 45:1
my right h. hath spanned the. 48:13
hath sworn by his right h. 62:8
that led them by the right h. 63:12
the signet on my right h. Jer 22:24
drawn back his right h. Lam 2:3
he stood on his right h. as an. 4
at right h. divination. Ezek 21:22
cup of Lord's right h. Hab 2:16
standing at his right h. Zech 3:1
if thy right h. offend thee. Mat 5:30
not left know what thy right h. 6:3
Son of man sitting on the right h. of
   power. Mark 14:62; Luke 22:69
to heaven, sat on right h. of God.
   Mark 16:19; Heb 1:3; 8:1
   10:12; 12:2; 1 Pet 3:22
man whose right h. was. Luke 6:6
he is on my right h. I. Acts 2:25
right h. of God exalted. 33; 5:31
he took him by the right h. and. 3:7
standing on right h. of God. 7:55, 56
is even at the right h. Rom 8:34
right h. in heavenly. Eph 1:20
sitteth on the right h. of. Col 3:1

in his right h. seven stars. Rev 1:16
   20; 2:1
laid right h. upon me, saying. 1:17
I saw in his right h. a book. 5:1, 7
receive mark in their right h. 13:16
   see left hand
to stretch forth or out hand
Abraham stretched forth his h. to
   slay. Gen 22:10
I will stretch out my h. on Egypt.
   Ex 3:20; 7:5; 9:15
stretch out thy h. over the sea.
   14:16; 26:7, 19
Moses stretched out his h. 14:21, 27
who can stretch forth hand against
   the Lord's anointed? 1 Sam 26:9
not afraid to stretch forth thy h.
   2 Sam 1:14
stretch forth thy hand. Ps 138:7
she stretcheth out her h. Pr 31:20
I will stretch out my h. Ezek 14:9
will I stretch out mine h. upon. 13
I will stretch out mine h. upon. 25:7
I will also stretch out mine h. 13
I will stretch out mine h. on the. 16
I will stretch out mine h. against.
   35:3
shall stretch forth his h. Dan 11:42
stretch out mine h. upon Judah.
   Zeph 1:4
stretch out his h. against Assyria.
   2:13
   see strong

thine or thy hand
blood from thy h. Gen 4:11
thy maid is in thy h., do to. 16:6
he said, lay not thine h. upon. 22:12
thy h. under my thigh. 24:2; 47:29
thy h. shall be in the neck. 49:8
what is that in thine h.? Ex 4:2
this rod in thine h. 17; 7:15; 17:5
stretch forth thine h. over. 8:5; 9:22
   10:12, 21; Mat 12:13; Mark 3:5
it shall be for a sign on thine h.
   Ex 13:9, 16; Deut 6:8
put not thine h. with. Ex 23:1
delivered Og into thy h. Num 21:34
in works of thy h. Deut 2:7; 14:29
   15:10; 23:20; 28:8, 12, 20
I have given into thy h. 2:24
Og and his people into thy h. 3:2
thy h. shall be first on him. 13:9
nought of cursed thing to thine h. 17
bind up money in thine h. 14:25
nor shut thine h. from thy. 15:7
thou shalt open thine h. wide to. 8
pluck the ears with thine h. 23:25
be no might in thine h. 28:32
in every work of thine h. 30:9
all the saints are in thy h. 33:3
I have given into thine h. Josh 6:2
for I will give Ai into thine h. 8:18
behold, we are in thine h. to. 9:25
slack not thy h. from thy. 10:6
kings of Canaan into thy h. 8
Sisera into thine h. Judg 4:7
the Midianites into thine h. 7:7
and Zalmunna in thine h.? 8:15
hold thy peace, lay thine h. 18:19
Benjamin into thine h. 20:28
priest, withdraw thy h. 1 Sam 14:19
what is under thine h.? give. 21:3
deliver Philistines into thine h.
   23:4; 2 Sam 5:19
I may eat of thine h. 2 Sam 13:10
stay thine h. 24:16; 1 Chr 21:15
let thine h., I pray thee, be against
   2 Sam 24:17; 1 Chr 21:15
hast fulfilled it with thine h.
   1 Ki 8:24; 2 Chr 6:15
of bread in thine h. 2 Ki 17:11
Syrians into thine h. 20:13, 28
hast let go out of thy h. a man. 42
take my staff in thine h. 2 Ki 4:29
take a present in thine h. 8:8
take this box of oil in thine h. 9:1
give me thine h. and he gave. 10:15
he said, put thine h. upon. 13:16
in thine h. is power and might. 29:12
for house cometh of thine h. 16
in thine h. is there not? 2 Chr 20:6
law which is in thine h. Ezra 7:14

hand (continued)

wisdom that is in *thine h. Ezra* 7:25
but put forth *thine h.* and touch.

Job 1:11; 2:5
himself put not forth *thine h.*   1:12
behold, he is in *thine h.* but.   2:6
can deliver out of *thine h.*   10:7
if iniquity be in *thine h.* put.   11:14
withdraw *thine h.* far from.   13:21
what receiveth he of *thine h.*?   35:7
O God, lift up *thine h. Ps* 10:12
spite, to requite it with *thy h.*   14
from men which are *thy h.*   17:14
thine h. shall find out all.   21:8
into *thine h.* I commit my.   31:5
my times are in *thy h.*: deliver.   15
for day and night *thy h.* was.   32:4
thy h. presseth me.   38:2
by blow of *thine h.*   39:10
why withdrawest thou *thy h.*? 74:11
thy h. be upon the man of *thy* right h.
   80:17
they are cut off from *thy h.*   88:5
thou openest *thy h.* 104:28; 145:16
know that this is *thy h.*   109:27
let *thine h.* help me.   119:173
laid *thine h.* on me.   139:5
even there shall *thy h.* lead.   10
send *thine h.* from above.   144:7
is in power of *thine h. Pr* 3:27
if thou hast stricken *thy h.*   6:1
if thought evil, lay *thy h.* upon. 30:32
withdraw not *thine h. Eccl* 7:18
whatsoever *thy h.* findeth to do. 9:10
evening withhold not *thine h.*   11:6
ruin be under *thy h. Isa* 3:6
when *thy h.* is lifted up, they. 26:11
I the Lord will hold *thine h.*   42:6
my inheritance into *thine h.*   47:6
I have taken out of *thy h.* cup. 51:22
found the life of *thine h.*   57:10
we are the work of *thy h.*   64:8
thine h. as a grape.   *Jer* 6:9
I sat alone because of *thy h.*   15:17
to take the cup at *thine h.*   25:28
take in *thy h.* the roll.   36:14
chains which were upon *thine h.* 40:4
his blood will I require at *thine h.*
   Ezek 3:18, 20; 33:8
smite with *thine h.* and.   6:11
and fill *thine h.* with coals.   10:2
I will give her cup into *thine h.* 23:31
took hold of thee by *thy h.*   29:7
shall become one in *thine h.*   37:17
to turn *thine h.* upon the.   38:12
he given into *thine h. Dan* 2:38
deliver us out of *thine h.*   3:17
thine h. shall he lift up on.   *Mi* 5:9
cut off witchcrafts out of *thine h.* 12
if *thy h.* or foot offend thee.
   Mat 18:8; *Mark* 9:43
reach *thy h.* and thrust. *John* 20:27
thine h. and counsel.   *Acts* 4:28
stretching forth *thine h.* to heal.   30

your hand

your h. are they delivered. *Gen* 9:2
take double money in *your h.* 43:12
your feet, staff in *your h. Ex* 12:11
of the land into *your h.*   23:31
rejoice in all ye put *your h.* to.
   Deut 12:7
deliver it into *your h. Josh* 8:7, 20
delivered them into *your h.*   10:19
Amorites into *your h.*   24:8, 11
Moabites into *your h. Judg* 3:28
Midianites into *your h.*   7:15
his blood of *your h.*?   *2 Sam* 4:11
be delivered into *your h.* 2 Chr 18:14
hath delivered them into *your h.* 28:9
required this at *your h.? Isa* 1:12
I am in *your h.*: do with. *Jer* 26:14
said, behold, he is in *your h.*   38:5
and fulfilled with *your h.*   44:25
be no more in *your h. Ezek* 13:21
deliver my people out of *your h.* 23
an offering at *your h. Mal* 1:10
should I accept this of *your h.*?   13
it with good will at *your h.*   2:13

handbreadth

a border of an *h.* round about.
   Ex 25:25; 37:12
a molten sea *h.* thick.   *1 Ki* 7:26
   2 Chr 4:5
made my days as an *h. Ps* 39:5

six cubits long, and an *h. Ezek* 40:5
the cubit is a cubit and an *h.*   43:13

hand broad

hooks an *h.* broad.   *Ezek* 40:43

handful

take thereout an *h.* of flour. *Lev* 2:2
   5:12; 6:15; 9:17*; *Num* 5:26
an *h.* of meal in a barrel.   *1 Ki* 17:12
there shall be an *h.* of.   *Ps* 72:16*
better is *h.* with quietness. *Eccl* 4:6
and as the *h.* after the.   *Jer* 9:22

handfuls

earth brought forth by *h. Gen* 41:47
take to you *h.* of ashes of.   *Ex* 9:8
fall also some *h.* of.   *Ruth* 2:16*
if dust of Samaria shall suffice for *h.*
   1 Ki 20:10
ye pollute me for *h.* of ? *Ezek* 13:19

handkerchiefs

were brought unto sick *h. Acts* 19:12

handle

father of such as *h.* the.   *Gen* 4:21
they that *h.* the pen of.   *Judg* 5:14
men that could *h.* shield.   *1 Chr* 12:8
   2 Chr 25:5
hands, but they *h.* not.   *Ps* 115:7
they that *h.* the law knew.   *Jer* 2:8
Lybians that *h.* the shield.   46:9
all that *h.* the oar, and. *Ezek* 27:29
h. me and see.   *Luke* 24:39
taste not, *h.* not.   *Col* 2:21

handled

that it may be *h.*   *Ezek* 21:11
him away shamefully *h. Mark* 12:4
our hands have *h.* of the. *1 John* 1:1

handleth

he that *h.* matter wisely.   *Pr* 16:20
cut off him that *h.* sickle. *Jer* 50:16
shall he stand that *h.*   *Amos* 2:15

handling

all of them *h.* swords.   *Ezek* 38:4
not *h.* the word of God.   *2 Cor* 4:2

handmaid

Sarai had an *h.* whose.   *Gen* 16:1
Zilpah to Leah's *h.*   29:24; 35:26
to be Rachel's *h.* 29:29; 30:4; 35:25
that son of thy *h.* may.   *Ex* 23:12
wine for me and thy *h. Judg* 19:19
spoken friendly to thy *h. Ruth* 2:13
answered, I am Ruth thine *h.*   3:9
on affliction of thine *h.*   *1 Sam* 1:11
count not thine *h.* for a daughter. 16
Hannah said, let thy *h.* find.   18*
let thy *h.* speak.   25:24
remember thy *h.*   31
let thy *h.* be a servant to wash.   41
thy *h.* had two sons.   *2 Sam* 14:6
hear the words of thy *h.*   20:17
didst swear to thy *h.*?   *1 Ki* 1:13
the Lord thy God to thy *h.*   17
she took my son while thine *h.* 3:20
thy *h.* hath not any thing. *2 Ki* 4:2
man of God, do not lie to thine *h.* 16
save the son of thy *h.*   *Ps* 86:16
and the son of thy *h.*   116:16
and an *h.* that is heir to.   *Pr* 30:23
caused every man his *h. Jer* 34:16
behold the *h.* of the.   *Luke* 1:38

handmaiden

the low estate of his *h. Luke* 1:48

handmaids

children to the two *h. Gen* 33:1
he put the *h.* and their children.   2
not like to one of thy *h. Ruth* 2:13
himself in eyes of *h.*   *2 Sam* 6:20
the *h.* to return for *h. Jer* 34:11
on the *h.* will I pour my spirit.
   Joel 2:29; *Acts* 2:18

hands

thyself under her *h.*   *Gen* 16:9
the *h.* are the *h.* of Esau.   27:22
h. were made strong by *h.* of. 49:24
but Moses' *h.* were.   *Ex* 17:12
thou shalt put all in the *h.* of. 29:24
h. and on his son's *h. Lev* 8:27
of memorial in her *h.*   *Num* 5:18
and shall put them on the *h.*   6:19
the work of men's *h. Deut* 4:28
   27:15; 2 Ki 19:18; 2 Chr 32:19

of the covenant were in my two *h.*
   Deut 9:15
I cast them out of my two *h.*   17
the *h.* of the witnesses shall.   17:7
through the work of your *h.*   31:29
delivered them into *h.* of. *Judg* 2:14
into *h.* of Midianites.   6:13
are *h.* of Zeba and Zalmunna ? 8:6, 15
delivered them out of *h.* of enemies.
   34; *1 Sam* 14:48
into *h.* of Philistines.   *Judg* 10:7
given Laish into your *h.*   18:10
and her *h.* were upon the.   19:27
nor deliver me into *h. 1 Sam* 30:15
let your *h.* be strong.   *2 Sam* 2:7
   Zech 8:9, 13
then the *h.* of all with. *2 Sam* 16:21
delivered them into the *h.* of.   23:6
they cannot be taken with *h.*   23:6
into the *h.* of the guard.   *1 Ki* 14:27
   2 Chr 12:10
poured water on the *h.*   *2 Ki* 3:11
skull and the palms of her *h.*   9:35
whom I brought into your *h.*   10:24
Asaph under the *h.* of.   *1 Chr* 25:2
under the *h.* of Jeduthun.   3
h. of their father.   6
let not your *h.* be weak.   *2 Chr* 15:7
weakened the *h.* of people. *Ezra* 4:4
strengthened the weak *h.*   *Job* 4:3
God hath turned me into the *h.* 16:11
who is he that will strike *h.*?   17:3
that hath clean *h.* shall be.   9
he that hath clean *h.*   *Ps* 24:4
in whose *h.* is mischief.   26:10
clap your *h.*   47:1
ye weigh the violence of your *h.* 58:2
shall stretch out her *h.* unto. 68:31
idols, the work of men's *h.*   115:4
   135:15; *Isa* 37:19
h. but handle not, feet.   *Ps* 115:7
lift up your *h.* in sanctuary.   134:2
me, O Lord, from the *h.* of.   140:4
folding of the *h.* to sleep.   *Pr* 6:10
   24:33
h. that shed innocent blood.   6:17
the recompence of man's *h.*   12:14
plucketh it down with her *h.*   14:1
a man striketh *h.* and.   17:18
one of them that strike *h.*   22:26
spider taketh hold with her *h.* 30:28
worketh willingly with her *h.* 31:13
h. to the spindle, her *h.* hold.   19
yea, she reacheth forth her *h.* to. 20
give her the fruit of her *h.* and.   31
them both *h.* full with.   *Eccl* 4:6*
her *h.* are as bands.   7:26
the idleness of *h.*   10:18
the work of the *h.* of a.   *S of S* 7:1
forth your *h.* I will hide my eyes from
   you; your *h.* are full.   *Isa* 1:15
worship work of their own *h.*   2:8
therefore shall all *h.* be faint.   13:7
idols which your own *h.* have.   31:7
strengthen ye the weak *h.*   35:3
thy work say, he hath no *h.*   45:9
h. are defiled with blood.   59:3
that spreadeth her *h.*   *Jer* 4:31
a tree, the work of the *h.* of.   10:3
and of the *h.* of the founder, blue. 9
cause them to fall by *h.* that.   19:7
weapons that are in your *h.*   21:4
the *h.* of evildoers, that none return.
   23:14; *Ezek* 13:22
not with works of your *h. Jer* 25:6, 7
shall pass under *h.* of him.   33:13
weakeneth *h.* of men of war, *h.* 38:4
upon all the *h.* shall be.   48:37
Zion spreadeth her *h.*   *Lam* 1:17
how esteemed as work of *h.*   4:2
that was overthrown, and no *h.*   6
h. of pitiful women have sodden. 10
h. shall be feeble. *Ezek* 7:17; 21:7
was cut out without *h. Dan* 2:34, 45
may do evil with both *h.*   *Mi* 7:3
all shall clap the *h.* over. *Nah* 3:19
in all labour of your *h. Hag* 2:17
of Zerubbabel laid. *Zech* 4:9
to eat with unwashen *h. Mat* 15:20
   Mark 7:2, 5
betrayed into *h.* of men. *Mat* 17:22
   26:45; *Mark* 9:31; *Luke* 9:44
having two *h.* to be cast into fire.
   Mat 18:8; *Mark* 9:43

h., another without *h.*   *Mark* 14:58
ye stretched forth no *h.* *Luke* 22:53
must be delivered into the *h.*   24:7
wicked *h.* have crucified. *Acts* 2:23
by *h.* of the apostles were.   5:12
in temples made with *h.*   48; 17:24
laying on of the apostles' *h.*   8:18
elders by the *h.* of Barnabas.   11:30
is worshipped with men's *h.*   17:25
gods which are made with *h.*   19:26
these *h.* have ministered to.   20:34
shall deliver him into the *h.*   21:11
house not made with *h.*   *2 Cor* 5:1
in flesh made by *h.*   *Eph* 2:11
circumcision made without *h.*
           Col 2:11
work with your own *h.* *1 Thes* 4:11
pray, lifting up holy *h.*   *1 Tim* 2:8
of *h.* of presbytery.   4:14; *Heb* 6:2
tabernacle not with *h.*   *Heb* 9:11
into holy place made with *h.*   24
fearful to fall into the *h.* of.   10:31
wherefore lift up the *h.*   12:12
cleanse your *h.* ye sinners. *Jas* 4:8
       see clap

his hands

his h. were hairy.   *Gen* 27:23
guiding *his h.*   48:14
Hur stayed up *his h.*   *Ex* 17:12
cast the tables out of *his h.*   32:19
his own *h.* shall bring.   *Lev* 7:30
and hath not rinsed *his h.* in.   15:11
his h. full of sweet incense.   16:12
Aaron shall lay both *his h.* on.   21
Balak smote *his h.*   *Num* 24:10
let *his h.* be sufficient.   *Deut* 33:7
and accept the work of *his h.*   11
for Moses had laid *his h.*   34:9
the deserving of *his h.*   *Judg* 9:16
both the palms of *his h.*   *1 Sam* 5:4
climbed up on *his h.* and his.   14:13
went and strengthened *his h.*   23:16
heard, *his h.* were feeble. *2 Sam* 4:1
spread *his h.* toward heaven.
  1 Ki 8:22; 38:54; *2 Chr* 6:12, 13, 29
with the work of *his h.*   *1 Ki* 16:7
put *his h.* upon his.   *2 Ki* 4:34
in not receiving at *his h.*   5:20
Elisha put *his h.* upon the.   13:16
who hath with *his h.*   *2 Chr* 6:4
with one of *his h.*   *Neh* 4:17
blessed the work of *his h. Job* 1:10
he woundeth, and *his h.* make.   5:18
and *his h.* shall restore their.   20:10
all are the works of *his h.*   34:19
for he clappeth *his h.* amongst.   37
snared in work of *his h.*   *Ps* 9:16
not the operation of *his h.*   28:5
by the skilfulness of *his h.*   78:72
his h. were delivered from.   81:6
the sea is his, and *his h.*   95:5
the works of *his h.* are verity. 111:7
his h. refuse to labour.   *Pr* 21:25
foldeth *his h.* together.   *Eccl* 4:5
his h. are as gold rings. *S of S* 5:14
the reward of *his h.* shall.   *Isa* 3:11
consider the operation of *his h.* 5:12
to altars, the work of *his h.*   17:8
his h. in midst of them. as he that
     swimmeth spreadeth *his h.*   25:11
that shaketh *his h.* from.   33:15
every man with *his h.* on? *Jer* 30:6
king heard the report, *his h.*   50:43
the deep lifted up *his h.*   *Hab* 3:10
his h. shall also finish.   *Zech* 4:9
he should put *his h.* on them.
     Mat 19:13; *Mark* 10:16
washed *his h.* before the. *Mat* 27:24
are wrought by *his h.*   *Mark* 6:2
put *his h.* on his eyes.   8:23, 25
shewed them *his h.* and feet.
     Luke 24:40; *John* 20:20
and he lifted up *his h.* *Luke* 24:50
given all things into *his h. John* 13:3
except I see in *his h.* the.   20:25
putting *his h.* on him.   *Acts* 9:17
Herod stretched forth *his h.*   12:1
and his chains fell off from *his h.* 7
wall, and escaped *his h. 2 Cor* 11:33
working with *his h.*   *Eph* 4:28
       see lay, laid

mine hands, my hands

in innocency of *my h.*   *Gen* 20:5

seen the labour of *my h. Gen* 31:42
I will spread abroad *my h.*
     Ex 9:29; *Ezra* 9:5
I put my life in *my h.*   *Judg* 12:3
according to cleanness of *my h.*
     2 Sam 22:21; *Ps* 18:20, 24
he teacheth *my h.* to war.
     2 Sam 22:35; *Ps* 18:34; 144:1
is no wrong in *mine h. 1 Chr* 12:17
O God, strengthen *my h.*   *Neh* 6:9
and if I make *my h.*   *Job* 9:30
any injustice in *mine h.*   16:17
blot hath cleaved to *mine h.*   31:7
there be iniquity in *my h.*   *Ps* 7:3
they pierced *my h.* and my.   22:16
I will wash *mine h.* in.   26:6
when I lift up *my h.* toward.   28:2
I will lift up *my h.* in thy name. 63:4
in vain, I have washed *my h.*   73:13
I have stretched out *my h.*   88:9
my h. will I lift to thy.   119:48
lifting up of *my h.* as the.   141:2
I stretch forth *my h.* to thee.   143:6
the works that *my h.*   *Eccl* 2:11
I rose, and *my h.*   *S of S* 5:5
Assyria the work of *my h. Isa* 19:25
he seeth the work of *mine h.*   29:23
concerning the work of *my h.*   45:11
even *my h.* have stretched out.   12
graven thee on palms of *my h.* 49:16
people also the work of *my h.*   60:21
I have spread out *my h.* all.   65:2
I will also smite *mine h. Ezek* 21:17
you out of *my h.*?   *Dan* 3:15
set me on the palms of *my h.* 10:10
behold *my h.* and my feet.
     Luke 24:39; *John* 20:27
but also *my h.* and head. *John* 13:9
stretched forth *my h.*   *Rom* 10:21
by putting on of *my h.*   *2 Tim* 1:6

our hands

concerning toil of *our h.*   *Gen* 5:29
have we brought in *our h.*   43:22
into *our h.* Og king of.   *Deut* 3:3
shall say, *our h.* have not shed. 21:7
delivered into *our h.* all. *Josh* 2:24
meat offering at *our h. Judg* 13:23
into *our h.* our enemy.   16:24
will give you into *our h. 1 Sam* 17:47
stretched out *our h.* to a. *Ps* 44:20
thou the work of *our h.* upon. 90:17
fame, *our h.* wax feeble.   *Jer* 6:24
heart with *our h.* to God. *Lam* 3:41
say to work of *our h.*   *Hos* 14:3
him away out of *our h.*   *Acts* 24:7
working with our own *h. 1 Cor* 4:12
our h. have handled.   *1 John* 1:1

right hands

they gave to me and Barnabas the
     right h. of fellowship.   *Gal* 2:9

their hands

him out of *their h.*   *Gen* 37:21, 22
shall put *their h.* on head. *Ex* 29:10
shall put *their h.* on the.   15, 19
shalt receive them of *their h.*   25
           Lev 8:28
Israel shall put *their h.*   *Num* 8:10
the Levites shall lay *their h.*   12
fruit of land in *their h.*   *Deut* 1:25
the elders shall wash *their h.*   21:6
Midianites into *their h.*   *Judg* 7:2
me not out of *their h.*   12:2
they cut off *their h.*   *2 Sam* 4:12
they clapped *their h.*   *2 Ki* 11:12
me to anger with all the works of
     their h.   22:17; *2 Chr* 34:25
their h. with vessels of.   *Ezra* 1:6
on and prospereth in *their h.*   5:8
their h. in the work of the.   6:22
they gave *their h.* that they. 10:19
strengthened *their h.* for. *Neh* 2:18
their h. shall be weakened.   6:9
gavest them into *their h.*   9:24
their h. cannot perform.   *Job* 5:12
strength of *their h.* profit me. 30:2
after work of *their h.*   *Ps* 28:4
have not found *their h.*   76:5
bear thee up in *their h.*   91:12
forth *their h.* to iniquity.   125:3
the spoils of *their h.*   *Isa* 25:11
act of violence is in *their h.*   59:6
shall enjoy work of *their h.*   65:22
works of *their* own *h.*   *Jer* 1:16

the works of *their h.*   *Jer* 25:14
           Lam 3:64
with works of *their h.*   *Jer* 32:30
delivered me into *their h. Lam* 1:14
their h. and wings.   *Ezek* 10:12
blood is in *their h.*   23:37, 45
violence that is in *their h. Jonah* 3:8
every work of *their h.*   *Hag* 2:14
with *their h.* they should bear thee.
     Mat 4:6; *Luke* 4:11
they wash not *their h.*   *Mat* 15:2
palms of *their h.* 26:67; *Mark* 14:65
except they wash *their h. Mark* 7:3
rubbing them in *their h.*   *Luke* 6:1
smote him with *their h.*   *John* 19:3
in the works of *their h.*   *Acts* 7:41
wonders to be done by *their h.* 14:3
and palms in *their h.*   *Rev* 7:9
not of the works of *their h.*   9:20
received his mark in *their h.*   20:4

thine *or* thy hands

sanctuary which *thy h.*   *Ex* 15:17
bless thee in all works of *thine h.*
     Deut 16:15; 24:19
afterward shall *thine h. Judg* 7:11
thy h. were not bound.   *2 Sam* 3:34
despise work of *thine h.*?   *Job* 10:3
thine h. have made and fashioned. 8
desire to work of *thine h.*   14:15
by pureness of *thine h.*   22:30
over the works of *thy h.*   *Ps* 8:6
triumph in the works of *thy h.* 92:4
heavens are work of *thy h.*   102:25
thy h. have made me and.   119:73
shalt eat labour of *thine h.*   128:2
the works of *thine* own *h.*   138:8
I muse on the work of *thy h.* 143:5
destroy work of *thine h.*   *Eccl* 5:6
and *thine h.* on thy head.   *Jer* 2:37
lift up *thy h.* for the life. *Lam* 2:19
smite *thine h.* together. *Ezek* 21:14
can *thine h.* be strong in the? 22:14
worship work of *thine h.*   *Mi* 5:13
let not *thine h.* be slack. *Zeph* 3:16
these wounds in *thine h.*? *Zech* 13:6*
Father, into *thy h.* I.   *Luke* 23:46
stretch forth *thy h.*   *John* 21:18
are the works of *thine h.*   *Heb* 1:10
him over the works of *thy h.*   2:7

handstaves

and shall burn the *h.*   *Ezek* 39:9

hand weapon

him with a *h. weapon. Num* 35:18

handwriting

blotting out the *h.*   *Col* 2:14*

handywork

firmament sheweth his *h.*   *Ps* 19:1

hang

Pharaoh shall *h.* thee.   *Gen* 40:19
h. them before the Lord. *Num* 25:4
if thou *h.* him on a tree. *Deut* 21:22
his life shall *h.* in doubt.   28:66
we will *h.* them up.   *2 Sam* 21:6
to speak to the king to *h. Esth* 6:4
then the king said, *H.* him.   7:9
there *h.* a thousand.   *S of S* 4:4
they shall *h.* upon him all. *Isa* 22:24
virgins of Jerusalem *h.*   *Lam* 2:10
take pin of it to *h.* any? *Ezek* 15:3
on these two *h.* all law.   *Mat* 22:40
saw venomous beast *h.*   *Acts* 28:4
lift up hands *h.* down.   *Heb* 12:12

hanged

h. the chief baker. *Gen* 40:22; 41:13
for he that is *h.* is.   *Deut* 21:23
and the king of Ai he *h.* *Josh* 8:29
the five kings *h.* he on.   10:26
Rechab and Baanah *h.* *2 Sam* 4:12
Ahithophel *h.* himself.   17:23
Absalom *h.*   18:10
seven sons of Saul *h.* they.   21:9
set up, let him be *h.*   *Ezra* 6:11
chamberlains were *h.*   *Esth* 2:23
they *h.* Haman.   7:10
they *h.* his ten sons.   9:14
we *h.* our harps on the.   *Ps* 137:2
princes are *h.* up by their. *Lam* 5:12
h. the shield and.   *Ezek* 27:10
h. their shields upon thy walls.   11
millstone were *h.* about.   *Mat* 18:6
     Mark 9:42; *Luke* 17:2
Judas went and *h.*   *Mat* 27:5

thieves who were *h.*   *Luke* 23:39
and *h.* on a tree.   *Acts* 5:30; 10:39

hangeth

and he *h.* the earth upon.   *Job* 26:7
is every one that *h.* on.   *Gal* 3:13

hanging

they were *h.* on trees.   *Josh* 10:26

hanging
(*Revised Versions substitute for
this the word* screen)
thou shalt make an *h.*   *Ex* 26:36
thou shalt make for the *h.* five.   37
h. for court gate.   27:16; 38:18
     39:40; 40:8, 33
the *h.* for the door at the.   35:15
     36:37; 39:38; 40:5, 28

hangings

h. of an hundred cubits. *Ex* 27:9; 11
     38:9, 11
shall be *h.* of fifty.   27:12; 38:12
the *h.* on either side of gate.   27:14
     15; 38:14, 15
the *h.* of court.   35:17; 38:9
     16, 18; 39:40; *Num* 3:26; 4:26
women wove *h.* for the.   2 *Ki* 23:7
blue *h.* fastened with.   *Esth* 1:6

Hannah

Elkanah's wife *H.* had.   1 *Sam* 1:2
H. why weepest thou ?   8
so *H.* rose up.   9
H. spake in her heart, only her.   13
Elkanah knew *H.*   19
after *H.* conceived.   20
but *H.* went not up.   22
H. prayed, and said.   2:1
the Lord visited *H.* so that.   21

Hanoch

sons of Midian, Ephah, *H.*
     Gen 25:4; 1 *Chr* 1:33
H. son of Reuben.   *Gen* 46:9
     Ex. 6:14; *Num* 26:5; 1 *Chr* 5:3

Hanun

H. his son reigned in.   2 *Sam* 10:1
kindness unto *H.*   2; 1 *Chr* 19:2
H. took David's servants, and.
     2 *Sam* 10:4; 1 *Chr* 19:4
the valley gate repaired *H.* *Neh* 3:13
H. sixth son of Zalaph repaired.   30

hap

and her *h.* was to light.   *Ruth* 2:3

haply

if *h.* the people had.   1 *Sam* 14:30
if *h.* he might find any. *Mark* 11:13
lest *h.* after he hath laid. *Luke* 14:29
lest *h.* ye be found to.   *Acts* 5:39
if *h.* they might feel after.   17:27
h. if they of Macedonia. 2 *Cor* 9:4*

happen

no punishment *h.* to.   1 *Sam* 28:10
there shall no evil *h.* to.   *Pr* 12:21
shew us what shall *h.*   *Isa* 41:22
what things should *h.*   *Mark* 10:32

happened

it was a chance that *h.*   1 *Sam* 6:9
as I *h.* by chance upon. 2 *Sam* 1:6
there *h.* to be there a man.   20:1
him of all that had *h.*   *Esth* 4:7
therefore this evil is *h.* to. *Jer* 44:23
of all things that had *h. Luke* 24:14
wonder at that which *h.*   *Acts* 3:10
blindness in part is *h.*   *Rom* 11:25*
now all things *h.* to.   1 *Cor* 10:11
the things which *h.* to me. *Phil* 1:12
some strange thing *h.*   1 *Pet* 4:12
is *h.* to them according. 2 *Pet* 2:22

happeneth

that one event *h.* to.   *Eccl* 2:14
as it *h.* to the fool, so it *h.*   15
wicked men to whom it *h.*   8:14
but time and chance *h.* to.   9:11

happier

but she is *h.* if she so.   1 *Cor* 7:40

happy

h. am I, for daughters.   *Gen* 30:13
h. art thou, O Israel.   *Deut* 33:29
h. thy men, *h.* thy servants.
     1 *Ki* 10:8; 2 *Chr* 9:7
h. is the man whom God.   *Job* 5:17
h. is man who hath quiver. *Ps* 127:5
h. shalt thou be, it shall be.   128:2

---

h. he be that rewardeth. *Ps* 137:8, 9
h. is that people that is in such a
     case, yea *h.* is that.   144:15
h. is he that hath God of.   146:5
h. is man that findeth.   *Pr* 3:13
h. is every one that retaineth.   18
h. is he that hath mercy on.   14:21
trusteth in the Lord, *h.* is he.   16:20
h. is the man that feareth.   28:14
he that keepeth the law, *h.* is. 29:18
are they *h.* that deal ?   *Jer* 12:1
now we call the proud *h.* *Mal* 3:15
know these things, *h.* *John* 13:17
I think myself *h.* king.   *Acts* 26:2
h. is he that condemneth. *Rom* 14:22
behold, we count them *h.* *Jas* 5:11
righteousness' sake, *h.*   1 *Pet* 3:14
for name of Christ *h.* are ye.   4:14

Haran, *a man*

Terah begat *H.*   *Gen* 11:26, 27
H. died before Terah.   28
Milcah, the daughter of *H.*   29
Terah took Lot the son of *H.* his. 31
Caleb's concubine, bare *H.* and
     Moza, and *H.* begat.   1 *Chr* 2:46
Shimei, *H.* Shelomith.   23:9

Haran, *a place*

Terah came to *H.*   *Gen* 11:31
Terah died in *H.*   32
at 75 years departed out of *H.* 12:4
souls that they had gotten in *H.*   5
flee to *H.*   27:43
from Beer-sheba toward *H.*   28:10
they said, of *H.* are we.   29:4
my fathers destroyed *H.* 2 *Ki* 19:12
     Isa 37:12

Harbonah

H. was one of the.   *Esth* 1:10; 7:9

hard

is any thing too *h.* for ?   *Gen* 18:14
travailed, and had *h.*   35:16, 17
their lives bitter with *h.*   *Ex* 1:14
h. causes they brought unto.   18:26
cause that is too *h.*   *Deut* 1:17
it shall not seem *h.* to thee.   15:18
if there arise matter too *h.* for. 17:8
laid upon us *h.* bondage.   26:6
of Zeruiah be too *h.*   2 *Sam* 3:39
Amnon thought it *h.* to do.   13:2
to prove him with *h.* questions.
     1 *Ki* 10:1; 2 *Chr* 9:1
thou hast asked a *h.*   2 *Ki* 2:10
as *h.* as a piece of the.   *Job* 41:24*
hast shewed thy people *h.*   *Ps* 60:3
thy wrath lieth *h.* on me.   88:7
long shall wicked speak *h.?*   94:4*
way of transgressors is *h. Pr* 13:15*
give thee rest from *h.*   *Isa* 14:3
there is nothing too *h.*   *Jer* 32:17
Lord: is there any thing too *h.?*   27
art not sent to a people of *h.*
     Ezek 3:5, 6
shewing *h.* sentences.   *Dan* 5:12*
that thou art an *h.* man. *Mat* 25:24
h. for them that trust. *Mark* 10:24
this is an *h.* saying.   *John* 6:60
h. for thee to kick. *Acts* 9:5; 26:14
things to say, and *h.*   *Heb* 5:11
which are things *h.* to.   2 *Pet* 3:16
all ungodly of their *h.*   *Jude* 15

hard, *adverb*

rump, shall he take off *h.* by. *Lev* 3:9
Abimelech went *h.* to.   *Judg* 9:52*
Israel pursued *h.* after.   20:45
h. after Philistines in. 1 *Sam* 14:22
followed *h.* upon Saul, and upon.
     31:2; 2 *Sam* 1:6; 1 *Chr* 10:2
Naboth had a vineyard *h.* 1 *Ki* 21:1
cut off garments *h.* by. 1 *Chr* 19:4*
my soul followeth *h.* after. *Ps* 63:8
the men rowed *h.* to.   *Jonah* 1:13
whose house joined *h.*   *Acts* 18:7

harden

I will *h.* Pharaoh's heart.   *Ex* 4:21
     7:3; 14:4
I will *h.* the hearts of the.   14:17
shalt not *h.* thy heart.   *Deut* 15:7
it was of Lord to *h.*   *Josh* 11:20
wherefore then do ye *h.?* 1 *Sam* 6:6
yea, I would *h.* myself.   *Job* 6:10*
h. not your hearts.   *Ps* 95:8
     Heb 3:8, 15; 4:7

---

hardened

Lord *h.* Pharaoh's heart.   *Ex* 7:13
   9:12; 10:1, 20, 27; 11:10; 14:8
Pharaoh's heart is *h.*   7:14*
was *h.*   22; 8:19; 9:7*, 35
he *h.* his heart.   8:15, 32; 9:34
Lord thy God *h.* his.   *Deut* 2:30
as Egyptians and Pharaoh *h.* their.
     1 *Sam* 6:6
they *h.* their necks.   2 *Ki* 17:14
Zedekiah *h.* heart from. 2 *Chr* 36:13
they and our fathers *h.* their necks.
     Neh 9:16; 17:29
who hath *h.* himself.   *Job* 9:4
she is *h.* against her young.   39:16†
hast thou *h.* our heart ?   *Isa* 63:17
hearkened not, but *h.*   *Jer* 7:26*
have *h.* their necks not to.   19:15*
when his mind was *h.*   *Dan* 5:20
for their heart was *h.*   *Mark* 6:52
have ye your heart yet *h.?*   8:17
blinded their eyes, *h.*   *John* 12:40
but when divers were *h.*   *Acts* 19:9
lest any of you be *h.*   *Heb* 3:13

hardeneth

a wicked man *h.* his.   *Pr* 21:29
he that *h.* his heart shall fall. 28:14
that being often reproved *h.*   29:1
whom he will he *h.*   *Rom* 9:18

harder

brother offended *h.* to.   *Pr* 18:19
have made their faces *h.*   *Jer* 5:3
h. than flint have I made. *Ezek* 3:9

hardhearted

house of Israel are *h.*   *Ezek* 3:7*

hardly

when Sarai dealt *h.*   *Gen* 16:6
when Pharaoh would *h.*   *Ex* 13:15
h. bestead and hungry.   *Isa* 8:21†
rich man shall *h.* enter. *Mat* 19:23*
     Mark 10:23; *Luke* 18:24
bruising him, *h.* departeth. *Luke* 9:39
h. passing it, we came. *Acts* 27:8*

hardness

dust groweth into *h.*   *Job* 38:38*
because of *h.* of your hearts.
     Mat 19:8; *Mark* 10:5
grieved for the *h.* of.   *Mark* 3:5
upbraided them with their *h.*   16:14
but after thy *h.* and.   *Rom* 2:5
endure *h.* as a good.   2 *Tim* 2:3*

hare

the *h.* is unclean to you.   *Lev* 11:6
     Deut 14:7

harlot

our sister as with *h.?*   *Gen* 34:31
her, he took her to be an *h.*   38:15
daughter in law hath played *h.*   24
priest shall not take an *h. Lev* 21:14
spies came into an *h.'s.*   *Josh* 2:1
only Rahab the *h.* shall live.   6:17
Jephthah was son of an *h. Judg* 11:1
Samson saw there an *h.* and.   16:1
him with attire of an *h.*   *Pr* 7:10
faithful city become an *h.?*   *Isa* 1:21
years shall Tyre sing as an *h.* 23:15
take an harp, thou *h.* that hast.   16
wanderest, playing the *h. Jer* 2:20
thou hast played the *h.* with.   3:1
tree, and there hath played *h.*   6
feared not, but went and played *h.* 8
playedst the *h.* because. *Ezek* 16:15
playedst *h.* thereon.   16
playedst *h.* with them.   28
hast not been as an *h.*   31
O *h.* hear the word.   35
thee to cease from playing the *h.* 41
Aholah played the *h.* when.   23:5
wherein she had played the *h.*   19
a woman that playeth the *h.*   44
mother hath played the *h. Hos* 2:5
thou shalt not play the *h.*   3:3
tho' Israel play the *h.,* let not. 4:15
have given a boy for an *h. Joel* 3:3
thy wife shall be an *h.*   *Amos* 7:17
return to hire of an *h.*   *Mi* 1:7
of the well favoured *h.*   *Nah* 3:4
the members of an *h.?*   1 *Cor* 6:15
that he who is joined to an *h.* is. 16
by faith the *h.* Rahab.   *Heb* 11:31
not Rahab the *h.* justified ? *Jas* 2:25

harlots

came two women h. *1 Ki* 3:16
keepeth company with h. *Pr* 29:3
assemble in h.' houses. *Jer* 5:7
whores, sacrifice with h. *Hos* 4:14
publicans and h. go. *Mat* 21:31
but the publicans and the h. 32
thy living with h. *Luke* 15:30
Babylon, mother of h. *Rev* 17:5

harm

this pillar unto me, for h. *Gen* 31:52
shall make amends for h. *Lev* 5:16
enemy, nor sought his h. *Num* 35:23
will no more do thee h. *1 Sam* 26:21
shall Sheba do more h. *2 Sam* 20:6
and there was no h. in. *2 Ki* 4:41
do my prophets no h. *1 Chr* 16:22
Ps 105:15
if he have done thee no h. *Pr* 3:30
him, and do him no h. *Jer* 39:12
do thyself no h. *Acts* 16:28
gained this h. 27:21
he felt no h. 28:5
saw no h. come to him. 6
spake any h. of these. 21

harm

will h. you, if followers ? *1 Pet* 3:13

harmless

wise as serpents and h. *Mat* 10:16
ye may be h., the sons. *Phil* 2:15
is holy, h., undefiled. *Heb* 7:26*

harness, *substantive*
(*Revised Versions substitute for
this the word armour*)
him that girdeth on h. *1 Ki* 20:11
joints of his h. 22:34; *2 Chr* 18:33
brought every man h. *2 Chr* 9:24

harness, *verb*
h. the horses, and get. *Jer* 46:4

harnessed

Israel went up h. out of. *Ex* 13:18*

Harod

pitched beside well of H. *Judg* 7:1

Harosheth, *see* **gentiles**

harp

of them that handle h. *Gen* 4:21
thee away with tabret and h. 31:27
of prophets with a h. *1 Sam* 10:5
is a cunning player on an h. 16:16
David took an h. and played. 23
prophesied with a h. to. *1 Chr* 25:3
take the timbrel and h. *Job* 21:12
h. also is turned to mourning. 30:31
praise Lord with the h.*Ps* 33:2;150:3
yea, upon the h. will I praise thee. 43:4
my dark sayings upon the h. 49:4
awake psaltery and h. 57:8; 108:2
sing with h. 71:22; 92:3; 98:5
147:7; 149:3
bring hither the pleasant h. 81:2
the h. and the viol are in. *Isa* 5:12
sound like an h. for Moab. 16:11
take an h. 23:16
the joy of the h. ceaseth. 24:8
at sound of h. *Dan* 3:5, 7, 10, 15
whether pipe or h. *1 Cor* 14:7

harped

known what is piped or h.? *1 Cor* 14:7

harpers

the voice of h. harping. *Rev* 14:2
the voice of h. shall be heard. 18:22

harps

all Israel played on h. *2 Sam* 6:5
made of almug trees h. *1 Ki* 10:12
we hanged our h. upon. *Ps* 137:2
be with tabrets and h. *Isa* 30:32
the sound of thy h. *Ezek* 26:13
every one of them h. *Rev* 5:8
harping with their h. 14:2
the h. of God. 15:2

see **cymbal**

harrow

or will he h. the valleys ? *Job* 39:10

harrows

under saws and h. of. *2 Sam* 12:31
with saws and h. of iron. *1 Chr* 20:3

hart

may eat flesh as of the h. *Deut* 12:15
14:5; 15:22

as the h. panteth after. *Ps* 42:1
lame man leap as an h. *Isa* 35:6

harts

ten fat oxen, besides h. *1 Ki* 4:23
princes become like h. *Lam* 1:6

harvest

(*This, the time for reaping, or the
ingathering of the crops, is used
both literally and figuratively in
Scripture. The day of judgement
is called the harvest time for the
world*)
while earth remaineth, h. *Gen* 8:22
went in days of wheat h. 30:14
neither be earing nor h. 45:6
keep the feast of h. *Ex* 23:16; 34:22
in earing time and in h. 34:21
when ye reap h. *Lev* 19:9; 23:10
22; *Deut* 24:19
own accord of h. not reap. *Lev* 25:5
in beginning of barley h. *Ruth* 1:22
my maidens till end of h. 2:21, 23
of Beth-shemesh reaping their h.
1 Sam 6:13
will set them to reap his h. 8:12
is it not wheat h. to-day ? 12:17
death in h. in barley h. *2 Sam* 21:9
her from beginning of barley h. 10
whose h. the hungry eateth. *Job* 5:5
gathereth her food in the h. *Pr* 6:8
he that sleepeth in h. causeth. 10:5
as rain in h. so honour is not. 26:1
according to joy in h. *Isa* 9:3
for the shouting for thy h. is. 16:9
but the h. shall be a heap in. 17:11
cloud of dew in the heat of h. 18:4
for afore the h. when the bud. 5
the h. of the river is her. 23:3
they shall eat up thy h. *Jer* 5:17
to us the appointed weeks of h. 24
the h. is past, summer is. 8:20
O Judah, he hath set an h. *Hos* 6:11
because h. of the field. *Joel* 1:11
put in the sickle, for the h. 3:13
yet three months to h. *Amos* 4:7
h. is plenteous, the. *Mat* 9:37
pray ye Lord of h. 38; *Luke* 10:2
grow together until h.: in time of h.
Mat 13:30
h. is end of the world, reapers. 39
in the sickle because h. *Mark* 4:29
said unto them, the h. *Luke* 10:2
cometh h.? the fields are white to h.
John 4:35
time is come, for the h. *Rev* 14:15

harvestman

it shall be as when the h. *Isa* 17:5
fall as handful after h. *Jer* 9:22

harvest time

overfloweth all *time* of h. *Josh* 3:15
in *time* of wheat h. *Judg* 15:1
to David in h. *time*. *2 Sam* 23:13
of snow in the *time* of h. *Pr* 25:13
handleth sickle in h. *time*. *Jer* 50:16
a little while *time* of her h. 51:33
in the *time* of h. I will. *Mat* 13:30

hast

Lot, h. thou here any besides ? whatsoever thou h. in. *Gen* 19:12
Esau said, H. thou but one ? 27:38
as a prince h. thou power. 32:28
Esau said, keep that thou h. 33:9
thy flock, and all that thou h. 45:10
and gather all that thou h. *Ex* 9:19
every firstling thou h. shall. 13:12
gold, and all thou h. is. *Deut* 8:13
makest thou ? what h.? *Judg* 18:3
and all that thou h. *1 Sam* 25:6
h. thou not here with? *2 Sam* 15:35
tell me, what h. in house. *2 Ki* 4:2
h. thou an arm like God ? *Job* 10:4
say not, Go, when thou h. *Pr* 3:28
what h. thou here ? whom h. thou ?
Isa 22:16
go and sell that thou h. *Mat* 19:21
Mark 10:21; *Luke* 18:22
thou h. that is thine. *Mat* 25:25
from whence then h.? *John* 4:11
to whom thou now h. is not. 18
thou h. words of eternal life. 6:68
said, thou h. a devil. 7:20; 8:48, 52

if I wash thee not, thou h. *John* 13:8
thou h. neither part nor. *Acts* 8:21
thou who h. the form of. *Rom* 2:20
h. thou faith ? have it to. 14:22
what h. thou that thou ? *1 Cor* 4:7
may say, thou h. faith. *Jas* 2:18
thou h. patience, and for. *Rev* 2:3
but this thou h. 6
thou h. a name to live. 3:1, 4
thou h. a little strength. 8
hold that fast which thou h. 11

haste, *substantive*
for Moses and Aaron in h. *Ex* 10:16
ye shall eat in h. with your. 12:11
out of land in h. 33; *Deut* 16:3
business required h. *1 Sam* 21:8
cast away in their h. *2 Ki* 7:15
they went up in h. to. *Ezra* 4:23
I said in my h., I am cut. *Ps* 31:22
I said in my h., All men. 116:11
shall not go out with h. *Isa* 52:12
Daniel before king in h. *Dan* 2:25
king rose up in h. and spake. 3:24
the king went in h. unto the. 6:19
in straightway with h. *Mark* 6:25
the hill country with h. *Luke* 1:39
the shepherds came with h. 2:16

haste

h. thee, escape thither. *Gen* 19:22
h. ye and go up to my. 45:9, 13
speed, h., stay not. *1 Sam* 20:38
h. thee, for Philistines have. 23:27
O my Strength, h. thee. *Ps* 22:19

see **haste**

hasted

young man, and he h. *Gen* 18:7
drink, my lord, and she h. 24:18, 20
and taskmasters h. them. *Ex* 5:13
people h. and passed. *Josh* 4:10
the king of Ai saw it. they h. 8:14
the ambush h. and set the city. 19
the sun h. not to go down. 10:13
liers in wait h. and. *Judg* 20:37
David h. *1 Sam* 17:48
Abigail h. 25:23, 42
except thou hadst h. and. 34
the witch at En-dor h. and. 28:24
who was of Bahurim, h. *2 Sam* 19:16
the prophet h. and took. *1 Ki* 20:41
they h. and put garments. *2 Ki* 9:13
yea, himself h. also. *2 Chr* 26:20
Haman h. to his house. *Esth* 6:12
they h. to bring Haman unto. 14
or if my foot hath h. to. *Job* 31:5
were troubled and h. away.
Ps 48:5; 104:7
Paul h. to be at. *Acts* 20:16

hasten

h. hither Micaiah the. *1 Ki* 22:9*
and see that ye h. the. *2 Chr* 24:5
sorrows multiplied that h. *Ps* 16:4*
I would h. my escape from. 55:8
or who else can h.? *Eccl* 2:25*
let him h. his work that. *Isa* 5:19
I the Lord will h. it in his. 60:22
I will h. my word to. *Jer* 1:12*

hastened, -eth

Abraham h. into the tent. *Gen* 18:6
angels h. Lot, saying, arise. 19:15
howbeit the Levites h. *2 Chr* 24:5
posts went out, being h. by king.
Esth 3:15; 8:14
captive exile h. to. *Isa* 51:14
I have not h. from. *Jer* 17:16

hasteth

as the eagle that h. *Job* 9:26*
drinketh up a river, and h. 40:23*
as a bird h. to snare. *Pr* 7:23
and he that h. with his feet. 19:2
he that h. to be rich, hath an. 28:22
the sun h. to the place. *Eccl* 1:5
fly as eagle that h. to eat. *Hab* 1:8
great day of the Lord h. *Zeph* 1:14

hastily

brought Joseph h. out. *Gen* 41:14
driving them out h. *Judg* 2:23
Abimelech called h. unto his. 9:54
and the man came in h. *1 Ki* 20:33*
may be gotten h. *Pr* 20:21

go not forth *h.* to strive, lest. *Pr* 25:8
Mary that she rose *h.*   *John* 11:31*

hasting
judgement, and *h.* righteousness.
                 Isa 16:5*
and *h.* unto the coming. *2 Pet* 3:12*

hasty
he that is *h.* of spirit.   *Pr* 14:29
every one that is *h.* only.   21:5
seest thou a man that is *h.*   29:20
let not thy heart be *h.*   *Eccl* 5:2
be not *h.* in thy spirit to be.   7:9
be not too *h.* to go out of his.   8:3
as the *h.* fruit before.   *Isa* 28:4*
why is decree so *h.?*   *Dan* 2:15*
that bitter and *h.* nation.   *Hab* 1:6

hatch
owl shall *h.* and gather.   *Isa* 34:15
they *h.* cockatrice' eggs, weave. 59:5

hatcheth
sitteth on eggs and *h.* not. *Jer* 17:11*

hate
This word is used in the Bible fre-
quently, as it is now, not for literal
hatred, but a dislike, or even a
lesser degree of love for one than
for another, Deut 21:15; Pr 13:24;
Luke 14:26.

gate of those that *h.*   *Gen* 24:60
Joseph will peradventure *h.*   50:15
shalt not *h.* thy brother. *Lev* 19:17
they that *h.* you shall reign.   26:17
them that *h.* thee flee. *Num* 10:35
repayeth them that *h.*   *Deut* 7:10
lay them upon them that *h.* 15;30:7
if any man *h.* his neighbour.   19:11
and go in unto her and *h.* her. 22:13
if the latter husband *h.* her.   24:3
the loins of them that *h.* him. 33:11
and love them that *h.?*   *2 Chr* 19:2
that *h.* thee shall be.   *Job* 8:22
shall find those that *h.* thee. *Ps* 21:8
they that *h.* the righteous.   34:21
they which *h.* us spoil you.   44:10
let them also that *h.* him flee. 68:1
they that *h.* thee have lifted.   83:2
and I will plague them that *h.* 89:23
ye that love the Lord *h.* evil. 97:10
he turned their heart to *h.*   105:25
them be turned back that *h.* 129:5
how long, fools, will ye *h.?* *Pr* 1:22
six things doth the Lord *h.*   6:16
Lord is to *h.* evil; pride do I *h.* 8:13
reprove not a scorner, lest he *h.* 9:8
brethren of the poor do *h.*   19:7
weary of thee, and so *h.* thee. 25:17
bloodthirsty *h.* the upright.   29:10
love and a time to *h.*   *Eccl* 3:8
unto will of them that *h. Ezek* 16:27
to them that *h.* thee.   *Dan* 4:19
h. him that rebuketh.   *Amos* 5:10
h. the evil, and love the good.   15
who *h.* the good, and love. *Mi* 3:2
love thy neighbour, *h.*   *Mat* 5:43
do good to them that *h.* you.   44
                 Luke 6:27
either he will *h.* the one.   *Mat* 6:24
                 Luke 16:13
shall betray and shall *h. Mat* 24:10
hand of all that *h.* us. *Luke* 1:71
are ye when men shall *h.* you. 6:22
h. not his father, and mother. 14:26
world cannot *h.* you, but. *John* 7:7
if the world *h.* you, ye know that it
  hated me.   15:18; *1 John* 3:13
ten horns, these shall *h. Rev* 17:16

I hate
there is one man, but I *h.* him.
      1 Ki 22:8; *2 Chr* 18:7
I *h.* the work of them.   *Ps* 101:3
I *h.* every false way. 119:104, 128
I *h.* vain thoughts.   113
I *h.* and abhor lying.   163
do not I *h.* them, O Lord? 139:21
I *h.* them with perfect hatred.   22
froward mouth do I *h.*   *Pr* 8:13
I *h.* robbery for burnt.   *Isa* 61:8
abominable thing that I *h. Jer* 44:4
I *h.* I despise your feast. *Amos* 5:21
I *h.* his palaces, therefore.   6:8
these are things that I *h. Zech* 8:17

what I *h.* that do I.   *Rom* 7:15
the Nicolaitans I *h.*   *Rev* 2:6, 15*

hate me
me, seeing ye *h. me?*   *Gen* 26:27
and fourth generation of them that *h.*
  me.   *Ex* 20:5; *Deut* 5:9
reward them that *h. me. Deut* 32:41
do not ye *h. me?*   *Judg* 11:7
thou dost *h. me.*   14:16
destroy them that *h. me.*
      2 Sam 22:41; *Ps* 18:40
I suffer of them that *h. me. Ps* 9:13
they *h. me* with cruel hatred. 25:19
let them wink that *h. me.*   35:19
that *h. me* wrongfully. 38:19; 69:4
all that *h. me* whisper.   41:7
upon me, in wrath *h. me.*   55:3*
from them that *h. me.*   69:14
they which *h. me* may see.   86:17
desire upon them that *h. me.* 118:7
all they that *h. me* love.   *Pr* 8:36

hated
Esau *h.* Jacob, because. *Gen* 27:41
the Lord saw Leah was *h.*   29:31
that I was *h.*   33
h. Joseph yet the more. 37:4, 5, 8
shot at him and *h.* him.   49:23*
and said, because the Lord *h.* us.
          Deut 1:27; 9:28
h. him not in times past.   4:42
         19:4, 6; *Josh* 20:5
one loved and another *h. Deut* 21:15
before the son of the *h.*   16
shall acknowledge the son of *h.* 17
thou hadst utterly *h.* her. *Judg* 15:2
and blind that are *h.*   *2 Sam* 5:8
Amnon *h.* Tamar.   13:15
Absalom *h.* Amnon.
from my strong enemy, and from
  them that *h.* me. 22:18; *Ps* 18:17
rule over them that *h.* them. *Esth* 9:1
would unto those that *h.* them.   5
destruction of him that *h. Job* 31:29
I have *h.* congregation of. *Ps* 26:5
I have *h.* them that regard.   31:6
put them to shame that *h.* us. 44:7
neither was it he that *h.* me. 55:12
saved them from him that *h.* 106:10
and they that *h.* them ruled.   41
they *h.* knowledge, and.   *Pr* 1:29
and say, how have I *h.*   5:12
man of wicked devices is *h.* 14:17
the poor is *h.* even of his own. 20
therefore I *h.* life.   *Eccl* 2:17
I *h.* labour.   18
been forsaken and *h.*   *Isa* 60:15
brethren that *h.* you said.   66:5
therefore have I *h.* mine. *Jer* 12:8
them that thou hast *h. Ezek* 16:37
sith thou hast not *h.* blood.   35:6
I *h.* them for wickedness. *Hos* 9:15
I loved Jacob, and *h.* Esau.
          Mal 1:3; *Rom* 9:13
ye shall be *h.*   *Mat* 10:22
     Mark 13:13; *Luke* 21:17
shall be *h.* of all nations. *Mat* 24:9
his citizens *h.* him, and. *Luke* 19:14
it *h.* me before it *h.* you. *John* 15:18
have both seen and *h.* both me. 25
written in their law, They *h.* me. 25
world hath *h.* them, because. 17:14
no man ever yet *h.* his.   *Eph* 5:29
righteousness and *h.*   *Heb* 1:9

hateful
iniquity be found to be *h.*   *Ps* 36:2
we were *h.* and hating.   *Tit* 3:3
every unclean and *h.* bird. *Rev* 18:2

hatefully
shall deal with thee *h. Ezek* 23:29

haters
the *h.* of Lord should.   *Ps* 81:15
backbiters, *h.* of God.   *Rom* 1:30

hatest
thine enemies, and *h.*   *2 Sam* 19:6
thou *h.* all workers of.   *Ps* 5:5
lovest righteousness, and *h.* 45:7
thou *h.* instruction, and.   50:17
into hand whom thou *h. Ezek* 23:28
thou *h.* the deeds of the.   *Rev* 2:6

hateth
if thou see ass of him that *h. Ex* 23:5

be slack to him that *h.*   *Deut* 7:10
every abomination he *h.*   12:31
any image which the Lord *h.* 16:22
daughter unto this man, he *h.* 22:16
me in his wrath, who *h.*   *Job* 16:9
shall even he that *h.* right?   34:17
loveth violence, his soul *h. Ps* 11:5
dwelt with him that *h.* peace. 120:6
and he that *h.* suretyship. *Pr* 11:15
but he that *h.* reproof is.   12:1
a righteous man *h.* lying, but. 13:5
he that spareth his rod *h.* his. 24
he that *h.* reproof shall die. 15:10
but he that *h.* gifts shall live. 27
he that *h.* dissembleth with. 26:24
a lying tongue *h.* those that. 28
he that *h.* covetousness.   28:16
is partner with a thief *h.* his. 29:24
feasts my soul *h.*   *Isa* 1:14
Lord saith, that he *h.*   *Mal* 2:16
one that doeth evil *h. John* 3:20
but me the world *h.* because.   7:7
that *h.* his life in this world. 12:25
world, therefore world *h.* you. 15:19
he that *h.* me *h.* my Father also. 23
he that *h.* his brother. *1 John* 2:9, 11
whosoever *h.* his brother is.   3:15
I love God, and *h.* his brother. 4:20

hath
h. he given all that he *h. Gen* 24:36
uncleanness he *h.*   *Lev* 22:5
no devoted thing of all he *h.* 27:28
h. the strength of. *Num* 23:22; 24:8
done away because he *h.* no.   27:4
inherit that which he *h. Deut* 21:16
a double portion of all he *h.* 17
woman and all she *h.*   *Josh* 6:21
burnt with fire, and all he *h.*   7:15
h. the Lord as great? *1 Sam* 15:21
thine handmaid *h.* not.   *2 Ki* 4:2
she *h.* no child, her husband is. 14
hedge about all he *h.*   *Job* 1:10
touch all he *h.*   11
behold, all that he *h.* is in thy. 12
all that a man *h.* will he give. 2:4
so the poor *h.* hope.   5:16
h. the rain a father?   38:28
righteous man *h.* is better. *Ps* 37:16
catch all that he *h.*   109:11
happy is the man *h.* his quiver. 127:5
happy he that *h.* God of.   146:5
despised and *h.* a servant. *Pr* 12:9
the sluggard desireth, and *h.* 13:4
maketh himself rich, yet *h.*   7
is life unto him who *h.* it.   16:22
stone in eyes of him that *h.* it. 17:8
he that *h.* it, shall abide.   19:23
who *h.* woe? who *h.* sorrow? who
  h. wounds?   23:29
yea, he *h.* neither child.   *Eccl* 4:8
for he *h.* not another to help.   10
for what *h.* the wise more?   6:8
neither *h.* he the power in the. 8:8
and she *h.* no breasts.   *S of S* 8:8
and his soul *h.* appetite.   *Isa* 29:8
he *h.* no hands.   45:9
and *h.* no light.   50:10
he *h.* no form nor comeliness. 53:2
he that *h.* no money, come.   55:1
prophet that *h.* a dream, let him tell,
  and he that *h.* my word. *Jer* 23:28
h. Israel no sons? *h.* he no?   49:1
deceiver which *h.* in flock. *Mal* 1:14
h. not where to lay head.   *Mat* 8:20
                Luke 9:58
he that *h.* ears to hear, let him hear.
  Mat 11:15; 13:9, 43; *Mark* 4:9
  Luke 8:8; 14:35; *Rev* 2:7
they say he *h.* a devil.   *Mat* 11:18
h. to him shall be given, who *h.* not,
  from him shall be taken that he *h.*
    13:12; 25:29; *Mark* 4:25
            Luke 19:26
selleth all that he *h.* and. *Mat* 13:44
whence *h.* this man? 56; *Mark* 6:2
h. Beelzebub, and.   *Mark* 3:22
because they said, he *h.* an.   30
and ye say, he *h.* a devil. *Luke* 7:33
              John 10:20
ruler over all that he *h. Luke* 12:44
forsaketh not all that he *h.*   14:33
whose superscription *h.* it?   20:24
h. a purse, he that *h.* no.   22:36

spirit *h*. not flesh and bones.
　　　　　　　Luke 24:39
he that *h*. the bride, is. *John* 3:29
he that believeth on the Son *h*. ever-
　lasting life. 36; 5:24; 6:47, 54
Father *h*. life in himself, so *h*. 5:26
h. one that judgeth him. 12:48
he that *h*. my commandments. 14:21
prince of this world *h*. nothing. 30
greater love *h*. no man than. 15:13
all things that the Father *h*. 16:15
delivered thee unto me, *h*. 19:11
what advantage then *h*.? *Rom* 3:1
by works, he *h*. whereof to. 4:2
h. not the potter power over? 9:21
the wife *h*. not power of. *1 Cor* 7:4
but every man *h*. his proper gift. 7
h. a psalm, *h*. a doctrine, *h*. a. 14:26
h. righteousness with unrighteous-
　ness? what communion.*2 Cor* 6:14
what concord. Christ? 15
what agreement *h*. temple of God? 16
according to that a man *h*. 8:12
desolate *h*. more children. *Gal* 4:27
nor idolater *h*. any. *Eph* 5:5
if any thinketh he *h*. *Phil* 3:4
builder *h*. more honour. *Heb* 3:3
man *h*. an unchangeable. 7:24
your confidence, which *h*. great. 10:35
a man say he *h*. faith, and ? *Jas* 2:14
denieth Son, same *h*. *1 John* 2:23
every man that *h*. this hope. 3:3
ye know that no murderer *h*. 15
whoso *h*. this world's good, and. 17
believed the love that God *h*. 4:16
no fear in love, because fear *h*. 18
believeth on Son of God *h*. 5:10
h. the Son *h*. life, *h*. not Son *h*. 12
not in the doctrine of Christ, *h*. not
　God. He that abideth *h*. *2 John* 9
that *h*. key of David. *Rev* 3:7
where she *h*. a place prepared. 12:6
because he knoweth that he *h*. 12
beast which *h*. the seven heads. 17:7
and there is the mind which *h*. 9
on such the second death *h*. 20:6

hating
provide men of truth, *h*. *Ex* 18:21
times past hateful, and *h*. *Tit* 3:3
h. even garment spotted by. *Jude* 23

hatred
if he thrust him off *h*. *Num* 35:20
h. wherewith he hated. *2 Sam* 13:15
hate me with cruel *h*. *Ps* 25:19
compassed me about with *h*. 109:3
they have rewarded me *h*. 5
I hate them with perfect *h*. I. 139:22
h. stirs up strifes, love. *Pr* 10:12
he that hideth *h*. with lying lips. 18
than a stalled ox, and *h*. 15:17
whose *h*. is covered by deceit. 26:26
knoweth either love or *h*. *Eccl* 9:1
their love, their *h*. and envy is. 6
destroy it for the old *h*. *Ezek* 25:15
thou hast had a perpetual *h*. 35:5
to envy thou hast used out of *h*. 11
iniquity, and for great *h*. *Hos* 9:7
but the prophet is *h*. in the house. 8
works of flesh; witchcraft, *h*. *Gal* 5:20

hats
in their hosen and *h*. *Dan* 3:21*

haughtily
neither shall ye go *h*. *Mi* 2:3

haughtiness
h. of men shall be bowed. *Isa* 2:11
and the *h*. of men shall be. 17
I will lay low the *h*. of the. 13:11
of the *h*. of Moab. 16:6; *Jer* 48:29

haughty
thine eyes are upon *h*. *2 Sam* 22:28
Lord, my heart is not *h*. *Ps* 131:1
an *h*. spirit before a fall. *Pr* 16:18
before destruction heart is *h*. 18:12
proud and *h*. scorner is his. 21:24
daughters of Zion are *h*. *Isa* 3:16
high hewn down, and *h*. 10:33*
the *h*. people of the earth. 24:4*
were *h*. before me, I. *Ezek* 16:50
no more be *h*. because. *Zeph* 3:11

haunt
his place where his *h*. *1 Sam* 23:22

---

men were wont to *h*. *1 Sam* 30:31
to be on all that *h*. it. *Ezek* 26:17

have
they *h*. all one language. *Gen* 11:6
h. ye another brother? 43:7
h. ye a father? 44:19
have brought all that they *h*. 46:32
thou shalt *h*. no other gods. *Ex* 20:3
　　　　　　　Deut 5:7
the priest shall *h*. it. *Lev* 7:7, 8
the sons of Aaron shall *h*. 10
and a just hin, shall ye *h*. 19:36
priest's daughter *h*. no child. 22:13
　　　　　　　Num 27:8, 9
whence should I *h*. flesh? *Num* 11:13
h. I now any power at all to? 22:38
peace he and his seed shall *h*. 25:13
that *h*. many, them that *h*. few. 35:8
voice of God, as we *h*.? *Deut* 5:26
father and all they *h*. *Josh* 2:13
though they *h*. iron chariots. 17:18
what *h*. you to do with Lord? 22:24
h. ye called us to take that we *h*.?
　　　　　　　Judg 14:15
h. taken my gods, and what *h*.? 18:24
I am too old to *h*. an husband, if I
　should *h*. an husband. *Ruth* 1:12
but we will *h*. a king. *1 Sam* 8:19
present to bring; what *h*. we? 9:7
utterly destroy all that they *h*. 15:3
what can he *h*. more but the? 18:8
h. I need of mad men, that ye *h*.?
　　　　　　　21:15
Amnon said, *h*. out all. *2 Sam* 13:9
they *h*. there with them their. 15:36
what *h*. I to do with you, ye? 16:10
I *h*. no son to keep my name. 18:18
what right *h*. I yet to cry? 19:28
said unto king, how long *h*. I to? 34
Israel said, we *h*. ten parts in. 43
h. thou respect unto. *1 Ki* 8:28
saying, What portion *h*. we? 12:16
I *h*. not a cake, but an handful. 17:12
king, I am thine, and all I *h*. 20:4
that I may *h*. it for a garden. 21:2
scattered as sheep that *h*. no. 22:17
h. her forth without. *2 Ki* 11:15
　　　　　　　2 Chr 23:14
this sign shalt thou *h*. *2 Ki* 20:9
shall any after thee *h*. *2 Chr* 1:12
from henceforth thou shalt *h*. 16:9
what *h*. I to do with thee? 35:21
he said, *H*. me away, for I am. 23
other men *h*. our lands. *Neh* 5:5
let it look for light but *h*. *Job* 3:9
O that I might *h*. my request. 6:8
then should I yet *h*. comfort. 10
what profit should we *h*. if? 21:15
they mar my path, they *h*. no. 30:13
profit shall I *h*. if be cleansed? 35:3
the Lord shall *h*. them. *Ps* 2:4
h. workers of iniquity? 14:4; 53:4
in pleasant places, I *h*. a. 16:6
say, Ah! so would we *h*. it. 35:25
whom *h*. I in heaven but? 73:25
sing to my God while I *h*. 104:33
a good understanding *h*. all. 111:10
they *h*. mouths; eyes *h*. they. 115:5
they *h*. ears; noses *h*. they. 6, 7
　　　　　　　135:16, 17
so shall I *h*. wherewith to. 119:42
great peace *h*. they which love. 165
praises unto my God while I *h*. 146:2
this honour *h*. all his saints. 149:9
lot, let us all *h*. one purse. *Pr* 1:14
shall beg in harvest and *h*. 20:4
shall *h*. him become his son. 29:21
and I *h*. not the understanding. 30:2
nor *h*. the knowledge of the holy. 3
they *h*. all one breath. *Eccl* 3:19
giveth life to them that *h*. it. 7:12
h. they any more a reward. 9:5
neither *h*. they any more portion. 6
we *h*. a little sister and. *S of S* 8:8
thou, O Solomon, must *h*. a. 12
gone, because they *h*. no. *Isa* 5:13
also shalt thou *h*. no rest. 23:12
h. a strong city, salvation will. 26:1
ye shall *h*. a song as in night. 30:29
blind that *h*. eyes, deaf that *h*. 43:8
h. not I the Lord? there is no. 45:21
in the Lord *h*. I righteousness. 24
children which thou shalt *h*. 49:20

---

hand shortened? *h*. I no? *Isa* 50:2
h. of my hand, ye shall lie down. 11
now therefore what *h*. I here? 52:5
dogs, which can never *h*. 56:11
for your shame you shall *h*. 61:7
h. eyes and see not; which *h*. ears,
　and hear not. *Jer* 5:21
people love to *h*. it so, what. 31
no flesh shall *h*. peace. 12:12
h. sons nor daughters in. 16:2
said, ye shall *h*. peace. 23:17; 29:7
plant vineyard, nor *h*. any. 35:7
he shall *h*. none to sit upon. 36:30
he shall *h*. his life for a prey. 38:2
to the which they *h*. a desire. 44:14
they will destroy till they *h*. 49:9
the nation which *h*. neither gates. 31
mind, therefore *h*. I hope. *Lam* 3:21
neither will I *h*. any pity. *Ezek* 5:11
　　　　　　　7:4; 8:18; 9:10
eye spare, neither *h*. ye pity. 9:5
h. I any pleasure that the? 18:23
I *h*. no pleasure in death. 32; 33:11
when iniquity shall *h*. 21:25, 29
any wisdom that I *h*. *Dan* 2:30
loose, and they *h*. no hurt. 3:25
shall *h*. a chain of gold. 5:7, 16
the king should *h*. no damage. 6:2
now they shall say, We *h*. *Hos* 10:3
unto you, ye shall not *h*. *Mi* 3:6
this shall they *h*. for. *Zeph* 2:10
but ye *h*. not enough. *Hag* 1:6
h. we not all one father? *Mal* 2:10
we *h*. Abraham to our father.
　　　　　Mat 3:9; *Luke* 3:8
thy coat, let him *h*. thy. *Mat* 5:40
love you, what reward *h*. ye? 46
they *h*. their reward. 6:2; 5:16
the foxes *h*. holes, birds *h*. nests.
　　　　　　8:20; *Luke* 9:58
what *h*. we to do with thee, Jesus?
　Mat 8:29; *Mark* 1:24; *Luke* 4:34
and he shall have more abundance.
　　　　　Mat 13:12; 25:29
it is not lawful for thee to *h*. her.
　　　　　14:4; *Mark* 6:18
we *h*. so much bread? *Mat* 15:33
how many loaves ye? 34
　　　　　Mark 6:38; 8:5
h. faith as a grain. *Mat* 17:20; 21:21
what shall I do, that I may *h*.? 19:16
followed thee what shall we *h*.? 27
h. poor always with you, but me ye *h*.
　26:11; *Mark* 14:7; *John* 12:8
need *h*. we of witnesses? *Mat* 26:65
h. nothing to do with that. 27:19
deliver him now, if he will *h*. him. 43
the whole *h*. no need of. *Mark* 2:17
long as they *h*. the bridegroom. 19
if any man *h*. ears to hear. 4:23
　　　　　7:16; *Rev* 13:9
so fearful, how is it ye *h*.? *Mark* 4:40
saying, It is because we *h*. 8:16
h. salt in yourselves, *h*. peace. 9:50
thou shalt *h*. treasure in heaven.
　　　　　10:21; *Luke* 18:22
shall *h*. whatsoever he. *Mark* 11:23
receive them, and ye shall *h*. 24
what thank *h*. ye? *Luke* 6:32, 33, 34
taken what he seemeth to. 8:18
which of you shall *h*. a friend? 11:5
alms of such things as ye *h*. 41
and after that *h*. no more. 12:4
which neither *h*. storehouse nor. 24
sell that ye *h*. and give alms. 33
I pray thee *h*. me excused. 14:18, 19
ever with me, all that I *h*. 15:31
we will not *h*. this man to. 19:14
Satan hath desired to *h*. you. 22:31
what communications ye *h*.? 24:17
flesh and bones, as ye see me *h*. 39
h. ye here any meat? 41; *John* 21:5
said, They *h*. no wine. *John* 2:3
what *h*. I to do with thee? 4
but *h*. everlasting life. 3:15, 16
answered and said, I *h*. no. 4:17
hath given the Son to *h*. life. 5:26
and ye *h*. not his word abiding. 38
I know that ye *h*. the love. 42
believeth on him, may *h*. 6:40
except ye eat his flesh, ye *h*. no. 53
tempting, that they might *h*. to. 8:6
he that followeth me, shall *h*. 12
h. one father even God. 41

I h. not a devil. John 8:49
ye were blind, ye should h. no. 9:41
I am come that they might h. 10:10
other sheep I h. which are not. 16
walk while ye h. light. 12:35, 36
might h. peace. In the world ye shall
h. tribulation: I h. overcome. 16:33
but ye h. a custom that I. 18:39
we h. a law. 19:7
we h. no king but Cesar. 15
that believing ye might h. life. 20:31
silver and gold h. I none, but such as
I h. Acts 3:6
said, Lord, what wilt thou h.? 9:6
in him we live, move, and h. 17:28
know that by this craft we h. 19:25
h. four men which h. a vow. 21:23
when Gentiles, which h. Rom 2:14
ye h. your fruit unto holiness. 6:22
if any man h. not the Spirit. 8:9
I will come, and Sara shall h. 9:9
and all members h. not the. 12:4
hast thou faith? h. to thyself. 14:22
I h. whereof I may glory. 15:17
but we h. the mind of. 1 Cor 2:16
are naked, and h. no certain. 4:11
instructors, yet h. ye not many. 15
that one should h. his father's. 5:1
is in you, which ye h. of God. 6:19
let every man h. his own wife, let
every woman h. her own. 7:2
yet such shall h. trouble in the. 28
they that h. wives be as though. 29
h. you without carefulness. 32
I think also that I h. the Spirit. 40
that we all h. knowledge. 8:1
h. we not power to eat? 9:4, 5, 6
if a man h. long hair, it is. 11:14
if a woman h. long hair, it is a. 15
we h. no such custom, nor the. 16
what, h. ye not houses to eat in? 22
eye not say to hand, I h. no. 12:21
h. all the gifts of healing? 30
h. not charity, I am become. 13:1
I h. all faith and h. not charity. 2, 3
your rejoicing which I h. 15:31
for some h. not the knowledge. 34
such trust h. we through. 2 Cor 3:4
seeing we h. this ministry, we. 4:1
out of that which ye h. 8:11
he may h. to give to him. Eph 4:28
h. no fellowship with the. 5:11
I h. you in my heart. Phil 1:7
but I h. all. 4:18
love which ye h. to all. Col 1:4
what great conflict I h. for you. 2:1
if any man h. a quarrel. 3:13
ye also h. a Master in. 4:1
ye suffered, as they h. 1 Thes 2:14
for all men h. not faith. 2 Thes 3:2
not because we h. not power. 9
who will h. all men to. 1 Tim 2:4
him with whom we h. to. Heb 4:13
seeing then that we h. a great. 14
by reason of use h. their senses. 5:14
which hope we h. as an. 6:19
we h. such a High Priest, set. 8:1
that this man h. somewhat also. 3
that ye h. in heaven a better. 10:34
with such things as ye h. 13:5
we h. an altar whereof they h. no. 10
here h. we no continuing city. 14
but let patience h. her. Jas 1:4
h. not faith of Christ with. 2:1
and h. not works, can faith? 14
even so faith, if it h. not works. 17
thou hast faith, and I h. works. 18
if ye h. bitter envy, and strife. 3:14
ye lust and h. not, ye desire to h. ye
fight and war, yet ye h. not. 4:2
above all things h. 1 Pet 4:8
we h. a more sure word. 2 Pet 1:19
a heart they h. exercised. 2:14
if we say, we h. no sin. 1 John 1:8
h. an Advocate with the Father. 2:1
but we h. an unction from the. 20
and this commandment h. we. 4:21
that ye may know that ye h. 5:13
this is the confidence that we h. 14
we h. the petitions we desired. 15
I h. no greater joy than. 3 John 4
Diotrephes, who loveth to h. the. 9
I h. the keys of hell. Rev 1:18
I h. somewhat against. 2:4; 14:20

and ye shall h. tribulation. Rev 2:10
to you, and to as many as h. not. 24
but what ye h. already, hold. 25
which h. not the seal of God. 9:4
h. the testimony of Jesus. 12:17
they h. no rest day nor night. 14:11
these h. one mind, and give. 17:13
brethren that h. the testimony. 19:10
liars shall h. their part in lake. 21:8
that they may h. right to tree. 22:14
see compassion, dominion

haven
dwell at the h. an h. Gen 49:13
them to their desired h. Ps 107:30
h. not commodious, an h. Acts 27:12

fair havens
place which is called fair h. Acts 27:8

having
h. his uncleanness. Lev 7:20; 22:3
h. her sickness. 20:18
h. a wen or scurvy. 22:22
into a trance, but h. Num 24:4, 16
stay for them from h. Ruth 1:13
h. a drawn sword in. 1 Chr 21:16
h. Judah and Benjamin. 2 Chr 11:12
mourning, and h. his. Esth 6:12
h. no guide, overseer. Pr 6:7
and h. neither bars nor. Ezek 38:11
pass ye away, h. thy. Mi 1:11
king cometh to thee, h. Zech 9:9
he taught as one h. Mat 7:29
h. soldiers under me. 8:9; Luke 7:8
were as sheep h. no shepherd.
Mat 9:36; Mark 6:34
rather than h. two hands or. Mat 18:8
rather than h. two eyes to be cast.
9; Mark 9:43
not h. wedding garment? Mat 22:12
if a man die, h. no children. 24
Luke 20:28
and h. no issue, left. Mat 22:25
woman h. an alabaster box. 26:7
Mark 14:3
h. nothing to eat, Jesus. Mark 8:1
h. eyes, see ye not? h. ears? 18
a fig tree h. leaves. 11:13
h. one son. 12:6
woman h. an issue of. Luke 8:43
man of you h. an hundred? 15:4
either what woman h. ten pieces? 8
but which of you, h. a servant? 17:7
how knows he letters, h.? John 7:15
Simon Peter h. a sword. 18:10
h. land, sold it, and. Acts 4:37
h. a good report of the Jews. 10:22
h. more perfect knowledge of. 24:22
h. not the law, are a law. Rom 2:14
h. then gifts differing according. 12:6
h. a matter against. 1 Cor 6:1
h. that standeth stedfast. 7:37
h. the same spirit of. 2 Cor 4:13
h. nothing, and yet possessing. 6:10
h. therefore these promises. 7:1
ye always h. all sufficiency in. 9:8
h. in a readiness to revenge. 10:6
but h. hope, when your faith is. 15
h. no hope. Eph 2:12
not h. spot or wrinkle. 5:27
h. your loins girt about. 6:14
h. a desire to depart. Phil 1:23
h. this confidence. 25
h. the same conflict. 30
h. the same love. 2:2
not h. my own righteousness. Col 3:9
h. made peace through. 1:20
h. nourishment ministered. 2:19
h. his children in. 1 Tim 3:4
h. the promise of the life that. 4:8
h. damnation, because they. 5:12
h. food and raiment, let. 6:8
h. this seal, the Lord. 2 Tim 2:19
h. a form of godliness, but. 3:5
they shall heap teachers, h. 4:3
h. faithful children, not. Tit 1:6
h. conversation honest. 1 Pet 2:12
h. a good conscience, they. 3:16
h. eyes full of adultery. 2 Pet 2:14
these be sensual, h. not. Jude 19
h. seven horns. Rev 5:6
h. every one harps. 8
I saw an angel, h. the seal of. 7:2
h. a golden censer. 8:3
h. breastplates. 9:17

h. seven heads. Rev 12:3
h. great wrath. 12
h. the everlasting gospel. 14:6
h. the harps of God. 15:2
h. a golden cup. 17:4
h. great power. 18:1
h. the key of the pit. 20:1
holy Jerusalem, h. the glory. 21:11

havock
as for Saul, he made h. of. Acts 8:3*

hawk
h. had in. Lev 11:16; Deut 14:15
doth the h. fly by thy? Job 39:26

hay
h. appeareth, and tender. Pr 27:25
the h. is withered away. Isa 15:6*
on this foundation, h. 1 Cor 3:12

Hazael
anoint H. to be king. 1 Ki 19:15
that escapeth the sword of H. 17
H. went to meet Elisha. 2 Ki 8:9
Ben-hadad died, and H. reigned. 15
went with Joram against H. 28
kept Ramoth-gilead because of H. 9:14
H. smote them in all coasts. 10:32
H. set his face to go up to. 12:17
sent the hallowed things to H. 18
Israel into the hand of H. 13:3
but H. oppressed Israel. 22
so H. died. 24
Ben-hadad son of H. cities. 25
fire into the house of H. Amos 1:4

hazel
took him rods of h. and. Gen 30:37*

Hazelelponi
of their sister was H. 1 Chr 4:3

Hazeroth
abode at H. Num 11:35; 33:17
removed from H. 12:16; 33:18

Hazor
Joshua took H. head of. Josh 11:10
and he burnt H. with fire. 11, 13
Kedesh and H. cities of. 15:23, 25
Ramah and H. cities of. 19:36
Jabin who reigned in H. Judg 4:2
raised a levy to build H. 1 Ki 9:15
king of Syria took H. 2 Ki 15:29
the kingdoms of H. Jer 49:28
O ye inhabitants of H. 30
and H. shall be a dwelling for. 33

he
he shall rule over thee. Gen 3:16
strive with man, for he is flesh. 6:3
he with whom it is found. 44:10
brother be greater than he. 48:19
art he whom thy brethren. 49:8
he shall be thy spokesman to the
people, and he shall be. Ex 4:16
and hardened his heart, he. 9:34
he hath put in his heart that he may
teach both he and. 35:34
he among the sons of. Lev 7:33
shall go out in jubile, he and. 25:54
cursed is he that. Num 24:9
came, he and all his. Deut 3:1
it is he that giveth power to. 8:18
cursed be he. 27:16
So to the end of the chapter
he that doth go with thee, he will.
31:6, 8
is not he thy Father that? 32:6
I, even I am he, and there is. 39
Isa 41:4; 43:10, 13; 46:4; 48:12
Lord your God is he. Josh 23:3, 10
what man is he will? Judg 10:18
I am he that came. 1 Sam 4:16
not a goodlier person than he. 9:2
this is he. 16:12
as his name is so is he. 25:25
two men better than he. 1 Ki 2:32
she and he and her house. 17:15
thou he that troubleth Israel? 18:17
is not that he whose places.
2 Ki 18:22; Isa 36:7
he in first year of reign. 2 Chr 29:3
where, and who is he? Job 9:24
who is he that will plead? 13:19
man dieth, and where is he?
20:7; Isa 63:11
thou art he that took me. Ps 22:9

he it is shall tread. *Ps* 60:12; 108:13
he that is our God is the God. 68:20
he is God, it is *he* that. 100:3
is *he* that giveth salvation. 144:10
Lord, happy is *he*. *Pr* 16:20; 29:18
he that is higher than. *Eccl* 5:8
untimely birth is better than *he*. 6:3
he sitteth on the circle. *Isa* 40:22
he that comforteth. 51:12; 52:6
John 18:5, 6, 8; *Rev* 1:18; 2:23
and said, it is not *he*. *Jer* 5:12
art not thou *he*, O Lord our? 14:22
the king is not *he* that can do. 38:5
he also shall be in derision. 48:26
art thou *he* of whom? *Ezek* 38:17
is more righteous than *he*. *Hab* 1:13
where is *he* that is born? *Mat* 2:2
this is *he* that was spoken of. 3:3
art thou *he* that should come? 11:3
Luke 7:19, 20
he that is not with me is against me,
and *he* that. *Mat* 12:30; *Luke* 11:23
Christ? whose son is *he*? *Mat* 22:42
he is in the desert, *he* is in. 24:26
the same is *he*. 26:48; *Mark* 14:44
is none other but *he*. *Mark* 12:32
he to whom the Son. *Luke* 10:22
and *he* from within shall. 11:7
who is *he* that gave thee this? 20:2
he that sitteth at meat, or *he*? 22:27
they said, *he* is not here, but. 24:6
we trusted *he* should have. 21
this was *he* of whom. *John* 1:15, 30
I that speak to thee, am *he*. 4:26
where is *he*? 7:11
is not this *he* they seek to kill? 25
believe not that I am *he*, ye. 8:24
then shall ye know that I am *he*. 28
they said, is not this *he*? 9:8
this is *he*, but *he* said, I am *he*. 9
who is *he*, Lord? 36
he that talketh with thee. 37
ye may believe that I am *he*. 13:19
they knew it was *he* who. *Acts* 3:10
this is *he* that was in church. 7:38
is not this *he* that destroyed? 9:21
Peter said, I am *he* whom. 10:21
he that was ordained of God. 42
ye that I am? I am not *he*. 13:25
he is not a Jew that is. *Rom* 2:28
he is a Jew that is one inwardly. 29
he that in these things. 14:18
are we stronger than *he*? *1 Cor* 10:22
that as *he* is Christ's. *2 Cor* 10:7
faithful is *he* that. *1 Thes* 5:24
he who now letteth will let, until *he*
be taken. *2 Thes* 2:7
son is *he* whom the father? *Heb* 12:7
he for our profit, that we might. 10
as *he* which hath called. *1 Pet* 1:15
we walk in light, as *he* is. *1 John* 1:7
when *he* shall appear, we may. 2:28
is righteous, even as *he* is. 3:7
dwelleth in him, and *he*. 24; 4:15
he that is in you, than *he* in. 4:4
because as *he* is, so are we in. 17
he that hath the Son, hath life; and
he that hath not the Son. 5:12
follow not evil, *he* that doeth good is
of God; *he* that doeth. *3 John* 11
holy is *he* that hath part. *Rev* 20:6
he that is unjust, *he* that is. 22:11

head

it shall bruise thy *h*. *Gen* 3:15
shall lift up thy *h*. 40:13, 19
on the *h*. of Joseph, and on the top of
the *h*. of him. 49:26; *Deut* 33:16
Aaron and his sons put their hands
upon *h*. *Ex* 29:10; *Lev* 4:4; 8:14
put hands upon the *h*. of the ram.
Ex 29:15, 19; *Lev* 8:18, 22
shall put hand on the *h*. *Lev* 1:4
shall lay his hand on the *h*. of. 3:2
hand on *h*. of sin offering. 4:29, 33
leprous, his plague is in his *h*. 13:44
shall be rent, and his *h*. bare. 45
not make baldness on their *h*. 21:5
shall not uncover his *h*. nor rend. 10
uncover the woman's *h*. *Num* 5:18
shall no razor come upon his *h*. 6:5
of his God is on his *h*. 7
shall shave his *h*. 9, 18; *Deut* 21:12
and he shall hallow his *h*. *Num* 6:11

---

on his *h*., blood on our *h*. *Josh* 2:19
she smote off Sisera's *h*. *Judg* 5:26
no razor shall come on his *h*. 13:5
Goliath's *h*. *1 Sam* 17:57
of Nabal on his own *h*. 25:39
thee keeper of my *h*. for ever. 28:2
cut off Saul's *h*. 31:9
earth upon his *h*. *2 Sam* 1:2; 15:32
blood be upon thy *h*. 1:16; *1 Ki* 2:37
and said, Am I a dog's *h*.? *2 Sam* 3:8
let it rest on the *h*. of Joab, and. 29
go over, and take off his *h*. 16:9
take thy master from thy *h*. to-day.
2 Ki 2:3, 5
unto his father, My *h*. my *h*. 4:19
if the *h*. of Elisha shall. 6:31
murderer sent to take away my *h*. 32
daughter of Jerusalem hath shaken
her *h*. 19:21; *Isa* 37:22
did lift up the *h*. of Jehoiachin.
2 Ki 25:27; *Jer* 52:31
his way on his *h*. *2 Chr* 6:23
are increased over our *h*. *Ezra* 9:6
reproach on their own *h*. *Neh* 4:4
return on his own *h*. *Esth* 9:25
Job arose, shaved his *h*. *Job* 1:20
yet will not I lift up my *h*. 10:15
I could shake my *h*. at you. 16:4
the lifter up of mine *h*. *Ps* 3:3
shall return on his own *h*. 7:16
out the lip, they shake the *h*. 22:7
thou anointest my *h*. with oil. 23:5
now shall my *h*. be lifted up. 27:6
iniquities are gone over mine *h*. 38:4
a shaking of the *h*. among. 44:14
is strength of mine *h*. 60:7; 108:8
God shall wound the *h*. of. 68:21
hate thee, have lift up the *h*. 83:2
therefore shall he lift up the *h*. 110:7
as for the *h*. of those that. 140:9
which shall not break my *h*. 141:5
blessings are on the *h*. of. *Pr* 10:6
blessing on the *h*. of him. 11:26
heap coals of fire on his *h*. 25:22
Rom 12:20
man's eyes are in his *h*. *Eccl* 2:14
hand is under my *h*. *S of S* 2:6; 8:3
my *h*. is filled with dew, my. 5:2
h. as most fine gold. 11
thy *h*. as Carmel. 7:5
whole *h*. is sick and heart. *Isa* 1:5
joy shall be on their *h*. 51:11
is it to bow down his *h*. as a? 58:5
helmet of salvation on his *h*. 59:17
and thine hands on thy *h*. *Jer* 2:37
O that my *h*. were waters. 9:1
fall grievously on the *h*. 23:19; 30:23
their way on their *h*. *Ezek* 9:10
h. was made bald, shoulder. 29:18
O king, thou art this *h*. *Dan* 2:38
recompense on your *h*. *Joel* 3:4, 7
pant after dust on the *h*. *Amos* 2:7
will bring baldness on every *h*. 8:10
cut them in the *h*. all of them. 9:1
no man did lift up his *h*. *Zech* 1:21
then set the crowns on the *h*. 6:11
thou swear by thy *h*. *Mat* 5:36
smote him on *h*. 27:30; *Mark* 15:19
she said, The *h*. of John. *Mark* 6:24
my *h*. with oil thou didst. *Luke* 7:46
but also my hands and his *h*. *John* 13:9
his *h*. covered, dishonoureth his *h*.
1 Cor 11:4
ought to have power on her *h*. 10
the *h*. to the feet, I have no. 12:21
and gave him as *h*. to the church.
Eph 1:22; 4:15; *Col* 1:18
not holding the *h*. from. *Col* 2:19
eyes flame of fire, and *h*. *Rev* 19:12
see **bald, beard, bow, bowed,
cover, covered, crown**

head *of the corner*

the *h. of the corner*. *Mat* 21:42
Mark 12:10; *Luke* 20:17
Acts 4:11; *1 Pet* 2:7

head, *for ruler, governor*

one rod shall be for the *h*. *Num* 17:3
he was *h*. over a people of a. 25:15
Lord will make thee *h*. *Deut* 28:13
he shall be the *h*. and thou shalt. 44
each one an *h*. of house. *Josh* 22:14
he shall be *h*. over all Gilead.
Judg 10:18; 11:8

---

shall I be your *h*.? *Judg* 11:9
the people made him *h*. 11
thou not made the *h*.? *1 Sam* 15:17
thou hast kept me to be *h*. of the
heathen. *2 Sam* 22:44; *Ps* 18:43
thou art exalted as *h*. *1 Chr* 29:11
h. of Damascus is Rezin, *h*. of.
Isa 7:8, 9
will cut off from Israel *h*. 9:14
and honourable, he is the *h*. 15
nor work which *h*. or tail, or. 19:15
art Gilead to me, *h*. of. *Jer* 22:6
themselves one *h*. *Hos* 1:11
woundedst the *h*. out of. *Hab* 3:13
thou didst strike through the *h*. 14
h. of every man is Christ; the *h*. of
the woman is the man; and the
h. of Christ is God. *1 Cor* 11:3
is the *h*. of the wife, even as Christ is
h. of the church, and. *Eph* 5:23
h. of all principality. *Col* 2:10

head, for *top, chief*

the *h*. of fat valleys. *Isa* 28:1, 4
they lie at the *h*. of all the. 51:20*
built high places at *h*. *Ezek* 16:25
choose it at the *h*. 21:19
king of Babylon stood at the *h*. of. 21

head with *hair* or *hairs*

hair is fallen off his *h*. *Lev* 13:40, 41
shave all his *hair* off his *h*. 14:9
locks of *hair* of his *h*. *Num* 6:5
and shalt take the *hair* of *h*. of. 18
the *hair* of his *h*. began. *Judg* 16:22
not an *hair* of his *h*. *1 Sam* 14:45
weighed *hair* of his *h*. *2 Sam* 14:26
plucked off *hair* of my *h*. *Ezra* 9:3
they are more than *hairs* of my *h*.
Ps 40:12; 69:4
the *hair* of thine *h*. *S of S* 7:5
nor was an *hair* of their *h*. *Dan* 3:27
hair of his *h*. like the pure. 7:9
hairs of your *h*. are numbered.
Mat 10:30; *Luke* 12:7
with *hairs* of her *h*. *Luke* 7:38, 44
not an *hair* of your *h*. perish. 21:18
not an *hair* fall from *h*. *Acts* 27:34
his *h*. and his *hairs* were. *Rev* 1:14

axe head

the *axe* slippeth. *Deut* 19:5
axe h. fell into water. *2 Ki* 6:5

bed's head

himself on the *bed's h*. *Gen* 47:31

hoary head

rise before the *hoary h*. *Lev* 19:32

spear's head

spear's h. weighed 600 shekels.
1 Sam 17:7; *2 Sam* 21:16

headbands

Lord will take away *h*. *Isa* 3:20*

headlong

of froward is carried *h*. *Job* 5:13
might cast him down *h*. *Luke* 4:29
falling *h*. he burst. *Acts* 1:18

heads

they bowed down their *h*. *Gen* 43:28
Ex 4:31
uncover not your *h*. lest. *Lev* 10:6
and put dust upon their *h*. *Josh* 7:6
Job 2:12
they lifted up their *h*. no. *Judg* 8:28
did God render upon their *h*. 9:57
it not be with the *h*. *1 Sam* 29:4
put ropes on our *h*. *1 Ki* 20:31
put ropes on their *h*. and came. 32
take ye the *h*. of your. *2 Ki* 10:6
they have brought the *h*. of the. 8
lift up your *h*. O ye gates. *Ps* 24:7, 9
caused men to ride over our *h*. 66:12
brakest the *h*. of the dragons. 74:13
thou brakest the *h*. of leviathan. 14
on me, they shaked their *h*. 109:25
their *h*. shall be baldness. *Isa* 15:2
everlasting joy on their *h*. 35:10
and covered their *h*. *Jer* 14:3
ashamed, they covered their *h*. 4
shall be on all their *h*. *Ezek* 7:18
their way on their *h*. 11:21; 22:31
their swords under their *h*. 32:27
have linen bonnets on their *h*. 44:18
they shall poll their *h*. 20

reviled, wagging their *h. Mat* 27:39
              Mark 15:29
up, and lift up your *h. Luke* 21:28
blood be upon your own *h. Acts* 18:6
on their *h.* were as it were. *Rev* 9:7
were like to serpents, and had *h.* 19
having seven *h.* and on his *h.* 13:1
his *h.* as it were wounded to. 3
seven *h.* are seven mountains. 17:9
they cast dust on their *h.* 18:19

heads for governors
and made them *h.* over. *Ex* 18:25
were *h.* of thousands. *Num* 11:16
take all the *h.* of the people. 25:4*
and Gad answered the *h. Josh* 22:21
Joshua called for their *h.* and. 23:2
the *h.* of Israel were. *1 Chr* 12:32
assembled all the *h.* to. *2 Chr* 5:2
certain of the *h.* of Ephraim. 28:12
shall wound the *h.* over. *Ps* 110:6
O *h.* of Jacob, and. *Mi* 3:1, 9
h. thereof judge for reward. 11

see **fathers**

headstone
is become the *h.* of the. *Ps* 118:22
bring forth the *h.* with. *Zech* 4:7†

heady
for men shall be *h.* *2 Tim* 3:4*

heal
h. her now, O God. *Num* 12:13
alive, I wound, I *h. Deut* 32:39
I will *h.* thee, and add. *2 Ki* 20:5
sign that the Lord will *h.* me ?
their sin, and will *h. 2 Chr* 7:14
O Lord, *h.* me, for my. *Ps* 6:2
h. my soul, for I have sinned. 41:4
h. the breaches thereof, for. 60:2
to kill, and a time to *h. Eccl* 3:3
smite and *h.* it, and he shall *h.* them.
              Isa 19:22
his ways, and will *h.* him. 57:18, 19
return, and I will *h.* your. *Jer* 3:22
h. me, O Lord, and I shall be. 17:14
I will *h.* thee of thy wounds. 30:17
breach is great, who can *h.* thee ?
              Lam 2:13
yet could he not *h.* you. *Hos* 5:13
he hath torn, and will *h.* us. 6:1
I will *h.* their backsliding, I. 14:4
he shall not *h.* that that. *Zech* 11:16
I will come and *h.* him. *Mat* 8:7
to *h.* all manner of sickness. 10:1
              Mark 3:15
h. the sick, cleanse the lepers.
    Mat 10:8; *Luke* 9:2; 10:9
is it lawful to *h.* on the sabbath days ?
    Mat 12:10; *Luke* 14:3
I should *h.* them. *Mat* 13:15
   John 12:40; *Acts* 28:27
whether he would *h.* on sabbath.
     Mark 3:2; *Luke* 6:7
he hath sent me to *h.* the. *Luke* 4:18
ye will surely say, Physician, *h.* 23
the Lord was present to *h.* 5:17
that he would come and *h.* his. 7:3*
would come down and *h. John* 4:47
forth thine hand to *h. Acts* 4:30

healed
God *h.* Abimelech and. *Gen* 20:17
him to be thoroughly *h. Ex* 21:19
the bile is *h. Lev* 13:18
the scall is *h.* 37
the plague of leprosy be *h.* 14:3, 48
thou canst not be *h. Deut* 28:27
then he shall be *h. 1 Sam* 6:3
have *h.* the waters. *2 Ki* 2:21
waters were *h.* 22
king Joram went to be *h.* in. 8:29
Joram was returned to be *h.* 9:15
           2 Chr 22:6
Lord hearkened and. *2 Chr* 30:20
thee, and thou hast *h.* me. *Ps* 30:2
sent his word, and *h.* them. 107:20
and convert, and be *h. Isa* 6:10
and with his stripes we are *h.* 53:5
have *h.* the hurt. *Jer* 6:14; 8:11
which refuseth to be *h.* 15:18
O Lord, and I shall be *h.* 17:14
balm, if so be she may be *h.* 51:8
h. Babylon, but she is not *h.* 9
not be bound up to be *h. Ezek* 30:21
neither have ye *h.* that which. 34:4

---

the waters shall be *h. Ezek* 47:8, 9
marishes thereof shall not be *h.* 11
I would have *h.* Israel. *Hos* 7:1
but they knew not that I *h.* 11:3
the palsy, and he *h. Mat* 4:24
speak, and my servant shall be *h.*
     Mat 8:8; *Luke* 7:7
multitudes followed him, he *h.*
     Mat 12:15; 14:14
that she may be *h.* and. *Mark* 5:23*
all, nor could be *h.* of. *Luke* 8:43
therefore come and be *h.* and. 13:14
when he saw that he was *h.* 17:15
touched his ear, and *h.* him. 22:51
he that was *h.* wist not. *John* 5:13
the man who was *h. Acts* 4:14
and they were *h.* every one. 5:16
that he had faith to be *h.* 14:9*
Paul prayed, and *h.* father of. 28:8
but let it rather be *h. Heb* 12:13
another, that ye may be *h. Jas* 5:16
whose stripes ye were *h. I Pet* 2:24
deadly wound was *h. Rev* 13:3, 12

healer
I will not be an *h. Isa* 3:7

healeth
the Lord that *h.* thee. *Ex* 15:26
who *h.* all thy diseases. *Ps* 103:3
he *h.* the broken in heart. 147:3
and he *h.* the stroke. *Isa* 30:26

healing, substantive
no *h.* for us, the time of *h. Jer* 14:19
is no *h.* of thy bruise. *Nah* 3:19*
Sun of righteousness arise with *h.*
            Mal 4:2
that had need of *h. Luke* 9:11
on whom this miracle of *h. Acts* 4:22
another the gift of *h. 1 Cor* 12:9, 28
have all the gifts of *h.?* 30
leaves of tree were for *h. Rev* 22:2

healing
thou hast no *h.* medicine. *Jer* 30:13
went about *h.* all manner. *Mat* 4:23
preaching gospel, and *h. Luke* 9:6
h. all that were oppressed of the.
         Acts 10:38

health
our father is in good *h. Gen* 43:28
Joab said, Art thou in *h.? 2 Sam* 20:9
who is the *h.* of my countenance.
      Ps 42:11†; 43:5†
thy saving *h.* may be known. 67:2
it shall be *h.* to thy navel. *Pr* 3:8
they are *h.* to all their flesh. 4:22
the tongue of the wise is *h.* 12:18
but a faithful ambassador is *h.* 13:17
sweet to the soul, and *h.* to. 16:24
thy *h.* shall spring forth. *Isa* 58:8
looked for a time of *h. Jer* 8:15
why is not the *h.* of my people ? 22
I will restore *h.* unto thee. 30:17
I will bring it *h.* and cure. 33:6
for this is for your *h. Acts* 27:34*
mayest be in *h.* as thy soul. *3 John* 2

heap, substantive
h. and did eat on the *h. Gen* 31:46
this *h.* be witness, and this pillar. 52
floods stood upright as an *h. Ex* 15:8
     Josh 3:13, 16; *Ps* 33:7; 78:13
shall be an *h.* for ever. *Deut* 13:16
over him a great *h.* of. *Josh* 7:26
burnt Ai, and made it an *h.* 8:28
raise on the king of Ai a great *h.* 29
down at the end of the *h. Ruth* 3:7
they laid very great *h. 2 Sam* 18:17
thy belly is like an *h.* of. *S of S* 7:2
shall be a ruinous *h. Isa* 17:1
harvest shall be an *h.* in the. 11*
thou hast made of a city an *h.* 25:2
builded on her own *h. Jer* 30:18
Rabbah shall be a desolate *h.* 49:2
make Samaria as an *h. Mi* 1:6
didst walk through the *h. Hab* 3:15
one came to an *h.* of. *Hag* 2:16

heap
I will *h.* mischiefs upon. *Deut* 32:23
I could *h.* up words. *Job* 16:4*
though he *h.* up silver as. 27:16
the hypocrites in heart. 36:13*
thou shalt *h.* coals of fire. *Pr* 25:22
           Rom 12:20
to gather and to *h.* up. *Eccl* 2:26

---

h. on wood, kindle fire. *Ezek* 24:10
for they shall *h.* dust. *Hab* 1:10
h. to themselves teachers. *2 Tim* 4:3

heaped
Tyrus *h.* up silver as. *Zech* 9:3
ye have *h.* treasure. *Jas* 5:3*

heapeth
he *h.* up riches, and. *Ps* 39:6
he *h.* unto him all people. *Hab* 2:5

heaps
them together on *h. Ex* 8:14
bone of an ass, *h.* on *h. Judg* 15:16
lay ye them in two *h. 2 Ki* 10:8
fenced cities into ruinous *h.* 19:25
and laid them by *h. 2 Chr* 31:6
month they began to lay the *h.* 7
princes came and saw the *h.* 8
revive stones out of the *h.? Neh* 4:2
are ready to become *h. Job* 15:28
have laid Jerusalem on *h. Ps* 79:1
make Jerusalem *h. Jer* 9:11; 26:18
way marks, make thee high *h.* 31:21
cast Babylon up as *h.* and. 50:26
and Babylon shall become *h.* 51:37
their altars are as *h.* in. *Hos* 12:11
Jerusalem shall become *h. Mi* 3:12

hear
(*This word is often used for listening to the word of God with a firm purpose to obey his commands. It is also used of God hearing prayer, in the sense of answering, or granting it*)
that all that *h.* will laugh. *Gen* 21:6
h. us, my lord, thou art a. 23:6
that the people may *h. Ex* 19:9
noise of them that sing do I *h.* 32:18
h. I pray you, ye sons. *Num* 16:8
rise up, Balak, and *h.* 23:18
and her father *h.* her vow. 30:4
h. the cause between. *Deut* 1:16
and I will make them *h.* my. 4:10
h. Israel the statutes. 5:1; 6:3; 9:1
  20:3; *Isa* 48:1; *Mark* 12:29
and *h.* all that the Lord. *Deut* 5:27
h. all these words which I. 12:28
if thou shalt *h.* say in one. 13:12
bring it, that we may *h.* 30:12, 13
that they may *h.* and fear Lord.
     31:12, 13; *Jer* 6:10
h. the words of the Lord. *Josh* 3:9
when ye hear the sound of trumpet.
   6:5; *Neh* 4:20; *Dan* 3:5, 15
h. O ye kings, give ear. *Judg* 5:3
why abodest, to *h.* bleatings of ? 16
riddle, that we may *h.* it. 14:13
for I *h.* of your evil. *1 Sam* 2:23
it is no good report that I *h.* 24
lowing of the oxen which I *h.* 15:14
how can I go ? if Saul *h.* it. 16:2
h. the words of thy handmaid. 25:24
          2 Sam 20:17
let my lord the king *h. 1 Sam* 26:19
no man deputed of the king to *h.*
          2 Sam 15:3
as soon as ye *h.* the sound of. 10
what thing soever thou shalt *h.* 35
send to me every thing that ye *h.* 36
h. likewise what Hushai saith. 17:5
woman cried out of city, *h.* 20:16
as soon as they *h.*, they shall be
obedient. 22:45; *Ps* 18:44
to *h.* the wisdom of Solomon.
  1 Ki 4:34; 10:8, 24; *2 Chr* 9:7, 23
    Mat 12:42; *Luke* 11:31
and *h.* thou in heaven. *1 Ki* 8:30
  32, 34, 36, 39, 43, 45, 49; *2 Chr* 6:21
saying, O Baal, *h.* us. *1 Ki* 18:26
made the host to *h.* a. *2 Ki* 7:6
h. the word of the great king. 18:28
           Isa 36:13
h. the words of Sennacherib.
    2 Ki 19:16; *Isa* 37:17
when thou shalt *h.* 1 Chr* 14:15
thou mayest *h.* prayer. *Neh* 1:6*
h. O our God, for we are. 4:4
and all that could *h.* with. 8:2
h. it, and know thou it. *Job* 5:27
h. diligently my speech. 13:17; 21:2
will God *h.* his cry ? 27:9
h. my words. 34:2
h. I beseech thee, and I will. 42:4

have mercy upon me, h.   *Ps* 4:1
   39:12; 54:2; 84:8; 102:1; 143:1
the Lord h. thee in the day.   20:1*
save, Lord, let the king h. us.   9*
h. O Lord, when I cry with.   27:7
h. O Lord, and have mercy.   30:10
h. this, all ye people, give ear.   49:1
make me to h. joy and.   50:7; 81:8
for who, say they, doth h.?   59:7
h. my cry, O God, attend to.   61:1
come, and h., all ye that fear.   66:16
h. groaning of the prisoner.   102:20
when they h. the words of.   138:4
me to h. thy lovingkindness.   143:8
my son, h. the instruction.   *Pr* 1:8
h. ye children, the instruction.   4:1
h. O my son, and receive. 10; 19:20
h. for I will speak of excellent.   8:6
h. instruction, and be wise.   33
cease to h. instruction.   19:27
bow thine ear, h. the words.   22:17
h. thou, my son, be wise.   23:19
and be more ready to h.   *Eccl* 5:1
it is better to h. the rebuke.   7:5
let us h. the conclusion of.   12:13
voice, cause me to h. it. *S of S* 8:13
h. O heavens, and give ear.   *Isa* 1:2
h. ye indeed, but.   6:9; *Mark* 4:12
when he bloweth, h. ye.   *Isa* 18:3
h. ye that are afar off what.   33:13
let the earth h. and all that.   34:1
h. ye deaf.   42:18
who will h. for time to come ?   23
or let them h. and say, It is.   43:9
assemble yourselves and h.   48:14
h. ye this, I have not spoken.   16
h. and your soul shall live.   55:3
                 John 5:25
shall I h. the sound of ?   *Jer* 4:21
therefore h. ye nations.   6:18
h. O earth.   19
h. ye the words of this.   11:2, 6
who refused to h.   10; 13:10
h. ye, give ear, for the Lord.   13:15
then I will cause thee to h.   18:2
caused my people to h. my.   23:22
if the princes h. that I have.   38:25
therefore h. counsel of. 49:20; 50:45
h. I pray you, all.   *Lam* 1:18
h. what I say.   *Ezek* 2:8
h. at my mouth.   3:17; 33:7
he that heareth, let him h.   3:27
lying to my people, that h.   13:19
h. what is the word that.   33:30
they h. thy words, but will not. 31, 32
O God, h. the prayer of. *Dan* 9:17*
O Lord, h. O Lord, forgive.   19
h. ye this, O priests.   *Hos* 5:1
h. this, ye old men.   *Joel* 1:2
h. this word that the Lord hath
   spoken. *Amos* 3:1; 4:1; 5:1; 8:4
h. all ye people, hearken.   *Mi* 1:2
I said, h. I pray you, O.   3:1, 9
h. ye, O mountains.   6:2
h. ye the rod and him.   9
all that h. the bruit of.   *Nah* 3:19
lest they should h. law.   *Zech* 7:12
the things which ye h.   *Mat* 11:4
lame walk, and deaf h.   5
         Mark 7:37; *Luke* 7:22
to h. those things that ye h.
       Mat 13:17; *Luke* 10:24
he said to multitude h.   *Mat* 15:10
beloved Son, h. him. 17:5; *Mark* 9:7
neglect to h. them, to h. *Mat* 18:17
are such as h. the word. *Mark* 4:18
          20; *Luke* 8:12, 13
heed what ye h. you that h. more.
                Mark 4:24
pressed on him to h.   *Luke* 5:1
multitudes came together to h.   15
which came to h. him, and to. 6:17
I say to you which h. love your.   27
heed therefore how ye h.   8:18
which h. the word and. 21; 11:28
but who is this of whom I h.?   9:9
publicans and sinners to h. him. 15:1
said, How is it that I h. this ? 16:2
and prophets let them h. them.   29
Lord said, h. what the unjust. 18:6
were very attentive to h. him. 19:48*
to him in temple, for to h. him. 21:38
as I h. I judge.   *John* 5:30

who can h. it ?   *John* 6:60
law judge a man before it h.?   7:51
wherefore would ye h. it again ? 9:27
sheep h. his voice, and he.   10:3
if any man h. my words.   12:47
and the word which ye h. is.   14:24
how h. we every man ?   *Acts* 2:8
this, which ye now see and h.   33
send for thee, and to h.   10:22
to h. all things that are.   33
desired to h. the word of God. 13:7
whole city came together to h.   44
by my mouth should h. the.   15:7
either to tell or to h. some.   17:21
ye h. Paul hath turned.   19:26
h. ye my defence which I make. 22:1
that thou wouldest h. us of.   24:4
Agrippa said, I would h.   25:22
but we desire to h. what.   28:22
I h. there be divisions. *1 Cor* 11:18
or else be absent, I may h. *Phil* 1:27
we h. that some walk. *2 Thes* 3:11
thyself and them that h. *1 Tim* 4:16
all the Gentiles might h. *2 Tim* 4:17
let every one be swift to h. *Jas* 1:19
we know that he h. us. *1 John* 5:15
than to h. my children.   *3 John* 4
blessed that h. words of.   *Rev* 1:3
which neither can see, nor h.   9:20

see ear, ears, voice

hear me

shall Pharaoh h. me ?   *Ex* 6:12
h. me, O Lord, h. me.   *1 Ki* 18:37
h. me, my brethren.   *1 Chr* 28:2
h. me, thou Jeroboam.   *2 Chr* 13:4
h. me, Asa.   15:2
and h. me, and h. me, O Judah. 20:20
h. me, ye Levites, sanctify.   29:5
I will shew thee, h. me, I. *Job* 15:17
O that one would h. me, my.   31:35
h. me when I call, O God.   *Ps* 4:1*
consider, and h. me, O Lord.   13:3*
upon thee, for thou wilt h. me. 17:6*
h. me, lest they should rejoice. 38:16
attend unto me, and h. me.   55:2*
thy right hand, and h. me.   60:5*
multitude of thy mercy h. me. 69:13*
trouble, h. me speedily.   17*; 143:7
God, my God will h. me.   *Mi* 7:7
I beseech thee, h. me.   *Acts* 26:3
also all that h. me, were such.   29
that will they not h. me. *1 Cor* 14:21

hear not, or not hear

wilt not h. but worship. *Deut* 30:17
the Lord will not h.   *1 Sam* 8:18*
and thou dost not h. me. *Job* 30:20*
surely God will not h. vanity. 35:13
Lord will not h. me.   *Ps* 66:18
the ear, shall he not h.?   94:9
many prayers, I will not h. *Isa* 1:15
      Jer 7:16; 11:14; 14:12
      Ezek 8:18; *Amos* 5:23
children that will not h. law. *Isa* 30:9
ear heavy that it cannot h.   59:1
he will not h.   2
when I spake ye did not h.   65:12
when I spake, they did not h.   66:4
                 Zech 1:4
have ears and h. not.   *Ezek* 12:2; *Mark* 8:18
but if ye will not h.   22:5; *Mal* 2:2
that they might not h.   *Jer* 17:23
        19:15; *Zech* 7:11
thou saidst, I will not h. *Jer* 22:21
praised the gods of silver, which see
   not, nor h. *Dan* 5:23; *Rev* 9:20
Lord, but he will not h.   *Mi* 3:4
I cry, and thou wilt not h. *Hab* 1:2
not receive you, nor h. *Mat* 10:14
if he will not h. thee, then.   18:17
if they h. not Moses.   *Luke* 16:31
even because ye cannot h. *John* 8:43
therefore h. them not, because.   47
I told you, and ye did not h.   9:27
but the sheep did not h. them. 10:8
soul which will not h.   *Acts* 3:23
will they not h. me.   *1 Cor* 14:21
do ye not h. the law ?   *Gal* 4:21

would not hear

besought us, we would not h.
               Gen 42:21
against the child, ye would not h. 22

thou wouldest not h.   *Ex* 7:16
Israel would not h. *Deut* 1:43; 3:26
   2 Ki 17:14; 18:12; *Neh* 9:29
               Zech 7:13
Amaziah would not h.   *2 Ki* 14:11
             2 Chr 25:20
this is the refreshing: yet they would
   not h.   *Isa* 28:12
might be for praise, they would not h.
          Jer 13:11; 29:19
he would not h.   36:25
I would not h.   *Zech* 7:13

hear now, or now hear

and he said, h. now my words.
       Num 12:6; 20:10
Saul said, h. now, ye.   *1 Sam* 22:7
h. now, thou son of Ahitub.   12
h. now my reasoning.   *Job* 13:6
h. me now, therefore, O.   *Pr* 5:7
and he said, h. ye now.   *Isa* 7:13
now h. O Jacob my servant.   44:1
h. now, thou that art given to. 47:8
therefore, h. now this, thou.   51:21
h. now this, O foolish.   *Jer* 5:21
h. now, Hananiah.   28:15
now, O Joshua.   *Zech* 3:8
h. not, I pray thee, O my.   37:20
h. ye now what the Lord.   *Mi* 6:1
which ye now see and h. *Acts* 2:33
in me, and now h. to be in. *Phil* 1:30

shall hear

the people shall h. and.   *Ex* 15:14
   Deut 13:11; 17:13; 19:20; 21:21
the Egyptians shall h. it. *Num* 14:13
ye shall h. small as well. *Deut* 1:17
who shall h. report of thee.   2:25
which shall h. all these statutes. 4:6
of the land shall h. of it.   *Josh* 7:9
and thou shalt h. what.   *Judg* 7:11
Israel shall h. that.   *2 Sam* 16:21
shall h. of thy great.   *1 Ki* 8:42
and he shall h. a rumour. *2 Ki* 19:7
               Isa 37:7
prayer to him, he shall h. *Job* 22:27
humble shall h. thereof.   *Ps* 34:2
cry, and the Lord h. my voice. 55:17
God shall h. and afflict them.   19
mine ears shall h. desire of.   92:11
they shall h. my words.   141:6
day shall the deaf h.   *Isa* 29:18
when he shall h. it he will.   30:19
thine ears shall h. a word.   21
shall h. all the good.   *Jer* 33:9
and the heaven shall h.   *Hos* 2:21
the earth shall h. the corn and.   22
by hearing, ye shall h.   *Mat* 13:14
             Acts 28:26
if he shall h. thee thou. *Mat* 18:15
ye shall h. of wars.   24:6
     Mark 13:7; *Luke* 21:9
dead shall h. voice of.   *John* 5:25
whatsoever he shall h. that.   16:13
him shall ye h. in all things.
        Acts 3:22; 7:37
said he, thou shalt h. him.   25:22
shall they h. without a.   *Rom* 10:14

will hear

speak unto us, we will h.   *Ex* 20:19
             Deut 5:27
if they cry, I will surely h. 22:23, 27
I will h. what the Lord.   *Num* 9:8
king will h. to deliver.   *2 Sam* 14:16
be thy God will h. the.   *2 Ki* 19:4
then will I h. from heaven.
       2 Chr 7:14; *Ps* 20:6
wilt h. and help. *2 Chr* 20:9; *Ps* 38:15
the Lord will h.   *Ps* 4:3
thou wilt h. me.   17:6
I will h. what God the Lord.   85:8
he also will h. their cry, and. 145:19
man will h. and increase.   *Pr* 1:5
the Lord will h. them.   *Isa* 41:17*
are yet speaking, I will h.   65:24
house of Judah will h.   *Jer* 36:3
whether they will h. or forbear.
       Ezek 2:5, 7; 3:11
I will h. the heavens.   *Hos* 2:21
God, my God will h. me.   *Mi* 7:7
I am their God and will h. them.
       Zech 10:6; 13:9
we will h. thee again of. *Acts* 17:32
for they will h. that thou.   21:22

I *will h.* thee, when thy. *Acts* 23:35
to the Gentiles, they *will h.*   28:28

hear *the word of the Lord.*
h. therefore *the word of the Lord.*
    1 Ki 22:19; *2 Chr* 18:18
    Jer 29:20; 42:15; *Amos* 7:16
Elisha said *h.* ye *word of the Lord.*
    2 Ki 7:1; *Jer* 17:20; 21:11
Hezekiah, *H. the word of Lord.*
    2 Ki 20:16; *Isa* 39:5
h. word of the Lord, ye rulers of
    Sodom.   *Isa* 1:10
h. the word of the Lord, ye scornful
    men.   28:14
h. word of Lord, ye that tremble. 66:5
h. word of Lord, O house of Jacob.
    Jer 2:4; 10:1
h. the word of the Lord, all ye of. 7:2
yet *h. word of the Lord,* O ye.   9:20
h. word of Lord, O kings of Judah.
    19:3; 22:2
earth, *h. the word of the Lord.* 22:29
h. the word of Lord, O ye nations.
    31:10
h. word of Lord, O Zedekiah.   34:4
h. the word of the Lord, all Judah.
    44:24, 26
of Israel, *h. the word of the Lord,* I
    will bring a.   *Ezek* 6:3; 36:1, 4
prophets *h.* ye *the word of the Lord.*
    13:2
O harlot, *h. the word of the Lord.*
    16:35
forest of the south, *H. the word of the*
    Lord.   20:47
Ammonites, *h. the word of the Lord.*
    25:3
shepherds, *h. the word of the Lord.*
    34:7, 9
dry bones, *h. the word of the Lord.*
    37:4
h. word of the Lord, ye children.
    Hos 4:1
Amaziah, *h.* thou *the word of the*
    Lord.   *Amos* 7:16

heard
because Lord hath *h.*   *Gen* 16:11
neither yet *h.* I of it, but.   21:26
because the Lord hath *h.* that. 29:33
aloud, and the Egyptians *h.*   45:2
God *h.* their groaning.   *Ex* 2:24
he hath *h.* your murmurings.   16:9
neither let it be *h.* out of thy. 23:13
sound shall be *h.* when he.   28:35
people *h.* these evil tidings.   33:4
let all that *h.* him lay.   *Lev* 24:14
complained, the Lord *h.* *Num* 11:1
against Moses, the Lord *h.* it. 12:2
they have *h.* thou art among. 14:14
nations which have *h.* the fame.   15
in the day that *h.* it.   30:7, 14
they *h.* that they were. *Josh* 9:16
Samuel cried, and the Lord *h.* him.
    1 Sam 7:9*
come, as thy servant hath *h.?* 23:11
hast not *h.* that Adonijah ? *1 Ki* 1:11
nor was any tool of iron *h.* in.   6:7
and prosperity exceedeth fame which
    I *h.*   10:7; *2 Chr* 9:6
hast thou not *h.* long ago?
    2 Ki 19:25; *Isa* 37:26
make one sound to be *h.* *2 Chr* 5:13
he was entreated and *h.* his. 33:13
the noise was *h.* afar.   *Ezra* 3:13
the joy of Jerusalem *h.* *Neh* 12:43
h. the secret of God ?   *Job* 15:8
of wrong, but I am not *h.*   19:7
but how little a portion is *h.* 26:14
when the ear *h.* me, then it. 29:11
the Lord hath *h.* my.   *Ps* 6:9
thou hast *h.* the desire of.   10:17
save me, for thou hast *h.*   22:21*
but when he cried *h.*   24; 34:6
    40:1; 120:1
I sought the Lord, and he *h.*   34:4*
but I as a deaf man *h.* not.   38:13
thou, O God, hast *h.* my vows. 61:5
verily God hath *h.* me, he.   66:19
cause judgement to be *h.*   76:8
therefore the Lord *h.* this and. 78:21
when God *h.* this, was wroth.   59
where I *h.* a language that I.   81:5
Zion *h.* and was glad, and.   97:8

their affliction, when he *h. Ps* 106:44
for thou hast *h.* me, and.   118:21*
lo, we *h.* of it at Ephratah.   132:6
cry himself, but not be *h.*   *Pr* 21:13
to be *h.* unto Laish.   *Isa* 10:30
have ye not *h.?* hath it not ?   40:21
hast thou not *h.* everlasting God ? 28
thou hast *h.* see all this, will ? 48:6
which they had not *h.* shall.   52:15
violence shall no more be *h.* in. 60:18
men have not *h.* what he hath. 64:4
weeping shall be no more *h.*   65:19
who hath *h.* such a thing ?   66:8
isles afar off, that have not *h.*   19
thou hast *h.* the sound.   *Jer* 4:19
wickedness, spoil is *h.* in her.   6:7
rising early, but ye *h.* not.   7:13
hearkened and *h.* but they.   8:6
ask the heathen, who hath *h.* 18:13
let cry be *h.* from houses when. 22
howling of the flock shall be *h.* 25:36
prophesied as ye have *h.*   26:11
h. every one should let his.   34:10
spoken, but they have not *h.* 35:17
the nations have *h.* of thy.   46:12
and the cry is *h.* among.   50:46
a rumour that shall be *h.* in. 51:46
they have *h.* that I sigh.   *Lam* 1:21
thou hast *h.* their reproach.   3:61
the nations *h.* of him.   *Ezek* 19:4
thy harps shall be no more *h.* 26:13
h. the sound of the trumpet.   33:5
and I *h.* but I understood. *Dan* 12:8
their congregation hath *h. Hos* 7:12
unto Lord, and he *h.* me. *Jonah* 2:2*
such as they have not *h.*   *Mi* 5:15
I *h.*, my belly trembled. *Hab* 3:16
Lord hearkened and *h.* it. *Mal* 3:16
ye have *h.* it was said.   *Mat* 5:21
    27, 33, 38, 43
they shall be *h.* for their much. 6:7
ye hear, and have not *h.* them.
    13:17; *Luke* 10:24
offended after they *h.*   *Mat* 15:12
when the king *h.* thereof.   22:7
ye have *h.* his blasphemy.   26:65
    Mark 14:64
but when they have *h.* *Mark* 4:15
and when they *h.* it they.   14:11
fear not, thy prayer is *h. Luke* 1:13
    Acts 10:31
have spoken, shall be *h. Luke* 12:3
when they *h.* it, they said.   20:16
what he hath *h.* that.   *John* 3:32
every man that hath *h.* of the. 6:45
on ground, as though he *h.* not. 8:6
since world began was it not *h.* 9:32
I thank thee that thou hast *h.* 11:41
ask them which *h.* me, what. 18:21
when Simon Peter *h.* that it. 21:7
for the promise ye have *h. Acts* 1:4
h. this, they were pricked.   2:37
many of them which *h.* the.   4:4
fear came on all them that *h.*   5:5
when the Gentiles *h.* this.   13:48
the same *h.* Paul speak, who. 14:9
which worshipped God, *h.* us. 16:14
and the prisoners *h.* them.   25*
h. this, they were baptized.   19:5
of what thou hast seen and *h.* 22:15
h. him concerning the faith.   24:24
of whom they have not *h. Rom* 10:14
but I say, have they not *h.?*   18
they that have not *h.* shall.   15:21
not seen, nor ear *h.*   *1 Cor* 2:9
h. of my conversation.   *Gal* 1:13
after that ye *h.* the word. *Eph* 1:13
h. of your faith in the Lord.   15
if so be ye have *h.* him and.   4:21
that ye had *h.* that he.   *Phil* 2:26
things ye have *h.* and seen.   4:9
since we *h.* of your faith.   *Col* 1:4
since day ye *h.* of it, and knew.   6
since day we *h.* it, do not cease.   9
things thou hast *h.* of me. *2 Tim* 2:2
to us by them that *h.* him. *Heb* 2:3
for some when they had *h.*   3:16
with faith in them that *h.*   4:2
offered up prayers, and was *h.* 5:7
h. of the patience of Job. *Jas* 5:11
ye *h.* that antichrist shall come.
    1 John 2:18; 4:3
have *h.* from the beginning.   2:24
    3:11; *2 John* 6

therefore how thou hast *h.* *Rev* 3:3
and all that are in them *h.*   5:13
I *h.* the number of them which. 7:4
I *h.* the number of the.   9:16
I *h.* the angel of the waters. 16:5
of trumpeters shall be *h.* no. 18:22
the voice of bride shall be *h.* no.   23
things, and *h.* them, when I *h.* 22:8

I have **heard**
Ishmael *I have h.* thee. *Gen* 17:20
dreamed a dream: *I have h.* say that
    thou canst.   41:15; *Dan* 5:14, 16
I have h. there is corn.   *Gen* 42:2
I have h. their cry.   *Ex* 3:7
I have h. the groaning.   6:5
I have h. the murmuring.   16:12
    Num 14:27
I have h. the voice of.   *Deut* 5:28
now *I have h.* that thou. *1 Sam* 25:7
word that *I have h.* is.   *1 Ki* 2:42
I have h. thy prayer thou hast. 9:3
    2 Ki 20:5; *2 Chr* 7:12; *Isa* 38:5
which thou hast prayed *I have h.*
    2 Ki 19:20
I also have h. thee, saith Lord.
    22:19; *2 Chr* 34:27
I have h. many such things. *Job* 16:2
I have h. the check of my.   20:3
I have h. of thee by the hearing. 42:5
for *I have h.* slander.   *Ps* 31:13
twice *I have h.* this, power.   62:11
that which *I have h.* of.   *Isa* 21:10
I have h. from the Lord a.   28:22
in an acceptable time have I *h.* 49:8*
    2 Cor 6:2
I have h. what prophets. *Jer* 23:25
I have h. Ephraim bemoaning. 31:18
I have h. you, behold, I will.   42:4
I have h. a rumour from.   49:14
know *I have h.* all.   *Ezek* 35:12
I have h. him and.   *Hos* 14:8*
Lord, *I have h.* thy speech. *Hab* 3:2
I have h. the reproach.   *Zeph* 2:8
those things *I have h.*   *John* 8:26
truth, which *I have h.* of God.   40
all things that *I have h.* of.   15:15
I have h. their groaning. *Acts* 7:34
Lord, *I have h.* by many of this. 9:13

heard joined with *voice*
h. voice of the Lord walking. *Gen* 3:8
I *h.* thy *voice*, and was afraid.   10
God *h.* the *voice* of the lad.   21:17
God hath *h.* my *voice*, and.   30:6
h. that I lifted up my *voice*.   39:15
then he *h.* the *voice* of. *Num* 7:89
we cried, he *h.* our *voice*.   20:16
the Lord *h.* the *voice* of. *Deut* 1:34
similitude, only he *h.* a *voice*.   4:12
v. of God as thou hast *h.*   33; 5:26
ye *h.* the *voice* out of the.   5:23
have *h.* his *voice* out of the.   24
and the Lord *h.* the *voice* of your. 28
we cried, the Lord *h.* our *voice*. 26:7
let not thy *voice* be *h.*   *Judg* 18:25
her *voice* was not *h.*   *1 Sam* 1:13
the Lord *h.* the *voice*.   *1 Ki* 17:22
voice was *h.* prayer.   *2 Chr* 30:27
was silence, I *h.* a *voice*.   *Job* 4:16
I have *h.* the *voice* of thy.   33:8
stay them when his *voice* is *h.* 37:4
Lord with my *voice*, he *h.*   *Ps* 3:4
the Lord hath *h.* the *voice* of.   6:8
I called, he *h.* my *voice* out of. 18:6
no speech where their *voice* is not *h.*
    19:3
because he hath *h.* the *voice*. 28:6
the *voice* of his praise to be *h.* 66:8
love the Lord, because he hath *h.* my
    voice.   116:1
voice of the turtle is *h.* *S of S* 2:12
h. the *voice* of the Lord.   *Isa* 6:8
their *voice* shall be *h.* even.   15:4
his glorious *voice* to be *h.*   30:30
nor cause his *voice* to be *h.*   42:2
to make your *voice* be *h.* on.   58:4
voice of weeping shall no more be *h.*
    65:19
a *voice* was *h.* upon the. *Jer* 3:21
h. a *voice* of a woman in.   4:31
voice of wailing is *h.* out of.   9:19
h. a *voice* of trembling.   30:5
a *voice* was *h.* in Ramah.   31:15
    Mat 2:18

hast *h.* my *voice,* hide.   *Lam* 3:56
and I *h.* a *voice* of one.   *Ezek* 1:28
ι *h.* behind me a *voice* of.   3:12
voice should no more be *h.*   19:9
cause their *voice* to be *h.*   27:30
I *h.* a man's *voice* between. *Dan* 8:16
yet *h.* I the *voice* of his words, when
    I *h.*   10:9
voice of thy messengers no more be
    h.   *Nah* 2:13
neither *h.* his *voice.*   *John* 5:37
h. a *voice,* saying, Saul, Saul.
    Acts 9:4; 22:7; 26:14
h. a *voice* saying to me, arise. 11:7
they *h.* not the *voice* of him.   22:9
which *voice* they that *h. Heb* 12:19
voice which came from heaven we *h.*
    2 Pet 1:18
I *h.* a great *voice.*   *Rev* 1:10; 16:1
    19:1; 21:3
the first *voice* I *h.* was as it.   4:1
I beheld, and *h.* the *voice* of.   5:11
I *h.* a *voice* in the midst of the.   6:6
I *h.* the *voice* of the fourth beast. 7
I *h.* a *voice* from the four.   9:13
I *h.* a *voice* from heaven.   10:4, 8
    14:2, 13; 18:4
and I *h.* a loud *voice,* saying. 12:10
I *h.* the *voice* of harpers.   14:2
I *h.* as it were the *voice* of a.   19:6

we have heard

we have h. how the Lord. *Josh* 2:10
as soon as *we had h.* these.   11
we have h. the fame of him.   9:9
thee according to all *we have h.*
    2 Sam 7:22; *1 Chr* 17:20
we have h. kings of Israel are.
    1 Ki 20:31
we have h. the fame thereof.
    Job 28:22; *Jer* 6:24
we have h. with our ears.   *Ps* 44:1
as *we have h.* so have we.   48:8
dark sayings which *we have h.* 78:3
we have h. of pride of Moab.
    Isa 16:6; *Jer* 48:29
we have h. songs, glory. *Isa* 24:16
we have h. a voice.   *Jer* 30:5
because *we have h.* reproach. 51:51
we have h. a rumour from.   *Ob* 1
for *we have h.* that God. *Zech* 8:23
we have h. him say, I. *Mark* 14:58
whatsoever *we have h.* done in
    Capernaum.   *Luke* 4:23
we ourselves have h. of his. 22:71
we believe, we have h.   *John* 4:42
we have h. out of the law.   12:34
speak things *we have h. Acts* 4:20
we have h. him speak.   6:11
we have h. him say, this Jesus. 14
we have h. that certain.   15:24
we have not h. whether there. 19:2
to things which *we have h. Heb* 2:1
that which *we have h. 1 John* 1:1, 3
message which *we have h.* of him. 5

heard joined with *word* or *words*
when he *h.* the *words* of. *Gen* 24:30
Abraham's servant *h.* their *words.* 52
and when Esau *h.* the *words.* 27:34
Jacob *h.* the *words* of Laban's. 31:1
when his master *h.* the *words.* 39:19
h. words of God.   *Num* 24:4, 16
heads of Israel *h.* words. *Josh* 22:30
for it hath *h.* all the *words* of. 24:27
when Zebul *h.* the *words. Judg* 9:30
Samuel *h.* all the *words.* *1 Sam* 8:21
Israel *h.* Goliath's *words.*   17:11
the same *words,* and David *h.*   23
words were *h.* which David.   31
the *word* that I have *h.* is good.
    1 Ki 2:42
Hiram *h.* Solomon's *words.*   5:7
when Ahab *h.* those *words.*   21:27
when the king *h.* words. *2 Ki* 6:30
be not afraid of *words* thou hast *h.*
    19:6; *Isa* 37:6
h. the *words* of book of law, he rent.
    2 Ki 22:11, 18; *2 Chr* 34:19
Asa *h.* these *words.*   *2 Chr* 15:8
I *h.* these *words,* I sat.   *Neh* 1:4
angry when I *h.* these *words.*   5:6
wept, when they *h. words.*   8:9
h. the *voice* of thy *words,* saying.
    Job 33:8

man's *words* are not *h.*   *Eccl* 9:16
the *words* of wise men are *h.* in. 17
words which God hath *h. Isa* 37:4
marked, and *h.* his *word. Jer* 23:18
ye have not *h.* my *words.*   25:8
city all the *words* ye have *h.* 26:12
all the princes *h.* his *words.*   21
them all the *words* he had *h.* 36:13
not afraid that *h.* these *words.*   24
Pashur *h.* the *words* Jeremiah. 38:1
Darius *h.* these *words.*   *Dan* 6:14
thy *words* were *h.,* and I am. 10:12
they *h.* these *words.*   *Mat* 22:22
as soon as Jesus *h.* the *word.*
    Mark 5:36
Jesus' feet, and *h.* his *words.*
    Luke 10:39
fell on them who *h. word. Acts* 10:44
h. unspeakable *words.*   *2 Cor* 12:4
ye *h.* the *word* of truth.   *Eph* 1:13
ye *h.* in the *word* of the.   *Col* 1:5
word which ye *h.* of us. *1 Thes* 2:13
sound *words* thou hast *h.* of me.
    2 Tim 1:13
h. intreated that *word. Heb* 12:19
the *word* ye have *h.* from the.
    1 John 2:7

heardest

and thou *h.* his words.   *Deut* 4:36
for thou *h.* in that day. *Josh* 14:12
h. what I spake against this place.
    2 Ki 22:19; *2 Chr* 34:27
and thou *h.* their cry by.   *Neh* 9:9
thou *h.* them from heaven.   27, 28
thou *h.* the *voice* of my.   *Ps* 31:22
my ways, and thou *h.* me.   119:26*
the day when thou *h.*   *Isa* 48:7
yea, thou *h.* not, yea, thou.   8
of hell I cried, thou *h. Jonah* 2:2

hearer

if any be a *h.* of the word. *Jas* 1:23
he being not a forgetful *h.* but.   25

hearers

the *h.* of the law are.   *Rom* 2:13
minister grace unto *h.*   *Eph* 4:29
the subverting of the *h.* *2 Tim* 2:14
doers of word, and not *h.*   *Jas* 1:22

hearest

Boaz to Ruth, *h.* thou ?   *Ruth* 2:8
h. thou men's words ? *1 Sam* 24:9
when *h.* sound in the.   *2 Sam* 5:24
when thou *h.* forgive.   *1 Ki* 8:30
    2 Chr 6:21
daytime, but thou *h.* not.   *Ps* 22:2*
thou that *h.* prayer, unto thee. 65:2
said unto him, *h.* thou ? *Mat* 21:16
h. thou not how many things ? 27:13
wind bloweth, and thou *h. John* 3:8
and I knew that thou *h.* me.   11:42

heareth

for that he *h.* your murmurings.
    Ex 16:7, 8
disallow her in day that he *h.*
    Num 30:5
when he *h.* the words of. *Deut* 29:19
for thy servant *h.*   *1 Sam* 3:9, 10
at which ears of every one that *h.*
    11; *2 Ki* 21:12; *Jer* 19:3
whosoever *h.* it will say. *2 Sam* 17:9
and he *h.* the cry of the. *Job* 34:28
cry, and the Lord *h.*   *Ps* 34:17
thus I was as a man that *h.* not. 38:14
Lord *h.* poor, and despiseth. 69:33
blessed is the man that *h. Pr* 8:34
a wise son *h.* his father's.   13:1
ransom his riches, but the poor *h.* 8
but he *h.* the prayer of the.   15:29
that *h.* the reproof of life.   31, 32
a matter before he *h.* it.   18:13
the man that *h.* speaketh.   21:28
lest he that *h.* it put thee.   25:10
h. cursing, and bewrayeth it. 29:24
there is none that *h.*   *Isa* 41:26
opening the ears, but he *h.* not. 42:20
shalt say, he that *h.*   *Ezek* 3:27
whosoever *h.* the sound of the. 33:4
whoso *h.* these sayings.   *Mat* 7:24
    26; *Luke* 6:47, 49
when any one *h.* word. *Mat* 13:19
is he that *h.* the word.   20, 22, 23

he that *h.* you *h.* me.   *Luke* 10:16
and *h.* him rejoiceth.   *John* 3:29
h. my word, and believeth.   5:24
that is of God *h.* God's words. 8:47
h. not sinners, but if any man be a
    worshipper of God, him he *h.* 9:31
one that is of the truth, *h.*   18:37
me above that he *h.* of.   *2 Cor* 12:6
and the world *h.* them. *1 John* 4:5
he that knoweth God *h.* us.   6
according to his will, he *h.* us. 5:14
let him that *h.* say, Come. *Rev* 22:17
I testify to every man that *h.*   18

hearing

law to Israel in their *h. Deut* 31:11
for in our *h.* the king. *2 Sam* 18:12
was neither voice nor *h.* *2 Ki* 4:31
hast spoken in my *h.*   *Job* 33:8
I have heard of thee by the *h.* 42:5
nor reprove after the *h.* of. *Isa* 11:3
I was bowed down at the *h.* 21:3
that stoppeth his ears from *h.* 33:15
to others he said in my *h. Ezek* 9:5
cried unto them in my *h.* O. 10:13
a famine of the word. *Amos* 8:11
to be reserved to the *h. Acts* 25:21*
entered into the place of *h.*   23
faith cometh by *h.* and *h. Rom* 10:17
the *h.?* if whole were it. *1 Cor* 12:17
or by the *h.* of faith.   *Gal* 3:2, 5
seeing ye are dull of *h.*   *Heb* 5:11

hearing, verb

the *h.* ear, the Lord.   *Pr* 20:12
turneth away the ear from *h.* 28:9
nor is the ear filled with *h. Eccl* 1:8
and *h.* they hear not.   *Mat* 13:13
by *h.* ye shall hear, and shall.   14
their ears dull of *h.*   15; *Acts* 28:27
    Heb 5:11
h. him were astonished.   *Mark* 6:2
h. them and asking.   *Luke* 2:46
Ananias *h.* these words.   *Acts* 5:5
h. and seeing the miracles which. 8:6
men stood, *h.* a voice, but.   9:7
many of the Corinthians *h.*   18:8
h. of thy love and faith.   *Philem* 5
Lot in seeing and *h.*   *2 Pet* 2:8

hearken

how shall Pharaoh *h.?*   *Ex* 6:30
if ye *h.* to these judgements.
    Deut 7:12
if ye will *h.* diligently to my. 11:13
if thou carefully *h.* to voice of. 15:5
    Jer 17:24
to him ye shall *h.*   *Deut* 18:15
if thou *h.* to commandments. 28:13
    1 Ki 11:38
as to Moses, so will we *h. Josh* 1:17
to *h.* than the fat of. *1 Sam* 15:22
for who will *h.* to you in ?   30:24
have thou respect to *h.* to cry.
    1 Ki 8:28
mayest *h.* to the prayer.   29, 52
    2 Chr 6:19, 20
shall we *h.* then to you ? *Neh* 13:27
Israel, if thou wilt *h.*   *Ps* 81:8
if ruler *h.* to lies, servants. *Pr* 29:12
them that hear shall *h.*   *Isa* 32:3
h. and hear for the time.   42:23
if so be they will *h.* and.   *Jer* 26:3
to *h.* to the prophets whom I.   5
pray to me, and I will *h.* unto. 29:12
not receive instruction to *h.* 35:13
refused to *h.,* stopped.   *Zech* 7:11
to *h.* unto you more than. *Acts* 4:19
knocked, a damsel came to *h.* 12:13*

hearken, imperatively

wives of Lamech, *h.* to.   *Gen* 4:23
my lord, *h.* to me.   23:15
h. to Israel your father.   49:2
rise up, *h.* unto me, thou son of.
    Num 23:18
h. O Israel, to statutes. *Deut* 4:1
take heed, and *h.* O Israel.   27:9
he cried, *h.* to me, ye.   *Judg* 9:7
h. to the supplication.   *1 Ki* 8:30
    2 Chr 6:21
he said, *h.* O people.   *1 Ki* 22:28
and he said, *h.* all ye.   *2 Chr* 18:27
h. ye, all Judah, and ye.   20:15
and *h.* to the pleadings of. *Job* 13:6

Job, *h.* unto me. *Job 32:10; 33:31*
h. to all my words. 33:1
h. unto me, ye men of. 34:10
let a wise man *h.* 34
h. to this, O Job. 37:14
h. I will teach you *Ps 34:11*
h. O daughter. 45:10
h. to me, therefore, O children.
  Pr 7:24; 8:32
hear my voice, *h.* and. *Isa 28:23*
come near, ye nations, *h.* 34:1; 49:1
h. to me, O house of Jacob. 46:3
  48:12; *Hos 5:1*
h. to me, stouthearted. *Isa 46:12*
h. to me, ye that follow after. 51:1
h. unto me, my people, give ear. 4
h. to me, ye that know. 7
h. diligently unto me, eat. 55:2
saying, *h.* to the sound. *Jer 6:17*
O Lord, *h.* and do; defer. *Dan 9:19*
h. O earth, and all that. *Mi 1:2*
he said, *h.* to me, every. *Mark 7:14*
ye men of Judah, *h.* to. *Acts 2:14*
men, brethren, and fathers, *h.* 7:2
saying, men and brethren, *h.* 15:13
h. my beloved brethren. *Jas 2:5*
  see **voice**

hearken not, or not **hearken**
if ye will *not h.*, to be. *Gen 34:17*
Pharaoh shall *not h.* to you. *Ex 7:4*
  22; 11:9
but if ye will *not h.* to me. *Lev 26:14*
  18, 21, 27
thou shalt *not h.* to that. *Deut 13:3*
not h. unto him, nor shall thine.
the man that will *not h.* to. 17:12
that whosoever will *not h.* 18:19
chastened, he will *not h.* to. 21:18
not h. to Balaam. 23:5; *Josh 24:10*
will *not h.* to thy words. *Josh 1:18*
yet they would *not h.* to. *Judg 2:17*
king of Edom would *not h.* 11:17
men of Gibeah would *not h.* 19:25
of Benjamin would *not h.* 20:13
elders said, *h. not* to him. *1 Ki 20:8*
did *not h.* but did after. *2 Ki 17:40*
h. not to Hezekiah. 18:31; *Isa 36:16*
Rehoboam would *not h.* *2 Chr 10:16*
spake, but they would *not h.* 33:10
if *not h.* hold thy peace, I. *Job 33:33*
not h. to the voice of. *Ps 58:5*
but my people would *not h.* 81:11
ear is uncircumcised, they *cannot h.*
  Jer 6:10
said, we will *not h.* 17; 44:16
shalt speak, they will *not h.* 7:27
they cry to me, I will *not h.* 11:11
that they may *not h.* to me. 16:12
if ye will *not h.* to me. 17:27
  26:4; *Ezek 20:39*
h. not to words of the prophets.
  Jer. 23:16; 27:9, 14, 16, 17; 29:8
counsel, wilt thou *not h.?* 38:15
not h. to thee, for they will *not h.*
  Ezek 3:7
rebelled, and would *not h.* 20:8
because they did *not h.* to him.
  Hos 9:17; Zech 1:4

hearkened
Abraham *h.* to Ephron. *Gen 23:16*
God *h.* to Leah. 30:17
God *h.* to Rachel. 22
to Hamor *h.* all that went out. 34:24
that Joseph *h.* not to her. 39:10
h. not to Moses. *Ex 6:9; 16:20*
Israel have not *h.* to me. 6:12
Pharaoh *h.* not to them. 7:13
  8:15, 19; 9:12
Lord *h.* to me. *Deut 9:19; 10:10*
these nations *h.* to observers. 18:14
h. to Joshua as to Moses. 34:9
  Josh 1:17
king of Ammonites *h.* *Judg 11:28*
the woman of Endor *h.* *1 Sam 28:21*
king *h.* not to people. *1 Ki 12:15*
  16; *2 Chr 10:15*
h. therefore to the word. *1 Ki 12:24*
Ben-hadah *h.* to king Asa. 15:20
  2 Chr 16:4
and the Lord *h.* to. *2 Ki 13:4*
king of Assyria *h.* to Asa. 16:9
Hezekiah *h.* to messengers. 20:13
Judah *h.* not to the law. 21:9

fathers *h.* not to words. *2 Ki 22:13*
Joash *h.* to princes. *2 Chr 24:17*
Amaziah *h.* not to the. 25:16
Lord *h.* to Hezekiah, and. 30:20
Josiah *h.* not to Pharaoh-necho. 35:22
and *h.* not to thy commandments.
  Neh 9:16, 29, 34; Jer 34:14
now when Mordecai *h.* *Esth 3:4*
that my people had *h.* *Ps 81:13*
and he *h.* diligently with. *Isa 21:7*
O that thou hadst *h.* to my. 48:18
they have not *h.* to my word.
  Jer 6:19; 7:24, 26; 25:3, 4, 7
  26:5; 29:19; 32:33; 34:17; 35:14
  15, 16; 36:31; 44:5
Irijah *h.* not to Jeremiah. 37:14
they would have *h.* to thee. *Ezek 3:6*
neither have we *h.* to thy. *Dan 9:6*
the Lord *h.* and heard it. *Mal 3:16*
  Jer 8:6
sirs, ye should have *h.* *Acts 27:21*
  see **voice**

hearkenedst
h. not to voice of Lord. *Deut 28:45*

hearkeneth
but whoso *h.* to me. *Pr 1:33*
he that *h.* to counsel is wise. 12:15

hearkening
angels *h.* to the voice of. *Ps 103:20*

heart
(The word heart is used in Scripture
as the seat of life or strength; hence
it means mind, soul, spirit, or one's
entire emotional nature and under-
standing. It is also used as the
centre or inner part of a thing)

Jacob's *h.* fainted, for. *Gen 45:26*
for ye know the *h.* of a. *Ex 23:9*
they shall be on Aaron's *h.* 28:30
whoso is of a willing *h.* let. 35:5
he filled with wisdom of *h.* 35
eyes, cause sorrow of *h.* *Lev 26:16*
discourage ye the *h.?* *Num 32:7*
they discouraged the *h.* of the. 9
there were such an *h.* *Deut 5:29*
smite with astonishment of *h.* 28:28
the Lord with gladness of *h.* 47
give thee there a trembling *h.* 65
Lord hath not given you an *h.* to. 29:4
h. of the people melt. *Josh 14:8*
great thoughts of *h.* *Judg 5:15*
there were great searchings of *h.* 16
the priest's *h.* was glad, he. 18:20
now Hannah, she spake in her *h.*
  1 Sam 1:13
that God gave him another *h.* 10:9
but the Lord looketh on the *h.* 16:7
let no man's *h.* fail because. 17:32
David's *h.* smote him, because. 24:5
no grief, nor offence of *h.* 25:31
and Nabal's *h.* was merry within. 36
she despised him in her *h.* *2 Sam 6:16*
  1 Chr 15:29
Amnon's *h.* is merry. *2 Sam 13:28*
that the king's *h.* was toward. 14:1
thrust darts through the *h.* 18:14
he bowed the *h.* of all men. 19:14
an understanding *h.* *1 Ki 3:9*
given thee an understanding *h.* 12
Solomon wisdom and largeness of *h.*
  4:29
the *h.* of David. 8:17; *2 Chr 6:7*
people went to tents glad of *h.*
  1 Ki 8:66; 2 Chr 7:10
communed with him of all that was
  in her *h.* *1 Ki 10:2; 2 Chr 9:1*
perfect, as was the *h.* of. *1 Ki 11:4*
shall the *h.* of this people. 12:27
h. of king of Assyria. *2 Ki 6:11*
into any man's *h.* 12:4; *2 Chr 29:31*
were not of double *h.* *1 Chr 12:33*
let the *h.* of them rejoice. 16:10
  Ps 105:3
I know thou triest the *h.* *1 Chr 29:17*
  18; *Jer 11:20*
came into Solomon's *h.* *2 Chr 7:11*
turned the *h.* of king of. *Ezra 6:22*
a thing as this in the king's *h.* 7:27
else but sorrow of *h.* *Neh 2:2*
when the *h.* of the king. *Esth 1:10*
forth that day with a glad *h.* 5:9
he is wise in *h.* and. *Job 9:4*

he taketh away the *h.* of. *Job 12:24†*
I caused the widow's *h.* to. 29:13
but the hypocrites in *h.* heap. 36:13
not any that are wise of *h.* 37:24
given understanding to *h.* 38:36*
and with double *h.* do. *Ps 12:2*
are right, rejoicing the *h.* 19:8
them that are of a broken *h.* 34:18
knoweth the secrets of the *h.* 44:21
arrows are sharp in the *h.* 45:5
in *h.* ye work wickedness. 58:2
the *h.* is deep. 64:6
have more than *h.* could wish. 73:7
a froward *h.* shall depart. 101:4
an high look, and a proud *h.* will. 5
glad the *h.* of man, bread, which
  strengtheneth man's *h.* 104:15
a *h.* that deviseth wicked. *Pr 6:18*
met him a woman subtle of *h.* 7:10
ye of an understanding *h.* 8:5
the wise in *h.* will receive. 10:8
h. of the wicked is little worth. 20
froward *h.* are abomination. 11:20
be servant to the wise of *h.* 29
but he that is of perverse *h.* 12:8
deceit is in the *h.* of them who. 20
heaviness in the *h.* of man. 25
hope deferred maketh the *h.* 13:12
the *h.* knoweth his own. 14:10
in laughter the *h.* is sorrowful. 13
backslider in *h.* be filled with. 14
a sound *h.* is the life of the flesh. 30
wisdom resteth in *h.* of him. 33
but the *h.* of the foolish doeth. 15:7
a merry *h.* maketh a cheerful countenance; but by sorrow of the *h.* 13
h. of him that hath understanding. 14
a merry *h.* hath a continual feast. 15
the *h.* of the righteous studieth. 28
of the eyes rejoiceth the *h.* 30
the preparation of *h.* in man. 16:1
proud in *h.* is an abomination. 5
a man's *h.* deviseth his way. 9
h. of wise teacheth his mouth. 23
seeing he hath no *h.* to it. 17:16
hath a froward *h.* findeth no. 20
a merry *h.* doeth good like a. 22
before destruction the *h.* of. 18:12
the *h.* of the prudent getteth. 15
many devices in a man's *h.* 19:21
counsel in *h.* of man is like. 20:5
the king's *h.* is in the hand of. 21:1
high look, and a proud *h.* is sin. 4
he that loveth pureness of *h.* 22:11
foolishness is bound in the *h.* 15
doth not he that pondereth *h.?* 24:12
and the *h.* of kings is. 25:3
singeth songs to an heavy *h.* 20
a wicked *h.* is like a potsherd. 26:23
perfume rejoice the *h.* 27:9
h. of man answereth to man. 19
that is of a proud *h.* stirreth. 28:25*
the *h.* of her husband doth. 31:11
sadness of countenance *h.* *Eccl 7:3*
the *h.* of the wise is in the house of
  mourning, the *h.* of fools. 4
and a gift destroyeth the *h.* 7*
wise man's *h.* discerneth both. 8:5
the *h.* of men is fully set in. 11
the *h.* of the sons of men is. 9:3
drink thy wine with merry *h.* 7
wise man's *h.* is at right hand, fool's
  h. at left. 10:2
make their *h.* fat. *Isa 6:10*
  Mat 13:15; Acts 28:27
pride and stoutness of *h.* *Isa 9:9*
punish fruit of the stout. 10:12
all hands faint, every man's *h.* 13:7
ye shall have gladness of *h.* 30:29
h. of rash shall understand. 32:4
to them that are of fearful *h.* 35:4
yet he laid it not to *h.* 42:25
a deceived *h.* hath turned. 44:20
and no man layeth it to *h.* 57:1
  Jer 12:11
and to revive the *h.* of the. *Isa 57:15*
uttering from the *h.* words of. 59:13
servants shall sing for joy of *h.*. but
ye shall cry for sorrow of *h.* 65:14
the *h.* of the king and princes. 5:23
people hath a rebellious. 5:23
Israel are uncircumcised in *h.* 9:26
triest the reins and the *h.* 11:20
the *h.* is deceitful above all. 17:9

I the Lord search the h.   Jer 17:10
that seest the reins and h.   20:12
long shall this be in the h.?   23:26
and I will give them an h. to.   24:7
be as the h. of a woman in her.
    48:41; 49:22
give them sorrow of h.   Lam 3:65
with their whorish h.   Ezek 6:9
I will take the stony h. out.   11:19
with lies ye made h. of the.   13:22
and make you a new h. and.   18:31
every h. shall melt, all hands.   21:7
rejoiced in h. with all thy.   25:6
vengeance with a despiteful h.   15*
for thee with bitterness of h. 27:31*
and I will give you an h. of.   36:26
strangers uncircumcised in h.   44:7
    9; Acts 7:51
let a beast's h. be given.   Dan 4:16
a man's h. was given to it.   7:4
wine take away the h.   Hos 4:11*
like a silly dove without h.   7:11*
h. melteth, and the knees. Nah 2:10
city that said in her h.   Zeph 2:15
not lay it to h. to give glory, because
ye do not lay it to h.   Mal 2:2
turn the h. of fathers, and h.   4:6
meek and lowly in h.   Mat 11:29
out of the abundance of the h. 12:34
    Luke 6:45
out of the treasure of the h.
    Mat 12:35; Luke 6:45
come forth from the h.   Mat 15:18
out of h. proceed evil thoughts.   19
    Mark 7:21
with hardness of h.   Mark 16:14
pondered them in her h.   Luke 2:19
kept these sayings in her h.   51
which in a good h. having.   8:15
O fools, slow of h. to believe. 24:25
devil having put into the h. John 13:2
eat with singleness of h.   Acts 2:46
were cut to the h.   5:33; 7:54
purpose of h. they would.   11:23
impenitent h. treasurest.   Rom 2:5
circumcision is that of the h.   29
ye have obeyed from the h.   6:17
with the h. man believeth unto. 10:10
entered into h. of man.   1 Cor 2:9
so decreed in his h. that he.   7:37
of much anguish of h. I.   2 Cor 2:4
written in fleshly tables of h.   3:3
appearance, and not in h.   5:12
earnest care in the h. of Titus. 8:16
will of God from the h.   Eph 6:6
but in singleness of h.   Col 3:22
in presence, not in h.   1 Thes 2:17
of the intents of the h.   Heb 4:12
us draw near with a true h.   10:22
h. be established with grace.   13:9
the hidden man of the h.   1 Pet 3:4
an h. exercised with.   2 Pet 2:14
she saith in her h. I sit.   Rev 18:7

heart
depths were congealed in h. Ex 15:8
h. of Egypt shall melt in.   Isa 19:1
so shall the Son of man be . . . in
    the h. of the earth.   Mat 12:40

heart with all
serve him with all your h. and with.
    Deut 11:13; Josh 22:5
    1 Sam 12:20, 24
love the Lord with all your h. and.
    Deut 13:3; 30:6; Mat 22:37
    Mark 12:30, 33; Luke 10:27
do them with all thy h.   Deut 26:16
return to the Lord with all thine h.
    30:2; Joel 2:12
told her all his h.   Judg 16:17, 18
walk before me with all their h.
    1 Ki 2:4; 8:23
return unto thee with all their h. and
    all. 8:48; 2 Ki 23:25; 2 Chr 6:38
followed me with all his h. 1 Ki 14:8
heed to walk with all.   2 Ki 10:31
walk before the Lord with all their h.
    23:3; 2 Chr 34:31
seek God of fathers with all their h.
    2 Chr 15:12
they had sworn with all their h.   15
sought the Lord with all his h. 22:9
he did it with all his h. and.   31:21
O Lord, with all my h.   Ps 86:12

Lord with all thy h., lean not. Pr 3:5
search for me with all your h.
    Jer 29:13
with the joy of all their h. Ezek 36:5
be glad with all the h.   Zeph 3:14
believest with all thy h.   Acts 8:37

see apply, broken, clean, evil,
    harden, hardened

his heart
imagination of his h.   Gen 6:5
Lord and grieved him at his h.   6
Lord said in his h.   8:21
Abraham in his h.   17:17
Esau said in his h., The days. 27:41
he will be glad in his h.   Ex 4:14
neither did he set his h. to.   7:23
that giveth willingly with his h. 25:2
of judgement upon his h.   28:29
he hath put in his h. that he. 35:34
made his h. obstinate.   Deut 2:30
multiply wives, that his h.   17:17
his h. be not lifted up above his. 20
avenger pursue, while his h.   19:6
heart faint as well as his h.   20:8
he is poor, and setteth his h. 24:15
that he bless himself in his h. 29:19
his h. was merry, he went. Ruth 3:7
his h. trembled for the. 1 Sam 4:13
laid up these words in his h. 21:12
it came to pass that his h.   25:37
David said in his h.   27:1
his h. trembled.   28:5
found in his h. to pray this prayer.
    2 Sam 7:27; 1 Chr 17:25
take the thing to his h. 2 Sam 13:33
which God had put in his h.
    1 Ki 10:24; 2 Chr 9:23
wives turned away his h.
    1 Ki 11:3, 4, 9
Jeroboam said in his h.   12:26
arrow went out at his h. 2 Ki 9:24
prepared not his h. to. 2 Chr 12:14
his h. was lifted up in ways.   17:6
his h. was lifted up to his.   26:16
that prepareth his h. to seek. 30:19
for his h. was lifted up.   32:25
himself for the pride of his h.   26
know all that was in his h.   31
Ezra prepared his h. to.   Ezra 7:10
foundest his h. faithful.   Neh 9:8
Haman thought in his h.   Esth 6:6
that durst presume in his h.   7:5
if he set his h. upon man. Job 34:14
his h. is as firm as a stone.   41:24
wicked boasteth of his h.'s. Ps 10:3
he hath said in his h.   6; 11:13
    14:1; 53:1
that speaketh truth in his h.   15:2
hast given him his h.'s desire. 21:2
the thoughts of his h. to all.   33:11
law of his God is in his h.   37:31
his h. gathereth iniquity to.   41:6
smooth, but war was in his h. 55:21
according to integrity of his h. 78:72
his h. is fixed, trusting in.   112:7
his h. is established, he shall not. 8
frowardness is in his h.   Pr 6:14
but that his h. may discover.   18:2
and his h. fretteth against.   19:3
thinketh in his h. so is he; eat and
    drink, saith he, but his h.   23:7
but he that hardeneth his h. 28:14
yea his h. taketh no rest. Eccl 2:23
him in the joy of his h.   5:20
day of gladness of his h. S of S 3:11
his h. was moved, and the h. Isa 7:2
neither doth his h. think so, but it is
    in his h. to destroy and.   10:7
his h. will work iniquity, to.   32:6
none considereth in his h.   44:19*
frowardly in the way of his h. 57:17*
but in h. he layeth his.   Jer 9:8
performed thoughts of his h. 23:20
engaged his h. to approach. 30:21*
performed the intents of his h.   24
heard the haughtiness of his h. 48:29
up his idols in his h.   Ezek 14:4, 7
his h. lifted up in his height. 31:10
    Dan 5:20
Daniel purposed in his h.   Dan 1:8
let his h. be changed.   4:16; 5:21
the king set his h. on Daniel.   6:14
shall magnify himself in his h.   8:25

his h. shall be lifted up.   Dan 11:12
his h. shall be against the holy.   28
that saith in his h., Who shall? Ob 3
adultery with her in his h. Mat 5:28
away that was sown in his h.   13:19
if evil servant shall say in his h.
    24:48; Luke 12:45
entereth not into his h.   Mark 7:19
shall not doubt in his h. but.   11:23
of his h.; an evil man out of the evil
    treasure of his h.   Luke 6:45
it came into his h. to.   Acts 7:23
standeth stedfast in his h. 1 Cor 7:37
thus are the secrets of his h.   14:25
as he purposeth in his h. 2 Cor 9:7

mine or my heart
the integrity of my h.   Gen 20:5
speaking in mine h. Rebekah. 24:45
imagination of mine h. Deut 29:19
word as it was in mine h. Josh 14:7
my h. is toward the.   Judg 5:9
said, My h. rejoiceth.   1 Sam 2:1
to that which is in mine h.   35
my eyes and mine h. shall be there.
    1 Ki 9:3; 2 Chr 7:16
went not mine h. with? 2 Ki 5:26
h. right as my h. is with thy h.? 10:15
to all that was in mine h.   30
if to help, mine h. shall. 1 Chr 12:17
mine h. to build an house of. 28:2
it is in mine h. to make. 2 Chr 29:10
what God had put in my h. to do.
    Neh 2:12; 7:5
thoughts of my h. are.   Job 17:11
God maketh my h. soft, and. 23:16
my h. shall not reproach me.   27:6
and mine h. walked after mine. 31:7
mine h. have been deceived by.   9
and my h. hath been secretly.   27
of the uprightness of my h.   33:3
at this also my h. trembleth.   37:1
hast put gladness in my h.   Ps 4:7
take counsel, sorrow in my h.   13:2
but I trusted, my h. shall rejoice.   5
my h. is glad.   16:9
thou hast proved mine h.   17:3
let the meditation of my h.   19:14
my h. is like wax.   22:14
try my reins and my h.   26:2
troubles of my h. are enlarged. 25:17
my h. shall not fear though.   27:3
my h. said to thee, Thy face, Lord. 8
my h. trusted in him, my h.   28:7
of the wicked saith in my h.   36:1
of the disquietness of my h.   38:8
my h. panteth, my strength faileth.
    10; Isa 21:4
my h. was hot within me.   39:3
yea, thy law is within my h.   40:8
hid thy righteousness within my h. 10
able to look up, therefore my h.   12
my h. is inditing a good matter. 45:1
the meditation of my h. be of.   49:3
my h. is sore pained within me. 55:4
my h. is fixed, O God, my h. is.
    57:7; 108:1
I will cry, when my h. is.   61:2
if I regard iniquity in my h.   66:18
reproach hath broken my h.   69:20
verily I have cleansed my h.   73:13
my h. was grieved, I was pricked. 21
my h. faileth, but God is the strength
    of my h.   26
my h. and flesh crieth out for. 84:2
unite my h. to fear thy name. 86:11
my h. is smitten and withered. 102:4
my h. is wounded within me. 109:22
word have I hid in mine h.   119:11
when thou shalt enlarge my h.   32
incline my h. to thy testimonies. 36
my h. be sound in thy statutes.   80
are the rejoicing of my h.   111
inclined mine h. to perform.   112
Lord, my h. is not haughty.   131:1
search me, and know my h. 139:23
incline not my h. to any evil.   141:4
my h. within me is desolate. 143:4
how hath my h. despised? Pr 5:12
can say, I have made my h.? 20:9
if thine heart be wise, my h.   23:15
I gave my h. to seek.   Eccl 1:13
my h. had great experience of.   16
I gave my h. to know wisdom.   17

heart (continued)

I said in *mine h.* I will prove thee.
  Eccl 2:1, 15; 3:17, 18
mine h. to give myself to wine, yet
  acquainting *mine h.* with. 2:3
I withheld not *my h.* from any. 10
to cause *my h.* to despair of all. 20
mine h. to know and search. 7:25
  8:9, 16
this I considered in *my h.* 9:1
hast ravished *my h.* *S of S* 4:9
I sleep, but *my h.* waketh. 5:2
my h. shall cry out for. *Isa* 15:5
day of vengeance is in *mine h.* 63:4
according to *mine h.* *Jer* 3:15
pained at *my h. my h.* maketh. 4:19
neither came it into *my h.* 7:31*
when I comfort myself, *my h.* 8:18
hast seen me and tried *mine h.* 12:3
joy and rejoicing of *mine h.* 15:16
his word was in *mine h.* as a. 20:9
mine h. is broken. 23:9
mine h. shall mourn. 48:31
therefore *mine h.* shall sound. 36
behold, *mine h.* is turned. *Lam* 1:20
my sighs are many, and *my h.* 22
mine eye affecteth *mine h.* 3:51
kept the matter in *my h.* *Dan* 7:28
mine h. is turned within. *Hos* 11:8
did *my h.* rejoice. *Acts* 2:26
to weep, and break *mine h.?* 21:13
continual sorrow in *my h.* *Rom* 9:2
my h.'s desire to God for Israel. 10:1
because I have you in *my h.* *Phil* 1:7
  see applied

one heart
was to give them *one h.* *2 Chr* 30:12
I will give them *one h.* *Jer* 32:39
  Ezek 11:19
believed were of *one h.* *Acts* 4:32

own heart
not after your *own h.* *Num* 15:39
sought man after his *own h.*
  1 Sam 13:14; *Acts* 13:22
according to thine *own h.* hast thou.
  2 Sam 7:21; *1 Chr* 17:19
man plague of his *own h.* *1 Ki* 8:38
had devised of his *own h.* 12:33
them out of thine *own h.* *Neh* 6:8
your *own h.* on your bed. *Ps* 4:4
according to thine *own h.* 20:4
shall enter into their *own h.* 37:15
I commune with my *own h.* and 77:6
trusteth in his *own h.* *Pr* 28:26
communed with mine *own h.*
  Eccl 1:16
thy *own h.* knoweth thou hast. 7:22
after imagination of their *own h.*
  Jer 9:14; 23:17
a vision of their *own h.* 23:16
prophesy the deceit of their *own h.*
  26; *Ezek* 13:17
of Israel in their *own h.* *Ezek* 14:5
but deceiveth his *own h.* *Jas* 1:26

our heart
have discouraged *our h.* *Deut* 1:28
for *our h.* shall rejoice. *Ps* 33:21
our h. is not turned back. 44:18
let us lift up *our h.* with. *Lam* 3:41
the joy of *our h.* is ceased. 5:15
our h. is faint. 17
did not *our h.* burn? *Luke* 24:32
our mouth is open, *our h.* *2 Cor* 6:11
if *our h.* condemn us. *1 John* 3:20
if *our h.* condemn us not, we. 21

perfect heart
let your *h.* be *perfect.* *1 Ki* 8:61
his *h.* was not *perfect.* 11:4; 15:3
Asa's *h.* was *perfect* with the Lord.
  15:14; *2 Chr* 15:17
have walked before thee with a *per-*
  fect h. *2 Ki* 20:3; *Isa* 38:3
came with *perfect h.* to. *1 Chr* 12:38
serve God with a *perfect h.* 28:9
with *perfect h.* they offered. 29:9
give Solomon my son a *perfect h.* 19
them whose *h.* is *perfect.* *2 Chr* 16:9
in fear of Lord with *perfect h.* 19:9
right, but not with a *perfect h.* 25:2
my house with *perfect h.* *Ps* 101:2

pure heart
ascend? that hath a *pure h.* *Ps* 24:4
blessed are the *pure* in *h.* *Mat* 5:8

is charity out of *pure h.* *1 Tim* 1:5
the Lord out of a *pure h.* *2 Tim* 2:22
another with a *pure h.* *1 Pet* 1:22

their heart
their h. failed them. *Gen* 42:28
their h. melted, neither was there
  spirit in them. *Josh* 5:1
thou hast turned *their h.* *1 Ki* 18:37
and prepare *their h.* *1 Chr* 29:18
utter words out of *their h.?* *Job* 8:10
thou hast hid *their h.* from. 17:4
wilt prepare *their h.* *Ps* 10:17
generation that set not *their h.* 78:8
they tempted God in *their h.* 18
their h. was not right with him. 37
people that do err in *their h.* 95:10
he turned *their h.* to hate. 105:25
he brought down *their h.* 107:12
their h. is as fat as grease. 119:70
imagine mischief in *their h.* 140:2
for *their h.* studieth. *Pr* 24:2
set the world in *their h.* *Eccl* 3:11
madness is in *their h.* while. 9:3
ears and understand with *their h.*
  Isa 6:10; *Mat* 13:15; *Acts* 28:27
their h. is far from me. *Isa* 29:13
  Mat 15:8; *Mark* 7:6
neither say they in *their h.* *Jer* 5:24
in the imagination of *their h.* 13:10
prophesy the deceit of *their h.* 14:14
is graven on table of *their h.* 17:1
their h. cried to Lord. *Lam* 2:18
up their idols in *their h.* *Ezek* 14:3
for *their h.* went after their. 20:16
that *their h.* may faint, ruins. 21:15
but *their h.* goeth after. 33:31
they set *their h.* on their. *Hos* 4:8
they have made ready *their h.* 7:6
not cried unto me with *their h.* 14
their h. is divided. 10:2
their h. was exalted. 13:6
I will rend the caul of *their h.* 8
men that say in *their h.* *Zeph* 1:12
their h. shall rejoice. *Zech* 10:7
Judah shall say in *their h.* 12:5
their h. was hardened. *Mark* 6:52
  Rom 1:21
the thought of *their h.* *Luke* 9:47
their h.; they should not see, nor
  understand with *their h.* *John* 12:40
were pricked in *their h.* *Acts* 2:37
the vail is upon *their h.* *2 Cor* 3:15
the blindness of *their h.* *Eph* 4:18

thine, thy heart
in the integrity of *thy h.* *Gen* 20:6
my plagues upon *thine h.* *Ex* 9:14
not hate thy brother in *thine h.*
  Lev 19:17
they depart from *thy h.* *Deut* 4:9
if thou seek him with all *thy h.* 29
consider it in *thine h.* 4:39; 8:5
love Lord with all *thine h.* 6:5
in *thine h.* these nations are more.
  7:17; 8:17; 18:21; *Jer* 13:22
know what was in *thine h.* *Deut* 8:2
then *thine h.* be lifted up, and. 14
speak not thou in *thine h.* after. 9:4
not for uprightness of *thine h.* 5
serve thy God with all *thy h.* 10:12
a thought in *thy* wicked *h.* 15:9
thine h. shall not be grieved. 10
fear of *thine h.* wherewith. 28:67
circumcise *thine h.* and the *h.* 30:6
is very nigh unto thee, in *thy h.* 14
if *thine h.* turn, so that thou. 17
when *thine h.* is not. *Judg* 16:15
and let *thine h.* be merry. 19:6, 9
  1 Ki 21:7
father said, Comfort *thine h.*
  Judg 19:8
why is *thy h.* grieved? *1 Sam* 1:8
thine shall be to grieve *thine h.* 2:33
tell thee all that is in *thine h.* 9:19
do all that is in *thine h.* *1 Sam* 14:7
  2 Sam 7:3; *1 Chr* 17:2
thee, according to *thy h.* *1 Sam* 14:7
pride and naughtiness of *thy h.* 17:28
reign over all that *thine h.*
  2 Sam 3:21
wickedness *thine h.* is. *1 Ki* 2:44
in *thine h.* to build. 8:18
  2 Chr 1:11; 6:8

Jehu said, Is *thine h.* right, as *my h.*
  is with *thy h.?* *2 Ki* 10:15
thine h. hath lifted thee up. 14:10
  2 Chr 25:19
because *thine h.* was tender.
  2 Ki 22:19; *2 Chr* 34:27
hast prepared *thine h.* *2 Chr* 19:3
thou shouldest set *thine h.* *Job* 7:17
things hast thou hid in *thine h.* 10:13
if thou prepare *thine h.* and. 11:13
why doth *thine h.* carry thee? 15:12
lay up his words in *thine h.* 22:22
shall strengthen *thine h.* *Ps* 27:14
give thee the desires of *thine h.* 37:4
thine h. to understanding. *Pr* 2:2
wisdom entereth into *thine h.* 10
my son, let *thine h.* keep my. 3:1
upon the table of *thine h.* 3; 7:3
he said, let *thine h.* retain. 4:4, 21
keep *thy h.* with all diligence. 23
them continually upon *thine h.* 6:21
after her beauty in *thine h.* 25
let not *thine h.* incline to her. 7:25
if *thine h.* be wise, my *h.* 23:15
let not *thine h.* envy sinners. 17
hear, my son, and guide *thine h.* 19
my son, give me *thine h.* 26
thine h. shall utter perverse. 33
let not *thine h.* be glad when. 24:17
let not *thine h.* be hasty to. *Eccl* 5:2
thy h. cheer thee; walk in ways of *thy*
  h. 11:9
remove sorrow from *thy h.* 10
thou hast said in *thine h.* *Isa* 14:13
thine h. shall meditate terror. 33:18
these things to *thy h.* 47:7; 57:11
that sayest in *thine h.* I am. 47:8, 10
shalt thou say in *thine h.* 49:21
O Jerusalem, wash *thine h.* *Jer* 4:14
because it reacheth unto *thine h.* 18
thine h. are not but for thy. 22:17
set *thine h.* toward the. 31:21
thine h. deceived thee. 49:16; *Ob* 2
pour out *thine h.* like. *Lam* 2:19
receive in *thine h.* hear. *Ezek* 3:10
how weak is *thine h.* saith. 16:30
can *thine h.* endure in days. 22:14
because *thine h.* is lifted up. 28:2, 5
hast set *thine h.* as the heart. 6
thine h. was lifted up because. 17
set *thine h.* upon all that I. 40:4
know the thoughts of *thy h.* *Dan* 2:30
hast not humbled *thine h.* 5:22
thou didst set *thine h.* to. 10:12
filled *thine h.* to lie. *Acts* 5:3
thou conceived this in *thine h.?* 4
for *thy h.* is not right in the. 8:21
thought of *thine h.* may. 22
say not in *thine h.*, Who? *Rom* 10:6
and shalt believe in *thine h.* that. 9

upright in heart
were more *upright in h.* *2 Chr* 29:34
saveth the *upright in h.* *Ps* 7:10
may shoot at the *upright in h.* 11:2
joy, ye that are *upright in h.* 32:11
righteousness to *upright in h.* 36:10
the *upright in h.* shall glory. 64:10
the *upright in h.* shall follow. 94:15
sown for the *upright in h.* 97:11

uprightness of heart
he walketh in *uprightness of h.*
  1 Ki 3:6; 9:4
I will praise thee with *uprightness of*
  h. *Ps* 119:7

whole heart
I will praise thee, O Lord, with my
  whole h. *Ps* 9:1; 111:1; 138:1
seek him with the *whole h.* 119:2
with my *whole h.* have I. 10
observe it with my *whole h.* 34
thy favour with my *whole h.* 58
thy precepts with my *whole h.* 69
I cried with my *whole h.* hear. 145
head is sick, the *whole h.* *Isa* 1:5
not turned with *whole h.* *Jer* 3:10
unto me with their *whole h.* 24:7
them in land with my *whole h.* 32:41

whose heart
whose h. stirred him up. *Ex* 35:21
  29; 36:2
all the women, *whose h.* 35:26
whose h. turneth away. *Deut* 29:18
whose h. is as the heart. *2 Sam* 17:10

whose h. thou knowest. *1 Ki* 8:39
     2 Chr 6:30
behalf of them *whose h. 2 Chr* 16:9
in *whose h.* are the ways. *Ps* 84:5
woman *whose h.* is snares and nets.
     Eccl 7:26
in *whose h.* is my law. *Isa.* 51:7
whose h. departeth from. *Jer* 17:5
whose h. walketh after. *Ezek* 11:21
whose h. the Lord. *Acts* 16:14

your **heart**
circumcise foreskin of *your h.*
   Deut 10:16; *Jer* 4:4
your h. be not deceived. *Deut* 11:16
lay up these my words in *your h.* 18
will turn away *your h. 1 Ki* 11:2
set *your h.* and soul. *1 Chr* 22:19
your h. shall live. *Ps* 22:26
he shall strengthen *your h.* 31:24
ye people, pour out *your h.* 62:8
if riches increase, set not *your h.* 10
your h. shall live that seek. 69:32
ye see this, *your h.* shall. *Isa* 66:14
and lest *your h.* faint. *Jer* 51:46
and rend *your h.* and not. *Joel* 2:13
you imagine evil in *your h. Zech* 7:10
there will *your h.* be also. *Mat* 6:21
     Luke 12:34
have ye *your h.* yet ? *Mark* 8:17
for the hardness of *your h.* 10:5
not *your h.* be troubled. *John* 14:1, 27
sorrow hath filled *your h.* 16:6
I will see you, and *your h.* shall. 22
in singleness of *your h. Eph* 6:5

hearted
many as were willing *h. Ex* 35:22
the stout *h.* are spoiled. *Ps* 76:5
all the merry *h.* do sigh. *Isa* 24:7
me to bind up the broken *h.* 61:1
of Israel are hard *h. Ezek* 3:7

faint **hearted**
is there that is *faint h.? Deut* 20:8

tender **hearted**
Rehoboam was young and *tender h.*
     2 Chr 13:7
and be kind one to another, *tender h.*
     Eph 4:32

wise **hearted**
unto all that are *wise h. Ex* 28:3
hearts of all that are *wise h.* 31:6
and every *wise h.* among you. 35:10
all the women that were *wise h.* 25
then wrought every *wise h.* man.
     36:1, 2, 8

hearth
make cakes upon the *h. Gen* 18:6
bones are burnt as an *h. Ps* 102:3*
to take fire from the *h. Isa* 30:14
a fire on the *h.* burning. *Jer* 36:22*
roll into fire that was on the *h.* 23*
of Judah like as of fire. *Zech* 12:6*

heartily
what ye do, do it *h.* as to. *Col* 3:23

hearts
they discouraged the *h. Num* 32:9
wherefore the *h.* of the. *Josh* 7:5
of men, whose *h.* God. *1 Sam* 10:26
so Absalom stole the *h. 2 Sam* 15:6
the *h.* of the men of Israel. 13
thou only knowest the *h. 1 Ki* 8:39
     2 Chr 6:30
the Lord searcheth all. *1 Chr* 28:9
the righteous God trieth the *h.*
    Ps 7:9; *Pr* 17:3
more then the *h.* of men ? *Pr* 15:11
but the Lord pondereth the *h.* 21:2
wine to those that be of heavy *h.*
     31:6*
mighty men's *h.* of Moab. *Jer* 48:41
I will also vex the *h. Ezek* 32:9
both these kings' *h.* shall. *Dan* 11:27
turn the *h.* of the fathers. *Luke* 1:17
that the thoughts of *h.* may be. 2:35
signs in the sun, men's *h.* 21:26
which knowest the *h.* of all men.
    Acts 1:24; 15:8
he that searcheth the *h. Rom* 8:27
by fair speeches deceive the *h.* 16:18
the counsels of the *h. 1 Cor* 4:5
searcheth the reins and *h. Rev* 2:23

our **hearts**
soon as we heard, *our h. Josh* 2:11
incline *our h.* to him. *1 Ki* 8:58
filling *our h.* with food. *Acts* 14:17
love of God is shed abroad in *our h.*
     Rom 5:5
of the Spirit in *our h. 2 Cor* 1:22
our epistle written in *our h.* 3:2
God hath shined in *our h.* 4:6
that you are in *our h.* to die. 7:3
God, who trieth *our h. 1 Thes* 2:4
our h. sprinkled from. *Heb* 10:22
and shall assure *our h. 1 John* 3:19

their **hearts**
a faintness into *their h. Lev* 26:36
if then *their* uncircumcised *h.* 41
their h. inclined to follow. *Judg* 9:3
when *their h.* were merry. 16:25
they were making *their h.* 19:22
thee with all *their h. 2 Chr* 6:14
such as set *their h.* to seek. 11:16
people had not prepared *their h.* to.
     20:33
my sons have cursed God in *their h.*
     Job 1:5
but mischief is in *their h. Ps* 28:3
he fashioneth *their h.* alike. 33:15
let them not say in *their h. Lev.* 34:25
said in *their h.,* Let us destroy. 74:8
gave them up to *their* own *h.* 81:12
that are upright in *their h.* 125:4
hath shut *their h.* they. *Isa* 44:18
and write my law in *their h.*
   Jer 31:33; *Heb* 8:10
put my fear in *their h. Jer* 32:40
out of *their* own *h. Ezek* 13:2
consider not in *their h. Hos* 7:2
yea, they made *their h. Zech* 7:12
and reasoning in *their h. Mark* 2:6
for the hardness of *their h.* 3:5
taketh away word sown in *their h.*
    4:15; *Luke* 8:12
in imagination of *their h. Luke* 1:51
heard laid them up in *their h.* 66
all men mused in *their h.* of. 3:15
in *their h.* turned back. *Acts* 7:39
through lust of *their h. Rom* 1:24
work of law written in *their h.* 2:15
their h. might be comforted. *Col* 2:2
always err in *their h. Heb* 3:10
God hath put in *their h. Rev* 17:17

your **hearts**
comfort ye *your h.* after. *Gen* 18:5
O Israel, let not *your h. Deut* 20:3
set *your h.* to all the words. 32:46
ye know in all *your h. Josh* 23:14
incline *your h.* to the Lord. 24:23
do ye harden *your h.? 1 Sam* 6:6
the Lord with all *your h.* and prepare
your h. to the Lord to serve. 7:3
ye dissembled in *your h. Jer* 42:20*
imagine evil in *your h. Zech* 8:17
think ye evil in *your h.? Mat* 9:4
if ye from *your h.* forgive not. 18:35
of the hardness of *your h.* 19:8
these things in *your h.? Mark* 2:8
what reason ye in *your h.? Luke* 5:22
God knoweth *your h.* 16:15
settle it in *your h.* not to. 21:14
lest at any time *your h.* be. 34
thoughts arise in *your h.?* 24:38
of his Son into *your h. Gal* 4:6
Christ may dwell in *your h. Eph* 3:17
melody in *your h.* to. 5:19; *Col* 3:16
that he might comfort *your h.* 6:22
keep *your h.* and minds. *Phil* 4:7
peace of God rule in *your h. Col* 3:15
your estate and comfort *your h.* 4:8
may establish *your h. 1 Thes* 3:13
comfort *your h.* and. *2 Thes* 2:17
Lord direct *your h.* into love. 3:5
if ye have strife in *your h. Jas* 3:14
your h. ye double minded. 4:8
ye have nourished *your h.* 5:5
be ye also patient, stablish *your h.* 8
the Lord God in *your h. 1 Pet* 3:15
day star arise in *your h. 2 Pet* 1:19

hearty
sweetness of a friend by *h. Pr* 27:9

heat
h., summer and winter. *Gen* 8:22
sat in the tent door in the *h.* of. 18:1

what meaneth the *h.* of ? *Deut* 29:24
be devoured with burning *h.* 32:24
slew Ammonites till *h. 1 Sam* 11:11
they came about the *h. 2 Sam* 4:5
but he gat no *h. 1 Ki* 1:1
my lord may get *h.* 2
drought and *h.* consume. *Job* 24:19
my bones are burnt with *h.* 30:30
hid from the *h.* thereof. *Ps* 19:6
together, then they have *h. Eccl* 4:11
a shadow in the daytime from the *h.*
    Isa 4:6; 25:4
like a clear *h.* on herbs, and like a
  cloud of dew on the. 18:4
h. in a dry place, even the *h.* 25:5
neither shall the *h.* nor sun. 49:10
shall not see when *h. Jer* 17:8
dead body shall be cast in the day to
  h. 36:30
in their *h.* I will make their. 51:39
and I went in the *h.* of. *Ezek* 3:14
borne the burden and *h. Mat* 20:12
blow, there will be *h. Luke* 12:55
came a viper out of the *h. Acts* 28:3
no sooner risen with a burning *h.*
     Jas 1:11
shall melt with fervent *h. 2 Pet* 3:10

heat
h. the furnace more. *Dan* 3:19

heated
more than wont to be *h. Dan* 3:19
adulterers, as an oven *h. Hos* 7:4

heath
he shall be like the *h.* in. *Jer* 17:6
flee, and be like the *h.* in the. 48:6

heathen
(*Most frequently this word merely
means the other nations as distinguished from the Hebrews, without
intending any reference to religion.
But it generally means idolaters.
The Revisions very frequently substitute the word* nations *for* heathen)
bondmen shall be of the *h.* round.
     Lev 25:44
forth in sight of the *h.* 26:45
be head of *h. 2 Sam* 22:44; *Ps* 18:43
to abominations of the *h. 2 Ki* 16:3
  17:15; 21:2; *2 Chr* 28:3; 36:14
walked in statutes of the. *2 Ki* 17:8
as did the *h.* whom the Lord. 11
deliver us from the *h. 1 Chr* 16:35
over all kingdoms of *h. 2 Chr* 20:6
the abominations of *h.* 33:2
made Judah to do worse than *h.* 9
from filthiness of the *h. Ezra* 6:21
Jews who were sold to *h. Neh* 5:8
because of the reproach of the *h.* 9
all the *h.* that were about us. 6:16
why do the *h.* rage ? *Ps* 2:1
     Acts 4:25
shall give thee the *h.* for thy. *Ps* 2:8
thou hast rebuked the *h.* thou. 9:5
the *h.* are sunk in the pit that. 15
arise, let the *h.* be judged in. 9:19
the *h.* are perished out of his. 10:16
Lord bringeth the counsel of *h.* 33:10
how thou didst drive out the *h.* 44:2
the *h.* raged, the kingdoms. 46:6
God reigneth over the *h.* 47:8
awake to visit all the *h.* 59:5
shalt have all the *h.* in derision. 8
he cast out the *h.* also. 78:55; 80:8
the *h.* are come into thine. 79:1
thy wrath upon the *h.* 6; *Jer* 10:25
the *h.* say, where is their God ? let
  him be known among *h. Ps* 79:10
     115:2
he that chastiseth the *h.* 94:10
openly shewed in the sight of *h.* 98:2
h. shall fear the name of the. 102:15
gave them the lands of the *h.* 105:44
gave them into hand of the *h.* 106:41
gave them heritage of the *h.* 111:6
the idols of the *h.* are silver. 135:15
execute vengeance upon the *h.* 149:7
the lords of the *h.* have. *Isa* 16:8
of the *h.* be not dismayed at signs of
  heaven, for the. *Jer* 10:2
ambassador is sent to the *h.* 49:14
seen that the *h.* entered. *Lam* 1:10
bring the worst of the *h. Ezek* 7:24

after the manners of *h.*   *Ezek* 11:12
polluted before the *h.*   20:9, 14, 22
ye say, we will be as the *h.*   32
be sanctified before the *h.* 41; 28:25
thee a reproach to the *h.*   22:4
inheritance in sight of the *h.*   16
gone a whoring after the *h.*   23:30
deliver thee for a spoil to *h.*   25:7
house of Judah is like to all the *h.* 8
it shall be the time of the *h.*   30:3
hand of the mighty one of *h.*   31:11
his shadow in midst of the *h.*   17
no more be a prey to the *h.*   34:28
neither bear the shame of the *h.*   29
possession to the residue of the *h.* 36:3
a derision to the residue of the *h.* 4
ye have borne the shame of the *h.* 6
when they entered unto the *h.*   20
h. know I am Lord.   23, 36; 37:28
  38:16; 39:7
and all the *h.* shall see my.   39:21
that the *h.* should rule.   *Joel* 2:17
and come, all ye *h.* and gather. 3:11
h. be wakened, and come up to valley
  of Jehoshaphat ... to judge all *h.* 12
possess remnant of all *h. Amos* 9:12
the Lord is near on all the *h. Ob* 15
all the *h.* drink continually.   16
execute fury upon the *h. Mi* 5:15
thou didst thresh the *h. Hab* 3:12
all the isles of the *h. Zeph* 2:11
destroy the strength of *h. Hag* 2:22
sore displeased with *h. Zech* 1:15
shall speak peace to the *h.*   9:10
the wealth of all the *h.* shall. 14:14
wherewith Lord will smite the *h.* 18
repetitions as the *h.* do.   *Mat* 6:7
let him be to thee as an *h.* 18:17*
in perils by the *h.*   2 *Cor* 11:26
we should go unto the *h.*   *Gal* 2:9
that God would justify the *h.* 3:8

among the **heathen**

among the h. and land.   *Lev* 26:33
  Jer 9:16; *Ezek* 20:23; 22:15
perish *among the h.* and. *Lev* 26:38
few in number *among h. Deut* 4:27
thee, O Lord, *among h.* and sing
  praises.   2 *Sam* 22:50; *Ps* 18:49
declare his glory *among h.*
  1 *Chr* 16:24; *Ps* 96:3
to us from *among the h. Neh* 5:17
it is reported *among the h.*   6:6
scattered us *among the h. Ps* 44:11
us a byword *among the h.*   14
I will be exalted *among the h.* 46:10
known *among the h.* in sight. 79:10
say *among the h.* that Lord. 96:10
were mingled *among the h.* 106:35
and gather us from *among h.*   47
judge *among the h.* he shall. 110:6
said *among the h.* Lord hath. 126:2
ask *among the h.*, who.   *Jer* 18:13
make thee small *among the h.* 49:15
she dwelleth *among the h. Lam* 1:3
said *among the h.* they shall. 4:15
shadow we shall live *among the h.* 20
have cast them far off *among the h.*
  Ezek 11:16
abominations *among the h.* 12:16
went forth *among the h.* 16:14
scatter them *among the h.* 36:19
profaned *among the h.* 21, 22, 23
you from *among the h.* 24, 37:21
reproach of famine *among the h.* 30
set my glory *among the h.* 39:21
be led into captivity *among h.* 28
a reproach *among the h. Joel* 2:19
ambassador sent *among the h. Ob* 1
made thee small *among the h.* 2
behold ye *among the h. Hab* 1:5
a curse *among the h. Zech* 8:13
be great *among the h. Mal* 1:11
name is dreadful *among the h.* 14
preach him *among the h. Gal* 1:16

heave

as ye do the *h.* offering, so shall ye *h.*
  it.   *Num* 15:20

heaved

is *h.* of the ram of.   *Ex* 29:27
ye have *h.* the best, *Num* 18:30, 32
  see **offering, shoulder**

heaven

This word is used of the abode of

*the redeemed after death and the
second resurrection. It is also
used for God, without whom there
would be no heaven.*

*It is sometimes used of the air,
as in the phrase* birds *or* fowls *of*
heaven. *And for the sky, wherein
the sun, moon, and stars are placed.*
the beginning God created *h. Gen* 1:1
and God called the firmament *h.* 8
lights in the firmament of *h.* 14, 15
fly in the open firmament of *h.* 20
and the windows of *h.* were. 7:11
windows of *h.* were stopped. 8:2
possessor of *h.* and earth. 14:19, 22
fire from the Lord out of *h.* 19:24
God called to Hagar out of *h.* 21:17
called to Abraham out of *h.* 22:11, 15
give thee of the dew of *h.* 27:28, 39
said, this is the gate of *h.* 28:17
blessings of *h.* above.   49:25
six days Lord made *h.* and earth.
  Ex 20:11; 31:17
as it were the body of *h.* in. 24:10
I will make your *h.* as. *Lev* 26:19
burned to the midst of *h. Deut* 4:11
I call *h.* and earth. 26; 30:19; 31:28
ask from the one side of *h.* to. 4:32
out of *h.* he made thee hear his. 36
behold, the *h.* and *h.* of heavens.
  10:14; *Ps* 115:16
water of the rain of *h. Deut* 11:11
he shut up *h.*   17; 1 *Ki* 8:35
  2 *Chr* 6:26; 7:13
multiplied as days of *h. Deut* 11:21
open the *h.* to give the rain. 28:12
h. that is over thy head shall. 23
scatter thee to the utmost part of *h.*
  30:4; *Neh* 1:9
precious things of *h.*   *Deut* 33:13
of Jeshurun rideth upon the *h.* 26
of *h.* shall he thunder.   1 *Sam* 2:10
taken up between *h.*   2 *Sam* 18:9
dropped on them out of *h.* 21:10
the foundations of *h.* moved. 22:8
h. and the *h.* of heavens cannot.
  1 *Ki* 8:27; 2 *Chr* 2:6; 6:18
when *h.* is shut up, and. 1 *Ki* 8:35
mean while the *h.* was black. 18:45
of all kingdoms, thou hast made *h.*
  2 *Ki* 19:15; 2 *Chr* 2:12; *Neh* 9:6
angel stood between *h.* 1 *Chr* 21:16
it is as high as *h.*   *Job* 11:8
h. shall reveal his iniquity. 20:27
is not God in height of *h.?* 22:12
walketh in the circuit of *h.* 14
the pillars of *h.* tremble at. 26:11
the hoary frost of *h.* who? 38:29
thou the ordinances of *h.?* 33
who can stay the bottles of *h.?* 37
forth is from the end of *h. Ps* 19:6
hear him from his holy *h.* 20:6
let *h.* and earth praise him. 69:34
he opened the doors of *h.* 78:23
given them of the corn of *h.* 24
to endure as the days of *h.* 89:29
h. is high above the earth. 103:11
them with the bread of *h.* 105:40
the Lord who made *h.* and earth.
  115:15; 121:2; 124:8; 134:3
  146:6; *Isa* 37:16; *Jer* 32:17
  Acts 4:24; 14:15; *Rev* 14:7
covereth *h.* with clouds. *Ps* 147:8
glory is above earth and *h.* 148:13
the *h.* for height, the earth. *Pr* 25:3
far, from the end of *h.*   *Isa* 13:5
who hath meted out *h.* with. 40:12
sing, O *h.* and be. 49:13; *Rev* 18:20
h. my throne, earth my footstool.
  Isa 66:1; *Acts* 7:49
cakes to the queen of *h. Jer* 7:18
not dismayed at the signs of *h.* 10:2
do not I fill *h.* and earth? 23:24
if *h.* above can be measured. 31:37
appointed ordinances of *h.* 33:25
to burn incense to queen of *h.* 44:17
  18, 19, 25
from the four quarters of *h.* 49:36
hath stretched out the *h.* by. 51:15
the *h.* and earth shall sing for. 48
swifter than eagles of *h. Lam* 4:19
me between earth and *h. Ezek* 8:3
I will cover the *h.* and make. 32:7
the lights of *h.* will I make dark. 8

be wet with dew of *h.*   *Dan* 4:15
  23, 25, 33; 5:21
his will in the army of *h.*   4:35
extol and honour the King of *h.* 37
thyself against the Lord of *h.* 5:23
the four winds of *h.* strove. 7:2
of man, came with clouds of *h.* 13
towards the four winds of *h.* 8:8
divided toward four winds of *h.* 11:4
buildeth his stories in *h. Amos* 9:6
the *h.* over you is stayed. *Hag* 1:10
as the four winds of *h. Zech* 2:6
ephah between earth and *h.* 5:9
not open windows of *h. Mal* 3:10
till *h.* and earth pass. *Mat* 5:18
neither swear by *h.*; for it is God's
  throne.   34; *Jas* 5:12
I thank thee, Father, Lord of *h.*
  Mat 11:25; *Luke* 10:21
swear by *h.* sweareth by. *Mat* 23:22
coming in the clouds of *h.* 24:30
  26:64; *Mark* 14:62
elect from one end of *h. Mat* 24:31
h. and earth shall pass away. 35
  Mark 13:31; *Luke* 21:33
the angels of *h.* but my. *Mat* 24:36
from utmost part of *h. Mark* 13:27
Jesus praying, the *h.*   *Luke* 3:21
when the *h.* was shut up.   4:25
I have sinned against *h.* 15:18, 21
it is easier for *h.* and earth. 16:17
for the powers of *h.* shall be. 21:26
hereafter ye shall see *h. John* 1:51
the *h.* must receive.   *Acts* 3:21
I saw *h.* opened, and a vessel.
  10:11; *Rev* 19:11
seeing he is Lord of *h. Acts* 17:24
prayed again, and the *h. Jas* 5:18
cometh down out of *h Rev* 3:12
h. departed as a scroll when. 6:14
an angel flying through the midst of *h.*
  8:13; 14:6
who created *h.* and the things. 10:6
have power to shut *h.* that. 11:6
voice out of the temple of *h.* 16:17
fell on men a great hail out of *h.* 21
rejoice over her, thou *h.* 18:20
fowls that fly in midst of *h.* 19:17
came down from God out of *h.* 20:9
earth and *h.* fled away, and. 11
a new *h.* and earth, the first *h.* 21:1
Jerusalem descending out of *h.* 10
  see **fowl, fowls**

from **heaven**

and the rain *from h.* was. *Gen* 8:2
rain bread *from h.* for you. *Ex* 16:4
I have talked with you *from h.*
  20:22; *Neh* 9:13
look down *from h.*   *Deut* 26:15
  Isa 63:15; *Lam* 3:50
as dust *from h.* shall it. *Deut* 28:24
cast great stones *from h. Josh* 10:11
they fought *from h.*   *Judg* 5:20
Lord thundered *from h.* 2 *Sam* 22:14
down *from h.* and there came down
  fire *from h.*   2 *Ki* 1:10, 12, 14
answered him *from h.* 1 *Chr* 21:26
hear thou *from h.*   2 *Chr* 6:21, 23
  27, 30
the fire came down *from h.* 7:1
then will I hear *from h.* and. 14
bread *from h.* for hunger. *Neh* 9:15
heardest them *from h.* 27, 28
of God is fallen *from h. Job* 1:16
the Lord looked down *from h.*
  Ps 14:2; 53:2
the Lord looketh *from h. Ps* 33:13
shall send *from h.* and save. 57:3
judgement to be heard *from h.* 76:8
O God, look down *from h.* 80:14
shall look down *from h.* 85:11
from h. did the Lord behold. 102:19
from h. O Lucifer!   *Isa* 14:12
as snow falleth *from h.* and. 55:10
Lord cast down *from h.*   *Lam* 2:1
came down *from h.*   *Dan* 4:13
an holy one coming down *from h.* 23
fell a voice *from h.* saying. 31
  Mat 3:17; *Luke* 3:22; *John* 12:28
shew them a sign *from h. Mat* 16:1
John, whence was it? *from h.* or of?
  21:25; *Mark* 11:30; *Luke* 20:4
for the angel descended *from h.*
  Mat 28:2; *Rev* 10:1; 18:1; 20:1

seeking of him a sign *from h.*
    Mark 8:11; *Luke* 11:16
fire to come down *from h. Luke* 9:54
as lightning fall *from h.* 10:18
fire and brimstone *from h.* 17:29
signs shall there be *from h.* 21:11
appeared an angel *from h.* 22:43
Spirit descending *from h. John* 1:32
came down *from h.* 3:13; 6:33
except it be given him *from h.* 3:27
he that cometh *from h.* is above. 31
he gave them bread *from h.* to. 6:31
gave you not that bread *from h.* 32
I came *from h.* not to do. 38, 42
came down *from h.* 41, 50, 51, 58
came a sound *from h. Acts* 2:2
a light *from h.* shined about him.
    9:3; 22:6; 26:13
sheet let down *from h.* 11:5
voice answered me again *from h.* 9
good, and gave us rain *from h.* 14:17
God is revealed *from h. Rom* 1:18
man is the Lord *from h. 1 Cor* 15:47
our house that is *from h. 2 Cor* 5:2
an angel *from h.* preach. *Gal* 1:8
wait for his Son *from h. 1 Thes* 1:10
himself shall descend *from h.* 4:16
Lord Jesus shall be revealed *from*
    h. 2 *Thes* 1:7
him that speaketh *from h. Heb* 12:25
gospel to you with the Holy Ghost
    sent down *from h.* 1 *Pet* 1:12
fell a great star *from h. Rev* 8:10
and I saw a star fall *from h.* 9:1
voice *from h.,* Seal up those things.
    10:4, 8; 11:12; 14:2, 13; 18:4
fire come down *from h.* 13:13

    see **God** *of heaven*

    host, or, *hosts of* **heaven**
seest the *host of h. Deut* 4:19
and worshipped the *host of h.* 17:3
Lord sitting on the throne and the
    host of h. 1 Ki 22:19; 2 *Chr* 18:18
Israel worshipped the *host of h.*
    2 *Ki* 17:16
Manasseh worshipped *host of h.*
    21:3; 2 *Chr* 33:3
built altars for the *host of h.*
    2 *Ki* 21:5; 2 *Chr* 33:5
vessels made for *host of h. 2 Ki* 23:4
that burnt incense to *host of h.* 5
made the *h.* of heavens with their
    host, and the *host of h. Neh* 9:6
all the *host of h.* shall be. *Isa* 34:4
them before the *host of h. Jer* 8:2
incense to all the *host of h.* 19:13
as the *host of h.* cannot be. 33:22
even to the *host of h. Dan* 8:10
them that worship *host of h.Zeph* 1:5
up to worship the *host of h. Acts* 7:42

    in **heaven**
nor likeness of any thing *in h.*
    Ex 20:4; *Deut* 5:8
what God *in h.* can do? *Deut* 3:24
that the Lord he is God *in h.* 4:39
in h. that thou shouldest say. 30:12
God he is God *in h. Josh* 2:11
is no God like thee *in h. 1 Ki* 8:23
    2 *Chr* 6:14
hear thou *in h.* 1 *Ki* 8:30, 32, 34
    36, 39, 43, 45, 49
make windows *in h.* 2 *Ki* 7:2, 19
all that is *in h.* and. 1 *Chr* 29:11
art not thou God *in h.?* 2 *Chr* 20:6
my witness *in h. Job* 16:19
the Lord's throne is *in h. Ps* 11:4
whom have I *in h.* but thee? 73:25
thy thunder was *in the h.* 77:18*
an east wind to blow *in the h.* 78:26
who *in h.* can be compared to? 89:6*
as a faithful witness *in h.* 37*
himself to behold things *in h.* 113:6
thy word is settled *in h.* 119:89
that did he *in h.* and earth. 135:6
for God is *in h.* and thou. *Eccl* 5:2
sword shall be bathed *in h. Isa* 34:5
the stork *in h.* knoweth her. *Jer* 8:7
there is a God *in h.* that. *Dan* 2:28
signs and wonders *in h.* and. 6:27
buildeth his stories *in h. Amos* 9:6
great is your reward *in h. Mat* 5:12
your Father who is *in h.* 16

of your Father who is *in h. Mat* 5:45
be perfect as your Father *in h.* 48
which art *in h.* 6:9; *Luke* 11:2
will be done on earth, as it is *in h.*
    Mat 6:10; *Luke* 11:2
yourselves treasures *in h. Mat* 6:20
shall your Father *in h.* give. 7:11
will of my Father *in h.* 21; 12:50
before my Father *in h.* 10:32
I deny before my Father *in h.*
but my Father which is *in h.* 16:17
shall be bound *in h.:* shall be loosed
    in h. 19; 18:18
in h. their angels do always behold
    the face of my Father *in h.* 18:10
for them of my Father *in h.* 19
thou shalt have treasure *in h.* 19:21
    Luke 18:22
are as the angels of God *in h.*
    Mat 22:30; *Mark* 12:25
your Father who is *in h. Mat* 23:9
sign of the Son of man *in h.* 24:30
all power is given to me *in h.* 28:18
will your Father *in h. Mark* 11:26
the powers that are *in h.* 13:32
no, not the angels which are *in h.* 32
reward is great *in h. Luke* 6:23
your names are written *in h.* 10:20
joy shall be *in h.* over one. 15:7
peace *in h.* and glory in. 19:38
Son of man who is *in h. John* 3:13
wonders *in h.* above and. *Acts* 2:19
whether *in h.* or in earth. 1 *Cor* 8:5
gather in one, things *in h. Eph* 1:10
of whom the whole family *in h.* 3:15
your master is *in h.* 6:9; *Col* 4:1
should bow, of things *in h. Phil* 2:10
is *in h.* from whence we look. 3:20
is laid up for you *in h. Col* 1:5
all things created that are *in h.* 16
him to reconcile all things *in h.* 20
ye have *in h.* a better. *Heb* 10:34
born which are written *in h.* 12:23
inheritance reserved *in h. 1 Pet* 1:4
there are three that bear record *in h.*
    1 *John* 5:7
door was opened *in h. Rev* 4:1
a throne was set *in h.* and one. 2
no man *in h.* or earth was. 5:3
creature *in h.* saying, Blessing. 13
was silence *in h.* 8:1
great voices *in h.* 11:15
temple of God was opened *in h.* 19
a great wonder *in h.* 12:1, 3
there was war *in h.:* Michael. 7
place found any more *in h.* 8
loud voice saying *in h.* 10; 19:1
them that dwell *in h.* 13:6
of the temple which is *in h.* 14:17
I saw another sign *in h.* great. 15:1
the tabernacle of testimony *in h.* 5
the armies that were *in h.* 19:14

    into **heaven**
take up Elijah *into h.* 2 *Ki* 2:1
up by a whirlwind *into h.* 11
if I ascend *into h.* thou. *Ps* 139:8
who hath ascended *into h.? Pr* 30:4
    Rom 10:6
said, I will ascend *into h. Isa* 14:13
was received up *into h. Mark* 16:19
angels were gone away *into h.*
    Luke 2:15
from them, carried up *into h.* 24:51
into h. taken from you *into h.* Jesus
    shall come ... go *into h. Acts* 1:11
looked up stedfastly *into h.* 7:55
was received up *into h.* 10:16; 11:10
into h. itself, to appear. *Heb* 9:24
who is gone *into h.* on. 1 *Pet* 3:22

    see **kingdom**

    heaven joined with *stars*
stars in the firmament of *h. Gen* 1:17
thy seed as *stars of h.* 22:17; 26:4
    Ex 32:13; 1 *Chr* 27:23; *Neh* 9:23
you are this day as *stars of h.*
    Deut 1:10; 10:22
whereas ye were as *stars of h.* 28:62
the *stars of h.* shall not. *Isa* 13:10
cover *h.* and make *stars. Ezek* 32:7
merchants as *stars of h. Nah* 3:16
the *stars* shall fall from *h.*
    Mat 24:29; *Mark* 13:25

and the *stars* of *h.* fell. *Rev* 6:13
the third part of *stars of h.* 12:4

    to **heaven**, *or unto* **heaven**
top may reach *unto h. Gen* 11:4
and the top of it reached *to h.* 28:12
the cities great and walled up *to h.*
    Deut 1:28; 9:1
thou lift up thine eyes *unto h.* 4:19
who shall go up for us *to h.?* 30:12
I lift up my hand *to h.* and. 32:40
smoke of the city ascended up *to h.*
    Josh 8:20
flame of the city ascended up *to h.*
    Judg 20:40
cry of city went up *to h.* 1 *Sam* 5:12
hands spread up *to h.* 1 *Ki* 8:54
that reacheth up *unto h.* 2 *Chr* 28:9
prayer came up even *unto h.* 30:27
Isaiah prayed and cried *to h.* 32:20
they mount up *to h. Ps* 107:26
her judgement reacheth *unto h.*
    Jer 51:9
height reached *to h. Dan* 4:11, 20
held up his left hand *unto h.* 12:7
they climb up *to h. Amos* 9:2
which art exalted *to h. Mat* 11:23
and looking up *to h.* 14:19
    Mark 6:41; *Luke* 9:16
looking up *to h.* he. *Mark* 7:34
much as his eyes *unto h. Luke* 18:13
and no man hath ascended up *to h.*
    John 3:13
Jesus lifted up his eyes *to h.* 17:1
caught up *to* the third *h.* 2 *Cor* 12:2
lifted up his hand *to h. Rev* 10:5
and they ascended up *to h.* 11:12
sins have reached *unto h.* 18:5

    toward **heaven**
look now *toward h. Gen* 15:5
sprinkle it *toward* the *h. Ex* 9:8
Moses sprinkled it up *toward h.* 10
thine hand *toward h.* 22; 10:21
forth his rod *toward h.* 9:23
forth his hand *toward h.* 10:22
flame went up *toward h. Judg* 13:20
Solomon spread forth his hands *to-*
    ward h. 1 *Ki* 8:22; 2 *Chr* 6:13
dust on their heads *toward h.*
    Job 2:12
as an eagle *toward h. Pr* 23:5
stedfastly *toward h. Acts* 1:10

    under **heaven**
let the waters *under h. Gen* 1:9
destroy all flesh from *under h.* 6:17
high hills *under* the whole *h.* 7:19
remembrance of Amalek from *under*
    h. Ex 17:14; *Deut* 25:19
thee on nations *under h. Deut* 2:25
divided to all nations *under h.* 4:19
their name from *under h.* 7:24; 9:14
out his name from *under h.* 29:20
of Israel from *under h.* 2 *Ki* 14:27
seeth *under* the whole *h. Job* 28:24
directeth it *under* the whole *h.* 37:3
is *under* the whole *h.* is mine. 41:11
all things done *under h. Eccl* 1:13
good they should do *under h.* 2:3
every purpose *under* the *h.* 3:1
out of one part *under h. Luke* 17:24
of every nation *under h. Acts* 2:5
none other name *under h.* • 4:12
every creature *under h. Col* 1:23

    heavenly
h. Father will forgive you. *Mat* 6:14
yet your *h.* Father feedeth them. 26
your *h.* Father knoweth that ye. 32
every plant my *h.* Father. 15:13
so shall my *h.* Father do also. 18:35
a multitude of the *h.* host. *Luke* 2:13
your *h.* Father shall give. 11:13
believe, if I tell you of *h. John* 3:12
not disobedient to the *h. Acts* 26:19
the *h.* such are they that are *h.*
    1 *Cor* 15:48
also bear the image of the *h.* 49
spiritual blessings in *h. Eph* 1:3
right hand in *h.* places. 1:20; 2:6
unto the powers in *h.* places. 3:10
preserve me to his *h.* 2 *Tim* 4:18
partakers of the *h. Heb* 3:1
and have tasted of the *h.* gift. 6:4
example and shadow of *h.* 8:5

h. things with better sacrifices.
       Heb 9:23
an *h.* country.   11:16
the *h.* Jerusalem.   12:22

heavens
thus the *h.* and the earth. *Gen* 2:1
generations of the *h.* and the earth in
 the day that the Lord made the *h.* 4
give ear, O *h.* I will speak.
     Deut 32:1; *Isa* 1:2
also his *h.* shall drop. *Deut* 33:28
earth trembled, the *h.* *Judg* 5:4
he bowed the *h.* and came.
    2 *Sam* 22:10; *Ps* 18:9
the heaven of *h.* cannot. 1 *Ki* 8:27
the Lord made the *h.* 1 *Chr* 16:26
 Neh 9:6; *Ps* 96:5; 102:25; 136:5
let the *h.* be glad, let. 1 *Chr* 16:31
then hear from the *h.* 2 *Chr* 6:25
       33, 35, 39
is grown up to the *h.* *Ezra* 9:6
spreadeth out the *h.* *Job* 9:8
man riseth not till the *h.* be. 14:12
yea, the *h.* are not clean in. 15:15
excellency mount up to the *h.* 20:6
Spirit he hath garnished the *h.* 26:13
look to the *h.* and see, and. 35:5
thou hast set thy glory above the *h.*
      Ps 8:1; 113:4
I consider thy *h.* the work. *Ps* 8:3
the *h.* declare the glory of God. 19:1
the Lord were the *h.* made. 33:6
shall call to the *h.* from above. 50:4
h. shall declare his righteousness. 6
exalted, O God, above *h.* 57:5, 11
        108:5
mercy is great unto the *h.* 57:10
        108:4
him that rideth upon the *h.* 68:4, 33
h. also dropped at the presence. 8
their mouth against the *h.* 73:9
thy *h.* shall praise thy wonders. 89:5
the *h.* are thine, the earth also. 11
let the *h.* rejoice, earth be glad.
    96:11; *Rev* 12:12
h. declare his righteousness. *Ps* 97:6
who stretchest out the *h.* 104:2
       Isa 40:22
mercy is great above the *h. Ps* 108:4
the heaven, even the *h.* are. 115:16
bow thy *h.* O Lord, and come. 144:5
praise ye the Lord from the *h.* 148:1
ye *h.* of *h.* and waters above the *h.* 4
he established the *h.* *Pr* 3:19
when he prepared the *h.* I was. 8:27
will shake the *h.* and earth. *Isa* 13:13
      Hag 2:6, 21
the *h.* shall be rolled. *Isa* 34:4
he that created the *h.* 42:5; 45:18
sing, O ye *h.* for the Lord. 44:23
Lord, that stretchest forth the *h.* 24
45:12; 51:13; *Jer* 10:12; *Zech* 12:1
drop down ye *h.* from above. *Isa* 45:8
hand hath spanned the *h.* 48:13
sing, O *h.* and be joyful, O. 49:13
clothe *h.* with blackness, I. 50:3
eyes to the *h.* and look, the. 51:6
that I may plant the *h.* and lay. 16
for as the *h.* are higher than. 55:9
thou wouldest rend the *h.* and. 64:1
behold, I create new *h.* and. 65:17
for as the new *h.* which I. 66:22
astonished, O ye *h.* and *Jer* 2:12
I beheld the *h.* and they had. 4:23
birds of the *h.* were fled. 25; 9:10
shall the earth mourn, *h.* 4:28
the *h.* and the earth shall perish, and
 from under these *h.* 10:11
or can the *h.* give showers? 14:22
from under *h.* of the Lord. *Lam* 3:66
that the *h.* were opened. *Ezek* 1:1
      Mat 3:16
known that the *h.* do. *Dan* 4:26
I will hear the *h.*, they. *Hos* 2:21
the *h.* shall tremble, sun. *Joel* 2:10
and the *h.* and the earth. 3:16
his glory covered the *h.* *Hab* 3:3
four spirits of the *h.* *Zech* 6:5
and the *h.* shall give their dew. 8:12
powers of the *h.* shall be. *Mat* 24:29
coming up, he saw the *h. Mark* 1:10
not ascended into the *h.* *Acts* 2:34
whom the *h.* must receive until. 3:21

behold, I see the *h.* opened *Acts* 7:56
h. are the work of thine. *Heb* 1:10
Priest that is passed into *h.* 4:14
Priest made higher than the *h.* 7:26
by word of God the *h.* 2 *Pet* 3:5
but the *h.* which are now, are. 7
h. shall pass away with a great. 10
wherein the *h.* being on fire. 12

in the heavens
that sitteth *in the h.* *Ps* 2:4
Lord also thundered *in the h.* 18:13
mercy, O Lord, is *in the h.* 36:5
shalt thou establish *in the h.* 89:2
prepared his throne *in the h.* 103:19
God is *in the h.* he hath done. 115:3
O thou that dwellest *in the h.* 123:1
light is darkened *in the h. Isa* 5:30*
a multitude of waters *in the h.*
     Jer 10:13; 51:16
hearts to God *in the h.* *Lam* 3:41
shew wonders *in the h.* *Joel* 2:30
a treasure *in the h.* *Luke* 12:33
hands, eternal *in the h.* 2 *Cor* 5:1
of the Majesty *in the h.* *Heb* 8:1
patterns of things *in the h.* 9:23

heavier
be *h.* than the sand of. *Job* 6:3
my stroke is *h.* than my. 23:2
a fool's wrath is *h.* than. *Pr* 27:3

heavily
so that drave them *h.* *Ex* 14:25
I bowed down *h.* as one. *Ps* 35:14*
on ancient hast thou *h.* laid. *Isa* 47:6

heaviness
sacrifice I rose from my *h. Ezra* 9:5*
I will leave off my *h.* *Job* 9:27*
heart, and I am full of *h. Ps* 69:20
soul melteth for *h.* 119:28
a foolish son is the *h.* of. *Pr* 10:1
h. in the heart of man. 12:25
the end of that mirth is *h.* 14:13
there shall be *h.* and. *Isa* 29:2*
of praise for spirit of *h.* 61:3
that I have great *h.* and. *Rom* 9:2*
come again to you in *h.* 2 *Cor* 2:1*
my brother was full of *h. Phil* 2:26*
your joy be turned into *h.* *Jas* 4:9
if need be, ye are in *h.* 1 *Pet* 1:6*

heavy
Moses' hands were *h.* *Ex* 17:12
for this thing is too *h.* for. 18:18
because it is too *h.* for. *Num* 11:14
was an old man and *h.* 1 *Sam* 4:18
was *h.* on them of Ashdod. 5:6, 11
the hair was *h.* on. 2 *Sam* 14:26
father's *h.* yoke lighter. 1 *Ki* 12:4
 10, 11, 14; 2 *Chr* 10:4, 10, 11, 14
sent to thee with *h.* 1 *Ki* 14:6
went to his house *h.* 20:43; 21:4
the bondage was *h.* *Neh* 5:18
shall my hand be *h.* *Job* 33:7
and night thy hand was *h.* *Ps* 32:4
h. burden they are too *h.* 38:4
singeth songs to an *h.* *Pr* 25:20
stone is *h.* and sand weighty. 27:3
wine to those that be of *h.* 31:6*
make their ears *h.*, shut. *Isa* 6:10
transgression thereof shall be *h.*24:20
and the burden thereof is *h.* 30:27*
carriages were *h.* loaden. 46:1*
this the fast, to undo the *h.*? 58:6*
neither his ear *h.* that it. 59:1
hath made my chain *h.* *Lam* 3:7
all ye that are *h.* laden. *Mat* 11:28
for they bind *h.* burdens. 23:4
sorrowful, and very *h.* 26:37*
for their eyes were very *h.* 43
    Mark 14:33*, 40*
were with him, were *h. Luke* 9:32

Heber
the sons of Beriah, *H. Gen* 46:17
      1 *Chr* 7:31
H. the Kenite. *Judg* 4:11, 17; 5:24
which was the son of *H. Luke* 3:35

Hebrew, language
written over him in *H. Luke* 23:38
      John 19:20
a pool called in the *H.* *John* 5:2
called in *H.* Gabbatha. 19:13
called in *H.* Golgotha. 17
Paul spake to them in *H.*
    Acts 21:40; 22:2

a voice saying in the *H.* *Acts* 26:14
in *H.* Abaddon. *Rev* 9:11
in the *H.* Armageddon. 16:16

Hebrew man
an *H.* man, be sold. *Deut* 15:12

Hebrew, servant
the *H.* servant came in. *Gen* 39:17
if thou buy an *H.* servant. *Ex* 21:2

Hebrew woman, women
a midwife to *H.* women. *Ex* 1:16
H. women are not as the. 19
thee a nurse of the *H.* women? 2:7
if any *H.* woman be. *Deut* 15:12

Hebrewess
man should let an *H.* *Jer* 34:9

Hebrew
told Abraham the *H.* *Gen* 14:13
see he hath brought in an *H.* 39:14
with us a young man, an *H.* 41:12
Egyptian smiting an *H.* *Ex* 2:11
H. or Hebrewess go free. *Jer* 34:9
I am an *H.* *Jonah* 1:9

Hebrews
out of the land of the *H. Gen* 40:15
might not eat with the *H.* 43:32
this is one of the *H.* *Ex* 2:6
two men of the *H.* strove. 13
God of the *H.* 3:18; 5:3; 7:16
     9:1, 13; 10:3
shout in camp of the *H.* 1 *Sam* 4:6
ye be not servants to the *H.* 9
let the *H.* hear. 13:3
lest the *H.* make swords. 19
behold the *H.* come forth. 14:11
the *H.* that were with the. 21
princes said, What do these *H.*? 29:3
Grecians against the *H.* *Acts* 6:1
they *H.* or Israelites? 2 *Cor* 11:22
an Hebrew of the *H.* *Phil* 3:5

Hebron, place
Sarah died in Kirjath-arba, the same
 is *H. Gen* 23:2; 35:27; *Josh* 14:15
     20:7; *Judg* 1:10
out of the vale of *H.* *Gen* 37:14
H. was built seven. *Num* 13:22
as he did to *H.* so he. *Josh* 10:39
Joshua gave to Caleb *H.* 14:13, 14
      Judg 1:20
them which were in *H.* 1 *Sam* 30:31
Go up? he said, Unto *H.* 2 *Sam* 2:1
David was king in *H.* 11; 5:5
   1 *Ki* 2:11; 1 *Chr* 29:27
Joab and his men came to *H.*
      2 *Sam* 2:32
to David were sons born in *H.* 3:2, 5
      1 *Chr* 3:1, 4
they buried Abner in *H.* 2 *Sam* 3:32
head of Ish-bosheth in *H.* 4:12
to *H.* and David made a league with
 them in *H.* 5:3; 1 *Chr* 11:3
wives after he was come from *H.*
      2 *Sam* 5:13
vowed to the Lord in *H.* 15:7
Absalom reigneth in *H.* 10
cities of Judah *H.* a. 1 *Chr* 6:57
with a perfect heart to *H.* 12:38
built Zorah, *H.* in. 2 *Chr* 11:10

Hebron, person
Amram, *H.* and Uzziel. *Ex* 6:18
 Num 3:19; 1 *Chr* 6:2, 18; 23:12
Mareshah father of *H.* 1 *Chr* 2:42
the sons of *H.* 43; 15:9; 23:19; 24:23

hedge
hast thou not made an *h.* *Job* 1:10
of slothful is an *h.* *Pr* 15:19
breaketh a *h.*, a serpent. *Eccl* 10:8*
I will take away the *h.* *Isa* 5:5
nor made up the *h.* for. *Ezek* 13:5*
man that should make up *h.* 22:30*
sharper than a thorn *h.* *Mi* 7:4
h. about it, digged for. *Mark* 12:1

hedge
behold, I will *h.* up thy. *Hos* 2:6

hedged
whom God hath *h.* in. *Job* 3:23
hath *h.* me about, I. *Lam* 3:7*
a vineyard, and *h.* it. *Mat* 21:33

hedges
amongst plants and *h.* 1 *Chr* 4:23

hast thou broken down her *h.?*
    Ps 80:12; 89:40
run to and fro by the *h.* *Jer* 49:3*
which camp in the *h.* *Nah* 3:17
the highways and *h.* *Luke* 14:23

heed
Amasa took no *h.* to. *2 Sam* 20:10
Jehu took no *h.* to. *2 Ki* 10:31
by taking *h.* according. *Ps* 119:9
wicked doer giveth *h.* *Pr* 17:4
preacher gave good *h.* *Eccl* 12:9*
diligently with much *h.* *Isa* 21:7
let us not give *h.* to any. *Jer* 18:18
h. to me, O Lord, and hearken. 19
he gave *h.* unto them. *Acts* 3:5
the people of Samaria gave *h.* 8:6
they gave *h.* to Simon from least. 10
neither give *h.* to fables. *1 Tim* 1:4
    Tit 1:14
h. to seducing spirits. *1 Tim* 4:1
give the more earnest *h.* *Heb* 2:1
see **take**

heel, -s
thou shalt bruise his *h.* *Gen* 3:15
hold on Esau's *h.* 25:26; *Hos* 12:3
that biteth the horses' *h. Gen* 49:17
settest a print on the *h. Job* 13:27*
gin shall take him by the *h.* 18:9
friend, hath lifted up his *h.* against
  me. *Ps* 41:9; *John* 13:18
when iniquity of my *h.* *Ps* 49:5
iniquity are thy *h.* made. *Jer* 13:22

Hege
unto the custody of *H.* *Esth* 2:3

heifer
take me an *h.* of three. *Gen* 15:9
bring me a red *h.* *Num* 19:2
burn the *h.* in his sight. 5
gather up the ashes of the *h.* 9
that city shall strike off *h.'s* neck. *Deut* 21:3
shall strike off *h.'s* neck. 4
wash hands over the *h.* 6
not plowed with my *h. Judg* 14:18
Lord said, Take an *h. 1 Sam* 16:2
out for Moab as an *h.* of. *Isa* 15:5*
Egypt is like a fair *h.* *Jer* 46:20
uttered their voice as an *h.* 48:34
ye are grown fat as an *h.* 50:11
back, as a backsliding *h. Hos* 4:16
Ephraim is as an *h.* that is. 10:11
the ashes of an *h.* *Heb* 9:13

height
the *h.* of the ark shall. *Gen* 6:15
ark of shittim wood, a cubit and a
  half be *h. Ex* 25:10, 23; 37:1, 10
h. of the altar shall. *Ex* 27:1; 38:1
h. of court shall be. 27:18; 38:18
h. of altar of incense. 30:2; 37:25
look not on the *h.* of. *1 Sam* 16:7
Goliath's *h.* was six cubits. 17:4
the *h.* of house of God. *1 Ki* 6:2
oracle twenty cubits in the *h.* 20
the *h.* of the one cherub was. 26
the *h.* of the house of Lebanon. 7:2
h. of the one chapiter was five. 16
the *h.* of the molten sea was. 23
h. of one base was three cubits. 27
with chariots I am come up to the *h.*
  of. *2 Ki* 19:23; *Isa* 37:24
the *h.* of one pillar was. *2 Ki* 25:17
it up a very great *h.* *2 Chr* 33:14
the *h.* of God's house. *Ezra* 6:3
is not God in the *h.* of heaven? and
  behold the *h.* of the. *Job* 22:12
Lord looked from *h.* of. *Ps* 102:19
the heaven for *h.,* and earth. *Pr* 25:3
in the depth, or in the *h.* *Isa* 7:11
come and sing in the *h.* *Jer* 31:12
O thou that holdest the *h.* 49:16
though she should fortify *h.* 51:53
in mountain of the *h.* of Israel.
    Ezek 17:23; 20:40
she appeared in her *h.* with. 19:11
therefore his *h.* was exalted. 31:5*
thou hast lifted up thyself in *h.* 10*
trees exalt themselves for *h.* 14*
fill the valleys with thy *h.* 32:5
image of gold whose *h. Dan* 3:1
saw and beheld a tree whose *h.* 4:10
and the *h.* thereof reached. 11, 20
whose *h.* was like the *h. Amos* 2:9
nor *h.* nor depth shall be. *Rom* 8:39

what is the *h.* of the love? *Eph* 3:18
breadth and *h.* of the city. *Rev* 21:16

heights
Lord, praise him in the *h. Ps* 148:1
I will ascend above the *h. Isa* 14:14

heinous
for this is an *h.* crime. *Job* 31:11

heir, -s
in my house is mine *h.* *Gen* 15:3
saying, This shall not be thine *h.* 4
Ishmael shall not be *h.* with. 21:10
we will destroy the *h.* *2 Sam* 14:7
an handmaid that is *h.* *Pr* 30:23
no sons? hath he no *h.?* *Jer* 49:1
be *h.* unto them that were his *h.* 2*
yet will I bring an *h.* *Mi* 1:15*
this is the *h.* *Mat* 21:38
    Mark 12:7; *Luke* 20:14
that he should be *h.* of. *Rom* 4:13
which are of the law be *h.* 14
children, then *h.;* *h.* of God, and
  joint-*h.* with Christ; if we. 8:17
ye are *h.* according to the. *Gal* 3:29
I say, that the *h.* as long as. 4:1
if a son, then an *h.* of God. 7
bondwoman shall not be *h.* 30
Gentiles should be fellow-*h. Eph* 3:6
h. according to the hope. *Tit* 3:7
whom he appointed *h.* of *Heb* 1:2
for them who shall be *h.* of. 14
God willing to shew unto the *h.* 6:17
h. of the righteousness by. 11:7
and Jacob, the *h.* with him of the. 9
h. of the kingdom he hath. *Jas* 2:5
as *h.* together of grace. *1 Pet* 3:7

Helam
the river came to *H.* *2 Sam* 10:16

Helbon
merchant in wine of *H. Ezek* 27:18

held
Joseph *h.* up his father's. *Gen* 48:17
when Moses *h.* up hand. *Ex* 17:11
the loops *h.* one curtain to. 36:12*
and *h.* the lamps in. *Judg* 7:20
Samson said unto lad that *h.* 16:26
she *h.* it, he measured. *Ruth* 3:15
Nabal *h.* a feast in his. *1 Sam* 25:36
for Joab *h.* back the. *2 Sam* 18:16
time Solomon *h.* a feast. *1 Ki* 8:65
sea *h.* three thousand. *2 Chr* 4:5
them *h.* both spears. *Neh* 4:16, 21
and with the other hand he *h.* 17
the king *h.* out the golden. *Esth* 5:2
if we have been sold, I had *h.* 7:4
my foot *h.* his steps, his *Job* 23:11
mouth must be *h.* in. *Ps* 32:9
thy mercy, O Lord, *h.* me up. 94:18
I *h.* him, and would not. *S of S* 3:4
the king is *h.* in the galleries. 7:5
took them captives, *h.* *Jer* 50:33
he *h.* up his right hand. *Dan* 12:7
h. a council against him. *Mat* 12:14
the men that *h.* Jesus. *Luke* 22:63
same man that was healed, *h.* Peter.
    Acts 3:11
part *h.* with Jews, part with. 14:4
dead wherein we were *h. Rom* 7:6
testimony which they *h.* *Rev* 6:9

held peace
at her, *h.* his *peace.* *Gen* 24:21
Jacob *h.* his *peace* until they. 34:5
and Aaron *h.* his *peace.* *Lev* 10:3
her husband *h.* his *peace* at her.
    Num 30:7; 11:14
Saul, he *h.* his *peace. 1 Sam* 10:27
people *h.* their *peace.* *2 Ki* 18:36
they *h.* their *peace,* and found.
    Neh 5:8
nobles *h.* their *peace. Job* 29:10
I was dumb, I *h.* my *peace. Ps* 39:2
h. their *peace. Isa* 36:21; *Mark* 3:4
    9:34; *Luke* 14:4; 20:26
have not I *h.* my *peace? Isa* 57:11
but Jesus *h.* his *peace. Mat* 26:63

Heldai
captivity even of *H.* *Zech* 6:10

Heli
which was the son of *H. Luke* 3:23

Helkath-hazzurim
place was called *H.* *2 Sam* 2:16

hell
*This word is generally used in the
Old Testament to translate the
Hebrew word* Sheol, *which really
means simply the place of the dead,
without reference to happiness or
the reverse, see* Gen 37:35; 42:38;
1 Sam 2:6; Job 14:13.
*In other passages there is an idea
of punishment. The American Revision retains the Hebrew word in
all places.*
In the New Testament the word
hell *is used to translate two words,*
[1] Hades, *generally meaning the
same as* Sheol, *the place of the dead,*
Acts 2:21; 1 Cor 15:55; Rev 20:13.
[2] Gehenna, *the place of retribution for evil deeds.*
Note.—*Where this last is the
meaning of a verse it is here starred.*

burn unto the lowest *h. Deut* 32:22
sorrows of *h.* compassed me.
    2 Sam 22:6; *Ps* 18:5
deeper than *h.* what canst? *Job* 11:8
h. is naked before him. 26:6
shall be turned into *h.* *Ps* 9:17
thou wilt not leave my soul in *h.*
    16:10; *Acts* 2:27
go down quick into *h.* *Ps* 55:15
my soul from the lowest *h.* 86:13
and the pains of *h.* gat hold. 116:3
if I make my bed in *h.* thou. 139:8
her steps take hold on *h.* *Pr* 5:5
her house is the way to *h.* 7:27
guests are in the depths of *h.* 9:18
h. and destruction are before. 15:11
depart from *h.* beneath. 24
shalt deliver his soul from *h.* 23:14
h. and destruction are never. 27:20
therefore *h.* hath enlarged. *Isa* 5:14
h. from beneath is moved. 14:9
shalt be brought down to *h.* 15
and with *h.* are we at. 28:15
debase thyself even unto *h.* 57:9
I cast him down to *h. Ezek* 31:16
they also went down unto *h.* 17
him out of the midst of *h.* 32:21
which are going down to *h.* with. 27
though they dig into *h. Amos* 9:2
out of the belly of *h. Jonah* 2:2
enlargeth his desire as *h. Hab* 2:5
shall be in danger of *h. Mat* 5:22*
body should be cast into *h.* 29*, 30*
to destroy soul and body in *h.*
    10:28*; *Luke* 12:5*
Capernaum brought down to *h.*
    Mat 11:23; *Luke* 10:15
gates of *h.* shall not. *Mat* 16:18
having two eyes, to be cast into *h.*
    18:9*; *Mark* 9:47*
twofold more child of *h. Mat* 23:15*
escape the damnation of *h.?* 33*
h. he lifted up his eyes. *Luke* 16:23
soul was not left in *h.* *Acts* 2:31
tongue is set on fire of *h. Jas* 3:6*
cast angels down to *h.* *2 Pet* 2:4*
and I have the keys of *h. Rev* 1:18
was Death, and *h.* followed. 6:8
death and *h.* delivered up the. 20:13
death and *h.* were cast into the. 14

helm
about with a small *h.* *Jas* 3:4*

helmet
he had a *h.* of brass. *1 Sam* 17:5, 38
and an *h.* of salvation. *Isa* 59:17
against shield and *h.* *Ezek* 23:24
they hanged the shield and *h.* 27:10
all of them with shield and *h.* 38:5
take *h.* of salvation, and. *Eph* 6:17
and for an *h.* the hope of. *1 Thes* 5:8

helmets
prepared spears and *h. 2 Chr* 26:14
forth with your *h.* *Jer* 46:4

help, *substantive*
I will make him an *h. Gen* 2:18
there was not found an *h.* meet. 20
father, said he, was my *h. Ex* 18:4
be thou an *h.* to him. *Deut* 33:7

upon the heavens in thy h. Deut 33:26
saved by Lord the shield of thy h. 29
they came not to the h. Judg 5:23
hot, ye shall have h. 1 Sam 11:9
gathered to ask h. of. 2 Chr 20:4
is not my h. in me ? Job 6:13
my hand, when I saw my h. 31:21
soul, there is no h. for him. Ps 3:2
the Lord send thee h. from. 20:2
thou hast been my h. leave. 27:9
waits for Lord, he is our h. 33:20
stand up for mine h. 35:2; 44:26
thou art my h. and my. 40:17; 70:5
praise him for the h. of his. 42:5
God is a very present h. in. 46:1
h. for vain is the h. 60:11; 108:12
because thou hast been my h. 63:7
my God, make haste for my h. 71:12
I have laid h. upon one that. 89:19
Lord had been my h. 94:17
he is their h. and their. 115:9, 10, 11
from whence cometh my h. 121:1
my h. cometh from Lord which. 2
our h. is in name of Lord. 124:8
man, in whom there is no h. 146:3
hath the God of Jacob for his h. 5
to whom will ye flee for h.? Isa 10:3
we flee for h. to be delivered. 20:6
nor be an h. nor profit, but. 30:5
that go down to Egypt for h. 31:1
against the h. of them that work. 2
failed for our vain h. Lam 4:17
holpen with a little h. Dan 11:34
but in me is thine h. Hos 13:9
having obtained h. of. Acts 26:22

help, *verb*
father, who shall h. thee. Gen 49:25
forbear to h. him, thou shalt surely
h. him. Ex 23:5*; Deut 22:4
let them rise and h. Deut 32:38
your brethren, and h. Josh 1:14
come unto me, and h. me. 10:4
us quickly, and save us, and h. us. 6
king of Gezer came up to h. 33
then h. me: then I will h. thee.
2 Sam 10:11; 1 Chr 19:12
Syrians feared to h. Ammon.
2 Sam 10:19; 1 Chr 19:19
woman said, H., O king. 2 Sam 14:4
2 Ki 6:26
come unto me to h. me. 1 Chr 12:17
day there came to David to h. 22
of Damascus came to h. 18:5
David commanded to h. 22:17
it is nothing with thee to h., h. us, O
Lord our God, we rest. 2 Chr 14:11
shouldest thou h. the ungodly. 19:2
then thou wilt hear and h.
for God hath power to h. and. 25:8
war with mighty power to h. 26:13
kings of Assyria to h. him. 28:16
Syria h. them, that they may h. 23
the Levites did h. them. 29:34
and his mighty men did h. him. 32:3
is the Lord our God, to h. us. 8
the men of his place h. Ezra 1:4
to require horsemen to h. 8:22
will he h. the evil doers. Job 8:20*
him that had none to h. him. 29:12
h. Lord. Ps 12:1
for there is none to h. 22:11
haste thee to h. me. 22:19; 38:22
40:13; 70:1
Lord shall h. them. 37:40
God shall h. her. 46:5
awake to h. me. 59:4
h. us, O God of salvation. 79:9
was none to h. 107:12; Isa 63:5
h. me, O Lord my God. Ps 109:26
my part with them that h. 118:7
h. thou me. 119:86
let thine hand h. me. 173
and let thy judgements h. me. 175
hath not another to h. Eccl 4:10
the Egyptians shall h. Isa 30:7
fear not, I will h. 41:10, 13, 14; 44:2
Lord God will h. me. 50:7, 9
army, which is come to h. Jer 37:7
people fell, and none did h. Lam 1:7
scatter all about to h. Ezek 12:14
out of hell with them that h. 32:21
princes came to h. me. Dan 10:13
his end, and none shall h. 11:45

him, saying, Lord h. me. Mat 15:25
on us and h. us. Mark 9:22
Lord, I believe, h. thou mine. 24
they should come and h. Luke 5:7
bid her therefore that she h. 10:40
into Macedonia, and h. us. Acts 16:9
crying out, men of Israel, h. 21:28
h. those women which. Phil 4:3
we may find grace to h. Heb 4:16

helped
Moses stood up and h. Ex 2:17
hath the Lord h. us. 1 Sam 7:12
following Adonijah, h. 1 Ki 1:7
and two kings that h. him. 20:16
and they were h. 1 Chr 5:20
but they h. them not, for the. 12:19
they h. David against the band. 21
when God h. the Levites that. 15:26
the Lord h. Jehoshaphat. 2 Chr 18:31
every one h. to destroy. 20:23
God h. him against the. 26:7
for he was marvellously h. till. 15
king of Assyria h. him not. 28:21
Shabbethai the Levite h. Ezra 10:15
officers of the king h. Esth 9:3
how hast thou h. him that ? Job 26:2
and I am h. Ps 28:7
brought low, and he h. me. 116:6
but the Lord h. me. 118:13
they h. every one his. Isa 41:6
day of salvation have I h. thee. 49:8
and they h. forward the. Zech 1:15
when he was come, h. Acts 18:27
the earth h. the woman. Rev 12:16

helper
nor was there any h. 2 Ki 14:26
my path, they have no h. Job 30:13
thou art the h. of the. Ps 10:14
Lord, be thou my h. 30:10
God is my h. 54:4
deliver him that hath no h. 72:12
and Zidon every h. Jer 47:4
salute Urbane, our h. Rom 16:9*
the Lord is my h. I will. Heb 13:6

helpers
among the mighty men, h. 1 Chr 12:1
and peace be to thine h. 18
the proud h. do stoop. Job 9:13
when all her h. shall be. Ezek 30:8
and Lubim were thy h. Nah 3:9
and Aquila my h. in. Rom 16:3*
but are h. of your joy. 2 Cor 1:24
we might be fellow-h. 3 John 8

helpeth
for thy God h. thee. 1 Chr 12:18
both he that h. shall fall. Isa 31:3
the Spirit also h. our. Rom 8:26
submit to every one that h. with us.
1 Cor 16:16

helping
the prophets of God h. Ezra 5:2
thou so far from me ? Ps 22:1
ye also h. together by. 2 Cor 1:11

helps
used h. undergirding. Acts 27:17
gifts of healings, h. 1 Cor 12:28

helve
head slippeth from the h. Deut 19:5

hem, -s
upon the h. of it thou shalt make.
Ex 28:33*, 34*; 39:24*, 25*, 26*
woman touched h. of his garment.
Mat 9:20*; 14:36*

Heman
wiser than Ethan, H. 1 Ki 4:31
Zerah, H. and Calcol. 1 Chr 2:6
H. a singer, son of Joel. 6:33
15:17, 19; 16:42
the sons of Asaph and of H. 25:1
4, 6; 2 Chr 5:12; 29:14; 35:15
H. God gave H. 14 sons. 1 Chr 25:6

hemlock
springeth up as h. in. Hos 10:4
of righteousness into h. Amos 6:12

hen
as a h. gathereth chickens.
Mat 23:37; Luke 13:34

Hen
crown shall be for H. Zech 6:14

hence
said, they are departed h. Gen 37:17
ye shall not go forth h. 42:15
carry up my bones from h. 50:25
Ex 13:19
go h. thrust you out h. Ex 11:1
depart and go h. thou and. 33:1
not with me, carry us not up h. 15
thee down quickly from h. Deut 9:12
h. out of Jordan twelve. Josh 4:3
depart not h. I pray thee. Judg 6:18
nor go h. but abide fast by. Ruth 2:8
get thee h. 1 Ki 17:3; Isa 36:10
Mat 4:10
O spare me, before I go h. Ps 39:13
take from h. thirty. Jer 38:10
he said, Get you h., walk. Zech 6:7
shall say, Remove h. to. Mat 17:20
cast thyself down from h. Luke 4:9
out, and depart h. 13:31; John 7:3
pass from h. to you. Luke 16:26
take things h.; make not. John 2:16
arise, let us go h. 14:31
my kingdom not h. 18:36
sir, if thou have borne him h. 20:15
the H. G. not many days h. Acts 1:5
I will send thee far h. unto. 22:21
come they not h. even ? Jas 4:1

henceforth
the ground not h. yield. Gen 4:12
neither must Israel h. Num 18:22
ye shall h. return no. Deut 17:16
shall h. commit no more. 19:20
I will not h. drive out. Judg 2:21
thy servant will h. not. 2 Ki 5:17
from h. thou shalt have. 2 Chr 16:9
about his people from h. Ps 125:2*
hope in the Lord from h. 131:3*
it with justice from h. Isa 9:7
h. there shall no more come. 52:1
mouth of thy seed's seed h. 59:21
thou shalt no more h. Ezek 36:12
in mount Zion from h. Mi 4:7
ye shall not see me h. Mat 23:39
I will not drink h. of this. 26:29
h. all generations shall. Luke 1:48
fear not, from h. thou shalt. 5:10
h. there shall be five in one. 12:52
h. ye know him, and. John 14:7
h. I call you not servants. 15:15
they speak h. to no man. Acts 4:17
I am clean, h. I will go unto. 18:6
that h. we should not. Rom 6:6*
should not h. live unto. 2 Cor 5:15*
h. know we no man, h. know. 16*
from h. let no man. Gal 6:17
h. be no more children. Eph 4:14*
that ye h. walk not as other. 17
h. there is laid up for. 2 Tim 4:8
h. expecting till enemies. Heb 10:13
who die in Lord, from h. Rev 14:13

henceforward
and h. among your. Num 15:23*
no fruit grow on thee h. Mat 21:19

Hephzi-bah
mother's name was H. 2 Ki 21:1
thou shalt be called H. Isa 62:4

herald
then an h. cried aloud. Dan 3:4

herb
the h. yielding seed. Gen 1:11, 12
I have given you every h. 29
made every h. 2:5
thou shalt eat the h. 3:18
even as the h. I have given. 9:3
hail smote every h. of. Ex 9:22, 25
the locusts eat every h. 10:12, 15
rain upon the tender h. Deut 32:2
were as the green h. 2 Ki 19:26
Isa 37:27
before any other h. Job 8:12
the bud of the tender h. 38:27*
wither as the green h. Ps 37:2
he causeth h. to grow for. 104:14
shall flourish like an h. Isa 66:14*

herbs
and with bitter h. eat it. Ex 12:8
Num 9:11
it as a garden of h. Deut 11:10
have it for garden of h. 1 Ki 21:2
into field to gather h. 2 Ki 4:39
and did eat up all the h. Ps 105:35

better is a dinner of h. *Pr* 15:17
and h. of the mountains are. 27:25
a clear heat upon h. *Isa* 18:4*
thy dew is as the dew of h. 26:19
I will dry up all their h. 42:15
how long the h. of every. *Jer* 12:4
is greatest among all h. *Mat* 13:32
    Mark 4:32
tithe all manner of h. *Luke* 11:42
who is weak eateth h. *Rom* 14:2
and bringeth forth h. *Heb* 6:7

herd, -s
Abraham ran to the h. *Gen* 18:7
Jacob divided his h. into two. 32:7
my lord also hath our h. 47:18
our flocks and h. will. *Ex* 10:9
your offering of the h. *Lev* 1:2
h. male or female. 3:1; *Num* 15:3
the tithe of the h. or. *Lev* 27:32
shalt kill of thy h. *Deut* 12:21
males that come of thy h. 15:19
Saul came after the h. *1 Sam* 11:5*
spared to take of his h. *2 Sam* 12:4
the h. in Sharon, h. in. *1 Chr* 27:29
Achor a place for the h. *Isa* 65:10
for young of the h. *Jer* 31:12
h. of cattle are perplexed. *Joel* 1:18
let not the h. nor flock. *Jonah* 3:7
there shall be no h. in. *Hab* 3:17
h. of swine feeding. *Mat* 8:30
  Mark 5:11; *Luke* 8:32
whole h. ran violently. *Mat* 8:32
  Mark 5:13; *Luke* 8:33
see flocks

herdman
prophet, but I was an h. *Amos* 7:14

herdmen
the h. of Abram and Lot. *Gen* 13:7
no strife between my h. and thy h. 8
h. of Gerar did strive with Isaac's h.
     26:20
chiefest of h. belonged. *1 Sam* 21:7
who was among the h. *Amos* 1:1

here
men said, hast thou h.? *Gen* 19:12
thy two daughters which are h. 15
therefore swear unto me h. by. 21:23
h. I am. 22:1, 7, 11; 27:1, 18; 31:11
 37:13; 46:2; *Ex* 3:4; *1 Sam* 3:4, 5
 6, 8, 16; *2 Sam* 1:7; 15:26; *Isa* 6:8
abide ye h. with the ass. *Gen* 22:5
I stand h! by the well. 24:13
set it h. before my brethren. 31:37
and h. also have I done. 40:15
one of your brethren h. with. 42:33
lo, h. is seed for you, ye shall. 47:23
Tarry ye h. for us, until. *Ex* 24:14
saying, Lo, we be h. *Num* 14:40
lodge h. this night, I will. 22:8, 19
h. seven altars, prepare h. 23:1, 29
go to war, and you sit h.? 32:6
we will build sheepfolds h. for. 16
who are all of us h. alive. *Deut* 5:3
after all the things we do h. 12:8
h. and with him that is not h. 29:15
cast lots for you h. *Josh* 18:6, 8
is there any man h.? *Judg* 4:20
and what hast thou h.? 18:3
lodge h. 19:9
behold, h. is my daughter. 24
give h. your advice and. 20:7
but abide h. fast by. *Ruth* 2:8
turn aside, sit down h. 4:1, 2
I am the woman that stood by thee h.
    1 Sam 1:26
hill and said, Is the seer h.? 9:11
behold, h. I am. 12:3; 22:12
    Isa 58:9
slay them h. and eat. *1 Sam* 14:34
Samuel said to Jesse, Are h.? 16:11
is there not h. under thine ? 21:8
h. wrapped in a cloth, none save h. 9
behold, we be afraid h. in. 23:3
what do these Hebrews h.? 29:3
tarry h. to-day. *2 Sam* 11:12
turn aside h. 18:30
be thou h. present. 20:4
h. be oxen. 24:22
nay, but I will die h. *1 Ki* 2:30
behold, Elijah is h. 18:8; 11:14
what doest thou h. Elijah? 19:9, 13
as thy servant was busy h. 20:40
not h. a prophet ? 22:7; *2 Ki* 3:11

Elijah said, Tarry h. *2 Ki* 2:2, 6
h. is Elisha. 3:11
why sit we h. until we die ? 7:3
lepers said, If we sit still h. 4
look there be h. none of the. 10:23
joy thy people present h. *1 Chr* 29:17
h. shall thy proud. *Job* 38:11
may say unto thee, H. we are. 35
this is my rest, h. will. *Ps* 132:14
behold, h. cometh a. *Isa* 21:9
thou h.? whom hast thou h.? 22:16
h. a little, and there. 28:10, 13
therefore, what have I h.? 52:5
Israel committeth h. *Ezek* 8:6, 17
gray hairs are h. and. *Hos* 7:9
a greater than Jonas is h. *Mat* 12:41
    Luke 11:32
a greater than Solomon is h.
   Mat 12:42; *Luke* 11:31
give me h. John Baptist's. *Mat* 14:8
we have h. but five loaves. 17
there be some standing h. 16:28
    Luke 9:27
to be h. let us make h. *Mat* 17:4
shall not be left h. one stone. 24:2
you, Lo, h. is Christ. 23; *Mark* 13:21
sit ye h. while I go and pray.
  Mat 26:36 *Mark* 14:32
tarry ye h. and watch. *Mat* 26:38
he is not h., he is risen. 28:6
  Mark 16:6; *Luke* 24:6
are not his sisters h.? *Mark* 6:3
stones and buildings are h. 13:1
heard done, do h. in thy. *Luke* 4:23
for we are h. in a desert place. 5:3
neither shall they say, Lo h.! 17:21
say to you, See h.; or, see there. 23
behold, h. is thy pound. 19:20
h. are two swords, he said. 22:38
unto them, Have ye h. any ? 24:41
there is a lad h. which. *John* 6:9
Lord, if thou hadst been h. 11:21, 32
h. is water. *Acts* 8:36
behold, I am h. Lord. 9:10
and h. he hath authority from. 14
are we all h. present before. 10:33
no harm: for we are all h. 16:28
who ought to have been h. 24:19
and all men which are h. 25:24
unto you all things done h. *Col* 4:9
h. men that die receive. *Heb* 7:8
for h. have we no continuing. 13:14
sit h. in a good place, or sit h. under.
    Jas 2:3
of your sojourning h. *1 Pet* 1:17
h. is the patience of the saints.
   Rev 13:10; 14:12
h. is wisdom; let him that. 13:18
h. are they that kept the. 14:12
and h. is the mind which hath. 17:9
see stand

hereafter
things that are to come h. *Isa* 41:23
h. also, if ye will not. *Ezek* 20:39
should come to pass h. *Dan* 2:29, 45
h. shall ye see the Son. *Mat* 26:64
man eat fruit of thee h. *Mark* 11:14
h. shall Son of man sit. *Luke* 22:69
I say, H. ye shall see. *John* 1:51
not now, thou shalt know h. 13:7
h. I will not talk much with. 14:30
pattern to them which h. *1 Tim* 1:16
things which shall be h. *Rev* 1:19
thee things which must be h. 4:1
there come two woes more h. 9:12

hereby
h. ye shall be proved, by. *Gen* 42:15
h. shall I know that ye are. 33
h. know that the Lord. *Num* 16:28
h. know that the living. *Josh* 3:10
nothing, yet am I not h. *1 Cor* 4:4
h. we do know that we. *1 John* 2:3
keepeth word, h. know we that. 5
h. perceive we the love of God. 3:16
h. we know that we are of. 19
and h. we know that he abideth. 24
h. know ye the Spirit of God. 4:2
h. know we the Spirit of truth. 6
h. know we that we dwell in him. 13

herein
only h. will the men. *Gen* 34:22*
h. thou hast done foolishly.
    2 Chr 16:9

h. is that saying true. *John* 4:37
h. is a marvellous thing, that. 9:30
h. is my Father glorified. 15:8
h. do I exercise myself. *Acts* 24:16
h. I give my advice, for. *2 Cor* 8:10
h. is love. *1 John* 4:10
h. is love made perfect. 17

heresies
(*This word never appears in the
New Testament in its strict
modern meaning, but means sects,
factions*)
also h. among you. *1 Cor* 11:19†
the flesh, wrath, strife, h. *Gal* 5:20
bring in damnable h. *2 Pet* 2:1

heresy
way which they call h. *Acts* 24:14*

heretick
an h. after the second. *Tit* 3:10*

heretofore
am not eloquent, neither h. *Ex* 4:10
straw to make brick as h. 5:7
not passed this way h. *Josh* 3:4
thou knewest not h. *Ruth* 2:11
not been such a thing h. *1 Sam* 4:7
which h. have sinned. *2 Cor* 13:2

hereunto
or who else can hasten h.? *Eccl* 2:25*
for even h. were ye. *1 Pet* 2:21

herewith
wast not satisfied h. *Ezek* 16:29
be meat in mine house, and prove
me now h. saith the. *Mal* 3:10

heritage
I will give it you for an h. *Ex* 6:8
and the h. appointed by. *Job* 20:29
the h. of oppressors which. 27:13
yea, I have a goodly h. *Ps* 16:6
give me the h. of those that. 61:5
people, they afflict thy h. 94:5
he may give them the h. of. 111:6
have I taken as an h. 119:111
lo, children are an h. of the. 127:3
and gave their land for an h.
  135:12; 136:21, 22
is the h. of the servants. *Isa* 54:17
I will feed thee with the h. 58:14
and ye made mine h. *Jer* 2:7
I give thee a goodly h.? 3:19
I have left mine h. 12:7
mine h. is as a lion. 8
mine h. is unto me as a speckled. 9
them again every man to his h. 15
discontinue from thine h. 17:4
O destroyers of mine h. 50:11
and give not thine h. to. *Joel* 2:17
plead with them for my h. 3:2
oppress a man and his h. *Mi* 2:2
feed the flock of thine h. 7:14
by the transgression of his h. 18
Esau's mountains and h. *Mal* 1:3
being lords over God's h. *1 Pet* 5:3*

heritages
to inherit the desolate h. *Isa* 49:8

Hermas, Hermes
salute *Hermas*, Patrobas, *Hermes*.
    Rom 16:14

Hermogenes
are Phygellus and H. *2 Tim* 1:15

Hermon
mount Sion, which is H. *Deut* 4:48
all mount H. Reuben. *Josh* 13:11
Tabor and H. shall. *Ps* 89:12
the dew of H. that descended. 133:3
top of Shenir and H. *S of S* 4:8

Hermonites
from the land of h. *Ps* 42:6

Herod
should not return to H. *Mat* 2:12
was there till the death of H. 15
H. slew all the children in. 16
for H. had laid hold on John. 14:3
    Mark 6:17
but when H.'s birthday was kept.
   Mat 14:6; *Mark* 6:21
H. feared John. *Mark* 6:20
beware of the leaven of H. 8:15
and H. being tetrarch. *Luke* 3:1
all the evils which H. had done. 19
H. heard of all that was done. 9:7

depart thence, for *H.*   *Luke* 13:31
Pilate sent Jesus to *H.*   23:7
H. was glad.   8
H. with his men of war set.   11
Pilate and *H.* were made.   12
no fault in this man, nor yet *H.*   15
both *H.* and Pilate.   *Acts* 4:27
H. vexed the church.   12:1
when *H.* would have brought.   6
out of the hand of *H.*   11
day *H.* made an oration to them. 21
had been brought up with *H.* 13:1
him to be kept in *H.'s.*   23:35

Herodians
see **sect**
their disciples, with *H.* saying, we.
  Mat 22:16; *Mark* 12:13
took counsel with the *H.* *Mark* 3:6

Herodias
John in prison for *H.'s* sake.
  Mat 14:3; *Mark* 6:17
the daughter of *H.* danced.
  Mat 14:6; *Mark* 6:22
H. had a quarrel.   *Mark* 6:19
reproved by John for *H.* *Luke* 3:19

Herodion
salute *H.* my kinsman. *Rom* 16:11

heron
the stork, the *h.* unclean. *Lev* 11:19
  Deut 14:18

herself
number to *h.* seven days. *Lev* 15:28
if she profane *h.* by playing. 21:9
if a woman bind *h.* by a. *Num* 30:3
she returned answer to *h.* *Judg* 5:29
bowed *h.* and travailed. *1 Sam* 4:19
Abigail bowed *h.* to the earth. 25:41
a woman washing *h.* *2 Sam* 11:2
she shall feign *h.* another. *1 Ki* 14:5
she lifteth up *h.* on high. *Job* 39:18
swallow found a nest for *h.* *Ps* 84:3
h. coverings of tapestry. *Pr* 31:22
hell hath enlarged *h.* *Isa* 5:14
screech owl find for *h.* a place. 34:14
as a bride adorneth *h.* with. 61:10
Israel hath justified *h.* *Jer* 3:11
of Zion that bewaileth *h.* 4:31
is feeble and turneth *h.* to. 49:24
maketh idols against *h.* *Ezek* 22:3
their idols she defiled *h.* 23:7
she hath wearied *h.* with lies. 24:12
she decked *h.* with her. *Hos* 2:13
Tyrus did build *h.* a. *Zech* 9:3
she said within *h.* If I. *Mat* 9:21
earth bringeth forth fruit of *h.*
  Mark 4:28
Elisabeth hid *h.* five. *Luke* 1:24
woman could in no wise lift up *h.*
  13:11
through faith Sarah *h.* *Heb* 11:11
Jezebel who calleth *h.* a. *Rev* 2:20
she hath glorified *h.* and lived. 18:7
and his wife hath made *h.* 19:7

see **himself**

Heshbon
Israel dwelt in *H.* *Num* 21:25
H. was the city of Sihon. 26
come into *H.* 27
a fire gone out of *H.* 28
H. is perished. 30
children of Reuben built *H.* 32:37
given Sihon king of *H.* *Deut* 2:24
while Israel dwelt in *H.* *Judg* 11:26
land of the king of *H.* *Neh* 9:22
like the fish pools of *H.* *S of S* 7:4
H. shall cry. *Isa* 15:4
for field of *H.* languish. 16:8
water thee with my tears, O *H.* 9
in *H.* they have devised. *Jer* 48:2
from cry of *H.* even to Elealeh. 34
stood under the shadow of *H.*, but a
  fire shall come out of *H.* 45
howl, O *H.* 49:3

see **Sihon**

Heth
Canaan begat Sidon and *H.*
  Gen 10:15; *1 Chr* 1:13
before the children of *H.* *Gen* 23:7
Abraham purchased of the sons of *H.*
  25:10; 49:32

because of the daughters of *H.*
  Gen 27:46

hew
h. thee two tables of stone. *Ex* 34:1
  Deut 10:1
shall *h.* down the graven. *Deut* 12:3
man goeth with neighbour to *h.* 19:5
they *h.* me cedar trees. *1 Ki* 5:6
and Hiram's builders did *h.* 18*
David set masons to *h.* *1 Chr* 22:2
Solomon told 80,000 to *h.* *2 Chr* 2:2
h. ye down trees and. *Jer* 6:6
cried aloud, *H.* down. *Dan* 4:14, 23

hewed
he *h.* two tables like the first.
  Ex 34:4; *Deut* 10:3
Saul *h.* oxen in pieces. *1 Sam* 11:7
and Samuel *h.* Agag in pieces. 15:33
h. stones to lay. *1 Ki* 5:17*
three rows of *h.* stone. 6:36; 7:12
measures of *h.* stones. 7:9, 11
buy *h.* stone to repair. *2 Ki* 12:12
thou hast *h.* thee out. *Isa* 22:16
my people have *h.* them. *Jer* 2:13
therefore have I *h.* them. *Hos* 6:5

hewer
h. of wood, unto drawer. *Deut* 29:11

hewers
be *h.* of wood and. *Josh* 9:21, 23
made them that day *h.* of wood. 27
80,000 *h.* in mountains. *1 Ki* 5:15
  2 Chr 2:18
money to masons and *h.* *2 Ki* 12:12
are *h.* with thee in. *1 Chr* 22:15
to thy servants the *h.* *2 Chr* 2:10
come against Egypt as *h.* *Jer* 46:22

heweth
boast against him that *h.*? *Isa* 10:5
that *h.* him out a sepulchre. 22:16
he *h.* him down cedars, and. 44:14

hewn
she hath *h.* out her seven. *Pr* 9:1
of stature shall be *h.* down. *Isa* 10:33
Lebanon is ashamed, and *h.* 33:9*
the rock whence ye are *h.* 51:1
h. down and cast into fire. *Mat* 3:10
  7:19; *Luke* 3:9
he had *h.* out in the rock. *Mat* 27:60
  Mark 15:46; *Luke* 23:53

see **stone**

Hezekiah, called **Ezekias**
H. Ahaz's son reigned. *2 Ki* 16:20
H. sent to the king of Assyria. 18:14
H. gave him all the silver in. 15
H. hath taken away. 22; *Isa* 36:7
let not *H.* deceive you. *2 Ki* 18:29
  2 Chr 32:15; *Isa* 36:14
hearken not to *H.* *2 Ki* 18:31, 32
  Isa 36:16
king *H.* heard it, he rent his.
  2 Ki 19:1; *Isa* 37:1
H. prayed. *2 Ki* 19:15; *2 Chr* 30:18
  Isa 37:15
H. was sick to death. *2 Ki* 20:1
  2 Chr 32:24; *Isa* 38:1
H. wept sore. *2 Ki* 20:3; *Isa* 38:3
turn again, tell *H.* *2 Ki* 20:5
Berodach sent a present to *H.* 12
  Isa 39:1
nothing, that *H.* shewed them not.
  2 Ki 20:13; *Isa* 39:2
H. said, Good is the word of the.
  2 Ki 20:19; *Isa* 39:8
H. slept with his fathers. *2 Ki* 20:21
  2 Chr 32:3
built what *H.* had destroyed.
  2 Ki 21:3; *2 Chr* 33:3
Neariah, *H.* and. *1 Chr* 3:23
came in days of *H.* and smote. 4:41
H. commanded to offer. *2 Chr* 29:27
H. rejoiced, and all the people. 30:21
the Lord hearkened to *H.* 30:20
H. spake comfortably to all. 22
H. gave the congregation 1000. 24
H. appointed the courses of. 31:2
then *H.* commanded to prepare. 11
rested on the words of *H.* 32:8
so shall not the God of *H.* deliver. 15
saved *H.* from Sennacherib. 22
H. rendered not again according. 25
not on them in the days of *H.* 26

H. prospered in all his. *2 Chr* 32:30
the children of Ater of *H.* *Ezra* 2:16
  Neh 7:21
which the men of *H.* copied. *Pr* 25:1
Manasseh the son of *H.* *Jer* 15:4
in days of *H.* 26:18; *Mi* 1:1
H. and all Judah put. *Jer* 26:19
to Hosea in days of *H.* *Hos* 1:1
Achaz begat *H.* *Mat* 1:9
H. begat Manasses. 10

Hezron
sons of Reuben, *H.* Carmi.
  Gen 46:9; *Ex* 6:14
son of Pharez, *H.* *Gen* 46:12
  Ruth 4:18; *1 Chr* 2:5; 4:1
H. begat Ram, Ram. *Ruth* 4:19
the sons of *H.* *1 Chr* 2:9
Caleb the son of *H.* 18
H. begat Segub. 21
after that *H.* was dead. 24
Jerahmeel the firstborn of *H.* 25

hid, *verb*
and Adam and his wife *h.* *Gen* 3:8
because I was naked, and I *h.* 10
Jacob *h.* them under the oak. 35:4
goodly child, she *h.* Moses. *Ex* 2:2
Moses slew the Egyptian, and *h.* 12
Moses *h.* his face, for he was. 3:6
Rahab *h.* the spies with. *Josh* 2:4, 6
because she *h.* messengers. 6:17, 25
and behold they are *h.* in the. 7:21
the five kings *h.* themselves. 10:16
Jotham was left, for he *h.* *Judg* 9:5
Samuel told Eli and *h.* *1 Sam* 3:18
Saul *h.* himself. 10:22
David *h.* himself. 20:24
Obadiah *h.* the. *1 Ki* 18:4, 13
and the Lord hath *h.* *2 Ki* 4:27
give thy son, she hath *h.* 6:29
and *h.* it, carried thence, and *h.* 7:8
h. him and his. 11:2; *2 Chr* 22:11
Ornan and four sons *h.* *1 Chr* 21:20
h. sorrow from mine eyes. *Job* 3:10
these things hast thou *h.* 10:13
thou hast *h.* their heart from. 17:4
young men saw me and *h.* 29:8
in net which they *h.* is their. *Ps* 9:15
neither hath he *h.* his face. 22:24
without cause they *h.* for me. 35:7
net that he hath *h.* catch himself. 8
I would have *h.* myself. 55:12
thy word have I *h.* in. 119:11*
the proud have *h.* a snare. 140:5
falsehood have we *h.* *Isa* 28:15
his hand, in quiver he *h.* me. 49:2
I *h.* not my face from shame. 50:6
and we *h.* as it were our. 53:3
in a little wrath I *h.* my face. 54:8
I *h.* me and was wroth, and. 57:17
your sins have *h.* his face. 59:2
for thou hast *h.* thy face from. 64:7
because they are *h.* from. 65:16
so I went and *h.* it by. *Jer* 13:5
from the place where I had *h.* it. 7
for they have *h.* snares for. 18:22
I have *h.* my face from this. 33:5
to take them, but the Lord *h.* 36:26
on these stones I have *h.* 43:10
have *h.* their eyes from. *Ezek* 22:26
h. I my face from them. 39:23, 24
thou hast *h.* from the wise.
  Mat 11:25; *Luke* 10:21
h. in three measures of meal.
  Mat 13:33; *Luke* 13:21
went and *h.* his lord's. *Mat* 25:18
I went and *h.* thy talent in the. 25
Elisabeth *h.* herself five. *Luke* 1:24
but Jesus *h.* himself. *John* 8:59
free man *h.* themselves. *Rev* 6:15

hid
suck of treasures *h.* in. *Deut* 33:19
and behold, it was *h.* in. *Josh* 7:22
the five kings are found *h.* 10:17
behold, he is *h.* now in. *2 Sam* 17:9
no matter *h.* from king. 18:13
  1 Ki 10:3; *2 Chr* 9:2
he was *h.* in house of God.
  2 Ki 11:3; *2 Chr* 22:12
Ahaziah was *h.* in. *2 Chr* 22:9
dig for it more than for *h.* *Job* 3:21
given to a man whose way is *h.*? 23
brooks, wherein the snow is *h.* 6:16
the thing that is *h.* bringeth. 28:11

seeing it is *h*. from eyes. *Job* 28:21
the waters are *h*. as with a. 38:30
belly thou fillest with *h*. *Ps* 17:14
nothing is *h*. from the heat. 19:6
searchest for her as for *h*. *Pr* 2:4
why sayest, My way is *h*. *Isa* 40:27
they are *h*. in prison houses. 42:22
nor their iniquity *h*. from. *Jer* 16:17
bound up, his sin is *h*. *Hos* 13:12*
h. that shall not be known. *Mat* 10:26
Mark 4:22; *Luke* 8:17; 12:2
this saying was *h*. *Luke* 9:45; 18:34
but now they are *h*. from. 19:42
beginning hath been *h*. in. *Eph* 3:9
mystery which hath been *h*. *Col* 1:26
in whom are *h*. all treasures. 2:3
and your life is *h*. with Christ. 3:3
by faith Moses was *h*. *Heb* 11:23

be hid
thy face shall I *be h*. *Gen* 4:14
thing *be h*. from. *Lev* 4:13; 5:3, 4
it *be h*. from the eyes. *Num* 5:13
shalt *be h*. from scourge. *Job* 5:21
darkness shall *be h*. in his. 20:26
of prudent men *be h*. *Isa* 29:14
repentance shall *be h*. *Hos* 13:14
though they *be h*. *Amos* 9:3
drunken, thou shalt *be h*. *Nah* 3:11
shall *be h*. in the day. *Zeph* 2:3
if our gospel *be h*. it is. *2 Cor* 4:3*

not be hid
on an hill *cannot be h*. *Mat* 5:14
he entered into an house, but he could
not be h. *Mark* 7:24
otherwise *cannot be h*. *1 Tim* 5:25

not hid
fathers, and *not h*. it. *Job* 15:18
iniquity have I *not h*. *Ps* 32:5
and my groaning is *not h*. 38:9
not h. thy righteousness. 40:10
and my sins are *not h*. from. 69:5
they are *not h*. from my face, neither
is iniquity hid from. *Jer* 16:17
Israel is *not h*. from me. *Hos* 5:3
saw that she was *not h*. *Luke* 8:47

Hiddekel
the third river is *H*. *Gen* 2:14
the side of the river *H*. *Dan* 10:4

hidden
if it be *h*. from him, he. *Lev* 5:2
it is not *h*. from thee. *Deut* 30:11
as an *h*. untimely birth. *Job* 3:16
number of years is *h*. to the. 15:20*
seeing times are not *h*. from. 24:1
in *h*. part shalt make me. *Ps* 51:6
wicked rise, a man is *h*. *Pr* 28:12
I will give thee *h*. riches. *Isa* 45:3
shewed thee new things, *h*. 48:6
how are his *h*. things sought! *Ob* 6
of these things are *h*. *Acts* 26:26
h. wisdom which God. *1 Cor* 2:7
will bring to light the *h*. things. 4:5
have renounced *h*. things. *2 Cor* 4:2
but let it be the *h*. man. *1 Pet* 3:4
I give to eat of the *h*. *Rev* 2:17

hidden ones
against thy *h*. ones. *Ps* 83:3

hide, substantive
his *h*. and flesh he. *Lev* 8:17*; 9:11*

hide
shall I *h*. from Abraham? *Gen* 18:17
we will not *h*. it from my. 47:18
she could not longer *h*. him. *Ex* 2:3
any ways *h*. their eyes. *Lev* 20:4
go astray, *h*. thyself. *Deut* 22:1, 4
lost things, thou mayest not *h*. 3
and *h*. yourselves there. *Josh* 2:16
tell what thou hast done, *h*. it. 7:19
to *h*. the wheat from. *Judg* 6:11
h. it not from me, if thou *h*.
1 Sam 3:17; *2 Sam* 14:18
secret place, and *h*. *1 Sam* 19:2
why should my father *h*.? 20:2
let me go, that I may *h*. myself. 5
the place where thou didst *h*. 19
h. thyself by the brook. *1 Ki* 17:3
chamber to *h*. 22:25; *2 Chr* 18:24
then will I not *h*. myself. *Job* 13:20
O that thou wouldest *h*. me. 14:13
he *h*. it under his tongue. 20:12

from his purpose, and *h*. *Job* 33:17
h. them in the dust together. 40:13
h. me under the shadow. *Ps* 17:8
h. me in his pavilion, in secret of his
tabernacle shall he *h*. me. 27:5*
thou didst *h*. thy face and I. 30:7
thou shalt *h*. them in secret. 31:20
and *h*. not thyself from my. 55:1
h. me from the secret counsel. 64:2
we will not *h*. them from their. 78:4
O Lord, wilt thou *h*. thyself? 89:46
h. not thy commandments. 119:19
I flee to thee to *h*. me. 143:9
h. my commandments. *Pr* 2:1*
I will *h*. my eyes from you. *Isa* 1:15
and *h*. thee in the dust, for. 2:10
they *h*. not their sin. 3:9
h. the outcasts. 16:3
h. thyself as it were for a. 26:20
to them that seek deep to *h*. 29:15
that thou *h*. not thyself from. 58:7
and *h*. it there in a hole. *Jer* 13:4
I commanded thee to *h*. there. 6
h. thee, thou, and Jeremiah. 36:19
ask thee a thing, *h*. nothing. 38:14
h. it not from us. 25
h. them in the clay. 43:9
h. not thine ear at my. *Lam* 3:56
no secret they can *h*. *Ezek* 28:3
garden of God could not *h*. 31:8
neither will I *h*. my face. 39:29
and shall *h*. a multitude. *Jas* 5:20
h. us from the face of him. *Rev* 6:16

see face

hide himself
doth not David *h*. himself?
1 Sam 23:19; 26:1
can any *h*. himself in? *Jer* 23:24
not be able to *h*. himself. 49:10
Jesus did *h*. himself. *John* 12:36

hide themselves
they that *h*. themselves. *Deut* 7:20
people did *h*. themselves in caves.
1 Sam 13:6
to *h*. themselves in field. *2 Ki* 7:12
the earth *h*. themselves. *Job* 24:4
iniquity may *h*. themselves. 34:22
they *h*. themselves, they. *Ps* 56:6
rise, men *h*. themselves. *Pr* 28:28
fled to *h*. themselves. *Dan* 10:7
h. themselves in top of. *Amos* 9:3

hidest
wherefore *h*. thou thy face?
Job 13:24; *Ps* 44:24; 88:14
why *h*. thyself in times? *Ps* 10:1
thou *h*. thy face, they are. 104:29
art a God that *h*. thyself. *Isa* 45:15

hideth
places where he *h*. *1 Sam* 23:23
he *h*. himself on the right. *Job* 23:9
when he *h*. his face, who? 34:29
who is he that *h*. counsel? 42:3
he *h*. his face, he will. *Ps* 10:11
yea, the darkness *h*. not. 139:12
he that *h*. hatred with. *Pr* 10:18
slothful *h*. his hand. 19:24*; 26:15*
man foreseeth and *h*. 22:3; 27:12
whosoever *h*. her, the. 27:16*
he that *h*. his eyes shall. 28:27
that *h*. his face from the. *Isa* 8:17
a man hath found, he *h*. *Mat* 13:44

hiding
by *h*. mine iniquity in. *Job* 31:33
my *h*. place. *Ps* 32:7; 119:114
shall overflow the *h*. *Isa* 28:17
man shall be as an *h*. place. 32:2
and there was the *h*. of. *Hab* 3:4

Hiel
H. the Beth-elite built. *1 Ki* 16:34

Higgaion
snared in his work *H*. *Ps* 9:16

high
[1] *Lofty, tall, elevated*, Deut 3:5;
Esth 5:14. [2] *Advanced*, Gen
29:7. [3] *Exalted in rank or
dignity*, Deut 26:19; Ps 62:9. [4]
Arrogant, boastful, Ps 18:27;
Isa 10:12. [5] *High places were
the altars built, according to custom, on conspicuous places. They
are usually thought of as places of*

idolatry, and certainly were such in
later times.
lo, it is yet *h*. day. *Gen* 29:7
Israel went out with *h*. hand.
Ex 14:8; *Num* 33:3
quails as it were two cubits *h*.
Num 11:31*
were fenced with *h*. walls. *Deut* 3:5
gods on the *h*. mountains. 12:2
and to make thee *h*. above. 26:19
get up above thee very *h*. 28:43*
till thy *h*. and fenced walls. 52
should say, our hand is *h*. 32:27*
at this house which is *h*. *1 Ki* 9:8
estate of a man of *h*. *1 Chr* 17:17
this house is *h*. shall be. *2 Chr* 7:21
a gallows be made of fifty cubits *h*.
Esth 5:14; 7:9
it is as *h*. as heaven. *Job* 11:8
he judgeth those that are *h*. 21:22
behold the stars, how *h*. 22:12
and the *h*. arm shall be. 38:15
he beholdeth all *h*. things. 41:34
wilt bring down *h*. looks. *Ps* 18:27*
give ear, both low and *h*. 49:2
men of *h*. degree are a lie. 62:9
also, O God, is very *h*. 71:19
built his sanctuary like *h*. 78:69*
strong is thy hand, *h*. is thy. 89:13
thou, Lord, art *h*. above earth. 97:9
99:2; 113:4
him that hath an *h*. look and. 101:5
for as the heaven is *h*. 103:11
I exercise in things too *h*. 131:1*
though the Lord be *h*. yet. 138:6
such knowledge, it is *h*. 139:6
let the *h*. praises of God be in. 149:6
praise him on *h*. sounding. 150:5
and as an *h*. wall in his. *Pr* 18:11
an *h*. look, and a proud heart. 21:4
wisdom is too *h*. for a fool. 24:7
afraid of that which is *h*. *Eccl* 12:5
on all cedars that are *h*. *Isa* 2:13
and upon all the *h*. mountains. 14
Lord sitting on a throne *h*. 6:1
the glory of his *h*. looks. 10:12
the *h*. ones of stature shall be. 33
of the *h*. ones that are on *h*. 24:21
the fortress of *h*. fort shall. 25:12
breach swelling out in an *h*. 30:13
my servant shall be very *h*. 52:13
for thus saith the *h*. and. 57:15
a glorious *h*. throne. *Jer* 17:12
waymarks, make thee *h*. 31:21*
thou makest thy nest *h*. 49:16
h. gates shall be burnt with. 51:58
their rings they were so *h*. *Ezek* 1:18
brought down the *h*. tree. 17:24
low, and abase him that is *h*. 21:26
behold the Assyrian was of *h*. 31:3
I will feed them on the *h*. 34:14
the two horns were *h*. *Dan* 8:3
whose habitation is *h*. that. *Ob* 3
against the *h*. towers. *Zeph* 1:16
sabbath day was an *h*. *John* 19:31
with an *h*. arm brought. *Acts* 13:17
mind not *h*. things. *Rom* 12:16
it is *h*. time. 13:11
casting down every *h*. *2 Cor* 10:5
for the prize of the *h*. *Phil* 3:14
had a wall great and *h*. *Rev* 21:12

see gate, God, hill, hills

most High
knowledge of *most H*. *Num* 24:16
when the *most H*. divided to the.
Deut 32:8
the *most H*. uttered. *2 Sam* 22:14
sing praise to the name of the Lord
most H. *Ps* 7:17; 9:2; 92:1
through mercy of the *most H*. 21:7
the tabernacle of the *most H*. 46:4
the Lord *most H*. is terrible. 47:2
pay thy vows to the *most H*. 50:14
against me, O thou *most H*. 56:2*
I will cry unto God *most H*. 57:2
knowledge in the *most H*.? 73:11
the right hand of the *most H*. 77:10
by provoking the *most H*. 78:17, 56
the children of the *most H*. 82:6
that thou art *most H*. over. 83:18
secret place of the *most H*. 91:1
thou hast made the *most H*. thy. 9
but thou, Lord, art *most H*. 92:8

the counsel of the *most H. Ps* 107:11
I will be like the *most H. Isa* 14:14
the face of the *most H. Lam* 3:35
of mouth of *most H.* proceedeth. 38
that the *most H.* ruleth. *Dan* 4:17
this is the decree of the *most H.* 24
most H. ruleth in kingdom. 25, 32
and I blessed the *most H.* and. 34
the saints of *most H.* shall. 7:18
was given to the saints of *most H.* 22
great words against the *most H.* 25
of the saints of the *most H.* 27
but not to the *most H. Hos* 7:16
called them to the *most H.* 11:7
the *most H.* dwelleth not. *Acts* 7:48

see mountain

on high

stretch wings on *h. Ex* 25:20; 37:9
of blue, to fasten it on *h.* 39:31*
God will set thee on *h. Deut* 28:1
hast lifted me up on *h. 2 Sam* 22:49
man who was raised up on *h.* 23:1
set Naboth on *h. 1 Ki* 21:9, 12
hast thou lifted up thine eyes on *h.?*
   2 Ki 19:22; *Isa* 37:23
kingdom was lifted up on *h.*
   1 Chr 14:2
praise God of Israel on *h.*
   2 Chr 20:19*
to set up on *h.* those. *Job* 5:11
and my record is on *h.* 16:19
of the Almighty from on *h.?* 31:2
she lifteth up herself on *h.* 39:18
up and make her nest on *h.?* 27
sakes therefore return on *h. Ps* 7:7
thou hast ascended on *h.* 68:18
O God, set me up on *h.* 69:29
lift not up your horn on *h.* 75:5
I will set him on *h.* because. 91:14
the Lord on *h.* is mightier. 93:4
setteth he the poor on *h.* 107:41
our God, who dwelleth on *h.?* 113:5
out a sepulchre on *h. Isa* 22:16
for the windows from on *h.* 24:18
host of high ones that are on *h.* 21
down them that dwell on *h.* 26:5
be poured on us from on *h.* 32:15
he dwelleth on *h.* 33:5
he shall dwell on *h.* 16
lift up your eyes on *h.* and. 40:26
voice to be heard on *h.* 58:4
shall roar from on *h. Jer* 25:30
deep set him up on *h. Ezek* 31:4*
may set his nest on *h. Hab* 2:9
lifted up his hands on *h.* 3:10
dayspring from on *h. Luke* 1:78
endued with power from on *h.* 24:49
he ascended up on *h. Eph* 4:8
of the Majesty on *h. Heb* 1:3

see place, places, priest, tower

higher

his king shall be *h. Num* 24:7
Saul was *h.* than any of. *1 Sam* 9:2
Jotham built *h.* gate of. *2 Ki* 15:35*
on the *h.* places, I even. *Neh* 4:13*
clouds, which are *h. Job* 35:5
to the rock that is *h.* than I. *Ps* 61:2
make him *h.* than kings. 89:27*
regardeth, and there be *h. Eccl* 5:8
are *h.* than earth, so my ways *h.* than
   your ways, thoughts. *Isa* 55:9
read Baruch in the *h. Jer* 36:10*
from the way of the *h. Ezek* 9:2*
for the galleries were *h.* than. 42:5
and this shall be the *h.* place. 43:13*
one horn *h.* than other. *Dan* 8:3
to thee, Friend, go up *h. Luke* 14:10
soul be subject to the *h. Rom* 13:1
an High Priest made *h. Heb* 7:26

highest

Lord thundered, the *H. Ps* 18:13
H. himself shall establish her. 87:5
nor the *h.* part of the dust. *Pr* 8:26*
she crieth upon the *h.* places. 9:3
is higher than the *h. Eccl* 5:8
and took the *h.* branch. *Ezek* 17:3
I will take of the *h.* branch. 22
from lowest chamber to the *h.* 41:7
saying, Hosanna in the *h. Mat* 21:9
   Mark 11:10
called the Son of the *H. Luke* 1:32
the power of the *H.* shall. 35
called the prophet of the *H.* 76

glory to God in the *h. Luke* 2:14
   19:38
shall be the children of the *H.* 6:35
sit not down in the *h.* room. 14:8
and love the *h.* seats in. 20:46*

highly

angel said, thou art *h. Luke* 1:28
that which is *h.* esteemed. 16:15*
Herod was *h.* displeased. *Acts* 12:20
think of himself more *h. Rom* 12:3
wherefore God also hath *h. Phil* 2:9
to esteem them very *h. 1 Thes* 5:13

highminded

be not *h.* but fear. *Rom* 11:20
   1 Tim 6:17
traitors, heady, *h. 2 Tim* 3:4*

highness

by reason of his *h.* I. *Job* 31:23*
that rejoice in my *h. Isa* 13:3*

highway, -s

and your *h.* shall be. *Lev* 26:22
by king's *h. Num* 20:17, 19; 21:22
   Deut 2:27
in days of Jael *h.* were. *Judg* 5:6
to kill the people in the *h.* 20:31
and draw them unto the *h.* 32
gleaned of them in the *h.* 45
kine went along the *h. 1 Sam* 6:12
wallowed in blood in *h. 2 Sam* 20:12
h. of fuller's field. *2 Ki* 18:17
   Isa 7:3; 36:2
h. of upright to depart. *Pr* 16:17
an *h.* for the remnant. *Isa* 11:16
shall be *h.* out of Egypt to. 19:23
h. lie waste, wayfaring man. 33:8
and an *h.* shall be there. 35:8
make in the desert a *h.* for. 40:3
and my *h.* shall be exalted. 49:11
cast up, cast up the *h.* 62:10
heart toward the *h. Jer* 31:21
shall say in all the *h. Amos* 5:16*
go therefore into the *h. Mat* 22:9
   Luke 14:23
Bartimaeus sat by *h. Mark* 10:46

Hilkiah

Eliakim son of *H. 2 Ki* 18:18
Eliakim son of *H.* to Hezekiah. 37
   Isa 36:22
saying, Go up to *H. 2 Ki* 22:4
H. gave book to. 8, 10; *2 Chr* 34:15
H. to enquire of the Lord for him.
   2 Ki 22:12; *2 Chr* 34:20
so *H.* went to Huldah. *2 Ki* 22:14
   2 Chr 34:22
commanded *H.* to bring *2 Ki* 23:4
Shallum begat *H.* and *H. 1 Chr* 6:13
H. son of Amaziah. 45
H. son of Meshullam. 9:11
H. the second son of Hosah. 26:11
H. the son of Shallum. *Ezra* 7:1
H. stood on Ezra's right. *Neh* 8:4
Seraiah the son of *H.* dwelt. 11:11
H. the priest went up with. 12:7
of *H.,* Hashabiah were priests. 21
servant Eliakim son of *H. Isa* 22:20
Jeremiah the son of *H. Jer* 1:1
son of *H.* was sent to Babylon. 29:3

hill

built an altar under the *h. Ex* 24:4*
which dwelt in that *h. Num* 14:45*
were ready to go up into the *h.*
   Deut 1:41*, 43*
circumcised Israel at *h. Josh* 5:3
they said, The *h.* is not. 17:16*
Joshua buried on the *h.* Gaash.
   24:30*; *Judg* 2:9
Eleazar was buried in *h. Josh* 24:33
Midianites were by *h. Judg* 7:1
house of Abinadab in *h. 1 Sam* 7:1
his servants went up the *h.* 9:11*
shalt come to *h.* of God. 10:5, 10
hid in *h.* of Hachilah. 23:19; 26:1
came down by covert of *h.* 25:20*
they were come to *h. 2 Sam* 2:24
much people came by the *h.* 13:34
Shimei went along on the *h.* 16:13
they hanged them in the *h.* 21:9*
Solomon built in the *h. 1 Ki* 11:7*
the *h.* Samaria, built on *h.* 16:24
to man of God to the *h. 2 Ki* 4:27
who shall ascend into the *h.? Ps* 24:3
remember thee from the *h.* 42:6

h. of God is as the *h.* of. *Ps* 68:15*
this is the *h.* which God. 16*
I will get me to the *h. S of S* 4:6
vineyard in a very fruitful *h. Isa* 5:1
shake his head against *h.* 10:32
be left an ensign on an *h.* 30:17
hosts shall fight for the *h.* 31:4
every mountain and *h.* shall. 40:4
hunt them from every *h. Jer* 16:16
measuring line upon the *h.* 31:39
holdest the height of the *h.* 49:16
gone from mountain to *h.* 50:6
make places about my *h. Ezek* 34:26
city that is set on an *h. Mat* 5:14
and every *h.* shall be. *Luke* 3:5
led him unto the brow of the *h.* 4:29
were come down from the *h.* 9:37*
the midst of Mars' *h. Acts* 17:22*

high hill, -s

all *high h.* under heaven. *Gen* 7:19
groves on every *high h. 1 Ki* 14:23
   2 Ki 17:10
is a *high h.* as the hill. *Ps* 68:15
why leap ye, ye *high h.?* this is. 16
high h. are a refuge for the. 104:18
every *high h.,* rivers. *Isa* 30:25
when on every *high h. Jer* 2:20, 23
remember groves on *high h.* 17:2
idols on every *high h. Ezek* 6:13
then they saw every *high h.* 20:28
wandered on every *high h.* 34:6

holy hill

on my *holy h.* of Zion. *Ps* 2:6
he heard me out of his *holy h.* 3:4
shall dwell in thy *holy h.?* 15:1
me, bring me to thy *holy h.* 43:3
worship at his *holy h.* the. 99:9

hill, with top

stand on *top* of the *h. Ex* 17:9
Hur, went to *top* of the *h.*
to go up to the *h. top. Num* 14:44
them to the *top* of an *h. Judg* 16:3*
David stood on *top* of an *h.*
   1 Sam 26:13*
Abner stood on the *top* of an *h.*
   2 Sam 2:25
little past the *top* of the *h.* 16:1*
sat on the *top* of an *h. 2 Ki* 1:9

hill country

inhabitants of *h. country. Josh* 13:6
of Aaron, Arba in *h. country.* 21:11
down into *h. country. Luke* 1:39
noised through all the *h. country.* 65

hills

of the everlasting *h. Gen* 49:26
and from the *h.* I behold. *Num* 23:9
out of the valleys and *h. Deut* 8:7
out of whose *h.* thou mayest. 9
it is a land of *h.* and valleys. 11:11
precious things of lasting *h.* 33:15
smote all country of *h. Josh* 10:40*
took all that land, the *h.* 11:16*
the gods of the *h. 1 Ki* 20:23, 28
all Israel scattered on the *h.* 22:17*
burnt incense on the *h. 2 Ki* 16:4
   2 Chr 28:4
thou made before the *h.? Job* 15:7
foundations also of the *h. Ps* 18:7*
cattle on a thousand *h.* are. 50:10
the little *h.* rejoice on every. 65:12
the little *h.* by righteousness. 72:3
h. were covered with shadow. 80:10*
strength of the *h.* is his also. 95:4
the *h.* melted like wax at. 97:5†
let the *h.* be joyful together. 98:8
springs, which run among *h.* 104:10*
he watereth the *h.* from his. 13*
he toucheth the *h.* and they. 32*
and the little *h.* skipped. 114:4, 6
I will lift up mine eyes to *h.* 121:1
mountains and all *h.* praise. 148:9
before the *h.* was I brought. *Pr* 8:25
skipping upon the *h. S of S* 2:8
be exalted above the *h. Isa* 2:2
day of the Lord shall be on all *h.* 14
did tremble, their carcases. 5:25
on all *h.* shall not come the. 7:25
who hath weighed the *h.* in? 40:12
and thou shalt make the *h.* 41:15
make waste mountains and *h.* 42:15
mountains shall depart. 54:10
the *h.* shall break forth. 55:12

blasphemed me upon the *h. Isa* 65:7
salvation hoped for from *h. Jer* 3:23
I beheld, and lo, the *h.* moved. 4:24
thy abominations on the *h.* 13:27
saith Lord to the *h. Ezek* 6:3; 36:4
in thy *h.* shall slain fall. 35:8
and say to the *h.* to the rivers. 36:6
burn incense on the *h. Hos* 4:13
and they shall say to the *h.* 10:8
and the *h.* shall flow with. *Joel* 3:18
wine, and all the *h. Amos* 9:13
be exalted above the *h. Mi* 4:1
arise, and let the *h.* hear thy. 6:1
the *h.* melt, and earth. *Nah* 1:5
perpetual *h.* did bow. *Hab* 3:6
great crashing from the *h. Zeph* 1:10
begin to say to the *h. Luke* 23:30

him

me he restored, and *h. Gen* 41:13
whosoever hath sinned, *h. Ex* 32:33
Caleb, *h.* will I bring. *Num* 14:24
to come near, even *h.* whom. 16:5
h. shalt thou serve, and to *h.*
Deut 10:20
the Lord hath chosen *h.* and. 18:5
see ye *h.* whom Lord. *1 Sam* 10:24
h. that dieth in city. *1 Ki* 14:11
16:4; 21:24
h. that pisseth against the wall.
21:21; *2 Ki* 9:8
they hid *h.* even *h.* and. *2 Ki* 11:2
and *h.* that followed her, kill. 15
h. shall ye fear, *h.* shall ye. 17:36
h. did outlandish women. *Neh* 13:26
h. they have hanged on. *Esth* 8:7
not *h.* that is deceived. *Job* 15:31
h. that had none to help *h.* 29:12
behold, who teacheth like *h.*? 36:22
thunder with a voice like *h.*? 40:9
Job shall pray for you, for *h.* 42:8
Lord hath set apart *h. Ps* 4:3
h. shall he teach in the way. 25:12
worship *h.* 45:11
h. that hath no helper. 72:12
h. will I cut off, *h.* that hath. 101:5
h. that soweth discord. *Pr* 6:19
h. shall the people curse. 24:24
a little folly *h.* that is in. *Eccl* 10:1
h. that offereth in the. *Jer* 48:35
and cut off from it *h. Ezek* 35:7
and *h.* that holdeth the. *Amos* 5:10
cut off *h.* that offereth. *Mal* 2:12
h. only shalt thou serve. *Mat* 4:10
Luke 4:8
confess me before men, *h.* will I confess also. *Mat* 10:32; *Luke* 12:8
h. will I deny before my. *Mat* 10:33
h. that sent me. 40; *Mark* 9:37
this is my Son, hear ye *h.*
Mat 17:5; *Acts* 3:22; 7:37
go tell *h.* between *h.* and. *Mat* 18:15
nor let *h.* in the field return.
24:18; *Mark* 13:6
h. they compelled to. *Mat* 27:32
let *h.* that readeth. *Mark* 13:14
let *h.* that is on the housetop. 15
h. that for sedition and. *Luke* 23:25
but *h.* they saw not. 24:24
whom he hath sent, *h. John* 5:38
come in his own name, *h.* ye. 43
h. hath God the Father sealed. 6:27
h. that cometh unto me, I will. 37
h. he heareth. 9:31
h. will my Father honour. 12:26
God shall also glorify *h.* in. 13:32
h. being delivered. *Acts* 2:23
h. God exalted. 5:31
h. God raised up the third. 10:40
h. would Paul have to go forth with
h. 16:3
whom ye worship *h.* declare. 17:23
h. that is weak in faith. *Rom* 14:1
let not *h.* that eateth, despise *h.* 3
defile temple, *h.* shall. *1 Cor* 3:17
h. that thinketh he standeth. 10:12
for he hath made *h.* to. *2 Cor* 5:21
let *h.* that is taught in the. *Gal* 6:6
let *h.* that stole steal no. *Eph* 4:28
h. therefore I hope to. *Phil* 2:23
receive *h.* therefore in the Lord. 29
h. whose coming is. *2 Thes* 2:9
might destroy *h.* that. *Heb* 2:14
sprang there of one, and *h.* 11:12

about him

his servants were standing *about h.*
1 Sam 22:6, 7
the footmen that stood *about h.* 17
wars which were *about h. 1 Ki* 5:3
compassed *about h.* to. *2 Chr* 18:31
made an hedge *about h.*? *Job* 1:10
let all round *about h. Ps* 76:11
in reverence of all *about h.* 89:7
all ye that are *about h. Jer* 48:17
a dismaying to all *about h.* 39
devour all round *about h.* 50:32
shall be round *about h. Lam* 1:17
scatter all that are *about h.* to help
him. *Ezek* 12:14
his graves are round *about h.*
32:22, 25, 26
great multitudes *about h. Mat* 8:18
multitude sat *about h. Mark* 3:32
the Jews round *about h. John* 10:24
each six wings *about h. Rev* 4:8

above him

shall be strong *above h. Dan* 11:5

after him

with his seed *after h. Gen* 17:19
his household *after h.* 18:19
be a statute for his seed *after h.*
Ex 28:43
shall be his son's *after h.* 29:29
that go a whoring *after h. Lev* 20:5
turn away from *after h. Num* 32:15
of blood pursue *after h. Josh* 20:5
fled, they pursued *after h. Judg* 1:6
they went *after h.* and took. 3:28
was gathered *after h.* 6:34, 35
armourbearer *after h. 1 Sam* 14:13
I went out *after h.* and. 17:35
saw that Saul came *after h.* 26:3
followed hard *after h. 2 Sam* 1:6
and all the people *after h.* 15:17
the people returned *after h.* 23:10
on the throne of my lord *after h.*
1 Ki 1:20, 27
to set up his son *after h.* 15:4
I will run *after h.* and. *2 Ki* 5:20
Jehu followed *after h.* and. 9:27
sent *after h.* to. 14:19; *2 Chr* 25:27
so that *after h.* was none like him.
2 Ki 18:5; 23:25
Zebadiah his son *after h. 1 Chr* 27:7
priest went in *after h. 2 Chr* 26:17
after h. repaired. *Neh* 3:16
So to the 31st verse
they that come *after h. Job* 18:20
he in his house *after h.* 21:21
every man shall draw *after h.* 33
a path to shine *after h.* 41:32
not descend *after h. Ps* 49:17
children are blessed *after h. Pr* 20:7
bring to see what shall be *after h.*
Eccl 3:22; 6:12
should find nothing *after h.* 7:14
what shall be *after h.* who? 10:14
after h. through the city. *Ezek* 9:5
sent a message *after h. Luke* 19:14
world is gone *after h. John* 12:19
much people *after h. Acts* 5:37
to him, and to his seed *after h.* 7:5
if haply they might feel *after h.* 17:27
which should come *after h.* 19:4

against him

man's hand *against h. Gen* 16:12
he prevailed not *against h.* 32:25
they conspired *against h.* 37:18
1 Ki 15:27; 16:9; *2 Ki* 14:19
15:10, 25; 21:23
which ye murmur *against h.*
Ex 16:8; *Num* 14:36; 16:11
an adversary *against h. Num* 22:22
man rise up *against h. Deut* 19:11
witness that to testify *against h.* 16
loins that rise *against h.* 33:11
a man over *against h. Josh* 5:13
lion roared *against h. Judg* 14:5
Philistines shouted *against h.* 15:14
Lord said, Go up *against h.* 20:23
battle was *against h. 2 Sam* 10:9
put forth *against h.* dried. *1 Ki* 13:4
to bear witness *against h.* 21:13
went up *against h. 2 Ki* 23:29
Lord sent *against h.* bands of. 24:2
to speak *against h. 2 Chr* 32:17
not prevail *against h. Esth* 6:13

movedst me *against h. Job* 2:3
have sinned *against h.* 8:4
hardened himself *against h.* 9:4
prevailest for ever *against h.* 14:20
thou strive *against h.*? 33:13
what doest thou *against h.*? 35:6
sinned yet more *against h. Ps* 78:17
messenger shall be sent *against h.*
Pr 17:11
if one prevail *against h. Eccl* 4:12
axe boast *against h.*, or saw magnify
itself *against h.*? *Isa* 10:15
are called forth *against h.* 31:4
that are incensed *against h.* 45:24
lift up a standard *against h.* 59:19
we shall prevail *against h. Jer* 20:10
for since I spake *against h.* I. 31:20
against h. that bendeth, let. 51:3
prophesy *against h.* and Egypt.
Ezek 29:2; 38:2
call for a sword *against h.* 38:21
I will plead *against h.* with. 22
have sinned *against h. Dan* 9:11
but he that cometh *against h.* 11:16
prepare war *against h. Mi* 3:5
I have sinned *against h.* 7:9
up a parable *against h.*? *Hab* 2:6
and held a counsel *against h.*
Mat 12:14; *Mark* 3:6
that cometh *against h. Luke* 14:31
they cried so *against h. Acts* 22:24
what they had *against h.* 23:30
priest desired favour *against h.* 25:3
to have judgement *against h.* 15
not bring *against h.* a. *Jude* 9
sinners have spoken *against h.* 15
make war *against h. Rev* 19:19

at him

the archers shot *at h. Gen* 49:23
Saul cast a javelin *at h. 1 Sam* 20:33
threw stones *at h.* and. *2 Sam* 16:13
shall clap their hands *at h. Job* 27:23
him that puffeth *at h. Ps* 12:5
the Lord shall laugh *at h.* 37:13
shall see and laugh *at h.* 52:6
do they shoot *at h.* and. 64:4
shut their mouths *at h. Isa* 52:15
south shall push *at h. Dan* 11:40
the mountains quake *at h. Nah* 1:5
they were offended *at h. Mark* 6:3
at *h.* they cast stones, and. 12:4
and they marvelled *at h.* 7:9
he marvelled *at h.* and. *Luke* 7:9
they could not come *at h.* for. 8:19
Jews then murmured *at h. John* 6:41
took up stones to cast *at h.* 8:59

before him

meat *before h.* to eat. *Gen* 24:33
messengers *before h.* to. 32:3
so went the present over *before h.* 21
and they cried *before h.* 41:43
they sat *before h.* 43:33
fell *before h.* 44:14
Lord passed by *before h. Ex* 34:6
have wept *before h. Num* 11:20
man straight *before h. Josh* 6:5
service of the Lord *before h.* 22:27
chased, he fled *before h. Judg* 9:40
wife wept *before h.* and. 14:16, 17
anointed is *before h. 1 Sam* 16:6
came to Saul and stood *before h.* 21
a shield went *before h.* 17:7
they fled *before h. 2 Sam* 10:13
1 Chr 19:14
eat and drink *before h. 2 Sam* 11:13
they set bread *before h.* 12:20
and fifty men to run *before h.*
15:1; *1 Ki* 1:5
2 Sam 22:24; *Ps* 18:23
harlots, stood *before h. 1 Ki* 3:16
Omri worse than all *before h.* 16:25
Ahab evil above all *before h.* 30, 33
men, sons of Belial, *before h.* 21:10
to the ground *before h. 2 Ki* 2:15
when called, stood *before h.* 4:12
prophets were sitting *before h.* 38
king sent a man from *before h.* 6:32
kings stood not *before h.* how? 10:4
kings that were *before h.* 17:2
nor any that were *before h.* 18:5
did, which were *before h.* 21:11
there was no king *before h.* 23:25

did eat bread continually before h.
2 Ki 25:29; Jer 52:33
and come before h. 1 Chr 16:29
fear before h. 30; Ps 96:9
Eccl 3:14; 8:12
before h. like Solomon. 1 Chr 29:5
to burn before h. sweet. 2 Chr 2:4, 6
kingdom was quiet before h. 14:5
chosen you to stand before h. 29:11
that wine was before h. Neh 2:1
make a request before h. Esth 4:8
proclaim before h. 6:9, 11
fall before h. 13
I will maintain my ways before h.
Job 13:15
shall not come before h. 16
are innumerable before h. 21:33
order my cause before h. 23:4
hell is naked before h. and. 26:6
judgement is before h. 35:14
is turned into joy before h. 41:22
cry came before h. Ps 18:6
brightness that was before h. 12
shall bow before h. 22:29
a fire shall devour before h. 50:3
pour out your heart before h. 62:8
that hate him flee before h. 68:1
God, sing and rejoice before h. 4
wilderness shall bow before h. 72:9
kings shall fall before h., nations
shall serve h. 11
righteousness shall go before h.
85:13
and majesty are before h. 96:6
worship the Lord, fear before h. 9
goeth before h. and burneth. 97:3
his chosen stood before h. 106:23
showed before h. my trouble. 142:2
rejoicing always before h. Pr 8:30
wisdom is before h. that hath. 17:24
reward with him, work before h.
Isa 40:10; 62:11
nations before h. are as. 40:17
gave nations before h. and. 41:2
to subdue nations before h. 45:1
supplications before h. Jer 42:9
wilt thou say before h. Ezek 28:9
shall groan before h. with. 30:24
10,000 stood before h. Dan 7:10
no beasts might stand before h. 8:4
no power in ram to stand before h. 7
none shall stand before h. 11:16
be overflown from before h. 22
shall I come before h.? Mi 6:6
keep silence before h. Hab 2:20
before h. went the pestilence. 3:5
a book of remembrance written before h. Mal 3:16
before h. be gathered. Mat 25:32
bowed the knee before h. 27:29
fell down before h. Mark 3:11; 5:33
before h. in the spirit. Luke 1:17
and righteousness before h. 75
means to lay him before h. 5:18
I have nothing to set before h. 11:6
that I am sent before h, John 3:28
Paul also before h. Acts 23:33
before h. whom he believed, even.
Rom 4:17
without blame before h. Eph 1:4
joy that was set before h. Heb 12:2
not ashamed before h. 1 John 2:28
assure our hearts before h. 3:19
first beast before h. Rev 13:12
wrought miracles before h. 19:20

behind him
in the tent door behind h. Gen 18:10
spear came out behind h.
2 Sam 2:23
his master's feet behind h.?
2 Ki 6:32
leave a blessing behind h. Joel 2:14
behind h. were red horses. Zech 1:8
diseased with an issue of blood came
behind h. Mat 9:20; Luke 8:44
leave his wife behind h. Mark 12:19
at his feet behind h. Luke 7:38

beside him
there is none beside h. Deut 4:35
his servants passed on beside h.
2 Sam 15:18
beside h. stood Mattithiah. Neh 8:4

between him
Lord made between h. Lev 26:46
shall discern between h. Mal 3:18
beyond him
an arrow beyond h. 1 Sam 20:36
by him
not let us pass by h. Deut 2:30
shall dwell in safety by h. 33:12
by h. children of Israel. Judg 3:15
all that stood by h. went out. 19
and by h. actions are. 1 Sam 2:3
that evil is determined by h. 20:7
of heaven standing by h. 1 Ki 22:19
we may enquire of the Lord by h.
2 Ki 3:11; 8:8
by h. the Lord had given. 5:1
hundred slain by h. 1 Chr 11:11
queen also sitting by h. Neh 2:6
the Ammonite was by h. 4:3
sweareth by h. shall glory. Ps 63:11
that are slain by h. Isa 27:7
by h. daily sacrifice was. Dan 8:11
sware by h. that liveth for ever.
12:7; Rev 10:6
rocks are thrown down by h. Nah 1:6
sweareth by h. who. Mat 23:21
sweareth by h. that sitteth. 22
Herod being reproved by h. shut up
John. Luke 3:19
heard all that was done by h. 9:7
things that were done by h. 13:17
all things were made by h. John 1:3
the world was made by h. and. 10
wonders God did by him. Acts 2:22
the faith which is by h. 3:16; 4:10
by h. all that believe. 13:39
following the Lord stood by h. 23:11
ye are enriched by h. 1 Cor 1:5
are all things, and we by h. 8:6
have been taught by h. Eph 4:21
for by h. were all things. Col 1:16
he is before all things, by h. all. 17
by h. to reconcile all things to himself
by h. 20
to God the Father by h. 3:17
are taken captive by h. 2 Tim 2:26
that come to God by h. Heb 7:25
by h. let us offer the sacrifice. 13:15
who by h. do believe in. 1 Pet 1:21
are sent by h. for punishment. 2:14

concerning him
made an oath con. h. Judg 21:5
word Lord hath spoken con. h.
2 Ki 19:21; Isa 37:22
so commanded con. h. Esth 3:2
a proclamation con. h. Dan 5:29
among people con h. John 7:12, 32
Jews did not believe con. h. 9:18
David speaketh con. h. Acts 2:25
enquire something con. h. 23:15
con. h. that hath so done. 1 Cor 5:3

see **fear**
for him
an help meet for h. Gen 2:18, 20
Joseph's father wept for h. 37:35
I will be surety for h. of. 43:9
no blood shed for h. Ex 22:2
blood shed for h. 3
accepted for h. to make atonement
for h. Lev 1:4; 4:26, 31; 5:13
14:18, 19, 20, 31; 15:15; 19:22
Num 5:8; 6:11; 15:28
shall ask counsel for h. Num 27:21
take no satisfaction for h. 35:32
lie in wait for h. and. Deut 19:11
his hands be sufficient for h. 33:7
he that will plead for h. Judg 6:31
shall entreat for h.? 1 Sam 2:25
how he laid wait for h. in. 15:2
them, and Saul sent for h. 17:31
enquired of Lord for h. 22:10, 15
sought no more again for h. 27:4
till the land for h. 2 Sam 9:10
for h. the kingdom, even for h.
1 Ki 2:22
saddled for h. the ass, to wit. 13:23
all Israel shall mourn for h. 14:13
very great burning for h. 2 Chr 16:14
people made no burning for h. 21:19
I have prepared for h. Esth 5:4
saw that he moved not for h. 7
there is nothing done for h. 6:3
gallows he had prepared for h. 4

talk deceitfully for h.? Job 13:7
did not I weep for h. that ? 30:25
there is no help for h. Ps 3:2
Lord, and wait patiently for h. 37:7
give to God a ransom for h. 49:7
prayer also be made for h. 72:15
as for h. that wanteth. Pr 9:4, 16
he shall gather it for h. that. 28:8
bowels were moved for h. S of S 5:4
the Lord and look for h. Isa 8:17
for h. he will save us. 25:9
a snare for h. that reproveth. 29:21
are all they that wait for h. 30:18
his arm shall rule for h. 40:10
what he hath prepared for h. that
waiteth for h. 64:4
shall not lament for h. Jer 22:18
my bowels are troubled for h. 31:20
to them that wait for h. Lam 3:25
Pharaoh make for h. in. Ezek 17:17
for h. I caused Lebanon to mourn for
h., and all the trees of the field
fainted for h. 31:15
so shalt thou do for h. that. 45:20
nor shall she be for h. Dan 11:17
where no gin is for h. Amos 3:5
Lord nor enquired for h. Zeph 1:6
shall mourn for h. be in bitterness
for h. Zech 12:10
not lawful for h. to eat. Mat 12:4
better for h. that a millstone. 18:6
Mark 9:42; Luke 17:2
when he looketh not for h.
Mat 24:50; Luke 12:46
Jesus had done for h. Mark 5:20
child Jesus, to do for h. Luke 2:27
they were all waiting for h. 8:40
went to make ready for h. 9:52
made unto God for h. Acts 12:5
for I look for h. with. 1 Cor 16:11
created by him and for h. Col 1:16
them that look for h. Heb 9:28

from him
and God went up from h. Gen 35:13
it be hid from h. when. Lev 5:3
by him, went out from h. Judg 3:19
locks, his strength went from h.
16:19
hid nothing from h. 1 Sam 3:18
retire from h. 2 Sam 11:15
went out from h. 13:9
thing would come from h. 1 Ki 20:33
were scattered from h. 2 Ki 25:5
the Lord turned from h. 2 Chr 12:12
turn from h. that he may. Job 14:6
he hid his face from h. Ps 22:24
the poor from h. that spoileth. 35:10
have hid myself from h. 55:12
waiteth on God: from h. 62:1
of the righteous from h. Isa 5:23
hid as it were our faces from h. 53:3
she go from h. and become. Jer 3:1
part of hand sent from h. Dan 5:24
ye take from h. burdens. Amos 5:11
and laid his robe from h. Jonah 3:6
from h. that would borrow of thee.
Mat 5:42
from h. shall be taken. 13:12
Mark 4:25; Luke 8:18
from h. that hath not shall be taken.
Mat 25:29; Luke 19:26
hour might pass from h. Mark 14:35
he taketh from h. all. Luke 11:22
I am from h. John 7:29
but will flee from h. 10:5
soon removed from h. Gal 1:6
if we turn away from h. Heb 12:25
of compassion from h. 1 John 3:17
commandment have we from h. 4:21
peace from h. which is. Rev 1:4

see **depart, departed**

in him
nations of earth shall be blessed in h.
Gen 18:18
for my name is in h. Ex 23:21
Shechem put confidence in h.
Judg 9:26
was no strength in h. 1 Sam 28:20
no fault in h. 29:3; John 19:4, 6
in h. will I trust. 2 Sam 22:3
Ps 91:2
he is a buckler to all that trust in h.
2 Sam 22:31; Isa 36:6

if wickedness be in *h*.   *1 Ki* 1:52
the wisdom of God was in *h*.   3:28
because in *h*. there is found.   14:13
there was no breath left in *h*. 17:17
put their trust in *h*.   *1 Chr* 5:20
me, yet will I trust in *h*.   *Job* 13:15
before him, trust thou in *h*.   35:14
that put their trust in *h*.   *Ps* 2:12
all those that trust in *h*.   18:30
my heart trusted in *h*. and I.   28:7
our heart shall rejoice in *h*.   33:21
    66:6; 149:2
man that trusteth in *h*.   34:8
none of them that trust in *h*.   22
trust also in *h*.; and he shall.   37:5
because they trust in *h*.   40
trust in *h*. at all times, ye.   62:8
shall be glad and trust in *h*.   64:10
men shall be blessed in *h*.   72:17
is no unrighteousness in *h*.   92:15
    John 7:18
perceivest not in *h*. lips.   *Pr* 14:7
them that put their trust in *h*. 30:5
shall not rejoice in *h*.   *Eccl* 4:16
bless themselves in *h*.   *Jer* 4:2
all them that trust in *h*.   46:25
his taste remained in *h*.   48:11
therefore will I hope in *h*. *Lam* 3:24
servants who trusted in *h*. *Dan* 3:28
nor any error or fault found in *h*.6:4
none understanding in *h*.   *Ob* 7
them that trust in *h*.   *Nah* 1:7
soul is not upright in *h*.   *Hab* 2:4
they were offended in *h*. *Mat* 13:57
do shew themselves in *h*.   14:2
no cause of death in *h*. *Luke* 23:22
in *h*. was life; and the life. *John* 1:4
whosoever believeth in *h*.   3:15, 16
    Acts 10:43
shall be in *h*. a well of.   *John* 4:14
dwelleth in me, and I in *h*.   6:56
    10:38; 15:5
his brethren believe in *h*.   7:5
there is no truth in *h*.   8:44
made manifest in *h*.   9:3
no light in *h*.   11:10
God is glorified in *h*.   13:31
if God be glorified in *h*.   32
in *h*. we live, move.   *Acts* 17:28
they believe in *h*. of.   *Rom* 10:14
in *h*. shall the Gentiles trust. 15:12
of man which is in *h*.   *1 Cor* 2:11
all things, we in *h*. 8:6; *1 John* 5:20
nay, but in *h*. was yea. *2 Cor* 1:19, 20
righteousness of God in *h*.   5:21
for we are weak in *h*. but.   13:4
chosen us in *h*.   *Eph* 1:4
gather together; even in *h*.   10
Christ, and be found in *h*. *Phil* 3:9
that in *h*. should all. *Col* 1:19; 2:9
so walk ye in *h*.   2:6
rooted and built up in *h*.   7
in *h*. dwelleth the fulness of the. 9
ye are complete in *h*. who is the. 10
I will put my trust in *h*. *Heb* 2:13
shall have no pleasure in *h*.   10:38
the truth is not in *h*.   *1 John* 2:4
in *h*. verily is love of God perfected,
    hereby know we that we are in *h*. 5
he that saith he abideth in *h*.   6
thing is true in *h*. and in you.   8
none occasion of stumbling in *h*. 10
the Father is in *h*.   15; 3:17
you, ye shall abide in *h*.   27, 28
man that hath this hope in *h*.   3:3
in *h*. is no sin.   5
who abideth in *h*. sinneth not.   6
for his seed remaineth in *h*. he.   9
hath eternal life abiding in *h*.   15
dwelleth in *h*. and he. 24; 4:13
    15, 16
confidence that we have in *h*.   5:14

into him

child's soul come into *h*. *1 Ki* 17:21
soul of the child came into *h*.   22
many devils were entered into *h*.
    Luke 8:30
Satan entered into *h*.   *John* 13:27
may grow up into *h*. in.   *Eph* 4:15

of him

Lord was entreated of *h*. *Gen* 25:21
beware of *h*. and obey.   *Ex* 23:21
not what is become of *h*.   32:1, 23

flesh of *h*. hath issue.   *Lev* 15:7, 33
    25:36
take thou no usury of *h*.   *Num* 35:33
but by the blood of *h*.   *Deut* 18:19
I will require it of *h*.   22; *2 Ki* 1:15
not be afraid of *h*.   *1 Sam* 17:32
heart fail because of *h*.   *2 Ki* 5:20
and take somewhat of *h*.   10:24
shall be for the life of *h*.   *1 Chr* 5:2
of *h*. came the chief.   *2 Chr* 28:23
they were the ruin of *h*.   33:13, 19
he was entreated of *h*.   *Ezra* 8:21
to seek of *h*. a right way.   *Job* 7:8
eye of *h*. hath seen me.   12:5
despised in the thought of *h*.   18:21
is the place of *h*. that knoweth.   23:15
consider, I am afraid of *h*.   *Ps* 37:7
not thyself because of *h*.   *Pr* 16:26
mouth craveth it of *h*.   23:24
wise child, shall have joy of *h*.   26:12; 29:20
take a pledge of *h*. for a.   27:13
shall the work say of *h*.   *Isa* 29:16
feet of *h*. bringeth good tidings.
    52:7; *Nah* 1:15
will not make mention of *h*. *Jer* 20:9
be not afraid of *h*. saith the.   42:11
as the punishment of *h*. *Ezek* 14:10
Babylon hath taken oath of *h*. 17:13
no pleasure in the death of *h*. 18:32
nations also heard of *h*. he.   19:4
in the hand of *h*. that slayeth. 28:9
take hold of skirt of *h*.   *Zech* 8:23
I will encamp because of *h*.   9:8
as it is written of *h*.   *Mat* 26:24
    Mark 9:13; 14:21
in a dream because of *h*. *Mat* 27:19
should tell no man of *h*. *Mark* 8:30
of *h*. shall Son of man be ashamed.
    38; *Luke* 9:26
of *h*. that taketh thy.   *Luke* 6:30
much given, of *h*. shall much. 12:48
ye of *h*. whom Father.   *John* 10:36
the justifier of *h*. that.   *Rom* 3:26
not of works but of *h*. that.   9:11
it is not of *h*. that willeth, but.   16
for of *h*. and through him.   11:36
of *h*. are ye in Christ.   *1 Cor* 1:30
shew forth praises of *h*.   *1 Pet* 2:9
ye may be found of *h*.   *2 Pet* 3:14
we have heard of *h*.   *1 John* 1:5
which we have received of *h*.   2:27
doeth righteousness is born of *h*. 29
all kindreds of the earth shall wail
    because of *h*.   *Rev* 1:7

on, or upon him

whatsoever is laid upon *h*.   *Ex* 21:30
his uncleanness upon *h*.   *Lev* 7:20
if her flowers be upon *h*. he.   15:24
and not suffer sin upon *h*.   19:17
his blood shall be upon *h*.   20:9
oil of his God is upon *h*.   21:12
spirit that was upon *h*.   *Num* 11:25
his iniquity shall be upon *h*.   15:31
seeing him not, cast it upon *h*. 35:23
shall be first upon *h*.   *Deut* 13:9
witnesses shall be first upon *h*. 17:7
written in this book upon *h*.   29:20
if any hand be upon *h*.   *Josh* 2:19
the Spirit of the Lord came upon *h*.
    Judg 3:10; 14:6, 19; 15:14
    Num 24:2; *1 Sam* 10:10; 19:23
Philistines be upon *h*.   *1 Sam* 18:17
I will come upon *h*.   *2 Sam* 17:2
an oath be laid upon *h*.   *1 Ki* 8:31
    2 Chr 6:22
saying, Lay hold on *h*.   *1 Ki* 13:4
shut the door upon *h*.   *2 Ki* 4:21
head of Elisha stand on *h*.   6:31
the people trode upon *h*. in. 7:17, 20
there was wrath upon *h*. *2 Chr* 32:25
Lord his God upon *h*.   *Ezra* 7:6, 9
set thy heart upon *h*.   *Job* 7:17
destroyer shall come upon *h*.   15:21
wicked shall come upon *h*.   20:22
and shall rain it upon *h*. while.   23
cometh, terrors are upon *h*.   25
when trouble cometh upon *h*.? 27:9
I will call upon *h*. as.   *Ps* 116:2
nigh to all that call upon *h*. 145:18
I will pour water upon *h*. *Isa* 44:3
of our peace was upon *h*.   53:5
seek the Lord, call ye upon *h*. 55:6
and he will have mercy upon *h*.   7
have mercy upon *h*.   *Jer* 31:20

will I spread upon *h*.   *Ezek* 12:13
be upon *h*., wickedness of the wicked
    shall be upon *h*.   18:20
gray hairs are here and there upon *h*.
    Hos 7:9
shall leave his blood upon *h*.   12:14
put my Spirit upon *h*.   *Mat* 12:18
and they spit upon *h*. and.   27:30
and on *h*. they laid the. *Luke* 23:26
it abode upon *h*.   *John* 1:32
remaining on *h*.   33
on *h*. is not condemned.   3:18; 5:24
    6:40; *Rom* 9:33; *1 Pet* 2:6
look on *h*. whom they.   *John* 19:37
Saul set his eyes on *h*.   *Acts* 13:9
not only to believe on *h*.   *Phil* 1:29
had mercy on *h*. and not on *h*.   2:27
took not on *h*. the nature.   *Heb* 2:16
that sat on *h*.   *Rev* 6:2, 5, 8; 19:11
and he set a seal upon *h*.   20:3

over him

thou shalt rule over *h*.   *Gen* 4:7
and confess over *h*. all.   *Lev* 16:21
thou shalt not rule over *h*. 25:43, 53
people wept again over *h*. *2 Sam* 3:34
they mourned over *h*.   *1 Ki* 13:30
burnt the king's house over *h*. 16:18
a wicked man over *h*.   *Ps* 109:6
spread their net over *h*. *Ezek* 19:8
times pass over *h*.   *Dan* 4:16, 23
made lamentation over *h*. *Acts* 8:2
no more dominion over *h*. *Rom* 6:9
let them pray over *h*.   *Jas* 5:14

through him

that all men through *h*.   *John* 1:7
that the world through *h*.   3:17
be saved from wrath, through *h*.
    Rom 5:9
than conquerors through *h*.   8:37
of him, through *h*. and to him. 11:36
through *h*. we have access. *Eph* 2:18
sent his Son, that we might live
    through *h*.   *1 John* 4:9

to, or unto him

to Seth, to *h*. also there.   *Gen* 4:26
Lord, who appeared unto *h*.   12:7
shall a child be born unto *h*.? 17:17
of which God had spoken to *h*. 21:2
unto *h*. hath he given all that. 24:36
unto *h*. shall the gathering.   49:10
thou shalt be to *h*.   *Ex* 4:16
not be to *h*. as an usurer.   22:25
it shall be a statute for ever unto *h*.
    28:43; 30:21
and to *h*. will I give the. *Deut* 1:36
raise up a Prophet, unto *h*.   18:15
to do to *h*. as he hath.   *Judg* 15:10
Lord hath done to *h*.   *1 Sam* 28:17
David, even so I do to *h*. *2 Sam* 3:9
wilt thou go to *h*. to-day? *2 Ki* 4:23
so it fell out unto *h*. for the.   7:20
even to *h*. and his sons. *2 Chr* 13:5
king, so shall ye say unto *h*.   34:26
to *h*. that is afflicted.   *Job* 6:14
what doest thou unto *h*.?   35:6
to *h*. that rideth on.   *Ps* 68:33
to *h*. shall be given of gold.   72:15
to *h*. that made great lights.   136:7
to *h*. that smote great kings, for.   17
one event to *h*. that sacrificeth, and to
    h. that sacrificeth not.   *Eccl* 9:2
people turneth not to *h*.   *Isa* 9:13
turn to *h*. from whom Israel.   31:6
they are counted to *h*. less.   40:17
will ye compare unto *h*.?   18
even to *h*. shall men come.   45:24
thus saith the Lord to *h*. whom. 49:7
to *h*. that is far off, and to *h*. 57:19
look, even to *h*. that is poor.   66:2
to *h*. that knocketh, it.   *Mat* 7:8
to *h*. that smiteth thee. *Luke* 6:29
whosoever hath, to *h*. shall be. 8:18
to *h*. that blasphemeth against. 12:10
living, for all live unto *h*.   20:38
then I go unto *h*. *John* 7:33; 16:5
to *h*. the porter openeth, the.   10:3
to *h*. they agreed, and.   *Acts* 5:40
to *h*. they had regard, because. 8:11
to *h*. give all the prophets.   10:43
now to *h*. that worketh.   *Rom* 4:4
to *h*. that worketh not, but.   5
even to *h*. who is raised.   7:4
and to *h*. are all things, to.   11:36

20

to h. that esteemeth, to h. Rom 14:14
now to h. that is of power to. 16:25
be to h. who speaketh a. 1 Cor 14:11
it was accounted to h. for. Gal 3:6
unto h. be glory in the. Eph 3:21
I will be to h. a Father. Heb 1:5
to h. that was able to save him. 5:7
it was imputed unto h. Jas 2:23
to h. that knoweth to do good, to h.
4:17
unto h. that loved us. Rev 1:5
to h. that overcometh. 2:7, 17; 3:21
to h. will I give power over. 2:26
will give unto h. that is athirst. 21:6

toward him
it was not toward h. Gen 31:2
anger was abated toward h. Judg 8:3
heart is perfect toward h. 2 Chr 16:9
stretch out thine hands toward h.
Job 11:13
lift up thy hands toward h. Lam 2:19
branches turned toward h. Ezek 17:6
your love toward h. 2 Cor 2:8

under him
stone and put it under h. Ex 17:12
mule that was under h. 2 Sam 18:9
helpers do stoop under h. Job 9:13
spread sackcloth and ashes under h.
Isa 58:5
the roots thereof were under h.
Ezek 17:6
all things put under h. 1 Cor 15:27
28; Heb 2:8

with him
saw that Lord was with h. Gen 39:3
I have given with h. Aholiab.
Ex 31:6; 38:23
with h. will I speak mouth to mouth.
Num 12:8; Jer 32:4
his God is with h. and. Num 23:21
with h. that standeth here with us,
also with h. that is. Deut 29:15
was no strange god with h. 32:12
and the Lord was with h.
1 Sam 3:19; 18:12, 14
the Lord is with h. 16:18
folly is with h. 25:25
Lord of hosts was with h.
2 Sam 5:10; 1 Chr 11:9
will I be, and with h. 2 Sam 16:18
Solomon held a feast, and all Israel
with h. 1 Ki 8:65; 2 Chr 7:8
word of Lord is with h. 2 Ki 3:12
his hand might be with h. 15:19
the Lord was with h. and he. 18:7
1 Chr 9:20; 2 Chr 1:1; 15:9
while ye be with h. 2 Chr 15:2
with h. fourscore priests of. 26:17
be more with us than with h. 32:7
with h. is an arm of flesh, with. 8
the Lord his God be with h. 36:23
Ezra 1:3
with h. 150 males. Ezra 8:3
with h. 200 males. 4
with h. 50 males. 6
with h. is wisdom. Job 12:13, 16
candle shall be put out with h. 18:6
acquaint thyself with h. and. 22:21
mercy shall be with h. Ps 89:24
I will be with h. in trouble. 91:15
and with h. is plenteous. 130:7
one brought up with h. Pr 8:30
that shall abide with h. Eccl 8:15
righteous, it shall be well with h.
Isa 3:10
wicked, it shall be ill with h. 11
his reward is with h. 40:10; 62:11
with h. also that is of a. 57:15
it was well with h. Jer 22:15, 16
he shall deal with h. Ezek 31:11
covenant was with h. of. Mal 2:5
art in the way with h. Mat 5:25
they should be with h. Mark 3:14
he might be with h. 5:18; Luke 8:38
hand of Lord was with h. Luke 1:66
this man was also with h. 22:56
miracles, except God be with h.
John 3:2
and make our abode with h. 14:23
but God was with h. Acts 7:9; 10:38
him is accepted with h. 10:35
crying, Away with h. 21:36

we are buried with h. by baptism.
Rom 6:4; Col 2:12
live with h. Rom 6:8; 2 Cor 13:4
1 Thes 5:10; 2 Tim 2:11
shall he not with h. give? Rom 8:32
will God bring with h. 1 Thes 4:14
we also shall reign with h.
2 Tim 2:12; Rev 20:6
the heirs with h. of the. Heb 11:9
when we were with h. 2 Pet 1:18
and I will sup with h. Rev 3:20
with h. 144,000 having his. 14:1
they that are with h. are. 17:14

within him
his soul within h. mourn. Job 14:22
the gall of asps within h. 20:14
layeth up deceit within h. Pr 26:24
his Holy Spirit within h. Isa 63:11
spirit of man within h. Zech 12:1

without him
and without h. was not. John 1:3

himself
set on for him by h. Gen 43:32
if he came in by h. he shall go out by
h. Ex 21:3
sin offering which was for h.
Lev 9:8; 16:6, 11
shall make an atonement for h.
16:11, 17, 24
to bring you near to h. Num 16:9
taken spoil, every man for h. 31:53
Lord hath chosen thee to h. Deut 7:6
14:2; 28:9; 29:13; 2 Sam 7:23
provided the first part for h.
Deut 33:21
let the Lord h. require. Josh 22:23
he h. turned again. Judg 3:19
David encouraged h. 1 Sam 30:6
Elijah h. went a day's journey, and
he requested for h. 1 Ki 19:4
God h. is with us for. 2 Chr 13:12
thrust him out, yea, h. hasted. 26:20
h. separated from the. Ezra 10:8
only on h. put not forth. Job 1:12
wise may be profitable to h. 22:2
will he delight h. in the ? 27:10
because he justified h. rather. 32:2
that he should delight h. with. 34:9
when he raiseth h. the. 41:25
him that is godly for h. Ps 4:3
the poor committeth h. unto. 10:14
net that he hath hid catch h. 35:8
he setteth h. in a way that is. 36:4
for God is judge h. 50:6
and the Highest h. shall. 87:5
but on h. shall his crown. 132:18
Lord hath chosen Jacob to h. 135:4
shall take wicked h. Pr 5:22
shall be watered also h. 11:25
h. rich, that maketh h. poor. 13:7
man shall be satisfied from h. 14:14
hath made all things for h. 16:4
that laboureth, laboureth for h. 26
he also shall cry h. but shall. 21:13
the evil, and hideth h. 22:3; 27:12
child left to h. bringeth. 29:15
beloved hath withdrawn h. S of S 5:6
the Lord h. shall give you. Isa 7:14
he hath spoken, and h. hath. 38:15
another shall call h. by the. 44:5
departeth from evil, maketh h. 59:15
make h. an everlasting name? 63:12
way of man is not in h. Jer 10:23
that is mad, and maketh h. 29:26
hath sworn by h. 51:14; Amos 6:8
prince prepare for h. Ezek 45:22
be cut off, but not for h. Dan 9:26
he hath withdrawn h. Hos 5:6
vine, bringeth forth fruit to h. 10:1
the mighty deliver h. Amos 2:14
swift of foot shall not deliver h. 15
h. shall reward thee. Mat 6:4
h. took our infirmities, bare. 8:17
he not root in h. but dureth. 13:21
he saved others; h. he cannot save.
27:42; Mark 15:31
said, He is beside h. Mark 3:21
let him deny h., and take up his cross.
8:34; Luke 9:23
love his neighbour as h. Mark 12:33
sent them, whither he h. Luke 10:1
spirits more wicked than h. 11:26
lord's will, and prepared not h. 12:47

he came to h. he said. Luke 15:17
nobleman went to receive for h. 19:12
saying, that he h. is Christ. 23:2
also h. waited for the kingdom. 51
the things concerning h. 24:27
Jesus h. stood in the midst of. 36
Jesus h. baptized not. John 4:2
God was his Father, making h. 5:18
I say, the Son can do nothing of h. 19
for as the Father hath life in h. 26
for he h. knew what he would. 6:6
when Jesus knew in h. that his. 61
and he h. seeketh to be known. 7:4
he that speaketh of h. seeketh. 18
him, he shall speak for h. 9:21
this spake he not of h. but. 11:51
God shall glorify him in h. 13:32
he shall not speak of h. but. 16:13
Father h. loveth you, because. 27
maketh h. a king, speaketh. 19:12
Jesus shewed h. again. 21:1, 14
durst no man join h. to. Acts 5:13
rose up Theudas, boasting h. 36
giving out that h. was some. 8:9
speaketh the prophet this ? of h.? 34
while Peter doubted in h. 10:17
when Peter was come to h. 12:11
he left not h. without witness. 14:17
while he answered for h. 25:8; 26:1
as he spake for h. Festus said. 26:24
was suffered to dwell for h. 28:16
think of h. more highly. Rom 12:3
to h., no man dieth to. 14:7
for even Christ pleased not h. 15:3
yet he h. is judged of. 1 Cor 2:15
but he h. shall be saved, yet. 3:15
let a man examine h., and so. 11:28
then shall the Son h. be. 15:28
reconciled us to h. by Jesus.
2 Cor 5:18, 19
man trust to h. let him of h. 10:7
for ye suffer if a man exalt h. 11:20
who gave h. for our sins. Gal 1:4
gave h. for me. 2:20
think h. to be something. 6:3
he have rejoicing in h. 4
to make in h. of twain. Eph 2:15
Jesus h. being the chief corner-. 20
hath given h. for us. 5:2
gave h. for it. 25
present it to h. a glorious church. 27
loveth h. 28
so love his wife, even as h. 33
reconcile all things to h. Col 1:20
sitteth, shewing h. that. 2 Thes 2:4
who gave h. a ransom. 1 Tim 2:6
h. for us, to purify to h. Tit 2:14
being condemned of h. 3:11
when he had by h. purged. Heb 1:3
he also h. likewise took part. 2:14
in that he h. hath suffered. 18
for that he h. also is compassed. 5:2
as for the people, so also for h. 3
no man taketh this honour to h. 4
Christ glorified not h. to be made. 5
he sware by h. 6:13
when he offered up h. 7:27
away sin by the sacrifice of h. 9:26
but committed h. to. 1 Pet 2:23
ought to walk, even as. 1 John 2:6
hath this hope, purifieth h. even. 3:3
believeth hath the witness in h. 5:10
nor doth he h. receive. 3 John 10
that no man knew but h. Rev 19:12
God h. shall be with them. 21:3

see **bowed, hide**

hin
(*A liquid measure of the Hebrews.
It was the sixth part of a Bath or
Ephah, and held about one gallon
and three pints*)

fourth part of an h. of oil. Ex 29:40
unto thee of oil olive an h. 30:24
a just ephah and h. shall. Lev 19:36
shall be of wine, fourth part of an h.
23:13; Num 15:4; 28:14
part of an h. of wine. Num 15:5
the third part of an h. of oil. 6
half an h. 7
drink sixth part of an h. Ezek 4:11
an h. of oil for an ephah. 45:24
46:5, 7, 11
third part of an h. of oil to. 46:14

hind, -s
Naphtali is a *h.* let loose. *Gen* 49:21
my feet like *hs.*' feet. and setteth me.
    2 Sam 22:34; *Ps* 18:33; *Hab* 3:19
thou mark when the *h.*? *Job* 39:1
of Lord maketh the *h.* *Ps* 29:9
her be as the loving *h.* *Pr* 5:19
I charge you by the *h.* of the field.
    S of S 2:7; 3:5
the *h.* calved in the field. *Jer* 14:5

hinder
h. me not, seeing the. *Gen* 24:56
let nothing *h.* thee from. *Num* 22:16
come and fight, and *h.* the. *Neh* 4:8*
away, who can *h.* him? *Job* 9:12
and shut up, who can *h.* him? 11:10
what doth *h.* me to be? *Acts* 8:36
should *h.* the gospel of. *1 Cor* 9:12
who did *h.* you, that? *Gal* 5:7

hinder *end*
Abner smote him with *h.* end of.
    2 Sam 2:23

hinder *part*
and his *h.* part toward. *Joel* 2:20
Jesus was in the *h.* part. *Mark* 4:38
the *h.* part was broken. *Acts* 27:41*

hinder *parts*
their *h.* parts were inward.
    1 Ki 7:25; *2 Chr* 4:4
enemies in the *h.* parts. *Ps* 78:66*

hinder *sea*
them toward the *h.* sea. *Zech* 14:8*

hindered
given, that they be not *h.* *Ezra* 6:8
were entering in, ye *h.* *Luke* 11:52
have been much *h.* *Rom* 15:22
have come, but Satan *h.* *1 Thes* 2:18
that your prayers be not *h. 1 Pet* 3:7

hindereth
is persecuted, and none *h. Isa* 14:6*

hindermost, *or* **hindmost**
put Rachel and Joseph *h. Gen* 33:2
shall go *h.* with their. *Num* 2:31
and smote the *h.* of thee. *Deut* 25:18
pursue, and smite the *h. Josh* 10:19
the *h.* of the nations. *Jer* 50:12

hinges
and the *h.* of gold for. *1 Ki* 7:50
door turneth upon his *h. Pr* 26:14

Hinnom
went up by valley of *H. Josh* 15:8
is in the valley of *H. 2 Ki* 23:10
incense in the valley of *H. 2 Chr* 28:3
to pass through fire in *H.* 33:6
the valley of the son of *H. Jer* 19:2
places in the valley of *H.* 32:35

hip
he smote them *h.* and. *Judg* 15:8

Hiram
H. king of Tyre sent messengers to.
    2 Sam 5:11; *1 Chr* 14:1
H. king of Tyre sent servants to Solo-
    mon, for *H.* was ever. *1 Ki* 5:1, 8
H. gave Solomon cedar trees. 10
Solomon gave *H.* 20,000. 11
peace between *H.* and Solomon. 12
Solomon sent and fetched *H.* 7:13
H. made the lavers, *H.* made. 40
H. came to see the cities. 9:12
H. sent in the navy his. 27
the navy of *H.* brought in. 10:11
at sea a navy, with the navy of *H.* 22

hire, *substantive*
God hath given me my *h. Gen* 30:18
and of such shall be my *h.* 32
when it shall come for thy *h.* 33
ringstraked shall be thy *h.* 31:8*
thing, it came for his *h. Ex* 22:15
shalt not bring the *h. Deut* 23:18
thou shalt give him his *h.* 24:15
to thee will I give *h. 1 Ki* 5:6
she shall turn to her *h. Isa* 23:17
and her *h.* shall be holiness to. 18
in that thou scornest *h. Ezek* 16:31
and thou also shalt give no *h.* 41
it of the *h.* of an harlot. return to
    the *h.* of an harlot. *Mi* 1:7
priests thereof teach for *h.* 3:11
no *h.* for man, nor any *h. Zech* 8:10
give them their *h. Mat* 20:8

labourer is worthy of his *h.*
    Luke 10:7
the *h.* of the labourers is. *Jas* 5:4

hire
h. a goldsmith, and he. *Isa* 46:6
went out to *h.* labourers. *Mat* 20:1

hired
h. thee with my son's. *Gen* 30:16
if it be an *h.* thing it. *Ex* 22:15
wages of him that is *h. Lev* 19:13
they *h.* against thee Balaam.
    Deut 23:4; *Neh* 13:2
Abimelech *h.* vain persons. *Judg* 9:4
Micah hath *h.* me, and I am. 18:4
that were full, have *h. 1 Sam* 2:5
Ammon to the Syrians. *2 Sam* 10:6
    1 Chr 19:7
king of Israel hath *h. 2 Ki* 7:6
h. masons and. *2 Chr* 24:12
Amaziah *h.* 100,000 mighty. 25:6
h. counsellors against. *Ezra* 4:5
Sanballat had *h.* him. *Neh* 6:12, 13
with a razor that is *h. Isa* 7:20
h. men are like fatted. *Jer* 46:21
up, Ephraim hath *h. Hos* 8:9
yea, though they have *h.* among. 10
no man hath *h.* us. *Mat* 20:7
when they came that were *h.* 9
Paul dwelt two years in his own *h.*
    house. *Acts* 28:30

hired *servant*
an *h.* servant not eat thereof.
    Ex 12:45; *Lev* 22:10
be meat for thy *h.* servant. *Lev* 25:6
but as an *h.* servant he shall be. 40
the time of an *h.* servant shall. 50
as a yearly *h.* servant shall he. 53
a double *h.* servant. *Deut* 15:18*
not oppress an *h.* servant. 24:14

hired *servants*
the ship with *h.* servants. *Mark* 1:20
many *h.* servants have. *Luke* 15:17
as one of thy *h.* servants. 19

hireling
days like the days of an *h.*? *Job* 7:1
as an *h.* looketh for the reward. 2
he shall accomplish as an *h.* 14:6
in three years as the years of an *h.*
    Isa 16:14; 21:16
those that oppress the *h. Mat* 3:5
he that is an *h.* and not. *John* 10:12
the *h.* fleeth, because he is an *h.* 13

hires
all the *h.* thereof shall. *Mi* 1:7

hirest
thou *h.* them, that they. *Ezek* 16:33

his
(*As the neuter possessive pronoun
its* was *hardly come into use in
1611 in the Authorised Version
(" King James's Version ")* was
translated, the possessive his *was
often used where modern usage
would require* its. *In these places
the Revisions change the pronoun
to the modern form*)
the seed should not be *h. Gen* 38:9
dead beast shall be *h. Ex* 21:34
another challengeth to be *h.*
    part, and it shall be *h. Lev* 27:15
hallowed thing shall be *h. Num* 5:10
the Lord will shew who are *h.* 16:5
and let my last end be like *h.* 23:10
of the firstborn is *h. Deut* 21:17
h. will I be, with him. *2 Sam* 18:18
for it was *h.* from the. *1 Ki* 2:15
a captain of *h.* conspired. *2 Ki* 15:25
is one law of *h.* to put. *Esth* 4:11
and the deceiver are *h. Job* 12:16
because it is none of *h.* 15:23 *(?)*
Lord, all ye saints of *h. Ps* 30:4
strength of the hills is *h.* also. 95:4
ye ministers of *h.* that do. 103:21
is mine, and I am *h. S of S* 2:16
passed by; *h.* it was. *Ezek* 16:15
then it shall be *h.* to the year. 46:17
wisdom and might are *h. Dan* 2:20
h. that did escape, nor have delivered
    up those of *h. Ob* 14
him increaseth that which is not *h.*
    Hab 2:6

is not mine, but *h.* that. *John* 7:16
baptized, he and all *h. Acts* 16:33
Spirit, he is none of *h. Rom* 8:9
knoweth them that are *h. 2 Tim* 2:19
works, as God did from *h. Heb* 4:10

hiss
(*Hiss, or hissing is generally used
in the Bible with the idea of contempt or scorn. Occasionally the
the word has the idea of anger*)
house every one shall *h. 1 Ki* 9:8
men shall *h.* him out of. *Job* 27:23
he will *h.* to them from. *Isa* 5:26
the Lord shall *h.* for the fly. 7:18
passeth thereby shall *h.* 49:17; 50:13
they *h.* at the daughter. *Lam* 2:15
thy enemies *h.* and gnash the. 16
the merchants shall *h. Ezek* 27:36
passeth by her shall *h. Zeph* 2:15
I will *h.* for them and. *Zech* 10:8

hissing
delivered them to *h. 2 Chr* 29:8
their land a perpetual *h. Jer* 18:16
make this city an *h.* 19:8
make them an *h.* 25:9, 18; 29:18
Babylon shall be an *h.* 51:37
inhabitants thereof an *h. Mi* 6:16

hit
and the archers *h.* him. *1 Sam* 31:3*
    1 Chr 10:3*

hither
angry that ye sold me *h. Gen* 45:5
it was not you that sent me *h.* 8
bring down my father *h.* 13
draw not nigh *h.*: put off. *Ex* 3:5
there came men in *h. Josh* 2:2
bring the description *h.* to me. 18:6
him, who brought thee *h.*? *Judg* 18:3
we will not turn aside *h.* 19:12
bring *h.* a burnt offering. *1 Sam* 13:9
Saul said, bring *h.* the ark. 14:18
bring me *h.* every man his ox. 34
let us draw near *h.* unto God. 36
bring *h.* Agag. 15:32
why camest thou *h.*? 17:28
Abiathar, bring *h.* the. 23:9; 30:7
I have brought them *h. 2 Sam* 1:10
hasten *h.* Micaiah. *1 Ki* 22:9*
Jordan divided *h.* and. *2 Ki* 2:8, 14
not bring in captives *h. 2 Chr* 28:13
which brought us up *h. Ezra* 4:2
his people return *h. Ps* 73:10
take a palm, and bring *h.* 81:2
let him turn in *h. Pr* 9:4, 16
draw near *h.* ye sons of. *Isa* 57:3
he said, bring them *h. Mat* 14:18
Jesus said, bring him *h.* to me.
    17:17; *Luke* 9:41
how camest thou in *h.*? *Mat* 22:12
bring in *h.* the poor. *Luke* 14:21
bring *h.* the fatted calf and. 15:23
bring *h.* and slay them. 19:27
colt tied, loose him, bring him *h.* 30
Rabbi, when camest thou *h.*?
    John 6:25
reach *h.* thy finger, reach *h.* 20:27
that came *h.* for that. *Acts* 9:21
call *h.* Simon, whose surname. 10:32
have brought *h.* these men. 19:37

see **come**

hitherto
behold, *h.* thou wouldest. *Ex* 7:16
Lord hath blessed me *h. Josh* 17:14
h. thou hast mocked. *Judg* 16:13
grief have I spoken *h. 1 Sam* 1:16
and saying, *h.* hath the Lord. 7:12
thou hast brought me *h. 2 Sam* 7:18
    1 Chr 17:16
thy father's servant *h. 2 Sam* 15:34
who *h.* waited in the. *1 Chr* 9:18
h. the greatest part kept. 12:29
h. shalt thou come, but. *Job* 38:11
h. have I declared thy. *Ps* 71:17
terrible from their beginning *h.*
    Isa 18:2, 7
my Father worketh *h. John* 5:17
h. have ye asked nothing. 16:24
to come, but was let *h. Rom* 1:13
for *h.* ye were not able. *1 Cor* 3:2

Hittite
the field of Ephron the *H. Gen* 25:9

daughter of Beeri the *H. Gen 26:34*
Elon the *H.* 36:2
Abraham bought of Ephron the *H.*
49:30; 50:13
I will drive out the *H. Ex 23:28*
33:2; 34:11
the *H.* and Amorite. *Josh 9:1; 11:3*
to Abimelech the *H. 1 Sam 26:6*
send me Uriah the *H. 2 Sam 11:6*
thy servant Uriah the *H.* 21, 24
hast killed Uriah the *H.* 12:9
taken the wife of Uriah the *H.* 10
Uriah the *H.* thirty-seven. 23:39
matter of Uriah the *H. 1 Ki 15:5*
thy mother an *H. Ezek 16:3, 45*

Hittites
unto thy seed have I given land of *H.*
Gen 15:20; Josh 1:4
Canaanites, the Amorites. *Ex 3:8, 17*
13:5; 23:23; *Deut 7:1; 20:17*
Josh 3:10; 12:8; 24:11; Judg 3:5
1 Ki 9:20; Neh 9:8
into the land of the *H. Judg 1:26*
Israel dwelt among the *H.* 3:5
loved women of the *H.* 11:1
hired the kings of the *H. 2 Ki 7:6*
left of *H.,* Solomon made. *2 Chr 8:7*
abominations of the *H. Ezra 9:1*

Hivite, much in **Hittite**

ho
to whom he said, *Ho. Ruth 4:1*
ho every one that thirsteth. *Isa 55:1*
ho, ho, come forth. *Zech 2:6*

hoar, *see* **frost, hairs, head**

hoary
think the deep to be *h. Job 41:32*

Hobab
Moses said to *H.* come. *Num 10:29*
of the children of *H. Judg 4:11*

hoised
they *h.* up the mainsail. *Acts 27:40**

hold, *substantive*
(*In the Old Testament the American
Revision renders this* stronghold)
they entered into a *h. Judg 9:46*
put them to the *h.* and set the h. 49
David in *h. 1 Sam 22:4; 24:22*
2 Sam 5:17; 23:14
abide not in the *h. 1 Sam 22:5*
came of Judah to *h. 1 Chr 12:16*
and put them in *h.* unto. *Acts 4:3**
is become the *h.* of every. *Rev 18:2*

see **strong**

hold
lift up the lad, *h.* him. *Gen 21:18*
that they may *h.* a feast. *Ex 5:1*
to let them go, and wilt *h.* 9:2
for we must *h.* a feast unto. 10:9
Lord will not *h.* 20:7; *Deut 5:11*
bring the vail, and *h.* it. *Ruth 3:15*
how should I *h.* up my ? *2 Sam 2:22*
his hand to ark of God, and took *h.* of
it, oxen shook it. 6:6; *1 Chr 13:9*
now therefore *h.* him. *1 Ki 2:9*
the king shall *h.* out. *Esth 4:11*
teach me, and I will *h. Job 6:24*
I know that thou wilt not *h.* 9:28
if I *h.* my tongue, I shall. 13:19
the righteous also shall *h.* on. 17:9
dart, the habergeon cannot *h.* 41:26
h. up my goings in thy. *Ps 17:5*
horror hath taken *h.* upon. 119:53
h. thou me up, and I shall. 117
and thy right hand shall *h.* 139:10
and her hands *h.* the. *Pr 31:19*
they all *h.* swords, being. *S of S 3:8*
I the Lord will *h.* thy. *Isa 41:13*
and I will *h.* thine hand. 42:6
broken cisterns, can *h. Jer 2:13*
astonishment hath taken *h.* 8:21
they shall *h.* the bow. 50:42
anguish took *h.* of him, and. 43
to make it strong to *h. Ezek 30:21*
might have *h.,* they had not *h.* 41:6
then shall he say, *H. Amos 6:10*
them, and *h.* themselves. *Zech 11:5*
else he will *h.* to the one. *Mat 6:24*
Luke 16:13
all *h.* John as a prophet. *Mat 21:26*
they have received to *h. Mark 7:4*

ye *h.* the tradition of men. *Mark 7:8*
who *h.* the truth in. *Rom 1:18**
receive him, and *h.* such. *Phil 2:29*
h. the traditions ye. *2 Thes 2:15*
if we *h.* the beginning. *Heb 3:14*
them that *h.* the doctrine. *Rev 2:14*
that *h.* doctrine of Nicolaitanes. 15

see **caught, take**

hold *fast*
he shall *h.* it *fast,* but. *Job 8:15*
my righteousness I *h. fast,* I. 27:6
they *h. fast* deceit, they. *Jer 8:5*
prove all things, *h. fast. 1 Thes 5:21*
h. fast the form of sound. *2 Tim 1:13*
if we *h. fast* the confidence. *Heb 3:6*
h. fast our profession. 4:14; 10:23
ye have already *h. fast. Rev 2:25*
h. fast and repent. 3:3
h. fast which thou hast. 11

hold *peace*
ye shall *h.* your *peace. Ex 14:14*
her father *h.* his *peace. Num 30:4*
husband altogether *h.* his *peace.* 14
h. thy *peace,* lay hand. *Judg 18:19*
h. thy *peace,* my sister. *2 Sam 13:20*
I know it, *h.* ye your *peace.*
2 Ki 2:3, 5
tidings, and we *h.* our *peace.* 7:9
saying, *H.* your *peace. Neh 8:11*
lies make men *h.* their *peace* ?
Job 11:3
altogether *h.* your *peace.* 13:5
h. your *peace,* let me alone. 13
mark well, *h.* thy *peace* and. 33:31
h. thy *peace,* and I will teach. 33
O God, *h.* not thy *peace,* be not still.
Ps 83:1; 109:1
will I not *h.* my *peace. Isa 62:1*
which shall never *h.* their *peace.* 6
wilt thou *h.* thy *peace* and ? 64:12
I cannot *h.* my *peace. Jer 4:19*
h. thy *p.* at the presence. *Zeph 1:7*
because they should *h.* their *peace.*
Mat 20:31; Mark 10:48; Luke 18:39
h. thy *peace* come out of him.
Mark 1:25; Luke 4:35
should *h.* their *peace. Luke 19:40*
to them to *h.* their *peace. Acts 12:17*
but speak, and *h.* not thy *peace.* 18:9
let the first *h.* his *peace. 1 Cor 14:30*

holden
there was not *h.* such a passover.
2 Ki 23:22*, 23*
if they be *h.* in cords. *Job 36:8**
thy right hand hath *h. Ps 18:35*
by thee have I been *h.* up. 71:6
thou hast *h.* me up by my. 73:23
shall be *h.* with the cords. *Pr 5:22*
I have long *h.* my peace. *Isa 42:14*
whose right hand I have *h.* to. 45:1
eyes were *h.* they. *Luke 24:16*
possible he should be *h. Acts 2:24*
yea, he shall be *h.* up. *Rom 14:4**

holdest
if thou altogether *h.* thy. *Esth 4:14*
wherefore *h.* thou me ? *Job 13:24*
h. my eyes waking, I. *Ps 77:4*
O thou that *h.* the height. *Jer 49:16*
h. thy tongue when the. *Hab 1:13*
thou *h. fast* my name. *Rev 2:13*

holdeth
and still he *h. fast* his. *Job 2:3*
h. back the face of his throne. 26:9
bless God who *h.* our. *Ps 66:9*
a man of understanding *h. Pr 11:12*
a fool when he *h.* his peace. 17:28
and none *h.* with me. *Dan 10:21*
I will cut off him that *h. Amos 1:5, 8*
that *h.* the seven stars. *Rev 2:1*

holding
shaketh his hands from *h. Isa 33:15*
I am weary with *h.* in, I. *Jer 6:11*
eat not, *h.* the tradition. *Mark 7:3*
h. forth the word of life. *Phil 2:16*
not *h.* the head, from. *Col 2:19*
h. faith and a good. *1 Tim 1:19*
h. the mystery of faith in a pure. 3:9
h. fast faithful word, as he. *Tit 1:9*
I saw four angels *h.* the. *Rev 7:1*

holds
have remained in their *h. Jer 51:30**
brought him into *h. Ezek 19:9**

see **strong**

hole
there shall be an *h.* in the. *Ex 28:32*
Jehoiada bored an *h.* in. *2 Ki 12:9*
put in his hand by the *h. S of S 5:4*
child shall play on the *h. Isa 11:8*
look to *h.* of the pit whence. 51:1
and hide it there in a *h.* of. *Jer 13:4*
I looked, behold a *h. Ezek 8:7*

holes
come forth out of the *h 1 Sam 14:11*
h. of the rocks. *Isa 2:19; 7:19*
all of them snared in *h.* 42:22
hunt them out of the *h. Jer 16:16*
her nest in sides of the *h.* 48:28
not move out of their *h. Mi 7:17**
lion filled his *h.* with prey. *Nah 2:12**
to put it in a bag with *h. Hag 1:6*
shall consume in their *h. Zech 14:12**
Jesus saith, The foxes have *h.*
Mat 8:20; Luke 9:58

holier
come not near, for I am *h. Isa 65:5*

holiest
which is called the *h. Heb 9:3*
the way into the *h.* was not yet. 8
enter into the *h.* by blood of. 10:19*

holily
are witnesses how *h. 1 Thes 2:10*

holiness
like thee, glorious in *h.? Ex 15:11*
h. to the Lord. 28:36*; 39:30*
Zech 14:20*, 21*
worship the Lord in the beauty of *h.*
1 Chr 16:29; Ps 29:2; 96:9
praise the beauty of *h. 2 Chr 20:21*
sanctified themselves in *h.* 31:18
at the remembrance of his *h.*
Ps 30:4*; 97:12
sitteth upon throne of his *h.* 47:8*
praised in mountain of his *h.* 48:1
hath spoken in his *h.* 60:6; 108:7
once I have sworn by my *h.* 89:35
h. becometh thine house, O. 93:5
be willing, in beauties of *h.* 110:3
and her hire shall be *h. Isa 23:18*
shall be called the way of *h.* 35:8
drink it in the courts of my *h.* 62:9*
from habitation of thy *h.* 63:15
the people of thy *h.* have. 18*
Israel was *h.* to the Lord. *Jer 2:3*
of the words of his *h.* 23:9
bless thee, O mountain of *h.* 31:23
God hath sworn by his *h. Amos 4:2*
mount Zion there shall be *h. Ob 17**
Judah hath profaned the *h. Mal 2:11*
might serve him in *h. Luke 1:75*
as though by our *h.* made. *Acts 3:12**
according to Spirit of *h. Rom 1:4*
servants to righteousness unto *h.*
6:19
ye have your fruit unto *h.* 22
perfecting *h.* in the fear. *2 Cor 7:1*
created in righteousness and *h.*
Eph 4:24
your hearts unblameable, in *h.*
1 Thes 3:13
us unto uncleanness, but to *h.* 4:7*
continue in faith and *h. 1 Tim 2:15*
in behaviour as becometh *h. Tit 2:3*
be partakers of his *h. Heb 12:10*
follow peace with men, and *h.* 14*

hollow
the *h.* of his thigh. *Gen 32:25, 32*
shalt make the altar *h.* with boards.
Ex 27:8; 38:7
plague be in walls with *h. Lev 14:37*
God clave in *h.* place. *Judg 15:19*
measured waters in *h. Isa 40:12*
the pillar, it was *h. Jer 52:21*

holpen (*American Revision,* helped)
have *h.* the children. *Ps 83:8*
thou, Lord, hast *h.* me. 86:17
and he that is *h.* shall. *Isa 31:3*
they shall be *h.* with a. *Dan 11:34*
hath *h.* his servant Israel. *Luke 1:54*

holy

[1] *Godly,* Deut 33:8; Ps 86:2.
[2] *Dedicated,* 2 Chr 31:6, *or sacred*
1 Cor 9:13. [3] *The holy place, the
inner room of the tabernacle or
temple where none but priests could
enter.* [4] *The Holy of Holies, the
innermost part of the house of God,
where only the High Priest entered,
and he but once a year, on the
Day of Atonement.*
thou standest is *h.* ground.   *Ex* 3:5
the rest of the *h.* sabbath.   16:23
to me a *h.* nation.   19:6; *1 Pet* 2:9
sabbath day to keep it *h.*   *Ex* 20:8
hallow in all their *h.* gifts.   28:38
and put the *h.* crown upon the. 29:6
because they are *h.*   33
because it is *h.*   34
make it an oil of *h.* ointment. 30:25
it is *h.* and it shall be *h.* unto.   32
tempered together, pure and *h.*   35
for it is *h.* unto you.   31:14, 15
upon Aaron the *h.* crown.   *Lev* 8:9
may put difference between *h.* 10:10
he shall put on the *h.* linen.   16:4
make atonement for the *h.*   33
Lord your God am *h.*   19:2; 21:8
be ye *h.*   20:7
for he is *h.* unto his God.   21:7
man sanctify his house to be *h.* 27:14
the tithe of the land is *h.* unto.   30
the priest shall take *h.*   *Num* 5:17
ye may remember, and be *h.* 15:40
all the congregation are *h.*   16:3
shew who are his, and who is *h.*   5
not redeem them, they are *h.* 18:17
sent Phinehas with the *h.*   31:6*
for there is none *h.* as.   *1 Sam* 2:2
vessels of the young men are *h.* 21:5
ark and the tabernacle, and all the *h.*
    1 Ki 8:4; *2 Chr* 5:5
I perceive this is an *h.*   *2 Ki* 4:9
bring the *h.* vessels into. *1 Chr* 22:19
I have prepared for the *h.*   29:3
go in, for they are *h.*   *2 Chr* 23:6
Levites which were *h.* to the Lord,
  put the *h.* ark into the.   35:3
the other *h.* offerings sod they in. 13
h. to the Lord, vessels are *h.* also.
    Ezra 8:28
the *h.* seed mingled themselves. 9:2
known unto them thy *h.*   *Neh* 9:14
hear him from his *h.* heaven. *Ps* 20:6
art *h.* O thou that inhabitest.   22:3
lift my hands towards thy *h.*   28:2
preserve my soul, for I am *h.* 86:2*
his *h.* arm hath gotten him.   98:1
his footstool, for he is *h.*   99:5
and worship at his *h.* hill.   9
remembered his *h.* promise. 105:42
the Lord is *h.* in all his.   145:17*
the knowledge of the *h.* is.   *Pr* 9:10
devoureth that which is *h.*   20:25
I the knowledge of the *h.*   30:3*
Jerusalem shall be called *h. Isa* 4:3
one cried, *H. h. h.* is the Lord.   6:3
h. seed shall be the substance.   13
worship in the *h.* mountain.   27:13
as when a *h.* solemnity is.   30:29
Lord hath made bare his *h.*   52:10
sabbath, the *h.* of the Lord.   58:13
thy *h.* cities are a wilderness. 64:10
our *h.* and beautiful house is.   11
the *h.* flesh is passed.   *Jer* 11:15
no difference between *h. Ezek* 22:26
increase them as the *h.* flock. 36:38*
they be *h.* chambers, where.   42:13
their garments, for they are *h.*   14
and lay them in the *h.*   44:19
shall teach difference between *h.* 23
an *h.* portion of the land.   45:1, 4
oblation of *h.* portion.   6, 7; 48:18
into the *h.* chambers of the.   46:19
for the priests shall be this *h.* 48:10
not sell firstfruits, for it is *h.*   14
shall offer the *h.* oblation.   20, 21
came in before me, in whom is the
  spirit of the *h. Dan* 4:8, 9, 18; 5:11
heart shall be against the *h.* 11:28
the *h.* covenant, intelligence with
  them that forsake the *h.*   30
h. flesh, and with his skirt touch
  bread or oil, shall it be *h.?Hag* 2:12

inherit Judah in the *h.*   *Zech* 2:12
Lord is raised up out of his *h.*   13
give not that which is *h.*   *Mat* 7:6
and all the *h.* angels with.   25:31
he was a just man and *h. Mark* 6:20
he shall come in his own glory, and
  of *h.* angels.   8:38; *Luke* 9:26
by the mouth of *h.* prophets.
    Luke 1:70; *Acts* 3:21
and to remember his *h. Luke* 1:72
male shall be called *h.* to.   2:23
h. Father, keep those.   *John* 17:11
against thy *h.* child.   *Acts* 4:27
done by name of thy *h.* child.   30
thou standest is *h.* ground.   7:33
warned from God by an *h.*   10:22
had promised in the *h.*   *Rom* 1:2
the commandment is *h.,* just.   7:12
fruit be *h.* if the root be *h.*   11:16
ye present your bodies a *h.*   12:1
salute one another with a *h.* kiss.
    16:16; *1 Cor* 16:20; *2 Cor* 13:12
    1 Thes 5:26; *1 Pet* 5:14
temple of God is *h.*   *1 Cor* 3:17
but now are they *h.*   7:14
that she may be *h.*   34
h. and without blame. *Eph* 1:4; 5:27
to present you *h.* and.   *Col* 1:22
put on, as the elect of God, *h.* 3:12
epistle be read to all *h.* *1 Thes* 5:27
lifting up *h.* hands.   *1 Tim* 2:8
hath called us with an *h.* *2 Tim* 1:9
hast known *h.* scriptures.   3:15*
bishop must be sober, *h.*   *Tit* 1:8
h. brethren, partakers of. *Heb* 3:1
priest became us, who is *h.*   7:26
h. in all conversation. *1 Pet* 1:15, 16
a *h.* priesthood, to offer up.   2:5
the *h.* women also who trusted. 3:5
we were with him in *h.* *2 Pet* 1:18
but *h.* men spake as moved by. 21
than to turn from the *h.*   2:21
words spoken before by the *h.* 3:2
what persons to be in all *h.*   11
things, saith he that is *h.*   *Rev* 3:7
H. h. h. Lord God Almighty.   4:8
How long, O Lord, *h.* and ?   6:10
tormented in presence of *h.*   14:10
not fear thee ? for thou art *h.*   15:4
rejoice over her, ye *h.*   18:20*
h. is he that hath part in first. 20:6
and he shewed me the *h.*   21:10
Lord God of the *h.* prophets. 22:6*
he that is *h.* let him be *h.* still.   11

see **convocation, habitation, hill**

holy day

day shall be an *h.* day.   *Ex* 35:2
this *day* is *h.* unto. *Neh* 8:9, 10, 11
them on sabbath or *h.* day.   10:31
multitude that kept *h.* day. *Ps* 42:4
thy pleasure on my *h.* day. *Isa* 58:13
in respect of an *h.* day.   *Col* 2:16*

see **garments**

Holy Ghost

*(American Revision substitutes for
this the words* Holy Spirit. *The
starred references here refer to
other changes)*

with child of the *H. Ghost. Mat* 1:18
conceived in her is of *H. Ghost.* 20
baptize you with *H. Ghost.*   3:11
    Mark 1:8; *Luke* 3:16
    John 1:33; *Acts* 1:5
blasphemy against the *H. Ghost.*
    Mat 12:31*; *Mark* 3:29
    Luke 12:10
speaketh against the *H. Ghost.*
    Mat 12:32
baptize in name of Father, Son, and
  H. Ghost.   28:19
David said by the *H. Ghost.*
    Mark 12:36; *Acts* 1:16
speak, but the *H. Ghost. Mark* 13:11
filled with *H. Ghost.*   *Luke* 1:15
the *H. Ghost* shall come upon.   35
and Elisabeth was filled with the *H.
  Ghost.*   41
Zacharias was filled with the *H.
  Ghost.*   67
Simeon; *H. Ghost* was upon.   2:25
revealed unto him by *H. Ghost.* 26
the *H. Ghost* descended in a.   3:22
being full of the *H. Ghost.*   4:1

H. Ghost shall teach you. *Luke* 12:12
for the *H. Ghost* was.   *John* 7:39*
who is the *H. Ghost.*   14:26
he saith, receive ye the *H. Ghost.*
    20:22; *Acts* 2:38
he through the *H. Ghost. Acts* 1:2
after that the *H. Ghost* is come.   8
filled with the *H. Ghost.* 2:4; 4:31
the promise of the *H. Ghost.*   2:33
Peter, filled with the *H. Ghost.* 4:8
heart to lie to the *H. Ghost.*   5:3
witnesses, so is also *H. Ghost.*   32
look out men full of *H. Ghost.* 6:3*
Stephen, a man full of *H. Ghost.* 5
ye always resist the *H. Ghost.* 7:51
he being full of *H. Ghost* looked. 55
might receive the *H. Ghost.*   8:15
and they received the *H. Ghost.* 17
when Simon saw that *H. Ghost.* 18
hands, he may receive *H. Ghost.* 19
be filled with the *H. Ghost.*   9:17
the comfort of the *H. Ghost.*   31
anointed Jesus with *H. Ghost.* 10:38
H. Ghost fell on all which.   44
poured the gift of the *H. Ghost.* 45
have received the *H. Ghost.*   47
H. Ghost fell on them as on. 11:15
shall be baptized with *H. Ghost.* 16
Barnabas, full of the *H. Ghost.* 24
the *H. Ghost* said, separate.   13:2
being sent forth by *H. Ghost.*   4
Paul, filled with the *H. Ghost.* 9
were filled with the *H. Ghost.* 52
giving them the *H. Ghost* as.   15:8
it seemed good to the *H. Ghost.* 28
were forbidden of *H. Ghost.*   16:6
the *H. Ghost* ? ... not heard whether
  there be any *H. Ghost.*   19:2
laid hands on them, the *H. Ghost.* 6
save that the *H. Ghost.*   20:23
over which *H. Ghost* hath made. 28
thus saith the *H. Ghost,* so. 21:11
well spake the *H. Ghost* by. 28:25
love of God is shed abroad in hearts
  by *H. Ghost.*   *Rom* 5:5
me witness in the *H. Ghost.*   9:1
God is joy in the *H. Ghost.* 14:17
through power of *H. Ghost.* 15:13
being sanctified by *H. Ghost.*   16
words which *H. Ghost.* *1 Cor* 2:13*
the temple of the *H. Ghost.*   6:19
Lord, but by the *H. Ghost.*   12:3
kindness, by *H. Ghost.* *2 Cor* 6:6
communion of the *H. Ghost.* 13:14
gospel came in *H. Ghost. 1 Thes* 1:5
word with joy of the *H. Ghost.*   6
thing keep by *H. Ghost. 2 Tim* 1:14
renewing of the *H. Ghost.* *Tit* 3:5
with gifts of the *H. Ghost. Heb* 2:4
as the *H. Ghost* saith, To-day. 3:7
made partakers of the *H. Ghost.* 6:4
the *H. Ghost* this signifying.   9:8
whereof the *H. Ghost* is a.   10:15
the *H. Ghost* sent down. *1 Pet* 1:12
moved by the *H. Ghost. 2 Pet* 1:21
Word, and the *H. Ghost. 1 John* 5:7
praying in the *H. Ghost.*   *Jude* 20

see **God**

most holy

place and the *most h.*   *Ex* 26:33
of the testimony in the *most h.* 34
be an altar *most h.*   29:37; 40:10
it is *most h.*   30:10
that they may be *most h.*   29
perfume shall be to you *most h.* 36
offering shall be Aaron's, it is *most h.*
    Lev 2:3, 10; 6:17; 10:12
the sin offering is *most h.* 6:25, 29
    10:17
trespass offering is *most h.*   7:1, 6
    14:13
bread of God, both of *most h.* 21:22
cakes of fine flour are *most h.* 24:9
devoted thing is *most h.* to.   27:28
be service about *most h.* *Num* 4:4
they approach the *most h.* things. 19
render to me shall be *most h.* 18:9
in the *most h.* place shalt thou.   10
them for the *most h.* place. *1 Ki* 6:16
made vessels for the *most h.* 7:50
brought the ark unto *most h.* place.
    8:6; *2 Chr* 5:7
sons for work of *most h. 1 Chr* 6:49

to sanctify *most h.*   *1 Chr* 23:13
made the *most h.* house. *2 Chr* 3:8
in the *most h.* house he made.   10
doors thereof for the *most h.*   4:22
Kore to distribute the *most h.* 31:14
not eat of the *most h.* things.
    Ezra 2:63; *Neh* 7:65
limit shall be *most h.* *Ezek* 43:12
near in the *most h.* place.   44:13
be the sanctuary and *most h.* 45:3
oblation be a thing *most h.*   48:12
weeks to anoint the *most h. Dan* 9:24
yourselves on your *most h. Jude* 20

holy *mountain, -s*
foundation is in the *h. mountains.*
    Ps 87:1
nor destroy in my *h. mountain.*
    Isa 11:9; 65:25
will I bring to my *h. mountain.* 56:7
shall inherit my *h. mountain.* 57:13
that forget my *h. mountain.* 65:11
beasts to my *h. mountain.* 66:20
in my *h. mountain* they. *Ezek* 20:40
wast upon the *h. mountain.* 28:14
turned from thy *h. mountain.*
    Dan 9:16
supplication for the *h. mountain.* 20
in glorious *h. mountain.*   11:45
alarm in my *h. mountain. Joel* 2:1
in Zion, my *h. mountain.*   3:17
drunk on my *h. mountain.* *Ob* 16
because of *h. mountain. Zeph* 3:11
Lord called *h. mountain. Zech* 8:3

holy *name*
to profane my *h. name.* *Lev* 20:3
profane not my *h. name.*   22:2
ye profane my *h. name.*   32
glory ye in his *h. name. 1 Chr* 16:10
    Ps 105:3
we give thanks to thy *h. name.*
    1 Chr 16:35; *Ps* 106:47
house for thy *h. name. 1 Chr* 29:16
trusted in his *h. name.* *Ps* 33:21
terrible *name,* for it is *h.*   99:3
bless the Lord, bless his *h. name.*
    103:1; 145:21
h. and reverend is his *name.* 111:9
    Luke 1:49
One, whose name is *h. Isa* 57:15
my *h. name* no more. *Ezek* 20:39
they profaned my *h. name.* 36:20
but I had pity for mine *h. name.* 21
sakes, but for my *h. name's* sake. 22
h. name known in ... not let them pollute my *h. name* any more. 39:7
will be jealous for my *h. name.*   25
my *h. name* shall Israel no. 43:7
they have defiled my *h. name* by. 8
to profane my *h. name. Amos* 2:7

holy *oil*
an *h.* anointing *oil.* *Ex* 30:25, 31
made the *h.* anointing *oil.*   37:29
was anointed with *h. oil. Num* 35:25
with my *h. oil* have I. *Ps* 89:20

holy *One*
Urim be with thy *h. one. Deut* 33:8*
words of the *H. One.* *Job* 6:10
in hell, nor suffer thine *H. One* to.
    Ps 16:10; *Acts* 2:27; 13:35
in vision to thy *h. one. Ps* 89:19*
and his *H. One* shall be. *Isa* 10:17
shall sanctify the *H. One* of. 29:23
I be equal ? saith the *H. One.* 40:25
I am the Lord your *H. One.* 43:15
Redeemer of Israel his *H. One.* 49:7
an *h. one* came down. *Dan* 4:13, 23
for I am the *H. One* in. *Hos* 11:9
from everlasting, O Lord my *H. One.*
    Hab 1:12
the *H. One* came from mount. 3:3
I know thee who thou art, the *H. One.*
    Mark 1:24; *Luke* 4:34
ye denied the *H. One.* *Acts* 3:14
unction from the *H. One. 1 John* 2:20

holy *One of Israel*
lifted thy eyes against the *H. One* of
  Isr. *2 Ki* 19:22; *Isa* 37:23
sing, O thou *H. One of Isr. Ps* 71:22
limited the *H. One of Isr.* 78:41
the *H. One of Isr.* is our king. 89:18
provoked the *H. One of Isr. Isa* 1:4
counsel of the *H. One of Isr.* 5:19
the word of the *H. One of Isr.* 24

the Lord, the *H. One of Isr. Isa* 10:20
    43:3; 45:11
great is the *H. One of Isr.* in. 12:6
have respect to *H. One of Isr.* 17:7
rejoice in the *H. One of Isr.* 29:19
cause the *H. One of Isr.* to. 12, 15
saith the *H. One of Isr.*   12, 15
not unto the *H. One of Isr.*   31:1
Redeemer, the *H. One of Isr.* 41:14
glory in the *H. One of Isr.*   16
and the *H. One of Isr.* hath.   20
your Redeemer, the *H. One of Isr.*
    43:14
is his name, the *H. One of Isr.* 47:4
saith thy Redeemer, the *H. One of*
  Isr.   48:17; 54:5
of *Isr.* and his *H. One.*   49:7
unto thee, for the *H. One of Isr.* 55:5
gold to the *H. One of Isr.*   60:9
the Zion of the *H. One of Isr.* 14
Babylon proud against the *H. One of*
  Isr.   *Jer* 50:29
sin against the *H. One of Isr.* 51:5
Lord, the *H. One in Isr. Ezek* 39:7

holy *ones*
the word of the *h. ones.* *Dan* 4:17

holy *people*
thou art an *h. people* to the Lord.
    Deut 7:6; 14:2, 21
thou mayest be an *h. people.* 26:19
establish thee an *h. people.* 28:9
call them, the *h. people. Isa* 62:12
and destroy the *h. people. Dan* 8:24
the power of the *h. people.* 12:7

holy *place*
in unto the *h. place.* *Ex* 28:29, 35
minister in the *h. place.* 43; 29:30
seeth his flesh in the *h. place.* 29:31
sweet incense for the *h. place.* 31:11
service in the *h. place.* 35:19; 39:1, 41
all the work of the *h. place.* 38:24*
with unleavened bread ... in *h. place.*
    Lev 6:16, 26; 7:6; 10:13; 24:9
wash that in the *h. place.*   6:27
reconcile withal in the *h. place.* 30
eaten sin offering in *h. place?* 10:17*
not brought in within *h. place.* 18*
slay burnt offering in *h. place.* 14:13*
not at all times into the *h. place.* 16:2
Aaron come into the *h. place.*   3
atonement for the *h. place.*   16
atonement in the *h. place.* 17, 27
end of reconciling the *h. place.* 20
when he went into the *h. place.* 23
flesh with water in the *h. place.* 24
place whereon thou standest is *h.*
    Josh 5:15
seen out in the *h. place.* *1 Ki* 8:8
priests come out of the *h. place.* 10
    2 Chr 5:11
charge of the *h. place. 1 Chr* 23:32
carry filthiness out of the *h. place.*
    2 Chr 29:5
burnt offerings in the *h. place.* 7
up to his *h.* dwelling-*place.* 30:27
stand in the *h. place* according. 35:5
us a nail in his *h. place. Ezra* 9:8
stand in his *h. place* ? *Ps* 24:3
make glad the *h. place.*   46:4
as in Sinai, in the *h. place.* 68:17
from the *place* of the *h. Eccl* 8:10
in the high and *h. place. Isa* 57:15
this is the most *h. place. Ezek* 41:4
place is *h.*   42:13
not go out of the *h. place.*   10
it shall be an *h. place* for the. 45:4
the abomination stand in *h. place.*
    Mat 24:15
blasphemous words against this *h.*
  place.   *Acts* 6:13
hath polluted this *h. place.* 21:28
once into the *h. place.* *Heb* 9:12
entered every year into *h. place.* 25

holy *places*
because *places* are *h.* *2 Chr* 8:11
out of thy *h. places.* *Ps* 68:35
h. places shall be defiled. *Ezek* 7:24
thy word toward the *h. places.* 21:2*
not entered into *h. places. Heb* 9:24

shall be **holy**
ye *shall be h.* men unto. *Ex* 22:31
toucheth altar *shall be h.* 29:37

toucheth them *shall be h.* *Ex* 30:29
    Lev 6:18
holy, and it *shall be h. Ex* 30:32, 37
tabernacle, and it *shall be h.* 40:9
flesh thereof *shall be h.* *Lev* 6:27
ye *shall be h.* for I am holy. 11:44
    45; 19:2; 20:26
fruit thereof *shall be h.* to. 19:24
the priests *shall be h.* unto. 21:6
they *shall be h.* to the Lord. 23:20
it is the jubile: it *shall be h.* 25:12
man giveth to Lord *shall be h.* 27:9
exchange thereof *shall be h.* 10, 33
field in the jubile *shall be h.*   21
the tenth *shall be h.* unto the. 32
Nazarite *shall be h.* unto. *Num* 6:5
doth choose he *shall be h.* 16:7
male shall eat it, it *shall be h.* 18:10
shall thy camp *be h.* *Deut* 23:14
towards east *shall be h.* *Jer* 31:40
holy portion *shall be h. Ezek* 45:1
then *shall* Jerusalem *be h. Joel* 3:17

holy *Spirit*
take not thy *h. Spirit.*   *Ps* 51:11
and vexed his *h. Spirit.* *Isa* 63:10
is he that put his *h. Spirit* ?   11
Father give *h. Spirit.* *Luke* 11:13
h. Spirit of promise. *Eph* 1:13
grieve not *h. Spirit* of God.   4:30
given us his *h. Spirit.* *1 Thes* 4:8

holy *temple*
toward thy *h. temple. Ps* 5:7; 138:2
the Lord is in his *h. temple.*   11:4
the goodness of thy *h. temple.* 65:4
h. temple have they defiled. 79:1
toward thy *h. temple.* *Jonah* 2:4
in unto thee, to thy *h. temple.*   7
Lord from his *h. temple.* *Mi* 1:2
Lord is in his *h. temple.* *Hab* 2:20
groweth to an *h. temple* in. *Eph* 2:21

holy *thing*
eat of the *h. thing.*   *Lev* 22:10
if a man eat of the *h. thing.*   14
thy estimation as an *h. thing.* 27:23
not touch any *h. thing. Num* 4:15*
to them a *thing* most *h. Ezek* 48:12
therefore that *h. thing.* *Luke* 1:35

holy *things*
bear iniquity of *h. things. Ex* 28:38
ignorance in the *h. things. Lev* 5:15
from the *h. things* of Israel. 22:2
that goeth unto the *h. things.*   3
h. things till he be clean. 4, 6, 12
shall afterward eat of the *h. things.* 7
shall not profane the *h. things.* 15
when they eat *h. things.*   16
not go in to see, when *h. things* are.
    Num 4:20
of *h. things* shall be his. 5:9; 18:19
shall ye pollute the *h. things.* 18:32
thy *h. things* take and. *Deu* 12:26
in purifying *h. things.* *1 Chr* 23:28
the tithe of *h. things.* *2 Chr* 31:6*
ordinances for *h. things. Neh* 10:33
the *h. things* to the Levites. 12:47
I require your *h. things. Ezek* 20:40
despised mine *h. things.*   22:8
have profaned my *h. things.*   26
not kept charge of my *h. things.* 44:8
near to any of my *h. things.* 13
minister about *h. things. I Cor* 9:13*

home
until her lord came *h.* *Gen* 39:16
bring these men *h.* slay and. 43:16*
beast not brought *h.* *Ex* 9:19
thou shalt bring her *h. Deut* 21:12
but he shall be free at *h. one.* 24:5
father's household *h.* to thee.
    Josh 2:18*
if ye bring me *h.* again. *Judg* 19:9
way, that thou mayest go *h.* 19:9
Lord hath brought me *h. Ruth* 1:21
went unto their own *h.* *1 Sam* 2:20
and bring their calves *h.* from. 6:7
men shut up their calves at *h.* 10
went *h.* to Gibeah. 10:26; 24:22
no more *h.* to his father's.
David sent *h.* to Tamar. *2 Sam* 13:7
the king doth not fetch *h.*   14:13
Ahithophel gat him *h.* to.   17:23
Lebanon, two months at *h. 1 Ki* 5:14
h. with me and refresh. 13:7, 15

and tarry at *h.* *2 Ki* 14:10
2 Chr 25:19
bring the ark of God *h.* *1 Chr* 13:12
so David brought not ark *h.* to. 13
the army of Ephraim to go *h.*: they
returned *h.* in great. *2 Chr* 25:10
Haman came *h.*, called. *Esth* 5:10
believe he will bring *h.* *Job* 39:12
she that tarried at *h.* *Ps* 68:12
good man is not at *h.* *Pr* 7:19
come *h.* at the day appointed. 20
man goeth to his long *h.* *Eccl* 12:5
that Gedaliah should carry him *h.*
Jer 39:14
abroad the sword, *h.* there. *Lam* 1:20
neither keepeth at *h.* *Hab* 2:5
when ye brought it *h.* I. *Hag* 1:9
servant lieth at *h.* sick. *Mat* 8:6
go *h.* to thy friends. *Mark* 5:19
farewell which are at *h.* *Luke* 9:61
he cometh *h.* he calleth his. 15:6
took her to his own *h.* *John* 19:27
went away to their own *h.* 20:10
and they returned *h.* *Acts* 21:6
hunger let him eat at *h.* *1 Cor* 11:34
ask their husbands at *h.* 14:35
at *h.* in the body. *2 Cor* 5:6
learn to show piety at *h.* *1 Tim* 5:4*
chaste, keepers at *h.* *Tit* 2:5

homeborn
be to him that is *h.* *Ex* 12:49
sister whether *born* at *h.* *Lev* 18:9
Israel a servant ? is he a *h.*? *Jer* 2:14

homer
(*A measure of capacity used in both
liquid and dry measure. It was
equal to ten ephahs or baths, or
approximately 9 gallons or 11
bushels. This word is frequently
confused with omer, which was
one-tenth of an ephah or about
5 pints*)
h. of barley seed at fifty. *Lev* 27:16
seed of an *h.* shall yield. *Isa* 5:10
shall be after the *h.* *Ezek* 45:11
the sixth part of an ephah of an *h.* 13
of a bath, for ten baths are an *h.* 14
for an *h.* and half an *h.* *Hos* 3:2

honest
is an *h.* and good heart. *Luke* 8:15
you seven men of *h.* *Acts* 6:3*
provide things *h.* in the. *Rom* 12:17*
providing *h.* things in. *2 Cor* 8:21*
should do that which is *h.* 13:7*
whatsoever things are *h.* *Phil* 4:8*
our conversation *h.* *1 Pet* 2:12*

honestly
let us walk *h.* as in day. *Rom* 13:13
may walk *h.* toward. *1 Thes* 4:12†
things willing to live *h.* *Heb* 13:18†

honesty
life in godliness and *h.* *1 Tim* 2:2*

honey
*Palestine is often referred to in
the Bible as a land flowing with
milk and honey, Ex* 3:8. *Bees are
still abundant even in the remote
parts of the wilderness, where
they deposit their honey in the
crevices of rocks or in hollow trees.
In some places the word which is
translated honey may mean a
decoction of the juice of the grape,
Gen* 43:11; *Ezek* 27:17. *Honey
was not to be used in sacrifices, Lev* 2:11; *but the firstfruits
of honey as of other things were to
be presented to the Lord, for the
use of his priests.*
carry a little *h.*, spices. *Gen* 43:11
like wafers made with *h.* *Ex* 16:31
no leaven. nor any *h.* *Lev* 2:11
a land of oil olive and *h.* *Deut* 8:8
2 Ki 18:32
he made him to suck *h.* *Deut* 32:13
there was *h.* in carcase. *Judg* 14:8, 9
what sweeter than *h.*? what ? 18
and there was *h.* upon. *1 Sam* 14:25
h. dropped. 26
I tasted a little *h.* 29, 43
brought *h.* and butter. *2 Sam* 17:29

take a cruse of *h.* and. *1 Ki* 14:3
brought firstfruits of *h.* *2 Chr* 31:5
see the brooks of *h.* and. *Job* 20:17
sweeter than *h.* *Ps* 19:10; 119:103
with *h.* out of the rock. 81:16
my son, eat *h.* *Pr* 24:13; 25:16
it is not good to eat much *h.* 25:27
h. and milk are under. *S of S* 4:11
my honeycomb with my *h.* 5:1
butter and *h.* shall he eat. *Isa* 7:15
for butter and *h.* shall everyone. 22
we have treasures of *h.* *Jer* 41:8
was in my mouth as *h.* for. *Ezek* 3:3
eat fine flour, *h.* and oil. 16:13 19
Judah traded in *h.* and balm. 27:17
and his meat was locusts and wild *h.*
Mat 3:4; *Mark* 1:6
in thy mouth sweet as *h.* *Rev* 10:9
see **floweth, flowing**

honeycomb
rod, and dipped it in a *h.* *1 Sam* 14:27
also than honey and *h.* *Ps* 19:10
strange woman drop as *h.* *Pr* 5:3
words are as an *h.* sweet. 16:24
eat the *h.* which is sweet. 24:13
full soul loatheth an *h.* 27:7
Thy lips drop as the *h.* *S of S* 4:11
I have eaten my *h.* with. 5:1
him a piece of an *h.* *Luke* 24:42

honour
to their assembly, my *h.* *Gen* 49:6*
will get me *h.* upon Pharaoh. *Ex* 14:17
when I have gotten me *h.* upon. 18
I will promote thee unto great *h.*
Num 22:17, 37
hath kept thee back from *h.* 24:11
shalt put some of thine *h.* 27:20
above all nations in *h.* *Deut* 26:19
shall not be for thine *h.* *Judg* 4:9
to pass, we may do thee *h.* 13:17
shall I be had in *h.* *2 Sam* 6:22
given thee riches and *h.* *1 Ki* 3:13
glory and *h.* are in his. *1 Chr* 16:27
can David say more for *h.* 17:18
both riches and *h.* come of. 29:12
in old age, full of riches and *h.* 28
not asked riches or *h.* *2 Chr* 1:11
thee riches, and wealth, and *h.* 12
had *h.* in abundance. 17:5; 18:1
nor shall it be for thy *h.* 26:18
had much riches and *h.* 32:27
of Jerusalem did him *h.* 33
the *h.* of his excellent. *Esth* 1:4
shall give to their husbands *h.* 20
h. hath been done Mordecai ? 6:3
light and gladness, joy and *h.* 8:16
sons come to *h.* he. *Job* 14:21
the enemy lay mine *h.* in. *Ps* 7:5*
crowned him with *h.* 8:5; *Heb* 2:7, 9
h. and majesty. *Ps* 21:5
loved the place where thine *h.* 26:8*
nevertheless man being in *h.* 49:12
in *h.* and understandeth not. 20
sing forth the *h.* of his name. 66:2*
thy mouth be filled with thy *h.* 71:8
h. and majesty are before him. 96:6
thou art clothed with *h.* 104:1
horn shall be exalted with *h.* 112:9
I will speak of the *h.* of thy. 145:5
h. have all his saints, praise. 149:9
left hand are riches and *h.* *Pr* 3:16
and she shall bring thee to *h.* 4:8
lest thou give thine *h.* to others. 5:9
riches and *h.* are with me. 8:18
a gracious woman retaineth *h.* 11:16
of the people is the king's *h.* 14:28*
before *h.* is humility. 15:33; 18:12
it is an *h.* for a man to cease. 20:3
followeth mercy, findeth *h.* 21:21
of the Lord are riches and *h.* 22:4
the *h.* of kings is to search. 25:2*
so *h.* is not seemly for a fool. 26:1
so is he that giveth *h.* to a fool. 8
h. shall uphold the humble. 29:23
and *h.* are her clothing. 31:25*
whom God hath given *h.* *Eccl* 6:2
that is in reputation for *h.* 10:1
h. before all nations of. *Jer* 33:9*
rewards and great *h.* *Dan* 2:6
I have built for the *h.* of my. 4:30*
mine *h.* and brightness returned. 36*
gave thy father glory and *h.* 5:18*
they shall not give the *h.* of. 11:21

father, where is mine *h.*? *Mal* 1:6
prophet is not without *h.* save in his.
Mat 13:57; *Mark* 6:4; *John* 4:44
receive not *h.* from men. *John* 5:41*
h. one of another, and seek not *h.* 44*
if I honour myself, my *h.* is. 8:54*
seek for glory and *h.* *Rom* 2:7
but *h.* to every man that. 10
lump to make one vessel to *h.* 9:21
kindly affectioned, in *h.* 12:10
render therefore *h.* to whom *h.* 13:7
we bestow more *h.* *1 Cor* 12:23, 24
by *h.* and dishonour, by. *2 Cor* 6:8*
not in any *h.* to satisfying. *Col* 2:23*
possess his vessel in *h.* *1 Thes* 4:4
the only wise God be *h.* *1 Tim* 1:17
counted worthy of double *h.* 5:17
own masters worthy of all *h.* 6:1
to whom be *h.* and power. 16
vessels, some to *h.* *2 Tim* 2:20, 21
builded, hath more *h.* *Heb* 3:3
no man taketh this *h.* to. 5:4
be found to praise, *h.* *1 Pet* 1:7
giving *h.* to the wife as to the. 3:7
from God the Father *h.* *2 Pet* 1:17
beasts give glory and *h.* *Rev* 4:9
to receive glory and *h.* 11; 5:12
h. power and might be to him. 5:13
7:12; 19:1
be glad, rejoice, and give *h.* 19:7*
bring their glory and *h.* 21:24, 26

honour, *verb*
h. thy father and thy mother.
Ex 20:12; *Deut* 5:16; *Mat* 15:4
19:19; *Mark* 7:10; 10:19
Luke 18:20; *Eph* 6:2
shalt not *h.* the person. *Lev* 19:15
thou shalt *h.* the face of the old. 32
they *h.* God and man. *Judg* 9:9
that *h.* me I will *h.* *1 Sam* 2:30
yet *h.* me now, I pray thee. 15:30
David doth *h.* thy father, that he.
2 Sam 10:3; *1 Chr* 19:3
whom the king delighteth to *h.*
Esth 6:6, 7, 9, 11
I will deliver him and *h.* *Ps* 91:15
h. Lord with thy substance. *Pr* 3:9
with their lips do *h.* me. *Isa* 29:13
the beast of the field shall *h.* 43:20
and shalt *h.* him, not doing. 58:13
I extol and *h.* the King. *Dan* 4:37
he *h.* the God . . . a god whom his
fathers knew not, shall he *h.* 11:38
and *h.* not his father or. *Mat* 15:6
should *h.* Son as they *h.* *John* 5:23
but I *h.* my Father, and ye. 8:49
if I *h.* myself, my *h.* is nothing. 54
him will my Father *h.* 12:26
h. widows that are. *1 Tim* 5:3
h. all men, fear God, *h.* *1 Pet* 2:17

honourable
Shechem was more *h.* *Gen* 34:19
sent princes more *h.* *Num* 22:15
the city a man of God, and he is an *h.*
man, all he saith. *1 Sam* 9:6
faithful as David, who is *h.* in. 22:14
was he not most *h.* of three ?
2 Sam 23:19; *1 Chr* 11:21
was more *h.* than the thirty, but. 23
now Naaman was *h.* with. *2 Ki* 5:1
Jabez was more *h.* than. *1 Chr* 4:9
behold, was *h.* among thirty. 11:25
had the earth, and the *h.* *Job* 22:8
king's daughters among thy *h.*
Ps 45:9
his work is *h.* and glorious. 111:3
doth take away the *h.* man. *Isa* 3:3
behave proudly against the *h.* 5
and their *h.* men are famished. 5:13
ancient and *h.* he is the head. 9:15
whose traffickers are the *h.* of. 23:8
bring into contempt all the *h.* of. 9
magnify the law and make it *h.* 42:21
thou hast been *h.* 43:4
the holy of the Lord *h.* 58:13
cast lots for her *h.* men. *Nah* 3:10
of Arimathaea an *h.* *Mark* 15:43*
lest a more *h.* man be. *Luke* 14:8
Jews stirred up the *h.* *Acts* 13:50*
also of *h.* women not a few. 17:12
ye are strong, ye are *h.* *1 Cor* 4:10
members we think less *h.* 12:23
marriage is *h.* in all. *Heb* 13:4

honoured

I will be *h.* upon Pharaoh. *Ex* 14:4
reproof shall be *h.*   *Pr* 13:18
on his master shall be *h.*   27:18
nor hast thou *h.* me with. *Isa* 43:23
all that *h.* her, despise. *Lam* 1:8
of the elders were not *h.*   5:12
I praised and *h.* him that. *Dan* 4:34
who also *h.* us with.   *Acts* 28:10
or one member be *h.*   *1 Cor* 12:26

honourest

and *h.* thy sons above. *1 Sam* 2:29

honoureth

but he *h.* them that fear. *Ps* 15:4
is better than he that *h.*   *Pr* 12:9
he that *h.* him hath mercy.   14:31
a son *h.* his father, where? *Mal* 1:6
and *h.* me with their lips.   *Mark* 7:6
he that *h.* not the Son, *h.* not the.   *John* 5:23
it is my Father that *h.* me, of. 8:54*

honours

honoured us with many *h. Acts* 28:10

hoods

I will take away the *h.*   *Isa* 3:23*

hoof

there shall not an *h.* be.   *Ex* 10:26
whatever parteth *h.* and. *Lev* 11:3
divide the *h.* but divideth not *h.*   4
divideth not the *h.*   5, 6; *Deut* 14:7
the swine, though he divide the *h.*   *Lev* 11:7, 26; *Deut* 14:6, 8

hoofs

were the horse *h.* broken. *Judg* 5:22
than an ox with *h.*   *Ps* 69:31
horses' *h.* shall be counted. *Isa* 5:28
of the stamping of the *h.* *Jer* 47:3
with *h.* of horses shall. *Ezek* 26:11
nor shall the *h.* of beasts.   32:13
I will make thy *h.* brass. *Mi* 4:13

hook

I will put my *h.* in thy nose.   *2 Ki* 19:28; *Isa* 37:29
thou draw leviathan with an *h.?*   *Job* 41:1, 2*
go, and cast an *h.* and. *Mat* 17:27

hooks

their *h.* shall be of gold.   *Ex* 26:32
  37; 36:36
the *h.* of the pillars shall be.   27:10
  11, 17; 38:10, 11, 12, 17, 19
their spears into pruning *h.* *Isa* 2:4
  Mi 4:3
off the sprigs with pruning *h.*   18:5
but I will put *h.* *Ezek* 29:4; 38:4
and within were *h.*, an hand. 40:43
beat your pruning *h.* into. *Joel* 3:10
take you away with *h.* *Amos* 4:2

hope

should say, I have *h.*, if. *Ruth* 1:12
there is *h.* in Israel. *Ezra* 10:2
fear, confidence, thy *h.?* *Job* 4:6
poor hath *h.*, and iniquity.   5:16
my days are spent without *h.*   7:6
hypocrite's *h.* shall perish. 8:13, 14*
be secure, because there is *h.* 11:1?
their *h.* shall be as the giving up. 20
for there is *h.* of a tree if it.   14:7
thou destroyest the *h.* of man. 19
what is *h.* of hypocrite though? 27:8
the *h.* of him is in vain.   41:9
might set their *h.* in. *Ps* 78:7
happy is he whose *h.* is in. 146:5
the *h.* of the righteous. *Pr* 10:28
h. of unjust men perisheth. 11:7
h. deferred maketh the.   13:12
but the righteous hath *h.*   14:32
thy son while there is *h.*   19:18
more *h.* of a fool than. 26:12; 29:20
to living, there is *h.* *Eccl* 9:4
is no *h. Isa* 57:10; *Jer* 2:25; 18:12
O the *h.* of Israel. *Jer* 14:8; 17:13
blessed is the man whose *h.* 17:7*
there is *h.* in the end, saith. 31:17
even the Lord, the *h.* of their. 50:7
therefore have I *h.* *Lam* 3:21
the dust, if so be there may be *h.* 29
she saw that her *h.* was. *Ezek* 19:5
our bones dried, our *h.* lost. 37:11
Achor for a door of *h. Hos* 2:15

the Lord will be the *h.* *Joel* 3:16*
hold ye prisoners of *h.* *Zech* 9:12
the *h.* of their gains. *Acts* 16:19
of the *h.* and resurrection of. 23:6
I have *h.* toward God which. 24:15
now I am judged for the *h.* 26:6
for which *h.'s* sake. I am accused. 7
h. that we should be saved. 27:20
for *h.* of Israel I am bound. 28:20
experience; experience, *h. Rom* 5:4
h. maketh not ashamed, because. 5
saved by *h.*: but *h.* seen is not *h.* 8:24
through patience might have *h.* 15:4
that ye may abound in *h.* through. 13
be partaker of his *h.* *1 Cor* 9:10
now abideth faith, *h.*, charity. 13:13
this life only we have *h.* in. 15:19
h. of you is stedfast. *2 Cor* 1:7
seeing that we have such *h.* 3:12
having *h.* when your faith is. 10:15
we thro' the Spirit wait for *h. Gal* 5:5
may know what is the *h.* *Eph* 1:18
having no *h.* and without God. 2:12
even as ye are called in one *h.* 4:4
for the *h.* laid up for you. *Col* 1:5
be not moved away from the *h.* 23
which is Christ in you, the *h.* of. 27
your patience of *h.* in. *1 Thes* 1:3
for what is our *h.* and joy? 2:19
even as others who have no *h.* 4:13
and for an helmet the *h.* of. 5:8
hath given us good *h.* *2 Thes* 2:16
Jesus, who is our *h.* *1 Tim* 1:1
looking for that blessed *h. Tit* 2:13
made heirs according to the *h.* 3:7
rejoicing of the *h.* firm to. *Heb* 3:6
to the full assurance of *h.* 6:11
who have fled to lay hold on *h.* 18
which *h.* we have as an anchor of. 19
bringing in of a better *h.* did. 7:19
us again to a lively *h.* *1 Pet* 1:3
that your faith and *h.* might be. 21
asketh a reason of the *h.* that. 3:15
man that hath this *h.* *1 John* 3:3

hope, *verb*

strength, that I should *h.?* *Job* 6:11*
didst make me *h.* when. *Ps* 22:9*
of courage, all ye that *h.* in. 31:24
h. in his mercy.   33:18; 147:11
on us, according as we *h.* in. 33:22
in thee, O Lord, do I *h.* 38:15
h. thou in God.   42:5, 11; 43:5
but I will *h.* continually. 71:14
thou hast caused me to *h.* 119:49
I *h.* in thy word. 81, 114; 130:5
let Israel *h.* in Lord. 130:7; 131:3
in the pit cannot *h.* for. *Isa* 38:18
therefore will I *h.* in him. *Lam* 3:24
good that a man should both *h.* 26
have made others to *h.* *Ezek* 13:6
if ye lend to them of whom ye *h.*   *Luke* 6:34
promise our tribes *h.* to. *Acts* 26:7
why doth he *h.* for? *Rom* 8:24
if we *h.* for that we see not. 25
him I *h.* to send presently. *Phil* 2:23
be sober, and *h.* to the. *1 Pet* 1:13

in **hope**

my flesh shall rest in *h.* *Ps* 16:9*
  Acts 2:26
against hope believed in *h. Rom* 4:18
and rejoice in *h.* of the glory. 5:2
hath subjected the same in *h.* 8:20
rejoicing in *h.* patient in. 12:12
may abound in *h.* through. 15:13
ploweth in *h.*; that thresheth in *h.*   *1 Cor* 9:10
in *h.* of eternal life which. *Tit* 1:2

my **hope**

is now *my h.?* as for *my h. Job* 17:15
and *my h.* hath he removed. 19:10
if I have made gold *my h.* or. 31:24
what wait I for? *my h.* is. *Ps* 39:7
for thou art *my h.* O Lord God. 71:5
  Jer 17:17
not be ashamed of *my h. Ps* 119:116
and *my h.* is perished. *Lam* 3:18*
according to *my h.* that in. *Phil* 1:20

hoped

enemies of the Jews *h.* *Esth* 9:1
confounded because they had *h.*   *Job* 6:20

have *h.* in thy judgements. *Ps* 119:43
I have *h.* in thy word.   74, 147
I have *h.* for thy salvation. 166
in vain is salvation *h.* for. *Jer* 3:23
he *h.* to have seen some. *Luke* 23:8
h. money should have. *Acts* 24:26
they did, not as we *h.* *2 Cor* 8:5
substance of things *h.* for. *Heb* 11:1

hopeth

charity *h.* all things. *1 Cor* 13:7

Hophni

two sons of Eli, *H. 1 Sam* 1:3; 4:4
H. and Phinehas shall both. 2:34
H. and Phinehas were slain. 4:11, 17

hoping

do good, and lend, *h.* *Luke* 6:35*
I write, *h.* to come. *1 Tim* 3:14

Hor, *see* **mount**

Horeb

came to the mountain of God, even
to *H.*   *Ex* 3:1; *1 Ki* 19:8
before thee on the rock in *H. Ex* 17:6
of ornaments by mount *H.* 33:6
spake to us in *H. Deut* 1:6; 4:15
stoodest before the Lord in *H.* 4:10
a covenant with us in *H.* 5:2; 29:1
also in *H.* ye provoked the. 9:8
desiredst of the Lord in *H.* 18:16
two tables which Moses put in ark at
H.   *1 Ki* 8:9; *2 Chr* 5:10
they made a calf in *H.* *Ps* 106:19
commanded unto him in *H. Mal* 4:4

Hor-hagidgad

encamped at *H.* *Num* 33:32
went from *H.*   33

Hormah

discomfited them to *H. Num* 14:45
called the name of place *H.* 21:3
you in Seir, even unto *H. Deut* 1:44
of Judah, Eltolad, *H. Josh* 15:30
out of Judah, Bethul, *H.* 19:4
the city was called *H.* *Judg* 1:17
them that were in *H. 1 Sam* 30:30
Shimei's sons dwelt at *H. 1 Chr* 4:30

horn

This word is often used meta-
phorically to signify strength and
honour, because horns are the chief
weapons and ornaments of the
animals which possess them; hence
they are also used as a type of vic-
tory. In the sense of honour, the
word stands both for the abstract,
Lam 2:3; *and so for supreme*
authority, or for the concrete,
Dan 7:8, *whence it comes to mean*
king or kingdom.

wont to push with his *h.* *Ex* 21:29
Hannah said, mine *h.* is. *1 Sam* 2:1
and he shall exalt the *h.* of. 10
fill thine *h.* with oil, go, I will. 16:1
Samuel took the *h.* of oil. 13
the *h.* of my salvation. *2 Sam* 22:3
  Ps 18:2
priest took an *h.* of oil. *1 Ki* 1:39
God, to lift up the *h.* *1 Chr* 25:5
I have defiled my *h.* in. *Job* 16:15
lift not up the *h.* *Ps* 75:4, 5
and in thy favour our *h.* 89:17
and in my name shall his *h.* 24
h. shalt thou exalt like a. 92:10
his *h.* shall be exalted with. 112:9
make the *h.* of David to. 132:17
he also exalteth the *h.* of. 148:14
h. of Moab is cut off. *Jer* 48:25
cut off all the *h.* of Israel. *Lam* 2:3
he hath set up the *h.* of thine. 17
I will cause the *h.* to. *Ezek* 29:21
little *h.*; in this *h.* *Dan* 7:8, 20
the great words which the *h.* 11
the same *h.* made war with the. 21
goat had a notable *h.* between. 8:5
he was strong, the great *h.* 8
of them came forth a little *h.* 9
the great *h.* that is between his. 21
lift up their *h.* over the. *Zech* 1:21
hath raised up an *h.* of. *Luke* 1:69

hornet

(*The large species of wasp, whose*
sting is very severe)

Lord will send the *h.* *Deut* 7:20
I sent the *h.* before you. *Josh* 24:12

hornets
I will send *h.* before thee. *Ex* 23:28

horns
in a thicket by his *h.* *Gen* 22:13
h. of it on the four corners, his *h.*
Ex 27:2; 30:2; 37:25; 38:2
put of the blood on the *h.* 29:12
Lev 4:7, 18, 25, 30, 34; 8:15; 9:9
16:18
shalt overlay the *h.* *Ex* 30:3; 37:26
make an atonement on *h.* of. 30:10
his *h.* are like the *h.* *Deut* 33:17
Joab caught hold on *h.* of. *1 Ki* 2:28
Zedekiah made *h.* of iron. 22:11
2 Chr 18:10
heard me from the *h.* of. *Ps* 22:21
than a bullock that hath *h.* 69:31
h. of the wicked will I cut off, but the
h. of the righteous shall. 75:10
bind the sacrifice to the *h.* 118:27
brought for a present *h.* *Ezek* 27:15
all the diseased with your *h.* 34:21
the altar and upward shall be four *h.*
43:15
fourth beast had ten *h.* *Dan* 7:7, 20
I considered the *h.*, three *h.* were. 8
the ten *h.* are ten kings that shall. 24
ram had two *h.*: the two *h.* were. 8:3
came to the ram which had two *h.* 6
the ram, and brake his two *h.* 7
two *h.* are the kings of Media. 20
have we not taken *h.* by. *Amos* 6:13
for I will make thy *h.* iron. *Mi* 4:13
he had *h.* coming out of. *Hab* 3:4
I saw, and behold, four *h. Zech* 1:18
the *h.* which have scattered. 19, 21
are come to cast out the *h.* 21
a Lamb having seven *h.* *Rev* 5:6
having seven heads and ten *h.* 12:3
beast having ten *h.* and on his *h.* 13:1
another beast had two *h.* like a. 11
coloured beast, having ten *h.* 17:3
hath the seven heads and ten *h.* 7
the ten *h.* thou sawest are. 12, 16
see **rams**

Horonaim
in the way of *H.* they shall. *Isa* 15:5
crying shall be from *H.* *Jer* 48:3
in going down of *H.* the enemies. 5
from Zoar to *H.* they uttered. 34

Horonite, *see* **Sanballat**

horrible
wicked he shall rain a *h.* *Ps* 11:6*
me up also out of a *h.* pit. 40:2
a *h.* thing is committed. *Jer* 5:30
virgin of Israel hath done a *h.* 18:13
seen in the prophets a *h.* 23:14
I have seen a *h.* thing in. *Hos* 6:10

horribly
be *h.* afraid, O ye heavens. *Jer* 2:12
their kings shall be *h.* *Ezek* 32:10

horror
a *h.* of great darkness. *Gen* 15:12
h. hath overwhelmed me. *Ps* 55:5
h. hath taken hold on me. 119:53*
h. shall cover them, and. *Ezek* 7:18

horse
*The most striking feature of the
notices of this animal in the Bible
is that it invariably means a war-
horse. The principal use of the
horse in war was in the chariot, and
because of the hilly nature of
Palestine only certain localities
allowed the use of chariots. The
possession of a large number of
horses, or their breeding, was forbidden in early times, Deut 17:16,
and was held to apply to later
periods as well. David first gathered a force of cavalry or chariots,
2 Sam 8:4, but Solomon was the
first to have them in great numbers,
1 Ki 4:26. They were not shod,
and those with naturally hard hoofs
were greatly desired, Isa 5:28.
Horses and chariots were used in
idolatrous processions, 2 Ki 23:11.*

adder that biteth the *h.* heels.
Gen 49:17
the *h.* and rider hath he. *Ex* 15:21
were *h.* hoofs broken. *Judg* 5:22
a *h.* for 150 shekels. *1 Ki* 10:29
2 Chr 1:17
Ben-hadad king escaped on *h.* with.
1 Ki 20:20
like the army lost, *h.* for *h.* 25
let *h.* the king rideth upon. *Esth* 6:8
let this *h.* be delivered to one. 9
take the apparel and *h.* as thou. 10
Haman the apparel and the *h.* 11
she scorneth the *h.* *Job* 39:18
hast thou given *h.* strength ? 19
be ye not as the *h.* or as. *Ps* 32:9
h. is a vain thing for safety. 33:17
the chariot and *h.* are cast. 76:6
not in the strength of the *h.* 147:10
the *h.* is prepared against. *Pr* 21:31
a whip for the *h.* a rod for the. 26:3
forth the chariot and *h.* *Isa* 43:17
through the deep, as a *h.* 63:13
as the *h.* rusheth into. *Jer* 8:6
will I break in pieces the *h.* 51:21
nor shall he that rideth *h. Amos* 2:15
a man riding upon a red *h. Zech* 1:8
and I will cut off the *h.* from. 9:10
made them as his goodly *h.* 10:3
I will smite every *h.* with. 12:4
shall be the plague of the *h.* 14:15
behold, a white *h.* *Rev* 6:2; 19:11
h. that was red. 6:4
a black *h.* 5
behold, a pale *h.* 8
blood came even to the *h.* 14:20
against him that sat on the *h.* 19:19
sword of him that sat on the *h.* 21

horseback
there went one on *h.* to. *2 Ki* 9:18
then he sent out a second on *h.* 19
and bring him on *h.* *Esth* 6:9
Haman brought him on *h.* 11
sent letters by posts on *h.* 8:10

horse gate
to entering of *h. gate.* *2 Chr* 23:15
above *h. gate* repaired. *Neh* 3:28
corner of the *h. gate.* *Jer* 31:40

horseleech
the *h.* hath two daughters. *Pr* 30:15

horseman
Joram said, take an *h.* *2 Ki* 9:17
h. lifteth up the bright. *Nah* 3:3

horsemen
Joseph chariots and *h.* *Gen* 50:9
the *h.* of Pharaoh pursued. *Ex* 14:9
me honour on Pharaoh and his *h.* 17
Pharaoh and *h.* went into sea. 15:19
Josh 24:6
your sons to be his *h.* *1 Sam* 8:11
Philistines gathered 6000 *h.* 13:5
lo, the *h.* followed hard. *2 Sam* 1:6
and David took 700 *h.* 8:14
David slew 40,000 *h.*, smote. 10:18
prepared chariots and *h.* *1 Ki* 1:5
Solomon had 12,000 *h.* 4:26; 10:26
store for his chariots, and cities for
his *h.* 9:19, 22; *2 Chr* 8:6, 9
escaped on an horse with his *h.* 20:20
chariots of Israel and *h.* *2 Ki* 2:12
leave to Jehoahaz but fifty *h.* 13:7
Joash said, O my father, the *h.* 14
in Egypt for chariots and *h.* 18:24
came up with 60,000 *h.* *2 Chr* 12:3
a huge host with many *h.* 16:8
ashamed to require *h.* *Ezra* 8:22
sent captains and *h.* with. *Neh* 2:9
chariot with a couple of *h. Isa* 21:7, 9
h. shall set themselves in array. 22:7
not bruise them with his *h.* 28:28*
and trust in *h.* because they. 31:1
put thy trust on Egypt for *h.* 36:9
flee for the noise of the *h.* *Jer* 4:29
get up, ye *h.* and stand with. 46:4
all of them *h.* riding. *Ezek* 23:6, 12
against Tyrus with *h.* 26:7
shake at the noise of the *h.* 10
Togarmah traded in fairs with *h.*
27:14*
thee forth, horses and *h.* 38:4
north shall come with *h. Dan* 11:40

I will not save them by horses, nor by
h. *Hos* 1:7
as *h.* so shall they run. *Joel* 2:4
h. shall spread themselves, and their
h. shall come from far. *Hab* 1:8
make ready *h.* threescore. *Acts* 23:23
morrow they left the *h.* to go. 32
number of the army of *h.* *Rev* 9:16

horses
bread in exchange for *h.* *Gen* 47:17
hand of Lord is upon the *h.* *Ex* 9:3
h. to himself, to the end that he
should multiply *h.* *Deut* 17:16
also and straw for the. *1 Ki* 4:28
they brought *h.* and mules. 10:25
2 Chr 9:24
Solomon had *h.* out of Egypt.
1 Ki 10:28; 2 Chr 1:16, 17; 9:28
find grass to save the *h.* *1 Ki* 18:5
and my *h.* are as thy *h.* 22:4
2 Ki 3:7
there appeared *h.* of fire. *2 Ki* 2:11
Naaman came with his *h.* and. 5:9
they left their *h.* and fled for. 7:7
but *h.* tied. 10
some take five of the *h.* 13
blood was sprinkled on the *h.* 9:33
brought Amaziah on *h.* 25:28
2 Chr 25:28
I will deliver thee 2000 *h.*
2 Ki 18:23; Isa 36:8
Josiah took away the *h.* *2 Ki* 23:11
h. were 736. *Ezra* 2:66; *Neh* 7:68
I have seen servants on *h. Eccl* 10:7
land is also full of *h.* *Isa* 2:7
their *h.'* hoofs shall be counted. 5:28
no, for we will flee upon *h.* 30:16
and stay on *h.* and trust in. 31:1
and their *h.* are flesh, and not. 3
his *h.* are swifter than. *Jer* 4:13
as fed *h.* in the morning. 5:8
they ride on *h.* set in array. 6:23
snorting of his *h.* was heard. 8:16
canst thou contend with *h.?* 12:5
harness the *h.* and get up, ye. 46:4
stamping of the hoofs of his *h.* 47:3
and they shall ride upon *h.* 50:42
cause the *h.* to come up as. 51:27
they might give him *h.* *Ezek* 17:15
horsemen riding on *h.* 23:6, 12
issue is like the issue of *h.* 20
all of them riding on *h.* 23; 38:15
the abundance of his *h.* 26:10
traded in thy fairs with *h.* 27:14
forth, and all thy army, *h.* 38:4
nor by battle, by *h.* *Hos* 1:7
not save, we will not ride on *h.* 14:3
as the appearance of *h.* *Joel* 2:4
have taken away your *h.* *Amos* 4:10
shall *h.* run upon the rock ? 6:12
that I will cut off thy *h.* *Mi* 5:10
their *h.* also are swifter. *Hab* 1:8
that thou didst ride on thy *h.* 3:8
walk through the sea with thy *h.* 15
I will overthrow the *h.* *Hag* 2:22
him there were red *h.* *Zech* 1:8
chariot red *h.*, in the second black *h.*
6:2
white *h.* in fourth chariot bay *h.* 3
h. go forth into the north country. 6
the riders on *h.* shall be. 10:5
on bells of *h.* HOLINESS UNTO
THE LORD. 14:20
we put bits in the *h.'* mouths. *Jas* 3:3
locusts were like *h.* *Rev* 9:7
h., the heads of *h.* as heads of. 17
buyeth the merchandise of *h.* 18:13
followed him upon white *h.* 19:14
may eat flesh of kings and *h.* 18
see **chariots**

hosanna
*An Hebrew word, meaning, Save,
we pray. It is taken from the
118th Psalm, and was the cry of the
multitudes as they thronged in our
Lord's triumphal procession into
Jerusalem, Mat 21:9, 15; Mark
11:9, 10; John 12:13.*

Hosea
*(One of the Minor Prophets. The
same name as* **Hoshea**)

hosen
men were bound in their *h. Dan* 3:21

Hoshea

H. son of Nun.   *Deut* 32:44
H. made a conspiracy.   *2 Ki* 15:30
H. son of Elah began to reign. 17:1
H. became Assyria's servant.   3
ninth year of H. Samaria. 6; 18:10
ruler of Ephraim was H. *1 Chr* 27:20
H. sealed the covenant.   *Neh* 10:23

hospitality

*This virtue has always been very
much esteemed by civilized peoples.
The Jewish laws with regard to
strangers are framed in accordance
with the spirit of hospitality,
Lev 19:33, 34, etc.; and before the
giving of the law there were many
instances of the entertaining of
strangers, Gen 18:2, 3; Heb 13:2.
It was more necessary in those
times of difficult travel and few
inns, but the spirit of modern
hospitality is the same.
In Apostolic times the virtue was
strongly enjoined on the followers
of Christ, although the higher
civilization and larger population
made it less of a necessity than in
patriarchal times.*

distributing, given to h. *Rom* 12:13
                                     1 Tim 3:2
but a lover of h. a lover.   *Tit* 1:8
use h. one to another.   *1 Pet* 4:9

host

two pence, gave them to h.*Luke* 10:35
Gaius mine h. and of.   *Rom* 16:23

host

*[1] The word very frequently
means camp or army. In these
passages, easily discovered by the
context, the Revisions use these
other words. [2] It means in some
cases merely a vast number.*

earth was finished, and all h. *Gen* 2:1
chief captain of his h.   21:22, 32
he said, This is God's h.   32:2
honoured on all his h.   *Ex* 14:4, 17
h. of Egyptians through pillar of fire
  and of cloud, and troubled h.   24
the waters covered all the h.   28
dew lay round about the h.   16:13
h. and those that were numbered.
Num 2:4, 6, 8, 11, 13, 15, 19, 21, 23
all that entered into h.   *Num* 4:3*
over the h. of Judah.   10:14
the h. of Issachar.   15
over h. of Zebulun.   18
over h. of Reuben.   19
over h. of Simeon.   19
wroth with the officers of h.   31:14
the officers of the h. came near.   48
war were wasted from h. *Deut* 2:14
to destroy them from among h.   15
when the h. goeth forth against. 23:9
pass through the h. and. *Josh* 1:11
the officers went through the h. 3:2
as captain of the h. of the Lord. 5:14
came again to Joshua to the h.   18:9
the captain of whose h.   *Judg* 4:2
and all the h. of Sisera fell on.   16
the h. of Midian was beneath.   7:8
arise, get thee down unto the h. 9, 10
cake of bread tumbled into the h. 13
and all the h. ran, and cried   21
up and smote the h., the h.   8:11
pursued and discomfited all the h. 12
Saul came into the h. *1 Sam* 11:11
there was trembling in the h. 14:15
the noise of the h. went on and. 19
the captain of Saul's h. was Abner. 50
David came as the h. was.   17:20
when Saul saw the h. of the.   28:5
deliver the h. of Israel to.   19
coming in with me in the h. is. 29:6
Lord shall smite the h. *2 Sam* 5:24
David had smitten all the h. of
  Hadadezer.   8:9; *1 Chr* 18:9
David smote Shobach captain of
  their h. *2 Sam* 10:18; *1 Chr* 19:18
Amasa captain of h.   *2 Sam* 17:25
if thou be not captain of h.   19:13
Joab was over all the h.   20:23
                                   1 Chr 18:15

these three brake through the h.
  2 Sam 23:16; *1 Chr* 11:18
son of Ner captain of h. of Israel
  and Amasa captain of h. *1 Ki* 2:32
Benaiah over the h.   35, 4:4
Omri captain of the h., king. 16:16
gathered all his h. together.   20:1
hand and carry me out of h.   22:34
was no water for the h.   *2 Ki* 3:9
spoken for to captain of the h.? 4:13
sent he horses and great h.   6:14
Ben-hadad gathered his h. and.   24
come and let us fall unto the h. 7:4
h. to hear the noise of a great h.   6
behold the captains of the h.   9:5
Sennacherib sent a great h.   18:17
Nebuchadnezzar came and his h.
                                     25:1
scribe of the h.   19; *Jer* 52:25
their fathers over the h. *1 Chr* 9:19
was a great h. like the h.   12:22
of all the captains of the h.   27:3
Zerah came with an h.   *2 Chr* 14:9
not relied, therefore is the h.   16:7
Ethiopians and Lubims a huge h.? 8
and carry me out of the h.   18:33
delivered a great h. into.   24:24
Uzziah had an h. of fighting.   26:11
Oded went out before the h.   28:9
though an h. should encamp. *Ps* 27:3
all h. of them made by breath. 33:6
by the multitude of an h.   16
Pharaoh and h. in Red sea.   136:15
hosts mustereth the h. of. *Isa* 13:4
Lord shall punish the h. of.   24:21
that bringeth out their h.   40:26
and all their h. have I.   45:12
destroy ye utterly all her h. *Jer* 51:3
speech, as noise of an h. *Ezek* 1:24
cast down some of the h. *Dan* 8:10
himself to the prince of the h.   11
an h. was given him against the. 12
to give the h. to be trodden.   13
the captivity of this h. shall. *Ob* 20
multitude of heavenly h. *Luke* 2:13
    see **heaven**

hostages

all the gold and silver and h. and.
    2 Ki 14:14; *2 Chr* 25:24

hosts

the h. of Lord went out.   *Ex* 12:41
of Canaan and all their h. *Josh* 10:5
                                     11:4
Zalmunna with their h.   *Judg* 8:5
sent the captains of the h. *1 Ki* 15:20
the Lord, all ye his h.   *Ps* 103:21
O God, go forth with h.?   108:11
all his angels, all his h.   148:2
a goodly heritage of the h. *Jer* 3:19
    see **God, Lord**

hot

when the sun waxed h.   *Ex* 16:21
there is a h. burning.   *Lev* 13:24
afraid of anger and h.   *Deut* 9:19
pursue, while his heart is h.   19:6
this our bread we took h. *Josh* 9:12
Lord was h. against Israel, and he.
          Judg 2:14*, 20*; 3:8*; 10:7*
not thine anger be h. against. 6:39*
time sun be h., ye.   *1 Sam* 11:9
put h. bread in day when it.   21:6
be opened till the sun be h. *Neh* 7:3
when it is h. they are.   *Job* 6:17
neither chasten in thy h. *Ps* 6:1; 38:1
my heart was h. within me.   39:3
he gave their flocks to h.   78:48
can one go upon h. coals? *Pr* 6:28
brass of it may be h.   *Ezek* 24:11
furnace was exceeding h. *Dan* 3:22
they are all h. as an oven.   *Hos* 7:7
seared with a h. iron.   *1 Tim* 4:2
thou art neither cold nor h.: I would
  thou wert cold or h. *Rev* 3:15, 16
    see **wax**, *verb*

hotly

thou hast so h. pursued. *Gen* 31:36

hottest

Uriah in forefront of h. *2 Sam* 11:15

hough

Lord said, thou shalt h.   *Josh* 11:6

houghed

h. their horses, burnt.   *Josh* 11:9
and David h. all the.   *2 Sam* 8:4

hour

*(The day was not divided into
hours by the ancient Hebrews.
Only the natural divisions of morning, noon, and evening were noted.
After the Exile there was a somewhat clearer division which, it is
supposed, was learned from the
Babylonians. The length of the
hour was dependent usually upon
the season, as people commonly
reckoned it as the twelfth part of
the natural day, from sunrise to
sunset, and this would differ according to season)*

was astonied for one h. *Dan* 4:19*
made whole from that h. *Mat* 9:22
made whole from that very h. 15:28
was cured from that very h. 17:18
about the third h. and saw.   20:3
about the sixth and ninth h.   5
the eleventh h.   6
have wrought but one h.   12
that h. knoweth no man.   24:36, 42
                               Mark 13:32
such an h. as ye think not.
   Mat 24:44, 50; *Luke* 12:40, 46
neither the day nor the h. *Mat* 25:13
could ye not watch one h.?   26:40
                               Mark 14:37
the h. is at hand, the.   *Mat* 26:45
h. was darkness over land to ninth h.
     27:45; *Mark* 15:33; *Luke* 23:44
about the ninth h. Jesus cried.
     Mat 27:46; *Mark* 15:34
be given you in that h. *Mark* 13:11
that if possible the h. might.   14:35
it was the third h. and they.   15:25
in that h. Jesus rejoiced. *Luke* 10:21
had known what h. the thief. 12:39
and when the h. was come.   22:14
but this is your h. and the power. 53
space of one h. after another.   59
for it was about tenth h.   *John* 1:39
Jesus saith, Woman, mine h. is. 2:4
it was about the sixth h. 4:6; 19:14
believe me, the h. cometh. 4:21, 23
he the h. when he began to amend,
  yesterday at seventh h.   52
h. is coming, and.   5:25, 28; 16:32
his h. was not yet come. 7:30; 8:20
the h. is come, Son.   12:23; 17:1
Father, save me from this h.: but for
  this cause came I to this h.   12:27
when Jesus knew that his h.   13:1
hath sorrow, because her h.   16:21
from that h. that disciple.   19:27
seeing it is third h. of.   *Acts* 2:15
h. of prayer being the ninth h. 3:1
about the ninth h. an angel.   10:3
up to pray about the sixth h.   9
ago I was fasting until this h.   30
make ready at the third h. of. 23:23
to this present h. both.   *1 Cor* 4:11
conscience of idol unto this h.   8:7
stand we in jeopardy every h.? 15:30
gave place, no not for an h. *Gal* 2:5
not know what h. I will.   *Rev* 3:3
I will keep thee from the h. of.   10
silence about space of half an h. 8:1
which were prepared for an h.   9:15
the h. of his judgement is come. 14:7
receive power as kings one h. 17:12
for in one h. is thy judgement. 18:10
in one h. so great riches come.   17
that great city in one h. she is. 19

same hour

the same h. be cast.   *Dan* 3:6, 15
the same h. was the thing.   4:33
the same h. came forth fingers. 5:5
was healed the same h.   *Mat* 8:13
it shall be given you the same h.
                      10:19; *Luke* 12:12
the same h. said Jesus.   *Mat* 26:55
that same h. cured many. *Luke* 7:21
scribes same h. sought to lay. 20:19
they rose up the same h.   24:33
that it was at the same h. *John* 4:53
he came out the same h. *Acts* 16:18
he took up the same h. of night. 33

the *same h.* I looked up. *Acts* 22:13
the *same h.* was there a. *Rev* 11:13

hours

are there not twelve *h.? John* 11:9
about space of thre *h.* *Acts* 5:7
about two *h.,* Great is Diana. 19:34

house

[1] *A place to dwell in,* Gen 19:3;
*hence used also of the body as the
dwelling place of the soul of man.*
2 Cor 5:1. [2] *The household, or
persons dwelling in the house,* Acts
10:2; Heb 11:7. [3] *Kindred or
lineage,* 2 Sam 7:18; Luke 1:27.
[4] *Wealth, riches, or estates,* Mat
23:14. [5] *The grave,* Job 30:23;
Isa 14:18. [6] *The house of God,
the building erected for the worship
of God, in which his spirit is most
frequently considered as dwelling.*
Judg 18:31; 2 Chr 5:14; 1 Tim 3:15.
Sodom compassed the *h.* *Gen* 19:4
to the *h.* of my master's.   24:27
I have prepared the *h.*   31
go to the *h.* of Bethuel, thy.   28:2
Lord blessed the Egyptian's *h.* 39:5
the Egyptians and the *h.* of.   45:2
frogs shall come into *h.* of. *Ex* 8:3
a lamb according to the *h.* of. 12:3*
not an *h.* where there was not.   30
carry of the flesh out of the *h.* 46
came out from Egypt, out of *h.* of
bondage. 13:3, 14; *Deut* 5:6; 6:12
shalt not covet neighbour's *h.*
Ex 20:17; *Deut* 5:21
command they empty *h.* *Lev* 14:36
priest shall go out of the *h.*   38
break down *h.* and mortar of *h.* 45
he that goeth into the *h.* shall. 46
he shall take to cleanse the *h.*   49
h. sold in walled city, not go. 25:30
if she vowed in her husband's *h.*
Num 30:10
redeemed you out of *h.* *Deut* 7:8
of the land of Egypt, from the *h.* of.
8:14; 13:5, 10; *Josh* 24:17
Judg 6:8; *Jer* 34:13; *Mi* 6:4
h. of him that hath his shoe loosed.
Deut 25:10
for her *h.* was upon the. *Josh* 2:15
neither shewed kindness to *h.* of.
Judg 8:35
h. of Millo made Abimelech.   9:6
let fire come from *h.* of Millo.   20
Ammon fought against the *h.*   10:9
may feel pillars whereon *h.*   16:26
the *h.* was full of men.   27
h. fell on the lords.   30
Micah had an *h.* of gods.   17:5
and they came unto the *h.*   18:13
no man receiveth me to *h.*   19:18
Belial beset the *h.* round.   22; 20:5
sworn unto *h.* of Eli.   *1 Sam* 3:14
brought the ark into the *h.*   5:2
and brought the ark into the *h.* 7:1
thee, where the seer's *h.* is.   9:18
Nabal was churlish, and of *h.*   25:3
certainly make my lord a sure *h.* 28
war between *h.* of Saul and *h.* of
David.   *2 Sam* 3:1
shew kindness to the *h.* of Saul.   8
let there not fail from the *h.* of. 29
came to the *h.* of Ish-bosheth, who. 4:5
lame shall not come into the *h.* 5:8
h. of Obed-edom, David brought ark
from his *h.* 6:11,12; *1 Chr* 13:14
I have not dwelt in any *h.*
2 Sam 7:6; *1 Chr* 17:5
he will make thee an *h.* *2 Sam* 7:11
to bless the *h.* of thy servant.
1 Chr 17:27
is left of the *h.* of Saul? *2 Sam* 9:1
I gave thee thy master's *h.*   12:8
now to thy brother Amnon's *h.* 13:7
a man of the family of the *h.*   16:5
who made me an *h.* as.   *1 Ki* 2:24
which he spake concerning the *h.* 27
and the whole *h.* he overlaid.   6:22
so Solomon finished the *h.*   9:25
Pharaoh, who gave him an *h.* 11:18
made an *h.* of his high places. 12:31
bring an evil on the *h.* of. 14:10, 14
Baasha smote all the *h.* of.   15:29

Zimri slew all the *h.* of. *1 Ki* 16:11
and he, and her *h.* did eat.   17:15
I will make thy *h.* like the *h.* 21:22
cry to king for her *h.* and. *2 Ki* 8:3
as did the *h.* of Ahab.   18, 27
2 Chr 21:6; 22:4
for the whole *h.* of Ahab. *2 Ki* 9:8
best, fight for your master's *h.* 10:3
h. of Baal was full from on end.   21
made the *h.* of Baal a draught *h.* 27
for all that was laid out for *h.* 12:12
h. of his precious things, all the *h.* of
his armour.   20:13; *Isa* 39:2
h. of which I said, My. *2 Ki* 23:27
every great man's *h.* he burnt. 25:9
of Salma; Ataroth the *h.* *1 Chr* 2:54*
sons, the *h.* of Asuppim.   26:15*
glory of Lord filled the *h.* *2 Chr* 7:1
Ezek 43:4, 5
chosen this place to myself for *h.* of.
2 Chr 7:12
so the *h.* of Ahaziah had no.   22:9
but against the *h.* wherewith. 35:21
that we went to the *h.* of. *Ezra* 5:8
let the *h.* be builded, the place. 6:3
and for the *h.* which I.   *Neh* 2:8
gather all virgins to the *h.* *Esth* 2:3
king did give *h.* of Haman.   8:1, 7
drinking wine in eldest brother's *h.*
Job 1:13, 18
and smote the corners of the *h.*   19
hath taken away a *h.* which.   20:19
for ye say, Where is the *h.* of ? 21:28
and to the *h.* appointed for.   30:23
shouldest know paths to the *h.* 38:20
whose *h.* I have made the.   39:6
my rock be for a *h.* of.   *Ps* 31:2
the sparrow hath found an *h.*   84:3
stork, fir trees are her *h.*   104:17
her *h.* inclineth to death.   *Pr* 2:18
young man went way to her *h.*   7:8
her feet abide not in her *h.*   11
her *h.* is the way to hell.   27
wisdom hath builded her *h.*   9:1
but the *h.* of the righteous shall. 12:7
the *h.* of the wicked shall be. 14:11
the Lord will destroy the *h.* of. 15:25
than an *h.* full of sacrifices.   17:1
h. and riches are inheritance. 19:14
dwell in corner of *h.* top. 21:9; 25:24
wisely considereth the *h.*   21:12
through wisdom is an *h.* built. 24:3
foot from thy neighbour's *h.*   25:17
nor go into brother's *h.* in day. 27:10
to go to *h.* of mourning, than *h.* of
feasting.   *Eccl* 7:2
through idleness of hands *h.* 10:18
when the keepers of the *h.*   12:3
the beams of our *h.* are. *S of S* 1:17
me to the banqueting *h.* his.   2:4
brought him into my mother's *h.* 3:4
bring thee into my mother's *h.*   8:2
woe to them that join *h.* to *h.,* field.
Isa 5:8
the *h.* was filled with smoke.   6:4
that opened not the *h.* of.   14:17*
so that there is no *h.*   23:1
every *h.* shut.   24:10
he will arise against the *h.* of. 31:2
and I will glorify the *h.* of.   60:7
our holy and beautiful *h.* is.   64:11
enter not into the *h.* of.   *Jer* 16:5
thou shalt not go into *h.* of.   8
h. of the king of Judah. 21:11; 22:1
go to the *h.* of the Rechabites. 35:2
to *h.* of Jonathan.   37:20; 38:26
rebellious *h.* yet shall have a.
Ezek 2:5; 3:9, 26, 27; 12:3
rebellious like that rebellious *h.* 2:8
he said to them, Defile the *h.* go. 9:7
the midst of a rebellious *h.*   12:2
in your days, O rebellious *h.*   25
say now to the rebellious *h.*   17:12
a parable to the rebellious *h.* 24:3
shew them the form of the *h.*   43:11
this is the law of *h.;* Upon the top. 12
so shall ye reconcile the *h.*   45:20
which he carried to the *h.*   *Dan* 1:2
blood of Jezreel on the *h.*   *Hos* 1:4
a fire into the *h.* of Hazael. *Amos* 1:4
that holdeth the sceptre from the *h.* 5
the winter *h.* with summer *h.* 3:15
or went into *h.* and leaned his. 5:19
the great *h.* and the little *h.* 6:11

I will rise against *h.* of.   *Amos* 7:9
drop not thy word against the *h.*   16
the *h.* of Esau shall be for.   *Ob* 18
heaps, and the mountain of the *h.*
Mi 3:12
let us go up to the *h.* of the.   4:2
works of the *h.* of Ahab.   *Nah* 1:14
out of the *h.* of thy gods.   1:14
enter into the *h.* of the thief, into *h.*
of him that sweareth.   *Zech* 5:4
family of the *h.* of Nathan.   12:12
and beat upon that *h.*   *Mat* 7:25, 27
Luke 6:48
when ye come into a *h.*   *Mat* 10:12
if *h.* be worthy, let.   13; *Luke* 10:5
every *h.* divided against itself.
Mat 12:25; *Mark* 3:25
how can one enter into a strong
man's *h.?* *Mat* 12:29; *Mark* 3:27
against good man of *h.* *Mat* 20:11*
your *h.* is left to you desolate.
Mat 23:38; *Luke* 13:25
man of the *h.* had known in what
watch.   *Mat* 24:43; *Luke* 12:39
h. divided against itself, that *h.*
Mark 3:25
that hath left *h.* or brethren. 10:29
is the guestchamber? say ye to the
good man of *h.* 14:14; *Luke* 22:11
that *h.* remain, go not from *h.* to *h.*
Luke 10:7
Martha, received him into her *h.* 38
not light candle and sweep *h.?* 15:8
h. was filled with odour. *John* 12:3
from heaven filled all *h.*   *Acts* 2:2
breaking bread from *h.* to *h.*   46*
every *h.* ceased not to teach. 5:42*
Simon a tanner, whose *h.* is.   10:6
entered into the man's *h.*   11:12
he came to the *h.* of Mary.   12:12
but the Jews assaulted the *h.*   17:5
whose *h.* joined hard to the.   18:7
they fled out of that *h.* naked. 19:16
publicly, and from *h.* to *h.*   20:20
entered into the *h.* of Philip.   21:8
greet the church in their *h.* *Rom* 16:5
1 Cor 16:19
which are of the *h.* of.   *1 Cor* 1:11*
ye know the *h.* of Stephanas.   16:15
earthly *h.* be dissolved, we have an *h.*
2 Cor 5:1
desiring to be clothed upon with *h.* 2*
wandering about from *h.* to *h.* and.
1 Tim 5:13
younger women guide the *h.*   14*
Lord give mercy to *h.* of. *2 Tim* 1:16
in a great *h.* there are vessels. 2:20
he who built the *h.* more honour than
Heb 3:3
h. is built by some man, he.   4
whose *h.* are we, if we hold fast. 6
receive him not into your *h.* nor.
2 John 10
see Aaron, born, build, built,
chief, David, door, dwell

house joined with *father*

get thee from thy *father's h.*
Gen 12:1
to wander from *father's h.*   20:13
took me from my *father's h.* 24:7
thou shalt go to my *father's h.*   38
wife for my son of my *father's h.* 40
portion for us in our *father's h.?*
31:14
at thy *father's h.* till Shelah be grown
. . . dwelt in her *father's h.* 38:11
made me forget my *father's h.* 41:51
my brethren and *father's h.*   46:31
in Egypt, he and his *father's h.* 50:22
a lamb, according to *h.* of their
fathers.   *Ex* 12:3
returned to her *father's h.* *Lev* 22:13
Israel by *h.* of their *fathers,* with.
Num 1:2, 18, 20, 22, 24
tribe, every one head of the *h.* of his
fathers.   1:4, 44; *Josh* 22:14
numbered by the *h.* of their *fathers.*
Num 1:45
pitch with ensign of their *father's h.*
2:2
children of Levi after the *h.* of their
fathers, by.   3:15, 20; 4:46
Gershon by *h.* of their *fathers.* 4:38

Merari after *h.* of their *fathers.*
          Num 4:42
according to *h.* of their *fathers*
   twelve rods.   17:2, 3
and *father's h.* bear iniquity of. 18:1
vow a vow, being in her *father's h.*
          30:3, 16
Reuben, Gad, according to the *h.* of
   their *fathers.*   34:14
whore in her *father's h. Deut* 22:21
kindness to my *father's h.* Josh 2:12
the least in my *father's h. Judg* 6:15
risen up against my *father's h.* 9:18
not inherit in our *father's h.* 11:2
burn thee and thy *father's h.* 14:15
all the *h.* of his *father* came. 16:31
went to his *father's h.*   19:2
brought him into her *father's h.* 3
plainly appear to *h.* of thy *father.*
          1 Sam 2:27
said the *h.* of thy *f.* should walk. 30
thee, and on all thy *father's h.?* 9:20
king will make his *father's h.* 17:25
no more home to his *father's h.* 18:2
king sent to call all his *father's h.*
          22:11
thou and all thy *father's h.* shall. 16
destroy my name out of *father's h.*
          24:21
rest on Joab and all his *father's h.*
          2 Sam 3:29
iniquity be on me, and on my *father's*
   h.   14:9
my *father's h.* were but dead. 19:28
pray thee, be against me and against
   my *father's h.* 24:17; *1 Chr* 21:17
innocent blood from me and *father's*
   h.   *1 Ki* 2:31
father's h. have troubled Israel.
          18:18
Hemath *father* of the *h.* of Rechab.
          1 Chr 2:55
h. of their *fathers* increased. 4:38
son of Guni, chief of *h.* of their
   fathers.   5:15, 24; 7:2, 7, 9, 40
with them after the *h.* of *fathers.* 7:4
chief in the *h.* of their *fathers.* 9:9
          13; 12:30
of Zadok, his *father's h.*   12:28
me before the *h.* of my *father.* 28:4
slain thy brethren of thy *father's h.*
          2 Chr 21:13
could not shew their *father's h.*
        Ezra 2:59; *Neh* 1:6
chief of *h.* of their *father. Ezra* 10:16
both I and my *father's h.*   *Neh* 1:6
thou and thy *father's h.* shall be destroyed.   *Esth* 4:14
forget thy people and thy *father's h.*
          Ps 45:10
take hold of his brother of the *h.* of
   his *father.*   *Isa* 3:6
bring on thy *father's h.* days. 7:17
throne to his *father's h.*   22:23
all the glory of his *father's h.*   24
the *h.* of thy *fathers* dealt treacherously.   *Jer* 12:6
send him to my *father's h.*
         Luke 16:27
not my *Father's h.* a house of merchandise.   *John* 2:16
Father's h. are many mansions. 14:2
nourished in his *father's h. Acts* 7:20

house of God
other but the *h. of God. Gen* 28:17
stone which I set shall be *God's h.* 22
drawers of water for *h. of God.*
         Josh 9:23
all the time *h. of God. Judg* 18:31
and went up to the *h. of God.* 20:18*
people came unto the *h. of God.* 26*
          21:2*
which one goeth up to *h. of God.* 31*
Azariah ruler of *h. of God.*
     1 Chr 9:11; *Neh* 11:11
governors of *h. of God. 1 Chr* 24:5
glory filled the *h. of God. 2 Chr* 5:14
with them hid in *h. of God.*   22:12
they set the *h. of God* in.   24:13
a carved image in the *h. of God.* 33:7
they burnt the *h. of God.*   36:19
to the *h.* of the great *God. Ezra* 5:8
let the *h. of God* be builded. 15; 6:7,

needed for the *h. of God? Ezra* 7:20
it be done for the *h.* of the *God.* 23
let us meet in *h. of God. Neh* 6:10
I said, Why is the *h. of God?* 13:11
I went with them to the *h. of God.*
        Ps 42:4; 55:14
olive tree in the *h. of God.*   52:8
be doorkeeper in *h. of God.* 84:10
thou goest to *h. of God. Eccl* 5:1
let us go up to the *h. of God.*
      Isa 2:3; *Mi* 4:2
is hated in the *h. of God. Hos* 9:8
withholden from *h. of God. Joel* 1:13
cut off from the *h. of God.*   16
to *h. of God* men to pray. *Zech* 7:2*
into the *h.* of *God,* and did eat the.
   Mat 12:4; *Mark* 2:26; *Luke* 6:4
to behave thyself in the *h. of God.*
        1 Tim 3:15
high priest over the *h. of God.*
        Heb 10:21
begin at the *h. of God. 1 Pet* 4:17

his house
Lord plagued Pharaoh and *his h.*
        Gen 12:17
of *his h.* were circumcised.   17:27
him overseer over *his h.*   39:4, 5
made me lord of all *his h.*   45:8
          Acts 7:10
atonement for *his h. Lev* 16:6, 11
a man shall sanctify *his h.*   27:14
sanctified it will redeem *his h.*   15
would give me *his h.* full of silver.
      Num 22:18; 24:13
let him go and return to *his h.*
      Deut 20:5, 6, 7, 8
him send her out of *his h.*   24:1
go into *his h.* to fetch his pledge. 10
became a snare to *his h. Judg* 8:27
with Jerubbaal and *his h.* 9:16, 19
spoken concerning *his h. 1 Sam* 3:12
I will judge *his h.* for ever.   13
Ramah, for there was *his h.*   7:17
Samuel buried Samuel in *his h.* 25:1
departed every one to *his h.*
        2 Sam 6:19
before thy father and *his h.*   21
pass, when the king sat in *his h.* 7:1
concerning *his h.*   25; *1 Chr* 17:23
went not down to *his h.* 11:9, 10, 13
fetched her to *his h.* became.   27
bring the king back to *his h.?* 19:11
it is for Saul and *his bloody h.* 21:1
silver nor gold of Saul, nor of *his h.* 4
his h. there shall be peace. *1 Ki* 2:33
building, and finished all *his h.* 7:1
man to *his h.* for thing. 12:24; 22:17
   1 Chr 16:43; *2 Chr* 11:4; 18:16
did eat bread in *his h.*   *1 Ki* 13:19
sword against Baasha and *his h.* 16:7
of Israel went to *his h.* 20:43; 21:4
Elisha sat in *his h.* and.   *2 Ki* 6:32
nothing in *his h.* Hezekiah.   20:13
it went evil with *his h. 1 Chr* 7:23
Saul, his sons, and all *his h.*   10:6
the ark remained in *his h.*   13:14
toward God and *his h. 2 Chr* 24:16
his h. be made a dunghill. *Ezra* 6:11
one repaired over against *his h.*
        Neh 3:28
out every man from *his h.*   5:13
to be over against *his h.*   7:3
an hedge about *his h.?*   *Job* 1:10
shall return no more to *his h.* 7:10
he shall lean on *his h.* it shall. 8:15
the increase of *his h.* shall.   20:28
pleasure hath he in *his h.?*   21:21
he buildeth *his h.* as a moth. 27:18
when the glory of *his h. Ps* 49:16
made him Lord of *his h.*   105:21
and riches shall be in *his h.*   112:3
give the substance of *his h. Pr* 6:31
        S of S 8:7
not depart from *his h.*   *Pr* 17:13
even punish that man and *his h.*
        Jer 23:34
oppress a man and *his h.*   *Mi* 2:2
evil covetousness to *his h. Hab* 2:9
in the midst of *his h.*   *Zech* 5:4
then he shall spoil *his h. Mat* 12:29
        Mark 3:27
to take any thing out of *his h.*
     Mat 24:17; *Mark* 13:15

not have suffered *his h. Mat* 24:43
he would come into *his h. Luke* 8:41
went down to *his h.* justified. 18:14
believed and *his* whole *h. John* 4:53
feared God with all *his h. Acts* 10:2
to send for thee into *his h.*   22
he had seen an angel in *his h.* 11:13
to him and to all in *his h.*   16:32
into *his h.* he rejoiced, believing in
   God with all *his h.*   34; 18:8
church which is in *his h.*   *Col* 4:15
faithful in all *his h.*   *Heb* 3:2, 5
an ark for the saving of *his h.* 11:7

house of Israel
let *h. of Israel* bewail.   *Lev* 10:6
be of *h. of Israel* that killeth an ox or
   lamb.   17:3, 8, 10; 22:18
all *h. of Israel* mourned. *Num* 20:29
h. of Israel lamented.   *1 Sam* 7:2
they mourned for the *h. of Israel.*
        2 Sam 1:12
all the *h. of Israel* played.   6:5
David and the *h. of Israel.*   15
the *h. of Israel* and Judah.   12:8
shall *h. of Israel* restore the.   16:3
kings of *h. of Israel* are. *1 Ki* 20:31
truth toward *h. of Israel.*   *Ps* 98:3
us, he will bless *h. of Israel.* 115:12
bless ye Lord, O *h. of Israel.* 135:19
vineyard of Lord is the *h. of Israel.*
        Isa 5:7
the *h. of Israel* shall possess. 14:2
remnant of the *h. of Israel.*   46:3
goodness toward *h. of Israel.*   63:7
families of *h. of Israel.*   *Jer* 2:4
as a thief, so is the *h. of Israel.*   26
Judah shall walk with *h. of Israel.*
        3:18
treacherously, *h. of Israel.* 20; 5:11
h. of Israel are uncircumcised. 9:26
the *h. of Israel* have broken.   11:10
for evil for evil, the *h. of Israel.* 17
cleave to me the whole *h. of Israel.*
        13:11
liveth, who led the *h. of Israel.* 23:8
I will sow the *h. of Israel.*   31:27
covenant with *h. of Israel.*   31, 33
I promised to the *h. of Israel.* 33:14
the *h. of Israel* was ashamed. 48:13
speak to *h. of Israel. Ezek* 3:1; 17:2
   20:27, 30; 24:21; 33:10; 36:22
get thee unto the *h. of Israel.*   3:4
thou art sent to the *h. of Israel.*   5
h. of Israel will not hearken to me,
   for all the *h. of Israel* are.   7
watchman to *h. of Israel.*   17; 33:7
be a sign to the *h. of Israel.*   4:3
iniquity of the *h. of Israel* upon.   4
bear iniquity of the *h. of Israel.*   5
a fire shall come forth into the *h. of*
   Israel.   5:4
abominations of the *h. of Israel.* 6:11
all the idols of the *h. of Israel.* 8:10
the ancients of *h. of Israel.*   11, 12
the iniquity of the *h. of Israel.*   9:9
ye said, O *h. of Israel,* for.   11:5
the *h. of Israel* wholly are they. 15
the *h. of Israel* said. 12:9, 27; 18:29
divination within *h. of Israel.* 12:24
hedge for the *h. of Israel.*   13:5
the writing of the *h. of Israel.*   9
h. of Israel that setteth up idols.
        14:4, 7
h. of Israel may go no more.   11
eyes to idols of *h. of Israel.* 18:6, 15
O *h. of Israel,* is not my way?   25
will I judge you, O *h. of Israel.*   30
ye die, O *h. of Israel?*   31; 33:11
but the *h. of Israel* rebelled.   20:13
O *h. of Israel,* go ye, serve ye every
   one his idols, if ye will not.   39
the *h. of Israel* serve me.   40
corrupt doings, O *h. of Israel.*   44
h. of Israel is to me become. 22:18
briar to the *h. of Israel.*   28:24
have gathered the *h. of Israel.*   25
staff of a reed to *h. of Israel.* 29:6
the confidence of *h. of Israel.*   16
the horn of the *h. of Israel* to.   21
that they, even the *h. of Israel.* 34:30
multiply all the *h. of Israel.*   36:10
when the *h. of Israel* dwelt in.   17
which the *h. of Israel* profaned.   21

your sakes, O *h. of Israel. Ezek* 36:22
for your ways, O *h. of Israel.* 32
be enquired of by the *h. of Israel.* 37
bones are whole *h. of Israel.* 37:11
write on it, for the *h. of Israel.* 16
months shall *h. of Israel* be. 39:12
the *h. of Israel* shall know I. 22
h. of Israel went into captivity. 23
mercy on whole *h. of Israel.* 25
poured my Spirit on *h. of Israel.* 29
thou seest to the *h. of Israel.* 40:4
shew house to the *h. of Israel.* 43:10
rebellious, even to *h. of Israel.* 44:6
caused the *h. of Israel* to fall. 12
of the seed of the *h. of Israel.* 7
for the whole *h. of Israel.* 45:6
land shall they give to *h. of Israel.* 8
reconciliation for the *h. of Israel.* 17
kingdom of *h. of Israel. Hos* 1:4
have mercy on the *h. of Israel.* 6
and hearken, ye *h. of Israel.* 5:1
horrible thing in *h. of Israel.* 6:10
h. of Israel compasseth me. 11:12
leave ten to *h. of Israel. Amos* 5:3
saith the Lord to the *h. of Israel.* 4
sacrifices 40 years, O *h. of Israel* ? 25
nations, to whom *h. of Israel.* 6:1
you a nation, O *h. of Israel.* 14
against thee in the *h. of Israel.* 7:10
I will sift the *h. of Israel.* 9:9
sins of the *h. of Israel. Mi* 1:5
princes of the *h. of Israel.* 3:1, 9
a curse, O *h. of Israel. Zech* 8:13
go to lost sheep of the *h. of Israel.*
                  Mat 10:6; 15:24
all the *h. of Israel* know. *Acts* 2:36
O *h. of Israel,* have ye offered ? 7:42
a new covenant with *h. of Israel.*
                  Heb 8:8, 10

house *of Jacob*
souls of *h. of Jacob.*   *Gen* 46:27
say to the *h. of Jacob.*   *Ex* 19:3
h. of Jacob from people. *Ps* 114:1
O *h. of Jacob,* let us walk. *Isa* 2:5
forsaken thy people, *h. of Jacob.* 6
his face from *h. of Jacob.* 8:17
escaped of the *h. of Jacob.* 10:20
cleave to the *h. of Jacob.* 14:1
Lord concerning *h. of Jacob.* 29:22
O *h. of Jacob* and Israel. 46:3
hear ye this, O *h. of Jacob.* 48:1
shew the *h. of Jacob* their sins. 58:1
word of Lord, O *h. of Jacob. Jer* 2:4
declare this in the *h. of Jacob.* 5:20
my hand to *h. of Jacob. Ezek* 20:5
testify to *h. of Jacob. Amos* 3:13
utterly destroy the *h. of Jacob.* 9:8
the *h. of Jacob* shall possess. *Ob* 17
h. of Jacob shall be a fire. 18
named the *h. of Jacob.*   *Mi* 2:7
pray, ye heads of the *h. of Jacob.* 3:9
reign over *h. of Jacob. Luke* 1:33

house *of Joseph*
men into *Joseph's h.*   *Gen* 43:17
h. of Joseph shall abide. *Josh* 18:5
the *h. of Joseph* went up. *Judg* 1:22
the *h. of Joseph* sent to descry. 23
hand of the *h. of Joseph.* 35
I am come the first this day of all the
  h. of Joseph.   *2 Sam* 19:20
charge of *h. of Joseph.*   *1 Ki* 11:28
break out like fire in *h. of Joseph.*
                  Amos 5:6
h. of Joseph shall be a flame. *Ob* 18
will save the *h. of Joseph. Zech* 10:6

house *of Judah*
David king over *h. of Judah.*
  2 Sam 2:4, 7, 11; *1 Chr* 2:84
I gave thee *h. of Judah. 2 Sam* 12:8
he assembled all the *h. of Judah.*
                1 Ki 12:21
speak to all the *h. of Judah.* 23
escaped of the *h. of Judah* take.
    2 Ki 19:30; *Isa* 37:31
ruler of *h. of Judah.*   *2 Chr* 19:11
behind the *h. of Judah. Neh* 4:16
a father to the *h. of Judah. Isa* 22:21
h. of Judah shall walk. *Jer* 3:18
the *h. of Judah* hath dealt. 5
the *h. of Judah* have broken. 11:10
for evil of the *h. of Judah* that. 17
I will pluck *h. of Judah.* 12:14
cleave to me the *h. of Judah.* 13:11

I will sow the *h. of Judah. Jer* 31:27
a new covenant with *h. of Judah.* 31
I promised to *h. of Judah.* 33:14
may be *h. of Judah* will hear. 36:3
bear the iniquity of *h. of Judah* forty
  days.   *Ezek* 4:6
light thing to *h. of Judah* ? 8:17
iniquity of *h. of Judah* is great. 9:9
Aha, against the *h. of Judah.* 25:3
the *h. of Judah* is like to all the. 8
dealt against the *h. of Judah.* 12
mercy upon *h. of Judah. Hos* 1:7
I will be to the *h. of Judah.* 5:12
young lion to the *h. of Judah.* 14
for remnant of *h. of Judah. Zeph* 2:7
a curse, O *h. of Judah. Zech* 8:13
to do well to the *h. of Judah.* 15
the fast shall be to *h. of Judah.* 10:3
Lord hath visited *h. of Judah.* 10:3
strengthen the *h. of Judah.*
eyes unto the *h. of Judah.* 12:4
covenant with *h. of Judah. Heb* 8:8

king's house
on roof of the *king's h. 2 Sam* 11:2
departed out of the *king's h.* 8
hear out of the *king's h.* 15:35
finished the *king's h.*   *1 Ki* 9:1
treasure of *king's h.* 14:26; 15:18
  2 Ki 16:8; *2 Chr* 12:9; 25:24
Zimri burnt the *king's h.* *1 Ki* 16:18
told it to the *king's h.*   *2 Ki* 7:11*
he burnt the *king's h.* 25:9
             Jer 39:8; 52:13
shall be at the *king's h. 2 Chr* 23:5
son was over the *king's h.* 26:21
portion out of *h. of the king.* 28:21
given out of the *king's h. Ezra* 6:4
maidens out of *king's h. Esth* 2:9
shalt escape in the *king's h.* 4:13
was great in the *king's h.* 9:4
give ear, O *h. of the king. Hos* 5:1

house *of Levi*
a man of the *h. of Levi.*   *Ex* 2:1
rod of Aaron for *h. of Levi* was.
                Num 17:8
the Lord, O *h. of Levi.*   *Ps* 135:20
family of the *h. of Levi. Zech* 12:13

in the house
of Esau that were in *h. Gen* 27:15
even all that was in the *h.* 29
blessing was on all in the *h.* 39:5
not what is with me in the *h.* 8
was heard in Pharaoh's *h.* 45:16
in one *h.* shall passover. *Ex* 12:46
of leprosy in a *h. Lev* 14:34, 35
again and break out in the *h.* 44
the plague be spread in the *h.* 44
he that lieth, that eateth in the *h.* 47
plague hath not spread in the *h.* 48
whoso with thee in the *h. Josh* 2:19
all that are with her in the *h.* 6:17
in the *h.* of Micah. *Judg* 17:4, 12
find rest, each in *h.* of. *Ruth* 1:9
she tarried a little in the *h.* 2:7
had a fat calf in the *h. 1 Sam* 28:24
sent to publish it in the *h.* of. 31:9
they put his armour in the *h.* 10
dwell in one *h. . . . .* of a child with her
  in the *h.*   *1 Ki* 3:17
any tool of iron heard in the *h.* 6:7
is found some good in the *h.* 14:13
drinking himself drunk in the *h.* 16:9
in the *h.*? thine handmaid hath not
  any thing in the *h.*   *2 Ki* 4:2
he returned, and walked in the *h.* 35
leaneth on my hand, bow in *h.* 5:18
and bestowed them in the *h.* 24
in *h.* of Nisroch. 19:37; *Isa* 37:38
a graven image in the *h. 2 Ki* 21:7
slew young men in the *h. 2 Chr* 36:17
had put them in the *h.* of. *Ezra* 1:7
search was made in the *h.* of. 6:1
the queen also in the *h.*? *Esth* 7:8
the gallows standeth in the *h.* of. 9
my songs in the *h.* of my. *Ps* 119:54
curse of Lord is in the *h. Pr* 3:33
thy labours be in the *h.* of a. 5:10
her feet abide not in her *h.* 7:11
in the *h.* of the righteous is. 15:6
wise is in *h.* of mourning . . . fools is
  in the *h.* of mirth.   *Eccl* 7:4
it may remain in the *h. Isa* 44:13

set their abominations *in the h.*
         Jer 7:30; 32:34
covenant before me *in the h.* 34:15
put him *in the h.* of Jonathan. 37:15
remain ten men in one *h. Amos* 6:9
in the h. of Aphrah roll. *Mi* 1:10*
of wickedness *in the h.* of. 6:10
I was wounded *in the h. Zech* 13:6
unto all that are *in the h. Mark* 5:15
that he was *in the h. Mark* 2:1
being *in the h.* he asked them. 9:33
in the h. his disciples asked. 10:10
in Bethany, *in the h.* of Simon. 14:3
nor abide *in any h.* but. *Luke* 8:27
abideth not *in the h.*   *John* 8:35
Mary sat still *in the h.* 11:20
enquire *in the h.* of Judas. *Acts* 9:11
Peter is lodged *in the h.* of. 10:32

house joined with *Lord*
shalt bring into the *h.* of the *Lord.*
  Ex 23:19; 34:26; *Neh* 10:35
of a dog into *h.* of *Lord. Deut* 23:18
treasury of *h.* of the *Lord. Josh* 6:24
going to *h.* of the *Lord. Judg* 19:18
up to the *h.* of the *Lord. 1 Sam* 1:7
unto *h.* of the *Lord.* 24; *2 Ki* 12:4
  9, 13; 22:4; *2 Chr* 34:14
came into *h.* of *Lord. 2 Sam* 12:20
of building *h.* of *Lord.*   *1 Ki* 3:1
foundation of *h.* of *Lord* laid. 6:37
  2 Chr 8:16; *Ezra* 3:11; *Zech* 8:9
made for *h.* of the *Lord. 1 Ki* 7:40
  45:51; *2 Chr* 4:16; 5:1; 24:14
cloud filled *h.* of *Lord. 1 Ki* 8:10, 11
  2 Chr 5:13; 7:2; *Ezek* 44:4
dedicated *h.* of the *Lord. 1 Ki* 8:63
he went up unto the *h.* of *Lord.*
          10:5; *2 Chr* 9:4
hid in the *h.* of *Lord* six. *2 Ki* 11:3
oath of them in *h.* of the *Lord.* 4
let her not be slain in *h.* of *Lord.* 15
             2 Chr 23:14
appointed officers over *h.* of *Lord.*
  2 Ki 11:18; *2 Chr* 23:18
brought from the *h.* of the *Lord.*
          2 Ki 11:19; 23:6
found in *h.* of the *Lord.* 12:10
  14:14; 16:8; 18:15
oversight of the *h.* of the *Lord.* 12:11
was not brought into *h.* of *Lord.* 16
turned he from *h.* of *Lord.* 16:18
shalt go up unto *h.* of *Lord.* 20:5
will heal me, and that I shall go up to
  the *h.* of the *Lord.* 8; *Isa* 38:22
covenant which were found in *h.* of
  Lord. 2 Ki 23:2, 24; *2 Chr* 34:17, 30
Sodomites that were by *h.* of *Lord.*
             2 Ki 23:7
entering in of *h.* of the *Lord.* 11
burnt the *h.* of the *Lord.* 25:9
             Jer 52:13
song in the *h.* of the *Lord. 1 Chr* 6:31
said, This is the *h.* of the *Lord.* 22:1
build the *h.* of the *Lord* thy God. 11
prepared for the *h.* of the *Lord.* 14
the work of the *h.* of the *Lord.* 23:4
minister in the *h.* of the *Lord. 2 Chr* 26:12
so the *h.* of the *Lord.*   *2 Chr* 8:16
he was cut off from *h.* of *Lord.*
         26:21; *Joel* 1:9
sanctify *h.* of the *Lord. 2 Chr* 29:5
cleanse the *h.* of the *Lord.* 15
the idol out of *h.* of *Lord.* 33:15
book of the law in *h.* of *Lord.* 34:15
polluted the *h.* of *Lord.* 36:14
beautify *h.* of the *Lord. Ezra* 7:27
will dwell in the *h.* of *Lord. Ps* 23:6
I may dwell in the *h.* of *Lord.* 27:4
planted in the *h.* of *Lord.* 92:13
vows in courts of *Lord's h.* 116:19
you out of the *h.* of *Lord.* 118:26
let us go into *h.* of the *Lord.* 122:1
because of the *h.* of *Lord* I will. 9
stand in the *h.* of the *Lord.* 134:1
             135:2
mountain of the *Lord's h.*   *Isa* 2:2
             Mi 4:1
up into *h.* of the *Lord.*   *Isa* 37:14
praise to *h.* of the *Lord. Jer* 17:26
governor in the *h.* of the *Lord.* 20:1
which was by *h.* of the *Lord.* 26:2
to worship in the *Lord's h.* 26:2
words in the *h.* of the *Lord.* 7

spake to me in *h.* of Lord. *Jer* 28:1
that stood in the *h.* of the *Lord.*   5
officers in the *h.* of the *Lord.* 29:26
Rechabites into *h.* of the *Lord.* 35:2
I cannot go into *h.* of *Lord.*   36:5
read in the *Lord's h.* upon the.   6
entry that is in *h.* of the *Lord.* 38:14
them to the *h.* of the *Lord.*   41:5
the sanctuaries of *Lord's h.*   51:51
a noise in the *h.* of the *Lord. Lam* 2:7
the time that the *Lord's h. Hag* 1:2
see court, door, gate, treasures,
vessels

mine, or *my* house
the steward of *my h.* is.   *Gen* 15:2
one born in *my h.* is mine heir.   3
be destroyed, I and *my h.*   34:30
thou shalt be over *my h.*   41:40
faithful in all *mine h.*   *Num* 12:7
things out of *mine h.   Deut* 26:13
my h. we will serve Lord. *Josh* 24:15
forth of doors of *my h.   Judg* 11:31
this man come into *mine h.*   19:23
kindness from *my h.   1 Sam* 20:15
fellow come into *my h.?*   21:15
what is my *h.* that thou hast?
   2 Sam 7:18; *1 Chr* 17:16
go into *mine h.* to eat? *2 Sam* 11:11
my h. be not so with God.   23:5
it is near to my *h.   1 Ki* 21:2
all in *mine h.* have they seen.
   2 Ki 20:15; *Isa* 39:4
settle him in *mine h.   1 Chr* 17:14
the grave is *mine h.   Job* 17:13
I will walk in *my h.* with. *Ps* 101:2
into the tabernacle of *my h.*   132:3
at the window of *my h.   Pr* 7:6
in *my h.* is neither bread.   *Isa* 3:7
them will I give in *mine h.*   56:5
in *my h.* of prayer, *mine h.* shall be
called an *h.* of.   7; *Mat* 21:13
   Mark 11:17; *Luke* 19:46
beloved to do in *mine h.? Jer* 11:15
forsaken *mine h.* I left mine.   12:7
in *my h.* have I found their.   23:11
I sat in *mine h.* and.   *Ezek* 8:1
done in midst of *mine h.*   23:39
to pollute it, even *my h.*   44:7
was at rest in *mine h.   Dan* 4:4
drive them out of *mine h. Hos* 9:15
why? because of *mine h. Hag* 1:9
shalt also judge *my h.   Zech* 3:7
I will encamp about *mine h.*   9:8
may be meat in *mine h.   Mal* 3:10
I will return into *my h.   Mat* 12:44
   Luke 11:24
them farewell at *my h.   Luke* 9:61
compel them, that *my h.*   14:23
hour I prayed in *my h.   Acts* 10:30
saying, Come into *my h.* and. 16:15

own house
servants born in *own h. Gen* 14:14
I provide for mine *own h.*   30:30
bring it unto thine *own h. Deut* 22:2
and come unto his *own h. Josh* 20:6
and dwelt in his *own h.   Judg* 8:29
person in his *own h.   2 Sam* 4:11
against thee out of thy *own h.* 12:11
own h. and not see my face, so Absalom returned to *own h.*   14:24
again in peace to his *own h.*   19:30
Joab buried in his *own h. 1 Ki* 2:34
an end of building his *own h.*   3:1
building his *own h.* 13 years.   7:1
a levy to build his *own h.*   9:15
own h. David.   12:16; *2 Chr* 10:16
thee into thine *own h.   1 Ki* 14:12
was buried in his *own h.*
   h.   2 Ki 21:18; *2 Chr* 33:20
slew the king in his *own h.*
   2 Ki 21:23; *2 Chr* 33:24
came in his heart to make in his *own
h.   2 Chr* 7:11
wherein Solomon had built the house
of the Lord and his *own h.*   8:1
bear rule in his *own h.   Esth* 1:22
troubleth his *own h.* shall. *Pr* 11:29
of gain troubleth his *own h.*   15:27
every one in his *own h.   Isa* 14:18
are the men of his *own h.   Mi* 7:6
run every man to his *own h. Hag* 1:9
a prophet is not without honour, save
in his *own h. Mat* 13:57; *Mark* 6:4

to his *own h.   Luke* 1:23; 5:25
Mary returned to her *own h.*   1:56
a great feast in his *own h.*   5:29
return to thy *own h.* and shew. 8:39
man went unto his *own h. John* 7:53
two years in his *own h. Acts* 28:30*
that ruleth well his *own h. 1 Tim* 3:4
know not how to rule his *own h.*   5
for those of his *own h.*   5:8
as a Son over his *own h.   Heb* 3:6

this house
greater in *this h.* than I.   *Gen* 39:9
and bring me out of *this h.*   40:14
this h. thou art building.   *1 Ki* 6:12
how much less *this h.* that I.   8:27
opened toward *this h.* 29; *2 Chr* 6:20
before thine altar in *this h.*
   1 Ki 8:31; *2 Chr* 6:22
make supplication to thee in *this h.*
   1 Ki 8:33, 42; *2 Chr* 6:24, 32
his hands towards *this h. 1 Ki* 8:38
hallowed *this h.* 9:3; *2 Chr* 7:16, 20
at *this h.* every one shall hiss.
   1 Ki 9:8; *2 Chr* 7:21
this h. which I have chosen.
   2 Ki 21:7; *2 Chr* 33:7
upon us we stand before *this h.* for
thy name is in *this h.   2 Chr* 20:9
founda.ion of *this h.* was. *Ezra* 3:12
who destroyed *this h.*   5:12
this h. was finished on third.   6:15
stand before me in *this h. Jer* 7:10
is *this h.* become a den of?   11
therefore will I do to *this h.*   14
enter in by the gates of *this h.* 22:4
this h. shall become a desolation.   5
will I make *this h.* like Shiloh. 26:6
this h. shall be like Shiloh.   9
me to prophesy against *this h.*   12
and *this h.* lie waste.   *Hag* 1:4
who is left that saw *this h.* in?   2:3
I will fill *this h.* with glory, saith.   7
the glory of *this* latter *h.* greater.   9
laid foundation of *this h. Zech* 4:9
say, Peace be to *this h. Luke* 10:5
is salvation come to *this h.*   19:9

thine or *thy* house
all *thy h.* into the ark.   *Gen* 7:1
been twenty years in *thy h.*   31:41
up and come into *thine h.   Ex* 8:3
that is clean in *thy h. Num* 18:11, 13
when thou sittest in *thine h.*
   Deut 6:7; 11:19
on the posts of *thy h.*   6:9; 11:20
an abomination into *thine h.*   7:26
he loveth thee and *thine h.*   15:16
bring her home to thine *h.*   21:12
remain in *thine h.* and bewail.   13
bring not blood upon *thine h.*   22:8
not have in *thine h.* divers.   25:14
given to thee and *thine h.*   26:11
are entered into *thine h. Josh* 2:3
shall go out of doors of *thy h.*   19
we will burn *thine h.* on. *Judg* 12:1
man that came into *thine h.*   19:22
woman that is come into *thine h.*
   Ruth 4:11
let *thy h.* be like the house.   12
that *thy h.* should walk. *1 Sam* 2:30
not be an old man in *thine h.*   31
the increase of *thine h.* shall die. 33
one in *thine h.* shall crouch to.   36
is honourable in *thine h.*   22:14
peace be to *thine h.* and to.   25:6
her, Go up in peace to *thine h.*   35
thine h. shall be established for.
   2 Sam 7:16
go down to *thy h.* and wash.   11:8
didst not thou go down to *thine h.?* 10
never depart from *thine h.*   12:10
go to *thine h.*   14:8; *1 Ki* 2:36
give me half *thine h.   1 Ki* 13:8
back with thee into *thine h.*   18
make *thy h.* like the *h.* of Jeroboam.
   16:3; 21:22
they shall search *thine h.*   20:6
set *thine h.* in order.   *2 Ki* 20:1
   Isa 38:1
what have they seen in *thine h.*
   2 Ki 20:15; *Isa* 39:4
all in *thine h.* shall be carried.
   2 Ki 20:17; *Isa* 39:6
come to *thy h.* in multitude. *Ps* 5:7

loved the habitation of *thy h. Ps* 26:8
satisfied with fatness of *thy h.*   36:8
no bullock out of *thy h.*   50:9
satisfied with goodness of *thy h.* 65:4
will go into *thy h.* with burnt. 66:13
zeal of *thine h.* hath eaten me up.
   69:9; *John* 2:17
holiness becometh *thine h. Ps* 93:5
fruitful vine by sides of *thine h.* 128:3
that are cast out to *thy h.   Isa* 58:7
thou shalt live and *thine h. Jer* 38:17
shut thyself within *thine h.*
   Ezek 3:24
blessing to rest in *thine h.*   44:30
consulted shame to *thy h. Hab* 2:10
arise, go unto *thine h.   Mat* 9:6
   Mark 2:11; *Luke* 5:24
the passover at *thy h.   Mat* 26:18
I entered *thine h.* thou. *Luke* 7:44
to-day I must abide at *thy h.*   19:5
thou and all *thy h.* shall be saved.
   Acts 11:14; 16:31
to the church in *thy h.   Philem* 2
   see tops

household, *or* households
he will command his *h.   Gen* 18:19
Jacob said to his *h.* Put away. 35:2
famine of your *h.* be gone.   42:33*
lest thou and thy *h.* come to. 45:11
take your father and your *h.* and. 18
nourished his father's *h.*   47:12
shall be food for your *h.*   24
man and his *h.* came.   *Ex* 1:1
if the *h.* be too little for the.   12:4
made an atonement for his *h.*
   Lev 16:17
every place, and your *h. Num* 18:31
wonders upon all his *h. Deut* 6:22*
swallowed them and their *h.*   11:6
rejoice, thou and thy *h.*   14:26
eat it before the Lord, thou and thy *h.*
   15:20
bring all thy father's *h.   Josh* 2:18
Rahab, her father's *h.* and all. 6:25
and the family shall come by *h.* 7:14
brought his *h.* man by man.   18
he feared his father's *h.   Judg* 6:27
life, with the lives of thy *h.* 18:25
evil is determined against his *h.*
   1 Sam 25:17*
man with his *h.*   27:3; *2 Sam* 2:3
Lord blessed him and all his *h.*
   2 Sam 6:11*
David returned to bless his *h.*   20
king went forth and all his *h.* 15:16
asses be for the king's *h.* to. 16:2
put his *h.* in order, and.   17:23*
to carry over the king's *h.*   19:18
Judah brought the king and his *h.* 41
Abishai was over the *h.   1 Ki* 4:6
victuals for the king and his *h.*   7
in giving food for my *h.*   5:9
Hiram wheat for food to his *h.*   11
Genubath was in Pharaoh's *h.* 11:20*
go and tell the king's *h.   2 Ki* 7:9
go and thine *h.* to sojourn.   8:1
Eliakim son of Hilkiah who was over
h.   18:18; 19:2; *Isa* 36:22; 37:2
principal *h.* being taken. *1 Chr* 24:6*
camels and a great *h.   Job* 1:3
milk for food of thy *h.   Pr* 27:27
and giveth meat to her *h.*   31:15
not afraid of the snow for her *h.:* for
all her *h.* are clothed with scarlet. 21
well to the ways of her *h.*   27
they call them of his *h.? Mat* 10:25
foes shall be they of his own *h.*   36
ruler over his *h.*   24:45; *Luke* 12:42
was baptized and her *h. Acts* 16:15
are of Aristobulus' *h.   Rom* 16:10
that be of the *h.* of Narcissus.   11
I baptized also the *h.* of. *1 Cor* 1:16
to them who are of the *h. Gal* 6:10
no more strangers, but of the *h.* of
God.   *Eph* 2:19
that are of Cesar's *h.   Phil* 4:22
salute the *h.* of.   *2 Tim* 4:19*

householder
so the servants of the *h. Mat* 13:27
unto a man that is an *h.*   52; 20:1
was a certain *h.* planted.   21:33

household servants
two of his *h.* servants.   *Acts* 10:7

household stuff

found of all thy *h. stuff ? Gen* 31:37
I cast out all the *h. stuff. Neh* 13:8

houses

carry corn for the famine of your *h.*
Gen 42:19
God, he made them *h.*   *Ex* 1:21†
heads of their fathers' *h.*   6:14
frogs from thee and thy *h.*   8:9, 11
and the frogs died out of the *h.*   13
swarms of flies into thy *h.*   21, 24
and cattle flee into the *h.*   9:20
fill thy *h.* and the *h.* of all thy servants, and the *h.* of all.   10:6
on the upper door post of the *h.* 12:7
blood be for a token upon the *h.*   13
away leaven out of your *h.*   15
no leaven found in your *h.*   19
destroyer to come in unto your *h.* 23
passed over and delivered our *h.* 27
h. of villages be counted. *Lev* 25:31
the *h.* of the cities of their.   32, 33
sum of the sons of Gershon throughout their *h.*   *Num* 4:22
swallowed them up and their *h.*
16:32*
according to their father's *h.*   17:6
we will not return unto our *h.* 32:18
to give thee *h.* full of all. *Deut* 6:11
when hast built goodly *h.* and. 8:12
dwellest in their cities and *h.*   19:1
Neh 9:25
hot provision out of our *h. Josh* 9:12
that there is in these *h. Judg* 18:14
men that were in the *h.* near.   22
he cried against the *h.*   *1 Ki* 13:32
they shall search the *h.* of thy. 20:6
put them in the *h.* of.   *2 Ki* 17:29
which sacrificed in the *h.* of the. 32
he brake down the *h.* of the.   23:7
the *h.* of the high places, Josiah. 19
he burnt all the *h.* of Jerusalem.
25:9; *Jer* 52:13
David made *h.* in city.   *1 Chr* 15:1
Solomon pattern of the *h.*   28:11
to overlay the walls of the *h.* 29:4
timber to floor the *h.*   *2 Chr* 34:11
and prepare yourselves by *h.* 35:4
your wives and your *h. Neh* 4:14
mortgaged our lands and *h.*   5:3
them their vineyards and *h.*   11
the people were few, and *h.* not. 7:4
we cast lots after the *h.* of our. 10:34
and feasted in their *h.*   *Job* 1:4
princes, who filled their *h.*   3:15
them that dwell in *h.* of clay.   4:19
he dwelleth in *h.* which no.   15:28
their *h.* are safe from fear, nor. 21:9
yet he filled their *h.* with.   22:18
the dark they dig through *h.*   24:16
that their *h.* shall continue. *Ps* 49:11
let us take the *h.* of God.   83:12*
fill our *h.* with spoil.   *Pr* 1:13
make they their *h.* in rocks.   30:26
I builded me *h.* I planted. *Eccl* 2:4
the poor is in your *h.*   *Isa* 3:14
of a truth, many *h.* shall. 5:9; 6:11
rock of offence to both *h.* of.   8:14
h. be spoiled, their wives.   13:16
their *h.* shall be full of doleful.   21
shall cry in their desolate *h.*   22
on the tops of their *h.* every.   15:3
the *h.* of Jerusalem, and the *h.* 22:10
yea. upon all the *h.* of joy in. 32:13
shall build *h.* and inhabit.   65:21
troops in the harlots' *h.*   *Jer* 5:7
as cage is full of birds, are their *h.* 27
and their *h.* shall be turned.   6:12
cry be heard from their *h.*   18:22
the *h.* of Jerusalem and the *h.* of.
19:13
build ye *h.* and dwell in.   29:5, 28
h. and fields shall be possessed.
32:15
h. on whose roofs they offered.   29
concerning *h.* of this city, and *h.* 33:4
they burnt the *h.* of the people. 39:8
I will kindle a fire in *h.* of. 43:12, 13
h. are turned to aliens.   *Lam* 5:2
shall possess their *h. Ezek* 7:24
it is not near, let us build *h.*   11:3
burn thine *h.* with fire. 16:41; 23:47
destroy thy pleasant *h.*   26:12

shall build *h.* and plant. *Ezek* 28:26
thee in the doors of the *h.*   33:30
shall be a place for their *h.*   45:4
your *h.* shall be made a dunghill.
Dan 2:5
their *h.* shall be made a dunghill.
3:29
I will place them in their *h.* saith.
Hos 11:11
climb up upon the *h.*   *Joel* 2:9
and summer house, *h.* of ivory shall
   perish, great *h.* shall. *Amos* 3:15
the *h.* of Achzib shall be.   *Mi* 1:14
and they covet *h.* and take.   2:2
cast out from their pleasant *h.*   9
which fill their masters' *h. Zeph* 1:9
h. shall become a desolation, they
   shall build *h.* but not inhabit.   13
in the *h.* of Ashkelon shall.   2:7
to dwell in your cieled *h.? Hag* 1:4
h. shall be rifled, and the. *Zech* 14:2
wear soft clothing are in kings' *h.*
Mat 11:8
one that hath forsaken *h.* or.   19:29
devour widows' *h.*   23:14*
Mark 12:40; *Luke* 20:47
fasting to their own *h.*   *Mark* 8:3*
receive me into their *h. Luke* 16:4
were possessors of *h.* sold. *Acts* 4:34
have ye not *h.* to eat in ? *1 Cor* 11:22
ruling their own *h.* well. *1 Tim* 3:12
they which creep into *h.*   *2 Tim* 3:6
who subvert whole *h.*   *Tit* 1:11

how

and *h.* saidst thou, she ? *Gen* 26:29
h. is it thou hast found it ?   27:20
Jacob said, *h.* dreadful is.   28:17
h. then can I do this great ?   39:9
h. then should we steal our ?   44:8
what shall we speak ? *h.* shall ?   16
h. shall I go to my father, lad ?   34
h. is that ye are come so ? *Ex* 2:18
h. then shall Pharaoh hear ?   6:12
and *h.* shall Pharaoh hearken ?   30
Moses told *h.* the Lord.   18:8
seen *h.* I bare you. 19:4; *Deut* 1:31
h. we are to encamp in. *Num* 10:31
h. shall I curse, whom God hath not
   cursed ? *h.*   23:8
h. goodly are thy tents, O !   24:5
h. can I myself bear ?   *Deut* 1:12
if thou shalt say, *H.* can I ?   7:17
h. the earth opened her mouth. 11:6
h. did these nations serve ?   12:30
h. he met thee by the way.   25:18
h. we have dwelt in Egypt, and *h.* we
   came through nations.   29:16
h. should one chase a.   32:30
h. shall we make a league with ?
Josh 9:7
h. shall we order the child, *h.* do to
   him ?   *Judg* 13:12
she said, *H.* canst thou say ? 16:15
they said, Tell us, *h.* was this ? 20:3
h. do for wives for them ? 21:7, 16
know *h.* the matter will. *Ruth* 3:18
said, *H.* shall this man ? *1 Sam* 10:27
see *h.* mine eyes have been. 14:29
h. can I go ? if Saul hear he.   16:2
h. went the matter, I.   *2 Sam* 1:4
h. knowest thou that Saul and ?   5
h. are the mighty fallen! 19, 25, 27
h. Joab did, *h.* the people did, and *h.*
11:7
h. then will he vex himself ? 12:18
I know not *h.* to go out.   *1 Ki* 3:7
h. do you advise, that I may ? 12:6
h. Jeroboam warred, and *h.*   14:19
h. I hid an hundred men of.   18:13
and see *h.* the man seeketh.   20:7
h. he seeketh a quarrel. *2 Ki* 5:7
two kings stood not, *h.* then ? 10:4
taught them *h.* they should,   17:28
h. then wilt thou turn away ? 18:24
Isa 36:9
heard long ago, *h.* I have done it.
2 Ki 19:25; *Isa* 37:26
h. I have walked before thee.
2 Ki 20:3; *Isa* 38:3
behold, I say, *H.* they. *2 Chr* 20:11
his prayer, and *H.* God was.   33:19
to know *h.* Esther did.   *Esth* 2:11
h. can I endure to see evil that ? 8:6

h. should a man be just ?   *Job* 9:2
and thou sayest, *H.* doth ?   22:13
h. hast thou helped him that is without power ? *h.* savest thou ?   26:2
h. little a portion is heard of !   14
h. say ye to my soul, Flee. *Ps* 11:1
h. thou didst drive out heathen, *h.*
44:2
say to God, *H.* terrible art thou. 66:3
h. doth God know ?   73:11
h. amiable are thy tabernacles. 84:1
h. short my time is.   89:47
O Lord, *h.* manifold are !   104:24
O *h.* love I thy law, it is.   119:97
h. sweet are thy words unto.   103
consider *h.* I love thy precepts. 159
h. he sware unto the Lord.   132:2
h. precious are thy thoughts. 139:17
a word in due season, *h.* good!
Pr 15:23
there is a generation, O *h.*   30:13
he knoweth not *h.* to go. *Eccl* 10:15
knowest not *h.* the bones.   11:5
h. fair is thy love, my sister, my
   spouse !   *S of S* 4:10; 7:6
I have put off my coat, *h.* shall ? 5:3
h. beautiful are thy feet with.   7:1
h. art thou fallen from !   *Isa* 14:12
shall say in that day, and *h.?*   20:6
for *h.* should my name be ?   48:11
h. to speak a word in season.   50:4
h. beautiful are the feet of him.
52:7; *Rom* 10:15
h. canst thou say, I am ?   *Jer* 2:23
I said, *h.* shall I put thee ?   3:19
h. shall I pardon thee for this ?   5:7
h. do ye say ?   8:8; 48:14
h. are we spoiled ?   9:19
to ask *h.* thou doest ?   15:5
h. can it be quiet, seeing the ? 47:7
h. is the hammer of the whole ? 50:23
h. doth city sit solitary.   *Lam* 1:1
h. weak is thy heart.   *Ezek* 16:30
if we pine away in sins, *h.?*   33:10
h. shall I give thee up, Ephraim ? *h.*
   deliver thee ? *h.* make ? *Hos* 11:8
h. do the beasts groan ? *Joel* 1:18
if thieves came to thee, *h.* art. *Ob* 5
h. is she become a desolation.
Zeph 2:15
h. do you see it now ?   *Hag* 2:3
h. great is his goodness! *Zech* 9:17
if light be darkness in.   *Mat* 6:23
h. wilt thou say to thy brother ? 7:4
if ye know *h.* to give good gifts.   11
Luke 11:13
take no thought *h.* or.   *Mat* 10:19
h. they might destroy him.   12:14
Mark 3:6; 11:18
h. shall his kingdom stand ?
Mat 12:26; *Luke* 11:18
h. can ye, being evil, speak? *Mat* 12:34
h. is it that ye do not understand that
   I spake it not ?   16:11
h. think ye ? if a man have.   18:12
h. soon is the fig tree.   21:20
h. camest thou in hither not ? 22:12
if call him Lord, *h.* is he his son ? 45
Luke 20:44
h. can ye escape the ? *Mat* 23:33
h. then shall the scriptures ? 26:54
h. is it that he eateth ? *Mark* 2:16
h. he went into house. 26; *Luke* 6:4
grow up, he knoweth not *h.*
Mark 4:27
he said, *H.* is it that ye have ?   40
h. hardly shall they that.   10:23
sought *h.* they might take him. 14:1
sought *h.* he might betray him.   11
Luke 22:4
h. shall this be, seeing I ? *Luke* 1:34
h. is it that ye sought me ?   2:49
take heed *h.* ye hear.   8:18
h. readest thou ?   10:26
and *h.* am I straitened till it. 12:50
h. is it that ye do not discern ?   56
he said, *h.* is it that I hear ? 16:2
remember *h.* he spake unto ? 24:6
h. he was known of them in.   35
h. can a man be born ?   *John* 3:4
h. can these things be ?   9
h. can ye believe ?   5:44
if not his writing, *h.* believe ?   47
h. can this man give us his ? 6:52

h. knoweth this man ? *John* 7:15
h. were thy eyes opened ? 9:10
h. opened eyes ? 26
h. loved him. 11:36
h. can we know the way ? 14:5
h. is it thou wilt manifest ? 22
finding nothing h. they. *Acts* 4:21
h. is it that ye have agreed ? 5:9
h. God by his hand would. 7:25
h. can I, except some man ? 8:31
told, h. he had seen the Lord. 9:27
h. God anointed Jesus of. 10:38
h. he had seen an angel. 11:13
h. he had opened the door. 14:27
let us go again, and see h. 15:36
h. I kept back nothing that. 20:20
h. so labouring, ye ought to. 35
h. shall God judge the ? *Rom* 3:6
h. we that are dead to sin ? 6:2
h. to perform what is good. 7:18
h. shall he not win freely ? 8:32
h. shall they call ? h. shall they believe ? h. shall they hear ? 10:14
h. he maketh intercession to. 11:2
h. unsearchable his judgements. 33
take heed h. he buildeth. *1 Cor* 3:10
unmarried careth h. he may. 7:32
that is married careth h. he. 33
she careth h. she may please. 34
h. shall it be known what is piped ?
14:7
h. shall be known what is spoken ? 9
h. say some that there is no ? 15:12
man will say, h. are the dead ? 35
h. with fear and. *2 Cor* 7:15
h. that in a great trial of. 8:2
know ye not h. that Jesus ? 13:5
h. turn ye again to weak ? *Gal* 4:9
ye see h. large a letter I have. 6:11
also may know h. I do. *Eph* 6:21
see h. it will go with me. *Phil* 2:23
h. to be abased, and know h. to. 4:12
h. ye ought to answer. *Col* 4:6
and h. ye turned to God. *1 Thes* 1:9
h. holily we behaved ourselves. 2:10
h. we exhorted you. 11
h. ye ought to walk. 4:1
should know h. to possess his. 4:4
h. ye ought to follow us. *2 Thes* 3:7
not h. to rule his own house, h. shall
he take care of the ? *1 Tim* 3:5
know h. thou oughtest to behave. 15
h. shall we escape if we ? *Heb* 2:3
now consider h. great this man. 7:4
ye see h. that by works. *Jas* 2:24
h. great a matter a little fire. 3:5
Lord knoweth h. to. *2 Pet* 2:9
h. dwelleth the love of ? *1 John* 3:17
h. can he love God whom he ? 4:20
h. that the Lord having. *Jude* 5
h. thou canst not bear them. *Rev* 2:2
h. thou hast received. 3:3

see do

how long
h. *long* wilt refuse to ? *Ex* 10:3
h. *long* shall this man be a snare ? 7
h. *long* refuse to keep my ? 16:28
h. *long* will this people provoke me ?
h. *long* will it be ere ? *Num* 14:11
h. *long* shall I bear with this ? 27
h. *long* are ye slack to ? *Josh* 18:3
Eli said, H. *long* wilt ? *1 Sam* 1:14
h. *long* wilt thou mourn for ? 16:1
Barzillai said, H. *long* ? *2 Sam* 19:34
h. *long* halt ye between ? *1 Ki* 18:21
for h. *long* shall thy journey be ?
Neh 2:6
h. *long* wilt thou not depart from ?
Job 7:19
h. *long* wilt thou speak ? h. *long* shall
words of thy mouth be like ? 8:2
h. *long* will it be ere you ? 18:2
h. *long* will ye vex my soul ? 19:2
h. *long* will you turn my glory into
shame ? h. *long* will ye ? *Ps* 4:2
vexed; but thou, O Lord, h. *long* ?
6:3
h. *long* wilt thou forget me ? 13:1
h. *long* shall I take counsel in my
soul ? h. *long* shall my enemy ? 2
Lord, h. *long* wilt thou look ? 35:17
h. *long* will ye imagine ? 62:3
among us that knoweth h. *long*. 74:9

h. *long* shall adversary ? *Ps* 74:10
h. *long* wilt thou be angry for ?
79:5; 80:4
h. *long* wilt thou judge unjustly ? 82:2
h. *long*, Lord, wilt thou hide ? 89:46
return, O Lord, h. *long* ? let. 90:13
the proud, Lord, h. *long* shall the
wicked, h. *long* shall ? 94:3
h. *long* shall they utter and ? 4
h. *long*, simple ones, will ? *Pr* 1:22
h. *long* wilt thou sleep, O ? 6:9
then said I, Lord, h. *long* ? *Isa* 6:11
h. *long* shall vain ? *Jer* 4:14
h. *long* shall I see standard ? 21
h. *long* shall land mourn ? 12:4
h. *long* shall this be in heart ? 23:26
baldness on Gaza, h. *long* wilt ? 47:5
O sword of the Lord, h. *long* ere ? 6
h. *long* shall be vision ? *Dan* 8:13
h. *long* shall it be to end of ? 12:6
h. *long* will it be ere they ? *Hos* 8:5
h. *long* shall I cry, and ? *Hab* 1:2
increaseth what not his, h. *long* ? 2:6
h. *long* wilt thou not have mercy on
Jerusalem ? *Zech* 1:12
h. *long* shall I be with you, h. *long*?
Mat 17:17; *Mark* 9:19; *Luke* 9:41
h. *long* is it ago since ? *Mark* 9:21
h. *long* dost thou make ? *John* 10:24
h. *long*, O Lord, holy and ? *Rev* 6:10

how many
h. *many* are mine iniquities and ?
Job 13:23
h. *many* are the days ? *Ps* 119:84
h. *many* loaves have ye ? *Mat* 15:34
Mark 6:38; 8:5
h. *many* baskets ye took up ?
Mat 16:9; *Mark* 8:19, 20
h. *many* things they. *Mark* 15:4
h. *many* hired servants. *Luke* 15:17
in h. *many* things he. *1 Tim* 1:18

how many times
h. *many times* shall I adjure thee ?
1 Ki 22:16; *2 Chr* 18:15

how much
h. *much* rather when. *2 Ki* 5:13
without prescribing h. *much*.
Ezra 7:22
h. *much* better is it to get. *Pr* 16:16
h. *much* better is thy love.
S of S 4:10
h. *much* is a man better ? *Mat* 12:12
h. *much* owest thou to ? *Luke* 16:5, 7
h. *much* every man hath. 19:15
h. *much* evil he hath. *Acts* 9:13
h. *much* he is the Mediator. *Heb* 8:6
of h. *much* sorer punishment. 10:29
h. *much* she hath glorified. *Rev* 18:7

how much less
contain thee, h. *much less* this
house ? *1 Ki* 8:27; *2 Chr* 6:18
h. *much less* shall your God ?
2 Chr 32:15
h. *much less* in them that dwell in
houses of clay ? *Job* 4:19
h. *much less* shall I answer ? 9:14
h. *much less* is man that is ? 25:6
h. *much less* to him that accepteth ?
34:19
h. *much less* shall it be meet for ?
Ezek 15:5

how much more
and h. *much more* after my death ?
Deut 31:27
h. *much more* if people ? *1 Sam* 14:30
h. *much more* then if we ? 23:3
h. *much more* when wicked men ?
2 Sam 4:11
h. *much more* now may this ? 16:11
h. *much more* abominable and ?
Job 15:16
h. *much more* then the hearts of ?
Pr 15:11
h. *much more* do his friends ? 19:7
h. *much more* when with a ? 21:27
h. *much more* when I send my four
sore judgements ? *Ezek* 14:21
h. *much more* shall your heavenly
Father ? *Mat* 7:11; *Luke* 11:13
h. *much more* shall call ? *Mat* 10:25
h. *much more* are ye better than ?
Luke 12:24

h. *much more* will he clothe you ?
Luke 12:28
h. *much more* their fulness ?
Rom 11:12
h. *much more* these which be ? 24
h. *much more* things that pertain to ?
1 Cor 6:3
brother to me, h. *much more* to ?
Philem 16

how oft, often
h. *oft* is the candle of the wicked put
out ? h. *oft* cometh ? *Job* 21:17
h. *oft* did they provoke ? *Ps* 78:40
h. *oft* shall my brother ? *Mat* 18:21
h. *often* would I have gathered thy
children as a. 23:37; *Luke* 13:34

howbeit
h. Sisera fled on his feet. *Judg* 4:17
h. the king of Ammonites. 11:28
h. the hair of his head began. 16:22
h. the name of the city was. 18:29
h. we may not give them wives of.
21:18
h. there is a kinsman. *Ruth* 3:12
h. yet protest solemnly. *1 Sam* 8:9
h. Asahel refused to. *2 Sam* 2:23
h. because by this deed hast. 12:14
h. he would not hearken. 13:14
h. he would not go, but blessed. 25
h. he attained not unto the first three.
23:19; *1 Chr* 11:21
h. the kingdom is turned. *1 Ki* 2:15
h. I believed not the words. 10:7
2 Chr 9:6
h. I will not rend all the kingdom.
1 Ki 11:13, 34
I have lacked nothing, h. let. 11:22
h. slingers went about in. *2 Ki* 3:25
h. Lord shewed me, that he. 8:10
h. from sins of Jeroboam, Jehu. 10:29
h. there were not made for. 12:13
h. high places were not taken away.
14:4; 15:35; *2 Chr* 20:33
h. every nation made. *2 Ki* 17:29
h. they did not hearken, but. 40
h. there was no reckoning. 22:7
h. the Lord God of Israel. *1 Chr* 28:4
h. the king of Israel stayed himself.
2 Chr 18:34
h. the Levites hastened it not. 24:5
h. he entered not into temple. 27:2
h. in business of ambassadors. 32:31
h. thou art just in all. *Neh* 9:33
h. our God turned the curse. 13:2
h. he will not stretch out. *Job* 30:24
h. he meaneth not so. *Isa* 10:7
h. I sent to you all my. *Jer* 44:4
h. this kind goeth not. *Mat* 17:21
h. Jesus suffered him. *Mark* 5:19
h. in vain do they worship me. 7:7
h. there came boats from. *John* 6:23
h. no man spake openly of. 7:13
h. we know this man whence he. 27
h. Jesus spake of his death. 11:13
h. when he the Spirit of truth. 16:13
h. many who heard the. *Acts* 4:4
h. the Most High dwelleth not. 7:48
h. he rose up and came into. 14:20
h. certain men clave to him. 17:34
h. we must be cast upon a. 27:26
h. they looked when he should have
swollen. 28:6
h. we speak wisdom. *1 Cor* 2:6
h. there is not in every man. 8:7
h. in the Spirit he speaketh. 14:2
h. in malice be children, in. 20
h. that was not first which. 15:46
h. wherein soever any is. *2 Cor* 11:21
h. when ye knew not God. *Gal* 4:8
h. for this cause I obtained mercy.
1 Tim 1:16
h. not all that came out of. *Heb* 3:16

howl
(American Revision usually sub-
stitutes the word wail*)*
h. ye, for the day of the. *Isa* 13:6
h. O gate. 14:31
Moab hath. 15:2, 3; 16:7
h. ye ships of Tarshish, for it. 23:1
pass over to Tarshish, h. ye. 6
make them to h. 52:5
h. for vexation. 65:14
lament and h. *Jer* 4:8; 48:20

h. ye shepherds. *Jer 25:34*
inhabitants of the land shall h. 47:2
I will h. for Moab. 48:31
they shall h. 39
h. O Heshbon. 49:3
h. for Babylon. 51:8
cry and h. son of man. *Ezek 21:12*
prophesy and say, H. ye, woe. 30:2
h. ye drinkers. *Joel 1:5*
h. yo vinedressers. 11
lament and h. ye ministers of. 13
I will wail and h., will go. *Mi 1:8*
h. ye inhabitants of. *Zeph 1:11*
h. fir tree, h. O ye oaks. *Zech 11:2*
ye rich men, weep and h. *Jas 5:1*

howled
not cried to me, when they h. on. *Hos 7:14*

howling
in waste h. wilderness. *Deut 32:10*
h. thereof is gone to Eglaim and. *Isa 15:8*
an h. of principal of the. *Jer 25:36*
h. from the second gate. *Zeph 1:10*
there is a voice of the h. *Zech 11:3*

howlings
songs of the temple shall be h. *Amos 8:3*

huge
and Lubims a h. host. *2 Chr 16:8*

humble
[1] *Not proud or assertive. The word does not have its modern sense of undue self-depreciation.* [2] *To humble is to humiliate.*
and he shall save the h. *Job 22:29*
not the cry of the h. *Ps 9:12**
O God, forget not the h. 10:12*
hast heard the desire of the h. 17*
the h. shall hear thereof and. 34:2
h. shall see this and be glad. 69:32
better be of a h. spirit. *Pr 16:19**
honour shall uphold the h. 29:23*
of a contrite and h. spirit, to revive the spirit of the h. *Isa 57:15*
but giveth grace to the h. *Jas 4:6; 1 Pet 5:5*

humble
refuse to h. thyself? *Ex 10:3*
to h. thee and to prove. *Deut 8:2, 16*
h. ye them, and do. *Judg 19:24*
my people shall h. *2 Chr 7:14*
because thou didst h. thyself. 34:27
go, h. thyself, and make. *Pr 6:3*
h. yourselves, sit down. *Jer 13:18*
shall h. himself. *Mat 18:4; 23:12*
my God will h. me. *2 Cor 12:21*
h. yourselves in the sight. *Jas 4:10*
h. yourselves under. *1 Pet 5:6*

humbled
if their uncircumcised hearts be h. *Lev 26:41*
h. thee and suffered thee. *Deut 8:3*
because thou hast h. her. 21:14
22:29
hath h. his neighbour's wife. 22:24
because hast h. thyself. *2 Ki 22:19*
princes and the king h. *2 Chr 12:6*
when the Lord saw that they h. 7
he h. himself, wrath turned. 7
divers of Asher and Zebulun h. 30:11
Hezekiah h. himself for pride. 32:26
Manasseh h. himself greatly. 33:12
graven images before he was h. 19
Amon h. not himself before the Lord, as Manasseh his father h. 23
Zedekiah h. not himself. 36:12
as for me, I h. my soul. *Ps 35:13**
looks of man shall be h. *Isa 2:11**
h., eyes of the lofty shall be h. 5:15
and the haughty shall be h. 10:33*
they are not h. even to. *Jer 44:10*
remembrance and is h. *Lam 3:20**
in thee have they h. *Ezek 22:10*
and another in thee hath h. 11
thou his son hast not h. *Dan 5:22*
he h. himself and became. *Phil 2:8*

humbledst
because thou h. thyself. *2 Chr 34:27*

humbleness
put on kindness, h. of. *Col 3:12*

21

humbleth
seest thou how Ahab h.? because he h. himself. *1 Ki 21:29*
he croucheth and h. *Ps 10:10**
who h. himself to behold. 113:6
man boweth, great man h. *Isa 2:9**
he that h. himself shall be exalted. *Luke 14:11; 18:14*

humbly
I h. beseech thee that. *2 Sam 16:4*
love mercy, and to walk h. *Mi 6:8*

humiliation
in his h. his judgement. *Acts 8:33*

humility
before honour is h. *Pr 15:33; 18:12*
by h. are riches, and honour. 22:4
Lord with all h. of mind. *Acts 20:19**
beguile you in a voluntary h. *Col 2:18*
wisdom in will worship and h. 23
another, clothed with h. *1 Pet 5:5*

hundred
Shem was an h. years. *Gen 11:10*
child be born to him that is an h.? 17:17; 21:5; *Rom 4:19*
Jacob bought for an h. pieces. *Gen 33:19; Josh 24:32*
hangings h. cubits long. *Ex 27:9, 11*
38:9, 11
the court shall be an h. cubits. 18
h. sockets were cast of the h. 38:27
five shall chase an h. and an h. put to. *Lev 26:8*
shall amerce him in an h. *Deut 22:19*
so Gideon and the h. men. *Judg 7:19*
ten of an h. of a 1000. 20:10
of Benjamin 25,000 and an h. 35
but an h. foreskins. *1 Sam 18:25*
2 Sam 3:14
an h. clusters of raisins. *1 Sam 25:18*
2 Sam 16:1
reserved for an h. chariots. *2 Sam 8:4; 1 Chr 18:4*
provision for one day h. *1 Ki 4:23*
house of the forest an h. cubits. 7:2
Obadiah took h. prophets. 18:4, 13
this before an h. men? *2 Ki 4:43*
Jehoahaz in bands, and put land to a tribute of an h. 23:33; *2 Chr 36:3*
least was over an h. *1 Chr 12:14*
Simeon seven thousand and one h. 25
Lord make his people an h. 21:3
Solomon made an h. *2 Chr 3:16*
made an h. basons of gold. 4:8
men for an h. talents of silver. 25:6
what shall we do for the h. talents? 9
Jotham an h. talents of silver. 27:5
brought an h. rams. 29:32
they gave one h. priests'. *Ezra 2:69*
offered at the dedication an h. 6:17
an h. talents of silver, h. measures of wheat and wine, and an h. 7:22
h. talents of gold, an h. 8:26
restore to them the h. *Neh 5:11*
more than an h. stripes. *Pr 17:10*
man beget an h. children. *Eccl 6:3*
though sinner do evil h. times. 8:12
h. years old, but the sinner being an h. years old shall. *Isa 65:20*
measured an h. cubits. *Ezek 40:19*
gate to gate an h. cubits. 23, 27
h. cubits long, an h. cubits broad. 47
house an h. cubits long. 41:13
place toward east, an h. cubits. 14
one side and other, an h. cubits. 15
the temple were an h. cubits. 42:8
shall leave an h., that which went forth by an h. shall. *Amos 5:3*
if a man have an h. sheep. *Mat 18:12; Luke 15:4*
owed him an h. pence. *Mat 18:28*
an h. measures of oil. *Luke 16:6*
thou? an h. measures of wheat. 7
myrrh and aloes, an h. *John 19:39*

hundredfold, see fold
one hundred and five
Seth lived one h. and five years. *Gen 5:6*

one hundred and ten
Joseph lived one h. and ten years. *Gen 50:22, 26*

Joshua died, being an h. and ten years old. *Josh 24:29; Judg 2:8*
Johanan an h. and ten. *Ezra 8:12*

one hundred and twelve
Uzziel an h. and twelve. *1 Chr 15:10*
Jorah, an h. and twelve. *Ezra 2:18*
Hariph, an h. and twelve. *Neh 7:24*

one hundred and nineteen
Terah h. and nineteen. *Gen 11:25*

one hundred and twenty
his days shall be h. and twenty years. *Gen 6:3*
the gold of the spoons was an h. and twenty shekels. *Num 7:86*
an h. and twenty years. *Deut 31:2*
Moses an h. and twenty years. 34:7
an h. and twenty talents of gold. *1 Ki 10:10; 2 Chr 9:9*
and brethren an h. and twenty. *1 Chr 15:5*
porch an h. and twenty. *2 Chr 3:4*
an h. and twenty priests. 5:12
kingdom an h. and twenty. *Dan 6:1*
names were about an h. and twenty. *Acts 1:15*

one hundred twenty two
men of Michmash, h. twenty two. *Ezra 2:27; Neh 7:31*

one hundred twenty three
Aaron an h. twenty three. *Num 33:39*
of captivity an h. twenty and three. *Ezra 2:21; Neh 7:32*

one hundred and twenty seven
Sarah was an h. twenty seven. *Gen 23:1*
reigned over an h. and twenty seven. *Esth 1:1; 8:9; 9:30*

one hundred and twenty eight
men of Anathoth h. twenty eight. *Ezra 2:23; Neh 7:27*
Asaph an h. twenty eight. *Ezra 2:41*
brethren an h. and twenty eight. *Neh 11:14*

one hundred and thirty
Adam lived h. thirty years. *Gen 5:3*
pilgrimage are an h. and thirty. 47:9
weight thereof was an h. and thirty. *Num 7:13, 19, 25*
charger weighing an h. and thirty. 85
brethren an h. and thirty. *1 Chr 15:7*
Jehoiada was an h. and thirty years. *2 Chr 24:15*

one hundred thirty three
Kohath an h. thirty three. *Ex 6:18*

one hundred thirty seven
Ishmael an h. and thirty seven. *Gen 25:17*
of Levi were h. and thirty seven. *Ex 6:16*
Amram were an h. thirty seven. 20

one hundred thirty eight
children of Shobai of Ater, h. thirty eight. *Neh 7:45*

one hundred thirty nine
of Shobai in all an h. thirty nine. *Ezra 2:42*

one hundred forty
Job an h. forty years. *Job 42:16*

one hundred forty four
the wall an h. forty four cubits. *Rev 21:17*

one hundred forty seven
Jacob an h. forty seven. *Gen 47:28*

one hundred forty eight
the children of Asaph h. forty eight. *Neh 7:44*

one hundred and fifty
waters prevailed an h. and fifty days. *Gen 7:24; 8:3*
and an horse for an h. and fifty. *1 Ki 10:29; 2 Chr 1:17*
sons' sons an h. and fifty. *1 Chr 8:40*
reckoned of males, an h. and fifty. *Ezra 8:3*
table an h. and fifty Jews. *Neh 5:17*

one hundred fifty three
net full of fishes an h. and fifty and three. *John 21:11*

one **hundred** *fifty six*
Magbish, and *h. fifty six. Ezra* 2:30
one **hundred** *sixty*
with him *h. sixty* males. *Ezra* 8:10
one **hundred** *sixty two*
Jared lived *h. sixty two* years.
Gen 5:18
one **hundred** *seventy two*
brethren *h. seventy two. Neh* 11:19
one **hundred** *seventy five*
life was an *h. seventy five. Gen* 25:7
one **hundred** *eighty*
of Isaac an *h.* and *eighty* years.
Gen 35:28
feast for an *h.* and *eighty* days.
Esth 1:4
one **hundred** *eighty two*
Lamech lived *h. eighty two* and.
Gen 5:28
one **hundred** *eighty seven*
Methuselah lived *h. eighty seven.*
Gen 5:25
one **hundred** *eighty eight*
of Beth-lehem an *h. eighty eight.*
Neh 7:26
hundred *thousand*
Judah were an *h. thous. Num* 2:9
the camp of Reuben an *h. thous.* 16
slew of Syrians *h. thous. 1 Ki* 20:29
to king of Israel an *h. thous.* lambs,
an *h. thous.* rams. *2 Ki* 3:4
from Hagarites an *h. thous.* men.
1 Chr 5:21
thousand and *h. thous.* 21:5
for house of Lord *h. thous.* 22:14
an *h. thous.* talents of iron. 29:7
he hired an *h. thous. 2 Chr* 25:6
one **hundred** *and eight thousand*
and an **hundred**
of camp of Ephraim, 108,100.
Num 2:24
an **hundred** *twenty thousand*
the Midianites 120,000. *Judg* 8:10
a sacrifice of an 120,000 sheep.
1 Ki 8:63; *2 Chr* 7:5
Gad, and Manasseh, 120,000.
1 Chr 12:37
slew in Judah in one day 120,000.
2 Chr 28:6
Nineveh were about 120,000 persons.
Jonah 4:11
an **hundred** *forty four thousand*
were sealed 144,000 of all. *Rev* 7:4
with him 144,000, having his. 14:1
learn that song but the 144,000. 3
an **hundred** *fifty thousand*
strangers in the land of Israel were
found 150,000. *2 Chr* 2:17
an **hundred** *eighty thousand*
with Benjamin 180,000. *1 Ki* 12:21
2 Chr 11:1
with Jehozabad were 180,000, for.
2 Chr 17:18
an **hundred** *eighty five thousand*
of the Lord smote of the Assyrians,
185,000. *2 Ki* 19:35; *Isa* 37:36
two **hundred**
begat Nahor *two h.* years. *Gen* 11:23
two h. she goats, and *two h.* 32:14
Achan saw *two h.* shekels. *Josh* 7:21
his mother took *two h. Judg* 17:4
slew of Philistines *two h.* men.
1 Sam 18:27
two h. abode by. 25:13; 30:10, 21
two h. loaves, *two h.* cakes. 25:18
weighed hair *two h.* 2 *Sam* 14:26
with Absalom went *two h.* 15:11
Ziba brought David *two h.* 16:1
pomegranates were *two h. 1 Ki* 7:20
Solomon made *two h.* targets. 10:16
2 Chr 9:15
burnt offerings *two h. 2 Chr* 29:32
were among them *two h. Ezra* 2:65
offered at dedication *two h.* 6:17
the fruit thereof *two h. S of S* 8:12
one lamb out of *two h. Ezek* 45:15
two h. pennyworth is not. *John* 6:7
make ready *two h.* soldiers, and
spearmen *two h.* *Acts* 23:23

two **hundred** *five*
the days of Terah were *two h. five*
years. *Gen* 11:32
two **hundred** *seven*
Reu lived *two h. seven. Gen* 11:21
two **hundred** *nine*
Peleg lived *two h. nine. Gen* 11:19
two **hundred** *twelve*
gates were *two h. twelve. 1 Chr* 9:22
two **hundred** *eighteen*
Obadiah *two h. eighteen. Ezra* 8:9
two **hundred** *twenty*
service of Levites *two h. twenty.*
Ezra 8:20
two **hundred** *twenty three*
Beth-el and Ai *two h. twenty three.*
Ezra 2:28
two **hundred** *thirty two*
of provinces *two h. thirty two.*
1 Ki 20:15
two **hundred** *forty two*
fathers *two h. forty two. Neh* 11:13
two **hundred** *forty five.*
their mules *two h.* and *forty five.*
Ezra 2:66; *Neh* 7:68
and *two h. forty five* singing men.
Neh 7:67
two **hundred** *fifty*
cinnamon *two h.* and *fifty,* of calamus *two h.* and *fifty. Ex* 30:23
two h. and *fifty* princes. *Num* 16:2
two h. and *fifty* censers. 17
consumed the *two h.* and *fifty.* 35
two h. and *fifty* that bare. *2 Chr* 8:10
north *two h. fifty. Ezek* 48:17
two **hundred** *seventy six*
ship *two h. seventy six* souls.
Acts 27:37
two **hundred** *eighty four*
in the holy city *two h. eighty four.*
Neh 11:18
two **hundred** *eighty eight*
songs *two h. eighty eight. 1 Chr* 25:7
two **hundred** *fifty thousand*
sheep *two h. fifty thous. 1 Chr* 5:21
three **hundred**
Enoch walked with God *three h.*
Gen 5:22
the ark shall be *three h.* 6:15
Benjamin *three h.* pieces of. 45:22
lapped were *three h.* men. *Judg* 7:6
and he retained those *three h.* 8
the *three h.* men that were. 8:4
coast of Arnon *three h.* years. 11:26
and caught *three h.* foxes. 15:4
spear weighed *three h.* shekels.
2 Sam 21:16
Abishai lifted up his spear against
three h. 23:18; *1 Chr* 11:11, 20
made *three h.* shields. *1 Ki* 10:17
Solomon had *three h.* 11:3
Hezekiah *three h.* talents. *2 Ki* 18:14
three h. shekels of gold. *2 Chr* 9:16
against Asa with *three h.* 14:19
passover offerings *three h.* 35:8
with Shechaniah *three h. Ezra* 8:5
the Jews slew *three h. Esth* 9:15
sold for *three h.* pence. *John* 12:5
three **hundred** *eighteen*
with *three h. eighteen* servants.
Gen 14:14
three **hundred** *twenty*
Harim *three h.* and *twenty.*
Ezra 2:32; *Neh* 7:35
three **hundred** *twenty three*
the children of Bezai 323. *Ezra* 2:17
Neh 7:23
three **hundred** *twenty eight*
of Hashum *three h. twenty eight.*
Neh 7:22
three **hundred** *forty five*
children of Jericho 345. *Ezra* 2:34
Neh 7:36
three **hundred** *fifty*
flood *three h. fifty* years. *Gen* 9:28

three **hundred** *sixty*
of Israel *three h. sixty* men died.
2 Sam 2:31
three **hundred** *sixty five*
Enoch's days were *three h. sixty*
five years. *Gen* 5:23
three **hundred** *seventy two*
the children of Shephatiah 372.
Ezra 2:4; *Neh* 7:9
three **hundred** *ninety*
to number of days 390. *Ezek* 4:5, 9
three **hundred** *thousand*
went out to war 300,000. *Num* 31:36
Israel were 300,000. *1 Sam* 11:8
2 Chr 14:8
with Adnah mighty men 300,000.
2 Chr 17:14
and Benjamin to be 300,000. 25:5
three **hundred** *and seven thou-*
sand five **hundred**
an army of 307,500. *2 Chr* 26:13
three **hundred** *and thirty seven*
thousand five **hundred**
pertained unto the congregation was
337,500 sheep. *Num* 31:43
four **hundred**
afflict them *four h.* years.
Gen 15:13; *Acts* 7:6
four h. shekels of silver. 23:15, 16
Esau cometh to thee with *four h.*
32:6; 33:1
found *four h.* virgins of. *Judg* 21:12
there were with David about *four h.*
men. *1 Sam* 22:2; 25:13; 30:10
save *four h.* young men on. 30:17
four h. pomegranates. *1 Ki* 7:42
prophets of the groves *four h.* 18:19
gathered of the prophets about *four*
h. and said. 22:6; *2 Chr* 18:5
brake down wall of Jerusalem *four h.*
cubits. *2 Ki* 14:13; *2 Chr* 25:23
of house for *h.* lambs. *Ezra* 6:17
to whom about *four h.* *Acts* 5:36
four **hundred** *and three*
Arphaxad lived 403. *Gen* 11:13
lived after he begat Eber 403. 15
four **hundred** *and ten*
second sort *four h. ten. Ezra* 1:10
four **hundred** *and twenty*
from thence gold, 420. *1 Ki* 9:28
four **hundred** *and thirty*
Eber lived 430 years. *Gen* 11:17
in Egypt 430 years. *Ex* 12:40, 41
law which was 430 years. *Gal* 3:17
four **hundred** *thirty five*
their camels were 435. *Ezra* 2:67
Neh 7:69
four **hundred** *and fifty*
prophets of Baal 450. *1 Ki* 18:19, 22
gave judges about *four h. fifty* years.
Acts 13:20
four **hundred** *fifty four*
Adin *four h. fifty four* *Ezra* 2:15
four **hundred** *sixty eight*
of Perez were 468 men. *Neh* 11:6
four **hundred** *eighty*
in 480 years Solomon. *1 Ki* 6:1
four **hundred** *thousand*
Benjamin 400,000. *Judg* 20:2, 17
array with 400,000 men. *2 Chr* 13:3
four **hundred** *seventy thousand*
Judah was 470,000 that. *1 Chr* 21:5
five **hundred**
Noah was *five h.* years. *Gen* 5:32
Shem lived after *five h.* years. 11:11
of pure myrrh *five h.* *Ex* 30:23
of cassia *five h.* shekels after. 24
levy one soul of *five h. Num* 31:28
offerings *five h.* oxen. *2 Chr* 35:9
Shushan *five h.* men. *Esth* 9:6, 12
five h. yoke of oxen, *five h.* she
asses. *Job* 1:3
he measured *five h.* reeds.
Ezek 42:16, 17, 18, 19, 20
be for the sanctuary *five h.* in length,
with *five h.* in breadth. 45:2
one owed *five h.* pence. *Luke* 7:41
above *five h.* brethren at. *1 Cor* 15:6

five **hundred** *and thirty*
gave *five h. and thirty* priests'.
            Neh 7:70
five **hundred** *and fifty*
five hundred fifty bare rule over.
            1 Ki 9:23
five **hundred** *thousand*
men of Judah were 500,000 men.
            2 Sam 24:9
slain of Israel 500,000 men.
            2 Chr 13:17
six **hundred**
Noah *six h.* years old when flood.
            Gen 7:6, 11
Pharaoh took *six h.*   *Ex* 14:7
slew with an ox goad *six h.*
            Judg 3:31
out of Eshtaol *six h.*   18:11, 16, 17
six h. Benjamites fled to.   20:47
Saul numbered the people *six h.*
         1 Sam 13:15; 14:2
spear head weighed *six h.*   17:7
David and his men about *six h.*
          23:13; 27:2; 30:9
all the Gittites were *six h.* men.
            2 Sam 15:18
six h. shekels of gold went to one
   target.   *1 Ki* 10:16; *2 Chr* 9:15
a chariot went for *six h.* shekels.
       1 Ki 10:29; *2 Chr* 1:17
Ornan *six h.* shekels.   *1 Chr* 21:25
house with gold to *six h.* talents.
            2 Chr 3:8
consecrated things were *six h.* oxen.
            29:33
six **hundred** *twenty one*
children of Ramah *six h. twenty one.*
       Ezra 2:26; *Neh* 7:30
six **hundred** *twenty three*
Bebai, *six h. twenty three. Ezra* 2:11
six **hundred** *twenty eight*
Bebai, *six h. twenty eight. Neh* 7:16
six **hundred** *forty two*
of Bani, *six h. forty two. Ezra* 2:10
Nekoda, *six h. forty two. Neh* 7:62
six **hundred** *forty eight*
Binnui, *six h. forty eight. Neh* 7:15
six **hundred** *and fifty*
weighed unto their hand *six h. fifty*
   talents.   *Ezra* 8:26
six **hundred** *fifty two*
Nekoda, *six h. fifty two. Ezra* 2:60
Arah, *six h. and fifty two. Neh* 7:10
six **hundred** *sixty six*
gold to Solomon in year 666 talents.
            1 Ki 10:14
of Adonikam, 666.   *Ezra* 2:13
and his number is 666.   *Rev* 13:18
six **hundred** *sixty seven*
of Adonikam, 667.   *Neh* 7:18
six **hundred** *seventy five*
tribute of sheep were 675. *Num* 31:37
six **hundred** *ninety*
Jeuel and brethren 690.   *1 Chr* 9:6
six **hundred** *thousand*
journeyed about 600,000.   *Ex* 12:37
for every man for 600,000.   38:26
numbered were 600,000. *Num* 1:46
people are 600,000 footmen.   11:21
six **hundred** *seventy five*
     thousand
prey was 675,000 sheep. *Num* 31:32
seven **hundred**
of Gibeah were *seven h.* chosen.
         Judg 20:15, 16
David took from him *seven h.*
            2 Sam 8:4
David slew men of *seven h.*   10:18
had *seven h.* wives.   *1 Ki* 11:3
Moab took *seven h.*   *2 Ki* 3:26
the Lord *seven h.* oxen. *2 Chr* 15:11
seven **hundred** *twenty one*
Lod, Hadid, Ono, 721.   *Neh* 7:37
seven **hundred** *twenty five*
Lod, Hadid, Ono, 725.   *Ezra* 2:33
seven **hundred** *thirty six*
their horses were 736.   *Ezra* 2:66
            Neh 7:68

seven **hundred** *forty three*
of Kirjath-arim, 743.   *Ezra* 2:25
seven **hundred** *forty five*
captive of the Jews 745.   *Jer* 52:30
seven **hundred** *sixty*
the children of Zaccai 760.
        Ezra 2:9; *Neh* 7:14
seven **hundred** *seventy five*
children of Arah, 775.   *Ezra* 2:5
seven **hundred** *seventy seven*
of Lamech were 777.   *Gen* 5:31
seven **hundred** *eighty two*
Methuselah lived 782.   *Gen* 5:26
eight **hundred**
he begat Seth lived 800.   *Gen* 5:4
after he begat Enoch lived 800.   19
his spear against 800.   *2 Sam* 23:8
eight **hundred** *seven*
after he begat Enos 807.   *Gen* 5:7
eight **hundred** *fifteen*
after he begat Cainan 815. *Gen* 5:10
eight **hundred** *twenty two*
that did work were 822. *Neh* 11:12
eight **hundred** *thirty*
he begat Jared 830 years. *Gen* 5:16
eight **hundred** *thirty two*
carried captive 832.   *Jer* 52:29
eight **hundred** *forty*
he begat Mahalaleel 840.   *Gen* 5:13
eight **hundred** *forty five*
children of Zattu were 845. *Neh* 7:13
eight **hundred** *ninety five*
Mahalaleel were 895.   *Gen* 5:17
nine **hundred**
Jabin had *nine h.*   *Judg* 4:3, 13
nine **hundred** *five*
days of Enos were 905.   *Gen* 5:11
nine **hundred** *ten*
days of Cainan 910 years. *Gen* 5:14
nine **hundred** *twelve*
days of Seth were 912.   *Gen* 5:8
nine **hundred** *twenty eight*
him Gabbai, Sallai, 928.   *Neh* 11:8
nine **hundred** *thirty*
that Adam lived were 930. *Gen* 5:5
nine **hundred** *forty five*
children of Zattu 945.   *Ezra* 2:8
nine **hundred** *fifty*
of Noah were 950 years. *Gen* 9:29
nine **hundred** *fifty six*
brethren according to generations
   956.   *1 Chr* 9:9
nine **hundred** *sixty two*
Jared were 962 years.   *Gen* 5:20
nine **hundred** *sixty nine*
days of Methuselah were 969 years.
            Gen 5:27
nine **hundred** *seventy three*
the children of Jedaiah 973.
       Ezra 2:36; *Neh* 7:39
hundreds
be rulers of *h.* and tens.   *Ex* 18:21
         25; *Deut* 1:15
was wroth with captains over *h.*
            Num 31:14
took gold of the captains of *h.*   54
will son of Jesse make you captains
   of *h.?*   *1 Sam* 22:7
the Philistines passed on by *h.* 29:2
set captains of *h.* over. *2 Sam* 18:1
all the people came out by *h.*   4
and set the rulers over *h. 2 Ki* 11:4
captains over *h.* did the priest give
   spears and.   10; *2 Chr* 23:9
with the captains of *h. 1 Chr* 13:1
which the captains over *h.*   26:26
the captains over the *h.*   28:1
then the captains of *h.* offered. 29:6
Jehoiada took captains of *h.*
            2 Chr 23:1
made them captains over *h.*   25:5
sat down in ranks by *h. Mark* 6:40
hunger, *substantive*
whole assembly with *h.*   *Ex* 16:3
serve thine enemies in *h. Deut* 28:48
they shall be burnt with *h.*   32:24

bread from heaven for their *h.*
            Neh 9:15
young lions do lack and suffer *h.*
            Ps 34:1C
an idle soul shall suffer *h. Pr* 19:15
he is like to die for *h.*   *Jer* 38:9*
see no war, nor have *h.* of.   42:14
that faint for *h.* in top of. *Lam* 2:19
than they that be slain with *h.*   4:9
be no more consumed with *h.*
            Ezek 34:29
and I perish with *h.*   *Luke* 15:17
been in *h.* and thirst.   *2 Cor* 11:27
given them to kill with *h.*   *Rev* 6:8
hunger, *verb*
he suffered thee to *h.*   *Deut* 8:3
shall not *h.* nor thirst.   *Isa* 49:10
blessed are they that *h.*   *Mat* 5:6
            Luke 6:21
are full, for ye shall *h.*   *Luke* 6:25
he that cometh to me shall never *h.*
            John 6:35
if thine enemy *h.* feed. *Rom* 12:20
we both *h.* and thirst.   *1 Cor* 4:11
and if any man *h.* let him eat. 11:34
they shall *h.* no more.   *Rev* 7:16
hungerbitten
his strength shall be *h.*   *Job* 18:12
hungered
he was afterwards an *h.*   *Mat* 4:2
            Luke 4:2
his disciples were an *h.*   *Mat* 12:1
did when he was an *h.* 3; *Mark* 2:25
returned into city, he *h. Mat* 21:18
for I vas an *h.* and ye gave.   25:35
Lord, when saw we thee an *h.?* 37, 44
for I was an *h.* and ye gave.   42
did when himself was an *h. Luke* 6:3
hungry
they that were *h.* ceased. *1 Sam* 2:5
the people is *h.,* weary. *2 Sam* 17:29
they know that we be *h.*   *2 Ki* 7:12
h. eateth up and taketh it. *Job* 5:5
withholden bread from the *h.*   22:7
away the sheaf from the *h.*   24:10
if I were *h.* I would not. *Ps* 50:12
h. and thirsty, their soul.   107:5
filleth the *h.* soul with goodness.   9
and there he maketh the *h.* to.   36
who giveth food to the *h.*   146:7
satisfy his soul when he is *h. Pr* 6:30
if thine enemy be *h.* give.   25:21
to the *h.* soul every bitter.   27:7
bestead and *h.:* when they shall be
   h., they shall fret.   *Isa* 8:21
snatch on right hand, and be *h.* 9:20
it shall even be as when a *h.*   29:8
empty the soul of the *h.*   32:6
yea, he is *h.* and his strength. 44:12
to deal thy bread to the *h.?*   58:7
draw out thy soul to the *h.*   10
shall eat, but ye shall be *h.*   65:13
his bread to the *h.*   *Ezek* 18:7, 16
from Bethany he was *h. Mark* 11:12
he hath filled the *h.* with. *Luke* 1:53
Peter became very *h.*   *Acts* 10:10
one is *h.* and another is. *1 Cor* 11:21
to be full and to be *h.*   *Phil* 4:12
hunt
(*Hunting as a matter of necessity,
whether for the extermination of
dangerous beasts or for procuring
food, betokens a rude and semi-
civilized state; as an amusement,
it indicates an advanced state.
As a pastoral people the Hebrews
did little hunting as a sport; and
their rules of eating prevented their
doing so for food, after the Law was
given*)
Esau went to field to *h.*   *Gen* 27:5
as when one doth *h.*   *1 Sam* 26:20
wilt thou *h.* the prey ? *Job* 38:39
evil shall *h.* violent man. *Ps* 140:11
the adulteress will *h.*   *Pr* 6:26
shall *h.* them from every. *Jer* 16:16
they *h.* our steps that we. *Lam* 4:18
will ye *h.* the souls ? *Ezek* 13:18
pillows wherewith ye there *h.*   20
h. every man his brother. *Mi* 7:2
hunted
in your hand to be *h.*   *Ezek* 13:21

hunter, -s

mighty *h*. before the Lord: even as
Nimrod the mighty *h*. Gen 10:9
Esau was a cunning *h*. 25:27
a roe from hand of the *h*. Pr 6:5
will I send for many *h*. Jer 16:16

huntest

yet thou *h*. my soul. 1 Sam 24:11
h. me as a fierce lion. Job 10:16

hunteth

which *h*. and catcheth. Lev 17:13

hunting

brother came in from *h*. Gen 27:30
roasteth not that which he took in *h*.
Pr 12:27

Hur

Moses, Aaron, *H*. went up. Ex 17:10
Aaron and *H*. stayed up his. 12
Aaron and *H*. are with you. 24:14
Bezaleel, the son of Uri, son of *H*.
31:2; 35:30; 38:22
they slew Evi, Rekem, Zur, *H*. and.
Num 31:8; Josh 13:21
of *H*. in mount Ephraim. 1 Ki 4:8
Ephratah, which bare *H*. 1 Chr 2:19
H. begat Uri. 20
sons of Caleb the son of *H*. 50
sons of Judah, *H*. Shobal. 4:1
sons of *H*. Ephratah, Ashur. 4
Rephaiah son of *H*. Neh 3:9

hurl

if *h*. at him by lying in. Num 35:20

hurleth

and as a storm *h*. him. Job 27:21*

hurling

right hand and left in *h*. 1 Chr 12:2*

hurt, substantive

a young man to my *h*. Gen 4:23
that thou wilt do us no *h*. 26:29
power of my hand to do you *h*. 31:29
he turn and do you *h*. Josh 24:20*
peace to thee, and no *h*. 1 Sam 20:21
behold, David seeketh thy *h*. 24:9
that rise to do *h*. be. 2 Sam 18:32
why meddle to thy *h*. that thou?
2 Ki 14:10; 2 Chr 25:19
why damage grow to *h*.? Ezra 4:22
such as sought their *h*. Esth 9:2
that sweareth to his *h*. Ps 15:4
that devise my *h*. 35:4; 70:2
ashamed that rejoice at my *h*. 26
my *h*. speak mischievous. 38:12
do they devise my *h*. 41:7
with reproach that seek my *h*. 71:13
brought to shame that seek my *h*. 24
for the owners to their *h*. Eccl 5:13
ruleth over another to his own *h*. 8:9
have healed *h*. of my people.
Jer 6:14; 8:11
walk after other gods to your *h*. 7:6
for *h*. of my people am I *h*. 8:21
woe is me for my *h*.! 10:19
to be removed for their *h*. 24:9*
and I will do you no *h*. 25:6
provoke me to your own *h*. 7
welfare of this people, but the *h*. 38:4
they have no *h*. Dan 3:25
I have done no *h*. 6:22
and no manner of *h*. was. 23
voyage will be with *h*. Acts 27:10

hurt, participle

if a beast be *h*. no man. Ex 22:10
if it be *h*. or die, the owner. 14
were good and we were not *h*.
1 Sam 25:15
whoso removeth stones shall be *h*.
Eccl 10:9
for the *h*. of my people am I *h*.
Jer 8:21
not be *h*. of second death. Rev 2:11

hurt, verb

suffered him not to *h*. me. Gen 31:7
men strive and *h*. woman. Ex 21:22
if one man's ox *h*. another's that. 35
neither have I *h*. one. Num 16:15
shepherds with us, we *h*. 1 Sam 25:7
thy wickedness may *h*. a. Job 35:8
whose feet *h*. with fetters. Ps 105:18
not *h*. nor destroy in all my holy.
Isa 11:9; 65:25
lest any *h*. it, I will keep it. 27:3

lions have not *h*. me. Dan 6:22
it shall not *h*. them. Mark 16:18
came out of him, and *h*. Luke 4:35
shall by any means *h*. you. 10:19
set on thee to thy *h*. Acts 18:10
see thou *h*. not the oil. Rev 6:6
given to *h*. earth and sea. 7:2
saying, *H*. not the earth, neither. 3
they should not *h*. the grass. 9:4
and their power was to *h*. men. 10
heads, and with them they do *h*. 19
if any *h*. them, fire proceedeth. 11:5

hurtful

this city is *h*. to kings. Ezra 4:15
David from the *h*. sword. Ps 144:10
be rich fall into *h*. lusts. 1 Tim 6:9

hurting

kept me from *h*. thee. 1 Sam 25:34

husband

a bloody *h*. art thou to. Ex 4:25, 26
as the woman's *h*. will lay. 21:22
that is betrothed to a *h*. Lev 19:20
Deut 22:23
his sister which hath had no *h*.
Lev 21:3; Ezek 44:25
if she had at all an *h*. Num 30:6
woman married to a *h*. Deut 22:22
and if the latter *h*. hate her or. 24:3
her former *h*. may not take her. 4
perform the duty of a *h*. 25:5
eye shall be evil toward *h*. 28:56
the *h*. of the woman slain. Judg 20:4
Naomi's *h*. died, she. Ruth 1:3
to have an *h*. if I should have an *h*. 12
the *h*. with the wife shall. Jer 6:11
although I was an *h*. to them. 31:32
with sackcloth for *h*. of. Joel 1:8
begat Joseph the *h*. of. Mat 1:16
she had lived with an *h*. Luke 2:36
I have no *h*. Thou hast well said, I
have no *h*. John 4:17
if *h*. be dead, she is loosed from her
h. Rom 7:2, 3
h. render to wife due benevolence,
also wife to the *h*. 1 Cor 7:3
also the *h*. hath not power of his. 4
let not the *h*. put away his wife. 11
woman who hath an *h*. that. 13
h. is sanctified by wife, and unbelieving wife is sanctified by *h*. 14
espoused you to one *h*. 2 Cor 11:2
than she which hath an *h*. Gal 4:27
the *h*. is head of wife as. Eph 5:23
bishop be blameless, *h*. of one wife.
1 Tim 3:2; Tit 1:6

her husband

fruit, and gave to *her h*. Gen 3:6
wife gave Hagar to *her h*. 16:3
not take a woman put away from *her
h*. Lev 21:7
hid from eyes of *her h*. Num 5:13
done trespass against *her h*. 27
aside to another instead of *her h*. 29
if *her h*. heard it, and. 30:7, 11, 14
if *her h*. disallow her on the day. 8
and if she vowed in *her h*.'s house. 10
if *her h*. hath utterly made. 12
her h. may establish it or make. 13
unto her, and be *her h*. Deut 21:13
her h.'s brother shall go in. 25:5
draweth near to deliver *her h*. 11
woman came and told *her h*.
Judg 13:6
Manoah *her h*. was not with her. 9
made haste, and shewed *her h*. 10
her h. arose and went after. 19:3
her two sons and *her h*. Ruth 1:5
each of you in the house of *her h*. 9
Naomi had kinsman of *her h*. 2:1
Elkanah *her h*. to her. 1 Sam 1:8, 23
she said unto *her h*. I will not go. 22
when she came up with *her h*. 2:19
father and *her h*. were dead. 4:19
because of *her h*. 21
she told not *her h*. 25:19
took her from *her h*. 2 Sam 3:15
her h. went with her along. 16
wife of Uriah heard that *her h*. was
dead, mourned for *her h*. 11:26
said to *her h*., Behold now. 2 Ki 4:9
hath no child, and *her h*. is old. 14
she called unto *her h*. and said. 22

wife is a crown to *her h*. Pr 12:4
heart of *her h*. doth safely. 31:11
her h. is known in the gates. 23
her h. also riseth up, and he. 28
wife departeth from *her h*. Jer 3:20
taketh strangers instead of *her h*.
Ezek 16:32
that loatheth *her h*. and her. 45
wife, neither am I *her h*. Hos 2:2
now Joseph *her h*. being. Mat 1:19
shall put away *her h*. Mark 10:12
marrieth her put away from *her h*.
Luke 16:18
buried her by *her h*. Acts 5:10
by law to *her h*. so long. Rom 7:2
if *her h*. be dead, she is free from. 3
woman have *her* own *h*. 1 Cor 7:2
and likewise the wife to *her h*. 3
let not wife depart from *her h*. 10
or be reconciled to *her h*. 11
how she may please *her h*. 34
the law as long as *her h*. liveth. 39
that she reverence *her h*. Eph 5:33
a bride adorned for *her h*. Rev 21:2

my husband

now therefore *my h*. Gen 29:32
this time will *my h*. be joined. 34
that thou hast taken *my h*.? 30:15
given my maiden to *my h*. 18
Leah said, Now will *my h*. dwell. 20
my h.'s brother refuseth. Deut 25:7
am a widow, *my h*. is dead.
2 Sam 14:5; 2 Ki 4:1
not leave to *my h*. a. 2 Sam 14:7
go and return to *my* first *h*. Hos 2:7

thy husband

desire shall be to *thy h*. Gen 3:16
instead of *thy h*. Num 5:19, 20
said to Samson's wife, entice *thy h*.
Judg 14:15
since death of *thy h*. Ruth 2:11
is it well with *thy h*.? 2 Ki 4:26
thy Maker is *thine h*. Isa 54:5
go, call *thy h*. John 4:16
he is not *thy h*. 18
that have buried *thy h*. Acts 5:9
thou shalt save *thy h*. 1 Cor 7:16

husbandman

Noah began to be an *h*. Gen 9:20
I break in pieces the *h*. Jer 51:23
alas! they shall call the *h*. Amos 5:16
no prophet, I am a *h*. Zech 13:5*
vine, my Father is the *h*. John 15:1
h. that laboureth must. 2 Tim 2:6
h. waiteth for precious. Jas 5:7

husbandmen

captain left of the poor to *h*.
2 Ki 25:12 ; Jer 52:16
Uzziah had *h*. also in. 2 Chr 26:10
dwell in Judah itself *h*. Jer 31:24
ashamed, O ye *h*. howl. Joel 1:11
let it out to *h*. and went into a far.
Mat 21:33; Luke 20:9
sent his servants to. Mat 21:34
Mark 12:2; Luke 20:10
when *h*. saw the son. Mat 21:38
Mark 12:7; Luke 20:14
what will he do to those *h*.?
Mat 21:40
his vineyard to other *h*. 41
might receive from *h*. Mark 12:2
he will come and destroy the *h*. 9

husbandry

Uzziah had husbandmen also: for he
loved *h*. 2 Chr 26:10
ye are God's *h*. ye are. 1 Cor 3:9

husbands

they may be your *h*.? Ruth 1:11
stay for them from having *h*.? 13
shall despise their *h*. in. Esth 1:17
wives shall give to their *h*. honour. 20
give your daughters to. Jer 29:6
which loathed their *h*. Ezek 16:45
thou hast had five *h*. John 4:18
let them ask their *h*. 1 Cor 14:35
yourselves to your *h*. Eph 5:22, 24
h. love your wives, even as Christ.
25; Col 3:19
yourselves to your own *h*. Col 3:18
let deacons be the *h*. 1 Tim 3:12
women to love their *h*. Tit 2:4
chaste, obedient to their own *h*. 5

subjection to your own *h*. *1 Pet* 3:1
ye *h*. dwell with them according. 7

Hushai
H. the Archite came. *2 Sam* 15:32
so *H*. David's friend came into. 37
H. came to Absalom and. 16:16
said to *H*., Is this thy kindness ? 17
call *H*. 17:5
for, said *H*. thou knowest thy. 8
the counsel of *H*. is better than. 14
then said *H*. to Zadok and to. 15
Baanah the son of *H*. *1 Ki* 4:16
and *H*. was the king's. *1 Chr* 27:33

husk, -s
kernels even to the *h*. *Num* 6:4
full ears of corn in the *h*. *2 Ki* 4:42
filled his belly with *h*. *Luke* 15:16

Huzzab
H. be led away captive. *Nah* 2:7

Hymenaeus
of whom is *H*. and. *1 Tim* 1:20
is *H*. and Philetus. *2 Tim* 2:17

hymn, -s
when they had sung an *h*. *Mat* 26:30
Mark 14:26
to yourselves in psalms and *h*.
Eph 5:19
one another in psalms and *h*. *Col* 3:16

hypocrisies
aside all malice and *h*. *1 Pet* 2:1

hypocrisy
(*A false assumption of virtue;
canting pretence of goodness or
religion. The word is frequently
used in the Bible with the meaning
of godlessness*)
iniquity, to practise *h*. *Isa* 32:6
within ye are full of *h*. *Mat* 23:28
knowing their *h*. said. *Mark* 12:15
of Pharisees, which is *h*. *Luke* 12:1
speaking lies in their. *1 Tim* 4:2
is pure and without *h*. *Jas* 3:17

hypocrite
the *h*.'s hope shall perish. *Job* 8:13*
for an *h*. shall not come. 13:16*
shall stir up himself against *h*. 17:8*
and the joy of the *h*. is but. 20:5*
what is the hope of the *h*.? 27:8*
h. reign not, lest the people. 34:30*
an *h*. with his mouth destroyeth.
Pr 11:9*
for every one is an *h*. *Isa* 9:17*
thou *h*., first cast out beam. *Mat* 7:5
thou *h*., cast beam out. *Luke* 6:42
thou *h*., doth not each one ? 13:15

hypocrites
congregation of *h*. shall. *Job* 15:34*
the *h*. in heart heap up. 36:13*
fearfulness hath surprised the *h*.
Isa 33:14*
not sound a trumpet, as *h*. *Mat* 6:2
prayest, thou shalt not be as *h*. 5
when ye fast, be not as the *h*. 16
ye *h*. well did Esaias prophesy. 15:7
Mark 7:6
O ye *h*. ye can discern the face of.
Mat 16:3; *Luke* 12:56
why tempt ye me, ye *h*.? *Mat* 22:18
scribes and Pharisees, *h*. ye shut up.
23:13, 14, 15, 23, 25, 27, 29
him his portion with the *h*. 24:51
scribes and Pharisees, *h*. *Luke* 11:44

hypocritical
with *h*. mockers in feasts. *Ps* 35:16*
him against an *h*. nation. *Isa* 10:6*

hyssop
(*A bushy herb in common use
among the Hebrews. It is not
known whether it was or was not
the shrub now known by the name*)
shall take a bunch of *h*. *Ex* 12:22
take cedar wood, scarlet, and *h*.
Lev 14:4, 6, 49, 51
cleanse the house with the *h*. 52
shall cast *h*. into midst. *Num* 19:6
a clean person shall take *h*. 18
cedar tree even unto the *h*. *1 Ki* 4:33
purge me with *h*. and I. *Ps* 51:7
spunge, and put it on *h*. *John* 19:29
he took blood with *h*. *Heb* 9:19

I

I
behold *I*, even *I*, do bring a flood.
Gen 6:17
I, behold *I*, establish my. 9:9
I shall be destroyed, *I* and. 34:30
shall *I*, thy mother and ? 37:10
and *I*, whither shall *I* go ? 30
in this house greater than *I*. 39:9
who am *I*, that *I* should go to ?
Ex 3:11
Lord is righteous, *I* and my. 9:27
and *I*, behold *I* will harden. 14:17
I thy father in law Jethro am. 18:6
I, behold *I*, have given with. 31:6
I, even *I*, will chastise. *Lev* 26:28
I, behold *I*, have taken the Levites.
Num 3:12; 18:6
nations more than *I*, how can *I*.?
Deut 7:17
I, even *I*, am he, there is no. 32:39
forty years old was *I*. *Josh* 14:7
I, even *I*, will sing to the. *Judg* 5:3
till *I* Deborah arose, that *I* arose. 7
when *I* blow, *I* and all that. 7:18
may bewail my virginity, *I*. 11:37
I and my people were at strife. 12:2
I came to Gibeah, *I* and my. 20:4
more righteous than *I*. *1 Sam* 24:17
I and my kingdom are. *2 Sam* 3:28
I, whither shall *I* cause my ? 13:13
I and my son Solomon be. *1 Ki* 1:21
I, even *I*, only remain a prophet.
18:22; 19:10, 14
who am *I*, and what my people that
we should ? *1 Chr* 29:14; *2 Chr* 2:6
what *I* and fathers have. *2 Chr* 32:13
I, even *I* Artaxerxes. *Ezra* 7:21
but so did not *I*, because. *Neh* 5:15
I also and my maidens. *Esth* 4:16
I only am escaped to tell thee.
Job 1:15, 16, 17, 19
condemneth thee, and not *I*. 15:6
refuse or choose, and not *I*. 34:33
rock that is higher than *I*. *Ps* 61:2
they are stronger than *I*. 142:6
hereunto more than *I*? *Eccl* 2:25
I am the rose of Sharon. *S of S* 2:1
I am my beloved's. 6:3; 7:10
I am a wall. 8:10
I and children. Lord hath given me.
Isa 8:18; *Heb* 2:13
I the Lord, the first; *I* am he.
Isa 41:4; 43:11, 25
I am with thee, for *I*. 41:10; 43:5
I am the first, *I* am the last. 44:6
48:12; *Rev* 1:17
who as *I* shall call, and ? *Isa* 44:7
I, even my hands have. 45:12
even to your old age *I* am he, *I*. 46:4
I am God, and there is none else, *I*. 9
I, even *I* have spoken, *I* have. 48:15
it was, there am *I*. 16; *Mat* 18:20
yet shall *I* be glorious in. *Isa* 49:5
I, even *I* am he. 51:12; 52:6
behold, it is *I*. 52:6
stand by thyself, for *I* am. 65:5
thou art stronger than *I*. *Jer* 20:7
behold *I*, even *I*, will utterly. 23:39
behold *I*, even *I*, am against thee.
Ezek 5:8
behold *I*, even *I*, will bring a. 5:8
behold *I*, even *I*, will search. 34:11
I, even *I*, will judge between fat. 20
I am their inheritance, *I* am. 44:28
when *I*, even *I* Daniel. *Dan* 8:15
I, even *I*, will tear, *I* will. *Hos* 5:14
Haggai spoke, *I* am with. *Hag* 1:13
I was but little displeased. *Zech* 1:15
I accept of your hands ? *Mal* 1:13
after me is mightier than *I*.
Mat 3:11; *Mark* 1:7
it is *I*, be not afraid. *Mat* 14:27
Mark 6:50; *John* 6:20
men say that *I* the Son ? *Mat* 16:13
two or three, there am *I* in. 18:20
in name, saying, *I* am Christ. 24:5
began to say, Lord, is it *I*? 26:22
offended, yet will not *I*. *Mark* 14:29
father and *I* sought thee. *Luke* 2:48
if *I* by Beelzebub cast out. 11:19
if *I* with the finger of God cast. 20

name saying, *I* am Christ. *Luke* 21:8
but *I* am among you as he. 22:27
that it is *I* myself, handle me. 24:39
he confessed, *I* am not the Christ.
John 1:20; 3:28
I knew him not. 33
I that speak am he. 4:26
I am not alone, but *I* and. 8:16
I am from above, *I* am not of. 23
I am he, *I* do nothing of myself. 28
verily, before Abraham was, *I*. 58
I and my Father are one. 10:30
the Father in me, and *I* in him. 38
17:21
and *I*, if *I* be lifted up, will. 12:32
if *I* then your Lord and. 13:14
I in my Father. 14:20
I go unto Father: for my Father is
greater than *I*. 28
abide in me, and *I* in you. 15:4
I in them. 17:23, 26
but *I* have known thee. 25
Pilate answered, am *I* a Jew ? 18:35
what was *I*, that *I* could ? *Acts* 11:17
I obtained this freedom; *I* was. 22:28
no more *I*, that do it. *Rom* 7:17, 20
I am of Paul, *I* of Apollos, *I* of.
1 Cor 1:12; 3:4
and *I*, brethren, when *I* came to. 2:1
and *I*, brethren, could not speak. 3:1
I would that all men even as *I*. 7:7
if they abide even as *I*. 8
yet not *I*, but Lord. 10
or *I* only and Barnabas, have. 9:6
I therefore so run, so fight *I*, not. 26
of me, even as *I* am of Christ. 11:1
I am what *I* am, yet not *I*. 15:10
whether it were *I* or they, so. 11
work of Christ, even as *I*. 16:10
Hebrews ? so am *I*. *2 Cor* 11:22
I am more. 23
I burn not ? 29
dead to the law, that *I*. *Gal* 2:19
I live, yet not *I*, but Christ liveth. 20
brethren, be as *I* am, for *I* am. 4:12
I, brethren, if *I* yet preach. 5:11
I should glory in cross, and *I* to. 6:14
I also, after *I* heard of. *Eph* 1:15
I therefore, prisoner of the Lord. 4:1
be ye holy, for *I* am. *1 Pet* 1:16
I love in the truth, and not *I* only.
2 John 1
I am Alpha and Omega. *Rev* 1:8
as many as *I* love, *I* rebuke. 3:19
as *I* also overcame. 21
I John saw. 21:2; 22:8
see thou do it not, *I* am thy. 22:9
I Jesus have sent my angel to testify
these things, *I* am the root and. 16

Ibhar
David's son *I*. *2 Sam* 5:15
1 Chr 3:6; 14:5

ice
blackish by reason of *ice*. *Job* 6:16
womb came the *ice* and frost. 38:29
forth his *ice* like morsels. *Ps* 147:17

Ichabod
child *I*., glory departed. *1 Sam* 4:21
Ahiah, the son of Ahitub, *I*. 14:3

Iconium
Barnabas came unto *I*. *Acts* 13:51
in *I*. they went both into the. 14:1
thither certain Jews from *I*. 19
of by the brethren at *I*. 16:2
which came to me at *I*. *2 Tim* 3:11

Iddo
Abinadab son of *I*. had. *1 Ki* 4:14
Joash his son, *I*. his. *1 Chr* 6:21
half tribe of Manasseh *I*. 27:21
acts of Solomon written in visions of
I. the. *2 Chr* 9:29; 12:15; 13:22
Zechariah son of *I*. prophesied.
Ezra 5:1; *Zech* 1:1, 7
prophesying of Zechariah son of *I*.
Ezra 6:14
I. the chief, and told them what they
should say to *I*. and his. 8:17
I. with priests went up. *Neh* 12:4

idle
[1] *One who is slothful or lazy,*
Ex 5:8, 17. [2] *One that would*

work, *but is not hired.* Mat 20:3, 6.
[3] *Unprofitable.* Mat 12:36.

they be *i.*; therefore they cry. *Ex* 5:8
are *i.* ye are *i.*: ye say, Let us go. 17
and *i.* soul shall suffer. *Pr* 19:15
every *i.* word that men. *Mat* 12:36
standing *i.* in marketplace. 20:3, 6
words seemed *i.* tales. *Luke* 24:11
they learn to be *i.* and not only *i.*
1 *Tim* 5:13

idleness
eateth not the bread of *i.* *Pr* 31:27
i. the house droppeth. *Eccl* 10:18
and abundance of *i.* *Ezek* 16:49*

idol
woe to the *i.* shepherd. *Zech* 11:17

idol
she made an *i.* in grove. *1 Ki* 15:13
2 *Chr* 15:16
he set the *i.* in house of. *2 Chr* 33:7
he took the *i.* out of the house. 15
say my *i.* hath done them. *Isa* 48:5
incense as if he blessed an *i.* 66:3
a despised broken *i.* *Jer* 22:28*
offered sacrifice to the *i.* *Acts* 7:41
we know an *i.* is nothing in world.
1 *Cor* 8:4; 10:19
some with conscience of the *i.* 8:7

idolater
a brother be an *i.* not to. *1 Cor* 5:11
an *i.* hath any inheritance. *Eph* 5:5

idolaters
with the covetous or *i.* *1 Cor* 5:10
i. shall not inherit the kingdom. 6:9
neither be ye *i.* as were some. 10:7
but *i.* shall have their part. *Rev* 21:8
without are murderers and *i.* 22:15

idolatries
walked in abominable *i.* *1 Pet* 4:3

idolatrous
Josiah put down the *i.* *2 Ki* 23:5

idolatry
is as iniquity and *i.* *1 Sam* 15:23*
city wholly given to *i.* *Acts* 17:16*
beloved, flee from *i.* *1 Cor* 10:14
works of the flesh are *i.* *Gal* 5:20
covetousness, which is *i.* *Col* 3:5

idols
turn ye not unto *i.* *Lev* 19:4
shall make no *i.* 26:1
carcases upon carcases of your *i.* 30
their *i.* wood and stone. *Deut* 29:17
in the house of their *i.* *1 Sam* 31:9
Asa removed the *i.* his. *1 Ki* 15:12
abominable in following *i.* 21:26
for they served *i.* *2 Ki* 17:12
2 *Chr* 24:18
Judah to sin with his *i.* *2 Ki* 21:11
Amon served the *i.* that his. 21
the *i.* that were spied in the. 23:24
carry tidings to their *i.* *1 Chr* 10:9
gods of the people are *i.* 16:26
Asa put away abominable *i.* out.
2 *Chr* 15:8
Josiah cut down all the *i.* in. 34:7*
gods of the nations are *i.* *Ps* 96:5
that boast themselves of *i.* 97:7
they served their *i.* that. 106:36
whom they sacrificed to the *i.* of. 38
their *i.* are silver. 115:4; 135:15
their land is full of *i.* *Isa* 2:8
the *i.* he shall utterly abolish. 20
cast away his *i.* of silver. 20; 31:7
hath found kingdoms of *i.* 10:10
i., so do to Jerusalem and her *i.*? 11
i. of Egypt shall be moved at. 19:1
they shall seek to the *i.* and to. 3
the makers of *i.* shall go to. 45:16
their *i.* were on the beasts. 46:1
inflaming yourselves with *i.* 57:5
her *i.* are confounded. *Jer* 50:2*
and they are mad upon their *i.* 38
I will cast down your slain men
before your *i.* *Ezek* 6:4, 5, 13
laid waste, your *i.* may be broken. 6
go a whoring after their *i.* 9
offer sweet savour to all their *i.* 13
the *i.* of Israel portrayed. 8:10
up their *i.* in their heart. 14:3, 4, 7
estranged from me through their *i.* 5
repent, and turn from your *i.* 6

i. of thy abominations. *Ezek* 16:36
eyes to the *i.* of Israel. 18:6, 15
hath lifted up his eyes to the *i.* 12
yourselves with *i.* of Egypt. 20:7, 18
nor did they forsake the *i.* of. 8
for their heart went after *i.* 16
their eyes went after father's *i.* 24
pollute yourselves with all your *i.*
20:31; 22:4; 23:7, 30, 37
my holy name no more with *i.* 20:39
city maketh *i.* against herself. 22:3
slain their children to their *i.* 23:39
ye shall bear the sins of your *i.* 49
I will destroy *i.* and will. 30:13
up your eyes towards your *i.* 33:25
i. wherewith they polluted it. 36:18
from *i.* will I cleanse you. 25; 37:23
astray from me after their *i.* 44:10
ministered to them before their *i.* 12
Ephraim is joined to *i.* *Hos* 4:17
gold have they made them *i.* 8:4
have made *i.* according to. 13:2
I to do any more with *i.* 14:8
i. thereof will I lay. *Mi* 1:7
therein to make dumb *i.* *Hab* 2:18
I have spoken vanity. *Zech* 10:2*
I will cut off names of the *i.* 13:2
from pollutions of *i.* *Acts* 15:20
from meats offered to *i.* 29; 21:25
thou that abhorrest *i.* *Rom* 2:22
things offered to *i.* *1 Cor* 8:1, 4, 10
10:19, 28; *Rev* 2:14, 20
carried away to dumb *i.* *1 Cor* 12:2
temple of God with *i.*? *2 Cor* 6:16
ye turned to God from *i.* *1 Thes* 1:9
keep yourselves from *i.* *1 John* 5:21
not worship devils and *i.* *Rev* 9:20

Idumea
shall come down on *I.* *Isa* 34:5, 6
I. shall be desolate. *Ezek* 35:15
have I spoken against all *I.* 36:5
followed him from *I.* *Mark* 3:8

if
she said, *if* it be so ? *Gen* 25:22
if he said thus. 31:8
if ye will be as we be. 34:15
if it must be so now, take of. 43:11
if so be the Lord will. *Josh* 14:12
if they say to us, Tarry. *1 Sam* 14:9
if we say thus, it is well. 20:7
2 *Sam* 15:26
if we say, *if* we sit still here; *if* they
save us, *if* they kill us. *2 Ki* 7:4
if ye be mine, *if* ye will. 10:6
if I be wicked. *Job* 9:29; 10:15
if it be not so. 24:25
if I have done this, *if* there. *Ps* 7:3
if they be prophets, *if.* *Jer* 27:18
take balm for her pain, *if* so. 51:8
if it be so, our God is. *Dan* 3:17
if it may be a lengthening. 4:27
if so be it yield, strangers. *Hos* 8:7
if thou be the Son of God. *Mat* 4:3
27:40; *Luke* 4:3
if it be thou, bid me come. *Mat* 14:28
let him deliver him, *if* he. 27:43
if thou wilt, thou canst. *Mark* 1:40
if we shall say, Of men. 11:32
if he be Christ. *Luke* 23:35, 39
John 10:24
if thou be not Elias. *John* 1:25
if the world hate you. 15:18
1 *John* 3:13
if thou let this man go. *John* 19:12
if it be of God ye cannot. *Acts* 5:39
if in this life only we. *1 Cor* 15:19
if a son, then an heir of. *Gal* 4:7
if any consolation, *if* any. *Phil* 2:1
if they shall enter. *Heb* 4:3, 5
if they had been of us. *1 John* 2:19

if not
if not I will know. *Gen* 18:21
if not tell me. 24:49
if not, blot me, I pray. *Ex* 32:32
if not, let fire come out. *Judg* 9:15, 20
and *if not*, I will take. *1 Sam* 2:16
if not, then we shall know it is. 6:9
if not, I pray thee. *2 Sam* 13:26
after his saying? *if not* speak. 17:6
but *if not*, it shall not. *2 Ki* 2:10
if not, where, and who ? *Job* 9:24
if not, hearken unto me, hold. 33:33
if not, be it known to. *Dan* 3:18

give me my price; *if not.* *Zech* 11:12
but *if not*, it shall turn. *Luke* 10:6
if not, after that thou shalt. 13:9

if now
if now I have found favour. *Gen* 18:3
O God, *if now* thou do. 24:42
if now ye will deal kindly with. 49
if now I have found grace in thy.
33:10; 47:29; *Ex* 34:9; *Judg* 6:17
if now thou didst receive it.
1 *Cor* 4:7

ignominy
and with *i.* reproach. *Pr* 18:3

ignorance
if a soul shall sin through *i.* *Lev* 4:2*
5:15; *Num* 15:24*, 27*, 28*, 29*
of Israel sin through *i.* *Lev* 4:13*
hath done somewhat through *i.* 22*
common people sin through *i.* 27*
forgiven them, for it is *i.* *Num* 15:25*
I wot that through *i.* ye. *Acts* 3:17
and the times of this *i.* God. 17:30
alienated through the *i.* *Eph* 4:18
to former lusts in your *i.* *1 Pet* 1:14
ye may put to silence *i.* of. 2:15

ignorant
foolish was I, and *i.*; I was. *Ps* 73:22
they are all *i.* they are. *Isa* 56:10*
though Abraham be *i.* of us. 63:16
that they were *i.* men. *Acts* 4:13
I would not have you *i.* brethren.
Rom 1:13; *1 Cor* 10:1; 12:1
2 *Cor* 1:8; *1 Thes* 4:13
i. of God's righteousness. *Rom* 10:3
should be *i.* of this mystery. 11:25
man be *i.* let him be *i.* *1 Cor* 14:38
not *i.* of Satan's devices. *2 Cor* 2:11
have compassion on the *i.* *Heb* 5:2
they are willingly *i.* of. *2 Pet* 3:5*
but, beloved, be not *i.* of this one. 8

ignorantly
soul that sinneth *i.* *Num* 15:28*
killeth his neighbour *i.* *Deut* 19:4*
ye *i.* worship, declare I. *Acts* 17:23
because I did it *i.* in. *1 Tim* 1:13

ill
kine came up *i.* favoured. *Gen* 41:3
4, 19, 20, 21
why dealt ye so *i.* with me ? 43:6
hath any *i.* blemish. *Deut* 15:21
it shall go *i.* with him. *Job* 20:26*
it went *i.* with Moses. *Ps* 106:32
the wicked, it shall be *i.* *Isa* 3:11
if it seem *i.* to thee to. *Jer* 40:4
his stink and his *i.* *Joel* 2:20
behaved themselves *i.* *Mi* 3:4*
love worketh no *i.* to. *Rom* 13:10

illuminated
ye were *i.* ye endured. *Heb* 10:32*

Illyricum
round about unto *I.* *Rom* 15:19

image
make man in our *i.* *Gen* 1:26, 27
9:6
a son in his own *i.* after his *i.* 5:3
nor rear up a standing *i.* *Lev* 26:1*
Deut 16:22*
Michal took an *i.* and. *1 Sam* 19:13*
behold there was an *i.* in bed. 16*
put away the *i.* of Baal. *2 Ki* 3:2*
they brake down the *i.* and. 10:27*
Manasseh set carved *i.* *2 Chr* 33:7
an *i.* was before mine. *Job* 4:16*
shalt despise their *i.* *Ps* 73:20
seat of the *i.* of jealousy. *Ezek* 8:3, 5
behold, a great *i.* stood. *Dan* 2:31
stone that smote *i.* became a. 35
the king made an *i.* of gold. 3:1
worship the golden *i.* 5, 10, 15
many days without an *i.* *Hos* 3:4*
whose is this *i.*? *Mat* 22:20
Mark 12:16; *Luke* 20:24
of the *i.* which fell down. *Acts* 19:35
glory of God into an *i.* *Rom* 1:23
to be conformed to the *i.* 8:29
bowed the knee to *i.* of Baal. 11:4
is the *i.* and glory of God. *1 Cor* 11:7
as we have borne the *i.* 15:49
changed into same *i.* *2 Cor* 3:18

the i. of God. 2 Cor 4:4; Col 1:15
after the i. of him that. Col 3:10
by his Son, the express i. Heb 1:3
a shadow, not the very i. of. 10:1
they should make an i. Rev 13:14
had power to give life unto the i. 15
man worship beast and his i. 14:9
rest, who worship beast and his i. 11
victory over beast and his i. 15:2
fell on them that worshipped i. 16:2
them that worshipped his i. 19:20
not worshipped beast nor his i. 20:4
see graven

molten image
made them a molten i. Deut 9:12
son to make a molten i. Judg 17:3
and worshipped molten i. Ps 106:19
for his molten i. is falsehood.
Jer 10:14; 51:17
graven and molten i. Hab 2:18

imagery
in the chambers of his i. Ezek 8:12

images
Rachel had stolen her father's i.
Gen 31:19* 34*
searched but found not the i. 35*
quite break down their i. Ex 23:24*
34:13*; Deut 7:5*; Num 33:52
I will cut down your i. Lev 26:30
make i. of your emerods. 1 Sam 6:5
they laid the i. of their emerods. 11
they left their i., David. 2 Sam 5:21
hast made molten i. to. 1 Ki 14:9
built them high places, i. and. 23*
i. out of house of Baal. 2 Ki 10:26
his i. brake they in pieces. 11:18
18:4*; 23:14*
set up i. 17:10*
they made molten i. 16
Josiah put away i. that were. 23:24*
broke down the i. 2 Chr 14:3, 5
Jehoiada brake i. 23:17
Hezekiah brake i. 31:1*
Ahaz made also molten i. 28:2
sacrificed to all the carved i. 33:22
down carved and molten i. 34:3, 4
not look to groves or i. Isa 17:8
the groves and i. shall not. 27:9
the ornament of molten i. 30:22
their molten i. are wind and. 41:29
he shall break the i. Jer 43:13*
idols confounded, her i. are. 50:2
altars desolate, and your i. Ezek 6:4
idols broken, and that your i. may. 6
but they made the i. of their. 7:20
madest to thyself i. of men. 16:17
of Babylon consulted with i. 21:21
the i. of the Chaldeans. 23:14
cause their i. to cease out of. 30:13
they have made goodly i. Hos 10:1*
their altars, spoil their i. 2*
have made their molten i. of. 13:2
the tabernacle of your i. Amos 5:26
graven and standing i. Mi 5:13*

image work
he made two cherubims of i. work.
2 Chr 3:10

imagination
(An old meaning of the word is a plotting or a devising of evil. Another, which is much used in the Bible, is stubbornness)
every i. of his heart was. Gen 6:5
the i. of man's heart is evil. 8:21
though I walk in the i. Deut 29:19*
for I know their i. 31:21
1 Chr 28:9
this for ever in the i. 1 Chr 29:18
the i. of his own heart. Jer 23:17*
scattered the proud in i. Luke 1:51

imaginations
Lord understandeth all i. 1 Chr 28:9
heart that deviseth wicked i. Pr 6:18
hast seen all their i. Lam 3:60*
thou hast heard all their i. 61*
became vain in their i. Rom 1:21*
casting down i. that. 2 Cor 10:5
see heart

imagine
do ye i. to reprove words? Job 6:26
the devices ye wrongfully i. 21:27

why do the people i. a? Ps 2:1
they seek my hurt and i. 38:12
how long will ye i. mischief? 62:3*
i. mischief in their heart. 140:2†
heart of them that i. evil. Pr 12:20*
yet do they i. mischief. Hos 7:15†
what do ye i. against? Nah 1:9†
let none i. evil against neighbour.
Zech 7:10†; 8:17†
why do the people i.? Acts 4:25

imagined
which they have i. Gen 11:6*
in devices they have i. Ps 10:2†
they i. mischievous device. 21:11†

imagineth
there is one that i. evil. Nah 1:11†
Imlah, see Micaiah; Immanuel, see Emmanuel

immediately
they i. left the ship and. Mat 4:22
i. his leprosy was cleansed. 8:3
Mark 1:42; Luke 5:13
i. received sight. Mat 20:34
Mark 10:52; Luke 18:43
i. the cock crew. Mat 26:74
Luke 22:60; John 18:27
i. the Spirit driveth him. Mark 1:12
he lifted her up, and i. the. 31
Satan cometh i. and taketh. 4:15
when affliction ariseth, i. they. 17
mouth was opened i. Luke 1:64
i. it fell. 6:49
i. her issue of blood staunched. 8:44
i. she was made straight. 13:13
kingdom of God should i. 19:11
and i. the man was made. John 5:9
Aeneas arose i. Acts 9:34
I sent i. to thee. 10:33
i. the angel of the Lord smote. 12:23
i. I conferred not with. Gal 1:16
and i. I was in the Spirit. Rev 4:2

immortal
King eternal, i., invisible. 1 Tim 1:17*

immortality
to them who seek for i. Rom 2:7*
mortal must put on i. 1 Cor 15:53
this mortal shall have put on i. 54
only hath i. dwelling. 1 Tim 6:16
who brought i. to light. 2 Tim 1:10*

immutability
the i. of his counsel. Heb 6:17

immutable
that by two i. things, in. Heb 6:18

impart
two coats, let him i. to. Luke 3:11
that I may i. to you some. Rom 1:11

imparted
nor hath he i. to her. Job 39:17
were willing to have i. 1 Thes 2:8

impediment
bring one that had i. in. Mark 7:32

impenitent
thou, after thy i. heart. Rom 2:5

imperious
work of an i. whorish. Ezek 16:30

implacable
without natural affection, i. Rom 1:31

implead
law is open, let them i. Acts 19:38*

importunity
of his i. he will rise and. Luke 11:8

impose
it shall not be lawful to i. Ezra 7:24

imposed
in carnal ordinances i. on. Heb 9:10

impossible
and nothing shall be i. Mat 17:20
with men this is i.; but. 19:26
Mark 10:27; Luke 18:27
for with God nothing shall be i.
Luke 1:37*; 18:27
it is i. that offences will. 17:1
it is i. for those who were. Heb 6:4*
it was i. for God to lie. 18
without faith it is i. to please. 11:6

impotent
a great multitude of i. John 5:3*
deed done to the i. man. Acts 4:9
there sat a man at Lystra i. in. 14:8

impoverish
shall i. thy fenced cities. Jer 5:17*

impoverished
Israel was greatly i. Judg 6:6*
he that is so i. chooseth. Isa 40:20
Edom saith, We are i. but. Mal 1:4*

imprisoned
they know that I i. Acts 22:19

imprisonment
death, banishment, or i. Ezra 7:26
of mockings, bonds, i. Heb 11:36

imprisonments
in stripes, in i., in tumults. 2 Cor 6:5

impudent
and with an i. face she. Pr 7:13
for they are i. children. Ezek 2:4
the house of Israel are i. 3:7*

impute
[1] To charge or credit another with, 2 Sam 19:19. [2] To ascribe vicariously, Rom 4:11. The Revisions frequently substitute reckon.
let not the king i. any. 1 Sam 22:15
let not my lord i. 2 Sam 19:19
the Lord will not i. sin. Rom 4:8

imputed
nor shall it be i. to him. Lev 7:18
blood shall be i. to that man. 17:4
righteousness might be i. Rom 4:11
i. to him for righteousness. 22, 23
Jas 2:23
shall be i. if we believe. Rom 4:24
but sin is not i. when there. 5:13

imputeth
blessed, to whom Lord i. not. Ps 32:2
God i. righteousness. Rom 4:6

imputing
pass over, i. his power. Hab 1:11*
Christ, not i. their trespasses unto.
2 Cor 5:19

in
and the Lord shut him in. Gen 7:16
I am in Father. John 14:10, 11, 20

inasmuch
i. as he hated him not. Deut 19:6
i. as thou followedst not. Ruth 3:10
i. as have done it to one. Mat 25:40
i. as ye did it not to one of the. 45
i. as both in bonds. Phil 1:7
i. as he who builded. Heb 3:3
i. as ye are partakers of. 1 Pet 4:13

incense
A rich perfume used in sacrifices, Ex 37:29.
shall burn a perpetual i. Ex 30:8
ye shall offer no strange i. thereon. 9
he made the pure i. of sweet. 37:29
set the altar of gold for i. 40:5
his censer, and put i. Lev 10:1
he shall put i. on the fire. 16:13
ten shekels full of i. Num 7:14, 86
put i. in them before Lord. 16:7, 17
the 250 men that offered i. 35
Moses said to Aaron, put on i. 46
on i. and made an atonement. 47
shall put i. before thee. Deut 33:10
the altars of i. took. 2 Chr 30:14
forsaken me, and burned i. 34:25
I will offer to thee the i. Ps 66:15
be set forth before thee as i. 141:2
i. is an abomination to me. Isa 1:13
not wearied thee with i. 43:23*
bring gold and i. and shew. 60:6*
sacrificeth and burneth i. on. 65:3
burneth i. as if he blessed. 66:3*
cometh there to me i.? Jer 6:20*
the gods to whom they offer i. 11:12
provoke me to anger, in offering i. 16
offerings and i. in their. 41:5*
and him that burneth i. to. 48:35
and a thick cloud of i. Ezek 8:11
thou hast set mine oil and i. 16:18
thou hast set mine i. and oil. 23:41
i. shall be offered to my. Mal 1:11
praying at time of i. Luke 1:10

given to him much *i.* to.   *Rev* 8:3
the smoke of thy *i.* ascended up.   4
  see **altar, burn, burnt**

sweet incense
spices for *sweet i.*   *Ex* 25:6
   35:8, 28; *Num* 4:16
to make oil and sweet *i.*   *Ex* 31:11
brought the oil and *sweet i.*   39:38
a censer, hands full of *sweet i.*
   Lev 16:12

incensed
are *i.* against thee be ashamed.
   Isa 41:11
all that are *i.* against him.   45:24

incline
i. your heart to Lord.   *Josh* 24:23
he may *i.* our hearts.   *1 Ki* 8:58
i. your ears to the words.   *Ps* 78:1
i. my heart unto thy testimonies.
   119:36
i. not my heart to any thing.   141:4
  see **ear**

inclined
i. to follow Abimelech.   *Judg* 9:3
Lord *i.* unto me, and heard my cry.
   Ps 40:1; 116:2
I have *i.* mine heart to.   119:112
nor *i.* mine ear to them.   *Pr* 5:13
nor *i.* ear. *Jer* 7:24, 26; 11:8; 17:23
   34:14
but ye have not *i.* your ear.   25:4
   35:15; 44:5

inclineth
her house *i.* to death.   *Pr* 2:18

inclose
we will *i.* her with cedar. *S of S* 8:9

inclosed
onyx stones *i.* in ouches. *Ex* 39:6, 13
Israel *i.* the Benjamites. *Judg* 20:43
they are *i.* in their own fat. *Ps* 17:10
of the wicked have *i.* me.   22:16
a garden *i.* is my sister. *S of S* 4:12*
he hath *i.* my ways with. *Lam* 3:9*
i. great multitude of fishes. *Luke* 5:6

inclosings
stones shall be set in gold in *i.*
   Ex 28:20*; 39:13*

incontinency
tempt you not for your *i.* *1 Cor* 7:5

incontinent
natural affection, *i.*   *1 Tim* 3:3*

incorruptible
the glory of the *i.* God. *Rom* 1:23
to obtain an *i.* crown. *1 Cor* 9:25
the dead shall be raised *i.* 15:52
us to an inheritance, *i.*   *1 Pet* 1:4
being born of *i.* seed, by the. 23

incorruption
it is raised in *i.*   *1 Cor* 15:42
neither doth corruption inherit *i.* 50
this corruptible must put on *i.* 53
corruptible shall have put on *i.* 54

increase, *substantive*
yield you the *i.* thereof. *Lev* 19:25
for thy cattle shall all the *i.* 25:7
take thou no usury of him or *i.* 36
usury, lend him victuals for *i.* 37
the land shall yield her *i.* 26:4
land shall not yield her *i.* or. 20
i. of the threshingfloor. *Num* 18:30
risen up in father's stead an *i.* 32:14
I will also bless the *i.* of thy kine.
   Deut 7:13; 28:4
shalt truly tithe all the *i.*   14:22
shall bring forth all tithe of the *i.* 28
shall bless thee in all thy *i.* 16:15
be the *i.* of thy kine.   28:18, 51
i. of thy house shall die. *1 Sam* 2:33
it yieldeth much *i.* to. *Neh* 9:37
i. of his house shall. *Job* 20:28
would root out all mine *i.* 31:12
earth shall yield her *i.* *Ps* 67:6
he gave also their *i.* to the. 78:46
and our land shall yield her *i.* 85:12
much *i.* is by the strength. *Pr* 14:4
and with the *i.* of his lips he. 18:20
not be satisfied with *i.* *Eccl* 5:10
of the *i.* of his government. *Isa* 9:7
firstfruits of his *i.* was. *Jer* 2:3
nor hath taken any *i.* *Ezek* 18:8, 17
upon usury, and taken *i.* 18:13; 22:12

---

earth shall yield her *i.* *Ezek* 34:27
ground shall give her *i.* *Zech* 8:12
but God gave the *i.* *1 Cor* 3:6, 7
maketh *i.* of the body to. *Eph.* 4:16
increaseth with *i.* of God. *Col* 2:19

increase, *verb*
by years thou shalt *i.* *Lev* 25:16
O Israel, that ye may *i.* *Deut* 6:3
lest beasts of the field *i.* on. 7:22
i. thy army, and come. *Judg* 9:29
he would *i.* Israel like. *1 Chr* 27:23
strange wives to *i.* *Ezra* 10:10
latter end should greatly *i.* *Job* 8:7
dost not *i.* thy wealth by. *Ps* 44:12
if riches *i.* set not your heart. 62:10
thou shalt *i.* my greatness. 71:21
in the world, they *i.* in riches. 73:12
the Lord shall *i.* you more. 115:14
a wise man will *i.* *Pr* 1:5; 9:9
that oppresseth poor to *i.* 22:16
they perish, the righteous *i.* 28:28
goods *i.* they are increased that.
   Eccl 5:11
there be many things that *i.* 6:11
meek shall *i.* their joy. *Isa* 29:19
and didst *i.* thy perfumes. 57:9
I will *i.* the famine on. *Ezek* 5:16
will *i.* it, and lay no famine. 36:29
I will *i.* them with men like a. 37
he shall *i.* with glory. *Dan* 11:39
commit whoredom, and shall not *i.*
   Hos 4:10
they shall *i.* as they have. *Zech* 10:8
unto Lord, *I.* our faith. *Luke* 17:5
he must *i.*, but I must. *John* 3:30
and *i.* the fruits of your. *2 Cor* 9:10
make you to *i.* in love. *1 Thes* 3:12
we beseech you, that ye *i.* 4:10*
they will *i.* to more. *2 Tim* 2:16*

increased
the waters *i.* and bare. *Gen* 7:17, 18
thou hadst, and it is now *i.* 30:30
Jacob *i.*   43
Israel *i.* abundantly. *Ex* 1:7
till thou be *i.* and inherit. 23:30
the host went on and *i.* *1 Sam* 14:19
people *i.* with Absalom. *2 Sam* 15:12
the battle *i.* that day. *1 Ki* 22:35
   2 Chr 18:34
house of their fathers *i.* *1 Chr* 4:38
for our iniquities are *i.* *Ezra* 9:6
are they *i.* that trouble me. *Ps* 3:1
that their corn and wine *i.* 4:7
glory of his house is *i.* 49:16
and he *i.* his people greatly. 105:24
years of thy life shall be *i.* *Pr* 9:11
I *i.* more than all before. *Eccl* 2:9
goods increase, they are *i.* that. 5:11
nation, and not *i.* the joy. *Isa* 9:3
thou hast *i.* the nation. 26:15
their backslidings are *i.* *Jer* 5:6
widows are *i.* above the sand. 15:8
take wives, that ye may be *i.* 29:6
because thy sins were *i.* 30:14, 15
i. in daughter of Judah. *Lam* 2:5*
and hast *i.* thy whoredoms.
   Ezek 16:26*; 23:14
wisdom hast thou *i.* thy riches. 28:5
and knowledge shall be *i.* *Dan* 12:4
were *i.* so they sinned. *Hos* 4:7*
according to fruit, he hath *i.* 10:1*
increase, as they have *i.* *Zech* 10:8
fruit, that sprang up and *i.* *Mark* 4:8
Jesus *i.* in wisdom and. *Luke* 2:52*
and the word of God *i.* *Acts* 6:7
Saul *i.* the more in strength. 9:22
churches *i.* in number daily. 16:5
when your faith is *i.* *2 Cor* 10:15*
rich, and *i.* with goods. *Rev* 3:17*

increasest
i. thine indignation upon. *Job* 10:17

increaseth
my affliction *i.* *Job* 10:16*
he *i.* the nations. 12:23
the tumult of those *i.* *Ps* 74:23*
scattereth, and yet *i.* *Pr* 11:24
she *i.* the transgressors. 23:28
man of knowledge *i.* strength. 24:5
he that by unjust gain *i.* his. 28:8*
multiplied, transgression *i.* 29:16
i. knowledge, *i.* sorrow. *Eccl* 1:18
no might, he *i.* strength. *Isa* 40:29

---

he daily *i.* lies and. *Hos* 12:1*
woe to him that *i.* that. *Hab* 2:6
body *i.* with the increase. *Col* 2:19

increasing
i. in the knowledge of God. *Col* 1:10

incredible
thought *i.* God should ? *Acts* 26:8

incurable
him with an *i.* disease. *2 Chr* 21:18
my wound is *i.* without. *Job* 34:6
why is my wound *i.*? *Jer* 15:18
thy bruise is *i.*   30:12
thy sorrow is *i.*   15
for her wound is *i.*; for it is. *Mi* 1:9

indebted
every one that is *i.* to us. *Luke* 11:4

indeed
wife shall bear a son *i.* *Gen* 17:19
yet *i.* she is my sister. 20:12
i. reign over us, shalt thou *i.*? 37:8
mother and brethren *i.* come. 10
for *i.* I was stolen away out. 40:15
if you will obey my voice *i.*
   Ex 19:5; 23:22
ye should *i.* have eaten it. *Lev* 10:18
hath the Lord *i.* spoken ? *Num* 12:2
if thou wilt *i.* deliver this. 21:2
am I not able *i.* to promote ? 22:37
i. the hand of the Lord. *Deut* 2:15
son of the hated, which is *i.* 21:16
i. I have sinned against. *Josh* 7:20
if thou wilt *i.* look on. *1 Sam* 1:11
but will God *i.* dwell on the earth ?
   1 Ki 8:27, *2 Chr* 6:18
thou hast *i.* smitten. *2 Ki* 14:10
wouldest bless me *i.* *1 Chr* 4:10
have sinned and done evil *i.* 21:17
i. that I have erred. *Job* 19:4
i. speak righteousness. *Ps* 58:1
hear ye *i.*, see ye *i.* but. *Isa* 6:9
for if ye do this thing *i.* *Jer* 22:4
I *i.* baptize. *Mat* 3:11; *Mark* 1:8
   Luke 3:16
that he was a prophet *i.* *Mark* 11:32
we *i.* justly. *Luke* 23:41
the Lord is risen *i.* 24:34
behold an Israelite *i.* *John* 1:47
that this is *i.* the Christ. 4:42
meat *i.*, my blood is drink *i.* 6:55
the rulers know *i.* that this is ? 7:26
then are ye my disciples *i.* 8:31
make you free, ye shall be free *i.* 36
that *i.* a notable miracle. *Acts* 4:16
law, neither *i.* can be. *Rom* 8:7
all things *i.* are pure, but *i.* 14:20
and *i.* bear with me. *2 Cor* 11:1
some *i.* preach Christ. *Phil* 1:15
you to me *i.* is not grievous. 3:1
i. have a shew of wisdom. *Col* 2:23
i. ye do it towards all. *1 Thes* 4:10
honour widows that are widows *i.*
   1 Tim 5:3
she that is a widow *i.* 5, 16
disallowed *i.* of men. *1 Pet* 2:4

indignation
great *i.* against Israel. *2 Ki* 3:27
Sanballat took great *i.* *Neh* 4:1
Haman was full of *i.* *Esth* 5:9
there increasest thine *i.* *Job* 10:17
pour out thy *i.* on them. *Ps* 69:24
he cast upon them wrath, *i.* 78:49
thine *i.* and thy wrath. 102:10
in their hand is mine *i.* *Isa* 10:5
for yet a little while, and the *i.* 25
even the Lord, and the weapons of
   his *i.* 13:5, *Jer* 50:25
hide thyself till the *i.* be. *Isa* 26:20
full of *i.* his tongue as fire. 30:27
with the *i.* of his anger. 30
for the *i.* of the Lord is on. 34:2
i. shall be known towards. 66:14
not be able to abide his *i.* *Jer* 10:10
for thou hast filled me with *i.* 15:17
despised in *i.* of his anger. *Lam* 2:6
I will pour out mine *i.* *Ezek* 21:31
not rained on in day of his *i.* 22:24
therefore I poured out mine *i.* 31
i. against holy covenant. *Dan* 11:30
will bear the *i.* of the Lord. *Mi* 7:9
who can stand before his *i.*? *Nah* 1:6
march through land in *i.* *Hab* 3:12
i. these seventy years. *Zech* 1:12

whom the Lord hath *i.*   *Mal* 1:4
they were moved with *i.*   *Mat* 20:24
they had *i.* saying, To what ?   26:8
ruler of synagogue answered with *i.*
             Luke 13:14
they were filled with *i.*   *Acts* 5:17*
obey unrighteousness, *i.*   *Rom* 2:8
what *i.*, yea, what fear ! *2 Cor* 7:11
looking for of fiery *i.*   *Heb* 10:27
into the cup of his *i.*   *Rev* 14:10

inditing
my heart is *i.* a good.   *Ps* 45:1*

industrious
man that he was *i.*   *1 Ki* 11:28

inexcusable
therefore thou art *i.* O.   *Rom* 2:1*

infallible
himself by many *i.* proofs. *Acts* 1:3

infamous
mock thee which art *i.*   *Ezek* 22:5

infamy
thine *i.* turn not away.   *Pr* 25:10
an *i.* of the people.   *Ezek* 36:3*

infant
slay man, woman, *i.*   *1 Sam* 15:3
no more thence an *i.* of. *Isa* 65:20

infants
as *i.* which never saw light. *Job* 3:16
i. shall be dashed in.   *Hos* 13:16
brought also *i.* to him. *Luke* 18:15

inferior
I am not *i.* to you.   *Job* 12:3; 13:2
another kingdom *i.* to thee. *Dan* 2:39
ye *i.* to other churches ? *2 Cor* 12:13

infidel
believeth with an *i.?*   *2 Cor* 6:15*
and is worse than an *i.*   *1 Tim* 5:8*

infinite
not thine iniquities *i.?*   *Job* 22:5*
his understanding is *i.*   *Ps* 147:5
her strength, and it was *i.* *Nah* 3:9

infirmities
himself took our *i.* and.   *Mat* 8:17
healed by him of their *i.* *Luke* 5:15
cured many of their *i.*   7:21; 8:2
Spirit also helpeth our *i.* *Rom* 8:26
strong ought to bear the *i.* of.   15:1
which concern mine *i.* *2 Cor* 11:30
I glory not, but in mine *i.*   12:5*, 9
I take pleasure in mine *i.*   10
wine for thine often *i.*   *1 Tim* 5:23
with the feeling of our *i.* *Heb* 4:15

infirmity
(*Disease or disability, ordinarily applied to the body, but in the Bible used frequently for mental or moral weakness*)
separation for her *i.*   *Lev* 12:2
this is mine *i.* but I will. *Ps* 77:10
a man will sustain his *i.* *Pr* 18:14
which had a spirit of *i.* *Luke* 13:11
thou art loosed from thine *i.*   12
an *i.* thirty-eight years. *John* 5:5
of the *i.* of your flesh. *Rom* 6:19
ye know how through *i.* I. *Gal* 4:13
also is compassed with *i.* *Heb* 5:2
high priests which have *i.*   7:28

inflame
continue till wine *i.* them. *Isa* 5:11

inflaming
i. yourselves with idols. *Isa* 57:5

inflammation
an *i.* of the burning.   *Lev* 13:28*
smite thee with an *i.* *Deut* 28:22

inflicted
punishment which was *i.* *2 Cor* 2:6

influences
canst thou bind the *i.?* *Job* 38:31*

infolding
a fire *i.* itself, and a.   *Ezek* 1:4

inform
to all that they *i.* thee. *Deut* 17:10*

informed
i. me, and talked with. *Deut* 9:22*
are *i.* of thee that thou teachest.
           Acts 21:21, 24
i. the governor.   24:1; 25:2, 15

ingathering
feast of the *i.* in the end. *Ex* 23:16

ingrafted
with meekness the *i.* word. *Jas* 1:21

inhabit
land which ye shall *i.*   *Num* 35:34
the wicked shall not *i.* *Pr* 10:30
villages that Kedar doth *i. Isa* 42:11
shall build houses and *i.*   65:21
shall not build, and another *i.*   22
shall *i.* the parched.   *Jer* 17:6
thou daughter, that dost *i.*   48:18
i. those wastes of Israel. *Ezek* 33:24
waste cities and *i.* them. *Amos* 9:14
houses, but not *i.* them. *Zeph* 1:13

inhabitant
great and fair without *i.*   *Isa* 5:9
cities be wasted without *i.*   6:11
Ephraim and the *i.* of Samaria. 9:9
cry out and shout, thou *i.* of.   12:6
the *i.* of this isle shall say in.   20:6
snare, are upon thee, O *i.* of. 24:17
i. shall not say, I am sick.   33:24
cities are burned without *i. Jer* 2:15
cities shall be laid waste without an *i.*
     4:7; 9:11; 26:9; 33:10; 34:22
gather thy wares, O *i.* of the. 10:17*
i. of the valley.   21:13
i. of Lebanon.   22:23
is a curse, without an *i.*   44:22
desolate, without *i.* 46:19; 51:29, 37
O *i.* of Aroer.   48:19
O *i.* of Moab.   43
be upon Babylon, shall the *i.* 51:35
I will cut off the *i.* from plain of Aven.
           Amos 1:5
I will cut off the *i.* from Ashdod.   8
i. of Saphir, of Zaanan. *Mi* 1:11
the *i.* of Maroth waited carefully. 12
O thou *i.* of Lachish, bind the.   13
will bring an heir to thee, O *i.*   15
destroy, that there shall be no *i.*
          Zeph 2:5
destroyed, so that there is none *i.* 3:6

inhabitants
he overthrew all the *i.*   *Gen* 19:25
take hold of the *i.*   *Ex* 15:14
all the *i.* of Canaan shall melt.   15
itself vomiteth out her *i. Lev* 18:25
proclaim liberty to all the *i.*   25:10
land that eateth up the *i. Num* 13:32
have withdrawn the *i. Deut* 13:13
thou shalt surely smite the *i.* of. 15
even the *i.* of the country. *Josh* 2:24
peace, save the *i.* of Gibeon.   11:19
drive out the *i.* 17:12; *Judg* 1:19, 27
no league with the *i.* of. *Judg* 2:2
the *i.* of the villages ceased.   5:7*
curse ye bitterly the *i.* thereof.   23
be head over all the *i.* of Gilead.
         10:18; 11:8
he upon the *i.* of Jabesh-gilead. 21:9
smite the *i.* of Jabesh-gilead.   10
buy it before the *i.* and. *Ruth* 4:4*
Elijah who was of the *i.* *1 Ki* 17:1*
i. were of small power. *2 Ki* 19:26
first *i.* that dwelt in.   *1 Chr* 9:2
the *i.* of mount Seir.   *2 Chr* 20:23
from under the *i.* thereof. *Job* 26:5
all the *i.* of world stand.   *Ps* 33:8
looketh on all the *i.* of the earth.   14
give ear, all ye *i.* of the world. 49:1
all the *i.* thereof are dissolved. 75:3
put down the *i.* like a.   *Isa* 10:13*
all the *i.* of the world, see ye.   18:3
be still, ye *i.* of the isle.   23:2, 6
and scattereth abroad the *i.*   24:1
the earth is defiled under the *i.*   5
therefore the *i.* of the earth are.   6
the *i.* of the world will learn. 26:9
have the *i.* of the world fallen. 18
behold man no more with the *i.* 38:11
i. thereof are as grasshoppers. 40:22
isles and *i.* sing to the Lord. 42:10
let the *i.* of the rock sing, let.   11
too narrow by reason of the *i.* 49:19
fill the *i.* with drunkenness. *Jer* 13:13
will I do to the *i.* thereof.   19:12
I will smite the *i.* of this city. 21:6
as Sodom, and the *i.* thereof. 23:14
for a sword upon the *i.* thereof. 25:29
            50:35

innocent blood on the *i.*   *Jer* 26:15
dwell deep, O *i.* of Dedan. 49:8, 30
the Lord will disquiet the *i.*   50:34
and my blood upon the *i.* of. 51:35
i. of the world would not. *Lam* 4:12
i. of Egypt shall know. *Ezek* 29:6
i. of earth are reputed as. *Dan* 4:35
i. thereof have spoken lies. *Mi* 6:12
I should make the *i.* thereof an.   16
come *i.* of many cities. *Zech* 8:20
the *i.* of one city shall go to.   21
the *i.* of the earth have. *Rev* 17:2
       see Jerusalem

inhabitants of the land
stink among the *i.* of *land. Gen* 34:30
I will deliver *i.* of *land.*   *Ex* 23:31
a covenant with *i.* of *land.* 34:12, 15
because of the *i.* of *land. Num* 32:17
shall drive out the *i.* of *land.* 33:52
       55; *2 Chr* 20:7
all the *i.* of the *land* faint. *Josh* 2:9
all the *i.* of *land* shall hear of.   7:9
to destroy all the *i.* of the *land.* 9:24
of old the *i.* of *land.*   *1 Sam* 27:8
he hath given *i.* of *land. 1 Chr* 22:18
forth on all *i.* of *land.*   *Jer* 1:14
will fling out the *i.* of *land.*   10:18
and the *i.* of *land* shall howl. 47:2
controversy with *i.* of *land. Hos* 4:1
the *i.* of the *land* tremble. *Joel* 2:1
no more pity *i.* of the *l. Zech* 11:6

inhabited
till they came to a land *i. Ex* 16:35
iniquities to a land not *i. Lev* 16:22
it shall never be *i.* nor. *Isa* 13:20
thou shalt be *i.*   44:26
formed it to be *i.*   45:18
the desolate cities to be *i.*   54:3
make thee a land not *i. Jer* 6:8
in a salt land and not *i.*   17:6
thee cities which are not *i.*   22:6
afterward it shall be *i.* as in. 46:26
it shall not be *i.*   50:13
no more *i.* for ever.   39
the cities that are *i.*   *Ezek* 12:20
set thee, that thou be not *i.* 26:20
nor shall it be *i.* forty years. 29:11
the cities shall be *i.* and the. 36:10
desolate places that are now *i.* 38:12
Jerusalem be *i.* as towns. *Zech* 2:4
and Askelon shall not be *i.*   9:5
Jerusalem shall be *i.* again. 12:6
it shall be lifted up, and *i.* in. 14:10
but Jerusalem shall be safely *i.*   11

inhabiters
woe, woe, woe, to *i.*   *Rev* 8:13
woe to the *i.* of the earth.   12:12

inhabitest
thou that *i.* the praises.   *Ps* 22:3

inhabiteth
houses that no man *i.*   *Job* 15:28
lofty One that *i.* eternity. *Isa* 57:15

inhabiting
be meat to the people *i.*   *Ps* 74:14

inherit
know that I shall *i.* it ?   *Gen* 15:8
and they shall *i.* it for ever. *Ex* 32:13
it to the Levites to *i.*   *Num* 18:24
names of tribes they shall *i.*   26:55
we will not *i.* on yonder side. 32:19
cause Israel to *i.* it.   *Deut* 1:38
Lord God giveth you to *i.*   12:10
he maketh his sons to *i.*   21:16
not *i.* in our father's.   *Judg* 11:2
them *i.* the throne of.   *1 Sam* 2:8
seed shall *i.* the earth.   *Ps* 25:13
that wait on the Lord shall *i.*   37:9
but the meek shall *i.* the earth.   11
           Mat 5:5
be blessed of him shall *i. Ps* 37:22
also of his servants shall *i.* it. 69:36
O God, for thou shalt *i.* all.   82:8
the wise shall *i.* glory.   *Pr* 3:35
cause those who love me to *i.* 8:21
own house, shall *i.* the wind. 11:29
the simple *i.* folly, but the.   14:18
to cause to *i.* the desolate. *Isa* 49:8
thy seed shall *i.* the Gentiles. 54:3*
and mine elect shall *i.* it, and. 65:9
my people Israel to *i. Jer* 12:14
doth their king *i.* Gad ?   49:1*
ye shall *i.* it, one as well. *Ezek* 47:14

the Lord shall *i*. Judah. *Zech* 2:12
shall *i*. everlasting life. *Mat* 19:29
i. the kingdom prepared for. 25:34
i. eternal life. *Mark* 10:17
    Luke 10:25; 18:18
unrighteous not *i*. the. *1 Cor* 6:9
neither shall extortioners *i*. 10
    Gal 5:21
cannot *i*. the kingdom of God, nor
  doth corruption *i*. *1 Cor* 15:50
who through faith *i*. the. *Heb* 6:12
called, that ye should *i*. *1 Pet* 3:9
he that overcometh shall *i*.*Rev* 21:7

inherit *land*
give thee this *land* to *i*. it. *Gen* 15:7
that thou mayest *i*. land. 28:4
ye shall *i*. their *land*. *Lev* 20:24
land ye shall *i*. by lot. *Num* 34:13
thou mayest *i*. his *land*. *Deut* 2:31
i.land Lord giveth thee. 16:20; 19:3
righteous shall *i*. the *land*. *Ps* 37:29
shall exalt thee to *i*. the *land*. 34
they *i*. the *land* for ever. *Isa* 60:21
border, whereby ye shall *i*. the *land*.
    Ezek 47:13

inheritance
any portion or *i*. for us ? *Gen* 31:14
of their brethren in their *i*. 48:6
in mountain of thine *i*. *Ex* 15:17
take them as an *i*. for. *Lev* 25:46
or given us *i*. of fields. *Num* 16:14
i. for I am thy part and thine *i*. 18:20
shall cause his *i*. to pass to. 27:8
i. to brethren. 9
i. to father's brethren. 10
our *i*. is fallen. 32:19, 32; 34:15
prince, to divide the land by *i*. 34:18
put to the *i*. of the tribe. 36:3, 4
Israel may enjoy the *i*. 8
nor *i*. remove from one tribe to. 9
a people of *i*. as ye are. *Deut* 4:20
destroy not thine *i*. 9:26
they are thine *i*. 29
Jacob is the lot of his *i*. 32:9
sacrifices of Lord their *i*. *Josh* 13:14
    18:7
God of Israel was their 13:33
by lot was their *i*. 14:2; *Ps* 78:55
Hebron therefore became the *i*. of.
    Josh 14:14
daughters of Manasseh had *i*. 17:6
every man to his *i*. 24:28; *Judg* 2:6
    21:24
i. for them that escaped. *Judg* 21:27
lest I mar mine own *i*. *Ruth* 4:6
thee captain over his *i*. *1 Sam* 10:1
from abiding in the *i*. of. 26:19
neither *i*. in son of Jesse. *2 Sam* 20:1
    1 Ki 12:16
that ye may bless the *i*. *2 Sam* 21:3
thy people and thy *i*. *1 Ki* 8:51, 53
give the *i*. of my fathers. 21:3, 4
the remnant of mine *i*. *2 Ki* 21:14
Canaan, the lot of your *i*. *1 Chr* 16:18
every one in his *i*. *Neh* 11:20
what *i*. of the Almighty? *Job* 31:2
is the portion of mine *i*. *Ps* 16:5
bless thine *i*. 28:9
chosen for his *i*. 33:12
their *i*. shall be for ever. 37:18
he shall choose our *i*. for us. 47:4
thou didst confirm thine *i*. 68:9
the rod of thine *i*., thou hast. 74:2
and was wroth with his *i*. 78:62
him to feed Israel his *i*. 71
heathen are come into thine *i*. 79:1
neither will he forsake his *i*. 94:14
Canaan, the lot of your *i*. 105:11
that I may glory with thine *i*. 106:5
he abhorred his own *i*. 40
good man leaveth an *i*. *Pr* 13:22
have part of the *i*. among. 17:2
house and riches are the *i*. of. 19:14
an *i*. may be gotten hastily. 20:21
wisdom is good with an *i*. *Eccl* 7:11
blessed be Israel mine *i*. *Isa* 19:25
I have polluted mine *i*. and. 47:6
sake, the tribes of thine *i*. 63:17
Israel is the rod of his *i*. *Jer* 10:16
    51:19
right of *i*. is thine, redemption. 32:8
i. is turned to strangers. *Lam* 5:2
thou shalt be their *i*. *Ezek* 36:12

for an *i*.: I am their *i*. *Ezek* 44:28
i. thereof shall be his son's.
    46:16, 17
shall not take of the people's *i*. 18
i. among you with tribes. 47:22, 23
let us seize on his *i*. *Mat* 21:38
and the *i*. shall be ours. *Mark* 12:7
    Luke 20:14
that he divide the *i*. *Luke* 12:13
to give you an *i*. among. *Acts* 20:32
and *i*. among them sanctified. 26:18
if the *i*. be of the law, it. *Gal* 3:18
we have obtained an *i*. *Eph* 1:11
which is the earnest of our *i*. 14
the riches of the glory of his *i*. in. 18
i. in the kingdom of Christ. 5:5
to be partakers of the *i*. of. *Col* 1:12
shall receive the reward of *i*. 3:24
as he hath by *i*. obtained. *Heb* 1:4
the promise of eternal *i*. 9:15
begotten us to an *i*. *1 Pet* 1:4

for **inheritance**
and take us *for* thine *i*. *Ex* 34:9
all the tenth in Israel *for* an *i*.
    Num 18:21, 26
shall be divided *for* an *i*. 26:53
33:54; 34:2; 36:2; *Deut* 4:21, 38
15:4; 19:10; *Josh* 13:6, 7, 32
14:1; 19:49, 51; *Ezek* 45:1
    47:22; 48:29
the Lord doth give thee *for* an *i*.
  Deut 20:16; 21:23; 24:4; 25:19
26:1; *Josh* 11:23; 13:6; 14:13
1 Ki 8:36; *2 Chr* 6:27; *Jer* 3:18
leave it *for* an *i*. for children.
    1 Chr 28:8; *Ezra* 9:12
give thee heathen *for* thine *i*. *Ps* 2:8
is given us *for* an *i*. *Ezek* 33:24
it shall be to them *for* an *i*. *L* 44:28
shall fall unto you *for* an *i*. 47:14
after receive *for* an *i*. *Heb* 11:8

no or none **inheritance**
thou shalt have no *i*. *Num* 18:20
23:24; 26:62; *Deut* 10:9; 14:27
29; 18:1, 2; *Josh* 13:14, 33; 14:3
no i. in the son of Jesse. *2 Chr* 10:16
he gave him *none i*. in it. *Acts* 7:5

inheritances
these are the *i*. Joshua. *Josh* 19:51

inherited
return till Israel have *i*. *Num* 32:18
children of Israel *i*. in. *Josh* 14:1
they *i*. the labour of. *Ps* 105:44
our fathers have *i*. lies. *Jer* 16:19
one, and he *i*. the land. *Ezek* 33:24
have *i*. the blessing. *Heb* 12:17

inheriteth
inheriting which he *i*. *Num* 35:8

inheritor
out of Judah an *i*. of my. *Isa* 65:9

iniquities
over the goat all the *i*. *Lev* 16:21
in the *i*. of their fathers shall. 26:39
our *i*. are increased over. *Ezra* 9:6
for our *i*. have we, our kings. 7
punished us less than our *i*. 13
Israel confessed the *i*. *Neh* 9:2
how many are mine *i*.? *Job* 13:23
thou makest me to possess the *i*. 26
great, and thine *i*. infinite. 22:5
and mine *i*. are gone over. *Ps* 38:4
i. have taken hold on me. 40:12
my sins, and blot out all *i*. 51:9
they search out *i*. 64:6
i. prevail against. 65:3
not against us former *i*. 79:8
hast set our *i*. before thee. 90:8
Lord, who forgiveth all thine *i*. 103:3
rewarded us according to our *i*. 10
if thou, Lord shouldest mark *i*. 130:3
redeem Israel from all his *i*. 8
his own *i*. shall take the. *Pr* 5:22
wearied me with thine *i*. *Isa* 43:24
but he was bruised for our *i*. 53:5
as for our *i*. we know them. 59:12
our *i*. like the wind have taken. 64:6
consumed us because of our *i*. 7
turned back to *i*. of their. *Jer* 11:10
O Lord, though our *i*. testify. 14:7
for *i*. of her priests that. *Lam* 4:13
multitude of thine *i*. *Ezek* 28:18

break off thine *i*. by. *Dan* 4:27
from our *i*. and understand. 9:13
for our sins, and for the *i*. of. 16
turn, he will subdue our *i*. *Mi* 7:19
bless in turning every one from his *i*.
    Acts 3:26
blessed are they whose *i*. *Rom* 4:7
hath remembered her *i*. *Rev* 18:5

their **iniquities**
bear on him all *their i*. *Lev* 16:22
fools because of *their i*. *Ps* 107:17
he shall bear *their i*. *Isa* 53:11
will pardon all *their i*. *Jer* 33:8
sinned, we have borne *their i*.
    Lam 5:7
their i. shall be on their. *Ezek* 32:27
may be ashamed of *their i*. 43:10
their i. will I remember no more.
    Heb 8:12; 10:17

your **iniquities**
shall ye bear *your i*. *Num* 14:34
for *your i*. have you sold. *Isa* 50:1
your i. separated between you. 59:2
your i. I will recompense. 65:7
your i. have turned away. *Jer* 5:25
pine away for *your i*. *Ezek* 24:23
loathe youselves for *your i*. 36:31
cleansed you from all *your i*. 33
punish you for all *your i*. *Amos* 3:2

iniquity
i. of the Amorites is not. *Gen* 15:16
thou be consumed in the *i*. of. 19:15
God hath found out the *i*. of. 44:16
visiting the *i*. of fathers. *Ex* 20:5
  34:7; *Num* 14:18; *Deut* 5:9
forgiving *i*. and transgression.
    Ex 34:7; *Num* 14:18
and pardon our *i*. and. *Ex* 34:9
therefore I do visit the *i*. *Lev* 18:25
an offering bringing *i*. to. *Num* 5:15
shall the man be guiltless from *i*. 31
pray thee, the *i*. of this people. 14:19
he hath not beheld *i*. in Jacob. 23:21
against a man for any *i*. *Deut* 19:15
God of truth and without *i*. 32:4
i. of Peor too little for ? *Josh* 22:17
judge for the *i*. which. *1 Sam* 3:13
the *i*. of Eli's house shall not. 14
and stubbornness is as *i*. 15:23*
if there be in me. I slay me. 20:8
upon me let this *i*. be. 25:24
    2 Sam 14:9
if there be *i*. in me, let. *2 Sam* 14:32
let not my lord impute *i*. to. 19:19
to take away *i*. of thy servant.
    24:10; *1 Chr* 21:8
for there is no *i*. with. *2 Chr* 19:7
they that plow *i*. reap. *Job* 4:8
poor hath hope, and *i*. stoppeth. 5:16
I pray you, let it not be *i*. 6:29*
is there *i*. in my tongue ? 30*
God exacteth less than thine *i*. 11:6
if *i*. be in thy hand, put it far. 14
for thy mouth uttereth thine *i*. 15:5
filthy is man which drinketh *i*. 16
thou shalt put away *i*. far. 22:23
it is an *i*. to be punished. 31:11, 28
innocent, nor is there *i*. in me. 33:9
if I have done *i*. I will do. 34:32
that they return from *i*. 36:10
take heed, regard not *i*. for this. 21
can say, Thou hast wrought *i*.? 23
O Lord, if there be *i*. in. *Ps* 7:3
behold, he travaileth with *i*. 14
whom the Lord imputeth not *i*. 32:2
thou forgavest the *i*. of my sin. 5
the words of his mouth are *i*. 36:3
thou dost correct man for *i*. 39:11
heart gathereth *i*. to itself. 41:6
when the *i*. of my heels shall. 49:5
behold I was shapen in *i*. and. 51:5
and have done abominable *i*. 53:1
they cast *i*. upon me, and in. 55:3
shall they escape by *i*.? 56:7
if I regard *i*. in my heart. 66:18
thou hast forgiven the *i*. of thy. 85:2
throne of *i*. have fellowship. 94:20
all *i*. shall stop her mouth. 107:42
let the *i*. of his fathers be. 109:14
they also do no *i*.: they walk. 119:3
let not any *i*. have dominion. 133
put forth their hands to *i*. 125:3
by mercy and truth *i*. *Pr* 16:6

of the wicked devoureth *i*. *Pr* 19:28
he that soweth *i*. shall reap. 22:8
of righteousness that *i*. *Eccl* 3:16
a people laden with *i*. a. *Isa* 1:4
it is *i*. even the solemn meeting. 13
woe to them that draw *i*. 5:18
i. is taken away, and thy sin. 6:7
prepare for the *i*. of their. 14:21
this *i*. shall not be purged. 22:14
by this shall the *i*. of Jacob. 27:9
all that watch for *i*. are cut off. 29:20
this *i*. shall be to you as a. 30:13
cry unto her, her *i*. is pardoned. 40:2
Lord hath laid on him the *i*. 53:6
for the *i*. of his covetousness. 57:17
fingers are defiled with *i*. 59:3
they bring forth *i*. 4
their works are works of *i*. 6
their thoughts are thoughts of *i*. 7
not wroth, nor remember *i*. 64:9
what is *i*. have your fathers ? *Jer* 2:5
thine *i*. is marked before me. 22
only acknowledge thine *i*. 3:13
the greatness of thine *i*. are. 13:22
we acknowledge the *i*. of our. 14:20
what is our *i*.? 16:10
i. hid from mine eyes. 17
for multitude of thine *i*. 30:14, 15
Hos 9:7
recompensest *i*. of fathers. *Jer* 32:18
the *i*. of Israel be sought for. 50:20
Babylon, be not cut off in her *i*. 51:6
not discovered thine *i*. *Lam* 2:14
for the punishment of the *i*. of. 4:6
thine *i*. is accomplished, he will visit
thine *i*. O daughter of Edom. 22
lay *i*. of the house of. *Ezek* 4:4
nor strengthen himself in *i*. 7:13
the *i*. of the house of Israel. 9:9
this was the *i*. of thy sister. 16:49
withdrawn his hand from *i*. 18:8
he shall not die for the *i*. of his. 17
repent, so *i*. shall not be your. 30
to remembrance your *i*. 21:23, 24
i. shall have an end. 25, 29; 35:5
wast perfect, till *i*. was found. 28:15
defiled thy sanctuaries by *i*. of. 18
house of Israel to fall into *i*. 44:12
make reconciliation for *i*. *Dan* 9:24
the *i*. of Ephraim was. *Hos* 7:1
against children of *i*. 10:9
ye reaped *i*. 13
find no *i*. in me. 12:8
is there *i*. in Gilead ? 11
the *i*. of Ephraim is bound up. 13:12
for thou hast fallen by thine *i*. 14:1
take away all *i*. and receive us. 2
woe to them that devise *i*. *Mi* 2:1
they build up Jerusalem with *i*. 3:10
who is a God like to thee, that
pardoneth *i*.? 7:18
why dost thou shew me *i*.? *Hab* 1:3
and thou canst not look on *i*. 13*
that establisheth a city by *i*. 2:12
Lord, he will not do *i*. *Zeph* 3:5
of Israel shall not do *i*. 13
I have caused thine *i*. to. *Zech* 3:4
I will remove the *i*. of that land. 9
i. was not found in his lips, did turn
many away from *i*. *Mal* 2:6
gather them which do *i*. *Mat* 13:41
ye are full of hypocrisy and *i*. 23:28
because *i*. shall abound, love. 24:12
field with the reward of *i*. *Acts* 1:18
thou art in the bond of *i*. 8:23
servants to *i*. unto *i*. *Rom* 6:19
rejoiceth not in *i*. but in. *1 Cor* 13:6
the mystery of *i*. doth. *2 Thes* 2:7*
Christ, depart from *i*. *2 Tim* 2:19
redeem us from all *i*. *Tit* 2:14
hast hated *i*. therefore God. *Heb* 1:9
tongue is a fire, a world of *i*.
Jas 3:6

see bear, commit, committed

his iniquity

his i. shall be upon him. *Num* 15:31
that man perished not alone in *his i*.
Josh 22:20
heavens shall reveal *his i*. *Job* 20:27
God layeth up *his i*. for his. 21:19
until *his i*. be found to be. *Ps* 36:2
die for *his i*. *Jer* 31:30; *Ezek* 3:18
19; 7:16; 18:26

the stumblingblock of *his i*.
Ezek 14:7, 14
shall die in *his i*. 18:18; 33:8, 9
he is taken away in *his i*. but. 33:6
was rebuked for *his i*. *2 Pet* 2:16*

mine iniquity

what is *mine i*. and ? *1 Sam* 20:1
I kept myself from *mine i*.
2 Sam 22:24; *Ps* 18:23
thou not take away *mine i*.? *Job* 7:21
thou enquirest after *mine i*. 10:6
not acquit me from *mine i*. 14
bag, thou sewest up *mine i*. 14:17
if I covered, by hiding *mine i*. 31:33
pardon *mine i*. for it is. *Ps* 25:11
faileth because of *mine i*. 31:10
and *mine i*. have I not hid. 32:5
for I will declare *mine i*. I. 38:18
me throughly from *mine i*. 51:2

their iniquity

pine away in *their i*. *Lev* 26:39
confess *their i*. and iniquity of. 40
the punishment of *their i*. 41, 43
cover not *their i*. let not. *Neh* 4:5
add iniquity unto *their i*. *Ps* 69:27
he forgave *their i*. 78:38
I will visit *their i*. 89:32
bring upon them *their i*. 94:23
brought low for *their i*. 106:43
punish wicked for *their i*. *Isa* 13:11
inhabitants of earth for *their i*. 26:21
people shall be forgiven *their i*. 33:24
now remember *their i*. *Jer* 14:10
I will recompense *their i*. 16:18
forgive not *their i*. nor blot. 18:23
punish that nation for *their i*. 25:12
for I will forgive *their i*. 31:34
cleanse them from all *their i*. 33:8
I may forgive *their i*. and sin. 36:3
punish his servants for *their i*. 31
thee the years of *their i*. *Ezek* 4:5
may consume away for *their i*. 17
the stumblingblock of *their i*. 7:19
14:3
bear the punishment of *their i*. 14:10
which bringeth *their i*. to. 29:16
went into captivity for *their i*. 39:23
set their heart on *their i*. *Hos* 4:8
Israel fall in *their i*. 5:5
he will remember *their i*. he. 9:9

work iniquity

with men that *work i*. *Ps* 141:4
help of them that *work i*. *Isa* 31:2
heart will *work i*. to practise. 32:6
a city of them that *work i*. *Hos* 6:8
from me, ye that *work i*. *Mat* 7:23

workers of iniquity

punishment to the *w. of i*. *Job* 31:3
company with the *w. of i*. 34:8
where the *w. of i*. may hide. 22
stand, thou hatest all *w. of i*. *Ps* 5:5
depart from me all ye *w. of i*. 6:8
Luke 13:27
have all *w. of i*. no ? *Ps* 14:4; 53:4
not away with the *w. of i*. 28:3
there are the *w. of i*. fallen. 36:12
envious against the *w. of i*. 37:1
deliver me from the *w. of i*. 59:2
insurrection of the *w. of i*. 64:2
all the *w. of i*. do flourish. 92:7
the *w. of i*. shall be scattered. 9
the *w. of i*. boast themselves. 94:4
stand up for me against the *w. of i*. 16
them forth with the *w. of i*. 125:5
from the gins of the *w. of i*. 141:9
destruction shall be to *w. of i*.
Pr 10:29; 21:15

injured

ye have not *i*. me at all. *Gal* 4:12

injurious

a persecutor and *i*. *1 Tim* 1:13

injustice

not for *i*. in my hands. *Job* 16:17

ink

I wrote them with *i*. *Jer* 36:18
written not with *i*. but. *2 Cor* 3:3
I would not write with *i*. *2 John* 12
3 John 13

inkhorn

with a writer's *i*. *Ezek* 9:2, 3, 11

inn

ass provender in the *i*. *Gen* 42:27*
we came to the *i*. we opened. 43:21*
by the way in the *i*., the. *Ex* 4:24*
no room for them in the *i*. *Luke* 2:7
brought him to an *i*. and took. 10:34

inner

cherubims in *i*. house. *1 Ki* 6:27
gave patterns of the *i*. *1 Chr* 28:11
to the king into the *i*. court. *Esth* 4:11
Esther stood in the *i*. court. 5:1
and the cloud filled the *i*. *Ezek* 10:3
end of measuring the *i*. house. 42:15
the gate of the *i*. court shall be. 46:1
thrust them into the *i*. *Acts* 16:24
with might in the *i*. man. *Eph* 3:16

see chamber

innermost

into the *i*. parts of the belly.
Pr 18:8; 26:22

innocency

in the *i*. of my hands. *Gen* 20:5
wash my hands in *i*. so. *Ps* 26:6
have washed my hands in *i*. 73:13
before him *i*. was found. *Dan* 6:22
be ere they attain to *i*.? *Hos* 8:5

innocent

the *i*. and the righteous. *Ex* 23:7
reward to slay the *i*. *Deut* 27:25
whoever perished being *i*.? *Job* 4:7
laugh at the trial of the *i*. 9:23
that thou wilt not hold me *i*. 28
i. shall stir up the hypocrite. 17:8
i. laugh them to scorn. 22:19
deliver the island of the *i*. 30
i. shall divide the silver. 27:17
I am *i*. nor is iniquity in me. 33:9
doth he murder the *i*. *Ps* 10:8
taketh reward against the *i*. 15:5
I shall be *i*. from the great. 19:13*
let us lurk privily for the *i*. *Pr* 1:11
toucheth her shall not be *i*. 6:29*
haste to be rich shall not be *i*. 28:20*
sayest, Because I am *i*. *Jer* 2:35
I am *i*. of the blood of. *Mat* 27:24

see blood

innocents

the blood of the poor *i*. *Jer* 2:34
place with the blood of *i*. 19:4

innumerable

after him, as there are *i*. *Job* 21:23
i. evils have compassed. *Ps* 40:12
are things creeping *i*. 104:25
grasshoppers, and are *i*. *Jer* 46:23
i. multitude gathered. *Luke* 12:1*
is by the sea shore *i*. *Heb* 11:12
an *i*. company of angels. 12:22

inordinate

corrupt in her *i*. love. *Ezek* 23:11*
fornication, *i*. affection. *Col* 3:8*

inquisition

shall make diligent *i*. *Deut* 19:18
when *i*. was made of the. *Esth* 2:23
he maketh *i*. for blood. *Ps* 9:12

inscription

found an altar with this *i*. *Acts* 17:23

inside

covered the walls on *i*. *1 Ki* 6:15

inspiration

i. of Almighty giveth. *Job* 32:8*
all scripture is given by *i*. *2 Tim* 3:16

instant

[1] *A short moment of time*, Isa
29:5. [2] *Very eager, or pressing*,
Luke 23:23.

yea, it shall be at an *i*. *Isa* 29:5
cometh suddenly at an *i*. 30:13
at what *i*. I speak. *Jer* 18:7, 9
she coming in that *i*. *Luke* 2:38*
and they were *i*. with loud. 23:23*
patient, continuing *i*. *Rom* 12:12*
preach the word, be *i*. *2 Tim* 4:2

instantly

they besought him *i*. *Luke* 7:4*
our twelve tribes *i*. *Acts* 26:7*

instruct

that he might *i*. thee. *Deut* 4:36
thy good Spirit to *i*. *Neh* 9:20
that contendeth *i*. him ? *Job* 40:2*

my reins also *i*. me in. *Ps* 16:7
I will *i*. thee and teach thee. 32:8
mother's house, who will *i*. *S of S* 8:2
his God doth *i*. him to. *Isa* 28:26
understand shall *i*. many. *Dan* 11:33
Lord, that he may *i*. *1 Cor* 2:16

instructed
led him about, he *i*. *Deut* 32:10*
Jehoiada the priest *i*. him. *2 Ki* 12:2
Chenaniah *i*. about the. *1 Chr* 15:22
that were *i*. in the songs of. 25:7
Solomon was *i*. for the. *2 Chr* 3:3*
behold thou hast *i*. many. *Job* 4:3
be *i*. ye judges of the. *Ps* 2:10
mine ear to them that *i*. *Pr* 5:13
the wise is *i*. he receiveth. 21:11
spake thus to me and *i*. *Isa* 8:11
who *i*. him, and taught him? 40:14
be *i*. O Jerusalem, lest my. *Jer* 6:8
after that I was *i*. I smote. 31:19
every scribe who is *i*. to. *Mat* 13:52
and she, being before *i*. of. 14:8*
wherein thou hast been *i*. *Luke* 1:4
man was *i*. in the way. *Acts* 18:25
his will, being *i*. out of. *Rom* 2:18
and in all things, I am *i*. *Phil* 4:12*

instructing
i. those that oppose *2 Tim* 2:25

instruction
the ears, and sealeth *i*. *Job* 33:16
seeing thou hatest *i*. and. *Ps* 50:17
to know wisdom and *i*. *Pr* 1:2
to receive the *i*. of wisdom. 3
despise wisdom and *i*. 7; 15:5
hear the *i*. of thy father. 1:8; 4:1
take fast hold of *i*., let her. 4:13
how have I hated *i*. and my. 5:12
he shall die without *i*. and. 23
and reproofs of *i*. are the. 6:23
receive my *i*. 8:10
hear *i*. and be wise. 33
give *i*. to a wise man and he. 9:9
way of life that keepeth *i*. 10:17*
loveth *i*. loveth knowledge. 12:1*
son heareth his father's *i*. 13:1
shall be to him that refuseth *i*. 18*
he that refuseth *i*. hateth his. 15:32*
the fear of the Lord is the *i*. of. 33
but the *i*. of fools is folly. 16:22*
hear counsel, and receive *i*. 19:20
cease to hear the *i*. that causeth. 27
apply thy heart to *i*. and. 23:12
buy the truth, also *i*. and. 23
upon it and received *i*. 24:32
not hear, nor receive *i*. *Jer* 17:23
not hearkened to receive *i*. 32:33
receive *i*. to hearken to my. 35:13
a reproach, a taunt, an *i*. *Ezek* 5:15
surely thou wilt receive *i*. *Zeph* 3:7*
all scripture is profitable for *i*.
2 Tim 3:16

instructor
Tubal-Cain, an *i*. of. *Gen* 4:22*
i. of foolish, a teacher. *Rom* 2:20*

instructors
ye have 10,000 *i*. in. *1 Cor* 4:15

instrument
smite him with an *i*. of. *Num* 35:16
sing to him with an *i*. of ten strings.
Ps 33:2; 92:3
new song, O God, on an *i*. 144:9
threshed with a threshing *i*. *Isa* 28:27
thee a sharp threshing *i*. 41:15
that bringeth forth an *i*. for. 54:16*
one that can play on an *i*. *Ezek* 33:32

instruments
i. of cruelty are in their. *Gen* 49:5*
pattern of all the *i*. *Ex* 25:9*
shall keep all the *i*. of. *Num* 3:8
they shall take all the *i*. of. 4:12*
sanctified all the *i*. 7:1*
with the holy *i*. 31:6*
make *i*. of war, and *i*. *1 Sam* 8:12
king Saul with *i*. of music. 18:6
their flesh with *i*. of oxen. *1 Ki* 19:21
to oversee all the *i*. of. *1 Chr* 9:29*
make a sound with musical *i*. 16:42
singing with loud *i*. to. *2 Chr* 30:21
Hanani with musical *i*. *Neh* 12:36
prepared for him the *i*. *Ps* 7:13
players on *i*. followed after. 68:25*
as the players on *i*. shall be. 87:7*

praise him with stringed *i*. *Ps* 150:4
as musical *i*. and that of. *Eccl* 2:8†
i. also of the churl are evil. *Isa* 32:7
my songs to the stringed *i*. 38:20
nor *i*. of music brought. *Dan* 6:18
Gilead with threshing *i*. *Amos* 1:3
and invent to themselves *i*. of. 6:5
singer on my stringed *i*. *Hab* 3:19
take thee *i*. of a foolish. *Zech* 11:15
yield members *i*. of unrighteousness,
members as *i*. of. *Rom* 6:13

insurrection
this city hath made *i*. *Ezra* 4:19
from the *i*. of the workers. *Ps* 64:2*
that had made *i*. who had committed
murder in the. *Mark* 15:7
Jews made *i*. with one. *Acts* 18:12*

integrity
in *i*. of my heart I have. *Gen* 20:5
I know that thou didst this in the *i*. 6
thy father walked in *i*. *1 Ki* 9:4
he holdeth fast his *i*. *Job* 2:3
dost thou still retain thine *i*. 9
I will not remove my *i*. from. 27:5
that God may know my *i*. 31:6
according to my *i*. that. *Ps* 7:8
i. and uprightness preserve. 25:21
I walked in my *i*. 26:1
I will walk in *i*. 11
thou upholdest me in my *i*. 41:12
he fed them according to *i*. 78:72
the *i*. of the upright shall. *Pr* 11:3
poor that walketh in his *i*. 19:1
just man walketh in his *i*. 20:7

intelligence
i. with them that forsake covenant.
Dan 11:30*
did not *i*. to go up. *Josh* 22:23*
ye *i*. to add more to. *2 Chr* 28:13
ye *i*. to bring this man's. *Acts* 5:28
what ye *i*. to do as touching. 35

intend

intended
for they *i*. evil against. *Ps* 21:11

intendest
i. thou to kill me, as the ? *Ex* 2:14

intending
which of you *i*. to build ? *Luke* 14:28
i. after Easter to bring. *Acts* 12:4
sailed to Assos, there *i*. to. 20:13

intent
to the *i*. the Lord might. *2 Sam* 17:14
to *i*. he might destroy. *2 Ki* 10:19
to the *i*. he might let. *2 Chr* 16:1
to the *i*. that I might. *Ezek* 40:4
to the *i*. that the living. *Dan* 4:17
not there to the *i*. ye. *John* 11:15
for what *i*. he spake this to. 13:28
and came hither for that *i*. *Acts* 9:21
I ask for what *i*. ye have ? 10:29
to the *i*. we should not. *1 Cor* 10:6
to the *i*. that now to the. *Eph* 3:10

intents
till he have performed *i*. *Jer* 30:24
is a discerner of the. *Heb* 4:12

intercession
and made *i*. for the. *Isa* 53:12
cry, nor make *i*. to me. *Jer* 7:16
let them now make *i*. to the. 27:18
Gemariah had made *i*. 36:25
but the Spirit maketh *i*. for us.
Rom 8:26, 27, 34
how he maketh *i*. to God. 11:2*
he ever liveth to make *i*. *Heb* 7:25

intercessions
that prayers and *i*. be. *1 Tim* 2:1

intercessor
he wondered that there was no *i*.
Isa 59:16

intermeddle
a stranger doth not *i*. *Pr* 14:10

intermeddleth
seeketh and *i*. with all. *Pr* 18:1*

intermission
ceaseth not without any *i*. *Lam* 3:49

interpret
none that could *i*. them. *Gen* 41:8
according to his dream he did *i*. 12
do all *i*.? *1 Cor* 12:30
except he *i*. 14:5

pray that he may *i*. *1 Cor* 14:13
let one *i*. 27

interpretation
[1] *A translation, or turning from
one language into another,* 1 Cor
12:10. [2] *The gift of explaining
visions and dreams, etc.,* Gen 40:8;
2 Pet 1:20.

each man according to the *i*. of his
dream. *Gen* 40:5; 41:11
the *i*. of it. 40:12, 18; *Dan* 4:24; 5:26
baker saw that the *i*. *Gen* 40:16
when Gideon heard the *i*. *Judg* 7:15
a proverb and the *i*. *Pr* 1:6*
we shall shew the *i*. *Dan* 2:4, 7, 36
the dream is certain, and the *i*. 45
and the *i*. thereof be to thy. 4:19
he will shew the *i*. 5:12
not shew the *i*. 15
and he made me to know the *i*. 7:16
Cephas, which is by *i*. a. *John* 1:42
of Siloam, which is by *i*. Sent. 9:7
by *i*. is called Dorcas. *Acts* 9:36
sorcerer, so is his name by *i*. 13:8
to another the *i*. of. *1 Cor* 12:10
every one of you hath an *i*. 14:26
being by *i*. king of. *Heb* 7:2
is of any private *i*. *2 Pet* 1:20

interpretations
Joseph said, do not *i*.? *Gen* 40:8
that thou canst make *i*. *Dan* 5:16

interpreted
as Joseph had *i*. *Gen* 40:22; 41:13
written and *i*. in the. *Ezra* 4:7*
being *i*. is, God with us. *Mat* 1:23
being *i*., Damsel, arise. *Mark* 5:41
which is, being *i*. the place of. 15:22
i. My God, my God, why hast? 34
being *i*. Master. *John* 1:38
which is, being *i*., the Christ. 41
is, being *i*. the son of. *Acts* 4:36

interpreter
and there is no *i*. of it. *Gen* 40:8
spake to them by an *i*. 42:23
i., one among a thousand. *Job* 33:23
but if there be no *i*. let. *1 Cor* 14:28

interpreting
i. of dreams was found. *Dan* 5:12

intreat
[1] *To supplicate or pray to,* Ex
8:8; Judg 13:8. [2] *To intercede,
or speak in one's behalf,* Gen 25:21;
1 Sam 2:25. [3] *To seek,* Pr 19:6.
i. for me to Ephron the. *Gen* 23:8
called for Moses, and said, the.
Ex 8:8, 28; 9:28; 10:17
when shall I *i*. for thee ? 8:9
I will *i*. the Lord that the flies. 29
i. me not to leave thee. *Ruth* 1:16
who shall *i*. for him ? *1 Sam* 2:25
i. the face of the Lord. *1 Ki* 13:6
among the people, shall *i*. *Ps* 45:12
many will *i*. the favour of. *Pr* 19:6
being defamed, we *i*. *1 Cor* 4:13
I *i*. thee also, true yoke-. *Phil* 4:3*
rebuke not, but *i*. him. *1 Tim* 5:1*

intreated
i. for his wife, Lord was *i*. *Gen* 25:21
out and *i*. the Lord. *Ex* 8:30; 10:18
then Manoah *i*. the Lord. *Judg* 13:8
after that God was *i*. *2 Sam* 21:14
Lord was *i*. for the land. 24:25
cried and he was *i*. of. *1 Chr* 5:20
prayed, and God was *i*. *2 Chr* 33:13
God, and he was *i*. of us. *Ezra* 8:23
I called, I *i*. him with. *Job* 19:16
though I *i*. for the children's. 17*
I *i*. thy favour with my. *Ps* 119:58
he shall be *i*. of them. *Isa* 19:22
his father out, and *i*. *Luke* 15:28
i. the word should not. *Heb* 12:19
from above is easy to be *i*. *Jas* 3:17
see also entreat, *etc*.

intreaties
the poor useth *i*. but the. *Pr* 18:23
praying us with much *i*. *2 Cor* 8:4

intruding
i. into things he hath not. *Col* 2:18*

invade
wouldest not let Israel *i*. *2 Chr* 20:10
will *i*. them with troops. *Hab* 3:16

invaded

the Philistines have *i*.   *1 Sam* 23:27
David and his men *i*. the.   27:8
the Amalekites *i*. the south.   30:1
bands of Moabites *i*. the land.   *2 Ki* 13:20
Philistines had *i*. the.   *2 Chr* 28:18

invasion

we made an *i*. on.   *1 Sam* 30:14

invent

i. instruments of music.   *Amos* 6:5*

invented

Uzziah made engines, *i*. by cunning
  men, to shoot arrows. *2 Chr* 26:15

inventions

vengeance of their *i*.   *Ps* 99:8*
him to anger with their *i*.   106:29*
whoring with their own *i*.   39*
out knowledge of witty *i*.   *Pr* 8:12*
have sought out many *i*.   *Eccl* 7:29

inventors

i. of evil things.   *Rom* 1:30

invisible

the *i*. things of him are.   *Rom* 1:20
the image of the *i*. God.   *Col* 1:15
heaven and earth, visible and *i*.   16
the King immortal, *i*.   *1 Tim* 1:17
as seeing him who is *i*.   *Heb* 11:27

invited

since I said, I have *i*.   *1 Sam* 9:24
Absalom *i*. all king's.   *2 Sam* 13:23
to-morrow am I *i*. to her.   *Esth* 5:12

inward

it in the fire; it is fret *i*.   *Lev* 13:55
their hinder parts were *i*.   *1 Ki* 7:25
and their faces were *i*.   *2 Chr* 3:13
my *i*. friends abhorred.   *Job* 19:19
who hath *i*. wisdom in the *i*.?   38:36
i. part is very wickedness.   *Ps* 5:9
i. thought is, that their houses. 49:11
desirest truth in the *i*. parts.   51:6
i. thought of every one of.   64:6
searching all the *i*. parts.   *Pr* 20:27
so do stripes the *i*. parts of the.   30
my *i*. parts sound for Kir-. *Isa* 16:11
my law in their *i*. parts.   *Jer* 31:33
your *i*. part is full of.   *Luke* 11:39
the law of God after *i*.   *Rom* 7:22
the *i*. man is renewed.   *2 Cor* 4:16
i. affection is more abundant.   7:15

inwardly

their mouth, but curse *i*.   *Ps* 62:4
but *i*. they are ravening.   *Mat* 7:15
is a Jew who is one *i*.   *Rom* 2:29

inwards

fat that covereth the *i*. *Ex* 29:13, 22
  Lev 3:3, 9, 14; 4:8; 7:3; 9:19
thou shalt wash the *i*.   *Ex* 29:17
  Lev 1:9, 13; 9:14
his *i*. and dung burn in.   *Lev* 4:11
the fat on the *i*. Moses burnt.   8:16
washed the *i*. and the legs with.   21

iron

(*The word is used :* [1] *Literally, of
the metal so named.* [2] *As a
symbol of hardness and strength*)
with an instrument of *i*.   *Num* 35:16
was a bedstead of *i*.   *Deut* 3:11
out of the *i*. furnace, out of Egypt.
  4:20; *1 Ki* 8:51; *Jer* 11:4
a land whose stones are *i*. *Deut* 8:9
not lift up any *i*. tool on.   27:5
is under thee shall be *i*.   28:23
put a yoke of *i*. on.   48; *Jer* 28:14
over which no man lift *i*. *Josh* 8:31
have chariots of *i*. 17:16; *Judg* 1:19
though they have *i*. chariots, and.
  Josh 17:18
hundred chariots of *i*. *Judg* 4:3, 13
weighed 600 shekels of *i*. *1 Sam* 17:7
under harrows of *i*.   *2 Sam* 12:31
  1 Chr 20:3
must be fenced with *i*. *2 Sam* 23:7
nor any tool of *i*. heard.   *1 Ki* 6:7
Zedekiah made him horns of *i*.
  22:11; *2 Chr* 18:10
and the *i*. did swim.   *2 Ki* 6:6
David prepared *i*. in.   *1 Chr* 22:3
i. for the things of *i*.   29:2, 7
graven with an *i*. pen.   *Job* 19:24
shall flee from the *i*. weapon.   20:24

i. is taken out of the earth. *Job* 28:2
bones are like bars of *i*.   40:18
he esteemeth *i*. as straw.   41:27
break them with a rod of *i*. *Ps* 2:9
they hurt, he was laid in *i*. 105:18*
being bound in *i*.   107:10
cut bars of *i*.   16
their nobles with fetters of *i*. 149:8
i. sharpeneth *i*. so a.   *Pr* 27:17
if the *i*. be blunt, and he. *Eccl* 10:10
thickets of forest with *i*. *Isa* 10:34
I will cut asunder the bars of *i*. 45:2
thy neck is an *i*. sinew, thy.   48:4
for *i*. I will bring silver, for stones *i*.
  60:17
thee this day an *i*. pillar.   *Jer* 1:18
shall *i*. break northern *i*.?   15:12
Judah is written with a pen of *i*. 17:1
make for them yokes of *i*.   28:13
i. pan, and set it for a wall of *i*.
  Ezek 4:3
was thy merchant with *i*.   27:12
Javan occupied with bright *i*.   19
his legs of *i*., feet part *i*. *Dan* 2:33
  34, 41, 42
then was the *i*. and clay broken. 35
kingdom shall be strong as *i*.   40
had great *i*. teeth, it.   7:7
beast, whose teeth were of *i*.   19
with instruments of *i*.   *Amos* 1:3
for I will make thy horn *i*. *Mi* 4:13
they came to the *i*. gate. *Acts* 12:10
seared with a hot *i*.   *1 Tim* 4:2
rule them with a rod of *i*. *Rev* 2:27
  12:5; 19:15
were breastplates of *i*.   *Rev* 9:9

see **brass**

irons

fill his skin with barbed *i*.? *Job* 41:7

is *there*

is there yet any portion ? *Gen* 31:14
God *is there* in heaven ? *Deut* 3:24
what nation *is there* so great ? 4:7, 8
who *is there* of all flesh that ?   5:26
man *is there* that hath ?   20:5; 7:8
is there any understanding.   32:28
is there any man ?   *Judg* 4:20
is there never a ?   14:3
who *is there* among all the ? 21:5, 8
neither *is there* any rock. *1 Sam* 2:2
and David said, *is there* not ? 17:29
nor *is there* any God beside thee.
  2 Sam 7:22; *Isa* 44:8
is there any that is left of Saul's ?
  2 Sam 9:1, 3
is there not here a prophet ? *1 Ki* 22:7
  2 Ki 3:11; *2 Chr* 18:6
in thy hand *is there* not ? *2 Chr* 20:6
who *is there* among you of all his
  people ?   36:23; *Ezra* 1:3
who *is there* being as I ? *Neh* 6:11
is there iniquity in ? *Job* 6:30; 33:9
is there any secret thing ?   15:11*
what profit *is there* in my blood ?
  Ps 30:9
is there a price in the ? *Pr* 17:16
is there any thing whereof it may be ?
  Eccl 1:10
what good *is there* to ?   5:11
nor *is there* any end of their
  treasures, nor *is there* any. *Isa* 2:7
nor *is there* knowledge to.   44:19
nor say, *Is there* not a lie in ?   20
is there no balm in Gilead, *is there* ?
  Jer 8:22
I am Lord, *is there* any thing ? 32:27
asked him, *Is there* any word ? 37:17
is there iniquity in Gilead ? surely
  they are vanity.   *Hos* 12:11
is there yet any with thee ?
  Amos 6:10
what man *is there* of you ? *Mat* 7:9
nor *is there* salvation in. *Acts* 4:12
what profit *is there* of ? *Rom* 3:1
is there unrighteousness with ? 9:14

there **is**

there is as it were a plague in.
  Lev 14:35
there is nothing at all.   *Num* 11:6
and *there is* no god.   *Deut* 32:39
yet *there is* both straw. *Judg* 19:19
there is a feast of the Lord. 21:19
for *there is* no restraint. *1 Sam* 14:6

that *there is* a God in. *1 Sam* 17:46
there is but a step between.   20:3
then come thou, for *there is*.   21
there is neither adversary. *1 Ki* 5:4
there is no God like thee in heaven.
  8:23; *2 Chr* 6:14
there is no man that sinneth not.
  1 Ki 8:46; *2 Chr* 6:36
behold, *there is* Ahijah.   *1 Ki* 14:2
there is yet one man.   22:8
there is a prophet in.   *2 Ki* 5:8
yet *there is* hope in Israel.
  Ezra 10:2; *Job* 11:18
there is a certain people. *Esth* 3:8
ye may know *there is* a. *Job* 19:29
shalt say, *There is* lifting up. 22:29
but *there is* a spirit in man.   32:8
fool hath said, *There is* no God.
  Ps 14:1; 53:1
in keeping them *there is* great. 19:11
there is no want to them that. 34:9
there is a river whose streams. 46:4
verily *there is* a reward for. 58:11
there is little Benjamin.   68:27
man, in whom *there is* no help. 146:3
there is that scattereth. *Pr* 11:24
there is that maketh himself. 13:7
the righteous *there is* favour. 14:9
there is a way that seemeth right.
  12; 16:25
in all labour *there is* profit.   23
there is an end.   23:18
there is a generation that curseth.
  30:11, 12, 13, 14
to every thing *there is* a. *Eccl* 3:1
there is a just man, *there is* a. 7:15
word of a king is, *there is*.   8:4
there is that neither day nor.   11:6
there is one event.   9:2
for to him *there is* hope.   4
me *there is* no Saviour. *Isa* 43:11
me *there is* no God. 44:6, 8; 45:5
there is no throne, O daughter. 47:1
there is no peace to wicked. 48:22
  57:21; *Jer* 6:14
because *there is* no water. *Isa* 50:2
there is no beauty.   53:2
but thou saidst, *There is* no hope.
  57:10; *Jer* 2:25; 18:12
there is hope in thy end. *Jer* 31:17
Jeremiah said, *There is*.   37:17
there is a conspiracy of. *Ezek* 22:25
there is Elam.   32:24
there is Edom, her kings.   29
because *there is* no shepherd. 34:5
there is a God that revealeth.
  Dan 2:28
there is a man in thy kingdom. 5:11
because *there is* no truth. *Hos* 4:1
there is no healing of. *Nah* 3:19
there is no resurrection. *Mat* 22:23
  Mark 12:18; *1 Cor* 15:12
there is none good but. *Mark* 10:18
and yet *there is* room. *Luke* 14:22
there is joy in presence of.   15:10
because *there is* no truth. *John* 8:44
stumbleth, because *there is*. 11:10
there is among you envying and.
  1 Cor 3:3
reported *there is* fornication.   5:1
to us *there is* but one God.   8:6
there is a natural body, *there is* a.
  15:44
against such *there is* no law. *Gal* 5:23
there is no respect of. *Col* 3:25
there is no fear in love. *1 John* 4:18
there is a sin unto death.   5:16
there is a sin not unto death.   17

see **none, one**

there **is not**

there is not aught left in. *Gen* 47:18
king's sons *there is* not. *2 Sam* 13:30
there is not among us.   *1 Ki* 5:6
there is not a God in. *2 Ki* 1:3, 6
to birth, and *there is* not.   19:3
upon earth *there is* not. *Job* 41:33
and *there is* not a second. *Eccl* 4:8
there is not one barren. *S of S* 6:6
there is not a greater. *Luke* 7:28
that *there is* not a wise. *1 Cor* 6:5
there is not in every man that. 8:7

Isaac

call his name *I*.   *Gen* 17:19; 21:3

will I establish with *I.* Gen 17:21
heir with my son, even *I.* 21:10
for in *I.* shall thy seed be called.
  12; *Rom* 9:7; *Heb* 11:18
take thine only son *I.* Gen 22:2
Abraham bound *I.* 9
take a wife for *I.* 24:4
appointed for *I.* 14
I. went out to meditate in the. 63
I. was comforted after his. 67
all that he had unto *I.* 25:5
his sons *I.* and Ishmael buried. 9
God bless·d *I.* 11
I. forty years old when he took. 20
I. intreated the Lord for his wife. 21
I. was sixty years old when. 26
I. loved Esau. 28
I. went to Abimelech king of. 26:1
I. was sporting with Rebekah his. 8
I. sowed and received an. 12
I.'s servants digged in valley and. 19
grief of mind to *I.* and Rebekah. 35
as *I.* had made an end of. 27:30
I. called Jacob, blessed him. 28:1
I. sent Jacob away, he went to. 5
except the fear of *I.* had. 31:42
the God of *I.* 32:9; *Ex* 3:6, 15, 16
  4:5; *I Ki* 18:36; *1 Chr* 29:18
  2 Chr 30:6; *Mat* 22:32
  Mark 12:26; *Luke* 20:37
  Acts 3:13; 7:32
Jacob came to *I.* Gen 35:27
I. gave up the ghost. 29
to the God of his father *I.* 46:1
God, before whom my father *I.* 48:15
let the name of my father *I.* 7
there they buried *I.* 49:31
he sware to *I.* 50:24
remembered his covenant with Abraham, with *I. Ex* 2:24; *Lev* 26:42
his seed and gave him *I. Josh* 24:3
I gave unto *I.* Jacob and Esau. 4
his oath unto *I. I Chr* 16:16; *Ps* 105:9
rulers over the seed of *I. Jer* 33:26
high places of *I.* shall be desolate.
  Amos 7:9
word against the house of *I.* 16
I., and *I.* begat Jacob. *Mat* 1:2
  Luke 3:34; *Acts* 7:8
shall sit down with *I.* in. *Mat* 8:11
when ye shall see *I.* in. *Luke* 13:28
conceived by our father *I.* was. *Rom* 9:10
we, brethren, as *I.* was. *Gal* 4:28
in tabernacles with *I.* and. *Heb* 11:9
Abraham offered up *I.* 17; *Jas* 2:21
by faith *I.* blessed Jacob. *Heb* 11:20

Isaiah *or* Esaias

Hezekiah sent Eliakim to *I.*
  2 Ki 19:2; *Isa* 37:2
Hezekiah was sick, *I.* came to him.
  2 Ki 20:1; *Isa* 38:1
and *I.* cried unto the Lord.
  2 Ki 20:11; *2 Chr* 32:20
acts did *I.* write. *2 Chr* 26:22; 32:32
I. hath walked naked. *Isa* 20:3
spoken by the prophet *E. Mat* 3:3
  4:14; 8:17; 12:17; 13:14
  Luke 3:4; *John* 1:23; 12:38
well did *E.* prophesy of you.
  Mat 15:7; *Mark* 7:6
him book of prophet *E. Luke* 4:17
because that *E.* said. *John* 12:39
these things said *E.* when he. 41
the eunuch read *E. Acts* 8:28, 30
spake the Holy Ghost by *E.* 28:25
E. also crieth concerning. *Rom* 9:27
E. said before, Except the Lord. 29
E. saith, Lord, who hath ? 10:16
E. is very bold, and saith, I. 20
again *E.* saith, There shall be. 15:12

Iscariot, *see* Judas

Ish-bosheth

Abner took *I.* and set. *2 Sam* 2:8
wroth for the words of *I.* 3:8
David sent messengers to *I.* 14
they brought the head of *I.* 4:8
but they took the head of *I.* 12

Ishmael

call his name *I.* Gen 16:11, 15
old when Hagar bare *I.* 16
said to God, O that *I.* might. 17:18
as for *I.* I have heard thee, I. 20
I. was 13 years old when. 25

his sons Isaac and *I.* buried.*Gen* 25:9
the generations of *I.* 12, 13, 16
  1 Chr 1:29, 31
years of the life of *I.* 137. *Gen* 25:17
went Esau unto *I.* and took. 28:9
I. came to Gedaliah. *2 Ki* 25:23
  Jer 40:8
I. came and ten men with him.
  2 Ki 25:25; *Jer* 41:1
Abraham, Isaac and *I.* *1 Chr* 1:28
and *I.* were sons of Azel. 8:38; 9:44
Zebadiah son of *I.* the. *2 Chr* 19:11
Jehoiada took *I.* into covenant. 23:1
I. Elasah, had taken. *Ezra* 10:22
Ammonites hath sent *I.* *Jer* 40:14
I will slay *I.* 15
for thou speakest falsely of *I.* 16
I. smote Gedaliah. 41:2
I. went forth to meet them. 6
then *I.* carried away captive. 10
then Johanan went to fight with *I.* 12
but *I.* escaped from Johanan. 15

Ishmaelites

let us sell him to the *I.* *Gen* 37:27
bought him of the hand of *I.* 39:1
because they were *I.* *Judg* 8:24
Edomites and *I.* confederate against.
  Ps 83:3

island

he shall deliver the *i.* of. *Job* 22:30
the wild beasts of the *i.* *Isa* 34:14
under a certain *i.* Clauda. *Acts* 27:16
must be cast on a certain *i.* 26
the *i.* was called Melita. 28:1
of the chief man of the *i.* 7
others who had diseases in the *i.* 9
every *i.* was moved out. *Rev* 6:14
every *i.* fled away, mountains. 16:20

islands

his people from the *i.* of. *Isa* 11:11
wild beasts of the *i.* shall. 13:22
keep silence before me, O *i.* 41:1
his praise in the *i.* 42:12
I will make the rivers *i.* and. 15
i. he will repay recompence. 59:18
wild beasts of the *i.* shall. *Jer* 50:39

isle

inhabitants of the *i.* say. *Isa* 20:6
be still, ye inhabitants of the *i.* 23:2
Tarshish, howl, inhabitants of the *i.* 6
through the *i.* to Paphos. *Acts* 13:6
which had wintered in the *i.* 28:11
I John was in the *i.* that is. *Rev* 1:9

isles

the *i.* of the Gentiles. *Gen* 10:5
laid a tribute on the *i.* *Esth* 10:1
the kings of the *i.* shall. *Ps* 72:10
let the multitude of the *i.* be. 97:1
ye the Lord in the *i.* of. *Isa* 24:15
he taketh up the *i.* as a very. 40:15
the *i.* saw it and feared, the. 41:5
the *i.* shall wait for his law. 42:4
the *i.* and the inhabitants thereof. 10
listen, O *i.* unto me, and. 49:1
the *i.* shall wait upon me. 51:5; 60:9
the *i.* afar off that have not. 66:19
over the *i.* of Chittim. *Jer* 2:10
the kings of the *i.* shall drink. 25:22
hear and declare it in the *i.* 31:10
shall not *i.* shake at ? *Ezek* 26:15
the *i.* tremble, the *i.* shall. 18
of the people for many *i.* 27:3
benches of ivory, brought out of *i.* 6
blue and purple from the *i.* of. 7
many *i.* were the merchandise. 15
inhabitants of the *i.* shall be. 35
dwell carelessly in the *i.* 39:6
turn his face to the *i.* *Dan* 11:18
the *i.* of the heathen. *Zeph* 2:11

Israel

be no more Jacob but *I.* *Gen* 32:28
but *I.* shall be thy name. 35:10
  1 Ki 18:31
I. dwelt in land of Egypt. *Gen* 47:27
and *I.* bowed himself upon the. 31
in thee shall *I.* bless, saying. 48:20
the shepherd, the stone of *I.* 49:24
I. is my son. *Ex* 4:22
obey his voice to let *I.* go ? 5:2
that we have let *I.* go from. 14:5
from *I.,* for Lord fighteth. 25
Lord saved *I.* that day from. 30

I. prevailed. *Ex* 17:11
Isaac, and *I.* thy servant. 32:13
her son and a man of *I.* *Lev* 24:10
good concerning *I.* *Num* 10:29
to the many thousands of *I.* 36
thus saith thy brother *I.,* Let. 20:14
I. vowed a vow unto the Lord. 21:2
then *I.* sang this song, Spring up. 17
defy *I.* 23:7
shall be said of *I.* What hath! 23
a Sceptre rise out of *I.* 24:17
Edom a possession, and *I.* 18
Phinehas went after man of *I.* 25:8
name be not put out of *I. Deut* 25:6
shall teach *I.* thy law, Jacob. 33:10
I. then shall dwell in safety. 28
when *I.* turned their backs. *Josh* 7:8
I. hath sinned. 11
took the mountain of *I.* 11:16
and *I.* he shall know. 22:22
I. served the Lord all days. 24:31
it came to pass when *I.* *Judg* 1:28
them I may prove *I.* 2:22; 3:1, 4
toward the governors of *I.* 5:9
I. was greatly impoverished by. 6:1
save *I.* 14, 15, 36, 37
lest *I.* vaunt themselves. 7:2
so that *I.* was sore distressed. 10:9
grieved for the misery of *I.* 16
because *I.* took away my land. 11:13
smote Benjamin before *I.* 20:35
I. was smitten. *1 Sam* 4:2, 10
I. is fled. 17
on whom is the desire of *I.?* 9:20
heard that *I.* also was had. 13:4
also the strength of *I.* will. 15:29
of the God of the armies of *I.* 17:45
the beauty of *I.* is slain. *2 Sam* 1:19
broughtest in *I.* 5:2; *1 Chr* 11:2
nation is like thy people *I.? 2 Sam* 7:23
the ark, and *I.* and Judah. 11:11
for *I.* had fled every man to. 19:8
Judah and *I.* were many. *1 Ki* 4:20
I. dwelt safely. 25; *Jer* 23:6
I. shall be a proverb among. *1 Ki* 9:7
he abhorred *I.* 11:25
so *I.* rebelled. 12:19
Lord shall smite *I.* as a reed. 14:15
art thou he that troubleth *I.?* 18:17
began to cut *I.* short. *2 Ki* 10:32
was put to the worse before *I.* 14:12
would blot out the name of *I.* 27
carried *I.* away into Assyria. 17:6
  23, 23
of Jacob, whom he named *I.* 34
the Lord concerning *I.* *1 Chr* 11:10
they of *I.* were a thousand. 21:5
the God of *I.* 29:18; *1 Ki* 18:36
  2 Chr 6:16; 30:6; *Jer* 31:1
because thy God loved *I.* 2 *Chr* 9:8
whether they were of *I.* *Ezra* 2:59
  Neh 7:61
for ever towards *I.* *Ezra* 3:11
to increase the trespass of *I.* 10:10
Jacob shall rejoice, *I.* shall be glad.
  Ps 14:7; 53:6
fear him, all ye seed of *I.* 22:23
redeem *I.* O God, out of all. 25:22
Lord, from the fountain of *I.* 68:26
heard this, he abhorred *I.* 78:59
would not hearken, *I.* would. 81:11
O that my people *I.* had walked. 13
that name of *I.* may be no more. 83:4
Judah was his sanctuary, *I.* 114:2
he that keepeth *I.* shall. 121:4
peace shall be upon *I.* 125:5; 128:6
I. hope in the Lord. 130:7; 131:3
Lord hath chosen *I.* for his. 135:4
together the outcasts of *I.* 147:2
let *I.* rejoice in him that made. 149:2
but *I.* doth not know nor. *Isa* 1:3
blessed be *I.* mine inheritance. 19:25
I. shall blossom and bud. 27:6
but thou *I.* art my servant. 41:8
who gave *I.* to robbers ? 42:24
have given *I.* to reproaches. 43:28
himself by the name of *I.* 44:5
for *I.* mine elect's sake, I. 45:4
I. shall be saved in Lord with. 17
in the Lord shall the seed of *I.* 25
called by the name of *I.* 48:1
though *I.* be not gathered, I. 49:5
to restore the preserved of *I.* 6
gathereth the outcasts of *I.* 56:8

I. acknowledge us not.   *Isa* 63:16
I. was holiness to the Lord. *Jer* 2:3
is *I.* a servant ?   14
the salvation of *I.*   3:23
I. is the rod of his.   10:16; 51:19
of *I.,* saviour in trouble. 14:8; 17:13
for was not *I.* a derision ?   48:27
hath *I.* no sons ? hath he no ?   49:1
I. shall be heir to them that were. 2
I. is a scattered sheep, lions. 50:17
I will bring *I.* again to his.   19
iniquity of *I.* be sought for and.   20
I. hath not been forsaken of.   51:5
Lord hath swallowed up *I. Lam* 2:5
you in the border of *I. Ezek* 11:10
wilt thou make a full end of *I.?*   13
I the Lord do sanctify *I.*   37:28
are gone from me, when *I.*   44:10
though thou *I.* play harlot. *Hos* 4:15
I. slideth back as a backsliding.   16
I. is not hid from me,   5:3; 6:10
I. shall fall.   5:5
I. shall cry to me, My God.   8:2
I. hath cast off the thing that.   3
I. is swallowed up.   8
I. shall know it.   9:7
I. hath forgotten his Maker.   14
I found *I.* like grapes in the.   9:10
I. is an empty vine.   10:1
I. shall be ashamed of his own.   6
the sin of *I.* be destroyed.   8
when *I.* was a child, then I.   11:1
how shall I deliver thee, *I.?*   8
I. served and kept sheep.   12:12
with them for my heritage I. *Joel* 3:2
I. shall surely be led. *Amos* 7:11, 17
Adullam the glory of *I.*   *Mi* 1:15
they shall smite the judge of *I. 5:1
holpen his servant *I.*   *Luke* 1:54
art thou a master of *I.? John* 3:10
that for the hope of *I.*   *Acts* 28:20
not all *I.* which are of *I. Rom* 9:6
concerning *I.* though number of *I.* 27
I. which followed the law of.   31
but I say, did not *I.* know ?   10:19
I. hath not obtained what he.   11:7
behold *I.* after the flesh. *I Cor* 10:18
on them and on *I.* of God. *Gal* 6:16
of the stock of *I.* of the.   *Phil* 3:5

see **children, congregation,
elders, God, Holy** One of Israel,
house

against **Israel**
Arad fought *ag. I.*   *Num* 21:1
Sihon fought *ag. I.*   23
is there any divination *ag. I.?* 23:23
anger of Lord was kindled *ag. I.* 25:3
  32:13; *Judg* 2:14, 20; 3:8; 10:7
2 Sam 24:1; *2 Ki* 13:3; *I Chr* 27:24
      2 Chr 28:13; *Ps* 78:21
of Canaan *ag. I.*   *Josh* 8:14; 11:5
Balak of Moab warred *ag. I.* 24:9
Eglon *ag. I.*   *Judg* 3:12
Midian *ag. I.*   6:2
Ammon made war *ag. I.* 11:4, 5, 20
Balak, did he ever strive *ag. I.?* 25
Philistines put themselves in array
against I.   *I Sam* 4:2; 7:7, 10
         31:1; *I Chr* 10:1
Ben-hadad *ag. I.*   *I Ki* 20:26
           2 Ki 6:8
Moab rebelled *ag. I.*   *2 Ki* 1:1
was great indignation *ag. I.* 3:27
yet the Lord testified *ag. I.* 17:13
stood up *against I.*   *I Chr* 21:1
Rehoboam went out *ag. I. 2 Chr* 11:1
words I have spoken *ag. I. Jer* 36:2
prophesy *ag. I.*   *Amos* 7:16
maketh intercession *ag. I. Rom* 11:2

all **Israel**
able men out of *all I.*   *Ex* 18:25
all I. round about fled. *Num* 16:34
all I. shall hear. *Deut* 13:11; 21:21
all I. stoned Achan with. *Josh* 7:25
all I. went a whoring. *Judg* 8:27
that his sons did to *all I. I Sam* 2:22
all I. knew that Samuel was.   3:20
word of Samuel came to *all I.* 4:1
lay it for a reproach on *all I.* 11:2
but *all I.* and Judah loved.   18:16
all I. had lamented Samuel.   28:3
to bring about *all I.*   *2 Sam* 3:12
all I. understood that it was not. 37

will do this thing before *all I.*
         2 Sam 12:12
in *all I.* none so much praised. 14:25
all I. shall hear that thou art. 16:21
all I. know thy father.   17:10
and *all I.* fled every one to.   18:17
speech of *all I.* is come to me. 19:11
the eyes of *all I.* are.   *I Ki* 1:20
thou knowest that *all I.* set.   2:15
all I. heard of the judgement.   3:28
king and *all I.* offered sacrifice. 8:62
all I. stoned Adoram with.   12:18
all I. shall mourn for him.   14:13
gather to me *all I.* unto.   18:19
I saw *all I.* scattered.
         2 Chr 18:16
David and *all I.* went to. *I Chr* 11:4
David and *all I.* played.   13:8
all I. brought up the ark of. 15:28
I have walked with *all I.*   17:6
all I. and the princes obeyed. 29:23
all I. forsook the law. *2 Chr* 12:1
hear me, Jeroboam, and *all I.* 13:4
God smote Jeroboam and *all I.* 15
ruin of him and of *all I.*   28:23
to make an atonement for *all I.*
      29:24; *Ezra* 6:17
all I. went out and brake. *2 Chr* 31:1
all I. dwelt in their cities. *Ezra* 2:70
          Neh 7:73
made *all I.* swear to do. *Ezra* 10:5
all I. gave the portions. *Neh* 12:47
belongeth to us, to *all I.* *Dan* 9:7
yea, *all I.* have transgressed.   11
the law of Moses for *all I. Mal* 4:4
not *all I.* which are of *I. Rom* 9:6
so *all I.* shall be saved, as it. 11:26

camp of **Israel**
went before the *camp* of *I. Ex* 24:19
Egyptians and the *camp* of *I.*   20
the *camp* of *I.* a curse. *Josh* 6:18
them without the *camp* of *I.*   23
out of the *camp* of *I.* am I escaped.
         2 Sam 1:3
came to the *camp* of *I.*   *2 Ki* 3:24

for **Israel**
God had done for *I.*   *Ex* 18:1, 8
Josh 24:31; *Judg* 2:7, 10; *I Ki* 8:66
Lord fought for *I.*   *Josh* 10:14, 42
left no sustenance for *I.*   *Judg* 6:4
cried unto Lord for *I.*   *I Sam* 7:9
made it an ordinance for *I.*   30:25
not any helper for *I.*   *2 Ki* 14:26
atonement for *I.* as Moses had.
    I Chr 6:49; 22:1; *Neh* 10:33
statute for *I.,* a law of God. *Ps* 81:4
salvation in Zion for *I.*   *Isa* 46:13
word of the Lord for *I. Zech* 12:1
my prayer to God for *I.*   *Rom* 10:1

from **Israel**
shalt be cut off *from I.*   *Ex* 12:15
       Num 19:13
be turned away *from I. Num* 25:4
put evil *from I.* *Deut* 17:12; 22:22
       Judg 20:13
one tribe cut off *from I. Judg* 21:6
the glory is departed *from I.*
       I Sam 4:21, 22
the cities taken *from I.* were.   7:14
away the reproach *from I.*   17:26
the plague was stayed *from I.*
       2 Sam 24:25
they separated *from I.* all the mixed
multitude.   *Neh* 13:3
cut off *from I.* head and.   *Isa* 9:14
for *from I.* was it also, the. *Hos* 8:6

in **Israel**
he had wrought folly in *I. Gen* 34:7
      Deut 22:21; *Josh* 7:15
       Judg 20:6, 10
Jacob, scatter them in *I. Gen* 49:7
strangers sojourn in *I.*   *Lev* 20:2
     22:18; *Ezek* 14:7
able to go forth to war in *I.*
     Num 1:3, 45; 26:2
heads of thousands in *I.* 1:16; 10:4
to me all the firstborn in *I.*   3:13
every thing devoted in *I.*   18:14
given all the tenth in *I.* for an.   21
nor seen perverseness in *I.*   23:21
abomination is wrought in *I.*
      Deut 17:4; 22:21
up his brother a name in *I.*   25:7

his name be called in *I. Deut* 25:10
arose not a prophet since in *I.* 34:10
Rahab dwelleth in *I.*   *Josh* 6:25
in *I.* till that I Deborah arose, that I
  arose a mother in *I.*   *Judg* 5:7
spear seen among 40,000 in *I.?* 8
in *I.* to lament Jephthah.   11:39
was no king in *I.*   17:6, 18:1
       19:1; 21:25
be priest to a family in *I.*   18:19
in *I.,* one tribe lacking in *I.?* 21:3
times in *I.* concerning redeeming,
  this was a testimony in *I. Ruth* 4:7
his name may be famous in *I.*   14
I will do a thing in *I.*   *I Sam* 3:11
beforetime in *I.* when a man.   9:9
wrought salvation in *I.* 11:13; 14:45
father's house free in *I.*   17:25
know that there is a God in *I.*   46
is my father's family in *I.*   18:18
who is like to thee in *I.?*   26:15
great man fallen in *I. 2 Sam* 3:38
ought to be done in *I.*   13:12
be as one of the fools in *I.*   13
put to death this day in *I.?* 19:22
and peaceable in *I.,* thou seekest to
  destroy a mother in *I.*   20:19
shalt thou kill any man in *I.* 21:4
cut off him that is shut up and left in
  I. I Ki 14:10; 21:21; *2 Ki* 9:8
that thou art God in *I.*   *I Ki* 18:36
left me seven thousand in *I.* 19:18
because there is not a God in *I.*
      2 Ki 1:3, 6, 16
that there is a prophet in *I.*   5:8
no God in all the earth but in *I.* 15
the prophet in *I.* telleth the.   6:12
for there was joy in *I. I Chr* 12:40
a man to be ruler in *I. 2 Chr* 7:18
because he had done good in *I.* 24:16
for them that are left in *I.*   34:21
Josiah made all present in *I.* to. 33
passover like to that kept in *I.* 35:18
made them an ordinance in *I.* 25
yet there is hope in *I.*   *Ezra* 10:2
Judah, his name is great in *I. Ps* 76:1
and he appointed law in *I.*   78:5
signs and for wonders in *I. Isa* 8:18
hath glorified himself in *I.*   44:23
committed villany in *I.*   *Jer* 29:23
set signs and wonders in *I.* 32:20
it as a proverb in *I.*   *Ezek* 12:23
          18:3
I am the holy One in *I.*   39:7
Gog a place of graves in *I.*   11
give them no possession in *I.* 44:28
every dedicated thing in *I.*   29
shall be his possession in *I.* 45:8
oblation for the prince in *I.*   16
he exalted himself in *I. Hos* 13:1
that is to be ruler in *I.*   *Mi* 5:2
is committed in *I.*   *Mal* 2:11
so great faith, no not in *I. Mat* 8:10
         Luke 7:9
it was never so seen in *I. Mat* 9:33
and rising of many in *I. Luke* 2:34
many widows were in *I.*   4:25
lepers in *I.*   27

see **king, kings**

land of **Israel**
no smith found in all the *land* of *I.*
       I Sam 13:19
little maid out of *land* of *I. I Ki* 5:2
came no more into *land* of *I.* 6:23
brethren left in *land* of *I. I Chr* 13:2
strangers that were in *land* of *I.*
    22:2; *2 Chr* 2:17; 30:25
idols through *land* of *I. 2 Chr* 34:7
the Lord to the *land* of *I. Ezek* 7:2
I will give you the *land* of *I.* 11:17
the Lord of the *land* of *I.* 12:19
enter into *land* of *I.* 13:9; 20:38
bring you into the *land* of *I.* 20:42
         37:12
prophesy against the *land* of *I.* 21:2
Aha, against the *land* of *I.* 25:3
with despite against *land* of *I.* 6
Judah and *land* of *I.* were. 27:17
shall come against *land* of *I.* 38:18
great shaking in the *land* of *I.* 19
brought me into *land* of *I.* 40:2
go into the *land* of *I.* for. *Mat* 2:20
and came into the *land* of *I.* 21

made Israel sin
Jeroboam made I. to sin. 1 Ki 14:16
  15:26, 30, 34; 16:19, 26; 22:52
Baasha made my people I. to sin.
          16:2, 13
Ahab made I. to sin. 21:22
son of Nebat who made I. to sin.
2 Ki 3:3; 10:29, 31; 13:2, 6, 11
  14:24; 15:9, 18, 24, 28; 23:15

men of Israel
called for all men of I. Josh 10:24
men of I. gathered. Judg 20:11
men of I. went out. 22
men of I. encouraged themselves. 22
the men of I. gave place to the. 36
men of I. were distressed that day.
       1 Sam 14:24
the men of I. fled from the. 31:1
beaten and the men of I. 2 Sam 2:17
hearts of the men of I. are. 15:13
whom the men of I. choose. 16:18
words of men of Judah fiercer than
  of the men of I. 19:43
men of I. were gone away. 23:9
down the chosen men of I. Ps 78:31
fear not, ye men of I. I. Isa 41:14
ye men of I. hear these. Acts 2:22
ye men of I. why marvel ? 3:12
ye men of I. take heed to. 5:35
Paul said, Men of I. give. 13:16
crying out, Men of I. help. 21:28

O Israel
these be thy gods, O I. Ex 32:4
are thy tabernacles, O I. Num 24:5
hearken, O I. Deut 4:1; 27:9
       Isa 48:12
hear, O I., the statutes. Deut 5:1
  6:3, 4; 9:1; 20:3; Ps 50:7
  81:8; Isa 44:1; Mark 12:29
happy art thou, O I. Deut 33:29
in the midst of thee, O I. Josh 7:13
every man to his tents, O I.
  2 Sam 20:1; 1 Ki 12:16
       2 Chr 10:16
behold thy gods, O I. 1 Ki 12:28
O I. trust thou in Lord. Ps 115:9
why speakest thou, O I.? Isa 40:27
O I. fear not. 43:1; Jer 30:10
       46:27
been weary of me, O I. Isa 43:22
O I. for thou art my servant, O.
  thou shalt not be. 44:21; 49:3
if thou wilt return, O I. Jer 4:1
       Hos 14:1
O I. thy prophets are. Ezek 13:4
rejoice not, O I. for joy. Hos 9:1
O I. thou hast sinned from. 10:9
O I. thou hast destroyed. 13:9
to meet thy God. O I. Amos 4:12
shout, O I. be glad and. Zeph 3:14

over Israel
Abimelech reigned three years over
      Judg 9:22
had dominion over I. 14:4
his sons judges over I. 1 Sam 8:1
reigned two years over I. 13:1
thee from being king over I. 13:26
Ish-bosheth Saul's son reigned over
  I. 2 Sam 2:10
throne of David over I.
  5:2, 3, 17; 6:21; 1 Chr 11:3
hosts is the God over I. 2 Sam 7:26
Solomon king over I. 1 Ki 1:34
Jeroboam king over I. 11:37
shall raise up a king over I. 14:14
Nadab reigned over I. 15:25
Elah reigned over I. 16:8
Omri king over I. 16
Ahab reigned over I. 29
Ahaziah reigned over I. 22:51
Jehoram reigned over I. 2 Ki 3:1
Jehu king over I. 9:3, 6, 12; 10:36
Jehoahaz reigned over I. 13:1
Jehoash reigned over I. 10
Zechariah reigned over I. 15:8
Menahem reigned over I. 15:17
Pekahiah reigned over I. 23
Hoshea reigned over I. 17:1
Chenaniah for outward business over
  I. 1 Chr 26:29
times that went over I. are. 29:30
his excellency is over I. Ps 68:34
preacher was king over I. Eccl 1:12

Israel joined with people
much people of I. died. Num 21:6
O Lord, to thy people I. Deut 21:8
and bless thy people I. 26:15
should bless people of I. Josh 8:33
before his people I. Judg 11:23
offerings of I. my people. 1 Sam 2:29
Saul captain over my people I. 9:16
made his people I. utterly. 27:12
I will save my people I. 2 Sam 3:18
to feed my people I. 5:2; 7:7
       1 Chr 11:2
for his people I.'s sake. 2 Sam 5:12
for my people I. that they may dwell
  and move no. 7:10; 1 Chr 17:9
to thyself thy people I. 2 Sam 7:24
not forsake my people I. 1 Ki 6:13
when thy people I. be smitten. 8:33
       2 Chr 6:24
what prayer soever be made by all
  thy people I. 1 Ki 8:38
fear thee, as do thy people I. 43
given rest to his people I. 56
because of his people I. 1 Chr 14:2
be ruler over my people I. 17:7
       2 Chr 6:5
earth is like thy people I. 1 Chr 17:21
people I. didst thou make. 22
shewed I. his people. 2 Chr 7:10
blessed Lord and his people I. 31:8
serve now the Lord your God and his
  people I. 35:3
all they of the people of I. Ezra 7:13
people of I. have not separated. 9:1
heritage to I. his people. Ps 135:12
people I. be as the sand. Isa 10:22
wickedness of my people I. Jer 7:12
which I caused my people I. 12:14
caused my people I. to err. 23:13
again the captivity of my people I.
  and Judah. 30:3; Amos 9:14
Edom by my people I. Ezek 25:14
your fruit to my people I. 36:8
will cause my people I. to walk. 12
when my people I. dwelleth. 38:14
come up against my people I. 16
the sin of my people I. Dan 9:20
go, prophesy unto my people I.
       Amos 7:15
is come upon my people I. 8:2
shall rule my people I. Mat 2:6
glory of thy people I. Luke 2:32
people of I. were gathered against.
       Acts 4:27
God of this people I. chose. 13:17
repentance to all people of I. 24

princes of Israel
the princes of I. being. Num 1:44
the princes of I. heads and princes of
  the tribes offered at the. 7:2, 84
princes of I. to help. 1 Chr 22:17
David assembled the princes of I.
      23:2; 28:1
princes of I. humbled. 2 Chr 12:6
slew divers of princes of I. 21:4
lamentation for the princes of I.
      Ezek 19:1
be upon all the princes of I. 21:12
the princes of I. were on thee. 22:6
it suffice you, O princes of I. 45:9

to or unto Israel
God spake unto I. in. Gen 46:2
hear and hearken unto I. 49:2
the Lord hath done to I. Ex 18:9
Joshua gave it for inheritance to I.
  Josh 11:23; 21:43
Lord ha'k given rest unto I. 23:1
he hath shewed unto I. Judg 8:35
what Amalek did to I. 1 Sam 15:2
that seemed good to I. 2 Sam 3:19
an adversary to I. 1 Ki 11:25
for a law, and to I. for an everlasting
  covenant. 1 Chr 16:17; Ps 105:10
a cause of trespass to I.? 1 Chr 21:3
I will give quietness to I. in. 22:9
ordinance for ever to I. 2 Chr 2:4
scribe of his statutes to I. Ezra 7:11
Lord had commanded to I. Neh 8:1
truly God is good to I. Ps 73:1
heritage unto I. 135:12; 136:22
sheweth his judgements to I. 147:19
as it was to I. in the day. Isa 11:16
a wilderness unto I.? Jer 2:31

a father to I. Ephraim is. Jer 31:9
I will be as the dew to I. Hos 14:5
to declare to I. his sin. Mi 3:8
the word of the Lord to I. Mal 1:1
day of his shewing unto I. Luke 1:80
be made manifest to I. John 1:31
restore the kingdom to I.? Acts 1:6
to give repentance to I. 5:31
God hath raised unto I. 13:23
to I. he saith, All day. Rom 10:21
in part is happened to I. 11:25

tribes of Israel
Dan shall judge as one of tribes of I.
      Gen 49:16
are the twelve tribes of I. 28
according to 12 tribes of I. Ex 24:4
through all tribes of I. to war.
      Num 31:4
to any of the other tribes of I. 36:3
every one of tribes of I. shall keep. 9
evil out of tribes of I. Deut 29:21
when the tribes of I. were. 33:5
men out of tribes of I. Josh 3:12
to number of tribes of I. 4:5, 8
brought I. by their tribes. 7:16
Joshua gave to the tribes of I. 12:7
fathers of tribes of I. divided. 19:51
princes through tribes of I. 22:14
Joshua gathered all tribes of I. 24:1
Dan not among tribes of I. Judg 18:1
chief of tribes of I. presented. 20:2
of an 100 out of all tribes of I. 10
tribes of I. came not up. 21:5, 8
a breach in the tribes of I. 15
him out of all tribes of I. 1 Sam 2:28
the smallest of the tribes of I. 9:21
Samuel caused all tribes of I. 10:20
made head of the tribes of I.? 15:17
came all the tribes of I. to David.
      2 Sam 5:1
word with any of tribes of I. 7:7
servant is of one of tribes of I. 15:2
spies through all the tribes of I. 10
strife through the tribes of I. 19:9
all the tribes of I. and number. 24:2
no city out of all the tribes of I. to
  build. 1 Ki 8:16; 2 Chr 6:5
Jerusalem out of all the tribes of I.
  1 Ki 11:32; 14:21; 2 Ki 21:7
    2 Chr 12:13; 33:7
out of all the tribes of I. 2 Chr 11:16
goats according to tribes of I.
      Ezra 6:17
made tribes of I. to dwell. Ps 78:55
I will take tribes of I. Ezek 37:19
the twelve tribes of I. 47:13, 21, 22
city out of all the tribes of I. 48:19
after the names of the tribes of I. 31
among tribes of I. have I. Hos 5:9
the eyes of all tribes of I. Zech 9:1
judging the twelve tribes of I.
  Mat 19:28; Luke 22:30
with names of twelve tribes of I.
      Rev 21:12

with Israel
Amalek fought with I. Ex 17:8
a covenant with thee and I. 34:27
have no inheritance with I. Deut 18:1
his judgements with I. 33:21
of Canaan fought with I. Josh 9:2
Gibeon made peace with I. 10:1
themselves together to fight with I.
  1 Sam 13:5; 28:1; 2 Sam 21:15
Syrians made peace with I.
      2 Sam 10:19
was very angry with I. 2 Ki 17:18
for Lord is not with I. 2 Chr 25:7
Lord will plead with I. Mi 6:2

Israelite
the I. was slain, Zimri. Num 25:14
the son of Ithra an I. 2 Sam 17:25
behold an I. indeed, in. John 1:47
I also am an I. of seed. Rom 11:1

Israelites
the cattle of the I. dead. Ex 9:7
I. born shall dwell in. Lev 23:42
all the I. passed over on. Josh 3:17
only divide it by lot to the. 13:6
destroyed of the I. Judg 20:21
servants did to all I. 1 Sam 2:14
I. went to the Philistines to. 13:20
turned to be with the. 14:21
all the I. lamented Samuel. 25:1

the *I*. pitched by a.   *1 Sam* 29:1
the *I*. were troubled at.   *2 Sam* 4:1
the *I*. rose and smote.   *2 Ki* 3:24
as all the multitude of the *I*.   7:13
inhabitants were the *I*.   *1 Chr* 9:2
who are *I*.; to whom.   *Rom* 9:4
are they *I*.? so am I.   *2 Cor* 11:22

Israelitish
the son of an *I*. woman.   *Lev* 24:10
I. woman's son blasphemed the.   11

Issachar
Leah called his name *I*.   *Gen* 30:18
Leah's son, *I*.   35:23
sons of *I*.   46:13; *1 Chr* 7:1
I. is a strong ass.   *Gen* 49:14
Israel's sons, *I*., Zebulun.   *Ex* 1:3
                                1 Chr 2:1
the princes of *I*., Nethaneel.
                        Num 1:8; 2:5; 7:18
I. and Joseph shall stand to bless.
                                Deut 27:12
rejoice, Zebulun and *I*. in.   33:18
they met together in *I*.   *Josh* 17:10
Manasseh had in *I*. and Asher.   11
the princes of *I*. were with Deborah,
even *I*. and also.   *Judg* 5:15
Tola a man of *I*. arose to.   10:1
was an officer in *I*.   *1 Ki* 4:17
Ahijah of the house of *I*.   15:27
they that were nigh to *I*. *1 Chr* 12:40
I. the seventh son of.   26:5
captain of *I*. Omri the son of.   27:18
of *I*. had not cleansed.   *2 Chr* 30:18
of Simeon, *I*. a portion. *Ezek* 48:25
by the border of *I*., Zebulun a.   26
south side, one gate of *I*., one.   33

tribe of **Issachar**
were numbered of the *tribe of I*.
                                Num 1:29
Judah shall be the *tribe of I*.   2:5
over the *tribe of I*. was.   10:15
of the *tribe of I*. to spy the.   13:7
prince of the *tribe of I*.   34:26
inheritance of the *tribe of I*.
                                Josh 19:23
lot out of the families of the *tribe of I*.
                    21:6, 28; *1 Chr* 6:62, 72
of *tribe of I*. were sealed.   *Rev* 7:7

issue
[1] *A passage, way, or outlet*, Ps
68:20. [2] *Children or posterity*,
Gen 48:6. [3] *A flux or running*,
Lev 12:7. [4] *To flow*, Ezek 47:8.
[5] *To come forth hastily and
violently*, Josh 8:22.

issue, *substantive*
i. which thou begettest.   *Gen* 48:6
the *i*. of her blood. *Lev* 12:7; 15:25
                    Mat 9:20; *Mark* 5:25
                            Luke 8:43, 44
running *i*.   *Lev* 15:2, 3; 22:4
hath the *i*.   15:8, 28
of Joab, one hath an *i*.   *2 Sam* 3:29
on him the offspring and *i*. *Isa* 22:24
whose *i*. is like the *i*.   *Ezek* 23:20
having no *i*. left his wife. *Mat* 22:25

issue
thy sons that *i*. from thee. *2 Ki* 20:18
                                Isa 39:7
these waters *i*. toward.   *Ezek* 47:8*

issued
other *i*. out of the city.   *Josh* 8:22
break forth as if it *i*.   *Job* 38:8
waters *i*. from under.   *Ezek* 47:1
because their waters *i*. out of.   12
a fiery stream *i*. and.   *Dan* 7:10
of their mouths *i*. fire. *Rev* 9:17, 18

issues
to God belong the *i*.   *Ps* 68:20
out of it are the *i*. of life. *Pr* 4:23

Italian
a centurion of the *I*. band. *Acts* 10:1

Italy
Jew lately come from *I*.   *Acts* 18:2
that we should sail into *I*.   27:1
they of *I*. salute you.   *Heb* 13:24

itch
will smite thee with *i*.   *Deut* 28:27

itching
teachers having *i*. ears.   *2 Tim* 4:3

22

Ithamar
Aaron's sons, Abihu, and *I*.
                    Ex 6:23; *1 Chr* 6:3
counted by the hand of *I*.   38:21
charge under hand of *I*.   *Num* 4:28
Ahimelech of sons of *I*.   *1 Chr* 24:3
chief men among the sons of *I*.   4
of the sons of *I*. Daniel.   *Ezra* 8:2
see **Eleazar**

Ithiel
I. son of Jesaiah dwelt.   *Neh* 11:7
man spake to *I*. even to *I*.   *Pr* 30:1

itself
the fruit tree, whose seed is in *i*.
                                Gen 1:11
the beast that dieth of *i*.   *Lev* 7:24
             17:15; 22:8; *Deut* 14:21
land *i*. vomiteth out.   *Lev* 18:25
nor reap what groweth of *i*.   25:11
                                Isa 37:30
undersetters were ot the base *i*.
                                1 Ki 7:34
darkness, as darkness *i*.   *Job* 10:22
gathereth iniquity to *i*.   *Ps* 41:6
even Sinai *i*. was moved at.   68:8
his heart may discover *i*.   *Pr* 18:2
wine when it moveth *i*. aright. 23:31
ointment which bewrayeth *i*.   27:16
the tender grass sheweth *i*.   25
shall axe boast *i*. against him that
heweth, saw magnify *i*., rod shake
i., staff lift up *i*.   *Isa* 10:15
your soul delight *i*. in fatness.   55:2
shall thy moon withdraw *i*.   60:20
shall dwell in Judah *i*.   *Jer* 31:24
a fire unfolding *i*. and.   *Ezek* 1:4
not eaten what dieth of *i*. 4:14; 44:31
be base, that it might not lift *i*. 17:14
nor exalt *i*. any more above.   29:15
it raised up *i*. on the one.   *Dan* 7:5
thought for the things of *i*. *Mat* 6:34
every kingdom divided against *i*.
             12:25; *Mark* 3:24, 25; *Luke* 11:17
branch cannot bear fruit of *i*.
                                John 15:4
together in a place by *i*.   20:7
i. could not contain the books. 21:25
Spirit *i*. beareth witness.   *Rom* 8:16
creature *i*. also shall be delivered. 21
Spirit *i*. maketh intercession for. 26
there is nothing unclean of *i*. 14:14
not even nature *i*. teach? *1 Cor* 11:14
charity vaunteth not *i*., is not. 13:4
charity doth not behave *i*.   5
every thing that exalts *i*. *2 Cor* 10:5
edifying of *i*. in love.   *Eph* 4:16
into heaven *i*. to appear.   *Heb* 9:24
good report of truth *i*.   *3 John* 12

Iturea
brother Philip tetrarch of *I*. *Luke* 3:1

Ivah
the gods of Hena and *I*.? *2 Ki* 18:34
is the king of *I*.?   19:13; *Isa* 37:13

ivory
king made a throne of *i*.   *1 Ki* 10:18
                                2 Chr 9:17
bringing gold, silver, and *i*.
                    1 Ki 10:22; *2 Chr* 9:21
the *i*. house which Ahab. *1 Ki* 22:39
out of the *i*. palaces.   *Ps* 45:8
his belly is as bright as *i*. *S of S* 5:14
thy neck is as a tower of *i*.   7:4
made thy benches of *i*.   *Ezek* 27:6
thee for a present horns of *i*.   15
houses of *i*. shall perish.   *Amos* 3:15
lie upon beds of *i*. and stretch.   6:4
man buyeth vessels of *i*.   *Rev* 18:12

J

Jaazaniah
J. came to Gedaliah.   *2 Ki* 25:23
J. of the house of the.   *Jer* 35:3
J. stood with his censer.   *Ezek* 8:11
J. and Pelatiah princes of.   11:1

Jabal
J. was the father of such.   *Gen* 4:20

Jabbok
passed over the ford *J*.   *Gen* 32:22

---

not to any place of river *J*. *Deut* 2:37
Reuben and Gad border to *J*.   3:16
Gilead to the river *J*.   *Josh* 12:2

Jabesh
told Saul the tidings of men of *J*.
                                1 Sam 11:5
shewed to the men of *J*. and.   9
came to *J*. and burned the.   31:12
their bones at *J*.   13; *1 Chr* 10:12
Shallum the son of *J*. conspired.
                                2 Ki 15:10
Shallum the son of *J*. began to.   13
smote Shallum the son of *J*.   14

Jabesh-gilead
none to the camp from *J*. *Judg* 21:8
smite the inhabitants of *J*.   10
found 400 young virgins of *J*.   12
Benjamites wives of women of *J*. 14
Nahash came and encamped against
J.   *1 Sam* 11:1
the inhabitants of *J*. heard.
                        31:11; *1 Chr* 10:12
men of *J*. were they that buried Saul.
                                2 Sam 2:4
bones of Saul from men of *J*. 21:12

Jabez
scribes who dwelt at *J*. *1 Chr* 2:55

Jabez
honourable than his brethren, mother
called his name *J*.   *1 Chr* 4:9
J. called on God of Israel, saying. 10

Jabin
when *J*. king of Hazor.   *Josh* 11:1
sold them into hand of *J*. *Judg* 4:2
peace between *J*. and the house.   17
God subdued that day, *J*. king.   23
of Israel prevailed against *J*.   24
do to them as unto *J*.   *Ps* 83:9

Jachin
he called the pillar on the right hand
J.   *1 Ki* 7:21; *2 Chr* 3:17

Jacinth
breastplates of fire, *J*.   *Rev* 9:17*
foundation of city was a *j*.   21:20

Jacob
he was called *J*.   *Gen* 25:26
J. was a plain man.   27
J. sod pottage.   29
J. gave Esau pottage.   34
the voice is *J*.'s.   27:22
J. was scarce gone out.   30
is not he rightly named *J*.?   36
Esau hated *J*.   41
if *J*. take a wife of Heth.   46
Isaac sent away *J*.   28:5
J. obeyed his father.   7
J. awaked out of sleep.   16
J. vowed a vow.   20
J. saw Rachel the daughter.   29:10
J. served seven years for Rachel. 20
and *J*. did so, and fulfilled her. 28
J. came out of the field in.   30:16
and *J*. took him rods of green.   37
were Laban's, the stronger *J*.'s.   42
J. hath taken all that was.   31:1
J. stole away unawares to Laban.   20
J. sware by the fear of his father. 53
J. sent messengers before.   32:3
J. saith, Thus have I sojourned.   4
then *J*. was greatly afraid.   7
say, They be thy servant *J*.'s.   18
J. was left alone, and there.   24
be no more *J*. but Israel.   28; 35:10
J. called the name of place.   32:30
J. looked, and behold, Esau.   33:1
J. journeyed to Succoth.   17
J. came to Shalem.   18
J. held his peace until they.   34:5
sons of *J*.   7, 13, 25; 35:26; 49:1, 2
                                1 Ki 18:31
J. came to Luz.   *Gen* 35:6
J. called the place Beth-el.   15
these are the generations of *J*. 37:2
J. rent his clothes, put sackcloth. 34
J.'s heart fainted, for he.   45:26
J. and all his seed came into.   46:6
that came with *J*. were sixty-six. 26
J. blessed Pharaoh.   47:10
the whole age of *J*.   28
the mighty God of *J*. 49:24; *Ex* 3:6
15, 16; 4:5; *2 Sam* 23:1; *Ps* 20:1

remembered his covenant with *J.*
    Ex 2:24; *Lev* 26:42
come, curse me *J.* and. *Num* 23:7
can count dust of *J* and number? 10
enchantment against *J.* it shall be
  said of *J.* and Israel, what ? 23
shall come a star out of *J.* 24:17
out of *J.* come he that shall have. 19
J. is the lot of his. *Deut* 32:9
they shall teach *J.* thy. 33:10
fountain of *J.* shall be on land. 28
Israel his servant, ye children of *J.*
  1 Chr 16:13; *Ps* 105:6
J. shall rejoice. *Ps* 14:7; 53:6
the name of the God of *J.* 20:1
all ye seed of *J.* glorify him. 22:23
command deliverances for *J.* 44:4
the god of *J.* 46:7, 11; 75:9; 76:6
  81:1, 4; 84:8; 94:7; 114:7; 132:2
  5; 146:5
the excellency of *J.* whom he loved.
  47:4; *Nah* 2:2
fire was kindled against *J. Ps* 78:21
he brought him to feed *J.* his. 71
for they have devoured *J.* and. 79:7
brought back the captivity of *J.* 85:1
gates of Zion more than all the dwellings of *J.* 87:2
J. sojourned in the land of. 105:23
the Lord hath chosen *J.* 135:4
the God of *J.* *Isa* 2:3; 41:21
Mi 4:2; *Mat* 22:32; *Mark* 12:26
  Luke 20:37; *Acts* 3:13; 7:32, 46
remnant of *J.* shall return. *Isa* 10:21
Lord will have mercy on *J.* 14:1
in that day the glory of *J.* shall. 17:4
shall cause them that come of *J.* 27:6
by this shall the iniquity of *J.* be. 9
sanctify the Holy One of *J.* 29:23
J. whom I have chosen, the. 41:8
fear not, thou worm *J.* and ye. 14
who gave *J.* for a spoil ? 42:24
therefore I have given *J.* to. 43:28
call himself by the name of *J.* 44:5
Lord hath redeemed *J.* 23; *Jer* 31:11
for *J.* my servant's sake. *Isa* 45:4
hath redeemed his servant *J.* 48:20
that formed me to bring *J.* 49:5
servant to raise up the tribes of *J.* 6
the mighty One of *J.* 26; 60:16
feed thee with heritage of *J.* 58:14
bring forth a seed out of *J.* 65:9
the portion of *J.* not like them.
  Jer 10:16; 51:19
they have eaten up *J.* and. 10:25
even the time of *J.'s* trouble. 30:7
fear thou not, O my servant *J.* 10
bring again the captivity of *J.* 18
sing with the gladness for *J.* 31:7
will I cast away the seed of *J.* 33:26
J. shall return to be in rest. 46:27
commanded concerning *J. Lam* 1:17
he burned against *J.* like a. 2:3
Judah shall plow, *J.* shall. *Hos* 10:11
I will punish *J.* 12:2
J. fled into Syria. 12
abhor the excellency of *J. Amos* 6:8
shall *J.* arise, for he is small ? 7:2, 5
sworn by the excellency of *J.* 8:7
for the transgression of *J.* *Mi* 1:5
hear, I pray you, O heads of *J.* 3:1
remnant of *J.* shall be among. 5:8
Esau *J.'s* brother ? yet I loved *J.*
  Mal 1:2
therefore, ye sons of *J.* are not. 3:6
Isaac begat *J.* 1:2
Matthan begat *J.* 15
sit down with Abraham, Isaac, and *J.*
  8:11
J. in kingdom of God. *Luke* 13:28
now *J.'s* well was there. *John* 4:6
Joseph called his father *J. Acts* 7:14
J. have I loved, but. *Rom* 9:13
turn away ungodliness from *J.* 11:26
in tabernacles with *J.* *Heb* 11:9
by faith Isaac blessed *J.* 20
J. blessed the sons of Joseph. 21

    see **house**

    in **Jacob**

I will divide them *in J. Gen* 49:7
not beheld iniquity *in J. Num* 23:21
know that God ruleth *in J. Ps* 59:13
established a testimony *in J.* 78:5

and righteousness *in J. Ps* 99:4
from transgression *in J. Isa* 59:20

    O Jacob

how goodly are thy tents, O *J.*!
  Num 24:5
that seek thy face, O *J. Ps* 24:6
why sayest thou, O *J.? Isa* 40:27
Lord that created thee, O *J.* 43:1
hast not called upon me, O *J.* 22
yet hear, O *J.* 44:1
fear not, O *J.* my servant. 2
  Jer 46:27, 28
remember these, O *J.* for. *Isa* 44:21
hearken unto me, O *J.* 48:12
I will surely assemble, O *J. Mi* 2:12

   to or unto **Jacob**

speak not to *J. Gen* 31:24, 29
God appeared unto *J.* and. 35:9
land which he sware to give to *J.*
  50:24; *Ex* 6:8; 33:1; *Num* 32:11
  Deut 6:10; 29:13; 30:20; 34:4
  Ezek 37:25
confirmed the same to *J.* for a law.
  1 Chr 16:17; *Ps* 105:10
shewed his word unto *J. Ps* 147:19
Lord sent a word unto *J. Isa* 9:8
declare unto *J.* his transgression.
  Mi 3:8
wilt perform truth to *J.* and. 7:20

    Jael

fled away to tent of *J. Judg* 4:17
J. took a nail of the tent and. 21
J. came out to meet Barak. 22
in days of *J.* the highways. 5:6
blessed above women shall *J.* 24

    Jah

extol him by his name *J. Ps* 68:4

    Jahaz

his people and came and fought at *J.*
  Num 21:23; *Deut* 2:32
  Judg 11:20
shall be heard even to *J. Isa* 15:4
to *J.* have they uttered. *Jer* 48:34

    Jahazah

out of Reuben *J.* given. *Josh* 21:36
judgement is come upon Holon and
  J. *Jer* 48:21

    Jailer

charging the *j.* to keep. *Acts* 16:23

    Jair

J. took the small towns. *Num* 32:41
  Deut 3:14
J. the Gileadite judged. *Judg* 10:3
J. died. 5
Segub begat *J.* *1 Chr* 2:22
Elhanan the son of *J.* slew. 20:5
Mordecai the son of *J.* *Esth* 2:5

    Jairus

J. a ruler of the synagogue.
  Mark 5:22; *Luke* 8:41

  Jakeh, *see* **Agur**

    Jambres

as Jannes and *J.* withstood Moses.
  2 Tim 3:8

    James

saw two brethren *J.* and John.
  Mat 4:21; *Mark* 1:19
J. the son of Zebedee. *Mat* 10:2
  Mark 3:17
J. the son of Alpheus. *Mat* 10:3
  Mark 3:18; *Acts* 1:13
and his brethren *J.* and Joses.
  Mat 13:55; *Mark* 6:3
after six days Jesus taketh Peter, *J.*
  and John. *Mat* 17:1; *Mark* 5:37
  9:2; 14:33; *Luke* 8:51
Mary mother of *J.* *Mat* 27:56
  Mark 15:40; 16:1; *Luke* 24:10
much displeased with *J. Mark* 10:41
Peter, *J.* and John asked him. 13:3
J. was astonished at. *Luke* 5:10
abode both Peter, *J.* and. *Acts* 1:13
Herod killed *J.* brother of. 12:2
Peter said, shew these things to *J.* 17
J. answered, saying, Hearken. 15:13
Paul went in with us unto *J.* 21:18
after that was seen of *J.* *1 Cor* 15:7
save *J.* the Lord's brother. *Gal* 1:19
J. perceived the grace given. 2:9
before certain came from *J.* did. 12

    jangling

turned aside to vain *j.* *1 Tim* 1:6

    Janna

Melchi the son of *J.* *Luke* 3:24

  Jannes, *see* **Jambres**

    Japheth

J. the sons of Noah. *Gen* 5:32
  6:10; 7:13; 9:18; *1 Chr* 1:4
Shem and *J.* took a garment and.
  Gen 9:23
God shall enlarge *J.* he shall. 27
unto *J.* were sons born. 10:1
  1 Chr 1:4, 5
Eber, brother of *J.* *Gen* 10:21

    Jareb

saw, and sent to king *J.* *Hos* 5:13
for a present to king *J.* 10:6

    Jared

begat *J.* *Gen* 5:15; *Luke* 3:37

    Jasher

written in the book of *J. Josh* 10:13
  2 Sam 1:18

    Jashubites

the family of the *J.* *Num* 26:24

    Jason

assaulted the house of *J. Acts* 17:5
they drew *J.* 6
whom *J.* hath received. 7
had taken security of *J.* 9
Lucius, *J.* and Sosipater. *Rom* 16:21

    jasper

fourth row an onyx and a *j.*
  Ex 28:20; 39:13
topaz, the diamond and *j. Ezek* 28:13
was to look upon like a *j.* *Rev* 4:3
light was like to a *j.* stone. 21:11
of the wall of city was of *j.* 18
stones, the first foundation was *j.* 19

    Javan

sons of Japheth, *J.,* Tubal. *Gen* 10:2
  1 Chr 1:5
those that escape to *J.* *Isa* 66:19
J. and Tubal were. *Ezek* 27:13, 19

    javelin

(*A variety of spear. Revisions
  use the general word* spear)
and Phinehas took a *j.* *Num* 25:7
there was a *j.* in Saul's hand.
  1 Sam 18:10; 19:9
Saul cast the *j.* for he said. 18:11
he smote the *j.* into the wall. 19:10

    jaw

an hollow place in the *j. Judg* 15:19*
canst thou bore his *j.?* *Job* 41:2

    jawbone

Samson found a new *j. Judg* 15:15
with the *j.* of an ass have. 16
he cast away the *j.* out of his. 17

    jaws

and I brake the *j.* of. *Job* 29:17
tongue cleaveth to my *j.* *Ps* 22:15
shall be a bridle in *j.* *Isa* 30:28
off the yoke on their *j.* *Hos* 11:4

    jaw teeth

their *j.* teeth as knives. *Pr* 30:14

    Jazer

saw the land of *J.* *Num* 32:1, 3
are come even unto *J.* *Isa* 16:8
I will bewail with weeping of *J.* 9

    jealous

Lord thy God am a *j.* God. *Ex* 20:5
  34:14; *Deut* 4:24; 5:9; 6:15
  Josh 24:19
j. of his wife. *Num* 5:14, 30
j. for Lord of hosts. *1 Ki* 19:10, 14
and will be *j.* for my. *Ezek* 39:25
will the Lord be *j.* for. *Joel* 2:18
God is *j.* and the Lord. *Nah* 1:2
I am *j.* for Jerusalem. *Zech* 1:14
was *j.* for Zion. 8:2
for I am *j.* over you. *2 Cor* 11:2

    jealousies

is law of *j.* when a wife. *Num* 5:29

    jealousy

(*In addition to its modern meaning,
this word also used to mean
zeal, solicitude*)
the spirit of *j.* come. *Num* 5:14, 30
for it is an offering of *j.* and. 15, 18

then priest shall take *j*. offering.
Num 5:25
consumed not Israel in my *j*. 25:11
j. shall smoke against. *Deut* 29:20
they provoked him to *j*. 32:16
1 Ki 14:22
moved me to *j*.: I will move them
to *j*. *Deut* 32:21
they moved him to *j*. *Ps* 78:58
how long. Lord, shall thy *j*.? 79:5
for *j*. is the rage of man. *Pr* 6:34
j. is cruel as the grave. *S of S* 8:6
he shall stir up *j*. like. *Isa* 42:13
seat of the image of *j*.? *Ezek* 8:3
gate of altar this image of *j*. in. 5
give thee blood in fury and *j*. 16:38
my *j*. shall depart from thee. 42
I will set my *j*. against thee. 23:25
in the fire of *j*. have I spoken. 36:5
6; 38:19
whose land devoured by fire of his *j*.
Zeph 1:18; 3:8
for Zion with great *j*. *Zech* 1:14; 8:2
provoke you to *j*. by them. *Rom* 10:19
Gentiles, to provoke them to *j*. 11:11
provoke the Lord to *j*.? *1 Cor* 10:22
over you with godly *j*. *2 Cor* 11:2

Jebusite
Canaan begat the *J*. *Gen* 10:16
1 Chr 1:14
drive out the *J*. *Ex* 33:2; 34:11
the threshingplace of Araunah the *J*.
2 Sam 24:16; *1 Chr* 21:15
Judah, and Ekron as a *J*. *Zech* 9:7

Jebusites
the *J*. dwell in the. *Num* 13:29
J. dwell with the children of Judah.
Josh 15:63
drive *J*. that inhabited. *Judg* 1:21
turn into this city of the *J*. 19:11
up and smiteth the *J*. *2 Sam* 5:8
see Hittites

Jeconiah
sons of Jehoiakim, *J*. *1 Chr* 3:16
the sons of *J*. Assir and. 17
away captive *J*. *Jer* 24:1; 27:20
will bring again to this place *J*. 28:4

Jedidiah
called Solomon *J*. *2 Sam* 12:24, 25

Jeduthun
Heman and *J*. to give. *1 Chr* 16:41
the sons of *J*. 42; 25:3; *2 Chr* 29:14
the king's order to *J*. *1 Chr* 25:6

Jegar-sahadutha
Laban called the heap *J*. *Gen* 31:47

Jehoahaz, *called* Ahaziah
J. son of Jehu reigned. *2 Ki* 10:35
J. son of Jehu began to reign. 13:1
people of the land took *J*. the son of
Josiah. 23:30; *2 Chr* 36:1
Pharaoh-necho took *J*. away.
2 Ki 23:34; *2 Chr* 36:4
never a son save *J*. *2 Chr* 21:17

Jehoash, *or* Joash
J. seven years old when. *2 Ki* 11:21
J. did what was right in sight. 12:2
J. sent all the hallowed things. 18
his servant slew *J*. in the house. 20
J. the son of Jehoahaz. 13:10
sent messengers to *J*. 14:8
J. slept with his fathers and. 16

Jehoiachin
J. was 18 years old. *2 Ki* 24:8
J. king of Judah went to. 12
up the head of *J*. 25:27; *Jer* 52:31
J. was eight years old. *2 Chr* 36:9

Jehoiada
Benaiah the son of *J*. *2 Sam* 8:18
20:23; 23:20, 22; *1 Chr* 11:22, 24
18:17
king sent Benaiah son of *J*. *1 Ki* 1:44
Benaiah the son of *J*. was over. 4:4
J. made a covenant. *2 Ki* 11:17
2 Chr 23:16
J. the priest instructed. *2 Ki* 12:2
J. was leader of the. *1 Chr* 12:27
after Ahithophel was *J*. a. 27:34
right all the days of *J*. *2 Chr* 24:2
after the death of *J*. came the. 17
remembered not the kindness *J*. 22
for the blood of the sons of *J*. 25

old gate repaired *J*. son. *Neh* 3:6
thee priest instead of *J*. *Jer* 29:26

Jehoiakim
turned his name to *J*. *2 Ki* 23:34
2 Chr 36:4
J. gave silver and gold. 2 Ki 23:35
J. became his servant three. 24:1
the Lord concerning *J*. *2 Ki* 22:18
J. sent men after Urijah into. 26:22
the roll which *J*. the king. 36:28
thus saith the Lord of *J*. king of. 30
Zedekiah did what was evil as *J*.
52:2
and the Lord gave *J*. *Dan* 1:2

Jehonadab
lighted on *J*. the son. *2 Ki* 10:15
Jehu and *J*. went into the house. 23

Jehoram
J. son of Jehoshaphat. *1 Ki* 22:50
2 Ki 8:16
J. the son of Ahab. *2 Ki* 1:17
Elishama and *J*. priests. *2 Chr* 17:8
J. went forth and smote the. 21:9
the Lord stirred up against *J*. 16
went with *J*. to war against. 22:5
Ahaziah went out with *J*. against. 7

Jehoshaphat
J. the son of Ahilud. *2 Sam* 8:16, 20
24; *1 Ki* 4:3; *1 Chr* 18:15
J. son of Paruah was. *1 Ki* 4:17
J. the son of Asa. 15:24; *2 Chr* 17:1
J. came down to Ahab. *1 Ki* 22:2
Ahab and *J*. sat each on his throne.
10; *2 Chr* 18:9
J. went up to Ramoth-gilead.
1 Ki 22:29; *2 Chr* 18:28
J. cried out. *1 Ki* 22:32
J. slept with his fathers. 50
let my servants go, but *J*. would. 49
I regard presence of *J*. *2 Ki* 3:14
look out there Jehu the son of *J*. 9:2
J. blew with trumpet. *1 Chr* 15:24
Lord was with *J*. because. *2 Chr* 17:3
they made no war against *J*. 10
J. waxed great exceedingly. 12
J. had riches and honour in. 18:1
J. feared and set himself to. 20:3
returned, and *J*. in the forefront. 27
after this did *J*. join with Ahaziah. 35
Eliezer prophesied against *J*. 37
walked in the ways of *J*. 21:12
said they, He is the son of *J*. 22:9
down to the valley of *J*. *Joel* 3:2
come up to the valley of *J*. 12

Jehoshua
Oshea, son of Nun, *J*. *Num* 13:16
Non his son, *J*. his son. *1 Chr* 7:27

Jehovah
by my name *J*. was I not. *Ex* 6:3
whose name alone is *J*. *Ps* 83:18
Lord *J*. is my strength. *Isa* 12:2
Lord *J*. is everlasting strength. 26:4

Jehovah-jireh
called the name of the place *J*.
Gen 22:14

Jehovah-nissi
name of the altar *J*. *Ex* 17:15

Jehovah-shalom
and called the altar *J*. *Judg* 6:24

Jehu
J. son of Hanani. *1 Ki* 16:1, 7, 12
J. son of Nimshi shalt thou. 19:16
J. slay; that escapeth sword of *J*. 17
look out there *J*. *2 Ki* 9:2
J. is king. 13
son of Nimshi conspired. 14
a watchman spied company of *J*. 17
driving is like the driving of *J*. 20
J. drew a bow with his full. 24
J. slew all that remained of. 10:11
Ahab served Baal, *J*. shall serve. 18
J. departed not from the sins. 29
J. took no heed to walk in the. 31
word which he spake to *J*. 15:12
Obed begat *J*. and *J*. *1 Chr* 2:38
J. son of Josibiah. 4:35
J. son of Azmaveth. 12:3
J. went out to meet. *2 Chr* 19:2
written in the book of *J*. son. 20:34
J. was executing judgement. 22:8
the blood of Jezreel on *J*. *Hos* 1:4

jeoparded
were people that *j*. their. *Judg* 5:18

jeopardy
went in *j*. of their lives. *2 Sam* 23:17
1 Chr 11:19
will fall to Saul, to *j*. *1 Chr* 12:19
with water, and were in *j*. *Luke* 8:23
and why stand we in *j*.? *1 Cor* 15:30

Jephthah
J. the Gileadite was a mighty... and
Gilead begat *J*. *Judg* 11:1
J. fled from his brethren, and. 3
J. uttered all his words before. 11
hearkened not to words of *J*. 28
the Spirit came on *J*. 29
J. vowed a vow. 30
to lament the daughter of *J*. 40
J. judged Israel six years, then died
J. 12:7
the Lord sent *J*. and. *1 Sam* 12:11
would fail me to tell of *J*. *Heb* 11:32

Jephunneh
Caleb the son of *J*. *Num* 13:6
the sons of Jether, *J*. *1 Chr* 7:38
see Caleb

Jerahmeel
Hezron, *J*. and Ram. *1 Chr* 2:9
the sons of *J*. 33
J. the son of Kish. 24:29
king commanded *J*. to. *Jer* 36:26

Jeremiah
Hamutal, the daughter of *J*. of.
2 Ki 23:31; 24:18; *Jer* 52:1
J. a mighty. *1 Chr* 5:24; 12:4, 10, 13
and *J*. lamented for. *2 Chr* 35:25
humbled not himself before *J*. 36:12
of Lord by the mouth of *J*. till land
enjoyed her. 21, 22; *Ezra* 1:1
Azariah, *J*. sealed the. *Neh* 10:2
Seraiah, *J*. went up with. 12:1
days of Joiakim, of *J*., Hananiah. 12
J. and Shemaiah went after. 34
the words of *J*. the son. *Jer* 1:1
the word that came to *J*. 7:1; 11:1
14:1; 18:1
devise devices against *J*. 18:18
Pashur smote *J*. and put him. 20:2
the Lord, What seest thou, *J*.? 24:3
people were gathered against *J*. 26:9
the hand of Ahikam was with *J*. 24
yoke from the prophet *J*. 28:10
why hast thou not reproved *J*.? 29:27
J. was shut up in court of. 32:2
J. spake all these words to. 34:6
Jaazaniah the son of *J*. 35:3
said, Go hide thee, thou and *J*. 36:19
Lord hid Baruch the scribe and *J*. 26
J. came in and went out. 37:4
so Irijah took *J*. and brought. 14
princes were wroth with *J*. 15
when *J*. was entered into the. 16
to commit *J*. into the court of. 21
they cast *J*. into the dungeon. 38:6
drew up *J*. with cords out of the. 13
the king sware secretly to *J*. 16
gave charge concerning *J*. 39:11
then went *J*. to Gedaliah son of. 40:6
J. wrote in a book all the evil. 51:60
thus far are the words of *J*. 64
was spoken by *J*. *Mat* 2:17; 27:9
others say Thou art *J*. or one. 16:14

Jericho
go view *J*. *Josh* 2:1
passed over right against *J*. 3:16
J. was straitly shut up. 6:1
I have given into thine hand *J*. 2
the man that buildeth the city *J*. 26
Joshua sent men from *J*. to. 7:2
to *J*. and the men of *J*. fought. 24:11
tarry at *J*. till your beard be grown.
2 Sam 10:5; *1 Chr* 19:5
days did Hiel build *J*. *1 Ki* 16:34
Lord hath sent me to *J*. *2 Ki* 2:4
Chaldees overtook him in the plains
of *J*. 25:5; *Jer* 39:5; 52:8
the captives to *J*. *2 Chr* 28:15
man went down to *J*. *Luke* 10:30
by faith the walls of *J*. *Heb* 11:30

Jeroboam
J. was a mighty man of. *1 Ki* 11:28
Solomon sought to kill *J*. and 40
J. dwelt in Egypt. 12:2

J. was come again.   *1 Ki* 12:20
J. built Shechem and dwelt.   25
J. ordained a feast in the eighth. 32
J. stood by the altar to burn.   13:1
after this J. returned not from. 33
became sin to the house of J.   34
at that time Abijah the son of J. 14:1
come in, thou wife of J.   6
bring evil upon the house of J.   10
him that dieth of J. shall the.   11
for he only of J. shall come to.   13
of the sins of J.   16; 15:30
between Rehoboam and J.   14:30
Baasha left not to J. any.   15:29
evil and walked in the way of J. 34
   2 Ki 10:31; 13:6; 14:24; 17:22
J. son of Joash sat on.   *2 Ki* 13:13
saved Israel by the hand of J. 14:27
J. drave Israel from following. 17:21
genealogies in days of J. *1 Chr* 5:17
J. had cast off Levites. *2 Chr* 11:14
golden calf which J. made for. 13:8
God smote J. and all Israel.   15
neither did J. recover strength.   20
prophesied in the days of J. *Hos* 1:1
          Amos 1:1
rise against house of J.   *Amos* 7:9
thus Amos saith, J. shall die.   11

Jeroboam joined with *Nebat*
J. son of *Nebat* lifted.   *1 Ki* 11:26
spake by Ahijah the Shilonite to J.
son of *Nebat*. 12:15; *2 Chr* 10:15
like house of J. the son of *Nebat*.
  1 Ki 16:3; 21:22; *2 Ki* 9:9
in all the way of J. the son of *Nebat*.
  1 Ki 16:26, 31; 22:52; *2 Ki* 3:3
Jehu departed not from the sins of J.
son of *Nebat*.   *2 Ki* 10:29; 13:2
  11; 14:24; 15:9, 18, 24, 28

Jerubbaal
he called him J. saying.   *Judg* 6:32
then J. (who is Gideon) rose up. 7:1
and J. went and dwelt in his.   8:29
they kindness to the house of J.   35
either that all sons of J. reign.   9:2
slew his brethren the sons of J.   5
if ye dealt well with J.   16
if sincerely with J.   19
is not he the son of J.?   28
the Lord sent J. and.   *1 Sam* 12:11

Jerubbesheth
Abimelech son of J.   *2 Sam* 11:21

Jerusalem, or **Hierusalem**
Jebusi, which is J.   *Josh* 18:28
          Judg 19:10
Goliath's head to J.   *1 Sam* 17:54
and his men went to J.   *2 Sam* 5:6
the shields of gold to J.   8:7
all the people returned to J.   12:31
shall bring me again to J.   15:8
carried the ark of God again to J. 29
my lord went out of J.   19:19
they came to J. at the end of. 24:8
stretched out his hand on J. to. 16
         1 Chr 21:15
of building the wall of J.   *1 Ki* 3:1
she came to J. with a very.   10:2
for J.'s sake which I have chosen.
   11:13; *2 Chr* 6:6
him and to establish J.   *1 Ki* 15:4
country, that Lord should deliver J.
  2 Ki 18:35; *Isa* 36:20
out of J. shall go forth a remnant.
  2 Ki 19:31; *Isa* 37:32
bring such evil upon J.   *2 Ki* 21:12
I will wipe J. as a man wipeth a. 13
blood till he had filled J.   16; 24:4
I will cast off J. when.   *2 Ki* 23:27
he carried away all J. and.   24:14
burnt all the houses of J.   25:9
not be poured on J.   *2 Chr* 12:7
came to J. with psalteries.   20:28
wrath was upon J.   24:18; 29:8
          32:25
altars in every corner of J.   28:24
spake against the God of J.   32:19
Josiah began to purge J. from. 34:3
to inquire concerning J.   *Ezra* 7:14
thou before the God of J.   19
so I came to J. *Neh* 2:11; 7:6; 13:7
merchants lodged without J.   13:20
Zion, build thou walls of J. *Ps* 51:18

the heathen have laid J. on. *Ps* 79:1
have they shed round about J.   3
J. is builded as a city.   122:3
pray for the peace of J. they.   6
mountains are round about J. 125:2
thou shalt see the good of J. 128:5
if I prefer not J. above my.   137:6
children of Edom in the day of J.   7
the Lord doth build up J. he.   147:2
comely, O my love, as J. *S of S* 6:4
he saw concerning J.   *Isa* 1:1; 2:1
for J. is ruined.   3:8
have purged the blood of J.   4:4
so will I do to J.   10:11
performed whole work on J.   12
numbered the houses of J.   22:10
Lord of hosts defend J.   31:5
thine eyes see J. a quiet.   33:20
speak ye comfortably to J.   40:2
give to J. one that bringeth.   41:27
that saith to J. Thou shalt.   44:26
of J. for Lord hath comforted his
  people, he hath redeemed J. 52:9
for J.'s sake I will not rest till. 62:1
give him no rest till he make J.   7
Zion is a wilderness, J. a.   64:10
for behold, I create J. a.   65:18
rejoice ye with J. and be glad. 66:10
and cry in the ears of J.   *Jer* 2:2
they shall call J. the throne of. 3:17
fro through the streets of J.   5:1
to flee out of the midst of J.   6:1
why then is this people of J.?   8:5
I will make J. heaps, and a.   9:11
words in the streets of J.   11:6
great pride of Judah and J.   13:9
Judah mourneth, the cry of J.   14:2
come from the places about J. 17:26
make void the counsel of J.   19:7
the houses of J. shall be defiled. 13
have seen in prophets of J. an. 23:14
J. shall become heaps.   26:18
          Mi 3:12
about J. shall flocks pass. *Jer* 33:13
in those days J. shall dwell.   16
let us go to J. for fear of.   35:11
till day that J. was taken.   38:28
brake down the walls of J.   39:8
the evil I have brought on J.   44:2
was kindled in the streets of J.   6
let J. come into your mind.   51:50
J. hath grievously sinned. *Lam* 1:8
J. is as a menstruous woman.   17
this is J.   *Ezek* 5:5
go through the midst of J.   9:4
son of man cause J. to know. 16:2
of Babylon is come to J.   17:12
sword may come to Judah in J. 21:20
right hand the divination for J.   22
gather you into the midst of J. 22:19
one that had escaped out of J. 33:21
flock of J. in her solemn.   36:38
being open toward J.   *Dan* 6:10
as hath been done upon J.   9:12
of the commandment to build J. 25
again the captivity of J.   *Joel* 3:1
then shall J. be holy.   17
J. shall dwell.   20
entered and cast lots upon J. *Ob* 11
are they not J.?   *Mi* 1:5
build up Zion with blood, J.   3:10
search J. with candles.   *Zeph* 1:12
not have mercy on J.?   *Zech* 1:12
I am jealous for J. and Zion.   14
comfort Zion, and choose J. 17; 2:12
horns which have scattered J.   1:19
goest thou ? I go to measure J.   2:2
J. shall be inhabited as towns.   4
I will dwell in the midst of J.   8:3
have I thought to do well to J.   15
behold, I will make J. a cup.   12:2
make J. a burdensome stone.   3
J. shall be safely inhabited.   14:11
the offering of J. shall be.   *Mal* 3:4
then went out to him J.   *Mark* 1:5
         Mat 5:35
neither swear by J.   *Mat* 5:35
to shew how he must go to J. 16:21
when he was come into J.   21:10
parents brought him to J. *Luke* 2:22
they turned back again to J.   45
a great multitude out of J.   6:17
as though he would go to J.   9:53
that a prophet perish out of J. 13:33

because he was nigh to J. *Luke* 19:11
ye shall see J. compassed.   21:20
J. shall be trodden down of the.   24
tarry ye in J. till ye be.   24:49
and they returned to J. with.   52
Jesus was coming to J. *John* 12:12
ye have filled J. with.   *Acts* 5:28
might bring them bound unto J. 9:2
bound in the Spirit to J.   20:22
tidings came that all J. was.   21:31
get thee quickly out of J.   22:18
him whether he would go to J.? 25:20
that my service for J.   *Rom* 15:31
your liberality unto J.   *1 Cor* 16:3
Agar answereth to J.   *Gal* 4:25
J. which is above is free.   26
the new J.   *Rev* 3:12; 21:2
the holy J.   21:10

see **dwell**

against **Jerusalem**
Judah had fought ag. J.   *Judg* 1:8
Shishak came ag. J.   *1 Ki* 14:25
         2 Chr 12:9
Sennacherib ag. J.   *2 Ki* 18:17
         2 Chr 32:2
the king of Babylon came ag. J.
  2 Ki 24:10; 25:1; *Jer* 34:1, 7
    39:1; 52:4; *Ezek* 24:2
Shimshai, wrote ag. J.   *Ezra* 4:8
to come and fight ag. J.   *Neh* 4:8
publish ag. J.   *Jer* 4:16
cast a mount ag. J.   6:6
that Tyrus hath said ag. J. *Ezek* 26:2
destroy nations that come ag. J.
    Zech 12:9; 14:12

at **Jerusalem**
dwelt with Judah at J.   *Josh* 15:63
came to his house at J.   *2 Sam* 20:3
sacrifice in house of the Lord at J.
  1 Ki 12:27; *2 Chr* 9:25; *Isa* 27:13
fathers dwelt at J.   *1 Chr* 9:34, 38
to build the house of the Lord at J.
  2 Chr 3:1; *Ezra* 1:2; 5:2
offered themselves to dwell at J.
         Neh 11:2
this time was not I at J.   13:6
because of thy temple at J. *Ps* 68:29
the Lord who dwelleth at J.   135:21
shall dwell in Zion at J.   *Isa* 30:19
into J., so we dwell at J.   *Jer* 35:11
also shall fight at J.   *Zech* 14:14
should accomplish at J.   *Luke* 9:31
Herod himself was also at J.   23:7
all nations, beginning at J.   24:47
nor yet at J. shall ye worship.
         John 4:21
all things that he did at J.   45
to all the dwellers at J.   *Acts* 1:19
against the church at J.   8:1
hath done to thy saints at J.   9:13
they that dwell at J. have.   13:27
be at J. the day of Pentecost. 20:16
so shall the Jews at J. bind. 21:11
but also to die at J. for the name. 13
to them of Damascus at J.   26:20
for the saints at J.   *Rom* 15:26

see **daughters**

from **Jerusalem**
Shimei had gone from J.   *1 Ki* 2:41
Hazael went away from J. *2 Ki* 12:18
carried into captivity from J. to.
  24:15; *Esth* 2:6; *Jer* 24:1; 27:20
        29:1; 52:29
the word of the Lord from J.
       Isa 2:3; *Mi* 4:2
take away from J. the stay. *Isa* 3:1
the Lord utter his voice from J.
       Joel 3:16; *Amos* 1:2
cut off the horse from J. *Zech* 9:10
waters shall go out from J.   14:8
followed him from J.   *Mat* 4:25
man went down from J. *Luke* 10:30
which was from J. about sixty. 24:13
should not depart from J. *Acts* 1:4
way that goeth down from J.   8:26
there came prophets from J.   11:27
from J. to Illyricum I.   *Rom* 15:19

in **Jerusalem**
dwell with Benjamin in J. *Judg* 1:21
feed thee with me in J. *2 Sam* 19:33
thee an house in J.   *1 Ki* 2:36
a light alway before me in J.   11:36
         15:4

worship before this altar in J.
2 Ki 18:22
Lord said, In J. will I put.   21:4
now Huldah dwelt in J. in.   22:14
these dwelt in J. 1 Chr 8:28, 32; 9:3
that they may dwell in J.   23:25
king made silver in J.   2 Chr 9:27
away the altars that were in J. 30:14
great joy in J. not the like in J.   26
house of the Lord which is in J.
Ezra 1:3
Israel, whose habitation is in J. 7:15
us a wall in Judah and in J.   9:9
no right nor memorial in J. Neh 2:20
let every one lodge in J.   4:22
bring one of ten to dwell in J.   11:1
Zion and his praises in J. Ps 102:21
that have been before me in J.
Eccl 1:16; 2:7, 9
that remaineth in J. be.   Isa 4:3
Lord of hosts shall reign in J. 24:23
scornful men that rule in J.   28:14
is in Zion, his furnace in J.   31:9
I will rejoice in J. and joy.   65:19
shall be comforted in J.   66:13
publish in J. and say.   Jer 4:5
which Manasseh did in J.   15:4
the staff of bread in J.   Ezek 4:16
in mount Zion and in J.   Joel 2:32
J. be inhabited in her place, even in
J.   Zech 12:6
every pot in J. shall be.   14:21
is committed in J.   Mal 2:11
a man in J. whose name. Luke 2:25
that looked for redemption in J.   38
Jesus tarried behind in J.   43
sinners above all that dwelt in J.
13:4
art thou only a stranger in J.? 24:18
in J. is the place where. John 4:20
shall be witnesses to me in J.
Acts 1:8; 10:39
the disciples multiplied in J.   6:7
hast testified of me in J.   23:11
which thing I also did in J.   26:10

inhabitants of **Jerusalem**
ye *inhabitants of* J. be not afraid.
2 Chr 20:15
Lord saved *inhabitants of* J. 32:22
inhabitants of J. did him honour. 33
inhabitants of J. did according to.
34:32
O *inhabitants of* J. judge. Isa 5:3
snare to *inhabitants of* J.   8:14
father to the *inhabitants of* J. 22:21
inhabitants of J. shall remain for.
Jer 17:25
and tell Judah and *inhabitants of* J.
35:13
to whom *inhabitants of* J. have said.
Ezek 11:15
I give the *inhabitants of* J. for. 15:6
the *inhabitants of* J. shall be my
strength.   Zech 12:5
the glory of the *inhabitants of* J.   7
shall defend the *inhabitants of* J.   8
pour upon *inhabitants of* J. the.   10
opened to the *inhabitants of* J. 13:1

O **Jerusalem**
vows in midst of thee, O J. Ps 116:19
stand within thy gates, O J.   122:2
if I forget thee, O J.   137:5
praise the Lord, O J.   147:12
O J. that bringest good. Isa 40:9
stand up, O J.   51:17
beautiful garments, O J.   52:1
arise, and sit down, O J.   2
O J. wash thy heart from. Jer 4:14
be thou instructed, O J. lest.   6:8
cut off thine hair, O J. and.   7:29
woe to thee, O J. Wilt thou not? 13:27
who have pity upon thee, O J.? 15:5
O J. J. thou that killest the prophets.
Mat 23:37; Luke 13:34

up to **Jerusalem**
up with the king to J. 2 Sam 19:34
for you to go up to J.   1 Ki 12:28
his face to go up to J.   2 Ki 12:17
Pekah came up to J. to war.   16:5
let him go up to J.   Ezra 1:3; 7:13
we go up to J.; Son of man.
Mat 20:18; Mark 10:33
Luke 18:31

the way going up to J.   Mark 10:32
ascending up to J.   Luke 19:28
Peter was come up to J.   Acts 11:2
go up to J. to the apostles.   15:2
he should not go up to J.   21:4, 12
wilt thou go up to J. and ?   25:9
neither went I up to J. to.   Gal 1:17
I went up to J. to see Peter and. 18
I went up to J. with Barnabas.   2:1

Jeshua
came with Zerubbabel, J. Ezra 2:2
stood up J. son of Jozadak.   3:2

Jeshurun
but J. waxed fat and.   Deut 32:15
he was king in J. when Israel. 33:5
none like to the God of J.   26
fear not, thou J. whom.   Isa 44:2

Jesse
Obed, he is the father of J.
Ruth 4:17; Mat 1:5
Obed begat J. and J. begat David.
Ruth 4:22; Mat 1:6
I will send thee to J.   1 Sam 16:1
he sanctified J. and his sons and.   9
I have seen a son of J. that is.   18
Saul sent messengers unto J.   19
I am the son of thy servant J. 17:58
hast chosen the son of J.   20:30
as long as the son of J. liveth.   31
will the son of J. give every.?   22:7
made a league with the son of J.   8
Doeg said, I saw the son of J.   9
and who is the son of J.?   25:10
inheritance in son of J. 2 Sam 20:1
1 Ki 12:16; 2 Chr 10:16
to David the son of J.   1 Chr 10:14
thine are we, thou son of J.   12:18
rod out of the stem of J.   Isa 11:1
shall be a root of J. 10; Rom 15:12
found David the son of J. Acts 13:22

Jesting
nor filthiness, nor j. not.   Eph 5:4

Jesus
J. for he shall save his people from.
Mat 1:21, 25; Luke 1:31; 2:21
J. was led up of the Spirit. Mat 4:1
from that time J. began to.   17
J. put forth his hand and.   8:3
when J. heard it, he marvelled.   10
do with thee, J. thou Son of God ?
29; Mark 1:24; 5:7; Luke 8:28
city came out to meet J. Mat 8:34
J. seeing their faith.   9:2
as J. sat at meat.   10
J. turned him about.   22
J. departed thence.   27
J. knew their thoughts.   12:25
these things spake J. to the.   13:24
Herod heard of the fame of J.   14:1
walked on the water, to go to J.   29
they saw no man save J. only.   17:8
Mark 9:8
J. rebuked the devil and. Mat 17:18
when come into the house, J.   19
J. called a little child to him.   18:2
two blind men heard that J.   20:30
J. had compassion on them.   34
is J. the prophet of Nazareth. 21:11
J. perceived their wickedness. 22:18
they might take J. by subtilty. 26:4
the disciples did as J. had.   19
J. took bread. 26; Mark 14:22
thou also wast with J.   Mat 26:69
71; Mark 14:67
remembered words of J. Mat 26:75
written, This is J. the king.   27:37
J. cried with a loud voice.   46
Mark 15:37
Joseph, who also himself was J.'
disciple.   Mat 27:57
fear not ye, I know ye seek J.
Mat 28:5; Mark 16:6
J. met them.   Mat 28:9
J. came and spake to them.   18
J. could no more enter. Mark 1:45
J. withdrew himself with his.   3:7
J. gave them leave.   5:13
J. suffered him not.   19
J. knowing that virtue had gone. 30
Elias and Moses talking with J.   9:4
then J. beholding him.   10:21

J. saw that he answered. Mark 12:34
bound J. and carried him.   15:1
in the midst before J.   Luke 5:19
what they might do to J.   6:11
who sat at J.' feet and heard. 10:39
Zacchaeus sought to see J. who. 19:3
bear the cross after J.   23:26
J. himself drew near and.   24:15
they said, Is not this J.? John 6:42
that is called J. made clay.   9:11
J. spake of his death.   11:13
J. wept.   35
sir, we would see J.   12:21
when J. knew that his hour.   13:1
leaning on J.' bosom.   23
whom seek ye ? they said, J.   18:7
officers that stood by struck J.   22
came J. forth, wearing crown. 19:5
there stood by the cross of J.   25
J. knowing that all things were.   28
took the body of J.   40
there laid they J.   42
knew not that it was J. 20:14; 21:4
of all that J. began to.   Acts 1:1
this same J. which is taken up.   11
was guide to them who took J.   16
this J. hath God raised up.   2:32
3:26; 5:30
hath glorified his Son J.   3:13
through J. resurrection from.   4:2
that they had been with J.   13
not to teach in the name of J.   18
against thy holy child J.   27
the name of thy holy child J.   30
not speak in the name of J.   5:40
this J. shall destroy this place. 6:14
he saw J. standing on the right. 7:55
Philip preached unto him J.   8:35
I am J. whom thou persecutest. 9:5
22:8; 26:15
even J., that appeared to thee. 9:17
at Damascus in the name of J.   27
how God anointed J. with.   10:38
raised to Israel a Saviour J.   13:23
there is another king, one J.   17:7
because he preached J. and the.   18
adjure you by J. whom Paul. 19:13
J. I know, and Paul I know, but. 15
had questions of one J. who.   25:19
persuading them concerning J. 28:23
of him that believeth in J. Rom 3:26
Spirit of him that raised up J.   8:11
by Spirit calleth J.   1 Cor 12:3
your servants for J.' sake. 2 Cor 4:5
the life of J. might be made.   10
we are delivered to death for J.   11
J. shall raise up us also by J.   14
that cometh, preach another J. 11:4
him as the truth is in J.   Eph 4:21
at name of J. every knee. Phil 2:10
J. who delivered us.   1 Thes 1:10
them that sleep in J. will God. 4:14
we see J. who was made. Heb 2:9
great high priest, J. son. 4:14; 6:20
was J. made surety of better.   7:22
the holiest by the blood of J. 10:19
looking unto J. the author of.   12:2
to J. the Mediator of the new.   24
wherefore J. suffered without. 13:12
confess J. is Son of God. 1 John 4:15
that J. is the Son of God.   5:5
that keep the faith of J.   Rev 14:12
with blood of martyrs of J.   17:6
beheaded for the witness of J.   20:4
I J. have sent mine angel to. 22:16

see **Christ**

Jesus joined with *Lord*
all the time the Lord J.   Acts 1:21
same J. both Lord and Christ. 2:36
Stephen saying, Lord J.   7:59
in the name of the Lord J.   8:16
boldly in the name of Lord J.   9:29
Grecians, preaching Lord J.   11:20
believe on the Lord J. Christ. 16:31
heard the word of the Lord J. 19:10
and the name of the Lord J. was. 17
the words of the Lord J.   20:35
Lord J. same night he.   1 Cor 11:23
no man can say that J. is Lord. 12:3
are ours in the day of the Lord J.
2 Cor 1:14
about the dying of Lord J.   4:10
the marks of Lord J.   Gal 6:17

who both killed Lord J. *1 Thes* 2:15
exhort you by the Lord J.   4:1
we gave you by Lord J.   2
Lord J. shall be revealed. *2 Thes* 1:7
from dead our Lord J.   *Heb* 13:20
knowledge of J. our Lord. *2 Pet* 1:2
even so, come Lord J.   *Rev* 22:20
   see grace, name

Jesus *said*
mind the word J. *said. Mark* 14:72
believed the word J. *said. John* 2:22
the same hour in which J. *said.* 4:53
when J. had thus *said*, he was. 13:21
yet J. *said* not unto him.   21:23

Jesus, for *Joshua*
with J. into possession.   *Acts* 7:45
if J. had given them rest.   *Heb* 4:8

Jesus
J. who is called Justus.   *Col* 4:11

Jethro, called *Reuel*
Moses kept the flock of J.   *Ex* 3:1
Moses returned to J. his.   4:18
when J. heard of all that God. 18:1
J. came with his sons and his wife. 5
I thy father in law J. am come.   6
J. rejoiced for the goodness.   9, 10
J. took a burnt offering and.   12

Jew
a certain J. whose name.   *Esth* 2:5
told them that he was a J.   3:4
do even so to Mordecai the J. 6:10
of them, to wit, of a J.   *Jer* 34:9
take hold of skirt of a J. *Zech* 8:23
is it that thou, being a J.? *John* 4:9
Pilate answered am I a J.?   18:35
for a man that is a J.   *Acts* 10:28
sorcerer, a J. named Bar-jesus. 13:6
certain J. named Aquila.   18:2
a J. named Apollos.   24
sons of Sceva a J.   19:14
Alexander a J.   33, 34
Paul a J.   21:39; 22:3
to the J. first.   *Rom* 1:16; 2:9, 10
behold, thou art called a J., and. 2:17
he is not a J.   28
he is a J. who is one inwardly.   29
what advantage then hath the J.? 3:1
no difference between the J. and.
   10:12; *Gal* 3:28; *Col* 3:11
to the J. I became as a J. *1 Cor* 9:20
if thou being a J. livest as. *Gal* 2:14

Jewel
as a *j.* of gold in a.   *Pr* 11:22
of knowledge are a precious *j.* 20:15
put a *j.* on thy forehead. *Ezek* 16:12*

Jewels
servant brought forth *j.*   *Gen* 24:53
shall borrow *j.* of gold.   *Ex* 3:22
   11:2; 12:35
they brought all *j.* of gold.   35:22
   Num 31:50
gold, even all wrought *j. Num* 31:51
put the *j.* of gold in. *1 Sam* 6:8, 15
riches and precious *j.*   *2 Chr* 20:25
for all manner of pleasant *j.* 32:27*
of it shall not be for *j.*   *Job* 28:17
comely with rows of *j. S of S* 1:10*
joints of thy thighs are like *j.*   7:1
bride adorneth herself with her *j.*
   Isa 61:10
taken thy *j.* of my gold. *Ezek* 16:17
shall take thy fair *j.*   39; 23:26
with earrings and *j.*   *Hos* 2:13
when I make up my *j. Mal* 3:17*

Jewess
Timotheus was son of a J. *Acts* 16:1
Felix' wife Drusilla was a J.   24:24

Jewish
not giving heed to J.   *Tit* 1:14

Jewry
my father brought out of J. *Dan* 5:13

Jews
king Rezin drave the J.   *2 Ki* 16:6
the J. are come up to.   *Ezra* 4:12
I asked concerning the J.   *Neh* 1:2
what do these feeble J.?   4:2
table one hundred and fifty J. 5:17
thou and the J. think to rebel. 6:6
I saw J. that married wives. 13:23
mourning among the J.   *Esth* 4:3

deliverance arise unto J.   *Esth* 4:14
Mordecai be of seed of the J.   6:13
laid his hand upon the J.   8:7
write ye for the J., in king's name. 8
J. had light, and gladness.   16, 17
for the fear of the J. fell upon.   17
officers of the king helped the J. 9:3
should not fail from among J.   28
was great among the J.   10:3
said, I am afraid of the J. *Jer* 38:19
captive 3023 of the J.   52:28, 30
near and accused the J.   *Dan* 3:8
is reported among the J. *Mat* 28:15
John's disciples and J.   *John* 3:25
the J. have no dealings with.   4:9
salvation is of the J.   22
feast of the J.   5:1
did the J. persecute Jesus.   16
J. sought the more to kill him.   18
the J. therefore strove among. 6:52
openly of him, for fear of J.   7:13
the J. did not believe that.   9:18
the J. took up stones again. 10:31
master, the J. of late sought.   11:8
when Jesus saw her and the J.   33
J. went away and believed.   12:11
I taught in temple, whither J. 18:20
not be delivered to the J.   36
of Jesus as the manner of J. 19:40
to none, but the J. only. *Acts* 11:19
Herod saw it pleased the J.   12:3
because or the J. that were.   16:3
these men being J. do trouble.   20
J. and Greeks heard the word. 19:10
certain of the vagabond J.   13
the J. laid wait for him.   20:3, 19
so shall the J. at Jerusalem. 21:11
certain of the J. banded.   23:12
this man was taken of the J.   27
certain J. from Asia found.   24:18
to the J. have done no wrong. 25:10
is he God of J. only ?   *Rom* 3:29
Christ, to the J. a.   *1 Cor* 1:23
to J. I became as a Jew, that.   9:20
of J. five times received. *2 Cor* 11:24
and not as do the J.   *Gal* 2:14
we who are J. by nature, and.   15
have suffered of the J. *1 Thes* 2:14
which say they are J. and are not.
   Rev 2:9; 3:9

see Gentiles
all the Jews
Haman sought to destroy all the J.
   Esth 3:6, 13
more than all the J.   4:13
go, gather all the J.   16
when all the J. in Moab. *Jer* 40:11
even all the J. returned out of.   12
Ishmael slew all the J. that.   41:3
the word concerning all the J. 44:1
all the J. except they wash, they.
   Mark 7:3
all the Jews to depart. *Acts* 18:2
this was known to all the J. 19:17
thou teachest all the J. to.   21:21
a good report of all the J.   22:12
of sedition among all the J.   24:5
manner of life at Jerusalem know all
the J.   26:4

King of the Jews
that is born King of the J.? *Mat* 2:2
Jesus, Art thou King of the J.?
   27:11; *Mark* 15:2; *Luke* 23:3
   John 18:33
Hail, King of the J.   *Mat* 27:29
   Mark 15:18; *John* 19:3
accusation, This is the King of the
Jews. *Mat* 27:37; *Mark* 15:26
   Luke 23:38; *John* 19:19
will ye that I release to you King of
the J.?   *Mark* 15:9; *John* 18:39
call the King of the J.? *Mark* 15:12
if thou be the King of the J. save
thyself.   *Luke* 23:37
the King of the J. but that he said, I
am King of the J.   *John* 19:21

Jezebel
Ahab took to wife J.   *1 Ki* 16:31
when J. cut off the prophets. 18:4
when J. slew the prophets of.   13
of Baal which eat at J.'s table.   19
Ahab told J. all that Elijah.   19:1
the elders did as J. had sent. 21:11

when J. heard Naboth.   *1 Ki* 21:15
dogs shall eat J.   23; *2 Ki* 9:10, 36
none like Ahab, whom J. *1 Ki* 21:25
avenge at the hand of J.   *2 Ki* 9:7
whoredoms of thy mother J.   22
J. shall be as dung upon face of field,
so they shall not say, this is J. 37
sufferest that woman J.   *Rev* 2:20

Jezreel, name of place and person
pitched in the valley of J. *Judg* 6:33
also took Ahinoam of J. *1 Sam* 25:43
by a fountain which is in J.   29:1
Ish-bosheth king over J. *2 Sam* 2:9
rode and went to J.   *1 Ki* 18:45
before Ahab to entrance of J.   46
a vineyard which was in J.   21:1
dogs shall eat Jezebel by the wall
of J.   23; *2 Ki* 9:10, 36
Joram went back to J.   *2 Ki* 8:29
   2 Chr 22:6
in a chariot and went to J. *2 Ki* 9:16
come to me to J. by to-morrow. 10:6
heads of the king's sons to J.   7
of the father of Etam, J. *1 Chr* 4:3
call his name J. for I will avenge the
blood of J. on house.   *Hos* 1:4
break bow of Israel in valley of J. 5
for great shall be the day of J.   11
wine and oil shall hear J.   2:22

Jezreelite, *see* Naboth
Joab
three sons of Zeruiah, J. *2 Sam* 2:18
should I hold up my face to J.?   22
J. also and Abishai pursued.   24
of Abner rest on the head of J. 3:29
so J. and Abishai his brother.   30
J. son of Zeruiah was.   8:16; 20:23
   1 Chr 11:6; 18:15; 27:34
demanded of Uriah how J. did.
   2 Sam 11:7
abide in tents, and my lord J.   11
David wrote a letter to J.   14
J. fought against Rabbah of. 12:26
J. put the words in widow's. 14:3
is not the hand of J. with thee ? 19
Absalom sent for J.   30
J.'s field is near.   30
J. killed Amasa.   20:9
woman said, Art thou J.?   17
the king's word prevailed against J.
   24:4; *1 Chr* 21:4
Adonijah conferred with J. *1 Ki* 1:7
moreover thou knowest what J. 2:5
J. fled to tabernacle of Lord.   28
six months J. remain, every. 11:16
Seraiah begat J.   *1 Chr* 4:14
J. led the army.   20:1
word was abominable to J.   21:6
all that Abner and J. had.   26:28
of children of Jeshua and J.
   Ezra 2:6; *Neh* 7:11
of the sons of J. Obadiah. *Ezra* 8:9

Joah
J. son of Asaph the recorder.
   2 Ki 18:18; *Isa* 36:3
J. son of Zimmah.   *1 Chr* 6:21
J. son of Obed-edom.   26:4

Joanna
which was the son of J.   *Luke* 3:27
J. the wife of Chuza, Herod's.   8:3
J. and Mary   24:10

Joash
that pertaineth to J. the.   *Judg* 6:11
sword of Gideon the son of J.   7:14
carry him back to Amon and J. the.
   1 Ki 22:26; *2 Chr* 18:25
Jehosheba stole J.   *2 Ki* 11:2
   2 Chr 22:11
J. the son of Jehoahaz.   *2 Ki* 13:9
J. the king of Israel wept over.   14
J. beat Ben-hadad three times.   25
of Jeroboam the son of J.   14:27
Becher, Zemira, and J.   *1 Chr* 7:8
J. the son of Shemaiah the.   12:3
over the cellars of oil was J.   27:28
J. remembered not the. *2 Chr* 24:22
executed judgement against J.   24

Job
the sons of Issachar, J.   *Gen* 46:13
Uz whose name was J.   *Job* 1:1
considered my servant J.?   8; 2:3
Satan said, Doth J. fear God?   1:9

J. sinned not with his lips.
Job 1:22; 2:10
Satan went and smote *J.* with. 2:7
three men ceased to answer *J.* 32:1
against *J.* was Elihu's wrath. 2
no answer and condemned *J.* 3
none of you that convinced *J.* 12
mark well, O *J.* hearken. 33:31
man is like *J.* who drinketh? 34:7
J. hath spoken without. 35
my desire is that *J.* may be tried. 36
doth *J.* open his mouth in vain?35:16
spoken as my servant *J.* hath. 42:7, 8
bullocks and go to my servant *J.* 8
the Lord also accepted *J.* 9
the Lord gave *J.* twice as much. 10
Lord blessed the latter end of *J.* 12
so fair as the daughters of *J.* 15
after this lived *J.* 140 years. 16
so *J.* died, being old and full. 17
Noah, Daniel and *J.* *Ezek* 14:14, 20
heard of the patience of *J. Jas* 5:11

Joel

Samuel's firstborn was *J.* *1 Sam* 8:2
Simeon, *J.* and Jehu. *1 Chr* 4:35
Reubenites, the sons of *J.* 5:4, 8
of the Gadites, *J.* the chief, and. 12
Heman, a singer, son of *J.* 6:33
Elkanah the son of *J.* a. 36
Michael, Obadiah and *J.* 7:3
J. and Mibhar were valiant. 11:38
of the sons of Gershom, *J.* 15:7
David called for Isaiah and *J.* 11
Laadan, the chief was *J.* 23:8
Jehuli, Zetham and *J.* 26:22
half tribe of Manasseh, *J.* 27:20
J. and Benaiah had. *Ezra* 10:43
J. son of Zichri was. *Neh* 11:9
word came to *J.* the son. *Joel* 1:1
spoken by the prophet *J.* *Acts* 2:16

Johanan

J. came to Gedaliah. *2 Ki* 25:23
Jer 40:8, 13
Josiah, the firstborn *J.* *1 Chr* 3:15
into the chamber of *J.* *Ezra* 10:6
but when *J.* heard of all. *Jer* 41:11
so *J.* obeyed not the voice of. 43:4

John son of *Zacharias*

J. had raiment of camel's hair.
Mat 3:4; *Mark* 1:6
came to be baptized, but *J.* *Mat* 3:14
when *J.* was cast into prison. 4:12
Mark 1:14
then came to him the disciples of *J.*
Mat 9:14; *Mark* 2:18; *Luke* 5:33
7:18; 11:1; *John* 3:25
J. had heard the works of Christ.
Mat 11:2; *Luke* 7:19
go and shew *J.* these things.
Mat 11:4; *Luke* 7:22
Jesus began to say concerning *J.*
Mat 11:7; *Luke* 7:24
the law prophesied till *J.* *Mat* 11:13
Luke 16:16
Herod beheaded *J.* *Mat* 14:10
Mark 6:16; *Luke* 9:9
all hold *J.* as a prophet. *Mat* 21:26
Mark 11:32; *Luke* 20:6
J. came in way of righteousness.
Mat 1:32
Herod feared *J.* knowing. *Mark* 5:20
thou shalt call his name *J.*
Luke 1:13, 60
mused in their hearts of *J.* 3:15
it was said, that *J.* was risen. 9:7
a man, whose name was *J.* *John* 1:6
and this is the record of *J.* 19, 32
next day *J.* seeth Jesus coming. 29
J. also was baptizing in Enon. 3:23
for *J.* was not yet cast into. 24
made more disciples than *J.* 4:1
sent to *J.* and he bare witness. 5:33
greater witness than that of *J.* 36
J. did no miracle; but all that *J.*
spake. 10:41
for *J.* truly baptized with water.
Acts 1:5; 11:16
J. had first preached before. 13:24
and as *J.* fulfilled his course, he. 25
see baptism, baptist

John *the apostle*

James and *J.* the sons of. *Mat* 4:21
10:2; *Mark* 1:19; 3:17

Jesus sent Peter and *J.* *Luke* 22:8
Peter and *J.* went up. *Acts* 3:1
lame man held Peter and *J.* 11
the boldness of Peter and *J.* 4:13
sent to Samaria Peter and *J.* 8:14
James the brother of *J.* 12:2
his angel to his servant *J.* *Rev* 1:1
J. to the seven churches which. 4
who also am your brother. 9:1
I *J.* saw the holy city. 21:2
see James

John

J. and Alexander. *Acts* 4:6

John, surnamed *Mark*

Peter came to house of *J.* *Acts* 12:12
with them *J.* whose surname. 25
and they had also *J.* to their. 13:5
J. departing from them, returned. 13
to take with them *J.* 15:37

join

they *j.* to our enemies. *Ex* 1:10
did Jehoshaphat *j.* *2 Chr* 20:35
and *j.* in affinity with. *Ezra* 9:14
hand *j.* in hand. *Pr* 11:21; 16:5
woe to them that *j.* house. *Isa* 5:8
the Lord shall *j.* his enemies. 9:11*
sons of stranger that *j.* 56:6
come, let us *j.* ourselves. *Jer* 50:5
j. them one to another. *Ezek* 37:17
they shall *j.* in the end. *Dan* 11:6
the rest durst no man *j.* *Acts* 5:13
go near and *j.* thyself to this. 8:29
Saul assayed to *j.* himself. 9:26

joined

kings were *j.* together in. *Gen* 14:3
they *j.* battle with them in the. 8*
will my husband be *j.* to me. 29:34
of Levi be *j.* to thee. *Num* 18:2, 4
they *j.* battle, Israel. *1 Sam* 4:2
day the battle was *j.* *1 Ki* 20:29
Jehoshaphat *j.* affinity. *2 Chr* 18:1
he *j.* with Ahaziah to. 20:36, 37
set up walls, and *j.* the. *Ezra* 4:12*
all the wall was *j.* *Neh* 4:6
j. should keep these days. *Esth* 9:27
let it not be *j.* to the days. *Job* 3:6*
Leviathan's scales are *j.* one. 41:17
the flakes of his flesh are *j.* 23
Assur also is *j.* with them. *Ps* 83:8
to him that is *j.* to all. *Eccl* 9:4
every one *j.* to them. *Isa* 13:15*
and the strangers shall be *j.* 14:1
thou shalt not be *j.* with them. 20
nor him that hath *j.* to the. 56:3
their wings were *j.* one. *Ezek* 1:9
were courts *j.* of forty. 46:22*
Ephraim is *j.* to idols. *Hos* 4:17
many nations shall be *j.* *Zech* 2:11
what God hath *j.* together.
Mat 19:6; *Mark* 10:9
he went and *j.* himself. *Luke* 15:15
about four hundred *j.* *Acts* 5:36
whose house *j.* hard to the. 18:7
ye be perfectly *j.* in. *1 Cor* 1:10
he which is *j.* to an harlot. 6:16
he that is *j.* to the Lord is one. 17
the whole body fitly *j.* *Eph* 4:16*
and shall be *j.* to his wife. 15:31*
see Baal-peor

joining, -s

prepared iron for the *j.* *1 Chr* 22:3*
j. to the wing of the. *2 Chr* 3:12

joint

thigh was out of *j.* *Gen* 32:25*
all my bones are out of *j.* *Ps* 22:14
is like a foot out of *j.* *Pr* 25:19
by that which every *j.* *Eph* 4:16

joint-heirs

heirs of God, and *j.*-heirs. *Rom* 8:17

joints

king of Israel between the *j.* of the.
1 Ki 22:34; *2 Chr* 18:33
the *j.* of thy thighs are. *S of S* 7:1†
that the *j.* of his loins. *Dan* 5:6
all the body by *j.* *Col* 2:19
to dividing asunder of *j.* *Heb* 4:12

Jonadab, *called Jehonadab*

J. was Amnon's friend. *2 Sam* 13:3
J. son of Rechab came. *2 Ki* 10:15
J. our father commanded. *Jer* 35:6

obeyed the voice of *J.* *Jer* 35:8, 18
J. shall not want a man to stand. 19

Jonah, *or* Jonas

spake by his servant *J.* *2 Ki* 14:25
J. rose to flee to Tarshish. *Jonah* 1:3
lots, and the lot fell upon *J.* 7
they cast *J.* into the sea, the. 15
J. was in the belly of the fish. 17
J. prayed. 2:1
the fish vomited out *J.* 10
J. went to Nineveh. 3:3
it displeased *J.* 4:1
the gourd to come up over *J.* 4:6
to it, but the sign of the prophet *J.*
Mat 12:39; 16:4; *Luke* 11:29, 30
as *J.* was three days in. *Mat* 12:40
repented at the preaching of *J.* 41
Simon son of *J.* lovest thou me ?
John 21:15, 16, 17

Jonathan

J. and his sons were. *Judg* 18:30
men were with *J.* in. *1 Sam* 13:2
with Saul and *J.* were swords. 22
knew not that *J.* was gone. 14:3
J. climbed up upon his hands. 13
J. heard not when his father. 27
though it be in *J.* my son, he. 39
I and *J.* my son will be on the. 40
J. was taken. 42
thou shalt surely die, *J.* 44
so the people rescued *J.* that he. 45
the soul of *J.* was knit with. 18:1
but *J.* Saul's son delighted. 19:2
J. spake good of David to Saul. 4
let not *J.* know this lest he. 20:3
do so and much more to *J.* 13
J. made a covenant with. 16
anger was kindled against *J.* 30
J. knew it was determined to. 33
J. cried after the lad. 37
J. and David knew. 39
J. arose and went to David. 23:16
the Philistines slew *J.* 31:2
1 Chr 10:2
Saul and *J.* his son. *2 Sam* 1:4
the bow of *J.* turned not back. 22
Saul and *J.* were lovely in. 23
distressed for thee, my brother *J.* 26
J. had a son that was lame. 4:4; 9:3
shew thee kindness for *J.'s* sake. 9:7
J. the son of Abiathar. 15:27, 36
1 Ki 1:42, 43
now *J.* and Ahimaaz. *2 Sam* 17:17
Mephibosheth the son of *J.* 21:7
took the bones of Saul and *J.* 12
J. the son of Shimea slew him. 21
1 Chr 20:7
of sons of Jashen, *J.* *2 Sam* 23:32
Jada, Jether and *J.* *1 Chr* 2:32
sons of Hashem, *J.* Ahiam. 11:34
also *J.* David's uncle was a. 27:32
Ebed the son of *J.* went. *Ezra* 8:6
only *J.* and Jehaziah were. 10:15
Joiada begat *J.* *Neh* 12:11
of Melicu, *J.* 14
Zechariah the son of *J.* with a. 35
in prison in the house of *J. Jer* 37:15
return to the house of *J.* 20; 38:26
Johanan and *J.* came to. 40:8
see David, Saul

Joppa

bring it by sea in floats to *J.*
2 Chr 2:16; *Ezra* 3:7
Jonah went down to *J.* *Jonah* 1:3
at *J.* a disciple named. *Acts* 9:36
it was known throughout all *J.* 42
Peter tarried many days in *J.* 43
send men to *J.* and call. 10:5, 32
certain brethren from *J.* 23
I was in the city of *J.* praying. 11:5

Joram, *called* Jehoram

Toi sent *J.* his son to. *2 Sam* 8:10
J. of Ahab, *J.* son of. *2 Ki* 8:16
Syrians wounded *J.* 28
J. went to Jezreel. 29
Jehoshaphat conspired against *J.*
9:14
a bow and smote *J.* between. 24
Jehosheba the daughter of *J.* 11:2
of the Levites, *J.* over. *1 Chr* 26:25
destruction of Ahaziah was of God
by coming to *J.* *2 Chr* 22:7
Josaphat begat *J.* and *J.* *Mat* 1:8

Jordan

him all the plain of *J.* Gen 13:11
go down to *J.* and goings out at the.
Num 34:12; Josh 13:27; 18:12
come to *J.* stand still in *J.* Josh 3:8
passeth over before you into *J.* 11
J. overfloweth all his banks in. 15
stones out of the midst of *J.* 4:3
priests, come ye up out of *J.* 17
God dried the waters of *J.* 23
Lord hath made *J.* a border. 22:25
they took the fords of *J.* Judg 3:28
7:24; 12:5
slew him at the passages of *J.* 12:6
king returned and came to *J.*
2 Sam 19:15
down to meet me at *J.* 1 Ki 2:8
in plain of *J.* did the king cast them
in clay ground. 7:46; 2 Chr 4:17
brook Cherith before *J.* 1 Ki 17:3, 5
Lord hath sent me to *J.* 2 Ki 2:6
they two stood by *J.* 7
Elisha stood by *J.* 13
go and wash in *J.* seven times. 5:10
dipped himself seven times in *J.* 14
let us go, we pray thee, to *J.* 6:2
went after the Syrians to *J.* 7:15
that he can draw up *J.* Job 40:23
thee from the land of *J.* Ps 42:6
sea fled, *J.* was driven. 114:3, 5
do in the swelling of *J.?* Jer 12:5
from the swelling of *J.* 49:19; 50:44
pride of *J.* is spoiled. Zech 11:3
were baptized of him in *J.* Mat 3:6
Mark 1:5, 9
cometh Jesus from Galilee to *J.*
Mat 3:13

beyond Jordan
Atad which is *beyond J.* Gen 50:10
Abel-mizraim, which is *beyond J.* 11
land that is *beyond J.* Deut 3:25
kings of Amorites *beyond J.*
Josh 9:10
gave them *beyond J.* 13:8; 18:7
Gilead abode *beyond J.* Judg 5:17
Zebulun and land of Naphtali *beyond*
J. in. Isa 9:1; Mat 4:15
in Bethabara *beyond J.* John 1:28
he that was with thee *beyond J.* 3:26

on the other side Jordan
Ebal, are they not *on other side J.?*
Deut 11:30
content and dwelt *on the other side*
J. Josh 7:7
and half the tribe *on the other side J.*
12:1; 13:27, 32; 14:3; 17:5; 22:4
on other side J. Bezer. 20:8
who dwelt *on the other side J.* 24:8
of Oreb, Zeeb *on other side J.*
Judg 7:25
Israel *on other side J.* oppressed.
10:8
on other side J. forsook. 1 Sam 31:7
of Merari cities *on other side J.*
1 Chr 6:78
on the other side J. 120,000. 12:37

on this side Jordan
is fallen *on this side J.* Num 32:19
32; 34:15; Josh 1:14, 15; 22:7
give three cities *on this side J.*
Num 35:14; Deut 4:41
on this side J. Moses. Deut 1:5
we took the land *on this side J.* 3:8
kings *on this side J.* Josh 9:1
1700 officers *this side J.* 1 Chr 26:30

over Jordan
I passed *over* this *J.* Gen 32:10
land, bring us not *over J.* Num 32:5
go all of you armed *over J.* 21
we will pass *over J.* armed. 32
passed *over J.* into the land. 33:51
35:10; Deut 12:10; 27:4, 12
thou shalt not go *over J.* Deut 3:27
4:21; 31:2
this land, I must not go *over J.* 4:22
pass *over J.* this day. 9:1; 11:31
go *over J.* thou and all. Josh 1:2
three days ye shall pass *over J.* 11
were passed clean *over J.* 3:17; 4:1
Israel came *over* this *J.* on. 4:22
brought this people *over J.* to. 7
ye went *over J.* and came. 24:11
Ammon passed *over J.* Judg 10:9

Hebrews went *over J.* 1 Sam 13:7
his men passed *over J.* 2 Sam 2:29
the people passed *over J.* 17:22
and all Israel passed *over J.* 24
conduct the king *over J.* 19:15, 31
they that passed *over J.* 1 Chr 12:15
David passed *over J.* against. 19:17

Jorim, Jose
Jose the son of Eliezer, the son of
Jorim. Luke 3:29

Josedech, see Joshua

Joseph
she called his name *J.* Gen 30:24
Jacob put Rachel and *J.* 33:2
the sons of Rachel, *J.* and Benjamin.
35:24; 46:19; 1 Chr 2:2
J. brought to his father. Gen 37:2
Israel loved *J.* 3
J. dreamed a dream. 5
his brethren sold *J.* 28
J. is rent in pieces. 33
but the Lord was with *J.* 39:2, 21
Egyptian's house for *J.'s* sake. 5
wife cast her eyes upon *J.* 7
J.'s master took him and put him. 20
butler told his dream to *J.* 40:9
not the chief butler remember *J.* 23
they brought *J.* out of the. 41:14
Pharaoh put his ring on *J.'s* hand. 42
J. 30 years old when he stood. 46
J. gathered corn as the sand of. 49
go to *J.* 41:55
J. knew his brethren. 42:8
J. is not. 36
the man did as *J.* bade. 43:17
J. made haste, for his bowels. 30
I am *J.* 45:3, 4
say, Thus saith thy son *J.* 9
they told him, saying, *J.* is. 26, 28
J. shall put his hand upon thine. 46:4
J. went up to meet Israel his. 29
J. nourished his father and. 47:12
all the Egyptians came to *J.* 15
die, and he called his son *J.* 29
one told Jacob, thy son *J.* 48:2
J. brought them from between. 12
Jacob blessed *J.* and said, God. 15
J. is a fruitful bough, even a. 49:22
blessings shall be on head of *J.* 26
J. went up to bury his father. 50:7
J. will peradventure hate us. 15
and they sent a messenger to *J.* 16
J. wept when they spake unto. 17
J. took an oath of the children. 25
new king which knew not *J.*
Ex 1:8; Acts 7:18
Moses took the bones of *J.* Ex 13:19
sons of *J.* Manasseh. Num 26:28, 37
these on Gerizim to bless, Judah, *J.*
Deut 27:12
of *J.* he said, Blessed of the. 33:13
blessing come upon head of *J.* 16
but the birthright was *J.'s.* 1 Chr 5:2
sons of Jacob and *J.* Ps 77:15
refused the tabernacle of *J.* 78:67
give ear, thou that leadest *J.* 80:1
this he ordained in *J.* for a. 81:5
even *J.* who was sold for a. 105:17
write for *J.* the stick. Ezek 37:16, 19
tribes of Israel, *J.* shall have. 47:13
one gate of *J.* one gate of. 48:32
be gracious to the remnant of *J.*
Amos 5:15
not grieved for the affliction of *J.* 6:6
near the ground that Jacob gave to *J.*
John 4:5
the patriarchs sold *J.* into. Acts 7:9
at the second time *J.* was made. 13
then *J.* called his father Jacob. 14
Jacob blessed sons of *J.* Heb 11:21
J. made mention of Israel's. 22
see house

Joseph with *tribe* and *children*
of the *children* of *J.* of Ephraim.
Num 1:10, 32
of the *tribe* of *J.* namely of. 13:11
princes of the *children* of *J.* 34:23
the *tribe* of the sons of *J.* hath. 36:5
the *children* of *J.* two tribes.
Josh 14:4; 16:4
the lot of *children* of *J.* fell. 16:1
the *children* of *J.* spake. 17:14, 16

---

dwelt the *children* of *J.* 1 Chr 7:29
of the *tribe* of *J.* were sealed 12,000.
Rev 7:8

Joseph, husband of *Mary*
Jacob begat *J.* the. Mat 1:16
mother Mary was espoused to *J.* 18
J. her husband being a just man. 19
J. did as angel of the Lord hath. 24
the Lord appeared to *J.* 2:13, 19
name was *J.* of house. Luke 1:27
J. also went up from Galilee. 2:4
as we supposed, the son of *J.* 3:23
this *J.'s* son? 4:22; John 1:45; 6:42

Joseph, the name of divers men
Issachar, Igal son of *J.* Num 13:7
of Asaph, Zaccur, *J.* 1 Chr 25:2, 9
Shallum, *J.* had taken. Ezra 10:42
of Shebaniah, *J.* was a. Neh 12:14
J. of Arimathaea, Jesus' disciple.
Mat 27:57, 59; Mark 15:43, 45
Luke 23:50; John 19:38
Janna, son of *J.* Luke 3:24, 26, 30
two, *J.* called Barsabas. Acts 1:23

Joses
James and *J.* Mat 13:55; Mark 6:3
Mary the mother of *J.* Mat 27:56
Mark 15:40, 47
J. by apostles was surnamed.
Acts 4:36

Joshua, called Jehoshua, and Oshea
J. discomfited Amalek. Ex 17:13
rehearse it in the ears of *J.* 14
rose up and his minister *J.* 24:13
when *J.* heard the noise of. 32:17
J. departed not out of the. 33:11
of the tribe of Ephraim, *Oshea* son
of Nun. Num 13:8
Oshea the son of Nun, Jehoshua. 16
save Caleb and *J.* 14:30, 38; 26:65
32:12
take thee *J.* 27:18
he set *J.* before Eleazar. 22
Eleazar and *J.* shall divide. 34:17
but *J.* shall go in. Deut 1:38; 31:3
charge *J.* and encourage him. 3:28
31:23
J. was full of the spirit of. 34:9
J. commanded officers. Josh 1:10
J. sent two men to spy secretly. 2:1
Lord said to *J.* 3:7; 5:9; 6:2
7:10; 8:18; 10:8
children of Israel did so as *J.* 4:8
day the Lord magnified *J.* in. 14
children, them *J.* circumcised. 5:7
J. fell on his face to the earth. 14
and *J.* did so. 15
so the Lord was with *J.* 6:27
J. rent his clothes. 7:6
pursued after *J.* 8:16
then *J.* built an altar to the. 30
which *J.* read not before all the. 35
then spake *J.* Sun, stand still. 10:12
their land did *J.* take at one. 42
J. did unto them as the Lord. 11:9
now *J.* was old and. 13:1; 23:1
so *J.* blessed Caleb and gave. 14:13
J. cast lots for them before. 18:10
gave an inheritance to *J.* 19:49
J. blessed the Reubenites. 22:6
J. gathered the tribes of. 24:1
so *J.* made a covenant with. 25
J. the servant of the Lord died. 29
Judg 2:8
days of *J.* and of elders that overlived *J.* Josh 24:31; Judg 2:7
into the field of *J.* 1 Sam 6:14, 18
which he spake by *J.* 1 Ki 16:34
in of the gate of *J.* 2 Ki 23:8
J. son of Josedech. Hag 1:1, 12, 14
2:2, 4
and he shewed me *J.* the. Zech 3:1
now *J.* was clothed with filthy. 3
stone that I have laid before *J.* 9
set them upon the head of *J.* 6:11

Josiah
a child shall be born, *J.* 1 Ki 13:2
the people made *J.* king. 2 Chr 21:24
2 Chr 33:25
J. was eight years old. 2 Ki 22:1

did J. take away. 2 Ki 23:19, 24
2 Chr 34:33
J. went. 2 Ki 23:29; 2 Chr 35:22
sons of J. were Johanan. 1 Chr 3:15
J. kept a passover. 2 Chr 35:1
keep such a passover as J. 18
in the 18th year of J. was this. 19
archers shot at king J. and. 23
and Jerusalem mourned for J. 24
lamented for J. . . men spake of J. 25
came in days of J. Jer 1:2; 3:6
Zephaniah in days of J. Zeph 1:1
go into the house of J. Zech 6:10
Amon begat J. Mat 1:10
J. begat Jechonias. 11

jot
one j. or tittle shall in. Mat 5:18

Jotham
J. youngest son of. Judg 9:5, 21
on them came the curse of J. 57
J. judged the people. 2 Ki 15:5
2 Chr 26:21
of Jahdai, Regem and J. 1 Chr 2:47
Azariah his son, J. his son. 3:12
genealogies in the days of J. 5:17
J. became mighty. 2 Chr 27:6
in the days of J. Isa 1:1; Hos 1:1
Mi 1:1
Ozias begat J. and J. Mat 1:9

journey
Lord hath made his j. Gen 24:21
Jacob went on his j. and. 29:1
after him seven days' j. 31:23
let us take our j. 33:12
Israel took his j. 46:1
they took their j. from. Ex 13:20
Israelites took their j. from. 16:1
a j. yet shall keep the. Num 9:10
is not in a j. and forbeareth to. 13
they first took their j. 10:13
there are eleven days' j. Deut 1:2
arise, take thy j. before the. 10:11
take victuals with you for your j.
Josh 9:11
by reason of the very long j. 13
the j. thou takest is not. Judg 4:9
Lord sent thee on a j. 1 Sam 15:18
thou not from thy j.? 2 Sam 11:10
or he is in a j. 1 Ki 18:27
the j. is great. 19:7
compass of seven days' j. 2 Ki 3:9
for how long shall thy j. be? Neh 2:6
man is gone a long j. Pr 7:19
nor scrip for your j. nor. Mat 10:10
take nothing for their j. Mark 6:8
Luke 9:3
a friend of mine in his j. Luke 11:6
the younger took his j. into a. 15:13
Jesus wearied with his j. John 4:6
might have a prosperous j. Rom 1:10
I trust to see you in my j. 15:24*
may bring me on my j. 1 Cor 16:6
and Apollos on their j. Tit 3:13
bring forward on their j. 3 John 6

day's journey
the quails fall a day's j. Num 11:31
himself went a day's j. 1 Ki 19:4
to enter city a day's j. Jonah 3:4
went a day's j. among. Luke 2:44
from Jerusalem a sabbath day's j.
Acts 1:12

see three days
journeyed
that as they j. they. Gen 11:2
Abram j. going on toward. 12:9, 20:1
Lot j. east. 13:11
Jacob j. to Succoth. 33:17
Israel j. toward Beth-el. 35:5
j. from Beth-el. 16
j. to the tower of Edar. 21
cloud not taken up, then they j. not.
Ex 40:37; Num 9:21
after that the children of Israel j.
Num 9:17, 18
charge of the Lord, and j. not. 19
commandment of Lord they j. 20, 23
j. not till Miriam was brought. 12:15
house of Micah as he j. Judg 17:8
as Saul j. he came near. Acts 9:3
which j. with him stood. 7; 26:13

journeying
make trumpets for j. of. Num 10:2

we are j. to the place. Num 10:29
as he was j. towards. Luke 13:22
in j. often, in perils. 2 Cor 11:26

journeyings
were the j. of Israel's. Num 10:28

journeys
Abram went on his j. Gen 13:3
j. according to the. Ex 17:1
cloud was taken up, they went on in
their j. 40:36; Num 10:12
for the cloud was upon the tabernacle through all their j. Ex 40:38
blow an alarm for their j. Num 10:6
these are the j. of Israel. 33:1, 2

joy, substantive
to meet Saul with j. 1 Sam 18:6
for there was j. in. 1 Chr 12:40
by lifting up the voice with j. 15:16
bring ark of the covenant with j. 25
now have I seen with j. the. 29:17
to Jerusalem with j. 2 Chr 20:27
noise of the shout of j. Ezra 3:13
of the house of God with j. 6:16
the feast seven days with j. 22
the j. of the Lord is. Neh 8:10
of Jerusalem was heard. j. 12:43
the Jews had light, j. Esth 8:16
sorrow to j. they should make them
days of feasting and j. 9:22*
this is the j. of his way. Job 8:19
the j. of the hypocrite is but. 20:5
widow's heart to sing for j. 29:13
he will see his face with j. 33:26
and sorrow is turned into j. 41:22*
presence is fulness of j. Ps 16:11
his tabernacles sacrifices of j. 27:6
but j. cometh in the morning. 30:5
I went with the voice of j. and. 42:4
unto God my exceeding j. 43:4
the j. of the whole earth is. 48:2
restore to me the j. of thy. 51:12
nations be glad and sing for j. 67:4
forth his people with j. 105:43
sow in tears shall reap in j. 126:5
Jerusalem above my chief j. 137:6
counsellors of peace is j. Pr 12:20
not intermeddle with his j. 14:10
folly is j. to him destitute. 15:21
a man hath j. by the answer of. 23
father of a fool hath no j. 17:21
it is j. to the just to do. 21:15
a wise child shall have j. 23:24
not my heart from j. Eccl 2:10
him wisdom, knowledge, and j. 26
God answereth him in the j. 5:20
way, eat thy bread with j. 9:7
the j. according to the j. Isa 9:3
Lord shall have no j. in their. 17*
with j. shall ye draw water. 12:3
is taken out of the plentiful. 16:10
j. of the harp ceaseth. 24:8
is darkened. 11
meek shall increase their j. 29:19
on all houses of j. 32:13
a j. of wild asses. 14
and rejoice even with j. and. 35:2
j. on their heads. 10; 51:11
break forth into j. 52:9
go out with j. 55:12
I will make thee a j. of many. 60:15
to give them the oil j. for. 61:3
everlasting j. shall be unto them. 7
my servants shall sing for j. 65:14
I create her people a j. 18
but he shall appear to your j. 66:5
rejoice for j. with her, all ye. 10
the word was to me the j. Jer 15:16
turn their mourning into j. 31:13
to me a name of j., a praise. 33:9
shall be heard the voice of j. 11
spakest, thou skippedst for j. 48:27*
j. is taken from the plentiful. 33
praise, the city of my j. 49:25
city, the j. of the whole. Lam 2:15
the j. of our heart is ceased. 5:15
take from them the j. Ezek 24:25
appointed, with the j. of all. 36:5
rejoice not, O Israel, for j. Hos 9:1
because j. is withered. Joel 1:12
rejoice over thee with j. Zeph 3:17
anon with j. receiveth it. Mat 13:20
Luke 8:13
for j. thereof goeth and. Mat 13:44

enter thou into the j. Mat 25:21, 23
leaped in my womb for j. Luke 1:44
in that day, and leap for j. 6:23
seventy returned again with j. 10:17
j. shall be in heaven over one. 15:7
there is j. in the presence of. 10
they yet believed not for j. 24:41
this my j. therefore is. John 3:29
to you, that my j. might remain in
you, and that your j. might. 15:11
sorrow shall be turned into j. 16:20
for j. that a man is born into. 21
and your j. no man taketh from. 22
ye shall receive, that your j. 24
might have my j. fulfilled. 17:13
make me full of j. with. Acts 2:28*
disciples filled with j. in the. 13:52
might finish my course with j. 20:24
kingdom of God is j. in. Rom 14:17
God fill you with all j. in. 15:13
may come to you with j. by the. 32
are helpers of your j. 2 Cor 1:24
that my j. is the j. of you all. 2:3
joyed we for the j. of Titus. 7:13
the abundance of their j. 8:2
Spirit is love, j. peace. Gal 5:22
making request with j. Phil 1:4
furtherance and j. of faith. 25
fulfil ye my j. 2:2
my j. and crown. 4:1
received the word with j. 1 Thes 1:6
what is our hope or j.? 2:19
ye are our j. 20
for the j. wherewith we joy. 3:9
I may be filled with j. 2 Tim 1:4
let me have j. of thee. Philem 20
who for the j. that was. Heb 12:2
they may do it with j. and. 13:17
count it j. when ye fall into. Jas 1:2
and your j. be turned into. 4:9
ye rejoice with j. 1 Pet 1:8
be glad also with exceeding j. 4:13
that your j. may be full. 1 John 1:4
2 John 12
I have no greater j. than. 3 John 4
you faultless with exceeding j.
Jude 24

see gladness
joy, verb
the king shall j. in thy. Ps 21:1
j. before thee according. Isa 9:3
I will rejoice and j. in my. 65:19
I will j. in the God of my. Hab 3:18
he will j. over thee with. Zeph 3:18
also j. in God through. Rom 5:11*
I j. and rejoice with. Philem 2:17
for the same cause also do ye j. 18
wherewith we j. for you. 1 Thes 3:9

great joy
the people rejoiced with great j.
1 Ki 1:40
David the king rejoiced with great j.
1 Chr 29:9
so there was great j. 2 Chr 30:26
them rejoice with great j. Neh 12:43
they rejoiced with great j. Mat 2:10
sepulchre with fear and great j. 28:8
good tidings of great j. Luke 2:10
to Jerusalem with great j. 24:52
and there was great j. in. Acts 8:8
they caused great j. to all. 15:3
for we have great j. in thy. Philem 7

shout, or shouted for joy
many shouted aloud for j. Ezra 3:12
sons of God shouted for j. Job 38:7
trust in thee rejoice: let them ever
shout for j. Ps 5:11; 35:27
shout for j. all ye that are. 32:11
the valleys shout for j. they. 65:13
thy saints shout for j. 132:9, 16

joyed
more j. we for the joy. 2 Cor 7:13

joyful
went to their tents j. 1 Ki 8:66
Lord hath made them j. Ezra 6:22
went forth that day j. Esth 5:9
let no j. voice come therein. Job 3:7
love thy name be j. in. Ps 5:11
soul shall be j. in the Lord. 35:9
shall praise thee with j. lips. 63:5
make a j. noise to God, all. 66:1
make a j. noise to the God of. 81:1

that know the *j.* sound.   *Ps* 89:15
make a *j.* noise to the rock of.   95:1
a *j.* noise to him.   2; 98:4; 100:1
make a *j.* noise before the.   98:6
let the hills be *j.* together before.   8*
the barren to be a *j.* mother.   113:9
let the children of Zion be *j.*   149:2
let the saints be *j.* in glory; let.   5*
of prosperity be *j.* but in.   *Eccl* 7:14
heavens, and be *j.* earth.   *Isa* 49:13
make them *j.* in my house of.   56:7
soul shall be *j.* in my God.   61:10
I am exceeding *j.* in all.   *2 Cor* 7:4*

joyfully
live *j.* with the wife.   *Eccl* 9:9
down and received him *j. Luke* 19:6
ye took *j.* the spoiling of. *Heb* 10:34

joyfulness
not the Lord with *j.*   *Deut* 28:47
to longsuffering with *j.*   *Col* 1:11

joying
with you in the spirit, *j.*   *Col* 2:5

joyous
art full of stirs, a *j.* city.   *Isa* 22:2
is this your *j.* city, whose.   23:7
houses of joy in the *j.* city.   32:13
no chastening seemeth to be *j.*
     Heb 12:11

jubile
cause trumpet of the *j.* to. *Lev* 25:9
j. it shall be holy to you.   10, 12
a *j.* shall that fiftieth year be.   11
in the year of *j.* ye shall return.   13
a field shall go out in the year of *j.*
     25:28; 27:21, 24
house shall not go out in the *j.* 25:30
they shall go out in the year of *j.*
     31, 33, 54
his field from year of *j.*   27:17, 18
j. then their inheritance. *Num* 36:4

Judah
called his name *j.*   *Gen* 29:35
sons of Leah, *J.* Issachar.   35:23
J. thought Tamar to be an.   38:15
J. acknowledged the signet and.   26
sons of *J.*   46:12; *Num* 26:19
     1 Chr 2:3; 4:1
Jacob sent *J.* before him. *Gen* 46:28
J. thou art he whom thy.   49:8
J. is a lion's whelp, he couched.   9
sceptre shall not depart *J.* until.   10
the sons of Israel, Levi, *J.*   *Ex* 1:2
     1 Chr 2:1
J. Nashan son of.   *Num* 1:7
the camp of *J.* shall pitch on.   2:3
numbered in the camp of *J.*   9
Simeon, Levi, *J.* shall. *Deut* 27:12
blessing of *J.* the voice of *J.*   33:7
brought the family of *J.*   *Josh* 7:17
J. shall abide in their coast.   18:5
the Lord said, *J.* shall go. *Judg* 1:2
the Lord was with *J.*   19
fight against *J.*   10:9
whom Tamar bare to *J.*   *Ruth* 4:12
search him out throughout all the
     thousands of *J.*   *1 Sam* 23:23
J. do shew kindness.   *2 Sam* 3:8
David reigned over *J.* seven.   5:5
the ark, Israel, and *J.* abide.   11:11
J. came to Gilgal to meet.   19:15
go number Israel and *J.*   24:1
captain of host of *J.*   *1 Ki* 2:32
J. and Israel were many, as.   4:20
J. and Israel dwelt safely.   25
of God out of *J.* by the word of the
     Lord to Beth-el. 13:1; *2 Ki* 23:17
J. did evil in the sight of. *1 Ki* 14:22
Abijam reigned over *J.*   15:1
reigned Asa over *J.*   9
went up against *J.*   17; *2 Chr* 16:1
Jehoshaphat began to reign over *J.*
     1 Ki 22:41
Lord would not destroy *J. 2 Ki* 8:19
Edom revolted from *J.*   20, 22
     2 Chr 21:8, 10
Ahaziah began to reign over *J.*
     2 Ki 9:29
to fall, thou and *J.* with thee.   14:10
     2 Chr 25:19
J. was put to the worse.
     2 Ki 14:12; *2 Chr* 25:22

Azariah restored Elath to *J.*
     2 Ki 14:22; *2 Chr* 26:2
to send against *J.* Rezin. *2 Ki* 15:37
testified against Israel and *J.*   17:13
J. kept not the commandments.   19
Manasseh made *J.* to sin. 21:11, 16
bringing such evil upon *J. 2 Ki* 21:12
his anger kindled against *J.*   23:26
     2 Chr 25:10
I will remove *J.* also.   *2 Ki* 23:27
bands of Chaldees against *J.*   24:2
of the Lord came this on *J.*   3
so *J.* was carried away.   25:21
     1 Chr 6:15
J. prevailed above his.   *1 Chr* 5:2
of *J.*, Elihu, one of David's.   27:18
for he hath chosen *J.* to be.   28:4
so they were before *J. 2 Chr* 13:13
children of Israel fled before *J.*   16
Asa commanded *J.* to seek.   14:4
took the groves out of *J.*   17:6
Jehoram compelled *J.* to.   21:11
hast made *J.* and Jerusalem.   13
wrath came upon *J.*   24:18; 28:9
     29:8; 32:25
Lord brought *J.* low, made *J.* 28:19
lambs for a sin offering for *J.* 29:21
all the congregation of *J.*   30:25
Manasseh commanded *J.* to. 33:16
Josiah began to purge *J.*   34:3, 5
sons of *J.* to set forward. *Ezra* 3:9
sent to enquire concerning *J.*   7:14
J. and Eliezer had taken.   10:23
wouldst send me to *J.*   *Neh* 2:5
convey me till I come into *J.*   7
the nobles of *J.* sent letters.   6:17
J. son of Senuah was second. 11:9
for *J.* rejoiced for the priests. 12:44
Gilead is mine, *J.*   *Ps* 60:7; 108:8
J. was his sanctuary, Israel.   114:2
he saw concerning *J.*   *Isa* 1:1; 2:1
Lord doth take from *J.* the stay. 3:1
J. is fallen.   8
let us go up against *J.*   7:6
that Ephraim departed from *J.*   17
pass through *J.* shall overflow. 8:8
together shall be against *J.*   9:21
together the dispersed of *J.*   11:12
J. shall be cut off; Ephraim shall not
     envy *J.* and *J.* not vex.   13
discovered the covering of *J.* 22:8
forth out of the waters of *J.* 48:1
and out of *J.* an inheritor of.   65:9
cities are thy gods, O *J.*   *Jer* 2:28
treacherous sister *J.* saw it. 3:7, 8
Egypt, and *J.* and Edom.   9:26
will I mar the pride of *J.*   13:9
J. shall be carried away captive. 19
J. mourneth.   14:2
hast thou utterly rejected *J.*   19
the sin of *J.* is written with.   17:1
I will void the counsel of *J.*   19:7
J. shall be saved.   23:6
do this to cause *J.* to sin.   32:35
I will cause the captivity of *J.* 33:7
I have spoken against *J.*   36:2
the Lord, ye remnant of *J.*   42:15
in mouth of any man of *J.*   44:26
sins of *J.* shall not be found. 50:20
J. hath not been forsaken of. 51:5
J. was carried away captive. 24:9
     Lam 1:3
sword may come to *J. Ezek* 21:20
J. and Israel were thy.   27:17
write upon it for *J.* and for. 37:16
of Reuben, a portion for *J.*   48:7
gate of Reuben, one gate of *J.*   31
harlot, yet let not *J.*   *Hos* 4:15
J. shall fall.   5:5
when *J.* saw his wound.   13
O *J.* what shall I do unto thee ? 6:4
J. shall plow, Jacob shall.   10:11
but *J.* ruleth yet with God.   11:12
also a controversy with *J.*   12:2
but *J.* shall dwell for ever. *Joel* 3:20
three transgressions of *J. Amos* 2:4
I will send a fire on *J.*. it shall.   5
incurable, it is come to *J.*   *Mi* 1:9
little among the thousands of *J.* 5:2
out mine hand upon *J.*   *Zeph* 1:4
have scattered *J.*   *Zech* 1:19, 21
Lord shall inherit *J.* his.   2:12
when I have bent *J.* for me.   9:13

save the tents of *J.* first. *Zech* 12:7
J. also shall fight at.   14:14
J. hath dealt treacherously; *J.* hath
     profaned the holiness. *Mal* 2:11
then shall the offering of *J.*   3:4
Jacob begat *J.*   *Mat* 1:2
J. begat Phares.   3
which was the son of *J.* *Luke* 3:33
our Lord sprang of *J.*   *Heb* 7:14

all Judah
but all Israel and all *J. 1 Sam* 18:16
33 years over all *J.*   *2 Sam* 5:5
all *J.* rejoiced at the. *2 Chr* 15:15
all *J.* stood before the Lord. 20:13
all *J.* did honour Hezekiah. 32:33
all *J.* and Jerusalem mourned. 35:24
all *J.* brought the tithe. *Neh* 13:12
give all *J.* to the king of. *Jer* 20:4
set my face to cut off all *J.*   44:11
see **Benjamin, Beth-lehem,**
     children, cities, daughter,
     daughters, house

in Judah
be afraid here in *J.*   *1 Sam* 23:3
the feast that is in *J.*   *1 Ki* 12:32
it came to pass in Jerusalem and *J.*
     2 Ki 24:20; *Jer* 52:3
cunning men that are with me in *J.*
     2 Chr 2:7
in *J.* things went well.   12:12
they taught in *J.* and had book. 17:9
Pekah slew in *J.* 120,000 in.   28:6
in *J.* hand of God was to give. 30:12
for them that are left in *J.*   34:21
the Jews that were in *J.*   *Ezra* 5:1
mercy to give us a wall in *J.*   9:9
saying, There is a king in *J. Neh* 6:7
I saw in *J.* some treading.   13:15
in *J.* is God known.   *Ps* 76:1
declare ye in *J.* publish in Jerusalem.
     Jer 4:5; 5:20
prosper, ruling any more in *J.* 22:30
shall be as a governor in *J. Zech* 9:7
every pot in *J.* be holiness.   14:21

     see **king, kings**

land of Judah
Lord shewed him all the *land of J.*
     Deut 34:2
went to return unto the *land of J.*
     Ruth 1:7
thee into the *land of J. 1 Sam* 22:5
remained in *land of J.*   *2 Ki* 25:22
garrisons in *land of J.*   *2 Chr* 17:2
the *land of J.* shall be a. *Isa* 19:17
shall be sung in the *land of J.* 26:1
speech in the *land of J.*   *Jer* 31:23
had nothing in the *land of J.*   39:10
committed in the *land of J.*   44:9
should return unto the *land of J.*   14
seer, into the *land of J. Amos* 7:12
horn over the *land of J.*   *Zech* 1:21
Bethlehem, in the *land of J. Mat* 2:6

men of Judah
men of *J.* said, Why are ? *Judg* 15:10
the men of *J.* anointed. *2 Sam* 2:4
the heart of all the men of *J.* 19:14
the words of the men of *J.*   43
men of *J.* clave to their king. 20:2
assemble the men of *J.* within.   4
men of *J.* were five hundred. 24:9
men of *J.* gave a shout. *2 Chr* 13:15
men of *J.* gathered.   *Ezra* 10:9
men of *J.* are his pleasant. *Isa* 5:7
your hearts, ye men of *J.*   *Jer* 4:4
is found among the men of *J.* 11:9
bring upon the men of *J.* all. 36:31
the sight of the men of *J.*   43:9
men of *J.* shall be consumed. 44:27
belongeth to the men of *J. Dan* 9:7

     see **princes**

tribe of Judah
Bezaleel of the *tribe of J.*   *Ex* 31:2
     35:30; 38:22
numbered of *tribe of J.*   *Num* 1:27
the prince of the *tribe of J.*   7:12
of the *tribe of J.* Caleb. 13:6; 34:19
Achan of *tribe of J.* took. *Josh* 7:1
and the *tribe of J.* was taken. 16, 18
lot of the *tribe of J.*   15:1, 20
Levites out of the *tribe of J.* 21:4, 9
     1 Chr 6:65
the *tribe of J.* only.   *1 Ki* 12:20

left but *tribe of J.* only.   *2 Ki* 17:18
but he chose the *tribe of J. Ps* 78:68
Lion of the *tribe of J.* hath. *Rev* 5:5
of the *tribe of J.* were sealed.   7:5

Judas
Joses, Simon, and *J.*   *Mat* 13:55
J. one of the twelve came, and a.
    26:47; *Mark* 14:43
   Luke 22:47; *John* 18:3, 5
then *J.* repented himself. *Mat* 27:3
some thought because *J. John* 13:29
J. said unto him, not Iscariot.   14:22
spake before concerning *J. Acts* 1:16
J. by transgression, fell.   25
after this man rose up *J.* of.   5:37
enquire in the house of *J.* for.   9:11
J. surnamed Barsabas.   15:22, 27
J. and Silas exhorted the.   32

Judas Iscariot
J. Iscariot, who betrayed him.
    Mat 10:4; *Mark* 3:19
   Luke 6:16; *John* 6:71; 13:2
J. Iscariot went to chief priests.
    Mat 26:14; *Mark* 14:10
Satan into *J. Iscariot.*   *Luke* 22:3
the sop to *J. Iscariot.*   *John* 13:26

Judea
into the province of *J.*   *Ezra* 5:8
in *J.* flee into mountains. *Mat* 24:16
    Mark 13:14; *Luke* 21:21
he left *J.* and departed.   *John* 4:3
depart hence and go into *J.* again.
    7:3; 11:7
in *J.* ye be witnesses. *Acts* 1:8
ye men of *J.* be this known.   9:31
had rest throughout *J.*   9:31
was published through *J.*   10:37
went down from *J.* to Cesarea. 12:19
received letters out of *J.*   28:21
that do not believe in *J. Rom* 15:31
on my way toward *J.*   *2 Cor* 1:16
churches which are in *J.* are in Christ.
    1 Thes 2:14

judge, *substantive*
shall not the *J.* of all ?   *Gen* 18:25
came, and will needs be a *j.*   19:9
who made thee a *j.* over us ? *Ex* 2:14
    Acts 7:27, 35
come to the *j.* that shall. *Deut* 17:9
will not hearken to the *j.*   12
that the *j.* shall cause him to.   25:2
the Lord was with the *j. Judg* 2:18
the *j.* was dead, they corrupted.   19
the Lord the *J.* be *j.* this.   11:27
if a man sin, the *j.*   *1 Sam* 2:25*
O that I were made *j.*   *2 Sam* 15:4
supplication to my *j.*   *Job* 9:15*
delivered for ever from my *j.*   23:7
to be punished by the *j.*   31:28
declare, for God is *j.*   *Ps* 50:6
a *j.* of the widows.   68:5
God is the *j.*   75:7
lift up thyself, thou *J.* of.   94:2
away from Jerusalem the *j. Isa* 3:2
I will cut off the *j.* from. *Amos* 2:3
shall smite the *J.* of Israel. *Mi* 5:1
prince asketh, and the *j.* asketh. 7:3
deliver thee to the *j.,* the *j.* deliver.
    Mat 5:25; *Luke* 12:58
man, who made me a *j.? Luke* 12:14
saying, There was in a city a *j.*   18:2
hear what the unjust *j.* saith.   6
be the *j.* of quick and. *Acts* 10:42
for I will be no *j.* of such.   18:15
hast been of many years a *j.*   24:10
the Lord, the righteous *j. 2 Tim* 4:8
come to God the *J.* of.   *Heb* 12:23
a doer of the law, but a *j. Jas* 4:11
behold, the *J.* standeth before.   5:9

judge, *verb, applied to God and Christ*
j. between me and thee.   *Gen* 16:5
    1 Sam 24:12, 15
God of their father *j.*   *Gen* 31:53
Lord look on you, and *j.*   *Ex* 5:21
Lord shall *j.* his people. *Deut* 32:36
   Ps 50:4; 135:14; *Heb* 10:30
Lord shall *j.* the ends.   *1 Sam* 2:10
hear and *j.* thy servants.   *1 Ki* 8:32
    2 Chr 6:23
cometh to *j.* the earth. *1 Chr* 16:33
    Ps 96:13; 98:9

wilt thou not *j.* them ?   *2 Chr* 20:12
sayest, Can he *j.* through ? *Job* 22:13
Lord shall *j.* the people righteously.
   Ps 7:8; 9:8; 50:4; 96:10
j. the fatherless and poor.   10:18
    Isa 11:4
j. me, O Lord.   *Ps* 7:8; 26:1; 35:24
    43:1; 54:1; *Lam* 3:59
arise, O God, *j.* the earth.   *Ps* 82:8
shall *j.* the world with righteousness.
   96:13; 98:9; *Acts* 17:31
shall *j.* among the heathen. *Ps* 110:6
God shall *j.* the righteous. *Eccl* 3:17
and he shall *j.* among the. *Isa* 2:4
the Lord standeth to *j.* the.   3:13
he shall not *j.* after the sight.   11:3
mine arm shall *j.* the people.   51:5
and will *j.* thee according. *Ezek* 7:3
I *j.* between cattle and cattle. 34:17
there will I sit to *j.* the.   *Joel* 3:12
j. among many people.   *Mi* 4:3
I hear, I *j.*: my judgement. *John* 5:30
I *j.* no man.   8:15
and yet if I *j.*   16
things to say and to *j.* of you.   26
I *j.* him not, I came not to *j.*   12:47
when God shall *j.* the.   *Rom* 2:16
how shall God *j.* the world ?   3:6
who shall *j.* quick and dead.
    2 Tim 4:1; *1 Pet* 4:5
and adulterers God will *j. Heb* 13:4
dost thou not *j.* and ?   *Rev* 6:10
in righteousness he doth *j.*   19:11

see further, I *will judge*

judge, *applied to man, or other things*
that they may *j.* betwixt. *Gen* 31:37
Dan shall *j.* his people as.   49:16
that Moses sat to *j.* the.   *Ex* 18:13
I *j.* between one and another.   16
small matter they shall *j.*   22
in righteousness shalt thou *j.* thy.
    Lev 19:15; *Deut* 1:16; 16:18
the congregation *j.*   *Num* 35:24
the judges may *j.* them. *Deut* 25:1
sin, the judge shall *j.*   *1 Sam* 2:25
make us a king to *j.* us.   8:5, 6, 20
heart to *j.* thy people: for who is able
   to *j.* this ?   *1 Ki* 3:9; *2 Chr* 1:10
throne where he might *j.*   *1 Ki* 7:7
mayest *j.* my people.   *2 Chr* 1:11
for ye *j.* not for man, but for.   19:6
set judges which may *j. Ezra* 7:25
do ye *j.* uprightly, O ye ?   *Ps* 58:1
he shall *j.* thy people with.   72:2
he shall *j.* the poor of.   4; *Pr* 3:9
how long will ye *j.* unjustly ? *Ps* 82:2
j. the fatherless, plead.   *Isa* 1:17
j. not the fatherless.   23; *Jer* 5:28
I *j.* I pray you betwixt me.   *Isa* 5:3
wilt thou *j.* them ? *Ezek* 20:4; 22:2
they shall *j.* thee.   23:24, 45; 24:14
Son of man, wilt *j.* Aholah ?   23:36
they shall *j.* it according to.   44:24
saviours come to *j.* the.   *Ob* 21
the heads thereof *j.* for.   *Mi* 3:11
then thou shalt also *j.*   *Zech* 3:7
j. not that ye be not.   *Mat* 7:1
what judgement ye *j.* 2; *Luke* 6:37
yea, and why *j.* ye not ? *Luke* 12:57
j. not according to the appearance,
   but *j.* righteous.   *John* 7:24
doth our law *j.* any man before ? 51
ye *j.* after flesh.   8:15
same shall *j.* him.   12:48
take and *j.* him according to. 18:31
j. ye.   *Acts* 4:19
j. yourselves unworthy.   13:46
for sittest thou to *j.* me after ? 23:3
if it fulfil the law, *j.* thee. *Rom* 2:27
j. him that eateth.   14:3
why dost thou *j.* thy brother ?   10
let us not *j.* one another, but *j.* 13
I *j.* not mine own self.   *1 Cor* 4:3
j. nothing before the time.   5
I to do to *j.* them that are without? do
   not ye *j.* them that are within? 5:12
not know that saints shall *j.?*   6:2
know ye not that we shall *j.?*   3
to *j.* who are least esteemed.   4
shall be able to *j.* between.   5*
j. ye what I say.   10:15
j. in yourselves.   11:13

we would *j.* ourselves. *1 Cor* 11:31*
speak, and the other *j.*   14:29*
because we thus *j.* that. *2 Cor* 5:14
let no man therefore *j.*   *Col* 2:16
but if thou *j.* the law.   *Jas* 4:11

I will judge
I told him that I *will j.*   *1 Sam* 3:13
receive, I *will j.* uprightly. *Ps* 75:2
I *will j.* thee according to thy ways.
    Ezek 7:3, 8, 27; 33:20
I *will j.* you in the border. 11:10, 11
I *will j.* thee as women that.   16:38
therefore I *will j.* you, O.   18:30
I *will j.* thee in the place.   21:30
I, even I, *will j.* between. 34:20, 22

will I judge
the nation they shall serve *will I j.*
    Gen 15:14; *Acts* 7:7
own mouth *will I j.* thee. *Luke* 19:22

judged
God hath *j.* me and.   *Gen* 30:6
j. the people, small matter they *j.*
    Ex 18:26
Othniel *j.* Israel.   *Judg* 3:10
Deborah *j.* Israel.   4:4
Tola *j.* Israel.   10:2
Jair *j.* Israel.   3
Jephthah *j. Israel.*   12:7
Ibzan *j.* Israel.   8
Elon *j.* Israel.   11
Abdon *j.* Israel.   14
Samson *j.* Israel.   15:20; 16:31
Eli *j.* Israel.   *1 Sam* 4:18
Samuel *j.* Israel.   7:6, 15, 16, 17
judgement the king had *j. 1 Ki* 3:28
of the judges that *j.*   *2 Ki* 23:22
let the heathen be *j.* in.   *Ps* 9:19
condemn him when he is *j.*   37:33
when he shall be *j.* let him. 109:7
j. the cause of the poor.   *Jer* 22:16
that shed blood are *j.*   *Ezek* 16:38
thou also who hast *j.* thy sisters. 52
and the wounded shall be *j.* 28:23
known, when I have *j.* thee.   35:11
to their doings I *j.* them.   36:19
our judges that *j.* us.   *Dan* 9:12
that ye be not *j.*   *Mat* 7:1
shall be *j.* 2; *Luke* 6:37
him, thou hast rightly *j.* *Luke* 7:43
prince of this world is *j. John* 16:11
if ye have *j.* me to be.   *Acts* 16:15
we would have *j.* according.   24:6
and there be *j.* of these.   25:9, 20
stand, where I ought to be *j.* 25:10
and am *j.* for the hope of the. 26:6
shall be *j.* by the law.   *Rom* 2:12
    Jas 2:12
overcome when thou art *j. Rom* 3:4
why yet am I also *j.* as a sinner ?   7
yet he himself is *j.* of. *1 Cor* 2:15
a small thing that I should be *j.* 4:3
I have *j.* already, as though I.   5:3
and if the world shall be *j.* by.   6:2
for why is my liberty *j.* of ? 10:29
judge we should not be *j.*   11:31
when we are *j.* we are chastened. 32
convinced of all, he is *j.* of.   14:24
she *j.* him faithful.   *Heb* 11:11*
be *j.* according to men.   *1 Pet* 4:6
time of the dead, that they should
   be *j.*   *Rev* 11:18
because thou hast *j.* thus.   16:5
righteous, for he hath *j.* the.   19:2
the dead were *j.* out of those. 20:12
were *j.* every man according to.   13

judgement
[1] *The sentence, or decision of a judge,* 1 Ki 3:28. [2] *The spirit of wisdom and prudence, enabling to know and discern right from wrong, and good from evil,* Ps 72:1. [3] *The righteous statutes and commandments of God,* Ps 119:7, 20. [4] *Justice and equity,* Isa 1:17; Luke 11:42. [5] *God's decrees and purposes concerning nations, or persons,* Rom 11:33. [6] *Courts of judgement,* Mat 5:21. [7] *The last judgement,* Mat. 25:31-46.

gods I will execute *j.*   *Ex* 12:12
according to this *j.* be it done. 21:31
after many, to wrest *j.*   23:2, 6

make the breastplate of *j*. *Ex* 28:15
names in breastplate of *j*. 29, 30
a statute of *j*. *Num* 27:11; 35:29
after the *j*. of Urim before the. 27:21
afraid of man, for the *j*. *Deut* 1:17
he doth execute the *j*. of the. 10:18
judge the people with just *j*. 16:18
not wrest *j*. 19
shew thee sentence of *j*. 17:9
according to the *j*. 11
thou shalt not pervert the *j*. 24:17
and they come unto *j*. 25:1
cursed be he that perverteth *j*. 27:19
for all his ways are *j*.; a God. 32:4†
if my hand take hold on *j*. I. 41
the congregation for *j*. *Josh* 20:6
up to Deborah for *j*. *Judg* 4:5
bribes and perverted *j*. *1 Sam* 8:3
David executed *j*. *2 Sam* 8:15
1 Chr 18:14
came to king for *j*. *2 Sam* 15:2, 6
understanding to discern *j*. *1 Ki* 3:11
all Israel heard of the *j*. the. 28
the porch of *j*. 7:7
so shall thy *j*. be. 20:40
took king and gave *j*. *2 Ki* 25:6
chief of fathers for *j*. *2 Chr* 19:8
cometh on us as the sword, *j*. 20:9
when Jehu was executing *j*. 22:8
executed *j*. against Joash. 24:24
let *j*. be executed. *Ezra* 7:26
all that knew law and *j*. *Esth* 1:13
doth God pervert *j*.? *Job* 8:3
if I speak of *j*. 9:19
but there is no *j*. 19:7
that ye may know there is a *j*. 29
do the aged understand *j*. 32:9
let us choose to us *j*. 34:4
will the Almighty pervert *j*. 8
yet *j*. is before him, trust. 35:14*
fulfilled the *j*. of the wicked, *j*. and
justice take hold on these. 36:17
awake for me to the *j*. thou. *Ps* 7:6
hath prepared his throne for *j*. 9:7
shall minister *j*. to the people. 8
the Lord is known by the *j*. he. 16
he loveth righteousness and *j*. 33:5†
37:28
he shall bring forth thy *j*. as. 37:6
and his tongue talketh of *j*. 30
shall judge thy poor with *j*. 72:2
thou didst cause *j*. to be heard. 76:8*
when God arose to *j*. to save the. 9
justice and *j*. are the. 89:14†; 97:2†
but *j*. shall return to. 94:15
also loveth *j*.; thou executest *j*. and.
99:4†
I will sing of mercy and *j*. to. 101:1
Lord executeth *j*. for. 103:6; 146:7
blessed are they that keep *j*. 106:3
Phinehas stood up and executed *j*. 30
the works are verity and *j*. 111:7
teach me good *j*. and. 119:66
I have done *j*. and justice. 121†
quicken me according to thy *j*. 149
for there are set thrones of *j*. 122:5
to execute upon them the *j*. 149:9
instruction of wisdom and *j*. *Pr* 1:3†
he keepeth the paths of *j*. and. 2:8†
then shalt thou understand *j*. 9†
the midst of the paths of *j*. 8:20
that is destroyed for want of *j*. 13:23
gift to pervert the ways of *j*. 17:23
an ungodly witness scorneth *j*. 19:28
that sitteth in the throne of *j*. 28:5
evil men understand not *j*. but. 28:5
the king by *j*. establisheth the. 29:4
every man's *j*. cometh from. 26
nor pervert the *j*. of any of. 31:5
the sun the place of *j*. *Eccl* 3:16
violent perverting of *j*. and. 5:8
man discerneth both time and *j*. 8:5
every purpose there is time and *j*. 6
seek *j*. *Isa* 1:17
it was full of *j*. 21
Zion shall be redeemed with *j*. 27†
purged Jerusalem by spirit of *j*. 4:4
and looked for *j*. 5:7†
and to establish it with *j*. 9:7
to turn aside the needy from *j*. 10:2†
execute *j*. 16:3; *Jer* 21:12; 22:3
Ezek 18:8; 45:9; *Zech* 7:9; 8:12
seeking *j*. *Isa* 16:5
for a spirit of *j*. 28:6

I will lay *j*. to the line. *Isa* 28:17†
for the Lord is a God of *j*. 30:18
then *j*. shall dwell in the. 32:16†
Lord hath filled Zion with *j*. 33:5†
the people of my curse to *j*. 34:5
taught him in the path of *j*.? 40:14
let us come near together to *j*. 41:1
he shall bring forth *j*. to the. 42:1
he shall bring forth *j*. unto truth. 3
he shall not fail, till he have set *j*. 4
from prison and from *j*. 53:8
keep ye *j*. and do justice. 56:1
Hos 12:6†
is no *j*. in their goings. *Isa* 59:8†
therefore is *j*. far from us. 9†
we look for *j*. but there is none. 11†
j. is turned away backward. 14†
him that there was no *j*. 15†
I the Lord love *j*. I hate. 61:8†
be any that executeth *j*. *Jer* 5:1
not the *j*. of their God. 4; 8:7*
they have known the *j*. of their. 5:5
if ye throughly execute *j*. 7:5
exercise *j*. and righteousness. 9:24†
correct me, but with *j*. not in. 10:24
execute *j*. in the morning. 21:12
branch shall execute *j*. 23:5; 33:15
to Riblah, where he gave *j*. upon
Zedekiah. 39:5; 52:9
and *j*. is come upon the. 48:21
thus far is the *j*. of Moab. 47
whose *j*. was not to drink. 49:12*
forsake her, for her *j*. reacheth. 51:9
for they had executed *j*. *Ezek* 23:10
I will set *j*. before them, they. 24
all whose ways are *j*. *Dan* 4:37
j. was set. 7:10
but the *j*. shall sit. 26
j. was given to the saints of the. 22
give ye ear, for *j*. is. *Hos* 5:1
thus *j*. springeth up as hemlock. 10:4
turn *j*. into wormwood. *Amos* 5:7
love the good, and establish *j*. in. 15
but let *j*. run down as waters and. 24
for ye have turned *j*. into gall. 6:12
is it not to know *j*.? *Mi* 3:1
I am full of *j*. 8
that abhor *j*. 9
and execute *j*. for me. 7:9
law is slacked, *j*. doth. *Hab* 1:4
j. shall proceed of themselves. 7
thou hast ordained them for *j*. 12
have wrought his *j*. *Zeph* 2:3
every morning doth he bring *j*. 3:5
where is the God of *j*.? *Mal* 2:17
in danger of the *j*. *Mat* 5:21, 22
with what *j*. ye judge, ye shall. 7:2
shew *j*. to the Gentiles. 12:18
till he send forth *j*. unto victory. 20
and have omitted *j*., mercy. 23:23†
pass over *j*. and love of. *Luke* 11:42†
but hath committed all *j*. *John* 5:22
him authority to execute *j*. also. 27
but judge righteous *j*. 7:24
j. I am come into this world. 9:39
now is the *j*. of this world. 12:31
reprove the world of *j*. 16:8, 11
in his humiliation his *j*. *Acts* 8:33
as he reasoned of *j*., Felix. 24:25
the Jews desiring to have *j*. 25:15
knowing the *j*. of God. *Rom* 1:32*
sure that the *j*. of God is. 2:2
that thou shalt escape the *j*. of? 3
and revelation of the righteous *j*. 5
for the *j*. was by one to. 5:16
j. came on all men to. 18
be joined together in *j*. *1 Cor* 1:10
should be judged of man's *j*. 4:3
token of the righteous *j*. *2 Thes* 1:5
open, going before to *j*. *1 Tim* 5:24
and of eternal *j*. *Heb* 6:2
after this the *j*. 9:27
certain fearful looking for of *j*. 10:27
j. without mercy, shewed no mercy,
mercy rejoiceth against *j*. *Jas* 2:13
we shall receive greater *j*. 3:1
that *j*. must begin at the. *1 Pet* 4:17
whose *j*. lingereth not. *2 Pet* 2:3*
angels reserved unto *j*. 4
to *j*. of the great day. *Jude* 6†
to execute *j*. 15
fear God, for the hour of his *j*. is
come. *Rev* 14:7
will shew thee *j*. of the great. 17:1

for in one hour is thy *j*. come.
Rev 18:10
and *j*. was given to them. 20:4
see bear, day

do judgement
to do justice and *j*. *Gen* 18:19†
1 Ki 10:9; *Pr* 21:3†; *Jer* 22:15
God was in him to do *j*. *1 Ki* 3:28
them to do justice and *j*. *2 Chr* 9:8
they refuse to do *j*. *Pr* 21:7†
it is joy to the just to do *j*. but. 15†
I will do *j*. on the graven images.
Jer 51:47
I will do *j*. on her graven images. 52

in judgement
unrighteousness in *j*. *Lev* 19:15, 35
the congregation in *j*. *Num* 35:12
not respect persons in *j*. *Deut* 1:17
matter too hard for thee in *j*. 17:8
ye that sit in *j*. and. *Judg* 5:10*
who is with you in *j*. *2 Chr* 19:6
come together in *j*. *Job* 9:32
excellent in power and in *j*. 37:23
shall not stand in *j*. *Ps* 1:5
the meek will he guide in *j*. 25:9
trangresseth not in *j*. *Pr* 16:10
overthrow the righteous in *j*. 18:5
have respect of persons in *j*. 24:23
hosts shall be exalted in *j*. *Isa* 5:16
him that sitteth in *j*. 28:6
they stumble in *j*. 7
behold princes shall rule in *j*. 32:1
that shall rise against thee in *j*. 54:17
Lord liveth in righteousness and in *j*.
Jer 4:2†
they stand in *j*. *Ezek* 44:24
betroth thee to me in *j*. *Hos* 2:19
oppressed and broken in *j*. 5:11
come near to you in *j*. *Mal* 3:5
Nineveh shall rise in *j*. *Mat* 12:41
queen of south shall rise in *j*. 42
Luke 11:31, 32
your love may abound in *j*. *Phil* 1:9*

into judgement
bringest me into *j*. with. *Job* 14:3
will he enter with thee into *j*.? 22:4
that he should enter into *j*. 34:23
enter not into *j*. with. *Ps* 143:2
God will bring thee into *j*. *Eccl* 11:9
bring every work into *j*. 12:14
Lord will enter into *j*. *Isa* 3:14

my judgement
taken away my *j*. *Job* 27:2*; 34:5*
my *j*. was as a robe. 29:14*
wilt thou also disannul my *j*.? 40:8
up thyself, awake to my *j*. *Ps* 35:23
my *j*. is passed over from. *Isa* 40:27
yet surely my *j*. is with Lord. 49:4
I will make my *j*. to rest for a. 51:4
heathen shall see my *j*. *Ezek* 39:21
and my *j*. is just. *John* 5:30
my *j*. is true. 8:16
yet I give my *j*. *1 Cor* 7:25
happier in my *j*. 40

judgement hall
Jesus to the hall of *j*. . . . . went not
into the *j*. hall. *John* 18:28*
Pilate entered into the *j*. hall. 33*
into the *j*. hall, and saith. 19:9*
kept in Herod's *j*. hall. *Acts* 23:35*

judgements
I will redeem you with great *j*.
Ex 6:6; 7:4
these are the *j*. thou shalt set. 21:1
told the people all the *j*. 24:3
gods the Lord executed *j*. *Num* 33:4
judge according to these *j*. 35:24
are the *j*. which the Lord. 36:13
if ye hearken to these *j*. *Deut* 7:12
they shall teach Jacob thy *j*. 33:10
he executed the *j*. of the Lord. 21
his *j*. were before me. *2 Sam* 22:23
Ps 18:22
remember *j*. of his mouth.
1 Chr 16:12; *Ps* 105:5
his *j*. are in all the earth.
1 Chr 16:14; *Ps* 105:7
but sinned against thy *j*. *Neh* 9:29
thy *j*. are far above out. *Ps* 10:5
the *j*. of the Lord are true. 19:9
thy *j*. are a great deep. 36:6
be glad because of thy *j*. 48:11

give the king thy *j.* O God. *Ps* 72:1
Judah rejoiced, because of thy *j.*
    97:8
learned thy righteous *j.* 119:7
with my lips I declared all *j. of.* 13
longing that it hath unto thy *j.* 20
thy *j.* have I laid before me. 30
away my reproach, for thy *j.* are. 39
I hoped in thy *j.* 43
I remembered thy *j.* 52
because of thy righteous *j.* 62, 164
I know, O Lord, that thy *j.* are. 75
I have not departed from thy *j.* 102
I will keep thy righteous *j.* 106
teach me thy *j.* 108
I am afraid of thy *j.* 120
art thou, and upright are thy *j.* 137
quicken me according to thy *j.* 156
every one of thy righteous *j.* 160
let my soul live, and let thy *j.* 175
his *j.* they have not known. 147:20
j. are prepared for. *Pr* 19:29
way of thy *j.* we waited. *Isa* 26:8
for when thy *j.* are in the earth. 9
me talk with thee of thy *j. Jer* 12:1*
nor done according to *j. Ezek* 5:7*
j. in midst of thee. 8; 10:15; 11:9
execute *j.* on thee in sight. 16:41
shall judge thee according to their *j.*
    23:24
I will execute *j.* on Moab. 25:11
executed *j.* on all those that. 28:26
I will execute *j.* in No. 30:14
thus will I execute *j.* in Egypt. 19
I will feed them with *j.* 34:16
by departing from thy *j. Dan* 9:5
thy *j.* are as the light that. *Hos* 6:5
hath taken away thy *j. Zeph* 3:15
unsearchable are his *j. Rom* 11:33
if ye have *j.* of things. *1 Cor* 6:4
j. are made manifest. *Rev* 15:4*
righteous are thy *j.* 16:7; 19:2

my **judgements**
ye shall do *my j.* I am. *Lev* 18:4
therefore keep *my j.* 5; 25:18
if your soul abhor *my j.* so. 26:15
because they despised *my j.* 43
constant to do *my j.* *1 Chr* 28:7
children walk not in *my j. Ps* 89:30
I will utter *my j.* against. *Jer* 1:16
she changed *my j.* into wickedness.
    Ezek 5:6
neither have kept *my j.* nor. 5:7
when I send *my* four sore *j.* 14:21
and ye shall keep *my j.* 36:27
judge it according to *my j.* 44:24

statutes and **judgements**
keep my *st. and* my *j. Lev* 18:5, 26
  20:22; *Deut* 11:1; 11:1; 26:16, 17
  30:16; *1 Ki* 2:3; 8:58; 9:4; 11:33
observe all my *st. and j. Lev* 19:37
  Deut 11:32; 12:1; *2 Chr* 7:17
these are the *st. and j.* Lord made.
    Lev 26:46; *Deut* 4:45
hearken to *st. and j. Deut* 4:1; 5:1
I have taught you *st. and j.* 4:5
hath *st. and j.* so righteous as all ? 8
commanded to teach *st. and j.* 14
  6:1; *Ezra* 7:10
I will speak the *st. and j. Deut* 5:31
thee, What mean the *st. and j.?* 6:20
forget Lord in not keeping his *st. and*
  j. 8:11; *Neh* 1:7
my *st. and* execute my *j. 1 Ki* 6:12
heed to fulfil *st. and j. 1 Chr* 22:13
come between *st. and j. 2 Chr* 19:10
thou gavest them right *st. and j.*
    Neh 9:13
a curse, to do all his *st. and j.* 10:29
sheweth his *st. and j.* to. *Ps* 147:19
refused my *j. and* my *st. Ezek* 5:6
not walked in my *st.* nor executed
  my *j.* 11:12; 20:13, 16, 21
walked in my *st. and j.* 18:9, 17
  20:19; 37:24
my *st. and* shewed my *j.* 20:11
st. of fathers, nor observe their *j.* 18
them *st.* not good, *and j.* 25
of Moses with *st. and j. Mal* 4:4

judgement seat
he was set down on *j. seat.*
  Mat 27:19; *John* 19:13

brought him to the *j. seat. Acts* 18:12
drave them from the *j. seat.* 16
beat Sosthenes before the *j. seat.* 17
I stand at Cesar's *j. seat.* 25:10
I sat on *j. seat.* 17
we shall all stand before the *j. seat*
  of Christ. *Rom* 14:10; *2 Cor* 5:10
draw you before *j. seats. Jas* 2:6

judges
shall bring him to the *j. Ex* 21:6*
and he shall pay as the *j.* 22
shall be brought to the *j.* 22:8*
both shall come before the *j.* 9*
Moses said to the *j.* Slay. *Num* 25:5
I charged your *j.* at that. *Deut* 1:16
j. shalt thou make in all. 16:18
stand before priests and *j.* 19:17
the *j.* shall make diligent. 18
thy elders and thy *j.* shall. 21:2
they come that the *j.* may. 25:1
enemies themselves being *j.* 32:31
their *j.* stood on this side. *Josh* 8:33
Joshua called for their heads and *j.*
    23:2; 24:1
Lord raised up *j.* *Judg* 2:16, 18
would not hearken to their *j.* 17
when the *j.* ruled a famine. *Ruth* 1:1
he made his sons *j.* *1 Sam* 8:1, 2
I commanded *j.* to be. *2 Sam* 7:11
from the days of the *j. 2 Ki* 23:22
word to any of the *j. 1 Chr* 17:6, 10
thousand were officers and *j.* 23:4
and his sons were for *j.* 26:29
Solomon spake to the *j. 2 Chr* 1:2
he set *j.* in the land. 19:5
said to the *j.* 6
set *j.* which may judge. *Ezra* 7:25
and with them the *j.* of every. 10:14
covereth the face of the *j. Job* 9:24
and he maketh the *j.* fools. 12:17
iniquity to be punished by *j.* 31:11
be instructed, ye *j.* of the. *Ps* 2:10
when *j.* are overthrown in. 141:6
princes, and all *j.* of the earth. 148:11
princes rule, and all *j.* of. *Pr* 8:16
I will restore thy *j.* as at. *Isa* 1:26
he maketh the *j.* of the earth. 40:23
sent to gather the *j.* *Dan* 3:2, 3
his words against our *j.* that. 9:12
they have devoured their *j. Hos* 7:7
where are thy *j.* of whom ? 13:10
her *j.* are evening wolves. *Zeph* 3:3
they shall be your *j.* *Mat* 12:27
    Luke 11:19
that he gave to them *j.* *Acts* 13:20
and are become *j.* of evil. *Jas* 2:4

judgest
be clear when thou *j.* *Ps* 51:4
Lord of hosts, that *j. Jer* 11:20
whosoever thou art that *j. Rom* 2:1
O man, that *j.* them which do. 3
that *j.* another man's servant ? 14:4
who art thou that *j.? Jas* 4:12

judgeth
seeing he *j.* those that. *Job* 21:22
for by them *j.* he the people. 36:31
God *j.* the righteous, is. *Ps* 7:11
verily he is a God that *j.* in. 58:11
in congregation of mighty, he *j.* 82:1
king that faithfully *j. Pr* 29:14
for the Father *j.* no man. *John* 5:22
there is one that *j.* 8:50
one that *j.* him. 12:48
he that is spiritual *j.* all. *1 Cor* 2:15
but he that *j.* me is the Lord. 4:4
that are without, God *j.* 5:13
he that *j.* his brother,. *Jas* 4:11
respect of persons *j.* *1 Pet* 1:17
committed himself to him that *j.* 2:23
strong is the Lord that *j.* *Rev* 18:8

judging
j. the people of the land. *2 Ki* 15:5
    2 Chr 26:21
satest in the throne *j.* right. *Ps* 9:4*
he shall sit *j.* and seeking. *Isa* 16:5
j. the twelve tribes. *Mat* 19:28
    Luke 22:30

juice
to drink wine of the *j. S of S* 8:2

jumping
noise of horses and the *j. Nah* 3:2†

juniper
and sat under a *j.* tree. *1 Ki* 19:4, 5
who cut up *j.* roots. *Job* 30:4*
the mighty with coals of *j. Ps* 120:4

Jupiter
called Barnabas, J. *Acts* 14:12
then the priests of J. brought. 13
image which fell down from J. 19:35

jurisdiction
he belonged to Herod's *j. Luke* 23:7

just
[1] *One who is righteous before*
God, Gen 6:9. [2] *Exact, accurate,*
Lev 19:36. [3] *Honest, upright,*
Luke 23:50. *The word is in most*
places replaced in the Revisions by
the word righteous.

Noah was a *j.* man. *Gen* 6:9
j. balances, *j.* weights, a *j.* ephah,
  and a *j.* hin shall ye have.
  Lev 19:36; *Deut* 25:15; *Ezek* 45:10
judge people with *j. Deut* 16:18
that is altogether *j.* shalt thou. 20
a God without iniquity, *j.* and. 32:4
over men must be *j.* *2 Sam* 23:3
thou art *j.* in all that is. *Neh* 9:33
mortal man be more *j.? Job* 4:17
but how should man be *j.* with ? 9:2
j. upright man is laughed to. 12:4
he may prepare it, but the *j.* 27:17
in this thou art not *j.* 33:12
end, but establish the *j.* *Ps* 7:9
wicked plotteth against the *j.* 37:12
the habitation of the *j.* *Pr* 3:33
the path of the *j.* is as the. 4:18
a *j.* man, and he will increase. 9:9
are upon the head of the *j.* 10:6
the memory of the *j.* is blessed. 7
tongue of the *j.* is as choice. 20
the mouth of the *j.* bringeth forth. 31
but *j.* weight is his delight. 11:1
but through knowledge shall the *j.* 9
but the *j.* shall come out of. 12:13
shall no evil happen to the *j.* 21
the sinner is laid up for the *j.* 13:22
a *j.* weight and balance are. 16:11
he that condemneth the *j.* is. 17:15
also to punish the *j.* is not good. 26
in his own cause seemeth *j.* 18:17
j. man walketh in his integrity. 20:7
joy to the *j.* to do judgement. 21:15
a *j.* man falleth seven times. 24:16
hate the upright, but the *j.* 29:10
man is an abomination to the *j.* 27
j. man that perisheth in. *Eccl* 7:15
not a *j.* man upon earth that. 20
there be *j.* men to whom it. 8:14
j. is uprightness, thou most upright
  dost weigh path of *j.* *Isa* 26:7
turn aside the *j.* for a thing. 29:21
I the Lord, a *j.* God, and a. 45:21
shed the blood of the *j.* *Lam* 4:13
but if a man be *j.* and. *Ezek* 18:5
he is *j.* he shall surely live. 9
ways of Lord right, *j. Hos* 14:9
they afflict the *j.* they. *Amos* 5:12
the *j.* shall live by faith. *Hab* 2:4
  Rom 1:17; *Gal* 3:11; *Heb* 10:38
j. Lord is in the midst. *Zeph* 3:5
j. and having salvation. *Zech* 9:9
husband, being a *j.* man. *Mat* 1:19
sendeth rain on the *j.* and on. 5:45
the wicked from among the *j.* 13:49
to do with that *j.* man. 27:19
innocent of the blood of this *j.* 24
knowing that he was a *j. Mark* 6:20
the wisdom of the *j. Luke* 1:17
Simeon was *j.* and devout. 2:25
the resurrection of the *j.* 14:14
over ninety and nine *j.* persons. 15:7
should feign themselves *j.* 20:20
Joseph was a good man and *j.* 23:50
and my judgement is *j. John* 5:30
the centurion a *j.* man. *Acts* 10:22
shall be resurrection both of *j.* 24:15
hearers of the law are *j. Rom* 2:13
whose damnation is *j.* 3:8
he might be *j.* 26
the commandment holy, *j.* 7:12
whatsoever things are *j. Phil* 4:8
give servants that which is *j. Col* 4:1

a bishop must be j., holy. *Tit* 1:8
received a j. recompence. *Heb* 2:2
spirits of j. men made perfect. 12:23
condemned and killed the j. *Jas* 5:6
Christ suffered, the j. *1 Pet* 3:18
delivered j. Lot, vexed. *2 Pet* 2:7
if we confess, he is j. to. *1 John* 1:9
j. and true are thy ways. *Rev* 15:3

most just
condemn him that is most j.?
Job 34:17

Just One
Holy One and the J. *Acts* 3:14
of the coming of the J. One. 7:52
his will, and see that J. One. 22:14

Justice
(*Uprightness, just treatment. The Revisions often change this word to righteousness*)

keep way of Lord to do j. *Gen* 18:19
he executeth j. of Lord. *Deut* 33:21
David executed j. *2 Sam* 8:15
1 Chr 18:14
judge, I would do j. *2 Sam* 15:4
Almighty pervert j.? *Job* 8:3
judgement and j. take hold. 36:17
is excellent in plenty of j. 37:23
do j. to the afflicted and. *Ps* 82:3
j. and judgement are habitation.
89:14
have done judgement and j. 119:121
receive the instruction of j. *Pr* 1:3
reign, and princes decree j. 8:15
seest the perverting of j. *Eccl* 5:8
establish his throne with j. *Isa* 9:7
keep ye judgement, and do j. 56:1
ask of me the ordinances of j. 58:2
none calleth for j. 59:4
neither doth j. overtake us. 9
j. standeth afar off, truth is. 14
execute judgement and j. in earth.
Jer 23:5
bless thee, O habitation of j. 31:23
the Lord, the habitation of j. 50:7
princes, execute judgement and j.
Ezek 45:9

see do **judgement**, *before*

justification
raised again for our j. *Rom* 4:25
gift is of many offences to j. 5:16
free gift came upon all men to j. 18

see **sanctify**

justified
a man full of talk be j.? *Job* 11:2
I know that I shall be j. 13:18
then can man be j. with God? 25:4
because he j. himself rather. 32:2
thou mightest be j. when. *Ps* 51:4
sight shall no man living be j. 143:2
they may be j. *Isa* 43:9
thou mayest be j. 26
all the seed of Israel be j. 45:25
backsliding Israel hath j. *Jer* 3:11
j. thy sisters in all. *Ezek* 16:51, 52
wisdom is j. of her children.
Mat 11:19; *Luke* 7:35
thy words thou shalt be j. *Mat* 12:37
and publicans j. God. *Luke* 7:29
this man went down j. rather. 18:14
are j. from all things from which ye
could not be j. by. *Acts* 13:39
doers of the law shall be j. *Rom* 2:13
mightest be j. in thy sayings. 3:4
shall no flesh be j. in his sight. 20
j. freely by his grace. 24; *Tit* 3:7
a man is j. by faith. *Rom* 3:28; 5:1
Gal 2:16; 3:24
if Abraham were j. by. *Rom* 4:2
being j. by faith we have peace. 5:1
being now j. by his blood, we. 9
he j. them he also glorified. 8:30
yet am I not hereby j. *1 Cor* 4:4
ye are j. in the name of Lord. 6:11
a man is not j. by the works of the
law. *Gal* 2:16; 3:11
whosoever of you is j. by law. 5:4
God manifest in the flesh, j. in the
spirit. *1 Tim* 3:16
our father j. by works? *Jas* 2:21
that by works a man is j. 24
was not Rahab the harlot j. by? 25

justifier
j. of him who believeth. *Rom* 3:26

justifieth
he that j. the wicked is. *Pr* 17:15
he is near that j. me. *Isa* 50:8
believeth on him that j. *Rom* 4:5
of God's elect? it is God that j. 8:33

justify
(*To show to be just or righteous ; to vindicate*)
I will not j. the wicked. *Ex* 23:7
then they shall j. the. *Deut* 25:1
if I j. myself, my own. *Job* 9:20
God forbid that I should j. 27:5
speak, for I desire to j. thee. 33:32
which j. the wicked for. *Isa* 5:23
my righteous servant j. many. 53:11
he willing to j. himself. *Luke* 10:29
are they which j. yourselves. 16:15
God shall j. circumcision. *Rom* 3:30
foreseeing that God would j. *Gal* 3:8

justifying
and j. the righteous. *1 Ki* 8:32
2 Chr 6:23

justle
the chariots shall j. one. *Nah* 2:4†

justly
Lord require but to do j.? *Mi* 6:8
indeed j. for we receive. *Luke* 23:41
how holily and j. we. *1 Thes* 2:10

Justus
Joseph, who was surnamed J. and.
Acts 1:23
certain man's house, named J. 18:7
Jesus, who is called J. *Col* 4:11

K

Kadesh
Enmishpat, which is K. *Gen* 14:7
to wilderness of Paran to K.
Num 13:26
behold, we are in K. a city. 20:16
me at water of Meribah in K. 27:14
Deut 32:51; *Ezek* 47:19; 48:28
of Zin, which is K. *Num* 33:36
abode in K. many days. *Deut* 1:46
shaketh the wilderness of K. *Ps* 29:8

Kadesh-barnea
I sent them from K. to see the land.
Num 32:8; *Deut* 9:23; *Josh* 14:7
them from K. to Gaza. *Josh* 10:41
concerning me and thee in K. 14:6

Kareah, *see* Johanan

Kedar
the son of Ishmael, K. *Gen* 25:13
1 Chr 1:29
I dwell in the tents of K. *Ps* 120:5
comely as the tents of K. *S of S* 1:5
glory of K. shall fail. *Isa* 21:16, 17
the villages that K. doth. 42:11
the flocks of K. shall be. 60:7
send to K. and consider. *Jer* 2:10
K., thus saith the Lord; Arise ye, go
up to K. 49:28
princes of K. occupied. *Ezek* 27:21

keep
[1] *To retain or hold fast.* 2 Tim
1:14. [2] *To defend and protect.*
Ps 127:1. [3] *To observe and
practise.* Ps 119:4; Acts 16:4. [4]
To celebrate, Mat 26:18. [5] *To
perform as a duty ; observe,* Mat
19:17.

the garden of Eden to k. *Gen* 2:15
and they shall k. the way of. 18:19
I am with thee, to k. thee. 28:15, 20
I will again feed and k. thy. 30:31
my brother, k. that thou hast. 33:9
and let them k. food in the. 41:35
whom the Egyptians k. *Ex* 6:5
shall k. it till the fourteenth. 12:6
k. it a feast to the Lord through.
14; 23:15; 34:18; *Lev* 23:41
that ye shall k. this service.
Ex 12:25; 13:5
of Israel shall k. it. 12:47
thou shalt k. this ordinance in. 13:10
sabbath day to k. it holy. 20:8
31:13, 14, 16; *Deut* 5:12, 15

money or stuff to k. *Ex* 22:7, 10
k. thee far from a false matter. 23:7
three times shalt thou k. a feast. 14
I send an Angel to k. thee in. 20
that delivered him to k. *Lev* 6:2, 4
ye shall k. my ordinances, I am the
Lord. 18:4, 30; 22:9; *Ezek* 11:20
shall k. my sabbaths. 19:3, 30
26:2; *Isa* 56:4
shall k. a feast seven days.
Lev 23:39; *2 Chr* 30:13
ye shall k. my judgements and.
Lev 25:18
Lord bless thee and k. *Num* 6:24
14th day at even ye shall k. it. 9:3
month at even they shall k. it. 11
thy sons shall k. your priests'. 18:7
ye shall k. a feast to the. 29:12
k. himself to inheritance. 36:7*, 9*
k. therefore and do them. *Deut* 4:6
5:1*
loved you, would k. the oath. 7:8
if ye k. them, the Lord shall k. 12
k. the feast of weeks to the. 16:10
shalt k. a solemn feast to Lord. 15
may learn to k. all the words. 17:19
k. thee from every wicked. 23:9
gone out of thy lips thou shalt k. 23*
k. therefore the words of this. 29:9
k. yourselves from the. *Josh* 6:18
set men by the cave, for to k. 10:18
to k. all that is written in the. 23:6
whether they will k. the. *Judg* 2:22
thou shalt k. fast by my. *Ruth* 2:21
he will k. the feet of his. *1 Sam* 2:9
Eleazar his son, to k. the ark. 7:1
women which were concubines to k.
2 Sam 15:16; 16:21; 20:3
no son to k. my name. 18:18
k. with thy servant David.
1 Ki 8:25; *2 Chr* 6:16
man to me and said, K. *1 Ki* 20:39
that thou wouldest k. me. *1 Chr* 4:10
which could k. rank. 12:33*, 38*
that thou mayest k. the law. 22:12
k. this for ever in imagination. 29:18
had no power to k. still the kingdom.
2 Chr 22:9*
ye purpose to k. under the. 28:10
for they could not k. it at. 30:3
assembly took counsel to k. other. 23
watch and k. them till. *Ezra* 8:29
to k. the dedication with. *Neh* 12:27
that the Levites should k. 13:22
nor k. they the king's. *Esth* 9:27
that they would k. those two. 9:27
that thou wouldest k. me. *Job* 14:13
though k. it still within. 20:13
k. them, O Lord. *Ps* 12:7; 31:20
k. me as the apple of the eye. 17:8
k. back thy servant also from presumptuous sins. 19:13
O k. my soul, and deliver me. 25:20
k. thy tongue from evil, and. 34:13
and k. his way. 37:34
I will k. my mouth. 39:1
my mercy will I k. for him. 89:28
his angels charge, to k. thee. 91:11
nor chide, nor will he k. his. 103:9
observe and k. his laws. 105:45
blessed are they that k. judgement.
106:3
barren woman to k. house. 113:9
blessed are they that k. his. 119:2
thou hast commanded us to k. 4
may live and k. thy word. 17, 101
teach me, and I shall k. it to. 33
I shall k. thy law. 34, 44
I have said, that I would k. 57
I am a companion of them that k. 63
I will k. thy precepts with. 69, 134
so shall I k. the testimony of thy. 88
I understand, because I k. thy. 100
k. thy righteous judgements. 106
therefore doth my soul k. them. 129
down my eyes, because they k. 136
save me, and I shall k. thy. 146
except the Lord k. the city. 127:1
k. me from the hands of the. 140:4
k. the door of my lips. 141:3
k. me from the snares they have. 9
understanding shall k. thee. *Pr* 2:11
thou mayest k. the paths of the. 20
my son, k. sound wisdom and. 3:21

Lord shall *k*. thy foot from. *Pr* 3:26
love wisdom, and she shall *k*.   4:6
k. instruction, let her not go, for. 13
k. my sayings in the midst of.   21
k. thy heart with all diligence.   23
and that thy lips may *k*.   5:2
when thou sleepest it shall *k*.   6:22
to *k*. thee from the evil woman.   24
my son, *k*. my words, and lay.   7:1
may *k*. thee from the strange.   5
for blessed are they that *k*.   8:32
he that doth *k*. his soul shall.   22:5
it is pleasant if thou *k*. them.   18
such as *k*. the law contend.   28:4
there is a time to *k*. and.   *Eccl* 3:6
k. thy foot when thou goest to.   5:1
k. the fruit thereof, two. *S of S* 8:12
wilt *k*. him in perfect.   *Isa* 26:3
I the Lord do *k*. it, I will *k*. it.   27:3
have called thee, I will *k*. thee. 42:6
k. not back.   43:6
k. ye judgement.   56:1
k. his anger to the end ?   *Jer* 3:5
and I will not *k*. anger for ever.   12
k. him as a shepherd doth.   31:10
I will *k*. nothing back from.   42:4
k. my judgements and do them.
    Ezek 20:19; 36:27
that they may *k*. the whole.   43:11
k. mercy and judgement. *Hos* 12:6
the doors of thy mouth.   *Mi* 7:5
k. thy feasts.   *Nah* 1:15
k. the munition.   2:1
shalt also *k*. my courts.   *Zech* 3:7
man taught me to *k*. cattle.   13:5*
k. the feast of tabernacles.   14:16
    18, 19
the priests' lips should *k*.   *Mal* 2:7
k. your own tradition.   *Mark* 7:9
his angels charge to *k*.   *Luke* 4:10
having heard the word *k*. it.   8:15
that hear the word and *k*. it.   11:28
thy enemies shall *k*. thee in.   19:43
if *k*. my saying shall. *John* 8:51, 52
but I know him, and *k*. his.   55
his life in this world shall *k*.   12:25
if a man love me he will *k*.   14:23
my saying, they will *k*. yours. 15:20
k. through thy name.   17:11
k. from the evil.   15
and to *k*. back part of the. *Acts* 5:3
for a man that is a Jew to *k*.   10:28
him to soldiers to *k*. him.   12:4
command them to *k*. the law.   15:5
ye must be circumcised, and *k*.   24
from which, if ye *k*. yourselves.   29
them the decrees for to *k*.   16:4
charging the jailer to *k*. them.   23
I must by all means *k*. this.   18:21
k. themselves from things.   21:25
a centurion to *k*. Paul.   24:23*
if thou *k*. the law.   *Rom* 2:25
k. the righteousness of law.   26
let us *k*. the feast.   *1 Cor* 5:8
not *k*. company.   11
decreed that he will *k*. his.   7:37
I *k*. under my body and bring. 9:27*
that ye *k*. the ordinances, as.   11:2
if ye *k*. in memory what I.   15:2*
and so will I *k*. myself. *2 Cor* 11:9
neither do circumcised *k*.   *Gal* 6:13
endeavouring to *k*. unity.   *Eph* 4:3
peace of God shall *k*.   *Phil* 4:7
who shall stablish and *k*. *2 Thes* 3:3
nor partaker of sins, *k*.   *1 Tim* 5:22
k. that which is committed to.   6:20
able to *k*. that which I have com-
    mitted unto him.   *2 Tim* 1:12
good thing committed to thee *k*.   14
and to *k*. himself unspotted. *Jas* 1:27
whosoever shall *k*. whole law.   2:10
k. yourselves from idols. *1 John* 5:21
k. yourselves in the love.   *Jude* 21
to him that is able to *k*. you.   24
blessed are they that hear and *k*.
    Rev 1:3
I will *k*. thee from the hour of. 3:10
of them who *k*. the sayings of. 22:9

keep alive

ark to *k*. them *alive*.   *Gen* 6:19, 20
to *k*. seed *alive* on the face of.   7:3
women, children *k*. *alive*. *Num* 31:18
full line to *k*. *alive*.   *2 Sam* 8:2

none can *k*. *alive* his own soul.
    Ps 22:29
deliver and *k*. them *alive* in.   33:19
preserve him and *k*. him *alive*.   41:2

keep charge

and *k*. the *charge* of the Lord.
    Ex 8:35; *1 Ki* 2:3
k. *charge* of tabernacle.   *Num* 1:53
    18:4; 31:30; *1 Chr* 23:32
they shall *k*. his *charge*.   *Num* 3:7
    8:26; 18:3; *Deut* 11:1
k. the *charge* of children of Israel.
    Num 3:8
k. *charge* of the sanctuary.   32
    18:5; *1 Chr* 23:32
to me, and *k*. my *charge*. *Ezek* 44:16
if thou wilt *k*. my *charge*. *Zech* 3:7

keep commandments

refuse ye to *k*. my *com*.?   *Ex* 16:28
to them that *k*. my *com*.   20:6
ye *k*. my *com*. and do them.
    Lev 22:31; *Deut* 4:40; 6:17; 7:11
if ye *k*. my *com*.   *Lev* 26:3
    Deut 11:22; 19:9; 28:9; 30:10
    1 Ki 3:14
may *k*. the *com*. of Lord. *Deut* 4:2
would fear me and *k*. my *com*. 5:29
thou wouldest *k*. his *com*.   8:2
thou shalt *k*. the *com*.   6; 11:1, 8
    13:4, 18
to *k*. the *com*. of the Lord.   10:13
    27:1; 30:16
avouched Lord to *k*. his *com*. 26:17
thee, that thou shouldest *k*. *com*. 18
hearkenedst not to *k*. his *com*. 28:45
to *k*. his *com*. to cleave. *Josh* 22:5
charge of Lord to *k*. his *com*. *1 Ki* 2:3
k. my *com*.   6:12; *2 Ki* 17:13
    Pr 4:4; 7:2
incline our hearts to *k*. his *com*.
    1 Ki 8:58
be perfect to *k*. his *com*.   61
if ye will not *k*. my *com*. I will. 9:6
if thou wilt *k*. my *com*.   11:38
    Neh 1:9; *John* 15:10
made a covenant to *k*. *com*.
    2 Ki 23:3; *2 Chr* 34:31
k. and seek for all the *com*. of the.
    1 Chr 28:8
a perfect heart to *k*. thy *com*. 29:19
of God, but *k*. his *com*.   *Ps* 78:7
delayed not to *k*. thy *com*.   119:60
for I will *k*. *com*. of my God.   115
let thy heart *k*. my *com*.   *Pr* 3:1
my son, *k*. thy father's *com*.   6:20
to *k*. the king's *com*.   *Eccl* 8:2
fear God and *k*. his *com*. this. 12:13
enter into life, *k*. the *com*. *Mat* 19:17
love me, *k*. my *com*.   *John* 14:15
love *com*. without spot. *1 Tim* 6:14
we do know that we know him if we
    k. his *com*.   *1 John* 2:3
receive, because we *k*. his *com*. 3:22
love God and *k*. his *com*.   5:2
love of God, that we *k*. his *com*.   3
her seed which *k*. *com*.   *Rev* 12:17
are they which *k*. the *com*.   14:12

see covenant

keep passover

k. *pass*. to Lord . . . be circumcised,
    then let him *k*. *pass*.   *Ex* 12:48
of Israel *k*. *pass*. in its season.
    Num 9:2, 4; *Deut* 16:1
    2 Ki 23:21
could not *k*. the *pass*.   *Num* 9:6
yet he shall *k*. *pass*.   10
ordinances of *pass*. they shall *k*. 12
and forbeareth to *k*. the *pass*.   13
if a stranger will *k*. the *pass*. to. 14
came to *k*. the *pass*. to. *2 Chr* 30:1
taken counsel, to *k*. *pass*. in the. 2
was prepared to *k*. *pass*.   35:16
kings of Israel *k*. such a *pass*.   18
say to him, I will *k*. *pass*. *Mat* 26:18

keep silence

who said, *K*. *silence*, and. *Judg* 3:19
not *k*. *silence*.   *Ps* 35:22; 83:1
come and not *k*. *silence*.   50:3
a time to *k*. *silence* and. *Eccl* 3:7
k. *silence* before me, O.   *Isa* 41:1
k. not *silence*.   62:6

behold, I will not *k*. *silence*. *Isa* 65:6
elders of daughter of Zion *k*. *silence*.
    Lam 2:10
prudent shall *k*. *silence*. *Amos* 5:13
let the earth *k*. *silence*.   *Hab* 2:20
let him *k*. *silence* in the. *1 Cor* 14:28
let your women *k*. *silence* in the. 34

keep statutes

if thou wilt *k*. all his *stat*. *Ex* 15:26
    Deut 30:10; *1 Ki* 9:4; 11:38
k. my *stat*. and judgements.
    Lev 18:5, 26; 19:19; 20:8, 22
    Ezek 44:24
thou shalt *k*. therefore his *stat*.
    Deut 4:10; 26:16
fear Lord to *k*. his *stat*.   6:2
avouched Lord to *k*. his *stat*. 26:17
hearkenedst not to *k*. his *stat*. 28:45
in my ways to *k*. my *stat*. 11:33
were directed to *k*. thy *stat*. *Ps* 119:5
I will *k*. thy *stat*., forsake.   8, 145
will turn and *k*. my *stat*. *Ezek* 18:21

keeper

Abel was a *k*. of sheep.   *Gen* 4:2
am I my brother's *k*.?   9
Joseph favour in sight of *k*.   39:21
the *k*. of the prison committed.   22
the *k*. of the prison looked not to. 23
left sheep with a *k*.   *1 Sam* 17:20
carriage in the hand of the *k*.   22
I will make thee *k*. of mine.   28:2
k. of the wardrobe.   *2 Ki* 22:14
    2 Chr 34:22
Asaph the *k*. of the king's. *Neh* 2:8
after him Shemaiah *k*. of the.   3:29
Hege *k*. of women. *Esth* 2:3, 8, 15
and as a booth that he *k*. *Job* 27:18
Lord is thy *k*., the Lord. *Ps* 121:5
they made me the *k*. of. *S of S* 1:6
the son of Shallum *k*. of *Jer* 35:4
k. of prison awaking. *Acts* 16:27*
the *k*. of the prison told this.   36*

keepers

a third part shall be *k*.   *2 Ki* 11:5
k. of the gates of the. *1 Chr* 9:19
when the *k*. of the house. *Eccl* 12:3
k. took away my vail. *S of S* 5:7
let out the vineyard to *k*.   8:11
as *k*. of the field are.   *Jer* 4:17
k. of charge of house.   *Ezek* 40:45
    46; 44:8, 14
for fear of him the *k*.   *Mat* 28:4
k. standing before doors. *Acts* 5:23
k. kept the prison.   12:6*
Herod examined the *k*.   19*
discreet, chaste, *k*. at home. *Tit* 2:5*

see door

keepest

who *k*. covenant and.   *1 Ki* 8:23
    2 Chr 6:14; *Neh* 9:32
orderly and *k*. the law.   *Acts* 21:24

keepeth

and he die not, but *k*.   *Ex* 21:18
faithful God which *k*. covenant.
    Deut 7:9; *Neh* 1:5
behold he *k*. the sheep. *1 Sam* 16:11
he *k*. back his soul from. *Job* 33:18
he *k*. all his bones, none. *Ps* 34:20
he that *k*. thee will not.   121:3, 4
Lord God, which *k*. truth.   146:6
he *k*. the paths of.   *Pr* 2:8
is in the way of life that *k*.   10:17*
he that *k*. his mouth *k*. 13:3; 21:23
righteousness *k*. him upright in. 13:6
k. his way preserveth. 16:17; 19:16
he that *k*. understanding.   19:8
that *k*. thy soul, doth not he. 24:12
whoso *k*. the fig tree shall.   27:18
whoso *k*. the law is a wise.   28:7
that *k*. company with harlots. 29:3
but a wise man *k*. it in till.   3
but he that *k*. the law, happy.   18
k. the commandments.   *Eccl* 8:5
nation which *k*. truth.   *Isa* 26:2
k. the sabbath from polluting it, and
    k. his hand from doing.   56:2, 6
that *k*. back his sword. *Jer* 48:10
he sitteth alone and *k*.   *Lam* 3:28
man, neither *k*. at home. *Hab* 2:5
a strong man armed *k*. *Luke* 11:21
yet none of you *k*. the. *John* 7:19
is not of God, because he *k*.   9:16

keeping

that hath my commandments and *k*. them. *John* 14:21
he that loveth me not, *k*. not. 24
I know him, and *k*. not. *1 John* 2:4
whoso *k*. his word, in him. 5; 3:24
he that is begotten of God *k*. 5:18
that overcometh and *k*. *Rev* 2:26
blessed is he that *k*. his. 16:15
blessed is he that *k*. sayings. 22:7

keeping

Lord God *k*. mercy for. *Ex* 34:7
k. the charge of the. *Num* 3:28, 38
forget not God, in not *k*. *Deut* 8:11
with them *k*. sheep. *1 Sam* 25:16
were porters *k*. the ward. *Neh* 12:25
and in *k*. of them is great. *Ps* 19:11
by *k*. of his covenant. *Ezek* 17:14
O Lord the great God, *k*. *Dan* 9:4
there were shepherds *k*. *Luke* 2:8
k. the commandments. *1 Cor* 7:19
commit the *k*. of their. *1 Pet* 4:19

Keilah

K. and Achzib, cities. *Josh* 15:44
Philistines fight against *K*.
1 Sam 23:1
arise, go down to *K*. 4
David saved *K*. 5
son of Ahimelech fled to *K*. 6
K. deliver me to Saul ? 11, 12
the ruler of the half part of *K*. repaired. *Neh* 3:17, 18

Kenaz, *see* Othniel

Kenites

seed have I given the *K*. *Gen* 15:19
Balaam looked on the *K*. *Num* 24:21
Saul said to the *K*. *1 Sam* 15:6
road against south of the *K*. 27:10

kept

Abraham *k*. my charge. *Gen* 26:5
with sheep, for she *k*. them. 29:9
nor hath he *k*. back any thing. 39:9
send one, and ye shall be *k*. 42:16
now Moses *k*. the flock. *Ex* 3:1
lay up for you to be *k*. until. 16:23
pot of manna *k*. for. 32, 33, 34
the owner hath not *k*. 21:29, 36
and it be *k*. close, and. *Num* 5:13
they *k*. the passover. 9:5
why are we *k*. back ? 7
then Israel *k*. the charge. 19, 23
bring Aaron's rod to be *k*. 17:10
k. for a water of separation. 19:9
Lord hath *k*. thee back. 24:11
which *k*. the charge of the. 31:47
k. them as the apple. *Deut* 32:10
they observed thy word, and *k*. 33:9
Israel *k*. the passover. *Josh* 5:10
k. me alive these 45 years. 14:10
ye have *k*. all that Moses. 22:2
ye have *k*. the charge of. 3
k. fast by the maidens. *Ruth* 2:23
time it hath been *k*. *1 Sam* 9:24
not *k*. the commandment. 13:13, 14
David said, Thy servant *k*. his. 17:34
k. themselves from women. 21:4
surely in vain have I *k*. all. 25:21
blessed be thou who hast *k*. me. 33
the Lord God hath *k*. me. 39
why hast thou not *k*. thy ? 26:15
because ye have not *k*. your. 16
the young man that *k*. *2 Sam* 13:34
I have *k*. the ways of the Lord. 22:22
Ps 18:21
I have *k*. myself from iniquity.
2 Sam 22:24; *Ps* 18:23
hast *k*. me to be head of the heathen.
2 Sam 22:44
not *k*. the oath of Lord ? *1 Ki* 2:43
thou hast *k*. for him this great. 3:6
k. with thy servant David my father.
8:24; *2 Chr* 6:15
Solomon *k*. not that the Lord.
1 Ki 11:10
thou hast not *k*. my covenant and. 11
because David *k*. my commandments. 34; 14:8
man of God from Judah not *k*.
2 Ki 17:19
Judah *k*. not the.
Hezekiah *k*. commandments. 18:6
the word of the Lord Saul *k*. not.
1 Chr 10:13
while David *k*. himself close. 12:1

Solomon *k*. the feast. *2 Chr* 7:8
k. the dedication of altar. 9
k. feast of unleavened bread.
30:21; *Ezra* 6:22
and they *k*. other seven days.
2 Chr 30:23
our fathers have not *k*. the. 34:21
Josiah and Israel *k*. the passover.
35:1, 17, 19
was no passover like to that *k*. 18
they *k*. also the feast of. *Ezra* 3:4
the dedication of this house. 6:16
children of the captivity *k*. the. 19
we have not *k*. the commandments.
Neh 1:7
they *k*. the feast seven days. 8:18
nor our fathers *k*. thy law. 9:34
days of Purim be *k*. *Esth* 9:28
ways have I *k*. and not. *Job* 23:11
k. close from the fowls of air. 28:21
I have *k*. me from paths. *Ps* 17:4
hast *k*. me alive. 30:3
a multitude that *k*. holy day. 42:4
they *k*. not the covenant of. 78:10
they tempted God, and *k*. not. 56
they *k*. his testimonies and. 99:7
have *k*. thy testimonies. 119:22, 167
I have *k*. thy law. 55
because I *k*. thy precepts. 56, 168
now have I *k*. thy word. 67
they *k*. not thy word. 158
eyes desired, I *k*. not. *Eccl* 2:10
riches *k*. for owners thereof. 5:13
vineyard have I not *k*. *S of S* 1:6
a holy solemnity is *k*. *Isa* 30:29
not *k*. my laws. *Jer* 16:11
and *k*. his precepts. 35:18
neither have *k*. my judgements.
Ezek 5:7; 20:21
hath *k*. my judgements. 18:9
hath *k*. my statutes. 19
ye have not *k*. the charge of. 44:8
that *k*. the charge of my. 15; 48:11
would, he *k*. alive, he set. *Dan* 5:19
I *k*. the matter in my heart. 7:28
for a wife, and *k*. sheep. *Hos* 12:12
and Edom *k*. his wrath. *Amos* 1:11
Judah hath not *k*. his. 2:4
statutes of Omri are *k*. *Mi* 6:16
as ye have not *k*. my ways.
Mal 2:9; 3:7
what profit is it that we have *k*.? 3:14
they that *k*. the swine. *Mat* 8:33
which have been *k*. secret. 13:35
Herod's birthday was *k*. 14:6
these have I *k*. from my youth.
19:20; *Luke* 18:21
nor was any thing *k*. secret, but.
Mark 4:22
and they *k*. that saying. 9:10
Luke 9:36
Mary *k*. these things. *Luke* 2:19, 51
he was *k*. bound with chains. 8:29
thy pound, which I have *k*. 19:20
but thou hast *k*. good. *John* 2:10
of my burying hath she *k*. this. 12:7
as I have *k*. my father's. 15:10
if they have *k*. my saying. 20
thine they were, and have *k*. 17:6
k. in thy name, those thou gavest me
I have *k*. 12
and spake to her that *k*. the. 18:16
saith the damsel that *k*. the door. 17
sold, and *k*. back part of. *Acts* 5:2
law, and have not *k*. it. 7:53
Eneas had *k*. his bed eight. 9:33
Peter was *k*. in prison. 12:5
keepers *k*. the prison. 6
I *k*. back nothing profitable. 20:20
and *k*. the raiment of them. 22:20
and he commanded him to be *k*.
23:35; 25:21
that Paul should be *k*. 25:4
the centurion *k*. them from. 27:43
with a soldier that *k*. him. 28:16
mystery *k*. secret since. *Rom* 16:25
I *k*. myself from being. *2 Cor* 11:9
the governor *k*. the city with. 32
we were *k*. under law. *Gal* 3:23
my course, I *k*. the faith. *2 Tim* 4:7
through faith Moses *k*. *Heb* 11:28
the hire that is *k*. back. *Jas* 5:4
who are *k*. by the power. *1 Pet* 1:5
by the same word are *k*. *2 Pet* 3:7

angels which *k*. not their. *Jude* 6
hast *k*. my word, and not. *Rev* 3:8
because thou hast *k*. the word. 10

kept silence

men gave ear, and *k*. sil. *Job* 29:21
great multitude, that I *k*. sil. 31:34
when I *k*. sil. my bones. *Ps* 32:3
hast thou done, and I *k*. sil. 50:21
the multitude *k*. sil. *Acts* 15:12
Hebrew, they *k*. the more sil. 22:2

kerchiefs

k. on head of every. *Ezek* 13:18
your *k*. will I tear, and deliver. 21

Kerioth

judgement is come on *K*. *Jer* 48:24
K. is taken. 41
devour the palaces of *K*. *Amos* 2:2

kernels

eat nothing from the *k*. *Num* 6:4

kettle

servant struck into the *k*. *1 Sam* 2:14

Keturah

wife, her name was *K*. *Gen* 25:1
children of *K*. 4; *1 Chr* 1:32, 33

key

therefore they took a *k*. *Judg* 3:25
k. of house of David lay. *Isa* 22:22
have taken away the *k*. *Luke* 11:52
saith he that hath the *k*. *Rev* 3:7
given *k*. of bottomless pit. 9:1; 20:1

keys

give the *k*. of kingdom. *Mat* 16:19
k. of hell and of death. *Rev* 1:18

kick

wherefore *k*. ye at my ? *1 Sam* 2:29
it is hard to *k*. against the pricks.
Acts 9:5; 26:14

kicked

but Jeshurun waxed-fat and *k*.
Deut 32:15

kid

(*Kid of the goats is frequently changed in Revisions to* he goat)
brethren killed a *k*. of. *Gen* 37:31
I will send thee a *k*. from. 38:17
not seethe *k*. in his mother's milk.
Ex 23:19; 34:26; *Deut* 14:21
bring his offering, a *k*. of the goats.
Lev 4:23, 28; 9:3; *Ezek* 43:22
45:23
or a *k*. for a sin offering. *Lev* 5:6
then ye shall sacrifice one *k*. 23:19
Num 7:16, 22, 28; 15:24; 28:15
30; 29:5, 11, 16, 19, 25
done for a lamb or a *k*. *Num* 15:11
and made ready a *k*. *Judg* 6:19
so Manoah took a *k*. with a. 13:19
Samson rent lion as a *k*. 14:6
visited his wife with a *k*. 15:1
an ass laden, and a *k*. *1 Sam* 16:20
lie down with the *k*. *Isa* 11:6
never gavest me a *k*. *Luke* 15:29

kidneys

thou shalt take the two *k*. and burn.
Ex 29:13, 22; *Lev* 3:4, 10, 15; 4:9
7:4; 8:16, 25
but fat and *k*. burnt on. *Lev* 9:10, 19
rams, with the fat of. *Deut* 32:14
the sword of Lord, with fat of *k*. of
rams. *Isa* 34:6

Kidron, *see* brook

kids

fetch me from thence two *k*.
Gen 27:9
she put the skins of the *k*. on. 16
take two *k*. of the goats. *Lev* 16:5
the *k*. of the goats for. *Num* 7:87
one carrying three *k*. *1 Sam* 10:3
two little flocks of *k*. *1 Ki* 20:27
Josiah gave lambs and *k*. *2 Chr* 35:7
feed thy *k*. beside the. *S of S* 1:8

kill

Cain, should *k*. him. *Gen* 4:15
they will *k*. me, but will save. 12:12
men of the place should *k*. me. 26:7
himself, purposing to *k*. thee. 27:42
and said, Let us not *k*. him. 37:21
a son, then ye shall *k*. him. *Ex* 1:16
thou to *k*. me ? 2:14; *Acts* 7:28
him, and sought to *k*. him. *Ex* 4:24

of Israel shall *k.* it. *Ex* 12:6, 21
to *k.* this whole assembly. 16:3
to *k.* us and our children. 17:3
thou shalt not *k.* 20:13*; *Deut* 5:17*
 Mat 5:21; *Rom* 13:9
steal an ox or sheep, and *k. Ex* 22:1
I will *k.* you with the sword. 24
k. bullock before the Lord. 29:11
 Lev 1:5; 4:4
then thou shalt *k.* the ram. *Ex* 29:20
shall *k.* it on the side of the altar.
 Lev 1:11; 16:15
and *k.* it at the door of the. 3:2
shall *k.* it before the tabernacle. 8, 13
k. it in the place where they *k.* 4:24
k. the burnt offering. 33; 7:2
k. the sin offering. 14:13; 16:11
he shall *k.* the lamb of the. 14:25
shall *k.* the one of the birds. 50
seed to Molech, and *k.* him not. 20:4
thou shalt *k.* the woman and the. 16
cow or ewe, ye shall not *k.* it. 22:28
thus with me, *k.* me. *Num* 11:15
if thou *k.* all this people as. 14:15
hast brought us to *k.* us in. 16:13
for now would I *k.* thee. 22:29
k. every male among the little ones,
 k. every woman that hath. 31:17
revenger of blood *k.* slayer. 35:27
should *k.* his neighbour unawares.
 Deut 4:42
thou mayest *k.* and eat flesh. 12:15
then thou shalt *k.* of thy herd. 21
but thou shalt surely *k.* him. 13:9
I *k.* and I make alive, I. 32:29
if Lord were pleased to *k. Judg* 13:23
saying, Surely we will not *k.* 15:13
it is day, we shall *k.* him. 16:2
they began to *k.* as at other times.
 20:31, 39
hear it, he will *k.* me. *1 Sam* 16:2
if he be able to *k.* me, then. 17:9
that they should *k.* David. 19:1
Saul my father seeketh to *k.* thee. 2
why should I *k.* thee? 17
bade me *k.* thee. 24:10
swear thou wilt neither *k.* me. 30:15
smite Amnon, then *k. 2 Sam* 13:28
that we may *k.* him, for the. 14:7
iniquity be in me, let him *k.* me. 32
nor for us shalt thou *k.* any. 21:4
Solomon sought to *k. 1 Ki* 11:40
and they shall *k.* me, and go. 12:27
am I God, to *k.* and? *2 Ki* 5:7
and if they *k.* us, we shall. 7:4
him that followeth her *k.* 11:15
k. the passover, sanctify. *2 Chr* 35:6
by posts to *k.* all Jews. *Esth* 3:13
a time to *k.* and a time. *Eccl* 3:3
and I will *k.* thy root. *Isa* 14:30
year to year, let them *k.* 29:1*
ye *k.* them that are fed. *Ezek* 34:3
shall *k.* shall be in danger. *Mat* 5:21
fear not them which *k.* the body.
 10:28; *Luke* 12:4
and they shall *k.* him. *Mat* 17:23
 Mark 9:31; 10:34
come let us *k.* him. *Mat* 21:38
 Mark 12:7; *Luke* 20:14
ye shall *k.* and crucify. *Mat* 23:34
deliver you up, and shall *k.* you. 24:9
take Jesus by subtilty and *k.* 26:4
to save life, or to *k.*? *Mark* 3:4
do not *k.* 10:19; *Luke* 18:20
 Jas 2:11
for Herod will *k.* thee. *Luke* 13:31
hither the fatted calf and *k.* it. 15:23
and scribes sought how to *k.* 22:2
Jews sought the more to *k.* him.
 John 5:18; 7:1
why go ye about to *k.* me? 7:19
who goeth about to *k.* thee? 20
he whom they seek to *k.*? 25
will he *k.* himself? 8:22
ye seek to *k.* me. 37, 40
not but to steal and *k.* 10:10
Jews took counsel to *k.* Paul.
 Acts 9:23; 26:21
day and night to *k.* him. 9:24
to him, Rise, Peter, *k.* and eat. 10:13
they went about to *k.* him. 21:31
near, are ready to *k.* him. 23:15
laying wait in the way to *k.* 25:3
soldiers' counsel was to *k.* 27:42

no adultery, yet if thou *k. Jas* 2:11
ye *k.* and desire to have, and. 4:2
I will *k.* her children. *Rev* 2:23
that they should *k.* one another. 6:4
power was given them to *k.* with. 8
that they should not *k.* them. 9:5
overcome them and *k.* them. 11:7

killed
Joseph's coat, and *k.* a kid.
 Gen 37:31
the beast hath *k.* a man. *Ex* 21:29
bullock shall be *k.* before. *Lev* 4:15
where the burnt offering is *k.* shall
the sin offering be *k.* before. 6:25
the ram be *k.* 8:19
one of the birds be *k.* 14:5
in the blood of the bird *k.* 6
ye have *k.* the people. *Num* 16:41
whosoever hath *k.* any person. 31:19
skirt of thy robe, and *k. 1 Sam* 24:11
take my flesh I have *k.* for. 25:11
woman hasted and *k.* the calf. 28:24
thou hast *k.* Uriah with. *2 Sam* 12:9
smote the Philistine and *k.* 21:17
and because he *k.* him. *1 Ki* 16:7
hast thou *k.* and also taken? 21:19
Pekah *k.* Pekahiah. *2 Ki* 15:25
David *k.* Shophach. *1 Chr* 19:18
Ahab *k.* sheep and. *2 Chr* 18:2
he slew those that had *k.* the. 25:3
so they *k.* the bullocks, rams. 29:22
the priests *k.* them and made. 24
k. the passover. 30:15; 35:1, 11
 Ezra 6:20
for thy sake are we *k. Ps* 44:22
k. her beasts, mingled. *Pr* 9:2
hast *k.* and not pitied. *Lam* 2:21
and be *k.* and be raised again.
 Mat 16:21; *Mark* 8:31; 9:31
beat one, and *k.* another. *Mat* 21:35
 Mark 12:5
oxen and my fatlings are *k. Mat* 22:4
are children of them that *k.* 23:31
Herodias would have *k. Mark* 6:19
k. him and cast him out of the. 12:8
the first day, when they *k.* 14:12
fathers *k.* them. *Luke* 11:47, 48
after he hath *k.* hath power. 12:5
hath *k.* the fatted calf. 15:27, 30
when the passover must be *k.* 22:7
k. the Prince of life. *Acts* 3:15
he *k.* James. 12:2
and would have *k.* himself. 16:27
drink till they had *k.* Paul. 23:12
Jews, and should have been *k.* 27
for thy sake we are *k.* all. *Rom* 8:36
Lord, they have *k.* thy prophets. 11:3
as chastened and not *k.* 2 Cor 6:9
who *k.* the Lord Jesus. *1 Thes* 2:15
ye have condemned and *k. Jas* 5:6
brethren who should be *k. Rev* 6:11
was the third part of men *k.* 9:18
the rest which were not *k.* by. 20
he must in this manner be *k.* 11:5
killeth with sword, must be *k.* 13:10
image of the beast, should be *k.* 15

killedst
to kill me, as thou *k.* the. *Ex* 2:14
forasmuch as thou *k. 1 Sam* 24:18

killest
Jerusalem, which *k.* the prophets.
 Mat 23:37; *Luke* 13:34

killeth
k. an ox, or lamb, or goat, in the
camp, or *k.* it out. *Lev* 17:3
k. any man shall surely be put to
death. 24:17, 21; *Num* 35:30
he that *k.* a beast. *Lev* 24:18, 21
k. any person unawares. *Num* 35:11
 15; *Deut* 19:4; *Josh* 20:3, 9
the Lord *k.* and maketh. *1 Sam* 2:6
man who *k.* him, king. 17:25; 26:27
wrath the foolish man. *Job* 5:2
the murderer *k.* the poor and. 24:14
of the slothful *k.* him. *Pr* 21:25
he that *k.* an ox, as if he. *Isa* 66:3
who *k.* you will think. *John* 16:2
letter *k.*, but the Spirit. *2 Cor* 3:6
he that *k.* with sword. *Rev* 13:10

killing
which aided him in *k. Judg* 9:24

charge of *k.* passover. *2 Chr* 30:17
oxen, and *k.* sheep. *Isa* 22:13
by swearing, lying, *k.* and. *Hos* 4:2
beating some, and *k. Mark* 12:5

kin
approach to any near of *k. Lev* 18:6
uncovereth his near *k.* 20:19
for his *k.* that is near, he. 21:2
if any of his *k.* come to. 25:25*, 49
the man is near of *k.* to. *Ruth* 2:20
the king is near of *k.* 2 Sam 19:42
not, but among his own *k. Mark* 6:4

kind, *substantive*
herb yielding seed, and the fruit tree
yielding fruit after his *k.*
 Gen 1:11, 12
forth abundantly after their *k.* and
every winged fowl after his *k.* 21
beast of earth after their *k.* 24
beast of the earth after his *k.* 25
k. and of cattle after their *k.*, every
creeping thing after his *k.* 6:20
cattle and fowl, after their *k.* 7:14
raven, hawk after his *k. Lev* 11:14
 15, 16, 19; *Deut* 14:14
and tortoise after his *k. Lev* 11:29
cattle gender with a diverse *k.* 19:19
instruments of every *k. 1 Chr* 28:14
sellers of all *k.* of ware. *Neh* 13:20
I planted trees of all *k. Eccl* 2:5
the multitude of all *k.* of. *Ezek* 27:12
and gathered of every *k. Mat* 13:47
this *k.* goeth not out but by prayer.
 17:21; *Mark* 9:29
there is one *k.* of flesh. *1 Cor* 15:39
that we should be a *k. Jas* 1:18
for every *k.* of beasts and birds. 3:7

kind
saying, If thou be *k.* to. *2 Chr* 10:7
God is *k.* to unthankful. *Luke* 6:35
suffereth long and is *k.* 1 Cor 13:4
be *k.* one to another. *Eph* 4:32

kindle
a contentious man to *k. Pr* 26:21*
k. in the thickets of the. *Isa* 9:18
k. a burning like the burning. 10:16
breath of the Lord doth *k.* it. 30:33
nor shall the flame *k.* upon. 43:2
never want a man to *k. Jer* 33:18*
fire and flame shall *k.* in. *Ob* 18

kindled
Potiphar's wrath was *k. Gen* 39:19
burning the Lord hath *k. Lev* 10:6
wrath of the Lord was *k. Num* 11:33
 Deut 11:17; *2 Ki* 22:13, 17
 Ps 106:40
coals were *k.* by it. *2 Sam* 22:9
 Ps 18:8
also *k.* his wrath against. *Job* 19:11
k. the wrath of Elihu, against Job
was his wrath *k.* because. 32:2
three friends was his wrath *k.* 3, 5
my wrath is *k.* against thee. 42:7
when his wrath is *k.* but. *Ps* 2:12
when their wrath is *k.* 124:3
the sparks that ye have *k. Isa* 50:11
wrath was *k.* in the cities. *Jer* 44:6
I the Lord have *k.* it. *Ezek* 20:48
my repentings are *k. Hos* 11:8
if it be already *k. Luke* 12:49
 see **anger, fire**

kindleth
his breath *k.* coals. *Job* 41:21
yea, he *k.* it, and baketh. *Isa* 44:15
a matter a little fire *k.*! *Jas* 3:5*

kindly
if you will deal *k.* with me.
 Gen 24:49; 47:29
Shechem spake *k.* to the. 34:3
Joseph spake *k.* to his. 50:21
deal *k.* and truly with. *Josh* 2:14
the Lord deal *k.* with you. *Ruth* 1:8
thou shalt deal *k.* with. *1 Sam* 20:8
spake *k.* to Jehoiachin. *2 Ki* 25:28
 Jer 52:32
be *k.* affectioned one. *Rom* 12:10*

kindness
this is thy *k.* thou shalt. *Gen* 20:13
according to the *k.* I have. 21:23
O Lord, shew *k.* to my master. 24:12
know that thou hast shewed *k.* 14
think on me, and shew *k.* 40:14

23

I have shewed you *k*. that ye will also
shew *k*. to my father's. *Josh* 2:12
nor shewed *k*. to house. *Judg* 8:35
not lett off his *k*. to living. *Ruth* 2:20
thou hast shewed more *k*. 3:10
ye shewed *k*. to Israel. *1 Sam* 15:6
thou shalt shew me the *k*. of. 20:14
thou shalt not cut off thy *k*. 15
this *k*. unto your lord. *2 Sam* 2:5
k. to you, I also will requite you this
k. because ye have done this. 6
against Judah shew *k*. to house. 3:8
that I may shew him *k*. for. 9:1
any, that I may shew the *k*. of. 3
shew thee *k*. for Jonathan's sake. 7
k. to Hanun son of Nahash, as his
father shewed *k*. 10:2; *1 Chr* 19:2
Absalom said, Is this thy *k*. to thy ?
2 Sam 16:17
shew *k*. to the sons of. *1 Ki* 2:7
kept for David this great *k*. 3:6
Joash remembered not *k*. of.
2 Chr 24:22
God gracious, of great *k*. *Neh* 9:17*
the maiden obtained *k*. of. *Esth* 2:9
me his marvellous *k*. *Ps* 31:21
for his merciful *k*. is great. 117:2
let thy merciful *k*. be for. 119:76
smite me, it shall be a *k*. 141:5
desire of a man is his *k*. *Pr* 19:22
in her tongue is the law of *k*. 31:26
with everlasting *k*. will I. *Isa* 54:8
but my *k*. shall not depart. 10
I remember thee, the *k*. of. *Jer* 2:2
for he is gracious, of great *k*.
Joel 2:13* *Jonah* 4:2*
people shewed us no little *k*.
Acts 28:2
by longsuffering, by *k*. *2 Cor* 6:6
in his *k*. toward us. *Eph* 2:7
put on *k*. humbleness of. *Col* 3:12
k. of God our Saviour. *Tit* 3:4
godliness brotherly *k*.; to *k*. charity.
2 Pet 1:7
see **lovingkindness**

kindred
God said, Get thee from thy *k*.
Gen 12:1; *Acts* 7:3
go to *k*. and take a wife.
Gen 24:4; 38:40
Lord who took me from my *k*. 7*
when thou comest to my *k*. if they. 41
the Lord said, Return to thy *k*. 31:3
13*; 32:9
ask'd us straitly of our *k*. 43:7
to my own land and *k*. *Num* 10:30
brought out all her *k*. *Josh* 6:23
of the *k*. of Elimelech. *Ruth* 2:3; 3:2
the *k*. of Saul 3000. *1 Chr* 12:29
Esther shewed not her people or *k*.
Esth 2:10, 20
to see the destruction of my *k*. 8:6
Elihu, of the *k*. of Ram. *Job* 32:2
men of thy *k*. said, Get. *Ezek* 11:15
none of thy *k*. called by. *Luke* 1:61
the *k*. of the high priest. *Acts* 4:6
Joseph's *k*. was made known. 7:13
Jacob to him and all his *k*. 14
dealt subtilly with our *k*. 19
redeemed us out of every *k*. and.
Rev 5:9
gospel to preach to every *k*. 14:6

kindreds
give to the Lord, ye *k*. *1 Chr* 16:28
Ps 96:7
all *k*. of nations shall. *Ps* 22:27
k. of the earth be blessed. *Acts* 3:25
k. of the earth shall wail. *Rev* 1:7
a great multitude of all *k*. 7:9
of *k*. shall see their dead. 11:9
was given him over all *k*. 13:7

kinds
creepeth after their *k*. *Gen* 8:19*
divers *k*. of spices. *2 Chr* 16:14
appoint over them four *k*. *Jer* 15:3
be according to their *k*. *Ezek* 47:10
dulcimer, and all *k*. of music.
Dan 3:5, 7, 10, 15
to another divers *k*. of. *1 Cor* 12:10
are, it may be, so many *k*. of. 14:10

kine
Is taken, [1] *Literally, for cows.*
Deut 7:13. [2] *Figuratively, for*

the *proud and wealthy rulers of
Israel*, *Amos* 4:4.

forty *k*. ten bulls, a. *Gen* 32:15
up seven well favoured *k*. 41:2, 18
seven other *k*. came out. 3, 4, 19, 20
seven good *k*. are seven years. 26
the seven thin ill favoured *k*. are. 27
bless the increase of thy *k*. *Deut* 7:13
blessed shall be the increase of thy
k. 28:4
cursed shall be the increase of thy *k*.
18
not leave the increase of thy *k*. 51
butter of *k*., milk of sheep. 32:14
milch *k*. and tie the *k*. *1 Sam* 6:7
took two *k*. 10
the *k*. took the straight way. 12
wood of cart, and offered the *k*. 14
butter, and cheese of *k*. *2 Sam* 17:29
hear ye this word, ye *k*. *Amos* 4:1

king
Melchizedek *k*. of Salem.
Gen 14:18; *Heb* 7:1
in Edom, before there reigned any *k*.
Gen 36:31; *1 Chr* 1:43
arose up a new *k*. over. *Ex* 1:8
the shout of a *k*. is. *Num* 23:21
and his *k*. shall be higher. 24:7
I will set a *k*. over me. *Deut* 17:14
shalt in any wise set him *k*. over. 15
bring thee, and thy *k*. which. 28:36
and he was *k*. in Jeshurun. 33:5
the children of a *k*. *Judg* 8:18
the trees went to anoint a *k*. 9:8
no *k*. in Israel, but every man did.
17:6; 18:1; 19:1; 21:25
give strength to his *k*. *1 Sam* 2:10
go make us a *k*. to judge us. 8:5
give us a *k*. 6
shew the manner of the *k*. 8:9, 11
cry in that day because of your *k*. 18
we will have a *k*. 19
that our *k*. may judge us, and. 20
and make them a *k*. 22
nay, but set a *k*. over us. 10:19
God save the *k*. 24; *2 Sam* 16:16
2 Ki 11:12; *2 Chr* 23:11
I have made a *k*. over. *1 Sam* 12:1
the *k*. walketh before you. 2
nay; but a *k*. shall reign over us: when
Lord your God was your *k*. 12
behold the *k*. whom ye have. 13
wickedness is great in asking a *k*. 17
our sins this evil, to ask us a *k*. 19
consumed, both you and your *k*. 25
sent me to anoint thee to be *k*. 15:1
rejected thee from being *k*. 23, 26
I have provided me a *k*. 16:1
let not the *k*. sin against his. 19:4
I should not fail to sit with *k*. 20:5
let not the *k*. impute any. 22:15
that thou shalt surely be *k*. 24:20
a feast like the feast of a *k*. 25:36
enemies of my lord the *k*. 29:8
he made Ish-bosheth *k*. *2 Sam* 2:9
what the *k*. did, pleased all. 3:36
not of the *k*. to slay Abner. 37
Lord had established him *k*. over.
5:12
him a mess of meat from *k*. 11:8
I anointed thee *k*. over. 12:7
I pray thee, speak to the *k*. 13:13
and the *k*. and his throne be. 14:9
of God so is my Lord the *k*. 17; 19:27
controversy, came to the *k*. 15:2
there is none deputed of the *k*. 3
abide with the *k*. for thou art. 19
in what place my lord the *k*. 21
this dead dog curse the *k*.? 16:9
flee, I will smite the *k*. only. 17:2
is no matter hid from the *k*. 18:13
k. saved us out of the hand of. 19:9
of all Israel is come to the *k*. 11
the *k*. should take it to his heart. 19
I know that I am this day *k*. 22
I yet to cry any more to the *k*.? 28
because the *k*. is near of kin. 42
we have ten parts in the *k*. 43
tower of salvation for his *k*. 22:51
Araunah as a *k*. give to *k*. 24:23
Adonijah said, I will be *k*. *1 Ki* 1:5
for Solomon shall be *k*. in my. 35
I will speak for thee to the *k*. 2:18

as *k*. hath said, so will thy. *1 Ki* 2:38
made thy servant *k*. instead of. 3:7
women spake before the *k*. 22
Israel heard the judgement the *k*. 28
k. and all Israel offered. 8:62
not any thing hid from the *k*. 10:3
lifted up his hand against *k*. 11:26
thou shalt reign and shalt be *k*. 37
who told me I should be *k*. 14:2
the Lord shall raise up a *k*. over. 14
conspired and hath slain the *k*. 16:16
blaspheme God and the *k*. 21:10
prophets declare good to the *k*. 22:13
2 Chr 18:12
there was then no *k*. in Edom: a
deputy was *k*. *1 Ki* 22:47
O man of God, *k*. said. *2 Ki* 1:9, 11
be spoken for to the *k*.? 4:13
lord on whose hand the *k*. 7:2
she went to cry to the *k*. for. 8:3
shewed that thou shalt be *k*. 13
Edom revolted, made a *k*. over. 20
we will not make any *k*. 10:5
with the *k*. as he goeth out and. 11:8
a covenant between the Lord and *k*.,
between the *k*. also and the. 17
had slain the *k*. his father. 14:5
2 Chr 25:3
brought the *k*. word. *2 Ki* 22:9
20; *2 Chr* 34:16, 28
Shaphan read it before the *k*.
2 Ki 22:10; *2 Chr* 34:18
they took the *k*. and brought him.
2 Ki 25:6; *Jer* 52:9
they dwelt with the *k*. *1 Chr* 4:23
Shemaiah wrote them before *k*. 24:6
worshipped the Lord and *k*. 29:20
hath made thee *k*. *2 Chr* 2:11; 9:8
so the *k*. hearkened not to. 10:15
for he thought to make him *k*. 11:22
him at the command of the *k*. 24:21
thou made of the *k*.'s counsel ? 25:16
be it known to the *k*. *Ezra* 4:12
13; 5:8
and pray for the life of *k*. and. 6:10
who will not do the law of the *k*. 7:26
who hath put in the *k*.'s heart to. 27
to require of the *k*. a band of. 8:22
was the *k*.'s cupbearer. *Neh* 1:11
will ye rebel against the *k*.? 2:19
mayest be their *k*. according to. 6:6
to preach, saying, There is a *k*. 7
nations was there no *k*. like him, God
made him *k*. over all Israel. 13:26
so I will go in unto the *k*. *Esth* 4:16
whom the *k*. delighteth to. 6:6, 7
as the word went out of the *k*. 7:8
who had spoken good for the *k*. 9
prevail, as a *k*. ready to. *Job* 15:24
bring him to the *k*. of terrors. 18:14
I sat chief, and dwelt as a *k*. in. 29:25
is it fit to say to the *k*., Thou ? 34:18
he is a *k*. over all children. 41:34
I set my *k*. upon my holy. *Ps* 2:6
hearken to my cry, my *K*. 5:2; 84:3
the Lord is *K*. for ever. 10:16; 29:10
deliverance giveth he to his *k*. 18:50
let the *k*. hear us when we call. 20:9
k. shall joy in thy strength. 21:1
for the *k*. trusteth in the Lord. 7
the *k*. of glory shall come. 24:7, 9
K. of glory ? the Lord strong. 8
the Lord of hosts, he is the *K*. 10
no *k*. saved by the multitude. 33:16
art my *K*. O God, command. 44:4
I have made touching the *k*. 45:1
so shall the *k*. greatly desire. 11
she shall be brought to the *k*. 14
sing praises to our *K*. 47:6
God is the *K*. 7
thou wilt prolong the *k*.'s life. 61:6
the *k*. shall rejoice in God. 63:11
the goings of my God, my *K*. 68:24
give the *k*. thy judgements. 72:1
God is my *K*. of old, working. 74:12
Holy One of Israel is our *k*. 89:18
noise before the Lord, the *K*. 98:6
the *k*.'s strength also loveth. 99:4
the *k*. sent and loosed him. 105:20
of Zion be joyful in their *K*. 149:2
of people is the *k*.'s honour. *Pr* 14:28
the *k*.'s favour is toward a wise. 35
and truth preserve the *k*. 20:28
for grace of his lips, the *k*. 22:11

fear thou the Lord, and *k*. *Pr* 24:21
the wicked flee from before the *k*. 25:5
the locusts have no *k*. yet go. 30:27
and a *k*. against whom there is. 31
what can the man do that cometh
  after the *k*.? *Eccl* 2:12
the *k*. himself is served by the. 5:9
where the word of a *k*. is, there. 8:4
O land, when thy *k*. is a child. 10:16
blessed when thy *k*. is the son. 17
curse not the *k*. no, not in thy. 20
the *k*. brought me into. *S of S* 1:4
while the *k*. sitteth at his table. 12
k. Solomon with the crown. 3:11
the *k*. is held in the galleries. 7:5
mine eyes have seen the *K*. *Isa* 6:5
let us set a *k*. in the midst of it. 7:6
curse their *k*. and their God. 8:21
and a fierce *k*. shall rule over. 19:4
according to days of one *k*. 23:15
for Tophet; yea, for the *k*. it. 30:33
behold, a *k*. shall reign in. 32:1
thine eyes shall see the *k*. 33:17
Lord is our *k*., he will save us. 22
your reasons, saith the *k*. of. 41:21
Creator of Israel, your *K*. 43:15
and thou wentest to the *k*. 57:9
the heart of *k*. shall perish. *Jer* 4:9
Lord in Zion ? is not her *k*. in ? 8:19
the true God, an everlasting *k*. 10:10
to the *k*. and queen, Humble. 13:18
a *K*. shall reign and prosper. 23:5
thus saith the Lord, of the *k*. 29:16
for the *k*. is not he that can do. 38:5
hast said to the *k*...to thee. 25
saith the *K*. whose name is the Lord.
  46:18; 48:15; 51:57
why doth their *k*. inherit Gad ? 49:1*
I will destroy from thence the *k*. 38
Lord hath despised the *k*. *Lam* 2:6
the *k*. shall mourn and. *Ezek* 7:27
taken the *k*. and the princes. 17:12
hath taken of the *k*.'s seed and. 13
k. dwelleth that made him *k*. 16
I will bring a *k*. of kings from. 26:7
k. shall be *k*. to them all. 37:22, 24
there is no *k*. asked such. *Dan* 2:10
none that can shew it before *k*. 11
before the *k*. and I will shew the *k*. 24
these men before the *k*. 3:13
is come upon my lord the *k*. 4:24
while the word was in the *k*.'s. 31
and honour the *K*. of heaven. 37
the *k*. saw the part of the hand. 5:5
assembled together to the *k*. 6:6
k. of fierce countenance shall. 8:23
and a mighty *k*. shall stand. 11:3
the *k*. shall do according to his. 36
many days without a *k*. *Hos* 3:4
seek the Lord, and David their *k*. 5
sent to *k*. Jareb. 5:13; 10:6
they made the *k*. glad with. 7:3
in the day of our *k*. princes made. 5
no *k*.; what then should a *k*. do ? 10:3
her *k*. is cut off, as the foam. 7
the Assyrian shall be his *k*. 11:5
I will be thy *k*.; give me a *k*. 13:10
I gave thee a *k*. in mine anger. 11
k. shall go into captivity. *Amos* 1:15
for it is the *k*.'s chapel, the *k*.'s. 7:13
and their *k*. shall pass. *Mi* 2:13
cry ? is there no *k*. in thee ? 4:9
k. shall perish from Gaza. *Zech* 9:5
thy *K*. cometh to thee. 9; *Mat* 21:5
into the hand of his *k*. *Zech* 11:6
shall be *k*. over all the earth. 14:9
even go up to worship the *K*. 16, 17
kingdom likened to a certain *k*.
  Mat 18:23; 22:2
k. came in to see the guests. 22:11
with haste to the *k*. *Mark* 6:25
what *k*. going to war against another
  k.? *Luke* 14:31
K. that cometh in name of. 19:38
he himself is Christ, a *K*. 23:2
to make him a *k*. *John* 6:15
thy *K*. cometh. 12:15
to him, Art thou a *k*. then ? 18:37
maketh himself a *k*. speaketh. 19:12
saith to the Jews, Behold your *K*. 14
crucify your *K*.? have no *k*. but. 15
till another *k*. arose, who. *Acts* 7:18
afterward they desired a *k*. 13:21
that there is another *k*. one. 17:7

the *k*. knoweth of these. *Acts* 26:26
now to the *K*., eternal. *1 Tim* 1:17
who is the *K*. of kings, and. 6:15
and not afraid of the *k*.'s. *Heb* 11:23
not fearing the wrath of the *k*. 27
to the *k*. as supreme. *1 Pet* 2:13
fear God, honour the *k*. 17
they had a *k*. over them. *Rev* 9:11
just are thy ways, thou *K*. 15:3
of lords, *K*. of kings. 17:14; 19:16
see **David, great, house, Jews**

king *of the Amorites, see* **Sihon**

king *of Assyria*
Pul the *k*. of A. came. *2 Ki* 15:19
exacted money to give *k*. of A. 20
from house of Lord to *k*. of A. 16:18
Hoshea *k*. of A. took Samaria. 17:6
k. of A. did carry away Israel. 18:11
thus saith great king the *k*. of A. 19
land out of hand of *k*. of A. 19:32
saith Lord concerning *k*. of A. 19:32
  Isa 37:33
turned heart of *k*. of A. to. *Ezra* 6:22
bring upon thee the *k*. of A. *Isa* 7:17
shave by *k*. of A. the head and. 20
k. of A. hath devoured. *Jer* 50:17
will punish Babylon as I punished *k*.
  of A. 18
shepherds slumber, O *k*. of A.
  Nah 3:18

see **Bashan, Babylon**

king *of Egypt*
midwives did not as *k*. of E. *Ex* 1:17
sure the *k*. of E. will not let. 3:19
them a charge to the *k*. of E. 6:13
k. of E. came not again any more
  ...pertained to *k*. of E. *2 Ki* 24:7
k. of E. came up. *2 Chr* 12:2
the *k*. of E. put him down. 36:3
k. of E. made Eliakim his brother. 4
so is the *k*. of E. to all that. *Isa* 36:6

see **Pharaoh**

king *of Israel*
after whom is the *k*. of Isr. come ?
  1 Sam 24:14
k. of Isr. is come out to. 26:20
glorious was the *k*. of Isr. to day!
  2 Sam 6:20
thee, go out to *k*. of Isr. *1 Ki* 20:31
not, save only with *k*. of Isr. 22:31
  2 Chr 18:30
they said, Surely it is *k*. of Isr.
  1 Ki 22:32; *2 Chr* 18:31
shew me which of us is for *k*. of Isr.?
  2 Ki 6:11
out of the hand of *k*. of Isr. 16:7
that it was not *k*. of. *2 Chr* 18:32
son of David *k*. of Isr. did build. 35:3
  Ezra 5:11
not Solomon *k*. of Isr. sin? *Neh* 13:26
saith the Lord, the *k*. of Isr. *Isa* 44:6
the *k*. of Isr. be cut off. *Hos* 10:15
k. of Isr. is in the midst. *Zeph* 3:15
if he be *k*. of Isr. let him descend.
  Mat 27:42; *Mark* 15:32
thou art the *k*. of Isr. *John* 1:49
blessed is the *k*. of Isr. 12:13

king *of Judah*
being then *k*. of J. *2 Ki* 8:16
to *k*. of J. which sent you to. 22:18
as for *k*. of J. who sent. *2 Chr* 34:26
to do with thee, thou *k*. of J.? 35:21
hear the word of the Lord O *k*. of J.
  Jer 34:4
thus shall ye say to *k*. of J. 37:7

king *of Moab*
Balak *k*. of M. brought. *Num* 23:7
the *k*. of M. warred. *Josh* 24:9
Israel served the *k*. of M. *Judg* 3:14
like manner sent to *k*. of M. 11:17
better than Balak *k*. of M.? 25
into hand of *k*. of M. *1 Sam* 12:9
father and mother to *k*. of M. 22:4
and Mesha *k*. of M. *2 Ki* 3:4
k. of M. rebelled against Israel. 5, 7
when the *k*. of M. saw battle. 26
and yokes to the *k*. of M. *Jer* 27:3

O king
Abner said, O *k*. I. *1 Sam* 17:55
therefore, O *k*. come down. 23:20

lord, O *k*. *1 Sam* 26:17; *2 Sam* 14:9
  22; 16:4; 19:26; *1 Ki* 1:13, 20, 24
  20:4; *2 Ki* 6:12, 26; 8:5
Tekoah said, Help, O *k*. *2 Sam* 14:4
I will be thy servant, O *k*. 15:34
O *k*. let not the army. *2 Chr* 25:7
extol thee, my God, O *k*. *Ps* 145:1
would not fear thee, O *k*.? *Jer* 10:7
O *k*. live for ever. *Dan* 2:4; 3:9
  5:10; 6:21
as for thee, O *k*. 2:29
thou O *k*. sawest an image. 31
thou O *k*. art a king of kings, for. 37
O *k*. hast made a decree. 3:10
deliver us out of thy hand, O *k*. 17
be it known to thee, O *k*. 18
true, O *k*. 24
it is thou, O *k*. 4:22
O *k*. let my counsel be. 27
O *k*. Nebuchadnezzar, to thee it. 31
O thou *k*., the most high God. 5:18
a petition save of thee, O *k*. 6:7
now, O *k*. establish the decree. 8
regardeth not thee, O *k*. 13
know, O *k*. 15
also before thee, O *k*. have I. 22
at midday, O *k*. I saw. *Acts* 26:13
O *k*. I was not disobedient. 19

king *of Persia*
as Cyrus, *k*. of P. hath. *Ezra* 4:3
till the reign of Darius *k*. of P. 5
Bishlam wrote unto Artaxerxes *k*. of
  P. 7; 6:14
mercy in sight of the *k*. of P. 9:9

see **Cyrus**

king *of Syria*
Ben-hadad *k*. of S. *1 Ki* 20:20
k. of S. will come up against. 22
captain of host of *k*. of S. *2 Ki* 5:1
k. of S. was sick. 8:7
k. of S. hath sent me to thee. 9
the *k*. of S. oppressed them. 13:4
k. of S. had destroyed them. 7
out of the hand of the *k*. of S. 16:7
hast relied on *k*. of S. the host of the
  k. of S. is escaped. *2 Chr* 16:7

see **Ben-hadad, Hazael, Rezin**

king *of Tyre*
Hiram *k*. of T. sent messengers to.
  2 Sam 5:11; *1 Chr* 14:1
the *k*. of T. sent servants. *1 Ki* 5:1
Hiram the *k*. of T. had. 9:11
sent to Huram the *k*. of T. *2 Chr* 2:3
Huram the *k*. of T. answered. 11

kingdom
ye shall be to me a *k*. *Ex* 19:6
Gad, Reuben, and Manasseh the *k*.
  of Sihon and the *k*. of. *Num* 32:33
  Deut 3:13; *Josh* 13:12, 21, 27, 30
took the *k*. of Og in. *Deut* 3:4
matter of *k*. he told. *1 Sam* 10:16
Samuel told the manner of the *k*. 25
renew the *k*. there. 11:14
Saul took *k*. 14:47
rent the *k*. of Israel. 15:28; 28:17
can he have more but the *k*.? 18:8
to translate the *k*. *2 Sam* 3:10
Israel shall restore me the *k*. 16:3
hath delivered the *k*. into hand. 8
thou knowest that the *k*. *1 Ki* 2:15
ask for him the *k*. for he is my. 22
not like made in any *k*. 10:20
  2 Chr 9:19
I will surely rend the *k*. from thee.
  1 Ki 11:11; 31:35
not rend away all *k*. 11:13, 34
to bring *k*. again to Rehoboam.
  12:21; *2 Chr* 11:1
k. return again to house. *1 Ki* 12:26
I rent the *k*. away from the. 14:8
no *k*. where my lord hath not. 18:10
dost thou now govern the *k*.? 21:7
as the *k*. was confirmed. *2 Ki* 14:5
with him, to confirm the *k*. 15:19
and turned the *k*. to David.
  1 Chr 10:14; 12:23
from one *k*. to another people.
  16:20; *Ps* 105:13
earth is thine, thine is the *k*. O Lord.
  1 Chr 29:11; *Ps* 22:28; *Mat* 6:13
think to withstand the *k*. *2 Chr* 13:8
and the *k*. was quiet before. 14:5

k. gave he to Jehoram. *2 Chr* 21:3
Jehoram was risen up to the *k.* 4
no power to keep still the *k.* 22:9
for a sin offering for the *k.* 29:21
no god of any nation or *k.* 32:15
not served thee in their *k. Neh* 9:35
which sat first in the *k. Esth* 1:14
thou art come to the *k.* for. 4:14
given to the half of the *k.* 5:3, 6; 7:2
shall fight, *k.* against *k. Isa* 19:2
Mat 24:7; *Mark* 13:8; *Luke* 21:10
call nobles thereof to *k. Isa* 34:12
the *k.* that will not serve thee. 60:12
Jer 27:8
I speak concerning a *k. Jer* 18:7
concerning a *k.*, to build and to. 9
he hath polluted the *k.* and. *Lam* 2:2
didst prosper into a *k. Ezek* 16:13
that the *k.* might be base. 17:14
shall be there a base *k.* 29:14
heaven hath given thee a *k. Dan* 2:37
shall God of heaven set up a *k.* 44
Most High ruleth in *k.* 4:17, 25, 32
O king, the *k.* is departed. 31
Daniel concerning the *k.* 6:4
take the *k.* and possess the *k.* 7:18
the saints possessed the *k.* 22
whose *k.* is an everlasting *k.* 27
give the honour of the *k.* 11:21
cause to cease the *k.* of. *Hos* 1:4
Lord are upon sinful *k. Amos* 9:8
the *k.* shall be the Lord's. *Ob* 21
k. shall come to daughter. *Mi* 4:8
the gospel of the *k. Mat* 4:23
9:35; 24:14
the children of the *k.* shall. 8:12
k. divided against itself is brought.
12:25; *Mark* 3:24; *Luke* 11:17
seed are children of *k. Mat* 13:38
shall shine as the sun in the *k.* 43
inherit the *k.* prepared for. 25:34
drink it new in my Father's *k.* 26:29
blessed be the *k.* of our. *Mark* 11:10
pleasure to give you *k. Luke* 12:32
to receive for himself a *k.* 19:12
having received the *k.* 15
I appoint unto you a *k.* as. 22:29
thou restore again the *k.? Acts* 1:6
have delivered up the *k. 1 Cor* 15:24
translated us into the *k. Col* 1:13
we receiving a *k.* that. *Heb* 12:28
heirs of the *k.* which he. *Jas* 2:5
an entrance ministered into everlasting *k. 2 Pet* 1:11
k. and patience of Jesus. *Rev* 1:9
have received no *k.* as yet. 17:12
to agree, and give their *k.* to. 17
see **establish, established,
throne**

kingdom *of God*
but seek ye first the *k. of God.*
Mat 6:33; *Luke* 12:31
k. of God is come unto. *Mat* 12:28
Luke 10:9, 11; 11:20
eye of a needle, than for a rich man
to enter into *k. of God. Mat* 19:24
Mark 10:23; *Luke* 18:24
harlots go into *k. of God. Mat* 21:31
k. of God shall be taken from. 43
preaching *k. of God. Mark* 1:14
Acts 8:12; 20:25; 28:31
k. of God is at hand. *Mark* 1:15
to know the mystery of *k. of God.*
4:11; *Luke* 8:10
so is the *k. of God* as if. *Mark* 4:26
whereunto shall liken *k. of God?*
30; *Luke* 13:18, 20
have seen *k. of God. Mark* 9:1
better to enter into the *k. of God.* 47
children, for of such is *k. of God.*
10:14; *Luke* 18:16
whoso shall not receive *k. of God.*
Mark 10:15; *Luke* 18:17
trust in riches to enter into *k. of God.*
Mark 10:24, 25; *Luke* 18:25
far from the *k. of God. Mark* 12:34
I drink it new in the *k. of God.* 14:25
which waited for the *k. of God.*
15:43; *Luke* 23:51
I must preach *k. of God. Luke* 4:43
poor, for yours is the *k. of God.* 6:20
that is least in the *k. of God.* 7:28
glad tidings of *k. of God.* 8:1
them to preach *k. of God.* 9:2, 60

and spake to them of *k. of God.*
Luke 9:11
of death, till they see *k. of God.* 27
back, is fit for the *k. of God.* 62
the prophets in the *k. of God.* 13:28
sit down in the *k. of God.* 29
shall eat bread in *k. of God.* 14:15
since that time the *k. of God.* 16:16
demanded when *k. of God.* 17:20
the *k. of God* cometh not with. 20
behold the *k. of God* is within. 21
children for *k. of God's* sake. 18:29
that *k. of God* should appear. 19:11
the *k. of God* is nigh at hand. 21:31
it be fulfilled in the *k. of God.* 22:16
I will not drink until *k. of God.* 18
cannot see the *k. of God. John* 3:3
cannot enter into the *k. of God.* 5
things pertaining to *k. of God.*
Acts 1:3; 8:12; 19:8
much tribulation enter into *k. of God.*
14:22
and testified *k. of God.* 28:23
k. of God is not meat. *Rom* 14:17
k. of God is not in word. *1 Cor* 4:20
shall not inherit the *k. of God.* 6:9
nor extortioners inherit *k. of God.*
10; *Gal* 5:21; *Eph* 5:5
cannot inherit *k. of God. 1 Cor* 15:50
workers unto the *k. of God. Col* 4:11
worthy of the *k. of God. 2 Thes* 1:5
come the *k. of our God. Rev* 12:10

kingdom *of heaven*
repent, for *k. of h.* is at hand.
Mat 3:2; 4:17; 10:7
in spirit, their's is *k. of h.* 5:3, 10
least in *k. of h.* great in *k. of h.* 19
no case enter into *k. of h.* 20; 18:3
Lord, shall enter into *k. of h.* 7:21
with Abraham in *k. of h.* 8:11
in *k. of h.* is greater than. 11:11
k. of h. suffereth violence, violent. 12
know mysteries of the *k. of h.* 13:11
the *k. of h.* is like. 24, 31, 33, 44, 45
47, 52; 18:23; 20:1; 22:2; 25:1, 14
to thee the keys of *k. of h.* 16:19
is the greatest in *k. of h.?* 18:1, 4
for ye shut up the *k. of h.* 23:13

his **kingdom**
the beginning of *his k. Gen* 10:10
his k. shall be exalted. *Num* 24:7
on the throne of *his k. Deut* 17:18
may prolong his days in *his k.* 20
he had exalted *his k. 2 Sam* 5:12
with him in *his k. 1 Chr* 11:10
for *his k.* was lifted up on high. 14:2
strengthened in *his k. 2 Chr* 1:1
to build a house for *his k.* 2:1, 12
again to Jerusalem into *his k.* 33:13
his k. ruleth over all. *Ps* 103:19
glorious majesty of *his k.* 145:12
that is born in his *k. Eccl* 4:14
upon *his k.* to order and. *Isa* 9:7
his k. is an everlasting. *Dan* 4:3
his k. from generation to generation.
34; 6:26; 7:14
his k. shall be broken and. 11:4
south shall come into *his k.* 9
how shall *his k.* stand? *Mat* 12:26
Luke 11:18
gather out of *his k.* all. *Mat* 13:41
Son of man coming in *his k.* 16:28
of *his k.* there shall be. *Luke* 1:33
hath called you to *his k. 1 Thes* 2:12
at his appearing and *his k. 2 Tim* 4:1
and *his k.* was full of. *Rev* 16:10

my **kingdom**
brought on me and *my k. Gen* 20:9
I and *my k.* are guiltless. *2 Sam* 3:28
settle him in *my k.* for. *1 Chr* 17:14
glory of *my k.* in my *k. Dan* 4:36
in every dominion of *my k.* 6:26
it to the half of *my k. Mark* 6:23
eat and drink at my table in *my k.*
Luke 22:30
my k. is not of this world, if *my k.*
were, but now *my k. John* 18:36

thy **kingdom**
but now *thy k.* shall. *1 Sam* 13:14
sceptre of *thy k.* a right sceptre.
Ps 45:6; *Heb* 1:8
speak of glory of *thy k. Ps* 145:11
thy k. is an everlasting kingdom. 13

thy k. shall be sure to. *Dan* 4:26
there is a man in *thy k.* 5:11
God numbered *thy k.* 26
thy k. is divided. 28
thy k. come, thy will be done.
Mat 6:10; *Luke* 11:2
on the left in *thy k. Mat* 20:21
thou comest to *thy k. Luke* 23:42

kingdoms
Lord do to all the *k. Deut* 3:21
be removed into all the *k.* of. 28:25
the head of all those *k. Josh* 11:10
you out of hand of all *k. 1 Sam* 10:18
reigned over all *k.* from. *1 Ki* 4:21
the God of all the *k.* of. *2 Ki* 19:15
all the *k.* may know. 19; *Isa* 37:20
went over all the *k. 1 Chr* 29:30
know the service of the *k. 2 Chr* 12:8
fear fell upon all the *k.* 17:10; 20:29
thou rulest over all the *k.* of. 20:6
all *k.* hath the Lord. 36:23; *Ezra* 1:2
thou gavest them *k.* and. *Neh* 9:22
the heathen raged, the *k. Ps* 46:6
sing unto God, ye *k.* of the. 68:32
thy wrath on the *k.* that have. 79:6
k. are gathered to serve. 102:22
smote all the *k.* of Canaan. 135:11
my hand hath found the *k. Isa* 10:10
the noise of the *k.* of nations. 13:4
Babylon the glory of *k.* 19; 47:5
man that did shake *k.?* 14:16
he shook the *k.* 23:11
God of all *k.* 37:16
and over the *k.* I have. *Jer* 1:10
and in all their *k.* none like. 10:7*
to be removed into all *k.* 15:4; 24:9
34:17
all the *k.* of the world shall. 25:26
prophesied against great *k.* 28:8
them a terror to all *k.* 29:18
all the *k.* fought against. 34:1
concerning Kedar and the *k.* 49:28
with thee will I destroy *k.* 51:20
call together against her the *k.* 27
be the basest of the *k. Ezek* 29:15
neither be divided into two *k.* 37:22
consume all these *k. Dan* 2:44
shall be diverse from all *k.* 7:23
four *k.* shall stand up out of. 8:22
better than these *k.? Amos* 6:2
and I will shew the *k.* thy. *Nah* 3:5
I may assemble the *k.* to. *Zeph* 3:8
throne of *k.* and I will destroy the
strength of the *k.* of. *Hag* 2:22
shewed him all the *k.* of world.
Mat 4:8; *Luke* 4:5
through faith subdued *k. Heb* 11:33
k. of this world become *k. Rev* 11:15

kingly
he was deposed from his *k.* throne.
Dan 5:20

kings
k. shall come out of thee. *Gen* 17:6
16; 35:11
these are the *k.* that reigned. 36:31
slew the *k.* of Midian. *Num* 31:8
hath done to these two *k. Deut* 3:21
he shall deliver their *k.* into. 7:24
five *k.* of Amorites. *Josh* 10:5
these five *k.* fled. 16
bring out those five *k.* 22
put your feet on necks of these *k.* 24
Joshua smote all their *k.* 40; 11:17
all these *k.* thirty and one. 12:24
seventy *k.* having their thumbs cut
off. *Judg* 1:7
hear, O ye *k.* 5:3
the *k.* came and fought. 19
time when *k.* go forth to. *2 Sam* 11:1
not be any among the *k. 1 Ki* 3:13
10:23; *2 Chr* 1:12; 9:22
Solomon over all the *k.* on. *1 Ki* 4:24
Ben-hadad and thirty-two *k.* 20:1
these three *k.* together. *2 Ki* 3:10
this is blood, the *k.* are surely. 23
hired against us the *k.* of the. 7:6
behold, two *k.* stood not before. 10:4
he reproved *k.* for them. *1 Chr* 16:21
Ps 105:14
k. sought the presence of. *2 Chr* 9:23
but not in the sepulchres of the *k.*
21:20; 21:25
burial which belonged to *k.* 26:23

the revenue of the *k.*   *Ezra* 4:13
this city hath been hurtful to *k.* 15
made insurrection against *k.*   19
there have been mighty *k.* over. 20
God destroy *k.* that shall.   6:12
Artaxerxes, king of *k.* to Ezra. 7:12
k. and priests have been delivered.
  9:7; *Neh* 9:24
little to us and our *k.*   *Neh* 9:32
nor have our *k.* or princes.   34
had I been at rest with *k.* *Job* 3:14
he looseth the bond of *k.*   12:18
with *k.* are they on the throne. 36:7
k. of the earth set themselves.
  Ps 2:2; *Acts* 4:26
be wise, therefore, O ye *k. Ps* 2:10
k.' daughters among thy.   45:9
lo, the *k.* were assembled.   48:4
k. of armies did flee apace. 68:12
when the Almighty scattered *k.* 14
shall *k.* bring presents to thee. 29
yea, all *k.* shall fall down.   72:11
he is terrible to the *k.* of.   76:12
make him higher than the *k.* 89:27
the *k.* of the earth shall fear. 102:15
he shall strike through *k.* in. 110:5
of thy testimonies before *k.* 119:46
nations, and slew mighty *k.* 135:10
which smote great *k.*   136:17, 18
all *k.* of the earth.   138:4; 148:11
that giveth salvation to *k.* 144:10
to bind their *k.* with chains. 149:8
by me *k.* reign, and princes. *Pr* 8:15
abomination for *k.* to commit. 16:12
righteous lips are the delight of *k.* 13
the diligent in business shall stand
  before *k.*   22:29
honour of *k.* to search a.   25:2
heart of *k.* is unsearchable.   3
the spider is in *k.*' palaces. 30:28
to that which destroyeth *k.* 31:3
it is not for *k.* O Lemuel, to drink. 4
the peculiar treasure of *k. Eccl* 2:8
be forsaken of both her *k. Isa* 7:16
my princes altogether *k.?*   10:8
raised all the *k.* of the nations. 14:9
all the *k.* of the nations lie in. 18
I am the son of ancient *k.*   19:11
Lord shall punish the *k.* of. 24:21
and made him ruler over *k.* 41:2
I will loose the loins of *k.* to. 45:1
k. shall see and arise, princes. 49:7
k. shall be thy nursing fathers. 23
the *k.* shall shut their mouths. 52:15
and *k.* to the brightness of. 60:3
their *k.* shall minister to thee. 10
thy gates open, that their *k.* 11
also suck the breast of *k.*   16
and all *k.* shall see thy glory. 62:2
they, their *k.* and princes. *Jer* 2:26
even *k.* that sit upon David's. 13:13
into the gates of this city, *k.* 17:25
k. sitting upon the throne of. 22:4
I made Judah and *k.* drink. 25:18
k. of Tyrus.   22
all the *k.* of Arabia.   24
the *k.* of Zimri.   25
all the *k.* of the north.   26
me to anger, they, their *k.* 32:32
burnings of former *k.* before. 34:5
as we, our *k.* and princes to. 44:17
your *k.* and princes burnt.   21
I will punish their *k.* and. 46:25
k. shall go into captivity.   49:3
many *k.* shall be raised up. 50:41
the spirit of *k.* of the Medes. 51:11
k. of the earth would not. *Lam* 4:12
their *k.* shall be sore afraid.
  Ezek 27:35; 32:10
I will lay thee before *k.* to. 28:17
there is Edom, her *k.* and. 32:29
their *k.* shall no more defile. 43:7
k. and setteth up *k.* *Dan* 2:21
these *k.* shall God set up a.   44
that your God is a Lord of *k.* 47
the four beasts are four *k.* 7:17
ten *k.*; he shall subdue three *k.* 24
spake in thy name to our *k.* 9:6
to our *k.* and princes belongs. 8
I remained there with the *k.* 10:13
stand up three *k.*   11:2
both these *k.*' hearts.   27
hot as an oven, all their *k. Hos* 7:7
they have set up *k.* but not. 8:4

---

they shall scoff at *k.* *Hab* 1:10
brought before governors and *k.* for
  my sake. *Mat* 10:18; *Mark* 13:9
  Luke 21:12
clothing are in *k.*' houses. *Mat* 11:8
of whom do *k.* of the earth ? 17:25
prophets and *k.* have. *Luke* 10:24
of Gentiles exercise.   22:25
a chosen vessel to bear my name before *k.*   *Acts* 9:15
ye have reigned as *k.* *1 Cor* 4:8
prayers be made for *k.* *1 Tim* 2:2
King of *k.*, Lord of lords.   6:15
  Rev 17:14; 19:16
from slaughter of the *k.* *Heb* 7:1
Christ the prince of the *k. Rev* 1:5
hath made us *k.* and priests.
  6*; 5:10*
k. of the earth hid themselves. 6:15
prophesy again before *k.* 10:11
way of the *k.* of east might. 16:12
spirits which go forth to the *k.* 14
whom *k.* of earth committed. 17:2
there are seven *k.*, five are fallen. 10
ten *k.* which receive power as *k.* 12
city which reigneth over *k.* of. 18
k. of earth have committed. 18:3
k. of earth who shall bewail her. 9
ye may eat the flesh of *k.* 19:18
k. of the earth gathered to make. 19
the *k.* of the earth do bring. 21:24

kings *of the Amorites*
two *k.* of Am.   *Deut* 4:47; 31:4
  Josh 2:10; 9:10; 24:12
when all *k.* of Am. heard. *Josh* 5:1
five *k.* of Am. gathered.   10:5, 6
see book, great

kings *of Israel*
book of the Chronicles of the *k.* of Isr.
 1 Ki 14:19; 15:31; 16:5, 14, 20
 27; 22:39; *2 Ki* 1:18; 10:34; 13:8
 12; 14:15, 28; 15:11, 15, 21, 26, 31
more than all *k.* of Isr. *1 Ki* 16:33
we heard that *k.* of Isr. are. 20:31
Jehoram walked in way of *k.* of Isr.
  2 Ki 8:18
Joash was buried with the *k.* of Isr.
  13:13; 14:16
Jeroboam slept with his fathers *k.* of
  Isr.   14:29
Ahaz walked in the way of the *k.* of
  Isr.   16:3
Hoshea did evil, but not as the *k.* of
  Isr.   17:2
Israel walked in the statutes of the
  k. of Isr.   8
away houses the *k.* of Isr. 23:19
passover in days of the *k.* of Isr. 22
written in book of *k.* of Isr. *1 Chr* 9:1
 2 Chr 16:11; 25:26; 27:7; 28:26
  32:32; 33:18
is mentioned in the book of the *k.* of
  Isr.   *2 Chr* 20:34; 35:27; 36:8
Ahaz was not brought into sepulchres
  of *k.* of Isr.   28:27
houses of Achzib shall be a lie to *k.* of
  Isr.   *Mi* 1:14

kings *of Judah*
Ziklag pertained to the *k.* of J.
  1 Sam 27:6
acts of Rehoboam in the Chronicles
 of the *k.* of J. *1 Ki* 14:29; 15:7, 23
 22:45; *2 Ki* 8:23; 15:6, 36; 16:19
 20:20; 21:17, 25; 23:28; 24:5
hallowed things the *k.* of J. had dedicated.   *2 Ki* 12:18, 19
written in the Chronicles of the *k.* of
 J.   14:18; *2 Chr* 25:26; 28:26
  32:32; 35:27; 36:8
like him of all the *k.* of J. *2 Ki* 18:5
priests *k.* of J. ordained.   23:5
took horses *k.* of J. had given. 11
beat down altars which *k.* of J. 12
passover in all days of *k.* of J. 22
floor houses *k.* of J. *2 Chr* 34:11
Isaiah in days of the *k.* of J. *Isa* 1:1
iron pillar against *k.* of J. *Jer* 1:18
bring out bones of the *k.* of J. 8:1
in gate, whereby *k.* of J.   17:19
word of Lord ye *k.* of J. 20; 19:3
burnt incense to gods *k.* of J. 19:4
houses of the *k.* of J. shall.   13
treasures of *k.* of J. will.   20:5

---

concerning houses of *k.* of J. *Jer* 33:4
wickedness of *k.* of J.?   44:9
word of Lord that came to Hosea in
 days of *k.* of J. *Hos* 1:1; *Mi* 1:1
  see kings *of Israel*

kinsfoik
my *k.* have failed and.   *Job* 19:14
Jesus among their *k.* *Luke* 2:44

kinsfoiks
left none of Baasha's *k.* *1 Ki* 16:11
Jehu slew Ahab's *k.* *2 Ki* 10:11*
shall be betrayed by *k. Luke* 21:16

kinsman
if the man have no *k.* to. *Num* 5:8
give his inheritance to his *k.* 27:11
Naomi had a *k.* his name. *Ruth* 2:1
thou art a near *k.*   3:9
near *k.*: a *k.* nearer than I. 12
to thee the part of a *k.* well; if not, I
 will do the part of a *k.* to. thee 13
behold the *k.* of whom Boaz. 4:1
the *k.* said, I cannot redeem it. 6
the *k.* said unto Boaz, Buy it. 8
not left thee this day without a *k.* 14
being his *k.* whose ear. *John* 18:26
salute Herodion my *k.* *Rom* 16:11

kinsmen
of kin one of our next *k. Ruth* 2:20
my lovers and *k.* stood. *Ps* 38:11
friends, brethren, nor *k. Luke* 14:12
called together his *k.* *Acts* 10:24
accursed, for my *k.* according to the.
  Rom 9:3
salute my *k.*   16:7
my *k.* salute you.   21

kinswoman
is my father's near *k.* *Lev* 18:12
she is thy mother's near *k.* 13
call understanding thy *k.* *Pr* 7:4

kinswomen
they are her near *k.* *Lev* 18:17

Kir
the people captive to K. *2 Ki* 16:9
in the night K. of Moab. *Isa* 15:1
Elam bare the quiver, K.   22:6
go into captivity to K. *Amos* 1:5
brought the Assyrians from K.? 9:7

Kir-haraseth
only in K. left they. *2 Ki* 3:25
for the foundations of K. *Isa* 16:7
inward parts shall sound for K. 11

Kiriathaim
smote Emims in Shavah K. *Gen* 14:5
saith Lord, K. is confounded and.
  Jer 48:1
judgement is come upon K. and. 23

Kirjath-arba
Sarah died in K. the. *Gen* 23:2
 Josh 14:15; 20:7; *Judg* 1:10

Kirjath-jearim
K. a city of the Hivites. *Josh* 9:17
was to Baalah, which is K. 15:9, 60
K. a city of Judah. 18:14; *1 Chr* 13:6
the men of K. came. *1 Sam* 7:1
ark of God from K. *1 Chr* 13:5
brought the ark from K. *2 Chr* 1:4

Kish
a man of Benjamin whose name was
 K.   *1 Sam* 9:1
asses of K. Saul's father. 3; 14:51
that is come to the son of K.? 10:11
and Saul the son of K. was. 21
Saul in sepulchre of K. *2 Sam* 21:14
K. the son of Gibeon. *1 Chr* 8:30
Ner begat K.   33
K. son of Mahli.   23:21
K. son of Abdi. *2 Chr* 29:12
of Shimei, son of K. *Esth* 2:5
them Saul the son of K. *Acts* 13:21

kiss, -es
*In the Bible times and countries
the kiss was given as a sign.* [1] *Of
reverence and subjection to a
superior,* 1 Sam 10:1. [2] *Of love
and affection,* Gen 27:26, 27;
1 Sam 20:41. [3] *Of idolatrous
reverence and adoration,* Hos 13:2.
the *k.* of an enemy are. *Pr* 27:6
k. me with the *k.* of. *S of S* 1:2
thou gavest me no *k.* *Luke* 7:45

Son of man with a *k*.? *Luke* 22:43
another with an holy *k*. *Rom* 16:16
greet with an holy *k*. *1 Cor* 16:20
                        2 Cor 13:12
brethren with an holy *k*. *1 Thes* 5:26
one another with a *k*. *1 Pet* 5:14

kiss, *verb*
come near now and *k*. *Gen* 27:26
not suffered me to *k*. my sons. 31:28
Amasa by beard to *k*. *2 Sam* 20:9
let me *k*. my father. *1 Ki* 19:20
k. the Son, lest he be angry. *Ps* 2:12
every man shall *k*. his. *Pr* 24:26
him *k*. me with kisses. *S of S* 1:2
I would *k*. thee, yea I should. 8:1
let men that sacrifice *k*. *Hos* 13:2
saying, Whomsoever I *k*. the same.
                Mat 26:48; *Mark* 14:44
not ceased to *k*. my feet. *Luke* 7:45
drew near to Jesus to *k*. him. 22:47

kissed
Jacob came near and *k*. *Gen* 27:27
Jacob *k*. Rachel and wept. 29:11
Laban *k*. Jacob. 13
Laban *k*. his sons and his. 31:55
Esau *k*. Jacob. 33:4
Joseph *k*. all his brethren. 45:15
Jacob *k*. and embraced. 48:10
on his father's face and *k*. him. 50:1
Moses in the mount and *k*. *Ex* 4:27
his father in law and *k*. him. 18:7
k. her daughters in law. *Ruth* 1:9
Orpah *k*. her mother in law. 14
poured oil and *k*. Saul. *1 Sam* 10:1
Jonathan and David *k*. one. 20:41
the king *k*. Absalom. *2 Sam* 14:33
Absalom *k*. any man that. 15:5
the king *k*. Barzillai, and. 19:39
which hath not *k*. him. *1 Ki* 19:18
mouth hath *k*. my hand. *Job* 31:27
righteousness and peace *k*. *Ps* 85:10
she caught him and *k*. him. *Pr* 7:13
hail, Master, and *k*. him. *Mat* 26:49
                        Mark 14:45
Mary *k*. his feet and. *Luke* 7:38
fell on his neck and *k*. him. 15:20
Paul's neck and *k*. him. *Acts* 20:37

kite
the *k*. after his kind unclean.
        Lev 11:14*; *Deut* 14:13*

Kittim
sons of Javan, Tarshish, K.
        Gen 10:4; *1 Chr* 1:7
see **Chittim**

knead
k. it, and make cakes. *Gen* 18:6
women *k*. their dough. *Jer* 7:18

kneaded
Endor took flour and *k*. *1 Sam* 28:24
Tamar took flour and *k*. *2 Sam* 13:8
the baker *k*. the dough. *Hos* 7:4

kneadingtroughs
frogs shall come into thy *k*. *Ex* 8:3
their *k*. being bound up in. 12:34

knee
before him, bow the *k*. *Gen* 41:43
every *k*. shall bow, every tongue.
        Isa 45:23; *Rom* 14:11; *Phil* 2:10
they bowed the *k*. before him.
        Mat 27:29*; *Mark* 15:19
who have not bowed the *k*. *Rom* 11:4

kneel
he made his camels *k*. *Gen* 24:11
let us *k*. before the Lord. *Ps* 95:6

kneeled
Solomon *k*. down on. *2 Chr* 6:13
Daniel *k*. three times. *Dan* 6:10
and Jesus *k*. down and. *Luke* 22:41
Stephen *k*. and cried with. *Acts* 7:60
Peter *k*. and prayed. 9:40
Paul *k*. and prayed. 20:36
and we *k*. down on the shore. 21:5

kneeling
Solomon rose up from *k*. *1 Ki* 8:54
a man *k*. to him saying. *Mat* 17:14
                        Mark 10:17
there came a leper *k*. *Mark* 1:40

knees
Bilhah shall bear on my *k*. *Gen* 30:3
out from between his *k*. 48:12

brought up on Joseph's *k*. *Gen* 50:23
shall smite thee in the *k*. *Deut* 28:35
on his *k*. to drink. *Judg* 7:5, 6
made Samson sleep on her *k*. 16:19
from kneeling on his *k*. *1 Ki* 8:54
put his face between his *k*. 18:42
k. which have not bowed. 19:18
third captain fell on his *k*. *2 Ki* 1:13
sat on his mother's *k*. till noon. 4:20
kneeled down on his *k*. *2 Chr* 6:13
I fell on my *k*. and spread. *Ezra* 9:5
why did the *k*. prevent? *Job* 3:12
strengthened the feeble *k*. 4:4
my *k*. are weak through. *Ps* 109:24
confirm the feeble *k*. *Isa* 35:3
and be dandled upon her *k*. 66:12
all *k*. shall be weak as water.
                        Ezek 7:17; 21:7
the waters were to the *k*. 47:4
his *k*. smote one against. *Dan* 5:6
kneeled on his *k*. three times. 6:10
an hand set me upon my *k*. 10:10
she is empty, and the *k*. *Nah* 2:10
bowing their *k*. worshipped him.
                        Mark 15:19
Simon Peter fell down at Jesus' *k*.
                        Luke 5:8
for this cause I bow my *k*. *Eph* 3:14
hang down and feeble *k*. *Heb* 12:12

knew
Adam *k*. Eve his wife. *Gen* 4:1, 25
Cain *k*. his wife. 17
Judah *k*. her no more. 38:26
Jephthah's daughter *k*. no man.
                        Judg 11:39
they *k*. her and abused her. 19:25
Elkanah *k*. Hannah his. *1 Sam* 1:19
but the king *k*. her not. *1 Ki* 1:4
Joseph *k*. her not, till. *Mat* 1:25

knew
Adam and Eve *k*. that. *Gen* 3:7
Noah *k*. what his younger. 9:24
Jacob *k*. it, and said, It is. 37:33
Onan *k*. the seed should not. 38:9
Joseph saw and *k*. his. 42:7, 8
and *k*. the knowledge. *Num* 24:16
from the day I *k*. you. *Deut* 9:24
a prophet whom the Lord *k*. 34:10
such as before *k*. nothing. *Judg* 3:2
Manoah *k*. that he was an. 13:21
they *k*. the voice of the. 18:3
all Israel *k*. that Samuel. *1 Sam* 3:20
Saul *k*. that the Lord was. 18:28
for if I *k*. then would I not. 20:9
Jonathan *k*. that it was. 33
only David and Jonathan *k*. 39
for the servant *k*. nothing of. 22:15
slay the priests, because they *k*. 17
David said to Abiathar, I *k*. it. 22
David *k*. that Saul secretly. 23:9
Saul *k*. David's voice, and. 26:17
he *k*. that valiant men. *2 Sam* 11:16
Obadiah *k*. Elijah, and. *1 Ki* 18:7
then Manasseh *k*. the. *2 Chr* 33:13
manner to all that *k*. law. *Esth* 1:13
O that I *k*. where I might! *Job* 23:3
because I *k*. that thou. *Isa* 48:4
shouldest say, Behold, I *k*. them. 7
I *k*. that thou wouldest deal very. 8
I formed thee, I *k*. thee. *Jer* 1:5
then I *k*. this was the word of. 32:8
Gedaliah, and no man *k*. it. 41:4
men which *k*. their wives. 44:15
I *k*. that they were the cherubims.
                        Ezek 10:20
he *k*. their desolate palaces. 19:7
he *k*. that the most high. *Dan* 5:21
when Daniel *k*. the writing was. 6:10
I *k*. thou art a gracious. *Jonah* 4:2
k. that it was the word of. *Zech* 11:11
profess I never *k*. you. *Mat* 7:23
when Jesus *k*. he withdrew. 12:15
Jesus *k*. their thoughts. 25; *Luke* 6:8
I *k*. thee that thou art an. *Mat* 25:24
he *k*. that for envy they. 27:18
speak because they *k*. *Mark* 1:34
ship, straightway they *k*. him. 6:54
k. he had spoken the parable. 12:12
the devils, for they *k*. *Luke* 4:41
servant which *k*. his lord's. 12:47
nor *k*. they the things that. 18:34
were opened, and they *k*. 24:31
but the servants *k*. *John* 2:9

not commit himself unto them, because he *k*. *John* 2:24
and testify, for he *k*. what was. 25
the father *k*. it was at the. 4:53
Jesus *k*. he had been long in. 5:6
for he himself *k*. what he. 6:6
Jesus *k*. that his disciples. 61
Jesus *k*. from the beginning who. 64
I *k*. that thou hearest me. 11:42
that if any man *k*. where he. 57
when Jesus *k*. that his hour. 13:1
for he *k*. who should betray him. 11
no man at the table *k*. for what. 28
Jesus *k*. that they were. 16:19
Judas which betrayed him *k*. 18:2
k. that it was he that *Acts* 3:10
which when the brethren *k*. 9:30
when Rhoda *k*. Peter's voice. 12:14
they *k*. all that his father was. 16:3
they *k*. that he was a Jew. 19:34
k. that he was a Roman. 22:29
which *k*. me from the beginning. 26:5
k. the island was called Melita. 28:1
that when they *k*. God. *Rom* 1:21
the princes of this world *k*. *1 Cor* 2:8
to be sin, who *k*. no sin. *2 Cor* 5:21
I *k*. a man in Christ. 12:2, 3
in you since ye *k*. grace of. *Col* 1:6
you *k*. what great conflict I. 2:1
though ye once *k*. this. *Jude* 5
written that no man *k*. *Rev* 19:12

knew *not*
place, and I *k*. it not. *Gen* 28:16
Jacob *k*. not that Rachel had. 31:32
Judah *k*. not she was his. 38:16
he *k*. not aught he had. 39:6
but they *k*. not him. 42:8
king which *k*. not Joseph. *Ex* 1:8
I *k*. not that thou stoodest.
                        Num 22:34
which thy fathers *k*. not. *Deut* 8:16
thy fathers *k*. not. 29:26; 32:17
a generation which *k*. not the Lord.
                        Judg 2:10
Manoah *k*. not that he was. 13:16
his father *k*. not that it was. 14:4
Benjamin *k*. not that evil. 20:34
of Eli *k*. not the Lord. *1 Sam* 2:12
people *k*. not that Jonathan. 14:3
the lad *k*. not any thing. 20:39
sent messengers after Abner, but
David *k*. it not. *2 Sam* 3:26
k. ye *not* they would shoot? 11:20
simplicity, and *k*. not any. 15:11
I saw a tumult, but I *k*. not. 18:29
a people which I *k*. not shall. 22:44
gathered gourds for they *k*. them
not. *2 Ki* 4:39
the rulers *k*. not whither. *Neh* 2:16
Job's friends *k*. him *not*. *Job* 2:12
the cause which I *k*. not I. 29:16
things which I *k*. not. 42:3
my charge things I *k*. not. *Ps* 35:11
against me, and I *k*. it not. 15
behold, we *k*. it not. *Pr* 24:12
blind by a way they *k*. not. *Isa* 42:16
set him on fire, yet he *k*. not. 25
and nations that *k*. not thee. 55:5
handle the law *k*. me not. *Jer* 2:8
k. not that they had devised. 11:19
other gods whom they *k*. not. 44:3
honour a god whom his fathers *k*.
not. *Dan* 11:38
made princes and I *k*. it not. *Hos* 8:4
but they *k*. not that I healed. 11:3
nations whom they *k*. not. *Zech* 7:14
and they *k*. him not. *Mat* 17:12
k. not till flood came. 24:39
his mother *k*. not of it. *Luke* 12:43
that *k*. not and did commit. 12:48
the world *k*. him not. *John* 1:10
I *k*. him not. 31, 33
governor *k*. not whence it was. 2:9
yet they *k*. not the scriptures. 20:9
k. not that it was Jesus. 14; 21:4
because they *k*. him *not*. *Acts* 13:27
more part *k*. not wherefore. 19:32
when it was day, they *k*. not. 27:39
world by wisdom *k*. not. *1 Cor* 1:21
howbeit then, when ye *k*. not God.
                        Gal 4:8
world knoweth us not, because it *k*.
him *not*. *1 John* 3:1

knewest

manna, which thou *k*. not. *Deut* 8:3
people which thou *k*. not. *Ruth* 2:11
thou *k*. that they dealt. *Neh* 9:10
then thou *k*. my path in. *Ps* 142:3
heardest not, yea, thou *k*. *Isa* 48:8
thy heart, thou *k*. all this. *Dan* 5:22
thou *k*. I reaped where. *Mat* 25:26
          Luke 19:22
thou *k*. not the time of. *Luke* 19:44
if thou *k*. the gift of God. *John* 4:10

knife

Abraham took the *k*. *Gen* 22:6, 10
took a *k*. and laid hold. *Judg* 19:29
put a *k*. to thy throat. *Pr* 23:2
take thee a sharp *k*. *Ezek* 5:1
and smite about it with a *k*. 2

knit

Israel were *k*. together. *Judg* 20:11
soul of Jonathan was *k*. *1 Sam* 18:1
my heart shall be *k*. *1 Chr* 12:17
I saw a sheet *k*. at the. *Acts* 10:11
hearts being *k*. together. *Col* 2:2
body *k*. together increaseth with. 19

knives

make thee sharp *k*. and. *Josh* 5:2
Joshua made him sharp *k*. and. 3
cut themselves with *k*. *2 Ki* 18:28
nine and twenty *k*. Cyrus. *Ezra* 1:9
jaw teeth as *k*. to devour. *Pr* 30:14

knock

k. and it shall be opened. *Mat* 7:7
          Luke 11:9
ye begin to *k*. at door. *Luke* 13:25
stand at the door and *k*. *Rev* 3:20

knocked

and as Peter *k*. at door. *Acts* 12:13

knocketh

of my beloved that *k*. *S of S* 5:2
to him that *k*. shall be opened.
         Mat 7:8; *Luke* 11:10
when he cometh and *k*. *Luke* 12:36

knocking

Peter continued *k*. and. *Acts* 12:16

knop, -s

his *k*. and his flowers. *Ex* 25:31, 34
           36; 37:17
with a *k*. and flower in. 25:33; 37:19
and *k*. branches of the same. 25:36
          37:17, 20, 22
cedar carved with *k*. *1 Ki* 6:18
were *k*. compassing it, *k*. cast. 7:24

know

God doth *k*. that your eyes. *Gen* 3:5
man is become as one of us, to *k*. 22
said to Abram, *K*. thy seed. 15:13
and see, and if not, I will *k*. 18:21
if thou restore her not, *k*. 20:7
make them *k*. the statutes. *Ex* 18:16
hast not let me *k*. whom thou. 33:12
they shall *k*. the land. *Num* 14:31
k. this day and. *Deut* 4:39; 11:2
to prove thee and *k*. what was. 8:2
fathers *k*. he might make thee *k*. 3
proveth you, to *k*. whether ye. 13:3
shall let your children *k*. *Josh* 4:22
and Israel he shall *k*. 22:22
k. whether they would. *Judg* 3:4
city of my people doth *k*. *Ruth* 3:11
she rose up before one could *k*. 14*
sit still, my daughter, till thou *k*. 18
this assembly shall *k*. *1 Sam* 17:47
he saith, Let not Jonathan *k*. 20:3
let no man *k*. any thing of. 21:2
k. and see that there is no. 24:11
therefore *k*. and consider. 25:17
Achish said to David, *k*. 28:1
surely thou shalt *k*. what thy. 2
to *k*. thy going out, to *k*. *2 Sam* 3:25
things to make thy servant *k*. 7:21
to *k*. all things that are in. 14:20
thy servant doth *k*. that I. 19:20
k. every man the plague. *1 Ki* 8:38
          2 Chr 6:29
he shall *k*. that there is. *2 Ki* 5:8
they *k*. that we be hungry. 7:12
k. now that there shall fall. 10:10
Issachar, to *k*. what Israel ought.
          1 Chr 12:32
my son, *k*. thou the God of. 28:9
ought ye not to *k*. that. *2 Chr* 13:5

k. that this city is a. *Ezra* 4:15
all such as *k*. the laws of thy. 7:25
Mordecai walked to *k*. *Esth* 2:11
k. what it was, and why it. 4:5
people *k*. whosoever shall come. 11
shalt *k*. thy tabernacle. *Job* 5:24
shalt *k*. that thy seed shall. 25
hear it, and *k*. thou it for thy. 27
nor shall his place *k*. him. 7:10
but of yesterday, and *k*. 8:9
k. therefore that God exacteth. 11:6
than hell, what canst thou *k*.? 8
to *k*. my transgression. 13:23
k. that God hath overthrown. 19:6
him, and he shall *k*. it. 21:19
sayest, How doth God *k*.? 22:13
do they that *k*. him not see? 24:1
one *k*. them, they are in terrors. 17
let us *k*. among ourselves. 34:4
dost thou *k*. when God ? 37:15
dost thou *k*. the balancings of ? 16
caused the dayspring to *k*. 38:12
that thou shouldest *k*. the paths. 20*
k. the Lord hath set apart. *Ps* 4:3
that *k*. thy name put their. 9:10
lovingkindness to them *k*. 36:10
Lord, make me to *k*. mine end. 39:4
be still, and *k*. that I am God. 46:10
part thou shalt make me to *k*. 51:6
k. that God ruleth in Jacob. 59:13
How doth God *k*.? 73:11
I thought to *k*. this. 16
Babylon to them that *k*. me. 87:4
blessed are they that *k*. the. 89:15
the place thereof shall *k*. it. 103:16
k. my heart, try me, and *k*. 139:23
no man that would *k*. me. 142:4
cause me to *k*. the way wherein. 143:8
k. wisdom and instruction. *Pr* 1:2
attend to *k*. understanding. 4:1
the lips of righteous *k*. what. 10:32
be thou diligent to *k*. the. *Eccl* 1:17
I gave my heart to *k*. 1:17
I applied my heart to *k*. 7:25
when I applied my heart to *k*. 8:16
though a wise man think to *k*. 17
the living *k*. they shall die, but. 5
but *k*. that God will bring thee. 11:9
before the child shall *k*. *Isa* 7:16
and all the people shall *k*. even. 9:9
Egyptians shall *k*. the Lord. 19:21
that they may see and *k*. 41:20
that we may *k*. the latter end. 22
all flesh shall *k*. that I am. 49:26
k. how to speak in season. 50:4
therefore my people shall *k*. 52:6
seek me, and delight to *k*. my. 58:2
thou shalt *k*. that I the Lord. 60:16
k. and see that it is an evil. *Jer* 2:19
see thy way in valley, *k*. what. 23
and *k*. O congregation, what is. 6:18
through deceit they refuse to *k*. 9:6
k. that for thy sake I have. 15:15
to *k*. my hand and my might, and
    they shall *k*. that my name. 16:21
deceitful, who can *k*. it ? 17:9
was not this to *k*. me ? saith. 22:16
give them an heart to *k*. me. 24:7
they shall all *k*. me. 31:34; *Heb* 8:11
go, hide thee, let no man *k*. *Jer* 36:19
he said, Let no man *k*. of. 38:24
and no man shall *k*. it. 40:15
Judah shall *k*. whose words. 44:28
k. that there hath been a prophet.
         Ezek 2:5; 33:33
k. that I the Lord hath spoken. 5:13
k. her abomination. 16:2; 20:4
they shall *k*. my vengeance. 25:14
all that *k*. thee shall be. 28:19
thus shall they *k*. that I am. 34:30
heathen shall *k*. 37:28; 39:23
givest knowledge to them who *k*.
          Dan 2:21
k. that the Most High. 4:25, 32
make me *k*. the interpretation. 7:16
k. the truth of the fourth beast. 19
make thee *k*. what shall be. 8:19
k. therefore and understand. 9:25
people that *k*. their God. 11:32
thou shalt *k*. the Lord. *Hos* 2:20
Israel shall *k*. it. 9:7
and thou shalt *k*. no god. 13:4
prudent, and he shall *k*. them. 14:9
is it not for you to *k*.? *Mi* 3:1

thou shalt *k*. that the Lord sent me.
          Zech 2:11; 4:9
shall *k*. that I have sent. *Mal* 2:4
let not thy left hand *k*. *Mat* 6:3
if ye *k*. how to give good gifts. 7:11
          Luke 11:13
see no man *k*. it. *Mat* 9:30
      Mark 5:43; 7:24; 9:30
it is given unto you to *k*. *Mat* 13:11
       Mark 4:11; *Luke* 8:10
k. that it [desolation] is near.
   Mat 24:33; *Mark* 13:29; *Luke* 21:20
k. this, if the goodman. *Mat* 24:43
          Luke 12:39
k. that this is indeed. *John* 4:42
if any do his will, he shall *k*. 7:17
do the rulers *k*. indeed. 26
and *k*. what he doeth ? 51
sheep follow him, for they *k*. 10:4
I *k*. my sheep. 14
thou shalt *k*. hereafter. 13:7
by this shall all men *k*. ye are. 35
behold, they *k*. what I said. 18:21
not for you to *k*. times. *Acts* 1:7
let all the house of Israel *k*. 2:36
shouldest *k*. his will and see. 22:14
they *k*. I imprisoned them that. 19
life from my youth *k*. all Jews. 26:4
I speak to them that *k*. *Rom* 7:1
but I say, Did not Israel *k*.? 10:19
neither can he *k*. them. *1 Cor* 2:14
nothing as he ought to *k*. 8:2
but I would have you *k*. that. 11:3
to *k*. the love of Christ. *Eph* 3:19
for this cause I sent to *k*. *1 Thes* 3:5
one should *k*. how to possess. 4:4
to *k*. them who labour among. 5:12
them which believe and *k*. *1 Tim* 4:3
this *k*. also that in last. *2 Tim* 3:1
they profess that they *k*. *Tit* 1:16
but wilt thou *k*. O vain ? *Jas* 2:20
let him *k*. he which converteth. 5:20
but what they *k*. naturally. *Jude* 10
all churches shall *k*. that. *Rev* 2:23
I will make them to *k*. that I. 3:9
see **certain, certainly, certainty**

I know

now *I k*. that thou art a. *Gen* 12:11
whereby shall *I k*. that I shall? 15:8
I k. that he will command. 18:19
I k. thou didst this in integrity. 20:6
now *I k*. that thou fearest. 22:12
thereby shall *I k*. that thou. 24:14
I k. it, my son, *I k*. 48:19
Lord said, *I k*. their sorrows. *Ex* 3:7
Aaron thy brother *I k*. he can. 4:14
I k. that ye will not yet fear. 9:30
I k. that the Lord is greater. 18:11
thou hast said, *I k*. thee. 33:12, 17
I k. their imagination. *Deut* 31:21
for *I k*. thy rebellion and thy. 27
I k. that after my death ye will. 29
I k. the Lord hath given. *Josh* 2:9
I k. that thou wilt save. *Judg* 6:37
now *k*. *I* that the Lord will. 17:13
I k. thy pride and. *1 Sam* 17:28
do not *I k*. thou hast chosen ? 20:30
till *I k*. what God will do for. 22:3
I k. well that thou shalt. 24:20
I k. that thou art good in my. 29:9
yea *I k*. it, hold you. *2 Ki* 2:3, 5
I k. that there is no God. 5:15
I k. the evil that thou wilt do. 8:12
I k. thy abode and. 19:27; *Isa* 37:28
I k. that thou triest. *1 Chr* 29:17
I k. that God hath. *2 Chr* 25:16
I k. it is so of a truth, but. *Job* 9:2
I k. that thou canst do every. 42:2
this *I k*. that thou favourest. 41:11
I k. all the fowls of the. 50:11
this *I k*. for God is for me. 56:9
I, O Lord, that thy. 119:75
for *I k*. the Lord is great and. 135:5
I k. the Lord will maintain. 140:12
I k. that there is no good. *Eccl* 3:12

I k. that whatsoever God. *Eccl* 3:14
I k. it shall be well with. 8:12
nor shall I k. the loss of. *Isa* 47:8
and I k. that I shall not. 50:7
I k. their works and their. 66:18
I k. the way of man is. *Jer* 10:23
given me knowledge, and I k. 11:18
for I k. the thoughts that I. 29:11
I k. and am a witness, saith. 23
I k. his wrath, saith the. 48:30
I k. things that come. *Ezek* 11:5
the dream, and I shall k. *Dan* 2:9
I k. Ephraim, and Israel. *Hos* 5:3
I did k. thee in the wilderness. 13:5
I k. your manifold. *Amos* 5:12
I k. that for my sake. *Jonah* 1:12
fear not ye, I k. that ye. *Mat* 28:5
I k. thee who thou art. *Mark* 1:24
Luke 4:34
whereby shall I k. this. *Luke* 1:18
I k. that Messias cometh. *John* 4:25
but I k. you. 5:42
I k. whence I came. 8:14
I k. that ye are Abraham's. 37
but I k. him. 55
one thing I k. 9:25
Father knoweth me, so I k. 10:15
I k. my sheep, and they follow. 27
I k. that what thou wilt ask. 11:22
Martha said, I k. that he shall. 24
I k. his commandment is. 12:50
I speak not of all, I k. whom. 13:18
now I k. of a surety. *Acts* 12:11
Jesus I k. and Paul I k. 19:15
I k. that ye shall see my face. 20:25
I k. this, that after my departing. 29
I will k. the uttermost of. 24:22
because I k. thee to be expert. 26:3
king Agrippa, I k. that thou. 27
I k. that in me dwelleth. *Rom* 7:18
I k. nothing by myself. *1 Cor* 4:4
I k. in part, then shall I k. as. 13:12
I k. the forwardness of. *2 Cor* 9:2
I k. this shall turn to. *Phil* 1:19
I k. that I shall abide with you. 25
be of good comfort, when I k. 2:19
I k. how to be abased, I k. 4:12
for I k. whom I have believed.
2 Tim 1:12
I k. him, and keepeth. *1 John* 2:4
I k. thy works. *Rev* 2:2, 9, 13, 19
3:1, 8, 15
I k. the blasphemy of them. 2:9

know not, or not **know**
is Abel ? he said, I k. not. *Gen* 4:9
I am old, I k. not the day. 27:2
I k. not the Lord, nor will. *Ex* 5:2
we k. not with what we must. 10:26
or if thou k. him not. *Deut* 22:2
Samuel did not yet k. *1 Sam* 3:7
give to men whom I k. not ? 25:11
I k. not how to go out. *1 Ki* 3:7
carry thee whither I k. not. 18:12
they k. not the manner. *2 Ki* 17:26
them that k. them not. *Ezra* 7:25
they shall not k. nor see. *Neh* 4:11
would I not k. my soul. *Job* 9:21*
knowest thou that we k. not ? 15:9
do ye not k. their tokens ? 21:29
they k. not the ways thereof. 24:13
the dark, they k. not the light. 16
for I k. not to give flattering. 32:22
great, and we k. him not. 36:26
for I k. not the numbers. *Ps* 71:15
they k. not, neither will they. 82:5
teacheth man, shall he not k.? 94:10
I will not k. a wicked person. 101:4
k. not at what they stumble. *Pr* 4:19
that thou canst not k. them. 5:6
doth not he k. it, and shall ? 24:12
k. not what to do in the end. 25:8
wicked regardeth not to k. it. 29:7
four things which I k. not. 30:18
dead k. not any thing. *Eccl* 9:5
if thou k. not, O fairest. *S of S* 1:8
Israel doth not k. nor. *Isa* 1:3
shall ye not k. it ? 43:19
there is no God; I k. not any. 44:8
thou shalt not k. from whence. 47:11
and thou didst not k. them. 48:6
they k. not, shall not k. peace. 59:8
for they k. not the way. *Jer* 5:4
other gods, whom ye k. not ? 7:9

k. not the judgements of. *Jer* 8:7
k. not me, saith the Lord. 9:3
the heathen that k. thee not. 10:25
into a land that they k. not. 14:18
22:28
dwelleth safely shalt thou not k. it ?
Ezek 38:14
she did not k. that I gave. *Hos* 2:8
they k. not to do right. *Amos* 3:10
k. not the thoughts of. *Mi* 4:12
unto you, I k. you not. *Mat* 25:12
Peter said, I k. not what thou sayest.
26:70; *Luke* 22:60
curse and swear, saying, I k. not.
Mat 26:72, 74; *Mark* 14:68, 71
Jesus said, Ye k. not. *Mark* 10:38
ye err, because ye k. not the. 12:24
seeing I k. not a man. *Luke* 1:34
I k. not whence you are. 13:25, 27
woman, I k. him not. 22:57
forgive them; for they k. not. 23:34
that they should not k. him. 24:16
standeth one among you whom ye k.
not. *John* 1:26
if I should say, I k. him not. 8:55
blind man said, I k. not. 9:12, 25
opened his eyes, we k. not. 21
for this fellow, we k. not from. 29
for they k. not the voice of. 10:5
Lord, we k. not whither thou. 14:5
because they k. not him that. 15:21
we k. not where they have laid. 20:2
I k. not where they have laid. 13
could not k. the certainty. *Acts* 21:34
for we k. not what we should pray
for. *Rom* 8:26
I k. not whether I baptized any other.
1 Cor 1:16
I determined not to k. any. 2:2
if I k. not the meaning of. 14:11
which k. not God. *1 Thes* 4:5
vengeance on them that k. not God.
2 Thes 1:8
k. not how to rule his. *1 Tim* 3:5
evil of things they k. not. *Jude* 10
shalt not k. what hour I. *Rev* 3:3

see, ye **know**
know *that I am the Lord*
ye shall k. *that I am the Lord.* *Ex* 6:7
16:12; *1 Ki* 20:28; *Ezek* 6:7, 13
7:4, 9; 11:10, 12; 12:20; 13:9, 14
21, 23; 14:8; 15:7; 20:38, 42, 44
23:49; 24:24; 25:5; 35:9; 36:11
37:6, 13; *Joel* 3:17
Egyptians shall k. *that I am Lord.*
Ex 7:5; 14:4, 18
thou shalt k. *I am Lord.* *Ex* 7:17
1 Ki 20:13; *Isa* 49:23; *Ezek* 16:62
22:16; 25:7; 35:4, 12
to the end that thou mayest k. *that I
am the Lord.* *Ex* 8:22
that ye may k. *that I am Lord.*
10:2; 31:13; *Ezek* 20:20
they shall k. *that I am the Lord.*
Ex 29:46; *Ezek* 6:10, 14; 7:27
12:15, 16; 24:27; 25:11, 17; 26:6
28:22, 23, 24, 26; 29:9, 16, 21
30:8, 19, 25, 26; 32:15; 33:29
34:27; 35:15; 36:38; 38:23
39:6, 28
that ye might k. *that I am the Lord.*
Deut 29:6
I will give them an heart to k. me
that I am the Lord. *Jer* 24:7
my sabbaths that they might k. *that
I am the Lord.* *Ezek* 20:12, 26
and the heathen shall k. *that I am
the Lord.* 36:23; 39:7
the house of Israel shall k. *that I am
the Lord.* 39:22

may, mayest, or might **know**
mayest k. there is none like God.
Ex 8:10; 9:14
mayest k. that the earth. 9:29
ye may k. the Lord doth put. 11:7
that I may k. what to do to. 33:5
thy way, that I may k. thee. 13
generations may k. that. *Lev* 23:43
may k. what the Lord. *Num* 22:19
that thou mightest k. that the Lord
he is God. *Deut* 4:35
ye may k. the way by. *Josh* 3:4
may k. that as I was with Moses. 7

people might k. the hand. *Josh* 4:24
Israel might k. to teach. *Judg* 3:2
we may k. whether our way. 18:5
tell me, that I may k. *Ruth* 4:4
that all the earth may k. there is a
God in Israel. *1 Sam* 17:46
1 Ki 8:43, 60; *2 Ki* 19:19
I may k. the number. *2 Sam* 24:2
this people may k. that. *1 Ki* 18:37
may k. thy name, and may k. that
this house is. *2 Chr* 6:33
his servants, that they may k. 12:8
that ye may k. there is. *Job* 19:29
be weighed, that God may k. 31:6
that all men may k. his work. 37:7
nations may k. themselves. *Ps* 9:20
measure of days, that may k. 39:4
generation to come might k. 78:6
that men may k. that thou. 83:18
may k. that this is thy hand. 109:27
I may k. thy testimonies. 119:125
draw nigh that we may k. *Isa* 5:19
may k. to refuse the evil. 7:15
that all may k. that thou art. 37:20
that we may k. ye are gods. 41:23
declared, that we may k. and. 26
ye may k. and believe me. 43:10
that thou mayest k. that I am. 45:3
that they may k. from the rising. 6
thou mayest k. and try. *Jer* 6:27
that ye may k. that my words. 44:29
flesh may k. that I have. *Ezek* 21:5
that heathen may k. me. 38:16
mightest k. the thoughts. *Dan* 2:30
intent that the living may k. 4:17
cast lots. that we may k. *Jonah* 1:7
ye may k. the righteousness. *Mi* 6:5
that ye may k. the Son of man.
Mat 9:6; *Mark* 2:10; *Luke* 5:24
ye may k. and believe. *Mark* 10:38
the world may k. 14:31; 17:23
might k. thee the only true God. 17:3
ye may k. that I find no fault. 19:4
may we k. what this new? *Acts* 17:19
all may k. that those things. 21:24
we might k. the things. *1 Cor* 2:12
that ye might k. the love. *2 Cor* 2:4
that I might k. the proof of you. 9
that ye may k. the hope. *Eph* 1:18
whom I sent, that ye might k. 6:22
may k. him and the power. *Phil* 3:10
may k. how to answer. *Col* 4:6
whom I sent, that he might k. 8
thou mayest k. how thou oughtest to
behave. *1 Tim* 3:15
may k. ye have eternal. *1 John* 5:13
that we may k. him that is true. 20

we **know**, *or* **know** *we*
Laban ? they said, We k. *Gen* 29:5
shall we k. the word ? *Deut* 18:21
we k. it is not his hand. *1 Sam* 6:9
nor k. we what to do. *2 Chr* 20:12
God is great, and we k. him not.
Job 36:26
our iniquities, we k. them. *Isa* 59:12
we k. if we follow on to. *Hos* 6:3
cry to me, My God, we k. thee. 8:2
we k. thou art true, and. *Mat* 22:16
Mark 12:14; *Luke* 20:21
we k. thou art a teacher. *John* 3:2
to thee, we speak that we do k. 11
we k. what we worship. 4:22
father and mother we k.? 6:42
howbeit, we k. whence this. 7:27
we k. that thou hast a devil. 8:52
we k. that this is our son and. 9:20
said to him, we k. that this man. 24
we k. that God spake to Moses. 29
now we k. that God heareth. 31
Lord we k. not whither thou goest,
and how can we k. the way ? 14:5
and we k. that his testimony. 21:24
we would k. what these. *Acts* 17:20
we k. it is every where. 28:22
we k. that what things. *Rom* 3:19
we k. that the law is spiritual. 7:14
we k. that the whole creation. 8:22
we k. that all things work. 28
we k. that we all have. *1 Cor* 8:1
we k. that an idol is nothing in. 4
we k. in part, and prophesy. 13:9
we k. that if our earthly. *2 Cor* 5:1
k. we no man after flesh, k. we. 16

we k. that the law is. *1 Tim 1:8*
for we k. him that hath. *Heb 10:30*
hereby we k. that we k. *1 John 2:3*
hereby k. we that we are in him. 5
we k. that it is the last time. 18
but we k. that when he shall. 3:2
we k. that we have passed from. 14
hereby we k. that we are of the. 19
hereby we k. that he abideth. 24
hereby k. we the spirit of. 4:6
hereby we k. that we dwell in. 13
by this we k. that we love the. 5:2
we k. that he heareth us, we k. that
  we have petitions that we. 15
we k. whosoever is born of God. 18
we k. that we are of God, and. 19
we k. that the Son of God is come,
  that we may k. him that. 5:20

ye know, or know ye
he said, K. ye Laban the ? *Gen 29:5*
ye k. that with all my power. 31:6
ye k. that my wife bare me. 44:27
at even ye shall k. the. *Ex 16:6*
ye k. the heart of a stranger. 23:9
ye shall k. my breach. *Num 14:34*
ye shall k. that the Lord. 16:28
ye shall k. the living God is among.
  Josh 3:10
and ye k. in all your hearts. 23:14
ye k. there is in these houses an
  ephod. *Judg 18:14*
k. ye that Ramoth is ? *1 Ki 22:3*
ye k. the man and his. *2 Ki 9:11*
what ye k. the same do. *Job 13:2*
k. ye that the Lord he is God.
  Ps 100:3
hearken, ye that k. *Isa 51:7*
k. ye for certain, if ye. *Jer 26:15*
all ye that k. his name, say. 48:17
ye shall k. that I have not done.
  Ezek 14:23
ye shall k. I the Lord have spoken.
  17:21; 37:14
ye shall k. that I am in. *Joel 2:27*
ye shall k. the Lord hath sent me.
  Zech 2:9; 6:15
ye shall k. them by their fruits.
  Mat 7:16, 20
ye k. that the princes of the Gentiles.
  20:25; *Mark 10:42*
ye k. that summer is nigh. *Mat 24:32*
  Mark 13:28; Luke 21:30
watch, for ye k. neither. *Mat 25:13*
k. ye not this parable ? *Mark 4:13*
k. ye that the kingdom of God.
  Luke 21:31
ye both k. me, and know. *John 7:28*
ye shall k. that I am he. 8:28
ye shall k. the truth. 32
k. ye nothing. 11:49
k. ye what I have done. 13:12
if ye k. these things, happy. 17
I go ye k. and the way ye k. 14:4
from henceforth ye k. him. 7, 17
ye shall k. I am in my Father. 20
ye k. that it hated me before. 15:18
as ye yourselves also k. *Acts 2:22*
ye k. how that it is unlawful. 10:28
brethren, ye k. how that a good. 15:7
ye k. that by this craft we. 19:25
ye k. from the first day that. 20:18
ye k. that ye were Gentiles. carried.
  1 Cor 12:2
ye k. your labour is not in. 15:58
brethren, ye k. the house of. 16:15
ye k. the grace of our Lord. *2 Cor 8:9*
I trust ye shall k. we are not. 13:6
k. ye that they which are of faith.
  Gal 3:7
ye k. how through infirmities. 4:13
ye k. that no whoromonger. *Eph 5:5*
ye k. the proof of him. *Phil 2:22*
as ye k. what manner. *1 Thes 1:5*
shamefully entreated, as ye k. 2:2
neither flattering words, as ye k. 5
ye k. how we exhorted and. 11
it came to pass, and ye k. 3:4
ye k. what commandments we. 4:2
and now ye k. what withholdeth.
  2 Thes 2:6
ye k. how when he would have inherited the blessing. *Heb 12:17*
k. ye that our brother. 13:23

ye k. that ye were not redeemed.
  1 Pet 1:18
put you in remembrance, though ye
  k. them. *2 Pet 1:12*
seeing ye k. these things. 3:17
ye k. all things. *1 John 2:20*
because ye k. it. 21
if ye k. he is righteous, ye k. 29
ye k. he was manifested to. 3:5
ye k. no murderer hath eternal. 15
hereby k. ye the Spirit of God. 4:2
and ye k. that our record. *3 John 12*

ye know not, or know ye not
k. ye not that there is a prince fallen?
  2 Sam 3:38
k. ye not what I and my fathers ?
  2 Chr 32:13
do ye not k. their tokens. *Job 21:29*
k. ye not what these things mean ?
  Ezek 17:12
Jesus said, Ye k. not what ye ask.
  Mat 20:22
ye k. not what hour your Lord. 24:42
K. ye not this parable ? *Mark 4:13*
ye err, because ye k. not. 12:24
watch, for ye k. not when. 13:33, 35
ye k. not what manner. *Luke 9:55*
standeth one among you, whom ye k.
  not. *John 1:26*
ye worship ye k. not what. 4:22
meat ye k. not of. 32
is true, whom ye k. not. 7:28
ye neither k. me nor my. 8:19
that ye k. not from whence. 9:
k. ye not that so many ? *Rom 6:3**
k. ye not to whom ye yield ? 16
k. ye not, brethren, for I speak. 7:1*
ye k. not that ye are the temple of
  God ? *1 Cor 3:16; 6:15, 19*
k. ye not that a little leaven ? 5:6
do ye not k. the saints shall ? 6:2
ye k. not that we shall judge ? 3
k. ye not, the unrighteous shall ? 9
ye k. not the which is ? 16
do ye not k. that they which ? 9:13
ye k. not that they which run ? 24
k. ye not yourselves ? *2 Cor 13:5*
ye k. not the friendship of ?
  Jas 4:4
ye k. not what shall be on the. 14
not written, because ye k. not the
  truth. *1 John 2:21*

knowest
thou k. my service that. *Gen 30:26*
thou k. how I have served thee. 29
thou k. any man of activity. 47:6
k. thou not yet that Egypt ? *Ex 10:7*
thou k. the people are set on. 32:22
for thou k. how we are. *Num 10:31*
thou k. the travel that hath. 20:14
Egypt, which thou k. *Deut 7:15*
the Anakims, whom thou k. 9:2
nation thou k. not, shall eat. 28:33
thou k. the thing that the. *Josh 14:6*
k. thou not Philistines ? *Judg 15:11*
woman said, Thou k. what Saul hath
  done. *1 Sam 28:9*
how k. thou that Saul ? *2 Sam 1:5*
k. thou not that it will be ? 2:26
thou k. Abner the son of Ner. 3:25
thou, Lord, k. thy servant. 7:20
  1 Chr 17:18
For, said Hushai, thou k. *2 Sam 17:8*
the king, thou k. it not. *1 Ki 1:18*
thou k. also what Joab did to. 2:5
thou k. what thou oughtest to do. 9
thou k. that the kingdom was. 15
thou k. all the wickedness. 44
whose heart thou k. thou only k. 8:39
  2 Chr 6:30
k. thou the Lord will ? *2 Ki 2:3, 5*
thou k. that thy servant did. 4:1
k. that I am not wicked. *Job 10:7*
thou k. that we know not ? 15:9
k. thou not this of old, since ? 20:4
therefore speak what thou k. 34:33
measures thereof, if thou k.? 38:5
earth, declare, if thou k. it all. 18
k. thou it, because thou wast ? 21
k. thou the ordinances of heaven ? 33
k. thou when the wild goats. 39:1, 2
not refrained, O Lord thou k.
  Ps 40:9; Jer 15:15

thou k. my foolishness. *Ps 69:5*
thou k. my downsitting and. 139:2
O Lord, thou k. it altogether. 4
k. not what a day may. *Pr 27:1*
k. not what evil shall. *Eccl 11:2*
k. not what is the way of the Spirit,
  even so thou k. not the works. 5
k. not whether shall prosper. 6
a nation that thou k. not. *Isa 55:5*
whose language thou k. not. *Jer 5:15*
but thou, O Lord, k. me. 12:3
land which thou k. not. 15:14; 17:4
desired woeful day, thou k. 17:16
thou k. all their counsel to. 18:23
thee things which thou k. not. 33:3
O Lord God, thou k. *Ezek 37:3*
k. thou wherefore I ? *Dan 10:20*
angel said, K. thou not ? *Zech 4:5, 13*
k. thou that Pharisees ? *Mat 15:12*
thou k. commandments. *Mark 10:19*
  Luke 18:20
deny that thou k. me. *Luke 22:34*
Nathanael said, Whence k. thou me ?
  John 1:48
art thou a master, and k. not ? 3:10*
Jesus said, What I do, thou k. 13:7
we are sure thou k. 16:30; 21:17
k. thou not I have power ? 19:10
thou k. that I love thee. 21:15, 16
which k. the hearts of. *Acts 1:24*
no wrong, as thou very well k. 25:10
k. his will, and approvest. *Rom 2:18*
what k. thou, O wife, k.? *1 Cor 7:16*
k. that all they in Asia. *2 Tim 1:15*
how he ministered to me, thou k. 18
and k. not that thou art. *Rev 3:17*
I said unto him, Sir, thou k. 7:14

knoweth
my lord k. the children. *Gen 33:13*
when he k. of it, he shall. *Lev 5:3, 4*
he k. thy walking through. *Deut 2:7*
no man k. of Moses' sepulchre. 34:6
Lord God of gods, he k. *Josh 22:22*
the iniquity which he k. *1 Sam 3:13*
thy father certainly k. that. 20:3
that also Saul my father k. 23:17
thy servant k. that I. *2 Sam 14:22*
all Israel k. thy father is a. 17:10
he k. vain men. he seeth. *Job 11:11*
he k. the day of darkness is. 15:23
he k. the way that I take. 23:10
there is a path which no fowl k. 28:7
God understandeth and k. the. 23
therefore he k. their works. 34:25
Lord k. way of righteous. *Ps 1:6*
the Lord k. the days of the. 37:18
for he k. the secrets of the. 44:21
is there any among us that k. 74:9
Lord k. the thoughts of man. 94:11
k. our frame, remembereth. 103:14
moon for seasons, the sun k. 104:19
but the proud he k. afar off. 138:6
that my soul k. right well. 139:14
woman is simple and k. *Pr 9:13*
heart k. his own bitterness. 14:10
poor, that k. to walk. *Eccl 6:8*
thine own heart k. thou hast. 7:22
no man k. either love or hatred. 9:1
the ox k. his owner, the ass. *Isa 1:3*
the stork k. her appointed. *Jer 8:7*
he understandeth and k. me. 9:24
k. what is in the darkness. *Dan 2:22*
Lord is good, he k. them. *Nah 1:7*
the unjust k. no shame. *Zeph 3:5*
your Father k. what. *Mat 6:8*
k. ye have need of. 32; *Luke 12:30*
no man k. the Son but the Father,
  nor any k. *Mat 11:27; Luke 10:22*
of that day k. no man. *Mat 24:36*
  Mark 13:32
ye justify, but God k. *Luke 16:15*
how k. this man letters ? *John 7:15*
when Christ cometh, no man k. 27
as the Father k. me. 10:15
nor k. him. 14:17
he saw it, and he k. that he. 19:35
God which k. the hearts. *Acts 15:8*
for the king k. of these things. 26:26
he k. what is the mind. *Rom 8:27*
k. the things of a man, even so the
  things of God k. no. *1 Cor 2:11*
he k. any thing, he k. nothing. 8:2
I love you not ? God k. *2 Cor 11:11*

knoweth

God k. I lie not.   2 Cor 11:31
I cannot tell, God k.   12:2, 3
the Lord k. them that.   2 Tim 2:19
him that k. to do good.   Jas 4:17
Lord k. how to deliver.   2 Pet 2:9
and k. all things.   1 John 3:20
he that k. God.   4:6
loveth is born of God, and k.   7
written, which no man k. Rev 2:17
because he k. that he hath.   12:12

who knoweth, or knoweth not
David our lord k. it not.   1 Ki 1:11
who k. whether thou art? Esth 4:14
who k. not such things?   Job 12:3
who k. not in all these, that the? 9
come to honour, he k. it not.   14:21
place of him that k. not God. 18:21
man k. not the price thereof. 28:13
in anger, yet he k. it not.   35:15*
riches, and k. not who.   Ps 39:6
who k. the power of thine?   90:11
a brutish man k. not, nor a fool. 92:6
k. not that it is for his life. Pr 7:23
but he k. not that the dead.   9:18
and who k. the ruin of them? 24:22
who k.whether he be wise? Eccl 2:19
who k. the spirit of man that? 3:21
for who k. what is good for?   6:12
who k. the interpretation of?   8:1
for he k. not that which shall be. 7
for man also k. not his time.   9:12
because he k. not how to go. 10:15
who seeth us? who k. us? Isa 29:15
and there, yet he k. not.   Hos 7:9
who k. if he will return? Joel 2:14
grow up, he k. not how. Mark 4:27
this people, who k. not.   John 7:49
walketh in darkness. k. not.   12:35
servant k. not what his lord. 15:15
k. not that Ephesians.   Acts 19:35
walketh in darkness, k. not. whither.
    1 John 2:11
therefore the world k. us not.   3:1
he that loveth not, k. not God. 4:8

knowing

ye shall be as gods, k.   Gen 3:5
my father David not k.   1 Ki 2:32
Jesus k. their thoughts.   Mat 9:4
    Luke 11:17
ye err, not k. scriptures. Mat 22:29
Jesus immediately k. in. Mark 5:30*
the woman k. what was done.   33
feared John, k. that he was.   6:20
but he k. their hypocrisy.   12:15
they laughed, k. that she. Luke 8:53
and one for Elias, not k. what.   9:33
Jesus k. the Father had.   John 13:3
Jesus k. all things that should. 18:4
Jesus k. that all things were. 19:28
none durst ask him, k. that it. 21:12
k. that God had sworn.   Acts 2:30
his wife not k. what was done.   5:7
he taught, k. only the baptism. 18:25
not k. the things that shall.   20:22
who k. the judgement of. Rom 1:32
not k. that the goodness of God. 2:4
k. that tribulation worketh.   5:3
k. this, that our old man is.   6:6
k. Christ being raised from dead.   9
the time, now it is high.   13:11
k. that as ye are partakers. 2 Cor 1:7
k. that he which raised Lord.   4:14
k. that whilst we are at home.   5:6
k. the terror of the Lord, we.   11
k. that a man is not.   Gal 2:16
k. that whatsoever good.   Eph 6:8
k. that your master is.   9; Col 4:1
k. that I am set for.   Phil 1:17
k. that of the Lord ye.   Col 3:24
k. beloved, your election. 1 Thes 1:4
k. this, that the law is.   1 Tim 1:9
is proud, k. nothing, but doting. 6:4
k. that they do gender.   2 Tim 2:23
k. of whom thou hast learned.   3:14
k. that he that is such.   Tit 3:11
k. that thou wilt do more. Philem 21
k. ye have in heaven a.   Heb 10:34
he went out, not k. whither.   11:8
k. this, that the trying of.   Jas 1:3
k. we shall receive greater.   18
blessing, k. that ye are.   1 Pet 3:9*
k. that the same afflictions are.   5:9
k. that shortly I must put. 2 Pet 1:14
k. this, that no prophecy. 2 Pet 1:20
k. there shall come scoffers in.   3:3

knowledge

tree of k. of good and.   Gen 2:9, 17
filled Bezaleel in k.   Ex 31:3; 35:31
sin come to his h.   Lev 4:23, 28
and knew the k. of the.   Num 24:16
thou shouldest take k.   Ruth 2:10
blessed be he that did take k.   19
the Lord is a God of k.   1 Sam 2:3
take k. of all the lurking.   23:23
shipmen that had k. of sea.
    1 Ki 9:27; 2 Chr 8:18
give me k. that I may.   2 Chr 1:10
but hast asked k.   11
k. is granted thee.   12
every one having k.   Neh 10:28
wise man utter vain k.?   Job 15:2
for we desire not the k. of.   21:14
shall any teach God k. seeing?   22
and my lips shall utter k.   33:3*
ear unto me, ye that have k.   34:2
I will fetch my k. from afar.   36:3
he that is perfect in k. is.   4; 37:16
night unto night sheweth k. Ps 19:2
is there k. in the most High? 73:11
he that teacheth man k. shall. 94:10
me good judgement and k.   119:66
such k. is too wonderful for.   139:6
that thou takest k. of him?   144:3
to give the young man k.   Pr 1:4
fear of Lord is the beginning of k.   7
fools hate k.   22
if thou criest after k.   2:3*
for that they hated k. and did.   29
out of his mouth cometh k. and. 2:6
and when k. is pleasant to thy.   10
his k. the depths are broken.   3:20
and that thy lips may keep k.   5:2
right to them that find k.   8:9
k. rather than gold.   10
and find out k.   12
k. of the holy is understanding. 9:10
wise men lay up k.: but the.   10:14
but through k. shall the just.   11:9
loveth instruction loveth k.   12:1
a prudent man concealeth k.   23
prudent man dealeth with k.   13:16
k. is easy to him that.   14:6
not in him the lips of k.   7
prudent are crowned with k.   18
the tongue of the wise useth k. 15:2
the lips of the wise disperse k.   7
hath understanding seeketh k.   14
he that hath k. spareth his.   17:27
the prudent getteth k. and the ear of
    the wise seeketh k.   18:15
and he will understand k.   19:25
to err from the words of k.   27
lips of k. are a precious jewel. 20:15
when the wise is instructed, he re-
    ceiveth k.   21:11
eyes of the Lord preserve k.   22:12
and apply thine heart unto my k. 17
excellent things in counsels and k. 20
thine ears to the words of k.   23:12
by k. shall the chambers be.   24:4
man of k. increaseth strength.   5
so shall the k. of wisdom be to.   14
by a man of k. the state.   28:2
wisdom, nor have k. of holy.   30:3
heart had experience of k. Eccl 1:16
he that increaseth k. increaseth.   18
is a man whose labour is in k.   2:21
God giveth to a man wisdom, k.   26
but the excellency of k. is.   7:12
nor k. in the grave, whither.   9:10
still taught the people k.   12:9
before the child shall have k. Isa 8:4
spirit of k. and of the fear.   11:2
whom shall he teach k.? them. 28:9
the rash shall understand k.   32:4
wisdom and k. shall be stability. 33:6
who taught him k.   40:14
nor is there k.   44:19
and maketh their k. foolish.   25
thy wisdom and thy k. hath.   47:10
by his k. my righteous.   53:11
which shall feed you with k. Jer 3:15
every man is brutish in his k.   10:14
    51:17
Lord hath given me k. of it.   11:18
favoured and cunning in k. Dan 1:4
God gave them k.   Dan 1:17
he giveth k. to them.   2:21
excellent spirit and k. were.   5:12
many run to and fro, and k.   12:4
destroyed for lack of k.: because thou
    hast rejected k., I will.   Hos 4:6
the earth filled with the k. Hab 2:14
priest's lips should keep k. Mal 2:7
that place had k. of him. Mat 14:35
k. of salvation by remission of sins.
    Luke 1:77
taken away the key of k.   11:52
marvelled and took k.   Acts 4:13
having more perfect k. of.   24:22
to retain God in their k.   Rom 1:28
which hast the form of k.   2:20
justified, for by law is the k.   3:20
zeal, but not according to k.   10:2
ye also are filled with all k.   15:14
in all utterance and all k.   1 Cor 1:5
we know that we all have k. K. 8:1
there is not in every man that k.   7
if any man see thee which hast k.   10
through thy k. shall thy weak.   11
to another the word of k. by the. 12:8
understand all mysteries and all k.
    13:2
whether there be k. it shall vanish. 8
speak to you by revelation or k. 14:6
the savour of his k.   2 Cor 2:14
to give the light of the k. of the.   4:6
by k., by longsuffering, by.   6:6
abound in faith, utterance, and k. 8:7
I be rude in speech, yet not in k. 11:6
give you wisdom in the k. Eph 1:17
ye may understand my k.   3:4*
love of Christ which passeth k.   19
we come in the unity of the k.   4:13
love may abound more in k. Phil 1:9
things but loss for k. of Christ.   3:8
ye might be filled with k.   Col 1:9
hid treasures of wisdom and k.   2:3
new man which is renewed in k. 3:10
all men to come to the k. 1 Tim 2:4
never able to come to k.   2 Tim 3:7
after we have received k. Heb 10:26
man, and endued with k.? Jas 3:13*
husbands dwell with them according
    to k.   1 Pet 3:7
through the k. of him.   2 Pet 1:3
add to virtue k. and to k.   5
nor unfruitful in the k. of our.   8
grow in grace and in the k. of. 3:18

knowledge of God
shalt thou find the k. of God. Pr 2:5
is no truth, nor k. of God. Hos 4:1
desired the k. of God more.   6:6
the riches both of the wisdom and k.
    of God.   Rom 11:33
have not the k. of God. 1 Cor 15:34
exalteth itself against k. of God.
    2 Cor 10:5
increasing in the k. of God. Col 1:10
through the k. of God.   2 Pet 1:2

knowledge of the Lord
the good k. of the Lord. 2 Chr 30:22*
full of the k. of the Lord.   Isa 11:9
escaped pollution through the k. of
    the Lord.   2 Pet 2:20

no knowledge
your children which in that day had
    no k.   Deut 1:39
have all the workers of iniquity no
    k.?   Ps 14:4; 53:4
captivity because they have no k.
    Isa 5:13
have no k. that set up their images.
    45:20
our soul, and thou takest no k. 58:3
do good, they have no k.   Jer 4:22

without knowledge
committed without k. of. Num 15:24
Job hath spoken without k. and.
    Job 34:35
multiplieth words without k. 35:16
perish by sword, and die without k.
    36:12
by words without k.   38:2; 42:3
the soul be without k.   Pr 19:2

known
nor had any man k. her. Gen 24:16
surely this thing is k.   Ex 2:14

if it be *k.* that the ox hath. *Ex* 21:36
for wherein shall it be *k.*   33:16
sin they have sinned is *k. Lev* 4:14
whether he hath seen or *k.* of it. 5:1
woman that hath *k.* man. *Num* 31:17
take wise men, and *k. Deut* 1:13, 15
be not *k.* who hath slain him. 21:1
which had *k.* the works. *Josh* 24:31
k. to you why his hand. *1 Sam* 6:3
let it be *k.* that thou art God in.
     1 Ki 18:36
it *k.* to the king. *Ezra* 4:12, 13; 5:8
enemies heard it was *k.* to. *Neh* 4:15
thing was *k.* to Mordecai. *Esth* 2:22
Lord is *k.* by the judgement. *Ps* 9:16
hast *k.* my soul in adversities. 31:7
God is *k.* in her palaces for. 48:3
thy way may be *k.* on earth. 67:2
thou hast *k.* my reproach. 69:19
in Judah is God *k.:* his name. 76:1
sea, thy footsteps are not *k.* 77:19
which we have heard and *k.* 78:3
be *k.* among the heathen in. 79:10
shall thy wonders be *k.* in ? 88:12
because he hath *k.* my name. 91:14
that have *k.* thy testimonies. 119:79
I have *k.* of old thou hast. 152
hast searched me, and *k.* me. 139:1
that perverteth his ways shall be *k.*
     Pr 10:9
a fool's wrath is presently *k.* 12:16
a child is *k.* by his doings. 20:11
her husband is *k.* in the gates. 31:23
a fool's voice is *k.* by. *Eccl* 5:3
and it is *k.* that it is man, nor. 6:10
excellent things, this is *k. Isa* 12:5
and the Lord shall be *k.* to. 19:21
their seed shall be *k.* among. 61:9
hand of the Lord shall be *k.* to. 66:14
they have *k.* the way of. *Jer* 5:5
then shall prophet be *k.* the. 28:9
saith Lord God, be it *k. Ezek* 35:32
     Acts 4:10; 13:38; 28:28
I will be *k.* in the eyes. *Ezek* 38:23
but if not, be it *k.* to thee. *Dan* 3:18
after thou shalt have *k.* the. 4:26
have I *k.* of all families. *Amos* 3:2
a day which shall be *k. Zech* 14:7
ye had *k.* what this meant. *Mat* 12:7
tree is *k.* by his fruit. 33; *Luke* 6:44
goodman of house had *k. Mat* 24:43
     Luke 12:39
prophet, he would have *k. Luke* 7:39
saying, If thou hadst *k.* in. 19:42
how he was *k.* of them in. 24:35
himself seeketh to be *k.* *John* 7:4
nor my Father: if ye had *k.* me, ye
 should have *k.* my. 8:19; 14:7
I know my sheep, and am *k.* 10:14
now they have *k.* 17:7
and have *k.* surely. 8
I have *k.* thee, these have *k.* 25
that disciple which was *k.* 18:15, 16
was *k.* to all dwellers. *Acts* 1:19
this *k.* unto you, and hearken. 2:14
but their laying await was *k.* of. 9:24
it was *k.* throughout all Joppa. 42
k. unto God are all his works. 15:18
this was *k.* to all the Jews and. 19:17
have *k.* the certainty. 22:30; 23:28
which may be *k.* of God. *Rom* 1:19
for who hath *k.* the mind of the
 Lord ?   11:34; *1 Cor* 2:16
for had they *k.* it. *1 Cor* 2:8
same is *k.* of him. 8:3
know, even as I also am *k.* 13:12
how shall it be *k.* what is piped? 14:7
how shall it be *k.* what is spoken? 9
Ye are our epistle, *k.* and. *2 Cor* 3:2
though we have *k.* Christ. 5:16
as unknown, and yet well *k.;* as. 6:9
have *k.* God or are *k.* of. *Gal* 4:9
might be *k.* by church the. *Eph* 3:10
let your moderation be *k. Phil* 4:5
thou hast fully *k.* my. *2 Tim* 3:10
from a child thou hast *k.* the. 15
preaching might be fully *k.* 4:17
because ye have *k.* him. *1 John* 2:13
we have *k.* and believed the. 4:16
that have *k.* the truth. *2 John* 1:1

made or *madest* **known**

Joseph *made* himself *k.* *Gen* 45:1
and *madest k.* to them. *Neh* 9:14

the Lord hath *made k.* his. *Ps* 98:2
make k. his ways to Moses. 103:7
that which is in the midst of fools is
 made k.   *Pr* 14:33
have *made k.* to thee this day. 22:19
made myself *k.* to. *Ezek* 20:5, 9
Arioch *made* the thing *k. Dan* 2:15
Daniel *made* the thing *k.* to. 17
hast *made k.* to me, *made k.* to. 23
God hath *made k.* to the king. 45
made k. that which shall surely be.
     Hos 5:9
Lord hath *made k.* to us. *Luke* 2:15
seen it, they *made k.* abroad. 17
I have *made k.* to you. *John* 15:15
made k. to me the ways. *Acts* 2:28
Joseph was *made k.* to his brethren;
 and Joseph's kindred *made k.* 7:13
made k. to all nations. *Rom* 16:26
made k. to us the mystery. *Eph* 1:9
how by revelation he *made k.* 3:3
requests be *made k.* to. *Phil* 4:6
we *make k.* the coming. *2 Pet* 1:16

make **known**

I will *make* myself *k.* *Num* 12:6
thou mayest *make k.* to me what I.
     1 Sam 28:15
make k. his deeds among people.
     1 Chr 16:8; *Ps* 105:1
in *making k.* all these great. 17:19
they should *make* them *k. Ps* 78:5
with my mouth will I *make k.* 89:1
that he might *make k.* his. 106:8
to *make k.* to sons of men. 145:12
I will *make k.* my words. *Pr* 1:23
the father to children shall *make k.*
 thy truth. *Isa* 38:19
to *make* thy name *k.* to thy. 64:2
I will *make* myself *k. Ezek* 35:11
I *make* my holy name *k.* in. 39:7
a man that will *make k. Dan* 2:25
art thou able to *make k.* to me ? 26
Lord *maketh k.* to the king. 28, 29
shall *make k.* the interpretation. 30
     5:15, 16, 17
midst of the years *make k. Hab* 3:2
God willing to *make k.* his power in.
     Rom 9:22
that he might *make k.* riches of. 23
to *make k.* the mystery of. *Eph* 6:19
Tychicus shall *make k.* to you. 21
whom God will *make k.* *Col* 1:27
shall *make k.* to you all things. 4:9

not **known**

I have two daughters which have *not*
 k. man. *Gen* 19:8; *Num* 31:18
     35; *Judg* 21:12
not be *k.* they had. *Gen* 41:21
and the plenty shall *not* be *k.* in. 31
Jehovah was I *not k.* *Ex* 6:3
with children which have *not k.*
     Deut 11:2; 31:13
to go after gods which ye have *not k.*
     11:28; 13:6, 13
nor thy fathers have *k.* 28:36, 64
as had *not k.* the wars. *Judg* 3:1
withs, so his strength was *not k.* 16:9
but make *not* thyself *k.* *Ruth* 3:3
let it *not* be *k.* that a woman. 14
and the thing was *not k. 2 Sam* 17:19
be *not k.* to be the wife. *1 Ki* 14:2
people whom I have *not k. Ps* 18:43
and thy footsteps are *not k.* 77:19
heathen that have *not k.* thee. 79:6
not k. my ways. 95:10; *Heb* 3:10
they have *not k.* them. *Ps* 147:20
he hath *not* seen the sun, nor *k.* any
 thing. *Eccl* 6:5
have ye *not k.?* *Isa* 40:21
hast thou *not k.?*
paths that they have *not k.* 42:16
have *not k.* nor understood. 44:18
though thou hast *not k.* me. 45:4, 5
foolish, they have *not k.* me. *Jer* 4:22
countries thou hast *not k. Ezek* 32:9
not make k. the dream. *Dan* 2:5, 9
they did *not make k.* to. 4:7; 5:8
they have *not k.* the Lord. *Hos* 5:4
their place is *not k.* *Nah* 3:17
for there is nothing hid that shall *not*
 be *k. Mat* 10:26; *Luke* 8:17; 12:2
they should *not* make him *k.*
     Mat 12:16; *Mark* 3:12

a stranger, and hast *not k.* the things
 which ? *Luke* 24:18
yet ye have *not k.* him. *John* 8:55
and yet hast thou *not k.* me. 14:9
because they have *not k.* the. 16:3
the world hath *not k.* thee. 17:25
of peace have they *not k. Rom* 3:17
I had *not k.* sin but by the law: for
 I had *not k.* 7:7
other ages was *not* made *k. Eph* 3:5
been better *not* to have *k. 2 Pet* 2:21
hath not seen nor *k.* him. *1 John* 3:6
which have *not k.* depths. *Rev* 2:24

Kohath

the sons of Levi, Gershon, *K.* and.
 Gen 46:11; *Ex* 6:16; *Num* 3:17
the sons of *K. Ex* 6:18; *Num* 3:19
 27, 29, 30; 16:1; *1 Chr* 6:2, 22, 61
life of *K.* were 133 years. *Ex* 6:18
sum of the sons of *K.* of. *Num* 4:2
service of the sons of *K.* 4, 15; 7:9
the sons of *K.* Uriel. *1 Chr* 15:5

Kohathites

off the family of the *K.* *Num* 4:18
Aaron numbered sons of *K.* 34, 37
the *K.* set forward bearing. 10:21
the lot came out for *K.* *Josh* 21:4
     1 Chr 6:54
sons of *K.* sanctified. *2 Chr* 29:12
the sons of the *K.* to set the. 34:12

Korah

Aholibamah bare *K.* *Gen* 36:5
duke *K.* 16, 18
sons of Izhar, *K.* Nepheg. *Ex* 6:21
     Num 16:1
take censers, *K.* and all. *Num* 16:6
K. gathered all the congregation. 19
from about the tabernacle of *K.* 24
that he be not as *K.* and as. 40
strove in the company of *K.* 26:9
the children of *K.* died not. 11
not in the company of *K.* 27:3
Esau, Joalam and *K.* *1 Chr* 1:35
sons of Hebron, *K.* 2:43
Amminadab his son, *K.* his. 6:22
son of *K.* and his brethren. 9:19
in the gainsaying of *K.* *Jude* 11

L

Laban

a brother, his name was *L. Gen* 24:29
flee thou to *L.* my brother. 27:43
a wife of the daughters of *L.* 28:2
know ye *L.?* 29:5
L. gave Rachel, Bilhah. 29
Jacob fed the rest of *L.'s* flocks. 30:36
so the feebler were *L.'s,* the. 42
beheld the countenance of *L.* 31:2
seen all that *L.* doth to thee. 12
Jacob stole away unawares to *L.* 20
God came to *L.* in a dream by. 24
L. searched all the tent, but. 34
Jacob chode with *L.* 36
L. kissed his sons. 55
I have sojourned with *L.* and. 32:4

Laban

between Paran and *L.* *Deut* 1:1

labour, *substantive*

God hath seen the *l.* *Gen* 31:42
travailed and had hard *l.* 35:16, 17
and looked on our *l.* *Deut* 26:7
out every man from his *l. Neh* 5:13
or wilt thou leave thy *l.? Job* 39:11
her *l.* is in vain without fear. 16
he gave their *l.* to locust. *Ps* 78:46
yet is their strength *l.* and. 90:10
man goeth to his *l.* until. 104:23
they inherited the *l.* of the people.
     105:44
down their heart with *l.* 107:12
let the stranger spoil his *l.* 109:11
thou shalt eat the *l.* of thy. 128:2
the *l.* of the righteous. *Pr* 10:16
he that gathereth by *l.* shall. 13:11
in all *l.* there is profit, but. 14:23
what profit hath a man of all his *l.?*
     Eccl 1:3
all things are full of *l.;* man. 8*
all my *l.* my portion of all my *l.* 2:10

I hated all my *l*. which I. *Eccl* 2:18
he have rule over all my *l*. 19
my heart to despair of the *l*. I. 20
a man whose *l*. is in wisdom. 21
what hath man of all his *l*. under? 22
soul enjoy good in *l*. 24; 3:13; 5:18
yet there is no end of all his *l*. 4:8
have a good reward for their *l*. 9
nothing of his *l*. which he may. 5:15
to rejoice in his *l*.; this is the gift. 19
all the *l*. of man is for his mouth. 6:7
shall abide with him of his *l*. 8:15
thy portion in thy *l*. under. 9:9
the *l*. of the foolish wearieth. 10:15
l. of Egypt shall come. *Isa* 45:14
spend your *l*. for that which? 55:2
shame devoured the *l*. of. *Jer* 3:24
came I forth to see *l*. and? 20:18
take away all thy *l*. *Ezek* 23:29
the land of Egypt for his *l*. 29:20*
though the *l*. of the olive. *Hab* 3:17
a drought on all the *l*. of. *Hag* 1:11
whereon ye bestowed no *l*. *John* 4:38
who bestowed much *l*. on. *Rom* 16:6
every man shall receive according to
his *l*. *1 Cor* 3:8
that your *l*. is not in vain. 15:58
lest I bestowed *l*. in vain. *Gal* 4:11
flesh, this is fruit of my *l*. *Phil* 1:22
my brother and companion in *l*. 2:25
remembering your *l*. of. *1 Thes* 1:3
for ye remember, brethren, our *l*. 2:9
you, and our *l*. be in vain. 3:5
but wrought with *l*. and. *2 Thes* 3:8
to forget your *l*. of love. *Heb* 6:10
I know thy works, and *l*. *Rev* 2:2

labour, *verb*

work, that they may *l*. *Ex* 5:9
days shalt thou *l*. 20:9; *Deut* 5:13
not all the people to *l*. *Josh* 7:3
a land, for which he did not *l*. 24:13
be a guard to us, and *l*. *Neh* 4:22
I be wicked, why then *l*.? *Job* 9:29
Lord build, they *l*. in vain. *Ps* 127:1
oxen may be strong to *l*. 144:14*
his hands refuse to *l*. *Pr* 21:25
L. not to be rich, cease from. 23:4*
he, For whom do I *l*.? *Eccl* 4:8
though a man *l*. to seek it out. 8:17
I will weep bitterly, *l*. not. *Isa* 22:4
they shall not *l*. in vain, nor. 65:53
the people shall *l*. in vain. *Jer* 51:58
under persecution we *l*. *Lam* 5:5*
be in pain, and *l*. to bring. *Mi* 4:10
that the people should *l*. *Hab* 2:13
come unto me all ye that *l*. *Mat* 11:28
l. not for the meat that. *John* 6:27
and Tryphosa who *l*. *Rom* 16:12
and *l*. working with our. *1 Cor* 4:12
we *l*. to be accepted of. *2 Cor* 5:9*
but rather *l*. working. *Eph* 4:28
whereunto I also *l*. striving. *Col* 1:29
to know them which *l*. *1 Thes* 5:12
therefore we both *l*. and. *1 Tim* 4:10
especially they that *l*. in word. 5:17
let us *l*. therefore to. *Heb* 4:11*

laboured

so we *l*. in the work. *Neh* 4:21
that which he *l*. for. *Job* 20:18
on the labour I had *l*. to. *Eccl* 2:11
all my labour wherein I have *l*. 19
yet to a man that hath not *l*. 21
of his heart wherein he hath *l*. 22
what profit hath he that hath *l*.? 5:16
thy sorceries wherein thou hast *l*.
Isa 47:12
to thee with whom thou hast *l*. 15
I said, I have *l*. in vain. 49:4
drink, for which thou hast *l*. 62:8
king *l*. to deliver Daniel. *Dan* 6:14
for which thou hast *l*. *Jonah* 4:10
other men *l*. and ye are. *John* 4:38
salute Persis, who *l*. *Rom* 16:12
but I *l*. more abundantly. *1 Cor* 15:10
I have not run nor *l*. in. *Phil* 2:16
help those that *l*. with me in. 4:3
and for my name's sake *l*. *Rev* 2:3

labourer

the *l*. is worthy of his hire. *Luke* 10:7
l. is worthy of his reward. *1 Tim* 5:18

labourers

harvest plenteous, but *l*. few.
Mat 9:37; *Luke* 10:2

pray the Lord that he will send *l*.
Mat 9:38; *Luke* 10:2
went out early to hire *l*. *Mat* 20:1
when he had agreed with the *l*. 2
call the *l*. 8
for we are *l*. together. *1 Cor* 3:9*
behold the hire of the *l*. *Jas* 5:4

laboureth

he that *l*. *l*. for himself. *Pr* 16:26*
in that wherein he *l*.? *Eccl* 3:9
one that helpeth and *l*. *1 Cor* 16:16
the husbandman that *l*. *2 Tim* 2:6

labouring

the sleep of a *l*. man. *Eccl* 5:12
l. ye ought to support. *Acts* 20:35
l. for you in prayer. *Col* 4:12*
l. night and day we. *1 Thes* 2:9

labours

of thy *l*. when thou hast gathered in
thy *l*. out of the field. *Ex* 23:16
all thy *l*. shall a nation. *Deut* 28:33
and thy *l*. be in the house. *Pr* 5:10
fast, ye exact all your *l*. *Isa* 58:3
I will deliver all their *l*. *Jer* 20:5*
in my *l*. shall they find no. *Hos* 12:8
I smote you in all the *l*. *Hag* 2:17
entered into their *l*. *John* 4:38
in tumults, in *l*. in. *2 Cor* 6:5
not boasting of other men's *l*. 10:15
in *l*. more abundant, in. 11:23
may rest from their *l*. *Rev* 14:13

lace

breastplate with *l*. of blue. *Ex* 28:28
thou shalt put it on a blue *l*. 37
tied it to a *l*. of blue to fasten. 39:31

Lachish

the Lord delivered *L*. *Josh* 10:32
the king of *L*. one. 12:11
Judah had *L*. 15:39
Amaziah fled to *L*. *2 Ki* 14:19
2 Chr 25:27
king of Assyria to *L*. *2 Ki* 18:14
Assyria sent Rab-shakeh from *L*.
with a great host. 17; *Isa* 36:2
Rehoboam built *L*. and. *2 Chr* 11:9
Babylon fought against *L*. *Jer* 34:7
O inhabitant of *L*. bind. *Mi* 1:13

lack, *substantive*

destroy for *l*. of fire? *Gen* 18:28
that gathered little had no *l*.
Ex 16:18; *2 Cor* 8:15
old lion perisheth for *l*. *Job* 4:11
ones wander for *l*. of meat. 38:41
my people are destroyed for *l*. of.
Hos 4:6
his life to supply your *l*. *Phil* 2:30
that ye may have *l*. of. *1 Thes* 4:12

lack, *verb*

there shall *l*. five of? *Gen* 18:28
not *l*. any thing in it. *Deut* 8:9
the young lions do *l*. *Ps* 34:10
to the poor shall not *l*. *Pr* 28:27
thy head *l*. no ointment. *Eccl* 9:8
have I kept, what *l*. I yet? *Mat* 19:20
if any of you *l*. wisdom. *Jas* 1:5

lacked

thou hast *l*. nothing. *Deut* 2:7
l. of David's servants. *2 Sam* 2:30
provided victual, they *l*. *1 Ki* 4:27
but what hast thou *l*. with me? 11:22
sustain them, they *l*. *Neh* 9:21
because it *l*. moisture. *Luke* 8:6
without purse, *l*. ye any? 22:35
any among them that *l*. *Acts* 4:34
more honour to that part which *l*.
1 Cor 12:24
ye were careful, but *l*. *Phil* 4:10

lackest

but one thing thou *l*. *Mark* 10:21
Luke 18:22

lacketh

there *l*. not one man of. *Num* 31:49
not fail one that *l*. bread. *2 Sam* 3:29
committeth adultery, *l*. *Pr* 6:32*
honoureth himself, and *l*. bread. 12:9
he that *l*. these things. *2 Pet* 1:9

lacking

thou suffer salt to be *l*. *Lev* 2:13
a lamb that hath any thing *l*. 22:23
should be one tribe *l*. in. *Judg* 21:3
there was nothing *l*. to. *1 Sam* 30:19

they shall fear no more, nor shall be *l*.
Jer 23:4
for that which was *l*. *1 Cor* 16:17
was *l*. to me the brethren. *2 Cor* 11:9
might perfect what is *l*. *1 Thes* 3:10

lad, -s

This word is used [1] *Of a boy of
about thirteen,* Gen 21:12, 17. [2]
Of a boy of about seventeen, Gen
37:2. [3] *Of a married man,* Gen
43:8 *compared with* 46:21. [4] *Of
a servant,* 1 Sam 20:36.

grievous because of the *l*. *Gen* 21:12
God heard the voice of the *l*. 17
arise, lift up the *l*. 18
she gave the *l*. drink. 19
God was with the *l*. and he. 20
I and the *l*. will go yonder. 22:5
lay not thine hand upon the *l*. 12
l. was with the sons of Bilhah. 37:2
send the *l*. with me, and we. 43:8
we said, The *l*. cannot leave. 44:22
the *l*. be not with us, his life is bound
up in the *l*.'s life. 30, 31, 34
became surety for the *l*. 32
abide instead of the *l*.; let the *l*. 33
who redeemed me, bless the *l*. 48:16
Samson said to the *l*. *Judg* 16:26
behold I will send a *l*. *1 Sam* 20:21
unto the *l*. Run, and as the *l*. ran. 36
Jonathan cried after the *l*. 37, 38
l. knew not any thing, only. 39
gave his artillery to his *l*. 40
a *l*. saw them and told. *2 Sam* 17:18
a *l*. here hath five barley. *John* 6:9

ladder

dreamed, and behold a *l*. *Gen* 28:12

lade

l. your beasts and go to. *Gen* 45:17
my father did *l*. you. *1 Ki* 12:11
ye *l*. men with grievous. *Luke* 11:46

laded

they *l*. their asses with the corn.
Gen 42:26; 44:13
those that *l*. wrought. *Neh* 4:17
l. us with such things. *Acts* 28:10*

laden

sent ten asses *l*. with. *Gen* 45:23
Jesse took an ass *l*. with bread.
1 Sam 16:20
a people *l*. with iniquity. *Isa* 1:4
labour and are heavy *l*. *Mat* 11:28
silly women, *l*. with sins. *2 Tim* 3:6

ladeth

woe to him that *l*. himself. *Hab* 2:6

lading

on the sabbath *l*. asses. *Neh* 13:15
damage not only of *l*. *Acts* 27:10

ladies

wise *l*. answered her, yea. *Judg* 5:29
shall *l*. of Persia and. *Esth* 1:18*

lady

no more be called a *l*. *Isa* 47:5†
and thou saidst, I shall be a *l*. 7†
the elder to the elect *l*. *2 John* 1
now I beseech thee, *l*., that we. 5

laid

and *l*. it on both their. *Gen* 9:23
Abraham took wood and *l*. it. 22:6
Jacob *l*. the rods before. 30:41
she went away, and *l*. by her. 38:19
right hand, and *l*. it on. 48:14
she *l*. it in the flags by. *Ex* 2:3
let more work be *l*. on the men. 5:9
he shall give whatsoever is *l*. 21:30
Egyptians *l*. on us hard. *Deut* 26:6
stalks of flax she had *l*. *Josh* 2:6
they took and *l*. them out. 7:23
blood be *l*. on Abimelech. *Judg* 9:24
took the child and *l*. it in. *Ruth* 4:16
l. a great heap of stones on Absalom.
2 Sam 18:17*
my son and *l*. it in her bosom, and *l*.
her dead child in my. *1 Ki* 3:20
an oath be *l*. on him. 8:31; *2 Chr* 6:22
the prophet *l*. the carcase. *1 Ki* 13:29
l. his carcase in his own grave. 30
he carried him up, and *l*. him. 17:19
she went and *l*. him on. *2 Ki* 4:21
Lord *l*. this burden on him. 9:25
took and *l*. it on the boil. 20:7

l. upon Israel in the. *2 Chr 24:9*
where they *l.* the meat. *Neh 13:5*
and my calamity *l.* in. *Job 6:2*
the snare is *l.* for him in. *18:10**
or who *l.* the corner-stone. *38:6*
and majesty hast *l.* on. *Ps 21:5*
out of the net they have *l.* for. *31:4*
like sheep they are *l.* in the. *49:14*
to be *l.* in the balance, they. *62:9*
they have *l.* Jerusalem on. *79:1*
l. me in the lowest pit. *88:6*
I have *l.* help upon one that. *89:19*
hurt with fetters. he was *l.* *105:18*
thy judgements have I *l.* *119:30*
wicked have *l.* a snare. *110; 141:19*
thou hast *l.* thine hand upon. *139:5*
they have privily *l.* a snare. *142:3*
he *l.* it upon my mouth. *Isa 6:7**
burned him, yet *l.* it. *42:25; 57:11*
thou hast very heavily *l.* *47:6*
Lord *l.* on him the iniquity of. *53:6*
I have *l.* a snare for thee. *Jer 50:24*
be thou *l.* with the uncircumcised.
　　　　　　　　　　 Ezek 32:19
when I have *l.* the land. *33:29*
spoken, saying, They are *l.* *35:12*
I drew them, and I *l.* *Hos 11:4*
garners are *l.* desolate. *Joel 1:17*
on clothes *l.* to pledge. *Amos 2:8*
they have *l.* a wound. *Ob 7*
he arose and *l.* his robe. *Jonah 3:6*
now gather, he hath *l.* siege. *Mi 5:1*
it is *l.* over with gold. *Hab 2:19*
from before a stone was *l.* *Hag 2:15*
the stone that I have *l.* *Zech 3:9*
for they *l.* the pleasant land. *7:14*
now the axe is *l.* to the root.
　　　　　　　Mat 3:10; Luke 3:9
l. it in his own new tomb. *Mat 27:60*
and her daughter *l.* on. *Mark 7:30*
Mary beheld where he was *l.* *15:47*
behold the place where they *l.* *16:6*
her firstborn, and *l.* *Luke 2:7*
Lazarus was *l.* at his gate. *16:20*
wherein never man before was *l.*
　　　　　　23:53; John 19:41
said, Where have ye *l.?* *John 11:34*
l. aside his garments, and. *13:4*
there is they Jesus therefore. *19:42*
not where they have *l.* him. *20:2, 13*
whom they *l.* at the gate. *Acts 3:2*
and *l.* the money at the. *4:37; 5:2*
l. them on beds and couches. *5:15*
when washed, they *l.* her in. *9:37*
David was *l.* to his fathers. *13:36*
nothing *l.* to his charge. *23:29*
l. many complaints they could. *25:7*
concerning the crime *l.* against. *16*
necessity is *l.* upon me. *1 Cor 9:16*
I pray it be not *l.* to. *2 Tim 4:16*
　　see **foundation**

laid *down*
before they were *l. down.* *Josh 2:8*
carried them, and *l.* them *down.* *4:8*
his feet and *l.* her *down.* *Ruth 3:7*
Eli was *l. down.* *1 Sam 3:2*
Samuel *l. down* to sleep. *3*
Amnon was *l. down.* *2 Sam 13:8*
did eat, and *l.* him *down.* *1 Ki 19:6*
Ahab came and *l.* him *down.* *21:4*
I *l.* me *down* and slept. *Ps 3:5*
since thou art *l. down* no feller is.
　　　　　　　　　　 Isa 14:8
up that I *l.* not *down.* *Luke 19:22*
l. them *down* at the. *Acts 4:35*
witnesses *l. down* their clothes. *7:58*
for my life *l. down* their. *Rom 16:4*
ie *l. down* his life for. *1 John 3:16*

laid *hand*
nobles he *l.* not his *hand.* *Ex 24:11*
Tamar *l.* her *hand* on. *2 Sam 13:19*
because he *l.* his *hand* on. *Esth 8:7*
l. not their *hand* on spoil. *9:10, 15, 16*
princes *l.* their *hand* on. *Job 29:9*
thou hast *l.* thine *hand.* *Ps 139:5*
my *hand* that I have *l.* *Ezek 39:21*
he *l.* his right *hand* upon. *Rev 1:17*

laid *hands*
his sons *l.* their *h.* *Lev 8:14, 18, 22*
Moses *l.* his *hands* on Joshua.
　　　　　Num 27:23; Deut 34:9
and they *l. hands* on her.
　　　　2 Ki 11:16; 2 Chr 23:15*

l. their *hands* on the he goats.
　　　　　　　 2 Chr 29:23
nor have *l. hands* on their. *Ob 13*
l. hands, and took him. *Mat 18:28*
and he *l.* his *hands* on them. *19:15*
they came and *l. hands* on Jesus.
　　　　　 26:50; Mark 14:46
save that he *l. hands* on. *Mark 6:5*
he *l.* his *hands* on every. *Luke 4:40*
he *l.* his *hands* on her, she. *13:13*
but no man *l. hands* on him.
　　　　　　 John 7:30, 44; 8:20
and they *l. hands* on the apostles.
　　　　　　　　 Acts 4:3; 5:18
and prayed, they *l. hands* on. *6:6*
then *l.* they their *hands* on. *8:17*
they *l.* their *hands* on Paul. *13:3*
when Paul had *l.* his *hands.* *19:6*
up the people, and *l. hands.* *21:27*
Paul *l. hands* on Publius'. *28:8*

laid *hold*
men *l. hold* on Lot's. *Gen 19:16*
took a knife, and *l. hold.* *Judg 19:29*
Saul *l. hold* on Samuel's skirt, and.
　　　　　　　　 1 Sam 15:27
l. hold on other gods. *2 Chr 7:22*
Herod had *l. hold* on John.
　　　　　 Mat 14:3; Mark 6:17
l. no *hold* on me. *Mat 26:55*
l. hold on Jesus. *57; Mark 14:51*
l. hold on one Simon. *Luke 23:26*
he *l. hold* on the dragon. *Rev 20:2*

laid *up*
she *l. up* his garments. *Gen 39:16*
Joseph *l. up* food in the. *41:48*
l. it *up* till the morning. *Ex 16:24*
Aaron *l. up* the pot of manna. *34*
Moses *l. up* the rods. *Num 17:7*
not this *l. up* in store ? *Deut 32:34*
Samuel *l.* it *up* before. *1 Sam 10:25*
David *l. up* these words. *21:12*
which thy fathers *l. up.* *2 Ki 20:17*
treasures were *l. up.* *Ezra 6:1*
thou hast *l. up* for them. *Ps 31:19*
wealth of sinners is *l. up.* *Pr 13:22*
fruits which I have *l. up.* *S of S 7:13*
at Michmash he *l. up.* *Isa 10:28*
that *l. up* shall they carry. *15:7*
shall not be treasured or *l. up.* *23:18*
which fathers *l. up* be carried. *39:6*
they *l. up* the roll in the. *Jer 36:20*
l. them *up* in their hearts. *Luke 1:66*
hast much goods *l. up* for. *12:19*
thy pound I have kept *l. up* in. *19:20*
for the hope which is *l. up.* *Col 1:5*
is *l. up* for me a crown. *2 Tim 4:8*

laid *wait*
l. wait against Shechem. *Judg 9:34*
l. wait all night for Samson. *16:2*
Amalek *l. wait* for him. *1 Sam 15:2*
Saul came and *l. wait* in the valley. *5*
l. wait at my neighbour's. *Job 31:9*
they *l. wait* for us in the wilderness.
　　　　　　　　　 Lam 4:19
when the Jews *l. wait* for him.
　　　　　　　 Acts 20:3; 23:30

laid *waste*
l. waste his dwelling place. *Ps 79:7*
Ar and Kir *l. waste.* *Isa 15:1*
Tyre, it is *l. waste.* *23:1*
your strength is *l. waste.* *23:14*
kings of Assyria *l. waste* all. *37:18*
pleasant things are *l. waste.* *64:11*
thy cities shall be *l. waste.* *Jer 4:7*
　　　　Ezek 6:6; 12:20; 19:7; 29:12
should this city be *l. waste* ?
　　　　　　　　　 Jer 27:17
now she is *l. waste.* *Ezek 26:2*
l. my vine *waste,* and. *Joel 1:7*
Israel shall be *l. waste.* *Amos 7:9*
say, Nineveh is *l. waste.* *Nah 3:7*
I *l.* his heritage *waste.* *Mal 1:3*

laidest
l. affliction on our loins. *Ps 66:11*
takest up that thou *l.* *Luke 19:21*

lain
he had *l.* in the grave. *John 11:17*
the body of Jesus had *l.* *20:12*
　　see **lien**

Laish
to spy the country of L. *Judg 18:14*
the name of the city was L. *29*
cause thy voice to be heard unto L.
　　　　　　　　 Isa 10:30

Laish, *person*
given to Phalti son of L. *1 Sam 25:44*
Ish-bosheth took her from the son of
L. *2 Sam 3:15*

lake
Jesus stood by the *l.* *Luke 5:1*
two ships standing by the *l.* *2*
over to the other side of the *l.* *8:22*
down a storm of wind on the *l.* *23*
violently down a steep place into *l.* *33*
were cast into a *l.* of fire. *Rev 19:20*
devil was cast into *l.* of fire. *20:10*
hell were cast into the *l.* of. *14*
not in the book of life, cast into *l.* *15*
their part in the *l.* burneth. *21:8*

lamb
(*The word is used most often
literally, of a young sheep. Jesus
is called the Lamb of God because
he was sacrificed for us, as was
the lamb in the Jewish ritual*)
where is the *l.* for a ? *Gen 22:7*
God will provide himself a *l.* *8*
to them every man a *l.* *Ex 12:3, 21*
your *l.* shall be without blemish. *5*
thou redeem with a *l.* *13:13; 34:20*
l. thou shalt offer in morning, and the
　other *l.* *29:39, 41; Num 28:4*
with a *l.* a tenth deal of. *Ex 29:40*
　　Num 28:21, 29; 29:4, 10, 15
if he offer a *l.* *Lev 3:7; 4:32; 5:6*
　　　　　　　 22:23; 23:12
as the fat of a *l.* is taken away. *4:35*
if not able to bring a *l.* *5:7; 12:8*
take a *l.* of the first year. *9:3*
　　　　 14:10; Num 6:12; 7:15, 21
the priest shall take the *l. Lev 14:12*
slay the *l.* *13, 25*
l. of trespass offering. *24*
that killeth an ox, or a *l.* or. *17:3*
offer a *l.* without blemish. *23:12*
one he *l.* of first year for a burnt
　offering, ewe *l.* of. *Num 6:14*
prepare with sacrifice for one *l.* *15:5*
thus done for one *l.* *11; 28:7, 13*
　　　　　　 14; Ezek 46:15
offered a sucking *l.* to. *1 Sam 7:9*
lion and bear and took a *l.* *17:34*
took the poor man's *l.* *2 Sam 12:4*
he shall restore the *l.* fourfold. *6*
shall dwell with the *l.* *Isa 11:6*
send ye the *l.* to the ruler of. *16:1*
l. to the slaughter. *53:7; Jer 11:19*
wolf and the *l.* shall feed. *65:25*
that sacrificeth a *l.* as if he. *66:3*
one *l.* out of flock for. *Ezek 45:15*
a *l.* of the first year thou. *46:13*
Lord will feed them as *l.* *Hos 4:16*
behold *l.* of God that. *John 1:29, 36*
l. dumb before the shearer. *Acts 8:32*
as of a *l.* without blemish. *1 Pet 1:19*
the elders stood a *l.* slain. *Rev 5:6*
beasts fell down before the *l.* *8*
saying, Worthy is the *l.* that was. *12*
glory, and power, be to the *l.* for. *13*
I saw when the *l.* opened one. *6:1*
hide us from the wrath of the *l.* *16*
multitude stood before the *l.* *7:9*
salvation to our God and to the *l.* *10*
white in the blood of the *l.* *14*
for the *l.* shall feed and lead. *17*
by the blood of the *l.* *12:11*
l. slain from the foundation. *13:8*
he had two horns like a *l.* and. *11*
I looked, and lo, a *l.* stood on. *14:1*
these are they that follow the *l.* *4*
presence of angels and the *l.* *10*
of Moses and song of the *l.* *15:3*
war with the *l.* and the *l.* shall. *17:14*
for the marriage of the *l.* is. *19:7*
the marriage supper of the *l.* *9*
I will shew thee the bride, the *l.'s*
　wife. *21:9*
the twelve apostles of the *l.* *14*
God Almighty and the *l.* are the. *22*
God did lighten it, and the *l.* is. *23*
but they are written in the *l.'s* book. *27*
of throne of God and of *l.* *22:1, 3*

lambs

did separate the *l.*   *Gen* 30:40
rams twelve, *l.* of the.   *Num* 7:87
sixty *l.*   88
fourteen *l.*   29:13, 17, 20, 23
for the bullocks, *l.* and rams. 29:18
with fat of *l.* and rams. *Deut* 32:14
spared the best of the *l. 1 Sam* 15:9
to Israel 100,000 *l.*   *2 Ki* 3:4
to the Lord a thousand *l. 1 Chr* 29:21
priests killed *l.* and.   *2 Chr* 29:22
burnt offerings two hundred *l.*   32
Josiah gave to the people *l.*   35:7
mayest buy speedily *l.*   *Ezra* 7:17
shall be as the fat of *l.*   *Ps* 37:20
little hills skipped like *l.*   114:4
ye little hills that skipped like *l.*   6
l. are for thy clothing.   *Pr* 27:26
delight not in blood of *l.*   *Isa* 1:11
then shall the *l.* feed after.   5:17
sword filled with blood of *l.*   34:6
he shall gather the *l.* with.   40:11
I will bring them like *l.*   *Jer* 51:40
occupied with thee in *l. Ezek* 27:21
ye shall drink the blood of *l.*   39:18
in the sabbath six *l.*   46:4
in new moons six *l.*   6
and meat offering for the *l.*   5, 7
eat the *l.* out of the flock. *Amos* 6:4
I send you forth as *l.*   *Luke* 10:3
to Peter, Feed my *l.*   *John* 21:15

five lambs

five l. of the first year.   *Num* 7:17
    23, 29, 35, 41, 47

seven lambs

Abraham set *seven* ewe *l. Gen* 21:28
what mean these *seven* ewe *l.* set? 29
these *seven* ewe *l.* thou shalt.   30
offer with bread *seven l. Lev* 23:18
seven l. of the first year without.
    Num 28:11, 19, 27; 29:2, 8, 36
a tenth deal throughout *seven l.*
    28:21, 29; 29:4, 10
they brought *seven l.*   *2 Chr* 29:21

two lambs

two l. of the first year offer.
    Ex 29:38; *Num* 28:3
day he shall take *two l. Lev* 14:10
then ye shall sacrifice *two l.* of. 23:19
and on the sabbath *two l.* Num 28:9

lame

a blind or *l.* man shall.   *Lev* 21:18
if it be *l.* thou shalt.   *Deut* 15:21
Jonathan had a son that was *l.* of his
feet.   *2 Sam* 4:4; 9:3, 13
away the blind and the *l.*   5:6
whosoever smiteth the *l.*
because thy servant is *l.*   19:26
to the blind, feet to the *l. Job* 29:15
legs of the *l.* are not equal. *Pr* 26:7
then is prey divided, the *l. Isa* 33:23
then shall the *l.* man leap as.   35:6
them the blind and the *l.*   *Jer* 31:8
offer the *l.* for sacrifice.   *Mal* 1:8
that which was torn and *l.*   13
the *l.* walk.   *Mat* 11:5; 15:31
    21:14; *Luke* 7:22
call the poor, the *l.* and. *Luke* 14:13
certain man. *l.* from womb. *Acts* 3:2
L man held Peter and John.   11
with palsies and that were *l.*   8:7
lest the *l.* be turned out. *Heb* 12:13

Lamech

Methusael begat *L.*   *Gen* 4:18
L. took two wives.   19
Methuselah begat *L.*   5:25
    1 Chr 1:3
Noe, which was son of *L. Luke* 3:36

lament

Israel went yearly to *l. Judg* 11:40*
and her gates shall *l.*   *Isa* 3:26
fishers also shall mourn and *l.* 19:8
l. for the teats and pleasant. 32:12*
for this *l.* and howl, for.   *Jer* 4:8
to *l.* nor bemoan them.   16:5, 6
they shall not *l.* for him.   22:18
l. thee saying, Ah Lord.   34:5
ye daughters of Rabbah, *l.* and. 49:3
rampart and the wall to *l. Lam* 2:8
they shall *l.* over Tyrus. *Ezek* 27:32
of the nations shall *l.* her.   32:16

l. like a virgin girded.   *Joel* 1:8
gird yourselves, and *l.* ye priests. 13
l. with a doleful lamentation, and.
    Mi 2:4
say, ye shall weep and *l. John* 16:20
kings of the earth shall *l. Rev* 18:9*

lamentable

king cried with a *l.* voice. *Dan* 6:20

lamentation

mourned with a sore *l. Gen* 50:10
lamented with this *l.*   *2 Sam* 1:17
their widows made no *l.*   *Ps* 78:64
in ashes, make bitter *l.*   *Jer* 6:26
and take up a *l.* on the high.   7:29
habitations of wilderness a *l.*   9:10
every one her neighbour *l.*   20
in Ramah *l.* and weeping.   31:15
    Mat 2:18
shall be *l.* generally on.   *Jer* 48:38
increased mourning and *l. Lam* 2:5
take thou up a *l.* for.   *Ezek* 19:1
this is a *l.* and shall be for a *l.*   14
they shall take up a *l.* for Tyrus.
    26:17; 27:2, 32
a *l.* upon the king of Tyrus.   28:12
take up a *l.* for Pharaoh.   32:2, 16
l. against you, O house.   *Amos* 5:1
shall call such as are skilful of *l.*   16
turn all your songs into *l.*   8:10
lament with a doleful *l.*   *Mi* 2:4
great *l.* over Stephen.   *Acts* 8:2

lamentations

Josiah in their *l.* and, behold, they are
written in the *l.*   *2 Chr* 35:25
was written therein *l.*   *Ezek* 2:10

lamented

people *l.* because the.   *1 Sam* 6:19
all the house of Israel *l.* after.   7:2
Israelites *l.* Samuel.   25:1; 28:3
David *l.* over Saul.   *2 Sam* 1:17
king *l.* over Abner and said.   3:33
and Jeremiah *l.* for.   *2 Chr* 35:25
die and not be *l.*   *Jer* 16:4; 25:33
to you, but ye have not *l. Mat* 11:17
company of people *l.*   *Luke* 23:27

lamp

In Bible times [1] *a small cup-
like vessel, usually of earthenware,
containing oil in which a cotton
wick floated. It gave a very faint
light.* [2] *A torch,* Judg 7:16, 20.
*The word is frequently used sym-
bolically, the special meaning
being easily gained from the context.*

a burning *l.* that passed. *Gen* 15:17
to cause the *l.* to burn.   *Ex* 27:20
ere *l.* went out. Samuel. *1 Sam* 3:3
thou art my *l.* O Lord. *2 Sam* 22:29
God gave him a *l.* in.   *1 Ki* 15:4
a *l.* despised in thought. *Job* 12:5*
thy word is a *l.* to my. *Ps* 119:105
I have ordained a *l.* for.   132:17
commandment is a *l.* the. *Pr* 6:23
l. of the wicked shall be put.   13:9
curseth his father, his *l.* shall. 20:20
salvation thereof as a *l.*   *Isa* 62:1
star burning as it were a *l. Rev* 8:10

lamps

light the *l.* thereof.   *Ex* 25:37; 40:4
dresseth the *l.* burn incense on. 30:7
when Aaron lighteth the *l.* at even. 8
and his *l.* with the oil for.   35:14
and they brought *l.* to Moses. 39:37
he lighted the *l.* before the Lord.
    40:25; *Num* 8:2, 3
l. to burn continually.   *Lev* 24:2
    2 Chr 13:11
order the *l.*   *Lev* 24:4
and cover his *l.*   *Num* 4:9
l. within the pitchers.   *Judg* 7:16
and held the *l.* in their left hand. 20
he made *l.* of gold.   *1 Ki* 7:49
    2 Chr 4:20, 21
of his mouth go burning *l. Job* 41:19
like the appearance of *l. Ezek* 1:13
and his eyes as *l.* of fire. *Dan* 10:6
which took their *l.*   *Mat* 25:1; 3:4
arose and trimmed their *l.*   7
give us of your oil; for our *l.*   8

seven lamps

make the *seven l.* thereof. *Ex* 25:37
his *seven l.* of pure gold.   37:23
seven l. shall give light.   *Num* 8:2
a candlestick and *seven l. Zech* 4:2
seven l. of fire burning.   *Rev* 4:5

lance

they that hold the *l.* are. *Jer* 50:42

lancets

cut themselves with *l.*   *1 Ki* 18:28

land

[1] *The earth, as distinguished
from sea,* Mat 23:15. [2] *One
particular country,* Mat 9:26. [3]
Arable ground, Gen 26:12. [4]
The inhabitants of a country, Isa
37:11. [5] *A certain possession,*
2 Sam 19:29; Acts 4:37.

gold of that *l.* is good.   *Gen* 2:12
out of that *l.* went forth Ashur. 10:11
get thee into a *l.* I will shew. 12:1
    Acts 7:3
and the *l.* was not able to. *Gen* 13:6
is not the whole *l.* before thee?   9
I will give thee and seed the *l.* 17:8
    28:13; 35:12
behold, my *l.* is before thee.   20:15
of the Canaanite, in whose *l.*   24:37
Isaac sowed in that *l.* and.   26:12
bought the *l.* so the *l.* became. 47:20
only the *l.* of the priests bought.   22
the *l.* was corrupted by.   *Ex* 8:24
so that *l.* was darkened.   10:15
days may be long upon the *l.*   20:12
goat bear iniquities into a *l.* not.
    Lev 16:22
and the *l.* is defiled.   18:25, 27
that the *l.* spue not you. 28; 20:22
then shall the *l.* keep.   25:2; 26:34
l. shall yield her fruit.   25:19; 26:4
l. shall not be sold, for the *l.*   25:23
l. of your enemies shall eat.   26:38
and I will remember the *l.*   42
the *l.* also shall be left of them.   43
see the *l.* what it is, and. *Num* 13:18
the *l.* is a *l.* that eateth up the.   32
surely they shall not see the *l.* 14:23
Caleb will I bring to the *l.*   24
when ye be come into the *l.* 15:2, 18
    Deut 17:14; 18:9; 26:1
delivered into thy hand his *l.*
    Num 21:34; *Deut* 3:2
country Lord smote is a *l.* for cattle.
    Num 32:4
blood defileth the *l.* and the *l.* 35:33
to him will I give the *l.*   *Deut* 1:36
accounted a *l.* of giants. 2:20; 3:13
a *l.* of wheat, and barley, and.   8:8
l. wherein eat bread, *l.* whose.   9
not able to bring them into the *l.* 9:28
to Jotbath, a *l.* of rivers.   10:7
a *l.* which the Lord thy God.   11:12
whole *l.* thereof is brimstone. 29:23
cast them into another *l.* as at.   28
he found him in a desert *l.*   32:10
he will be merciful to his *l.*   43
blessed of the Lord be his *l.*   33:13
Lord shewed him all the *l.*   34:1
saying, Go view the *l.*   *Josh* 2:1
Lord hath given you the *l.* 9; 21:43
Joshua took all that *l.*   11:16, 23
and the *l.* had rest from war. 14:15
given you a *l.* for which ye did. 24:13
l. had rest forty.   *Judg* 3:11; 5:31
l. had rest fourscore years.   30
to fight against me in my *l.*   11:12
ye shall come to a large *l.*   18:10
day of the captivity of the *l.*   30
hath troubled the *l.*   *1 Sam* 14:29
David the king of the *l.*?   21:11
saying, Whose is the *l.*? *2 Sam* 3:12
restore thee all the *l.* of Saul.   9:7
entreated for the *l.*   21:14; 24:25
them the *l.* of Cabul.   *1 Ki* 9:13
victuals, and gave him *l.*   11:18
cry to the king for her *l.*   *2 Ki* 8:3
since the day that she left the *l.*   6
manner of the God of *l.*   17:26, 27
take you to a *l.* of corn and wine.
    18:32; *Isa* 36:17
hath any of the gods delivered at all
his *l.*   *2 Ki* 18:33; *Isa* 36:18

neither move any more out of the *l.*
     2 Ki 21:8; *2 Chr* 33:8
the king of Egypt came no more out
     of his *l.*   *2 Ki* 24:7
left of the poor of the *l.*   25:12
     Jer 52:16
and the *l.* was wide.   *1 Chr* 4:40
Gath, who were born in that *l.*   7:21
pluck them out of my *l.*   *2 Chr* 7:20
make walls, while the *l.* is.   14:7
when he had purged the *l.*   34:8
that ye may eat the good of *l.*
     Ezra 9:12; *Isa* 1:19
nor brought we any *l.*   *Neh* 5:16
l. behold, we are servants in.   9:36
if my *l.* cry against me.   *Job* 31:38
for correction, or his *l.,* or for.   37:13
barren *l.* his dwellings.   39:6
are perished out of his *l.*   *Ps* 10:16
remember them from the *l.* of.   42:6
got not the *l.* in possession.   44:3
root these out of the *l.* of the.   52:5
deep root, and it filled the *l.*   80:9
be on the faithful of the *l.*   101:6
destroy all the wicked of the *l.*   8
called for a famine on the *l.*   105:16
the *l.* brought forth frogs in.   30
despised the pleasant *l.*   106:24
l. was polluted with blood.   38
he turneth the fruitful *l.* into. 107:34
thirsts after thee as a thirsty *l.* 143:6
into the *l.* of uprightness.   10
that tilleth his *l.* shall be.   *Pr* 12:11
     28:19
for the transgression of a *l.*   28:2
woe to thee, O *l.* when.   *Eccl* 10:16
blessed art thou, O *l.* when thy.   17
if one look unto the *l.*   *Isa* 5:30
l. that thou abhorrest shall be.   7:16
all *l.* shall become briers.   24
l. of Zebulun, *l.* of Naphtali.   9:1
     Mat 4:15
thro' wrath of the Lord is *l. Isa* 9:19
come to destroy the whole *l.*   13:5
break the Assyrian in my *l.*   14:25
woe to the *l.* shadowing with.   18:1
whose *l.* the rivers have spoiled. 2, 7
blessing in the midst of the *l.* 19:24
the desert, from a terrible *l.*   21:1
l. of Chittim it is revealed.   23:1
the *l.* shall be utterly emptied. 24:3
darkened, the mirth of the *l.*   11
l. of trouble and anguish.   30:6
of a great rock in a weary *l.*   32:2
the *l.* of my people shall come.   13
behold the *l.* that is very.   33:17
the *l.* thereof shall become.   34:9
thirsty *l.* springs of water.   35:7
these from the *l.* of Sinim.   49:12
the *l.* of thy destruction be too.   19
he was cut off out of the *l.* of. 53:8
pillar against the whole *l. Jer* 1:18
wentest after me, in a *l.* that.   2:2
led us through a *l.* of deserts, a *l.* 6
ye entered, ye defiled my *l.*   7; 3:9
young lions made his *l.* waste. 2:15
I give thee a pleasant *l.?*   3:19
for the whole *l.* is spoiled.   4:20
serve strangers in a *l.* that is.   5:19
make thee a *l.* not inhabited.   6:8
l. trembled at the sound.   8:16
l. perisheth and is burnt.   9:12
we have forsaken the *l.*   19
let us cut him off from *l.*   11:19
the *l.* mourn, herbs wither ?   12:4
from the one end of the *l.* even to. 12
bring again every man to his *l.*   15
brought Israel from *l.* of the north.
     16:15; 31:16
because they defiled my *l.*   16:18
inhabit wilderness into a salt *l.* 17:6
the *l.* whereunto they desire.   22:27
is profaneness gone forth into the *l.*
     23:15
I will bring on that *l.* all my.   25:13
very time of my *l.* come.   27:7
all the *l.* is before me.   40:4
and they cry hath filled the *l.*   46:12
the king of Babylon and his *l.*   50:18
for it is the *l.* of graven images.   38
a dry *l.,* a *l.* wherein no man. 51:43
her whole *l.* shall be confounded. 47
l. is full of bloody.   *Ezek* 7:23
filled the *l.* with violence.   8:17

l. is full of blood, and city. *Ezek* 9:9
the *l.* sinneth against me.   14:13
bring a sword on *l.*   17
a pestilence into *l.*   19
took also of the seed of the *l.*   17:5
hath taken the mighty of the *l.*   13
shall come forth out of one *l.*   21:19
thou art the *l.* is not cleansed. 22:24
in the gap before me for the *l.*   30
will I leave thee upon the *l.*   32:4
I bring the sword upon a *l.*   33:2
seeth the sword come upon the *l.*   3
l. is given us for inheritance.   24
have appointed my *l.* into their. 36:5
thou *l.* devourest up men, and.   13
like a cloud to cover the *l.* 38:9, 16
I will go up to the *l.* of unwalled. 11
I will bring thee against my *l.*   16
they may cleanse the *l.*   39:12
thus shall they cleanse the *l.*   16
shall be the border of the *l.*   47:15
he shall stand in the glorious *l.*
     Dan 11:16, 41
shall the *l.* mourn and.   *Hos* 4:3
for a nation is come up upon my *l.*
     Joel 1:6
the *l.* is as the garden of Eden.   2:3
the Lord be jealous for his *l.*   18
fear not, O *l.* be glad.   21
and parted my *l.*   3:2
she is forsaken upon her *l. Amos* 5:2
the *l.* is not able to bear all.   7:10
make the poor of the *l.* to fail   8:4
shall not the *l.* tremble for this ?   8
hosts is he that toucheth the *l.*   9:5
all things from off the *l.*   *Zeph* 1:2
whole *l.* shall be devoured by fire. 18
praise and fame in every *l.*   3:19*
Ho, ho, flee from the *l.* of. *Zech* 2:6
remove the iniquity of that *l.* in. 3:9
up, as an ensign upon his *l.*   9:16
l. shall mourn, every family.   12:12
unclean spirit to pass out of *l.*   13:2
in all the *l.* two parts therein.   8
all the *l.* shall be turned as a.   14:10
shall be a delightsome *l.*   *Mal* 3:12
went abroad into all that *l. Mat* 9:26
for the *l.* of Sodom.   10:15; 11:24
ye compass sea and *l.* to.   23:15
was darkness over all the *l.*   27:45
     Mark 15:33
sea, and be alone on the *l. Mark* 6:47
neither fit for the *l.* nor. *Luke* 14:35
a great famine in that *l.*   15:14
the ship was at the *l.*   *John* 6:21
Peter drew the net to *l.* full.   21:11
having *l.* sold it, and.   *Acts* 4:37
tell me whether ye sold the *l.* for? 5:8
day, they knew not the *l.*   27:39
into the sea, and get to *l.*   43
that they escaped all safe to *l.*   44
see **Benjamin, Canaan, Chal-**
     deans, darkness, desolate,
     divide, divided, inhabitants,
     inherit, Israel, Judah, strange

dry **land**

let *dry l.* appear.   *Gen* 1:9
called *dry l.* earth.   10
that was in the *dry l.* died.   7:22
water on *dry l.* and the waters shall
     become blood on *dry l.*   *Ex* 4:9
Lord made the sea *dry l.*   14:21
Israel walked on *dry l.*   29; 15:19
     Neh 9:11
the priests' feet were lifted up on *dry*
     l.   *Josh* 4:18
came over this Jordan on *dry l.*   22
longeth for thee in a *dry l. Ps* 63:1
he turned the sea into *dry l.*   66:6
rebellious dwell in a *dry l.*   68:6
and his hands formed the *dry l.* 95:5
I will make *dry l.* springs. *Isa* 41:18
of nations shall be a *dry l. Jer* 50:12
her cities are a *dry l.* and.   51:43
lest I set her as a *dry l.*   *Hos* 2:3
who made sea and *dry l. Jonah* 1:9
vomited out Jonah on the *dry l.* 2:10
shake the sea and *dry l. Hag* 2:6
the Red sea as by *dry l. Heb* 11:29

see **dwelt, Egypt, good**

in the **land**

Canaanite dwelt then in *the l.*
     Gen 13:7

shall be fruitful in the *l. Gen* 26:22
plenty not be known in the *l.*   41:31
and ye shall traffiick in the *l.*
     42:34
for to sojourn in the *l.* are.   47:4
go ye, sacrifice to your God in the *l.*
     Ex 8:25
Lord shall do this thing in the *l.* 9:5
they are entangled in the *l.*   14:3
give peace in the *l.* and.   *Lev* 26:6
ye may do them in the *l. Deut* 4:14
go well with thee in the *l.*   5:16
that ye may prolong days in the *l.*
     11:9, 21; 25:15
hath given thee rest in the *l.* 25:19
bless thee in the *l.* 28:8, 11; 30:16
as long as ye live in the *l.*   31:13
no magistrate in the *l.*   *Judg* 18:7
and if he be in the *l.* I. *1 Sam* 23:23
made judge in the *l.*   *2 Sam* 15:4
if there be famine in the *l. 1 Ki* 8:37
     2 Chr 6:28
long as they live in the *l. 2 Chr* 6:31
set judges in the *l.*   19:5
wonder that was done in the *l.* 32:31
nor is it found in the *l.* of. *Job* 28:13
goodness of the Lord in the *l.* of the.
     Ps 27:13
devise deceitful matter in the *l.*
     35:20
the synagogues of God in the *l.* 74:8
walk before the Lord in the *l.* 116:9
thou art my portion in the *l.* 142:5
shall every one eat in the *l. Isa* 7:22
in the *l.* of uprightness he.   26:10
not see the Lord in the *l.* of.   38:11
them in the *l.* serve me. *Ezek* 20:40
I shall set glory in the *l.* of.   26:20
caused terror in the *l.* of the living.
     32:23; 24:32
make them one nation in the *l.* 37:22
in the *l.* shall be his possession. 45:8
there is no truth in the *l. Hos* 4:1
up a Shepherd in the *l. Zech* 11:16
great distress in the *l. Luke* 21:23
by faith he sojourned in the *l.* of.
     Heb 11:9

our **land**

buy us and *our l.* for bread, and we
     and *our l.*   *Gen* 47:19
and *our l.* shall yield her. *Ps* 85:12
turtle is heard in *our l. S of S* 2:12
the Assyrian shall come into *our l.*
     Mi 5:5
us when he cometh into *our l.*   6

own **land**

Jethro went into his *own l. Ex* 18:27
     Num 10:30
a true report I heard in mine *own l.*
     1 Ki 10:6; *2 Chr* 9:5
carried out of their *own l. 2 Ki* 17:23
take you to a land like your *own l.*
     18:32; *Isa* 36:17
shall return to his *own l. 2 Ki* 19:7
with shame to his *own l. 2 Chr* 32:21
every one to his *own l.*   *Isa* 13:14
and set them in their *own l.*   14:1
fall by the sword in his *own l.*   37:7
they that dwell in their *own l.*
     Jer 23; 27:11
Egypt, into their *own l.* 37:7; 42:12
flee every one to his *own l.*   50:16
them into their *own l. Ezek* 34:13
     36:24; 37:14, 21; 39:28
Israel dwelt in their *own l.*   36:17
captive out of their *own l. Amos* 7:11
see **people, possess, possession**

their **land**

people sold not their *l.*   *Gen* 47:22
ye shall inherit *their l. Lev* 20:24
no inheritance in *their l. Num* 18:20
not give you of *their l. Deut* 2:5, 9
bring thee, and give thee *their l.* 4:38
     Judg 6:9
we took *their l.* and gave it.
     Deut 29:8; *Josh* 10:42
Lord rooted them out of *their l.*
     Deut 29:28
and pray unto thee toward *their l.*
     1 Ki 8:48
sin and heal *their l.*   *2 Chr* 7:14
flaming fire in *their l.*   *Ps* 105:32

and gave *their l.* for an heritage.
       Ps 135:12; 136:21
their l. is full of silver.   *Isa* 2:7
their l. also is full of idols.   8
their l. shall be soaked with.   34:7
I will pluck them out of *their l.*
       Jer 12:14
bring them again into *their l.* 16:15
forsaken, though *their l.* was. 51:5
shall be safe in *their l.* *Ezek* 34:27
they dwelt safely in *their l.* 39:26
will plant them on *their l. Amos* 9:15

this land
the Lord said, Unto thy seed I will
give *this l. Gen* 12:7; 15:18; 24:7
      48:4; *Ex* 32:13
thee again into *this l.* *Gen* 12:5
get thee out from *this l.* and. 31:13
will bring you out of *this l.* 50:24
brought us unto *this l.* *Num* 14:3
then he will bring us into *this l.* 8
this l. be given to thy servants. 32:5
this l. shall be your possession. 22
this l. shall fall to you. 34:2, 13
      Josh 13:2
but I must die in *this l. Deut* 4:22
and he hath given us *this l.* 26:9
      Josh 1:13
Lord done thus to *this l.? Deut* 29:24
  27; *I Ki* 9:8; 2 *Chr* 7:21
the inhabitants of *this l.* *Judg* 2:2
Lord said, Go up against *this l.*
      2 *Ki* 18:25; *Isa* 36:10
come again into *this l.* 2 *Chr* 30:9
sword shall not be in *this l. Jer* 14:15
that begat them in *this l.* 16:3
and small shall die in *this l.* 6
I will cast you out of *this l.* 13
he shall see *this l.* no more. 22:12
will bring them again to *this l.* 24:6
bring them against *this l.* 25:9
and *this* whole *l.* shall be a. 11
prophesied against *this l.* 26:20
be possessed again in *this l.* 32:15
and I will plant them in *this l.* 41
Babylon shall destroy *this l.* 36:29
come against you, nor *this l.* 37:10
if ye will abide in *this l.* I. 42:10
we will not dwell in *this l.* 13
pluck up even *this* whole *l.* 45:4
to us is *this l.* given in. *Ezek* 11:15
this l. shall fall unto you for. 47:14
this is the *l.* which ye shall. 48:29
removed him into *this l. Acts* 7:4

thy land
years thou shalt sow *thy l. Ex* 23:10
cast their young in *thy l.* 26
they shall not dwell in *thy l.* 33
nor shall any man desire *thy l.* 34:24
let me pass through *thy l. Num* 21:22
      Deut 2:27; *Judg* 11:17, 19
bless the fruit of *thy l.* *Deut* 7:13
bury him; that *thy l.* be not. 21:23
give the rain to *thy l.* in. 28:12
shall be the fruit of *thy l.* 18, 42
do great things for *thy l.* 2 *Sam* 7:23
famine come to thee in *thy l.?* 24:13
been favourable to *thy l.* *Ps* 85:1
fill the breadth of *thy l.* *Isa* 8:8
thou hast destroyed *thy l.* 14:20
through *thy l.* as a river, O. 23:10
no more be heard in *thy l.* 60:18
thy l. be termed desolate; the Lord
delighteth in thee, and *thy l.* 62:4
set darkness upon *thy l. Ezek* 32:8
thy l. shall be divided. *Amos* 7:17
cut off the cities of *thy l. Mi* 5:11
the gates of *thy l.* shall. *Nah* 3:13

your land
bought you and *your l.* *Gen* 47:23
when ye reap the harvest of *your l.*
      Lev 19:9; 23:22
which they begat in *your l.* 25:45
and dwell in *your l.* safely. 26:5
nor the sword go through *your l.* 6
for *your l.* shall not yield her. 20
you go to war in *your l.* *Num* 10:9
get into *your l.* 22:13
this shall be *your l.* 34:12
give you rain of *your l. Deut* 11:14
his hand from off *your l.* 1 *Sam* 6:5
strange gods in *your l.* *Jer* 5:19

---

remove you far from *your l. Jer* 27:10
is *your l.* a desolation and. 44:22

landed
we had *l.* at Caesarea. *Acts* 18:22
into Syria, and *l.* at Tyre. 21:3

landing
l. at Syracuse we. *Acts* 28:12*

landmark, -s
not remove thy neighbour's *l.*
      Deut 19:14; *Pr* 22:28; 23:10
removeth neighbour's *l. Deut* 27:17
some remove the *l.* and. *Job* 24:2

lands
dearth was in all *l.* *Gen* 41:45
left but our bodies and *l.* 47:18
wherefore they sold not their *l.* 22
restore those *l.* again. *Judg* 11:13
the kings of Assyria have done to all
l.   2 *Ki* 19:11; *Isa* 37:11
David went into all *l.* 1 *Chr* 14:17
the manner of other *l.* 2 *Chr* 13:9
fear fell on all *l.* round about. 17:10
as the gods of other *l.* have. 32:17
separated from people of *l. Ezra* 9:1
with the people of those *l.* 2, 11
have mortgaged our *l.* *Neh* 5:3, 4
men have our *l.* and vineyards. 5
I pray you, this day their *l.* 11
separated from people of the *l.* 10:28
they call their *l.* after their. *Ps* 49:11
a joyful noise, all ye *l.* 66:1; 100:1
and gave them the *l.* of. 105:44
hand, to scatter them in the *l.* 106:27
gathered them out of the *l.* 107:3
brought up Israel from *l. Jer* 16:15
all these *l.* to Nebuchadnezzar. 27:6
into a land which is the glory of all *l.*
      Ezek 20:6, 15
them out of their enemies' *l.* 39:27
hath forsaken houses, *l. Mat* 19:29
      Mark 10:29
an hundredfold, *l.* *Mark* 10:30
were possessors of *l.* sold. *Acts* 4:34

lanes
go out quickly into the *l. Luke* 14:21

language
whole earth was of one *l. Gen* 11:1
one, and they have all one *l.* 6
and there confound their *l.* 7, 9
speak in the Syrian *l.* 2 *Ki* 18:26
      Isa 36:11
Rab-shakeh cried in the Jews' *l.*
      2 *Ki* 18:28; *Isa* 36:13
could not speak in the Jews' *l.* but
according to the *l.* of. *Neh* 13:24
to every people after their *l.*
      Esth 1:22; 3:12; 8:9
no *l.* where their voice is. *Ps* 19:3
where I heard a *l.* that I. 81:5
from a people of strange *l.* 114:1
five cities speak the *l.* of. *Isa* 19:18
a nation, whose *l.* thou. *Jer* 5:15
not sent to a people of hard *l.*
      Ezek 3:5, 6
I decree, every *l.* that. *Dan* 3:29
turn to the people a pure *l. Zeph* 3:9
them speak in his own *l.* *Acts* 2:6

languages
O people, nations, and *l.* *Dan* 3:4
all *l.* fell down and worshipped. 7
Nebuchadnezzar to all *l.* 4:1
all *l.* trembled and feared. 5:19
Darius to all *l.* 6:25
all people, nations, and *l.* 7:14
ten men out of all *l.* *Zech* 8:23

languish
for the fields of Hebron *l. Isa* 16:8
spread nets on waters shall *l.* 19:8
haughty people of the earth do *l.* 24:4
gates of Judah *l.* and. *Jer* 14:2
that dwelleth therein shall *l. Hos* 4:3

languished
and wall to lament, *l.* *Lam* 2:8

languisheth
the world *l.* and fadeth. *Isa* 24:4
the vine *l.* 33:9
the earth mourneth and *l.* 33:9
she that hath borne seven *l. Jer* 15:9
the oil *l.* *Joel* 1:10
the fig tree *l.* 12
l. and Carmel, the flower *l. Nah* 1:4

---

languishing
Lord will strengthen him on the bed
of *l.* *Ps* 41:3

lanterns
Judas cometh with *l.* *John* 18:3

Laodicea
conflict I have for them at *L. Col* 2:1
zeal for them that are in *L.* 4:13
salute brethren which are in *L.* 15
likewise read the epistle from *L.* 16

Laodiceans
read in the church of the *L. Col* 4:16
angel of church of the *L.* *Rev* 3:14

lap
wild gourds, his *l.* full. 2 *Ki* 4:39
I shook my *l.* and said. *Neh* 5:13
the lot is cast into the *l.* *Pr* 16:33

lapped
the number that *l.* were. *Judg* 7:6
the Lord said, By them that *l.* I. 7

lappeth
that *l.* of the water as. *Judg* 7:5

large
the land, behold it is *l. Gen* 34:21
them into a good and *l.* land. *Ex* 3:8
shall come into a *l.* land. *Judg* 18:10
he brought me forth also into a *l.*
place. 2 *Sam* 22:20; *Ps* 18:19
the work is great and *l.* *Neh* 4:19
the city was *l.* and great. 7:4*
have not served thee in the *l.* 9:35
set my feet in a *l.* room. *Ps* 31:8
and set me in a *l.* place. 118:5
he will toss thee into a *l. Isa* 22:18
shall thy cattle feed in *l.* 30:23
ordained, he made it deep and *l.* 33
I will build *l.* chambers. *Jer* 22:14*
sister's cup deep and *l. Ezek* 23:32
as a lamb in a *l.* place. *Hos* 4:16
they gave *l.* money to. *Mat* 28:12
will shew you a *l.* upper room.
      Mark 14:15; *Luke* 22:12
ye see how *l.* a letter I. *Gal* 6:11
the length is as *l.* as. *Rev* 21:16*

largeness
God gave Solomon *l.* 1 *Ki* 4:29

lasciviousness
heart of men proceed *l. Mark* 7:22
not repented of the *l.* 2 *Cor* 12:21
of the flesh are manifest, *l. Gal* 5:19
given themselves over to *l. Eph* 4:19
walked in *l.*, lusts, excess. *I Pet* 4:3
grace of our God into *l.* *Jude* 4

last
(*Frequently used where modern
writers would use* latter)
shall overcome at the *l. Gen* 49:19*
my *l.* end be like his. *Num* 23:10
why are ye the *l.* to bring the king
back? 2 *Sam* 19:11, 12
now these be the *l.* words of. 23:1
for by the *l.* words of. 1 *Chr* 23:27
David the king, first and *l.* 29:29
of Solomon, first and *l.* 2 *Chr* 9:29
of Rehoboam, first and *l.* 12:15
the acts of Asa, first and *l.* 16:11
acts of Jehoshaphat, first and *l.* 20:34
acts of Amaziah, first and *l.* 25:26
the acts of Uzziah, first and *l.* 26:22
the acts of Ahaz, first and *l.* 28:26
Josiah's deeds, first and *l.* 35:27
the *l.* sons of Adonikam. *Ezra* 8:13
from the first day to the *l. Neh* 8:18
and thou mourn at the *l. Pr* 5:11*
the *l.* it biteth like a serpent. 23:32
the Lord, the first, and with the *l.*
  Isa 41:4; 44:6; 48:12; *Rev* 1:11
      17; 2:8; 22:13
he shall not see our *l.* end. *Jer* 12:4
at *l.* Nebuchadnezzar hath. 50:17
remembered not her *l.* *Lam* 1:9
at the *l.* Daniel came in. *Dan* 4:8
and the higher came up *l.* 8:3
what shall be in the *l.* end. 19
I will slay the *l.* of them. *Amos* 9:1
l. state of that man is worse.
      Mat 12:45; *Luke* 11:26
many that are first shall be *l.* and the
l. first. *Mat* 19:30; 20:16
      Mark 10:31; *Luke* 13:30
beginning from the *l.* to. *Mat* 20:8

l. have wrought one hour. *Mat* 20:12
I will give to this *l.* even as unto. 14
l. of all he sent his son, saying.
       21:37*; *Mark* 12:6
l. of all the woman died. *Mat* 22:27
    Mark 12:22; *Luke* 20:32*
at the *l.* came two false. *Mat* 26:60*
the *l.* error shall be worse. 27:64
desire to be first, the same shall be *l.*
       Mark 9:35
hast paid the *l.* mite. *Luke* 12:59
the eldest even to the *l.* *John* 8:9
set forth us the apostles *l.* *1 Cor* 4:9
and *l.* of all he was seen of. 15:8
the *l.* enemy is death. 26
the *l.* Adam. 45
changed in a moment, at the *l.* 52
at *l.* your care of me. *Phil* 4:10*
the *l.* works to be more. *Rev* 2:19
having the seven *l.* plagues. 15:1
seven vials full of the seven *l.* 21:9

last day, days
befall you in the *l.* days. *Gen* 49:1
come to pass in *l.* days. *Isa* 2:2
    Mi 4:1; *Acts* 2:17
should raise it up at the *l.* day.
    John 6:39, 40, 44, 54
in the *l.* day, the great day. 7:37
he shall rise again at the *l.* day. 11:24
judge him in the *l.* day. 12:48
in *l.* days perilous times. *2 Tim* 3:1
hath spoken in these *l.* days by his
    Son. *Heb* 1:2
treasure for the *l.* days. *Jas* 5:3
come in *l.* days scoffers. *2 Pet* 3:3

last time, times
revealed in the *l.* time. *1 Pet* 1:5
manifest in these *l.* times for. 20
is the *l.* time: are there many anti-
    christs . . . it is the *l.* time.
    1 John 2:18
be mockers in the *l.* time. *Jude* 18

lasted
wept while the feast *l.* *Judg* 14:17

lasting
things of the *l.* hills. *Deut* 33:15

latchet
nor the *l.* of their shoes. *Isa* 5:27
the *l.* of whose shoes. *Mark* 1:7
    Luke 3:16

late
is vain for you to sit up *l.* *Ps* 127:2
of *l.* my people is risen up. *Mi* 2:8
the Jews of *l.* sought to. *John* 11:8

lately
Aquila a Jew *l.* come. *Acts* 18:2

Latin
written in Hebrew, and Greek, and *L.*
    Luke 23:38*; *John* 19:20

latter
the voice of the *l.* sign. *Ex* 4:8
give thee the first rain, and *l.* rain.
    Deut 11:14
if her *l.* husband hate her or. 24:3
stand at the *l.* day. *Job* 19:25
their mouth as for the *l.* rain. 29:23
as a cloud of the *l.* rain. *Pr* 16:15
mayest be wise in the *l.* end. 19:20
and there hath been no *l.* *Jer* 3:3
both the former and *l.* rain in. 5:24
in the *l.* years thou shalt. *Ezek* 38:8
in the *l.* time of their. *Dan* 8:23
not be as the former or the *l.* 11:29
as the *l.* and former rain. *Hos* 6:3
l. rain in the first month. *Joel* 2:23
beginning of the *l.* growth. *Amos* 7:1
the glory of the *l.* house. *Hag* 2:9
the time of the *l.* rain. *Zech* 10:1
that in the *l.* times. *1 Tim* 4:1
    see **days, end**

lattice
cried through the *l.* *Judg* 5:28
fell down through the *l.* *2 Ki* 1:2
shewing himself through the *l.*
    S of S 2:9

laud
praise the Lord, and *l.* *Rom* 15:11

laugh
(*Used both for the laugh of joy
and the laugh of derision*)
wherefore did Sarah *l.?* *Gen* 18:13
24

said, Nay, but thou didst *l.* *Gen* 18:15
hath made me to *l.*, all will *l.* 21:6
and famine thou shalt *l.* *Job* 5:22
he will *l.* at the trial of the. 9:23*
and the innocent *l.* them to. 22:19
in the heavens shall *l.* *Ps* 2:4
all they that see me *l.* me to. 22:7
the Lord shall *l.* at him, for. 37:13
righteous also shall *l.* at him. 52:6
but thou, O Lord, shalt *l.* at. 59:8
and our enemies *l.* among. 80:6
will *l.* at your calamity. *Pr* 1:26
whether he rage or *l.* there is. 29:9
weep, and a time to *l.* *Eccl* 3:4
ye that weep, ye shall *l.* *Luke* 6:21
woe unto you that *l.* now! for ye. 25

laughed
Abraham *l.* *Gen* 17:17
Sarah *l.* in herself. 18:12
Sarah denied, saying, I *l.* not. 15
daughter of Zion hath *l.* *2 Ki* 19:21
    Isa 37:22
they *l.* them to scorn. *2 Chr* 30:10
they *l.* us to scorn, and. *Neh* 2:19
just and upright man is *l.* *Job* 12:4
if I *l.* on them, they. 29:24
thou shalt be *l.* to scorn. *Ezek* 23:32
they *l.* him to scorn. *Mat* 9:24
    Mark 5:40; *Luke* 8:53

laugheth
he *l.* at the shaking of. *Job* 41:29

laughing
till he fill thy mouth with *l.* *Job* 8:21

laughter
our mouth filled with *l.* *Ps* 126:2
even in *l.* the heart is. *Pr* 14:13
I said of *l.* It is mad. *Eccl* 2:2
sorrow is better than *l.* 7:3
so is *l.* of the fool. 6
let your *l.* be turned to. *Jas* 4:9

launch
he said to Simon, *L.* out. *Luke* 5:4*

launched
go over, and they *l.* forth. *Luke* 8:22
after we had *l.* *Acts* 21:1*; 27:2*, 4*

laver
make a *l.* of brass. *Ex* 30:18
the *l.* and his foot. 28; 31:9
    35:16; 39:39
he made the *l.* of brass and. 38:8
thou shalt set the *l.* 40:7
and he set the *l.* 30
anoint the *l.* and his foot. 11
he anointed both the *l.* and. *Lev* 8:11
under the *l.* were undersetters.
    1 Ki 7:30
l. was forty baths, and every *l.* 38
Ahaz removed the *l.* *2 Ki* 16:17

lavers
then made he ten *l.* of. *1 Ki* 7:38
Hiram make the *l.* and shovels. 40
l. on the bases. 43; *2 Chr* 4:6, 14

lavish
l. gold out of the bag. *Isa* 46:6

law
(*When used alone it most frequently refers to the Mosaic Law,
and, in the New Testament, the
additions to that Law made by the
Jewish teachers*)
Joseph made it a *l.* over. *Gen* 47:26
l. to him that is homeborn. *Ex* 12:49
    Lev 24:22; *Num* 15:16, 29
I will give thee a *l.* and. *Ex* 24:12
to the sentence of the *l.* *Deut* 17:11
hand went a fiery *l.* for them. 33:2
Moses commanded us a *l.* even. 4
according to all the *l.* *Josh* 1:7
stones a copy of the *l.* of Moses. 8:32
he read the words of the *l.* 34
take heed to the *l.*
    2 Ki 17:13, 37; 21:8
nor do after the *l.* and. *2 Ki* 17:34
perform the words of the *l.* 23:24
according to all the *l.* of Moses. 25
to Jacob for a *l.* *1 Chr* 16:17
that thou mayest keep the *l.* 22:12

Judah to do the *l.* *2 Chr* 14:4
l. and commandment. 19:10
in their place according to *l.* 30:16
in every work, and in the *l.* 31:21
do according to the whole *l.* 33:8
heard the words of the *l.* 34:19
ready scribe in the *l.* *Ezra* 7:6; 12:21
according to the *l.* of thy God. 14
will not do the *l.* of God and *l.* of. 26
be done according to the *l.* 10:3
the priest brought the *l.* *Neh* 8:2
the people to understand the *l.* 7
when they heard the words of *l.* 9
together to understand the *l.* 13
themselves to *l.* of God. 10:28
an oath to walk in God's *l.* 29
into them the portions of the *l.* 12:44
when they had heard the *l.* 13:3
was according to the *l.* *Esth* 1:8
queen Vashti according to *l.?* 15
one *l.* of his to put him to death. 4:11
which is not according to the *l.* 16
receive the *l.* from his. *Job* 22:22
in his *l.* he meditates day. *Ps* 1:2
l. of his God is in his heart. 37:31
he appointed a *l.* in Israel. 78:5
and they refused to walk in his *l.* 10
was a *l.* of the God of Jacob. 81:4
frameth mischief by a *l.* 94:20
the same to Jacob for a *l.* 105:10
the *l.* of thy mouth is better. 119:72
forsake not the *l.* of thy mother.
    Pr 1:8; 6:20
is a lamp, and the *l.* is light. 6:23
l. of the wise is a fountain. 13:14
the *l.* praise the wicked, but such as
    keep the *l.* contend with. 28:4
keepeth the *l.* is a wise son. 7
away his ear from hearing the *l.* 9
but he that keepeth the *l.* 29:18
they drink and forget the *l.* 31:5
her tongue is the *l.* of kindness. 26
and give ear to the *l.* of. *Isa* 1:10
out of Zion shall go forth the *l.* 2:3
    Mi 4:2
seal the *l.* *Isa* 8:16
to the *l.* and the testimony. 20
the isles shall wait for his *l.* 42:4
the Lord will magnify the *l.* 21
were they obedient to his *l.* 24
for a *l.* shall proceed from me. 51:4
they that handle the *l.* *Jer* 2:8
the *l.* shall not perish from. 18:18
was sealed according to *l.* 32:11
obeyed, nor walked in his *l.* 44:23
the *l.* is no more, prophets. *Lam* 2:9
the *l.* shall perish from. *Ezek* 7:26
concerning the *l.* of his God. *Dan* 6:5
according to *l.* of the Medes. 12, 15
thou hast forgotten the *l.* *Hos* 4:6
therefore the *l.* is slacked. *Hab* 1:4
done violence to the *l.* *Zeph* 3:4
priests concerning the *l.* *Hag* 2:11
they should hear the *l.* *Zech* 7:12
the *l.* of truth was in his. *Mal* 2:6
and they should seek the *l.* at. 7
caused many to stumble at the *l.* 8
ways, but have been partial in *l.* 9
remember the *l.* of Moses my. 4:4
am come to destroy the *l.* *Mat* 5:17
shall in no wise pass from the *l.* 18
any man will sue thee at the *l.* 40
the *l.* prophesied until John. 11:13
    Luke 16:16
have ye not read in the *l.?* *Mat* 12:5
the great commandment in *l.* 22:36
commandments have all the *l.* 40
the weightier matters of the *l.* 23:23
after the custom of the *l.* *Luke* 2:27
there were doctors of the *l.* 5:17
than for one tittle of the *l.* to. 16:17
l. was given by Moses. *John* 1:17
of whom Moses in the *l.* did. 45
give you the *l.* and yet none of you
    keepeth the *l.?* Why go ye ? 7:19
l. of Moses should not be broken. 23
people who knoweth not the *l.* 49
doth our *l.* judge any man before? 51
Moses in the *l.* commanded. 8:5
is it not written in your *l.?* 10:34
we have heard out of the *l.* 12:34
what is written in their *l.* 15:25
judge him according to your *l.* 18:31
we have a *l.* and by our *l.* he. 19:7

Gamaliel, a doctor of the *l. Acts* 5:34
blasphemous words against *l.* 6:13
received the *l.* by angels. 7:53
reading of the *l.* and prophets. 13:15
could not be justified by the *l.* 39
to command them to keep the *l.* 15:5
circumcised and keep the *l.* 24
God contrary to the *l.* 18:13
but if it be a question of your *l.* 15
the *l.* is open. 19:38
zealous of the *l.* 21:20
thou thyself keepest the *l.* 24
man that teacheth against the *l.* 28
to the manner of the *l.* 22:3
devout man according to the *l.* 12
me after the *l.* and commandest me
to be smitten contrary to *l.?* 23:3
have judged according to our *l.* 24:6
nor against the *l.* of the Jews. 25:8
persuading them out of the *l.* 28:23
without *l.:* . . . have sinned in the *l.*
shall be judged by the *l. Rom* 2:12
not the hearers of the *l.* are just. 13
Gentiles, which have not *l.*, do by
nature things contained in *l.*, these,
having not *l.*, are a *l.* unto. 14
shew the work of the *l.* written.
called a Jew, and restest in the *l.* 17
being instructed out of the *l.* 18
the form of the truth in *l.* 20
makest thou boast of the *l.* through
breaking the *l.* dishonourest ? 23
profiteth if thou keep the *l.* but if thou
be a breaker of the *l.* 25
keep the righteousness of the *l*
it fulfil the *l.* judge thee who by circumcision dost trangress the *l.* 27
what things soever the *l.* saith. 3:19
l. no flesh be justified, for by the *l.* is
the knowledge. 20, 28; *Gal* 2:16
righteousness of God is witnessed by
the *l. Rom* 3:21
by what *l.* excluded ? by the *l.* 27
void the *l.?* we establish the *l.* 31
promise was not through the *l.* 4:13
for if they which are of the *l.* 14
l. worketh wrath, for where no *l.* 15
not to that only which is of the *l.* 16
l. sin was in the world, but sin is not
imputed when there is no *l.* 5:13
the *l.* entered, that the offence. 20
speak to them which know the *l.*, the
l. hath dominion over a man. 7:1
the *l.* to her husband; if he be dead,
she is loosed from the *l.* 2, 3
ye also are become dead to the *l.* 4
of sins which were by the *l.* 5
now we are delivered from the *l.* 6
is the *l.* sin ? I had not known sin, but
by *l.* nor lust, except *l.* had said. 7
for without the *l.* sin was dead. 8
the *l.* is holy, and commandment. 12
the *l.* is spiritual. 14
the *l.* is good. 16; *1 Tim* 1:8
I find then a *l. Rom* 7:21
I delight in the *l.* of God. 22
l. warring against the *l.* of my mind,
bringing me into captivity to *l.* 23
I serve *l.* of God: flesh *l.* of sin. 25
l. of life made me free from the *l.* 8:2
for what the *l.* could not do, in. 3
righteousness of the *l.* might be. 4
carnal mind is not subject to the *l.* 7
pertaineth the giving of the *l.* 9:4
Israel followed after the *l.* of. 31
sought it by the works of the *l.* 32
Christ is the end of the *l.* for. 10:4
righteousness which is of the *l.* 5
loveth another, hath fulfilled *l.* 13:8
love is the fulfilling of the *l.* 10
dare any of you go to *l.? 1 Cor* 6:1
brother goeth to *l.* with brother. 6
because ye go to *l.* one with. 7
wife is bound by the *l.* as long. 7:39
saith not the *l.* the same also ? 9:8
obedience, as also saith the *l.* 14:34
sin, and strength of sin is the *l.* 15:56
not justified by the works of the *l.*
Gal 2:16
I through the *l.* am dead to the *l.* 19
righteousness come by the *l.* then. 21
Spirit by the works of the *l.?* 3:2
doeth he it by the works of the *l.?* 5
as are of the works of the *l.* 10

no man is justified by the *l. Gal* 3:11
l. is not of faith, but the man. 12
redeemed us from the curse of *l.* 13
covenant in Christ, the *l.* cannot. 17
if the inheritance be of the *l.* not. 18
wherefore then serveth the *l.?* 19
l. . . . promises? if a *l.* had been given,
righteousness had been by the *l.* 21
the *l.* was our schoolmaster to. 24
tell me, do ye not hear the *l.? 4:21
he is a debtor to do the whole *l.* 5:3
of you are justified by the *l.* 4
all the *l.* is fulfilled in one word. 14
against such there is no *l.* 23
bear ye, and so fulfil the *l.* of. 6:2
nor themselves keep the *l.* but. 13
abolished in his flesh the *l. Eph* 2:15
as touching the *l.* a. *Phil* 3:5
touching the righteousness in the *l.* 6
mine own righteousness, of the *l.* 9
to be teachers of the *l. 1 Tim* 1:7
the *l.* is not made for a righteous. 9
contentions about the *l. Tit* 3:9
people according to the *l. Heb* 7:5
it the people received the *l.* 11
of necessity a change of the *l.* 12
not after the *l.* of a carnal. 16
for the *l.* made nothing perfect. 19
l. maketh men high priests, but word
of the oath which was since *l.* 28
priests offer gifts according to *l.* 8:4
had spoken according to the *l.* 9:19
are by the *l.* purged with blood. 22
the *l.* having a shadow of good. 10:1
he that despised Moses' *l.* died. 28
into perfect *l.* of liberty. *Jas* 1:25
if ye fulfil the royal *l.* 2:8
and are convinced of the *l.* as. 9
shall keep the whole *l.* 10
thou art a transgressor of the *l.* 11
they that shall be judged by the *l.* 12
evil of the *l.* and judgeth the *l.* 4:11
sin transgresseth also the *l.* for sin is
the transgression of *l. 1 John* 3:4

see book

law of the Lord
that the *Lord's l.* may be. *Ex* 13:9
Jehu took no heed to walk in *l.* of
Lord. 2 Ki 10:31
Rehoboam forsook *l.* of *Lord* and.
2 Chr 12:1
be encouraged in the *l.* of *Lord.* 31:4
Josiah's goodness according to the *l.*
of *Lord.* 35:26
prepared his heart to seek the *l.* of
Lord. *Ezra* 7:10
his delight is in the *l.* of *L. Ps* 1:2
the *l.* of the *Lord* is perfect. 19:7
who walk in the *l.* of the *Lord.* 119:1
cast away the *l.* of *Lord. Isa* 5:24
will not hear the *l.* of the *Lord.* 30:9
l. of the *Lord* is with us. *Jer* 8:8
despised the *l.* of the *Lord. Amos* 2:4
according to the *l.* of *Lord. Luke* 2:39

my law
will walk in *my l.* or no. *Ex* 16:4
children walk in *my l.* 2 Chr 6:16
O my people, to *my l. Ps* 78:1
if his children forsake *my l.* 89:30
forget not *my l.* but keep. *Pr* 3:1
forsake not *my l.* 4:2
keep *my l.* as the apple. 7:2
in whose heart is *my l. Isa* 51:7
not hearkened unto *my l. Jer* 6:19
they have forsaken *my l.* 9:13
and have not kept *my l.* 16:11
not hearken to walk in *my l.* 26:4
put *my l.* in their inward parts. 31:33
feared nor walked in *my l.* 44:10
her priests have violated *my l.*
Ezek 22:26
trespassed against *my l. Hos* 8:1
to him the great things of *my l.* 12

this law
this shall be the *l.* of leper. *Lev* 14:2
execute on her *this l. Num* 5:30
this is the ordinance of the *l.* 31:21
Moses to declare *this l. Deut* 1:5
all *this l.* which I set before you. 4:8
shall write him a copy of *this l.* 17:18
to keep all the words of *this l.* 19
them the words of *this l.* 27:3, 8

confirmeth not the words of *this l.*
Deut 27:26
not observe words of *this l.* 28:58
all the words of *this l.* 29:29; 31:12
Moses wrote *this l.* 31:9
thou shalt read *this l.* 11
of writing the words of *this l.* in. 24
children to do the words of *this l.*
32:46
read the words of *this l. Josh* 8:34

this is the **law**
this is the l. of the burnt offering.
Lev 6:9; 7:37
this is the l. of meat offering. 6:14
this is the l. of sin offering. 25
this is the l. of the trespass. 7:1
this is the l. of the beasts. 11:46
this is the l. of her that hath. 12:7
this is the l. of the plague of leprosy.
13:59; 14:32, 57
this is the l. for all manner. 14:54
this is the l. of him that hath an
issue. 15:32
this is the l. of jealousies. *Num* 5:29
this is the l. of the Nazarite. 6:13
this is the l. when a man dieth. 19:14
this is the l. which Moses. *Deut* 4:44
this is the l. of the house. *Ezek* 43:12
this is the l. and prophets. *Mat* 7:12

thy **law**
shall teach Israel thy *l. Deut* 33:10
they cast *thy l.* behind. *Neh* 9:26
bring them again to *thy l.* 29
kings, nor our princes kept *thy l.* 34
yea, *thy l.* is within my. *Ps* 40:8
teachest him out of *thy l.* 94:12
things out of *thy l.* 119:18
way of lying, and grant me *thy l.* 29
give me understanding, and I shall
keep *thy l.* 34
I keep *thy l.* continually for ever. 44
have I not declined from *thy l.* 51
the wicked that forsake *thy l.* 53
thy name, and kept *thy l.* 55
but I have not forgotten *thy l.* 61
is fat, but I delight in *thy l.* 70
I may live, for *thy l.* is my delight.
77, 92, 174
pits, which are not after *thy l.* 85
O how I love *thy l.* 97
yet do I not forget *thy l.* 109
but *thy l.* do I love. 113, 163
made void *thy l.* 126
down, because they keep not *thy l.*
136
and *thy l.* is the truth. 142
are far from *thy l.* 150
peace have they who love *thy l.* 165
not, nor walked in *thy l. Jer* 32:23
have transgressed *thy l. Dan* 9:11

under the **law**
them that are *under the l. Rom* 3:19
for ye are not under the *l.* 6:14
because we are not *under l.* 15
under the l. as *under the l.* that I
. . . that are *under the l. 1 Cor* 9:20
without law to God, but *under l.* 21
we were kept *under the l. Gal* 3:23
made *under the l.* 4:4
redeem them that were *under l.* 5
ye that desire to be *under the l.* 21
if ye be led of the Spirit, ye are not
under the l. 5:18

without **law**
a long season, Israel hath been *without l.* 2 Chr 15:3
as many as sinned *without l.* perish
without l. *Rom* 2:12
righteousness of God *without l.* 3:21
for *without l.* sin was dead. 7:8
I was alive *without* the *l.* once. 9
that are *without l.*, as *without l.*, not
without l. to God. *1 Cor* 9:21

written in the **law**
as it is *w.* in the *l.* of Moses.
1 Ki 2:3; *2 Chr* 23:18; 25:4; 31:3
Ezra 3:2; *Neh* 10:34, 36
Dan 9:13; *Luke* 2:23
do according to all *w.* in the *l.*
1 Chr 16:40; *2 Chr* 35:26
found *w.* in the *l.* that. *Neh* 8:14
oath that is *w.* in *l.* of. *Dan* 9:11

what is *w.* in the *l.?*   *Luke* 10:26
fulfilled, which were *w.* in *l.*   24:44
things that are *w.* in *l.*   *Acts* 24:14
it is *w.* in the *l.*   *1 Cor* 9:9
in the *l.* it is *w.*   14:21

lawful
shall not be *l.* to impose. *Ezra* 7:24
shall the *l.* captive be ? *Isa* 49:24
do that which is *l.*   *Ezek* 18:5
    21:27; 33:14, 19
the son hath done that which is *l.*
    18:19; 33:16
do what is not *l.*   *Mat* 12:2
    Mark 2:24; *Luke* 6:2
was not *l.* for him to eat. *Mat* 12:4
    Mark 2:26; *Luke* 6:4
l. to heal on the sabbath? *Mat* 12:10
  12; *Mark* 3:4; *Luke* 6:9; 14:3
it is not *l.* for thee to have her.
    Mat 14:4; *Mark* 6:18
is it *l.* for man to put away wife ?
    Mat 19:3; *Mark* 10:2
l. to give tribute to ? *Mat* 22:17
    Mark 12:14; *Luke* 20:22
it is not *l.* to put them in the treasury.
    Mat 27:6
not *l.* for thee to carry. *John* 5:10
not *l.* for us to put any man. 18:31
which are not *l.* to receive. *Acts* 16:21
shall be determined in a *l.* 19:39
is it *l.* for you to scourge ? 22:25
all things are *l.* unto me:all things *l.*
for me.   *1 Cor* 6:12; 10:23
is not *l.* for a man to. *2 Cor* 12:4

lawfully
good, if a man use it *l.*   *1 Tim* 1:8
yet is not crowned, except he strive *l.*
    2 Tim 2:5

lawgiver
l. from between his feet. *Gen* 49:10*
digged the well by direction of the *l.*
    Num 21:18*
in a portion of the *l.*   *Deut* 33:21
Judah is my *l.*   *Ps* 60:7*; 108:8*
the Lord is our *l.* and. *Isa* 33:22
there is one *l.* who is able. *Jas* 4:12

lawless
the law is for the *l.* and. *1 Tim* 1:9

laws
my statutes and my *l.*   *Gen* 26:5
refuse ye to keep my *l.?*   *Ex* 16:28
I do make them know the *l.* 18:16
teach them ordinances and *l.* 20
l. which the Lord made. *Lev* 26:46
know the *l.* of thy God. *Ezra* 7:25
thou gavest them true *l.* *Neh* 9:13
commandedst them statutes and *l.* 14
written among the *l.* of. *Esth* 1:19
their *l.* are diverse from all people,
   neither keep they the king's *l.* 3:8
they might keep his *l.* *Ps* 105:45
have transgressed the *l.* *Isa* 24:5
shew them all the *l.* *Ezek* 43:11
hear all the *l.* 44:5
they shall keep my *l.* 24
to change times and *l.* *Dan* 7:25
we obeyed to walk in his *l.* 9:10
I will put my *l.* into their. *Heb* 8:10
put my *l.* into their hearts. 10:16

lawyer
(*One skilled in the interpretation
of the Mosaic Law*)
one that was a *l.* asked him.
    Mat 22:35; *Luke* 10:25
bring Zenas the *l.* and. *Tit* 3:13

lawyers
l. rejected the counsel. *Luke* 7:30
then answered one of the *l.* 11:45
woe unto you, *l.* 46, 52
Jesus spake to *l..* 14:3

lay, *as with a woman*
the firstborn *l.* with her father.
    Gen 19:33, 34, 35
and Jacob *l.* with Leah. 30:16
Shechem *l.* with Dinah. 34:2
Reuben went and *l.* with. 35:22
man that *l.* with woman. *Deut* 22:22
the man only that *l.* with her. 25
man that *l.* with her give fifty. 29
Eli heard they *l.* with. *1 Sam* 2:22
she came, and he *l.* with her.
    2 Sam 11:4; 12:24

Amnon forced Tamor and *l.*
    2 Sam 13:14
for in her youth they *l.* *Ezek* 23:8

lay
tale of bricks ye shall *l.*   *Ex* 5:8
as woman's husband will *l.* 21:22
neither shalt thou *l.* upon. 22:25
and *l.* the wood in order. *Lev* 1:7
the priests shall *l.* the parts. 8, 12
thou shalt *l.* the frankincense. 2:15
and *l.* the burnt offering in. 6:12
Lord, *l.* not the sin upon. *Num* 12:11
l. them on them that hate. *Deut* 7:15
shall *l.* the fear of you upon. 11:25
l. not innocent blood to thy. 21:8*
l. thee an ambush for the city.
    Josh 8:2
Samson *l.* till midnight. *Judg* 16:3
behold, a woman *l.* at his. *Ruth* 3:8
and Samuel *l.* till the. *1 Sam* 3:15
and *l.* it for a reproach on. 11:2
Saul *l.* in the trench, people. 26:5, 7
Ish-bosheth, who *l.* on a. *2 Sam* 4:5*
lamb eat of his meat, and *l.* 12:3
David *l.* all night on the. 16; 13:31
l. my bones beside his. *1 Ki* 13:31
l. it on wood and put no fire. 18:23
and as he *l.* and slept under. 19:5
Ahab fasted and *l.* in. 21:27
he went up and *l.* upon. *2 Ki* 4:34
l. ye them in two heaps at. 10:8
long as she *l.* desolate. *2 Chr* 36:21
many *l.* in sackcloth and. *Esth* 4:3
the dew *l.* all night. *Job* 29:19
he will not *l.* on man more. 34:23*
let him *l.* mine honour in. *Ps* 7:5
they that seek my life, *l.* 38:12
found a nest, where she may *l.* 84:3
and the living will *l.* it to. *Eccl* 7:2
woe to them that *l.* field. *Isa* 5:8
to *l.* the land desolate. 13:9
    Ezek 33:28
I will *l.* low haughtiness. *Isa* 13:11
key of house of David *l.* on. 22:22
fortress shall he *l.* low. 25:12
behold, I will *l.* in Zion a. 28:16
judgement will I *l.* to the line. 17*
that *l.* a snare for him that. 29:21
staff which the Lord shall *l.* 30:32
there shall the great owl *l.* 34:15
a lump of figs, and *l.* it for. 38:21
thou didst not *l.* these things. 47:7
I will *l.* thy stones with fair. 54:11
I will *l.* stumblingblocks. *Jer* 6:21
    Ezek 3:20
take thee a tile, and *l.* it. *Ezek* 4:1
l. siege against it. 2, 3
l. the iniquity of the house of. 4
I will *l.* bands upon thee. 8
I will *l.* my vengeance on. 25:14, 17
I will *l.* thee before kings. 28:17
l. thy flesh on the mountains. 32:5
and I will *l.* no famine upon. 36:29
be tilled, whereas it *l.* desolate. 34
I will *l.* sinews upon you. 37:6
there *l.* the most holy things. 42:13
    14; 44:19
O Lord, *l.* not on us. *Jonah* 1:14
idols thereof will I *l.* *Mi* 1:7
l. it to heart, I will send a curse upon
  you; because ye do not *l.* *Mal* 2:2
hath not where to *l.* his head.
    Mat 8:20; *Luke* 9:58
and lay them on men's. *Mat* 23:4
see the place where the Lord *l.* 28:6
the sick of the palsy *l.* *Mark* 2:4
shall *l.* thee even with. *Luke* 19:44*
l. impotent folk, blind. *John* 5:3
it was a cave, and a stone *l.* 11:38
Lord, *l.* not this sin to. *Acts* 7:60
l. on you no greater burden. 15:28
and no small tempest *l.* on. 27:20
l. any thing to the charge. *Rom* 8:33
I *l.* in Sion a stumblingstone. 9:33
let every one *l.* by him. *1 Cor* 16:2
l. aside every weight. *Heb* 12:1
wherefore *l.* apart all. *Jas* 1:21
I *l.* in Sion a chief. *1 Pet* 2:6

see **foundation**

lay down
before they *l. down* men. *Gen* 19:4
and Lot perceived not when she *l.
down.* 33, 35

Jacob *l. down* in that place. *Gen* 28:11
he *l. down* as a lion. *Num* 24:9
he *l. down* at her feet. *Judg* 5:27
his feet, and *l.* thee *down.* *Ruth* 3:4
lie down, and Samuel went and *l.
down.* *1 Sam* 3:5, 9
Saul *l. down* naked all that. 19:24
Jonadab said, *L.* thee *down* on thy.
    2 Sam 13:5
so Amnon *l. down* and made. 6
l. down now, put me in surety with.
    Job 17:3*
l. me down in peace. *Ps* 4:8
young lions *l.* them *down.* 104:22
thy mother *l. down.* *Ezek* 19:2*
l. themselves down on clothes.
    Amos 2:8
and I *l. down* my life for my sheep.
    John 10:15, 17
l. it *down* of myself, have power to *l.*
  it *down.* 18
I will *l. down* my life for. 13:37, 38
that a man *l. down* his life. 15:13
to *l. down* our lives. *1 John* 3:16

lay hand
l. not thy *hand* on the lad. *Gen* 22:12
shed no blood, *l.* no *hand.* 37:22
l. my *hand* upon Egypt. *Ex* 7:4
l. his *hand* on the head of his offering. *Lev* 3:2, 8
l. his *hand* on the head of the peace.
    13; 4:24
he shall *l.* his *hand* on the bullock's
head. 4:4, 15
he shall *l.* his *hand* on the sin offering. 29, 33
l. thy *hand* on Joshua. *Num* 27:18
l. thy *hand* upon thy mouth, and go.
    Judg 18:19
to *l.* *hand* on the king. *Esth* 2:21
to *l.* *hand* on such as sought. 9:2
daysman might *l.* his *hand.* *Job* 9:33
mark me, and *l.* your *hand.* 21:5
I will *l.* my *hand* on my mouth. 40:4
l. thy *hand* upon him. 41:8
thought evil, *l.* *hand* upon. *Pr* 30:32
l. their *hand* on Edom. *Isa* 11:14
shall *l.* their *hand* on their mouth.
    Mi 7:16
and *l.* thy *hand* on her. *Mat* 9:18

lay hands
Aaron shall *l.* both his *hands* on.
    Lev 16:21
him *l.* their *hands* on head. 24:14
the Levites *l.* their *h.* *Num* 8:12
I will *l. hands* on you. *Neh* 13:21
scorn to *l.* *hands* on. *Esth* 3:6
they sought to *l. hands* on him.
    Mat 21:46; *Luke* 20:19
come and *l.* thy *hands.* *Mark* 5:23
l. hands on the sick, and they. 16:18
shall *l. hands* on you. *Luke* 21:12
on whomsoever I *l. hands.* *Acts* 8:19
l. hands suddenly on. *1 Tim* 5:22

lay hold
shall his father *l. hold.* *Deut* 21:19
and *l. hold* on her, and lie. 22:28
l. thee *hold* on the wood. *2 Sam* 2:21
hand, saying, *L. hold* on. *1 Ki* 13:4
life to them that *l. hold.* *Pr* 3:18
I sought to *l. hold* on folly. *Eccl* 2:3
shall roar, and *l. hold* on. *Isa* 5:29
they shall *l. hold* on bow. *Jer* 6:23
l. hold on his neighbour. *Zech* 14:13
will he not *l. hold* on it ? *Mat* 12:11
out to *l. hold* on him. *Mark* 3:21
they sought to *l. hold* on him. 12:12
l. hold on eternal life. *1 Tim* 6:12, 19
to *l. hold* on the hope. *Heb* 6:18

lay up
l. up corn under the hand. *Gen* 41:35
l. up manna for you till. *Ex* 16:23
l. up a pot of manna to be kept. 33
l. them *up* in tabernacle. *Num* 17:4
l. them *up* without the camp. 19:9
l. up these my words. *Deut* 11:18
shall *l.* it *up* within thy gates. 14:28
l. up his words in thy. *Job* 22:22
then shalt *l.* *up* gold as dust and. 24
l. up my commandments. *Pr* 7:1
wise men *l. up* knowledge. 10:14
l. not *up* for yourselves treasures
upon earth. *Mat* 6:19

l. up for yourselves treasures in
heaven.　　　　　　*Mat 6:20*
children not to *l. up* for. *2 Cor 12:14*

lay wait

from such as *l.* in *wait.*　*Ezra 8:31*
that *l. wait* for my soul.　*Ps 71:10*
let us *l. wait* for blood.　*Pr 1:11*
l. wait for their own blood.　18
l. not *wait* against the.　24:15
they *l. wait* as he that.　*Jer 5:26*

lay waste

that shouldest be to *l. waste.*
　　　2 Ki 19:25; Isa 37:26
I will *l.* it *waste,* it shall.　*Isa 5:6*
I will *l.* thy cities *waste. Ezek 35:4*

layest

thou *l.* the burden of.　*Num 11:11*
l. thou a snare for my ? *1 Sam 28:9*

layeth

God *l.* up his iniquity.　*Job 21:19*
soul crieth out, yet God *l.*　24:12*
the sword of him that *l.* at.　41:26
he *l.* up the depth in.　*Ps 33:7*
l. the beams of his chambers. 104:3
he *l.* up wisdom for the.　*Pr 2:7*
with knowledge, but a fool *l.* 13:16*
dissembleth, and *l.* up deceit. 26:24
l. her hands to the spindle.　31:19
the lofty city he *l.* low to. *Isa 26:5*
blessed is the man that *l.*　56:2*
perisheth, and no man *l.* it to. 57:1
but in heart he *l.* his wait. *Jer 9:8*
l. it to heart.　　　　12:11
Lord *l.* the foundation.　*Zech 12:1*
he that *l.* up treasure.　*Luke 12:21*
he *l.* it on his shoulders.　15:5

laying

hurl at him by *l.* wait.　*Num 35:20*
him any thing without *l.* wait.　22
commune of *l.* snares.　*Ps 64:5*
l. aside the commandment of God.
　　　　　　Mark 7:8
l. wait for him, and.　*Luke 11:54*
l. on of the apostles'.　*Acts 8:18*
but their *l.* wait was known.　9:24*
kinsmen heard of their *l.* in. 23:16
l. wait in the way to kill him. 25:3
with *l.* on of the hands. *1 Tim 4:14*
l. up in store a good foundation. 6:19
not *l.* again the foundation. *Heb 6:1*
doctrine of baptisms, and of *l.* on. 2
l. aside all malice, guile. *1 Pet 2:1*

Lazarus

certain beggar named *L. Luke 16:20*
seeth *L.* in Abraham's bosom.　23
send *L.* that he may dip the tip.　24
likewise *L.* received evil things.　25
Mary whose brother *L.* *John 11:2*
Jesus loved *L.*　　　　　5
our friend *L.* sleepeth.　　11
L. is dead.　　　　　　14
he cried, *L.* come forth.　　43
L. was one of them that sat.　12:2
came that they might see *L.*　9
when he called *L.* out of grave.　17

lead, *substantive*

sank as *l.* in the mighty.　*Ex 15:10*
l. that may abide fire.　*Num 31:22*
graven with iron and *l.*　*Job 19:24*
l. is consumed of the fire. *Jer 6:29*
they are led *l.* in the midst. *Ezek 22:18*
as they gather *l.* so will I gather. 20
with iron, tin, and *l.* Tarshish. 27:12
lifted up a talent of *l.*　*Zech 5:7*
he cast the weight of *l.* on the.　8

lead

I will *l.* on softly as the. *Gen 33:14*
a pillar of cloud to *l.*　*Ex 13:21*
go, *l.* the people to the place. 32:34
l. them out and bring. *Num 27:17*
whither the Lord shall *l.* you.
　　　　Deut 4:27; 28:37
shall make captains to *l.* the.　20:9
so the Lord alone did *l.* him. 32:12
Barak, *l.* thy captivity.　*Judg 5:12*
they may *l.* them away. *1 Sam 30:22*
find compassion before them that *l.*
　　　　　　2 Chr 30:9
pillar of cloud to *l.*　*Neh 9:19*
l. me, O Lord, in thy.　*Ps 5:8*
l. me in thy truth.　　25:5
l. me in a plain path.　27:11

for thy name's sake *l.* me.　*Ps 31:3*
light and truth, let them *l.* me.　43:3
l. me into Edom ?　60:9*; 108:10
l. me to the rock that is.　61:2
l. them forth with workers of. 125:5
there shall thine hand *l.* me. 139:10
l. me in the way everlasting.　24
l. me into the land of.　143:10
goest, it shall *l.* thee.　*Pr 6:22*
l. in way of righteousness.　8:20*
l. thee to my mother's.　*S of S 8:2*
l. thee cause thee to err.　*Isa 3:12*
a little child shall *l.* them.　11:6
the king of Assyria *l.*　20:4
gently *l.* those that are with. 40:11
I will *l.* them in paths not.　42:16
hath mercy on them, shall *l.*　49:10
I will *l.* him, and restore.　57:18
so didst thou *l.* thy people.　63:14
with supplications will I *l.* *Jer 31:9*
shall *l.* Zedekiah to Babylon.　32:5
maids *l.* her, as with voice. *Nah 2:7*
l. us not into temptation.
　　Mat 6:13; *Luke 11:4*
if the blind *l.* the blind.　*Mat 15:14*
　　　　　　Luke 6:39
when they shall *l.* you. *Mark 13:11*
take him and *l.* him away.　14:44
loose his ox and *l.* him. *Luke 13:15*
seeking some to *l.* him.　*Acts 13:11*
have we not power to *l.*? *1 Cor 9:5*
we may *l.* a quiet life.　*1 Tim 2:2*
l. captive silly women.　*2 Tim 3:6*
to *l.* them out of the land. *Heb 8:9*
shall feed and *l.* them.　*Rev 7:17*

leader

Jehoiada was *l.* of the. *1 Chr 12:27*
David consulted with captains and
every *l.*　　　　　13:1
I have given him a *l.*　*Isa 55:4*

leaders

angel which cut off *l.*　*2 Chr 32:21*
the *l.* of this people.　*Isa 9:16*
they be blind *l.* of the. *Mat 15:14*

leadest

that *l.* Joseph like a flock.　*Ps 80:1*

leadeth

turned to the way that *l.* *1 Sam 13:17*
he *l.* counsellors away.　*Job 12:17*
he *l.* princes away spoiled, and.　19
he *l.* me beside the still.　*Ps 23:2*
he *l.* me in the paths of.　3
l. him into the way that.　*Pr 16:29*
Lord thy God which *l.*　*Isa 48:17*
wide is the way that *l.* to. *Mat 7:13*
narrow is the way that *l.* to life.　14
Jesus *l.* them into a high. *Mark 9:2*
he calleth his sheep and *l. John 10:3*
the iron gate that *l.*　*Acts 12:10*
the goodness of God *l.* to. *Rom 2:4*
he that *l.* shall go into.　*Rev 13:10*

leaf

her mouth was an olive *l.* *Gen 8:11*
sound of a shaken *l.*　*Lev 26:36*
wilt thou break a *l.* driven to and
fro ?　　　　　*Job 13:25*
his *l.* also shall not wither. *Ps 1:3*
be as an oak, whose *l.*　*Isa 1:30*
their host fall as a *l.*　34:4
we all do fade as a *l.*　64:6
no grapes, the *l.* shall. *Jer 8:13*
but her *l.* shall be green, and.　17:8
l. shall not fade, the *l.* *Ezek 47:12*

league

(*The Revisions frequently change
this word to* covenant)

make therefore a *l.*　*Josh 9:6, 11*
Joshua made a *l.* with the.　15, 16
no *l.* with the inhabitants. *Judg 2:2*
my son hath made a *l.* *1 Sam 22:8*
king David made a *l.*　*2 Sam 5:3*
Solomon made a *l.*　*1 Ki 5:12*
is a *l.* between me and thee.　15:19
go break thy *l.* with.　*2 Chr 16:3*
be in *l.* with the stones.　*Job 5:23*
men of the land that is in *l.* shall.
　　　　　　Ezek 30:5
after the *l.* he shall work. *Dan 11:23*

Leah

elder daughter was *L.*　*Gen 29:16*
L. was tender eyed, but Rachel.　17
in the morning, behold it was *L.*　25

the Lord saw that *L.*　*Gen 29:31*
L. conceived and bare.　32; 30:19
out of the field, *L.* met him.　30:16
Jacob called Rachel and *L.*　31:4
Jacob put *L.* and her children.　33:2
Dinah the daughter of *L.* went. 34:1
L.; Reuben, Simeon.　35:23; 46:15
Abraham, there I buried *L.*　49:31
make this woman like *L. Ruth 4:11*

lean

kine came out of the river *l.*fleshed.
　　　　　　Gen 41:3, 19
the *l.*fleshed eat up the.　4, 20
land is, whether fat or *l. Num 13:20*
being the king's son *l.* *2 Sam 13:4*
of his flesh shall wax *l.*　*Isa 17:4*
between fat cattle and *l. Ezek 34:20*

lean, *verb*

I may *l.* on the pillars.　*Judg 16:26*
on which if a man *l.*　*2 Ki 18:21*
　　　　　　Isa 36:6
shall *l.* on his house.　*Job 8:15*
l. not to thine own.　*Pr 3:5*
yet will they *l.* on the Lord. *Mi 3:11*

leaned

behold, Saul *l.* upon.　*2 Sam 1:6*
on whose hand the king *l.* *2 Ki 7:2*
when they *l.* on thee.　*Ezek 29:7*
l. his hand on the wall.　*Amos 5:19*
who also *l.* on his breast. *John 21:20*

leaneth

not fail one that *l.* on. *2 Sam 3:29*
l. on my hand in the.　*2 Ki 5:18*

leaning

that cometh up *l.* on.　*S of S 8:5*
there was *l.* on Jesus'. *John 13:23*
Jacob worshipped, *l.* on. *Heb 11:21*

leanness

my *l.* rising up in me.　*Job 16:8*
gave request, but sent *l. Ps 106:15*
among his fat ones *l.*　*Isa 10:16*
but I said, My *l.*, my *l.*, woe. 24:16*

leap

all the rams which *l.* on. *Gen 31:12*
have legs to *l.* withal.　*Lev 11:21*
and of Dan, he shall *l.* *Deut 33:22*
and sparks of fire *l.* out. *Job 41:19*
why *l.* ye, ye high hills ? *Ps 68:16*
then shall the lame man *l.* *Isa 35:6*
of chariots shall they *l.*　*Joel 2:5*
shall punish those that *l.* *Zeph 1:9*
in that day, and *l.* for joy. *Luke 6:23*

leaped

the rams which *l.* upon. *Gen 31:10*
by my God, *l.* over a wall.
　　　　2 Sam 22:30; Ps 18:29
they *l.* upon the altar.　*1 Ki 18:26*
babe *l.* in her womb. *Luke 1:41, 44*
stand upright, and he *l.* *Acts 14:10*
he in whom evil spirit was, *l.* 19:16

leaping

Michal saw David *l.*　*2 Sam 6:16*
behold he cometh *l.* on.　*S of S 2:8*
l. up, stood and walked.　*Acts 3:8*

learn

that they may *l.* to fear me.
　　　　Deut 4:10; 14:23
that ye may *l.* them, and keep. 5:1
therein, that he may *l.* to fear. 17:19
shalt not *l.* to do after the.　18:9
they may hear, and *l.* and.　31:12
that their children may *l.* to.　13
I might *l.* thy statutes. *Ps 119:71, 73*
lest thou *l.* his ways.　*Pr 22:25*
l. to do well, seek.　*Isa 1:17*
neither shall they *l.* war. 2:4; *Mi 4:3*
the inhabitants of world shall *l.*
righteousness.　　*Isa 26:9*
not the wicked *l.* righteousness.
murmured shall *l.* doctrine. 29:24†
l. not the way of heathen. *Jer 10:2*
if they will diligently *l.* ways. 12:16
but go and *l.* what that. *Mat 9:13*
l. of me, for I am meek and. 11:29
l. a parable of the fig tree.　24:32
　　　　　　Mark 13:28
l. in us not to think.　*1 Cor 4:6*
one by one, that all may *l.*　14:31
if they will *l.* any thing, let them. 35
would *l.* of you, received ye ? *Gal 3:2*

l. not to blaspheme.   *1 Tim* 1:20*
let the woman *l.* in silence.   2:11
let them *l.* first to shew piety.   5:4
and withal they *l.* to be idle.   13
let ours *l.* to maintain.   *Tit* 3:14
no man could *l.* that song. *Rev* 14:3

learned

tarry, for I have *l.* by.   *Gen* 30:27*
among the heathen, and *l.* *Ps* 106:35
l. thy righteous judgements.   119:7
I neither *l.* wisdom, nor.   *Pr* 30:3
deliver to one that is *l.*   *Isa* 29:11
is not *l.* he saith, I am not *l.*   12
given me tongue of the *l.* he wakeneth mine ear to hear as *l.*   50:4*
it *l.* to catch the prey. *Ezek* 19:3, 6
every man that hath *l.*   *John* 6:45
man letters, having never *l.*   7:15
Moses was *l.* in all.   *Acts* 7:22*
the doctrine ye have *l.*   *Rom* 16:17
have not so *l.* Christ.   *Eph* 4:20
those things ye have *l.* and. *Phil* 4:9
l., therewith to be content.   11
as ye *l.* of Epaphras our.   *Col* 1:7
in the things thou hast *l.* knowing of
   whom thou hast *l.*   *2 Tim* 3:14
though ye were a son, yet *l.* *Heb* 5:8

learning

will hear and increase *l.*   *Pr* 1:5
man, and he will increase in *l.*   9:9
of the lips increaseth *l.*   16:21
the heart of the wise addeth *l.*   23
whom they might teach *l.*   *Dan* 1:4
God gave them skill in all *l.*   17
Festus said, Much *l.*   *Acts* 26:24
were written for our *l.*   *Rom* 15:4
ever *l.* and never able.   *2 Tim* 3:7

leasing

long will ye seek after *l.?*   *Ps* 4:2*
destroy them that speak *l.*   5:6*

least

[1] *The smallest quantity,* Num
11:32. [2] *Most humble and lowly,*
Luke 9:48. [3] *The meanest person, or one of the least judgement,
skill, and experience,* Judg 6:15.
not worthy of the *l.* of.   *Gen* 32:10
gathered *l.* gathered.   *Num* 11:32
l. in my father's house.   *Judg* 6:15
my family, the *l.* of.   *1 Sam* 9:21
one captain of *l.* of.   *2 Ki* 18:24
l. of flock shall draw them.
   Jer 49:20*; 50:45*
not the *l.* grain fall upon. *Amos* 9:9
art not the *l.* among the princes of
   Judah.   *Mat* 2:6
of these *l.* commandments, shall be
   called the *l.* in the kingdom.   5:19
that is *l.* in the kingdom of heaven, is
   greater.   11:11*; *Luke* 7:28*
is the *l.* of all seeds.   *Mat* 13:32*
have done it to the *l.*   25:40, 45
he that is *l.* among you. *Luke* 9:48
not able to do that which is *l.*   12:26
faithful in the *l.*: unjust in.   16:10
them to judge who are *l.* *1 Cor* 6:4*
for I am the *l.* of the apostles. 15:9
who am less than the *l.*   *Eph* 3:8

see greatest

at the least
damsel abide with us, *at the l.*
   Gen 24:55
at the l. such as before.   *Judg* 3:2
if kept themselves *at l.* *1 Sam* 21:4*
hadst known *at l.* in.   *Luke* 19:42
that *at the l.* the shadow of Peter.
   Acts 5:15

leather
man, girt with a girdle of *l.* *2 Ki* 1:8

leathern
John had a *l.* girdle.   *Mat* 3:4

leave

[1] *Permission,* Num 22:13; Mark
5:13. [2] *To depart from,* John
16:28. [3] *Farewell,* Acts 18:18.
[4] *To lay down,* Mat 5:24.

leave, substantive
refuseth to give me *l.*   *Num* 22:13
asked *l.* of me.   *1 Sam* 20:6, 28
certain days obtained I *l.* *Neh* 13:6
Jesus gave them *l.*   *Mark* 5:13

Pilate gave him *l.* to.   *John* 19:38
Paul took his *l.* of the.   *Acts* 18:18
when we had taken our *l.* one. 21:6
l. I went to Macedonia. *2 Cor* 2:13

leave

l. father and mother and. *Gen* 2:24
   Mat 19:5; *Mark* 10:7; *Eph* 5:31
let me *l.* with thee some of the folk.
   Gen 33:15
l. one of your brethren here. 42:33
not *l.* his father, if he *l.*   44:22
let no man *l.* manna till.   *Ex* 16:19
what they *l.* the beasts of.   23:11
not *l.* any of the peace offering.
   Lev 7:15; 22:30
shall put off garments and *l.*   16:23
thou shalt *l.* them for the poor.
   19:10; 23:22
l. none of the passover.   *Num* 9:12
he said, *L.* us not, I pray.   10:31
will yet again *l.* them in the. 32:15
not *l.* thee either corn.   *Deut* 28:51
of children which he shall *l.*   54
and *l.* them in the lodging. *Josh* 4:3*
olive said, Should I *l.* my ? *Judg* 9:9
vine said, Should I *l.* my vine ?   13
Entreat me not to *l.*   *Ruth* 1:16
lest my father *l.* caring.   *1 Sam* 9:5
Saul said, Let us not *l.* a.   14:36
if I *l.* of all that pertain to.   25:22
shall not *l.* to my husband neither
   name nor.   *2 Sam* 14:7
let him not *l.* us nor.   *1 Ki* 8:57
shall eat and shall *l.*   *2 Ki* 4:43
did he *l.* of the people but fifty. 13:7
this good land, and *l.* it. *1 Chr* 28:8
to *l.* us a remnant to.   *Ezra* 9:8
l. it for an inheritance to your.   12
I pray you let us *l.* off this. *Neh* 5:10
the work cease whilst I *l.* it ?   6:3
would *l.* the seventh year.   10:31*
wilt thou *l.* thy labour ? *Job* 39:11
thou wilt not *l.* my soul in hell.
   Ps 16:10; *Acts* 2:27
they *l.* their substance to. *Ps* 17:14
thou hast been my help, *l.* me not.
   27:9; 119:121
they die and *l.* their wealth. 49:10
O God, my trust, *l.* not my. 141:8
l. the paths of uprightness. *Pr* 2:13
l. off contention, before it be. 17:14
I should *l.* it to the man. *Eccl* 2:18
yet shall he *l.* it for his portion.   21
if ruler rise up against thee, *l.* 10:4
will ye *l.* your glory ?   *Isa* 10:3
shall *l.* your name for a curse. 65:15
I might *l.* my people, and.   *Jer* 9:2
called by thy name, *l.* us not. 14:9
riches, he shall *l.* them in.   17:11
will a man *l.* the snow of ?   18:14
child and suckling, to *l.* you.   44:7
l. the cities, and dwell in.   48:28
not *l.* some gleaning grapes ?   49:9
thy fatherless children, I will.   11
and *l.* thee naked and bare.
   Ezek 16:39; 23:29
will turn thee, *l.* but a.   39:2*
l. the stump of his. *Dan* 4:15, 23, 26
he *l.* his blood upon him. *Hos* 12:14
return, and *l.* a blessing. *Joel* 2:14
l. an hundred, shall *l.*   *Amos* 5:3
who *l.* off righteousness in the.   7*
would they not *l.* grapes ?   *Ob* 5
it shall *l.* them neither.   *Mal* 4:1
I there thy gift before.   *Mat* 5:24
doth he not *l.* the ninety and nine ?
   18:12; *Luke* 15:4
to have done, and not *l.* *Mat* 23:23
and *l.* his wife, and *l.* *Mark* 12:19
they shall not *l.* in thee. *Luke* 19:44
my peace I *l.* with you. *John* 14:27
I *l.* the world and go to the.   16:28
ye shall *l.* me alone, yet I am not. 32
not reason we should *l.*   *Acts* 6:2
her, let her not *l.* him.   *1 Cor* 7:13
I will never *l.* thee, nor. *Heb* 13:5*
the court *l.* out, and.   *Rev* 11:2

I will, or will I leave
if I say, I will *l.* off my. *Job* 9:27
I will *l.* my complaint upon. 10:1*
yet *will I l.* a remnant.   *Ezek* 6:8
but I *will l.* a few.   12:16
I *will l.* you there, and melt. 22:20*

I will *l.* thee thrown into. *Ezek* 29:5 †
I will *l.* thee upon the land.   32:4
I will *l.* in midst of thee. *Zeph* 3:12

I will not leave
I will not *l.* thee until I. *Gen* 28:15
as the Lord liveth, I will not *l.* thee.
   2 Ki 2:2; 4:30
As thy soul liveth, I will not *l.* 2:4, 6
Lord *I will not l.* him in.   *Ps* 37:33
I will not *l.* thee together. *Jer* 30:11
   46:28
I will not *l.* you comfortless.
   John 14:18

leaved
before him the two-*l.* gates. *Isa* 45:1

leaven
*A piece of dough salted and soured,
to ferment and relish a mass of
dough for bread,* Hos 7:4; 1 Cor 5:6.
*The word is also used figuratively in
the New Testament for teachings.*
ye shall put away *l.*   *Ex* 12:15, 19
neither shall be *l.* seen in all. 13:7
blood of my sacrifice with *l.*   34:25
shall be made with *l.*   *Lev* 2:11
it shall not be baken with *l.*   6:17
eat meat offering without *l.*   10:12
they shall be baken with *l.*   23:17
of thanksgiving with *l.*   *Amos* 4:5
kingdom of heaven is like *l.*
   Mat 13:33; *Luke* 13:21
the *l.* of the Pharisees. *Mat* 16:6
   11; *Mark* 8:15; *Luke* 12:1
not beware of the *l.*   *Mat* 16:12
little *l.* leaveneth the whole lump.
   1 Cor 5:6; *Gal* 5:9
purge out therefore the old *l.* that.
   1 Cor 5:7
let us keep the feast, not with old *l.* 8

leavened
for whosoever eateth *l.* *Ex* 12:15, 19
shall eat nothing *l.* in all your.   20
their dough before it was *l.*   34, 39
there shall no *l.* be eaten.   13:3, 7
after he hath kneaded the dough till
   it be *l.*   *Hos* 7:4
till the whole was *l.*   *Mat* 13:33
   Luke 13:21

see bread

leaveneth
little leaven *l.* the whole lump.
   1 Cor 5:6; *Gal* 5:9

leaves
sewed fig *l.* and made.   *Gen* 3:7
when they cast their *l.*   *Isa* 6:13*
read three or four *l.*   *Jer* 36:23
it shall wither in all the *l. Ezek* 17:9
l. thereof fair.   *Dan* 4:12, 21
shake off his *l.*   14
nothing thereon but *l.*   *Mat* 21:19
   Mark 11:13
his branch putteth forth *l.*
   Mat 24:32; *Mark* 13:28
l. were for the healing of. *Rev* 22:2

leaves for doors
the two *l.* of the one door. *1 Ki* 6:34
two *l.* apiece, two *l.* for. *Ezek* 41:24

leaveth
the ostrich *l.* her eggs.   *Job* 39:14
a good man *l.* an.   *Pr* 13:22
like a sweeping rain which *l.*   28:3
idol shepherd, that *l.*   *Zech* 11:17
then the devil *l.* him.   *Mat* 4:11
the hireling *l.* the sheep. *John* 10:12

leaving
Jesus *l.* Nazareth, dwelt. *Mat* 4:13
thieves departed, *l.*   *Luke* 10:30
men *l.* the natural use.   *Rom* 1:27
l. the principles of the.   *Heb* 6:1*
Christ suffered for us, *l.* *1 Pet* 2:21

Lebanon
goodly mountain and *L.* *Deut* 3:25
that dwelt in mount *L.*   *Judg* 3:3
ten thousand a month to *L.* *1 Ki* 5:14
the forest of *L.*   7:2; 10:17, 21
was in *L.* sent to cedar in *L.* give thy.
   2 Ki 14:9; *2 Chr* 25:18
I am come up to the sides of *L.*
   2 Ki 19:23; *Isa* 37:24
skill to cut timber in *L.* *2 Chr* 2:8
L. and Sirion like a.   *Ps* 29:6

thereof shall shake like *L*. *Ps* 72:16
shall grow like a cedar in *L*. 92:12
Solomon made a chariot of the wood
   of *L*.   *S of S* 3:9
from *L*. my spouse, from *L*.   4:8
garments is like the smell of *L*. 11
waters, and streams from *L*.   15
his countenance is as *L*.   5:15
thy nose is as the tower of *L*. 7:4
L. shall fall.   *Isa* 10:34
L. shall be turned into a. 29:17
L. is ashamed.   33:9
the glory of *L*. shall be given. 35:2
L. is not sufficient to burn for. 40:16
the glory of *L*. shall come. 60:13
leave the snow of *L*.? *Jer* 18:14
Gilead and the head of *L*. 22:6
go up to *L*. and cry, lift up thy. 20
longwinged, came to *L*. *Ezek* 17:3
and I caused *L*. to mourn. 31:15
cast forth his roots as *L*. *Hos* 14:5
his smell as *L*.   6
the scent as the wine of *L*. 7
Bashan and the flower of *L*. *Nah* 1:4
violence of *L*. shall cover. *Hab* 2:17
them into the land of *L*. *Zech* 10:10
open thy doors, O *L*. that fire. 11:1
    see cedars

Lebbaeus
L. whose surname was Thaddaeus.
    Mat 10:3

led
the way, the Lord *l*. me. *Gen* 24:27
blessed the Lord, who had *l*. me. 48
Moses *l*. flock to backside. *Ex* 3:1
God *l*. them not through the. 13:17
but God *l*. them about, through. 18
thou in mercy hast *l*. forth. 15:13
Lord *l*. thee forty years. *Deut* 8:2
who *l*. thee through that great. 15
I have *l*. you forty years in. 29:5
l. him about, he instructed. 32:10*
l. him through all land. *Josh* 24:3
enemies, which *l*. them. *1 Ki* 8:48*
but Elisha *l*. them to. *2 Ki* 6:19
Joab *l*. forth the power. *1 Chr* 20:1
and Amaziah *l*. forth. *2 Chr* 25:11
in the day he *l*. them. *Ps* 78:14
he *l*. them on safely, so that. 53
l. them through the depths as through
   a. 106:9; 136:16; *Isa* 63:13
he *l*. them forth by right. *Ps* 107:7
I have *l*. thee in right. *Pr* 4:11
they that are *l*. of them. *Isa* 9:16
they thirsted not when they *l*. 48:21
for ye shall be *l*. forth in. 55:12
that *l*. them by the right hand. 63:12
where is the Lord that *l*. us? *Jer* 2:6
hath forsaken God, when he *l*. 17
the place whither they have *l*. 22:12
the Lord liveth which *l*. the. 23:8
he hath *l*. me into darkness. *Lam* 3:2
and *l*. them with him. *Ezek* 17:12*
who caused them to be *l*. 39:28
l. me about to the outer. 47:2
also I *l*. you 40 years. *Amos* 2:10
Israel shall surely be *l*. captive. 7:11
and Huzzab shall be *l*. *Nah* 2:7*
then was Jesus *l*. of the Spirit.
    Mat 4:1; *Luke* 4:1
they *l*. him to Caiaphas the high.
    Mat 26:57; *Mark* 14:53
    Luke 22:54; *John* 18:13
they *l*. him to Pontius Pilate the.
    Mat 27:2, 31; *Mark* 15:16, 20
    Luke 22:54; *John* 18:13
the blind man and *l*. *Mark* 8:23*
l. Jesus to the brow. *Luke* 4:29
they shall be *l*. away captive. 21:24
and *l*. him into their council. 22:66
the whole multitude *l*. him. 23:1*
two other malefactors were *l*. 32
l. them out as far as Bethany. 24:50
l. Jesus unto the hall. *John* 18:28
he was *l*. as a sheep to. *Acts* 8:32
they *l*. Saul by the hand. 9:8; 22:11
as Paul was to be *l*. into. 21:37*
as many as are *l*. by the. *Rom* 8:14
idols. even as ye were *l*. *1 Cor* 12:2
but if ye be *l*. by the Spirit. *Gal* 5:18
silly women, *l*. away. *2 Tim* 3:6
being *l*. away with the error of the
   wicked, fall from. *2 Pet* 3:17*

leddest
wast he that *l*. out Israel.
    2 Sam 5:2; *1 Chr* 11:2
l. them in the day by a. *Neh* 9:12
thou *l*. thy people like. *Ps* 77:20
l. into the wilderness. *Acts* 21:38

ledges
were between the *l*. *1 Ki* 7:28
the *l*. and borders thereof were. 35*
on plates of the *l*. he graved. 36*

leeks
we remember the *l*. *Num* 11:5

lees
a feast of wine on the *l*. *Isa* 25:6
hath settled on his *l*. *Jer* 48:11
men settled on their *l*. *Zeph* 1:12

left
had *l*. communing with. *Gen* 18:33
who hath not *l*. destitute my. 24:27
Judah, and *l*. bearing. 29:35; 30:9
other company which is *l*. 32:8
l. all that he had in Joseph's. 39:6
he *l*. his garment in. 12, 13, 15, 18
Joseph gathered corn till he *l*. 41:49
at the eldest, and *l*. at the. 44:12
not enough *l*. but our bodies. 47:18
little ones *l*. they in Goshen. 50:8
why is it that ye have *l*.? *Ex* 2:20
l. his servants and his cattle. 9:21
herb, all that the hail *l*. 10:12, 15
there shall not an hoof be *l*. 26
but some of them *l*. of it till. 16:20
nor sacrifice of passover be *l*. 34:25
l. of the meat offering. *Lev* 2:10
Ithamar, his sons that were *l*. 10:12
are *l*. of you shall pine away. 26:39
the land also shall be *l*. of them. 43
not *l*. a man of them. *Num* 26:65
Josh 8:17; *Judg* 4:16; *Hos* 9:12
we *l*. none to remain. *Deut* 2:34
Josh 10:33, 37, 39, 40; 11:8, 11, 14
ye shall be *l*. few in number among
   the heathen. *Deut* 4:27; 28:62
    Isa 24:6; *Jer* 42:2
that are *l*. be destroyed. *Deut* 7:20
he hath nothing *l*. him in. 28:55
there is none shut up or *l*. 32:36
and *l*. them without the camp of.
    Josh 6:23*
they *l*. the city open, and. 8:17
he *l*. nothing undone of all. 11:15
was none of the Anakims *l*. 22
ye have not *l*. your brethren. 22:3
of nations which Joshua *l*. when.
    Judg 2:21
the Lord *l*. those nations. 23; 3:1
l. no sustenance for Israel. 6:4
Jotham the youngest son was *l*. 9:5
she was *l*., and her two. *Ruth* 1:3, 5
was minded to go, then she *l*. 18
how thou hast *l*. thy father. 2:11
eat and was sufficed, and *l*. 14
Lord hath not *l*. thee this day. 4:14
that is *l*. in thy house. *1 Sam* 2:36
the stump of Dagon was *l*. 5:4
that *l*.! set before thee and eat. 9:24*
thy father hath *l*. the care. 10:2
two of them were not *l*. 11:11
David rose up and *l*. sheep. 17:20
David *l*. his carriage in the hand. 22
not been *l*. any that pisseth. 25:34
David *l*. neither man nor. 27:9*
they *l*. their images. *2 Sam* 5:21
any *l*. of the house of Saul? 9:1
sons, there is not one of them *l*. 13:30
quench my coal which is *l*. 14:7
l. ten concubines. 15:16; 16:21
shall not be *l*. so much as one. 17:12
their children that were *l*. *1 Ki* 9:21
    2 Chr 8:8
cut off him that is shut up and *l*.
    1 Ki 14:10; *2 Ki* 9:8
he *l*. not Jeroboam any. *1 Ki* 15:29
l. Baasha not one that pisseth. 16:11
there was no breath *l*. in. 17:17
and *l*. his servant. 19:3
I only am *l*. 10
yet I have *l*. me 7000. 18
he *l*. oxen and ran. 19
they did eat and *l*. *2 Ki* 4:44
they arose and *l*. tents. 7:7
all that are *l*. 13

since the day she *l*. the land even.
    2 Ki 8:6
Jehu slew all, till he *l*. him. 10:11
so that there was not a man *l*. 21
for there was not any *l*. nor. 14:26
they *l*. the commandments of. 17:16
lift up thy prayer for the remnant that
   are *l*. 19:4; *Isa* 37:4
nothing shall be *l*. saith. *2 Ki* 20:17
l. of the poor of the land. 25:12
    Jer 39:10; 52:16
our brethren that are *l*. *1 Chr* 13:2
for the Levites *l*. their. *2 Chr* 11:14
I have also *l*. you in the hand. 12:5
was never a son *l*. him. 21:17
and they *l*. the house of Lord. 24:18
l. Joash in great diseases. 25:12
enough to eat, and have *l*. 31:10
God *l*. him to try him, that he. 32:31
enquire for them that are *l*. 34:21
concerning the Jews which had *l*.
    Neh 1:2
the remnant that are *l*. are. 3
there was no breach *l*. therein. 6:1
it shall go ill with him that is *l*. 26
was not one of them *l*. *Ps* 106:11
a child *l*. to himself. *Pr* 29:15
Zion is *l*. as a cottage in a. *Isa* 1:8
except Lord had *l*. us. 9; *Rom* 9:29
he that is *l*. in Zion shall. *Isa* 4:3
butter and honey shall every one eat
   that is *l*. 7:22
gathereth eggs that are *l*. 10:14
for the remnant that shall be *l*. 11:16
yet gleaning grapes shall be *l*. 17:6
in the city is *l*. desolation. 24:12
till ye be *l*. as a beacon on. 30:17
shall be *l*. saith the Lord. 39:6
I *l*. my heritage. *Jer* 12:7
to the sword. 31:2
how is the city of praise not *l*.! 49:25
let nothing of her be *l*. 50:26
shall be *l*. a remnant. *Ezek* 14:22
nor *l*. her whoredoms brought. 23:8
cut him off and have *l*. him. 31:12
the kingdom shall not be *l*. to other.
    Dan 2:44
worm *l*. the locust hath *l*. *Joel* 1:4
who is *l*. that saw this house in her
   glory? *Hag* 2:3
part shall be *l*. therein. *Zech* 13:8
l. their nets. *Mat* 4:20
they *l*. their ships. 22
he touched her, and the fever *l*. her.
    8:15; *Mark* 1:31
took up of the meat that was *l*.
    Mat 15:37; *Mark* 8:8
he *l*. his wife to his brother.
    Mat 22:25; *Mark* 12:20
your house is *l*. unto you. *Mat* 23:38
there shall not be *l*. one stone upon.
    24:2; *Mark* 13:2; *Luke* 21:6
one shall be taken, and other *l*.
    Mat 24:40, 41; *Luke* 17:34, 35, 36
Jesus *l*. them, and prayed the third.
    Mat 26:44
l. all and followed. *Mark* 10:28
no man that hath *l*. house. 29
    Luke 18:28, 29
had her, and *l*. no seed. *Mark* 12:22
he *l*. all, rose up, and. *Luke* 5:28
that my sister hath *l*. me to. 10:40
woman then *l*. her waterpot.
    John 4:28
at the seventh hour the fever *l*. 52
that his soul was not *l*. in. *Acts* 2:31
l. not himself without witness. 14:17
captain. they *l*. beating of Paul. 21:32
and Felix *l*. Paul. 24:27; 25:14
we thought good to be *l*. *1 Thes* 3:1
the cloak that I *l*. at. *2 Tim* 4:13
Trophimus have I *l*. sick at. 20
this cause I *l*. thee at Crete. *Tit* 1:5
he *l*. nothing that is not. *Heb* 2:8
us fear. lest a promise being *l*. 4:1
the angels which *l*. their. *Jude* 6
thou hast *l*. thy first love. *Rev* 2:4
    see alone, hand

left *off*
l. off to build the city. *Gen* 11:8
l. off talking with him, and. 17:22
not *l*. off his kindness. *Ruth* 2:20

Baasha *l. off* building. *1 Ki* 15:21
2 Chr 16:5
they *l. off* speaking. *Job* 32:15*
he hath *l. off* to be wise. *Ps* 36:3
so they *l. off* speaking. *Jer* 38:27
since we *l. off* to burn incense. 44:18
have *l. off* to take heed. *Hos* 4:10

left *corner*
guard stood to the *l. corner* about.
2 Ki 11:11

lefthanded
raised Ehud, a man *l.* *Judg* 3:15
seven hundred chosen men *l.* 20:16

left *pillar*
he set up the *l. pillar.* *1 Ki* 7:21

left *side*
five bases on the *l. side.* *1 Ki* 7:39
five candlesticks on the *l. side.* 49
with his weapon from right to *l. side.*
2 Chr 23:10
had the face of an ox on the *l. side.*
Ezek 1:10
lie also on thy *l. side,* and lay. 4:4
olive tree upon *l. side.* *Zech* 4:3, 11

leg, -s
with fire his head and *l.* *Ex* 12:9
wash the inwards and his *l.* 29:17
Lev 9:14
his head, and his *l.* burn. *Lev* 4:11
he washed the inwards and *l.* 8:21
which have *l.* above their feet. 11:21
shall smite thee in the knees and *l.*
Deut 28:35
of brass upon his *l.* *1 Sam* 17:6
pleasure in the *l.* of a man. *Ps* 147:10
the *l.* of the lame are not. *Pr* 26:7
his *l.* are as pillars of. *S of S* 5:15
take away ornaments of *l. Isa* 3:20*
make bare the *l.* uncover the. 47:2*
his *l.* of iron, his feet. *Dan* 2:33
two *l.,* or piece of an ear. *Amos* 3:12
their *l.* might be broken. *John* 19:31
and brake the *l.* of the first. 32
he was dead, brake not his *l.* 33

Legion
my name is *L.* for we are many.
Mark 5:9; *Luke* 8:30

legions
me more than twelve *l.* *Mat* 26:53

leisure
had no *l.* so much as to. *Mark* 6:31

Lemuel
the words of king *L.* *Pr* 31:1
not for kings, O *L.* to drink. 4

lend
if thou *l.* money to any. *Ex* 22:25
not *l.* him thy victuals. *Lev* 25:37*
shalt *l.* to many nations. *Deut* 15:6
thou shalt surely *l.* him sufficient. 8
thou shalt not *l.* upon usury. 23:19
to a stranger thou mayest *l.* 20
thou dost *l.* thy brother any. 24:10
the man to whom thou dost *l.* 11
thou shalt *l.* to many nations. 28:12
l. to thee, thou shalt not *l.* him. 44
if ye *l.* to them of whom ye . . . for
sinners also *l.* to sinners.
Luke 6:34
your enemies, do good and *l.* 35
and say to him, Friend, *l.* me. 11:5

lender
is servant to the *l.* *Pr* 22:7
as with the *l.* so with. *Isa* 24:2

lendeth
every creditor that *l.* *Deut* 15:2
merciful, and *l.*; his seed. *Ps* 37:26
man sheweth favour and *l.* 112:5
pity on the poor *l.* to Lord. *Pr* 19:17

length
through the land in the *l. Gen* 13:17
he is thy life, and the *l. Deut* 30:20
l. of days, understanding. *Job* 12:12
even *l.* of days for ever. *Ps* 21:4
for *l.* of days shall they. *Pr* 3:2
l. of days is in her right hand. 16
and to see what is the *l. Zech* 2:2
l. of the roll is twenty cubits. 5:2
be able to comprehend. *Eph* 3:18
l. as large as the breadth. *Rev* 21:16

at length
him become his son *at l.* *Pr* 29:21
if now at *l.* I may have a journey.
Rom 1:10

lengthen
then will I *l.* thy days. *1 Ki* 3:14
l. thy cords and strengthen. *Isa* 54:2

lengthened
that thy days may be *l. Deut* 25:15*

lengthening
a *l.* of thy tranquillity. *Dan* 4:27

lent
they *l.* to them such as. *Ex* 12:36*
thing that is *l.* on usury. *Deut* 23:19
I *l.* him to the Lord, he shall be *l.*
1 Sam 1:28*
for the loan which is *l.* to. 2:20†
I have not *l.* on usury nor have men *l.*
me. *Jer* 15:10

lentiles
gave Esau pottage of *l.* *Gen* 25:34
piece of ground full of *l.* *2 Sam* 23:11
see beans

leopard
(*A large and ferocious spotted
animal*)
the *l.* shall lie down with. *Isa* 11:6
a *l.* watch over their cities. *Jer* 5:6
can the *l.* change his spots? 13:23
and lo, another like a *l.* *Dan* 7:6
I will be to them as a *l.* *Hos* 13:7
the beast was like to a *l.* *Rev* 13:2

leopards
the mountains of the *l.* *S of S* 4:8
horses are swifter than *l.* *Hab* 1:8

leper
l. in whom the plague is. *Lev* 13:45
shall be the law of the *l.* in. 14:2
the leprosy be healed in the *l.* 3
man of the seed of Aaron is a *l.* 22:4
out of the camp every *l.* *Num* 5:2
from the house of Joab, one that is a
l. *2 Sam* 3:29
Naaman was a *l.* *2 Ki* 5:1
recover the *l.* 6
went from his presence a *l.* as. 27
Azariah was a *l.* to the day. 15:15
the king was a *l.* *2 Chr* 26:21
him, for they said, He is a *l.* 23
and behold, there came a *l.*
Mat 8:2; *Mark* 1:40
in the house of Simon the *l.*
Mat 26:6; *Mark* 14:3

lepers
when the *l.* came to the. *2 Ki* 7:8
heal the sick, cleanse *l.* *Mat* 10:8
the lame walk, the *l.* are cleansed.
11:5; *Luke* 7:22
many *l.* were in Israel. *Luke* 4:27
met him ten men that were *l.* 17:12

leprosy
skin like the plague of *l.* *Lev* 13:2
it is a plague of *l.* 3, 8, 11, 15, 25
27, 30, 42, 49
when the plague of *l.* is in a man. 9
if a *l.* break out. 12
if the *l.* covered his flesh. 13
as the *l.* appeareth in the skin. 43
that the plague of *l.* is in. 47
this is the law of the plague of *l.*
59; 14:54, 55, 57
if the plague of *l.* be healed. 14:3
him that is to be cleansed from *l.* 7
him in whom is the plague of *l.* 32
heed in the plague of *l.* *Deut* 24:8
recover him of his *l.* *2 Ki* 5:3, 7
mayest recover him of his *l.* 6
the *l.* of Naaman shall cleave. 27
the *l.* rose up in his. *2 Chr* 26:19
his *l.* was cleansed. *Mat* 8:3
Mark 1:42; *Luke* 5:13
behold, a man full of *l.* *Luke* 5:12
see fretting

leprous
behold, his hand was *l.* *Ex* 4:6
l. man is unclean. *Lev* 13:44
Miriam became *l.* behold she was *l.*
Num 12:10
there were four *l.* men. *2 Ki* 7:3
and Uzziah was *l.* in. *2 Chr* 26:20

less
some more, some *l.* *Ex* 16:17
the poor shall not give *l.* than. 30:15
word of the Lord to do *l. Num* 22:18
to few thou shalt give *l.* inheritance.
26:54; 33:54
thy servant knew nothing *l.* or more.
1 Sam 22:15
Abigail told him nothing *l.* 25:36
punished us *l.* than our. *Ezra* 9:13
exacteth *l.* than iniquity. *Job* 11:6
much *l.* do lying lips a. *Pr* 17:7
much *l.* for a servant to rule. 19:10
all nations are counted *l.* *Isa* 40:17
when it is sown is *l.* *Mark* 4:31
mother of James the *l.* 15:40
members we think *l.* *1 Cor* 12:23
the more I love, the *l.* *2 Cor* 12:15
l. than the least of all. *Eph* 3:8
and that I may be the *l.* *Phil* 2:28
the *l.* is blessed of better. *Heb* 7:7

lesser
made the *l.* light to rule. *Gen* 1:16
for the treading of *l.* *Isa* 7:25*
l. settle to the greater. *Ezek* 43:14

lest
ye touch it, *l.* ye die. *Gen* 3:3
Lev 10:6, 7, 9; *Num* 18:32
l. we be scattered abroad. *Gen* 11:4
l. thou say, I have made. 14:23
l. thou be consumed in the. 19:15
l. I die. 19; 26:9
l. he come and smite me. 32:11
l. he die, as his brethren did. 38:11
Deut 20:5, 6, 7
let her take it to her, *l. Gen* 38:23
l. thou and thy household. 45:11
go, *l.* he fall on us with. *Ex* 5:3
l. peradventure the people. 13:17
l. they break through to the. 19:21
sanctify, *l.* the Lord break forth. 22
let not God speak with us, *l.* 20:19
I will not go, *l.* I consume thee. 33:3
shall not go in to see, *l.* they die.
Num 4:20; 18:22
l. ye perish quickly. *Deut* 1:11
l. he cry against thee to. 24:15
l. if he should exceed and. 25:3
let them live, *l.* wrath. *Josh* 9:20
shall be a witness, *l.* ye deny. 24:27
l. Israel vaunt themselves. *Judg* 7:2
let him not know, *l.* he. *1 Sam* 20:3
l. I take the city, and. *2 Sam* 12:28
l. he take thee away. *Job* 36:18
l. I deal with you after your. 42:8
kiss the Son, *l.* he be angry. *Ps* 2:12
lighten mine eyes, *l.* I sleep. 13:3
consider this, *l.* I tear you. 50:22
l. thou dash thy foot. 91:12
Mat 4:6; *Luke* 4:11
Moses stood, *l.* he should. *Ps* 106:23
grant not, *l.* they exalt. 140:8
l. I be like them that go down. 143:7
reprove not a scorner, *l.* he. *Pr* 9:8
love not sleep, *l.* thou come. 20:13
l. thou learn his ways, and. 22:25
l. the Lord see it, and it. 24:18
l. thou know not what to do. 25:8
l. he that heareth it, put thee to. 10
l. he be weary of thee, and so. 17
answer not a fool, *l.* thou also. 26:4
add not to his words, *l.* he. 30:6
l. I be full and deny thee, or *l.* 9
l. they see with their eyes. *Isa* 6:10
Acts 28:27
l. any hurt it, I will keep it. *Isa* 27:3
not mockers, *l.* your bands. 28:22
l. thou shouldest say, My idol hath.
48:5, 7
be not dismayed, *l.* I. *Jer* 1:17
l. my fury come forth. 4:4; 21:12
instructed, *l.* my soul depart. 6:8
cause me not to return, *l.* I. 37:20
l. I strip her naked, and. *Hos* 2:3
seek the Lord, *l.* he break. *Amos* 5:6
as an adamant, *l.* they. *Zech* 7:12
l. I come and smite the. *Mal* 4:6
l. we should offend, go. *Mat* 17:27
l. there be not enough for us. 25:9
take heed, *l.* any man. *Mark* 13:5
l. coming suddenly, he find you. 36
watch and pray, *l.* ye enter. 14:38
l. they should believe. *Luke* 8:12

l. your hearts be overcharged.
              Luke 21:34
sin no more, *l.* a worse.   *John* 5:14
they went out *l.* they should.   18:28
l. ye be found to fight.   *Acts* 5:39
beware therefore, *l.* that.   13:40
take heed, *l.* he spare not thee.
              Rom 11:21, 44
l. we hinder the gospel. *1 Cor* 9:12
standeth take heed *l.* he fall.   10:12
l. Satan should get.   *2 Cor* 2:11
l. I should be exalted above.   12:7
l. by any means I should.   *Gal* 2:2
considering thyself, *l.* thou.   6:1
not of works, *l.* any man.   *Eph* 2:9
l. any man beguile you.   *Col* 2:4
provoke not children, *l.* they.   3:21
l. being lifted up with.   *1 Tim* 3:6
l. at any time we should let them slip.
              Heb 2:1
l. there be in any an evil heart. 3:12
l. any of you be hardened.   13
l. any man fall after the same. 4:11
l. ye be weary and faint in.   12:3
l. what is lame be turned out.   13
l. any man fail of the grace.   15
grudge not, *l.* ye be.   *Jas* 5:9
swear not, *l.* ye fall into.   12
beware, *l.* ye also being. *2 Pet* 3:17
keepeth his garments, *l.* *Rev* 16:15

let
*(Used occasionally in the now
     obsolete sense of* hinder)
Naphtali is a hind *l.*   *Gen* 49:21
king of Egypt will not *l.* you go.
   Ex 3:19; 4:21; 7:14; 8:32; 9:7
        17, 35; 10:20, 27; 11:10
after that he will *l.* you go.   3:20
l. my people go. 5:1; 7:16; 8:1, 20
           9:1, 13; 10:3
why do ye *l.* the people from ?   5:4*
I will *l.* you go.   8:28; 9:28; 13:17
why have we *l.* Israel go ?   14:5
and Moses *l.* his father in law. 18:27
shall he *l.* her be redeemed.   21:8
l. him go free for his eye,   26, 27
seventh year thou shalt *l.* it.   23:11
hast not *l.* me know whom.   33:12
and shall *l.* the living bird. *Lev* 14:7
not *l.* seed pass through.   18:21*
not *l.* cattle gender with a.   19:19
thou shalt *l.* him go.   *Deut* 15:12
thou shalt not *l.* him go away.   13
and all therein, he *l.* none remain.
          Josh 10:28*, 30*
so Joshua *l.* the people.   24:28*
they *l.* the man go and.   *Judg* 1:25
Saul would *l.* him go no. *1 Sam* 18:2
to-morrow I will *l.*   *2 Sam* 11:12
I pray thee, *l.* Tamar my.   13:6
Elijah said, *L.* none of.   *1 Ki* 18:40
thou wouldest not *l.*   *2 Chr* 20:10
queen did *l.* no man.   *Esth* 5:12
even that he would *l.* loose. *Job* 6:9
my righteousness I will not *l.*   27:6
l. not those that wait on thee be
ashamed, *l.* not those.   *Ps* 69:6
and *l.* Satan stand at his right. 109:6
l. me not wander from thy.   119:10
and would not *l.* him go. *S of S* 3:4
l. out the vineyard to keepers. 8:11
work, and who shall *l.* it ? *Isa* 43:13
those will I *l.* remain.   *Jer* 27:11
I will not *l.* them pollute. *Ezek* 39:7
planted a vineyard and *l.* *Mat* 21:33
     Mark 12:1; *Luke* 20:9
answer me nor *l.* me.   *Luke* 22:68*
the Jews cried, If thou *l. John* 19:12
ship could not bear up, we *l.* her.
           Acts 27:15*
you, but was *l.* hitherto. *Rom* 1:13*
who now letteth, will *l.* *2 Thes* 2:7*
lest at any time we should *l. Heb* 2:1
     see **alone**

let *down*
l. down thy pitcher, I pray thee.
       Gen 24:14; 18:46
when he *l. down* his hands, Amalek.
            Ex 17:11
Rahab *l.* them *down.* *Josh* 2:15, 18
Michal *l.* David *down.* *1 Sam* 19:12
the man was *l. down.*   *2 Ki* 13:21
they *l. down* Jeremiah.   *Jer* 38:6

they stood they *l. down* their wings.
          Ezek 1:24, 25
they *l. down* the bed wherein.
      Mark 2:4; *Luke* 5:19
and *l. down* your nets.   *Luke* 5:4
at thy word I will *l. down* the net. 5
and *l.* him *down* in a basket.
      Acts 9:25; *2 Cor* 11:33
l. down to the earth.   *Acts* 10:11
had *l. down* the boat.   27:30

letter
David wrote a *l.* to.   *2 Sam* 11:14
I will send a *l.* to the.   *2 Ki* 5:5
now when this *l.* is come to thee. 6
as soon as this *l.* cometh to.   10:2
Hezekiah received the *l.*   19:14
          Isa 37:14
the *l.* was written in.   *Ezra* 4:7
Rehum wrote a *l.* against.   8
now this is the copy of the *l.*   7:11
            5:6, 7
a *l.* to Asaph the keeper.   *Neh* 2:8
sent to me with an open *l.* in.   6:5
wrote to confirm this *l.* of. *Esth* 9:29
the words of the *l.* that.   *Jer* 29:1
Zephaniah priest read this *l.* in.   29
Claudius wrote a *l.* to.   *Acts* 23:25
the governor had read the *l.* he. 34
l. dost transgress the law. *Rom* 2:27
circumcision of heart, not in the *l.* 29
serve, not in the oldness of the *l.* 7:6
ministers not of the *l.*   *2 Cor* 3:6
you sorry with *l.* I do not repent. 7:8
ye see how large a *l.* I.   *Gal* 6:11*
shaken by word or by *l. 2 Thes* 2:2
I have written a *l.* to.   *Heb* 13:22

letters
l. in Ahab's name.   *1 Ki* 21:8, 9
Jehu wrote *l.* and sent.   *2 Ki* 10:1
Babylon sent *l.* to Hezekiah.   20:12
Hezekiah wrote *l.* also. *2 Chr* 30:1
so the posts went with the *l.*   6
Sennacherib wrote *l.* to rail on. 32:17
let *l.* be given me to thee.   *Neh* 2:7
sent *l.* to Tobiah, and *l.* came. 6:17
and Tobiah sent *l.* to put me.   19
Ahasuerus sent *l.* to the. *Esth* 1:22
the *l.* were sent by posts. 3:13; 8:10
to reverse *l.* devised by Haman. 8:5
Mordecai sent *l.* to all.   9:20, 30
because thou hast sent *l. Jer* 29:25
was written in *l.* of.   *Luke* 23:38
how knoweth this man *l.? John* 7:15
of him *l.* to Damascus.   *Acts* 9:2
the apostles wrote *l.* after.   15:23*
I received *l.* to the brethren.   22:5
we neither received *l.* out of.   28:21
shall approve by your *l. 1 Cor* 16:3
we *l.* of commendation.   *2 Cor* 3:1
as if I would terrify you by *l.*   10:9
for his *l.* are weighty and.   10
such as we are in word, by *l.*   11

lettest
l. such words go out of.   *Job* 15:13
with a cord thou *l.* down ?   41:1*
now *l.* thou thy servant. *Luke* 2:29

letteth
he that *l.* him go, his life. *2 Ki* 10:24
strife is as when one *l.* out. *Pr* 17:14
only he that now *l.* will. *2 Thes* 2:7*

letting
deal deceitfully in not *l.* the people.
            Ex 8:29

Levi
was his name called *L. Gen* 29:34
the sons of *L.*   46:11; *Ex* 6:16
          Num 3:17
Simeon, *L.* are brethren. *Gen* 49:5
years of the life of *L.*   *Ex* 6:16
upon you, ye sons of *L. Num* 16:7
Jochebed, daughter of *L.*   26:59
L. hath no part with his. *Deut* 10:9
priests the sons of *L.* shall.   21:5
L. he said, Let thy Thummim. 33:8
made priests which were not of *L.*
            1 Ki 12:31
but *L.* and Benjamin.   *1 Chr* 21:6
none of the sons of *L.*   *Ezra* 8:15
bless Lord, O house of *L. Ps* 135:20
the sons of Zadok among the sons of
L.   *Ezek* 40:46

of Judah, one gate of *L. Ezek* 48:31
family of the house of *L. Zech* 12:13
covenant might be with *L. Mal* 2:4
corrupted the covenant of *L.*   8
purify the sons of *L.*   3:3
L. the son of Alpheus.   *Mark* 2:14
Matthat, which was the son of *L.*
          Luke 3:24, 29
he saw a publican named *L.*   5:27
L. made him a great feast in his. 29
L. who received tithes.   *Heb* 7:9

tribe of **Levi**
not number *tribe of L.*   *Num* 1:49
bring the *tribe of L.* near and.   3:6
tribe of L. bring, that they.   18:2
separated the *tribe of L. Deut* 10:8
tribe of L. shall have no part nor.
       18:1; *Josh* 13:14, 33
Moses' sons were named of the *tribe
   of L.*   *1 Chr* 23:14
of *tribe of L.* were sealed. *Rev* 7:7

leviathan
thou draw out *l.* with ?   *Job* 41:1
heads of *l.* in pieces.   *Ps* 74:14
l. thou hast made to play.   104:26
punish *l.* even *l.* that crooked serpent.   *Isa* 27:1

Levite
is not Aaron the *l.* thy ?   *Ex* 4:14
rejoice before the Lord your God,
   ye and the *l.*   *Deut* 12:12, 18
      16:11, 14; 26:11, 13
l. shall come and eat. 14:29; 26:12
if a *l.* come from any of thy.   18:6
a young man a *l.*   *Judg* 17:7, 9
so the *l.* went in.   10
the *l.* was content to dwell.   11
Micah consecrated the *l.*   12
a *l.* to my priest.   13
voice of the young man the *l.*   18:3
certain *l.* sojourning on mount. 19:1
the *l.* said, I came into Gibeah. 20:4
on Jahaziel *l.* came.   *2 Chr* 20:14
Cononiah the *l.* was ruler.   31:12
Kore the *l.* over the freewill.   14
Shabbethai the *l.* helped. *Ezra* 10:15
likewise a *l.* came and. *Luke* 10:32
Barnabas a *l.* having.   *Acts* 4:36

Levites
of the fathers of the *l.*   *Ex* 6:25
for the service of the *l.*   38:21
cities of *l.* may redeem. *Lev* 25:32
the cities of the *l.* are their.   33
l. not numbered.   *Num* 1:47; 2:33
shalt appoint the *l.* over the.   1:50
the *l.* shall take it down.   51
the *l.* shall pitch.   53
and thou shalt give the *l.*   3:9
I have taken the *l.* : the *l.* shall. 12
chief over chief of the *l.*   32
were numbered of the *l.* 39; 4:46
and thou shalt take the *l.* for me.
      3:41, 45; 8:14
shalt give wagons unto the *l.*   7:5
take the *l.* from Israel and.   8:6
bring the *l.* before tabernacle. 9, 10
Aaron shall offer the *l.* before the. 11
after that shall the *l.* go in.   15, 22
this is it that belongeth unto the *l.* 24
thou do to the *l.* touching their.   26
the *l.* to do service.   18:6, 23
tithes I have given to the *l.*   24
give to the *l.* cities round.   35:2, 8
minister, as his brethren the *l.* do.
          Deut 18:7
to the *l.* he gave none.   *Josh* 14:3
gave these cities to the *l.*   21:3, 8
all the cities of the *l.* were.   41
l. took down the ark.   *1 Sam* 6:15
Zadok and the *l.* were. *2 Sam* 15:24
the children of the *l.*   *1 Chr* 15:15
when God helped the *l.* that.   26
l. wrote them before the king. 24:6
the *l.* which were singers stood.
       2 Chr 5:12; 7:6
the *l.* left their suburbs and.   11:14
cast out the sons of Aaron and *l.* 13:9
also the *l.* shall be officers.   19:11
the *l.* shall compass the king. 23:6, 7
the *l.* hastened it not.   24:5
hear me, ye *l.* sanctify now.   29:5
spake comfortably to the *l.*   30:22
of the *l.* there were scribes.   34:13

Josiah said to *l.* which. *2 Chr 35:3*
of the *l.* gave to the *l.* 500 oxen. 9
l. prepared for themselves. 14, 15
set the *l.* in their courses. *Ezra 6:18*
after him repaired the *l.* *Neh 3:17*
l. caused people to understand. 8:7
the *l.* stilled the people, saying. 11
the overseer of the *l.* was. 11:22
dedication they sought the *l.* 12:27
portions of *l.* had not been given
them, for the *l.* were fled. 13:10
defiled the priesthood of the *l.* 29
I will multiply the *l.* *Jer 33:22*
l. that are gone shall bear iniquity.
Ezek 44:10
went not astray when the *l.* 48:11

priests and Levites
shalt come to *p.* the *l.* *Deut 17:9*
to do all that *p.* and *l.* shall. 24:8
p. and *l.* bearing the ark. *Josh 3:3*
p. and *l.* brought up ark. *1 Ki 8:4*
p. and *l.* shall be porters. *2 Chr 23:4*
p. and *l.* were more upright. 29:34
p. and *l.* were ashamed, and. 30:15
l. and the *p.* praised the Lord. 21
then the *p.* and *l.* blessed the. 27
questioned with the *p.* and *l.* 31:9
gave willingly to the *p.* and *l.* 35:8
so *p.* and *l.* dwelt in. *Ezra 2:70*
for the *p.* and *l.* were purified. 6:20
went up of the *p.* and the *l.* 7:7
p. and *l.* have not separated. 9:1
made the *p.* and *l.* to swear. 10:5
our princes, *l.* and *p.* *Neh 9:38*
we cast lots among *p.* and *l.* 10:34
p. and *l.* purified themselves. 12:30
Judah rejoiced for the *p.* and *l.* 44
take of them for *p.* and *l.* *Isa 66:21*
p. and *l.* not want a man. *Jer 33:18*
with *l.* the *p.* my ministers. 21
the *p.* and *l.* that kept. *Ezek 44:15*
the Jews sent *p.* and *l.* *John 1:19*

Levitical
if perfection were by the *L.* *Heb 7:11*

levy, *substantive*
Solomon raised a *l.* of. *1 Ki 5:13*
and Adoniram was over the *l.* 14
reason of the *l.* Solomon raised. 9:15

levy, *verb*
l. a tribute to the Lord. *Num 31:28*
did Solomon *l.* a tribute. *1 Ki 9:21**

lewd
ashamed of thy *l.* way. *Ezek 16:27*
unto Aholibah, the *l.* women. 23:44
l. fellows of baser sort. *Acts 17:5**

lewdly
l. defiled his daughter. *Ezek 22:11*

lewdness
they have committed *l.* *Judg 20:6*
she hath wrought *l.* *Jer 11:15*
I have seen the *l.* of thy. 13:27
shalt not commit this *l.* *Ezek 16:43*
thou hast borne thy *l.* and. 58
in midst of thee they commit *l.* 22:9
calledst to remembrance *l.* 23:21
I make thy *l.* to cease. 27, 48
shall be discovered, both thy *l.* 29
therefore bear thou also thy *l.* and. 35
shall recompense your *l.* on you. 49
in thy filthiness is *l.* 24:13
now will I discover her *l.* *Hos 2:10*
murder in way, they commit *l.* 6:9
a matter of wicked *l.* *Acts 18:14**

liar
who will make me a *l.?* *Job 24:25*
l. giveth ear to a naughty. *Pr 17:4*
poor man is better than a *l.* 19:22
and thou be found a *l.* 30:6
altogether to me as a *l.?* *Jer 15:18**
he is a *l.* and the father. *John 8:44*
I shall be a *l.* like to. 55
and every man a *l.* *Rom 3:4*
sinned, we make him a *l.* *1 John 1:10*
l. and truth is not in him. 2:4; 4:20
who is a *l.* but he that denieth? 2:22
not God, hath made him a *l.* 5:10

liars
shall be found *l.* to thee. *Deut 33:29*
in haste, all men are *l.* *Ps 116:11*
the tokens of the *l.* *Isa 44:25*

---

a sword is upon the *l.* *Jer 50:36**
law is made for *l.* for. *1 Tim 1:10*
the Cretians are alway *l.* *Tit 1:12*
and hast found them *l.* *Rev 2:2*
all *l.* shall have their part in. 21:8

liberal
l. soul shall be made fat. *Pr 11:25*
vile person shall not be called *l.*
Isa 32:5†
the *l.* deviseth *l.* things, and by *l.* 8
for your *l.* distribution. *2 Cor 9:13**

liberality
your *l.* to Jerusalem. *1 Cor 16:3**
to the riches of their *l.* *2 Cor 8:2*

liberally
furnish him *l.* out of. *Deut 15:14*
who giveth to all men *l.* *Jas 1:5*

Libertines
called synagogue of the *L.* *Acts 6:9*

liberty
ye shall proclaim *l.* *Lev 25:10*
and I will walk at *l.* *Ps 119:45*
he sent me to proclaim *l.* *Isa 61:1*
to proclaim *l.* *Jer 34:8*
in my sight, in proclaiming *l.* 15
his servant whom he had set at *l.* 16*
not hearkened to me in proclaiming
l. : I proclaim a *l.* for you. 17
be his to the year of *l.* *Ezek 46:17*
l. them that are bruised. *Luke 4:18*
Paul, and let him have *l.* *Acts 24:23**
man might have been set at *l.* 26:32
gave him *l.* to go to his friends. 27:3*
glorious *l.* of children of. *Rom 8:21*
she is at *l.* to marry. *1 Cor 7:39**
take heed lest this *l.* of yours. 8:9
for why is my *l.* judged of? 10:29
where the Spirit of the Lord is, there
is *l.* *2 Cor 3:17*
privily, to spy out our *l.* *Gal 2:4*
stand fast in the *l.* wherewith. 5:1*
called unto *l.*; only use not *l.* 13*
Timothy is set at *l.* *Heb 13:23*
looketh into the law of *l.* *Jas 1:25*
shall be judged by the law of *l.* 2:12
as free, and not using *l.* *1 Pet 2:16**
they promise them *l.* *2 Pet 2:19*

Libnah
pitched in *L.* *Num 33:20*
removed from *L.* 21
passed to *L.* *Josh 10:29*
gave *L.* to Levites. 21:13
then *L.* revolted. *2 Ki 8:22*
2 Chr 21:10
found the king of Assyria warring
against *L.* *2 Ki 19:8; Isa 37:8*
Hammutal, daughter of Jeremiah of
L. *2 Ki 23:31; 24:18; Jer 52:1*

Libya
L. shall fall with them. *Ezek 30:5*
parts of *L.* about Cyrene. *Acts 2:10*

Libyans
L. that handled the shield. *Jer 46:9*
L. and Ethiopians shall. *Dan 11:43*

lice
that dust may become *l.* *Ex 8:16*
smote dust, it became *l.* in man. 17
so with their enchantments to bring
forth *l.*: so there were *l.* upon. 18
l. in all their coasts. *Ps 105:31*

licence
given him *l.* Paul stood. *Acts 21:40**
accused have *l.* to answer. 25:16**

lick
now shall this company *l.* *Num 22:4*
dogs *l.* thy blood, even. *1 Ki 21:19*
his enemies shall *l.* dust *Ps 72:9*
l. up the dust of thy feet. *Isa 49:23*
l. up the dust like a serpent. *Mi 7:17*

licked
fire *l.* up the water in. *1 Ki 18:38*
dogs *l.* the blood of Naboth. 21:19
and the dogs *l.* up his blood. 22:38
the dogs came and *l.* his sores.
Luke 16:21

licketh
lick up all, as the ox *l.* *Num 22:4*

lid
bored a hole in the *l.* *2 Ki 12:9*

---

lie
drink wine, we will *l.* *Gen 19:32*
go thou in, and *l.* with him. 34
he shall *l.* with thee to-night. 30:15
she said, Come *l.* with me. 39:7, 12
2 Sam 13:11
he came in unto me to *l.* *Gen 39:14*
if a man *l.* with a maid. *Ex 22:16*
man shall *l.* with seed. *Lev 15:18*
if a man *l.* with her at all. 24
not *l.* carnally with thy. 18:20
shalt not *l.* with mankind. 22
nor *l.* with beasts. 23
l. with his daughter in law. 20:12
if *l.* with mankind. 13
if *l.* with a beast. 15
if a man *l.* with a woman having. 18
man *l.* with his uncle's wife. 20
if a man *l.* with her. *Num 5:13*
man find her, and *l.* *Deut 22:23*
if the man force her, and *l.* with. 25
damsel not betrothed, and *l.* with. 28
betroth a wife, and another *l.* 28:30
go to *l.* with my wife? *2 Sam 11:11*
shall *l.* all night betwixt. *S of S 1:13*

lie
I will *l.* with my fathers. *Gen 47:30**
let the ground *l.* still. *Ex 23:11*
curses in this book shall *l.* on him.
Deut 29:20
went to *l.* in ambush. *Josh 8:9*, 12
all thy wants *l.* on me. *Judg 19:20*
mark the place where he shall *l.*
Ruth 3:4
let her *l.* in thy bosom. *1 Ki 1:2*
I *l.* among them that are. *Ps 57:4*
like slain that *l.* in the grave. 88:5
if two *l.* together they have heat.
Eccl 4:11
beasts of the desert shall *l.* there.
Isa 13:21
kings of the nations *l.* in. 14:18*
thy sons *l.* at the head of all. 51:20
the young and old *l.* on. *Lam 2:21*
l. thou also upon thy left. *Ezek 4:4*
l. again on thy right side. 6
shalt *l.* 390 days. 9
shalt *l.* in the midst of the. 31:18
they *l.* uncircumcised. 32:21, 30
shall not *l.* with the mighty. 27
l. with the slain. 28
l. with uncircumcised. 29
shall they *l.* in a good fold. 34:14
come, *l.* all night in. *Joel 1:13*
that *l.* on beds of ivory. *Amos 6:4*
when Jesus saw him *l.* he. *John 5:6*
Peter seeth the linen clothes *l.* 20:6

lie down
before a beast, to *l. down* thereto.
Lev 18:23; 20:16
ye shall *l. down* and none. 26:6
Israel shall not *l. down. Num 23:24*
cause him to *l. down. Deut 25:2*
Boaz went to *l. down* at. *Ruth 3:7*
tarry this night, *l. down* until. 13
Eli said, I called not, *l. down* again.
1 Sam 3:5, 6, 9
even he went to *l. down.* *2 Sam 11:13*
when I *l. down* I say, When? *Job 7:4*
thou shalt *l. down* and none. 11:19
which shall *l. down* with him. 20:11
they shall *l. down* alike in. 21:26
the rich man shall *l. down.* 27:19
he maketh me *l. down* in. *Ps 23:2*
l. down and thy sleep be. *Pr 3:24*
leopard shall *l. down.* *Isa 11:6*
their young ones shall *l. down.* 7
and the needy shall *l. down.* 14:30
for flocks which shall *l. down.* 17:2
the calf feed and *l. down.* 27:10
power shall *l. down* together. 43:17
ye shall *l. down* in sorrow. 50:11
place for herds to *l. down.* 65:10
we *l. down* in our shame. *Jer 3:25*
shepherds causing their flocks to *l.
down.* 33:12
cause them to *l. down. Ezek 34:15*
them to *l. down* safely. *Hos 2:18*
l. down in the evening. *Zeph 2:7*
flocks shall *l. down.* 14
for beasts to *l. down* in. 15
Israel shall feed and *l. down.* 3:13

lie in wait

if a man *l.* not in wait.   *Ex* 21:13
neighbour and *l.* in wait. *Deut* 19:11
l. in wait against the city . *Josh* 8:4
l. in wait in the field.   *Judg* 9:32
saying, Go and *l. in wait* in.   21:20
hast stirred up my servant to *l. in
wait.*   *1 Sam* 22:8, 13
in the covert to *l. in wait. Job* 38:40
for lo, they *l. in wait.*   *Ps* 59:3
the wicked are to *l. in wait. Pr* 12:6
oven, whiles they *l. in wait. Hos* 7:6
all *l. in wait* for blood.   *Mi* 7:2
l. in wait for him more. *Acts* 23:21
whereby they *l. in wait* to. *Eph* 4:14

lie waste

the highways *l. waste.*   *Isa* 33:8
it shall *l. waste.*   34:10
and this house *l. waste.*   *Hag* 1:4

lie, verb

soul *l.* to his neighbour.   *Lev* 6:2*
ye shall not steal, nor *l.*   19:11
a man, that he should *l. Num* 23:19
Strength of Israel will not *l.* nor.
         1 Sam 15:29
my lord, do not *l.* to thy. *2 Ki* 4:16
is evident to you if I *l.*   *Job* 6:28
should I *l.* against my right.   34:6
sworn that I will not *l. Ps* 89:35
faithful witness will not *l. Pr* 14:5
children that will not *l. Isa* 63:8*
walking in falsehood do *l. Mi* 2:11
shall speak and not *l.*   *Hab* 2:3
filled thy heart to *l.?*   *Acts* 5:3
I say the truth in Christ, I *l.* not.
      Rom 9:1; *1 Tim* 2:7
Lord knoweth I *l.* not. *2 Cor* 11:31
to you, behold I *l.* not.   *Gal* 1:20
l. not one to another.   *Col* 3:9
God, that cannot *l.,* promised. *Tit* 1:2
impossible for God to *l.*   *Heb* 6:18
glory not, *l.* not against.   *Jas* 3:14
have fellowship with him and walk in
   darkness, we *l.* and.   *1 John* 1:6
say they are Jews, but do *l. Rev* 3:9

lie, substantive

men of high degree are a *l. Ps* 62:9
the proud have forged a *l.*   119:69
a *l.* in my right hand ?   *Isa* 44:20
they prophesy a *l.* to you to remove.
    Jer 27:10, 14, 15*, 16; 29:21
this people to trust in a *l.*   28:15
caused you to trust in a *l.*   29:31
whilst they divine a *l. Ezek* 21:29
houses of Achzib shall be a *l.* to.
         Mi 1:14
for the diviners have seen a *l.* and.
         Zech 10:2
when he speaketh a *l.* he. *John* 8:44
truth of God into a *l.*   *Rom* 1:25
more abounded through my *l.*   3:7
they should believe a *l. 2 Thes* 2:11
ye know that no *l.* is.   *1 John* 2:21
you of all things, and is no *l.*   27
whatsoever maketh a *l. Rev* 21:27
whosoever loveth and maketh a *l.*
         22:15

lied

prophet, but he *l.* unto.   *1 Ki* 13:18
they *l.* unto him with.   *Ps* 78:36
afraid, that thou hast *l. Isa* 57:11
thou hast not *l.* unto men. *Acts* 5:4

lien, or lain

one might have *l.* with. *Gen* 26:10
if no man have *l.* with. *Num* 5:19
if some man have *l.* with thee.   20
woman that hath *l. Judg* 21:11
for now should I have *l. Job* 3:13
though ye have *l.* among. *Ps* 68:13
thou hast not been *l.* with. *Jer* 3:2

liers in wait

there were *l. in* ambush. *Josh* 8:14
Shechem set *l. in wait. Judg* 9:25
there were *l. in wait* abiding. 16:12
Israel set *l. in wait* round. 20:29
the *l. in wait* came forth.   33
l. in wait hasted and rushed.   37
they trusted in the *l. in wait.*   36

lies

thou hast told me *l. Judg* 16:10, 13
should thy *l.* make men ? *Job* 11:3*
ye are forgers of *l.*   13:4

---

such as turn aside to *l.*   *Ps* 40:4
and go astray, speaking *l.*   58:3
they delight in *l.,* they curse.   62:4
the mouth that speaketh *l.* 63:11
that telleth *l.* shall not tarry. 101:7
hates a false witness that speaketh *l.*
         Pr 6:19
but a false witness will utter *l.* 14:5
deceitful witness speaketh *l.*   25
and he that speaketh *l.* shall. 19:5
speaketh *l.* shall perish.   9
if a ruler hearken to *l.* his.   29:12
far from me vanity and *l.*   30:8
prophet that teacheth *l. Isa* 9:15
pride of Moab, but his *l.*   16:6*
we have made *l.* our refuge. 28:15
sweep away the refuge of *l.*   17
your lips have spoken *l.,* your. 59:3
they trust in vanity, and speak *l.*   4
bend their tongues like their bow for
   l.   *Jer* 9:3
taught their tongue to speak *l.*   5
prophesy *l.*   14:14; 23:25, 26
fathers have inherited *l.*   16:19
thou hast prophesied *l.*   20:6
adultery, and walk in *l.*   23:14
to err by their *l.* and lightness.   32
his *l.* shall not so affect it. 48:30*
spoken vanity and seen *l. Ezek* 13:8
upon the prophets that divine *l.*   9
my people that hear your *l.*   19
with *l.* ye have made the.   22
divining *l.* unto them, saying. 22:28
hath wearied herself with *l.* 24:12*
speak *l.* at one table. *Dan* 11:27
princes gladg with their *l.* *Hos* 7:3
yet they have spoken *l.* against. 10:13
eaten the fruit of *l.* because. 10:13
compasseth me about with *l.* 11:12
increaseth *l.* and desolation. 12:1
and their *l.* caused them. *Amos* 2:4
thereof have spoken *l.*   *Mi* 6:12
bloody city, it is full of *l.* *Nah* 3:1
image, and a teacher of *l. Hab* 2:18
Israel shall not speak *l.* *Zeph* 3:13
speakest *l.* in the name. *Zech* 13:3
speak *l.* in hypocrisy.   *1 Tim* 4:2

liest

the land whereon thou *l. Gen* 28:13
when thou *l.* down. *Deut* 6:7; 11:19
Get thee up; wherefore *l.* thou thus
   upon thy face ?   *Josh* 7:10*
l. down, shalt not be afraid. *Pr* 3:24

lieth

doest not well, sin *l.*   *Gen* 4:7*
of the deep that *l.* under.   49:25*
found that which was lost, and *l.*
   concerning it.   *Lev* 6:3
he that *l.* in the house.   14:47
every bed whereon he *l.* is.   15:4
every thing that she *l.* upon shall be
   unclean.   20, 26
all the bed whereon he *l.*   24, 33
sabbaths, as long as it *l.* 26:34, 35
sabbaths, while she *l.* desolate.   43
his great strength.   *Judg* 16:5
wherein thy great strength *l.*   6, 15
l. under the shady trees. *Job* 40:21
he *l.* he shall rise no more. *Ps* 41:8
thy wrath *l.* hard on me, thou. 88:7
my servant *l.* at home sick. *Mat* 8:6
my daughter *l.* at point. *Mark* 5:23
as much as *l.* in you, live. *Rom* 12:8
the whole world *l.* in. *1 John* 5:19

lieth down

it shall be when he *l.* down. *Ruth* 3:4
so man *l.* down and riseth. *Job* 14:12
that *l.* down in the midst. *Pr* 23:34

lieth in wait

l. in wait secretly as a lion: *l. in wait*
   to catch the poor.   *Ps* 10:9*
and *she l. in wait* at every. *Pr* 7:12
she also *l. in wait* as for a.   23:28

lieth waste

the place of my fathers' sepulchres
   l. waste.   *Neh* 2:3
you see how Jerusalem *l. waste.*   17

lieth, as with a woman

whoso *l.* with a beast.   *Ex* 22:19
whoso *l.* carnally with a. *Lev* 19:20
man that *l.* with his father's. 20:11
lie with mankind as he *l.* with.   13

---

cursed be he that *l.* with. *Deut* 27:20
l. with beast.   21
l. with his sister.   22
l. with his mother in law   23
her that *l.* in thy bosom.   *Mi* 7:5

lieutenants

(Revised Versions, satraps)
king's commissions to *l.*   *Ezra* 8:36
commanded the king's *l. Esth* 3:12
had commanded to the *l.*   8:9
all the rulers and *l.* helped.   9:3

life

[1] *Literally, animate existence, as
distinguished from dead matter,*
Gen 1:20. [2] *Conscious existence
with the powers derived from it,*
Job 3:20. [3] *The existence of the
soul after the death of the body,*
John 5:29. *Other passages correspond with modern uses of the
word, or are derived from these
heads.*

creature that hath *l.*   *Gen* 1:20
every thing wherein there is *l.*   30
into his nostrils the breath of *l.*   2:7
the tree of *l.* in the midst.   9; 3:22
keep the way of the tree of *l.*   3:24
wherein is the breath of *l.* 6:17; 7:22
flesh with the *l.* shall ye not eat.
     9:4; *Lev* 17:14
man will I require *l.* of man. *Gen* 9:5
according to time of *l.*   18:10*, 14*
these were the years of the *l.*   23:1
the years of Abraham's *l.*   25:7
by the *l.* of Pharaoh.   42:15, 16
send me before to preserve *l.* 45:5
not attained to the years of *l.* 47:9
of the *l.* of Levi were 137.   *Ex* 6:16
years of the *l.* of Kohath.   18
l. of Amram.   20
shall give *l.* for *l.* 21:23; *Deut* 19:21
for the *l.* of the flesh is.   *Lev* 17:11
the other in her *l.* time.   18:18
blood is the *l.;* and thou mayest not
   eat the *l.* with flesh. *Deut* 12:23
tree of the field is man's *l.*   20:19
taketh a man's *l.* to pledge.   24:6
I have set before thee *l.* 30:15, 19
         Jer 21:8
it is not a vain thing, because it is
   your *l.*   *Deut* 32:47
the men answered, Our *l. Josh* 2:14
up in the bundle of *l.*   *1 Sam* 25:29
for the *l.* of his brother.   *2 Sam* 14:7
whether in death or *l.* there.   15:21
for thyself long *l.* nor asked the *l.* of.
    1 Ki 3:11; *2 Chr* 1:11
time of *l.* thou shalt. *2 Ki* 4:16*, 17*
left camp, and fled for their *l.*   7:7
they may pray for the *l. Ezra* 6:10
Jews to stand for their *l. Esth* 8:11
why is *l.* given to the bitter in soul ?
         Job 3:20
thou hast granted me *l.* and. 10:12
and no man is sure of *l.*   24:22
owners thereof to lose their *l.* 31:39
the Almighty hath given me *l.* 33:4
he preserveth not the *l.* of the. 36:6
their *l.* is among the unclean.   14
shew me the path of *l.*   *Ps* 16:11
he asked *l.* of thee, thou.   21:4
in his favour is *l.:* weeping. 30:5†
man is he that desireth *l.?*   34:12
with thee is the fountain of *l.* 36:9
thou wilt prolong the king's *l.* 61:6
kindness is better than *l.*   63:3
who holdeth our soul in *l.*   66:9
but gave their *l.* over to the. 78:50
with long *l.* will I satisfy him. 91:16
the blessing, even *l.* for.   133:3
which taketh away the *l.*   *Pr* 1:19
nor take hold of the paths of *l.* 2:19
long *l.* and peace shall they.   3:2
she is a tree of *l.* to them that.   18
so shall they be *l.* to thy soul.   22
they are *l.* to those that find.   4:22
for out of it are the issues of *l.*   23
shouldest ponder the path of *l.*   5:6
of instruction are the way of *l.* 6:23
will hunt for the precious *l.*   26
whoso findeth me findeth *l.* and. 8:35
the righteous is a well of *l.* 10:11
is in the way of *l.* that keepeth. 17

the righteous is a tree of *l.* Pr 11:30
righteous regardeth the *l.* of. 12:10
in the way of righteousness is *l.* 28
the ransom of a man's *l.* are. 13:8
desire cometh, it is a tree of *l.* 12
law of the wise is a fountain of *l.* 14
of the Lord is a fountain of *l.* 14:27
a sound heart is the *l.* of the flesh. 30
wholesome tongue is a tree of *l.* 15:4
way of *l.* is above to the wise. 24
reproof of *l.* abideth among. 31
of the king's countenance is *l.* 16:15
understanding is wellspring of *l.* 22
death and *l.* are in the power. 18:21
followeth mercy, findeth *l.* 21:21
are riches, honour, and *l.* 22:4
good all the days of her *l.* 31:12
good they should do all the days of
their *l.* Eccl 2:3
therefore I hated *l.* 17
wisdom giveth *l.* 7:12
in all these things is the *l.* Isa 38:16
sing songs all the days of our *l.* 20
found the *l.* of thy hand. 57:10*
and death shall be chosen rather
than *l.* Jer 8:3
into the hand of those that seek their
l. 21:7; 34:20, 21
I set before you the way of *l.* 21:8
dismayed before their enemies, before them that seek their *l.* 49:37
lift up thy hands for the *l.* Lam 2:19
strengthened the hands of wicked,
by promising him *l.* Ezek 13:22*
walk in the statutes of *l.* 33:15
perish for this man's *l.* Jonah 1:14
my covenant was with him of *l.* and
peace. Mal 2:5
which sought the child's *l.* Mat 2:20
take no thought for your *l.* 6:25
Luke 12:22
to enter into *l.* halt or maimed.
Mat 18:8; Mark 9:43, 45
enter into *l.* with one eye. Mat 18:9
if wilt enter into *l.* keep. Mat 19:17
is it lawful to save *l.* or to kill?
Mark 3:4; Luke 6:9
all the days of our *l.* Luke 1:75
for a man's *l.* consisteth not. 12:15
the *l.* is more than meat. 23
in him was *l.* and the *l.* John 1:4
believeth not, shall not see *l.* 3:36
Father hath *l.* in himself, so hath he
given to the Son to have *l.* 5:26
good, to the resurrection of *l.* 29
to me that ye might have *l.* 40; 10:10
giveth *l.* unto the world. 6:33
I am the bread of *l.* 35, 48
which I will give for the *l.* of the. 51
and drink his blood, ye have no *l.* 53
words I speak to you, they are *l.* 63
but shall have the light of *l.* 8:12
resurrection and the *l.* 11:25; 14:6
believing ye might have *l.* 20:31
known to me the ways of *l.* Acts 2:28
killed the Prince of *l.* whom. 3:15
seeing he giveth to all *l.* 17:25
the manner of *l.* from my youth. 26:4
be no loss of any man's *l.* 27:22
in *l.* by one, Jesus Christ. Rom 5:17
all men to justification of *l.* 18
should walk in newness of *l.* 6:4
the Spirit of *l.* in Christ Jesus. 8:2
to be spiritually minded is *l.* 6
the Spirit is *l.* because of. 10
that neither death nor *l.* 38
the receiving the be but *l?* 11:15
the world, or *l..* or death. 1 Cor 3:22
things without *l.* giving sound. 14:7
we despaired even of *l.* 2 Cor 1:8
the savour of *l.* unto *l.* 2:16
killeth, but the Spirit giveth *l.* 3:6
that the *l.* of Jesus might be. 4:10
death worketh in us, but *l.* in you. 12
might be swallowed up of *l.* 5:4
the *l.* which I now live. Gal 2:20
which could have given *l.* 3:21*
alienated from the *l.* Eph 4:18
whether it be by *l.* or by. Phil 1:20
holding forth the word of *l.* 2:16
l. is hid with Christ in God. Col 3:3
when Christ who is our *l.* shall. 4
may lead a peaceable *l.* 1 Tim 2:2
having the promise of *l.* 4:8

the promise of *l.* in Christ. 2 Tim 1:1
and he hath brought *l.* to light. 10
fully known my manner of *l.* 3:10
beginning of days, nor end of *l.*
Heb 7:3
after the power of an endless *l.* 16
receive the crown of *l.* Jas 1:12
for what is your *l.?* it is even. 4:14
as being heirs together of the grace
of *l.* 1 Pet 3:7
for he that will love *l.* and see. 10
for the time past of our *l.* may. 4:3
all things pertaining to *l.* 2 Pet 1:3
handled the word of *l.* 1 John 1:1
for the *l.* was manifested, and we. 2
pride of *l.* is not of the Father. 2:16
hath Son hath *l.*; and he that hath not
the Son of God hath not *l.* 5:12
he shall give him *l.* for them. 16
I give to eat of the tree of *l.* Rev 2:7
I will give thee a crown of *l.* 10
of the creatures that had *l.* died. 8:9
Spirit of *l.* from God entered. 11:11
he had power to give *l.* to. 13:15*
to thirsty of the water of *l.* 21:6
me a pure river of water of *l.* 22:1
tree of *l.* bare twelve manner of. 2
have right to the tree of *l.* 14
let him take the water of *l.* 17

see book, eternal, everlasting

his life
seeing his *l.* is bound. Gen 44:30
for the ransom of his *l.* Ex 21:30
read therein all the days of his *l.*
Deut 17:19
feared him all the days of his *l.*
Josh 4:14
father adventured his *l.* Judg 9:17
they which he slew in his *l.* 16:30
put his *l.* in his hand. 1 Sam 19:5
was come out to seek his *l.* 23:15
this word against his *l.* 1 Ki 2:23
he arose and went for his *l.* 19:3
thy life be for his *l.* 20:39, 42
his *l.* shall be for the life. 2 Ki 10:24
the temple to save his *l.* Neh 6:11
to make request for his *l.* Esth 7:7
all that a man hath will he give for
his *l.* Job 2:4
he is in thy hand, but save his *l.* 6
and his *l.* from perishing by. 33:18
his *l.* abhorreth bread. 20
his *l.* to destroyers. 22
he will deliver, and his *l.* shall. 28
not that it is for his *l.* Pr 7:23
his mouth, keepeth his *l.* 13:3
man to rejoice and do good in his *l.*
Eccl 3:12
man that prolongeth his *l.* 7:15
labours all the days of his *l.* 15
Moab, his *l.* shall be. Isa 15:4
his *l.* shall be to him for a prey.
Jer 21:9; 38:2
hand of them that seek his *l.* 44:30
to warn, to save his *l.* Ezek 3:18
himself in iniquity of his *l.* 7:13
tremble, every man for his *l.* 32:10
findeth his *l.* shall lose it: he that
loseth his *l.* shall find it. Mat 10:39
16:25; Mark 8:35; Luke 9:24
17:33; John 12:25
to give his *l.* a ransom for many.
Mat 20:28; Mark 10:45
hate not his own *l.* also. Luke 14:26
good Shepherd giveth his *l.* for.
John 10:11
that a man lay down his *l.* for. 15:13
for his *l.* is taken from. Acts 8:33
trouble not yourselves, his *l.* 20:10
shall be saved by his *l.* Rom 5:10
regarding his *l.* to supply. Phil 2:30
he laid down his *l.* 1 John 3:16

see days

my life
shewed in saving my *l.* Gen 19:19
of my *l.*:what good shall my *l.?* 27:46
my *l.* is preserved. 32:30
fed me all my *l.* 48:15
I put my *l.* in my hands. Judg 12:3
what is my *l.* or my father's family?
1 Sam 18:18
that he seeketh my *l.?* 20:1
he that seeketh my *l.* seeketh. 22:23

my *l.* be much set by. 1 Sam 26:24
layest thou a snare for my *l.?* 28:9
I put my *l.* in my hand, and. 21
because my *l.* is yet whole in me.
2 Sam 1:9
my son of my bowels seeketh my *l.*
16:11
falsehood against my *l.* 18:13
now, take away my *l.* 1 Ki 19:4
they seek my *l.* to take it away.
10, 14; Rom 11:3
let my *l.* be precious. 2 Ki 1:13, 14
let my *l.* be given me at my petition.
Esth 7:3
I should prolong my *l.* Job 6:11
O remember that my *l.* is but. 7:7
chooseth death rather than my *l.* 15
yet I would despise my *l.* 9:21
my soul is weary of my *l.* 10:1
wherefore do I put my *l.* in ? 13:14
let him tread down my *l.* Ps 7:5
follow me all the days of my *l.* 23:6
gather not my *l.* with bloody. 26:9
Lord is the strength of my *l.* 27:1
house of the Lord all days of my *l.* 4
my *l.* is spent with grief. 31:10
they devised to take away my *l.* 13
seek after my *l.* lay snares. 38:12
my prayer to the God of my *l.* 42:8
preserve my *l.* from fear of the. 64:1
and my *l.* draweth nigh to. 88:3
my *l.* hath smitten my *l.* to the. 143:3
cut off like a weaver my *l.* Isa 38:12
cut off my *l.* in dungeon. Lam 3:53
Lord, thou hast redeemed my *l.* 58
hast brought up my *l.* Jonah 2:6
take, I beseech thee, my *l.* 4:3
and I lay down my *l.* for the sheep.
John 10:15
me, because I lay down my *l.* 17
Lord, I will lay down my *l.* 13:37
nor count I my *l.* dear. Acts 20:24

this life
have their portion in this *l.* Ps 17:14
good for a man in this *l.* Eccl 6:12
this is thy portion in this *l.* and. 9:9
are choked with the cares of.
Luke 8:14
hearts overcharged with the cares
of this *l.* 21:34
speak all words of this *l.* Acts 5:20
that pertain to this *l.* 1 Cor 6:3
of things pertaining to this *l.* 4
if in this *l.* only we have hope. 15:19
entangleth himself with affairs of
this *l.* 2 Tim 2:4
eternal life, and this *l.* 1 John 5:11

thy life
Escape for thy *l.*; look. Gen 19:17
dead which sought thy *l.* Ex 4:19
thy *l.* shall hang in doubt before thee,
no assurance of thy *l.* Deut 28:66
thee, and thou lose thy *l.* Judg 18:25
thee a restorer of thy *l.* Ruth 4:15
if thou save not thy *l.* 1 Sam 19:11
seeketh my life seeketh thy *l.* 22:23
thy *l.* was much set by this. 26:24
enemy that sought thy *l.* 2 Sam 4:8
which this day saved thy *l.* 19:5
thou mayest save thy *l.* 1 Ki 1:12
if I make not thy *l.* as the life. 19:2
peradventure he will save thy *l.* 20:31
if he be missing thy *l.* be. 39, 42
who redeemeth thy *l.* Ps 103:4
and the years of thy *l.* shall be.
Pr 4:10; 9:11
keep her, for she is thy *l.* 4:13
and the years of thy *l.* shall. 9:11
will I give people for thy *l.* 43:4
they will seek thy *l.* Jer 4:30
of the men that seek thy *l.* 11:21
22:25; 38:16
thy *l.* shall be for a prey to thee.
39:18; 45:5
wilt thou lay down thy *l.?* John 13:38

to or unto life
he had restored to *l.* 2 Ki 8:1, 5
the righteous tendeth to *l.* Pr 10:16
as righteousness tendeth to *l.* 11:19
fear of the Lord tendeth to *l.* 19:23
the way that leadeth unto *l.* Mat 7:14
but is passed from death unto *l.*
John 5:24; 1 John 3:14

granted repentance unto *l*. *Acts* 11:18
ordained to *l*.   *Rom* 7:10
their dead raised to *l*.   *Heb* 11:35

lift

To lift up the eyes, frequently means to direct and make known our desires to God by prayer, Ps 121; 123:1. To lift up the head, is [1] To restore a person to his former dignity, Gen 40:13. [2] To recover former strength and courage, so as to oppress others, Judg 8:28. [3] To rejoice and be glad, Luke 21:28. [4] To be advanced above others, and obtain a complete victory over them, Ps 27:6. To lift up the hand, is [1] To swear, or by oath to confirm a thing, Gen 14:22. [2] To bless, Lev 9:22. [3] To pray, Ps 28:2. [4] To rise in rebellion, 2 Sam 18:28; 20:21. [5] To oppress, threaten, injure, or wrong in any way, Job 31:21.

Hath lift up his heel against me, Ps 41:9. Hath behaved himself insolently, contemptuously and injuriously towards me. It is a phrase taken from an unruly horse, who kicks at one who owns and feeds him.

Lift up his horn, Ps 75:4. Carry not yourselves arrogantly, scornfully, or maliciously towards me or any of God's people.

Lift up thy feet, Ps 74:3. Come speedily to our help, and for our deliverance.

To lift up one's self in height, that is to grow proud, insolent, and oppressive, Ezek 31:10.

the ark was *l*. up above.   *Gen* 7:17
l. up the lad, and hold him in. 21:18
shall *l*. up thine head.   40:13, 19
if thou *l*. up a tool on it.   *Ex* 20:25
Lord *l*. up his countenance upon thee.
                                         Num 6:26
wherefore then *l*. ye up ?   16:3
l. up himself as a young lion. 23:24
shalt help him to *l*.   *Deut* 22:4
not *l*. up an iron tool. 27:5; *Josh* 8:31
he *l*. up his spear against 800.
                                         2 Sam 23:8
l. up thy prayer for the remnant.
                                     2 Ki 19:4; *Isa* 37:4
l. up head of Jehoiachin. *2 Ki* 25:27
were to *l*. up the horn.   *1 Chr* 25:5
I blush to *l*. up my face.   *Ezra* 9:6
if righteous, yet will I not *l*. up.
                                         Job 10:15
then shalt thou *l*. up thy face.
                                     11:15; 22:26
l. up the light of thy.   *Ps* 4:6
arise, O Lord, in thine anger, *l*. 7:6
l. up your heads, O ye gates, be *l*.
                                         24:7, 9
unto thee, O Lord, do I *l*. up my soul.   25:1; 86:4; 143:8
hear, when I *l*. up my hands. 28:2
feed them also, and *l*. them up.   9*
l. up thy feet to perpetual.   74:3
and to the wicked, *l*. not up. 75:4, 5
the floods *l*. up their waves.   93:3
l. up thyself, thou judge of.   94:2
shall he *l*. up the head.   110:7
if they fall, the one will *l*. *Eccl* 4:10
not *l*. up sword against nation.
                                     Isa 2:4; *Mi* 4:3
he will *l*. up an ensign.   *Isa* 5:26
as if staff should *l*. up itself. 10:15
smite, and shall *l*. up his staff. 24
so shall *l*. it up after the manner. 26
l. ye up a banner upon the.   13:2*
now will I rise, now will I *l*. 33:10
Lord shall *l*. up a standard. 59:19*
l. up a standard for the.   62:10
nor *l*. up cry nor prayer for them.
                                     Jer 7:16; 11:14
they shall *l*. up a shout.   51:14
let us *l*. up our heart.   *Lam* 3:41
it might not *l*. itself up. *Ezek* 17:14
and shall *l*. up the buckler.   26:8
so that no man did *l*. up his head.
                                         Zech 1:21

will he not *l*. it out on the sabbath ?
                                         Mat 12:11
in no wise *l*. up herself. *Luke* 13:11
l. up your heads; for your.   21:28
and he shall *l*. you up.   *Jas* 4:10*
                                    see eyes

lift hand or hands

I have *l*. up mine hand. *Gen* 14:22
shall no man *l*. up his hand.   41:44
I *l*. up my h., and say. *Deut* 32:40
l. up thine hand, forget.   *Ps* 10:12
when I *l*. up my hands toward. 28:2
I will *l*. up my hands in thy.   63:4
my h. will I *l*. up to thy.   119:48
l. up your hands in sanctuary. 134:2
I will *l*. up mine hand to the Gentiles.   *Isa* 49:22
l. up thy hands toward.   *Lam* 2:19
wherefore *l*. up the h.   *Heb* 12:12

lift voice

Hagar *l*. up her voice.   *Gen* 21:16
canst thou *l*. up thy voice ? *Job* 38:34
l. up thy voice, O daughter.
                                         Isa 10:30*
they shall *l*. up their voice. 24:14
l. up thy voice with strength. 40:9
not cry, nor *l*. up his voice.   42:2
and cities *l*. up their voice.   11
shall *l*. up the voice.   52:8
cry, spare not, *l*. up thy voice 58:1
cry, and *l*. up thy voice. *Jer* 22:20
to *l*. up the voice with. *Ezek* 21:22

lifted

Lot *l*. up his eyes and.   *Gen* 13:10
Abraham *l*. up his eyes. 18:2; 22:13
Esau *l*. up voice.   27:38
and Jacob *l*. up his voice.   29:11
I *l*. up mine eyes, saw. 31:10; 33:1
l. up Joseph out of the pit.   37:28
as I *l*. up my voice.   39:18
Pharaoh *l*. up the head of.   40:20
l. up the rod and smote waters.
                                 Ex 7:20; 14:16
Aaron *l*. up his hand.   *Lev* 9:22
the congregation *l*. up.   *Num* 14:1
Moses *l*. up his hand and.   20:11
then thy heart be *l*. up. *Deut* 8:14
that his heart be not *l*. above. 17:20
of the priests' feet were *l*. *Josh* 4:18
the people *l*. up their voice and wept.
                             Judg 2:4; 21:2; *1 Sam* 11:4
so they *l*. up their heads. *Judg* 8:28
Jotham *l*. up his voice and.   9:7
Orpah and Ruth *l*. up their voice and wept.   *Ruth* 1:9, 14
Saul *l*. up his voice and wept.
                                     1 Sam 24:16
David and people *l*. up voice. 30:4
                                     2 Sam 3:32
king's sons came and *l*. *2 Sam* 13:36
Sheba hath *l*. up his hand.   20:21
also hast *l*. me up on high.   22:49
he *l*. up his spear against 300. 23:18
                                     1 Chr 11:11
Jeroboam *l*. up hand against king.
                                     1 Ki 11:26, 27
he *l*. up his face to the.   *2 Ki* 9:32
thine heart hath *l*. thee.   14:10
his kingdom was *l*. up. *1 Chr* 14:2*
and singers *l*. up voice. *2 Chr* 5:13
his heart was *l*. up in the ways. 17:6
heart was *l*. up to destruction.
                                     26:16; 32:25
l. up their voice and wept. *Job* 2:12
if I have *l*. up my hand against. 31:21
or *l*. up myself when evil found. 29
who hath not *l*. up his soul. *Ps* 24:4
shall my head be *l*. up above. 27:6
for thou hast *l*. me up.   30:1
                                        102:10
hath *l*. up his heel against me. 41:9
                                     John 13:18
as he *l*. up axes upon the. *Ps* 74:5
they that hate thee have *l*. up. 83:2
floods have *l*. up their voice. 93:3
therefore he *l*. up his hand. 106:26
and their eyelids are *l*. up. *Pr* 30:13
day of the Lord of hosts shall be on every one that is *l*. up. *Isa* 2:12
on cedars that are high and *l*. up. 13
mountains *l*. up.   14
sitting on a throne high and *l*. up. 6:1
when thy hand is *l*. up they.   26:11

against whom hast thou *l*. up thine eyes on high ?   *Isa* 37:23
her judgement is *l*. up to. *Jer* 51:9
creatures were *l*. up.   *Ezek* 1:19
wheels were *l*. up.   20, 21; 10:17*
so the Spirit *l*. me up and.   3:14
Spirit *l*. me up between the earth.
                                     8:3; 11:1
l. up their wings. 10:16, 19; 11:22
and *l*. up my hand to the.   20:5, 6
yet *l*. up mine hand in the.   15, 23
into the land for the which I *l*. up mine hand.   28, 42; 47:14
because thine heart is *l*. up.   28:2
                                     5, 17; 31:10*
thus saith the Lord, I have *l*. 36:7
have I *l*. up my hand against. 44:12
when his heart was *l*. up. *Dan* 5:20
but hast *l*. up thyself against.   23
the first beast was *l*. up from.   7:4
then I *l*. up mine eyes.   8:3; 10:5
thine hand shall be *l*. up. *Mi* 5:9
his soul which is *l*. up is. *Hab* 2:4*
deep *l*. up his hands on high. 3:10
which *l*. up their horn.   *Zech* 1:21
behold, there was *l*. up a.   5:7
they *l*. up the ephah between.   5:9
the stones of a crown, *l*. up.   9:16
the land shall be *l*. up.   14:10
by the hand, and *l*. her up. *Mark* 1:31
but Jesus *l*. him up, and.   9:27
he *l*. up his eyes on his. *Luke* 6:20
a certain woman *l*. up her.   11:27
ten lepers *l*. up their voices.   17:13
and he *l*. up his hands and.   24:50
l. up the serpent in the wilderness,
. . . the Son of man be *l*. *John* 3:14
when ye have *l*. up the Son.   8:28
I, if I be *l*. up, will draw all. 12:32
Son of man must be *l*. up.   34
Peter *l*. up his voice.   *Acts* 2:14
l. up their voice to God with.   4:24
they *l*. up their voices saying. 14:11
and then *l*. up their voices.   22:22
being *l*. up with pride.   *1 Tim* 3:6
the angel *l*. up his hand. *Rev* 10:5

lifter

my glory, and the *l*. up.   *Ps* 3:3

liftest

thou *l*. me up to the wind. *Job* 30:22
l. me up from the gates.   *Ps* 9:13
l. above those that rise up.   18:48
and *l*. up thy voice for.   *Pr* 2:3

lifteth

bringeth low, and *l*. up. *1 Sam* 2:7, 8
thine heart *l*. thee up.   *2 Chr* 25:19
what time the ostrich *l*. *Job* 39:18
wind which *l*. up the.   *Ps* 107:25
he, the needy out of the.   113:7
the Lord *l*. up the meek.   147:6*
when he *l*. up an ensign.   *Isa* 18:3
that *l*. himself up in his.   *Jer* 51:3
horseman *l*. up his bright. *Nah* 3:3*

lifetime

Absalom in his *l*. had.   *2 Sam* 18:18
thou in thy *l*. receivedst. *Luke* 16:25
were all their *l*. subject. *Heb* 2:15

lifting

Abishai chief, for *l*. up. *1 Chr* 11:20
sounding, by *l*. up the voice. 15:16
answered, Amen, with *l*.   *Neh* 8:6
shalt say, There is *l*. up. *Job* 22:29
l. up of my hands as.   *Ps* 141:2
hast done foolishly in *l*.   *Pr* 30:32
shall mount up like the *l*. *Isa* 9:18
at *l*. up of thyself nations were. 33:3
men pray every where, *l*. *1 Tim* 2:8

light

morning was *l*.. the men. *Gen* 44:3
of the house, till it was *l*. *Judg* 19:26
them till the morning *l*. *1 Sam* 14:36
night shall be *l*. about.   *Ps* 139:11
when morning is *l*. they.   *Mi* 2:1
evening time it shall be *l*. *Zech* 14:7

light

our soul loatheth this *l*. *Num* 21:5
and my burden is *l*.   *Mat* 11:30
our *l*. affliction worketh. *2 Cor* 4:17

light

hired vain and *l*. persons. *Judg* 9:4
her prophets are *l*. and.   *Zeph* 3:4

light, *adj.*
Asahel was *l.* of foot.   *2 Sam* 2:18

light, *adv.*
cursed that setteth *l.*   *Deut* 27:16
they set *l.* by father.   *Ezek* 22:7
but made *l.* of it, and.   *Mat* 22:5

light *thing*
seemeth it a *l. thing ?*   *1 Sam* 18:23
it had been a *l. thing.*   *1 Ki* 16:31
a *l. thing* in sight of Lord. *2 Ki* 3:18
it is a *l. thing* for the shadow. 20:10
l. thing that thou shouldest. *Isa* 49:6
a *l. thing* they commit ? *Ezek* 8:17

light
there be *l.* and there was *l. Gen* 1:3
God saw the *l.*   4
God called the *l.* day.   5
the greater *l.* to rule . . . lesser *l.* 16
Israel had *l.* in their.   *Ex* 10:23
pillar gave *l.* by night to these. 14:20
offering, oil for the *l.*   25:6; 27:20
   35:8, 14, 28; 39:37; *Lev* 24:2
pertaineth oil for the *l. 2 Sam* 21:17*
as ye have *l.* depart.   *1 Sam* 29:10
thou quench not the *l. 2 Sam* 21:17*
he shall be as the *l.* of the.   23:4
l. was against *l.* in.   *1 Ki* 7:4, 5
my servant may have a *l.*   11:36*
nor pillar of fire by night to shew
   them *l.*   *Neh* 9:19
the Jews had *l.*, joy.   *Esth* 8:16
neither let the *l.* shine.   *Job* 3:4
let it look for *l.* but have none.   9
as infants which never saw *l.*   16
l. given to him in misery.   20, 23
without order, where the *l.*   10:22
bringeth out to *l.* the shadow. 12:22
they groan in the dark without *l.* 25
the *l.* of the wicked shall be.   18:5
the *l.* shall be dark in his.   6
l. shall shine on thy ways.   22:28
those that rebel against the *l.* 24:13
the murderer rising with the *l.* 14
daytime, they know not the *l.*   16
upon whom doth not his *l.?*   25:3
that is hid bringeth he to *l.*   28:11
and his life shall see the *l.*   33:28
to be enlightened with the *l.* of. 30
behold he spreadeth his *l.*   36:30
with clouds the covereth *l.* and. 32*
the *l.* of his cloud to shine ? 37:15*
men see not the bright *l.* in.   21
wicked their *l.* is withholden. 38:15
where is way where *l.* dwelleth ? 19
by what way is the *l.* parted ?   24
his neesings a *l.* doth shine.   41:18
lift up the *l.* of thy.   *Ps* 4:6
Lord is my *l.* and my salvation. 27:1
forth thy righteousness as *l.*   37:6
l. of mine eyes, it also is gone. 38:10
they shall never see *l.*   49:19
thou hast prepared the *l.*   74:16
all the night with a *l.* of fire. 78:14
l. is sown for the righteous. 97:11
who covereth thyself with *l.* 104:2
Lord, who hath shewed us *l.* 118:27
thy word is a lamp, and a *l.* 119:105
entrance of thy words giveth *l.* 130
darkness and *l.* are both.   139:12
sun, and all ye stars of *l.*   148:3
just is as the shining *l.*   *Pr* 4:18
is a lamp, the law is *l.*   6:23
l. of righteous rejoiceth, but. 13:9
the *l.* of the eyes rejoiceth. 15:30
truly the *l.* is sweet.   *Eccl* 11:7
while the sun or the *l.* be not. 12:2
put darkness for *l.* and *l.*   *Isa* 5:20
the *l.* is darkened in the heavens.
it is because there is no *l.*   8:20*
a great *l.; on them hath *l.* shined. 9:2
l. of Israel shall be for fire. 10:17
moon shall not cause her *l.* to shine.
   13:10; *Mat* 24:29; *Mark* 13:24
l. of moon be as *l.* of sun, *l.* of sun as
   the *l.* of seven days. *Isa* 30:26
my judgement to rest for a *l.*   51:4
we wait for *l.* but behold.   59:9
be to thee an everlasting *l.*   60:19
heavens, and they had no *l. Jer* 4:23
I will take from them the *l.*   25:10
sun for a *l.* by day, and ordinances of
   the moon and stars for *l.*   31:35
and the *l.* dwelleth with. *Dan* 2:22

l. and understanding.   *Dan* 5:11, 14
thy judgements as *l.* that.   *Hos* 6:5
bring me forth to the *l.*   *Mi* 7:9
brightness was as the *l.*   *Hab* 3:4
at the *l.* of thine arrows they.   11
bring judgement to *l.*   *Zeph* 3:5
in that day the *l.* shall. *Zech* 14:6
in darkness saw great *l.*   *Mat* 4:16
ye are the *l.* of the world.   5:14
it giveth *l.* unto all that are in. 15*
let your *l.* so shine before men.   16
l. of body is the eye, if eye . . . full
   of *l.*   6:22*; *Luke* 11:34*, 36
raiment was white as the *l. Mat* 17:2
a *l.* to lighten Gentiles. *Luke* 2:32
enter in may see the *l.* 8:16; 11:33
wiser than the children of *l.*   16:8
and life was the *l.* of men. *John* 1:4
to bear witness of that *l.*   7, 8
that was the true *l.* which.   9
condemnation, that *l.* is come. 3:19
that doeth evil hateth the *l.*   20
doeth truth cometh to the *l.*   21
a shining *l.*: and ye were willing for
   a season to rejoice in his *l.*   5:35*
I am the *l.* of the world, he that followeth me shall have *l.* 8:12; 9:5
because he seeth the *l.*   11:9
stumbleth, because there is no *l.* 10
yet a little while is the *l.*   12:35
ye have *l.*, believe in the *l.* that. 36
I am come a *l.* into the world.   46
shined about him a *l.*   *Acts* 9:3
l. shined in the prison, and. 12:7
I have set thee to be a *l.* to. 13:47
he called for a *l.* and sprang. 16:29
there shone a great *l.* round.   22:6
were with me saw indeed the *l.*   9
not see for the glory of that *l.*   11
O king, I saw in the way a *l.* 26:13
should shew *l.* to the people and. 23
a *l.* of them which are in. *Rom* 2:19
put on the armour of *l.*   13:12
who will bring to *l.* hidden. *1 Cor* 4:5
lest the *l.* of the gospel. *2 Cor* 4:4
who commanded *l.* to shine out.   6
transformed into an angel of *l.* 11:14
now are ye *l.* in the Lord: walk as
   children of *l.*   *Eph* 5:8
made manifest by the *l.*: for whatsoever doth make manifest is *l.* 13
inheritance of saints in *l.*   *Col* 1:12
ye are all children of the *l.* and day.
   1 Thes 5:5
dwelling in *l.* no man.   *1 Tim* 6:16
and immortality to *l.*   *2 Tim* 1:10
into his marvellous *l.*   *1 Pet* 2:9
take heed, as unto a *l.* that shineth
   in a dark place.   *2 Pet* 1:19*
God is *l.* and in him.   *1 John* 1:5
the *l.* of a candle shall. *Rev* 18:23
her *l.* was like a stone most. 21:11
lighten it, and the Lamb is the *l.* 23*
l. of the sun, the Lord giveth *l.* 22:5
see **countenance, darkness**

give **light**
and let them be to *give l. Gen* 1:15
and God set the stars to *give l.*   17
of fire to *give* them *l.*   *Ex* 13:21
the lamps may *give l.* over against.
   25:37; *Num* 8:2
he promised to *give* him alway a *l.*
   2 Ki 8:19*; *2 Chr* 21:7*
to *give* them *l.* in the way. *Neh* 9:12
and fire to *give l.* in the. *Ps* 105:39
stars of heaven shall not *give* their *l.*
   Isa 13:10
I will *give* thee for a *l.* to. 42:6; 49:6
nor shall the moon *give l.* to thee.
   60:19; *Ezek* 32:7
it *giveth l.* unto all in the house.
   Mat 5:15; *Luke* 11:36
to *give* the *l.* of the knowledge of.
   2 Cor 4:6
Christ shall *give* thee *l. Eph* 5:14*

in the **light**
that I may walk in the *l. Ps* 56:13
come, let us walk in the *l. Isa* 2:5
walk in the *l.* of your fire.   50:11*
the light, believe in the *l. John* 12:36
we walk in the *l.* as he is in the *l.*
   1 John 1:7
he that saith he is in the *l.*, and. 2:9

brother, abideth *in the l. 1 John* 2:10
saved shall walk in *l.*   *Rev* 21:24

thy **light**
in *thy l.* shall we see light. *Ps* 36:9
O send out *thy l.* and thy truth. 43:3
then shall *thy l.* break forth. *Isa* 58:8
then shall *thy l.* rise in obscurity. 10
arise, shine, for *thy l.* is come. 60:1
the Gentiles shall come to *thy l.*   3
the sun shall be no more *thy l.*   19
Lord shall be *thy* everlasting *l.*   20

light, -ed
shall *l.* the lamps.   *Ex* 25:37; 40:4
he *l.* the lamps before the Lord.
   40:25; *Num* 8:3
for thou wilt *l.* my candle. *Ps* 18:28
nor do men *l.* a candle.   *Mat* 5:15
no man when he hath *l.* a candle.
   Luke 8:16; 11:33
doth not *l.* a candle, and ?   15:8
nor shall the sun *l.* on.   *Rev* 7:16*

light (*to come upon*)
her hap was to *l.* on a.   *Ruth* 2:3
and we will *l.* on him. *2 Sam* 17:12

lighted (*came down*)
she saw Isaac, she *l.* off. *Gen* 24:64
and she *l.* off her ass.   *Josh* 15:18
   Judg 1:14
Sisera *l.* off his chariot. *Judg* 4:15
Abigail hasted and *l.* off the ass.
   1 Sam 25:23
Naaman *l.* down from.   *2 Ki* 5:21

lighted (*came upon*)
Jacob *l.* on a certain.   *Gen* 28:11
Jehu *l.* on Jehonadab.   *2 Ki* 10:15
word to Jacob and it *l.* on. *Isa* 9:8

lighten
the Lord will *l.* my.   *2 Sam* 22:29
that our God may *l.* our. *Ezra* 9:8
l. mine eyes, lest I sleep. *Ps* 13:3
a light to *l.* the Gentiles. *Luke* 2:32
glory of God did *l.* it.   *Rev* 21:23

lighten
peradventure he will *l.*   *1 Sam* 6:5
cast wares into the sea, to *l.* it of.
   Jonah 1:5

lightened
looked unto him and were *l. Ps* 34:5
the lightnings *l.* the world.   77:18
earth was *l.* with his glory. *Rev* 18:1
see **enlightened**

lightened
being tossed, next day they *l.* ship.
   Acts 27:18*, 38

lighteneth
Lord *l.* both their eyes.   *Pr* 29:13
for as lightning that *l.*   *Luke* 17:24

lighter
make heavy yoke which he put upon
   us. *1 Ki* 12:4, 9, 10; *2 Chr* 10:10
altogether *l.* than vanity.   *Ps* 62:9

lightest
say to him, When thou *l. Num* 8:2

lighteth
when Aaron *l.* the lamps.   *Ex* 30:8
the true light which *l.*   *John* 1:9

lighteth
axe head slippeth and *l. Deut* 19:5

lighting
Lord shall shew the *l.* down of his
   arm.   *Isa* 30:30
like a dove, and *l.* on him. *Mat* 3:16

lightly
one might *l.* have lien. *Gen* 26:10
when at first he *l.* afflicted. *Isa* 9:1*
and all the hills moved *l. Jer* 4:24*
can *l.* speak evil of me. *Mark* 9:39*
see **esteemed**

lightness
l. of her whoredoms she. *Jer* 3:9
my people to err by their *l.*   23:32*
minded, did I use *l.? 2 Cor* 1:17*

lightning
he sent *l.* and discomfited them.
   2 Sam 22:15
he made a way for the *l. Job* 28:26
he directeth his *l.* to the ends. 37:3
who divided a way for the *l.* 38:25
cast forth *l.* and scatter. *Ps* 114:6

out of fire went forth *l.*   *Ezek* 1:13
ran as the appearance of *l.*   14
face as the appearance of *l. Dan* 10:6
his arrow shall go forth as the *l.*
    Zech 9:14
as *l.* cometh out of the east.
    Mat 24:27; *Luke* 17:24
his countenance was as *l. Mat* 28:3
I beheld Satan as *l.* fall. *Luke* 10:18

lightnings
thunders, *l.* and thick.   *Ex* 19:16
all the people saw the *l.* and. 20:18
canst thou send *l.* that ? *Job* 38:35
he shot out *l.* and.   *Ps* 18:14
l. lighted the world.   77:18; 97:4
he maketh *l.* for the rain.   135:7
he maketh *l.* with rain. *Jer* 10:13
    51:16
chariots shall run like the *l. Nah* 2:4
out of throne proceeded *l. Rev* 4:5
were voices, thunderings, and *l.* 8:5
    11:19
l. and a great earthquake.   16:18

lights
be *l.* in the firmament.   *Gen* 1:14
let them be for *l.* in firmament.   15
God made two great *l.* greater.   16
windows of narrow *l.*   *1 Ki* 6:4*
that made great *l.* for. *Ps* 136:7
all the bright *l.* will I make dark.
    Ezek 32:8
girded, your *l.* burning.*Luke* 12:35*
l. in the upper chamber. *Acts* 20:8
whom ye shine as *l.* in. *Phil* 2:15
from the Father of *l.*   *Jas* 1:17

lign aloes
as the trees of *l. a.* which. *Num* 24:6

ligure
(*Revised Versions,* jacinth)
the third row a *l.,* an agate and an
  amethyst.   *Ex* 28:19; 39:12*

like
Sodom was *l.* the land.   *Gen* 13:10
who is *l.* unto thee ?   *Ex* 15:11
Deut 33:29; *1 Ki* 8:23; *2 Chr* 6:14
    Ps 35:10; 71:19
manna was *l.* coriander. *Ex* 16:31
the glory of the Lord was *l.*   24:17
make any ointment *l.* it.   30:32
compoundeth any thing *l.* it.   33
of each shall there be a *l.* weight.   34
hew two tables *l.* unto the first. 34:1
    Deut 10:1, 3
my last end be *l.* his.   *Num* 23:10
hath been heard *l.* it. *Deut* 4:32
lest thou be a cursed thing *l.* it. 7:26
set king over me *l.* all nations.
    17:14; *1 Sam* 8:5, 20
they shall have *l.* portions to eat.
    Deut 18:8
prophet of thy brethren *l.* me.   15
    Acts 3:22; 7:37
raise a prophet from brethren *l.*
  thee.   *Deut* 18:18
l. the overthrow of Sodom.   29:23
not a prophet *l.* unto Moses. 34:10
no day *l.* that before. *Josh* 10:14
countenance *l.* an angel. *Judg* 13:6
brake them from his arms *l.*   16:12
I shall become weak and *l.* any.   17
though I be not *l.* to one of thy.
    Ruth 2:13
woman *l.* Rachel and *l.* Leah.   4:11
let thy house be *l.* the house.   12
nor is there any rock *l.*   *1 Sam* 2:2
be strong, quit yourselves *l.* men. 4:9
    1 Cor 16:13
staff of his spear was *l.* a.   17:7
Nabal held a feast *l.* the feast. 25:36
a valiant man, and who is *l.* 26:15
l. to name of great men. *2 Sam* 7:9
what one nation in earth is *l.?*   23
he maketh my feet *l.* hinds'. 22:34
none *l.* thee before thee. nor after
  thee arise *l.* thee.   *1 Ki* 3:12, 13
there was not the *l.* made in. 10:20
Jeroboam ordained a feast *l.* 12:32
l. the house of Jeroboam.   16:3, 7
    21:22; *2 Ki* 9:10
ariseth a little cloud *l. 1 Ki* 18:44*
number thee an army *l.* the.   20:25
pitched before them *l.* two little.   27

word *l.* word of one of those.
   1 Ki 22:13; *2 Chr* 18:12
but not *l.* his father and *l.*   *2 Ki* 3:2
his flesh came again *l.* flesh of a. 5:14
l. the house of Baasha son of.   9:9
made them *l.* dust by threshing. 13:7
yet not *l.* David his father.   14:3
   16:2; *2 Chr* 28:1
the Lord charged they should not do
  l. them.   *2 Ki* 17:15
take you to a land *l.* your own.
    18:32; *Isa* 36:17
l. to him was there no king.
    2 Ki 23:25; *Neh* 13:26
host *l.* the host of God. *1 Chr* 12:22
would increase Israel *l.* stars. 27:23
over a people *l.* the dust. *2 Chr* 1:9
no burning for him *l.* burning. 21:19
be not ye *l.* your fathers and.   30:7
l. to the abominations of the.   33:2
there was no passover *l.* to.   35:18
to grave *l.* as a shock of. *Job* 5:26
hast thou not curdled me *l.?*   10:10
though man be born *l.* a wild. 11:12
he maketh them to stagger *l.* 12:25
your remembrances *l.*   13:12*
he cometh forth *l.* a flower.   14:2
who drinketh iniquity *l.* water. 15:16
he runneth upon me *l.* a giant. 16:14
he shall perish for ever *l.* his. 20:7
they send their little ones *l.* 21:11
what man is *l.* Job, who ?   34:7
power: who teacheth *l.* him ? 36:22
gird up now thy loins *l.* a man. 38:3
    40:7
hast thou an arm *l.* God ? or. 40:9
on earth there is not his *l.* 41:33
ye have not spoken right *l.* my. 42:8
he shall be *l.* a tree planted. *Ps* 1:3
ungodly are not so, but are *l.*   4
lest he tear my soul *l.* a lion.   7:2
out *l.* water, my heart *l.* wax. 22:14
I become *l.* them that go down. 28:1
I am forgotten, I am *l.* a.   31:12
thy righteousness is *l.* the.   36:6
shall be soon cut down *l.* grass. 37:2
spreading himself *l.* a green bay. 35
beauty to consume *l.* a moth. 39:11
thou hast given us *l.* sheep. 44:11
man is *l.* the beasts that. 49:12, 20
tongue is *l.* a sharp razor.   52:2
but I am *l.* a green olive tree.   8
O that I had wings *l.* a dove ! 55:6
l. the poison of a serpent, *l.*   58:4
make a noise *l.* a dog.   59:6, 14
whet their tongue *l.* a sword. 64:3
he shall come down *l.* rain. 72:6
neither plagued *l.* other men. 73:5
leddest thy people *l.* a flock. 77:20
    78:52
unfaithfully *l.* their fathers. 78:57
their blood have shed *l.* water. 79:3
thereof *l.* the goodly cedars. 80:10
shall die *l.* men, and fall *l.* one. 82:7
make them *l.* a wheel.   83:13
who is a strong Lord *l.* unto thee ?
    89:8; 113:5; *Mi* 7:18
flourish *l.* the palm tree, he shall
  grow *l.* a cedar in.   *Ps* 92:12
heart withered *l.* grass. 102:4, 11
I am *l.* a pelican, *l.* an owl of the.   6
shall wax old *l.* a garment.   26
l. as a father pitieth his. 103:13
out the heavens *l.* a curtain. 104:2
the dry places *l.* a river. 105:41
stagger *l.* a drunken man. 107:27
l. water, and *l.* oil into. 109:18
they that make them are *l.* to them.
    115:8; 135:18
we were *l.* them that dream. 126:1
lest I be *l.* them that go down. 143:7
man is *l.* to vanity, his days. 144:4
l. wool, hoar frost *l.* ashes. 147:16
l. the bars of a castle.   *Pr* 18:19
counsel in the heart of man is *l.* 20:5
biteth *l.* a serpent, stingeth *l.* 23:32
unfaithful man is *l.* a broken tooth.
    25:19
l. a city broken down, and.   28
fool, lest thou be *l.* to him.   26:4
my beloved is *l.* a roe.   *S of S* 2:9
turn, my beloved, and be thou *l.* a roe.
    17; 8:14

cometh *l.* pillars of smoke ? *S of S* 3:6
thy teeth are *l.* a flock of sheep. 4:2
thy lips *l.* scarlet, temples *l.* a.   3
thy neck is *l.* the tower of David.   4
breasts are *l.* two young.   5; 7:3
his lips *l.* lilies dropping sweet. 5:13
my soul made me *l.* chariots.   6:12
joints of thy thighs are *l.* jewels. 7:1
l. a goblet, thy belly is *l.* wheat.   2
stature *l.* a palm tree.   7
smell of thy nose *l.* apples.   8
would have been *l.* unto Gomorrah.
    Isa 1:9; *Rom* 9:29
red *l.* crimson, shall be.   *Isa* 1:18
inhabitants *l.* a valiant man. 10:13
lion shall eat straw *l.* the ox.   11:7
and shall be an highway, *l.* as it.   16
art thou become *l.* to us ?   14:10
I will be *l.* the most High.   14
out *l.* an abominable branch.   19
sound *l.* an harp for Moab.   16:11
in that day shall Egypt be *l.* 19:16
l. as my servant Isaiah hath.   20:3
will toss thee *l.* a ball into a. 22:18
l. a woman with child that.   26:17
breath of the Lord *l.* a stream. 30:33
Sharon is *l.* a wilderness.   33:9
I have cut off *l.* a weaver my. 38:12
l. a crane or swallow so did I.   14
will I cry *l.* a travailing.   42:14
to whom will ye compare me that we
  may be *l.?*   46:5
wicked are *l.* the troubled sea. 57:20
lift up thy voice *l.* a trumpet.   58:1
be *l.* a watered garden, and *l.*   11
for the wall *l.* the blind.   59:10
all *l.* bears, and mourn sore *l.*   11
enemy shall come in *l.* a flood.   19
l. him that treadeth in the.   63:2
our iniquities *l.* wind have.   64:6
peace to her *l.* a river.   66:12
lest my fury come forth *l.* fire.
    Jer 4:4; 21:12
l. as ye have forsaken me.   5:19
portion of Jacob is not *l.* them. 10:16
I was *l.* a lamb brought to.   11:19
for he shall be *l.* the heath in.   17:6
word *l.* fire and *l.* a hammer? 23:29
make this house *l.* Shiloh.   26:6, 9
Zion shall be plowed *l.* a field.   18
l. Zedekiah and *l.* Ahab.   29:22
were added besides to them many *l.*
  words.   36:32
he is *l.* to die with hunger.   38:9
Egypt is *l.* a very fair heifer. 46:20
flee, be *l.* the heath in the.   48:6
be *l.* the dove that maketh nest.   28
shall come *l.* a lion.   49:19; 50:44
is *l.* me, who will appoint ? 49:19
of Jacob is not *l.* them.   51:19
not do any more the *l.*   *Ezek* 5:9
l. as I have done, so shall.   12:11
and doeth *l.* to any of.   18:10
the house of Judah is *l.* to all. 25:8
thou *l.* in thy greatness ?   31:2, 18
nor any tree was *l.* unto him in his.   8
month shall he do the *l.*   45:25
form of the fourth is *l.* the Son of
  God.   *Dan* 3:25
made *l.* the beasts, *l.* oxen.   5:21
one *l.* the Son of man came.   7:13
shall be *l.* people, *l.* priest. *Hos* 4:9
princes *l.* them that remove.   5:10
they *l.* men have transgressed. 6:7
I am *l.* a green fir tree, from. 14:8
hath not been ever the *l.*   *Joel* 2:2
lest he break out *l.* fire. *Amos* 5:6
instruments of music *l.* David. 6:5
l. as the Lord of hosts.   *Zech* 1:6
the governors of Judah *l.* a.   12:6
l. a dove, and lighting.   *Mat* 3:16
   Mark 1:10; *Luke* 3:22; *John* 1:32
be not ye therefore *l.* unto. *Mat* 6:8
was not arrayed *l.* one of these.
    29; *Luke* 12:27
l. children sitting in the market.
    Mat 11:16; *Luke* 7:32
it was restored whole *l. Mat* 12:13
kingdom is *l.* to a grain of mustard.
   13:31; *Mark* 4:31; *Luke* 13:19
kingdom of heaven is *l.* leaven.
    Mat 13:33; *Luke* 13:21
is *l.* unto treasure.   *Mat* 13:44
is *l.* unto a merchant.   45

is *l.* unto a net.   *Mat* 13:47
is *l.* an householder.   52; 20:1
of heaven is *l.* unto a certain.   22:2
second is *l.* unto it. 39; *Mark* 12:31
l. to whited sepulchres. *Mat* 23:27
countenance was *l.* lightning.   28:3
shew you to whom he is *l. Luke* 6:47
and to what are they *l.?*   7:31
are *l.* unto children.   32
what is the kingdom of God *l.?* 13:18
never man spake *l.* this. *John* 7:46
I shall be a liar *l.* unto you.   8:55
others said, He is *l.* him.   9:9
l. a lamb dumb before. *Acts* 8:32
God gave them the *l.* gift.   11:17
we also are men of *l.* passions. 14:15
Godhead is of *l.* gold or silver. 17:29
workmen of *l.* occupation.   19:25
l. to corruptible man.   *Rom* 1:23
l. as Christ was raised up from. 6:4
fashioned *l.* unto his body. *Phil* 3:21
suffered *l.* things of.   *1 Thes* 2:14
it behoved him to be made *l.* unto
   his brethren.   *Heb* 2:17
all points tempted *l.* as we are. 4:15
but made *l.* unto the Son of God. 7:3
that wavereth is *l.* a wave. *Jas* 1:6
he is *l.* a man beholding his.   23
Elias was a man subject to *l.*   5:17
l. figure whereunto even baptism doth
   now save us.   *1 Pet* 3:21*
obtained *l.* precious faith. *2 Pet* 1:1
we shall be *l.* him.   *1 John* 3:2
one *l.* the Son of man, clothed.
        Rev 1:13; 14:14
saying, Who is *l.* to the beast? 13:4
he had two horns *l.* a lamb, and. 11
three unclean spirits *l.* frogs. 16:13
city is *l.* to this great city?   18:18

like, *verb*
if the man *l.* not to.   *Deut* 25:7, 8
did not *l.* to retain God. *Rom* 1:28

like *manner*
did in *l.* man. with their.   *Ex* 7:11
in *l.* man. thou shalt deal.   23:11
in *l.* man. shalt thou do with his ass.
        Deut 22:3
in *l.* man. they sent to king of Moab.
        Judg 11:17
Samuel in *l.* man.   *1 Sam* 19:24
Sanballat sent in *l.* man. *Neh* 6:5
shall die in *l.* man.   *Isa* 51:6
ye in *l.* man. when ye. *Mark* 13:29
in *l.* man. did their fathers unto the
   prophets.   *Luke* 6:23
third took her, in *l.* man.   20:31
shall so come in *l.* man. *Acts* 1:11
in *l.* man. that women adorn.
        1 Tim 2:9
in *l.* man. giving themselves to fornication.   *Jude* 7

none **like**
there is *none l.* the Lord our God.
  Ex 8:10; 9:14; *Deut* 33:26
  2 Sam 7:22; *1 Chr* 17:20
none l. the hail.   *Ex* 9:24
none l. cry of Egypt.   11:6
none l. Saul among all. *1 Sam* 10:24
David said, There is *none l.*   21:9
was *none l.* Solomon.   *1 Ki* 3:12
none l. Ahab.   21:25
after there was *none l.* Hezekiah.
        2 Ki 18:5
there is *none l.* him in. *Job* 1:8; 2:3
among the gods *none l.* unto thee.
   Ps 86:8; *Jer* 10:6, 7
I am God, and there is *none l.* me.
        Isa 46:9
is great, so that *none* is *l.* it. *Jer* 30:7
was found *none l.* Daniel. *Dan* 1:19

such **like**
and doeth not *such l.* *Ezek* 18:14
many other *such l.* things ye do.
        Mark 7:8, 13
drunkenness and such *l.* *Gal.* 5:21

like *wise*
I in *l. wise* will tell you. *Mat* 21:24

liked
of my father he *l.* me. *1 Chr* 28:4*

liken
to whom then will ye *l.* God?
     Isa 40:18, 25; 46:5

---

thing shall I *l.* to thee?   *Lam* 2:13
doeth them, I will *l.* him. *Mat* 7:24
whereunto shall I *l.* this generation?
     11:16; *Luke* 7:31
whereunto shall we *l.* the kingdom?
     Mark 4:30; *Luke* 13:20

likeness
who can be *l.* unto the Lord? *Ps* 89:6
l. the daughter of Zion.   *Jer* 6:2*
l. to a foolish man who. *Mat* 7:26
kingdom of heaven is *l.*   13:24
      18:23; 25:1

likeness
let us make man after our *l.*
     Gen 1:26; 5:1
Adam begat a son in his own *l.*   5:3
not make the *l.* of any.   *Ex* 20:4
a graven image, the *l.* of male or.
   Deut 4:16, 17, 18, 23*, 25*; 5:8
when I awake with thy *l. Ps* 17:15
l. will ye compare to him? *Isa* 40:18
l. of four living creatures. *Ezek* 1:5
as for the *l.* of their faces. 10; 10:22
l. of lamps.   1:13
the four had one *l.*   16; 10:10
the *l.* of the firmament was.   1:22
l. of a throne.   26; 10:1
the *l.* of the glory of the Lord.   1:28
lo, a *l.* as of fire.   8:2
l. of the hands of a man.   10:21
gods are come down in the *l.* of men.
       Acts 14:11
in the *l.* of his death, we shall be also
   in the *l.* of his.   *Rom* 6:5
God sending his Son in the *l.*   8:3
made in the *l.* of men.   *Phil* 2:7

likeminded
God of patience grant you to be *l.*
     Rom 15:5*
that ye be *l.*   *Phil* 2:2*
I have no man *l.* who will care.   20

liketh
(*American Version*, pleaseth)
shall dwell where it *l.* *Deut* 23:16
also for the Jews as it *l.* *Esth* 8:8
for this *l.* you, O children. *Amos* 4:5

likewise
l. shalt thou do with thine oxen.
       Ex 22:30
gods, even so will I do *l. Deut* 12:30
maidservant thou shalt do *l.* 15:17
lost goods shalt thou do *l.*   22:3
look on me, and do *l.*   *Judg* 7:17
and they prophesied *l. 1 Sam* 19:21
fell *l.* on his sword, and died.   31:5
let us hear *l.* what he. *2 Sam* 17:5
l. did he for all his strange wives.
       1 Ki 11:8
l. fled before Abishai. *1 Chr* 19:15
praise every morning and *l.*   23:30
I *l.* might exact of them. *Neh* 5:10
my maidens will fast *l.* *Esth* 4:16
l. the fool and brutish.   *Ps* 49:10
God shall *l.* destroy thee for.   52:5
l. hast cursed others.   *Eccl* 7:22
they be quiet, and *l.* many. *Nah* 1:12
l. shall also Son of man. *Mat* 17:12
so *l.* shall my heavenly Father. 18:35
the sixth hour, and did *l.*   20:5
l. received every man a penny.   10
to the second and said *l.*   21:30
and they did unto them *l.*   36
l. the second and third died.   22:26
       Mark 12:21
so *l.* when ye see these things.
     Mat 24:33; *Luke* 21:31
l. he that had received two talents.
       Mat 25:17
l. also said all his disciples. 26:35
       Mark 14:31
l. the chief priests mocked.
    Mat 27:41; *Mark* 15:31
gave thanks *l.* to the Lord. *Luke* 2:38
let him do *l.*   3:11
do ye also to them *l.*   6:31
go and do thou *l.*   10:37
ye shall all *l.* perish.   13:3, 5
l., whoever forsaketh not all.   14:33
l. joy shall be in heaven.   15:7, 10
l. Lazarus received evil.   16:25
so *l.* when ye shall have done. 17:10
l. also the cup after supper.   22:20

---

also doeth the Son *l.*   *John* 5:19
prophets have *l.* foretold. *Acts* 3:24
l. the men leaving the.   *Rom* 1:27
l. reckon yourselves to be.   6:11
l. the Spirit helpeth our.   8:26
and *l.* also the wife to.   *1 Cor* 7:3
other Jews dissembled *l.*   *Gal* 2:13
l. the good works of.   *1 Tim* 5:25
young men *l.* exhort to.   *Tit* 2:6
he also himself *l.* took.   *Heb* 2:14
arm yourselves *l.* with.   *1 Pet* 4:1
l. these filthy dreamers.   *Jude* 8
shone not, and the night *l. Rev* 8:12

liking
their young are in good *l. Job* 39:4
he see your faces worse *l. Dan* 1:10

lilies
wrought with flowers of *l.*
    1 Ki 7:26; *2 Chr* 4:5
feedeth among the *l. S of S* 2:16; 6:3
roes which feed among the *l.*   4:5
his lips like *l.* dropping sweet. 5:13
like wheat set about with *l.*   7:2
consider the *l.* how they grow.
    Mat 6:28; *Luke* 12:27

lily
Sharon, and *l.* of valleys. *S of S* 2:1
as the *l.* among thorns, so is my.   2
Israel shall grow as the *l. Hos* 14:5

lily *work*
chapiters were of *l.* work. *1 Ki* 7:19
top of the pillars was *l.* work.   22

lime
be as the burnings of *l.* *Isa* 33:12
of king of Edom to *l.*   *Amos* 2:1

limit
l. thereof shall be most. *Ezek* 43:12

limited
they *l.* the Holy One.   *Ps* 78:41*

limiteth
l. a certain day, saying.   *Heb* 4:7*

line
bind this *l.* of scarlet.   *Josh* 2:18
she bound the scarlet *l.* in the.   21
measured Moab with a *l.*; with one
   full *l.* to keep alive.   *2 Sam* 8:2
a *l.* of twelve cubits.   *1 Ki* 7:15
a *l.* of thirty cubits.   23; *2 Chr* 4:2
stretch over Jerusalem *l. 2 Ki* 21:13
who hath stretched the *l.? Job* 38:5
their *l.* is gone out through. *Ps* 19:4
them an inheritance by *l.*   78:55
precept must be upon precept; *l.*
   upon *l.,* *l.* upon *l.* *Isa* 28:10, 13
judgement will I lay to the *l.*   17
shall stretch out on it the *l.*   34:11
hath divided it to them by *l.*   44:13*
he marketh it out with a *l.* 44:13*
the measuring *l.* shall. *Jer* 31:39
hath stretched out a *l.* *Lam* 2:8
a man that had the *l.* of flax.
       Ezek 40:3
the man that had the *l.* went. 47:3
land shall be divided by *l. Amos* 7:17
a *l.* shall be stretched. *Zech* 1:16
a man with a measuring *l.* in. 2:1
not to boast in another man's *l.*
      2 Cor 10:16*

lineage
because he was of the *l.* of David.
       Luke 2:4*

linen
garment mingled of *l.* and woollen.
    Lev 19:19*; *Deut* 22:11
on him an ephod of *l.*   *1 Chr* 15:27
wrapped him in *l.*   *Mark* 15:46
       Luke 23:53
angels clothed in pure and white *l.*
       Rev 15:6*

linen, *adj.*
make them *l.* breeches.   *Ex* 28:42
put on *l.* garment and *l.* breeches.
      Lev 6:10; 16:4
whether woollen or *l.* garment.
     13:47, 48, 52, 59
Aaron shall put off the *l.*   16:23
l. clothes and *l.* garments.   32
      Ezek 44:17, 18
Samuel ministered with a *l.* ephod.
       1 Sam 2:18

that did wear a l. ephod. *1 Sam 22:18*
David was girded with a l. ephod.
2 Sam 6:14
l. yarn ... merchants received the l.
1 Ki 10:28*; 2 Chr 1:16*
get thee a l. girdle, put. *Jer 13:1*
wrapped it in a l. cloth. *Mat 27:59*
John 19:40
a l. cloth cast about his. *Mark 14:51*
left the l. cloth and fled naked. 52
Peter beheld the l. clothes.
Luke 24:12; John 20:6
John saw the l. clothes. *John 20:5*
see **fine**

lines
with two l. measured. *2 Sam 8:2*
l. are fallen in pleasant. *Ps 16:6*

lingered
while Lot l. the men. *Gen 19:16*
except we had l. surely we. 43:10

lingereth
whose judgement l. not. *2 Pet 2:3*

lintel
and strike the l. and two. *Ex 12:22*
when he seeth blood on the l. he. 23
l. and side posts were. *1 Ki 6:31*
smite l. that the posts. *Amos 9:1**

lintels
lodge in the upper l. of it. *Zeph 2:14*

lion
(*This word is often used as a
synonym of strength and power*)
Judah couched as a l. *Gen 49:9*
Israel lay down as a l., as a great l.
Num 24:9
Gad dwelleth as a l. *Deut 33:20*
of l. there was a swarm of bees and
honey in carcase of l. *Judg 14:8*
what is stronger than a l.? 18
a l. and took a lamb. *1 Sam 17:34*
is as the heart of a l. *2 Sam 17:10*
slew a l. in the midst of a pit. 23:20*
1 Chr 11:22
a l. met him by the way and slew him,
the l. also stood by. *1 Ki 13:24*
l. standing by the carcase. 25, 28
hath delivered him to the l. 26
art departed from me, a l. shall slay
thee; a l. found him and. 20:36
roaring of the l., and the voice of the
fierce l. *Job 4:10*
huntest me as a fierce l. 10:16
nor the fierce l. passed by it. 28:8
hunt the prey for the l.? 38:39
lest he tear my soul like a l. *Ps 7:2*
he lieth in wait secretly as a l. 10:9
like a l. that is greedy of his. 17:12
gaped on me as a roaring l. 22:13
save me from the l.'s mouth. 21
thou shalt tread on the l. 91:13
king's wrath is as the roaring of a l.
Pr 19:12
king is as the roaring of a l. 20:2
the slothful saith, There is a l. 22:13
there is a l. in the way, a l. 26:13
the righteous are bold as a l. 28:1
l. which is strongest among. 30:30
dog is better than a dead l. *Eccl 9:4*
their roaring shall be like a l.
Isa 5:29
l. shall eat straw like the ox. 11:7
65:25
he cried, A l.: My lord, I stand. 21:8
no l. shall be there, nor. 35:9
as a l. so will he break all 38:13
your prophets like a l. *Jer 2:30*
l. is come up from his thicket. 4:7
a l. out of the forest shall slay. 5:6
my heritage is to me as a l. in. 12:8
forsaken his covert as the l. 25:38
shall come up like a l. 49:19; 50:44
as a l. in secret places. *Lam 3:10*
and the face of a l. on. *Ezek 1:10*
third was the face of a l. 10:14
prophets like a roaring l. 22:25
the first was like a l. and. *Dan 7:4*
will be to Ephraim as a l. *Hos 5:14*
he shall roar like a l. when. 11:10
I will be to them as l. 13:7
I will devour as a l. 8
cheek teeth of a great l. *Joel 1:6*
will a l. roar when he? *Amos 3:4*

l. hath roared, who will not? *Amos 3:8*
taketh out of mouth of l. 12
of Jacob shall be as a l. *Mi 5:8*
l. did tear in pieces enough for his.
Nah 2:12
out of the mouth of the l. *2 Tim 4:17*
the devil as a roaring l. *1 Pet 5:8*
first beast was like a l. *Rev 4:7*
the l. of the tribe of Judah. 5:5
loud voice, as when a l. roareth. 10:3
mouth as the mouth of a l. 13:2
see **bear**

old lion
as an old l. who shall rouse him?
Gen 49:9
the old l. perisheth for. *Job 4:11*
come the young and old l.? *Isa 30:6*
lion, even old l. walked. *Nah 2:11*

young lion
up himself as a young l. *Num 23:24*
behold, a young l. roared. *Judg 14:5*
young l. lurking in secret. *Ps 17:12*
young l. shalt thou trample. 91:13
calf and young l. lie down. *Isa 11:6*
like the young l. roaring on. 31:4
became a young l. and learned to
catch the prey. *Ezek 19:3, 6*
another, and made him a young l. 5
thou art like a young l. of the. 32:2
face of a young l. was towards. 41:19
as a young l. to the house of Judah.
Hos 5:14
will a young l. cry out of his den, if he
has taken nothing? *Amos 3:4*
Jacob as a young l. among the flocks.
Mi 5:8

lioness
what is thy mother? A l. *Ezek 19:2*

lionesses
lion strangled for his l. *Nah 2:12*

lionlike
slew two l. men of Moab.
2 Sam 23:20*; 1 Chr 11:22*

lions
Saul and Jonathan stronger than l.
2 Sam 1:23
on the borders were l., oxen: beneath
the l. were. *1 Ki 7:29*
cherubims, l. and palm trees. 36
two l. stood beside the stays. 10:19
2 Chr 9:18
twelve l. stood on the one side.
1 Ki 10:20; 2 Chr 9:19
the Lord sent l. among. *2 Ki 17:25*
therefore he hath sent l. among. 26
were like faces of l. *1 Chr 12:8*
rescue my darling from l. *Ps 35:17*
my soul is among l.: I lie even. 57:4
look from top of Amana, from the l.'
dens. *S of S 4:8*
l. upon him that escapeth. *Isa 15:9*
the l. have driven Israel. *Jer 50:17*
roar together like l. 51:38
she lay down among l. *Ezek 19:2*
went up and down among the l. 6
the l. had the mastery. *Dan 6:24*
Daniel from the power of the l. 27
the dwelling of the l.? *Nah 2:11*
her princes within are roaring l.
Zeph 3:3
faith stopped the mouths of l.
Heb 11:33
were as the teeth of l. *Rev 9:8*
the horses were as the heads of l. 17
see **den**

lion's whelp, whelps
Judah is a l. whelp. *Gen 49:9*
Dan is a l. whelp. *Deut 33:22*
the stout l. whelps are. *Job 4:11*
l. whelps have not trodden it. 28:8
they shall yell as l. whelps. *Jer 51:38*

young lions
teeth of the young lions are. *Job 4:10*
the appetite of the young l.? 38:39
the young l. do lack and. *Ps 34:10*
great teeth of the young l. 58:6
young l. roar after their prey. 104:21
shall roar like young l. *Isa 5:29*
young l. roared upon him. *Jer 2:15*
whelps among young l. *Ezek 19:2*
with all the young l. shall. 38:13

the feedingplace of the young l.?
Nah 2:11
sword shall devour thy young l. 13
voice of the roaring of young l.
Zech 11:3

lip
put a covering on his l. *Lev 13:45*
they shoot out the l. *Ps 22:7*
the l. of truth shall be. *Pr 12:19*

lips
of uncircumcised l. *Ex 6:12, 30*
aught out of her l. *Num 30:6; 8:12*
heart, only her l. moved. *1 Sam 1:13*
with flattering l. do they. *Ps 12:2*
shall cut off all flattering l. 3
our l. are our own, who is lord? 4
goeth not out of feigned l. 17:1
let lying l. be put to silence. 31:18
behold, swords are in their l. 59:7
for the words of their l. let. 12
praise thee with joyful l. 63:5
soul, O Lord, from lying l. 120:2
adders' poison is under their l. 140:3
mischief of their own l. cover. 9
and perverse l. put far. *Pr 4:24*
l. of a strange woman drop as. 5:3
with flattering of her l. she. 7:21
in the l. of him that hath. 10:13
hideth hatred with lying l. is a. 18
the l. of the righteous feed many. 21
the l. of righteous know what is. 32
lying l. are an abomination. 12:22
but the l. of the wise shall. 14:3
when perceivest not in him the l. 7
the talk of the l. tendeth only to. 23
the l. of the wise disperse. 15:7
a divine sentence is in the l. 16:10
righteous l. are the delight of. 13
sweetness of the l. increaseth. 21
doer giveth heed to false l. 17:4
less do lying l. become a prince. 7
the l. of knowledge are a. 20:15
and their l. talk of mischief. 24:2
burning l. are like a potsherd. 26:23
l. of a fool will swallow himself.
Eccl 10:12
causing the l. of those asleep to.
S of S 7:9
undone, a man of unclean l.... of
a people of unclean. *Isa 6:5*
for with stammering l. will. 28:11
this people with their l. do. 29:13
I create the fruit of the l. 57:19
your l. have spoken lies. 59:3
l. of those that rose. *Lam 3:62*
cover your l. nor eat. *Ezek 24:22*
taken up in the l. of talkers. 36:3
render the calves of our l. *Hos 14:2*
seers shall cover their l. *Mi 3:7*
priest's l. should keep. *Mal 2:7*
honoureth me with their l.
Mat 15:8; Mark 7:6
of asps is under their l. *Rom 3:13*
other l. will I speak to. *1 Cor 14:21*
fruit of our l. giving. *Heb 13:15*

his lips
pronouncing with his l. *Lev 5:4*
did not Job sin with his l. *Job 2:10*
O that God would open his l. 11:5
from commandment of his l. 23:12
the request of his l. *Ps 21:2*
spake unadvisedly with his l. 106:33
he that refraineth his l. *Pr 10:19*
by transgression of his l. 12:13
openeth wide his l. shall have. 13:3
wise addeth learning to his l. 16:23
in his l. there is as a burning fire. 27
moving his l. he bringeth evil. 30
shutteth his l. is a man of. 17:28
his l. are the snare of his soul. 18:7
with the increase of his l. shall. 20
he that is perverse in his l. 19:1
that flattereth with his l. 20:19
for grace of his l. the king. 22:11
shall kiss his l. that giveth. 24:26
hateth dissembleth with his l. 26:24
his l. like lilies dropping. *S of S 5:13*
with breath of his l. shall. *Isa 11:4*
his l. are full of indignation. 30:27
was not found in his l. *Mal 2:6*
his l. that they speak. *1 Pet 3:10*

my lips
to the pleading of *my l.*   *Job* 13:6
moving of *my l.* should assuage. 16:5
my l. shall not speak wickedness.
                       27:4
I will speak, I will open *my l.* 32:20
my l. shall utter knowledge.   33:3
up their names into *my l. Ps* 16:4
lo, I have not refrained *my l.*   40:9
open thou *my l.*   51:15
my l. shall praise thee.   63:3
I will pay vows, which *my l.*   66:14
my l. shall greatly rejoice.   71:23
thing that is gone out of *my l.* 89:34
with *my l.* have I declared. 119:13
my l. shall utter thy praise.   171
Lord, keep the door of *my l.* 141:3
the opening of *my l. Pr* 8:6
is an abomination to *my l.*   7
which came out of *my l. Jer* 17:16
the sons of men touched *my l.*
                Dan 10:16
I heard, *my l.* quivered.   *Hab* 3:16

thy lips
which is gone out of *thy l.* perform.
              Deut 23:23
I will put my bridle in *thy l.*
     2 Ki 19:28; *Isa* 37:29
fill *thy l.* with rejoicing.   *Job* 8:21
thy l. own l. testify against thee. 15:6
the word of *thy l.* I have.   *Ps* 17:4
keep *thy l.* from speaking.   34:13
grace is poured into *thy l.*   45:2
thy l. may keep knowledge. *Pr* 5:2
withal be fitted in *thy l.*   22:18
rejoice when *thy l.* speak.   23:16
deceive not with *thy l.*   24:28
praise thee, and not *thine* own *l.* 27:2
thy l. are like a thread. *S of S* 4:3
thy l. O my spouse, drop as the. 11
this hath touched *thy l.*   *Isa* 6:7
cover not *thy l.* and eat. *Ezek* 24:17

liquor
nor shall he drink any *l.*   *Num* 6:3
a round goblet, which wanteth not *l.*
              S of S 7:2*

liquors
offer the first of thy *l.*   *Ex* 22:29

listed
done unto him whatsoever they *l.*
    Mat 17:12; *Mark* 9:13

listen
l. O isles, unto me, and.   *Isa* 49:1

listeth
wind bloweth where it *l.*   *John* 3:8
whithersoever the governor *l.*
              Jas 3:4*

litters
bring your brethren in chariots and *l.*
              Isa 66:20

little
l. water, I pray you.   *Gen* 18:4
let me drink a *l.* water of.   24:17
it was but *l.* thou hadst.   30:30
a *l.* way to Ephrath.   35:16; 48:7
buy us a *l.* food.   43:2; 44:25
a *l.* balm, a *l.* honey.   43:11
if the household be too *l.*   *Ex* 12:4
he that gathered *l.* had no lack. 16:18
              2 Cor 8:15
by *l.* and *l.* I will drive them out.
    Ex 23:30; *Deut* 7:22
and gather but *l.* in.   *Deut* 28:38
Dan went out too *l.* for. *Josh* 19:47
is the iniquity of Peor too *l.?* 22:17
give me *l.* water to drink. *Judg* 4:19
              1 Ki 17:10
that she tarried a *l.* in.   *Ruth* 2:7
mother made him a *l.*   *1 Sam* 2:19
because I tasted a *l.* of this honey.
           14:29, 43
when thou wast *l.* in thine.   15:17
save one *l.* ewe lamb. *2 Sam* 12:3
if that had been too *l.* I would.   8
thy servant will go a *l.* way. 19:36*
brasen altar was too *l.*   *1 Ki* 8:64
my *l.* finger thicker than.   12:10
             2 Chr 10:10
and a *l.* oil in a cruse.   *1 Ki* 17:12
make a *l.* cake.   13
there ariseth a *l.* cloud like.   18:44
like two *l.* flocks of kids.   20:27

25

l. children out of the city mocked.
           2 Ki 2:23†
away captive a *l.* maid.   5:2
Ahab served Baal a *l.* but.   10:18
a *l.* space, give us a *l.*   *Ezra* 9:8
all the trouble seem *l.*   *Neh* 9:32
and my ear received a *l. Job* 4:12*
that I may take comfort a *l.*   10:20
but how *l.* a portion is heard ? 26:14
suffer me a *l.* and I will shew. 36:2
wrath is kindled but a *l.*   *Ps* 2:12*
made him a *l.* lower than the angels.
        8:5 ; *Heb* 2:7
l. that righteous man hath. *Ps* 37:16
l. hills rejoice on every side. 65:12*
there is *l.* Benjamin, with.   68:27
l. hills by righteousness.   72:3*
l. hills skipped like lambs. 114:4, 6
a *l.* sleep, a *l.* slumber, a *l.* folding.
        Pr 6:10; 24:33
heart of the wicked is *l.*   10:20
better is a *l.* with the fear of. 15:16
better is a *l.* with righteousness. 16:8
four things that are *l.* on the. 30:24
sweet, whether he eat *l. Eccl* 5:12
there was a *l.* city, and few.   9:14
so doth a *l.* folly him that is in. 10:1
take us the foxes, the *l. S of S* 2:15
was but a *l.* that I passed.   3:4
we have a *l.* sister, and she.   8:8
hide thyself for a *l.* moment till.
              Isa 26:20
here a *l.* and there a *l.*   28:10, 13
the isles as a very *l.* thing.   40:15
in a *l.* wrath I hid my face.   54:8*
I will be to them a *l. Ezek* 11:16
but as if that were a very *l.* 16:47
and sent out her *l.* rivers.   31:4*
up another *l.* horn.   *Dan* 7:8; 8:9
shall be holpen with a *l.* help. 11:34
they shall sorrow a *l. Hos* 8:10*
the *l.* house with clefts. *Amos* 6:11
l. among the thousands.   *Mi* 5:2
sown much, and bring in *l. Hag* 1:6
for much, and lo, it came to *l.*   9
was but a *l.* displeased. *Zech* 1:15
clothe you, O ye of *l.* faith? *Mat* 6:30
    8:26; 16:8; *Luke* 12:28
O thou of *l.* faith.   *Mat* 14:31
seven, and a few *l.* fishes.   15:34
he went a *l.* further.   26:39
         Mark 1:19; 14:35
my *l.* daughter lieth at. *Mark* 5:23
to whom *l.* is forgiven, the same
loveth *l.!*   *Luke* 7:47*
fear not, *l.* flock.   12:32
he was *l.* of stature.   19:3
been faithful in a very *l.*   19:17
of them may take a *l.*   *John* 6:7
put the apostles forth a *l. Acts* 5:54
man alive, and were not a *l.* 20:12
barbarians shewed us no *l.* 28:2*
a *l.* leaven leaveneth the whole lump.
     1 Cor 5:6; *Gal* 5:9
could bear with me a *l. 2 Cor* 11:1
that I may boast myself a *l.*   16
bodily exercise profiteth *l. 1 Tim* 4:8
use a *l.* wine for thy.   5:23
who was made a *l.* lower. *Heb* 2:9
tongue is a *l.* member. . . a *l. Jas* 3:5
vapour that appeareth for a *l.* 4:14
thou hast a *l.* strength.   *Rev* 3:8
rest a *l.* season.   6:11
be loosed a *l.* season.   20:3
see **book, chambers, child,**
children

little one, or ones
a *l.* one, is it not a *l.* one ? *Gen* 19:20
l. ones took thy captive.   34:29
we, and thou, and our *l.* ones. 43:8
l. one, and his brother is dead. 44:20
out of Egypt for your *l.* ones. 45:19
carried their *l.* ones.   46:5
food for your *l.* ones.   47:24
l. ones left thou in Goshen.   50:8
will nourish you and your *l.* ones. 21
go, and your *l.* ones.   *Ex* 10:10, 24
l. ones, them will I bring. *Num* 14:31
Midian captives and *l.* ones.   31:9
every male among the *l.* ones.   17
build cities for our *l.* ones.   32:16
our *l.* ones shall dwell in.   17, 26
we destroyed men, women, and *l.*
ones.   *Deut* 2:34

the women and *l.* ones. *Deut* 20:14
Joshua read before the women and *l.*
ones.   *Josh* 8:35
put the *l.* ones before.   *Judg* 18:21
over and all the *l.* ones. *2 Sam* 15:22
Judah stood before Lord and *l.* ones.
            2 Chr 20:13
genealogy of all their *l.* ones. 31:18
right way for our *l.* ones. *Ezra* 8:21
cause to perish *l.* ones.   *Esth* 8:11
their *l.* ones like a flock. *Job* 21:11
that dasheth thy *l.* ones.   *Ps* 137:9
a *l.* one shall become a. *Isa* 60:22
nobles sent their *l.* ones.   *Jer* 14:3
her *l.* ones have caused a cry. 48:4
my hand on the *l.* ones. *Zech* 13:7
give to drink to one of these *l.* ones.
            Mat 10:42
whoso shall offend one of these *l.*
ones.   18:6; *Mark* 9:42
despise not one of these *l.* ones.
            Mat 18:10
of these *l.* ones should perish.   14
that he should offend one of these *l.*
ones.   *Luke* 17:2

little while
exalted for a *l.* while.   *Job* 24:24
yet a *l.* while and wicked. *Pr* 37:10
l. while and indignation. *Isa* 10:25
a very *l.* while, and Lebanon. 29:17
possessed it but a *l.* while.   63:18
l. while and her harvest. *Isa* 51:33
yet a *l.* while and I will avenge the
blood.   *Hos* 1:4
a *l.* while and I will shake. *Hag* 2:6
and after a *l.* while another saw him.
          Luke 22:58
yet a *l.* while and I am with you.
      John 7:33; 13:33
a *l.* while is the light.   12:35
yet *l.* while, and the world.   14:19
a *l.* while, and ye shall not see me,
and again a *l.* while. 16:16, 17, 19
a *l.* while ? we cannot tell.   18
for yet a *l.* while and he. *Heb* 10:37

live
they shall sell the *l.* ox.   *Ex* 21:35
a seraphim, having a *l.* coal. *Isa* 6:6

see **goat**

live
tree of life, and *l.* for.   *Gen* 3:22
and my soul shall *l.* because. 12:13
O that Ishmael might *l.!*   17:18
escape, and my soul shall *l.*   19:20
for thee, and thou shall *l.*   20:7
by sword shalt thou *l.* and.   27:40
thy goods, let him not *l.*   31:32
Joseph said, This do, and *l.*   42:18
Joseph, doth my father yet *l.?* 45:3
daughter, then she shall *l. Ex* 1:16
no man see me and *l.*   33:20
he shall *l.* in them, I am.   *Lev* 18:5
   Neh 9:29; *Ezek* 20:11, 13, 21
upon serpent, shall *l.*   *Num* 21:8
alas, who shall *l.* when God ? 24:23
all the days they shall *l. Deut* 4:10
people hear, as thou hast, and *l.?* 33
word of the Lord doth man *l.*   8:3
days that ye *l.* on the earth.   12:1
to one of these cities and *l.*   19:5
learn to fear Lord as long as ye *l.*
      31:13; *1 Ki* 8:40
let Reuben *l.* and not die. *Deut* 33:6
only Rahab harlot shall *l. Josh* 6:17
league with them to let them *l.* 9:15
we will let them *l.* lest wrath. 20, 21
not only while I *l.* shew. *1 Sam* 20:14
l. thou and thy children.   *2 Ki* 4:7
they save us alive, we shall *l.*   7:4
ways so long as they *l.* *2 Chr* 6:31
if a man die, shall he *l.? Job* 14:14
wherefore do the wicked *l.?* 21:7
your heart shall *l.* for ever. *Ps* 22:26
still *l.* and not see corruption. 49:9
will I bless thee while I *l.*   63:4
hearts shall *l.* that seek God. 69:32
he shall *l.*   72:15
I shall not die but *l.*   118:17
understanding, and I shall *l.* 119:144
let my soul *l.* and it shall.   175
I *l.* will I praise the Lord.   146:2
commandments and *l.*   *Pr* 4:4; 7:2

forsake the foolish and *l.* *Pr* 9:6
he that hateth gifts shall *l.* 15:27
if a man *l.* many years. *Eccl* 6:3, 6
　　　　　　　　　　　　　　11:8
madness is in their heart while they *l.*
　　　　　　　　　　　　　　9:3
l. joyfully with the wife whom. 9
thy dead men shall *l.* *Isa* 26:19
by these things men *l.*: make me
　to *l.* 38:16
hear, and your soul shall *l.* 55:3
he that falleth to Chaldeans, shall *l.*
　　Jer 21:9; 27:12, 17; 38:2, 17
obey . . . and thy soul shall *l.* 38:20
his shadow we shall *l.* *Lam* 4:20
he shall surely *l.* *Ezek* 3:21; 18:9
　　　　　17; 33:13, 15, 16
when thou wast in thy blood, *L.* 16:6
kept all my statutes, shall surely *l.*
　　　　　18:19, 21, 22; 20:11, 25
shall he *l.* 18:24
turn yourselves and *l.* 32; 33:11
on us, how should we then *l.?* 33:10
is lawful and right, he shall *l.* 19
Son of man, can these bones *l.?* 37:3
enter you, and ye shall *l.* 5, 6, 14
which liveth and moveth shall *l.*;
　every thing shall *l.* whither. 47:9
revive us, we shall *l.* in. *Hos* 6:2
seek me, and ye shall *l.* *Amos* 5:4, 6
me to die than to *l.* *Jonah* 4:3, 8
the just shall *l.* by his faith.
　　　　　Hab 2:4; *Rom* 1:17
l. with their children. *Zech* 10:9
man shall not *l.* by bread alone.
　　　　　Mat 4:4; *Luke* 4:4
lay thy hand upon her, and she shall *l.*
　　　　　Mat 9:18; *Mark* 5:23
they which *l.* delicately. *Luke* 7:25
this do, and thou shalt *l.* 10:28
of dead, for all *l.* unto him. 20:38
dead shall hear voice of the Son of
　God, and *l.* *John* 5:25
sent me, and I. by Father: so he
　that eateth me, even shall *l.* 6:57
he were dead, yet he shall *l.* 11:25
because I *l.* ye shall *l.* also. 14:19
in him we *l.* and move. *Acts* 17:28
not fit that he should *l.* 22:22
that are dead to sin, *l.* *Rom* 6:2
we believe that we shall also *l.* 8
we are debtors, not to *l.* after. 8:12
ye *l.* after flesh ye shall die . . . mor-
　tify deeds of body, ye shall *l.* 13
doeth these things shall *l.* by them.
　　　　　10:5; *Gal* 3:12
if possible, *l.* peaceably. *Rom* 12:18*
l. we *l.* to the Lord; whether we *l.*
　therefore or die, we are. 14:8
they *l.* of the things of. *1 Cor* 9:13*
preach gospel, should *l.* of gospel. 14
l. are delivered to death. *2 Cor* 4:11
as dying, and behold we *l.* 6:9
in our hearts to die and *l.* with. 7:3
we shall *l.* with him by the. 13:4
brethren, be of one mind, *l.* in. 11
Gentiles to *l.* as Jews. *Gal* 2:14
dead to the law, that I might *l.* 19
I *l.*. yet not I, but Christ liveth in me,
　the life I now *l.* in flesh, I *l.* by. 20
the just shall *l.* by faith. 3:11
　　　　　　　　Heb 10:38
if we *l.* in the Spirit, let. *Gal* 5:25
for me to *l.* is Christ. *Phil* 1:21
if I *l.* in the flesh, this is fruit. 22
now we *l.* if ye stand. *1 Thes* 3:8
died, that we should *l.* 5:10
if dead, we shall also *l.* *2 Tim* 2:11
all that will *l.* godly shall suffer. 3:12
that we should *l.* soberly. *Tit* 2:12
to Father of spirits and *l.?* *Heb* 12:9
things willing to *l.* honestly. 13:18
if the Lord will we shall *l.* *Jas* 4:15
should *l.* to righteousness. *1 Pet* 2:24
no longer should *l.* in the flesh. 4:2
but *l.* according to God in spirit. 6
ensample to those that *l.* *2 Pet* 2:6
escaped from them that *l.* in. 18
his Son, that we might *l.* *1 John* 4:9
had the wound and did *l.* *Rev* 13:14

see for ever

as I live

as truly *as I l.*, earth. *Num* 14:21, 28

---

so long *as I l.* *Job* 27:6; *Ps* 104:33
　　　　　　　　　　　　116:2
As I l. saith the Lord. *Isa* 49:18
　Jer 22:24; *Ezek* 5:11; 14:16, 18
　20; 16:48; 17:16, 19; 18:3; 20:3
　33; 33:11, 27; 34:8; 35:6, 11
　　　Zeph 2:9; *Rom* 14:11
As I l. saith the king. *Jer* 46:18

may, might, or mayest **live**

that we *may l.* and not die.
　　Gen 42:2; 43:8; 47:19
that he *may l.* with thee. *Lev* 25:35
no usury, that thy brother *may l.* 36
to them that they *may l.* *Num* 4:19
for to do to them, that ye *may l.*
　Deut 4:1; 5:33; 8:1; 30:6, 16
one of these cities he *might l.* 4:42
follow, that thou *mayest l.* 16:20
that thou and thy seed *may l.* 30:19
that the child *may l.* *2 Sam* 12:22
bread, that you *may l.* *2 Ki* 18:32
sceptre, that he *may l.* *Esth* 4:11
bountifully, that I *may l.* *Ps* 119:17
mercies come to me, that I *may l.* 77
to thy word, that I *may l.* 116
dwell in tents, that ye *may l.* many.
　　　　　　　　　　Jer 35:7
slain, that they *may l.* *Ezek* 37:9
not evil, that ye *may l.* *Amos* 5:14
and thou *mayest l.* long. *Eph* 6:3

not live

the mountain shall *not l.* *Ex* 19:13
not suffer a witch to *l.* 22:18
not l. by bread only, but by the word.
　Deut 8:3; *Mat* 4:4; *Luke* 4:4
sure that he could *not l.* *2 Sam* 1:10
is wanting he shall *not l.* *2 Ki* 10:19
set house in order, thou shalt *not l.*
　　　　　20:1; *Isa* 38:1
I loath it, I would *not l.* *Job* 7:16
wicked shall *not l.* half. *Ps* 55:23
dead, they shall *not l.* *Isa* 26:14
souls that should *not l.* *Ezek* 13:19
then live ? he shall *not l.* 18:13
whereby they should *not l.* 20:25
to him, thou shalt *not l.* *Zech* 13:3
cast out children, that they might *not*
　l. *Acts* 7:19
crying, that he ought *not* to *l.* 25:24
vengeance suffereth *not* to *l.* 28:4
not l. to themselves. *2 Cor* 5:15

lived

his son, while he yet *l.* *Gen* 25:6
Jacob *l.* in the land of Egypt. 47:28
and Caleb *l.* still. *Num* 14:38
beheld the serpent of brass he *l.* 21:9
the voice of God and *l.* *Deut* 5:26
if Absalom had *l.* and. *2 Sam* 19:6
before Solomon his father while he
　yet *l.* *1 Ki* 12:6; *2 Chr* 10:6
Amaziah *l.* after death of Jehoash.
　　2 Ki 14:17; *2 Chr* 25:25
while he *l.* he blessed. *Ps* 49:18
breath came into them, and they *l.*
　　　　　　　　Ezek 37:10
had *l.* with a husband. *Luke* 2:36
l. in all good conscience. *Acts* 23:1
sect of our religion I *l.* a. 26:5
ye also walked sometime, when ye
　l. in them. *Col* 3:7
ye have *l.* in pleasure. *Jas* 5:5
how much she hath *l.* *Rev* 18:7, 9
they *l.* with Christ. 20:4
the rest *l.* not again. 5

lively

Hebrew women are *l.* *Ex* 1:19
but my enemies are *l.* *Ps* 38:19
received the *l.* oracles. *Acts* 7:38*
us again to a *l.* hope. *1 Pet* 1:3*
ye, as *l.* stones, are built up a. 2:5*

liver

the caul above the *l.* *Ex* 29:13, 22
　Lev 3:4, 10, 15; 4:9; 7:4; 8:16
　　　　　　25; 9:10, 19
strike through his *l.* *Pr* 7:23
my *l.* is poured upon. *Lam* 2:11
he looked in the *l.* *Ezek* 21:21

see caul

lives

your blood of your *l.* *Gen* 9:5
to save your *l.* by a great. 45:7
thou hast saved our *l.*: let us. 47:25

---

they made their *l.* bitter. *Ex* 1:14
deliver our *l.* from death. *Josh* 2:13
were sore afraid of our *l.* 9:24
that jeoparded their *l.* *Judg* 5:18
thou lose thy life with *l.* of. 18:25
Saul and Jonathan lovely in their *l.*
　　　　　　　　2 Sam 1:23
saved *l.* of thy sons, wives. 19:5
that went in jeopardy of their *l.*
　　　　23:17; *1 Chr* 11:19
and stood for their *l.* *Esth* 9:16
they lurk privily for their *l.* *Pr* 1:18
fall by them which seek their *l.*
　　　　　　Jer 19:7; 46:26
seek their *l.* shall straiten them. 19:9
flee, save your *l..* be like the. 48:6
with the peril of our *l.* *Lam* 5:9
their *l.* were prolonged. *Dan* 7:12
Son of man is not come to destroy
　men's *l.* *Luke* 9:56
hazarded their *l.* for our. *Acts* 15:26
will be with damage of our *l.* 27:10
to lay down our *l.* for. *1 John* 3:16
they loved not their *l.* to. *Rev* 12:11

livest

Levite as long as thou *l.* *Deut* 12:19
if thou being a Jew *l.* after. *Gal* 2:14
a name that thou *l.* and. *Rev* 3:1

liveth

that *l.* shall be meat for. *Gen* 9:3
talk with man, and he *l.* *Deut* 5:24
have lent him to the Lord as long as
　he *l.* *1 Sam* 1:28
for as long as son of Jesse *l.* 20:31
thus shalt say to him that *l.* 25:6
as God *l.* unless thou. *2 Sam* 2:27
as my lord the king *l.* surely. 15:21
Lord *l.* blessed be my rock. 22:47
　　　　　　　　Ps 18:46
this is my son that *l.* *1 Ki* 3:23
Elijah said, See thy son *l.* 17:23
that my Redeemer *l.* *Job* 19:25
as God *l.* who hath taken. 27:2
what man that *l.* and shall ? *Ps* 89:48
shalt swear, the Lord *l.* *Jer* 4:2
though they say, The Lord *l.* they. 5:2
swear by my name, the Lord *l.* 12:16
no more be said, The Lord *l.* 16:14
　　　　　　　15; 23:7, 8
Egypt, saying, The Lord *l.* 44:26
every thing that *l.* and. *Ezek* 47:9
nor swear, the Lord *l.* *Hos* 4:15
Thy God, O Dan, *l.*; and, The manner
　of Beer-sheba *l.* *Amos* 8:14
Jesus said, Go thy way, thy son *l.*
　　　　　　John 4:50, 51, 53
whosoever *l.* and believeth in. 11:26
that he *l.* he *l.* to God. *Rom* 6:10
over man as long as he *l.* 7:1, 2
so if while her husband *l.* she be. 3
for none of us *l.* or dieth to. 14:7
wife is bound as long as her husband
　l. *1 Cor* 7:39
l. by the power of God. *2 Cor* 13:4
yet not I, but Christ *l.* *Gal* 2:20
she that *l.* in pleasure is dead while
　she *l.* *1 Tim* 5:6*
it is witnessed that he *l.* *Heb* 7:8
he ever *l.* to make intercession. 25
no strength while testator *l.* 9:17
I am he that *l.* and was. *Rev* 1:18

see for ever

as the Lord **liveth**

as the Lord l. if ye have saved.
　　　　　　　　Judg 8:19
part of kinsman, *as the Lord l.*
　　　　　　　　Ruth 3:13
for, *as the Lord l.*,. . . . though it be in
　Jonathan. *1 Sam* 14:39
as the Lord l. 45; 19:6; 20:21
　25:26; 26:10, 16; 28:10; 29:6
　2 Sam 4:9; 12:5; 14:11; *1 Ki* 1:29
　2:24; *2 Ki* 5:20; *2 Chr* 18:13
　　　　　　　　Jer 38:16
as the Lord l. there is but a step.
　　　　　　　　1 Sam 20:3
as the Lord God of Israel l. 25:34
　　　　　1 Ki 17:1; 18:15
as the Lord l. and as my lord the
　king *l.* *2 Sam* 15:21
as the Lord thy God l. *1 Ki* 17:12
　　　　　　　　18:10

as the Lord l. and thy soul liveth.
2 Ki 2:2, 4, 6; 4:30
as the Lord of hosts *l.* before whom
I stand. *3*:14; 5:16

as thy soul liveth
as thy soul l. I am the woman who
stood praying. *1 Sam* 1:26
Abner said, *As thy soul l. O.* 17:55
as soul l. there is but one step. 20:3
as thy soul l. seeing Lord. 25:26
as thy soul l. I will not do this thing.
2 Sam 11:11
as thy soul l. none can turn to the
right hand or left. 14:19
as thy soul l., I will not leave thee.
So they went. *2 Ki* 2:2

living
[1] *One who is alive, or enjoys life,*
1 Ki 3:22. [2] *Of a well, or water
always running,* John 4:10; 7:38.
[3] *Spiritual,* Rom 12:1. [4] *A
person's wealth, goods, or estate,*
Luke 15:12.

having dominion over every *l.* thing.
Gen 1:28
man became a *l.* soul. 2:7
Eve, mother of all *l.* 3:20
every *l.* thing of all flesh, two. 6:19
and every *l.* substance I have. 7:4
and every *l.* substance was. 23
Noah and every *l.* thing. 8:1
any more every thing *l.* 21
of any *l.* thing which is in the water.
Lev 11:10
as for the *l.* bird, he shall take it.
14:6, 7, 53
not made abominable by any *l.* 20:25
he stood between the dead and the *l.*
Num 16:48
off his kindness to the *l. Ruth* 2:20
shut up *l.* in widowhood. *2 Sam* 20:3
the *l.* is my son, the dead thy son.
1 Ki 3:22, 23
divide the *l.* child in two, and. 25
l. child was, give her the *l.* 26
king said, Give her the *l.* child. 27
in whose hand is soul of every *l.*
thing. *Job* 12:10
is hid from the eyes of all *l.* 28:13
house appointed for all *l.* 30:23
enlightened with light of *l.* 33:30
of the Lord in land of *l. Ps* 27:13
thee out of the land of the *l.* 52:5
walk in the light of the *l.* 56:13
away both *l.,* and in his wrath. 58:9*
blotted out of the book of the *l.* 69:28
I will walk before the Lord in the
land of the *l.* 116:9
thou art my portion in the land of the
l. 142:5
in thy sight shall no man *l.* be justified. 143:2
the desire of every *l.* thing. 145:16
dead, more than the *l. Eccl* 4:2
I considered all the *l.* under the. 15
knoweth to walk before the *l.* 6:8
end of all men, and the *l.* will lay. 7:2
joined to all the *l.,* for a dog is. 9:4
for the *l.* know that they shall die. 5
a well of *l.* water. *S of S* 4:15
is written among the *l.* in. *Isa* 4:3
seek to their God for the *l.* to. 8:19
Lord in the land of the *l.* 38:11
the *l.* the *l.* he shall praise thee. 19
out of the land of the *l.* 53:8
forsaken fountain of *l.* waters.
Jer 2:13; 17:13
off from the land of the *l.* 11:19
wherefore doth a *l.* man? *Lam* 3:39
glory in the land of the *l.* 26:20
caused terror in the land of the *l.*
32:23, 24, 25, 26, 27, 32
I have more than any *l. Dan* 2:30
to the intent that the *l.* may. 4:17
l. waters shall go out. *Zech* 14:8
not the God of the dead, but of the *l.*
Mat 22:23; *Mark* 12:27
Luke 20:38
she had, even all her *l. Mark* 12:44
woman had spent all her *l. Luke* 8:43
he divided unto them his *l.* 15:12

substance with riotous *l.*
Luke 15:13, 30
why seek ye the *l.* among? 24:5
given thee *l.* water. *John* 4:10
whence hast thou that *l.* water? 11
I am the *l.* bread which came. 6:51
as the *l.* Father hath sent me. 57
shall flow rivers of *l.* water. 7:38
your bodies a *l.* sacrifice. *Rom* 12:1
be Lord both of dead and *l.* 14:9
first man Adam was made a *l.* soul.
1 Cor 15:45
l. in the world, are ye? *Col* 2:20
l. in malice, envy, and. *Tit* 3:3
enter by a new and *l. Heb* 10:20
coming as to a *l.* stone. *1 Pet* 2:4
Lamb shall lead them to *l. Rev* 7:17*
every *l.* soul died in the sea. 16:3

see bird, creature, God

lizard
the *l.,* snail, and mole. *Lev* 11:30

lo
l. Sarah thy wife shall. *Gen* 18:10
l. it is yet high day, water ye. 29:7
l. I die. 50:5
l. I come in a cloud. *Ex* 19:9
l. we be here, and will. *Num* 14:40
l. the Lord hath kept thee. 24:11
I did but taste honey, and *l.* I must
die. *1 Sam* 14:43
l. I have sinned and. *2 Sam* 24:17
strength, *l.* he is strong. *Job* 9:19
away, and *l.* he was not. *Ps* 37:36
l. I come. 40:7
l. we heard it at Ephratah. 132:6
l. the man that made not God. 52:7
l. they that are far from. 73:27
l. thine enemies, for *l.* thine. 92:9
l. this only have I found. *Eccl* 7:29
l. the winter is past. *S of S* 2:11
l. this is our God, we. *Isa* 25:9
the earth, and *l.* it was. *Jer* 4:23
I beheld, and *l.* there was no. 25
l. certainly in vain made he it. 8:8
for *l.* I begin to bring evil. 25:29
when *l.* he had given. *Ezek* 17:18
for *l.* it cometh. 30:9
l. it will come. 33:33
for *l.* they are gone. *Hos* 9:6
l. the days shall come. *Amos* 4:2
ye looked for much, and *l. Hag* 1:9
and *l.* the heavens were. *Mat* 3:16
l., here is Christ, or there. 24:23
l. I have told you. 28:7
l. I am with you. 20
Satan bound, *l.* these. *Luke* 13:16
l. nothing worthy of death. 23:15
unworthy, *l.* we turn to. *Acts* 13:46
l. I come to do thy will. *Heb* 10:7, 9

loaden
carriages were heavy *l. Isa* 46:1*

loadeth
Lord, who daily *l.* us. *Ps* 68:19*

loaf
(*A loaf in Palestine in Bible times
was a round, flat, crisp cake of
dough baked on the hearth*)
one *l.* of bread, one cake. *Ex* 29:23
every one a *l.* of bread. *1 Chr* 16:3
they more than one *l. Mark* 8:14

Lo-ammi
call his name *L.* for ye. *Hos* 1:9

loan
for the *l.* which is lent. *1 Sam* 2:20†

loath, see lothe

loaves
take ten *l.* and run. *1 Sam* 17:17
made haste and took 200 *l.* 25:18
take with thee ten *l. 1 Ki* 14:3
the man of God 20 *l. 2 Ki* 4:42
have here but five *l. Mat* 14:17
and he took the five *l.*
Mark 6:38; *Luke* 9:13
said, How many *l.* have ye?
Mat 15:34; *Mark* 6:38; 8:5
he took the seven *l.* and the fishes.
Mat 15:36; *Mark* 8:6
the five *l.* of the 5000. *Mat* 16:9
nor the seven *l.* of the 4000. 10
eat of the *l.* were 5000. *Mark* 6:44
not the miracle of the *l.* 52
Friend, lend me three *l. Luke* 11:5

who hath five barley *l. John* 6:9
Jesus took the *l.* and distributed. 11
fragments of the barley *l.* 13
because ye did eat of the *l.* 26

see bread

wave loaves
shall bring two *wave l. Lev* 23:17

lock
myrrh on the handles of the *l.*
S of S 5:5*

locked
the doors and *l.* them. *Judg* 3:23
doors of the parlour were *l.* 24

locks
let the *l.* of the hair of his. *Num* 6:5
seven *l.* of my head. *Judg* 16:13
to shave off the seven *l.* 19
set up doors, and *l.* thereof.
Neh 3:3*, 6*, 13*, 14*, 15*
doves' eyes within thy *l. S of S* 4:1*
pomegranate within thy *l.* 3*
my *l.* are filled with the drops. 5:2
his *l.* are bushy, and black as. 11
thy temples within thy *l.* 6:7*
uncover thy *l.,* make bare. *Isa* 47:2
nor suffer their *l.* to. *Ezek* 44:20

see bars

locust
(*An insect of the grasshopper
family, which travels in swarms,
and commits great ravages on
vegetation. It has been used as
food from the earliest times, and
resembles the shrimp in taste. At
the present time it is eaten by only
the poorest people*)
remained not one *l.* in. *Ex* 10:19
l. after his kind, and bald *l.* ye.
Lev 11:22
all thy trees shall the *l. Deut* 28:42
if there be in the land *l. 1 Ki* 8:37
2 Chr 6:28
also their labour to the *l. Ps* 78:46
tossed up and down as the *l.* 109:23
l. eaten, and that which *l. Joel* 1:4
restore the years that the *l.* 2:25

locusts
to-morrow I will bring *l. Ex* 10:4
hand over Egypt for the *l.* 12
the east wind brought the *l.* 13
no such *l.* 14
the west wind took away the *l.* 19
l. shall consume it. *Deut* 28:38
if I command the *l.* to. *2 Chr* 7:13
he spake, and *l.* came. *Ps* 105:34
the *l.* have no king, yet. *Pr* 30:27
running to and fro of *l. Isa* 33:4
thyself many as the *l. Nah* 3:15
thy crowned are as the *l.* and. 17
his meat was *l.* and wild honey.
Mat 3:4; *Mark* 1:6
came out of the smoke *l. Rev* 9:3
shapes of *l.* were like to horses. 7

lodge
daughter of Zion is left as a *l.* in garden. *Isa* 1:8

lodge
the house for us to *l.* in. *Gen* 24:23
enough, and room to *l.* 25
them, *l.* here this night. *Num* 22:8
place where ye shall *l. Josh* 4:3
l. here, that thy heart. *Judg* 19:9
to *l.* in Gibeah or in Ramah. 13, 15
20:4
the old man said, Only *l.* not. 19:20
thou lodgest I will *l. Ruth* 1:16
thy father will not *l. 2 Sam* 17:8
l. not this night in the plains. 16
let every one *l.* within. *Neh* 4:22
why *l.* ye about the wall? 13:21
they cause the naked to *l. Job* 24:7*
stranger did not *l.* in street. 31:32
my beloved, let us *l. S of S* 7:11
of Arabia shall ye *l. Isa* 21:13
and *l.* in monuments, and eat. 65:4
shall thy vain thoughts *l.? Jer* 4:14
beasts shall *l.* in upper. *Zeph* 2:14
birds of the air come and *l.* in.
Mat 13:32; *Mark* 4:32
with whom we should *l. Acts* 21:16

lodged
Jacob l. there that same. Gen 32:13
and himself l. that night in the. 21
into harlot's house, and l. Josh 2:1*
he and all Israel, and l. there. 3:1
over to the place where they l. 4:8
came to the camp, and l. in. 6:11
but Joshua l. that night among. 8:9
of Micah, they l. there. Judg 18:2
eat and drink, and l. there. 19:4
urged him, therefore he l. 7
into a cave, and l. there. 1 Ki 19:9
they l. round about the. 1 Chr 9:27
merchants l. without. Neh 13:20
righteousness l. in it, but. Isa 1:21
to Bethany and l. there. Mat 21:17
Simon were l. there. Acts 10:18
called he them in, and l. them. 23
Publius l. us three days. 28:7*
l. she have l. strangers. 1 Tim 5:10*

lodgest
Ruth said, Where thou l. Ruth 1:16

lodgeth
l. with one Simon a. Acts 10:6

lodging
leave them in the l. Josh 4:3
them to his house to l. Judg 19:15
have taken up their l. at. Isa 10:29
the wilderness a l. place. Jer 9:2
many to him into his l. Acts 28:23
prepare me also a l. Philem 22

lodgings
I will enter into the l. 2 Ki 19:23

loft
and carried him into a l. 1 Ki 17:19*
Eutychus fell down from the third l.
Acts 20:9*

loftily
corrupt, they speak l. Ps 73:8

loftiness
l. of man shall be bowed. Isa 2:17
the pride of Moab, his l. Jer 48:29

lofty
haughty, nor mine eyes l. Ps 131:1
a generation, O how l. are l Pr 30:13
the l. looks of man shall. Isa 2:11
5:15
Lord be on every one that is l. 12*
the l. city he layeth low to. 26:5
on a l. mountain hast thou. 57:7
thus saith high and l. One. 15

log
(A measure; two-thirds of a pint)
the priest shall take a l. of oil.
Lev 14:10, 12, 24
shall take some of the l. of oil. 15
then he shall take a l. of oil. 21

loins
(The word is used often in the phrase to gird up the loins, which means to prepare for active work, since the eastern peoples commonly wore flowing garments and when they wished to be active tucked them up out of the way)
shall come out of thy l. Gen 35:11
put sackcloth upon his l. 37:34
the souls which came out of his l.
46:26; Ex 1:5
eat it, with your l. girded. Ex 12:11
breeches reach from the l. 28:42
smite through the l. of. Deut 33:11
sword fastened on his l. 2 Sam 20:8
the girdle about his l. 1 Ki 2:5
son shall come forth of thy l. 8:19
2 Chr 6:9
thicker than my father's l. 1 Ki 12:10
2 Chr 10:10
Elijah girded up his l. 1 Ki 18:46
put sackcloth on our l. 20:31
girded sackcloth on their l. 32
girt with girdle of leather about his l.
2 Ki 1:8; Mat 3:4; Mark 1:6
gird up thy l. 2 Ki 4:29; 9:1
Job 38:3; 40:7; Jer 1:17
he girdeth the l. of kings. Job 12:18
if his l. have not blessed me. 31:20
his strength is in his l. 40:16
my l. are filled with a. Ps 38:7
affliction upon our l. 66:11
and make their l. continually. 69:23

girdeth her l. with strength. Pr 31:17
girdle of their l. be loosed. Isa 5:27
shall be the girdle of his l. 11:5
sackcloth from off thy l., put. 20:2
are my l. filled with pain. 21:3
gird sackcloth upon your l. 32:11
I will loose the l. of kings to. 45:1
girdle and put it upon thy l. Jer 13:1
as the girdle cleaveth to the l. 11
man with his hands on his l. 30:6
and upon the l. shall be. 48:37
appearance of his l. upward.
Ezek 1:27
l. downward, fire; from his l. 8:2
sigh with the breaking of thy l. 21:6
with girdles upon their l. 23:15
thou madest all their l. to be. 29:7
have linen breeches on their l. 44:18
the waters were to the l. 47:4
so the joints of his l. were. Dan 5:6
l. were girded with fine gold. 10:5
bring sackcloth on your l. Amos 8:10
make thy l. strong. Nah 2:1
pain is in all l. 10
of his l. he would raise. Luke 12:35
having your l. girt about. Acts 2:30
they came out of the l. of. Eph 6:14
for he was yet in the l. of his. Heb 7:5
wherefore gird up the l. 1 Pet 1:13

Lois
in thy grandmother L. 2 Tim 1:5

long
fed me all my life l. Gen 48:15
trumpet soundeth l. Ex 19:13, 19
that thy days may be l. on. 20:12
when the cloud tarried l. Num 9:19
ye dwelt l. enough. Deut 1:6; 2:3
and shalt have remained l. 4:25
if the way be too l. for thee. 14:24
overtake him, because way is l. 19:6
make great plagues and of l. 28:59
when they make a l. blast. Josh 6:5
old, by reason of the very l. 9:13
ye dwelt in the wilderness a l. 24:7*
there was l. war between. 2 Sam 3:1
and hast not asked l. life. 1 Ki 3:11
2 Chr 1:11
for a l. season Israel. 2 Chr 15:3
l. life will I satisfy him. Ps 91:16
forty years l. was I grieved. 95:10
my soul l. dwelt with him. 120:6
plowers made l. their furrows. 129:3
those that have been l. dead. 143:3
and l. life shall they. Pr 3:2*
the goodman is gone a l. 7:19
that tarry l. at the wine. 23:30
by l. forbearing is a prince. 25:15
man goeth to his l. home. Eccl 12:5
my elect shall l. enjoy. Isa 65:22
this captivity is l.: build. Jer 29:28
shall the women eat their children of
a span l.? Lam 2:20*
a great eagle l.-winged. Ezek 17:3
his branches became l. because. 31:5
suffer their locks to grow l. 44:20
time appointed was l. Dan 10:1*
not stay l. in the place of. Hos 13:13
repented l. ago in sackcloth and.
Mat 11:21
and for pretence make l. prayers.
23:14; Mark 12:40; Luke 20:47
who go in l. clothing. Mark 12:38
Luke 20:46
sitting clothed in a l. Mark 16:5
avenge, though he bear l. Luke 18:7*
to see him of a l. season. 23:8
as Paul was l. preaching. Acts 20:9*
l. after there arose a tempest. 27:14
but after l. abstinence Paul. 21
if a man have l. hair. 1 Cor 11:14
if a woman have l. hair it is a. 15
that thou mayest live l. Eph 6:3
if I tarry l. that thou. 1 Tim 3:15
the husbandman hath l. Jas 5:7*
see ago, cubits, day

long, verb
which l. for death, but. Job 3:21
grant me thing that I l. for! 6:8
for I l. to see you, that. Rom 1:11
by their prayer which l. 2 Cor 9:14
how greatly I l. after you. Phil 1:8

as long as
as l. as she is put apart. Lev 18:19
enjoy sabbaths, as l. as it. 26:34, 35
as l. as the cloud abode. Num 9:18
forsake not the Levite as l. as thou.
Deut 12:19
fear the Lord as l. as you live. 31:13
lent to the Lord, as l. as. 1 Sam 1:28
as l. as son of Jesse liveth. 20:31
any thing as l. as we were. 25:15
as l. as he sought the Lord he
prospered. 2 Chr 26:5
as l. as she lay desolate she. 36:21
fear thee as l. as sun and. Ps 72:5
be continued as l. as the sun. 17
to the Lord as l. as I live. 104:33
call upon him as l. as I live. 116:2
as l. as they, and as broad as they.
Ezek 42:11*
as l. as bridegroom is with them.
Mat 9:15; Mark 2:19
as l. as I am in the world. I am the.
John 9:5*
dominion over a man as l. as he.
Rom 7:1
wife is bound as l. as her. 1 Cor 7:39
heir as l. as he is a child. Gal 4:1
daughters ye are as l. as. 1 Pet 3:6*
as l. as I am in this tabernacle.
2 Pet 1:13

so long
is his chariot so l. in? Judg 5:28
found in thy servant, so l. 1 Sam 29:8
so l. as the whoredoms. 2 Ki 9:22
they may fear thee so l. 2 Chr 6:31
so l. as I see Mordecai. Esth 5:13
shall not reproach me so l. Job 27:6
peace so l. as the moon. Ps 72:7
that he tarried so l. Luke 1:21
bound to her husband so l. Rom 7:2
to-day, after so l. a time. Heb 4:7

long time
been there a l. time. Gen 26:8
dwelt in Egypt a l. time. Num 20:15
besiege a city a l. time. Deut 20:19
war a l. time with kings. Josh 11:18
a l. time after that Joshua. 23:1*
ark abode the time was l. 1 Sam 7:2
woman that had l. time. 2 Sam 14:2
not done it of a l. time. 2 Chr 30:5*
l. time holden my peace. Isa 42:14
and forsake us so l. time. Lam 5:20
after a l. time the lord of those servants. Mat 25:19; Luke 20:9
which had devils l. time. Luke 8:27
into a far country for a l. time. 20:9
that he had been a l. time. John 5:6
have I been so l. time with? 14:9
because of l. time he had. Acts 8:11
l. time abode they with. 14:3, 28
judgement of l. time. 2 Pet 2:3*

long while
he talked a l. while till. Acts 20:11

longed
David l. to go forth. 2 Sam 13:39
David l. and said, O that one. 23:15
1 Chr 11:17
behold, I have l. after. Ps 119:40
l. for thy commandments. 131
I have l. for thy salvation. 174
for he l. after you all. Phil 2:26
brethren dearly beloved and l. 4:1

longest
thou sore l. after thy. Gen 21:30

longer
she could no l. hide him. Ex 2:3
you go, and ye shall stay no l. 9:28
could not any l. stand. Judg 2:14
he tarried l. than the. 2 Sam 20:5
wait for the Lord any l.? 2 Ki 6:33
the measure thereof is l. Job 11:9
Lord could no l. bear. Jer 44:22
for thou mayest be no l. Luke 16:2
desired him to tarry l. Acts 18:20
he ought not to live any l. 25:24
dead to sin, live any l. Rom 6:2
no l. under a schoolmaster. Gal 3:25
when we could no l. forbear.
1 Thes 3:1, 5
drink no l. water, but. 1 Tim 5:23
that he no l. live the rest. 1 Pet 4:2
should be time no l. Rev 10:6

longeth

my son Shechem *l.* for.   *Gen* 34:8
because thy soul *l.* to.   *Deut* 12:20
my flesh *l.* for thee in.   *Ps* 63:1
my soul *l.* for the courts of.   84:2

longing

fail with the *l.* for them.   *Deut* 28:32
satisfieth the *l.* soul.   *Ps* 107:9
my soul breaketh for the *l.*   119:20

longsuffering

Lord God merciful and gracious, *l.*
  Ex 34:6*; *Num* 14:18*
  Ps 86:15*; *2 Pet* 3:9
O Lord, take me not away in thy *l.*
  Jer 15:15
thou the riches of, *l.*   *Rom* 2:4
endured with much *l.* vessels.   9:22
by knowledge, by *l.*   *2 Cor* 6:6
of the Spirit is love, *l.*   *Gal* 5:22
l., forbearing one another.   *Eph* 4:2
strengthened to all *l.* with.   *Col* 1:11
as elect of God, meekness, *l.*   3:12
Christ might shew all *l.*   *1 Tim* 1:16
fully known my faith, *l.*   *2 Tim* 3:10
rebuke, exhort with all *l.* and.   4:2
when *l.* of God waited.   *1 Pet* 3:20
l. of our Lord is salvation. *2 Pet* 3:15

look, -s

bring down high *l.*   *Ps* 18:27
that hath a high *l.* I will not.   101:5
a proud *l.,* a lying tongue. *Pr* 6:17*
high *l.* and proud heart is sin.   21:4
the lofty *l.* of man shall be. *Isa* 2:11
punish the glory of his high *l.* 10:12
dismayed at their *l.*   *Ezek* 2:6; 3:9
whose *l.* was more stout. *Dan* 7:20

look, verb

l. from the place where. *Gen* 13:14
l. towards heaven, and tell.   15:5
thy life, *l.* not behind thee.   19:17
l. ye so sadly to-day ?   40:7
now let Pharaoh *l.* out a man. 41:33
Jacob said, Why *l.* ye one ?   42:1
l. to it; for evil is.   *Ex* 10:10
and their faces shall *l.*   25:20
l. that thou make them after.   40
then the priest shall *l.*   *Lev* 13:39
priest shall *l.* and behold.   53, 56
shall *l.* if the plague.   14:3, 39, 44
l. not to the stubborness. *Deut* 9:27
thine eyes shall *l.* and fail.   28:32
ruddy, and goodly to *l. 1 Sam* 16:12
l. how thy brethren fare.   17:18
go up now, *l.* toward.   *1 Ki* 18:43
I would not *l.* toward.   *2 Ki* 3:14
l. when messenger cometh.   6:32
l. out there Jehu, and go in.   9:2
l. even out best and meetest.   10:3
l. there be none of the servants.   23
come, let us *l.* one another.   14:8
God of our fathers *l.*   *1 Chr* 12:17
let it *l.* for light, but.   *Job* 3:9
therefore shall no man *l.*   20:21*
l. to heavens and see, and.   35:5
my prayer to thee, and *l.*   *Ps* 5:3*
that I am not able to *l.* up.   40:12
as the eyes of servants *l.* up.   123:2
let thine eyes *l.* right on.   *Pr* 4:25
to know thy flocks, and *l.* well. 27:23
l. out at the windows.   *Eccl* 12:3
l. from top of Amana.   *S of S* 4:8
if one *l.* unto the land.   *Isa* 5:30
on the land, I will *l.* for him.   8:17
curse their king and God, and *l.*   21
they shall *l.* unto earth, and.   22
in that day shall a man *l.*   17:7
he shall not *l.* to the altars.   8
l. away from me; I will weep. 22:4
l. in that day to the armour.   8
l. not to the Holy One of Israel. 31:1
hear ye deaf, *l.* ye blind, that. 42:18
l. unto me, and be saved, all. 45:22
l. to the rock whence ye are.   51:1
l. to Abraham your father and to.   2
they all *l.* to their own way. 56:11*
we *l.* for judgement, but.   59:11
but to this man will I *l.* that.   66:2
and while ye *l.* for light.   *Jer* 13:16
take and *l.* well to him, do.   39:12
come with me and I will *l.* well. 40:4
mighty ones are fled, and *l.*   46:5
the fathers shall not *l.* back.   47:3

all of them princes to *l. Ezek* 23:15
remembrance when they *l.*   29:16
who *l.* to other gods, and.   *Hos* 3:1
I will *l.* again towards.   *Jonah* 2:4
I will *l.* unto the Lord.   *Mi* 7:7
but none shall *l.* back.   *Nah* 2:8
or do we *l.* for another ?   *Mat* 11:3
  Luke 7:19, 20
hands on eyes, and made him *l.* up.
  Mark 8:25
things begin, then *l.* up. *Luke* 21:28
search and *l.*: for out of. *John* 7:52
l. ye out seven men of.   *Acts* 6:3
be a question of words, *l.* ye.   18:15
I *l.* for him with the brethren.
  1 Cor 16:11
Israel could not stedfastly *l.* to the
  end.   *2 Cor* 3:13
while we *l.* not at things which. 4:18
from whence we *l.* for.   *Phil* 3:20
to them that *l.* for him.   *Heb* 9:28
angels desire to *l.* into.   *1 Pet* 1:12
we *l.* for new heavens.   *2 Pet* 3:13
seeing ye *l.* for such things, be.   14
l. to yourselves, that we.   *2 John* 8
and no man was able to *l.*   *Rev* 5:3
worthy to read the book nor *l.*   4

look down

l. down from thy holy.   *Deut* 26:15
l. down, behold, and visit. *Ps* 80:14
righteousness shall *l. down.*   85:11
l. down from heaven, and. *Isa* 63:15
till Lord *l. down* and behold from
  heaven.   *Lam* 3:50

look on, or upon

be in cloud, and I will *l. upon* it.
  Gen 9:16
art a fair woman to *l. upon.*   12:11
Rebekah was very fair to *l. upon.*
  24:16; 26:7
afraid to *l. upon* God.   *Ex* 3:6
Lord *l. upon* you and judge.   5:21
and Moses did *l. upon* all.   39:43
l. on the plague in the skin of the
  flesh.   *Lev* 13:3, 21, 25, 26, 31
  32, 34, 43, 50
the priest shall *l. on* him.   3, 5, 6
  27, 36
the priest shall *l. upon* it.   14:48
for a fringe, that ye may *l. upon* it.
  Num 15:39
Gideon said, *L. on* me. *Judg* 7:17
if thou wilt indeed *l. on. 1 Sam* 1:11
l. not *on* his countenance or.   16:7
l. upon such a dead dog. *2 Sam* 9:8
very beautiful to *l upon.*   11:2
Lord will *l. on* my affliction. 16:12
Lord *l. upon* it and require it.
  2 Chr 24:22
queen was fair to *l. on. Esth* 1:11
be content, *l. upon* me.   *Job* 6:28
l. on every one that is proud. 40:12
stare and *l. upon* me.   *Ps* 22:17
l. upon mine affliction and.   25:18*
how long wilt thou *l. on* ?   35:17
and *l. upon* the face of thine.   84:9
l. thou *upon* me, and be.   119:132*
let thine eyes *l.* right on.   *Pr* 4:25
l. not thou *upon* the wine.   23:31
l. not *upon* me, because I am black.
  S of S 1:6
return, that we may *l. upon.*   6:13
narrowly *l. upon* thee.   *Isa* 14:16
l. upon Zion.   33:20
l. upon the earth beneath.   51:6
forth and *l. upon* the carcases. 66:24
let our eye *l. upon* Zion.   *Mi* 4:11
l. upon thee, shall flee.   *Nah* 3:7
purer eyes than to *l. upon* iniquity.
  Hab 1:13
mayest *l. upon* their nakedness. 2:15
l. upon me whom they pierced.
  Zech 12:10
I beseech thee, *l. upon. Luke* 9:38
your eyes, and *l. upon. John* 4:35
l. upon him whom they pierced.
  19:37
Peter and John said, *L. on* us.
  Acts 3:4, 12*
l. upon things after outward appearance.   *2 Cor* 10:7
l. not every man *on* his.   *Phil* 2:4
he that sat was to *l. upon. Rev* 4:3

looked

God *l.* on the earth and it. *Gen* 6:12
the men rose up, and *l.*   18:16
his wife *l.* back.   19:26
l. out at a window.   26:8
the Lord hath *l.* upon my.   29:32
the keeper of the prison *l.* not. 39:23
Joseph *l.* on them, behold they. 40:6
Moses went and *l.* on.   *Ex* 2:11
he *l.* this way and that way.   12
and God *l.* upon the children.   25
Lord had *l.* on their affliction.   4:31
  Deut 26:7
the Lord *l.* on the host of. *Ex* 14:24
l. toward the wilderness.   16:10
the people *l.* after Moses till. 33:8
Aaron *l.* on Miriam.   *Num* 12:10
l. towards the tabernacle.   16:42
he *l.* on Amalek, he took up. 24:20
l. on the Kenites, and took up.   21
when the men of Ai *l.*   *Josh* 8:20
mother of Sisera *l.* out. *Judg* 5:28
the Lord *l.* upon him, and said. 6:14
Manoah and his wife *l.* on. 13:19, 30
Benjamites *l.* behind them.   20:40
they had *l.* into the ark. *1 Sam* 6:19
I have *l.* on my people.   9:16
the watchmen of Saul *l.* and. 14:16
when they were come, he *l.*   16:6
the Philistines *l.* about, and.   17:42
Saul *l.* behind him, David stood.
  24:8; *2 Sam* 1:7
Abner *l.* behind him.   *2 Sam* 2:20
Michal *l.* through a window.   6:16
they *l.* but there was none.   22:42
servant went up and *l.*   *1 Ki* 18:43
turned back and *l.* on.   *2 Ki* 2:24
the people *l.* and behold he.   6:30
Jezebel painted, and *l.* out at. 9:30
l. one another in the face at.   14:11
when Judah *l.* back.   *2 Chr* 13:14
l. on him, and behold he was. 26:20
sight of all who *l.* on her. *Esth* 2:15
troops of Tema *l.,* Sheba. *Job* 6:19
the Lord *l.* to see if any.   *Ps* 14:2
l. to him, and were lightened. 34:5
God *l.* down on the children of. 53:2
l. down from his sanctuary. 102:19
l. they shaked their heads.   109:25
because the sun hath *l. S of S* 1:6*
he *l.* that it should bring. *Isa* 5:2
he *l.* for judgement, but behold.   7
ye have not *l.* to the maker.   22:11
terrible things which we *l.* not. 64:3
we *l.* for peace, no good came.
  Jer 8:15; 14:19
certainly this is the day that we *l.* for.
  Lam 2:16
whither the head *l.* they. *Ezek* 10:11
consulted with images, he *l.*   21:21
let our countenance be *l. Dan* 1:13
not have *l.* on the day.   *Ob* 12
thou shouldest not have *l.* on.   13
ye *l.* for much, and lo it. *Hag* 1:9
when he *l.* round about. *Mark* 3:5
  5:32; 10:23
he *l.* up to heaven, and blessed. 6:41
he *l.* and said, I see men as.   8:24
they *l.* they saw the stone.   16:4
l. on me to take away. *Luke* 1:25
to all that *l.* for redemption.   2:38
likewise a Levite came and *l.* 10:32
the Lord turned, and *l.*   22:61
then the disciples *l.* one. *John* 13:22
while they *l.* stedfastly. *Acts* 1:10
after they had *l.* a great while. 28:6*
for he *l.* for a city which. *Heb* 11:10
which we have *l.* upon. *1 John* 1:1

looked with eyes

Jacob lifted up his *eyes* and *l.*
  Gen 33:1
lifted up their *eyes* and *l.*   37:25
I lifted up mine *eyes* and *l. Dan* 10:5
Zechariah lifted his *eyes* and *l.*
  Zech 2:1; 5:9; 6:1

I looked

have *I* also here *l.* after. *Gen* 16:13
I l. and behold ye had sinned.
  Deut 9:16
when *I l.* for good, then. *Job* 30:26
I l. for some to take pity. *Ps* 69:20
I l. on my right hand, and.   142:4
at the window, *I l.* through. *Pr* 7:6

l l. upon it, and received. *Pr* 24:32
I l. on all the works that. *Eccl* 2:11
I l. that it should bring forth grapes.
Isa 5:4
and *I l.* and there was none to. 63:5
I l. and behold. *Ezek* 1:4; 2:9; 8:7
10:1, 9; 44:4
I Daniel *l.* and behold. *Dan* 12:5
I have *l.* and behold a candlestick.
Zech 4:2
and the same hour *I l.* up. *Acts* 22:13
I l. and behold. *Rev* 4:1; 6:8; 14:1
14; 15:5

lookest
thou *l.* narrowly to all. *Job* 13:27*
why *l.* on them that deal ? *Hab* 1:13

looketh
if leprosy cover wheresoever priest *l.*
Lev 13:12*
when he *l.* on the serpent. *Num* 21:8
Pisgah, which *l.* toward. 20; 23:28
man *l.* on the outward. *1 Sam* 16:7
as an hireling *l.* for the. *Job* 7:2
l. to the ends of the earth. 28:24
he *l.* on men, and if any say. 33:27*
the Lord *l.* from heaven. *Ps* 33:13
he *l.* on all the inhabitants of. 14
he *l.* on the earth, and it. 104:32
the prudent *l.* well to. *Pr* 14:15
she *l.* well to the ways of. 31:27
he *l.* forth at the window. *S of S* 2:9
that *l.* forth as the morning ? 6:10
as the tower which *l.* toward. 7:4
when he that *l.* upon it. *Isa* 28:4
the door that *l.* toward. *Ezek* 8:3
gate which *l.* eastward. 11:1; 40:6
22*; 43:1; 44:1; 46:1, 12; 47:2
gate of the court that *l.* 40:20
l. on a woman to lust. *Mat* 5:28
lord come when that servant *l.* not
for him. 24:50; *Luke* 12:46
l. into the perfect law of. *Jas* 1:25

looking
three oxen *l.* toward the north.
1 Ki 7:25
Michal *l.* out at a window, saw
David. *1 Chr* 15:29
three oxen *l.* toward the south.
2 Chr 4:4
mine eyes fail with *l.* upward.
Isa 38:14
l. up to heaven, he blessed.
Mat 14:19; *Luke* 9:16
and *l.* up to heaven, he. *Mark* 7:34
there were also women *l.* on. 15:40
l. round about them all. *Luke* 6:10
and *l.* back, is fit for the. 9:62
hearts failing them for *l.* 21:26*
John *l.* on Jesus saith. *John* 1:36
l. in, saw linen clothes lying. 20:5
l. stedfastly on him, saw. *Acts* 6:15
they ready, *l.* for a promise. 23:21
l. for that blessed hope. *Tit* 2:13
but a certain fearful *l.* for. *Heb* 10:27
l. unto Jesus the author and. 12:2
l. diligently, lest any fail of the. 15
l. for the coming of the. *2 Pet* 3:12
l. for the mercy of our Lord. *Jude* 21

lookingglass, -es
(*Properly, as in Revisions, mirror,
mirrors, as they were made of
polished metal, not of glass*)
laver and foot of *l.-glasses.* *Ex* 38:8
sky as a molten *l.-glass.* *Job* 37:18

loops
make *l.* of blue. *Ex* 26:4, 5
l. shalt thou make. 5, 10
put taches in the *l.* 11
made *l.* of blue. 36:11
fifty *l.* made he. 12, 17

loose
Naphtali is a hind let *l.* *Gen* 49:21
let the living bird *l.* into. *Lev* 14:7
he would let *l.* his hand and cut me.
Job 6:9
they have let *l.* the bridle. 30:11
lo I see four men *l.* *Dan* 3:25

loose, verb
and *l.* his shoe from. *Deut* 25:9
l. thy shoe from off thy. *Josh* 5:15
canst thou *l.* the bands of ? *Job* 38:31

l. those that are appointed to death.
Ps 102:20
go and *l.* the sackcloth. *Isa* 20:2
I will *l.* the loins of kings. 45:1
O Jerusalem, *l.* thyself from. 52:2
to *l.* the bands of wickedness. 58:6
and now behold I *l.* thee. *Jer* 40:4
whatsoever ye *l.* on earth.
Mat 16:9; 18:18
an ass tied and colt, *l.* and bring.
21:2; *Acts* 11:2, 4; *Luke* 19:30
why do ye *l.* him ? *Luke* 19:31, 33
Jesus said, *L.* him. *John* 11:44
shoes of his feet I am not worthy to
l. *Acts* 13:25
been given, that he might *l.* 24:26
who is worthy to *l.* the seals? *Rev* 5:2
hath prevailed to *l.* the seven. 5
l. the four angels bound in. 9:14

loosed
that the breastplate be not *l.*
Ex 28:28; 39:21
him that hath his shoe *l.* *Deut* 25:10
his bands *l.* from off. *Judg* 15:14
because he *l.* my cord. *Job* 30:11
l. the bands of the wild ass ? 39:5
the king sent and *l.* him. *Ps* 105:20
thy servant, thou hast *l.* 116:16
silver cord be *l.* or bowl. *Eccl* 12:6
girdle of their loins be *l.* *Isa* 5:27
tacklings are *l.* they could. 33:23
hasteneth that he may be *l.* 51:14
joints of his loins were *l.* *Dan* 5:6
thou shalt loose on earth, shall be *l.*
in heaven. *Mat* 16:19; 18:18
with compassion, and *l.* him. 18:27*
the string of his tongue was *l.*
Mark 7:35; *Luke* 1:64
woman, thou art *l.* from. *Luke* 13:12
ought not this woman to be *l.?* 16
raised up, having *l.* the. *Acts* 2:24
when Paul and his company *l.* 13:13
every one's bands were *l.* 16:26
on the morrow he *l.* him from. 22:30
hearkened, and not have *l.* 27:21
l. the rudder bands, and hoised. 40
be dead, she is *l.* from. *Rom* 7:2*
art thou *l.* from wife ? *1 Cor* 7:27
the four angels were *l.* *Rev* 9:15
after that he must be *l.* a. 20:3, 7

looseth
he *l.* the bond of kings. *Job* 12:18
food to hungry, the Lord *l.* *Ps* 149:7

loosing
what do ye, *l.* the colt ? *Mark* 11:5
as they were *l.* the colt. *Luke* 19:33
l. from Troas, we came. *Acts* 16:11*
l. thence, they sailed close. 27:13

lop
behold the Lord shall *l.* *Isa* 10:33

Lord
(*This word means, in general, one
with power and authority, a master
or ruler. The Hebrew word trans-
literated Jehovah is usually rendered in the Old Testament by
LORD written in small capitals.
This the American Revision
changes to Jehovah. Otherwise the
word is used for Jesus Christ, for
the Holy Spirit, for a husband, and
for any one whom it was desired to
address deferentially*)
too hard for the *L.?* *Gen* 18:14
the *L.* before whom I walk. 24:40
we saw certainly the *L.* 26:28
again, then shall the *L.* be. 28:21
L. was with Joseph. 39:2, 21, 23
who is the *L.* that I should obey ?
Ex 5:2
and the *L.* did so, and there. 8:24
the earth is the *L.'s.* 9:29; *Ps* 24:1
1 Cor 10:26
the *L.* be so with you, as I. *Ex* 10:10
because of that which the *L.* 13:8
beast the male shall be the *L.'s.* 12
be unto thee holy for the *L.* 30:37
on the *L.'s* side? let him come. 32:26
for *L.* whose name is jealous. 34:14
all the fat is the *L.'s.* *Lev* 3:16
Aaron shall cast one lot for the *L.*
16:8; 25:4; 27:2

thou *L.* art among this people, that
thou *L.* art seen face. *Num* 14:14
therefore the *L.* will not be. 43
are given as a gift for the *L.* 18:6
that I may know what the *L.* 22:19
all that the *L.* speaketh that. 23:26
the *L.* hath kept thee back. 24:11
brought oblation for the *L.* 31:50
for they have wholly followed the *L.*
32:12; *Deut* 1:36
so shall the *L.* do to all kingdoms.
Deut 3:21
know that the *L.* he is God. 4:35
39; *1 Ki* 18:39
I stood between the *L.* and you.
Deut 5:5
heaven of heavens is the *L.'s.* 10:14
L. of lords, a great God, a. 17
ye have seen all that the *L.* 29:2
L. hath not given you an heart to. 4
hath the *L.* done thus to this land ?
24; *1 Ki* 9:8; *2 Chr* 7:21
L. shall do to them as he did to Sihon.
Deut 31:4
do ye thus requite the *L.?* 32:6
to flight, except the *L.* had. 30
O people, saved by the *L.* 33:29
swear unto me by the *L.* *Josh* 2:12
1 Sam 24:21
even the *L.* of all the. *Josh* 3:11, 13
the *L.* do to all your enemies. 10:25
if so be the *L.* will be with me. 14:12
the *L.* was with Judah. *Judg* 1:19
and the *L.* was with the house. 22
which knew not the *L.* 2:10
is not the *L.* gone out before ? 4:14
if the *L.* be with us, why is ? 6:13
meet me shall surely be the *L.* 11:31
now know I that the *L.* will. 17:13
L. do so to me and more. *Ruth* 1:17
1 Sam 20:13
the *L.* be with you. *Ruth* 2:4
2 Chr 20:17; *2 Thes* 3:16
none holy as the *L.* *1 Sam* 2:2
pillars of the earth are the *L.'s.* 8
it is the *L.* let him do what seemeth.
3:18; *John* 21:7
Samuel grew, and the *L.*
1 Sam 3:19; 18:12, 14; *2 Ki* 18:7
1 Chr 9:20
this great thing which the *L.* will do.
1 Sam 12:16
the *L.* be with thee. 17:37; 20:13
1 Chr 22:11, 16
the *L.* be between thee and me.
1 Sam 20:23, 42
L. art become their God.
2 Sam 7:24; *1 Chr* 17:22
L. do what seemeth him good.
2 Sam 10:12; *1 Chr* 19:13
if the *L.* be God, follow. *1 Ki* 18:21
if the *L.* do not help. *2 Ki* 6:27
what should I wait for the *L.?* 33
and see my zeal for the *L.* 10:16
am I now come up without the *L.?*
18:25; *Isa* 36:10
for great is the *L.* *1 Chr* 16:25
Ps 48:1; 145:3
now *L.* thou art God. *1 Chr* 17:26
that which is thine for the *L.* 21:24
for man, but for the *L.* *2 Chr* 19:3
and the *L.* shall be with the good. 11
Manasseh knew that the *L.* 33:13
even that thou art *L.* alone. *Neh* 9:6
Isa 37:20
L. hath set apart the godly. *Ps* 4:3
nation, whose God is the *L.* 33:12
my bones say, *L.* who is ? 35:10
for he is thy *L.*; worship. 45:11
if I regard iniquity, the *L.* will. 66:18
for thou *L.* art good, ready. 86:5
thou *L.* art most high for ever. 92:8
97:9
know ye that the *L.* he is God. 100:3
do thou for me, O God the *L.*
109:21; 140:7
they may know that thou *L.* 109:27
gracious is the *L.* and. 116:5
this is the *L.'s* doing; it is. 118:23
God is the *L.* 27
if it had not been the *L.* 124:1, 2
L. shouldest mark iniquity. 130:3
find out a place for the *L.* 132:5
lest the *L.* see it, and it. *Pr* 24:18

thee, and say, Who is the *L.? Pr* 30:9
but shall stay upon the *L. Isa* 10:20
L. shall be known to Egypt. 19:21
the *L.* will be to us a place. 33:21
did not the *L.*, he against whom we
sinned ? 42:24
sing, O heavens, for the *L.* 44:23
the *L.* will go before you. 52:12
where is the *L.* that brought us up
out of Egypt ? *Jer* 2:6, 8
for they are not the *L.'s.* 5:10
is not the *L.* in Zion ? is not? 8:19
know that my name is the *L.* 16:21*
if so be that the *L.* will deal. 21:2
called, The *L.* our Righteousness.
23:6; 33:16
saying, Know the *L.* 31:34
Heb 8:11
the *L.* the hope of their. *Jer* 50:7
remember the *L.* afar off. 51:50
for the *L.* will not cast. *Lam* 3:31
till the *L.* look down, and. 50
possess it, whereas the *L.* was there.
Ezek 35:10
your God is a *L.* of kings. *Dan* 2:47
face to shine, for the *L.'s* sake. 9:17
thou shalt know the *L. Hos* 2:20
have not known the *L.* 5:4
they shall walk after the *L.* 11:10
his reproach shall his *L.* 12:14
fear not, for the *L.* will. *Joel* 2:21
be evil in the city, and *L. Amos* 3:6
so the *L.* shall be with you. 5:14
kingdom shall be the *L.'s. Ob* 21
L. on the head of them. *Mi* 2:13
the *L.* and say, Is not the *L.?* 3:11
the *L.* shall reign over them in. 4:7
and what doth the *L.* require ? 6:8
that swear by the *L.* and. *Zeph* 1:5
when eyes of man shall be toward
the *L. Zech* 9:1
the *L.* shall be seen over them. 14
then shall the *L.* go forth. 14:3
in that day shall there be one *L.* 9
that saith, *L. L.* shall enter into the
kingdom. *Mat* 7:21, 22
L. if thou wilt, thou canst make.
8:2; *Luke* 5:12
L. save us. *Mat* 8:25
they said, Yea, *L.* 9:28; 13:51*
L. save me. 14:30
saying, *L.* help me. 15:25
she said, Truth, *L.:* yet the dogs. 27
L. that our eyes may. 20:33
L. hath need of. 21:3; *Mark* 11:3
Luke 19:31, 34
doth David call him *L.? Mat* 22:43
45; *Mark* 12:37; *Luke* 20:44
not what hour your *L. Mat* 24:42
whom his *L.* shall find so doing.
46; *Luke* 12:43
the *L.* of that servant shall come.
Mat 24:50; *Luke* 12:46
L. L. open to us. *Mat* 25:11
enter into the joy of thy *L.* 21
L. when saw thee an hungered ?
37, 44
L. is it I ? 26:22
the place where the *L.* lay. 28:6
Son of man is *L.* of sabbath.
Mark 2:28; *Luke* 6:5
how great things the *L. Mark* 5:19
L. I believe, help thou. 9:24*
John 9:38; 11:27
L. that I might receive my sight.
Mark 10:51*
L. working with them. *Mark* 16:20
ready a people for the *L. Luke* 1:17
thus *L.* dealt with me, to take. 25
Saviour, which is Christ the *L.* 2:11
why call ye me *L., L. I.* 9:57, 61
a man said to him, *L. I.* 9:57, 61
L. teach us to pray, as John. 11:1
L. let it alone this year, till. 13:8
apostles said unto the *L.* 17:5
where, *L.?* 37
L. remember me when thou. 23:42*
saying, The *L.* is risen indeed. 24:34
L., to whom shall we go ? *John* 6:68
she said, No man, *L.* 8:11
who is he, *L.*, that I might ? 9:36
they said to him, *L.* come. 11:34
ye call me Master and *L.* 13:13
L. who is it ? 25

they have taken the *L.* out. *John* 20:2
we have seen the *L.* 25
ask him, knowing it was the *L.* 21:12
Peter saith, *L.* what shall this ? 21
whom ye crucified, both *L. Acts* 2:36
L. thou art God. 4:24
now *L.* behold threatenings. 29
who art thou, *L.?* 9:5; 26:15
and said, What is it, *L.?* 10:4
Not so *L.*, for I have never. 14; 11:8
Jesus Christ, he is *L.* of all. 10:36
I said, What shall I do, *L.?* 22:10
short work will the *L. Rom* 9:28
same *L.* over all is rich unto. 10:12
he might be *L.* of the dead. 14:9
not have crucified the *L. 1 Cor* 2:8
the *L.* gave to every man. 3:5
he that judgeth me is the *L.* 4:4
to you, if the *L.* will. 19; *Jas* 4:15
body is for the *L. 1 Cor* 6:13
yet not I, but the *L.* 7:10
of administrations, but the same *L.*
12:5
second man is the *L.* 15:47*
be present with the *L. 2 Cor* 5:8
I speak it not after the *L.* 11:17
one *L.*, one faith, one. *Eph* 4:5
even as the *L.* the church. 5:29*
that Jesus Christ is *L. Phil* 2:11
the *L.* is at hand. 4:5
we ever be with the *L. 1 Thes* 4:17
the King of kings, and *L. 1 Tim* 6:15
that call on the *L. 2 Tim* 2:22
out of them all the *L.* delivered. 3:11
which the *L.* shall give me. 4:8
notwithstanding the *L.* stood. 17
began to be spoken by the *L. Heb* 2:3
saying, Know the *L.:* for all. 8:11
and the *L.* shall raise. *Jas* 5:15
one day is with the *L. 2 Pet* 3:8
Michael said, The *L.* rebuke. *Jude* 9
our *L.* was crucified. *Rev* 11:8
become the kingdoms of our *L.* 15
for he is *L.* of lords. 17:14; 19:16

*see anointed, appeared, bless,
blessed, called, cast out,
chosen, choose, commanded,
fear, feared, give, given, liveth,
made, rejoice, shewed, smite*

against the Lord

sinned *ag. the L.* your. *Ex* 10:16
Josh 7:20; *2 Sam* 12:13
murmurings *ag. the L. Ex* 16:7, 8
have trespassed *ag. the L.* 5:19
Num 5:6; 31:16
commit trespass *ag. the L. Lev* 6:2
only rebel not *ag. the L. Num* 14:9
Josh 22:19
together *ag. the L. Num* 16:11
27:3; *Ps* 2:2; *Acts* 4:26
we have spoken *ag. the L. Num* 21:7
when they strove *ag. the L.* 26:9
ye have sinned *ag. the L.* 32:23
Jer 40:3; 44:23
have sinned *ag. the L. Deut* 1:41
1 Sam 7:6; *Jer* 8:14
ye have been rebellious *ag. the L.*
9:7, 24; 31:27
might rebel this day *ag. the L.*
Josh 22:16
ye rebel this day *ag. the L.* 18
if in transgression *ag. the L.* 22
we should rebel *ag. the L.* 22
committed this trespass *ag. the L.* 31
if a man sin *ag. the L. 1 Sam* 2:25
sin *ag. the L.* in ceasing to. 12:23
the people sin *ag. the L.* in. 14:33
and eat, and sin not *ag. the L.* 34
Israel had sinned *ag. the L.* their
God. *2 Ki* 17:7
things not right *ag. the L.* God. 9
transgression he committed *ag. the
L. 1 Chr* 10:13
because they had transgressed *ag.
the L. 2 Chr* 12:2
warn them that they trespass not *ag.
the L.* 19:10
offended already *ag. the L.* 28:13
transgressed sore *ag. the L.* 19
he trespass yet more *ag. the L.* 22
rulers take counsel *ag. the L. Ps* 2:2
heart fretteth *ag. the L. Pr* 19:3
wisdom nor counsel *ag. the L.* 21:30

doings are *ag. the L. Isa* 3:8
iniquity to utter error *ag. the L.* 32:6
and lying *ag. the L.* 59:13
taught rebellion *ag. the L. Jer* 28:16
29:32
he magnified himself *ag. the L.* 48:26
42
because they have sinned *ag. the L.*
50:7
shoot at Babylon: for she hath sinned
ag. the L. 14, 29
hast striven *ag. the L.* 24; *Zeph* 1:17
up thyself *ag. the L. Dan* 5:23
treacherously *ag. the L. Hos* 5:7
do ye imagine *ag. the L.? Nah* 1:9
that imagineth evil *ag. the L.* 11

before the Lord

mighty hunter *bef. the L. Gen* 10:9
well watered, *bef. the L.* 13:10
of Sodom were sinners *bef. the L.* 13
Abraham stood yet *bef. the L.* 18:22
eat and bless thee *bef. the L.* 27:7
come near *bef. the L. Ex* 16:9
lay it up *bef. the L.* to be kept. 33
1 Sam 10:25
males appear *bef. the L. Ex* 23:17
34:24; *Deut* 16:16; *1 Sam* 1:22
order the lamps *bef. the L.*
Ex 27:21; 40:25
bear their names *bef. the L.* 28:12
for a memorial *bef. the L.* 29
30:16; *Num* 31:54
sprinkle seven times *bef. the L.*
Lev 4:6, 17; 14:16, 27
a fire out from *bef. the L.* 9:24
they died *bef. the L.* 10:2; *Num* 3:4
bring her near, set her *bef. the L.*
Num 5:16, 18, 30
remembered *bef. the L.* your. 10:9
of salt for ever *bef. the L.* 18:19
and hang them up *bef. the L.* 25:4
their cause *bef. the L.* 27:5
I fell down *bef. the L. Deut* 9:18
must eat them *bef. the L.* 12:18
which stand there *bef. the L.* 18:7
both shall stand *bef. the L.* 19:17
cursed be the man *bef. the L.* that
buildeth. *Josh* 6:26
words *bef. L.* in Mizpeh. *Judg* 11:11
bef. the L. is your way. 18:6
all the people sat there *bef. the L.*
20:26; *2 Sam* 7:18
sin of men was very great *bef. the
L. 1 Sam* 2:17
witness against me *bef. the L.* 12:3
reason with you *bef. the L.* 7
that day detained *bef. the L.* 21:7
men, cursed be they *bef. L.* 26:19
bef. the L. which chose. *2 Sam* 6:21
them in the hill *bef. the L.* 21:9
Hezekiah spread it *bef. the L.*
2 Ki 19:14; *Isa* 37:14
is subdued *before the L. 1 Chr* 22:18
did eat and drink *bef. the L.* 29:22
bef. the L. for he cometh to judge.
Ps 96:13; 98:9
let them be *bef. the L.* 109:15
I will walk *bef. the L.* in. 116:9
destruction are *bef. the L. Pr* 15:11
that dwell *bef. the L. Isa* 23:18
supplications *bef. the L. Jer* 36:7
to eat bread *bef. the L. Ezek* 44:3
not our prayer *bef. the L. Dan* 9:13
shall I come *bef. the L. Mi* 6:6
O all flesh, *bef. the L. Zech* 2:13
to pray *bef. the L.* 7:2; 8:21, 22
mournfully *bef. the L. Mal* 3:14
charging them *bef. the L. 2 Tim* 2:14
accusation *bef. the Lord. 2 Pet* 2:11

from the Lord

gotten a man *from the L. Gen* 4:1
fire *from the L.* 19:24
proceedeth *from the L.* 24:50
forth a wind *from the L. Num* 11:31
came out a fire *from the L.* 16:35
wrath gone out *from the L.* 46
evil spirit *from the L.* troubled him.
1 Sam 16:14; 19:9
a deep sleep *from the L.* 26:12
it was his *from the L. 1 Ki* 2:15
peace for ever *from the L.* 33
the blessing *from the L. Ps* 24:5
adversaries *from the L.* 109:20

my help cometh *from the L.*
     Ps 121:2
of the tongue is *from the L. Pr* 16:1
prudent wife is *from the L.* 19:14
but every man's judgement cometh
  from the L.   29:26
their counsel *from the L. Isa* 29:15
my way is hid *from the L.* 40:27
word came to Jeremiah *from the L.*
  Jer 7:1; 11:1; 18:1; 21:1; 26:1
  27:1; 30:1; 32:1; 34:1, 8, 12
  35:1; 36:1; 40:1
heart departeth *from the L.* 17:5
is there any word *from the L.?* 37:17
heard a rumour *from the L.* 49:14
no vision *from the L.* *Lam* 2:9
hope is perished *from the L.* 3:18
get ye far *from the L. Ezek* 11:15
word that cometh *from the L.* 33:30
whoredom, departing *from the L.*
  Hos 1:2
a rumour *from the L.* arise. *Ob* 1
evil came down *from the L. Mi* 1:12
Jacob shall be as dew *from the L.* 5:7
turned back *from the L. Zeph* 1:6
tumult *from the L.* shall. *Zech* 14:13
told her *from the L.* *Luke* 1:45
we are absent *from the L. 2 Cor* 5:6

Lord *God*
blessed be the *L. God. Gen* 9:26
Abram said, *L. God,* what wilt? 15:2
L. God, whereby shall I know? 8
the *L. God* of my master. 24:27
I am the *L. God* of Abraham. 28:13
the *L. God* of Israel. *Ex* 32:27
Josh 9:18, 19; 10:40, 42; 13:14
  33; 14:14
the *L. God* merciful and. 34:6
Joshua said, Alas, O *L. God.*
  Josh 7:7
L. God of gods, the *L. God* of. 22:22
ye to do with the *L. God* of? 24
the *L. God* of Israel. 24:2; *Judg* 4:6
5:3, 5; 11:21, 23; 21:3; *Ruth* 2:12
1 Sam 2:30; 14:41; 20:12; 23:10
25:32, 34; *1 Ki* 1:30; *1 Chr* 23:25
  24:19
alas, O *L. God,* because. *Judg* 6:22
O *L. God,* remember me only. 16:28
who is able to stand before this holy
  L. God? *1 Sam* 6:20
L. God of hosts was with him.
  2 Sam 5:10
who am I, O *L. God,* and? 7:18
manner of man, O *L. God*? 19
for thou, *L. God,* knowest thy. 20
thou art great, O *L. God.* 22
the *L. God* of my lord the king.
  1 Ki 1:36
king said, Blessed be the *L. God.*
  48; 8:15; *1 Chr* 16:36; 29:10
good thing toward the *L. God.*
  1 Ki 14:13
As the *L. God* of Israel liveth. 17:1
may know thou art *L. God.* 18:37
  2 Ki 19:19
where is *L. God* of Elijah? *2 Ki* 2:14
state of a man of high degree, O *L.*
  God. *1 Chr* 17:17
fight ye not against *L. God* of fathers.
  2 Chr 13:12
house of the *L. God* of fathers. 24:18
for thy honour from *L. God.* 26:18
spake more against *L. God.* 32:16
thou art the *L. God,* who didst choose
  Abram. *Neh* 9:7
redeemed me, O *L. God* of. *Ps* 31:5
L. God of Israel from everlasting to.
  41:13; 72:18; 106:48; *Luke* 1:68
L. God might dwell. *Ps* 68:18
thou art my hope, O *L. God.* 71:5
for *L. God* is a sun and. 84:11
I will hear what the *L. God.* 85:8
heard from the *L. God. Isa* 28:22
for the *L. God* will help me. 50:7, 9
for *L. God* shall slay thee. 65:15
saying, The *L. God* liveth. *Jer* 44:26
As I live, saith the *L. God.*
  Ezek 5:11, 14, 16
I am the *L. God.* 13:9; 23:49; 24:24
thus it was, saith the *L. God.* 16:19
Woe unto thee, saith the *L. God.* 23
to his ways, saith the *L. God.* 18:30

to pass, saith the *L. God. Ezek* 21:7
no more, saith the *L. God.* 13
forgotten me, saith the *L. God.* 22:12
wrought for me, saith the *L. God.* 29:20
your God, saith the *L. God.* 34:31
am the Lord, saith the *L. God.* 36:23
sakes do I this, saith the *L. God.* 32
and I answered, O *L. God.* 37:3
spoken it, saith the *L. God.* 39:5
  23:34; 26:14; 28:10
it is done, saith the *L. God.* 6
accept you, saith the *L. God.* 43:27
face unto the *L. God* to. *Dan* 9:3
even *L. God* of hosts is. *Hos* 12:5
Philistines shall perish, saith *L. God.*
  Amos 1:8
L. God will do nothing, but. 3:7
the *L. God* hath spoken, who? 8
liketh you, saith the *L. God.* 4:5
L. God of hosts is he that. 9:5
let the *L. God* be witness. *Mi* 1:2
L. God is my strength. *Hab* 3:19
sanctify the *L. God* in. *1 Pet* 3:15
holy, holy, *L. God* Almighty. *Rev* 4:8
  11:17; 16:7
thy works, *L. God* Almighty. 15:3
for strong is the *L. God* who. 18:8
for the *L. God* omnipotent. 19:6
the *L. God* and the Lamb. 21:22
the *L. God* giveth them light. 22:5

see **fathers**

Lord *his God*
besought the *L. his God. Ex* 32:11
against the commandments of the *L.*
  his God. *Lev* 4:22
L. his God is with him. *Num* 23:21
learn to fear the *L. his G. Deut* 17:19
in name of the *L. his God.* 18:7
encouraged himself in *L. his G.*
  1 Sam 30:6
an house unto the name of *L. his G.*
  1 Ki 5:3
heart was not perfect with *L. his G.*
  11:4; 15:3
L. his God give a lamp in. 15:4
the sight of *L. his God. 2 Ki* 16:2
L. his God was with him. *2 Chr* 1:1
right in eyes of the *L. his God.* 14:2
Asa cried unto the *L. his God.* 11
when they saw that *L. his G.* 15:9
Uzziah transgressed against the *L.*
  his G. 26:16
his ways before *L. his God.* 27:6
L. his G. delivered Ahaz. 28:5
Hezekiah wrought right before *L.*
  his God. 31:20
Manasseh in affliction besought *L.*
  his God. 33:12
repair house of the *L. his God.* 34:8
evil in sight of *L. his God.* 36:5, 12
the *L. his G.* be with him, and. 23
to hand of *L. his G.* *Ezra* 7:6
happy he whose hope is in the *L. his*
  God. *Ps* 146:5
prayed to the *L. his God. Jonah* 2:1
of the name of *L. his God. Mi* 5:4

Lord *my God*
the word of *L. my God. Num* 22:18
L. my God commanded. *Deut* 4:5
again voice of *L. my God.* 18:16
hearkened to voice of *L. my God.*
  26:14
followed the *L. my God. Josh* 14:8
offerings to *L. my God. 2 Sam* 24:24
O *L. my G. 1 Ki* 3:7; 8:28; 17:20, 21
  1 Chr 21:17; *2 Chr* 6:19; *Ps* 7:1, 3
  13:3; 30:2, 12; 35:24; 38:15
  40:5; 86:12; 109:26; *Jonah* 2:6
  Hab 1:12
the *L. my God* hath given. *1 Ki* 5:4
house unto the name of the *L. my*
  God. 5; *1 Chr* 22:7; *2 Chr* 2:4
hand of the *L. my God. Ezra* 7:28
out my hands to the *L. my God.* 9:5
the *L. my God* will. *Ps* 18:28
for thou art *L. my God.* *Jer* 31:18
I prayed unto the *L. my God. Dan* 9:4
supplication before *L. my God.* 20
L. my God, Feed the flock. *Zech* 11:4
and the *L. my God* shall come. 14:5

Lord *our God*
sacrifice to *L. our God. Ex* 3:18; 5:3
  8:27; 10:25

there is none like to *L. our God.*
  Ex 8:10; *Ps* 113:5
to serve the *L. our God.* *Ex* 10:26
L. our God spake unto. *Deut* 1:6
all that wilderness, as the *L. our God*
  commanded us. 19, 41; 6:20
which *L. our God* doth give unto us.
  1:20, 25; 2:29
L. our God delivered him. 2:33
unto whatsoever *L. our God.* 37
so nigh to them, as *L. our God.* 4:7
L. our God made a covenant. 5:2
the *L. our God* hath shewed. 24
hear the voice of the *L. our God.* 25
hear all that the *L. our God.* 27
O Israel, *L. our God* is one Lord.
  6:4; *Mark* 12:29
to fear *L. our God.* *Deut* 6:24
to do before *L. our God.* 25
day before the *L. our God.* 29:15
things belong to the *L. our God.* 29
you before the *L. our God. Josh* 18:6
the altar of *L. our God.* 22:19, 29
L. our God, he it is that brought us
  up. 24:17
the people said, The *L. our God.* 24
whomsoever *L. our God. Judg* 11:24
cry to the *L. our God* for. *1 Sam* 7:8
L. our God be with us. *1 Ki* 8:57
words be nigh unto *L. our God.* 59
we trust Lord *our God. 2 Ki* 18:22
O *L. our God,* save thou us. 19:19
that it be of *L. our God. 1 Chr* 13:2
the *L. our God* made a breach. 15:13
he is the *L. our God*; his judgements. 16:14; *Ps* 105:7
O *L. our God.* *1 Chr* 29:16
  2 Chr 14:11; *Ps* 99:8; 106:47
  Isa 26:13; 37:20; *Jer* 14:22
  Dan 9:15
keep the charge of the *L. our God.*
  2 Chr 13:11
have sought the *L. our God.* 14:7
iniquity with the *L. our God.* 19:7
but with us is the *L. our God.* 32:8
L. our God shall deliver us. 11
been shewed from the *L. our God.*
  Ezra 9:8
name of the *L. our God.* *Ps* 20:7
beauty of the *L. our God.* 90:17
yea, the *L. our God* shall cut. 94:23
exalt ye the *L. our God.* 99:5, 9
for the *L. our God* is holy. 9
for he is the Lord *our God.* 105:7
house of the *L. our God.* 122:9
wait on the *L. our God.* 123:2
come to thee, for thou art the *L. our*
  God. *Jer* 3:22
L. our God is the salvation. 23
sinned against the *L. our God* . . . not
  obeyed voice of *L. our God.* 25
doeth *L. our God* these things? 5:19
let us now fear the *L. our God.* 24
for the *L. our God* hath put. 8:14
committed against the *L. our God.*
  16:10
us in the name of *L. our God.* 26:16
up to Zion, to the *L. our God.* 31:6
pray now to *L. our God* for us.
  37:3; 42:20
the voice of the *L. our God.* 42:6
the *L. our God* hath not sent. 43:2
vengeance of *L. our God.* 50:28
Zion the work of *L. our God.* 51:10
to the *L. our God* belong. *Dan* 9:9
obeyed voice of the *L. our God.* 10
for the *L. our God* is righteous in. 14
in the name of the *L. our G. Mi* 4:5
afraid of the *L. our God.* 7:17
as *L. our God* shall call. *Acts* 2:39
power to the *L. our God.* *Rev* 19:1

Lord *their God*
may serve *L. their God.* *Ex* 10:7
  2 Chr 34:33; *Jer* 30:9
know that I am the *L. their God.*
  Ex 29:46; *Ezek* 28:26; 34:30
  39:22, 28
break covenant, I am *L. their God.*
  Lev 26:44; *Zech* 10:6
forgat *L. their God.* *Judg* 3:7
  8:34; *1 Sam* 12:9; *Jer* 3:21
because they forsook *L. their God.*
  1 Ki 9:9; *Jer* 22:9

Israel had sinned against the *L. their*
  God.   2 *Ki* 17:7
right against the *L. their God.*   9
did not believe in the *L. their God.* 14
left all the commandments of the *L.*
  their God.   16
Judah kept not commandments of
  the *L. their God.*   19
obeyed not voice of the *L. their God.*
       18:12; *Jer* 7:28
were consecrated to the *L. their*
  God.   2 *Chr* 31:6
sacrifice unto *L. their God.*   33:17
words of the *L. their God* for which
  the *L. their God* had.   *Jer* 43:1
they shall go and seek the *L. their*
  God.   50:4; *Hos* 3:5
save them by *L. their God. Hos* 1:7
not return to the *L. their God.*   7:10
obeyed the voice of the *L. their God.*
       Hag 1:12
L. their God shall save. *Zech* 9:16
he turn to *L. their God. Luke* 1:16

Lord thy God
I am the *L. thy God.*   *Ex* 20:2
 Ps 81:10; *Isa* 51:15; *Hos* 12:9
       13:4
for I the *L. thy God* am a jealous
  God.   *Ex* 20:5; *Deut* 5:9
L. thy God hath been.   *Deut* 2:7
L. thy God is a consuming fire. 4:24
L. thy God is a merciful God.   31
that the *L. thy God,* he is God. 7:9
L. thy God is among.   21; 23:14
so the *L. thy God* chasteneth.   8:5
not do so to the *L. thy God.*   12:31
for the *L. thy God* is with thee. 20:1
say before the *L. thy God.* 26:5, 13
fear this fearful name, the *L. thy*
  God.   28:58
L. thy God is with thee. *Josh* 1:9
only the *L. thy God* be with.   17
L. thy God will be with thee.
       2 *Sam* 14:17
Araunah said, The *L. thy God.* 24:23
face of the *L. thy God.*   1 *Ki* 13:6
as the *L. thy God* liveth I have not a
  cake.   17:12; 18:10
L. thy God, the Holy One. *Isa* 43:3
because of the *L. thy God.*   55:5
pray for us to the *L. thy God. Jer* 42:2
that the *L. thy God* may shew us. 3
where is the *L. thy God ? Mi* 7:10
the *L. thy God* in midst. *Zeph* 3:17
thou shalt not tempt the *L. thy God.*
  Mat 4:7; *Luke* 4:12

Lord your God
holy, for I the *L. your God. Lev* 19:2
Lord your God hath multiplied you.
       Deut 1:10
L. your God he shall fight. 30; 3:22
not tempt the *L. your God.*   6:16
L. your God is God of gods.   10:17
L. your God is he that goeth.   20:4
L. your God is God in.   *Josh* 2:11
the *L. your God* is he that hath fought
  for you.   23:3, 10
when *L. your God* was your king.
       1 *Sam* 12:12
L. your God ye shall fear. 2 *Ki* 17:39
is not the *L. your God* with you ?
       1 *Chr* 22:18
believe in *L. your God.* 2 *Chr* 20:20
sent me to *L. your God. Jer* 42:20
ye know that I am the *L. your God.*
       Joel 3:17
prophet shall the *L. your God* raise.
       Acts 3:22; 7:37
see, I am the **Lord** your God

Lord of hosts
O *L. of hosts.*   1 *Sam* 1:11
Ps 59:5; 84:1, 3, 12; 2 *Sam* 7:27
       Jer 11:20; 20:12
name of the *L. of hosts.* 2 *Sam* 6:2
the *L. of hosts* is God over.   7:26
Elijah said, As *L. of hosts* liveth.
     1 *Ki* 18:15; 2 *Ki* 3:14
the zeal of the *L. of hosts* shall do.
  2 *Ki* 19:31; *Isa* 9:7; 37:32
greater, for the *L. of h.* 1 *Chr* 11:9
the *L. of h.* God of Israel.   17:24
L. of hosts, he is the King. *Ps* 24:10
the *L. of h.* is with us.   46:7, 11

in city of *L. of hosts.*   *Ps* 48:8
the Lord, the *L. of hosts. Isa* 1:24
the day of the *L. of hosts.*   2:12
Holy, holy is the *L. of hosts.*   6:3
seen the King, the *L. of hosts.*   5
sanctify the *L. of hosts* himself. 8:13
for the *L. of hosts* hath purposed.
       14:27; 23:9
swear to the *L. of hosts.*   19:18
L. of hosts is his name. 47:4; 48:2
  51:15; 54:5; *Jer* 10:16; 31:35
     32:18; 50:34; 51:19
king, whose name is the *L. of hosts.*
     Jer 46:18; 48:15
L. of hosts saith, I will punish. 46:25
is it not of the *L. of hosts ? Hab* 2:13
I am with you, saith *L. of hosts.*
       Hag 2:4
the *L. of hosts* thought. *Zech* 1:6
the *L. of hosts* sent me. 2:9, 11; 4:9
wrath from the *L. of hosts.*   7:12
not hear, saith the *L. of hosts.*   13
and to seek the *L. of hosts.*   8:21
come to seek the *L. of hosts.*   22
the King, *L. of hosts.*   14:16, 17
be holiness unto the *L. of hosts.*   21
I am a great King, saith *L. of hosts.*
       Mal 1:14

see, saith the Lord
I the Lord
for I the *L. your God* am holy.
     Lev 19:2; 20:26; 21:8
for I the *L.* do sanctify him.   21:15
     23; 22:9, 16
I the *L.* have said it, I will do it.
     Num 14:35; *Ezek* 21:17
I the *L.* do keep it, I will. *Isa* 27:3
I the *L.* the first, and with.   41:4
when the needy seek, I the *L.*   17
I the *L.* have called thee in.   42:6
I the *L.* which call thee by.   45:3
I the *L.* do all these things.   7
I the *L.* created it.   8
I the *L.* speak righteousness.   19
who hath told ? have not I the *L.?* 21
that I the *L.* am thy Saviour. 60:16
I the *L.* will hasten it in his time. 22
for I the *L.* love judgement.   61:8
I the *L.* search the heart. *Jer* 17:10
I the *L.* have spoken it. *Ezek* 5:13
  15; 17; 17:21; 21:32; 22:14
     24:14; 26:14; 30:12
I the *L.* will answer him.   14:4, 7
I the *L.* have deceived that.   9
I *L.* have brought down, I *L.*   17:24
I the *L.* have kindled it.   20:48
I the *L.* have drawn forth.   21:5
I the *L.* will be their God.   34:24
know that I the *L.* their God.   30
I the *L.* do build, I the *L.*   36:36
I the *L.* have performed it.   37:14
I the *L.* do sanctify Israel.   28

I am the Lord
I am the *L.* that brought. *Gen* 15:7
I am the *L. Ex* 6:2, 6, 8, 29; 12:12
  Lev 18:5, 6, 21; *Num* 3:13
     Isa 43:11; 45:8
I am the *L.* thy God which. *Ex* 20:2
I am *L.* which hallow you. *Lev* 22:32
I am *L.:* that is my name. *Isa* 42:8
shall say, I am the *L.'s.*   44:5
knoweth that I am the *L. Jer* 9:24
behold, I am the *L.* the God. 32:27
I am the *L.,* I change not. *Mal* 3:6
see know

I am the Lord your God
ye shall know that I am *L. your God.*
     Ex 6:7; 16:12
I am the *L. your God. Lev* 11:44
  18:30;   19:3;   20:7;   23:22
  Judg 6:10; *Ezek* 20:5, 7, 19, 20
       Joel 2:27

Lord Jesus, see Jesus

in the Lord
he believed in the *L.*   *Gen* 15:6
children of Reuben, Gad; ye have no
  part in the *L.*   *Josh* 22:25, 27
rejoiceth in the *L.,* mine horn is exalted in the *L.*   1 *Sam* 2:1
put your trust in the *L.*   *Ps* 4:5
in the *L.* put I my trust.   11:1
     26:1; 31:6; 73:28

all ye that hope in the *L. Ps* 31:24
be glad in the *L.*   32:11
make her boast in the *L.*   34:2
be joyful in the *L.*   35:9
delight also thyself in the *L.*   37:4
       Isa 58:14
rest in the *L.*   *Ps* 37:7
in the *L.* will I praise his.   56:10
righteous shall be glad in the *L.*
     64:10; 104:34
trust in the *L.* with all thine heart.
       Pr 3:5
putteth his trust in the *L.*   29:25
in the *L.* Jehovah is.   *Isa* 26:4
increase their joy in the *L.*   29:19
shall be saved in the *L.*   45:17
in the *L.* have I righteousness.   24
in the *L.* shall all the seed of.   25
in the *L.* is the salvation. *Jer* 3:23
she trusted not in the *L.*   *Zeph* 3:2
be my strength in the *L. Zech* 12:5
many believed in the *L. Acts* 9:42
speaking boldly in the *L.*   14:3
ye receive her in the *L. Rom* 16:2
greet Amplias in the *L.*   8
who laboured much in the *L.*   12
salute Rufus, chosen in the *L.*   13
I Tertius salute you in the *L.*   22
glorieth, let him glory in the *L.*
     1 *Cor* 1:31; 2 *Cor* 10:17
and faithful in the *L.*   1 *Cor* 4:17
called in the *L.*   7:22
whom she will; only in the *L.*   39
are ye not my work in the *L.?*   9:1
seal of apostleship are ye in the *L.* 2
without the man, in the *L.*   11:11
labour is not in vain in the *L.* 15:58
an holy temple in the *L. Eph* 2:21
and testify in the *L.*   4:17
now are ye light in the *L.*   5:8
obey your parents in the *L.*   6:1
brethren, be strong in the *L.*   10
faithful minister in the *L.*   21
brethren in the *L.* waxing. *Phil* 1:14
I trust in the *L.* I shall come.   2:24
receive him therefore in the *L.*   29
stand fast in the *L.* 4:1; 1 *Thes* 3:8
the same mind in the *L.*   *Phil* 4:2
rejoice in the *L.* alway.   4
but I rejoiced in the *L.* greatly.   10
own husbands in the *L.*   *Col* 3:18
is a fellow-servant in the *L.*   4:7
thou hast received in the *L.*   17
which are over you in *L.* 1 *Thes* 5:12
confidence in the *L.*   2 *Thes* 3:4
in the flesh and in the *L. Philem* 16
joy of thee in the *L.:* refresh my
  bowels in the *L.*   20
dead which die in the *L.*   *Rev* 14:13
see rejoice, trust

Lord is
the *L. is* in this place.   *Gen* 28:16
the *L. is* righteous, I and my people
  wicked.   *Ex* 9:27; 2 *Chr* 12:6
L. is my strength and.   *Ex* 15:2
the *L. is* a man of war, the *L. is.*   3
I know that *L. is* greater than. 18:11
the *L. is* with us, fear.   *Num* 14:9
the *L. is* longsuffering. 18; *Nah* 1:3
go not up, for the *L. is. Num* 14:42
holy every one, and the *L. is.*   16:3
the *L. is* his inheritance. *Deut* 10:9
the *L. is* their inheritance.   18:2
witness, that *L. is* God. *Josh* 22:34
and said, The *L. is* with thee.
     Judg 6:12; *Luke* 1:28
for the *L. is* a God of.   1 *Sam* 2:3
L. is with David. 16:18; 2 *Sam* 7:3
seeing *L. is* departed. 1 *Sam* 28:16
he said, The *L. is* my rock.
     2 *Sam* 22:2; *Ps* 18:2
know that *L. is* God.   1 *Ki* 8:60
L. is the God of the hills.   20:28
the *L. is* our God.   2 *Chr* 13:10
the *L. is* with you while ye.   15:2
L. is known by judgement. *Ps* 9:16
L. is king for ever and ever.   10:16
the *L. is* in his holy temple.   11:4
because the *L. is* his refuge.   14:6
the *L. is* the portion of mine.   16:5
the *L. is* my shepherd, I shall.   23:1
the *L. is* my light and my salvation, the
L. is the strength of my life.   27:1

the *L. is* my strength.
Ps 28:7; 118:14
the *L. is* their strength, and he. 28:8
O taste and see that the *L. is.* 34:8
for the *L.* most high *is* terrible. 47:2
L. is our defence and Holy. 89:18
to shew that *L. is* upright. 92:15
the *L. is* clothed with strength. 93:1
the *L. is* my defence and. 94:22
the *L. is* a great God. 95:3; 96:4
99:2; 135:5
the *L. is* good. 100:5; 34:8; 135:3
145:9; *Jer* 33:11; *Lam* 3:25
Nah 1:7
L. is merciful and gracious.
Ps 103:8; 111:4; 145:8
the *L. is* high. 113:4
the *L. is* on my side. 118:6
the *L. is* thy keeper, the *L. is.* 121:5
so the *L. is* round about his. 125:2
L. is righteous. 129:4; 145:17
Lam 1:18; *Dan* 9:14
the *L. is* nigh to all them. *Ps* 145:18
L. is far from the wicked. *Pr* 15:29
the *L. is* the maker of them. 22:2
L. is a God of judgement. *Isa* 30:18
the *L. is* exalted. 33:5
L. is our judge, our. 22
L. is well pleased for his. 42:21
the *L. is* the true God. *Jer* 10:10
whose hope the *L. is.* 17:7
the *L. is* with me. 20:11
the *L. is* my portion. *Lam* 3:24
the city, the *L. is* there. *Ezek* 48:35
maketh the stars the *L. is* his name.
Amos 5:8; 9:6
L. is in his holy temple. *Hab* 2:20
the just *L. is* in the midst thereof.
Zeph 3:5, 15
fight, because *L. is* with. *Zech* 10:5
shall say, The *L. is* my God. 13:9
the *L. is* risen indeed. *Luke* 24:34
the *L. is* that Spirit. 2 *Cor* 3:17
known, the *L. is* at hand. *Phil* 4:5
the *L. is* the avenger of. 1 *Thes* 4:6
but the *L. is* faithful. 2 *Thes* 3:3
the *L. is* my helper, I. *Heb* 13:6
L. is very pitiful, and. *Jas* 5:11
tasted that *L. is* gracious. 1 *Pet* 2:3
L. is not slack concerning. 2 *Pet* 3:9

my Lord
said, Oh, not so, *my* L. *Gen* 19:18
Moses said. O *my* L. I. *Ex* 4:10
O *my* L. send by hand of whom. 13
let the power of *my* L. *Num* 14:17
saith *my* L. to his servant ? *Josh* 5:14
O *my* L. if he. L. be with us.
Judg 6:13
O *my* L. wherewith shall I ? 15
O *my* L. let the man of God. 13:8
to the L. thou art *my* L. *Ps* 16:2
stir up thyself, my God, *my* L. 35:23
John 20:28
the L. said to *my* L. *Ps* 110:1
Mat 22:44; *Mark* 12:36
Luke 20:42; *Acts* 2:34
a lion : *My* L. I stand. *Isa* 21:8
but Zion said. *My* L. hath. 49:14
O *my* L. by the vision. *Dan* 10:16
of *my* L. talk with this *my* L.? 17
and I said, Let *my* L. speak. 19
O *my* L. what shall be end of ? 12:8
said I, O *my* L. what are these ?
Zech 1:9; 4:4; 6:4
knowest thou ? No, *my* L. 4:5, 13
the mother of *my* L. *Luke* 1:43
have taken away *my* L. *John* 20:13
of Christ Jesus *my* L. *Phil* 3:8

O Lord
for thy salvation, O L. *Gen* 49:18
who is like to thee, O L.? *Ex* 15:11
return, O L. unto Israel. *Num* 10:36
Ps 6:4
O L. hast given me. *Deut* 26:10
O L. what shall I say ? *Josh* 7:8
thine enemies perish, O L. *Judg* 5:31
O L. turn counsel of. 2 *Sam* 15:31
thou art my lamp, O L. and. 22:29
be it far from me, O L. that. 23:17
O L. there is none like. 1 *Chr* 17:20
O L. is greatness, thine, O L. 29:11
help us, O L. our God ; O L. thou
art our God. 2 *Chr* 14:11

arise, O L.; save me. *Ps* 3:7
lead me, O L. 5:8
O L. heal me. 6:2
but thou, O L. how long ? 3
arise, O L. 7:6; 9:19; 10:12; 17:13
judge me, O L. according. 7:8; 26:1
O L. our L. 8:1, 9
I will praise thee, O L. 9:1
O L.: consider my trouble. 13
31:9; 86:3; 123:3
O L. my strength. 18:1; 19:14
be not thou far from me, O L. 22:19
35:22
hear, O L. 27:7; 30:10; 39:12
69:16; 86:6; 102:1; 119:145
140:6
I trusted in thee, O L. I said. 31:14
gods none like to thee, O L. 86:8
teach me thy way, O L. I walk. 1
25:4; 27:11
not unto us, O L. not unto. 115:1
O L. thy commandments. 119:151
hear my prayer, O L. 143:1, 7
Isa 37:17; *Dan* 9:19
O L. thou art my God. *Isa* 25:1
O L. art our Father. 63:16; 64:8
O L. thou art great. *Jer* 10:6
so be it, O L. 11:5
but thou, O L. knowest me. 12:3
O L. art in the midst of us. 14:9
O L. the hope of Israel. 17:13
heal me, O L. and I shall be. 14
see, O L., and consider ; for I am
become vile. *Lam* 1:11; 2:20
thou, O L. remainest for ever. 5:19
turn us unto thee, O L. we. 21
we beseech thee, O L. *Jonah* 1:14
O L. thou hast ordained. *Hab* 1:12
O L. revive thy work in. 3:2
O L. thou Son of David. *Mat* 15:22
20:30, 31
I am a sinful man, O L. *Luke* 5:8
thou art worthy, O L. to. *Rev* 4:11
saying, How long, O L.? 6:10
who shall not fear thee, O L.? 15:4
O L. which art, and wast. 16:5

see Lord God
anger of the Lord
anger of the L. was kindled against
Moses. *Ex* 4:14
anger of the L. was kindled against
Israel. *Num* 11:10; 25:3
Josh 7:1; *Judg* 2:14, 20; 3:8
1-0:7; 2 *Sam* 24:1; 2 *Ki* 13:3
Isa 5:25
anger of the L. kindled against
Aaron. *Num* 12:9
that the fierce *anger of L.* may. 25:4
augment yet the *anger of L.* 32:14
lest the *anger of L.* be. *Deut* 6:15
so will *anger of L.* be. 7:4
anger of the L. was smoked. 29:20
anger of L. be kindled against you.
Josh 23:16
anger of L. kindled against Uzzah.
2 *Sam* 6:7; 1 *Chr* 13:10
through *anger of the L.* it came to.
2 *Ki* 24:20; *Jer* 52:3
anger of the L. kindled against
Amaziah. 2 *Chr* 25:15
fierce *anger of the L.* is not turned
back from us. *Jer* 4:8
of the fierce *anger of the L.* 12:13
anger of the L. shall not return till.
23:20; 30:24
his soul from *anger of the L.* 51:45
in day of *L.'s anger* none. *Lam* 2:22
anger of L. hath divided them. 4:16
before the fierce *anger of L. Zeph* 2:2
hid in day of the *anger of the L.* 3
see commandment, congrega-
tion, counsel, day, eyes, face,
fear, feast, glory, hand, house,
knowledge, law

mouth of the Lord
word that proceedeth out of mouth
of L. *Deut* 8:3
counsel at *mouth of L. Josh* 9:14
disobeyed *mouth of L.* 1 *Ki* 13:21
for the *mouth of L.* hath spoken it.
Isa 1:20; 40:5; 58:14; *Jer* 9:12
Mi 4:4

by a new name, which the *mouth of*
the L. shall name. *Isa* 62:2
speak not out of *mouth of the L.*
Jer 23:16

name of the Lord
Abram called on the *name of the L.*
Gen 12:8
she called the *name of L.* 16:13
Isaac called on *name of L.* 26:25
shall not take *name of L.* in vain.
Ex 20:7; *Deut* 5:11
proclaim *name of the L.* *Ex* 33:19
proclaimed the *name of the L.* 34:5
woman's son blasphemed the *name*
of the L. *Lev* 24:11, 16
minister in *name of L. Deut* 18:5, 7
speaketh in the *name of the L.* 22
chosen to bless in *name of L.* 21:5
art called by the *name of L.* 28:10
publish *name of L.*: ascribe. 32:3
thy servants are come because of
name of the L. *Josh* 9:9
in *name of L.* of hosts. 1 *Sam* 17:45
both of us in *name of L.* 20:42
called by *name of the L.* 2 *Sam* 6:2
blessed the people in the *name of L.*
18; 1 *Chr* 16:2
no house built to the *name of the L.*
1 *Ki* 3:2; 5:3, 5; 8:17, 20
1 *Chr* 22:7, 19; 2 *Chr* 2:1, 4; 6:10
Sheba heard concerning *name of L.*
1 *Ki* 10:1
altar in the *name of the L.* 18:32
that which is true in *name of L.* 22:16
2 *Chr* 18:15
cursed them in *name of the L.*
2 *Ki* 2:24
which he spake in *name of L.*
1 *Chr* 21:19; 2 *Chr* 33:18
blessed be the *name of the L.*
Job 1:21; *Ps* 113:2
sing praises to *name of L. Ps* 7:17
remember *name of the L.* our. 20:7
shall fear the *name of the L.* 102:15
to declare *name of the L.* in. 21
praise the *name of L.* 113:1; 135:1
148:5, 13; *Joel* 2:26
rising of sun *L.'s name* is. *Ps* 113:3
called I upon *name of L.* 116:4
in the *name of L.* will I destroy.
118:10, 11, 12
cometh in the *name of the L.* 26
thanks unto *name of the L.* 122:4
our help is in *name of L.* 124:8
we bless you in *name of L.* 129:8
name of L. is a strong. *Pr* 18:10
place of the *name of the L. Isa* 18:7
glorify the *name of the L.* in. 24:15
name of L. cometh from far. 30:27
which swear by *name of L.* 48:1
let him trust in *name of the L.* 50:10
and to love the *name of L.* to. 56:6
they fear the *name of L.* 59:19
and gold to *name of the L.* 60:9
all nations gathered to *name of the*
L. *Jer* 3:17
prophesy not in the *name of L.* 11:21
prophesied in the *name of L.* 26:9
he hath spoken to us in the *name of*
L. 16; 44:16
Urijah that prophesied in the *name of*
the L. 26:20
mention of *name of L.* *Amos* 6:10
will walk in *name of Lord. Mi* 4:5
majesty of the *name of the L.* 5:4
trust in *name of the L. Zeph* 3:12
lies in *name of the L. Zech* 13:3
that cometh in the *name of L.*
Mat 21:9; 23:39; *Mark* 11:9, 10
Luke 13:35; 19:38; *John* 12:13
spake boldly in *name of the L.* Jesus.
Acts 9:29
to be baptized in *name of L.* 10:48
to call over them the *name of the L.*
19:13
and the *name of the L.* Jesus. 17
to die for the *name of L.* 21:13
sins, calling on *name of L.* 22:16
that the *name of L.* Jesus may be
glorified. 2 *Thes* 1:12
command you in the *name of L.* 3:6
have spoken in *name of L. Jas* 5:10
with oil in the *name of the L.* 14

of the Lord

of the *L.* to harden.   *Josh* 11:20
asked him *of the L.*   *1 Sam* 1:20
them in the ears *of the L.*   8:21
Saul said, Blessed be ye *of L.* 23:21
     2 Sam 2:5
his name Jedidiah because *of the L.*
     2 Sam 12:25
the saying *of the L.*   *1 Ki* 15:29
this evil is *of the L.*   *2 Ki* 6:33
man of God and enquire *of L.*   8:8
saying *of the L.* to Elijah.   10:17
we may enquire *of L.*   *2 Chr* 18:7
go, enquire *of the L.* for me.   34:21
I will say *of the L.* He.   *Ps* 91:2
disposing thereof is *of the L.*
     Pr 16:33
man's goings are *of the L.*   20:24
safety is *of L.*   21:31
worship, because *of the L.* *Isa* 49:7
O arm *of the L.* awake as.   51:9
pray thee, *of the L.* for us. *Jer* 21:2
it is *of the L.'s* mercies. *Lam* 3:22
salvation is *of the L.*   *Jonah* 2:9
the will *of L.* be done.   *Acts* 21:14
I have received *of the L.* *1 Cor* 11:23
opened to me *of the L.* *2 Cor* 2:12
shall he receive *of the L.* *Eph* 6:8
knowing that *of the L.* *Col* 3:24
may find mercy *of the L.* *2 Tim* 1:18
receive any thing *of the L.* *Jas* 1:7
seen the end *of the L.*   5:11
longsuffering *of the L.* *2 Pet* 3:15

see angel

prophet and *prophets* of the Lord

Samuel established to be a *p. of the*
L.   *1 Sam* 3:20
Jezebel cut off *p. of the L.* *1 Ki* 18:4
Jezebel slew the *p. of the L.*   13
I only remain a *p. of the L.*   22
is there not here a *p. of the L.* to?
     22:7; *2 Ki* 3:11; *2 Chr* 18:6
a *p. of the L.* was there. *2 Chr* 28:9

see sabaoth, sabbath

servant, servants of the Lord

Moses the *s. of the L.* died there.
     Deut 34:5
death of Moses *s. of the L. Josh* 1:1
which Moses the *s. of the L.* commanded.   1:13; 8:31, 33; 11:12
     22:2, 5; *2 Ki* 18:12
which Moses the *s. of the L.* gave.
     Josh 1:15; 12:6; 13:8; 18:7; 22:4
Moses the *s. of the L.* smite.   12:6
s. of L. sent me from Kadesh.   14:7
Joshua son of Nun the *s. of the L.*
died.   24:29; *Judg* 2:8
blood of all the *s. of the L. 2 Ki* 9:7
here none of the *s. of the L.*   10:23
Moses *s. of the L.* made. *2 Chr* 1:3
to commandment of Moses the *s. of*
the L.   24:6
praise the Lord, praise, O ye *s. of the*
L.   *Ps* 113:1; 135:1
bless Lord, O all ye *s. of L.*   134:1
blind or deaf as the *L.'s s. Isa* 42:19
heritage of the *s. of the L.*   54:17
and the *s. of the L.* must not strive.
     2 Tim 2:24

sight of the Lord

Er was wicked in *s. of L.* and he slew
him.   *Gen* 38:7
been accepted in *s. of L. Lev* 10:19
do that which is good in *s. of L.*
     Deut 6:18; 12:28
do what is right in *s. of the L.* 12:25
21:9; *2 Ki* 12:2; 14:3; 15:3, 24
18:3; 22:2; *2 Chr* 20:32; 24:2
25:2; 26:4; 27:2; 29:2; 34:2
wickedness is great ye have done in
the *s. of L.*   *1 Sam* 12:17
     1 Ki 21:25; *2 Ki* 21:6
a light thing in *s. of L.*   *2 Ki* 3:18
did not what was right in *s. of L.* 16:2
     2 Chr 28:1
precious in *s. of L.* is death of his
saints.   *Ps* 116:15
that doeth evil, is good in *s. of L.*
     Mal 2:17
great in *the s. of the L. Luke* 1:15
not only in *s. of the L. 2 Cor* 8:21

humble yourselves in the *s. of the L.*
     Jas 4:10

see evil

Spirit of the Lord

S. of L. came on Othniel. *Judg* 3:10
S. of L. came on Gideon.   6:34
S of L. came on Jephtha.   11:29
S. of L. began to move Samson.
     13:25; 14:6, 19; 15:14
S. of L. will come on Saul.
     1 Sam 10:6
S. of L. came upon David.   16:13
S. of L. departed from.   14
S. of L. spake by me.   *2 Sam* 23:2
S. of L. shall carry thee. *1 Ki* 18:12
went *S. of the L.* from me to speak
unto?   22:24; *2 Chr* 18:23
S. of the L. hath taken.   *2 Ki* 2:16
Jahaziel came *S. of L. 2 Chr* 20:14
S. of L. shall rest upon.   *Isa* 11:2
S. of L. bloweth upon it.   40:7
who hath directed *S. of L.?*   13
the *S. of L.* shall lift.   59:19
S. of L. is upon me, because the.
     61:1; *Luke* 4:18
S. of L. caused him to rest. *Isa* 63:14
carried in *S. of L.*   *Ezek* 11:5
     37:1
house of Jacob, is the *S. of L.? Mi* 2:7
full of power by the *S. of L.*   3:8
agreed to tempt *S. of L.*   *Acts* 5:9
the *S. of L.* caught away Philip. 8:39
where the *S. of L.* is, there is liberty.
     2 Cor 3:17
glory, even as by the *S. of L.*   18

temple of the Lord

by a post of the *t. of L.*   *1 Sam* 1:9
lamp of God went out in the *t. of the*
L.   3:3
people into *t. of L.*   *2 Ki* 11:13
gold off from doors of *t. of L.* 18:16
bring out of the *t. of L.* vessels. 23:4
Solomon had made in *t. of L.* 24:13
Uzziah went into *t. of L. 2 Chr* 26:16
not into the *t. of L.*   27:2
uncleanness found in *t. of L.* 29:16
foundation of the *t. of L. Ezra* 3:6
laid foundation of *t. of L.*   10
The *t. of L.,* The *t. of L. Jer* 7:4
were set before the *t. of the L.* 24:1
t. of L. were 25 men, with their backs
toward *t. of L.* and. *Ezek* 8:16
stone was laid in *t. of L. Hag* 2:15
and he shall build the *t. of the L.*
     Zech 6:12; 13:15
for a memorial in *t. of L.*   6:14
Zacharias went into *t. of L. Luke* 1:9

voice of the Lord

and obey *v. of L.*   *Deut* 30:8
     Jer 26:13; 38:20
obeyed not the *v. of L.*   *Josh* 5:6
     1 Sam 28:18; *1 Ki* 20:36; *Jer* 3:25
     7:28; 42:13, 21; 43:4, 7; 44:23
     Dan 9:10
thou not obey *v. of L.? 1 Sam* 15:19
yea, I have obeyed the *v. of the L.* 20
in obeying the *v. of the L.*   22
the *v. of the L.* is upon.   *Ps* 29:3
the *v. of the L.* is powerful.   4
the *v. of the L.* divideth the.   7
v. of L. shaketh the wilderness.   8
v. of the L. maketh the hinds.   9
not to the *v. of the L.*   106:25
I heard the *v. of the L.*   *Isa* 6:8
v. of the L. shall Assyrians.   30:31
a *v. of the L.* that rendereth   66:6
v. of the L. our God that it may be
well . . . obey the *v. of L. Jer* 42:6
the *L.'s v.* crieth unto the.   *Mi* 6:9
people obeyed *v. of the L. Hag* 1:12
diligently obey the *v. of L. Zech* 6:15
v. of L. came to Moses. *Acts* 7:31

way of the Lord

command his household to keep *w.*
of L.   *Gen* 18:19
will keep the *w. of L. Judg* 2:22
Amon walked not in the *w. of L.*
     2 Ki 21:22
who walk in *w. of the L.* *Ps* 119:1
w. of the L. is strength.   *Pr* 10:29
prepare ye *w. of the L.*   *Isa* 40:3
     Mat 3:3; *Mark* 1:3; *Luke* 3:4

know not *way of the L.*   *Jer* 5:4
they have known *way of the L.*   5
the *w. of the L.* is not equal.
     Ezek 18:25, 29; 33:17, 20
make straight *way of L. John* 1:23
instructed in *w. of L.*   *Acts* 18:25

ways of the Lord

for I have kept the *w. of L.*
     2 Sam 22:22; *Ps* 18:21
lifted up in *w. of L.*   *2 Chr* 17:6
sing in the *w. of the L.*   *Ps* 138:5
the *w. of the L.* are right. *Hos* 14:9
cease to pervert the right *w. of the*
L.   *Acts* 13:10

word of the Lord

feared the *w. of the L.*   *Ex* 9:20
regarded not the *w. of the L.* left. 21
according to *w. of the L. Num* 3:16
51; 4:45; 36:5; *Deut* 34:5
Josh 8:27; 19:50; 22:9; *1 Ki* 12:24
13:26; 14:18; 16:12, 34; 17:5, 16
22:38; *2 Ki* 1:17; 4:44; 7:16
     9:26; 14:25
he hath despised the *w. of the L.*
     Num 15:31
beyond the *w. of L.* my God. 22:18
to shew you the *w. of L. Deut* 5:5
w. of L. was precious.   *1 Sam* 3:1
w. of the L. yet revealed to.   7
hast rejected the *w. of the L.* 15:23, 26
the *w. of L.* is tried.   *2 Sam* 22:31
     Ps 18:30
might fulfil *w. of the L.*   *1 Ki* 2:27
     2 Chr 36:21
to the *w. of the L.* and returned.
     1 Ki 12:24; *2 Chr* 11:4; *Jer* 37:2
a man of God by *w. of L. 1 Ki* 13:1
the altar in the *w. of the L.*   2
man of God had given by *w. of L.* 5
charged me by *w. of L.* saying.   9
angel spake by *w. of L.* saying.   18
disobedient unto the *w. of L.*   26
he cried by the *w. of the L.*   32
according to the *w. of L.*   14:18
w. of the L. in my mouth.   17:24
prophet said, in *w. of L.,* Smite.
     20:35
enquire, I pray thee, at *w. of L.*
     22:5; *2 Chr* 18:4
Jehoshaphat said, *W. of L. 2 Ki* 3:12
this is *w. of L.*   9:36
nothing of the *w. of the L.* fall. 10:10
this was the *w. of L.*   15:12
good is the *w. of L.* 20:19; *Isa* 39:8
according to *w. of L.*   *2 Ki* 23:16
24:2; *1 Chr* 11:3, 10; 12:23
15:15; *Jer* 13:2; 32:8; *Jonah* 3:3
against *w. of the L.*   *1 Chr* 10:13
of king by *w. of L.*   *2 Chr* 30:12
not kept the *w. of the L.*   34:21
that *w. of L.* might be accomplished.
     36:22; *Ezra* 1:1
for the *w. of L.* is right.   *Ps* 33:4
by *w. of L.* were heavens made.   6
word came, the *w. of L.*   105:19
and the *w. of L.* from Jerusalem.
     Isa 2:3; *Mi* 4:2
the *w. of L.* was to them.   28:13
see ye the *word of the L.* *Jer* 2:31
w. of the L. is to them a reproach.
     6:10; 20:8
have rejected the *w. of L.*   8:9
to me, Where is the *w. of L.?* 17:15
to this day the *w. of L.* hath.   25:3
if the *w. of L.* be with them.   27:18
that this was the *word of the L.* 32:8
the *w. of L.* that came to Hosea.
     Hos 1:2
wander to seek *w. of L. Amos* 8:12
w. of L. is against you.   *Zeph* 2:5
this is *w. of the L.* to Zerubbabel.
     Zech 4:6
w. of the L. in the land of Hadrach.
     9:1; 12:1; *Mal* 1:1
poor of the flock knew that it was *w.*
of L.   *Zech* 11:11
Peter remembered *w. of L.*
     Luke 22:61; *Acts* 11:16
preached the *w. of L.*   *Acts* 8:25
     13:49; 15:35, 36; 16:32
glorified the *w. of the L.*   13:48
heard the *w. of the L.* Jesus. 19:10

sounded out the *w. of L. 1 Thes* 1:8
say to you by the *w. of the L.* 4:15
pray that the *w. of the L.* may have
　free course. *2 Thes* 3:1
w. of L. endureth for. *1 Pet* 1:25
　words of the Lord
Moses told people all *w. of L.*
　Ex 24:3; *Num* 11:24
Moses wrote all the *w. of L.* and.
　Ex 24:4
heard all the *w. of the L. Josh* 24:27
told people *w. of the L. 1 Sam* 8:10
the voice of the *w. of the L.* 15:1
came by *w. of L.* to cleanse the.
　2 Chr 29:15
w. of the L. are pure. *Ps* 12:6
Baruch wrote all *w. of L. Jer* 36:4
roll thou hast written *w. of L.* 6, 8
of the book all the *w. of the L.* 11
hearing the *w. of the L. Amos* 8:11
　see **came, hear**
　work of the Lord
see the *w. of the L.* *Ex* 34:10
regard not the *w. of L.* *Isa* 5:12
cursed that doeth the *w. of L.*
　Jer 48:10
this is the *w. of L.* 50:25
declare the *w. of L.* 51:10
abounding in the *w. of the L.*
　1 Cor 15:58
he worketh the *w. of the L.* 16:10
　works of the Lord
known all the *w. of the L. Josh* 24:31
seen all the great *w. of the L.*
　Judg 2:7
regard not the *w. of the L. Ps* 28:5
come, behold the *w. of the L.* 46:8
I will remember the *w. of the L.* 77:11
these see the *w. of the L.* 107:24
the *w. of L.* are great. 111:2
declare *w. of L.* 118:17
　wrath of the Lord
w. of L. was kindled. *Num* 11:33
the *L.'s w.* be kindled. *Deut* 11:17
for great is the *w. of L. 2 Ki* 22:13
　2 Chr 34:21
the *w. of L.* turned. *2 Chr* 12:12
the *w. of L.* was upon Judah. 29:8
so that the *w. of the L.* 32:26
until *w. of the L.* arose. *Ps* 106:40
was *w. of the L.* kindled. *Ps* 106:40
through the *w. of the L. Isa* 9:19
remove in the *w. of the L.* 9:19
because of *w. of the L. Jer* 50:13
gold shall not be able to . . . day of *w.*
　of the L. Ezek 7:19; *Zeph* 1:18
　see **praise**
　Lord *said*
L. said in his heart. *Gen* 8:21
he hearkened not as the *L. said.*
　Ex 7:13; 22; 8:15, 19; *Deut* 9:3
　Judg 2:15; 6:27
is that which the *L. said. Ex* 16:23
all the words the *L. said.* 24:3
all *L. said* we will do. 7; *Num* 32:31
place of which *L. said. Num* 10:29
as the *L. said* to him by the. 16:40
for the *L.* had said, They shall. 26:65
as the *L.* hath said. *Deut* 31:3
　Josh 14:12; *Joel* 2:32
all the *L. said* to Moses. *Josh* 11:23
thing that the *L. said.* 14:6
what is the thing that *L. said* to thee ?
　1 Sam 3:17
tell thee what the *L. said.* 15:16
day of which the *L. said* to thee. 24:4
because the *L.* said to him, Curse
　David. *2 Sam* 16:10
L. said he would dwell. *1 Ki* 8:12
　2 Chr 6:1
nations, concerning which *L. said* to
　Israel. *1 Ki* 11:2
L. said not that he would blot out.
　2 Ki 14:27
whereof the *L.* had said, Ye. 17:12
which *L.* said in Jerusalem. 21:4, 7
　2 Chr 33:4
Solomon had made in temple as the
　L. said. *2 Ki* 24:13
the *L.* hath said unto me. *Ps* 2:7
the *L.* said unto my Lord. 110:1
　Mat 22:44; *Mark* 12:36
　Luke 20:42; *Acts* 2:34

then *said* the *L.* *Isa* 7:3; 8:3
　Ezek 44:2; *Hos* 3:1; *Jonah* 4:10
　Luke 20:13
for so *L.* said unto me, I. *Isa* 18:4
thus hath *L.* said unto me. 21:16
　Jer 4:27; 6:6
L. said, Forasmuch. *Isa* 29:13
rest, I the *L.* have said. *Ezek* 21:17
said the *L.* in a vision. *Acts* 9:10
the word of *L.* how he said. 11:16

　saith the **Lord**
thus *saith* the *L.* *Ex* 4:22; 5:1
　7:17; *1 Sam* 2:27; *2 Sam* 12:11
　24:12
what the *L. saith,* that will I speak.
　Num 24:13
thus *saith* the *L.* God of. *Josh* 7:13
　24:2; *Judg* 6:8; *2 Sam* 12:7
but now the *L. saith,* Be it far from
　me. *1 Sam* 2:30
saith L. of hosts. 15:2; *2 Sam* 7:8
　1 Chr 17:7; *Jer* 6:9; 7:3, 21
L. saith, that will I speak. *1 Ki* 22:14
not be purged, *saith* the *L. Isa* 22:14
　Jer 5:14; 35:17; 49:5; 50:31
now will I rise, *saith* the *L.*; now
　will I be exalted. *Isa* 33:10
　Ps 12:5
now *saith* the *L.* that formed me.
　Isa 49:5
saith the *L.* that hath mercy. 54:10
for I am with thee, *saith* the *L.*
　Jer 1:8. 19; 30:11
fear is not in thee, *saith* the *L.* 2:19
yet return unto me, *saith* the *L.* 3:1
if thou wilt return, *saith* the *L.* 4:1
fear ye not me, *saith L.* 5:22
I have seen it, *saith L.* 7:11
evil, they know not me, *saith* the *L.*
　9:3
to know me ? *saith* the *L.* 22:16
I a God at hand, *saith* the *L.*? 23:23
I shall not see him, *saith* the *L.* 24
even forsake you, *saith* the *L.* 33
not sent him, *saith* the *L.* 27:15
not sent them, *saith* the *L.* 29:9
L. saith and the Lord hath not sent
　them. *Ezek* 13:6, 7
I am against you, *saith L.* 8
thus it was, *saith L.* 16:19
be no more, *saith* the *L.* God. 21:13
and I am your God *saith L.* 34:31
it is done, *saith* the *L.* God. 39:8
accept you, *saith* the *L.* God. 43:27
is it not even thus, O Israel ? *saith*
　the *L.* *Amos* 2:11
this liketh you, *saith* the *L.* 4:5
shall not be, *saith L.* 7:3
called by my name, *saith L.* 9:12
the *L. saith,* Arise thou. *Mi* 6:1
behold, I am against thee, *saith* the
　L. *Nah* 2:13; 3:5
wait ye upon me, *saith L. Zeph* 3:8
why ? *saith L.* of hosts. *Hag* 1:9
I am with you, *saith L.* 13
for I, *saith* the *L.* will be. *Zech* 2:5
but by my Spirit, *saith* the *L.* 4:6
loved you, *saith* the *L.* *Mal* 1:2
this of your hand, *saith* the *L.* 13
great King, *saith* the *L.* of hosts. 14
fear not me, *saith* the *L. of.* 3:5
now herewith, *saith* the *L. of.* 10
shall be mine, *saith* the *L. of.* 17
shall do this, *saith* the *L. of.* 4:3
saith the *L.* who doeth. *Acts* 15:17
I will repay, *saith* the *L. Rom* 12:19
hear me for all this, *saith* the *L.*
　1 Cor 14:21
ye separate, *saith* the *L. 2 Cor* 6:17
regarded them not, *saith* the *L.*
　Heb 8:9
I will recompense, *saith* the *L.* 10:30
and the ending, *saith* the *L. Rev* 1:8
　see **live, saved**

　Lord joined with *seek*
thence thou shalt *seek L. Deut* 4:29
heart rejoice, that *seek L.*
　1 Chr 16:10; *Ps* 105:3
seek the *L.* and his strength.
　1 Chr 16:11; *Ps* 105:4
set your heart to *seek* the *L.*
　1 Chr 22:19; *2 Chr* 11:16

his heart to *seek* the *L. 2 Chr* 12:14
Judah to *seek* the *L.* God. 14:4
a covenant to *seek* the *L.* 15:12
would not *seek* the *L.* God. 13
set himself to *seek* the *L.* 20:3
Judah they came to *seek L.* 4
were come to *seek* the *L. Ezra* 6:21
praise the *L.* that *seek. Ps* 22:26
they that *seek* the *L.* shall not want
　any good. 34:10
that *seek L.* understand. *Pr* 28:5
neither do they *seek L. Isa* 9:13
　31:1; *Hos* 7:10
ye that *seek* the *L.* look to. *Isa* 51:1
seek ye *L.* while he may be. 55:6
shall go and *seek* the *L. Jer* 50:4
return and *seek* the *L. Hos* 3:5
with their herds to *seek* the *L.* 5:6
to *seek* the *L.* till he come. 10:12
seek the *L.* and ye shall live, lest.
　Amos 5:6
seek ye the *L.* all ye meek. *Zeph* 2:3
go to *seek* the *L.* of hosts. *Zech* 8:21
people shall come to *seek* the *L.* 22
the *L.* whom ye *seek* shall suddenly
　come. *Mal* 3:1
of men might *seek* the *L. Acts* 15:17
seek the *L.* if haply they might. 17:27

　Lord joined with *sent*
the *L. sent* him forth from the gar-
　den. *Gen* 3:23
the *L. sent* us to destroy it. 19:13
words of *L.* who had *sent. Ex* 4:28
L. God of the Hebrews *sent.* 7:16
and *L. sent* thunder and hail. 9:23
that the *L.* hath *sent* me. *Num* 16:28
death, then *L.* hath not *sent.* 29
cried, the *L. sent* an angel. 20:16
the *L. sent* fiery serpents. 21:6
L. sent you from Kadesh-barnea.
　Deut 9:23
wonders which the *L. sent.* 34:11
the *L. sent* a prophet. *Judg* 6:8
then the *L. sent* Moses. *1 Sam* 12:8
and the *L. sent* Jerubbaal. 11
the *L. sent* thunder. 18
L. sent me to anoint thee. 15:1
the *L. sent* thee on a journey. 18
way which the *L. sent* me. 20
the *L.* hath *sent* thee away. 20:22
L. sent Nathan to David. *2 Sam* 12:1
L. sent pestilence on Israel. 24:15
　1 Chr 21:14
tarry, for the *L.* hath *sent* me to
　Beth-el. *2 Ki* 2:2
L. hath *sent* me to Jericho. 4
L. sent me to Jordan. 6
therefore the *L. sent* lions. 17:25
the *L. sent* against him bands. 24:2
the *L. sent* an angel. *2 Chr* 32:21
L. sent a word into Jacob. *Isa* 9:8
L. sent him to prophesy. *Jer* 19:14
L. hath *sent* to you all his servants.
　25:4
drink to whom the *L.* had *sent* me. 17
L. sent me to prophesy. 26:12, 15
L. hath truly *sent* him. 28:9
the *L.* hath not *sent* thee. 15
L. hath not *sent* them. *Ezek* 13:6
the *L. sent* out a great wind into.
　Jonah 1:4
L. their God had *sent* him. *Hag* 1:12
L. hath *sent* to walk to. *Zech* 1:10
know *L.* of hosts hath *sent* me 2:9
　11; 4:9; 6:15
words which *L.* hath *sent.* 7:12
Saul, the *L.* Jesus hath *sent* me.
　Acts 9:17
the *L.* hath *sent* his angel. 12:11

　serve the **Lord**
let the men go, that they may *serve*
　the *L.* their God. *Ex* 10:7
Pharaoh said, Go *serve* the *L.* your
　God. 8; 11:24; 12:31
take to *serve* the *L.* our God . . . until
　what we must *serve* the *L.* 10:26
ye shall *serve* the *L.* your. 23:25
to *serve* the *L.* thy God. *Deut* 10:12
fear and *serve* the *L.* *Josh* 24:14
seem evil unto you to *serve* the *L.* 15
will we *serve* the *L.*; he is our God.
　18, 21, 24
Joshua said, Ye cannot *serve L.* 19

ye have chosen you the *L.* to *serve*
him. *Josh* 24:22
serve the L. with all your heart.
1 Sam 12:20
if the Lord shall bring me again, then
will I *serve the L.* *2 Sam* 15:8
but yield, and *serve the L.* your God.
2 Chr 30:8; 35:3
Judah to *serve the L.* 33:16; 34:33
serve the L. with fear. *Ps* 2:11
serve the L. with gladness. 100:2
gathered to *serve the L.* 102:22
for ye *serve the L.* Christ. *Col* 3:24

Lord *spake*
name of *L.* that *spake* to. *Gen* 16:13
L. spake, saying, I will. *Lev* 10:3
in the day the *L. spake* with Moses.
Num 3:1; 9:1
as the *L. spake* unto Moses. 5:4
whereof *L. spake* to Moses. 21:16
L. spake to you out of the midst of
fire. *Deut* 4:12
similitude in the day the *L. spake.* 15
these words the *L. spake* to. 5:22
the words which the *L. spake.* 9:10
commandments which *L. spake.* 10:4
the *L. spake* this word to. *Josh* 14:10
this mountain whereof *L. spake.* 12
Samuel did that which the *L. spake.*
1 Sam 16:4
L. may continue his word which he
spake. *1 Ki* 2:4
word of the *L.* which he *spake.* 2:27
as the *L. spake* to David my. 5:5
L. hath performed word he *spake.*
8:20; *2 Ki* 10:10
perform his saying, which the *L.
spake.* *1 Ki* 12:15; *2 Chr* 10:15
to the word of the *L.* which he *spake.*
1 Ki 13:26; 14:18; 16:12, 34
17:16; 22:38; *2 Ki* 10:10; 24:2
the *L.* which he *spake* by his servant
Ahijah. *1 Ki* 15:29; *2 Ki* 10:17
spake the L. saying, The dogs shall
eat Jezebel. *1 Ki* 21:23
word of *L.* which he *spake.*
2 Ki 9:36
L. which he *spake* to Jehu. 15:12
L. spake by his servants. 21:10
L. spake unto Gad. *1 Chr* 21:9
L. spake to Manasseh. *2 Chr* 33:10
moreover, the *L. spake.* *Isa* 7:10
L. spake also unto me again. 8:5
for the *L. spake* thus to me with. 11
time *spake* the *L.* by Isaiah. 20:2
words that the *L. spake.* *Jer* 30:4
the word that the *L. spake.* 50:1
L. hath done that which he *spake.*
51:12
L. spake unto the fish. *Jonah* 2:10
then *spake* the *L.* to Paul. *Acts* 18:9

Lord joined with *spoken*
Abram departed as *L.* had *spoken.*
Gen 12:4; 21:1; 24:51; *Ex* 9:12
35; *Deut* 6:19
words the *L.* had *spoken.* *Ex* 4:30
all that the *L.* hath *spoken.* 19:8
gave in commandment all that the *L.*
had *spoken.* 34:32
statutes *L.* hath *spoken.* *Lev* 10:11
for *L.* had *spoken* to Moses, saying.
Num 1:48; 15:22
the *L.* hath *spoken* good. 10:29
hath the *L.* indeed *spoken* only by
Moses? 12:2
what hath the *L. spoken*? 23:17
L. hath not *spoken.* *Deut* 18:21, 22
failed not aught which *L.* had *spoken.*
Josh 21:45
L. have done the good he hath
spoken. *1 Sam* 25:30
now then do it, for the *L.* hath
spoken. *2 Sam* 3:18
for thou, O *L.* hath *spoken* it. 7:29
sign which *L.* hath *spoken.* *1 Ki* 13:3
for the *L.* hath *spoken* it. 14:11
Isa 21:17; 22:25; 24:3; 25:8
Joel 3:8; *Ob* 18
after the *L.* had *spoken* these words
to Job. *Job* 42:7
the *L.* hath *spoken,* and called the
earth. *Ps* 50:1

for thus hath the *L. spoken* to me.
Isa 31:4
L. will do this thing that he hath
spoken. 38:7
mouth of *L.* hath *spoken.* *Jer* 9:12
proud, for the *L.* hath *spoken.* 13:15
say, What hath *L. spoken*? 23:35, 37
L. hath *spoken* against nation. 27:13
destroyed, as *L.* hath *spoken.* 48:8
I the *L.* have *spoken* it. *Ezek* 5:13
15, 17; 17:21, 24; 21:32; 22:14
24:14; 26:14; 30:12; 34:24
36:36; 37:14
when the *L.* hath not *spoken.* 22:28
for I have *spoken* it, saith *L.*
26:5; 28:10; 39:5
hear this word that the *L.* hath
spoken. *Amos* 3:1
the *L.* God hath *spoken,* who? 8
L. of hosts hath *spoken* it. *Mi* 4:4
fulfilled which was *spoken* of the *L.*
Mat 1:22; 2:15
so then after the *L.* had *spoken* to
them. *Mark* 16:19
had seen the *L.* and that he had
spoken. *Acts* 9:27
at the first began to be *spoken* by the
L. *Heb* 2:3

to or *unto the* **Lord**
I have lift up my hands *to L.* most
high. *Gen* 14:22
I have taken on me to speak *to the L.*
18:27, 31
let us go, and do sacrifice *to L.*
Ex 5:17; 8:8, 29
we must hold a feast *to L.* 10:9
12:14; *Num* 29:12
sing *to the L. Ex* 15:1, 21; *Judg* 5:3
1 Chr 16:23; *Ps* 13:6; 30:4; 68:32
95:1; 96:1, 2; 98:1, 5; 104:33
147:7; 149:1; *Isa* 12:5; 42:10
Jer 20:13
for to-day is a sabbath *to the L.*
Ex 16:25; 35:2; *Lev* 25:2
sacrificeth save *unto the L. Ex* 22:20
holy *unto the L.* 30:10; 31:15
Lev 23:20; 27:21, 30, 32
Num 6:8; *Ezra* 8:28
We have sinned; pray *unto L.*
Num 21:7; *Jer* 29:7; *Acts* 8:24
do *to the L.* in feasts. *Num* 29:39
not do so *to the L.* thy. *Deut* 12:31
I have opened my mouth *to the L.*
Judg 11:35, 36
dedicated the silver *to the L.* 17:3
not up *to the L.* to Mizpeh. 21:8
Hannah prayed *to the L. 1 Sam* 1:10
and he prayed *to the L.* 8:6
is no restraint *to the L.* 14:6
hang them up *to the L. 2 Sam* 21:6
being priest *to the L.* *1 Ki* 2:27
Elisha shut door, prayed *to the L.*
2 Ki 4:33; 6:18
Hezekiah clave *to the L.* 18:6
unto the wall, and prayed *to L.* 20:2
2 Chr 32:24; *Isa* 37:15; 38:2
passover holden *to the L. 2 Ki* 23:23
but poured it out *to L. 1 Chr* 11:18
give thanks *to L.,* call upon his name.
16:8, 41; *Ps* 92:1
burn *to L.* morning and. *2 Chr* 13:11
bring *to the L.* the collection. 24:9
but yield yourselves *to the L.* 30:8
salvation belongeth *to the L. Ps* 3:8
they cried *unto the L.* 18:41
and *to the L.* I made. 30:8; 142:1
compared *to L.* be likened *to L.?*
89:6
shall I render *to the L.* for? 116:12
I said *to the L.* Thou art my. 140:6
abomination *to the L.* *Pr* 3:32
11:1, 20; 12:22; 15:8, 9, 26; 16:5
17:15; 20:10, 23
commit thy works *to L.* 16:3
giveth to poor lendeth *to L.* 19:17
vow a vow *to the L.* *Isa* 19:21
even *to the L.* and he shall heal. 22
shall be holiness *to L.* 23:18
Jer 2:3; *Zech* 14:20
to the L. for a name. *Isa* 55:13
joined himself *to the L.* 56:3, 6
acceptable day *to the L.* 58:5
Jeremiah prayed *to the L. Jer* 32:16

to take heed *to the L.* *Hos* 4:10
Jonah prayed *to the L.* *Jonah* 4:2
their gain *unto the L.* and their substance *unto the L.* of. *Mi* 4:13
therefore I will look *to the L.* I. 7:7
shall be known *to the L.* *Zech* 14:7
but shalt perform *to the L.* *Mat* 5:33
to present him *to the L.* *Luke* 2:22
shall be called holy *to the L.* 23
the more added *to the L. Acts* 5:14
they would cleave *to the L.* 11:23
they ministered *unto the L.* 13:2
commended them *to the L.* 14:23
judged me faithful *to the L.* 16:15
eateth, eateth *to the L.* *Rom* 14:6
live *to the L.*; we die *to the L.* 8
their own selves *to the L. 2 Cor* 8:5
is acceptable *to the L.* *Eph* 5:10
submit yourselves, as *to the L.* 22
6:7; *Col* 3:23

see **cry, cried, give, turn**

lord, as applied to *man*
after I am old, my *l.* *Gen* 18:12
nay, my *l.* hear me. 23:11
my *l.* hearken to me. 15
Drink, my *l.*; and she hasted. 24:18
be *l.* over thy brethren, let. 27:29
I have made him thy *l.* 37
let it not displease my *l.* 31:35
shall ye speak to my *l.* Esau. 32:4
I have sent to tell my *l.* that I. 5
it is a present sent to my *l.* Esau. 18
his garment, until his *l.* 39:16*
had offended their *l.* the king. 40:1
nay, my *l.* but to buy food. 42:10
who is the *l.* of the land. 30, 33
is not this it, in which my *l.?* 44:5
should we steal out of thy *l.'s* house.8
will be my *l.'s* bondmen. 9
we told him the words of my *l.* 24
and he hath made me *l.* of all. 45:8
God hath made me *l.* of all. 9
my *l.* how that there is nothing left
in sight of my *l.* but our. 47:18
anger of my *l.* wax hot. *Ex* 32:22
and said, My *l.* Moses. *Num* 11:28
my *l.* I beseech thee, lay not. 12:11
as my *l.* commandeth. 32:25, 27
the Lord commanded my *l.* 36:2
their *l.* was fallen down. *Judg* 3:25
Turn in, my *l.,* turn in to me. 4:18
fell down where her *l.* was. 19:26
and her *l.* rose up in morning. 27
favour in thy sight, my *l. Ruth* 2:13
l. I am of a sorrowful. *1 Sam* 1:15
O my *l.* as thy soul liveth, my *l.* 26
here I am, my *l.* 22:12
Saul, saying, My *l.* the king. 24:8
on me, my *l.* on me let this. 25:24
let not my *l.* regard this man. 25
seek evil to my *l.* be as Nabal. 26
young men that follow my *l.* 27
shall have dealt with my *l.* 31
not kept thy *l.* the king? 26:15
David said, It is my voice, my *l.* 17
why doth my *l.* thus pursue after? 18
fight against enemies of my *l.* 29:8
them hither to my *l.* *2 Sam* 1:10
I will gather all Israel to my *l.* 3:21
according to all that my *l.* hath. 9:11
Uriah slept with all the servants of
his *l.* 11:9, 13
let not my *l.* suppose they. 13:32
handmaid speak to my *l.* 14:12
angel of God, so is my *l.* 17
none can turn from aught my *l.* 19
l. is wise according to wisdom. 20
dead dog curse my *l.* the king. 16:9
Cushi said, Tidings, my *l.* 18:31
let not my *l.* impute iniquity to me,
the day my *l.* the king. 19:19
first to go down to meet my *l.* 20
my *l.* is come again in peace. 30
be a burden to my *l.* 35
go over with my *l.* 37
take thou thy *l.'s* servants, and. 20:6
my *l.* the king may see it, but why
doth my *l.* delight in? 24:3
let my *l.* take and offer what. 22
that my *l.* the king may. *1 Ki* 1:2
thing done by my *l.* the king? 27
the Lord God of my *l.* the king. 36
the Lord hath been with my *l.* 37

as my *l.* the king hath said. *1 Ki* 2:38
O my *l.* I and this woman. 3:17
O my *l.* give her the living child. 26
fled from his *l.* Hadadezer. 11:23
art thou that my *l.* Elijah ? 18:7
was it not told my *l.* what I did ? 13
Go tell thy *l.* Behold Elijah is. 14
my *l.* I am thine, and all. 20:4
tell my *l.* all thou didst send for. 9
pleasant as my *l.* seeth. *2 Ki* 2:19
nay, my *l.* do not lie to thine. 4:16
did I desire a son of my *l.?* 28
would God my *l.* were with the. 5:3
went in and told his *l.* saying. 4
servants said, None, my *l.* 6:12
saying, Help, my *l.* O king. 26
then a *l.* on whose hand. 7:2*, 17*
my *l.* O king, this is the woman. 8:5
said, Why weepeth my *l.?* 12
forth to the servants of his *l.* 9:11
thee, give pledges to my *l.* 18:23*
cunning men of my *l.* *2 Chr* 2:14
the counsel of my *l.* *Ezra* 10:3
our own, who is *l.* over us ? *Ps* 12:4
Ah *l.*, or Ah his glory. *Jer* 22:18; 34:5
now, I pray thee, my *l.* 37:20
my *l.* the king, these men. 38:9
I fear my *l.* the king. *Dan* 1:10
is no king nor *l.* that asked. 2:10
my *l.* the dream be to them. 4:19
decree which is come upon my *l.* 24
servant above his *l.* *Mat* 10:24
that the servant be as his *l.* 25
L., have patience with me. 18:26
they came and told their *l.* all. 31
my *l.* delayeth his coming. 24:48
Luke 12:45
his *l.* said unto him, Well done.
Mat 25:21, 23
men that wait for their *l.* *Luke* 12:36
that servant shewed his *l.* 14:21
my *l.* taketh away from me. 16:3
and he said to the first, How much
owest thou unto my *l.?* 5
not what his *l.* doeth. *John* 15:15
servant is not greater than his *l.* 20
thing to write to my *l.* *Acts* 25:26
a servant, though *l.* of all. *Gal* 4:1
Abraham, calling him *l.* *1 Pet* 3:6

lords
Behold now, my *l.*, turn in. *Gen* 19:2
consumed *l.* of high places of Arnon.
Num 21:28
is Lord of *l.* *Deut* 10:17
1 Tim 6:15; *Rev* 17:14
five *l.* of the Philistines. *Josh* 13:3
Judg 3:3
l. of the Philistines. *Judg* 16:5
and the house fell upon the *l.* 30
they gathered *l.* of the Philistines.
1 Sam 5:8, 11
plague on you all, and on your *l.* 6:4
l. of the Philistines went after 12
l. of the Philistines went up. 7:7
the *l.* passed on by hundreds. 29:2
nevertheless, the *l.* favour thee not. 6
that thou displease not the *l.* 7
offerings which *l.* offered. *Ezra* 8:25*
the *l.* of the heathen. *Isa* 16:8
other *l.* have had dominion. 26:13
say my people, We are *l.? Jer* 2:31*
great *l.* renowned, all. *Ezek* 23:23*
my counsellors and I. *Dan* 4:36
feast to a thousand of his *l.* 5:1
thy *l.* have drunk wine in them. 23
with his own signet and of his *l.* 6:17
made a supper to his *l.* *Mark* 6:21
gods many, and *l.* many. *1 Cor* 8:5
nor as being *l.* over God's. *1 Pet* 5:3

lordship
kings of Gentiles exercise *l.*
Mark 10:42; *Luke* 22:25

Lo-ruhamah
God said, Call her name *L. Hos* 1:6
weaned *L.* she conceived and. 8

lose
run on thee, and thou *l. Judg* 18:25
mules alive, that we *l.* *1 Ki* 18:5
caused sorrow to *l.* life. *Job* 31:39
shalt vomit up, and *l.* *Pr* 23:8
to get, and a time to *l.* *Eccl* 3:6
findeth his life shall *l.* it. *Mat* 10:39
16:25; *Mark* 8:35; *Luke* 9:24

he shall in no wise *l.* his reward.
Mat 10:42; *M'rk* 9:41
and *l.* his own soul. *Mat* 16:26*
Mark 8:36*; *Luke* 9:25
if he *l.* one sheep. *Luke* 15:4
if she *l.* one piece. 8
whosoever shall *l.* his life. 17:33
Father's will I should *l. John* 6:39
loveth his life shall *l.* it. 12:25
look to yourselves, we *l.* *2 John* 8

loseth
and he that *l.* his life. *Mat* 10:39

loss
torn, I bare the *l.* of. *Gen* 31:39
pay for the *l.* of time. *Ex* 21:19
nor shall I know the *l. Isa* 47:8
come in one day *l.* of children. 9
gained this harm and *l. Acts* 27:21
there shall be no *l.* of any man's. 22
burned, he shall suffer *l. 1 Cor* 3:15
I counted *l.* for Christ. *Phil* 3:7
and I count all things but *l.* for Christ,
for whom I suffered the *l.* of. 8

lost
for any manner of *l.* thing. *Ex* 22:9
Deut 22:3
found that which was *l.* *Lev* 6:3
restore the *l.* thing he found. 4
the days that were before shall be *l.*
Num 6:12*
with all *l.* thing of thy brother's.
Deut 22:3
asses of Kish, Saul's father, were *l.*
1 Sam 9:3
as for thine asses that were *l.* 20
army like that thou hast *l. 1 Ki* 20:25
astray like a *l.* sheep. *Ps* 119:176
thou hast *l.* the other. *Isa* 49:20*
seeing I have *l.* my children. 21*
people hath been *l.* sheep. *Jer* 50:6
saw that her hope was *l. Ezek* 19:5
sought that which was *l.* 34:4
I will seek that which was *l.* 16
they say, Our hope is *l.*, we. 37:11
if the salt have *l.* his savour.*Mat* 5:13
Mark 9:50; *Luke* 14:34
rather to the *l.* sheep. *Mat* 10:6
not sent but to the *l.* sheep. 15:24
Son of man is come to save that which
was *l.* 18:11; *Luke* 19:10
go after that which is *l. Luke* 15:4
found my sheep which was *l.* 6
found the piece which I had *l.* 9
this my son was *l.* 24
thy brother was *l.* 32
Gather up fragments that nothing
be *l.* *John* 6:12
none of them is *l.* but the. 17:12
them thou gavest me, I have *l.* 18:9
our gospel is hid, to them that are *l.*
2 Cor 4:3*

lot
*Many things were decided in
olden times by casting lots, and the
term was used in rather a figurative
sense in connection with other
things. As examples, lots were
cast,* [1] *To find out a person,*
1 Sam 14:41; *Jonah* 1:7. [2] *To
divide lands,* Num 26:55, 56. [3]
To choose a church officer, Acts
1:26. [4] *To order and regulate
the courses of men in office,* 1 Chr
24:5; 25:8. [5] *To decide a controversy,* Ps 22:8.
one *l.* for Lord, other for scapegoat.
Lev 16:8, 9, 10
land shall be divided by *l.*
Num 26:55; *Ezek* 48:29
divide the land by *l.* *Num* 33:54
36:2; *Josh* 13:6; *Ezek* 47:22
land ye shall inherit by *l. Num* 34:13
Jacob is the *l.* of his. *Deut* 32:9
was the *l.* of the tribe. *Josh* 15:1
the *l.* of Joseph. 16:1
was a *l.* for Manasseh. 17:1
thou given me but one *l.?* 14
thou shalt not have one *l.* only. 17
l. of the tribe of Benjamin. 18:11
and the second *l.* came forth. 19:1
the third *l.* came for the children. 10
fourth *l.* came out to Issachar. 17

fifth *l.* to Asher. *Josh* 19:24
sixth *l.* to Naphtali. 32
seventh *l.* came for tribe of Dan. 40
l. for families of Kohathites. 21:4
1 Chr 6:54
Gershon had by *l.* *Josh* 21:6
gave by *l.* to the Levites. 8
my *l.* to fight against Canaanites,
likewise go . . . into thy *l. Judg* 1:3
we will go up by *l.* against it. 20:9
God, give a perfect *l.* *1 Sam* 14:41
Merari were given by *l.* *1 Chr* 6:63
I give the land of Canaan, the *l.* of.
16:18; *Ps* 105:11
they were divided by *l.* *1 Chr* 24:5
first *l.* came forth to Jehoiarib. 7
first *l.* came forth for Asaph. 25:9
Pur, that is *l.* before. *Esth* 3:7
cup, thou maintainest my *l. Ps* 16:5
shall not rest on the *l.* of the. 125:3
cast in thy *l.* among us. *Pr* 1:14
l. is cast into lap, but disposing. 16:33
l. causeth contentions to cease. 18:18
l. of them that rob us. *Isa* 17:14
and he hath cast the *l.* for. 34:17
stones of the stream are thy *l.* 57:6
this is thy *l.* from me. *Jer* 13:25
bring it out, let no *l.* fall. *Ezek* 24:6
stand in thy *l.* at end. *Dan* 12:13
none that shall cast a cord by *l.*
Mi 2:5
his *l.* was to burn incense. *Luke* 1:9
the *l.* fell on Matthias. *Acts* 1:26
no *l.* or part in this matter. 8:21
their land to them by *l.* 13:19*

Lot
Haran begat *L.* *Gen* 11:27
Terah took *L.* 31
L. went with him. 12:4; 13:1
L. had flocks. 13:5
strife between herdmen of Abram
and *L.* 7
L. chose him all the plain of. 11
they took *L.* prisoner. 14:12
L. sat in the gate of Sodom; *L.* 19:1
pulled *L.* into house. 10
the angels hastened *L.* 15
God sent *L.* out of the midst of. 29
both the daughters of *L.* were. 36
I have given Ar to the children of *L.*
Deut 2:9, 19
holpen the children of *L.* *Ps* 83:8
was in the days of *L.* *Luke* 17:28
remember *L.*'s wife. 32
delivered just *L.* vexed. *2 Pet* 2:7

lothe (loathe)
Egyptians shall *l.* to drink. *Ex* 7:18
I *l.* it, I would not live. *Job* 7:16
l. themselves for evils. *Ezek* 6:9
ye shall *l.* yourselves in your. 20:43
l. yourselves for your iniquities.
36:31

lothed (loathed)
hath thy soul *l.* Zion ? *Jer* 14:19
soul *l.* them, their soul. *Zech* 11:8*

lotheth (loatheth)
soul *l.* this light bread. *Num* 21:5
full soul *l.* an honeycomb. *Pr* 27:7
l. her husband and her. *Ezek* 16:45

lothing (loathing)
wast cast out to the *l.* *Ezek* 16:5*

lothsome (loathsome)
month, till it be *l.* to you. *Num* 11:20
skin is broken and become *l. Job* 7:5
are filled with a *l.* disease. *Ps* 38:7
a wicked man is *l.* and. *Pr* 13:5

lots
cast *l.* between me and Jonathan.
1 Sam 14:42
cast *l.* over against. *1 Chr* 24:31
parted garments, casting *l.*
Mat 27:35; *Mark* 15:24
they gave forth their *l.* *Acts* 1:26
see cast

loud
l. instruments to Lord. *2 Chr* 30:21
people shouted with a *l.* *Ezra* 3:13
the singers sang *l.* with. *Neh* 12:12
cried with a *l.* cry. *Esth* 4:1
play skilfully with a *l.* *Ps* 33:3
make a *l.* noise and rejoice. 98:4*
praise him on *l.* cymbals. 150:5

she is *l.* and stubborn.   *Pr* 7:11*
angel cried with a *l.* cry.   *Rev* 14:18

loud joined with *voice*
I cried with a *l. voice.*   *Gen* 39:14
voice of the trumpet exceeding *l.*
      Ex 19:16
speak with a *l. voice.*   *Deut* 27:14
wept with a *l. voice.*   *2 Sam* 15:23
blessed congregation with a *l. voice.*
      1 Ki 8:55
sware to the Lord with a *l. voice.*
      2 Chr 15:14
to praise Lord with a *l. voice.* 20:19
      Luke 19:37
many wept with a *l. voice. Ezra* 3:12
answered with a *l. voice.*   10:12
his friend with a *l. voice. Pr* 27:14
they cry with a *l. voice. Ezek* 8:18
he cried with a *l. voice,* saying.   9:1
spake out with a *l. voice. Luke* 1:42
unclean spirit cried with a *l. voice.*
      8:28; *Acts* 8:7
back and with a *l. voice. Luke* 17:15
said with a *l. voice,* Stand. *Acts* 14:10
Festus said with a *l. voice.*   26:24
proclaiming with a *l. voice. Rev* 5:2*
with a *l. voice,* Worthy is.   12*
angel saying with a *l. voice,* Woe,
   woe.   8:13*; 14:7*, 9*, 15*
a *l. voice* saying in heaven.   12:10*

loud *voices*
instant with *l.* voices.   *Luke* 23:23

louder
trumpet waxed *l.* and *l.*   *Ex* 19:19

love
*In a number of verses in the
Authorized Version of the New
Testament the word* charity *is
used where the true meaning is*
love. *In the 17th century when the
Bible was translated the word*
charity *had this meaning, which
the French* cher, chère, *from the
same root (Latin,* carus, *dear)
still retains. As charity now often
means something quite different,
both the Revisions substitute for it
the word which expresses the true
idea—*love. *These references are :*
1 Cor 8:1; 13:1, 2, 3, 4, 8, 13; 14:1;
16:14; Col. 3:14; 1 Thes 3:6;
2 Thes 1:3; 1 Tim 1:5; 2:15; 4:12;
2 Tim 2:22; 3:10; 1 Pet 4:8; 5:14;
2 Pet 1:7; 3 John 6; Jude 12;
Rev 2:19. See also Rom 14:15.

a few days for the *l.*   *Gen* 29:20
passing the *l.* of women. *2 Sam* 1:26
greater than the *l.* he had.   13:15
be thou ravished always with her *l.*
      Pr 5:19
let us take our fill of *l.* till.   7:18
hatred stirreth up strifes, but *l.* 10:12
dinner of herbs where *l.* is.   15:17
a transgression seeketh *l.*   17:9
rebuke is better than secret *l.*   27:5
no man knoweth either *l.*   *Eccl* 9:1
also their *l.* and hatred is now.   6
banner over me was *l.*   *S of S* 2:4
apples, for I am sick of *l.*   5; 5:8
thereof being paved with *l.*   3:10
how pleasant art thou, O *l.!*   7:6
l. is strong as death, jealousy.   8:6
many waters cannot quench *l.:* if a
   man would give all . . . for *l.*   7
I remember thee, the *l.*   *Jer* 2:2
trimmest thy way to seek *l.?*   33
loved thee with everlasting *l.*   31:3
time was the time of *l. Ezek* 16:8
corrupt in her inordinate *l.*   23:11*
came to her into bed of *l.*   17
mouth they shew much *l.*   33:31
Daniel into tender *l.*   *Dan* 1:9*
l. of Lord toward Israel.   *Hos* 3:1
I drew them with bands of *l.*   11:4
l. of many shall wax cold. *Mat* 24:12
if ye have *l.* one to.   *John* 13:35
greater *l.* hath no man than.   15:13
l. wherewith thou hast loved. 17:26
who shall separate us from the *l.* of
   Christ ?   *Rom* 8:35
let *l.* be without dissimulation. 12:9
affectioned with brotherly *l.*   10

l. worketh no ill, therefore *l.*
      Rom 13:10
I beseech you for the *l.* of the. 15:30
you may know the *l.*   *2 Cor* 2:4
that ye would confirm your *l.*   8
l. of Christ constraineth us.   5:14
Holy Ghost, by *l.* unfeigned.   6:6
prove the sincerity of your *l.*   8:8
churches the proof of your *l.*   24
and the God of *l.* shall be.   13:11
faith which worketh by *l.*   *Gal* 5:6
but brethren, by *l.* serve one.   13
fruit of the Spirit is *l.,* joy.   22
after I heard of your *l.*   *Eph* 1:15
l. of Christ, passeth knowledge. 3:19
and *l.* with faith, from God.   6:23
that your *l.* may abound.   *Phil* 1:9
other of *l.* doth preach Christ.   17
therefore any comfort of *l.*   2:1
likeminded, having the same *l.*   2
l. which ye have to all the saints.
      Col 1:4
who declared to us your *l.* in.   8
your labour of *l.*   *1 Thes* 1:3
touching brotherly *l.,* ye need.   4:9
breastplate of faith and *l.*   5:8
they received not the *l. 2 Thes* 2:10
abundant with faith and *l. 1 Tim* 1:14
the *l.* of money is the root.   6:10
righteousness, *l.,* patience.   11
not given the spirit of fear, but of *l.*
      2 Tim 1:7
yet for *l.'s* sake I rather beseech
   thee.   *Philem* 9
work and labour of *l.*   *Heb* 6:10
to provoke unto *l.* and to.   10:24
let brotherly *l.* continue.   13:1
to unfeigned *l.* of the.   *1 Pet* 1:22
the *l.* of the Father is. *1 John* 2:15
behold what manner of *l.* the.   3:1
let us love one another, for *l.*   4:7
God is *l.*   8
herein is *l.* not that we loved God. 10
l. that God hath to us; God is *l.* 16
herein is our *l.* made perfect.   17
there is no fear in *l.;* perfect *l.*   18
this is *l.,* that we walk after. *2 John* 6
mercy to you, peace and *l.*   *Jude* 2
hast left thy first *l.*   *Rev* 2:4

love, *verb*
l. thy neighbour as.   *Lev* 19:18, 34
   Mat 19:19; 22:39; *Mark* 12:31
l. the Lord thy God with.   *Deut* 6:5
   10:12; 11:1, 13, 22; 19:9; 30:6
God, which keepeth covenant with
   them that *l.* him.   7:9; *Dan* 9:4
he will *l.* thee, bless thee. *Deut* 7:13
delight in thy fathers to *l.*   10:15
l. therefore the stranger, for ye.   19
know whether ye *l.* the Lord.   13:3
command thee to *l.* Lord thy. 30:16
that thou mayest *l.* the Lord.   20
take heed to *l.* the Lord your God.
      Josh 22:5; 23:11
l. him be as the sun.   *Judg* 5:31
king's servants *l.* thee. *1 Sam* 18:22
shouldest thou *l.* them ? *2 Chr* 19:2
mercy for them that *l.* him. *Neh* 1:5
how long will ye *l.* vanity ?   *Ps* 4:2
let them that *l.* thy name be.   5:11
I will *l.* thee, O Lord my.   18:1
O *l.* the Lord, all ye saints.   31:23
l. thy salvation say.   40:16; 70:4
they that *l.* his name shall.   69:36
ye that *l.* the Lord, hate evil. 97:10
usest to do to those that *l.* 119:132
great peace have they who *l.*   165
shall prosper that *l.* thee.   122:6
preserveth them that *l.* him.   45:20
long, ye simple, will ye *l.?*   *Pr* 1:22
l. wisdom, and she shall keep.   4:6
all they that hate me, *l.* death. 8:36
a wise man and he will *l.* thee.   9:8
kings *l.* him that speaketh.   16:13
that *l.* it shall eat the fruit.   18:21
a time to *l.* and a time.   *Eccl* 3:8
therefore do the virgins *l. S of S* 1:3
than wine, the upright *l.* thee.   4
to serve and *l.* the name.   *Isa* 56:6
the Lord *l.* judgement.   61:8
Jerusalem all ye that *l.* her.   66:10
and my people *l.* to have.   *Jer* 5:31
l. a woman beloved, *l.*   *Hos* 3:1

her rulers with shame, do *l. Hos* 4:18
drive them out, I will *l.* them.   9:15
I will *l.* them freely, for mine. 14:4
hate evil and *l.* the good. *Amos* 5:15
hate the good and *l.* the.   *Mi* 3:2
to *l.* mercy and to walk.   6:8
l. no false oath.   *Zech* 8:17
l. the truth.   19
it hath been said, L. thy. *Mat* 5:43
but I say, L. your enemies.   44
      Luke 6:27, 35
if ye *l.* them which *l.* you.
   5:46; *Luke* 6:32
they *l.* to pray standing. *Mat* 6:5
hate the one and *l.* the other.   24
      Luke 16:13
l. the Lord thy God with all thy heart.
   Mat 22:37; *Mark* 12:30, 33
      Luke 10:27
l. the uppermost rooms. *Mat* 23:6
scribes, who *l.* to go.   *Mark* 12:38
which of them will *l.?*   *Luke* 7:42
ye *l.* greetings in the markets.
      Luke 11:43; 20:46
will *l.* him and manifest. *John* 14:21
l. me, my Father will *l.* him.   23
my commandment, That ye *l.* one
   another.   15:12, 17
the world would *l.* his own.   19
for good, to them *l.* God. *Rom* 8:28
owe nothing to any, but to *l.*   13:8
shalt *l.* thy neighbour as thyself.
   Rom 13:9; *Gal* 5:14; *Jas* 2:8
prepared for them that *l. 1 Cor* 2:9
if any man *l.* God the same is.   8:3
husbands, *l.* your wives, as Christ
   also. *Eph* 5:25, 28, 33; *Col* 3:19
grace be with all them that *l.* our
   Lord Jesus.   *Eph* 6:24
are taught of God to *l. 1 Thes* 4:9
but to all them that *l. 2 Tim* 4:8
teach young women to *l.*   *Tit* 2:4
greet them that *l.* us in the.   3:15
Lord promised to them that *l.* him.
      Jas 1:12; 2:5
whom having not seen ye *l. 1 Pet* 1:8
see ye *l.* one another with a.   22
l. the brotherhood.   2:17
l. as brethren.   3:8
he that will *l.* life.   10
l. not the world, if any man *l.* the.
      1 John 2:15
from the beginning that we should *l.*
   3:11; 4:7, 11; *2 John* 5
to life, because we *l.*   *1 John* 3:14
l. one another, as he gave us.   23
if we *l.* one another, God.   4:12
l. him, because he first loved us.   19
can he *l.* God whom he hath not ? 20
loveth God, *l.* his brother also.   21
l. the children of God, when we *l.* 5:2

love of God
ye pass over judgement and *l.* of
   God.   *Luke* 11:42
not *l.* of God in you.   *John* 5:42
l. of God is shed abroad. *Rom* 5:5
separate us from the *l.* of God. 8:39
l. of God be with you. *2 Cor* 13:14
hearts into the *l.* of God. *2 Thes* 3:5
kindness and *l.* of God.   *Tit* 3:4
the *l.* of God perfected. *1 John* 2:5
hereby perceive we *l.* of God.   3:16
dwelleth the *l.* of God in him ?   17
was manifested the *l.* of God.   4:9
this is *l.* of God that we keep.   5:3
keep yourselves in the *l.* of God.
      Jude 21

his love
Lord did not set *his l.*   *Deut* 7:7
because he hath set *his l. Ps* 91:14
in *his l.* and in his pity he. *Isa* 63:9
will rest in *his l.* he will. *Zeph* 3:17
and abide in *his l.*   *John* 15:10
but God commendeth *his l. Rom* 5:8
if love one another *his l. 1 John* 4:12

in love
clave unto these in *l.*   *1 Ki* 11:2
in *l.* to my soul delivered. *Isa* 38:17
to you with a rod, or in *l. 1 Cor* 4:21
as ye abound in your *l.* to. *2 Cor* 8:7
be without blame before him in *l.*
      Eph 1:4
rooted and grounded in *l.*   3:17

forbearing one another *in l. Eph* 4:2
the truth *in l.* may grow up to. 15
to edifying of itself *in l.* 16
walk *in l.* as Christ hath loved. 5:2
being knit together *in l.* *Col* 2:2
you to increase *in l.* *1 Thes* 3:12
esteem them highly *in l.* 5:13
in faith and *l.* which is. *2 Tim* 1:13
he that dwelleth *in l.* *1 John* 4:16
no fear *in l.*: he that feareth is not
made perfect *in l.* 18
Father *in* truth and *l.* *2 John* 3

my love
for *my l.* they are mine. *Ps* 109:4
rewarded me hatred for *my l.* 5
compared thee, O *my l. S of S* 1:9
behold, thou art fair, *my l.* 15; 4:1
as lily, so is *my l.* among. 2:2
my l. till he please. 7; 3:5; 8:4
rise up, *my l.* 2:10, 13
all fair, *my l.*; there is no spot. 4:7
open to me, *my l.* my dove. 5:2
beautiful, O *my l.* as Tirzah. 6:4
continue ye in *my l.* *John* 15:9
abide in *my l.* 10
my l. be with you all in Christ Jesus.
1 Cor 16:24

thy love
thy l. was wonderful. *2 Sam* 1:26
for *thy l.* is better. *S of S* 1:2; 4:10
we will remember *thy l.* more. 1:4
how fair is *thy l.* my sister! 4:10
hearing of *thy l.* and faith. *Philem* 5
joy and consolation in *thy l.* 7
hast left *thy* first *l.* *Rev* 2:4

I love
savoury meat, such as *I l. Gen* 27:4
if servant shall say, *I l.* *Ex* 21:5
canst thou say, *I l.* thee? *Judg* 16:15
I l. Tamar my brother. *2 Sam* 13:4
I l. the Lord, because. *Ps* 116:1
O how *I l.* thy law. 119:97
thy law do *I l.* 113, 163
therefore *I l.* thy testimonies. 119
I l. thy commands above gold. 127
consider how *I l.* thy precepts. 159
thy testimonies *I l.* exceedingly. 167
I l. them that *l.* me. *Pr* 8:17
world may know that *I l. John* 14:31
knowest that *I l.* thee. 21:15, 16, 17
the more *I l.* you, the. *2 Cor* 12:15
if a man say, *I l.* God. *1 John* 4:20
I l. in the truth. *2 John* 1; *3 John* 1
as *I l.* I rebuke and. *Rev* 3:19

love me
my husband will *l. me.* *Gen* 29:32
showing mercy to thousands of them
that *l. me.* *Ex* 20:6; *Deut* 5:10
I love them that *l. me.* *Pr* 8:17
cause those that *l. me* to inherit. 21
Father ye would *l. me.* *John* 8:42
doth my Father *l. me.* 10:17
if ve *l. me,* keep my. 14:15
if a man *l. me,* he will keep. 23

love not
l. not sleep, lest thou. *Pr* 20:13
if any man *l. not* the. *1 Cor* 16:22
because I *l.* you *not*? *2 Cor* 11:11
l. not the world. *1 John* 2:15
let us *not l.* in word. 3:18

loved
Rebekah to wife, and *l.* *Gen* 24:67
Isaac *l.* Esau, but Rebekah *l.* 25:28
meat such as his father *l.* 27:14
Jacob *l.* Rachel more. 29:18, 30
Shechem *l.* Dinah, and spake. 34:3
Israel *l.* Joseph more than. 37:3, 4
because he *l.* thy fathers. *Deut* 4:37
but because the Lord *l.* you. 7:8
23:5; 33:3
Samson *l.* a woman in. *Judg* 16:4
Elkanah *l.* Hannah. *1 Sam* 1:5
Saul *l.* David. 16:21
Jonathan *l.* David as his own soul.
18:1, 3; 20:17
Israel and Judah *l.* David. 18:16
Saul's daughter, *l.* David. 20
Lord *l.* Solomon, and. *2 Sam* 12:24
son of David, *l.* Tamar. 13:1
than love wherewith he *l.* her. 15
Solomon *l.* the Lord. *1 Ki* 3:3
because the Lord *l.* Israel. 10:9
2 Chr 9:8

Solomon *l.* many strange. *1 Ki* 11:1
the Lord *l.* his people. *2 Chr* 2:11
Rehoboam *l.* Maacah. *2 Chr* 11:21
Uzziah had husbandmen, he *l.* 26:10
the king *l.* Esther above. *Esth* 2:17
they whom I *l.* are turned against.
Job 19:19
excellency of Jacob whom he *l.*
Ps 47:4
the mount Zion which he *l.* 78:68
as he *l.* cursing, so let it. 109:17
heaven whom they have *l.* *Jer* 8:2
thus have they *l.* to wander. 14:10
them that thou hast *l.* *Ezek* 16:37
thou hast *l.* a reward on. *Hos* 9:1
their abominations were according
as they *l.* 10
was a child, then I *l.* him. 11:1
wherein hast thou *l.* us.? *Mal* 1:2
holiness of Lord which he *l.* 2:11
beholding him, *l.* him. *Mark* 10:21
forgiven, for she *l.* much. *Luke* 7:47
God so *l.* the world. *John* 3:16
Jesus *l.* Martha, and her sister. 11:5
Jews, behold how he *l.* him. 36
for they *l.* praise of men more. 12:43
having *l.* his own, he *l.* them to. 13:1
disciple whom Jesus *l.* 23; 19:26
20:2; 21:7, 20
he that loveth me shall be *l.* 14:21
if ye *l.* me, ye would rejoice. 28
Father *l.* me, so have I *l.* you. 15:9
loveth you, because ye *l.* 16:27
l. them, as thou hast *l.* me. 17:23
love wherewith thou hast *l.* me. 26
more than conquerors through him
that *l.* us. *Rom* 8:37
love you, the less I be *l.* *2 Cor* 12:15
l. me, and gave himself. *Gal* 2:20
great love wherewith he *l. Eph* 2:4
as Christ also *l.* us. 5:2
Christ *l.* the church. 25
Father, which hath *l.* us. *2 Thes* 2:16
Demas having *l.* this. *2 Tim* 4:10
hast *l.* righteousness. *Heb* 1:9
Balaam *l.* the wages of. *2 Pet* 2:15
l. God, but that he *l.* us. *1 John* 4:10
if God so *l.* us. 11
because he first *l.* us. 19
to him that *l.* us and. *Rev* 1:5
l. not their lives to the death. 12:11

I have loved
I have *l.* the habitation. *Ps* 26:8
commandments *I have l.* 119:47, 48
I have l. thee, therefore. *Isa* 43:4
I have l. strangers, and. *Jer* 2:25
I have l. thee with an everlasting
love. 31:3
I have l. you, yet ye say. *Mal* 1:2
as *I have l.* you, that ye also love.
John 13:34; 15:12
Father loved me, so have I *l.* 15:9
written, Jacob *I have l.* *Rom* 9:13
make them know that *I have l.*
Rev 3:9

lovedst
thou *l.* their bed where. *Isa* 57:8
l. me before foundation. *John* 17:24

lovely
and Jonathan were *l.* *2 Sam* 1:23
he is altogether *l.* O. *S of S* 5:16
them as a very *l.* song. *Ezek* 33:32
whatsoever things are *l.* *Phil* 4:8

lover
for Hiram was ever a *l.* *1 Ki* 5:1
l. and friend hast thou. *Ps* 88:18
a *l.* of hospitality, a *l.* of good men.
Tit 1:8*

lovers
my *l.* and friends stand. *Ps* 38:11
the harlot with many *l.* *Jer* 3:1
thy *l.* will despise thee, they. 4:30
go up and cry, for all thy *l.* 22:20
thy *l.* shall go into captivity. 22
all thy *l.* have forgotten thee. 30:14
l. hath none to comfort. *Lam* 1:2
called for my *l.* but they deceived. 19
thy gifts to all thy *l.* *Ezek* 16:33
discovered with thy *l.* and idols. 36
I will gather thy *l.* 37
doted on her *l.* 23:5

her into the hand of her *l. Ezek* 23:9
behold, I will raise up thy *l.* 22
I will go after my *l.* *Hos* 2:5
shall follow her *l.*
her lewdness in the sight of *l.* 10
these rewards that my *l.* have. 12
and she went after her *l.* and. 13
Ephraim hath hired *l.* 8:9
be *l.* of their own selves. *2 Tim* 3:2
l. of pleasures more than *l.* of. 4

loves
us solace ourselves with *l.* *Pr* 7:18
will I give thee my *l.* *S of S* 7:12

lovest
son Isaac whom thou *l.* *Gen* 22:2
thou dost but hate me, and *l.* me not.
Judg 14:16
thou *l.* thine enemies. *2 Sam* 19:6
thou *l.* righteousness. *Ps* 45:7
thou *l.* evil more than good. 52:3
thou *l.* all devouring words. 4
with wife whom thou *l.* *Eccl* 9:9
he whom thou *l.* is sick. *John* 11:3
Simon, son of Jonas, *l.* thou me ?
21:15, 16, 17

loveth
for thy father, such as he *l. Gen* 27:9
little one, and his father *l.* him. 44:20
Lord *l.* the stranger in. *Deut* 10:18
go away because he *l.* thee. 15:16
daughter in law who *l.* *Ruth* 4:15
and him that *l.* violence. *Ps* 11:5
Lord *l.* righteousness. 7; 33:5
what man is he that *l.* many days ?
34:12
Lord *l.* judgement. 37:28; 99:4
the Lord *l.* gates of Zion. 87:2
word is very pure, therefore thy servant *l.* 119:140
The Lord *l.* the righteous. 146:8
the Lord *l.* he correcteth. *Pr* 3:12
l. instruction, *l.* knowledge. 12:1
but he that *l.* him, chasteneth. 13:24
he *l.* him that followeth after. 15:9
a scorner *l.* not one that. 12
a friend *l.* at all times. 17:17
l. transgression that *l.* strife. 19
he that getteth wisdom *l.* his. 19:8
l. pleasure, he that *l.* wine. 21:17
he that *l.* pureness of heart. 22:11
whoso *l.* wisdom rejoiceth his. 29:3
that *l.* silver, he that *l.* *Eccl* 5:10
O thou whom my soul *l. S of S* 1:7
bed I sought him whom my soul *l.* 3:1
seek him whom my soul *l.*
saw ye him whom my soul *l.*? 3
I found him whom my soul *l.* 4
every one *l.* gifts and. *Isa* 1:23
Ephraim as heifer *l.* to. *Hos* 10:11
he is a merchant, he *l.* to. 12:7
l. father or mother, he that *l.* son or
daughter more than me. *Mat* 10:37
he *l.* our nation. *Luke* 7:5
the same *l.* little. 47
the Father *l.* the Son, and hath given
all things. *John* 3:35; 5:20
l. his life shall lose it. 12:25
commandments, he it is that *l.* me,
he that *l.* me, *me* shall be. 14:21
he that *l.* me not, keepeth not. 24
Father himself *l.* you, because. 16:27
he that *l.* another hath. *Rom* 13:8
for God *l.* a cheerful giver. *2 Cor* 9:7
that *l.* his wife, *l.* himself. *Eph* 5:28
for whom the Lord *l.* he. *Heb* 12:6
he that *l.* his brother. *1 John* 2:10
he that *l.* not his brother, is not of
God. 3:10
l. not his brother, abideth in death.
14; 4:8, 20
every one that *l.* is born of God. 4:7
that he who *l.* God, love his. 21
that *l.* him that begat, *l.* him. 5:1
Diotrephes *l.* to have. *3 John* 9
l. and maketh a lie. *Rev* 22:15

loving
let her be as the *l.* hind. *Pr* 5:19
l. favour rather than silver. 22:1
lying down, *l.* to slumber. *Isa* 56:10

lovingkindness
thy marvellous *l.* *Ps* 17:7; 92:2
thy *l.* is before mine eyes. 26:3
how excellent is thy *l.* O God! 36:7

O continue thy *l.* to them. *Ps* 36:10
I have not concealed thy *l.*   40:10
let thy *l.* continually preserve.   11
the Lord will command his *l.*   42:8
we have thought of thy *l.* O.   48:9
mercy on me according to thy *l.* 51:1
because thy *l.* is better than.   63:3
O Lord, for thy *l.* is good.   69:16
l. be declared in the grave ?   88:11
l. will I not utterly take.   89:33
to shew forth thy *l.* in the.   92:2
who crowneth thee with *l.* and. 103:4
shall understand *l.* of Lord. 107:43
quicken me after thy *l.* 119:88, 159
hear my voice according to thy *l.* 149
praise thy name for thy *l.* 138:2
cause me to hear thy *l.* in.   143:8
the Lord which exercise *l.*   *Jer* 9:24
taken away my peace, even *l.*   16:5
with *l.* have I drawn thee.   31:3
shewest *l.* unto thousands.   32:18
betroth thee to me in *l.*   *Hos* 2:19

lovingkindnesses
Lord thy mercies and *l.*   *Ps* 25:6
where are thy former *l.?*   89:49
mention the *l.* of the Lord according
   to the multitude of his *l. Isa* 63:7

low
shalt come down very *l. Deut* 28:43
the Lord bringeth *l.*   *1 Sam* 2:7
sycamore trees in the *l.* *2 Chr* 9:27
Uzziah had much cattle in *l.*   26:10
Philistines invaded cities of *l.* 28:18
on high those that be *l.*   *Job* 5:11
look on proud, and bring him *l.* 40:12
high and *l.* rich and poor.   *Ps* 49:2
surely men of *l.* degree.   62:9
remembered us in our *l.*   136:23
pride shall bring him *l.*   *Pr* 29:23
rich sit in *l.* place.   *Eccl* 10:6
sound of the grinding is *l.*   12:4
will lay *l.* the haughtiness. *Isa* 13:11
fort of thy walls shall he lay *l.* 25:12
the lofty city he layeth it *l.* to. 26:5
thy speech shall be *l.* out of.   29:4
city shall be *l.* in a *l.* place.   32:19
I called on thy name out of *l.* dungeon.   *Lam* 3:55
spreading vine of *l.*
that I have exalted the *l.* tree. *Ezek* 17:6   24
exalt him that is *l.*, abase.   21:26
shall set thee in the *l.* parts. 26:20*
regarded *l.* estate of his. *Luke* 1:48
hath exalted them of *l.* degree.   52
condescend to men of *l.*   *Rom* 12:16
let the brother of *l.* degree. *Jas* 1:9
but the rich in that he is made *l.* 10

see **brought**

lower
l. second and third stories. *Gen* 6:16
if rising be in sight *l.*   *Lev* 13:20
it be no *l.* than the skin.   21, 26
set in the *l.* places the.   *Neh* 4:13
made him a little *l.* than the angels.
   Ps 8:5; *Heb* 2:7, 9
shall go into the *l.* parts of the. 63:9
put *l.* in presence of prince. *Pr* 25:7
waters of the *l.* pool.   *Isa* 22:9
Shout, ye *l.* parts.   44:23
bottom even to the *l.*   *Ezek* 43:14
descended first into the *l.*   *Eph* 4:9

lower *parts of the earth*
[1] *The valleys,* Isa 44:23. [2]
The state of the dead, Ps 63:9.
[3] *The mother's womb,* Ps 139:15.
[4] *The earth, as the lowest part
of the visible world, or the grave
and state of the dead,* Eph 4:9.

lowest
shall burn to the *l.* hell. *Deut* 32:22†
made priests *l.*   *1 Ki* 12:31; 13:33
   2 Ki 17:32
my soul from the *l.* hell. *Ps* 86:13†
thou hast laid me in the *l.* pit. 88:6
curiously wrought in the *l.*   139:15
increased from the *l.*   *Ezek* 41:7
straitened more than the *l.*   42:6
shame to take *l.* room. *Luke* 14:9
sit down in the *l.* room.   10

loweth
wild ass bray, or *l.* the ox ? *Job* 6:5

26

---

lowing
along the highway *l.*   *1 Sam* 6:12
then the *l.* of the oxen ?   15:14

lowliness
that ye walk with all *l.*   *Eph* 4:2
but in *l.* of mind, let each. *Phil* 2:3

lowly
yet hath he respect to *l.*   *Ps* 138:6
but he giveth grace to *l.*   *Pr* 3:34
then cometh shame, but with *l.* 11:2
humble spirit with the *l.*   16:19*
he is just, *l.* and riding. *Zech* 9:9
for I am meek and *l.*   *Mat* 11:29

lowring
for the sky is red and *l.*   *Mat* 16:3

Lucas
Marcus, Demas, *L.* my. *Philem* 24

Lucifer
fallen from heaven, O *L. Isa* 14:12

Lucius
L. of Cyrene was a.   *Acts* 13:1
L. Jason and Sosipater. *Rom* 16:21

lucre
Samuel's sons turned after *l.,* took.
   1 Sam 8:3
greedy of filthy *l.*   *1 Tim* 3:3, 8
not be given to filthy *l.*   *Tit* 1:7
they ought not for filthy *l.*   11
feed flock not for filthy *l.* *1 Pet* 5:2

Luke
L. the beloved physician. *Col* 4:14
only *L.* is with me.   *2 Tim* 4:11

lukewarm
because thou art *l.*   *Rev* 3:16

lump
take a *l.* of figs and lay. *2 Ki* 20:7*
   Isa 38:21*
of the same *l.* one vessel. *Rom* 9:21
firstfruit be holy the *l.* is.   11:16
a little leaven leaveneth the whole *l.*
   1 Cor 5:6; *Gal* 5:9
that ye may be a new *l.*   *1 Cor* 5:7

lunatick
and those which were *l. Mat* 4:24*
mercy on my son, for he is *l.* 17:15*

lurk
come, let us *l.* privily.   *Pr* 1:11
l. privily for their own lives.   18

lurking
knowledge of all the *l.* *1 Sam* 23:23
he sitteth in the *l.* places. *Ps* 10:8
as it were a young lion *l.* in.   17:12

lust
(*Formerly often used with a
general meaning of pleasure, desire, with no idea of evil*)
my *l.* shall be satisfied.   *Ex* 15:9
asking meat for their *l.*   *Ps* 78:18
not estranged from their *l.*   30
to their own hearts' *l.*   81:12*
burned in their *l.* one.   *Rom* 1:27
not known *l.* except the law.   7:7*
ye shall not fulfil *l.* of flesh. *Gal* 5:16
not in *l.* of concupiscence. *1 Thes* 4:5
he is drawn of his own *l.*   *Jas* 1:14
l. hath conceived, it bringeth.   15
that is in world through *l.* *2 Pet* 1:4
that walk after flesh in the *l.* of. 2:10
l. of the flesh, the *l.* of. *1 John* 2:16
world passeth away, and the *l.* 17

lust, *verb*
l. not after her beauty.   *Pr* 6:25
on a woman to *l.* after her. *Mat* 5:28
not *l.* after evil things.   *1 Cor* 10:6
ye *l.* and have not, ye kill. *Jas* 4:2

lusted
buried the people that *l. Num* 11:34
but they *l.* exceedingly. *Ps* 106:14
not lust as they also *l.* *1 Cor* 10:6
fruits thy soul *l.* after.   *Rev* 18:14

lusteth
what thy soul *l.* after.   *Deut* 12:15
   20, 21; 14:26
flesh *l.* against the Spirit. *Gal* 5:17
dwelleth in us *l.* to envy. *Jas* 4:5

lusting
mixed multitude fell a *l. Num* 11:4

---

lusts
the *l.* of other things.   *Mark* 4:19
and the *l.* of your father. *John* 8:44
gave them up to uncleanness through
   l.   *Rom* 1:24
obey it in the *l.* thereof.   6:12
provision for flesh, to fulfil *l.* 13:14
have crucified flesh with *l. Gal* 5:24
our conversation in tne *l.* of. *Eph* 2:3
according to the deceitful *l.*   4:22
into foolish and hurtful *l.* *1 Tim* 6:9
flee youthful *l.* but.   *2 Tim* 2:22
silly women led away with *l.*   3:6
own *l.* shall they heap teachers. 4:3
that denying worldly *l.*   *Tit* 2:12
disobedient, serving divers *l.*   3:3
not hence, even of your *l.?*   *Jas* 4:1
ye may consume it on your *l.*   3
according to former *l.*   *1 Pet* 1:14
abstain from fleshly *l.* that.   2:11
no longer should live to the *l.*   4:2
in lasciviousness, *l.* excess of.   3
they allure through the *l. 2 Pet* 2:18
walking after their own *l.*   3:3
complainers, walking after *l. Jude* 16
walk after their own ungodly *l.*   18

lusty
Moab 10,000 men, all *l.*   *Judg* 3:29

Luz
the city was called *L.* at the first.
   Gen 28:19; *Judg* 1:23
Jacob came to *L.* in the. *Gen* 35:6
Almighty appeared to me at *L.* 48:3

Lycaonia
and Derbe, cities of *L.*   *Acts* 14:6
voices, saying in the speech of *L.* 11

Lydda
down to the saints at *L.* *Acts* 9:32
dwelt at *L.* turned to the Lord.   35
forasmuch as *L.* was nigh.   38

Lydia
L. shall fall with them.   *Ezek* 30:5

Lydia
L. whose heart the Lord. *Acts* 16:14
entered into the house of *L.*   40

lying
hated them that regard *l.* vanities,
   but I trust in the Lord. *Ps* 31:6
let the *l.* lips be put to silence. 18
thou lovest *l.* rather than.   52:3
and for cursing and *l.* which. 59:12
spoken against me with *l.*   109:2
remove from me the way of *l.* 119:29
I hate and abhor *l.* but thy law. 163
soul, O Lord, from *l.* lips.   120:2
hateth a proud look, a *l.*   *Pr* 6:17
that hideth hatred with *l.* lips. 10:18
but a *l.* tongue is but for a.   12:19
l. lips are abomination to the.   22
a righteous man hateth *l.* but a
   wicked man is loathsome.   13:5
much less do *l.* lips become a. 17:7
getting of treasures by a *l.*   21:6
a *l.* tongue hateth those.   26:28
rebellious people, *l.*   *Isa* 30:9
wicked devices with *l.* words. 32:7
in transgressing and *l.* against. 59:13
trust ye not in *l.* words.   *Jer* 7:4
behold, ye trust in *l.* words that.   8
because have spoken *l.* words. 29:23
vanity and *l.* divination. *Ezek* 13:6
spoken a *l.* divination ?   7
by your *l.* to my people that.   19
ye have prepared *l.* words. *Dan* 2:9
by swearing, *l.* and killing. *Hos* 4:2*
that observe *l.* vanities forsake.
   Jonah 2:8
away *l.* speak truth.   *Eph* 4:25
whose coming is with *l.* *2 Thes* 2:9

lying *spirit*
l. spirit in the mouth of all his.
   1 Ki 22:22; *2 Chr* 18:21
Lord hath put a *l.* spirit in prophets.
   1 Ki 22:23; *2 Chr* 18:22

lying, *verb*
three flocks of sheep *l.* *Gen* 29:2
him that hateth thee, *l.*   *Ex* 23:5
if one be found slain, *l.* *Deut* 21:1
my path and *l.* down.   *Ps* 139:3
sleeping, *l.* down, loving. *Isa* 56:10

man sick of the palsy, *l.* *Mat* 9:2
where the damsel was *l.* *Mark* 5:40
babe *l.* in a manger. *Luke* 2:12, 16
then *l.* on Jesus' breast. *John* 13:25*
he saw the linen clothes *l.* yet. 20:5
napkin not *l.* with the linen. 7

lying *in wait*
rose up from *l. in wait.* *Judg* 9:35
now there were men *l. in wait.* 16:9
as a bear *l. in wait,* as. *Lam* 3:10
me by the *l. in wait* of Jews.
  Acts 20:19
when Paul's kinsmen heard of their
  l. in wait. 23:16

lying *with*
l. with Jacob's daughter. *Gen* 34:7
kill woman that hath known man by *l.*
  with him. *Num* 31:17
not known man by *l. with* him, keep
  alive. 18; *Judg* 21:12
women had not known man by *l.*
  with him. *Num* 31:35
if a man be found *l. with. Deut* 22:22

Lysanias
reign of Tiberius, *L.* *Luke* 3:1

Lysias
L. unto the most excellent Felix.
  Acts 23:26

Lystra
were ware of it, and fled unto *L.*
  Acts 14:6
a certain man at *L.* impotent. 8
Paul came to *L.* 16:1
by the brethren at *L.* 2
afflictions which came unto me at *L.*
  2 Tim 3·11

M

Maachah
Reumah Nahor's concubine bare *M.*
  Gen 22:24
M. mother of Absalom. *2 Sam* 3:3
  1 Chr 3:2
M. the mother of Abijam, the daugh-
  ter of. *1 Ki* 15:2, 10; *2 Chr* 11:22
M. Caleb's concubine. *1 Chr* 2:48
M. the wife of Machir bare. 7:16
Hanan the son of *M.* 11:43

Maaseiah
Zichri slew *M.* *2 Chr* 28:7
Rehum and *M.* sealed. *Neh* 10:25
Zephaniah the son of *M. Jer* 21:1
  29:25; 37:3
Lord of Zedekiah son of *M.* 29:21
Neriah son of *M.* 32:12; 51:59
above the chamber of *M.* son. 35:4

Maath
which was the son of *M. Luke* 3:26

Macedonia
come over into *M.* and. *Acts* 16:9
Timotheus were come from *M.* 18:5
when he had passed through *M.* 19:21
hath pleased them of *M. Rom* 15:26
were come into *M.* *2 Cor* 7:5
bestowed on the churches of *M.* 8:1
boast of you to them of *M.* 9:2
lest if they of *M.* find you. 4
brethren which came from *M.* 11:9
to all that believe in *M. 1 Thes* 1:7
sounded the word, not only in *M.* 8
the brethren that are in *M.* 4:10

Machir
M. the son of Manasseh.
  Gen 50:23; *Num* 32:39
M. begat Gilead. *Num* 26:29; 27:1
  36:1; *Josh* 17:1
Moses gave Gilead unto *M.*
  Num 32:40; *Deut* 3:15
out of *M.* came down. *Judg* 5:14
M. the son of Ammiel. *2 Sam* 9:4
  5; 17:27

Machpelah
give me cave of *M.* *Gen* 23:9, 17
buried Sarah in the cave of *M.* 19
buried Abraham in *M.* 25:9
buried Jacob in *M.* 49:30; 50:13

mad
be *m.* for the sight of. *Deut* 28:34
feigned himself *m.* *1 Sam* 21:13
servants. Ye see the man is *m.* 14

this *m.* fellow to thee ? *2 Ki* 9:11
m. against me are sworn. *Ps* 102:8
I said of laughter, It is *m. Eccl* 2:2
maketh a wise man *m.* 7:7*
that maketh diviners *m.* *Isa* 44:25
be moved, and be *m.* *Jer* 25:16
for every man that is *m.* put. 29:26
they are *m.* upon their idols. 50:38
therefore the nations are *m.* 51:7
fool, the spiritual man is *m. Hos* 9:7
he hath a devil and is *m. John* 10:20
to Rhoda, Thou art *m.* *Acts* 12:15
being exceedingly *m.* against them.
  26:11
learning doth make thee *m.* 24
I am not *m.* most noble Festus. 25
not say that ye are *m.? 1 Cor* 14:23

made
who *m.* thee prince over us ?
  Ex 2:14; *Acts* 7:27
hath *m.* man's mouth ? *Ex* 4:11
m. his servants and cattle flee. 9:20
after he had *m.* it a molten. 32:4
Aaron had *m.* them naked. 25
m. them gods of gold. 31; *Hos* 8:4
of Israel *m.* all the work. *Ex* 39:42
why have ye *m.* us to come from
  Egypt ? *Num* 20:5
and calf which he had *m. Deut* 9:21
Joshua and Israel *m.* as if. *Josh* 8:15
went and *m.* as if they had been. 9:4
m. the heart of the people. 14:8
altar which our fathers *m.* 22:28
m. Samson sleep upon. *Judg* 16:19
Samson *m.* the Philistines. 25, 27
away the gods which I *m.* 18:24
his sons *m.* themselves vile.
  1 Sam 3:13*
that Samuel *m.* his sons judges. 8:1
have *m.* a king over you. 12:1
wast thou not *m.* the head ? 15:17
sword hath *m.* women childless. 33
Whither have ye *m.* road ? 27:10
m. himself sick. *2 Sam* 13:6*
calves that he had *m. 1 Ki* 12:32
idols which his fathers *m.* 15:12
she had *m.* an idol in a grove. 13
streets as my fathers *m.* 20:34
they *m.* him king and. *2 Ki* 11:12
so Urijah the priest *m.* it. 16:11
yet his father *m.* him. *1 Chr* 26:10
art thou *m.* of the king's counsel ?
  2 Chr 25:16
for Ahab *m.* Judah naked. 28:19
set the idol he had *m.* in the. 33:7
Josiah *m.* all present to serve. 34:33
whom he *m.* governor. *Ezra* 5:14
we *m.* our prayer unto. *Neh* 4:9
Ahasuerus *m.* her queen. *Esth* 2:17
they *m.* it a day of feasting. 9:17, 18
wast thou *m.* before the ? *Job* 15:7
m. a pit, and is fallen into pit he *m.*
  Ps 7:15
are sunk into the pit they *m.* 9:15
is the man that *m.* not God. 52:7
I *m.* me great works. *Eccl* 2:4
I *m.* me gardens. 5
I *m.* me pools of water. 6
they *m.* me the keeper. *S of S* 1:6
he *m.* the pillars of silver. 3:10
my soul *m.* me like chariots. 6:12
their own fingers *m.* *Isa* 2:8
is this the man that *m.* earth? 14:16
for we have *m.* lies our refuge. 28:15
of him that *m.* it, he *m.* me not. 29:16
which your hands have *m.* unto. 31:7
they have *m.* them crooked. 59:8
gods that have not *m.* *Jer* 10:11
have *m.* my pleasant portion a wilderness. 12:10
vessel that *m.* was marred in hand
  of potter, so he *m.* it again. 18:4
had *m.* that the prison. 37:15
which Asa the king had *m.* 41:9
Nebuchadnezzar *m.* me an. 51:34
ye *m.* the heart of the. *Ezek* 13:22*
the king dwelleth that *m.* 17:16
m. their sweet savour. 20:28
ye have *m.* your iniquity to be. 21:24
waters *m.* him great, deep set. 31:4
thy father *m.* master of. *Dan* 5:11
yet *m.* we not prayer before. 9:13

princes have *m.* him sick. *Hos* 7:5
the workman *m.* it, therefore. 8:6
the god which ye *m.* *Amos* 5:26
they *m.* their hearts as. *Zech* 7:12
thy faith hath *m.* thee whole.
  Mat 9:22; *Mark* 5:34; 10:52
  Luke 8:48; 17:19
have *m.* commandment of God of
  none effect. *Mat* 15:6
prayer, but ye have *m.* it a den of.
  21:13; *Mark* 11:17; *Luke* 19:46
m. them other five talents. *Mat* 25:16
who *m.* me a judge ? *Luke* 12:14
and his name hath *m.* *Acts* 3:16
as for Saul, he *m.* havock of. 8:3*
who had *m.* this conspiracy. 23:13
they hoised up sail, and *m.* 27:40
m. free from law of sin. *Rom* 8:2
concerning faith have *m. 1 Tim* 1:19
law *m.* nothing perfect. *Heb* 7:19
believeth not, hath *m.* God a liar.
  1 John 5:10
m. them white in blood. *Rev* 7:14
m. all nations drink of wine. 14:8
  see **covenant, end, fire**

made, referring to *God, Lord,*
  Christ
God *m.* the firmament. *Gen* 1:7
m. two great lights, he *m.* stars.
  16; *Ps* 136:7, 9
m. the beast of the earth. *Gen* 1:25
every thing that he had *m.* 31
from all his work he had *m.* 2:2
God *m.* the earth and heavens. 4
  Ex 20:11; 31:17; *Ps* 146:6
  Isa 45:18; *Jer* 10:12
m. to grow every tree. *Gen* 2:9
m. he a woman. 22
in the likeness of God *m.* 5:1; 9:6
Lord he had *m.* man. 6:6, 7
God *m.* a wind to pass over. 8:1
Sarah said, God hath *m.* me. 21:6
m. his journey prosperous. 24:21
Lord hath *m.* room for us. 26:22
the Lord *m.* all Joseph did. 39:3, 23
God hath *m.* me to forget. 41:51
God hath *m.* me a father. 45:8
feared God, he *m.* houses. *Ex* 1:21
Lord *m.* the sea dry land. 14:21
I *m.* Israel to dwell in. *Lev* 23:43
Lord your God and I have *m.* 26:13
he *m.* them wander in. *Num* 32:13
for the Lord *m.* his heart. *Deut* 2:30
out of heaven he *m.* thee to. 4:36
the Lord hath *m.* thee as. 10:22
m. the water of the Red sea. 11:4
nations which he hath *m.* 26:19
m. thee, and established thee. 32:6
he *m.* him ride, he *m.* suck. 13
then he forsook God which *m.* 15
Lord *m.* Jordan border. *Josh* 22:25
m. him have dominion. *Judg* 5:13*
the Lord had *m.* a breach in. 21:15
and *m.* them dwell in. *1 Sam* 12:8
Lord repented that he had *m.* 15:35
Lord had *m.* a breach. *2 Sam* 6:8*
he *m.* darkness pavilions. 22:12
thy gentleness hath *m.* me great. 36
  Ps 18:35
who hath *m.* me a house. *1 Ki* 2:24
Lord loved Israel, therefore he *m.*
  10:9; 14:7; 16:2; *2 Chr* 1:11
but the Lord *m.* the heavens.
  1 Chr 16:26; *Neh* 9:6; *Ps* 33:6
  96:5; 121:2; 124:8; 134:3
Lord had *m.* them to rejoice.
  2 Chr 20:27
he sought the Lord, God *m.* 26:5
Lord had *m.* them joyful.
  Ezra 6:22; *Neh* 12:43
thy hands have *m.* me. *Job* 10:8
he hath *m.* me weary, thou hast *m.* 16:7
he hath *m.* me a byword of. 17:6
he *m.* a decree for the rain. 28:26
that *m.* me in the womb make. 31:15
the Spirit of God *m.* me, and. 33:4
m. him can make his sword. 40:19
hast not *m.* my foes to. *Ps* 30:1
what desolations he hath *m.* in. 46:8
the sea is his and he *m.* it. 95:5
he *m.* us. 100:3
darkness, and *m.* it dark. 105:28

the day the Lord hath *m. Ps* 118:24
thy hands have *m.* me and. 119:73
that by wisdom *m.* the heavens.
   136:5; *Acts* 14:15
m. Israel pass through. *Ps* 136:14
he hath *m.* a decree which. 148:6
rejoice in him that *m.* him. 149:2
the Lord *m.* all things. *Pr* 16:4
the Lord hath *m.* even both. 20:12
he hath *m.* every thing. *Eccl* 3:11
I found that God hath *m.* man. 7:29
he that *m.* them will not. *Isa* 27:11
he hath *m.* Tophet deep and. 30:33
thus saith the Lord that *m.* 44:2
he *m.* intercession for the. 53:12
things hath mine hand *m.* 66:2
lo, certainly in vain *m.* he it. *Jer* 8:8
Lord *m.* thee priest instead. 29:26
and hast *m.* thee a name as. 32:20
as the Lord liveth, that *m.* 38:16
he hath *m.* me desolate and faint.
   Lam 1:13; 3:11
the Lord hath *m.* my strength. 1:14
my skin hath he *m.* old. 3:4
hath *m.* my chain heavy. 7
m. my paths crooked. 9
he hath *m.* me drunken with. 15
I *m.* nations to shake at. *Ezek* 31:16
fear God who hath *m.* sea. *Jonah* 1:9
I *m.* their streets waste. *Zeph* 3:6
he *m.* them male and female.
   Mat 19:4; *Mark* 10:6
did not he that *m.* that? *Luke* 11:40
was not any thing *m.* *John* 1:3
Jesus *m.* more disciples. 4:1
he *m.* water wine. 46
he that *m.* me whole said. 5:11
m. clay of the spittle. 9:6; 11:14
m. himself the Son of God. 19:7
know that God hath *m.* *Acts* 2:36
know that God *m.* choice. 15:7
God that *m.* the world and. 17:24
hath *m.* of one blood all nations. 26
the Holy Ghost hath *m.* you. 20:28
m. foolish the wisdom. *1 Cor* 1:20
m. us able ministers of. *2 Cor* 3:6
hath *m.* him to be sin for us. 5:21
Christ hath *m.* us free. *Gal* 5:1
he hath *m.* us accepted. *Eph* 1:6
God hath *m.* us sit together. 2:6
he is our peace who hath *m.* 14
but *m.* himself of no. *Philem* 2:7
who hath *m.* us meet to. *Col* 1:12
he *m.* a shew of them openly. 2:15
by whom also he *m.* *Heb* 1:2
for when God *m.* promise to. 6:13
and hath *m.* us kings and. *Rev* 1:6
and worship him that *m.* 14:7

I have, or *have I* **made**

living substance *I have m. Gen* 7:4
lest thou say, *I have m.* 14:23
a father of nations *have I m.* thee.
   17:5; *Rom* 4:17
Isaac said, Behold, *I have m.* him thy
  lord. *Gen* 27:37
see *I have m.* thee a god. *Ex* 7:1
I have m. thee a great name.
   2 Sam 7:9; *1 Chr* 17:8
I have m. supplication. *1 Ki* 8:59
I have m. provision. *1 Chr* 29:19
I Darius *have made* a decree.
   Ezra 6:11, 12
I have m. my bed in. *Job* 17:13
if *I have m.* gold my hope. 31:24
I have m. the wilderness. 39:6
things which *I have m. Ps* 45:1
who can say, *I have m.* my ? *Pr* 20:9
I have m. their shouting. *Isa* 16:10
the sighing thereof *have I m.* 21:2
yea, *I have m.* him. 43:7; 46:4
I have m. the earth, and created.
   45:12; *Jer* 27:5
the souls which *I have m. Isa* 57:16
behold *I have m.* thee a. *Jer* 1:18
but *I have m.* Esau bare. 49:10
behold, *I have m.* thy face strong.
   Ezek 3:8, 9
I have m. thee a watchman to. 17
whom *I have* not *m.* sad. 13:22
and *I have m.* the dry tree. 17:24
have I m. thee a reproach. 22:4
I have m. it for myself. 29:3, 9
I have m. him fair by multitude. 31:9

image which *I have m. Dan* 3:15
I have m. the stink of camps to.
   Amos 4:10
I have m. thee small among the.
   Obad 2
have *I m.* you contemptible. *Mal* 2:9
because *I have m.* a man every whit
  whole.. *John* 7:23
yet *have I m.* myself. *1 Cor* 9:19

thou hast **made**

plant them in the place which *thou
  hast m. Ex* 15:17
thou hast m. an atonement for. 29:36
this oath which *thou hast m.*
  swear. *Josh* 2:17, 20
thou hast m. thy servant king instead of David. *1 Ki* 3:7
supplication that *thou hast m.* 9:3
thou hast m. heaven and earth.
  2 Ki 19:15; *Isa* 37:16; *Jer* 32:17
word came, saying, Thou *hast m.*
  great wars. *1 Chr* 22:8
thou hast m. an hedge. *Job* 1:10
remember that *thou hast m.* 10:9
thou hast m. desolate all my. 16:7
thou hast m. him little lower than
  angels. *Ps* 8:5
thou hast m. me the head of. 18:43
thou hast m. him most blessed. 21:6
thou hast m. my mountain. 30:7
behold, *thou hast m.* my days. 39:5
thou hast m. the earth to tremble.
   60:2
thou hast m. us drink the wine. 3
thou hast m. summer and. 74:17
all nations whom *thou hast m.* 86:9
thou hast m. me an abomination to
  them. 88:8
thou hast m. all his enemies. 89:42
thou hast m. his glory to cease. 44
hast thou m. all men in vain? 47
thou hast m. the Lord thy habitation. 91:9
thou, Lord, *hast m.* me glad. 92:4
wisdom *hast thou m.* them. 104:24
Leviathan, whom *thou hast m.* 26
thou hast m. me wiser than. 119:98
for *thou hast m.* of a city. *Isa* 25:2
but *thou hast m.* me to serve. 43:24
O Lord, why *hast thou m.* us to err
  from thy ways? 63:17
where are thy gods that *thou hast m.*
  thee? *Jer* 2:28
wait on thee, for *thou hast m.* 14:22
thou hast m. us as the offscouring
  and refuse. *Lam* 3:45
nor *hast thou m.* up the hedge in the
  house. *Ezek* 13:5
thou hast m. thee an high place in
  every street. 16:24
thou hast m. thy beauty to be. 25
thy idols which *thou hast m.* 22:4
at thy dishonest gain which *thou
  hast m.* 13
but one hour, and *thou hast m.* them
  equal to us. *Mat* 20:12
why *hast thou m.* me thus. *Rom* 9:20
thou hast m. us to our God kings and
  priests. *Rev* 5:10

made *haste*

Rebekah *m. haste* and. *Gen* 24:46
Joseph *m. haste.* 43:30
Moses *m. haste.* *Ex* 34:8
Manoah's wife *m. haste. Judg* 13:10
David *made h.* *1 Sam* 23:26
Abigail *m. haste.* 25:18
nurse *m. haste* to flee. *2 Sam* 4:4
I *m.* haste, and delayed. *Ps* 119:60
Zacchaeus *m. haste.* *Luke* 19:6
 see **Israel, sin, known**

made *manifest*

secret that shall not be *m. manifest.*
   Luke 8:17
he should be *m. manifest. John* 1:31
his deeds may be *m. manifest.* 3:21
God should be *m. manifest* in. 9:3
I was *m. manifest* to them that
  asked not. *Rom* 10:20
m. manifest to all nations for the
  obedience of faith. 16:26
every man's work shall be *m. manifest.* *1 Cor* 3:13

are approved may be *m. manifest.*
   1 Cor 11:19
secrets of his heart *m. manifest.*
   14:25
life of Jesus should be *m. manifest.*
   2 Cor 4:10, 11
been throughly *m. manifest.* 11:6
m. manifest by the light. *Eph* 5:13
but now is *m. manifest* to. *Col* 1:26
now *m. manifest* by the appearing of
  Christ. *2 Tim* 1:10
way into the holiest was not yet *m.*
  manifest. *Heb* 9:8
went out, that they they might be *m.*
  manifest. *1 John* 2:19
judgements are *m. manifest.*
   Rev 15:4

made *peace*

and Joshua *m. peace* with them.
   Josh 9:15; 10:1, 4
was not a city that *m. peace* with
  Israel. 11:19
of Hadarezer were smitten, they *m.*
  peace. *2 Sam* 10:19; *1 Chr* 19:19
Jehoshaphat *m. peace.* *1 Ki* 22:44

made *ready*

m. ready the present. *Gen* 43:25
Joseph *m. ready* his chariot. 46:29
m. ready his chariot, and. *Ex* 14:6
in and *m. ready* a kid. *Judg* 6:19
till we have *m. ready* a kid. 13:15
m. ready before it was. *1 Ki* 6:7
chariot was *m. ready.* *2 Ki* 9:21
m. ready for the building. *1 Chr* 28:2
afterward they *m. ready* for themselves. *2 Chr.* 35:14
his bow and *m.* it *ready. Ps* 7:12
have *m. ready* their heart. *Hos* 7:6
the disciples *m. ready. Mat* 26:19
  Mark 14:16; *Luke* 22:13
they *m. ready* Peter but. *Acts* 10:10
boast of things *m. ready. 2 Cor* 10:16
wife hath *m.* herself ready. *Rev* 19:7

made *speed*

Rehoboam *m. speed* to get.
   1 Ki 12:18; *2 Chr* 10:18

made *void*

hath utterly *m. void. Num* 30:12
thou hast *m. void* covenant. *Ps* 89:39
they have *m. void* thy law. 119:126
be heirs, faith is *m. void. Rom* 4:14

made, *passively*

hands were *m.* strong. *Gen* 49:24
may be *m.* unclean. *Lev* 22:5
shall bear all that is *m.* for them.
   Num 4:26
that is *m.* of the vine tree. 6:4
what supplication be *m.* *1 Ki* 8:38
   2 Chr 6:29
ears attend to prayer *m. 2 Chr* 6:40
let there be search *m.* in. *Ezra* 5:17
and arch was *m.* in the house. 6:1
lct house be *m.* a dunghill. 11
gallows be *m.* of fifty. *Esth* 5:14
I am *m.* to possess months. *Job* 7:3
his like on earth, who is *m.* 41:33
when one is *m.* rich. *Ps* 49:16
fearfully and wonderfully *m.* 139:14
the righteous is *m.* plain. *Pr* 15:19
the simple is *m.* wise. 21:11
trust in Lord shall be *m.* fat. 28:25
cannot be *m.* straight. *Eccl* 1:15
countenance the heart is *m.* 7:3
a feast is *m.* for laughter. 10:19
which shall be *m.* as grass. *Isa* 51:12
shall earth be *m.* to bring forth. 66:8
a vessel that cannot be *m. Jer* 19:11
the word of the Lord was *m.* 20:8
his heart was *m.* like. *Dan* 5:21
these stones be *m.* bread. *Mat* 4:3
and the rent is *m.* worse. 9:16
   Mark 2:21
and payment to be *m. Mat* 18:25
is *m.* ye make him twofold. 23:15
there was a cry *m.* behold. 25:6
rather a tumult was *m.* 27:24
the sepulchre be *m.* sure. 64
sabbath was *m.* for man. *Mark* 2:27
a recompence be *m.* thee. *Luke* 14:12
Pilate and Herod were *m.* 23:12
m. by him, and without him was not
  any thing *m.* that was *m. John* 1:3
the world was *m.* by him. 10

Word was *m.* flesh, and. *John* 1:14
the water that was *m.* wine.   2:9
wilt thou be *m.* whole?   5:6
Behold, thou art *m.* whole.   14
ye shall be *m.* free.   8:33
might be *m.* blind.   9:39
that they may be *m.* perfect.   17:23
distribution was *m.* to.   *Acts* 4:35
prayer *m.* without ceasing.   12:5
promise which was *m.*   13:32; 26:6
prayer was wont to be *m.*   16:13
they be no gods which are *m.* 19:26
Jesus who was *m.* of the. *Rom* 1:3
by the things that are *m.*   20
thy circumcision is *m.*   2:25
were *m.* sinners, many *m.*   5:19
being *m.* free from sin.   6:18, 22
that which is good, *m.* death. 7:13
we had been *m.* like to Sodom. 9:29
the mouth confession is *m.*   10:10
let their table be *m.* a snare.   11:9
thy brother is *m.* weak.   14:21
cross of Christ be *m.*   *1 Cor* 1:17
are in Christ, who of God is *m.*   30
m. a spectacle to the world.   4:9
we are *m.* as filth of world.   13
I am *m.* all things to all men. 9:22
have been all *m.* to drink.   12:13
in Christ shall all be *m.* alive. 15:22
first man Adam was *m.* a living soul,
    last Adam was *m.* a.   45
which was *m.* glorious. *2 Cor* 3:10
an house not *m.* with hands.   5:1
might be *m.* the righteousness. 21
my strength is *m.* perfect in. 12:9
are ye now *m.* perfect by? *Gal* 3:3
Christ redeemed us, being *m.*   13
his seed were the promises *m.*   16
to whom the promise was *m.*   19
sent his Son, *m.* of a woman, *m.* 4:4
circumcision in flesh *m.*   *Eph* 2:11
were far off, are *m.* nigh by the. 13
whereof I was *m.* a minister.   3:7
    Col 1:23, 25
and was *m.* in the likeness. *Phil* 2:7
m. conformable to his death.   3:10
m. peace through blood. *Col* 1:20
with the circumcision *m.*   2:11
the law is not *m.* for a.   *1 Tim* 1:9
and giving of thanks be *m.* for. 2:1
grace, we should be *m.* heirs. *Tit* 3:7
being *m.* so much better. *Heb* 1:4
it behoved him to be *m.* like.   2:17
for we are *m.* partakers of.   3:14
himself to be *m.* an high priest. 5:5
being *m.* perfect, he became the. 9
m. like to the Son of God.   7:3
m. of necessity a change.   12
m. not after law of a carnal.   16
an oath was *m.* priest.   20
those priests were *m.* without.   21
Jesus was *m.* a surety of a better. 22
there was a tabernacle *m.*   9:2
a perfect tabernacle not *m.*   11
not entered into holy places *m.*   24
is a remembrance *m.* of sins. 10:3
expecting till his enemies be *m.* 13
ye were *m.* a gazingstock.   33
were not *m.* of things which. 11:3
weakness which are *m.* strong. 34
us should not be *m.* perfect.   40
the spirits of just men *m.*   12:23
rich, in that he is *m.* low. *Jas* 1:10
by works was faith *m.* perfect. 2:22
m. after similitude of God.   3:9
m. head of the corner.   *1 Pet* 2:7
but these *m.* to be taken. *2 Pet* 2:12
they were *m.* bitter.   *Rev* 8:11
been *m.* drunk with wine of.   17:2

madest
thou *m.* him to have dominion over.
    Ps 8:6
visit the branch that thou *m.* 80:15
son of man, whom thou *m.*   17
m. to thyself images of. *Ezek* 16:17
thou *m.* all their loins to be. 29:7
neither *m.* it grow.   *Jonah* 4:10
art not thou that Egyptian which *m.*
    an uproar?   *Acts* 21:38
thou *m.* him a little lower. *Heb* 2:7

madman
fellow to play the *m.*   *1 Sam* 21:15
as a *m.* who casteth.   *Pr* 26:18

madmen
have I need of *m.?*   *1 Sam* 21:15
O *m.* the sword shall.   *Jer* 48:2

madness
shall smite thee with *m.* *Deut* 28:28
heart to know wisdom and *m.*
    Eccl 1:17
to behold wisdom and *m.*   2:12
wickedness of folly, and *m.*   7:25
m. is in their heart, while.   9:3
his talk is mischievous *m.*   10:13
horse and rider with *m.* *Zech* 12:4
were filled with *m.*   *Luke* 6:11
dumb ass forbade the *m.* *2 Pet* 2:16

Magdala
into the coasts of *M.*   *Mat* 15:39

magician
such things at any *m.*   *Dan* 2:10

magicians
and called for the *m.*   *Gen* 41:8
I told this to the *m.* but none. 24
m. of Egypt did so in like manner.
    Ex 7:11, 22; 8:7, 18
the *m.* said to Pharaoh, This. 8:19
m. could not stand before.   9:11
ten times better than all *m.* *Dan* 1:20
king commanded to call the *m.* 2:2
the secret cannot the *m.* shew. 27
then came in the *m.* but did not. 4:7
master of the *m.* tell me.   9
father made master of the *m.* 5:11

magistrate
was no *m.* in the land.   *Judg* 18:7
goest to the *m.* give.   *Luke* 12:58

magistrates
set *m.* and judges, who. *Ezra* 7:25
bring you to the *m.*   *Luke* 12:11*
Paul and Silas to the *m.* *Acts* 16:20
m. commanded to beat them.   22
the *m.* sent the serjeants.   35, 36
told these words to the *m.*   38
in mind to obey *m.* and.   *Tit* 3:1*

magnifical
the house must be exceeding *m.*
    1 Chr 22:5

magnificence
m. should be destroyed. *Acts* 19:27

magnified
thou hast *m.* thy mercy. *Gen* 19:19
Lord *m.* Joshua in sight. *Josh* 4:14
let thy name be *m.*   *2 Sam* 7:26
    1 Chr 17:24
and the Lord *m.* Solomon.
    1 Chr 29:25; *2 Chr* 1:1
Hezekiah was *m.* in sight of all.
    2 Chr 32:23*
say, Let the Lord be *m.*   *Ps* 35:27
say continually, The Lord be *m.*
    40:16; 70:4
thou hast *m.* thy word above. 138:2
for he *m.* himself against the Lord.
    Jer 48:26, 42; *Dan* 8:11
the enemy hath *m.* himself. *Lam* 1:9
and *m.* themselves against their bor-
    der.   *Zeph* 2:8
m. themselves against people.   10
Lord will be *m.* from the. *Mal* 1:5
but the people *m.* them. *Acts* 5:13
name of Lord Jesus was *m.* 19:17
Christ be *m.* in my body. *Phil* 1:20

magnify
[1] *To declare and shew forth one's
greatness and glory,* Luke 1:46.
[2] *To increase one's esteem, reputation, and authority,* Josh 3:7;
4:14; 1 Chr 29:25.
day will I begin to *m.* thee. *Josh* 3:7
thou shouldest *m.* him?   *Job* 7:17
if indeed ye will *m.* yourselves. 19:5
remember that thou *m.* his.   36:24
O *m.* the Lord with me.   *Ps* 34:3
clothed with shame that *m.* 35:26
my foot slippeth, they *m.*   38:16
did *m.* himself against me.   55:12
m. him with thanksgiving.   69:30
Shall the saw *m.* itself?   *Isa* 10:15
he will *m.* the law and make. 42:21
thus will I *m.* myself.   *Ezek* 38:23
and he shall *m.* himself.   *Dan* 8:25
the king shall *m.* himself.   11:36
shall *m.* himself above all.   37

they *m.* not themselves.   *Zech* 12:7
soul doth *m.* the Lord.   *Luke* 1:46
tongues, and *m.* God.   *Acts* 10:46
I am an apostle, I *m.*   *Rom* 11:13*

Magog
the son of Japheth, *M.*   *Gen* 10:2
    1 Chr 1:5
against the land of *M.*   *Ezek* 38:2
I will send a fire on *M.* and.   39:6
to gather Gog and *M.*   *Rev* 20:8

Mahanaim
called name of place *M.*   *Gen* 32:2
out of Gad to Levites, *M.*
    Josh 21:38; *1 Chr* 6:80
Ish-bosheth to *M.*   *2 Sam* 2:8
then David came to *M.*   17:24, 27
provided sustenance at *M.*   19:32
Shimei cursed me when I went to *M.*
    1 Ki 2:8
the son of Iddo had *M.*   4:14

Maher-shalal-hash-baz
in the roll concerning *M.*   *Isa* 8:1
then said Lord, Call his name *M.* 3

Mahlon
Elimelech's sons, *M.*   *Ruth* 1:2
M. and Chilion died also both.   5
have bought all that was *M.*   4:9
wife of *M.* have I purchased.   10

maid
(*The Revisions frequently substitute for this word the word*
handmaid. *The handmaids or
maidservants of those days were
usually slaves*)
go in unto my *m.* Hagar. *Gen* 16:2
behold, thy *m.* is in thy hand.   6
Hagar, Sarai's *m.* whence?   8
Laban gave Zilpah his *m.*   29:24
Bilhah, to be Rachel's *m.*   29
m. Bilhah, go in unto her.   30:3
Rachel's *m.* conceived.   7
gave Zilpah her *m.*   9
Zilpah, Leah's *m.* bare Jacob. 10, 12
she sent her *m.* to fetch.   *Ex* 2:5
the *m.* went and called the.   8
smite his *m.* with a rod.   21:20
or the eye of his *m.* that it.   26
if a man entice a *m.* not.   22:16*
shall be meat for thy *m.* *Lev* 25:6
I came to her, I found her not a *m.*
    Deut 22:14*, 17*
away captive a little *m.* *2 Ki* 5:2
thus said the *m.* that is of Israel.   4
m. was fair and beautiful. *Esth* 2:7
should I think upon a *m.?* *Job* 31:1
way of a man with a *m.* *Pr* 30:19
with *m.* so with mistress. *Isa* 24:2
m. forget her ornaments? *Jer* 2:32
the young man and the *m.*   51:22
father go in to the same *m.* *Amos* 2:7
for the *m.* is not dead.   *Mat* 9:24
by the hand, and the *m.* arose.   25
another *m.* saw him.   26:71
    Mark 14:69; *Luke* 22:56
called, saying, *M.,* arise. *Luke* 8:54

maid child
if she bear a *m. child.*   *Lev* 12:5

maiden
I have given my *m.* to.   *Gen* 30:18
is my daughter a *m.*   *Judg* 19:24
on young man or *m.*   *2 Chr* 36:17
every *m.* to the king.   *Esth* 2:13
as the eyes of a *m.* to her mistress.
    Ps 123:2
and mother of the *m.*   *Luke* 8:51

maidens
her *m.* walked along by.   *Ex* 2:5
abide here fast by my *m.* *Ruth* 2:8
that thou go out with his *m.*   22
kept fast by the *m.* of Boaz.   23
they found *m.* going to. *1 Sam* 9:11
I and my *m.* will fast.   *Esth* 4:16
thou bind him for thy *m.?* *Job* 41:5
their *m.* were not given.   *Ps* 78:63
young men and *m.* praise.   148:12
hath sent forth her *m.*   *Pr* 9:3
maintenance for thy *m.*   27:27
giveth a portion to her *m.*   31:15
I got me servants and *m.* *Eccl* 2:7
m. of seed of Israel.   *Ezek* 44:22*
begin to beat menservants and *m.*
    Luke 12:45

maids

preferred her and her *m.*   *Esth* 2:9
my *m.* count me for a.   *Job* 19:15
ravished the *m.* in cities.   *Lam* 5:11
slay utterly both *m.* and.   *Ezek* 9:6
her *m.* shall lead her with.   *Nah* 2:7
young men cheerful, and new wine
the *m.*   *Zech* 9:17

maidservant

the firstborn of the *m.*   *Ex* 11:5
thy *m.* shall do no work.   20:10
     Deut 5:14
not covet thy neighbour's wife, nor
m.   *Ex* 20:17
sell his daughter to be a *m.*   21:7
if he smite out his *m.'s* tooth.   27
if an ox push a *m.* he shall give.   32
that thy *m.* may rest as.   *Deut* 5:14
desire thy neighbour's *m.*   21
eat them, thou and thy *m.*   12:18
     16:11, 14
to thy *m.* thou shalt do.   15:17
son of his *m.* king.   *Judg* 9:18
despise cause of my *m.*   *Job* 31:13
his *m.* go free.   *Jer* 34:9, 10

maidservants

Abram had *m.* and she asses.
     Gen 12:16; 24:35
Abimelech's wife and *m.*   20:17
had much cattle and *m.*   30:43
entered into the two *m.'* tents.   31:33
rejoice, ye and your *m.*   *Deut* 12:12
he shall take your *m.*   *1 Sam* 8:16
of the *m.* shall I be had.   *2 Sam* 6:22
time to receive *m.?*   *2 Ki* 5:26

mail

he was armed with a coat of *m.*
     1 Sam 17:5, 38

maimed

blind or *m.* ye shall not.   *Lev* 22:22
them those that were *m.*   *Mat* 15:30
wondered when they saw the *m.*   31
better to enter into life *m.*   18:8*
     Mark 9:43
makest a feast, call *m.*   *Luke* 14:13
bring in hither the poor and *m.*   21

main

hoised up the *m.*-sail.   *Acts* 27:40*

maintain

[1] *To support and preserve,* 1 Chr
26:27; Ps 16:5. [2] *To defend
by argument,* Job 13:15. [3] *To
persevere in,* Tit 3:8, 14.
m. their cause.   *1 Ki* 8:45, 49, 59
     2 Chr 6:35, 39
they dedicate to *m.* the house of the
Lord.   *1 Chr* 26:27*
I will *m.* mine own ways.   *Job* 13:15
Lord will *m.* the cause of.   *Ps* 140:12
careful to *m.* good works.   *Tit* 3:8
learn to *m.* good works for uses.   14

maintained

for thou hast *m.* my right.   *Ps* 9:4

maintainest

portion, and thou *m.* my lot.   *Ps* 16:5

maintenance

have *m.* from the king.   *Ezra* 4:14*
the *m.* for thy maidens.   *Pr* 27:27

majesty

is the power and *m.*   *1 Chr* 29:11
upon him such royal *m.*   25
shewed the honour of his *m.*   *Esth* 1:4
with God is terrible in *m.*   *Job* 37:22
deck thyself now with *m.*   40:10
honour and *m.* hast thou.   *Ps* 21:5
voice of the Lord is full of *m.*   29:4
with thy glory and *m.*   45:3
in thy *m.* ride.   4
reigneth, he is clothed with *m.*   93:1
honour and *m.* are before him.   96:6
clothed with honour and *m.*   104:1
speak of the honour of thy *m.*   145:5
to make known the glorious *m.*   12
hide thee for the glory of his *m.*
     Isa 2:10; 19:21
they shall sing for the *m.* of.   24:14
behold the *m.* of the Lord.   26:10
ornament he set it in *m.*   *Ezek* 7:20

for the honour of my *m.*   *Dan* 4:30
excellent *m.* was added unto me.   36
Nebuchadnezzar thy father *m.*   5:18
the *m.* he gave him, all people.   19
feed in *m.* of the name.   *Mi* 5:4
on the right hand of *m. Heb* 1:3; 8:1
eyewitnesses of his *m.*   *2 Pet* 1:16
wise God be glory and *m.*   *Jude* 25

make

let us *m.* man.   *Gen* 1:26
I will *m.* him an help.   2:18
and a tree to be desired to *m.*   3:6
m. coats of skins.   21
m. thee an ark.   6:14
let us *m.* brick.   11:3
let us *m.* us a name.   4
I will *m.* of thee a great nation.
     12:2; 21:18; 46:3; *Ex* 32:10
let us *m.* a name, lest.   *Gen* 12:4
I will *m.* thy seed as the dust.   13:16
I will *m.* thee exceeding fruitful.
     17:6; 48:4
m. Ishmael fruitful, I will.   17:20
let us *m.* our father drink wine.
     19:32, 34
I will *m.* thy seed as the stars.   26:4
Isaac said, *M.* me savoury.   27:4
bless thee, and *m.* thee fruitful. 28:3
I will *m.* thy seed as the sand.   32:12
m. ye marriages with us and.   34:9
ye *m.* me to stink among the.   30
go to Beth-el, and *m.* there an.   35:1
m. there an altar unto God.   3
m. mention of me to Pharaoh. 40:14
land *m.* thy father to dwell.   47:6
God *m.* thee as Ephraim and. 48:20
they say to us, *M.* brick.   *Ex* 5:16
m. your count for the lamb.   12:4
m. them know the statutes.   18:16
not *m.* unto thee any graven image.
     20:4; *Lev* 26:1; *Deut* 5:8
not *m.* with me gods of.   *Ex* 20:23
an altar of earth shalt thou *m.*   24
if thou wilt *m.* me an altar.   25
m. full restitution.   22:3, 5, 6, 12
m. no mention of other gods. 23:13
     Josh 23:7
I will *m.* enemies turn.   *Ex* 23:27
shall not dwell, lest they *m.* thee. 33
m. me a sanctuary.   25:8
so shall ye *m.* it.   9
shalt *m.* holy garments.   28:2, 4
garments which they shall *m.*   4
for Aaron's sons thou shalt *m.*   40
m. them linen breeches.   42
m. him an altar of shittim.   30:1
m. it an oil of holy ointment.   25
perfume, you shall not *m.* like.   37
that they *m.* all that.   31:6; 35:10
up, *m.* us gods which shall go before
us.   32:1, 23; *Acts* 7:40
I will *m.* of thee a great.   *Ex* 32:10
I will *m.* my goodness pass.   33:19
and *m.* thy sons go a whoring. 34:16
m. no molten gods.   17; *Lev* 19:4
neither man nor woman *m. Ex* 36:6
he shall *m.* amends for.   *Lev* 5:16
not *m.* yourselves abominable.
     11:43; 20:25
not *m.* any cuttings in your.   19:28
not *m.* baldness.   21:5; *Deut* 14:1
I will *m.* you fruitful.   *Lev* 26:9
I will *m.* your heaven as iron.   22
beasts, which shall *m.* you few.   22
man shall *m.* a singular vow.   27:2
the Lord *m.* thee a curse, *m.* thy.
     Num 5:21
he shall not *m.* himself unclean. 6:7
the Lord *m.* his face to shine.   25
so *m.* themselves clean.   8:7
let us *m.* a captain, and return. 14:4
will *m.* of thee a greater nation.   12
thou *m.* thyself a prince.   16:13
if the Lord *m.* a new thing.   30
let them *m.* them broad plates.   38
I will *m.* to cease from me.   17:5
m. thee a fiery serpent, and.   21:8
he shall *m.* her vow of none.   30:8
ye shall *m.* it go through fire.   31:23
Lord *m.* you a thousand.   *Deut* 1:11
I will *m.* them rulers over you.   13
I will *m.* them hear my words.   4:10
ye *m.* you a graven image.   16, 23

nor shalt thou *m.* marriages.
     Deut 7:3
m. thee know that man liveth.   8:3
if it *m.* thee answer of peace. 20:11
if it will *m.* no peace with thee.   12
m. thee high above all nations. 26:19
shall *m.* thee plenteous. 28:11; 30:9
Lord shall *m.* thee the head.   13
m. the remembrance of.   32:26
I kill, and I *m.* alive, I wound.   39
thou shalt *m.* thy way.   *Josh* 1:8
m. yourselves accursed, and *m.* the
camp of Israel a curse.   6:18
m. confession.   7:19; *Ezra* 10:11
so shall your children *m. Josh* 22:25
m. marriages with them.   23:12
Samson, that he may *m. Judg* 16:25
m. the woman like Rachel and Leah.
     Ruth 4:11
provoked her sore, to *m. 1 Sam* 1:6
m. them inherit the throne.   2:8
ye *m.* the Lord's people to.   2:24
to *m.* yourselves fat with.   29
ye shall *m.* images of your.   6:5
m. a new cart.   7
m. us a king to judge us.   8:5
hearken to them, and *m.*   22
because it hath pleased the Lord to
m. you his.   12:22; *1 Chr* 17:22
Lord will *m.* my lord.   *1 Sam* 25:28
I will *m.* thee keeper of mine.   28:2
m. this fellow return that he.   29:4
will *m.* thee an house.   *2 Sam* 7:11
things, to *m.* thy servant know.   21
to *m.* him a name.   23
and *m.* thyself sick.   13:5
should I *m.* thee go up and ? 15:20
all my desire, though he *m.* it. 23:5
m. his throne greater.   *1 Ki* 1:37
God *m.* the name of Solomon.   47
did I not *m.* thee to swear ?   2:42
prayer which thy servant shall *m.*
     8:29; *2 Chr* 6:21
pray, and *m.* supplication to thee in.
     1 Ki 8:33, 47; *2 Chr* 6:24
I will *m.* him prince all. *1 Ki* 11:34
m. the yoke lighter.   12:9, 10
     2 Chr 10:10
m. thy house like the house of.
     1 Ki 16:3; 21:22; *2 Ki* 9:9
and after *m.* for thee.   *1 Ki* 17:13
if I *m.* not thy life as the life. 19:2
us *m.* a little chamber.   *2 Ki* 4:10
am I God to kill and to *m.* alive ? 5:7
let us *m.* a place, where we.   6:2
if Lord would *m.* windows. 7:2, 19
m. him arise up, and anoint.   9:2
we will not *m.* any king, do.   10:5
m. an agreement with me.   18:31
     Isa 36:16
nor will I *m.* feet of Israel move.
     2 Ki 21:8
m. his son or daughter to pass.
     23:10; *Ezek* 20:31
all Israel to *m.* him king.
     1 Chr 11:10; 12:31, 38
m. thee a name of greatness. 17:21
Lord *m.* his people 100 times. 21:3
he liked me to *m.* me king.   28:4
thine hand it is to *m.* great. 29:12
m. it a proverb among.   *2 Chr* 7:20
thought to *m.* him king.   11:22
God shall *m.* thee fall before.   25:8
I *m.* a decree what ye shall do.
     Ezra 6:8; 7:13, 21
branches of thick trees to *m.* booths.
     Neh 8:15
the king to *m.* supplication. *Esth* 4:8
Haman stood up to *m.* request.   7:7
m. them days of feasting and.   9:22
and his hands *m.* whole.   *Job* 5:18
m. thy supplication to.   8:5; 22:27
and if I *m.* my hands never.   9:30
should thy lies *m.* men hold ?   11:3
m. me to know my transgression.
     13:23
that ye *m.* yourselves strange. 19:3
now, who will *m.* me a liar ? 24:25
made me in womb *m.* him ? 31:15
quietness, who then can *m.* ? 34:29
they *m.* the oppressed to cry.   35:9
can *m.* his sword to approach. 40:19
will he *m.* many supplications ? 41:3
m. thy way straight before.   *Ps* 5:8

night _m._ I my bed to swim. _Ps_ 6:6
_m._ them as a fiery oven in. 21:9
shalt _m._ them turn their back. 12
_m._ me hope when on breasts. 22:9
_m._ thy face shine on thy servant.
31:16; 119:135
my soul shall _m._ her boast in. 34:2
_m._ me to know mine end. 39:4
_m._ me not the reproach of the. 8
_m._ no tarrying. 40:17; 70:5
will _m._ all his bed. 41:3
I will _m._ thy name to be. 45:17
the streams shall _m._ glad the. 46:4
in hidden part shalt _m._ me. 51:6
_m._ me to hear joy and gladness. 8
wings will I _m._ my refuge. 57:1
sing forth his name, _m._ his. 66:2
ye people, _m._ the voice of his. 8
thine enemies _m._ a tumult. 83:2
_m._ their nobles like Oreb. 11
O my God, _m._ them like a wheel. 13
valley of Baca, _m._ it a well. 84:6
will _m._ him my firstborn. 89:27
his seed also will I _m._ to endure. 29
_m._ us glad, according to the. 90:15
until I _m._ thine enemies thy. 110:1
Mat 22:44; _Mark_ 12:36
Luke 20:43; _Acts_ 2:35; _Heb_ 1:13
they that _m._ them are like unto.
_Ps_ 115:8; 135:18
_m._ me to understand the. 119:27
_m._ me go in the path of thy. 35
there will I _m._ the horn of. 132:17
if I _m._ my bed in hell, thou. 139:8
to the Lord did I _m._ my. 142:1
go humble thyself, and _m._ _Pr_ 6:3
fools _m._ a mock at sin, but. 14:9
and with good advice _m._ war. 20:18
after vows to _m._ enquiry. 25
_m._ thee know the certainty. 22:21
_m._ no friendship with an angry. 24
riches certainly _m._ themselves. 23:5
be wise, and _m._ my heart glad. 27:11
yet _m._ they their houses. 30:26
who can _m._ that straight ? _Eccl_ 7:13
nor _m._ thyself over wise. 16
when ye _m._ many prayers. _Isa_ 1:15
wash you, _m._ you clean. 16
_m._ me not a ruler. 3:7
_m._ the heart of this people fat. 6:10
let us _m._ a breach therein. 7:6
the Lord of hosts shall _m._ 10:23
and shall _m._ him of quick. 11:3
_m._ men go over dry shod. 15
_m._ mention that his name is. 12
will _m._ a man more precious. 13:12
_m._ thy shadow as the night. 16:3
Lord _m._ to all people a feast. 25:6
that he may _m._ peace with me. 27:5
_m._ to understand doctrine ? 28:9
that _m._ a man an offender. 29:21
to _m._ empty the soul of the. 32:6
wilt thou recover me and _m._ 38:16
_m._ straight in the desert a. 40:3
Mat 3:3; _Mark_ 1:3; _Luke_ 3:4
I will _m._ the wilderness. _Isa_ 41:18
I will _m._ the rivers islands. 42:15
I will _m._ darkness light before. 16
he will magnify and _m._ the law. 21
_m._ a way in the wilderness. 43:19
they that _m._ a graven image. 44:9
_m._ the crooked places straight. 45:2
_m._ peace and create evil, I the. 7
they shall _m._ supplication. 14
to whom will ye _m._ me equal ? 46:5
_m._ bare the leg, uncover the. 47:2
_m._ his way prosperous. 48:15
_m._ all my mountains a way. 49:11
_m._ the rivers a wilderness. 50:2
I will _m._ my judgements to rest. 51:4
they that rule over them, _m._ 52:5
when thou shalt _m._ his soul. 53:10
_m._ thy windows of agates. 54:12
I will _m._ them joyful in my. 56:7
_m._ ye a wide mouth ? 57:4
to _m._ your voice to be heard. 58:4
Lord shall _m._ fat thy bones. 11
I will _m._ the place of my feet. 60:13
_m._ thee an eternal excellency. 15
I will also _m._ thy officers peace. 17
till he _m._ Jerusalem a praise. 62:7
_m._ them drunk in my fury. 63:6
_m._ himself an everlasting name. 12
people to _m._ thyself a glorious. 14

to _m._ thy name known to thy. _Isa_ 64:2
as new earth which I will _m._ 66:22
shalt thou _m._ thyself fair. _Jer_ 4:30
_m._ my words in thy mouth. 5:14
_m._ thee mourning, as for an. 6:26
nor _m._ intercession to me. 7:16
_m._ Jerusalem heaps and den. 9:11
he turn it, and _m._ it gross. 13:16
_m._ thee a fenced brasen wall. 15:20
a man _m._ gods to himself. 16:20
good to the potter for it. 18:4
_m._ void counsel of Judah. 19:7
even _m._ this city as Tophet. 12
_m._ thee a terror to thyself. 20:4
I will _m._ thee a wilderness. 22:6
prophets, they _m._ you vain. 23:16
_m._ this house like Shiloh. 26:6
_m._ thee bonds and yokes, put. 27:2
now _m._ intercession to the Lord. 15
I will _m._ them like vile figs. 29:17
Lord _m._ thee like Zedekiah. 22
I will _m._ you be removed. 34:17
_m._ her cakes to worship her ? 44:19
_m._ ye him drunken: for he. 48:26
I will _m._ thee small among. 49:15
_m._ thee a burnt mountain. 51:25
and _m._ her springs dry. 36
_m._ them drunken. 39
I will _m._ drunk her princes. 57
_m._ bread thereof. _Ezek_ 4:9
_m._ a chain. 7:23
_m._ him a sign and a proverb. 14:8
I will _m._ my fury toward. 16:42
and _m._ you a new heart. 18:31
should we then _m._ mirth ? 21:10
that should _m._ up the hedge. 22:30
_m._ no mourning for the dead. 24:17
_m._ her like the top of a. 26:4, 14
I will _m._ thee a terror, thou. 21
_m._ the stars thereof dark. 32:7, 8
I will _m._ them and places. 34:26
_m._ them one stick, shall be. 37:19
_m._ them one nation in the land. 22
_m._ them keepers of charge. 44:14
shall _m._ thee to eat grass as oxen.
Dan 4:25, 32
_m._ this man to understand the vision.
8:16; 10:14
weeks to _m._ reconciliation for. 9:24
fall to _m._ them white. 11:35
shall go utterly to purge and _m._ 44
I _m._ her as a wilderness. _Hos_ 2:3
_m._ a wall, that she shall not find. 6
_m._ them to lie down safely. 18
_m._ the king glad with their. 7:3
_m._ Ephraim ride, Judah. 10:11
how shall I _m._ thee as Admah ? 11:8
_m._ thee dwell in tabernacles. 12:9
nor will I _m._ you a reproach.
Joel 2:19
_m._ the poor of the land to. _Amos_ 8:4
_m._ gardens, and eat fruit. 9:14
that _m._ my people err. _Mi_ 3:5
her that halted a remnant. 4:7
I will _m._ thee sick in smiting. 6:13
I will _m._ thy grave, for. _Nah_ 1:14
filth on thee, and _m._ thee vile. 3:6
_m._ thyself many, as the canker-. 15
write the vision, and _m._ _Hab_ 2:2
_m._ my feet like hinds' feet. 3:19
shall _m._ even a speedy riddance.
Zeph 1:18
for I will _m._ you a name. 3:20
I will _m._ thee as a signet. _Hag_ 2:33
_m._ bright clouds. _Zech_ 10:1
I will _m._ Jerusalem a cup of. 12:2
I _m._ Jerusalem a burdensome. 3
did not he _m._ one ? yet. _Mal_ 2:15
when I _m._ up my jewels. 3:17
_m._ her a publick example. _Mat_ 1:19
I will _m._ you fishers of men. 4:19
Mark 1:17
_m._ one hair white or black. _Mat_ 5:36
Lord, if thou wilt, thou canst _m._ me.
8:2; _Mark_ 1:40; _Luke_ 5:12
_m._ the tree good, or the. _Mat_ 12:33
let us _m._ here three tabernacles.
17:4; _Mark_ 9:5; _Luke_ 9:33
for pretence _m._ long prayers.
Mat 23:14; _Mark_ 12:40
to _m._ one proselyte, and. _Mat_ 23:15
ye _m._ clean the outside of the cup.
25; _Luke_ 11:39
I will _m._ thee ruler. _Mat_ 25:21

your way, _m._ it as sure. _Mat_ 27:65
why _m._ ye this ado ? _Mark_ 5:39
can ye _m._ children of ? _Luke_ 5:34
did he not _m._ that which is ? 11:40
consent began to _m._ excuse. 14:18
_m._ me as one of thy hired. 15:19
_m._ friends of the mammon of. 16:9
_m._ straight the way of. _John_ 1:23
_m._ not my Father's house. 2:16
by force to _m._ him a king. 6:15
the truth shall _m._ you free. 8:32
if the Son _m._ you free, ye shall. 36
dost thou _m._ us to doubt ? 10:24
will come and _m._ our abode. 14:23
_m._ me full of joy with. _Acts_ 2:28
him, arise and _m._ thy bed. 9:34
to _m._ thee a minister and a. 26:16
much learning doth _m._ thee mad. 24
_m._ the faith of God without effect.
Rom 3:3
do we then _m._ void the law ? 31
power to _m._ one vessel unto. 9:21
short work will the Lord _m._ 28
_m._ not provision for the flesh. 13:14
God is able to _m._ him stand. 14:4
things which _m._ for peace. 19
to _m._ a certain contribution. 15:26
and _m._ them the members. _1 Cor_ 6:15
meat _m._ my brother to offend. 8:13
temptation also _m._ a way to. 10:13
if I _m._ you sorry, who ? _2 Cor_ 2:2
_m._ up beforehand your bounty. 9:5
able to _m._ all grace abound. 8
did I _m._ gain of you by any ? 12:17
_m._ myself a transgressor. _Gal_ 2:18
_m._ the promise of none effect. 3:17
desire to _m._ a fair show in. 6:12
to _m._ in himself of twain. _Eph_ 2:15
the Lord _m._ you to increase in love.
1 Thes 3:12
_m._ ourselves an ensample to you.
2 Thes 3:9
scriptures which are able to _m._ thee
wise unto salvation. _2 Tim_ 3:15
_m._ full proof of thy ministry. 4:5
to _m._ the Captain of their. _Heb_ 2:10
to _m._ reconciliation for the sins. 17
liveth to _m._ intercession. 7:25
_m._ all things according to. 8:5
could not _m._ him that did. 9:9
_m._ comers thereunto perfect. 10:1
_m._ straight paths for your. 12:13
_m._ you perfect in every good. 13:21
of them that _m._ peace. _Jas_ 3:18
the God of all grace _m._ _1 Pet_ 5:10
_m._ your calling and. _2 Pet_ 1:10
we _m._ him a liar, his. _1 John_ 1:10
I will _m._ them worship. _Rev_ 3:9
_m._ a pillar in the temple of my. 12
eat it, and it shall _m._ thy belly. 10:9
shall _m._ war against them. 11:7
went to _m._ war with the. 12:17
saying, Who is able to _m._ war ? 13:4
that they should _m._ an image. 14
he doth judge and _m._ war. 19:11
behold, I _m._ all things new. 21:5
see **afraid, atonement, covenant,**
desolate, desolation, end, fire,
good, known, mention, noise

make haste

come on them, _m._ haste. _Deut_ 32:35
and said, _M._ haste and do as I have.
Judg 9:48
is before you, _m._ haste. _1 Sam_ 9:12
me to _m._ haste. _2 Chr_ 35:21
cause Haman to _m._ haste.
Esth 5:5; 6:10
for this I _m._ haste. _Job_ 20:2
_m._ haste to help me, O Lord, my.
_Ps_ 38:22; 40:13; 70:1; 71:12
I am poor and needy, _m._ haste unto
me. 70:5; 141:1
they _m._ haste to shed blood.
_Pr_ 1:16; _Isa_ 59:7
_m._ haste, my beloved. _S of S_ 8:14
he that believeth shall not _m._ haste.
Isa 28:16
thy children shall _m._ haste. 49:17
let them _m._ haste, and. _Jer_ 9:18
_m._ haste to the wall. _Nah_ 2:5
said, Zacchaeus, _m._ haste _Luke_ 19:5
_m._ haste and get quickly out.
Acts 22:18

make manifest

m. manifest the counsels. *1 Cor 4:5*
doth m. manifest is light. *Eph 5:13*
that I may m. it manifest. *Col 4:4*

make ready

m. ready three measures. *Gen 18:6*
m. ready, for these men. 43:16
and Joram said, M. ready. *2 Ki 9:21*
m. ready their arrow on. *Ps 11:2*
m. ready thine arrows. 21:12
the trumpet to m. ready. *Ezek 7:14*
there m. ready for us. *Mark 14:15*
Luke 22:12
to m. ready a people. *Luke 1:17*
m. ready, wherewith I may sup. 17:8
m. ready 200 soldiers to. *Acts 23:23*

make speed

m. speed, haste. *1 Sam 20:38*
m. speed to depart. *2 Sam 15:14*
let him m. speed and. *Isa 5:19*

make waste

m. your cities waste. *Lev 26:31*
will m. waste mountains. *Isa 42:15*
will m. Jerusalem waste. *Ezek 5:14*
m. land of Egypt utterly waste.
29:10; 30:12

maker, or makers

more pure than his M.? *Job 4:17*
in so doing my M. will soon. 32:22
where is God my M.? 35:10
righteousness to my M. 36:3
before the Lord our M. *Ps 95:6*
oppresseth the poor, reproacheth his
M. *Pr 14:31*
mocketh the poor reproacheth his M.
17:5
rich and poor, Lord is the M. 22:2
the m. of it as a spark. *Isa 1:31**
shall a man look to his M. 17:7
ye have not looked to the m. 22:11*
that striveth with his M. 45:9
Holy One of Israel and his M. 11
confusion that are m. of idols. 16
forgettest the Lord thy M. 51:13
thy m. is thy husband, and. 54:5
saith the Lord the M. *Jer 33:2*
hath forgotten his M. *Hos 8:14*
graven image that m. hath graven,
m. of his work ? *Hab 2:18*
builder and M. is God. *Heb 11:10*

makest

and what m. thou in ? *Judg 18:3*
m. me possess the iniquities of my
youth. *Job 13:26*
is it gain to him that thou m.? 22:3
thou only m. me to dwell. *Ps 4:8*
m. his beauty to consume. 39:11
thou m. us to turn back. 44:10
thou m. us a reproach to our. 13
thou m. us a byword among. 14
m. the outgoings of morning. 65:8
m. the earth soft with showers. 10
thou m. us a strife to our. 80:6
thou m. darkness, and it. 104:20
that thou m. account of him ? 144:3
m. thy flock to rest at. *S of S 1:7*
fashioneth it, what m. thou ? *Isa 45:9*
that m. thy nest in cedars. *Jer 22:23*
thou m. this people to trust. 28:15
thou m. thy high place. *Ezek 16:31*
and m. men as the fishes. *Hab 1:14*
bottle to him, and m. him. 2:15
when thou m. a dinner. *Luke 14:12*
but when thou m. a feast, call. 13
prophets are dead, whom m. thou
thyself ? *John 8:53*
because thou being a man m. 10:33
and m. thy boast of God. *Rom 2:17*
m. thy boast of the law. 23

maketh

who m. the dumb, or deaf ? *Ex 4:11*
priest that m. atonement clean.
Lev 7:7; 14:11
blood that m. an atonement. 17:11
that m. his son to pass. *Deut 18:10*
against the city that m. war. 20:20
he m. his sons to inherit. 21:16
m. merchandise of him. 24:7
cursed be the man that m. 27:15
cursed be he that m. the blind. 18
oath which the Lord m. with. 29:12
Lord killeth and m. *1 Sam 2:6*

the Lord m. poor, and m. rich.
1 Sam 2:7
God m. my way perfect.
2 Sam 22:33; Ps 18:32
he m. my feet like hinds' feet.
2 Sam 22:34; Ps 18:33
m. sore, and bindeth up. *Job 5:18*
Lord m. Arcturus, Orion. 9:9
he m. the judges fools. 12:17
he m. to stagger. 25
he m. collops of fat on his. 15:27
God m. my heart soft, and. 23:16
he m. peace in his high places. 25:2
booth that the keeper m. 27:18
m. us wiser than the fowls. 35:11
m. small the drops of water. 36:27
m. the deep to boil like a pot. 41:31
he m. a path to shine after him. 32
when he m. inquisition. *Ps 9:12*
he m. me to lie down in green. 23:2
Lord m. the hinds to calve 29:9
he m. the devices of people of. 33:10
blessed is the man that m. the. 40:4
he m. wars to cease to the end. 46:9
who m. the clouds his chariot. 104:3
m. his angels spirits. 4; *Heb 1:7*
wine that m. glad heart. *Ps 104:15*
m. the storm a calm, the. 107:29
he m. the hungry to dwell. 36
m. him families like a flock. 41
he m. the barren woman to. 113:9
m. lightnings for rain, bringeth. 135:7
who m. grass to grow on the. 147:8
he m. peace in thy borders. 14
a wise son m. a glad father. *Pr 10:1*
15:20
but the hand of the diligent m. 10:4
blessing of the Lord, it m. rich. 22
m. ashamed is as rottenness. 12:4
heart of a man m. it to stoop, but a
good word m. it glad. 25
m. himself rich, yet hath nothing,
there is that m. himself. 13:7
hope deferred m. the heart sick. 12
a merry heart m. a cheerful. 15:13
good report m. the bones fat. 30
he m. even his enemies to be. 16:7
a man's gift m. room for. 18:16
wealth m. many friends, but. 19:4
she m. herself coverings. 31:22
she m. fine linen and selleth it. 24
the work that God m. *Eccl 3:11*
oppression m. a wise man mad. 7:7
wisdom m. his face to shine. 8:1
not works of God, who m. all. 11:5
Lord m. the earth empty. *Isa 24:1*
he m. the judges of the earth. 40:23
which m. a way in the sea. 43:16
he m. a god, and worshippeth it.
44:15, 17; 46:6
I am the Lord that m. all. 44:24
he m. diviners mad. 25
watereth earth, and m. it. 55:10
m. himself a prey. 59:15
he m. lightnings. *Jer 10:13; 51:16*
cursed be the man that m. 17:5
m. himself a prophet. 29:26, 27
m. idols against herself. *Ezek 22:3*
but m. his petition three. *Dan 6:13*
that m. desolate. 11:31; 12:11
that m. the morning. *Amos 4:13*
seek him that m. the seven stars. 5:8
sea, and m. it dry. *Nah 1:4*
he m. his sun to rise on. *Mat 5:45*
he m. both deaf to hear. *Mark 7:37*
m. himself a king. *John 19:12*
Aeneas, Jesus Christ m. *Acts 9:34*
hope m. not ashamed. *Rom 5:5*
Spirit m. intercession. 8:26, 27, 34
m. intercession to God. 11:2
who m. thee to differ ? *1 Cor 4:7*
he that m. me glad, but ? *2 Cor 2:2*
m. manifest the savour of his. 14
it m. no matter to me. *Gal 2:6*
m. increase of the body. *Eph 4:16*
m. men high priests, but the word of
. . . the law m. the Son. *Heb 7:28*
he m. fire come down. *Rev 13:13*
whatsoever m. a lie. 21:27; 22:15

maketh haste

m. haste to be rich. *Pr 28:20*

making

m. confession to the. *2 Chr 30:22*

testimony of Lord is sure, m. wise.
Ps 19:7
of m. many books there. *Eccl 12:12*
walking and m. a tinkling. *Isa 3:16*
that brought tidings, m. *Jer 20:15*
m. ephah small, and the. *Amos 8:5*
m. the word of God of. *Mark 7:13*
m. himself equal with. *John 5:18*
as poor, yet m. many. *2 Cor 6:10*
give thanks for you, m. mention of.
Eph 1:16; 1 Thes 1:2; Philem 4
new man. so m. peace. *Eph 2:15*
m. melody in your heart. 5:19
you m. request with joy. *Phil 1:4*
m. them an ensample. *2 Pet 2:6*
compassion, m. a difference. *Jude 22*

making

wares of thy m. *Ezek 27:16, 18*

Malcham

by the Lord and by M. *Zeph 1:5*

Malchus

servant's name was M. *John 18:10*

male

every m. circumcised. *Gen 17:23*
34; 15:22, 24
for the passover a m. of. *Ex 12:5*
the m. shall be the Lord's. 13:12
34:19; *Luke 2:23*
a m. without blemish. *Lev 1:3, 10*
4:23; 22:19
every m. among the priests. 7:6
thy estimation shall be of the m. 27:3
5, 6, 7
every m. by their polls. *Num 1:2*
every m. from 20 years old. 20
every m. from a month old. 3:15
now kill every m. among. 31:17
smite every m. thereof. *Deut 20:13*
destroy every m. *Judg 21:11*
he had smitten every m. in Edom.
1 Ki 11:15, 16
hath in his flock a m. *Mal 1:14*
see female

male children

were the m. children of. *Josh 17:2*

malefactor

if he were not a m. *John 18:30**

malefactors

there were two m. *Luke 23:32*
they crucified him, and the m. 33
one of the m. railed on him. 39

males

Levi slew all the m. *Gen 34:25*
m. be circumcised. *Ex 12:48*
to the Lord all being m. 13:15
three times a year all thy m. shall appear before. 23:17; *Deut 16:16*
all the m. of Aaron. *Lev 6:18, 29*
number of all m. from a month old.
Num 3:22; 28:34; 26:62
the firstborn of the m. 3:40, 43
Midianites, and slew the m. 31:7
all firstling m. sanctify. *Deut 15:19*
m. that came out of Egypt died.
Josh 5:4
their genealogy of m. *2 Chr 31:16*
to all the m. among priests. 19
by genealogy of the m. *Ezra 8:3*

malice

not with leaven of m. *1 Cor 5:8*
howbeit in m. be ye children. 14:20
from you with all m. *Eph 4:31*
also put off all these; m. *Col 3:8*
living in m. and envy. *Tit 3:3*
laying aside all m. *1 Pet 2:1**

malicious

prating against us with m. *3 John 10**

maliciousness

all unrighteousness, m. *Rom 1:29*
liberty for a cloke of m. *1 Pet 2:16**

malignity

murder, debate, m. *Rom 1:29*

mallows

cut up m. by the bushes. *Job 30:4*

mammon

ye cannot serve God and m.
Mat 6:24; Luke 16:13
make friends of m. of. *Luke 16:9*
if not faithful in unrighteous m. 11

Mamre

Abram dwelt in the plain of *M*.
    Gen 13:18; 14:13
Eshcol, *M*. let them take. 14:24
appeared to Abraham in *M*. 18:1
Machpelah before *M*. 23:17, 19
    49:30; 50:13
Jacob came to Isaac to *M*. 35:27

man

[1] *A human being*, 1 Cor 10:13.
[2] *The human race; mankind*,
Job 5:7. [3] *The adult male, as
distinguished from a woman or a
child*, Acts 4:22.

God said, Let us make *m*. in our
  image. *Gen* 1:26, 27; 9:6
God formed *m*. of the dust. 2:7
it is not good that *m*. should. 18
they were both naked, the *m*. 25
the *m*. is become as one of us. 3:22
not always strive with *m*. 6:3
I will destroy *m*. whom I have. 7
curse the ground for *m*.'s sake. 8:21
m.'s blood, by *m*. shall his. 9:6
which have not known *m*. 19:8
    Num 31:35
restore the *m*. his wife. *Gen* 20:7
the *m*. wondering at her held. 24:21
Laban ran out to the *m*. to. 29
what *m*. is this that walketh ? 65
give her to another *m*. 29:19
by the *m*. whose these are. 38:25
arise, go again to the *m*. 43:13
the *m*. in whose hand cup. 44:17
that ye have left the *m*.? *Ex* 2:20
content to dwell with the *m*. 21
who hath made *m*.'s mouth ? 4:11
upon *m*., flesh shall it not be. 30:32
m. that brought us out of. 32:1, 23
be imputed to that *m*. and that *m*.
  shall be cut off from. *Lev* 17:4
m. bring his wife to. *Num* 5:15
but the *m*. that is clean, and. 9:13
the *m*. Moses was very meek. 12:3
the *m*. shall be put to death. 15:35
    Deut 22:25
m. whom the Lord doth. *Num* 16:7
but *m*. that shall be unclean. 19:20
day that God created *m*. *Deut* 4:32
God doth talk with *m*. and he. 5:24
m. doth not live by bread only, but.
  8:3; *Mat* 4:4; *Luke* 4:4
tree of the field is *m*.'s. *Deut* 20:19
and they shall come *m*. by m.
    Josh 7:14, 17, 18
but they let go the *m*. *Judg* 1:25
I will shew thee the *m*. whom. 4:22
for as the *m*. is, so is his. 8:21
me they honour God and *m*. 9:9
cheereth God and *m*. 13
what *m*. will fight against ? 10:18
m. hath appeared that came. 13:10
the *m*. spakest to the woman ? 11
and as another *m*. 16:7, 11, 17
bring forth the *m*. that came. 19:22
the *m*. took her on an ass and. 28
m. was Elimelech. *Ruth* 1:2; 2:19
for the *m*. will not be in rest. 3:18
m. of thine whom I. *1 Sam* 2:33
m. came in hastily, and told. 4:14
a *m*. of God. and he is an honourable *m*. 9:6
behold the *m*. whom I spake. 17
if the *m*. should yet come. 10:22
Lord seeth not as *m*. seeth. 16:7
what be done to the *m*.? 17:26
lo, ye see the *m*. is mad. 21:14
anger kindled against the *m*. said to
  Nathan, the *m*. that. *2 Sam* 12:5
David, Thou art the *m*. 7
come out, thou bloody *m*. 16:7*, 8
the *m*. thou seekest is as if. 17:3
m. that consumed us, and. 21:5
the *m*. who was raised up on. 23:1
slew every one his *m*. *1 Ki* 20:20
when *m*. turned again. *2 Ki* 5:26
I will bring you to the *m*. 6:19
you know the *m*. and his. 9:11
tell the *m*. that sent you. *2 Chr* 34:23
Levites, *m*. by *m*. 38,000. *1 Chr* 23:3
the palace is not for *m*. but. 29:1
let not *m*. prevail. *2 Chr* 14:11

for ye judge not for *m*. but.
    2 Chr 19:6
what shall be done unto the *m*.?
    Esth 6:6, 7, 9
m. be more just than ? *Job* 4:17
yet *m*. is born to trouble, as. 5:7
happy is the *m*. whom God. 17
appointed time for *m*. on earth ? 7:1
what is *m*. that thou shouldest ? 17
  15:14; *Ps* 8:4; 144:3; *Heb* 2:6
but how should *m*. be just ? *Job* 9:2
or seest thou as *m*. seeth ? 10:4
days of *m*.? years as *m*.'s days ? 5
vain *m*. would be wise, though *m*.
    11:12
m. that is born of a woman. 14:1
m. dieth and wasteth away, *m*. 10
so *m*. lieth down, and riseth not. 12
first *m*. that was born ? 15:7
what is *m*. that he should be ? 14
abominable and filthy is *m*. 16
m. was first placed on the. 20:4
me is my complaint to *m*.? 21:4
can *m*. be justified with God ? 25:4
m. that is a worm, and son of *m*. 6
but there is a spirit in *m*. 32:8
God thrusteth him down, not *m*. 13
that God is greater than *m*. 33:12
God speaketh, yet *m*. perceiveth it
  not. 14
that he may withdraw *m*. from purpose, and hide pride from *m*. 17
if a messenger, to shew to *m*. 23
worketh God often with *m*. 29
m. is like Job, who drinketh ? 34:7
his heart upon *m*. if he gather. 14
for he will not lay on *m*. more. 23
arise, O Lord, let not *m*. *Ps* 9:19
that the *m*. of earth may no. 10:18
what *m*. is he that feareth ? 25:12
what *m*. is he that desireth ? 34:12
when thou dost correct *m*. 39:11
m. being in honour. 49:12, 20
I will not be afraid what *m*. 56:11
m. did eat angels' food, he. 78:25
thy hand be on the *m*. of. 80:17
what *m*. is he that liveth ? 89:48
thou turnest *m*. to destruction. 90:3
that teacheth *m*. knowledge ? 94:10
for *m*. his days are as grass. 103:15
m. goeth forth to his work. 104:23
I will not fear what *m*. can. 118:6
than put confidence in *m*. 8
m. is like to vanity, his days. 144:4
from *m*. that speaketh. *Pr* 2:12
come as an armed *m*. 6:11; 24:34
preparations of the heart in *m*. 16:1
m.'s goings are of the Lord, how can
  a *m*.? 20:24
so is the *m*. that deceiveth. 26:19
things full of labour, *m*. *Eccl* 1:8
can the *m*. do that cometh ? 2:12
hath *m*. of all his labour ? 22
it is known that it is *m*. 6:10
what is *m*. better ? 11
what is good for *m*.? 11
because *m*. goeth to his long. 12:5
from *m*. whose breath is. *Isa* 2:22
I said, I shall behold *m*. no. 38:11
the *m*. that executeth my. 46:11
it is not in *m*. to direct. *Jer* 10:23
I am the *m*. that hath. *Lam* 3:1
cows' dung for *m*.'s dung.
    Ezek 4:15
judgement between *m*. and *m*. 18:8
be changed from *m*.'s. *Dan* 4:16
O *m*. greatly beloved. 10:19
for I am God, and not *m*. *Hos* 11:9
declareth to *m*. what is. *Amos* 4:13
that tarrieth not for *m*. *Mi* 5:7
he hath shewed thee, O *m*. 6:8
the *m*. of wisdom shall see. 9
the wicked devoureth *m*. *Hab* 1:13
I will cut off the *m*. *Zeph* 1:3
the *m*. whose name is. *Zech* 6:12
m. taught me to keep cattle. 13:5*
awake, O sword, against *m*. that. 7
Lord will cut off the *m*. *Mal* 2:12
what *m*. is there of you, if his son ?
    Mat 7:9; 12:11; *Luke* 15:4
and they defile the *m*. *Mat* 15:18
let not *m*. put asunder. 19:6
    Mark 10:9
I do not know the *m*. *Mat* 26:72, 74

sabbath was made for *m*. not *m*.
    Mark 2:27
colt tied, whereon never *m*. sat. 11:2
he said, *M*. thy sins are. *Luke* 5:20
m. who made me a judge ? 12:14
fear not God, nor regard *m*. 18:4
Peter said, *M*., I am not. 22:58
Peter said, *M*., I know not. 60
he asked, whether the *m*. was. 23:6
never *m*. was laid. 53; *John* 19:41
knew what was in *m*. *John* 2:25
what *m*. is that which said ? 5:12
not testimony from *m*. 34
which none other *m*. did. 15:24
unto them, Behold the *m*. 19:5
for the *m*. was above. *Acts* 4:22
how can I, except some *m*.? 8:31
himself, or of some other *m*.? 34
the *m*. in whom the evil. 19:16
what *m*. is there that knoweth ? 35
m. that owneth this girdle. 21:11
Jews laid wait for the *m*. 23:30
I would also hear the *m*. 25:22
inexcusable, O *m*. *Rom* 2:1
thinkest thou, O *m*. 3
of God after the inward *m*. 7:22
O wretched *m*. that I am, who ? 24
but O *m*. who art thou that ? 9:20
the *m*. who doeth. 10:5; *Gal* 3:12
with heart *m*. believeth. *Rom* 10:10
what *m*. knoweth the things of a *m*.?
    1 Cor 2:11
how knowest thou, O *m*.? 7:16*
such as is common to *m*. 10:13
head of the woman is the *m*. 11:3
m. is not of the woman. 8
but woman for the *m*. 9
m. without the woman, nor the
  woman without the *m*. 11
the *m*. also by the woman. 12
by *m*. came death, by *m*. 15:21
the first *m*. Adam was made. 45
the first *m*. is of the earth, earthy;
  the second *m*. is the Lord. 47
outward *m*. perish, yet the inward *m*.
  is renewed day by. *2 Cor* 4:16
not of men, neither by *m*. *Gal* 1:1
I preached is not after *m*. 11
of twain one new *m*. *Eph* 2:15
his Spirit in the inner *m*. 3:16
that ye put on new *m*. created. 4:24
new *m*. which is renewed. *Col* 3:10
despiseth not *m*. but God. *1 Thes* 4:8
men, the *m*. Christ Jesus. *1 Tim* 2:5
usurp authority over the *m*. 12
Saviour toward *m*. appeared. *Tit* 3:4
house is built by some *m*. *Heb* 3:4
Lord pitched, and not *m*. 8:2
I will not fear what *m*. shall. 13:6
a double minded *m*. is unstable in
  all his ways. *Jas* 1:8
wilt thou know, O vain *m*.? 2:20
let it be the hidden *m*. *1 Pet* 3:4
see **beast, blessed, cursed, each,
  evil, foolish, good, old, poor,
  rich, understanding**

a man

not *a m*. to till the ground. *Gen* 2:5
shall *a m*. leave his father. 24
Mat 19:5; *Mark* 10:7; *Eph* 5:31
I have gotten *a m*. from the Lord.
    Gen 4:1
slain *a m*. to my wounding. 23
if *a m*. can number the dust. 13:16
there is not *a m*. to come in. 19:31
dead man; she is *a m*.'s wife. 20:3
Esau a cunning hunter, *a m*. 25:27
there wrestled *a m*. with him. 32:24
let Pharaoh look out *a m*. discreet
  and wise. 41:33
a m. in whom the Spirit of God. 38
wot ye not such *a m*. as I can ? 44:15
in their anger they slew *a m*. 49:6
face, as *a m*. speaketh. *Ex* 33:11
plague of leprosy is in *a m*. *Lev* 13:9
if *a m*. do he shall live. 18:5
  Neh 9:29; *Ezek* 20:11, 13, 21
and *a m*. of Israel strove. *Lev* 24:10
caused a blemish in *a m*. 20
no devoted thing *a m*. shall. 27:28
be *a m*. of every tribe. *Num* 1:4
tribe shall ye send *a m*. 13:2
a m. that gathered sticks. 15:32

is law when a m. dieth. Num 19:14
God is not a m. that he should lie.
    23:19; 1 Sam 15:29
among these there was not a m. of.
    Num 26:64
was not left a m. save Caleb. 65
a m. over the congregation. 27:16
take thee Joshua, a m. in whom. 18
Lord bare thee, as a m. Deut 1:31
after the cubit of a m. 3:11
that as a m. chasteneth his son. 8:5
shall not rise against a m. 19:15
take ye out of every tribe a m.
    Josh 3:12; 4:2, 4
a m. over against him with. 5:13
shall not a m. of them stand. 10:8
hearkened to the voice of a m. 14
Arba was a great m. among. 14:15
not a m. of all their enemies. 21:44
the spies saw a m. Judg 1:24
escaped not a m. 3:29
was not a m. left. 4:16
was a m. that told a dream. 7:13
save the sword of Gideon a m. 14
Tola a m. of Issachar. 10:1
she called a m. 16:19
a m. plucked off his shoe. Ruth 4:7
I will send thee a m. 1 Sam 9:16
there shall not a m. be put. 11:13
the Lord hath sought him a m. 13:14
not leave a m. of them. 14:36
a m. who is a cunning player. 16:16
provide me a m. that can play. 17
choose you a m. for you, let. 17:8
give me a m. that we may fight. 10
such that a m. cannot speak. 25:17
and there escaped not a m. 30:17
as a m. falleth before. 2 Sam 3:34
prince and a great m. is fallen. 38
a m. enquired at the oracle. 16:23
happened to be there a m. 20:1*
and shew thyself a m. 1 Ki 2:2
not fail thee a m. on throne. 4; 8:25
a m. turned aside, and brought a m.
    20:39
a m. whom I appointed to. 42
came a m. to meet us. 2 Ki 1:6
a m. from Baal-shalisha. 4:42
not a m. left that came not. 10:21
as they were burying a m.. 13:21
shall be a m. of rest. 1 Chr 22:9
there shall not fail thee a m.
    2 Chr 6:16; 7:18
a m. to seek the welfare. Neh 2:10
should such a m. as I flee? 6:11
all that a m. hath will he. Job 2:4
why is light given to a m.? 3:23
shall a m. be more pure than? 4:17
he is not a m. as I am, that. 9:32
and should a m. full of talk? 11:2
he shutteth up a m. 12:14
if a m. die. 14:14
one might plead for a m. with God,
    as a m. pleadeth for. 16:21
can a m. be profitable to God? 22:2
done against a nation or a m. 34:29
thy wickedness may hurt a m. 35:8
if a m. speak he shall be swallowed.
    37:20
gird up now thy loins like a m. 38:3
    40:7
I was as a m. that. Ps 38:14
but it was thou, a m. mine. 55:13
imagine mischief against a m.? 62:3
a m. was famous according. 74:5
a m. that hath no strength. 88:4
he sent a m. before them. 105:17
pleasure in the legs of a m. 147:10
strive not with a m. Pr 3:30
for jealousy is the rage of a m. 6:34
there is a way that seemeth right
    unto a m. 14:12; 16:25
all ways of a m. are clean. 16:2
a m.'s ways please the Lord. 7
how can a m. understand? 20:24
a m. given to appetite. 23:2
so a contentious m. to kindle. 26:21
so is a m. that wandereth. 27:8
as the furnace, so is a m. to. 21
when the wicked rise a m. 28:12
he that rebuketh a m. shall find. 23
seest thou a m. that is hasty? 29:20
a m. whose labour is in wisdom and
    knowledge, yet to a m. Eccl 2:21

God giveth to a m. that is good.
    Eccl 2:26
for this a m. is envied of his. 4:4
a m. to whom God hath given. 6:2
who can tell a m. what shall? 12
a m. cannot tell what shall. 10:14
if a m. live many years. 11:8
if a m. would give all. S of S 8:7
I am a m. of unclean lips. Isa 6:5
a m. more precious than. 13:12
at that day shall a m. look. 17:7
than that a m. can stretch. 28:20
that make a m. an offender. 29:21
a m. shall be an hiding place. 32:2
not meet thee as a m. 47:3
he is a m. of sorrows and. 53:3
for a m. to afflict his soul? 58:5
an ox, is as if he slew a m. 66:3
forsaken, and not a m. Jer 4:29
places, if ye can find a m. 5:1
why shouldest thou be as a m.? 14:9
that thou hast borne me a m. 15:10
a m. made gods to himself? 16:20
a m. that shall not prosper. 22:30
I am like a m. whom wine. 23:9
see whether a m. doth travail? 30:6
a woman shall compass a m. 31:22
David shall never want a m. 33:17
shall the priests want a m. 18
Jonadab shall not want a m. 35:19
man put in array like a m. to. 50:42
good for a m. to hope. Lam 3:26
it is good for a m. that he bear. 27
complain, a m. for punishment. 39
sought for a m. among. Ezek 22:30
art a m. and not God. 28:2, 9
people of the land take a m. 33:2
not a m. on earth that. Dan 2:10
found a m. of the captives. 25
there is a m. in thy kingdom. 5:11
stand as a m. and a m.'s heart. 7:4
O Daniel, a m. greatly. 10:11
robbers wait for a m. Hos 6:9
there shall not be a m. left. 9:12
drew them with cords of a m. 11:4
a m. and his father go. Amos 2:7
as if a m. did flee from a lion. 5:19
a m. and his house, even a m. Mi 2:2
if a m. walking in spirit and. 11
a m.'s enemies are the men of his
    own house. 7:6; Mat 10:36
as a m. spareth his own. Mal 3:17
I am a m. under authority. Mat 8:9
    Luke 7:8
to set a m. at variance. Mat 10:35
how much is a m. better? 12:12
spirit is gone out of a m. 43
the mouth defileth a m. 15:11
unwashen hands defileth not a m. 20
is it lawful for a m. to put away?
    19:3; Mark 10:2
if a m. die having no. Mat 22:24
the city, to such a m. and say to him.
    26:18; Mark 14:13; Luke 22:10
seeing I know not a m.? Luke 1:34
depart, for I am a sinful m. 5:8
which a m. took and cast. 13:19
to be guest with a m. that is. 19:7
there was a m. sent from. John 1:6
after me cometh a m. who is. 30
except a m. be born again. 3:3, 5
how can a m. be born when? 4
a m. can receive nothing, except. 27
come, see a m. which told me. 4:29
I have made a m. whole. 7:23
a m. that hath told you the. 8:40
a m. that is called Jesus. 9:11
how can a m. a sinner, do such? 16
a m. makest thyself God. 10:33
if a m. love me, he will keep. 14:23
for joy that a m. is born into. 16:21
Jesus a m. approved of. Acts 2:22
I myself also am a m. 10:26
I found David, a m. after. 13:22
not believe, though a m. declare. 41
there stood a m. of Macedonia. 16:9
I am a m. who am a Jew. 21:39
preachest a m. should. Rom 2:21
sayest, a m. should not commit. 22
I speak as a m. 3:5
dominion over a m. 7:1
let a m. so account of us. 1 Cor 4:1
it is required, that a m. be found. 2
every sin that a m. doeth is. 6:18

it is good for a m. not to touch.
    1 Cor 7:1
I say that it is good for a m. so. 26
say I these things as a m.? or. 9:8
a m. indeed ought not to. 11:7
if a m. have long hair, it is a. 14
but let a m. examine himself. 28
when I became a m., I put. 13:11
sufficient to such a m. is. 2 Cor 2:6
according to that a m. hath. 8:12
if a m. bring you into bondage, if a m.
    smite. 11:20
I knew a m. in Christ caught. 12:2, 3
which it is not lawful for a m. 4
a m. is not justified by. Gal 2:16
brethren, if a m. be overtaken. 6:1
think himself to be. 3
found in fashion as a m. Phil 2:8
the law is good, if a m. 1 Tim 1:8
if a m. desire the office of a. 3:1
if a m. know not how to rule his. 5
if a m. also strive for. 2 Tim 2:5
if a m. therefore purge himself. 21
a m. that is a heretic. Tit 3:10
he is like a m. beholding. Jas 1:23
if there come a m. with a gold. 2:2
what profit, though a m. say. 14
a m. may say, Thou hast faith. 18
ye see how that by works a m. 24
Elias was a m. subject to like. 5:17
if a m. for conscience. 1 Pet 2:19
for of whom a m. is. 2 Pet 2:19
if a m. say, I love God. 1 John 4:20
beast had a face as a m. Rev 4:7
scorpion, when he striketh a m. 9:5

a certain man

a cer. m. found him. Gen 37:15
a cer. m. saw it, and. 2 Sam 18:10
a cer. m. drew a bow at a venture.
    1 Ki 22:34; 2 Chr 18:33
a cer. m. had two sons. Mat 21:28
    Luke 15:11
a cer. m. went down. Luke 10:30
the ground of a cer. rich m. 12:16
a cer. m. had a fig tree planted. 13:6
a cer. m. made a great supper.
    14:16
there was a cer. m. which had. 16:1
a cer. blind m. sat by the way. 18:35
a cer. noble-m. went into a. 19:12
a cer. m. planted a vineyard. 20:9
a cer. noble-m. whose son was sick.
    John 4:46
a cer. m. was sick, named. 11:1
a cer. m. lame from his. Acts 3:2
a cer. m. named Ananias, sold. 5:1
a cer. m. called Simeon, who. 8:9
there he found a cer. m. 9:33
there was a cer. m. in Caesarea. 10:1
there sat a cer. m. at Lystra. 14:8
entered into a cer. m.'s house. 18:7
a cer. m. named Demetrius. 19:24
a cer. m. left in bonds. 25:14

any man

a virgin, nor had any m. known her.
    Gen 24:16
if thou knowest any m. of activity.
    47:6
if any m. have any. Ex 24:14
nor let any m. be seen through. 34:3
nor shall any m. desire thy land. 24
any m. hath a running. Lev 15:2
if any m.'s seed of copulation go. 16
if any m. lie with her at all, he. 24
killeth any m. shall surely. 24:17
any m. giveth the priest. Num 5:10
if any m.'s wife go aside, and. 12
if any m. die very suddenly. 6:9
the dead body of any m. 19:11, 13
if a serpent had bitten any m. 21:9
if any m. hate his neighbour and.
    Deut 19:11
witness rise up against any m. 16
blood on thy house, if any m. 22:8
be any m. among you that is not
    clean. 23:10
not any m. be able to stand before.
    Josh 1:5
remain courage in any m. 2:11
when any m. doth enquire, Is there
    any m. here? Judg 4:20
weak and be like any other m. 16:17
no business with any m. 18:7, 28

that when any *m.* offered sacrifice.
1 Sam 2:13
if any *m.* said, Fail not to burn. 16
taken aught at any *m.'s* hand. 12:4
when any *m.* that had a controversy.
2 Sam 15:2
it was so, that when any *m.* came. 5
shall any *m.* be put to death. 19:22
for us shalt thou kill any *m.* 21:4
if any *m.* trespass. *1 Ki* 8:31
what supplication soever be made
by any *m.* 38; *2 Chr* 6:29
if thou meet any *m.* *2 Ki* 4:29
chose I any *m.* to be ruler. *2 Chr* 6:5
nor told I any *m.* what God put in my
heart. *Neh* 2:12
let me not accept any *m.* *Job* 32:21
more brutish than any *m.* *Pr* 30:2
marred more than any *m.* *Isa* 52:14
in mouth of any *m.* *Jer* 44:26
come not near any *m.* on. *Ezek* 9:6
ask a petition of any god or *m.*
Dan 6:7, 12
if any *m.* sue thee at law. *Mat* 5:40
knoweth any *m.* the Father. 11:27
nor shall any *m.* hear his voice. 12:19
if any *m.* will come after me. 16:24
Luke 9:23
if any *m.* say aught to you, say.
Mat 21:3; *Mark* 11:3; *Luke* 19:31
carest thou for any *m.* *Mat* 22:16
nor durst any *m.* from that day. 46
if any *m.* say, Lo, here is Christ.
24:23; *Mark* 13:21
nothing to any *m.* but go. *Mark* 1:44
if any *m.* hath ears to hear. 4:23
7:16; *Rev* 13:9
neither could any *m.* tame. *Mark* 5:4
not that any *m.* should know it. 9:30
if any *m.* desire to be first, the. 35
take heed, lest any *m.* deceive. 13:5
nor said any thing to any *m.* 16:8
art bidden of any *m.* to. *Luke* 14:8
if any *m.* come to me, and hate. 26
taken any thing from any *m.* 19:8
if any *m.'s* brother die, having. 20:28
hath any *m.* brought him aught to
eat? *John* 4:33
not that any *m.* hath seen. 6:46
if any *m.* eat of this bread he. 51
if any *m.* do his will he shall. 7:17
if any *m.* thirst, let him come. 37
doth our law judge any *m.?* 51
never in bondage to any *m.* 8:33
if any *m.* did confess that he. 9:22
if any *m.* be a worshipper of. 31
that any *m.* opened the eyes of. 32
by me, if any *m.* enter in, he. 10:9
nor shall any *m.* pluck them out. 28
if any *m.* walk in the day. 11:9
if any *m.* knew where he were. 57
if any *m.* serve me, let him. 12:26
if any *m.* hear my words. 47
that any *m.* should ask thee. 16:30
for us to put any *m.* to death. 18:31
not call any *m.* common. *Acts* 10:28
can any *m.* forbid water, these? 47
matter against any *m.* law. 19:38
me disputing with any *m.* 24:12
Romans to deliver any *m.* 25:16
shall be no loss of any *m.'s* life. 27:22
if any *m.* have not the Spirit of.
Rom 8:9
if any *m.* build on this. *1 Cor* 3:12
if any *m.'s* work abide. 14
if any *m.'s* work be burnt. 15
if any *m.* defile the temple of. 17
if any *m.* among you seemeth. 18
any *m.* that is called a brother. 5:11
is any *m.* called, being circumcised?
7:18
if any *m.* think that he knoweth. 8:2
if any *m.* love God. 3
if any *m.* see thee which hast. 10
that any *m.* should make my. 9:15
if any *m.* say that this is offered.
10:28
any *m.* seem to be contentious. 11:16
if any *m.* hunger let him. 34
any *m.* speak in an unknown. 14:27
if any *m.* think himself to be a. 37
if any *m.* be ignorant, let him. 38
if any *m.* love not the Lord. 16:22
if any *m.* be in Christ. *2 Cor* 5:17

if any *m.* trust to himself that.
2 Cor 10:7
lest any *m.* should think of. 12:6
if any *m.* preach any other. *Gal* 1:9
not of works, lest any *m.* *Eph* 2:9
whatsoever good thing any *m.* 6:8
lest any *m.* should beguile. *Col* 2:4
beware lest any *m.* spoil you. 8
if any *m.* hath a quarrel. 3:13
none render evil for evil to any *m.*
1 Thes 5:15
did eat any *m.'s* bread. *2 Thes* 3:8
if any *m.* obey not our word. 14
any *m.* teach otherwise. *1 Tim* 6:3
lest any *m.* fall after. *Heb* 4:11
but if any *m.* draw back, my. 10:38
lest any *m.* fail of the grace. 12:15
nor tempteth any *m.* *Jas* 1:13
if any *m.* among you seem. 26
if any *m.* offend not in word. 3:2
if any *m.* speak, let him.
1 Pet 4:11
yet if any *m.* suffer as christian. 16
if any *m.* sin, we have. *1 John* 2:1
if any *m.* love the world, the. 15
and ye need not that any *m.* 27
if any *m.* see his brother sin. 5:16
if any *m.* hear my voice. *Rev* 3:20
if any *m.* will hurt them, fire. 11:5
if any *m.* worship the beast. 14:9
if any *m.* shall add to these. 22:18
if any *m.* shall take away from. 19

man child

every *m. child* shall be circumcised.
Gen 17:10, 12
the uncircumcised *m. child* shall. 14
born a *m. child*, then. *Lev* 12:2
handmaid a *m. child.* *1 Sam* 1:11
said, There is a *m. child* conceived.
Job 3:3; *Jer* 20:15
she was delivered of a *m. child.*
Isa 66:7; *Rev* 12:5
brought forth a *m. child. Rev* 12:13

every man

on earth, and every *m.* *Gen* 7:21
at hand of every *m.'s* brother. 9:5
hand be against every *m.* and every
m.'s hand. 16:12
to restore every *m.'s* money. 42:25
every *m.'s* money was in his sack.
35; 43:21
look down every *m.* his sack. 44:11
and laded every *m.* his ass, and. 13
Joseph cried, Cause every *m.* 45:1
the Egyptians sold every *m.* 47:20
every *m.* and his household. *Ex* 1:1
for they cast down every *m.* 7:12
let every *m.* borrow of his. 11:2
take to them every *m.* a lamb. 12:3
every *m.* according to his eating. 4
16:16; 18:21
that which every *m.* must eat. 12:16
abide ye every *m.* in his place. 16:29
every *m.* that giveth it. 25:2
give every *m.* a ransom for. 30:12
every *m.* a sword by his side, slay
every *m.* his brother, every *m.* his.
32:27
stood every *m.* at his tent door. 33:8
they worshipped every *m.* in his. 10
came every *m.* from his work. 36:4
a bekah for every *m.* that is. 38:26
fear every *m.* his mother. *Lev* 19:3
ye shall return every *m.* 25:10, 13
pitch every *m.* by his standard.
Num 1:52; 2:2, 17
every *m.'s* hallowed things. 5:10
give to every *m.* according to. 7:5
take every *m.* his censer. 16:17
they took every *m.* his censer. 18
write thou every *m.'s* name. 17:2
took every *m.* his rod. 9
men of war had taken spoil, every *m.*
31:53
Israel inherited every *m.* his. 32:18
pass over every *m.* armed. 27, 29
judge righteously between every *m.*
Deut 1:16
shall ye return every *m.* to his. 3:20
not do every *m.* what is right. 12:8
every *m.* shall give as he. 16:17
every *m.* shall die for his own sin.
Deut 24:16; *2 Ki* 14:6; *2 Chr* 25:4

every *m.* of you a stone. *Josh* 4:5
ascend every *m.* straight. 6:5, 20
every *m.* to his inheritance. 24:28
Judg 2:6
to every *m.* a damsel or. *Judg* 5:30
go every *m.* unto his place. 7:7, 8
and he put a trumpet in every *m.'s.*
16
set every *m.'s* sword against his fellow. 22; *1 Sam* 14:20
give me every *m.* his earrings.
Judg 8:24, 25
the people cut down every *m.* 9:49
every *m.* did what was right in.
17:6; 21:25
catch you every *m.* his wife. 21:21
every *m.* to his tribe, every *m.* to. 24
every *m.* into his tent. *1 Sam* 4:10
Samuel said, Go ye every *m.* 8:22
every *m.* his ox, every *m.* his. 14:34
that break away every *m.* 25:10
David said, Gird you on every *m.* 13
the Lord render to every *m.* his
righteousness. 26:23; *2 Chr* 6:30
grieved every *m.* for his sons.
1 Sam 30:6
save to every *m.* his wife and. 22
they went out every *m.* *2 Sam* 13:9
every *m.* gat him upon his mule. 29
that every *m.* which hath any. 15:4
covered every *m.* his head, and. 30
for Israel hath fled every *m.* 19:3
Sheba said, Every *m.* to his. 20:1
dwelt safely every *m.* in. *1 Ki* 4:25
every *m.* the plague of heart. 8:38
give to every *m.* according to his.
39; *Job* 34:11; *Jer* 17:10
brought every *m.* his present.
1 Ki 10:25; *2 Chr* 9:24
not go up, return every *m.* to his.
1 Ki 12:24; 22:17, 36; *2 Chr* 11:4
take the kings, every *m.* *1 Ki* 20:24
thence every *m.* a beam. *2 Ki* 6:2
every *m.* with his weapons. 11:8
Judah fled every *m.* to their. 14:12
and then eat ye every *m.* of. 18:31
God shake out every *m.* *Neh* 5:13
do according to every *m.'s.* *Esth* 1:8
every *m.* should bear rule in his. 22
and every *m.* shall draw. *Job* 21:23
the hand of every *m.* that. 37:7
every *m.* at his best state is vanity.
Ps 39:5, 11
every *m.* walketh in a vain shew. 6
renderest to every *m.* according to
his work. 62:12; *Pr* 24:12
every *m.* is a friend to. *Pr* 19:6
every *m.* shall kiss his lips. 24:26
every *m.'s* judgement cometh. 29:26
eat every *m.* the flesh. *Isa* 9:20
therefore every *m.'s* heart shall.
13:7
in that day every *m.* shall cast. 31:7
every *m.* is brutish in knowledge.
Jer 10:14; 51:17
turn every *m.* from his evil way.
26:3; 35:15; 36:3
for every *m.* that is mad, and. 29:26
teach no more every *m.* his neighbour. 31:34; *Heb* 8:11
in proclaiming liberty every *m.* to his
neighbour. *Jer* 34:15, 17
rise up every *m.* in his tent. 37:10
deliver ye every *m.* his soul. 51:45
with every *m.* his censer. *Ezek* 8:11
every *m.* in the chambers. 12
every *m.* with his destroying. 9:1, 2
away every *m.* his abominations. 20:7
they did not every *m.* cast away. 8
every *m.* shall tremble for. 32:10
not scattered every *m.* from. 46:18
every *m.* that shall hear. *Dan* 3:10
that every *m.* that shall ask. 6:12
mariners cried every *m.* *Jonah* 1:5
sit still every *m.* under. *Mi* 4:4
hunt every *m.* his brother. 7:2
and ye run every *m.* to his own
house. *Hag* 1:9
every *m.* his neighbour. *Zech* 3:10
every *m.* with his staff in his. 8:4
speak every *m.* truth to his neighbour. 16; *Eph* 4:25
why do we deal treacherously every
m.? *Mal* 2:10

shall reward *every m.* according to.
  Mat 16:27; *Rom* 2:6; *Rev* 22:12
received *every m.* a penny.
               Mat 20:9, 10
he gave to *every m.* according. 25:15
saw *every m.* clearly.   *Mark* 8:25
and gave to *every m.* his work. 13:34
casting lots, what *every m.*   15:24
give to *every m.* that.   *Luke* 6:30
every m. presseth into it.   16:16
much *every m.* had gained.   19:15
which lighteth *every m.*   *John* 1:9
every m. at beginning doth set. 2:10
every m. that hath heard and. 6:45
ye shall be scattered *every m.* 16:32
how hear we *every m.* in? *Acts* 2:8
parted to all men, as *every m.* had
  need.   45; 4:35
every m. determined to send. 11:29
peace to *every m.* that.   *Rom* 2:10
be true, but *every m.* a liar.   3:4
as God dealt to *every m.* the. 12:3
every m. be fully persuaded. 14:5
Lord gave to *every m.I Cor* 3:5; 7:17
every m.'s work shall be made. 3:13
then shall *every m.* have praise. 4:5
nevertheless, let *every m.* have. 7:2
but *every m.* hath his proper gift. 7
let *every m.* abide in the.   20, 24
there is not in *every m.* that.   8:7
let *every m.* seek another's. 10:24*
know that the head of *every m.* 11:3
Spirit is given to *every m.* to. 12:7
every m. in his order, Christ. 15:23
commending ourselves to *every m.*
                2 Cor 4:2
I testify again to *every m. Gal* 5:3
let *every m.* prove his own work. 6:4
for *every m.* shall bear his own. 5
look not *every m.* on his. *Phil* 2:4
teaching *every m.* in all wisdom; to
  present *every m.*   *Col* 1:28
ye ought to answer *every m.*   4:6
taste death for *every m. Heb* 2:9
but *every m.* is tempted. *Jas* 1:14
let *every m.* be swift to hear.   19
who judgeth according to *every m.'s*
  work.   *1 Pet* 1:17
to give reason to *every m.* that. 3:15
every m. hath received the gift. 4:10
every m. that hath this hope in him.
             1 John 3:3
judged *every m.* according to their
  works.   *Rev* 20:13
I testify to *every m.* that heareth.
             22:18

man of God
Moses the *m. of God. Deut* 33:1
             Josh 14:6
woman told, saying, A *m, of God*
  came to the.   *Judg* 13:6
let the *m. of God* come again to. 8
a *m. of God* to Eli. *1 Sam* 2:27
is in this city a *m. of God.*   9:6
present to bring the *m. of God.* 7
give to the *m. of God* to tell us. 8
Shemaiah the *m. of God. 1 Ki* 12:22
a *m. of God* out of Judah.   13:1
m. of God who was disobedient. 26
do with thee, O *m. of God?* 17:18
I know that thou art a *m. of God.* 24
m. of God and spake to Ahab. 20:28
thou *m. of God,* king said, Come
  down.   *2 Ki* 1:9, 11
O *m. of God,* I pray thee, let my life
  be precious.   13
she came and told *m. of God.* 4:7
this is *m. of God.*
thou *m. of God,* do not lie to.   16
that I may run to *m. of God.*   22
she came unto the *m. of God.* 25, 27
O thou *m. of God,* there is death. 40
brought the *m. of God* bread.   42
to the saying of *m. of God.*   5:14
of Elisha, the *m. of God.*   20: 8:4
to place which *m. of God.*   6:10
when the servant of the *m. of God.*
              15
lord answered the *m. of God.* 7:2, 19
trode on him as the *m. of God* said.
            17, 18
after the saying of *m. of God.* 8:2
m. of God is come hither.   7

the *m. of God* wept.   *2 Ki* 8:11
and go, meet the *m. of God.*   8
and the *m. of God* was wroth. 13:19
word which the *m. of God.* 23:16
it is the sepulchre of *m. of God.* 17
Moses *m. of God.* *1 Chr* 23:14
      2 Chr 30:16; *Ezra* 3:2
David the *m. of God.* *2 Chr* 8:14
       Neh 12:24, 36
came a *m. of God* to Amaziah.
         2 Chr 25:7
m. of God answered, The Lord is. 9
of Igdaliah a *m. of God. Jer* 35:4
thou, O *m. of God,* flee. *1 Tim* 6:11
that the *m. of God* may be perfect.
         2 Tim 3:17
     •   •

mighty **man**
Lord is with thee, thou *mighty m.*
        Judg 6:12
now Jephthah was a *mighty m.* 11:1
a kinsman of a *mighty m.* of. *Ruth* 2:1
Benjamite, a *mighty m.* of power
        1 Sam 9:1
David a *mighty m.* and a man of
  war.   16:18; *2 Sam* 17:10
Jeroboam was a *mighty m.*
         1 Ki 11:28
Naaman was also a *mighty m.*
         2 Ki 5:1
Ismaiah a *mighty m.* among.
        1 Chr 12:4
Eliada a *mighty m.* of valour.
       2 Chr 17:17
Zichri, a *mighty m.* of.   28:7
as for the *mighty m.* he. *Job* 22:8
a *mighty m.* is not delivered by.
       Ps 33:16
thou in mischief, O *mighty m.* 52:1
Lord awaked like a *mighty m.* 78:65
in the hand of a *mighty m.* 127:4
take away the *mighty m. Isa* 3:2
mighty m. shall be humbled. 5:15
the sword, not of a *mighty m.* 31:8
go forth as a *mighty m.*   42:13
nor let the *mighty m.* glory. *Jer* 9:23
shouldest be as a *mighty m.* 14:9
nor *mighty m.* escape.   46:6
mighty m. stumbled.   12
the *mighty m.* shall cry. *Zeph* 1:14
as sword of a *mighty m. Zech* 9:13
Ephraim shall be like a *mighty m.*
        10:7

no **man**
no m. is with us, see. *Gen* 31:50
without thee shall *no m.* lift. 41:44
stood *no m.* while Joseph made. 45:1
saw that there was *no m. Ex* 2:12
let *no m.* leave of it till the. 16:19
let *no m.* go out of his place on. 29
hurt or driven away, *no m.*   22:10
no m. did put on him his. 33:4
shall *no m.* see me and live. 20
no m. shall come up with thee. 34:3
there shall be *no m.* in. *Lev* 16:17
no m. that hath a blemish. 21:21
no m. shall sanctify it, it is. 27:26
if *no m.* hath lain with. *Num* 5:19
no m. able to stand before thee.
     Deut 7:24; 11:25
oppressed, and *no m.* shall save.
       28:29, 68
no m. knoweth of his sepulchre. 34:6
no m. hath been able to stand before.
       Josh 23:9
daughter knew *no m. Judg* 11:39
no m. that took them to his house.
      19:15, 18
virgins that had known *no m.* 21:12
for by strength shall *no m. 1 Sam* 2:9
let them if there be *no m.*   11:3
let *no m.'s* heart fail because. 17:32
no m. know any thing of. 21:2
and *no m.* saw nor knew it. 26:12
no m. deputed of king. *2 Sam* 15:3
for there is *no m.* that sinneth not.
   1 Ki 8:46; *2 Chr* 6:36
behold, there was *no m.* in camp.
      2 Ki 7:5, 10
let him alone, let *no m.* move. 23:18
no m. do them wrong, he reproved.
   1 Chr 16:21; *Ps* 105:14
queen did let *no m.* come. *Esth* 5:12
may *no m.* reverse.   8:8

no m. could withstand. *Esth* 9:2
shall *no m.* make thee ashamed?
       Job 11:3
in houses which *no m.*   15:28
therefore shall *no m.* look. 20:21
he riseth, and *no m.* is sure. 24:22
where *no m.* is, wherein there is no
  m.   38:26
I am a worm, and *no m. Ps* 22:6
there was *no m.* 142:4; *Isa* 41:28
     59:16; *Jer* 4:25
in thy sight shall *no m.* be justified.
     Ps 143:2
and *no m.* regarded.   *Pr* 1:24
the pit, let *no m.* stay him. 28:1
flee when *no m.* pursueth.   17
no m. hath power over. *Eccl* 8:8
no m. knoweth either love.   9:1
no m. remembered that same. 15
no m. shall spare his. *Isa* 9:19
no m. may come in.   24:10
he regardeth *no m.*   33:8
when I came, was there *no m.* 50:2
and *no m.* layeth it to heart. 57:1
      Jer 12:11
so that *no m.* went. *Isa* 60:15
and where *no m.* dwelt. *Jer* 2:6
no m. repented.   8:6
for *no m.* of his seed shall. 22:30
this is Zion, whom *no m.* 30:17
go hide, and let *no m.* know. 36:19
Zedekiah said, Let *no m.* 38:24
and *no m.* shall know it. 40:15
no m. knew it.   41:4
and *no m.* dwelleth. 44:2; 51:43
no m. shall abide there. 49:18, 33
      50:40
ask bread, and *no m.* *Lam* 4:4
no m. may pass through. *Ezek* 14:15
no m. shall enter in by this. 44:2
yet let *no m.* strive or. *Hos* 4:4
is scattered, and *no m. Nah* 3:18
so that there is *no m.* *Zeph* 3:6
so that *no m.* did lift up. *Zech* 1:21
that *no m.* passed through nor. 7:14
no m. can serve two masters.
    Mat 6:24; *Luke* 16:13
tell *no m.*   *Mat* 8:4; 16:20
  Mark 7:36; *Luke* 5:14; 9:21
see that *no m.* know it. *Mat* 9:30
  Mark 5:43; 7:24; 8:30; 9:9
no m. knoweth the Son, but the
  Father. *Mat* 11:27; *Luke* 10:22
saw *no m.* save Jesus. *Mat* 17:8
tell the vision to *no m.* till the. 9
no m. was able to answer. 22:46
call *no m.* father on the earth. 23:9
that day and hour knoweth *no m.*
    24:36; *Mark* 13:32
no m. that hath left house.
   Mark 10:29; *Luke* 18:29
no m. eat fruit of thee. *Mark* 11:14
that thou carest for *no m.* 12:14
do violence to *no m.* *Luke* 3:14
salute *no m.*   10:4
with the husks, and *no m.* 15:16
no m. hath seen God. *John* 1:18
      1 John 4:12
no m. can do these miracles.*John* 3:2
no m. hath ascended up to.   13
for the Father judgeth *no m.* 5:22
no m. can come to me. 6:44, 65
but *no m.* laid hands. 7:30, 44; 8:20
he said, No *m.* Lord.   8:11
I judge *no m.*   15
the night cometh when *no m.* 9:4
no m. taketh it from me. 10:18
no m. is able to pluck them out. 29
no m. at the table knew. 13:28
no m. cometh to the Father. 14:6
greater love hath *no m.* 15:13
and your joy *no m.* taketh. 16:22
let *no m.* dwell therein. *Acts* 1:20
that they speak to *no m.* 4:17
of the rest durst *no m.* join. 5:13
we had opened, we found *no m.* 23
voice, but seeing *no m.* 9:7, 8
no m. shall set on thee to. 18:10
preaching kingdom of God, *no m.*
     28:31
recompense to *no m. Rom* 12:17
owe *no m.* any thing, but. 13:8
and *no m.* dieth to himself. 14:7
that *no m.* put a stumblingblock. 13

of God knoweth no m.   1 Cor 2:11
himself is judged of no m.   15
other foundation can no m. lay. 3:11
let no m. deceive himself.   18, 21
let no m. seek his own, but.   10:24
henceforth know we no m. after the
   flesh.   2 Cor 5:16
no m., we have corrupted no m. 7:2
God accepteth no m.   Gal 2:6
but that no m. is justified by.   3:11
let no m. deceive you.   Eph 5:6
   2 Thes 2:3
for no m. ever yet hated.   Eph 5:29
no m. likeminded, who.   Phil 2:20
let no m. beguile you of.   Col 2:18
that no m. go beyond.   1 Thes 4:6
suddenly on no m.   1 Tim 5:22
at my first answer no m. 2 Tim 4:16
to speak evil of no m.   Tit 3:2
no m. taketh this honour.   Heb 5:4
no m. gave attendance at.   7:13
without which no m. shall see. 12:14
let no m. say when he is.   Jas 1:13
the tongue can no m. tame, it.   3:8
little children, let no m.   1 John 3:7
a new name, which no m.   Rev 2:17
he that shutteth, and no m.   3:7
and no m. can shut it.   8
that no m. take thy crown.   11
and no m. was able to open. 5:3, 4
multitude which no m. could.   7:9
that no m. might buy or sell. 13:17
no m. could learn that song.   14:3
no m. was able to enter into.   15:8
no m. buyeth their merchandise.
   18:11
a name written, that no m.   19:12

of man
of m. will I require life of m. Gen 9:5
all the firstborn of m.   Ex 13:13
   Num 18:15
afraid of the face of m.   Deut 1:17
is this the manner of m.? 2 Sam 7:19
not fall into the hands of m.   24:14
   1 Chr 21:13
what manner of m. was he ? 2 Ki 1:7
no man there, nor voice of m.   7:10
days as the days of m.?   Job 10:5
destroyest the hope of m.   14:19
for vain is the help of m.   Ps 60:11
   108:12
wrath of m. shall praise thee. 76:10
the ways of m. are before.   Pr 5:21
the spirit of m. will sustain.   18:14
the discretion of m. deferreth. 19:11
the desire of m. is his kindness.   22
so the heart of m. answereth. 27:19
fear of m. bringeth a snare.   29:25
not the understanding of m.   30:2
way of a m. with a maid.
all the labour of m. is.   Eccl 6:7
misery of m. is great upon.   8:6
this is the whole duty of m.   12:13
after the figure of a m., according to
   the beauty of a m.   Isa 44:13
shouldest be afraid of a m.   51:12
I know the way of m. is.   Jer 10:23
aside the right of a m.   Lam 3:35
they four had the face of a m.
   Ezek 1:10; 10:14
no foot of m. shall pass.   29:11
neither shall the foot of m.   32:13
appearance of a m. Dan 8:15; 10:18
when the eyes of m. shall. Zech 9:1
who formeth the spirit of m.   12:1
of m. is this that the winds. Mat 8:27
Mark 4:41; Luke 8:25
of m. be so with his wife. Mat 19:10
he said, Come out of the m.
   Mark 5:8; Luke 8:29
nor of the will of m. but. John 1:13
any should testify of m.   2:25
voice of a god, not of m. Acts 12:22
upon every soul of m.   Rom 2:9
the blessedness of the m.   4:6
entered into heart of m.   1 Cor 2:9
knoweth the things of a m. save the
   spirit of m. which is in him, so. 11
judged of you, or of m.   4:3
woman is the glory of the m.   11:7
but the woman is of the m.   8, 12
neither received it of m.   Gal 1:12
wrath of m. worketh not.   Jas 1:20

forgetteth what manner of m. Jas 1:24
all the glory of m. as.   1 Pet 1:24
old time by the will of m. 2 Pet 1:21
is the number of a m.   Rev 13:18
to the measure of a m.   21:17

one man
we all one m.'s sons. Gen 42:11, 13
two homers for one m.   Ex 16:22
if one m.'s ox hurt another's. 21:35
this people as one m.   Num 14:15
shall one m. sin, and wilt ?   16:22
lacketh not one m. of us.   31:49
one m. shall chase a.   Josh 23:10
Midianites as one m.   Judg 6:16
priest to the house of one m.   18:19
was gathered as one m.   20:1
all the people arose as one m.   8
if one m. sin against.   1 Sam 2:25
as the heart of one m. 2 Sam 19:14
there is yet one m. Micaiah.
   1 Ki 22:8; 2 Chr 18:7
gathered together as one m.
   Ezra 3:1; Neh 8:1
as one m. mocketh.   Job 13:9
one m. among a thousand have.
   Eccl 7:28
one m. ruleth over another.   8:9
shall take hold of one m.   Isa 4:1
one m. was clothed with. Ezek 9:2
one m. should die for the people.
   John 11:50; 18:14
by one m. sin entered into. Rom 5:12
grace, which is by one m. Jesus. 15
if by one m.'s offence death.   17
as by one m.'s disobedience many.
one m. esteemeth one day.   14:5
been the wife of one m.   1 Tim 5:9

son of man
nor son of m. that he   Num 23:19
and the son of m. which.   Job 25:6
may profit the son of m.   35:8
and son of m. that thou visitest.
   Ps 8:4; Heb 2:6
on son of m. whom thou. Ps 80:17
son of m. that thou makest.   144:3
trust in the son of m.   146:3
not afraid of the son of m. Isa 51:12
blessed is the son of m. that.   56:2
nor shall son of m. dwell in it.
   Jer 49:18, 33; 50:40
any son of m. pass thereby.   51:43
hast thou seen this, O son of m.?
   Ezek 8:15, 17
sigh therefore, thou son of m.   21:6
one like the Son of m.   Dan 7:13
   Rev 1:13; 14:14
Son of m. hath not where to lay.
   Mat 8:20; Luke 9:58
Son of m. hath power on earth to.
   Mat 9:6; Mark 2:10; Luke 5:24
not gone over, till the Son of m. be.
   Mat 10:23
the Son of m. came eating.   11:19
   Luke 7:34
Son of m. is Lord even of sabbath.
   Mat 12:8; Mark 2:28; Luke 5:5
whosoever speaketh against the Son of
   m.   Mat 12:32; Luke 12:10
shall Son of m. be three. Mat 12:40
good seed is the Son of m.   13:37
the Son of m. shall send forth.   41
say, that I, the Son of m. am ? 16:13
until the Son of m. be risen again.
   17:9; Mark 9:9
the Son of m. shall be betrayed.
   Mat 17:22; 20:18; 26:2, 45
   Mark 14:41; Luke 9:44
also the coming of the Son of m.
   Mat 24:27, 37, 39; Luke 17:26
see Son of m. coming.   Mat 24:30
   Mark 13:26; Luke 21:27
hour ye think not Son of m. cometh.
   Mat 24:44; Luke 12:40
when the Son of m. shall. Mat 25:31
the Son of m. goeth.   26:24
   Mark 14:21; Luke 22:22
Son of m. be ashamed. Mark 8:38
written of the Son of m.   9:12
the Son of m. is delivered.   10:33
10:33; Luke 24:7
Son of m. is as a man. Mark 13:34*
for the Son of m.'s sake. Luke 6:22

the Son of m. must suffer.
   Luke 9:22, 26
S. of man is not come to destroy. 56
so shall Son of m. be to this generation.   11:30; 17:24
him shall the Son of m. confess. 12:8
of the days of the Son of m.   17:22
when the Son of m. cometh.   18:8
the Son of m. is come to seek. 19:10
stand before the Son of m.   21:36
betrayest thou the Son of m.? 22:48
descending on Son of m. John 1:51
even the Son of m. which is.   3:13
even so must the Son of m. be.   14
because he is the Son of m.   5:27
which the Son of m. shall give. 6:27
eat the flesh of the Son of m.   53
ye shall see the Son of m. ascend. 62
when ye have lifted up the Son of
   m. then shall.   8:28
Son of m. should be glorified. 12:23
Son of m. must be lifted up, who is
   this Son of m.?   34
now is the Son of m. glorified. 13:31
see the Son of m. standing. Acts 7:56

see **son**

that man
even that m. shall be cut off from.
   Lev 17:9
I will set my face against that m.
   20:3, 5; Ezek 14:8
brought not offering that m. shall.
   Num 9:13
stone that m. or.   Deut 17:5, 12
elders shall take that m. and. 22:18
so shall it be done to that m.   25:9
shall smoke against that m.   29:20
that m. perisheth not.   Josh 22:20
and that m. was perfect.   Job 1:1
for the end of that m. is.   Ps 37:37
blessed is that m. who maketh. 40:4
this and that m. was born in.   87:5
for bread that m. will.   Pr 28:21
that m. be as cities Lord. Jer 20:16
I will even punish that m.   23:34
last state of that m. is worse.
   Mat 12:45; Luke 11:26
woe to that m. by whom. Mat 18:7
that m. by whom the Son of man is
   ... good were it for that m.   26:24
   Mark 14:21; Luke 22:22
to do with that just m. Mat 27:19
by that m. whom he hath ordained.
   Acts 17:31
evil for that m. who.   Rom 14:20
that m. of sin be revealed, the son
   of perdition.   2 Thes 2:3
note that m. and have no.   3:14
let not that m. think he.   Jas 1:7

this man
wilt thou go with this m.? Gen 24:58
he that toucheth this m. or.   26:11
how long shall this m. be ? Ex 10:7
gave my daughter to this m. to wife.
   Deut 22:16
seeing this m. is come. Judg 19:23
to this m. do not so vile a thing. 24
this m. went up early.   1 Sam 1:3
said, How shall this m. save ? 10:27
seen this m. that is come ?   17:25
not my lord regard this m.   25:25
how this m. seeketh.   1 Ki 20:7
to me, and said, Keep this m.   39
this m. sends to me to.   2 Ki 5:7
mercy in sight of this m. Neh 1:11
this m. Mordecai waxed. Esth 9:4
this m. was the greatest. Job 1:3
this m. made not God.   Ps 52:7
this m. was born there.   87:4, 5, 6
is this the m. that made ? Isa 14:16
this m. will I look, even to.   66:2
is this m. Coniah a despised broken
   idol ?   Jer 22:28
Lord, Write ye this m. childless. 30
saying, This m. is worthy. 26:11, 16
let this m. be put to death, this m.
   seeketh not the welfare of.   38:4
make this m. understand. Dan 8:16
not perish for this m.'s life. Jonah 1:14
this m. shall be the peace. Mi 5:5
I say to this m. Go, and he. Mat 8:9
scribes said, This m. blasphemeth.
   9:3; Mark 2:7

whence hath *this m.* this wisdom ?
       Mat 13:54; *Mark* 6:2
some said, This *m.* calleth.
       Mat 27:47
I know not *this m.* of. *Mark* 14:71
this m. was the Son of God. 15:39
this m. if he were a prophet.
       Luke 7:39
say to thee, Give *this m.* place. 14:9
saying, This *m.* began to build. 30
this m. receiveth sinners, and. 15:2
I tell you, *this m.* went down. 18:14
will not have *this m.* to reign. 19:14
said, This *m.* was also with. 22:56
I find no fault in *this m.* 23:4, 14
away with *this m.* 18
but *this m.* hath done nothing. 41
this m. went to Pilate and. 52
this m. give us his flesh ? *John* 6:52
how knoweth *this m.* letters ? 7:15
howbeit, we know *this m.* whence. 27
never man spake like *this m.* 46
Master, who did sin, *this m.*? 9:2
neither hath *this m.* sinned, nor. 3
this m. is not of God, he keepeth. 16
praise God, we know that *this m.* 24
if *this m.* were not of God he. 33
all that John spake of *this m.* 10:41
this m. which opened the eyes of
  blind, caused that *this m.*? 11:37
what do we ? for *this m.* doeth. 47
art not thou one of *this m.*'s ? 18:17
bring ye against *this m.*? 29
not *this m.* but Barabbas, now. 40
if let *this m.* go, thou art not. 19:12
and what shall *this m.* do ? 21:21
this m. purchased a field. *Acts* 1:18
had made *this m.* to walk. 3:12, 16
even by him doth *this m.* stand. 4:10
intend to bring *this m.*'s blood. 5:28
after *this m.* rose up Judas of. 37
this m. ceaseth not to speak. 6:13
saying, This *m.* is the great. 8:10
I heard of *this m.* how much. 9:13
of *this m.*'s seed hath God. 13:23
through *this m.* is preached to. 38
this m. was instructed in way. 18:25
this is the *m.* that teacheth all. 21:28
this m. is a Roman. 22:26
find no evil in *this m.* 23:9
this m. was taken of the Jews.
       23:27
this m. a pestilent fellow. 24:5
accuse *this m.* if there be any. 25:5
ye see *this m.* about whom. 24
this m. doeth nothing worthy. 26:31
this m. might have been set at. 32
this m. is a murderer. 28:4
this m. was counted worthy. *Heb* 3:3
now consider how great *this m.* 7:4
this m. because he continueth. 24
that *this m.* have somewhat. 8:3*
this m. after he had offered. 10:12
this m. shall be blessed. *Jas* 1:25
but deceiveth, *this m.*'s religion. 26

man of war

the Lord is a *m. of war.* *Ex* 15:3
son of Manasseh, was a *m. of war.*
       Josh 17:1
David a *m. of war.* *1 Sam* 16:18
  2 Sam 17:8; *1 Chr* 28:3
Goliath was a *m. of war* from his.
       1 Sam 17:33
take away the *m. of war.* *Isa* 3:2
jealousy like a *m. of war.* 42:13

wicked man

if the *wicked m.* be worthy to be.
       Deut 25:2
wicked m. travaileth. *Job* 15:20
the portion of a *wicked m.* from.
       20:29; 27:13
set thou a *wicked m.* over. *Ps* 109:6
a *wicked m.* walketh with. *Pr* 6:12
he that rebuketh a *wicked m.* 9:7
when a *wicked m.* dieth, his. 11:7
a *wicked m.* is loathsome, and. 13:5
a *wicked m.* taketh a gift out. 17:23
wicked m. hardeneth his face. 21:29
lay not wait, O *wicked m.* 24:15
a *wicked m.* that prolongeth his.
       Eccl 7:15
wicked m. shall die in iniquity.
       Ezek 3:18

which *wicked m.* doeth. *Ezek* 18:24
when a *wicked m.* turneth from. 27
O *wicked m.* thou shalt surely die,
  that *wicked m.* shall die in. 33:8

wise man

m. discreet and *wise.* *Gen* 41:33
for thou art a *wise m.* *1 Ki* 2:9
David's uncle, was a *wise m.*
       1 Chr 27:32
a *wise m.* utter vain ? *Job* 15:2
I cannot find one *wise m.* 17:10
let a *wise m.* hearken to me. 34:34
a *wise m.* will hear and. *Pr* 1:5
rebuke a *wise m.* and he will. 9:8
give instruction to a *wise m.* he. 9
a *wise m.* feareth, and. 14:16
a *wise m.* will pacify wrath. 16:14
entereth more into a *wise m.* 17:10
a *wise m.* scaleth the city of. 21:22
seest thou a *m. wise* in his ? 26:12
a *wise m.* contendeth with. 29:9
but a *wise m.* keepeth it in. 11
the *wise m.*'s eyes are in. *Eccl* 2:14
and how dieth the *wise m.*? 16
whether he shall be *wise m.* or. 19
maketh a *wise m.* mad. 7:7
who is as the *wise m.*? 8:1
a *wise m.*'s heart discerneth time. 5
though a *wise m.* think to know. 17
found in it a poor *wise m.* 9:15
a *wise m.*'s heart is at his right. 10:2
the words of a *wise m.*'s mouth. 12
who is the *wise m.* that ? *Jer* 9:12
let not the *wise m.* glory in. 23
liken him to a *wise m.* *Mat* 7:24
a not *wise m.* amongst. *1 Cor* 6:5
who is a *wise m.* endued ? *Jas* 3:13

man joined with woman

the *m.* said, the *woman* whom thou.
       Gen 3:12
dead *m.*, for the *woman* thou. 20:3
every *m.* and *woman.* *Ex* 35:29
let no *m.* nor *woman* make. 36:6
if a *m.* or *woman* have. *Lev* 13:29
if *m.* or *woman* have in the skin. 38
woman also with whom the *m.* 15:18
issue of the *m.* and *woman.* 33
if *m.* lie with a *woman.* 20:18
a *m.* or *woman* that hath a familiar
  spirit. 27
when *m.* or *woman* shall commit any
  sin. *Num* 5:6
when either *m.* or *woman* shall. 6:2
kill *woman* that hath known *m.*
       31:17; *Judg* 21:11
m. or *woman* that hath. *Deut* 17:2
bring forth that *m.* or *woman.* 5
woman . . . that pertaineth to a *m.* nor
  shall *m.* put on a *woman's.* 22:5
if a *m.* . . . with a *woman*, both *m.* that
  lay with *woman*, and *woman.* 22
be among you *m.* or *woman.* 29:18
utterly destroyed both *m.* and
  woman. *Josh* 6:21
but slay both *m., woman.* *1 Sam* 15:3
David left neither *m.* nor *woman*
  alive. 27:9, 11
m. and *woman* a loaf. *1 Chr* 16:3
m. or *woman* shall die. *2 Chr* 15:13
whether *m.* or *woman* come to the
  king. *Esth* 4:11
from you, *m.* and *woman.* *Jer* 44:7
in pieces *m.* and *woman.* 51:22
of the *woman* is the *m.* *1 Cor* 11:3
woman is the glory of the *m.* 7
the *m.* is not of the *woman*, but
  woman of the *m.* 8
nor is the *m.* without the *woman.* 11
as *woman* is of the *m.* so is the *m.* by
  the *woman.* 12
if any *m.* or *woman.* *1 Tim* 5:16

young man

I have slain a *young m.* *Gen* 4:23
Abraham gave it to a *young m.* 18:7*
the *young m.* deferred not to. 34:19
was with us a *young m.* an. 41:12
Joshua a *young m.* *Ex* 33:11
there ran a *young m.* *Num* 11:27
destroy both the *young m.* and.
       Deut 32:25
caught a *young m.* of the men of Succoth. *Judg* 8:14

hastily to the *young m.* and his *young
  m.* thrust him through. *Judg* 9:54
young m. of Beth-lehem-judah. 17:7
the *young m.* became his priest. 12
knew the voice of the *young m.* 18:3
Saul was a choice *young m.* and.
       1 Sam 9:2
Jonathan said to the *young m.* 14:1
whose son art thou, *young m.*?
       17:58
I say thus to the *young m.* 20:22*
David, I am *young m.* of. 30:13
David said to the *young m.* that told.
       2 Sam 1:5, 13
bring the *young m.* Absalom. 14:21
for my sake with the *young m.* 18:5
young m. Absalom safe ? 29, 32
enemies be as that *young m.* is. 32
Solomon seeing *young m.* indus-
  trious. *1 Ki* 11:28
the eyes of the *young m.* *2 Ki* 6:17
so the *young m.* even *young m.* went
  to Ramoth. 9:4
and Zadok, a *young m. 1 Chr* 12:28
compassion on *young m. 2 Chr* 36:17
wherewith shall *young m.*? *Ps* 119:9
to *young m.* knowledge. *Pr* 1:4
discerned a *young m.* void of. 7:7
rejoice, O *young m.* in. *Eccl* 11:9
as *young m.* marrieth a. *Isa* 62:5
break in pieces the *young m.* and
  maid. *Jer* 51:22
speak to this *young m. Zech* 2:4
young m. said, All these. *Mat* 19:20
followed him a certain *young m.*
       Mark 14:51
saw a *young m.* sitting on the. 16:5
Young m. I say unto thee, arise.
       Luke 7:14
clothes at *young m.*'s feet. *Acts* 7:58
young m. named Eutychus. 20:9
brought the *young m.* alive. 12*
bring this *young m.* to the. 23:17, 18
captain then let the *young m.* 22

Manaen

M. who had been brought. *Acts* 13:1

Manasseh

called the firstborn *M.* *Gen* 41:51
thy two sons *M.* and Ephraim. 48:5
God make thee as Ephraim and *M.* 20
and he set Ephraim before *M.* 20
of *M.* Gamaliel was. *Num* 1:10
Gamaliel prince of *M.* offered. 7:54
these are the families of *M.* 26:34
       27:1
married into the family of *M.* 36:12
the thousands of *M.* *Deut* 33:17
two tribes, *M.* Ephraim. *Josh* 14:4
the male children of *M.* 17:2
Zelophehad son of *M.* had no. 3
there fell ten portions to *M.* 5
the daughters of *M.* had an. 6
M. had in Issachar, Beth-shean. 11
children of *M.* could not drive out. 12
my family is poor in *M.* *Judg* 6:15
Jonathan son of Gershom, son of *M.*
       18:30
M. his son reigned. *2 Ki* 20:21
       2 Chr 32:33
and *M.* seduced them to do more
  evil. *2 Ki* 21:9
M. shed innocent blood, till he. 16
the altars *M.* made did Josiah. 23:12
M. had provoked him withal. 26
for the sins of *M.* this came. 24:3
dwelt of the children of *M. 1 Chr* 9:3
fell some of *M.* to David. 12:19
strangers out of *M.* fell. *2 Chr* 15:9
letters to Ephraim and *M.* 30:1
yet divers of *M.* humbled. 11
cut down the groves in *M.* 31:1
M. made Judah and Jerusalem. 33:9
Lord spake to *M.* he would not. 10
the captains took *M.* among. 11
then *M.* knew that the Lord he. 13
humbled not himself, as *M.* 23
so did Josiah in the cities of *M.* 34:6
M. had taken strange wives.
       Ezra 10:30, 33
Gilead is mine, *M.* *Ps* 60:7; 108:8
before *M.* stir up thy strength. 80:2
M. shall eat Ephraim. *Isa* 9:21
removed, because of *M.* *Jer* 15:4

side a portion for *M.*   *Ezek* 48:4
Ezekias begat *M.* and *M. Mat* 1:10
     tribe of **Manasseh**
numbered of the *tribe of M.* 32,200.
         Num 1:35
tribe of M. and the captain of the
   children of *M.*   2:20; 10:23
of the *tribe of M.*, Gaddi.   13:11
to half *tribe of M.* the kingdom of
   Og.   32:33
half *tribe of M.* have received. 34:14
for the *tribe of M.*, Hanniel.   23
half *tribe of M.* passed.   *Josh* 4:12
nine tribes and half *tribe of M.* 13:7
tribe of M. this was possession of
   half *tribe of M.*   29; 12:6; 18:7
also a lot for the *tribe of M.*   17:1
gave Golan out of the *tribe of M.*
         20:8; 21:27
the half *tribe of M.* built.   22:10
Gad, and half *tribe of M. 1 Chr* 5:18
tribe of M. to the Levites. 6:70, 71
half *tribe of M.* 18,000 to.   12:31
rulers over Gad half *tribe of M.*
     26:32; 27:20, 21
tribe of M. were sealed.   *Rev* 7:6
       mandrakes
(*The Hebrew word for mandrake*
means love-plant, and it is supposed
to have power to excite vuluptuous-
ness. Its roots are forked and
sometimes bear a resemblance to a
human being. It is a powerful
narcotic)
Reuben found *m.*   Rachel said, Give
   me of thy *m.*   *Gen* 30:14
son's *m.* also ?   Therefore he shall
   lie with thee for thy son's *m.*   15
hired thee with my son's *m.*   16
m. give a smell, and at. *S of S* 7:13
       Maneh
shekels shall be your *M. Ezek* 45:12
       manger
laid him in a *m.*   *Luke* 2:7
shall find him in a *m.*   12
found the babe lying in a *m.*   16
       manifest
that God might have.   *Eccl* 3:18*
love him, and *m.* myself. *John* 14:21
m. thyself to us, and not unto ?   22
the miracle in. to all.   *Acts* 4:16
known of God is *m.* in.   *Rom* 1:19
m. counsels of hearts.   *1 Cor* 4:5
it is *m.* that he is excepted.   15:27
makes *m.* the savour of. *2 Cor* 2:14
works of the flesh are *m.*   *Gal* 5:19
my bonds in Christ are *m. Phil* 1:13
that I may make it *m.*   *Col* 4:4
a *m.* token of righteous. *2 Thes* 1:5
God was *m.* in the flesh. *1 Tim* 3:16
good works of some are *m.*   5:25*
their folly shall be *m.*   *2 Tim* 3:9
creature that is not *m.*   *Heb* 4:13
but was *m.* in these last. *1 Pet* 1:20
children of God are *m.* *1 John* 3:10
       see **made**
       manifestation
waiteth for the *m.* of the. *Rom* 8:19
the *m.* of the Spirit is.   *1 Cor* 12:7
but by *m.* of the truth.   *2 Cor* 4:2
       manifested
hid which shall not be *m. Mark* 4:22
miracles did Jesus, and *m.* forth his
   glory.   *John* 2:11
I have *m.* thy name unto the.   17:6
the righteousness of God is *m.*
        Rom 3:21
but hath in due time *m.*   *Tit* 1:3
the life was *m.* and we. *1 John* 1:2
that he was *m.* to take away.   3:5
purpose was the Son of God *m.*   8
in this was *m.* the love of God.   4:9
       manifestly
are *m.* declared to be.   *2 Cor* 3:3
       manifold
in thy *m.* mercies forsookest them
   not.   *Neh* 9:19
according to *m.* mercies gavest.   27
O Lord, how *m.* are thy ! *Ps* 104:24
I know your *m.* transgressions and
   sins.   *Amos* 5:12

shall not receive *m.*   *Luke* 18:30
might be known the *m.*   *Eph* 3:10
ye are in heaviness through *m.*
   temptations.   *1 Pet* 1:6
good stewards of the *m.* grace. 4:10
       mankind
shall not lie with *m.* as.   *Lev* 18:22
if a man lie with *m.* as.   20:13
is the breath of all *m.*   *Job* 12:10
them that defile with *m. 1 Tim* 1:10
hath been tamed of *m.*   *Jas* 3:7
       manna
(*The word means* "*what is this ?* "
It was the food by which Israel was
sustained during the 40 *years in*
the wilderness. There is a modern
substance now called manna, but it
does not answer all the conditions)
to another, it is *m.*   *Ex* 16:15
put a homer full of *m.* therein.   33
Israel did eat *m.* forty years.   35
nothing besides this *m. Num* 11:6
the *m.* was as coriander seed.   7
fell upon camp the *m.* fell on it.   9
and fed thee with *m. Deut* 8:3, 16
     Neh 9:20; *Ps* 78:24
m. ceased, they had *m.*   *Josh* 5:12
our fathers did eat *m. John* 6:31, 49
not as your fathers did eat *m.*   58*
golden pot that had *m.*   *Heb* 9:4
give to eat of the hidden *m. Rev* 2:17
       manner
two *m.* of people shall.   *Gen* 25:23
was of all *m.* of bake-meats. 40:17
their lives bitter in all *m.*   *Ex* 1:14
no *m.* of work shall be done. 12:16
all *m.* of trespass, any *m.*   22:9*
in wisdom, and in all *m.* of. 31:3, 5
   35:31, 33, 35; 36:1; *1 Chr* 28:21
burnt offering according to *m.*
     Lev 5:10*; *Num* 9:14*
no *m.* of fat of ox or sheep. *Lev* 7:23
no *m.* of blood.   26, 27; 17:10, 14
law for all *m.* of plague.   14:54
ye shall do no *m.* of work.   23:31
ye shall have one *m.* of law.   24:22
       Num 15:16*
she be taken with the *m. Num* 5:13
offering according to the *m.*   15:24*
do no *m.* of servile work.   28:18
saw no *m.* of similitude. *Deut* 4:15
this is the *m.* of the release.   15:2
that lieth with any *m.* of beast. 27:21
what *m.* of men were they? *Judg* 8:18
now this was the *m.* in.   *Ruth* 4:7*
and shew them the *m.* of the king.
      1 Sam 8:9, 11
Samuel told the people the *m.* 10:25
bread is in a *m.* common.   21:5*
so will be his *m.* all the while. 27:11
is this the *m.* of man ? *2 Sam* 7:19
what *m.* of man was he ? *2 Ki* 1:7
by a pillar, as the *m.* was.   11:14
know not the *m.* of the God.   17:26
let him teach them the *m.* of God. 27
all *m.* of measure.   *1 Chr* 23:29
for so was the king's *m.*   *Esth* 1:13
abhorreth all *m.* of meat. *Ps* 107:18
full, affording all *m.* of store. 144:13
at our gates are all *m.* *S of S* 7:13
shall feed after their *m.*   *Isa* 5:17*
this hath been thy *m.*   *Jer* 22:21
and no *m.* of hurt was.   *Dan* 6:23
the *m.* of Beer-sheba.   *Amos* 8:14
and healing all *m.* of sickness.
      Mat 4:23; 10:1
shall say all *m.* of evil against. 5:11
What *m.* of man is this, that even
   wind? 8:27; *Mark* 4:41; *Luke* 8:25
all *m.* of sin shall be forgiven to.
      Mat 12:31
what *m.* of stones are ! *Mark* 13:1
what *m.* of salutation.   *Luke* 1:29
saying, What *m.* of child shall ?   66
have known what *m.* of woman. 7:39
ye know not what *m.* of spirit.   9:55
ye tithe mint, rue, and all *m.*   11:42
what *m.* of communications ?   24:17
what *m.* of saying is this ? *John* 7:36
m. of the Jews is to bury.   19:40*
Paul, as his *m.* was, went. *Acts* 17:2*
ye know after what *m.* I have. 20:18
to the perfect *m.* of the law.   22:3

it is not *m.* of Romans. *Acts* 25:16*
my *m.* of life from my youth.   26:4
wrought in me all *m.* of.   *Rom* 7:8
sorry after a godly *m.*   *2 Cor* 7:9*
m. of men we were.   *1 Thes* 1:5
what *m.* of entering in we had.   9
known my *m.* of life.   *2 Tim* 3:10*
assembling, as the *m.*   *Heb* 10:25*
forgetteth what *m.* of man. *Jas* 1:24
m. of time the Spirit.   *1 Pet* 1:11
holy in all *m.* of conversation.   15
what *m.* of persons.   *2 Pet* 3:11
behold what *m.* of love. *1 John* 3:1
in this *m.* be killed.   *Rev* 11:5
which bare twelve *m.* of fruits. 22:2
       see **like**
     after the **manner**
Sarah *after the m.* of women.
      Gen 18:11
to come in to us *after the m.* 19:31
after the former m. when.   40:13
deal with her *after the m.*   *Ex* 21:9
number, *after the m.*   *Num* 29:18
city *after the same m.*   *Josh* 6:15
careless, *after the m.* of. *Judg* 18:17
turned and spake *after the same m.*
      1 Sam 17:30
after the m. of the nations.
   2 *Ki* 17:33; 2 *Chr* 13:9
and I answered them *after the same*
   m.   *Neh* 6:4
after the m. of Egypt.   *Isa* 10:24
      Amos 4:10
polluted *after the m.*   *Ezek* 20:30
after the m. of Babylonians. 23:15
after the m. of adulteresses, and
   after the m. of women.   45*
after the m. of the purifying of the.
      John 2:6
circumcised *after the m. Acts* 15:1*
I speak *after the m.* of men.
   Rom 6:19; *1 Cor* 15:32; *Gal* 3:15
after the same m. also he took the
   cup.   *1 Cor* 11:25
being a Jew, livest *after the m.* of.
      Gal 2:14*
     after this **manner**
far from thee to do *after this m.*
      Gen 18:25
saying, *After this m.* did thy. 39:19
he sent *after this m.* ten asses. 45:23
after this m. ye shall offer daily.
      Num 28:24
spoken *after this m.*   *2 Sam* 17:6
after this m. will I mar.   *Jer* 13:9
after this m. therefore pray ye.
      Mat 6:9
one *after this m.* and.   *1 Cor* 7:7
after this m. in old time. *1 Pet* 3:5
     on this **manner**
saying, On *this m.* shall ye speak to.
      Gen 32:19
told Saul, saying, On *this m.* spake
   David.   *1 Sam* 18:24
on *this m.* did Absalom. *2 Sam* 15:6
one said on *this m.*, another on that
   m.   *1 Ki* 22:20; *2 Chr* 18 19
persuade you on *this m.* 2 *Chr* 32:15
       manners
shall not walk in the *m. Lev* 20:23*
do after the former *m.* *2 Ki* 17:34†
have done after the *m. Ezek* 11:12*
suffered he their *m.*   *Acts* 13:18†
corrupt good *m.*   *1 Cor* 15:33†
God in divers *m.* spake.   *Heb* 1:1
       Manoah
M. intreated the Lord.   *Judg* 13:8
God hearkened to the voice of *M.* 9
M. arose and went after his wife. 11
M. knew not that he was an angel. 16
M. took a kid, and offered it.   19
M. and his wife looked on it.   20
M. knew that he was an angel.   21
in the buryingplace of *M.*   16:31
       manservant
not do any work, thou nor thy *m.*
     Ex 20:10; *Deut* 5:14
not covet thy neighbour's *m.*
     Ex 20:17; *Deut* 5:21
smite out his *m.*'s tooth.   *Ex* 21:27
if the ox shall push a *m.* he shall. 32

must eat them, thou and thy *m.*
    Deut 12:18
rejoice, thou and *m.*
    16:11, 14
despise cause of my *m.*   *Job* 31:13
let his *m.* go free.   *Jer* 34:9, 10

mansions
house are many *m.*   *John* 14:2

manslayer
ye shall appoint for *m.*   *Num* 35:6
the *m.* die not, until he stand.   12

manslayers
law was made for *m.*   *1 Tim* 1:9

mantle
Sisera with a *m.*   *Judg* 4:18*
and covered with a *m.* *1 Sam* 28:14
wrapped his face in his *m. 1 Ki* 19:13
Elijah cast his *m.* upon Elisha.   19
Elijah took his *m.* and.   *2 Ki* 2:8
Elisha took Elijah's *m.* that. 13, 14
heard this, I rent my *m. Ezra* 9:3, 5
arose and rent his *m.*   *Job* 1:20
rent every one his *m.·*   2:12
confusion, as with a *m.* *Ps* 109:29

mantles
I will take away the *m.*   *Isa* 3:22

many
thou shalt be a father of *m.* nations.
    Gen 17:4, 5; *Rom* 4:17, 18
he made him a coat of *m.* colours.
    Gen 37:3; 23:32
to gaze, and *m.* perish.   *Ex* 19:21
Moses sat, Return, O Lord, to the
  m. thousands of.   *Num* 10:36
whether they be few or *m.*   13:18
to *m.* thou shalt give more.   26:54
divided between *m.* and few.   56
have *m.* cities, shall give *m.*   35:8
hath cast out *m.* nations. *Deut* 7:1
lend to *m.* nations. 15:6; 28:12
and *m.* evils shall befall. 31:17, 21
and chariots very *m.*   *Josh* 11:4
m. were overthrown.   *Judg* 9:40
the destroyer which slew *m.* 16:24
she that hath *m.* children. *1 Sam* 2:5
the Lord to save by *m.* or few. 14:6
Judah and Israel were *m. 1 Ki* 4:20
they were exceeding *m.*   7:47
dress it first, for ye are *m.* 18:25
witchcrafts are so *m.* *2 Ki* 9:22
Rehabiah were very *m. 1 Chr* 23:17
hath given me *m.* sons.   28:5
Rehoboam desired *m.* *2 Chr* 11:23
to help whether with *m.*   14:11
there were *m.* in congregation. 30:17
m. of Ephraim and Manasseh. 18
we are *m.* that have. *Ezra* 10:13
and our daughters are *m.* *Neh* 5:2
there were *m.* in Judah sworn. 6:18
and feared God above *m.*   7:2
among *m.* nations was no king. 13:26
and *m.* lay in sackcloth. *Esth* 4:3
thou hast instructed *m.*   *Job* 4:3
yea, *m.* shall make suit unto. 11:19
m. are they that rise up.   *Ps* 3:1
there be *m.* that say of my. 2; 4:6
consider mine enemies, they are *m.*
    25:19; 56:2
heard the slander of *m.*   31:13
m. sorrows shall be to the. 32:10
m. are the afflictions of the. 34:19
better than the riches of *m.* 37:16
m. shall see it and fear, and. 40:3
delivered, for there were *m.* 55:18
I am a wonder to *m.*; but thou. 71:7
m. are my persecutors.   119:157
years of thy life shall be *m. Pr* 4:10
for she hath cast down *m.*   7:26
the righteous feed *m.*   10:21
the rich hath *m.* friends.   14:20
wealth maketh *m.* friends.   19:4
for transgression of land *m.* are. 28:2
his eyes, shall have *m.* a curse. 27
darkness shall be *m.*   *Eccl* 11:8
trust in chariots because they are *m.*
    Isa 31:1
knowledge shall he justify *m.* 56:11
he bare the sin of *m.* and made. 12
slain of the Lord shall be *m.* 66:16
their transgressions are *m. Jer* 5:6
for our backslidings are *m.* 14:7
for we are left but few of *m.* 42:2
he made *m.* to fall.   46:16

---

for my sighs are *m.* my. *Lam* 1:22
but we are *m.*; the land. *Ezek* 33:24
by peace shall destroy *m. Dan* 8:25
m. stand up against the king. 11:14
understand shall instruct *m.* 33
utterly to make away *m.* 44
m. that sleep in the dust shall. 12:2
m. shall run to and fro, and. 4
Ephraim hath made *m.* *Hos* 8:11
be quiet, and likewise *m. Nah* 1:12
inhabitants of *m.* cities. *Zech* 8:20
but did turn *m.* away.   *Mal* 2:6
and *m.* there be that go. *Mat* 7:13
m. will say to me in that day. 22
m. shall come from the east. 8:11
he did not *m.* mighty works. 13:58
m. that are first shall be last.
    19:30; *Mark* 10:31
for *m.* be called, but few chosen.
    Mat 20:16; 22:14
for *m.* shall come in my name, and
  shall deceive *m.* 24:5; *Mark* 13:6
    Luke 21:8
love of *m.* shall wax. *Mat* 24:12
this is my blood, shed for *m.* 26:28
they appear to *m.*   27:53
name is Legion, for we are *m.*
    Mark 5:9; *Luke* 8:30
m. shall he turn to Lord. *Luke* 1:16
fall and rising of *m.* in Israel. 2:34
m. widows were in Israel. 4:25
m. lepers were in Israel. 27
and devils also came out of *m.* 41
her sins which are *m.*   7:47
great supper, and bade *m.* 14:16
are they among so *m.? John* 6:9
m. therefore of his disciples. 60, 66
and *m.* resorted to him, and. 10:41
for all so *m.*, the net was not. 21:11
I have heard by *m.* of this. *Acts* 9:13
where *m.* were gathered. 12:12
m. brought their books. 19:19
m. of the saints did I shut up. 26:10
m. be dead . . . the grace of God hath
  abounded unto *m.*   *Rom* 5:15
m. were made sinners, *m.* be. 19
so we, being *m.* are one body. 12:5
she hath been a succourer of *m.* 16:2
not *m.* wise, not *m.* mighty are.
    1 Cor 1:26
yet have ye not *m.* fathers. 4:15
there be gods *m.* and lords *m.* 8:5
but with *m.* God was not. 10:5
we being *m.* are one bread. 17
seeking the profit of *m.*   33
m. are weak and *m.* sleep. 11:30
not one member, but *m.* 12:14
great door, and there are *m.* 16:9
may be given by *m.*   *2 Cor* 1:11
punishment was inflicted of *m.* 2:6
m. which corrupt the word. 17
m. redound to glory.   4:15
as poor, yet making *m.* rich. 6:10
zeal hath provoked very *m.* 9:2
and profited above *m.* *Gal* 1:14
and to seeds, as of *m.*   3:16
m. brethren waxing confident by.
    Phil 1:14
m. walk, of whom I have told. 3:18
bringing *m.* sons to glory. *Heb* 2:10
they truly were *m.* priests. 7:23
offered to bear the sins of *m.* 9:28
sprang of one, so *m.* as stars. 11:12
my brethren be not *m.* *Jas* 3:1
m. shall follow pernicious. *2 Pet* 2:2
are there *m.* antichrists. *1 John* 2:18
because *m.* false prophets are. 4:1
see **believed, days, how, waters**

after many
cause to decline *after m.* *Ex* 23:2

as many as
and *as m. as* were willing. *Ex* 35:22
as m. as had not known. *Judg* 3:1
as m. as came to the place stood.
    2 Sam 2:23
as m. as were of free. *2 Chr* 29:31
as m. as ye find bid to. *Mat* 22:9
and gathered together *as m. as.* 10
as m. as touched him. *Mark* 6:56
rise and give *as m. as* he needeth.
    Luke 11:8
but *as m. as* received him. *John* 1:12
give eternal life to *as m. as.* 17:2

---

even to *as m. as* the Lord. *Acts* 2:39
as m. as have spoken have. 3:24
fear came upon *as m. as* heard. 5:11
and *as m. as* obeyed him. 36, 37
were astonished, *as m. as.* 10:45
as m. as were ordained to. 13:48
as m. as have sinned without law,
  and *as m. as* have. *Rom* 2:12
for *as m. as* are led by the Spirit.
    8:14
as m. as are of the works. *Gal* 3:10
as m. as desire to make a fair shew
  in the flesh.   6:12
and *as m. as* walk according. 16
as m. as be perfect be. *Phil* 3:15
and for *as m. as* have not. *Col* 2:1
as m. servants as are. *1 Tim* 6:1
but to *as m. as* have not. *Rev* 2:24
as m. as I love I rebuke. 3:19
cause that *as m. as* would not. 13:15

many people
people of the land now are *m. Ex* 5:5
a *people* great and *m.* *Deut* 2:21
the *people* are too *m.* . . . yet too *m.*
  for me.   *Judg* 7:2, 4
Lord had smitten *m.* of the *people.*
    1 Sam 6:19
m. of the *people* are fallen and dead.
    2 Sam 1:4
but the *people* are *m.* *Ezra* 10:13
m. people of land became. *Esth* 8:17
m. people shall go and say. *Isa* 2:3
judge and rebuke *m. people.* 4
multitude of *m. people.* 17:12
m. people of a strange. *Ezek* 3:6
without *m. people* to pluck it. 17:9
vex the hearts of *m. people.* 32:9
I will make *m. people* amazed. 10
and *m. people* with thee. 38:9, 15
judge among *m. people.* *Mi* 4:3
beat in pieces *m. people.* 13
shall be in midst of *m. people.* 5:7
m. people shall come. *Zech* 8:22
thou must prophesy before *m.* *peo-*
  ples, nations and tongues.
    Rev 10:11

many things
I have heard *m.* such *things.*
    Job 16:2
and *m.* such *things* are with. 23:14
there be *m. things* that. *Eccl* 6:11
seeing *m. things*, but. *Isa* 42:30
spake *m. things* to them. *Mat* 13:3
suffer *m. things* of the elders and
  chief priests. 16:21; *Mark* 8:31
  9:12; *Luke* 9:22; 17:25
make thee ruler over *m. things.*
    Mat 25:21, 23
hearest thou not how *m. things* they
  witness? 27:13; *Mark* 15:4
have suffered *m. things* this day in a
  dream.   *Mat* 27:19
suffered *m. things* of many physicians.   *Mark* 5:26
he did *m. things*, and heard. 6:20
m. things there be, as washing of
  cups.   7:4, 8, 13
accused him of *m. things.* 15:3
thou art troubled about *m. things.*
    Luke 10:41
to speak of *m. things.* 11:53
I have *m. things* to say. *John* 8:26
    16:12
there are *m.* other *things.* 21:25
that I ought to do *m. things* contrary.
    Acts 26:9
diligent in *m. things.* *2 Cor* 8:22
suffered so *m. things.* *Gal* 3:4
in how *m. things* he. *2 Tim* 1:18
have *m. things* to say. *Heb* 5:11
in *m. things* we offend. *Jas* 3:2
having *m. things* to write to you.
    2 John 12; *3 John* 13

many a time
m. a time turned he his. *Ps* 78:38
m. a time have they afflicted me.
    129:1, 2

many times
how *m. times* shall I adjure thee?
    1 Ki 22:16
m. times didst deliver them.
    Neh 9:28; *Ps* 106:43

many *years*
if there be yet *m.* years. *Lev* 25:51
that was builded *m.* years ago.
            Ezra 5:11
yet *m.* years didst thou. *Neh* 9:30
children, and live *m.* years. *Eccl* 6:3
man live *m.* years, and rejoice. 11:8
m. days and years shall. *Isa* 32:10
prophesied *m.* years. *Ezek* 38:17
done these so *m.* years. *Zech* 7:3
hast goods laid up for *m.* years.
            Luke 12:19
he said, Lo, these *m.* years. 15:29
of *m.* years a judge. *Acts* 24:10
now after *m.* years I came to. 17
a great desire *m.* years. *Rom* 15:23

mar
nor *m.* the corners of. *Lev* 19:27
lest I *m.* mine own. *Ruth* 4:6
images of your mice that *m.* the
   land. *1 Sam* 6:5
and *m.* every good. *2 Ki* 3:19
they *m.* my path, they. *Job* 30:13
I *m.* the pride of Judah. *Jer* 13:9

Mara
not Naomi, call me *M.* *Ruth* 1:20

Marah
not drink of waters of *M.* *Ex* 15:23
days, and pitched in *M.* *Num* 33:8
removed from *M.* and came. 9

Maran-atha
(*An Aramaic or Syriac expression
used by St. Paul at the conclusion of
his First Epistle to the Corinthians,
1 Cor 16:22, meaning our Lord
cometh*)

marble
I have prepared *m.* in. *1 Chr* 29:2
pillars of *m.*: pavement of red, blue,
   white, and black *m.* *Esth* 1:6
his legs are as pillars of *m.* set.
            S of S 5:15
the vessels of *m.* no man. *Rev* 18:12

march
thou didst *m.* through. *Ps* 68:7
shall *m.* with an army. *Jer* 46:22
m. every one on his ways. *Joel* 2:7
which shall *m.* through. *Hab* 1:6
didst *m.* through the land. 3:12

marched
behold, the Egyptians *m.* *Ex* 14:10

marchedst
when thou *m.*, the earth. *Judg* 5:4

Marcus
M. sister's son to Barnabas. *Col* 4:10
M. saluteth. *Philem* 24; *1 Pet* 5:13

mariners
of Zidon were thy *m.* *Ezek* 27:8*
ships of the sea with their *m.* were. 9
thy *m.* shall fall into the midst of. 27
the *m.* shall come down from. 29
then the *m.* were afraid. *Jonah* 1:5

marishes
miry places and marishes *m.* shall. *Ezek* 47:11

Mark
John, surnamed *M.* *Acts* 12:12
John, whose surname was *M.* 25
Barnabas took *M.* and. 15:39
take *M.* and bring. *2 Tim* 4:11

mark, *substantive*
the Lord set a *m.* upon. *Gen* 4:15*
though I shot at a *m.* *1 Sam* 20:20
hast thou set me as a *m.* against
   thee? *Job* 7:20; 16:12; *Lam* 3:12
set a *m.* on the men. *Ezek* 9:4
any man on whom is the *m.* 6
I press toward the *m.* *Phil* 3:14*
all to receive a *m.* *Rev* 13:16
save he that had the *m.* 17
if any man receive his *m.* 14:9
whosoever receiveth his *m.* 11
his image, and over his *m.* 15:2
sore on them that had the *m.* 16:2
that received *m.* of beast. 19:20
nor received his *m.* upon their. 20:4

mark, *verb*
thou shalt *m.* the place. *Ruth* 3:4
m. when Amnon's heart is merry.
            2 Sam 13:28

m. how this man. *1 Ki* 20:7
the prophet said, *M.* and see. 22
m. and afterwards we will. *Job* 18:2
m. me and be astonished, and. 21:5
m. well, O Job, hearken to me. 33:31
canst thou *m.* when the hinds? 39:1
m. the perfect man. *Ps* 37:37
m. well her bulwarks. 48:13
they *m.* my steps, when they. 56:6
if thou, Lord, shouldest *m.* 130:3
m. well, *m.* the entering. *Ezek* 44:5
m. them who cause. *Rom* 16:17
m. them who walk so. *Phil* 3:17

marked
as she prayed, Eli *m.* *1 Sam* 1:12
hast thou *m.* the old way? *Job* 22:15
which they had *m.* in the day. 24:16
yet thine iniquity is *m.* *Jer* 2:22
who hath *m.* his word and? 23:18
m. how they chose rooms. *Luke* 14:7

markest
if I sin, then thou *m.* *Job* 10:14

market
they traded in thy *m.* *Ezek* 27:13*
            17*, 19*, 25*
standing idle in the *m.* *Mat* 20:3
they come from the *m.* *Mark* 7:4*
salutations in the *m.* places. 12:38
sitting in the *m.* place. *Luke* 7:32
is a pool at Jerusalem by the sheep
   m. *John* 5:2*
them into the *m.* place. *Acts* 16:19
he disputed in the *m.* daily. 17:17*

marketh
my feet in stocks, he *m.* *Job* 33:11
the carpenter *m.* it out. *Isa* 44:13

markets
(*Revisions,* marketplaces)
children sitting in the *m.* *Mat* 11:16
love greetings in the *m.* 23:7
         Luke 11:43; 20:46

marks
ye shall not print any *m.* *Lev* 19:28
I bear in my body the *m.* *Gal* 6:17

marred
his visage was so *m.* *Isa* 52:14
girdle was *m.* *Jer* 13:7
the vessel was *m.* 18:4
m. their vine branches. *Nah* 2:2
the bottles will be *m.* *Mark* 2:22

marriage
(*The word marriage is used* [1]
literally; and [2] *figuratively to
represent the union of God with
his people or of Christ with his
church*)
her duty of *m.* shall he. *Ex* 21:10
were not given to *m.* *Ps* 78:63*
a king who made a *m.* *Mat* 22:2
come to the *m.* 4
all ye find, bid to the *m.* 9
not given in *m.* but as the angels.
   22:30; *Mark* 12:25; *Luke* 20:35
given in *m.* until day. *Mat* 24:38
went in with him to the *m.* 25:10
they did eat, they were given in *m.*
          Luke 17:27; 20:34
there was a *m.* in Cana. *John* 2:1
Jesus and his disciples to the *m.* 2
her in *m.* doeth well, but he that
   giveth her not in *m.* *1 Cor* 7:38
m. is honourable in all. *Heb* 13:4
m. of the Lamb is come. *Rev* 19:7
called to the *m.* supper of Lamb. 9

marriages
and make ye *m.* with us. *Gen* 34:9
neither shalt thou make *m.* *Deut* 7:3
else if he shall make *m.* *Josh* 23:12

married
Lot spake to them that *m.* *Gen* 19:14
if *m.* his wife shall go out. *Ex* 21:3
if *m.* to a stranger, she. *Lev* 22:12
woman whom he had *m.* *Num* 12:1
if they be *m.* to the sons of. 36:3
m. to their father's brothers'. 11
lying with a woman *m.* *Deut* 22:22
m. when sixty years old. *1 Chr* 2:21
Abijah *m.* fourteen. *2 Chr* 13:21
Jews that had *m.* wives. *Neh* 13:23
woman when she is *m.* *Pr* 30:23

of desolate than of *m.* *Isa* 54:1
in thee, thy land shall be *m.* 62:4
children, for I am *m.* to. *Jer* 3:14
hath *m.* the daughter of. *Mal* 2:11
the first when he had *m.* *Mat* 22:25
for he had *m.* her. *Mark* 6:17
be *m.* to another, committeth. 10:12
I have *m.* a wife, and. *Luke* 14:20
they drank, they *m.* wives. 17:27
husband liveth, she be *m.* *Rom* 7:3
dead, that ye should be *m.* 4
to the *m.* I command. *1 Cor* 7:10
he that is *m.* 33
she that is *m.* careth for. 34
to be *m.* to whom she will, only. 39

marrieth
young man *m.* a virgin. *Isa* 62:5
m. her who is put away, doth.
     Mat 19:9; *Luke* 16:18

marrow
(*A soft tissue which fills the
cavities of most bones; hence, the
choicest of food*)
are moistened with *m.* *Job* 21:24
be satisfied as with *m.* *Ps* 63:5
it shall be health and *m.* *Pr* 3:8
feast of fat things full of *m.* *Isa* 25:6
asunder of joints and *m.* *Heb* 4:12

marry
brother's wife, and *m.* *Gen* 38:8*
m. to whom they think best...father's
   tribe shall they *m.* *Num* 36:6
wife of dead shall not *m.* *Deut* 25:5
so shall thy sons *m.* thee. *Isa* 62:5
m. her that is divorced committeth.
    Mat 5:32; 19:9; *Mark* 10:11
so, it is not good to *m.* *Mat* 19:10
his brother shall *m.* his wife. 22:24
they neither *m.* nor are given. 30
    Mark 12:25; *Luke* 20:35
let them *m.*, for it is better to be.
          1 Cor 7:9
if thou *m.* if a virgin *m.*: she hath. 28
he sinneth not, let them *m.* 36
forbidding to *m.* and. *1 Tim* 4:3
to wax wanton, they will *m.* 5:11
the younger women *m.*, bear. 14

marrying
do this great evil in *m.* *Neh* 13:27
they were *m.* and giving. *Mat* 24:38

Mars' hill
in the midst of *M.* hill. *Acts* 17:22

mart
Tyre, and she is a *m.* of. *Isa* 23:3

Martha
a woman named *M.* *Luke* 10:38
M. was cumbered about. 40
M. M. thou art careful. 41
Mary and her sister *M.* *John* 11:1
now Jesus loved *M.* Mary, and. 5
Jesus was in that place where *M.* 30
made him a supper, and *M.* 12:2

martyr
blood of thy *m.* Stephen. *Acts* 22:20*
wherein Antipas was my faithful *m.*
          Rev 2:13*

martyrs
drunken with blood of *m.* *Rev* 17:6

marvel
no *m.*; for Satan himself. *2 Cor* 11:14

marvel
if thou seest, *m.* not at. *Eccl* 5:8
and all men did *m.* *Mark* 5:20
m. not that I said, Ye must be born.
         John 3:7
greater works, that ye may *m.* 5:20
m. not at this. 28
done one work, and ye *m.* 7:21
men of Israel, why *m.* *Acts* 3:12
I *m.* that ye are so soon. *Gal* 1:6
m. not if the world. *1 John* 3:13
wherefore didst thou *m.?* *Rev* 17:7*

marvelled
and the men *m.* one. *Gen* 43:33
they saw it, and so they *m.* *Ps* 48:5
when Jesus heard it, he *m.* *Mat* 8:10
the men *m.* 27
m. and glorified God. 9:8*, 33
disciples saw it, they *m.* 21:20

they *m.*, and left him. *Mat 22:22*
   Mark 12:17; Luke 20:26
that the governor *m.* *Mat 27:14*
   Mark 15:5, 44
m. because of their unbelief.
   Mark 6:6
people *m.* that he tarried. *Luke 1:21*
his name is John, and they *m.* 63
Joseph and his mother *m.* at. 2:33
Jesus heard these things he *m.* 7:9
Pharisee saw it, he *m.* 11:38
disciples *m.* he talked. *John 4:27*
Jews *m.*, How knoweth this ? 7:15
m. saying, Are not these ? *Acts 2:7*
they *m.* and took knowledge. 4:13

marvellous
who doeth *m.* things. *Job 5:9*
thou shewest thyself *m.* upon. 10:16
thy *m.* lovingkindness. *Ps 17:7*
he hath shewed me his *m.* 31:21
m. things did he in the sight. 78:12
for he hath done *m.* things. 98:1
Lord's doing; it is *m.* in our eyes.
   118:23; *Mat 21:42; Mark 12:11*
shall speak *m.* things. *Dan 11:36*
will I shew unto him *m.* *Mi 7:15*
if it be *m.* should it be *m.? Zech 8:6*
herein is a *m.* thing. *John 9:30*
darkness into his *m.* light. *1 Pet 2:9*
heaven, great and *m.* *Rev 15:1*

marvellous work
proceed to do a *m. work. Isa 29:14*

marvellous works
remember his *m.* works.
   1 Chr 16:12; Ps 105:5
declare his *m.* works. *1 Chr 16:24*
forth all thy *m.* works. *Ps 9:1*
great and *m.* are thy works. 139:14
   Rev 15:3

marvellously
he was *m.* helped till. *2 Chr 26:15*
God thundereth *m.* with. *Job 37:5*
regard, and wonder *m.* *Hab 1:5*

marvels
I will do *m.* such as have. *Ex 34:10*

Mary
Joseph the husband of *M. Mat 1:16*
his mother *M.* was espoused. 18
take unto thee *M.* thy wife. 20
saw the young child with *M.* 2:11
mother called *M.?* 13:55; *Mark 6:3*
M. the mother of James. *Mat 27:56*
   Mark 15:40, 47; 16:1
virgin's name was *M.* *Luke 1:27*
fear not, *M.* 30
heard the salutation of *M.* 41
M. abode three months. 56
went to be taxed with *M.* his. 2:5
shepherds found *M.* and the. 16
but *M.* kept all these things in. 19
had a sister called *M.* 10:39
M. hath chosen that good part. 42
the town of *M.* *John 11:1*
but *M.* sat still. 20
she called *M.* her sister secretly. 28
M. took a pound of ointment. 12:3
M. the wife of Cleophas. 19:25
M. stood without at the. 20:11
Jesus saith to her, *M.* She turned. 16
in prayer with *M.* *Acts 1:14*
Peter came to house of *M.* 12:12
greet *M.* who bestowed. *Rom 16:6*

Mary Magdalene
women were there, among whom
   was *M. Magdalene.* *Mat 27:56*
   Mark 15:40; John 19:25
M. Magdalene sitting. *Mat 27:61*
came *M. Magdalene* to see the
   sepulchre. 28:1; *John 20:1*
M. Magdalene and Mary the.
   Mark 16:1; Luke 24:10
he appeared first to *M. Magdalene.*
   Mark 16:9
M. Magdalene told the. *John 20:18*

masons
Hiram sent to David *m. 2 Sam 5:11*
   1 Chr 14:1
gave money to *m.* and hewers of.
   2 Ki 12:12; 22:6; Ezra 3:7
he set *m.* to hew. *1 Chr 22:2*
they hired *m.* to repair. *2 Chr 24:12*
27

Massah
name of the place *M.* *Ex 17:7*
shall not tempt the Lord, as ye tempted him in *M.* *Deut 6:16; 9:22*
whom thou didst prove at *M.* 33:8

mast, -s
lieth on the top of a *m.* *Pr 23:34*
not strengthen their *m.* *Isa 33:23*
Lebanon to make *m.* *Ezek 27:5*

master
Joseph's *m.* put him in. *Gen 39:20*
if she please not her *m.* *Ex 21:8*
give to their *m.* thirty shekels. 32
m. of the house shall be. 22:8
and spake to the *m.* of. *Judg 19:22*
the *m.* of the house went out. 23
David sent messengers to salute our
   m. *1 Sam 25:14*
determined against our *m.* 17
have not kept your *m.* 2 Sam 2:7*
m. Saul is dead. *2 Sam 2:7**
   1 Ki 22:17
these have no *m.* *2 Chr 18:16*
he cried, Alas, *m.* for it *2 Ki 6:5*
drink, and go to their *m.* 23
and they went to their *m.* 23
seeing your *m.'s* sons are with. 10:2
look out the best of your *m.'s* sons. 3
take the heads of your *m.'s* sons. 6
ye say to your *m.* 19:6; *Isa 37:6*
and Chenaniah, *m.* of. *1 Chr 15:27*
servant, so with his *m.* *Isa 24:2*
king spake to the *m.* *Dan 1:3*
m. of the magicians. 4:9; 5:11
and if I be a *m.* where is ? *Mal 1:6*
the Lord will cut off the *m.* 2:12*
m. I will follow thee. *Mat 8:19*
eateth your *m.* with publicans ? 9:11
they have called the *m.* 10:25
m. we would see a sign from. 12:38
fall from their *m.'s* table. 15:27
they said, Doth not your *m.?* 17:24
m. we know that thou art true.
   22:16; *Mark 12:14*
one is your *m.*, even. *Mat 23:8*, 10
the *m.* saith, My time is at. 26:18
M. is it I ? 25*
Hail, *m.* and kissed him. 49*
   *Mark 14:45**
why troublest thou the *m.* any more ?
   Mark 5:35
m. it is good for us to be here. 9:5*
   Luke 9:33
m. what shall I do ? *Mark 10:17*
   Luke 10:25
for ye know not when the *m.*
   Mark 13:35
the publicans said, *M.?* *Luke 3:12*
m. say on. 7:40
saying, *M.* we perish. 8:24
is dead; trouble not the *m.* 49
when once *m.* of the house. 13:25
thou a *m.* in Israel ? *John 3:10**
the *m.* is come and calleth. 11:28
ye call me *M.* and ye say. 13:13
if I then your *m.* have washed. 14
believed the *m.* of ship. *Acts 27:11*
knowing your *m.* is in heaven.
   Eph 6:9; Col 4:1
meet for the *m.'s* use. *2 Tim 2:21*

his master
under the thigh of *his m.* *Gen 24:9*
of *his m.*, for goods of *his m.* 10
Joseph was in house of *his m.* 39:2
when *his m.* heard the words. 19
if *his m.* have given him. *Ex 21:4*
his m. shall bore his ear through. 6
to *his m.* the servant which is escaped from *his m.* *Deut 23:15*
servant said to *his m.* *Judg 19:11*
the arrows and came to *his m.*
   1 Sam 20:38
servants break away every one from
   his m. 25:10
reconcile himself to *his m.* 29:4*
a great man with *his m.* *2 Ki 5:1*
went in, and stood before *his m.* 25
not the sound of *his m.'s* feet ? 6:32
departed and came to *his m.* 8:14
Zimri peace, who slew *his m.?* 9:31
his m. hath sent to reproach God.
   19:4; *Isa 37:4*

will fall to *his m.* Saul. *1 Chr 12:19*
servant is free from *his m.* *Job 3:19*
that waiteth on *his m.* *Pr 27:18*
accuse not a servant to *his m.* 30:10
ass knoweth *his m.'s* crib. *Isa 1:3*
servant honoureth *his m.* *Mal 1:6*
the disciple is not above *his m.*
   Mat 10:24; Luke 6:40
disciple be as *his m.* *Mat 10:25*
perfect shall be as *his m.* *Luke 6:40*
his own *m.* he standeth. *Rom 14:4**

my master
my m. Abraham shew kindness to
   my m. *Gen 24:12, 27, 42, 48*
shewed kindness to *my m.* 24:14
the Lord hath blessed *my m.* 35
Lord hath appointed for *my m.* 44
deal truly and kindly with *my m.* 49
send me away to *my m.* 54, 56
servant had said, It is *my m.* 65
my m. wotteth not what. 39:8
shall say, I love *my m.* *Ex 21:5*
should do this to *my m. 1 Sam 24:6**
my m. left me because I fell. 30:13
me into the hands of *my m.* 15
my m. goeth into house of. *2 Ki 5:18*
my m. hath spared Naaman. 20
my m. hath sent me, saying. 22
and he said, Alas, *my m.*, how ? 6:15
I conspired against *my m.* 10:9
turn away one captain of the least of
   my m.'s servants. 18:24; *Isa 36:9*
hath *my m.* sent me to thy master ?
   2 Ki 18:27; Isa 36:12
I pray thee, to *my m.* *Isa 36:8*

thy master
be *thy m.'s* son's wife. *Gen 24:51*
rise up early with *thy m.'s* servants.
   1 Sam 29:10
I give *thy m.'s* son all. *2 Sam 9:9*
thy m.'s house, *thy m.'s* wives. 12:8
where is *thy m.'s* son ? 16:3
away *thy m.* to-day. *2 Ki 2:3, 5*
we pray thee, and seek *thy m.* 16
the house of Ahab *thy m.* 9:7
master sent me to *thy m.* and. 18:27

masterbuilder
as wise *m.* I have laid. *1 Cor 3:10*

masteries
if a man also strive for *m.*, yet is he
   not crowned. *2 Tim 2:5*

masters
children shall be her *m.* *Ex 21:4*
eyes of servants look to their *m.*
   Ps 123:2
refresheth soul of his *m.* *Pr 25:13*
as nails fastened by *m.* of. *Eccl 12:11*
them to say to their *m.* *Jer 27:4*
their *m.*, Let us drink. *Amos 4:1**
who fill their *m.'s* houses. *Zeph 1:9*
no man can serve two *m.* *Mat 6:24*
   Luke 16:13
neither be ye called *m.* *Mat 23:10*
her *m.* much gain. *Acts 16:16*
her *m.* saw the hope of their gains. 19
to them that are your *m.* *Eph 6:5*
   Col 3:22; Tit 2:9; 1 Pet 2:18
ye *m.* do the same things to them.
   Eph 6:9; Col 4:1
count their *m.* worthy. *1 Tim 6:1*
believing *m.*, let them not despise. 2
be not many *m.* knowing. *Jas 3:1**

mastery
them that shout for *m.* *Ex 32:18*
the lions had the *m.* of. *Dan 6:24*
that striveth for the *m. 1 Cor 9:25**

mate
every one with her *m.* *Isa 34:15*
fail, none shall want her *m.* 16

matrix
set apart unto the Lord all that
   openeth the *m.* *Ex 13:12, 15*
all that openeth the *m.* is. 34:19
firstborn that open the *m. Num 3:12*
every thing that openeth *m.* 18:15

Mattan
slew *M.* priest of Baal. *2 Ki 11:18*
   2 Chr 23:17

Mattathias
which was the son of *M. Luke 3:25*

matter

him concerning that *m.*   *Gen* 24:9
small *m.* that thou hast taken. 30:15
when they have a *m.* they. *Ex* 18:16
every great *m.* they shall bring to
   thee, but every small *m.* they. 22
but every small *m.* they judged. 26
keep thee far from a false *m.* 23:7
that died about the *m.* of Korah.
      Num 16:49
you in *m.* of Peor, in *m.*   25:18
trespass in the *m.* of Peor.   31:16
arise a *m.* too hard.   *Deut* 17:8
mouth of three witnesses *m.*   19:15
how the *m.* will fall out. *Ruth* 3:18
m. of the kingdom he. *1 Sam* 10:16
touching the *m.* thou and I.   20:23
and David knew the *m.*   39
how went the *m.?* I pray. *2 Sam* 1:4
no *m.* hid from the king.   18:13
they ended the *m.*   20:18
the *m.* is not so.   21
at all times as the *m.*   *1 Ki* 8:59*
save in the *m.* of Uriah the.   15:5
for every *m.* pertaining. *1 Chr* 26:32
served the king in any *m.*   27:1
from command in any *m.* *2 Chr* 8:15
see ye hasten the *m.*   24:5
to cease, till the *m.*   *Ezra* 5:5
sat down to examine the *m.* 10:16
have *m.* for evil report. *Neh* 6:13
inquisition was made of the *m.*
      Esth 2:23
seeing the root of the *m. Job* 19:28
answer, for I am full of *m.*   32:18*
heart is inditing a good *m.* *Ps* 45:1
themselves in an evil *m.*   64:5*
spirit concealeth the *m.* *Pr* 11:13
that handleth a *m.* wisely.   16:20*
that repeateth a *m.* separateth. 17:9
that answereth a *m.* before.   18:13*
kings is to search out a *m.*   25:2
marvel not at the *m.*   *Eccl* 5:8
wings shall tell the *m.*   10:20
the conclusion of the *m.*   12:13
the *m.* was not perceived. *Jer* 38:27
inkhorn, reported the *m. Ezek* 9:11
whoredoms a small *m.?*   16:20
can shew the king's *m. Dan* 2:10
known to us the king's *m.*   23
end of the *m.:* I kept the *m.*   7:28
understand the *m.* and.   9:23
to blaze abroad the *m. Mark* 1:45
him again of the same *m.*   10:10
Peter rehearsed the *m. Acts* 11:4
came to consider of this *m.*   15:6
Gallio said, If it were a *m.* of. 18:14
if Demetrius have a *m.*   19:38
the uttermost of your *m.*   24:22
any of you having a *m.? 1 Cor* 6:1
might be ready as a *m. 2 Cor* 9:5
it were, it maketh no *m. Gal* 2:6
defraud brother in any *m. 1 Thes* 4:6
great a *m.* a little fire! *Jas* 3:5*

this matter

speak no more to me of *this m.*
      Deut 3:26
his neighbour, so is *this m.*   22:26
who will hearken to you in *this m.?*
      1 Sam 30:24
ye angry for *this m.? 2 Sam* 19:42
answer concerning *this m. Ezra* 5:5
pleasure to us concerning *this m.* 17
arise, for *this m.* belongeth.   10:4
sat trembling because of *this m.* 9
were employed about *this m.*   15
seen concerning *this m. Esth* 9:26
Melzar consented to them in *this m.*
      Dan 1:14
to answer thee in *this m.*   3:16
this m. is by the decree of.   4:17*
part nor lot in *this m. Acts* 8:21
hear thee again of *this m.*   17:32
approved yourselves clear in *this m.*
      2 Cor 7:11

matters

if any have *m.* let him. *Ex* 24:14*
if arise *m.* of controversy. *Deut* 17:8
son of Jesse that is prudent in *m.*
      1 Sam 16:18*
end of telling the *m. 2 Sam* 11:19
Absalom said, See thy *m.* are. 15:3
thou any more of thy *m.?*
      19:29

you in *m.* of the Lord, and Zebadiah
   for all the king's *m. 2 Chr* 19:11
Pethahiah in all *m.* concerning.
      Neh 11:24
whether Mordecai's *m. Esth* 3:4
the *m.* of the fastings.   9:31, 32
not account of his *m. Job* 33:13
thus devise deceitful *m. Ps* 35:20*
exercise myself in great *m.*   131:1
in *m.* of wisdom he found. *Dan* 1:20
and told the sum of the *m.*   7:1
omitted the weightier *m. Mat* 23:23
be no judge of such *m. Acts* 18:15
any thing concerning other *m.* 19:39
there be judged of these *m.*   25:20
judge the smallest *m.? 1 Cor* 6:2
a busybody in other men's *m.*
      1 Pet 4:15

Matthew

a man named *M.* and saith. *Mat* 9:9
Philip, Thomas, and *M.* the.   10:3
   Mark 3:18; *Luke* 6:15; *Acts* 1:13

Matthias

called Barsabas, and *M. Acts* 1:23
the lot fell on *M.* and he was.   26

mattock

sharpen every man his axe and *m.*
      1 Sam 13:20
be digged with the *m. Isa* 7:25

mattocks

had a file for the *m. 1 Sam* 13:21
Josiah with their *m. 2 Chr* 34:6*

maul

false witness, is a *m. Pr* 25:18

maw

two cheeks and the *m. Deut* 18:3

may

seeing I go whither I *m.* return thou.
      2 Sam 15:20
she said, If I *m.* but touch. *Mat* 9:21
if this cup *m.* not pass away.   26:42
as I *m.* so say, Levi also. *Heb* 7:9

may be

that it *m.* be well with. *Gen* 12:13
it *m.* be that I may obtain.   16:2
that the Lord's law *m.* be. *Ex* 13:9
that his fear *m.* be before.   20:20
of all meat which *m.* be. *Lev* 11:34
for his sister a virgin he *m.* be. 21:3
that it *m.* be an holy.   23:21
m. be for a memorial. *Num* 10:10
the possession *m.* be ours.   32:32
m. be well with you. *Deut* 5:33; 6:3
   18; 22:7; *Ruth* 3:1; *Jer* 7:23
m. be to thee a God. *Deut* 29:13
m. be there for a witness.   31:26
it *m.* be a witness between us.
      Josh 22:27
it *m.* be the Lord will. *1 Sam* 14:6
m. be a snare, Philistines *m.* be.
      18:21
it *m.* be that the king. *2 Sam* 14:15
it *m.* be Lord will look on.   16:12
m. be Lord thy God will hear.
      2 Ki 19:4; *Isa* 37:4
m. be before thee for. *1 Chr* 17:27
that ye *m.* be strong. *Ezra* 9:12
it *m.* be that my sons have sinned.
      Job 1:5
consume them, that they *m.* not be.
      Ps 59:13
that Israel *m.* be no more.   83:4
our sons *m.* be as plants.   144:12
that our garners *m.* be full.   13
that our oxen *m.* be strong.   14
that thy trust *m.* be in. *Pr* 22:19
whereof it *m.* be said, See this is
   new.   *Eccl* 1:10
that it *m.* be for the time. *Isa* 30:8
the Lord waiteth that he *m.* be. 18
that we *m.* be like.   46:5
I *m.* be glorified.   60:21
name *m.* be no more. *Jer* 11:19
it *m.* be the house of Judah. 36:3
it *m.* be they will present their. 7
that it *m.* be well with us.   42:6
take balm, if so be she *m.*   51:8
put his mouth in the dust; if so be
   there *m.* be hope. *Lam* 3:29
it *m.* be they will consider.
      Ezek 12:3
that they *m.* be my people.   14:11

it *m.* be a lengthening. *Dan* 4:27
that they *m.* be cut off. *Hos* 8:4
it *m.* be the Lord will. *Amos* 5:15
it *m.* be ye shall be hid. *Zeph* 2:3
that ye *m.* be children of. *Mat* 5:45
that thine alms *m.* be in secret. 6:4
it *m.* be they will reverence him.
      Luke 20:13
the inheritance *m.* be ours.   14
ye *m.* be the children. *John* 12:36
there ye *m.* be also.   14:3
that they *m.* be one.   17:11, 21, 22
that the love *m.* be in them.   26
that he *m.* be wise. *1 Cor* 3:18
that ye *m.* be a new lump.   5:7
that she *m.* be holy in body.   7:34
are, it *m.* be, so many kinds.   14:10
be subject, that God *m.* be.   15:28
m. be that I will winter.   16:6
see that he *m.* be with you.   10
power *m.* be of God. *2 Cor* 4:7
so there *m.* be a performance. 8:11
your abundance *m.* be a supply. 14
as I said, ye *m.* be ready.   9:3
that it *m.* be well with thee. *Eph* 6:3
that ye *m.* be blameless. *Phil* 2:15
that I *m.* be of good comfort.   19
I *m.* be the less sorrowful.   28
charge that they *m.* be. *1 Tim* 5:7
man of God *m.* be. *2 Tim* 3:17
that they *m.* be found in. *Tit* 1:13
that ye *m.* be perfect. *Jas* 1:4

mayest

with all thy heart thou *m. Acts* 8:37

mayest be

thou *m.* be a multitude. *Gen* 28:3
m. be to us instead of. *Num* 10:31
m. be an holy people. *Deut* 26:19
thou *m.* be their king. *Neh* 6:6
that thou *m.* be justified. *Job* 40:8
that thou *m.* be feared. *Ps* 130:4
sing songs, that thou *m.* be. *Isa* 23:16
that thou *m.* be my salvation. 49:6
that thou *m.* be saved. *Jer* 4:14
that thou *m.* be bound up.   30:13
for thou *m.* be no longer. *Luke* 16:2

Mazzaroth

canst thou bring forth *M.? Job* 38:32

me

serpent beguiled *me.*   *Gen* 3:13
put in ward both *me* and.   41:10
me restored, and him he hanged. 13
me have ye bereaved of.   42:36
there is none like *me* in. *Ex* 9:14
they have rejected *me. 1 Sam* 8:7
when Joab sent *me* thy. *2 Sam* 18:29
me, even my thy servant. *1 Ki* 1:26
thyself to another than *me. Isa* 57:8
let not *me* be dismayed. *Jer* 17:18
me, and who will appoint *me?* 50:44
know no God but *me. Hos* 13:4
mother more than *me. Mat* 10:37
receiveth *me,* and he that receiveth
   me.   40; *Mark* 9:37; *John* 13:20
why callest thou *me* good ?
      Mat 19:17; *Luke* 18:19
me ye have not always. *Mat* 26:11
      Mark 14:7; *John* 12:8
he that despiseth *me,* despiseth him
   that sent *me.*   *Luke* 10:16
would have believed *me. John* 5:46
world cannot hate *me,* but *me.*   7:7
ye neither know *me,* nor my.   8:19
though ye believe not *me.*   10:38
yet hast thou not known *me* ?   14:9
hateth *me* hateth my Father.   15:23
hated both *me* and my Father.   24
known the Father nor *me.*   16:3
O Father, glorify thou *me.*   17:5
me ? ask them who heard *me.* 18:21
if well, why smitest thou *me* ?   23
he that delivered *me* to thee. 19:11
Simon, son of Jonas, lovest thou
   me ?   21:15, 16, 17
Saul, why persecutest thou *me* ?
      Acts 9:4; 22:7
what advantageth it *me* ? *1 Cor* 15:32

about me

like the nations that are *about me.*
      Deut 17:14
children were *about me. Job* 29:5
came round *about me* daily. *Ps* 88:17
night shall be light *about me.* 139:11

the earth was *about me. Jonah* 2:6
shone a great light *about me.*
          Acts 22:6; 26:13

above me

thy sons *above me.*   *1 Sam* 2:29

after me

hotly pursued *after me.* *Gen* 31:36
them, Follow *after me.*   *Judg* 3:28
to armourbearer, Come *after me.*
          1 Sam 14:12
not cut off my seed *after me.* 24:21
Solomon shall reign *after me.*
       1 Ki 1:13, 17, 30
Adonijah shall reign *after me.* 24
man that shall be *after me. Eccl* 2:18
shall there be *after me.* *Isa* 43:10
when thou wentest *after me. Jer* 2:2
after me is mightier.   *Mat* 3:11
  Mark 1:7; *John* 1:15, 27, 30
he that followeth not *after me.*
     Mat 10:38; *Luke* 14:27
that will come *after me. Mat* 16:24
     Mark 8:34; *Luke* 9:23
cometh one *after me.*   *Acts* 13:25
that asked not *after me. Rom* 10:20

against me

from sinning *ag. me.*   *Gen* 20:6
all these things are *ag. me.* 42:36
ye thought evil *ag. me.*   50:20
make thee sin *ag. me.*   *Ex* 23:33
sinned *ag. me,* him will I blot. 32:33
they trespassed *ag. me. Lev* 26:40
murmur *ag. me.*   *Num* 14:27, 29
gathered together *ag. me.*   35
abide over *ag. me.*   22:5
thou stoodest *ag. me.*   34
ye trespassed *ag. me. Deut* 32:51
 Ezek 17:20; 20:27, 38; 39:23, 26
anger be hot *ag. me.*   *Judg* 6:39
vaunt themselves *ag. me.*   7:2
doest me wrong to war *ag. me.* 11:27
Lord is gone out *ag. me. Ruth* 1:13
witness *ag. me* before. *1 Sam* 12:3
he arose *ag. me* I caught. 17:35
you have conspired *ag. me.* 22:8, 13
stirred thee up *ag. me.*   26:19
I pray thee, be *ag. me. 2 Sam* 24:17
seeketh a quarrel *ag. me. 2 Ki* 5:7
thy witnesses *ag. me.*   *Job* 10:17
writest bitter things *ag. me.* 13:26
which is a witness *ag. me.* 16:8
I loved are turned *ag. me.* 19:19
will he plead *ag. me* with.   23:6
opposest thyself *ag. me.*   30:21
if my land cry *ag. me,* or. 31:38
findeth occasions *ag. me.* 33:10
many that rise up *ag. me.* *Ps* 3:1
           18:39, 48
are risen up *ag. me.* 27:12; 54:3
their mouth wide *ag. me.*   35:21
ag. me do they devise my hurt,
   whisper *ag. me.*   41:7
they are mad *ag. me,* they are sworn
   ag. me.   102:8
did sit and speak *ag. me.* 119:23
he that sinneth *ag. me.* *Pr* 8:36
have rebelled *ag. me.*   *Isa* 1:2
    Ezek 2:3; 20:8, 13, 21
it crieth out *ag. me.*   *Jer* 12:8
ag. me he is turned.   *Lam* 3:3
their imaginations *ag. me.*   60
so they sinned *ag. me.* *Hos* 4:7
ag. me, spoken lies *ag. me.* 7:13
assemble and rebel *ag. me.* 14
imagine mischief *ag. me.*   15
O my people, testify *ag. me. Mi* 6:3
rejoice not *ag. me,* O mine.   7:8
have been stout *ag. me. Mal* 3:13
he that is not with me is *ag. me.*
     Mat 12:30; *Luke* 11:23
my brother sin *ag. me?*   18:21
up his heel *ag. me.*   *John* 13:18
have no power at all *ag. me.* 19:11
if they had aught *ag. me. Acts* 24:19

at me

thrust sore *at me* to fall. *Ps* 118:13
are ye angry *at me?*   *John* 7:23

before me

all flesh is come *bef. me. Gen* 6:13
thee . . . righteous *bef. me.*   7:1
walk *bef. me,* and be thou perfect.
 17:1; *1 Sam* 2:30; *1 Ki* 2:4
    8:25; 9:4; *2 Chr* 7:17

a vine was *bef. me.*   *Gen* 40:9
shalt have no other gods *bef. me.*
     Ex 20:3; *Deut* 5:7
none shall appear *bef. me* empty.
    Ex 23:15; 34:20
way is perverse *bef. me. Num* 22:32
go up *bef. me* to the high. *1 Sam* 9:19
go down *bef. me* to Gilgal. 10:8
I pray thee, stand *bef. me.* 16:22
go on *bef. me,* behold I come. 25:19
all his judgements were *bef. me.*
   2 Sam 22:23; *Ps* 18:22; 119:30
as thou hast walked *bef. me.*
    1 Ki 8:25; *2 Chr* 6:16
may have a light *bef. me. 1 Ki* 11:36
humbleth himself *bef. me.* 21:29
because thou hast wept *bef. me.*
   2 Ki 22:19; *2 Chr* 34:27
plainly read *bef. me.*   *Ezra* 4:18
former governors that were *bef. me.*
          Neh 5:15
the queen also *bef. me?* *Esth* 7:8
able to stand *bef. me?* *Job* 41:10
the Lord always *bef. me.* *Ps* 16:8
thou preparest a table *bef. me.* 23:5
is continually *bef. me.*   38:17
while the wicked is *bef. me.* 39:1
been continually *bef. me.*   50:8
my sin is ever *bef. me.*   51:3
endure as the sun *bef. me.* 89:36
all that have been *bef. me.*
       Eccl 1:16; 2:7, 9
which is mine. is *bef. me.* S of S 8:12
come to appear *bef. me.* *Isa* 1:12
silence *bef. me,* O islands. 41:1
there was no god. 43:10
walls are continually *bef. me.* 49:16
spirit should fail *bef. me.* 57:16
behold, it is written *bef. me.* 65:6
shall remain *bef. me.* saith. 66:22
thine iniquity is marked *bef. me.*
          Jer 2:22
bef. me continually is grief. 6:7
and come and stand *bef. me.* 7:10
Samuel stood *bef. me,* yet. 15:1
thou shalt stand *bef. me.*   19
prophets that have been *bef. me.*
          28:8
have only done evil *bef. me.* 32:30
priests shall not want a man *bef. me.*
       33:18; 35:19
had made a covenant *bef. me.* 34:15
will stand *bef. me?* 49:19; 50:44
elders of Judah sat *bef. me.*
          Ezek 8:1
the elders of Israel sat *bef. me.*
        14:1; 20:1
their way was *bef. me* as.   36:17
shall stand *bef. me* to offer. 44:15
Daniel came in *bef. me. Dan* 4:8
is come up *bef. me.*   *Jonah* 1:2
violence are *bef. me.*   *Hab* 1:3
and nation *bef. me.*   *Hag* 2:14
shall prepare the way *bef. me.*
    Mal 3:1; *Mat* 11:10
and slay them *bef. me. Luke* 19:27
preferred *bef. me,* for he was *bef.*
   me.   *John* 1:15; 27:30
another steppeth down *bef. me.* 5:7
all that ever came *bef. me.* 10:8
of these things *bef. me. Acts* 25:9
were in Christ *bef. me. Rom* 16:7
were apostles *bef. me.* *Gal* 1:17

behind me

turn thee *behind me.* *2 Ki* 9:18, 19
heard *behind me* a voice. *Ezek* 3:12
get thee *behind me,* Satan, thou.
   Mat 16:23; *Mark* 8:33; *Luke* 4:8

beside me

arose and took my son from *beside*
   me.   *1 Ki* 3:20
beside me there is no Saviour.
         Isa 43:11; *Hos* 13:4
and *beside me* there is no God.
     Isa 44:6; 45:5, 6, 21
and none else *beside me.* 47:8, 10

between me

make *betw. me* and.   *Gen* 9:12, 13
that is *betw. me* and every. 15, 17
no strife *betw. me* and thee. 13:8
Lord judge *betw. me* and thee.
    16:5; *1 Sam* 24:12, 15

I will make my covenant *betw. me*
   and thee. *Gen* 17:2, 7, 10, 11
is that *betw. me* and thee ? 23:15
witness *betw. me* and. 31:41, 48
Lord watch *betw. me* and thee. 49
God is witness *betw. me* and. 50
keep, for it is a sign *betw. me* and.
  Ex 31:13, 17; *Ezek* 20:12, 20
cast lots *betw. me.*   *1 Sam* 14:42
there is but a step *betw. me.* 20:3
saying, Lord be *betw. me* and. 42
there is a league *betw. me* and thee.
    1 Ki 15:19; *2 Chr* 16:3
judge, I pray you, *betw. me. Isa* 5:3
and the wall *betw. me.* *Ezek* 43:8

by me

Rachel died *by me* in.   *Gen* 48:7
there is a place *by me.* *Ex* 33:21
shalt not pass *by me.* *Num* 20:18
stand thou here *by me.* *Deut* 5:31
by me they honour God. *Judg* 9:9
as he spake *by me.*   *1 Sam* 28:17
the Lord spake *by me. 2 Sam* 23:2
Lord not spoken *by me. 1 Ki* 22:28
        2 Chr 18:27
the trumpet was *by me.* *Neh* 4:18
he goeth *by me,* and I. *Job* 9:11
by me kings reign.   *Pr* 8:15
by me princes rule.   16
by me thy days shall be.   9:11
which are borne *by me.* *Isa* 46:3
but not *by me.*   54:15
up kings, but not *by me. Hos* 8:4
thou mightest be profited *by me.*
     Mat 15:5; *Mark* 7:11
even he shall live *by me. John* 6:57
I am the door: *by me* if any. 10:9
to the Father but *by me.*   14:6
an angel stood *by me.* *Acts* 27:23
hath wrought *by me.* *Rom* 15:18
of God preached *by me. 2 Cor* 1:19
which is made sorry *by me.* 2:2
that *by me* preaching. *2 Tim* 4:17

concerneth, concerning me

to Moses *conc. me.*   *Josh* 14:6
word he spake *conc. me.* *1 Ki* 2:4
doth not prophesy good *conc. me.*
         22:8, 18
will perfect that which *conc. me.*
         Ps 138:8
a prophet to enquire *conc. me.*
         Ezek 14:7
for the things *conc. me. Luke* 22:37
written in Psalms *conc. me.* 24:44
thy testimony *conc. me. Acts* 22:18

for me

entreat *for me* to Ephron. *Gen* 23:8
         Ex 8:28
reserved a blessing *for me?*
         Gen 27:36
wilt do this thing *for me.* 30:31
my righteousness answer *for me.* 33
which I have digged *for me.* 50:5
and nurse it *for me.*   *Ex* 2:9
take the Levites *for me. Num* 3:41
it is too heavy *for me.*   11:14
for they are too mighty *for me.* 22:6
song may be a witness *for me.*
        Deut 31:19
as *for me* and my house. *Josh* 24:15
too many *for me* to give. *Judg* 7:2
this thing be done *for me.* 11:37
get her *for me* to wife. 14:2, 3
and wine also *for me.*   19:19
as *for me. 1 Sam* 12:23; *1 Chr* 22:7
   28:2; 29:17; *Job* 21:4; *Ps* 5:7
       17:15; 35:13
thou valiant *for me.* *1 Sam* 18:17
what God will do *for me.* 22:3
none of you that is sorry *for me.* 8
better *for me* than to escape. 27:1
the sons of Zeruiah be too hard *for*
   me.   *2 Sam* 3:39
shalt thou build an house *for me.* 7:5
if Syrians be too strong *for me.*
     10:11; *1 Chr* 19:12
good *for me* to have. *2 Sam* 14:32
mayest thou defeat. 15:34
they were too strong *for me.* 22:18
         Ps 18:17
pray *for me,* that my hand be.
         1 Ki 13:6
in and dress it *for me.*   17:12

not thy riding *for me*.   *2 Ki* 4:24
the brasen altar be *for me* to. 16:15
enquire of the Lord *for me*.   22:13
             2 Chr 34:21
was prepared *for me* daily. *Neh* 5:18
graves are ready *for me*.   *Job* 17:1
thing appointed *for me*.   23:14
waited *for me* as for the rain. 29:23
things too wonderful *for me*. 42:3
art a shield *for me*.   *Ps* 3:3
awake *for me*.   7:6
net they have laid privily *for me*.
  31:4; 35:7; 119:110; 140:5
        141:9; 142:3
as *for me*.   41:12; 55:16; 69:13
  Isa 59:21; *Jer* 17:16; 26:14
  40:10; *Ezek* 9:10; *Dan* 2:30
        7:28; 10:17
this I know, God is *for me*. *Ps* 56:9
performeth all things *for me*. 57:2
hast been a shelter *for me*. 61:3
it was too painful *for me*. 73:16
rise up *for me*, who will stand up for
  me ?   94:16
but do thou *for me*, O God. 109:21
it is good *for me*.   119:71
the proud digged pits *for me*. 85
wicked have waited *for me* to. 95
things too high *for me*.   131:1
is too wonderful *for me*. 139:6
food convenient *for me*. *Pr* 30:8
things too wonderful *for me*. 18
undertake *for me*.   *Isa* 38:14
set it in order *for me* ?   44:7
the place is too strait *for me*. 49:20
not be ashamed that wait *for me*. 23
the isles shall wait *for me*. 60:9
of them that asked not *for me*. 65:1
search *for me* with all. *Jer* 29:13
any thing too hard *for me* ? 32:27
they wrought *for me*. *Ezek* 29:20
thou shalt abide *for me*. *Hos* 3:3
better *for me* to die. *Jonah* 4:3, 8
execute judgement *for me*. *Mi* 7:9
bent Judah *for me*.   *Zech* 9:13
and give *for me* and. *Mat* 17:27
weep not *for me*, but. *Luke* 23:28
pray ye to the Lord *for me*. *Acts* 8:24
intent ye have sent *for me*. 10:29
prayers to God *for me*. *Rom* 15:30
are lawful *for me*. *1 Cor* 6:12; 10:23
it were better *for me* to die. 9:15
and gave himself *for me*. *Gal* 2:20
for me, that utterance. *Eph* 6:19
laid up *for me* a crown. *2 Tim* 4:8

from **me**

I pray thee, *from me*.   *Gen* 13:9
thine only son *from me*.   22:12
steal away *from me* ?   31:27
take thy daughters *from me*. 31
kept back any thing *from me*. 39:9
the one went out *from me*. 44:28
if ye take this also *from me*. 29
every man to go out *from me*. 45:1
get thee *from me*, see. *Ex* 10:28
tell me, hide it not *from me*.
    Josh 7:19; *1 Sam* 3:17
strength will go *from me*. *Judg* 16:17
why should my father hide this thing
  from me ?   *1 Sam* 20:2
said, Have out all men *from me*.
        2 Sam 13:9
put this woman out *from me*. 17
far be it *from me*.   20:20
this thing is *from me*. *1 Ki* 12:24
went Spirit of Lord *from me*. 22:24
        2 Chr 18:23
Lord hath hid it *from me*. *2 Ki* 4:27
offended, return *from me*. 18:14
I chased him *from me*. *Neh* 13:28
driven quite *from me* ? *Job* 6:13
his rod away *from me*.   9:34
thine hand far *from me*. 13:21
put my brethren far *from me*. 19:13
of the wicked is far *from me*. 21:16
mine integrity *from me*. 27:5
hide thy face *from me* ? *Ps* 13:1
away his statutes *from me*. 18:22
O Lord, be not far *from me*. 35:22
light of eyes, gone *from me*. 38:10
thy stroke away *from me*. 39:10
tender mercies *from me*. 40:11
take not Holy Spirit *from me*. 51:11

turned his mercy *from me*. *Ps* 66:20
hidest thou thy face *from me* ? 88:14
hide not thy face *from me* in trouble.
      102:2; 143:7
commandments *from me*. 119:19
away my vail *from me*. *S of S* 5:7
turn away thine eyes *from me*. 6:5
look away *from me*, I will. *Isa* 22:4
age is removed *from me*. 38:12
a law shall proceed *from me*. 51:4
anger shall turn *from me*. *Jer* 2:35
shalt not turn away *from me*. 3:19
of thy measures *from me*. 13:25
hide nothing *from me*. 38:14
from me shall spoilers come. 51:53
warning *from me*. *Ezek* 3:17; 33:7
are all estranged *from me*. 14:5
separateth himself *from me*. 7
go no more astray *from me*. 11
went astray *from me* after. 44:10
Israel went astray *from me*. 15
thing is gone *from me*. *Dan* 2:5, 8
Israel is not hid *from me*. *Hos* 5:3
for they have fled *from me*. 7:13
bent to backsliding *from me*. 11:7
like a fir tree, *from me* is thy. 14:8
take away *from me* the noise of.
        Amos 5:23
let this cup pass *from me*. *Mat* 26:39
    Mark 14:36; *Luke* 22:22
not pass away *from me*. *Mat* 26:42
my lord taketh *from me*. *Luke* 16:3
man taketh it *from me*. *John* 10:18
all in Asia be turned away *from me*.
        2 Tim 1:15

see depart, departed

in **me**

it is not *in me*.   *Gen* 41:16
if there be iniquity *in me*.
  1 Sam 20:8; *2 Sam* 14:32
life is yet whole *in me*. *2 Sam* 1:9
because he delighted *in me*. 22:20
        Ps 18:19
is not my help *in me* ? *Job* 6:13
the matter is found *in me*. 19:28
would put strength *in me*. 23:6
my breath is *in me*. 27:3
saith, It is not *in me*. 28:14
nor is there iniquity *in me*. 33:9
to mine integrity *in me*. *Ps* 7:8
arrows stick fast *in me*. 38:2
I pour out my soul *in me*. 42:4
why art thou disquieted *in me* ? 5
be any wicked way *in me*. 139:24
fury is not *in me*, who. *Isa* 27:4
trust *in me* shall possess. 57:13
have fathers found *in me* ? *Jer* 2:5
hast put thy trust *in me*. 39:18
thy widows trust *in me*. 49:11
soul is humbled *in me*. *Lam* 3:20
innocency found *in me*. *Dan* 6:22
no strength *in me*. 10:8, 17
find none iniquity *in me*. *Hos* 12:8
thyself, but *in me* is thy help. 13:17
shall not be offended *in me*.
      Mat 11:6; *Luke* 7:23
little ones which believe *in me*.
    Mat 18:6; *Mark* 9:42
be accomplished *in me*. *Luke* 22:37
he dwelleth *in me*, and I. *John* 6:56
he that believeth *in me*. 11:25, 26
believe also *in me*. 14:1
Father that dwelleth *in me*. 10
ye *in me*, and I in you. 20
prince hath nothing *in me*. 30
every branch *in me*. 15:2
abide *in me*. 4
he that abideth *in me*. 5
if a man abide not *in me* he is. 6
if ye abide *in me*. 7
in me ye might have peace. 16:33
as thou, Father, art *in me*. 17:21
I in them, and thou *in me*, that. 23
any evil doing *in me*. *Acts* 24:20
by faith that is *in me*. 26:18
no cause of death *in me*. 28:18
as *in me* is, I am ready. *Rom* 1:15
wrought *in me* all manner of. 7:8
sin working death *in me* by. 13
but sin that dwelleth *in me*. 17, 20
that *in me* dwelleth no good thing. 18
truth of Christ is *in me*. *2 Cor* 11:10
proof of Christ speaking *in me*. 13:3

to reveal his Son *in me*. *Gal* 1:16
and they glorified God *in me*. 24
was mighty *in me* towards. 2:8
but Christ liveth *in me*. 20
conflict which ye saw *in me*, and now
  hear to be *in me*. *Phil* 1:30
heard and seen *in me*, do. 4:9
which worketh *in me*. *Col* 1:29
that *in me* Christ Jesus. *1 Tim* 1:16

of **me**

of me, He is my brother. *Gen* 20:13
he will accept of *me*. 32:20
men say not *of me*, A woman slew.
        Judg 9:54
take knowledge *of me*. *Ruth* 2:10
Saul shall despair *of me*. *1 Sam* 27:1
then dost thou ask *of me* ? 28:16
this thing is done *of me*. *2 Chr* 11:4
not spoken *of me* the thing. *Job* 42:7
ask *of me*, and I shall give. *Ps* 2:8
in thy book it is written *of me*. 40:7
        Heb 10:7
enemies speak evil *of me*. *Ps* 41:5
triumph thou because *of me*. 60:8
and Israel would none *of me*. 81:11
not take counsel *of me*. *Isa* 30:1
thou make an end *of me*. 38:12, 13
weary *of me*, O Israel. 43:22
not be forgotten *of me*. 44:21
and their righteousness *of me*. 54:17
they ask *of me* the ordinances. 58:2
are gone forth *of me*. *Jer* 10:20
sent you to enquire *of me*. 37:7
come to enquire *of me* ? *Ezek* 20:3
say *of me*, Doth he not speak ? 49
more than me, is not worthy *of me*.
        Mat 10:37, 38
and learn *of me*, for I am. 11:29
ye shall be offended because *of me*
  this night. 26:31; *Mark* 14:27
whoso shall be ashamed *of me*.
    Mark 8:38; *Luke* 9:26
lightly speak evil *of me*. *Mark* 9:39
virtue is gone out *of me*. *Luke* 8:46
do in remembrance *of me*. 22:19
Jew, askest drink *of me* ? *John* 4:9
beareth witness *of me*. 5:32, 37
they which testify *of me*. 39
for Moses wrote *of me*. 46
this voice came not because *of me*.
        12:30
he shall testify *of me*. 15:26
did others tell it thee *of me* ? 18:34
promise ye have heard *of me*.
        Acts 1:4
as thou hast testified *of me*. 23:11
be ye followers *of me*. *1 Cor* 4:16
      11:1; *Phil* 3:17
this do in remembrance *of me*.
      1 Cor 11:24, 25
he was seen *of me* also. 15:8
the salutation *of me* Paul. 16:21
        Col 4:18
think *of me* above that which he . . .
  or heareth *of me*. *2 Cor* 12:6
which is preached *of me*. *Gal* 1:11
care *of me* hath flourished. *Phil* 4:10
the testimony *of me* his. *2 Tim* 1:8
which thou hast heard *of me*. 13
thou hast heard *of me*, commit. 2:2
had compassion *of me*. *Heb* 10:34

on **me**, or *upon* **me**

I have taken *upon me*. *Gen* 18:27, 31
thou hast brought on *me*. 20:9
I shall bring a curse *upon me*. 27:12
upon me be thy curse, my son. 13
custom of women is *upon me*. 31:35
think *on me* when it shall be. 40:14
ye will not fall *upon me*. *Judg* 15:12
all thy wants lie *upon me*. 19:20
come down *upon me*. *1 Sam* 13:12
upon me, my lord, *upon me*. 25:24
the iniquity be *on me*. *2 Sam* 14:9
set their faces *on me*. *1 Ki* 2:15
I pray thee, be *on me*. *1 Chr* 21:17
writing by his hand *upon me*. 28:19
hand of the Lord *upon me*.
    Ezra 7:28; *Neh* 2:8, 18
think *upon me*, my God. *Neh* 5:19
feared is come *upon me*. *Job* 3:25
fear came *upon me*. 4:14
be content, look *upon me*. 6:28

thine eyes are *upon me.* *Job* 7:8
thyself marvellous *upon me.* 10:16
runneth *upon me* like a giant. 16:14
have pity *upon me,* O ye. 19:21
have mercy *upon me.* *Ps* 4:1; 6:2
   9:13; 25:16; 27:7; 30:10; 31:9
   51:1; 86:16
look and stare *upon me.* 22:17
thy hand was heavy *upon me.* 32:4
the Lord thinketh *upon me.* 40:17
they cast iniquity *upon me.* 55:3
thy vows are *upon me.* 56:12
hath set his love *upon me.* 91:14
he shall call *upon me.* 15
look thou *upon me.* 119:132
laid thine hand *upon me.* 139:5
look not *upon me,* sun hath looked
   upon me. *S of S* 1:6
hast not called *upon me.* *Isa* 43:22
the isles shall wait *upon me.* 51:5
Spirit of the Lord God is *upon me.*
   61:1; *Luke* 4:18
these things *upon me?* *Jer* 13:22
cast a stone *upon me.* *Lam* 3:53
Lord was strong *upon me. Ezek* 3:14
the hand of the Lord was there *upon
   me.* 22; 33:22; 37:1; 40:1
hand fell there *upon me.* 8:1
Spirit of the Lord fell *upon me.* 11:5
therefore wait ye *upon me. Zeph* 3:8
then cried he *upon me.* *Zech* 6:8
flock that waited *upon me.* 11:11
they shall look *upon me* whom they
   pierced. 12:10
have mercy *upon me.* *Mat* 15:22
   Mark 10:47, 48; *Luke* 18:38, 39
wrought a good work *upon me.*
   Mat 26:10; *Mark* 14:6
days wherein he looked *on me.*
   Luke 1:25
that believeth *on me.* *John* 6:35
   47; 7:38; 12:44, 46; 14:12
they believe not *on me.* 16:9
who shall believe *on me.* 17:20
things come *upon me.* *Acts* 8:24
reproaches of them that reproached
   thee fell *on me.* *Rom* 15:3
necessity is laid *upon me. 1 Cor* 9:16
cometh *upon me* daily. *2 Cor* 11:28
of Christ may rest *upon me.* 12:9
God had mercy *on me.* *Phil* 2:27
right hand *upon me.* *Rev* 1:17

see call

over me

to Pharaoh, Glory *over me.* *Ex* 8:9
will set a king *over me.* *Deut* 17:14
settest a watch *over me.* *Job* 7:12
enemy be exalted *over me. Ps* 13:2
let them not have dominion *over me.*
   19:13; 119:133
enemies triumph *over me.* 25:2
doth not triumph *over me.* 41:11
billows are gone *over me.* 42:7
banner *over me* was love. *S of S* 2:4
waves passed *over me.* *Jonah* 2:3

to or unto me

blood crieth *unto me.* *Gen* 4:10
to me thou hast given no seed. 15:3
said he not *unto me?* 20:5
swear *unto me* by God. 21:23
spake the man *unto me.* 24:30
wherefore come ye *to me?* 26:27
Lord hath brought it *to me.* 27:20
thou hast done *unto me?* 29:25
hath given them *to me.* 31:9
unto me, Return to thy country. 32:9
what ye shall say *unto me.* 34:11, 12
shew kindness *unto me.* 40:14
brethren are come *unto me.* 46:31
the cry of the children of Israel
   come *unto me.* *Ex* 3:9
bloody husband art thou *to me.* 4:25
feast *unto me* in the wilderness. 5:1
take you *to me* for a people. 6:7
have not hearkened *unto me.* 12
sanctify *unto me* all firstborn. 13:2
criest thou *unto me?* 14:15
matter, they come *unto me.* 18:16
peculiar treasure *unto me.* 19:5
ye shall be *unto me* a kingdom. 6
they cry at all *unto me.* 22:23, 27
sons shalt thou give *unto me.* 29

shall be holy men *unto me.* *Ex* 22:31
that he may minister *unto me.* 28:1
   3; 29:1; 30:30; 40:13; *Jer* 33:22
   Ezek 43:19
let him come *unto me.* *Ex* 32:26
thou sayest *unto me.* 33:12
present thyself there *to me.* 34:2
for *unto me* Israel are. *Lev* 25:55
raise up a prophet like *unto me*
   Deut 18:15; *Acts* 3:22; 7:37
to me belongeth vengeance and
   recompence. *Deut* 32:35
are ye come *unto me?* *Judg* 11:7
as they did *unto me,* so have. 15:11
and be *unto me* a father. 17:10
Lord do so *to me,* and. *Ruth* 1:17
   2 Sam 3:35; 19:13; *1 Ki* 2:23
cry is come *unto me.* *1 Sam* 9:16
anoint *unto me* him whom. 16:3
and *to me* they ascribed but. 18:8
very pleasant hast thou been *unto
   me.* *2 Sam* 1:26
he shall not return *to me.* 12:23
man might come *unto me.* 15:4
what Joab did *to me.* *1 Ki* 2:5
so let the gods do *to me* and more.
   19:2; 20:10
Lord saith *unto me* that will. 22:14
send *unto me* to recover a man of his
   leprosy. *2 Ki* 5:7
let him come now *to me.* 8
God do so *to me.* 6:31
thus and thus spake he *to me.* 9:12
and come *to me* to Jezreel. 10:6
tell the man that sent you *to me.*
   22:15; *2 Chr* 34:23
ark of God home *to me?* *1 Chr* 13:12
prophesy good *unto me.* *2 Chr* 18:17
extended mercy *unto me.* *Ezra* 7:28
then were assembled *unto me.* 9:4
but if ye turn *unto me.* *Neh* 1:9
afraid of is come *unto me.* *Job* 3:25
nights are appointed *to me.* 7:3
do not two things *unto me.* 13:20
unto me men gave ear. 29:21
declare *unto me.* 40:7; 42:4
lines are fallen *unto me.* *Ps* 16:6
incline thine ear *unto me.*
   17:6; 31:2; 102:2
turn thee *unto me.* 25:16
merciful *unto me.* 26:11; 41:4, 10
   56:1; 57:1; 86:3; 119:58, 132
be not silent *to me.* 28:1
he inclined *unto me.* 40:1; 77:1
what flesh can do *unto me.* 56:4
what man can do *unto me.* 11; 118:6
wilt hearken *unto me.* 81:8
he shall cry *unto me,* Thou. 89:26
wilt thou come *unto me?* 101:2
when they said *unto me,* Let. 122:1
are thy thoughts *unto me!* 139:17
thee, make haste *unto me.* 141:1
whoso hearkeneth *unto me* shall
   dwell safely. *Pr* 1:33
will do so to him as he hath done *to
   me.* 24:29
as to the fool, so it happeneth even *to
   me.* *Eccl* 2:15
bundle of myrrh is my beloved *unto
   me.* *S of S* 1:13, 14
abomination *unto me.* *Isa* 1:13
they are a trouble *unto me.* 14
he calleth to me out of Seir. 21:11
shall be *unto me* as Ariel. 29:2
unto me, for I have redeemed. 44:22
look *unto me,* and be saved. 45:22
unto me every knee shall bow. 23
let him come near *to me.* 50:8
as the waters of Noah *to me.* 54:9
come not near *to me,* I am. 65:5
return, O Israel, *unto me.* *Jer* 4:1
though they shall cry *unto me.* 11:11
mine heritage is *unto me.* 12:8, 9
that they might be *unto me.* 13:11
thy word was *unto me* the joy. 15:16
be altogether *unto me* as a liar? 18
them *unto me* as Sodom. 23:14
this city hath been *to me* a. 32:31
shall be *to me* a name of joy. 33:9
who shall come *unto me?* 49:4
the violence done *to me* be. 51:35
shall be like *unto me.* *Lam* 1:21
as thou hast done *unto me.* 22
thou hast borne *unto me. Ezek* 16:20

house of Israel is *to me.* *Ezek* 22:18
they have done *unto me.* 23:38
she is turned *unto me.* 26:2
office of a priest *unto me.* 44:13
to me to minister *unto me.* 15
is not revealed *to me.* *Dan* 2:30
my reason returned *unto me;* lords
   sought *unto me.* 4:36
betroth thee *unto me.* *Hos* 2:19, 20
and I will sow her *unto me* in. 23
I bought her *to me* for fifteen 3:2
thou shalt be no priest *to me.* 4:6
them that calleth *unto me.* 7:7
they have not cried *unto me* with. 14
Israel shall cry *unto me.* 8:2
as Ethiopians *unto me?* *Amos* 9:7
shall come forth *unto me.* *Mi* 5:2
shall be a light *unto me.* 7:8
see what he will say *unto me.*
   Hab 2:1
yet ye turned not *to me.* *Hag* 2:17
turn ye *unto me,* saith. *Zech* 1:3
at all fast *unto me,* even *to me?* 7:5
and comest thou *to me?* *Mat* 3:14
to me in that day, Lord. 7:22
come *unto me* all ye that. 11:28
bring them *to me.* 14:18; 17:17
   21:2; *Mark* 9:19
forbid them not to come *unto me.*
   Mat 19:14; *Mark* 10:14
and ye came *unto me.* *Mat* 25:36
ye have done it *unto me.* 40
not to these, ye did it not *to me.* 45
all power is given *unto me.* 28:18
it be *unto me* according. *Luke* 1:38
for that is delivered *unto me.* 4:6
whoso cometh *to me.* 6:47; 14:26
all things are delivered *unto me.* 10:22
God be merciful *to me* a. 18:13
come *to me* to have life. *John* 5:40
he that cometh *to me.* 6:35, 37
no man can come *to me.* 44, 65
of the Father cometh *unto me.* 45
let him come *to me* and. 7:37
I will draw all men *unto me.* 12:32
the Father said *unto me.* 50
speakest thou not *unto me?* 19:10
be witnesses *unto me.* *Acts* 1:8
known *unto me* the ways of life. 2:28
he is a chosen vessel *unto me.* 9:15
vessel descend, and it came even *to
   me.* 11:5
a voice speaking *unto me.* 26:14
made death *unto me?* *Rom* 7:13
the grace given *unto me.* 12:23
   1 Cor 3:10
things are lawful *unto me. 1 Cor* 6:12
should be so done *unto me.* 9:15
woe is *unto me* if I preach not. 16
gospel is committed *unto me.* 14:11
be a barbarian *unto me.* 11
a great door and effectual is open
   unto me. 16:9; *2 Cor* 2:12
was lacking *to me.* *2 Cor* 11:9
maketh no matter *to me.* *Gal* 2:6
and have given them *to me.* 4:15
unto me who am less. *Eph* 3:8
for *to me* to live is Christ. *Phil* 1:21
to me indeed is not grievous. 3:1
but what things were gain *to me.* 7
been a comfort *unto me.* *Col* 4:11
not *to me* only. *2 Tim* 4:8
is profitable *to me.* 11
now profitable to thee and *to me.*
   Philem 11
especially *to me.* 16
thou owest *to me* thyself. 19
belongeth *unto me,* saith. *Heb* 10:30
what man shall do *unto me.* 13:6

toward me

countenance is not *toward me* as.
   Gen 31:5
thy mercy *toward me.* *Ps* 86:13
all his benefits *toward me.* 116:12
I am my Beloved's, his desire is
   toward me. *S of S* 7:10
fear *toward me* is taught. *Isa* 29:13
bowels and mercies *toward me.*
   63:15
high God hath wrought *toward me.*
   Dan 4:2
fervent mind *toward me.* *2 Cor* 7:7
of service *toward me.* *Phil* 2:30

under **me**
enlarged my steps *under me.*
     2 Sam 22:37; *Ps* 18:36
thou hast subdued *under me.*
     2 Sam 22:40; *Ps* 18:39
bringeth down the people *under me.*
     2 Sam 22:48; *Ps* 18:47
was *under me* to pass.   *Neh* 2:14
my people *under me.*   *Ps* 144:2
having soldiers *under me. Mat* 8:9
          Luke 7:8

with **me**
it may be well *with me. Gen* 12:13
if God will be *with me* and keep.
     28:20; *Josh* 14:12
thy cattle was *with me. Gen* 30:29
God hath been *with me.*   31:5
discern thou what is thine *with me.*
                    32
and she said, Lie *with me.*   39:7
     12, 14; *2 Sam* 13:11
send lad *with me.*   *Gen* 43:8
lad be not *with me.*   44:34
why chide ye *with me? Ex* 17:2
not make *with me* gods of.   20:23
thy presence go not *with me.* 33:15
deal thus *with me,* kill. *Num* 11:15
laid up in store *with me? Deut* 32:34
and there is no God *with me.*   39
the people that are *with me. Josh* 8:5
if thou wilt go *with me. Judg* 4:8
I and all that are *with me.*   7:18
hast thou to do *with me?*   11:12
when thy heart is not *with me.* 16:15
behold, the silver is *with me.* 17:2
dwell *with me.*   10
as ye have dealt *with me. Ruth* 1:8
why will ye go *with me?*   11
eat *with me* to-day. *1 Sam* 9:19
if he be able to fight *with me.* 17:9
but *with me* thou shalt be in safeguard.   22:23
hast dealt well *with me.*   24:18
and thy sons be *with me.*   28:19
wentest not *with me? 2 Sam* 19:25
feed thee *with me* in Jerusalem. 33
made *with me* an everlasting. 23:5
hand might be *with me. 1 Chr* 4:10
even so deal *with me. 2 Chr* 2:3
are *with me* in Judah.   7
God, who is *with me.*   35:21
but it is not so *with me. Job* 9:35
sea saith, It is not *with me.* 28:14
Almighty was yet *with me.*   29:5
that was at peace *with me. Ps* 7:4
thou art *with me.*   23:4
his song shall be *with me.*   42:8
made a covenant *with me.*   50:5
there were many *with me.* 55:18
they may dwell *with me.* 101:6
for they are ever *with me.* 119:98
honour are *with me,* yea. *Pr* 8:18
come *with me* from Lebanon.
                  S of S 4:8
shall make peace *with me. Isa* 27:5
who will contend *with me?* 50:8
there was none *with me.*   63:3
the Lord is *with me.* *Jer* 20:11
do *with me* as seemeth good. 26:14
none holdeth *with me. Dan* 10:21
then it was better *with me. Hos* 2:7
have ye to do with me ? *Joel* 3:4
walked *with me* in peace. *Mal* 2:6
he that is not *with me* is against me,
   he that gathereth not *with me.*
      Mat 12:30; *Luke* 11:23
Lord, have patience *with me,* and I
   will pay thee all. *Mat* 18:26, 29
not thou agree *with me* for ? 20:13
and watch *with me.*   26:38, 40
my children are *with me* in bed.
                  Luke 11:7
saying, Rejoice *with me.* 15:6, 9
                Phil 2:18
thou art ever *with me. Luke* 15:31
hand ... is *with me* on the table. 22:21
have continued *with me.*   22:28
thou be *with me* in paradise. 23:43
that sent me is *with me. John* 8:29
thou hast no part *with me.* 13:8
he that eateth bread *with me.* 18
have been *with me* from the. 15:27
because the Father is *with me.* 16:32
that they also be *with me.* 17:24

that were *with me.* *Acts* 20:34
with me saw the light.   22:9, 11
evil is present *with me.* *Rom* 7:21
strive *with me* in your.   15:30
but *with me* it is a very. *1 Cor* 4:3
of God that was *with me.*   15:10
I go, they shall go *with me.*   16:4
that *with me* there should be yea.
                 2 Cor 1:17
served *with me* in the. *Phil* 2:22
see how it will go *with me.*   23
women, who laboured *with me.* 4:3
no church communicated *with me.* 15
only Luke is *with me. 2 Tim* 4:11
none stood *with me.*   16
the Lord stood *with me* and.   17
have retained *with me. Philem* 13
walk *with me* in white. *Rev* 3:4
sup with him, and he *with me.* 20
to sit *with me* in my throne.   21
and my reward is *with me.* 22:12

within **me**
arrows of the Almighty are *within
   me.*   *Job* 6:4
reins be consumed *within me.* 19:27
spirit *within me* constraineth. 32:18
heart was hot *within me.* *Ps* 39:3
soul is cast down *within me.* 42:6
why disquieted *within me ?* 11; 43:5
a right spirit *within me.*   51:10
of my thoughts *within me.* 94:19
all that is *within me* bless. 103:1
my spirit was overwhelmed *within
   me.*   142:3; 143:4
with my spirit *within me. Isa* 26:9
my heart *within me* is broken.
                 Jer 23:9
my heart is turned *within me.*
      Lam 1:20; *Hos* 11:8
soul fainted *within me.* *Jonah* 2:7

without **me**
without me they shall. *Isa* 10:4
for *without me* ye can. *John* 15:5

meadow
and they fed in a *m.* *Gen* 41:2*

meadows
came even out of the *m. Judg* 20:33*

meal
an ephah of barley *m.* *Num* 5:15
bring *m.* and cast it into. *2 Ki* 4:41
were nigh brought *m.* *1 Chr* 12:40
millstones and grind *m.* *Isa* 47:2
the bud shall yield no *m.* *Hos* 8:7

see **barrel, measures**

mealtime
at *m.* come thou hither. *Ruth* 2:14

mean, *verb*
what *m.* these seven ? *Gen* 21:9
what *m.* ye by this ? *Ex* 12:26
thy son asketh what *m.? Deut* 6:20
ask, what *m.* ye by ? *Josh* 4:6, 21
what *m.* ye that ye beat ? *Isa* 3:15
what these things *m.? Ezek* 17:12
what *m.* ye, that ye use this proverb ?
                    18:2
from the dead should *m. Mark* 9:10
this vision should *m.* *Acts* 10:17
know what these things *m.* 17:20
what *m.* ye to weep and ? 21:13*
I *m.* not that other men. *2 Cor* 8:13

mean, *adjective*
stand before *m.* men. *Pr* 22:29
m. man boweth down. *Isa* 2:9
m. man shall be brought down. 5:13
sword not of a *m.* man shall. 31:8*
a citizen of no *m.* city. *Acts* 21:39

meanest
what *m.* thou by all this drove I met ?
                 Gen 33:8
what *m.* thou by these ? *2 Sam* 16:2
                Ezek 37:18
what *m.* thou, O sleeper ? *Jonah* 1:6

meaneth
what *m.* the heat of ? *Deut* 29:24
what *m.* the noise ? *1 Sam* 4:6, 14
what *m.* then this bleating ? 15:14
howbeit he *m.* not so. *Isa* 10:7
and learn what that *m.* *Mat* 9:13
had known what this *m.*   12:7
to another, What *m.* this ? *Acts* 2:12

meaning
had sought for the *m.* *Dan* 8:15*
not the *m.* of the voice. *1 Cor* 14:11

meaning
we launched, *m.* to sail. *Acts* 27:2*

means
that will by no *m.* clear the guilty.
      Ex 34:7; *Num* 14:18
broken by the *m.* of the. *Judg* 5:22*
by what *m.* we may prevail. 16:5
but doth he devise *m. 2 Sam* 14:14
by any *m.* he be missing. *1 Ki* 20:39
by this *m.* thou shalt have no portion.   *Ezra* 4:16
by any *m.* redeem his. *Ps* 49:7
for by *m.* of a whorish. *Pr* 6:26*
bear rule by their *m.* *Jer* 5:31
this hath been by your *m.* *Mal* 1:9
by no *m.* come out thence. *Mat* 5:26
they sought *m.* to bring. *Luke* 5:18
nothing shall by any *m.* hurt. 10:19*
by what *m.* he now seeth. *John* 9:21
we be examined, by what *m. Acts* 4:9
must by all *m.* keep this feast. 18:21
if by any *m.* they might attain. 27:12
by any *m.* I might have a. *Rom* 1:10
by any *m.* I may provoke. 11:14
take heed, lest by any *m. 1 Cor* 8:9
that I might by all *m.* save. 9:22
lest by any *m.* when I have.   27
by *m.* of many, thanks. *2 Cor* 1:11
lest by any *m.* as the serpent. 11:3
lest by any *m.* I should run in vain.
                 Gal 2:2
if by any *m.* I attain to. *Phil* 3:11
some *m.* the tempter. *1 Thes* 3:5
deceive you by any *m. 2 Thes* 2:3*
peace always by all *m.*   3:16*
that by *m.* of death. *Heb* 9:15*
deceiveth them by *m.* *Rev* 13:14*

meant
but God *m.* it unto good. *Gen* 50:20
what these things *m.* *Luke* 15:26
pass by, he asked what it *m.* 18:36

mean time
in the *m. time* when there were
   gathered.   *Luke* 12:1

mean while
m. while the heaven. *1 Ki* 18:45*
in *m. while* his disciples. *John* 4:31
their thoughts *m. while* accusing.
                 Rom 2:15*

measure
curtains shall have one *m. Ex* 26:2, 8
no unrighteousness in *m. Lev* 19:35
and a just *m.* shalt. *Deut* 25:15
cubits one *m.*   *1 Ki* 6:25
bases had one *m.*   7:37
a *m.* of fine flour. *2 Ki* 7:1, 16, 18
the *m.* thereof is longer. *Job* 11:9
weigheth the waters by *m.* 28:25
make me to know the *m.* *Ps* 39:4
tears to drink in great *m.* 80:5
her mouth without *m.* *Isa* 5:14
in *m.* when it shooteth forth. 27:8
dust of earth in a *m.*   40:12
correct thee in *m. Jer* 30:11; 46:28
the end is come. and *m.* of. 51:13
drink water by *m.* *Ezek* 4:11, 16
and scant *m.* that is. *Mi* 6:10
m. ye mete, it shall be measured.
   Mat 7:2; *Mark* 4:24; *Luke* 6:38
fill ye up the *m.* of your. *Mat* 23:32
were amazed beyond *m. Mark* 6:51
beyond *m.* astonished. 7:37; 10:26
good *m.* pressed down. *Luke* 6:38
giveth not the Spirit by *m. John* 3:34
dealt to every man the *m. Rom* 12:3
were pressed out of *m.* *2 Cor* 1:8
not boast of things without our *m.* but
   to *m.* of the rule. 10:13, 14, 15
stripes above *m.,* in prisons. 11:23
should be exalted above *m.* 12:7*
beyond *m.* I persecuted. *Gal* 1:13
according to the *m.* of the. *Eph* 4:7
m. of the stature of the fulness. 13
the effectual working in the *m.* 16
a voice saying, A *m.* of. *Rev* 6:6
to the *m.* of a man, that is. 21:17

measure, *verb*
shall *m.* from without. *Num* 35:5
shall *m.* to their cities. *Deut* 21:2

I will *m*. their former.   *Isa* 65:7
them *m*. the pattern.   *Ezek* 43:10
a measuring line to *m*.   *Zech* 2:2
m. the temple of God.   *Rev* 11:1
court leave out and *m*. not.   2
golden reed to *m*. the city.   21:15

measured

m. six measures of barley. *Ruth* 3:15
m. with a line, with two lines *m*. he.
     2 *Sam* 8:2
m. waters in hollow ?   *Isa* 40:12
heaven above can be *m*.   *Jer* 31:37
sand of the sea cannot be *m*.   33:22
he *m*. the breadth of.   *Ezek* 40:5
m. the threshold.   6
he *m*. also the porch.   8, 9
he *m*. the entry.   11
m. the gate.   13, 24
m. the wall.   41:5
he *m*. the house.   13
he *m*. the length of the building.   15
he *m*. the east side with.   42:16
he *m*. north side.   17, 18, 19
he *m*. a thousand cubits.   47:3, 4
be as sand of sea which cannot be *m*.
     Hos 1:10
he stood and *m*. the earth. *Hab* 3:6
measure ye mete, it shall be *m*. to.
     Mat 7:2; *Mark* 4:24; *Luke* 6:38
he *m*. the city.   *Rev* 21:16
he *m*. the wall.   17

measures

three *m*. of fine meal.   *Gen* 18:6
not have divers *m*.   *Deut* 25:14
Abigail took five *m*. of. *1 Sam* 25:18
provision for one day was thirty *m*.
of flour, and sixty *m*. of. *1 Ki* 4:22
20 thousand *m*. of wheat, and twenty
m. of pure oil.   5:11; *2 Chr* 2:10
m. of hewed stones. *1 Ki* 7:9, 11*
contain two *m*. of seed.   18:32
for all manner of *m*. *1 Chr* 23:29
done to an hundred *m*.   *Ezra* 7:22
who hath laid the *m*.?   *Job* 38:5
divers *m*. are like.   *Pr* 20:10
is the portion of thy *m*. *Jer* 13:25
the arches according to these *m*.
     Ezek 40:24, 29
gate according to these *m*.   28, 32
are the *m*. of the altar.   43:13
the *m*. of the profane place.   48:16
to an heap of twenty *m*.   *Hag* 2:16
leaven, which a woman hid in three
m. of meal. *Mat* 13:33; *Luke* 13:21
an hundred *m*. of oil.   *Luke* 16:6
he said, An hundred *m*. of wheat. 7
see barley

measuring

the *m*. line shall yet go. *Jer* 31:39
man with a *m*. reed.   *Ezek* 40:3, 5
he had made an end of *m*.   42:15
he measured with *m*. reed.   16, 17
     18, 19
a man with a *m*. line in.   *Zech* 2:1
they *m*. themselves.   *2 Cor* 10:12

meat

[1] *Food of any sort, especially
any solid food. The Revisions
generally change the word to food.*
[2] *Flesh, as distinct from fish,
fowl, or vegetables and grains.*

to you it shall be for *m*.   *Gen* 1:29
I have given every herb for *m*.   30
every moving thing shall be *m*.   9:3
savoury *m*. such as I love.   27:4, 7
Esau also made savoury *m*.   31
bread and *m*. for his father.   45:23
of all *m*. which may be. *Lev* 11:34
his house, shall eat of his *m*. 22:11*
she shall eat of her father's *m*.   13*
sabbath of land shall be *m*. 25:6, 7
buy *m*. of them for money. *Deut* 2:6
thou shalt sell me *m*. for money.   28
destroy trees not for *m*.   20:20
kings gathered their *m*.   *Judg* 1:7
out of the eater came forth *m*. 14:14
sit with the king at *m*. *1 Sam* 20:5
Jonathan did eat no *m*. the.   34
cause David to eat *m*. *2 Sam* 3:35
there followed him a mess of *m*. 11:8
eat of his own *m*. and drank. 12:3*
let Tamar dress the *m*. in.   13:5*

she saw the *m*. of his table.
     1 Ki 10:5; *2 Chr* 9:4
strength of that *m*. forty. *1 Ki* 19:8
were nigh brought *m*.   *1 Chr* 12:40
they gave *m*. and drink.   *Ezra* 3:7
are as my sorrowful *m*.   *Job* 6:7
the mouth taste his *m*.?   12:11
m. in his bowels is turned.   20:14
shall none of his *m*. be left.   21*
juniper roots for their *m*.   30:4
soul abhorreth dainty *m*.   33:20
words, as the mouth tasteth *m*. 34:3
he giveth *m*. in abundance.   36:31
they wander for lack of *m*.   38:41
my tears have been my *m*. *Ps* 42:3
given us like sheep for *m*.   44:11
wander up and down for *m*.   59:15
gave me also gall for my *m*. 69:21
thou gavest him to be *m*.   74:14
tempted God by asking *m*.   78:18
he sent them *m*. to the full.   25
but while their *m*. was yet in.   30
the young lions seek their *m*. 104:21
thou mayest give them their *m*. 27
abhorreth all manner of *m*. 107:18
he hath given *m*. to them.   111:5
them *m*. in due season.   145:15
ant provideth her *m*. in.   *Pr* 6:8
for they are deceitful *m*.   23:3
when he is filled with *m*.   30:22
yet they prepare their *m*. in the. 25
giveth *m*. to her household. 31:15
no more give thy corn to be *m*. for
thine enemies.   *Isa* 62:8
dust shall be the serpent's *m*. 65:25
pleasant things for *m*.   *Lam* 1:11
while they sought their *m*.   19
children, they were their.   4:10
m. shall be by weight.   *Ezek* 4:10
my *m*. which I gave thee.   16:19
I have given thee for *m*. to beasts.
     29:5; 34:5, 8
that they may not be *m*.   34:10
grow trees for *m*., fruit for *m*. 47:12
would not defile himself with the
king's *m*.   *Dan* 1:8†
king who hath appointed your *m*. 10
and in it was *m*. for all.   4:12, 21
part of his *m*., shall destroy. 26†
and I laid *m*. unto them. *Hos* 11:4
not *m*. cut off before ?   *Joel* 1:16
portion fat, *m*. plenteous. *Hab* 1:16
fields shall yield no *m*.   3:17
if one do touch any *m*.?   *Hag* 2:12
in that ye say, His *m*.   *Mal* 1:12
tithes, that there may be *m*.   3:10
and his *m*. was locusts.   *Mat* 3:4
life more than *m*.?   6:25; *Luke* 12:23
as Jesus sat at *m*. in. *Mat* 9:10; 26:7
     Mark 2:15; 14:3; 16:14
     Luke 24:30
workman is worthy of his *m*.
     Mat 10:10
which sat with him at *m*.   14:9
took up of the broken *m*.   15:37*
     Mark 8:8*
to give them *m*. in due season.
     Mat 24:45; *Luke* 12:42
I was an hungered, and ye gave me
m.   *Mat* 25:35
hungered, and ye gave me no *m*. 42
that hath *m*., let him do. *Luke* 3:11
commanded to give her *m*.   8:55
except we should go and buy *m*. 9:13
presence of them that sit at *m*. 14:10
servant, Go and sit down to *m*. 17:7
greater, he that sitteth at *m*.? 22:27
he said, Have ye here any *m*.?
     24:41; *John* 21:5
were gone to buy *m*.   *John* 4:8
m. to eat that ye know not of.   32
my *m*. is to do the will of him.   34
labour not for the *m*. which perisheth,
but for that *m*. which.   6:27
my flesh is *m*. indeed, my.   55
they did eat their *m*. with. *Acts* 2:46
when he had received *m*. he.   9:19
jailor set *m*. before them.   16:34
them all to take *m*.   27:33, 34
they also took some *m*.   36
be grieved with thy *m*., destroy not
him with thy *m*. for.   *Rom* 14:15
for the kingdom of God is not *m*. 17*
for *m*. destroy not the work of.   20

milk, and not with *m*.   *1 Cor* 3:2
m. commendeth us not to God. 8:8
if any man see thee sit at *m*. in.   10
if *m*. make my brother to offend. 13
did eat the same spiritual *m*. 10:3
let no man judge you in *m*. *Col* 2:16
of milk, not of strong *m*. *Heb* 5:12*
but strong *m*. belongeth to them. 14*
who for one morsel of *m*. sold. 12:16
see fowls

meat offering

(*This offering did not contain
flesh, but was usually a preparation
of flour with spices and other in-
gredients. The Revisions usually
change the word to meal offering*)

according to *m*. off. of.   *Ex* 29:41
offer no *m*. off. thereon.   30:9
Moses offered the *m*. off.   40:29
offer a *m*. off. *Lev* 2:1, 4, 5, 7, 14
remnant of *m*. off.   3, 10; 5:13
law of the *m*. off.   6:14; 7:37
deals of flour for a *m*. off.   14:10
pertaineth daily *m*. off.   *Num* 4:16
fine flour mingled with oil for *m*. off.
     7:13, 19; 28:12, 13
m. off. two tenths.   15:6; 28:9, 12
the *m*. off. of the morning.   28:8
when ye bring a new *m*. off.   26
besides his *m*. off. and burnt offering.
     29:6, 22, 25, 34
to offer thereon *m*. off. *Josh* 22:23
took a kid with a *m*. off. *Judg* 13:19
not have received a *m*. off.   23
m. off. was offered.   *2 Sam* 3:20*
wheat for the *m*. off.   *1 Chr* 21:23
for continual *m*. off.   *Neh* 10:33
thou offered a *m*. off.   *Isa* 57:6
they lay the *m*. off.   *Ezek* 42:13
they shall eat the *m*. off.   44:29
prepare the *m*. off.   45:17, 24
do like according to the *m*. off.   25
m. off. shall be an ephah for a ram.
     46:5
a *m*. off. and an ephah for a bullock.
     7, 11
they prepare the *m*. off. and.   15
m. off. and the drink offering is cut
off.   *Joel* 1:9
the *m*. off. and drink offering is withholden.   13
leave a blessing, even a *m*. off. 2:14

meat offerings

do for your *m*. off.   *Num* 29:39
build an altar for the *m*. off. *Josh* 22:29
because altar was too little to receive
m. off.   *1 Ki* 8:64; *2 Chr* 7:7
lambs with their *m*. off. *Ezra* 7:17
they laid their *m*. off.   *Neh* 13:5
Judah to bring *m*. off.   *Jer* 17:26
want a man to kindle *m*. off. 33:18
princes to give *m*. off. *Ezek* 45:17
though ye offer *m*. off. *Amos* 5:22

meats

desire thou his dainty *m*. *Pr* 23:6*
draught, purging all *m*. *Mark* 7:19
m. offered to idols.   *Acts* 15:29*
m. for the belly, and the belly for a.
     1 Cor 6:13
to abstain from *m*., which. *1 Tim* 4:3
which stood only in *m*.   *Heb* 9:10
established with grace, not *m*. 13:9

Medad

told Moses, Eldad and *M*. prophesy
in camp.   *Num* 11:26, 27

meddle

m. not with them of mount Seir.
     Deut 2:5*
m. not with the children of.   19*
why *m*. to thy hurt ?   *2 Ki* 14:10
     2 Chr 25:19
m. not with him that.   *Pr* 20:19
m. not with them that are.   24:21

meddled

contention before it be *m*. *Pr* 17:14*

meddleth

that *m*. with strife not. *Pr* 26:17*

meddling

forbear thee from *m*.   *2 Chr* 35:21
but every fool will be *m*.   *Pr* 20:3*

Mede, -s

cities of the *M.*   *2 Ki* 17:6; 18:11
the province of the *M.*   *Ezra* 6:2
among the laws of the *M. Esth* 1:19
I will stir up *M.* against them.
     Isa 13:17; *Jer* 51:11
all the kings of the *M.*   *Jer* 25:25
kingdom is given to the *M. Dan* 5:28
the law of the *M.*   6:8, 12, 15
Ahasuerus of the seed of the *M.* 9:1
year of Darius the *M.*   11:1

Media

power of Persia and *M.*   *Esth* 1:3
seven princes of Persia and *M.*   14
the ladies of *M.* shall say this.   18
book of the kings of *M.*   10:2
O *M.* all the sighing.   *Isa* 21:2
two horns are kings of *M. Dan* 8:20

mediator

(*This word, when applied to Moses,
has the meaning of intermediary.
When applied to Christ it has
somewhat of that meaning, with
probably a little of the meaning of
intercessor*)
angels in the hand of a *m. Gal* 3:19
a *m.* is not a *m.* of one, but.   20
one *m.* between God.   *1 Tim* 2:5
he is the *m.* of a better.   *Heb* 8:6
for this cause he is *m.* of.   9:15
and to Jesus the *m.* of the.   12:24

medicine

heart doeth good like a *m. Pr* 17:22
thereof shall be for *m. Ezek* 47:12*

medicines

thou hast no healing *m.*   *Jer* 30:13
in vain shalt thou use many *m.* 46:11

meditate

Isaac went out to *m.*   *Gen* 24:63
shalt *m.* therein day.   *Josh* 1:8
in his law doth he *m.* day.   *Ps* 1:2
and *m.* on thee in the night.   63:6
I will *m.* also of all thy work. 77:12
will *m.* in thy precepts. 119:15, 78
did *m.* in thy statutes.   23
I will *m.* in thy statutes.   48
night watches, that I might *m.*   148
I *m.* on all thy works, I muse. 143:5
heart shall *m.* terror.   *Isa* 33:18*
not to *m.* before what ye shall
answer.   *Luke* 21:14
m. upon these things.   *1 Tim* 4:15

meditation

my words, consider my *m.*   *Ps* 5:1
let the *m.* of my heart be.   19:14
the *m.* of my heart shall be.   49:3
my *m.* of him shall be sweet. 104:34
I love thy law, it is my *m.*   119:97
for thy testimonies are my *m.*   99

meek

(*Gentle, kind, not easily provoked,
ready to yield rather than cause
trouble; but not used in the Bible
in the bad sense of tamely submissive and servile*)
man Moses was very *m. Num* 12:3
the *m.* shall eat and.   *Ps* 22:26
m. will he guide in judgement. 25:9
m. shall inherit the earth.   37:11
God arose to save all the *m.* 76:9
the Lord lifteth up the *m.*   147:6
he will beautify the *m.* with. 149:4
equity, for the *m.* of.   *Isa* 11:4
the *m.* shall increase their.   29:19
preach good tidings to the *m.* 61:1
aside the way of the *m. Amos* 2:7
seek ye the Lord, all ye *m. Zeph* 2:3
blessed are the *m.*   *Mat* 5:5
for I am *m.* and lowly.   11:29
thy king cometh to thee, *m.*   21:5
the ornament of a *m.*   *1 Pet* 3:4

meekness

because of truth and.   *Ps* 45:4
seek *m.* shall be hid.   *Zeph* 2:3
come in the spirit of *m.*? *1 Cor* 4:21†
by the *m.* of Christ.   *2 Cor* 10:1
fruit of the Spirit is *m.*   *Gal* 5:23
restore in the spirit of *m.*   6:1
with all lowliness and *m. Eph* 4:2
put on therefore *m.*, longsuffering.
     Col 3:12

---

faith, love, patience, *m. 1 Tim* 6:11
in *m.* instructing those. *2 Tim* 2:25
gentle, shewing all *m.*   *Tit* 3:2
receive with *m.* the ingrafted word.
     Jas 1:21
him shew his works with *m.*   3:13
of your hope with *m.*   *1 Pet* 3:15

meet

(*As an adjective, fit, suitable*)
I will make an help *m. Gen* 2:18
found an help *m.* for Adam.   20
Moses said, It is not *m.*   *Ex* 8:26
pass over, all that are *m.* for war.
     Deut 3:18*
m. for the necks of them. *Judg* 5:30
it was not *m.* to see the king's dishonour.   *Ezra* 4:14
surely it is *m.* to be said. *Job* 34:31*
more than is *m.*   *Pr* 11:24
do with me as seemeth *m.* to you.
     Jer 26:14*
to whom it seemed *m.* to me. 27:5*
is it *m.* for any work? *Ezek* 15:4*
it was *m.* for no work.   5
fruits *m.* for repentance. *Mat* 3:8*
it is not *m.* to take the children's
bread.   15:26; *Mark* 7:27
it was *m.* we should make merry.
     Luke 15:32
do works *m.* for repentance.
     Acts 26:20*
receiving that recompence which was
m.   *Rom* 1:27*
am not *m.* to be called an. *1 Cor* 15:9
if it be *m.* that I go also.   16:4
is *m.* for me to think this. *Phil* 1:7*
made us *m.* to be partakers. *Col* 1:12
bound to thank God for you, as it is
m.   *2 Thes* 1:3
he shall be vessel *m.*   *2 Tim* 2:21
herbs *m.* for them by.   *Heb* 6:7
m. to stir you up.   *2 Pet* 1:13*

meet

Sodom went out to *m. Gen* 14:17
them, and ran to *m.* them.   18:2
Lot seeing them, rose up to *m.* 19:1
servant ran to *m.* Rebekah.   24:17
what man walketh to *m.* us?   65
Laban ran to *m.* Jacob.   29:13
Leah went out to *m.* Jacob.   30:16
Esau cometh to *m.* thee. 32:6; 33:4
Joseph went up to *m.* Israel. 46:29
Aaron cometh forth to *m.*   *Ex* 4:14
go into wilderness to *m.* Moses. 27
Moses went out to *m.* his.   18:7
brought forth the people to *m.* 19:17
if thou *m.* thine enemy's ox.   23:4
there I will *m.* with thee.   25:22
   29:42, 43; 30:6, 36; *Num* 17:4
Balak went out to *m. Num* 22:36
Lord will come to *m.* me.   23:3
stand here, while I *m.* the Lord.   15
went forth to *m.* them without. 31:13
lest the pursuers *m.* you. *Josh* 2:16*
with you, and go to *m.* them.   9:11
Jael went out to *m.* Sisera.
     Judg 4:18, 22
they came up to *m.* Gideon.   6:35
out of the doors to *m.* me.   11:31
his daughter came to *m.* him.   34
father of damsel rejoiced to *m.* 19:3
that they *m.* thee not in any other
field.   *Ruth* 2:22
shall *m.* thee three men. *1 Sam* 10:3
m. a company of prophets.   5
Saul went to *m.* Samuel.   13:10
Samuel rose up early to *m.*   15:12
Philistine drew nigh to *m.*   17:48
the women came to *m.* Saul.   18:6
sent thee this day to *m.* me.   25:32
to *m.* David and to *m.* people. 30:21
Michal came out to *m. 2 Sam* 6:20
David sent to *m.* the men.   10:5
     1 Chr 19:5
Archite came to *m.* him. *2 Sam* 15:32
Mephibosheth came to *m.*   19:24
Shimei came down to *m.*   *1 Ki* 2:8
Solomon rose up to *m.*   19
went to *m.* Ahab, to *m.* Elijah. 18:16
arise, go down to *m.* Ahab.   21:18
go up to *m.* messengers.   *2 Ki* 1:3
there came a man to *m.* us.   6
what man came up to *m.* you?   7

---

prophets came to *m.* Elisha. *2 Ki* 2:15
run now, I pray thee, to *m.* her. 4:26
if thou *m.* any man, salute.   29
the chariot to *m.* him.   5:21, 26
go *m.* the man of God.   8:8
Hazael went to *m.* him.   9
horseman, and send to *m.*   9:17
one on horseback to *m.* him.   18
Jonadab coming to *m.* him.   10:15
Ahaz went to *m.* the king.   16:10
let us *m.* together.   *Neh* 6:2, 10
they *m.* with darkness.   *Job* 5:14
the horse goeth on to *m.*   39:21
came I forth to *m.* thee.   *Pr* 7:15
bear robbed of her whelps *m.* 17:12
rich and poor *m.* together.   22:2
poor and deceitful *m.* together. 29:13
go forth to *m.* Ahaz.   *Isa* 7:3
hell is moved for thee to *m.*   14:9
beasts of desert shall also *m.* 34:14
vengeance, and I will not *m.*   47:3*
went forth to *m.* them.   *Jer* 41:6
messenger run to *m.* another. 51:31
I will *m.* them as a bear bereaved.
     Hos 13:8
prepare to *m.* thy God. *Amos* 4:12
angel went out to *m.*   *Zech* 2:3
city came out to *m.* Jesus. *Mat* 8:34
to *m.* the bridegroom.   25:1
cometh, go ye out to *m.* him.   6
there shall *m.* you a man.
     Mark 14:13; *Luke* 22:10
with ten thousand to *m. Luke* 14:31
people went forth to *m. John* 12:13
to *m.* us as far as Appii-forum.
     Acts 28:15
clouds to *m.* the Lord. *1 Thes* 4:17

meetest

look out the best of your.   *2 Ki* 10:3
m. him that rejoiceth.   *Isa* 64:5

meeteth

Esau my brother *m.* him.   *Gen* 32:17
slay murderer when he *m.* him.
     Num 35:19, 21

meeting

would dwell in *M.*   *Judg* 1:27
afraid at *m.* of David.   *1 Sam* 21:1
even the solemn *m.*   *Isa* 1:13

Megiddo

would dwell in *M.*   *Judg* 1:27
Canaan fought by waters of *M.* 5:19
pertained Taanach and *M. 1 Ki* 4:12
raised a levy to build *M.*   9:15
Ahaziah fled to *M.* and.   *2 Ki* 9:27
Josiah was slain at *M.*   23:29, 30
     2 Chr 35:22

Megiddon

in the valley of *M.*   *Zech* 12:11

Melchi

which was the son of *M. Luke* 3:24

Melchizedek

king *M.* brought forth.   *Gen* 14:18
priest for ever after the order of *M.*
     Ps 110:4; *Heb* 5:6, 10; 6:20
     7:17, 21
this *M.* king of Salem.   *Heb* 7:1
loins of his father, when *M.*   10
should rise after the order of *M.* 11
after the similitude of *M* ariseth. 15

melody

make sweet *m.* sing.   *Isa* 23:16
found therein, the voice of *m.* 51:3
I will not hear the *m.*   *Amos* 5:23
making *m.* in your heart.   *Eph* 5:19

melons

we remember the *m.*   *Num* 11:5

melt

(*Frequently used in the old sense
of to be prostrate because of fear*)
of Canaan shall *m.*   *Ex* 15:15
things, our hearts did *m. Josh* 2:11
made the heart of the people *m.* 14:8
lion, shall utterly *m.*   *2 Sam* 17:10
let them *m.* away as waters. *Ps* 58:7
with his teeth, and *m.* away. 112:10
every man's heart shall *m.* *Isa* 13:7
     Ezek 21:7
the heart of Egypt shall *m. Isa* 19:1
behold, I will *m.* them.   *Jer* 9:7
m. it; so will I *m.* you. *Ezek* 22:20
the land, and it shall *m. Amos* 9:5

all hills shall m. *Amos* 9:13; *Nah* 1:5
and the elements shall m. with heat.
2 Pet 3:10*, 12

melted
when sun waxed hot, it m. *Ex* 16:21
their heart m. *Josh* 5:1
hearts of Israel m. 7:5
the mountains m. before. *Judg* 5:5*
multitude m. away. *1 Sam* 14:16
my heart is m. in midst. *Ps* 22:14
his voice, and the earth m. 46:6
the hills m. like wax. 97:5
their soul m. 107:26
mountains shall be m. *Isa* 34:3
ye shall be m. in the. *Ezek* 22:21
as silver is m. in the midst. 22

melteth
as a snail which m., let. *Ps* 58:8
as wax m. so let wicked perish. 68:2
my soul m. for heaviness. 119:28
out his word and m. them. 147:18
workman m. a graven. *Isa* 40:19†
burnt, the founder m. *Jer* 6:29
the heart of Nineveh m. *Nah* 2:10

melting
as when the m. fire. *Isa* 64:2

member
(*Generally used in the archaic
sense of limb, or other part of the
body. In this sense it is often
also used figuratively*)
that hath his privy m. *Deut* 23:1
body is not one m. but. *1 Cor* 12:14
if they were all one m., where? 19
whether one m. suffer; one m. 26
the tongue is a little m. *Jas* 3:5

members
my m. are as a shadow. *Job* 17:7
in thy book all my m. *Ps* 139:16
thy m. should perish. *Mat* 5:29, 30
nor your m. as instruments.*Rom* 6:13
as ye yielded your m. servants. 19
sins did work in our m. 7:5
another law in my m. .... law of sin
which is in my m. 23
many m. in one body, and all m.
have not the same office. 12:4
every one m. one of another. 5
bodies are the m. of Christ? shall
I then take the m. of? *1 Cor* 6:15
body hath many m. and all m. 12:12
now hath God set the m. in. 18
are they many m., yet one body. 20
m. which seem more feeble. 22
but that the m. should have. 25
one member suffer, all the m. 26
ye are the body of Christ, and m. 27
for we are m. one of. *Eph* 4:25
m. of his body, of his flesh. 5:30
mortify your m. which are. *Col* 3:5
so is tongue among our m. *Jas* 3:6
lusts that war in your m. 4:1

memorial
this is my m. unto all. *Ex* 3:15
shall be to you for a m. 12:14
it shall be for a m. between. 13:9
write this for a m. in a book. 17:14
stones of m. to the children. 28:12
for a m. before the Lord. 29; 39:7
money may be for a m. 30:16
burn the m. of it on altar. *Lev* 2:2
9:16; 5:12; 6:15; *Num* 5:26
a m. of blowing trumpets.
Lev 23:24; *Num* 10:10
on the bread for a m. *Lev* 24:7
for it is an offering of m. *Num* 5:15
priest put the offering of m. 18
took brasen censers to be a m. 16:40
gold of the captains for m. 31:54
stones shall be for a m. *Josh* 4:7
ye have no portion nor m. *Neh* 2:20
nor the m. of them perish. *Esth* 9:28
their m. is perished. *Ps* 9:6
and thy m. throughout all. 135:13
the Lord is his m. *Hos* 12:5
crowns be for a m. in. *Zech* 6:14
this be told for a m. of her.
Mat 26:13; *Mark* 14:9
alms are come up for a m. *Acts* 10:4

memory
he may cut off the m. *Ps* 109:15
utter the m. of thy great. 145:7

m. of the just is blessed. *Pr* 10:7
m. of them is forgotten. *Eccl* 9:5
and made all their m. to. *Isa* 26:14
if ye keep in m. what. *1 Cor* 15:2

Memphis
M. shall bury them. *Hos* 9:6

men
then began m. to call on. *Gen* 4:26
when m. began to multiply on. 6:1
looked, and lo, three m. stood. 18:2
the m. of the city, m. of Sodom. 19:4
where are m. which came into? 5
only to these m. do nothing. 8
smote the m. 11
power with God and m. 32:28
m. are peaceable with us. 34:21
only herein will the m. consent. 22
we are true m. 42:11, 31
bring these m. home. 43:16
said, Up, follow after the m. 44:4
m. are shepherds, for their. 46:32
saved the m.-children. *Ex* 1:17, 18
go now ye that are m. and. 10:11
thrice in the year shall m. 34:23
Aaron took these m. *Num* 1:17
all the people are m. of great. 13:32
m. that did bring evil report. 14:37
put out the eyes of these m.? 16:14
if these m. die the common death. 29
God said, What m. are these? 22:9
said to Balaam, Go with the m. 35
slay ye every one his m. that. 25:5
not one of these m. shall. *Deut* 1:35
to cease from among m. 32:26
Reuben live, let not his m. 33:6
there came m. in hither. *Josh* 2:2
bring forth the. 3; *1 Sam* 11:12
because he feared the m. *Judg* 6:27
Penuel answered as the m. 8:8
should give bread to thy m. 15
m. say not of me, A woman. 9:54
there were m. lying in wait. 16:2
therefore deliver us the m. 20:13
with the Lord and m. *1 Sam* 2:26
he smote the m. of the city. 5:9
m. that died not were smitten. 12
hearest thou m.'s words? 24:9
but the m. were very good. 25:15
m. the sons of Zeruiah. *2 Sam* 3:39
and let us play the m. for. 10:12
but dead men before my. 19:28
he that ruleth over m. must. 23:3
two lionlike m. of. 20; *1 Chr* 11:22
happy thy m. that hear. *1 Ki* 10:8
m. come out of Samaria. 20:17
now the m. did diligently. 33
open the eyes of these m. *2 Ki* 6:20
they reckoned not with m. 12:15
the m. of Babylon ... m. of Cuth.
Nergal, m. of Hamath. 17:30
hath he not sent me to the m.?
18:27; *Isa* 36:12
what said these m.? *2 Ki* 20:14
Isa 39:3
drink blood of these m.? *1 Chr* 11:19
let m. say among the nations. 16:31
m. were greatly ashamed. 19:5
will God dwell with m.? *2 Chr* 6:18
the m. expressed by name. 28:15
and the m. did the work. 34:12
let m. of his place help. *Ezra* 1:4
to cause these m. to cease. 4:21
expenses be given to these m. 6:8
nor m. of the guard. *Neh* 4:23
other m. have our lands and. 5:5
sleep falleth on m. *Job* 4:13; 33:15
they are gone away from m. 28:4
if the m. of my tabernacle. 31:31
m. do therefore fear him. 37:24
themselves to be but m. *Ps* 9:20
m. which are thy hand, from. 17:14
m. will praise thee when. 49:18
m. of low degree are vanity, m. 62:9
hast received gifts for m. 68:18
and m. shall be blessed in. 72:17
as other m., neither are they plagued
like other m. 73:5
but ye shall die like m. 82:7
that m. may know that thou. 83:18
O that m. would praise the Lord.
107:8, 15, 21, 31
on our side, when m. rose. 124:2
m. shall speak of the might. 145:6

m. do not despise a thief. *Pr* 6:30
to you, O m. I call. 8:4
m. depart from evil. 16:6
most m. proclaim each his own. 20:6
which the m. of Hezekiah. 25:1
m. to search their own glory. 27
when the wicked rise, m. hide. 28:28
God doeth it that m. may. *Eccl* 3:14
m. shall fall by the sword. *Isa* 3:25
the Lord have removed m. 6:12
thing for you to weary m.? 7:13
now the Egyptians are m. 31:3
by these things m. live. 38:16
wherefore I will give m. for. 43:4
even to him shall m. come. 45:24
and shew yourselves m. 46:8
that m. may bring to thee. 60:11
m. shall call you the ministers. 61:6
m. have not heard, nor. 64:4
set a trap, they catch m. *Jer* 5:26
horses set in array, as m. for. 6:23
neither can m. hear the voice. 9:10
let their m. be put to death. 18:21
I will give the m. that transgressed
my covenant. 34:18
m. have done evil to prophet. 38:9
to Gedaliah, they and their m. 40:8
then the m. shall cry and. 47:2
arise ye, and spoil the m. of. 49:28
surely I will fill thee with m. 51:14
m. call the perfection. *Lam* 2:15
m. that devise mischief. *Ezek* 11:2
these m. set up their idols. 14:3
though these three m., Noah, Daniel,
Job. 14, 16, 18
sent for m. to come from. 23:40
I will deliver thee to the m. 25:4, 10
ye are m., and I am God. 34:31
mountains with his slain m. 35:8
multiply m. upon you. 36:10, 37
m. have not regarded. *Dan* 3:12
fire slew those m. that took. 22
these m., upon whose bodies fire. 27
drive thee from m. 4:25, 32
m. we shall not find occasion. 6:5
that m. fear before the God. 26
but they like m. trangressed the
covenant. *Hos* 6:7
m. that were at peace. *Ob* 7
pass securely, as m. averse. *Mi* 2:8
man's enemies are the m. of. 7:6
makest m. as the fishes. *Hab* 1:14
they are m. wondered at. *Zech* 3:8
had sent their m. to pray. 7:2
but lo, I will deliver the m. 11:6
light so shine before m. *Mat* 5:16
shall teach m. so, shall be called. 19
do not your alms before m. 6:1
they may appear to m. to fast. 16
thou appear not unto m. to fast. 18
that m. should do to you, do ye even
so to them. 7:12; *Luke* 6:31
given such power to m. *Mat* 9:8
whoso shall confess me before m.
10:32; *Luke* 12:8
whoso shall deny me before m.
Mat 10:33; *Luke* 12:9
but while m. slept, his enemy.
Mat 13:25
whom do m. say that I am? 16:13
Mark 8:27
ye appear righteous to m. *Mat* 23:28
and said, I see m. as. *Mark* 8:24
with m. it is impossible. 10:27
Luke 18:27
good will toward m. *Luke* 2:14
thou shalt catch m. 5:10
shall rise up with the m. of. 11:31
to whom m. have committed. 12:48
I am not as other m. as. 18:11
not honour from m. *John* 5:41
manifested thy name to the m. 17:6
of these m. which have companied.
Acts 1:21
others said, These m. are full. 2:13
what shall we do to these m.? 4:16
thou hast not lied unto m. 5:4
the m. ye put in prison there in. 25
obey God rather than m. 29
to do, as touching these m. 35
refrain from these m. 38
Spirit said, Behold three m. 10:19
also are m. of like passions. 14:15
m. that hazarded their lives. 15:26

these *m.* are servants of. *Acts* 16:17
serjeants, saying, Let those *m.* go. 35
brought hither these *m.* 19:37
also of yourselves shall *m.* 20:30
of offence toward God and *m.* 24:16
m. with *m.* working. *Rom* 1:27
condescend to *m.* of low. 12:16
we are made a spectacle unto world
  and to angels and *m.* *1 Cor* 4:9
for he speaketh not to *m.* 14:2
but in understanding he *m.* 20
with *m.* of other tongues and lips. 21
we persuade *m.* *2 Cor* 5:11
for I mean not that other *m.* 8:13
persuade *m.*? or seek to please *m.?*
  Gal 1:10
he gave gifts unto *m.* *Eph* 4:8
so ought *m.* to love their wives. 5:28
to Lord and not to *m.* 6:7; *Col* 3:23
not as pleasing *m.* but. *1 Thes* 2:4
I will that *m.* pray every. *1 Tim* 2:8
m. shall be lovers of. *2 Tim* 3:2
priest taken from among *m. Heb* 5:1
for *m.* verily swear by the. 6:16
here *m.* that die receive tithes. 7:8
as it is appointed unto *m.* 9:27
to the spirits of just *m.* 12:23
therewith curse we *m.* *Jas* 3:9
judged according to *m.* *1 Pet* 4:6
but holy *m.* of God. *2 Pet* 1:21
for there are certain *m.* crept. *Jude* 4
only those *m.* which have. *Rev* 9:4
their power was to hurt *m.* 10
redeemed from among *m.* 14:4
not since *m.* were on the earth. 16:18
tabernacle of God is with *m.* 21:3
see **brethren, chief, chosen,
evil, great, Israel, Judah, old,
rich, righteous, singing**

all men

all the *m.* of his house. *Gen* 17:27
all the *m.* are dead. *Ex* 4:19
die the common death of *all m.*
  Num 16:29
all the *m.* that followed. *Deut* 4:3
said, Have out *all m.* *2 Sam* 13:9
was wiser than *all m.* *1 Ki* 4:31
all m. may know his work. *Job* 37:7
all m. shall fear, and. *Ps* 64:9
thou made *all m.* in vain ? 89:47
I said in my haste, All *m.* 116:11
that is the end of *all m. Eccl* 7:2
so with *all* the *m.* that set. *Jer* 42:17
I set *all m.* every one against his
  neighbour *Zech* 8:10
ye shall be hated of *all m. Mat* 10:22
  Mark 13:13; *Luke* 21:17
all m. cannot receive. *Mat* 19:11
tho' *all m.* shall be offended. 26:33
all m. seek thee. *Mark* 1:37
all m. did marvel. 5:20
all m. counted John a. 11:32
all m. speak well of you. *Luke* 6:26
sinners above *all m.* that dwelt. 13:4
that *all m.* through him. *John* 1:7
himself, because he knew *all m.* 2:24
the same baptizeth, and *all m.* 3:26
all m. should honour the Son. 5:23
if we let alone, *all m.* will. 11:48
I will draw *all m.* unto me. 12:32
by this shall *all m.* know that. 13:35
Lord, who knowest the hearts of *all*
  m. *Acts* 1:24
all m. glorified God for what. 4:21
but now commandeth *all m.* 17:30
hath given assurance to *all m.* 31
all the *m.* were about twelve. 19:7
burned their books before *all m.* 19
pure from the blood of *all m.* 20:26
be his witness to *all m.* 22:15
death passed upon *all m. Rom* 5:12
on *all m.* to condemnation, the free
  gift came on *all m.* to. 18
honest in the sight of *all m.* 12:17
live peaceably with *all m.* 18
is come abroad to *all m.* 16:19
I would that *all m.* were. *1 Cor* 7:7
for though I be free from *all m.* 9:19
I am made all things to *all m.* 22
even as I please *all m.* in. 10:33
of *all m.* most miserable. 15:19
known and read of *all m. 2 Cor* 3:2
let us do good to *all m.* *Gal* 6:10

to make *all m.* see what is. *Eph* 3:9
let your moderation be known to *all*
  m. *Phil* 4:5
and contrary to *all m.* *1 Thes* 2:15
abound in love toward *all m.* 3:12
be patient toward *all m.* 5:14
follow that which is good to *all m.* 15
all m. have not faith. *2 Thes* 3:2
thanks be made for *all m. 1 Tim* 2:1
who will have *all m.* to be saved. 4
who is the Saviour of *all m.* 4:10
but be gentle to *all m.* *2 Tim* 2:24
shall be made manifest to *all m.* 3:9
man stood with me, but *all m.* 4:16
God hath appeared to *all m. Tit* 2:11
shewing all meekness to *all m.* 3:2
follow peace with *all m. Heb* 12:14
God, that giveth to *all m.* *Jas* 1:5
Honour *all m.*, Love the. *1 Pet* 2:17
hath good report of *all m. 3 John* 12

in men

let no man glory in *m.* *1 Cor* 3:21

like men

quit yourselves *like m.* *1 Sam* 4:9
  1 Cor 16:13
but ye shall die *like m.* *Ps* 82:7
like m. have transgressed. *Hos* 6:7
yourselves *like* unto *m.* that wait for
  their lord. *Luke* 12:36

mighty men

mighty m. which were of old.*Gen* 6:4
mighty m. of Moab. *Ex* 15:15
the *mighty m.* of valour. *Josh* 1:14
Jericho and the *mighty m.* 6:2
thirty thousand *mighty m.* 8:3
m. of Gibeon were *mighty.* 10:2
ascended from Gilgal with *mighty m.*
  of valour. 7
bows of the *mighty m.* *1 Sam* 2:4
Joab and all the host of the *mighty m.*
  2 Sam 10:7; 20:7; *1 Chr* 19:8
mighty m. were on his right hand.
  2 Sam 16:6
his *m.,* that they be *mighty m.* 17:8
be names of the *mighty m.* 23:8
Eleazar one of the three *mighty m.* 9
the three *mighty m.* brake. 16, 17
name among three *mighty m.* 22
the *mighty m.* were not with Adonijah. *1 Ki* 1:8
the *mighty m.* and Solomon. 10
exacted of all *mighty m. 2 Ki* 15:20
carried away all the *mighty m.* 24:14
these were *mighty m.* of valour.
  1 Chr 5:24; 7:7, 9, 1., 40
sons of Ulam were *mighty m.* 8:40
the chief of the *mighty m.* 11:10, 11
were among the *mighty m.* 12:1
were all *mighty m.* of valour. 21, 25
  30; 26:6, 31
mighty m. submitted themselves to
  Solomon. 29:24
battle against Abijah, being
  m. 2 Chr 13:3; 14:8; 17:13, 14, 16
an hundred thousand *mighty m.* 25:6
counsel with his *mighty m.* 32:3
angel cut off all the *mighty m.* 21
their brethren *mighty m. Neh* 11:14
break in pieces *mighty m. Job* 34:24
more than ten *mighty m. Eccl* 7:19
all shields of *mighty m. S of S* 4:4
mighty m. of Kedar *Isa* 21:17
quiver is an open sepulchre, they are
  mighty m. *Jer* 5:16
king, with all his *mighty m.* 26:21
recovered *mighty m.* of war. 41:16
let *mighty m.* come forth. 46:9
we are *mighty m.* 48:14
hearts of *mighty m.* of Moab. 41
heart of *mighty m.* of Edom. 49:22
sword is upon her *mighty m.* 50:36
mighty m. of Babylon have. 51:30
mighty m. are taken, their bows. 56
I will make drunk her *mighty m.* 57
under foot my *mighty m. Lam* 1:15
table with *mighty m.* *Ezek* 39:20
mighty m. to bind. *Dan* 3:20
trust in the multitude of thy *mighty*
  m. *Hos* 10:13
shall run like *mighty m.* *Joel* 2:7
wake up the *mighty m.* 3
thy *mighty m.* O Teman. *Ob* 9
the shield of his *mighty m. Nah* 2:3

as *mighty m.* that tread. *Zech* 10:5
mighty m. hid themselves in the
  dens. *Rev* 6:15
eat the flesh of *mighty m.* 19:18

of men

saw the daughters *of m.* *Gen* 6:2
came in to the daughters *of m.* 4
none devoted *of m.* *Lev* 27:29
whether it be *of m.* *Num* 18:15
prey both *of m.* and beasts. 31:11
what manner *of m.* were. *Judg* 8:18
went with a band *of m.* *1 Sam* 10:26
him with the rod *of m.* *2 Sam* 7:14
spied a band *of m.* *2 Ki* 13:21
places with the bones *of m.* 23:14
they took away *of m.* *1 Chr* 5:21
the band *of m.* had slain. *2 Chr* 22:1
O thou Preserver *of m.?* *Job* 7:20
then he openeth the ears *of m.* 33:16
concerning the works *of m. Ps* 17:4
but I am a reproach *of m.* 22:6
haughtiness *of m.* shall be bowed
  down. *Isa* 2:11
the haughtiness *of m.* shall be made
  low. 17
taught by the precept *of m.* 29:13
workmen, they are *of m.* 44:11
fear ye not the reproach *of m.* 51:7
is despised and rejected *of m.* 53:3
carcases *of m.* shall fall. *Jer* 9:22
with the dead bodies *of m.* 33:5
to thyself images *of m. Ezek* 16:17
eat not the bread *of m.* 24:17, 22
traded the persons *of m.* in. 27:13
no more bereave them *of m.* 36:12
cities be filled with flocks *of m.* 38
mingle with the seed *of m. Dan* 2:43
Most High . . . *of m.* and setteth up
  . . . basest *of m.* 4:17, 25, 32; 5:21
by reason of multitude *of m.*
  Mi 2:12; *Zech* 2:4
make you fishers *of m.* *Mat* 4:19
trodden under foot *of m.* 5:13
they may have glory *of m.* 6:2
seen *of m.* 5; 23:5
beware *of m.* 10:17
for doctrines, commandments *of m.*
  15:9; *Mark* 7:7
but the things that be *of m.*
  Mat 16:23; *Mark* 8:33
betrayed into hands *of m. Mat* 17:22
  Mark 9:31; *Luke* 9:44; 24:7
made eunuchs *of m.* *Mat* 19:12
baptism of heaven or *of m.?* 21:25
if we say *of m.* 26; *Mark* 11:30
  32; *Luke* 20:4, 6
regardest not person *of m.*
  Mat 22:16; *Mark* 12:14
be called *of m.* Rabbi. *Mat* 23:7
out of the heart *of m.* *Mark* 7:21
life was the light *of m.* *John* 1:4
they loved the praise *of m.* 12:43
Judas received a band *of m.* 18:3
to whom a number *of m. Acts* 5:36
if this work be *of m.* it will. 38
come down in likeness *of m.* 14:11
the residue *of m.* might seek. 15:17
honourable women, and *of m.* 17:12
unrighteousness *of m.* *Rom* 1:18
judge the secrets *of m.* 2:16
whose praise is not *of m.* 29
brethren, I speak after the manner
  of m. 6:19; *Gal* 3:15
Christ is approved *of m. Rom* 14:18
stand in the wisdom *of m. 1 Cor* 2:5
learn in us not to think *of m.* 4:6
be not the servants *of m.* 7:23
speak with tongues *of m.* and. 13:1
if, after the manner *of m.*, I. 15:32
things in the sight *of m. 2 Cor* 2:1
Paul an apostle, not *of m.* *Gal* 1:1
doctrine, by sleight *of m. Eph* 4:14
made in the likeness *of m. Phil* 2:7
after the tradition *of m.* *Col* 2:8
and doctrines *of m.* 22
manner *of m.* we were. *1 Thes* 1:5
nor *of m.* sought we glory. 2:6
it not as the word *of m.* 13
disputings *of m.* of. *1 Tim* 6:5
commandments *of m.* *Tit* 1:14
disallowed indeed *of m. 1 Pet* 2:4
to silence ignorance of foolish *m.* 15
no longer live to the lusts *of m.* 4:2

receive the witness of m. *1 John* 5:9
were as the faces of m. *Rev* 9:7
slay the third part of m. 15, 18
were slain of m. 7000. 11:13
fire come down in sight of m. 13:13
of slaves and souls of m. 18:13

see children

sons of men

ye sons of m. how long will ye turn
my glory into ? *Ps* 4:2; 58:1
thee, before the sons of m. 31:19
beholdeth all the sons of m. 33:13
I lie among the sons of m. 57:4
to make known to sons of m. 145:12
and my delights were with the sons
of m. *Pr* 8:31
travail hath God given to the sons
of m. *Eccl* 1:13; 3:10
good for sons of m. 2:3
delights of the sons of m. 8
the estate of the sons of m. 18
which befalleth the sons of m. 19
heart of sons of m. is set in. 8:11
the heart of the sons of m. 9:3
so are the sons of m. snared. 12
more than the sons of m. *Isa* 52:14
ways of the sons of m. *Jer* 32:19
driven from the sons of m. *Dan* 5:21
similitude of the sons of m. 10:16
joy is withered away from the sons of
m. *Joel* 1:12
nor waiteth for the sons of m. *Mi* 5:7
be forgiven to sons of m. *Mark* 3:28
not known to sons of m. *Eph* 3:5

men of war

taken sum of m. of w. *Num* 31:49
till m. of w. came out of Egypt were.
Deut 2:14, 16; *Josh* 5:6
the city, ye m. of w. *Josh* 6:3
drew sword, all these were m. of w.
Judg 20:17
set over the m. of w. *1 Sam* 18:5
they were m. of w. and chief captains.
1 Ki 9:22; *2 Chr* 8:9
and all the m. of w. fled.
2 Ki 25:4; *Jer* 52:7
took an officer set over m. of w.
2 Ki 25:19; *Jer* 52:25
Gadites m. of w. came to. *1 Chr* 12:8
these m. of w. came to Hebron. 38
set battle in array with m. of w.
2 Chr 13:3
and the m. of w. were in. 17:13
the hands of m. of w. *Jer* 38:4
Ishmael slew m. of w. 41:3
Johanan took the m. of w. 16
all the m. of w. shall be cut off.
49:26; 50:30
m. of w. are affrighted. 51:32
Phut were thy m. of w. *Ezek* 27:10
all thy m. of w. that are in thee. 27
at my table with m. of w. 39:20
climb wall like m. of w. *Joel* 2:7
all the m. of w. draw near. 3:9
Herod with his m. of w. *Luke* 23:11

wicked men

but the m. of Sodom were wicked.
Gen 13:13
tents of these wicked m. *Num* 16:26
then answered all the wicked m.
1 Sam 30:22
as a man falleth before wicked m.
2 Sam 3:34*
when wicked m. have slain. 4:11
marked old way that wicked m. have
trodden. *Job* 22:15
walketh with wicked m. 34:8
he striketh them as wicked m. 26
of his answers for wicked m. 36
there be wicked m. to whom it
happeneth. *Eccl* 8:14
people are found wicked m. *Jer* 5:26
destroy those wicked m. *Mat* 24:41
be delivered from wicked m.
2 Thes 3:2

wise men

Pharaoh called for all wise m.
Gen 41:8; *Ex* 7:11
wise m. that wrought. *Ex* 36:4
take ye wise m. and. *Deut* 1:13
chief of your tribes, wise m. 15

king said to wise m. *Esth* 1:13
then said Haman's wise m. 6:13
which wise m. have told. *Job* 15:18
hear my words, O ye wise m. 34:2
he seeth that wise m. die. *Ps* 49:10
wise m. lay up knowledge. *Pr* 10:14
he that walketh with wise m. 13:20
but wise m. turn away wrath. 29:8
the words of wise m. are. *Eccl* 9:17
where are thy wise m.? *Isa* 19:12
the wisdom of their wise m. 29:14
turneth wise m. backward. 44:25
the wise m. are ashamed. *Jer* 8:9
as among all the wise m. of. 10:7
Babylon, and on her wise m. 50:35
make drunken her wise m. 51:57
thy wise m. O Tyrus. *Ezek* 27:8
wise m. thereof were thy calkers. 9
destroy all the wise m. of. *Dan* 2:12
cannot the wise m. shew unto. 27
decree to bring in all the wise m. 4:6
king spake to the wise m. 5:7
even destroy the wise m. out. *Ob* 8
came wise m. from east. *Mat* 2:1
he had privily called the wise m. 7
was mocked of wise m. 16
I send wise m. 23:34
not many wise m. called. *1 Cor* 1:26
speak as to wise m.; judge ye. 10:15

men joined with women

both m. and women brought bracelets. *Ex* 35:22
destroyed the m. and women and.
Deut 2:34; *Josh* 8:25
thousand m. and women. *Judg* 9:49
fled all the m. and women. 51
m. and women, upon the roof about
3000 m and women. 16:27
well to the women as m. *2 Sam* 6:19
brought the law before m. and
women. *Neh* 8:2, 3
Jeremiah said to the m. and women.
Jer 44:20
added to Lord both m. and women.
Acts 5:14
Saul haling m. and women. 8:3
baptized, both m. and women. 12
whether m. or women he might
bring them bound. 9:2
prison both m. and women. 22:4

men, women and children, see children

ye men

hearken unto me, ye m. *Judg* 9:7
ye m. of understanding. *Job* 34:10
ye m. of Galilee. *Acts* 1:11
ye m. of Judea. 2:14
ye m. of Israel. 5:35
ye m. and brethren, if ye. 13:15
ye m. of Athens. 17:22
ye m. of Ephesus, what man? 19:35

young men

that which the young m. *Gen* 14:25
Moses sent young m. *Ex* 24:5
Joshua one of the young m.
Num 11:28
young m. that were spies. *Josh* 6:23
so used the young m. *Judg* 14:10
charged the young m. *Ruth* 2:9
followedst not young m. 3:10
the sin of the young m. *1 Sam* 2:17
your goodliest young m. 8:16
the young m. kept themselves. 21:4
and the vessels of the young m. 5
ask thy young m. and they. 25:8
handmaid saw not the young m. 25
let one of the young m. come. 26:22
save 400 young m. which rode. 30:17
David called one of the young m.
2 Sam 1:15
let the young m. arise and. 2:14
hold on one of the young m. 21
have slain all the young m. 13:32
and ten young m. that bare. 18:15
consulted with young m. *1 Ki* 12:8
spake after counsel of young m.
2 Chr 10:8, 14
by young m. of princes. *1 Ki* 20:14
send, I pray thee, one of the young
m. *2 Ki* 4:22*
there be come two young m. 5:22
their young m. wilt thou slay. 8:12
slew their young m with. *2 Chr* 36:17

it fell upon the young m. *Job* 1:19
the young m. saw me, and hid. 29:8
consumed their young m. *Ps* 78:63
praise the Lord, young m. 148:12
the glory of young m. is. *Pr* 20:29
no joy in their young m. *Isa* 9:17
bows also shall dash young m. 13:18
do I nourish up young m. 23:4
young m. shall be discomfited. 31:8
young m. shall utterly fall. 40:30
pour fury on assembly of young m.
Jer 6:11
to cut off the young m. from. 9:21
the young m. shall die by. 11:22
against the mother of the young m.
15:8
let their young m. be slain. 18:21
young m. and old rejoice. 31:13
his chosen young m. are gone. 48:15
her young m. shall fall in the streets.
49:26; 50:30
spare ye not her young m. 51:3
assembly to crush my young m.
Lam 1:15
my virgins and young m. are. 18
the young m. and old lie on. 2:21
took the young m. to grind. 5:13
the young m. have ceased from. 14
all of them desirable young m.
Ezek 23:6, 12, 23
young m. of Aven shall fall. 30:17
your young m. shall see visions.
Joel 2:28; *Acts* 2:17
and of your young m. *Amos* 2:11
your young m. have I slain. 4:10
your young m. shall faint. 8:13
the young m. cheerful. *Zech* 9:17
and the young m. laid. *Mark* 14:51
and the young m. arose. *Acts* 5:6
the young m. came in and found. 10
young m. likewise exhort. *Tit* 2:6
I write to you, young m. because.
1 John 2:13, 14

Menahem

M. smote Shallum in. *2 Ki* 15:14
M. smote Tiphsah. 16
M. exacted money. 20

mend

brass to m. the house. *2 Chr* 24:12
gave it the workmen to m. 34:10

mending

James and John, with Zebedee,
their nets. *Mat* 4:21; *Mark* 1:19

Mene

M. M. God hath numbered thy.
Dan 5:25, 26

menpleasers

not with eye service, as m. *Eph* 6:6
Col 3:22

menservants

Abram had m. and. *Gen* 12:16
Abimelech gave m. to. 20:14
God hath given my master m. 24:35
Jacob had m. and camels. 30:43
32:5
shall not go out as m. do. *Ex* 21:7
rejoice before Lord, ye and your m.
Deut 12:12
king will take you m. *1 Sam* 8:16
is it a time to receive m.? *2 Ki* 5:26
shall begin to beat the m. *Luke* 12:45

see two

menstealers

law is made for m. *1 Tim* 1:10

menstruous

cast them away as a m. *Isa* 30:22*
Jerusalem is as a m. *Lam* 1:17*
near to a m. woman. *Ezek* 18:6

mention

m. of me unto Pharaoh. *Gen* 41:14
make no m. of other gods. *Ex* 23:13
Josh 23:7
he made m. of the ark. *1 Sam* 4:18
no m. shall be made of coral or of
pearls. *Job* 28:18
m. of thy righteousness. *Ps* 71:16
m. of Rahab and Babylon. 87:4
make m. that his name. *Isa* 12:4
that maketh m. thereof shall. 19:17
by thee only we will make m. 26:13

mention

make m. of God of Israel. *Isa 48:1*
from bowels hath he made m. 49:1
ye that make m. of the Lord. 62:6
make ye m. to nations. *Jer 4:16*
I will not make m. of him. 20:9
we may not make m. of. *Amos 6:10*
I make m. of you always. *Rom 1:9*
Eph 1:16; 1 Thes 1:2
making m. of thee always. *Philem 4*
Joseph made m. of the. *Heb 11:22*

mention

I will m. the lovingkindnesses of.
Isa 63:7
burden of the Lord shall ye m. no
more. *Jer 23:36*

mentioned

these cities, which are m. *Josh 21:9*
these m. by name. *1 Chr 4:38*
Jehu is m. in the book. *2 Chr 20:34**
sister Sodom was not m. *Ezek 16:56*
his transgressions shall not be m.
18:22*
his righteousness shall not be m. 24*
none of his sins shall be m. 33:16*

Mephibosheth

son, his name was M. *2 Sam 4:4*
but M. shall eat bread at. 9:10, 11
M. had a young son Micha ... of
Ziba were servants to M. 12
are all that pertained unto M. 16:4
wentest thou not with me, M.? 19:25
but the king spared M. the. 21:7
sons of Rizpah, Armoni and M. 8

Merab

Saul's eldest daughter M.
1 Sam 14:49; 18:17
M. should have been given. 18:19

Merari

Gershon, Kohath, M. *Gen 46:11*
Ex 6:16; Num 3:17; 1 Chr 6:1, 16
23:6
sons of M. *Ex 6:19; Num 3:20*
1 Chr 6:19, 29; 23:21; 24:26
charge of the sons of M. *Num 3:36*
were numbered of M. 4:42
M. set forward. 10:17
oxen given to the sons of M. 7:8
cities given to M. *Josh 21:7, 40*
1 Chr 6:63, 77

merchandise

thou shalt not make m. *Deut 21:14*
and maketh m. of him. 24:7
m. of it is better than the m. *Pr 3:14*
perceiveth that her m. is good. 31:18
her m. shall be holiness. *Isa 23:18*
the m. of Ethiopia shall come. 45:14
make a prey of thy m. *Ezek 26:12*
were in thee to occupy thy m. 27:9
isles were the m. of thy hands. 15*
by the multitude of thy m. 28:16*
farm, another to his m. *Mat 22:5*
make not my Father's house an house
of m. *John 2:16*
feigned words make m. *2 Pet 2:3*
no man buyeth their m. *Rev 18:11*
the m. of gold, and silver. 12

merchant

current money with m. *Gen 23:16*
she is like the m. ships. *Pr 31:14*
deliverest girdles to the m. 24
all powders of the m. *S of S 3:6*
against the m. city. *Isa 23:11**
art a m. of the people. *Ezek 27:3*
Tarshish was thy m. by reason. 12
Syria was thy m. 16, 18, 20*
he is a m., the balances. *Hos 12:7**
for all the m. people. *Zeph 1:11**

merchantman, men

passed by Midianites m. *Gen 37:28*
he had of the m. *1 Ki 10:15*
like a m. seeking. *Mat 13:45*

merchants

traffic of spice m. *1 Ki 10:15*
the king's m. received linen yarn.
28; *2 Chr 1:16*
besides that which m. *2 Chr 9:14*
the goldsmiths and the m. *Neh 3:32*
so the m. lodged without. 13:20
part him among the m.? *Job 41:6*
m. of Zidon replenished. *Isa 23:2*
city, whose m. are princes. 8
thy m. they shall wander. 47:15*

crept the twigs, he set it in a city of
m. *Ezek 17:4*
Meshech, were thy m. 27:13
Judah and Israel thy m. 17
in these were thy m. 21
m. of Sheba. 22, 23
there were thy m. in all sorts. 24
m. shall hiss at thee. 36
m. of Tarshish. 38:13
hast multiplied thy m. *Nah 3:16*
for the m. of the earth. *Rev 18:3*
the m. of the earth shall weep. 11
for thy m. were the great men. 23

Mercurius

called Paul, M., because. *Acts 14:12*

mercies

of the least of thy m. *Gen 32:10*
for his m. are great. *2 Sam 24:14*
1 Chr 21:13
remember the m. of David thy servant. *2 Chr 6:42*
in thy manifold m. *Neh 9:19*
according to thy m. thou gavest. 27
deliver according to thy m. 28
m. thou didst not consume. 31
according to thy m. blot out. *Ps 51:1*
in the multitude of thy m. 69:13
according to thy tender m. 16
I will sing of the m. of Lord. 89:1
not multitude of thy m. 106:7
according to multitude of his m. 45
let thy m. come also to me. 119:41
with great m. will I gather. *Isa 54:7*
sure m. of David. 55:3; *Acts 13:34*
on them according to his m. *Isa 63:7*
where is thy zeal and thy m.? 15*
I have taken away my m. *Jer 16:5*
shew m. to you, that he may. 42:12
it is of the Lord's m. we. *Lam 3:22*
according to multitude of his m. 32
desire m. concerning. *Dan 2:18*
to the Lord our God belong m. 9:9
righteousness, but thy great m. 18
betroth thee unto me in m. *Hos 2:19*
to Jerusalem with m. *Zech 1:16*
I beseech you by the m. *Rom 12:1*
the Father of m. and. *2 Cor 1:3*
if any fellowship of the Spirit, if any
bowels and m. *Phil 2:1**
put on therefore, holy and beloved,
bowels of m. *Col 3:12**

tender mercies

remember, O Lord, thy *tender m.*
Ps 25:6; 51:1
withhold not thy *tender m.* 40:11
in anger shut up his *tender m.* 77:9
let thy *tender m.* speedily. 79:8
crowneth thee with *tender m.* 103:4
let thy *tender m.* come unto. 119:77
great are thy *tender m.* O Lord. 156
tender m. are over all his. 145:9
tender m. of the wicked. *Pr 12:10*

merciful

Lord being m. unto Lot. *Gen 19:16*
Lord God, m. and gracious, *Ex 34:6**
be m. O Lord, to thy. *Deut 21:8**
and will be m. to his land. 32:43*
with the m. thou wilt shew thyself m.
2 Sam 22:26; Ps 18:25
of Israel are m. kings. *1 Ki 20:31†*
God is gracious and m. *2 Chr 30:9*
pardon, gracious and m. *Neh 9:17**
and be m. to me. *Ps 26:11; 41:4*
10; 56:1; 57:1; 86:3; 119:58, 132
the righteous is ever m. 37:26*
be not m. to any wicked. 59:5
God be m. to us, and bless us. 67:1
Lord is m. and gracious. 103:8*
for his m. kindness is great. 117:2
let thy m. kindness be for. 119:76
the m. man doeth good. *Pr 11:17†*
m. men are taken away. *Isa 57:1†*
Return, for I am m. saith. *Jer 3:12*
he is gracious and m. *Joel 2:13†*
that thou art a m. God. *Jonah 4:2**
blessed are the m.: for they. *Mat 5:7*
be ye m. as your Father also is m.
Luke 6:36
publican saying, God be m. 18:13
be a m. High Priest. *Heb 2:17*
m. to their unrighteousness. 8:12
see God

mercy

*(Compassion; pity for the unde-
serving and the guilty. Used of
both God and man. The word is
frequently changed in the Revisions
to lovingkindness)*
not destitute of his m. *Gen 24:27*
and God give you m. before. 43:14
keeping m. for thousands. *Ex 34:7*
Dan 9:4
Lord is longsuffering and of great m.
Num 14:18; Ps 103:11; 145:8
covenant and m. *Deut 7:9, 12*
my m. shall not depart. *2 Sam 7:15*
1 Chr 17:13; Ps 89:24
m. and truth be with. *2 Sam 15:20*
keepest covenant and m. *1 Ki 8:23*
Neh 1:5; 9:32
m. endureth for ever. *1 Chr 16:34*
41; *2 Chr 5:13; 7:3, 6; 20:21*
Ezra 3:11; Ps 106:1; 107:1
118:1; 136:1, *to the end*
Jer 33:11
extended m. to me. *Ezra 7:28*
extended m. to us in sight of. 9:9
grant him m. in the sight. *Neh 1:11*
correction or for m. *Job 37:13*
and through the m. of. *Ps 21:7*
goodness and m. shall follow. 23:6
the paths of the Lord are m. 25:10
that trusteth in Lord, m. shall. 32:10
them that hope in his m. 33:18
I trust in the m. of God for. 52:8
God shall send forth his m. 57:3
the God of my m. shall prevent me.
59:10, 17
O prepare m. and truth. 61:7
O Lord, belongeth m. 62:12
which hath not turned his m. 66:20
is his m. clean gone for ever? doth
m. fail? 77:8
m. and truth are met together. 85:10
art plenteous in m. 86:5, 15; 103:8
I said, m. shall be built up. 89:2
m. and truth shall go before. 14
my m. will I keep for him for. 28
he hath remembered his m. 98:3
the Lord is good, his m. is. 100:5
sing of m. and judgement. 101:1
the m. of the Lord is from. 103:17
there be none to extend m. 109:12
with the Lord there is m. and. 130:7
in those that hope in his m. 147:11
let not m. and truth forsake. *Pr 3:3*
he that hath m. on the poor. 14:21*
m. and truth shall be to them. 22
he that honoureth God hath m. 31
by m. and truth iniquity is. 16:6
m. and truth preserve the king ... is
upholden by m. 20:28; *Isa 16:5*
he that followeth after m. *Pr 21:21*
he that hath m. on them. *Isa 49:10*
saith the Lord that hath m. 54:10
in my favour have I had m. on. 60:10
are cruel, and have no m. *Jer 6:23*
there is no truth, nor m. *Hos 4:1†*
for I desired m. and not sacrifice.6:6†
reap in m. 10:12†
keep m. and wait on God. 12:6†
the fatherless findeth m. 14:3
they forsake their own m. *Jonah 2:8†*
do justly, and to love m. *Mi 6:8†*
because he delighteth in m. 7:18
perform the m. to Abraham. 20
in wrath remember m. *Hab 3:2*
merciful, shall obtain m. *Mat 5:7*
omitted judgement and m. 23:23
m. is on them that fear. *Luke 1:50*
in remembrance of his m. 54
to perform the m. promised to. 72
remission through the tender m. 78
his glory on vessels of m. *Rom 9:23*
have now obtained m. 11:30
your m. they also may obtain m. 31
might glorify God for his m. 15:9
that hath obtained m. *1 Cor 7:25*
as we have received m. *2 Cor 4:1*
peace be on them, and m. *Gal 6:16*
God who is rich in m. *Eph 2:4*
death, but God had m. on. *Phil 2:27*
m. and peace from God. *1 Tim 1:2*
2 Tim 1:2; Tit 1:4; 2 John 3
I obtained m. because I. *1 Tim 1:13*
for this cause I obtained m. 16

Lord give *m*. to house. *2 Tim* 1:16
that he may find *m*. of the Lord. 18
but according to his *m*. *Tit* 3:5
that we may obtain *m*. *Heb* 4:16
Moses' law died without *m*. 10:28*
judgement without *m*. that shewed
no *m*. and *m*. rejoiceth. *Jas* 2:13
wisdom from above, full of *m*. 3:17
Lord is pitiful, and of tender *m*. 5:11
to his abundant *m*. hath. *1 Pet* 1:3
m. but now have obtained *m*. 2:10
m. to you, peace and love. *Jude* 2
looking for the *m*. of Lord Jesus. 21

have mercy

have m. upon me. *Ps* 4:1; 6:2
9:13; 25:16; 27:7; 30:10; 31:9
51:1; 86:16
shalt *have m*. on Zion. 102:13
have m. on us. 123:2, 3
his sins surely *have m*. *Pr* 28:13
neither *have m*. on their fatherless.
Isa 9:17*
Lord will *have m*. on Jacob. 14:1*
will not *have m*. on them. 27:11*
he may *have m*. on you. 30:18
for God will *have m*. upon. 49:13*
with kindness will I *have m*. 54:8
and he will *have m*. on him. 55:7
nor *have m*. but destroy them.
Jer 13:14*; 21:7
have m. on his dwelling-. 30:18*
I will surely *have m*. on. 31:20
33:26; *Ezek* 39:25; *Hos* 1:7; 2:23
he may *have m*. on you. *Jer* 42:12
no more *have m*. on the house of
Israel. *Hos* 1:6; 2:4
wilt thou not *have m*.? *Zech* 1:12
bring them again, for I *have m*. 10:6
I will *have m*. and not sacrifice.
Mat 9:13; 12:7
Son of David, *have m*. on me. 9:27
15:22; 20:30, 31; *Mark* 10:47, 48
Luke 18:38, 39
Lord, *have m*. on my son. *Mat* 17:15
Abraham, *have m*. on. *Luke* 16:24
Jesus, Master, *have m*. on. 17:13
I will *have m*. on whom I will *have*
m. *Rom* 9:15, 18
that he might *have m*. on all. 11:32

mercy

mercy joined with *shew, shewed*
sheweth, shewing
Lord was with Joseph, and *shewed*
him *m*. *Gen* 39:21*
shewing m. to thousands. *Ex* 20:6
Deut 5:10
I will *shew m*. on whom I will *shew*
m. *Ex* 33:19
no covenant, nor *shew* them *m*.
Deut 7:2
may turn and *shew* thee *m*. 13:17
shew us city, and we will *shew* thee
m. *Judg* 1:24
sheweth m. to his anointed.
2 Sam 22:51; *Ps* 18:50
shewed to thy servant David .
great *m*. *1 Ki* 3:6; *2 Chr* 1:8
shewest m. to thy servants.
2 Chr 6:14
righteous *sheweth m*. *Ps* 37:21*
shew us thy *m*. O Lord, and. 85:7
remembered not to *shew m*. 109:16
didst *shew* them no *m*. *Isa* 47:6
cruel, and will not *shew m*. *Jer* 50:42
thy sins by *shewing m*. *Dan* 4:27
judgement, and *shew m*. *Zech* 7:9
Lord *shewed* great *m*. *Luke* 1:58
he that *shewed m*. on him. 10:37
God that *sheweth m*. *Rom* 9:16
sheweth m. with cheerfulness. 12:8
judgement without *m*. that hath
shewed no *m*. *Jas* 2:13

thy mercy

magnified *thy m*. to me. *Gen* 19:19
in *thy m*. hast led forth. *Ex* 15:13
the greatness of *thy m*. *Num* 14:19
according to *thy m*. *Neh* 13:22
in multitude of *thy m*. *Ps* 5:7
save me for *thy m*.'s sake. 6:4; 31:16
trusted in *thy m*. my heart. 13:5
according to *thy m*. remember. 25:7
rejoice in *thy m*. for thou. 31:7
let *thy m*. O Lord, be upon. 33:22
thy m. O Lord, is in the. 36:5

redeem us, for *thy m*.'s sake. *Ps* 44:26
for *thy m*. is great unto the. 57:10
I will sing aloud of *thy m*. 59:16
in the multitude of *thy m*. 69:13
shew us *thy m*. O Lord. 85:7
great is *thy m*. 86:13
O satisfy us early with *thy m*. 90:14
thy m. O Lord, held me up. 94:18
thy m. is great above heavens. 108:4
because *thy m*. is good. 109:21
save me according to *thy m*. 26
for *thy m*. and for thy truth's. 115:1
earth is full of *thy m*. 119:64
servant according to *thy m*. 124
thy m. endureth for ever. 138:8
and of *thy m*. cut off mine. 143:12

mercy seat

(*The golden covering of the ark of
the covenant, in which the tables
of the law were deposited*)
make a *m*. *seat* of gold. *Ex* 25:17
the cherubims covering the *m*. *seat*
with their wings. 20; *Heb* 9:5
m. *seat* between the cherubims.
Ex 25:22; *Lev* 16:2; *Num* 7:89
shalt put the *m*. *seat* upon the ark.
Ex 26:34; 40:20
made the *m*. *seat* of pure gold. 37:6
incense may cover *m*. *seat*. *Lev* 16:13
David gave Solomon the pattern of
the *m*. *seat*. *1 Chr* 28:11

Meribah

name of the place *M*. *Ex* 17:7
water of *M*. *Num* 20:13; 27:14
rebelled at water of *M*. 20:24
Deut 32:51; 33:8
thee at the waters of *M*. *Ps* 81:7

Merodach

Babylon taken, *M*. is. *Jer* 50:2

Merodach-baladan

M. sent letters and a. *Isa* 39:1

Merom

at the waters of *M*. *Josh* 11:5, 7

Meroz

Curse ye *M*. said angel. *Judg* 5:23

merrily

go in *m*. with the king. *Esth* 5:14

merry

they drank and were *m*. *Gen* 43:34
grapes, and made *m*. *Judg* 9:27*
when their hearts were *m*. 16:25
and let thine heart be *m*. 19:6
that thine heart may be *m*. 9
were making their hearts *m*. 22
Boaz, his heart was *m*. *Ruth* 3:7
Nabal's heart was *m*. *1 Sam* 25:36
Amnon's heart is *m*. *2 Sam* 13:28
Israel were making *m*. *1 Ki* 4:20
and let thine heart be *m*. 21:7
people away *m*. in heart. *2 Chr* 7:10*
heart of the king was *m*. *Esth* 1:10
m. heart maketh cheerful. *Pr* 15:13
he that is of a *m*. heart hath. 15*
a *m*. heart doeth good like a. 17:22
than to eat and be *m*. *Eccl* 8:15
drink thy wine with a *m*. heart. 9:7
laughter, wine maketh *m*. 10:19*
all the *m*.-hearted do sigh. *Isa* 24:7
them that make *m*. *Jer* 30:19
dances of them that make *m*. 31:4
eat, drink, and be *m*. *Luke* 12:19
let us eat and be *m*. 15:23, 24
I might make *m*. with my friends. 29
it was meet we should make *m*. 32
is any *m*.? let him sing. *Jas* 5:13*
over them and make *m*. *Rev* 11:10

Meshach, see Abed-nego

Meshech

M. the son of Japheth. *Gen* 10:2
1 Chr 1:5
Shem, Elam, and *M*. *1 Chr* 1:17
that I sojourn in *M*. *Ps* 120:5
Tubal and *M*. were thy. *Ezek* 27:13
there is *M*. 32:26
chief prince of *M*. 38:2, 3
the chief prince of *M*. and. 39:1

Mesopotamia

Eliezer went to *M*. to. *Gen* 24:10
they hired Balaam of *M*. *Deut* 23:4
Chushan-rishathaim king of *M*.
Judg 3:8
Lord delivered the king of *M*. 10

sent to hire chariots out of *M*.
1 Chr 19:6
the dwellers in *M*. we hear. *Acts* 2:9
God appeared to Abraham in *M*. 7:2

message

Ehud said, I have a *m*. from God.
Judg 3:20
had heard this *m*. *1 Ki* 20:12
that sendeth a *m*. by a fool. *Pr* 26:6
Haggai in the Lord's *m*. *Hag* 1:13
his citizens sent a *m*. *Luke* 19:14*
this is the *m*. which we have heard.
1 John 1:5; 3:11

messenger

sent a *m*. to Joseph. *Gen* 50:16*
the *m*. said, Israel. *1 Sam* 15:13
m. to David, saying. *2 Sam* 15:13
then Jezebel sent a *m*. *1 Ki* 19:2
the *m*. went to call Micaiah. 22:13
2 Chr 18:12
ere *m*. came to him, Elisha said,
When the *m*. cometh. *2 Ki* 6:32
the *m*. came to them, but. 9:18
there came a *m*. to Job. *Job* 1:14
a *m*. an interpreter of a. 33:23*
a wicked *m*. falleth into. *Pr* 13:17
a cruel *m*. shall be sent. 17:11
so is a faithful *m*. to them. 25:13
deaf, as my *m*. that I sent? *Isa* 42:19
one *m*. shall run to meet. *Jer* 51:31
unto whom a *m*.was sent. *Ezek* 23:40
Haggai, the Lord's *m*. *Hag* 1:13
for he is the *m*. of the Lord. *Mal* 2:7
will send my *m*. even the *m*. of. 3:1
Mat 11:10; *Mark* 1:2; *Luke* 7:27
the *m*. of Satan, to. *2 Cor* 12:7
in labour, but your *m*. *Phil* 2:25

messengers

Jacob sent *m*. before him. *Gen* 32:3
Moses sent *m*. from Kadesh.
Num 20:14; *Deut* 2:26
Israel sent *m*. unto Sihon, saying.
Num 21:21
Balak sent *m*. to Balaam. 22:5
spake I not also to thy *m*.? 24:12
Rahab hid the *m*. *Josh* 6:17, 25
Joshua sent *m*. to Achan's. 7:22
Gideon sent *m*. through. *Judg* 6:35
Jephthah sent *m*. to king. 11:12, 14
came the *m*. to Gibeah. *1 Sam* 11:4
Saul sent *m*. to Jesse, and. 16:19
Saul sent *m*. to David. 19:11, 14
15, 20, 21
David sent *m*. to salute our. 25:14
Abigail went after the *m*. 42
m. to Jabesh-gilead. *2 Sam* 2:5
Abner sent *m*. to David on. 3:12
David sent *m*. to Ish-bosheth. 14
Joab sent *m*. after Abner. 26
Hiram sent *m*. to David. 5:11
1 Chr 14:1
David sent *m*. to Bath-sheba, and.
2 Sam 11:4
Joab sent *m*. to David. 12:27
Ben-hadad sent *m*. to. *1 Ki* 20:2
go up to meet the *m*. *2 Ki* 1:3
sent *m*. to enquire of Baal-zebub. 16
Amaziah sent *m*. to Jehoash. 14:8
Ahaz sent *m*. to Tiglath-pileser. 16:7
Hoshea had sent *m*. to So. 17:4
Sennacherib sent *m*. to Hezekiah.
19:9; *Isa* 37:9
by thy *m*. hast thou reproached.
2 Ki 19:23
David sent *m*. to comfort Hanun.
1 Chr 19:2
sent to them by his *m*. *2 Chr* 36:15
but they mocked the *m*. of God. 16
wrath of a king is as *m*. *Pr* 16:14
what shall one answer *m*.? *Isa* 14:32
swift *m*. to nation scattered. 18:2
Hezekiah received letter from *m*.
37:14
the counsel of his *m*. 44:26
and thou didst send thy *m*. 57:9*
send by the hand of the *m*. *Jer* 27:3
sent *m*. unto them into. *Ezek* 23:16
in that day shall *m*. go forth. 30:9
the voice of thy *m*. be no. *Nah* 2:13
and when the *m*. of John. *Luke* 7:24
and sent *m*. before his face. 9:52
they are the *m*. of the. *2 Cor* 8:23
Rahab had received *m*. *Jas* 2:25

mess, or messes
sent *m.* to them, but Benjamin's *m.*
  five times so much.   *Gen* 43:34
a *m.* of meat.   *2 Sam* 11:8

Messiah
(*Literally, the Anointed One. It means the expected king and deliverer of the Hebrews, who should free them from the yoke of aliens, and make them a great nation ruling over the whole world. Christ is the same word in the Greek. Jesus of Nazareth, believed by his followers to be this long-promised Messiah of the Jews, is for that reason called Christ. The first promise of the Messiah, although not using that name, is that to Eve in Gen 3:15. The same promise was, in varying phraseology, repeated to many individuals through the ages, notably to Abraham and David*)
to build Jerusalem unto the *M.* the
  Prince.   *Dan* 9:25*
and after 62 weeks shall *M.* be. 26*
found *M.* which is Christ. *John* 1:41
woman saith, I know that *M.* 4:25

met
and the angels of God *m. Gen* 32:1
thou by this drove I *m.?*   33:8
God of the Hebrews hath *m.* with us.
            Ex 3:18; 5:3
the Lord *m.* him, and sought. 4:24
Aaron went and *m.* Moses in.   27
they *m.* Moses and Aaron who. 5:20
God *m.* Balaam.   *Num* 23:4, 16
because they *m.* you not. *Deut* 23:4
          Neh 13:2
Amalek *m.* thee by way. *Deut* 25:18
all these kings were *m.* *Josh* 11:5
of prophets *m.* Saul. *1 Sam* 10:10
behold, Abigail *m.* David.   25:20
Ziba *m.* David with. *2 Sam* 16:1
Absalom *m.* the servants of. 18:9
a lion *m.* him.   *1 Ki* 13:24
Elijah *m.* Obadiah, and he. 18:7
Ahaziah *m.* Jehu.   *2 Ki* 9:21*
Jehu *m.* with the brethren. 10:13
mercy and truth are *m.* *Ps* 85:10
there *m.* him a woman.   *Pr* 7:10
a lion, and bear *m.* him. *Amos* 5:19
behold, Jesus *m.* them, saying. 28:9
where two ways *m.*   *Mark* 11:4*
much people *m.* him.   *Luke* 9:37
         John 12:18
there *m.* him ten men. *Luke* 17:12
then Martha went and *m.* him.
       John 11:20, 30
Cornelius *m.* him, and. *Acts* 10:25
damsel possessed *m.* us.   16:16
he disputed with them that *m.* 17:17
place where two seas *m.*   27:41
who *m.* Abraham.   *Heb* 7:1
when Melchizedek *m.* him.   10

mete
when they did *m.* it with. *Ex* 16:18
I will *m.* out valley. *Ps* 60:6; 108:7
with what measure ye *m.* it shall be.
  Mat 7:2; *Mark* 4:24; *Luke* 6:38

meted
go to a nation *m.* out. *Isa* 18:2, 7
m. out heaven with a span. 40:12

meteyard
no unrightequsness in *m. Lev* 19:35

Metheg-ammah
David took *M.* from.   *2 Sam* 8:1

Methuselah
Enoch begat *M.*   *Gen* 5:21
M. begat Lamech.   25
days of *M.* were 969 years.   27
Henoch, *M.* Lamech.   *1 Chr* 1:3
which was the son of *M. Luke* 3:37

Micah
mount Ephraim called *M. Judg* 17:1
man *M.* had an house of gods. 5
M. consecrated the Levite for. 12
thus dealeth *M.*   18:4
they set up *M.*'s graven image. 31
M. his son, Reaia his. *1 Chr* 5:5
Merib-baal begat *M.* 8:34; 9:40

---

sons of *M.* were Pithon, and Melech.
    1 Chr 8:35; 9:41
Mattaniah the son of *M.*   9:15
Abdon the son of *M.* *2 Chr* 34:20
M., Rehob, sealed the. *Neh* 10:11
M. the Morasthite prophesied in.
    Jer 26:18; *Mi* 1:1

Micaiah
M. the son of Imlah.   *1 Ki* 22:8, 9
        2 Chr 18:8
Zedekiah smote *M.* on. *1 Ki* 22:24
Take *M.*, and carry him back to
  Amon.   26; *2 Chr* 18:23, 25

mice
five golden *m.*   *1 Sam* 6:4, 18
images of your emerods and *m.* 5

Michael
M. one of the chief.   *Dan* 10:13
none holdeth with me but *M.* 21
at that time shall *M.* stand. 12:1
yet *M.* the archangel.   *Jude* 9
M. and angels fought.   *Rev* 12:7

Michaiah
mother was *M.* of Uriel. *2 Chr* 13:2
Jehoshaphat sent *M.* to teach. 17:7
son of *M.* to give. *Neh* 12:35, 41
M. heard what Baruch. *Jer* 36:11, 13

Michal
younger daughter *M.* *1 Sam* 14:49
M. Saul's daughter.   18:20, 28
so *M.* let David down.   19:12
M. took an image and laid.   13
Saul had given *M.* David's. 25:44
thou first bring *M.* *2 Sam* 3:13
deliver me my wife *M.* whom. 14
M. Saul's daughter looked . . . and
  despised.   6:16; *1 Chr* 15:29
M. had no child to.   *2 Sam* 6:23
king took five sons of *M.*   21:8

midday
when *m.* was past.   *1 Ki* 18:29
from morning to *m.*   *Neh* 8:3
at *m.* O king, I saw in. *Acts* 26:13

middle
beginning of *m.* watch. *Judg* 7:19
there come people by the *m.* 9:37
hold of the two *m.* pillars. 16:29
of the *m.* of a sling. *1 Sam* 25:29
their garments in the *m.* *2 Sam* 10:4
the king did hallow the *m.* of the
  court.   *1 Ki* 8:64; *2 Chr* 7:7
gone into the *m.* court. *2 Ki* 20:4
princes sat in the *m.* gate. *Jer* 39:3
were a wheel in the *m. Ezek* 1:16
broken down the *m.* wall. *Eph* 2:14

middlemost
higher than the *m.*   *Ezek* 42:5, 6

Midian
dwelt in the land of *M.* *Ex* 2:15
Jethro priest of *M.* heard all. 18:1
said to the elders of *M. Num* 22:4
Zur of a chief house in *M.* 25:15
go and avenge the Lord of *M.* 31:3
they slew the kings of *M.* beside. 8
Israel took all the women of *M.* 9
delivered them to *M.* *Judg* 6:1, 2
hand hath God delivered *M.* 7:14
delivered us from *M.* 8:22; 9:17
M. subdued before Israel. 28
Edomites arose out of *M. 1 Ki* 11:18
the yoke, as in day of *M.* *Isa* 9:4
the slaughter of *M.* at Oreb. 10:26
the dromedaries of *M.* shall. 60:6
curtains of the land of *M. Hab* 3:7

Midianites
by *M.* merchantmen.   *Gen* 37:28
the *M.* sold him into Egypt to. 36
vex *M.* and smite them. *Num* 25:17
avenge Israel of the *M.*   31:2
to the Lord because of *M. Judg* 6:7
and thou shalt smite the *M.* 16
Israel pursued after the *M.* 7:23
princes of the *M.* Oreb, Zeeb. 25
wentest to yield with the *M.* 8:1
do to them as to the *M.* *Ps* 83:9

Midianitish
brought a *M.* woman. *Num* 25:6
of the *M.* woman was Cozbi. 15

midnight
at *m.* will I go into the. *Ex* 11:4
at *m.* the Lord smote the. 12:29

---

till *m.* and rose at *m.*   *Judg* 16:3
at *m.* the man was afraid. *Ruth* 3:8
she arose at *m.* and.   *1 Ki* 3:20
shall be troubled at *m.* *Job* 34:20
at *m.* I will rise to.   *Ps* 119:62
at *m.* there was a cry. *Mat* 25:6
come at even, or *m.* *Mark* 13:35
at *m.* and say, Lend me. *Luke* 11:5
and at *m.* Paul and. *Acts* 16:25
continued his speech till *m.* 20:7

midst
dry through *m.* of sea. *Ex* 14:16
  Num 33:8; *Neh* 9:11; *Ps* 136:14
take sickness from *m.* *Ex* 23:25
mountain burnt to the *m. Deut* 4:11
evil away from the *m.* of thee. 13:5
raise up a Prophet from *m.* 18:15
from the *m.* of the furnace of iron.
          1 Ki 8:51
brook that ran through the *m.* of.
        2 Chr 32:4
m. thereof being paved. *S of S* 3:10
purged blood from the *m.* *Isa* 4:4
breath shall reach to the *m.* 30:28
take away from the *m.* of thee. 58:9
proceed from the *m.* of. *Jer* 30:21
come from the *m.* of Sihon. 48:45
through the *m.* of the city. *Ezek* 9:4
glory went up from *m.* of city. 11:23
I will cut him off from *m.* 14:8, 9
m. of it is burnt, is it meet? 15:4
have filled the *m.* of thee.   28:16
I will bring forth a fire from *m.* of. 18
of the *m.* of the fire.   *Dan* 3:26
judge from *m.* thereof. *Amos* 2:3
passing through the *m.* *Luke* 4:30
about the *m.* of the feast. *John* 7:14
going through the *m.* of them. 8:59
angel flying through the *m. Rev* 8:13

in the midst
be a firmament *in the m.* *Gen* 1:6
the tree of life *in the m.* 2:9; 3:3
Abram divided them *in the m.* 15:10
wonders I will do *in the m. Ex* 3:20
I am the Lord *in the m.* of. 8:22
overthrew Egyptians *in the m.* 14:27
walked on dry land *in the m.* of sea.
           29; 15:19
for I will not go up *in the m.* 33:3
in the m. of their uncleanness.
        Lev 16:16
set forward *in the m.* of camp.
        Num 2:17
defile not the camp *in the m.* 5:3
and the city shall be *in the m.* 35:5
        Ezek 48:15
acts which he did *in the m.* of.
        Deut 11:3
swallowed them up *in the m.* 6
separate three cities *in the m.* 19:2
God walketh *in the m.* of. 23:14
priests stood firm *in the m.* of
  Jordan.   *Josh* 3:17; 4:10
set up twelve stones *in the m.* 4:9
accursed thing *in the m.* of. 7:13
are hid in the earth *in the m.* 21
anointed him *in the m. 1 Sam* 16:13
was yet alive *in the m. 2 Sam* 18:14
stood *in the m.* of the ground. 23:12
a lion *in the m.* of a pit in time. 20
they were *in the m.* of Samaria.
        1 Ki 6:20
their garments *in the m. 1 Chr* 19:4
till we come *in the m.* *Neh* 4:11
it is melted *in the m.* of. *Ps* 22:14
will declare thy name: *in the m.* of
  the congregation. 22; *Heb* 2:12
God is *in the m.* of her, she. *Ps* 46:5
mischief *in the m.*   55:10
wickedness *in the m.*   11
enemies roar *in the m.* of. 74:4
working salvation *in the m.* 12
and he let it fall *in the m.* 78:28
take me not away *in the m.* 102:24
rule thou *in the m.* of thine. 110:2
pay vows *in the m.* of thee. 116:19
I walk *in the m.* of trouble. 138:7
keep them *in the m.* of. *Pr* 4:21
I was in all evil *in the m.* 5:14
I lead *in the m.* of the paths. 8:20
which is *in the m.* of fools. 14:33
he that lieth down *in the m.* 23:34
the way of a ship *in the m.* 30:19

a tower in the m. of it.   Isa 5:2
I dwell in the m. of a people.   6:5
forsaking in the m. of the land.   12
set a king in the m. of it, the.   7:6
Holy One in the m. 12:6; Hos 11:9
in the m. of the noon day. Isa 16:3
blessing in the m. of the land. 19:24
fountains in the m. of thee.   41:18
oppression in the m. of her. Jer 6:6
is in the m. of deceit.   9:6
O Lord, art in the m. of us.   14:9
in the m. of his days.   17:11
in the m. of the people.   37:12
the just in the m. of her. Lam 4:13
in the m. of the nations. Ezek 5:5
will execute judgement in the m.   8
fall in the m. of you.   6:7; 11:7
in the m. of Babylon he.   17:16
sheddeth blood in the m.   22:3
ye shall be melted in the m.   21
as silver is melted in the m. of.   22
many widows in the m. thereof.   25
her princes in the m. thereof.   27
thus have they done in the m. 23:39
for spreading of nets in the m. 26:5
be glorified in the m. of thee. 28:22
profaned in the m. of them. 36:23
sanctuary in the m. of them. 37:26
my sanctuary shall be in the m. 28
dwell in the m. of Israel. 43:7, 9
and the prince in the m.   46:10
men walking in the m.   Dan 3:25
in the m. of the week.   9:27
whoredoms is in the m.   Hos 5:4
I am in the m. of Israel. Joel 2:27
conspired in the m.   Amos 7:10
remnant be in the m. of. Mi 5:7, 8
thy casting down shall be in the m.
    of thee.   6:14
people in the m. of thee. Nah 3:13
in the m. of the years.   Hab 3:2
lie down in the m. of her. Zeph 2:14
just Lord is in the m. thereof.   3:5
I will leave in the m. of thee a.   12
king of Israel, even the Lord, is in the
    m. of thee.   15, 17
glory in the m. of her.   Zech 2:5
will dwell in the m. of thee. 10, 11
remain in the m. of his house. 5:4
sitteth in the m. of the ephah.   7
in the m. of Jerusalem.   8:3, 8
mount of Olives shall cleave in the
    m. thereof.   14:4
sheep in the m. of wolves. Mat 10:16
ship was in the m. of the sea. 14:24
    Mark 6:47
set a little child in the m. of them.
    Mat 18:2; Mark 9:36
am I in the m. of them. Mat 18:20
in the m. of the doctors. Luke 2:46
rise, and stand forth in the m.   6:8
let them which are in the m. 21:21
the vail was rent in the m.   23:45
Jesus himself stood in the m.
    24:36; John 20:19, 26
had set her in the m. John 8:3, 9
one, and Jesus in the m.   19:18
Peter stood up in the m. Acts 1:15
falling, he burst asunder in the m. 18
then Paul stood up in the m. 17:22
blameless in the m. of a. Phil 2:15
in the m. of the seven candlesticks.
    Rev 1:13; 2:1
in the m. of the Paradise of.   2:7
in the m. of the throne were.   4:6
in the m. of the throne stood.   5:6
    7:17

into the midst
Israel went into the m.   Ex 14:22
and Moses went into the m. 24:18
I will come into the m. of thee. 33:5
Aaron ran into the m. Num 16:47
blood ran into the m. 1 Ki 22:35
Mordecai went into the m. of the
    city.   Esth 4:1
carried into the m. of sea. Ps 46:2
into the m. whereof they are. 57:6
I will assemble them into the m.
    Jer 21:4
cast it into the m. of river. 51:63
into the m. of the fire. Ezek 5:4
I will gather you into the m. 22:19
into the m. of a fiery. Dan 3:6
and he cast it into the m. Zech 5:8

out of the midst
sent Lot out of the m. Gen 19:29
angel appeared out of the m. of a
    bush.   Ex 3:2
God called to him out of the m. of
    bush.   4; 24:16
spake unto you out of the m. of fire.
    Deut 4:12; 15, 33, 36; 5:4, 22, 24
take him a nation out of the m. 4:34
take out of the m. of Jordan twelve
    stones.   Josh 4:3, 8
they took them out of the m.   7:23
cometh out of the m. of pit. Isa 24:18
depart, go out of the m. of her. 52:11
    Jer 50:8; 51:6, 45
forth out of the m. of it. Ezek 11:7
I will bring thee out of the m. 29:4
to him out of the m. of hell. 32:21
eat calves out of the m. Amos 6:4
cut off horses out of the m. Mi 5:10
pluck up groves out of the m. 14
take away out of the m. Zeph 3:11

midwive
the m. said unto Rachel. Gen 35:17
the m. bound on his hand a. 38:28
ye do the office of a m. Ex 1:16

midwives
but the m. feared God. Ex 1:17, 21
are delivered ere the m. come. 19
God dealt well with the m. 20

might, substantive
art my firstborn, my m. Gen 49:3
this people in thy m. Num 14:13
according to thy m. Deut 3:24
love thy God with all thy m. 6:5
the m. of mine hand hath. 8:17
be no m. in thine hand. 28:32
goeth forth in his m. Judg 5:31
go in this thy m. 6:14
bowed with his m. 6:14
danced with all his m. 2 Sam 6:14
Asa, and all his m. 1 Ki 15:23
Baasha, and his m. 16:5
Omri and his m. 27
Jehoshaphat and his m. that. 22:45
Jehu and all his m. 2 Ki 10:34
Jehoahaz and his m. 13:8
acts of Jehoash and his m. 14:15
Hezekiah and his m. 20:20
to the Lord with all his m. 23:25
captive all the men of m. 24:16
men of m. came to David. 1 Chr 12:8
for the house with all my m. 29:2
in thine hand is power and m. 12
    2 Chr 20:6
acts of David ... with all his reign
    and his m. 1 Chr 29:30
we have no m. against. 2 Chr 20:12
his power and m. Esth 10:2
none of the men of m. Ps 76:5
men shall speak of the m. 145:6
to do, do it with thy m. Eccl 9:10
the spirit of counsel and m. Isa 11:2
near, acknowledge my m. 33:13
by the greatness of his m. 40:26
no m. he increaseth strength. 29
mighty man glory in his m. Jer 9:23
and thy name is great in m. 10:6
cause them to know my m. 16:21
break the chief of their m. 49:35
m. hath failed, they became. 51:30
ashamed of their m. Ezek 32:30
for wisdom and m. are. Dan 2:20
O God, who hast given me m. 23
that I have built by the m. 4:30
full of judgement and m. Mi 3:8
be confounded at all their m. 7:16
not by m. nor by power, but. Zech 4:6
far above all m., power. Eph 1:21
strengthened with m. 3:16; Col 1:11
and in power of his m. Eph 6:10
whereas angels, which are greater in
    m. 2 Pet 2:11
m. be unto out God. Rev 7:12

might be
I would it m. be according to.
    Gen 30:34
tent, that it m. be one. Ex 36:18
it m. be above the curious. 19:21
that I m. be their God. Lev 26:45
fear me, that it m. be. Deut 5:29
that he m. be the king's. 1 Sam 18:27
that my name m. be. 1 Ki 8:16

windows, m. this thing be. 2 Ki 7:2
silver, that his hand m. be. 15:19
my name m. be there. 2 Chr 6:5, 6
m. not be as their fathers. Ps 78:8
that they m. be unto me. Jer 13:11
in good soil, that it m. be. Ezek 17:8
that ye m. be a possession to. 36:3
that my covenant m. be. Mal 2:4
prayed that he m. be with him.
    Mark 5:18; Luke 8:38
what m. this parable be? Luke 8:9
that your joy m. be full. John 15:11
m. be the father of them. Rom 4:11
that it m. be of grace. 16
m. be Lord both of dead and. 14:9
m. not be chargeable. 2 Thes 3:8
though I m. be much bold. Philem 8
m. be a merciful Priest. Heb 2:17
we m. be partakers of his. 12:10
and hope m. be in God. 1 Pet 1:21

see fulfilled

mightier
for thou art much m. Gen 26:16
children of Israel are m. Ex 1:9
nation and m. than they. Num 14:12
    Deut 4:38; 7:1; 9:1, 14; 11:23
the Lord on high is m. Ps 93:4
contend with him that is m. Eccl 6:10
he that cometh after me is m. than I.
    Mat 3:11; Mark 1:7; Luke 3:16

mighties
one of the three m. 1 Chr 11:12
these things did these three m. 19
had a name among the three m. 24

mightily
that ye may increase m. Deut 6:3
Jabin m. oppressed Israel. Jude 4:3
came m. on Samson. 14:6; 15:14
the Lord shall m. roar. Jer 25:30
let man and beast cry m. Jonah 3:8
fortify thy power m. Nah 2:1
m. convinced the Jews. Acts 18:28
so m. grew the word of God. 19:20
which worketh in me m. Col 1:29
cried m. saying, Babylon. Rev 18:2

mighty
he was a m. hunter. Gen 10:9
become a great and m. nation. 18:18
hear us: thou art a m. prince. 23:6
of Israel waxed m. Ex 1:7, 20
be no more m. thunderings. 9:28
the Lord turned a m. strong. 10:19
as lead in the m. waters. 15:10
nor shall honour the person of the m.
    Lev 19:15
people, for they are too m. Num 22:6
he brought them out with m. power.
    Deut 4:37; 9:29
shall destroy them with a m. 7:23
great nation, m. and populous. 26:5
have dominion over the m. Judg 5:13
help of the Lord against the m. 23
hand of these m. gods. 1 Sam 4:8
how are m. fallen! 2 Sam 1:19, 25
the shield of the m. is vilely. 21
the slain, from fat of the m. 22
m. of the land carried. 2 Ki 24:15
Nimrod was m. 1 Chr 1:10
Zadok was m. 12:28
Benaiah was m. 27:6
Abijah was m. 2 Chr 13:21
made war with m. power. 26:13
so Jotham became m. 27:6
there have been m. kings. Ezra 4:20
mercy to me before m. princes. 7:28
repaired to house of the m. Neh 3:16
a stone in the m. waters. 9:11
the poor from the there. Job 5:15
from the hand of the m.? 6:23
he is wise in heart, and m. 9:4
and he overthroweth the m. 12:19
the strength of the m. 21
the wicked m. in power? 21:7
draweth also the m. with. 24:22
the m. shall be taken away. 34:20
by reason of the arm of the m. 35:9
he raiseth himself, the m. 41:25
and m., Lord m. in battle. Ps 24:8
give to the Lord, O ye m. 29:1
sword on thy thigh, O most m. 45:3
for lo, the m. are gathered. 59:3
his voice, and that a m. voice. 68:33

enemies wrongfully are *m.*   *Ps* 69:4
thou driest up *m.* rivers.   74:15
in the congregation of the *m.*   82:1
among sons *m.* can be likened ? 89:6
thou hast a *m.* arm.   13
laid help upon one that is *m.*   19
bosom the reproach of the *m.*   50
mightier than the *m.* waves.   93:4
make his *m.* power known.   106:8
his seed shall be *m.* upon.   112:2
sharp arrows of the *m.* with.   120:4
nations, and slew *m.* kings. 135:10
he that is slow to anger is better than
   the *m.*   *Pr* 16:32
the lot parteth between the *m.* 18:18
scaleth the city of the *m.*   21:22
for their Redeemer is *m.*   23:11*
m. shall fall in the war   *Isa* 3:25
that are *m.* to drink wine.   5:22
his *m.* wind shall he shake.   11:15
like the rushing of *m.* waters. 17:12
away with a *m.* captivity.   22:17
prey be taken from the *m.*?   49:24
in righteousness, *m.* to save.   63:1
a *m.* and an ancient nation. *Jer* 5:15
great in counsel and *m.*   32:19
shew thee great and *m.* things. 33:3
hath also taken the *m.*   *Ezek* 17:13
by the swords of the *m.* will.   32:12
the strong among the *m.* shall.   21
shall not lie with the *m.* that.   27
with a great and *m.* army.   38:15
eat the flesh of the *m.* and.   39:18
how great and *m.* are his. *Dan* 4:3
his power shall be *m.* but not. 8:24
a *m.* king shall stand up that. 11:3
a very great and *m.* army.   25
the *m.* deliver himself. *Amos* 2:14
courageous among the *m.*   2:16
I know your *m.* sins.   5:12
righteousness as a *m.* stream.   24
a *m.* tempest in the sea. *Jonah* 1:4
howl, because the *m.*   *Zech* 11:2
most of his *m.* works.   *Mat* 11:20
if the *m.* works which were.   21, 23
this man these *m.* works ?   13:54
he did not many *m.* works there.   58
               Mark 6:5
Baptist risen; therefore *m.* works do
   shew forth. *Mat* 14:2; *Mark* 6:14
m. works are wrought by. *Mark* 6:2
he that is *m.* hath done. *Luke* 1:49
he hath put down the *m.* from.   52
amazed at *m.* power of God.   9:43
there arose a *m.* famine in.   15:14
praised God for the *m.* works. 19:37
who was a prophet *m.* in deed. 24:19
as of a rushing *m.* wind. *Acts* 2:2
Moses was *m.* in words and.   7:22
Apollos, *m.* in the scriptures. 18:24
Gentiles obedient through *m.* signs.
               Rom 15:19
not many *m.* not many.   *1 Cor* 1:26
weak, to confound things *m.*   27
weapons of our warfare are *m.*
   through God.   *2 Cor* 10:4
is not weak, but *m.* in you.   13:3
same was *m.* in me toward. *Gal* 2:8
working of his *m.* power. *Eph* 1:19
Jesus shall be revealed with his *m.*
   angels.   *2 Thes* 1:7
shaken of a *m.* wind.   *Rev* 6:13
I saw another *m.* angel. 10:1; 18:21
so *m.* an earthquake and.   16:18
Alas, Babylon, that *m.* city !   18:10
voice of *m.* thunderings.   19:6
see **acts, God, hand, man, men**

mighty *one*
Nimrod began to be a *m.* one.
               Gen 10:8
the *m.* one of Israel.   *Isa* 1:24
     30:29; 49:26; 60:16
Lebanon shall fall by *m.* one. 10:34
Lord hath a *m.* and strong one. 28:2
me as a *m.* terrible one. *Jer* 20:11
him into hand of *m.* one. *Ezek* 31:11

mighty *ones*
prancing of their *m.* ones. *Judg* 5:22
I have called my *m.* ones. *Isa* 13:3
their *m.* ones are beaten. *Jer* 46:5
thither cause thy *m.* ones. *Joel* 3:11

Milcah
M. daughter of Haran.   *Gen* 11:29

M. also bare children. *Gen* 22:20, 23
Bethuel son of *M.* the wife.   24:15
daughter's name was *M. Num* 26:33

milch
thirty *m.* camels with.   *Gen* 32:15
make a new cart, take two *m.* kine.
           2 Sam 6:7, 10

Milcom
Solomon went after *M.*   *1 Ki* 11:5
they have worshipped *M.* god.   33
had builded for *M.*   *2 Ki* 23:13

mildew, *see* **blasting**

mile
compel thee to go a *m.*   *Mat* 5:41

Miletum
have I left at *M.* sick.   *2 Tim* 4:20

Miletus
next day we came to *M. Acts* 20:15
from *M.* he sent to Ephesus to.   17

milk
*An important article of food in the
East. Not only the milk of cows,
but also that of sheep,* Deut 32:14,
of camels, Gen 32:15, *and of goats,*
Pr 27:27, *was used. The latter
was most highly esteemed.*

took butter and *m.*   *Gen* 18:8
teeth shall be white with *m.* 49:12
butter of kine and *m. Deut* 32:14
Jael opened a bottle of *m. Judg* 4:19
water, and she gave him *m.*   5:25
poured me out as *m.*?   *Job* 10:10
his breasts are full of *m.*   21:24
thou shalt have goats' *m. Pr* 27:27
the churning of *m.* bringeth.   30:33
honey and *m.* are under. *S of S* 4:11
drunk my wine with my *m.*   5:1
his eyes washed with *m.* and.   12
for abundance of *m.* that. *Isa* 7:22
are weaned from the *m.*   28:9
come, buy wine and *m.* without. 55:1
thou shalt suck the *m.* of.   60:16
were whiter than *m.*   *Lam* 4:7
fruit, and drink thy *m. Ezek* 25:4
hills shall flow with *m.*   *Joel* 3:18
I have fed you with *m.*   *1 Cor* 3:2
flock, and eateth not of the *m.*? 9:7
such as have need of the *m. Heb* 5:12
that useth *m.* is a babe.   13
desire sincere *m.* of word. *1 Pet* 2:2
see **flowing**

milk
that ye may *m.* out and. *Isa* 66:11

mill, -s
that is behind the *m.*   *Ex* 11:5
ground the manna in *m. Num* 11:8
shall be grinding at the *m. Mat* 24:41

millet
take lentiles, *m.* and.   *Ezek* 4:9

millions
be thou mother of thousands of *m.*
           Gen 24:60

Millo
all the house of *M.*   *Judg* 9:6
let fire devour the house of *M.*   20
built round about from *M. 2 Sam* 5:9
of the levy to build *M.*   *1 Ki* 9:15
did Solomon build *M.*   24; 11:27
Joash in the house of *M. 2 Ki* 12:20

millstone
no man shall take the *m. Deut* 24:6
woman cast a piece of *m. Judg* 9:53
          2 Sam 11:21
a piece of the nether *m. Job* 41:24
a *m.* were hanged about his neck.
   Mat 18:6; *Mark* 9:42; *Luke* 17:2
a stone like a great *m. Rev* 18:21
sound of a *m.* shall be heard.   22

millstones
the *m.* and grind meal.   *Isa* 47:2
away the sound of the *m. Jer* 25:10

mincing
wanton eyes, walking and *m. Isa* 3:16

mind, *substantive*
a grief of *m.* to Isaac. *Gen* 26:35
m. of the Lord might. *Lev* 24:12*
all the desire of his *m. Deut* 18:6
give they sorrow of *m.*   28:65*
shalt call them to *m.* among.   30:1
him with a willing *m.*   *1 Chr* 28:9

---

people had a *m.* to work.   *Neh* 4:6
but he is in one *m.* who ? *Job* 23:13
dead man out of *m.*   *Ps* 31:12
with a wicked *m.*   *Pr* 21:27
all his *m.* but a wise man.   29:11*
perfect peace, whose *m.*   *Isa* 26:3
bring it again to *m.* O ye.   46:8
shall not come into *m.*   65:17
covenant shall not come to *m.*
            Jer 3:16
and came it not into his *m.*? 44:21
his *m.* was hardened.   *Dan* 5:20*
then shall his *m.* change. *Hab* 1:11
clothed, and in his right *m.*
   Mark 5:15; *Luke* 8:35
called to *m.* the words. *Mark* 14:72
Mary cast in her *m.*   *Luke* 1:29
neither be ye of doubtful *m.*   12:29
received word with all readiness of
   m.   *Acts* 17:11
serve with humility of *m.*   20:19
given up to a reprobate *m. Rom* 1:28
with the *m.* I serve the law.   7:25
carnal *m.* is enmity against.   8:7
he knoweth what is the *m.* of.   27
who hath known the *m.* of ?   11:34
be of the same *m.* one toward. 12:16
fully persuaded in his own *m.*   14:5
with one *m.* glorify God.   15:6
together in the same *m.*   *1 Cor* 1:10
known the *m.* of the Lord ? . . . but
   we have the *m.* of Christ.   2:16
your fervent *m.* toward me. *2 Cor* 7:7
there be first a willing.   8:12*
brethren, be of one *m.*   13:11
        Phil 1:27*; 2:2
desires of the flesh and *m. Eph* 2:3
walk in vanity of their *m.*   4:17
in lowliness of *m.* let each. *Phil* 2:3
let this *m.* be in you which.   5
that they be of the same *m.*   4:2
puffed up by his fleshly *m. Col* 2:18
humbleness of *m.*, meekness. 3:12*
not soon shaken in *m.*   *2 Thes* 2
God hath given us the spirit of a
   sound *m.*   *2 Tim* 1:7*
their *m.* and conscience.   *Tit* 1:15
put them in *m.* to be subject.   3:1
put my laws into their *m. Heb* 8:10
be ye all of one *m.*   *1 Pet* 3:8
likewise with the same *m.*   4:1
not for lucre, but of a ready *m.* 5:2
here is the *m.* which hath. *Rev* 17:9
these have one *m.* and shall give. 13
see **alienated**
   mine or *my* **mind**
not done them of *mine* own *m.*
          Num 16:28
good or bad of *mine* own *m.* 24:13
that which is in *my m.*   *1 Sam* 2:35
was in *my m.* to build. *1 Chr* 22:7*
my m. could not be toward. *Jer* 15:1
nor came it into *my m.* 19:5; 32:35
this I recall to *my m.*   *Lam* 3:21
another law warring against the law
   of *my m.*   *Rom* 7:23
   thy **mind**
not *thy m.* on the asses. *1 Sam* 9:20
be according to *thy m.*? *Job* 34:33
things come into *thy m. Ezek* 38:10
thoughts came into *thy m. Dan* 2:29
love the Lord thy God with all *thy m.*
   Mat 22:37; *Mark* 12:30
          Luke 10:27
without *thy m.* would.   *Philem* 14
   your **mind**
if it be *your m.* I should. *Gen* 23:8
let Jerusalem come into *your m.*
          Jer 51:50
that come into *your m. Ezek* 11:5
which cometh into *your m.* 20:32
by renewing of *your m. Rom* 12:2
of *your* ready *m.*   *2 Cor* 8:19
forwardness of *your m.*   9:2
in the spirit of *your m.*   *Eph* 4:23
sometime alienated and enemies in
   your m.   *Col* 1:21
up the loins of *your m. 1 Pet* 1:13

mind, *verb*
are after flesh, *m.* things. *Rom* 8:5
m. not high things, but.   12:16
nevertheless let us *m. Phil* 3:16
for many walk, who *m.* earthly.   19

minded

stedfastly *m.* to go with. *Ruth* 1:18
Joash was *m.* to repair. *2 Chr* 24:4
which are *m.* of their own free will.
Ezra 7:13
Joseph was *m.* to put. *Mat* 1:19
for to be carnally *m.* is death, but to
be spiritually *m.* is. *Rom* 8:6*
be not high-*m.* but fear. 11:20
grant you to be like *m.* one. 15:5
this confidence I was *m.* *2 Cor* 1:15
when I was thus *m.* did I use. 17
will be no otherwise *m.* *Gal* 5:10
that ye be like *m.* having. *Phil* 2:2
no man like *m.* who will care. 20
be thus *m.* if in any thing ye be otherwise *m.* God will reveal. 3:15
comfort the feeble-*m.* *1 Thes* 5:14
the rich be not high-*m.* *1 Tim* 6:17
shall be heady, high-*m.* *2 Tim* 3:4
exhort to be sober *m.* *Tit* 2:6
a double *m.* man is unstable. *Jas* 1:8
your hearts, ye double *m.* 4:8

mindful

be ye *m.* always of his. *1 Chr* 16:15*
our fathers were not *m.* of. *Neh* 9:17
what is man, that thou art *m.* of him,
and son of man ? *Ps* 8:4; *Heb* 2:6
be *m.* of his covenant. *Ps* 111:5
Lord hath been *m.* of us, he. 115:12
not been *m.* of the rock. *Isa* 17:10
being *m.* of thy tears. *2 Tim* 1:4*
if they had been *m.* of that country.
Heb 11:15
m. of the words spoken. *2 Pet* 3:2

minding

Paul *m.* himself to go afoot.
Acts 20:13

minds

and speak your *m.* *Judg* 19:30
be chafed in their *m.* *2 Sam* 17:8
if it be your *m.* let none go forth.
2 Ki 9:15
they set their *m.* *Ezek* 24:25*
with despiteful *m.* to cast it. 36:5*
and made their *m.* evil. *Acts* 14:2
they changed their *m.* and said. 28:6
but their *m.* were blinded. *2 Cor* 3:14
world hath blinded the *m.* 4:4
your *m.* should be corrupted. 11:3
God shall keep your *m.* *Phil* 4:7
men of corrupt *m.* *1 Tim* 6:5
2 Tim 3:8
in their *m.* will I write. *Heb* 10:16
wearied and faint in your *m.* 12:3*
I stir up your pure *m.* by. *2 Pet* 3:1

mine

that thou seest is *m.* *Gen* 31:43
m. as Reuben and Simeon shall be *m.*
48:5
firstborn, both of man and beast, it is
m. *Ex* 13:2; 34:19; *Num* 3:13
for all the earth is *m.* *Ex* 19:5
Ps 50:12
that ye should be *m.* *Lev* 20:26
Isa 43:1
the land is *m.* for ye are. *Lev* 25:23
the Levites shall be *m.* *Num* 3:12
45; 8:14
of children of Israel are *m.* 8:17
Joab's field is near *m.* *2 Sam* 14:30
the kingdom was *m.* *1 Ki* 2:15
let it be neither *m.* nor thine. 3:26
gold, and wives, are *m.* 20:3
if ye will be *m.* and if. *2 Ki* 10:6
is under heaven is *m.* *Job* 41:11
myself from *m.* iniquity. *Ps* 18:23
beast of the forest is *m.* 50:10
wild beasts of field are *m.* 11
Gilead is *m.* and Manasseh is *m.*
60:7; 108:8
counsel is *m.* and sound. *Pr* 8:14
my beloved is *m.* and I am his.
S. of S. 2:16; 6:3
my vineyard, which is *m.* 8:12
word shall stand, *m.* or. *Jer* 44:28
thee, thou becamest *m.* *Ezek* 16:8
souls are *m.*; soul of son is *m.* 18:4
and they were *m.* 23:4
when she was *m.* 5
the river is *m.* 29:9
these countries be *m.* 35:10
is *m.* and the gold is *m.* *Hag* 2:8

28

they shall be *m.* saith. *Mal* 3:17
heareth sayings of *m.* *Mat* 7:24
heareth these sayings of *m.* and. 26
my right hand and on my left, is not
m. to give. 20:23; *Mark* 10:40
for a friend of *m.* in his journey is
come to me. *Luke* 11:6
Jesus saith, *M.* hour. *John* 2:4
my doctrine is not *m.* 7:16
am known of *m.* 10:14
word which ye hear is not *m.* 14:24
he shall receive of *m.* 16:14
that the Father hath are *m.* 15
m. are thine, and thine are *m.* 17:10
vengeance is *m.*, I will repay.
Rom 12:19
in every prayer of *m.* *Phil* 1:4

mingle

men of strength to *m.* *Isa* 5:22
m. with the seed of. *Dan* 2:43

mingled

there was fire *m.* with. *Ex* 9:24
sow thy field with *m.* *Lev* 19:19
holy seed have *m.* *Ezra* 9:2
and *m.* my drink with. *Ps* 102:9
m. among the heathen. 106:35
she hath *m.* her wine. *Pr* 9:2
the wine which I have *m.* 5
Lord hath *m.* a perverse. *Isa* 19:14
cup to all *m.* people. *Jer* 25:20, 24
a sword on all the *m.* people. 50:37
Ezek 30:5
gave him vinegar *m.* *Mat* 27:34
gave him wine *m.* with. *Mark* 15:23
blood Pilate had *m.* *Luke* 13:1
followed hail and fire *m.* *Rev* 8:7
as it were a sea of glass *m.* 15:2

minish, -ed

(*American Revision,* diminish)
ye shall not *m.* aught of. *Ex* 5:19
are *m.* and brought low. *Ps* 107:39

minister

Used in the Bible mainly in the
archaic sense of one who serves,
waits on, or attends another, Ex
24:13; 1 Ki 10:5. It is applied, [1]
To Christ, when comparing him
with the Hebrew high priest, Heb
8:2. [2] To those who were to
care for the work of the gospel,
1 Cor 14:1. [3] To magistrates,
Rom 13:6. [4] To the angels, Ps
104:4.

rose, and his *m.* Joshua. *Ex* 24:13
spake to Joshua, Moses' *m.* *Josh* 1:1
let him be your *m.* *Mat* 20:26
Mark 10:43
book again to the *m.* *Luke* 4:20*
also John to their *m.* *Acts* 13:5*
to make thee a *m.* and a. 26:16
the *m.* of God to thee. *Rom* 13:4, 6
Christ was a *m.* of the. 15:8
I should be the *m.* of Jesus to. 16
is Christ the *m.* of sin ? *Gal* 2:17
whereof I was made a *m.* *Eph* 3:7
Col 1:23, 25
Tychicus, a faithful *m.* of the Lord.
Eph 6:21; *Col* 4:7
who is for you a faithful *m.* *Col* 1:7
brother and *m.* of God. *1 Thes* 3:2
a good *m.* of Christ. *1 Tim* 4:6
a *m.* of the sanctuary. *Heb* 8:2

minister, verb

m. to me in the priest's. *Ex* 28:1
3, 4, 41; 29:1, 44; 30:30; 31:10
35:19; 39:41; 40:13, 15
shall be upon Aaron to *m.* 28:35
when they come to altar to *m.* 43
29:30; 30:20
I will sanctify Aaron to *m.* 29:44
he presented them to *m.* *Lev* 7:35
whom he shall consecrate to *m.*
16:32; *Num* 3:3
m. with their brethren. *Num* 8:26
tribe of Levi to *m.* to. *Deut* 10:8
to stand to *m.* in the name. 18:5, 7
God hath chosen them to *m.* 21:5
child did *m.* to the. *1 Sam* 2:11
could not stand to *m.* because of the.
1 Ki 8:11; *2 Chr* 5:14
chosen to *m.* before him. *1 Chr* 15:2

to *m.* and to give thanks. *1 Chr* 23:13
2 Chr 31:2
priests which *m.* are. *2 Chr* 13:10
he shall *m.* judgement to. *Ps* 9:8
rams of Nebaioth shall *m.* *Isa* 60:7
their kings shall *m.* to thee. 10
multiply Levites that *m.* *Jer* 33:22
which come near to *m.* *Ezek* 40:46
41:15, 16
stand before them to *m.* 44:11
not to be ministered unto, but to *m.*
Mat 20:28; *Mark* 10:45
sick, and did not *m.*? *Mat* 25:44
his acquaintance to *m.* to him.
Acts 24:23
I go to *m.* to the saints. *Rom* 15:25
duty is to *m.* to them in carnal. 27
they which *m.* about holy. *1 Cor* 9:13
both *m.* bread for your. *2 Cor* 9:10*
that it may *m.* grace. *Eph* 4:29*
which *m.* questions. *1 Tim* 1:4
angels sent to *m.* to. *Heb* 1:14*
to the saints, and do *m.* 6:10
but to us they did *m.* the. *1 Pet* 1:12
even so *m.* the same one to. 4:10
if any man *m.* let him do it as. 11

ministered

Eleazar and Ithamar *m.* *Num* 3:4
Deut 10:6
Samuel *m.* before. *1 Sam* 2:18; 3:1
his servant that *m.* *2 Sam* 13:17
Abishag *m.* to David. *1 Ki* 1:4, 15
after Elijah, and *m.* to him. 19:21
snuffers, and all vessels wherewith
they *m.* *2 Ki* 25:14; *Jer* 52:18
m. to them before their. *Ezek* 44:12
thousand thousands *m.* *Dan* 7:10
angels came and *m.* to him.
Mat 4:11; *Mark* 1:13
she arose and *m.* unto them.
Mat 8:15; *Mark* 1:31
which *m.* to him of their substance.
Luke 8:3
as they *m.* and fasted. *Acts* 13:2
these hands have *m.* to my. 20:34
epistle of Christ *m.* by us. *2 Cor* 3:3
having nourishment *m.* *Phil* 2:25
how many things he *m.* *2 Tim* 1:18
stead he might have *m.* *Philem* 13
m. to the saints, and. *Heb* 6:10
an entrance shall be *m.* *2 Pet* 1:11*

ministereth

now he that *m.* seed. *2 Cor* 9:10
he that *m.* to you the Spirit. *Gal* 3:5*

ministering

charge of *m.* vessels. *1 Chr* 9:28*
gates of house, *m.* to. *Ezek* 44:11
women followed Jesus *m.* to him.
Mat 27:55
let us wait on our *m.* *Rom* 12:7
m. the gospel. 15:16
on us the *m.* to the saints. *2 Cor* 8:4
for as touching *m.* to the saints. 9:1
are they not all *m.* spirits ? *Heb* 1:14
priest standeth daily *m.* 10:11

ministers

the attendance of his *m.* *1 Ki* 10:5
2 Chr 9:4
to impose toll on *m.* *Ezra* 7:24*
bring unto us *m.* for house. 8:17
ye *m.* of his that do. *Ps* 103:21
who maketh his *m.* a flaming fire.
104:4; *Heb* 1:7
men shall call you the *m.* *Isa* 61:6
covenant be broken with David my
servant, and with my *m.* *Jer* 33:21
be *m.* in my sanctuary. *Ezek* 44:11
holy portion for the *m.* of. 45:4
the Lord's *m.* mourn. *Joel* 1:9
howl, ye *m.* 13
m. weep between the porch. 2:17
beginning were *m.* of word. *Luke* 1:2
God's *m.* attending. *Rom* 13:6
m. by whom ye believed. *1 Cor* 3:5
us as of the *m.* of Christ. 4:1
who made us able *m.* *2 Cor* 3:6
approving ourselves as the *m.* 6:4
no great thing, if his *m.* also be transformed as the *m.* of. 11:15
are they *m.* of Christ ? I am more. 23

ministration
as the days of his m.   Luke 1:23
neglected in the daily m.   Acts 6:1
but if the m. of death.   2 Cor 3:7
m. of the Spirit be rather ?   8, 9
by the experiment of this m.   9:13

ministry
instruments of the m.   Num 4:12
came to do the service of the m.   47
praised by their m.   2 Chr 7:6
similitudes, by the m. of the prophets.   Hos 12:10
obtained part of this m.   Acts 1:17
that may take part of this m.   25
we will give ourselves to m.   6:4
they had fulfilled their m.   12:25
might finish my course, and m. 20:24
God had wrought by his m.   21:19
or m., let us wait on our. Rom 12:7
to the m. of saints.   1 Cor 16:15
seeing we have this m.   2 Cor 4:1
hath given to us the m. of.   5:18
giving no offence, that the m.   6:3
for work of the m. for.   Eph 4:12
take heed to the m. thou.   Col 4:17
putting me into the m.   1 Tim 1:12*
make full proof of thy m. 2 Tim 4:5
profitable to me for the m.   11
he obtained a more excellent m.   Heb 8:6
with blood the vessels of the m. 9:21

minstrel, -s
me a m. when m. played. 2 Ki 3:15
when Jesus saw the m.   Mat 9:23*

mint
pay tithe of m. anise.   Mat 23:23
ye tithe m. and all.   Luke 11:42

miracle
(An event beyond the power of any known physical laws to produce; a supernatural occurrence produced by the power of God ; a marvel, wonder. In the Revisions the word is generally rendered in the Old Testament wonder, or mighty work ; and in the New Testament sign)
speak, saying, Shew a m.   Ex 7:9
considered not the m.   Mark 6:52
no man which shall do a m.   9:39
hoped to have seen some m. done.   Luke 23:8
this is the second m.   John 4:54
and said, John did no m.   10:41
a notable m. hath been.   Acts 4:16
forty years on whom this m.   22

miracles
which have seen.   Num 14:22
that have not seen his m. Deut 11:3
seen those signs and great m.   29:3
where be all his m. our. Judg 6:13
beginning of m. did.   John 2:11
when they saw the m. he did.   23
no man can do these m. except.   3:2
because they saw his m.   6:2
not because ye saw the m.   26
will he do more m. than ?   7:31
that is a sinner do such m.?   9:16
for this man doeth many m.   11:47
he had done so many m.   12:37
approved of God by m.   Acts 2:22
Stephen did great m. among.   6:8
hearing and seeing the m.   8:6
wondered, beholding the m.   13
declaring what m. God had.   15:12
God wrought special m. by.   19:11
another the working m. 1 Cor 12:10
after that m.   28
are all workers of m.?   29
he that worketh m. among. Gal 3:5
them witness with m.   Heb 2:4
by the means of those m. Rev 13:14
spirits of devils working m.   16:14
false prophet that wrought m. 19:20

mire
I did stamp them as m. of the.   2 Sam 22:43; Isa 10:6; Mi 7:10
rush grow up without m.?   Job 8:11
he hath cast me into the m.   30:19
pointed things on the m.   41:30
I sink in deep m. where.   Ps 69:2
deliver me out of the m.: let me.   14

whose waters cast up m.   Isa 57:20
was no water, but m.   Jer 38:6
thy feet are sunk in the m.   22
and fine gold as the m.   Zech 9:3
tread their enemies in m. of.   10:5
her wallowing in the m. 2 Pet 2:22

Miriam
M. took a timbrel.   Ex 15:20
M. and Aaron spake.   Num 12:1
M. became leprous white.   10
M. was shut up seven days.   15
M. died there.   20:1
were born Aaron, Moses, M. 26:59
remember what God did to M. by. the way   Deut 24:9
thee Moses, Aaron, and M.   Mi 6:4

mirth
sent thee away with m.   Gen 31:27
away to make great m.   Neh 8:12
us desired of us m.   Ps 137:3
and the end of that m.   Pr 14:13
I will prove thee with m.   Eccl 2:1
I said of m. What doeth it ?   2
of fools is in the house of m.   7:4
then I commended m. because. 8:15
m. of tabrets the joy of   Isa 24:8
joy is darkened, the m. of the.   11
the voice of m. from.   Jer 7:34
16:9; 25:10; Hos 2:11
we then make m.?   Ezek 21:10

miry
me out of the m. clay.   Ps 40:2
the m. places shall not. Ezek 47:11
iron mixed with m.   Dan 2:41, 43

miscarrying
give them a m. womb.   Hos 9:14

mischief
(Very frequently used to mean wickedness, iniquity)
for he said, Lest some m. Gen 42:4
if m. befall him by the way in which ye go.   38; 44:29
depart, and yet no m.   Ex 21:22
for m. did he bring them out. 32:12*
people that are set on m.   22*
that Saul practised m.   1 Sam 23:9
art taken in thy m.   2 Sam 16:8
m. that Hadad did.   1 Ki 11:25
see how this man seeketh m.   20:7
some m. will come upon us. 2 Ki 7:9*
they thought to do me m.   Neh 6:2
Esther besought to put away m. of.   Esth 8:3
conceive m. and bring.   Job 15:35
he conceived m. brought.   Ps 7:14
his m. shall return upon his.   16
under his tongue is m. and.   10:7
thou beholdest m. and spite, to.   14
hands is m., their hand is.   26:10
which speak peace, but m.   28:3
the wicked deviseth m.   36:4*
why boastest thyself in m.?   52:1
m. and sorrow are in the.   55:10
imagine m. against a man ?   62:3
the throne, which frameth m.? 94:20
nigh that follow after m.   119:150*
let the m. of their own lips.   140:9
except they have done m.   Pr 4:16
he deviseth m. continually.   6:14*
be swift in running to m.   18
sport to a fool to do m.   10:23*
he that seeketh m. it shall.   11:27
wicked shall be filled with m.   12:21
messenger falleth into m.   13:17*
perverse tongue falleth into m.   17:20
and their lips talk of m.   24:2
wicked shall fall into m.   16*; 28:14
therefore m. shall fall.   Isa 47:11
in vanity, they conceive m.   59:4
m. shall come upon m.   Ezek 7:26
are the men that devise m.   11:2*
kings' hearts shall be to do m.   Dan 11:27
yet do they imagine m.   Hos 7:15
full of all m. thou child. Acts 13:10*

mischiefs
I will heap m. on them. Deut 32:23
thy tongue deviseth m.   Ps 52:2*
imagine m. in their heart.   140:2

mischievous
imagined a m. device.   Ps 21:11
that seek my hurt, speak m.   38:12
he shall be called a m.   Pr 24:8
the end of his talk is m. Eccl 10:13
man uttereth his m. desire.   Mi 7:3

miserable
Job said, m. comforters.   Job 16:2
of all men most m.   1 Cor 15:19*
knowest not that thou art m. Rev 3:17

miserably
he will m. destroy those. Mat 21:41

miseries
Jerusalem remembered in days of her m.   Lam 1:7
howl for your m. that shall. Jas 5:1

misery
was grieved for the m.   Judg 10:16
given to him that is in m.? Job 3:20
thou shalt forget thy m.   11:16
remember his m. no more. Pr 31:7
the m. of a man is great.   Eccl 8:6
mine affliction and m.   Lam 3:19
destruction and m. are.   Rom 3:16

Mishael
of Uzziel, M. Elzaphan and Zithri.   Ex 6:22; Lev 10:4
Ezra's left hand stood M. Neh 8:4
children of Judah, M.   Dan 1:6

miss
hair breadth and not m. Judg 20:16
if thy father at all m.   1 Sam 20:6

missed
thou shalt be m.   1 Sam 20:18
neither m. any thing as long. 25:15
nothing was m. of all that.   21

missing
neither was there aught m. unto them.   1 Sam 25:7
any means he be m.   1 Ki 20:39

mist
up a m. from the earth.   Gen 2:6
there fell on him a m.   Acts 13:11
to whom the m. of darkness is.   2 Pet 2:17*

mistress
her m. was despised in.   Gen 16:4
I flee from my m. Sarai.   8
return to thy m.   9
son of the m. of house.   1 Ki 17:17
her m. Would God my lord. 2 Ki 5:3
maiden to hand of her m.   Ps 123:2
that is heir to her m.   Pr 20:23
the maid so with her m.   Isa 24:2
m. of witchcrafts, that.   Nah 3:4

misused
they despised m. and. 2 Chr 36:16*

mite, -s
a widow threw in two m.   Mark 12:42; Luke 21:2
paid the very last m.   Luke 12:59

mitre
they shall make a m.   Ex 28:4, 39
39:28
a blue lace upon the m. 28:37; 39:31
shalt put the m. upon his head. 29:6
the holy crown on the m.   Lev 8:9
linen m. shall he be attired.   16:4
a fair m. on his head, so they set a fair m.   Zech 3:5

mixed
a m. multitude went up.   Ex 12:38
the m. multitude fell a.   Num 11:4
they separated from Israel all m.   Neh 13:3
that go to seek m. wine.   Pr 23:30
thy wine m. with water.   Isa 1:22
the iron m. with miry.   Dan 2:41
Ephraim m. himself among. Hos 7:8
not being m. with faith.   Heb 4:2*

mixture
wine red, it is full of m.   Ps 75:8
Nicodemus, and brought a m. of myrrh and aloes.   John 19:39
is poured out without m. Rev 14:10

Mizar
thee from the hill of M.   Ps 42:6

Mizpah
the heap was called M.   Gen 31:49

those stones Geba of Benjamin, and
  M.   *1 Ki* 15:22; *2 Chr* 16:6
son of Nethaniah came to Gedaliah
  to *M.*   *2 Ki* 25:23; *Jer* 41:1
men of Gibeon and *M.*   *Neh* 3:7
Shallum ruler of *M.*   15
Ezer ruler of *M.*   19
went to Gedaliah to *M.*   *Jer* 40:6
behold, I will dwell at *M.*   10
the Jews that were at *M.*   41:3
carried away captive from *M.*   14
been a snare on *M.*   *Hos* 5:1

Mizpeh

Dilean and *M.* cities.   *Josh* 15:38
M. Chephirah, cities of.   18:26
and encamped in *M.*   *Judg* 10:17
uttered all his words in *M.*   11:11
gathered to the Lord in *M.*   20:1
up to the Lord to *M.* shall die.   21:5
gather all Israel to *M.*   *1 Sam* 7:5
judged Israel in *M.*   6, 16
the people to the Lord to *M.*   10:17
David went thence to *M.*   22:3

Mnason

M. an old disciple.   *Acts* 21:16

Moab

daughter's son was *M.*   *Gen* 19:37
smote Midian in field of *M.*   36:35
   1 Chr 1:46
take hold on men of *M.*   *Ex* 15:15
woe to thee, *M.*   *Num* 21:29
   Jer 48:46
M. was sore afraid, and *M.* was
  distressed.   *Num* 22:3
smite the corners of *M.*   24:17
whoredom with daughters of *M.* 25:1
through the coast of *M.*   *Deut* 2:18
Moses died in the land of *M.*   34:5
slew of *M.* about 10,000. *Judg* 3:29
so *M.* was subdued under the.   30
served gods of Syria and *M.*   10:6
took not away the land of *M.* 11:15
into the country of *M.*   *Ruth* 1:2
took wives of the women of *M.*   4
Saul fought against *M.* and Ammon.
   1 Sam 14:47
David smote *M.* and.   *2 Sam* 8:2
slew two lionlike men of *M.*   23:20
the abomination of *M.*   *1 Ki* 11:7
M. rebelled against.   *2 Ki* 1:1
wilt thou go with me against *M.?* 3:7
kings are slain, therefore *M.*   23
had the dominion in *M.* *1 Chr* 4:22
gold he brought from *M.*   18:11
M. came against Jehoshaphat.
   2 Chr 20:1
behold, how the children of *M.*   10
had married wives of *M.* *Neh* 13:23
M. is my washpot.   *Ps* 60:8; 108:9
M. is confederate against thee. 83:6
lay their hand upon *M.*   *Isa* 11:14
the burden of *M.* Ar of *M.* laid waste.
   15:1; 16:13; *Jer* 48:1; *Ezek* 25:8
   Amos 2:2
heart shall cry out for *M.*   *Isa* 15:5
we have heard the pride of *M.* 16:6
   Jer 48:29
like an harp for *M.*   *Isa* 16:11
and the glory of *M.* shall be.   14
M. shall be trodden down.   25:10
I will punish Egypt, Judah, and *M.*
   Jer 9:26
I made Edom and *M.* to.   25:21
Jews returned from *M.*   40:11
shall be no more praise of *M.* 48:2
give wings to *M.* that it may flee. 9
M. hath been at ease from his.   11
tell ye it in Arnon, that *M.* is.   20
M. shall wallow in his vomit.   26
gladness is taken from land of *M.* 33
how hath *M.* turned the back!   39
bring again the captivity of *M.*   47
send a fire upon *M.*   *Amos* 2:2
M. shall be as Sodom.   *Zeph* 2:9
   see **king**

Moabite

a *M.* shall not enter into the congregation.   *Deut* 23:3; *Neh* 13:1
Ithmah the *M.* a valiant. *1 Chr* 11:46

Moabites

is the father of the *M.*   *Gen* 19:37
said, Distress not the *M.*   *Deut* 2:9

---

delivered the *M.* to you.   *Judg* 3:28
M. became David's servants and.
   2 Sam 8:2; *1 Chr* 18:2
loved women of the *M.*   *1 Ki* 11:1
Chemosh god of the *M.*   33
he will deliver the *M.*   *2 Ki* 3:18
rose up and smote the *M.*   24
the bands of the *M.* invaded. 13:20
sent against him bands of *M.*   24:2
abominations of the *M.*   *Ezra* 9:1

Moabitess, see Ruth

mock

[1] *To deride or laugh at,* 2 *Chr*
30:10. [2] *To speak in jest,* *Gen*
19:14. [3] *To disappoint, deceive,*
Num 22:29.
Hebrew to *m.* us.   *Gen* 39:14, 17
mocketh, do ye so *m.* him. *Job* 13:9
after I have spoken, *m.* on.   21:3
I will *m.* when your fear.   *Pr* 1:26
fools make a *m.* at sin.   14:9
deliver me, and they *m.*   *Jer* 38:19
adversary did *m.* at her.   *Lam* 1:7
m. thee who art infamous. *Ezek* 22:5
deliver him to Gentiles to *m.* him.
   Mat 20:19
they shall *m.* him and. *Mark* 10:34
behold, begin to *m.* him. *Luke* 14:29

mocked

seemed as one that *m.* to. *Gen* 19:14
thou hast *m.* me.   *Num* 22:29
hast *m.* me, and told me lies.
   Judg 16:10, 13, 15.
at noon, Elijah *m.*   *1 Ki* 18:27
out of the city *m.* Elisha. *2 Ki* 2:23
them to scorn and *m.* *2 Chr* 30:10
but they *m.* the messengers.   36:16
wroth, and *m.* the Jews. *Neh* 4:1
I am as one *m.* of his.   *Job* 12:4*
saw that he was *m.* he. *Mat* 2:16
they bowed the knee and *m.* 27:29
   31; *Mark* 15:20
be *m.* and spitefully. *Luke* 18:32
men that held Jesus *m.* him. 22:63
Herod *m.* him.   23:11
the soldiers also *m.* him.   36
the resurrection, some *m. Acts* 17:32
deceived, God is not *m.*   *Gal* 6:7

mocker

wine is a *m.*, strong drink. *Pr* 20:1

mockers

are there not *m.* with me ? *Job* 17:2
with hypocritical *m.*   *Ps* 35:16
be not *m.* lest bands be. *Isa* 28:22*
not in the assembly of. *Jer* 15:17*
be *m.* in the latter times.   *Jude* 18

mockest

when thou *m.* shall no man. *Job* 11:3

mocketh

as one *m.* another, do.   *Job* 13:9*
he *m.* at fear, and is not.   39:22
m. poor reproacheth his.   *Pr* 17:5
eye that *m.* at his father.   30:17
a derision, every one *m.* me. *Jer* 20:7

mocking, -s

saw the son of Hagar *m.* *Gen* 21:9
I made thee a *m.* to all. *Ezek* 22:4
the chief priests *m.*   *Mat* 27:41
   Mark 15:31
m. said. These men are. *Acts* 2:13
had trial of cruel *m.*   *Heb* 11:36

moderately

you the former rain *m.* *Joel* 2:23*

moderation

m. be known to all men. *Phil* 4:5*

modest

themselves in *m.* apparel. *1 Tim* 2:9

moist

shall he eat *m.* grapes. *Num* 6:3*

moistened

and his bones are *m.* *Job* 21:24*

moisture

my *m.* is turned into.   *Ps* 32:4
because it lacked *m.*   *Luke* 8:6

mole

lizard, snail, and *m.* are. *Lev* 11:30*

Molech

pass through fire to *M.*   *Lev* 18:21
that giveth of his seed to *M.* shall
  surely be.   20:2; 3, 4; *Jer* 32:35
built an high place for *M. 1 Ki* 11:7
son pass through to *M.*   *2 Ki* 23:10

moles, see bats

mollified

neither bound up, nor *m.*   *Isa* 1:6

Moloch

have borne the tabernacle of *M.*
   Amos 5:26; *Acts* 7:43

molten

after he had made *m.* calf.   *Ex* 32:4
   8; *Deut* 9:12, 16; *Neh* 9:18
shalt make thee no *m.* gods.
   Ex 34:17; *Lev* 19:4
chapters of *m.* brass.   *1 Ki* 7:16
he made a *m.* sea.   23
undersetters *m.*   30
their spokes were all *m.*   33
and brass is *m.* out of.   *Job* 28:2
sky is strong, and as a *m.*   37:18
filthiness of it may be *m. Ezek* 24:11
the mountains shall be *m.*   *Mi* 1:4

moment

midst of thee in a *m.*   *Ex* 33:5
that I may consume them in a *m.*
   Num 16:21, 45
try him every *m.*   *Job* 7:18
hypocrite is but for a *m.*   20:5
and in a *m.* they go down to. 21:13
in a *m.* shall they die, people. 34:20
anger endureth but a *m.*   *Ps* 30:5
into desolation as in a *m.*   73:19
tongue is but for a *m.*   *Pr* 12:19
as it were for a *m.*   *Isa* 26:20
I will water it every *m.*   27:3
two things shall come in a *m.* 47:9
small *m.* have I forsaken.   54:7
I hid my face from thee for a *m.* 8
my curtains in a *m.*   *Jer* 4:20
was overthrown in a *m.*   *Lam* 4:6
and shall tremble at every *m.*
   Ezek 26:16; 32:10
kingdoms of world in a *m. Luke* 4:5
all be changed in a *m.* *1 Cor* 15:52
which is but for a *m.*   *2 Cor* 4:17

money

*(Coined money was unknown until
late in Bible times. Gold and silver
in the form of rings or ingots were
weighed in payment where we
would count coins)*
give it for as much *m.*   *Gen* 23:9*
I will give thee *m.* for the field. 13*
quite devoured also our *m.*   31:15
to restore every man's *m.*   42:25
he espied his *m.*   27
my *m.* is restored.   28
double *m.* in your hand.   43:12, 15
fear not, I had your *m.*   23
and put every man's *m.* in his. 44:1
Joseph gathered all the *m.*   47:14
for *m.* faileth.   15
how that our *m.* is spent.   18
go out free without *m.*   *Ex* 21:11
for he is his *m.*   21
be laid on him a sum of *m.*   30*
and divide the *m.*   35*
deliver to his neighbour *m.*   22:7
if thou lend *m.* to any of my.   25
shalt take the atonement *m.*   30:16
not give him *m.* on usury.
   Lev 25:37; *Deut* 23:19
took the redemption *m.* *Num* 3:49
meat and water for *m. Deut* 2:6, 28
turn it into *m.*   14:25
shalt bestow that *m.*   26
not sell her at all for *m.*   21:14
they took no gain of *m.* *Judg* 5:19
lords of Philistines brought *m.* 16:18
yet he restored the *m.* to his. 17:4
the worth of it in *m.*   *1 Ki* 21:2
is it a time to receive *m.?* *2 Ki* 5:26
m. of the dedicated things.   12:4
therefore receive no more *m.*   7
m. in the chest, and told the *m.* that
  was found   10; *2 Chr* 24:11
trespass *m.* and sin *m.*   *2 Ki* 12:16
Menahem exacted the *m.* of.   15:20
Jehoiakim gave *m.* to.   23:35

gave m. also to masons. *Ezra 3:7*
buy speedily with this m. *7:17*
we have borrowed m. *Neh 5:4*
servants might exact of them m. *10*
of the sum of m. Haman. *Esth 4:7*
the fruits without m. *Job 31:39*
also gave him a piece of m. *42:11*
put not out his m. to usury. *Ps 15:5*
he hath taken a bag of m. *Pr 7:20*
for wisdom and m. is a. *Eccl 7:12*
wine maketh merry, but m. *10:19*
redeemed without m. *Isa 52:3*
no m., come, buy without m. *55:1*
wherefore spend ye m. for that? *2*
I weighed him the m. *Jer 32:9, 10*
men shall buy fields for m. and. *44*
drunken our water for m. *Lam 5:4*
thereof divine for m. *Mi 3:11*
received the tribute m. *Mat 17:24**
thou shalt find a piece of m. *27**
shew me the tribute m. *22:19*
earth, and hid his lord's m. *25:18*
to have put my m. to the exchangers,
and at my. *27; Luke 19:23*
large m. to the soldiers. *Mat 28:12*
so they took m. and did as they. *15*
they took no m. in their purse.
Mark 6:8; Luke 9:3
the people cast m. into. *Mark 12:41*
and promised to give him m. *14:11*
Luke 22:5
changers of m. sitting. *John 2:14*
he poured out changers' m. *15*
brought the m. and laid. *Acts 4:37*
sorcerer offered them m. *8:18*
but Peter said, Thy m. perish. *20**
he hoped that m. should have. *24:26*
the love of m. is the root. *1 Tim 6:10*
see **brought**

moneychangers
overthrew tables of m. and seats of
them. *Mat 21:12; Mark 11:15*

monsters
even the sea m. draw out. *Lam 4:3**

month
(The Jews reckoned by the year of 360 days, and in all probability made an adjustment by adding a thirteenth month occasionally. They had two New Years, the Civil, in Tisri (October), and the Sacred, in Abib or Nisan, the month in which they left Egypt under Moses. The following table gives the months in order, beginning with the Sacred New Year. The numbers in parentheses are those of the months according to the civil reckoning; and the modern names given are approximately the corresponding months according to our calendar. The exact period in modern terms differs each year)

(7)	1. Nisan, Abib,		April.
(8)	2. Iar, Zif,		May.
(9)	3. Sivan,		June.
(10)	4. Tammuz,		July.
(11)	5. Ab,		Aug.
(12)	6. Elul,		Sept.
(1)	7. Tisri, Ethanim,		Oct.
(2)	8. Marchesvan,		Nov.
(3)	9. Chisleu (Kislev),		Dec.
(4)	10. Tebeth,		Jan.
(5)	11. Sebat,		Feb.
(6)	12. Adar,		Mar.

Answering to our

Laban space of a m. *Gen 29:14*
ye out in the m. Abib. *Ex 13:4*
keep the feast in the m. Abib. *23:15*
m. Abib thou camest out. *34:18*
Deut 16:1; Josh 5:10
if it be from a m. old to. *Lev 27:6*
every male from m. old. *Num 3:15*
22, 28, 34, 39, 40, 43; 26:62
a m. or year that the cloud. *9:22*
flesh, even a whole m. *11:20, 21*
from a m. old shalt thou. *18:16*
the burnt offering of every m. *28:14*
29:6*
thine house a full m. *Deut 21:13*
each man his m. made provision.
1 Ki 4:7, 27
a m. they were in Lebanon. *5:14*

in the m. Zif. *1 Ki 6:37*
in the m. Bul. *38*
feast in m. Ethanim. *8:2*
in m. Chisleu. *Neh 1:1*
in m. Nisan. *2:1; Esth 3:7*
m. Elul. *Neh 6:15*
Jews gathered in m. Adar.
Esth 9:15, 17, 19, 21
m. which was turned from. *22*
in her m. they shall find. *Jer 2:24*
now shall a m. devour. *Hos 5:7**
I cut off in one m. *Zech 11:8*
prepared for a day and m. *Rev 9:15*
yielded her fruit every m. *22:2*
see **first**

second **month**
in *second* m. the fountains were.
Gen 7:11
second m. was the earth dried. *8:14*
wilderness of Sin in *second* m.
Ex 16:1
in *second* m. take sum. *Num 1:1*
in *second* m. shall keep passover.
9:11; 2 Chr 30:2
of *second* m. cloud was taken up.
Num 10:11
second m. Solomon began to build.
1 Ki 6:1; 2 Chr 3:2
the course of *second* m. *1 Chr 27:4*
second m. began Zerubbabel to.
Ezra 3:8
third **month**
in *third* m. came into wilderness of.
Ex 19:1
captain for *third* m. *1 Chr 27:5*
gathered at Jerusalem in the *third*
m. *2 Chr 15:10*
in *third* m. they began to lay. *31:7*
king's scribes were called in *third* m.
Esth 8:9
in *third* m. word of Lord. *Ezek 31:1*

fourth **month**
fourth m. the famine. *2 Ki 25:3*
fourth captain for *fourth* m. was.
1 Chr 27:5
fourth m. the city was. *Jer 39:2*
in *fourth* m. the famine was. *52:6*
in *fourth* m. Ezekiel saw. *Ezek 1:1*
fast of the *fourth* m. *Zech 8:19*
see **fifth**

sixth **month**
captain for *sixth* m. *1 Chr 27:9*
in *sixth* m. the elders of. *Ezek 8:1*
in *sixth* m. word of Lord. *Hag 1:1*
in *sixth* m. they did work in. *15*
in *sixth* m. the angel. *Luke 1:26*
this is the *sixth* m. with her, who. *36*
see **seventh**

eighth **month**
in *eighth* m. came word. *Zech 1:1*

ninth **month**
the *ninth* m. the people. *Ezra 10:9*
in the *ninth* m. they. *Jer 36:9*
winter house in the *ninth* m. *22*
in *ninth* m. came word. *Hag 2:10*
from the *ninth* m. consider it. *18*
to Zechariah in *ninth* m. *Zech 7:1*

tenth **month**
waters decreased until the *tenth* m.
Gen 8:5
sat down in *tenth* m. *Ezra 10:16*
to the king in *tenth* m. *Esth 2:16*
tenth m. came Nebuchadnezzar.
Jer 39:1; 52:4
in *tenth* m. came word. *Ezek 24:1*
29:1
in the *tenth* m. one that had escaped.
33:21

eleventh **month**
in the *eleventh* m. Moses. *Deut 1:3*
in *eleventh* m. came word. *Zech 1:7*

twelfth **month**
Haman to the *twelfth* m. *Esth 3:7*
thirteenth day of the *twelfth* m. *13*
8:12; 9:1
twelfth m. Evil-merodach. *Jer 52:31*
in *twelfth* m. the word of. *Ezek 32:1*

this **month**
this m. shall be beginning. *Ex 12:2*
this m. shall take every man a. *3*

keep this service in *this* m. *Ex 13:5*
Num 9:3; 28:17
tenth day of *this* m. an. *Num 29:7*
this m. Israel assembled. *Neh 9:1*

monthly
the m. prognosticators. *Isa 47:13*

months
in beginnings of your m. *Num 10:10*
in beginnings of m. offer a. *28:11*
burnt offering through the m. *14*
let me alone two m. *Judg 11:37*
at the end of two m. she returned. *39*
was with her father four m. *19:2*
in the rock Rimmon four m. *20:47*
ark was in country of Philistines
seven m. *1 Sam 6:1*
Philistines a year and four m. *27:7*
over Judah seven years and six m.
2 Sam 2:11; 5:5; 1 Chr 3:4
ark was with Obed-edom three m.
2 Sam 6:11
Jerusalem at end of nine m. *24:8*
and two m. they were. *1 Ki 5:14*
for six m. did Joab remain. *11:16*
reigned over Israel six m. *2 Ki 15:8*
by month through the m. *1 Chr 27:1*
twelve m. purified, six m. with oil of
myrrh, six m. with. *Esth 2:12*
into the number of the m. *Job 3:6*
so am I made to possess m. of. *7:3*
number of his m. are with. *14:5*
when the number of his m. *21:21*
O that I were as in m. past, as. *29:2*
canst thou number the m. that ? *39:2*
seven m. Israel shall be. *Ezek 39:12*
after the end of seven m. shall. *14*
new fruit according to his m. *47:12*
at the end of twelve m. *Dan 4:29*
and hid herself five m. *Luke 1:24*
heaven was shut up three years and
six m. *4:25; Jas 5:17*
are yet four m. then. *John 4:35*
there a year and six m. *Acts 18:11*
observe days, and m. *Gal 4:10*
tormented five m. *Rev 9:5, 10*
under foot forty-two m. *11:2*
him to continue forty-two m. *13:5*
see **three**

monuments
people which lodge in the m.
Isa 65:4*

moon
put forth by the m. *Deut 33:14*
m. in valley of Ajalon. *Josh 10:12*
m. and it shineth not. *Job 25:5*
when I consider the m. *Ps 8:3*
and peace so long as the m. *72:7*
established for ever as the m. *89:37*
he appointeth the m. for. *104:19*
while the sun, m. or stars. *Eccl 12:2*
fair as m., clear as the. *S of S 6:10*
round tires like the m. *Isa 3:18*
see **sun**

new **moon**
is the *new* m. *1 Sam 20:5, 18*
it is neither *new* m. *2 Ki 4:23*
trumpet in the *new* m. *Ps 81:3*
that from one *new* m. to. *Isa 66:23*
in the day of *new* m. it. *Ezek 46:1*
in the day of *new* m. offer a. *6*
will the *new* m. be gone ? *Amos 8:5*
in respect of the *new* m. *Col 2:16*

new **moons**
sacrifices in the *new* m. *1 Chr 23:31*
2 Chr 2:4; 31:3; Ezra 3:5
Neh 10:33; Ezek 46:3
new m. and sabbaths I. *Isa 1:13*
your *new* m. and feasts my soul. *14*
offerings in the *new* m. *Ezek 45:17*
to cease her *new* m. *Hos 2:11*

Mordecai
M. came up with Zerubbabel.
Ezra 2:2; Neh 7:7
Jew, whose name was M. *Esth 2:5*
M. sat in the king's gate. *19, 21*
the thing was known to M. *22*
Haman saw that M. bowed not. *3:5*
shewed him the people of M. *6*
M. rent his clothes, and put. *4:1*
told Esther the words of M, *9*
Esther bade them return M. *15*
so long as I see M. the Jew. *5:13*

more

gallows made, that M. Esth 5:14
honour hath been done to M.? 6:3
make haste, and do even so to M. 10
Haman had made for M. 7:9
his ring and gave it to M. Esther set
M. over the house of Haman. 8:2
M. went out from the king in. 15
because the fear of M. fell. 9:3
M. the Jew was next to king. 10:3

more

Jacob loved Rachel m. Gen 29:30
riches m. than that they might. 36:7
Israel loved Joseph m. than all. 37:3
brethren hated him yet the m. 5, 8
Israel are m. than we. Ex 1:9
the m. they afflicted them, the m. 12
let there m. work be laid upon. 5:9
Pharaoh sinned yet m. and. 9:34
yet will I bring one plague m. 11:1
they gathered some m. some. 16:17
rich shall not give m. nor. 30:15
add the fifth part m. thereto. Lev 6:5
shut him up seven days m. 13:5
33, 54
you seven times m. 26:18, 21
firstborn which are m. Num 3:46
princes m. honourable than. 22:15
word of Lord. to do less or m. 18
what the Lord will say to me m. 19
thou shalt give the m. 26:54; 33:54
a thousand times m. Deut 1:11
on you, not because ye were m. 7:7
nations are m. than I. 17; 20:1
add three cities m. for thee. 19:9
were m. which died. Josh 10:11
corrupted themselves m. Judg 2:19
m. than they which he slew. 16:30
and what have I m.? 18:24
Lord do so to me and m. Ruth 1:17
1 Sam 14:44; 2 Sam 3:35; 19:13
shewed m. kindness in. Ruth 3:10
God do so to thee and m. 1 Sam 3:17
what can ye have m. but the ? 18:8
and much m. to Jonathan. 20:13
knew nothing less or m. 22:15
said, Thou art m. righteous. 24:17
m. do God to the enemies. 25:22
she told him nothing less or m. 36
to Abner, and m. also. 2 Sam 3:9
David took him m. concubines. 5:13
I will yet be m. vile than. 6:22
what can David say m. unto ? 7:20
we have also m. right in. 19:43
God do so to me, and m. also.
1 Ki 2:23; 20:10; 2 Ki 6:31
Ahab did m. to provoke. 1 Ki 16:33
gods to me, and m. also. 19:2
there is not a vessel m. 2 Ki 4:6
m. than they that be with them.
6:16; 2 Chr 32:7
seduced them to do m. evil. 2 Ki 21:9
his people so many m. 1 Chr 21:3
there were m. chief men found. 24:4
put m. to your yoke. 2 Chr 10:11
m. spoil than they could. 20:25
Lord is able to give thee m. 25:9
intend to add m. to our sins. 28:13
Ahaz did trespass yet m. against. 22
the Levites were m. upright. 29:34
his servants spake m. against. 32:16
Amon trespassed m. and m. 33:23
whatsoever m. shall be. Ezra 7:20
yet ye bring m. wrath. Neh 13:18
Esther obtained favour m. than all.
Esth 2:17
delight to do honour m. than ? 6:6
dig for it m. than for hid. Job 3:21
m. than my necessary food. 23:12
nor regardeth the rich m. 34:19
for he will not lay on man m. 23
saidst, My righteousness is m. 35:2
teacheth us m. than the beasts. 11
latter end of Job m. than. 42:12
m. than when their corn. Ps 4:7
m. to be desired are they. 19:10
thy thoughts are m. than can. 40:5
iniquities are m. than the hairs. 12
lovest evil m. than good. 52:3
that hate me are m. than hairs. 69:4
yet praise thee m. and m. 71:14
they have m. than heart could. 73:7
they sinned yet m. against. 78:17
gates of Zion m. than all. 87:2

increase you m. and m. Ps 115:14
I have m. understanding. 119:99
understand m. than the ancients. 100
m. than they that watch for. 130:6
wisdom is m. precious. Pr 3:15
shineth m. and m. unto the. 4:18
there is that withholdeth m. 11:24
a reproof entereth m. into a. 17:10
there is m. hope of a fool than of him.
26:12; 29:20
I increased m. than all. Eccl 2:9
remembrance of wise m. than. 16
or who can hasten hereunto m.? 25
the dead m. than the living. 4:2
and be m. ready to hear than. 5:1
remember thy love m. S of S 1:4
what is thy beloved m.? 5:9
what could be done m. to ? Isa 5:4
afterward did m. grievously. 9:1
I will bring m. upon Dimon. 15:9
his visage so marred m. than. 52:14
for m. are the children of the. 54:1
Israel justified herself m. Jer 3:11
because they are m. than the. 46:23
changed judgements into wickedness
m. than nations. Ezek 5:6
because he multiplied m. than the. 7
thou wast corrupted m. than they in
all thy ways. 16:47, 51, 52; 23:11
not for any wisdom that I have m.
than any living. Dan 2:30
the furnace seven times m. 3:19
continue m. years than the king. 11:8
knowledge of God m. Hos 6:6
now they sin m. and m. and. 13:2
wicked devoureth man m. Hab 1:13
what is m. than these. Mat 5:37
brethren only, what do you m.? 47
is not the life m. than meat ? 6:25
Luke 12:23
of m. value than many sparrows.
Mat 10:31; Luke 12:7
loveth father or mother m. Mat 10:37
and m. than a prophet. 11:9
seven spirits m. wicked than. 12:45
he shall have m. abundance. 13:12
he rejoiceth m. of that sheep. 18:13
take with thee one or two m. 16
they should have received m. 20:10
cried the m. Have mercy. 31; 27:23
Mark 10:48; 15:14; Luke 18:39
give me m. than twelve. Mat 26:53
to you that hear shall m. Mark 4:24
m. he charged them, so much the m.
7:36
poor widow cast in m. than all.
12:43; Luke 21:3
have been sold for m. Mark 14:5
what thou spendest m. Luke 10:35
of him they will ask m. 12:48
not receive manifold m. in. 18:30
many m. believed. John 4:41
Jews sought the m. to kill. 5:18
will he do m. miracles than ? 7:31
praise of men m. than. 12:43
that it may bring forth m. fruit. 15:2
Simon, lovest thou me m.? 21:15
to hearken to you m. Acts 4:19
believers were the m. added. 5:14
but Saul increased the m. in. 9:22
the m. part knew not why. 19:32
it is m. blessed to give. 20:35
there were m. than forty. 23:13, 21
believed the master m. than. 27:11
served the creature m. Rom 1:25
if the truth of God hath m. 3:7
we are m. than conquerors. 8:37
that I might gain the m. 1 Cor 9:19
I speak with tongues m. than. 14:18
so I rejoiced the m. 2 Cor 7:7
I boast the m. 10:8
am m.; in prisons m. frequent. 11:23
the desolate hath many m. Gal 4:27
love may abound m. and m.
Phil 1:9; 1 Thes 4:10
trust in the flesh, I m. Phil 3:4
God, abound m. and m. 1 Thes 4:1
lovers of pleasure m. 2 Tim 3:4
also do m. than I say. Philem 21
I m. say? time would fail. Heb 11:32
much m. shall not we escape. 12:25
yet once m. I shake not the. 26, 27
he giveth m. grace. Jas 4:6
m. sure word of prophecy. 2 Pet 1:19

and the last to be m. Rev 2:19
there come two woes m. 9:12

see **abundantly**

any **more**

returned not again any m. Gen 8:12
curse the ground any m. 21; 9:11
nor shall thy name any m. 17:5
not any m. be called Jacob. 35:10
deal deceitfully any m. Ex 8:29
neither shall there be any m. 9:29
a cry, none like it any m. 11:6
man nor woman make any m. 36:6
not be redeemed any m. Lev 27:20
be no wrath any m. Num 18:5
voice of the Lord any m. Deut 5:25
see this great fire any m. 18:16
had Israel manna any m. Josh 5:12
nor will I be with you any m. 7:12
any m. sons in my womb ? Ruth 1:11
Saul shall despair to seek me any m.
1 Sam 27:1
children of wickedness afflict any m.
2 Sam 7:10
feared to help Ammon any m.
10:19; 1 Chr 19:19
speakest thou any m.? 2 Sam 19:29
make the feet of Israel move any m.
2 Ki 21:8; 2 Chr 33:8
nor shall his place know him any m
Job 7:10; 20:9
I will not offend any m. 34:31
neither have they any m. Eccl 9:5
be stricken any m.? Isa 1:5
nor shall they learn war any m. 2:4
Mi 4:3
teachers be removed any m.
Isa 30:20
be termed desolate any m. 62:4
that be done any m. Jer 3:16
nor walk any m. after imagination. 17
stretch forth my tent any m. 10:20
I will not speak any m. in. 20:9
not return thither any m. 22:11
ruling any m. in Judah. 30
shall not sorrow any m. at. 31:12
thrown down any m. for ever. 40
themselves of them any m. 34:10
not do any m. the like. Ezek 5:9
words be prolonged any m. 12:28
shalt give no hire any m. 16:41
never open thy mouth any m. 63
shall not return any m. 21:5
not remember Egypt any m. 23:27
from thy filthiness any m. 24:13
thou shall be a terror, and never shalt
be any m. 27:36; 28:19
nor shall exalt itself any m. 29:15
nor foot of man trouble them any m.
32:13; 37:23
none of them any m. there. 39:28
hide my face any m. from them. 29
nor say any m. to the work. Hos 14:3
what I to do any m. with idols ? 8
pass through her any m. Joel 3:17
not again pass by them any m.
Amos 7:8; 8:2
prophesy not again any m. at. 7:13
not see evil any m. Zeph 3:15
durst any ask him any m. Mat 22:46
not any m. one loaf. Mark 8:14
they saw no man any m. save. 9:8
nor can they die any m. Luke 20:36
I will not eat any m. thereof. 22:16
let us not judge one another any m.
Rom 14:13
be spoken to any m. Heb 12:19
shall they thirst any m. Rev 7:16
place in heaven found any m. 12:8
buyeth her merchandise any m. 18:11
nor shall there be any m. pain. 21:4

much **more**

people being much m. Ex 36:5
much m. the wicked and. Pr 11:31
as this day, and much m. Isa 56:12
not much m. clothe you ? Mat 6:30
so much m. went a fame. Luke 5:15
I say unto you, and much m. 7:26
much m. being now justified by his.
Rom 5:9
much m. being reconciled, we. 10
much m. they that receive. 17
grace did much m. abound. 20
much m. doth ministration. 2 Cor 3:9

much m. that which remaineth.
    2 Cor 3:11
proved *much m.* diligent.   8:22
are *much m.* bold to.   *Phil* 1:14
have obeyed, now *much m.*   2:12
so *much m.* as you see day.
    Heb 10:25
much m. shall not we escape. 12:25
being *much m.* precious. *1 Pet* 1:7

no **more**
waters shall *no m.*   *Gen* 9:15
be called *no m.* Jacob.   32:28
Judah knew her again *no m.*   38:26
ye shall see my face *no m.*   44:23
    Ex 10:28
no m. give the people.   *Ex* 5:7
see thy face again *no m.*   10:29
ye shall see them again *no m.* 14:13
shall *no m.* offer their.   *Lev* 17:7
fifty they shall serve *no m. Num* 8:25
speak *no m.* to me of this. *Deut* 3:26
Lord spake, and added *no m.*   5:22
circumcise, and be *no m.* stiff-. 10:16
do *no m.* such wickedness.   13:11
    17:13
henceforth return *no m.*   17:16
thou shalt see it *no m.* again. 28:68
I am 120 years, I can *no m. Jo.* 31:2
God will *no m.* drive out. *Josh* 23:13
up their heads *no m.*   *Judg* 8:28
I will deliver you *no m.*   10:13
was *no m.* sad.   *1 Sam* 1:18
talk *no m.* so exceeding proudly. 2:3
came *no m.* into the coast of.   7:13
and Samuel came *no m.* to.   15:35
let him go *no m.* home to his. 18:2
return, for I will *no m.* do.   26:21
and he sought *no m.* again.   27:4
and answereth me *no m.*   28:15
after Israel *no m.*   *2 Sam* 2:28
dwell in a place of their own, and
    move *no m.*   7:10; *1 Chr* 17:9
shalt go *no m.* out with us to battle.
    2 Sam 21:17
there was *no m.* spirit in her.
    1 Ki 10:5; *2 Chr* 9:4
Elisha saw Elijah *no m.*   *2 Ki* 2:12
bands of Syria came *no m.*   6:23
no m. of her than the skull.   9:35
shall *no m.* carry the tabernacle.
    1 Chr 23:26
us build, that we be *no m. Neh* 2:17
no m. on the sabbath.   13:21
Vashti came *no m.*   *Esth* 1:19
she came *no m.* in to the king. 2:14
eyes shall *no m.* see good. *Job* 7:7
shall see me *no m.*   8
shall come up *no m.*   9
return *no m.* to his house.   10
till the heavens be *no m.*   14:12
saw him shall see him *no m.*   20:9
shall be *no m.* remembered.   24:20
they answered *no m.*   32:15, 16
iniquity, I will do *no m.*   34:32
the battle, do *no m.*   41:8
earth may *no m.* oppress. *Ps* 10:18
I go hence, and be *no m.*   39:13
he shall rise up *no m.*   41:8
see not signs, there is *no m.*   74:9
and be favourable *no m.*   77:7
name of Israel be *no m.* in.   83:4
thou rememberest *no m.*   88:5
thereof shall know it *no m.* 103:16
let the wicked be *no m.* 104:35
so is the wicked *no m.* *Pr* 10:25
remember his misery *no m.*   31:7
king, who will *no m.* be. *Eccl* 4:13
bring *no m.* vain oblations. *Isa* 1:13
shall *no m.* stay on him that. 10:20
driven away, and be *no m.*   19:7
there is *no m.* strength.   23:10
no m. rejoice.   12
the earth shall *no m.* cover. 26:21
shall weep *no m.*   30:19
vile person shall be *no m.*   32:5
I shall behold man *no m.*   38:11
shalt *no m.* be called tender. 47:1
shalt *no m.* be called the lady.   5
shalt *no m.* drink it again.   51:22
no m. come into thee the uncircum-
    cised.   52:1
violence shall *no m.* be heard. 60:18
the **sun** shall be *no m.* thy light. 19

sun shall *no m.* go down. *Isa* 60:20
thou shalt *no m.* be termed.   62:4
I will *no m.* give thy corn to.   8
weeping shall be *no m.* heard. 65:19
there shall be *no m.* thence an.   20
will come *no m.* unto thee. *Jer* 2:31
they shall say *no m.* The ark.   3:16
no m. be called Tophet. 7:32; 19:6
his name may be *no m.*   11:19
shall *no m.* be said, The Lord liveth.
    16:14; 23:7
shall return *no m.*   22:10
see this land *no m.*   12
fear *no m.* nor be dismayed.   23:4
of Lord shall ye mention *no m.*   36
fall and rise *no m.* because of. 25:27
teach *no m.* every man his neighbour,
    and I . . . their sin *no m.*   31:34
should be *no m.* a nation.   33:24
shall see this place *no m.*   42:18
name shall be *no m.* named. 44:26
saith Lord, Is wisdom *no m.?* 49:7
it shall *no m.* be inhabited. 50:39
law is *no m.* her prophets. *Lam* 2:9
he will *no m.* carry thee away. 4:22
no m. any vain vision. *Ezek* 12:24
and my word shall be *no m.*   25
the wall is *no m.*   13:15
and they shall be *no m.* in.   21
ye shall see *no m.* vanity.   23
go *no m.* astray.   14:11
and will be *no m.* angry.   16:42
that his voice should be *no m.* 19:9
ye my holy name *no m.*   20:39
it shall be *no m.* saith. 21:13, 27
shalt be *no m.* remembered.   32
speak, and be *no m.* dumb.   24:27
thou shalt be *no m.* built.   26:14
shalt be *no m.*   21
he *no m.* a pricking brier.   28:24
they shall *no m.* rule over.   29:15
shall be *no m.* the confidence of. 16
there shall be *no m.* a prince. 30:13
shall be *no m.* a prey. 34:22, 28, 29
shalt devour men *no m.*   36:14
shall be *no m.* two nations.   37:22
house of Israel *no m.* defile.   43:7
my princes shall *no m.* oppress. 45:8
I will *no m.* have mercy. *Hos* 1:6
shalt call me *no m.* Baali.   2:16
they shall *no m.* be remembered. 17
out, I will love them *no m.*   9:15
I will *no m.* make you a. *Joel* 2:19
fallen, she shall *no m.* rise. *Amos* 5:2
they shall *no m.* be pulled out. 9:15
have *no m.* soothsayers. *Mi* 5:12
thou shalt *no m.* worship work. 13
I will afflict thee *no m.*   *Nah* 1:12
a command that *no m.* of thy.   14
the wicked shall *no m.* pass.   15
thy messengers shall *no m.*   2:13
shalt *no m.* be haughty. *Zeph* 3:11
I will *no m.* pity the. *Zech* 11:6
shall *no m.* be remembered. 13:2
be *no m.* utter destruction. 14:11
be *no m.* the Canaanite in the.   21
they are *no m.* twain, but one.
    Mat 19:6; *Mark* 10:8
and ye suffer him *no m. Mark* 7:12
and enter *no m.* into him.   9:25
I will drink *no m.* of the fruit. 14:25
exact *no m.* than what. *Luke* 3:13
we have *no m.* but five loaves. 9:13
after that have *no m.* that.   12:4
thou art made whole, sin *no m.*
    John 5:14; 8:11
back, and walked *no m.* with.   6:66
the world seeth me *no m.*   14:19
no m. can ye, except ye abide. 15:4
Father, and ye see me *no m.* 16:10
no m. the anguish, for joy.   21
when I shall *no m.* speak in.   25
now I am *no m.* in the world. 17:11
eunuch saw him *no m. Acts* 8:39
now *no m.* to return to corruption.
    13:34
shall see my face *no m.* 20:25, 38
dieth *no m.*; death hath *no m.*
    Rom 6:9
now then it is *no m.* I that. 7:17, 20
no m. of works: otherwise grace is
    no m. grace.   11:6
know we him *no m.*   *2 Cor* 5:16
it is *no m.* of promise. *Gal* 3:18

thou art *no m.* a servant. *Gal* 4:7
ye are *no m.* strangers. *Eph* 2:19
we be *no m.* children tossed.   4:14
let him that stole steal *no m.*   28
iniquities I will remember *no m.*
    Heb 8:12; 10:17
had *no m.* conscience of sins. 10:2
no m. offering for sin.   18, 26
overcometh shall go *no m. Rev* 3:12
no m., neither thirst any more. 7:16
find them *no m.* at all.   18:14
be heard *no m.* in thee.   22, 23
deceive the nations *no m.*   20:3
no m. sea.   21:1
no m. death.   4
no m. curse.   22:3

moreover
m. by them is thy servant. *Ps* 19:11
he said, *M.* there shall be. *Isa* 39:8
thou hast *m.* multiplied. *Ezek* 16:29
m. this is their resemblance.
    Zech 5:6
mockings, *m.* of bonds. *Heb* 11:36

Moriah
into the land of *M.*   *Gen* 22:2
the house of Lord in *M.*   *2 Chr* 3:1

morning
m. arose, the angels.   *Gen* 19:15
servants rose up in the *m.*   24:54
they rose betimes in the *m.*   26:31
the *m.* behold it was Leah.   29:25
came in unto them in the *m.*   40:6
in the *m.* he shall devour.   49:27
thee to Pharaoh in the *m. Ex* 7:15
in the *m.* the east wind.   10:13
to his strength in the *m.*   14:27
in the *m.* ye shall see the glory. 16:7
shall give you in the *m.* bread. 8, 12
in the *m.* the dew lay round.   13
one lamb thou shalt offer in the *m.*
    29:39; *Num* 28:4
meat offering of the *m.*   *Ex* 29:41
m. and come up in the *m.*   34:2
nor sacrifice be left to the *m.*   25
altar all night to the *m.*   *Lev* 6:9
taken up in the *m.*   *Num* 9:21
Balaam rose in the *m.* and. 22:21, 22
in *m.,* would God it were. *Deut* 28:67
death whilst it is yet *m. Judg* 6:31
in the *m.* when it is day, we. 16:2
her lord rose in the *m.* and. 19:27
Israel rose up in the *m.*   20:19
as the light of the *m.* when the sun
    riseth, even a *m.*   *2 Sam* 23:4
was up in the *m.* word came. 24:11
considered it in the *m.*   *1 Ki* 3:21
name of Baal from *m.* to noon. 18:26
some laboured from *m.*   *Neh* 4:21
he read therein from *m.* to.   8:3
seek me in the *m.* but.   *Job* 7:21
shine forth, and be as the *m.* 11:17
m. is to them as the shadow. 24:17
hast thou commanded the *m.?* 38:12
like eyelids of the *m.*   41:18
thou hear in the *m.,* O Lord; in the *m.*
    will I direct my prayer. *Ps* 5:3
but joy cometh in the *m.*   30:5
dominion over them in the *m.* 49:14
sing of thy mercy in the *m.*   59:16
in the *m.* shall my prayer.   88:13
in the *m.* they are like grass. 90:5
in the *m.* it flourisheth and.   6
the dawning of the *m.* 119:147
they that watch for the *m.* 130:6
if I take the wings of the *m.* 139:9
thy lovingkindness in the *m.* 143:8
and princes eat in the *m. Eccl* 10:16
in *m.* sow thy seed, and in the. 11:6
looketh forth as the *m.? S of S* 6:10
O Lucifer, son of the *m. Isa* 14:12
before the *m.* he is not.   17:14
the watchman said, The *m.* 21:12
for *m.* by *m.* shall it pass. 28:19
he wakeneth *m.* by *m.* he.   50:4
thy light break forth as the *m.* 58:8
were as fed horses in the *m. Jer* 5:8
hear the cry in the *m.*   20:16
execute judgement in the *m.* 21:12
the *m.* is come on thee. *Ezek* 7:7*
the *m.* is gone forth, the rod. 10*
in the *m.* came the word of.   12:8
I spake to the people in the *m.* : . . .
I did in the *m.* as I was.   24:18

came to me in the *m.*   *Ezek* 33:22
is prepared as the *m.*   *Hos* 6:3
for your goodness is as a *m.*   4
m. it burneth as a flaming fire. 7:6
a *m.* shall the king of Israel. 10:15*
as the *m.* spread upon the. *Joel* 2:2*
maketh the *m.* darkness. *Amos* 4:13
the shadow of death into the *m.* 5:8
a worm when the *m.* rose. *Jonah* 4:7
when the *m.* is light.   *Mi* 2:1
in the *m.* it will be foul. *Mat* 16:3
when *m.* was come, the elders. 27:1
the *m.* as they passed. *Mark* 11:20
the cockcrowing, or in *m.*   13:35
   see **cloud, evening**

early in the **morning**
Abraham gat up *early in m.*
   Gen 19:27; 21:14; 22:3
Abimelech rose *early in the m.* 28:8
Jacob rose up *early in m.*   28:18
Laban rose *early in m.,* kissed. 31:55
rise up *early in m.,* stand. *Ex* 8:20
   9:13
Moses rose *early in m.* 24:4; 34:4
Joshua rose *early in m.*   *Josh* 3:1
   6:12; 7:16; 8:10
city rose *early in the m.* *Judg* 6:28
Gideon rose *early in m.*   38
Levite rose *early in m.*   19:5, 8
they rose up *early in the m.*
   1 Sam 1:19; 29:11; *2 Ki* 3:22
   19:35; *2 Chr* 20:20; *Isa* 37:36
Samuel rose *early in m. 1 Sam* 15:12
David rose *early in m.*   17:20
wherefore rise up *early in the m.* 29:10
Job rose up *early in the m. Job* 1:5
friend, rising *early in m.* *Pr* 27:14
rise *early in m.* to follow. *Isa* 5:11
arose *early in m.* they were. 37:36
king Darius rose very *early in m.*
   Dan 6:19
went *early in m.* to hire. *Mat* 20:1
early in m. came to sepulchre.
   Mark 16:2; *Luke* 24:1*
the people came *early in m.*
   Luke 21:38; *John* 8:2
entered into the temple *early in m.*
   Acts 5:21*

every **morning**
gathered manna *every m. Ex* 16:21
thereon sweet incense *every m.* 30:7
free offerings *every m.*   36:3
burn wood on it *every m. Lev* 6:12
opening *every m.* pertaineth to.
   1 Chr 9:27
to stand *every m.* to thank. 23:30
they burn to the Lord *every m.*
   2 Chr 13:11
visit him *every m.*   *Job* 7:18
been chastened *every m.* *Ps* 73:14
be thou our arm *every m. Isa* 33:2
mercies are new *every m. Lam* 3:23
prepare a lamb *every m. Ezek* 46:13
meat offering *every m.*   14
every m. a burnt offering.   15
your sacrifices *every m. Amos* 4:4
every m. doth he bring judgement to
light.   *Zeph* 3:5

morning *light*
let us spoil them until *m. light.*
   1 Sam 14:36
pertain to him by *m. light.* 25:22
told him nothing until *m. light.* 36
over Jordan by *m. light. 2 Sam* 17:22
if we tarry until *m. light.* *2 Ki* 7:9

morning *star and stars*
when *m.* stars sang together.
   Job 38:7
give him the *m. star.* *Rev* 2:28
I am the bright and *m. star.* 22:10

until the **morning**
let nothing of it remain *until the m.*
   Ex 12:10; 16:19; 23:18; 29:34
   Lev 7:15; *Num* 9:12
at the door *until the m.* *Ex* 12:22
left of it *until the m.*   16:20
to be kept *until the m.*   23
not abide *until the m. Lev* 19:13
flesh remain *until the m. Deut* 16:4
her all night *until the m. Judg* 19:25
lie down *until the m.* *Ruth* 3:13
she lay *until the m.*   14
Samuel lay *until the m. 1 Sam* 3:15

heed to thyself *until m. 1 Sam* 19:2
kings in two heaps *until m. 2 Ki* 10:8
fill of love *until the m.* *Pr* 7:18
I reckoned *until the m.* *Isa* 38:13

morning *watch*
in *m. watch* the Lord. *Ex* 14:24
of host in *m. watch.* *1 Sam* 11:11

morrow
Lord did that thing on the *m. Ex* 9:6
on *m.* the remainder. *Lev* 7:16; 19:6
none of it until the *m.* 22:30*
on *m.* after sabbath the priest. 23:11
ye shall count from the *m.* after. 15
on *m.* the congregation. *Num* 16:41
manna ceased on *m.* after. *Josh* 5:12
on the *m.* he took a thick. *2 Ki* 8:15
not the bones till the *m.* *Zeph* 3:3
no thought for the *m.,* for the *m.*
shall take thought for. *Mat* 6:34
to depart on the *m.* *Acts* 20:7
know not what shall be on the *m.*
   Jas 4:14

to-morrow
to-m. shall this sign be. *Ex* 8:23
to-m. the Lord shall do this. 9:5
to-m. is the rest of the holy. 16:23
sanctify them to-day and *to-m.* 19:10
Aaron said, *To-m.* is a feast. 32:5
sanctify yourselves against *to-m.* ye.
   Num 11:18; *Josh* 7:13
to-m. the Lord will shew. *Num* 16:5*
be thou, they and Aaron *to-m.* 16
to-m. Lord will do wonders. *Josh* 3:5
to-m. he will be wroth with. 22:18
to-m. get you early on. *Judg* 19:9
go up, for then I will. 20:28
to-m. by that time sun. *1 Sam* 11:9
to-m. is the new moon. 20:5, 18
to-m. shalt thou and thy. 28:19
my servants to thee *to-m. 1 Ki* 20:6
we will eat my son *to-m. 2 Ki* 6:28
to-m. a measure of fine flour be. 7:1
to Jezreel by *to-m.* this time. 10:6
to-m. go ye down against them.
   2 Chr 20:16, 17
I will do *to-m.* as the king. *Esth* 5:8
to-m. am I invited to her with. 12
to-m. I will give, when. *Pr* 3:28
boast not thyself *to-m.* thou. 27:1
let us eat, for *to-m.* we die.
   Isa 22:13; *1 Cor* 15:32
to-m. shall be as this day. *Isa* 56:12
to-m. is cast into the oven. *Mat* 6:30
   Luke 12:28
cures to-day and *to-m.* *Luke* 13:32
I must walk to-day and *to-m.* 33
to-m. said he, thou shalt. *Acts* 25:22
to-day or *to-m.* we will go. *Jas* 4:13

morsel
I will fetch a *m.* of bread. *Gen* 18:5
heart with a *m.* of bread. *Judg* 19:5
eat bread, and dip thy *m. Ruth* 2:14
or have eaten my *m.* *Job* 31:17
better is a dry *m.* and. *Pr* 17:1
the *m.* thou hast eaten shalt. 23:8
who for one *m.* sold his. *Heb* 12:16*
   see **bread**

morsels
forth his ice like a *m.* *Ps* 147:17

mortal
m. man be more just ? *Job* 4:17
reign in your *m.* body. *Rom* 6:12
shall also quicken your *m.* 8:11
this *m.* must put on. *1 Cor* 15:53, 54
manifest in our *m.* flesh. *2 Cor* 4:11

mortality
m. might be swallowed. *2 Cor* 5:4

mortally
smite his neighbour *m. Deut* 19:11

mortar
mills, or beat it in a *m. Num* 11:8
bray a fool in a *m.* *Pr* 27:22

morter (*mortar*)
slime had they for *m.* *Gen* 11:3
made them serve in *m.* *Ex* 1:14
take other *m.* and plaster. *Lev* 14:42
and shall break down the *m.* of. 45
upon princes as upon *m. Isa* 41:25
lo, others daubed it with untempered
   m. Ezek 13:10, 11, 14, 15; 22:28
clay, and tread the *m. Nah* 3:14

mortgaged
also said, We have *m.* *Neh* 5:3

mortify
if ye *m.* deeds of body. *Rom* 8:13†
m. your members which. *Col* 3:5†

Moses
called his name *M.*   *Ex* 2:10
M. feared, and said, This thing. 14
sought to slay *M.* but *M.* fled. 15
called to him and said, *M. M.* 3:4
M. hid his face, he was afraid. 6
anger was kindled against *M.* 4:14
go to meet *M.*   27
M. returned unto the Lord. 5:22
according to the word of *M.* 8:13, 31
   9:12, 35; 12:35
M. stretched forth his hand. 10:22
M. was very great.   11:3
the Lord and his servant *M.* 14:31
the people murmured against *M.*
   15:24; 17:3
they hearkened not to *M.* 16:20
M. cried to the Lord.   17:4
M. did so. 6; *Num* 17:11
M.' hands were heavy. *Ex* 17:12
M. built an altar.   15
M. sat to judge.   18:13
M. went up unto God.   19:3
M. returned the words of the. 8
called *M.* up to mount Sinai. 19:20
M. drew near unto the thick. 20:21
M. alone shall come near. 24:2
M. wrote all the words of the. 4
and *M.* went into the midst of. 18
as for *M.* we wot not what. 32:1, 23
M. besought the Lord.   11
M.' anger waxed hot.   19
the Lord talked with *M.* 33:9
M. went up.   34:4
M. put the vail upon his face. 34:35
M. did look on all work; *M.* 39:43
M. was not able to enter. 40:35
M. sought the goat of. *Lev* 10:16
the blasphemer to *M.*   24:11
as the Lord spake to *M. Num* 5:4
the people cried to *M.,* and *M.* 11:2
M. heard people weep through. 10
indeed spoken only by *M.?* 12:2
M. was very meek above all. 3
M. is not so, who is faithful in. 7
ark and *M.* departed not out. 14:44
when *M.* heard it, he fell upon. 6
M. laid up the rods before the. 17:7
the people chode with *M.* 20:3
against God and against *M.* 21:5
M. made a serpent of brass and. 9
Midianitish woman in sight of *M.*
   25:6
M. sent them to war, them. 31:6
M. was wroth with the officers. 14
M. wrote their goings out by. 33:2
M. charged the people. *Deut* 27:11
M. wrote this law.   31:9
M. wrote this song, and taught. 22
wherewith *M.* the man of God. 33:1
M. the servant of the Lord. 34:5
since in Israel like to *M.* 10
as I was with *M.* so I. *Josh* 1:5; 3:7
as we hearkened to *M.* so. 1:17
Joshua, as they feared *M.* 4:14
Lord spake this word to *M.* 14:10
as I was in the day *M.* sent me. 11
as it is written in the law of *M.*
   1 Ki 2:3; *2 Ki* 23:25; *2 Chr* 23:18
   Ezra 3:2; *Dan* 9:11, 13
   Luke 24:44; *1 Cor* 9:9
the two tables which *M.* *1 Ki* 8:9
M. the man of God. *1 Chr* 23:14
the son of *M.* was ruler. 26:24
known his ways unto *M. Ps* 103:7
he sent *M.* his servant. 105:26
they envied *M.* also in the. 106:16
had not *M.* stood before him. 23
so that it went ill with *M.* for. 32
the right hand of *M.* *Isa* 63:12
though *M.* and Samuel. *Jer* 15:1
remember the law of *M.* *Mal* 4:4
appeared *M.* and Elias talking with.
   Mat 17:3; *Mark* 9:4; *Luke* 9:30
let us make one tabernacle for *M.*
   Mat 17:4; *Mark* 9:5
did *M.* then command ? *Mat* 19:7
M. suffered you to put away. 8

Pharisees sit in *M.'* seat. *Mat* 23:2
did *M.* command you ? *Mark* 10:3
M. wrote. If a man's brother die.
      12:19; *Luke* 20:28
M. and the prophets. *Luke* 16:29
if they hear not *M.* and the. 31
dead are raised, *M.* shewed. 20:37
beginning at *M.* and all the prophets,
he expounded. 24:27
law was given by *M.* *John* 1:17
have found him of whom *M.* 45
as *M.* lifted up the serpent. 3:14
one accuseth you, even *M.* 5:45
had ye believed *M.* ye had. 46
M. gave you not that bread. 6:32
did not *M.* give you the law ? 7:19
not because it is of *M.* but of. 22
that the law of *M.* should not. 23
disciple, we are *M.'* disciples. 9:28
we know that God spake unto *M.* 29
for *M.* truly said unto. *Acts* 3:22
blasphemous words against *M.* 6:11
change the customs which *M.* 14
in which time *M.* was born. 7:20
then *M.* trembled and durst not. 32
this *M.* whom they refused, did. 35
M. that said unto Israel. 37
be justified by the law of *M.* 13:39
circumcised after manner of *M.* 15:1
them to keep the law of *M.* 5
M. hath in every city them that. 21
the Jews to forsake *M.* 21:21
things which *M.* did say. 26:22
out of the law of *M.* and. 28:23
from Adam to *M.* *Rom* 5:14
M. describeth righteousness of. 10:5
all baptized to *M.* in. *1 Cor* 10:2
not behold the face of *M.* *2 Cor* 3:7
not as *M.* who put a vail over. 13
when *M.* is read, the vail is. 15
and Jambres withstood *M.* *2 Tim* 3:8
M. was faithful in all. *Heb* 3:2, 5
worthy of more glory than *M.* 3
that came out of Egypt by *M.* 16
which tribe *M.* spake nothing. 7:14
for when *M.* had spoken. 9:19
that despised *M.'* law. 10:28
by faith *M.* was hid three. 11:23
M. refused to be called son of. 24
M. said, I exceedingly fear. 12:21
about the body of *M.* *Jude* 9
song of *M.* and the Lamb. *Rev* 15:3
see **Aaron, book, commanded,
law**

most

m. men proclaim every. *Pr* 20:6
m. of mighty works. *Mat* 11:20
them will love him *m.?* *Luke* 7:42
that he to whom he forgave *m.* 43
sorrowing *m.* of all for. *Acts* 20:38
it be by two, or at *m.* *1 Cor* 14:27

mote

m. that is in thy brother's eye, but
not beam ? *Mat* 7:3; *Luke* 6:41
let me pull out the *m.* *Mat* 7:4
to cast out the *m.* out of thy brother's
eye. 5; *Luke* 6:42

moth

are crushed before the *m.* *Job* 4:19
buildeth his house as a *m.* 27:18
beauty to consume like a *m.* *Ps* 39:11
the *m.* shall eat them up. *Isa* 50:9
                51:8
I be to Ephraim as a *m.* *Hos* 5:12
treasures, where *m.* and rust doth
corrupt. *Mat* 6:19
neither *m.* nor rust corrupt. 20
      Luke 12:33

motheaten

garment that is *m.* *Job* 13:28
your garments *m.* *Jas* 5:2

mother

was the *m.* of all living. *Gen* 3:20
shall be a *m.* of nations. 17:16
told them of her *m.'s* house. 24:28
brother and *m.* precious things. 53
thou the *m.* of thousands of. 60
lest he smite the *m.* with. 32:11
called the child's *m.* *Ex* 2:8
to take a wife and her *m.* *Lev* 20:14
Deborah arose a *m.* *Judg* 5:7
m. of Sisera looked out. 28
go, return each to her *m.'s. Ruth* 1:8

to Zeruiah, Joab's *m.* *2 Sam* 17:25
seekest to destroy a *m.* in. 20:19
be set for the king's *m.* *1 Ki* 2:19
child, she is the *m.* thereof. 3:27
away the king's *m.* *2 Ki* 24:15
and to be a joyful *m.* *Ps* 113:9
doth not bless their *m.* *Pr* 30:11
the only one of her *m.* *S of S* 6:9
of your *m.'s* divorcement ? *Isa* 50:1
your *m.* shall be sore. *Jer* 50:12
as is the *m.* so is the. *Ezek* 16:44
your *m.* was an Hittite, father. 45
women the daughters of one *m.* 23:2
plead with your *m.* for she. *Hos* 2:2
their *m.* hath played the harlot. 5
m. was dashed in pieces upon. 10:14
up against her *m.* a man's enemies.
  Mi 7:6; *Mat* 10:35; *Luke* 12:53
saw Peter's wife's *m.* sick.
      Mat 8:14; *Luke* 4:38
instructed of her *m.* *Mat* 14:8
brought it to her *m.* 11; *Mark* 6:28
born from their *m.'s* womb.
                Mat 19:12
m. of Zebedee's children. 20:20
the *m.* of my Lord should ? *Luke* 1:43
the *m.* of Jesus was there. *John* 2:1
                Acts 1:14
house of Mary *m.* of. *Acts* 12:12
Jerusalem which is the *m. Gal* 4:26
the *m.* of harlots. *Rev* 17:5

see **father**

his **mother**

his m. took him a wife. *Gen* 21:21
into *his m.* Sarah's tent, and . . . after
the death of *his m.* 24:67
brought them to *his m.* 27:14
brought mandrakes to *his m.* 30:14
brother Benjamin, *his m.'s* son. 43:29
he alone is left of *his m.* 44:20
seethe a kid in *his m.'s* milk.
  Ex 23:19; 34:26; *Deut* 14:21
take *his m.'s* daughter. *Lev* 20:17
his m.'s name was Shelomith. 24:11
out of *his m.'s* womb. *Num* 12:12
the daughter of *his m. Deut* 27:22
Abimelech went to *his m.'s. Judg* 9:1
he said to *his m.* 17:2
he restored it to *his m.* 3
his m. made him a little. *1 Sam* 2:19
and *his m.* bare him. *1 Ki* 1:6
his m. he removed from. 15:13
Elijah delivered him to *his m.* 17:23
walked in the way of *his m.* 22:52
lad, Carry him to *his m.* *2 Ki* 4:19
his m. called his name. *1 Chr* 4:9
his m. was his counsellor. *2 Chr* 22:3
mourneth for *his m.* *Ps* 35:14
sin of *his m.* be blotted out. 109:14
is weaned of *his m.* 131:2
is the heaviness of *his m. Pr* 10:1
foolish man despiseth *his m.* 15:20
a child left bringeth *his m.* 29:15
prophecy that *his m.* taught. 31:1
forth of *his m.'s* womb. *Eccl* 5:15
crown wherewith *his m. S of S* 3:11
whom *his m.* comforteth. *Isa* 66:13
his m. was espoused. *Mat* 1:18
young child and *his m.* 2:13, 20
his m. stood without. 12:46
      Mark 3:31; *Luke* 8:19
js not this the carpenter's son ? is
not *his m.* called Mary? *Mat* 13:55
with Holy Ghost from *his m.'s* womb.
              Luke 1:15
his m. said, He shall be called. 60
Joseph and *his m.* knew not. 2:43*
but *his m.* kept these sayings. 51
the only son *of his m.* and. 7:12
he delivered him to *his m.* 15
second time into *his m.'s* womb ?
              John 3:4
his m. stood by the cross of. 19:25
saw *his m.* he saith to *his m.* 26
man lame from *his m.'s* womb.
         Acts 3:2; 14:8
salute Rufus and *his m. Rom* 16:13

mother in law

lieth with his *m.* in law. *Deut* 27:23
kissed her *m.* in law. *Ruth* 1:14
hast done to thy *m.* in law. 2:11
Ruth dwelt with her *m.* in law. 23
all that her *m.* in law bade. 3:6

go not empty to thy *m.* in law.
               Ruth 3:17
riseth up against the *m.* in law.
  Mi 7:6; *Mat* 10:35; *Luke* 12:53

my **mother**

the daughter of *my m.* *Gen* 20:12
even the sons of *my m.* *Judg* 8:19
Nazarite from *my m.'s* womb. 16:17
to her, Ask on, *my m.* *1 Ki* 2:20
naked came I out of *my m.'s. Job* 1:21
up the doors of *my m.'s* womb. 3:10
the worm, Thou art *my m.* 17:14
guided her from *my m.'s* womb. 31:18
when on *my m.'s* breasts. *Ps* 22:9
thou art my God from *my m.'s.* 10
and in sin did *my m.* conceive. 51:5
become an alien to *my m.'s.* 69:8
he that took me out of *my m.'s.* 71:6
hast covered me in *my m.'s.* 139:13
beloved in sight of *my m.* *Pr* 4:3
my m.'s children were angry with me.
            S of S 1:6
brought him to *my m.'s* house. 3:4
sucked the breasts of *my m.* 8:1
bring thee into *my m.'s* house. 2
the bowels of *my m.* he. *Isa* 49:1
woe is me, *my m.* that. *Jer* 15:10
not the day wherein *my m.* 20:14
or that *my m.* might have been. 17
Jesus said, Who is *my m.?*
      Mat 12:48; *Mark* 3:33
behold *my m.* and my brethren.
      Mat 12:49; *Mark* 3:34
my m. and my brethren are these.
            Luke 8:21
separated me from *my m.'s.*
            Gal 1:15

thy **mother**

thy m.'s sons bow down. *Gen* 27:29
shall I and *thy m.* come to ? 37:10
nakedness of *thy m.* *Lev* 18:7
nakedness of daughter of *thy m.* 9
not uncover nakedness of sister of
thy m. 13; 20:19
the son of *thy m.* entice. *Deut* 13:6
so shall *thy m.* be childless among.
            1 Sam 15:33
to the confusion of *thy m.'s.* 20:30
whoredoms of *thy m.* *2 Ki* 9:22
thou slanderest *thine* own *m.'s* son.
            Ps 50:20
forsake not the law of *thy m.*
            Pr 1:8; 6:20
and despise not *thy m.* 23:22
thy m. brought thee forth. *S of S* 8:5
cast thee out, and *thy m.* *Jer* 22:26
father an Amorite, *thy m. Ezek* 16:3
thy m.'s daughter that loatheth. 45
and say, What is *thy m.?* 19:2
thy m. is like a vine in thy. 10
and I will destroy *thy m.* *Hos* 4:5
behold *thy m.* and my brethren.
      Mat 12:47; *Mark* 3:32
      Luke 8:20; *John* 19:27
dwelt in *thy m.* Eunice. *2 Tim* 1:5

mothers

shall be thy nursing *m.* *Isa* 49:23
Lord, concerning their *m. Jer* 16:3
m. where is corn and wine? soul was
poured out into their *m.' Lam* 2:12
we are fatherless, our *m.* are. 5:3
hundredfold, sisters, *m. Mark* 10:30
for murderers of *m.* *1 Tim* 1:9
elder women as *m.;* younger. 5:2

motions

the *m.* of sins did work. *Rom* 7:5*

mouldy

bread of provision was dry and *m.*
            Josh 9:5, 12

mount, -ing

though his excellency in. *Job* 20:6
doth the eagle *m.* up at thy ? 39:27
they *m.* up to heaven. *Ps* 107:26
shall *m.* up as the lifting. *Isa* 9:18*
by the *m.* of Luhith shall. 15:5
they shall *m.* up with wings. 40:31
though Babylon should *m.* up to.
            Jer 51:53
when the cherubims lifted up wings
to *m.* up. *Ezek* 10:16, 19

mount

(This word very frequently means hill country, and is so rendered by the Revisions)

sacrifice on the *m.*	*Gen* 31:54
encamped at the *m.* of.	*Ex* 18:5
whoso toucheth the *m.* shall.	19:12
Moses went down from the *m.*	14
	32:15; 34:29
thick cloud upon the *m.*	16; 24:15
m. Sinai on a smoke.	18
bounds about the *m.*	23
Lord abode upon *m.* Sinai.	24:16
devouring fire on the top of *m.*	17
Lord gave Moses on *m.* Sinai.	31:18
brake them beneath the *m.*	32:19
in the morning to *m.* Sinai.	34:2
man be seen through all the *m.*	3
departed from the *m.*	*Num* 10:33
and came unto *m.* Hor.	20:22
bring up to *m.* Hor.	25
Aaron died in *m.* Hor.	28
point out for you in this *m.*	*Deut* 1:6
long enough in this *m.*	*Deut* 1:6
go to the *m.* of the Amorites.	7
the *m.* burned with fire.	9:15
shall stand upon *m.* Ebal.	27:13
get thee to *m.* Nebo, which.	32:49
shined forth from *m.* Paran.	33:2
draw towards *m.* Tabor.	*Judg* 4:6
depart early from *m.* Gilead.	7:3
gat him up to *m.* Zalmon.	9:48
up by the ascent of *m.*	*2 Sam* 15:30
the top of the *m.* where he.	32*
to Horeb, the *m.* of God.	*1 Ki* 19:8
go and stand on the *m.* before.	11
on right hand the *m.*	*2 Ki* 23:13
go to the *m.* and fetch.	*Neh* 8:15
down also on *m.* Sinai.	9:13
of goats from *m.* Gilead.	*S of S* 4:1
the *m.* of the daughter of Zion.	
	Isa 10:32; 16:1
I will sit on the *m.* of the.	14:13
shall worship in the holy *m.*	27:13
siege against thee with a *m.*	29:3
hew ye trees, and cast a *m.* against.	
	Jer 6:6; *Ezek* 4:2; 21:22; 26:8
north shall cast up a *m.*	*Dan* 11:15
understanding out of *m.* Esau.	*Ob* 8
come to judge the *m.* of Esau.	21
Holy One from *m.* Paran.	*Hab* 3:3
in wilderness of *m.* Sinai.	*Acts* 7:30
the one from the *m.* Sinai.	*Gal* 4:24
Agar is *m.* Sinai in Arabia.	
not come to the *m.*	*Heb* 12:18

see **Carmel, Ephraim, Gerizim Gilboa, Seir, Zion**

before the **mount**

Israel camped *before the m.*	*Ex* 19:2
the flocks feed *before the m.*	34:3

in, or into the **mount**

in the m. of the Lord.	*Gen* 24:14
overtook Jacob in the *m.* Gilead.	
	31:23
and tarried all night *in the m.*	54
met him *in the m.* of God.	*Ex* 4:27
go not up *into the m.*	19:12
Lord said to Moses, Come up to me *into the m.*	24:12; *Deut* 10:1
Moses went up *into the m.* of God.	
	Ex 24:13, 15, 18
Moses was *in the m.* forty days.	
	24:18; *Deut* 9:9; 10:10
their pattern shewed thee *in the m.*	
Ex 25:40; 26:30; 27:8; *Heb* 8:5	
get thee up *into m.*	*Num* 27:12
die *in the m.* as Aaron died *in m.* Hor.	
	Deut 32:50
altar to Lord *in m.* Ebal.	*Josh* 8:30
the sepulchres *in the m.*	*2 Ki* 23:16
to build house of Lord *in m.* Moriah.	
	2 Chr 3:1
rise up as *in m.* Perazim.	*Isa* 28:21
spake to him *in m.* Sinai.	*Acts* 7:38
with him *in the holy m.*	*2 Pet* 1:18

mount *of Olives*

stand on the *m.* of Olives, and the *m.* of Olives shall cleave.	*Zech* 14:4
they were come to the *m.* of Olives.	
	Mat 21:1; *Luke* 19:29
and as he sat upon *m.* of Olives.	
	Mat 24:3; *Mark* 13:3

---

sung an hymn, they went out into *m.* of Olives.	*Mat* 26:30
	Mark 14:26; *Luke* 22:39
descent of *m.* of Olives.	*Luke* 19:37
and abode in *m.* of Olives.	21:37
went unto *m.* of Olives.	*John* 8:1
returned from the *m.* of Olives.	
	Acts 1:12

mountain

(Used as now both literally and figuratively for a great mass, or a vast quantity. The Revisions frequently change it to hill, or hill country)

A Catalogue of the most famous mountains mentioned in Scripture

Abarim, *on the East of Jordan, in* Moab. Nebo *and* Pisgah *were parts of this,* Num 27:12; Deut 34:1.

Ararat, *on which Noah's ark rested,* Gen 8:4.

Bashan, *probably a whole district of hill country.*

Carmel, *on the Mediterranean Sea on the border of Phoenicia,* 1 Ki 18:20-42.

Ebal, *in Samaria near Shechem,* Deut 11:26-29.

Gerizim, *separated by a valley from Ebal,* Deut 11:26-29.

Gilboa, *on which King Saul met his death,* 1 Sam 31:1.

Gilead, *a mountainous region east of Jordan.*

Hermon, *probably the scene of the Transfiguration,* Mat 17:1.

Hor, *on which Aaron died,* Num 20:25, 27.

Hor *(another),* Num 34:7, 8. *Probably Lebanon.*

Horeb or Sinai, *the Mount of God, or of the Law.*

Lebanon, *the most important range in Syria, to the north,* Josh 1:4; 1 Ki 5:2-7.

Moab, *Mts. of, a general term for the hill country east of Jordan.*

Moriah, *the site of the temple in Jerusalem.*

Nebo (Pisgah), *the place of Moses' death,* Deut. 34:1.

Olivet *or* Mt. *of* Olives, *near Jerusalem, associated much with our Saviour.*

Seir, *the mountainous district east of the Dead Sea,* Gen 14:6.

Sinai. *See* Horeb.

Tabor, *on the Plain of Esdraelon,* Judg 4:6-15; 19:22.

Zion *or* Sion, *one the mountains on which Jerusalem was built, the south-east corner.*

remained fled to the *m.*	*Gen* 14:10
escape to the *m.*	19:17
I cannot escape to the *m.*	19
came to the *m.* of God.	*Ex* 3:1
Egypt, shall serve God on this *m.*	12
to him out of the *m.* saying.	19:3
people saw the *m.* smoking.	18
up into top of the *m.*	*Num* 14:40
ye are come to the *m.*	*Deut* 1:20
ye have compassed this *m.*	2:3
goodly *m.* and Lebanon.	3:25
the *m.* burnt with fire.	4:11; 5:23
call the people to the *m.*	33:19
get ye to the *m.* and hide.	*Josh* 2:16
plain and *m.* of Israel.	11:16
give me this *m.*	14:12
the *m.* shall be thine.	17:18
drave out the inhabitants of the *m.*	
	Judg 1:19
forced children of Dan into *m.*	34
on a *m.* on the one side, and Israel stood on a *m.* on.	*1 Sam* 17:3
this side of the *m.* and David and his men on that side of the *m.*	23:26
cast him on some *m.*	*2 Ki* 2:16
the *m.* was full of horses.	6:17
surely the *m.* falling.	*Job* 14:18
flee as a bird to your *m.*?	*Ps* 11:1
thou hast made my *m.* to.	30:7
brought to this *m.* his right.	78:54

---

the *m.* of the Lord's house established.	*Isa* 2:2; *Mi* 4:1
let us go up to the *m.* of the Lord.	
	Isa 2:3; *Mi* 4:2
a beacon on top of a *m.*	*Isa* 30:17
goeth with a pipe to *m.* of Lord.	29
every *m.* shall be made low.	40:4
	Luke 3:5
hunt them from every *m.*	*Jer* 16:16
O my *m.* in the field, I will give.	17:3
the *m.* of the house as high places of.	
	26:18; *Mi* 3:12
people have gone from *m.*	*Jer* 50:6
O *m.* saith the Lord . . . and I will make thee a burnt *m.*	51:25
eyes are dim, because of *m.* of Zion.	
	Lam 5:18
Lord stood on the *m.*	*Ezek* 11:23
as profane out of *m.* of God.	28:16
the house on top of the *m.*	43:12
stone became a great *m.*	*Dan* 2:35
the stone was cut out of the *m.*	45
to thee from *m.* to *m.*	*Mi* 7:12
go up to *m.*, bring wood.	*Hag* 1:8
who art thou, O great *m.*?	*Zech* 4:7
m. of the Lord, the holy *m.*	8:3
half of *m.* shall remove.	14:4
he went up into a *m.*	*Mat* 5:1
	14:23; 15:29; *Mark* 3:13; 6:46
	Luke 6:12; 9:28; *John* 6:3, 15
come down from the *m.*	*Mat* 8:1
them into an high *m.* apart.	17:1
down from the *m.*	9; *Mark* 9:9
a grain of mustard, shall say to this *m.*	*Mat* 17:20; 21:21; *Mark* 11:23
into a *m.* where Jesus.	*Mat* 28:16
swine feeding on *m.*	*Luke* 8:32
as a beast touch the *m.*	*Heb* 12:20
every *m.* and island were.	*Rev* 6:14
as it were a great *m.* burning.	8:8

see **holy**

high mountain

banner upon the *high m.*	*Isa* 13:2
upon every *high m.* rivers.	30:25
get thee up into the *high m.*	40:9
on a lofty and *high m.* hast.	57:7
gone up upon every *high m.*	*Jer* 3:6
plant it on a *high m.*	*Ezek* 17:22
set me on a very *high m.*	40:2
taketh him up into an exceeding *high m.* and.	*Mat* 4:8; *Luke* 4:5
Peter, James, and John, and bringeth into *high m.*	*Mat* 17:1; *Mark* 9:2
in the Spirit to *high m.*	*Rev* 21:10

in the, or in this **mountain**

Zoar, and dwelt *in the m.*	*Gen* 19:30
plant them *in the m.*	*Ex* 15:17
go up *into the m.*	*Num* 13:17
up *in this m.* Abarim.	*Deut* 32:49
he blew a trumpet *in the m.* of.	
	Judg 3:27
David remained *in a m.*	*1 Sam* 23:14
80,000 to hew *in the m.*	*2 Chr* 2:2
God is to be praised *in the m.* of.	
	Ps 48:1
in this m. shall the Lord.	*Isa* 25:6
he will destroy *in this m.* the face.	7
in this m. shall the hand of.	10
in the m. of Israel I.	*Ezek* 17:23
ye kine, that are *in the m.*	*Amos* 4:1
woe to them that trust *in the m.*	6:1
worshipped *in this m.*	*John* 4:20
neither *in this m.* nor Jerusalem.	21

mountains

m. were covered.	*Gen* 7:20
ark rested on the *m.*	8:4
in tenth month tops of the *m.*	5
departed from the *m.*	*Num* 33:48
destroy places on the high *m.*	
	Deut 12:2
the Anakims from the *m.*	*Josh* 11:21
the *m.* melted from.	*Judg* 5:5
go up and down on the *m.*	11:37
her virginity upon the *m.*	38
ye *m.* of Gilboa, let.	*2 Sam* 1:21
strong wind rent the *m.*	*1 Ki* 19:11
as the roes on the *m.*	*1 Chr* 12:8
all Israel scattered on the *m.*	
	2 Chr 18:16
which removeth the *m.*	*Job* 9:5
he overturneth the *m.* by the.	28:9
m. bring forth food.	40:20
is like the great *m.*	*Ps* 36:6

though the *m.* be carried into. *Ps* 46:2
though the *m.* shake with the. 3
strength setteth fast the *m.* 65:6
the *m.* shall bring peace. 72:3
glorious than *m.* of prey. 76:4
flames setteth the *m.* on fire. 83:14
before the *m.* were brought. 90:2
waters stood above the *m.* 104:6
they go up by the *m.*; go down by. 8
m. skipped like rams. 114:4, 6
as the *m.* are round about. 125:2
that descended on the *m.* 133:3
touch the *m.* and they shall. 144:5
grass to grow on the *m.* 147:8
m. and all hills praise the. 148:9
before the *m.* were settled. *Pr* 8:25
leaping on the *m.* *S of S* 2:8
be like a roe on the *m.* 17; 8:14
look from Amana and the *m.* 4:8
the day of the Lord shall be upon
all the high *m.* *Isa* 2:14
and on my *m.* tread him. 14:25
up an ensign on the *m.* 18:3
the *m.* shall be melted with. 34:3
who hath weighed the *m.*? 40:12
thou shalt thresh the *m.* and. 41:15
and I will make waste *m.* 42:15
into singing, ye *m.* 44:23; 49:13
make all my *m.* a way. 49:11
how beautiful upon the *m.* are the
feet of him that. 52:7; *Nah* 1:15
for the *m.* shall depart. *Isa* 54:10
m. shall break forth before. 55:12
the *m.* might flow down at. 64:1, 3
burnt incense on the *m.* 65:7
out of Judah an inheritor of my *m.* 9
I beheld the *m.* and. *Jer* 4:24
for the *m.* will I take up a. 9:10
stumble on the dark *m.* 13:16
from the *m.* bringing offerings. 17:26
vines on the *m.* of Samaria. 31:5
as Tabor among the *m.* so. 46:18
turned them away on the *m.* 50:6
pursued us on the *m.* *Lam* 4:19
set thy face toward the *m. Ezek* 6:2
and say, Ye *m.* of Israel, hear the. 3
shall be on the *m.* like doves. 7:16
not eaten upon the *m.* 18:6, 15
but hath eaten upon the *m.* 11
no more be heard on the *m.* 19:9
in thee they eat upon the *m.* 22:9
upon the *m.* his branches. 31:12
I will lay thy flesh on the *m.* 32:5
the *m.* of Israel shall be. 33:28
wandered through all the *m.* 34:6
feed them on the *m.* of Israel. 13, 14
I will fill his *m.* with his slain. 35:8
spoken against the *m.* of Israel. 12
m. of Israel, and say, Ye *m.* of Israel,
hear the word of the. 36:1, 4
but ye, O *m.* of Israel, shall shoot. 8
one nation on the *m.* of Israel. 37:22
out against the *m.* of Israel. 38:8
m. shall be thrown down. 20
I will call for a sword against him
throughout all my *m.* 21
and will bring thee on the *m.* 39:2
thou shalt fall on the *m.* of Israel. 4
even a great sacrifice on the *m.* 17
morning spread upon the *m. Joel* 2:2
m. shall drop down new wine. 3:18
assemble yourselves on the *m.* of.
Amos 3:9
he that formeth the *m.* the. 4:13
the *m.* shall drop sweet wine. 9:13
the *m.* shall be molten. *Mi* 1:4
arise, contend thou before the *m.* 6:1
hear ye, O ye *m.* the Lord's. 2
the *m.* quake at him. *Nah* 1:5
people scattered on the *m.* 3:18
m. were scattered, the hills. *Hab* 3:6
m. saw thee, and they trembled. 10
a drought on the *m.* *Hag* 1:11
between the *m.* of brass. *Zech* 6:1
and laid his *m.* waste. *Mal* 1:3
goeth into the *m.* and. *Mat* 18:12
be in Judæa flee into the *m.* 24:16
that I could remove *m.* 1 *Cor* 13:2
the *m.* were not found. *Rev* 16:20
heads are seven *m.* on which. 17:9

in the **mountains**
to slay them in the *m.* *Ex* 32:12
pitched *in m.* of Abarim. *Num* 33:47

not to the cities *in the m. Deut* 2:37
kings that dwell *in the m. Josh* 10:6
made them dens *in the m. Judg* 6:2
as doth hunt a partridge *in the m.*
1 *Sam* 26:20
hewers *in the m.* 1 *Ki* 5:15
made high places *in m.* 2 *Chr* 21:11
had vine dressers *in the m.* 26:10
multitude *in the m.* like. *Isa* 13:4
day he was *in the m.* *Mark* 5:5
in deserts and *in the m. Heb* 11:38

of the **mountains**
tops *of the m.* were seen. *Gen* 8:5
offer him on one of *m.* I will. 22:2
Balak brought me out of the *m.*
Num 23:7
foundations of the *m.* *Deut* 32:22
things of the ancient *m.* 33:15
liers in wait for him in top of the
m. *Judg* 9:25
down from the top of the *m.* thou
seest the shadow of the *m.* as. 36
I am come up to height of *m.*
2 *Ki* 19:23; *Isa* 37:24
with the showers of the *m. Job* 24:8
range of the *m.* is his pasture. 39:8
I know all the fowls of the *m.*
Ps 50:11
of corn on top of the *m.* 72:16
and herbs of the *m.* *Pr* 27:25
shall be established in top of the *m.*
Isa 2:2; *Mi* 4:1
as the chaff of the *m.* *Isa* 17:13
left to the fowls of the *m.* 18:6
shout from the top of the *m.* 42:11
the multitude of the *m.* *Jer* 3:23
cities of the *m.* shall flocks. 33:13
be in the tops of the *m. Ezek* 6:13
sounding again of the *m.* 7:7
on the tops of the *m.* *Hos* 4:13
chariots on tops of the *m. Joel* 2:5
to the bottom of the *m.* *Jonah* 2:6
flee to the valley of the *m. Zech* 14:5
in the rocks of the *m.* *Rev* 6:15

to the **mountains**
I will get me to the *m.* *S of S* 4:6
and crying to the *m.* *Isa* 22:5
thus saith the Lord to the *m.*
Ezek 6:3; 36:4
thy blood even to the *m.* 32:6
man, prophesy to the *m.* 36:1, 6
they shall say to the *m.* *Hos* 10:8
nigh to the *m.* a herd. *Mark* 5:11
let them that be in Judaea flee to the
m. 13:14; *Luke* 21:21
begin to say to *m.* Fall on us.
Luke 23:30; *Rev* 6:16

mounts
(*American Revision.* mounds)
m. are come to the city. *Jer* 32:24
houses thrown down by the *m.* 33:4
him, by casting up *m.* *Ezek* 17:17

mourn
Abraham came to *m.* *Gen* 23:2
how long wilt thou *m.*? 1 *Sam* 16:1
rend clothes, and *m.* 2 *Sam* 3:31
came into the city to *m.* 1 *Ki* 13:29
all Israel shall *m.* for him. 14:13
holy to the Lord, *m.* not. *Neh* 8:9
an appointment to *m.* *Job* 2:11
that those which *m.* may be. 5:11
soul within him shall *m.* 14:22
I *m.* in my complaint. *Ps* 55:2*
and thou *m.* at the last. *Pr* 5:11
bear rule, the people *m.* 29:2*
a time to *m.* and a time. *Eccl* 3:4
gates shall lament and *m.* *Isa* 3:26
of Kir-hareseth shall ye *m.* 16:7
the fishers also shall *m.* 19:8
I did *m.* as a dove. 38:14
we roar like bears, we *m.* 59:11
sent me to comfort all that *m.* 61:2
m. in Zion, give beauty for ashes. 3
all ye that *m.* for her. 66:10
for this shall earth *m.* *Jer* 4:28
how long shall the land *m.*? 12:4
my heart shall *m.* for men. 48:31
ways of Zion do *m.* *Lam* 1:4
let not the seller *m.* *Ezek* 7:12
the king shall *m.* and the prince. 27
yet neither shalt thou *m.* nor. 24:16
ye shall pine away and *m.* one. 23

I caused Lebanon to *m.* *Ezek* 31:15
therefore shall the land *m. Hos* 4:3
for the people shall *m.* over. 10:5
the Lord's ministers *m.* *Joel* 1:9
of the shepherds shall *m.* *Amos* 1:2
every one *m.* that dwelleth. 8:8; 9:5
shall *m.* for him as one mourneth.
Zech 12:10
and the land shall *m.* every. 12
blessed are they that *m.* *Mat* 5:4
children of bridechamber *m.*? 9:15
all the tribes of the earth *m.* 24:30
that laugh, for ye shall *m. Luke* 6:25
afflicted, and *m.* and weep. *Jas* 4:9
the merchants shall weep and *m.*
Rev 18:11

mourned
Jacob *m.* for his son. *Gen* 37:34
Egyptians *m.* for Jacob. 50:3, 10
people heard these evil tidings, they
m. *Ex* 33:4; *Num* 14:39
the congregation *m.* *Num* 20:29
nevertheless, Samuel *m.* for Saul.
1 *Sam* 15:35
and they *m.* for Saul. 2 *Sam* 1:12
Bath-sheba *m.* for Uriah. 11:26
David *m.* for his son. 13:37
as one that had long time *m.* 14:2
m. over the man of God. 1 *Ki* 13:30
all Israel *m.* for Jeroboam's. 14:18
Ephraim their father *m.* 1 *Chr* 7:22
and all Judah *m.* for. 2 *Chr* 35:24
m. for the transgression. *Ezra* 10:6
I sat down and *m.* *Neh* 1:4
when ye fasted and *m.* *Zech* 7:5
we have *m.* unto you, and ye have.
Mat 11:17; *Luke* 7:32
told them as they *m.* *Mark* 16:10
and have not rather *m.* 1 *Cor* 5:2

mourner
feign thyself to be a *m.* 2 *Sam* 14:2

mourners
that comforteth the *m.* *Job* 29:25
m. go about the streets. *Eccl* 12:5
restore comforts to him and his *m.*
Isa 57:18
be to them as bread of *m. Hos* 9:4

mourneth
behold, the king *m.* 2 *Sam* 19:1
I bowed as one that *m.* *Ps* 35:14
mine eye *m.* by reason of. 88:9*
the earth *m.* *Isa* 24:4; 33:9
the new wine *m.* 24:7
being desolate *m.* to me. *Jer* 12:11
Judah *m.* and the gates. 14:2
of swearing the land *m.* 23:10
the land *m.* for the corn. *Joel* 1:10
m. for his firstborn. *Zech* 12:10

mournfully
that we have walked *m.* *Mal* 3:14

mourning, *substantive*
days of *m.* for my father. *Gen* 27:41
and when the days of his *m.* 50:4
made a *m.* for his father Jacob. 10
m.. this is a grievous *m.* 11
eaten thereof in my *m. Deut* 26:14
so the days of *m.* for Moses. 34:8
when the *m.* was past. 2 *Sam* 11:27
that day was turned into *m.* 19:2
there was great *m.* among. *Esth* 4:3
was turned to them from *m.* 9:22
to raise up their *m.* *Job* 3:8
my harp also is turned to *m.* 30:31
thou hast turned my *m.* *Ps* 30:11
to go to the house of *m.* *Eccl* 7:2
wise is in the house of *m.* 4
the Lord did call to *m.* *Isa* 22:12
and sorrow and *m.* shall flee. 51:11
and the days of thy *m.* shall. 60:20
them the oil of joy for *m.* 61:3
make thee *m.* as for. *Jer* 6:26
enter not into the house of *m.* 16:5
turn their *m.* into joy. 31:13
daughter of Judah *m.* *Lam* 2:5
our dance is turned into *m.* 5:15
written lamentations, *m.* and woe.
Ezek 2:10
make no *m.* for the dead. 24:17
I caused a *m.* 31:15
with weeping and *m.* *Joel* 2:12
the husbandmen to *m.* *Amos* 5:16

turn your feasts into *m.* and I will
 make it as the *m.* of an. *Amos* 8:10
came not forth in the *m. Mi* 1:11
m. in Jerusalem, as *m. Zech* 12:11
great *m.*, Rachel weeping. *Mat* 2:18
us your desire, your *m. 2 Cor* 7:7
laughter be turned into *m. Jas* 4:9
in one day death and *m. Rev* 18:8

mourning, *verb*
to the grave to my son *m. Gen* 37:35
I pray thee, put on *m. 2 Sam* 14:2
hasted to his house *m. Esth* 6:12
went *m.* without the sun. *Job* 30:28
I am troubled, I go *m. Ps* 38:6
why go I *m.* because of oppression?
 42:9; 43:2
call for the *m.* women. *Jer* 9:17
in *m.* to comfort them for. 16:7
all of them *m.* for their iniquities.
 Ezek 7:16
I Daniel was *m.* 3 weeks. *Dan* 10:2
will make a *m.* as the owls. *Mi* 1:8

mouse
weasel and *m.* shall be. *Lev* 11:29
abomination, and the *m. Isa* 66:17

mouth
and lo, in her *m.* was. *Gen* 8:11
and enquire at her *m.* 24:57
stone was upon the well's *m.* 29:2
stone from the well's *m.* 3, 10
his money was in his sack's *m.*
 42:27; 43:12, 21
who hath made man's *m.? Ex* 4:11
be to thee instead of a *m.* 16
will I speak *m.* to *m. Num* 12:8
the earth open her *m.* and. 16:30
put a word in Balaam's *m.* 23:5
put to death by the *m.* of witnesses.
 35:30; *Deut* 17:6; 19:15
roll great stones on the *m.*
 Josh 10:18, 27
open *m.* of cave, and bring out. 22
Eli marked her *m. 1 Sam* 1:12
the words in her *m. 2 Sam* 14:3, 19
a covering over the well's *m.* 17:19
every *m.* that hath not. *1 Ki* 19:18
prophets declare good to the king
 with one *m.* 22:13
a lying spirit in *m.* of his prophets.
 22, 23; *2 Chr* 18:21, 22
Necho from *m.* of God. *2 Chr* 35:22
word of the Lord by the *m.* of Jeremiah. 36:21, 22; *Ezra* 1:1
went out of the king's *m. Esth* 7:8
iniquity stoppeth her *m. Job* 5:16
doth not the *m.* taste? 12:11*; 34:3*
there was no answer in the *m.* 32:5
out of the *m.* of babes hast. *Ps* 8:2
 Mat 21:16
save me from the lion's *m. Ps* 22:21
whose *m.* must be held in. 32:9*
the *m.* of the righteous. 37:30
in whose *m.* are no reproofs. 38:14
but *m.* that speaketh lies. 63:11
let not the pit shut her *m.* 69:15
iniquity shall stop her *m.* 107:42
m. of wicked, of deceitful. 109:2
then was our *m.* filled with. 126:2
scattered at the grave's *m.* 141:7
whose *m.* speaketh vanity. 144:8, 11
from thee a froward *m. Pr* 4:24
and her *m.* is smoother than oil. 5:3
walketh with froward *m.* 6:12; 10:32
the froward *m.* do I hate. 8:13
violence covereth the *m.* of. 10:6, 11
the *m.* of the foolish is near. 14
the *m.* of the just bringeth. 31
the city is overthrown by *m.* 11:11
the *m.* of the upright shall. 12:6
in the *m.* of the foolish is a. 14:3
the *m.* of fools poureth out. 15:2
the *m.* of fools feedeth on. 14
the *m.* of the wicked poureth out. 28
the words of a man's *m.* are. 18:4
a fool's *m.* is his destruction. 7
m. of the wicked devoureth. 19:28
the *m.* of a strange woman. 22:14
so is a parable in the *m.* 26:7, 9
and a flattering *m.* worketh ruin. 28
eateth, and wipeth her *m.* 30:20
words of a wise man's *m. Eccl* 10:12
Israel with open *m. Isa* 9:12
an evil doer, and every *m.* 17

make ye a wide *m.? Isa* 57:4
Spirit not depart out of *m.* 59:21
shall speak with him *m.* to *m.*
 Jer 32:4; 34:3
Baruch wrote from *m.* of Jeremiah.
 36:4, 27, 32; 45:1
goeth forth out of our *m.* 44:17
no more named in *m.* of any. 26
out of the *m.* of Most. *Lam* 3:38
to open the *m.* in the slaughter.
 Ezek 21:22
thee the opening of the *m.* 29:21
came near to the *m.* of. *Dan* 3:26
word was in the king's *m.* 4:31
brought, and laid on the *m.* of. 6:17
it had three ribs in *m.* of it. 7:5
there was a *m.* speaking. 8, 20
of Baalim out of her *m. Hos* 2:17
taketh out of the *m. Amos* 3:12
shall even fall into the *m. Nah* 3:12
of lead on the *m.* of it. *Zech* 5:8
out of the *m.* of God. *Mat* 4:4
abundance of the heart the *m.* 12:34
goeth into the *m.* defileth not. 15:11
in the *m.* of two or three witnesses
 every word. 18:16; *2 Cor* 13:1
as he spake by *m.* of his. *Luke* 1:70
for I will give you a *m.* and. 21:15
Holy Ghost spake by *m.* of David.
 Acts 1:16; 4:25
by *m.* of all his prophets. 3:18, 21
you the same things by *m.* 15:27
them to smite him on the *m.* 23:2
m. is full of cursing. *Rom* 3:14
that every *m.* may be stopped. 19
with the *m.* confession is. 10:10
that ye may with one *m.* 15:6
muzzle the *m.* of the ox. *1 Cor* 9:9*
I was delivered out of *m. 2 Tim* 4:17
out of the same *m. Jas* 3:10
given to him a *m. Rev* 13:5
the spirits came out of *m.* of. 16:13
 see **Lord**

his **mouth**
his m.: I will be with *his m. Ex* 4:15
put a word in *his m. Num* 23:16
proceedeth out of *his m.* 30:2
put my words in *his m. Deut* 18:18
no man put his hand to *his m.*
 1 Sam 14:26, 27
delivered it out of *his m.* 17:35
there is tidings in *his m. 2 Sam* 18:25
and fire out of *his m.* devoured.
 22:9; *Ps* 18:8
spake with *his m.* to David.
 1 Ki 8:15; *2 Chr* 6:4
he put *his m.* on *his m. 2 Ki* 4:34
judgements of *his m. 1 Chr* 16:12
by the breath of *his m. Job* 15:30
be sweet in *his m.* 20:12
keep it still within *his m.* 13
pray thee, the law from *his m.* 22:22
esteemed the words of *his m.* 23:12
sound that goeth out of *his m.* 37:2
draw up Jordan into *his m.* 40:23
out of *his m.* go burning. 41:19
and a flame goeth out of *his m.* 21
his m. is full of cursing. *Ps* 10:7
made by breath of *his m.* 33:6
words of *his m.* are iniquity. 36:3
man that openeth not *his m.* 38:13
words of *his m.* are smoother. 55:21
remember the judgements of *his m.*
 105:5
his m. cometh knowledge. *Pr* 2:6
hypocrite with *his m.* 11:9
good by the fruit of *his m.* 12:14
eat good by the fruit of *his m.* 13:2
he that keepeth *his m.* keepeth. 3
joy by the answer of *his m.* 15:23
his m. transgresseth not. 16:10
of the wise teacheth *his m.* 23
for himself, for *his m.* craveth. 26
and *his m.* calleth for strokes. 18:6
satisfied with the fruit of *his m.* 20
not so much as bring it to *his m.*
 19:24; 26:15
but *his m.* shall be filled. 20:17
whoso keepeth *his m.* 21:23
labour of a man is for *his m. Eccl* 6:7
beginning of words of *his m.* 10:13
with the kisses of *his m. S of S* 1:2
his m. is most sweet, this is. 5:16

earth with the rod of *his m. Isa* 11:4
was any deceit in *his m.* 53:9
peaceably with *his m. Jer* 9:8
ear receive the word of *his m.* 20
write all these words at *his m.* 36:17
bring out of *his m.* that. 51:44
putteth *his m.* in the dust. *Lam* 3:29
cleaveth to the roof of *his m.* 4:4
his blood out of *his m. Zech* 9:7
law of truth was in *his m. Mal* 2:6
should seek the law at *his m.* 7
and *his m.* was opened. *Luke* 1:64
words proceeded out of *his m.* 4:22
abundance of heart *his m.* 6:45
catch somewhat out of *his m.* 11:54
have heard of *his own m.* 22:71
filled a spunge and put it to *his m.*
 John 19:29
hear the voice of *his m. Acts* 22:14
with the spirit of *his m. 2 Thes* 2:8
guile found in *his m. 1 Pet* 2:22
out of *his m.* went a sharp sword.
 Rev 1:16; 19:15, 21
cast out of *his m.* water. 12:15
the dragon cast out of *his m.* 16
and *his m.* was as the m uth. 13:2

my **mouth**
my m. that speaketh. *Gen* 45:12
the word God putteth in *my m.*
 Num 22:38; 23:12
the words of *my m. Deut* 32:1
my m. is enlarged over. *1 Sam* 2:1
I will not refrain *my m. Job* 7:11
mine own *m.* shall condemn. 9:20
strengthen you with *my m.* 16:5
my servant with *my m.* 19:16
fill *my m.* with arguments. 23:4
my m. hath kissed my hand. 31:27
neither have I suffered *my m.* 30
tongue hath spoken in *my m.* 33:2
will lay my hand upon *my m.* 40:4
purposed that *my m. Ps* 17:3
words of *my m.* be acceptable. 19:14
shall continually be in *my m.* 34:1
I said, I will keep *my m.* 39:1
he hath put a new song in *my m.* 40:3
hear this, *my m.* shall speak. 49:3
and *my m.* shall shew forth. 51:15
give ear to the words of *my m.* 54:2
my m. shall praise thee with. 63:5
my m. hath spoken, when I. 66:14
I cried to him with *my m.*, he. 17
let *my m.* be filled with thy. 71:8
my m. shall shew forth thy. 15
ears to the words of *my m.* 78:1
I will open *my m.* in a parable. 2
with *my m.* will I make known. 89:1
praise the Lord with *my m.* 109:30
word of truth out of *my m.* 119:43
sweeter than honey to *my m.* 103
freewill offerings of *my m.* 108
cleave to the roof of *my m.* 137:6
O Lord, before *my m.* 141:3
my m. shall speak praise. 145:21
nor decline from the words of *my m.*
 Pr 4:5; 5:7
attend to the words of *my m.* 7:24
for *my m.* shall speak truth. 8:7
the words of *my m.* are in. 8
he laid the coal on *my m. Isa* 6:7
and have not asked at *my m.* 30:2
my m. it hath commanded. 34:16
word is gone out of *my m.* 45:23
things went forth out of *my m.* 48:3
my m. like a sharp sword. 49:2
word that goeth out of *my m.* 55:11
hand and touched *my m. Jer* 1:9
shalt be as *my m.* 15:19
written from *my m.* 36:6
in *my m.* like honey for. *Ezek* 3:3
hear the word at *my m.* 17; 33:7
abominable flesh into *my m.* 4:14
flesh nor wine in *my m. Dan* 10:3
by the words of *my m. Hos* 6:5
open *my m.* in parables. *Mat* 13:35
time entered into *my m. Acts* 11:8
the Gentiles by *my m.* should. 15:7
I may open *my m.* boldly. *Eph* 6:19
with the sword of *my m. Rev* 2:16
I will spue thee out of *my m.* 3:16
the book was in *my m.* sweet. 10:10

mouth with *opened*
earth *opened* her *m.* to. *Gen* 4:11

earth *opened* her *m*. and swallowed.
Num 16:32; 26:10; *Deut* 11:6
opened the *m*. of ass. *Num* 22:28
I have *opened* my *m*. *Judg* 11:35, 36
opened Job his *m*. and. *Job* 3:1
and they *opened* their *m*. wide.
29:23; *Ps* 35:21
now I have *opened* my *m*. *Job* 33:2
I *opened* not my *m*. *Ps* 39:9
m. of the deceitful are *opened*. 109:2
I *opened* my *m*. and panted. 119:131
hell hath *opened* her *m*. *Isa* 5:14
there was none that *opened* m. 10:14
yet he *opened* not his *m*. 53:7
I *opened* my *m*. and he caused me.
Ezek 3:2
thy *m*. be *opened* to him which is.
24:27; 33:22
opened my *m*. and spake. *Dan* 10:16
opened his *m*. and taught. *Mat* 5:2
when thou hast *opened* his *m*. 17:27
his *m*. was *opened* immediately.
Luke 1:64
like a lamb dumb, so *opened* he not
his *m*. *Acts* 8:32
Philip *opened* his *m*. 35
Peter *opened* his *m*. 10:34
our *m*. is *opened* to you. *2 Cor* 6:11
earth *opened* her *m*. and helped.
Rev 12:16
he *opened* his *m*. in blasphemy. 13:6

mouth with **openeth**
dumb man that *openeth* not his *m*.
Ps 38:13
a fool *openeth* not his *m*. *Pr* 24:7
openeth her *m*. with wisdom. 31:26

their **mouth**
their hand to *their m*. *Judg* 7:6
thy manna from *their m*. *Neh* 9:20
the poor from *their m*. *Job* 5:15
gaped upon me with *their m*. 16:10
laid their hand on *their m*. 29:9
cleaved to the roof of *their m*. 10
no faithfulness in *their m*. *Ps* 5:9
with *their m*. they speak. 17:10
O God, in *their m*.: break out. 58:6
they belch out with *their m*. 59:7
for the sin of *their m*. and words. 12
they bless with *their m*. but. 62:4
their m. against the heavens. 73:9
flatter him with *their m*. 78:36
praises of God be in *their m*. 149:6
draw near me with *their m*. *Isa* 29:13
cut off from *their m*. *Jer* 7:28
thou art near in *their m*. far. 12:2
enemies have opened *their m*.
Lam 2:16
with *their m*. they shew much love.
Ezek 33:31
my flock from *their m*. 34:10
is deceitful in *their m*. *Mi* 6:12
lay their hand on *their m*. 7:16
tongue found in *their m*. *Zeph* 3:13
shall consume away in *their m*.
Zech 14:12
nigh to me with *their m*. *Mat* 15:8
their m. speaketh great. *Jude* 16
power is in *their m*. and. *Rev* 9:19
fire proceedeth out of *their m*. 11:5
and in *their m*. was found. 14:5

thy **mouth**
I will be with *thy m*. *Ex* 4:12, 15
Lord's law may be in *thy m*. 13:9
of other gods out of *thy m*. 23:13
promised with *thy m*. *Deut* 23:23
word is nigh to thee, in *thy m*. 30:14
Rom 10:8
not depart out of *thy m*. *Josh* 1:8
where is now *thy m*.? *Judg* 9:38
if thou hast opened *thy m*. 11:36
lay thine hand upon *thy m*. 18:19
Pr 30:32
thy m. hath testified. *2 Sam* 1:16
thou spakest with *thy m*. *1 Ki* 8:24
2 Chr 6:15
word in *thy m*. is truth. *1 Ki* 17:24
words of *thy m*. be like a *Job* 8:2
till he fill *thy m*. with laughing. 21
thy m. uttereth thine iniquity. 15:5
thine own m. condemneth thee. 6
such words go out of *thy m*. 13
my covenant in *thy m*. *Ps* 50:16
thou givest *thy m*. to evil. 19

open *thy m*. *Ps* 81:10
who satisfieth *thy m*. with. 103:5†
all the judgements of *thy m*. 119:13
the law of *thy m*. is better. 72
the testimony of *thy m*. 88
hear the words of *thy m*. 138:4
snared with the words of *thy m*.
Pr 6:2
praise thee, and not *thine* own *m*.
27:2
open *thy m*. for the dumb, in. 31:8
open *thy m*., judge righteously. 9
be not rash with *thy m*. *Eccl* 5:2
suffer not *thy m*. to cause thy. 6
roof of *thy m*. like the. *S of S* 7:9
I have put my words in *thy m*.
Isa 51:16; *Jer* 1:9
my words which I put in *thy m*. shall
not depart out of *thy m*. *Isa* 59:21
my words in *thy m*. fire. *Jer* 5:14
open *thy m*. and eat. *Ezek* 2:8
tongue cleave to roof of *thy m*. 3:26
I will open *thy m*. and thou shalt. 27
was not mentioned by *thy m*. 16:56
never open *thy m*. any more. 63
set the trumpet to *thy m*. *Hos* 8:1
keep doors of *thy m*. *Mi* 7:5
out of *thine* own *m*. will I judge.
Luke 19:22
if thou confess with *thy m*. *Rom* 10:9
it shall be in *thy m*. sweet. *Rev* 10:9

your **mouth**
proceeded out of *your m*. *Num* 32:24
not arrogancy come out of *your m*.
1 Sam 2:3
lay your hand on *your m*. *Job* 21:5
thus with *your m*. ye have boasted.
Ezek 35:13
is cut off from *your m*. *Joel* 1:5
no corrupt communication proceed
out of *your m*. *Eph* 4:29; *Col* 3:8

mouths
song, put it in their *m*. *Deut* 31:19
not be forgotten out of *m*. of. 21
they gaped upon me with their *m*.
Ps 22:13
meat was yet in their *m*. 78:30
they have *m*. but they speak not.
115:5; 135:16
there any breath in their *m*. 135:17
kings shut their *m*. at. *Isa* 52:15
ye and wives have spoken with your
m. *Jer* 44:25
enemies opened their *m*. *Lam* 3:46
hath shut the lions' *m*. *Dan* 6:22
putteth not into their *m*. *Mi* 3:5
deceivers, whose *m*. must. *Tit* 1:11
stopped the *m*. of lions. *Heb* 11:33
put bits in the horses' *m*. *Jas* 3:3
their *m*. issued fire. *Rev* 9:17, 18

move
[1] *To change position*, 2 *Ki* 21:8.
[2] *To rouse, or influence*, Deut
32:21; Judg 13:25. [3] *To affect,
as by pity or other feeling*, Ruth
1:19.
not a dog *m*. his tongue. *Ex* 11:7
that *m*. in the waters. *Lev* 11:10
not *m*. a sickle into. *Deut* 23:25
I will *m*. them to jealousy. 32:21
Spirit of the Lord began to *m*.
Judg 13:25
may dwell and *m*. no more.
2 *Sam* 7:10; *2 Ki* 21:8*
let no man *m*. his bones. *2 Ki* 23:18
with nails that it *m*. not. *Jer* 10:4
m. out of their holes. *Mi* 7:17*
will not *m*. them. *Mat* 23:4
for in him we live, *m*. *Acts* 17:28
none of these things *m*. me. 20:24

moveable
her ways are *m*., canst not. *Pr* 5:6*

moved
the Spirit of God *m*. on. *Gen* 1:2
all flesh died that *m*. on the. 7:21
have *m*. me to jealousy. *Deut* 32:21
none *m*. his tongue. *Josh* 10:21
she *m*. him to ask of her father a
field. 15:18; *Judg* 1:14
that all the city was *m*. *Ruth* 1:19
heart, only her lips *m*. *1 Sam* 1:13
the king was much *m*. *2 Sam* 18:33

foundations of heaven *m*. 2 *Sam* 22:8
m. David against them. 24:1
world shall be stable, that it be not *m*.
1 Chr 16:30; *Ps* 93:1; 96:10
dwell, and shall be *m*. no. *1 Chr* 17:9
God *m*. them to depart. 2 *Chr* 18:31
they have *m*. sedition. *Ezra* 4:15
saw that Mordecai *m*. not. *Esth* 5:9
at this my heart is *m*. *Job* 37:1
flesh, they cannot be *m*. 41:23
I shall not be *m*. *Ps* 10:6; 16:8
30:6; 62:2, 6
those rejoice when I am *m*. 13:4
these things shall never be *m*. 15:5
foundations of the hills *m*. 18:7†
in Lord, and shall not be *m*. 21:7
she shall not be *m*. God shall. 46:5
the kingdoms were *m*. 6
suffer the righteous to be *m*. 55:22
suffereth not our feet to be *m*. 66:9
m. at the presence of God. 68:8*
they *m*. him to jealousy. 78:58
reigneth, let the earth be *m*. 99:1
surely he shall not be *m*. 112:6
not suffer thy foot to be *m*. 121:3
righteous shall not be *m*. *Pr* 12:3
and my bowels were *m*. *S of S* 5:4
the posts of the door *m*. *Isa* 6:4
heart was *m*. as trees are *m*. 7:2
and there was none that *m*. 10:14
hell from beneath is *m*. for. 14:9
the idols of Egypt shall be *m*. 19:1
earth is broken down, and *m*. 24:19
image that shall not be *m*. 40:20
it should not be *m*. 41:7
all the hills *m*. lightly. *Jer* 4:24
they shall drink, and be *m*. 25:16*
whose waters are *m*. as. 46:7*, 8*
earth is *m*. at the noise of. 49:21*
Babylon the earth is *m*. 50:46*
he was *m*. with choler. *Dan* 8:7
king of the south shall be *m*. 11:11
was *m*. with compassion. *Mat* 9:36
14:14; 18:27; *Mark* 1:41; 6:34
m. with indignation. *Mat* 20:24
all the city was *m*. saying. 21:10*
but the chief priests *m*. *Mark* 15:11*
that I should not be *m*. *Acts* 2:25
patriarchs, *m*. with envy. 7:9
but the Jews *m*. with envy. 17:5
the city was *m*. and people. 21:30
be not *m*. from the hope. *Col* 1:23
that no man be *m*. by. *1 Thes* 3:3
Noah *m*. with fear. *Heb* 11:7
kingdom which cannot be *m*. 12:28*
they spake as *m*. by. 2 *Pet* 1:21
mountain and island *m*. *Rev* 6:14

movedst
though thou *m*. me against him.
Job 2:3

mover
found this fellow a *m*. of sedition.
Acts 24:5

moveth
living creature that *m*. *Gen* 1:21
every thing that *m*. on earth. 28
be on all that *m*. on earth. 9:2*
of every creature that *m*. *Lev* 11:46
Behemoth *m*. his tail. *Job* 40:17
thing that *m*. praise him. *Ps* 69:34
when it *m*. itself aright. *Pr* 23:31*
m. whithersoever the rivers come.
Ezek 47:9*

moving, *substantive*
the *m*. of my lips should. *Job* 16:5*
blind, waiting for the *m*. *John* 5:3

moving
the waters bring forth *m*. *Gen* 1:20
every *m*. thing shall be meat. 9:3
m. his lips; he bringeth. *Pr* 16:30*

mower
wherewith the *m*. filleth. *Ps* 129:7

mowings
growth after the king's *m*. *Amos* 7:1

mown
rain upon the *m*. grass. *Ps* 72:6

much
for thou art *m*. mightier. *Gen* 26:16
it is a night to be *m*. *Ex* 12:42
he that gathered *m*. 16:18; 2 *Cor* 8:15
if the scab spread *m*. abroad.
Lev 13:7, 22, 27, 35

soul of people was *m.* *Num* 21:4
shall carry *m.* seed out. *Deut* 28:38
return with *m.* riches. *Josh* 22:8
it grieveth me *m.* for. *Ruth* 1:13
a *m.* greater slaughter. *1 Sam* 14:30
his name was *m.* set by. 18:30
but Jonathan delighted *m.* in. 19:2
as thy life was *m.* set by this day, so
let my life be *m.* set by. 26:24
had understanding exceeding *m.*
1 Ki 4:29
Jehu shall serve him *m.* *2 Ki* 10:18
m. wickedness in sight of Lord. 21:6
of Ophel he built *m.* *2 Chr* 27:3
Manasseh wrought *m.* evil in. 33:6
it is a time of *m.* rain. *Ezra* 10:13
it yieldeth *m.* increase. *Neh* 9:37
mine hand had gotten *m.* 31:25
m. less do lying lips. *Pr* 17:7
m. less for a servant to have. 19:10
whether he eat little or *m.* *Eccl* 5:12
he hath *m.* sorrow and wrath. 17
sinner destroyeth *m.* good. 9:18
thou take thee *m.* sope [soap].
Jer 2:22
it containeth *m.* *Ezek* 23:32
shew *m.* love. 33:31
fruit thereof was *m.* *Dan* 4:12, 21
ye have sown *m.* *Hag* 1:6
ye looked for *m.* 9
not *m.* better than they? *Mat* 6:26
where they had not *m.* earth. 13:5
Mark 4:5
might have been sold for *m.*
Mat 26:9
sins are forgiven, for she loved *m.*
Luke 7:47
m. is given, of him shall *m.* be required . . . committed *m.* 12:48
is faithful also in *m.*: unjust in least
is unjust in *m.* 16:10
forth *m.* fruit. *John* 12:24; 15:5
I will not talk *m.* with you. 14:30
her masters *m.* gain. *Acts* 16:16
them *m.* which had believed. 18:27
Festus said, *M.* learning doth. 26:24
m. every way. *Rom* 3:2
laboured *m.* in the Lord. 16:12
out of *m.* affliction I. *2 Cor* 2:4
m. rather be in subjection. *Heb* 12:9
m. more shall not we escape. 25
the righteous availeth *m.* *Jas* 5:16
I wept *m.* because no man. *Rev* 5:4
see how much, **how** much less,
how *much more,* much **more,**
people

as much
as m. money as it is worth.
Gen 23:9
mess was five times *as m.* 43:34
fill sacks with food *as m.* 44:1
twice *as m.* as they gather daily.
Ex 16:5, 22
sons have, one *as m.* as. *Lev* 7:10
for *as m.* as the Lord. *Josh* 17:14
take *as m.* as thy soul. *1 Sam* 2:16
cut wood *as m.* as. *2 Chr* 2:16
gave Job twice *as m.* as. *Job* 42:10
joy in testimonies, *as m. Ps* 119:14
to receive *as m.* again. *Luke* 6:34
likewise of fishes *as m. John* 6:11
as m. as in me is, I am. *Rom* 1:15
in *as m.* as I am the apostle. 11:13
as m. as lieth in you, live. 12:18
in *as m.* as not without an oath.
Heb 7:20

so much
remained not *so m.* *Ex* 14:28
sweet cinnamon half *so m.* 30:23
poor and cannot get *so m. Lev* 14:21
not give you *so m.* as a. *Deut* 2:5
none to be *so m.* praised as Absalom.
2 Sam 14:25
there shall not be left *so m.* 17:12
the spoil, it was *so m.* *2 Chr* 20:25
will not *so m.* as bring it. *Pr* 19:24
eat *so m.* as is sufficient for. 25:16
why gaddest thou *so m.? Jer* 2:36
have we spoken *so m.? Mal* 3:13
we have *so m.* bread? *Mat* 15:33
was no room, no, not *so m.* as about.
Mark 2:2
not *so m.* as eat. 3:20; 6:31
so m. more a great deal they. 7:36

so m. the more went there a fame.
Luke 5:15
have ye not read *so m.* as this? 6:3
would not lift up *so m.* as his. 18:13
he cried *so m.* the more, Have. 39
sold it for *so m.* she said, Yea, for so
m. *Acts* 5:8
no inheritance, not *so m.* as to. 7:5
not *so m.* as heard whether. 7:7
not *so m.* as named. *1 Cor* 5:1
being made *so m.* better. *Heb* 1:4
by *so m.* Jesus made surety. 7:22
so m. more as ye see day. 10:25
if *so m.* as a beast touch. 12:20
so m. torment and sorrow. *Rev* 18:7

too much
sufficient, and *too m.* *Ex* 36:7
them, ye take *too m.* *Num* 16:3, 7
the part of children of Judah was *too
m.* for them. *Josh* 19:9
too m. for you to go up to. *1 Ki* 12:28
arise *too m.* contempt. *Esth* 1:18

very much
corn as sand, *very m.* *Gen* 41:49
very m. cattle went up. *Ex* 12:38
remaineth *very m.* land. *Josh* 13:1
with *very m.* cattle, *very m.* 22:8
Sheba came with *very m.* *1 Ki* 10:2
innocent blood *very m.* *2 Ki* 21:16
David *very m.* brass. *1 Chr* 18:8
away *very m.* spoil. *2 Chr* 14:13
given him substance *very m.* 32:29
people transgressed *very m.* 36:14
I am afflicted *very m. Ps* 119:107
summer fruits *very m.* *Jer* 40:12

mufflers
away the chains, the *m.* *Isa* 3:19

mulberry trees
upon them over against the *m. trees.*
2 Sam 5:23; *1 Chr* 14:14
the sound in tops of the *m. trees.*
2 Sam 5:24; *1 Chr* 14:15

mule
gat him upon his *m.* *2 Sam* 13:29
Absalom rode on a *m.,* the. 18:9
to ride on my *m.* *1 Ki* 1:33; 38:44
not as the horse or *m.* *Ps* 32:9
plague of the horse, of the *m.*
Zech 14:15

mules
Anah that found *m.* in. *Gen* 36:24*
brought horses and *m.,* a rate year
by year. *1 Ki* 10:25; *2 Chr* 9:24
grass to save the *m.* *1 Ki* 18:5
to thy servant two *m.* *2 Ki* 5:17
brought bread on camels and on *m.*
1 Chr 12:40
their *m.* were 245. *Ezra* 2:66
Neh 7:68
sent letters by riders on *m.*
Esth 8:10*, 14*
your brethren on *m.* *Isa* 66:20
traded in thy fairs with *m.*
Ezek 27:14

multiplied
Israel grew and *m.* *Gen* 47:27
Ex 1:7, 20
more afflicted, they *m.* *Ex* 1:12
my wonders may be *m.* in. 11:9
your God hath *m.* you. *Deut* 1:10
m. and all that thou hast is *m.* 8:13
that your days may be *m.* 11:21
I *m.* his seed, and gave. *Josh* 24:3
their cattle were *m.* *1 Chr* 5:9
if his children be *m.* it is. *Job* 27:14
if thy transgressions are *m.* 35:6
their sorrows shall be *m.* *Ps* 16:4
hate me wrongfully are *m.* 38:19
them, so that they are *m.* 107:38
thy days shall be *m.* *Pr* 9:11
wicked are *m.* transgression. 29:16
thou hast *m.* the nation. *Isa* 9:3
for our transgressions are *m.* 59:12
when ye be *m.* they shall. *Jer* 3:16
m. more than the nations. *Ezek* 5:7*
ye have *m.* your slain in. 11:6
thou hast *m.* thy whoredoms.
23:19
m. thy fornication. 16:29
m. thine abominations. 51

faint, and ruins be *m.* *Ezek* 21:15
his boughs were *m.* 31:5
m. your words. 35:13
peace be *m.* to you. *Dan* 4:1; 6:25
1 Pet 1:2; *2 Pet* 1:2; *Jude* 2
I *m.* her silver and gold. *Hos* 2:8
Judah hath *m.* fenced cities. 8:14
I have *m.* visions, and used. 12:10
hast *m.* thy merchants. *Nah* 3:16
when the number of the disciples
was *m.* *Acts* 6:1, 7
people grew and *m.* in Egypt. 7:17
the fear of the Lord were *m.* 9:31
word of God grew and *m.* 12:24

multipliedst
children also *m.* thou as. *Neh* 9:23

multiplieth
he *m.* my wounds without. *Job* 9:17
he *m.* words against God. 34:37
m. words without knowledge. 35:16

multiply
be fruitful and *m.* *Gen* 1:22, 28
8:17; 9:7; 35:11
I will *m.* thy sorrow. 3:16
when men began to *m.* on. 6:1
I will *m.* Hagar's seed. 16:10; 17:20
and I will *m.* thee. 17:2; 48:4
I will *m.* thy seed. 22:17; 26:4, 24
Heb 6:14
bless thee, and *m.* thee. *Gen* 28:3
deal wisely with them; lest they *m.*
Ex 1:10
I will *m.* my signs and. 7:3
lest the beast of the field *m.* 23:29
whom thou saidst, I will *m.* 32:13
Lev 26:9; *Deut* 7:13; 13:17
28:63; 30:5
that ye may live and *m.* and go in
and possess. *Deut* 8:1; 30:16
the king shall not *m.* horses. 17:16
neither shall he *m.* wives, nor. 17
did all their family *m.* *1 Chr* 4:27
I shall *m.* my days as. *Job* 29:18
I will *m.* them, they shall. *Jer* 30:19
so will I *m.* the seed of David. 33:22
I have caused thee to *m.* *Ezek* 16:7
I will *m.* men. 36:10
m. man and beast. 11
I will *m.* the fruit of the tree. 30
I will place them and *m.* 37:26
Gilgal *m.* transgression. *Amos* 4:4
and *m.* your seed sown. *2 Cor* 9:10

multiplying
in *m.* I will multiply. *Gen* 22:17
Heb 6:14

multitude
[1] *A great company or number of
persons or things,* Gen 30:30; 48:4.
[2] *The common people,* Mat 9:33.
[3] *The whole assembly, both common people and senators,* Acts
23:7. [4] *The church, or a company of the faithful,* Acts 15:12, 22;
21:22. [5] *Great store, or plenty,*
Ps 5:7; Hos 9:7. [6] *Much variety,*
Eccl 5:3, 7.

not numbered for *m.* *Gen* 16:10
32:12; *1 Ki* 3:8
God Almighty make thee a *m.*
Gen 28:3*
now increased unto a *m.* 30:30
I will make of thee a *m.* of people.
48:4*; 16:19
a mixed *m.* went up also. *Ex* 12:38
thou shalt not follow a *m.* 23:2
according to the *m.* of. *Lev* 25:16
mixed *m.* fell a lusting. *Num* 11:4
ye are as the stars for *m. Deut* 1:10
10:22; 28:62; *Heb* 11:12
as sand on sea shore for *m.*
Josh 11:4; *Judg* 7:12; *1 Sam* 13:5
2 Sam 17:11; *1 Ki* 4:20
grasshoppers for *m.* *Judg* 6:5; 7:12
m. melted away. *1 Sam* 14:16
he dealt among the whole *m.* of
Israel. *2 Sam* 6:19
could not be told for *m.* *1 Ki* 8:5
they are as all the *m.* *2 Ki* 7:13
hast said, With the *m.* of my chariots.
19:23; *Isa* 37:24
people like dust for *m.* *2 Chr* 1:9
we go against this *m.* 14:11

the *m.* were dead bodies. *2 Chr* 20:24
for a *m.* had not cleansed.   30:18
be not afraid of all the *m.*   32:7
from Israel the mixed *m. Neh* 13:3
Haman told of the *m.*   *Esth* 5:11
Mordecai accepted of the *m.*   10:3
should not the *m.* of words? *Job* 11:2
and *m.* of years should teach.   32:7
by reason of *m.* of oppressions. 35:9
he scorneth the *m.* of the city. 39:7*
I will come in the *m.* of.   *Ps* 5:7
cast them out in *m.* of their.   10
no king saved by the *m.* of.   33:16
I had gone with the *m.* to the. 42:4
that boast themselves in *m.*   49:6
according to the *m.* of thy.   51:1
rebuke the *m.* of bulls, with. 68:30
O God, in the *m.* of thy.   69:13
turn to me, according to the *m.* of. 16
deliver me not to the *m.* of.   74:19
in the *m.* of my thoughts.   94:19
they remembered not *m.* of.   106:7
and repented, according to *m.*   45
praise him among the *m.*   109:30
in the *m.* of words.   *Pr* 10:19
in the *m.* of counsellors. 11:14; 24:6
in *m.* of people is the king's. 14:28
in *m.* of counsellors they are. 15:22
gold, and a *m.* of rubies.   20:15
the *m.* of business, a fool's voice is
known by the *m.* of.   *Eccl* 5:3
in the *m.* of dreams there are.   7
to what purpose is the *m.? Isa* 1:11
m. dried up with thirst.   5:13
m. and pomp shall descend.   14
woe to *m.* of many people.   17:12
so *m.* of nations be that fight. 29:8
when *m.* of shepherds is called. 31:4
shall come on thee for *m.* of.   47:9
stand now with the *m.* of thy.   12
thou art wearied in the *m.* of thy. 13
m. of camels shall cover thee. 60:6
according to *m.* of his loving. 63:7
is a *m.* of waters. *Jer* 10:13*; 51:16*
yea, they have called a *m.*   12:6*
I have wounded thee for *m.*   30:14
I will punish the *m.* of No.   46:25*
afflicted her, for *m.* of.   *Lam* 1:5
compassion according to *m.* of. 3:32
wrath is on all the *m. Ezek* 7:12, 14
touching the whole *m.* thereof.   13
answer him according to the *m.* 14:4
by reason of the *m.*   27:12, 18, 33
the *m.* of the wares.   16, 18
Pharaoh and all his *m.* 31:18; 32:32
Elam and her *m.*   32:24
Tubal and all her *m.*   26
bury Gog, and all his *m.*   39:11
words like voice of a *m. Dan* 10:6
north shall set forth a *m.*   11:13
for *m.* of thine iniquity.   *Hos* 9:7
thou didst trust in the *m.*   10:13
there is a *m.* of slain.   *Nah* 3:3
the *m.* of the whoredoms of.   4
he feared the *m.*   *Mat* 14:5; 21:46
I have compassion on the *m.* 15:32
                          Mark 8:2
thou seest the *m.* thronging thee.
                Mark 5:31; *Luke* 8:45
was with the angel a *m. Luke* 2:13
together an innumerable *m.*   12:1
him in the absence of the *m.*   22:6
yet spake, behold, a *m.*   47
whole *m.* of them arose.   23:1
a *m.* being present in.   *John* 5:13
not able to draw it for the *m.* 21:6
m. that believed were of. *Acts* 4:32
saying pleased the whole *m.*   6:5
the *m.* rose up together.   21:22
m. must needs come together. 21:22
and shall hide a *m.* of sins. *Jas* 5:20
shall cover the *m.* of sins. *I Pet* 4:8

see **great**

multitudes
draw her and all her *m. Ezek* 32:20
m. in the valley of decision. *Joel* 3:14
dumb spake; and the *m.   Mat* 9:33
when he saw the *m.* he was.   36
m. cried, saying, Hosanna to. 21:9
m. were added both of.   *Acts* 5:14
Jews saw the *m.* they were.   13:45
the waters are *m.*   *Rev* 17:15

see **great**

munition
against her and her *m.*   *Isa* 29:7*
keep the *m.*, watch the.   *Nah* 2:1†

munitions
his defence shall be *m.*   *Isa* 33:16

murder
[1] *The taking away of a man's
life unlawfully,* Mark 15:7. [2]
*All cruelty in thought, word, or
deed,* Mat 19:18; 1 John 3:15.
(*Intentional murder was always
punished with death, but accidental
murder, among the Hebrews, was
only punished by banishment. Cities
of refuge were appointed for man-
slaughter,whither a man might retire,
and continue in safety, till the death
of the high priest; then the offender
was at liberty to return to his own
city, and his own house, if he
pleased. But as for the murderer,
he was put to death without any
remission, and the kinsmen of the
murdered person might kill him
with impunity*)
in secret doth he the.   *Ps* 10:8
they slay the widow, and *m.*   94:6
ye steal, *m.* and commit ? *Jer* 7:9
so priests *m.* in the way.   *Hos* 6:9

murder
thou shalt do no *m.*   *Mat* 19:18
who had committed *m.*   *Mark* 15:7
and for *m.* was cast. *Luke* 23:19, 25
full of envy, *m.* debate.   *Rom* 1:29

murderer
he is a *m.*: the *m.* shall surely be put
to death.   *Num* 35:16, 17, 18, 21
of blood shall slay the *m.*   19, 21
m. shall be put to death by.   30
no satisfaction for the life of a *m.* 31
see how this son of a *m. 2 Ki* 6:32
m. rising with the light.   *Job* 24:14
his children to the *m.*   *Hos* 9:13
he was a *m.* from the.   *John* 8:44
ye desired a *m.* to be.   *Acts* 3:14
no doubt this man is a *m.*   28:4
of you suffer as a *m.*   *I Pet* 4:15
his brother is a *m.*; ye know that no
m. hath eternal life.   *I John* 3:15

murderers
the children of the *m.*   *2 Ki* 14:6
lodged in it, but now *m.*   *Isa* 1:21
wearied, because of *m.*   *Jer* 4:31
and destroyed those *m.*   *Mat* 22:7
have been now the *m.*   *Acts* 7:52
led 4000 men that were *m.*   21:38
law made for *m.* of fathers and.
                             I Tim 1:9
m. shall have their part.   *Rev* 21:8
are whoremongers and *m.*   22:15

murders
out of the heart proceed *m.*
                 Mat 15:19; *Mark* 7:21
the flesh are envyings, *m. Gal* 5:21
repented they of their *m.* *Rev* 9:21

murmur
that ye *m.* against us ?   *Ex* 16:7
murmurings ye *m.*   8; *Num* 14:27
the congregation to *m.*   *Num* 14:36
what is Aaron, that ye *m.?*   16:11
of Israel, whereby they *m.*   17:5
Jesus said, *M.* not among. *John* 6:43
neither *m.* as some of. *I Cor* 10:10

murmured
the people *m.*   *Ex* 15:24; 17:3
congregation of Israel *m.* against.
             16:2; *Num* 14:2; 16:41
years old, which have *m. Num* 14:29
ye *m.* in your tents.   *Deut* 1:27
all the congregation *m.*   *Josh* 9:18
believed not, but *m.* in.   *Ps* 106:25
they that *m.* shall learn. *Isa* 29:24
received a penny, they *m. Mat* 20:11
and they *m.* against her. *Mark* 14:5
and Pharisees *m.*   *Luke* 5:30
m. saying, This man receiveth. 15:2
m. that he was gone to be.   19:7
Jews *m.* at him, because. *John* 6:41
he knew that his disciples *m.* 61
heard that the people *m.*   7:32
as some of them *m.*   *I Cor* 10:10

murmurers
m. complainers, walking.   *Jude* 16

murmuring
m. among the people.   *John* 7:12
a *m.* of Grecians against.   *Acts* 6:1

murmurings
he heareth your *m.*   *Ex* 16:7, 8, 9
                     12; *Num* 14:27
your *m.* are not against us. *Ex* 16:8
cease the *m.* of Israel.   *Num* 17:5
shalt quite take away their *m.*   10
do all things without *m.*   *Phil* 2:14

murrain
be a very grievous *m.*   *Ex* 9:3

muse
I *m.* on the work of thy.   *Ps* 143:5

mused
men *m.* in their hearts.   *Luke* 3:15*

music
to meet king Saul with *m.I Sam* 18:6
with instruments of *m. 1 Chr* 15:16
               2 Chr 5:13; 23:13; 34:12
Levites with instruments of *m.*
                            2 Chr 7:6
daughters of *m.* shall be. *Eccl* 12:4
rising, I am their *m.*   *Lam* 3:63*
have ceased from their *m.*   5:14
ye hear the sound of cornet, and
all kinds of *m. Dan* 3:5, 7, 10, 15
neither were instruments of *m.* 6:18
invent instruments of *m.*   *Amos* 6:5
elder son heard *m.* and. *Luke* 15:25

musical
with *m.* instruments.   *1 Chr* 16:42
with the *m.* instruments.   *Neh* 12:36
as *m.* instruments, and.   *Eccl* 2:8†

musicians
voice of *m.* shall be.   *Rev* 18:22

musing
while I was *m.* the fire.   *Ps* 39:3

must
m. I needs bring thy son ? *Gen* 24:5
it *m.* not be so done in our.   29:26
thou *m.* come in to me.   30:16
if it *m.* be so.   43:11
it *m.* be put in water.   *Lev* 11:32
seven days ye *m.* eat.   23:6
he *m.* do after the law.   *Num* 6:21
m. we fetch you water out of ? 20:10
m. I not take heed to speak ? 23:12
Lord speaketh that I *m.* do.   26
by what way we *m.* go.   *Deut* 1:22
I *m.* die in this land, I *m.*   4:22
thou *m.* eat them before.   12:18
approach that thou *m.* die.   31:14
way by which ye *m.* go.   *Josh* 3:4
thou *m.* offer it to the.   *Judg* 13:16
there *m.* be an inheritance.   21:17
a little, and lo I *m.* die. *1 Sam* 14:43
ruleth over men *m.*   *2 Sam* 23:3
shall touch them *m.* be fenced.   7
he sleepeth, and *m.* be. *1 Ki* 18:27
hast said, so *m.* we do.   *Ezra* 10:12
they *m.* needs be borne.   *Jer* 10:5
fulfilled, that thus it *m.? Mat* 26:54
new wine *m.* be put into new bottles.
             Mark 2:22; *Luke* 5:38
Son of man *m.* suffer many things.
                      Mark 8:31; 9:12
say the scribes that Elias *m.?* 9:11
of wars, be ye not troubled, for such
things *m.* be.   13:7; *Luke* 21:9
gospel *m.* first be published.
                          Mark 13:10
m. be about my Father's. *Luke* 2:49
I *m.* preach kingdom of God. 4:43
I bought ground, and *m.* go. 14:18
Zacchaeus, to-day I *m.* abide. 19:5
day when the passover *m.*   22:7
the things written *m.* be. 37; 24:44
he *m.* release one to them.   23:17
Son of man *m.* be delivered.   24:7
ye *m.* be born again.   *John* 3:7
the serpent, so *m.* the Son of.   14
m. increase, but I *m.* decrease. 30
and he *m.* needs go through.   4:4
God is a spirit, *m.* worship him. 24
I *m.* work the works of him.   9:4
sheep I have, them also I *m.* 10:16
knew not that he *m.* rise again. 20:9

m. have been fulfilled. *Acts* 1:16
m. one be ordained to be a. 22
other name whereby we *m.* 4:12
told thee what thou *m.* do. 9:6
m. through much tribulation. 14:22
ye *m.* be circumcised and. 15:24
said, Sirs, what *m.* I do to ? 16:30
I *m.* by all means keep this. 18:21
the multitude *m.* needs come. 21:22
so *m.* thou bear witness also. 23:11
fear not, thou *m.* be brought. 27:24
we *m.* be cast on a certain island. 26
wherefore ye *m.* needs. *Rom* 13:5
m. ye needs go out of. *1 Cor* 5:10
there *m.* also be heresies. 11:19
for he *m.* reign till he hath. 15:25
for we *m.* all appear. *2 Cor* 5:10
I *m.* needs glory, I will glory. 11:30
a bishop then *m.* be blameless.
 1 Tim 3:2; *Tit* 1:7
he *m.* have a good report. *1 Tim* 3:7
likewise *m.* deacons be grave. 8
husbandman *m.* be first. *2 Tim* 2:6
the servant of the Lord *m.* not. 24
it remaineth that some *m. Heb* 4:6
there *m.* be the death of the. 9:16
cometh to God, *m.* believe that. 11:6
as they that *m.* give account. 13:17
shew thee things which *m. Rev* 4:1
if any will hurt, he *m.* in this. 11:5
that he *m.* be loosed a little. 20:3
to shew things which *m.* shortly. 22:6

mustard seed, see grain

mustered
he took the scribe which *m.* the
 people. *2 Ki* 25:19; *Jer* 52:25

mustereth
the Lord *m.* the host of. *Isa* 13:4

mutter, -ed
that peep, and that *m. Isa* 8:19
tongue hath *m.* perverseness. 59:3

mutual
comforted by the *m.* faith. *Rom* 1:12

muzzle
thou shalt not *m.* the ox. *Deut* 25:4
 1 Cor 9:9; *1 Tim* 5:18

Myra
M. a city of Lycia. *Acts* 27:5

myrrh
bearing balm and *m. Gen* 37:25
the man a present, *m.*, nuts. 43:11
pure *m.* five hundred. *Ex* 30:23
six months with oil of *m. Esth* 2:12
thy garments smell of *m. Ps* 45:8
perfumed my bed with *m. Pr* 7:17
a bundle of *m.* is my. *S of S* 1:13
perfumed with *m.* and. 3:6
get me to the mountain of *m.* 4:6
m. and aloes with all the chief. 14
I have gathered my *m.* with. 5:1
with *m.*, my fingers with sweet *m.* 5
lilies, dropping sweet smelling *m.* 13
to him gifts, gold and *m. Mat* 2:11
wine mingled with *m. Mark* 15:23
brought a mixture of *m. John* 19:39

myrtle
fetch *m.* olive branches. *Neh* 8:15
in the wilderness the *m. Isa* 41:19
brier shall come up the *m.* 55:13

myrtle trees
and he stood among the *m. trees.*
 Zech 1:8, 10, 11

myself
because naked, and hid *m. Gen* 3:10
by *m.* have I sworn, in blessing.
 22:16; *Isa* 45:23; *Jer* 22:5; 49:13
brought you unto *m. Ex* 19:4
I sanctified them for *m. Num* 8:17
I the Lord will make *m.* known. 12:6
not able to bear you *m. Deut* 1:9. 12
go out and shake *m. Judg* 16:20
I cannot redeem it for *m. Ruth* 4:6
I forced *m.* therefore. *1 Sam* 13:12
that I may hide *m.* in the field. 20:5
kept me from avenging *m.* 25:33
go forth with you *m. 2 Sam* 18:2
kept *m.* from mine iniquity. 22:24
shew *m.* unto him. *1 Ki* 18:15
I will disguise *m.* 22:30
 2 Chr 18:29
I bow *m.* in the house of. *2 Ki* 5:18

---

chosen this place to *m. 2 Chr* 7:12
I consulted with *m.* and. *Neh* 5:7
come with the king but *m. Esth* 5:12
do honour more than to *m.* 6:6
harden *m.* in sorrow. *Job* 6:10
so that I am a burden to *m.* 7:20
if I justify *m.* 9:20
I will comfort *m.* 27
if I wash *m.* with snow water. 30
leave my complaint upon *m.* 10:1
will I not hide *m.* from thee. 13:20
mine error remained with *m.* 19:4
whom I shall see for *m.* and eyes. 27
or have eaten my morsel *m.* 31:17
or if I lift up *m.* when evil found. 29
wherefore I abhor *m.* and. 42:6
I behaved *m.* as though he had been.
 Ps 35:14
glory, I *m.* awake early. 57:8; 108:2
I will behave *m.* wisely in. 101:2
but I give *m.* to prayer. 109:4
I will delight *m.* in thy. 119:16
delight *m.* in thy commandments. 47
thy judgement and comforted *m.* 52
nor do I exercise *m.* in. 131:1
behaved and quieted *m.* as child. 2
heart to give *m.* to wine. *Eccl* 2:3
labour wherein I have shewed *m.* 19
now will I lift up *m. Isa* 33:10
people have I formed for *m.* 43:21
abroad the earth by *m.* 44:24
comfort *m.* against sorrow. *Jer* 8:18
I *m.* will fight against you. 21:5
will answer him by *m. Ezek* 14:7
in the day I made *m.* known. 20:5, 9
river is mine, I have made it for *m.*
 29:3
will make *m.* known amongst. 35:11
I magnify *m.* and sanctify *m.* 38:23
nor did I anoint *m.* at all. *Dan* 10:3
bow *m.* before the high God. *Mi* 6:6
heard, I trembled in *m. Hab* 3:16
separated *m.* as I have. *Zech* 7:3
I *m.* worthy to come. *Luke* 7:7
I *m.*; handle me and see. 24:39
if I bear witness of *m. John* 5:31
know whether I speak of *m.* 7:17
I am not come of *m.* but he that. 28
though I bear record of *m.* 8:14
I am one that bear witness of *m.* 18
know that I do nothing of *m.* 28
nor came I of *m.* but he sent me. 42
if I honour *m.* my honour is. 54
I lay it down of *m.* 10:18
spoken of *m.*; Father sent me. 12:49
again, and receive you unto *m.* 14:3
that I speak, I speak not of *m.* 10
love him, and manifest *m.* to him. 21
for their sakes I sanctify *m.* 17:19
stand up, I *m.* also am. *Acts* 10:26
count I my life dear unto *m.* 20:24
more cheerfully answer for *m.* 24:10
herein do I exercise *m.* to have. 16
I would hear the man *m.* 25:22
I verily thought with *m.* I. 26:9
I could wish that *m.* were. *Rom* 9:3
I have reserved to *m.* 7000. 11:4
and I *m.* also am persuaded. 15:14
succourer of many, and of *m.* 16:2
for I know nothing by *m. 1 Cor* 4:4
I have in a figure transferred to *m.* 6
that all men were even as I *m.* 7:7
yet have I made *m.* servant. 9:19
lest that I *m.* should be cast. 27
now I Paul *m.* beseech. *2 Cor* 10:1
an offence in abasing *m.*? 11:7
kept *m.* from being burdensome. 9
receive me, that I may boast *m.* a. 16
of *m.* I will not glory but. 12:5
m. was not burdensome to you. 13
I make *m.* a transgressor. *Gal* 2:18
I also *m.* shall come. *Phil* 2:24
not *m.* to have apprehended. 3:13
receive Onesimus as *m. Philem* 17

Mysia
come to *M. Acts* 16:7
they passing by *M.* came to Troas. 8

mysteries
*(Something secret, hidden, not
 known to all)*
you to know the *m.* of the kingdom.
 Mat 13:11; *Luke* 8:10
as stewards of the *m. 1 Cor* 4:1

---

though I understand all *m. 1 Cor* 13:2
the Spirit he speaketh *m.* 14:2

mystery
know the *m.* of kingdom. *Mark* 4:11
be ignorant of this *m. Rom* 11:25
the revelation of the *m.* 16:25
wisdom of God in a *m. 1 Cor* 2:7
I shew you a *m.*; We shall. 15:51
made known to us the *m. Eph* 1:9
made known to me the *m.* 3:3
knowledge in the *m.* of Christ. 4
what is the fellowship of the *m.* 9
this is a great *m.* but I speak. 5:32
boldly, to make known the *m.* of.
 6:19; *Col* 1:26, 27; 4:3
acknowledgement of the *m. Col* 2:2
the *m.* of iniquity doth. *2 Thes* 2:7
holding *m.* of faith in. *1 Tim* 3:9
great is the *m.* of godliness. 16
the *m.* of the seven stars. *Rev* 1:20
m. of God should be finished. 10:7
m., Babylon the great. 17:5
m. of the woman. 7

N

Naaman
Benjamin, *N.* and. *Gen* 46:21
the son of Bela, *N. Num* 26:40
 1 Chr 8:4
N. captain of Syria. *2 Ki* 5:1
N. was wroth and went away. 11
my master hath spared *N.* the. 20
the leprosy of *N.* shall cleave. 27
was cleansed, saving *N. Luke* 4:27

Naamathite, see Zophar

Naashon, or Nahshon
Elisheba the sister of *N. Ex* 6:23
N. son of Amminadab. *Num* 1:7
 2:3; 10:14
offered the first day was *N.* 7:12
this was the offering of *N.* son. 17
Amminadab begat *N.* and *N.* begat.
 Ruth 4:20; *1 Chr* 2:10, 11
 Mat 1:4
which was the son of *N. Luke* 3:32

Nabal
name of the man was *N. 1 Sam* 25:3
N. did shear his sheep. 4
go to *N.* and greet him. 5
N. is his name, and folly is. 25
Lord smote *N.* that he died. 38
returned the wickedness of *N.* 39
Abigail *N.*'s wife. 27:3; 30:5
 2 Sam 2:2; 3:3

Naboth
N. the Jezreelite had. *1 Ki* 21:1
give thee vineyard of *N.* the. 7
set *N.* on high. 9, 12
heard *N.* was stoned. 14
Ahab heard that *N.* was dead. 16
Ahab is in the vineyard of *N.* 18
dogs licked the blood of *N.* 19
him in the portion of *N. 2 Ki* 9:21, 25
seen yesterday the blood of *N.* 26

Nadab
the sons of Aaron, *N.* Abihu.
 Ex 6:23; *Lev* 10:1
N. and Abihu, seventy. *Ex* 24:1, 9
N. and Abihu died. *Num* 3:4; 26:61
N. son of Jeroboam reigned.
 1 Ki 14:20; 15:25
N. son of Shammai. *1 Chr* 2:28
the sons of *N.* 30
Baal and *N.* the sons. 8:30; 9:36

Nagge
was the son of *N. Luke* 3:25

Nahash
N. came up against Jabesh.
 1 Sam 11:1; 12:12
shew kindness to Hanun the son of
 N. 2 Sam 10:2; *1 Chr* 19:2
the daughter of *N. 2 Sam* 17:25
Shobi son of *N.* brought beds. 27

Nahor
Serug begat *N. Gen* 11:22
N. lived 29 years. 24; *1 Chr* 1:26
Terah begat Abraham, *N.* and Haran.
 Gen 11:26, 27

N.'s wife Milcah. Gen 11:29
hath born children to thy brother N.
	22:20, 23; 24:15, 24
went to the city of N. 24:10
God of Abraham and N. 31:53

nail
(A finger-nail; a tent-peg, usually of wood; a metal pin, perhaps of gold)
n. of tent, and smote n. Judg 4:21
Sisera lay dead, the n. was. 22
she put her hand to the n. 5:26
give us a n. in his holy. Ezra 9:8
I will fasten him as a n. Isa 22:23
shall the n. that is fastened be. 25
out of him came the n. Zech 10:4

nailing
took it out of the way, n. Col 2:14

nails
her head, and pare her n. Deut 21:12
iron in abundance for n. 1 Chr 22:3
the weight of the n. 2 Chr 3:9
n. fastened by the. Eccl 12:11
he fastened his idol with n.
	Isa 41:7; Jer 10:4
his n. were grown like. Dan 4:33
fourth beast, whose n. were. 7:19
into the print of the n. John 20:25

Nain
into a city called N. Luke 7:11

Naioth
Samuel and David dwelt at N.
	1 Sam 19:18, 19, 22
Saul went to N. 23
David fled from N. 20:1

naked
[1] Altogether unclothed or un-covered, Gen 2:25; 3:7. [2] With few clothes on, having put off the greatest part of them, 1 Sam 19:24; John 21:7. [3] Not clothed with the righteousness of Christ, Rev 3:17. [4] Destitute of all worldly goods, Job 1:21. [5] Discovered, known, and manifest, Job 26:6; Heb 4:13.
they were n. and were. Gen 2:25
knew that they were n. 3:7, 10, 11
people were n. for Aaron had made them n. to their. Ex 32:25*
Saul lay down n. all. 1 Sam 19:24
spoil clothed all the n. 2 Chr 28:15
Ahaz made Judah n. and. 19*
n. came I out of my mother's womb, and n. shall I return. Job 1:21
thou hast stripped the n. of. 22:6
they cause the n. to lodge. 24:7, 10
hell is n. before him and. 26:6
n. shall he return, to go. Eccl 5:15
when thou seest the n. Isa 58:7
shalt make thyself n. Lam 4:21
hath covered the n. Ezek 18:7, 16
lest I strip her n. and set. Hos 2:3
shall flee away n. in. Amos 2:16
I will go stripped and n. Mi 1:8
having thy shame n. 11*
bow was made quite n. Hab 3:9
I was n. and ye clothed. Mat 25:36
	43
when saw we thee n. and? 38, 44
linen cloth about his n. Mark 14:51
linen cloth, fled from them n. 52
Peter was n. and cast. John 21:7
fled out of that house n. Acts 19:16
present hour we are n. 1 Cor 4:11
we shall not be found n. 2 Cor 5:3
but all things are n. to. Heb 4:13
if a brother or sister be n. Jas 2:15
poor, and blind, and n. Rev 3:17
garments, lest he walk n. 16:15
make her desolate and n. 17:16
	see bare

nakedness
and Ham saw the n. of. Gen 9:22
n., they saw not their father's n. 23
to see the n. of the land. 42:9, 12
thy n. be not discovered. Ex 20:26
breeches to cover their n. 28:42
none shall uncover their n. Lev 18:6
the n. of father or mother. 7, 8, 11
	15; 20:11

the n. of thy sister. Lev 18:9
n. of thy son's daughter. 10
n. of father's wife's daughter. 11
n. of father's sister. 12
n. of mother's sister. 13; 20:19
n. of father's brother. 18:14
n. of daughter in law. 15
n. of thy brother's wife, it is thy brother's. 16
n. of a woman and her daughter. 17
n. of a woman as long as. 19; 20:18
sister's n. and she see his n. 20:17
uncovered his uncle's n. 20
uncovered his brother's n. 21
serve thine enemies in n. Deut 28:48
of thy mother's n. 1 Sam 20:30
thy n. shall be uncovered. Isa 47:3
they have seen her n. Lam 1:8
I covered thy n., yea. Ezek 16:8
thy n. discovered through. 36
	23:18
and will discover thy n. 16:37
discovered their father's n. 22:10
these discovered her n. and. 23:10
the n. of thy whoredom shall. 29
flax given to cover her n. Hos 2:9
shew the nations thy n. Nah 3:5
mayest look on their n. Hab 2:15
who shall separate us from the love of Christ? shall n. Rom 8:35
often, in cold and n. 2 Cor 11:27
that the shame of thy n. Rev 3:18

name
Name is frequently used to de-signate the entire person, his individuality and his power. This is usually the case when the refer-ence is to God.
The word is also used to mean a race, as descended from some one man.
that was the n. thereof. Gen 2:19
call the n. of the city after n. 4:17
and called their n. Adam. 5:2
let us make us a n. lest we. 11:4
therefore the n. of the city. 19:22
the n. of the city was Luz. 28:19
shall be called after the n. of. 48:6
whose n. is Jealous. Ex 34:14
neither profane the n. of thy God.
	Lev 18:21; 19:12; 21:6; 22:2, 32
n. of one Eldad, of the. Num 11:26
write thou every man's n. 17:2
the n. of the Israelite that. 25:14
n. of Midianitish woman slain. 15
why should n. of our father? 27:4
Nobah, after his own n. 32:42
shalt destroy their n. Deut 7:24
and blot out their n. from. 9:14
bring up an evil n. on her. 22:14
he hath brought up an evil n. 19
firstborn shall succeed in n. 25:6
to raise up to his brother a n. 7
to make thee high in n. and in. 26:19
this glorious and fearful n. 28:58
nor make mention of n. Josh 23:7
man's n. with whom I. Ruth 2:19
raise up the n. of the dead. 4:5, 10
neighbours gave it a n. 17
n. of the man was Nabal. 1 Sam 25:3
they spake to Nabal in the n. of. 9
whose n. is called by the. n. of the Lord. 2 Sam 6:2
a great n. like the n. of the great men in the earth. 7:9; 1 Chr 17:8
God redeemed to make him a n.
	2 Sam 7:23; 1 Chr 17:21
David gat him a n. when. 2 Sam 8:13
to my husband neither n. nor. 14:7
Abishai had the n. among. 23:18
Benaiah, and had the n. among three mighty men. 22; 1 Chr 11:20, 24
n. of Solomon better than thy n. and his throne greater. 1 Ki 1:47
chose to put his n. there. 14:21
	2 Chr 12:13
call ye on the n. of your gods.
	1 Ki 18:24, 25
wrote letters in Ahab's n. 21:8
not blot out the n. of. 2 Ki 14:27
and was called after their n.
	Ezra 2:61; Neh 7:63
prophesied in the n. of. Ezra 5:1

and gavest him the n. of. Neh 9:7
so didst thou get thee a n. as. 10
the king in Mordecai's n. Esth 2:22
for the Jews in the king's n. 8:8
he shall have no n. in the. Job 18:17
thou hast put out their n. Ps 9:5
the n. of the God of Jacob. 20:1
in the n. of God we will set up. 5
if we have forgotten the n. 44:20
I will praise the n. of God. 69:30
the n. of Israel be no more. 83:4
whose n. alone is Jehovah. 18
let them praise thy great m. 99:3
n. be blotted out. 109:13
Lord's n. is to be praised. 113:3
the n. of the wicked. Pr 10:7
n. of the Lord is a strong. 18:10
good n. is rather to be chosen. 22:1
lest I take the n. of my God. 30:9
a good n. is better than. Eccl 7:1
off from Babylon the n. Isa 14:22
it shall be to the Lord for a n. 55:13
them a n.. an everlasting n. 56:5
whose n. is holy. 57:15
called by a new n. 62:2
himself an everlasting n. 63:12
to make thyself a glorious n. 14
n. for a curse to my chosen, and call his servants by another n. 65:15
seed and your n. remain. 66:22
that they might be to me for a n.
	Jer 13:11; 33:9
which hast made thee a n. 32:20
this is the n. wherewith she. 33:16
saith the King, whose n. is the Lord.
	46:18; 48:15; 51:57
n. thereof is called Bamah.
	Ezek 20:29
son of man, write thee the n. 24:2
the n. of the city shall be. 48:35
blessed be the n. of God. Dan 2:20
Daniel came, according to the n. 4:8
call her n. Lo-ruhamah. Hos 1:6
be remembered by their n. 2:17
saith Lord, whose n. is. Amos 5:27
every one in the n. of his god, we will walk in the n. of our. Mi 4:5
I will cut off the n. of the. Zeph 1:4
make you a n. and a praise. 3:20
whose n. is the Branch. Zech 6:12
prophet in the n. of a prophet, a righteous man in n. of. Mat 10:41
give a cup of water only in n. 42
baptizing them in the n. 28:19
kindred is called by this n. Luke 1:61
saying, His n. is John. 63
shall cast out your n. as evil. 6:22
from God, whose n. was. John 1:6
not believed in the n. of the. 3:18
I am come in my Father's n. 5:43
I do in my Father's n. 10:25
be baptized in the n. of. Acts 2:38
in the n. of Jesus Christ, rise up. 3:6
by what power or n. have ye? 4:7
there is none other n. under. 12
henceforth to no man in this n. 17, 18
may be done by the n. of Jesus. 30
should not teach in this n. 5:28, 40
preaching, concerning the n. 8:12
them that called on this n. 9:21
boldly in the n. of Jesus. 27
their lives for the n. of Jesus. 15:26
said, In the n. of Jesus. 16:18
they were baptized in the. 19:5
contrary to the n. of Jesus of. 26:9
for the n. of God is. Rom 2:24
ye baptized in the n.? 1 Cor 1:13
in the n. of our Lord Jesus. 5:4
	Eph 5:20
are justified in the n. of. 1 Cor 6:11
far above every n. that. Eph 1:21
him a n. above every n. Phil 2:9
at the n. of Jesus every knee. 10
do all in the n. of Lord. Col 3:17
that the n. of God be not. 1 Tim 6:1
the n. of Christ, depart. 2 Tim 2:19
obtained a more excellent n. Heb 1:4
blaspheme that worthy n.? Jas 2:7
if reproached for the n. 1 Pet 4:14
should believe on n. of his Son.
	1 John 3:23; 5:13
a n. written, which no. Rev 2:17
thou hast a n. that thou livest. 3:1
I will write on him the n. of. 12

the *n.* of the star is called. *Rev* 8:11
n. in the Hebrew tongue is.   9:11
and on his heads the *n.* of.   13:1
his Father's *n.* written in.   14:1
blasphemed the *n.* of God.   16:9
was a *n.* written, Mystery.   17:5
a *n.* written no man knew but. 19:12
on his thigh a *n.* written, King of. 16

see **called**

name, *verb*
shalt anoint to me him whom I *n.*
     1 Sam 16:3
bring him up whom I shall *n.*   28:8
mouth of the Lord shall *n. Isa* 62:2

by **name,** or *by the name*
I appeared *by the n.* of God. *Ex* 6:3
called *by n.* Bezaleel.   31:2; 35:30
I know thee *by n.*   33:12, 17
by n. ye shall reckon.   *Num* 4:32
cities mentioned *by n. Josh* 21:9
of Gath, Goliath *by n. 1 Sam* 17:23
Sheba, son of Bichri *by n.* hath lifted
   up his hand.   *2 Sam* 20:21
be born, Josiah *by n.*   *1 Ki* 13:2
these written *by n.*   *1 Chr* 4:41
which were expressed *by n.*   12:31
   16:41; *2 Chr* 28:15; 31:19
she were called *by n.*   *Esth* 2:14
by the n. of Jacob, and surname himself *by the n.*   *Isa* 44:5; 48:1
which call thee *by thy n.*   45:3
calleth his own sheep *by n. John* 10:3
by the n. of Jesus this.   *Acts* 4:10
I beseech you *by the n. 1 Cor* 1:10
our friends salute thee. Greet the
   friends *by n.*   *3 John* 14
see **expressed**

his **name**
shall say, What is *his n.?*   *Ex* 3:13
     Pr 30:4
the Lord is *his n.*   *Ex* 15:3
   Jer 33:2; *Amos* 5:8; 9:6
not hold him guiltless that taketh *his*
   n. in vain.   *Ex* 20:7; *Deut* 5:11
every stone with *his n.* shall they be.
     Ex 28:21; 39:14
Jair called them after *his* own *n.*
     Deut 3:14
and shalt swear by *his n.*   6:13
to bless in *his n.* to this day.   10:8
     1 Chr 23:13
shall choose to put *his n. Deut* 12:5
   21; *1 Ki* 14:21; *2 Chr* 12:13
choose to cause *his n. Deut* 12:11
choose to place *his n.* there.   14:23
     16:6, 11; 26:2
shall choose to set *his n.*   14:24
that *his n.* be not put out.   25:6
his n. shall be called in Israel.   10
Lord shall blot out *his n.*   29:20
neither told he me *his n. Judg* 13:6
his n. may be famous.   *Ruth* 4:14
for *his* great *n.'s* sake. *1 Sam* 12:22
   Ps 23:3; 106:8; *1 John* 2:12
     3 John 7
so that *his n.* was much. *1 Sam* 18:30
as *his n.* is, so is he, Nabal is *his n.*
     25:25
give thanks to Lord, call upon *his n.*
   1 Chr 16:8; *Ps* 105:1; *Isa* 12:4
give the glory due to *his n.*
   1 Chr 16:29; *Ps* 29:2; 96:8
God that caused *his n.*   *Ezra* 6:12
let us exalt *his n.*   *Ps* 34:3; 66:2
when shall he die and *his n.?*   41:5
the heavens by *his n.* Jah.   68:4
they that love *his n.* shall.   69:36
his n. shall endure for ever.   72:17
and blessed be *his* glorious *n.*   19
his n. is great in Israel.   76:1
bless *his n.*   96:2; 100:4
among them that call on *his n.* 99:6
holy and reverend is *his n.*   111:9
sing praises to *his n.* for it.   135:3
praise *his n.,* for *his n.* alone. 148:13
praise *his n.* in the dance.   149:3
haughty scorner is *his n.*   *Pr* 21:24
his n. shall be covered.   *Eccl* 6:4
shall call *his n.* Immanuel. *Isa* 7:14
     Mat 1:23
and *his n.* shall be called. *Isa* 9:6
make mention that *his n.* is   12:4

the Lord of hosts is *his n. Isa* 47:4
   48:2; 51:15; 54:5; *Jer* 10:16
   31:35; 32:18; 50:34; 51:19
his n. should not have been cut off.
     Isa 48:19
his n. may be no more. *Jer* 11:19
speak any more in *his n.*   20:9
this is *his n.* whereby he.   23:6
all ye that know *his n.* say.   48:17
God of hosts is *his n.*   *Amos* 4:13
shall walk up and down in *his n.*
     Zech 10:12
shall be one Lord, and *his n.*   14:9
thought on *his n.* a book. *Mal* 3:16
shalt call *his n.* Jesus.   *Mat* 1:23
     Luke 1:31; 2:21
his n. shall the Gentiles. *Mat* 12:21
for *his n.* was spread. *Mark* 6:14
thou shalt call *his n.* *Luke* 1:13
remission of sins should be preached
     24:47
that believe on *his n.* *John* 1:12
many believed in *his n.* when. 2:23
shall come in *his* own *n.*   5:43
might have life through *his n.* 20:31
his n. through faith in *his n.* hath.
     Acts 3:16
worthy to suffer for *his n.*   5:41
through *his n.* shall receive.   10:43
sorcerer, for so is *his n.*   13:8
them a people for *his n.*   15:14
all nations for *his n. Rom* 1:5
ye shewed towards *his n. Heb* 6:10
giving thanks to *his n.*   13:15
not blot out *his n.* but will confess
   his n.   *Rev* 3:5
and *his n.* that sat on him.   6:8
hath *his n.* Apollyon.   9:11
to blaspheme *his n.*   13:6
number of *his n.*   17; 15:2
receiveth the mark of *his n.*   14:11
and *his n.* shall be in their.   22:4
see **holy, Lord**

my **name**
dost ask after *my n.?*   *Gen* 32:29
let *my n.* be named on them.   48:16
this is *my n.* for ever.   *Ex* 3:15
raised the up, that *my n.*   9:16
where I record *my n.* I will.   20:24
provoke him not, for *my n.*   23:21
swear by *my n.* falsely. *Lev* 19:12
Molech, to profane *my* holy *n.* 20:3
my n. on the children. *Num* 6:27
shall speak in *my n. Deut* 18:19 20
thou thus after *my n.?* *Judg* 13:18
wilt not destroy *my n. 1 Sam* 24:21
Nabal, and greet him in *my n.* 25:5
an house for *my n. 2 Sam* 7:13
   1 Ki 5:5; 8:18, 19; *1 Chr* 22:10
lest I take the city, and it be called
   after *my n.*   *2 Sam* 12:28
I have no son to keep *my n.* 18:18
my n. might be therein. *1 Ki* 8:16
   29; 11:36; *2 Ki* 21:4, 7; *2 Chr* 6:5
     6; 7:16; 33:4, 7
have hallowed for *my n. 1 Ki* 9:7
not build an house to *my n.*
     1 Chr 22:8; 28:3
it was in thine heart to build an house
   for *my n.*   *2 Chr* 6:8
build the house for *my n.*   9
I have sanctified for *my n.*   7:20
I have chosen to set *my n.* there.
     Neh 1:9; *Jer* 7:12
in *my n.* shall his horn. *Ps* 89:24
he hath known *my n.*   91:14
they shall sanctify *my n. Isa* 29:23
sun shall they call on *my n.* 41:25
I am the Lord, that is *my n.*   42:8
for *my n.'s* sake will I defer. 48:9
should *my n.* be polluted ?   11
made mention of *my n.*   49:1
my n. continually every day. 52:5
my people shall know *my n.*   6
cast you out for *my n.'s* sake. 66:5
they prophesy lies in *my n.*
   Jer 14:14, 15; 23:25
know that *my n.* is The Lord. 16:21
to forget *my n.* as their fathers have
   forgotten *my n.* for Baal.   23:27
a lie in *my n.*   27:15; 29:9, 21, 23
turned and polluted *my n.*   34:16
sworn by *my* great *n., my n.* no. 44:26

but I wrought for *my n.'s* sake.
     Ezek 20:9, 14, 22, 44
sanctify *my* great *n.*   36:23
shall call on *my n.* I.   *Zech* 13:9
priests, that despise *my n. Mal* 1:6
my n. shall be great among Gentiles,
   and . . . shall be offered to *my n.* 11
my n. is dreadful among.   14
heart, to give glory unto *my n.*   2:2
and was afraid before *my n.*   5
to you that fear *my n.* shall.   4:2
hated of all men for *my n.'s* sake.
   Mat 10:22; 24:9; *Mark* 13:13
     Luke 21:17
receive a child in *my n.*   *Mat* 18:5
   Mark 9:37; *Luke* 9:48
gathered together in *my n.Mat* 18:20
forsaken houses for *my n.'s.*   19:29
many shall come in *my n.*   24:5
   Mark 13:6; *Luke* 21:8
saying, *My n.* is Legion. *Mark* 5:9
do a miracle in *my n.*   9:39
cup of water to drink in *my n.*   41
in *my n.* shall they cast out. 16:17
rulers for *my n.'s* sake. *Luke* 21:12
ye shall ask in *my n.*   *John* 14:13
   14; 15:16; 16:23, 24, 26
whom he will send in *my n.*   14:26
will they do for *my n.'s* sake. 15:21
vessel to bear *my n.*   *Acts* 9:15
he must suffer for *my n.'s* sake. 16
Gentiles upon whom *my n.* is. 15:17
my n. might be declared. *Rom* 9:17
I baptized in *mine* own *n. 1 Cor* 1:15
and for *my n.'s* sake hast. *Rev* 2:3
thou holdest fast *my n.* and.   13
and hast not denied *my n.*   3:8
see **called**

thy **name**
and make *thy n.* great.   *Gen* 12:2
thy n. Abram, but *thy n.* shall. 17:5
what is *thy n.?* 32:27, 29; *Judg* 13:17
thy n. shall be no more called Jacob.
     Gen 32:28; 35:10; *1 Ki* 18:31
Pharaoh to speak in *thy n. Ex* 5:23
thou do to *thy* great *n.? Josh* 7:9
thy n. be magnified.   *2 Sam* 7:26
will sing praise to *thy n.*   22:50
   Ps 9:2; 18:49; 61:8; 66:4; 92:1
Solomon better than *thy n. 1 Ki* 1:47
turn and confess *thy n.*   8:33
     2 Chr 6:24, 26
but cometh for *thy n.'s* sake.
     1 Ki 8:41; *2 Chr* 6:32
shall hear of *thy* great *n. 1 Ki* 8:42
earth may know *thy n.;* this house is
   called by *thy n.*   43; *2 Chr* 6:33
house I built for *thy n.*   *1 Ki* 8:44
   48; *2 Chr* 6:34, 38
thy n. may be magnified. *1 Chr* 17:24
praise *thy n.*   29:13; *Ps* 44:8
wouldest put *thy n.* there. *2 Chr* 6:20
in *thy n.* we go against this. 14:11
a sanctuary for *thy n.*   20:8
before this house, for *thy n.* is.   9
who desire to fear *thy n. Neh* 1:11
blessed be *thy* glorious *n.*   9:5
let them that love *thy n.*   *Ps* 5:11
how excellent is *thy n.* in.   8:1, 9
they that know *thy n.* will.   9:10
I will declare *thy n.* to my brethren.
     22:22; *Heb* 2:12
for *thy n.'s* sake pardon. *Ps* 25:11
for *thy n.'s* sake lead me and. 31:3
through *thy n.* will we tread. 44:5
I will make *thy n.* to be.   45:17
according to *thy n.* so is.   48:10
I will wait on *thy n.*   52:9
save me by *thy n.*   54:1
heritage of those that fear *thy n.* 61:5
will lift up my hands in *thy n.* 63:4
defiled dwelling place of *thy n.* 74:7
enemy blaspheme *thy n.?*   10
people have blasphemed *thy n.*   18
needy praise *thy n.*   21
thy n. is near, thy works.   75:1
that have not called on *thy n.* 79:6
     Jer 10:25
for the glory of *thy n.* and purge away
   our sins for *thy n.'s* sake. *Ps* 79:9
we will call upon *thy n.*   80:18
may seek *thy n.* O Lord.   83:16
come and glorify *thy n.*   86:9, 12

29

unite my heart to fear *thy n.* Ps 86:11
shall rejoice in *thy n.* 89:12, 16
O Lord, for *thy n.'s* sake. 109:21
but unto *thy n.* give glory. 115:1
I have remembered *thy n.* 119:55
do to those that love *thy n.* 132
thy n. O Lord, endureth. 135:13
n. for thy lovingkindness: for thou
hast ... word above all *thy n.* 138:2
take *thy n.* in vain. 139:20
shall give thanks to *thy n.* 140:13
that I may praise *thy n.* 142:7
O Lord, for *thy n.'s* sake. 143:11
I will bless *thy n.* for ever. 145:1, 2
praise *thy n.* for ever. 2; Isa 25:1
thy n. is as ointment. S of S 1:3
our soul is to *thy n.* Isa 26:8
will make mention of *thy n.* 13
thy n. is from everlasting. 63:16
make *thy n.* known to thine. 64:2
none that calleth on *thy n.* is. 7
art great and *thy n.* is. Jer 10:6
Lord calleth *thy n.* a green. 11:16
do thou it for *thy n.'s* sake. 14:7
do not abhor us for *thy n.'s* sake. 21
sent letters in *thy n.* to all. 29:25
I called upon *thy n.* Lam 3:55
prophets spake in *thy n.* Dan 9:6
wisdom shall see *thy n.* Mi 6:9
that no more of *thy n.* be. Nah 1:14
have we despised *thy n.?* Mal 1:6
hallowed be *thy n.* Mat 6:9
Luke 11:2
in *thy n.* have we cast out. Mat 7:22
he asked him, What is *thy n.?*
Mark 5:9; Luke 8:30
casting out devils in *thy n.* Mat 9:38
Luke 9:49
subject through *thy n.* Luke 10:17
Father, glorify *thy n.* John 12:28
I have manifested *thy n.* 17:6, 26
keep through *thine* own *n.* 11, 12
bind all that call on *thy n.* Acts 9:14
and sing unto *thy n.* Rom 15:9
to them that fear *thy n.* Rev 11:18
not fear and glorify *thy n.?* 15:4
see called

named, -eth
silver which he had *n.* Gen 23:16
Is not he rightly *n.* Jacob? 27:36
my name be *n.* on them. 48:16
n. the child Ichabod. 1 Sam 4:21
Jacob whom he *n.* Israel. 2 Ki 17:34
Moses' sons *n.* of the. 1 Chr 23:14
what hath been, is *n.* Eccl 6:10
ye shall be *n.* the priests. Isa 61:6
name shall no more be *n.* Jer 44:26
which are *n.* chief of. Amos 6:1
that art *n.* of the house. Mi 2:7
Jesus was so *n.* of the. Luke 2:21
twelve, whom he *n.* apostles. 6:13
not where Christ was *n.* Rom 15:20
such fornication not *n.* 1 Cor 5:1
every name that is *n.* Eph 1:21
family in heaven and earth is *n.* 3:15
covetousness, let it not be once *n.*
5:3
let every one that *n.* 2 Tim 2:19

namely
sore evil, *n.* riches kept. Eccl 5:13
razor that is hired, *n.* Isa 7:20
the second is like, *n.* Mark 12:31

names
Adam gave *n.* to all cattle. Gen 2:20
called their *n.* after the *n.* 26:18
make no mention of the *n.* of other.
Ex 23:13; Deut 12:3
grave on them the *n.* of children of.
Ex 28:9, 21
bear their *n.* before the. 12, 29
the number of their *n.* Num 1:2
n. of the men that shall stand. 5
number of *n.* of the Levites. 3:43
n. of the men which Moses. 13:16
n. of men which shall divide. 34:17
the *n.* of mighty men. 2 Sam 23:8
what are the *n.* of the man? Ezra 5:4
nor take up their *n.* into. Ps 16:4
lands after their own *n.* 49:11
the stars; he calleth them all by
their *n.* 147:4; Isa 40:26
n. of them were Aholah. Ezek 23:4
I will take away the *n.* of. Hos 2:17

cut off the *n.* of the idols. Zech 13:2
your *n.* are written in. Luke 10:20
the number of the *n.* 120. Acts 1:15
question of words and *n.* 18:15
whose *n.* are in the book. Phil 4:3
thou hast a few *n.* in Sardis. Rev 3:4
whose *n.* are not written. 13:8; 17:8
I saw a woman full of *n.* 17:3
n. written thereon, *n.* of the. 21:12
in them the *n.* of twelve apostles. 14

Naomi
Elimelech's wife was *N.* Ruth 1:2
is this *N.?* 19
call me not *N.*, call me Mara. 20
N. had a kinsman of her. 2:1
buyest the field of hand of *N.* 4:5
bought all at the hand of *N.* 9
there is a son born to *N.* 17

Naphtali
called his name *N.* Gen 30:8
Rachel's handmaid. Dan, *N.* 35:25
sons of *N.* 46:24; Num 1:42
26:48; 1 Chr 7:13
N. is a hind let loose. Gen 49:21
Israel, *N.* Gad, and Asher. Ex 1:4
of *N.* Ahira was prince. Num 1:15
2:29; 7:78
Ebal to curse; Dan, *N.* Deut 27:13
of *N.* he said, O *N.* satisfied. 33:23
sixth lot came out to *N.* Josh 19:32
in Galilee, in mount *N.* 20:7
nor did *N.* drive out the. Judg 1:33
called Zebulun and *N.* to. 4:10
Zebulun and *N.* jeoparded. 5:18
Gideon sent messengers to *N.* 6:35
themselves together out of *N.* 7:23
was officer in *N.* 1 Ki 4:15
Ben-hadad smote *N.* 15:20
2 Chr 16:4
carried *N.* captive to. 2 Ki 15:29
N. brought bread on. 1 Chr 12:40
captain of *N.* was Jerimoth. 27:19
Josiah in *N.* brake. 2 Chr 34:6
princes of Zebulun and *N.* Ps 68:27
afflicted the land of *N.* Isa 9:1
a portion for *N.* Ezek 48:3
one gate of *N.* 34
dwelt in the borders of *N.* Mat 4:13
the land of *N.* by the way of. 15
tribe of Naphtali
the *tribe of N.* 53,400 Num 1:43
host of the *tribe of N.* Ahira. 10:27
of the *tribe of N.* Nahbi. 13:14
of the *tribe of N.* Pedaheel. 34:28
inheritance of *tribe of N.* Josh 19:39
cities out of *tribe of N.* 21:32
1 Chr 6:62, 76
widow's son of *tribe of N.* 1 Ki 7:14
tribe of N. were sealed. Rev 7:6

napkin
I have kept in a *n.* Luke 19:20
bound about with a *n.* John 11:44
n. that was about his head. 20:7

narrow
Lord stood in a *n.* way. Num 22:26
mount Ephraim be too *n.* Josh 17:15
made windows of *n.* 1 Ki 6:4*
strange woman is a *n.* pit. Pr 23:27
destruction shall be too *n.* Isa 49:19*
n. is the way which. Mat 7:14*

narrowed
in wall he made *n.* rests. 1 Ki 6:6*

narrower
covering *n.* than he can. Isa 28:20

narrowly
thou lookest *n.* to all. Job 13:27*
shall *n.* look upon thee. Isa 14:16

Nathan
son of David, *N.* 2 Sam 5:14
N. the prophet. 7:2
so did *N.* speak. 7:17
the Lord sent *N.* 12:1, 25
Igal son of *N.* one of David's. 23:36
but *N.* the prophet he. 1 Ki 1:10
talked with David, *N.* came in. 22
let Zadok and *N.* anoint him king. 34
Azariah son of *N.* was over. 4:5
Artai begat *N.* and. 1 Chr 2:36
Joel the brother of *N.* a. 11:38
written in the book of *N.* 29:29
Solomon in book of *N.* 2 Chr 9:29

Ahava for *N.* and Ariel. Ezra 8:16
Shelemiah, *N.* had taken. 10:39
of the house of *N.* Zech 12:12
which was the son of *N.* Luke 3:31

Nathanael
Philip findeth *N.* John 1:45
N. of Cana. 21:2

nation
[1] *All the inhabitants of a particular country,* Deut 4:34. [2] *A country or kingdom,* Ex 34:10; Rev 7:9. [3] *Countrymen, natives of the same stock,* Acts 26:4. [4] *The heathen or Gentiles,* Isa 55:5.

also that *n.* they serve. Gen 15:14
wilt thou slay a righteous *n.?* 20:4
bondwoman I will make a *n.* 21:13
a *n.* and kings shall come. 35:11
Egypt, since it became a *n.* Ex 9:24
ye shall be unto me an holy *n.* 19:6
1 Pet 2:9
to sell her to a strange *n.* Ex 21:8*
that this *n.* is thy people. 33:13
have not been done in any *n.* 34:10
nor any of your *n.* commit abominations. Lev 18:26*
walk in the manners of the. 20:23
I will make of thee a great *n.*
Num 14:12; Deut 9:14
assayed to take him a *n.* from the
midst of another *n.?* Deut 4:34
thy land shall a *n.* eat up. 28:33
bring thee and thy king to a *n.* 36
bring a *n.* against thee. 49
a *n.* of fierce countenance shall. 50
are a *n.* void of counsel. 32:28
what *n.* like thy people? 2 Sam 7:23
1 Chr 17:21
n. whither my lord hath not sent ...
took an oath of the *n.* 1 Ki 18:10
every *n.* made gods. 2 Ki 17:29
they went from *n.* to *n.* 1 Chr 16:20
n. was destroyed of *n.* 2 Chr 15:6
no god of any *n.* or kingdom. 32:15
it be done against a *n.* Job 34:29
blessed is *n.* whose God. Ps 33:12
my cause against an ungodly *n.* 43:1
cut them off from being a *n.* 83:4
they went from one *n.* to. 105:13
rejoice in gladness of thy *n.* 106:5
dealt so with any *n.* 147:20
righteousness exalteth a *n.* Pr 14:34
ah sinful *n.*, a people laden. Isa 1:4
n. shall not lift up sword against *n.*
2:4; Mi 4:3
thou hast multiplied the. Isa 9:3
against an hypocritical *n.* 10:6
messengers of the *n.?* 14:32
swift messengers, to a *n.* scattered
and peeled, a *n.* meted. 18:2, 7
open that the righteous *n.* may. 26:2
increased the *n.* O Lord, the *n.* 15
to him whom the *n.* abhorreth. 49:7
give ear to me, O my *n.* 51:4
thou shalt call a *n.* thou. 55:5
seek me, as a *n.* that did. 58:2
the *n.* that will not serve thee. 60:12
small one become a strong *n.* 22
a *n.* that was not called by. 65:1
or shall a *n.* be born at once? 66:8
n. changed their gods? Jer 2:11
avenged on such a *n.* 5:9, 29; 9:9
n. on you from far ... it is a mighty
n., it is an ancient *n.* 5:15
a *n.* that obeyeth not the. 7:28
pluck up and destroy that *n.* 12:17
speak concerning a *n.* to. 18:7, 9
if that *n.* against whom I have. 8
punish that *n.* for their. 25:12; 27:8
shall go forth from *n.* to *n.* 25:32
n. which will not serve. 27:8, 13
cease from being a *n.* 31:36; 33:24
cut off Moab from being a *n.* 48:2
get you up to the wealthy *n.* 49:31
no *n.* whither Elam shall. 36
out of the north cometh a *n.* 50:3
have watched for a *n.* Lam 4:17
Israel, a rebellious *n.* Ezek 2:3
I will make them one *n.* 37:22
four kingdoms shall stand up out of
the *n.* Dan 8:22
never was since there was a *n.* 12:1
for a *n.* is come up upon. Joel 1:6

raise up against you a n. *Amos* 6:14
was cast off a strong n. *Mi* 4:7
that bitter and hasty n. *Hab* 1:6
gather together, O n. *Zeph* 2:1
woe to the n. of the Cherethites. 5
so is this people and n. *Hag* 2:14
even this whole n. have. *Mal* 3:9
given to a n. bringing *Mat* 21:43
n. shall rise against n. 24:7
 Mark 13:8; *Luke* 21:10
for he loveth our n. *Luke* 7:5
this fellow perverting the n. 23:2
come and take our n. *John* 11:48
one man die, that the whole n. 50
Jesus should die for that n. 51
and not for that n. only, but. 52
thine own n. hath delivered. 18:35
devout men out of every n. *Acts* 2:5
the n. to whom they shall be. 7:7
good report among all the n. 10:22
to come to one of another n. 28
but in every n. he that feareth. 35
deeds are done to this n. 24:2
thou hast been a judge to this n. 10
I came to bring alms to my n. 17
at first among mine own n. 26:4
aught to accuse my n. of. 28:19
my equals in my own n. *Gal* 1:14*
crooked and perverse n. *Phil* 2:15*
redeemed us out of every n. *Rev* 5:9
gospel to preach to every n. 14:6

see foolish

nations

(*Revisions, frequently* peoples)
were the n. divided. *Gen* 10:32
Tidal king of n. made war. 14:1*, 9*
shalt be a father of many n. 17:4
 5; *Rom* 4:17, 18
and I will make n. of thee.
 Gen 17:6; 35:11; 48:19
she shall be a mother of n. 17:16
two n. are in thy womb. 25:23
and let n. bow down to thee. 27:29
cast out the n. before thee. *Ex* 34:24
 Deut 4:38; 7:22; 8:20
the n. are defiled. *Lev* 18:24
as it spued out the n. 28
reckoned among the n. *Num* 23:9
Israel shall eat up the n. 24:8
Amalek was the first of the n. 20
fear of thee on the n. *Deut* 2:25
wisdom in sight of the n. 4:6
scatter you among n. 27; *Neh* 1:8
hath cast out many n. *Deut* 7:1
to possess n. greater. 9:1; 11:23
God shall cut off n. 12:29; 19:1
lend to many n. 15:6; 28:12
set thee on high above all n. 28:1
Most High divided to the n. 32:8
rejoice, O ye n. with his people.
the Lord left those n. *Judg* 2:23
redeemed from the n. 2 *Sam* 7:23
of the n. concerning. 1 *Ki* 11:2
after the manner of n. 2 *Ki* 17:33
hath any of the gods of the n.? 18:33
 19:12; 2 *Chr* 32:13, 14; *Isa* 36:18
say among the n., The. 1 *Chr* 16:31
driving out n. from before. 17:21
after the manner of n. 2 *Chr* 13:9
among many n. was no. *Neh* 13:26
the n.: he enlargeth the n. *Job* 12:23
n. may know themselves. *Ps* 9:20
kindreds of n. shall worship. 22:27
Lord is governor among the n. 28
subdue the n. under our feet. 47:3
sing to thee among the n. 57:9; 108:3
his eyes behold the n. 66:7
let the n. be glad. 67:4
gods of the n. are idols. 96:5
their seed among the n. 106:27
they did not destroy the n. 34
the people curse, n. shall. *Pr* 24:24
shall judge among the n. *Isa* 2:4
an ensign to the n. from far. 5:26
in his heart to cut off n. 10:7
set up an ensign for the n. 11:12
he that ruled the n. in anger. 14:6
which didst weaken the n. 12
kings of the n. lie in glory. 18
Sihor, she is a mart of n. 23:3
the n. were scattered. 33:3
ye n. to hear. 34:1; *Jer* 31:10
n. are as a drop of a. *Isa* 40:15

shall he sprinkle many n. *Isa* 52:15
n. that knew not thee, shall. 55:5
yea, those n. shall be utterly. 60:12
that the n. may tremble at. 64:2
those that escape to the n. 66:19
thee a prophet to the n. *Jer* 1:5
this day set thee over the n. 10
n. shall bless themselves in. 4:2
make ye mention to n., publish. 16
therefore hear ye n. 6:18; 31:10
fear thee, O King n.? 10:7
the n. shall not be able to abide. 10
many n. shall pass by this city. 22:8
n. shall serve themselves of them.
 25:14; 27:7
a controversy with the n. 25:31
n. have heard of thy shame. 46:12
ye among the n. Babylon is. 50:2
hindermost of the n. shall be a. 12
cry is heard among the n. 46
n. have drunken of her wine, n. 51:7
I break in pieces the n. 20
prepare the n. against her, call. 27
astonishment among the n. 41
n. the n. shall not flow together. 44
city that was great among n. *Lam* 1:1
my judgements into wickedness,
 more than the n. *Ezek* 5:6, 7
thee a reproach among the n. 14
remnant escape among the n. 6:8
remember me among the n. 9
scatter them among the n. 12:15
the n. also heard of him. 19:4
n. set against him on every side. 8
I will cause many n. to come. 26:3
shall become a spoil to the n. 5
strangers upon thee, the terrible of
 the n. 28:7; 30:11; 31:12
I will scatter Egyptians among n.
 29:12; 30:23
no more rule over the n. 29:15
I made n. shake at the sound. 31:16
thou art like a lion of the n. 32:2
the daughters of the n. shall. 16, 18
thou hast said, These two n. 35:10
land hast bereaved thy n. 36:13
shall be no more two n. 37:22
forth out of the n. 38:8, 12
known in the eyes of many n. 23
sanctified in sight of many n. 39:27
have hired among the n. *Hos* 8:10
wanderers among the n. 9:17
scattered among the n. *Joel* 3:2
are named chief of n. *Amos* 6:1
many n. shall come and say. *Mi* 4:2
he shall rebuke strong n. afar off. 3
also many n. are gathered. 11
the n. shall see, be confounded. 7:16
that selleth n. through. *Nah* 3:4
I will shew the n. thy nakedness. 5
not spare continually to slay n.
 Hab 1:17
hast spoiled many n. 2:8
and drove asunder the n. 3:6
I have cut off the n. *Zeph* 3:6
is to gather the n. 8
many n. shall be joined. *Zech* 2:11
and strong n. shall come to. 8:22
of all the languages of the n. 23
things do the n. seek. *Luke* 12:30
earth shall be distress of n. 21:25
destroyed seven n. in. *Acts* 13:19
I give power over the n. *Rev* 2:27
prophesy before many n. 10:11
n. shall see their dead bodies. 11:9
and the n. were angry, thy. 18
was given him over all n. 13:7
cities of the n. fell. 16:19
waters thou sawest are n. 17:15
that he should deceive the n. 20:3
n. of them which are saved. 21:24
the honour of the n. into it. 26
for the healing of the n. 22:2

see great

all nations

hath divided to all n. *Deut* 4:19
thee high above all n. 26:19; 28:1
a byword among all n. 28:37
his fame was in all n. 1 *Ki* 4:31
fear of David on all n. 1 *Chr* 14:17
marvellous works among all n. 16:24
Hezekiah magnified in sight of all n.
 2 *Chr* 32:23

saving health among all n. *Ps* 67:2
kings fall down, all n. shall. 72:11
men blessed in him, all n. shall. 17
for thou shalt inherit all n. 82:8
all n. shall come and worship. 86:9
Lord is high above all n. 113:4
praise the Lord, all ye n. 117:1
all n. compassed me about. 118:10
all n. shall flow unto it. *Isa* 2:2
vail that is over all n. 25:7
indignation of Lord is on all n. 34:2
all n. before him are as nothing.
 40:17
I will gather all n. and languages.
 66:18; *Joel* 3:2
your brethren out of all n. *Isa* 66:20
and all n. shall serve him.
 Jer 27:7; *Dan* 7:14
sift the house of Israel among all n.
 Amos 9:9
but gathereth to him all n. *Hab* 2:5
n. and the desire of all n. *Hag* 2:7
I will gather all n. *Zech* 14:2
punishment of all n. that come. 19
all n. shall call you blessed. *Mal* 3:12
ye shall be hated of all n. *Mat* 24:9
kingdom shall be preached to all n.
 24:14; *Mark* 13:10; *Luke* 24:47
 Rom 16:26
shall be gathered all n. *Mat* 25:32
go ye, and teach all n. 28:19
be called of all n. the. *Mark* 11:17
away captive into all n. *Luke* 21:24
suffered of all n. to walk. *Acts* 14:16
one blood all n. of men. 17:26
the faith among all n. *Rom* 1:5
all n. for obedience of faith. 16:26
shall all n. be blessed. *Gal* 3:8
a multitude of all n. stood. *Rev* 7:9
was to rule all n. with a rod. 12:5
she made all n. drink of the wine.
 14:8; 18:3
all n. shall come and worship. 15:4
sorceries were all n. deceived. 18:23

all the nations

all the n. of earth be blessed.
 Gen 18:18; 22:18; 26:4
above all the n. on earth. *Deut* 14:2
set a king over me, as all the n.
 17:14; 1 *Sam* 8:5, 20
to mind among all the n. *Deut* 30:1
will gather thee from all the n. 3
into hell, and all the n. *Ps* 9:17
stretched out on all the n. *Isa* 14:26
the multitude of all the n. 29:7, 8
laid waste all the n. and. 37:18
let all the n. be gathered. 43:9
bare his holy arm in eyes of all the n.
 52:10
spring forth before all the n. 61:11
and all the n. shall be gathered.
 Jer 3:17
prophesied against all the n. 25:13
cause all the n. to drink it. 15
made all the n. drink. 17
this city a curse to all the n. 26:6
will gather you from all the n. 29:14
reproach among all the n. 18; 44:8
and honour before all the n. 33:9
make a full end of all the n. 46:28
them among all the n. *Zech* 7:14
destroy all the n. that come. 12:9
left of all the n. that came. 14:16

these nations

if thou say, These n. are more than I.
 Deut 7:17
for wickedness of these n. 9:4, 5
Lord drive out all these n. 11:23
How did these n. serve? 12:30
these n. hearkened to. 18:14
cities which are not of these n. 20:15
among these n. shalt thou. 28:65
you serve the gods of these n. 29:18
Lord will destroy these n. 31:3
Lord hath done to these n. *Josh* 23:3
divided to you by lot these n. 4
that ye come not among these n. 7
to the remnant of these n. 12
no more drive out any of these n. 13
these n. the Lord left. *Judg* 3:1
so these n. feared Lord. 2 *Ki* 17:41
these n. are uncircumcised. *Jer* 9:26
bring them against these n. 25:9

these n. shall serve king. *Jer* 25:11
of iron on neck of *these* n.   28:14

native
more see his n. country. *Jer* 22:10

nativity
died in the land of his n. *Gen* 11:28
left the land of thy n.   *Ruth* 2:11
go to the land of our n.   *Jer* 46:16
thy n. is of the land of. *Ezek* 16:3
as for thy n. in the day thou.   4
judge thee in land of thy n.   21:30*
Chaldea, the land of their n.   23:15

natural
not dim, nor his n. force. *Deut* 34:7
without n. affection.   *Rom* 1:31
     2 *Tim* 3:3
if God spared not the n. branches.
     Rom 11:21, 24
n. man receiveth not.   *1 Cor* 2:14
sown a n. body. There is a n. 15:44
first that which is n.   46
his n. face in a glass.   *Jas* 1:23
these as n. brute beasts. *2 Pet* 2:12*

naturally
who will n. care for your state.
     Phil 2:20*
know n. as brute beasts. *Jude* 10

nature
[1] *Natural endowment or instinct,*
Rom 2:14. [2] *Birth, or natural
descent,* Gal 2:15. [3] *The existing system of things in the world,*
1 Cor 11:14. [4] *The physical con-
stitution or existence; the vital
powers,* Heb 2:16. [5] *The state
of the unregenerate soul,* Eph. 2:3
change to that against n. *Rom* 1:26
do by n. the things contained.   2:14
shall not uncircumcision by n.?   27
olive tree, which is wild by n. and
wert graffed contrary to n.   11:24
not even n. itself teach ? *1 Cor* 11:14
who are Jews by n. and.   *Gal* 2:15
service unto them, which by n.   4:8
by n. children of wrath.   *Eph* 2:3
took not on him the n.   *Heb* 2:16*
on fire the course of n.   *Jas* 3:6
partakers of the divine n. *2 Pet* 1:4

naught, or **nought**
serve me for n.?   *Gen* 29:15
n. of the cursed thing. *Deut* 13:17
and thou givest him n.   15:9
rejoice to bring you to n.   28:63*
pleasant, but the water n. *2 Ki* 2:19
their counsel to n.   *Neh* 4:15
doth Job fear God for n.? *Job* 1:9
wicked shall come to n.   8:22
mountain falling cometh to n. 14:18
pledge from thy brother for n. 22:6
counsel of heathen to n.   *Ps* 33:10
sellest thy people for n.   44:12
set at n. all my counsel. *Pr* 1:25
n., it is n. saith the buyer.   20:14
counsel, it shall come to n. *Isa* 8:10
terrible one is brought to n.   29:20
aside the just for a thing of n.   21
as nothing, as a thing of n.   41:12
nothing, and your work of n.   24
have spent my strength for n.   49:4
ye have sold yourselves for n. 52:3
people is taken away for n.   5
vision, and a thing of n.   *Jer* 14:14
Beth-el shall come to n. *Amos* 5:5
rejoice in a thing of n.   6:13
would shut the doors for n.? . . . fire
on mine altar for n.   *Mal* 1:10
he must suffer many things, and be
set at n. *Mark* 9:12; *Luke* 23:11
this is the stone set at n. *Acts* 4:11
scattered, and brought to n.   5:36
of men, it will come to n.   38
in danger to be set at n.   19:27
set at n. thy brother ?   *Rom* 14:10
to bring to n. things.   *1 Cor* 1:28
wisdom of this world that cometh to
n.   *1 Cor* 2:6
any man's bread for n. *2 Thes* 3:8
so great riches come to n. *Rev* 18:17

naughtiness
I know thy pride, and the n. of thy.
     1 Sam 17:28

be taken in their own n. *Pr* 11:6*
and superfluity of n.   *Jas* 1:21

naughty
a n. person walketh.   *Pr* 6:12*
and a liar giveth ear to a n.   17:4*
other basket had very n. figs.
     Jer 24:2*

Naum
which was the son of N. *Luke* 3:25

navel
his force is in the n.   *Job* 40:16*
it shall be health to thy n. *Pr* 3:8
thy n. is like a round. *S of S* 7:2†
wast born, thy n. was. *Ezek* 16:4

naves
their n. and spokes.   *1 Ki* 7:33*

navy
Solomon made a n. of. *1 Ki* 9:26
Hiram sent in the n. his.   27
the n. of Hiram brought gold. 10:11
king Solomon had at sea a n. of.   22

nay
for he will not say thee n. *1 Ki* 2:17
not n. for I will not say thee n.   20*
communication be yea, yea, n. n.
     Mat 5:37; *Jas* 5:12
I tell you N.; but rather. *Luke* 12:51
I tell you N., but except ye. 13:3, 5
he said, N. father Abraham.   16:30
n. verily, but let them. *Acts* 16:37
by law of works ? n. but. *Rom* 3:27
n. but O man, who art thou ?   9:20
should be yea, yea, n. n. *2 Cor* 1:17
toward you was not yea and n.   18
Jesus Christ . . . was not yea, n. 19

Nazarene
he shall be called a N. *Mat* 2:23

Nazarenes
of the sect of the N. *Acts* 24:5

Nazareth
dwelt in a city called N. *Mat* 2:23
this is Jesus of N. 21:11; *Mark* 1:24
   10:47; *Luke* 4:34; 18:37; 24:19
also with Jesus of N. *Mark* 14:67
ye seek Jesus of N.   16:6
Gabriel was sent to N. *Luke* 1:26
Jesus came to N. and. 2:51; 4:16
Jesus of N.   *John* 1:45; 18:5, 7
  19:19; *Acts* 2:22; 4:10; 6:14
     22:8
good thing come out of N.? *John* 1:46
of Jesus of N. rise up. *Acts* 3:6
God anointed Jesus of N.   10:38
to the name of Jesus of N.   26:9

Nazarite
(*Among the ancient Hebrews, a
person who was consecrated to
God, and pledged never to cut the
hair, drink wine, or touch a corpse
during the period of the vow.
This could be taken for a limited
period, or for life. The Revisions
change the spelling to* Nazirites)
a vow of a N. to separate. *Num* 6:2
the law of the N. when.   13, 21
the N. shall shave the head of.   18
put them on the hands of the N.   19
after that the N. may drink.   20
the child shall be a N. to God.
     Judg 13:5, 7; 16:17

Nazarites
her N. purer than snow. *Lam* 4:7*
of your young men for N. *Amos* 2:11
ye gave the N. wine to drink.   12

Neapolis
next day we came to N. *Acts* 16:11

near
this city is n. to flee to. *Gen* 19:20
Jacob went n. to Isaac.   27:22
bring it n., he brought it n.   25
Jacob went n. and rolled.   29:10
thou shalt be n. to me, thou. 45:10
he brought them n. and.   48:10
land of Philistines, although that was
n.   *Ex* 13:17
any that is n. of kin. *Lev* 18:6
thy father's n. kinswoman.   12
thy mother's n. kinswomen. 13, 17
for he uncovereth his n. kin. 20:19

his kin n. to him he may be defiled.
     Lev 21:2
bring the tribe of Levi n. *Num* 3:6
bring her n. and set her.   5:16
to bring you n. to himself. 16:9, 10
cometh n. the tabernacle.   17:13
in plains of Moab, n. Jericho. 26:3
go thou n. and hear all. *Deut* 5:27
not plant a grove of trees n. 16:21
men n. Micah's house. *Judg* 18:22
not that evil was n. them.   20:34
the man is n. of kin to. *Ruth* 2:20
spread skirt, for thou art a n. 3:9, 12
Joab's field is n. mine. *2 Sam* 14:30
because the king is n. of kin. 19:42
land of enemy far or n.   *1 Ki* 8:46
     2 *Chr* 6:36
thy vineyard, because it is n. to.
     1 Ki 21:2
one is so n. another, no. *Job* 41:16
for trouble is n.   *Ps* 22:11
thy name is n.   75:1
thou art n. O Lord, thy.   119:151
horn of Israel, a people n.   148:14
through the street, n. her. *Pr* 7:8
the mouth of the foolish is n. 10:14
is a neighbour that is n.   27:10
that are n. acknowledge. *Isa* 33:13
tell ye, and bring them n.   45:21
bring n. my righteousness.   46:13
he is n. that justifieth me.   50:8
my righteousness is n. my.   51:5
upon the Lord while he is n.   55:6
my salvation is n. to come.   56:1
peace be to him that is n.   57:19
thou art n. in their mouth. *Jer* 12:2
kings of the north far and n. 25:26
our end is n., our days. *Lam* 4:18
he that is n. shall fall. *Ezek* 6:12
day of trouble is n.   7:7; 30:3
who say, It is not n., let us.   11:3
be n. and far shall mock thee. 22:5
to Israel that are n.   *Dan* 9:7
the day of the Lord is n.   *Ob* 15
     Zech 1:16
know that it is n. even. *Mat* 24:33
that summer is n.   *Mark* 13:28
together his n. friends. *Acts* 10:24

see **came, come, draw, drew**

nearer
there is a kinsman n.   *Ruth* 3:12
our salvation n. than. *Rom* 13:11

Nebaioth
the son of Ishmael, N. *Gen* 25:13
     1 *Chr* 1:29
rams of N. shall minister. *Isa* 60:7

Nebat, *see* **Jeroboam**

Nebo
Elealeh and N. is a land. *Num* 32:3
the children of Reuben built N.   38
get thee up unto mount N.
     Deut 32:49; 34:1
in Aroer, even unto N.   1 *Chr* 5:8
the children of N. *Ezra* 2:29; 10:43
the men of the other N.   *Neh* 7:33
Moab shall howl over N. *Isa* 15:2
N. stoopeth.   46:1
woe unto N.   *Jer* 48:1
is come upon Dibon and N.   22

**Nebuchadnezzar, Nebuchad-
rezzar**
in his days N. came up. *2 Ki* 24:1
  25:1; *2 Chr* 36:6; *Jer* 39:1; 52:4
for the people whom N. *2 Ki* 25:22
carried away Judah by N. *1 Chr* 6:15
     Jer 24:1; 29:1; 52:28
Cyrus brought forth the vessels N.
     Ezra 1:7; 5:14; 6:5
which will not serve N. *Jer* 27:8
I break the yoke of N.   28:11
that they may serve N. king.   14
deliver them into hand of N.   29:21
this city into the hand of N.   32:28
N. gave charge concerning.   39:11
I will take N. my servant.   43:10
N. king of Babylon shall.   49:28
last this N. hath broken.   50:17
N. hath devoured me, he.   51:34
I will bring on Tyrus N. *Ezek* 26:7
I will give the land of Egypt to N.
     29:19; 30:10
N. dreamed.   *Dan* 2:1

N. the king made an image. *Dan* 3:1
N. was full of fury. 19
N. was astonished. 24
came upon the king *N.* 4:28, 33
at end of days I *N.* lifted up mine. 34
I *N.* praise and extol. 37
most high God gave *N.* a. 5:18

Nebuzar-adan
N. captain of guard. 2 *Ki* 25:8
N. left of the poor of. *Jer* 39:10

necessary
his words more than *n.* *Job* 23:12
was *n.* that the word first. *Acts* 13:46
greater burden than these *n.* 15:28
with such things as were *n.* 28:10*
which seem feeble are *n.* 1 *Cor* 12:22
I thought it *n.* to exhort. 2 *Cor* 9:5
I supposed it *n.* to send. *Phil* 2:25
good works for *n.* uses. *Tit* 3:14
n. patterns should be. *Heb* 9:23

necessities
have ministered to my *n.* *Acts* 20:34
ministers of God in *n.* 2 *Cor* 6:4
I take pleasure in *n.*, in. 12:10

necessity
[1] *Something that must needs
be, when it is contrary to its very
nature and principles to be otherwise,* Heb 9:16. [2] *Poverty, or
want of temporal good things,*
Rom 12:13. [3] *Force or constraint,* 2 Cor 9:7.
of *n.* he must release. *Luke* 23:17
distributing to the *n.* *Rom* 12:13
having no *n.* and hath. 1 *Cor* 7:37
for *n.* is laid upon me, yea. 9:16
not grudgingly, or of *n.* 2 *Cor* 9:7
once and again to my *n.* *Phil* 4:16
not be as it were of *n.* *Philem* 14
made of *n.* a change of. *Heb* 7:12
n. this man have somewhat. 8:3
there must of *n.* be the death. 9:16

neck
skins on smooth of his *n.* *Gen* 27:16
break the yoke from off thy *n.* 40
Esau fell on his *n.* and. 33:4
gold chain about Joseph's *n.* 41:42
Ezek 16:11; *Dan* 5:7, 16, 29
fell on Benjamin's *n.* and. *Gen* 45:14
Jacob's *n.*; he wept on his *n.* 46:29
thy hand shall be on the *n.* 49:8
break his *n.* *Ex* 13:13; 34:20
off his head from his *n.* *Lev* 5:8
strike off the heifer's *n.* *Deut* 21:4
a yoke of iron upon thy *n.* 28:48
and his *n.* brake, and. 1 *Sam* 4:18
Zedekiah stiffened his *n.* 2 *Chr* 36:13
hardened their *n.* and. *Neh* 9:29
on him, even on his *n.* *Job* 15:26
he hath taken me by the *n.* 16:12
hast thou clothed his *n.* with? 39:19
in his *n.* remaineth strength. 41:22
speak not with a stiff *n.* *Ps* 75:5
be chains about thy *n.* *Pr* 1:9
bind them about thy *n.* 3:3; 6:21
life and grace to thy *n.* 3:22
thy *n.* is comely with. *S of S* 1:10
thy *n.* is like the tower of. 4:4
my heart with one chain of thy *n.* 9
thy *n.* is a tower of ivory. 7:4
reach even to the *n.* *Isa* 8:8
be taken from off thy *n.* 10:27
to the midst of the *n.* 30:28
thy *n.* is an iron sinew. 48:4
from the bands of thy *n.* 52:2
as if he cut off a dog's *n.* 66:3
not, made their *n.* stiff. *Jer* 17:23
and put them on thy *n.* 27:2
will not put *n.* under yoke of. 8, 11
the yoke from off Jeremiah's *n.*
28:10, 12
I have put a yoke on the *n.* 14
break his yoke from off thy *n.* 30:8
are come upon my *n.* *Lam* 1:14
over on her fair *n.* *Hos* 10:11
the foundation unto the *n.* *Hab* 3:13
a millstone were hanged about his *n.*
Mat 18:6; *Mark* 9:42; *Luke* 17:2
his father fell on his *n.* *Luke* 15:20
put a yoke on the *n.* *Acts* 15:10
they fell on Paul's *n.* and. 20:37
see harden

necks
put your feet on the *n.* *Josh* 10:24
for the *n.* of them that. *Judg* 5:30
were on their camel's *n.* 8:21, 26
given me *n.* of enemies.
2 *Sam* 22:41*; *Ps* 18:40*
the nobles put not their *n.* *Neh* 3:5
walk with stretched forth *n.* *Isa* 3:16
bring your *n.* under yoke. *Jer* 27:12
n. are under persecution. *Lam* 5:5
to bring thee on the *n.* *Ezek* 21:29
shall not remove your *n.* *Mi* 2:3
life laid down their own *n.* *Rom* 16:4

necromancer
found among you a *n.* *Deut* 18:11

need
him sufficient for his *n.* *Deut* 15:8
have I *n.* of madmen? 1 *Sam* 21:15
much as thou shalt *n.* 2 *Chr* 2:16
ye shall not *n.* to fight in. 20:17
and let what they have *n.* *Ezra* 6:9
so he shall have no *n.* *Pr* 31:11
I have *n.* to be baptized. *Mat* 3:14
Father knoweth what things ye have
n. of. 6:8, 32; *Luke* 12:30
that be whole *n.* not a physician.
Mat 9:12; *Mark* 2:17; *Luke* 5:31
they *n.* not depart, give. *Mat* 14:16
the Lord hath *n.* of them. 21:3
Mark 11:3; *Luke* 19:31, 34
n. have we of witnesses? *Mat* 26:65
Mark 14:63; *Luke* 22:71
David did when he had *n.* *Mark* 2:25
healed them that had *n.* *Luke* 9:11
over just persons which *n.* 15:7
things we have *n.* of. *John* 13:29
as every man had *n.* *Acts* 2:45; 4:35
her in what she hath *n.* *Rom* 16:2
if *n.* so require, let him. 1 *Cor* 7:36
to the hand, I have no *n.* 12:21
our comely parts have no *n.* 24
or *n.* we epistles of ? 2 *Cor* 3:1
to abound and to suffer *n.* *Phil* 4:12
God shall supply all your *n.* 19
so that we *n.* not speak. 1 *Thes* 1:8
of brotherly love ye *n.* not that. 4:9
of the times ye have no *n.* that. 5:1
grace to help in time of *n.* *Heb* 4:16
have *n.* that one teach you again;
such as have *n.* of milk. 5:12
what *n.* that another priest? 7:11
for ye have *n.* of patience. 10:36
though now, if *n.* be. 1 *Pet* 1:6
ye *n.* not that any man. 1 *John* 2:27
and see his brother have *n.* 3:17
I am rich, and have *n.* *Rev* 3:17
the city had no *n.* of sun. 21:23
and they *n.* no candle, nor. 22:25

needed
he *n.* not that any should. *John* 2:25
as though he *n.* any thing. *Acts* 17:25

needest, -eth
Jacob said What *n.* it. *Gen* 33:15
give him as many as he *n.* *Luke* 11:8
is washed, *n.* not save. *John* 13:10
and *n.* not that any man. 16:30
to give to him that *n.* *Eph* 4:28
a workman that *n.* not. 2 *Tim* 2:15
who *n.* not daily to offer. *Heb* 7:27

needful
shall be *n.* for the house. *Ezra* 7:20
one thing is *n.* and Mary. *Luke* 10:42
n. to circumcise them. *Acts* 15:5
the flesh is more *n.* for you. *Phil* 1:24
these things which are *n.* *Jas* 2:16
it was *n.* for me to write. *Jude* 3

needle
for a camel to go through the eye of
a *n.* *Mat* 19:24; *Mark* 10:25
Luke 18:25

needlework
an hanging wrought with *n.*
Ex 26:36; 27:16; 36:37; 38:18
make the girdle of *n.* 28:39; 39:29
divers colours of *n.* *Judg* 5:30
brought in raiment of *n.* *Ps* 45:14

needs
must *n.* be circumcised. *Gen* 17:13
said, This one fellow will *n.* 19:9
must I *n.* bring thy son again ? 24:5
thou wouldest *n.* be gone. 31:30
we must *n.* die. and. 2 *Sam* 14:14

must *n.* be borne, because. *Jer* 10:5
it must *n.* be that offences. *Mat* 18:7
for such things must *n.* *Mark* 13:7
ground, and I must *n.* *Luke* 14:18
n. go through Samaria. *John* 4:4
this scripture must *n.* *Acts* 1:16
must *n.* have suffered. 17:3
the multitude must *n.* come. 21:22
ye must *n.* be subject. *Rom* 13:5
must *n.* go out of world. 1 *Cor* 5:10
if I must *n.* glory. 2 *Cor* 11:30

needy
open thy hand to the *n.* *Deut* 15:11
servant that is poor and *n.* 24:14
they turn the *n.* out of. *Job* 24:4
killeth the poor and *n.* 14
the *n.* shall not alway. *Ps* 9:18
for the sighing of the *n.* now. 12:5
the poor and *n.* 35:10; 72:4, 13
bow, to cast down the *n.* 37:14
I am poor and *n.*, make. 40:17; 70:5
he shall deliver the *n.* 72:12; 82:4
the poor and *n.*, save the *n.* 72:13
let the poor and *n.* praise. 74:21
justice to the afflicted and *n.* 82:3
deliver the poor and *n.* rid from. 4
for I am poor and *n.* 86:1; 109:22
the poor and *n.* man. 109:16
he lifteth the *n.* out of the. 113:7
devour the *n.* from. *Pr* 30:14
cause of the poor and *n.* 31:9
forth her hands to the *n.* 20
to turn aside the *n.* *Isa* 10:2
n. shall lie down in safety. 14:30
been a strength to the *n.* in. 25:4
steps of the *n.* shall tread. 26:6
when the *n.* speaketh right. 32:7
when the poor and *n.* seek. 41:17
and the right of *n.* do. *Jer* 5:28
cause of the poor and *n.* 22:16
the hands of the *n.* *Ezek* 16:49
oppressed the poor and *n.* 18:12
vexed the poor and *n.* 22:29
Bashan, which crush the *n.* *Amos* 4:1
O ye that swallow up the *n.* 8:4
buy the *n.* for a pair of shoes. 6

neesings
by his *n.* a light doth. *Job* 41:18†

neglect
n. to hear them, tell it to the church,
but if he *n.* to hear. *Mat* 18:17*
n. not the gift that. 1 *Tim* 4:14
how shall we escape, if *n.*? *Heb* 2:3

neglected
their widows were *n.* *Acts* 6:1

neglecting
n. the body, not in any. *Col* 2:23*

negligent
my sons, be not now *n.* 2 *Chr* 29:11
not be *n.* to put you in. 2 *Pet* 1:12*

Nehelamite, *see* **Shemaiah**

Nehemiah
N. came with Zerubbabel. *Ezra* 2:2
Neh 7:7
the words of *N.* the son. *Neh* 1:1
N. son of Azbuk repaired. 3:16
N. which is the. 8:9; 10:1
Israel in the days of *N.* 12:47

Nehushtan
the brasen serpent *N.* 2 *Ki* 18:4

neighbour
[1] *One who dwells or is placed
near to another,* 2 Ki 4:3. [2]
*Every man, to whom we have an
opportunity of doing good,* Mat
22:39. [3] *A fellow-labourer, of
one and the same people,* Acts 7:27.
[4] *One who does us good, and who
pities and relieves us in distress,*
Luke 10:36.
every woman borrow of her *n.*
Ex 3:22; 11:2
hath given it to a *n.* 1 *Sam* 15:28
better is a *n.* that is near. *Pr* 27:10
the *n.* and his friends. *Jer* 6:21
and teach every one her *n.* 9:20
was *n.* to him that fell. *Luke* 10:36

neighbour. *adjective*
overthrow of Sodom and Gomorrah
and the *n.* *Jer* 49:18; 50:40

his neighbour

and *his* n. take a lamb. *Ex* 12:4
come on *his* n. to slay him. 21:14
if a man deliver to *his* n. 22:7
hand to *his* n.'s goods. 8, 11
deliver to *his* n. an ass or ox. 10
if borrow aught of *his* n. and it. 14
camp, slay every man *his* n. 32:27
or hath deceived *his* n. *Lev* 6:2
adultery with *his* n.'s wife, shall.
    20:10; *Deut* 22:24
cause a blemish in *his* n. *Lev* 24:19
should kill *his* n. *Deut* 4:42; 19:4
lendeth aught to *his* n. he shall not
    exact of *his* n. or his. 15:2
if any hate *his* n. and lie. 19:11
a man riseth against *his* n. 22:26
removeth *his* n.'s landmark. 27:17.
cursed be he that smiteth *his* n. 24
shoe, and gave to *his* n. *Ruth* 4:7
trespass against *his* n. *1 Ki* 8:31
man sin against *his* n. *2 Chr* 6:22
one mocked of *his* n. *Job* 12:4
as a man pleadeth for *his* n. 16:21
speak vanity with *his* n. *Ps* 12:2
nor doeth evil to *his* n. 15:3*
privily slandereth *his* n. 101:5
goeth in to *his* n.'s wife. *Pr* 6:29
his mouth destroyeth *his* n. 11:9
despiseth *his* n. 12; 14:21
is more excellent than *his* n. 12:26
poor is hated even of *his* n. 14:20
a violent man enticeth *his* n. 16:29
but *his* n. cometh and. 18:17
separated from *his* n. 19:4*
his n. findeth no favour. 21:10
false witness against *his* n. 25:18
man that deceiveth *his* n. 26:19
that flattereth *his* n. spreadeth. 29:5
a man is envied of *his* n. *Eccl* 4:4
oppressed every one by *his* n. *Isa* 3:5
fight every one against *his* n. 19:2
they helped every one *his* n. 41:6
neighed after *his* n.'s wife. *Jer* 5:8
between a man and *his* n. 7:5
every one of *his* n., trust not. 9:4
deceive every one *his* n. 5
speak peaceably to *his* n. 8
every man to *his* n. 22:8; 23:35
useth *his* n.'s service without. 22:13
tell every one to *his* n. 23:27
words every one from *his* n. 30
teach no more every man *his* n.
    31:34; *Heb* 8:11*
liberty to *his* n. *Jer* 34:15, 17
defiled *his* n.'s wife. *Ezek* 18:6, 15
hath defiled *his* n.'s wife. 11; 22:11
    33:26
that giveth *his* n. drink. *Hab* 2:15
call every man *his* n. *Zech* 3:10
every one against *his* n. 8:10
every man the truth to *his* n. 16
imagine evil against *his* n. 17
love *his* n. as himself. *Mark* 12:33
he that did *his* n. wrong. *Acts* 7:27
worketh no evil to *his* n. *Rom* 13:10
let every one please *his* n. 15:2
speak every man truth with *his* n.
    Eph 4:25

my neighbour

wait at *my* n.'s door. *Job* 31:9
to Jesus, Who is *my* n.? *Luke* 10:29

thy neighbour

not bear false witness against *thy* n.
    Ex 20:16; *Deut* 5:20
take *thy* n.'s raiment to. *Ex* 22:26
carnally with *thy* n.'s wife. *Lev* 18:20
thou shalt not defraud *thy* n. 19:13
shalt thou judge *thy* n. 15
stand against the blood of *thy* n. 16
in any wise rebuke *thy* n. 17
love *thy* n. as thyself. 18
buyest aught of *thy* n. 25:14, 15
or covet *thy* n.'s wife. *Deut* 5:21
thou shalt not remove *thy* n.'s. 19:14
comest into *thy* n.'s vineyard. 23:24
and given it to *thy* n. *1 Sam* 28:17
give them to *thy* n. *2 Sam* 12:11
say not to *thy* n. Go. *Pr* 3:28
devise not evil against *thy* n. 29
be not witness against *thy* n. 24:28
when *thy* n. hath put thee to. 25:8
debate *thy* cause with *thy* n. 9

withdraw thy foot from *thy* n.'s.
    Pr 25:17
shalt love *thy* n. *Mat* 5:43; 19:19
    22:39; *Mark* 12:31; *Luke* 10:27
    Rom 13:9; *Gal* 5:14; *Jas* 2:8

neighbours

that they were their n. *Josh* 9:16
her n. gave it a name. *Ruth* 4:17
borrow vessels abroad of all thy n.
    2 Ki 4:3
speak peace to their n. *Ps* 28:3
reproach among all my n. 31:11
us a reproach to our n. 44:13
become a reproach to our n. 79:4
render unto our n. sevenfold. 12
makest us a strife to our n. 80:6
he is a reproach to his n. 89:41
against all my evil n. *Jer* 12:14
adultery with their n.' wives. 29:23
his seed is spoiled and his n. 49:10
fornication with Egypt, thy n.
    Ezek 16:26
gained of thy n. by extortion. 22:12
the Assyrians her n. 23:5, 12
n. and her cousins heard. *Luke* 1:58
a supper, call not thy rich n. 14:12
together his friends and n. 15:6, 9
n. and they who before had seen him
    blind. *John* 9:8

neighed

n. after his neighbour's wife. *Jer* 5:8

neighing, -s

land trembled at the n. *Jer* 8:16
seen thine adulteries and n. 13:27

neither

the tree, shall ye touch. *Gen* 3:3
fight in. with small nor. *1 Ki* 22:31
n. tell I you by what. *Mat* 21:27

(Most frequently this means son's son, grandchild, and is so rendered in Revisions)

neither have son nor n. *Job* 18:19*
from Babylon son and n. *Isa* 14:22*

nephews

forty sons and thirty n. *Judg* 12:14*
have children or n. *1 Tim* 5:4*

Ner

N. begat Kish. *1 Chr* 8:33; 9:36, 39
    see Abner

Nereus

salute Julia, *N.* and. *Rom* 16:15

Nergal

Cuth made *N.* their god. *2 Ki* 17:30

Neriah, see Baruch

nest

thou puttest thy n. in a. *Num* 24:21
if a bird's n. chance to. *Deut* 22:6
as an eagle stirreth up her n. 32:11
I shall die in my n. *Job* 29:18
command, make n. on high? 39:27
swallow hath found a n. *Ps* 84:3
wandereth from her n. *Pr* 27:8
hath found as n. riches. *Isa* 10:14
bird cast out of the n. 16:2
the great owl made her n. 34:15
thy n. in the cedars. *Jer* 22:23
the dove makes her n. in the. 48:28
thy n. as high as the eagle. 49:16
set thy n. among the stars. *Ob* 4
he may set his n. on high. *Hab* 2:9

nests

the birds make their n. *Ps* 104:17
fowls of heaven made their n.
    Ezek 31:6
and the birds of the air have n.
    Mat 8:20; *Luke* 9:58

net

(A woven fabric for catching fish or birds; hence a snare, trap. It is also used figuratively, as for difficulties in which one is caught; or the traps set by one's enemies)

he is cast into a n. by. *Job* 18:8
compassed me with his n. 19:6
in the n. they hid, is. *Ps* 9:15
draweth him into his n. 10:9
pluck my feet out of n. 25:15; 31:4
they have hid for me their n. 35:7
let his n. that he hath hid catch. 8

they have prepared a n. for. *Ps* 57:6
thou broughtest us into the n. 66:11
they have spread a n. by. 140:5
surely in vain the n. *Pr* 1:17
the wicked desireth the n. of. 12:12
that flattereth spreadeth a n. 29:5
fishes are taken in an evil n.
    Eccl 9:12
as a wild bull in a n. *Isa* 51:20
he hath spread a n. *Lam* 1:13
my n. will I spread on him.
    Ezek 12:13; 17:20
nations shall spread their n. 19:8
I will spread out my n. over. 32:3
ye have been a n. spread. *Hos* 5:1
I will spread my n. upon them. 7:12
hunt his brother with a n. *Mi* 7:2
catch them in their n. *Hab* 1:15
therefore they sacrifice to their n. 16
therefore empty their n.? 17
casting n. into the sea. *Mat* 4:18
    Mark 1:16
of heaven is like a n. cast. *Mat* 13:47
I will let down the n. *Luke* 5:5
multitude of fishes, and their n. 6
the n. on the right side. *John* 21:6
came in a ship, dragging the n. with. 8
n. to land, yet was not the n. 11

Nethaneel

N. the son of Zuar was prince.
    Num 1:8; 2:5; 7:18, 23; 10:15
N. the fourth son of. *1 Chr* 2:14
N. and Amasai blew with. 15:24
the son of *N.* the scribe, one. 24:6
Obed-edom, Joah and *N.* 26:4
Jehoshaphat sent *N.* to. *2 Chr* 17:7
N. gave to the Levites for. 35:9
Ishmael, *N.* had taken. *Ezra* 10:22
in days of Joiakim *N.* *Neh* 12:21
N. with musical instruments. 36

Nethaniah

Ishmael son of *N.* *2 Ki* 25:23, 25
    Jer 40:8; 41:1
Asaph, Joseph and *N.* *1 Chr* 25:2
fifth lot came forth to *N.* he. 12
Levites to teach, even *N.* *2 Chr* 17:8
princes sent the son of *N. Jer* 36:14
Ishmael the son of *N.* slew. 41:2
but Ishmael the son of *N.* escaped. 15

nether

they stood at the n. part. *Ex* 19:17
no man shall take n. millstone to.
    Deut 24:6*
gave her the upper springs and the n.
    Josh 15:19; *Judg* 1:15
built Gezer and Beth-horon the n.
    1 Ki 9:17; *1 Chr* 7:24
as a piece of n. millstone. *Job* 41:24
delivered to death to n. parts.
    Ezek 31:14
be comforted in the n. parts. 16
shalt be brought down to n. parts. 18
them down to the n. parts. 32:18
Elam gone down to the n. parts. 24

nethermost

the n. chamber was. *1 Ki* 6:6

Nethinims

inhabitants were the *N.* *1 Chr* 9:2
the *N.* went up with. *Ezra* 2:43
N. and the children of Solomon's
    servant were 392. 58; *Neh* 7:60
the *N.* went to Jerusalem. *Ezra* 7:7
not lawful to impose toll on *N.* 24
to Iddo and brethren the *N.* 8:17
the *N.* whom David appointed. 20
N. dwelt in Ophel. *Neh* 3:26; 11:21
the *N.* had separated from. 10:28
and Gispa were over the *N.* 11:21

nets

n. of checker work. *1 Ki* 7:17
wicked fall into their own n.
    Ps 141:10
heart is snares and n. *Eccl* 7:26
they that spread n. shall. *Isa* 19:8
spreading of n. in the. *Ezek* 26:5
place to spread n. on. 14; 47:10
James and John mending their n.
    Mat 4:21; *Mark* 1:19; *Luke* 5:2
they forsook their n. *Mark* 1:18
your n. for a draught. *Luke* 5:4

nettles

under the n. they were. *Job* 30:7

network (cont.)

and n. had covered the. *Pr* 24:31
n. and brambles in the. *Isa* 34:13
n. shall possess the. *Hos* 9:6
shall be the breeding of n. *Zeph* 2:9

network

grate of n. of brass. *Ex* 27:4; 38:4
round about on n. *1 Ki* 7:18, 42
n. on the chapiters. *Jer* 52:22
all the pomegranates on n. were. 23

networks

the two n. upon the. *1 Ki* 7:41
pomegranates for the two n. 42
they that weave n. shall. *Isa* 19:9*

never

kine, such as I n. saw. *Gen* 41:19
the fire shall n. go out. *Lev* 6:13
upon which n. came yoke. *Num* 19:2
the poor shall n. cease. *Deut* 15:11
n. break my covenant. *Judg* 2:1
is there n. a woman among ? 14:3
green withs that were n. dried. 16:7
if bind with new ropes that n. 11
sword shall n. depart. *2 Sam* 12:10
he n. prophesieth good. *2 Chr* 18:7
was n. a son left him, save. 21:17
infants which n. saw light. *Job* 3:16
make my hands n. so clean. 9:30
n. eateth with pleasure. 21:25
I shall n. be in adversity. *Ps* 10:6
his face, he will n. see it. 11
these things shall n. be moved. 15:5
in prosperity I said, I shall n. 30:6
in thee do I trust, let me n. 31:1
they shall n. see light. 49:19
Lord will n. suffer righteous. 55:22
O Lord, let me n. be put to. 71:1
I will n. forget thy precepts. 119:93
the righteous shall n. be. *Pr* 10:30
destruction are n. full, so the eyes of
a man are n. satisfied. 27:20
three things that are n. 30:15
Babylon n. be inhabited. *Isa* 13:20
the seed of evil doers shall n. 14:20
no city, it shall n. be built. 25:2
are greedy dogs which can n. 56:11
watchmen that shall n. hold. 62:6
we are thine: Thou n. barest. 63:19
their confusion shall n. *Jer* 20:11
David shall n. want a man. 33:17
n. open thy mouth. *Ezek* 16:63
Tyrus shall n. be found. 26:21
terror and n. shall be. 27:36; 28:19
a kingdom that shall n. *Dan* 2:44
trouble, such as n. was. 12:1
my people shall n. be ashamed.
Joel 2:26, 27
I will n. forget any of. *Amos* 8:7
they shall fall and n. rise. 14
judgement dcth n. go. *Hab* 1:4
profess unto them, I n. *Mat* 7:23
it was n. so seen in Israel. 9:33
have ye n. read, Out of the mouth of
babes ? 21:16, 42; *Mark* 2:25
Peter said, Yet will I n. *Mat* 26:33
he answered him to n. a word. 27:14
we n. saw it on this. *Mark* 2:12
Holy Ghost, hath n. forgiveness. 3:29
into fire that n. shall be. 9:43, 45
colt tied, whereon n. man sat.
11:2; *Luke* 19:30
good for that man if he had n. been
born. *Mark* 14:21
n. gavest me a kid to. *Luke* 15:29
the wombs that n. bare. 23:29
wherein n. man before was laid. 53
John 19:41
I give, shall n. thirst. *John* 4:14
shall n. hunger, and he that believeth
on me shall n. thirst. 6:35
man, having n. learned ? 7:15
n. man spake like this man. 46
and we were n. in bondage. 8:33
he shall n. see death. 51, 52; 10:28
11:26
thou shalt n. wash my feet. 13:8
I have n. eaten any. *Acts* 10:14
being a cripple, who n. had. 14:8
charity n. faileth, but. *1 Cor* 13:8
n. able to come to. *2 Tim* 3:7
n. with those sacrifices. *Heb* 10:1
the same sacrifices which can n. 11
I will n. leave thee, nor forsake. 13:5
things ye shall n. fall. *2 Pet* 1:10

never so

charming n. so wisely. *Ps* 58:5

never so much

ask me n. so m. dowry. *Gen* 34:12

nevertheless

n. in the day when I. *Ex* 32:34
n. these ye shall not eat. *Lev* 11:4
Deut 14:7
n. a fountain or pit shall. *Lev* 11:36
n. the people be strong. *Num* 13:28
n. the ark of the covenant. 14:44
n. the firstborn of man shalt. 18:15
n. the Kenite shall be wasted. 24:22
n. it shall be purified with. 31:23
n. the Lord thy God. *Deut* 23:5
n. children of Israel expelled not.
Josh 13:13
n. my brethren that went up. 14:8
n. the inhabitants of. *Judg* 1:33
n. the Lord raised up judges. 2:16
n. the people refused. *1 Sam* 8:19
n. Samuel mourned for Saul. 15:35
n. Saul spake not any thing. 20:26
n. the lords favour thee not. 29:6
n. David took the strong. *2 Sam* 5:7
n. a lad saw them and told. 17:18
n. he would not drink thereof. 23:16
n. thou shalt not build. *1 Ki* 8:19
n. for David's sake did the. 15:4
n. Asa his heart was perfect. 14
n. in his old age he was. 23
n. the high places were not. 22:43
n. if thou see me when. *2 Ki* 2:10
n. he cleaved to the sins of. 3:3
n. they departed not from sins. 13:6
n. the priests of the high. 23:9
n. David took the castle. *1 Chr* 11:5
n. the king's word prevailed. 21:4
n. they shall be his. *2 Chr* 12:8
n. the heart of Asa was. 15:17
n. there are good things found. 19:3
n. divers of Asher humbled. 30:11
n. the people did sacrifice in. 33:17
n. Josiah would not turn. 35:22
n. we made our prayer. *Neh* 4:9
n. they were disobedient. 9:26
n. for thy mercies' sake thou. 31
n. him did outlandish women. 13:26
n. Haman refrained. *Esth* 5:10
n. thou heardest my. *Ps* 31:22
n. man being in honour. 49:12
n. I am continually with thee. 73:23
n. they did flatter him with. 78:36
n. my lovingkindness will I not. 89:33
n. he saved them for his. 106:8
n. he regarded their affliction. 44
n. the counsel of the Lord. *Pr* 19:21
n. the poor man's wisdom. *Eccl* 9:16
n. the dimness shall not be. *Isa* 9:1
n. in those days I will not. *Jer* 5:18
n. the hand of Ahikam was. 26:24
n. hear thou this word that. 28:7
n. Elnathan and Delaiah. 36:25
n. if thou warn the. *Ezek* 3:21
n. I will remember my. 16:60
n. mine eye spared them. 20:17
n. I withdrew my hand, and. 22
n. if thou warn the wicked. 33:9
n. leave the stump of. *Dan* 4:15
n. the men rowed hard. *Jonah* 1:13
n. for the oath's sake. *Mat* 14:9
from me, n. not as I will, but. 26:39
n. hereafter ye shall see the. 64
n. not what I will. *Mark* 14:36
Luke 22:42
n. at thy word I will. *Luke* 5:5
n. I must walk to-day. 13:33
n. when Son of man cometh. 18:8
Lazarus is dead, n. let. *John* 11:15
n. among the chief rulers. 12:42
n. I tell you the truth; it is. 16:7
n. he left not himself. *Acts* 14:17
n. the centurion believed. 27:11
n. death reigned from. *Rom* 5:14
n. I have written more boldly. 15:15
n. to avoid fornication. *1 Cor* 7:2
n. such shall have trouble in. 28
n. he that standeth stedfast. 37
n. we have not used this. 9:12
n. neither is the man. 11:11
n. when it shall turn. *2 Cor* 3:16
n. God comforteth those that. 7:6
n. being crafty, I caught. 12:16

new

n. I live, yet not I, but. *Gal* 2:20
n. what saith scripture, cast. 4:30
n. let every one so love his wife.
Eph 5:33
n. to abide in the flesh. *Phil* 1:24
n. whereto we have already. 3:16
n. I am not ashamed. *2 Tim* 1:12
n. the foundation of God. 2:19
n. it yieldeth peaceable. *Heb* 12:11
n. we look for new. *2 Pet* 3:13
n. I have somewhat. *Rev* 2:4

new

[1] *Fresh, newly made,* Judg
15:13; Mat 9:17. [2] *Sweet, as*
new wine, not yet fermented,
Joel 1:5. [3] *Undressed, as cloth,*
Mat 9:16.

there arose up a n. king. *Ex* 1:8
offer a n. meat offering. *Lev* 23:16
Num 28:26
old, because of the n. *Lev* 26:10
Lord make a n. thing. *Num* 16:30
what man is there that hath built a n.
house ? *Deut* 20:5; 22:8
when taken a n. wife, he shall. 24:5
sacrificed to devils, to n. 32:17
bottles of wine were n. *Josh* 9:13
they chose n. gods, then. *Judg* 5:8
they bound him with n. cords. 15:13
16:11, 12
make a n. cart, and. *1 Sam* 6:7
set the ark on a n. cart. *2 Sam* 6:3
1 Chr 13:7
being girded with a n. *2 Sam* 21:16
clad with a n. garment. *1 Ki* 11:29
Ahijah caught the n. garment. 30
bring a n. cruse, and. *2 Ki* 2:20
stood in the n. court. *2 Chr* 20:5
it is ready to burst like n. *Job* 32:19
a n. song. *Ps* 33:3; 96:1; 98:1
144:9; 149:1; *Isa* 42:10
put a n. song in my mouth. *Ps* 40:3
is no n. thing under the. *Eccl* 1:9
whereof may be said, This is n.? 10
all pleasant fruits, n. *S of S* 7:13
behold n. things do. *Isa* 42:9; 48:6
behold, I will do a n. thing. 43:19
be called by a n. name. 62:2
n. heavens and a n. 65:17; 66:22
the n. gate of the Lord's house.
Jer 26:10; 36:10
the Lord hath created a n. 31:22
mercies are n. every. *Lam* 3:23
I will put a n. spirit within you.
Ezek 11:19; 36:26
a n. heart and n. spirit. 18:31
shall bring forth n. fruit. 47:12
a piece of n. cloth to an. *Mat* 9:16*
Mark 2:21*; *Luke* 5:36
but they put n. wine into n. bottles.
Mat 9:17; *Mark* 2:22; *Luke* 5:38
of his treasure things n. *Mat* 13:52
for this is my blood of the n. 26:28
Mark 14:24; *Luke* 22:20
1 Cor 11:25
until I drink it n. with you.
Mat 26:29; *Mark* 14:25
body in his own n. tomb. *Mat* 27:60
saying, What n. doctrine? *Mark* 1:27
speak with n. tongues. 16:17
a n. commandment give. *John* 13:34
a n. sepulchre, wherein. 19:41
what this n. doctrine is ? *Acts* 17:19
to tell or to hear some n. thing. 21
ye may be a n. lump. *1 Cor* 5:7
able ministers of the n. *2 Cor* 3:6
in Christ, he is a n. creature; behold,
all things are become n. 5:17
but a n. creature. *Gal* 6:15
of twain, one n. man. *Eph* 2:15
put on the n. man. 4:24; *Col* 3:10
the Mediator of the n. *Heb* 9:15
by a n. and living way hath. 10:20
as n. born babes desire. *1 Pet* 2:2
n. heavens and a n. *2 Pet* 3:13
I write no n. commandment unto.
1 John 2:7
a n. commandment I write. 8
I wrote a n. commandment. *2 John* 5
n. name written, which. *Rev* 2:17
n. Jerusalem. 3:12; 21:2
I will write my n. name. 3:12
and they sung a n. song. 5:9; 14:3

n. heaven and a n. earth. *Rev 21:1*
I make all things n.   5
   see **covenant, moon**

new *wine*
offering of the n. wine. *Neh 10:39*
chamber where the n. wine.   13:5
brought tithe of n. wine unto the. 12
burst out with n. wine.   *Pr 3:10*
the n. wine mourneth, the. *Isa 24:7*
as the n. wine is found in.   65:8
wine and n. wine take.   *Hos 4:11*
n. wine shall fail in her.   9:2
the n. wine is cut off.   *Joel 1:5*
n. wine is dried up.   10
mountains shall drop n. wine.   3:18
drought on the n. wine.   *Hag 1:11*
n. wine shall make the maids cheerful.   *Zech 9:17*
n. wine into old bottles, but n. wine.
    Mat 9:17; Mark 2:22; Luke 5:37
men are full of n. wine.   *Acts 2:13*

newly
gods that came n. up. *Deut 32:17**
but n. set the watch.   *Judg 7:19*

newness
should walk in n. of life. *Rom 6:4*
we should serve in n. of spirit.   7:6

news
so is good n. from afar. *Pr 25:25*

next
bear at this set time n. *Gen 17:21*
neighbour n. take a lamb. *Ex 12:4*
stood up all the n. day. *Num 11:32*
inheritance to his kinsman n. 27:11
the city which is n. to. *Deut 21:3*
the elders of the city n. to the.   6
is one of our n. kinsmen. *Ruth 2:20*
and I shall be n. to thee. *1 Sam 23:17*
them to the evening of n. day. 30:17
Elkanah that was n. *2 Chr 28:7*
Mordecai was n. to king. *Esth 10:3*
worm the n. day smote. *Jonah 4:7*
the n. day that followed. *Mat 27:62*
us go into the n. towns. *Mark 1:38*
the n. day John seeth. *John 1:29*
in hold unto the n. day. *Acts 4:3*
the n. day Moses shewed.   7:26
be preached n. sabbath.   13:42, 44

Nicanor
Stephen, Philip and N. *Acts 6:5*

Nicodemus
N. a ruler of the Jews. *John 3:1*
N. came to Jesus by.   7:50; 19:39

Nicolaitanes
hatest the deeds of the N. *Rev 2:6*
hold the doctrine of the N.   15

Nicopolis
to come unto me to N. *Tit 3:12*

Niger
Simeon who was called N. *Acts 13:1*

nigh
virgin that is n. to him. *Lev 21:3*
any that is n. of kin may.   25:49
him, but not n., a star. *Num 24:17*
hath God so n. to them. *Deut 4:7*
gods of the people n. to the.   13:7
if thy brother be not n.   22:2
the word is n. unto thee.   30:14
         Rom 10:8
wherefore approached ye so n.?
      2 Sam 11:20, 21
my words be n. to the. *1 Ki 8:59*
Lord is n. unto them that. *Ps 34:18*
his salvation is n. them that.   85:9
the Lord is n. unto all that. 145:18
day of the Lord is n. *Joel 2:1*
ye know that summer is n.
     Mat 24:32; Luke 21:30
that it is n. even at the. *Mark 13:29*
desolation thereof is n. *Luke 21:20*
your redemption draweth n.   28
kingdom of God is n. at hand.   31
a feast of Jews was n. *John 6:4*
passover was n. at hand.   11:55
sepulchre was n. at hand.   19:42
n. by the blood of Christ. *Eph 2:13*
peace to them that were n.   17
sick. n. unto death. *Phil 2:27*
is rejected, is n. unto. *Heb 6:8*
   see **came, draw**

night
[1] *The time while the sun is
below our horizon,* Ex 12:30, 31;
Mat 27:64. [2] *A time of ignorance and unbelief,* Rom 13:12.
[3] *Adversity and affliction,* Isa
21:12. [4] *Death.* John 9:4.
darkness he called n.   *Gen 1:5*
lights, to divide the day from n. 14
lesser light to rule the n.   16
tarry all n.   19:2; *Num 22:19*
         Judg 19:6, 9
men which came in to thee this n.?
         Gen 19:5
drink wine that n.   33, 34, 35
tarried all n.   24:54; 28:11; 31:54
         32:13, 21
appeared to Isaac the same n. 26:24
shall lie with thee to-n.   30:15, 16
each man his dream in one n. 40:5
         41:11
Israel in visions of the n.   46:2
and at n. he shall divide.   49:27*
eat the flesh that n. roast. *Ex 12:8*
the land of Egypt this n.   12
n. to be much observed to the Lord,
   this is that n. of the Lord to be. 42
not near the other all n.   14:20
the burning on the altar all n. *Lev 6:9*
not abide with thee all n.   19:13
the people stood up all that n.
        Num 11:32
and the people wept that n.   14:1
to them, Lodge here this n. 22:8, 19
God came to Balaam at n.   20
shall no leavened bread remain all n.
        Deut 16:4
body shall not remain all n. 21:23
came men in hither to-n. *Josh 2:2*
that n. for it was dry on. *Judg 6:40*
all n. and were quiet all n.   16:2
man would not tarry that n.   19:10
and abused her all the n. until.   25
an husband also to-n. *Ruth 1:12*
Boaz winnoweth barley to-n.   3:2
cried to the Lord all n. *1 Sam 15:11*
Lord hath said to me this n.   16
fled and escaped that n.   19:10
if thou save not thy life to-n.
        19:11
rose up and went away that n. 28:25
men of Jabesh went all n.   31:12
men walked all n.   *2 Sam 2:29*
Joab and his men went all n.   32
away through the plain all n.   4:7
David went and lay all n.   12:16
pursue after David this n.   17:1
lodge not this n. in the plain.   16
tarry one with thee this n.   19:7
that n. the angel of the. *2 Ki 19:35*
that n. did God appear. *2 Chr 1:7*
n. could not the king sleep. *Esth 6:1*
let the n. perish in which it. *Job 3:3*
let that n. be solitary.   7
the visions of the n.   4:13
arise, and the n. be gone ?   7:4
and the dew lay all n. on my. 29:19
desire not the n. when people. 36:20
all the n. make I my bed. *Ps 6:6*
n. unto n. sheweth knowledge. 19:2
may endure for a n., but joy. 30:5
he led them all n. with a. 78:14
forth thy faithfulness every n. 92:2
darkness, and it is n. 104:20
even the n. shall be light. 139:11
the black and dark n. *Pr 7:9*
ariseth also while it is yet n. 31:15
shall lie all n. between my breasts.
        S of S 1:13
with the drops of n.   5:2
continue until n. till wine. *Isa 5:11*
make thy shadow as the n.   16:3
the n. of my pleasure he. 21:4*
what of the n.? what of the n.?   11
morning cometh, and also the n.   12
shall be a dream of a n.   29:7
aside to tarry for a n. *Jer 14:8*
secret revealed in a n. *Dan 2:19*
in that n. was Belshazzar.   5:30
king passed the n. fasting.   6:18
baker sleepeth all the n. *Hos 7:6*
howl, come, lie all n. in. *Joel 1:13*
the day dark with n. *Amos 5:8*
up in a n. perished in a n. *Jonah 4:10*
therefore n. shall be to you. *Mi 3:6*

fourth watch of n. Jesus went to.
    Mat 14:25; Mark 6:48
be offended because of me this n.
     Mat 26:31; Mark 14:27
this n. before cockcrow. *Mat 26:34*
we have toiled all n. *Luke 5:5*
continued all n. in prayer to.   6:12
this n. thy soul shall be.   12:20
in that n. two shall be in.   17:34
at n. he went out and abode. 21:37
the n. cometh when no. *John 9:4*
went out, and it was n.   13:30
that n. they caught nothing.   21:3
the same n. Peter was. *Acts 12:6*
the same hour of the n.   16:33
n. following the Lord stood. 23:11
soldiers at third hour of the n.   23
stood by me this n. the angel. 27:23
the n. is far spent, the. *Rom 13:12*
the same n. in which. *1 Cor 11:23*
we are not of the n. nor. *1 Thes 5:5*
there shall be no n. there.
      Rev 21:25; 22:5

by **night**
to Abimelech in a dream *by n.*
        Gen 20:3
to Laban in a dream *by n.*   31:24
stolen by day, or stolen *by n.*   39
consumed me, and the frost *by n.* 40
Moses and Aaron *by n.*   *Ex 12:31*
before them *by n.* in a.   13:21, 22
     14:20; 40:38; *Neh 9:12*
appearance of fire *by n.* *Num 9:16*
cloud taken up by day or *by n.* 21
in fire *by n.* to shew. *Deut 1:33*
forth out of Egypt *by n.*   16:1
that chanceth him *by n.*   23:10
Joshua sent them away *by n.*
        Josh 8:3
that he did it *by n.* *Judg 6:27*
up *by n.* thou and thy people. 9:32
house round about *by n.*   20:5
after Philistines *by n.* *1 Sam 14:36*
Abishai came to people *by n.* 26:7
Saul came to the woman *by n.* 28:8
beasts of the field *by n.* *2 Sam 21:10*
Lord appeared to Solomon *by n.*
     1 Ki 3:5; 2 Chr 7:12
by n. and compassed. *2 Ki 6:14*
rose *by n.* and smote Edomites.
     8:21; *2 Chr 21:9*
all the men of war fled *by n.*
     2 Ki 25:4; Jer 52:7
not be afraid of terror *by n. Ps 91:5*
nor the moon smite thee *by n.* 121:6
that *by n.* stand in the house. 134:1
moon and stars to rule *by n.* 136:9
        Jer 31:35
candle goeth not out *by n. Pr 31:18*
by n. on my bed I. *S of S 3:1*
of a flaming fire *by n.* *Isa 4:5*
let us go *by n.* and destroy. *Jer 6:5*
forth out of the city *by n.*   39:4
if thieves *by n.* they will.   49:9
I saw in my vision *by n.* *Dan 7:2*
if robbers *by n.* came to thee. *Ob 5*
and his mother *by n.* *Mat 2:14*
lest his disciples come *by n.*   27:64
        28:13
watch over their flock *by n. Luke 2:8*
Nicodemus came to Jesus *by n.*
      John 3:2; 19:39
the angel *by n.* opened. *Acts 5:19*
they took Paul *by n.* and let. 9:25
sent away Paul and Silas *by n.* 17:10
   see **day**

in the **night**
his servants rose *in the n. Ex 12:30*
dew fell on the camp *in the n.*
        Num 11:9
child died *in the n.* *1 Ki 3:19*
king arose *in the n.* and. *2 Ki 7:12*
I arose *in the n.* *Neh 2:12*
I went up *in the n.*   15
in the n. they may be a guard. 4:22
yea, *in the n.* will they come. 6:10
noonday, as *in the n.* *Job 5:14*
in the n. the murderer. 24:14
stealeth him away *in the n.* 27:20
overturneth them *in the n.* 34:25
who giveth songs *in the n.?* 35:10
instruct me *in the n.* seasons.
        Ps 16:7

nighthawk

hast visited me in the n.   Ps 17:3
I cry in the n. season, and.   22:2
and in the n. his song shall.   42:8
my sore ran in the n. and.   77:2
to remembrance my song in the n. 6
are but as a watch in the n.   90:4
fire to give light in the n.   105:39
thy name in the n.   119:55
taketh not rest in the n.   Eccl 2:23
because of fear in the n.   S of S 3:8
in the n. Ar and Kir of.   Isa 15:1
have I desired thee in the n.   26:9
have a song as in the n.   30:29
at noonday as in the n.   59:10*
shall be cast out in the n.   Jer 36:30
she weepeth sore in the n.   Lam 1:2
cry out in the n.   2:19
fall with thee in the n.   Hos 4:5
if a man walk in the n.   John 11:10
a vision appeared to Paul in the n.
   Acts 16:9; 18:9
as a thief in the n.   1 Thes 5:2
   2 Pet 3:10
sleep in the n. are drunken in the n.
   1 Thes 5:7

nighthawk

owl and n. ye shall not eat.
   Lev 11:16; Deut 14:15

nights

rain forty days, forty n. Gen 7:4, 12
wearisome n. are appointed. Job 7:3
set in my ward whole n.   Isa 21:8
see days

nightwatches

meditate on thee in the n.   Ps 63:6
mine eyes prevent the n.   119:148

Nimrod

Cush begat N.   Gen 10:8
   1 Chr 1:10
as N. the mighty hunter.   Gen 10:9
land of Assyria and N.   Mi 5:6

Nimshi, see Jehu

nine

fifth day n. bullocks.   Num 29:26
Lord commanded to give to the n.
   34:13; Josh 13:7; 14:2
Og's bedstead was n.   Deut 3:11
Joab came to Jerusalem at end of n.
months.   2 Sam 24:8
n. parts to dwell in other. Neh 11:1
but where are the n.?   Luke 17:17
see hundred

nineteen

David's servants n. men. 2 Sam 2:30

nineteenth

in the n. year of Nebuchadnezzar.
   2 Ki 25:8; Jer 52:12

ninety

Enos lived n. years, and. Gen 5:9
shall Sarah, that is n. years? 17:17
of the building in cubits. Ezek 41:12

ninety-five

children of Gibbar n.-five. Ezra 2:20
children of Gibeon n.-five. Neh 7:25

ninety-six

Israel n.-six rams.   Ezra 8:35
n.-six pomegranates.   Jer 52:23

ninety-eight

Eli was n.-eight years. 1 Sam 4:5
the children of Ater n.-eight.
   Ezra 2:16; Neh 7:21

ninety-nine

Abram was n.-nine years. Gen 17:1
was n.-nine years old when he. 24
doth he not leave the n. and nine?
   Mat 18:12, 13; Luke 15:4, 7

Nineveh

went and builded N.   Gen 10:11
Sennacherib dwelt at N. 2 Ki 19:36
   Isa 37:37
go to N.   Jonah 1:2; 3:2
now N. was an exceeding great. 3:3
should not I spare N.?   4:11
the burden of N.   Nah 1:1
N. is like a pool.   2:8
N. is laid waste, who will?   3:7
N. a desolation, and.   Zeph 2:13
N. shall rise in judgement and con-
demn.   Mat 12:41; Luke 11:32

Ninevites

a sign unto the N.   Luke 11:30

ninth

of old fruit till the n. year. Lev 25:22
in n. year of Hoshea Samaria taken.
   2 Ki 17:6; 18:10
in the n. year of Zedekiah.   25:1
   Jer 39:1; 52:4; Ezek 24:1
Elzabad the n. captain. 1 Chr 12:12
the n. lot came forth to.   24:11
n. captain for the n. month.   27:12
the sixth and n. hour.   Mat 20:5
was darkness over all the land unto
the n. hour.   27:45; Mark 15:33
n. hour Jesus gave up the ghost.
   Mat 27:46; Mark 15:34
prayer, being the n. hour. Acts 3:1
a vision about the n. hour.   10:3, 30
n. foundation was a.   Rev 21:20
see day, month

Nisan

in the month N.   Neh 2:1
first month N.   Esth 3:7

Nisroch

worshipping in the house of N. his.
   2 Ki 19:37; Isa 37:38

nitre

as vinegar upon n. so is.   Pr 25:20
wash thee with n. and.   Jer 2:22*

no

let there be no strife.   Gen 13:8
me thou hast given no seed.   15:3
that thou wilt do us no hurt.   26:29
shed no blood, and lay no.   37:22
there was no harlot in.   38:21, 22
no interpreter.   40:8
we are no spies.   42:11, 31, 34
have no pasture.   47:4; Lam 1:6
is no straw given to.   Ex 5:16, 18
that no swarms of flies.   8:22
no work shall be done.   12:16
   Lev 16:29; 23:3, 7, 21, 28, 31
   Num 29:1; Deut 16:8
seven days no leaven shall be.
   Ex 12:19; 13:3, 7
were no graves in Egypt.   14:11
gathered little had no lack.   16:18
hurt a woman, and no.   21:12
there shall no blood be shed.   22:2
no gift; gift blindeth the wise. 23:8
thou shalt make no covenant.   32
ye shall offer no strange.   30:9
that there be no plague amongst. 12
for thou shalt worship no.   34:14
make thee no molten gods.   17
ye shall kindle no fire in your. 35:3
ye shall burn no leaven.   Lev 2:11
put no oil upon it.   5:11
ye shall eat no fat.   7:23
ye shall eat no manner of blood.
   26; 17:12, 14
touch no hallowed thing.   12:4
be no white hairs therein. 13:21, 26
no black hair.   31
there be no yellow hair.   32
do no unrighteousness.   19:15, 35
that there be no wickedness. 20:14
but there shall no stranger.   22:13
shall be no blemish therein.   21
houses which have no walls.   25:31
take thou no usury of him.   36
ye shall make you no idols.   26:1
no devoted thing shall.   27:28
if the man have no.   Num 5:8
there be no witness against.   13
and shall drink no vinegar.   6:3
there shall no razor come upon. 5
he shall come at no dead body. 6
that no stranger come near.   16:40
Zelophehad had no sons. 26:33; 27:3
   4; Josh 17:3; 1 Chr 23:22; 24:28
if a man die and no son. Num 27:8
and if he have no daughter.   9
be not as sheep that have no   17
   Ezek 34:5; Mat 9:36
no satisfaction for the life of a murderer.   Num 35:31, 32
saw no similitude.   Deut 4:12, 15
thine eye shall have no pity.   7:16
Levi hath no part with.   10:9; 14:27
   29; 18:1; Josh 14:4; 18:7
there shall be no poor.   Deut 15:4
if it will make no peace.   20:12

there shall be no might. Deut 28:32
nations thou shalt find no ease.   65
children in whom is no faith. 32:20
there was no day like.   Josh 10:14
no part in the Lord.   22:25, 27
there was no king in Israel.
   Judg 17:6; 18:1; 21:25
there was no magistrate.   18:7
where there is no want.   10; 19:19
no deliverer.   18:28
for it is no good report. 1 Sam 2:24
there was no open vision.   3:1
take it, for there is no other.   21:9
because he had no pity. 2 Sam 12:6
no such thing ought to be.   13:12
if he say, I have no delight.   15:26
I have no son to keep my.   18:18
Sheba said, We have no part. 20:1
there is no God like.   1 Ki 8:23
he would prophesy no good.   22:18
there is no God in Israel. 2 Ki 1:16
because Ahaziah had no son.   17
Jehu took no heed to walk.   10:31
Sheshan had no sons.   1 Chr 2:34
do my prophets no harm.   16:22
   Ps 105:15
that have no shepherd. 2 Chr 18:16
   Zech 10:2
there is no iniquity with. 2 Chr 19:7
we have no might against.   20:12
people made no burning for.   21:19
there was no passover like.   35:18
till there was no remedy.   36:16
that there should be no.   Ezra 9:14
ye have no portion in.   Neh 2:20
no king like Solomon.   13:26
he put no trust in his.   Job 4:18
in seven there shall no evil.   5:19
see no good.   9:25
that no eye had seen me.   10:18
and there can be no opening. 12:14
wander where there is no way.   24
physicians of no value.   13:4
let my cry have no place.   16:18
he shall have no name in.   18:17
servant, he gave me no.   19:16
no eye shall see me.   24:15
have no helper.   30:13
there is no help for him.   Ps 3:2
spirit there is no guile.   32:2
there is no want to them.   34:9
there is no fear of God.   36:1
in fear where no fear was.   53:5
they have no changes.   55:19
no good will he withhold.   84:11
there shall no evil befall thee. 91:10
there is no unrighteousness.   92:15
do no iniquity, they walk.   119:3
in whom there is no help.   146:3
shall no evil happen to.   Pr 12:21
seeing he hath no heart to it. 17:16
there is no wisdom against.   21:30
they had no comforter.   Eccl 4:1
is no work in the grave.   9:10
my love, there is no.   S of S 4:7
sister, and she hath no breasts. 8:8
there is no soundness in it.   Isa 1:6
field, till there be no place.   5:8
it is because there is no light. 8:20
government there shall be no.   9:7
none of these shall fail.   34:16
to them that have no might.   40:29
beside me there is no saviour. 43:11
no peace to wicked.   48:22; 57:21
in darkness, and hath no light. 50:10
hath no form nor comeliness.   53:2
no weapon formed against.   54:17
and he that hath no money.   55:1
there is no hope.   57:10; Jer 2:25
there is no judgement.   Isa 59:8
that there was no intercessor.   16
which are yet no gods.   Jer 2:11
received no correction.   30
when there is no peace. 6:14; 8:11
cruel, and have no mercy.   6:23
looked for peace, but no good. 8:15
   14:19
and there is no breath in them.
   10:14; 51:17
wherein is no pleasure. 22:28; 48:38
I will do you no hurt.   25:6
do him no harm.   39:12
shall see no war.   42:14
spoiler shall come, and no.   48:8

no sons ? hath he *no* heir ? *Jer* 49:1
she had *no* comforter. *Lam* 1:9
peace, and there was *no* peace.
     Ezek 13:10, 16
I have *no* pleasure in death of him.
     18:32; 33:11
yet had he *no* wages, nor.   29:18
is *no* other god that can. *Dan* 3:29
because there is *no* truth. *Hos* 4:1
thou shalt be *no* priest to me.   6
shall say, We have *no* king.   10:3
I was *no* prophet. *Amos* 7:14
there is *no* answer of God. *Mi* 3:7
is there *no* king in thee ?   4:9
there is *no* healing of thy. *Nah* 3:19
things that have *no* ruler. *Hab* 1:14
unjust knoweth *no* shame. *Zeph* 3:5
love *no* false oath. *Zech* 8:17
no oppressor shall pass.   9:8
I have *no* pleasure in you. *Mal* 1:10
ye shall in *no* case enter. *Mat* 5:20
thou shalt by *no* means come.   26
take therefore *no* thought.
     10:19; *Mark* 13:11; *Luke* 12:11, 22
there is *no* resurrection. *Mat* 22:23
     Mark 12:18; *Acts* 23:8
     1 Cor 15:12, 13
days, *no* flesh be saved. *Mark* 13:20
need *no* repentance. *Luke* 15:7
I find *no* fault in him.   23:4, 14
     John 18:38; 19:4, 6
I have *no* husband. *John* 4:17
ye have *no* life.   6:53
of Galilee ariseth *no* prophet. 7:52
ye should have *no* sin.   9:41
there is *no* light in him.   11:10
if I wash thee not, thou hast *no*. 13:8
now they have *no* cloak for. 15:22
we have *no* king but Caesar. 19:15
no difference between. *Acts* 15:9
for I will be *no* judge of.   18:15
written they observe *no*.   21:25
Jews have I done *no* wrong. 25:10
the people shewed us *no* little. 28:2
for there is *no* difference. *Rom* 3:22
for where *no* law is, no. 4:15; 5:13
flesh dwelleth *no* good thing. 7:18
them that are *no* people.   10:19
love worketh *no* ill to his.   13:10
that *no* flesh glory. *1 Cor* 1:29
no certain dwelling place.   4:11
I will eat *no* flesh while the. 8:13
there hath *no* temptation.   10:13
we have *no* such custom.   11:16
I have *no* need of thee.   12:21
no charity.   13:2
if there be *no* interpreter.   14:28
for us, who knew *no* sin. *2 Cor* 5:21
giving *no* offence in any thing. 6:3
I pray to God that ye do *no* evil. 13:7
against such there is *no* law. *Gal* 5:23
have *no* fellowship. *Eph* 5:11
but made himself of *no*. *Phil* 2:7
and have *no* confidence in.   3:3
which have *no* hope. *1 Thes* 4:13
and have *no* company. *2 Thes* 3:14
shall proceed *no* further. *2 Tim* 3:9
could swear by *no* greater. *Heb* 6:13
no place have been sought.   8:7
without shedding of blood is *no*. 9:22
have *no* pleasure in him.   10:38
no chastening for the present. 12:11
found *no* place of repentance.   17
have we *no* continuing city. 13:14
whom is *no* variableness. *Jas* 1:17
and have *no* works, can faith ? 2:14
who did *no* sin, nor. *1 Pet* 2:22
no prophecy of private. *2 Pet* 1:20
in him is *no* darkness. *1 John* 1:5
if we say, we have *no* sin, we.   8
in him is *no* sin.   3:5
there is *no* fear in love.   4:18
I have *no* greater joy. *3 John* 4
mouth was found *no* guile. *Rev* 14:5
received *no* kingdom as yet. 17:12
no widow, and shall see no.   18:7
found *no* place for them.   20:11
no temple therein.   21:22
no need of the sun.   23
no night there, they need *no*. 25; 22:5
see **bread, child, children, in-**
heritance, knowledge, man,
more, power, water, wise,
wrath

---

no *rain*
that there be *no rain*. *Deut* 11:17
     1 Ki 8:35; *2 Chr* 6:26; 7:13
there had been *no rain* in land.
     1 Ki 17:7; *Jer* 14:4
they rain *no rain* upon it. *Isa* 5:6
hath been *no* latter *rain*. *Jer* 3:3
even upon them shall be *no rain*.
     Zech 14:17
and if Egypt that have *no rain*.   18

no *rest*
but the dove found *no rest*. *Gen* 8:9
my sinews take *no rest*. *Job* 30:17
or laugh there is *no rest*. *Pr* 29:9
shalt thou have *no rest*. *Isa* 23:12
no rest till he establish.   62:7
sighing, and find *no rest*. *Jer* 45:3
heathen she findeth *no rest*. *Lam* 1:3
give thyself *no rest*.   2:18
we have *no rest*.   5:5
I had *no rest* in my spirit. *2 Cor* 2:13
our flesh had *no rest*.   7:5
they have *no rest* day.   *Rev* 14:11

no *strength*
no strength in Saul. *1 Sam* 28:20
arm that hath *no strength*. *Job* 26:2
man that hath *no strength*. *Ps* 88:4
there remained *no strength* in me.
     Dan 10:8, 17
I have retained *no strength*.   16
it is of *no strength* at all. *Heb* 9:17

no *where*
they were *no where*. *1 Sam* 10:14

no, *opposite of yes*
not let you go, *no* not by. *Ex* 3:19
whether walk in my law or *no*. 16:4
     Deut 8:2
here, thou shalt say, No. *Judg* 4:20
no, but we will bind thee.   15:13
no, my lord, I am of. *1 Sam* 1:15
no, not when the Lord hath.   20:15
no, but he would put strength in me.
     Job 23:6
no, not gold, nor the forces.   36:19
there is none that doeth good, *no*, not
one.   *Ps* 14:3; 53:3
curse not king, *no* not. *Eccl* 10:20
no, for we will flee. *Isa* 30:16
no, for I have loved. *Jer* 2:25
no, but we will go into the.   42:14
thee ? he shall say, No. *Amos* 6:10
answered and said, No. *Hag* 2:12
knowest what these be, I said, No.
     Zech 4:5, 13
so great faith, not *no*t in Israel.
     Mat 8:10; *Luke* 7:9
to this time, *no*, nor ever. *Mat* 24:21
no not the angels, but my.   36
no room, *no* not so much. *Mark* 2:2
bind him, *no* not with chains.   5:3
tribute to Caesar, or *no* ? *Luke* 20:22
no nor yet Herod: for I sent. 23:15
that Prophet? he said, No. *John* 1:21
whether he be a sinner or *no*.   9:25
meat? they answered, No.   21:5
no not so much as to set. *Acts* 7:5
than they? *no*, in no wise. *Rom* 3:9
none righteous, *no* not one.   10, 12
with such an one, *no* not. *1 Cor* 5:11
no, not one that shall be able.   6:5
place by subjection, *no*. *Gal* 2:5

No
I will punish *N*. *Jer* 46:25
     Ezek 30:14, 15, 16
better than populous *N*.? *Nah* 3:8

Noadiah
N. the son of Binnui. *Ezra* 8:33
think on the prophetess *N*. *Neh* 6:14

Noah, Noe
N. saying, This same. *Gen* 5:29
Lamech begat *N*.   30
N. found grace.   6:8
these are generations of *N*. 9; 10:1
     32; *1 Chr* 1:4
N. only remained alive. *Gen* 7:23
God remembered *N*. and every. 8:1
N. opened the window of the ark. 6
N. builded an altar to the Lord. 20
N. awoke from his wine.   9:24
the days of *N*.   29
this is as the waters of *N*. *Isa* 54:9

---

these three, *N*. Daniel, Job.
as it was in the days of *N*.
     Mat 24:37; *Luke* 17:26
was the son of *N*. *Luke* 3:36
by faith, *N*. being warned. *Heb* 11:7
waited in the days of *N*. *1 Pet* 3:20
spared not the old world, but saved
N.   *2 Pet* 2:5

Noah
of Zelophehad were *N*. *Num* 26:33
     27:1; 36:11; *Josh* 17:3

Nob
David came to *N*. *1 Sam* 21:1
son of Jesse coming to *N*.   22:9
to call the priests in *N*.   11
Doeg smote *N*. the city of.   19
of Benjamin dwelt at *N*. *Neh* 11:32
yet shall he remain at *N*. *Isa* 10:32

noble
whom the *n*. Asnapper. *Ezra* 4:10
king's most *n*. princes. *Esth* 6:9
planted thee a *n*. vine. *Jer* 2:21
Bereans more *n*. than. *Acts* 17:11
always, most *n*. Felix. 24:3; 26:25
how that not many *n*. *1 Cor* 1:26

nobleman
n. went into a far country. *Luke* 19:12
n. whose son was sick. *John* 4: 46, 49

nobles
on the *n*. of Israel he. *Ex* 24:11
the *n*. of the people. *Num* 21:18
dominion over the *n*. *Judg* 5:13
letters to the *n*. in his city. *1 Ki* 21:8
Jehoiada took the *n*. *2 Chr* 23:20
as yet told it to the *n*. *Neh* 2:16
the *n*. put not their necks.   3:5
and I rebuked the *n*. and the.   5:7
the *n*. of Judah sent letters.   6:17
mine heart to gather the *n*.   7:5
their brethren, their *n*.   10:29
I contended with the *n*. of.   13:17
the *n*. held their peace. *Job* 29:10
make their *n*. like Oreb. *Ps* 83:11
bind their *n*. with fetters.   149:8
by me princes rule, and *n*. *Pr* 8:16
king is the son of *n*. *Eccl* 10:17
into the gates of the *n*. *Isa* 13:2
they shall call the *n*. to the. 34:12
brought down all their *n*.   43:14
n. sent their little ones to. *Jer* 14:3
carried captive in. of Judah. 27:20
and their *n*. shall be of.   30:21
king of Babylon slew all the *n*. of
Judah.   39:6
of the king and his *n*. *Jonah* 3:7
Assyria, thy *n*. shall dwell. *Nah* 3:18

noise
the people heard the *n*. *Ex* 20:18*
he said, There is a *n*. of war. 32:17
but the *n*. of them that sing.   18
not shout nor make any *n*. *Josh* 6:10
delivered from the *n*. *Judg* 5:11
what meaneth the *n*. of this shout ?
     1 Sam 4:6, 14
n. in the host of Philistines. 14:19*
wherefore is this *n*. of ? *1 Ki* 1:41
is the *n*. that ye have heard.   45
n. of chariots, and a *n*. of. *2 Ki* 7:6
Athaliah heard a *n*. of guard. 11:13
     2 Chr 23:12
a *n*. with psalteries. *1 Chr* 15:28
discern *n*. of joy, from *n*. *Ezra* 3:13
any understand the *n*. *Job* 36:29*
n. thereof sheweth concerning it. 33
attentively the *n*. of his voice. 37:2
skilfully with a loud *n*. *Ps* 33:3
deep calleth at the *n*. of thy.   42:7
my complaint, and make a *n*. 55:2*
they make a *n*. like a dog. 59:6, 14
stilleth the *n*. of the seas, in. 65:7*
make a joyful *n*. to God. 66:1; 81:1
     95:1, 2; 98:4*, 6; 100:1
Lord is mightier than the *n*. 93:4*
battle is with confused *n*. *Isa* 9:5*
n. of a multitude in the mountains, a
tumultuous *n*. of the.   13:4
the *n*. of thy viols is brought. 14:11
which make a *n*. like the *n*. 17:12*
n. of them that rejoice endeth. 24:8
he who fleeth from the *n*. of fear. 18
thou shalt bring down the *n*. 25:5
visited of the Lord with great *n*. 29:6

nor abase himself for the *n. Isa* 31:4
at the *n.* of the tumult the.   33:3
a voice of *n.* from the city.   66:6*
heart maketh a *n.* in me. *Jer* 4:19*
the city shall flee for the *n.*   29
behold, the *n.* of the bruit.   10:22*
with the *n.* of a great tumult. 11:16
a *n.* shall come to the ends.   25:31
king of Egypt is but a *n.*   46:17
at the *n.* of the stamping of.   47:3
at the *n.* of their fall, at the cry the *n.*
    was heard in the Red sea.   49:21
the *n.* of taking of Babylon.   50:46
a *n.* of their voice is uttered. 51:55
enemy made *n.* in house. *Lam* 2:7
I heard the *n.* of their wings, like the
    n. of great.   *Ezek* 1:24; 43:2
the *n.* of the wheels, the *n.* of. 3:13
the land was desolate by the *n.* 19:7
thy walls shall shake at the *n.* 26:10
I will cause the *n.* of my songs.   13
as I prophesied, there was a *n.* 37:7
n. of chariots, like the *n.* of fire.
                      Joel 2:5
take from me the *n.* of. *Amos* 5:23
they shall make a great *n. Mi* 2:12
the *n.* of a whip, *n.* of.   *Nah* 3:2
the *n.* of a cry from the. *Zeph* 1:10
drink and make a *n.*   *Zech* 9:15
people making a *n.*   *Mat* 9:23*
pass away with great *n. 2 Pet* 3:10
I heard as it were the *n. Rev* 6:1*

noised
Joshua, his fame was *n. Josh* 6:27
it was *n.* that he was.   *Mark* 2:1
all these sayings were *n. Luke* 1:65
when this was *n.* abroad. *Acts* 2:6*

noisome
deliver thee from the *n.* pestilence.
                      Ps 91:3
when I send the sword and *n.* beast.
             Ezek 14:21†
fell a *n.* and grievous.   *Rev* 16:2

none
this is *n.* other but the. *Gen* 28:17
n. of you shall go out.   *Ex* 12:22
put *n.* of these diseases.   15:26
7th day, in it there shall be *n.* 16:26
to gather, and they found *n.*   27
shalt have *n.* other gods before me.
           20:3; *Deut* 5:7
n. shall appear before me empty.
       Ex 23:15; 34:20
n. shall approach to any. *Lev* 18:6
there shall *n.* be defiled.   21:1
shall leave *n.* of it until morrow.
       22:30; *Num* 9:12
and if the man have *n. Lev* 25:26
shall lie down, and *n.* shall.   26:6
flee when *n.* pursueth.   17, 36, 37
sons of Kohath he gave *n. Num* 7:9
n. that came out of Egypt.   32:11
we destroyed, and left *n. Deut* 2:34
   3:3; *Josh* 8:22; 10:28, 30, 33
                       11:8
will put *n.* of diseases of. *Deut* 7:15
be given, and *n.* to rescue.   28:31
thou shalt have *n.* assurance.   66
n. went out of Jericho, *n. Josh* 6:1
n. of you be freed from being.   9:23
n. moved his tongue against. 10:21
came *n.* to the camp.   *Judg* 21:14
there is *n.* holy as.   *1 Sam* 2:2
let *n.* of his words fall.   3:19
beware that *n.* touch. *2 Sam* 18:12
all vessels of pure gold; *n.* were of
   silver.   *1 Ki* 10:21; *2 Chr* 9:20
proclamation, *n.* was exempted.
                    1 Ki 15:22
blessing, I will receive *n. 2 Ki* 5:16
n. but Elisha tells the king of. 6:12
shall be *n.* to bury Jezebel.   9:10
let *n.* go forth or escape. 15; 10:25
till Jehu left Ahab *n.*   10:11
the prophets of Baal, let *n.* be.   19
look there be *n.* of the servants.   23
n. ought to carry ark of. *1 Chr* 15:2
honour, such as *n.* of.   *2 Chr* 1:12
he might let *n.* go out or.   16:1
so that *n.* is able to withstand. 20:6
they were dead bodies fallen, *n.* 24
which was unclean should. 23:19
found there *n.* of the sons. *Ezra* 8:15

n. of us put off our clothes. *Neh* 4:23
drinking according to law, *n.* did
   compel.   *Esth* 1:8
n. might enter the king's gate.   4:2
sat down, and *n.* spake.   *Job* 2:13
let it look for light but have *n.*   3:9
n. shall make him afraid.   11:19
           Jer 30:10; 46:27
tabernacle, because it is *n. Job* 18:15
shall *n.* of his meat be left.   20:21
him that had *n.* to help him. 29:12
but *n.* saith, Where is God ? 35:10
they cry, but *n.* giveth answer.   12
wickedness till thou find *n. Ps* 10:15
n. can keep alive his own.   22:29
let *n.* that wait on thee be.   25:3
n. that trust in him shall.   34:22
law in his heart, *n.* of his.   37:31
n. of them can redeem his.   49:7
and there be *n.* to deliver.   50:22
comforters, but found *n.*   69:20
and let *n.* dwell in their tents.   25
n. of the men of might found. 76:5
Israel would *n.* of me.   81:11
let there be *n.* to extend. 109:12
and ye would *n.* of my.   *Pr* 1:25
they would *n.* of my counsel.   30
n. that go unto her return.   2:19
envy not, and choose *n.* of his. 3:31
bear twins, and *n.* is.   *S of S* 4:2
they shall burn and *n.*   *Isa* 1:31
n. shall be weary, *n.* shall.   5:27
carry it away safe, and *n.* shall. 29
persecuted, and *n.* hindereth. 14:6
n. shall be alone in his.   31
n. shall make them afraid.   17:2
                    Zeph 3:13
and *n.* shall shut, *n.* open. *Isa* 22:22
n. shall pass through it.   34:10
they shall call the nobles but *n.*   12
no one shall fail, *n.* shall want.   16
n. delivereth, and *n.* saith.   42:22
n. considereth in his heart. 44:19
I am, and *n.* else beside.   47:8, 10
n. seeth me.   10
n. shall save thee.   15
n. considering that righteous. 57:1
n. calleth for justice, nor.   59:4
I called, *n.* did answer.   66:4
that *n.* can quench it. *Jer* 4:4; 21:12
for the beasts, and *n.* shall.   7:33
burnt up, so that *n.* can pass. 9:10
a wilderness that *n.* passeth.   12
shall fall as dung, and *n.* shall.   22
cities shall be shut, and *n.* 13:19
shall have *n.* to bury them. 14:16
and *n.* doth return from.   23:14
that *n.* should serve himself. 34:9
n. should serve themselves.   10
to this day they drink *n.* but. 35:14
n. to sit on the throne of.   36:30
n. shall remain or escape. 42:17
n. shall return, but such as. 44:14
n. shall tread with shouting. 48:33
n. shall gather up him that. 49:5
land desolate, and *n.* shall. 50:3
arrows, *n.* shall return in vain.   9
and there shall be *n.*   20
camp against it, let *n.* thereof.   29
shall fall, and *n.* shall raise.   32
that *n.* shall remain in it. 51:62
                   Ezek 7:11
n. to comfort her.   *Lam* 1:2, 17
n. come to the solemn feasts.   4
fell, and *n.* did help her.   7
there is *n.* to comfort me.   21
but *n.* goeth to the battle. *Ezek* 7:14
peace, and there shall be *n.*   25
n. of my words shall be.   12:28
n. followeth thee to commit. 16:34
hath spoiled *n.* by violence. 18:7
for a man, but found *n.*   22:30
n. of his sins shall be.   33:16
mountains desolate, that *n.*   28
and *n.* did search or seek.   34:6
dwell safely, and *n.* make afraid. 28
   39:26; *Mi* 4:4; *Nah* 2:11
and have left *n.* of them. *Ezek* 39:28
n. found like Daniel.   *Dan* 1:19
n. stay his hand, or say to him. 4:35
the vision, but *n.* understood it. 8:27
n. shall stand before him. 11:16
shall come to his end, and *n.*   45
n. of the wicked shall.   12:10

n. shall deliver her out of my hands.
          Hos 2:10; 5:14
they called, *n.* at all would.   11:7
Lord your God, and *n.*   *Joel* 2:27
there be *n.* to quench it. *Amos* 5:6
n. that shall cast a cord by lot.
                     Mi 2:5
will say, *n.* evil can come.   3:11
he teareth in pieces, and *n.*   5:8
they cry, Stand, but *n.*   *Nah* 2:8
let *n.* of you imagine evil.
           Zech 7:10; 8:17
let *n.* deal treacherously. *Mal* 2:15
dry places, seeking rest and findeth *n.*
       Mat 12:43; *Luke* 11:24
witnesses came, yet found *n.*
       Mat 26:60; *Mark* 14:55
impart to him that hath *n. Luke* 3:11
to *n.* of them was Elias sent.   4:26
n. of them was cleansed save.   27
n. of them shall taste of.   14:24
n. is good, save one, that. 18:19
n. of you keepeth the law. *John* 7:19
if I had not done the works *n.* 15:24
n. is lost but the son of.   17:12
thou gavest me, I have lost *n.* 18:9
silver and gold have I *n. Acts* 3:6
he was fallen on *n.* of them.   8:16
Pray, that *n.* of these things.   24
the word to *n.* but Jews.   11:19
Gallio cared for none of.   18:17
n. of these things move me.   20:24
he should forbid *n.* of his.   24:23
if there be *n.* of these things. 25:11
n. other than the prophets.   26:22
not the Spirit, he is *n.*   *Rom* 8:9
n. of us liveth, and *n.* dieth.   14:7
I thank God, I baptized *n. 1 Cor* 1:14
whom *n.* of the princes of this.   2:8
wives be as though they had *n.* 7:29
but I have used *n.* of these.   9:15
give *n.* offence to the Jews. 10:32
and *n.* of them is without. 14:10
of the apostles saw I *n.*   *Gal* 1:19
see that *n.* render evil. *1 Thes* 5:15
give *n.* occasion to.   *1 Tim* 5:14
let *n.* of you suffer as a. *1 Pet* :15
fear *n.* of these things.   *Rev* 2:10

see **effect, like**

there is **none**
there is n. greater in.   *Gen* 39:9
there is n. that can interpret. 41:15
there is n. so discreet and wise.   39
Lord is God, *there is n.* else.
   Deut 4:35, 39; *1 Ki* 8:60; *Isa* 45:5
  6, 14, 18, 22; 46:9; *Mark* 12:32
for *there is n.* to redeem. *Ruth* 4:4
there is n. holy as the Lord; *there*
   is n. beside.   *1 Sam* 2:2
there is n. that sheweth me, *there*
   is n.   22:8
a shadow, *there is n.* abiding.
              1 Chr 29:15
there is n. that can deliver.
       Job 10:7; *Ps* 7:2; 71:11
they are corrupt, *there is n.* that.
       Ps 14:1, 3; 53:1, 3; *Rom* 3:12
for *there is n.* to help.   *Ps* 22:11
there is n. on earth I desire. 73:25
seek water, *there is n.*   *Isa* 41:17
there is n. sheweth, *there is n.*   26
there is n. that can deliver. 43:13
and *there is n.* to guide. 51:18
judgement, but *there is n.* 59:11
and *there is n.* that calleth on. 64:7
there is n. to stretch.   *Jer* 10:20
there is n. to plead.   30:13
there is n. that doth deliver us.
                    Lam 5:8
there is n. that holdeth. *Dan* 10:21
there is n. of them that. *Hos* 7:7
is forsaken, *there is n.*   *Amos* 5:2
there is n. upright among. *Mi* 7:2
that said in her heart, I am, and
   there is n.   *Zeph* 2:15
but *there is n.* warm.   *Hag* 1:6
there is n. good but one. *Mat* 19:17
                  Mark 10:18
there is n. other commandment.
                  Mark 12:31
there is n. of thy kindred. *Luke* 1:61
there is n. other name.   *Acts* 4:12
there is n. righteous, no. *Rom* 3:10

there is n. that understandeth, *there
is* n. seeketh God.　　　*Rom* 3:11
there is n. other God.　　*1 Cor* 8:4

there was **none**
there was n. of men.　　*Gen* 39:11
there was n. that could interpret.
　　　　　　　　　　41:8
but *there was* n. that could.　　24
until *there was* n. left.　*Num* 21:35
and *there was* n. to save. *Deut* 22:27
there was n. to part them.
　　　　　　　　2 Sam 14:6
there was n. to be so much praised
　as Absalom.　　　　　　25
they looked, but *there was* n. to save.
　　　22:42; *Ps* 18:41
there was n. that followed the house.
　　　1 Ki 12:20; *2 Ki* 17:18
to have pity, but *there was* n.
　　　　　　　　　Ps 69:20
and *there was* n. to bury them. 79:3
and *there was* n. to help.　107:12
when as yet *there was* n. of. 139:16
there was n. moved the. *Isa* 10:14
there was n. to answer.　　50:2
winepress alone, and of the people
　there was n. with me.　　63:3
and I wondered that *there was* n. 5
there was n. that could deliver.
　　　　　　　　　Dan 8:7

noon
shall dine with me at n.　*Gen* 43:16
against Joseph came at n.　　　25
tarried until after n.　　*Judg* 19:8
who lay on a bed at n.　*2 Sam* 4:5
on Baal even until n.　　*1 Ki* 18:26
at n. Elijah mocked them, and.　27
and they went out at n.　　20:16
he sat on her knees till n. *2 Ki* 4:20
at n. will I pray, and.　　*Ps* 55:17
thy flock to rest at n.　　*S of S* 1:7
arise, let us go up at n.　　*Jer* 6:4
the sun to go down at n. *Amos* 8:9
about n. there shone.　　*Acts* 22:6

noonday
thou shalt grope at n.　*Deut* 28:29
they grope in the n. as in. *Job* 5:14
be clearer than the n.　　　11:17
bring forth judgement as n. *Ps* 37:6
destruction that wasteth at n.　91:6
as the night, in midst of n. *Isa* 16:3
darkness shall be as the n.　58:10
we stumble at n. as in the.　59:10
have brought a spoiler at n. *Jer* 15:8
drive out Ashdod at n.　*Zeph* 2:4

noontide
hear the shouting at n.　*Jer* 20:16

Noph
the princes of *N.* are.　*Isa* 19:13
the children of *N.* have.　*Jer* 2:16
publish in *N.*　　　　　46:14
for *N.* shall be waste.　　19
I will cause their images to cease out
　of *N.*　　　　　*Ezek* 30:13
N. shall have distresses daily.　16

north
spread abroad to the n.　*Gen* 28:14
three oxen looking toward the n.
　　　1 Ki 7:25; *2 Chr* 4:4
were toward the n.　　*1 Chr* 9:24
he stretcheth out the n.　*Job* 26:7
and cold cometh out of the n.　37:9
cometh out of the n.: with God is. 22
the sides of the n., the city. *Ps* 48:2
n. and south, thou hast.　　89:12
turneth about to the n.　*Eccl* 1:6
if the tree fall toward the n.　11:3
sit in the sides of the n.　*Isa* 14:13
I will say to the n. Give up.　43:6
pot's face is toward the n. *Jer* 1:13
out of n. an evil break forth. 14; 4:6
　　　　　　　　　46:20
of the kingdoms of the n.　　15
these words toward the n.　3:12
together out of the land of the n. 18
for evil appeareth out of the n.　6:1
led Israel out of the n. country.
　　　　　　　23:8; 31:8
take all the families of the n.　25:9
all the kings of the n. far and.　26
stumble and fall toward the n. 46:6
sacrifice in the n. country.　10

delivered to people of n.　*Jer* 46:24
waters rise up out of the n.　47:2
out of n. cometh up a nation.　50:3
whirlwind came out of n.　*Ezek* 1:4
mine eyes the way toward the n. 8:5
toward the n. sat women weeping. 14
all faces from south to n.　　20:47
all flesh from south to n. will. 21:4
princes of the n. all of them. 32:30
the prospect toward the n. 40:44, 46
door was toward the n. 41:11; 42:4
and building toward the n.　42:1
their doors n.　　　　　4
chambers toward the n.　11, 13
chambers looked toward the n. 46:19
this holy oblation toward the n. 48:10
suburbs shall be toward the n.　17
come to the king of the n. *Dan* 11:6
more years than the king of the n. 8
fight with the king of the n.　11
the king of the n. shall return.　13
the king of the n. shall cast. 15, 40
but tidings out of the n. shall.　44
his hand against the n.　*Zeph* 2:13
black horses go into the n. *Zech* 6:6
quieted my spirit in the n.　　8
shall remove toward the n.　14:4
n. were three gates.　　*Rev* 21:13

from the **north**
gathered *from the* n.　　*Ps* 107:3
　Isa 49:12; *Jer* 16:15; 23:8
from the n. a smoke.　　*Isa* 14:31
I raised up one *from the* n.　41:25
evil *from the* n. and great. *Jer* 4:6
　6:22; 10:22; 50:9, 41; 51:48
a king of kings *from the* n. *Ezek* 26:7
to come up *from the* n. parts.　39:2
wander *from the* n. to the east.
　　　　　　　　Amos 8:12
from the land of *the* n.　*Zech* 2:6
from the n. and sit.　　*Luke* 13:29

north border
and this shall be your n. border.
　　　　　　　Num 34:7, 9

north quarter
Judah's border in n. quarter.
　　　　　　　　Josh 15:5
Togarmah of n. quarter. *Ezek* 38:6

north side
tabernacle on the n. side.　*Ex* 26:20
put the table on the n. side.　35
for n. side hangings of 100 cubits.
　　　　　　　27:11; 38:11
Dan shall be on n. side. *Num* 2:25
pitched on n. side of Ai. *Josh* 8:11
on the n. side of them.　*Judg* 7:1
feast on the n. side of Beth-el. 21:19
altar on n. side of altar. *2 Ki* 16:14
the n. side 500 reeds. *Ezek* 42:17
of the city on the n. side.　48:30

northern
break the n. iron, and.　*Jer* 15:12
remove from you the n.　*Joel* 2:20

northward
lift up thine eyes n. and eastward.
　　　　Gen 13:14; *Deut* 3:27
tabernacle n. without.　　*Ex* 40:22
the side of the altar n.　*Lev* 1:11
mountain, turn you n.　*Deut* 2:3
rock was situate n.　　*1 Sam* 14:5
lot came out n.　　　*1 Chr* 26:14
n. were four Levites a day.　17
n. was this image of.　　*Ezek* 8:5
brought me out of the gate n.　47:2
three gates n.; one gate of.　48:31

nose
that hath a flat n. shall.　*Lev* 21:18
put my hook in thy n.　*2 Ki* 19:28
　　　　　　　　Isa 37:29
his n. pierceth through.　*Job* 40:24
canst thou put a hook into his n.?
　　　　　　　　41:2
the wringing of the n.　*Pr* 30:33
thy n. is as the tower.　*S of S* 7:4
smell of thy n. like apples.　8*
a smoke in my n., a fire. *Isa* 65:5
the branch to their n.　*Ezek* 8:17
they shall take away thy n.　23:25

nose jewels
take away their tinkling ornaments,
　the rings and n. jewels. *Isa* 3:21

noses
n. have they, but they.　*Ps* 115:6
it shall stop the n.　*Ezek* 39:11*

nostrils
God breathed into man's n. *Gen* 2:7
all in whose n. was breath of.　7:22
with blast of thy n. waters. *Ex* 15:8
it come out at your n.　*Num* 11:20
went a smoke out of his n.
　　　　2 Sam 22:9; *Ps* 18:8
the blast of the breath of his n.
　　　　2 Sam 22:16; *Ps* 18:15
by breath of his n. they.　*Job* 4:9*
Spirit of God is in my n.　27:3
glory of his n. is terrible.　39:20*
out of his n. goeth smoke.　41:20
whose breath is in his n.　*Isa* 2:22
the breath of our n.　　*Lam* 4:20
stink of your camps to come into
　your n.　　　　*Amos* 4:10

not
I will afflict, but n. for.　*1 Ki* 11:39
upon me, and I am n.　　*Job* 7:8
he knoweth it n.　14:21; 35:15
n. unto us, O Lord, n.　*Ps* 115:1
to thy testimonies, and n.　119:36
the wicked are n.　　　*Pr* 12:7
buy the truth and sell it n.　23:23
riches are n. for ever. doth.　27:24
n. be an healer, make me n. *Isa* 3:7
n. as I have done to Samaria.　10:11
Moab, but his lies shall n.　16:6
but n. of me, n. of my spirit.　30:1
chosen thee, and n. cast.　41:9
thou shalt n. be forgotten.　44:21
let go my captives, n. for.　45:13
but n. in truth and.　　48:1
they may forget, yet will I n. 49:15
peace, and thou fearest me n. 57:11
of them that sought me n.　65:1
a wind, n. to fan.　　*Jer* 4:11
and they are n.　　　10:20
I commanded, but they did them n.
　　　　　　　　11:8
leave us n.　　　　　14:9
I sent them n. neither have.　14, 15
　　23:32; 29:9, 31; *Ezek* 13:6
and n. for good. *Jer* 21:10; 39:16
and n. out of the mouth.　23:16
of peace, and n. of evil.　29:11
n. of peace.　　　　30:5
because they were n.　　31:15
　　　　　　　　Mat 2:18
darkness, but n. into light. *Lam* 3:2
have sinned, and are n.　5:7
things shall n. come. *Ezek* 16:16
but n. by thy covenant.　61
n. according to your wicked. 20:44
art a man, and n. God.　28:2
they will n. do them.　33:31, 32
I do n. this for your sakes. 36:22, 32
shall be mighty, but n. by. *Dan* 8:24
but n. for himself.　　9:26
shall n. stand.　　　11:25
ye are n. my people, I will n. *Hos* 1:9
they return, but n. to the Most. 7:16
it shall n. be, saith.　*Amos* 7:3, 6
shall speak, and n. lie.　*Hab* 2:3
be ye n. as your fathers. *Zech* 1:4
n. by might nor power, but by.　4:6
I am the Lord, I change n.　*Mal* 3:6
be n. like hypocrites. *Mat* 6:5, 8, 16
and it fell n.　　　　7:25
and doeth them n.　　26
n. as the scribes.　29; *Mark* 1:22
have mercy, and n. *Mat* 9:13; 12:7
shall n. be forgiven to men.
　　　　　12:31, 32; *Luke* 12:10
saying, Lord, this shall n. *Mat* 16:22
but it shall n. be so among.　20:26
came n. to be ministered unto.　28
said, I go, sir, and went n.　21:30
but do n. ye after their works. 23:3
to have done, and n. to leave.　23
the end is n. yet.　　24:6
let him n. come down.　17
clothed me n., ye visited me n. 25:43
n. to one of these, did it n. to me. 45
n. on the feast day, lest there. 26:5
n. as I will, but as thou wilt.　39
　　　　　　　　Mark 14:36
see ye n.? hear ye n.? do ye n.
　remember?　　*Mark* 8:18

so it shall *n*. be among. *Mark* 10:43
but me ye have *n*. always. 14:7
he were the Christ or *n*. *Luke* 3:15
be healed, and *n*. on the. 13:14
I am *n*. as other men are. 18:11
woman, I know him *n*. 22:57
Peter said, Man, I am *n*. 58
I am *n*. the Christ. *John* 1:20; 3:28
n. because of thy saying. 4:42
ye will *n*. come to me, that ye. 5:40
I know ye have *n*. the love. 42
ye seek me *n*. because ye saw. 6:26
I came down, *n*. to do mine. 38
for I am *n*. alone, but I and the
  Father that sent me. 8:16; 16:32
I am *n*. of this world. 23
hireling, and *n*. the shepherd. 10:12
ye believe *n*., because ye are *n*. 26
said I *n*. unto thee, if thou? 11:40
this spake he, *n*. of himself, but. 51
and *n*. for that nation only. 52
this he said, *n*. that he cared. 12:6
I judge him *n*. for I came in. 47
Lord, *n*. my feet only, but. 13:9
ye are clean, but *n*. all. 10
if it were *n*. so. 14:2
Judas, *n*. Iscariot, . . . and *n*. unto? 22
I call you *n*. servants, but. 15:15
n. away, the Comforter will *n*. 16:7
for he shall *n*. speak of himself. 13
saying, *N*. this man. 18:40
touch me *n*. 20:17
n. to speak at all in the. *Acts* 4:18
have *n*. kept it. 7:53
he opened *n*. his mouth. 8:32
and shewed him, *n*. to all. 10:41
it is the voice of a god, and *n*. 12:22
I am *n*. he. 13:25
he be *n*. far from every one. 17:27
hold *n*. thy peace. 18:9
n. knowing the things that. 20:22
wolves enter in, *n*. sparing. 29
for I am ready *n*. to be. 21:13
I wist *n*. that he was the. 23:5
n. the hearers of the law. *Rom* 2:13
these having *n*. the law, are a. 14
and *n*. in the letter. 29
but *n*. before God. 4:2
to him that worketh *n*. but. 5
n. in circumcision, but. 10
and *n*. as it was by one that. 5:16
n., what I would, that do I *n*. 7:15
but ye are *n*. in the flesh, but. 8:9
how shall he *n*. with him give? 32
n. of the Jews only, but of. 9:24
was said, Ye are *n*. my people. 26
have they *n*. heard? yes. 10:18
n. to think of himself more. 12:3
ought to bear, and *n*. to please. 15:1
to preach, *n*. where Christ was. 20
to whom *n*. only I give thanks. 16:4
things which are *n*. *1 Cor* 1:28
eye hath *n*. seen, nor ear heard. 2:9
n. with meat. 3:2
ye *n*. carnal, and walk as men? 3, 4
n. to think of men above that. 4:6
and I will know, *n*. the speech. 19
n. with old leaven. 5:8
n. before the saints. 6:1
yet *n*. I, but the Lord. 7:10
to the rest speak I, *n*. the Lord. 12
am I *n*. an apostle? am I *n*. free?
  have I *n*. seen? 9:1
I therefore so run, *n*. as. 26
conscience, I say, *n*. thine. 10:29
have ye *n*. houses to eat in? 11:22
I am *n*. the eye, I am *n*. of. 12:16
yet *n*. I, but the grace of God. 15:10
n. as many which corrupt. *2 Cor* 2:17
n. with ink, *n*. in tables of. 3:3
n. that we are sufficient of. 5
n. as Moses, which put a vail. 13
we faint *n*. 4:1, 16
may be of God, and *n*. of us. 7
n. forsaken, cast down, but *n*. 9
we have an house *n*. made. 5:1
we walk by faith, *n*. by sight. 7
in appearance and *n*. in heart. 12
God comforted us, *n*. by his. 7:7
I rejoice, *n*. that ye were made. 9
I did it *n*. for his cause that had. 12
and this they did, *n*. as we hoped. 8:5
and *n*. according to that he hath *n*. 12

dare *n*. make ourselves. *2 Cor* 10:12
walked we *n*. in same spirit? 12:18
Paul an apostle, *n*. of men. *Gal* 1:1
I live, yet *n*. I. 2:20
and *n*. in another. 6:4
through faith, and that *n*. *Eph* 2:8
n. of works. 9
n. as fools, but as wise. 5:15
as to the Lord, and *n*. to men. 6:7
for we wrestle *n*. against flesh. 12
it is given to you, *n*. only. *Phil* 1:29
have obeyed, *n*. as in my. 2:12
and *n*. on him only, but on. 27
found in him, *n*. having mine. 3:9
n. as though I had already. 12
n. holding the head, from. *Col* 2:19
touch *n*. taste *n*. handle *n*. 21
on things above, *n*. on things. 3:2
to the Lord, and *n*. unto men. 23
that it was *n*. in vain. *1 Thes* 2:1
ye received it *n*. as word of. 13
therefore let us *n*. sleep as do. 5:6
all men have *n*. faith. *2 Thes* 3:2
n. because we have *n*. power.
n. given to wine, *n*. *1 Tim* 3:3
n. according to our works. *2 Tim* 1:9
 Tit 3:5
and *n*. to me only, but. *2 Tim* 4:8
please them, *n*. answering. *Tit* 2:9
n. now as a servant. *Philem* 16
n. without an oath, he. *Heb* 7:20
Lord pitched, and *n*. man. 8:2
n. without blood, which he. 9:7
n. made with hands, *n*. of this. 11
evidence of things *n*. seen. 11:1
died, *n*. having received the. 13
us should *n*. be made perfect. 40
then are ye bastards, *n*. sons. 12:8
n. with grief. 13:17
be a hearer, and *n*. a doer. *Jas* 1:23
n. by faith only. 2:24
offend *n*. in word. 3:2
yet ye have *n*., because ye ask *n*. 4:2
and doeth it *n*., to him it is sin. 17
n. a people, had *n*. *1 Pet* 2:10
be subject, *n*. only to the good. 18
reviled *n*. again, he threatened *n*. 23
better for them *n*. to. *2 Pet* 2:21
same hath *n*. the Father. *1 John* 2:23
n. as Cain. 3:12
n. that we loved God. 4:10
hath *n*. the Son, hath *n*. life. 5:12
there is a sin *n*. unto death. 17
these be sensual, having *n*. *Jude* 19
are apostles, and are *n*. *Rev* 2:2, 9
see thou do it *n*. 19:10; 22:9

see **able, afraid, ashamed, answered, believe, confounded, departed, fear, few, find, forsaken, give, given, hear, hearken, hid, is, knew, know, no, obey, obeyed, passed, see, seek, so, will, would**

if not

I will go down, and *if n*. *Gen* 18:21
and *if n*. tell me, that I. 24:49
if n. blot me, I pray, out. *Ex* 32:32
if n. let fire come. *Judg* 9:15, 20
and *if n*. I will take it. *1 Sam* 2:16
but *if n*. then we shall know. 6:9
if n. let Amnon go. *2 Sam* 13:26
if n.; speak thou. 17:6
but *if n*. it shall not be. *2 Ki* 2:10
if n. where, and who is he? *Job* 9:24
if n. hearken to me, hold. 33:33
and *if n*. forbear. *Zech* 11:12
if n. it shall turn to you. *Luke* 10:6
and *if n*. then thou shalt. 13:9

or not

journey prosperous *or n*. *Gen* 24:31
is Lord among us, *or n*.? *Ex* 17:7
word come to pass *or n*. *Num* 11:23
be wood therein *or n*. 13:20
fathers did keep it, *or n*. *Judg* 2:22

notable

(*Worthy of notice; remarkable*)
the goat had a *n*. horn. *Dan* 8:5
for it came up four *n*. ones. 8
had then a *n*. prisoner. *Mat* 27:16
before that *n*. day of the. *Acts* 2:20
a *n*. miracle hath been done. 4:16

note, -d

write it, and *n*. it in a. *Isa* 30:8*
that is *n*. in scripture. *Dan* 10:21*
n. that man, and have. *2 Thes* 3:14

note

of *n*. among the apostles. *Rom* 16:7

nothing

now *n*. will be restrained. *Gen* 11:6
only unto these men do *n*. for. 19:8
as we have done to thee *n*. 26:29
here also have I done *n*. to. 40:15
n. die that is the children's. *Ex* 9:4
let *n*. of it remain until. 12:10
ye shall eat *n*. leavened in. 20
gathered much, had *n*. over. 16:18
 2 Cor 8:15
if he have *n*. then he shall. *Ex* 23:3
there shall *n*. cast their young. 26
eat *n*. that is made of. *Num* 6:4
touch *n*. of theirs, lest ye be. 16:26
let *n*. hinder thee from. 22:16
lacked *n*. *Deut* 2:7; *Neh* 9:21
thou shalt save alive *n*. *Deu* 20:36
to the damsel thou shalt do *n*. 22:26
because he hath *n*. left him. 28:55
Joshua left *n*. undone. *Josh* 11:15
at the least such as before knew *n*.
  thereof. *Judg* 3:2
he rent him, and had *n*. in his. 14:6
Samuel told, and hid *n*. *1 Sam* 3:18
my father will do *n*. but will. 20:2
servant knew *n*. of all this. 22:15
n. was missed of all. 25:21; 30:19
she told him *n*. less or more. 36
poor man had *n*. save. *2 Sam* 12:3
that which doth cost me *n*. 24:24
victuals, they lacked *n*. *1 Ki* 4:27
there was *n*. in the ark save. 8:9
silver was *n*. accounted of in. 10:21
he answered *n*. 11:22; *Luke* 23:35
tell me *n*. but that which is true.
  1 Ki 22:16; *2 Chr* 18:15
fall *n*. to earth of word. *2 Ki* 10:10
n. in his house that he. 20:13
be carried into Babylon, *n*. shall be
  left. 17; *Isa* 39:2, 6
n. hid from Solomon. *2 Chr* 9:2
ye have *n*. to do with us. *Ezra* 4:3
they found *n*. to answer. *Neh* 5:8
we will restore, and require *n*. 12
for whom *n*. is prepared. 8:10
so that they lacked *n*. 9:21
Esther required *n*. but. *Esth* 2:15
yet all this availeth me *n*. 5:13
let *n*. fail of all that thou. 6:10
they go to *n*. and perish. *Job* 6:18
for ye are *n*. 21
of yesterday, and know *n*. 8:9
make my speech *n*. worth. 24:25
he hangeth the earth upon *n*. 26:7
it profiteth a man *n*. that he should
  delight himself with. 34:9
tried me and shalt find *n*. *Ps* 17:3
and mine age is as *n*. before. 39:5
he shall carry *n*. away. 49:17
who love thy law, and *n*. 119:165
simple, and knoweth *n*. *Pr* 9:13
of wickedness profit *n*. 10:2
desireth, and hath *n*. 13:4; 20:4
maketh himself rich, yet hath *n*. 13:7
if thou hast *n*. to pay, why? 22:27
whatsoever God doeth, *n*. *Eccl* 3:14
and he shall take *n*. of his. 5:15
so that he wanteth *n*. for his. 6:2
man should find *n*. after him. 7:14
all her princes shall be *n*. *Isa* 34:12
are as *n*. they are counted to him less
  than *n*. and vanity. 40:17; 41:29
the princes to *n*. 40:23; 41:11, 12
lest thou bring me to *n*. *Jer* 10:24
done *n*. of all that thou. 32:23
thee a thing, hide *n*. from me. 38:14
left of the poor which had *n*. 39:10
I will keep *n*. back from you. 42:4
destroy her utterly, let *n*. 50:26
is it *n*. to you, all ye? *Lam* 1:12
prophets that have seen *n*. *Ezek* 13:3
earth reputed as *n*. *Dan* 4:35
a wilderness, yea, and *n*. *Joel* 2:3
will a young lion cry out if he have
  taken *n*.? *Amos* 3:4
take up a snare, and have taken *n*. 5
surely the Lord will do *n*. 7

in comparison of it as n.? *Hag* 2:3
they have n. to eat. *Mat* 15:32
Mark 6:36; 8:1, 2
n. shall be impossible to you.
Mat 17:20; *Luke* 1:37
he found n. thereon but leaves.
Mat 21:19; *Mark* 11:13
answerest thou n.? *Mat* 26:62
he answered n. 27:12; *Mark* 14:60
61; 15:3, 4, 5
n. to do with that just. *Mat* 27:19
saw that he could prevail n. 24
see thou say n. to any. *Mark* 1:44
and had spent all, and was n. 5:26
take n. for their journey. 6:8
Luke 9:3
forth by n. but by prayer. *Mark* 9:29
those days he did eat n. *Luke* 4:2
toiled all night and taken n. 5:5
John 21:3
they had n. to pay, he. *Luke* 7:42
and n. shall by any means. 10:19
I have n. to set before him. 11:6
and lo, n. worthy of death. 23:15
Acts 23:29; 25:25; 26:31
man hath done n. amiss. *Luke* 23:41
man can receive n. except. *John* 3:27
Son can do n. of himself. 5:19, 30
gather, that n. be lost. 6:12
I should lose n. 39
quickeneth, the flesh profiteth n. 63
and they say n. unto him. 7:26
I do n. of myself. 8:28
he could do n. 9:33
ye know n. at all. 11:49
how ye prevail n.? behold. 12:19
this world hath n. in me. 14:30
for without me ye can do n. 15:5
that day ye shall ask me n. 16:23
have ye asked n. in my name. 24
in secret have I said ... 18:20
could say n. against it. *Acts* 4:14
finding n. how they might. 21
and go with them, doubting n. 10:20
11:12
be quiet, and do n. ras..ly. 19:36
I kept back n. that was. 20:20
that those things are n. 21:24
we will eat n. until we have. 23:14
fasting, having taken n. 27:33
to n. the understanding. *1 Cor* 1:19
I know n. by myself. 4:4
judge n. before the time. 5
he knoweth n. yet as he ought. 8:2
for though I preach, I have n. 9:16
not charity, I am n. 13:2; *2 Cor* 12:11
charity, it profiteth me n. *1 Cor* 13:3
having n. yet possessing. *2 Cor* 6:10
for we can do n. against. 13:8
in confidence added n. *Gal* 2:6
heir when a child, differeth n. 4:1
Christ shall profit you n. 5:2
n. be done through strife. *Phil* 2:3
every creature is good, n. *1 Tim* 4:4
doing n. by partiality. 5:21
proud, knowing n. 6:4
brought n. and we can carry n. out 7
n. be wanting unto them. *Tit* 3:13
thy mind would I do n. *Philem* 14
he left n. that is not put. *Heb* 2:8
Moses spake n. concerning. 7:14
for the law made n. perfect. 19
and entire, wanting n. *Jas* 1:4
let him ask in faith, n. wavering. 6
they went forth taking n. *3 John* 7

for nothing
shall go out free *for* n. *Ex* 21:2
that is profitable *for* n. *Isa* 44:10
was profitable *for* n. *Jer* 13:7, 10
salt have lost his savour, it is good
for n. *Mat* 5:13
lend, hoping *for* n. again. *Luke* 6:35
be careful *for* n. but by prayer.
Phil 4:6

in nothing
their time *in* n. else. *Acts* 17:21
receive damage by us *in* n. *2 Cor* 7:9
in n. am I behind chiefest, though I
be n. 12:11
in n. I shall be ashamed. *Phil* 1:20
and *in* n. terrified by your. 28

is nothing
there *is* n. at all beside. *Num* 11:6

is n. else save the sword. *Judg* 7:14
there *is* n. better than. *1 Sam* 27:1
and said, There *is* n. *1 Ki* 18:43
there *is* n. among my treasures.
2 Ki 20:15; *Isa* 39:4
it *is* n. with thee to help. *2 Chr* 14:11
this *is* n. else but sorrow. *Neh* 2:2
said, There *is* n. done. *Esth* 6:3
there *is* n. hid from the. *Ps* 19:6
there *is* n. froward or. *Pr* 8:8
there *is* n. better for a man.
Eccl 2:24; 3:22
begetteth a son. and there *is* n. 5:14
there *is* n. too hard. *Jer* 32:17
is n. covered that shall. *Mat* 10:26
Mark 4:22; *Luke* 12:2
swear by temple, it *is* n. *Mat* 23:16
swear by the altar, it *is* n. 18
there *is* n. from without a man that
can defile. *Mark* 7:15
myself, my honour *is* n. *John* 8:54
that there *is* n. unclean. *Rom* 14:14
is n., uncircumcision *is* n. *1 Cor* 7:19
we know that an idol *is* n. 8:4
when he *is* n. he deceiveth. *Gal* 6:3
are defiled *is* n. pure. *Tit* 1:15

of nothing
of n. your work nought. *Isa* 41:24
ye may have lack of n. *1 Thes* 4:12
increased, and have need of n.
Rev 3:17

notwithstanding
n. they hearkened not to. *Ex* 16:20
1 Sam 2:25; *2 Ki* 17:14
n. if he continue a day. *Ex* 21:21
n. ye would not go up. *Deut* 1:26
n. in thy days I will. *1 Ki* 11:12
n. I have spoken unto. *Jer* 35:14
n. being warned of God. *Mat* 2:22
n. he that is least in kingdom. 11:11
n. lest we should offend. 17:27
n. be sure of this that. *Luke* 10:11
n. in this rejoice, that spirits. 20
n. whether in pretence or. *Phil* 1:18
n. have well done, that ye. 4:14
n. she shall be saved in. *1 Tim* 2:15
n. Lord stood with me. *2 Tim* 4:17
n. ye give not those things. *Jas* 2:16
n. I have a few things. *Rev* 2:20

nought, *see* **naught**

nourish
[1] *To feed or maintain*, Gen 47:12.
[2] *To educate or bring up*, Acts
7:21. [3] *To instruct*, 1 Tim 4:6.
[4] *To cherish and comfort*, Ruth
4:15; Jas 5:5.
will I n. thee. *Gen* 45:11; 50:21
that man shall n. young. *Isa* 7:21†
nor do I n. up young men, nor. 23:4
an ash, the rain doth n. it. 44:14

nourished
Joseph n. his father. *Gen* 47:12
he brought and n. up. *2 Sam* 12:3
I have n. and brought up. *Isa* 1:2
she n. her whelps among. *Ezek* 19:2
n. in his father's house. *Acts* 7:20
Pharaoh's daughter n. him. 21
their country was n. by the. 12:20*
n. up in words of faith. *1 Tim* 4:6
have n. your hearts as in. *Jas* 5:5
n. for a time, times. *Rev* 12:14

nourisher
he shall be n. of thy old. *Ruth* 4:15

nourisheth
n. his flesh, as the Lord. *Eph* 5:29

nourishing
so n. them three years. *Dan* 1:5

nourishment
joints and bands having n. *Col* 2:19*

novice
not a n. lest being lifted. *1 Tim* 3:6

now
Adam said, This is n. *Gen* 2:23
I will go down n. and see. 18:21
n. will we deal worse with. 19:9
n. I know that thou fearest. 22:12
thou art n. the blessed of the. 26:29
what shall I do n. to thee? 27:37
n. will I praise the Lord. 29:35
Laban, and stayed there till n. 32:4

if it be so n. do this. *Gen* 43:11
so n. it was not you that sent. 45:8
about cattle from youth till n. 46:34
not such hail been in Egypt even till
n. *Ex* 9:18
go n. ye that are men, and. 10:11
yet n. if thou wilt forgive. 32:32
heal her n. O God, I. *Num* 12:13
this people from Egypt till n. 14:19
I shall see him, but not n. 24:17
Lord's host am I n. come. *Josh* 5:14
tell me n. what thou hast done. 7:19
are ye come to me n.? *Judg* 11:7
n. I know that the Lord will. 17:13
thou shalt give it me n. *1 Sam* 2:16
but n. the Lord saith, Be it far. 30
honour me I pray thee. 15:30
what have I n. done? 17:29
son, let us not all n. go. *2 Sam* 13:25
I n. also be thy servant. 15:34
let us n. fall into the hand. 24:14
cut off, but what? even n. *1 Ki* 14:14
it is enough, n. O Lord, take. 19:4
he said, Why are ye n. turned back?
2 Ki 1:5
was her's since she went till n. 8:6
know n. there shall fall to. 10:10
am I n. come up without the Lord.
18:25; *Isa* 36:10
n. have I brought it to pass.
2 Ki 19:35; *Isa* 37:26
remember n. how I have walked.
2 Ki 20:3; *Isa* 38:3
it n. known to the king. *Ezra* 4:13
even till n. hath it been building. 5:16
n. for a little space grace been. 9:8
n. there is hope in Israel. 10:2
put forth thy hand. *Job* 1:11; 2:5
n. it is come upon thee. 4:5
for n. ye are nothing, ye see. 6:21
lay down n. 17:3
where is n. my hope? 15
and if it be not so n. 24:25
n. I am their son. 30:9
heard of thee, but n. my eye. 42:5
n. will I arise, saith the. *Ps* 12:5
n. know I that the Lord saveth. 20:6
n. Lord, what wait I for, my. 39:7
why heathen say, Where is n.? 115:2
save n. I beseech thee, O. 118:25
but n. have I kept thy word. 119:67
do this n. my son, and. *Pr* 6:3
n. she is without, n. in the. 7:12
go to n. *Eccl* 2:1
that which n. is shall all be. 16
what hath been is n. 3:15
I will rise n. and go. *S of S* 3:2
n. go to, I will tell you. *Isa* 5:5
but n. the Lord hath spoken. 16:14
let them tell thee n. 19:12
what aileth thee n. that thou? 22:1
n. will I rise, n. will I lift up. 33:10
but n. O Lord, thou art our. 64:8
n. what hast thou to do? *Jer* 2:18
n. will I give sentence against. 4:12
the word of the Lord let it n. 17:15
turn n. every one from his. 25:5
ask ye n. and see whether a. 30:6
ye were n. turned, and had. 34:15
return ye n. every man from. 35:15
woe is me n.! for the Lord hath. 45:3
Daniel, to thee am I n. *Dan* 10:11
it better with me than n. *Hos* 2:7
and n. they sin more and more. 13:2
turn ye n. from your evil. *Zech* 1:4
n. have I seen with mine eyes. 9:8
prove me n. herewith. *Mal* 3:10
n. all this was done. *Mat* 1:22
days of John the Baptist, till n. 11:12
Sleep on n. 26:45
thinkest that I cannot n. pray. 53
let him n. come down from. 27:42
let him deliver him n. 43
so that the ship was n. *Mark* 4:37
n. lettest thy servant. *Luke* 2:29
which n. of these three was? 10:36
all things are n. ready. 14:17
but n. he that hath a purse. 22:36
draw out n. and bear. *John* 2:8
hast kept the good wine until n. 10
he whom thou n. hast is not. 4:18
hour cometh, and n. is. 23; 5:25
blind, how then doth he n. see? 9:19
what I do thou knowest not n. 13:7

now

ye cannot bear them n. *John* 16:12
ye n. therefore have sorrow. 22
lo, n. speakest thou plainly. 29
n. are we sure. 30
do ye n. believe ? 31
I kept them, and n. come I. 17:13
this is n. the third time that. 21:14
shed forth this which ye n. *Acts* 2:33
n. when they heard this, were. 37
and n. Lord, behold their. 4:29
n. I know of a surety, the Lord. 12:11
n. as soon as it was day. 18
n. why tarriest thou ? arise. 22:16
the Gentiles, to whom n. I. 26:17
but n. being made free. *Rom* 6:22
n. then it is no more I that do it.7:17
n. it is high time to awake. 13:11
n. ye are full, n. ye are. *1 Cor* 4:8
n. are they holy. 7:14
n. I know in part. 13:12
for I will not see you n. by. 16:7
said before, so say I n. *Gal* 1:9
do I n. persuade men or God ? 10
I n. live in the flesh, I live. 2:20
n. made perfect by the flesh ? 3:3
desire to be present with you n. 4:20
but as then, even so it is n. 29
n. to principalities. *Eph* 3:10
were darkness, but n. are ye. 5:8
from the first day until n. *Phil* 1:5
obeyed, but n. much more. 2:12
but n. ye also put off. *Col* 3:8
n. we live, if ye stand. *1 Thes* 3:8
promise of the life that n. *1 Tim* 4:8
for I am n. ready to be. *2 Tim* 4:6
not n. as a servant, but. *Philem* 16
n. we see not yet all things. *Heb* 2:8
go to n. ye that say, to-day.*Jas* 4:13
go to n., ye rich men, weep and. 5:1
though n. ye see him not. *1 Pet* 1:8
but are n. the people of God. 2:10
because the true light n. *1 John* 2:8
n. are we the sons of God, it. 3:2
and even n. already is it in the. 4:3

now therefore
n. *therefore* restore the. *Gen* 20:7
n. *therefore* my husband. 29:32
n. *therefore* and let us slay. 37:20
n. *therefore* fear Lord. *Josh* 24:14
n. *therefore* behold king ye have.
1 Sam 12:13
n. *therefore* stand and see this. 16
shall I not *therefore* n. require ?
2 Sam 4:11
n. *therefore* let my life. *2 Ki* 1:14
n. *therefore* advise thyself, what
word I shall bring. *1 Chr* 21:12
send me n. *therefore* a man cunning
to work in gold. *2 Chr* 2:7
n. *therefore*, O God. *Neh* 6:9
n. *therefore* be content. *Job* 6:28
be wise n. *therefore*, O ye kings.
Ps 2:10
n. *therefore* be not mockers.
Isa 28:22
n. *therefore* what have I here ? 52:5
n. *therefore* amend your. *Jer* 26:13
n. *therefore* why hast thou not reproved Jeremiah ? 29:27
n. *therefore* know certainly. 42:22
n. *therefore*, O our God. *Dan* 9:17
therefore also n. saith the Lord.
Joel 2:12
therefore n. shall they go captive.
Amos 6:7
n. *therefore* hear thou word. 7:16
n. *therefore* are we all present.
Acts 10:33
n. *therefore* why tempt ye ? 15:10
n. *therefore* depart, and go. 16:36
n. *therefore* there is a fault.
1 Cor 6:7
n. *therefore* perform. *2 Cor* 8:11
n. *therefore* ye are no more.
Eph 2:19

number, substantive
I being few in n. they. *Gen* 34:30
for it was without n. 41:49
lamb according to n. *Ex* 12:4
gather manna, according to n. 16:16
nothing barren, n. of thy days. 23:26
n. of years after the jubile, the n.
of years of the. *Lev* 25:15, 16, 50

shall make you few in n. *Lev* 26:22
n. of their names. *Num* 1:2, 18, 22
n. of males from. 3:22, 28, 34, 40, 43
odd n. of them is to be redeemed. 48
your whole n. from twenty. 14:29
after the n. of days ye searched. 34
n. ye shall prepare . . . to every one
according to their n. 15:12
who can count the n. of fourth ? 23:10
offerings shall be according to their
n. 29:18; 21:24, 27, 30, 33, 37
of their portion was in n. 31:36
left few in number among heathen.
Deut 4:27; 28:62
ye were more in n. than. 7:7
him to be beaten by a certain n. 25:2
according to the n. of Israel. 32:8
every man of you a stone, according
to n. *Josh* 4:5, 8
they and their camels without n.
Judg 6:5; 7:12
the n. of them that lapped. 7:6
to the n. of them that danced. 21:23
the n. of the lords of the. *1 Sam* 6:4
to the n. of all the cities. 18
went over by n. twelve. *2 Sam* 2:15
and toes twenty-four in n. 21:20
may know the n. of the people. 24:2*
Joab gave up the sum of the n.
12 stones according to n. *1 Ki* 18:31
n. was in the days of. *1 Chr* 7:2
the n. of them after their. 9*, 40
the n. of mighty men whom. 11:11
and silver, there is no n. 22:16
their n. by their polls, man. 23:3
set feasts by n. 31
n. of the workmen. 25:1
the n. that were instructed in. 7
but David took not the n. of. 27:23
people were without n. *2 Chr* 12:3
the whole n. of the chief of. 26:12
n. of the burnt offerings. 29:32
a great n. of priests sanctified. 30:24
is the n. of the vessels. *Ezra* 1:9
the n. of the men of the people. 2:2
daily burnt offerings by n 3:4
according to the n. of tribes. 6:17
by n. and by weight of. 8:34
the n. of those slain in Shushan.
Esth 9:11
offered according to the n. *Job* 1:5
let it not come into the n. 3:6
things without n. 5:9; 9:10
n. of his months are with thee. 14:5
the n. of years is hidden in. 15:20
is there any n. of his armies ? 25:3
declare to him the n. of my. 31:37
pieces mighty men without n. 34:24*
neither can the n. of his years. 36:26
n. of thy days is great. 38:21
were but a few men in n. *Ps* 105:12
caterpillars, and that without n. 34
are more in n. than the sand. 139:18
he telleth the n. of the stars. 147:4
queens and virgins without n.
S of S 6:8
residue of n. of archers. *Isa* 21:17
bringeth out their host by n. 40:26
furnish the drink offering to that n.
65:11*
n. of thy cities are thy gods. *Jer* 2:28
forgotten me days without n. 32
n. of thy cities, n. of streets. 11:13
a small n. that escape sword. 44:28
the n. of the days. *Ezek* 4:4; 5:9
thou shalt take a few in n. and. 5:3
understood by books the n. *Dan* 9:2
n. of Israel shall be as the sand.
Hos 1:10; *Rom* 9:27
up strong and without n. *Joel* 1:6
is a great n. of carcases. *Nah* 3:3*
Judas, being of the n. of. *Luke* 22:3
the men sat down, in n. 5000.
John 6:10; *Acts* 4:4
the n. of the names. *Acts* 1:15*
to Theudas a n. of men. 5:36
when the n. of disciples. 6:1, 7
a great n. believed and. 11:21
were increased in n. daily. 16:5
dare not make ourselves of the n.
2 Cor 10:12
not a widow be taken into the n.
1 Tim 5:9*
n. of them was 10,000. *Rev* 5:11

I heard the n. of them which. *Rev* 7:4
the n. of the army of the. 9:16
n. of his name. 13:17
count the n. of the beast; for it is
the n. of a man; and his n. is 666. 18
had victory over n. of beast. 15:2
n. of Gog is as the sand of. 20:8

number, verb
if a man can n. the dust. *Gen* 13:16
if thou be able to n. them. 15:5
he shall n. seven days for. *Lev* 15:13
shall n. to herself seven days. 28
seventh sabbath shall ye n. 23:16
thou shalt n. seven sabbaths. 25:8
Aaron shall n. them by. *Num* 1:3
only thou shalt not n. the tribe. 49
n. the children of Levi. 3:15
n. all the firstborn of the males. 40
till 50 years old n. them. 4:23, 30
of Merari thou shalt n. them. 29
Moses and Aaron did n. them. 37, 41
shalt thou n. begin to n. *Deut* 16:9
n. and see who is gone. *1 Sam* 14:17
to say, Go n. Israel. *2 Sam* 24:1
go now and n. the people. 2, 4
1 Chr 21:2
n. thee an army like. *1 Ki* 20:25
David to n. Israel. *1 Chr* 21:1
Joab began to n. but he. 27:24
who can n. the clouds ? *Job* 38:37
canst thou n. the months ? 39:2
So teach us to n. our days. *Ps* 90:12
therefore will I n. you. *Isa* 65:12*
which no man could n. *Rev* 7:9

numbered
thy seed also be n. *Gen* 13:16
it shall not be n. for. 16:10; 32:12
them that are n. *Ex* 30:13, 14
n. of the congregation. 38:25, 26
n. them in the wilderness. *Num* 1:19
those that were n. 21, 23, 44, 46; 2:4
13, 15, 19, 21, 23, 26, 28, 30
the Levites were not n. 1:47; 2:33
all that were n. in the camp. 2:9
were n. in camp of Reuben. 16
n. of Ephraim. 24
n. in camp of Dan. 31
Moses n. them. 3:16, 42
n. of the Levites were 22,000. 3:39
they n. of the sons of the. 4:34, 37
n. of the Gershonites. 38, 41
n. of the sons of Merari. 42, 45
these whom Moses and Aaron n. 45
and over them that were n. 7:2
in wilderness, all that were n. 14:29
these were n. of the children. 26:51
n. of the Levites. 57
Moses and Eleazar n. 63
Joshua rose early and n. *Josh* 8:10*
of Benjamin were n. *Judg* 20:15
he n. them in Bezek. *1 Sam* 11:8
Saul n. people in Telaim. 15:4
David n. the people. *2 Sam* 24:10
smote him after he had n. 24:10
people that cannot be n. *1 Ki* 3:8
sheep and oxen that could not be n.
8:5; *2 Chr* 5:6
then he n. the princes. *1 Ki* 20:15*
Ben-haded n. the Syrians. 26*
Israel were n. and were like. 27
and king Jehoram n. all. *2 Ki* 3:6
the people to be n. *1 Chr* 21:17
were n. from thirty years. 23:3, 27
Solomon n. all the. *2 Chr* 2:17
n. them from twenty years old. 25:5
Cyrus n. the vessels. *Ezra* 1:8
more than can be n. *Ps* 40:5
is wanting cannot be n. *Eccl* 1:15
ye have n. the houses of. *Isa* 22:10
he was n. with the transgressors; and
he bare. 53:12; *Mark* 15:28
as the host of heaven cannot be n.
Jer 33:22
God hath n. thy kingdom. *Dan* 5:26
sand, which cannot be n. *Hos* 1:10
hairs of your head are all n.
Mat 10:30; *Luke* 12:7
for he was n. with us. *Acts* 1:17
Matthias was n. with the eleven. 26

numberest
when thou n. that there be no plague
when thou n. *Ex* 30:12
for now thou n. my steps. *Job* 14:16

numbering
corn until he left *n*. Gen 41:49
after the *n*. wherewith. 2 Chr 2:17

numbers
these are the *n*. of the. 1 Chr 12:23
are the *n*. of them. 2 Chr 17:14
for I know not the *n*. Ps 71:15

Nun, *see* **Joshua**

nurse, *substantive*
Rebekah and her *n*. Gen 24:59
but Deborah, Rebekah's *n*. 35:8
call to thee a *n*. of Hebrew? Ex 2:7
the child, and became *n*. Ruth 4:16
n. took him up and fled. 2 Sam 4:4
they hid him and his *n*. 2 Ki 11:2
2 Chr 22:11
were gentle, as a *n*. 1 Thes 2:7

nurse
she may *n*. the child. Ex 2:7
child away, and *n*. it for me. 9

nursed
took the child, and *n*. it. Ex 2:9
thy daughters shall be *n*. Isa 60:4*

nursing
carry them in thy bosom, as a *n*.
Num 11:12
kings shall be thy *n*. fathers, queens
thy *n*. mothers. Isa 49:23

nurture
bring them up in the *n*. of. Eph 6:4*

nuts
carry down a present, *n*. Gen 43:11
into the garden of *n*. S of S 6:11

Nymphas
salute *N*. and the church. Col 4:15

O

oak
hid the gods under the *o*. Gen 35:4
Deborah was buried under an *o*. 8
up there under an *o*. Josh 24:26
angel of the Lord sat under an *o*.
Judg 6:11
mule went under an *o*. 2 Sam 18:9
Absalom hanged in an *o*. 10
alive in the *o*. 14
man of God under an *o*. in. 1 Ki 13:14
their bones under *o*. in. 1 Chr 10:12
as an *o*. whose leaf fadeth. Isa 1:30
teil tree, or *o*. whose substance. 6:13
he taketh the cypress and *o*. 44:14
idols under every thick *o*. Ezek 6:13

oaks
be ashamed of the *o*. Isa 1:29
day of the Lord on all the *o*. 2:13
of *o*. of Bashan have they. Ezek 27:6
burn incense upon the hills under *o*.
Hos 4:13
was strong as the *o*. Amos 2:9
fir tree, howl, O ye *o*. Zech 11:2

oar
all that handle the *o*. Ezek 27:29

oars
shall go no galley with *o*. Isa 33:21
Bashan they made thy *o*. Ezek 27:6

oath
(*A solemn appeal to God to witness the truth of a declaration.
It is also used of a solemn affirma-
tion not invoking the Deity. The
modern use of the word for profanity is not found in the Bible*)
Oaths were forbidden to be taken
by the Israelites. [1] Idolatrously,
in the name of any false gods, or in
the name of inanimate things,
Josh 23:7; Jas 5:12. [2] Deceitfully, Jer 42:5, 20. [3] Falsely,
Lev 6:3; 19:12. [4] Rashly, Lev
5:4; Mat 14:7.
clear from this my *o*. Gen 24:8, 41
o. which I sware to Abraham. 26:3
Deut 7:8; Ps 105:9; Jer 11:5
let there be now an *o*. betwixt us.
Gen 26:28
Joseph took an *o*. of children. 50:25
o. of the Lord shall be. Ex 22:11

shall pronounce with an *o*. Lev 5:4
shall charge her by an *o*. Num 5:19*
Lord make thee a curse and an *o*. 21
an *o*. to bind his soul. 30:2, 10
every binding *o*. to afflict soul. 13
his *o*. which the Lord maketh with.
Deut 29:12
you only do I make this *o*. Josh 2:17
blameless of this thine *o*. 2:17
be on us, because of the *o*. 9:20
Israel had made a great *o*. Judg 21:5
people feared the *o*. 1 Sam 14:26
charged them with the *o*. 27, 28
king spared Mephibosheth, because
of *o*. 2 Sam 21:7
hast thou not kept the *o*.? 1 Ki 2:43
o. be laid on him, and the *o*. come.
8:31; 2 Chr 6:22
he took an *o*. of the. 1 Ki 18:10
Jehoiada took an *o*. of. 2 Ki 11:4
be mindful of his *o*. to. 1 Chr 16:16
Judah rejoiced at the *o*. 2 Chr 15:15
Nehemiah took an *o*. of. Neh 5:12
they entered into an *o*. to walk. 10:29
in regard of the *o*. of God. Eccl 8:2
as he that feareth an *o*. 9:2
which hast despised the *o*.
Ezek 16:59; 17:18, 19
hath taken an *o*. of him. 17:13
that made him king, whose *o*. 16
us, and *o*. written in law. Dan 9:11
love no false *o*. for this. Zech 8:17
he promised with an *o*. Mat 14:7
for the *o*.'s sake. 9; Mark 6:26
he denied with an *o*. Mat 26:72
the *o*. which he sware. Luke 1:73
sworn with an *o*. to him. Acts 2:30
bound themselves with an *o*. 23:21*
an *o*. for confirmation is. Heb 6:16
God confirmed it by an *o*. 17
an *o*. he was made priest. 7:20, 21
the *o*. which was since the law. 28
the earth, nor any other *o*. Jas 5:12

oaths
them that have sworn *o*. Ezek 21:23
naked, according to the *o*. Hab 3:9
to the Lord thine *o*. Mat 5:33

Obadiah
Ahab called *O*., now *O*. 1 Ki 18:3
O. took an hundred prophets. 4
as *O*. was in the way, behold. 7
so *O*. went to meet Ahab, and. 16
son of Izrahiah, *O*. 1 Chr 3:21
son of Izrahiah, *O*. 7:3
O. son of Azel. 8:38; 9:44
O. the son of Shemaiah, the. 9:16
of Gadites men of might, *O*. 12:9
Ishmaiah son of *O*. 27:19
to his princes, to *O*. to. 2 Chr 17:7
Jahath and *O*. the Levites. 34:12
O. son of Jehiel went up. Ezra 8:9
O. sealed. Neh 10:5
O. was a porter. 12:25
the vision of *O*. Thus saith. Ob 1

Obed
called his name *O*. Ruth 4:17
Boaz begat *O*. 21; 1 Chr 2:12
Mat 1:5
Ephlal begat *O*. 1 Chr 2:37
O. one of David's valiant. 11:47
Shemaiah begat *O*. 26:7
took Azariah son of *O*. 2 Chr 23:1
which was the son of *O*. Luke 3:32

Obed-edom
the ark into the house of *O*.
2 Sam 6:10, 11; 1 Chr 13:13, 14
Lord blessed the house of *O*.
2 Sam 6:11, 12; 1 Chr 13:14
ark from house of *O*. into city of.
2 Sam 6:12; 1 Chr 15:25
O. a porter. 1 Chr 15:18, 24
O. with harp. 21
O.; and Jeiel with psalteries. 16:5
O. with their brethren, *O*. also. 38
sons of *O*. 26:4, 8
sons of *O*. fit for service. 6
the lot southward fell to *O*. 15
vessels found with *O*. 2 Chr 25:24

obedience
(*Subjection to the authority of
another, whether to God or to a
human being. In the Bible the*

*word is used most often in the sense
of subjection to the will of God, and
to his commands. It is used in
speaking of Jesus, who always
did the will of God.
It is also used of hearts and inanimate things, which are subject
to God's controlling power*)
for *o*. to the faith among. Rom 1:5
by the *o*. of one shall many. 5:19
of sin to death, or of *o*. unto. 6:16
your *o*. is come abroad unto. 16:19
known to all nations for the *o*. 26
women are commanded to be under
o. 1 Cor 14:34*
he remembereth the *o*. 2 Cor 7:15
bringing every thought to the *o*. 10:5
all disobedience, when your *o*. 6
confidence in thy *o*. Philem 21
learned he *o*. by the things. Heb 5:8
through sanctification of the Spirit to
o. 1 Pet 1:2

obedient
we will do, and be *o*. Ex 24:7
that Israel may be *o*. Num 27:20
shall be *o*. to his voice. Deut 4:30
because ye would not be *o*. 8:20*
strangers shall be *o*. 2 Sam 22:45
reprover upon an *o*. ear. Pr 25:12
if *o*. ye shall eat the good. Isa 1:19
nor were they *o*. to his law. 42:24
priests were *o*. to the faith. Acts 6:7
to make Gentiles *o*. Rom 15:18*
know whether ye be *o*. 2 Cor 2:9
servants, be *o*. to your masters.
Eph 6:5; Tit 2:9*
Christ became *o*. unto. Phil 2:8
wives, be *o*. Tit 2:5*
children, be *o*. 1 Pet 1:14

obeisance
(*A bodily movement in token of
respect and submission*)
your sheaves made *o*. Gen 37:7
eleven stars made *o*. to me. 9
bowed and made *o*. to Joseph. 43:28
Moses did *o*. to his. Ex 18:7
fell down and did *o*. 2 Sam 1:2
the woman of Tekoah did *o*. 14:4
man came nigh to do him *o*. 15:5
Bath-sheba did *o*. to king. 1 Ki 1:16
the princes of Judah made *o*. to the
king. 2 Chr 24:17

obey
(*Revisions frequently substitute
for this the word hearken*)
Gen 27:8, 13, 43
therefore, my son, *o*. my voice.
Lord, that I should *o*. him? Ex 5:2
now if ye will *o*. my voice. 19:5
o. his voice. 23:21
if thou shalt indeed *o*. his voice. 22
ye *o*. commands of Lord. Deut 11:27
o. his voice. 13:4; 27:10; 30:2, 8
1 Sam 12:14
thou mayest *o*. his voice. 30:20
Lord's voice will we *o*. Josh 24:24
to *o*. voice of Samuel. 1 Sam 8:19
to *o*. is better than sacrifice. 15:22
and refused to *o*. neither. Neh 9:17
if they *o*. and serve him. Job 36:11
hear, they shall *o*. me. Ps 18:44
eye that despiseth to *o*. Pr 30:17
of Ammon shall *o*. them. Isa 11:14
o. my voice, and I will be your God.
Jer 7:23; 11:4, 7
o. the voice of the Lord your God.
26:13; 38:20; Zech 6:15
Rechabites *o*. their. Jer 35:14
o. the voice of Lord our God ... well
with us when we *o*. the. 42:6
dominions shall serve and *o*. him.
Dan 7:27
is this, that even winds and sea *o*.?
Mat 8:27; Mark 4:41; Luke 8:25
the unclean spirits *o*. Mark 1:27
plucked up, and it shall *o*. Luke 17:6
ought to *o*. God rather. Acts 5:29
hath given to them that *o*. him. 32
that *o*. unrighteousness. Rom 2:8
that ye should *o*. it in the. 6:12
yourselves servants to *o*., his servants
ye are to whom ye *o*. 16

children, o. your parents.   *Eph* 6:1
    Col 3:20
servants, o. in all things.   *Col* 3:22
put them in mind to o.   *Tit* 3:1
salvation to all that o. him. *Heb* 5:9
o. them that have the rule.   13:17
bits in horses' mouths, that they may
o.   *Jas* 3:3

not obey, obey not
if ye will *not* o. the commandments.
  Deut 11:28; 28:62; *1 Sam* 12:15
  Job 36:12; *Jer* 12:17; 18:10
will *not* o. the voice. *Deut* 21:18, 20
didst thou *not* o.?   *1 Sam* 15:19
will *not* o. the Lord.   *Jer* 42:13
might *not* o. thy voice.   *Dan* 9:11
our fathers would *not* o.   *Acts* 7:39
and do *not* o. the truth.   *Rom* 2:8
who hath bewitched you, that ye
  should *not* o.?   *Gal* 3:1; 5:7
vengeance on them that o. *not* the
  gospel.   *2 Thes* 1:8
if any man o. *not* our word.   3:14
if any o. *not* the word.   *1 Pet* 3:1
be of them that o. *not* gospel ? 4:17

obeyed
all nations be blessed, because thou
  hast o.   *Gen* 22:18; 26:5
that Jacob o. his father.   28:7
have o. my voice in all.   *1 Sam* 15:20
Saul said, I have o.   24
I feared the people, and o.   24
handmaid hath o. thy voice.   28:21
all Israel o. Solomon.   *1 Chr* 29:23
they o. the words of.   *2 Chr* 11:4
then they o. and let.   *Jer* 34:10
thus have we o. the voice.   35:8, 10
because ye o. the commandment. 18
neither have we o. voice.   *Dan* 9:10
the people o. the voice.   *Hag* 1:12
many as o. Theudas.   *Acts* 5:36, 37
have o. from heart that.   *Rom* 6:17
ye have o., not as in my presence
  only.   *Phil* 2:12
by faith Abraham o.   *Heb* 11:8
Sarah o. Abraham.   *1 Pet* 3:6

not obeyed
because they o. not.   *Josh* 5:6
but ye have *not* o. my voice.
  Judg 2:2; 6:10
thou hast *not* o. the voice. *1 Ki* 20:36
because they o. *not* the.   *2 Ki* 18:12
not o. the voice of my teachers.
  Pr 5:13
ye have *not* o. my voice.   *Jer* 3:13
  25; 42:21; 43:4, 7; 44:23
have *not* o. my voice.   9:13; 11:8
  17:23; 32:23; 40:3; *Dan* 9:10, 14
she o. *not* the voice.   *Zeph* 3:2
not all o. the gospel.   *Rom* 10:16

obeyedst
because thou o. not the voice of.
  1 Sam 28:18
that thou o. *not* my voice. *Jer* 22:21

obeyeth
who that o. the voice ?   *Isa* 50:10
this is a nation that o.   *Jer* 7:28
cursed be the man that o. not. 11:3

obeying
their fathers o., but they. *Judg* 2:17
in sacrifice, as in o.   *1 Sam* 15:22
your souls in o. the truth. *1 Pet* 1:22

object
and o. if they had aught. *Acts* 24:19

oblation
(*An offering. From the Latin
oblatus, offered*)
an o. of a meat offering baken.
  Lev 2:4, 5, 7, 13
as for o. of the firstfruits.   2:12
if his o. be a sacrifice of.   3:1
offer one out of the whole o.   7:14
he shall bring his o. to the Lord. 29
that will offer his o. for all.   22:18
every o. of theirs shall.   *Num* 18:9
we have brought an o. for.   31:50
Egyptians shall do o.   *Isa* 19:21
impoverished that he hath no o. 40:20
offereth an o. as if he offered.   66:3
they offer an o. I will.   *Jer* 14:12†
o. shall be the priest's.   *Ezek* 44:30

divide the land, offer an o. *Ezek* 45:1
this is the o. ye shall offer. 13; 48:9
  20, 21
give this o. for the prince in.   45:16
they should offer an o. to. *Dan* 2:46
time of the evening o.   9:21
shall cause o. to cease.   27

oblations
Israel to offer their o.   *Lev* 7:38
to distribute the o. of.   *2 Chr* 31:14
bring no more vain o. unto. *Isa* 1:13
require the firstfruits of your o.
  Ezek 20:40
every sort of your o. shall be. 44:30

obscure
lamp shall be put out in o. darkness.
  Pr 20:20*

obscurity
blind shall see out of o.   *Isa* 29:18
then shall thy light rise in o. 58:10*
we wait for light, but behold o. 59:9*

observation
God cometh not with o. *Luke* 17:20

observe
(*Frequently means to keep, or to
celebrate, and is so rendered in the
Revisions*)
ye shall o. the feast of unleavened.
  Ex 12:17, 24; *Deut* 16:1
o. the sabbath.   *Ex* 31:16
o. thou that which I command thee.
  34:11; *Deut* 12:28; 24:8
o. feast of weeks.   *Ex* 34:22
nor shall ye use enchantments, o.
  times.   *Lev* 19:26
ye shall o. all my statutes.   37
  2 Chr 7:17; *Neh* 1:5; *Ps* 105:45
  Ezek 37:24
sacrifice shall ye o.   *Num* 28:2
o. the feast of tabernacles seven
  days.   *Deut* 16:13
men did diligently o.   *1 Ki* 20:33
whoso is wise, and will o. *Ps* 107:43
o. it with my whole heart.   119:34
and let thine eyes o.   *Pr* 23:26*
crane and swallow o. time. *Jer* 8:7
neither o. their judgements nor.
  Ezek 20:18
as a leopard by the way will I o.
  them.   *Hos* 13:7*
that o. lying vanities,   *Jonah* 2:8
teaching them to o. all. *Mat* 28:20
customs not lawful to o. *Acts* 16:21
Gentiles o. no such thing.   21:25
ye o. days, and months.   *Gal* 4:10
then o. these things.   *1 Tim* 5:21

see do

observed
father o. the saying.   *Gen* 37:11*
it is a night to be much o. *Ex* 12:42
not o. commandments. *Num* 15:22
Levi o. thy word, kept. *Deut* 33:9
when Joab o. city, he. *2 Sam* 11:16
Manasseh o. times.   *2 Ki* 21:6
  2 Chr 33:6
I heard him, and o. him. *Hos* 14:8
feared John and o. him. *Mark* 6:20*
have I o. from my youth.   10:20

observer
not be found an o. of times.
  Deut 18:10*

observers
nations hearkened to o. of times.
  Deut 18:14*

observest
things, but thou o. not.   *Isa* 42:20

observeth
he that o. the wind shall. *Eccl* 11:4

obstinate
God made his heart o.   *Deut* 2:30
I knew that thou art o.   *Isa* 48:4

obtain
I may o. children by.   *Gen* 16:2
and shall o. favour of.   *Pr* 8:35
they shall o. joy and gladness.
  Isa 35:10; 51:11
he shall o. the kingdom. *Dan* 11:21
accounted worthy to o. *Luke* 20:35*
they may o. mercy.   *Rom* 11:31
so run that ye may o. *1 Cor* 9:24*
they do it to o. a corruptible. 25*

but to o. salvation by.   *1 Thes* 5:9
may o. salvation which. *2 Tim* 2:10
that we may o. mercy.   *Heb* 4:16*
that they might o. a better.   11:35
desire to have, and cannot o. *Jas* 4:2

obtained
after certain days I o.   *Neh* 13:6*
Esther o. kindness.   *Esth* 2:9
she o. grace.   17
her that had not o. mercy. *Hos* 2:23
o. part of this ministry. *Acts* 1:17*
with a great sum o. I this.   22:28
o. help of God I continue.   26:22
supposing that they had o.   27:13
Israel hath not o. that which he seeketh for . . . hath o. it.   *Rom* 11:7
ye have now o. mercy through.   30
one that hath o. mercy.   *1 Cor* 7:25
have o. an inheritance.   *Eph* 1:11*
o. mercy, because I did it ignorantly.
  1 Tim 1:13, 16
o. a more excellent name. *Heb* 1:4
he had patiently endured, he o. 6:15
o. a more excellent ministry.   8:6
having o. eternal redemption.   9:12
elders o. a good report.   11:2*, 39*
Abel o. witness that he was.   4*
who o. promises, stopped.   11:33
not o. mercy, but now have o.
  1 Pet 2:10
have o. like precious.   *2 Pet* 1:1

see favour

obtaining
to o. of the glory of.   *2 Thes* 2:14

occasion
may seek o. against us.   *Gen* 43:18
mayest do as thou shalt find o.
  Judg 9:33; *1 Sam* 10:7
Samson sought o. against.   14:4
great o. to enemies.   *2 Sam* 12:14
which thou shalt have o. *Ezra* 7:20
o. who can turn her away ? *Jer* 2:24
not have o. any more.   *Ezek* 18:3
sought to find o. and could find none
  o.   *Dan* 6:4, 5
sin taking o. by the.   *Rom* 7:8, 11
put not an o. to fall in his.   14:13
we give you o. to glory.   *2 Cor* 5:12
by o. of the frowardness of.   8:8*
cut off o. from them which desire o.
  11:12
use not liberty for an o. *Gal* 5:13
younger give none o. to. *1 Tim* 5:14
o. of stumbling in him. *1 John* 2:10

occasioned
I have o. the death of. *1 Sam* 22:22

occasions
and give o. of speech against her.
  Deut 22:14*, 17*
findeth o. against me.   *Job* 33:10

occupation
shall say, What is your o.?
  Gen 46:33; 47:3; *Jonah* 1:8
for by o. they were tentmakers.
  Acts 18:3*
with the workmen of like o.   19:25

occupied
the gold that was o.   *Ex* 38:24*
ropes that never were o. *Judg* 16:11*
Syria o.   *Ezek* 27:16*
Dan and Javan o.   19*
Arabia o.   21*
Sheba o. in thy fairs.   22*
profited them that have o. *Heb* 13:9

occupiers
o. of thy merchandise. *Ezek* 27:27†

occupieth
he that o. the room of. *1 Cor* 14:16*

occupy
with mariners o. thy. *Ezek* 27:9†
servants, o. till I come. *Luke* 19:13*

occurrent
adversary nor evil o.   *1 Ki* 5:4

Ocran, *see* Pagiel

odd
the o. number is to be.   *Num* 3:48

Oded
came on Azariah son of O. *2 Chr* 15:1
prophet of the Lord, called O.   28:9

30

odious

made themselves o.   *1 Chr 19*:6
for an o. woman when.   *Pr 30*:23

odour

house was filled with o.   *John 12*:3
an o. of a sweet smell.   *Phil 4*:18

odours

savour of your sweet o.   *Lev 26*:31
in a bed of sweet o.   *2 Chr 16*:14
oil of myrrh and sweet o.   *Esth 2*:12
so· shall they burn o. for thee.
    Jer 34:5*
offer sweet o. to Daniel.   *Dan 2*:46
golden vials full of o.   *Rev 5*:8
no man buyeth their o.   *18*:13

offence

[1] *Any thing that a man finds in his way, that may occasion him to stumble or fall, whether physically or morally. The Revisions often translate it* stumblingblock, *or* occasion of stumbling. [2] *A sin, or trespass.*

o. of heart to my lord.   *1 Sam 25*:31
but a rock of o. to both.   *Isa 8*:14
till they acknowledge their o.
    Hos 5:15
Satan, thou art o. to me.   *Mat 16*:23
man by whom the o. cometh.   *18*:7
a conscience void of o.   *Acts 24*:16
o. so also is the free gift, for
    through the o. of.   *Rom 5*:15, 18
by one man's o. death reigned.   17
the law entered that the o.   20
stumbling stone, and rock of o. *9*:33
that man who eateth with o.   *14*:20
give none o. in any thing.
    1 Cor 10:32; *2 Cor 6*:3
an o. in abasing myself ? *2 Cor 11*:7
then is the o. of the cross. *Gal 5*:11
may be without o. till.   *Phil 1*:10
a rock of o. to them.   *1 Pet 2*:8

offences

yielding pacifieth great o. *Eccl 10*:4
because of o., for it must needs be
    that o.   *Mat 18*:7; *Luke 17*:1
was delivered for our o.   *Rom 4*:25
of many o. unto justification.   *5*:16
mark them which cause o.   *16*:17

offend

[1] *To commit any sin in thought, word, or deed,* Jas 3:2. [2] *To displease, thus the Pharisees were offended at Christ,* Mat 15:12. [3] *To be scandalized, or made to stumble by the example of another,* 1 Cor 8:13.

I will not o. any more.   *Job 34*:31
I should o. against generation of.
    Ps 73:15
law, nothing shall o. them. *119*:165
all that devour him shall o. *Jer 2*:3
adversaries said, We o. not.   *50*:7
harlot, let not Judah o.   *Hos 4*:15
pass over and o.   *Hab 1*:11
if thy right eye o. thee.   *Mat 5*:29
if thy right hand o. thee. 30; *18*:8, 9
    Mark 9:43, 45, 47
gather all things that o.   *Mat 13*:41
lest we should o. them, go.   *17*:27
whoso shall o. one of these little
    ones. 18:6; *Mark 9*:42; *Luke 17*:2
them, doth this o. you ? *John 6*:61
my brother o. . . . lest he o. *1 Cor 8*:13
yet o. in one point, he.   *Jas 2*:10
we o. all. If any man o. not.   *3*:2

offended

and what have I o. thee ? *Gen 20*:9
    Jer 37:18
the butler and baker had o.   *40*:1
saying, I have o.; return. *2 Ki 18*:14
we have o. against the. *2 Chr 28*:13
a brother o. is harder.   *Pr 18*:19
Edom hath greatly o.   *Ezek 25*:12
when Ephraim o. in Baal. *Hos 13*:1
blessed is he whosoever shall not be
    o.   *Mat 11*:6; *Luke 7*:23
persecution ariseth . . . by and by he
    is o.   *Mat 13*:21; *Mark 4*:17
and they were o. in him. *Mat 13*:57
    Mark 6:3

---

the Pharisees were o.   *Mat 15*:12
shall many be o. and betray.   *24*:10
all ye shall be o. because of.   *26*:31
all men shall be o. because of thee.
    Mat 26:33; *Mark 14*:29
that ye should not be o.   *John 16*:1
against Caesar have I o. *Acts 25*:8
whereby thy brother is o. *Rom 14*:21
who is o. and I burn ? *2 Cor 11*:29

offender

that make a man an o.   *Isa 29*:21
if I be an o. or have.   *Acts 25*:11

offenders

I and my son Solomon shall be
    counted o.   *1 Ki 1*:21

offer

(Revisions commonly use the word sacrifice, as having a more definite meaning)

not delay to o. the first.   *Ex 22*:29
not o. the blood.   *23*:18; *34*:25
shalt o. every day a bullock. *29*:36
thou shalt o. on altar two lambs. 38
one lamb thou shalt o. in the morn-
    ing.   39, 41; *Num 28*:4, 8
shall o. no strange incense. *Ex 30*:9
every one that did o. silver.   *35*:24
o. a male without blemish.
    Lev 1:3; *3*:6; *22*:19, 20
will o. a meat offering to the Lord.
    2:1, 14; *23*:16; *Num 6*:17
offerings thou shalt o. salt. *Lev 2*:13
if he o. a peace offering, he shall o.
    3:1, 6; *9*:2; *19*:5
if he o. a lamb for his. *3*:7; *14*:12
the goat he shall o. before.   *3*:12
o. a young bullock. 4:14; *Num 15*:24
o. that for sin offering. *Lev 5*:8; *9*:7
the sons of Aaron shall o.   *6*:14, 22
    14:19; *15*:15, 30; *Num 6*:11
o. of it all the fat.   *Lev 7*:3
it is for a thanksgiving. *12*; *22*:29
Israel to o. their oblations to.   38
o. their sacrifice to devils.   *17*:7
bringeth it not to the door to o.   9
eaten the same day ye o. it.   *19*:6
bread of their God they do o. *21*:6
blemish shall not come nigh to o.   21
o. for a freewill offering.   *22*:23
they o. their offering.   *Num 7*:11
shall o. the Levites.   *8*:11, 13, 15
kept back, that we may not o.?   *9*:7
shalt o. the third part of an.   *15*:7
if a stranger will o. an offering.   14
o. an heave offering.   *19*; *18*:24
    26, *28*, *29*
come near to o. incense.   *16*:40
shall ye observe to o. to me.   *28*:2
of your months ye shall o.   11
after this manner ye shall o.   24
shall choose, there o.   *Deut 12*:14
priest's due from them that o. *18*:3
o. sacrifices of righteousness.
    33:19; *Ps 4*:5
he made an end to o.   *Judg 3*:18
o. a great sacrifice to Dagon. *16*:23
Elkanah went up to o. *1 Sam 1*:21
her husband to o. sacrifice.   *2*:19
did I choose him my priest to o.? 28
I o. thee three things. *2 Sam 24*:12
    1 Chr 21:10
on thee shall he o. priests. *1 Ki 13*:2
should be able to o. so willingly.
    1 Chr 29:14, 17
vessels to o. withal.   *2 Chr 24*:14
o. sacrifices of sweet. *Ezra 6*:10
of blood will I not o.   *Ps 16*:4
will I o. in his tabernacle.   *27*:6
o. to God thanksgiving, pay. *50*:14
then shall they o. bullocks.   *51*:19
o. to thee burnt sacrifices.   *66*:15
Sheba and Seba shall o. gifts. *72*:10
I will o. the sacrifice of.   *116*:17
wentest thou up to o.   *Isa 57*:7
to whom they o. incense. *Jer 11*:12
when ye o. your gifts. *Ezek 20*:31
when ye o. my bread, the.   *44*:7
they shall o. to me the fat and.   15
ye shall o. an oblation to the Lord.
    45:1, 13; *48*:9
should o. an oblation.   *Dan 2*:46
o. wine offerings to Lord. *Hos 9*:4
o. a sacrifice of.   *Amos 4*:5

---

that which they o. there.   *Hag 2*:14
ye o. polluted bread.   *Mal 1*:7
if ye o. the blind, o. it now to.   8
o. to the Lord an offering in.   *3*:3
come and o. thy gift.   *Mat 5*:24
o. gift Moses commanded.   *8*:4
    Mark 1:44; *Luke 5*:14
smiteth on one cheek, o. *Luke 6*:29
if shall ask an egg, will he o.? *11*:12
that he may o. both gifts. *Heb 5*:1
for himself to o. for sins.   3
needeth not to o. sacrifice, first. 7:27
to o.: it is of necessity that this man
    have somewhat also to o.   *8*:3
nor yet that he should o.   *9*:25
o. sacrifice of praise to God. *13*:15
to o. spiritual sacrifices. *1 Pet 2*:5
he should o. it with prayers. *Rev 8*:3
see burnt offerings

offered

Jacob o. sacrifice on the mount.
    Gen 31:54; *46*:1
every man o. an offering. *Ex 35*:22
he slew the goat, and o. *Lev 9*:15
Nadab and Abihu o. strange fire.
    10:1; *16*:1; *Num 3*:4; *26*:61
the princes o. for the dedication.
    Num 7:2, 10
Aaron o. them as an offering. *8*:21
250 men that o. incense.   *16*:35
Balak o. oxen and sheep.   *22*:40
    23:2, 4, 14, 30
people willingly o.   *Judg 5*:2, 9
Manoah took a kid and o.   *13*:19
was that Elkanah o.   *1 Sam 1*:4
when any o. the priest's.   *2*:13
David o. peace. *2 Sam 6*:17; *24*:25
and all Israel o.   *1 Ki 8*:62, 63
Jeroboam o. in Beth-el.   *12*:32, 33
the people o. yet in the high. *22*:43
meat offering was o.   *2 Ki 3*:20
to the altar and o.   *16*:12
with the rulers o.   *1 Chr 29*:6
rejoiced for that they o. willingly. 9
Asa o. to the Lord of. *2 Chr 15*:11
Amaziah willingly o. himself. *17*:16
all that was willingly o.   *Ezra 1*:6
some of fathers o. freely for.   *2*:68
o. at the dedication of this.   *6*:17
his counsellors freely o. to the. *7*:15
Israel there present had o.   *8*:25
they o. a ram of the flock.   *10*:19
willingly o. themselves. *Neh 11*:2
day they o. great sacrifices.   *12*:43
hast o. a meat offering.   *Isa 57*:6
as if he o. swine's blood.   *66*:3
o. incense unto Baal.   *Jer 32*:29
o. there their sacrifices. *Ezek 20*:28
cause the reproach o.   *Dan 11*:18
have ye o. to me sacrifices and
    offerings ?   *Amos 5*:25
o. a sacrifice to Lord. *Jonah 1*:16
every place incense be o. *Mal 1*:11
Simon o. them money.   *Acts 8*:18
abstain from meats o. to idols.
    15:29; *21*:25
an offering should be o. for. *21*:26
things o. unto idols. *1 Cor 8*:1, 4, 7
    10; *10*:19, 28
if I be o. on the service. *Phil 2*:17
am now ready to be o. *2 Tim 4*:6
he had o. up prayers.   *Heb 5*:7
this he did once, when he o.   7:27
not without blood, which he o. 9:7
were o. gifts.   9
o. himself without spot to God. 14
Christ was once o. to bear the. 28
by faith Abel o. to God a more. 11:4
Abraham, when tried, o. up. 17
justified by works when he o.
    Jas 2:21

offereth

priest that o. it for sin. *Lev 6*:26
be imputed to him that o. it.   7:18
for he o. the bread of thy God. 21:8
whoso o. praise glorifieth. *Ps 50*:23
he that o. oblation as if. *Isa 66*:3

offering

(*From earliest times in all known peoples and races, a sacrifice, generally by fire, was held to be pleasing to the God they wor- shipped, whether a heathen*

divinity or the true God. Sacrifices were, therefore, not originated
by the Israelites, but regulated for
them by the law. They were
public, as the regular sacrifices of
the tabernacle or temple, or were
private, as expressive of thanks for
some blessing or sorrow for some
sin. As the laws of the sacrifices
occupy practically the whole of
Leviticus and are touched upon in
other books also, the details are too
long for a concordance, and should
be studied in a Bible Dictionary)

Cain brought an o. unto.   Gen 4:3
respect to Abel and to his o.   4
o. of every man, take my o. Ex 25:2
o. which ye shall take.   3; 35:5
an half shekel shall be the o. 30:13
an o. to the Lord to make.   15
ye shall bring your o. of.   Lev 1:2
o. to Lord be of fowls.   14
o. of fine flour.   2:1
no meat o. shall be made.   11
his hand on the head of his o. 3:2, 8
lamb for his o.   7; Num 6:14
and if his o. be a goat.   Lev 3:12
                              4:23, 28
o. of Aaron and of his sons.   6:20
o. be a vow, or a voluntary o. 7:16
an o. of jealousy, an o.   Num 5:15
princes offered their o. before. 7:10
offer their o. each prince on his. 11
Levites before the Lord for an o.
                              8:11, 21
o. of the Lord in his appointed. 9:13
respect not thou their o.   16:15
kick ye at mine o.?   1 Sam 2:29
purged with sacrifice nor o.   3:14
stirred thee up against me, let him
  accept an o.   26:19
o. of evening sacrifice.   1 Ki 18:29
bring an o. and come.   1 Chr 16:29
                              Ps 96:8
Israel shall bring the o.   Neh 10:39
I have not caused thee to serve with
  an o.   Isa 43:23
make his soul an o. for sin.   53:10
your brethren for an o.   66:20
provocation of their o.   Ezek 20:28
my dispersed bring my o.   Zeph 3:10
nor will I accept an o.   Mal 1:10
an o.: should I accept this?   13
that he regardeth not the o.   2:13
offer to the Lord an o. in.   3:3
the o. up of Gentiles.   Rom 15:16
o. and a sacrifice to God.   Eph 5:2
o. thou wouldest not.   Heb 10:5, 8
through the o. of the body of.   10
by one o. he hath perfected for.   14
there is no more o. for sin.   18
see burnt offering, free offering,
  meat offerings, burnt, drink,
  fire, free, made, make

offering, verb
as Samuel was o. the.   1 Sam 7:10
David made an end of o.
                   2 Sam 6:18; 1 Chr 16:2
Jehu had made an end of o.
                           2 Ki 10:25
o. according to commandment of
  Moses.   2 Chr 8:13
made an end of o., the king.   29:29
seven days, o. peace offerings. 30:22
of Aaron were busied in o.   35:14
priests o. willingly for the. Ezra 7:16
me to anger in o. to Baal. Jer 11:17
and o. him vinegar.   Luke 23:36
every priest o. often the. Heb 10:11

heave offering
shoulder of the heave o.   Ex 29:27
oblation for an heave o.   Lev 7:14
offer up an heave o. Num 15:19, 20
of first of dough give an heave o. 21
they offer as an heave o.   18:24
Lord's heave o. to Aaron.   28
to Eleazar for an heave o. of. 31:29
which was the Lord's heave o.   41
  see burnt offering

peace offering
sacrifice of peace o. Lev 3:1, 3, 6, 9

sin offering
shalt thou burn, it is a sin o. Ex 29:14
    Lev 4:21, 24; 5:9, 11, 12
the blood of the sin o.   Ex 30:10
bullock without blemish for a sin o.
    Lev 4:3; 16:3, 27; Num 8:8
priest shall take of the blood of sin o.
                          Lev 4:25; 5:9
hand on the head of the sin o., slay
  the sin o. in the place.   4:29, 33
a lamb for a sin o.   32; Num 6:14
a kid of goats for a sin o.   Lev 5:6
    9:3; 16:5, 15, 27; 23:19
which is for the sin o. first.   5:8
bring fine flour for a sin o.   11
is the law of the sin o. 6:25; 7:37
as the sin o. is, so is.   7:7; 14:13
thee a young calf for a sin o.   9:2
sought goat of the sin o.   10:16
why have ye not eaten sin o. in?   17
a turtle dove for a sin o.   12:6
fat of the sin o. shall be.   16:25
kid of the goats for a sin o. Num 7:16
    22, 28; 15:24; 28:15; 29:5
sin o. should be made.   2 Chr 29:24
he goats for a sin o.   Ezra 8:35
sin o. hast thou not required. Ps 40:6
a bullock for a sin o.   Ezek 43:19
day offer a kid for a sin o.   22
every day a goat for a sin o.   25
he shall offer his sin o.   44:27
meat offering and sin o.   29
where priest shall boil sin o. 46:20

trespass offering
shall bring his trespass o. Lev 5:6
without blemish for trespass o.   5
atonement with the ram of the trespass o.   16, 18; 6:6; 19:21, 22
in the day of his trespass o.   6:5
law of trespass o.   7:37
he lamb for trespass o.   14:12
    21, 24, 25; Num 6:12
trespass o. is most holy. Lev 14:13
any wise return him a trespass o.
                          1 Sam 6:3
shall be the trespass o.?   4, 8, 17
two tables to slay the trespass o. on.
                    Ezek 40:39; 42:13
eat the trespass o. and every. 44:29
priests shall boil trespass o. 46:20

wave offering
wave them for a wave o.   Ex 29:24
    26; Lev 7:30; 8:27, 29; 9:21
    10:15; 14:12, 24; 23:20
                          Num 6:20
the breast of the wave o. Ex 29:27
sheaf of the wave o.   Lev 23:15

wood offering
cast lots for the wood o. Neh 10:34
wood o. at times appointed. 13:31

offerings
if his o. be of the flocks. Lev 1:10
o. thou shalt offer salt.   2:13
with chief of all the o.   1 Sam 2:29
no dew nor fields of o.   2 Sam 1:21
people brought in the o. 2 Chr 31:12
the priests for passover.   35:8, 9
other holy o. sod they in pots.   13
should bring the firstfruits of o.
                          Neh 10:37; 12:44
remember all thy o.   Ps 20:3
with o. and incense.   Jer 41:5
will I require your o.   Ezek 20:40
sacrifice flesh for mine o. Hos 8:13
me o. forty years?   Amos 5:25
o. of Judah and Jerusalem. Mal 3:4
robbed thee? in tithes and o.   8
cast in unto the o.   Luke 21:4
bring alms to my nation and o.
                          Acts 24:17
  see burnt, drink, free
         made by fire

heave offerings
charge of mine heave o.   Num 18:8
shall bring your heave o. Deut 12:6

offerings of the Lord
men abhorred the o. of the Lord.
                          1 Sam 2:17

peace offerings
shalt sacrifice thereon thy peace o.
                          Ex 20:24
sacrificed peace o. of oxen.   24:5

heave offering of peace o. Ex 29:28
people brought peace o. and.   32:6
from the bullock of peace o. Lev 4:10
as fat of peace o.   26, 31, 35; 6:12
law of sacrifice of peace o.   7:11
                              13, 37
and a ram for peace o.   9:4, 18
out of the sacrifice of peace o. 10:14
offer them for peace o. 17:5; 23:19
offer a sacrifice of peace o.   19:5
                              22:21
a lamb for peace o.   Num 6:14
a ram for peace o.   17
peace o., two oxen, five lambs.
    7:17, 23, 29, 35, 41; 29:39
sacrifice of your peace o.   10:10
Joshua sacrificed peace o. Josh 8:31
offer peace o., let the Lord.   22:23
all Israel offered peace o.
                          Judg 20:26; 21:4
I will come and offer peace o.
                          1 Sam 10:8; 11:15
David offered peace o.   2 Sam 6:17
    24:25; 1 Chr 21:26
Solomon offered peace o. 1 Ki 3:15
                          8:63; 9:25
appointed priests for peace o.
                          2 Chr 31:2
Manasseh offered peace o.   33:16
I have peace o. with me.   Pr 7:14
peace o. to make reconciliation.
                          Ezek 45:15, 17
priest prepare peace o.   46:2
prince his peace o.   12
not regard peace o. of.   Amos 5:22

sin offerings
sin o. to make an.   Neh 10:33

thank offerings
bring thank o. to house. 2 Chr 29:31
sacrificed thereon thank o.   33:16

wave offerings
all the wave o. I have.   Num 18:11

wine offerings
wine o. to be pleasing.   Hos 9:4

office
me he restored to mine o. Gen 41:13
do the o. of a midwife.   Ex 1:16
to the o. of Eleazar.   Num 4:16*
they waited on their o.   1 Chr 6:32
ordain in their set o.   9:22
chief porters were in their set o. 26
brought to the king's o. 2 Chr 24:11
in their set o. they sanctified. 31:18
o. was to distribute to. Neh 13:13*
let another take his o.   Ps 109:8
near to do o. of priest. Ezek 44:13
I magnify mine o.   Rom 11:13*
have not the same o.   12:4
if a man desire the o.   1 Tim 3:1
the o. of a deacon.   10*, 13
who receive the o. of the. Heb 7:5

priest's office
minister to me in the priest's o.
    Ex 28:1, 3, 4, 41; 29:1, 44; 30:30
    35:19; 40:13, 15; Lev 7:35
    16:32*; Num 3:3
priest's o. shall be theirs. Ex 29:9*
in the priest's o.   31:10; 39:41
ministered in priest's o.   Num 3:4*
thy sons keep your priest's o. 18:7*
son ministered in the priest's o.
                          Deut 10:6
executed priest's o. in. 1 Chr 6:10
cast them off from executing priest's
  o.   2 Chr 11:14
while Zacharias executed the priest's
  o.   Luke 1:8

officer
Potiphar an o. of Pharaoh.
                          Gen 37:36; 39:1
and Zebul his o.?   Judg 9:28
Nathan, was the principal o. 1 Ki 4:5
Geber, son of Uri, was the only o. 19
Ahab called an o. and said.   22:9
king appointed an o.   2 Ki 8:6
Nebuzaradan took an o. out. 25:19
judge deliver thee to the o. and the
  cast.   Mat 5:25; Luke 12:58

officers
wroth with two of his o.   Gen 40:2
Joseph asked Pharaoh's o. Why? 7
let Pharaoh appoint o. over. 41:34*

offices

the o. of Israel cried to.   Ex 5:15
the o. did see that they were in.   19
gather unto me the o.   Num 11:16
                                 Deut 31:28
I made them o. among.   Deut 1:15
judges and o. shalt thou.   16:18
the o. shall speak to his o.   20:5, 8
and give to his o.   1 Sam 8:15
Nathan, over the o.   1 Ki 4:5
Solomon had twelve o. over.   7
place where the o. were.   28
chief of Solomon's o.   5:16; 9:23
Jehoiada commanded o. 2 Ki 11:15*
appointed o. over the house.   18
                             2 Chr 23:18
went out with his o.   2 Ki 24:12
the o. and mighty men carried.   15
six thousand were o.   1 Chr 23:4
Chenaniah and his sons were for o.
                                   26:29
Solomon's o. 250 that.   2 Chr 8:10
the Levites shall be o. before. 19:11
the o. of the king helped. Esth 9:3*
I will make thine o. peace. Isa 60:17
be o. in the house of.   Jer 29:26
the chief priests sent o.   John 7:32
the o. answered, Never man.   46
Judas having received o.   18:3
o. took Jesus.   12
one of the o. struck Jesus.   22
the o. found them not in. Acts 5:22

offices
into one of the priests' o. 1 Sam 2:36
priests according to o.   1 Chr 24:3*
waited on their o.   2 Chr 7:6
my good deeds for o.   Neh 13:14*

offscouring
hast made us as the o.   Lam 3:45
are the o. of all things.   1 Cor 4:13

offspring
thy o. as the grass of.   Job 5:25
their o. is established before. 21:8
and his o. shall not be satisfied. 27:14
yea, let my o. be rooted out.   31:8*
hang on him the o. and.   Isa 22:24
my blessing upon thine o.   44:3
the o. of thy bowels like the. 48:19
o. shall be known among the. 61:9
seed of the blessed, and o.   65:23
are also his o.   Acts 17:28, 29
I am the Root and the O. Rev 22:16

oft
as o. as he passed by.   2 Ki 4:8
how o. cometh their destruction?
                               Job 21:17
how o. did they provoke him. Ps 78:40
the Pharisees fast o.?   Mat 9:14
for o. times he falleth into the fire,
  and o. into.   17:15; Mark 9:22
o. shall my brother sin?   Mat 18:21
except they wash o. eat not. Mark 7:3
I punished them o. in.   Acts 26:11
do ye as o. as ye drink. 1 Cor 11:25
in deaths o.   2 Cor 11:23
for he o. refreshed me.   2 Tim 1:16
up rain that cometh o.   Heb 6:7

often
that being o. reproved.   Pr 29:1
feared the Lord spake o.   Mal 3:16
how o. would I have gathered thee.
              Mat 23:37; Luke 13:34
o. bound with fetters.   Mark 5:4
disciples of John fast o.?   Luke 5:33
for as o. as ye eat this. 1 Cor 11:26
journeyings o., in perils. 2 Cor 11:26
watchings o., in fastings o.   27
of whom I have told you o. Phil 3:18
a little wine for thine o. infirmities.
                              1 Tim 5:23
should offer himself o.   Heb 9:25
then he must o. have suffered.   26
to smite the earth as o.   Rev 11:6

oftener
Felix sent for him o.   Acts 24:26

oftentimes
worketh God o. with.   Job 33:29
o. also thine own heart.   Eccl 7:22
for o. it had caught him. Luke 8:29
for Jesus he o. resorted.   John 18:2
that o. I purposed to.   Rom 1:13
have o. proved diligent.   2 Cor 8:22
and o. offering the same. Heb 10:11

Og
to them as he did to O.   Deut 31:4
heard what you did to O.   Josh 2:10
the cities of O. pertaining.   13:21
in the country of O.   1 Ki 4:19
          see Bashan

oil
*The most common oil in use was
that made from the olive berry.
This was used [1] as food, Ex 29:2.
[2] As a cosmetic, for anointing the
body after a bath, etc., Ps 104:15.
[3] Medicinal, as referred to in
Isa 1:6; Luke 10:34; Jas 5:14.
[4] For light, Ex 27:20. [5] Ritual,
in the anointing of kings and
priests, Lev 8:12. [6] In offerings.*
Jacob poured o.   Gen 28:18; 35:14
take o. for the light.   Ex 25:6
                         35:14; 39:37
tempered with o.   29:2, 40
shalt make it an o. of holy.   30:25
pour o. upon it.   Lev 2:1, 6
flour mingled with o.   4, 5; 14:10
  21; 23:13; Num 6:15; 7:13, 19
  25, 31, 37. 43, 49, 55, 61, 67, 73, 79
      8:8; 28:13; 29:3, 9, 14
thy meat offering put o. upon it.
                        Lev 2:15; 6:21
shall burn part of the o.   2:16
he shall put no o. on it.   5:11
                             Num 5:15
meat offering mingled with o.
              Lev 7:10; 9:4; 14:10
shall offer cakes mingled with o.
                    7:12; Num 6:15
his right finger in the o. Lev 14:16
rest of the o. that is in.   17, 18, 29
all the o. vessels.   Num 4:9
was as the taste of fresh o.   11:8
fourth part of an hin of o.   15:4
third part of an hin of o.   6
o. for one bullock, and o.   28:12
not anoint thyself with o. Deut 28:40
                   2 Sam 14:2; Mi 6:15
made him suck o. out of the flinty
  rock.   Deut 32:13
let Asher be acceptable, . . . and dip
  his foot in o.   33:24
Samuel took a vial of o. 1 Sam 10:1
horn with o. and go.   16:1, 13
priest took an horn of o.   1 Ki 1:39
Hiram twenty measures of o.   5:11
o. in a cruse.   17:12
nor cruse of o. fail.   14, 16
house save a pot of o.   2 Ki 4:2
the o. stayed.   6
go sell the o. and pay thy debt. 7
box of o. go to Ramoth-gilead. 9:1, 3
he poured the o. on his head.   6
over the cellars of o.   1 Chr 27:28
gave drink and o. to them. Ezra 3:7
with o. of myrrh.   Esth 2:12
which make o. within.   Job 24:11
poured me out rivers of o.   29:6
my head with o.   Ps 23:5
words were softer than o.   55:21
and o. to make his face.   104:15
come like o. into his bones.   109:18
kindness, an excellent o.   141:5
is smoother than o.   Pr 5:3
and o. in the dwelling of.   21:20
to give to them the o. of joy. Isa 61:3
we have treasures of o.   Jer 41:8
flour, honey, and o.   Ezek 16:13, 19
hast set mine o. and incense.   18
Judah traded in honey and o.   27:17
their rivers to run like o.   32:14
ordinance of o., bath of o.   45:14
ephah for a ram, an hin of o.   24
give me my bread and o.   Hos 2:5
Assyrians, and o. is carried.   12:1
with 10,000 rivers of o.   Mi 6:7
empty the golden o. out.   Zech 4:12
the foolish took no o.   Mat 25:3
the wise took o.   4
give us of your o.   8
my head with o. thou.   Luke 7:46
an hundred measures of o.   16:6
*see anointed, anointing, beaten,
log*

wine with oil
best of the o. and w.   Num 18:12

bless thy w. and thy o.   Deut 7:13
gather thy w. and o.   11:14
tithe of thy w. and o.   12:17; 14:23
the firstfruits of w. and o.   18:4
                            2 Chr 31:5
not leave thee either w. or o.
                            Deut 28:51
oversee the w. and o.   1 Chr 9:29
nigh brought w. and o.   12:40
20,000 baths of w. and o.
                         2 Chr 2:10, 15
in strong holds o. and w.   11:11
storehouses for w. and o.   32:28
give w. and o. according.   Ezra 6:9
of w. and 100 baths of o.   7:22
restore w. and o. that ye. Neh 5:11
firstfruits of w. and o.   10:37
offering of the corn, new w. and o. 39
tithes of corn, new w. and o. 13:5, 12
that loveth w. and o. shall not be
  rich.   Pr 21:17
to Lord for w. and o.   Jer 31:12
w. and summer fruits and o. 40:10
drought on new w. and o. Hag 1:11
touch bread, w. or o. shall ?   2:12
poured in o. and w.   Luke 10:34
hurt not the w. and the o.   Rev 6:6
no man buyeth their w. and o. 18:13

oiled
one cake of o. bread.   Ex 29:23
                             Lev 8:26

oil olive
pure o. olive beaten for.   Ex 27:20
unto thee of o. olive an hin. 30:24
unto thee pure o. olive.   Lev 24:2
land of o. olive, and honey.
              Deut 8:8; 2 Ki 18:32

oil tree
wilderness, the o. tree.   Isa 41:19

ointment
*(This word often means oil and is so
put in the Revisions)*
make oil of holy o. and o. Ex 30:25*
house of his precious things and
  precious o.   2 Ki 20:13; Isa 39:2
the o. of the spices.   1 Chr 9:30*
sea to boil like pot of o.   Job 41:31
it is like the precious o.   Ps 133:2
o. and perfume rejoice.   Pr 27:9
the o. of his right hand.   16
is better than precious o.   Eccl 7:1
and let thy head lack no o.   9:8
dead flies cause the o. of.   10:1
thy name is as o. poured. S of S 1:3
nor mollified with o.   Isa 1:6
thou wentest to the king with o. 57:9
a box of precious o.   Mat 26:7
                     Mark 14:3; Luke 7:37
o. might have been sold for much.
                    Mat 26:9; John 12:5
hath poured out this o.   Mat 26:12
waste of the o. made ?   Mark 14:4
his feet with o.   Luke 7:38, 46
anointed the Lord with o. John 11:2
o. and anointed the feet of Jesus,
  house . . . odour of the o.   12:3

ointments
savour of thy good o.   S of S 1:3
the smell of thine o. is better. 4:10
anoint themselves with the chief o.
                             Amos 6:6
prepared spices and o.   Luke 23:56
their odours and o.   Rev 18:13

old
Noah was 500 years o.   Gen 5:32
Noah was 600 years o. when.   7:6
Shem was 100 years o. and.   11:10
Abraham 75 years o. when.   12:4
a ram of three years o.   15:9
Abram was fourscore and six years
  o. when Hagar bare.   16:16
he that is eight days o. shall. 17:12
that is an hundred years o.   17
Abraham 99 years o. when.   24
Ishmael thirteen years o. when. 25
Abraham and Sarah were o.   18:11
waxed o. my lord being o. also. 12
of surety bear a child, who am o.? 13
compassed the house, o. and. 19:4
our father is o.   31
Isaac being eight days o.   21:4
Abraham 100 years o.   5

Sarah was 127 years o. *Gen* 23:1
Abraham was o. 24:1
Isaac 40 years o. when took. 25:20
Isaac was 60 years o. when she. 26
Esau forty years o. when he. 26:34
when Isaac was o., he called Esau.
27:1, 2; 35:29
Joseph being 17 years o. was. 37:2
Pharaoh said to Jacob, How o.? 47:8
couched as an o. lion, who. 49:9
Joseph died, being 110 years o.
50:26
Moses was eighty years o. and Aaron
eighty-three years o. when. *Ex* 7:7
our young and our o. with sons. 10:9
are numbered from twenty years o.
30:14; 38:26; *Num* 1:3, 18; 14:29
1 *Chr* 23:27; 2 *Chr* 25:5; 31:17
Ezra 3:8
it is an o. leprosy in the. *Lev* 13:11
shall eat o. fruit. 25:22
shall eat o. store. 26:10
the male from 20 years o. even. 27:3
from five even to twenty years o. 5
month o. to five years o. 6
male, from a month o. *Num* 3:15
22, 28, 34, 39, 40, 43
from thirty years o. to fifty. 4:3
23:20; 1 *Chr* 23:3
Levites from 25 years o. *Num* 8:24
redeemed, from month o. 18:16
23,000 from month o. and. 26:62
Aaron was 123 years old. 33:39
thy raiment waxed not o. *Deut* 8:4
29:5; *Neh* 9:21
not regard the person of the o.
Deut 28:50
I am 120 years o. this day. 31:2
Moses was an 120 years o. 34:7
eat of the o. corn. *Josh* 5:11, 12
men and women, young and o. 6:21
they took o. sacks. 9:4
o. shoes on their feet. 5, 13
Joshua was o. and. 13:1; 23:1, 2
forty years o. was I, when. 14:7
this day eighty-five years o. 10
Joshua died, being 110 years o.
24:29; *Judg* 2:8
too o. to have a husband. *Ruth* 1:12
now Eli was very o. 1 *Sam* 2:22
Eli was ninety and eight years o. 4:15
Samuel was o., he made. 8:1, 5; 12:2
Saul's son was forty years o. when.
2 *Sam* 2:10
lame, and five years o. 4:4
David thirty years o. when he. 5:4
now Barzillai was eighty years o.
19:32, 35
king David was o. 1 *Ki* 1:1, 15
1 *Chr* 23:1
Solomon was o. his wives. 1 *Ki* 11:4
dwelt an o. prophet in. 13:11
child, and her husband is o. 2 *Ki* 4:14
married when sixty years o.
1 *Chr* 2:21
males from three years o. and.
2 *Chr* 31:16
destroy all the Jews, young and o.
Esth 3:13
wicked live, become o.? *Job* 21:7
am young, and ye are very o. 32:6
my bones waxed o. through. *Ps* 32:3
young, and now am o. 37:25
now when I am o. O God. 71:18
when o. he will not depart. *Pr* 22:6
remove not o. landmark. 23:10
thy mother when she is o. 22
wise child than an o. king. *Eccl* 4:13
pleasant fruits new and o. *S of S* 7:13
an heifer of three years o. *Isa* 15:5
Jer 48:34
young and o. naked. *Isa* 20:4
they shall wax o. as garment. 50:9
the o. waste places. 58:12; 61:4
child shall die 100 years o., but the
sinner being 100 years o. 65:20
ask for the o. paths. *Jer* 6:16
thence o. clouts, o. rags. 38:11, 12
break in pieces young and o. 51:22
the young and o. lie on. *Lam* 2:21
my skin hath he made o. 3:4
slay utterly o. and young. *Ezek* 9:6
said to her that was o. in adulteries.
23:43

destroy it for o. hatred. *Ezek* 25:15
you after your o. estates. 36:11
kingdom, being 62 years o. *Dan* 5:31
with calves of year o. *Mi* 6:6
children from two years o. *Mat* 2:16
new cloth unto an o. garment. 9:16
new wine into o. bottles. 17
Mark 2:21, 22; *Luke* 5:36, 37
out of his treasure things new and o.
Mat 13:52
Jesus twelve years o. *Luke* 2:42
for he saith, The o. is better. 5:39
one of the o. prophets is risen. 9:8
man be born when he is o.? *John* 3:4
thou art not yet fifty years o. 8:57
be o. another shall lead thee. 21:18
above forty years o. *Acts* 4:22
was full forty years o. 7:23
Mnason, an o. disciple. 21:16
went about 100 years o. *Rom* 4:19
purge out therefore the o. 1 *Cor* 5:7
the feast, not with o. leaven. 8
of the O. Testament. 2 *Cor* 3:14
o. things are passed away, all. 5:17
and o. wives' fables. 1 *Tim* 4:7
not taken under sixty years o. 5:9
he hath made the first o. That which
decayeth and waxeth o. *Heb* 8:13
purged from his o. sins. 2 *Pet* 1:9
God spared not the o. world. 2:5
o. commandment is word. 1 *John* 2:7
o. serpent, called the devil. *Rev* 12:9
the dragon, that o. serpent. 20:2
see **wax**

days of **old**, *see of* **old**

old *age*
buried in a good o. age. *Gen* 15:15
Abraham a son of his o. age. 21:2, 7
Abraham died in a good o. age. 25:8
Joseph was the son of his o. age.
37:3; 44:20
Gideon died in a good o. age.
Judg 8:32
nourisher in thine o. age. *Ruth* 4:15
Asa in o. age was. 1 *Ki* 15:23
David died in a good o. age, full of
days and honour. 1 *Chr* 29:28
in whom o. age perished. *Job* 30:2
not off in the time of o. age. *Ps* 71:9
bring forth fruit in o. age. 92:14
to your o. age I am he. *Isa* 46:4
conceived a son in her o. age.
Luke 1:36

old *gate*, *see* **gate**

old *man*
Abraham died an o. man. *Gen* 25:8
the o. man of whom ye spake ? 43:27
we have a father, an o. man. 44:20
honour face of o. man. *Lev* 19:32
there came an o. man from his work.
Judg 19:16
o. man said, Whither goest? 17, 20
spake to the o. man. 22
not be an o. man in thy house.
1 *Sam* 2:31, 32
Eli was an o. m. 4:18
Jesse was an o. m. 17:12
an o. man cometh up, and. 28:14
compassion on o. man. 2 *Chr* 36:17
nor o. man that hath not. *Isa* 65:20
I am an o. man, my wife. *Luke* 1:18
our o. man is crucified. *Rom* 6:6
put off the o. man which. *Eph* 4:22
ye have put off the o. man. *Col* 3:9

old *men*
Rehoboam consulted with the o.
men. 1 *Ki* 12:6
forsook counsel of o. men. 8, 13
2 *Chr* 10:6, 8, 13
o. men and children. *Ps* 148:12
the crown of o. men. *Pr* 17:6
beauty of o. men is the grey. 20:29
dance, young men and o. *Jer* 31:13
hear this, ye o. men, and. *Joel* 1:2
o. men shall dream dreams. 2:28
Acts 2:17
o. men and women dwell. *Zech* 8:4

of **old**
of o., men of renown. *Gen* 6:4
those nations were of o. 1 *Sam* 27:8
Ham had dwelt there of o. 1 *Chr* 4:40
of o. there were chief. *Neh* 12:46

knowest thou not this *of o.*? *Job* 20:4
mercies have been ever *of o.* *Ps* 25:6
thou didst in the times *of o.* 44:1
even he that abideth *of o.* 55:19
heavens which were *of o.* 68:33
which hast purchased *of o.* 74:2
for God is my king *of o.* working. 12
I have considered the days *of o.* 77:5
remember thy wonders *of o.* 11
I will utter dark sayings *of o.* 78:2
thy throne is established *of o.* 93:2
of o. hast laid the foundation. 102:25
thy judgements *of o.* O Lord. 119:52
testimonies I have known *of o.* 152
I remember the days *of o.* 143:5
Isa 63:11
me before his works *of o.* *Pr* 8:22
counsels *of o.* are faithfulness and.
Isa 25:1
for Tophet is ordained *of o.* 30:33
consider the things *of o.* 43:18
former things *of o.*: I am God. 46:9
awake, as in generations *of o.* 51:9
not I held my peace even *of o.*? 57:11
carried them all the days *of o.* 63:9
prophets before me and thee *of o.*
Jer 28:8
Lord hath appeared *of o.* to. 31:3
be inhabited as in days *of o.* 46:26
she had in the days *of o.* *Lam* 1:7
he commanded in days *of o.* 2:17
as they that be dead *of o.* 3:6
Lord, renew our days as *of o.* 5:21
down with people *of o.* *Ezek* 26:20
build it as in days *of o.* *Amos* 9:11
forth have been from *of o.* *Mi* 5:2
in Bashan, as in the days *of o.* 7:14
to our fathers from the days *of o.* 20
Nineveh is *of o.* like a pool. *Nah* 2:8
pleasant to the Lord, as in the days
of o. *Mal* 3:4
the heavens were *of o.* 2 *Pet* 3:5
who were *of o.* ordained to. *Jude* 4

old *time*
giants dwelt there in o. time.
Deut 2:20
o. time set in thy inheritance. 19:14
fathers dwelt on other side in o. time.
Josh 24:2
to speak in o. time. 2 *Sam* 20:18
moved sedition of o. time. *Ezra* 4:15
been already of o. time. *Eccl* 1:10
of o. time I have broken. *Jer* 2:20
bring thee down with people of o.
time. *Ezek* 26:20
I have spoken in o. time. 38:17
said by them of o. time. *Mat* 5:21
27, 33
Moses of o. time hath. *Acts* 15:21
in o. time holy women. 1 *Pet* 3:5
prophecy came not in o. time by man.
2 *Pet* 1:21

old *way*
o. way which wicked men. *Job* 22:15

oldness
should not serve in o. of. *Rom* 7:6

olive
(*Olives are one of the most common trees of Palestine, and the uses
of the tree are many. The tree is
often used as a figure for Israel*)
in mouth was an o. leaf. *Gen* 8:11
for thine o. shall cast. *Deut* 28:40
the mount, and fetch o. *Neh* 8:15
off his flower as the o. *Job* 15:33
children like o. plants. *Ps* 128:3
the labour of the o. shall. *Hab* 3:17
be these two o. branches? *Zech* 4:12
can fig tree, my brethren, bear o.
berries? *Jas* 3:12
see **oil**

olives
foxes burnt up the vineyards and o.
Judg 15:5
shalt tread the o. but shalt. *Mi* 6:15
see **mount**

Olivet
by ascent to mount O. 2 *Sam* 15:30
returned from the mount called O.
Acts 1:12

olive tree

beatest thine o. tree. *Deut* 24:20
o. tree, Reign over us. *Judg* 9:8
the o. tree said. Should I leave ? 9
two cherubims of o. tree. *1 Ki* 6:23
he made doors of o. tree. 31, 32
posts of o. tree. 33
like a green o. tree in the. *Ps* 52:8
shaking of an o. tree. *Isa* 17:6; 24:13
thy name a green o. tree. *Jer* 11:16
shall be as the o. tree. *Hos* 14:6
as yet the o. tree hath not. *Hag* 2:19
of the fatness of o. tree. *Rom* 11:17
o. tree, graffed in a good o. tree. 24

wild olive tree

thou being wild o. tree. *Rom* 11:17

olive trees

o. trees which thou plantedst not.
Deut 6:11
thou shalt have o. trees, but. 28:40
over the o. trees was Baal-hanan.
1 Chr 27:28
o. trees increased, palmer-. *Amos* 4:9
two o. trees by it on the. *Zech* 4:3
are the two o. trees. *Rev* 11:4

oliveyard

shalt thou do with thy o. *Ex* 23:11

oliveyards

and o. which ye planted not, do ye
eat. *Josh* 24:13; *Neh* 9:25
king shall take your o. *1 Sam* 8:14
to receive money and o.? *2 Ki* 5:26
pray, to them their o. *Neh* 5:11

Olympas

salute Julia, O. and all. *Rom* 16:15

omitted

o. weightier matters. *Mat* 23:23*

omnipotent

Lord God o. reigneth. *Rev* 19:6*

Omri

all Israel made O. king. *1 Ki* 16:16
half followed O. 21
but O. wrought evil. 25
Ahab son of O. did evil in the. 30
Athaliah daughter of O. *2 Ki* 8:26
2 Chr 22:2
O. son of Becher. *1 Chr* 7:8
O. son of Imri. 9:4
O. son of Michael. 27:18
for statutes of O. are kept. *Mi* 6:16

On

priest of O. *Gen* 41:45, 50; 46:20
O. the son of Peleth. *Num* 16:1

Onan

and called his name O. *Gen* 38:4
O. knew that the seed should. 9
sons of Judah, Er, O. 46:12
Num 26:19; *1 Chr* 2:3
Er and O. died in the. *Num* 26:19

once

speak yet but this o. *Gen* 18:32
forgive my sin only this o. *Ex* 10:17
atonement . . . altar of incense o. a.
30:10; *Lev* 16:34; *Heb* 9:7, 12
let us go up at o. and. *Num* 13:30
not consume them at o. *Deut* 7:22
go round the city o. *Josh* 6:3, 11, 14
this o.: prove but this o. *Judg* 6:39
come up o. 16:18
strengthen me this o. 28
let me smite him to the earth at o.
1 Sam 26:8*
o. in three years came the navy of
Tarshish. *1 Ki* 10:22; *2 Chr* 9:21
he saved himself not o. *2 Ki* 6:10
o. in ten days all store of. *Neh* 5:18
merchants lodged o. or twice. 13:20
God speaks o., yea twice. *Job* 33:14
o. have I spoken, but I will. 40:5
God hath spoken o. *Ps* 62:11
down the carved work at o. 74:6
in sight when o. art angry ? 76:7
o. have I sworn by my. 89:35
perverse shall fall at o. *Pr* 28:18
destroy and devour at o. *Isa* 42:14
shall a nation be born at o.? 66:8
out the inhabitants at o. *Jer* 10:18
be clean ? when shall it o. be ? 13:27
behold, I will o. cause. 16:21
yet o. it is a little while, and I will
shake. *Hag* 2:6; *Heb* 12:26

when o. the master of. *Luke* 13:25
they cried all at o. saying. 23:18
died, he died unto sin o. *Rom* 6:10
I was alive without the law o. 7:9
above 500 brethren at o. *1 Cor* 15:6
rods, o. was I stoned. *2 Cor* 11:25
the faith he o. destroyed. *Gal* 1:23
let it not be o. named. *Eph* 5:3
ye sent o. and again to. *Phil* 4:16
have come to you o. *1 Thes* 2:18
who were o. enlightened. *Heb* 6:4
this he did o. when he offered. 7:27*
but now o. in end of the world. 9:26*
it is appointed to men o. to die. 27
Christ was o. offered to bear sins.
28; 10:10
that the worshippers o. purged. 10:2
o. more signifieth the. 12:27
hath suffered o. for our. *1 Pet* 3:18
o. longsuffering of God waited. 20
the faith o. delivered to. *Jude* 3*
though ye o. knew this. 5

one

[1] One only, there being no other
of that kind, 1 Tim 2:5; Heb 10:14.
[2] The very same, Gen 11:1; 40:5;
1 Sam 6:4. [3] Some body, any
one, 2 Sam 23:15.

cleave to his wife, and they shall be o.
flesh. *Gen* 2:24; *Mat* 19:5
Mark 10:8; *1 Cor* 6:16
hast thou but o. blessing? *Gen* 27:38
not give our sister to o. that. 34:14
o. is not. 42:13, 32
o. went out from me. 44:28
yet will bring o. plague. *Ex* 11:1
in o. house shall it be eaten. 12:46
o. law shall be to him that is home-.
49; *Lev* 24:22; *Num* 15:16, 29
drive them out in o. year. *Ex* 23:29
every o. of the curtains shall have o.
measure. 26:2; 36:9, 15
o. tabernacle. 26:6; 36:13
o. loaf of bread, o. cake, and o.
29:23
then he shall be guilty in o. of these.
Lev 5:4, 5, 13
o. of your own country. 16:29; 17:15
bake your bread in o. oven. 26:26
if they blow but with o. *Num* 10:4
I have not taken o. as. 16:15
o. rod shall be for the head. 17:3
of the tribe shall be wife to o. 36:8
I took twelve men, o. of. *Deut* 1:23
o. of these cities. 4:42; 19:5, 11
o. witness shall not rise up. 19:15
be free at home o. year. 24:5
should o. chase a thousand ? 32:30
Joshua took at o. time. *Josh* 10:42
Jericho o., the king of Ai o. 12:9
Jerusalem o., king of Hebron o. 10
but o. lot and o. portion ? 17:14
thou shalt not have o. lot only. 17
that o. reign over you ? *Judg* 9:2
what o. is there of the tribes ? 21:8
o. plague was on you all. *1 Sam* 6:4
o., for Gaza o., for Askelon o. 17
and they came out with o. 11:7
son in law by o. of the twain. 18:21
what o. nation is like ? *2 Sam* 7:23
with o. full line to keep alive. 8:2
there will not tarry o. with. 19:7
slew at o. time. 23:8; *1 Chr* 11:11
O that o. would give me to drink.
2 Sam 23:15; *1 Chr* 11:17
given me o. to sit on. *1 Ki* 1:48
I ask o. petition of thee, deny. 2:16
were of o. measure, o. size. 6:25
there hath not failed o. word. 8:56
o. tribe to thy son. 11:13, 32, 36
prophets declare good to the king
with o. mouth. 22:13; *2 Chr* 18:12
carry thither o. of the. *2 Ki* 17:27
o. of the priests came and. 28
will turn away face of o. captain.
18:24; *Isa* 36:9
for asking counsel of o. *1 Chr* 10:13
o. of the least was over an. 12:14
worship before o. altar. *2 Chr* 32:12
Hanani, o. of my brethren. *Neh* 1:2
bring o. of ten to dwell. 11:1
he cannot answer him o. *Job* 9:3
o. dieth in his full strength. 21:23

he is in o. mind, and who ? *Job* 23:13
if an interpreter o. among. 33:23
be not afraid when o. is. *Ps* 49:16
fall like o. of the princes. 82:7
I have laid help on o. that is. 89:19
sing us o. of the songs of Zion. 137:3
let us all have o. purse. *Pr* 1:14
is like o. that taketh a dog. 26:17
o. generation passeth away. *Eccl* 1:4
that o. event happeneth to. 2:14
yea, they have all o. breath. 3:19
all go unto o. place, all are. 20; 6:6
two better than o. 4:9
how can o. be warm ? 11
if o. prevail against him, two. 12
counting o. by o. to find out. 7:27
but o. sinner destroyeth much. 9:18
are given from o. shepherd. 12:11
with o. of thy eyes, with o. chain of
thy neck. *S of S* 4:9
but o.; she is the only o. 6:9
vineyard shall yield o. bath. *Isa* 5:10
what shall o. answer messengers of
nation ? 14:32
o. shall be called the city of. 19:18
to the days of o. king. 23:15
shall be gathered o. by o. 27:12
o. thousand shall flee at the rebuke
of o. 30:17
no o. of these shall fail. 34:16
I have raised up o. from the. 41:25
I will give Jerusalem o. that. 27
o. shall say, I am the Lord's. 44:5
surely, shall o. say, in Lord. 45:24
o. saith, Destroy it not, a. 65:8
they four had o. likeness. *Ezek* 1:16
brought up o. of her whelps. 19:3
come forth out of o. land. 21:19
that they took both o. way. 23:13
that o. that had escaped. 33:21
Abraham was o.: we are many. 24
as a lovely song of o. 32
will set up o. shepherd. 34:23; 37:24
shall become o. in thy hand. 37:17
make them o. stick. 19
o. nation, o. king. 22
o. gate of Reuben. 48:31
o. gate of Joseph. 32
but o. decree for you. *Dan* 2:9
Daniel was astonied for o. hour. 4:19
o. like the Son of. 7:13; 10:16, 18
the covenant for o. week. 9:27
out of a branch shall o. stand. 11:7
o. shall certainly come and. 10
they shall speak lies at o. table. 27
Israel shall appoint themselves o.
head. *Hos* 1:11
cities wandered to o. city. *Amos* 4:8
remain ten men in o. house. 6:9
the Lord with o. consent. *Zeph* 3:9
on o. stone shall be seven. *Zech* 3:9
three shepherds in o. month. 11:8
be o. Lord, and his name o. 14:9
did not he make o.? And wherefore
o.? *Mal* 2:15
the voice of o. crying in. *Mat* 3:3
Mark 1:3; *Luke* 3:4; *John* 1:23
o. jot, or o. tittle shall not pass.
Mat 5:18
whoso shall break o. of these. 19
that o. of thy members. 29, 30
canst not make o. hair white. 36
which of you can add o. cubit ? 6:27
was not arrayed like o. of these. 29
Luke 12:27
shall give to drink to o. *Mat* 10:42
you shall have o. sheep ? 12:11
Elias; and Jeremias, or o. of. 16:14
Mark 6:15; 8:28; *Luke* 9:8, 19
o. for thee, o. for Moses, and o. for.
Mat 17:4; *Mark* 9:5; *Luke* 9:33
shall offend o. of these. *Mat* 18:6
Mark 9:42; *Luke* 17:2
heed ye despise not o. *Mat* 18:10
o. of these little ones should. 14
if not hear, then take with thee o. 16
none good but o. 19:17; *Mark* 10:18
Luke 18:19
last have wrought but o. hour.
Mat 20:12
they beat o. and killed another. 21:35
went their ways, o. to his farm. 22:5
they will not move them with o. of
their fingers. 23:4; *Luke* 11:46

for *o.* is your Master. *Mat* 23:8, 10
o. is your Father. 9
he gave to *o.* five talents, to. 25:15
he that had received the *o.* 18, 24
as ye have done it to *o.* 40
did it not to *o.* of the least. 45
o. of you shall betray me. 26:21
Mark 14:18; *John* 13:21
could ye not watch with me *o.* hour ?
Mat 26:40; *Mark* 14:37
they more than *o.* loaf. *Mark* 8:14
whoever shall receive *o.* of. 9:37
o. casting out devils. 38; *Luke* 9:49
ask of you *o.* question. *Mark* 11:29
having yet *o.* son, he sent him. 12:6
to say, *o.* by *o.*, Is it I ? 14:19
at the feast he released *o.* 15:6
Luke 23:17
o. mightier than I. *Luke* 3:16
I say to *o.*, Go, and he goeth. 7:8
he had *o.* only daughter, and. 8:42
there shall be five in *o.* house. 12:52
joy in heaven over *o.* 15:7, 10
to pass, than *o.* tittle of the. 16:17
if *o.* went from the dead. 30, 31
to see *o.* of the days of the. 17:22
sell his garment, and buy *o.* 22:36
standeth *o.* among you. *John* 1:26
o. of you is a devil. 6:70
have done *o.* work. 7:21
went out *o.* by *o.* beginning at. 8:9
I am *o.* that bear witness of. 18
they said, We have *o.* Father. 41
be *o.* fold, and *o.* shepherd. 10:16
I and my Father are *o.* 30
in *o.* the children of God. 11:52
he hath *o.* that judgeth him. 12:48
that they may be *o.* 17:11, 21, 22
they may be made perfect in *o.* 23
thou not *o.* of this man's ? 18:17, 25
o. be ordained to be. *Acts* 1:22
of *o.* heart and of *o.* soul. 4:32
go and enquire for *o.* Saul of. 9:11
there cometh *o.* after me. 13:25
there is another king, *o.* Jesus. 17:7
God hath made of *o.* blood all. 26
except it be for this *o.* voice. 24:21
had questions of *o.* Jesus. 25:19
Paul had spoken *o.* word. 28:25
for a righteous man will *o.* die.
Rom 5:7
for if through the offence of *o.* 15
by *o.* that sinned, for the judgement
was by *o.* to condemnation. 16
death reigned by *o.*; . . . they shall
reign in life by *o.*, Jesus Christ. 17
by the offence of *o.*; . . . even so by
the righteousness of *o.* 18
so by obedience of *o.* shall many. 19
Rebekah also had conceived by *o.*
9:10
o. saith, I am of Paul. *1 Cor* 3:4
planteth and that watereth are *o.* 8
such fornication, that *o.* have. 5:1
there is none other God but *o.* 8:4
but *o.* God, and *o.* Lord Jesus. 6
all run, but *o.* receiveth the. 9:24
are *o.* bread and *o.* body. 10:17
o. is hungry. 11:21
to *o.* is given by the Spirit the. 12:8
o. Spirit are baptized into *o.* body. 13
o. that believeth not, or *o.* 14:24
let *o.* interpret. 27
for ye may all prophesy *o.* by *o.* 31
was seen of me as of *o.* born. 15:8
if *o.* died for all, then. *2 Cor* 5:14
I have espoused you to *o.* 11:2
received I forty stripes save *o.* 24
of good comfort, be of *o.* mind.
13:11; *Phil* 2:2; *1 Pet* 3:8
Rev 17:13
but as of *o.*, And to thy seed, which
is Christ. *Gal* 3:16
ye are all *o.* in Christ. 28
law is fulfilled in *o.* word. 5:14
gather together in *o.* all things.
Eph 1:10
who hath made both *o.* 2:14
o. new man. 15
both have access by *o.* Spirit. 18
as ye are called in *o.* hope of. 4:4
o. faith, *o.* Lord, *o.* baptism. 5
o. God and Father of all. 6
with *o.* spirit, with *o.* *Phil* 1:27

the husband of *o.* wife. *1 Tim* 3:2
Tit 1:6
bishop, *o.* that ruleth well. *1 Tim* 3:4
be the husbands of *o.* wife. 12
o. of themselves, even a. *Tit* 1:12
but *o.* in a certain place. *Heb* 2:6
that are sanctified are all of *o.* 11
ye have need that *o.* teach you. 5:12
but this man after he had offered *o.*
sacrifice. 10:12
by *o.* offering he hath perfected. 14
sprang there even of *o.* so. 11:12
for *o.* morsel of meat sold. 12:16
no city, but we seek *o.* to. 13:14
yet offend in *o.* point, he is. *Jas* 2:10
if any err, and *o.* convert him. 5:19
these three are *o.* *1 John* 5:7
these agree in *o.* 8
o. woe is past, there. *Rev* 9:12
o. of his heads as wounded. 13:3
on the cloud *o.* sat like unto. 14:14
power as kings *o.* hour. 17:12
in *o.* hour is thy judgement. 18:10
in *o.* hour so great riches come. 17
that great city, for in *o.* hour. 19
several gate was of *o.* pearl. 21:21
see accord, another, day, every,
God, heart, little, man,
mighty, people

as one

man is become *as o.* of us. *Gen* 3:22
seemed *as o.* that mocked. 19:14
Dan shall judge *as o.* of the. 49:16
shall be *as o.* that is born in the land.
Ex 12:48; *Lev* 19:34; 24:22
let her not be *as o.* dead. *Num* 12:12
Gibeon a great city, *as o.* *Josh* 10:2
young man was to him *as o.* of his.
Judg 17:11
this Philistine shall be *as o.* of them.
1 Sam 17:36
as when *o.* doth hunt a partridge.
26:20
uncovered *as o.* of the. *2 Sam* 6:20
he shall eat at my table *as o.* 9:11
thou shalt be *as o.* of the fools. 13:13
the king speaketh this *as o.* 14:13
not be left so much *as o.* 17:12
as o. was felling a beam. *2 Ki* 6:5
and singers were *as o.* *2 Chr* 5:13
speakest *as o.* of the foolish women.
Job 2:10
I am *as o.* mocked of his. 12:4
he counteth me to him *as o.* 19:11
as o. that mourneth for. *Ps* 35:14
then the Lord awaked *as o.* 78:65
hast broken Rahab, *as o.* 89:10
I rejoice *as o.* that findeth. 119:162
thy poverty *as o.* that. *Pr* 6:11; 24:3
as the *o.* dieth, so dieth. *Eccl* 3:19
for why should I be *as o.*? *S of S* 1:7
then was I in his eyes *as o.* 8:10
as o. that gathereth eggs. *Isa* 10:14
thy voice *as o.* that hath a. 29:4
as o. whom his mother. 66:13
I will break *as o.* breaketh. *Jer* 19:11
mourn *as o.* in bitterness. *Zech* 12:10
as o. having authority. *Mat* 7:29
Mark 1:22
or *as o.* of the prophets. *Mark* 6:15
he was *as o.* dead. 9:26
as o. of thy hired servants. *Luke* 15:19
as o. that perverteth the people. 23:14
as o. that hath obtained. *1 Cor* 7:25
so fight I, not *as o.* that. 9:26

is one

the people *is o.* *Gen* 11:6
the dream *is o.* 41:25, 26
this *is o.* of the Hebrew. *Ex* 2:6
the Lord our God *is o.* Lord.
Deut 6:4; *Mark* 12:29
Boaz *is o.* of our next. *Ruth* 2:20
in this place *is o.* greater. *Mat* 12:6
it *is o.* of the twelve. *Mark* 14:20
he is not a Jew that *is o.* *Rom* 2:28
a Jew who *is o.* inwardly. 29
seeing it *is o.* God who shall. 3:30
unto the Lord *is o.* spirit. *1 Cor* 6:17
as body *is o.* and hath many. 12:12
glory of the celestial *is o.* and. 15:40
not a mediator of one, but God *is o.*
Gal 3:20
who *is o.* of you. *Col* 4:9, 12

not one

if they give *not* thee *o.* *Gen* 24:41
remained *not o.* *Ex* 8:31; 10:19
cattle of Israel died *not o.* 9:6, 7
where there was *not o.* dead. 12:30
shall *not o.* of these men. *Deut* 1:35
was *not o.* city too strong for. 2:36
is *not o.* of them left. *2 Sam* 13:30
there be *not o.* small stone. 17:13
he left him *not o.* that. *1 Ki* 16:11
out of an unclean, *not o.* *Job* 14:4
and did *not o.* fashion us in ? 31:15
shall *not o.* be cast down at the ? 41:9
there is none that doeth good, *not o.*
Ps 14:3; 53:3; *Rom* 3:12
was *not o.* feeble person. *Ps* 105:37
strong in power, *not o.* *Isa* 40:26
take heed ye despise *not o.* of these
little ones. *Mat* 18:10
none righteous, no *not o.* *Rom* 3:10
no *not o.* that shall be able. *1 Cor* 6:5
for the body is *not o.* member. 12:14

one in reference to *other*

o. was Adah, of *other* Zillah. *Gen* 4:19
the *o.* from the *other*. 13:11
o. end of Egypt to the *other*. 47:21
o. Shiphrah, of the *other*. *Ex* 1:15
o. came not near the *other*. 14:20
hands on *o.* side, and the *other*. 17:12
o. Gershom, of the *other*. 18:3
o. for a sin offering, the *other* for a.
Lev 5:7; 12:8; *Num* 6:11; 8:12
o. lot for the Lord, *other*. *Lev* 6:8
o. Eldad, the *other*. *Num* 11:26
o. lamb in morning, the *other* at. 28:4
o. side of heaven to *other*. *Deut* 4:32
o. end of earth to *other*. 13:7; 28:64
o. pillar and of the *other*. *Judg* 16:29
o. was Orpah, of *other*. *Ruth* 1:4
o. Hannah, the *other*. *1 Sam* 1:2
o. Baanah, of the *other*. *2 Sam* 4:2
men, *o.* rich, the *other* poor. 12:1
o. saith, This is my son: the *other*
saith, Nay. *1 Ki* 3:23
half to *o.* and half to the *other*. 25
pitched *o.* against the *other*. 20:29
o. hand wrought, with *other*. *Neh* 4:17
o. dieth, so dieth the *other*. *Eccl* 3:19
the *o.* over against the *other*. 7:14
Lord shall devour from *o.* end of the
land to the *other*. *Jer* 12:12; 25:33
o. basket had good figs, *other*. 24:2
go thee *o.* way or other. *Ezek* 21:16
o. horn was higher than the *other*.
Dan 8:3
o. on this side of river, the *other*. 12:5
o. I called Beauty, the *other*.
Zech 11:7
o. and love the *other*, or hold to the *o.*
and despise the *other*. *Mat* 6:24
Luke 16:13
the *o.* on thy right hand, and the *other*
on. *Mat* 20:21; *Mark* 10:37
o. end of heaven to *other*. *Mat* 24:31
o. taken, the *other* left. 40, 41
Luke 17:34, 35, 36
thieves, the *o.* on his right hand, the
other. *Mark* 15:27; *Luke* 23:33
o. cheek, offer the *other*. *Luke* 6:29
o. owed 500 pence, the *other*. 7:41
o. part, shineth to the *other*. 17:24
the *o.* a Pharisee, the *other*. 18:10
o. angel at the head, *other* at the.
John 20:12
departed asunder *o.* from *other*.
Acts 15:39
o. part Sadducees, the *other*. 23:6
defraud ye *not o.* the other. *1 Cor* 7:5
to *o.* the savour of life, to *other* of.
2 Cor 2:16
o. by bondmaid, *other*. *Gal* 4:22
contrary, the *o.* to the *other*. 5:17
and *o.* is, the *other* is not yet come.
Rev 17:10

there is one

trespass offering, *there is o.* *Lev* 7:7
there is o. tribe cut off. *Judg* 21:6
there is o. law of his to put. *Esth* 4:11
there is o. alone, and there. *Eccl* 4:8
there is o. event to righteous. 9:2
this is an evil, that *there is o.*
if ye will not, *there is o.* *Dan* 2:9
there is o. come out of thee. *Nah* 1:11

there is o. God. *Mark* 12:32
    1 Tim 2:5; *Jas* 2:19
there is o. that accuseth. *John* 5:45
there is o. that seeketh and. 8:50
there is o. kind of flesh. *1 Cor* 15:39
there is o. glory of sun, another. 41
there is o. lawgiver, who. *Jas* 4:12

one *of them*
as *o. of them* opened his sack.
    Gen 42:27
not so much as *o. of them. Ex* 14:28
have I hurt *o. of them. Num* 16:15
if *o. of them* die, and. *Deut* 25:5
thou art *o. of them* that. *Judg* 11:35
shall be as *o. of them. 1 Sam* 17:36
lacked not *o. of them. 2 Sam* 17:39
I am *o. of them* that are. 20:19
three things, choose *o. of them.*
    24:12; *1 Chr* 21:10
Baal, let not *o. of them* escape.
    1 Ki 18:40
life as the life of *o. of them.* 19:2
like the word of *o. of them.* 22:13
not *o. of them* is broken. *Ps* 34:20
every *o. of them* is gone back. 53:3
as a snail let every *o. of them.* 58:8
of every *o. of them* is deep. 64:6
o. of them in Zion appeareth. 84:7
there was not *o. of them* left. 106:11
be not thou *o. of them* that strike.
    Pr 22:26
the labour of the foolish wearieth
  every *o. of them. Eccl* 10:15
yet every *o. of them* doth curse me.
    Jer 15:10
things, every *o. of them. Ezek* 11:5
out of *o. of them* came forth. *Dan* 8:9
even thou wast as *o. of them. Ob* 11
o. of them sold for a farthing.
    Mat 10:29; *Luke* 12:6
have 100 sheep, and *o. of them* be
  gone. *Mat* 18:12; *Luke* 15:4
surely thou art *o. of them.*
    Mat 26:73; *Mark* 14:69, 70
o. of them when he saw. *Luke* 17:15
o. of them may take a little. *John* 6:7
Jesus by night, being *o. of them.* 7:50
Lazarus was *o. of them* that sat. 12:2
seeing *o. of them* suffer. *Acts* 7:24
and there stood up *o. of them.* 11:28

one *thing*
not *o. thing* hath failed. *Josh* 23:14
this is *o. thing,* therefore I said it.
    Job 9:22
o. thing have I desired of the Lord.
    Ps 27:4
o. thing befalleth them. *Eccl* 3:19
I will ask you *o. thing. Mat* 21:24
    Luke 6:9; 20:3
o. thing thou lackest. *Mark* 10:21
    Luke 18:22
but *o. thing* is needful. *Luke* 10:42
o. thing I know, that. *John* 9:25
some cried *o. thing,* some another.
    Acts 19:32; 21:34
this *o. thing* I do, I press. *Phil* 3:13
ignorant of this *o. thing. 2 Pet* 3:8

wicked **one**
then cometh the *wicked o. Mat* 13:19
the children of the *wicked o.* 38
ye have overcome the *wicked o.*
    1 John 2:13, 14
Cain, who was of that *wicked o.* 3:12
and that *wicked o.* toucheth. 5:18

ones
my sanctified *o.* I have also called my
  mighty *o.* for mine. *Isa* 13:3
came up four notable *o. Dan* 8:8
face to enter, and upright *o.* 11:17

Onesimus
O. a faithful and beloved. *Col* 4:9
beseech thee for my son *O. Philem* 10

Onesiphorus
mercy to the house of *O. 2 Tim* 1:16
and the household of *O.* 4:19

onions
we remember the *o.* and the garlick.
    Num 11:5

only
thoughts of his heart are *o. Gen* 6:5
Noah *o.* remained alive, and. 7:23
o. to these men do nothing. 19:8

thy son, thine *o.* son Isaac. *Gen* 22:2
withheld thy son, thine *o.* son. 12, 16
o. bring not my son thither. 24:8
o. obey my voice, and go. 27:13
o. herein will the men. 34:22, 23
o. in the throne will I be. 41:40
o. the land of priests. 47:22, 26
remain in the river *o. Ex* 8:9, 11
I will let you go, *o.* ye shall not. 28
o. this once, that he may take away
  from me this death *o.* 10:17
o. let your flocks and your herds. 24
every man must eat, that *o.* 12:16
o. he shall pay for the loss. 21:19
to any, save to the Lord *o.* 22:20
for that is his covering, *o.* it is. 27
o. he shall not go in unto the vail.
    Lev 21:23
o. the firstling of the beasts, it. 27:26
o. thou shalt not number. *Num* 1:49
hath the Lord indeed *o.* spoken ? 12:2
rebel not ye against the Lord *o.* 14:9
o. they shall not come nigh. 18:3
I will *o.* go through on my feet.
    20:19; *Deut* 2:28
o. the word that I shall. *Num* 22:35
o. the gold and the silver. 31:22
o. marry to the family of their. 36:6
o. take heed to thyself. *Deut* 4:9
saw no similitude, *o.* ye heard. 12
man doth not live by bread *o.* 8:3
o. the Lord had a delight in. 10:15
o. ye shall not eat the blood. 12:16
    23; 15:23
the man *o.* that lay with her. 22:25
shalt be above *o.* not beneath. 28:13
thou shalt be *o.* oppressed. 29, 33
nor with you *o.* I make this. 29:14
o. be thou strong and very.
    Josh 1:7, 18
o. Lord thy God be with thee. 17
o. that day compassed the city. 6:15
o. Rahab shall live. 17
burned Hazor *o.* 11:13
shalt not have one lot *o.* 17:17
might *o.* know to teach. *Judg* 3:2
if dew be on the fleece *o.* and. 6:37
let it not be dry *o.* upon the. 39, 40
deliver us *o.* we pray thee. 10:15
and she was his *o.* child. 11:34
I pray thee, *o.* this once. 16:28
the man said, *O.* lodge not. 19:20
Hannah *o.* moved her lips. *1 Sam* 1:13
o. the Lord establish his word. 23
o. the stump of Dagon was left. 5:4
and serve him *o.* 7:3, 4; *Mat* 4:10
    Luke 4:8
o. fear the Lord, and. *1 Sam* 12:24
o. be thou valiant for me. 18:17
not *o.* while I live, shew. 20:14
o. Jonathan and David knew. 39
o. Amnon is dead. *2 Sam* 13:32, 33
and I will smite the king *o.* 17:2
deliver him *o.* and I will. 20:21
returned after him *o.* to spoil. 23:10
o. the people sacrificed in. *1 Ki* 3:2
Gebar was the *o.* officer who. 4:19
followed David, but Judah *o.* 12:20
David did that *o.* which was. 14:8
he *o.* of Jeroboam shall come. 13
save *o.* in the matter of Uriah. 15:5
I *o.* am left, and they. 19:10, 14
fight not, save *o.* with the. 22:31
worshippers of Baal *o. 2 Ki* 10:23
left but the tribe of Judah *o.* 17:18
art the Lord, even thou *o.* 19:19
    Isa 37:20
o. the Lord give thee. *1 Chr* 22:12
save *o.* to burn sacrifice. *2 Chr* 2:6
thou *o.* knowest the hearts of. 6:30
yet to the Lord their God *o.* 33:17
not done wrong to king *o. Esth* 1:16
o. on himself put not forth. *Job* 1:12
I *o.* am escaped to tell. 15, 16, 17, 19
o. do not two things to me. 13:20
against a nation, or a man *o.* 34:29
thou, Lord, *o.* makest me. *Ps* 4:8
against thee *o.* have I sinned. 51:4
he *o.* is my rock and my. 62:2, 6
o. consult to cast him down. 4
my soul, wait thou *o.* upon God. 5
righteousness, even thine *o.* 71:16
God of Israel *o.* doth wondrous. 72:18
o. with thine eyes shalt thou. 91:8

tender and *o.* beloved in. *Pr* 4:3
let them be *o.* thine own, and. 5:17
the righteous is *o.* good. 11:23
o. by pride cometh contention. 13:10
the talk of the lips tendeth *o.* 14:23
evil man seeketh *o.* rebellion. 17:11
tend *o.* to plenteousness, *o.* to. 21:5
o. have I found, that God. *Eccl* 7:29
the *o.* one of her mother. *S of S* 6:9
o. let us be called by thy. *Isa* 4:1
we will *o.* make mention of. 26:13
it shall be a vexation *o.* to. 28:19
o. acknowledge thine. *Jer* 3:13
make mourning as for an *o.* son.
    6:26; *Amos* 8:10
o. done evil, *o.* provoked. *Jer* 32:30
and evil, an *o.* evil. *Ezek* 7:5
they *o.* shall be delivered. 14:16, 18
they shall *o.* poll their heads. 44:20
you *o.* have I known of all families.
    Amos 3:2
salute your brethren *o. Mat* 5:47
Lord, speak the word *o.* 8:8
give a cup of cold water *o.* 10:42
not lawful for him to eat, but *o.* 12:4
they might *o.* touch hem of. 14:36
they saw no man, save Jesus *o.* 17:8
    Mark 9:8
nothing thereon but leaves *o.*
    Mat 21:19
shall not *o.* do this which is done. 21
in heaven, but my Father *o.* 24:36
forgive sins, but God *o.? Mark* 2:7
Jesus saith, Be not afraid, *o.* believe.
    5:36; *Luke* 8:50
for journey, save a staff *o. Mark* 6:8
he is a dead man, *o.* son. *Luke* 7:12
one *o.* daughter. 8:42
he is my *o.* child. 9:38
art thou *o.* a stranger in. 24:18
not *o.* because he had broken sabbath.
    John 5:18
honour that cometh from God *o.*
  die, not for that nation *o.* 11:52
came not for Jesus' sake *o.* but. 12:9
not my feet *o.* but also. 13:9
know thee the *o.* true God. 17:3
they were baptized in. *Acts* 8:16
the word to none but Jews *o.* 11:19
Apollos taught, knowing *o.* 8:25
not *o.* our craft is in danger to. 19:27
ready not to be bound *o.* but to. 21:13
o. that they keep themselves from. 25
o. would to God, that not *o.* 26:29
not *o.* do same, but have. *Rom* 1:32
is he God of Jews *o.? is* 3:29
this blessedness on circumcision *o.?*
    4:9, 12
not to that *o.* which is of law. 16
not *o.* so, but we glory in. 5:3, 11
not *o.* they, but ourselves. 8:23
he called, not of Jews *o.* but. 9:24
ye must be subject, not *o.* for. 13:5
to whom not *o.* I give thanks. 16:4
to God *o.* wise be glory. 27
    1 Tim 1:17; *Jude* 25
o. in the Lord. *1 Cor* 7:39
I *o.* and Barnabas. 9:6
came word of God to you *o.?* 14:36
if in this life *o.* we have hope. 15:19
us, not by his coming *o. 2 Cor* 7:7
have begun not *o.* to do. 8:10
not that *o.* but was also chosen. 19
not *o.* in sight of Lord, but in. 21
heard *o.,* he who persecuted. *Gal* 1:23
o. would that we should. 2:10
this *o.* would I learn of you. 3:2
not *o.* when I am present. 4:18
o. use not liberty for an occasion. 5:13
o. lest they should suffer. 6:12
every name named, not *o. Eph* 1:21
o. let your conversation be. *Phil* 1:27
is given not *o.* to believe on him. 29
obeyed, not as in my presence *o.* 2:12
God had mercy not on him *o.* 27
no church communicated with me,
  but ye *o.* 4:15
o. are my fellow-workers. *Col* 4:11
gospel came not in word *o. 1 Thes* 1:5
to you not gospel of God *o.* 2:8
o. he who now letteth. *2 Thes* 2:7
not *o.* idle, but tattlers. *1 Tim* 5:13
is the blessed and *o.* Potentate. 6:15
who *o.* hath immortality. 16

not to me *o.* *2 Tim* 4:8
o. Luke is with me. 11
which stood *o.* in meats. *Heb* 9:10
I shake unto the earth *o.* 12:26
word, and not hearers *o.* *Jas* 1:22
by works, and not faith *o.* 2:24
not *o.* to good and gentle. *1 Pet* 2:18
not for our sins *o.* *1 John* 2:2
not by water *o.* 5:6
love in the truth, and not I *o.* *2 John* 1
denying the *o.* Lord God. *Jude* 4
but *o.* those which have. *Rev* 9:4
thee ? for thou *o.* art holy. 15:4

see begotten

onward
cloud was taken up, Israel went *o.*
Ex 40:36

onycha
take thee spices, *o.* and. *Ex* 30:34

onyx
fourth row a beryl and an *o.*
Ex 28:20; 39:13
wisdom cannot be valued with the *o.*
Job 28:16
the topaz and the *o.* was. *Ezek* 28:13

see stones

open, *adjective*
and fowl that may fly in *o.* *Gen* 1:20
Tamar sat in an *o.* place by. 38:14*
every *o.* vessel not covered is unclean.
Num 19:15
the man whose eyes are *o.* hath.
24:3, 4, 15
left Ai *o.* and pursued. *Josh* 8:17
was no *o.* vision. *1 Sam* 3:1†
carved with *o.* flowers. *1 Ki* 6:18
29:32, 35
eyes may be *o.* towards this house.
8:29, 52; *2 Chr* 6:20, 40; 7:15
eyes be *o.*, ear attentive. *Neh* 1:6
Sanballat with an *o.* letter sent. 6:5
as wicked men in the *o.* *Job* 34:26
their throat is an *o.* sepulchre.
Ps 5:9; *Rom* 3:13
righteous, his ears are *o.* *Ps* 34:15
fool layeth *o.* his folly. *Pr* 13:16
o. rebuke is better than secret. 27:5
devour Israel with *o.* mouth. *Isa* 9:12
windows from on high are *o.* 24:18
gate shall be *o.* continually. 60:11
quiver is an *o.* sepulchre. *Jer* 5:16
both what was sealed and *o.* 32:11
eyes are *o.* on all the ways. 19
many bones in *o.* valley. *Ezek* 37:2
his windows being *o.* in chamber to
Jerusalem. *Dan* 6:10
gates shall be set wide *o.* *Nah* 3:13
see heaven *o.*, angels. *John* 1:51
seeing prison doors *o.* *Acts* 16:27
the law is *o.* and there are. 19:38
we all with *o.* face beholding.
2 Cor 3:18*
mouth is *o.* to you, our heart. 6:11
some men's sins are *o.* *1 Tim* 5:24*
put him to an *o.* shame. *Heb* 6:6
his ears are *o.* to their. *1 Pet* 3:12
I have set before thee an *o.* *Rev* 3:8
in his hand a little book *o.* 10:2, 8

see field, fields

open, *verb*
(*This word is frequently used in a
figurative sense*)
if a man shall *o.* a pit. *Ex* 21:33
of such as *o.* every womb. *Num* 8:16
if earth *o.* her mouth, and. 16:30
thou shalt *o.* thy hand wide.
Deut 15:8, 11
answer of peace, and *o.* to thee. 20:11
Lord shall *o.* to thee his good. 28:12
o. mouth of cave and. *Josh* 10:22
then *o.* door and flee. *2 Ki* 9:3
and he said, *O.* the window. 13:17
God would *o.* his lips. *Job* 11:5
I will *o.* my lips, and answer. 32:20
doth Job *o.* his mouth in vain. 35:16
who can *o.* the doors of his ? 41:14
I will *o.* my dark saying. *Ps* 49:4
I will *o.* my mouth in a parable. 78:2
o. thy mouth wide and I will. 81:10
o. to me the gates of. 118:19
o. thy mouth for the dumb. *Pr* 31:8
o. thy mouth, judge righteously. 9

o. to me, my sister, my. *S of S* 5:2
I rose up to *o.* to my beloved. 5
he shall *o.*, and none shall shut, shut
and none shall *o.* *Isa* 22:22
o. the gates, that the righteous. 26:2
doth he *o.* and break clods ? 28:24
I will *o.* rivers in high places. 41:18
to *o.* blind eyes, to bring out. 42:7
o. before him the two leaved. 45:1
let the earth *o.*, let them bring. 8
be shut up, none shall *o.* *Jer* 13:19
o. her storehouses, cast her. 50:26
o. thy mouth and eat that. *Ezek* 2:8
I speak with thee, I will *o.* thy. 3:27
confounded and never *o.* 16:63
o. the mouth in the slaughter. 21:22
I will *o.* the side of Moab. 25:9
I will *o.* your graves, and cause. 37:12
one shall *o.* him the gate. 46:12
o. thy doors, O Lebanon. *Zech* 11:1
will not *o.* you windows. *Mal* 3:10
I will *o.* my mouth in. *Mat* 13:35
Lord, *o.* to us. 25:11; *Luke* 13:25
he knocketh, they may *o.* *Luke* 12:36
Paul was about to *o.* his. *Acts* 18:14
that I may *o.* my mouth. *Eph* 6:19
that God would *o.* to us door. *Col* 4:3
is worthy to *o.* the book ? *Rev* 5:2
no man was able to *o.* book. 3
no man was found worthy to *o.* and. 4
Root of David prevailed to *o.* book. 5
to take the book, and *o.* seals. 9

see eyes

opened
windows of heaven were *o.* *Gen* 7:11
Noah *o.* the window of the ark. 8:6
God *o.* Leah's womb. 29:31
he *o.* Rachel's. 30:22
Joseph *o.* all storehouses. 41:56
one of them *o.* his sack. 42:27
43:21; 44:11
when she had *o.* ark. *Ex* 2:6
earth *o.* her mouth, and swallowed.
Num 16:32; *Ps* 106:17
o. not the doors, they *o.* *Judg* 3:25
she *o.* a bottle of milk and. 4:19
her lord *o.* doors, went out. 19:27
and Elisha *o.* the door. *2 Ki* 9:10
they *o.* not to him, therefore. 15:16
Hezekiah *o.* doors of. *2 Chr* 29:3
not gates of Jerusalem be *o.* *Neh* 7:3
Ezra *o.* book; when he *o.* it. 8:5
charged gates not to be *o.* till. 13:19
o. my doors to traveller. *Job* 31:32
the gates of death been *o.?* 38:17*
mine ears hast thou *o.* *Ps* 40:6
though he had *o.* the doors. 78:23
he *o.* the rock, and the. 105:41
I *o.* to my beloved. *S of S* 5:6
that *o.* not the house of. *Isa* 14:17*
time that thine ear was not *o.* 48:8
Lord God hath *o.* mine ear, not. 50:5
thee have I *o.* my cause. *Jer* 20:12*
Lord hath *o.* his armoury. 50:25
that the heavens were *o.* *Ezek* 1:1
Mat 3:16; *Mark* 1:10*; *Luke* 3:21
Acts 7:56
thou hast *o.* thy feet to. *Ezek* 16:25
when I have *o.* your graves. 37:13
gate shall not be *o.*, no man. 44:2
new moon it shall be *o.* 46:1
was set, the books were *o.* *Dan* 7:10
rivers shall be *o.*, palace. *Nah* 2:6
shall be a fountain *o.* to. *Zech* 13:1
when they had *o.* their. *Mat* 2:11
knock, and it shall be *o.* unto you. 7:7
Luke 11:9, 10
the graves were *o.* and many bodies
arose. *Mat* 27:52
Ephphatha, that is, Be *o.* *Mark* 7:34
his ears were *o.* 35
when he *o.* book, he found. *Luke* 4:17
o. to us the scriptures. 24:32
then *o.* he their understanding. 45
the angel by night *o.* the. *Acts* 5:19
but when we had *o.* we found. 23
Peter saw heaven *o.* and a. 10:11
the iron gate which *o.* 12:10
o. not the gate, but ran in. 14
when they had *o.* the door. 16
he had *o.* the door of faith. 14:27
Lydia, whose heart the Lord *o.* 16:14
immediately all the doors were *o.* 26

door and effectual is *o.* unto me.
1 Cor 16:9; *2 Cor* 2:12
are naked and *o.* to him. *Heb* 4:13
a door was *o.* in heaven. *Rev* 4:1
the Lamb *o.* one of the seals. 6:1
had *o.* the second. 3, 5, 7, 9, 12; 8:1
he *o.* the bottomless pit, and. 9:2
the temple of God was *o.* 11:19
of the testimony was *o.* 15:5
I saw heaven *o.* and behold. 19:11
were *o.*: the book of life was *o.* 20:12

see days, mouth

openest
thou *o.* thy hand, they are. *Ps* 104:28
o. thine hand and satisfiest. 145:16

openeth
whatsoever *o.* the womb. *Ex* 13:2
set apart all that *o.* 12, 15; 34:19
Num 3:12; 18:15; *Luke* 2:23
the rich man *o.* his eyes. *Job* 27:19
he *o.* ears of men, and sealeth. 33:16
he *o.* their ear to discipline. 36:10
I as a dumb man that *o.* *Ps* 38:13
he that *o.* wide his lips. *Pr* 13:3
o. not his mouth in the gate. 24:7
she *o.* her mouth with wisdom. 31:26
brought as a lamb, so he *o.* *Isa* 53:7
the fire, all that *o.* womb. *Ezek* 20:26
the porter *o.*; sheep hear. *John* 10:3
he that *o.* and no man shutteth, and
shutteth and no man *o.* *Rev* 3:7

opening
o. ears, but he heareth not. *Isa* 42:20
o. and alleging that Christ. *Acts* 17:3

opening, -s
o. of house of God. *1 Chr* 9:27
a man, there can be no *o.* *Job* 12:14
in the *o.* of the gates. *Pr* 1:21*
and the *o.* of my lips shall be. 8:6
proclaim the *o.* of the prison. *Isa* 61:1
I will give thee the *o.* of. *Ezek* 29:21

openly
harlot that was *o.* by the way side ?
Gen 38:21*
hath he *o.* shewed. *Ps* 98:2
thy Father shall reward thee *o.*
Mat 6:4, 6, 18
spake that saying *o.* *Mark* 8:32
seeketh to be known *o.* *John* 7:4
to the feast, not *o.* but in secret. 10
no man spake of him *o.* for fear. 13
Jesus walked no more *o.* 11:54
I spake *o.* to the world. 18:20
raised up, and shewed him *o.*
Acts 10:40
they have beaten us *o.* 16:37
shew of them *o.* triumphing. *Col* 2:15

operation
they regard not the *o.* *Ps* 28:5
nor consider the *o.* of his. *Isa* 5:12
the faith of the *o.* of God. *Col* 2:12*

operations
there are diversity of *o.* *1 Cor* 12:6*

Ophel
much on the wall of O. *2 Chr* 27:3
Manasseh compassed about O. 33:14
Nethinims dwelt in O. *Neh* 3:26
11:21
repaired to the wall of O. 27

Ophir
Joktan begat O. *Gen* 10:29
1 Chr 1:23
they came to O. and fetched gold.
1 Ki 9:28; *2 Chr* 8:18; 9:10
brought from O. great. *1 Ki* 10:11
made ships to go to O. for. 22:48
talents of gold of O. *1 Chr* 29:4
lay up the gold of O. *Job* 22:24
valued with the gold of O. 28:16
the queen in gold of O. *Ps* 45:9
precious than wedge of O. *Isa* 13:12

opinion
durst not shew you mine *o.* *Job* 32:6
I also will shew you mine *o.* 10, 17

opinions
halt ye between two *o.?* *1 Ki* 18:21

opportunity
he sought *o.* to betray him.
Mat 26:16; *Luke* 22:6

as we have o. let us do good. *Gal* 6:10
careful, but ye lacked o.   *Phil* 4:10
they might have had o. to. *Heb* 11:15

oppose
instructing those that o.   *2 Tim* 2:25

opposed
when they o. themselves.   *Acts* 18:6

opposest
thy strong hand thou o.   *Job* 30:21*

opposeth
o. and exalteth himself.   *2 Thes* 2:4

oppositions
avoiding o. of science.   *1 Tim* 6:20

oppress
the Egyptians o. them.   *Exod* 3:9
vex nor o. a stranger.   22:21; 23:9
ye shall not o. one. *Lev* 25:14*, 17*
shalt not o. servant that. *Deut* 23:16
thou shalt not o. an hired.   24:14
Moabites did o. you.   *Judg* 10:12
thee that thou shouldest o.? *Job* 10:3
earth may no more o.   *Ps* 10:18
from the wicked that o. me.   17:9†
good, let not proud o. me.   119:122
nor o. the afflicted in.   *Pr* 22:22
will feed them that o. thee. *Isa* 49:26
if ye o. not the stranger.   *Jer* 7:6
I will punish all that o. them.   30:20
princes shall no more o.   *Ezek* 45:8
merchant, he loveth to o.   *Hos* 12:7
ye kine of Bashan which o. *Amos* 4:1
they o. a man and his house.   *Mi* 2:2
o. not the widow nor the.   *Zech* 7:10
witness against those that o. *Mal* 3:5
do not rich men o. you ?   *Jas* 2:6

oppressed
thou shalt be only o. *Deut* 28:29, 33
by reason of them that o. *Judg* 2:18
Jabin o. Israel.   4:3
out of the hand of the Egyptians, and
of all that o.   6:9; *1 Sam* 10:18
Philistines and Ammon o. *Judg* 10:8
whose ox have I taken ? whom have
I o.?   *1 Sam* 12:3
thou hast not defrauded, nor o. us. 4
Assyria o. them.   *2 Ki* 13:4
king of Syria o. Israel.   22
Asa o. some of the people the same
time.   *2 Chr* 16:10
because he hath o. and.   *Job* 20:19
they made the o. to cry.   35:9*
will be a refuge for the o.   *Ps* 9:9
judge the fatherless and o.   10:18
      103:6; 146:7
not the o. return ashamed.   74:21
enemies o. them, brought.   106:42
the tears of such as were o. *Eccl* 4:1
learn to do well, seek judgement,
relieve o.   *Isa* 1:17
the people shall be o. every.   3:5
O thou o. virgin, daughter.   23:12
O Lord, I am o., undertake.   38:14
Assyrian o. them without.   52:4
he was o. and afflicted, yet he.   53:7
fast ? to let the o. go free.   58:6
Israel and Judah were o.   *Jer* 50:33
hath not o. any, but. *Ezek* 18:7*, 16*
because he hath o.   12*
he cruelly o.   18
they have o. the stranger.   22:29
Ephraim is o. and broken.   *Hos* 5:11
o. in the midst thereof.   *Amos* 3:9
avenged him that was o.   *Acts* 7:24
Jesus healed all that were o.   10:38

oppresseth
against him that o. you.   *Num* 10:9
he fighting daily o. me.   *Ps* 56:1
he that o. the poor. *Pr* 14:31; 22:16
a poor man that o. the poor.   28:3

oppressing
go from the o. sword.   *Jer* 46:16
for fear of the o. sword.   50:16
woe to o. city, she obeyed. *Zeph* 3:1

oppression
I have seen o. wherewith.   *Ex* 3:9
and looked on our o.   *Deut* 26:7
the Lord saw the o. of.   *2 Ki* 13:4
openeth their ears in o.   *Job* 36:15
for the o. of the poor.   *Ps* 12:5*
o. of the enemy.   42:9; 43:2; 55:3
forgettest our o.   44:24

trust not in o.   *Ps* 62:10
speak wickedly concerning o.   73:8
brought low through o.   107:39
me from the o. of man.   119:134
seest the o. of the poor.   *Eccl* 5:8
o. maketh a wise man mad.   7:7*
but behold o.   *Isa* 5:7
because ye trust in o.   30:12
thou shalt be far from o.   54:14
speaking o. and revolt.   59:13
she is wholly o. in the midst. *Jer* 6:6
eyes and heart are for o.   22:17
they dealt by o. with.   *Ezek* 22:7
people of the land have used o.   29
not take inheritance by o.   46:18

oppressions
of the multitude of o.   *Job* 35:9
I considered the o. done.   *Eccl* 4:1
despiseth the gain of o.   *Isa* 33:15

oppressor
not the voice of the o.   *Job* 3:18*
of years is hidden to the o.   15:20
break in pieces the o.   *Ps* 72:4
envy not o., choose none.   *Pr* 3:31*
wanteth understanding is an o. 28:16
broken the rod of his o.   *Isa* 9:4
how hath the o. ceased!   14:4
because of the fury of the o.   51:13
deliver him that is spoiled out of the
hand of the o.   *Jer* 21:12; 22:3
of the fierceness of the o.   25:38
no o. shall pass through.   *Zech* 9:8
out of him came every o.   10:4*

oppressors
this is the heritage of o.   *Job* 27:13
strangers risen and o. seek. *Ps* 54:3
leave me not to mine o.   119:121
on the side of their o. there. *Eccl* 4:1
children are their o., women. *Isa* 3:12
they shall rule over their o.   14:2
the o. are consumed out of.   16:4
cry to Lord because of the o.   19:20

oracle
[1] *A place of communication from
God, as the Jewish Holy of Holies*,
1 Ki 6:16. [2] *The word of God,
the Scriptures*, Acts 7:38. *The
word, in the sense in which it is used
in Greek history, is not found in the
Bible, although there are instances
where the thing itself seems referred
to in other words*.
had enquired at the o. of God.
      2 Sam 16:23
for it within, for the o.   *1 Ki* 6:16
the ark of Lord into the o.   8:6
should burn before the o. *2 Chr* 4:20
my hands toward thy holy o. *Ps* 28:2

oracles
who received the lively o.   *Acts* 7:38
committed the o. of God.   *Rom* 3:2
principles of the o. of God. *Heb* 5:12
speak as the o. of God.   *1 Pet* 4:11

oration
Herod made an o. to them.
      Acts 12:21

orator
from Judah the eloquent o. *Isa* 3:3*
certain o. named Tertullus. *Acts* 24:1

orchard
an o. of pomegranates.   *S of S* 4:13

orchards
I made me gardens and o. *Eccl* 2:5*

ordain
[1] *To command or enjoin*, 1 Cor
9:14. [2] *To appoint or design to
a certain end or use*, Rom 7:10.
[3] *To choose or set apart for an
office or employment*, Mark 3:14.
David and Samuel did o. *1 Chr* 9:22
I will o. a place for my people. 17:9*
Lord, thou wilt o. peace.   *Isa* 26:12
so o. I in all churches.   *1 Cor* 7:17
thou shouldest o. elders.   *Tit* 1:5*

ordained
an offering that was o. in. *Num* 28:6
Jeroboam o. a feast. *1 Ki* 12:32, 33
idolatrous priests o.   *2 Ki* 23:5
Jeroboam o. priests for. *2 Chr* 11:15*
offer the offerings as it was o. 23:18*

instruments o. by David. *2 Chr* 29:27
o. the feast of Purim.   *Esth* 9:27
mouth of babes hast thou o. *Ps* 8:2*
the stars which thou hast o.   3
this he o. in Joseph for a.   81:5*
I have o. a lamp for mine.   132:17
Tophet is o. of old, he.   *Isa* 30:33*
I o. thee to be a prophet.   *Jer* 1:5*
king had o. to destroy.   *Dan* 2:24*
O Lord, thou hast o. them. *Hab* 1:12
Jesus o. twelve to be.   *Mark* 3:14*
I have o. that ye should. *John* 15:16*
one o. to be witness with. *Acts* 1:22*
o. of God to be the judge of.   10:42
as many as were o. to eternal. 13:48
when they had o. them elders. 14:23*
decrees that were o. of apostles. 16:4
he will judge the world by that man
whom he hath o.   17:31
which was o. to life.   *Rom* 7:10
powers that be, are o. of God. 13:1
hidden wisdom which God o.
      1 Cor 2:7*
the Lord hath o. that they.   9:14
the law was o. by angels.   *Gal* 3:19
which God hath before o. *Eph* 2:10*
I am o. a preacher and.   *1 Tim* 2:7*
priest is o. for men. *Heb* 5:1*; 8:3*
things were thus o., the priests. 9:6*
who were of old o. to this.   *Jude* 4*

ordaineth
he o. his arrows against.   *Ps* 7:13*

order
priests of second o.   *2 Ki* 23:4
according to their o.   *1 Chr* 6:32
him not after the due o.   15:13*
the o. commanded to them.   23:31*
according to the o. of David. 25:2, 6
      2 Chr 8:14*
darkness, without any o.   *Job* 10:22
priest for ever, after the o. *Ps* 110:4
      Heb 5:6, 10; 6:20; 7:11, 17, 21
given o. to churches of.   *1 Cor* 16:1
joying and beholding your o.   *Col* 2:5
not be called after o. of.   *Heb* 7:11

in order
Abraham laid wood in o.   *Gen* 22:9
two tenons in o.   *Ex* 26:17*
lamps set in o.   39:37
in o. the things that are to be set in o.
      40:4; *Lev* 1:7, 8, 12; 6:12; 24:8
and he set bread in o.   *Ex* 40:23
stalks of flax she had laid in o. upon
the roof.   *Josh* 2:6
put his house in o.   *2 Sam* 17:23
Elijah put wood in o.   *1 Ki* 18:33
set thine house in o.   *2 Ki* 20:1
      Isa 38:1
shew bread also set they in o.
      2 Chr 13:11
house of the Lord set in o.   29:35
set thy words in o. before. *Job* 33:5
reckoned up in o. to thee.   *Ps* 40:5
I will set them in o. before.   50:21
the preacher set in o.   *Eccl* 12:9
who declare it, and set it in o.?
      Isa 44:7
chambers were thirty in o. *Ezek* 41:6
in hand to set forth in o. *Luke* 1:1, 3
served before God in his o.   8
country of Phrygia in o.   *Acts* 18:23
the rest will I set in o.   *1 Cor* 11:34
be done decently and in o.   14:40
shall rise in his o., Christ.   15:23
I left thee to set in o.   *Tit* 1:5

order, verb
Aaron and sons shall o. it. *Ex* 27:21
      Lev 24:3, 4*
shall we o. the child ?   *Judg* 13:12
who shall o. the battle ? *1 Ki* 20:14*
o. my cause before him.   *Job* 23:4
teach us, for we cannot o.   37:19
o. my steps in thy word. *Ps* 119:133
his kingdom to o. it.   *Isa* 9:7*
o. ye the buckler and the. *Jer* 46:3*

ordered, -eth
to Lord in the o. place.   *Judg* 6:26*
covenant o. and sure.   *2 Sam* 23:5
now, I have o. my cause.   *Job* 13:18
steps of a good man are o. *Ps* 37:23*
to him who o. his conversation. 50:23

orderings

their *o.* under Aaron. *1 Chr* 24:19

orderly

walkest *o.* and keepest. *Acts* 21:24

ordinance

[1] *Any decree, statute, or law, made by civil governors,* 1 Pet 2:13.
[2] *A law, statute, or commandment of God,* Lev 18:4. *The Revisions frequently substitute the words* charge *or* statute.

Lord the feast of the passover, for an
  o. *Ex* 12:14, 24, 43; 13:10
for them a statute and an *o.* 15:25
according to *o.* of passover. *Num* 9:14
  2 Chr 35:13
to you for an *o.* for ever. *Num* 10:8
o. shall be for you in your. 15:15
and to thy sons by an *o.* for ever.
  18:8*; *2 Chr* 2:4
o. of law the Lord. *Num* 19:2; 31:21
and he set them an *o.* *Josh* 24:25
made it an *o.* for ever. *1 Sam* 30:25
and made them an *o.* *2 Chr* 35:25
after the *o.* of David. *Ezra* 3:10*
the law, changed the *o.* *Isa* 24:5
forsook not the *o.* of their God. 58:2
concerning the *o.* of oil. *Ezek* 45:14
an offering by a perpetual *o.* 46:14
that we have kept his *o.?* *Mal* 3:14
resisteth the *o.* of God. *Rom* 13:2
to every *o.* of man. *1 Pet* 2:13

ordinances

shalt teach them *o.* and. *Ex* 18:20
shall ye walk in their *o.* *Lev* 18:3
ye shall keep mine *o.* 4, 30; 22:9
  2 Chr 33:8; *Ezek* 11:20; 43:11
  1 Cor 11:2*
the *o.* of the passover. *Num* 9:12, 14
do they after their *o.* *2 Ki* 17:34
o. which he wrote for you. 37
made *o.* for us to charge. *Neh* 10:32
guide Arcturus? knowest thou the *o.?*
  Job 38:33; *Jer* 31:35; 33:25
they kept the *o.* that he. *Ps* 99:7
according to thine *o.* 119:91
the *o.* of justice, delight. *Isa* 58:2
if those *o.* depart from. *Jer* 31:36
he said, These are the *o.* *Ezek* 43:18
o. of the house of the Lord. 44:5
are gone away from mine *o.* *Mal* 3:7
Zacharias and Elisabeth walking in all
  commandments and *o.* *Luke* 1:6
law of commandments contained in *o.*
  Eph 2:15
the handwriting of *o.* *Col* 2:14
in the world, are ye subject to *o.?* 20
the first covenant had *o.* of. *Heb* 9:1
stood in carnal *o.* imposed on. 10

ordinary

diminished thine *o.* food. *Ezek* 16:27

Oreb

slew princes of Midian, Zeeb, O.
  Judg 7:25; 8:3
nobles like O. and Zeeb. *Ps* 83:11
Midian at the rock of O. *Isa* 10:26

organ, -s

(*Not the organ as we know it, but a perforated wind instrument, a pipe. It may be the ancient pipes of Pan, known to the Greeks. The Revisions translate it by the word* pipe)

father of such as handle *o.* *Gen* 4:21
rejoice at sound of the *o.* *Job* 21:12
o. turned into voice of them. 30:31
with the timbrel and *o.* *Ps* 150:4

Orion

who maketh O. and Pleiades.
  Job 9:9; *Amos* 5:8
or canst thou loose the bands of O.?
  Job 38:31

ornament

an *o.* of grace to thy head. *Pr* 1:9*
to thine head an *o.* of grace. 4:9*
an *o.* of fine gold, so is a wise. 25:12
ye shall defile *o.* of thy. *Isa* 30:22*
clothe thee with them all as with an *o.*
  49:18
the beauty of his *o.* he set. *Ezek* 7:20
even the *o.* of a meek. *1 Pet* 3:4*

ornaments

no man did put on him his *o.* *Ex* 33:4
now put off thy *o.* from thee. 5, 6
Gideon took *o.* that. *Judg* 8:21*
rings that he requested, beside *o.* 26*
Saul, who put *o.* on your. *2 Sam* 1:24
shall take away tinkling *o.* *Isa* 3:18*
bonnets, and the *o.* of the legs. 20*
decketh himself with *o.* 61:10*
can maid forget her *o.* or ? *Jer* 2:32
deckest thee with *o.* of gold. 4:30
art come to excellent *o.* *Ezek* 16:7
decked thee with *o.*, put bracelets. 11
deckedst thyself with *o.* 23:40

Ornan

the threshingfloor of O.
  1 Chr 21:15, 18, 28
and O. turned back, and saw. 20
David gave to O. for the place. 25

Orpah

the name of the one was O. *Ruth* 1:4
O. kissed Naomi, but Ruth. 14

orphans

we are *o.*, our mothers. *Lam* 5:3

Oshea, *see* Joshua

osprey, ossifrage

(*Revisions,* the gier eagle)
eagle, *osp.* and *ossif.* not eat.
  Lev 11:13; *Deut* 14:12

ostrich

wings and feathers to *o.?* *Job* 39:13*

ostriches

become cruel, like *o.* in. *Lam* 4:3

other

Noah stayed yet *o.* *Gen* 8:10, 12
is none *o.* but the house. 28:17
me yet *o.* seven years. 29:27, 30
if thou take *o.* wives beside. 31:50
then the *o.* company that is left. 32:8
seven *o.* kine came up. 41:3, 19
send away your *o.* brother. 43:14
o. money have we brought down. 22
was turned again as his *o.* *Ex* 4:7
they asked each *o.* of their. 18:7
the *o.* lamb offer thou at even. 29:41
  Num 28:8
ye shall not make any *o.* *Ex* 30:32
put off his garments, and put on *o.*
  Lev 6:11; *Ezek* 42:14; 44:19
fat be used in any *o.* use. *Lev* 7:24
take *o.* stones and *o.* mortar. 14:42
take a wife beside the *o.* in. 18:18
separated you from *o.* 20:24, 26
and the *o.* did set up. *Num* 10:21
he went not as at *o.* times. 24:1
they gave *o.* names to the. 32:38
married to any of the *o.* tribes. 36:3
all *o.* cities they took. *Josh* 11:19
came to me the *o.* day. *Judg* 13:10
and he like any *o.* man. 16:17
I will go out as at *o.* times. 20
began to kill as at *o.* times. 20:31
Lord called as at *o.* times, Samuel.
  1 Sam 3:10
with his hand as at *o.* times. 18:10
Saul sat on his seat as at *o.* 20:25
for there is no *o.* save. 21:9
evil is greater than *o.* *2 Sam* 13:16
to keep *o.* seven days. *2 Chr* 30:23
Hezekiah from hand of all *o.* 32:22
for the *o.* half of them held. *Neh* 4:16
for *o.* men have our lands and. 5:5
flag withereth before any *o.* herb.
  Job 8:12
out of the way, as all *o.* 24:24
in trouble as *o.* men, neither are they
  plagued like *o.* men. *Ps* 73:5
and peace kissed each *o.* 85:10
more rest than the *o.* *Eccl* 6:5
o. lords have had. *Isa* 26:13
after thou hast lost the *o.* 49:20
in thee from *o.* women. *Ezek* 16:34
none *o.* can shew it. *Dan* 2:11
not be left to *o.* people. 44
joy, O Israel, as *o.* people. *Hos* 9:1
where is any *o.* to save ? 13:10
he saw *o.* two brethren. *Mat* 4:21
cheek, turn to him the *o.* also. 5:39
restored whole as *o.* 12:13
  Mark 3:5; *Luke* 6:10
then he taketh seven *o.* spirits.
  Mat 12:45; *Luke* 11:26

o. fell into good ground. *Mat* 13:8
  Mark 4:8; *Luke* 8:8
o. servants more. *Mat* 21:36; 22:4
he will let out his vineyard to *o.* 21:41
and not to leave *o.* undone. 23:23
  Luke 11:42
came also the *o.* virgins. *Mat* 25:11
and made them *o.* five talents. 16
and the lusts of *o.* *Mark* 4:19
and many *o.* things there be. 7:4, 8
o. commandment is greater. 12:31
God, and there is none *o.* but. 32
preach kingdom of God to *o.* cities.
  Luke 4:43
Lord appointed *o.* seventy also. 10:1
or else while the *o.* is yet a. 14:32
that I am not as *o.* men. 18:11
down justified rather than the *o.* 14
o. things blasphemously. 22:65
o. men laboured. *John* 4:38
o. sheep I have. 10:16
not done works none *o.* man. 15:24
went out that *o.* disciple. 18:16
there are many *o.* things. 21:25
to speak with *o.* tongues *Acts* 2:4
and with many *o.* words. 40
salvation in any *o.* none *o.* name under
  heaven whereby we must be. 4:12
of himself, or of some *o.* man.? 8:34
nor *o.* creature, shall be. *Rom* 8:39
any *o.* commandment, it is. 13:9
whether I baptized any *o.* *1 Cor* 1:16
o. foundation can no man lay. 3:11
lead about sister, as well as *o.* 9:5
every one taketh before *o.* 11:21
but the *o.* is not edified. 14:17
of *o.* tongues and *o.* lips I. 21
speak, and let the *o.* judge. 29
of wheat, or some *o.* grain. 15:37
for I mean not that *o.* *2 Cor* 8:13
not boasting of *o.* men's. 10:15
I robbed *o.* churches to do. 11:8
I write to them and to all *o.* 13:2
o. apostles saw I none. *Gal* 1:19
and the *o.* Jews dissembled. 2:13
which in *o.* ages was not. *Eph* 3:5
that ye walk not as *o.* Gentiles. 4:17
but the *o.* preach Christ. *Phil* 1:17
let each esteem *o.* better than. 2:3
if any *o.* thinketh that he might. 3:4
with Clement and with *o.* my. 4:3
charity toward each *o.* *2 Thes* 1:3
teach no *o.* doctrine. *1 Tim* 1:3
be any *o.* thing contrary to. 10
partaker of *o.* men's sins. 5:22
swear by any *o.* oath. *Jas* 5:12
as a busybody in *o.* *1 Pet* 4:15
they wrest, as they do *o.* *2 Pet* 3:16
on you none *o.* burden. *Rev* 2:24
by reason of the *o.* voices. 8:13

see God, gods, one, side

others

of the earth shall *o.* grow. *Job* 8:19
o. bow down upon her. 31:10
shall set *o.* in their stead. 34:24
them in the open sight of *o.* 26
leave their wealth to *o.* *Ps* 49:10
give thine honour to *o.* *Pr* 5:9
likewise hast cursed *o.* *Eccl* 7:22
yet will I gather *o.* to him. *Isa* 56:8
shall be turned to *o.* *Jer* 6:12
I will give their wives unto *o.* 8:10
and they have made *o.* *Ezek* 13:6
o. daubed it with untempered. 10
was diverse from all *o.* *Dan* 7:19
kingdom shall be plucked up for *o.*
  11:4
do ye more than *o.?* *Mat* 5:47
o. say, that thou art Jeremias. 16:14
  Mark 6:15; 8:28; *Luke* 9:8, 19
he saw *o.* standing idle. *Mat* 20:3
o. cut down branches from trees.
  21:8; *Mark* 11:8
o. smote him with the palms of.
  Mat 26:67
will give vineyard to *o.* *Mark* 12:9
  Luke 20:16
He saved *o.*; himself he cannot save.
  Mark 15:31; *Luke* 23:35
o. which ministered to. *Luke* 8:3
did *o.* tell it thee of me ? *John* 18:34
if I be not an apostle to *o.? 1 Cor* 9:2
if *o.* be partakers of this power. 12

I have preached to o. *1 Cor 9:27*
not thine own, but of the o. 10:29
by my voice I might teach o 14:19
or need we, as some o., epistles of
commendation? *2 Cor 3:1*
of the forwardness of o. 8:8
children of wrath, even as o. *Eph 2:3*
also on the things of o. *Phil 2:4*
nor yet of o. sought we. *1 Thes 2:6*
that ye sorrow not, as o. which. 4:13
let us not sleep as do o. but. 5:6
sin rebuke, that o. may. *1 Tim 5:20*
be able to teach o. also. *2 Tim 2:2*
every year with blood of o. *Heb 9:25*
o. were tortured, not. 11:35
o. had trial of cruel mockings. 36
o. save with fear, pulling. *Jude 23*

otherwise
o. I should have wrought falsehood
against mine own. *2 Sam 18:13*
o. it shall come to pass. *1 Ki 1:21*
they eat passover o. *2 Chr 30:18*
lest o. they should. *Ps 38:16*
o. have no reward of. *Mal 6:1*
o. grace is no more grace; then is it
no more grace: o. *Rom 11:6*
toward thee goodness: o. thou. 22
if o. yet as a fool. *2 Cor 11:16*
will be none o. minded. *Gal 5:10*
any thing you be o. minded *Phil 3:15*
and they that are o. *1 Tim 5:25*
if any man teach o. and consent. 6:3
o. it is of no strength at. *Heb 9:17*

Othniel
O. son of Kenaz took it. *Josh 15:17*
Judg 1:13
Lord raised a deliverer, O. *Judg 3:9*
O. died. 11
sons of Kenaz, O. Seraiah, sons of O.
1 Chr 4:13
captain was Heldai of O. 27:15

ouches
(*Ornaments set with jewels.
American Revision changes to setting except in starred reference*)
set the stones in o. of gold.
Ex 28:11; 39:6, 13
shalt make o. of gold. 28:13
fasten wreathen chains to the o.
14; 39:18*
fasten in the two o. 28:25

ought, see owed
ought
that o. not to be done. *Gen 20:9*
34:7; *Lev 4:2, 27*
no such thing o. to be. *2 Sam 13:12*
to know what Israel o. *1 Chr 12:32*
none o. to carry the ark but. 15:2
o. ye not to know Lord. *2 Chr 13:5*
o. ye not to walk in the ? *Neh 5:9*
to him who o. to be feared. *Ps 76:11*
these o. ye to have done.
Mat 23:23; Luke 11:42
desolation standing where it o. not.
Mark 13:14
hour what ye o. to say. *Luke 12:12*
days in which men o. to work. 13:14
o. not this man to be loosed ? 16
that men o. always to pray. 18:1
O fools, o. not Christ to ? 24:26
the place where men o. *John 4:20*
o. to wash one another's feet. 13:14
and by our law he o. to die. 19:7
we o. to obey God. *Acts 5:29*
o. not to think the Godhead. 17:29
ye o. to be quiet, and to do. 19:36
how so labouring ye o. 20:35
that they o. not to circumcise. 21:21
who o. to have been here. 24:19
judgement seat, where I o. to. 25:10
crying, that he o. not to live. 24
that I o. to do many things. 26:9
what to pray for as we o. *Rom 8:26*
more highly than he o. 12:3
we o. to bear the infirmities of. 15:1
nothing as he o. to know. *1 Cor 8:2*
o. not to cover his head. 11:7
the woman o. to have power. 10
of whom I o. to rejoice. *2 Cor 2:3*
ye o. rather to forgive him. 7
I o. to have been commended. 12:11

the children o. not to lay up.
2 Cor 12:14
so o. men to love their. *Eph 5:28*
may speak boldly, as I o. to speak.
6:20; *Col 4:4*
know how ye o. to answer. *Col 4:6*
how ye o. to walk. *1 Thes 4:1*
know how ye o. to follow. *2 Thes 3:7*
speaking things which they o. not.
1 Tim 5:13
teaching things which they o. not.
Tit 1:11
we o. to give the more. *Heb 2:1*
he o. for people and for himself. 5:3
for when for the time ye o. 12
these things o. not so to be. *Jas 3:10*
for that ye o. to say. If the. 4:15
persons o. ye to be ? *2 Pet 3:11*
o. himself also to walk. *1 John 2:6*
o. to lay down our lives for. 3:16
if God loved us, we o. also. 4:11
we therefore o. to receive. *3 John 8*

ought, substantive
(*Practically everywhere the Revisions have changed this to
aught*)
he knew not o. that he had. *Gen 39:6*
there is not o. left, but our bodies.
47:18
ye shall not diminish o. thereof.
Ex 5:8; 11:19
thou shalt not carry forth o. 12:46
if a man borrow o. of his. 22:14
o. of flesh of the consecrations. 29:34
beareth o. of carcase. *Lev 11:25*
if o. remain unto third day. 19:6
if thou sellest o. or buyest o. 25:14
redeem o. of his tithes. 27:31
if o. be committed by. *Num 15:24*
the soul that doeth o. 30
when she vowed, or uttered o. 30:6
add or diminish o. from it. *Deut 4:2*
lendeth o. to his neighbour. 15:2
neither have I taken away o. for any
unclean use, nor given o. 26:14
there failed not o. of any. *Josh 21:45*
if o. but death part thee. *Ruth 1:17*
nor hast thou taken o. *1 Sam 12:4*
that ye have not found o. in. 5
neither was there o. missing. 25:7
we will not give them o. 30:22
if I taste bread or o. *2 Sam 3:35*
whoso saith o. to thee. 14:10
none can turn from o. my lord. 19
that thy brother hath o. *Mat 5:23*
if any man say o. to you, ye. 21:3
him no more to do o. *Mark 7:12*
and asked him if he saw o. 8:23
if ye have o. against any. 11:25
brought him o. to eat ? *John 4:33*
neither said any that o. *Acts 4:32*
and object, if they had o. 24:19
that I had o. to accuse my. 28:19
if he oweth thee o. put to. *Philem 18*

oughtest
what thou o. to do to him. *1 Ki 2:9*
thou o. to have put my. *Mat 25:27*
thee what thou o. to do. *Acts 10:6*
how thou o. to behave. *1 Tim 3:15*

our, see brother, father, Lord
ours
saying, The water is o. *Gen 26:20*
from our father that is o. 31:16
every beast of theirs be o.? 34:23
side Jordan may be o. *Num 32:32*
Ramoth in Gilead is o. *1 Ki 22:3*
ancient high places are o. *Ezek 36:2*
and inheritance shall be o.
Mark 12:7; Luke 20:14
Jesus, both theirs and o. *1 Cor 1:2*
ye also are o. in the day. *2 Cor 1:14*
let o. also learn to maintain. *Tit 3:14*

ourselves
and bow down o.? *Gen 37:10*
how shall we clear o.? 44:16
o. will go ready armed. *Num 32:17*
for a prey unto o. *Deut 2:35; 3:7*
we will discover o. *1 Sam 14:8*
we o. together will build. *Ezra 4:3*
that we might afflict o. before. 8:21
among o. what is good. *Job 34:4*
let us take to o. houses. *Ps 83:12*

made us, and not we o. *Ps 100:3*
come, let us solace o. *Pr 7:18*
falsehood have we hid o. *Isa 28:15*
we will fill o. with strong. 56:12
come let us join o. to. *Jer 50:5*
we o. have heard. *Luke 22:71*
John 4:42
we will give o. to prayer. *Acts 6:4*
we have bound o. under a. 23:14
we o. groan within o. *Rom 8:23*
bear and not to please o. 15:1
if we would judge o. *1 Cor 11:31*
wherewith we o. are. *2 Cor 1:4*
that we should not trust in o. 9
again to commend o. to you ? 3:1
not that we are sufficient of o. to
think any thing as of o., but our. 5
commending o. to every man's. 4:2
for we preach not o. but Christ Jesus
the Lord, and o. your servants. 5
for we commend not o. again. 5:12
whether we be beside o. it is. 13
in all things approving o. 6:4
let us cleanse o. from all. 7:1
or compare o. with some. 10:12
we stretch not o. beyond. 14
think ye we excuse o.? 12:19
we o. also are found. *Gal 2:17*
how holily we behaved o.
1 Thes 2:10
so that we o. glory in. *2 Thes 1:4*
we behaved not o. disorderly. 3:7
make o. an ensample unto you. 9
for we o. were sometimes. *Tit 3:3*
the assembling of o. *Heb 10:25*
we deceive o., the truth. *1 John 1:8*

out
o. of ground made Lord. *Gen 2:9*
she was taken o. of man. 23
for o. of it wast thou taken. 3:19
your sin will find you o. *Num 32:23*
as for the earth, o. of it. *Job 28:5*
o. of the mouth of babes. *Ps 8:2*
foundations of the earth are o. 82:5
thou teachest o. of thy law. 94:12
blessed you o. of house. 118:26
keep thy heart, for o. of it. *Pr 4:23*
candle goeth not o. by night. 31:18
sinners thereof o. of it. *Isa 13:9*
see o. of obscurity, o. of. 29:18
shall be saved o. of it. *Jer 30:7*
and o. of them shall proceed. 19
behold I will seek o. *Ezek 34:11*
that they bear them not o. into. 46:20
yet o. of thee shall he come forth to.
Mi 5:2; Mat 2:6
o. of him came forth. *Zech 10:4*
o. of the abundance of. *Mat 12:34*
o. of good treasure: . . . o. of evil. 35
o. of the heart proceed evil. 15:19
they were astonished o. *Mark 10:26*
nor enter to take any thing o. 13:15
o. of whom he had cast seven. 16:9
o. of thine own mouth. *Luke 19:22*
I have chosen you o. *John 15:19*
devout men, o. of every. *Acts 2:5*
both o. of the law, and o. 28:23
seen o. of me, as of one born o. of due
time. *1 Cor 15:8*
for o. of much affliction. *2 Cor 2:4*
be a performance o. of that. 8:11
recover themselves o. of. *2 Tim 2:26*
but o. of them all the Lord. 3:11
instant in season, o. of season. 4:2
o. of same mouth proceedeth blessing and cursing. *Jas 3:10*
see **camp, captivity, city, darkness, way, Zion**

outcast
they called thee an o. *Jas 30:17*

outcasts
he gathereth o. of Israel. *Ps 147:2*
Isa 56:8
he shall assemble the o. *Isa 11:12*
hide the o. 16:3
let my o. dwell with thee. 4
the o. in the land of Egypt. 27:13
whither the o. of. Elam. *Jer 49:36*

outer
into the o. court. *Ezek 46:21*
way without to the o. gate. 8:16
be cast into o. darkness. *Mat 8:12*
22:13; 25:30

outgoings
the o. of it were at the sea.
    Josh 17:9; 19:39
o. of it shall be thine.   18
the o. of the border were.   18:19
o. thereof are in the valley.   19:14
the o. of their border were.   22, 33
thou makest the o. of the.   Ps 65:8

outlandish
(This word formerly meant strictly
out-landish; i.e. anything which
was from another country with
other customs, hence strange, as the
Revisions put it)
even o. women caused Solomon to
sin.   Neh 13:26

outlived
elders that o. Joshua.   Judg 2:7

outrageous
cruel and anger is o.   Pr 27:4†

outrun
disciple did o. Peter.   John 20:4

outside
Gideon went to o. of the. Judg 7:11
and when I come to the o. of.   17
came to the o. of the camp.   19
and so on o. toward the. 1 Ki 7:9
behold a wall on the o. Ezek 40:5
make clean o. of the cup.
    Mat 23:25; Luke 11:39
o. of them may be clean also.   26

outstretched
out with an o. arm.   Deut 26:8
against you with an o. hand. Jer 21:5
made the earth by my o. arm. 27:5

outward
for man looketh on the o. 1 Sam 16:7
Chenaniah for the o. 1 Chr 26:29
Levites for o. business. Neh 11:16
come into the o. court. Esth 6:4
me into the o. court. Ezek 40:17
which appear beautiful o. Mat 23:27
nor circumcision,which is o. Rom 2:28
though our o. man perish. 2 Cor 4:16
on things after o. appearance? 10:7
not that o. adorning of. 1 Pet 3:3

outwardly
ye o. appear righteous. Mat 23:28
for he is not a Jew which is one o.
    Rom 2:28

outwent
afoot thither, and o.   Mark 6:33

oven
(The word frequently means
furnace)
offering baken in the o. Lev 2:4; 7:9
be unclean, whether it be o. 11:35
bake your bread in one o. 26:26
make them as a fiery o. Ps 21:9
skin was black like an o. Lam 5:10
adulterers, as an o. heated. Hos 7:4
made ready their heart like an o. 6
are all hot as an o., have devoured. 7
that shall burn as an o. Mal 4:1
grass, which to-morrow is cast into
the o. Mat 6:30; Luke 12:28

ovens
frogs shall come into thine o. Ex 8:3

over
first red, all o. like an. Gen 25:25
lord o. thy brethren, let them. 27:29
Pharaoh said, Thou shalt be o. 41:40
gathered much had nothing o.
    Ex 16:18; 2 Cor 8:15
what remaineth o. lay up. Ex 16:23
the mercy seat o. the testimony.
    30:6; Heb 9:5
the cherubims covered o. the mercy
seat. Ex 37:9
cloud was taken up from o. 40:36
one be killed o. running water.
    Lev 14:5; 6:50
shalt appoint Levites o. Num 1:50
o. and above them that were. 3:49
trumpets o. burnt offerings. 10:10
let the Lord set a man o. 27:16
dominion o. the nobles, o. Judg 5:13
and go to be promoted o. the trees.
    9:9, 11, 13
o. Saul and Jonathan. 2 Sam 1:17, 24

king o. Gilead, o. Ashurites, o. Jezreel, o. Ephraim and o. 2 Sam 2:9
Edom made a king o. 2 Ki 8:20
o. and above all I have. 1 Chr 29:3
increased o. our heads. Ezra 9:6
not watch o. my sin? Job 14:16
he is a king o. the children. 41:34
my cup runneth o. Ps 23:5
deliver me not o. to the will. 27:12
but he hath not given me o. 118:18
his tender mercies are o. all. 145:9
neither make thyself o. wise.
    Eccl 7:16
past, rain is o. and gone. S of S 2:11
set thee o. nations and o. Jer 1:10
he setteth up o. it the basest of men.
    Dan 4:17
king thought to set him o. the. 6:3
people shall mourn o. it. Hos 10:5
shall be dark o. them. Mi 3:6
thee ruler o. many. Mat 25:21, 23
together, and running o. Luke 6:38
more joy o. one sinner. 15:7, 10
this man to reign o. us. 19:14
thou authority o. ten cities. 17
he beheld city, and wept o. it. 41
appoint o. this business. Acts 6:3
hath dominion o. a man. Rom 7:1
the potter power o. the clay ? 9:21
given o. to lasciviousness. Eph 4:19
authority o. the man. 1 Tim 2:12
eyes of the Lord are o. 1 Pet 3:12
to him will I give power o. Rev 2:26
see all, him, Jordan, Israel, me,
    thee, them, us, you

over against
candlestick o. against table.
    Ex 26:35; 40:24
o. against candlestick. Num 8:2*, 3*
come on them o. against mulberry.
    2 Sam 5:23; 1 Chr 14:14
pitched one o. against. 1 Ki 20:29
one to be o. against house. Neh 7:3
set one o. against the. Eccl 7:14*
line shall yet go forth o. against it.
    Jer 31:39*
go into village o. against. Mat 21:2
    Mark 11:2; Luke 19:30
and Mary sitting o. against the
sepulchre. Mat 27:61

overcame
evil spirit was, o. them. Acts 19:16
even as I also o. and am. Rev 3:21
and they o. him by the blood. 12:11

overcharge
that I may not o. you all. 2 Cor 2:5*

overcharged
lest your hearts be o. Luke 21:34

overcome
o. him, but he shall o. Gen 49:19*
that cry for being o. Ex 32:18
we are well able to o. it. Num 13:30
peradventure I be able to o. 22:11*
Ahaz, could not o. him. 2 Ki 16:5
eyes, for they have o. me. S of S 6:5
head of them that are o. with wine.
    Isa 28:1
man whom wine hath o. Jer 23:9
a stronger shall o. him. Luke 11:22
I have o. the world. John 16:33
and mightest o. when. Rom 3:4*
be not o. of evil, but o. evil. 12:21
of whom a man is o., of same is he
brought. 2 Pet 2:19
for if they are again entangled therein and o. 20
o. the wicked one. 1 John 2:13, 14
ye are of God and have o. them. 4:4
beast shall o. witnesses. Rev 11:7
the saints, and to o. them. 13:7
and the Lamb shall o. them. 17:14

overcometh
of God, o. the world: this is victory
that o. world, even. 1 John 5:4
who is he that o. world, but he? 5
to him that o. will I give. Rev 2:7
he that o. shall not be hurt. 11
to him that o. will I give to eat. 17
to him that o. will I give power. 26
he that o. shall be clothed. 3:5
him that o. will I make pillar. 12
to him that o. will I grant. 21
he that o. shall inherit all. 21:7

overdrive
if men should o. them all. Gen 33:13

overflow
of Red sea to o. them. Deut 11:4
where the floods o. me. Ps 69:2
let not water flood o. me, nor. 15*
pass through Judah, o. Isa 8:8
consumption decreed shall o. 10:22
waters shall o. hiding place. 28:17
rivers they shall not o. thee. 43:2
north shall o. the land. Jer 47:2
one shall certainly come and o.
    Dan 11:10; 26:40
fats shall o. with wine and oil.
    Joel 2:24; 3:13

overflowed
rock, and streams o. Ps 78:20
world being o. with water. 2 Pet 3:6

overfloweth
Jordan o. all his banks. Josh 3:15

overflowing
bindeth the floods from o. Job 28:11*
water course for o. of waters. 38:25
flood of mighty waters o. Isa 28:2
when the o. scourge shall. 15, 18
his breath as an o. stream. 30:28
north shall be an o. flood. Jer 47:2
be an o. shower. Ezek 13:11, 13
I will rain on him an o. rain. 38:22
o. of the water passed. Hab 3:10*

overflown
Jordan when it had o. 1 Chr 12:15†
whose foundation was o. Job 22:16
flood shall they be o. Dan 11:22*

overlaid
shittim wood o. with gold. Ex 26:32
o. the staves of shittim wood. 38:6
died, because she o. it. 1 Ki 3:19
he o. the doors of them. 2 Chr 4:9
belly is as bright ivory o. S of S 5:14

overlay
shalt o. ark with pure gold.
    Ex 25:11, 24; 30:3
o. the horns of the altar with brass.
    27:2; 38:2

see gold

overlaying
the o. of their chapiters. Ex 38:17
o. of their chapiters and fillets. 19

overlived
elders that o. Joshua. Josh 24:31*

overmuch
be not righteous o. Eccl 7:16
be not o. wicked. 17
be swallowed up with o. sorrow.
    2 Cor 2:7

overpass
they shine:they o. the deeds. Jer 5:28

overpast
until these calamities be o. Ps 57:1
until indignation be o. Isa 26:20

overplus
let him restore the o. Lev 25:27

overran
by plain and o. Cushi. 2 Sam 18:23

overrunning
with an o. flood he will. Nah 1:8

oversee
some appointed to o. 1 Chr 9:29*
and 3600 to o. them. 2 Chr 2:2

overseer
he made him o. over. Gen 39:4, 5
Joel was their o. Neh 11:9
Zabdiel was o. 14
o. of Levites was Uzzi. 22
Jezrahiah was o. 12:42
the ant having no guide, o. Pr 6:7

overseers
let Pharaoh appoint o. Gen 41:34
Solomon set 3600 o. of the work.
    2 Chr 2:18
o. under hand of Cononiah. 31:13*
o. of all them that wrought. 34:12, 13
money into hand of o. 17
H. G. hath made you o. Acts 20:28

overshadow
Highest shall o. thee. Luke 1:35
of Peter might o. them. Acts 5:15

overshadowed
a cloud o. them. Mat 17:5
Mark 9:7; Luke 9:34

oversight
peradventure it was an o. Gen 43:12
have the o. of them. Num 3:32
pertaineth the o. of all the. 4:16*
of them that had the o. 2 Ki 12:11
22:5, 9; 2 Chr 34:10
had the o. of the gates. 1 Chr 9:23
o. of outward business. Neh 11:16
o. of the chamber of the house. 13:4*
taking o. not by constraint. 1 Pet 5:2

overspread
was the whole earth o. Gen 9:19

overspreading
for the o. of abominations. Dan 9:27*

overtake
up, when thou dost o. Gen 44:4
I will pursue, I will o. Ex 15:9
lest avenger of blood o. Deut 19:6
shall come and o. thee. 28:2
these curses shall o. thee. 15, 45
them, for ye shall o. them. Josh 2:5
Shall I o. them? Pursue: for thou
shalt surely o. them. 1 Sam 30:8
lest Absalom o. us. 2 Sam 15:14
neither doth justice o. us. Isa 59:9
ye feared shall o. you. Jer 42:16
she shall not o. her lovers. Hos 2:7
Gibeah did not o. them. 10:9
not o. nor prevent us. Amos 9:10
behold, the plowman shall o. 13
should o. you as a thief. 1 Thes 5:4

overtaken
mine enemies and o. Ps 18:37
brethren, if a man be o. Gal 6:1

overtaketh
while sword o. thee. 1 Chr 21:12

overthrew
God o. these cities. Gen 19:25, 29
Lord o. the Egyptians. Ex 14:27
Ps 136:15
Lord o. in his anger. Deut 29:23
as when God o. Sodom. Isa 13:19
Jer 50:40; Amos 4:11
be as the cities Lord o. Jer 20:16
Jesus o. tables of the. Mat 21:12
Mark 11:15; John 2:15

overthrow
I will not o. this city. Gen 19:21
thou shalt utterly o. them. Ex 23:24
ye shall o. their altars. Deut 12:3*
sent to spy it out and o. 2 Sam 10:3
battle more strong, and o. it. 11:25
David hath sent to o. them in the. 1 Chr 19:3
his hand to o. them in the. Ps 106:26
to o. their seed also among the. 27
who have purposed to o. him. 140:4*
the violent man to o. him. 11
not good to o. righteous. Pr 18:5*
I will o. the throne of kingdoms, I
will o. the chariots. Hag 2:22
of God, ye cannot o. it. Acts 5:39
and o. the faith of some. 2 Tim 2:18

overthrow, substantive
out of the midst of the o. Gen 19:29
as in the o. of Sodom. Deut 29:23
Jer 49:18
the cities with an o. 2 Pet 2:6

overthroweth
princes, and o. the mighty. Job 12:19
but wickedness o. the. Pr 13:6
God o. the wicked for. 21:12
he o. the words of the. 22:12
but he that receiveth gifts o. 29:4

overthrown
hast o. them that rose up. Ex 15:7
and many were o. Judg 9:40*
when some of them be o. at the first.
2 Sam 17:9*
Ethiopians were o. 2 Chr 14:13*
that God hath o. me. Job 19:6
judges are o. in stony places.
Ps 141:6
city is o. by the mouth. Pr 11:11
the wicked are o., and are not. 12:7
house of wicked shall be o. 14:11
your land is desolate, as o. Isa 1:7
but let them be o. before. Jer 18:23
sin of Sodom, that was o. Lam 4:6

countries shall be o. Dan 11:41
I have o. some of you. Amos 4:11
and Nineveh shall be o. Jonah 3:4
o. in the wilderness. 1 Cor 10:5

overtook
they o. Jacob in the. Gen 31:23
Laban o. Jacob. 25
the steward o. them. 44:6
Egyptians o. them. Ex 14:9
Micah o. the children. Judg 18:22
but the battle o. the men. 20:42*
the army of Chaldees o. 2 Ki 25:5
Jer 39:5; 52:8
all her persecutors o. her. Lam 2:3

overturn
waters, they o. earth. Job 12:15
I will o., o., o. it, until. Ezek 21:27

overturned
tent that it fell and o. it. Judg 7:13*

overturneth
which o. the mountains. Job 9:5
o. the mountains by the roots. 28:9
knoweth their works and o. 34:25

overwhelm
ye o. fatherless, dig a pit. Job 6:27*

overwhelmed
and horror hath o. me. Ps 55:5
when my heart is o. lead me. 61:2
and my spirit was o. 77:3; 142:3
143:4
but the sea o. their enemies. 78:53
then the waters had o. us. 124:4

owe
o. no man any thing. Rom 13:8

owed
o. him 10,000 talents. Mat 18:24
and found one which o. him an. 28
the one o. 500 pence. Luke 7:41

owest
pay me that thou o. Mat 18:28
how much o. thou unto my lord?
Luke 16:5, 7
thou o. to me even thine. Philem 19

oweth
hath wronged thee, or o. Philem 18

owl
(While different sorts of owls are
found in Palestine, the word so
translated more often means some
other bird or animal, usually the
ostrich)
o. and cuckow unclean. Lev 11:16*
Deut 14:15*, 16
the little o. and cormorant.
Lev 11:17; Isa 34:11, 15*
I am like an o. of desert. Ps 102:6

owls
(Revisions in all cases, ostriches)
companion to o., a brother. Job 30:29
the wild beasts shall lie there, and o.
Isa 13:21; 34:13; Jer 50:39
the dragons and the o. shall. 43:20
a mourning as the o. Mi 1:8

own
man in his o. image. Gen 1:27
begat a son in his o. likeness. 5:3
shall come of thine o. bowels. 15:4
I may go to mine o. place. 30:25
four parts shall be your o. 47:24
dead shall be his o. Ex 21:36
of the best of his o. field shall. 22:5
he shall offer it of his own. Lev 1:3
his o. hands shall bring the. 7:30
palm of his o. left hand. 14:15, 26
theirs is thine o. nakedness. 18:10
nor any of your o. nation, nor. 26
groweth of its o. accord. 25:5
and he shall return to his o. 41
his o. camp, by his o. Num 1:52
them of mine o. mind. 16:28; 24:13
sinners against their o. souls. 16:38
he called it after his o. name. 32:42
Deut 3:14
shall keep himself to his o. Num 36:9
eat grapes at thine o. Deut 23:24
sleep in his o. raiment. 24:13
every man shall be put to death for
o. sin. 16; 2 Ki 14:6; 2 Chr 25:4
fruit of thine o. body. Deut 28:53
nor knew he his o. children. 33:9

even among their o. stuff. Josh 7:11
from their o. doings. Judg 2:19
saying, Mine o. hand hath. 7:2
went to their o. home. 1 Sam 2:20
ark go again to his o. place. 5:11
wast little in thine o. sight. 15:17
avenging with thine o. hand. 25:26
base in mine o. sight. 2 Sam 6:22
dwell in a place of their o. 7:10
did eat of his o. meat, and. 12:3
to battle in thine o. person. 17:11
falsehood against mine o. life. 18:13
word against his o. life. 1 Ki 2:23
blood on his o. head. 32, 37
carcase in his o. grave. 13:30
laid him upon his o. bed. 17:19
made gods of their o. 2 Ki 17:29
and of thine o. have. 1 Chr 29:14
store we prepared, is all thine o. 16
his way on his o. head. 2 Chr 6:23
reproach on his o. head. Neh 4:4
should return on o. head. Esth 9:25
perish for ever like his o. Job 20:7
let them fall by their o. Ps 5:10
our lips are our o.: who is ? 12:4
God, even our o. God, shall. 67:6
he gave them their o. desire. 78:29
up to their o. hearts' lust. 81:12
their o. iniquity, and shall cut them
off in their o. wickedness. 94:23
let them be only thy o. Pr 5:17
for mine o. sake. Isa 37:35; 43:25
48:11
o. pleasure, nor o. words. 58:13
my river is mine o. Ezek 29:3
to his o. righteousness. 33:13
now their o. doings have. Hos 7:2
forsake their o. mercy. Jonah 2:8
what I will with mine o.? Mat 20:15
hate not his o. life also. Luke 14:26
you that which is your o.? 16:12
o., his o. received him not. John 1:11
a lie, he speaketh of his o. 8:44
an hireling, whose o. the sheep. 10:12
having loved his o. that were in. 13:1
the world would love his o. 15:19
every man to his o. 16:32
as though by our o. power. Acts 3:12
thine o.? was it not in thine o.? 5:4
purchased with his o. blood. 20:28
he considered not his o. Rom 4:19
he that spared not his o. Son. 8:32
to his o. master he standeth. 14:4
ye are not your o. for ye. 1 Cor 6:19
every man have his o. wife. 7:2
let no man seek his o. but. 10:24
conscience, I say, not thine o. 29
charity seeketh not her o. 13:5
for all seek their o. things. Phil 2:21
having mine o. righteousness. 3:9
provide not for his o., his o. 1 Tim 5:8
a prophet of their o. Tit 1:12
but by his o. blood he. Heb 9:12
our sins in his o. blood. Rev 1:5
see counsel, country, eyes, heart,
house, land, people, self,
selves, soul, way, ways, will

owner
but the o. of the ox. Ex 21:28
testified to his o., his o. shall. 29
the o. of the pit shall make it. 34
and his o. hath not kept him in. 36
o. of it shall accept thereof. 22:11
make restitution to the o. 12
o. thereof not being with it. 14
but if o. thereof be with it, not. 15
after name of Shemer, o. 1 Ki 16:24
ox knoweth his o., the ass. Isa 1:3
centurion believed the o. Acts 27:11

owners
or have caused the o. to. Job 31:39
life of o. thereof. Pr 1:19
there to the o. thereof? Eccl 5:11
a sore evil, riches kept for o. 13
the o. said, Why loose? Luke 19:33

owneth
o. the house shall tell. Lev 14:35
bind man that o. this. Acts 21:11

ox
shalt not covet thy neighbour's ox.
Ex 20:17; Deut 5:21
if ox gore a man. Ex 21:28, 29, 32

if *ox* were wont to push. *Ex* 21:29, 36
if *ox* push a manservant or. 32
if an *ox* or ass shall fall into a pit. 33
if a man shall steal an *ox*. 22:1
whether it be *ox* or ass, he shall. 4
trespass for an *ox*. 9
deliver an *ox* to keep. 10
enemy's *ox* going astray. 23:4
that thine *ox* and thine ass. 12
every firstling of an *ox* or. 34:19
no manner of fat of *ox* or. *Lev* 7:23
what man soever killeth an *ox*. 17:3
each of princes an *ox*. *Num* 7:3
as the *ox* licketh up the grass. 22:4
thine *ox* shall do no work. *Deut* 5:14
the *ox*, the sheep, and goat. 14:4
whether it be *ox* or sheep. 18:3
thy brother's *ox* go astray. 22:1
thy brother's *ox* fall down. 4
shalt not plow with an *ox* and ass. 10
thou shalt not muzzle the *ox*. 25:4
  1 Cor 9:9; *1 Tim* 5:18
thine *ox* shall be slain. *Deut* 28:31
they destroyed *ox* and sheep.
  Josh 6:21; *1 Sam* 15:15
600 men with an *ox* goad. *Judg* 3:31
they left neither sheep nor *ox*. 6:4
Samuel said, Whose *ox* or ass have
  I taken ? *1 Sam* 12:3
every man his *ox* and sheep. 14:34
me daily one *ox*, six sheep. *Neh* 5:18
or loweth the *ox* over ? *Job* 6:5
they take the widow's *ox* for. 24:3
eateth grass as an *ox*. 40:15
Lord better than an *ox*. *Ps* 69:31
glory into similitude of an *ox*. 106:20
goeth after her as an *ox*. *Pr* 7:22
is by strength of the *ox*. 14:4
better than a stalled *ox*, and. 15:17
the *ox* knoweth his owner. *Isa* 1:3
lion shall eat straw like the *ox*. 11:7
thither the feet of the *ox*. 32:20
that killeth an *ox*, as if he. 66:3
a lamb or an *ox* brought. *Jer* 11:19
had the face of an *ox*. *Ezek* 1:10
of you loose his *ox* on. *Luke* 13:15
shall have an *ox* or an ass. 14:5

wild ox
wild ox and chamois. *Deut* 14:5*

oxen
Abram had sheep, and *o. Gen* 12:16
gave Abraham sheep and *o*. 20:14
gave Abimelech sheep and *o*. 21:27
Jacob said thus, I have *o*. 32:5
Jacob took Shechem's *o*. 34:28*
hand of Lord is upon the *o. Ex* 9:3*
sacrifice thereon thine *o*. 20:24
shall restore five *o.* for one. 22:1
thou do with thine *o.* and sheep. 30
princes brought twelve *o. Num* 7:3
four *o.* he gave to the sons of. 7
and eight *o.* he gave to the sons. 8
Balak offered *o.* and sheep. 22:40
prepare me here seven *o*. 23:1*
money for *o.* or sheep. *Deut* 14:26
Joshua took Achan, his *o. Josh* 7:24
yoke of *o.* in pieces, and sent them
  . . . done to his *o. 1 Sam* 11:7
which yoke of *o.* might plow. 14:14*
the people took sheep and *o*. 32
Agag and the best of the *o*. 15:9
lowing of *o.* which I hear ? 14
spared the best of the sheep and *o*. 15
Doeg smote the *o.* and sheep. 22:19
took away the sheep, and *o*. 27:9
Uzza took hold of it, for *o. 2 Sam* 6:6
David sacrificed *o.* and fatlings. 13
be *o.* for burnt sacrifice. 24:22
the threshingfloor and *o*.
Adonijah slew sheep and *o*.
  1 Ki 1:9, 19, 25
provision, 10 fat *o.* 100 sheep. 4:23
one sea, 12 *o.* under it. 7:25, 44
  2 Chr 4:4, 15
sacrificing sheep and *o. 1 Ki* 8:5
a sacrifice to the Lord of 22,000 *o*.
  and 120,000. 63; *2 Chr* 7:5
plowing with twelve yoke of *o*.
  1 Ki 19:19
Elisha left the *o.* and ran. 20
he took a yoke of *o.* and slew. 21
to receive sheep and *o.? 2 Ki* 5:26
bread on mules and on *o. 1 Chr* 12:40

of the spoil 700 *o. 2 Chr* 15:11
Ahab killed sheep and *o.* for. 18:2
consecrated things were 600 *o.* 29:33
they brought in the tithes of *o.* 31:6
passover three hundred *o*. 35:8
3000 camels, 500 yoke of *o. Job* 1:3
the *o.* were plowing, and the. 14
1000 yoke of *o.* 1000 asses. 42:12
to have dominion over *o. Ps* 8:7
that our *o.* may be strong. 144:14
where no *o.* are the crib. *Pr* 14:4
for the sending forth of *o. Isa* 7:25
joy and gladness, slaying *o*. 22:13
the *o.* and asses shall eat. 30:24
husbandman and his *o. Jer* 51:23
they shall make thee to eat grass as *o*.
  Dan 4:25, 32, 33; 5:21
one plow there with *o.? Amos* 6:12
my *o.* and my fatlings. *Luke* 14:19
bought five yoke of *o. John* 2:14
temple those that sold *o*. 15
out, the sheep and the *o*.
  Acts 14:13
God take care for *o.? 1 Cor* 9:9

Ozem
O., sixth son of Jesse. *1 Chr* 2:15

Ozias
Joram begat *O. Mat* 1:8
O. begat Joatham. 9

P

Paarai
P. the Arbite, a mighty. *2 Sam* 23:35

paces
when gone six *p.* he. *2 Sam* 6:13

pacify, -ed, -eth
was king's wrath *p. Esth* 7:10
wise man will *p.* the wrath. *Pr* 16:14
a gift in secret *p.* anger. 21:14
p. great offences. *Eccl* 10:4*
when I am *p.* toward. *Ezek* 16:63*

Padan-aram
daughter of Bethuel of *P. Gen* 25:20
Isaac sent Jacob away to *P*. 28:6
Jacob was gone to *P*. 7
what he had gotten in *P*. 31:18
Jacob when he came from *P*. 35:9
sons born to him in *P*. 26; 46:15

paddle
shalt have a *p.* on thy. *Deut* 23:13

Pagiel
P. son of Ocran, prince of Asher.
  Num 1:13; 7:72

paid
custom, was *p.* them. *Ezra* 4:20
this day have I *p.* vows. *Pr* 7:14
so he *p.* fare thereof. *Jonah* 1:3
not come out thence till thou hast *p*.
  uttermost. *Mat* 5:26; *Luke* 12:59
received tithes, *p.* tithes. *Heb* 7:9

pain
(Used as now of great discomfort
either of mind or body)
flesh on him shall have *p. Job* 14:22
man travaileth with *p*. 15:20
he is chastened also with *p*. 33:19*
mine affliction and my *p. Ps* 25:18
p. as a woman in travail. 48:6
  Isa 13:8; 26:17
my loins filled with *p. Isa* 21:3
child, we have been in *p*. 26:18
before her *p.* came, she was. 66:7
taken hold of us, and *p.* as of a
  woman in. *Jer* 6:24; 22:23
put themselves to *p.* but. 12:13
why is my *p.* perpetual ? 15:18
it shall fall with *p.* on head. 30:23*
Babylon, take balm for her *p*. 51:8
great *p.* shall be in Ethiopia.
  Ezek 30:4, 9
Sin shall have great *p.*, No shall. 16
be in *p.* and labour in. *Mi* 4:10
p. is in all loins, faces. *Nah* 2:10
creation travaileth in *p. Rom* 8:22
their tongues for *p. Rev* 16:10
nor shall there be any more *p*. 21:4
  see pangs

pained
my heart is sore *p.* within. *Ps* 55:4
p. at report of Tyre. *Isa* 23:5
I am *p.* at my very heart. *Jer* 4:19
people shall be much *p. Joel* 2:6
travailing in birth, and *p. Rev* 12:2

painful
it was too *p.* for me. *Ps* 73:16

painfulness
in weariness and *p.*, in. *2 Cor* 11:27

pains
she travailed, for her *p. 1 Sam* 4:19
and the *p.* of hell gat. *Ps* 116:3
having loosed *p.* of death. *Acts* 2:24
they blasphemed, because of their *p*.
  Rev 16:11

painted
Jezebel *p.* her face, and. *2 Ki* 9:30
cieled with cedar, and *p. Jer* 22:14

paintedst
thou *p.* thy eyes. *Ezek* 23:40

painting
rentest thy face with *p. Jer* 4:30*

pair
offer a *p.* of turtle doves. *Luke* 2:24
he had a pair of balances. *Rev* 6:5

palace
Revisions usually replace this by
castle or court, *as the word generally
suggests a fortified house. The
word occasionally includes the
entire city,* Esth 9:12; *again, it is
restricted to a part of the royal
apartments,* 1 Ki 16:18. *It is
applied to the temple in Jerusalem
in* 1 Chr 29:1.
Zimri burnt the king's *p. 1 Ki* 16:18
vineyard hard by the *p*. 21:1
Pekaiah in the *p. 2 Ki* 15:25
shall be eunuchs in *p.* of king. 20:18
p. is not for man, but. *1 Chr* 29:1
a perfect heart to build the *p*. 19
terraces to the king's *p. 2 Chr* 9:11
maintenance from the *p. Ezra* 4:14
at Achmetha, in the *p.* a roll. 6:2
as I was in Shushan the *p. Neh* 1:1
beams for the gates of the *p*. 2:8
I gave Hanani, ruler of the *p*. 7:2
young virgins to the *p. Esth* 2:3
decree was given in Shushan, the *p*.
  3:15; 8:14
500 men in Shushan the *p*. 9:12
enter into the king's *p. Ps* 45:15
after the similitude of a *p*. 144:12
build on her a *p.* of silver. *S of S* 8:9
hast made a *p.* of strangers. *Isa* 25:2
flourishing in my *p. Dan* 4:4
king went to his *p.* and passed. 6:18
he shall plant his *p.* between. 11:45
ye shall cast them into *p. Amos* 4:3*
and *p.* shall be dissolved. *Nah* 2:6
Jesus afar off to the high priest's *p*.
  Mat 26:58; *Mark* 14:54
strong man keepeth his *p. Luke* 11:21
bonds are manifest in all the *p*.
  Phil 1:13*

palaces
and burnt all the *p. 2 Chr* 36:19
of myrrh, out of ivory *p. Ps* 45:8
God is known in her *p.* for. 48:3
bulwarks, consider her *p*. 13
his sanctuary like high *p*. 78:69*
prosperity within thy *p*. 122:7
spider is in king's *p. Pr* 30:28
cry in their pleasant *p. Isa* 13:22
p. shall be forsaken. 32:14
thorns come up in her *p*. 34:13
and let us destroy her *p. Jer* 6:5
come and is entered into our *p.* 9:21
devour the *p.* of Jerusalem. 17:27
consume the *p.* of Ben-hadad. 49:27
swallowed up all her *p. Lam* 2:5
knew their desolate *p. Ezek* 19:7
they shall set their *p.* in thee. 25:4*
in *p.* at Ashdod, in *p.* of Egypt.
  Amos 3:9
violence and robbery in their *p*. 10
thy *p.* shall be spoiled. 11
I hate his *p*. 6:8
when he shall tread in our *p. Mi* 5:5
  see devour

pale

his face now wax *p*. *Isa* 29:22
behold a *p*. horse: and his name was
Death. *Rev* 6:8

paleness

all faces turned into *p*. *Jer* 30:6

Palestina

(*This word refers to the land of
the Philistines and not to the whole
of what we know as Palestine.
Revisions change to* Philistia)

sorrow on men of P. *Ex* 15:14
rejoice not, thou whole P. *Isa* 14:29
thou whole P. art dissolved. 31

palm

pour it into *p*. of his. *Lev* 14:15, 26
struck Jesus with the *p*. *John* 18:22

palm branches

to mount and fetch *p. b*. *Neh* 8:15

palmerworm

(*The English word is one used for
a variety of caterpillar. It is not
however known to which variety the
word refers*)

what the *p*. left, the locust. *Joel* 1:4
the years that *p*. hath eaten. 2:25
the *p*. devoured them. *Amos* 4:9

palms

both the *p*. of his hands. *1 Sam* 5:4
they found skull and *p*. *2 Ki* 9:35
I have graven thee on *p*. of my hands
Isa 49:16
on the *p*. of my hands. *Dan* 10:10
smote him with the *p*. of their hands.
Mat 26:67; *Mark* 14:65*
and *p*. in their hands. *Rev* 7:9

palm tree

(*The palm, especially the date-
palm, is one of the most important
trees in the East. The fruit is the
daily food of millions ; wine is made
of the sap ; the seeds are made into
a food for camels ; the fibres of the
leaf-stems are woven into ropes
and rigging ; the tall trunk is a
valuable timber ; its leaves are
made into many different articles.)
The palm is also used as a symbol
of victory, Rev* 7:9.

under the *p*. of Deborah. *Judg* 4:5
shall flourish like the *p*. *Ps* 92:12
stature is like to a *p*. *S of S* 7:7
go up to the *p*., I will take hold. 8
they are upright as the *p*. *Jer* 10:5
man was toward the *p*. *Ezek* 41:19
the *p*. and the apple tree. *Joel* 1:12

palm trees

where were seventy *p*. *Ex* 15:27
take you branches of *p*. *Lev* 23:40
city of *p*. unto Zoar. *Deut* 34:3
out of the city of *p*. *Judg* 1:16
and possessed city of *p*. 3:13
carved figures of *p*. *1 Ki* 6:29, 32, 35
7:36; *2 Chr* 3:5; *Ezek* 40:16
them to the city of *p*. *2 Chr* 28:15
took branches of *p*. *John* 12:13

palsies

many taken with *p*., healed. *Acts* 8:7

palsy

(*An old word for the various sorts
of paralysis*)

and those that had the *p*. *Mat* 4:24
9:2; *Mark* 2:3; *Luke* 5:18
lieth at home sick of the *p*. *Mat* 8:6
faith, said to the sick of the *p*., Son.
9:2; *Mark* 2:5
Jesus saith to the sick of *p*., Arise.
Mark 2:10; *Luke* 5:24
Aeneas, who was sick of the *p*.
Acts 9:33

Pamphylia

Paphos to Perga in P. *Acts* 13:13
John departed from P. 15:38
sailed over the sea of P. 27:5

pan

meat offering baken in a *p*. *Lev* 2:5
in a *p*. it shall be made with oil. 6:21
all that is dressed in *p*. shall be. 7:9
priest's servant stuck it into the *p*.
1 Sam 2:14.

Tamar took a *p*. and. *2 Sam* 13:9
take unto thee an iron *p*. *Ezek* 4:3

pangs

p. and sorrows shall take. *Isa* 13:8
p. have taken hold on me, as *p*. 21:3
woman crieth out in her *p*. 26:17
thou be when *p*. come. *Jer* 22:23
as the heart of a woman in her *p*.
48:41; 49:22
and *p*. as of a woman in travail.
50:43; *Mi* 4:9

pannag

traded in thy market, *p*. *Ezek* 27:17

pans

thou shalt make *p*. to. *Ex* 27:3
they baked manna in *p*. *Num* 11:8*
over the things made in the *p*.
1 Chr 9:31; 23:29
offerings sod they in *p*. *2 Chr* 35:13

pant

that *p*. after the dust of. *Amos* 2:7

panted

I opened my mouth and *p*. *Ps* 119:131
my heart *p*., fearfulness. *Isa* 21:4

panteth

my heart *p*., my strength. *Ps* 38:10*
as hart *p*. so *p*. my soul after. 42:1

paper

(*The meaning in the Bible is
either the papyrus, made into a
sort of paper, or some preparation of
skin*)

the *p*. reeds by the. *Isa* 19:7*
not write with *p*. and ink. *2 John* 12

Paphos

through the isle unto P. *Acts* 13:6, 13

paps

lewdness for the *p*. of. *Ezek* 23:21
blessed are *p*. which. *Luke* 11:27
blessed are the *p*. which never. 23:29
and girt about the *p*. with. *Rev* 1:13

parable

(*The word comes from the Greek
parabolé which means a placing
beside. It is therefore the placing
of one subject by another as an
illustration. Especially is it used
for the illustration of spiritual things
by familiar earthly objects or inci-
dents. In the Bible the word is used
more generally than elsewhere,
being applied even to short proverbs*)
The prophets made use of Parables, to give a stronger impression
to prince and people of the threatenings or of the promises they made
to them. Nathan reproved David
under the parable of a rich man that
had taken away and killed the lamb
of a poor man, 2 Sam 12:2, 3, etc.
Jotham, son of Gideon, proposed to
the men of Shechem, the parable
of the bramble, whom the trees had
a mind to choose for their king,
Judg 9:7, 8, etc.
Our Saviour in the gospels often
speaks to the people in parables,
Mat 13:10, 13, etc. He made use
of them to veil the truth from those
who were not willing to see it.
Those who really desired to know
would not rest till they had found
out the meaning. This is given by
Jesus as an illustration of Isa 6:9, 10.

Balaam took up his *p*. and said.
Num 23:7; 24:3, 15, 20, 21, 23
took up his *p*., Rise up, Balak. 23:18
Job continued his *p*. *Job* 27:1; 29:1
incline mine ear to a *p*. *Ps* 49:4
my mouth, in a *p*., I will utter. 78:2
so is a *p*. in the mouth. *Pr* 26:7, 9
speak a *p*. to the house. *Ezek* 17:2
utter a *p*. to the rebellious. 24:3
one shall take up a *p*. *Mi* 2:4
shall not all these take up a *p*. against
him! *Hab* 2:6
the *p*. of the sower. *Mat* 13:18
another *p*. put he. 24, 31, 33; 21:33
without a *p*. spake. 13:34; *Mark* 4:34
the *p*. of the tares. *Mat* 13:36; 15:15

learn a *p*. of the fig tree. *Mat* 24:32
Mark 13:28; *Luke* 21:29
they asked him of *p*. *Mark* 4:10
7:17; *Luke* 8:9
know ye not this *p*.? *Mark* 4:13
he had spoken the *p*. against them.
12:12; *Luke* 20:19
he spake a *p*. to them. *Luke* 5:36
6:39; 8:4; 12:16; 13:6; 14:7
15:3; 18:1, 9; 19:11; 20:9; 21:29
John 10:6
this *p*. to us, or to all ? *Luke* 12:41

parables

doth he not speak *p*.? *Ezek* 20:49
spake many things to them in *p*.
Mat 13:3, 13, 34; 22:1; *Mark* 3:23
4:2, 13, 33; 12:1
will ye know all *p*.? *Mark* 4:13
but others in *p*. that. *Luke* 8:10

paradise

thou be with me in *p*. *Luke* 23:43
was caught up into *p*. *2 Cor* 12:4
midst of the *p*. of God. *Rev* 2:7

paramours

she doted upon their *p*. *Ezek* 23:20

Paran

Ishmael dwelt in the wilderness of P.
Gen 21:21
the wilderness of P. *Num* 10:12
12:16; 13:3, 26; *1 Sam* 25:1
shined from mount P. *Deut* 33:2
Holy One came from P. *Hab* 3:3

Parbar

the causeway, two at P. *1 Chr* 26:18

parcel

Jacob bought a *p*. of a field.*Gen*33:19
Josh 24:32; *John* 4:5
Naomi selleth a *p*. of land. *Ruth* 4:3
p. of ground full. *1 Chr* 11:13*, 14*

parched

the *p*. ground shall. *Isa* 35:7*
but he shall inhabit the *p*. *Jer* 17:6
see **corn**

parchments

but especially the *p*. *2 Tim* 4:13

pardon

he will not *p*. your. *Ex* 23:21
p. our iniquity and our sin. 34:9
Num 14:19
I pray thee, *p*. my sin. *1 Sam* 15:25
in this thing the Lord *p*. *2 Ki* 5:18
which Lord would not *p*. 24:4
the good Lord *p*. *2 Chr* 30:18
thou art a God ready to *p*. *Neh* 9:17
why dost thou not *p*. my ? *Job* 7:21
for thy name's sake *p*. *Ps* 25:11
for he will abundantly *p*. *Isa* 55:7
and I will *p*. it. *Jer* 5:1
how shall I *p*. thee for this ? 7
I will *p*. all their iniquities. 33:8
for I will *p*. them whom. 50:20

pardoned

I have *p*. according to. *Num* 14:20
that her iniquity is *p*. *Isa* 40:2
rebelled, thou hast not *p*. *Lam* 3:42

pardoneth

to thee, that *p*. iniquity ? *Mi* 7:18

pare

her head and *p*. her nails. *Deut* 21:12

parents

rise up against their *p*. and cause.
Mat 10:21; *Mark* 13:12
when the *p*. brought in. *Luke* 2:27
her *p*. were astonished, but. 8:56
man that hath left *p*. or wife. 18:29
ye shall be betrayed both by *p*. 21:16
sin, this man or his *p*.? *John* 9:2
these words spake his. 22, 23
proud, disobedient to *p*. *Rom* 1:30
2 Tim 3:2
not to lay up for the *p*. *2 Cor* 12:14
children, obey your *p*. *Eph* 6:1
Col 3:20
learn to requite their *p*. *1 Tim* 5:4
three months of his *p*. *Heb* 11:23

parlour

sitting in a summer *p*. *Judg* 3:20*
Ehud shut the doors of the *p*. 23*
Samuel brought them into the *p*.
1 Sam 9:22*

parlours
David gave Solomon a pattern of *p.*
　　　　　　　　　1 Chr 28:11*

Parmenas
Timon, *P.*, and Nicolas.　*Acts* 6:5

part, *noun*
they stood at the nether *p. Ex* 19:17
the breast, it shall be thy *p.*　29:26
p. of the beaten corn, *p. Lev* 2:16
right shoulder for his *p.*　　　7:33
consecration was Moses' *p.*　8:29
if any *p.* of their carcase.　11:37, 38
his hair fallen off from the *p.*　13:41
nor have *p.* among them. *Num* 18:20
　　　　Deut 10:9; 12:12; 14:27, 29
　　　　　　18:1; *Josh* 14:4; 18:7
I am thy *p.* and thine.　*Num* 18:20
might see utmost *p.* of the people.
　　　　　　Num 22:41; 23:13
he provided the first *p. Deut* 33:21
the *p.* of Judah was.　*Josh* 19:9
have no *p.* in the Lord.　22:25, 27
her hap was to light on a *p. Ruth* 2:3
unto thee the *p.* of a kinsman.　3:13
tarried in the utmost *p. 1 Sam* 14:2
our *p.* shall be to deliver.　3:20
as his *p.* is that goeth down to battle,
　so shall his *p.* be that.　30:24
we have no *p.* in David. *2 Sam* 20:1
come to uttermost *p.*　*2 Ki* 7:5, 8
on thy *p.* to set riders.　18:23
　　　　　　　　　Isa 36:8
greatest *p.* had kept.　*1 Chr* 12:29
went into the inner *p. 2 Chr* 29:16
cast out to the uttermost *p. Neh* 1:9
restore the hundredth *p.* of.　5:11
I will answer also my *p. Job* 32:17
their inward *p.* is very.　*Ps* 5:9
in hidden *p.* shalt make me.　51:6
Lord taketh my *p.* with them. 118:7
nor highest *p.* of the dust.　*Pr* 8:26
rejoicing in the habitable *p.* of.　31
shall have *p.* of inheritance.　17:2
fly that is in the utmost *p. Isa* 7:18
from utmost *p.* of earth.　24:16
he burneth *p.* thereof in the fire, with
　p. thereof he eateth.　44:16, 19
drink sixth *p.* of an hin. *Ezek* 4:11
leave but the sixth *p.* of thee.　39:2
sixth *p.* of an ephah of æn.　45:13
it shall be the prince's *p.* to.　17
a meat offering the sixth *p.*　46:14
p. iron, and *p.* clay. *Dan* 2:33, 41, 42
the king saw *p.* of the hand. 5:5, 24
arms shall stand on his *p.*　11:31
great deep, did eat up a *p. Amos* 7:4
he was in the hinder *p.* of. *Mark* 4:38
is not against us, is on our *p.*　9:40
hath chosen that good *p. Luke* 10:42
inward *p.* is full of ravening. 11:39
as lightning that lighteneth out of one
　p. shining to other *p.*　17:24
hast no *p.* with me.　*John* 13:8
four parts, every soldier a *p.* 19:23
and had obtained *p.* of.　*Acts* 1:17
that he may take *p.* of this.　25
Ananias kept back *p.* of the price,
　and brought a certain *p.*　5:2, 3
thou hast neither *p.* nor lot in. 8:21
p. held with the Jews, *p.* with. 14:4
the chief city of that *p.* of.　16:12*
more *p.* knew not wherefore.　19:32
perceived that the one *p.*　23:6
the more *p.* advised to depart. 27:12
honour to that *p.* which. *1 Cor* 12:24
of whom the greater *p.* remain. 15:6
what was lacking on your *p.*　16:17
what *p.* he that believeth. *2 Cor* 6:15
the measure of every *p. Eph* 4:16
he of the contrary *p.* may.　*Tit* 2:8
himself likewise took *p. Heb* 2:14*
on their *p.* he is evil spoken of, but
　on your *p.* he is.　*1 Pet* 4:14
holy that hath *p.* in the.　*Rev* 20:6
all liars shall have their *p.*　21:8
God shall take away his *p.*　22:19

part, *verb*
thou *p.* the meat offering.　*Lev* 2:6
if aught but death *p.*　*Ruth* 1:17
they shall *p.* alike.　*1 Sam* 30:24
was none to *p.* them.　*2 Sam* 14:6
shall they *p.* him among ?　*Job* 41:6
they *p.* my garments.　*Ps* 22:18
31

in **part**
blindness *in p.* is happened.
　　　　　　　　　Rom 11:25
we know *in p.* and we prophesy *in p.*
　　　　　　　　　1 Cor 13:9
then that which is *in p.* shall be.　10
I know *in p.* but then shall I know. 12
acknowledged us *in p.*　*2 Cor* 1:14
hath not grieved me but *in p.*　2:5

third **part**
flour mingled with the *third p.* of an.
　　　　Num 15:6; 28:14; *Ezek* 46:14
shalt offer the *third p.* of. *Num* 15:7
David sent a *third p.*　*2 Sam* 18:2
a *third p.* that enter in.　*2 Ki* 11:5
a *third p.* of you shall be porters.
　　　　　　　　　2 Chr 23:4
with *third p.* of shekel.　*Neh* 10:32
fire a *third p.*, a *third p.*, smite about
　it, a *third p.*　　*Ezek* 5:2, 12
third p. shall be left.　*Zech* 13:8
the *third p.* through the fire.　9
third p. of the trees.　*Rev* 8:7
and the *third p.* of the sea.　8
third p. of creatures died, *third p.* 9
it fell upon the *third p.* of.　10
third p. of the waters became.　11
third p. of the sun, moon, and stars,
　was smitten . . . for a *third p.*　12
for to slay the *third p.* of men. 9:15
was the *third p.* of men killed.　18
his tail drew *third p.* of the.　12:4

fourth **part**
flour mingled with the *fourth p.* of.
　　　　Ex 29:40; *Num* 15:4; 28:5
fourth p. of an hin of wine for a.
　Lev 23:13; *Num* 15:5; 28:7, 14
have here the *fourth p.* of a shekel.
　　　　　　　　　1 Sam 9:8
olive tree *fourth p.* of.　*1 Ki* 6:33
the *fourth p.* of a cab.　*2 Ki* 6:25
read one *fourth p.*; another *fourth p.*
　　　　　　　　　Neh 9:3
over *fourth p.* of earth.　*Rev* 6:8

fifth **part**
up *fifth p.* of the land. *Gen* 41:34
give *fifth p.* to Pharaoh.　47:24, 26
shall add the *fifth p. Lev* 5:16; 6:5
　22:14; 27:13, 19, 27, 31; *Num* 5:7
posts were a *fifth p.*　*1 Ki* 6:31

tenth **part**
an homer is the *tenth p.*　*Ex* 16:36
offering the *tenth p.* of an ephah.
　　　Lev 5:11; 6:20; *Num* 28:5
tenth p. of an ephah of.　*Num* 5:15
shall offer even the *tenth p.*　18:26
may contain *tenth p.*　*Ezek* 45:11
ye shall offer the *tenth p.* of a.　14
Abraham gave a *tenth p.*　*Heb* 7:2
tenth p. of the city fell.　*Rev* 11:13

partaker
and hast been *p.* with.　*Ps* 50:18
should be *p.* of his hope. *1 Cor* 9:10
that I might be *p.* thereof.　23
if I by grace be *p.* why am I ? 10:30
neither be *p.* of other.　*1 Tim* 5:22
be thou *p.* of afflictions. *2 Tim* 1:8*
the husbandman must be first *p.* 2:6
who am also a *p.* of the glory.
　　　　　　　　　1 Pet 5:1
is *p.* of his evil deeds.　*2 John* 11

partakers
not been *p.* in blood.　*Mat* 23:30
if Gentiles have been made *p.* of.
　　　　　　　　　Rom 15:27
others be *p.* of this power. *1 Cor* 9:12
who wait at altar, are *p.*　13
for we are all *p.* of that one.　10:17
are not they which eat of ?　18
be *p.* of the Lord's table, and.　21
are *p.* of the sufferings.　*2 Cor* 1:7
and *p.* of his promise in.　*Eph* 3:6
be not ye therefore *p.* with.　5:7
ye all are *p.* of my grace. *Phil* 1:7
meet to be *p.* of inheritance. *Col* 1:12
are *p.* of the benefit.　*1 Tim* 6:2
as the children are *p.* of. *Heb* 2:14*
brethren, *p.* of the heavenly.　3:1
for we are made *p.* of Christ.　14
were made *p.* of the Holy Ghost. 6:4
chastisement, whereof all are *p.* 12:8
might be *p.* of his holiness.　10

as ye are *p.* of Christ's.　*1 Pet* 4:13
p. of the divine nature.　*2 Pet* 1:4
that ye be not *p.* of her.　*Rev* 18:4

partakest
with them *p.* of root.　*Rom* 11:17

parted
the river was *p.* into.　*Gen* 2:10
a chariot *p.* them.　*2 Ki* 2:11
the waters *p.* hither and.　14
what way is the light *p.? Job* 38:24
scattered, and *p.* my land. *Joel* 3:2
crucified him, and *p.* his garments.
　　　Mat 27:35; *Mark* 15:24
　　　Luke 23:34; *John* 19:24
blessed them, was *p.*　*Luke* 24:51
p. them to all men, as.　*Acts* 2:45

parteth
whatsoever *p.* the hoof.　*Lev* 11:3
　　　　　　　　　Deut 14:6
the lot *p.* between the.　*Pr* 18:18

Parthians
P., we hear them speak in. *Acts* 2:9

partial
but have been *p.* in law.　*Mal* 2:9*
are ye not then *p.* in ?　*Jas* 2:4*

partiality
observe these things, doing nothing
　by *p.*　　　*1 Tim* 5:21
without *p.* and without.　*Jas* 3:17*

particular
Christ, members in *p.* *1 Cor* 12:27*
every one of you in *p.* so. *Eph* 5:33*

particularly
Paul declared *p.* what.　*Acts* 21:19*
we cannot now speak *p.*　*Heb* 9:5*

parties
cause of both *p.* shall.　*Ex* 22:9

parting
king of Babylon stood at the *p.* of the
　way.　　　*Ezek* 21:21

partition
and he made a *p.* by.　*1 Ki* 6:21*
broken down middle wall of *p.*
　　　　　　　　　Eph 2:14

partly
be *p.* strong, *p.* broken.　*Dan* 2:42
divisions, I *p.* believe it. *1 Cor* 11:18
p. whilst ye were made a . . . by
　afflictions, *p.* whilst ye. *Heb* 10:33

partner
whoso is *p.* with thief.　*Pr* 29:24
Titus, he is my *p.* and.　*2 Cor* 8:23
if count me a *p.* receive. *Philem* 17

partners
they beckoned to their *p.*　*Luke* 5:7
James and John who were *p.*　10

partridge
one doth hunt a *p.* in.　*1 Sam* 26:20
as the *p.* sitteth on eggs.　*Jer* 17:11

parts
four *p.* shall be your.　*Gen* 47:24
Aaron's sons shall lay the *p.* in.
　　　　　　　　　Lev 1:8
any thing lacking in his *p.*　22:23
the prey into two *p.*　*Num* 31:27
of the land into three *p.*　*Deut* 19:3
if any be driven to utmost *p.*　30:4
they shall divide it into seven *p.*
　　　　　　　　　Josh 18:5, 6, 9
emerods in their secret *p. 1 Sam* 5:9*
ten *p.* in the king.　*2 Sam* 19:43
divided into two *p.*　*1 Ki* 16:21
two *p.* keep watch.　*2 Ki* 11:7*
and nine *p.* to dwell in.　*Neh* 11:1
lo, these are *p.* of his.　*Job* 26:14
I will not conceal his *p.* nor.　41:12*
uttermost *p.* of earth for.　*Ps* 2:8
shall go into lower *p.* of the.　63:9
that dwell in utmost *p.*　65:8
divided the Red sea into *p.*　136:13
uttermost *p.* of the sea.　139:9
into innermost *p.*　*Pr* 18:8; 26:22
will discover their secret *p. Isa* 3:17
lower *p.* of the earth.　44:23
passed between the *p. Jer* 34:18, 19
in the low *p.* of earth.　*Ezek* 26:20
delivered to the nether *p.* of earth.
　　　　　　　　　31:14, 18
in nether *p.* of earth.　16; 32:18, 24

we are cut off for our *p. Ezek* 37:11*
out of the north *p.* 38:15; 39:2
length as one of the other *p.* 48:8
saith the Lord, two *p.* therein shall be
cut off. *Zech* 13:8
turned aside into the *p. Mat* 2:22
came from uttermost *p.* 12:42
Luke 11:31
and made four *p. John* 19:23
he had gone over those *p. Acts* 20:2
more place in those *p. Rom* 15:23
uncomely *p.* have more. *1 Cor* 12:23
for our comely *p.* have no need. 24
descended first into lower *p. Eph* 4:9
city was divided into three *p.*
Rev 16:19
see **back, hinder, inward**

Pashur
P. the son of Malchijah. *1 Chr* 9:12
Neh 11:12
the children of P. *Ezra* 2:38; 10:22
Neh 7:41
P. sealed. *Neh* 10:3
P. the son of Immer. *Jer* 20:1, 2
Lord called not thy name P. but. 3
P. go into captivity. 6
Zedekiah sent unto him P. 21:1
son of P. and P. the son of. 38:1

pass
after that ye shall *p.* on. *Gen* 18:5
shortly bring it to *p.* 41:32
will make my goodness *p. Ex* 33:19
father to *p.* to them. *Num* 27:7, 8
ye shall *p.* before your. *Josh* 1:14
he said to people, P. on. 6:7
bid the servants *p. 1 Sam* 9:27
Jesse made Abinadab *p.* 16:8
Jesse made seven of his sons *p.* 10
no place for the beast to *p. Neh* 2:14
brooks they *p.* away. *Job* 6:15
waters that *p.* away. 11:16
troubled, and *p.* away. 34:20
every one of them *p.* away. *Ps* 58:8
lips he bringeth evil to *p. Pr* 16:30
the simple *p.* on and are punished.
22:3; 27:12
grounded staff shall *p. Isa* 30:32
shall gallant ship *p.* thereby. 33:21
now have I brought it to *p.* 37:26
have given shall *p.* away. *Jer* 8:13
I will make thee to *p.* with. 15:14
the flocks shall *p.* again under. 33:13
nor doth any son of man *p.* 51:43
cause barber's razor to *p. Ezek* 5:1
cause you to *p.* under rod. 20:37
whom dost thou *p.* in beauty? 32:19
p. ye unto Calneh and. *Amos* 6:2
p. ye away, thou inhabitant. *Mi* 1:11
and their king shall *p.* before. 2:13
the day *p.* as the chaff. *Zeph* 2:2
thy iniquity to *p.* from. *Zech* 3:4
Till heaven and earth *p.,* one tittle
shall in no wise *p. Mat* 5:18
Father, let this cup *p.* from me.
26:39; *Mark* 14:35
would *p.* from hence to you cannot;
nor can they *p.* to. *Luke* 16:26*
for he was to *p.* that way. 19:4
if she *p.* the flower of her. *1 Cor* 7:36
grass he shall *p.* away. *Jas* 1:10
p. time of your sojourning here.
1 Pet 1:17
heavens shall *p.* away. *2 Pet* 3:10
see **came, come**

pass by
my hand while I *p.* by. *Ex* 33:22
not let us *p.* by him. *Deut* 2:30
Shammah to *p.* by. *1 Sam* 16:9
all they that *p.* by the. *Ps* 80:12
all that *p.* by the way spoil. 89:41
many nations shall *p.* by. *Jer* 22:8
all ye that *p.* by, behold. *Lam* 1:12
all that *p.* by clap their hands. 2:15
sight of all that *p.* by. *Ezek* 5:14
and caused me to *p.* by them. 37:2
caused me to *p.* by four. 46:21
I will not again *p.* by. *Amos* 7:8; 8:2
garments of them that *p.* by. *Mi* 2:8
that no man might *p.* by. *Mat* 8:28
hearing the multitude *p.* by.
Luke 18:36
and to *p.* by you into. *2 Cor* 1:16

not **pass**
we will *not p.* through. *Num* 20:17
thou shalt *not p.* by me. 18
his bounds he *cannot p. Job* 14:5
my way, that I *cannot p.* 19:8
decree, which shall *not p. Ps* 148:6
waters should *not p. Pr* 8:29
decree, that it *cannot p. Jer* 5:22
that shall *not p.* away. *Dan* 7:14
generation shall *not p. Mat* 24:34
Mark 13:30; *Luke* 21:32
my word shall *not p. Mat* 24:35
Mark 13:31; *Luke* 21:33

pass *not*
my lord, *p. not* away. *Gen* 18:3
beware that thou *p. not.* *2 Ki* 6:9
avoid it, *p. not* by it. *Pr* 4:15
seek not Beth-el, *p. not.* *Amos* 5:5

pass *over*
wind to *p.* over the earth. *Gen* 8:1
will not *p.* over this heap. 31:52
p. over before me, and put. 32:16
let my lord *p.* over before. 33:14
blood, I will *p.* over you. *Ex* 12:13, 23
stone, till thy people *p.* over. 15:16
but thy servants will *p.* over.
Num 32:27, 29, 32
if they will not *p.* over. 30
thou art to *p.* over through Ar.
Deut 2:18
p. over Arnon. 24
until I shall *p.* over Jordan. 29
ye shall *p.* over armed before. 3:18
thou art to *p.* over Jordan. 9:1; 11:31
27:2; *Josh* 1:11; 3:6, 14; 4:5
p. over into the land. *Josh* 22:19
not a man to *p.* over. *Judg* 3:28
we will *p.* over to Gibeah. 19:12
behold, we will *p.* over unto these
men. *1 Sam* 14:8
Ittai, Go and *p.* over. *2 Sam* 15:22
plains, but speedily *p.* over. 17:16
they may not *p.* over. *Ps* 104:9
it is a glory to *p.* over. *Pr* 19:11
p. over to Tarshish. *Isa* 23:6
p. over to Chittim. 12
by morning shall *p.* over. 28:19
he shall *p.* over to his strong. 31:9
unclean shall not *p.* over. 35:8
uncover the thigh, *p.* over. 47:2
way for ransomed to *p.* over. 51:10
for *p.* over the isles of. *Jer* 2:10
yet can they not *p.* over it. 5:22
river that I could not *p.* over.
Ezek 47:5
times *p.* over him. *Dan* 4:16, 25
the north shall *p.* over. 11:40
change, he shall *p.* over. *Hab* 1:11
and *p.* over judgement. *Luke* 11:42

pass *through*
I will *p.* through all thy. *Gen* 30:32
I will *p.* through land. *Ex* 12:12
the Lord will *p.* through to smite. 23
seed *p.* through the fire. *Lev* 18:21
Deut 18:10; *2 Ki* 17:17
let us, I pray them, *p.* through thy.
Num 20:17
let me *p.* through thy land. 21:22
Deut 2:27
not suffer Israel to *p.* through.
Num 21:23; *Judg* 11:20
ye are to *p.* through the coasts.
Deut 2:4
only I will *p.* through on my feet. 28
p. through the host and. *Josh* 1:11
p. through brickkiln. *2 Sam* 12:31
the land to *p.* through it. *1 Ki* 18:6
to *p.* through the fire. *2 Ki* 16:3
21:6; 23:10; *2 Chr* 33:6
Jer 32:35; *Ezek* 20:26, 31
caused them to *p.* through the sea.
Ps 78:13; 136:14
shall *p.* through Judah. *Isa* 8:8*
p. through it hardly bestead. 21
as whirlwinds in the south *p.* through,
so it cometh. 21:1
p. through thy land as a river. 23:10
scourge shall *p.* through. 28:15, 18
none shall *p.* through it for. 34:10
that none can *p.* through. *Jer* 9:10
prayers should not *p.* through
Lam 3:44
also shall *p.* through to thee. 4:21

pestilence and blood shall *p.* through
thee. *Ezek* 5:17
beasts *p.* through land, no man may
p. through. 14:15; 29:11; 33:28
passengers that *p.* through. 39:15
one shall come, *p.* through, and overflow. *Dan* 11:10
stranger shall *p.* through. *Joel* 3:17
I will *p.* through thee. *Amos* 5:17
when he shall *p.* through. *Nah* 1:12
no more *p.* through thee. 15
no oppressor shall *p.* through them.
Zech 9:8
p. through Macedonia. *1 Cor* 16:5

passage
refused to give Israel *p. Num* 20:21
altar at the *p.* of Israel. *Josh* 22:11*
garrison of Philistines went out to *p.*
1 Sam 13:23
they are gone over the *p. Isa* 10:29

passages
slew him at the *p.* of Jordan.
Judg 12:6*
between the *p.* there. *1 Sam* 14:4
and cry from the *p. Jer* 22:20*
to shew Babylon that the *p.* 51:32

passed
a lamp that *p.* between. *Gen* 15:17
have *p.* thy borders. *Num* 20:17
ye have not *p.* this way. *Josh* 3:4
the seven priests *p.* on before. 6:8
in all the way we went, among all
people through whom we *p.* 24:17
Ehud escaped and *p. Judg* 3:26
Saul is gone about and *p.* on.
1 Sam 15:12
Philistines *p.* on by hundreds. 29:2
David's servants *p.* on. *2 Sam* 15:18
it fell, that Elisha *p.* to. *2 Ki* 4:8
Gehazi *p.* on before them, and. 31
Solomon *p.* all the kings. *2 Chr* 9:22
then a spirit *p.* before. *Job* 4:15
my days are *p.* away as the. 9:26
and no stranger *p.* among. 15:19
his thick clouds *p. Ps* 18:12
yet he *p.* away, and lo. 37:36
all our days are *p.* away in. 90:9
was but a little that I *p. S of S* 3:4
come to Aiath, he is *p. Isa* 10:28
he pursued them, and *p.* 41:3
and the holy flesh is *p. Jer* 11:15
and *p.* between the parts. 34:18, 19
hath *p.* the time appointed. 46:17
nor smell of fire had *p. Dan* 3:27
the king went and *p.* the night. 6:18
hath not thy wickedness *p.? Nah* 3:19
now the time is far *p. Mark* 6:35
but is *p.* from death unto life.
John 5:24; *1 John* 3:14
so death *p.* on all men. *Rom* 5:12
high priest that is *p. Heb* 4:14
first earth were *p.* away. *Rev* 21:1
former things are *p.* away. 4

passed *by*
there *p.* by Midianites. *Gen* 37:28
Lord *p.* by before him. *Ex* 34:6
nations which ye *p.* by. *Deut* 29:16
behold, men *p.* by and. *1 Ki* 13:25
the Lord *p.* by. 19:11
Elijah *p.* by Elisha.
as the king *p.* by he cried. 20:39
that as oft as he *p.* by. *2 Ki* 4:8
the king *p.* by on the wall. 6:30
and there *p.* by a wild beast. 14:9
2 Chr 25:18
fierce lion *p.* by it. *Job* 28:8
for lo, the kings *p.* by. *Ps* 48:4
when I *p.* by and saw. *Ezek* 16:6
on every one that *p.* by. 15, 25
in sight of all that *p.* by. 36:34
of the waters *p.* by. *Hab* 3:10
heard that Jesus *p.* by. *Mat* 20:30
they that *p.* by reviled him. 27:39
Mark 15:29
as he *p.* by he saw Levi. *Mark* 2:14
would have *p.* by them. 6:48
in the morning as they *p.* by. 11:20
Simon who *p.* by to bear. 15:21
he *p.* by on the other side.
Luke 10:31, 32
through midst of them, so *p.* by.
John 8:59
as I *p.* by and beheld. *Acts* 17:23

passed *over*

and *p.* over the river.   *Gen* 31:21
for with my staff I *p.* over.   32:10
who *p.* over houses of.   *Ex* 12:27
when ye are *p.* over Jordan.
    Num 33:51; *Deut* 27:3
they *p.* over right against. *Josh* 3:16
all the Israelites *p.* over on.   17
people were clean *p.* over.   4:1, 11
people hasted and *p.* over.   10
the ark *p.* over.   11
Reubenites and Gadites *p.* over.   12
Gideon *p.* over and 300.   *Judg* 8:4
Ammon *p.* over Jordan.   10:9
Jephthah *p.* over to fight.   11:29, 32
the battle *p.* over to.   *1 Sam* 14:23
David *p.* over with 600 men.   27:2
men *p.* over Jordan.   *2 Sam* 2:29
Ittai *p.* over.   15:22
king and people *p.* over.   23
my judgement is *p.* over. *Isa* 40:27
could not be *p.* over.   *Ezek* 47:5
but I *p.* over upon her.   *Hos* 10:11
and waves *p.* over me.   *Jonah* 2:3

passed *through*

Abram *p.* through the.   *Gen* 12:6
land which we *p.* through. *Num* 14:7
p. through midst of the sea.   33:8
p. through mount Ephraim.*1 Sam* 9:4
posts *p.* through country of.
    2 Chr 30:10
they *p.* through the gate.   *Mi* 2:13
that no man *p.* through.   *Zech* 7:14
he *p.* through the midst of Samaria.
    Luke 17:11
as Peter *p.* through all quarters.
    Acts 9:32
p. through one street.   12:10
all our fathers *p.* through the sea.
    1 Cor 10:1
p. through the Red sea. *Heb* 11:29

passedst

why *p.* thou over to fight ? *Judg* 12:1

passengers

she standeth to call *p.*   *Pr* 9:15*
I will give Gog valley of *p.*: it shall
   stop noses of the *p.* *Ezek* 39:11*
to bury with *p.* those that.   14*
when *p.* see a man's bone.   15*

passest

kingdoms whither thou *p. Deut* 3:21
on land whither thou *p.* over. 30:18
if thou *p.* on, thou shalt. *2 Sam* 15:33
day thou *p.* over the.   *1 Ki* 2:37
when thou *p.* through waters.*Isa* 43:2

passeth

every one that *p.*   *Ex* 30:13, 14
while my glory *p.* by.   33:22
whatsoever *p.* under the. *Lev* 27:32
even the Lord *p.* over.   *Josh* 3:11
every one that *p.* by it shall be.
    1 Ki 9:8; *2 Chr* 7:21
of God, which *p.* by us.   *2 Ki* 4:9
money of every one that *p.*   12:4
he *p.* on also, but I.   *Job* 9:11
against him, and he *p.*   14:20
and my welfare *p.* away.   30:15
but the wind *p.* and cleanseth. 37:21
whatever *p.* through seas.   *Ps* 8:8
are a wind that *p.* away.   78:39
for the wind *p.* over it.   103:16
as a shadow that *p.* away.   144:4
as whirlwind *p.* so is.   *Pr* 10:25
he that *p.* by and meddleth.   26:17
one generation *p.* away.   *Eccl* 1:4
be as chaff that *p.* away.   *Isa* 29:5
a land that no man *p. Jer* 2:6; 9:12
as stubble that *p.* away.   13:24
every one that *p.* shall be astonished.
    18:16; 19:8
cut off from it him that *p. Ezek* 35:7
as early dew that *p.* away. *Hos* 13:3
God that *p.* by transgression.*Mi* 7:18
every one that *p.* by her. *Zeph* 2:15
streets waste, that none *p.* by.   3:6
because of him that *p.* by. *Zech* 9:8
told him that Jesus *p.* by. *Luke* 18:37
fashion of this world *p.* away.
    1 Cor 7:31; *1 John* 2:17
love of Christ which *p.*   *Eph* 3:19
the peace of God which *p.* understanding.   *Phil* 4:7

passing

we are *p.* from Beth-lehem-judah.
    Judg 19:18
thy love to me *p.* love. *2 Sam* 1:26
the people had done *p.* out.   15:24
as king of Israel was *p.*   *2 Ki* 6:26
p. through valley of Baca.   *Ps* 84:6
p. through the street near.   *Pr* 7:8
and *p.* over he will preserve. *Isa* 31:5
p. through land to bury. *Ezek* 39:14
he *p.* through midst of.   *Luke* 4:30
shadow of Peter *p.* by.   *Acts* 5:15
Philip *p.* through, preached.   8:40
they *p.* by Mysia, came down. 16:8
and hardly *p.* Crete we came.   27:8

passion

(*In the singular, the suffering and
death of Christ. In the plural it
means desires*)

himself alive after his *p.*   *Acts* 1:3

passions

men of like *p.* with you. *Acts* 14:15
man subject to like *p.* as.   *Jas* 5:17

passover

*This word comes from the Hebrew
verb, pasach, which signifies to
pass, to leap, or skip over. They
gave the name of Passover to the
feast which was established in
commemoration of the coming
forth out of Egypt, because the
night before their departure, the
destroying angel, who slew the
firstborn of the Egyptians, passed
over the Israelites, who were marked
with the blood of the lamb which
was killed the evening before; and
which for this reason was called
the Paschal Lamb.
The feast was kept for seven days,
from the 14th to the 21st Nisan,
corresponding to our March-
April. As the beginning of the
month was dependent on the moon
there was nearly a month's difference between the possible times of
beginning. This is the reason
for the varying dates of our Easter,
which must, as the commemoration
of Christ's resurrection, be determined by the date of the Passover.
There were many rules as to the
Passover Supper, some given in
Exodus being for the first celebration only.*

it is the Lord's *p.*, ye.   *Ex* 12:11
  27; *Lev* 23:5; *Num* 28:16
kill the *p.*   *Ex* 12:21
this is ordinance of the *p.*   43
they kept the *p.* at even. *Num* 9:5
on the morrow of the *p.* *Num* 33:3
    Josh 5:10
sacrifice the *p.* to Lord. *Deut* 16:2, 6
thou mayest not sacrifice *p.*   5
holden such a *p.* from days of judges,
  nor in days of kings. *2 Ki* 23:22
wherein this *p.* was holden.   23
then they killed *p.* in second month.
  2 Chr 30:15; 35:1, 11; *Ezra* 6:20
    Mark 14:12; *Luke* 22:7
yet did they eat *p.*   *2 Chr* 30:18
Josiah kept a *p.* unto the Lord. 35:1
    17:19; *Ezra* 6:19
Josiah gave all for *p. 2 Chr* 35:7, 8, 9
they roasted *p.* with fire.   13
ye shall have *p.* a feast. *Ezek* 45:21
prepare for thee to eat *p.? Mat* 26:17
    Mark 14:12; *Luke* 22:8, 11
and they made ready *p.* *Mat* 26:19
    Mark 14:16; *Luke* 22:13
desired to eat this *p.*   *Luke* 22:15
p. was at hand.   *John* 2:13; 11:55
was in Jerusalem at the *p.*   2:23
Jerusalem before *p.* to purify. 11:55
six days before *p.* to Bethany. 12:1
that they might eat the *p.*   18:28
release to you one at the *p.*   39
preparation of the *p.*   19:14
Christ our *p.* is sacrificed. *1 Cor* 5:7
thro' faith he kept the *p.* *Heb* 11:28
    see **feast, keep**

passovers

charge of killing of *p.*   *2 Chr* 30:17

past

days of mourning were *p.* *Gen* 50:4
    2 Sam 11:27
with horn in time *p.*   *Ex* 21:29, 36
go along, until we be *p.* *Num* 21:22
Emims dwelt therein in times *p.*
    Deut 2:10
now of the days which are *p.*   4:32
hated him not in times *p.* 42; 19:4, 6
bitterness of death is *p. 1 Sam* 15:32
his presence as in times *p.*   19:7
for David in time *p.* to be king.
    2 Sam 3:17
also in time *p.* when Saul was. 5:2
David was a little *p.* the top.   16:1
when midday was *p.*   *1 Ki* 18:29
was ruler in time *p.*   *1 Chr* 9:20
which doeth great things *p. Job* 9:10
secret, until thy wrath be *p.*   14:13
my days are *p.*, my purposes. 17:11
O that I were as in months *p.*   29:2
as yesterday when it is *p.* *Ps* 90:4
requireth that which is *p. Eccl* 3:15
for lo the winter is *p.*   *S of S* 2:11
the harvest is *p.*, the.   *Jer* 8:20
the time is now *p.*, send. *Mat* 14:15
sabbath was *p.*, Mary.   *Mark* 16:1
the voice was *p.*, Jesus. *Luke* 9:36
when they were *p.* first. *Acts* 12:10
who in times *p.* suffered all. 14:16
fast was now already *p.*, Paul. 27:9
for remission of sins that are *p.*
    Rom 3:25
for as ye in times *p.* have.   11:30
and his ways are *p.* finding out 33
old things *p.* away; all. *2 Cor* 5:17
my conversation in time *p. Gal* 1:13
persecuted us in times *p.*   23
I have also told you in time *p.* 5:21
in time *p.* ye walked.   *Eph* 2:2
our conversation in times *p.*   3
who being *p.* feeling have.   4:19
that resurrection is *p.*   *2 Tim* 2:18
who in time *p.* was to.   *Philem* 11
who spake in time *p.* to.   *Heb* 1:1
to conceive seed, when she was *p.*
    11:11
p. were not a people.   *1 Pet* 2:10
for the time *p.* of our life may. 4:3
darkness is *p.*, true.   *1 John* 2:8
one woe is *p.*   *Rev* 9:12
the second woe is *p.*   11:14

pastor

(*The original meaning of this word
was shepherd, and in this sense it
is sometimes used in the Bible.
The Eastern shepherd must both
protect and feed his sheep—so
there is a derived meaning of
spiritual leader, minister, one given
charge of a church of Christ, to care
for spiritual interests of the people
and feed their souls with spiritual
food. This meaning also is found
in the Bible*)

hastened from being a *p. Jer* 17:16*

pastors

p. also transgressed.   *Jer* 2:8*
I will give you *p.* according.   3:15*
for *p.* are become brutish.   10:21*
many *p.* have destroyed my. 12:10*
wind shall eat up all thy *p.*   22:22*
woe to the *p.* that destroy.   23:1*
thus saith Lord against *p.* that.   2*
and he gave some *p.*   *Eph* 4:11

pasture

thy servants have no *p.*   *Gen* 47:4
they went to seek *p.*   *1 Chr* 4:39
they found fat *p.*   40
because there was *p.*   41
of the mountains is his *p. Job* 39:8
why doth thine anger smoke against
  sheep of thy *p.?*   *Ps* 74:1
so we sheep of thy *p.* well.   79:13
people of his *p.*   95:7; 100:3
wild asses, a *p.* of flocks. *Isa* 32:14
scatter sheep of my *p.*   *Jer* 23:1
hath spoiled their *p.*   25:36
like harts that find no *p.* *Lam* 1:6
them in a good *p.*, a fat *p. Ezek* 34:14

small thing to have eaten good *p.*
       Ezek 34:18
ye my flock, the flock of my *p.*, are. 31
according to their *p.* so. *Hos* 13:6
because they have no *p.* *Joel* 1:18
go in and out and find *p.* *John* 10:9

pastures
twenty oxen out of *p.*   *1 Ki* 4:23
to lie down in green *p.*   *Ps* 23:2
they drop upon the *p.* of.   65:12
p. are clothed with flocks.   13
cattle shall feed in large *p. Isa* 30:23
p. shall be in all high places. 49:9*
down residue of your *p. Ezek* 34:18
one lamb out of flock of fat *p.* 45:15
fire hath devoured *p. Joel* 1:19, 20
for the *p.* of the wilderness. 2:22

Patara
Rhodes we came unto *P. Acts* 21:1

pate
come down upon his own *p. Ps* 7:16

path
[1] *A beaten way by which men can walk,* Gen 49:17. [2] *The regular methods by which one lives, or shows his character. This is used of both God and man.*

Dan a serpent, an adder in *p.* that.
       Gen 49:17
the Lord stood in a *p. Num* 22:24*
there is a *p.* which no fowl. *Job* 28:7
mar my *p.* they set forward. 30:13
he maketh a *p.* to shine. 41:32
thou wilt shew me the *p. Ps* 16:11
thy way, lead me in a plain *p.* 27:11
thy way in sea, thy *p.* is. 77:19
make me to go in *p.* of thy. 119:35
lamp, and a light to my *p.* 105
thou compassest my *p.* and. 139:3
then thou knewest my *p.* 142:3
thy foot from their *p.* *Pr* 1:15
understand every good *p.* 2:9
enter not into the *p.* of the. 4:14
the *p.* of the just is as the. 18
ponder the *p.* of thy feet, and. 26
thou shouldest ponder the *p.* 5:6
thou dost weigh the *p.* of. *Isa* 26:7
the way, turn aside out of *p.* 30:11
and taught him in the *p.* 40:14
a *p.* in the mighty waters. 43:16
walk every one in his *p. Joel* 2:8

Pathros
of his people from *P.* *Isa* 11:11
return into the land of *P. Ezek* 29:14
will make *P.* desolate, I will. 30:14

paths
the *p.* of their way are. *Job* 6:18
so are the *p.* of all that forget. 8:13
narrowly to all my *p.* 13:27
he hath set darkness in my *p.* 19:8
neither abide they in the *p.* 24:13
in stocks, marketh all my *p.* 33:11
that thou shouldest keep the *p.*38:20
through the *p.* of the seas. *Ps* 8:8
I have kept me from the *p.* 17:4
hold up my goings in thy *p.* that. 5
he leadeth me in the *p.* of. 23:3
O Lord, teach me thy *p.* 25:4
p. of the Lord are mercy. 10
and thy *p.* drop fatness. 65:11
he keepeth *p.* of judgement. *Pr* 2:8
leave *p.* of uprightness to walk. 13
they froward in their *p.* 15
her *p.* incline unto the dead. 18
nor take they hold of the *p.* of life. 19
thou mayest keep the *p.* of the. 20
he shall direct thy *p.* 3:6
all her *p.* are peace. 17
I have led thee in right *p.* 4:11
go not astray in her *p.* 7:25
in places of *p.* 8:2
I lead in the midst of the *p.* 20
and we will walk in his *p. Isa* 2:3
       Mi 4:2
destroy the way of thy *p. Isa* 3:12
I will lead them in *p.* they. 42:16
he called, the restorer of *p.* 58:12
destruction are in their *p.* 59:7
have made them crooked. 8

way, and ask for old *p.* *Jer* 6:16
from ancient *p.* to walk in *p.* 18:15
made my *p.* crooked. *Lam* 3:9
wall, she shall not find her *p. Hos* 2:6
make his *p.* straight. *Mat* 3:3
   Mark 1:3; *Luke* 3:4
straight *p.* for your feet. *Heb* 12:13

pathway
in the *p.* thereof there is. *Pr* 12:28

patience
servant worshipped him, saying,
Lord, have *p.* with. *Mat* 18:26, 29
bring forth fruit with *p. Luke* 8:15
in your *p.* possess ye your. 21:19
tribulation worketh *p. Rom* 5:3
and *p.* experience, and. 4
do we with *p.* wait for it. 8:25
we through *p.* and comfort. 15:4
the God of *p.* grant you to be. 5
as ministers of God in much *p.*
       2 Cor 6:4
wrought among you in all *p.* 12:12
with all might to all *p.* *Col* 1:11
remembering your *p.* of. *1 Thes* 1:3
glory in you for your *p.* *2 Thes* 1:4
and follow after love, *p. 1 Tim* 6:11
hast fully known my *p.* *2 Tim* 3:10
be sound in faith, in *p.* *Tit* 2:2
who through faith and *p. Heb* 6:12
ye have need of *p.* that after. 10:36
let us run with *p.* the race set. 12:1
of your faith worketh *p.* *Jas* 1:3
but let *p.* have her perfect work. 4
husbandman hath long *p.* for it. 5:7
for an example of *p.* 10
have heard of *p.* of Job. 11
to temperance *p.*; to *p.* *2 Pet* 1:6
companion in *p.* of Jesus. *Rev* 1:9
I know thy *p.* 2:2, 19
and thou hast *p.* 3
hast kept word of my *p.* 3:10
the *p.* of the saints. 13:10; 14:12

patient
p. in spirit is better than. *Eccl* 7:8
who by *p.* continuance. *Rom* 2:7
rejoicing in hope, *p.* in. 12:12
be *p.* toward all men. *1 Thes* 5:14*
and unto the *p.* waiting. *2 Thes* 3:5
not greedy of lucre, but *p.*
   1 Tim 3:3*; *2 Tim* 2:24*
be *p.* brethren. *Jas* 5:7
be ye also *p.* 8

patiently
Lord, and wait *p.* for him. *Ps* 37:7
I waited *p.* for the Lord, and. 40:1
beseech thee to hear me *p. Acts* 26:3
after he had *p.* endured. *Heb* 6:15
buffeted for faults ye take it *p.* . . . .
 suffer, ye take it *p.* *1 Pet* 2:20

Patmos
isle that is called *P.* *Rev* 1:9

patriarch
(*This name is given to the heads, or princes of the family, chiefly to those that lived before Moses. The name Patriarch comes from the Greek word,* Patriarches, *which signifies* Head of a family)
speak of the *p.* David. *Acts* 2:29
p. Abraham paid tithes. *Heb* 7:4

patriarchs
Jacob begat the twelve *p. Acts* 7:8
p. moved with envy sold Joseph. 9

patrimony
cometh from sale of his *p. Deut* 18:8

pattern
after the *p.* of all the. *Ex* 25:9
thou make them after their *p.* 40
candlestick was made after the *p.*
       Num 8:4
behold the *p.* of the altar. *Josh* 22:28
to Urijah the *p.* of altar. *2 Ki* 16:10
David gave Solomon *p. 1 Chr* 28:11
      12, 18, 19
let them measure the *p. Ezek* 43:10
that in me first Jesus Christ might
 shew for a *p.* *1 Tim* 1:16*
thyself a *p.* of good works. *Tit* 2:7*
according to *p.* I shewed. *Heb* 8:5

patterns
necessary that the *p.* of. *Heb* 9:23*

Paul
Saul, called *P.* filled. *Acts* 13:9
religious proselytes follow *P.* 43
P. waxed bold. 46
raised persecution against *P.* 50
the same heard *P.* 14:9
P. Mercurius, was chief speaker. 12
having stoned *P.* drew him out. 19
P. thought not good to take. 15:38
P. chose Silas. 40
him would *P.* have to go. 16:3
a vision appeared to *P.* in the. 9
to the things spoken of *P.* 14
followed *P.* 17
but *P.* being grieved. 18
P. and Silas prayed, and sang. 25
but *P.* cried, saying, Do thyself. 28
P. as his manner was, went. 17:2
consorted with *P.* and Silas.
brethren sent *P.* away. 10, 14
while *P.* waited at Athens. 16
P. was pressed in spirit, and. 18:5
Lord spake to *P.* in the night. 9
miracles by the hands of *P.* 19:11
P. I know. 15
P. purposed in spirit to go to. 21
this *P.* hath persuaded. 26
P. preached unto them, ready. 20:7
P. went down, and embracing. 10
wept sore, and fell on *P.'s* neck. 37
said to *P.* through the Spirit. 21:4
Agabus took *P.'s* girdle and. 11
the day following *P.* went in. 18
took *P.* and drew him out of. 30
saw soldiers, they left beating *P.* 32
P. stood on the stairs. 40
P. beholding. 23:1
lest *P.* should have been pulled. 10
be of good cheer, *P.* 11
not eat till they had killed *P.* 12, 14
P. prayed me to bring this. 18
soldiers brought *P.* to Antipatris. 31
informed governor against *P.* 24:1
that money should have been given
 him of *P.* 26
Felix left *P.* bound. 27
one Jesus, whom *P.* affirmed. 25:19
Festus said, *P.* thou art. 26:24
Julius courteously entreated *P.* 27:3
saying, Fear not, *P.* 24
P. besought them all to take meat. 33
the centurion, willing to save *P.* 43
but *P.* was suffered to dwell. 28:16
I am of *P.* *1 Cor* 1:12; 3:4
is Christ divided ? was *P.?* 1:13
who then is *P.?* 3:5
whether *P.,* or Apollos, or. 22
the salutation of me *P.* 16:21
    Col 4:18; *2 Thes* 3:17
come to you, even I *P. 1 Thes* 2:18
such an one as *P.* the aged. *Philem* 9
as our beloved brother *P. 2 Pet* 3:15

Paulus
the deputy Sergius *P.* *Acts* 13:7

paved
as it were a *p.* work. *Ex* 24:10
midst thereof being *p. S of S* 3:10

pavement
he put the sea on a *p.* *2 Ki* 16:17
Israel bowed themselves upon the *p.*
       2 Chr 7:3
the beds were on a *p.* *Esth* 1:6
p. made for the court, thirty chambers were upon the *p. Ezek* 40:17
p. by the side of the gates, was the
 lower *p.* 18
over against the *p.* was gallery. 42:3
a place called the *p.* *John* 19:13

pavilion, -s
he made darkness his *p.*
   2 Sam 22:12; *Ps* 18:11
kings drinking in *p.* *1 Ki* 20:12
drinking himself drunk in *p.* 16
he shall hide me in his *p. Ps* 27:5
keep them secretly in a *p.* 31:20
spread his royal *p.* *Jer* 43:10

paw
delivered me out of *p. 1 Sam* 17:37

paweth
the horse *p.* in the valley. *Job* 39:21

paws
whatsoever goeth on *p.* *Lev* 11:27

pay

only he shall *p*. for loss. *Ex* 21:19
and he shall *p*. as the judges. 22
he shall surely *p*. ox for ox. 36
found, let him *p*. double. 22:7, 9
p. according to the dowry. 17
water, I will *p*. for it. *Num* 20:19
vow, shall not slack to *p*. *Deut* 23:21
me go and *p*. my vow. 2 *Sam* 15:7
p. a talent of silver. 1 *Ki* 20:39
sell oil, and *p*. thy debt. 2 *Ki* 4:7
did Solomon make to *p*. tribute.
2 *Chr* 8:8
did children of Ammon *p*. to. 27:5
will they not *p*. toll and. *Ezra* 4:13
will *p*. 10,000 talents. *Esth* 3:9; 4:7
thou shalt *p*. thy vows. *Job* 22:27
I will *p*. my vows. *Ps* 22:25; 66:13
116:14, 18
and *p*. thy vows to the Most. 50:14
vow and *p*. to the Lord your. 76:11
given, will he *p*. again. *Pr* 19:17
if thou hast nothing to *p*. why? 22:27
defer not to *p*. it, *p*. that. *Eccl* 5:4
that thou shouldest vow and not *p*. 5
I will *p*. that which I have vowed.
Jonah 2:9
doth not your master *p*.? *Mat* 17:24
as he had not to *p*., his lord forgave
him. 18:25, 27; *Luke* 7:42
I will *p*. thee all. *Mat* 18:26, 29
p. me that thou owest. 28
till he should *p*. debt. 30
till he should *p*. all that was due. 34
for ye *p*. tithe of mint, anise. 23:23
p. ye tribute also. *Rom* 13:6

payeth

borroweth and *p*. not. *Ps* 37:21

payment

all to be sold, and *p*. *Mat* 18:25

peace

(*This word is used in the Bible as we use it to-day. It was, however, much used as a salutation, with no stress on the meaning, although that meaning was most probably the origin of its use in that way*)

Pharaoh an answer of *p*. *Gen* 41:16
I will give *p*. in land. *Lev* 26:6
the Lord lift up his countenance and
give thee *p*. *Num* 6:26
give to him my covenant of *p*. 25:12
Sihon with words of *p*. *Deut* 2:26
city, proclaim *p*. to it. 20:10
if it make thee answer of *p*. 11
if it will make no *p*. with thee. 12
thou shalt not seek their *p*. 23:6
I shall have *p*. though I walk. 29:19
was *p*. between Jabin. *Judg* 4:17
there was *p*. between Israel and.
1 *Sam* 7:14
well, thy servant shall have *p*. 20:7
there is *p*. to thee, no hurt. 21
throne shall there be *p*. 1 *Ki* 2:33
Solomon had *p*. on all sides. 4:24
there was *p*. between Hiram. 5:12
whether they come for *p*. 20:18
let him say, Is it *p*.? 2 *Ki* 9:17, 18
what hast thou to do with *p*.? 19, 22
p. so long as her witchcrafts? 22
she said, Had Zimri *p*., who slew? 31
is it not good, if *p*. be in my days?
20:19; *Isa* 39:8
I will give *p*. to Israel. 1 *Chr* 22:9
there was no *p*. to him. 2 *Chr* 15:5
beyond the river, *p*. *Ezra* 4:17
unto Darius the king, all *p*. 5:7
to Ezra perfect *p*. 7:12
nor seek their *p*. or their. 9:12
letters with words of *p*. *Esth* 9:30
Mordecai, speaking *p*. to all. 10:3
beasts of field shall be at *p*. *Job* 5:23
with him, and be at *p*. 22:21
maketh *p*. in his high places. 25:2
him that was at *p*. with. *Ps* 7:4
which speak *p*. to neighbours. 28:3
bless his people with *p*. 29:11
do good, seek *p*. and pursue it.
34:14; 1 *Pet* 3:11
they speak not *p*. but they devise.
Ps 35:20
themselves in abundance of *p*. 37:11

end of the upright man is *p*. *Ps* 37:37
such as be at *p*. with him. 55:20
the mountains shall bring *p*. 72:3
in days abundance of *p*. so long. 7
he will speak *p*. to his people. 85:8
righteousness and *p*. have kissed. 10
great *p*. have they which. 119:165
dwelt with him that hateth *p*. 120:6
I am for *p*., but when I speak they. 7
pray for *p*. of Jerusalem. 122:6
but *p*. shall be upon Israel. 125:5
shalt see *p*. upon Israel. 128:6
he maketh *p*. in thy borders. 147:14
pleasantness, her paths *p*. *Pr* 3:17
to the counsellors of *p*. is joy. 12:20
maketh his enemies to be at *p*. 16:7
of war, and a time of *p*. *Eccl* 3:8
The Prince of P. *Isa* 9:6
of the increase of his *p*. no end. 7
thou wilt ordain *p*. for us. 26:12
p. with me, and he shall make *p*. 27:5
righteousness shall be *p*. 32:17
the ambassadors of *p*. shall. 33:7
for *p*. I had great bitterness. 38:17
I make *p*. and create evil. 45:7
then had thy *p*. been as river. 48:18
no *p*. to the wicked. 22; 57:21
feet of him that publisheth *p*. 52:7
Nah 1:15
the chastisement of our *p*. *Isa* 53:5
nor shall covenant of my *p*. 54:10
shall be *p*. of thy children. 13
with joy, led forth with *p*. 55:12
he shall enter into *p*. 57:2
fruit of the lips; P. *p*. to him. 19
the way of *p*. they know not. 59:8
Rom 3:17
I will make thine officers *p*. *Isa* 60:17
behold, I will extend *p*. to her. 66:12
ye shall have *p*. whereas. *Jer* 4:10
P. *p*. when there is no *p*. 6:14; 8:11
we looked for *p*. but no. 8:15; 14:19
if in land of *p*. they wearied. 12:5
sword devour, no flesh shall have *p*. 12
you assured *p*. in this place. 14:13
I have taken away my *p*. from. 16:5
prophet which prophesied of *p*. 28:9
seek *p*. of the city whither. 29:7
thoughts of *p*., and not of evil. 11
a voice of fear, and not of *p*. 30:5
reveal to them abundance of *p*. 33:6
hast removed my soul far from *p*.
Lam 3:17
they shall seek *p*. there. *Ezek* 7:25
P. and there was no *p*. 13:10, 16
them a covenant of *p*. 34:25; 37:26
by *p*. he shall destroy. *Dan* 8:25*
men at *p*. with thee have. *Ob* 7
with their teeth and cry P. *Mi* 3:5
this man shall be the *p*. when. 5:5
I will give *p*. saith the Lord. *Hag* 2:9
counsel of *p*. be between. *Zech* 6:13
nor was there any *p*. to him. 8:10
execute judgement of truth and *p*. 16
love *p*. 19
shall speak *p*. to the heathen. 9:10
with him of life and *p*. *Mal* 2:5
worthy, let your *p*. come upon it; if
not, let your *p*. return. *Mat* 10:13
am come to send *p*. on earth. 34
he arose and said to the sea, *p*. be
still. *Mark* 4:39
have *p*. one with another. 9:50
feet into the way of *p*. *Luke* 1:79
and on earth *p*., good will. 2:14
if son of *p*. be there, your *p*. 10:6
to give *p*. on the earth? 12:51
desireth conditions of *p*. 14:32
p. in heaven, and glory in. 19:38
things which belong to thy *p*. 42
p. I leave with you, my *p*. *John* 14:27
that in me ye might have *p*. 16:33
preaching *p*. by Jesus Christ.
Acts 10:36
Blastus their friend desired *p*. 12:20
p. from God the Father. *Rom* 1:7
1 *Cor* 1:3; 2 *Cor* 1:2; *Gal* 1:3
Eph 1:2; *Phil* 1:2
but *p*. to every man that. *Rom* 2:10
justified, we have *p*. with God. 5:1
spiritually minded is life and *p*. 8:6
that preach the gospel of *p*. 10:15
kingdom of God is joy and *p*. 14:17
follow the things that make for *p*. 19

fill you with all joy and *p*. *Rom* 15:13
hath called us to *p*. 1 *Cor* 7:15
but author of *p*. as in. 14:33
Spirit is love, joy, *p*. *Gal* 5:22
for he is our *p*. *Eph* 2:14
so making *p*. 15
Christ came and preached *p*. 17
the Spirit in the bond of *p*. 4:3
preparation of gospel of *p*. 6:15
p. of God, which passeth. *Phil* 4:7
grace and *p*. from God. *Col* 1:2
1 *Thes* 1:1; 2 *Thes* 1:2; 1 *Tim* 1:2
2 *Tim* 1:2; *Tit* 1:4; *Philem* 3
2 *John* 3
let the *p*. of God rule in. *Col* 3:15
when they shall say, P. 1 *Thes* 5:3
be at *p*. among themselves. 13
Lord of *p*. give you *p*. 2 *Thes* 3:16
follow *p*. with all men. 2 *Tim* 2:22
Heb 12:14
Salem, that is, king of *p*. *Heb* 7:2
and received spies in *p*. 11:31
p. of them that make *p*.? *Jas* 3:18
p. from him that is, was. *Rev* 1:4
was given to him to take *p*. 6:4

see **held, hold, made, offerings**

peace *be*

and he said, P. *be* to you. *Gen* 43:23
Lord, said, P. *be* to thee. *Judg* 6:23
and the old man said, P. *be*. 19:20
p. *be* to thee, *p*. *be* to house, *p*. *be*.
1 *Sam* 25:6
p. *be* to thee, and *p*. *be*. 1 *Chr* 12:18
p. *be* within thy walls. *Ps* 122:7
I will now say, P. *be* within thee. 8
p. *be* multiplied to you. *Dan* 4:1
6:25; 1 *Pet* 1:2; 2 *Pet* 1:2; *Jude* 2
p. *be* to thee, be strong. *Dan* 10:19
first say, P. *be* to this. *Luke* 10:5
he saith, P. *be* to you. 24:36
John 20:19, 21, 26
p. *be* on them, and mercy. *Gal* 6:16
p. *be* to brethren, and. *Eph* 6:23
p. *be* with you all. 1 *Pet* 5:14
p. *be* to thee, our friends. 3 *John* 14

God of **peace**

the *God of p*. be with. *Rom* 15:33
the *God of p*. shall bruise. 16:20
God of p. shall be with you.
2 *Cor* 13:11; *Phil* 4:9
very *God of p*. sanctify. 1 *Thes* 5:23
now the *God of p*. make. *Heb* 13:20

in **peace**

sent thee away *in p*. *Gen* 26:29
departed from Isaac *in p*. 31
to my father's house *in p*. 28:21
as for you, get you up *in p*. 44:17
at Makkedah, *in p*. *Josh* 10:21
when I come again *in p*. *Judg* 8:9
when I return *in p*. whatever. 11:31
Abner went *in p*. 2 *Sam* 3:21, 22
he is gone *in p*. 23
return to the city *in p*. and. 15:27
so all the people shall be *in p*. 17:3
until the day he came *in p*. 19:24
king is come again *in p*. 30
the blood of war *in p*. 1 *Ki* 2:5
return every man *in p*. 22:17
2 *Chr* 18:16
in prison until I come *in p*.
1 *Ki* 22:27; 2 *Chr* 18:26
if thou return at all *in p*. 1 *Ki* 22:28
2 *Chr* 18:27
shalt be gathered to thy grave *in p*.
2 *Ki* 22:20; 2 *Chr* 34:28
returned *in p*. 2 *Chr* 19:1
tabernacle shall be *in p*. *Job* 5:24
I will lay me down *in p*. *Ps* 4:8
my soul *in p*. from the battle. 55:18
keep him in perfect *p*. *Isa* 26:3
in the *p*. thereof shall ye. *Jer* 29:7
but thou shalt die *in p*. 34:5
he walked with me *in p*. *Mal* 2:6
thy servant depart *in p*. *Luke* 2:29
palace his goods are *in p*. 11:21
conduct him forth *in p*. 1 *Cor* 16:11
be of one mind, live *in p*. 2 *Cor* 13:11
depart *in p*., be ye. *Jas* 2:16
righteousness is sown *in p*. 3:18
found of him *in p*. 2 *Pet* 3:14

see **go**

peaceable

these men are p. with. Gen 34:21
of them that are p. in 2 Sam 20:19
wide, quiet, and p. 1 Chr 4:40
my people dwell in a p. Isa 32:18
the p. habitations are. Jer 25:37
lead a quiet and p. life. 1 Tim 2:2*
it yieldeth the p. fruit. Heb 12:11
above is pure, p., gentle. Jas 3:17

peaceably

speak p. to him. Gen 37:4
restore those lands again p.
Judg 11:13
send some to call p. to the. 21:13
comest thou p.? 1 Sam 16:4
he said, P. 5; 1 Ki 2:13
if ye be come p. to me. 1 Chr 12:17
one speaketh p. to his. Jer 9:8
he shall come in p. Dan 11:21*, 24*
live p. with all men. Rom 12:18

peacemakers

blessed are the p. for they. Mat 5:9

peacocks

navy came, bringing p. 1 Ki 10:22
2 Chr 9:21
the goodly wings to p.? Job 39:13*

pearl

(Pearls were considered by the
ancients among the most precious
of gems and were highly esteemed
as ornaments. This is probably
the reason the word is used metaphorically for anything of great
value, and especially for wise
sayings)
he found one p. of great. Mat 13:46
gate was of one p. Rev 21:21

pearls

be made of coral or p. Job 28:18*
neither cast ye your p. Mat 7:6
man seeking goodly p. 13:45
not with gold, or p. or. 1 Tim 2:9
decked with gold and p. Rev 17:4
the merchandise of. 18:12, 16
twelve gates were twelve p. 21:21

peculiar

be a p. treasure to me. Ex 19:5†
to be a p. people. Deut 14:2†
26:18†; 1 Pet 2:9*
chosen Israel for his p. treasure.
Ps 135:4†
I gathered the p. treasure. Eccl 2:8
purify to himself p. people. Tit 2:14*

pedigree

they declared their p. Num 1:18

peeled

nation scattered and p. Isa 18:2*, 7*
every shoulder was p. Ezek 29:18†

peep

to wizards that p. and. Isa 8:19*

peeped

opened the mouth or p. Isa 10:14*

Pekah

P. conspired against. 2 Ki 15:25
in days of P. came Tiglath-pileser. 29
a conspiracy against P. 15:30
against Judah came P. 37; 16:5
P. slew in Judah 120,000. 2 Chr 28:6
Rezin and P. went towards. Isa 7:1

Pekahiah

P. son of Manahem. 2 Ki 15:22, 23

Pelatiah

Hananiah, P. of Judah. 1 Chr 3:21
having for their captian P. 4:42
P. and Hanan sealed. Neh 10:22
P. the son of Benaiah. Ezek 11:13

pelican

swan and p. unclean. Lev 11:18
Deut 14:17
I am like a p. of the. Ps 102:6

pen

they that handle the p. Judg 5:14*
graven with an iron p. Job 19:24
my tongue is the p. of a. Ps 45:1
write in it with a man's p. Isa 8:1
p. of the scribes is in vain. Jer 8:8
is written with a p. of iron. 17:1
I will not with ink and p. 3 John 13

pence

(The denarius, worth about 16 or
17 cents, or between 8d. and 9d.,
was the usual wage of an un-
skilled labourer for one day.
American Revision changes to
shillings)
owed him an hundred p. Mat 18:28
sold for more than 300 p.
Mark 14:5; John 12:5
the one owed 500 p. the. Luke 7:41
on morrow he took out two p. 10:35

Peniel

the name of the place P. Gen 32:30

penknife

Jehudi cut roll with a p. Jer 36:23

penny

with labourers for a p. Mat 20:2
they received every man a p. 9
not agree with me for a p.? 13
brought unto him a p. 22:19
he said, Bring me a p. Mark 12:15
Luke 20:24
of wheat for a p. and three measures
of barley for a p. Rev 6:6

pennyworth

two hundred p. of bread. Mark 6:37
two hundred p. is not. John 6:7

Pentecost

This word is derived from the
Greek word Pentecoste, fiftieth, because the feast of Pentecost was
celebrated the fiftieth day after the
sixteenth of Nisan, which was the
second day of the feast of the passover. The Hebrews call it the
Feast of Weeks, Ex 34:22, because
it was kept seven weeks after the
passover.
It was the Jewish harvest-home.
when the day of P. was. Acts 2:1
at Jerusalem the day of P. 20:16
tarry at Ephesus until P. 1 Cor 16:8

Penuel

as Jacob passed over P. Gen 32:31
Gideon went up thence to P. and.
Judg 8:8
he beat down the tower of P. 17
then Jeroboam went and built P.
1 Ki 12:25
P. the father of Gedor. 1 Chr 4:4
Iphediah and P. the sons of. 8:25

penury

lips tendeth only to p. Pr 14:23
she of her p. hath cast. Luke 21:4*

people

(The Revisions often change the
singular to the plural. In this case
it has more distinctly the idea of
nations or of people grouped
together. In the New Testament
the singular is more often changed
to multitude)
let p. serve thee, and. Gen 27:29
he also shall become a p. 48:19
I will take you for a p. and be to you
a God. Ex 6:7; Deut 4:20
2 Sam 7:24; Jer 13:11
thou art a stiffnecked p. Ex 33:3, 5
34:9; Deut 9:6
I separated you from other p.
Lev 20:24, 26
thou art undone, O p. Num 21:29
a p. come out from Egypt. 22:5, 11
head over a p. in Midian. 25:15
did ever p. hear voice? Deut 4:33
chosen thee to be a special p. 7:6
chosen thee to be a peculiar p. 14:2
a p. more than thou, be not. 20:1
shall be given to another p. 28:32
may establish thee for a p. to. 29:13
with those that are not a p. 32:21
who is like to thee, O p.? 33:29
gone back to her p. Ruth 1:15
ye make the Lord's p. 1 Sam 2:24
to us, to slay us and our p. 5:10
let it slay us not, and our p. 11
went to redeem for a p. 2 Sam 7:23
afflicted p. thou wilt save. 22:28
Ps 18:27

a p. I knew not shall serve me.
2 Sam 22:44; Ps 18:43
hearken, O p. every one. 1 Ki 22:28
the p., that they should be the Lord's
p. 2 Ki 11:17; 2 Chr 23:16
from one kingdom to another p.
1 Chr 16:20; Ps 105:13
valiantly for our p. 1 Chr 19:13
made me king over a p. 2 Chr 1:9
letters to every p. after. Esth 1:22
3:12; 8:9; Neh 13:24
Esther had not shewed her p. nor.
Esth 2:10
there is a certain p. scattered. 3:8
request before him for her p. 4:8
when p. are cut off in. Job 36:20
ye p. pour out your hearts. Ps 62:8
O bless our God, ye p. 66:8
a p. that do err. 95:10
from a p. of a strange. 114:1
happy is that p. 144:15
a p. near to him. 148:14
a reproach to any p. Pr 14:34
wicked ruler over the poor p. 28:15
ants are a p. not strong. 30:25
a p. laden with iniquity. Isa 1:4
give ear to the law, ye p. of. 10
be broken, that it be not a p. 7:8
should not a p. seek unto? 8:19
is a p. of no understanding. 27:11
this is a rebellious p. 30:9; 65:2
I will give p. for thy life. 43:4
bring forth the blind p. that. 8
a p. that provoketh me to. 65:3
a rejoicing, and her p. a joy. 18
a p. cometh from the north.
Jer 6:22; 50:41
destroyed from being a p. 48:42
her p. fell into the hand. Lam 1:7
and there shall be, like p. Hos 4:9
O Israel, for joy as other p. 9:1
tell us, of what p. art? Jonah 1:8
it shall be exalted, and p. Mi 4:1
there shall come p. Zech 8:20
to make ready a p. Luke 1:17
to take out of them a p. Acts 15:14
by them that are no p. Rom 10:19
to himself a peculiar p. Tit 2:14
they shall be to me a p. Heb 8:10
but ye are a peculiar p. 1 Pet 2:9
p. of God, time past were not a p. 10
redeemed us out of every p. Rev 5:9

all people

treasure above all p. Ex 19:5
Deut 7:6, 14; 10:15; Ps 99:2
the fewest of all p. Deut 7:7
scatter thee among all p. 28:64
came of all p. to hear. 1 Ki 4:34
all p. may know thy name. 8:43
2 Chr 6:33
byword among all p. 1 Ki 9:7
are diverse from all p. Esth 3:8
was published to all p. 14; 8:13
fear of them fell upon all p. 9:2
O clap your hands, all ye p. Ps 47:1
wonders among all p. 96:3
all ye nations, praise him, all ye p.
117:1; 148:11; Rom 15:11
to all p. a feast of fat. Isa 25:6
covering cast over all p. 7
called house of prayer for all p. 56:7
hear, I pray you, all p. 18; Mi 1:2
all p. and nations feared. Dan 5:19
all p. and nations should. 7:14
all p. will walk each in. Mi 4:5
heapeth unto him all p. Hab 2:5
a praise among all p. of earth.
Zeph 3:20
a burdensome stone for all p.
Zech 12:3*
tidings of joy, which shall be to all p.
Luke 2:10
before the face of all p. 31

all the people

all the p. of Sodom compassed.
Gen 19:4
he and all the p. with him. 35:6
that sold to all the p. of. 42:6
get thee out, and all the p. Ex 11:8
all the p. stand by thee from. 18:14
out of all the p. able men. 21

all the p. answered.   Ex 19:8; 24:3
come down in sight of all the p.   11
all the p. saw thunderings.   20:18
glory of the Lord appeared to all the
   p.   Lev 9:23
and before all the p. I will.   10:3
that all the Lord's p. were prophets.
   Num 11:29
and all the p. we saw are.   13:32
all the p. were in ignorance.   15:26
afterwards the hand of all the p.
   Deut 13:9; 17:7
all the p. shall hear and fear.   17:13
all the p. shall say, Amen.   27:15
   16, 17, 18, 19, 20, 21
all the p. of the earth shall.   28:10
that all the p. of the earth. Josh 4:24
all the p. that came out were. 5:4, 5
all the p. shall shout.   6:5
let not all the p. go: 7:3
from before us all the p.   24:18
house fell upon all the p. Judg 16:30
and all the p. arose as one.   20:8
him among all the p.   1 Sam 10:24
all the p. wept.   11:4
all the p. feared greatly.   12:18
because the soul of all the p.   11:4
all the p. stood, and.   2 Sam 2:28
Abner's grave, all the p. wept. 3:32, 34
and all the p. took notice of it.   36
bring back all the p. unto thee, so all
   the p. shall be in peace.   17:3
and all the p. were at strife.   19:9
woman went to all the p. in.   20:22
separate them from all p. 1 Ki 8:53
that all the p. of the earth may.   60
handfuls for all the p.   20:10
all the p. stood to the covenant.
   2 Ki 23:3
all the p. said, Amen.   1 Chr 16:36
all the p. will be wholly at.   28:21
king and all the p. offered. 2 Chr 7:4
may judge all the p.   Ezra 7:25
in sight of all p. for he was above all
      Neh 8:5
so the Levites stilled all the p.   11
O God, let all the p.   Ps 67:3, 5
and all the p. see his glory.   97:6
blessed be the Lord God of Israel: let
   all the p. say, Amen.   106:48
is no end of all the p.   Eccl 4:16
to speak to all the p.   Jer 26:8
all the p. were gathered against.   9
all the p. fought against.   34:1
a covenant with all the p.   8, 10
the hands of all the p.   38:4
all the p. obeyed the voice of. 43:4
all the p. are gone.   Ezek 31:12
when all the p. heard the.   Dan 3:7
covenant I made with all the p.
   Zech 11:10
a cup of trembling to all the p. 12:2
the Lord will smite all the p.   14:12
base before all the p.   Mal 2:9
unto him before all the p. Luke 8:47
all the p. rejoiced for the.   13:17
all the p. when they saw, gave. 18:43
all the p. were very attentive. 19:48
but if we say, Of men, all the p. 20:6
favour with all the p.   Acts 2:47
reputation among all the p.   5:34
not to all the p. but unto witnesses.
   10:41
of repentance to all the p.   13:24
stirred up all the p. and laid. 21:27
all the p., he sprinkled both book and
   all the p.   Heb 9:19

among the people
off from among the p.   Lev 18:29
be a curse among the p. Num 5:27
yourselves among the p. 1 Sam 14:34
ye brutish among the p.   Ps 94:8
know thee among the p. Ezek 28:19
understand among the p. Dan 11:33
they say among the p.   Joel 2:17
sow them among the p. Zech 10:9
all manner of disease among the p.
   Mat 4:23; 9:35
be an uproar among the p.   26:5
murmuring among the p. John 7:12
was a division among the p.   43
be destroyed from among the p.
   Acts 3:23

no further among the p.   Acts 4:17
wrought among the p.   5:12; 6:8
Paul ran in among the p.   14:14
false prophets also among the p.
   2 Pet 2:1
see **common, foolish, many,
men**

people of God
assembly of the p. of God. Judg 20:2
thing against p. of God. 2 Sam 14:13
p. of the God of Abraham.   Ps 47:9
a rest to the p. of God.   Heb 4:9
affliction with p. of God.   11:25
but are now p. of God.   1 Pet 2:10
see **great**

his people
be cut off from his p.   Gen 17:14
   Ex 30:33, 38; 31:14; Lev 7:20, 21
   25, 27; 17:4, 9; 19:8; 23:29
   Num 9:13; 15:30
was gathered to his p.   Gen 25:8
Ishmael was gathered to his p.   17
Isaac was gathered to his p.   35:29
Dan shall judge his p. as one of.
   49:16, 33
depart from his p.   Ex 8:29, 31
Amalek and his p.   17:13
Moses and for Israel his p.   18:1
blood, I will cut him off from among
   his p. Lev 17:10; 20:3, 6; 23:30
for the dead among his p.   21:1
profane his seed among his p.   15
gathered to his p.   Num 20:24, 26
delivered him into thy hand, and all
   his p.   21:34, 35; Deut 2:33
Og and all his p.   Deut 3:2, 3
thee to be his peculiar p.   26:18
for Lord's portion is his p.   32:9
shall judge his p.   36; Ps 135:14
with his p. he will be merciful to his
   . . . his p. Deut 32:43; Rom 15:10
was gathered to his p.   Deut 32:50
and bring Judah to his p.   33:7
Ai, the king and his p.   Josh 8:1
Amorites before his p.   Judg 11:23
Lord had visited his p.   Ruth 1:6
forsake his p. for his great name's
   . . . make you his p. 1 Sam 12:22
to be king over all his p.   15:1
make his p. Israel utterly to. 27:12
David executed justice to all his p.
   2 Sam 8:15; 1 Chr 18:14
people shall go for his p. 1 Ki 20:42
The Lord make his p. a hundred
   times so many more. 1 Chr 21:3
land is subdued before Lord and his
   p.   22:18
God hath given rest to his p. 23:25
Lord hath loved his p.   2 Chr 2:11
Lord hath blessed his p.   31:10
that could deliver his p.? 32:14, 15
to Manasseh and his p.   33:10
had compassion on his p.   36:15
wrath of Lord arose against his p. 16
who among you of all his p. go up. 23
   Ezra 1:3
seeking wealth of his p.   Esth 10:3
nor nephew among his p. Job 18:19
captivity of his p.   Ps 14:7; 53:6
give strength to his p.; the Lord will
   bless his p. with.   29:11; 68:35
that he may judge his p.   50:4
therefore his p. return hither. 73:10
he provide flesh for his p.?   78:20
he gave his p. over also to.   62
him to feed Jacob his p.   71
will speak peace to his p. and. 85:8
will not cast off his p.   94:14
we are his p.   100:3
he increased his p. greatly. 105:24
turned their heart to hate his p.   25
he brought forth his p.   43
wrath of the Lord kindled against
   his p.   106:40; Isa 5:25
shewed his p. the power. Ps 111:6
he sent redemption to his p.: holy. 9
with the princes of his p.   113:8
the presence of all his p. 116:14, 18
the Lord round about his p.   125:2
his p. through the wilderness. 136:16
exalteth the horn of his p.   148:14
Lord taketh pleasure in his p. 149:4
with the ancients of his p. Isa 3:14

and the heart of his p.   Isa 7:2
remnant of his p. left.   11:11
highway for the remnant of his p. 16
the poor of his p. shall trust.   14:32
the rebuke of his p. shall he.   25:8
beauty to residue of his p.   28:5
bindeth up breach of his p.   30:26
hath comforted his p.   49:13; 52:9
pleadeth the cause of his p.   51:22
separated me from his p.   56:3
days of old, Moses and his p. 63:11
and serve him and his p.   Jer 27:12
return every one to his p.   50:16
not good among his p.   Ezek 18:18
he and his p. with him.   30:11
be jealous and pity his p.   Joel 2:18
answer and say to his p.   19
Lord will be the hope of his p. 3:16
controversy with his p.   Mi 6:2
them as a flock of his p.   Zech 9:16
Jesus: he shall save his p. Mat 1:21
hath visited and redeemed his p.
   Luke 1:68
knowledge of salvation to his p.   77
and that God hath visited his p. 7:16
hath God cast away his p.? Rom 11:1
God hath not cast away his p.   2
Lord shall judge his p. Heb 10:30
they shall be his p., and God. Rev 21:3
see **holy, Israel**

people of the land
himself to p. of the l. Gen 23:7, 12
that sold to all p. of the land. 42:6
p. of the l. are many, ye.   Ex 5:5
p. of the l. shall stone him. Lev 20:2
if p. of the land do hide their.   4
neither fear ye p. of the l. Num 14:9
all p. of the l. rejoiced and blew with
   trumpets.   2 Ki 11:14, 20
Jotham judged p. of the land. 15:5
   2 Chr 26:21
p. of the l. slew all them that had
   killed Amon, and p. of the l. made.
   2 Ki 21:24; 2 Chr 33:25
p. of l. took Jehoahaz and anointed
   him.   2 Ki 23:30; 2 Chr 36:1
was no bread for p. of the l.
   2 Ki 25:3; Jer 52:6
mustered p. of the l. and sixty men of
   p. of land. 2 Ki 25:19; Jer 52:25
gods of p. of the land. 1 Chr 5:25
p. of l. weakened hands.   Ezra 4:4
wives of the p. of the land.   10:2
from the p. of the land.   11
daughters to p. of the l. Neh 10:30
if the p. of the l. bring ware.   31
many of the p. of the l. Esth 8:17
iron pillar against p. of l. Jer 1:18
all the p. of the land which. 34:19
hands of p. of the land. Ezek 7:27
p. of the l. have used oppression.
   22:29
if p. of the land take man to. 33:2
and all the p. of the land shall. 39:13
p. of the land shall give this. 45:16
prince prepare for p. of the land. 22
p. of the l. shall worship at.   46:3
when p. of the land shall come.   9
spake to the p. of the land. Dan 9:6
be strong, all ye p. of the l. Hag 2:4
speak to all the p. of the land.
   Zech 7:5

much people
Edom came out against him with
   much p.   Num 20:20
they went with much p. Josh 11:4
came much p. by way. 2 Sam 13:34
at Jerusalem much p. 2 Chr 30:13
there was gathered much p.   32:4
praise thee among much p. Ps 35:18
much p. gathered unto. Mark 5:21
Jesus went with him, and much p. 24
Jesus saw much p., was moved. 6:34
much p. of Jews knew. John 12:9
next day much p. took branches. 12
and drew away much p. Acts 5:37
and much p. was added unto. 11:24
for I have much p. in this city. 18:10
hath turned away much p.   19:26
I heard a voice of much p. Rev 19:1

my people
sons of my p. give I it. Gen 23:11
to thy word shall all my p.   41:10

to be gathered to *my p. Gen* 49:29
I have seen the affliction of *my p.*
　　　　　Ex 3:7; *Acts* 7:34
mayest bring forth *my p.Ex* 3:10; 7:4
let *my p.* go. 5:1; 7:16; 8:1, 20
　　　　　9:1, 13; 10:3
frogs from me and from *my p.* 8:8
wilt not let *my p.* go. 21; 10:4
land in which *my p.* dwell. 8:22, 23
thou thyself against *my p.* 9:17
I and *my p.* are wicked. 27
you forth from among *my p.* 12:31
money to any of *my p.* 22:25
I will be your God, ye shall by *my p.*
　　　　　Lev 26:12 *Jer* 11:4; 30:22
behold I go unto *my p. Num* 24:14
my p. were at great strife. *Judg* 12:2
a woman among all *my p.?* 14:3
a riddle to children of *my p.* 16
people shall be *my p. Ruth* 1:16
for all the city of *my p.* doth. 3:11
captain over *my p.* that he may serve
　　my p. . . . on *my p. 1 Sam* 9:16
I will save *my p. 2 Sam* 3:18
I took thee to be ruler over *my p.* 7:8
　　　　　2 Chr 6:5
art, *my p.* as thy people. *1 Ki* 22:4
　　　2 Ki 3:7; *2 Chr* 18:3
the captain of *my p. 2 Ki* 20:5
I commanded to feed *my p.*
　　　　　1 Chr 17:6
David said, Hear me, *my p.* 28:2
who am I, and what *my p.?* 29:14
thou mayest judge *my p. 2 Chr* 1:11
brought forth *my p.* out of Egypt. 6:5
pestilence among *my p.* 7:13
if *my p.* shall humble themselves. 14
let *my p.* be given me at. *Esth* 7:3
for we are sold, I and *my p.* to. 4
see evil shall come to *my p.* 8:5
who eat up *my p.* as. *Ps* 14:4; 53:4
hear, O *my p.* I will. 50:7; 81:8
slay them not, least *my p.* 59:11
I will bring *my p.* again. 68:22
give ear, O *my p.* to my law. 78:1
but *my p.* would not hearken. 81:11
O that *my p.* had hearkened. 13
my shield, who subdueth *my p.* 144:2
but Israel not know, *my p. Isa* 1:3
as for *my p.,* children are their oppressors, O *my p.* they which. 3:12
what mean ye that ye beat *my p.?* 15
my p. are gone into captivity. 5:13
right from poor of *my p.* 10:2
O *my p.* that dwellest in Zion. 24
blessed be Egypt, *my p.* and. 19:25
come, *my p.* enter thou into. 26:20
my p. shall dwell in a. 32:18
comfort ye, comfort ye *my p.* 40:1
drink to *my p.* my chosen. 43:20
I was wroth with *my p.* 47:6
hearken unto me, *my p.* and. 51:4
say to Zion, Thou art *my p.* 16
my p. went down into Egypt. 52:4
saith Lord, that *my p.* is taken. 5
therefore *my p.* shall know my. 6
for transgression of *my p.* was. 53:8
out of the way of *my p.* 57:14
shew *my p.* their transgression. 58:1
surely they are *my p.,* children. 63:8
Sharon a fold for *my p.* that. 65:10
Jerusalem, and joy in *my p.* 19
of a tree, are the days of *my p.* 22
but *my p.* have changed. *Jer* 2:11
for *my p.* have committed two. 13
why say *my p.,* We are lords? 31
yet *my p.* have forgotten. 32; 18:15
for *my p.* is foolish, they have. 4:22
for among *my p.* are found. 5:26
and *my p.* love to have it so. 31
for a fortress among *my p.* 6:27
and ye shall be *my p.* 7:23
my p. know not the judgement. 8:7
that I might leave *my p.* and go. 9:2
diligently learn the ways of *my p.* as
　　they taught *my p.* to. 12:16
I will destroy *my p.,* since they. 15:7
the pastors that feed *my p.* 23:2
if they had caused *my p.* to hear. 22
cause *my p.* to forget my name. 27
cause *my p.* to err by their lies. 32
they shall be *my p.* 24:7; 31:1, 33
32:38; *Ezek* 11:20; 36:28; 37:23
　　　　　27; *Zech* 8:8

behold good that I will do for *my p.*
　　　　　Jer 29:32
my p. shall be satisfied with. 31:14
they have despised *my p.* 33:24
my p. hath been lost sheep. 50:6
my p. go ye out of midst of her.
　　　　　51:45; *Rev* 18:4
derision to all *my p.* and. *Lam* 3:14
be in assembly of *my p. Ezek* 13:9
have seduced *my p.* 10
Will ye hunt the souls of *my p.?* 18
among *my p.* by lying to my. 19
I will deliver *my p.* out of. 21, 23
off from the midst of *my p.* 14:8
but that they may be *my p.* and. 11
sword shall be upon *my p.* 21:12
even house of Israel are *my p.* 34:20
my p., I will open your. 37:12, 13
up against *my p.* Israel. 38:16
they shall teach *my p.* the. 44:23
shall no more oppress *my p.* 45:8
exactions from *my p.* saith Lord. 9
that *my p.* be not scattered. 18
God, are ye not *my p.? Hos* 1:9, 10
them which were not *my p.* 2:23
my p. are destroyed for lack. 4:6
they eat up the sin of *my p.* 8
my p. ask counsel at their stocks. 12
returned the captivity of *my p.* 6:11
my p. are bent to backsliding. 11:7
my p. shall never be. *Joel* 2:26, 27
with them there for *my p.* 3:2
they have cast lots for *my p.* 3
sinners of *my p.* shall die. *Amos* 9:10
into the gate of *my p. Ob* 13
come to the gate of *my p. Mi* 1:9
changed the portion of *my p.* 2:4
of late *my p.* is risen up as an. 8
the women of *my p.* have ye. 9
eat the flesh of *my p.* and flay. 3:3
prophets that make *my p.* err. 5
O *my p.* what have I done? 6:3, 5
bear the reproach of *my p.* 16
they reproached *my p. Zeph* 2:8
the residue of *my p.* shall spoil. 9*
nations shall be *my p. Zech* 2:11
I will save *my p.* from the east. 8:7
I will say, It is *my p.* and. 13:9
I will call them *my p.,* which were
　　not *my p. Rom* 9:25
it was said, Ye are not *my p.* 26
they shall be *my p. 2 Cor* 6:16

see daughter

of the **people**
two manner *of p.* shall. *Gen* 25:23
one *of the p.* might lightly. 26:10
the gathering of *the p.* be. 49:10
all the heads *of the p. Num* 25:4
take the sum *of the p.* from. 26:4
twelve men out *of the p. Josh* 4:2
he was higher than any *of the p.*
　　　　　1 Sam 9:2; 10:23
for there is a sacrifice *of the p.* 9:12
none *of the p.* tasted any food. 14:24
then answered one *of the p.* 28
of the p. to destroy king. 26:15
nor did he leave *of the p. 2 Ki* 13:7
of the p. of those countries. *Ezra* 3:3
there was great cry *of the p. Neh* 5:1
and some *of the p.* dwelt in. 7:73
the tumult *of the p. Ps* 65:7
judge the poor *of the p.* 72:4
one chosen out *of the p.* 89:19
a present *of a p.* scattered. *Isa* 18:7
for a covenant *of the p.* 42:6
to rest for a light *of the p.* 51:4
and *of the p.* there was none. 63:3
prince not take *of the p. Ezek* 46:18
boil the sacrifice *of the p.* 24
and many *of the p. John* 7:31
because *of the p.* that stand. 11:42
punish, because *of the p. Acts* 4:21
himself, and errors *of the p. Heb* 9:7
they *of the p.* shall see their dead.
　　　　　Rev 11:9

see ears, elders

one **people**
one *p.* shall be stronger. *Gen* 25:23
with you, and become one *p.* 34:16
dwell with us, to be one *p.* 22

own **people**
fault is in thine *own p. Ex* 5:16
virgin of his *own p. Lev* 21:14

went to redeem to be his *own p.*
　　　　　1 Chr 17:21
deliver their *own p. 2 Chr* 25:15
forget also thine *own p. Ps* 45:10
made his *own p.* to go forth. 78:52
man turn to his *own p. Isa* 13:14
us go again to our *own p. Jer* 46:16

the **people**
behold *the p.* is one. *Gen* 11:6
why do ye let *the p.* from their work?
　　　　　Ex 5:4
behold, *the p.* of the land now. 5
and *the p.* bowed the head. 12:27
God led *the p.* about. 13:18
was told that *the p.* fled. 14:5
the p. feared the Lord, and. 31
the p. shall hear and be afraid. 15:14
till *the p.* pass over which thou. 16
the p. murmured, saying, What? 24
the p. rested on the seventh. 16:30
there was no water for *the p.* 17:1
the p. did chide. 2; *Num* 20:3
there shall come water out of it, that
　　the p. may drink. *Ex* 17:6
thou for *the p.* to God-ward. 18:19
the p. may hear when I speak. 19:9
Moses brought forth *the p.* out. 17
charge *the p.,* lest they break. 21
let not *the p.* break through. 24
when *the p.* saw it, they. 20:18, 21
neither shall *the p.* go up. 24:2
blood and sprinkled it on *the p.* 8
atonement for thyself and *the p.*
　　　　　Lev 9:7
offering for *the p.* 15, 18; 16:15
Moses and Aaron blessed *the p.* 9:23
the p. complained. *Num* 11:1
the p. cried to Moses. 2
and see *the p.* that dwelleth. 13:18
the p. be strong. 28
Caleb stilled *the p.* 30
the p. wept that night. 14:1
the p. mourned. 39
the p. spake against God and. 21:5
lo, *the p.* shall dwell alone. 23:9
behold, *the p.* shall rise up as. 24
gather me *the p.* together. *Deut* 4:10
priest's due from *the p.* 18:3
yea, he loved *the p.* 33:3
he shall push *the p.* 17
call *the p.* to the mountain. 19
the p. hasted and passed. *Josh* 4:10
so *the p.* shouted. 6:20
let *the p.* depart. 24:28
the p. that are with thee are too
　　many. *Judg* 7:2, 4
up thou, and *the p.* that are. 9:32
custom with *the p.* was. *1 Sam* 2:13
so *the p.* sent to Shiloh to. 4:4
did they not let *the p.* go? 6:6
the p. refused to obey the voice. 8:19
for *the p.* will not eat until. 9:13
the p. said to Saul, Shall Jonathan
　　die? so *the p.* rescued. 14:45
for *the p.* spared the best. 15:15
the p. took of the spoil, sheep. 21
the p. answered after. 17:27, 30
David distressed, for *the p.* 30:6
that *the p.* are fled from. *2 Sam* 1:4
the p. have made me afraid. 14:15
for *the p.* increased. 15:12
and *the p.* piped with pipes. *1 Ki* 1:40
for *the p.* went to worship. 12:30
the p. that followed Omri . . . *the p.*
　　that followed Tibni. 16:22
the p. answered him not. 18:21
pour out for *the p.* that. *2 Ki* 4:41
he said, Give *the p.* that they. 43
the p. trode upon him in the. 7:17
between the king and *the p.* 11:17
as yet *the p.* did sacrifice. 12:3
　　　　　14:4; 15:4, 35
the p. held their peace. 18:36
Lord for me and for *the p.* 22:13
the p. were without. *2 Chr* 12:3
as yet *the p.* had not prepared.
　　　　　20:33; 30:3
and *the p.* did yet corruptly. 27:2
Lord hearkened to Hezekiah and
　　healed *the p.* 30:20
since *the p.* began to bring. 31:10
the p. rested on the words. 32:8
and *the p.* transgressed. 36:14

but *the p.* are many.   *Ezra* 10:13
for *the p.* had a mind to.   *Neh* 4:6
and *the p.* did according to.   5:13
city was large, but *the p.* were.   7:4
the p. stood in their place.   8:7
so *the p.* went and brought palm.   16
the p. blessed all that offered.   11:2
had shewed him *the p.*   *Esth* 3:6
the p. also, to do with them as.   11
the p. of also the king's provinces.   4:11
no doubt but ye are *the p.*   *Job* 12:2
hypocrite reign not, lest *the p.*   34:30
why do *the p.* imagine?   *Ps* 2:1
blessed are *the p.* whom he.   33:12
how thou didst afflict *the p.*   44:2
arrows, whereby *the p.* fall.   45:5
therefore shall *the p.* praise.   17
in thine anger cast down *the p.*   56:7
let *the p.* praise thee.   67:3, 5
blessed is *the p.* that know.   89:15
we are *the p.* of his pasture.   95:7
he shall judge *the p.* with his truth.   96:13
he shall judge *the p.* with equity.   98:9
the Lord reigneth, let *the p.*   99:1
his deeds among *the p.*   105:1
no counsel is, *the p.* fall.   *Pr* 11:14
withholdeth corn, *the p.*   26; 24:24
the p. rejoiced, *the p.* mourn.   29:2
is no vision, *the p.* perish.   18
the p. shall be oppressed.   *Isa* 3:5
the p. that walked in darkness.   9:2
the p. turneth not to him that.   13
and *the p.* shall be as the fuel.   19
against *the p.* of my wrath.   10:6
the p. shall take them and.   14:2
it shall be as with *the p.* so.   24:2
for *the p.* shall dwell in Zion.   30:19
the p. shall be forgiven their.   33:24
my sword shall come on *the p.*   34:5
the p. is grass. The grass.   40:7
the p. in whose heart is my.   51:7
I will tread down *the p.* in.   63:6
the p. of thy holiness have.   18
the p. that shall say, The burthen.   *Jer* 23:34
the p. which were left of sword.   31:2
and went out among *the p.*   37:4
so he dwelt among *the p.*   39:14
dwell with him among *the p.*   40:5, 6
woe to thee, O Moab, *the p.* of.   48:46
the p. shall labour in vain.   51:58
gather you from *the p.*   *Ezek* 11:17
I will bring you out from *the p.*   20:34; 34:13
cut the off from *the p.*   25:7
bring thee down with *the p.*   26:20
see sword come, and *the p.*   33:6
they come unto thee as *the p.*   31
these are *the p.* of the Lord.   36:20
thou shalt fall, and *the p.* that.   39:4
things which are for *the p.*   42:14
slay the sacrifice for *the p.*   44:11
shall not sanctify *the p.* with.   19
the p. of the prince.   *Dan* 9:26
the p. that know their God.   11:32
the p. that doth not understand.   *Hos* 4:14
for *the p.* thereof shall mourn.   10:5
and *the p.* shall be gathered.   10
the p. shall be much pained.   *Joel* 2:6
the p. of Syria shall go.   *Amos* 1:5
trumpet be blown, and *the p.*?   3:6
so *the p.* of Nineveh.   *Jonah* 3:5
that *the p.* shall labour in the fire, and *the p.* shall weary.   *Hab* 2:13
against *the p.* of Lord.   *Zeph* 2:10
the p. did fear before.   *Hag* 1:12
the p. against whom Lord hath indignation.   *Mal* 1:4
the p. that sat in darkness.   *Mat* 4:16
we fear *the p.* for all hold John as a prophet.   21:26; *Mark* 11:32
and *the p.* were in expectation.   *Luke* 1:21
as *the p.* were in expectation.   3:15
the p. sought him.   4:42
the p. pressed upon him.   5:1
when returned, *the p.* gladly.   8:40
Whom say *the p.* that I am?   9:18
feared *the p.*   20:19; 22:2
he stirreth up *the p.*   23:5
one that perverteth *the p.*   14
the p. saw that Jesus.   *John* 6:24

but he deceiveth *the p.*   *John* 7:12
should die for *the p.*   11:50; 18:14
the p. magnified them.   *Acts* 5:13
the p. with one accord gave.   8:6
the p. gave shout, saying, It.   12:22
the p. saw what Paul had.   14:11
scarce restrained they *the p.*   18
persuaded *the p.* and stoned.   19
delivering thee from *the p.*   26:17
nothing against *the p.*   28:17
as for *the p.* so also.   *Heb* 5:3; 7:27
for under it *the p.* received.   7:11
that he might sanctify *the p.*   13:12
Lord having saved *the p.*   *Jude* 5

this people

I will give this *p.* favour.   *Ex* 3:21
so evil entreated this *p.*?   5:22
hath done evil to this *p.*   23
what shall I do to this *p.*?   17:4
thou wilt wear away, both thou and this *p.*   18:18
all this *p.* shall also go to their.   23
I have seen this *p.*   32:9
what did this *p.* unto thee?   21
this *p.* have sinned a great sin.   31
sayest to me, Bring up this *p.*   33:12
the burden of all this *p.* on me.   *Num* 11:11
have I conceived all this *p.*?   12
flesh to give unto all this *p.*   13
able to bear all this *p.* alone.   14
long will this *p.* provoke me?   14:11
thou art among this *p.*   14
if thou shalt kill all this *p.* as.   15
was not able to bring this *p.*   16
this *p.*, as thou hast forgiven this *p.*   21:2
indeed deliver this *p.*   21:2
I pray thee, curse this *p.*   22:6, 17
what this *p.* shall do to thy.   24:14
ye shall destroy all this *p.*   32:15
go over before this *p.*   *Deut* 3:28
voice of the words of this *p.*   5:28
saying, I have seen this *p.*   9:13
stubbornness of this *p.*   27
thou must go with this *p.*   31:7
this *p.* will rise up and go.   16
to this *p.* thou shalt.   *Josh* 1:6
because this *p.* have.   *Judg* 2:20
would to God this *p.* were.   9:29
this the *p.* thou hast despised?   38
evil doings by this *p.*   *1 Sam* 2:23
Lord and this *p.*, choose.   *2 Sam* 16:18
that I may answer this *p.*   *1 Ki* 12:6, 9; *2 Chr* 10:6, 9
a servant to this *p.* this.   *1 Ki* 12:7
if this *p.* go up to do sacrifice ... the heart of this *p.* shall turn.   27
I should be king over this *p.*   14:2
O Lord, that this *p.* may.   18:37
I pray thee, smite this *p.*   *2 Ki* 6:18
come in before this *p.*   *2 Chr* 1:10
was heavy on this *p.*   *Neh* 5:18
that I have done for this *p.*   19
Go.and tell this *p.*, Hear.   *Isa* 6:9
make the heart of this *p.* fat.   10; *Mat* 13:15; *Acts* 28:26, 27
this *p.* refuseth the waters.   *Isa* 8:6
walk in the way of this *p.*   11
to whom this *p.* shall say.   12
the leaders of this *p.* cause.   9:16
this *p.* was not till Assyrian.   23:13
tongue will speak to this *p.*   28:11
men, that rule this *p.*   14
this *p.* draw near me with.   29:13
work among this *p.*   14
but this is a *p.* robbed and.   42:22
this *p.* have I formed for.   43:21
greatly deceived this *p.*   *Jer* 4:10
words fire and this *p.* wood.   5:14
this *p.* hath a revolting heart.   23
I will bring evil on this *p.*   6:19
stumblingblocks before this *p.*   21
pray not thou for this *p.*   7:16; 11:14; 14:11
carcases of this *p.* meat for.   7:33
why is this *p.* of Jerusalem?   8:5
I will feed even this *p.* with.   9:15
this evil *p.* who refuse to.   13:10
could not be toward this *p.*   15:1
away my peace from this *p.*   16:5
even so will I break this *p.*   19:11
they shall not profit this *p.*   23:32
and when this *p.* shall ask thee.   33

makest this *p.* to trust.   *Jer* 28:15
a man to dwell among this *p.*   29:32
great evil upon this *p.*   32:42
considerest not what this *p.*   33:24
this *p.* have not hearkened.   35:16
pronounced against this *p.*   36:7
offended against this *p.*?   37:18
seeketh not welfare of this *p.*   38:4
the prophet of this *p.*   *Mi* 2:11
this *p.* say, The time is.   *Hag* 1:2
Haggai said, So is this *p.*   2:14
the remnant of this *p.*   *Zech* 8:6
I will not be to this *p.* as in.   11
cause the remnant of this *p.*   12
this *p.* draweth nigh with.   *Mat* 15:8
this *p.* honoureth me.   *Mark* 7:6
buy meat for this *p.*   *Luke* 9:13
be wrath upon this *p.*   21:23
but this *p.* who knoweth.   *John* 7:49
the God of this *p.* chose.   *Acts* 13:17
lips I will speak to this *p.*   *1 Cor* 14:21

thy people

thou delivered *thy p.*   *Ex* 5:23
frogs upon *thy p.*   8:3, 4
swarms of flies upon *thy p.*   21
all my plagues upon *thy p.*   9:14
that I smite thee and *thy p.*   15
till *thy p.* pass over, O Lord.   15:16
nor shalt curse the ruler of *thy p.*   22:28; *Acts* 23:5
the poor of *thy p.* may eat.   *Ex* 23:11
that this nation is *thy p.*   33:13
I and *thy p.* have found grace.   16
covenant before all *thy p.*   34:10
talebearer among *thy p.*   *Lev* 19:16
and an oath among *thy p.*   *Num* 5:21
this people shall do to *thy p.*   24:14
shalt be gathered to *thy p.*   27:13; 31:2; *Deut* 32:50
for *thy p.* have corrupted.   *Deut* 9:12
destroy not *thy p.*   26
yet they are *thy p.* and inheritance.   29; *Neh* 1:10
return with thee to *thy p.*   *Ruth* 1:10
thy p. shall be my people.   16
like *thy p.* ... before *thy p.* and thy children.
thou?   *2 Sam* 7:23; *1 Chr* 17:21
in the midst of *thy p.*   *1 Ki* 3:8
heart to judge *thy p.*   9; *2 Chr* 1:10
if *thy p.* go out to battle.   *1 Ki* 8:44
forgive *thy p.* that have sinned.   50; *2 Chr* 6:34, 39
they be *thy p.*   *1 Ki* 8:51
thy p. for his people.   20:42
I am as thou art, my people as *thy p.*, my.   22:4; *2 Ki* 3:7
thy hand be on *thy p.*   *1 Chr* 21:17
thoughts of heart of *thy p.*   29:18
with a plague will the Lord smite *thy p.* .. and thy children.   *2 Chr* 21:14
thy blessing is upon *thy p.*   *Ps* 3:8
save *thy p.* and bless.   28:9; *Jer* 31:7
sellest *thy p.* for nought.   *Ps* 44:12
shewed *thy p.* hard things.   60:3
wentest forth before *thy p.*   68:7
he shall judge *thy p.* with.   72:2
thine arm redeemed *thy p.*   77:15
thou leddest *thy p.* like a flock.   20
so we *thy p.* will give thee.   79:13
angry against prayer of *thy p.*?   80:4
crafty counsel against *thy p.*   83:3
forgiven the iniquity of *thy p.*   85:2
revive us, that *thy p.* may rejoice.   6
they break in pieces *thy p.*   94:5
thou bearest to *thy p.*   106:4
thy p. shall be willing in the.   110:3
thou hast forsaken *thy p.*   *Isa* 2:6
bring on thee and *thy p.* days.   7:17
destroyed thy land and *thy p.*   14:20
thy p. shall be all righteous.   60:21
so didst thou lead *thy p.*   63:14
we are *thy p.*   64:9
hear, thou and *thy p.*   *Jer* 22:2
will ye die, thou and *thy p.*?   27:13
get thee to *thy p.* and.   *Ezek* 3:11
set thy face against the daughters of *thy p.*   13:17
he shall slay *thy p.* with.   26:11
speak to children of *thy p.*   33:2, 12
children of *thy p.* say, The way.   17
the children of *thy p.* still are.   30
when the children of *thy p.*   37:18
thy p. are become a.   *Dan* 9:16

thy city and *thy p.* are.   *Dan* 9:19
are determined upon *thy p.*   24
what shall befall *thy p.*   10:14
standeth for the children of *thy p.*
   and at that time *thy p.* shall. 12:1
thy p. as they that strive.   *Hos* 4:4
tumult arose among *thy p.*   10:14
spare *thy p.*   *Joel* 2:17
feed *thy p.*   *Mi* 7:14
thy p. in the midst of.   *Nah* 3:13
thy p. is scattered on the.   18
forth for salvation of *thy p. Hab* 3:13

to or *unto the* **people**
be spokesman *to the p.*   *Ex* 4:16
he said, What is this thing that thou
   doest *to the p.?*   18:14
go *to the p.*   19:10
thou shalt set bounds *to the p.*   12
down from mount *to the p.*   14, 25
priest shall speak *to the p. Deut* 20:2
officers shall speak *to the p.*   5, 8
loaves of bread *to the p. Judg* 8:5
shall come *to a p.* secure. 18:10, 27
and art come *to a p.*   *Ruth* 2:11
all the words *to the p. 1 Sam* 8:10
Abishai came *to the p.* by.   26:7
David cried *to the p.* and *to.*   14
David came near *to the p.*   30:21
thy God add *to the p. 2 Sam* 24:3
hearkened not *to the p. 1 Ki* 12:15
Elijah came *to the p.* and.   18:21
Elisha gave *to the p.* and.   19:21
he said, Give *to p.* that.   *2 Ki* 4:42
Athaliah came *to the p.*   11:13
   2 Chr 23:12
to carry tidings *to the p. 1 Chr* 10:9
Josiah gave *to the p. 2 Chr* 35:7*
princes gave willingly *unto the p.* 8
said I *to the p.* Lodge.   *Neh* 4:22
were chargeable *to the p.*   5:15
minister judgement *to the p. Ps* 9:8
shall bring peace *to the p.*   72:3
breath *to the p.* upon it.   *Isa* 42:5
set up my standard *to the p.* 49:22
for a witness *to the p.*, a leader and
   commander *to the p.*   55:4
so I spake *to the p.* in.   *Ezek* 24:18
kingdom be given *to the p. Dan* 7:27
shall sell them *to the p.* far. *Joel* 3:8
cometh up *to the p.* he.   *Hab* 3:16
I will turn *to the p.* a.   *Zeph* 3:9
Lord's message *to the p. Hag* 1:13
talked *to the p.*, behold. *Mat* 12:46
was wont to release *to the p.* 27:15
began to speak *to the p. Luke* 7:24
as they spake *to the p.*   *Acts* 4:1
speak in the temple *to the p.* 5:20
which gave alms *to the p.* and. 10:2
us to preach *to the p.*   42
bring Peter forth *to the p.*   12:4
who are his witnesses *to the p.* 13:31
to bring them out *to the p.*   17:5
have entered in *to the p.*   19:30
made his defence *to the p.*   33
suffer me to speak *to the p.* 21:39
beckoned with the hand *to the p.* 40
suffer, and shew light *to the p.* 26:23

peoples
prophesy before many *p. Rev* 10:11
waters thou sawest are *p.*   17:15

Peor
Balaam to top of *P.*   *Num* 23:28
beguiled you in the matter of *P.*
   25:18; 31:16
iniquity of *P.* too little ? *Josh* 22:17

peradventure
(*Perhaps, supposing, possibly*)
p. there be fifty righteous. *Gen* 18:24
p. there shall lack five of the.   28
p. there be forty.   29, 30, 31
I will speak this once, *p.* ten.   32
p. the woman shall not.   24:5, 39
Jacob said. My father *p.*   27:12
p. thou wouldest take by.   31:31
I will see his face, *p.* he will. 32:20
for he said, Lest, *p.*, mischief. 42:4
carry it again, *p.* it was an.   43:12
lest *p.* I see evil shall come. 44:34
Joseph will *p.* hate us, and.   50:15
lest *p.* the people repent.   *Ex* 13:17
p. I shall make an atonement. 32:30
curse this people, *p.* I. *Num* 22:6, 11

p. the Lord will come to. *Num* 23:3
p. it will please God that thou.   27
men of Israel said, *P.* ye. *Josh* 9:7
p. he will lighten his hand. *1 Sam* 6:5
p. he can shew us our way that. 9:6
p. we may find grass to.   *1 Ki* 18:5
or *p.* he sleepeth, and must be.   27
go out to the king, *p.* he will. 20:31
lest *p.* the Spirit of Lord. *2 Ki* 2:16
watched for halting, *p.*   *Jer* 20:10
p. for a good man some.   *Rom* 5:7
p. God will give them.   *2 Tim* 2:25

perceive
given you a heart to *p. Deut* 29:4
this day we *p.* the Lord. *Josh* 22:31
that ye may *p.* your.   *1 Sam* 12:17
p. if Absalom had lived. *2 Sam* 19:6
I *p.* that this is an holy.   *2 Ki* 4:9
but I *p.* him not.   *Job* 9:11
I cannot *p.* him.   23:8
to *p.* the words of.   *Pr* 1:2
I *p.* that there is nothing. *Eccl* 3:22
and see ye indeed, but *p.*   *Isa* 6:19
speech than thou canst *p.*   33:9
shall see, and shall not *p. Mat* 13:14
   Mark 4:12; *Acts* 28:26
do ye not *p.* that whatsoever entereth
   into the man ?   *Mark* 7:18
he said, *p.* ye not yet, neither ? 8:17
I *p.* that virtue is gone. *Luke* 8:46
p. that thou art a prophet. *John* 4:19
p. ye how ye prevail nothing ? 12:19
I *p.* thou art in the gall. *Acts* 8:23
I *p.* God is no respecter of.   10:34
I *p.* in all things ye are too. 17:22
p. the same epistle made. *2 Cor* 7:8
hereby *p.* we the love.   *1 John* 3:16

perceived
he *p.* not when she lay down.
   Gen 19:33, 35
when Gideon *p.* he was. *Judg* 6:22
Eli *p.* that Lord had.   *1 Sam* 3:8
Saul *p.* that it was Samuel. 28:14
David *p.* that the Lord had.
   2 Sam 5:12; *1 Chr* 14:2
David *p.* that the child. *2 Sam* 12:19
Joab *p.* the king's heart was. 14:1
captains of chariots *p.* that it was.
   1 Ki 22:33; *2 Chr* 18:32
lo. I *p.* that God had.   *Neh* 6:12
they *p.* that this work was.   16
I *p.* portions of Levites had. 13:10
when Mordecai *p.* all.   *Esth* 4:1
hast thou *p.* the breadth ? *Job* 38:18
I *p.* that this also is vexation of.
   Eccl 1:17
I myself *p.* that one event.   2:14
nor *p.* by the ear what God. *Isa* 64:4
who hath *p.* and heard. *Jer* 23:18
for the matter was not *p.*   38:27
p. that he spake of them. *Mat* 21:45
   Luke 20:19
Jesus *p.* their wickedness. *Mat* 22:18
Jesus *p.* in spirit that.   *Mark* 2:8
they *p.* that he had seen. *Luke* 1:22
Jesus *p.* their thoughts.   5:22
was hid, that they *p.* it not.   9:45
but he *p.* their craftiness.   20:23
Jesus *p.* they would make him a
   king.   *John* 6:15
they *p.* that they were unlearned.
   Acts 4:13
when Paul *p.* that one part.   23:6
when James *p.* the grace. *Gal* 2:9

perceivest
p. not in him lips of.   *Pr* 14:7
but *p.* not beam that is. *Luke* 6:41

perceiveth
are brought low, but he *p. Job* 14:21
once, yet man *p.* it not.   33:14
p. that her merchandise. *Pr* 31:18

perceiving
p. that he had answered. *Mark* 12:28
Jesus *p.* the thought.   *Luke* 9:47
and *p.* he had faith to.   *Acts* 14:9

perdition
lost but the son of.   *John* 17:12
an evident token of *p.*   *Phil* 1:28
sin be revealed, son of *p. 2 Thes* 2:3
men in destruction and *p. 1 Tim* 6:9
who draw back to *p.*   *Heb* 10:39
and *p.* of ungodly men.   *2 Pet* 3:7*

the beast was, and is not, and shall
   go into *p.*   *Rev* 17:8, 11

perfect
Noah was *p.*   *Gen* 6:9
and be thou *p.*   17:1
offering shall be *p.*   *Lev* 22:21
thou shalt be *p.* with.   *Deut* 18:13
a *p.* weight, a *p.* measure.   25:15
Saul said, Give a *p.* lot. *1 Sam* 14:41
he maketh my way *p. 2 Sam* 22:33
   Ps 18:32
tongs made he of *p.* gold. *2 Chr* 4:21
king, to Ezra, *p.* peace.   *Ezra* 7:12
that man was *p.* and upright.
   Job 1:1, 8; 2:3
not cast away a *p.* man.   8:20
if I say, I am *p.*   9:20
though I were *p.*   21
he destroyeth the *p.* and the.   22
thou makest thy ways *p.*   22:3
mark the *p.* man, his end. *Ps* 37:37
shoot in secret at the *p.*   64:4
myself wisely in a *p.* way.   101:2
he that walketh in a *p.* way shall. 6
Lord will *p.* what concerneth. 138:8
I hate them with *p.* hatred. 139:22
p. shall remain in it.   *Pr* 2:21
shineth more and more unto *p.* 4:18
righteousness of the *p.* shall. 11:5
wilt keep him in *p.* peace. *Isa* 26:3
for it was *p.* through. *Ezek* 16:14
said, I am of *p.* beauty.   27:3
made thy beauty *p.*   11; 28:12
thou wast *p.* in thy ways.   28:15
p. even as your Father is *p. Mat* 5:48
if thou wilt be *p.* go and sell. 19:21
had *p.* understanding.   *Luke* 1:3*
may be made *p.* in one. *John* 17:23
him this *p.* soundness.   *Acts* 3:16
to the *p.* manner of law.   22:3*
having more *p.* knowledge of. 24:22*
is that *p.* will of God.   *Rom* 12:2
among them that are *p.* *1 Cor* 2:6†
my strength is made *p. 2 Cor* 12:9
be *p.*, be of good comfort, be. 13:11
are ye made *p.* by flesh ?   *Gal* 3:3
till we come to *p.* man.   *Eph* 4:13*
I were already *p.*   *Phil* 3:12
let us, as many as be *p.* be.   15
every man *p.* in Christ.   *Col* 1:28
may stand *p.* and complete in. 4:12
might *p.* that lacking in. *1 Thes* 3:10
man of God may be *p. 2 Tim* 3:17
make Captain of their salvation *p.*
   Heb 2:10
being made *p.* he became Author. 5:9
for law made nothing *p.* but.   7:19
him that did the service *p.*   9:9
greater and more *p.* tabernacle. 11
make the comers thereunto *p.* 10:1
should not be made *p.*   11:40
spirits of just men made *p.* 12:23
God make you *p.* in every. 13:21
let patience have her *p.* work, that
   ye may be *p.* and.   *Jas* 1:4
every good and *p.* gift is from.   17
whoso looketh into the *p.* law.   25
by works was faith made *p.*   2:22
in word, same is a *p.* man.   3:2
suffered, make you *p. 1 Pet* 5:10
is our love made *p.*   *1 John* 4:17
p. love casteth out fear, because fear
   hath torment . . . not made *p.* 18

see **heart**
is perfect
He the Rock, his work is *p. Deut* 32:4
as for God, his way is *p.*
   2 Sam 22:31; *Ps* 18:30
he that is *p.* in knowledge.
   Job 36:4; 37:16
law of the Lord is *p.*   *Ps* 19:7
when the bud is *p.*   *Isa* 18:5
who is blind as he that is *p.* ? 42:19*
which is in heaven is *p.*   *Mat* 5:48
every one that is *p.* shall. *Luke* 6:40
when that which is *p.*   *1 Cor* 13:10

perfected
house of God was *p.*   *2 Chr* 8:16
and work was *p.* by them.   24:13
thy builders have *p.*   *Ezek* 27:4
babes thou hast *p.* praise. *Mat* 21:16
third day I shall be *p. Luke* 13:32
by one offering he hath *p. Heb* 10:14*

is the love of God *p.*   *1 John* 2:5
another, his love is *p.* in us.   4:12

perfecting
p. holiness in the fear.   *2 Cor* 7:1
for *p.* of the saints, for.   *Eph* 4:12

perfection
out the Almighty to *p.?*   *Job* 11:7
nor prolong the *p.* thereof.   15:29*
he searcheth out all *p.*   28:3*
out of Zion, the *p.* of.   *Ps* 50:2
I have seen an end of *p.*   119:96
upon thee in their *p.*   *Isa* 47:9*
city that men call the *p.* of. *Lam* 2:15
and bring no fruit to *p.*   *Luke* 8:14
we wish, even your *p.*   *2 Cor* 13:9
let us go on to *p.*   *Heb* 6:1
if *p.* were by the Levitical.   7:11

perfectly
we shall consider it *p.*   *Jer* 23:20
were made *p.* whole.   *Mat* 14:36
way of God more *p.*   *Acts* 18:26
something more *p.*   23:15*, 20*
he *p.* joined together in. *1 Cor* 1:10
for yourselves know *p.*   *1 Thes* 5:2

perfectness
which is the bond of *p.*   *Col* 3:14

perform
(*Generally used with the idea of
carrying out to completion something that had been promised, or
what had been commanded*)
I will *p.* the oath which I sware.
   Gen 26:3; *Deut* 9:5; *Luke* 1:72
thou art not able to *p.*   *Ex* 18:18
all that enter in to *p.*   *Num* 4:23*
he commanded you to *p. Deut* 4:13
gone out of thy lips shalt *p.*   23:23
and *p.* duty of a husband's.   25:5
not *p.* duty of my husband's.   7
if he will *p.* the part of.   *Ruth* 3:13
in that day I will *p.* against Eli.
   1 Sam 3:12
that the king will *p.*   *2 Sam* 14:15
then I will *p.* my word.   *1 Ki* 6:12
that he might *p.* his saying.   12:15
   2 Chr 10:15
to *p.* the words of this covenant.
   2 Ki 23:3, 24; *2 Chr* 34:31
if it please the king to *p. Esth* 5:8
their hands cannot *p.*   *Job* 5:12
they are not able to *p.*   *Ps* 21:11
that I may daily *p.* my vows.   61:8
I have sworn, and I will *p.* 119:106
I have inclined my heart to *p.*   112
Lord of hosts will *p.* this.   *Isa* 9:7
vow to the Lord, and *p.* it.   19:21
Cyrus my shepherd shall *p.*   44:28
hasten my word to *p.* it.   *Jer* 1:12
I may *p.* the oath which I.   11:5
Lord *p.* thy words thou hast.   28:6
I will *p.* my good word toward you.
   29:10; 33:14
ye will *p.* your vows.   44:25
word, and will *p.* it.   *Ezek* 12:25
thou wilt *p.* the truth.   *Mi* 7:20
keep thy solemn feasts, *p. Nah* 1:15
thou shalt *p.* to the Lord. *Mat* 5:33
he was able also to *p.*   *Rom* 4:21
how to *p.* that which is good.   7:18
now therefore *p.* the.   *2 Cor* 8:11
he will *p.* it until the day.   *Phil* 1:6

performance
be a *p.* of those things.   *Luke* 1:45
so may be a *p.* also out. *2 Cor* 8:11*

performed
Saul hath not *p.* my.   *1 Sam* 15:11
I have *p.* the commandment.   13
they *p.* all that the king. *2 Sam* 21:14
Lord hath *p.* his word.   *1 Ki* 8:20
   2 Chr 6:10 *Neh* 9:8
Vashti hath not *p.*   *Esth* 1:15
kingdom it shall be *p.*   5:6; 7:2
to thee shall the vow be *p. Ps* 65:1
when the Lord hath *p.*   *Isa* 10:12
p. the thoughts.   *Jer* 23:20; 30:24
who have not *p.* words.   34:18
words of Jonadab are *p.*   35:14, 16
purpose of the Lord shall be *p.* 51:29
have spoken and *p.* it. *Ezek* 37:14
these things shall be *p.* *Luke* 1:20
when they had *p.* all things by. 2:39
when I have *p.* this, I. *Rom* 15:28

performeth
every man that *p.* not.   *Neh* 5:13
he *p.* the thing that is.   *Job* 23:14
I will cry to God that *p.*   *Ps* 57:2
that *p.* the counsel of his. *Isa* 44:26

performing
sacrifice in *p.* a vow.   *Num* 15:3, 8

perfume, -s
thou shalt make it a *p. Ex* 30:35, 37
ointment and *p.* rejoice.   *Pr* 27:9
thou didst increase thy *p. Isa* 57:9

perfumed
I have *p.* my bed with.   *Pr* 7:17
cometh *p.* with myrrh ? *S of S* 3:6

Perga
company came to *P.*   *Acts* 13:13
preached the word in *P.*   14:25

Pergamos
send it to *P.* and Thyatira. *Rev* 1:11
to the angel of the church in *P.* 2:12

perhaps
if *p.* thy thought may.   *Acts* 8:22
lest *p.* such a one be.   *2 Cor* 2:7*
p. he therefore departed. *Philem* 15

peril
bread with *p.* of our lives. *Lam* 5:9
shall famine, *p.,* or sword ? *Rom* 8:35

perilous
in last days *p.* times.   *2 Tim* 3:1*

perils
in *p.* of waters, in *p.* of robbers, in *p.*
by countrymen, in *p.* by heathen,
in *p.* in city, in *p.* in wilderness, in
p. in sea, in *p.* among false
brethren.   *2 Cor* 11:26

perish
that the land *p.* not.   *Gen* 41:36
and many of them *p.*   *Ex* 19:21
eye of his maid, that it *p.*   21:26
die, we *p.,* we all *p.*   *Num* 17:12
latter end shall be that he *p.* 24:20
lest ye *p.* quickly from. *Deut* 11:17
a Syrian ready to *p.* was.   26:5
until thou *p.* quickly.   28:20, 22
   Josh 23:13
let all thine enemies *p.*   *Judg* 5:31
shall descend into battle, and *p.*
   1 Sam 26:10
and to cause to *p.*   *Esth* 3:13; 7:4
and if I *p.* I *p.*   4:16
to cause to *p.* all power.   8:11
nor the memorial of them *p.* 9:28
let the day *p.* wherein I.   *Job* 3:3
by the blast of God they *p.*   4:9
they *p.* for ever, without any.   20
way go to nothing and *p.*   6:18
him that was ready to *p.*   29:13
any *p.* for want of clothing.   31:19
lest he be angry, and ye *p. Ps* 2:12
of the poor shall not *p.*   9:18
and the brutish person *p.*   49:10
like the beasts that *p.*   12, 20
so let the wicked *p.*   68:2; 83:17
they *p.* at the rebuke of thy. 80:16
in that day his thoughts *p.* 146:4
when the wicked *p. Pr* 11:10; 28:28
no vision, the people *p.*   29:18*
to him that is ready to *p.*   31:6
but those riches *p.* by.   *Eccl* 5:14
all their memory to *p.*   *Isa* 26:14
which were ready to *p.*   27:13
the law shall not *p.*   *Jer* 18:18
you out, and ye should *p.* 27:10, 15
remnant in Judah should *p.* 40:15
I will cause thee to *p. Ezek* 25:7
and fellows should not *p. Dan* 2:18
on us that we *p.* not. *Jonah* 1:6; 3:9
O Lord, let us not *p.* for this.   14
members should *p. Mat* 5:29, 30
saying, Lord, save us, we *p.* 8:25
   Luke 8:24
out, and the bottles *p.*   *Mat* 9:17
little ones should *p.*   18:14
carest thou not that we *p.? Mark* 4:38
that a prophet *p.* out. *Luke* 13:33
have bread enough, and I *p.* 15:17
not an hair of your head *p.* 21:18
whoso believeth in him should not *p.*
   John 3:15, 16
the whole nation *p.* not.   11:50

thy money *p.* with thee.   *Acts* 8:20
despisers, and wonder, and *p.* 13:41
cross is to them that *p.* foolishness.
   1 Cor 1:18
Christ in them that *p.*   *2 Cor* 2:15
but though our outward man *p.* 4:16
which all are to *p.* with.   *Col* 2:22
unrighteousness in them that *p.*
   2 Thes 2:10
that any should *p.* but.   *2 Pet* 3:9

    shall **perish**
ye *shall p.* among the heathen.
   Lev 26:38
also *shall p.* for ever.   *Num* 24:24
ye *shall* soon utterly *p.*   *Deut* 4:26
   8:19, 20; 30:18; *Josh* 23:16
I *shall* one day *p.* by.   *1 Sam* 27:1
house of Ahab *shall p.*   *2 Ki* 9:8
hypocrite's hope *shall p.*   *Job* 8:13
his remembrance *shall p.*   18:17
   20:7; 36:12
all flesh *shall p.* together.   34:15
way of the ungodly *shall p. Ps* 1:6
wicked *shall p.*   37:20
are far from thee *shall p.*   73:27
thine enemies *shall p.*   92:9
shall p. but thou shalt endure. 102:26
desire of the wicked *shall p.* 112:10
expectation of wicked *shall p.*
   Pr 10:28; 11:7
that speaketh lies *shall p.*   19:9
a false witness *shall p.* but.   21:28
their wise men *shall p.*   *Isa* 29:14
strive with thee *shall p.*   41:11
not serve thee *shall p.*   60:12
heart of the king *shall p.*   *Jer* 4:9
friend *shall p.*   6:21
gods *shall p.*   10:11, 15; 51:18
valley also *shall p.* and plain.   48:8
but the law *shall p.* from. *Ezek* 7:26
the Philistines *shall p.*   *Amos* 1:8
flight *shall p.* from the swift.   2:14
and the houses of ivory *shall p.* 3:15
and the king *shall p.*   *Zech* 9:5
take the sword *shall p.*   *Mat* 26:52
and bottles *shall p.*   *Luke* 5:37
ye *shall* all likewise *p.*   13:3, 5
sheep *shall* never *p.* nor. *John* 10:28
sinned without law, *shall p.* without.
   Rom 2:12
shall weak brother *p.?*   *1 Cor* 8:11
they *shall p.* but thou.   *Heb* 1:11
and *shall p.* in their.   *2 Pet* 2:12

perished
p. from the congregation. *Num* 16:33
Heshbon is *p.* even to Dibon.   21:30
that man *p.* not alone.   *Josh* 22:20
weapons of war *p.!*   *2 Sam* 1:27
whoever *p.* being innocent. *Job* 4:7
in whom old age was *p.*   30:2
their memorial is *p.*   *Ps* 9:6
the heathen are *p.* out of.   10:16
as Sisera and Jabin, which *p.* 83:10
I should have *p.* in mine.   119:92
their envy is *p.*   *Eccl* 9:6
truth is *p.*   *Jer* 7:28
riches that hath gotten are *p.* 48:36
is counsel *p.* from the prudent ? 49:7
strength and hope is *p.*   *Lam* 3:18
harvest of the field is *p.*   *Joel* 1:11
which came up and *p.*   *Jonah* 4:10
is thy counsellor *p.?*   *Mi* 4:9
the good man is *p.* out of.   7:2
herd of swine ran and *p. Mat* 8:32
p. between the altar.   *Luke* 11:51
he also *p.* and as many. *Acts* 5:37
asleep in Christ are *p. 1 Cor* 15:18
harlot Rahab *p.* not.   *Heb* 11:31
overflowed with water *p. 2 Pet* 3:6
and *p.* in the gainsaying. *Jude* 11

perisheth
lion *p.* for lack of prey.   *Job* 4:11
hope of unjust men *p.*   *Pr* 11:7
there is a just man that *p. Eccl* 7:15
righteous *p.* and no man. *Isa* 57:1
for what the land *p.* and. *Jer* 9:12
people of Chemosh *p.*   48:46
for the meat which *p.*   *John* 6:27
of the fashion of it *p.*   *Jas* 1:11
more precious than gold *p. 1 Pet* 1:7

perishing
his life from *p.* by sword. *Job* 33:18

Perizzite

the *P.* dwelled then in. *Gen* 13:7
and I will drive out the *P.* *Ex* 33:2
          34:11
when the *P.* and Hivite. *Josh* 9:1
Jabin sent to the *P.* and. 11:3

Perizzites

given to thy seed the land of the *P.*
  Gen 15:20; *Ex* 3:8, 17; 23:23
to stink among the *P.* *Gen* 34:30
wood in the land of the *P. Josh* 17:15
Lord delivered the *P.* to Judah.
        Judg 1:4, 5
Israel dwelt among the *P.* 3:5
Solomon made the *P.* *2 Chr* 8:7
abominations of *P.* *Ezra* 9:1

perjured

for liars and *p.* persons. *1 Tim* 1:10*

permission

I speak this by *p.* not by. *1 Cor* 7:6

permit

awhile, if the Lord *p.* *1 Cor* 16:7
will we do, if God *p.* *Heb* 6:3

permitted

Agrippa said, Thou art *p. Acts* 26:1
it is not *p.* to women. *1 Cor* 14:34

pernicious

follow their *p.* ways. *2 Pet* 2:2*

perpetual

[1] *Continual, or uninterrupted,*
Ezek 35:5. [2] *Final,* Ps 9:6.
[3] *Lasting to the end of the world,*
Gen 9:12. [4] *During the con-
tinuance of the legal dispensation,*
Ex 29:9; 30:8.

token of the covenant for *p. Gen* 9:12
priest's office be theirs for a *p.*
  statute. *Ex* 29:9
a *p.* incense before the Lord. 30:8
keep the sabbath for a *p.* 31:16
a *p.* statute not to eat fat. *Lev* 3:17
a *p.* meat offering for Aaron. 6:20
Aaron's by a *p.* statute. 24:9
not be sold, for it is their *p.* 25:34
a *p.* statute, that he. *Num* 19:21
destructions are come to a *p. Ps* 9:6*
lift up thy feet to the *p.* 74:3
he put them to a *p.* reproach. 78:66
by a *p.* decree, that it. *Jer* 5:22
people slidden back by a *p.?* 8:5
why is my pain *p.* and my ? 15:18
land desolate and *p.* hissing. 18:16
bring upon you a *p.* shame. 23:40
make them *p.* desolations. 25:9, 12*
the cities thereof shall be *p.* 49:13
let us join to the Lord in a *p.* 50:5*
may sleep a *p.* sleep. 51:39, 57
hast had a *p.* hatred. *Ezek* 35:5
thee *p.* desolations. 9: *Zeph* 2:9
p. ordinance to the Lord. *Ezek* 46:14
he beheld, and the *p.* hills. *Hab* 3:6*

perpetually

my heart shall be there *p.*
  1 Ki 9:3; *2 Chr* 7:16
his anger did tear *p.* *Amos* 1:11

perplexed

city Shushan was *p.* *Esth* 3:15
the herds of cattle are *p. Joel* 1:18
Herod was *p.* *Luke* 9:7
as they were *p.* 24:4
p. but not in despair. *2 Cor* 4:8

perplexity

for it is a day of *p.* *Isa* 22:5
now shall be their *p.* *Mi* 7:4
on earth distress of nations. with *p.*
  Luke 21:25

persecute

why do ye *p.* me as God ? *Job* 19:22
why *p.* we him, seeing the root ? 28
all them that *p.* me. *Ps* 7:1*
let the enemy *p.* my soul. 5*
wicked in his pride doth *p.* 10:2*
deliver me from them that *p.* 31:15
against them that *p.* me. 35:3*
angel of the Lord *p.* them. 6*
they *p.* him whom thou hast. 69:26
p. and take him, there is. 71:11*
so *p.* them with thy tempest. 83:15*
execute judgement on them that *p.*
  me. 119:84

they *p.* me wrongfully. *Ps* 119:86
be confounded that *p.* me. *Jer* 17:18
I will *p.* them with the sword. 29:18*
p. and destroy them in. *Lam* 3:66*
when men shall *p.* you. *Mat* 5:11
pray for them which *p.* you. 44
when they *p.* you in one city. 10:23
ye shall *p.* them from city. 23:34
they shall *p.* *Luke* 11:49; 21:12
did the Jews *p.* Jesus. *John* 5:16
me, they will also *p.* you. 15:20
bless them which *p.* you. *Rom* 12:14

persecuted

curses on them that *p.* *Deut* 30:7
because he *p.* the poor. *Ps* 109:16
princes have *p.* me without. 119:161
enemy hath *p.* my soul. 143:3
nations in anger is *p.* *Isa* 14:6
covered with anger, and *p.* us.
  Lam 3:43*
blessed which are *p.* for. *Mat* 5:10
so *p.* they, the prophets before. 12
if they have *p.* me, they. *John* 15:20
have not your fathers *p.?* *Acts* 7:52
p. this way unto the death. 22:4
I *p.* them even to strange. 26:11
reviled, we bless; being *p.* we suffer
  it. *1 Cor* 4:12
because I *p.* the church of God.
  15:9; *Gal* 1:13
are *p.* but not forsaken. *2 Cor* 4:9*
he which *p.* us in times. *Gal* 1:23
born after the flesh *p.* him. 4:29
have killed the Lord and *p.* us.
  1 Thes 2:15*
dragon *p.* woman that. *Rev* 12:13

persecutest

Saul, Saul, why *p.* thou me ?
  Acts 9:4; 22:7; 26:14
I am Jesus, whom thou *p.* 9:5; 22:8
  26:15

persecuting

zeal, *p.* the church. *Phil* 3:6

persecution

our necks are under *p.* *Lam* 5:5*
for when *p.* ariseth. *Mat* 13:21
  Mark 4:17
at that time there was great *p.*
  Acts 8:1
scattered abroad upon the *p.* 11:19*
and raised *p.* against Paul and. 13:50
p. or sword, separate us ? *Rom* 8:35
why do I yet suffer *p.?* *Gal* 5:11
suffer *p.* for cross of Christ. 6:12
live godly shall suffer *p. 2 Tim* 3:12

persecutions

lands, with *p.* *Mark* 10:30
I take pleasure in *p.* for. *2 Cor* 12:10
your faith in all your *p.* *2 Thes* 1:4
my *p.* at Antioch, what *p. 2 Tim* 3:11

persecutor

who was before a *p.* *1 Tim* 1:13

persecutors

their *p.* thou threwest. *Neh* 9:11*
his arrows against the *p.* *Ps* 7:13*
many are my *p.* 119:157
deliver me from my *p.* 142:6
and revenge me of my *p. Jer* 15:15
therefore my *p.* shall stumble. 20:11
all her *p.* overtook her. *Lam* 1:3
our *p.* are swifter than the. 4:19*

perseverance

thereunto with all *p.* *Eph* 6:18

Persia

the reign of the kingdom of *P.*
  2 Chr 36:20
a feast to the power of *P. Esth* 1:3
the seven princes of *P.* which. 14
the ladies of *P.* shall say to. 18
of *P.* and Lud were. *Ezek* 27:10
P. Ethiopia, and Libya with. 38:5
kings of Media and *P.* *Dan* 8:20
prince of *P.* withstood me; and I remained with the kings of *P.* 10:13
to fight with the prince of *P.* 20
stand up yet three kings in *P.* 11:2
  see **king**

Persians, *see* **Medes**

Persis

salute *P.* which laboured. *Rom* 16:12

person

Joseph was a goodly *p.* *Gen* 39:6
no uncircumcised *p.* *Ex* 12:48
nor honour the *p.* *Lev* 19:15
any sin, that *p.* be guilty. *Num* 5:6
for an unclean *p.* shall take. 19:17
clean *p.* shall take hyssop and. 18
whatsoever unclean *p.* toucheth. 22
whosoever hath killed any *p.* 31:19
  35:11, 15, 30; *Josh* 20:3 9
not testify against any *p. Num* 35:30
unclean and clean *p.* *Deut* 15:22
to slay an innocent *p.* 27:25
shall not regard the *p.* 28:60
a goodlier *p.* than he. *1 Sam* 9:2
David a comely *p.* 16:18
I have accepted thy *p.* 25:35
have slain a righteous *p. 2 Sam* 4:11
nor doth God respect any *p.* 14:14
go to battle in thine own *p.* 17:11
shall save the humble *p. Job* 22:29
in whose eyes a vile *p.* *Ps* 15:4*
fool and the brutish *p.* perish. 49:10
will not know a wicked *p.* 101:4
not one feeble *p.* among. 105:37
naughty *p.* walketh with. *Pr* 6:12
shall be called mischievous *p.* 24:8
violence to the blood of any *p.* 28:17
the vile *p.* shall be no more. *Isa* 32:5†
vile *p.* will speak villany. 6†
Johanan took every *p.* *Jer* 43:6
that were near the king's *p.* 52:25
the loathing of thy *p.* *Ezek* 16:5
if sword come and take any *p.* 33:6
come at no dead *p.* 44:25
shall stand up a vile *p. Dan* 11:21
regardest not *p.* of men. *Mat* 22:16
  Mark 12:14
of the blood of this just *p. Mat* 27:24
from you that wicked *p. 1 Cor* 5:13
forgave I it in the *p.* *2 Cor* 2:10
p. hath inheritance in. *Eph* 5:5
express image of his *p.* *Heb* 1:3
or profane *p.* as Esau, who. 12:16
saved Noah, the eighth *p. 2 Pet* 2:5

persons

give me *p.* and take the. *Gen* 14:21
to number of your *p.* *Ex* 16:16
p. shall be for the Lord. *Lev* 27:2
shall sprinkle it upon *p. Num* 19:18
both of the *p.*, beeves, asses. 31:28
thirty and two thousand *p.* in all. 35
which regardeth not *p. Deut* 10:17
into Egypt with seventy *p.* 22
Jerubbaal which were 70 *p. Judg* 9:2
Abimelech hired vain and light *p.* 4
slew threescore and ten *p.* 5, 18
to kill of Israel about 30 *p.* 20:39
which were about 30 *p. 1 Sam* 9:22
Doeg slew on that day 85 *p.* 22:18
the death of all the *p.* 22
king's sons being 70 *p.* *2 Ki* 10:6
king's sons and slew 70 *p.* 7
I have not sat with vain *p. Ps* 26:4†
followeth vain *p. Pr* 12:11; 28:19
from Jerusalem 832 *p.* *Jer* 52:29
away captive of Jews 745 *p.* 30
forts to cut off many *p.* *Ezek* 17:17
they traded the *p.* of men. 27:13
more than 120,000 *p.* *Jonah* 4:11
are treacherous *p.* *Zeph* 3:4
over ninety-nine just *p.* *Luke* 15:7
with the devout *p.* *Acts* 17:17
us by means of many *p.* *2 Cor* 1:11
made for perjured *p.* *1 Tim* 1:10*
what manner of *p.* ought ? *2 Pet* 3:11
having men's *p.* in admiration.
  Jude 16
  see **respect**

persuade

who shall *p.* Ahab, to ? *1 Ki* 22:20*
I will *p.* him. 21*
thou shalt *p.* him and prevail. 22*
doth not Hezekiah *p.? 2 Chr* 32:11
beware, lest Hezekiah *p.* *Isa* 36:18
will *p.* him and secure. *Mat* 28:14
we *p.* men. *2 Cor* 5:11
do I now *p.* men ? *Gal* 1:10†

persuaded

Ahab *p.* Jehoshaphat. *2 Chr* 18:2
forbearing a prince *p.* *Pr* 25:15
the chief priests *p.* the. *Mat* 27:20

will not be *p.* if one rose. *Luke* 16:31
for they be *p.* that John was. 20:6
p. them to continue in. *Acts* 13:43
who *p.* the people, and having. 14:19
Paul *p.* the Jews and the. 18:4
this Paul hath *p.* much people. 19:26
when he would not be *p.* 21:14
I am *p.* none of these things. 26:26
being *p.* that what he had promised.
Rom 4:21
p. that nothing can separate us. 8:38
let every man be fully *p.* in. 14:5
I know and am *p.* there is. 14
I myself also am *p.* of you. 15:14
I am *p.* that in thee. *2 Tim* 1:5
I am *p.* that he is able to keep. 12
are *p.* better things of you. *Heb* 6:9
seen them afar off, were *p.* of. 11:13

persuadest
almost thou *p.* me to. *Acts* 26:28*

persuadeth
when Hezekiah *p.* you. *2 Ki* 18:32
Paul *p.* men to worship. *Acts* 18:13

persuading
p. things concerning. *Acts* 19:8
p. them concerning Jesus. 28:23

persuasion
this *p.* cometh not of him. *Gal* 5:8

pertain
peace offerings *p.* to Lord. *Lev* 7:20
and eat of the sacrifice which *p.* 21
if I leave all that *p.* *1 Sam* 25:22
in those things which *p.* *Rom* 15:17
things *p.* to this life. *1 Cor* 6:3
things that *p.* to life. *2 Pet* 1:3

pertained
the half that *p.* to the. *Num* 31:43
buried in a hill that *p.* *Josh* 24:33
an oak that *p.* to Joash. *Judg* 6:11
of all that *p.* to Nabal. *1 Sam* 25:21
which *p.* to Ish-bosheth. *2 Sam* 2:15
all that *p.* to Obed-edom. 6:12
master's son all that *p.* to Saul. 9:9
all that *p.* to Mephibosheth. 16:4
vessels that *p.* to house. *1 Ki* 7:48
all that *p.* to the king. *2 Ki* 24:7
morning *p.* to them. *1 Chr* 9:27
cities which *p.* to Judah. *2 Chr* 12:4
abominations *p.* to Israel. 34:33

pertaineth
which *p.* to cleansing. *Lev* 14:32
to the office of Eleazar *p.* *Num* 4:16
not wear what *p.* to a man. *Deut* 22:5
Ziklag *p.* to the kings. *1 Sam* 27:6
it *p.* not to thee, Uzziah. *2 Chr* 26:18
to whom *p.* the adoption. *Rom* 9:4
he *p.* to another tribe. *Heb* 7:13

pertaining
half Gilead and cities *p.* *Josh* 13:31
every matter *p.* to God. *1 Chr* 26:32
things *p.* to kingdom of God. *Acts* 1:3
of things *p.* to this life. *1 Cor* 6:4
priest in things *p.* to God. *Heb* 2:17
for men in things *p.* to God. 5:1
not make him perfect, as *p.* to. 9:9

perverse
because thy way is. *Num* 22:32
are a *p.* and crooked. *Deut* 32:5
thou son of the *p.* *1 Sam* 20:30
cannot my taste discern *p.* things?
Job 6:30*
shall also prove me *p.* 9:20
p. lips put far from thee. *Pr* 4:24
is nothing froward or *p.* in. 8:8
he that is a *p.* heart shall. 12:8
p. in his ways despiseth him. 14:2
that hath *p.* tongue falleth. 17:20
than he that is *p.* in his lips. 19:1
thine heart shall utter *p.* 23:33*
than he that is *p.* in his ways. 28:6
he that is *p.* in his ways shall. 18
hath mingled a *p.* spirit. *Isa* 19:14
O *p.* generation. *Mat* 17:17
Luke 9:41
arise, speaking *p.* things. *Acts* 20:30
midst of a *p.* nation. *Phil* 2:15
p. disputings of men of. *1 Tim* 6:5*

perversely
what servant did *p.* *2 Sam* 19:19
and have done *p.* *1 Ki* 8:47
they dealt *p.* with me. *Ps* 119:78*

perverseness
neither hath he seen *p.* *Num* 23:21
but *p.* of transgressors. *Pr* 11:3
but *p.* therein is a breach in. 15:4
ye trust in *p.* and stay. *Isa* 30:12
tongue hath muttered *p.* 59:3*
the land is full of blood, and the city
full of *p.* *Ezek* 9:9*

pervert
a gift doth *p.* words of. *Deut* 16:19
shalt not *p.* the judgement. 24:17*
doth God *p.* judgement? *Job* 8:3
nor will the Almighty *p.* 34:12
to *p.* ways of judgement. *Pr* 17:23
and *p.* the judgement of any. 31:5
you, ye that *p.* equity. *Mi* 3:9
not cease to *p.* right? *Acts* 13:10
and would *p.* the gospel. *Gal* 1:7

perverted
took bribes, *p.* judgement. *1 Sam* 8:3
I have *p.* what was right. *Job* 33:27
and knowledge, it hath *p.* *Isa* 47:10
they have *p.* their way. *Jer* 3:21
ye have *p.* the words of the. 23:36

perverteth
the gift *p.* the words of. *Ex* 23:8
cursed be he that *p.* *Deut* 27:19*
but he that *p.* his ways. *Pr* 10:9
the foolishness of a man *p.* 19:3*
this man as one that *p.* people.
Luke 23:14

perverting
if thou seest the violent *p.* *Eccl* 5:8*
found this fellow *p.* the. *Luke* 23:2

pestilence
he fall on us with *p.* or. *Ex* 5:3
smite thee and thy people with *p.*
9:15
send the *p.* among you. *Lev* 26:25
smite them with the *p.* *Num* 14:12
the Lord shall make *p.* *Deut* 28:21
there be three days' *p.* *2 Sam* 24:13
1 Chr 21:12
the Lord sent a *p.* on Israel.
2 Sam 24:15; *1 Chr* 21:14
in the land of famine, *p.* *1 Ki* 8:37
2 Chr 6:28; 7:13; 20:9
their life over to the *p.* *Ps* 78:50
thee from the noisome *p.* 91:3
nor for the *p.* that walketh in. 6
I will consume them by *p.* *Jer* 14:12
24:10; 27:8
of this city shall die by *p.* 21:6
Zedekiah from the *p.* 7
in city shall die by *p.* 9; 38:2
Why die by the sword and *p.?* 27:13
prophesied of war and of *p.* 28:8
will send upon them the *p.* 29:17
them with the famine and *p.* 18
the city is given because of the *p.*
32:24, 36
liberty for you to the *p.* 34:17
Egypt shall die by the *p.* 42:17, 22
punished Jerusalem by the *p.* 44:13
shall die with the *p.* *Ezek* 5:12
p. and blood shall pass through. 17
sword, famine, and the *p.* 6:11
that is far off shall die by the *p.* 12
a sword without, *p.* and. 7:15
few men of them from the *p.* 12:16
or if I send a *p.* into that land. 14:19
I send the *p.* to cut off man. 21
I will send to her *p.* and blood. 28:23
in caves shall die of the *p.* 33:27
plead against him with *p.* and. 38:22
sent among you the *p.* *Amos* 4:10
before him went the *p.* *Hab* 3:5

pestilences
and there shall be *p.* *Mat* 24:7
Luke 21:11

pestilent
this man a *p.* fellow. *Acts* 24:5

pestle
in a mortar with a *p.* *Pr* 27:22

Peter
when *P.* was come down out of the
ship. *Mat* 14:29
I say, That thou art *P.* 16:18
he said to *P.*, Get thee behind me. 23
Mark 8:33

he taketh *P.* James and. *Mat* 17:1
26:37; *Mark* 5:37; 9:2; 14:33
Luke 8:51; 9:28
they that received tribute money
came to *P.* *Mat* 17:24
P. followed him to the high. 26:58
P. remembered words of Jesus. 75
Mark 14:72
tell his disciples and *P.* *Mark* 16:7
and looked upon *P.* *Luke* 22:61
city of Andrew and *P.* *John* 1:44
whose ear *P.* cut off. 18:26
P. was grieved because he. 21:17
in those days *P.* stood. *Acts* 1:15
seeing *P.* and John about to go. 3:3
P. filled with the Holy Ghost. 4:8
when they saw the boldness of *P.* 13
at least the shadow of *P.* might. 5:15
the apostles sent unto them *P.* 8:14
the disciples had heard that *P.* 9:38
P. put them all forth, and. 40
Rise, *P.* kill and eat. 10:13; 11:7
while *P.* spake these words. 10:44
as many as came with *P.* 45
further to take *P.* also. 12:3
P. was sleeping between two. 6
the angel of the Lord smote *P.* 7
as *P.* knocked at the door of. 13
what was become of *P.* 18
up to Jerusalem to see *P.* *Gal* 1:18
circumcision was committed to *P.*
2:7
wrought effectually in *P.* to the. 8
I said unto *P.* before them all. 14

Simon **Peter**
saw *Simon* called *P.* *Mat* 4:18
first *Simon*, who is called *P.* 10:2
Simon he surnamed *P.* *Mark* 3:16
Simon P. fell down at. *Luke* 5:8
Simon, whom he also named *P.* 6:14
cometh he to *Simon P.* *John* 13:6
and cometh to *Simon P.* 20:2
Jesus saith to *Simon P.*, *Simon*. 21:15
one *Simon*, whose surname is *P.*
Acts 10:5, 32; 11:13

petition
Israel grant thee thy *p.* *1 Sam* 1:17
Lord hath given me my *p.* which. 27
now I ask one *p.* of thee. *1 Ki* 2:16
I desire one small *p.* of thee, say. 20
the king said, What is thy *p.?*
Esth 5:6; 7:2; 9:12
then Esther said, My *p.* and. 5:7
if it please the king to grant my *p.* 8
let my life be given me at my *p.* 7:3
ask a *p.* of any god. *Dan* 6:7, 12
his *p.* three times a day. 13

petitions
the Lord fulfil all thy *p.* *Ps* 20:5
we know we have the *p.* *1 John* 5:15

Phalec
which was the son of *P.* *Luke* 3:35

Pharaoh
Sarai before *P.* *Gen* 12:15
plagued *P.* and his house. 17
Potiphar an officer of *P.* 39:1
P. was wroth against two. 40:2
shall *P.* lift up thine head. 13, 19
make mention of me to *P.* 14
P. dreamed. 41:1
so *P.* awoke. 4, 7
God shall give *P.* answer of. 16
let *P.* do this. 34
I am *P.* and without thee. 44
people cried to *P.* 55
by the life of *P.* 42:15, 16
thou art as *P.* 44:18
made me a father to *P.* 45:8
I will go up and shew *P.* 46:31
P. and went out from *P.* 47:10
and we will be *P.'s* servants. 25
of the priests became not *P.'s.* 26
in the ears of *P.* saying. 50:4
when *P.* heard, he sought. *Ex* 2:15
and I will send thee to *P.* 3:10
all those wonders before *P.* 4:21
P. said, Who is the Lord that? 5:2
officers came and cried unto *P.* 15
since I came to *P.* to speak. 23
see what I will do to *P.* 6:1
how then shall *P.* hear me? 12, 30
I have made thee a god to *P.* 7:1

I will harden P.'s heart.　　Ex 7:3
　　　13, 14, 22; 8:19; 9:12
stand before P.　　　8:20; 9:13
P. sent for Moses.　　　9:27
bring one plague more upon P. 11:1
did all these wonders before P.　10
from the firstborn of P.　　12:29
when P. had let people go.　13:17
will be honoured upon P.　14:4, 17
covered all the host of P.　　28
made affinity with P.　　1 Ki 3:1
an house for P.'s daughter.　　7:8
favour in the sight of P.　　11:19
them from under P.　　2 Ki 17:7
so is P. to all that trust in him.
　　　　　18:21; Isa 36:6
to commandment of P.　2 Ki 23:35
signs and wonders on P.　Neh 9:10
tokens and wonders on P.　Ps 135:9
overthrew P. and his host.　136:15
of horses in P.'s chariots. S of S 1:9
how say ye to P. I am.　　Isa 19:11
themselves in strength of P.　30:2
the strength of P. shall be your.　3
P. and his servants.　　Jer 25:19
broken for fear of P.'s army. 37:11
did cry, P. king of Egypt.　46:17
word that came, before that P. 47:1
P. with his army not.　Ezek 17:17
set thy face against P. king.　29:2
I am against thee, P. king. 3; 30:22
broken the arm of P.　30:21, 24, 25
this is P. and his multitude.　31:18
take up a lamentation for P.　32:2
kindred made known to P. Acts 7:13
P.'s daughter took him up and.　21
for scripture saith to P.　Rom 9:17
the son of P.'s daughter. Heb 11:24

Pharaoh-hophra
will give P. into hand of. Jer 44:30

Pharaoh-nechoh
P. went against Assyria. 2 Ki 23:29
P. put Jehoahaz in bands at.　33
P. make Eliakim king.　　34
he taxed to give money to P.　35
word to Jeremiah against P. Jer 46:2

Pharez
name was called P.　　Gen 38:29
sons of Judah, P. and.　　46:12
　1 Chr 2:4; Mat 1:3; Luke 3:33
and the sons of P. were Hezron and
　Hamul. Gen 46:12; Num 26:20, 21
　　Ruth 4:18; 1 Chr 2:5; 9:4
be like the house of P.　　Ruth 4:12

Pharisee
*The Pharisees were a religious
party or school among the Jews at
the time of Christ, so called from
the Aramaic form of the Hebrew
perushim, the separated ones. This
name may have been given them
by their enemies, as they usually
called themselves Haberim, associates.
They were formalists, very
patriotic but bigoted in their
patriotism as in their religion.
Their political influence was great,
though they were only about
6000 to 7000 in number.
Jesus denounced the Pharisees
for their hypocrisy, which was
shown by their care for the minutest
formalities imposed by the traditions
of the elders, but not for the
mind and heart which should
correspond. They were ambitious,
arrogant, and proudly self-righteous,
all of which qualities were contrary
to the teachings of Jesus. This
explains in part their intense
hostility to him. And their influence
over the people, who had
come to believe as they did, led to
their demand for the crucifixion of
Jesus.*

thou blind p. cleanse.　Mat 23:26
a certain p. besought.　Luke 11:37
went to pray, one a p. the.　18:10
the p. stood and prayed thus.　11
one in the council, a p. Acts 5:34
I am a p. the son of a p.　　23:6

after the most straitest sect of our
　religion I lived a p.　Acts 26:5
as touching the law, a p.　Phil 3:5

Pharisees
righteousness of the p.　Mat 5:20
why do we and the p. fast oft ? 9:14
　　　　　　　Mark 2:18
p. said, He casteth out devils.
　　　　　　　Mat 9:34
knowest thou that the p.?　15:12
beware of the leaven of the p. 16:6
　　11; Mark 8:15; Luke 12:1
the p. also came to him.　Mat 19:3
the scribes and p. sit in.　23:2
scribes and p. hypocrites. 13, 14, 15
　23, 25, 27, 29; Luke 11:42, 43, 44
the scribes and p.　Luke 5:30; 15:2
the scribes and p. watched.　6:7
but the p. rejected the counsel. 7:30
now do ye p. make clean.　11:39
p. who were covetous, heard. 16:14
sent were of the p.　　John 1:24
there was a man of the p.　3:1
p. and priests sent officers.　7:32
have any of the rulers or p.?　48
the p. gathered a council.　11:47
p. had given a commandment.　57
certain of sect of the p.　Acts 15:5
arose a dissension between p. and
　Sadducees.　　　23:7
there is no resurrection, but the p. 8

Pharpar, see Abana

Phebe
I commend unto you P.　Rom 16:1

Phenice
travelled as far as P.　Acts 11:19
Barnabas passed through P.　15:3
finding ship sailing over to P.　27:12
they might attain to P.　27:12

Philadelphia
write and send it unto P.　Rev 1:11
to the angel of the church in P.　3:7

Philetus, see Hymenaeus

Philip
P. and Bartholomew.　Mat 10:3
　Mark 3:18; Luke 6:14; Acts 1:13
for Herodias' sake his brother P.'s
　Mat 14:3; Mark 6:17; Luke 3:19
P. tetrarch of Iturea.　Luke 3:1
Jesus findeth P. and.　John 1:43
now P. was of Bethsaida, the.　44
P. findeth Nathanael, and saith.　45
the same came to P. and.　12:21
P. telleth Andrew; Andrew and P. 22
Hast thou not known me, P.?　14:9
P. the deacon.　　　Acts 6:5
the Spirit said to P.　　8:29
P. went down to Samaria.　5
to those things which P. spake.　6
believed P. preaching things.　12
Simon continued with P. and.　13
P. ran to him, and heard him read. 30
the Lord caught away P.　39
we entered into the house of P. 21:8

Philippi
from Neapolis we came to P. of
　Macedonia.　　　Acts 16:12
we sailed away from P. and.　20:6
we were shamefully entreated at P.
　　　　　　　1 Thes 2:2

Philistia
P. triumph thou because.　Ps 60:8
behold P. and Tyre, this man.　87:4
Moab my washpot, over P.　108:9

Philistim
out of whom came P.　Gen 10:14
　　　　　　　1 Chr 1:12

Philistine
am not I a P.?　　1 Sam 17:8
servant will fight with this P.　32
the P. cursed David.　　43
David smote the P. in his.　49
sword of Goliath the P. 21:9; 22:10
Abishai smote the P.　2 Sam 21:17

Philistines
sojourned in the P.s' land. Gen 21:34
Isaac had flocks, and the P.　26:14
P. stopped the wells.　15, 18
not through the land of P. Ex 13:17
the borders of P. not.　Josh 13:2
Ekron five lords of P.　3; Judg 3:3

Shamgar slew of the P.　Judg 3:31
served the gods of the P.　10:6
into the hands of the P.　7; 13:1
you from Egyptians and P.　11
an occasion against the P　14:4
be more blameless than the P.　15:3
the P. came up and burnt her.　6
that the P. are rulers over us ?　11
Samson judged Israel in the days of
　the P.　　　　20
the P. be upon thee. 16:9, 12, 14, 20
the P. took Samson and put out.　21
at once avenged of the P.　28
Samson said, Let me die with P. 30
went out against the P.　1 Sam 4:1
Lord smitten us before the P.?　3
yourselves like men, O ye P.!　9
the P. took the ark of God and. 5:1
the ark was in the land of P.　6:1
P. have brought again the ark.　21
us out of the hand of the P.　7:8
the P. drew near to battle.　10
the P. were subdued, and came. 13
the P. will come down upon. 13:12
Israelites went down to the P.　20
and let us go over to the P.　14:1
noise in the host of the P. went on. 19
was sore war against the P. all. 52
the P. saw their champion.　17:51
from chasing after the P.　53
hand of the P. be on him. 18:17, 21
then the princes of the P. went.　30
David fought with the P.　19:8
　　　　23:5; 2 Sam 21:15
from following the P.　1 Sam 24:1
escape into land of the P.　27:1
for the P. make war against.　28:15
displease not lords of the P.　29:7
P. followed hard upon Saul.　31:2
　　　　　　　1 Chr 10:2
sent into land of the P. 1 Sam 31:9
all the P. came up to.　2 Sam 5:17
shall I go up to the P.?　19
David smote the P.　25; 8:1
gold got from P.　　8:12
Eleazar smote the P.　23:10
Shammah slew P.　　12
brake through the host of the P.　16
sojourned in land of the P. 2 Ki 8:2
Jehoram the spirit of P. 2 Chr 21:16
helped Uzziah against the P.　26:7
P. had invaded the cities of.　28:18
P. with the inhabitants.　Ps 83:7
soothsayers like the P.　Isa 2:6
Syrians before, and the P.　9:12
shall fly on shoulders of the P. 11:14
the kings of the P. shall. Jer 25:20
the Lord came against the P.　47:1
for the Lord will spoil the P.　4
to the daughters of P. Ezek 16:27
because the P. have dealt.　25:15
stretch mine hand upon the P.　16
the remnant of the P.　Amos 1:8
go down to Gath of the P.　6:2
have not I brought the P.?　9:7
plain shall possess the P.　Ob 19
O land of the P. I will.　Zeph 2:5
cut off the pride of the P. Zech 9:6
see daughters

Philologus
salute P. Julia, and.　Rom 16:15

philosophers
certain p. encountered.　Acts 17:18

philosophy
man spoil you through p.　Col 2:8

Phinehas
Eleazar's wife bare him P.　Ex 6:25
P. hath turned my wrath from Israel.
　　　　　　　Num 25:11
Moses sent them and P. to.　31:6
Israel sent P. to the.　Josh 22:13
in a hill that pertained to P.　24:33
P. stood before the ark. Judg 20:28
Hophni and P. the priests. 1 Sam 1:3
Hophni and P. shall both die.　2:34
thy two sons Hophni and P.　4:11
P.'s wife was with child, near.　19
son of P. the Lord's priest.　14:3
Eleazar begat P.　　1 Chr 6:4
P. begat Abishua.　　50
P. son of Eleazar was ruler.　9:20

Abishua son of *P.* the son. *Ezra* 7:5
of the sons of *P.* Gershom went. 8:2
was Eleazar the son of *P.* 33
then stood up *P.* and. *Ps* 106:30

Phlegon
salute Asyncritus, *P.* *Rom* 16:14

Phrygia
had gone throughout *P.* *Acts* 16:6
over all the country of *P.* 18:23

Phurah
he went down with *P.* *Judg* 7:11

Phygellus, see Hermogenes

phylacteries
The same as frontlets. *They
were strips of parchment on which
were written four passages of
Scripture, Ex 13:2–10, 11–17;
Deut 6:4–9, 13–23. These were
put in cases of black calfskin and
bound on the forehead and the
arm, in obedience to their understanding of Ex 13:16. The Pharisees
affected to have the cases of their
phylacteries broader than the other
Jews wore, as a badge of distinction, and through ostentation, which
is what our Saviour denounced.*
made broad their *p.* *Mat* 23:5

physician
*(These were not like our phy-
sicians, as the science had not pro-
gressed far. But they were healers,
according to their ability. The
word is also used of healers of the
mind, comforters, and also of
embalmers, as having to do with
the human body)*
is there no balm in Gilead; is there
no *p.* there ? *Jer* 8:22
that be whole need not a *p.* but the.
Mat 9:12; *Mark* 2:17; *Luke* 5:31
p. heal thyself. *Luke* 4:23
Luke the *p.* *Col* 4:14

physicians
his servants the *p.* to embalm his
father; the *p.* *Gen* 50:2
to the Lord, but *p.* *2 Chr* 16:12
ye are all *p.* of no value. *Job* 13:4
had suffered many things of *p.*
Mark 5:26; *Luke* 8:43

pick
the ravens shall *p.* it out. *Pr* 30:17

pictures
shall destroy all their *p. Num* 33:52*
of gold in *p.* of silver. *Pr* 25:11*
Lord on all pleasant *p.* *Isa* 2:16*

piece
he laid one *p.* against. *Gen* 15:10
beaten out of one *p.* *Ex* 37:7*
trumpets of a whole *p. Num* 10:2*
woman cast a *p.* of a millstone upon.
Judg 9:53*; *2 Sam* 11:21
crouch to him for a *p.* of silver, that
I may eat a *p.* of. *1 Sam* 2:36
they gave him a *p.* of a cake. 30:12
to every one a *p.* of flesh.
2 Sam 6:19; *1 Chr* 16:3
was a *p.* of ground full of lentiles.
2 Sam 23:11
mar every good *p.* *2 Ki* 3:19, 25
repaired the other *p.* *Neh* 3:11
next Ezer another *p.* 19, 20, 21, 24
27, 30
as hard as a *p.* of the. *Job* 41:24*
every man also gave him a *p.* 42:11
brought to buy a *p.* of bread. *Pr* 6:26
for a *p.* of bread that man. 28:21
temples are a *p.* of pomegranate.
S of S 4:3; 6:7
daily a *p.* of bread. *Jer* 37:21
every good *p.*, the thigh. *Ezek* 24:4
bring it out *p.* by *p.*, let no lot fall. 6
mouth of lion, a *p.* of ear. *Amos* 3:12
p. was rained on, and the *p.* 4:7
no man putteth a *p.* of new cloth to.
Mat 9:16; *Mark* 2:21; *Luke* 5:36
find a *p.* of money. *Mat* 17:27*
I have bought a *p.* of a. *Luke* 14:18
if she lose one *p.* she doth. 15:8
for I have found the *p.* that 9
him a *p.* of a broiled fish. 24:42

pieces
passed between those *p. Gen* 15:17
thy brother 1000 *p.* of silver. 20:16
bought for 100 *p.* of money. 33:19
Josh 24:32
Joseph for twenty *p.* of silver. 37:28
Joseph is rent in *p.* 33; 44:28
to Benjamin thirty *p.* of silver. 45:22
if it be torn in *p.* let. *Ex* 22:13
have the two shoulder *p.* 28:7
on the shoulder *p.* 25; 39:4, 18
part the meat offering in *p. Lev* 2:6
Moses burnt the *p.* and fat. 8:20
burnt offering with the *p.* 9:13
Abimelech seventy *p.* of silver.
Judg 9:4
give thee 1100 *p.* of silver. 16:5
concubine into twelve *p.* 19:29
a yoke of oxen in *p.* *1 Sam* 11:7
Samuel hewed Agag in *p.* 15:33
new garment in twelve *p. 1 Ki* 11:30
to Jeroboam, Take thee ten *p.* 31
a strong wind brake in *p.* the. 19:11
Elisha rent his clothes in two *p.*
2 Ki 2:12
with him 6000 *p.* of gold. 5:5
sold for eighty *p.* of silver. 6:25
images of Baal in *p.* 11:18; 23:14
brake in *p.* the brasen serpent. 18:4
of Baal, and brake the images in *p.*
2 Chr 23:17; 31:1; 34:4; *Mi* 1:7
also shaken me in *p.* *Job* 16:12
his bones as strong *p.* of. 40:18*
rending in *p.* while none. *Ps* 7:2
lest I tear you in *p.* 50:22
submit with *p.* of silver. 68:30
heads of Leviathan in *p.* 74:14
the fruit bring 1000 *p.* *S of S* 8:11
ye beat my people to *p.*? *Isa* 3:15
that goeth out shall be torn in *p.*?
Jer 5:6
breaketh the rock in *p.* 23:29
aside and pulled me in *p. Lam* 3:11
that which is torn in *p. Ezek* 4:14
pollute me for a *p.* of bread ? 13:19
gather the *p.* thereof into. 24:4
brake the image in *p. Dan* 2:34, 45
forasmuch as iron breaketh in *p.* 40
brake all their bones in *p.* 6:24
devoured and brake in *p.* 7:7, 19
to me for fifteen *p.* of silver. *Hos* 3:2
who chop my people in *p.* *Mi* 3:3
thou shalt beat in *p.* many. 4:13
as a lion teareth in *p.* and none. 5:8
lion did tear in *p.* enough. *Nah* 2:12
for my price thirty *p.* *Zech* 11:12
I took the thirty *p.* of silver. 13
Mat 27:6, 9
what woman having ten *p.* of silver ?
Luke 15:8
price 50,000 *p.* of silver. *Acts* 19:19
lest Paul be pulled in *p.* 23:10
broken *p.* of the ship. 27:44*

see **break, broken, cut, dash,
dashed**

pierce
he shall *p.* them through. *Num* 24:8*
a man lean, it will go into his hand
and *p.* it. *2 Ki* 18:21; *Isa* 36:6
a sword shall *p.* through. *Luke* 2:35

pierced
when she had *p.* through. *Judg* 5:26
my bones are *p.* in me. *Job* 30:17
they *p.* my hands and. *Ps* 22:16
look on me whom they have *p.*
Zech 12:10; *John* 19:37
the soldiers *p.* his side. *John* 19:34
and *p.* themselves with. *1 Tim* 6:10
they also which *p.* him. *Rev* 1:7

pierceth
behemoth's nose *p.* *Job* 40:24

piercing
punish the *p.* serpent. *Isa* 27:1*
word of God is quick, *p.* *Heb* 4:12

piercings
that speaketh like the *p.* *Pr* 12:18

piety
let them learn to shew *p. 1 Tim* 5:4

pigeon, see young

Pi-hahiroth, see Baal-zephon

Pilate
they delivered him to Pontius *P.*
Mat 27:2; *Mark* 15:1
P. saw that he could. *Mat* 27:24
so that *P.* marvelled. *Mark* 15:5, 44
so *P.* willing to content the. 15
Pontius *P.* being governor. *Luke* 3:1
whose blood *P.* had mingled. 13:1
same day *P.* and Herod were. 23:12
this man went to *P.* and begged. 52
P. then went out to them. *John* 18:29
entered into the judgement hall. 33
when *P.* heard that, he was. 19:8
from thenceforth *P.* sought to. 12
P. wrote a title, and put it on. 19
Joseph besought *P.* and *P.* gave. 38
ye denied him in the presence of *P.*
Acts 3:13
against Jesus, Herod and *P.* 4:27
yet desired they *P.* that he. 13:28
who before *P.* witnessed. *1 Tim* 6:13

pile
the *p.* of it is fire and. *Isa* 30:33
make the *p.* for fire. *Ezek* 24:9

pilgrimage
years of my *p.* are 130 years . . . the
days of their *p.* *Gen* 47:9
them the land of their *p.* *Ex* 6:4*
in the house of my *p.* *Ps* 119:54

pilgrims
were strangers and *p.* *Heb* 11:13
I beseech you, as *p.* *1 Pet* 2:11

pillar
*(That which supports, either
actually or metaphorically. The
word is used of the cloud and fire
which led the Israelites through the
wilderness. It is also used in
other places where the form is
intended, not the idea of support)*
and became a *p.* of salt. *Gen* 19:26
Jacob set it up for a *p.* 28:18, 22
35:14
thou anointedst the *p.* 31:13
behold this *p.* 51
and this *p.* be witness. 52
Jacob set a *p.* upon Rachel's grave,
that is the *p.* 35:20
cloudy *p.* descended and. *Ex* 33:9
people saw the cloudy *p.* stand. 10
king, by the plain of the *p. Judg* 9:6
the flame arose with a *p.* 20:40
up a *p.*: he called the *p.* *2 Sam* 18:18
the right *p.*, the left *p.* *1 Ki* 7:21
king stood by *p.* *2 Ki* 11:14; 23:3
2 Chr 23:13
in day by a cloudy *p.* *Neh* 9:12
to them in the cloudy *p.* *Ps* 99:7
and a *p.* at the border. *Isa* 19:19
thee this day an iron *p.* *Jer* 1:18
the height of one *p.* was. 52:21
church, the *p.* and ground of the
truth. *1 Tim* 3:15
that overcometh will I make a *p.*
Rev 3:12

see **cloud, fire**

pillars
an altar and twelve *p.* *Ex* 24:4
hang the vail upon four *p.* 26:32
for the hanging five *p.* 37; 36:38
the 20 *p.*; hooks of the *p.* of silver.
27:10, 11; 38:10, 11, 12, 17
their *p.* ten. 27:12
their *p.* three. 14, 15; 38:14, 15
p. shall be four. 27:16
sockets for *p.* were of brass. 38:17
Samson between the *p. Judg* 16:25
the *p.* of the earth are. *1 Sam* 2:8
he cast two *p.* of brass. *1 Ki* 7:15
made of the almug trees *p.* 10:12
cut off gold from the *p.* *2 Ki* 18:16
brake in pieces the *p.* of brass and.
25:13, 16; *Jer* 52:17, 20
to rings and *p.* of marble. *Esth* 1:6
and the *p.* thereof tremble. *Job* 9:6
26:11
dissolved, I bear up the *p.* *Ps* 75:3
hewn out her seven *p.* *Pr* 9:1
cometh like *p.* of smoke ? *S of S* 3:6
he made the *p.* thereof of silver. 10
legs are as *p.* of marble set. 5:15
fire, and *p.* of smoke. *Joel* 2:30

Cephas who seemed to be *p. Gal 2:9*
his feet were as *p.* of fire. *Rev 10:1*

pilled
(*Revisions substitute the modern form* peeled)
Jacob *p.* white strakes. *Gen 30:37*
he set rods which he had *p.*   38

pillow, -s
put stones for his *p. Gen 28:11*
that he had put for his *p.*   18
a *p.* of goats' hair. *1 Sam 19:13, 16*
women that sew *p.* and. *Ezek 13:18*
I am against your *p.*   20
in the ship asleep on a *p. Mark 4:38*

pilots
O Tyrus, were thy *p. Ezek 27:8*
sound of the cry of thy *p.*   28

pin
with a *p.* . . . Samson awaked and
  went away with *p.* of. *Judg 16:14*
a *p.* of the vine tree ? *Ezek 15:3*

pine
p. away, in iniquities of their fathers
  shall they *p.* away. *Lev 26:39*
fetch olive and *p. Neh 8:15**
these *p.* away, stricken. *Lam 4:9*
ye shall *p.* away for. *Ezek 24:23*
if sins be upon us, and we *p. 33:10*

pineth
his teeth, and *p.* away. *Mark 9:18*

pine tree
p. and box tree together. *Isa 41:19*
the *p.* and box tree shall come. 60:13

pining
he will cut me off with *p. Isa 38:12**

pinnacle
setteth him on a *p.* of temple.
  Mat 4:5; Luke 4:9

pins
make all the *p.* of the tabernacle.
  Ex 27:19; 35:18; 38:20, 31; 39:40
their sockets, their *p.* and their cords.
  Num 3:37; 4:32

pipe, -s
of prophets with *p.*   *1 Sam 10:5*
the people piped with *p.*   *1 Ki 1:40*
the harp and *p.* are in. *Isa 5:12*
when one goeth with a *p.*   30:29
sound for Moab like *p. Jer 48:36*
workmanship of thy *p. Ezek 28:13*
and seven *p.* to the seven. *Zech 4:2*
through the golden *p.* empty.   12*
life, whether *p.* or harp. *1 Cor 14:7*

piped
people *p.* with pipes.   *1 Ki 1:40*
saying, We have *p.* unto you.
  Mat 11:17; Luke 7:32
be known what is *p.?*   *1 Cor 14:7*

pipers
voice of *p.* shall be. *Rev 18:22**

Pisgah
Balaam to the top of P. *Num 23:14*
get thee up into the top of P.
  Deut 3:27; 34:1
plain, under the springs of P.   4:29

Pisidia
came to Antioch in P. *Acts 13:14*
had passed throughout P.   14:24

piss
drink own *p.* with you. *2 Ki 18:27**
  Isa 36:12*
(*This word is used metaphorically for deep trouble, and for the depths of hell*)
was full of slime *p. Gen 14:10*
us cast him into some *p.* 37:20*, 24
owner of the *p.* shall. *Ex 21:34*
a *p.* wherein is water. *Lev 11:36*
quick into the *p. Num 16:30, 33*
hid themselves in *p.*   *1 Sam 13:6*
is now hid in some *p. 2 Sam 17:9*
cast Absalom into a great *p.*   18:17
Benaiah slew a lion in a *p.*   23:20
  1 Chr 11:22
Jehu slew them at the *p. 2 Ki 10:14*
down to the bars of the *p. Job 17:16*
back his soul from the *p.* 33:18, 30
from going down into the *p.* 24, 28

sunk down into the *p.*   *Ps 9:15*
them that go down into *p.*   28:1
not go down to the *p.*   30:3
blood, when I go down to the *p.?*   9
hid from me their net in a *p.*   35:7
up out of an horrible *p.*   40:2
to the *p.* of destruction.   55:23
let not the *p.* shut her mouth. 69:15
with them that go down into *p.* 88:4
hast laid me in the lowest *p.*   6
the proud have digged *p.*   119:85
let them be cast into deep *p.* 140:10
like unto them that go down into the
  p.   143:7 *Pr* 1:12
strange women is a deep *p. Pr 22:14*
woman is a narrow *p.*   23:27
fall himself into his own *p.*   28:10
a man shall flee to the *p.*; let no. 17
down to the sides of the *p. Isa 14:15*
to the stones of the *p.*   19
fear, and the *p.* and the snare. 24:17
  Jer 48:43, 44
cometh out of the midst of *p. Isa 24:18*
prisoners are gathered in the *p.*   22
water withal out of the *p.*   30:14*
hast delivered it from the *p.*   38:17
they that go down into the *p.*   18
he should not die in the *p.*   51:14
led us through a land of *p. Jer 2:6*
they came to the *p.* and found. 14:3†
into the midst of the *p.*   41:7
the *p.* which Asa made for fear.   9
anointed taken in their *p. Lam 4:20*
was taken in their *p. Ezek 19:4, 8*
with them that descend into the *p.*
  26:20; 28:8; 31:14, 16; 32:18, 24
     25, 29, 30
are set in the sides of the *p.* 32:23
of nettles and salt *p. Zeph 2:9*
prisoners out of the *p. Zech 9:11*
if it fall into a *p.* on sabbath.
  Mat 12:11; Luke 14:5*

see **bottomless, dig, digged**

pitch
p. it within and without with *p.*
  Gen 6:14
with slime and with *p.*   *Ex 2:3*
turned to *p.*, and the land thereof shall
  become burning *p. Isa 34:9*

pitch, *verb*
Israel shall *p.* every man. *Num 1:52*
the Levites shall *p.* round the.   53
man shall *p.* by his own standard. 2:2
camp of Judah *p.*   3
the Gershonites *p.*   3:23
sons of Kohath *p.*   29
Merari shall *p.*   35
you out a place to *p.* in. *Deut 1:33*
Joshua did *p.* twelve stones.
  Josh 4:20
nor shall the Arabian *p. Isa 13:20*
shepherds shall *p.* their. *Jer 6:3*

pitched
(*American Revision changes this word, when used intransitively, to* encamped)
Abram *p.* his tent, and. *Gen 12:8*
Lot *p.*   13:12
Isaac *p.* in valley.   26:17, 25
Jacob *p.* in mount, Laban *p.*   31:25
Jacob *p.* his tent before.   33:18
from Sin, Israel *p.* in. *Ex 17:1*
come to desert, and had *p.*   19:2
Moses took tabernacle, *p.* it.   33:7
when tabernacle is *p. Num 1:51*
so they *p.* by their standards. 2:34
at commandment of the Lord they *p.*
     9:18
the people *p.* in the wilderness. 12:16
Israel *p.* in Oboth.   21:10
p. in Ije-abarim.   11
Israel *p.* in Succoth.   33:5
they *p.* in Etham.   6
ambush *p.* on north side. *Josh 8:11*
set ark in tabernacle David had *p.*
  2 Sam 6:17
Israel and Absalom *p.* in land. 17:26
Israel *p.* before them. *1 Ki 20:27, 29*
Nebuchadnezzar *p.* against it.
  2 Ki 25:1; Jer 52:4
a place for the ark, and *p.* for it a
  tent. *1 Chr 15:1; 16:1; 2 Chr 1:4*
tabernacle which Lord *p. Heb 8:2*

pitcher, -s
let down *p.* I pray thee. *Gen 24:14*
Rebekah came with her *p.*   15, 45
empty *p.* and lamps within the *p.*
  Judg 7:16
they brake *p.* that were in.   19, 20
or the *p.* be broken at. *Eccl 12:6*
esteemed as earthen *p.? Lam 4:2*
man bearing a *p.* of water.
  Mark 14:13; Luke 22:10

pitied
also to be *p.* of all. *Ps 106:46*
and the Lord hath not *p. Lam 2:2*
  17, 21; 3:43
none eye *p.* thee, to do. *Ezek 16:5*

pitieth
like as a father *p.* his children, so
  the Lord *p.* them that. *Ps 103:13*
I will profane what your soul *p.*
  Ezek 24:21

pitiful
hands of *p.* women have. *Lam 4:10*
that the Lord is very *p. Jas 5:11*
love as brethren, be *p.*   *1 Pet 3:8**

pity
thine eye shall have no *p. Deut 7:16*
because he had no *p. 2 Sam 12:6*
to the afflicted, *p.* should. *Job 6:14**
have *p.* on me, *p.* on me.   19:21
looked for some to take *p. Ps 69:20*
that hath *p.* on poor. *Pr 19:17*
they shall have no *p.* on. *Isa 13:18*
in his love and in his *p.* he.   63:9
for who shall have *p.* upon ? *Jer 15:5*
nor have *p.* nor mercy.   21:7
nor will I have *p. Ezek 5:11; 7:4, 9*
  8:18; 9:10
eye spare, neither have ye *p.*   9:5
but I had *p.* for mine holy.   36:21
Edom did cast off all *p. Amos 1:11*
had *p.* on the gourd. *Jonah 4:10*
as I had *p.* on thee. *Mat 18:33**

pity, *verb*
nor shall thine eye *p.* him. *Deut 13:8*
  19:13, 21
thine eye shall not *p.*   25:12
for him that will *p.* the poor. *Pr 28:8*
I will not *p.* nor spare. *Jer 13:14*
Lord will *p.* his people. *Joel 2:18*
their own shepherds *p. Zech 11:5*
for I will no more *p.* inhabitants.   6

place
Lord said, Look from *p. Gen 13:14*
destroy and not spare the *p.?* 18:24
spare the *p.* for their sakes.   26
thou shalt shew at every *p.*   20:13
third day Abraham saw the *p.* 22:4
I may go unto mine own *p.*   30:25
into prison, the *p.* where.   40:3
p. whereon thou standest is holy.
  Ex 3:5; Josh 5:15
this people shall go to their *p.* in
  peace. *Ex 18:23*
to bring thee into the *p.* I.   23:20
he shall cast it by the *p. Lev 1:16*
first *p.* went standard. *Num 10:14*
ye shall eat it in every *p.* ye. 18:31
every *p.* whereon the soles of your.
  Deut 11:24; Josh 1:3
p. the Lord God shall choose.
  Deut 12:5, 14; 16:16
thy burnt offering in every *p.* 12:13
if the *p.* be too far.   21; 14:24
through thy land to my *p. Judg 11:19*
men of Israel gave *p.* to.   20:36
thou shalt mark the *p. Ruth 3:4*
and one of the same *p. 1 Sam 10:12*
went to their own *p.*   14:46
and David's *p.* was empty. 20:25, 27
and died in the same *p. 2 Sam 2:23*
in what *p.* my lord the king. 15:21
pit, or in some other *p.*   17:9
come upon him in some *p.*   12
to this day Absalom's *p.*   18:18*
eyes may be open toward *p. 1 Ki 8:29*
strike his hand over the *p. 2 Ki 5:11*
behold, *p.* where we dwell is.   6:1
grant me the *p.* of. *1 Chr 21:22*
to Ornan for the *p.* 600 shekels. 25
the priests stood in their *p.*
  2 Chr 30:16; 35:10
sons of Asaph, were in their *p.* 35:15

p. of my father's sepulchre. *Neh* 2:3
there was no *p.* for beast under. 14
in what *p.* ye hear sound of. 4:20
and Levites in their *p.* 13:11
her maids to the best *p.* *Esth* 2:9
deliverance from another *p.* 4:14
consumed out of their *p.* *Job* 6:17
shake the earth out of her *p.* 9:6
let my cry have no *p.* 16:18
where is the *p.* of understanding ?
28:12, 20
and he knoweth the *p.* thereof. 23
people are cut off in their *p.* 36:20
for darkness, where is the *p.*? 38:19
the wicked in their *p.* 40:12*
the *p.* where thine honour. *Ps* 26:8
my foot standeth in an even *p.* 12
thou art my hiding *p.* 32:7; 119:114
from the *p.* of his habitation. 33:14
the *p.* thereof shall know it. 103:16
the *p.* of judgement, in *Eccl* 3:16
all go unto one *p.* ; all are of. 20; 6:6
to field, till there be no *p.* *Isa* 5:8
shall remove out of her *p.* 13:13
and bring them to their *p.* 14:2
so that there is no *p.* clean. 28:8
barley and rye in their *p.*? 25
in every *p.* where grounded. 30:32*
p. is too strait for me, give *p.* 49:20
enlarge the *p.* of thy tent. 54:2
I will make the *p.* of my feet. 60:13
where is the *p.* of my rest ? 66:1
go ye now unto my *p.* *Jer* 7:12
till there be no *p.* 32; 19:11
glorious throne is the *p.* of. 17:12
waters come from another *p.* 18:14*
p. where they did offer. *Ezek* 6:13
p. of my throne shall Israel. 43:7
he shall burn it in the appointed *p.* 21
that no *p.* was found. *Dan* 2:35
the *p.* of his sanctuary was. 8:11
go and return to my *p.* *Hos* 5:15
dead bodies in every *p.* *Amos* 8:3
their *p.* is not known. *Nah* 3:17
p. shall not be found. *Zech* 10:10
again in her own *p.* 12:6; 14:10
be offered in every *p.* *Mal* 1:11
come, see the *p.* where the Lord lay.
Mat 28:6; *Mark* 16:6
in what *p.* soever ye. *Mark* 6:10
p. where it was written. *Luke* 4:17
two and two unto every *p.* 10:1
a Levite, when he was at the *p.* 32
to thee, Give this man *p.* 14:9
Jerusalem is the *p.* of. *John* 4:20
because my word hath no *p.* 8:37*
two days still in the same *p.* 11:6
Romans shall take away our *p.* 48
betrayed him, knew the *p.* 18:2
with one accord in one *p.* *Acts* 2:1
when they had prayed, the *p.* 4:31
the *p.* whereon thou standest. 7:33
or what is the *p.* of my rest ? 49
the *p.* of scripture which he. 8:32
rather give *p.* unto wrath. *Rom* 12:19
but now having no more *p.* 15:23
with all that in every *p.* call on Jesus
Christ. *1 Cor* 1:2
come together into one *p.* 11:20*
church be come into one *p.* 14:23*
his knowledge in every *p.* *2 Cor* 2:14
to whom we gave *p.* . . . no. *Gal* 2:5
nor give *p.* to the devil. *Eph* 4:27
in every *p.* your faith God-ward.
1 Thes 1:8
in another *p.*, Thou a priest. *Heb* 5:6
no *p.* should have been sought. 8:7
he found no *p.* of repentance. 12:17
the same *p.* sweet water. *Jas* 3:11*
nor was their *p.* found any. *Rev* 12:8
fly into wilderness to her *p.* 14
and there was found no *p.* 20:11
see **dwelling, holy,** *most* **holy**

a place
a *p.* where king's prisoners were.
Gen 39:20
appoint thee a *p.* to flee. *Ex* 21:13
behold, there is a *p.* by me. 33:21
place was a *p.* for cattle. *Num* 32:1
search you out a *p.* to pitch your.
Deut 1:33
a *p.* without the camp. 23:12
give him a *p.* in the city. *Josh* 20:4
32

where he could find a *p.* *Judg* 17:8
a *p.* where is no want of. 18:10
Saul set him up a *p.* *1 Sam* 15:12*
my servants to such a *p.* 21:2
let them give me a *p.* in. 27:5
a *p.* for Israel, that they may dwell in
a *p.* *2 Sam* 7:10; *1 Chr* 17:9
assigned Uriah to a *p.* *2 Sam* 11:16
I set there a *p.* for ark. *1 Ki* 8:21
1 Chr 15:1
let us make us a *p.* *2 Ki* 6:2
in such a *p.* shall be my camp. 8
beware thou pass not such a *p.* 9
I have built a *p.* for thy. *2 Chr* 6:2
there is a *p.* for gold. *Job* 28:1
until I find out a *p.* for. *Ps* 132:5
have a *p.* of refuge. *Pr* 14:26
a *p.* of refuge from rain. *Isa* 4:6
Lord will be to us a *p.* of. 33:21
for herself a *p.* of rest. 34:14
and within my walls a *p.* 56:5*
Achor a *p.* for the herds. 65:10
a *p.* for the spreading. *Ezek* 26:5, 14
I will give to Gog a *p.* of. 39:11
she is become a *p.* for. *Zeph* 2:15
that is to say, a *p.* of a skull.
Mat 27:33 ; *John* 19:17
found colt in a *p.* where. *Mark* 11:4*
I go to prepare a *p.* *John* 14:2, 3
in a certain *p.* testified. *Heb* 2:6*
he spake in a certain *p.* of the. 4:4*
called to go out into a *p.* he. 11:8
hath a *p.* prepared of God. *Rev* 12:6
into a *p.* called Armageddon. 16:16
see **choose**

high place
went up to an high *p.* *Num* 23:3*
is a sacrifice to-day in high *p.*
1 Sam 9:12
prophets coming from high *p.* 10:5
an end, Saul came to high *p.* 13
that was great high *p.* *1 Ki* 3:4
1 Chr 16:39
Solomon built an high *p.* *1 Ki* 11:7
high *p.* that Jeroboam . . . the high
p., burnt the high *p.* *2 Ki* 23:15
went to the high *p.* *2 Chr* 1:3
journey to high *p.* at Gibeon. 13
is weary on the high *p.* *Isa* 16:12
made a high *p.* in every street.
Ezek 16:24, 25, 31
the high *p.* whereunto ye go ? 20:29

his place
and Abraham returned to his *p.*
Gen 18:33
rose up and returned to his *p.* 31:35
neither rose from his *p.* *Ex* 10:23
in his *p.*, none go out of his *p.* 16:29
bright spot stay in his *p.* *Lev* 13:23
every man in his *p.* by. *Num* 2:17
Balaam rose up and returned to his
p. 24:25
to the gate of his *p.* *Deut* 21:19
be not cut off from his *p.* *Ruth* 4:10
laid down in his *p.* *1 Sam* 3:2
went and lay down in his *p.* 9
set Dagon in his *p.* again. 5:3
ark go down to his own *p.* 11; 6:2
go and see his *p.* where. 23:22
and Saul returned to his *p.* 26:25
that he may go again to his *p.* 29:4
ark of the Lord in his *p.* *2 Sam* 6:17
returned to his own *p.* 19:39
priests brought ark to his *p.*
1 Ki 8:6; *2 Chr* 5:7
every man out of his *p.* *1 Ki* 20:24
ark of the Lord to his *p.* *1 Chr* 15:3
and gladness are in his *p.* 16:27
chest to his *p.* again. *2 Chr* 24:11
king stood in his *p.* and made. 34:31
let men of his *p.* help. *Ezra* 1:4
for house of God to set it in his *p.*
2:68; 5:15; 6:7
every one from his own *p.* *Job* 2:11
neither shall his *p.* know him. 7:10
if he destroy him from his *p.* 8:18
is removed out of his *p.* 14:18
rock be removed out of his *p.*? 18:4
nor shall his *p.* any more. 20:9
hurleth him out of his *p.* 27:21
hands and hiss him out of his *p.* 23
is removed out of his *p.* 37:1
dayspring to know his *p.* 38:12

diligently consider his *p.* *Ps* 37:10
wandereth from his *p.* *Pr* 27:8
the sun hasteth to his *p.* *Eccl* 1:5
Lord cometh out of his *p.* *Isa* 26:21
his *p.* of defence shall be. 33:16
set him in his *p.*; from his *p.* shall he
not remove. 46:7
he is gone from his *p.* *Jer* 4:7
feed every one in his *p.* 6:3
glory of Lord from his *p.* *Ezek* 3:12
Lord cometh out of his *p.* *Mi* 1:3
worship every one from his *p.*
Zeph 2:11
grow up out of his *p.* *Zech* 6:12
thy sword into his *p.* *Mat* 26:52
might go to his own *p.* *Acts* 1:25
candlestick out of his *p.* *Rev* 2:5

in the place
not, am I in the *p.* of God ? *Gen* 50:19
plant them in the *p.* *Ex* 15:17
kill it in the *p.* where they kill.
Lev 4:24, 29, 33; 6:25; 7:2
in the *p.* of the boil there. 13:19
in the *p.* where the cloud. *Num* 9:17
inheritance be in the *p.* 33:54
twelve stones in the *p.* *Josh* 4:9
drunk water in the *p.* *1 Ki* 13:22
in the *p.* where dogs licked. 21:19
in the *p.* that David. *2 Chr* 3:1
sore broken us in the *p.* *Ps* 44:19
and stand not in the *p.* *Pr* 25:6
in the *p.* where the tree. *Eccl* 11:3
but he shall die in the *p.* *Jer* 22:12
38:9; 42:22
in the *p.* where the king dwelleth.
Ezek 17:16
judge thee in the *p.* where. 21:30
that in the *p.* where it was said.
Hos 1; 10; *Rom* 9:26
not stay long in the *p.* of. *Hos* 13:13
in the *p.* where crucified. *John* 19:41

of the place
men of the *p.* asked him; lest men
of *p.* should kill. *Gen* 26:7
all the men of the *p.* 29:22
the name of the *p.* Peniel. 32:30
name of *p.* Succoth. 33:17
name of *p.* Beth-el. 35:15
name of the *p.* Massah. *Ex* 17:7
name of the *p.* Taberah. *Num* 11:3
of the *p.* twelve stones. *Josh* 4:3
name of the *p.* Gilgal. 5:9
of *p.* called valley of Achor. 7:26
the men of the *p.* were. *Judg* 19:16
Naomi went forth out of the *p.*
Ruth 1:7
called name of the *p.* Perez-uzzah.
2 Sam 6:8
pattern of the *p.* of. *1 Chr* 28:11
name of the *p.*, valley. *2 Chr* 20:26
breadth of the *p.* left. *Ezek* 41:11
raise them out of the *p.* *Joel* 3:7
end of the *p.* thereof. *Nah* 1:1

that place
called *that p.* Beer-sheba. *Gen* 21:31
that *p.* Jehovah-jireh. 22:14
called name of that *p.* Beth-el. 28:19
name of that *p.* Mahanaim. 32:2
asked men of that *p.* 38:21
name of that *p.* Kibroth. *Num* 11:34
of them out of that *p.* *Deut* 12:3
the sentence they of that *p.* 17:10
name of that *p.* Bochim. *Judg* 2:5
that *p.* Ramath-lehi. 15:17
called that *p.* Selah-. *1 Sam* 23:28
that *p.* was called Helkath-hazzurim.
2 Sam 2:16
called that *p.* Baal-perazim. 5:20
1 Chr 14:11
that *p.* is called Perez-. *1 Chr* 13:11
men of that *p.* had. *Mat* 14:35
ye depart from that *p.* *Mark* 6:10
multitude being in that *p.* *John* 5:13
was in that *p.* where Martha. 11:30
both we and they of that *p.*
Acts 21:12

this place
bring them out of this *p.* *Gen* 19:12
we will destroy this *p.* 13
get out of this *p.* 14
fear of God is not in this *p.* 20:11
Lord is in this *p.* 28:16

dreadful is *this p.*   Gen 28:17
no harlot in *this p.*   38:21, 22
God hath given me in *this p.*   48:9
brought you out from *this p. Ex* 13:3
us unto *this* evil *p.*   Num 20:5
bare thee till ye came to *this p.*
     Deut 1:31; 9:7; 11:5
he hath brought us into *this p.* 26:9
when ye came unto *this p.*   29:7
makest thou in *this p.?*   *Judg* 18:3
prayer toward *this p. 1 Ki* 8:29, 30
  35; *2 Chr* 6:20, 21, 26, 40; 7:15
nor drink water in *this p. 1 Ki* 13:8, 16
come not against *this p. 2 Ki* 18:25
I will bring evil on *this p.* 22:16, 17
   20; *2 Chr* 34:24, 25, 28
and have chosen *this p. 2 Chr* 7:12
this the *p.* of him that. *Job* 18:21
innocent blood in *this p.*   *Jer* 7:6
be poured out on *this p.*   20
you assured peace in *this p.* 14:13
sons nor daughters in *this p.* 16:2
cause to cease out of *this p.* the. 9
will bring evil upon *this p.* 19:3
they estranged *this p.,* filled *this p.* 4
that *this p.* shall no more be. 6
thus will I do unto *this p.* 12; 40:2
went forth out of *this p.* 22:11; 24:5
restore you to *this p.* 27:22; 32:37
I will bring to *this p.* all. 28:3, 6
I will bring again to *this p.* 4
you to return to *this p.* 29:10
again be heard in *this p.* the. 33:10
ye shall see *this p.* no more. 42:18
punish you in *this p.* 44:29
hast spoken against *this p.* 51:62
this is the *p.* where the priests shall
  boil the offering. *Ezek* 46:20
of Baal from *this p.*   *Zeph* 1:4
in *this p.* will I give peace. *Hag* 2:9
in *this p.* one greater. *Mat* 12:6
into *this p.* of torment. *Luke* 16:28
from Galilee to *this p.* 23:5
shall destroy *this p.*   *Acts* 6:14
forth and serve me in *this p.* 7:7
against the law and *this p.* 21:28
and in *this p.* again, if they. *Heb* 4:5

thy place
restore thee to *thy p.*   Gen 40:13*
flee thou to *thy p.*   *Num* 24:11
return to *thy p.* and. *2 Sam* 15:19
rise against thee, leave not *thy p.*
     Eccl 10:4
shalt remove from *thy p. Ezek* 12:3
     38:15

to or *unto* the place
Abram went *unto the p.* Gen 13:3, 4
went *unto the p.* of which. 22:3, 9
to bring you *unto the p.*   *Ex* 3:8
lead people *unto the p.* of. 32:34
journeying *to the p.* of. *Num* 10:29
go up *to the p.* which Lord. 14:40
carried stones *to the p.*   *Josh* 4:8
come *to the p.* where. *1 Sam* 20:19
as many as came *to the p.* stood.
     2 Sam 2:23
sent *to the p.* which man. *2 Ki* 6:10
bring ark *to the p.* that. *1 Chr* 15:12
I will bring them *to the p. Neh* 1:9
they go *to the p.* that. *Ps* 104:8
present brought *to the p.*   *Isa* 18:7
I will do *to the p.* which I. *Jer* 7:14
will bring you again *to the p.* 29:14
was entered *into the p.* *Acts* 25:23

place, verb
and *p.* such over them. *Ex* 18:21
in the *p.* which he shall choose to *p.*
    Deut 14:23; 16:2, 6, 11; 26:2
and *p.* them in the house. *Ezra* 6:5
and I will *p.* salvation in. *Isa* 46:13
I shall *p.* you in your. *Ezek* 37:14, 26
shall *p.* the abomination. *Dan* 11:31
p. them in their houses. *Hos* 11:11*
bring them again to *p.* them.*Zech* 10:6

placed
God *p.* at east of the.   Gen 3:24
Joseph *p.* his father and his. 47:11
Jeroboam *p.* in Beth-el. *1 Ki* 12:32
and *p.* them in Halah. *2 Ki* 17:6
and *p.* them in the cities of. 24, 26
he *p.* in the chariot cities. *2 Chr* 1:14
he made tables, *p.* them in the. 4:8

he *p.* forces in all the.   *2 Chr* 17:2
of old, since man was *p.*   *Job* 20:4
the tent which he had *p.*   *Ps* 78:60
that they may be *p.* alone. *Isa* 5:8*
which *p.* sand for the.   *Jer* 5:22
eagle *p.* it by the great. *Ezek* 17:7

places
will keep thee in all *p.*   Gen 28:15
in all *p.* where I record.   *Ex* 20:24
utterly destroy all the *p. Deut* 12:2
abode in their *p.* till.   *Josh* 5:8
delivered in the *p.* of.   *Judg* 5:11
to one of these *p.* to lodge. 19:13
Israel in all those *p.*   *1 Sam* 7:16
sent presents to all the *p.* 30:31
in all the *p.* wherein? *2 Sam* 7:7
put down priests in *p.*   *2 Ki* 23:5
he filled their *p.* with the bones. 16
from all *p.* whence ye.   *Neh* 4:12
in lower *p.* and on higher *p.* 13
Levites out of all their *p.* 12:27
where are the dwelling *p.?Job* 21:28*
dens and remain in their *p.* 37:8*
he sitteth in lurking *p.* of. *Ps* 10:8
fallen to me in pleasant *p.* 16:6
afraid out of their close *p.* 18:45
set them in slippery *p.* 73:18
the dark *p.* of the earth are. 74:20
all his works, in all *p.* 103:22
they ran in the dry *p.* like. 105:41
he shall fill the *p.* with the. 110:6
she standeth in the *p.* of. *Pr* 8:2*
that art in the secret *p. S of S* 2:14
dwell in quiet resting *p. Isa* 32:18
straight, and rough *p.* plain. 40:4
I will make the crooked *p.* 45:2
a wind from those *p.* shall. *Jer* 4:12
in all *p.* whither I have. 8:3; 29:14
from *p.* about Jerusalem. 17:26
to be a taunt and a curse in all *p.* 24:9
take witnesses in the *p.* 32:44
Jews returned out of all *p.* 40:12
give for a prey in all *p.* 45:5
he hath destroyed his *p.* *Lam* 2:6
deliver them out of all *p. Ezek* 34:12
I will make the *p.* round my hill. 26
he said, These are the *p.* of. 46:24*
but the miry *p.* thereof. 47:11
of bread in all your *p.*   *Amos* 4:6
I will give thee *p.* to walk. *Zech* 3:7
he walketh through dry *p.*
     Mat 12:43; *Luke* 11:24
some fell on stony *p. Mat* 13:5, 20
famines and earthquakes in divers *p.*
   24:7; *Mark* 13:8; *Luke* 21:11
we accept it in all *p.*   *Acts* 24:3
blessed us in heavenly *p.*   *Eph* 1:3
at his own right hand in heavenly *p.* 20
together in heavenly *p.* in Christ. 2:6
to powers in heavenly *p.* might. 3:10
Christ are manifest in all *p. Phil* 1:13
island moved out of their *p. Rev* 6:14

see desolate, holy

high places
will destroy your *high p. Lev* 26:30
consumed lords of *high p.* of.
     Num 21:28
up into the *high p.* of Baal. 22:41
pluck down all their *high p.* 33:52
made him ride on *high p. Deut* 32:13
tread upon their *high p.* 33:29
their lives in the *high p. Judg* 5:18
people hide themselves in *high p.*
     1 Sam 13:6*
of Israel slain in *high p. 2 Sam* 1:19
thou wast slain in thy *high p.* 25
setteth me on my *high p.* 22:34
     Ps 18:33
people sacrificed in *high p. 1 Ki* 3:2
   2 *Ki* 17:32; *2 Chr* 33:17
incense in *high p.*   *1 Ki* 3:3; 22:43
  2 *Ki* 12:3; 15:4, 35; 16:4; 17:11
made an house of *high p. 1 Ki* 12:31
in Beth-el the priests of *high p.* 32
offer the priests of the *high p.* 13:2
all the houses of the *high p.* 32
the lowest of the people priests of
  the *high p.* 33; *2 Ki* 17:32
but the *high p.* were.   *1 Ki* 15:14
  22:43; *2 Ki* 12:3; 14:4; 15:4, 35
in houses of *high p.*   *2 Ki* 17:29
removed the *high p.* 18:4, 22
burn incense in the *high p.* 23:5

defiled the *high p.*... and brake down
  the *high p.* of gates. *2 Ki* 23:8, 13
  2 *Chr* 31:1; 32:12; *Isa* 36:7
priests of *high p.* came.   *2 Ki* 23:9
all the priests of the *high p.* 20
ordained priests for *high p.*
     2 Chr 11:15
Asa took away the *high p.* 14:3, 5
the *high p.* were not taken away.
     15:17; 20:33
took away the *high p.* 17:6
Jehoram made *high p.* 21:11
Ahaz made *high p.* 28:25
purge Jerusalem from *high p.* 34:3
peace in his *high p.*   *Job* 25:2
provoked him with their *high p.*
     Ps 78:58
on the top of the *high p.*   *Pr* 8:2
seat in the *high p.* of the city. 9:14
is gone up to the *high p.*   *Isa* 15:2
I will open rivers in *high p.* 41:18*
pastures shall be in all *high p.* 49:9*
cause thee to ride on *high p.* 58:14
thine eyes to the *high p.*   *Jer* 3:2*
a voice was heard on the *high p.* 21*
a dry wind in the *high p.* of. 4:11*
a lamentation in the *high p.* 7:29
come up on all the *high p.* 12:12
did stand in the *high p.* 14:6*
I will give thy *high p.* for sin. 17:3
become as the *high p.* of the forest.
     26:18; *Mi* 3:12
I will cause to cease in Moab him
  that offereth in *high p. Jer* 48:35
I will destroy your *high p. Ezek* 6:3
deckedst thy *high p.* with. 16:16
break down thy *high p.* 39
the ancient *high p.* are ours. 36:2
the *high p.* of Aven. *Hos* 10:8
treadeth on *high p.* of earth.
     Amos 4:13; *Mi* 1:3
the *high p.* of Isaac shall. *Amos* 7:9
what are the *high p.* of? *Mi* 1:5
to walk on mine *high p.* *Hab* 3:19
wickedness in *high p.* *Eph* 6:12

see built

waste places
waste *p.* of fat ones shall. *Isa* 5:17
comfort all her *waste p.* 51:3
sing together, ye *waste p.* 52:9
build the old *waste p.* 58:12

plague
and I will *p.* them that. *Ps* 89:23*

plague, substantive
yet I will bring one *p.*   *Ex* 11:1
the *p.* shall not be on you to. 12:13
there be no *p.* among them. 30:12
when the hair in the *p. Lev* 13:3, 17
if the *p.* spread not in. 5, 6; 14:48
a *p.* then priest shall see the *p.*
  13:30, 31, 32, 50, 51, 55; 14:37
he is a leprous man, his *p.* is. 13:44
and shut up it that hath the *p.* 50
or woof, it is a spreading *p.* 57*
if *p.* be departed from them. 58
there is as it were a *p.* in. 14:35
be no *p.* among Israel. *Num* 8:19
people with a very great *p.* 11:33
died by the *p.* before the Lord. 14:37
wrath is gone out, the *p.* 16:46, 47
the *p.* was stayed. 48, 50; 25:8
that died in the *p.* 16:49; 25:9
every *p.* which is not. *Deut* 28:61
not cleansed, although there was *p.*
     Josh 22:17
one *p.* was on you all. *1 Sam* 6:4
that *p.* may be stayed. *2 Sam* 24:21
     1 Chr 21:22
whatever *p.* or sickness. *1 Ki* 8:37
shall know every man the *p.* of. 38
with a great *p.* will the. *2 Chr* 21:14
nor any *p.* come nigh.   *Ps* 91:10
p. brake in upon them. 106:29
judgement, so *p.* was stayed. 30
this shall be the *p.* *Zech* 14:12, 18
she was healed of that *p. Mark* 5:29
and be whole of thy *p.* 34
because of the *p.* of hail. *Rev* 16:21

plagued
the Lord *p.* Pharaoh.   Gen 12:17
Lord *p.* the people for. *Ex* 32:35*
p. Egypt, and afterwards. *Josh* 24:35

that they should be *p.*   *1 Chr* 21:17
nor are they *p.* like other.   *Ps* 73:5
all the day have I been *p.*   14

plagues

Pharaoh with great *p.*   *Gen* 12:17
this time send all my *p.*   *Ex* 9:14
bring seven times more *p.* on you.
    Lev 26:21
make thy *p.* wonderful. *Deut* 28:59
when they see the *p.* of.   29:22
smote Egyptians with *p.*   *1 Sam* 4:8
and hiss because of all the *p. Jer* 19:8
    49:17; 50:13
O death, I will be thy *p. Hos* 13:14
to touch him, as many as had *p.*
    Mark 3:10
cured many of their *p. Luke* 7:21
were not killed by these *p. Rev* 9:20
to smite earth with *p.*   11:6
who hath power over these *p.*   16:9
that ye receive not of her *p.*   18:4
therefore shall her *p.* come in one. 8
God shall add to him the *p.*   22:18
    see seven

plain, adjective

Jacob was a *p.* man.   *Gen* 25:27
lead me in a *p.* path.   *Ps* 27:11
they are *p.* to him that.   *Pr* 8:9
of the righteous is made *p.*   15:19*
when he made *p.* the face. *Isa* 28:25
straight, and rough places *p.*   40:4
come on the *p.* country. *Jer* 48:21
write the vision, make it *p. Hab* 2:2
loosed, and he spake *p. Mark* 7:35

plain, substantive

they found a *p.* in the land. *Gen* 11:2
and Lot beheld all the *p.* of.   13:10
chose him all the *p.* of Jordan.   11
Lot dwelt in cities of the *p.*   12
Abram came and dwelt in the *p.* 18*
    14:13*
neither stay thou in all the *p.*   19:17
those cities in all the *p.*   25
Joshua took the valley and the *p.*
    Josh 11:16*
made Abimelech king by *p.* of pillar.
    Judg 9:6*
the Ammonites to the *p.*   11:33*
come to the *p.* of Tabor. *1 Sam* 10:3*
his men were in the *p.*   23:24*
men walked through *p. 2 Sam* 2:29*
Rechab gat them through the *p.* 4:7*
I will tarry in the *p.* till I hear. 15:28*
ran by the way of the *p.*   18:23
in *p.* of Jordan did king.   *1 Ki* 7:46
against them in the *p.*   20:23, 25
king went towards the *p. 2 Ki* 25:4*
    Jer 52:7
repaired the priests of *p. Neh* 3:22
they shall come from *p.* bringing
burnt offerings.   *Jer* 17:26*
against thee, O rock of the *p.* 21:13
p. shall be destroyed, as Lord. 48:8
go forth in the *p.*   *Ezek* 3:22, 23
vision that I saw in the *p.*   8:4

plainly

if the servant *p.* say, I.   *Ex* 21:5
words of this law very *p. Deut* 27:8
did I *p.* appear unto the house of thy
father?   *1 Sam* 2:27*
he told us *p.* that the asses.   10:16
letter hath been *p.* read. *Ezra* 4:18
stammerers shall speak *p. Isa* 32:4
if the Christ, tell us *p. John* 10:24
to them *p.*, Lazarus is dead.   11:14
shew you *p.* of the Father.   16:25
now speakest thou *p.* and.   29
such things declare *p. Heb* 11:14*

plainness

hope, we use great *p.*   *2 Cor* 3:12*

plains

Lord appeared in the *p. Gen* 18:1*
Israel pitched in *p.* of Moab.
    Num 22:1; 33:48
who numbered Israel in the *p.* 26:63
spoil unto the camp in the *p.*   31:12
the Lord spake to Moses in the *p.*
    33:50; 35:1
Lord commanded in the *p.*   36:13
Moses went up from the *p.* of Moab.
    Deut 34:1
Israel wept for Moses in the *p.*   8

---

lodge not in the *p.* of. *2 Sam* 17:16*
Chaldees overtook him in the *p.*
    2 Ki 25:5; *Jer* 39:5; 52:8
trees in the low *p.*   *1 Chr* 27:28
sycamores in low *p.*   *2 Chr* 9:27
had much cattle in the *p.*   26:10

plaister, substantive

lay it for a *p.* on boil.   *Isa* 38:21†
wrote on the *p.* of the wall. *Dan* 5:5†

plaister, verb

take mortar and shall *p.* house.
    Lev 14:42†
and *p.* them with *p.*   *Deut* 27:2†, 4

plaistered

if the plague come again after it is *p.*
    Lev 14:43†
spread after the house was *p.*   48†

plaiting

adorning let it not be *p.*   *1 Pet* 3:3

planes

fitteth the image with *p. Isa* 44:13

planets

incense to sun, moon, *p.*   *2 Ki* 23:5

planks

the floor with *p.* of fir.   *1 Ki* 6:15*
were thick *p.* on face.   *Ezek* 41:25*
chambers of house, and thick *p.* 26*

plant, substantive

Lord God made every *p.*   *Gen* 2:5
bring forth boughs like *p. Job* 14:9
of Judah his pleasant *p.*   *Isa* 5:7
thou shalt make thy *p.* grow. 17:11
before him as a tender *p.*   53:2
turned into degenerate *p. Jer* 2:21
for them a *p.* of renown. *Ezek* 34:29*
every *p.* my Father hath. *Mat* 15:13

plant, verb

p. them in mount of thy.   *Ex* 15:17
shalt not *p.* a grove.   *Deut* 16:21
thou shalt *p.* a vineyard. 28:30, 39
moreover, I will *p.* them.
    2 Sam 7:10; *1 Chr* 17:9
a sign unto thee, Ye shall *p.* vineyards, and eat the fruits. *2 Ki* 19:29
    Isa 37:30; 65:21; *Ezek* 28:26
    Amos 9:14
fields, and *p.* vineyards. *Ps* 107:37
shalt *p.* pleasant plants.   *Isa* 17:10
I will *p.* in the wilderness.   41:19
that I may *p.* heavens, and lay. 51:16
shall not *p.* and another eat.   65:22
set thee to build and to *p. Jer* 1:10
kingdom to build and to *p.*   18:9
I will *p.* and not pluck. 24:6; 42:10
p. gardens, and eat the fruit. 29:5, 28
shall *p.* vines on the mountains. 31:5
over them to build and to *p.*   28
I will *p.* them in this land.   32:41
nor shall you sow seed, nor *p.* 35:7
I will *p.* it on a high. *Ezek* 17:22, 23
Lord build and *p.* that.   - 36:36
he shall *p.* tabernacles. *Dan* 11:45
I will *p.* them upon their. *Amos* 9:15
they shall *p.* vineyards, but not drink
the wine thereof.   *Zeph* 1:13

plantation

it by furrows of her *p.*   *Ezek* 17:7

planted

the Lord God *p.* a garden. *Gen* 2:8
Noah *p.* a vineyard.   9:20
Abram *p.* a grove.   21:33
trees which Lord hath *p. Num* 24:6
that hath *p.* a vineyard? *Deut* 20:6
of oliveyards ye *p.* not. *Josh* 24:13
like a tree *p.* by the rivers.
    Ps 1:3; *Jer* 17:8
heathen, and *p.* the vine. *Ps* 80:8
which thy right hand hath *p.*   15
those that be *p.* in the house. 92:13
he that *p.* the ear, shall he?   94:9
whom the Lord hath *p.*   104:16
I *p.* me vineyards.   *Eccl* 2:4
I *p.* trees.   5
to pluck up that which is *p.*   3:2
p. it with the choicest vine. *Isa* 5:2
yea, they shall not be *p.* nor. 40:24
I had *p.* thee a noble vine. *Jer* 2:21
for the Lord of hosts that *p.* 11:17
thou hast *p.* them, they have. 12:2
what I have *p.* I will pluck up. 45:4

---

p. it in a fruitful field. *Ezek* 17:5, 8
yea, behold, being *p.* shall it?   10
p. by the waters: she was.   19:10
now she is *p.* in the wilderness. 13
Ephraim is *p.* in a.   *Hos* 9:13
p. pleasant vineyards.   *Amos* 5:11
every plant, which my heavenly
Father hath not *p.*   *Mat* 15:13
man *p.* a vineyard.   21:33
    Mark 12:1; *Luke* 20:9
a fig tree *p.* in vineyard. *Luke* 13:6
and be thou *p.* in the sea.   17:6
they bought, they sold, they *p.*   28
if we have been *p.* together in his
death.   *Rom* 6:5*
I have *p.*, Apollos.   *1 Cor* 3:6

plantedst

which thou *p.* not.   *Deut* 6:11
out heathen and *p.* them.   *Ps* 44:2

planters

p. shall plant, and eat.   *Jer* 31:5

planteth

her hands she *p.* vineyard. *Pr* 31:16
he *p.* an ash, and the.   *Isa* 44:14
he that *p.* any thing.   *1 Cor* 3:7
he that *p.* and he that watereth.   8
who *p.* a vineyard and eateth?   9:7

planting

branch of my *p.* work.   *Isa* 60:21
they might be called the *p.*   61:3

plantings

I will make Samaria as *p.* of. *Mi* 1:6

plants

that dwell among *p.*   *1 Chr* 4:23*
thy children like olive *p. Ps* 128:3
that our sons may be as *p.*   144:12
thy *p.* as an orchard. *S of S* 4:13*
broken down principal *p.*   *Isa* 16:8
shalt thou plant pleasant *p.*   17:10
thy *p.* are gone over sea. *Jer* 48:32*
rivers running round about his *p.*
    Ezek 31:4*

plat

in this *p.*, now take and cast him into
the *p.* of ground.   *2 Ki* 9:26

plate

thou shalt make a *p.*   *Ex* 28:36
made the *p.* of holy crown.   39:30
he put the golden *p.*   *Lev* 8:9

plates

beat gold into thin *p.*   *Ex* 39:3
of censers broad *p.*   *Num* 16:38
were made broad *p.* for a.   39*
base had *p.* of brass.   *1 Ki* 7:30*
silver spread into *p.* is.   *Jer* 10:9

platted

had *p.* a crown of thorns. *Mat* 27:29*
    Mark 15:17*; *John* 19:2*

platter

clean outside of the *p.* but within.
    Mat 23:25; *Luke* 11:39

play

the people rose up to *p.*   *Ex* 32:6
    1 Cor 10:7
to *p.* the whore in her. *Deut* 22:21
shall *p.* with his hand. *1 Sam* 16:16
now a man that can *p.* well.   17
this fellow to *p.* the madman. 21:15
let young men arise and *p.* before.
    2 Sam 2:14
will I *p.* before the Lord.   6:21
us *p.* the men for our people. 10:12
the beasts of the field *p. Job* 40:20
p. with him as with a bird?   41:5
p. skilfully with a loud.   *Ps* 33:3
leviathan whom thou madest to *p.*
therein.   104:26
sucking child shall *p.* cn.   *Isa* 11:8
and can *p.* well on an.   *Ezek* 33:32

played

and his concubine *p.*   *Judg* 19:2
David *p.* with his hand.
    1 Sam 16:23; 18:10; 19:9
women answered one another as
they *p.*   18:7
I have *p.* the fool, and have. 26:21
David and all Israel *p. 2 Sam* 6:5
    1 Chr 13:8
pass when the minstrel *p. 2 Ki* 3:15
hast *p.* the whore with. *Ezek* 16:28
    see harlot

player
who is a cunning p. 1 Sam 16:16

players
the p. on instruments. Ps 68:25*
as well the singers as the p. 87:7*

playeth
as to a woman that Ezek 23:44

playing
seen a son of Jesse cunning in p.
1 Sam 16:18
David dancing and p. 1 Chr 15:29
were the damsels p. Ps 68:25
boys and girls p. in the. Zech 8:5

plea
too hard between p. and p. Deut 17:8

plead
ye p. for Baal ? he that will p. for.
Judg 6:31†
saying, Let Baal p. against him. 32†
set me a time to p.? Job 9:19*
who is he that will p. with? 13:19*
O that one might p. for a man. 16:21*
p. against me my reproach. 19:5
will he p. against me with his ? 23:6*
seek judgement, p. for the widow.
Isa 1:17
Lord standeth up to p. and. 3:13†
let us p. together, declare. 43:26
by fire will the Lord p. 66:16
p. with you, and with your children's
children will I p. Jer 2:9†, 35*
wherefore will ye p. with me ? 29
righteous art thou, O Lord, when I p.
with thee. 12:1†
Lord will p. with all flesh, 25:31†
will p. with him there. Ezek 17:20†
I p. with you face to face. 20:35†
so will I p. with you, saith the. 36†
I will p. against him with. 38:22†
p. with your mother, p. Hos 2:2†
I will p. with them for my people.
Joel 3:2†
Lord will p. with Israel. Mi 6:2
see cause

pleaded
Lord that p. the cause. 1 Sam 25:39
hast p. causes of my soul. Lam 3:58
like as I p. with your fathers in the.
Ezek 20:36*

pleadeth
with God, as a man p. Job 16:21†
that p. cause of his people. Isa 51:22
justice, nor any p. for truth. 59:4

pleading
hearken to the p. of my lips. Job 13:6

pleasant
every tree grow that is p. Gen 2:9
was p. to the eyes, and a tree. 3:6*
saw the land that it was p. 49:15
Saul and Jonathan were p. in their
lives. 2 Sam 1:23
Jonathan, very p. hast thou. 26
whatever is p. they. 1 Ki 20:6
situation of this city is p. 2 Ki 2:19
made treasuries for p. jewels.
2 Chr 32:27*
fallen to me in p. places. Ps 16:6
bring hither the p. harp with. 81:2
they despised the p. land. 106:24
how p. for brethren to dwell. 133:1
to his name, for it is p. 135:3
147:1
when knowledge is p. to. Pr 2:10
the loving hind and p. roe. 5:19
bread eaten in secret is p. 9:17
words of the pure are p. 15:26
p. words are as honeycomb. 16:24
for it is p. if thou keep them. 22:18
shall be filled with all p. riches. 24:4
p. it is for the eyes to behold the sun.
Eccl 11:7
my beloved, yea p. S of S 1:16
an orchard with p. fruits. 4:13*
come and eat his p. fruits. 16*
fair and p. art thou, O love. 7:6
are all manner of p. fruits. 13
Lord upon all p. pictures. Isa 2:16
men of Judah his p. plant. 5:7
shall cry in their p. palaces. 13:22
shalt thou plant p. plants. 17:10
they lament for p. fields. 32:12

thy borders of p. stones. Isa 54:12†
p. things are laid waste. 64:11
I give thee a p. land ? Jer 3:19
my p. portion a desolate. 12:10
p. places of the wilderness. 23:10
shall fall like a p. vessel. 25:34
dear son ? is he a p. child ? 31:20†
she remembered all her p. Lam 1:7
spread his hand on her p. things. 10
they have given their p. things. 11
slew all that were p. to the eye. 2:4
they shall destroy thy p. houses.
Ezek 26:12
song of one that hath p. voice. 33:32
great toward the p. land. Dan 8:9*
ate no p. bread, nor came flesh. 10:3
honour a god with p. things. 11:38
p. places nettles shall. Hos 9:6
Ephraim is planted in a p. place. 13
your temples my p. things. Joel 3:5†
ye planted p. vineyards. Amos 5:11
ye cast out from p. houses. Mi 2:9
glory out of all the p. Nah 2:9†
laid the p. land desolate. Zech 7:14
offering of Jerusalem be p. Mal 3:4

pleasantness
her ways are ways of p. Pr 3:17

please
if she p. not her master. Ex 21:8
peradventure it will p. God that
thou mayest curse. Num 23:27
if it p. my father to. 1 Sam 20:13
let it p. thee to bless the house.
2 Sam 7:29; 1 Chr 17:27
if it p. I will give thee. 1 Ki 21:6
if thou p. they will be thy servants.
2 Chr 10:7
if it p. the king, and if thy servant
have found. Neh 2:5, 7; Esth 1:19
3:9; 5:8; 7:3; 8:5; 9:13
if p. God to destroy me. Job 6:9
his children shall seek to p. 20:10
this also shall p. the Lord. Ps 69:31
man's ways p. the Lord. Pr 16:7
nor awake my love till he p.
S of S 2:7; 3:5; 8:4
p. themselves in children. Isa 2:6
accomplish that which I p. 55:11
choose the things that p. me. 56:4
those things that p. him. John 8:29
in the flesh cannot p. God. Rom 8:8
and not to p. ourselves. 15:1
let every one p. his neighbour. 2
careth how he may p. 1 Cor 7:32
p. his wife. 33
how she may p. her husband. 34
p. all men in all things. 10:33
do I seek to p. men ? Gal 1:10
p. not God are contrary. 1 Thes 2:15
ought to walk and to p. God. 4:1
may p. him who hath chosen him.
2 Tim 2:4
and to p. them well in all things.
Tit 2:9
but without faith it is impossible to
p. him. Heb 11:6

pleased
Esau seeing daughters of Canaan p.
not Isaac. Gen 28:8
and thou wast p. with me. 33:10
and their words p. Hamor. 34:18
it p. Pharaoh well and his. 45:16
Balaam saw it p. the Lord. Num 24:1
the saying p. me well. Deut 1:23
Israel ... it p. them. Josh 22:30
if Lord were p. to kill us. Judg 13:23
he talked with her, and she p. 14:7
it p. Lord to make you his people.
1 Sam 12:22
it p. Saul that Michal loved. 18:20
it p. David to be the king's. 26
what the king did p. all. 2 Sam 3:36
saying p. Absalom well, and. 17:4
if all we had died, then it had p. 19:6
Solomon's speech p. the. 1 Ki 3:10
Solomon gave, p. not Hiram. 9:12
the thing p. the king. 2 Chr 30:4*
Neh 2:6; Esth 1:21; 2:4
the maiden p. the king. Esth 2:9
the thing p. Haman, he caused. 5:14
be p. O Lord, to deliver. Ps 40:13
be p. with sacrifices. 51:19

he hath done whatsoever he p.
Ps 115:3; 135:6; Jonah 1:14
yet it p. the Lord to bruise. Isa 53:10
it p. Darius to set over. Dan 6:1
will Lord be p. with thousands of
rams ? Mi 6:7
offer it, will he be p.? Mal 1:8
daughter of Herodias danced before
them, and p. Mat 14:6; Mark 6:22
saying p. whole multitude. Acts 6:5
because Herod saw it p. the. 12:3
for even Christ p. not. Rom 15:3
hath p. them of Macedonia. 26, 27
it p. God by foolishness. 1 Cor 1:21
and she be p. to dwell with him. 7:12
and if he be p. to dwell with her. 13
set members as it hath p. him. 12:18
a body as it hath p. him. 15:38
for if I yet p. men, I. Gal 1:10
when it p. God to reveal his Son. 15
it p. Father that in him all. Col 1:19
testimony, that he p. God. Heb 11:5

well pleased
Lord is well p. for his. Isa 42:21
beloved Son, in whom I am well p.
Mat 3:17; 12:18; 17:5; Mark 1:11
Luke 3:22; 2 Pet 1:17
them God was not well p. 1 Cor 10:5
sacrifices God is well p. Heb 13:16

men pleasers
not with eye service, as men p.
Eph 6:6; Col 3:22

pleaseth
do to her as it p. thee. Gen 16:6
dwell where it p. thee. 20:15
for she p. me well. Judg 14:3
maiden which p. the king. Esth 2:4
p. God shall escape. Eccl 7:26
he doeth whatsoever p. him. 8:3

pleasing
if I be p. in his eyes. Esth 8:5
shall they be p. to him. Hos 9:4
worthy of the Lord to all p. Col 1:10
so we speak, not as p. 1 Thes 2:4
those things that are p. 1 John 3:22

well-pleasing
acceptable, well-p. to God. Phil 4:18
obey, for this is well-p. Col 3:20
working in you that which is well-p.
in his sight. Heb 13:21

pleasure
after I am waxed old, shall I have
p.? Gen 18:12
thy fill at thine own p. Deut 23:24
I know thou hast p. in. 1 Chr 29:17
king send his p. to us. Ezra 5:17
to Lord God, and do his p. 10:11
over our cattle at their p. Neh 9:37
according to every man's p. Esth 1:8
what p. hath he in his house after ?
Job 21:21
dieth, and never eateth with p. 25
is it any p. to Almighty that ? 22:3
that hath p. in wickedness. Ps 5:4
hath p. in the prosperity. 35:27
good in thy good p. to Zion. 51:18
for thy servants take p. in. 102:14
bless Lord ye ministers of his, that
do his p. 103:21
to bind his princes at his p. 105:22
all them that have p. therein. 111:2
he taketh not p. in the legs. 147:10
the Lord taketh p. in them that. 11
Lord taketh p. in his people. 149:4
he that loveth p. shall. Pr 21:17
therefore enjoy p. Eccl 2:1
he hath no p. in fools. 5:4
thou shalt say, I have no p. 12:1
the night of my p. he. Isa 21:4
shall perform all my p. 44:28
stand, I will do all my p. 46:10
he will do his p. on Babylon. 48:14
p. of the Lord shall prosper. 53:10
day of your fast ye find p. 58:3
p. on my holy day, and call the sabbath a delight ... thine own p. 13
up the wind at her p. Jer 2:24
a vessel wherein is no p.? 22:28
at liberty at their p. to return. 34:16
like a vessel wherein is no p. 48:38
whom thou hast taken p. Ezek 16:37

have I any *p.* that the wicked die?
　　　　Ezek 18:23, 32; 33:11
a vessel wherein is no *p.* *Hos* 8:8
and I will take *p.* in it. *Hag* 1:8
I have no *p.* in you. *Mal* 1:10
Father's good *p.* to give. *Luke* 12:32
Felix, willing to shew the Jews a *p.*
　　left Paul. *Acts* 24:27*
willing to do the Jews a *p.* 25:9*
but have *p.* in them that. *Rom* 1:32
therefore I take *p.* in infirmities.
　　　　　　　2 Cor 12:10
good *p.* of his will. *Eph* 1:5, 9
and to do of his good *p.* *Phil* 2:13
fulfil the good *p.* of. *2 Thes* 1:11
believed not, but had *p.* in. 2:12
but she that liveth in *p.* *1 Tim* 5:6
in sacrifices thou hast no *p.*
　　　　　　　Heb 10:6, 8
my soul shall have no *p.* in him. 38
us after their own *p.* 12:10
ye have lived in *p.* on earth. *Jas* 5:5
that count it *p.* to riot. *2 Pet* 2:13
for thy *p.* they are and. *Rev* 4:11

pleasures
spend their years in *p.* *Job* 36:11
at thy right hand are *p.* *Ps* 16:11
drink of river of thy *p.* 36:8
thou that art given to *p.* *Isa* 47:8
are choked with the *p.* *Luke* 8:14
lovers of *p.* more than. *2 Tim* 3:4
serving divers lusts and *p.* *Tit* 3:3
than to enjoy the *p.* of sin. *Heb* 11:25

pledge
wilt thou give me a *p.?* *Gen* 38:17
what *p.* shall I give thee ? 18
Judah sent to receive his *p.* 20
take thy neighbour's raiment to *p.*
　　　　　　　Ex 22:26
or upper millstone to *p.* for he taketh
　　a man's life to *p.* *Deut* 24:6
into his house to fetch his *p.* 10, 11
shalt not sleep with his *p.* 12, 13
a widow's raiment to *p.* 17
how thy brethren fare, take their *p.*
　　　　　　　1 Sam 17:18
hast taken a *p.* from thy brother.
　　　　　　　Job 22:6
take the widow's ox for a *p.* 24:3
and they take a *p.* of the poor. 9
take *p.* for a strange woman.
　　　　Pr 20:16; 27:13
to the debtor his *p.* *Ezek* 18:7, 16
hath not restored the *p.,* shall he ? 12
if the wicked restore the *p.,* he. 33:15
on clothes laid to *p.* by. *Amos* 2:8

pledges
I pray thee, give *p.* to the king of
　Assyria. *2 Ki* 18:23; *Isa* 36:8

Pleiades
Arcturus, Orion, and *P.* *Job* 9:9
the sweet influences of *P.?* 38:31

plenteous
fifth part in the *p.* years. *Gen* 41:34
in the *p.* years the earth brought. 47
shall make thee *p.* *Deut* 28:11; 30:9
gold as *p.* as stones. *2 Chr* 1:15
art *p.* in mercy to all. *Ps* 86:5, 15
gracious, and *p.* in mercy. 103:8
with him is *p.* redemption. 130:7
bread shall be fat and *p.* *Isa* 30:23
fat, and their meat *p.* *Hab* 1:16
the harvest truly is *p.* *Mat* 9:37

plenteousness
the seven years of *p.* *Gen* 41:53*
of the diligent tend to *p.* *Pr* 21:5

plentiful
didst send a *p.* rain. *Ps* 68:9
out of the *p.* field. *Isa* 16:10*
and I brought you to a *p.* *Jer* 2:7
is taken from the *p.* field. 48:33*

plentifully
how hast thou *p.* declared ! *Job* 26:3
and *p.* rewardeth. *Ps* 31:23
rich man brought forth *p.* *Luke* 12:16

plenty
God give thee *p.* of corn. *Gen* 27:28
seven years of great *p.* 41:29
all the *p.* shall be forgotten in. 30
and the *p.* shall not be known. 31
a pit, wherein there is *p.* *Lev* 11:36*

Ophir *p.* of almug trees. *1 Ki* 10:11
to eat, have left *p.* *2 Chr* 31:10
shalt have *p.* of silver. *Job* 22:25*
excellent in power and in *p.* 37:23
barns be filled with *p.* *Pr* 3:10
land shall have *p.* of bread. 28:19
had we *p.* of victuals. *Jer* 44:17
shall eat in *p.* and praise. *Joel* 2:26

plotteth
wicked *p.* against the just. *Ps* 37:12

plough
put his hand to the *p.* *Luke* 9:62

plow
shalt not *p.* with an ox. *Deut* 22:10
yoke of oxen might *p.* *1 Sam* 14:14*
they that *p.* iniquity. *Job* 4:8
sluggard will not *p.* *Pr* 20:4
doth the plowman *p.?* *Isa* 28:24
Judah shall *p.* Jacob. *Hos* 10:11
one *p.* there with oxen ? *Amos* 6:12
plougheth should *p.* in hope.
　　　　　　　1 Cor 9:10

plowed, -ers
not *p.* with my heifer. *Judg* 14:18
the plowers *p.* on my. *Ps* 129:3
Zion shall be *p.* as a field. *Jer* 26:18
　　　　　　　Mi 3:12
ye have *p.* wickedness. *Hos* 10:13

ploweth
that *p.* should plow in. *1 Cor* 9:10

plowing, verb
Elisha, who was *p.* *1 Ki* 19:19
the oxen were *p.* and the. *Job* 1:14
having a servant *p.* *Luke* 17:7

plowing
and the *p.* of the wicked. *Pr* 21:4*

plowman
doth the *p.* plow all day ? *Isa* 28:24
the *p.* shall overtake the. *Amos* 9:13

plowmen
alien shall be your *p.* *Isa* 61:5
the *p.* were ashamed. *Jer* 14:4

plowshares
shall beat their swords into *p.*
　　　　　Isa 2:4; *Mi* 4:3
beat your *p.* into swords. *Joel* 3:10

pluck
shall *p.* away his crop. *Lev* 1:16
and quite *p.* down their. *Num* 33:52*
then thou mayest *p.* the ears with.
　　　　　　　Deut 23:25
then will I *p.* them up. *2 Chr* 7:20
p. the fatherless from. *Job* 24:9
he shall *p.* my feet out. *Ps* 25:15
p. thee out of thy dwelling. 52:5
thy right hand, *p.* it out of. 74:11
pass by the way do *p.* her. 80:12
to *p.* up what is planted. *Eccl* 3:2
p. out the house of Judah. *Jer* 12:14
I will utterly *p.* up and destroy. 17
a kingdom, to *p.* it up. 18:7
and yet would I *p.* thee. 22:24
and not *p.* them up. 24:6; 42:10
watched over them to *p.* up. 31:28
I have planted I will *p.* up. 45:4
without many people to *p.* *Ezek* 17:9
p. off thine own breasts. 23:34
Who *p.* off the skin from. *Mi* 3:2
I will *p.* up thy groves out of. 5:14
if thy right eye offend thee, *p.* it out.
　　Mat 5:29; 18:9; *Mark* 9:47
began to *p.* the ears of corn.
　　　　Mat 12:1; *Mark* 2:23
nor shall any *p.* them. *John* 10:28
no man is able to *p.* them out. 29

plucked
was an olive leaf *p.* off. *Gen* 8:11
and he *p.* his hand out. *Ex* 4:7
ye shall be *p.* from off. *Deut* 28:63
a man *p.* off his shoe. *Ruth* 4:7
p. the spear out of Egyptian's hand.
　　　　2 Sam 23:21; *1 Chr* 11:23
I *p.* off the hair of my. *Ezra* 9:3
I cursed them, and *p.* off. *Neh* 13:25
p. the spoil out of his. *Job* 29:17
my cheeks to them that *p.* *Isa* 50:6
wicked are not *p.* away. *Jer* 6:29
after I have *p.* them out. 12:15
it shall not be *p.* up, nor. 31:40
she was *p.* up in fury. *Ezek* 19:12

the wings thereof were *p.* *Dan* 7:4
three of the first horns *p.* up. 8
for his kingdom shall be *p.* 11:4
as a firebrand *p.* out of. *Amos* 4:11
is not this a brand *p.?* *Zech* 3:2
the chains had been *p.* *Mark* 5:4
his disciples *p.* ears of corn. *Luke* 6:1
be thou *p.* up by the root. 17:6
would have *p.* out your own eyes.
　　　　　　　Gal 4:15
twice dead, *p.* up by the roots.
　　　　　　　Jude 12

plucketh
the foolish *p.* it down. *Pr* 14:1

plumbline
behold the Lord stood upon a wall
　made by a *p.* with a *p.* *Amos* 7:7
and I said, A *p.* . . . Behold, I will set
　a *p.* in the midst of my people. 8

plummet
over Jerusalem the *p.* *2 Ki* 21:13
righteousness to the *p.* *Isa* 28:17
shall see the *p.* in hand. *Zech* 4:10

plunge
yet shalt thou *p.* me in the. *Job* 9:31

poets
of your own *p.* have said. *Acts* 17:28

point
p. out for you mount. *Num* 34:7*
p. out your border. 8*
p. out your east border. 10*

point, substantive
I am at the *p.* to die. *Gen* 25:32
is written with the *p.* of. *Jer* 17:1
my daughter lieth at the *p.* of death.
　　　　　　　Mark 5:23
was at the *p.* of death. *John* 4:47
offend in one *p.* is guilty. *Jas* 2:10

pointed
he spreadeth sharp *p.* *Job* 41:30*

points
in all *p.* as he came so. *Eccl* 5:16
but was in all *p.* tempted. *Heb* 4:15

poison
with the *p.* of serpents. *Deut* 32:24
their wine is *p.* of dragons. 33
the *p.* whereof drinketh. *Job* 6:4
he shall suck *p.* of asps. 20:16
their *p.* is like the *p.* of. *Ps* 58:4
like a serpent, adders' *p.* is. 140:3
the *p.* of asps is under. *Rom* 3:13
is an evil, full of deadly *p.* *Jas* 3:8

pole
set it upon a *p.* *Num* 21:8*
Moses put it on a *p.* 9*

policy
through his *p.* shall cause craft to.
　　　　　　　Dan 8:25

polished
p. after the similitude. *Ps* 144:12*
he hath made me a *p.* shaft. *Isa* 49:2
in colour to *p.* brass. *Dan* 10:6*

polishing
Nazarites purer, their *p.* *Lam* 4:7

poll, -s
of their names, every male by the *p.*
　Num 1:2; 18:20, 22; *1 Chr* 23:3
　　　　　　　24
take five shekels a piece by the *p.*
　　　　　　　Num 3:47

poll
only *p.* their heads. *Ezek* 44:20†
make thee bald, and *p.* *Mi* 1:16†

polled
p. his head, at year's end he *p.*
　　　　　　　2 Sam 14:26†

pollute
neither shall ye *p.* the. *Num* 18:32*
so shall ye not *p.* the land. 35:33
called by name, to *p.* it. *Jer* 7:30
p. my secret place. *Ezek* 7:21*, 22*
will ye *p.* me among my ? 13:19*
ye *p.* yourselves with idols. 20:31
　　　　　　　23:30; 36:18
p. ye my holy name. 20:39*; 39:7*
in my sanctuary to *p.* it. 44:7*
shall *p.* the sanctuary. *Dan* 11:31*

polluted
upon it, thou hast *p.* it. *Ex* 20:25

Josiah *p*. the altar.   2 *Ki* 23:16
the priests *p*. the house. 2 *Chr* 36:14
therefore were they as *p*.
     Ezra 2:62; *Neh* 7:64
and the land was *p*. with. *Ps* 106:38
I was wroth, I have *p*.   *Isa* 47:6*
how should my name be *p*.? 48:11*
thou say, I am not *p*.?   *Jer* 2:23
that land be greatly *p*.?   3:1, 2
turned and *p*. my name.   34:16*
he hath *p*. the kingdom. *Lam* 2:2*
they have *p*. themselves with. 4:14
my soul hath not been *p*. *Ezek* 4:14
nor be *p*. with all their.   14:11
I saw thee *p*. in thine own blood.
     16:6*, 22*
that it should not be *p*. 20:9*, 14, 22
they greatly *p*.   13*, 16*, 21*, 24*
I *p*. them in their own gifts. 26*
are ye *p*. after the manner of ? 30
was *p*. with the Babylonians. 23:17
Gilead is a city that is *p*. *Hos* 6:8*
all that eat thereof shall be *p*. 9:4
shalt die in a *p*. land.   *Amos* 7:17*
it is *p*., it shall destroy you. *Mi* 2:10
that is filthy and *p*.   *Zeph* 3:1
her priests have *p*. sanctuary. 4*
p. bread upon mine altar, and say,
   Wherein have we *p*. thee ? *Mal* 1:7
the table of the Lord is *p*.   12
p. this holy place.   *Acts* 21:28

polluting
sabbath from *p*. it.   *Isa* 56:2, 6

pollution
have they humbled her that was set
   apart for *p*.   *Ezek* 22:10

pollutions
abstain from *p*. of idols. *Acts* 15:20
escaped *p*. of the world. 2 *Pet* 2:20

pollux, *see* sign

pomegranate
*A kind of apple, covered without
with a reddish rind, and red within,
which opens lengthways, and shews
red grains within, full of juice like
wine, with little kernels. God
gave orders to Moses to put embroidered pomegranates, with
golden bells between, at the bottom
of the high priest's blue robe or
ephod,* Ex 28:33, 34.

a golden bell and a *p*. upon the hem.
     Ex 28:34; 39:26
Saul tarried under a *p*. tree.
     1 Sam 14:2
thy temples are like a piece of *p*.
     S of S 4:3; 6:7
to drink of juice of my *p*.   8:2
the *p*. tree and all trees. *Joel* 1:12
p. hath not brought forth. *Hag* 2:19

pomegranates
thou shalt make *p*. of blue.
     Ex 28:33; 39:24, 25
they brought of the *p*. *Num* 13:23
of seed, figs, vines, or *p*.   20:5
a land of *p*., oil olive.   *Deut* 8:8
chapiters on top with *p*. 1 *Ki* 7:18*
2 *Ki* 25:17; 2 *Chr* 3:16; *Jer* 52:22
plants are an orchard of *p*. with.
     S of S 4:13
whether the *p*. budded. 6:11; 7:12

pommels
the pillars and *p*. of the. 2 *Chr* 4:12*

pomp
and their *p*. shall descend. *Isa* 5:14
thy *p*. is brought down to.   14:11
p. of the strong to cease. *Ezek* 7:24*
the *p*. of her strength shall cease.
     30:18*; 33:28*
shall spoil the *p*. of Egypt. 32:12*
when Agrippa was come, and Bernice,
   with great *p*.   *Acts* 25:23

ponder
p. the path of thy feet.   *Pr* 4:26*
shouldest *p*. the path of life.   5:6*

pondered
Mary *p*. them in her heart. *Luke* 2:19

pondereth
ways of man, the Lord *p*. *Pr* 5:21*
Lord *p*. the heart.   21:2*
he that *p*. the heart.   24:12*

ponds
thy hand on their *p*.   *Ex* 7:19*; 8:5
purposes, that make *p*. *Isa* 19:10*

Pontius, *see* Pilate

Pontus
dwellers in P.   *Acts* 2:9; 18:2
     1 *Pet* 1:1

pool
the one side of the *p*.   2 *Sam* 2:13
hanged them up over the *p*.   4:12
washed chariot in *p*. of. 1 *Ki* 22:38
stood by the conduit of the upper *p*.
     2 *Ki* 18:17; *Isa* 7:3; 36:2
made a *p*. and conduit. 2 *Ki* 20:20
went on to the king's *p*.   *Neh* 2:14
repaired the wall of the *p*.   3:15
the waters of the lower *p*. *Isa* 22:9
ditch for the water of the old *p*.   11
ground shall become a *p*.   35:7
the wilderness a *p*. of water.   41:18
Nineveh of old is like a *p*. of water.
     Nah 2:8
by the sheep market a *p*. *John* 5:2
an angel went down into the *p*.   4
no man to put me into the *p*.   7
wash in the *p*. of Siloam.   9:7, 11

pools
thy hand on all their *p*.   *Ex* 7:19
rain also filleth the *p*.   *Ps* 84:6
I made me *p*. of water.   *Eccl* 2:6
make it for the *p*. of water. *Isa* 14:23
and I will dry up the *p*. and.   42:15

poor
*(Used in the Bible both of those
poor in this world's goods, and of
those spiritually poor)*
after them seven *p*. kine. *Gen* 41:19
that the *p*. of thy people. *Ex* 23:11
p. shall not give less than.   30:15
if he be *p*. and cannot. *Lev* 14:21
leave them for the *p*. and.   19:10
respect the person of the *p*.   15
if thy brother be waxen *p*.   25:25
     35, 39, 47
there be no *p*. among you. *Deut* 15:4
for the *p*. shall never cease out. 11
not young men, *p*. or rich. *Ruth* 3:10
the Lord maketh *p*. and. 1 *Sam* 2:7
p. out of the dust.   8; *Ps* 113:7
rich, and the other *p*. 2 *Sam* 12:1
the guard left of the *p*. of. 2 *Ki* 25:12
     Jer 39:10; 40:7; 52:15, 16
the *p*. from the sword. *Job* 5:15
so the *p*. hath hope, and.   16
seek to please the *p*.   20:10
oppressed and forsaken the *p*.   19
the *p*. of the earth hide.   24:4
and they take a pledge of the *p*.   9
the murderer killeth the *p*.   14
because I delivered the *p*.   29:12
soul grieved for the *p*.?   30:25
if I withheld the *p*. from.   31:16
seen any *p*. without covering.   19
the rich more than the *p*.   34:19
they cause the cry of the *p*.   28
he delivereth the *p*. in affliction.
     36:15*; *Ps* 72:12
the expectation of the *p*.   *Ps* 9:18
pride doth persecute the *p*.   10:2
are privily set against the *p*.   8
wait secretly to catch the *p*.   9
that the *p*. may fall by his.   10*
the *p*. committeth himself to.   14
for the oppression of the *p*. I. 12:5
the counsel of the *p*.   14:6
delivereth the *p*. from him.   35:10
their bow to cast down the *p*. 37:14
but I am *p*.   40:17; 69:29; 70:5
     86:1; 109:22
he that considereth the *p*.   41:1
both low and high, rich and *p*. 49:2
of thy goodness for the *p*.   68:10
Lord heareth *p*. and despiseth. 69:33
he shall judge the *p*. of.   72:4
he shall spare the *p*.   13
let the *p*. and needy praise. 74:21
defend the *p*.   82:3
deliver the *p*. and needy.   4
yet setteth he *p*. on high. 107:41
at the right hand of the *p*. 109:31
will satisfy her *p*. with.   132:15
maintain the right of the *p*. 140:12

he becometh *p*. that dealeth. *Pr* 10:4
the destruction of the *p*. is.   15
that maketh himself *p*.   13:7
his riches, but the *p*. heareth.   8
in the tillage of the *p*. but.   23
the *p*. is hated even of his.   14:20
he that hath mercy on the *p*.   21
p. reproacheth his maker; he that
   honoureth him hath mercy on *p*. 31
whoso mocketh the *p*.   17:5
the *p*. useth entreaties, but.   18:23
the *p*. is separated from his.   19:4
all brethren of the *p*. do hate him. 7
his ears at the cry of the *p*.   21:13
the rich and *p*. meet together. 22:2
the rich ruleth over the *p*. and the. 7
oppresseth the *p*. to increase.   16
for him that will pity the *p*.   28:8
the *p*. that hath understanding.   11
ruler over the *p*. people.   15
the cause of the *p*.   29:7, 13
that faithfully judgeth the *p*.   14
lest I be *p*. and steal, and.   30:9
as swords, to devour the *p*.   14
and plead the cause of the *p*. 31:9
his kingdom, becometh *p*. *Eccl* 4:14
the oppression of the *p*.   5:8
what hath the *p*. that knoweth ? 6:8
the spoil of the *p*. is in. *Isa* 3:14
that ye grind faces of the *p*.?   15
take away the right from the *p*. 10:2
cause it to be heard to Laish, O *p*. 30
shall he judge the *p*.   11:4
the firstborn of the *p*. shall.   14:30
and the *p*. of his people shall.   32*
even the feet of the *p*. shall.   26:6
p. among men shall rejoice.   29:19
to destroy the *p*. with lying.   32:7*
when the *p*. and needy seek.   41:17
bring the *p*. that are cast out.   58:7
blood of the *p*. innocents. *Jer* 2:34
these are *p*.; they are foolish.   5:4
delivered the soul of the *p*.   20:13
he judged the cause of the *p*. 22:16
strengthen hand of the *p*. *Ezek* 16:49
hath oppressed *p*. and needy. 18:12
taken off his hand from the *p*.   17
and they have vexed the *p*.   22:29
they sold the *p*. for a pair. *Amos* 2:6
the dust on the head of the *p*.   7
which oppress the *p*. and crush. 4:1
your treading is on the *p*.   5:11
turn aside the *p*. in the gate.   12
even to make the *p*. of the land. 8:4
that we may buy the *p*. for silver. 6
was to devour the *p*.   *Hab* 3:14
the *p*. people shall trust. *Zeph* 3:12
and oppress not the widow nor *p*.
     Zech 7:10
I will feed even you, O *p*.   11:7
the *p*. of the flock that waited.   11
blessed are the *p*. in spirit. *Mat* 5:3
p. have the gospel preached.   11:5
for ye have the *p*. always with you.
     26:11; *Mark* 14:7; *John* 12:8
a certain *p*. widow.   *Mark* 12:42
p. widow hath cast. 43; *Luke* 21:3
blessed be ye *p*. for yours. *Luke* 6:20
call the *p*. the maimed.   14:13, 21
that he cared for the *p*. *John* 12:6
a contribution for the *p*. *Rom* 15:26
as *p*. yet making many. 2 *Cor* 6:10
yet for your sakes he became *p*. 8:9
should remember the *p*. *Gal* 2:10
hath not God chosen the *p*.? *Jas* 2:5
but ye have despised the *p*.   6
knowest not that thou art *p*. *Rev* 3:17
he causeth rich and *p*. to.   13:16

is poor
of my people that *is p*.   *Ex* 22:25
thou shalt not oppress hired servant
   that *is p*.   *Deut* 24:14
for he *is p*. and setteth his heart. 15
behold, my family *is p*. *Judg* 6:15
better *is* the *p*. that walketh in his integrity, than he. *Pr* 19:1; 28:6
rob not poor because he *is p*.   22:22
better *is* a *p*. and wise child, than
   an old.   *Eccl* 4:13
to him that *is p*. and of a. *Isa* 66:2

poor man
countenance a *p*. *man* in.   *Ex* 23:3

if a *p. man*, harden not. *Deut* 15:7
if a *man* be *p.*, sleep not with. 24:12
seeing I am a *p. man.* 1 *Sam* 18:23
p. man had nothing. 2 *Sam* 12:3
but took the *p. man's* ewe lamb. 4
this *p. man* cried, and the. *Ps* 34:6
the *p.* and needy *man.* 109:16
and a *p. man* is better than a liar.
        Pr 19:22
pleasure shall be a *p. man.* 21:17
a *p. man* that oppresseth poor. 28:3
the *p.* and deceitful *man.* 29:13
a *p.* wise man, yet no man remembered that same *p. man. Eccl* 9:15
the *p. man's* wisdom is despised. 16
a *p. man* in vile raiment. *Jas* 2:2

to the poor
to the *p.* and stranger. *Lev* 23:22
of sending gifts to the *p. Esth* 9:22
I was a father to the *p. Job* 29:16
but he giveth right to the *p.* 36:6
he hath given to the *p. Ps* 112:9
        2 *Cor* 9:9
of his bread to the *p. Pr* 22:9
giveth to the *p.* shall not lack. 28:27
out her hand to the *p.* 31:20
been a strength to the *p. Isa* 25:4
by shewing mercy to the *p. Dan* 4:27
sell all, and give to the *p. Mat* 19:21
        Mark 10:21
sold for much, and given to the *p.*
   Mat 26:9; *Mark* 14:5; *John* 12:5
the gospel to the *p. Luke* 4:18; 7:22
and distribute to the *p.* 18:22
half of my goods I give to the *p.* 19:8
give something to the *p. John* 13:29
my goods to feed the *p.* 1 *Cor* 13:3
say to the *p.*, Stand thou. *Jas* 2:3

thy poor
the judgement of *thy p. Ex* 23:6
hand from *thy p.* brother. *Deut* 15:7
be evil against *thy p.* brother. 9
thine hand wide to *thy p.* 11
he shall judge *thy p. Ps* 72:2
congregation of *thy p.* for ever. 74:19

poorer
if he be *p.* than thy. *Lev* 27:8

poorest
none remained, save *p.* 2 *Ki* 24:14

poplar, -s
took rods of green *p. Gen* 30:37
incense under oaks and *p. Hos* 4:13

populous
great, mighty, and *p. Deut* 26:5
art thou better than *p.* No? *Nah* 3:8

porch
forth through the *p. Judg* 3:23
Solomon pattern of *p.* 1 *Chr* 28:11
shut up doors of the *p.* 2 *Chr* 29:7
month came they to the *p.* 17
between the *p.* and altar. *Ezek* 8:16
enter by way of *p.* of the gate. 44:3
        46:2, 8
priests weep between *p. Joel* 2:17
gone out into the *p. Mat* 26:71
the *p.*; and cock crew. *Mark* 14:68
temple in Solomon's *p. John* 10:23
together in Solomon's *p. Acts* 3:11
one accord in Solomon's *p.* 5:12

porches
with the temple and *p. Ezek* 41:15
Bethesda, having five *p. John* 5:2

Porcius
P. Festus came into. *Acts* 24:27

porter
(*Revisions render this doorkeeper*)
talled to the *p.* and said. 2 *Sam* 18:26
lepers called to the *p.* 2 *Ki* 7:10
Zechariah was *p.* of door. 1 *Chr* 9:21
and Kore the *p.* toward. 2 *Chr* 31:14
and commanded the *p. Mark* 13:34
to him the *p.* openeth. *John* 10:3

porters
the *p.* were Shallum. 1 *Chr* 9:17
and Jehiel the *p.* 15:18
and Hosah to be *p.* 16:38
the sons of Jeduthun were *p.* 42
four thousand were *p.* 23:5
the divisions of the *p.* 26:1, 12, 19

the *p.* by their courses. 2 *Chr* 8:14
p. waited at every gate. 35:15
p. and Nethinims went up. *Ezra* 7:7
the Levites and *p.* dwelt. *Neh* 7:73

portion
let them take their *p. Gen* 14:24
any *p.* or inheritance for us? 31:14
priest had a *p.* assigned, and did
   eat their *p.* 47:22
I have given thee one *p.* above. 48:22
have given it them for *p. Lev* 6:17
this is the *p.* of the anointing. 7:35
of Israel's half take thou one *p.*
        Num 31:30, 36
Moses took one *p.* of fifty for the. 47
by giving him a double *p. Deut* 21:17
for Lord's *p.* is his people. 32:9
in a *p.* of the lawgiver was. 33:21
given me but one *p.?* *Josh* 17:14
but to Hannah he gave a worthy *p.*
        1 *Sam* 1:5
Samuel said, Bring the *p.* which. 9:23
what *p.* have we in David? 1 *Ki* 12:16
        2 *Chr* 10:16
let a double *p.* of thy. 2 *Ki* 2:9
dogs shall eat Jezebel in *p.* of Jezreel. 9:10, 36, 37
Joram met him in *p.* of Naboth. 21
in the *p.* of Naboth's field. 25
Ahaz took a *p.* out of. 2 *Chr* 28:11
Hezekiah appointed king's *p.* 31:3
to give the *p.* of the priests. 4, 16
no *p.* on this side the river. *Ezra* 4:16
p. nor right in Jerusalem. *Neh* 2:20
that a certain *p.* should be. 11:23
and porters, every day his *p.* 12:47
the *p.* of a wicked man. *Job* 20:29
p. is cursed in the earth. 24:18
little a *p.* is heard of? 26:14*; 27:13
for what *p.* of God is there? 31:2
be the cup of their cup. *Ps* 11:6
the Lord is the *p.* of mine. 16:5
from men who have their *p.* 17:14
shall be a *p.* for foxes. 63:10
God is my *p.* 73:26
art my *p.* O Lord. 119:57; 142:5
giveth a *p.* to her maidens. *Pr* 31:15*
was my *p.* of all my labour. *Eccl* 2:10
shall he leave it for his *p.* 21
should rejoice, for that is his *p.* 3:22
        5:18; 9:9
him power to take his *p.* 5:19
nor have they any more *p.* for. 9:6
give a *p.* to seven, and also. 11:2
this is the *p.* of them. *Isa* 17:14
I will divide him a *p.* with. 53:12
among smooth stones of the stream
   is thy *p.* 57:6
they shall rejoice in their *p.* 61:7
the *p.* of Jacob is not like them.
     Jer 10:16; 51:19
my *p.* under foot, they have made
   my pleasant *p.* a desolate. 12:10
this is the *p.* of thy measures. 13:25
every day a *p.* until the day. 52:34
the Lord is my *p.* saith. *Lam* 3:24
shall offer an holy *p. Ezek* 45:1, 4
a *p.* shall be for prince on one. 7
to the coast of Hethlon, a *p.* 48:1
border of Dan a *p.* of Asher. 2
a *p.* for Naphtali. 3
a *p.* for Manasseh. 4
not defile himself with *p. Dan* 1:8
his *p.* be with the beasts. 4:15, 23
feed of the *p.* of his meat. 11:26
changed the *p.* of my people. *Mi* 2:4
by them their *p.* is fat. *Hab* 1:16
shall inherit Judah his *p. Zech* 2:12
shall appoint him his *p. Mat* 24:51
to give them their *p.* in. *Luke* 12:42
will appoint him his *p.* with. 46
give me the *p.* of goods that. 15:12

portions
they shall have like *p.* to eat.
        Deut 18:8
ten *p.* to Manasseh. *Josh* 17:5
sons and daughters *p.* 1 *Sam* 1:4
to give *p.* to all the. 2 *Chr* 31:19
eat the fat, and send *p. Neh* 8:10, 12
p. for the priests. 12:44
p. of the singers. 47
that the *p.* of the Levites had. 13:10
a day of sending *p.* to. *Esth* 9:19, 22

Joseph shall have two *p. Ezek* 47:13
against the *p.* for the prince. 48:21
devour them with their *p. Hos* 5:7

possess
thy seed shall *p.* the gate. *Gen* 22:17
        24:60
let us go up at once and *p.* it, for we.
     Num 13:30; *Deut* 1:21
next kinsman shall *p.* it. *Num* 27:11
I give it, they shall *p.* it. *Deut* 1:39
begin to *p.* that thou mayest. 2:31
ye shall *p.* greater nations. 11:23†
   12:2†, 29†; 18:14†; 31:3†
thou passest over Jordan to *p.* it.
        30:18; 31:13†
Esau mount Seir to *p.* it. *Josh* 24:4
shouldest thou *p.* it? *Judg* 11:23
wilt not thou *p.* what Chemosh? 24
he is gone down to *p.* 1 *Ki* 21:18
to *p.* months of vanity. *Job* 7:3
thou makest me *p.* iniquities. 13:26
and bittern shall *p.* it. *Isa* 34:11, 17
shall *p.* their houses. *Ezek* 7:24
shall be mine, we will *p.* 35:10
my people Israel to *p.* thee. 36:12
the saints shall *p.* the. *Dan* 7:18
for silver, nettles shall *p. Hos* 9:6
p. the remnant of Edom. *Amos* 9:12
shall *p.* their possessions. *Ob* 17
shall *p.* mount Esau, and Benjamin
   p. Gilead. 19
captivity of Israel shall *p.* that . . .
   and Jerusalem shall *p.* the. 20
the Chaldeans to *p.* the. *Hab* 1:6
my people shall *p.* them. *Zeph* 2:9
will cause remnant to *p. Zech* 8:12
give tithes of all that I *p. Luke* 18:12
in patience *p.* ye your souls. 21:19
know how to *p.* vessel. 1 *Thes* 4:4

possess with land
I will give you their *land* to *p.*
    Lev 20:24; *Num* 33:53
     Deut 3:18; 5:31; 17:14
shall *p.* it, I will bring into *land.*
        Num 14:24
go in and *p.* the *land.* *Deut* 1:8
     4:1; 6:18; 8:1; 9:5, 23; 10:11
       11:31; *Josh* 1:11
land whither ye go to *p.* it. *Deut* 4:5
   14, 26; 5:33; 6:1; 7:1; 11:10, 11
        29; 23:20
go over and *p.* that good *land.* 4:22
brought me to *p.* this *land.* 9:4
giveth not this *land* to *p.* for thy. 6
be strong and *p.* the *land.* 11:8
land which Lord God of thy fathers
   giveth thee to *p.* 12:1; 15:4
     19:2, 14; 21:1; 25:19
consumed from off *land* thou goest
   to *p.* 28:21
plucked from off the *land* whither
   thou goest to *p.* it. 63
ye slack to *p.* the *land*? *Josh* 18:3
and ye shall *p.* their *land.* 23:5
that ye might *p.* their *land.* 24:8
every man to *p.* the *land.* *Judg* 2:6
to enter to *p.* the *land.* 18:9
may *p.* this good *land.* 1 *Chr* 28:8
to *p.* is an unclean *land.* *Ezra* 9:11
they should *p.* the *land. Neh* 9:15
them in to *p.* the *land.* 23
p. them in the *land* of the Lord.
        Isa 14:2
do not rise nor *p.* the *land.* 21
trust in me shall *p.* the *land.* 57:13
land shall they *p.* the double. 61:7
return to *land* and *p.* it. *Jer* 30:3
shall ye *p.* the *land*? *Ezek* 33:25, 26
I brought you to *p. land.* *Amos* 2:10

possessed
Israel *p.* Sihon's *land. Num* 21:24
and people, and have *p.* the *land.* 35
     Deut 3:12; 4:47; *Neh* 9:22
to *land* thy fathers *p.* *Deut* 30:5
brethren have *p.* the *land. Josh* 1:15
they *p.* their *land* on the other. 12:1
yet very much *land* to be *p.* 13:1
Dan took Leshem and *p.* it. 19:47
they *p.* it and dwelt. 21:43; 22:9
Eglon king of Moab *p. Judg* 3:13
Israel *p.* all the *land* of. 11:21, 22
men of Ava *p.* Samaria. 2 *Ki* 17:24
for thou hast *p.* my reins. *Ps* 139:13

Lord *p.* me in the beginning. *Pr* 8:22
people hath *p.* it a little. *Isa* 63:18
vineyards shall be *p.* *Jer* 32:15*
they came in and *p.* it, but obeyed. 23
time came that saints *p.* *Dan* 7:22
told them by what means he that was
  p. was healed. *Luke* 8:36
none said that aught he *p.* *Acts* 4:32
a damsel *p.* with a spirit of. 16:16
as though they *p.* not. *I Cor* 7:30
  see devils

possessest
into land and *p.* it. *Deut* 26:1

possesseth
every daughter that *p.* *Num* 36:8
man's life consists not in things he *p.*
  Luke 12:15

possessing
as having nothing, yet *p.* *2 Cor* 6:10

possession
I will give all the land of Canaan for
  an everlasting. *Gen* 17:8; 48:4
give me a *p.* of a buryingplace.
  23:4, 9, 18, 20; 49:30; 50:13
Isaac had *p.* of flocks, of herds. 26:14
Edom in the land of their *p.* 36:43
and gave them a *p.* in the land. 47:11
Canaan, which I give to you for a *p.*
  Lev 14:34
ye shall return every man to his *p.*
  25:10, 13, 27, 28, 41; *Deut* 3:20
sold away some of his *p. Lev* 25:25
the Levites' *p.* shall go out in. 33
strangers shall be your *p.* 45, 46
sanctify some part of his *p.* 27:16
p. thereof shall be the priest's. 21
return to whom the *p.* of the land. 24
be a *p.,* Seir also a *p.* *Num* 24:18
to the lot shall the *p.* be. 26:56*
give us a *p.* among brethren. 27:4
daughters of Zelophehad give a *p.* 7
given to thy servants for *p.* 32:5
this land shall be your *p.* before. 22
Levites of their *p.* cities. 35:2, 8
return to the land of his *p.* 28
given mount Seir to Esau for a *p.*
  Deut 2:5
given Ar to Lot for a *p.* 9, 19
in land of his *p.* Lord gave them. 12
swallowed up all in their *p.* 11:6
which I gave Israel for a *p.* 32:49
for a *p.* to Reubenites. *Josh* 12:6
get ye into the land of your *p.* 22:4
to Manasseh Moses had given a *p.* 7
returned to the land of their *p.* 9
if your *p.* be unclean, take *p.* 19
take *p.* of the vineyard. *I Ki* 21:15
killed, and also taken *p.?* 19
cast out of thy *p.* *2 Chr* 20:11
dwelt every one in his *p.* *Neh* 11:3
parts of earth for thy *p.* *Ps* 2:8
got not the land in *p.* by their. 44:3
may dwell and have it in *p.* 69:35
take the houses of God in *p.* 83:12
the upright have good things in *p.*
  Pr 28:10*
I will make it a *p.* for. *Isa* 14:23
is this land given in *p.* *Ezek* 11:15
thee to men of the east for *p.* 25:4
high places are ours in *p.* 36:2
appointed my land into their *p.* 5
no *p.* in Israel, I am their *p.* 44:28
inheritance out of his own *p.* 46:18
with Sapphira sold a *p.* *Acts* 5:1
give it to him for a *p.* 7:5
with Jesus into *p.* of Gentiles. 45
redemption of the purchased *p.*
  Eph 1:14

possessions
and get you *p.* therein. *Gen* 34:10
Israel had *p.* therein and. 47:27
shall have *p.* among you. *Num* 32:30
you to the land of your *p. Josh* 22:4
whose *p.* were in Carmel. *I Sam* 25:2
that dwelt in their *p.* *I Chr* 9:2
the Levites left their *p.* 2 *Chr* 11:14
provided *p.* of flocks and. 32:29
I had great *p.* of great. *Eccl* 2:7
Jacob shall possess their *p.* *Ob* 17
for he had great *p.* *Mat* 19:22
  Mark 10:22
and sold their *p.* and. *Acts* 2:45
in the same quarters were *p.* 28:7*

possessor
most high God *p.* of. *Gen* 14:19, 22

possessors
whose *p.* slay them, and. *Zech* 11:5
as many as were *p.* of. *Acts* 4:34

possible
with God all things are *p. Mat* 19:26
  Mark 10:27
if *p.,* shall deceive the very elect.
  Mat 24:24; *Mark* 13:22
if *p.* let this cup pass from me.
  Mat 26:39; *Mark* 14:35
all things are *p.* to him. *Mark* 9:23
all things are *p.* to thee. 14:36
  Luke 18:27
was not *p.* he should be. *Acts* 2:24
if *p.* be at Jerusalem the day. 20:16
if it be *p.* live peaceably. *Rom* 12:18
p. ye would have plucked. *Gal* 4:15
not *p.* the blood of bulls. *Heb* 10:4

post, -s
(The old meaning of courier)
so the *p.* went with the letters from.
  2 *Chr* 30:6; *Esth* 3:13, 15; 8:10
p. rode on mules and. *Esth* 8:14
days are swifter than a *p.* *Job* 9:25
one *p.* shall run to meet. *Jer* 51:31

post
Eli sat on a seat by a *p.* *I Sam* 1:9*
on each *p.* were palm. *Ezek* 40:16

posterity
to preserve you a *p.* in. *Gen* 45:7*
or if any of your *p.* be. *Num* 9:10
I will take away the *p.* *I Ki* 16:3
take away the *p.* of Ahab. 21:21*
yet their *p.* approve. *Ps* 49:13*
his *p.* be cut off and blotted 109:13
not be divided to his *p.* *Dan* 11:4
your *p.* with fishhooks. *Amos* 4:2

posts
on the *p.* of thy house. *Deut* 6:9*
Samson took the two *p.* *Judg* 16:3
all the doors and *p.* were. *I Ki* 7:5
waiting at the *p.* of my doors.
  Pr 8:34
the *p.* of the door moved. *Isa* 6:4*
behind the *p.* thou set up thy. 57:8
the *p.* had one measure. *Ezek* 40:10
setting of their *p.* by my *p.* 43:8*
smite the lintel, that the *p.* may.
  Amos 9:1*

  see door
  side posts
strike the blood on the two side *p.*
  Ex 12:7, 22
seeth the blood on the side *p.* 23
lintel and side *p.* were a. *I Ki* 6:31

*(The English word is used to
translate a number of Hebrew
words, some of which have different
meanings. These are substituted
for pot in the Revisions)*
take a *p.* and put an. *Ex* 16:33
be sodden in a brazen *p. Lev* 6:28*
put the broth in a *p.* *Judg* 6:19
into the caldron or *p.* *I Sam* 2:14
thing, save a *p.* of oil. *2 Ki* 4:2
set on great *p.* 38
there is death in the *p.* 40
meal into the *p.,* no harm in the *p.* 41
as out of a seething *p.* *Job* 41:20
the deep to boil like a *p.* 31*
the fining *p.* is. *Pr* 17:3; 27:21
I see a seething *p.* *Jer* 1:13*
saith Lord, Set on a *p.* *Ezek* 24:3*
woe to bloody city, to the *p.* whose. 6
in pieces, as for the *p.* *Mi* 3:3
every *p.* in Jerusalem. *Zech* 14:21
wherein was the golden *p. Heb* 9:4

  water-pot
then left her *water-p.* *John* 4:28

potentate
the blessed and only *P. I Tim* 6:15

Potiphar
the Midianites sold Joseph to *P.*
  Gen 37:36; 39:1

Poti-pherah
the daughter of *P.* *Gen* 41:45, 50

pots
made the *p.* and shovels. *Ex* 38:3
oven, or rangers for *p.* *Lev* 11:35
p. and shovels of brass. *I Ki* 7:45
  2 Chr 4:16
Huram made the *p.* *2 Chr* 4:11
holy offerings sod they in *p.* 35:13
before your *p.* can feel the. *Ps* 58:9
ye have lien among the *p.* 68:13*
were delivered from the *p.* 81:6*
Rechabites *p.* full of wine. *Jer* 35:5*
washing of cups and *p. Mark* 7:4, 8
  see flesh
  water-pots
set there six *water-p.* *John* 2:6
Jesus saith to them, Fill *water-p.* 7

potsherd, -s
(A broken piece of earthenware)
him a *p.* to scrape himself. *Job* 2:8
my strength is dried up like a *p.*
  Ps 22:15
are like a *p.* covered. *Pr* 26:23*
let the *p.* strive with *p.* of. *Isa* 45:9

pottage
Jacob sod *p.* and Esau. *Gen* 25:29
feed me with *p.* 30
Jacob gave Esau *p.* 34
seethe *p.* for sons of the. *2 Ki* 4:38
shred them into the pot of *p.* 39
as they were eating the *p.* they. 40
skirt do touch bread or *p. Hag* 2:12

potter
in pieces like a *p.'s* vessel. *Ps* 2:9
it as the breaking of the *p.'s* vessel.
  Isa 30:14; *Jer* 19:11; *Rev* 2:27
down to the *p.'s* house. *Jer* 18:2
go and get a *p.'s* earthen bottle. 19:1
of the hands of the *p.* *Lam* 4:2
said, Cast it unto the *p. Zech* 11:13
them for the *p.'s* field. *Mat* 27:10
  see clay

potters
these were the *p.* and. *I Chr* 4:23

pound, -s
three *p.* of gold went. *I Ki* 10:17
treasure 5000 *p.* of silver. *Ezra* 2:69
treasure 2200 *p.* of silver. *Neh* 7:71
the rest gave 2000 *p.* of silver. 72
to his servants ten *p.* *Luke* 19:13
thy *p.* hath gained ten *p.* 16
hath gained five *p.* 18
behold, here is thy *p.* 20
take from him the *p.* 24
he hath ten *p.* 25
then Mary took a *p.* of. *John* 12:3
aloes about a 100 *p.* weight. 19:39

pour
shall take and *p.* water on. *Ex* 4:9
shall *p.* the anointing oil on. 29:7
thou shalt *p.* the blood of the bullock.
  12; *Lev* 4:7, 18, 25, 30, 34
nor *p.* drink offerings. *Ex* 30:9
he shall *p.* oil on the. *Lev* 2:1, 6
p. it into the palm of his. 14:15, 26
p. it on head of him that is to. 18
they shall *p.* out the dust that. 41
he shall *p.* out blood thereof. 17:13
he shall *p.* no oil upon. *Num* 5:15
he shall *p.* water out of his. 24:7*
p. blood out as water. *Deut* 12:16
  24; 15:23
take the flesh, and *p.* out. *Judg* 6:20
p. water on the burnt. *I Ki* 18:33
p. out the oil into those. *2 Ki* 4:4
p. out for the people, that they. 41
and *p.* the oil on Jehu's head. 9:3
p. down rain according. *Job* 36:27*
p. out my soul. *Ps* 42:4
ye people, *p.* out your heart. 62:8
p. out thine indignation on. 69:24
p. out thy wrath on the heathen 79:6
I will *p.* out my Spirit unto you.
  Pr 1:23; *Isa* 44:3; *Joel* 2:28, 29
  Acts 2:17, 18
I will *p.* water on him. *Isa* 44:3
skies *p.* down righteousness. 45:8
I will *p.* it out on the children abroad.
  Jer 6:11
and to *p.* out drink offerings. 7:18
p. out thy fury on heathen. 10:25
I will *p.* their wickedness. 14:16
p. out their blood by force. 18:21*

to p. out drink offerings to the queen
  of heaven.   Jer 44:17, 18, 19, 25
p. out thine heart like.   Lam 2:19
now will I shortly p. out.   Ezek 7:8
  14:19; 20:8, 13, 21; 30:15
I will p. out mine indignation. 21:31
       Zeph 3:8
set on the pot and p.   Ezek 24:3
I will p. out my wrath.   Hos 5:10
I will p. down the stones.   Mi 1:6
p. on house of David.   Zech 12:10
if I will not p. you out.   Mal 3:10
p. out the vials of wrath of. Rev 16:1

poured
Jacob p. oil on the top.   Gen 28:18
Jacob p. a drink offering.   35:14
the rain was not p. on   Ex 9:33
upon flesh shall it not be p.   30:32
where ashes are p. he.   Lev 4:12
Moses p. anointing oil on.   8:12
he p. the blood at the bottom. 15; 9:9
head the anointing oil was p.   21:10
to be p. to the Lord for a. Num 28:7
sacrifices shall be p. out. Deut 12:27
but I have p. out my soul. 1 Sam 1:15
drew water, and p. it out.   7:6
Samuel p. oil on Saul's head. 10:1
Tamar p. them out.   2 Sam 13:9
David would not drink thereof, but p.
  it out unto.   23:16; 1 Chr 11:18
rent, and ashes p. out.   1 Ki 13:3, 5
p. water on the hands.   2 Ki 3:11
vessels to her, and she p. out.   4:5
they p. out for the men to eat.   40
and Ahaz p. his drink offering. 16:13
my wrath not be p. out. 2 Chr 12:7
wrath that is p. out on us.   34:21
wrath shall be p. out on this place. 25
my roarings are p. out like. Job 3:24
not thou p. me out as milk ? 10:10
rock p. me out rivers of oil.   29:6
my soul is p. out upon me.   30:16
I am p. out like water.   Ps 22:14
grace is p. into thy lips.   45:2
clouds p. out water, skies.   77:17
I p. out my complaint before. 142:2
as ointment p. forth.   S of S 1:3
they p. out a prayer.   Isa 26:16
Lord hath p. on you the spirit. 29:10
till the spirit be p. on us from. 32:15
he hath p. on him the fury of. 42:25
hath p. out his soul to death. 53:12
hast p. out a drink offering.   57:6
my fury shall be p. out.   Jer 7:20
they have p. out drink offerings.
       19:13; 32:29
so shall it [fury] be p. out.   42:18
mine anger was p. forth.   44:6
when we p. drink offerings to.   19
he p. out his fury like fire.
       Lam 2:4; 4:11
my liver is p. upon earth.   11
their soul was p. out.   12
of the sanctuary are p. out.   4:1
filthiness was p. out.   Ezek 16:36
p. out their drink offerings.   20:28
with fury p. out will I rule.   33, 34
that I the Lord have p. out.   22:22
therefore I p. out mine.   31
p. their whoredom upon her.   23:8
she p. it not on the ground to. 24:7
wherefore I p. out my fury.   36:18
p. out my spirit on the house. 39:29
therefore the curse is p.   Dan 9:11
and that determined shall be p.   27
as waters that are p. down. Mi 1:4
fury is p. out like fire.   Nah 1:6
their blood shall be p. out. Zeph 1:17
p. ointment on his head.   Mat 26:7
  12; Mark 14:3
he p. out the changers' money.
       John 2:15
on the Gentiles was p.   Acts 10:45
wine of wrath of God p. Rev 14:10*
went and p. out his vial. 16:2, 3, 4
       8, 10, 12, 17

pouredst
p. out thy fornications. Ezek 16:15

poureth
he p. contempt on princes. Job 12:21
       Ps 107:40
he p. out my gall upon.   Job 16:13
eye p. out tears unto God.   20

wine is red, and he p.   Ps 75:8
but mouth of fools p. out.   Pr 15:2
the mouth of the wicked p. out.   28
p. out waters on the.   Amos 5:8; 9:6
he p. water into a bason. John 13:5

pouring
in p. thy fury on Jerusalem ? Ezek 9:8
his wounds, p. in oil.   Luke 10:34

pourtray
and p. upon it the city.   Ezek 4:1

pourtrayed
all the idols of Israel p.   Ezek 8:10
men p. on the wall, the images of the
  Chaldeans p. with.   23:14

poverty
all thou hast come to p.   Gen 45:11
so thy p. come as an armed man.
       Pr 6:11; 24:34
destruction of poor is their p. 10:15
but it tendeth to p.   11:24*
p. be to him that refuseth.   13:18
sleep, lest thou come to p.   20:13
and glutton come to p.   23:21
persons, shall have p. enough. 28:19
considereth not that p. shall come. 22
give me neither p. nor riches.   30:8
let him drink and forget his p.   31:7
their deep p. abounded to. 2 Cor 8:2
became poor, that ye through his p. 9
I know thy works and p.   Rev 2:9

powder
calf and ground it to p.   Ex 32:20
the rain of thy land p.   Deut 28:24
grove to p., cast the p.   2 Ki 23:6
the altar to p.   15; 2 Chr 34:7
it will grind him to p.   Mat 21:44*
       Luke 20:18*

powders
perfumed with all the p.   S of S 3:6

power
(Generally for rule, or authority ;
  frequently for might and strength)
hast thou p. with God.   Gen 32:28*
dignity, excellency of p.   49:3
break the pride of your p. Lev 26:19
have I now any p. to say ? Num 22:38
brought thee with thy mighty p.
       Deut 4:37
it is he that giveth thee p. to.   8:18
see'th that their p. is gone.   32:36
is my strength and p.   2 Sam 22:33
the inhabitants were of small p.
       2 Ki 19:26
Joab led forth the p.   1 Chr 20:1
thine is the p. and glory.   29:11
       Mat 6:13
in thine hand is p.   1 Chr 29:12
       2 Chr 20:6
God hath p. to help.   2 Chr 25:8
siege, and all his p. with him. 32:9
cease by force and p.   Ezra 4:23
his p. and wrath against all.   8:22
nor is it in our p. to redeem them.
       Neh 5:5
he made a feast to p. of.   Esth 1:3
perish the p. of the people.   8:11
the Jews hoped to have p.   9:1
redeem in war from the p. Job 5:20
also the mighty with his p.   24:22
helped him that is without p.   26:2
he divided the sea with his p.   12
the thunder of his p. who can ?   14
God exalteth by his p.   36:22
conceal his parts nor his p.   41:12
my darling from the p. of.   Ps 22:20
redeem my soul from the p. 49:15
p. belongeth unto God.   62:11
mountains girded with p.   65:6
he ruleth by his p. for ever.   66:7
he giveth strength and p. to. 68:35
by his p. he brought in the south
  wind.   78:26
who knoweth the p. of thine ? 90:11
his mighty p. to be known. 106:8
he shewed his people the p. 111:6
in the firmament of his p. 150:1
oppressors there was p.   Eccl 4:1
and hath given him p. to eat.   5:19
God giveth him not p. to eat.   6:2
word of a king is, there is p.   8:4
no man hath p. over the spirit.   8
their inhabitants were of small p.
       Isa 37:27

he giveth p. to the faint.   Isa 40:29
bringeth forth the army and p. 43:17
from the p. of the flame.   47:14
the earth by his p. Jer 10:12; 51:15
were in thee to their p.   Ezek 22:6
and the pride of her p. shall.   30:6
God hath given thee p.   Dan 2:37
Daniel from the p. of lions.   6:27
ran in fury of his p.   8:6
but not in his p.   22
p. shall be mighty, but not by his p. 24
not retain the p. of the arm.   11:6
he shall stir up his p. and his.   25
but he shall have p. over the.   43
to scatter the p. of the holy.   12:7
he had p. with God.   Hos 12:3
yea, he had p. over the angel.   4
I will ransom them from the p. 13:14
in the p. of their hand.   Mi 2:1
I am full of p. by the Spirit of.   3:8
imputing this his p. unto. Hab 1:11
delivered from the p. of evil.   2:9
there was the hiding of his p.   3:4
not by might, nor by my p. Zech 4:6
Lord will smite her p. in the sea. 9:4
Son of man hath p. on earth to.
  Mat 9:6; Mark 2:10; Luke 5:24
had given such p. to men. Mat 9:8
gave p. against unclean spirits. 10:1
       Luke 9:1
coming in the clouds with p.
  Mat 24:30; Luke 21:27
sitting on right hand with p.
  Mat 26:64; Mark 14:62
all p. is given unto me in heaven and
  in earth.   Mat 28:18
to heal sicknesses.   Mark 3:15
kingdom of God come with p.   9:1
p. of the Highest shall.   Luke 1:35
the devil said, All this p. will.   4:6
for his word was with p.   32
p. he commandeth unclean spirits. 36
the p. of the Lord was present. 5:17
I give you p. to tread on serpents,
  and over all the p. of the.   10:19
fear him that hath p. to cast.   12:5
they might deliver him to p.   20:20
and the p. of darkness.   22:53
until ye be endued with p.   24:49
to them gave he p. to become sons
  of God.   John 1:12*
I have p. to lay it down, and p. 10:18
thou hast given him p. over.   17:2
I have p. to crucify thee, p. to. 19:10
the Father hath put in his own p.
       Acts 1:7*
shall receive p. after Holy Ghost. 8
as though by our own p. or.   3:12
they asked, By what p. have ye ? 4:7
was it not in thine own p.?   5:4
faith and p., did great wonders. 6:8
saying, Give me also this p.   8:19
Jesus with Holy Ghost and p. 10:38
from the p. of Satan to God. 26:18
be the Son of God with p. Rom 1:4
his eternal p. and Godhead.   20
hath not the potter p. over ? 9:21
willing to make his p. known.   22
resisteth the p., resisteth.   13:2
then not be afraid of the p.?   3
through p. of the Holy Ghost. 15:13
wonders, by the p. of the Spirit. 19
that is of p. to establish you. 16:25*
of the Spirit and p.   1 Cor 2:4
know, not the speech, but the p. 4:19
with the p. of our Lord Jesus.   5:4
brought under the p. of any.   6:12
will raise us up by his own p.   14
wife and husband have not p. of. 7:4
but hath p. over his own will.   37
we p. to eat and to drink ?   9:4*
p. to lead about a sister, a wife ? 5*
not p. to forbear working ?   6
if others be partakers of this p. over
  you, we have not used this p.   12
the woman ought to have p. on. 11:10
put down all authority and p. 15:24
that the excellency of p. 2 Cor 4:7
p. yea, and beyond their p.   8:3
that the p. of Christ may rest. 12:9
according to the p. God hath. 13:10
his p. toward us, according to the
  working of his mighty p. Eph 1:19*
far above all principality, p. and. 21

prince of the *p.* of the air. *Eph* 2:2
by the effectual working of his *p.* 3:7
to the *p.* that worketh in us. 20
I may know the *p.* of his. *Phil* 3:10
according to his glorious *p. Col* 1:11*
us from the *p.* of darkness. 13
of all principality and *p.* 2:10
from the glory of his *p.* 2 *Tim* 1:9
the work of faith with *p.* 11
working of Satan with all *p.* 2:9
not *p.* but to make ourselves. 3:9
whom be honour and *p.* 1 *Tim* 6:16
God hath given us spirit of *p.*
     2 *Tim* 1:7
of godliness, but denying the *p.* 3:5
things by word of his *p. Heb* 1:3
him that had *p.* of death. 2:14
after the *p.* of an endless life. 7:16
as his divine *p.* hath given. 2 *Pet* 1:3
known the *p.* of our Lord. 16
to the only wise God our Saviour be
     glory and *p.*   *Jude* 25
I give *p.* over the nations. *Rev* 2:26
to receive honour and *p.* 4:11; 5:12
blessing, honour, glory, and *p.* 5:13
p. was given to him that sat on. 6:4
p. was given them over fourth. 8
honour, *p.*, and might be unto. 7:12
given *p.* as scorpions have *p.* 9:3
and their *p.* was to hurt men. 10
for their *p.* is in their mouth. 19
give *p.* to my two witnesses. 11:3
p. to shut heaven, *p.* over waters. 6
the *p.* of his Christ come. 12:10
gave him *p.* and his seat. 13:2, 4
p. was given to him to. 5, 7
he exerciseth all the *p.* of the. 12
had *p.* to give life. 15
had *p.* over fire. 14:18
filled with smoke from his *p.* 15:8
p. was given him to scorch. 16:8
blasphemed God who hath *p.* over. 9
receive *p.* as kings one hour. 17:12
shall give their *p.* and strength. 13
glory, honour, and *p.*, unto the. 19:1

     see **great** *power*

     power *of God*
the scriptures, nor the *p.* of God.
     Mat 22:29; *Mark* 12:24
all amazed at the mighty *p.* of God.
     Luke 9:43*
the right hand of *p.* of God. 22:69
this man is the great *p.* of God.
     Acts 8:10*
gospel is the *p.* of God. *Rom* 1:16
are saved, it is the *p.* of God.
     1 *Cor* 1:18
Christ the *p.* of God, and. 24
stand but by the *p.* of God. 2:5
of truth, by the *p.* of God. 2 *Cor* 6:7
liveth by *p.* of God, but we shall live
     with him by *p.* of God. 13:4
of the afflictions of the gospel, ac-
     cording to the *p.* of God. 2 *Tim* 1:8
kept by the *p.* of God. 1 *Pet* 1:5

     in power
it is *in p.* of my hand. *Gen* 31:29
become glorious *in p. Ex* 15:6
the wicked mighty *in p.*? *Job* 21:7
he is excellent *in p.* and in. 37:23
when it is *in p.* of thy. *Pr* 3:27
death and life are *in the p.* 18:21
that he is strong *in p.* not. *Isa* 40:26
slow to anger, great *in p. Nah* 1:3
go before him *in the p.* of Elias.
     Luke 1:17
in the p. of the Spirit. 4:14
kingdom of God not in word, but *in*
     p. 1 *Cor* 4:20
in weakness, it is raised *in p.* 15:43
be strong *in* the Lord and *p. Eph* 6:10
came in word, and also *in p.*
     1 *Thes* 1:5
greater *in p.* and might. 2 *Pet* 2:11

     my power
all *my p.* I have served. *Gen* 31:6
to shew in thee *my p. Ex* 9:16
My p. hath gotten me. *Deut* 8:17
built by the might of *my p. Dan* 4:30
that I might shew *my p. Rom* 9:17
that I abuse not *my p.* in. 1 *Cor* 9:18*

     no **power**
sell her he shall have *no p. Ex* 21:8
shall have *no p.* to stand. *Lev* 26:37
men of Ai had *no p.* to. *Josh* 8:20
people had *no p.* to weep. 1 *Sam* 30:4
with them that have *no p.* 2 *Chr* 14:11
house of Ahaziah had *no p.* to. 22:9
or have I *no p.* to deliver ? *Isa* 50:2
bodies the fire had *no p. Dan* 3:27
there was *no p.* in the ram to. 8:7
no p. against me, except. *John* 19:11
for there is *no p.* but. *Rom* 13:1
second death hath *no p. Rev* 20:6

     thy **power**
out by *thy* mighty *p. Deut* 9:29
all that he hath is in *thy p. Job* 1:12
sing, and praise *thy p. Ps* 21:13
scatter them by *thy p.* 59:11
will sing of *thy p.* 16
to see *thy p.* and thy glory. 63:2
through greatness of *thy p.* 66:3
and *thy p.* to every one that. 71:18
to the greatness of *thy p.* 79:11
be willing in day of *thy p.* 110:3
they shall talk of *thy p.* 145:11
fortify *thy p.* mightily. *Nah* 2:1

     powerful
Lord is *p.* full of majesty. *Ps* 29:4
for his letters, say they, are *p.*
     2 *Cor* 10:10*
word of God is quick, *p. Heb* 4:12*

     powers
p. of heaven be shaken. *Mat* 24:29
     Mark 13:25; *Luke* 21:26
when brought before *p. Luke* 12:11*
nor *p.* can separate from. *Rom* 8:38
the *p.* that be are ordained of. 13:1
p. in heavenly places. *Eph* 3:10
against principalities and *p.* 6:12
p. were created by him. *Col* 1:16
having spoiled *p.* he made a. 2:15
in mind to be subject to *p. Tit* 3:1*
tasted the *p.* of the world. *Heb* 6:5
on right hand of God, *p.* 1 *Pet* 3:22

     practices
heart exercised with covetous *p.*
     2 *Pet* 2:14*

     practise
not to *p.* wicked works. *Ps* 141:4*
person shall *p.* hypocrisy. *Isa* 32:6
destroy, prosper, and *p. Dan* 8:24*
morning is light, they *p.* it. *Mi* 2:1

     practised
that Saul secretly *p.* mischief.
     1 *Sam* 23:9*
the little horn *p.* and. *Dan* 8:12*

     praise
(*Most frequently used with regard
to praise rendered to God. The
verb is frequently changed in the
Revisions to bless, or give thanks*)
he is thy *p.* and he is. *Deut* 10:21
to make thee high in *p.* and. 26:19
I will sing *p.* to the Lord. *Judg* 5:3
     Ps 7:17; 9:2; 57:7; 61:8; 104:33
we may glory in thy *p.* 1 *Chr* 16:35
as taught to sing *p.* 2 *Chr* 23:13
above all blessing and *p. Neh* 9:5
of David were songs of *p.* 12:46
shew forth all thy *p. Ps* 9:14
my *p.* shall be of thee in the. 22:25
that my glory may sing *p.* 30:12
p. is comely for the upright. 33:1
his *p.* shall be continually in. 34:1
tongue shall speak of thy *p.* 35:28
even *p.* to our God. 40:3
with voice of *p.* 42:4
so is thy *p.* to the ends of. 48:10
offereth *p.* glorifieth me. 50:23
mouth shall shew forth thy *p.* 51:15
p. waiteth for thee, O God. 65:1
honour, make his *p.* glorious. 66:2
and make the voice of his *p.* 8
my *p.* shall be continually of. 71:6
let my mouth be filled with thy *p.* 8
we will shew forth thy *p.* 79:13
rejoice and sing *p.* 98:4
enter into his courts with *p.* 100:4
declare his *p.* in Jerusalem. 102:21
who can shew forth all his *p.*? 106:2
then they sang his *p.* 12
triumph in thy *p.* 47

give *p.* even with my glory. *Ps* 108:1
O God of my *p.* 109:1
his *p.* endureth. 111:10
lips shall utter *p.* when. 119:171
before the gods will I sing *p.* 138:1
my mouth shall speak the *p.* 145:21
p. is comely. 147:1
sing *p.* on the harp. 7
the *p.* of all his saints. 148:14
sing his *p.* in the congregation. 149:1
so is a man to his *p. Pr* 27:21
I will not give my *p.* to. *Isa* 42:8
sing his *p.* from the end of the. 10
let them declare his *p.* in the. 12
they shall shew forth my *p.* 43:21
my *p.* will I refrain for thee. 48:9
thou shalt call thy gates *P.* 60:18
the garment of *p.* for the spirit. 61:3
will cause righteousness and *p.* 11
till he made Jerusalem a *p.* in. 62:7
might be to me for a *p. Jer* 13:11
O Lord, for thou art my *p.* 17:14
bringing sacrifices of *p.* 26; 33:11
it shall be to me a joy, a *p.* 33:9
there shall be no more *p.* of. 48:2
how is the city of *p.* not left? 49:25
how is the *p.* of whole earth ? 51:41
earth was full of his *p. Hab* 3:3
will get them *p.* and fame. *Zeph* 3:19
make you a *p.* among all people. 20
thou hast perfected *p. Mat* 21:16
saw it, gave *p.* to God. *Luke* 18:43
unto him, Give God the *p. John* 9:24
p. of men more than *p.* of. 12:43
whose *p.* is not of men. *Rom* 2:29
thou shalt have *p.* of same. 13:3
every man have *p.* of God. 1 *Cor* 4:5
whose *p.* is in the gospel. 2 *Cor* 8:18
to *p.* of glory of his grace. *Eph* 1:6
to *p.* of glory who first. 12, 14
unto the *p.* of God. *Phil* 1:11
if there be any *p.* think on. 4:8
of the church will I sing *p. Heb* 2:12
him let us offer sacrifice of *p.* 13:15
faith might be found to *p.* 1 *Pet* 1:7
and for the *p.* of them that do. 2:14
to whom be *p.* and dominion. 4:11

     praise, *verb*
whom thy brethren shall *p. Gen* 49:8
fruit holy to *p.* the Lord. *Lev* 19:24
instruments I made to *p.* 1 *Chr* 23:5
and *p.* thy glorious name. 29:13
Levites to *p.* before the. 2 *Chr* 8:14
that should *p.* the beauty. 20:21
began to sing and to *p.* 22
to *p.* in the gates of the tents. 31:2
so will we sing and *p. Ps* 21:13
ye that fear the Lord, *p.* him. 22:23
pit, shall the dust *p.* thee ? 30:9
hope in God, for I shall yet *p.* him.
     42:5, 11; 43:5
God we boast, and *p.* thy name. 44:8
shall the people *p.* thee. 45:17
men will *p.* thee, when doest. 49:18
my lips shall *p.* thee. 63:3
mouth shall *p.* thee. 5
let the people *p.* thee. 67:3
let all the people *p.* thee. 5
heaven and the earth *p.* him. 69:34
I will yet *p.* thee more and. 71:14
let the poor and needy. 74:21
wrath of man shall *p.* thee. 76:10
dead arise and *p.* thee ? 88:10
the heavens shall *p.* thy. 89:5
p. thy great and terrible name. 99:3
p. him in the assembly of. 107:32
p. him, O ye servants of the Lord.
     113:1; 135:1
the dead *p.* not the Lord. 115:17
seven times a day do I *p.* 119:164
let my soul live and it shall *p.* 175
I will *p.* thy name for thy. 138:2
of the earth shall *p.* thee. 4
out of prison that I may *p.* 142:7
one generation shall *p.* thy. 145:4
all thy works shall *p.* thee. 10
p. the Lord, Jerusalem. 147:12
p. ye the Lord, *p.* him in the. 148:1
p. him, all his angels, *p.* him, ye. 2
p. him, sun and moon, *p.* him. 3
p. him, ye heavens of heavens.
p. his name in the dance. 149:3
p. God in his sanctuary, *p.* 150:1

p. him for his mighty acts, *p.* him.
    Ps 150:2
p. him with trumpet.   3
p. him with timbrel.   4
p. him upon the loud and.   5
let another man *p.* thee.   *Pr* 27:2
they that forsake the law *p.* the. 28:4
let her own works *p.* her in.   31:31
the grave cannot *p.* thee. *Isa* 38:18
the living he shall *p.* thee, as.   19
publish, *p.* ye and say.   *Jer* 31:7
I thank and *p.* thee, O.   *Dan* 2:23
I *p.* extol, and honour the king. 4:37
p. the name of the Lord. *Joel* 2:26
disciples began to *p.* God with loud.
    Luke 19:37
now I *p.* you that ye.   *1 Cor* 11:2
I declare, I *p.* you not.   17, 22
saying, P. our God, all ye. *Rev* 19:5

    I will, or *will I* **praise**
Leah said, Now will I *p.*   *Gen* 29:35
I will *p.* Lord according.   *Ps* 7:17
I will *p.* thee, O Lord, with my whole
  heart.   9:1; 111:1; 138:1
congregation will I *p.* thee.   22:22
with my song will I *p.* him.   28:7
I will give thee thanks, I will *p.* 35:18
    57:9; 108:3; 109:30
on the harp will I *p.* thee.   43:4
I will *p.* thee for ever, because. 52:9
I will *p.* thy name, O Lord.   54:6
in God I will *p.* his word.   56:4, 10
I will *p.* the name of God.   69:30
I will also *p.* thee with the.   71:22
I will *p.* thee, O Lord my.   86:12
I will go into them, and will *p.* 118:19
I will *p.* thee, for thou hast heard. 21
thou art my God, and I will *p.*   28
I will *p.* thee with uprightness. 119:7
I will *p.* thee, for I am wonderfully
  made.   139:14
I will *p.* thy name for ever.   145:2
I will *p.* thee, though.   *Isa* 12:1
I will *p.* thy name, thou hast. 25:1

praise *ye the Lord,* or **praise**
    the Lord
p. ye the Lord, for the avenging of
  Israel.   *Judg* 5:2
Levites to *p.* the Lord.   *1 Chr* 16:4
morning to *p.* the Lord.   23:20
with a harp to *p.* the Lord.   25:3
stood up to *p.* the Lord. *2 Chr* 20:19
p. the Lord, for his mercy.   21
cymbals to *p.* the Lord.   *Ezra* 3:10
they shall *p.* the Lord.   *Ps* 22:26
p. the Lord with harp, sing.   33:2
be created shall *p.* the Lord. 102:18
p. ye the Lord.   104:35; 106:1, 48
  111:1; 112:1; 113:1, 9; 115:18
  116:19; 117:2; 135:1; 146:1, 10
  147:20; 148:1, 14; 149:1, 9
    150:1, 6; *Jer* 20:13
Oh that men would *p.* the Lord.
    Ps 107:8, 15, 21, 31
I will greatly *p.* the Lord.   109:30
I will *p.* the Lord.   118:19
p. the Lord; for Lord is good. 135:3
while I live will I *p.* the Lord. 146:2
p. ye the Lord, for it is good. 147:1
p. the Lord, O Jerusalem, praise. 12
p. the Lord from the earth.   148:7
p. the Lord, call upon his. *Isa* 12:4
eat it, and *p.* the Lord.   62:9
p. the Lord of hosts, for. *Jer* 33:11
p. the Lord, all ye Gentiles.
    Rom 15:11

    praised
the people *p.* their god. *Judg* 16:24
none *p.* as Absalom.   *2 Sam* 14:25
the Lord is worthy to be *p.*   22:4
    Ps 18:3
Lord is great and greatly to be *p.*
  1 Chr 16:25; *Ps* 48:1; 96:4; 145:3
the people *p.* the Lord. *1 Chr* 16:36
and four thousand *p.* the Lord.
  23:5; *2 Chr* 7:3; *Neh* 5:13
of music *p.* the Lord.   *2 Chr* 5:13
David *p.* by the ministry.   7:6
Levites and priests *p.* the.   30:21
when they *p.* the Lord.   *Ezra* 3:11
and daily shall be *p.*   *Ps* 72:15
of sun Lord's name is to be *p.* 113:3
feareth Lord shall be *p.*   *Pr* 31:30

I *p.* the dead more than.   *Eccl* 4:2
and concubines *p.* her.   *S of S* 6:9
where our fathers *p.* thee. *Isa* 64:11
I *p.* and honoured him.   *Dan* 4:34
they *p.* the gods of gold and. 5:4, 23
and Zacharias spake and *p.* God.
    Luke 1:64

    praises
like thee, fearful in *p.?*   *Ex* 15:11
sing *p.* to thy name.   *2 Sam* 22:50
    Ps 18:49; 92:1; 135:3
Levites to sing *p.* to the Lord, and
  they sang *p.* with.   *2 Chr* 29:30
sing *p.* to the Lord that.   *Ps* 9:11
thou that inhabitest *p.* of Israel. 22:3
yea, I will sing *p.* to God.   27:6
  47:6; 68:32; 75:9; 108:3
God is king, sing ye *p.* with.   47:7
I will render *p.* unto.   56:12; 144:9
sing to God, sing *p.* to his.   68:4
generation to come *p.* of Lord. 78:4
I will sing *p.* to my God while. 146:2
for it is good to sing *p.* to.   147:1
let them sing *p.* to him.   149:3
let the high *p.* of God be in their. 6
shew forth the *p.* of Lord. *Isa* 60:6
mention of the *p.* of the Lord. 63:7
prayed and sang *p.* to.   *Acts* 16:25
shew forth the *p.* of him. *1 Pet* 2:9

    praiseth
husband also, and he *p.*   *Pr* 31:28

    praising
one sound to be heard in *p.* the Lord.
    2 Chr 5:13
Athaliah heard the people *p.* 23:12
they sang by course in *p.* *Ezra* 3:11
they will be still *p.* thee.   *Ps* 84:4
heavenly host *p.* God.   *Luke* 2:13
the shepherds returned, *p.* God. 20
in the temple *p.* God.   24:53
eat with gladness, *p.* God. *Acts* 2:47
and leaping, and *p.* God.   3:8, 9

    prancing
the noise of the *p.* horses. *Nah* 3:2

    prancings
broken by means of *p.*   *Judg* 5:22

    prating
but a *p.* fool shall fall.   *Pr* 10:8, 10
p. against us with.   *3 John* 10

    pray
(Revisions frequently change to
    beseech)
and shall *p.* for thee.   *Gen* 20:7
Samuel said, I will *p.*   *1 Sam* 7:5
p. for thy servants to the.   12:19
that I should sin in ceasing to *p.* 23
found in his heart to *p.* this prayer.
    2 Sam 7:27; *1 Chr* 17:25
when they shall *p.* toward. *1 Ki* 8:30
  35, 42, 44, 48; *2 Chr* 6:26, 34, 38
p. that my hand may be. *1 Ki* 13:6
shall *p.* and make.   *2 Chr* 6:24, 32
and turn and *p.* in the land of.   37
if my people shall *p.* and.   7:14
and *p.* for the life of.   *Ezra* 6:10
hear the prayer which I *p.* *Neh* 1:6
what profit should we have, if we *p.*
  unto him?   *Job* 21:15
p. to God, and he will be.   33:26
my servant Job shall *p.* for.   42:8
God, for to thee will I *p.*   *Ps* 5:2
and at noon will I *p.*   55:17*
p. for the peace of Jerusalem. 122:6
come to his sanctuary to *p.* *Isa* 16:12
p. to a god that cannot save. 45:20
p. not thou for this people. *Jer* 7:16
    11:14; 14:11
seek peace of the city, *p.* to.   29:7
ye shall *p.* to me, and I will.   12
p. now to the Lord.   37:3; 42:2, 20
behold, I will *p.* to the Lord.   42:4
they sent men to *p.*   *Zech* 7:2*
go speedily to *p.* before.   8:21*, 22*
and *p.* for them that despitefully.
    Mat 5:44; *Luke* 6:27
they love to *p.* standing.   *Mat* 6:5
p. to thy Father which is in.   6
when ye *p.* use not vain.   7
after this manner *p.* ye, Our.   9
p. ye the Lord of the harvest.   9:38
    Luke 10:2

he went . . . apart to *p.*   *Mat* 14:23
  Mark 6:46; *Luke* 6:12; 9:28
his hands on them and *p.* *Mat* 19:13
p. your flight be not in winter.
    24:20; *Mark* 13:18
sit ye here while I go and *p.* yonder.
    Mat 26:36; *Mark* 14:32
watch and *p.* that ye enter not.
  Mat 26:41; *Mark* 13:33; 14:38
    Luke 21:36; 22:40, 46
thinkest thou I cannot *p.? Mat* 26:53
to *p.* him to depart.   *Mark* 5:17
things ye desire when ye *p.*   11:24
Lord, teach us to *p.* as.   *Luke* 11:1
he said to them, When ye *p.* say.   2
that men ought always to *p.*   18:1
went up into the temple to *p.*   10
p. the Father.   *John* 14:16; 16:26
I *p.* for them, I *p.* not for.   17:9
I *p.* not that thou take them.   15
neither *p.* I for these alone, but. 20
p. God, if perhaps the.   *Acts* 8:22
Simon said, P. ye to the Lord.   24
up on the housetop to *p.*   10:9
not what we should *p.* for. *Rom* 8:26
a woman *p.* uncovered ? *1 Cor* 11:13
wherefore let him *p.* that he. 14:13
for if I *p.* in unknown tongue.   14
I will *p.* with spirit, *p.* with.   15
ambassadors for Christ, we *p.* you
  be reconciled.   *2 Cor* 5:20
now I *p.* to God, that ye do.   13:7
this I *p.* that your love.   *Phil* 1:9
we do not cease to *p.* for.   *Col* 1:9
p. without ceasing.   *1 Thes* 5:17
I *p.* God your whole spirit be.   23
brethren, *p.* for us.   25; *2 Thes* 3:1
    Heb 13:18
wherefore we *p.* always. *2 Thes* 1:11
I will that men *p.* every.   *1 Tim* 2:8
I *p.* God it be not laid to. *2 Tim* 4:16
is any afflicted ? let him *p.* *Jas* 5:13
p. over him, anointing him.   14
confess your faults, and *p.* one.   16
I do not say that he shall *p.* for it.
    1 John 5:16*

    prayed
Abraham *p.* and God healed Abime-
  lech.   *Gen* 20:17
when Moses *p.* the fire.   *Num* 11:2
and Moses *p.* for the people.   21:7
    Deut 9:26
I *p.* for Aaron also the.   *Deut* 9:20
Hannah *p.* to Lord.   *1 Sam* 1:10, 21
for this child I *p.*   27
Samuel *p.* unto the Lord.   8:6
Elisha *p.* unto the Lord.   *2 Ki* 4:33
    6:17, 18
Hezekiah *p.*   19:15; 20:2
  2 Chr 30:18; 32:24
that which thou *p.* to me.
    2 Ki 19:20; *Isa* 37:21
Isaiah *p.*   *2 Chr* 32:20
Manasseh *p.*   33:13
now when Ezra had *p.*   *Ezra* 10:1
    Neh 1:4; 2:4
the captivity when Job *p.* *Job* 42:10
Jeremiah *p.*   *Jer* 32:16
Jonah *p.*   *Jonah* 2:1; 4:2
Daniel *p.* three times. *Dan* 6:10; 9:4
p. let this cup pass from. *Mat* 26:39
  42:44; *Mark* 14:35, 39; *Luke* 22:41
a solitary place and *p.*   *Mark* 1:35
he *p.* him that he might be.   5:18
Jesus *p.* him he would thrust out a.
    Luke 5:3
into the wilderness and *p.*   16
as he *p.* his countenance was. 9:29
the Pharisee stood and *p.*   18:11
but I have *p.* that thy faith.   22:32
being in an agony he *p.* more.   44
his disciples *p.* him.   *John* 4:31
the disciples *p.* and said. *Acts* 1:24
when they *p.* they laid their.   4:31
Peter and John when come *p.*   8:15
Peter *p.*   9:40
Cornelius *p.* always.   10:2, 30
then they *p.* him to tarry.   48
they had fasted and *p.* 13:3; 14:23
man of Macedonia *p.* him.   16:9
at midnight Paul and Silas *p.*   25
Paul kneeled down and *p.*   20:36
kneeled down on shore and *p.* 21:5
while I *p.* in the temple, I.   22:17

Paul p. me to bring this young.
    Acts 23:18
to whom Paul entered in and p. 28:8
Elias p. that it might.   Jas 5:17
and he p. again, and the heaven. 18

prayer

heart to pray this p.   2 Sam 7:27
have respect to the p.   1 Ki 8:28
hearken to the p. 29; 2 Chr 6:19, 20
p. shall be made by any man.
    1 Ki 8:38; 2 Chr 6:29
hear their p.   1 Ki 8:45, 49
    2 Chr 6:35, 39, 40
end of praying this p.   1 Ki 8:54
lift up thy p. for remnant. 2 Ki 19:4
    Isa 37:4
be attent to the p.   2 Chr 7:15
their p. came to his holy.   30:27
Manasseh's p. unto God. 33:18, 19
thou mayest hear the p.   Neh 1:6
nevertheless we made our p.   4:9
yea thou restrainest p.   Job 15:4
thou shalt make thy p. to him. 22:27
O thou that hearest p.   Ps 65:2
p. shall be made for him.   72:15
how long be angry against p.? 80:4
he will regard the p. of the destitute,
    and not despise their p.   102:17
but I give myself unto p.   109:4
and let his p. become sin.   7
the p. of the upright is.   Pr 15:8
heareth the p. of the righteous.   29
his p. shall be abomination.   28:9
poured out a p. when.   Isa 26:16
joyful in my house of p.: for mine
    house shall be called an house of p.
    56:7; Mat 21:13; Mark 11:17
    Luke 19:46
cry nor p. for them. Jer 7:16; 11:14
that our p. should not pass. Lam 3:44
I set my face to the Lord, to seek by
    p.   Dan 9:3
yet make we not our p. before.   18
now, O our God, hear the p. of.   17
a p. of Habakkuk the.   Hab 3:1
howbeit, this kind goeth not out but
    by p.   Mat 17:21; Mark 9:29
Zacharias, thy p. is.   Luke 1:13
temple at the hour of p.   Acts 3:1
ourselves continually to p.   6:4
Cornelius, thy p. is heard.   10:31
p. was made without ceasing.   12:5
we went out where p. was.   16:13*
as we went to p. a certain.   16
give yourselves to p.   1 Cor 7:5
helping together by p.   2 Cor 1:11
by their p. for you, which.   9:14
praying always with all p. Eph 6:18
always in every p. of mine. Phil 1:4
my salvation through your p.   19
in every thing by p. let requests. 4:6
by the word and p.   1 Tim 4:5
the p. of faith shall save. Jas 5:15
the effectual p. of a righteous.   16*
sober, and watch unto p.   1 Pet 4:7
    see **heard**

    in **prayer**

the thanksgiving in p.   Neh 11:17
speaking in p. Gabriel.   Dan 9:21
whatever ye ask in p.   Mat 21:22
all night in p. to God.   Luke 6:12
with one accord in p.   Acts 1:14
continuing instant in p.   Rom 12:12
continue in p. and watch.   Col 4:2

    my **prayer**

also my p. is pure.   Job 16:17
have mercy upon me, and hear my p.
    Ps 4:1; 17:1; 39:12; 54:2
in the morning will I direct my p. 5:3
the Lord will receive my p.   6:9
and my p. returned to mine.   35:13
and my p. to the God of my.   42:8
give ear unto my p. O God.   55:1
O God, attend to my p. 61:1; 64:1*
    84:8; 86:6; 102:1; 143:1
attended to the voice of my p. 66:19
hath not turned away my p.   20
my p. is unto thee in an.   69:13
let my p. come before thee.   88:2
in the morning shall my p.   13
let my p. be set before thee.   141:2
for yet my p. shall be in their.   5
he shutteth out my p.   Lam 3:8

my p. came in to thee.   Jonah 2:7
brethren, my p. to God.   Rom 10:1

prayers

p. of David, son of.   Ps 72:20
when ye make many p.   Isa 1:15
pretence make long p.   Mat 23:14
    Mark 12:40; Luke 20:47
Anna continued in p.   Luke 2:37
disciples of John make p.?   5:33
breaking of bread and in p. Acts 2:42
thy p. and alms are come up.   10:4
make mention of you always in my p.
    Rom 1:9; Eph 1:16; 1 Thes 1:2
    2 Tim 1:3; Philem 4
strive with me in your p. Rom 15:30
fervently for you in p.   Col 4:12
I exhort that p. be made. 1 Tim 2:1
continueth in p. night and day.   5:5
I trust through your p. I.   Philem 22
when he had offered up p. Heb 5:7
heirs of life, that your p.   1 Pet 3:7
his ears are open to their p. but.   12
full of odours, which are the p. of
    saints.   Rev 5:8
he should offer it with the p.   8:3
the smoke which came with the p. 4

prayest

when thou p. be not.   Mat 6:5, 6

prayeth, -ing

as Hannah continued p.   1 Sam 1:12
woman that stood p. by thee.   26
hearken to prayer which thy servant
    1 Ki 8:28; 2 Chr 6:19, 20
Solomon had made an end of p.
    1 Ki 8:54; 2 Chr 7:1
he worshippeth it and p.   Isa 44:17
and found Daniel p.   Dan 6:11
while I was speaking and p.   9:20
ye stand p. forgive.   Mark 11:25
people were p. without.   Luke 1:10
and Jesus p., the heaven.   3:21
he was alone p., his disciples.   9:18
as he was p. in certain place.   11:1
behold he p.   Acts 9:11
I was at Joppa p.   11:5
were gathered together p.   12:12
every man p. with his.   1 Cor 11:4
every woman that p. uncovered.   5
spirit p. but my understanding. 14:14
p. us with much entreaty. 2 Cor 8:4
p. always with all prayer. Eph 6:18
p. always for you.   Col 1:3
p. also for us.   4:3
night and day p. exceedingly that we
    might see your face. 1 Thes 3:10
but ye, beloved, p. in the.   Jude 20

preach

(*To proclaim or publish abroad*)
prophets to p. of thee.   Neh 6:7
the Lord hath anointed me to p. good
    tidings.   Isa 61:1
p. to it the preaching.   Jonah 3:2
time Jesus began to p.   Mat 4:17
p. saying, The kingdom of God. 10:7
what ye hear, that p. ye upon.   27
he departed thence to p. in.   11:1
John did p. the baptism.   Mark 1:4
that I may p. there.   38; Luke 4:43
he might send them forth to p.
    Mat 3:14; Luke 9:2
to p. deliverance to. Luke 4:18, 19
go thou and p. the kingdom.   9:60
they ceased not to p.   Acts 5:42
he commanded us to p. to.   10:42
and p. unto you that ye should. 14:15
in every city them that p. him. 15:21
forbidden by Holy Ghost to p.   16:6
Jesus whom I p. to you is.   17:3
word of faith which we p. Rom 10:8
and how shall they p. except ?   15
we p. Christ crucified.   1 Cor 1:23
though I p. gospel, I have nothing to
    glory, woe is me if I p. not. 9:16
I or they, so we p. and so.   15:11
we p. not ourselves, but. 2 Cor 4:5
that I might p. him among. Gal 1:16
the gospel which I p. among the. 2:2
if I yet p. circumcision.   5:11
should p. among Gentiles. Eph 3:8
some indeed p. Christ of. Phil 1:15
the one p. Christ of contention.   16
whom we p., warning.   Col 1:28
p. the word, be instant.   2 Tim 4:2

preached

I have p. righteousness in.   Ps 40:9
poor have the gospel p.   Mat 11:5
p. saying, There cometh.   Mark 1:7
he p. in their synagogues.   39
many were gathered, he p. the.   2:2
went and p. that men should.   6:12
went forth and p. every where. 16:20
many other things p. he.   Luke 3:18
he p. in the synagogues of.   4:44
time the kingdom of God is p. 16:16
remission of sin should be p.   24:47
who before was p. to you. Acts 3:20
p. through Jesus resurrection.   4:2
p. Christ to Samaria.   8:5
p. the word of the Lord, p.   25
p. Jesus to eunuch.   35
Philip p. in all cities till he came. 40
Saul p. Christ in synagogues.   9:20
Barnabas told how Saul had p.   27
the baptism which John p.   10:37
they p. the word of God in.   13:5
when John had first p. before.   24
through this man is p. to you.   38
these words might be p. the next. 42
had p. the word in Perga.   14:25
and visit where we have p.   15:36
word was p. of Paul at Berea. 17:13
because he p. Jesus and the.   18
Paul p., ready to depart on.   20:7
lest when I have p. to.   1 Cor 9:27
keep in memory what I p.   15:2
if Christ be p. that he rose from. 12
Jesus who was p. among you by us.
    2 Cor 1:19
Jesus, whom we have not p.   11:4
than that we have p. to you. Gal 1:8
p. peace to you who were. Eph 2:17
Christ is p. and I therein. Phil 1:18
which was p. to every.   Col 1:23
p. to Gentiles, believed. 1 Tim 3:16
but the word p. did not.   Heb 4:2
they to whom it was first p.   6
went and p. to the spirits. 1 Pet 3:19
    see **gospel**

preacher

the words of the p. the son. Eccl 1:1
of vanities, saith the p. all. 2; 12:8
I the p. was king over Israel.   2:12
have I found, saith the p.   7:27
because p. was wise, he still.   12:9
p. sought to find out acceptable. 10
how hear without a p.?   Rom 10:14
whereunto I am ordained a p.
    1 Tim 2:7; 2 Tim 1:11
but saved Noah, a p. of.   2 Pet 2:5

preachest, -eth, -ing

preach to it the p. that I. Jonah 3:2
in those days came John p. Mat 3:1
    Luke 3:3
p. the gospel of the. Mat 4:23; 9:35
rise in judgement, because they re-
    pented at p.   12:41; Luke 11:32
Jesus came into Galilee p. the
    gospel.   Mark 1:14
p. and shewing glad.   Luke 8:1
they went through the towns p.   9:6
went every where p. the.   Acts 8:4
p. the things concerning the.   12
p. peace by Jesus Christ, he. 10:36
p. the word to none but to.   11:19
to the Greeks, p. the Lord.   20
continued in Antioch p.   15:35
by Jesus, whom Paul p.   19:13
Paul was long p., Eutychus.   20:9
among whom I have gone p.   25
p. the kingdom of God.   28:31
p. a man should not steal. Rom 2:21
according to the p. of Jesus.   16:25
for the p. of the cross.   1 Cor 1:18
by the foolishness of p. to save.   21
my p. was not with enticing.   2:4
not risen, then is our p. vain. 15:14
far as to you, p. gospel. 2 Cor 10:14
that cometh p. another Jesus.   11:4
he p. the faith which.   Gal 1:23
p. might be fully known. 2 Tim 4:17
hath in due times manifested his
    word through p.   Tit 1:3

precept, -s

commandedst them p.   Neh 9:14*
hast commanded us to keep thy p.
    Ps 119:4

I will meditate in thy *p.* *Ps* 119:15, 78
understand the way of thy *p.* 27
I have longed after thy *p.* 40
for I seek thy *p.* 45
because I kept thy *p.* 56, 100, 168
them that keep thy *p.* 63, 69, 134
I forsook not thy *p.* 87
I will never forget thy *p.* 93
for I have sought thy *p.* 94
thro' thy *p.* I get understanding. 104
yet I erred not from thy *p.* 110
esteem all thy *p.* to be right. 128
yet do not I forget thy *p.* 141
consider how I love thy *p.* 159
for I have chosen thy *p.* 173
for *p.* must be upon *p.*, *p.* upon *p.*
    Isa 28:10, 13
taught by the *p.* of men. 29:13*
have kept all Jonadab's *p.* *Jer* 35:18
by departing from thy *p.* *Dan* 9:5
for the hardness of your heart he
wrote you this *p.* *Mark* 10:5*
had spoken every *p.* *Heb* 9:19*

precious
to Rebekah's mother *p.* *Gen* 24:53
for the *p.* things of *Deut* 33:13
p. fruits brought forth by sun. 14
p. things of the lasting hills. 15
for *p.* things of the earth, and. 16
word of the Lord was *p.* *1 Sam* 3:1
because my soul was *p.* in. 26:21
let my life be *p.* in. *2 Ki* 1:13, 14
shewed them the *p.* things. 20:13
    Isa 39:2
and *p.* jewels which. *2 Chr* 20:25
gave them gifts of *p.* things. 21:3
their hands with *p.* things. *Ezra* 1:6
two vessels of fine copper, *p.* 8:27
eye seeth every *p.* thing. *Job* 28:10
cannot be valued with the *p.* onyx. 16
of their soul is *p.* *Ps* 49:8*
and *p.* shall their blood be. 72:14
p. in the sight of Lord is the. 116:15
goeth forth bearing *p.* seed. 126:6*
it is like *p.* ointment on the. 133:2
how *p.* also are thy thoughts. 139:17
find all *p.* substance. *Pr* 1:13
wisdom is more *p.* than rubies. 3:15
adulteress will hunt for the *p.* 6:26
substance of a diligent man is *p.*
    12:27
of knowledge are *p.* jewel. 20:15
chambers filled with all *p.* and. 24:4
good name is better than *p.* *Eccl* 7:1
I will make a man *p.* *Isa* 13:12
I lay in Zion a *p.* corner stone.
    28:16; *1 Pet* 2:6
thou wast *p.* in my sight. *Isa* 43:4
take the *p.* from the vile. *Jer* 15:19
I will deliver all the *p.* things. 20:5
the *p.* sons of Zion. *Lam* 4:2
treasure and *p.* things. *Ezek* 22:25
Dedan was thy merchant in *p.* 27:20
with their *p.* vessels of. *Dan* 11:8
power over all *p.* things of Egypt. 43
woman, having an alabaster box of
very *p.* *Mat* 26:7; *Mark* 14:3
waiteth for the *p.* fruit. *Jas* 5:7
faith much more *p.* than gold.
    1 Pet 1:7
but with the *p.* blood of Christ. 19
stone, chosen of God, and *p.* 2:4
therefore which believe, he is *p.* 7
like *p.* faith with us. *2 Pet* 1:1
great and *p.* promises. 4
buyeth their *p.* vessels. *Rev* 18:12
was like unto a stone most *p.* 21:11

predestinate
(*Revisions,* foreordain)
did foreknow, he did *p.* *Rom* 8:29
and whom he did *p.* them. he 30

predestinated
(*Revisions,* foreordained)
p. us to the adoption of. *Eph* 1:5
being *p.* according to the purpose. 11

preeminence
a man hath no *p.* above. *Eccl* 3:19
things he might have the *p.* *Col* 1:18
loveth to have the *p.* *3 John* 9

prefer
if I *p.* not Jerusalem. *Ps* 137:6

preferred, -ing
p. her and her maidens. *Esth* 2:9*
Daniel was *p.* above the. *Dan* 6:3*
cometh after me is *p.* before me.
    John 1:15*, 27*
who is *p.* before me, for he was. 30*
in honour *p.* one. *Rom* 12:10
observe, without *p.* *1 Tim* 5:21*

premeditate
neither do ye *p.*: but whatsoever
shall be given you. *Mark* 13:11

preparation
now make *p.* for it. *1 Chr* 22:5
torches in the day of *p.* *Nah* 2:3
followed the day of *p.* *Mat* 27:62
    Mark 15:42; *Luke* 23:54
    John 19:14, 31, 42
p. of the gospel of peace. *Eph* 6:15

preparations
p. of the heart in man. *Pr* 16:1

prepare
my God, and I will *p.* *Ex* 15:2*
on sixth day they shall *p.* that. 16:5
for a drink offering *p.* *Num* 15:5
or for a ram *p.* thou for a meat. 6
the number that ye shall *p.* 12
Balaam said, *P.* me seven oxen. 23:1
build me seven altars, and *p.* 29
thou shalt *p.* thee a way. *Deut* 19:3
p. you victuals to pass. *Josh* 1:11
we said, Let us now *p.* to. 22:26
p. your hearts to the Lord. *1 Sam* 7:3
say to Ahab, *P.* chariot. *1 Ki* 18:44
to *p.* shewbread every. *1 Chr* 9:32
O Lord God, *p.* their heart. 29:18
to *p.* me timber in. *2 Chr* 2:9
p. chambers in house of. 31:11
and *p.* yourselves. 35:4
sanctify yourselves, and *p.* 6
banquet that I shall *p.* *Esth* 5:8
p. thyself to the search. *Job* 8:8*
if thou *p.* thine heart toward. 11:13*
though he *p.* raiment as clay. 27:16
he may *p.* it. 17
thou wilt *p.* their heart. *Ps* 10:17
they *p.* themselves without. 59:4
O *p.* mercy and truth, which. 61:7
that they *p.* a city for. 107:36
p. thy work without. *Pr* 24:27
yet they *p.* their meat in. 30:25
p. slaughter for his. *Isa* 14:21
p. the table, watch in the. 21:5
of him that crieth, *P.* ye the way of
the Lord. 40:3; *Mal* 3:1; *Mat* 3:3
    Mark 1:2, 3; *Luke* 3:4; 7:27
workman to *p.* a graven. *Isa* 40:20
shall say, Cast ye up, *p.* the. 57:14
p. ye the way of the people. 62:10
p. a table for that troop. 65:11
p. ye war against her, arise. *Jer* 6:4
and *p.* them for the day of. 12:3
I will *p.* destroyers against. 22:7
say ye, Stand fast and *p.* thee. 46:14
set up watchmen, *p.* the. 51:12
blow the trumpet, *p.* nations. 27
thou shalt *p.* thy bread. *Ezek* 4:15
p. thee stuff for removing. 12:3
I will *p.* thee to blood, and blood. 35:6
p. for thyself, thou and all. 38:7
p. every day a goat, they shall also *p.*
    43:25
shall *p.* the sin offering. 45:17
on that day shall prince *p.* 22; 46:12
a meat offering. 45:24; 46:7, 14
shall *p.* his burnt offering. 46:2, 13
they shall *p.* the lamb and. 15
p. war, wake up. *Joel* 3:9
p. to meet thy God. *Amos* 4:12
even *p.* war against him. *Mi* 3:5
messenger, who shall *p.* *Mat* 11:10
we *p.* for thee to eat the passover?
    26:17; *Mark* 14:12; *Luke* 22:8, 9
in his ways. *Luke* 1:76
I go to *p.* a place for. *John* 14:2, 3
who shall *p.* himself to the battle?
    1 Cor 14:8
but withal *p.* me also a. *Philem* 22

prepared
I *p.* the house and room. *Gen* 24:31
neither had they *p.* any. *Ex* 12:39
into the place I have *p.* 23:30
Sihon be built and *p.* *Num* 21:27*

I have *p.* seven altars. *Num* 23:4
Absalom *p.* chariots. *2 Sam* 15:1
Adonijah *p.* *1 Ki* 1:5
they *p.* timber. 5:18
the oracle he *p.* in the house. 6:19
he *p.* provision and sent. *2 Ki* 6:23
brethren had *p.* for. *1 Chr* 12:39
David *p.* a place for ark of God. 15:1
    3:12; *2 Chr* 1:4; 3:1
David *p.* iron in abundance for the
nails. *1 Chr* 22:3
David *p.* abundantly before his.
    5, 14; 29:2
work of Solomon was *p.* *2 Chr* 8:16
Rehoboam *p.* not his heart. 12:14
Jehoshaphat *p.* his heart to. 19:3
for as yet the people had not *p.* 20:33
Uzziah *p.* shields and spears. 26:14
Jotham *p.* his ways before the. 27:6
Ahaz cast away we have *p.* 29:19
that God had *p.* the people. 36
they *p.* chambers in the house. 31:11
the service was *p.* 35:10, 16
when Josiah had *p.* the temple. 7:10
Ezra had *p.* his heart. *Ezra* 7:10
now that which was *p.* *Neh* 5:18
for whom nothing is *p.* 8:10
p. for him a great chamber. 13:5
to the banquet that I have *p.*
    Esth 5:4, 12; 6:14
on gallows Haman *p.* 6:4; 7:10
p. it, yea, and searched. *Job* 28:27
when I *p.* my seat in the. 29:7
he *p.* for him the instruments of.
    Ps 7:13
p. his throne for judgement. 9:7
p. a net for my steps. 57:6
of thy goodness for the. 68:10
thou hast *p.* the light and. 74:16
the Lord hath *p.* his throne. 103:19
when he *p.* the heavens. *Pr* 8:27
judgements are *p.* for scorners. 19:29
horse is *p.* against the day. 21:31
of old, for the king it is *p.* *Isa* 30:33
eye seen what he hath *p.* 64:4*
bed, and a table *p.* *Ezek* 23:41
of the pipes was *p.* in thee. 28:13
be thou *p.* and prepare for. 38:7
for ye have *p.* lying words. *Dan* 2:9
gold which they *p.* for Baal. *Hos* 2:8
his going forth is *p.* as the. 6:3
now the Lord had *p.* a. *Jonah* 1:17
God *p.* a gourd. 4:6
God *p.* a worm. 7
God *p.* a vehement east wind. 8
the defence shall be *p.* *Nah* 2:5
for the Lord hath *p.* a. *Zeph* 1:7
shall be given to them for whom it is
p. *Mat* 20:23; *Mark* 10:40
I have *p.* my dinner. *Mat* 22:4
inherit the kingdom *p.* 25:34
into fire *p.* for devil. 41
a large upper room *p.* *Mark* 14:15
ready a people *p.* for. *Luke* 1:17
which thou hast *p.* before face. 2:31
his Lord's will, but *p.* not. 12:47
they *p.* spices, and rested the.
    23:56; 24:1
he had afore *p.* to glory. *Rom* 9:23
things God hath *p.* for. *1 Cor* 2:9
vessel *p.* unto every. *2 Tim* 2:21
body hast thou *p.* me. *Heb* 10:5
Noah *p.* an ark to the saving. 11:7
their God, for he hath *p.* for. 16
and the seven angels *p.* *Rev* 8:6
the locusts were like to horses *p.* 9:7
which were *p.* for an hour, a day. 15
and the woman hath a place *p.* 12:6
kings of east may be *p.* 16:12
the holy city, *p.* as a bride for. 21:2

preparedst
thou *p.* room before it. *Ps* 80:9

preparest
when thou *p.* a bullock. *Num* 15:8
thou *p.* a table before me. *Ps* 23:5
earth, thou *p.* them corn. 65:9*

prepareth
that *p.* his heart to. *2 Chr* 30:19
their belly *p.* deceit. *Job* 15:35
who *p.* rain for earth. *Ps* 147:8

preparing
p. him a chamber in. *Neh* 13:7
while the ark was *p.* *1 Pet* 3:20

presbytery
laying on of hands of p. *1 Tim 4:14*

prescribed, -ing
salt without p. how. *Ezra 7:22*
grievousness which they have p. *Isa 10:1*

presence
hid themselves from p. *Gen 3:8*
Cain went out from the p. of. *4:16*
gone from the p. of Isaac. *27:30*
brethren were troubled at his p. *45:3*
why should we die in thy p.? *47:15*
out from Pharaoh's p. *Ex 10:11*
my p. shall go with tnee. *33:14*
if thy p. go not with me, carry. *15*
Israel departed from the p. *35:20*
shall be cut off from my p. *Lev 22:3*
Moses went from the p. *Num 20:6*
avoided out of his p. *1 Sam 18:11*
slipped away out of Saul's p. *19:10*
to play the madman in my p. *21:15*
as I served in thy father's p. so will
I be in thy p. *2 Sam 16:19*
from the p. of Solomon. *1 Ki 12:2*
I regard p. of Jehoshaphat. *2 Ki 3:14*
went out from his p. a leper. *5:27*
neither cast them from his p. *13:23*
cast them out from his p. *24:20*
that were in the king's p. *25:19**
honour are in his p. *1 Chr 16:27*
trees sing at the p. of God. *33**
the king sought the p. of. *2 Chr 9:23*
before this house in thy p. *20:9*
altars of Baalim in his p. *34:4*
before sad in his p. *Neh 2:1*
Mordecai went from the p. *Esth 8:15*
Satan went from the p. *Job 1:12; 2:7*
I am troubled at his p. *23:15*
fall and perish at thy p. *Ps 9:3*
in thy p. is fulness of joy. *16:11*
come forth from thy p. *17:2*
them in the secret of thy p. *31:20*
cast me not away from thy p. *51:11*
perish at the p. of God. *68:2*
Sinai moved at the p. of God. *8*
come before his p. with. *95:2*
hills melted like wax at the p. *97:5*
before his p. with singing. *100:2*
tremble, thou earth, at the p. *114:7*
shall I flee from thy p.? *139:7*
upright shall dwell in thy p. *140:13*
go from the p. of a foolish. *Pr 14:7*
devour your land in your p. *Isa 1:7*
Egypt shall be moved at his p. *19:1*
angel of his p. saved them. *63:9*
that mountains might flow (flowed)
down at thy p. *64:1, 3*
nations may tremble at thy p. *2*
the cities broken down at p. *Jer 4:26*
will ye not tremble at my p.? *5:22*
cast you out of my p. *23:39; 52:3*
men shall shake at my p. *Ezek 38:20*
Jonah rose to flee from the p. of. *Jonah 1:3*
men knew he fled from the p. *10*
earth is burnt at his p. *Nah 1:5*
hold thy peace at the p. *Zeph 1:7*
eaten and drunk in thy p. *Luke 13:26*
times of refreshing come from the p. *Acts 3:19*
they departed from the p. of. *5:41*
should glory in his p. *1 Cor 1:29*
who in p. am base. *2 Cor 10:1*
letters weighty, but his bodily p. *10*
have obeyed, not as in my p. only. *Phil 2:12*
being taken from you in p. not in
heart. *1 Thes 2:17*
destruction from the p. *2 Thes 1:9*
present you faultless before p. of his
glory. *Jude 24*

in the **presence**
he shall dwell in *the* p. of. *Gen 16:12*
in *the* p. of my people I give. *23:11*
in *the* p. of the children of Heth. *18*
Ishmael died in *the* p. of all. *25:18*
brother's wife come unto him in *the*
p. of the elders. *Deut 25:9*
should I not serve in *the* p. of his
son? *2 Sam 16:19*
Solomon stood in *the* p. *1 Ki 8:22*
against Naboth, in *the* p. of. *21:13*
these cast lots in *the* p. *1 Chr 24:31*

in the p. of Ahasuerus. *Esth 1:10*
a table *in the* p. of mine. *Ps 23:5*
now *in the* p. of all his. *116:14, 18*
become surety *in the* p. *Pr 17:18*
put not forth thyself *in the* p. *25:6*
than be put lower *in the* p. of. *7*
Hananiah spake *in the* p. *Jer 28:1*
in the p. of people. *11*
in the p. of witnesses. *32:12*
I am Gabriel, that stand *in the* p. of
God. *Luke 1:19*
worship *in the* p. of them. *14:10*
joy *in the* p. of the angels. *15:10*
signs did Jesus *in the* p. *John 20:30*
denied him *in the* p. of. *Acts 3:13*
soundness *in the* p. of you all. *16*
he gave thanks to God *in the* p. *27:35*
in the p. of our Lord. *1 Thes 2:19*
appear *in the* p. of God. *Heb 9:24*
in the p. of holy angels, *in the* p. *Rev 14:10*

present, *substantive*
he took a p. for Esau. *Gen 32:13, 18*
I will appease him with the p. *20*
so went the p. over before him. *21*
if I have found grace in thy sight,
then receive my p. at. *33:10*
carry down the man a p. *43:11*
men took the p. *15*
they made ready the p. *25*
brought him the p. in their hand. *26*
Israel sent a p. to Eglon. *Judg 3:15*
he brought the p. *17*
made an end to offer the p. *18*
come and bring forth my p. *6:18*
not a p. for the man of. *1 Sam 9:7*
a p. of the spoil of the. *30:26*
a p. to his daughter. *1 Ki 9:16**
they brought every man his p. *10:25*
2 Chr 9:24
sent thee a p. of silver. *1 Ki 15:19*
the king said, Take a p. *2 Ki 8:8*
so Hazael went ... and took a p. *9*
sent it for a p. to the king of. *16:8*
brought no p. to the king. *17:4*
make an agreement by a p. *18:31**
Isa 36:16*
sent letters and a p. to Hezekiah. *2 Ki 20:12; Isa 39:1*
a p. brought to Lord of. *Isa 18:7*
a p. of ivory and ebony. *Ezek 27:15*
carried to Assyria for a p. *Hos 10:6*

present, *adjective*
the people p. with him. *1 Sam 13:15*
loaves, or what there is p. *21:3*
and be thou here p. *2 Sam 20:4*
Israel were numbered, and were all
p. *1 Ki 20:27**
people p. here to offer. *1 Chr 29:17*
priests p. were sanctified. *2 Chr 5:11*
Israel p. at Jerusalem. *30:21*
all p. went out and brake the. *31:1*
all that were p. to stand. *34:32**
and all Israel p. offered. *Ezra 8:25*
the Jews p. in Shushan. *Esth 4:16*
God is a very p. help in. *Ps 46:1*
power of the Lord was p. *Luke 5:17*
there were p. at that season. *13:1*
manifold more in this p. life. *18:30*
being yet p. with you. *John 14:25*
and all elders were p. *Acts 10:33*
received us because of p. rain. *28:2*
to will is p. with me, but. *Rom 7:18*
would do good, evil is p. with. *21*
sufferings of this p. time. *8:18*
nor things p. nor things to come. *38*
1 Cor 3:22
even at this p. time there. *Rom 11:5*
even to this p. hour we both hunger. *1 Cor 4:11*
but p. in spirit, have judged as
though I were p. *5:3*
good for the p. distress. *7:26*
greater part remain to this p. *15:6*
willing rather to be p. *2 Cor 5:9*
that whether p. or absent. *9**
that I may not be bold when p. *10:2*
was p. with you and wanted. *11:9*
I foretell, as if I were p. the. *13:2*
I write, lest being p. I should. *10*
might deliver us from this p. world. *Gal 1:4*

not only when I am p. with. *Gal 4:18*
I desire to be p. with you. *20*
loved this p. world. *2 Tim 4:10*
godly in this p. world. *Tit 2:12*
figure for the time then p. *Heb 9:9*
for the p. seemeth joyous. *12:11*
be established in the p. truth. *2 Pet 1:12**

present, -ed, *verb*
Joseph p. himself to his. *Gen 46:29*
he p. five of his brethren to. *47:2*
and p. thyself there to me. *Ex 34:2*
meat offering, when it is p. *Lev 2:8*
in the day when he p. them. *7:35*
Aaron's sons p. to him the. *9:12, 18*
and they p. the burnt offering. *13*
the priest shall p. the man. *14:11**
the two goats, and p. them. *16:7**
the scapegoat shall be p. *10*
p. himself before the priest. *27:8**
then he shall p. the beast. *11**
and p. the tribe of Levi. *Num 3:6**
p. yourselves before the. *Deut 31:14*
p. themselves before God. *Josh 24:1*
it under oak, and p. it. *Judg 6:19*
the tribes of Israel p. *20:2*
now p. yourselves. *1 Sam 10:19*
Goliath the Philistine p. *17:16*
sons of God came to p. *Job 1:6*
Satan came to p. himself. *2:1*
will p. their supplication. *Jer 36:7*
I p. my supplication before. *38:26*
ye sent to p. your supplication. *42:9*
they p. the provocation. *Ezek 20:28*
do not p. our supplications. *Dan 9:18*
they p. to him gifts, gold. *Mat 2:11*
they brought him to p. *Luke 2:22*
called the saints, p. her. *Acts 9:41*
they p. Paul also before. *23:33*
that ye p. your bodies a. *Rom 12:1*
by Jesus and p. us with. *2 Cor 4:14*
that I may p. you as a chaste. *11:2*
he might p. it to himself. *Eph 5:27*
to p. you holy and. *Col 1:22*
we may p. every man perfect. *28*
is able to p. you faultless. *Jude 24**

presenting
p. my supplication before. *Dan 9:20*

presently
let them not fail to burn the fat p. *1 Sam 2:16*
a fool's wrath is p. known. *Pr 12:16*
and p. the fig tree. *Mat 21:19**
he shall p. give me more. *26:53**
him I hope to send p. *Phil 2:23**

presents
brought him no p. *1 Sam 10:27*
they brought p. and. *1 Ki 4:21*
gave Shalmanezer p. *2 Ki 17:3*
p. to Jehoshaphat. *2 Chr 17:5, 11*
p. to Hezekiah. *32:23**
kings shall bring p. unto. *Ps 68:29*
and the isles shall bring p. *72:10*
let all bring p. to him that. *76:11*
give p. to Moresheth-gath. *Mi 1:14**

preserve
that we may p. seed. *Gen 19:32, 34*
send me before you to p. life. *45:5*
God sent me to p. you a posterity. *7*
that he might p. us alive. *Deut 6:24*
thou shalt p. them from. *Ps 12:7*
p. me, O God, for in thee do. *16:1*
and uprightness p. me. *25:21*
my hiding place, shalt p. me. *32:7*
let thy truth continually p. me. *40:11*
Lord will p. him and keep. *41:2*
mercy and truth which may p. *61:7*
p. my life from fear of enemy. *64:1*
p. thou those that are. *79:11*
p. my soul, for I am holy. *86:2*
p. thee from all evil, he shall p. thy. *121:7**
p. thy going out and coming in. *8**
p. me from violent man. *140:1, 4*
discretion shall p. thee. *Pr 2:11**
and she shall p. thee. *4:6*
lips of the wise shall p. them. *14:3*
mercy and truth p. king. *20:28*
eyes of Lord p. knowledge. *22:12*
he will p. Jerusalem. *Isa 31:5*
I will p. thee, and give thee. *49:8*
thy children, I will p. *Jer 49:11*

preserved

lose his life shall *p*. it. *Luke* 17:33
the Lord will *p*. me unto his heavenly
  kingdom. *2 Tim* 4:18*

preserved, -eth
God, and my life is *p*. *Gen* 32:30
and *p*. us in all the way. *Josh* 24:17
us, who hath *p*. us. *1 Sam* 30:23
Lord *p*. David whithersoever he.
  2 Sam 8:6*; *1 Chr* 18:6*, 13*
thy visitation hath *p*. my. *Job* 10:12
as in days when God *p*. me. 29:2*
he *p*. not the life of the wicked. 36:6
for the Lord *p*. the faithful. *Ps* 31:23
his saints; they are *p*. for. 37:28
he *p*. the souls of his saints. 97:10
the Lord *p*. the simple. 116:6
Lord *p*. all them that love. 145:20
the Lord *p*. the strangers. 146:9
p. the way of his saints. *Pr* 2:8
keepeth his way *p*. his soul. 16:17
to restore the *p*. of Israel. *Isa* 49:6
by a prophet was he *p*. *Hos* 12:13
new wine into new bottles, and both
  are *p*. *Mat* 9:17; *Luke* 5:38
soul and body *p*. blameless.
  1 Thes 5:23
and *p*. in Jesus Christ, and. *Jude* 1

preserver
thee, O thou *p*. of men ? *Job* 7:20*

preservest
thou Lord hast made . . . and thou *p*.
  Neh 9:6
thou *p*. man and beast. *Ps* 36:6

presidents
three *p*.; Daniel was first. *Dan* 6:2
this Daniel was preferred above *p*. 3
the *p*. sought to find occasion. 4
these *p*. and princes assembled. 6, 7

press
[1] *To squeeze*, *Gen* 40:11. [2]
To crowd, *Luke* 8:45. [3] *To urge*,
Gen 19:3. [4] *A crowd or throng*,
Luke 19:3.

could not come nigh for the *p*.
  Mark 2:4; *Luke* 8:19
came in *p*. behind him. *Mark* 5:27
Jesus turned him about in the *p*. 30
not see Jesus for the *p*. *Luke* 19:3

press
(*Wine press*)
for the *p*. is full, the fats. *Joel* 3:13
fifty vessels out of the *p*. *Hag* 2:16
see wine

press, -ed, -eth
Lot *p*. on the two angels. *Gen* 19:3
they *p*. sore on Lot, and came near. 9
took the grapes and *p*. them. 40:11
Delilah *p*. him daily. *Judg* 16:16
Absalom *p*. him. *2 Sam* 13:25, 27
posts *p*. on by the king's. *Esth* 8:14
and thy hand *p*. me sore. *Ps* 38:2
were their breasts *p*. *Ezek* 23:3
I am *p*. under you as a cart is *p*.
  Amos 2:13
p. on him for to touch. *Mark* 3:10
people *p*. to hear the word. *Luke* 5:1
measure, *p*. down and shaken. 6:38
throng thee and *p*. thee. 8:45
every man *p*. into it. 16:16*
Paul was *p*. in spirit, and. *Acts* 18:5*
were *p*. above measure. *2 Cor* 1:8*
I *p*. toward the mark. *Phil* 3:14

presses
thy *p*. shall burst with. *Pr* 3:10
tread out no wine in their *p*.*Isa* 16:10

pressfat
when one came to the *p*. *Hag* 2:16*

presume
prophet who shall *p*. to. *Deut* 18:20*
he that durst *p*. in his. *Esth* 7:5

presumed
they *p*. to go up to hill. *Num* 14:44

presumptuous
servant also from *p*. sins. *Ps* 19:13
p. are they, selfwilled. *2 Pet* 2:10*

presumptuously
if a man come *p*. on his. *Ex* 21:14
the soul that doeth aught *p*.
  Num 15:30*; *Deut* 17:12

went *p*. up into the hill. *Deut* 1:43
shall hear, and do no more *p*. 17:13
prophet hath spoken it *p*. 18:22

pretence
for a *p*. make long prayers.
  Mat 23:14; *Mark* 12:40
every way, whether in *p*. or in truth,
  Christ is preached. *Phil* 1:18

prevail
upward did the waters *p*. *Gen* 7:20
peradventure I shall *p*. *Num* 22:6
by what means we may *p*. *Judg* 16:5
strength shall no man *p*. *1 Sam* 2:9
if I *p*. against him, then ye. 17:9
great things and shalt still *p*. 26:25
thou shalt persuade him, and *p*.
  1 Ki 22:22; *2 Chr* 18:21
O Lord, let not man *p*. *2 Chr* 14:11
thou shalt not *p*. against. *Esth* 6:13
they shall *p*. against him. *Job* 15:24
robber shall *p*. against him. 18:9*
arise, O Lord, let not man *p*. *Ps* 9:19
with our tongue will we *p*. 12:4
iniquities *p*. against me. 65:3
if one *p*. against him. *Eccl* 4:12
to war, but could not *p*. *Isa* 7:1
to pray, but he shall not *p*. 16:12
he shall *p*.against his enemies.42:13*
if so be thou mayest *p*. 47:12
they shall not *p*. against thee, for.
  Jer 1:19; 15:20; 20:11
toss, yet can they not *p*. 5:22
will be enticed, and we shall *p*. 20:10
who shall deal against him and shall
  p. *Dan* 11:7
gates of hell shall not *p*. *Mat* 16:18
Pilate saw he could *p*. nothing. 27:24
perceive ye how ye *p*. nothing.
  John 12:19

prevailed
the waters *p*. and. *Gen* 7:18, 19
the waters *p*. on the earth. 24
with my sister and have *p*. 30:8
when he saw he *p*. not against. 32:25
as a prince hast thou power with God
  and men, and hast *p*. 28
the famine *p*. over them. 47:20
blessings of thy father have *p*. 49:26
Israel *p*.: when he let down his hand,
  Amalek *p*. *Ex* 17:11
of the house of Joseph *p* *Judg* 1:35
Othniel's hand *p*. against. 3:10
Israel *p*. against Jabin. 4:24
Midian *p*. against Israel. 6:2
David *p*. over Goliath. *1 Sam* 17:50
the men *p*. against us. *2 Sam* 11:23
king's word *p*. against Joab. 24:4
that followed Omri *p*. *1 Ki* 16:22
the famine *p*. in the city. *2 Ki* 25:3
for Judah *p*. above his. *1 Chr* 5:2
p. against Hamath-zobah. *2 Chr* 8:3
Judah *p*. because they relied. 13:18
p. against the Ammonites. 27:5
lest mine enemy say, I have *p*.
  Ps 13:4
they have not *p*. against me. 129:2
thou art stronger than I, and hast *p*.
  Jer 20:7
friends have *p*. against thee. 38:22
I weep because the enemy *p*.
  Lam 1:16
the same horn *p*. against. *Dan* 7:21
power over angel and *p*. *Hos* 12:4
have deceived thee and *p*. *Ob* 7
of the chief priests *p*. *Luke* 23:23
in whom the evil spirit was, leaped
  on them and *p*. *Acts* 19:16
so grew word of God and *p*. 20
of David hath *p*. to open. *Rev* 5:5
dragon and his angels *p*. not. 12:8

prevailest
p. for ever against him. *Job* 14:20

prevaileth
into my bones, and it *p*. *Lam* 1:13

prevent
(*Usually used in its original sense
of going before, either actually or
symbolically*)
why did the knees *p*. me ? *Job* 3:12*
my mercy shall *p*. me. *Ps* 59:10†
mercies speedily *p*. us. 79:8†
morning shall my prayer *p*. 88:13*

eyes *p*. nightwatches. *Ps* 119:148*
The evil shall not *p*. us. *Amos* 9:10
we shall not *p*. them who are asleep.
  1 Thes 4:15*

prevented
the snares of death *p*. me.
  2 Sam 22:6*; *Ps* 18:5*
they *p*. me in the day of my calamities. 19*; *Ps* 18:18*
days of affliction *p*. me. *Job* 30:27*
who hath *p*. me that I ? 41:11*
I *p*. the dawning of. *Ps* 119:147†
they *p*. with their bread. *Isa* 21:14*
Jesus *p*. him, saying, Simon, of.
  Mat 17:25*

preventest
thou *p*. him with blessings. *Ps* 21:3†

prey
from the *p*. my son. *Gen* 49:9
he shall devour the *p*. 27
that our wives and children shall be
  a *p*.? *Num* 14:3, 31; *Deut* 1:39
lie down till he eat of *p*. *Num* 23:24
captives and *p*. to Moses. 31:12
take the sum of the *p*. that. 26
and divide the *p*. into two parts. 27
booty being the rest of the *p*. 32
only the cattle we took for a *p*. to.
  Deut 2:35; 3:7; *Josh* 8:2, 27; 11:14
divided the *p*.; to Sisera a *p*.
  Judg 5:30
give me the earrings of his *p*. 8:24
man the earrings of his *p*. 25
Judah shall become a *p*. *2 Ki* 21:14
a *p*. in the land of captivity. *Neh* 4:4
take the spoil of them for a *p*.
  Esth 3:13; 8:11
on the *p*. they laid not. 9:15, 16
perisheth for lack of *p*. *Job* 4:11
eagle that hasteth to the *p*. 9:26
as wild asses; rising betimes for a *p*.
  24:5*
wilt thou hunt the *p*. for ? 38:39
thence she seeketh the *p*. 39:29
like a lion greedy of his *p*. *Ps* 17:12
than the mountains of *p*. 76:4
lions roar after their *p*. 104:21
not given us for a *p*. to their. 124:6
lieth in wait as for a *p*. *Pr* 23:28
roar and lay hold of the *p*. *Isa* 5:29
that widows may be their *p*. 10:2
the *p*. of an hypocritical nation. 6
young lion roaring on his *p*. 31:4
the *p*. of a great spoil divided. 33:23
for a *p*. and none delivereth. 42:22
p. be taken from the mighty ? 49:24
the *p*. of the terrible shall be. 25
he that departeth from evil a *p*.59:15
his life shall be to him for a *p*.
  Jer 21:9; 38:2; 39:18; 45:5
p. on thee will I give for a *p*. 30:16
hands of strangers for *p*. *Ezek* 7:21
it learned to catch the *p*. 19:3
like wolves ravening the *p*. 22:27
make a *p*. of thy merchandise. 26:12
take her spoil, and take her *p*. 29:19
because my flock became a *p*. 34:8
flock shall no more be a *p*. 22, 28
to the cities that became a *p*. 36:4
minds, to cast it out for a *p*. 5
to take a spoil and a *p*. 38:12, 13
scatter among them the *p*. *Dan* 11:24
will lion roar when no *p*.? *Amos* 3:4
lion filled his holes with *p*. *Nah* 2:12
I will cut off thy *p*. from. 13
city, the *p*. departeth not. 3:1
that I rise up to the *p*. *Zeph* 3:8

price
[1] *The sum asked for a thing
when selling it*, *2 Sam* 24:24. [2]
The worth or value of a thing,
Job 28:18. [3] *Wages or hire*,
Zech 11:12.

thou shalt increase the *p*. . . . . thou
shalt diminish the *p*. of. *Lev* 25:16, 50
shall give him again the *p*. of. 52
not bring *p*. of a dog. *Deut* 23:18*
I will buy it at a *p*. *2 Sam* 24:24
  1 Chr 21:22, 24
merchants received the linen yarn at
  a *p*. *1 Ki* 10:28; *2 Chr* 1:16
man knoweth not the *p*. *Job* 28:13, 15
p. of wisdom is above rubies. 18

prices

increase wealth by their *p.* *Ps* 44:12
a *p.* in hand of a fool ? *Pr* 17:16
goats are the *p.* of the field. 27:26
virtuous woman, for her *p.* 31:10
go my captives not for *p.* *Isa* 45:13
buy wine and milk without *p.* 55:1
to the spoil without *p.* *Jer* 15:13
p. weighed for my *p.* *Zech* 11:12*
a goodly *p.* that I was prized at. 13
one pearl of great *p.* *Mat* 13:46
because it is the *p.* of blood. 27:6
took *p.* of him that was valued. 9
kept back part of the *p.* *Acts* 5:2, 3
they counted the *p.* of them. 19:19
for ye are bought with a *p.*
　　　　　1 Cor 6:20; 7:23
in sight of God of great *p.* *1 Pet* 3:4

prices

brought *p.* of the things. *Acts* 4:34

pricked

I was *p.* in my reins. *Ps* 73:21
they were *p.* in their heart. *Acts* 2:37

pricking

a *p.* briar to Israel. *Ezek* 28:24

pricks

those that remain be *p.* *Num* 33:55
it is hard to kick against the *p.*
　　　　Acts 9:5*; 26:14*

pride

I will break the *p.* of. *Lev* 26:19
I know thy *p.* and. *1 Sam* 17:28
humbled himself for *p.* *2 Chr* 32:26
that he may hide *p.* from man.
　　　　　Job 33:17
they cry because of the *p.* 35:12
his scales are his *p.* shut up. 41:15
king over all children of *p.* 34
the wicked in his *p.* *Ps* 10:2
through *p.* of his countenance. 4
hide them from the *p.* of man. 31:20*
let not the foot of *p.* come. 36:11
let them be taken in their *p.* 59:12
p. compasseth them as chain. 73:6
p. . . . do I hate. *Pr* 8:13
when *p.* cometh. 11:2
by *p.* cometh contention. 13:10
the foolish is a rod of *p.* 14:3
p. goeth before destruction. 16:18
man's *p.* shall bring him low. 29:23
in the *p.* of their hearts. *Isa* 9:9
p. of Moab, even of his haughtiness
　　and his *p.* 16:6; *Jer* 48:29
stain the *p.* of all glory. *Isa* 23:9
shall bring down their *p.* 25:11
woe to the crown of *p.* 28:1, 3
I will mar the *p.* of Judah. *Jer* 13:9
my soul shall weep for your *p.* 17
the *p.* of thy heart hath. 49:16
blossomed, *p.* hath. *Ezek* 7:10
iniquity of thy sister Sodom, *p.* 16:49
not mentioned in the day of thy *p.* 56
and the *p.* of her power shall. 30:6
those that walk in *p.* he is. *Dan* 4:37
mind was hardened in *p.* 5:20
the *p.* of Israel doth testify.
　　　　Hos 5:5; 7:10
p. of thine heart hath deceived. *Ob* 3
they have for their *p.* *Zeph* 2:10
them away that rejoice in thy *p.* 3:11
the *p.* of the Philistines. *Zech* 9:6
the *p.* of Assyria shall be. 10:11
the *p.* of Jordan is spoiled. 11:3
the heart proceedeth *p.* *Mark* 7:22
lifted up *p.* he fall into. *1 Tim* 3:6
the *p.* of life, is not of. *1 John* 2:16

priest

There were priests in every
nation, since the term is used of all
who have charge of the religious
life of a people. The Jewish priesthood as a definite body, dated from
the appointment of Aaron and his
sons as Priests of Jehovah at the
time of the Exodus. At about the
same time the entire tribe of Levi
was set apart to do the non-priestly
duties of the tabernacle, and the
religious services. The priests
were all descendants of Aaron, the
legal head of the house of Aaron in
each generation being High Priest.

The priestly duties included the
instruction of the people, sanitary
and medicinal care for their welfare,
and the services at the house of
God.

Jesus Christ, as the fulfilment
of the old dispensation, is called the
High Priest of those who have
accepted him.

p. of the most high God. *Gen* 14:18
　　　　　Heb 7:1
p. of Midian had seven. *Ex* 2:16
that son that is *p.* in his stead.
　　　　29:30; *Lev* 16:32
the *p.* shall burn it all on the altar.
Lev 1:9, 13, 17; 2:2, 9, 16; 3:11
　　16; 4:10, 31, 35; 7:5, 31
the *p.* shall lay them in order. 1:12
when it is presented to the *p.* 2:8
if the *p.* that is anointed do sin. 4:3
the *p.* shall dip his finger. 6, 17
the *p.* shall make an atonement. 4:20
　26; 5:6; 6:7; 12:8; 15:15, 30
　　　　16:30; 19:22
p. shall take of blood. 4:25; 30, 34
he shall bring them to the *p.* 5:8
the remnant shall be the *p.'s.* 13
p. shall put on his linen. 6:10
p. shall have to himself the skin. 7:8
it shall be the *p.'s* that offereth it. 9
　　　　　14; 14:13
the *p.* shall look on the plague. 13:3
5, 6, 17, 20, 21, 25, 26, 27, 30, 31, 32
p. shall look on him and pronounce
　unclean. 13:8, 11, 20, 22, 25, 30, 44
the *p.* shall shut him up. 4, 5, 31, 33
the *p.* shall pronounce him clean.
　　　　13:6, 17, 23, 28, 34
brought to the *p.* 13:9
come to the *p.* 16; 14:2
p. that maketh him clean. 14:11
the *p.* shall dip his right finger. 16
the house, shall come and tell *p.* 35
the *p.* shall pronounce the house. 48
if the daughter of a *p.* profane. 21:9
if the *p.* buy any soul with. 22:11
if *p.'s* daughter be married. 12, 13
a sheaf of firstfruits to the *p.* 23:10
the *p.* shall wave it before the. 11
p. shall value him, according. 27:8
possession thereof shall be *p.'s.* 21
trespass be recompensed to the *p.*
　　　　　Num 5:8
man shall bring wife to the *p.* 15
the *p.* shall execute upon her. 30
this is holy for the *r.* with the. 6:20
p. shall wash and be unclean. 19:7
in land till death of high *p.* 35:32
will not hearken to *p.* *Deut* 17:12
the *p.'s* due from people. 18:3
are come nigh to battle, the *p.* 20:2
go to the *p.* in those days. 26:3
sons who became his *p.* *Judg* 17:5
and be unto me a father and a *p.* 10
seeing I have a Levite to my *p.* 13
Micah hired me, and I am his *p.* 18:4
a father and a *p.* : better a *p.* unto one
　man, or a *p.* unto a tribe ? 19
all that the *p.* took for. *1 Sam* 2:14
give flesh to roast for the *p.* 15
choose him out of Israel to be my *p.*
　　　　　28
I will raise me up a faithful *p.* 35
while Saul talked to the *p.* 14:19
said the *p.*, Let us draw near to. 36
the *p.* answered, There is no. 21:4
p. gave them hallowed bread. 6
Abiathar from being *p.* *1 Ki* 2:27
p. had said, Let her not be slain.
　　　　　2 Ki 11:15
the same may be a *p.* of them that
　are no gods. *2 Chr* 13:9
Israel without a teaching *p.* 15:3
till there stood up a *p.* *Ezra* 2:63
　　　　　Neh 7:65
a *p.* for ever after the order of.
Ps 110:4; *Heb* 5:6; 7:17, 21
Uriah the *p.* and Zechariah. *Isa* 8:2
as with people, so with the *p.* 24:2
p. and prophet have erred. 28:7
from prophet to the *p.* every one
　dealeth falsely. *Jer* 6:13; 8:10
prophet and *p.* go to a land. 14:18
law shall not perish from *p.* 18:18

prophet and *p.* are profane. *Jer* 23:11
prophet and *p.* shall. 33, 34
thee *p.* instead of Jehoiada. 29:26
despised the king and the *p.* *Lam* 2:6
shall the *p.* and prophets be slain ? 20
but the law shall perish from the *p.*
　　　　　Ezek 7:26
near to do the office of a *p.* 44:13
nor shall any *p.* drink wine when. 21
a widow that had a *p.* before. 22
to the *p.* the first of your dough. 30
p. shall not eat of any thing. 30
that strive with the *p.* *Hos* 4:4
thou shalt be no *p.* to me. 6
shall be, like people, like *p.* 9
the *p.* of Beth-el sent to. *Amos* 7:10
and he shall be *p.* on. *Zech* 6:13
the *p.'s* lips should keep. *Mal* 2:7
go thy way, shew thyself to the *p.*
　　Mat 8:4; *Mark* 1:44; *Luke* 5:14
p. named Zacharias. *Luke* 1:5
there came down a certain *p.* 10:31
the *p.* of Jupiter brought oxen and
　garlands. *Acts* 14:13
abideth a *p.* continually. *Heb* 7:3
what need another *p.* should rise ? 11
Melchizedek ariseth another *p.* 15
not without oath he was made *p.* 20
on earth, he should not be a *p.* 8:4
every *p.* standeth daily. 10:11

see chief

high priest

high *p.* shalt not uncover. *Lev* 21:10
city of refuge till the death of the
　high *p.* *Num* 35:25; *Josh* 20:6
much money in chest, the high *p.*
　came. *2 Ki* 12:10; *2 Chr* 24:11
to Hilkiah the high *p.* *2 Ki* 22:4
Eliashib the high *p.* rose up. *Neh* 3:1
Joshua the high *p.* standing.
　　　　　Zech 3:1, 8; 6:11
to the palace of the high *p.*
　　　　Mat 26:3; *Luke* 22:54
struck servant of high *p.* *Mat* 26:51
　　　　Luke 22:50; *John* 18:10
led him to Caiaphas the high *p.*
　　　　Mat 26:57; *John* 18:24
the high *p.* rent his clothes.
　　Mat 26:65; *Mark* 14:63
days of Abiathar high *p.* *Mark* 2:26
Caiaphas being high *p.* *John* 11:49
　　　　　51; 18:13
disciple was known to high *p.* 18:15
answerest thou the high *p.* so ? 22
of the kindred of high *p.* *Acts* 4:6
said high *p.*, Are these things ? 7:1
Saul went to the high *p.* and. 9:1
high *p.* doth bear me witness. 22:5
revilest thou God's high *p.* ? 23:4
might be a faithful high *p.* *Heb* 2:17
consider Apostle, High P. of. 3:1
great high *p.* that is passed. 4:14
not an high *p.* which cannot be. 15
every high *p.* is ordained. 5:1
Christ glorified not himself to be an
　high *p.* 5
an high *p.* after the order. 10; 6:20
such an high *p.* became us. 7:26
we have such an high *p.* who. 8:1
high *p.* is ordained to offer gifts. 3
into second went high *p.* alone. 9:7
Christ being come an high *p.* of. 11
as high *p.* entereth holy place. 25
having an high *p.* over house. 10:21
into sanctuary by high *p.* 13:11

see office

priesthood

anointing shall be an everlasting *p.*
　　　　Ex 40:15; *Num* 25:13
and seek ye the *p.* also ? *Num* 16:10
shall bear iniquity of your *p.* 18:1
for *p.* of the Lord is their. *Josh* 18:7
therefore were they, as polluted, put
　from the *p.* *Ezra* 2:62; *Neh* 7:64
the *p.*, the covenant of *p.* *Neh* 13:29
who receive the office of *p.* *Heb* 7:5
were by the Levitical *p.* 11
the *p.* being changed, there. 12
spake nothing concerning the *p.* 14
this man hath an unchangeable *p.* 24
an holy *p.* *1 Pet* 2:5
ye are a royal *p.* 9

priests

land of *p*. bought he not, for the *p*.
  had portion assigned. *Gen* 47:22
except land of *p*. only, not.   26
be to me a kingdom of *p*.   *Ex* 19:6
the *p*. shall sprinkle. *Lev* 1:11; 3:2
males among the *p*. shall eat. 6:29
unto one of his sons the *p*.   13:2
make an atonement for the *p*. 16:33
holy to the Lord for the *p*.   23:20
shall stand before *p*. *Deut* 19:17
p. that bare the ark stood. *Josh* 3:17
where the *p*.' feet stood.   4:3, 9
the *p*. bare seven trumpets. 6:4, 13
p. took up the ark of the Lord. 12
were *p*. to tribe of Dan. *Judg* 18:30
Hophni and Phinehas. *1 Sam* 1:3
nor the *p*. of Dagon tread on. 5:5
Philistines called for the *p*. 6:2
king said, Turn and slay the *p*. 22:17
Doeg, Turn thou and fall on the *p*. 18
that Saul had slain the Lord's *p*. 21
and the *p*. took up the ark. *1 Ki* 8:3
made *p*. of the lowest. 12:31; 13:33
on thee shall he offer the *p*. of. 13:2
Jehu slew Ahab's *p*., he. *2 Ki* 10:11
call me all Baal's *p*., let none. 19
p. had not repaired breaches. 12:6
carry thither one of the *p*. ye. 17:27
put down idolatrous *p*. of king. 23:5
slew all the *p*. of the high places. 20
sea was for *p*. to wash in. *2 Chr* 4:6
p. sounding with trumpets. 5:12
p. could not stand to minister. 14
let thy *p*. be clothed with. 6:41
appointed the courses of the *p*. 8:14
ordained *p*. for high places. 11:15
have ye not cast out the *p*.? 13:9
p. with trumpets to cry alarm. 12
into house of Lord save the *p*. 23:6
with him fourscore *p*. of the. 26:17
Uzziah was wroth with the *p*. 19
p. were too few, they could. 29:34
p. had not sanctified. 30:3
Josiah burnt bones of the *p*. 34:5
Josiah set *p*. in their charges. 35:2
to the *p*. for passover offerings. 8
set the *p*. in their divisions. *Ezra* 6:18
and killed the passover for *p*. 20
offering of the people and *p*. 7:16
and our *p*. been delivered into. 9:7
as yet told it to the *p*. *Neh* 2:16
repaired the *p*., men of the plain. 3:22
hath come on us and our *p*. 9:32
we nor our *p*. kept thy law. 34
laid the offerings of the *p*. 13:5
their *p*. fell by the sword. *Ps* 78:64
Moses and Aaron among his *p*. 99:6
let thy *p*. be clothed with. 132:9
clothe her *p*. with salvation. 16
he sent elders of it, covered. *Isa* 37:2
but ye shall be named the *p*. of. 61:6
against the *p*. thereof. *Jer* 1:18
p. said not, Where is the Lord ? 2:8
Israel ashamed; their kings, *p*. 26
p. shall be astonished. 4:9
p. bare rule by their means. 5:31
bones of the *p*. they shall bring. 8:1
fill the *p*. with drunkenness. 13:13
I will satiate the souls of the *p*. 31:14
me to anger, they and their *p*. 32:32
into captivity with his *p*. 48:7; 49:3
her *p*. sigh, her virgins. *Lam* 1:4
p. and elders gave up the ghost. 19
for the iniquities of her *p*. 4:13
respected not persons of *p*. 16
her *p*. violated my law. *Ezek* 22:26
said, This chamber is for *p*. 40:45
shall be for the *p*. 45:4; 48:10, 11
hear this, O *p*.; and hearken, the
  house of Israel. *Hos* 5:1
p. murder in the way by. 6:9
p., the Lord's ministers, mourn.
  Joel 1:9, 13; 2:17
p. thereof teach for hire. *Mi* 3:11
I will cut off names of *p*. *Zeph* 1:4
her *p*. have polluted the. 3:4
ask *p*. concerning the law. *Hag* 2:11
O *p*. that despise my name. *Mal* 1:6
O ye *p*., this commandment is. 2:1
only for the *p*. to eat. *Mat* 12:4
p. in temple profane the sabbath, and.
  5; *Mark* 2:26; *Luke* 6:4
not lawful to eat but for *p*. *Mark* 2:26
33

shew yourselves to the *p*. *Luke* 17:14
the *p*. and captain came. *Acts* 4:1
company of *p*. were obedient. 6:7
sons of Sceva chief of the *p*. 19:14
those *p*. were made without an oath.
  Heb 7:21
they truly were many *p*. 23
seeing there are *p*. that offer. 8:4
p. went always into the first. 9:6
hath made us kings and *p*. to God.
  Rev 1:6; 5:10
be *p*. of God and of Christ. 20:6
see chief, Levites, office

high priests

and Caiaphas being high *p*. *Luke* 3:2
daily as those high *p*. to. *Heb* 7:27
for the law maketh men high *p*. 28

prince

This name is given, [1] *To God,
who is the supreme Ruler and
Governor,* Dan 8:11. [2] *To Christ,
who is called the* Prince of Peace,
Isa 9:6; the Prince of Life, Acts
3:15; the Prince of the kings of the
earth, Rev 1:5. [3] *To the chief
of the priests, called the princes of
the sanctuary,* Isa 43:28. [4] *To
men of princely excellency and
worth,* Eccl 10:7. [5] *To the
nobles, counsellors, and officers in
a kingdom,* Isa 10:8. [6] *To the
chief, or principal men of families,
or tribes,* Num 17:6. [7] *To the
devil, called the prince of this
world, John 12:31; who boasts of
having all the kingdoms of the
earth at his disposal, Mat 4:9.*

thou art a mighty *p*. *Gen* 23:6
as a *p*. hast power with God. 32:28
when Shechem, *p*. of the. 34:2
who made thee a *p*. over ? *Ex* 2:14
each *p*. shall offer on. *Num* 7:11
thyself altogether a *p*. over. 16:13
for each *p*. a rod, even twelve. 17:6
Cozbi the daughter of a *p*. 25:18
take one *p*. of every tribe to. 34:18
of each chief house a *p*. *Josh* 22:14
is a *p*. fallen in Israel ? *2 Sam* 3:38
I will make him a *p*. all. *1 Ki* 11:34
p. over my people. 14:7; 16:2
Sheshbazzar *p*. of Judah. *Ezra* 1:8
where is house of the *p*.? *Job* 21:28
as a *p*. would I go near unto. 31:37
but in want of people is destruction
  of *p*. *Pr* 14:28
much less do lying lips a *p*. 17:7
put lower in presence of the *p*. 25:7
by long forbearing is a *p*. 15*
p. that wanteth understanding. 28:16
how beautiful are thy feet, O *p*.'s
  daughter. *S of S* 7:1
the P. of Peace. *Isa* 9:6
Seraiah was a quiet *p*. *Jer* 51:59*
the *p*. shall be clothed. *Ezek* 7:27
this burden concerneth the *p*. 12:10
p. shall bear on his shoulder. 12
profane wicked *p*. of Israel. 21:25
son of man, say to *p*. of Tyrus. 28:2
be no more a *p*. of Egypt. 30:13
David a *p*. among them. 34:24
David shall be their *p*. for. 37:25
against Gog, the land of Magog, the
  chief *p*. of. 38:2, 3; 39:1
this gate is for the *p*.; the *p*. 44:3
and a portion shall be for the *p*. 45:7
it shall be the *p*.'s part to give. 17
shall the *p*. prepare a bullock. 22
p. shall enter by the porch. 46:2
the burnt offering that the *p*. shall. 4
and when the *p*. shall enter he. 8
and the *p*. in the midst of them. 10
p. prepares a voluntary burnt. 12
if the *p*. give a gift to any of his. 16
after, it shall return to the *p*. but. 17
p. shall not take of the people's. 18
residue shall be for the *p*. on. 48:21
to whom *p*. of the eunuchs. *Dan* 1:7
requested of *p*. of the eunuchs. 8
favour with the *p*. of the eunuchs. 9
magnified himself even to *p*. 8:11
up against the *p*. of princes. 25
unto the Messiah the P. 9:25
people of the *p*. that shall come. 26

p. of Persia withstood me. *Dan* 10:13
p. of Persia, *p*. of Grecia come. 20
with me, but Michael your *p*. 21
but a *p*. for his own behalf. 11:18
also the *p*. of the covenant. 22
Michael stand up, the great *p*. 12:1
Israel shall abide without *p*. *Hos* 3:4
the *p*. and the judge ask. *Mi* 7:3
casteth out devils by *p*. of devils.
  Mat 9:34; 12:24; *Mark* 3:22
p. of this world shall be. *John* 12:31
the *p*. of this world cometh. 14:30
the *p*. of this world is judged. 16:11
killed P. of life, whom. *Acts* 3:15
hath God exalted to be a P. 5:31
p. of the power of the air. *Eph* 2:2
Jesus Christ the P. of. *Rev* 1:5*

princes

the *p*. also of Pharaoh. *Gen* 12:15
twelve *p*. shall Ishmael beget. 17:20
  25:16
a wagon for two *p*. *Num* 7:3
the *p*. offered. 10
rose up 250 *p*. 16:2
the *p*. digged a well. 21:18
and the *p*. of Moab abode with. 22:8
Balak sent yet again *p*. more. 15
p. of the congregation. *Josh* 9:15
whom Moses smote with *p*. 13:21*
with Phinehas ten *p*. sent to. 22:14
kings, give ear, O ye *p*. *Judg* 5:3
and the *p*. of Issachar were with. 15
the two *p*. of the Midianites. 7:25
he described the *p*. of Succoth. 8:14
poor, to set them among *p*. *1 Sam* 2:8
p. of the Philistines were worth. 29:4
young men of the *p*. *1 Ki* 20:14
p. in their families. *1 Chr* 4:38
p. and people will be at thy. 28:21*
left spoil before the *p*. *2 Chr* 28:14
do the commandment of *p*. 30:12
p. gave a thousand bullocks. 24
p. gave willingly to the people. 35:8
treasures of his *p*. brought. 36:18
all the king's mighty *p*. *Ezra* 7:28
hand of the *p*. hath been chief. 9:2
according to the counsel of *p*. 10:8
our *p*. kept thy law. *Neh* 9:34
our *p*. Levites, and priests seal. 38
he made a feast to all his *p*.
  Esth 1:3; 2:18
advanced him above the *p*. 5:11
of one of the king's noble *p*. 6:9
with *p*. that had gold. *Job* 3:15
leadeth *p*. away spoiled. 12:19*
he poureth contempt on *p*. and. 21
the *p*. refrained talking, and. 29:9
is it fit to say to *p*., Ye are ? 34:18*
accepteth not the persons of *p*. 19
thou mayest make *p*. in all the earth.
  Ps 45:16
p. of the people are gathered. 47:9
the *p*. of Zebulun, the *p*. 68:27
p. shall come out of Egypt. 31
he shall cut off the spirit of *p*. 76:12
and fall like one of the *p*. 82:7
to bind his *p*. at his pleasure. 105:22
he poureth contempt upon *p*. 107:40
set him with *p*. even with the *p*. 113:8
than to put confidence in *p*. 118:9
p. also did sit and speak. 119:23
p. have persecuted me without. 161
put not your trust in *p*. nor in. 146:3
p. and all judges of the earth. 148:11
by me *p*. decree justice. *Pr* 8:15
p. rule. 16
it is not good to strike *p*. 17:26*
a servant to rule over *p*. 19:10
many are the *p*. thereof. 28:2
not for *p*. to drink strong drink. 31:4
p. walking as servants. *Eccl* 10:7
thy *p*. eat in the morning. 16
blessed art thou, when thy *p*. eat. 17
thy *p*. are rebellious. *Isa* 1:23
give children to be their *p*. 3:4
enter into judgement with the *p*. 14
are not my *p*. altogether kings ? 10:8
p. of Zoan fools, *p*. of. 19:11, 13
ye *p*. and anoint the shield. 21:5
Tyre, whose merchants are *p*. 23:8
his *p*. were at Zoan, his. 30:4
his *p*. shall be afraid of the. 31:9
and *p*. shall rule in judgement. 32:1

all her *p*. shall be nothing. *Isa* 34:12
bringeth the *p*. to nothing. 40:23
come upon *p*. as on mortar. 41:25*
I have profaned the *p*. 43:28
p. also shall worship because. 49:7
brasen walls against the *p*. *Jer* 1:18
they, their kings and *p*. are. 2:26
the heart of the *p*. shall be. 4:9
bring out the bones of his *p*. 8:1
kings and *p*. sitting on throne. 17:25
the king of Judah and his *p*. 24:8
the *p*. said, This man is not worthy to
die. 26:16
they and their kings and *p*. 32:32
his *p*. I will give to their. 34:21
p. were wroth with Jeremiah. 37:15
to the king of Babylon's *p*. 38:17
if *p*. hear that I have talked. 25
incense that ye and your *p*. 44:21
Chemosh and his *p*. go. 48:7; 49:3
will destroy from thence *p*. 49:38
a sword is on her *p*. and her. 50:35
I will make drunk her *p*. and. 51:57
p. are become like harts. *Lam* 1:6
polluted the kingdom and *p*. 2:2
p. are among the Gentiles. 9
p. are hanged up by hand. 5:12
p. like wolves ravening. *Ezek* 22:27
all of them *p*. to look to. 23:15
Edom and her *p*. with their. 32:29
there the *p*. of the north, all. 30
ye shall drink blood of the *p*. 39:18
my *p*. shall no more oppress. 45:8
to gather together the *p*. *Dan* 3:2*
set over the kingdom 120 *p*. 6:1*
Daniel preferred above the *p*. 3*
p. sought to find occasion against. 4*
stand up against prince of *p*. 8:25
who spake in thy name to our *p*. 9:6
confusion of face to our *p*. and. 8
Michael one of the chief *p*. 10:13
one of his *p*. shall be strong. 11:5
make *p*. glad with lies. *Hos* 7:3
p. have made him sick with wine. 5
their *p*. shall fall by the sword. 16
have made *p*. and I knew it not. 8:4
for the burthen of the king of *p*. 10
all their *p*. are revolters. 9:15
give me a king and *p*. 13:10
their king shall go into captivity, he
and his *p*. *Amos* 1:15
hear, ye *p*. of Israel. *Mi* 3:1*, 9
the *p*. shall be a scorn. *Hab* 1:10
I will punish the *p*. and. *Zeph* 1:8
p. within her are roaring lions. 3:3
p. of Gentiles exercise. *Mat* 20:25*
wisdom of the *p*. of this. *1 Cor* 2:6*
none of the *p*. of this world knew. 8*

all the princes
carried away all the *p*. *2 Ki* 24:14
all the *p*. submitted. *1 Chr* 29:24
and destroyed all the *p*. *2 Chr* 24:23
done wrong to all the *p*. *Esth* 1:16
seat above all the *p*. that were. 3:1
all their *p*. as Zabah. *Ps* 83:11
Jeremiah spake to all the *p*. and.
Jer 26:12
read it in ears of all the *p*. 36:21
all the *p*. of the sea. *Ezek* 26:16
will slay all the *p*. *Amos* 2:3

see Israel

princes of Judah
p. of Judah on wall. *Neh* 12:31
there is *p*. of Judah. *Ps* 68:27
slew all the *p*. of Judah. *Jer* 52:10
p. of Judah are like to. *Hos* 5:10
not least among *p*. of Judah. *Mat* 2:6

princess
p. among the provinces. *Lam* 1:1

princesses
Solomon had . . . wives, *p*. *1 Ki* 11:3

principal
also unto thee *p*. spices. *Ex* 30:23*
even restore it in the *p*. *Lev* 6:5*
his trespass with the *p*. *Num* 5:7*
son of Nathan was *p*. *1 Ki* 4:5*
the *p*. scribe of the host. *2 Ki* 25:19*
Jer 52:25*
one *p*. household taken. *1 Chr* 24:6*
priests, even *p*. fathers cast. 31*
Mattaniah *p*. to begin. *Neh* 11:17*
wisdom is the *p*. thing. 4:7

broken down *p*. plants. *Isa* 16:8*
cast in the *p*. wheat and. 28:25*
wallow in the ashes, ye *p*. *Jer* 25:34
no way to flee, nor the *p*. of flock. 35
against him eight *p*. men. *Mi* 5:5
p. men of the city entered with.
Acts 25:23

principality, -ties
your *p*. shall come down. *Jer* 13:18*
angels, *p*. nor powers be able to.
Rom 8:38
far above all *p*. and power. *Eph* 1:21
that now to *p*. might be known. 3:10
we wrestle against *p*. and. 6:12
p. were created by him. *Col* 1:16
the head of all *p*. and power. 2:10
having spoiled *p*. he made a shew. 15
in mind to be subject to *p*. *Tit* 3:1

principles
one teach you the first *p*. *Heb* 5:12
leaving the *p*. of the doctrine. 6:1

print
ye shall not *p*. any marks. *Lev* 19:28

print, substantive
*thou settest a *p*. on heels. *Job* 13:27*
in his hands *p*. of nails, and put my
finger into the *p*. of. *John* 20:25

printed
Oh that my words were *p*. *Job* 19:23*

Priscilla, see Aquila

prison
(*The prisons of Bible times were
generally windowless dungeons,
below ground; sometimes a cave or
pit was used for the purpose. The
prisoners were bound, or chained*)
Potiphar put Joseph in *p*. *Gen* 39:20
keeper of the *p*. committed to. 22
and baker in *p*. where Joseph. 40:3
bound in the house of your *p*. 42:19
put this fellow in *p*. *1 Ki* 22:27
2 Chr 18:26
bound Hoshea in *p*. *2 Ki* 17:4
brought Jehoiachin out of *p*. 25:27
and changed his *p*. garments. 29
Jer 52:31, 33
Palal repaired by the court of the *p*.
Neh 3:25*
my soul out of *p*. to praise. *Ps* 142:7
for out of *p*. he cometh. *Eccl* 4:14
shall be shut up in the *p*. *Isa* 24:22
bring out prisoners from the *p*. 42:7*
all of them hid in *p*. houses. 22
taken from *p*. and judgement. 53:8*
to proclaim opening of the *p*. 61:1
shouldest put him in *p*. *Jer* 29:26*
Jeremiah . . . in court of *p*. 32:2*
Jews that sat in court of the *p*. 12*
he was shut up in court of the *p*. 33:1*
37:21*; 38:6*, 28*; 39:15
they had not put him into *p*. 37:4
put him in *p*. in Jonathan's. 15
took Jeremiah out of the *p*. 39:14*
he put Zedekiah in *p*. till his. 52:11
John was cast into *p*. *Mat* 4:12*
and thou be cast into *p*. 5:25
Luke 12:58
John heard in *p*. the works. *Mat* 11:2
put him in *p*. for Herodias'. 14:3
he sent and beheaded John in *p*. 10
Mark 6:27
cast him into *p*. till he. *Mat* 18:30
in *p*. and ye came unto me. 25:36
thee in *p*. and came to thee? 39, 44
after John was put in *p*. *Mark* 1:14*
sent and bound John in *p*. 6:17
that he shut up John in *p*. *Luke* 3:20
thee both to *p*. and to death. 22:33
murder was cast into *p*. 23:19, 25
for John was not yet cast into *p*.
John 3:24
put apostles in common. *Acts* 5:18*
by night opened the *p*. doors. 19
sent to the *p*. 21*
found them not in the *p*. 22
committed them to *p*. 8:3
Peter was put in *p*. 12:4
he was kept in *p*. 5
light shined in the *p*. 7*
Lord brought him out of *p*. 17
Paul and Silas cast into *p*. 16:23

the inner *p*. *Acts* 16:24
seeing the *p*. doors open. 27*
saints did I shut up in *p*. 26:10
preached to spirits in *p*. *1 Pet* 3:19
cast some of you into *p*. *Rev* 2:10
Satan be loosed out of his *p*. 20:7

see gate

prison house
grind in the *p*. house. *Judg* 16:21
for Samson out of the *p*. house. 25
Hanani in a *p*. house. *2 Chr* 16:10
bring them that sit in darkness out
of the *p*. house. *Isa* 42:7

prisoner
let sighing of the *p*. come. *Ps* 79:11
to hear groaning of the *p*. 102:20
release to the people a *p*. *Mat* 27:15
then a notable 16; *Mark* 15:6
Paul *p*. called me to him. *Acts* 23:18
unreasonable to send a *p*. 25:27
was I delivered *p*. to Romans. 28:17
Paul, the *p*. of Jesus. *Eph* 3:1
4:1; *Philem* 1:9
not ashamed of me his *p*. *2 Tim* 1:8

see fellow

prisoners
where king's *p*. were. *Gen* 39:20
committed to Joseph all the *p*. 22
took some of Israel *p*. *Num* 21:1*
there the *p*. rest together. *Job* 3:18
despiseth not his *p*. *Ps* 69:33
the Lord looseth the *p*. 146:7
bow down under the *p*. *Isa* 10:4
opened not the house of his *p*. 14:17
shall lead the Egyptians *p*. 20:4*
be gathered together as *p*. 24:22
to bring out the *p*. from the. 42:7
mayest say to the *p*., Go forth. 49:9*
crush under feet the *p*. *Lam* 3:34
forth thy *p*. out of the pit. *Zech* 9:11
strong hold, ye *p*. of hope. 12
and the *p*. heard them. *Acts* 16:25
supposing that the *p*. had fled. 27
Paul and certain other *p*. 27:1
soldiers' counsel was to kill the *p*. 42
delivered the *p*. to captain. 28:16

prisons
delivering you into *p*. *Luke* 21:12
delivering into *p*. men. *Acts* 22:4
in *p*. more frequent, in deaths oft.
2 Cor 11:23

private
no prophecy is of any *p*. *2 Pet* 1:20

privately
disciples came *p*. saying. *Mat* 24:3
Jesus went into a ship *p*.
Mark 6:32*; *Luke* 9:10*
Andrew ask him *p*. *Mark* 9:28; 13:3
his disciples and said *p*. *Luke* 10:23
with Paul's kinsman *p*. *Acts* 23:19
but *p*. to them that were. *Gal* 2:2

privily
he sent to Abimelech *p*. *Josh* 9:31*
cut off Saul's skirt *p*. *1 Sam* 24:4
his eyes are *p*. set against the poor.
Ps 10:8
that they may *p*. shoot at. 11:2*
pull me out of net laid *p*. for me.
31:4; 142:3
commune of laying snares *p*. 64:5
p. slandereth his neighbour. 101:5
let us lurk *p*. for the. *Pr* 1:11
lurk *p*. for their own lives. 18
to put her away *p*. *Mat* 1:19
Herod, when he had *p*. called. 2:7
do they thrust us out *p*.? *Acts* 16:37
who came in *p*. to spy out. *Gal* 2:4
who shall *p*. bring in. *2 Pet* 2:1

privy
his *p*. member cut off. *Deut* 23:1
thy heart is *p*. to. *1 Ki* 2:44
into their *p*. chambers. *Ezek* 21:14
his wife also being *p*. to it. *Acts* 5:2

prize
but one receiveth the *p*. *1 Cor* 9:24
toward the mark for the *p*. *Phil* 3:14

prized
goodly price that I was *p*. *Zech* 11:13

proceed
the six branches that *p*. *Ex* 25:35
nor any word *p*. out of. *Josh* 6:10

seed which shall *p*. out. *2 Sam* 7:12
but I will *p*. no further. *Job* 40:5
p. to do a marvellous. *Isa* 29:14
give ear, for a law shall *p*. 51:4
for they *p*. from evil to evil. *Jer* 9:3
of them shall *p*. thanksgiving. 30:19
governor shall *p*. from midst. 21
and dignity shall *p*. of themselves.
Hab 1:7
things which *p*. out of the mouth defile the man. *Mat* 15:18
out of the heart *p*. 19; *Mark* 7:21
corrupt communication *p*. *Eph* 4:29
they shall *p*. no further. *2 Tim* 3:9

proceeded
whatever *p*. out of her. *Num* 30:12
do that which hath *p*. out. 32:24
do that which *p*. out of. *Judg* 11:36
Elihu also *p*. and said. *Job* 36:1
gracious words which *p*. *Luke* 4:22
I *p*. forth from God. *John* 8:42
he *p*. further to take Peter. *Acts* 12:3
which sword *p*. out of. *Rev* 19:21

proceedeth
thing *p*. from the Lord. *Gen* 24:50
that *p*. out of his mouth. *Num* 30:2
by every word that *p*. out of the
mouth of God. *Deut* 8:3; *Mat* 4:4
wickedness *p*. from. *1 Sam* 24:13
an error which *p*. from. *Eccl* 10:5
out of most High *p*. not. *Lam* 3:38
wrong judgement *p*. *Hab* 1:4*
Spirit of truth which *p*. *John* 15:26
same mouth *p*. blessing. *Jas* 3:10
fire *p*. out of their mouth. *Rev* 11:5

proceeding
water of life *p*. out of. *Rev* 22:1

process
in *p*. of time Cain. *Gen* 4:3
in *p*. of time Shuah Judah's. 38:12
in *p*. of time the king. *Ex* 2:23*
in *p*. of time, Ammon. *Judg* 11:4*

proclaim
I will *p*. the name of. *Ex* 33:19
feast of the Lord ye shall *p*.
Lev 23:2, 4, 21, 37
p. liberty. 25:10
p. peace unto it. *Deut* 20:10
go to *p*. in the ears of. *Judg* 7:3
p. a fast, and set Naboth. *1 Ki* 21:9
Jehu said, P. a solemn. *2 Ki* 10:20*
p. that they fetch pine. *Neh* 8:15
p. before him, Thus shall. *Esth* 6:9
most men *p*. their own. *Pr* 20:6
he hath sent me to *p*. liberty. *Isa* 61:1
to *p*. the acceptable year. 2
go and *p*. these words. *Jer* 3:12
11:6; 19:2
stand in gate of the Lord, and *p*. 7:2
a covenant to *p*. liberty. 34:8
I *p*. a liberty for you to sword. 17
p. ye this among Gentiles. *Joel* 3:9
and *p*. and publish the. *Amos* 4:5

proclaimed
and *p*. the name of. *Ex* 34:5, 6
they caused it to be *p*. 36:6
p. a fast, set Naboth. *1 Ki* 21:12
assembly, and they *p*. it. *2 Ki* 10:20
the man of God *p*. who *p*. 23:16, 17
feared and *p*. a fast. *2 Chr* 20:3
I *p*. a fast there at the river Ahava.
Ezra 8:21
Haman *p*. before him. *Esth* 6:11
p. thy salvation cometh. *Isa* 62:11
they *p*. a fast before Lord. *Jer* 36:9
they *p*. a fast, and put. *Jonah* 3:5
p. and published through Nineveh. 7
p. upon the housetops. *Luke* 12:3

proclaimeth, -ing
the heart of fools *p*. *Pr* 12:23
in *p*. liberty every. *Jer* 34:15, 17
I saw a strong angel *p*. *Rev* 5:2

proclamation
Aaron made *p*. and said. *Ex* 32:5
king Asa made a *p*. *1 Ki* 15:22
went a *p*. throughout the host. 22:36
Joash made a *p*. through. *2 Chr* 24:9
p. throughout all Israel. 30:5
Cyrus made a *p*. throughout all his
kingdom. 36:22; *Ezra* 1:1
Ezra and princes made *p*. *Ezra* 10:7
Belshazzar made *p*. *Dan* 5:29

procure
thus might we *p*. great. *Jer* 26:19*
prosperity that I *p*. unto it. 33:9

procured
hast thou not *p*. this to ? *Jer* 2:17
thy doings have *p*. these. 4:18

procureth
seeketh good *p*. favour. *Pr* 11:27*

produce
p. your cause, saith Lord. *Isa* 41:21

profane
(*As an adjective it means not holy,
sometimes having merely the idea
of secular.*
*As a verb it means to treat with
contempt, usually referring to sacred
things. At times it simply means
to make common*)
shall not take a wife that is *p*.
Lev 21:7, 14
prophets and priests are *p*. *Jer* 23:11
thou *p*. wicked prince of Israel.
Ezek 21:25*
difference between holy and *p*.
22:26*; 44:23*
thee as *p*. out of mountain. 28:16
between sanctuary and the *p*. 42:20*
shall be a *p*. place for city. 48:15*
made for unholy and *p*. *1 Tim* 1:9
refuse *p*. and old wives' fables. 4:7
avoid *p*. and vain babblings. 6:20
2 Tim 2:16
any *p*. person, as Esau. *Heb* 12:16

profane, verb
neither shalt thou *p*. name. *Lev* 18:21
19:12; 20:3; 21:6; 22:2, 32
his people to *p*. himself. 21:4
any priest, if she *p*. herself. 9
shall not *p*. the sanctuary of. 12, 23
nor shall he *p*. his seed among. 15
if they do *p*. my ordinance. 22:9
not *p*. holy things of Israel. 15
and *p*. the sabbath day. *Neh* 13:17
to my sanctuary to *p*. *Ezek* 23:39
I will *p*. my sanctuary. 24:21
maid, to *p*. my holy name. *Amos* 2:7
priests in the temple *p*. *Mat* 12:5
hath gone about to *p*. the. *Acts* 24:6

profaned
p. the hallowed things. *Lev* 19:8
thou hast *p*. his crown. *Ps* 89:39
I have *p*. the princes of. *Isa* 43:28
p. my sabbaths. *Ezek* 22:8; 23:38
p. my holy things, I am *p*. 22:26
sanctuary, when it was *p*. 25:3
they *p*. my holy name, when. 36:20
name which Israel had *p*. 21, 22, 23
but ye have *p*. it, in that. *Mal* 1:12
Judah hath *p*. the holiness. 2:11

profaneness
for from the prophets of Jerusalem
is *p*. gone forth. *Jer* 23:15†

profaneth
she *p*. her father, she. *Lev* 21:9

profaning
wrath by *p*. the sabbath. *Neh* 13:18
by *p*. the covenant of our. *Mal* 2:10

profess
I *p*. this day to the Lord. *Deut* 26:3
will I *p*. I never knew. *Mat* 7:23
they *p*. that they know. *Tit* 1:16

professed, -ing
p. themselves to be wise. *Rom* 1:22
glorify God for your *p*. *2 Cor* 9:13*
women *p*. godliness. *1 Tim* 2:10
hath *p*. a good profession. 6:12*
some *p*. have erred concerning. 21

profession
hast professed a good *p*. *1 Tim* 6:12
the High Priest of our *p*. *Heb* 3:1*
let us hold fast our *p*. 4:14*10:23*

profit, substantive
what *p*. shall this do ? *Gen* 25:32
what *p*. is it if we slay ? 37:26
it is not for the king's *p*. *Esth* 3:8
p. should we have if we? *Job* 21:15
might their strength *p*. me ? 30:2
what *p*. if I be cleansed from? 35:3
p. is there in my blood ? *Ps* 30:9
in all labour there is *p*. *Pr* 14:23

what *p*. hath a man of all his labour ?
Eccl 1:3; 3:9; 5:16
there was no *p*. under the sun. 2:11
moreover the *p*. of the earth. 5:9
by wisdom there is *p*. to. 7:11*
nor be any help nor *p*. *Isa* 30:5
things wherein is no *p*. *Jer* 16:19
what *p*. that we have kept ? *Mal* 3:14
what *p*. is there of circumcision ?
Rom 3:1
I speak for your own *p*. *1 Cor* 7:35
own *p*. but the *p*. of many. 10:33
about words to no *p*. *2 Tim* 2:14
chasteneth us for our *p*. *Heb* 12:10

profit, verb
things which cannot *p*. *1 Sam* 12:21
thy righteousness may *p*. *Job* 35:8
wickedness *p*. nothing. *Pr* 10:2
riches *p*. not in the day. 11:4
were ashamed of people that could
not *p*. *Isa* 30:5, 6
delectable things shall not *p*. 44:9
thou shalt be able to *p*. 47:12
Lord which teacheth thee to *p*. 48:17
for they shall not *p*. thee. 57:12
after things that do not *p*. *Jer* 2:8
glory for that which doth not *p*. 11
in lying words that cannot *p*. 7:8
to pain, but shall not *p*. 12:13
they shall not *p*. this people. 23:32
what *p*. if he gain the ? *Mark* 8:36
every man to *p*. withal. *1 Cor* 12:7
tongues, what shall I *p*. you ? 14:6
Christ shall *p*. you nothing. *Gal* 5:2
preached did not *p*. them. *Heb* 4:2
doth it *p*., my brethren ? *Jas* 2:14
things needful, what doth it *p*.? 16

profitable
can a man be *p*. to God, as wise is *p*.
to himself ? *Job* 22:2
wisdom is *p*. to direct. *Eccl* 10:10
image that is *p*. for nothing. *Isa* 44:10
girdle was *p*. for nothing. *Jer* 13:7
p. for thee that one of thy members
perish. *Mat* 5:29, 30
I kept back nothing *p*. to. *Acts* 20:20
godliness is *p*. to all. *1 Tim* 4:8
all scripture is *p*. for. *2 Tim* 3:16
Mark is *p*. to me for the. 4:11*
these things are *p*. to men. *Tit* 3:8
but now *p*. to thee and. *Philem* 11

profited, -eth
have sinned, and it *p*. not. *Job* 33:27
it *p*. nothing to delight in God. 34:9
what *p*. the graven image ? *Hab* 2:18
a gift by whatever thou mightest be
p. *Mat* 15:5; *Mark* 7:11
is a man *p*. if he gain ? *Mat* 16:26
spirit quickeneth, flesh *p*. *John* 6:63
circumcision *p*. if thou. *Rom* 2:25
not charity, it *p*. nothing. *1 Cor* 13:3
I *p*. in the Jews' religion. *Gal* 1:14*
for bodily exercise *p*. little. *1 Tim* 4:8
not *p*. them that have been occupied.
Heb 13:9

profiting
that thy *p*. may appear. *1 Tim* 4:15*

profound
revolters are *p*. to make. *Hos* 5:2*

progenitors
the blessings of my *p*. *Gen* 49:26

prognosticators
let monthly *p*. stand up. *Isa* 47:13

prolong, -ed
ye shall not *p*. your days. *Deut* 4:26
30:18
that thou mayest *p*. thy days upon
the earth. 4:40; 5:16*, 33; 6:2
11:9; 17:20; 22:7
through this thing ye shall *p*. 32:47
that I should *p*. my life ? *Job* 6:11*
the wicked shall not *p*. the. 15:29*
wilt *p*. the king's life. *Ps* 61:6
the state shall be *p*. *Pr* 28:2
covetousness, shall *p*. his days. 16
though a sinner's days be *p*.*Eccl* 8:12
neither shall the wicked *p*. his. 13
her days shall not be *p*. 13:22
see his seed, he shall *p*. his. 53:10
days are *p*. and vision. *Ezek* 12:22
I will speak, and word shall come to
pass, it shall be no more *p*. 25*

none of my words be *p*. *Ezek* 12:28*
yet their lives were *p*. for. *Dan* 7:12

prolongeth
fear of the Lord *p*. days. *Pr* 10:27
wicked man that *p*. his life. *Eccl* 7:15

promise
The word in the New Testament
is often taken for those promises
that God made to Abraham and the
other patriarchs of sending the
Messiah. It is in this sense that the
apostle Paul commonly uses the
word promise, Rom 4:13, 14; Gal
3:16. The Holy Spirit of promise,
Eph 1:13, is the Holy Ghost, which
God has promised to those that
shall believe in him. The first
commandment with promise is
Honour thy father and mother,
Eph 6:2. To which God has added
this promise, that their days shall
be long upon the earth, Ex 20:12.

know my breach of *p*. *Num* 14:34*
failed one word of good *p*. *1 Ki* 8:56
let thy *p*. to David be. *2 Chr* 1:9
do according to this *p*. *Neh* 5:12
not this *p*. even thus be he shaken
   out. People did . . . to *p*.   13
doth his *p*. fail for ? *Ps* 77:8
he remembered his holy *p*. 105:42*
I send *p*. of my Father. *Luke* 24:49
wait for the *p*. of Father. *Acts* 1:4
received *p*. of Holy Ghost.   2:33
p. is to you and to your children. 39
the time of the *p*. drew nigh. 7:17
to his *p*. hath raised a Saviour. 13:23
the *p*. made to fathers, God hath. 32
looking for a *p*. from thee.   23:21
for hope of the *p*. made of God. 26:6
to which *p*. our tribes, serving God. 7
p. that he shall be the heir. *Rom* 4:13
the *p*. is made of none effect.   14
p. might be sure to all the seed.   16
he staggered not at the *p*.   20
but children of the *p*. counted.   9:8
this is word of *p*. at this time.   9
that we might receive *p*. *Gal* 3:14
make the *p*. of none effect.   17
if of law, it is no more of *p*.: but God
   gave it to Abraham by *p*.   18
to whom the *p*. was made.   19
p. by faith of Jesus Christ might. 22
ye heirs according to the *p*.   29
we are the children of *p*.   4:28
with that Holy Spirit of *p*. *Eph* 1:13
strangers from covenants of *p*. 2:12
Gentiles be partakers of his *p*. 3:6
first commandment with *p*.   6:2
having the *p*. of the life. *1 Tim* 4:8
according to the *p*. of life. *2 Tim* 1:1
lest a *p*. left us of entering. *Heb* 4:1
for when God made *p*. to.   6:13
patiently endured, he obtained *p*. 15
to shew unto the heirs of *p*.   17
the *p*. of eternal life. 9:15; 10:36
sojourned in land of *p*. . . . heirs with
   him of the same *p*.   11:9
and these all received not the *p*. 39
saying, Where is the *p*. of ? *2 Pet* 3:4
is not slack concerning his *p*.   9
according to his *p*. we look for. 13
p. that he hath promised. *1 John* 2:25

promise, *verb*
while they *p*. liberty. *2 Pet* 2:19

promised
according as he hath *p*. *Ex* 12:25
to the place the Lord *p*. *Num* 14:40
the Lord bless you as he hath *p*.
     Deut 1:11; 15:6
increase as the Lord *p*. thee.   6:3
bring them to the land he *p*. 9:28
is his inheritance, as he *p*.   10:9*
enlarge thy border, as he *p*.   12:20
give thee the land he *p*. to give.
     19:8; 27:3
that which thou hast *p*. to God. 23:23
peculiar people, as he *p*. thee. 26:18
live, as the princes had *p*. *Josh* 9:21*
rest to your brethren, as he *p*. 22:4*
possess their land, as Lord *p*. 23:5*
for you, as he hath *p*. you.   10*
things are come the Lord *p*. you. 15*

hast *p*. this goodness to. *2 Sam* 7:28
me an house, as he *p*. *1 Ki* 2:24
Solomon wisdom, as he *p*.   5:12
throne of Israel as the Lord *p*. 8:20
rest to people, as he *p*. by Moses. 56
as I *p*. to David thy father.   9:5
as he *p*. to give a light. *2 Ki* 8:19
     2 Chr 21:7
hast *p*. this goodness. *1 Chr* 17:26
the throne as Lord *p*. *2 Chr* 6:10
which thou hast *p*. David.   15, 16
thou hadst *p*. to fathers. *Neh* 9:23*
that Haman had *p*. to pay. *Esth* 4:7
will bring on them all the good I *p*.
     Jer 32:42; 33:14*
Herod *p*. with oath to. *Mat* 14:7
p. to give him money. *Mark* 14:11
mercy *p*. to our fathers. *Luke* 1:72*
he *p*. to betray him unto them. 22:6*
he *p*. to give it to him. *Acts* 7:5
which he had *p*. afore. *Rom* 1:2
that what he *p*. he was able to. 4:21
eternal life, *p*. before world. *Tit* 1:2
he is faithful that *p*. *Heb* 10:23
judged him faithful that had *p*. 11:11
he hath *p*. saying, Yet once.   12:26
Lord *p*. to them. *Jas* 1:12; 2:5
this is the promise that he hath *p*. us,
   even eternal. *1 John* 2:25

promisedst
David that thou *p*. him. *1 Ki* 8:24, 25
and *p*. that they should go into the
   land. *Neh* 9:15*

promises
to whom pertain the *p*. *Rom* 9:4
to confirm the *p*. made to the. 15:8
all *p*. of God in him are. *2 Cor* 1:20
having therefore these *p*. dearly. 7:1
to his seed were *p*. made. *Gal* 3:16
law against the *p*. of God ?   21
and patience inherit *p*. *Heb* 6:12
blessed him that had the *p*.   7:6
was established upon better *p*. 8:6
died, not having received *p*.   11:13
had received the *p*., offered up. 17
who through faith obtained *p*.   33
great and precious *p*. *2 Pet* 1:4

promising
wicked way, by *p*. life. *Ezek* 13:22*

promote
I will *p*. thee to great honour.
     Num 22:17; 24:11
am I not able indeed to *p*. thee ? 37
and she shall *p*. thee. *Pr* 4:8

promoted
p. over the trees. *Judg* 9:9*, 11*, 13*
the king had *p*. him. *Esth* 5:11
then the king *p*. Shadrach. *Dan* 3:30

promotion
p. cometh neither from. *Ps* 75:6*
shame shall be the *p*. of the. *Pr* 3:35

pronounce
man shall *p*. with an oath. *Lev* 5:4*
priest shall *p*. him unclean. 13:3, 6
     8, 11, 15, 20, 22, 25, 27, 30, 44
shall *p*. him clean. 13:13, 17, 23, 28
     34, 37; 14:7
law, to *p*. it clean or unclean. 13:59
priest shall *p*. the house clean. 14:48
could not frame to *p*. it. *Judg* 12:6

pronounced
but he *p*. this prophecy. *Neh* 6:12
the Lord hath *p*. evil.   16:10; 19:15
p. this great evil.   35:17; 40:2
nation against whom I *p*. turn. 18:8*
word which I have *p*. against. 25:13
Lord will repent of evil he *p*. 26:13
repented of the evil he had *p*.   19
for I have *p*. the word, saith. 34:5*
Lord hath *p*. against this people. 36:7
Jeremiah *p*. all these words. 18, 31

pronouncing
if a soul swear, *p*. to do. *Lev* 5:4*

proof
I might know the *p*. of you. *2 Cor* 2:9
shew ye to them the *p*. of your. 8:24
ye seek a *p*. of Christ speaking. 13:3
but ye know the *p*. of him. *Phil* 2:22
full *p*. of thy ministry. *2 Tim* 4:5†

proofs
alive by many infallible *p*. *Acts* 1:3

proper
(Used with the old meaning of
one's own; still retained in the
French propre)
mine own *p*. good. *1 Chr* 29:3*
called in their *p*. tongue. *Acts* 1:19*
hath his *p*. gift of God. *1 Cor* 7:7
saw he was a *p*. child. *Heb* 11:23*

prophecies
but whether *p*., they. *1 Cor* 13:8
according to the *p*. that. *1 Tim* 1:18

prophecy
in the *p*. of Ahijah. *2 Chr* 9:29
when Asa heard *p*. of Obed. 15:8
he pronounced this *p*. *Neh* 6:12
p. man spake to Ithiel. *Pr* 30:1*
p. that his mother taught him. 31:1*
in them is fulfilled the *p*. of Esaias.
     Mat 13:14
p., by the same Spirit. *1 Cor* 12:10
though I have the gift of *p*. and. 13:2
the gift given thee by *p*. *1 Tim* 4:14
more sure word of *p*. *2 Pet* 1:19
no *p*. of scripture is of private. 20
p. came not in old time by the will. 21
hear the words of this *p*. *Rev* 1:3
rain not in the days of their *p*. 11:6
for the testimony of Jesus is the
   spirit of *p*.   19:10
keepeth the sayings of this *p*. 22:7
sayings of the *p*. of this book.   10
that heareth words of the *p*. of. 18
take from the words of this *p*.   19

prophesied
they *p*. and did not. *Num* 11:25
Eldad and Medad they *p*. in.   26
of God came upon Saul, and he *p*.
     1 Sam 10:10, 11; 18:10; 19:23, 24
messengers of Saul also *p*. 19:20, 21
they *p*. until the evening. *1 Ki* 18:29
prophets *p*. before them. 22:10, 12
     2 Chr 18:9
sons of Asaph *p*. *1 Chr* 25:2
the sons of Jeduthun who *p*.   3
Eliezer *p*. against. *2 Chr* 20:37
Haggai and Zechariah *p*. *Ezra* 5:1
prophets *p*. by Baal. *Jer* 2:8
Pashur heard that Jeremiah *p*. 20:1
and all to whom thou *p*. lies.   6
the prophets of Samaria *p*.   23:13
not spoken to them, yet they *p*. 21
all that Jeremiah hath *p*.   25:13
why hast thou *p*. in the name of ? 26:9
he hath *p*. against this city. 11, 20
Micah *p*. in days of Hezekiah. 18
Urijah *p*.   20
perform the words thou hast *p*. 28:6
p. against many countries.   8
Shemaiah hath *p*. to you.   29:31
prophets which *p*. to you ?   37:19
when I *p*. Pelatiah died. *Ezek* 11:13
so I *p*. as I was commanded, and as
   I *p*.   37:7, 10
who *p*. I would bring thee.   38:17
be ashamed when they *p*. *Zech* 13:4
Lord, have we not *p*.? *Mat* 7:22
prophets and law *p*. until John. 11:13
well hath Esaias *p*. of you. *Mark* 7:6
Zacharias *p*. saying. *Luke* 1:67
Caiaphas *p*. that Jesus. *John* 11:51
spake with tongues and *p*. *Acts* 19:6
I would rather that ye *p*. *1 Cor* 14:5
Enoch also *p*. of these things. *Jude* 14

prophesieth
he never *p*. good to me. *2 Chr* 18:7
prophet which *p*. of peace. *Jer* 28:9
p. of times far off. *Ezek* 12:27
him through when he *p*. *Zech* 13:3
that *p*. with her head. *1 Cor* 11:5
he that *p*. speaketh unto men. 14:3
he that *p*. edifieth the church.   4
greater is he that *p*. than he.   5

prophesy, *verb*
Eldad and Medad do *p*. *Num* 11:27
they shall *p*. *1 Sam* 10:5
thou shalt *p*.   6
doth not *p*. good of me. *1 Ki* 22:8
would not *p*. good. 18; *2 Chr* 18:17
who should *p*. with harps. *1 Chr* 25:1
p. not right things, *p*. *Isa* 30:10

the prophets *p.* falsely.   *Jer* 5:31
p. not in the name of the Lord. 11:21
prophets *p.* lies, they *p.* false.   14:14
concerning the prophets that *p.*   15
people to whom they *p.* shall be.   16
Tophet, whither Lord sent to *p.* 19:14
not to the prophets that *p.*   23:16
that *p.* lies in my name.   25; 26:32
    27:10, 14, 15, 16; 29:9, 21
p. against the inhabitants of.   25:30
Lord sent me to *p.* against.   26:12
why dost *p.* and say, I will ?   32:3
shalt *p.* against Jerusalem. *Ezek* 4:7
p. against the mountains. 6:2; 36:1
p. against them, *p.* O son.   11:4
p. against prophets that *p.* 13:2, 17
p. against the forest of the.   20:46
p. against land of Israel.   21:2, 9
son of man, *p.* and smite thy.   14
p. and say concerning.   28 ; 25:2
p. against Zidon.   28:21
p. against Pharaoh.   29:2
p. against Egypt.   30:2
p. against the shepherds of.   34:2
p. against mount Seir.   35:2
p. concerning the land of.   36:6
p. upon these bones.   37:4
p. to the wind.   9
p. against Gog.   38:2, 14; 39:1
your sons shall *p.*   *Joel* 2:28
    Acts 2:17, 18
commanded the prophets, saying, P.
    not.   *Amos* 2:12; *Mi* 2:6
who can but *p.*?   *Amos* 3:8
eat bread and *p.*   7:12
Go *p.* to my people Israel.   15
p. not again at Beth-el.   13
I will *p.* to thee of wine.   *Mi* 2:11
that when any shall yet *p.* then his
    father.   *Zech* 13:3
well did Esaias *p.* of you. *Mat* 15:7
p. thou Christ.   26:68; *Mark* 14:65
    Luke 22:64
virgins, which did *p.*   *Acts* 21:9
whether prophecy, let us *p. Rom* 12:6
know in part, and we *p.*   *1 Cor* 13:9
rather that ye may *p.*   14:1
if all *p.*   24
we may all *p.* one by one.   31
covet to *p.*   39
thou must *p.* again before. *Rev* 10:11
my two witnesses shall *p.*   11:3

prophesying
had made an end of *p. I Sam* 10:13
company of the prophets *p.*   19:20
prospered through *p.* of.   *Ezra* 6:14
man *p.* having his head. *1 Cor* 11:4
except by *p.* or by doctrine.   14:6
p. serveth not for them that.   22
despise not *p.*, prove. *1 Thes* 5:20

prophet
Ordinarily this word is understood
as meaning one who foretells
future events. It meant, at the time
our English Bible was translated,
also a preacher—and prophesying
meant preaching. A meaning of
the word less often recognized, but
really as common, is one who tells
—a forth-teller—who speaks for
another, most usually for God.
It is in this sense that many Bible
characters are called prophets, as
for example, Aaron, Moses, and
Jesus Christ. Those prophets who
wrote their prophecies, which are
preserved to us in our Bible, are
divided into two groups : four
major prophets—Isaiah, Jeremiah,
Ezekiel and Daniel—and 12 minor
prophets, whose names are given
to the last 12 books of the Old
Testament. There are also a
number of prophets named in the
Old Testament who were important
in their day, but who left no writings
behind them. The most important
of these are Elijah and Elisha,
whose deeds are related in 1 Ki
17–21; 2 Ki 1–9, 13. The periods
of the prophecies preserved to us
are in some cases a little uncertain.

*The following is, at least, approxi-
mately correct.*

1. Isaiah *began to prophesy near the
time of the death of Uzziah, king of
Judah. He continued to prophesy
to the reign of Manasseh, who
caused him to be put to death.*

2. Jeremiah *began in the thirteenth
year of the reign of Josiah king of
Judah. He continued to prophesy
till the taking of Jerusalem by the
Chaldeans ; and it is thought he
died two years after in Egypt;
Baruch was his disciple and ama-
nuensis.*

3. Ezekiel *was carried captive to
Babylon, along with Jeconiah king
of Judah. 11 years before the destruction of Jerusalem. He
preached during the captivity for
about 22 years. We do not know
when he died.*

4. Daniel *was taken into Chaldea
in the third year of Jehoiakim king
of Judah, and prophesied at Babylon to the end of the captivity.*

5. Hosea *prophesied under Jeroboam II. king of Israel, and his suc-
cessors, perhaps to the destruction
of Samaria.*

6. Joel *prophesied under Josiah
about the same time as Jeremiah.*

7. Amos *began to prophesy the
second year before the earthquake,
which was in the reign of king
Uzziah, about six years before the
death of Jeroboam II. king of
Israel.*

8. Obadiah *dwelt in Judea, probably after the taking of Jerusalem,
and before the desolation of Idumea.*

9. Jonah *lived in the kingdom of
Israel under the kings Joash and
Jeroboam II. about the same time
as Hosea, Isaiah, and Amos.*

10. Micah *lived under Jotham,
Ahaz, and Hezekiah, kings of
Judah; he was contemporary with
Isaiah, but began later to prophesy.*

11. Nahum *appeared in Judah
under the reign of Hezekiah, and
after the expedition of Sennacherib.*

12. Habakkuk *lived in Judea during the reign of Jehoiakim, before
the coming of Nebuchadnezzar into
the country.*

13. Zephaniah *appeared at the
beginning of the reign of Josiah,
and before the twenty-eighth year
of this prince.*

14. Haggai *was the great prophet
of the Return to Jerusalem, and the
rebuilding of the temple. He is
supposed to have been an old man,
as Hag 2:3 is taken to mean that
he had seen the old temple before
its destruction by Nebuchadnezzar.*

15. Zechariah *prophesied in Judea
at the same time as Haggai, and
continued to prophesy after him,
being younger.*

16. Malachi, *the author of the last
book in the Old Testament, lived
about the time of Nehemiah's
second visit to Jerusalem. Nothing
whatever is known of him.*

Aaron shall be thy *p.*   *Ex* 7:1
but the *p.* which shall presume.
    Deut 18:20, 22
p. Gad said to David.   *1 Sam* 22:5
word of the Lord came to the *p.*
    2 Sam 24:11
call me Nathan the *p.*   *1 Ki* 1:32
sent with him Nathan the *p.*   34
Ahijah the *p.* found Jeroboam. 11:29
an old *p.* in Beth-el.   13:11, 25
p. whom he had brought back.   23
p. took up the carcase of the man of
    God, and the old *p.* came to.   29
by *p.* Jehu came the word. 16:7, 12
Elijah the *p.* came near and said. 18:36
p. came to king of Israel.   20:22

my lord were with the *p.*   *2 Ki* 5:3
p. had bid thee do some great.   13
Elisha the *p.* telleth what thou. 6:12
young man the *p.* went to.   9:4
Isaiah the *p.* cried to Lord.   20:11
with bones of *p.* that came out. 23:18
came Shemaiah the *p.*   *2 Chr* 12:5
in the story of the *p.* Iddo.   13:22
the prophecy of the *p.* Oded.   15:8
a writing from Elijah the *p.*   21:12
then the *p.* forbare, and said. 25:16
the *p.* Isaiah prayed and cried. 32:20
from the days of Samuel the *p.* 35:18
not himself before Jeremiah *p.* 36:12
Haggai the *p.* prophesied. *Ezra* 5:1
prophesying of Haggai the *p.*   6:14
there is no more any *p.*   *Ps* 74:9
Lord doth take away the *p. Isa* 3:2
the *p.* that teacheth lies.   9:15
priest and *p.* have erred.   28:7
from the *p.* even unto the priest
    dealeth falsely.   *Jer* 6:13; 8:10
nor shall word perish from *p.* 18:18
both *p.* and priests are profane. 23:11
p. that hath a dream set him.   28
the *p.* Jeremiah said, Amen.   28:6
p. which prophesieth of peace, when
    the word of the *p.* shall . . . *p.*   9
so Hananiah the *p.* died the.   17
Baruch and Jeremiah the *p.*   36:26
nor his servants hearken to *p.*   37:2
take up Jeremiah the *p.* out.   38:10
shall the *p.* be slain ?   *Lam* 2:20
they seek a vision of *p. Ezek* 7:26
and cometh to the *p.* I will.   14:4
if *p.* be deceived, I the Lord have de-
    ceived that *p.*   9
punishment of the *p.* shall be.   10
p. also shall fall with thee. *Hos* 4:5
the *p.* is a fool.   9:7
p. is a snare of a fowler.   8*
I was no *p.* nor *p.*'s son. *Amos* 7:14
he shall even be the *p.*   *Mi* 2:11
prayer of Habakkuk the *p. Hab* 3:1
he shall say, I am no *p.*   *Zech* 13:5
will send you Elijah the *p. Mal* 4:5
spoken by the *p.* Isaiah.   *Mat* 1:22
    2:15; 3:3; 4:14; 8:17; 21:4
    Luke 3:4; *John* 1:23; 12:38
    Acts 28:25
thus it is written by the *p. Mat* 2:5
spoken by Jeremy the *p.*   17; 27:9
but the sign of the *p.* Jonas. 12:39
    Luke 11:29
spoken by the *p.*   *Mat* 13:35
    27:35
Jesus the *p.* of Nazareth of.   21:11
spoken of by Daniel the *p.*   24:15
    Mark 13:14
child be called *p.* of the Highest.
    Luke 1:76
to him book of the *p.* Esaias.   4:17
no *p.* is accepted in his own.   24
in the time of Eliseus the *p.*   27
not a greater *p.* than John.   7:28
of a truth this is the *p.*   *John* 7:40
out of Galilee ariseth no *p.*   52
was spoken by the *p.* Joel. *Acts* 2:16
made with hands, as saith *p.*   7:48
he read Esaias the *p.*   8:28, 30
of whom speaketh the *p.* this ?   34
judges until Samuel the *p.*   13:20
the ass forbad the madness of the
    p.   *2 Pet* 2:16

    see **priest, Lord**

a prophet
restore man his wife, for he is a *p.*
    Gen 20:7
if there be a *p.* among.   *Num* 12:6
arise a *p.* or dreamer.   *Deut* 13:1
I will raise up a *p.* from among.
    18:15, 18; *Acts* 3:22; 7:37
when a *p.* speaketh in.   *Deut* 18:22
arose not a *p.* in Israel like.   34:10
sent a *p.* to the children.   *Judg* 6:8
established to be a *p.*   *1 Sam* 3:20
now called a *p.* was called.   9:9
he said, I am a *p.* also.   *1 Ki* 13:18
I, even I only remain a *p.* of. 18:22
anoint Elisha to be a *p.*   19:16
there came a *p.* unto Ahab.   20:13
is there not here a *p.* of the Lord ?
    22:7; *2 Ki* 3:11; *2 Chr* 18:6

prophet

there is a p. in Israel. 2 Ki 5:8
sent a p. to Amaziah. 2 Chr 25:15
a p. of Lord was there, Oded. 28:9
thee a p. to the nations. Jer 1:5
maketh himself a p. 29:26, 27
there hath been a p. Ezek 2:5; 33:33
cometh to a p. to enquire of. 14:7
by a p. the Lord brought Israel out of
  Egypt, and by a p. Hos 12:13
a p. in the name of a p. shall receive
  a p.'s reward. Mat 10:41
went ye out for to see ? a p.? 11:9
a p. is not without honour save. 13:57
  Mark 6:4; John 4:44
they accounted him as a p. Mat 14:5
  21:26; Mark 11:32; Luke 20:6
they took him for a p. Mat 21:46
others said, That it is a p. Mark 6:15
a great p. is risen. Luke 7:16
this man, if he were a p. would. 39
cannot be that a p. perish out. 13:33
Jesus, who was a p. mighty. 24:19
perceive that thou art a p. John 4:19
the blind man said, He is a p. 9:17
being a p. and knowing. Acts 2:30
a certain p. named Agabus. 21:10
think himself to be a p. 1 Cor 14:37
a p. of their own land. Tit 1:12

false prophet
a false p., a Jew named. Acts 13:6
out of mouth of false p. Rev 16:13
taken, with him the false p. 19:20
where beast and false p. are. 20:10

that prophet
to the words of that p. Deut 13:3
that p. or that dreamer. 5; 18:20
have deceived that p. Ezek 14:9
Art thou that p.? John 1:21, 25
this is of a truth that p. that. 6:14
will not hear that p. Acts 3:23

prophetess
Miriam p. took a timbrel. Ex 15:20
and Deborah a p. judged. Judg 4:4
went to Huldah the p. 2 Ki 22:14
  2 Chr 34:22
think on the p. Noadiah. Neh 6:14
p. and she conceived a son. Isa 8:3
there was one Anna a p. Luke 2:36
who called herself a p. Rev 2:20

prophets
Lord's people were p. Num 11:29
meet a company of p. 1 Sam 10:5
company of p. met him. 10
prophesied among the p. 11
is Saul among the p.? 12; 19:24
answered him not by p. 28:6, 15
Obadiah hid 100 p. by 50. 1 Ki 18:4
Jezebel slew the p. 13
gather p. of Baal 450. 19, 22
take the p. of Baal, let none. 40
have slain p. with the sword. 19:10
  14; Neh 9:26
of Israel gathered the p. 1 Ki 22:6
a lying spirit in p. 22; 2 Chr 18:21
to p. of thy father, and p. 2 Ki 3:13
Josiah went and p., to house. 23:2
believe his p. so shall. 2 Chr 20:20
Yet he sent p. to them. 24:19
they misused his p. 36:16
were the p. of God helping. Ezra 5:2
appointed p. to preach. Neh 6:7
by thy Spirit in thy p. 9:30
trouble that hath come on our p. 32
the p. and seers hath he. Isa 29:10
say to the p., Prophesy not. 30:10
  Amos 2:12
and p. prophesied by Baal. Jer 2:8
their priests and p. are ashamed. 26
sword hath devoured your p. 30
the p. shall wonder. 4:9
p. become wind. 5:13
p. prophesy falsely, and.
bring out the bones of the p. 8:1
will fill p. with drunkenness. 13:13
the p. say, Ye shall not see. 14:13
p. prophesy lies in my name. 14
sword and famine shall those p. 15
folly in the p. of Samaria. 23:13
seen in p. an horrible thing. 14
from p. is profaneness gone forth. 15
I have not sent these p., yet. 21

I have heard what the p. Jer 23:25
p. of deceit of their own heart. 26
the p. that steal my word. 30, 31
priests and p. heard Jeremiah. 26:7
p. and people took Jeremiah. 8
the p., This man is worthy to die. 11
hearken not to your p. 27:9, 16
ye and the p. might perish. 15
if they be p. and word of Lord. 18
p. that have been before me. 28:8
Jeremiah sent to the p. 29:1
saith the Lord, Let not your p. 8
Lord hath raised us up p. in. 15
they and their p. provoke me. 32:32
where are now your p.? 37:19
her p. also find no vision. Lam 2:9
thy p. have seen vain things. 14
for the sins of her p. that have. 4:13
prophesy against the p. Ezek 13:2
Woe unto the foolish p. 3
O Israel, thy p. are like foxes. 4
my hand shall be upon the p. that. 9
there is a conspiracy of her p. 22:25
p. daubed them with untempered. 28
I have hewed them by p. Hos 6:5
I have spoken by p. and. 12:10
raised up of your sons p. Amos 2:11
and commanded the p. saying. 12
sun shall go down over p. Mi 3:6
p. thereof divine for money. 11
her p. are light and. Zeph 3:4
to whom the former p. Zech 1:4
the p. do they live for ever ? 5
Lord hath cried by former p. 7:7
word Lord sent by former p. 12
I will cause the p. to pass out. 13:2
the p. shall be ashamed, each. 4
so persecuted they the p. Mat 5:12
  Luke 6:23
not come to destroy the law and the
  p. Mat 5:17
for this is the law and the p. 7:12
many p. have desired to see. 13:17
  Luke 10:24
on these hang all the law and.
  Mat 22:40
of them who killed the p. 23:31
I send unto you p. 34; Luke 11:49
thou that killest the p. Mat 23:37
written in p., Behold I. Mark 1:2
as he spake by his holy p.
  Luke 1:70; 2 Pet 3:2
and p. were until John. Luke 16:16
They have Moses and p. 29, 31
slow to believe what the p. 24:25
found him of whom the p. John 1:45
Abraham is dead, and p. 8:52, 53
by the mouth of his p. Acts 3:18, 21
p. came from Jerusalem to. 11:27
in church at Antioch certain p. 13:1
after reading of law and the p. 15
which is spoken of in the p. 40
Judas and Silas being p. 15:32
things written in law and p. 24:14
none other things than p. did. 26:22
Agrippa, believest thou the p.? 27
promised afore by his p. Rom 1:2
witnessed by law and the p. 3:21
Lord, they have killed thy p. 11:3
apostles, secondarily p. 1 Cor 12:28
are all p.? 29
let p. speak two or three. 14:29
on foundation of the p. Eph 2:20
as it is now revealed to his p. 3:5
and he gave some p. and. 4:11
killed Lord, and own p. 1 Thes 2:15
spake to fathers by the p. Heb 1:1
take, my brethren, the p. Jas 5:10
which salvation the p. 1 Pet 1:10
two p. tormented them. Rev 11:10
rejoice, ye holy apostles and p. 18:20
in her was found blood of p. and. 24
for I am of thy brethren the p. 22:9

all the prophets
he had slain all the p. 1 Ki 19:1
throne, and all the p. prophesied.
  22:10, 12; 2 Chr 18:9, 11
call all the p. of Baal. 2 Ki 10:19
against Israel by all the p. 17:13
all the p. prophesied until. Mat 11:13
that blood of all the p. Luke 11:50
see all the p. in kingdom. 13:28

all the p. he expounded. Luke 24:27
all the p. from Samuel. Acts 3:24
to him give all the p. witness. 10:43

false prophets
false p. in sheep's. Mat 7:15
many false p. shall rise. 24:11, 24
  Mark 13:22
their fathers to false p. Luke 6:26
there were false p. also. 2 Pet 2:1
because many false p. 1 John 4:1

my prophets
mine anointed, and do my p. no.
  1 Chr 16:22; Ps 105:15

of the prophets
company of the p. met. 1 Sam 10:10
saw the company of the p. 19:20
man of the sons of the p. 1 Ki 20:35
that he was of the p. 41
words of the p. 22:13; 2 Chr 18:12
sons of the p. at Beth-el. 2 Ki 2:3
the sons of the p. at Jericho. 5
sons of the p. went to view afar. 7
sons of the p. said, The spirit. 15
woman of wives of sons of the p. 4:1
pottage for the sons of the p. 38
think of the rest of the p. Neh 6:14
because of the p. ell my. Jer 23:9
to the words of the p. 16; 27:14
this be in the heart of the p.? 23:26
by ministry of the p. Hos 12:10
by the mouth of the p. Zech 8:9
Elias or one of the p. Mark 16:14
  Mark 6:15; 8:28
ye build the tombs of the p.
  Mat 23:29; Luke 11:47
them in blood of the p. Mat 23:30
of the p. might be fulfilled 26:56
one of the p. was risen. Luke 9:8, 19
ye are children of the p. Acts 3:25
written in the book of the p. 7:42
of the p. have not your fathers? 52
reading of the law and the p. 13:15
they knew not voice of the p. 27
to this agree words of the p. 15:15
concerning Jesus out of the p. 28:23
by scriptures of the p. Rom 16:26
spirits of the p. are subject to the
  prophets. 1 Cor 14:32
on the foundation of the p. Eph 2:20
fail me to tell of the p. Heb 11:32
shed the blood of the p. Rev 16:6
Lord God of the holy p. sent. 22:6

servants the prophets
blood of my serv. the p. 2 Ki 9:7
I sent by my serv. the p. 17:13
Lord said by all his serv. the p. 23
spake by his serv. the p. 21:10; 24:2
commanded by serv. the p. Ezra 9:11
sent you my serv. the p. Jer 7:25
  25:4; 29:19; 35:15
to the words of my serv. the p. 26:5
spoken by my serv. the p. Ezek 38:17
hearkened to serv. the p. Dan 9:6
set before us by his serv. the p. 10
his secret to his serv. the p. Amos 3:7
which I commanded my serv. the p.
  Zech 1:6
declared to his serv. the p. Rev 10:7
give reward to serv. the p. 11:18

propitiation
hath set forth to be a p. Rom 3:25
and he is the p. 1 John 2:2; 4:10

proportion
according to the p. 1 Ki 7:36*
not conceal his comely p. Job 41:12†
according to p. of faith. Rom 12:6

proselyte
*This term comes from the Greek
word, Proselytos, which signifies
a stranger, one that comes from
abroad, or from another place.
The Hebrew word Ger or Necher,
has the same signification. It
means a convert to Judaism from
among the Gentiles.
The Talmud distinguishes between
Proselytes of the Gate, and Proselytes of Righteousness. The first
are those who dwelt in the land of
Israel and were not bound by circumcision. The term is derived*

from the expression the stranger that is within thy gates, Ex 20:10, etc.

The Proselytes of Righteousness *are those that were converted to Judaism, who received circumcision, and observed the whole law of Moses. They were therefore perfect Israelites.*

compass sea and land to make one *p.*   Mat 23:15
Nicholas a *p.* of Antioch.   Acts 6:5

proselytes
Jews and *p.*, we do hear. Acts 2:10
Jews and religious *p.* followed Paul.   13:43

prospect
chambers whose *p.* was. Ezek 40:44
p. to the north.   46
p. to the east.   42:15; 43:4

prosper
his angel and *p.* thee. Gen 24:40
if now thou do *p.* my way.   42
that Joseph did to *p.*   39:3, 23
but it shall not *p.*   Num 14:41
not *p.* in thy ways. Deut 28:29
that ye may *p.*   29:9; Josh 1:7*
    1 Ki 2:3
Go up to Ramoth-gilead and *p.*
  1 Ki 22:12, 15; 2 Chr 18:11, 14
son, the Lord *p.* thee. 1 Chr 22:11
shalt thou *p.* if thou takest heed. 13
fight ye not, for ye shall not *p.*
    2 Chr 13:12
prophets, so shall ye *p.*   20:20
Why transgress ye, that ye cannot *p.?*
    24:20
Lord God made Uzziah to *p.*   26:5
p., I pray thee, thy servant. Neh 1:11
God of heaven, he will *p.* us.   2:20
tabernacles of robbers *p.* Job 12:6
whatsoever he doeth shall *p.* Ps 1:3
ungodly who *p.* in the world. 73:12*
they shall *p.* that love thee. 122:6
his sins, shall not *p.*   Pr 28:13
whether shall *p.*   Eccl 11:6
pleasure of Lord shall *p.* Isa 53:10
formed against thee shall *p.*   54:17
shall *p.* in the thing whereunto. 55:11
thou shalt not *p.* in them. Jer 2:37
yet they *p.*   5:28
they shall not *p.*   10:21; 20:11
doth the way of wicked *p.?*   12:1
not *p.* in his days, for no man of his seed shall *p.*   22:30
a King shall reign and *p.*   23:5*
with Chaldeans ye shall not *p.* 32:5
are chief, her enemies *p.*   Lam 1:5
thou didst *p.*   Ezek 16:13
shall it *p.?*   17:9, 10
shall he *p.?* shall he escape *?* 17:15
destroy wonderfully and *p.* Dan 8:24
shall cause craft to *p.* in his hand. 25
lies, but it shall not *p.*   11:27, 36
all that thou mayest *p.*   3 John 2

prospered
seeing the Lord hath *p.* Gen 24:56
the hand of Israel *p.* Judg 4:24*
demanded how war *p.* 2 Sam 11:7
Hezekiah *p.* 2 Ki 18:7; 2 Chr 31:21
    32:30
Solomon *p.*   1 Chr 29:23
Asa *p.*   2 Chr 14:7
Jews *p.* through the prophesying of Haggai.   Ezra 6:14
against him and hath *p.?* Job 9:4
Daniel *p.* in the reign of. Dan 6:28
truth to the ground and it *p.*   8:12
lay by, as God hath *p.*   1 Cor 16:2

prospereth
work *p.* in their hands. Ezra 5:8
fret not because of him that *p.*
    Ps 37:7
a gift, whithersoever it turneth it *p.*
    Pr 17:8
health, even as thy soul *p.* 3 John 2

prosperity
thou shalt not seek their *p.* Deut 23:6
shall say to him that liveth in *p.*
    1 Sam 25:6
and *p.* exceedeth fame. 1 Ki 10:7
in *p.*, the destroyer shall. Job 15:21

shall spend their days in *p.* Job 36:11
in my *p.* I said, I shall.   Ps 30:6
Lord hath pleasure in the *p.* of. 35:27
when I saw the *p.* of wicked. 73:3
I beseech thee, send now *p.* 118:25
peace be within thy walls, *p.* 122:7
the *p.* of fools shall.   Pr 1:32
in the day of *p.* be joyful. Eccl 7:14
I spake to thee in thy *p.* Jer 22:21
all the *p.* that I procure to.   33:9*
far from peace, I forgat *p.* Lam 3:17
my cities through *p.* shall. Zech 1:17
when Jerusalem in *p.*   7:7

prosperous
Lord made his journey *p.* Gen 24:21
Joseph, he was a *p.* man.   39:2
thou make thy way *p.*   Josh 1:8
way we go shall be *p.* Judg 18:5
would make the habitation of thy righteousness *p.*   Job 8:6
he shall make his way *p.* Isa 48:15
for the seed shall be *p.* Zech 8:12*
I might have a *p.* journey. Rom 1:10

prosperously
Solomon *p.* effected all. 2 Chr 7:11
majesty ride *p.* because.   Ps 45:4

prostitute
do not *p.* thy daughter. Lev 19:29*

protection
rise up and be your *p.* Deut 32:38

protest, -ed
the man did solemnly *p.* Gen 43:3
hearken, yet *p.* solemnly. 1 Sam 8:9
and I *p.* unto thee.   1 Ki 2:42
I earnestly *p.* to your.   Jer 11:7
the angel of the Lord *p.* Zech 3:6
I *p.* by your rejoicing. 1 Cor 15:31

protesting
p. saying, Obey my voice. Jer 11:7

proud
p. helpers do stoop.   Job 9:13*
he smiteth through the *p.*   26:12*
shall thy *p.* waves be stayed. 38:11
behold *p.* and abase him.   40:11
look on *p.*, bring him low.   12
that speaketh *p.* things. Ps 12:3*
plentifully rewardeth the *p.*   31:23
man who respecteth not the *p.* 40:4
the *p.* are risen against me.   86:14
render a reward to the *p.*   94:2
him that hath a *p.* heart will I. 101:5
thou hast rebuked the *p.*   119:21
p. have had me greatly in derision. 51
p. have forged a lie against me. 69
let *p.* be ashamed, for they dealt. 78
the *p.* digged pits for me, not. 85
let not the *p.* oppress me.   122
filled with contempt of the *p.* 123:4
the *p.* waters had gone over. 124:5
the *p.* he knoweth afar off. 138:6
p. have hid a snare for me. 140:5
Lord hateth a *p.* look.   Pr 6:17
destroy the house of the *p.* 15:25
one *p.* in heart is abomination. 16:5
to divide the spoil with the *p.* 19
an high look and *p.* heart is. 21:4
p. scorner ... deals in *p.* wrath. 24
p. heart stirreth up strife.   28:25*
patient better than the *p.* Eccl 7:8
Lord on every one that is *p.* Isa 2:12
arrogancy of the *p.* to cease. 13:11
the *p.* wrath of Moab.
be not *p.*: for the Lord.   Jer 13:15
p. men answered Jeremiah.   43:2
Moab, he is exceeding *p.*   48:29
she hath been *p.*   50:29
O thou most *p.*   31
most *p.* shall stumble and fall. 32
he is a *p.* man, neither.   Hab 2:5
we call the *p.* happy.   Mal 3:15
p. as stubble.
he hath scattered the *p.* Luke 1:51
despiteful, *p.*, boasters. Rom 1:30
he is *p.*, knowing nothing. 1 Tim 6:4
covetous, boasters, *p.*   2 Tim 3:2
God resisteth the *p.*   Jas 4:6
    1 Pet 5:5

proudly
dealt *p.* he was above.   Ex 18:11
no more so exceeding *p.* 1 Sam 2:3
thou knewest that they dealt *p.*
    Neh 9:10, 16, 29

their mouth they speak *p.* Ps 17:10
which speak grievous things *p.* 31:18
child shall behave *p.*   Isa 3:5
shouldest thou have spoken *p.* Ob 12

prove
[1] *To try and examine*, 2 Cor 13:5.
[2] *To show to be true by argument*,
Acts 9:22; Rom 3:9.   [3] *To find true*, Eccl 7:23.
that I may *p.* them.   Ex 16:4
    Deut 8:16
God is come to *p.* you. Ex 20:20
humble thee, and to *p.* Deut 8:2
whom thou didst *p.* at Massah 33:8
that through them I may *p.* Israel.
    Judg 2:22; Isa 3:1, 4
let me *p.* thee but this once with fleece.   Judg 6:39
she came to *p.* Solomon. 1 Ki 10:1
    2 Chr 9:1
it shall *p.* me perverse. Job 9:20
O Lord, and *p.* me.   Ps 26:2
I will *p.* thee with mirth. Eccl 2:1
p. thy servants, I beseech. Dan 1:12
bring the tithes, *p.* me now herewith.
    Mal 3:10
oxen, I go to *p.* them. Luke 14:19
this he said to *p.* him. John 6:6
neither can they *p.* the things.
    Acts 24:13; 25:7
p. what is that good will. Rom 12:2
to *p.* the sincerity of your. 2 Cor 8:8
p. your own selves, know ye ? 13:5
let every man *p.* his own. Gal 6:4
p. all things; hold fast. 1 Thes 5:21

proved
hereby ye shall be *p.*   Gen 42:15
that your words may be *p.*   16
and there he *p.* them.   Ex 15:25
he had not *p.* his sword, David said,
I have not *p.* them. 1 Sam 17:39
thou hast *p.* my heart.   Ps 17:3
thou, O God, hast *p.* us.   66:10
p. thee at waters of Meribah. 81:7
fathers *p.* me and saw my.   95:9
this have I *p.* by wisdom. Eccl 7:23
and *p.* them ten days.   Dan 1:14
we before *p.* both Jews.   Rom 3:9
ye have often *p.* diligent. 2 Cor 8:22
these also be first *p.*   1 Tim 3:10
p. me, and saw my works. Heb 3:9

provender
we have both straw and *p.* Gen 24:25
the man gave straw and *p.* for.   32
opened sack to give his ass *p.* 42:27
the man gave their asses *p.*   43:24
there is both straw and *p.* Judg 19:19
him and gave *p.* to the asses.   21*
asses shall eat clean *p.*   Isa 30:24

proverb
(*This word has in the Bible, besides its ordinary modern use, that of a short parable, or a saying with a hidden meaning*)
a *p.* and a byword.   Deut 28:37
a *p.*, Is Saul among ? 1 Sam 10:12
as saith *p.* of the ancients.   24:13
Israel shall be a *p.* and.   1 Ki 9:7
will I make to be a *p.* 2 Chr 7:20
I became a *p.* to them.   Ps 69:11
understand a *p.* and words. Pr 1:6
take up this *p.* against. Isa 14:4*
deliver them to be a *p.* Jer 24:9
what is that *p.* ye have? Ezek 12:22
I will make this *p.* cease ... no more
use it as a *p.* in.   23; 18:2, 3
will make him a sign, and a *p.* 14:8
these take up a taunting *p.* Hab 2:6
surely say this *p.*, Physician heal thyself.   Luke 4:23*
thou plainly, and no *p.* John 16:29†
according to the *p.*   2 Pet 2:22

proverbs
that speak in *p.* say.   Num 21:27
spake three thousand *p.* 1 Ki 4:32
the *p.* of Solomon.   Pr 1:1; 10:1
    25:1
preacher set in order many *p.*
    Eccl 12:9
every one that useth *p.* Ezek 16:44
I have spoken in *p.* ... I shall no more speak in *p.* John 16:25†

proveth

for Lord your God p. you. Deut 13:3

provide

God will p. himself a lamb. Gen 22:8
when shall I p. for mine own? 30:30
shalt p. out of the people able men.
   Ex 18:21
p. me a man that can play well.
   1 Sam 16:17
men whom David did p. 2 Chr 2:7
can he p. flesh for his? Ps 78:20
p. neither gold nor silver. Mat 10:9
p. yourselves bags. Luke 12:33
and p. them beasts to set. Acts 23:24
p. things honest in sight. Rom 12:17
but if any p. not for his. 1 Tim 5:8

provided

he p. the first part. Deut 33:21
I have p. me a king. 1 Sam 16:1
he had p. the king of. 2 Sam 19:32
which p. victuals for. 1 Ki 4:7, 27
Hezekiah p. possessions of flocks.
   2 Chr 32:29
corn, when thou hast p. Ps 65:9
whose shall those things be, which
   thou hast p.? Luke 12:20*
God having p. better. Heb 11:40

providence

to this nation by thy p. Acts 24:2

provideth

p. for the raven his food. Job 38:41
p. her meat in summer. Pr 6:8

providing

p. for honest things. 2 Cor 8:21*

province, -s

by the princes of the p. 1 Ki 20:14
   15, 17, 19
hurtful to kings and p. Ezra 4:15
found in the p. of the Medes. 6:2
gold thou canst find in the p. 7:16
are the children of the p. 11:3
these are the chief of the p. 11:3
reigned over 127 p. Esth 1:1
wrong to people in all p. 16, 22
appoint officers in all the p. 2:3
king made a release to the p. 18
a people scattered in all p. of. 3:8
sent by posts to all the king's p. 13
all the people of the king's p. 4:11
127 p. and do every p. 8:9
in all p. of king Ahasuerus. 12
fame went through all the p. 9:4
they done in the rest of the p. 12
these days should be kept through
   every p. 28
the treasure of the p. Eccl 2:8
oppression in a p. marvel not. 5:8
princess among the p. Lam 1:1
against him from the p. Ezek 19:8
Daniel ruler over the p. Dan 2:48
image in the p. of Babylon. 3:1
promoted Shadrach in the p. of. 30
at Shushan in the p. of Elam. 8:2
on the fattest places of the p. 11:24
asked of what p. he was. Acts 23:34
Festus was come into the p. 25:1

proving

Saul p. that this is very. Acts 9:22
p. what is acceptable to. Eph 5:10

provision

give them p. for the way. Gen 42:25
gave them p. for the way. Josh 9:5
all the bread of their p. Josh 9:5
bread we took hot for our p. 12
each man made p. 1 Ki 4:7
Solomon's p. for one day was. 22
he prepared great p. 2 Ki 6:23
for which I have made p. 1 Chr 29:19
abundantly bless her p. Ps 132:15
appointed them a daily p. Dan 1:5*
make not p. for the flesh. Rom 13:14

provocation

Israel sin by his p. 1 Ki 15:30
for the p. wherewith Ahab. 21:22
because of the p., Manasseh.
   - 2 Ki 23:26
had wrought great p. Neh 9:18, 26
eye continue in their p.? Job 17:2
harden not your hearts as in p.
   Ps 95:8*; Heb 3:8, 15
hath been to me as a p. Jer 32:31
presented p. of offering. Ezek 20:28

provoke

obey his voice, and p. Ex 23:21
will this people p. me? Num 14:11*
if ye p. and break. Deut 31:20*
that p. God are secure. Job 12:6
how oft did they p. him? Ps 78:40*
their doings are against Lord, to p.
   the eyes of his glory. Isa 3:8
do they p. me to anger? Jer 7:19
in that ye p. me to wrath. 44:8
began to urge and p. Luke 11:53
I will p. you to jealousy by them that
   are no people. Rom 10:19
for to p. them to jealousy. 11:11, 14
do we p. the Lord to? 1 Cor 10:22
ye fathers, p. not your children to
   wrath. Eph 6:4
they had heard, did p. Heb 3:16
to p. to love and to good. 10:24
see anger

provoked

nor shall any of them that p. me see.
   Num 14:23*
these men have p. the Lord. 16:30*
in Horeb ye p. the Lord. Deut 9:8
at Taberah and Massah ye p. 22
her adversary also p. 1 Sam 1:6
so she p. her, therefore she wept. 7
Judah p. him to jealousy. 1 Ki 14:22
Manasseh had p. him. 2 Ki 23:26
Satan p. David to number Israel.
   1 Chr 21:1*
our fathers had p. God. Ezra 5:12
tempted and p. the most high God.
   Ps 78:56*
but p. him at the sea. 106:7*
they p. him with their own. 29
because they p. the spirit. 33*, 43
when your fathers p. Zech 8:14
charity is not easily p. 1 Cor 13:5
your zeal p. very many. 2 Cor 9:2*

provokedst

forget not how thou p. Deut 9:7

provoketh

whoso p. him to anger. Pr 20:2
people that p. me to anger. Isa 65:3
where was image which p. Ezek 8:3

provoking

because of p. his sons. Deut 32:19
groves, p. Lord to anger. 1 Ki 14:15
Baasha in p. the Lord. 16:7, 13
by p. the most High. Ps 78:17*
desirous of vain glory, p. Gal 5:26

prudence

son endued with p. 2 Chr 2:12*
I wisdom dwell with p. Pr 8:12*
abounded in all wisdom and p.
   Eph 1:8

prudent

David p. in matters. 1 Sam 16:18
p. man covereth shame. Pr 12:16
p. man concealeth knowledge. 23
every p. man dealeth with. 13:16
wisdom of the p. is to. 14:8
the p. man looketh well to his. 15
p. are crowned with knowledge. 18
he that regardeth reproof is p. 15:5
in heart shall be called p. 16:21
the heart of the p. getteth. 18:15
a p. wife is from the Lord. 19:14
p. man foreseeth evil. 22:3; 27:12
take away the p. and the. Isa 3:2*
woe to them that are p. in. 5:21
I have done it, for I am p. 10:13*
understanding of their p. men. 29:14
counsel perished from p.? Jer 49:7
who is p. and he shall? Hos 14:9
the p. shall keep silence. Amos 5:13
hid these things from p. Mat 11:25*
   Luke 10:21*
Sergius Paulus, a p. Acts 13:7*
understanding of the p. 1 Cor 1:19

prudently

my servant shall deal p. Isa 52:13*

prune

six years shalt thou p. Lev 25:3
not sow thy field nor p. 4

pruned

waste, it shall not be p. Isa 5:6

pruning

beat spears into p. hooks. Isa 2:4
   Mi 4:3
beat your p. hooks into. Joel 3:10

psalm

delivered first this p. 1 Chr 16:7
take a p. Ps 81:2
with the voice of a p. 98:5
written in the second p. Acts 13:33
saith also in another p., Thou. 35
how is it every one of you hath a p.?
   1 Cor 14:26

psalmist

David, sweet p. of Israel. 2 Sam 23:1

psalms

sing p. to him. 1 Chr 16:9*
   Ps 105:2*
noise to him with p. Ps 95:2
David saith in book of p. Luke 20:42
written in p. concerning me. 24:44
written in the book of p. Acts 1:20
speaking to yourselves in p. and.
   Eph 5:19
admonishing one another in p. and.
   Col 3:16
any merry? let him sing p. Jas 5:13*

psaltery

of prophets with a p. 1 Sam 10:5
sing to him with the p. Ps 33:2
   144:9
awake p. and harp. 57:8; 108:2
praise thee with the p. 71:22; 92:3
pleasant harp with the p. 81:2
trumpet, the p. and harp. 150:3
when ye hear sound of the p.
   Dan 3:5, 7, 10, 15

public

to make her a p. example. Mat 1:19

publican, -s

*A tax-gatherer. The taxes were
farmed by the Roman Senate to the
highest bidders. These delegated
their duties to others, the one condition being that they should raise
as much money as possible.
They were especially detested by
the Jews, not so much on account
of their frequent dishonesty, but
because they were paid servants of
the hated Romans. They were
therefore considered as traitors
and apostates.*
the p. the same? Mat 5:46, 47*
many p. sat with him. 9:10
   Mark 2:15; Luke 5:29
eateth master with p. and sinners?
   Mat 9:11; Mark 2:16; Luke 5:30
and Matthew the p. Mat 10:3
a friend of p. 11:19; Luke 7:34
as an heathen and a p. Mat 18:17
p. go into the kingdom of God. 21:31
p. and the harlots believed. 32
came p. to be baptized. Luke 3:12
saw a p. named Levi sitting. 5:27
p. justified God, being baptized. 7:29
then drew near to him the p. 15:1
one a Pharisee, and other a p. 18:10
thank thee, I am not as this p. 11
p. standing afar off, said, God. 13
Zacchaeus was chief among p. 19:2

publicly

p. convinced the Jews. Acts 18:28
have taught you p. 20:20

publish

I will p. name of Lord. Deut 32:3*
to p. it in the house. 1 Sam 31:9*
p. it not in streets of. 2 Sam 1:20
should p. that they bring. Neh 8:15
may p. with the voice. Ps 26:7*
p. in Jerusalem. Jer 4:5
p. against Jerusalem. 16
declare this, p. it in Judah. 5:20
p. ye and say, O Lord, save. 31:7
p. in Migdol, p. in Noph. 46:14
p. and conceal not, Babylon. 50:2
p. in palaces of Ashdod. Amos 3:9
proclaim and p. free offerings. 4:5
began to p. it much. Mark 1:45; 5:20

published

king's decree be p. through all.
   Esth 1:20, 22

Haman's decree was *p*.
    Esth 3:14; 8:13
company that *p*. it.   *Ps* 68:11*
caused it to be *p*. through Nineveh.
    Jonah 3:7
a great deal they *p*. it. *Mark* 7:36
gospel must first be *p*.   13:10
he went and *p*. through. *Luke* 8:39
that word which was *p*. *Acts* 10:37
word of the Lord was *p*. 13:49*

publisheth
that *p*. peace, that *p*. *Isa* 52:7
voice *p*. affliction from. *Jer* 4:15
feet of him that *p*. peace. *Nah* 1:15

Publius
the father of P. lay sick. *Acts* 28:8

Pudens
greeteth thee and P. *2 Tim* 4:21

puffed up
no one of you be *p*. up. *1 Cor* 4:6
some are *p*. up, as though I. 18
speech of them that are *p*. up. 19
are *p*. up, and have not rather. 5:2
vaunteth not itself, is not *p*. up. 13:4
vainly *p*. up by his fleshly. *Col* 2:18

puffeth at
enemies, he *p*. at them. *Ps* 10:5
safety from him that *p*. at him. 12:5

puffeth up
knowledge *p*. up, charity. *2 Cor* 8:1

Pul
P. king of Assyria came against
  Israel . . . gave P. *2 Ki* 15:19
stirred up the spirit of P. *1 Chr* 5:26
those that escape to P. *Isa* 66:19

pull, -ed
Noah *p*. the dove to him. *Gen* 8:9*
but the men *p*. Lot into the. 19:10*
Jeroboam could not *p*. *1 Ki* 13:4
let timber be *p*. down. *Ezra* 6:11
p. me out of net they have. *Ps* 31:4*
from thy state shall *p*. *Isa* 22:19
set thee to *p*. down and destroy.
    Jer 1:10*; 18:7*
p. them out like sheep for. 12:3
them and not *p*. down. 24:6; 42:10
p. me in pieces, hath. *Lam* 3:11
shall he not *p*. up ? *Ezek* 17:9
shall no more be *p*. up. *Amos* 9:15*
ye *p*. off the robe with. *Mi* 2:8*
p. away the shoulder. *Zech* 7:11
Let me *p*. out the mote out of thine
  eye. *Mat* 7:4*; *Luke* 6:42*
I will *p*. down my barns. *Luke* 12:18
and will not *p*. out on the ? 14:5*
have been *p*. in pieces. *Acts* 23:10*

pulling
mighty to the *p*. down. *2 Cor* 10:4*
others save with fear, *p*. *Jude* 23*

pulpit
stood upon *p*. of wood. *Neh* 8:4

pulse
beans and parched *p*. *2 Sam* 17:28
let them give *p*. to eat. *Dan* 1:12, 16

punish
p. you seven times more for your
  sins. *Lev* 26:18, 24
to *p*. the just is not good. *Pr* 17:26
p. the stout heart of king. *Isa* 10:12
I will *p*. world for their evil. 13:11
Lord shall *p*. host of high ones. 24:21
Lord cometh to *p*. inhabitants. 26:21
sword shall *p*. leviathan. 27:1
I will *p*. all them that are circumcised. *Jer* 9:25
I will *p*. men of Anathoth. 11:22
say when he shall *p*. thee ? 13:21*
will *p*. you according to fruit. 21:14
I will even *p*. that man. 23:34
p. king of Babylon. 25:12; 50:18
will *p*. that nation. 27:8
I will *p*. Shemaiah. 29:32
p. all that oppress them. 30:20
p. Jehoiakim and his seed. 36:31
I will *p*. them in Egypt, as I *p*. 44:13
sign that I will *p*. you in this. 29
I will *p*. the multitude of No. 46:25
and I will *p*. Bel in Babylon. 51:44
will *p*. them for their ways. *Hos* 4:9
I will not *p*. your daughters. 14

p. Jacob according to his. *Hos* 12:2
I will *p*. you for your iniquities.
    Amos 3:2
day I will *p*. the princes. *Zeph* 1:8
I will *p*. all those that leap on. 9
I will *p*. men that are settled. 12
I thought to *p*. when your fathers.
    Zech 8:14*
how they might *p*. them. *Acts* 4:21

punished
he shall be surely *p*. *Ex* 21:20, 22
he shall not be *p*. for he is his. 21
thou hast *p*. less than. *Ezra* 9:13
it is an iniquity to be *p*. by judges.
    Job 31:11, 28
when scorner is *p*., simple. *Pr* 21:11
but the simple pass on and are *p*.
    22:3; 27:12
as I have *p*. Jerusalem. *Jer* 44:13
I have *p*. the king of Assyria. 50:18
howsoever I *p*. them. *Zeph* 3:7
shepherds, I *p*. the goats. *Zech* 10:3
to bring them bound to Jerusalem to
  be *p*. *Acts* 22:5
I *p*. them oft in every. 26:11
be *p*. with everlasting. *2 Thes* 1:9
day of judgement to be *p*. *2 Pet* 2:9

punishment
my *p*. is greater than. *Gen* 4:13
than accept the *p*. of their iniquity.
    Lev 26:41, 43
Saul sware, No *p*. shall. *1 Sam* 28:10
and a strange *p*. to the workers of.
    Job 31:3*
great wrath shall suffer *p*. *Pr* 19:19
a man for *p*. of his sins. *Lam* 3:39
p. of my people is greater than the *p*.
  of Sodom. 4:6
the *p*. of thine iniquity is. 22
bear *p*. of their iniquity, *p*. of
  prophets as *p*. of. *Ezek* 14:10*
I will not turn away the *p*. *Amos* 1:3
    6, 9, 11, 13; 2:1, 4, 6
the *p*. of Egypt. *Zech* 14:19
go into everlasting *p*. *Mat* 25:46
to such a man is this *p*. *2 Cor* 2:6
of how much sorer *p*. *Heb* 10:29
sent by him for the *p*. *1 Pet* 2:14

punishments
wrath bringeth the *p*. *Job* 19:29
to execute *p*. upon the. *Ps* 149:7

pur
they cast *p*. that is, the lot. *Esth* 3:7
Haman had cast *p*. for to. 9:24
Purim, after the name of *p*. 26

see Purim

purchase, *substantive*
p. of field and cave. *Gen* 49:32
evidence of the *p*. *Jer* 32:11
I gave evidence of *p*. to. 12, 14, 16

purchase, -ed
field Abraham *p*. of. *Gen* 25:10
which thou hast *p*. *Ex* 15:16
if a man *p*. of the Levites. *Lev* 25:33*
Ruth have I *p*. to be my. *Ruth* 4:10
congregation thou hast *p*. *Ps* 74:2
his right hand had *p*. 78:54
this man *p*. a field with iniquity.
    Acts 1:18*
gift of God may be *p*. by. 8:20*
which he hath *p*. with his own. 20:28
redemption of the *p*. *Eph* 1:14*
office of deacon well, *p*. *1 Tim* 3:13*

pure
that they bring the *p*. oil. *Ex* 27:20
    Lev 24:2
take *p*. myrrh. *Ex* 30:23
with *p*. frankincense. 34
the *p*. candlestick. 31:8; 39:37
    Lev 24:4
set cakes on the *p*. table. *Lev* 24:6
thou shalt put *p*. frankincense on. 7
didst drink the *p*. blood. *Deut* 32:14*
with the *p*. thou wilt shew thyself *p*.
    2 Sam 22:27; *Ps* 18:26
measures of *p*. oil. *1 Ki* 5:11
set on the *p*. table. *2 Chr* 13:11
all were *p*. and killed. *Ezra* 6:20
shall a man be more *p*.? *Job* 4:17
if thou wert *p*. and upright. 8:6
hast said, My doctrine is *p*. 11:4
also my prayer is *p*. 16:17

stars are not *p*. in his sight. *Job* 25:5
words of the Lord are *p*. *Ps* 12:6
commandment of Lord is *p*. 19:8
word is very *p*.: therefore I. 119:140
the words of the *p*. are. *Pr* 15:26
say, I am *p*. from my sin ? 20:9
whether his work be *p*. 11
the *p*. his work is right. 21:8
every word of God is *p*. 30:5*
generation that are *p*. in their. 12
head like the *p*. wool. *Dan* 7:9
shall I count them *p*.? *Mi* 6:11
turn to the people a *p*. *Zeph* 3:9
in every place a *p*. offering. *Mal* 1:11
I am *p*. from the blood. *Acts* 20:26
all things indeed are *p*. *Rom* 14:20
whatsoever things are *p*. *Phil* 4:8
mystery of faith in a *p*. *1 Tim* 3:9
of sins, keep thyself *p*. 5:22
with a *p*. conscience. *2 Tim* 1:3
to the *p*. all things are *p*., but to . .
  nothing is *p*. *Tit* 1:15
our bodies washed with *p*. water.
    Heb 10:22
p. religion and undefiled. *Jas* 1:27
wisdom from above is first *p*. 3:17
I stir up your *p*. minds. *2 Pet* 3:1
himself even as he is *p*. *1 John* 3:3
angels clothed in *p*. linen. *Rev* 15:6
a *p*. river of water of life. 22:1

see heart, gold

purely
I will *p*. purge away. *Isa* 1:25

pureness
it is delivered by the *p*. *Job* 22:30
he that loveth *p*. of heart. *Pr* 22:11
approving ourselves, by *p*. *2 Cor* 6:6

purer
Nazarites *p*. than snow. *Lam* 4:7
thou art of *p*. eyes than. *Hab* 1:13

purge
Josiah began to *p*. Judah. *2 Chr* 34:3
p. me with hyssop. *Ps* 51:7
transgressions thou shalt *p*. 65:3†
and *p*. away our sins for thy. 79:9†
and purely *p*. away thy. *Isa* 1:25
I will *p*. from among. *Ezek* 20:38
shalt thou cleanse and *p*. it. 43:20*
seven days shall they *p*. altar. 26*
shall fall to *p*. them. *Dan* 11:35*
and *p*. them as gold. *Mal* 3:3*
he will throughly *p*. his floor, and.
    Mat 3:12*; *Luke* 3:17*
p. out therefore the old. *1 Cor* 5:7
if a man therefore *p*. *2 Tim* 2:21
p. your conscience from. *Heb* 9:14*

purged
Eli's house shall not be *p*. *1 Sam* 3:14
when he had *p*. the land. *2 Chr* 34:8
and truth, iniquity is *p*. *Pr* 16:6
shall have *p*. the blood of. *Isa* 4:4
taken away, and thy sin *p*. 6:7†
iniquity shall not be *p*. 22:14†
the iniquity of Jacob be *p*. 27:9†
have *p*. thee, and thou wast not *p*.,
  thou shalt not be *p*. *Ezek* 24:13†
when he had by himself *p*. our sins.
    Heb 1:3*
are by the law *p*. by blood. 9:22*
the worshippers once *p*. 10:2*
hath forgotten he was *p*. *2 Pet* 1:9*

purgeth
beareth fruit, he *p*. it. *John* 15:2*

purging
draught, *p*. all meats. *Mark* 7:19*

purification, -s
it is a *p*. for sin. *Num* 19:9*
burnt heifer of *p*. for sin. 17*
according to *p*. of the. *2 Chr* 30:19
the ward of their *p*. *Neh* 12:45
their things for *p*. be. *Esth* 2:3
so were the days of their *p*. 12
when days of her *p*. were. *Luke* 2:22
the accomplishment of the days of *p*.
    Acts 21:26

purified
and *p*. the altar, and. *Lev* 8:15
the Levites were *p*. *Num* 8:21
    Ezra 6:20
shall be *p*. with water. *Num* 31:23
Bath-sheba was *p*. from. *2 Sam* 11:4

purifier

are pure words, as silver p. Ps 12:6
many shall be p. and. Dan 12:10
from Asia found me p. Acts 24:18
things in the heavens be p. Heb 9:23
seeing ye have p. your. 1 Pet 1:22

purifier

as refiner and p. of silver. Mal 3:3

purifieth

dead body and p. not. Num 19:13
that hath this hope p. 1 John 3:3

purify

shall p. himself with. Num 19:12, 19
and shall not p. himself. 20
p. yourselves and your captives. 31:19
p. all your raiment, and all made. 20
by reason of breakings they p. Job 41:25
they p. themselves in. Isa 66:17
seven days shall they p. Ezek 43:26
and he shall p. the sons. Mal 3:3
went to Jerusalem to p. John 11:55
take and p. thyself. Acts 21:24
and p. to himself a people. Tit 2:14
p. your hearts, ye double. Jas 4:8

purifying

the blood of her p. Lev 12:4
when the days of her p. are. 6
sprinkle water of p. on. Num 8:7*
office was in p. all holy. 1 Chr 23:28
with other things for p. of women. Esth 2:12
after the manner of the p. John 2:6
arose a question about p. 3:25
sanctifieth to the p. of. Heb 9:13

purifying, verb

p. their hearts by faith. Acts 15:9
and the next day p. himself. 21:26

Purim

(Plural form of Hebrew pur, a lot. The annual festival instituted to commemorate the preservation of the Jews in Persia from the massacre designed by Haman. Haman, in his superstition, cast lots to determine the favourable day for the massacre)
called these days P. Esth 9:26
that these days of P. should. 28
this sacred letter of P. 29, 31
Esther confirmed these P. 32

purity

example in faith, in p. 1 Tim 4:12
younger as sisters, with all p. 5:2

purloining

not p. but shewing all good. Tit 2:10

purple

offering, blue, p. and scarlet. Ex 25:4
curtains of fine linen and p. 26:1
wires, to work in the p. 39:3
and spread a p. cloth. Num 4:13
p. raiment was on kings. Judg 8:26
cunning to work in p. 2 Chr 2:7, 14
the vail of blue, and p. and. 3:14
cords of fine linen and p. Esth 1:6
with garment of linen and p. 8:15
clothing is silk and p. Pr 31:22
covering of it of p. S of S 3:10
hair of thine head like p. 7:5
and p. is their clothing. Jer 10:9
p. was that which covered thee. Ezek 27:7
in thy fairs with emeralds, p. 16
clothed him with p. Mark 15:17
they took off the p. from him. 20
rich man clothed in p. Luke 16:19
put on him a p. robe. John 19:2
forth wearing the p. robe.
Lydia, a seller of p. Acts 16:14
woman was arrayed in p. Rev 17:4
buyeth the merchandise or p. 18:12
that was clothed in p. and scarlet. 16

purpose

handfuls of p. for her. Ruth 2:16*
to frustrate their p. Ezra 4:5
they made for the p. Neh 8:4
withdraw man from his p. Job 33:17
every p. is established. Pr 20:18
and a time to every p. Eccl 3:1, 17
8:6

to what p. is multitude? Isa 1:11
this is the p. that is purposed. 14:26
shall help in vain, and to no p. 30:7
to what p. cometh to me incense? Jer 6:20
Nebuchadnezzar conceived a p. 49:30
for every p. of the Lord shall stand. 51:29
that p. be not changed. Dan 6:17
To what p. is this waste? Mat 26:8
with p. of heart, they. Acts 11:23
appeared to thee for this p. 26:16
that they had obtained their p. 27:13
centurion kept them from their p. 43
called according to his p. Rom 8:28
that the p. of God according to. 9:11
even for this same p. have I. 17
according to p. of him. Eph 1:11
according to the eternal p. in. 3:11
to you for the same p. 6:22; Col 4:8
according to his own p. 2 Tim 1:9
thou hast fully known my p. 3:10
for this p. Son of God. 1 John 3:8

purpose, -ed, verb

I p. to build an house. 1 Ki 5:5
p. to keep under Judah. 2 Chr 28:10
Sennacherib p. to fight against. 32:2
I am p. my mouth shall. Ps 17:3
who have p. to overthrow my. 140:4
as I have p., so shall it. Isa 14:24
this is the purpose p. upon the. 26
the Lord hath p., who shall? 27
what the Lord hath p. upon. 19:12
Lord hath p. to stain the pride. 23:9
p. it, and I will also do it. 46:11
I have p. it, and will not. Jer 4:28
repent me of the evil which I p. 26:3
will hear all evil which I p. to. 36:3
purposes that he hath p. 49:20
50:45
Lord hath p. to destroy. Lam 2:8
Daniel p. in his heart not. Dan 1:8
Paul p. in spirit to go to. Acts 19:21
Paul p. to return through. 20:3*
oftentimes I p. to come. Rom 1:13
things I p., do I p. according to the flesh? 2 Cor 1:17
will which he hath p. in. Eph 1:9
eternal purpose which he p. in. 3:11

purposes

days are past, my p. are. Job 17:11
without counsel p. are. Pr 15:22
broken in the p. thereof. Isa 19:10
hear counsel of the Lord and p. Jer 49:20; 50:45

purposeth

every man as he p. in his. 2 Cor 9:7

purposing

comfort himself, p. to kill. Gen 27:42

purse

lot, let us have one p. Pr 1:14
carry neither p. nor scrip. Luke 10:4
I sent you without p. and. 22:35
he that hath a p., let him take it. 36

purses

nor brass in your p. Mat 10:9
take no money in their p. Mark 6:8

pursue

they did not p. after. Gen 35:5
enemy said, I will p., I. Ex 15:9
lest the avenger of blood. Deut 19:6; Josh 20:5
they shall p. thee until thou perish. Deut 28:22, 45
p. after them, ye shall. Josh 2:5
Ai were called together to p. 8:16
stay not, but p. after your. 10:19
whom dost thou p.? 1 Sam 24:14
a man is risen to p. thee. 25:29
doth my lord thus p. me? 26:18
shall I p. after this troop? 30:8
arise and p. after David. 2 Sam 17:1
servants, p. after Sheba. 20:6, 7
flee while enemies p. thee? 24:13
p. the dry stubble? Job 13:25
terrors p. my soul as the. 30:15*
seek peace and p. it. Ps 34:14
they that p. you be swift. Isa 30:16
the sword shall p. thee. Jer 48:2
blood shall p. thee. Ezek 35:6
enemy shall p. him. Hos 8:3

because Edom did p. his brother with the sword. Amos 1:11
darkness shall p. his. Nah 1:8

pursued

Abram p. them to Dan and Hobah. Gen 14:14, 15
brethren p. Jacob. 31:23, 36
the Egyptians p. after Israel. Ex 14:8
9:23; Deut 11:4; Josh 24:6
p. the spies. Josh 2:7
they of Ai p. 8:16, 17
p. after Adoni-bezek. Judg 1:6
Barak p. after chariots. 4:16, 22
Gideon p. after. 7:23, 25; 8:12
Israel p. Benjamin unto. 20:45
Israel p. the Philistines. 1 Sam 7:11
17:52
Saul p. David. 23:25
David p. Amalekites. 30:10
Asahel p. after Abner. 2 Sam 2:19
Joab p. Abner. 24
Joab p. Israel no more. 28
so Joab and Abishai p. 20:10
I have p. mine enemies. 22:38
Ps 18:37
fled, and Israel p. after. 1 Ki 20:20
army of Chaldees p. the king. 2 Ki 25:5; Jer 39:5; 52:8
Abijah p. after. 2 Chr 13:19
Asa and people p. Ethiopians. 14:13
he p. them, and passed. Isa 41:3
they p. us upon the mountains, they laid wait for us. Lam 4:19*

pursuer, -s

lest p. meet you. Josh 2:16
until the p. returned, the p. 22
turned back upon the p. 8:20
without strength before p. Lam 1:6

pursueth

flee when none p. you. Lev 26:17
shall fall when none p. 36, 37
faint, yet p. them. Judg 8:4
I am p. Zebah and Zalmunna. 5
Saul returned from p. 1 Sam 23:28
Joab came from p. a. 2 Sam 3:22
returned from p. after Israel. 18:16
your god is p. or on a. 1 Ki 18:27*
turned back from p. Jehoshaphat. 22:33; 2 Chr 18:32
he that p. evil, p. it to. Pr 11:19
p. sinners, to the righteous. 13:21
he p. them with words, yet. 19:7
wicked flee when no man p. 28:1

purtenance

his head, legs, and p. Ex 12:9*

push

ox were wont to p. Ex 21:29*, 36*
if the ox p. a manservant or. 32*
with them he shall p. Deut 33:17
with these thou shalt p. Syrians. 1 Ki 22:11; 2 Chr 18:10
they p. away my feet. Job 30:12
through thee will we p. down our enemies. Ps 44:5
king of south p. at him. Dan 11:40*

pushed

p. all the diseased with. Ezek 34:21

pushing

I saw the ram p. westward. Dan 8:4

put

there God p. the man. Gen 2:8, 15
I will p. enmity between thee. 3:15
p. thy hand under my thigh. 24:2, 9
47:29
and I p. the earring upon her. 24:47
p. them upon Jacob her. 27:15
she p. the skins of the kids. 16
Jacob p. the stones for his. 28:11
p. stone again on well's mouth. 29:3
p. own flocks by themselves. 30:40
when cattle were feeble, he p. not. 42
Rachel p. them in the camels'. 31:34
p. space betwixt drove and. 32:16
Tamar p. off her widow's. 38:14
all he had p. into Joseph's hand. 39:4
that they should p. me into. 40:3
p. them altogether in ward. 42:17
Joseph shall p. his hand on. 46:4
p. thy right hand upon his. 48:18
p. off thy shoes from off thy feet. Ex 3:5; Isa 20:2; Acts 7:33

shall *p.* them on your sons. *Ex* 3:22
Lord said, *P.* now thy hand in. 4:6
speak to him, and *p.* words in. 15
to *p.* a sword in their hand. 5:21
I will *p.* a division between. 8:23
may know the Lord doth *p.* 11:7
will *p.* none of these diseases. 15:26
p. an homer full of manna. 16:33
p. his beast in another man's. 22:5
whether he have *p.* his hand. 8
an oath that he hath not *p.* his. 11
p. not thine hand with wicked. 23:1
thou shalt *p.* all in the hands of. 29:24
p. of the perfume before the. 30:36
p. every man his sword by his side. 32:27
now *p.* off thy ornaments. 33:5
p. thee in a cleft of the rock. 22
he *p.* all on Aaron's and. *Lev* 8:27
nor *p.* a stumblingblock. 19:14
p. the blasphemer in ward. 24:12
p. ten thousand to flight. 26:8
Deut 32:30
shall *p.* my name on the. *Num* 6:27
spirit which is on thee, and *p.* 11:17
the Lord would *p.* his Spirit. 29
serpent of brass, and *p.* it on a. 21:9
Lord *p.* word in Balaam's. 23:5, 16
thou shalt *p.* them in ark. *Deut* 10:2
p. the tables in the ark. 5:1
thou shalt *p.* the blessing on. 11:29
place he shall choose to *p.* 12:5, 21
ye shall rejoice in all ye *p.* 7
p. my words in his mouth. 18:18
thou shalt not *p.* any grapes. 23:24
p. it even among their. *Josh* 7:11
I *p.* my life in my hands. *Judg* 12:3
p. me into one of the priests' offices.
1 Sam 2:36
he will *p.* your asses to work. 8:16
no man *p.* his hand to his. 14:26
and David *p.* them off him. 17:39
p. Goliath's armour in his tent. 54
did *p.* his life in his hand. 19:5
I have *p.* my life in my hand. 28:21
Lord *p.* them under the soles.
1 Ki 5:3
to *p.* my name there. 9:3; 11:36
14:21
of the calves *p.* he in Dan. 12:29
on wood, and *p.* no fire under. 18:23
king, *P.* this fellow in prison. 22:27
he *p.* his mouth upon. *2 Ki* 4:34
king's son, they *p.* the crown. 11:12
p. thine hand upon bow, he *p.* 13:16
will *p.* hook in thy nose. 19:28
Isa 37:29
Jerusalem will I *p.* my name. 21:7
2 Chr 6:20; 12:13; 33:7
that have *p.* their lives. *1 Chr* 11:19
he *p.* his hand to the ark. 13:10
and the angel *p.* up his sword. 21:27
house have I *p.* the ark. *2 Chr* 6:11
the king of Egypt *p.* him down. 36:3
Cyrus *p.* the decree in writing. 22
Ezra 1:1
destroy kings that *p.* *Ezra* 6:12
p. such a thing in the king's heart.
7:27
what God had *p.* in. *Neh* 2:12
nobles *p.* not their necks to. 3:5
that every one *p.* them off. 4:23
Tobiah would have *p.* me in fear.
6:14, 19
decree drew near to be *p.* *Esth* 9:1
behold, he *p.* no trust in. *Job* 4:18
wherefore do I *p.* my life in ? 13:14
p. me in a surety with me. 17:3
p. my brethren far from me. 19:13
but he would *p.* strength in me. 23:6
p. wisdom in inward parts. 38:36
canst thou *p.* an hook into his ? 41:2
thou hast *p.* gladness in. *Ps* 4:7
p. all things under his feet. 8:6
1 Cor 15:25, 27; *Eph* 1:22; *Heb* 2:8
p. in fear, O Lord, that. *Ps* 9:20
thou hast *p.* off my sackcloth. 30:11
let the lying lips be *p.* to. 31:18
he hath *p.* a new song in my. 40:3
p. to shame. 14; 44:7; 53:5
hast cast off and *p.* us to shame. 44:9
p. thou my tears into thy. 56:8
he *p.* them to a perpetual. 78:66
lover and friend hast thou *p.* 88:18

it is better to trust in the Lord than
to *p.* confidence in man. *Ps* 118:8
than to *p.* confidence in princes. 9
O Lord, *p.* me not to shame. 119:31
p. a knife to thy throat. *Pr* 23:2
when thy neighbour hath *p.* 25:8
lest he that heareth it *p.* thee. 10
then must he *p.* to more. *Eccl* 10:10
I have *p.* off my coat, how shall I *p.?*
S of S 5:3
my beloved *p.* in his hand by. 4
that *p.* darkness for light. *Isa* 5:20
p. down the inhabitants. 10:13
weaned child *p.* his hand on. 11:8
I have *p.* my Spirit upon him. 42:1
Mat 12:18
p. me in remembrance. *Isa* 43:26
thou shalt not be able to *p.* 47:11
I have *p.* my words in thy mouth
and covered thee. 51:16; *Jer* 1:9
p. it into the hand of them. *Isa* 51:23
to bruise him, he hath *p.* 53:10
words I *p.* in thy mouth shall. 59:21
where is he that *p.* his Spirit ? 63:11
how shall I *p.* thee among ? *Jer* 3:19
our God hath *p.* us to silence. 8:14
have *p.* themselves to pain. 12:13
will *p.* my law in their inward. 31:33
my fear in their hearts. 32:40
O sword, *p.* up thyself into. 47:6
they *p.* the branch to. *Ezek* 8:17
I will *p.* a new spirit within. 11:19
36:26, 27; 37:14
comeliness I had *p.* upon thee. 16:14
priests have *p.* no difference. 22:26
I will *p.* hooks in thy jaws. 29:4; 38:4
I will *p.* a fear in Egypt. 30:13
and *p.* breath in you, and ye. 37:6
would, he *p.* down. *Dan* 5:19
p. in the sickle, for the. *Joel* 3:13
I will *p.* them together. *Mi* 2:12
trust not a friend, *p.* ye not. 7:5
where they have been *p.* *Zeph* 3:19
wages to *p.* it in a bag. *Hag* 1:6
light candle and *p.* it. *Mat* 5:15
nor do men *p.* new wine into. 9:17
let no man *p.* asunder. 19:6
Mark 10:9
p. the Sadducees to. *Mat* 22:34
p. my money to exchangers. 25:27
p. up again thy sword. 26:52
John 18:11
not lawful to *p.* them into. *Mat* 27:6
p. his hands on them. *Mark* 10:16
p. down mighty from. *Luke* 1:52
best robe, *p.* it on him, and *p.* 15:22
none to *p.* me into pool. *John* 5:7
he *p.* clay upon mine eyes. 9:15
p. it upon hyssop, and *p.* it to. 19:29
p. my finger into the print. 20:25
Father hath *p.* in his own. *Acts* 1:7
they *p.* the apostles in hold. 4:3
p. them in common prison. 5:18
the men whom ye *p.* in prison. 25
seeing ye *p.* the word of God. 13:46
and *p.* no difference between. 15:9
to *p.* a yoke upon the neck. 10
p. a stumblingblock. *Rom* 14:13
he shall have *p.* down. *1 Cor* 15:24
till he *p.* all his enemies under. 25
God, which *p.* the same earnest care.
2 Cor 8:16
that ye *p.* off the old man. *Eph* 4:22
Col 3:9
ye also *p.* off all these. *Col* 3:8
if thou *p.* the brethren in remembrance. *1 Tim* 4:6; *2 Tim* 2:14
wherefore I *p.* thee in. *2 Tim* 1:6
p. them in mind to be subject. *Tit* 3:1
if he oweth, *p.* that on. *Philem* 18
to angels hath he not *p.* *Heb* 2:5
p. him to an open shame. 6:6
p. my laws into their mind. 8:10
p. my laws into their hearts. 10:16
we *p.* bits in the horses'. *Jas* 3:3
ye may *p.* to silence. *1 Pet* 2:15
to *p.* you always in. *2 Pet* 1:12
knowing that I must *p.* off this. 14
p. you also in remembrance. *Jude* 5
I will *p.* on you none. *Rev* 2:24
God hath *p.* in their hearts. 17:17

put away
p. away the strange gods. *Gen* 35:2

p. away the leaven out. *Ex* 12:15
nor take a woman *p. away. Lev* 21:7
p. away guilt of innocent blood.
Deut 19:13; 21:9
he may not *p. away* all his days.
22:19, 29
p. away the strange gods. *Josh* 24:14
23; *Judg* 10:16; *1 Sam* 7:3
Eli said, *p. away* thy. *1 Sam* 1:14
Saul had *p. away.* 28:3
Saul whom I *p. away.* *2 Sam* 7:15
Lord hath *p. away* thy sin. 12:13
Jehoram *p. away* the. *2 Ki* 3:2
did Josiah *p. away.* 23:24
Asa *p. away* the abominable idols.
2 Chr 15:8
covenant to *p. away* the wives.
Ezra 10:3
they gave their hands to *p. away.* 19
in thine hand, *p.* it *away. Job* 11:14
p. away iniquity from thy. 22:23
I did not *p. away* his statutes from.
Ps 18:22
p. not thy servant *away.* 27:9
p. away mine acquaintance. 88:8
p. away from thee a froward. *Pr* 4:24
have *p. away* ? for transgressions is
your mother *p. away. Isa* 50:1
if a man *p. away* his wife. *Jer* 3:1
I had *p.* her away and given her. 8
if thou wilt *p. away* thine. 4:1
let them *p. away* their. *Ezek* 43:9
take her that is *p. away.* 44:22
let her *p. away* her whoredoms.
Hos 2:2
p. far *away* the evil day. *Amos* 6:3
to *p.* her away privily. *Mat* 1:19
shall *p. away* his wife. 5:31, 32
19:9; *Mark* 10:11; *Luke* 16:18
man to *p. away* his wife ? *Mark* 10:2
if a woman shall *p. away* her. 12
p. away from you that wicked person. *1 Cor* 5:13
husband *p. away* his wife. 7:11, 12
I *p. away* childish things. 13:11
evil speaking be *p. away. Eph* 4:31
some having *p. away.* *1 Tim* 1:19
to *p. away* sin by the. *Heb* 9:26
see death, evil

put forth
lest he *p. forth* and take. *Gen* 3:22
Noah *p. forth* his hand and took. 8:9
men *p. forth* their hand and. 19:10
p. forth thine hand and. *Ex* 4:4
precious things *p. forth. Deut* 33:14
Ehud *p. forth* his left. *Judg* 3:21
angel *p. forth* the end of staff. 6:21
I will now *p. forth* a riddle. 14:12, 13
Samson *p. forth* and took. 15:15
Jonathan *p. forth* rod. *1 Sam* 14:27
servants not *p. forth* to slay. 22:17
not *p. forth* mine hand against. 24:10
Uzzah *p. forth* his hand to the ark of
God. *2 Sam* 6:6; *1 Chr* 13:9
Absalom *p. forth* his hand.
2 Sam 15:5
ye not *p. forth* my hand. 18:12
and his hand, which he *p. forth*
against him, dried up. *1 Ki* 13:4
p. forth thine hand now and touch
all that he hath. *Job* 1:11; 2:5
upon himself *p.* not *forth* thy. 12
p. forth his hands against. *Ps* 55:20
lest the righteous *p. forth.* 125:3
and understanding *p. forth* her voice?
Pr 8:1
p. not *forth* thyself in presence. 25:6
Lord *p. forth* his hand and touched.
Jer 1:9
p. forth form of an hand. *Ezek* 8:3
Son of man, *p. forth* a riddle. 17:2
Jesus *p. forth* his hand and. *Mat* 8:3
Mark 1:41; *Luke* 5:13
people were *p. forth,* he. *Mat* 9:25
parable *p.* he *forth.* 13:24, 31
Luke 14:7
to *p.* the apostles *forth. Acts* 5:34
but Peter *p.* them all *forth.* 9:40

put on
and raiment to *p.* on. *Gen* 28:20
Tamar *p.* on garments of her. 38:19
priest, shall *p.* them on. *Ex* 29:30
no man did *p.* on him his. 33:4

the priest shall *p. on* his. *Lev* 6:10
he shall *p. on* other garments. 11
p. on the holy linen coat. 16:4
he shall *p. on* his garments. 24
consecrated to *p. on* garment. 21:10
p. on incense, and go. *Num* 16:46
nor a man *p. on* a woman's.
　　　　　　　　　　Deut 22:5
weep for Saul, who *p. on. 2 Sam* 1:24
I pray *p. on* now mourning. 14:2
Joab's garment he had *p. on.* 20:8
but *p.* thou on thy robes. *1 Ki* 22:30
　　　　　　　　　　2 Chr 18:29
able to *p. on* armour. *2 Ki* 3:21
Mordecai *p. on* sackcloth. *Esth* 4:1
Esther *p. on* her royal apparel. 5:1
the just shall *p.* it on. *Job* 27:17
I *p.* on righteousness, and it. 29:14
how shall I *p.* it on? *S of S* 5:3
p. on strength. *Isa* 51:9; 52:1
p. on thy beautiful garments. 52:1
he *p.* on righteousness as a breast-
　plate, he *p.* on garments. 59:17
and *p.* it on thy loins. *Jer* 13:1, 2
and *p.* on the brigandines. 46:4
p. on thy shoes upon thy. *Ezek* 24:17
p. on other garments. 42:14; 44:19
Nineveh *p.* on sackcloth. *Jonah* 3:5
nor what ye shall *p.* on. *Mat* 6:25
　　　　　　　　　　Luke 12:22
they *p.* on the ass and. *Mat* 21:7
and *p.* on him a scarlet robe. 27:28
platted a crown of thorns. they *p.* it
　on his head. 29; *Jer* 19:2
them *p.* a spunge on a reed.
　　Mat 27:48; *Mark* 15:36
sandals, not *p.* on two coats.
　　　　　　　　　　Mark 6:9
p. on him the best robe. *Luke* 15:22
a title and *p.* it on cross. *John* 19:19
p. on armour of light. *Rom* 13:12
but *p.* ye on the Lord Jesus. 14
corruptible must *p.* on. *1 Cor* 15:53
shall have *p.* on immortality. 54
Christ, have *p.* on Christ. *Gal* 3:27
that ye *p.* on the new man.
　　　　　　Eph 4:24; *Col* 3:10
p. on whole armour of. *Eph* 6:11
p. on therefore as elect. *Col* 3:12
p. on charity, which is the bond. 14

put out
one *p. out* his hand. *Gen* 38:28
p. out the remembrance. *Ex* 17:14
fire shall not be *p. out.* *Lev* 6:12
p. out of the camp every leper.
　　　　　　　　　　Num 5:2, 4
and female shall ye *p. out.* 3
wilt thou *p. out* the eyes? 16:14
the Lord will *p. out* those. *Deut* 7:22
name be not *p. out* of Israel. 25:6
the Philistines *p. out* Samson's eyes.
　　　　　　　　　　Judg 16:21
p. now this woman out. *2 Sam* 13:17
he *p. out* his hand and. *2 Ki* 6:7
p. out the eyes of Zedekiah.
　　25:7; *Jer* 39:7; 52:11
have *p. out* the lamps. *2 Chr* 29:7
wicked shall be *p. out.* *Job* 18:5
and his candle be *p. out.* 6; 21:17
　　Pr 13:9; 20:20; 24:20
hast *p. out* their name. *Ps* 9:5
when I *p.* thee *out* I will cover
　heaven. *Ezek* 32:7
when he had *p.* them all out.
　　Mark 5:40; *Luke* 8:54
p. out of the stewardship. *Luke* 16:4
he should be *p. out* of the synagogue.
　　　　　　　　　　John 9:22
lest they should be *p. out* of the
　synagogue. 12:42
p. you *out* of the synagogues. 16:2

put trust
come and *p.* your *trust* in my shadow.
　　　　　　　　　　Judg 9:15
p. thy *trust* on Egypt. *2 Ki* 18:24
　　　　　　　　　　Isa 36:9
p. their *trust* in him. *1 Chr* 5:20
p. your *trust* in the Lord. *Ps* 4:5
p. their *trust* in thee rejoice. 5:11
my God, in thee do I *p.* my *trust.* 7:1
　　16:1; 25:20; 71:1
thy name, will *p. trust* in thee. 9:10

in the Lord *p.* I my *trust.* *Ps* 11:1
　　　　　　31:1; 71:1
savest them which *p.* their *trust.* 17:7
p. their *trust* under the shadow. 36:7
in God I have *p.* my *trust,* I. 56:4
I have *p.* my *trust* in the Lord. 73:28
p. not your *trust* in princes. 146:3
that *p.* their *trust* in him. *Pr* 30:5
hast *p.* thy *trust* in me. *Jer* 39:18
p. in *trust* with gospel. *1 Thes* 2:4
I will *p.* my *trust* in him. *Heb* 2:13

put, *participle*
Joseph was *p.* in a coffin. *Gen* 50:26
the vessel, it must be *p. Lev* 11:32
but if any water be *p.* on seed. 38
shall be *p.* apart seven days. 15:19
as long as she is *p.* apart. 18:19
nor feet *p.* in fetters. *2 Sam* 3:34
the kings having *p.* on their robes.
　　　　　　　　　　1 Ki 22:10
Judah was *p.* to the worse.
　2 Ki 14:12; *2 Chr* 25:22
the Syrians saw that they were *p.* to
　the worse. *1 Chr* 19:16, 19
neither was the number *p.* in. 27:24
every device shall be *p. 2 Chr* 2:14
Israel be *p.* to the worse. 6:24
were *p.* from the priesthood.
　　　　　Ezra 2:62; *Neh* 7:64
be *p.* to shame that seek after my.
　　　　　　　　　　Ps 35:4; 83:17
be *p.* to confusion, that desire. 70:2
let me never be *p.* to confusion. 71:1
shouldest be *p.* lower. *Pr* 25:7
nothing can be *p.* to it. *Eccl* 3:14
shalt not be *p.* to shame. *Isa* 54:4
ride, every one *p.* in array. *Jer* 50:42
have been *p.* to shame. *Zeph* 3:19
is *p.* in to fill it up. *Mat* 9:16
John was *p.* in prison. *Mark* 1:14
new wine must be *p.* into new bottles.
　　　　　2:22; *Luke* 5:38
no man having *p.* his hand to plough.
　　　　　　　　　　Luke 9:62
Judas bare what was *p.* in. *John* 12:6
devil having now *p.* into the. 13:2
that is not *p.* under him, but now we
　see not yet all things *p. Heb* 2:8
bodies to be *p.* in graves. *Rev* 11:9

Puteoli
came the next day to *P. Acts* 28:13

putrifying
bruises, and *p.* sores. *Isa* 1:6*

puttest
p. thy nest in a rock. *Num* 24:21
bless all thou *p.* thine hands to.
　　　　　Deut 12:18; 15:10
thou *p.* on me will I bear. *2 Ki* 18:14
thou *p.* my feet in stocks. *Job* 13:27
p. away the wicked like dross.
　　　　　　　　　　Ps 119:119
that *p.* thy bottle to him. *Hab* 2:15*

putteth
who *p.* any on a stranger. *Ex* 30:33
word that God *p.* in my. *Num* 22:38
woman *p.* forth her hand. *Deut* 25:11
graven image, and *p.* it in a. 27:15
as he that *p.* off harness. *1 Ki* 20:11
he *p.* no trust in his saints. *Job* 15:15
he *p.* forth his hand upon. 28:9
he *p.* my feet in the stocks. 33:11
p. not out his money to. *Ps* 15:5
God *p.* down one and setteth. 75:7
that *p.* his trust in Lord. *Pr* 28:25
who *p.* his trust in the Lord. 29:25
fig tree *p.* forth her. *S of S* 2:13*
p. his trust in me shall. *Isa* 57:13
as a shepherd *p.* on. *Jer* 43:12
he *p.* his mouth in dust. *Lam* 3:29
p. the stumblingblock. *Ezek* 14:4, 7
he that *p.* not into their. *Mi* 3:5
no man *p.* new cloth. *Mat* 9:16
　　　　　　　　　　Luke 5:36
tender and *p.* forth leaves ye know.
　　　Mat 24:32; *Mark* 13:28
no man *p.* new wine into old.
　　　　　Mark 2:22; *Luke* 5:37
immediately he *p.* in sickle.
　　　　　　　　　　Mark 4:29
no man *p.* a candle under. *Luke* 8:16
no man, when he hath lighted a
　candle, *p.* it in a secret place. 11:33

whoso *p.* away his wife. *Luke* 16:18
when he *p.* forth his own. *John* 10:4

putting
p. it on Hagar's shoulder. *Gen* 21:14
p. them upon the head. *Lev* 16:21
p. their hand to their mouth and.
　　　　　　　　　　Judg 7:6
p. forth of the finger. *Isa* 58:9
he hateth *p.* away. *Mal* 2:16
Ananias *p.* his hand. *Acts* 9:12, 17
they drew Alexander, Jews *p.* 19:33
as *p.* you in mind. *Rom* 15:15
p. away lying, speak truth. *Eph* 4:25
in *p.* off the body of the sins. *Col* 2:11
p. on the breastplate of. *1 Thes* 5:8
p. me into the ministry. *1 Tim* 1:12
by *p.* on of my hands. *2 Tim* 1:6
not *p.* on of apparel, but. *1 Pet* 3:3
not *p.* away the filth of the flesh. 21
to stir you up by *p.* you. *2 Pet* 1:13

Q

quails
　God gave quails *to the Israelites
upon two occasions:* First, *in the
wilderness of Sin, or Zin, a few days
after they had passed over the Red
Sea,* Ex 16:13. *The second time
was at the encampment, called in
Hebrew, Kibroth-hataavah, or the
graves of lust,* Num 11:31, 32.
at even *q.* came up. *Ex* 16:13
the Lord brought *q. Num* 11:31
and they gathered the *q.* 32
and he brought *q. Ps* 105:40

quake
earth shall *q.* before. *Joel* 2:10
the mountains *q.* at him. *Nah* 1:5
earth did *q.* and rocks. *Mat* 27:51
I exceedingly fear and *q. Heb* 12:21

quaked
whole mount *q.* greatly. *Ex* 19:18
host trembled, and the earth *q.*
　　　　　　　　　　1 Sam 14:15

quaking
eat thy bread with *q. Ezek* 12:18
but a great *q.* fell on them. *Dan* 10:7

quantity
on him vessels of small *q. Isa* 22:24*

quarrel
a sword shall avenge *q. Lev* 26:25*
see how he seeketh a *q. 2 Ki* 5:7
Herodias had a *q.* against John.
　　　　　　　　　　Mark 6:19*
if any man have a *q. Col* 3:13*

quarries
Ehud turned from the *q. Judg* 3:19
escaped and passed beyond *q.* 26

quarter
all people from every *q. Gen* 19:4
this was the west *q. Josh* 18:14
shall wander to his *q. Isa* 47:15
for his gain from his *q.* 56:11
to him from every *q. Mark* 1:45
see **south**

quarters
no leaven in thy *q. Ex* 13:7*
fringes on the four *q. Deut* 22:12*
in four *q.* were porters. *1 Chr* 9:24*
winds from four *q.* of. *Jer* 49:36
as Peter passed through all *q.*
　　　　　　　　　　Acts 9:32*
Jews which were in those *q.* 16:3*
in same *q.* were possessions. 28:7*
nations in four *q.* of earth. *Rev* 20:8*

Quartus
Q. a brother saluteth. *Rom* 16:23

quaternions
Peter to four *q.* of soldiers. *Acts* 12:4

queen
[1] *A sovereign princess, or chief
ruler of a kingdom,* 1 Ki 10:1.
[2] *The queen of heaven, a term
applied to the moon by idolatrous
moon-worshippers,* Jer 44:17, 25.
*They set up altars to her upon the
platforms or roofs of their houses*

oɪ the corners of the streets, near
their doors, and in groves. They
offered cakes to her kneaded up with
oil and honey, and made libations
to her with wine and other liquors.
q. of Sheba heard of the fame of.
      1 Ki 10:1; 2 Chr 9:1
q. had seen all Solomon's wisdom.
      1 Ki 10:4
no such spices as these the *q.* of
  Sheba gave.   10; *2 Chr 9:9*
king Solomon gave *q.* of Sheba all
  her desire. *1 Ki 10:13; 2 Chr 9:12*
Hadad the sister of the. *q.1 Ki 11:19*
Asa removed Maachah from being *q.*
     15:13; *2 Chr 15:16*
salute children of the *q. 2 Ki 10:13*
the *q.* sitting by him.   *Neh 2:6*
Vashti the *q.* made a feast. *Esth 1:9*
to bring the *q.*   11
the *q.* refused to come.   12
shall we do to the *q.* Vashti ? 15
q. hath not done wrong to the. 16
deed of *q.* shall come abroad. 18
have heard the deed of the *q.* 18
that pleaseth the king be *q.* 2:4
Esther *q.* instead of Vashti. 17
the *q,* exceedingly grieved. 4:4
what wilt thou, *q.* Esther ? 5:3
q. let no man to the banquet. 12
what is thy petition, *q.* Esther ? *7:2*
was afraid before king and *q.* 6
request to the *q.* for his life. 7
will he force *q.* also before me ? 8
house of Haman to Esther the *q.* 8:1
as Mordecai and Esther the *q.* 9:31
did stand the *q.* in gold. *Ps 45:9*
say to the king and *q.,* Humble yourselves.   *Jer 13:18**
incense to the *q.* of heaven. 44:17, 25
q. came into the banquet-. *Dan 5:10*
q. of the south shall rise up in the.
    Mat 12:42; Luke 11:31
Candace *q.* of Ethiopians. *Acts 8:27*
I sit a *q.* and am no widow. *Rev 18:7*

queens
there are threescore *q. S of S 6:8, 9*
q. thy nursing mothers. *Isa 49:23*

quench
shall *q.* my coal.   *2 Sam 14:7*
that thou *q.* not the light of. 21:17
asses *q.* their thirst.   *Ps 104:11*
waters cannot *q.* love. *S of S 8:7*
none shall *q.* them.   *Isa 1:31*
flax shall he not *q.* 42:3; *Mat 12:20*
lest my fury come forth, and burn
  that none can *q.* it. *Jer 4:4; 21:12*
none to *q.* it in Beth-el. *Amos 5:6*
able to *q.* the fiery darts. *Eph 6:16*
q. not Spirit, despise. *1 Thes 5:19*

quenched
Moses prayed, fire was *q.*
    Num 11:2*; 2 Chr 34:25
wrath shall not be *q.* *2 Ki 22:17*
they are *q.* as the fire. *Ps 118:12*
it shall not be *q.* night. *Isa 34:10*
they are *q.* as tow.   43:17
nor shall their fire be *q.* 66:24
my fury shall burn, and shall not be
  q.   *Jer 7:20; 17:27*
flame shall not be *q. Ezek 20:47, 48*
that never shall be *q. Mark 9:43, 45*
where the fire is not *q.* 44, 46, 48
q. the violence of fire. *Heb 11:34*

question, *substantive*
lawyer asked him a *q.* *Mat 22:35*
I will ask you one *q.* *Mark 11:29*
no man after that durst ask him any
  q.   12:34; *Luke 20:40*
there arose a *q.* between. *John 3:25*
apostles about this *q.* *Acts 15:2*
q. of words and names. 18:15
in danger to be called in *q.* 19:40*
I am called in *q.* 23:6; 24:21
no *q.* for conscience. *1 Cor 10:25, 27*

question, *verb*
began to *q.* him.   *Mark 8:11*
scribes, What *q.* ye with them ? 9:16

questioned, -ing
Hezekiah *q.* priests. *2 Chr 31:9*
q. among themselves. *Mark 1:27*
q. what rising from the dead. 9:10

and scribes *q.* with them. *Mark 9:14*
Pilate *q.* with him in. *Luke 23:9*

questions
to prove him with *q.* *1 Ki 10:1*
told her all her *q.* 3; *2 Chr 9:1, 2*
durst any ask him more *q. Mat 22:46*
and asking them *q.* *Luke 2:46*
accused of *q.* of their law. *Acts 23:29*
had certain *q.* against him. 25:19
doubted of such manner of *q.* 20*
I know thee to be expert in *q.* 26:3
which minister *q.* rather. *1 Tim 1:4*
but doting about *q.* and strifes. 6:4
but unlearned *q.* avoid. *2 Tim 2:23*
     Tit 3:9

quick
(*Very frequently used with the
  old meaning of* living)
there be *q.* raw flesh. *Lev 13:10*
the *q.* flesh that burneth have a. 24
down *q.* into the pit. *Num 16:30**
go down *q.* into hell. *Ps 55:15**
swallowed us up *q.* 124:3*
him of *q.* understanding. *Isa 11:3**
judge of the *q.* and dead. *Acts 10:42**
shall judge the *q.* and the dead.
  2 Tim 4:1; 1 Pet 4:5
the word of God is *q.* *Heb 4:12**

quicken
(*To bring back to life, either
literally, as to restore life to the
body, or figuratively, to stimulate
the spirit which was deadened*)
thou shalt *q.* me again. *Ps 71:20*
q. us, and we will call on thy. 80:18
q. me according to thy word.
  119:25, 107, 149, 154, 156
turn me from vanity, *q.* me in. 37
q. me in thy righteousness. 40
q. me after thy. 88, 159
q. me, O Lord, for thy. 143:11
shall also *q.* your mortal. *Rom 8:11*

quickened
thy word hath *q.* me. *Ps 119:50*
thy precepts thou hast *q.* me. 93
thou sowest, is not *q.* *1 Cor 15:36*
you hath he *q.,* who were. *Eph 2:1*
hath *q.* us together with Christ. 5
    Col 2:13
but *q.* by the Spirit. *1 Pet 3:18*

quickeneth
as the Father *q.* them; even so the
  Son *q.* whom.   *John 5:21*
it is the Spirit that *q.* 6:63
even God who *q.* the dead. *Rom 4:17*
God, who *q.* all things. *1 Tim 6:13*

quickening
was made a *q.* spirit. *1 Cor 15:45*

quickly
ready *q.* three measures. *Gen 18:6*
hast found it so *q.* my son ? 27:20
aside *q.* out of the way. *Ex 32:8*
  Deut 9:12, 16; Judg 2:17
put on incense and go *q. Num 16:46*
shalt thou destroy them *q. Deut 9:3*
get thee down *q.*   12
lest ye perish *q.*   11:17
till thou perish *q.* because of. 28:20
pursue *q.* for ye shall. *Josh 2:5*
the ambush arose *q.* out of. 8:19
come up to us *q.* and save us. 10:6
shall perish *q.* from off the. 23:16
thou shalt go down *q.* *1 Sam 20:19*
send *q.* and tell David. *2 Sam 17:16*
went both of them away *q.* 18
David, Arise and pass *q.* over. 21
king said, Come down *q. 2 Ki 1:11*
fetch *q.* Micaiah the. *2 Chr 18:8*
threefold cord is not *q.* *Eccl 4:12*
with thine adversary *q.* *Mat 5:25*
go *q.* and tell his disciples. 28:7
they departed *q.* with. 8; *Mark 16:8*
go *q.* into the streets. *Luke 14:21*
sit down *q.* and write fifty. 16:6
Mary arose *q.* and came. *John 11:29*
That thou doest, do *q.* 13:27
saying, Arise up *q.* *Acts 12:7*
get thee *q.* out of Jerusalem. 22:18
I will come to thee *q. Rev 2:5, 16*
behold, I come *q.* 3:11; 22:7, 12
behold third woe cometh *q.* 11:14
Surely I come *q.* Even so. 22:20

quicksands
should fall into the *q.* *Acts 27:17**

quiet
laid wait and were *q.* *Judg 16:2*
Zidonians, *q.* and secure. 18:7
to a people that were at *q.* 27
rejoiced, and the city was in *q.*
  2 Ki 11:20; 2 Chr 23:21
land was wide and *q.* *1 Chr 4:40*
land was *q.* ten years. *2 Chr 14:1*
the kingdom was *q.* before. 5; 20:30
should I have been *q.* *Job 3:13*
neither was I *q.,* yet trouble. 26
being wholly at ease and *q.* 21:23
against them that are *q. Ps 35:20*
glad, because they be *q.* 107:30
hearkeneth to me shall be in *q.*
    Pr 1:33
wise men are heard in *q. Eccl 9:17*
Take heed and be *q.;* fear. *Isa 7:4*
earth is at rest, and is *q.* 14:7
shall dwell in *q.* resting places. 32:18
Jerusalem a *q.* habitation. 33:20
and be in rest and *q.* *Jer 30:10*
long will it be ere thou be *q.?* 47:6
how be *q.* seeing the Lord hath ? 7
sorrow on sea, it cannot be *q.* 49:23
Seraiah was a *q.* prince. 51:59*
I will be *q.* and will be. *Ezek 16:42*
though they be *q.* they. *Nah 1:12**
ye ought to be *q.* and do. *Acts 19:36*
that ye study to be *q.* *1 Thes 4:11*
lead a *q.* and peaceable. *1 Tim 2:2*
a meek and *q.* spirit. *1 Pet 3:4*

quieted
behaved and *q.* myself. *Ps 131:2*
these *q.* my spirit in the. *Zech 6:8*

quieteth
when he *q.* the earth. *Job 37:17**

quietly
took Abner to speak *q. 2 Sam 3:27*
q. wait for the salvation. *Lam 3:26*

quietness
was in *q.* forty years. *Judg 8:28**
I will give *q.* to Israel. *1 Chr 22:9*
not feel *q.* in his belly. *Job 20:20*
when he giveth *q.* who can ? 34:29
dry morsel and *q.*   *Pr 17:1*
better is an handful with *q. Eccl 4:6*
in *q.* and confidence shall. *Isa 30:15*
effect of righteousness, is 32:17
thee we enjoy great *q.* *Acts 24:2**
we exhort that with *q. 2 Thes 3:12*

quit
he that smote him be *q.* *Ex 21:19*
owner of the ox shall be *q.* 28
will be *q.* of thine oath. *Josh 2:20**
q. yourselves like men. *1 Sam 4:9*
    1 Cor 16:13

quite
q. devoured also our. *Gen 31:15*
thou shalt *q.* break down. *Ex 23:24**
q. take away their murmurings.
    Num 17:10*
and *q.* pluck down all their. 33:52*
and he is *q.* gone. *2 Sam 3:24*
and is wisdom driven *q.?* *Job 6:13*
bow was made *q.* naked. *Hab 3:9*

quiver
therefore take thy *q.* and. *Gen 27:3*
q. rattleth against him. *Job 39:23*
man that hath his *q.* full. *Ps 127:5*
Elam bare the *q.* with. *Isa 22:6*
in his *q.* hath he hid me. 49:2
q. is as an open sepulchre. *Jer 5:16*
arrows of his *q.* to enter. *Lam 3:13*

quivered
when I heard, my lips *q.* *Hab 3:16*

R

Rabbah, *or* **Rabbath**
is it not in *R.* of the children of ?
    Deut 3:11
Israel besieged *R.* *2 Sam 11:1*
Joab fought against *R.* and. 12:26
Shobi of *R.* brought beds. 17:27
Joab smote *R.* and. *1 Chr 20:1*

an alarm to be heard in *R. Jer 49:2*
cry, ye daughters of *R.*, gird with. 3
sword may come to *R. Ezek 21:20*
I will make *R.* a stable for. 25:5
a fire in the wall of *R. Amos 1:14*

Rabbi
(*A title of respect meaning master, teacher, given by the Jews to their teachers and spiritual leaders, and often addressed to our Lord. Another form of the title was* Rabboni. *The titles were used with different degrees of honour—the lowest being* rab, master *; second,* rabbi, *my master ; and greatest of all,* rabboni, *my lord, master.*
The term rab *was also used in Babylonia and Assyria to mean* chief—*as* Rab-mag, *the chief of the magi, etc.*)

called of men, *r. r. Mat 23:7*
be not ye called *r.*, for one is. 8
R. where dwellest thou ? *John 1:38*
R. thou art the Son of God. 49
R. we know thou art a teacher. 3:2
R. he that was with thee. 26
they said, *R.* when camest ? 6:25

Rabboni
Mary saith, *John 20:16*
R., [R.V.] that I may receive my sight. *Mark 10:51*

Rab-shakeh
(*Properly a title of a court officer*)
the king of Assyria sent *R.*
2 Ki 18:17; Isa 36:2
they told him the words of *R.*
2 Ki 18:37; Isa 36:22
God will hear the words of *R.*
2 Ki 19:4; Isa 37:4

raca
(*A term of reproach and contempt meaning empty, and hence worthless. It is a weaker word than* fool)
shall say to his brother, *R. Mat 5:22*

race
strong man to run a *r. Ps 19:5**
the *r.* is not to the swift. *Eccl 9:11*
run in a *r.* run all. *1 Cor 9:24*
run with patience the *r. Heb 12:1*

Rachel
Jacob told *R.* that he. *Gen 29:12*
name of the younger was *R.* 16
R. was beautiful and well. 17
Jacob loved *R.* 18, 30
R. was barren. 31
seven years for *R.* 20, 25
Laban gave him *R.* his. 28
R. bare no children, *R.* envied. 30:1
kindled against *R.*: he said. 2
God remembered *R.* and opened. 22
R. had stolen her father's. 31:19, 34
then Laban went into *R.*'s tent. 33
Jacob put *R.* and Joseph. 33:2
R. died. 35:19; 48:7
sons of *R.* 35:24; 46:19, 22
make the woman like *R. Ruth 4:11*
find two men by *R.*'s. *1 Sam 10:2*
R. weeping. *Jer 31:15; Mat 2:18*

rafters
cedar, and our *r.* of fir. *S of S 1:17*

Ragau
was the son of *R. Luke 3:35*

rage, substantive
turned away in a *r. 2 Ki 5:12*
I know thy *r.* against me. 19:27
Isa 37:28
Asa was in a *r.* with. *2 Chr 16:10*
and ye have slain them in a *r.* 28:9
swalloweth the ground with *r.*
Job 39:24
cast abroad *r.* of thy wrath. 40:11*
thyself because of *r.* of. *Ps 7:6*
jealousy is *r.* of a man. *Pr 6:34*
Nebuchadnezzar commanded in his *r.* to bring. *Dan 3:13*
they shall fall for the *r. Hos 7:16*

rage, verb
why do the heathen *r.? Ps 2:1*
Acts 4:25
whether he *r.* or laugh. *Pr 29:9*
ye horses, *r.* ye chariots. *Jer 46:9*
chariots shall *r.* in streets. *Nah 2:4*

raged
heathen *r.*, the kingdoms. *Ps 46:6*

rageth
fool *r.* and is confident. *Pr 14:16**

ragged
tops of the *r.* rocks. *Isa 2:21*

raging
thou rulest the *r.* of the sea. *Ps 89:9*
strong drink is *r. Pr 20:1**
sea ceased from her *r. Jonah 1:15*
wind and *r.* of the water. *Luke 8:24*
r. waves of the sea foaming. *Jude 13*

rags
clothe a man with *r. Pr 23:31*
all our righteousnesses are as filthy *r. Isa 64:6**
took old rotten *r. Jer 38:11*
put *r.* under thine arm holes. 12

Rahab, person, place
entered into house of *R. Josh 2:1*
only *R.* shall live. 6:17
Joshua saved *R.* 25
make mention of *R. Ps 87:4*
thou hast broken *R.* in pieces. 89:10
not it that hath cut *R.? Isa 51:9*
Salmon begat Booz of *R. Mat 1:5*
by faith the harlot *R. Heb 11:31*
was not *R.* also justified ? *Jas 2:25*

rail
he wrote letters to *r. 2 Chr 32:17*

railed
our master *r.* on them. *1 Sam 25:14**
they that passed by *r. Mark 15:29*
one of malefactors *r.* on. *Luke 23:39*

railer
keep not company with *r. 1 Cor 5:11**

railing, adjective
angels bring not *r. 2 Pet 2:11*
Michael durst not bring against him a *r.* accusation. *Jude 9*

railing
cometh envy, strife, *r. 1 Tim 6:4*
not rendering *r.* for *r. 1 Pet 3:9**

raiment
the servant gave *r.* to. *Gen 24:53*
Rebekah took goodly *r.* of. 27:15
Isaac smelled his *r.* and. 27
Lord will give me *r.* to put. 28:20
shaved, and changed his *r.* 41:14
gave to each man changes of *r.*, but to Benjamin five changes of *r.* 45:22
borrow of the Egyptians *r. Ex 3:22*
12:35
her food and *r.* shall he not. 21:10
trespass for sheep, for *r.* 22:9
thy neighbour's *r.* to pledge. 26, 27
unclean beast falls on *r. Lev 11:32*
purify all your *r.* all. *Num 31:20*
thy *r.* waxed not old. *Deut 8:4*
loveth stranger, giving him *r.* 10:18
she shall put *r.* of her captivity. 21:13
lost *r.* restore, and all lost. 22:3
that he may sleep in his *r.* 24:13
not take a widow's *r.* to pledge. 17
to your tents with much *r. Josh 22:8*
a dagger under his *r. Judg 3:16*
purple *r.* that was on kings. 8:26
and put thy *r.* upon thee. *Ruth 3:3*
himself and put on *r. 1 Sam 28:8*
with him ten changes of *r. 2 Ki 5:5*
the lepers carried thence *r.* and. 7:8
Solomon, gold, and *r. 2 Chr 9:24*
the queen sent *r.* to clothe. *Esth 4:4*
and though he prepare *r. Job 27:16*
to king in *r.* of needlework. *Ps 45:14*
cast out as the *r.* of. *Isa 14:19**
and I will stain all my *r.* 63:3
thy *r.* was of fine linen. *Ezek 16:13*
thee with change of *r. Zech 3:4**
his *r.* of camels' hair. *Mat 3:4*
and the body more than *r.* 6:25
Luke 12:23
why take ye thought for *r.? Mat 6:28*

a man clothed in soft *r.*
Mat 11:8; Luke 7:25
his *r.* white as light. *Mat 17:2*
Mark 9:3; Luke 9:29
put his own *r.* on him. *Mat 27:31*
his *r.* was white as snow. 28:3
who stripped him of *r. Luke 10:30*
they parted his *r.* and cast lots.
23:34; *John 19:24*
Paul shook his *r.* and. *Acts 18:6*
I kept the *r.* of them that. 22:20
having food and *r.* let us. *1 Tim 6:8**
a poor man in vile *r. Jas 2:2*
be clothed in white *r. Rev 3:5*
buy white *r.* that thou mayest. 18
elders clothed in white *r.* 4:4

rain
Palestine has its rainy season and its dry season. During the latter the brooks dry up, and the first rains are very welcome. Early rain meant the autumn rain, Deut 11:14, *and latter rain that of the Spring,* Pr 16:15.

r. was upon the earth. *Gen 7:12*
r. from heaven was restrained. 8:2
the *r.* was not poured on. *Ex 9:33*
Pharaoh saw the *r.* ceased. 34
I will give you *r.* in due season.
Lev 26:4; Deut 11:14; 28:12
land drinks water of *r. Deut 11:11*
heaven that there be no *r.* 17
1 Ki 8:35; 2 Chr 6:26; 7:13
make *r.* of thy land. *Deut 28:24*
my doctrine shall drop as the *r.* 32:2
on the Lord to send *r. 1 Sam 12:17*
sent thunder and *r.* that day. 18
no dew nor *r.* upon. *2 Sam 1:21*
by clear shining after *r.* 23:4
give *r.* upon thy land. *1 Ki 8:36*
2 Chr 6:27
shall not be dew nor *r. 1 Ki 17:1*
because there had been no *r.* 7
till that day the Lord send *r.* 14
shew to Ahab, I will send *r.* 18:1
a sound of abundance of *r.* 41
that the *r.* stop thee not. 44
and there was a great *r.* 45
not see wind, nor see *r. 2 Ki 3:17*
trembling for the great *r. Ezra 10:9*
and it is a time of much *r.* 13
giveth *r.* upon the earth. *Job 5:10*
he made a decree for *r.* and. 28:26
waited for me as for the *r.* 29:23
clouds pour down *r.* 36:27
to small *r.* and to great *r.* of. 37:6
hath *r.* a father ? or who hath ? 38:28
didst send a plentiful *r. Ps 68:9*
down like *r.* on mown grass. 72:6
the *r.* also filleth the pools. 84:6
he gave them hail for *r.* and. 105:32
he maketh lightnings for the *r.* 135:7
Lord, who prepareth *r.* for. 147:8
clouds and wind without *r. Pr 25:14*
the north wind driveth away *r.* 23
as snow in summer, and *r.* in. 26:1
poor, is like a sweeping *r.* 28:3
if clouds be full of *r. Eccl 11:3*
clouds return after the *r.* 12:2
winter is past, *r.* is over. *S of S 2:11*
a covert from storm and *r. Isa 4:6*
clouds they *r.* no *r.* on it. 5:6
then shall he give the *r.* of. 30:23
as ash, and *r.* doth nourish it. 44:14
as the *r.* cometh down. 55:10
the Lord that giveth *r. Jer 5:24*
lightnings with *r.* 10:13; 51:16
for there was no *r.* 14:4
vanities of Gentiles can cause *r.?* 22
bow in cloud in day of *r. Ezek 1:28*
I will *r.* an overflowing *r.* 38:22*
shall make us as the *r. Hos 6:3*
to come down for your *r. Joel 2:23*
withholden the *r.* from you. *Amos 4:7*
upon them shall be no *r. Zech 14:17*
go not up, that have no *r.* 18
he sendeth *r.* on just and. *Mat 5:45*
r. descended, and floods. 7:25, 27
did good, and gave us *r. Acts 14:17*
because of the present *r.* 28:2
which drinketh in the *r. Heb 6:7*
and the heaven gave *r. Jas 5:18*
see **latter**

rain, verb
Lord had not caused it to r. Gen 2:5
cause it to r. forty days. 7:4
I will cause it to r. Ex 9:18
I will r. bread from heaven. 16:4
God shall r. his fury. Job 20:23
cause it to r. on the earth. 38:26
wicked he shall r. snares. Ps 11:6
that they r. no rain on it. Isa 5:6
r. an overflowing rain. Ezek 38:22
r. righteousness on you. Hos 10:12
I caused it to r. on one city. Amos 4:7
earnestly it might not r. Jas 5:17
that it r. not in days of. Rev 11:6

rainbow
there was a r. round. Rev 4:3
I saw an angel, and a r. was. 10:1

rained
Lord r. upon Sodom. Gen 19:24
the Lord r. hail on land. Ex 9:23
had r. down manna. Ps 78:24, 27
the land not r. upon. Ezek 22:24
one piece was r. upon; and the piece
  whereupon it r. not. Amos 4:7
the same day it r. fire. Luke 17:29
it r. not for three years. Jas 5:17

rainy
dropping in a r. day. Pr 27:15

raise
marry her, and r. up seed. Gen 38:8
shalt not r. a false report. Ex 23:1
God will r. up a prophet. Deut 18:15
  18; Acts 3:22; 7:37
refuseth to r. up to brother a name.
  Deut 25:7
r. thereon a great heap. Josh 8:29
to r. up the name of. Ruth 4:5, 10
I will r. me up a faithful priest.
  1 Sam 2:35
I will r. up evil. 2 Sam 12:11
elders went to him to r. him. 17
Lord shall r. up a king. 1 Ki 14:14
I will r. up thy seed. 1 Chr 17:11
who are ready to r. up their mourning. Job 3:8
his troops r. up their way. 19:12
they r. up against me ways of. 30:12
merciful to me, and r. me. Ps 41:10
they shall r. up a cry of. Isa 15:5
I will r. forts against thee. 29:3
I will r. up decayed places. 44:26
my servant to r. up tribes. 49:6
r. up foundations of many. 58:12
they shall r. up the former. 61:4
r. to David a righteous. Jer 23:5
their king, whom I will r. up. 30:9
I will r. against Babylon. 50:9
none shall r. him up. 32
r. a destroying wind. 51:1
I will r. up thy lovers. Ezek 23:22
I will r. up for them a plant. 34:29
third day he will r. us up. Hos 6:2
I will r. them out of the. Joel 3:7
there is none to r. her up. Amos 5:2
I will r. a nation against you. 6:14
I will r. up the tabernacle of David,
  and I will r. up his ruins. 9:11
we shall r. against him. Mi 5:5
there are that r. up strife. Hab 1:3
I will r. up the Chaldeans. 6
I will r. up a shepherd. Zech 11:16
to r. up children to Abraham.
  Mat 3:9; Luke 3:8
cleanse lepers, r. dead. Mat 10:8
marry his wife, and r. up seed.
  22:24; Mark 12:19; Luke 20:28
in three days I will r. it. John 2:19
will r. it up again. 6:39, 40, 44, 54
he would r. up Christ to. Acts 2:30
incredible that God should r.? 26:8
will also r. up us by his. 1 Cor 6:14
r. up us also by Jesus. 2 Cor 4:14
accounting God was able to r. him
  up. Heb 11:19
Lord shall r. him up. Jas 5:15

raised
I r. thee up to shew my power.
  Ex 9:16; Rom 9:17
children whom r. over. Josh 5:7
they r. over him a great heap. 7:26
Lord r. up judges. Judg 2:16, 18
Lord r. up a deliverer. 3:9, 15

man who was r. up. 2 Sam 23:1
Solomon r. up a levy of Israel.
  1 Ki 5:13; 9:15
and r. it up to the towers.
  2 Chr 32:5; 33:14
whose spirit God r. to. Ezra 1:5
not awake, nor be r. out. Job 14:12
I r. thee up under. S of S 8:5
it r. up from their thrones. Isa 14:9
the Assyrian r. up the palaces. 23:13
who r. up the righteous man. 41:2
I have r. up one from north. 25
r. him up in righteousness. 45:13
a great nation shall be r. Jer 6:22
a great whirlwind shall be r. 25:32
Lord hath r. us up prophets. 29:15
many kings shall be r. from. 50:41
Lord r. up the spirit of kings. 51:11
a bear r. up itself on. Dan 7:5
I r. up of your sons for. Amos 2:11
is r. up out of his holy. Zech 2:13
when I have r. up thy sons. 9:13
Joseph being r. from sleep. Mat 1:24
the dead are r. up. 11:5; Luke 7:22
killed, and r. up again the third day.
  Mat 16:21; 17:23; Luke 9:22
hath r. up an horn of. Luke 1:69
now that the dead are r. 20:37
Lazarus whom he r. John 12:1, 9, 17
God hath r. up. Acts 2:24, 32; 3:15
  26; 4:10; 5:30; 10:40; 13:30, 33
  34; 17:31; Rom 10:9; 1 Cor 6:14
  2 Cor 4:14; Gal 1:1; Eph 1:20
angel r. up Peter. Acts 12:7
he r. up David. 13:22
God r. to Israel a Saviour. 23
the Jews r. persecution against. 50
if we believe on him that r. Rom 4:24
r. again for our justification. 25
like as Christ was r. from dead. 6:4
Christ being r. from the dead. 9
him who is r. from the dead. 7:4
Spirit of him that r. up Jesus . . .
  he that r. up Christ. 8:11
r. up Christ; whom he r. 1 Cor 15:15
rise not, then is not Christ r. 16
if Christ be not r. your faith. 17
will say, How are the dead r.? 35
corruption, r. in incorruption. 42, 52
r. in glory, it is r. in power. 43
natural body, r. a spiritual body. 44
hath r. us up together in. Eph 2:6
operation of God who r. Col 2:12
his Son, whom he r. 1 Thes 1:10
remember Jesus was r. 2 Tim 2:8
their dead r. to life Heb 11:35
God that r. him up from the dead.
  1 Pet 1:21

raiser
stand up a r. of taxes. Dan 11:20

raiseth
he r. poor out of the dust.
  1 Sam 2:8; Ps 113:7
when he r. himself. Job 41:25
and r. stormy wind. Ps 107:25
he r. those that be bowed down.
  145:14; 146:8
as Father r. up the dead. John 5:21
trust in God which r. 2 Cor 1:9

raising
baker who ceaseth from r. Hos 7:4
nor found they me r. up. Acts 24:12

raisins
hundred clusters of r. 1 Sam 25:18
Egyptians two clusters of r. 30:12
with 100 bunches of r. 2 Sam 16:1
brought bunches of r. 1 Chr 12:40

ram
take a r. of three years. Gen 15:9
a r. caught in a thicket. 22:13
take one r. Ex 29:15
thou shalt slay the r. 16
burn the whole r. 18; Lev 8:21
it is a r. of consecration. Ex 29:22
  27, 31; Lev 8:22
eat the flesh of the r. Ex 29:32
take r. for burnt offering. Lev 9:2
r. for peace offering.
r. for trespass offering. 19:21
beside r. of atonement. Num 5:8
thus shall it be done for one r. 15:11
guilty, they offered a r. Ezra 10:19

shall offer a r. Ezek 43:23, 25
an ephah for a r. 45:24; 46:5, 7, 11
the prince shall offer a r. 46:4
new moon six lambs and a r. 6
I saw a r. which had two horns.
  Dan 8:3
I saw the r. pushing westward. 4
the goat ran to the r. that had. 6
come close to the r.: there was no
  power in the r.: none to deliver r. 7
the r. having two horns are. 20

Ram
Hezron begat R. and R. begat.
  Ruth 4:19; 1 Chr 2:9, 10
Jerahmeel, R. Bunah. 1 Chr 2:25
the sons of R. the firstborn. 27
Buzite of the kindred of R. Job 32:2

Ramah, Rama
R. a city of the tribe. Josh 18:25
Deborah dwelt between R. Judg 4:5
Elkanah came to his house in R.
  1 Sam 1:19; 2:11
Samuel's return was to R. 7:17
  15:34; 16:13
all the elders came unto R. 8:4
David fled, and came to R. 19:18
Saul went to R. 22, 23
Saul abode in R. 22:6
buried in his house at R. 25:1; 28:3
Baasha built R. 1 Ki 15:17
  2 Chr 16:1
Baasha left off building of R.
  1 Ki 15:21; 2 Chr 16:5
wounds the Syrians had given Joram
  at R. 2 Ki 8:29; 2 Chr 22:6
children of R. and Geba six hundred.
  Ezra 2:26; Neh 7:30
Benjamin dwelt at R. Neh 11:33
R. is afraid, Gibeah of. Isa 10:29
voice was heard in R. Jer 31:15
  Mat 2:18
merchants of R. were. Ezek 27:22
blow ye the trumpet in R. Hos 5:8

Ramoth-gilead
R. in Gilead of the Gadites, a city.
  Deut 4:43; Josh 20:8; 21:38
Geber was officer in R. 1 Ki 4:13
know ye that R. is ours? 22:3
wilt thou go with me to battle to R.?
  4; 2 Chr 18:3
shall I go against R.? 1 Ki 22:6
  15; 2 Chr 18:14
saying, Go up to R. and prosper.
  1 Ki 22:12; 2 Chr 18:11
Joram went against Hazael in R.
  2 Ki 8:28; 2 Chr 22:5
take this box of oil, and go to R.
  2 Ki 9:1
now Joram had kept R. 14
Gad to the Levites, R. 1 Chr 6:80

rampart
he made the r. and the wall. Lam 2:8
then populous No, whose r. Nah 3:8

rams
r. which leaped. Gen 31:10*, 12*
the r. of thy flock have I not. 38
Esau 200 ewes and 20 r. 32:14
r. of breed of Bashan. Deut 32:14
hearken than fat of r. 1 Sam 15:22
100,000 r. with wool. 2 Ki 3:4
to the Lord 1000 r. 1 Chr 29:21
Arabians brought 7700 r. 2 Chr 17:11
r. for offerings of the God. Ezra 6:9
dedication of the house 200 r. 17
with this money r., lambs. 7:17
offered ninety-six r. for a sin. 8:35
with the fat of r. Ps 66:15; Isa 34:6
mountains skipped like r. Ps 114:4, 6
the burnt offerings of r. Isa 1:11
is filled with fat of kidneys of r. 34:6
the r. of Nebaioth shall. 60:7
to the slaughter like r. Jer 51:40
occupied with thee in r. Ezek 27:21
I judge between the r. and. 34:17
ye shall drink the blood of r. 39:18
pleased with thousands of r. Mi 6:7
see battering, seven

rams' horns
bear before the ark seven trumpets
  of r. horns. Josh 6:4, 6, 8, 13
a long blast with the r. horns. 5

rams' skins
r. skins dyed red, and.   Ex 25:5
   26:14; 35:7; 36:19; 39:34

ran
Abraham r. to meet them. Gen 18:2
Abram r. to the herd.   7
servant r. to meet Rebekah. 24:17
Rebekah r. to the well to.   20
damsel r. and told her mother's. 28
r. out to the man to the well.   29
and Rachel r. and told her.   29:12
Laban r. to meet Jacob and.   13
Esau r. to meet him.   33:4
the fire r. along upon.   Ex 9:23
r. a young man and.   Num 11:27
Aaron r. into midst of the.   16:47
messenger r. to Aaron's. Josh 7:22
the ambush r. into Ai, and set. 8:19
all the host of Midian r. Judg 7:21
Jothan r. away, and fled.   9:21
Manoah's wife r. and shewed. 13:10
Samuel r. to Eli, and.   1 Sam 3:5
a man of Benjamin r. out of the. 4:12
and they r. and fetched Saul. 10:23
David r. into the army and.   17:22
David r. and stood upon the.   51
as the lad r. he shot an arrow. 20:36
Cushi bowed himself to Joab and r.
       2 Sam 18:21
Ahimaaz r. by the plain and.   23
servants of Shimei r.   1 Ki 2:39
the water r. round about the. 18:35
Elijah r. before Ahab to Jezreel. 46
Elisha left the oxen and r.   19:20
the blood r. into the midst of. 22:35
my sore r. in the night.   Ps 77:2*
waters r. in the dry places. 105:41
the ointment that r. down.   133:2
sent them, yet they r.   Jer 23:21
the living creatures r.   Ezek 1:14
r. out waters on the right side. 47:2
goat r. to the ram in fury.   Dan 8:6
herd of swine r. violently. Mat 8:32*
     Mark 5:13*; Luke 8:33*
one r. and filled a spunge.
     Mat 27:48; Mark 15:36
many knew him, and r. Mark 6:33
r. through that whole region.   55
his father r. and fell on. Luke 15:20
Zacchaeus r. before and climbed. 19:4
then arose Peter and r. to the. 24:12
so they r. both together. John 20:4
the people r. together.   Acts 3:11
they r. upon Stephen with.   7:57*
Philip r. to the chariot.   8:30
knew Peter's voice, she r. in. 12:14
Paul and Barnabas r. in.   14:14*
the people r. together and.   21:30
captain took soldiers and r.   32
they r. the ship aground and. 27:41
they r. greedily after the error of
    Balaam.   Jude 11

rang
that the earth r. again.   1 Sam 4:5
so that the city r. again.   1 Ki 1:45

range
the r. of the mountains.   Job 39:8

ranges
or r. for pots, they shall. Lev 11:35
that cometh within r. let. 2 Ki 11:8*
have her forth without the r.   15*
     2 Chr 23:14*

ranging
as a roaring lion, and a r. bear.
       Pr 28:15

rank
ears came up upon one stalk, r. and
   good.   Gen 41:5
devoured the seven r. ears.   7
forth in the second r.   Num 2:16
go forward in the third r.   24
50,000 could keep r.   1 Chr 12:33
men of war that could keep r.   38

ranks
against light in three r. 1 Ki 7:4, 5
shall not break their r.   Joel 2:7
they sat down in r. by.   Mark 6:40

ransom, substantive
(A price paid for freedom)
give for the r. of his life. Ex 21:30*
every man a r. for his soul.   30:12
from pit, I have found a r. Job 33:24

a great r. cannot deliver. Job 36:18
give to God a r. for him.   Ps 49:7
he will not regard any r.   Pr 6:35
r. of a man's life are his riches. 13:8
the wicked shall be a r. for.   21:18
I gave Egypt for thy r.   Isa 43:3
Son of man came to give his life a r.
     Mat 20:28; Mark 10:45
who gave himself r. for all. 1 Tim 2:6

ransom
r. them from power of.   Hos 13:14

ransomed
r. of the Lord shall return. Isa 35:10
the sea a way for the r. to.   51:10*
redeemed Jacob and r.   Jer 31:11

Rapha, and Raphu
Palti son of Raphu.   Num 13:9
Rapha, father of Eleasah. 1 Chr 8:37

rare
it is a r. thing that the king. Dan 2:11

rase
r. it, r. it, even to the.   Ps 137:7

rash
be not r. with thy mouth.   Eccl 5:2

rashly
quiet, and do nothing r.   Acts 19:36

rate
gather certain r. every day. Ex 16:4
brought mules at a r.   1 Ki 10:25
     2 Chr 9:24
a daily r. for every.   2 Ki 25:30
even after a certain r.   2 Chr 8:13*

rather
if we have not r. done it. Josh 22:24
much r. when he saith to. 2 Ki 5:13
chooseth death r. than life. Job 7:15
       Jer 8:3
he justified himself r.   Job 32:2
this hast thou chosen r.   36:21
and lying r. than to speak. Ps 52:3
r. be a doorkeeper in house. 84:10
receive knowledge r. than. Pr 8:10
to understanding r. than silver. 16:16
meet a man, r. than a fool.   17:12
a good name r. than great riches,
   loving favour r. than silver. 22:1
go r. to the lost sheep of. Mat 10:6
r. fear him that is able to.   28
r. than having two hands to.   18:8
r. than having two eyes to.   9
but go ye r. to them that sell. 25:9
but that r. tumult was made. 27:24
nothing bettered, but r. Mark 5:26
should r. release Barabbas.   15:11
r. rejoice, your names. Luke 10:20
r. blessed are they that hear. 11:28
but r. give alms of such things as. 41
but r. seek ye kingdom of God. 12:31
give peace ? Nay r. division.   51
will not r. say unto him.   17:8
justified r. than the other.   18:14
men loved darkness r. than light.
       John 3:19
obey God r. than men.   Acts 5:29
not r. let us do evil, that. Rom 3:8
yea, r. that is risen again.   8:34
r. through their fall salvation. 11:11
avenge not, but r. give place. 12:19
another, but judge this r.   14:13
puffed up, and have not r. 1 Cor 5:2
why do ye not r. take wrong ?   6:7
if made free, use it r.   7:21
over you, are not we r.?   9:12
desire r. that ye may.   14:1, 5
had r. speak five words with my. 19
so that ye ought r. to forgive him.
       2 Cor 2:7
ministration of the Spirit be r.   3:8
willing r. to be absent from.   5:8
therefore I will r. glory in.   12:9
God, or r. known of God. Gal 4:9
steal no more, but r. let. Eph 4:28
not named, but r. giving of.   5:4
with works of darkness, but r.   11
r. to the furtherance of. Phil 1:12
minister questions r.   1 Tim 1:4
exercise thyself r. to godliness. 4:7
but r. do them service.   6:2
yet for love's sake I r. Philem 9
choosing r. to suffer.   Heb 11:25
r. be in subjection to the.   12:9

but let it r. be healed.   Heb 12:13
but I beseech you the r. to.   13:19
r. give diligence to.   2 Pet 1:10

rattleth
quiver r. against him.   Job 39:23

rattling
noise of the r. of wheels. Nah 3:2

raven, -s
Noah sent forth a r.   Gen 8:7
every r. is unclean.   Lev 11:15
     Deut 14:14
I have commanded the r. 1 Ki 17:4
and the r. brought Elijah bread.   6
who provideth for the r. his food ?
     Job 38:41; Ps 147:9
the r. of the valley.   Pr 30:17
his locks bushy, and black as a r.
       S of S 5:11
the owl and the r. shall. Isa 34:11
consider the r.: they.   Luke 12:24

ravening
upon me as a r. lion.   Ps 23:13
like a roaring lion r.   Ezek 22:25
her princes are like wolves r., the 27
they are r. wolves.   Mat 7:15
inward part is full of r. Luke 11:39*

ravenous
r. beast shall go up.   Isa 35:9
calling a r. bird from the east. 46:11
give thee to the r. birds. Ezek 39:4

ravin
shall r. as a wolf.   Gen 49:27
filled his dens with r.   Nah 2:12

ravished
and be thou r. always.   Pr 5:19
why wilt thou be r. with a strange? 20
thou hast r. my heart.   S of S 4:9
the wives of Babylon shall be r.
       Isa 13:16
r. the women in Zion.   Lam 5:11
Jerusalem shall be r.   Zech 14:2

raw
eat not of it r. nor sodden. Ex 12:9
if there be quick r. flesh. Lev 13:10
when the r. flesh appeareth.   14
priest see r. flesh, for r. flesh is. 15
have sodden flesh, but r. 1 Sam 2:15

razor
shall no r. come upon his head.
     Num 6:5; Judg 13:5; 16:17
       1 Sam 1:11
thy tongue like a sharp r.   Ps 52:2
shave with a r. hired.   Isa 7:20
take thee a barber's r.   Ezek 5:1

reach
a tower whose top may r. Gen 11:4
linen breeches shall r.   Ex 28:42
your threshing shall r. to the vintage,
   and your vintage shall r. Lev 26:5
border shall r. to the sea. Num 34:11
head r. unto the clouds. Job 20:6
he shall r. even to the neck. Isa 8:8
breath shall r. to the midst.   30:28
thy plants r. to the sea.   Jer 48:32
mountains shall r. to Azal. Zech 14:5
r. hither thy finger, and r. thy hand.
       John 20:27
a measure to r. even.   2 Cor 10:13

reached
the ladder's top r. to. Gen 28:12
he r. her parched corn. Ruth 2:14
the tree grew, and the height thereof
   r. to heaven.   Dan 4:11, 20
as though we r. not to. 2 Cor 10:14
Babylon's sins have r.   Rev 18:5

reacheth
slain in a rage that r. up. 2 Chr 28:9
thy faithfulness r. to the.   Ps 36:5
thy truth r. to the clouds.   108:4
yea, she r. her hands to.   Pr 31:20
sword r. unto the soul.   Jer 4:10
because it r. to thine heart.   18
judgement r. to heaven.   51:9
greatness r. to heaven.   Dan 4:22

reaching
r. forth to those things. Phil 3:13*

read
he r. in the audience.   Ex 24:7
he r. all the words of the law.
       Josh 8:34, 35

when king had r. letter. *2 Ki* 5:7
Hezekiah received and r. the. 19:14
Shaphan r. book of law. 22:8, 10
Josiah r. in their ears all the words.
   23:2; *2 Chr* 34:30
curses in the book r. *2 Chr* 34:24
letter hath been plainly r. *Ezra* 4:18
king's letter was r. they made. 23
he r. the book of the law before the
   water gate. *Neh* 8:3, 8; 13:1
unto the last day he r. the law. 8:18
in their place and r. in the law. 9:3
book of the records was r. *Esth* 6:1
the letter, and r. it. *Isa* 37:14
Zephaniah the priest r. *Jer* 29:29
then r. Baruch the words of. 36:10
Jehudi r. it in ears of the king. 21
when he r. three or four leaves. 23
have ye not r.? *Mat* 12:3; 19:4
  21:16; 22:31; *Mark* 2:25; 12:10
   26; *Luke* 6:3
this title r. many of. *John* 19:20
the eunuch r. Esaias. *Acts* 8:28
place of scripture which he r. 32
prophets are r. every sabbath day.
   13:27; 15:21
which when they had r. 15:31
when the governor had r. 23:34
our epistle, known and r. *2 Cor* 3:2
when Moses is r. the vail is upon. 15
when this epistle is r. *Col* 4:16
that this epistle be r. *1 Thes* 5:27

read
the king shall r. therein. *Deut* 17:19
thou shalt r. this law before. 31:11
r. this, I pray thee. *Isa* 29:11, 12
book of the Lord and r. 34:16
go and r. in the roll thou. *Jer* 36:6
they said, Sit down now and r. 15
comest to Babylon and shalt r. 51:61
whosoever shall r. writing. *Dan* 5:7
king's wise men, they could not r. 8
gifts to thyself, yet I will r. 17
did ye never r. in the ? *Mat* 21:42
and stood up for to r. *Luke* 4:16
heard him r. Esaias. *Acts* 8:30
write none other things than what ye
  r. *2 Cor* 1:13
ye r. ye may understand. *Eph* 3:4
likewise r. the epistle. *Col* 4:16
worthy to r. the book. *Rev* 5:4

readest
written in law, how r.? *Luke* 10:26
Philip said, Understandest thou what
  thou r.? *Acts* 8:30

readeth
he may run that r. it. *Hab* 2:2
abomination, whoso r. let him understand. *Mat* 24:15; *Mark* 13:14
blessed is he that r. and. *Rev* 1:3

readiness
received the word with r. *Acts* 17:11
there was a r. to will. *2 Cor* 8:11
having a r. to revenge all. 10:6

reading
them to understand the r. *Neh* 8:8
r. in book of words of the. *Jer* 36:8
hast made an end of r. this. 51:63
after the r. of the law. *Acts* 13:15
vail untaken away in r. *2 Cor* 3:14
give attendance to r. *1 Tim* 4:13

ready
be almost r. to stone me. *Ex* 17:4
be r. against the third. 19:11, 15
be r. in the morning, and. 34:2
we will go r. armed. *Num* 32:17
r. to go up into the hill. *Deut* 1:41
a Syrian r. to perish was my. 26:5
the city, but be ye all r. *Josh* 8:4
five sheep r. dressed. *1 Sam* 25:18
thy servants are r. to. *2 Sam* 15:15
thou hast no tidings r.? 18:22
Ezra was a r. scribe in. *Ezra* 7:6
art a God r. to pardon. *Neh* 9:17
r. against that day. *Esth* 3:14; 8:13
who are r. to raise up. *Job* 3:8
is r. to slip with his feet. 12:5
day of darkness is r. at hand. 15:23
prevail as a king r. to battle. 24
are r. to become heaps. 28
the graves are r. for me. 17:1
and destruction shall be r. 18:12

3-4

blessing of him r. to perish. *Job* 29:13
my belly is r. to burst like. 32:19
for I am r. to halt, and. *Ps* 38:17
tongue is pen of a r. writer. 45:1
art good, and r. to forgive. 86:5
I am afflicted, and r. to die. 88:15
to deliver those that are r. *Pr* 24:11
drink to him that is r. to. 31:6
be more r. to hear than. *Eccl* 5:1*
shall come who were r. to perish.
   Isa 27:13
shall be as a breach r. to fall. 30:13
stammerers be r. to speak. 32:4
Lord was r. to save me: we. 38:20
It is r. for the soldering. 41:7
as if he were r. to destroy. 51:13
now if ye be r. to fall. *Dan* 3:15
and all things are r. *Mat* 22:4
then saith he, The wedding is r. 8
   Luke 14:17
therefore be ye also r. *Mat* 24:44
   Luke 12:40
they that were r. went in. *Mat* 25:10
spirit is r. but the flesh. *Mark* 14:38*
servant sick, and r. to die. *Luke* 7:2*
Lord, I am r. to go with. 22:33
your time is alway r. *John* 7:6
to them, r. to depart. *Acts* 20:7*
I am r. not to be bound only. 21:13
come near, are r. to kill him. 23:15
are r., looking for a promise. 21
r. to preach the gospel. *Rom* 1:15
of your r. mind. *2 Cor* 8:19
that Achaia was r. a year ago. 9:2
that, as I said, ye may be r. 3
same might be r. as a matter. 5
third time I am r. to come. 12:14
in good works, r. to. *1 Tim* 6:18
now r. to be offered. *2 Tim* 4:6*
put them in mind to be r. to. *Tit* 3:1
waxeth old, is r. to vanish. *Heb* 8:13*
r. to be revealed in. *1 Pet* 1:5
be r. always to give an answer. 3:15
account to him that is r. to. 4:5
not filthy lucre, but of a r. mind. 5:2
things that are r. to die. *Rev* 3:2
woman which was r. to be. 12:4*
  see made, make

realm
the r. of Jehoshaphat. *2 Chr* 20:30
r. who are minded to go. *Ezra* 7:13
there be wrath against the r.? 23
better than all in his r. *Dan* 1:20
thought to set him over the r. 6:3
Darius, king over the r. of the. 9:1
he shall stir up all against r. 11:2

reap
and when ye r. . . . shall not wholly
  r. the. *Lev* 19:9; 23:10, 22
of itself thou shalt not r. 25:5
shall neither sow nor r. 11
eyes be on the field they r. *Ruth* 2:9
set your servants to r. *1 Sam* 8:12
in third year sow and r. *2 Ki* 19:29
   Isa 37:30
wickedness r. the same. *Job* 4:8
they r. every one his corn. 24:6*
in tears shall r. in joy. *Ps* 126:5
iniquity, shall r. vanity. *Pr* 22:8
the clouds, shall not r. *Eccl* 11:4
wheat, but shall r. thorns. *Jer* 12:13
shall r. the whirlwind. *Hos* 8:7
righteousness, r. in mercy. *Mi* 6:15
sow, but shalt not r. 6:15
the fowls of the air r. not. *Mat* 6:26
   Luke 12:24
thou knewest I r. where. *Mat* 25:26
r. whereon ye bestowed. *John* 4:38
if we shall r. your carnal. *1 Cor* 9:11
sparingly shall r. sparingly . . . bountifully shall r. bountifully. *2 Cor* 9:6
man soweth, that shall he r. *Gal* 6:7
of the flesh r. corruption . . . of the
  Spirit r. life everlasting. 8
in due season we shall r. if we. 9
in thy sickle, and r.: for the time is
  come for thee to r. *Rev* 14:15

reaped
wickedness, ye r. iniquity. *Hos* 10:13
labourers, which r. down . . . cries
  of them which r. are. *Jas* 5:4
sickle, the earth was r. *Rev* 14:16

reaper
the plowman shall overtake the r.
   Amos 9:13

reapers
Ruth gleaned after the r. *Ruth* 2:3
Boaz said to the r., The Lord be. 4
let me glean after the r. 7
to his father to the r. *2 Ki* 4:18
to the r., Gather the tares. *Mat* 13:30
enemy is devil, and r. are the. 39

reapest
riddance when thou r. *Lev* 23:22
r. that thou didst not. *Luke* 19:21

reapeth
harvestman r. the ears. *Isa* 17:5
r. receiveth wages, that both he that
  soweth and he that r. *John* 4:36
one soweth and another r. 37

reaping
of Beth-shemesh were r. *1 Sam* 6:13
hard man, r. where thou hast not.
   Mat 25:24; *Luke* 19:22

reason
[1] *That faculty whereby we judge
of things,* Dan 4:36. [2] *Proof,
ground, or argument,* 1 Pet 3:15.
[3] *To dispute, or argue,* Mat 16:8;
Mark 8:16.
this is the r. of the levy. *1 Ki* 9:15
that can render a r. *Pr* 26:16
I applied to search the r. *Eccl* 7:25
same time my r. returned. *Dan* 4:36
It is not r. that we should leave the
  word of God. *Acts* 6:2
O ye Jews, r. would that I. 18:14
that asketh you a r. of. *1 Pet* 3:15

by reason
plenty not known *by* r. *Gen* 41:31
land of Canaan fainted *by* r. 47:13
Israel sighed *by* r. of the. *Ex* 2:23
I heard their cry *by* r. of their. 3:7
corrupted *by* r. of the flies. 8:24
unclean *by* r. of a dead body.
   Num 9:10
hallowed things given *by* r. of. 18:8
shall bear no sin *by* r. of it. 32
afraid *by* r. of the fire. *Deut* 5:5
shoes are become old *by* r. *Josh* 9:13
for their groanings *by* r. *Judg* 2:18
Ahijah's eyes were set *by* r. of age.
   1 Ki 14:4
minister *by* r. of cloud. *2 Chr* 5:14
be not afraid *by* r. of this great. 20:15
by r. of the sickness. 21:15, 19
blackish, *by* r. of the ice. *Job* 6:16
is dim *by* r. of sorrow. 17:7
by r. of his highness I could. 31:23
by r. of oppressions . . . they cry out
by r. of the arm. 35:9
we cannot order speech *by* r. 37:19
by r. of breakings they purify. 41:25
roared *by* r. of disquietness. *Ps* 38:8
blasphemeth *by* r. of enemy. 44:16
man that shouteth *by* r. of. 78:65
mourneth *by* r. of affliction. 88:9
if *by* r. of strength they be. 90:10
by r. of my groaning my. 102:5
not plow *by* r. of cold. *Pr* 20:4
by r. of the inhabitants. *Isa* 49:19
by r. of many waters. *Ezek* 19:10
terrors *by* r. of sword shall. 21:12*
by r. of the abundance of his. 26:10
Tyrus corrupted *by* r. of thy. 28:17
by r. of transgression. *Dan* 8:12
I cried *by* r. of my affliction.
   Jonah 2:2
noise *by* r. of multitude. *Mi* 2:12
sea arose *by* r. of a. *John* 6:18
by r. of him many believed. 12:11
by r. of him who subjected same.
   Rom 8:20
by r. of the glory that. *2 Cor* 3:10
by r. hereof he ought to. *Heb* 5:3
who *by* r. of use have senses. 14
to continue *by* r. of death. 7:23
by r. of whom the way of. *2 Pet* 2:2
by r. of the other voices. *Rev* 8:13
darkened *by* r. of the smoke. 9:2
rich *by* r. of the costliness. 18:19

reason, *verb*
that I may r. with you. *1 Sam* 12:7*
my words to r. with you. *Job* 9:14

and desire to r. with God. *Job 13:3*
he r. with unprofitable talk? *15:3*
and let us r. together. *Isa 1:18*
why r. ye among yourselves?
 Mat 16:8; Mark 2:8; 8:17
Pharisees began to r. *Luke 5:21*
Jesus said to them, What r. ye? *22*

reasonable
living sacrifice, which is your r. service. *Rom 12:1†*

reasoned
and they r. among. *Mat 16:7; 21:15*
 Mark 8:16; 11:31; Luke 20:5
perceived that they so r. *Mark 2:8*
husbandmen r. among. *Luke 20:14**
while they r. Jesus himself. *24:15*
three sabbaths Paul r. *Acts 17:2*
he r. in the synagogue every. *18:4*
Paul r. with Jews at Ephesus. *19*
as he r. of righteousness and. *24:25*

reasoning
hear my r. and hearken. *Job 13:6*
were certain scribes r. *Mark 2:6*
heard them r. together. *12:28*
arose a r. among them. *Luke 9:46*
Jews departed, and had great r.
 Acts 28:29

reasons
and gave ear to your r. *Job 32:11*
Bring forth your r., saith. *Isa 41:21*

Rebekah
Bethuel begat R. *Gen 22:23*
R. came to. *24:15*
R. is before thee. *51*
they sent away R. *59*
they blessed R. *60*
Isaac took R. *67; 25:20*
R. loved Jacob. *25:28*
lest men kill me for R. *26:7*
a grief of mind to R. *35*
words of Esau were told to R. *27:42*
that he was R.'s son. *29:12*
R.'s nurse died. *35:8*
Isaac and R. his wife. *49:31*
R. had conceived by. *Rom 9:10*

rebel
r. not against the Lord. *Num 14:9*
doth r. he shall die. *Josh 1:18*
an altar that ye might r. *22:16*
seeing that ye r. to-day against. *18*
r. not against the Lord, nor r. *19*
God forbid that we should r. *29*
and not r. against Lord. *1 Sam 12:14*
not obey the Lord, but r. *15*
will ye r. against the king? *Neh 2:19*
thou and the Jews think to r. *6:6*
that r. against the light. *Job 24:13*
if ye refuse and r. *Isa 1:20*
assemble for corn, and r. *Hos 7:14*

rebelled
thirteenth year they r. *Gen 14:4*
ye r. against my words. *Num 20:24*
 27:14; Deut 1:26, 43; 9:23
so Israel r. against the house of.
 1 Ki 12:19; 2 Chr 10:19
Moab r. against. *2 Ki 1:1, 3, 5, 7*
Hezekiah r. against Assyria. *18:7*
Jehoiakim r. against. *24:1*
Zedekiah r. *20; 2 Chr 36:13*
 Jer 52:3
Jeroboam hath r. *2 Chr 13:6*
were disobedient, and r. *Neh 9:26*
they have r. against thee. *Ps 5:10*
r. not against his word. *105:28*
because they r. against the. *107:11*
children, and they have r. *Isa 1:2*
r. and vexed his Holy Spirit. *63:10*
I have r. *Lam 1:18*
I have grievously r. *20*
r.: thou hast not pardoned. *3:42*
to a nation that hath r. *Ezek 2:3*
r. in sending his ambassadors. *17:15*
but they r. against me. *20:8, 13, 21*
we have r. by departing. *Dan 9:5*
mercies, though we have r. against. *9*
Samaria hath r. against. *Hos 13:16*

rebellest
On whom dost thou trust, that thou
r.? *2 Ki 18:20; Isa 36:5*

rebellion
know thy r. and thy stiff. *Deut 31:27*
shall know if it be in r. *Josh 22:22*

r. is as the sin of. *1 Sam 15:23*
that r. hath been made. *Ezra 4:19*
and in their r. appointed. *Neh 9:17*
addeth r. unto his sin. *Job 34:37*
evil man seeketh only r. *Pr 17:11*
thou hast taught r. *Jer 28:16; 29:32*

rebellious
r. against Lord. *Deut 9:7, 24; 31:27*
a stubborn and r. son. *21:18*
this our son is stubborn and r. *20*
the perverse r. woman. *1 Sam 20:30*
building the r. and. *Ezra 4:12, 15*
let not the r. exalt. *Ps 66:7*
r. dwell in a dry land. *68:6*
yea, for the r. also. *18*
and a r. generation. *78:8*
thy princes are r. *Isa 1:23*
woe to the r. children, saith. *30:1*
this is a r. people. *9*
I was not r. *50:5*
spread out my hands to a r. *65:2*
hath been r. against me. *Jer 4:17*
hath a revolting and r. heart. *5:23*
I send thee to a r. nation. *Ezek 2:3*
they are a r. house. *5, 6, 7; 3:9, 26*
 27; 12:2, 3
be not thou r. like that r. house. *2:8*
in the midst of a r. house. *12:2*
say now to the r. house. *17:12; 44:6*
parable to the r. house. *24:3*

rebels
for a token against the r. *Num 17:10*
said, Hear now, ye r. *20:10*
from among you the r. *Ezek 20:38*

rebuke, substantive
shall send on thee r. *Deut 28:20*
this is a day of r. *2 Ki 19:3*
 Isa 37:3
at thy r., at the blast of. *Ps 18:15*
at thy r. both chariot and. *76:6*
they perish at the r. of thy. *80:16*
at thy r. they fled, they. *104:7*
scorner heareth not r. *Pr 13:1*
but the poor heareth not r. *8**
r. is better than secret love. *27:5*
better to hear r. of. *Eccl 7:5*
the r. of his people shall. *Isa 25:8*
thousand shall flee at r. of one, at r.
 of five shall ye flee. *30:17*
behold, at my r. I dry up the. *50:2*
full of the r. of thy God. *51:20*
to render his r. with flames. *66:15*
for thy sake I suffered r. *Jer 15:15*
be desolate in the day of r. *Hos 5:9*
without r. in midst of a. *Phil 2:15*

rebuke
any wise r. thy neighbour. *Lev 19:17*
glean them, and r. her not. *Ruth 2:16*
God look thereon, and r. *1 Chr 12:17*
O Lord, r. me not. *Ps 6:1; 38:1*
r. the company of spearmen. *68:30*
r. a wise man, and he. *Pr 9:8*
to them that r. him shall. *24:25*
he shall r. many nations. *Isa 2:4**
 *Mi 4:3**
but God shall r. them. *Isa 17:13*
not wroth with, nor r. thee. *54:9*
Lord r. thee, even the Lord that hath
 chosen Jerusalem, r. *Zech 3:2*
I will r. the devourer. *Mal 3:11*
Peter began to r. him. *Mat 16:22*
 Mark 8:32
brother trespass, r. him. *Luke 17:3*
said, Master, r. thy disciples. *19:39*
r. not an elder, but. *1 Tim 5:1*
them that sin, r. before all. *20**
r., exhort with all long. *2 Tim 4:2*
r. them sharply. *Tit 1:13; 2:15*
said, The Lord r. thee. *Jude 9*
as many as I love, I r. *Rev 3:19*

rebuked
God hath seen and r. *Gen 31:42*
his father r. him, and said. *37:10*
and I r. the nobles and. *Neh 5:7**
hast r. the heathen, thou. *Ps 9:5*
he r. the Red sea also, and it. *106:9*
thou hast r. the proud that. *119:21*
he r. the wind. *Mat 8:26*
 Mark 4:39; Luke 8:24
Jesus r. the devil; and. *Mat 17:18*
his disciples r. them. *19:13*
 Mark 10:13; Luke 18:15

multitude r. blind men. *Mat 20:31*
and Jesus r. him. *Mark 1:25; 9:25*
 Luke 4:35; 9:42
Jesus r. Peter, saying. *Mark 8:33*
over her and r. the fever. *Luke 4:39*
turned, and r. James and John. *9:55*
went before r. the blind man. *18:39*
thief answering r. him. *23:40*
when thou art r. of him. *Heb 12:5*
but Balaam was r. for. *2 Pet 2:16*

rebuker
though I have been a r. of. *Hos 5:2*

rebukes
when thou with r. dost. *Ps 39:11*
execute judgements in furious r.
 Ezek 5:15; 25:17

rebuketh
he that r. a wicked man. *Pr 9:7*
he that r. a man, shall find. *28:23*
hate him that r. in gate. *Amos 5:10*
r. sea, and maketh it dry. *Nah 1:4*

rebuking
foundations of world discovered at
 the r. of the Lord. *2 Sam 22:16*
r. them, suffered them. *Luke 4:41*

recall
this I r. to mind. *Lam 3:21*

receipt
Matthew sitting at the r. *Mat 9:9**
 Mark 2:14; Luke 5:27**

receive
[1] *To take what is given, paid, or
put into one's hands,* 2 Sam 18:12;
2 Ki 5:26. [2] *To entertain, lodge,
or harbour,* Acts 28:2, 7. [3] *To
bear with, or suffer,* 2 Cor 11:16.
[4] *To hearken to,* Pr 2:1. [5] *To
believe,* Mat 11:14; John 1:12.
[6] *To admit one to be a member
of the church,* Rom 14:1. [7] *To
be endued with,* Acts 1:8.
thou shalt r. the wave. *Ex 29:25*
your tithes which you r. *Num 18:28*
shall r. of thy words. *Deut 33:3*
which thou shalt r. of. *1 Sam 10:4*
though I should r. a thousand
 shekels. *2 Sam 18:12*
thou shalt r. the cedar. *1 Ki 5:9*
shall we r. good of God? *Job 2:10*
shall I r. of the Almighty. *27:13*
Lord will r. my prayer. *Ps 6:9*
he shall r. the blessing from. *24:5*
my soul, for he shall r. me. *49:15*
afterward r. me to glory. *73:24*
I shall r. the congregation. *75:2*
if thou wilt r. my words. *Pr 2:1*
the wise in heart will r. *10:8*
I r. comfort in these? *Isa 57:6**
thou shalt r. sisters. *Ezek 16:61*
ye shall r. of me gifts. *Dan 2:6*
Ephraim shall r. shame. *Hos 10:6*
r. of you his standing. *Mi 1:11**
thou wilt r. instruction. *Zeph 3:7*
shall r. a prophet's reward . . . r. a
 righteous man's. *Mat 10:41*
blind r. their sight, lame walk. *11:5*
if ye will r. it, this is Elias. *14*
shall r. one such little child. *18:5*
 Mark 9:37; Luke 9:48
said, All men cannot r. *Mat 19:11*
r. an hundredfold. *29; Mark 10:30*
is right, that shall ye r. *Mat 20:7*
ye ask, believing, ye shall r. *21:22*
that they might r. fruits of it. *34*
ye shall r. the greater damnation.
 23:14; Mark 12:40; Luke 20:47
r. the word with gladness.
 Mark 4:16; Luke 8:13
as hear the word and r. *Mark 4:20*
Lord, that I might r. my sight. *10:51*
 Luke 18:41
pray, believe that ye r. *Mark 11:24*
might r. from the husbandmen. *12:2*
city ye enter, and they r. *Luke 10:8*
may r. me into their houses. *16:4*
may r. you into everlasting. *9*
for we r. the due reward of. *23:41*
own name, him ye will r. *John 5:43*
can ye believe, which r. honour? *44*
on sabbath r. circumcision. *7:23*
Spirit, which they that believe on him
 should r.: Holy Ghost was not. *39*

I will come again, and r. *John* 14:3
r. of mine, and shew it to you. 16:14
ask and ye shall r. that your joy. 24
shall r. power after that. *Acts* 1:8
ye shall r. gift of Holy Ghost. 2:38
Jesus, whom heavens must r. 3:21
they might r. the Holy Ghost. 8:15
hands, may r. the Holy Ghost. 19
that he might r. his sight. 9:12
that thou mightest r. thy sight. 17
shall r. remission of sins. 10:43
that they may r. forgiveness. 26:18
r. abundance of grace. *Rom* 5:17
resist shall r. to themselves. 13:2
that ye r. her in the Lord, as. 16:2
shall r. his own reward. *1 Cor* 3:8
if his work abide, he shall r. 14
if thou didst r. it, why dost thou ? 4:7
the church may r. edifying. 14:5
that every one may r. *2 Cor* 5:10
touch not unclean thing, and I will r.
6:17
r. damage by us in nothing. 7:9
that we would r. the gift. 8:4
if ye r. another spirit ye have. 11:4
that we might r. promise. *Gal* 3:14
that we might r. the adoption. 4:5
the same shall he r. of. *Eph* 6:8
ye shall r. the reward of. *Col* 3:24
he shall r. for the wrong he. 25
shouldest r. him for ever. *Philem* 15
sons of Levi, who r. office. *Heb* 7:5
here men that die r. tithes. 8
which are called might r. promise.
9:15; 10:36
after r. for an inheritance. 11:8
think he shall r. any thing. *Jas* 1:7
he shall r. the crown of life. 12
shall r. greater condemnation. 3:1
until he r. early and latter rain. 5:7
ye shall r. a crown of glory. *1 Pet* 5:4
shall r. the reward of. *2 Pet* 2:13
we ask, we r. of him. *1 John* 3:22
if we r. the witness of men. 5:9
that we r. a full reward. *2 John* 8
if any man r. his mark in. *Rev* 14:9
but r. power as kings one hour. 17:12

receive, *imperatively*
then r. my present at. *Gen* 33:10
r. I pray thee, the law. *Job* 22:22
and r. my sayings. *Pr* 4:10
r. my instruction. 8:10; 19:20
let your ear r. the word. *Jer* 9:20
all my words r. in thine. *Ezek* 3:10
him, r. us graciously. *Hos* 14:2*
that is able, let him r. it. *Mat* 19:12
Jesus saith, R. thy sight. *Luke* 18:42
Acts 22:13
R. ye the Holy Ghost. *John* 20:22
Lord Jesus, r. my spirit. *Acts* 7:59
weak in the faith r. ye. *Rom* 14:1
r. ye one another, as Christ. 15:7
r. us, we have wronged. *2 Cor* 7:2
yet as a fool r. me. 11:16
r. him in the Lord with. *Phil* 2:29
Marcus, if he come, r. him. *Col* 4:10
r. him that is mine own. *Philem* 12*
if thou count me a partner, r.'him. 17
r. with meekness. *Jas* 1:21

receive, *negatively*
said, I will r. none. *2 Ki* 5:16
r. no more money of your. 12:7
shall we r. good, and shall we not r.
evil ? *Job* 2:10
might not hear nor r. instruction.
Jer 17:23
will ye not r. instruction to ? 35:13
r. no more reproach of. *Ezek* 36:30
not r. you nor hear. *Mat* 10:14
Mark 6:11; *Luke* 9:5
shall not r. the kingdom of God as a.
Mark 10:15; *Luke* 18:17
not r. him, because his. *Luke* 9:53
and they r. you not, go into. 10:10
who shall not r. manifold. 18:30
and ye r. not our witness. *John* 3:11
a man can r. nothing, except it. 27
I r. not testimony from man. 5:34
I r. not honour from men. 41
in my Father's name, ye r. me not. 43
whom the world cannot r. 14:17
will not r. thy testimony. *Acts* 22:18
that thou didst not r.? *1 Cor* 4:7

that ye r. not the grace. *2 Cor* 6:1
against an elder r. not. *1 Tim* 5:19
ye ask and r. not, because. *Jas* 4:3
r. him not into your house. *2 John* 10
neither doth he himself r. *3 John* 10
ye r. not of her plagues. *Rev* 18:4

to receive
to r. brother's blood. *Gen* 4:11
to r. his pledge from woman's. 38:20
his pans to r. his ashes. *Ex* 27:3
gone up to r. the tables. *Deut* 9:9
altar before the Lord was too little
to r. *1 Ki* 8:64; *2 Chr* 7:7
is it a time to r. money, to r. garments ? *2 Ki* 5:26
priest consented to r. no more. 12:8
to r. instruction of wisdom. *Pr* 1:3
refused to r. correction. *Jer* 5:3
not hearkened to r. instruction. 32:33
not room enough to r. it. *Mal* 3:10
to r. it, let him r. it. *Mat* 19:12
no room to r. them. *Mark* 2:2
of whom ye hope to r. *Luke* 6:34
nobleman went to r. for. 19:12
not lawful for us to r. *Acts* 16:21
the disciples to r. him. 18:27
blessed to give than to r. 20:35
therefore ought to r. such. *3 John* 8
worthy, O Lord, to r. glory. *Rev* 4:11
worthy is Lamb to r. power. 5:12
causeth to r. a mark in their. 13:16

received
Isaac r. the same year an. *Gen* 26:12
and Aaron r. them at. *Ex* 32:4
and they r. of Moses all the. 36:3
Miriam be r. in again. *Num* 12:14
r. commandment to bless. 23:20
two tribes and half r. 34:14, 15
put to the inheritance of the tribe
whereunto they are r. 36:3, 4
the Gadites have r. their. *Josh* 13:8
not r. their inheritance. 18:2
would not have r. burnt offering.
Judg 13:23
have I r. any bribe ? *1 Sam* 12:3*
David r. of Abigail that she. 25:35
merchants r. linen yarn at a price.
1 Ki 10:28; *2 Chr* 1:16
Hezekiah r. the letter. *2 Ki* 19:14
Isa 37:14
then David r. them. *1 Chr* 12:18
Mordecai r. it not. *Esth* 4:4
mine ear r. a little thereof. *Job* 4:12
thou hast r. gifts for. *Ps* 68:18
it, and r. instruction. *Pr* 24:32
hath r. of the Lord's hand. *Isa* 40:2
your children, they r. no. *Jer* 2:30
not r. usury nor increase. *Ezek* 18:17
she r. not correction. *Zeph* 3:2
freely ye r., freely give. *Mat* 10:8
which r. seed by the way side. 13:19
r. seed into stony. 20, 22, 23
they that r. tribute money. 17:24
they r. every man a penny. 20:9, 10
and when they had r. it, they. 11
immediately their eyes r. sight. 34
r. five talents. 25:16
r. two talents. 17
had r. one talent. 18
should have r. mine own with. 27
things which they r. *Mark* 7:4
he r. his sight. 10:52; *Luke* 18:43
Acts 9:18
myrrh: but he r. it not. *Mark* 15:23
he was r. up into heaven. 16:19
Acts 1:9
woe to rich, for ye have r. *Luke* 6:24
the people gladly r. him. 8:40
r. them and spake to them. 9:11
come, that he should be r. up. 51
Martha r. him into her house. 10:38
because he hath r. him safe. 15:27
Zacchaeus came down and r. 19:6
returned, having r. kingdom. 15
own, his own r. him not. *John* 1:11
to as many as r. him, to them. 12
out of fulness have all we r. grace. 16
the hath r. testimony, hath. 3:33
Galileans r. him, having seen. 4:45
willingly r. him into the ship. 6:21
washed, and I r. sight. 9:11
how he had r. his sight. 15

that he had r. his sight . . . him that
had r. his sight. *John* 9:18
this commandment I r. of my. 10:18
he then having r. the sop. 13:30
words, and they have r. them. 17:8
Judas having r. band of men. 18:3
when Jesus had r. vinegar. 19:30
and a cloud r. him out. *Acts* 1:9
and having r. of the Father. 2:33
they that gladly r. his word. 41
feet and ancle bones r. 3:7
who r. the lively oracles to. 7:38
who have r. law by angels, and. 53
Samaria had r. the word of. 8:14
them, they r. the Holy Ghost. 17
r. meat, he was strengthened. 9:19
the vessel was r. again up. 10:16
which have r. the Holy Ghost. 47
that Gentiles had r. the word. 11:1
they were r. of the church. 15:4
having r. such charge, thrust. 16:24
hither also; whom Jason hath r. 17:7
Bereans r. the word with all. 11
have ye r. the Holy Ghost ? 19:2
ministry which I have r. of. 20:24
brethren r. us gladly. 21:17
from which I r. letters to. 22:5
having r. authority from the. 26:10
barbarians kindled a fire and r. 28:2
Publius r. us. 7
we neither r. letters out of Judaea. 21
Paul r. all that came. 30
by whom we have r. grace. *Rom* 1:5
r. the sign of circumcision. 4:11
by whom we have now r. the. 5:11
Spirit of bondage . . . but ye have r.
Spirit of adoption. 8:15
for God hath r. him. 14:3
another, as Christ also r. us. 15:7
have r. not the spirit of. *1 Cor* 2:12
as if thou hadst not r. it ? 4:7
I r. of the Lord, that which. 11:23
which also ye have r. 15:1
which I r. 3
as we have r. mercy. *2 Cor* 4:1
and trembling ye r. him. 7:15
spirit, which ye have not r. 11:4
five times r. I forty stripes. 24
gospel than that ye have r. *Gal* 1:9
I r. it not of man, neither was. 12
r. ye the Spirit by works of the ? 3:2
but r. me as an angel of God. 4:14
things ye have r. and seen. *Phil* 4:9
as ye have r. Christ, so. *Col* 2:6
whom, ye r. commandments. 4:10
ministry thou hast r. in Lord. 17
having r. the word in. *1 Thes* 1:6
r. word, ye r. it not as word. 2:13
as ye have r. of us how ye ought. 4:1
because they r. not the love of truth.
2 Thes 2:10
tradition which he r. of us. 3:6
in world, r. up into glory. *1 Tim* 3:16
God hath created to be r. 4:3
creature is good, if it be r. with. 4
transgression r. just recompence of.
Heb 2:2
r. tithes of Abraham and. 7:6*
under it the people r. the law. 11
sin wilfully after we have r. 10:26
faith Sarai r. strength to. 11:11
died, not having r. the promises. 13
he that r. promises offered up. 17
from whence also he r. him in. 19
had r. the spies. 31; *Jas* 2:25
women r. their dead. *Heb* 11:35
all having obtained a good report
through faith. r. not the promise. 39
vain conversation r. by tradition.
1 Pet 1:18*
as every one hath r. the gift. 4:10
r. from God the Father. *2 Pet* 1:17
anointing ye have r. *1 John* 2:27
as we have r. a command. *2 John* 4
even as I r. of my Father. *Rev* 2:27
how thou hast r. and heard. 3:3
who have r. no kingdom as yet. 17:12
had r. the mark of the beast. 19:20
had not r. the mark, reigned. 20:4

receivedst
thy lifetime r. thy good. *Luke* 16:25

receiver
scribe ? where is the r.? *Isa* 33:18*

receiveth
no man that r. me to. *Judg 19:18*
what r. he of thine hand ? *Job 35:7*
wise is instructed, he r. knowledge.
　　　　　　　　　　Pr 21:11
r. gifts, overthroweth it. 29:4*
that r. not correction. *Jer 7:28*
or r. offering with good. *Mal 2:13*
every one that asketh, r. *Mat 7:8*
　　　　　　　　　Luke 11:10
he that r. you r. me. and he that r. me
　　r. him that. *Mat 10:40; John 13:20*
he that r. a prophet . . . he that r. a
　righteous man. *Mat 10:41*
heareth word, and anon r. it. 13:20
little child in my name, r. me. 18:5
whoso shall receive me, r. not me,
　but him. *Mark 9:37; Luke 9:48*
this man r. sinners. *Luke 15:2*
no man r. his testimony. *John 3:32*
he that reapeth r. wages, and. 4:36
that rejecteth me, and r. not. 12:48
but one r. the prize. *1 Cor 9:24*
for the earth r. blessing. *Heb 6:7*
tithes, but there he r. them. 7:8
Levi who r. tithes, payed tithes. 9
every son whom he r. 12:6
saving he that r. it. *Rev 2:17*
whosoever r. the mark of. 14:11

receiveth not
r. not the things of God. *1 Cor 2:14*
Diotrephes r. us not. *3 John 9*

receiving
spared Naaman, in not r. *2 Ki 5:20*
and r. a commandment. *Acts 17:15*
r. in themselves that. *Rom 1:27*
shall r. of them be but life ? 11:15
concerning giving and r. *Phil 4:15*
we r. a kingdom which. *Heb 12:28*
r. the end of your faith. *1 Pet 1:9*

Rechab
R. the son of Rimmon. *2 Sam 4:2, 5*
R. escaped. 6
on Jehonadab son of R. *2 Ki 10:15*
son of R. went into the house of. 23
father of the house of R. *1 Chr 2:55*
Malchiah son of R. *Neh 3:14*
Jonadab the son of R. *Jer 35:6*
　see **Jonadab**

Rechabites
go to the house of the R. *Jer 35:2*

reckon
he shall r. with him that. *Lev 25:50*
shall r. to him the worth. 27:18, 23
by name ye shall r. the. *Num 4:32*
r. to him seven days. *Ezek 44:26*
when he had begun to r. *Mat 18:24*
r. yourselves to be dead. *Rom 6:11*
I r. that the sufferings of this. 8:18

reckoned
your heave offering r. *Num 18:27*
people shall not be r. among. 23:9
for Beeroth also was r. to. *2 Sam 4:2*
they r. not with the men. *2 Ki 12:15*
genealogy is not to be r. by birth-
　right. *1 Chr 5:1*
genealogy of generations was r. 7
all these were r. by genealogies. 17
　7:5, 7; 9:1, 22; 2 Chr 31:19
Azara 2:62; 8:3; Neh 7:5, 64
to us cannot be r. up. *Ps 40:5*
I r. till morning that. *Isa 38:13*
he was r. amongst the. *Luke 22:37*
reward is not r. of grace. *Rom 4:4*
faith was r. to Abraham. 9
how was it then r.? 10

reckoneth
lord r. with them. *Mat 25:19*

reckoning
there was no r. made. *2 Ki 22:7*
they were in one r. *1 Chr 23:11*

recommended
whence they had been r. *Acts 14:26*
being r. to the grace of God. 15:40*

recompence, *noun*
　(An equivalent given or received.
Now spelled recompense, both
noun and verb)
vengeance and r. *Deut 32:35*
vanity shall be his r. *Job 15:31*
the r. of a man's hand. *Pr 12:14*

will come with a r. *Isa 35:4*
r. to his enemies, to the islands r.
　　　　　　　　　　59:18
Lord that rendereth r. to his. 66:6
he will render to her a r. *Jer 51:6*
render to them a r. *Lam 3:64*
days of r. are come. *Hos 9:7*
will ye render me a r.? *Joel 3:4*
I will return your r. on your own. 7
bid thee, and a r. be. *Luke 14:12*
that r. of their error. *Rom 1:27*
let their table be made a r. to. 11:9
now for a r. in the same. *2 Cor 6:13*
transgression received a just r. of.
　　　　　　　　　　Heb 2:2
hath great r. of reward. 10:35
respect to the r. of reward. 11:26

recompences
year of r. for controversy. *Isa 34:8*
Lord God of r. shall surely. *Jer 51:56*

recompense, *verb*
he shall r. his trespass. *Num 5:7*
if he have no kinsman to r. the. 8*
the Lord r. thy work. *Ruth 2:12*
should the king r. me ? *2 Sam 19:36*
he will r. it, whether. *Job 34:33*
I will r. evil. *Pr 20:22*
I will r. into their bosom. *Isa 65:6*
first I will r. their iniquity. *Jer 16:18*
will r. according to their deeds.
　　　　　　　　25:14; Hos 12:2
r. work. *Jer 50:29*
r. abominations. *Ezek 7:3, 8*
r. thy ways. 4, 9; 9:10; 11:21; 16:43
oath and my covenant I will r. 17:19
they shall r. your lewdness. 23:49
if ye r. me, speedily will. *Joel 3:4*
for they cannot r. thee. *Luke 14:14*
r. to no man evil for evil. *Rom 12:17*
to r. tribulation to them. *2 Thes 1:6*
that hath said, I will r. *Heb 10:30*

recompensed
let the trespass be r. to. *Num 5:8*
cleanness of my hands hath he r. me.
　2 Sam 22:21, 25; Ps 18:20, 24
the righteous shall be r. *Pr 11:31*
shall evil be r. for good ? *Jer 18:20*
their own way have I r. *Ezek 22:31*
be r. at the resurrection. *Luke 14:14*
and it shall be r. to him. *Rom 11:35*

recompensest
thou r. iniquity of fathers. *Jer 32:18*

recompensing
by r. his way upon his. *2 Chr 6:23*

reconcile
brought to r. withal. *Lev 6:30*
should he r. himself ? *1 Sam 29:4*
shall ye r. the house. *Ezek 45:20*
r. both to God by cross. *Eph 2:16*
by him to r. all things. *Col 1:20*

reconciled
first be r. to thy brother. *Mat 5:24*
enemies we were r. to. *Rom 5:10*
be r. to her husband. *1 Cor 7:11*
who hath r. us to himself. *2 Cor 5:18*
we pray you be ye r. to God. 20
enemies, yet now hath he r. *Col 1:21*

reconciliation
to make a r. upon it. *Lev 8:15*
they made r. with their blood.
　　　　　　　　　2 Chr 29:24
one lamb to make r. *Ezek 45:15*, 17
to make r. for iniquity. *Dan 9:24*
to us the ministry of r. *2 Cor 5:18*
committed unto us the word of r. 19
to make r. for the sins. *Heb 2:17*

reconciling
an end of r. holy place. *Lev 16:20*
if casting away be r. *Rom 11:15*
God was in Christ, r. *2 Cor 5:19*

record
(Witness, usually in Revisions)
where I r. my name. *Ex 20:24*
I call heaven and earth to r.
　　　　　　　　　Deut 30:19; 31:28
appointed Levites to r. *1 Chr 16:4*
faithful witnesses to r. *Isa 8:2*
I take you to r. this day. *Acts 20:26*

record, *substantive*
and therein was a r. *Ezra 6:2*

behold, my r. is on high. *Job 16:19*
this is the r. of John. *John 1:19*
John bare r. saying, I saw. 32, 34
r. of thyself, thy r. is not. 8:13
r. of myself, yet my r. is true. 14
people with him, bare r. 12:17
that saw bare r. and his r. is. 19:35
I bare them r. that. *Rom 10:2*
I call God for a r. *2 Cor 1:23*
to their power I bear r., yea. 8:3
I bear you r., if it had. *Gal 4:15*
God is my r., how greatly. *Phil 1:8*
I bear him r. that he. *Col 4:13*
that bear r. in heaven. *1 John 5:7*
believeth not r. God gave of his Son.
　　　　　　　　　　10
this is the r. that God hath. 11
we bare r. and our r. is. *3 John 12*
who bare r. of the Word. *Rev 1:2*

recorded
Levites were r. chief of. *Neh 12:22*

recorder
Jehoshaphat was r. *2 Sam 8:16*
　20:24; 1 Ki 4:3; 1 Chr 18:15
Joah the son of Asaph the r.
　　　　2 Ki 18:18; Isa 36:3, 22
Joah son of Joahaz r. to repair.
　　　　　　　　　2 Chr 34:8

records
search in the book of r. *Ezra 4:15*
to bring the book of r. *Esth 6:1*

recount
he shall r. his worthies. *Nah 2:5*

recover
why did ye not r. them ? *Judg 11:26*
without fail r. all. *1 Sam 30:8*
went to r. his border. *2 Sam 8:3*
whether I shall r. *2 Ki 1:2*
the prophet would r. him of. 5:3
Naaman, that thou mayest r. 6
send to me to r. a man. 7
hand over place, and r. the leper. 11
enquire by him, shall I r.? 8:8, 9
thou mayest r. 10
that shouldest surely r. 14
nor did Jeroboam r. *2 Chr 13:20*
that they could not r. 14:13
that I may r. strength. *Ps 39:13*
to r. the remnant of. *Isa 11:11*
so wilt thou r. me and. 38:16
plaister, and he shall r. 21
and I will r. my wool. *Hos 2:9*
sick, and they shall r. *Mark 16:18*
that they may r. themselves out of
　the snare. *2 Tim 2:26*

recovered
David r. all the. *1 Sam 30:18*, 19
aught of good we have r. 22
Joash beat him, and r. *2 Ki 13:25*
he warred, and r. Damascus. 14:28
Rezin king of Syria r. Elath. 16:6
laid it on the boil, and he r. 20:7
was sick, and was r. *Isa 38:9; 39:1*
the health of my people r.? *Jer 8:22*
took the people he had r. 41:16

recovering
to preach r. of sight to. *Luke 4:18*

red
first came out r. all over. *Gen 25:25*
Feed me with that same r. 30
his eyes shall be r. with. 49:12
rams' skins dyed r. *Ex 25:5; 26:14*
　　　　　35:7; 36:19; 39:34
was found r. skins of rams. 35:23
bring thee a r. heifer. *Num 19:2*
saw the water r. as blood. *2 Ki 3:22*
on a pavement of r., blue. *Esth 1:6*
in hand of Lord is cup and wine
　is r. 75:8
look not on the wine when it is r.
　　　　　　　　　Pr 23:31
though your sins be r. *Isa 1:18*
A vineyard of r. wine. 27:2
art thou r. in thine apparel ? 63:2
shield of his mighty men is made r.
　　　　　　　　　Nah 2:3
a man riding on a r. horse and behind
　him were there r. *Zech 1:8*
in first chariot were r. horses. 6:2
will be fair weather, for sky is r.
　　　　　　　　　Mat 16:2, 3

another horse that was r.   *Rev* 6:4
a great r. dragon, seven.   12:3

Red *sea*

locusts into the R. sea.   *Ex* 10:19
by the way of the R sea.   13:18
drowned in the R. sea.   15:4
Israel from the R. sea.   22
bounds from the R. sea.   23:31
wilderness by the R. sea. *Num* 14:25
did he in the R. sea.?   21:14*
journey by the R. sea.   *Deut* 1:40
made the R. sea to overflow.   11:4
Lord dried up the R. sea. *Josh* 2:10
your God did to the R. sea.   4:23
pursued after to the R. sea.   24:6
their cry by the R. sea.   *Neh* 9:9
provoked him at the R. sea. *Ps* 106:7
he rebuked the R. sea, and it.   9
terrible things by the R. sea.   22
divided the R. sea in parts.   136:13
and his host in the R. sea.   15
was heard in the R. sea.   *Jer* 49:21
wonders in the R. sea.   *Acts* 7:36
they passed through the R. sea.
              Heb 11:29

reddish

a bright spot somewhat r. *Lev* 13:19
                 24:43
a white r. sore, it is a leprosy. 13:42
plague be r. in garment or.   49
with hollow strakes, r.   14:37

redeem

[1] *To buy again something that had been sold, by paying back the price to him that bought it,* Lev 25:25; 27:20. [2] *To deliver and bring out of bondage those who were kept prisoners by their enemies,* Deut 7:5; 32:6; Luke 1:68; 1 Tim 2:6; Tit 2:14.

To redeem time, *Eph* 5:16. *To embrace and improve every opportunity of doing good.*

I will r. you with a stretched. *Ex* 6:6
firstling of ass shall r. 13:13; 34:20
of my children I r.   15; 34:20
his kin come to r. it.   *Lev* 25:25*
if he have none to r. it.   26
he may r. it.   29
the cities may the Levites r.   32
his brethren may r. him.   48
or any of kin may r. him.   49
but if he will at all r. it, then. 27:13
his house will r. it.   15, 19, 20, 31
of man shalt thou r.   *Num* 18:15
from a month old shalt thou r.   16
goat thou shalt not r.   17
wilt r. it, if not, I will r. it. *Ruth* 4:4
cannot r. it for myself, r. thou it.   6
whom God went to r. to himself ?
     2 Sam 7:23; *1 Chr* 17:21
our power to r. them.   *Neh* 5:5
in famine he shall r. thee. *Job* 5:20
to r. me from the hand of.   6:23
r. Israel, O God, out of all. *Ps* 25:22
r. me and be merciful unto.   26:11
r. us for thy mercies' sake.   44:26
none of them can r. his brother. 49:7
but God will r. my soul from.   15
draw nigh to my soul, and r. it. 69:18
r. their soul from deceit.   72:14
he shall r. Israel from all his. 130:8
shortened that it cannot r.? *Isa* 50:2
I will r. thee out of hand. *Jer* 15:21
will r. them from death. *Hos* 13:14
Lord shall r. thee from.   *Mi* 4:10
to r. them that were under. *Gal* 4:5
that he might r. us from.   *Tit* 2:14

redeemed

the angel which r. me.   *Gen* 48:16
people whom thou hast r. *Ex* 15:13
then shall he let her be r.   21:8
with a bondmaid not r.   *Lev* 19:20
if a house in a city be not r.   25:30
houses of villages may be r.   31
to a stranger may be r. again.   48
if he be not r. then go out in.   54
sold the field, it shall not be r. 27:20
an unclean beast not r. then.   27
no devoted thing shall be r.   28, 29
and the change shall not be r.   33
those be r. that are more. *Num* 3:46
those that are to be r. from.   18:16

the Lord hath r. you out of the.
     Deut 7:8; 15:15; 24:18
thy people thou hast r.   9:26
Lord which r. you out of house. 13:5
Israel, whom thou hast r.   21:8
Lord hath r. my soul.   *2 Sam* 4:9
                1 Ki 1:29
whom thou hast r. out of Egypt.
  1 Chr 17:21; *Neh* 1:10; *Ps* 77:15
ability have r. the Jews.   *Neh* 5:8
thou hast r. me, O Lord.   *Ps* 31:5
my soul which thou hast r.   71:23
thine inheritance thou hast r.   74:2
he r. them from the hand of. 106:10
let the r. of the Lord say so, whom he
     hath r.   107:2
hath r. us from our enemies. 136:24
Zion shall be r. with.   *Isa* 1:27
the Lord, who r. Abraham.   29:22
no lion there, but the r. shall. 35:9
fear not, I have r. thee, thou. 43:1
for I have r. thee.   44:22
the Lord hath r. Jacob.   23; 48:20
                Jer 31:11
the r. of the Lord shall.   *Isa* 51:11
ye shall be r. without money. 52:3
r. Jerusalem.   9
holy people r. of Lord.   62:12
year of my r. is come.   63:4
in pity he r. them.   9
Lord, thou hast r. my life. *Lam* 3:58
though I r. them, yet they. *Hos* 7:13
I r. thee out of the house.   *Mi* 6:4
for them, I have r. them. *Zech* 10:8
visited and r. his people. *Luke* 1:68
he who should have r. Israel. 24:21
Christ r. us from the curse. *Gal* 3:13
ye were not r. with.   *1 Pet* 1:18
thou hast r. us to God.   *Rev* 5:9
the 144,000 which were r.   14:3*
these were r. from among men.   4*

redeemedst

which thou r. to thee.   *2 Sam* 7:23

Redeemer

I know that my R. liveth. *Job* 19:25
my strength and my R.   *Ps* 19:14
the high God was their R.   78:35
their R. is mighty, he.   *Pr* 23:11
thy R. the Holy One of Israel.
        Isa 41:14; 54:5
thus saith the Lord your R.   43:14
thus saith the Lord, his R. the. 44:6
saith the Lord thy R.   24; 48:17
             49:7; 54:8
as for our R., the Lord of.   47:4
I the Lord am thy R. 49:26; 60:16
R. shall come to Zion, to.   59:20
art our Father, our R.   63:16
their R. is strong, the.   *Jer* 50:34

redeemeth

the Lord r. the souls.   *Ps* 34:22
who r. life from destruction. 103:4

redeeming

the manner in Israel concerning r.
               Ruth 4:7
r. time, because the days are evil.
        Eph 5:16; *Col* 4:5

redemption

grant a r. for the land.   *Lev* 25:24
give again the price of his r. 51, 52
Moses took the r. money. *Num* 3:49
r. of their soul is precious. *Ps* 49:8
he sent r. to his people.   111:9
with him there is plenteous r. 130:7
right of r. is thine.   *Jer* 32:7, 8
to them that looked for r. *Luke* 2:38
look up, for your r. draweth. 21:28
the r. that is in Christ.   *Rom* 3:24
to wit, the r. of our body.   8:23
to us sanctification and r. *1 Cor* 1:30
in whom we have r. through his
     blood.   *Eph* 1:7; *Col* 1:14
until the r. of purchased. *Eph* 1:14
are sealed unto the day of r.   4:30
obtained eternal r. for us. *Heb* 9:12
for r. of the transgressions that. 15

redness

who hath r. of eyes ?   *Pr* 23:29

redound

that grace might r. to.   *2 Cor* 4:15*

reed

[1] *A plant growing in fens and watery places,* Job 40:21. [2] *A staff or rod of a reed, which was put in our Saviour's hand at his passion, by way of derision, instead of a sceptre,* Mat 27:29. [3] *A Jewish measure of six cubits three inches, or three yards three inches,* Ezek 40:3.

smite Israel as a r.   *1 Ki* 14:15
upon the staff of this bruised r.
     2 Ki 18:21; *Isa* 36:6
a bruised r. shall he not break.
        Isa 42:3; *Mat* 12:20
a staff of r. to Israel.   *Ezek* 29:6
a man with a measuring r.   40:3
with measuring r. 42:16, 17, 18, 19
a r. shaken ? *Mat* 11:7; *Luke* 7:24
put a r. in his right hand. *Mat* 27:29
smote him with a r. 30; *Mark* 15:19
put the spunge on a r. and gave.
     Mat 27:48; *Mark* 15:36
given me a r. like a rod.   *Rev* 11:1
had a golden r. to measure.   21:15
he measured with the r. 12,000.   16

reeds

he lieth in covert of the r. *Job* 40:21
the r. and flags shall.   *Isa* 19:6, 7*
of dragons shall be r.   35:7
the r. they have burnt.   *Jer* 51:32
he measured east side . . . five hundred r.   *Ezek* 42:16, 17, 18, 19
the length 25,000 r.   45:1

reel

they r. to and fro.   *Ps* 107:27
earth shall r. to and fro. *Isa* 24:20*

refine

I will r. them as silver.   *Zech* 13:9

refined

for the altar r. gold.   *1 Chr* 28:18
seven thousand talents of r. silver.
               29:4
wines on the lees well r.   *Isa* 25:6
behold, I have r. thee, but not. 48:10
refine them, as silver is r. *Zech* 13:9

refiner

he is like a r.'s fire, and.   *Mal* 3:2
shall sit as a r. and purifier.   3

reformation

until the time of r.   *Heb* 9:10

reformed

and if ye will not be r.   *Lev* 26:23

refrain

then Joseph could not r. himself.
               Gen 45:1
I will not r. my mouth.   *Job* 7:11
my son, r. thy foot.   *Pr* 1:15
there is a time to r. from.   *Eccl* 3:5
I will r. for thee that I.   *Isa* 48:9
wilt thou r. thyself for these ? 64:12
r. voice from weeping.   *Jer* 31:16
I say to you, R. from.   *Acts* 5:38
let him r. his tongue.   *1 Pet* 3:10

refrained

Joseph r. himself and.   *Gen* 43:31
Haman r. himself.   *Esth* 5:10
princes r. talking, and.   *Job* 29:9
I have not r. my lips.   *Ps* 40:9
I have r. my feet from.   119:101
still, and r. myself.   *Isa* 42:14
they have not r. their feet. *Jer* 14:10

refraineth

that r. his lips is wise.   *Pr* 10:19

refresh

with me and r. thyself.   *1 Ki* 13:7
Julius suffered Paul to r. *Acts* 27:3
brother, r. my bowels.   *Philem* 20

refreshed

stranger may be r.   *Ex* 23:12
he rested and was r.   31:17
Saul was r. and well.   *1 Sam* 16:23
r. themselves there.   *2 Sam* 16:14
speak that I may be r.   *Job* 32:20
I may with you be r.   *Rom* 15:32
for they r. my spirit.   *1 Cor* 16:18
spirit, was r. by you.   *2 Cor* 7:13
Onesiphorus oft r. me.   *2 Tim* 1:16
of the saints are r. by.   *Philem* 7

refresheth
for he r. the soul of.   *Pr* 25:13

refreshing
this is r., yet they would. *Isa* 28:12
times of r. shall come.   *Acts* 3:19

refuge
Cities of refuge. *In order to provide for the security of those, who unawares and without any design should kill a man, the Lord commanded Moses to appoint six cities of refuge, that the manslayer might retire thither, and have time to prepare for justification before the judges, so that the kinsman of the deceased might not pursue him thither and kill him. Of these cities there were three on each side Jordan : those on the west of Jordan were Kedesh of Naphtali, Hebron, and Shechem. Those beyond Jordan were Bezer, Golan, and Ramoth-gilead, Josh 20:7, 8. These cities were to be easy of access, and to have smooth and good roads to them, and bridges where there should be occasion. When there were any cross-roads, they took care to set up posts with an inscription, directing the way to the city of refuge. This city was to be well supplied with water and all kind of provisions. The case then came before the judges, that if possible he might clear himself. If he was found innocent, he dwelt safely in the city to which he had retired ; if otherwise, he was put to death, according to the severity of the law. Though he was found innocent, he was not therefore immediately set at liberty, but he was obliged to dwell in this city, without going out of it, till the death of the high priest : And if before this time he should any where go out of the city, the avenger of blood might safely kill him,* Num 35:25, 26, **27**, etc.*

shall ye have for r. *Num* 35:13, 15
eternal God is thy r.   *Deut* 33:27*
your r. from avenger.   *Josh* 20:3
high tower and my r. *2 Sam* 22:3
a r. for the oppressed, a r. *Ps* 9:9*
poor, because the Lord is his r. 14:6
God is our r.   46:1, 7, 11
God is known for a r.   48:3
thy wings I will make my r. 57:1
thou hast been my r. in the. 59:16
my r. is in God.   62:7
God is a r. for us.   8
thou art my strong r. 71:7; 142:5
he is my r.   91:2, 9
God is rock of my r.   94:22
high hills a r. for wild goats. 104:18
r. failed me.   142:4
thou art my r. and portion.   5
shall have a place of r. *Pr* 14:26
a place of r.   *Isa* 4:6
to the needy a r.   25:4
we have made lies our r. 28:15
hail shall sweep away the r. 17
O Lord, my r. in the day. *Jer* 16:19
who have fled for r. to lay. *Heb* 6:18

refuse
that was vile and r.   *1 Sam* 15:9
thou hast made us as r. *Lam* 3:45
sell the r. of wheat.   *Amos* 8:6

refuse, verb
if thou r. to let them go. *Ex* 4:23
            8:2; 9:2; 10:4
long wilt thou r. to humble ? 10:3
r. ye to keep my ?   16:28
if her father utterly r. to give. 22:17
whether thou r. or choose. *Job* 34:33
be wise, and r. it not.   *Pr* 8:33
they r. to do judgement.   21:7
slothful, his hands r. to labour. 25
if ye r., shall be devoured. *Isa* 1:20
may know to r. the evil. 7:15, 16
they r. to return.   *Jer* 8:5
they r. to know me.   9:6

evil people which r. to. *Jer* 13:10
if they r. to take the cup.   25:28
if thou r. to go forth, this. 38:21
if I be an offender, I r. *Acts* 25:11
but r. profane and old. *1 Tim* 4:7
the younger widows r.   5:11
see that ye r. not him. *Heb* 12:25

refused
Jacob r. to be comforted. *Gen* 37:35
r. and said to master's wife. 39:8
Jacob r. to remove his hand. 48:19
Edom r. to give Israel. *Num* 20:21
people r. to obey the. *1 Sam* 8:19
look not on him for I have r. 16:7*
Saul r. and said, I will not. 28:23
Asahel r. to turn aside. *2 Sam* 2:23
but Amnon r. to eat.   13:9
man r. to smite him. *1 Ki* 20:35
vineyard he r. to give thee. 21:15
him to take it, but he r. *2 Ki* 5:16
and r. to obey.   *Neh* 9:17
queen Vashti r. to come. *Esth* 1:12
that my soul r. to touch. *Job* 6:7
my soul r. to be comforted. *Ps* 77:2
they r. to walk in his law. 78:10
he r. tabernacle of Joseph.   67
stone which the builders r. 118:22*
I have called and ye r. *Pr* 1:24
when thou wast r. saith. *Isa* 54:6*
they r. to receive correction, they r.
              Jer 5:3
their fathers who r. to hear. 11:10
Rachel r. to be comforted. 31:15
all that took them r. to let. 50:33
for they have r. my. *Ezek* 5:6*
because they r. to return. *Hos* 11:5
but they r. to hearken. *Zech* 7:11
this Moses whom they r. *Acts* 7:35
nothing to be r. if it be. *1 Tim* 4:4
by faith Moses r. to be. *Heb* 11:24
r. him that spake on earth. 12:25

refusedst
thou r. to be ashamed.   *Jer* 3:3

refuseth
r. to let the people go. *Ex* 7:14
Lord r. to give me leave. *Num* 22:13
Balaam r. to come with us.   14
brother r. to raise up name.*Deut* 25:7
but he that r. reproof. *Pr* 10:17*
shame shall be to him that r. 13:18
that r. instruction despiseth. 15:32
this people r. the waters. *Isa* 8:6
my wound which r. to be. *Jer* 15:18

regard, noun
in r. of the oath of God. *Eccl* 8:2
to him they had r. because he had.
            Acts 8:11*

regard, verb
[1] *To look upon with compassion,*
Deut 28:50. [2] *To think of, consider, or lay to heart,* Isa 5:12.
[3] *To have respect for,* 2 Ki 3:14.
[4] *To hear and answer,* Ps 102:17.
[5] *To observe,* Rom 14:6.

r. not your stuff.   *Gen* 45:20
let them not r. vain.   *Ex* 5:9
r. not them that have. *Lev* 19:31*
which shall not r. person. *Deut* 28:50
nor did she r. it.   *1 Sam* 4:20
let not my lord r. this man. 25:25
r. not this, he is thy. *2 Sam* 13:20*
were it not that I r.   *2 Ki* 3:14
that day, let not God r. it. *Job* 3:4
nor will the Almighty r. it. 35:13
take heed, r. not iniquity. 36:21
they r. not the works of. *Ps* 28:5
I have hated them that r. 31:6
if I r. iniquity in my heart. 66:18
shall the God of Jacob r. it. 94:7*
he will r. the prayer of the. 102:17
thou mayest r. discretion. *Pr* 5:2*
will not r. any ransom, nor. 6:35
they r. not work of Lord. *Isa* 5:12
who will not r. silver.   13:17
will no more r. them. *Lam* 4:16
r. God of his fathers, nor r. any.
            Dan 11:37
r. the peace offering. *Amos* 5:22
behold, r. and wonder. *Hab* 1:5
will he r. your persons ? *Mal* 1:9*
not God, nor r. man. *Luke* 18:4
to Lord he doth not r. it. *Rom* 14:6

regarded
he that r. not the word. *Ex* 9:21
voice, nor any that r. *1 Ki* 18:29
thou hast r. me as. *1 Chr* 17:17
he r. their affliction. *Ps* 106:44
my hand, and no man r. *Pr* 1:24
O king, have not r. thee. *Dan* 3:12
he r. the low estate of. *Luke* 1:48*
feared not God, neither r. man. 18:2
and I r. them not.   *Heb* 8:9

regardest
thou r. not princes. *2 Sam* 19:6*
I stand up and thou r. *Job* 30:20
r. not the persons of men.
    Mat 22:16; *Mark* 12:14

regardeth
mighty and terrible, that r. not.
           Deut 10:r17
nor r. the rich more. *Job* 34:19
r. the crying of the driver. 39:7*
a righteous man r. the life. *Pr* 12:10
he that r. reproof shall be. 13:18
but he that r. reproof is.   15:5
wicked r. not to know cause. 29:7*
higher than the highest r. *Eccl* 5:8
he that r. the clouds shall not. 11:4
cities, he r. no man.   *Isa* 33:8
Daniel r. not thee, O king. *Dan* 6:13
he r. not the offering *Mal* 2:13
he that r. a day, r. it to. *Rom* 14:6

regarding
ever without any r. it. *Job* 4:20
nor r. his life to supply. *Phil* 2:30*

regeneration
Or the new birth, is the change and renovation of the soul by the Spirit and grace of God, John 3:5, 6.
in the r. when the Son of. *Mat* 19:28
us by the washing of r. *Tit* 3:5

region
all the r. of Argob. *Deut* 3:4, 13
in all r. of Dor.   *1 Ki* 4:11*
dominion over all the r.   24
then went to him all the r. *Mat* 3:5
sat in r. and shadow of death. 4:16
throughout all the r. about Galilee.
   Mark 1:28; *Luke* 4:14; 7:17
whole r. round about. *Mark* 6:55
Philip tetrarch of the r. *Luke* 3:1
published throughout r. *Acts* 13:49
they fled to the r. that lieth. 14:6
gone throughout r. of Galatia. 16:6

regions
throughout the r. of Judaea. *Acts* 8:1
gospel in r. beyond you. *2 Cor* 10:16
stop me in the r. of Achaia. 11:10
came into the r. of Syria. *Gal* 1:21

register
these sought their r.   *Ezra* 2:62
            Neh 7:64
a r. of the genealogy.   *Neh* 7:5*

rehearse
r. it in ears of Joshua. *Ex* 17:14
r. righteous acts of Lord. *Judg* 5:11

rehearsed
r. them in the ears of. *1 Sam* 8:21
they r. David's words.   17:31
Peter r. the matter from. *Acts* 11:4*
they r. all that God had done. 14:27

Rehoboam
R. the son of Solomon reigned.
   1 Ki 11:43; 14:21; *2 Chr* 9:31
R. consulted with the old men.
     1 Ki 12:6; *2 Chr* 10:6
R. reigned over them. *1 Ki* 12:17
         2 Chr 10:17
to bring the kingdom again to R.
    1 Ki 12:21; *2 Chr* 11:1
their heart shall turn again to R.
          1 Ki 12:27
war between R. and. 14:30; 15:6
R. was Solomon's son. *1 Chr* 3:10
           Mat 1:7
they made R. strong. *2 Chr* 11:17
R. loved Maachah daughter of. 21
R. made Abijah the son of.   22
against R. when R. was young. 13:7

Rehoboth
builded Nineveh and R. *Gen* 10:11
the name of the well R.   26:22
Saul of R. reigned. 36:37; *1 Chr* 1:48

Rehum
R. came with Zerubbabel.   Ezra 2:2
     Neh 12:3
R. the chancellor wrote.   Ezra 4:8
the king sent an answer to R. and. 17
letter was read before R.   23
R. the son of Bani.   Neh 3:17
R. of chief of the people.   10:25

reign
(*Used of temporal sovereigns; of God as spiritual ruler; and symbolically of sin or righteousness. Revisions frequently change to rule*)
Solomon's r. over Israel.   1 Ki 6:1
in 8th year of his r.   2 Ki 24:12
their cities to the r.   1 Chr 4:31
David's acts with all his r.   29:30
till r. of the kingdom.   2 Chr 36:20
priests recorded to r.   Neh 12:22
king in 7th year of his r.   Esth 2:16
year of the r. of Tiberius. Luke 3:1

reign, *verb*
thou indeed r. over us ?   Gen 37:8
Lord shall r. for ever.   Ex 15:18
     Ps 146:10
that hate you shall r.   Lev 26:17
thou shalt r. over many nations, but they shall not r.   Deut 15:6
70 r. over you, or one r.?   Judg 9:2
trees said, R. thou.   8, 10, 12, 14
that I should not r. over. 1 Sam 8:7
manner of king that shall r.   9, 11
Lord said, This same shall r.   9:17
shall Saul r. over us ?   11:12
but a king shall r. over us.   12:12
thou mayest r. over all. 2 Sam 3:21
that Adonijah doth r.?   1 Ki 1:11
shall r. after me.   1:13, 17, 30
Adonijah shall r. after me ?   1:24
faces on me, that I should r.   2:15
take thee, and thou shalt r.   11:37
Zimri did r. seven days in.   16:15
hast made to r. in his.   2 Chr 1:8
Behold, the king's son shall r.   23:3
that the hypocrite r. not.   Job 34:30
by me kings r. and princes. Pr 8:15
prison he cometh to r.   Eccl 4:14
of hosts shall r. in Zion. Isa 24:23
behold, a king shall r. in.   32:1
shalt thou r. because ?   Jer 22:15
a king shall r. and prosper.   23:5
should not have a son to r.   33:21
the Lord shall r. over them.   Mi 4:7
that Archelaus did r.   Mat 2:22
shall r. over house of.   Luke 1:33
will not have this man to r.   19:14
would not that I should r. over.   27
shall r. in life by one.   Rom 5:17
even so might grace r. unto life.   21
let not sin r. in your mortal.   6:12
shall rise to r. over Gentiles. 15:12
would to God ye did r. that we might r.   1 Cor 4:8
for he must r. till he put all.   15:25
if we suffer, we shall r. 2 Tim 2:12
and we also shall r.   Rev 5:10
and he shall r. for ever and.   11:15
they shall r. with him 1000 years.20:6
they shall r. for ever and ever. 22:5

see began

reigned
r. in Edom before any king r. over.
     Gen 36:31; 1 Chr 1:43
when Abimelech had r.   Judg 9:22
Saul r. one year, and when he r.
     1 Sam 13:1
Saul's son r. two years. 2 Sam 2:10
David r. forty years over.   5:4
David r. seven years in Hebron. 5
   1 Ki 2:11; 1 Chr 3:4; 29:27
David r. over Israel.   2 Sam 8:15
     1 Chr 18:14; 29:26
Hanun his son r. in his stead.
     2 Sam 10:1; 1 Chr 19:1
whose stead thou hast r. 2 Sam 16:8
and Solomon.   1 Ki 4:21; 11:42
   1 Chr 29:28; 2 Chr 9:30, 31
Rezon r. in Damascus.   1 Ki 11:24
r. over Syria.   29
Rehoboam r. 43; 12:17; 2 Chr 9:31
     10:17

Abijam his son r.   1 Ki 14:31
     2 Chr 12:16; 13:2
and Asa r. in his stead.   1 Ki 15:8
     9, 10; 2 Chr 14:1
Jehoshaphat his son r.   1 Ki 15:24
     2 Chr 17:1; 20:31
Nadab r.   1 Ki 15:25
Baasha r.   28, 29
Elah r.   16:6
Zimri r. in his stead.   10
Omri r.   22, 23
Omri died, and Ahab his son r.   28
Ahaziah, Ahab's son, r.   22:40, 51
     2 Ki 8:24, 26; 2 Chr 22:1, 2
Jehoshaphat r. 25 years. 1 Ki 22:42
     2 Chr 20:31
Jehoram r.   1 Ki 22:50; 2 Ki 3:1
     8:17; 2 Chr 21:5, 20
son that should have r.   2 Ki 3:27
Hazael r.   8:15
Jehoahaz r.   10:35
Jehu r.   36
Jehoash r. forty years in.   12:1
Amaziah r.   21; 14:1
     2 Chr 24:27; 25:1
Ben-hadad r.   2 Ki 13:24
Jeroboam r.   14:16, 23
Zachariah r.   29
Azariah r.   15:2; 2 Chr 26:3
and Jotham r.   2 Ki 15:7, 33
     2 Chr 26:23; 27:1, 8
Shallum r.   2 Ki 15:10, 13
Menahem son of Gadi r.   14, 17
Pekahiah his son r.   22, 23
Pekah r.   25, 27
Hoshea r.   30
Ahaz r.   15:38; 16:2; 2 Chr 28:1
Hezekiah r.   2 Ki 16:20; 18:2
     2 Chr 28:27; 29:1
Esarhaddon r. in his stead.
     2 Ki 19:37; Isa 37:38
Manasseh r.   2 Ki 20:21; 21:1
     2 Chr 32:33; 33:1
Amon r. in his stead.
     2 Ki 21:18, 19; 2 Chr 33:20, 21
Josiah r. in his stead.   2 Ki 21:26
     22:1; 2 Chr 34:1
Jehoahaz r. three months. 2 Ki 23:31
     2 Chr 36:2
Jehoiakim r. eleven years.
     2 Ki 23:36; 2 Chr 36:5
Jehoiachin r. in his.   2 Ki 24:6, 8
     2 Chr 36:8, 9
Zedekiah r. 2 Ki 24:18; 2 Chr 36:11
     Jer 37:1; 52:1
and Athaliah r. over.   2 Chr 22:12
Ahasuerus r. from India.   Esth 1:1
touching Shallum which r. Jer 22:11
death r. from Adam to.   Rom 5:14
man's offence death r. by one.   17
r. unto death, so might grace reign.21
ye have r. as kings.   1 Cor 4:8
great power, and hast r.   Rev 11:17
lived and r. with Christ.   20:4

reignest
thou r. over all, and in. 1 Chr 29:12

reigneth
ye and the king that r.   1 Sam 12:14
Absalom r. in Hebron.   2 Sam 15:10
Adonijah r.   1 Ki 1:18
the Lord r.   1 Chr 16:31; Ps 96:10
     97:1; 99:1
God r. over the heathen.   Ps 47:8
Lord r., he is clothed with.   93:1
for a servant when he r.   Pr 30:22
unto Zion, Thy God r.   Isa 52:7
which r. over the kings.   Rev 17:18
Lord God omnipotent r.   19:6

reigning
I have rejected him from r. over.
     1 Sam 16:1

reins
Kidneys *or* loins. *The Hebrews ascribe to the reins knowledge, joy, pain, pleasure : so in scripture it is often said, that God searcheth the hearts and the reins, Ps 7:9; Jer 17:10; 20:12.*
cleaveth my r. asunder.   Job 16:13
though my r. be consumed.   19:27
my r. also instruct me in the.   16:7
examine me, O Lord, try my r. 26:2

thus I was pricked in my r. Ps 73:21
thou hast possessed my r.   139:13
yea, my r. shall rejoice.   Pr 23:16
the girdle of his r.   Isa 11:5
that triest the r.   Jer 11:20
and far from their r.   12:2
I try the r.   17:10
that seest the r.   20:12
arrow to enter into my r.   Lam 3:13
he who searcheth the r.   Rev 2:23

reject
I will r. thee, that thou.   Hos 4:6
he would not r. her.   Mark 6:26
ye r. the commandment of.   7:9
and second admonition, r.   Tit 3:13

rejected
not r. thee, but they r.   1 Sam 8:7
ye have this day r. your God. 10:19
hast r. the word of the Lord, he hath
r. thee from being king. 15:23, 26
I have r. him from being king. 16:1
they r. his statutes.   2 Ki 17:15
Lord r. all the seed of Israel.   20
is despised and r. of men. Isa 53:3
for the Lord hath r. thy.   Jer 2:37
r. my law.   6:19
because the Lord hath r. them.   30
Lord hath r. the generation of. 7:29
lo, they have r. the word of.   8:9
hast thou utterly r. Judah ?   14:19
but thou hast utterly r. us. Lam 5:22
because thou hast r.   Hos 4:6
stone which builders r.   Mat 21:42
     Mark 12:10; Luke 20:17
he shall be r. of the elders.
     Mark 8:31; Luke 9:22
lawyers r. the counsel.   Luke 7:30
but he must first be r. of.   17:25
ye despised not, nor r.   Gal 4:14
thorns and briars r.   Heb 6:8
inherited blessing, was r.   12:17

rejecteth
that r. me, receiveth not. John 12:48

rejoice
ye shall r. in all.   Deut 12:7; 14:26
thou shalt r. in thy feast.   16:14
bless thee, therefore thou shalt r. 15
thou shalt r. in every good.   26:11
Lord will r. over you.   28:63; 30:9
r. O ye nations, with his.   32:43
he said, R. Zebulun, in thy.   33:18
r. ye in Abimelech.   Judg 9:19
Philistines gathered to r.   16:23
I r. in thy salvation.   1 Sam 2:1
thou sawest it, and didst r.   19:5
let the heart of them r. that seek.
     1 Chr 16:10; Ps 105:3
let the fields r. and all. 1 Chr 16:32
and let thy saints r.   2 Chr 6:41
made them to r.   20:27; Neh 12:43
and he shall not r.   Job 20:18
they r. at the sound of the.   21:12
fear, r. with trembling.   Ps 2:11
all that put their trust in thee r. 5:11
I will r. in thy salvation.   9:14
those that trouble me r. when. 13:4
my heart shall r. in thy salvation. 5
Jacob shall r. and Israel.   14:7
we will r. in thy salvation.   20:5*
how greatly shall he r.!   21:1
hast not made my foes to r.   30:1
for our heart shall r. in him.   33:21
my soul shall r. in his.   35:9
enemies wrongfully r. over me.   19
and let them not r. over me.   24
let them be ashamed that r.   26
lest they should r. over me.   38:16
let mount Zion r.; let Judah.   48:11
bones thou hast broken may r.   51:8
the righteous shall r. when.   58:10
in holiness, I will r.   60:6; 108:7
in shadow of thy wings will I r. 63:7
but the king shall r. in God.   11
morning and evening to r.   65:8
the little hills r.   12*
there did we r.   66:6
righteous r. yea, exceedingly. 68:3
r. before him.   4
my lips shall greatly r.   71:23
revive us, that thy people may r. 85:6
r. the soul of thy servant.   86:4
Tabor and Hermon shall r.   89:12

in thy name shall they r. Ps 89:16
made all his enemies to r. 42
let the heavens r. 96:11
trees of the wood r. 12*
Lord reigneth, let the earth r. 97:1
make a loud noise, r. and sing. 98:4*
Lord shall r. in his works. 104:31
that I may r. in gladness of thy. 106:5
righteous shall see it and r. 107:42
ashamed, let thy servant r. 109:28
I r. at thy word, as one. 119:162
let Israel r. in him that. 149:2
who r. to do evil, and. Pr 2:14
r. with the wife of thy youth. 5:18
wise, mine heart shall r. 23:15
yea, my reins shall r. when. 16
righteous shall greatly r. 24
she that bare thee shall r. 25
r. not when thine enemy. 24:17
ointment and perfume r. the. 27:9
righteous men do r., there. 28:12*
are in authority, people r. 29:2
righteous doth sing and r. 6
shall r. in time to come. 31:25*
a man to r. and do good. Eccl 3:12
should r. in his works. 22; 5:19
come after, shall not r. in him. 4:16
live many years, and r. in them. 11:8
r. O young man, in thy youth. 9
and r. in Rezin and. Isa 8:6
as men r. when they divide. 9:3
them that r. in my highness. 13:3*
yea, the fir trees r. at thee. 14:8
r. not thou, whole Palestina. 29
Thou shalt no more r. O virgin. 23:12
the noise of them that r. 24:8
poor among men shall r. in. 29:19
the desert shall r. 35:1
shall blossom and r. 2
for confusion they shall r. in. 61:7
as a bridegroom, so shall God r. 62:5
my servants shall r., but ye. 65:13
I will r. in Jerusalem, and. 19
r. ye with Jerusalem, and. 66:10
see this, your heart shall r. 14
virgin r. in the dance, and I will make
them r. from their. Jer 31:13
I will r. over them to do. 32:41
that they may r. and sleep. 51:39
thine enemy to r. over. Lam 2:17
let not the buyer r. nor. Ezek 7:12
r. at the inheritance of. 35:15
r. not, O Israel, for joy. Hos 9:1
ye which r. in a thing. Amos 6:13
r. not against me, O mine. Mi 7:8
take away them that r. Zeph 3:11
the Lord will r. over thee with. 17
r. O daughter of Zion. Zech 2:10
r. greatly, O daughter of Zion. 9:9
and their heart shall r. as. 10:7
and many shall r. at his. Luke 1:14
r. ye that day, and leap for. 6:23
in this r. not, rather r. because. 10:20
r. with me, for I have found. 15:6, 9
of the disciples began to r. 19:37
that reapeth may r. John 4:36
willing for a season to r. in. 5:35
if ye loved me, ye would r. 14:28
weep, but the world shall r. 16:20
you, and your heart shall r. 22
therefore did my heart r. Acts 2:26*
r. in hope of the glory. Rom 5:2
r. with them that do r. and. 12:15
he saith, R. ye Gentiles. 15:10
they that r. as though. 1 Cor 7:30
all the members r. with it. 12:26
of whom I ought to r. 2 Cor 2:3
now I r. not that ye were. 7:9
I r. that I have confidence in. 16
r. thou barren that. Gal 4:27
do r. yea, and will r. Phil 1:18
that I may r. in the day of. 2:16*
if I be offered, I joy and r. 17
same cause do ye joy and r. 18
see him again, ye may r. 28
we worship God, and r. in. 3:3*
now r. in my sufferings. Col 1:24
r. evermore. 1 Thes 5:16
let the brother of low degree r.
Jas 1:9*
now ye r. in your boastings. 4:16
wherein ye greatly r. 1 Pet 1:6
r. with joy unspeakable and. 8
but r. in as much as ye are. 4:13

on earth shall r. over. Rev 11:10
therefore r. ye heavens, and. 12:12
r. over her, thou heaven. 18:20
see glad

rejoice *before the Lord*
shall r. before the Lord. Lev 23:40
Deut 12:12, 18; 16:11; 27:7

rejoice *in the Lord*
r. in the Lord, O ye righteous.
Ps 33:1; 97:12
r. in the Lord, glory in. Isa 41:16
I will greatly r. in the Lord. 61:10
of Zion, r. in the Lord. Joel 2:23
yet I will r. in the Lord. Hab 3:18
heart shall r. in the Lord. Zech 10:7
brethren, r. in the Lord. Phil 3:1
r. in the Lord alway, and. 4:4

rejoiced
Jethro r. for all goodness. Ex 18:9
the Lord r. over you to. Deut 28:63
rejoice for good, as he r. over. 30:9
father of the damsel r. Judg 19:3
men of Beth-shemesh r. 1 Sam 6:13
the men of Israel r. greatly. 11:15
the people r. so that the. 1 Ki 1:40
Hiram r. greatly at Solomon's. 5:7
the people r. when Joash made king.
2 Ki 11:14, 20; 2 Chr 23:13, 21
people r. and David r. 1 Chr 29:9
all Judah r. at the oath. 2 Chr 15:15
princes and all the people r. 24:10
Hezekiah r. and all people. 29:36
of Israel and Judah r. 30:25
great sacrifices and r.: the wives
also, and children r. Neh 12:43
for Judah r. for the priests. 44
the city of Shushan r. Esth 8:15*
if I r. because my wealth. Job 31:25
if I r. at the destruction of. 29
in mine adversity they r. Ps 35:15
the daughters of Judah r. 97:8
I have r. in the way of. 119:14
for my heart r. in all. Eccl 2:10
I r. not in the assembly. Jer 15:17
ye r. O destroyers of mine. 50:11
the Ammonites r. Ezek 25:6
the priests that r. on it. Hos 10:5
nor shouldest thou have r. Ob 12
the star, they r. with joy. Mat 2:10
my spirit hath r. in God. Luke 1:47
they r. with Elisabeth. 58
in that hour Jesus r. in spirit. 10:21
the people r. for the things. 13:17
your father Abraham r. to. John 8:56
r. in the works of their. Acts 7:41
which, when had read, they r. 15:31
the jailer r. believing in God. 16:34
as though they r. not. 1 Cor 7:30
so that I r. the more. 2 Cor 7:7
I r. in the Lord greatly. Phil 4:10
I r. greatly that I found. 2 John 4
3 John 3

rejoiceth
My heart r. in the Lord. 1 Sam 2:1
horse r. in his strength. Job 39:21
and my glory r. Ps 16:9
and r. as a strong man to. 19:5
therefore my heart greatly r. 28:7
well with righteous, city r. Pr 11:10
the light of the eyes r. the heart. 13:9
light of the eyes r. the heart. 15:30
whoso loveth wisdom r. his. 29:3
that r. shall descend into. Isa 5:14
as bridegroom r. over bride. 62:5
thou meetest him that r. and. 64:5
when the whole earth r. Ezek 35:14
I say to you, he r. more. Mat 18:13
bridegroom r. greatly. John 3:29
r. not in iniquity, but r. 1 Cor 13:6
and mercy r. against. Jas 2:13*

rejoicest
doest evil, then thou r. Jer 11:15

rejoicing
come up from thence r. 1 Ki 1:45
burnt offerings with r. 2 Chr 23:18
fill thy lips with r. Job 8:21*
his statutes are right, r. Ps 19:8
r. shall they be brought to. 45:15
declare his works with r. 107:22*
voice of r. is in tabernacle. 118:15
they are the r. of my heart. 119:111
doubtless come again with r. 126:6

I was his delight, r. always. Pr 8:30
r. in the habitable part of his. 31
I create Jerusalem a r. Isa 65:18
word was to me the r. Jer 15:16
their r. was to devour. Hab 3:14
this is the r. city that. Zeph 2:15
it on his shoulders r. Luke 15:5
r. that they were counted worthy.
Acts 5:41
eunuch went on his way r. 8:39
r. in hope, patient in. Rom 12:12
I protest by your r. 1 Cor 15:31
our r. is this, testimony. 2 Cor 1:12*
that we are your r. even as ye. 14*
as sorrowful, yet always r. 6:10
then shall he have r. Gal 6:4
that your r. may be. Phil 1:26*
is our crown of r.? 1 Thes 2:19*
the r. of the hope firm. Heb 3:6
all such r. is evil. Jas 4:16*

release
seven years make a r. Deut 15:1
manner of the r.: it is the Lord's r. 2
the year of r. is at hand. 9
of the year of r. in feast. 31:10
he made a r. to provinces. Esth 2:18

release, *verb*
that lendeth shall r. it. Deut 15:2
with thy brother, hand shall r. 3
was wont to r. a prisoner. Mat 27:15
Luke 23:17; John 18:39
will ye that I r. unto you ? Mat 27:17
21; Mark 15:9; John 18:39
that he should rather r. Barabbas.
Mark 15:11; Luke 23:18
chastise him, and r. him. Luke 23:16
willing to r. Jesus, spake again. 20
I have power to r. thee ? John 19:10
Pilate sought to r. him. 12

released
then r. he Barabbas to. Mat 27:26
Mark 15:15; Luke 23:25
now at that feast he r. Mark 15:6

relied
because they r. on the. 2 Chr 13:18
r. on Syria, and hast not r. 16:7

relief
determined to send r. Acts 11:29

relieve
then thou shalt r. him. Lev 25:35*
r. the oppressed. Isa 1:17
things for meat to r. soul. Lam 1:11*
the comforter that should r. is 16*
while they sought meat to r. 19*
widows let them r. them; that it may
r. them that are. 1 Tim 5:16

relieved
if she have r. afflicted. 1 Tim 5:10

relieveth
he r. the fatherless and. Ps 146:9*

religion
straitest sect of our r. Acts 26:5
conversation in Jews' r. Gal 1:13
profited in the Jews' r. above. 14
heart, this man's r. is vain. Jas 1:26
pure r. and undefiled before God. 27

religious
r. proselytes followed. Acts 13:43*
among you seem to be r. Jas 1:26

rely
because thou didst r. 2 Chr 16:8

remain
r. a widow at thy. Gen 38:11
that the frogs r. in. Ex 8:9, 11
let nothing of it r. until the. 12:10
nor fat of my sacrifice r. 23:18
if the flesh of consecrations r. 29:34
if aught r. till third day. Lev 19:6
that which is sold shall r. 25:28
to the years that r. 27:18
those which ye let r. Num 33:55
all, we left none to r. Deut 2:34
nor shall any of the flesh r. 16:4
those which r. shall hear and. 19:20
she shall r. in thine house. 21:13
his body shall not r. all night on. 23
and cattle shall r. Josh 1:14*
neither did there r. any more. 2:11
let none of them r. 8:22; 10:28, 30

by lot these nations that r. *Josh* 23:4
among these nations that r.   7
ye cleave to these nations that r.   12
why did Dan r. in ships ? *Judg* 5:17
wives for them that r.   21:7, 16
shalt r. by the stone.   *1 Sam* 20:19
six months did Joab r.   *1 Ki* 11:16
even I only, r. a prophet of.   18:22*
five of the horses that r.   *2 Ki* 7:13
for we r. yet escaped.   *Ezra* 9:15*
shall he r. in the tomb.   *Job* 21:32*
those that r. of him shall.   27:15
the beasts go to dens and r.   37:8
would I r. in wilderness.   *Ps* 55:7*
perfect shall r. in the land.   *Pr* 2:21
shall r. in congregation of.   21:16*
as yet shall he r. at Nob. *Isa* 10:32*
righteousness shall r. in the.   32:16*
which r. among the graves.   65:4*
earth shall r. before me, so shall your
   seed and your name r.   66:22
residue of them that r. of.   *Jer* 8:3
and this city shall r. for ever.   17:25
residue of Jerusalem that r.   24:8
those will I let r. still in.   27:11
concerning vessels that r.   19*, 21
the palace shall r. after the.   30:18
hands of men that r.   38:4
none shall r.   42:17; 44:14; 51:62
evil, to leave you none to r.   44:7
none of them shall r.   *Ezek* 7:11
and they that r. shall be.   17:21
shall fowls of heaven r.   31:13*
men to bury those that r. of.   39:14
r. ten men in one house.   *Amos* 6:9
delivered those that did r.   *Ob* 14
flying roll shall r. in.   *Zech* 5:4*
all the families that r. shall.   12:14
in same house r. eating.   *Luke* 10:7
the fragments that r.   *John* 6:12
that my joy might r. in you.   15:11
that your fruit should r.   16*
that the bodies should not r.   19:31
let her r. unmarried.   *1 Cor* 7:11
of whom the greater part r.   15:6
we which are alive and r. till the
   coming of the Lord. *1 Thes* 4:15*
alive and r. shall be caught up. 17*
cannot be shaken may r. *Heb* 12:27
have heard r. in you. *1 John* 2:24*
which r ready to die.   *Rev* 3:2

remainder

thou shalt burn the r.   *Ex* 29:34
the r. shall Aaron and.   *Lev* 6:16
on the morrow also the r. shall. 7:16
but the r. on the third day shall. 17
neither name nor r.   *2 Sam* 14:7
the r. of wrath shalt.   *Ps* 76:10

remained

Noah only r. alive, and. *Gen* 7:23*
and they that r. fled to the.   14:10
flies, there r. not one.   *Ex* 8:31
there r. not any green thing.   10:15
there r. not one locust in all.   19
r. not so much as one chariot. 14:28
r. two of the men in.   *Num* 11:26
because he should have r.   35:28
their inheritance r. in house.   36:12
Og, king of Bashan, r.   *Deut* 3:11
when thou shalt have r. long. 4:25*
the rest who r. entered. *Josh* 10:20
in Gath there r. Anakims.   11:22
who r. of remnant of giants.   13:12
there r. of Israel seven tribes. 18:2
the Levites which r. of. 21:20, 26*
there r. with Gideon.   *Judg* 7:3
they which r. were scattered so that
   two not left.   *1 Sam* 11:11
David r. in a mountain.   23:14
David and his men r. in the. 24:3*
Tamar r. desolate in. *2 Sam* 13:20
Sodomites which r. he. *1 Ki* 22:46
Jehu slew all that r. *2 Ki* 10:11, 17
and there r. the grove also.   13:6
that r., he set Gedaliah.   25:22*
the ark r. in Obed-edom. *1 Chr* 13:14
my wisdom r. with me.   *Eccl* 2:9
these defenced cities r.   *Jer* 34:7
there r. but wounded men.   37:10
Jeremiah had r. many days in. 16
he r. in the court of the.   21; 38:13
people that r. in the city. 39:9; 52:15

away captive them that r. *Jer* 41:10
taste r. in him, his scent.   48:11
mighty men have r. in their.   51:30
Lord's anger none r.   *Lam* 2:22
I r. there astonished.   *Ezek* 3:15*
r. no strength in me. *Dan* 10:8, 17
and I r. there with the kings of. 13
in Sodom it would have r. *Mat* 11:23
fragments that r. twelve baskets.
   14:20; *Luke* 9:17; *John* 6:13
beckoned, r. speechless. *Luke* 1:22
while it r. was it not ?   *Acts* 5:4
forepart stuck fast, and r.   27:41

remainest

thou, O Lord, r. for ever.
   Lam 5:19*; *Heb* 1:11*

remaineth

while earth r. seed time. *Gen* 8:22
which r. to you from.   *Ex* 10:5
that which r. until morning.   12:10
that which r. over lay it up.   16:23
that r. of the flesh and.   *Lev* 8:32
take the meat offering that r. 16:16*
do for the tabernacle that r. 16:16*
destroy him that r.   *Num* 24:19*
stones that r. to this day. *Josh* 8:29
there r. yet much land to be.   13:1
this is land that yet r.: all Geshuri. 2
he made him that r.   *Judg* 5:13*
which stone r. unto.   *1 Sam* 6:18
Jesse said, There r. yet the.   16:11
ark r. under curtains.   *1 Chr* 17:1*
my error r. with myself.   *Job* 19:4
answers there r. falsehood.   21:34
in his neck r. strength.   41:22*
he that r. in Jerusalem.   *Isa* 4:3
he that r. in this city.   *Jer* 38:2*
Tyrus every helper that r.   47:4
he that r. and is besieged. *Ezek* 6:12
so my Spirit r. among.   *Hag* 2:5*
he that r. even he shall.   *Zech* 9:7*
therefore your sin r.   *John* 9:41
it r. that they that have wives be.
     1 Cor 7:29*
that which r. is glorious. *2 Cor* 3:11
until this day r. the same vail.   14
his righteousness r. for ever.   9:9*
seeing it r. that some.   *Heb* 4:6
there r. therefore a rest to.   9
there r. no more sacrifice for. 10:26
for his seed r. in him. *1 John* 3:9*

remaining

the cloud tarried, r. on. *Num* 9:22*
till none was left r. to Og. *Deut* 3:3
he left none r. *Josh* 10:33, 37, 39
     40; 11:8
were r. of the families of the. 21:40
be destroyed from r. in the coasts of
   Israel.   *2 Sam* 21:5
he left Ahab none r.   *2 Ki* 10:11
who r. in the chambers. *1 Chr* 9:33*
nor shall have any r.   *Job* 18:19
shall not be any r. of.   *Ob* 18
shalt see the Spirit r.   *John* 1:33*

Remaliah

fierce anger of son of R.   *Isa* 7:4
the son of R. hath taken evil.   5
head of Samaria is R.'s son.   9
rejoice in Resin and R.'s son.   8:6

remedy

there was no r.   *2 Chr* 36:16
he be broken without r.   *Pr* 6:15
be destroyed, and without r.   29:1

remember

did not butler r. Joseph. *Gen* 40:23
Moses said, R. this day.   *Ex* 13:3
r. sabbath day to keep it holy. 20:8
r. Abraham, Isaac, and Israel. 32:13
     Deut 9:27
we r. the fish which we. *Num* 11:5
r. all the commandments.   15:39
r. and do my commandments.   40
r. that thou wast a servant in the.
  Deut 5:15; 15:15; 16:12; 24:18, 22
thou shalt r. what the Lord.   7:18
thou shalt r. all the way the.   8:2
r. the Lord giveth thee power.   18
r. how thou provokedst the.   9:7
r. that thou wast a bondman in.
     15:15; 16:12; 24:18, 22
r. the day when thou camest.   16:3

r. what the Lord thy God did.
     Deut 24:9
r. what Amalek did to thee.   25:17
r. the days of old, consider.   32:7
r. word which Moses.   *Josh* 1:13
r. that I am your bone.   *Judg* 9:2
Abigail said, Then r. *1 Sam* 25:31
let the king r. the Lord. *2 Sam* 14:11
neither do thou r. what thy.   19:19
r. when I and thou rode.   *2 Ki* 9:25
r. how I have walked before thee.
     20:3; *Isa* 38:3
r. his marvellous works.
     1 Chr 16:12; *Ps* 105:5
r. the mercies of David. *2 Chr* 6:42
r. the word thou.   *Neh* 1:8
r. the Lord, which is great.   4:14
r. them that have defiled.   13:29
r. who ever perished ?   *Job* 4:7
O r. that my life is wind.   7:7
r. that thou hast made me.   10:9
r. it as waters that pass.   11:16
r. that thou magnify his work. 36:24
hand upon him, r. the battle.   41:8
r. all thy offerings and.   *Ps* 20:3
will r. the name of the Lord.   7*
all ends of the world shall r. 22:27
r. thy mercies, they have.   25:6
r. not the sins of my youth, r. thou. 7
r. thy congregation which thou. 74:2
r. this, that the enemy hath.   18
r. how the foolish man.   22
O r. not against us former.   79:8
r. how short my time is.   89:47
r. Lord the reproach of thy.   50
and to those that r. his.   103:18
r. the word unto thy servant. 119:49
Lord, r. David, and all his.   132:1
r. O Lord, children of Edom. 137:7
let him drink, and r. his.   *Pr* 31:7
not much r. the days.   *Eccl* 5:20
let him r. days of darkness.   11:8
r. now thy Creator in the days. 12:1
we will r. thy love.   *S of S* 1:4*
r. ye not the former things ?
     Isa 43:18; 46:9
own sake I will not r. thy sins. 43:25
r. these, O Jacob and Israel. 44:21
r. this, and shew yourselves. 46:8
neither didst r. the latter end. 47:7
shalt not r. the reproach of.   54:4
meetest those that r. thee.   64:5
not wroth, neither r. iniquity.   9
neither shall they r. it.   *Jer* 3:16
he will now r. their iniquity.   14:10
r., break not thy covenant with.   21
their children r. their altars.   17:2
r. that I stood before thee.   18:20
I do earnestly r. him still.   31:20
did not the Lord r. them ?   44:21
escaped, r. the Lord afar off. 51:50
O Lord, what is come.   *Lam* 5:1
then shalt r. thy ways. *Ezek* 16:61
     20:43; 36:31
mayest r. and be confounded. 16:63
shalt not r. Egypt any more. 23:27
will he r. their iniquity.   *Hos* 8:13
therefore he will r. iniquity.   9:9
r. now what Balak.   *Mi* 6:5
in wrath r. mercy.   *Hab* 3:2
r. the law of Moses my.   *Mal* 4:4
neither r. the five loaves. *Mat* 16:9
     Mark 8:18
sir, we r. that deceiver. *Mat* 27:63
to r. his holy covenant. *Luke* 1:72
r. that thou in thy lifetime.   16:25
r. Lot's wife.   17:32
r. how he spake to you.   24:6
r. the word that I said. *John* 15:20
time shall come ye may r.   16:4
r. that by the space of. *Acts* 20:31
r. words of the Lord Jesus, how. 35
would that we should r. *Gal* 2:10
r. that ye being in time. *Eph* 2:11
r. my bonds. Grace be. *Col* 4:18
for ye r. brethren our. *1 Thes* 2:9
r. ye not that I told ? *2 Thes* 2:5
r. that Jesus Christ. *2 Tim* 2:8
r. them that are in bonds. *Heb* 13:3
r. them which have the rule over. 7
r. the words spoken of. *Jude* 17
r. from whence thou art fallen.
     Rev 2:5
r. how thou hast received.   3:3

I remember

saying, *I* do *r*. my faults. *Gen* 41:9
I r. that which Amalek. *1 Sam* 15:2*
when *I r*. I am afraid. *Job* 21:6
when *I r*. these, I pour. *Ps* 42:4
when *I r*. thee upon my bed. 63:6
if *I* do not *r*. thee, let my. 137:6
I r. the days of old, I muse. 143:5
I r. thee, the kindness of. *Jer* 2:2
consider not that *I r*. all. *Hos* 7:2

I will remember

I will r. my covenant. *Gen* 9:15, 16
Lev 26:42; *Ezek* 16:60
I will for their sakes *r*. *Lev* 26:45
therefore *will I r*. thee. *Ps* 42:6
but *I will r*. the years of the. 77:10
I will r. the works, *I will r*. thy. 11*
I will r. their sin no more. *Jer* 31:34
Heb 8:12; 10:17
I will r. his deeds which. *3 John* 10

remember me

r. me, that I may be. *Judg* 16:28
handmaid, and *r. me*. *1 Sam* 1:11
r. me, O God. *Neh* 13:14, 22, 31
a set time, and *r. me*. *Job* 14:13
r me for thy goodness'. *Ps* 25:7
r. me with the favour that. 106:4
knowest, *r. me*, and visit. *Jer* 15:15
escape of you shall *r. me*. *Ezek* 6:9
r. me in far countries. *Zech* 10:9
Lord, *r. me* when thou comest into
thy kingdom. *Luke* 23:42
that ye *r. me* in all. *1 Cor* 11:2

remembered

God *r*. Noah. *Gen* 8:1
God *r*. Abraham. 19:29
God *r*. Rachel. 30:22
Joseph *r*. the dreams. 42:9
God *r*. his covenant. *Ex* 2:24; 6:5
shall be *r*. before the. *Num* 10:9
children of Israel *r*. not. *Judg* 8:34
the Lord *r*. Hannah. *1 Sam* 1:19
thus Joash *r*. not the. *2 Chr* 24:22
Ahasuerus *r*. Vashti. *Esth* 2:1
days of Purim should be *r*. 9:28
sinner shall be no more *r*. *Job* 24:20
thy name to be *r*. in all. *Ps* 45:17
I r. God and was troubled. 77:3
they *r*. that God was their. 78:35
for he *r*. that they were but flesh. 39
they *r*. not his hand, when he. 42
he *r*. his mercy toward the. 98:3
he hath *r*. his covenant for. 105:8
for he *r*. his holy promise. 42
they *r*. not the multitude of. 106:7
he *r*. for them his covenant, and. 45
iniquity of his fathers be *r*. 109:14
because that he *r*. not to shew. 16
wonderful works to be *r*. 111:4
I r. thy judgements of old. 119:52
I have *r*. thy name, O Lord. 55
who *r*. us in our low estate. 136:23
we wept, when we *r*. Zion. 137:1
yet no man *r*. that same. *Eccl* 9:15
that thou mayest be *r*. *Isa* 23:16
thou hast not *r*. me, nor laid. 57:11
then he *r*. the days of old. 63:11
heavens shall not be *r*. 65:17
name may be no more *r*. *Jer* 11:19
Jerusalem *r*. in the days. *Lam* 1:7
r. not his footstool in the day. 2:1
his righteousness shall not be *r*.
Ezek 3:20; 33:13
thou hast not *r*. the days. 16:22, 43
your iniquity to be *r*. 21:24
thou shalt be no more *r*. 32
Ammonites may not be *r*. 25:10
they shall no more be *r*. *Hos* 2:17*
Zech 13:2
and *r*. not the brotherly. *Amos* 1:9
fainted, *I r*. the Lord. *Jonah* 2:7
Peter *r*. the words of Jesus.
Mat 26:75; *Luke* 22:61
they *r*. his words, and. *Luke* 24:8
his disciples *r*. that it. *John* 2:17
risen, they *r*. that he had said. 22
was glorified, then they *r*. 12:16
then *r*. I the word of. *Acts* 11:16
hath *r*. her iniquities. *Rev* 18:5

rememberest

the slain whom thou *r*. no. *Ps* 88:5
there *r*. that thy brother. *Mat* 5:23

remembereth

maketh inquisition, he *r*. *Ps* 9:12
frame, he *r*. we are but dust. 103:14
she *r*. not her last end. *Lam* 1:9
she *r*. no more anguish. *John* 16:21
whilst he *r*. the obedience. *2 Cor* 7:15

remembering

r. mine affliction and. *Lam* 3:19
r. without ceasing your. *1 Thes* 1:3

remembrance

I will put out the *r*. *Ex* 17:14
bringing iniquity to *r*. *Num* 5:15
out the *r*. of Amalek. *Deut* 25:19
make the *r*. of them to cease. 32:26
keep my name in *r*. *2 Sam* 18:18
to call my sin to *r*.? *1 Ki* 17:18
his *r*. shall perish from. *Job* 18:17
in death is no *r*. of thee. *Ps* 6:5
give thanks at *r*. of his holiness.
30:4*; 97:12*
to cut off the *r*. of them from. 34:16
a psalm of David, to bring to *r*.
38:*title*; 70:*title*
call to *r*. my song in the night. 77:6
that Israel be no more in *r*. 83:4
thy *r*. unto all generations. 102:12*
righteous in everlasting *r*. 112:6
there is no *r*. of former. *Eccl* 1:11
no *r*. of wise more than fool. 2:16
our soul is to the *r*. of. *Isa* 26:8*
put me in *r*., let us plead. 43:26
hast thou set up thy *r*. 57:8*
soul hath them still in *r*. *Lam* 3:20
call to *r*. the iniquity. *Ezek* 21:23
I say that ye are come to *r*. 24
calling to *r*. the days of 23:19, 21
bringeth their iniquity to *r*. 29:16
a book of *r*. was written. *Mal* 3:16
Peter calling to *r*. saith. *Mark* 11:21
he hath holpen Israel in *r*. *Luke* 1:54
this do in *r*. of me. 22:19
1 Cor 11:24
bring all things to your *r*. *John* 14:26
thine alms are had in *r*. *Acts* 10:31
who shall bring you into *r*. *1 Cor* 4:17
as oft as ye drink it, in *r*. of. 11:25
God upon every *r*. of you. *Phil* 1:3
good *r*. of us always. *1 Thes* 3:6
put the brethren in *r*. *1 Tim* 4:6*
that I have *r*. of thee. *2 Tim* 1:3
when I call to *r*. the unfeigned. 5*
I put the in *r*. that thou stir. 6
of these things put them in *r*. 2:14
there is a *r*. of sins. *Heb* 10:3
but call to *r*. the former days. 32
to put you always in *r*. *2 Pet* 1:12
Jude 5
stir you up by putting you in *r*.
2 Pet 1:13
have these things always in *r*. 15
pure minds by way of *r*. 3:1
great Babylon came in *r*. *Rev* 16:19

remembrances

your *r*. are like to ashes. *Job* 13:12

remission

many, for the *r*. of sins. *Mat* 26:28
baptism of repentance for *r*. of sins.
Mark 1:4; *Luke* 3:3
salvation by *r*. of sins. *Luke* 1:77
that *r*. should be preached in. 24:47
baptized for *r*. of sins. *Acts* 2:38
believeth shall receive *r*. of. 10:43
for the *r*. of sins that. *Rom* 3:25*
shedding of blood is no *r*. *Heb* 9:22
where *r*. is, there no more. 10:18

remit, -ed

sins ye *r*. they are *r*. *John* 20:23*

remnant

the *r*. of meat offering. *Lev* 2:3
r. shall be the priest's as. 5:13
the *r*. of the oil that is. 14:18
only Og remained of *r*. of giants.
Deut 3:11; *Josh* 12:4; 13:12
his eye evil toward *r*. *Deut* 28:54
if ye cleave to the *r*. of. *Josh* 23:12
Gibeonites were of *r*. *2 Sam* 21:2
speak to the *r*. of the. *1 Ki* 12:23
I will take away the *r*. of. 14:10
of Sodomites, Jehoshaphat. 22:46
lift up thy prayer for the *r*.
2 Ki 19:4; *Isa* 37:4

the *r*. that is escaped shall yet take
root. *2 Ki* 19:30; *Isa* 37:31
shall go forth a *r*. *2 Ki* 19:31
Isa 37:32
I will forsake the *r*. of. *2 Ki* 21:14
the *r*. did Nebuzar-adan. 25:11
he will return to the *r*. *2 Chr* 30:6
the *r*. of their brethren. *Ezra* 3:8
Lord to leave us a *r*. to escape. 9:8
so that there should be no *r*. 14
the *r*. that are left of the. *Neh* 1:3
the *r*. of them the fire. *Job* 22:20
had left us a very small *r*. *Isa* 1:9
set his hand, to recover the *r*. 11:11
an highway for the *r*. of his. 16
cut off from Babylon the *r*. 14:22
and he shall slay thy *r*. 30
I will bring lions on the *r*. of. 15:9
the *r*. shall be very small. 16:14
shall cease from *r*. of Syria. 17:3
hearken, all the *r*. of the house. 46:3
glean the *r*. of Israel. *Jer* 6:9
there shall be no *r*. of them. 11:23
it shall be well with thy *r*. 15:11
will gather the *r*. of my flock. 23:3
the *r*. of Ashdod did drink of. 25:20
O Lord, save thy people, the *r*. 31:7
Nebuzar-adan carried away *r*. 39:9
king of Babylon had left a *r*. 40:11
Jews be scattered, and *r*. of. 15
Johanan took the *r*. 41:16; 43:5
the Lord, even for all this *r*. 42:2
word of Lord, ye *r*. of Judah. 15
O ye *r*. of Judah, go ye not. 19
I will take the *r*. of Judah. 44:12
so that none of the *r*. of Judah. 14
the *r*. shall know whose words. 28
Lord will spoil *r*. of country of. 47:4
Ashkelon is cut off, with the *r*. 5
the whole *r*. of thee. *Ezek* 5:10
yet will I leave a *r*. that ye. 6:8
make an end of the *r*.? 11:13
therein shall be left a *r*. 14:22
and thy *r*. shall fall by the. 23:25
I will destroy the *r*. of the. 25:16
in the *r*. whom the Lord. *Joel* 2:32
the *r*. of the Philistines. *Amos* 1:8
God will be gracious to the *r*. 5:15
that they may possess the *r*. of. 9:12
I will surely gather the *r*. *Mi* 2:12
make her that halted, a *r*. 4:7
the *r*. of his brethren shall. 5:3
the *r*. of Jacob, in the midst. 7
the *r*. of Jacob shall be among. 8
the transgression of the *r*. 7:18
the *r*. of the people shall. *Hab* 2:8
and I will cut off the *r*. *Zeph* 1:4
for the *r*. of house of Judah. 2:7
the *r*. of my people shall possess. 9
the *r*. of Israel shall not do. 3:13
all the *r*. of the people. *Hag* 1:12
stirred up the spirit of the *r*. 14
marvellous in eyes of *r*. *Zech* 8:6
I will cause *r*. of this people. 12
the *r*. took his servants. *Mat* 22:6
Esaias also crieth, a *r*. *Rom* 9:27
at this time also there is a *r*. 11:5
the *r*. were affrighted. *Rev* 11:13
to make war with the *r*. 12:17
the *r*. were slain with the. 19:21

remove

father's hand to *r*. it. *Gen* 48:17
inheritance of Israel *r*. *Num* 36:7, 9
shalt not *r*. thy neighbour's land.
Deut 19:14
then ye shall *r*. from. *Josh* 3:3
then would I *r*. Abimelech. *Judg* 9:29
so David would not *r*. *2 Sam* 6:10
the Lord said, I will *r*. *2 Ki* 23:27
came on Judah, to *r*. them. 24:3
I any more *r*. Israel. *2 Chr* 33:8
some *r*. the landmarks. *Job* 24:2
I will not *r*. mine integrity. 27:5*
of the wicked *r*. me. *Ps* 36:11*
r. thy stroke away from me. 39:10
r. from me reproach. 119:22*
r. from me the way of lying, and. 29
turn not, *r*. thy foot from. *Pr* 4:27
r. thy way far from her, and. 5:8
r. not the ancient landmark. 22:28
23:10
r. from me vanity and lies. 30:8
therefore *r*. sorrow. *Eccl* 11:10

the earth shall r. out of. *Isa 13:13**
from his place shall he not r. 46:7
then shalt thou not r. *Jer 4:1*
prophesy a lie, to r. you far. 27:10
that I should r. it from. 32:31
they shall r., they shall depart. 50:3*
r. out of the midst of Babylon. 8*
r. by day, thou shalt r. *Ezek 12:3*
saith the Lord, R. the diadem. 21:26
r. violence and spoil. 45:9
they were like them that r. *Hos 5:10*
but I will r. the northern. *Joel 2:20*
that ye might r. them from their. 3:6
ye shall not r. your necks. *Mi 2:3*
I will r. the iniquity of. *Zech 3:9*
half the mountain shall r. 14:4
r. hence, and it shall r. *Mat 17:20*
r. this cup from me. *Luke 22:42*
faith, so that I could r. *1 Cor 13:2*
or else I will r. thy candlestick.
Rev 2:5*

removed
*(In speaking of the journeying in
the wilderness the Revisions have
changed this word to journeyed)*
Noah r. the covering. *Gen 8:13*
Abram r. to Rehoboth. 12:8
Isaac r. from thence. 26:22
Jacob r. the he goats that. 30:35
and Joseph r. the people to. 47:21
the Lord r. the swarms. *Ex 8:31*
the angel of God r. and went. 14:19
the people saw it and r. and. 20:18*
people r. from Hazeroth. *Num 12:16*
they r. and pitched in the. 21:12, 13
Israel r. from Rameses. 33:5
they r. from Etham. 7, 9, 10
they r. from the Red sea. 11
r. from Alush. 14
r. from the desert of Sinai. 16
r. from Libnah. 21
r. from mount Shapher. 24
r. from Haradah. 25
r. from Makheloth. 26
r. from Tarah. 28
r. from Bene-jaakan. 32
r. from Jotbathah. 34
they r. from Ezion-gaber. 36
r. from Kadesh. 37
r. from Dibon-gad. 46
r. from Almon-diblathaim. 47
r. into all kingdoms. *Deut 28:25**
they r. from Shittim. *Josh 3:1*
when the people r. to pass over. 14
hand is not r. from you. *1 Sam 6:3*
Saul r. David from him. 18:13
he r. Amasa out of. *2 Sam 20:12**
Asa r. the idols. *1 Ki 15:12*
Maachah his mother, he r. from
being queen. 13; *2 Chr 15:16*
the high places were not r.
1 Ki 15:14*; 2 Ki 15:4, 35
Ahaz r. the laver. *2 Ki 16:17*
Lord r. Israel out of his sight.
17:18, 23; 23:27
nations which thou hast r. 17:26*
Hezekiah r. the high places. 18:4
r. the burnt offerings. *2 Chr 35:12*
and the rock is r. out. *Job 14:18*
shall the rock be r. out? 18:4
and mine hope hath he r. 19:10*
so would he have r. thee. 36:16*
though the earth be r. *Ps 46:2**
I r. his shoulder from. 81:6
so far hath he r. our. 103:12
it should not be r. for ever. 104:5*
Zion, which cannot be r. 125:1*
shall never be r. *Pr 10:30*
till the Lord have r. men. *Isa 6:12*
I have r. the bounds of. 10:13
Madmenah is r.: the inhabitants. 31*
in the sure place shall be r. 22:25*
the earth shall be r. like. 24:20*
thou hast r. it far to all ends. 26:15*
but have r. their heart far. 29:13
teachers be r. to a corner. 30:20*
of the stakes shall be r. 33:20*
mine age is r. from me as. 38:12*
the hills shall be r.: my kindness ...
shall not be r. saith. 54:10
I will cause them to be r. *Jer 15:4**
I will deliver them to be r. 24:9*
29:18*; 34:17*

sinned, therefore she is r. *Lam 1:8**
and thou hast r. my soul far. 3:17
their gold shall be r. *Ezek 7:19**
I will give them to be r. and. 23:46*
uncleanness of a r. woman. 36:17*
banquet of them shall be r.
Amos 6:7*
how hath he r. it from me! *Mi 2:4*
day shall the decree be far r. 7:11
if ye shall say, Be thou r.
he r. Abraham into this land.
Acts 7:4
when he had r. him, he raised. 13:22
are so soon r. from him. *Gal 1:6*

removeth
cursed he he that r. his neighbour's
landmark. *Deut 27:17*
which r. the mountains. *Job 9:5*
he r. away the speech of the. 12:20
whoso r. stones shall be. *Eccl 10:9**
seasons, he r. kings. *Dan 2:21*

removing
r. from thy flock all the. *Gen 30:32*
seeing I am a captive r. *Isa 49:21**
prepare the stuff for r. *Ezek 12:3, 4*
signifieth the r. of those. *Heb 12:27*

Remphan
star of your god R. *Acts 7:43*

rend
that ephod should not r. *Ex 39:23*
neither r. your clothes. *Lev 10:6*
priest shall r. the plague out. 13:56
I will surely r. the kingdom.
1 Ki 11:11; 12:31
howbeit, I will not r. away. *I Ki 11:13*
I will r. the kingdom. 31; 14:8
didst r. thy clothes. *2 Chr 34:27*
a time to r. and a time. *Eccl 3:7*
oh! that thou wouldest r. *Isa 64:1*
wind shall r. it. *Ezek 13:11, 13*
thou didst break and r. all. 29:7
and I will r. the caul. *Hos 13:8*
r. your heart, and not. *Joel 2:13*
turn again and r. you. *Mat 7:6*
let us not r. it, but cast. *John 19:24*

render
every offering they r. *Num 18:9*
I will r. vengeance to. *Deut 32:41*
he will r. vengeance to his. 43
evil of men of Shechem did God r.
upon their heads. *Judg 9:57**
Lord r. to every man. *1 Sam 26:23*
r. to every man according to his.
2 Chr 6:30
for he will r. unto man. *Job 33:26**
of a man shall he r. to him. 34:11
r. to them their desert. *Ps 28:4*
they that r. evil for good. 38:20
I will r. praises unto thee. 56:12
and r. to our neighbour. 79:12
lift up thyself, r. a reward. 94:2
what shall I r. to the Lord? 116:12
and shall not he r. to every man?
Pr 24:12; Rom 2:6
say not, I will r. to man. *Pr 24:29*
than seven men that can r. 26:16
Lord will come, to r. his. *Isa 66:15*
he will r. to Babylon. *Jer 51:6, 24*
r. to them a recompence. *Lam 3:64*
so will we r. the calves. *Hos 14:2*
will ye r. me a recompence? *Joel 3:4*
I declare, that I will r. *Zech 9:12*
r. him the fruits in. *Mat 21:41*
r. unto Caesar. 22:21; *Mark 12:17*
Luke 20:25
r. therefore to all their. *Rom 13:7*
let husband r. to wife. *1 Cor 7:3*
what thanks can we r.? *1 Thes 3:9*
see that none r. evil for evil. 5:15

rendered
thus God r. wickedness. *Judg 9:56**
the king of Moab r. to. *2 Ki 3:4*
Hezekiah r. not. *2 Chr 32:25*
man's hands be r. to him. *Pr 12:14*

renderest
r. to every man according. *Ps 62:12*

rendereth
a voice of the Lord that r. *Isa 66:6*

rendering
not r. evil for evil, or. *1 Pet 3:9*

rendest
though thou r. thy face. *Jer 4:30*

rending
lest he tear my soul, r. *Ps 7:2*

renew
r. the kingdom there. *1 Sam 11:14*
and r. a right spirit. *Ps 51:10*
that wait on Lord shall r. *Isa 40:31*
the people r. their strength. 41:1
O Lord, r. our days. *Lam 5:21*
if they fall away, to r. *Heb 6:6*

renewed
Asa r. the altar. *2 Chr 15:8*
and my bow was r. *Job 29:20*
so that thy youth is r. *Ps 103:5*
inward man is r. day. *2 Cor 4:16*
and be r. in the spirit. *Eph 4:23*
the new man, which is r. *Col 3:10*

renewest
thou r. thy witnesses. *Job 10:17*
and thou r. the face. *Ps 104:30*

renewing
be transformed by the r. *Rom 12:2*
he saved us by the r. *Tit 3:5*

renounced
have r. the hidden. *2 Cor 4:2*

renown
giants of old, men of r. *Gen 6:4*
in congregation, men of r. *Num 16:2*
thy r. went forth among. *Ezek 16:14*
harlot because of thy r. 15
raise up for them a plant of r. 34:29
it shall be to them a r. 39:13
and hast gotten thee r. *Dan 9:15*

renowned
these were the r. of. *Num 1:16**
evildoers shall never be r.
Isa 14:20*
and great lords, and r. *Ezek 23:23*
the r. city which was strong. 26:17

rent, *substantive*
a girdle there shall be a r. *Isa 3:24**
and the r. is made worse.
Mat 9:16; Mark 2:21
the new maketh a r. *Luke 5:36*

rent, *verb*
Joseph is without doubt r. in pieces.
Gen 37:33
ephod, that it be not r. *Ex 28:32*
bottles, old and r. *Josh 9:4, 13*
Samson r. the lion as he would have
r. a kid, and he had. *Judg 14:6*
Saul r. the skirt of. *1 Sam 15:27*
Lord hath r. the kingdom. 28; 28:17
Tamar r. her garment. *2 Sam 13:19*
Hushai came with his coat r. 15:32
the earth r. with the. *1 Ki 1:40*
Ahijah r. Jeroboam's new. 11:30
the altar shall be r. 13:3
altar was r. 5
and a strong wind r. the. 19:11
he r. Israel from the. *2 Ki 17:21*
when I heard this, I r. *Ezra 9:3*
having r. my garment and my. 5
then Job arose, and r. *Job 1:20*
Job's friends r. every one. 2:12
and the cloud is not r. under. 26:8
were not afraid, nor r. *Jer 36:24*
and No shall be r. *Ezek 30:16*
veil of temple was r. in twain.
Mat 27:51; Mark15:38; Luke 23:45
spirit cried, and r. him. *Mark 9:26*
see **clothes**

repaid
righteous, good shall be r. *Pr 13:21*

repair
let the priests r. the breaches of the.
2 Ki 12:5; 22:5, 6; 2 Chr 24:4*
34:8, 10
r. ye not the breaches? *2 Ki 12:7*
neither r. the breaches of the. 8
stone to r. the breaches. 12; 25:5, 6
money to r. the house. *2 Chr 24:5*
hired carpenters to r. the house. 12*
reviving to r. the house. *Ezra 9:9*
shall r. the waste cities. *Isa 61:4*

repaired
Benjamin r. cities, and. *Judg 21:23**
Solomon r. the breaches. *1 Ki 11:27*

Elijah r. the altar of the. *1 Ki* 18:30
the priests had not r. *2 Ki* 12:6
and r. therewith the house of. 14
and Joab r. the rest of. *1 Chr* 11:8
Hezekiah r. the doors of. *2 Chr* 29:3
Hezekiah r. Millo in the. 32:5*
Manasseh r. the altar of. 33:16*
next to them r. *Neh* 3:4, 5, 7, 8
      10, 12, 19
after him r. 6, 17, 18, 20, 22, 23, 24

repairer
thou shalt be called the r. *Isa* 58:12

repairing
concerning the r. of. *2 Chr* 24:27*

repay
he will r. him to his face. *Deut* 7:10
who shall r. him that? *Job* 21:31
that I should r. him? 41:11
deeds he will r. fury, and to the
islands he will r. *Isa* 59:18
again, I will r. thee. *Luke* 10:35
vengeance is mine, I will r., saith the
Lord. *Rom* 12:19
written it, I will r. it. *Philem* 19

repayeth
and r. them that hate. *Deut* 7:10

repeateth
he that r. matter. *Pr* 17:9*

repent
(Repent or repentance *is used of
regret and sorrow for having done
some deed. It is not always used
for godly repentance, which means
such sorrow as shall cause a complete change of action. Judas repented of his betrayal of Jesus,
Mat* 27:8, *but did not change his
life. When the word is used in
regard to God it is in a figure of
speech, which speaks of him almost as if human; and since his
actions are changed, attributes to
him the feelings which, in a man,
would cause such a change)*
lest the people r. *Ex* 13:17
turn from thy fierce wrath, and r. of
this. 32:12
man, that he should r. *Num* 23:19
the Lord shall r. for his. *Deut* 32:36
will not r.: for he is not a man, that
he should r. *1 Sam* 15:29
if they r. in captivity. *1 Ki* 8:47
I abhor myself, and r. *Job* 42:6
let it r. thee concerning. *Ps* 90:13
and will not r. 110:4; *Heb* 7:21
he will r. himself. *Ps* 135:14
and will not r. *Jer* 4:28
I will r. of the evil. 18:8; 26:13
if it do evil, then I will r. of. 18:10
that I may r. 26:3
for I r. of the evil. 42:10
r. and turn. *Ezek* 14:6; 18:30
spare, neither will I r. 24:14
knoweth if he will return and r.?
    Joel 2:14; *Jonah* 3:9
saying, R., for the kingdom of
heaven. *Mat* 3:2; 4:17
Jesus preaching, r. ye. *Mark* 1:15
preached that men should r. 6:12
except ye r. ye shall. *Luke* 13:3, 5
from the dead, they will r. 16:30
thy brother r. forgive him. 17:3, 4
r. and be baptized. *Acts* 2:38
r. ye therefore and be. 3:19
r. of this thy wickedness. 8:22
commandeth all men to r. 17:30
that they should r. and. 26:20
I do not r. though I did r. *2 Cor* 7:8
and r. . . . except thou r. *Rev* 2:5
r. or else I will come unto. 16
space to r. of her fornication. 21
except they r. of their deeds. 22
thou hast received, and r. 3:3
be zealous therefore and r. 19

repentance
r. shall be hid from mine. *Hos* 13:14
bring forth fruits meet for r.
    Mat 3:8; *Luke* 3:8
baptize with water unto r. *Mat* 3:11
to call sinners to r. 9:13; *Mark* 2:17
    Luke 5:32

did preach baptism of r. *Mark* 1:4
    Luke 3:3; *Acts* 13:24; 19:4
99 which need no r. *Luke* 15:7
that r. and remission of sins. 24:47
God exalted for to give r. *Acts* 5:31
Gentiles granted r. to life. 11:18
Greeks r. towards God. 20:21
and do works meet for r. 26:20
God leadeth thee to r. *Rom* 2:4
calling of God are without r. 11:29
that ye sorrowed to r. *2 Cor* 7:9
godly sorrow worketh r. to. 10
will give them r *2 Tim* 2:25
the foundation of r. *Heb* 6:1
to renew them again to r. 6
found no place of r. though. 12:17
that all should come to r. *2 Pet* 3:9

repented
it r. the Lord, that he. *Gen* 6:6
the Lord r. of the evil. *Ex* 32:14
    2 Sam 24:16; *1 Chr* 21:15
    Jer 26:19
it r. the Lord because. *Judg* 2:18
Israel r. for Benjamin. 21:6, 15
the Lord r. that he made Saul king.
    1 Sam 15:35
the Lord r. according to. *Ps* 106:45
no man r. him of his. *Jer* 8:6
Lord overthrew, and r. not. 20:16
that I was turned, I r. 31:19
the Lord r. for this. *Amos* 7:3, 6
God r. of the evil that. *Jonah* 3:10
punish you, and I r. not. *Zech* 8:14
because they r. not. *Mat* 11:20
they would have r. long ago.
    21; *Luke* 10:13
men of Nineveh shall rise because
they r. *Mat* 12:41; *Luke* 11:32
not, but afterward he r. *Mat* 21:29
ye, when ye had seen it, r. not. 32
Judas r. himself, and brought. 27:3
not to be r. of. *2 Cor* 7:10
many that have not r. of the. 12:21
repent, and she r. not. *Rev* 2:21
these plagues, yet r. not. 9:20
neither r. of their murders. 21
blasphemed and r. not. 16:9, 11

repentest
art a gracious God, and r. thee of the
evil. *Jonah* 4:2

repenteth
for it r. me that I have. *Gen* 6:7
it r. me that I have set. *1 Sam* 15:11
slow to anger, and r. *Joel* 2:13
over one sinner that r. *Luke* 15:7, 10

repenting
I am weary with r. *Jer* 15:6

repentings
my heart is turned, r. are. *Hos* 11:8

repetitions
use not vain r. as heathen. *Mat* 6:7

Rephaim
Philistines spread themselves in valley of R. *2 Sam* 5:18, 22; 23:13
    1 Chr 11:15; 14:9
ears in the valley of R. *Isa* 17:5

Rephaims
smote the R. in Ashteroth. *Gen* 14:5
have I given the land of R. 15:20

Rephidim
Israel pitched in R. *Ex* 17:1
    Num 33:14
fought with Israel in R. *Ex* 17:8
they were departed from R.
    19:2; *Num* 33:15

replenish
and r. the earth. *Gen* 1:28; 9:1

replenished
be r. from the east. *Isa* 2:6*
of Zidon have r. Tyre. 23:2
r. every sorrowful soul. *Jer* 31:25
r., now she is laid waste. *Ezek* 26:2
thou wast r. and made very. 27:25

repliest
O man, who art thou that r. against
God? *Rom* 9:20

report
(*Of good report*, of good reputation,
Acts 6:3)
to his father their evil r. *Gen* 37:2
shalt not raise a false r. *Ex* 23:1

brought up an evil r. *Num* 13:32
did bring up the evil r. died. 14:37
who shall hear r. of thee. *Deut* 2:25
It is no good r. I hear. *1 Sam* 2:24
it was a true r. I heard. *1 Ki* 10:6
    2 Chr 9:5
matter for an evil r. *Neh* 6:13
and a good r. maketh. *Pr* 15:30*
as at the r. concerning Egypt, so . . .
at the r. of Tyre. *Isa* 23:5
vexation only to understand r. 28:19*
who hath believed our r.? 53:1†
    John 12:38; *Rom* 10:16
Babylon hath heard the r. *Jer* 50:43*
seven men of honest r. *Acts* 6:3
Cornelius was of good r. 10:22*
Ananias, having a good r. of. 22:12
by evil r. and good r. as. *2 Cor* 6:8
things are of good r. *Phil* 4:8
must have a good r. of. *1 Tim* 3:7*
elders obtained a good r. *Heb* 11:2*
obtained a good r. through faith. 39*
Demetrius hath a good r. *3 John* 12*

report, *verb*
r. say they, and we will r. it.
    Jer 20:10
he will r. that God is. *1 Cor* 14:25

reported
it is r. among heathen. *Neh* 6:6
be r. to king according to these. 7
also they r. his good deeds. 19
despise their husbands, when it
shall be r. *Esth* 1:17
which had the inkhorn, r. *Ezek* 9:11
this saying is commonly r. *Mat* 28:15
r. all that chief priests. *Acts* 4:23
Timotheus was well r. of. 16:2
as we be slanderously r. *Rom* 3:8
it is r. that there is. *1 Cor* 5:1
a widow, well r. of for. *1 Tim* 5:10
that are now r. to you. *1 Pet* 1:12

reproach
[1] *Scorn or derision*, Neh 2:17;
5:9. [2] *Shame or disgrace*,
Pr 6:33. [3] *Censure or blame*,
Isa 51:7. [4] *Injury, either in
word or deed*, 2 Cor 12:10.

rolled away r. of Egypt. *Josh* 5:9
taketh away the r. *1 Sam* 17:26
in great affliction and r. *Neh* 1:3
and turn their r. upon their. 4:4
because of the r. of heathen. 5:9
make me not the r. of the. *Ps* 39:8
save me from r. of him. 57:3
for thy sake I have borne r. 69:7
r. hath broken my heart, I am. 20
let them be covered with r. 71:13
he put them to a perpetual r. 78:66
their r. wherewith they. 79:12
remember the r. of thy servants, how
I bear in my bosom the r. 89:50
remove from me r. and. 119:22
r. shall not be wiped away. *Pr* 6:33
and with ignominy cometh r. 18:3
that causeth shame and r. 19:26
strife and r. shall cease. 22:10*
to take away our r. *Isa* 4:1
fear ye not the r. of men. 51:7*
not remember the r. of thy. 54:4
an everlasting r. on you. *Jer* 23:40
because I did bear the r. of. 31:19
because we have heard r. 51:51
he is filled full with r. *Lam* 3:30
thou hast heard their r. O Lord. 61
consider and behold our r. 5:1
as at the time of thy r. *Ezek* 16:57
concerning r. of Ammonites. 21:28
nor shalt thou bear r. of the. 36:15
that ye receive no more r. 30
the r. offered by him to cease, without his own r. *Dan* 11:18
and his r. shall his Lord. *Hos* 12:14
not thine heritage to r. *Joel* 2:17
shall bear r. of my people. *Mi* 6:16
I have heard the r. of Moab. *Zeph* 2:8
r. of it was a burden. 3:18
I speak as concerning r. *2 Cor* 11:21*
good report lest fall into r. *1 Tim* 3:7
both labour and suffer r. 4:10*
esteeming the r. of Christ. *Heb* 11:26
without the camp, bearing his r. 13:13

reproach, verb
glean, and r. her not. Ruth 2:15
whom king of Assyria hath sent to r.
　2 Ki 19:4*, 16; Isa 37:4*, 17*
that they might r. me. Neh 6:13
my heart shall not r. me. Job 27:6
mine enemies r. me. Ps 42:10
the adversary r. me ? 74:10
mine enemies r. me all day. 102:8
when men shall r. you. Luke 6:22

a reproach
that were a r. to us. Gen 34:14
and lay it for a r. upon. 1 Sam 11:2
that we be no more a r. Neh 2:17
he that taketh not up a r. Ps 15:3
a r. of men, and despised. 22:6
I was a r. among all mine. 31:11
thou makest us a r. to our. 44:13
a r. to our neighbours. 79:4
he is a r. to his neighbours. 89:41
I became also a r. to them. 109:25
sin is a r. to any people. Pr 14:34
people that were a r. Isa 30:5
word of Lord is to them a r. Jer 6:10
word of Lord was made a r. 20:8
to be a r. and a proverb. 24:9; 29:18
　42:18; 44:8, 12
Bozrah shall become a r. and. 49:13
I will make thee a r. Ezek 5:14
Jerusalem shall be a r. and a. 15
I have made thee a r. unto. 22:4
people are become a r. Dan 9:16
no more make you a r. Joel 2:19

my reproach
hath taken away my r. Gen 30:23
the cause of my r. 1 Sam 25:39
plead against me my r. Job 19:5
heard the check of my r. 20:3
when I wept, that was my r. Ps 69:10
known my r. and my shame. 19
turn away my r. which I. 119:39
to take away my r. Luke 1:25

reproached
whom hast thou r.? 2 Ki 19:22*
　Isa 37:23*
by thy messengers thou hast r. the.
　2 Ki 19:23* Isa 37:24
ten times have ye r. me. Job 19:3
not an enemy that r. me. Ps 55:12
that r. thee, are fallen upon me.
　69:9; Rom 15:3
that the enemy hath r. Ps 74:18
have r. thee, O Lord. 79:12
thine enemies have r. O Lord, they
　have r. the footsteps. 89:51
have r. my people. Zeph 2:8
r. and magnified themselves. 10
if ye be r. for Christ. 1 Pet 4:14

reproaches
r. of them that reproached thee.
　Ps 69:9; Rom 15:3
I have given Israel to r. Isa 43:28*
I take pleasure in r. 2 Cor 12:10*
made a gazingstock by r. Heb 10:33

reproachest
Master, thou r. us also. Luke 11:45

reproacheth
aught presumptuously, r. the Lord.
　Num 15:30*
voice of him that r. and. Ps 44:16
how the foolish man r. thee. 74:22
to answer him that r. me. 119:42
　Pr 27:11
oppresseth poor r. his Maker.
　Pr 14:31; 17:5

reproachfully
smitten me on the cheek r. Job 16:10
none occasion to speak r. Tim 5:14*

reprobate
r. silver shall men call. Jer 6:30*
over them to a r. mind. Rom 1:28
r. concerning the faith. 2 Tim 3:8
to every good work r. Tit 1:16

reprobates
you, except ye be r. 2 Cor 13:5
shall know that we are not r. 6
honest, though we be as r. 7

reproof
astonished at his r. Job 26:11*
turn you at my r. Pr 1:23

ye would none of my r. Pr 1:25
despised my r. 30
my heart depised r. 5:12
but he that refuseth r. erreth. 10:17
but he that hateth r. is brutish. 12:1
he that regardeth r. shall be. 13:18
that regardeth r. is prudent. 15:5
he that hateth r. shall die. 10
heareth the r. of life, abideth. 31
he that heareth r. getteth. 32
r. entereth more into a wise. 17:10*
the rod and r. give wisdom. 29:15
is profitable for r. 2 Tim 3:16

reproofs
in whose mouth are no r. Ps 38:14
r. of instruction are way. Pr 6:23

reprove
r. the words of Rab-shakeh.
　2 Ki 19:4*; Isa 37:4*
doth your arguing r.? Job 6:25
do ye imagine to r. words ? 26
he will surely r. you if ye. 13:10
will he r. thee for fear of ? 22:4
I will not r. thee for burnt. Ps 50:8
I will r. thee, and set them. 21
let him r. me, it shall be an. 141:5
r. not a scorner, lest he. Pr 9:8
and r. one that hath. 19:25
lest he r. thee, and thou be. 30:6
neither r. after the hearing. Isa 11:3†
and r. with equity for the meek. 4†
backslidings shall r. thee. Jer 2:19
let no man strive nor r. Hos 4:4
he will r. the world of. John 16:8*
but rather r. them. Eph 5:11
r., rebuke, exhort with. 2 Tim 4:2

reproved
she was r. Gen 20:16*
Abraham r. Abimelech. 21:25
he r. kings for their sakes.
　1 Chr 16:21; Ps 105:14
often r. hardeneth his neck. Pr 29:1
not r. Jeremiah ? Jer 29:27*
answer when I am r. Hab 2:1*
Herod being r. by John. Luke 3:19
lest deeds should be r. John 3:20
all things that are r. are. Eph 5:13

reprover
wise r. upon an obedient. Pr 25:12
shalt not be to them a r. Ezek 3:26

reproveth
he that r. God, let him. Job 40:2*
he that r. a scorner. Pr 9:7
scorner loveth not one that r. 15:12
snare for him that r. Isa 29:21

reputation
that is in r. for wisdom. Eccl 10:1*
Gamaliel had in r. among. Acts 5:34*
which were of r. Gal 2:2*
but made himself of no r. Phil 2:7*
therefore, hold such in r. 29*

reputed
wherefore are we r. vile ? Job 18:3*
all the inhabitants are r. Dan 4:35

request, -s
desire a r. of you. Judg 8:24
king shall perform the r. 2 Sam 14:15
fulfilled the r. of his servant 22
granted him all his r. Ezra 7:6
what dost thou make r.? Neh 2:4
to make r. before him. Esth 4:8
what is thy r.? 5:3,6; 7:2; 9:12
my request at my r. 7:3
Haman stood up to make r. 7
O that I might have my r.! Job 6:8
hast not withholden r. Ps 21:2
he gave them their r. but. 106:15
r. for a prosperous. Rom 1:10
every prayer making r. Phil 1:4
let your r. be made known. 4:6

requested
earrings that he r. Judg 8:26
Elijah r. that he might. 1 Ki 19:4
Jabez what he r. 1 Chr 4:10
he r. of the prince. Dan 1:8
Daniel r. of the king. 2:49

require
your blood will I r. . . . hand of man
　will I r. the life of man. Gen 9:5
of my hand didst thou r. it. 31:39
of my hand shalt thou r. him. 43:9

what doth the Lord r.? Deut 10:12
　Mi 6:8
I will r. it of him. Deut 18:19
Lord will surely r. it of thee. 23:21
let Lord himself r. it. Josh 22:23
　1 Sam 20:16
but one thing I r. of. 2 Sam 3:13
shall not I r. his blood ? 4:11
whatsoever thou shalt r. 19:38
as the matter shall r. 1 Ki 8:59
my Lord r. this thing ? 1 Chr 21:3
look on it, and r. it. 2 Chr 24:22
Ezra shall r. of you. Ezra 7:21
to r. of the king a band. 8:22
and r. nothing of them. Neh 5:12
thou wilt not r. it. Ps 10:13
but his blood will I r. at thine hand.
　Ezek 3:18, 20; 33:6, 8
and there will I r. your. 20:40
and I will r. my flock at. 34:10
the Jews r. a sign. 1 Cor 1:22
if need so r., let him do what. 7:36

required
behold, his blood is r. Gen 42:22
such things as they r. Ex 12:36*
business r. haste. 1 Sam 21:8
when he r. they set. 2 Sam 12:20
every day's work r. 1 Chr 16:37
as duty of every day r. 2 Chr 8:14
　Ezra 3:4
why hast thou not r. of the ? 24:6
yet r. not I the bread. Neh 5:18
she r. nothing but what. Esth 2:15
and sin offering hast thou not r.
　Ps 40:6
and they that wasted us, r. 137:3
two things I have r. of thee. Pr 30:7*
who hath r. this at your ? Isa 1:12
r. of this generation. Luke 11:50, 51
this night thy soul shall be r. 12:20
of him shall be much r. 48
I might have r. mine own. 19:23
that it should be as they r. 23:24*
it is r. in stewards that. 1 Cor 4:2

requirest
will do all that thou r. Ruth 3:11*

requireth
God r. that which is past. Eccl 3:15*
rare thing that the king r. Dan 2:11

requiring
r. that he might be crucified.
　Luke 23:23

requite
Joseph will certainly r. Gen 50:15
do ye thus r. Lord ? Deut 32:6
and I will r. you this. 2 Sam 2:6
it may be the Lord will r. me. 16:12
I will r. thee in this. 2 Ki 9:26
beholdest to r. it with. Ps 10:14*
raise me up that I may r. 41:10
God shall surely r. Jer 51:56
let them learn to r. their. 1 Tim 5:4

requited
so God hath r. me. Judg 1:7
r. me evil for good. 1 Sam 25:21*

requiting
judge thy servants by r. 2 Chr 6:23

rereward
standard of Dan was r. Num 10:25
r. came after the ark. Josh 6:9, 13
David passed on in r. 1 Sam 29:2
God will be your r. Isa 52:12
glory of Lord shall be thy r. 58:8

rescue
have none to r. them. Deut 28:31
r. my soul from their. Ps 35:17
and none shall r. him. Hos 5:14

rescued
the people r. Jonathan. 1 Sam 14:45
David r. his two wives. 30:18
came I with an army, and r. him.
　Acts 23:27

rescueth
he delivereth and r. and. Dan 6:27

resemblance
this is their r. through. Zech 5:6

resemble
I r. kingdom of God ? Luke 13:18*

resembled
each one r. the children. Judg 8:18

reserve

will he r. his anger for ever ? Jer 3:5*
pardon them whom I r. 50:20*
to r. the unjust to the. 2 Pet 2:9*

reserved

thou not r. a blessing ? Gen 27:36
the most holy things r. Num 18:9
r. not to each his wife. Judg 21:22*
mother, that she had r. Ruth 2:18*
David r. horses for 100 chariots.
2 Sam 8:4; 1 Chr 18:4
wicked is r. to the day. Job 21:30
which I have r. against time. 38:23
but when Paul had appealed to be r.
Acts 25:21*
I have r. to myself 7000. Rom 11:4*
inheritance r. in heaven. 1 Pet 1:4
delivered them to be r. 2 Pet 2:4
mist of darkness is r. for ever. 17
the heavens and earth are r. 3:7
r. in everlasting chains. Jude 6*
to whom is r. the blackness. 13

reserveth

he r. to us the weeks of. Jer 5:24
r. wrath for his enemies. Nah 1:2

residue

locusts shall eat the r. Ex 10:5
r. of the sons of Kohath. 1 Chr 6:66
the r. of Israel were in. Neh 11:20
the r. of archers shall. Isa 21:17
Lord shall be a diadem to r. of. 28:5
I am deprived of the r. 38:10
r. thereof he maketh a god. 44:17
shall I make the r. thereof. 19
death chosen by all the r. Jer 8:3
r. of them will I deliver to. 15:9
and the r. of Jerusalem. 24:8
saith, concerning the r. of. 27:19
Jeremiah sent to r. of elders. 29:1
r. of the princes of Babylon. 39:3
Ishmael carried captive the r. 41:10
and the r. of the people that. 52:15
destroy all r. of Israel ? Ezek 9:8
thy r. shall be devoured. 23:25
tread the r. of your pastures. 34:18
possession unto r. of heathen. 36:3
a derision to the r. of the heathen. 4
I spoken against r. of heathen. 5
the r. in length over against. 48:18
the r. shall be for the prince. 21
and stamped the r. Dan 7:7, 19
r. of my people shall. Zeph 2:9
speak to Joshua and the r. Hag 2:2
I will not be to the r. Zech 8:11
r. of the people shall not be. 14:2
yet had he r. of spirit. Mal 2:15
and told it to the r. Mark 16:13
that the r. might seek. Acts 15:17

resist

Satan standing at his right hand to r.
Zech 3:1*
that ye r. not evil. Mat 5:39
shall not be able to r. Luke 21:15*
not able to r. the spirit. Acts 6:10*
always r. the Holy Ghost as. 7:51
they that r. shall receive. Rom 13:2*
these also r. the truth. 2 Tim 3:8*
r. the devil and he will. Jas 4:7
just, and he doth not r. you. 5:6
whom r. stedfast in the. 1 Pet 5:9*

resisted

who hath r. his will ? Rom 9:19*
have not yet r. unto blood. Heb 12:4

resisteth

whosoever r. the power, r. ordinance.
Rom 13:2*
God r. the proud. Jas 4:6; 1 Pet 5:5

resolved

I am r. what to do, when. Luke 16:4

resort

r. ye thither to us, God. Neh 4:20
I may continually r. Ps 71:3
the people r. to him. Mark 10:1*
whither Jews always r. John 18:20*

resorted

and Levites r. to him. 2 Chr 11:13
multitudes r. to him. Mark 2:13
and many r. to him. John 10:41*
Jesus ofttimes r. thither. 18:2
women who r. thither. Acts 16:13*

respect

(Respect of persons. Favour or partiality toward the rich or powerful)
the Lord had r. to Abel. Gen 4:4
to Cain, he had not r. 5
God looked, and had r. Ex 2:25*
for I will have r. unto. Lev 26:9
yet have thou r. unto the prayer.
1 Ki 8:28; 2 Chr 6:19
and the Lord had r. 2 Ki 13:23
is no iniquity nor r. of persons with
God. 2 Chr 19:7; Rom 2:11
Eph 6:9; Col 3:25
have r. unto covenant. Ps 74:20
when I have r. to all thy. 119:6
I will have r. unto thy ways. 15
I will have r. unto thy statutes. 117
yet hath he r. unto the lowly. 138:6
not good to have r. of persons in
judgement. Pr 24:23; 28:21
have r. to the Holy One. Isa 17:7
had r. to him that fashioned. 22:11
had no glory in this r. 2 Cor 3:10
not that I speak in r. of. Phil 4:11
let none judge you in r. of. Col 2:16
Moses had r. to. Heb 11:26*
faith with r. of persons. Jas 2:1
ye have r. to him that weareth. 3*
if ye have r. to persons, ye. 9
without r. of persons. 1 Pet 1:17

respect, verb

shalt not r. the person. Lev 19:15
Moses said, R. not thou. Num 16:15
ye shall not r. persons in judgement.
Deut 1:17; 16:19
neither doth God r. any person.
2 Sam 14:14*
nor shall r. that which. Isa 17:8

respected

they r. not the persons. Lam 4:16

respecter

God is no r. of persons. Acts 10:34

respecteth

he r. not any that are. Job 37:24*
blessed is man that r. not. Ps 40:4

respite

saw that there was r. Ex 8:15
Give us seven days' r. 1 Sam 11:3

rest

(This word includes freedom from oppression by the enemy, and peace of spirit, as well as the ordinary meanings)
Issachar saw that r. was. Gen 49:15
to-morrow the r. of holy. Ex 16:23
the seventh is the sabbath of r. 31:15
35:2; Lev 16:31; 23:3, 32; 25:4
thee, and I will give thee r. Ex 33:14
a year of r. to the land. Lev 25:5
until the Lord have given r.
Deut 3:20; Josh 1:13
not as yet come to the r. Deut 12:9
when he giveth you r. from. 10
thy God hath given thee r. 25:19
the sole of thy foot have r. 28:65
given your brethren r. Josh 1:15
the land had r. from war. 14:15
Judg 3:11; 5:31
the Lord gave them r. round about.
Josh 21:44; 2 Chr 15:15
God hath given r. Josh 22:4
Lord had given r. 23:1
land had r. eighty years. Judg 3:30
Lord grant you may find r. Ruth 1:9
shall I not seek r. for thee ? 3:1
for this man will not be in r. till. 18
Lord had given him r. 2 Sam 7:1
1 Ki 5:4; 8:56; 2 Chr 14:6, 7
after that the ark had r. 1 Chr 6:31
man of r. and I will give him r. 22:9
hath he not given you r.? 18
God of Israel hath given r. 23:25
to build a house of r. 28:2
for his God gave him r. 2 Chr 20:30
but after they had r. they. Neh 9:28
the Jews had r. from. Esth 9:16
slept, then had I been at r. Job 3:13
and there the weary be at r. 17
not in safety, neither had I r. 26*
shalt take thy r. in safety. 11:18

r. together is in the dust. Job 17:16
neither is there any r. in. Ps 38:3*
would I fly away and be at r. 55:6
that thou mayest give him r. 94:13*
should not enter into my r. 95:11
return to thy r. O my soul. 116:7
arise, O Lord, into thy r., thou. 132:8
this is my r. for ever, here will. 14
son, he shall give thee r. Pr 29:17
his heart taketh not r. in. Eccl 2:23
this hath more r. than. 6:5
and his r. shall be glorious. Isa 11:10
give thee r. from thy sorrow. 14:3
whole earth is at r. 7; Zech 1:11
Lord said, I will take my r. Isa 18:4
this is r. wherewith ye cause. 28:12
in returning and r. shall ye. 30:15
find for herself a place of r. 34:14*
where is the place of my r.? 66:1
find r. for your souls. Jer 6:16
return and be in r. 30:10*; 46:27
that he may give r. to land. 50:34
go to them that are at r. Ezek 38:11*
Nebuchadnezzar was at r. Dan 4:4
for this is not your r. Mi 2:10
Damascus shall be the r. Zech 9:1
and I will give you r. Mat 11:28
ye shall find r. to your souls. 29
seeking r. and. 12:43; Luke 11:24
sleep on now, and take your r.
Mat 26:45; Mark 14:41
of taking r. in sleep. John 11:13
what is place of my r.? Acts 7:49
then had the churches r. 9:31*
who are troubled r. with. 2 Thes 1:7
not enter into my r. Heb 3:11, 18
being left us of entering into r. 4:1
have believed do enter into r. 3
if they shall enter into my r. 5
for if Jesus had given them r. 8
remaineth a r. to the people of. 9
he that is entered into his r. hath. 10
labour to enter into that r. 11
see no

rest

Jacob fed r. of Laban's. Gen 30:36
the names of the r. on. Ex 28:10
the r. of the blood shall. Lev 5:9
the r. of the oil that. 14:17, 29
beside the r. of them. Num 31:8
being the r. of the prey. 32*
the r. of Gilead gave I. Deut 3:13
r. entered into fenced. Josh 10:20
r. bowed down to drink. Judg 7:6
the r. have we utterly. 1 Sam 15:15
the r. of the people he delivered to.
2 Sam 10:10; 1 Chr 19:11
the r. fled to Aphek to. 1 Ki 20:30
and thy children of the r. 2 Ki 4:7
Joab repaired the r. of. 1 Chr 11:8
Jeduthun and the r. chosen. 16:41
the r. of the money. 2 Chr 24:14
nor told it to the r. that. Neh 2:16
r. of our enemies heard I had. 6:1
r. of the people also cast lots. 11:1
what have done in the r.? Esth 9:12
the r. to their babes. Ps 17:14
r. of trees of his forest. Isa 10:19
r. of the land shall give. Ezek 45:8
should not perish with r. Dan 2:18
let the r. eat the flesh of. Zech 11:9
r. said, Let us see if. Mat 27:49
ye thought for the r.? Luke 12:26
the eleven and to all the r. 24:9
said to Peter and the r. Acts 2:37
of r. durst no man join. 5:13
and the r., they escaped all. 27:44
election obtained it, and r. Rom 11:7
r. speak I, not the Lord. 1 Cor 7:12
r. will I set in order when I. 11:34
not live r. of his time to. 1 Pet 4:2
and to the r. in Thyatira. Rev 2:24
the r. that were not killed. 9:20
r. of the dead lived not again. 20:5
see acts

rest, verb

wash your feet, and r. Gen 18:4
ye make them r. from. Ex 5:5
year thou shalt let it r. 23:11
seventh day thou shalt r. 12; 34:21
and in harvest thou shalt r. 34:21
then shall the land r. Lev 26:34
did not r. in your sabbaths. 35

thy maidservant may r. *Deut* 5:14
feet of the priests shall r. *Josh* 3:13
let it r. on the head of. *2 Sam* 3:29
have caused thee to r. from. 7:11
neither the birds to r. on them. 21:10
the spirit of Elijah doth r. *2 Ki* 2:15
we r. on thee, in thy. *2 Chr* 14:11*
there the prisoners r. *Job* 3:18*
that he may r. till he shall. 14:6
my flesh shall r. in hope. *Ps* 16:9*
Acts 2:26*
r. in the Lord, and wait. *Ps* 37:7
rod of wicked shall not r. on. 125:3
nor will he r. content. *Pr* 6:35
thy flock to r. at noon. *S of S* 1:7
all of them shall r. in the. *Isa* 7:19
the Spirit of the Lord shall. 11:2
shall the hand of the Lord r. 25:10
may cause the weary to r. 28:12
screech owl also shall r. 34:14
I will make my judgement to r. 51:4
enter into peace, they shall r. 57:2
troubled sea, when it cannot r. 20
Jerusalem's sake I will not r. 62:1
the Lord caused him to r. 63:14
went to cause him to r. *Jer* 31:2
put up into thy scabbard, r. 47:6
will cause my fury to r. *Ezek* 5:13
16:42; 21:17; 24:13
cause the blessing to r. 44:30
for thou shalt r. and. *Dan* 12:13
that I might r. in the day. *Hab* 3:16
he will r. in love, he will. *Zeph* 3:17
desert place, and r. a. *Mark* 6:31
there, your peace shall r. *Luke* 10:6
of Christ may r. on me. *2 Cor* 12:9
God did r. seventh day. *Heb* 4:4
they r. not day and night. *Rev* 4:8
that they should r. yet for a. 6:11
that they may r. from their. 14:13

rested
he r. on seventh day. *Gen* 2:2, 3
Ex 20:11; 31:17
the ark r. *Gen* 8:4
locusts r. in Egypt. *Ex* 10:14
the people r. on the seventh. 16:30
cloud abode, they r. *Num* 9:18*, 23*
cloud r. in the wilderness. 10:12*
when it r. he said, Return, O. 36
when spirit r. upon them. 11:25, 26
and the land r. from. *Josh* 11:23
the chambers r. on the. *1 Ki* 6:10
people r. on the words. *2 Chr* 32:8
day of the same r. *Esth* 9:17, 18
wherein the Jews r. from their. 22
bowels boiled and r. not. *Job* 30:27
they r. sabbath day. *Luke* 23:56

restest
thou art a Jew, and r. in. *Rom* 2:17

resteth
in safety, whereon he r. *Job* 24:23
wisdom r. in heart of him. *Pr* 14:33
for anger r. in the bosom. *Eccl* 7:9
Spirit of God r. upon. *1 Pet* 4:14

resting
to search out a r. place. *Num* 10:33
into thy r. place. *2 Chr* 6:41
spoil not his r. place. *Pr* 24:15
shall dwell in r. places *Isa* 32:18
forgotten their r. place. *Jer* 50:6

restitution
make full r. *Ex* 22:3, 5, 6, 12
his substance shall r. be. *Job* 20:18
until the times of the. *Acts* 3:21*

restore
[1] *To give back again*, Gen 20:14;
Judg 11:13. [2] *To bring back to
the first state or condition*, Gen
40:13; Isa 1:26; Acts 1:6. [3] *To
recover, or get again*, 2 Ki 14:25.
[4] *To heal or cure*, Mat 12:13.
r. the man his wife, and if thou r. her.
Gen 20:7
Pharaoh will r. thee to thy. 40:13
to r. every man's money. 42:25
he shall r. five oxen for. *Ex* 22:1*
found, he shall r. double. 4*
he shall r. that which he. *Lev* 6:4
he shall even r. it in the principal. 5
killeth a beast, he shall r. 24:21*
and r. the overplus to whom. 25:27
but if he be not able to r. it to. 28*

congregation shall r. *Num* 35:25
thou shalt r. again. *Deut* 22:2
therefore r. those lands. *Judg* 11:13
I will r. it. 17:3; *1 Sam* 12:3
1 Ki 20:34
I will r. thee all the land. *2 Sam* 9:7
he shall r. the lamb fourfold. 12:6
shall house of Israel r. me. 16:3
r. all that was hers. *2 Ki* 8:6
r. I pray you, to them. *Neh* 5:11
we will r. 12
and his hands shall r. *Job* 20:10
laboured for, shall he r. 18
r. to me the joy of thy. *Ps* 51:12
if he be found, he shall r. *Pr* 6:31
I will r. thy judges as. *Isa* 1:26
spoil, and none saith r. 42:22
to r. the preserved of Israel. 49:6
I will lead and r. comforts. 57:18
I will r. them to this. *Jer* 27:22
I will r. health to thee, and. 30:17
if the wicked r. pledge. *Ezek* 33:15
command to r. and to. *Dan* 9:25
I will r. to you the years. *Joel* 2:25
Elias shall come and r. *Mat* 17:11
have taken any thing, I r. *Luke* 19:8
Lord, wilt thou r. kingdom ? *Acts* 1:6
r. such an one in the spirit. *Gal* 6:1

restored
Abimelech r. him Sarah. *Gen* 20:14
he r. the chief butler to his. 40:21
me he r. to mine office, him. 41:13
my money is r. and it is in. 42:28
shall not be r. to thee. *Deut* 28:31
r. 1100 shekels. *Judg* 17:3, 4
from Israel were r. *1 Sam* 7:14
that my hand may be r. to me: the
king's hand was r. *1 Ki* 13:6
son he had r. to life. *2 Ki* 8:1, 5
he built and r. Elath to Judah.
14:22; *2 Chr* 26:2
r. coast of Israel from. *2 Ki* 14:25
the cities Huram had r. *2 Chr* 8:2*
brought to Babylon be r. *Ezra* 6:5
I r. that which I took not. *Ps* 69:4
but hath r. to the debtor. *Ezek* 18:7
violence, hath not r. pledge. 12
hand was r. whole like as the.
Mat 12:13; *Mark* 3:5; *Luke* 6:10
his sight was r. and he. *Mark* 8:25
that I may be r. to you. *Heb* 13:19

restorer
he shall be to thee a r. *Ruth* 4:15
shall be called r. of paths. *Isa* 58:12

restoreth
he r. my soul, he leadeth. *Ps* 23:3
Elias cometh first and r. *Mark* 9:12

restrain
dost thou r. wisdom ? *Job* 15:8†
wrath shalt thou r. *Ps* 76:10*

restrained
rain from heaven was r. *Gen* 8:2
and now nothing will be r. 11:6*
Sarai said, Lord hath r. me. 16:2
were r. from bringing. *Ex* 36:6
sons vile, and he r. not. *1 Sam* 3:13
toward me, are they r.? *Isa* 63:15
I r. the floods thereof. *Ezek* 31:15
these sayings, scarce r. *Acts* 14:18

restrainest
thou r. prayer before God. *Job* 15:4

restraint
there is no r. to the Lord. *1 Sam* 14:6

rests
he made narrowed r. *1 Ki* 6:6*

resurrection
(*The rising from the dead and
living again was a belief which was
held by many Israelites, although
it was not universal. It was a
more important article of faith
among the Christians, as Paul
argued in 1 Cor 15*)
Sadducees, who say there is no r.
Mat 22:23; *Mark* 12:18
Acts 23:8; *1 Cor* 15:12
in the r. whose wife ? *Mat* 22:28
Mark 12:23; *Luke* 20:33
in the r. they neither. *Mat* 22:30
as touching the r. have ye ? 31
out of the graves after his r. 27:53

recompensed at the r. *Luke* 14:14
deny any r. 20:27
the children of the r. 36
good to the r. of life: evil, to the r. of
damnation. *John* 5:29
brother shall rise in the r. 11:24
Jesus said, I am the r. and the. 25
witness with us of his r. *Acts* 1:22
David spake of r. of Christ. 2:31
preached through Jesus the r. 4:2
witness of the r. of the Lord. 33
he preached Jesus and the r. 17:18
heard of the r., some mocked. 32
of the hope and r. I am called. 23:6
shall be a r. of the dead. 24:15
Touching r. of the dead. 21
declared by the r. from. *Rom* 1:4
in the likeness of his r. 6:5
but if there be no r. of. *1 Cor* 15:13
by man came the r. 21
so is the r. of the dead. 42
know the power of his r. *Phil* 3:10
if I might attain to the r. of. 11
that the r. is past. *2 Tim* 2:18
of r. from the dead, and. *Heb* 6:2
they might obtain a better r. 11:35
hope, by r. of Jesus. *1 Pet* 1:3
save us, by r. of Jesus Christ. 3:21
this is the first r. *Rev* 20:5
he that hath part in the first r. 6

retain
still r. thine integrity ? *Job* 2:9*
he said, Let thine heart r. *Pr* 4:4
strong men r. riches. 11:16†
no man hath power to r. *Eccl* 8:8
she shall not r. the power. *Dan* 11:6
whose soever sins ye r. *John* 20:23
did not like to r. God. *Rom* 1:28*

retained
Gideon r. those 300. *Judg* 7:8
the damsel's father r. him. 19:4
and I r. no strength. *Dan* 10:8, 16
sins ye retain, they are r. *John* 20:23
whom I would have r. *Philem* 13

retaineth
every one that r. her. *Pr* 3:18
gracious woman r. honour. 11:16†
he r. not his anger for ever. *Mi* 7:18

retire
hottest battle, and r. *2 Sam* 11:15
toward Zion: r., stay not. *Jer* 4:6*

retired
Israel r. in battle. *Judg* 20:39*
they r. from the city. *2 Sam* 20:22*

return, *substantive*
meet Abram after his r. *Gen* 14:17
Samuel's r. was to. *1 Sam* 7:17
at r. of year Syria. *1 Ki* 20:22, 26

return
(*Frequently means* turn again, *or*
repent)
till thou r. to the ground: for dust
thou art . . . thou r. *Gen* 3:19
r. to thy mistress and. 16:9
I will certainly r. to thee. 18:10, 14
r. to land of thy kindred. 31:3, 13
Lord, which saidst unto me, R. 32:9
let me r. to my brethren. *Ex* 4:18
Lord said unto Moses, Go r. 19
lest people repent, and r. to. 13:17
shall r. to his possession. *Lev* 25:10
13, 27, 28
r. unto his own family. 41
the field shall r. to him. 27:24
r. Lord, to the many thousands.
Num 10:36
let us make a captain, and r. 14:4
the Lord said, R. unto Balak. 23:5
then afterward ye shall r. 32:22
slayer shall r. into the land of his.
35:28; *Josh* 20:6
r. every man to his possesssion.
Deut 3:20; *Josh* 1:15
cause people r. to Egypt. *Deut* 17:16
let him r. to his house. 20:5, 6, 7, 8
God will r. and gather thee. 30:3
thou shalt r. and obey the voice. 8
now r. ye, and get you. *Josh* 22:4
saying, R. with much riches. 8
and afraid, let him r. *Judg* 7:3
when I r. from the children of. 11:31

she might r. from Moab. *Ruth* 1:6
Naomi said, Go, r. to her mother's. 8
surely he will r. with thee to. 10
r. thou after thy sister in law. 15
r. him trespass offering. *1 Sam* 6:3
jewels of gold which ye r. him. 8
Saul said, Come, let us r. 9:5
said Saul, R. my son David. 26:21
said, Make this fellow r. 29:4, 7
ere thou bid people r.? *2 Sam* 2:26
said Abner to him, Go, r. 3:16
till beards be grown, then r. 10:5
     1 Chr 19:5
goest thou also with us ? r.
     2 Sam 15:19
I go whither I may, r. thou. 20
if thou r. to the city and say. 34
they said, R. thou and all thy. 19:14
see what answer I shall r. 24:13
shall r. his blood. *1 Ki* 2:32, 33
Lord shall r. thy wickedness. 44
so r. to thee with all their. 8:48
R. every man to his house. 12:24
kingdom r. to the house of David. 26
go, r. on thy way to the. 19:15
let them r. every man to his house.
     22:17; *2 Chr* 11:4; 18:16
r. at all in peace. *1 Ki* 22:28
     2 Chr 18:27
offended, r. from me. *2 Ki* 18:14
king of Assyria shall r. to his own
     land. 19:7, 33; *Isa* 37:7, 34
let the shadow r. *2 Ki* 20:10
shall r. and confess. *2 Chr* 6:24
if they r. to thee with all their. 38
that we may r. answer to. 10:9
fellow in the prison until I r. 18:26
he will r. to you. 30:6
if ye r. unto him. 9
said, When wilt thou r.? *Neh* 2:6
whence ye shall r. unto us. 4:12
r. Mordecai this answer. *Esth* 4:15
device r. upon his own head. 9:25
naked shall I r. thither. *Job* 1:21
r. yea, r. again, my. 6:29
he shall r. no more to his. 7:10
shall r. out of darkness. 15:22
as for you all, do ye r. and. 17:10
if thou r. to the Almighty. 22:23
he shall r. to the days of his. 33:25
commandeth that they r. from. 36:10
r. O Lord, deliver my soul. *Ps* 6:4
let mine enemies r. and be. 10
for their sakes therefore r. 7:7
his mischief shall r. upon his. 16
they r. at evening. 59:6
and let them r.
therefore his people r. hither. 73:10
let not oppressed r. ashamed. 74:21
r. we beseech thee, O God. 80:14
thou sayest, R. ye children. 90:3
r. O Lord, how long ? 13
judgement shall r. unto. 94:15
they die, and r. to their dust. 104:29
r. to thy rest, O my soul. 116:7
none that go unto her r. *Pr* 2:19
a stone, it will r. on him. 26:27
whence rivers come, thither they r.
     Eccl 1:7
naked shall he r. to go as he. 5:15
nor the clouds r. after the rain. 12:2
dust shall r. to the earth, and spirit r.
     to God. 7
r. r. O Shulamite, r. r. *S of S* 6:13
yet in it a tenth shall r. *Isa* 6:13
remnant shall r. to God. 10:21, 22
watchman said . . . R., come. 21:12
the ransomed of the Lord shall r.
     35:10; 51:11
r. unto me, for I have. 44:22
r. for thy servant's sake. 63:17
r. to her again ? yet r. *Jer* 3:1
R. thou backsliding Israel. 12
r. ye backsliding children. 22
if thou wilt r., r. unto me. 4:1
I will r. and have compassion. 12:15
if thou r. let them r. unto thee, but r.
     not thou unto them. 15:19
r. ye every one from. 18:11; 35:15
for he shall r. no more. 22:10
that none doth r. from his. 23:14
shall r. with their whole heart. 24:7
and Jacob shall r. 30:10; 46:27
great company shall r. thither. 31:8

that ye may r., every man. *Jer* 36:3
it may be they will r. every. 7
Pharaoh's army shall r. to. 37:7
that they should r. into . . . for none
     shall r. but such. 44:14, 28
none shall r. in vain. 50:9
when Sodom and Samaria shall r.
     . . . daughters shall r. *Ezek* 16:55
wicked should r. from ways ? 18:23
after it shall r. to the prince. 46:17
I r. to fight with Persia. *Dan* 10:20
and shall r. into his own land. 11:9
     10, 28
the king of the north shall r. 13
time appointed he shall r. and. 29
he shall be grieved and r. 30
I will go and r. to my first. *Hos* 2:7
the children of Israel r. 3:5
I will r. and take away my corn. 9
r. but not to the most High. 7:16
visit their sins they shall r. 8:13; 9:3
his reproach shall his Lord r. 12:14
dwell under his shadow shall r. 14:7
who knoweth if he will r.? *Joel* 2:14
I r. recompence on your head. 3:4, 7
thy reward shall r. upon. *Ob* 15
they shall r. to the hire. *Mi* 1:7
remnant of his brethren shall r. 5:3
Edom saith, We will r. *Mal* 1:4
R. to me, and I will r. to you, saith
     Lord . . . Wherein shall we r.? 3:7
shall ye r. and discern between. 18
r. into my house. 12:44; *Luke* 11:24
is in the field, r. back. *Mat* 24:18
r. to thine own house. *Luke* 8:39
when he will r. from wedding. 12:36
after this I will r. and. *Acts* 15:16
I will again r. to you, if God. 18:21

to return

when thou goest *to r.* *Ex* 4:21
were it not better *to r.*? *Num* 14:3
nor cause the people *to r.* *Deut* 17:16
went *to r.* unto Judah. *Ruth* 1:7
not to leave thee, or *to r.* from. 16
David rose early *to r.* *1 Sam* 29:11
to r. answer to this. *2 Chr* 10:6, 9
appointed a captain *to r.* *Neh* 9:17
they have refused *to r.* *Jer* 5:3; 8:5
     Hos 11:5
to the land where they desire *to r.*
     Jer 22:27; 44:14
in causing you *to r.* 29:10; 30:3
     32:44; 33:7, 11, 26; 34:22; 42:12
caused the servants *to r.* 34:11, 16
cause me not *to r.* 37:20; 38:26
shall I cause it *to r.*? *Ezek* 21:30
cause them *to r.* to Pathros. 29:14
caused me *to r.* to the brink. 47:6
because they refused *to r.* *Hos* 11:5
went to receive a kingdom and *to r.*
     Luke 19:12
more *to r.* to corruption. *Acts* 13:34
to r. through Macedonia. 20:3

return unto the Lord

and shalt r. *unto the Lord. Deut* 30:2
if ye r. *unto the Lord.* *1 Sam* 7:3
r. *unto the Lord,* he shall. *Isa* 19:22
let him r. *unto the Lord,* he. 55:7
let us r. *unto the Lord,* for. *Hos* 6:1
they do not r. *unto the Lord.* 7:10
O Israel, r. *unto the Lord* thy. 14:1

not return

will *not r.* to our houses. *Num* 32:18
Samuel said, I will *not r.* with thee.
     1 Sam 15:26
he shall *not r.* to me. *2 Sam* 12:23
I may *not r.* with thee. *1 Ki* 13:16
before I go whence I shall *not r.*
     Job 10:21; 16:22
forth, and r. *not* unto them. 39:4
gone out, and shall *not r.* *Isa* 45:23
it shall *not r.* to me void, but. 55:11
turn away, and *not r.*? *Jer* 8:4
destroy, since they r. *not* from. 15:7
he shall *not r.* thither. 22:11, 27
the anger of the Lord shall *not r.*
     23:20; 30:24
for seller shall *not r.* . . . multitude
     which shall *not r.* *Ezek* 7:13
that he should *not r.* from his. 13:22
my sword *not r.* any more. 21:5

thy cities shall *not r.* and. *Ezek* 35:9
he shall *not r.* by the way. 46:9
they do *not r.* to the Lord. *Hos* 7:10
he shall *not r.* into Egypt. 11:5
I will *not r.* to destroy Ephraim. 9
warned they should *not r.* *Mat* 2:12
let him likewise *not r.* *Luke* 17:31

returned

waters r. from off earth. *Gen* 8:3
the dove r. to him. 9
the dove r. not again. 12
Abraham r. unto his place. 18:33
Abraham r. to his young men. 22:19
Joseph r. again, communed. 42:24
we had r. this second time. 43:10
money that was r. in our sacks. 18
Moses r. to the Lord. *Ex* 5:22; 32:31
the sea r. to his strength. 14:27, 28
r. words of people to Lord. 19:8*
she is r. to her father's. *Lev* 22:13
Balaam rose up, and r. *Num* 24:25
till pursuers be r. *Josh* 2:16, 22
that waters of Jordan r. 4:18
of Reuben and Gad r. 22:9
the princes r. from Reuben. 32
judge was dead they r. *Judg* 2:19
yea, she r. answer to herself. 5:29
there r. of the people 22,000. 7:3
Gideon r. from battle before. 8:13
Gideon's daughter r. to her. 11:39
the Benjamites r. to their. 21:23
so Naomi and Ruth r. *Ruth* 1:22
they r. to Ekron same. *1 Sam* 6:16
David r. from slaughter of. 17:57
the Lord hath r. the. 25:39
the sword of Saul r. *2 Sam* 1:22
Go, return, and he r. 3:16
then David r. to bless his. 6:20
Lord r. on thee all the blood of. 16:8
thou seekest, is as if all r. 17:3
king r. and came to Jordan. 19:15
people r. after him only to. 23:10
r. not by way that he. *1 Ki* 13:10
Jeroboam r. not from his evil way. 33
Elisha r. and walked. *2 Ki* 4:35
he r. to man of God, he and. 5:15
r. home in great anger. *2 Chr* 25:10
Sennacherib r. with shame of. 32:31
thus they r. us answer. *Ezra* 5:11
we r. all of us to the wall. *Neh* 4:15
when they r. and cried unto. 9:28
my prayer r. into mine. *Ps* 35:13
they r. and enquired early. 78:34
so sun r. ten degrees. *Isa* 38:8
unto me. But she r. not. *Jer* 3:7
they r. with their vessels. 14:3
Jews r. out of all places. 40:12
creatures ran, and r. as. *Ezek* 1:14
they r. not when they went. 17
and have r. to provoke me to. 8:17
when I had r. behold, at the. 47:7
understanding r. unto me. *Dan* 4:34
at the same time my reason r. 36
when I r. the captivity of. *Hos* 6:11
yet have ye not r. to me. *Amos* 4:6
     8, 9, 10, 11
they r. and said, Like as. *Zech* 1:6
thus saith the Lord; I am r. to. 16
no man passed through nor r. 7:14
I am r. to Zion, and will dwell. 8:3
morning as he r. into. *Mat* 21:18
when he r. he found. *Mark* 14:40
Mary r. to her own house. *Luke* 1:56
shepherds r. glorifying God. 2:20
Jesus full of the Holy Ghost r. 4:1
Jesus r. in power of the Spirit. 14
into the ship and r. back again. 8:37
when Jesus r. the people gladly. 40
the apostles, when they were r. 9:10
the seventy r. again with joy. 10:17
that r. to give glory to God. 17:18
r. having received kingdom. 19:15
smote their breasts and r. 23:48
they r. and prepared spices. 56
r. from sepulchre and told. 24:9
they rose same hour, and r. to. 33
they worshipped him, and r. to. 52
then r. they to Jerusalem. *Acts* 1:12
found them not, they r. 5:22
the apostles r. to Jerusalem. 8:25
Barnabas and Saul r. from. 12:25
John r. to Jerusalem. 13:13
they r. again to Lystra and. 14:21

took ship, and they r. home. *Acts* 21:6
and r. to the castle.   23:32
I r. again unto Damascus. *Gal* 1:17
opportunity to have r.   *Heb* 11:15
now r. to Shepherd of.   *1 Pet* 2:25

returneth
his breath goeth, he r.   *Ps* 146:4
r. to his vomit, so a fool r. *Pr* 26:11
the wind r. according to.   *Eccl* 1:6
rain r. not thither, but.   *Isa* 55:10
him that r. I will cut off. *Ezek* 35:7
because of him that r.   *Zech* 9:8

returning
in r. and rest shall ye.   *Isa* 30:15
r., found servant whole.   *Luke* 7:10
r. and sitting in chariot. *Acts* 8:28
met Abraham r. from.   *Heb* 7:1

Reuben
and called his name R.   *Gen* 29:32
R. went in the days of wheat. 30:14
that R. went and lay with.   35:22
R., Jacob's firstborn.   23; 46:8
     49:3; *Num* 26:5; *1 Chr* 5:1
R. said unto them, Shed. *Gen* 37:22
R. returned to the pit; Joseph. 29
the sons of R.   46:9; *Ex* 6:14
   Num 16:1; 32:1, 37; *Deut* 11:6
       Josh 4:12; *1 Chr* 5:3, 18
as R. and Simeon, they.   *Gen* 48:5
standard of the camp of R.
              Num 2:10; 10:18
numbered in the camp of R.   2:16
prince of the children of R.   7:30
Moses gave to children of R. 32:33
                    Josh 13:23
mount Ebal to curse; R. *Deut* 27:13
let R. live, and not die.   33:6
to the stone of Bohan the son of R.
              Josh 15:6; 18:17
sent to the children of R.   22:13
for the divisions of R. *Judg* 5:15, 16
a portion for R.   *Ezek* 48:6
one gate of R.   31

tribe of Reuben
of the *tribe of R.*; Elizur. *Num* 1:5
the *tribe of R.* were numbered. 21
of the *tribe of R.*, Shammua. 13:4
the *tribe of R.* have received. 34:14
out of the *tribe of R.*, Gad and.
 Josh 20:8; 21:36; *1 Chr* 6:63, 78
of *tribe of R.* were sealed. *Rev* 7:5

Reubenites
the families of the R.   *Num* 26:7
cities gave I to the R.   *Deut* 3:12
    16; 29:8; *Josh* 12:6; 13:8
spake to the R.   *Josh* 1:12; 22:1
Hazael smote the R.   *2 Ki* 10:33
the prince of the R.   *1 Chr* 5:6
Tiglath-pilneser carried away R. 26
Adina a captain of the R.   11:42
his brethren over the R.   26:32
ruler of the R. was Eliezer. 27:16

reveal
shall r. his iniquity.   *Job* 20:27
I will r. them abundance.   *Jer* 33:6
couldest r. this secret.   *Dan* 2:47
to whomsoever the Son will r. him.
                Mat 11:27; *Luke* 10:22
grace, to r. his Son in me. *Gal* 1:16
God shall r. even this.   *Phil* 3:15

revealed
but things r. to us.   *Deut* 29:29
of the Lord r. to him.   *1 Sam* 3:7
the Lord r. himself to Samuel.   21
hast r. to thy servant.   *2 Sam* 7:27
it was r. in mine ears.   *Isa* 22:14
from Chittim it is r. to them. 23:1
glory of the Lord shall be r.   40:5
to whom is the arm of the Lord r.?
                  53:1; *John* 12:38
righteousness is near to be r.
                           Isa 56:1
for unto thee have I r.   *Jer* 11:20
then was the secret r. to. *Dan* 2:19
this secret is not r. to me for. 30
a thing was r. to Daniel, and. 10:1
nothing covered, that shall not be r.
                Mat 10:26; *Luke* 12:2
and r. them to babes.   *Mat* 11:25
                           Luke 10:21
and blood hath not r. it.   *Mat* 16:17
it was r. to Simeon by.   *Luke* 2:26
35

of many hearts may be r. *Luke* 2:35
when the Son of man is r.   17:30
righteousness of God r.   *Rom* 1:17
the wrath of God is r. from.   18
glory which shall be r. in us. 8:18
God hath r. them to us.   *1 Cor* 2:10
because it shall be r. by fire. 3:13
if any thing be r. to another. 14:30
should afterwards be r.   *Gal* 3:23
as it is now r. to his holy. *Eph* 3:5
Lord Jesus shall be r.   *2 Thes* 1:7
first, and that man of sin be r. 2:3
he might be r. in his time.   6
that wicked one be r., whom.   8
salvation, ready to be r.   *1 Pet* 1:5
unto whom it was r. that not.   12
when his glory shall be r.   4:13
of the glory that shall be r.   5:1

revealer
your God is a God of gods, a r. of
 secrets.   *Dan* 2:47

revealeth
a talebearer r.   *Pr* 11:13; 20:19
he r. the deep and secret. *Dan* 2:22
God in heaven that r. secrets.   28
that r. secrets maketh known.   29
he r. his secrets to his.   *Amos* 3:7

revelation
(*A revealing; in the Bible mainly
the revealing by God of his character
or deeds*)
and r. of the righteous.   *Rom* 2:5
according to r. of mystery.   16:25
speak to you either by r. *1 Cor* 14:6
every one of you hath a r., hath. 26
by the r. of Jesus Christ. *Gal* 1:12
and I went up by r. and.   2:2
Spirit of wisdom and r.   *Eph* 1:17
how that by r. he made.   3:3
grace brought at the r.   *1 Pet* 1:13
the r. of Jesus Christ.   *Rev* 1:1

revelations
come to visions and r.   *2 Cor* 12:1
exalted through abundance of r.   7

revellings
works of the flesh are r.   *Gal* 5:21
when ye walked in lusts, r. *1 Pet* 4:3

revenge
(*Most frequently found where
avenge is used in modern English.
Revisions make this change*)
O Lord, r. me of my.   *Jer* 15:15
in a readiness to r. all. *2 Cor* 10:6

revenge, *substantive*
and we shall take our r.   *Jer* 20:10
Philistines have dealt by r.
                           Ezek 25:15
r. it wrought in you.   *2 Cor* 7:11

revenged
because Edom r.   *Ezek* 25:12

revenger
the r. shall slay the. *Num* 35:19, 21
judge between slayer and r.   24
slayer out of the hand of the r. 25
if r. find him without, and r. kill. 27
minister of God, a r.   *Rom* 13:4

revengers
thou wouldest not suffer the r.
                           2 Sam 14:11

revenges
from the beginning of r. *Deut* 32:42

revengeth
the Lord r. and is furious. *Nah* 1:2

revenging
by the r. of the blood of. *Ps* 79:10

revenue
endamage the r. of kings. *Ezra* 4:13*
my r. is better than.   *Pr* 8:19
harvest of the river is her r. *Isa* 23:3

revenues
but in the r. of the wicked. *Pr* 15:6
than great r. without right.   16:8
be ashamed of your r.   *Jer* 12:13*

reverence
(*Where this word is used in connection with men alone it is with
the old meaning of deference, or
of an act of homage, or merely*

obeisance. *When used with reference to God it means godly fear and
awe*)
r. my sanctuary.   *Lev* 19:30; 26:2
servants in gate r.   *Esth* 3:2
They will r. my son.   *Mat* 21:37
the wife see that she r.   *Eph* 5:33

reverence, *substantive*
Mephibosheth did r. to. *2 Sam* 9:6*
and did r. to king.   *1 Ki* 1:31*
nor did him r.   *Esth* 3:2, 5
to be had in r. of all.   *Ps* 89:7*
we gave them r.   *Heb* 12:9
serve God with r.   28

reverend
holy and r. is his name.   *Ps* 111:9

reverse
hath blessed, and I cannot r. it.
                           Num 23:20
let it be written, to r.   *Esth* 8:5
with king's ring, may no man r.   8

revile
(*To use abusive language of any
sort*)
thou shalt not r. the gods. *Ex* 22:28
ye when men shall r. you. *Mat* 5:11*

reviled
that passed by r. him.   *Mat* 27:39
crucified with him r.   *Mark* 15:32*
they r. him, and said.   *John* 9:28
being r. we bless, being. *1 Cor* 4:12
when he was r., r. not.   *1 Pet* 2:23

revilers
nor r. shall inherit.   *1 Cor* 6:10

revilest
they said, R. thou God's? *Acts* 23:4

revilings
neither be afraid of their r. *Isa* 51:7
and the r. of Ammon.   *Zeph* 2:8

revive
(*To make to live again, or to have
new life*)
will they r. the stones?   *Neh* 4:2
wilt thou not r. us again? *Ps* 85:6*
thou wilt r. me, thou shalt.   138:7
to r. spirit of the humble, and to r.
 the heart of the contrite. *Isa* 57:15
after two days will he r. us. *Hos* 6:2
they shall r. as corn, and grow. 14:7
Lord, r. thy work in.   *Hab* 3:2

revived
spirit of Jacob r.   *Gen* 45:27
came again, and he r.   *Judg* 15:19
soul came, and he r.   *1 Ki* 17:22
bones of Elisha, he r.   *2 Ki* 13:21
commandment came, sin r. *Rom* 7:9
both died, rose, and r.   14:9*

reviving
to give us a little r.   *Ezra* 9:8, 9

revolt
speaking oppression and r. *Isa* 59:13

revolt, *verb*
also did Libnah r.   *2 Chr* 21:10
ye will r. more and more.   *Isa* 1:5

revolted
in his days Edom r.   *2 Ki* 8:20, 22
                        2 Chr 21:8, 10
Libnah r. at the same.   *2 Ki* 8:22
Israel have deeply r.   *Isa* 31:6
this people, they are r.   *Jer* 5:23

revolters
are all grievous r.   *Jer* 6:28
r. are profound to make.   *Hos* 5:2
all their princes are r.   9:15

revolting
this people hath a r. and. *Jer* 5:23

reward
thy exceeding great r.   *Gen* 15:1
for it is your r. for.   *Num* 18:31
God, who taketh not r.   *Deut* 10:17
cursed that taketh r. to slay. 27:25
a full r. be given thee.   *Ruth* 2:12
have given him a r.   *2 Sam* 4:10
it me with such a r.   19:36
I will give thee a r.   *1 Ki* 13:7
Bring to me? or Give a r.? *Job* 6:22*
as an hireling looketh for r.   7:2*

nor taketh r. against. *Ps* 15:5
in keeping of them is r. 19:11
desolate for a r. of their. 40:15*
there is a r. for the righteous. 58:11
let them be turned back for r. 70:3*
see the r. of the wicked. 91:8
render a r. to the proud. 94:2*
let this be the r. of mine. 109:20
the fruit of the womb is his r. 127:3
righteousness, a sure r. *Pr* 11:18
a r. in the bosom strong wrath. 21:14*
then there shall be a r. 24:14
there shall be no r. to the evil. 20
they have a good r. for. *Eccl* 4:9
neither have they any more a r. 9:5
the r. of his hands shall. *Isa* 3:11
justify the wicked for r. 5:23
his r. is with him, and his work
before him. 40:10; 62:11
let go my captives, not for r. 45:13
captain gave Jeremiah a r. *Jer* 40:5
thou givest r., and no r. *Ezek* 16:34*
hast loved a r. upon every. *Hos* 9:1*
thy r. shall return upon thine. *Ob* 15*
heads thereof judge for r. *Mi* 3:11
and judge asketh for a r. 7:3
great is your r. in heaven. *Mat* 5:12
 Luke 6:23
love you, what r. have ye? *Mat* 5:46
otherwise ye have no r. of your. 6:1
they have their r. 2, 5, 16
shall receive a prophet's r. . . . a
 righteous man's r. 10:41
he shall in no wise lose his r. 42
 Mark 9:41
but do good, and your r. *Luke* 6:35
for we receive the due r. 23:41
field with r. of iniquity. *Acts* 1:18
r. not reckoned of grace. *Rom* 4:4
every man shall receive his own r.
 1 Cor 3:8
work abide he shall receive a r. 14
thing willingly, I have a r. 9:17
what is my r. then? verily, that. 18
beguile you of your r. *Col* 2:18
ye shall receive the r. of the. 3:24
the labourer is worthy of his r.
 1 Tim 5:18*
recompence of r. *Heb* 2:2
 10:35; 11:26
r. of unrighteousness. *2 Pet* 2:13*
that we receive a full r. *2 John* 8
after error of Balaam for r. *Jude* 11
thou shouldest give r. *Rev* 11:18
and my r. is with me. 22:12

reward, verb
I will r. them that hate. *Deut* 32:41
wherefore the Lord r. *1 Sam* 24:19
the Lord shall r. the. *2 Sam* 3:39
I say, how they r. us. *2 Chr* 20:11
he shall r. evil to mine. *Ps* 54:5
the Lord shall r. thee. *Pr* 25:22
will r. them their doings. *Hos* 4:9
Father himself shall r. thee openly.
 Mat 6:4, 6, 18
shall r. every man according. 16:27
Lord r. him according. *2 Tim* 4:14*
r. her, even as she. *Rev* 18:6*

rewarded
have ye r. evil for good? *Gen* 44:4
thou hast r. me good . . . I have r.
 thee evil. *1 Sam* 24:17
Lord r. me according to my righteousness. *2 Sam* 22:21; *Ps* 18:20
your work shall be r. *2 Chr* 15:7
if I have r. evil to him. *Ps* 7:4
they r. me evil for good. 35:12
 109:5
nor r. us according to our. 103:10
the commandment be r. *Pr* 13:13
for they have r. evil to. *Isa* 3:9
thy work shall be r., saith. *Jer* 31:16
reward her even as she r. *Rev* 18:6*

rewarder
r. of them that diligently. *Heb* 11:6

rewardeth
he r. him and he shall. *Job* 21:19
plentifully r. proud doer. *Ps* 31:23
happy he that r. thee, as thou. 137:8
whoso r. evil for good. *Pr* 17:13
both r. the fool, and r. 26:10*

rewards
with the r. of divination. *Num* 22:7
followeth after r. *Isa* 1:23
of me gifts and r. honour. *Dan* 2:6
said, Give thy r. to another. 5:17
are my r. that my lovers. *Hos* 2:12*

Rezin
Lord began to send against Judah R.
 2 Ki 15:37; 16:5; *Isa* 7:1
that time R. recovered. *2 Ki* 16:6
took Damascus and slew R. 9
the children of R., children of Nekoda
 and Gazzam. *Ezra* 2:48; *Neh* 7:50
fear not the fierce anger of R. *Isa* 7:4
and the head of Damascus is R. 8
as the people rejoice in R. 8:6
set up the adversaries of R. 9:11

Rhegium
compass and came to R. *Acts* 28:13

Rhesa
who was the son of R. *Luke* 3:27

Rhoda
a damsel named R. *Acts* 12:13

Rhodes
we came unto R. *Acts* 21:1

rib, -s
God took one of his r. *Gen* 2:21
the r. which God had taken. 22
Asahel under the fifth r. *2 Sam* 2:23*
Joab smote Abner and Amasa under
 the fifth r. 3:27*; 20:10*
smote Ish-bosheth under fifth r. 4:6*
beast had three r. in the. *Dan* 7:5

ribband
the borders a r. of blue. *Num* 15:38*

rich
Abram very r. in cattle. *Gen* 13:2
I have made Abram r. 14:23
r. shall not give more, nor. *Ex* 30:15
and if a stranger wax r. *Lev* 25:47
young men poor or r. *Ruth* 3:10
poor and maketh r. *1 Sam* 2:7
men in one city, one r. *2 Sam* 12:1
he shall not be r. neither. *Job* 15:29
nor regardeth the r. more. 34:19
the r. shall entreat. *Ps* 45:12
hear this, both r. and poor. 49:2
be not afraid when one is made r. 16
of the diligent maketh r. *Pr* 10:4
blessing of the Lord, maketh r. 22
there is that maketh himself r. 13:7
poor is hated, but the r. hath. 14:20
but the r. answereth roughly. 18:23
wine and oil shall not be r. 21:17
r. and poor meet together, Lord. 22:2
the r. ruleth over the poor, and. 7
he that giveth to the r. shall. 16
labour not to be r.: cease from. 23:4
perverse, though he be r. 28:6
he that maketh haste to be r. 20, 22
abundance of the r. will not suffer.
 Eccl 5:12
and the r. sit in low place. 10:6
curse not the r. in thy. 20
with the r. in his death. *Isa* 53:9
are great, and waxen r. *Jer* 5:27
in chests of r. apparel. *Ezek* 27:24
Yet I am become r. *Hos* 12:8
be the Lord, for I am r. *Zech* 11:5
were r., cast in much. *Mark* 12:41
r. he hath sent empty. *Luke* 1:53
but woe unto you that are r. for. 6:24
is not r. toward God. 12:21
call not thy r. neighbours. 14:12
sorrowful, for he was very r. 18:23
Zacchaeus . . . and he was r. 19:2
same Lord is r. to all. *Rom* 10:12
full, now ye are r. *1 Cor* 4:8
yet making many r. *2 Cor* 6:10
though he was r. yet he became
 poor, that ye might be r. 8:9
God who is r. in mercy. *Eph* 2:4
they that will be r. fall. *1 Tim* 6:9
charge them that are r. in this. 17
that they do good, and be r. in. 18
let the r. rejoice in that. *Jas* 1:10
chosen the poor, r. in faith? 2:5
poverty, but thou art r. *Rev* 2:9
because thou sayest, I am r. 3:17
buy gold, that thou mayest be r. 18
he causeth the r. and poor to. 13:16

merchants of earth are waxed r.
 Rev 18:3, 15, 19

rich man or men
r. man had exceeding. *2 Sam* 12:2
a traveller to the r. man. 4
r. man shall lie down. *Job* 27:19
the r. man's wealth is his strong.
 Pr 10:15; 18:11
the r. man is wise in his. 28:11
let not the r. man glory. *Jer* 9:23
the r. men thereof are full. *Mi* 6:12
r. man shall hardly enter. *Mat* 19:23
than for a r. man to enter into. 24
 Mark 10:25; *Luke* 18:25
came a r. man of Arimathaea.
 Mat 27:57
the ground of a r. man. *Luke* 12:16
there was a certain r. man. 16:1
a r. man was clothed in purple. 19
fell from the r. man's table. 21
the r. man also died and was. 22
and saw the r. men casting. 21:1
so also shall the r. man. *Jas* 1:11
do not r. men oppress you? 2:6
go to now, ye r. men, weep. 5:1
great men, and r. men. *Rev* 6:15

richer
the fourth shall be far r. *Dan* 11:2

riches
the r. God hath taken. *Gen* 31:16
r. were more than they might. 36:7
return with much r. to. *Josh* 22:8
enrich with great r. *1 Sam* 17:25
neither hast asked r. *1 Ki* 3:11
 2 Chr 1:11
given thee both r. and. *1 Ki* 3:13
Solomon exceeded all the kings of
 the earth for r. 10:23; *2 Chr* 9:22
both r. and honour. *1 Chr* 29:12
David died full of days, r. and. 28
Jehoshaphat had r. and honour.
 2 Chr 17:5; 18:1
found r. with dead bodies. 20:25
Hezekiah had exceeding much r.
 32:27
r. of his glorious kingdom. *Esth* 1:4
them of the glory of his r. 5:11
he swallowed down r. *Job* 20:15
will he esteem thy r.? no, not. 36:19
is better than the r. of. *Ps* 37:16
he heapeth up r. and knoweth. 39:6
boast themselves in their r. 49:6
trusted in the abundance of r. 52:7
if r. increase, set not your. 62:10
ungodly, they increase in r. 73:12
earth is full of thy r. 104:24
wealth and r. shall be in. 112:3
rejoiced as much as in all r. 119:14
and in her left hand r. *Pr* 3:16
r. and honour are with me. 8:18
r. profit not in the day of wrath. 11:4
and strong men retain r. 16
trusteth in his r. shall fall. 28
poor, yet hath great r. 13:7
of a man's life are his r. 8
crown of the wise is their r. 14:24
and r. are the inheritance of. 19:14
is rather to be chosen than r. 22:1
by the fear of the Lord are r. 4
the poor to increase his r. 16
r. certainly make themselves. 23:5
be filled with all pleasant r. 24:4
for r. are not for ever, and. 27:24
give me neither poverty nor r. 30:8
his eye satisfied with r. *Eccl* 4:8
even r. kept for the owners. 5:13
those r. perish by evil travail. 14
to whom God hath given r. 19; 6:2
r. to men of understanding. 9:11
the r. of Damascus shall. *Isa* 8:4
hand found as a nest the r. 10:14
they will carry their r. on. 30:6
I will give thee hidden r. of. 45:3
eat the r. of the Gentiles. 61:6
rich man glory in his r. *Jer* 9:23
so he that getteth r. and not. 17:11
because r. that he hath gotten. 48:36
make a spoil of thy r. *Ezek* 26:12
multitude of all kind of r. 27:12
 18, 27, 33
thou hast gotten r. 28:4
increased thy r., and thine heart is
 lifted up because of thy r. 5

through his r. shall stir up. *Dan* 11:2
north shall come with much r. 13
them the prey, spoil and r. 24
return into his land with great r. 28
deceitfulness of r. choke. *Mat* 13:22
       Mark 4:19; *Luke* 8:14
hardly they that have r. *Mark* 10:23
how hard is it for them that trust in
  r. to enter ! 24; *Luke* 18:24
your trust the true r.? *Luke* 16:11
or despisest thou the r. of? *Rom* 2:4
he might make known the r. 9:23
be the r. of the world, and the diminishing of them the r. of. 11:12
O the depth of the r. of the. 33
abounded to the r. of their. *2 Cor* 8:2
redemption according to r. *Eph* 1:7
what the r. of the glory of his. 18
that he might shew exceeding r. 2:7
preach unsearchable r. of Christ. 3:8
grant you according to the r. 16
according to his r. in glory. *Phil* 4:19
what the r. of the glory. *Col* 1:27
love, and unto all the r. of the. 2:2
nor trust in uncertain r. *1 Tim* 6:17
reproach of Christ greater r. than.
       Heb 11:26
your r. are corrupted. *Jas* 5:2
to receive power and r. *Rev* 5:12
in one hour so great r. are. 18:17

richly
of Christ dwell in you r. *Col* 3:16
living God, who giveth r. *1 Tim* 6:17

rid
that he might r. him out. *Gen* 37:22
I will r. you out of their. *Ex* 6:6
I will r. evil beasts out. *Lev* 26:6*
r. them out of the hand. *Ps* 82:4*
send thine hand, r. me. 144:7*, 11*

riddance
thou shalt not make clean r. of thy.
       Lev 23:22*
he shall make even speedy r. of.
       Zeph 1:18*

ridden
ass, which thou hast r.? *Num* 22:30

riddle
put forth a r. to you. *Judg* 14:12
  13, 14, 15, 16, 17, 18, 19
Son of man, put orth a r. *Ezek* 17:2

ride
to r. in the second chariot. *Gen* 41:43
he made him r. on high. *Deut* 32:13
ye that r. on white asses. *Judg* 5:10
for king's household to r. *2 Sam* 16:2
saddle an ass that I may r. 19:26
cause Solomon to r. upon my mule.
       1 Ki 1:33, 38, 44
him to r. in his chariot. *2 Ki* 10:16
to r. upon the wind. *Job* 30:22
and in thy majesty r. *Ps* 45:4
thou hast caused men to r. 66:12
but ye said, We will r. *Isa* 30:16
I will cause thee to r. on the. 58:14
they r. on horses. *Jer* 6:23; 50:42
I will make Ephraim to r. *Hos* 10:11
we will not r. upon horses. 14:3
that thou didst r. upon. *Hab* 3:8
chariots, and those that r. *Hag* 2:22

rider
so that his r. shall fall. *Gen* 49:17
horse and r. thrown. *Ex* 15:1, 21
the horse and his r. *Job* 39:18
break in pieces horse and his r....
  the chariot and his r. *Jer* 51:21
I will smite his r. with. *Zech* 12:4

riders
if thou be able to set r. on.
  2 Ki 18:23; *Isa* 36:8
letters by r. on mules. *Esth* 8:10
the horses and their r. *Hag* 2:22
the r. on horses shall be. *Zech* 10:5

rideth
what saddle he r. on shall. *Lev* 15:9
who r. upon the heaven. *Deut* 33:26
horse that king r. upon. *Esth* 6:8
that r. on the heavens. *Ps* 68:4, 33
Lord r. on a swift cloud. *Isa* 19:1
that r. the horse deliver. *Amos* 2:15

ridges
waterest the r. thereof. *Ps* 65:10*

---

riding
Balaam was r. on his ass. *Num* 22:22
slack not thy r. for me. *2 Ki* 4:24
kings shall enter r. in chariots.
       Jer 17:25; 22:4
young men, horsemen r. on horses.
       Ezek 23:6, 12
great lords, all of them r. 23
people with thee r. on horses. 38:15
a man r. on a red horse. *Zech* 1:8
thy king cometh: r. upon an ass. 9:9

rie, or rye
(*Properly spelt, a variety of wheat*)
wheat and r. not smitten. *Ex* 9:32
cast in wheat, barley and r. *Isa* 28:25

rifled
houses r. and the women. *Zech* 14:2

right, substantive
shall not the Judge of all the earth
  do r.? *Gen* 18:25
of Zelophehad speak r. *Num* 27:7
r. of firstborn is his. *Deut* 21:17
redeem thou my r. to. *Ruth* 4:6
what r. have I to cry? *2 Sam* 19:28
we have also more r. in David. 43
no portion nor r. in Jerusalem.
       Neh 2:20
thou hast done r., but we have. 9:33
should I lie against my r.? *Job* 34:6
he that hateth r. govern? 17
but he giveth r. to the poor. 36:6
maintained my r.: judging. *Ps* 9:4*
hear the r. O Lord, attend to. 17:1
the Lord will maintain the r. 140:12
revenues without r. *Pr* 16:8
and they love him that speaketh r. 13
away the r. from poor. *Isa* 10:2
when the needy speaketh r. 32:7
the r. of the needy do. *Jer* 5:28
getteth riches, and not by r. 17:11
the r. of redemption is thine. 32:7, 8
to turn aside r. of a man. *Lam* 3:35
he come whose r. it is. *Ezek* 21:27
turn poor from their r. *Amos* 5:12
turn stranger from his r. *Mal* 3:5
they have no r. to eat. *Heb* 13:10
they may have r. to the tree of life.
       Rev 22:14

right, adjective
led me in the r. way. *Gen* 24:48
God of truth, just and r. *Deut* 32:4
do as seemeth good and r. *Josh* 9:25
frame to pronounce it r. *Judg* 12:6
the good and r. way. *1 Sam* 12:23
matters are good and r. *2 Sam* 15:3
is thy heart r. as my heart? *2 Ki* 10:15
things that were not r. 17:9
to seek of him a r. *Ezra* 8:21*
thou gavest them r. *Neh* 9:13
and the things seem r. *Esth* 8:5
how forcible are r. words! *Job* 6:25*
not lay on man more than r. 34:23
this to be r. that thou saidst? 35:2*
statutes of Lord are r. *Ps* 19:8
sceptre of thy kingdom is a r. 45:6*
O God, renew a r. spirit. 51:10
led them forth by the r. way. 107:7*
thy judgements are r. 119:75*
thy precepts are r. 128
I have led thee in r. paths. *Pr* 4:11*
my lips shall be r. things. 8:6
they are all r. to them that find. 9
thoughts of the righteous are r. 12:5*
way which seemeth r. 14:12; 16:25
work be pure, and whether r. 20:11
lips shall speak r. things. 23:16
his lips that giveth a r. answer. 24:26
considered every r. work. *Eccl* 4:4*
say, Prophesy not to us r. things.
       Isa 30:10
declare things that are r. 45:19
I had planted thee wholly a r. seed.
       Jer 2:21
evil, and their force is not r. 23:10
and had done r. in my sight. 34:15
ways of the Lord are r. *Hos* 14:9
for they know not to do r. *Amos* 3:10
clothed, and in his r. mind.
       Mark 5:15; *Luke* 8:35
hast answered r.: this. *Luke* 10:28
r. in sight of God. *Acts* 4:19
thy heart is not r. in the sight. 8:21

---

not cease to pervert the r. *Acts* 13:10
forsaken the r. way. *2 Pet* 2:15

right, adv.
people passed over r. *Josh* 3:16

see foot, hand

is right
and do that which is r. in his sight.
  Ex 15:26; *1 Ki* 11:38
thou shalt do that which is r.
  Deut 6:18; 12:25; 21:9
whatsoever is r. in own eyes. 12:8
doest that which is r. 28; 13:18
walked to do that is r. *1 Ki* 11:33
which is r. in my eyes. *2 Ki* 10:30
of me thing that is r. *Job* 42:7, 8
word of the Lord is r. *Ps* 33:4
the way of a fool is r. in. *Pr* 12:15
every way of man is r. in his. 21:2
as for the pure, his work is r. 8
man do that which is r. *Ezek* 18:5
done that which is lawful and r. 19
  21:27; 33:14, 16, 19
whatsoever is r. I will. *Mat* 20:4
judge ye not what is r.? *Luke* 12:57
in the Lord: this is r. *Eph* 6:1

was right
that which was r. in his own eyes.
       Judg 17:6; 21:25
David to do that only which was r.
       1 Ki 14:8; 15:5
Asa did that which was r. 15:11
       2 Chr 14:2
Jehoshaphat doing that which was r.
  1 Ki 22:43; *2 Chr* 20:32
Jehoash did that which was r.
  2 Ki 12:2; *2 Chr* 24:2
Amaziah did that which was r.
  2 Ki 14:3; *2 Chr* 25:2
Azariah did that which was r.
  2 Ki 15:3; *2 Chr* 26:4
Jotham did that which was r.
  2 Ki 15:34; *2 Chr* 27:2
Ahaz did not that which was r.
       2 Ki 16:2
Hezekiah did that which was r. 18:3
       2 Chr 29:2
Josiah did that which was r.
  2 Ki 22:2; *2 Chr* 34:2
the thing was r. in eyes. *1 Chr* 13:4
I have perverted that which was r.
       Job 33:27
their heart was not r. *Ps* 78:37
which came out of my lips was r.
       Jer 17:16*

right cheek
smite thee on the r. cheek. *Mat* 5:39

right corner
round from the r. corner. *2 Ki* 11:11

right early
God shall help her, and that r. early.
       Ps 46:5

right forth
driven every man r. forth. *Jer* 49:5

right on
let thine eyes look r. on. *Pr* 4:25
call passengers who go r. on. 9:15

right pillar
he set up the r. pillar. *1 Ki* 7:21

right well
my soul knoweth r. well. *Ps* 139:14

righteous
(*Frequently changed in the Revisions to upright*)
for thee have I seen r. *Gen* 7:1
wilt thou destroy the r. with? 18:23
if there be fifty r. wilt? 24, 26, 28
that be far from thee to slay r. 25
slay also a r. nation? 20:4
hath been more r. than I. 38:26
innocent and r. slay not. *Ex* 23:7
perverteth the words of the r. 8
       Deut 16:19
the death of the r. *Num* 23:10
that hath judgements so r. *Deut* 4:8
they shall justify the r. 25:1
       2 Chr 6:23
the r. acts of the Lord. *Judg* 5:11
       1 Sam 12:7
art more r. than I. *1 Sam* 24:17
have slain a r. person. *2 Sam* 4:11

two men more r. than he. *1 Ki* 2:32
justifying the r. to give him. 8:32
Jehu said, Ye be r. *2 Ki* 10:9
Lord God of Israel, thou art r.
    Ezra 9:15; *Neh* 9:8
where were the r. cut off? *Job* 4:7
whom, though I were r., yet. 9:15
if I be r. yet will I not lift. 10:15
that he should be r.? 15:14
r. also shall hold on his way. 17:9
to Almighty, that thou art r.? 22:3
the r. see it, and are glad. 19
    Ps 107:42
there the r. might dispute. *Job* 23:7
was r. in his own eyes. 32:1
Job hath said, I am r. 34:5
if thou be r. 35:7
withdraweth not his eyes from the r.
    36:7; *Ps* 34:15
that thou mayest be r. *Job* 40:8*
the congregation of the r. *Ps* 1:5
Lord knoweth way of the r. 6
for thou wilt bless the r. with. 5:12
for the r. God trieth the hearts. 7:9
God judgeth the r., God is angry. 11
what can the r. do? 11:3
Lord trieth the r. 5
God is in the generation of the r. 14:5
judgements of Lord are true and r.
    19:9; 119:7, 62, 106, 160, 164
contemptuously against the r. 31:18
be glad . . . and rejoice, ye r. 32:11
rejoice in the Lord, O ye r. 33:1
    97:12
the r. cry, and the Lord. 34:17
afflictions of r.: Lord delivereth. 19
they that hate the r. shall. 21
that favour my r. cause. 35:27
the Lord upholdeth the r. 37:17
but the r. sheweth mercy. 21
yet have I not seen r. forsaken. 25
the r. shall inherit the land. 29
the mouth of the r. speaketh. 30
the wicked watcheth the r. 32
but the salvation of the r. is of. 39
the r. also shall see, and fear. 52:6
he shall never suffer the r. to. 55:22
the r. shall rejoice when he. 58:10
verily there is a reward for the r. 11
r. shall be glad in the Lord. 64:10
but let the r. be glad, let them. 68:3
not be written with the r. 69:28
in his days shall r. flourish. 72:7
horns of r. shall be exalted. 75:10
the r. shall flourish like the. 92:12
gather against soul of the r. 94:21
light is sown for r. and. 97:11
of compassion and r. 112:4; 116:5
the r. shall be in everlasting. 6
the tabernacles of the r. 118:15
this gate, into which the r. shall. 20
sworn that I will keep thy r. 119:106
r. art thou, O Lord. 137; *Jer* 12:1
thy testimonies are r. *Ps* 119:138
not rest upon the lot of the r. lest the
    r. put forth their hands. 125:3
the r. shall give thanks to. 140:13
let the r. smite me, it shall. 141:5
the r. shall compass me. 142:7
the Lord is r. in all his ways. 145:17
the Lord loveth the r., he. 146:8
sound wisdom for the r. *Pr* 2:7
mayest keep the paths of the r. 20
but his secret is with the r. 3:32
the Lord will not suffer the r. 10:3
labour of the r. tendeth to life. 16
the lips of the r. feed many. 21
but the desire of the r. shall. 24
but the r. is an everlasting. 25
hope of the r. shall be gladness. 28
the r. shall never be removed. 30
the lips of the r. know what is. 32
r. is delivered out of trouble. 11:8
when it goeth well with the r. 10
but the seed of the r. shall be. 21
the desire of the r. is only good. 23
r. shall flourish as a branch. 28
the fruit of the r. is a tree of life. 30
behold, r. shall be recompensed. 31
but the root of the r. shall not. 12:3
thoughts of the r. are right, but. 5
the house of the r. shall stand. 7
root of the r. yieldeth fruit. 12
the r. is more excellent than his. 26

the light of the r. rejoiceth. *Pr* 13:9
but to the r. good shall be. 21
the r. eateth to the satisfying of. 25
among the r. there is favour. 14:9
bow at the gates of the r. 19
r. hath hope in his death. 32
in the house of the r. is much. 15:6
way of the r. is made plain. 19
the heart of the r. studieth to. 28
heareth the prayer of the r. 29
r. lips are the delight of kings. 16:13
overthrow the r. in judgement. 18:5
the r. runneth into it, and is safe. 10
shall be a ransom for the r. 21:18
r. giveth, and spareth not. 26
father of the r. shall greatly. 23:24
against the dwelling of the r. 24:15
to the wicked, Thou art r. 24
r. are bold as a lion. 28:1
whoso causeth the r. to go astray. 10
wicked perish, the r. increase. 28
when the r. are in authority. 29:2
the r. doth sing and rejoice. 6
the r. considereth the cause of. 7
but the r. shall see their fall. 16
God shall judge the r. *Eccl* 3:17
be not r. over much, neither. 7:16
according to the work of the r. 8:14
the r. and the wise are in the. 9:1
there is one event to the r. and. 2
say ye to the r., that it shall. *Isa* 3:10
the righteousness of the r. 5:23
songs, even glory to the r. 24:16
open ye, that the r. nation. 26:2
that we may say, He is r. 41:26
my r. servant shall justify. 53:11
r. perisheth . . . none considering
    that the r. is taken away from. 57:1
thy people also shall be all r. 60:21
r. art thou, O Lord, when. *Jer* 12:1
O Lord, that triest the r. 20:12
raise to David a r. branch. 23:5
have made the r. sad. *Ezek* 13:22
are more r. than thou. 16:52
righteousness of the r. shall. 18:20
but when the r. turneth. 24; 33:18
cut off r. and wicked. 21:3, 4
r. shall not deliver him, nor shall the
    r. be able to live. 33:12
when I say to the r. he shall live. 13
they sold r. for silver. *Amos* 2:6
compass about the r. *Hab* 1:4
him that is more r. than he. 13
discern between the r. *Mal* 3:18
not come to call the r., but sinners.
    Mat 9:13; *Mark* 2:17; *Luke* 5:32
then shall the r. shine. *Mat* 13:43
ye outwardly appear r. to. 23:28
garnish the sepulchres of r. 29
all r. blood shed on earth, from blood
    of r. Abel to Zacharias. 35
r. answer, Lord, when saw? 25:37
r. shall go into life eternal. 46
and they were both r. *Luke* 1:6
who trusted they were r. and. 18:9
appearance, but judge r. *John* 7:24
O r. Father, the world hath. 17:25
and revelation of the r. *Rom* 2:5
it is written, There is none r. 3:10
of one, many be made r. 5:19
a manifest token of r. *2 Thes* 1:5
it is a r. thing with God to. 6
the Lord, the r. Judge. *2 Tim* 4:8
witness that he was r. *Heb* 11:4
of Lord are over the r. *1 Pet* 3:12
if r. scarcely be saved. 4:18
Lot vexed his r. soul. *2 Pet* 2:8
advocate, Jesus Christ the r.
    1 John 2:1
if ye know that he is r., ye. 29
righteousness is r. as he is r. 3:7
were evil, and his brother's r. 12
Thou art r. O Lord. *Rev* 16:5
O Lord, true and r. are. 7; 19:2
he that is r. let him be r. 22:11
    see **Lord** *is*

righteous man, or men
a little that a r. man hath. *Ps* 37:16
the mouth of a r. man. *Pr* 10:11
a r. man regardeth the life. 12:10
a r. man hateth lying, but. 13:5
a r. man wisely considereth. 21:12
a r. man falling down before. 25:26

when r. men do rejoice. *Pr* 28:12
who raised up the r. man. *Isa* 41:2
when a r. man doth turn. *Ezek* 3:20
    18:26
if thou warn the r. man. 3:21
and the r. men, they shall. 23:45
r. man in the name of a r. man shall
    receive a r. man's. *Mat* 10:41
many r. men have desired. 13:17
this was a r. man. *Luke* 23:47
for a r. man will one die. *Rom* 5:7
law not made for r. man. *1 Tim* 1:9
prayer of a r. man availeth. *Jas* 5:16
for that r. man dwelling. *2 Pet* 2:8

righteously

hear causes, and judge r.
    Deut 1:16; *Pr* 31:9
judge the people r. *Ps* 67:4*; 96:10*
he that walketh r. shall. *Isa* 33:15
Lord, that judgest r. *Jer* 11:20
live soberly, r. and godly. *Tit* 2:12
to him that judgeth r. *1 Pet* 2:23

righteousness

*(The quality of being right or just.
This idea makes plain the difference
indicated by Paul between the righteousness of the law and the righteousness of God and Christ)*
and it shall be our r. if. *Deut* 6:25
it shall be r. to thee before. 24:13
shall offer sacrifices of r. 33:19
put on r., it clothed me. *Job* 29:14
ascribe r. to my Maker. 36:3
offer the sacrifices of r. *Ps* 4:5
Lord loveth r. 11:7; 33:5
he that worketh r. shall never. 15:2
he leadeth me in paths of r. 23:3
and r. from the God of his. 24:5
I have preached r. in the. 40:9
truth, and meekness, and r. 45:4
lovest r. and hatest. 7; *Heb* 1:9
hand, O God, is full of r. *Ps* 48:10
pleased with sacrifices of r. 51:19
lying, rather than to speak r. 52:3
speak r. O congregation? 58:1
judge thy people with r. 72:2
peace, and little hills by r. 3
r. and peace have kissed. 85:10
and r. shall look down from. 11
r. shall go before him, and set. 13
judgement shall return unto r. 94:15
judge the world with r. 96:13; 98:9
r. is the habitation of his. 97:2
executest r. in Jacob. 99:4; 103:6
blessed is he that doeth r. 106:3
open to me the gates of r., I. 118:19
the r. of thy testimonies is. 119:144
all thy commandments are r. 172
priests be clothed with r., thy. 132:9
understand r. and judgement. *Pr* 2:9
yea, durable riches and r. are. 8:18
I lead in the way of r. in midst. 20
but r. delivereth. 10:2; 11:4
the r. of the perfect shall. 11:5
r. of upright shall deliver. 6
to him that soweth r. shall be. 18
as r. tendeth to life, so he that. 19
truth, sheweth forth r. 12:17
in the way of r. is life, and. 28
r. keepeth him that is upright. 13:6
r. exalteth a nation. 14:34
that followeth after r. 15:9
better is a little with r. than. 16:8
throne is established by r. 12
if found in the way of r. 31
he that followeth after r. and mercy
    findeth life, r. and honour. 21:21
and the place of r. that. *Eccl* 3:16
r. lodged in it, but now. *Isa* 1:21
the city of r. 26
and her converts with r. 27
which take away the r. of the. 5:23
decreed shall overflow with r. 10:22
with r. shall he judge the poor. 11:4
r. shall be the girdle of his loins. 5
judgement, and hasting r. 16:5
of the world will learn r. 26:9
yet will he not learn r. 10
r. will I lay to the plummet. 28:17
and r. shall remain in the. 32:16
the work of r. shall be peace, and
    the effect of r. quietness and. 17
Zion with judgement and r. 33:5

and let skies pour down r. and let r.
  spring up together.   *Isa 45:8*
I the Lord speak r., I declare.   19
in tne Lord have I r.   24*
ye tnat are far from r.   46:12
ye that follow after r.   51:1
ye that know r.   7
r. is of me, saith the Lord.   54:17
me as a nation that did r.   58:2
put on r. as a breastplate.   59:17
officers peace, thine exactors r. 60:17
might be called trees of r.   61:3
covered me with robe of r.   10
so Lord will cause r. and praise.   11
until the r. thereof go forth as.   62:1
that rejoiceth and worketh r.   64:5
the Lord which exercise r.   *Jer 9:24*
execute ye judgement and r.   22:3
the Lord our r.   23:6; 33:16
the branch of r. to grow up to David,
  and he shall execute r.   33:15
hath brought forth our r.   51:10
own souls by their r. *Ezek 14:14, 20*
the r. of the righteous shall be. 18:20
r. of the righteous shall not.
break off thy sins by r.   *Dan 4:27*
O Lord, r. belongeth unto thee. 9:7
to bring in everlasting r. and.   24
they that turn many to r. shall. 12:3
till he come and rain r.   *Hos 10:12*
and who leave off r.   *Amos 5:7*
let r. run down as a mighty.   24
ye have turned the fruit of r.   6:12
that ye may know the r.   *Mi 6:5*
seek r., seek meekness.   *Zeph 2:3*
shall the Sun of r. arise.   *Mal 4:2*
becometh us to fulfil all r. *Mat 3:15*
that hunger and thirst after r.   5:6
except your r. exceed the r.   20
John came in the way of r.   21:32
in r. before him all days. *Luke 1:75*
reprove the world of sin and of r.
    John 16:8
of r., because I go to my Father. 10
worketh r. is accepted.   *Acts 10:35*
thou enemy of all r. wilt thou ? 13:10
as he reasoned of r. and.   24:25
therein is the r. of God. *Rom 1:17*
if uncircumcision keep the r. 2:26*
commend the r. of God.   3:5
the r. of God without the law.   21
r. of God which is by faith of.   22
to whom God imputeth r.   4:6
a seal of r. of faith, that r. might. 11
promise was through the r.   13
which receive gift of r. shall. 5:17
so by r. of one the free gift came. 18
so might grace reign through r.   21
instruments of r. to God.   6:13
death, or of obedience unto r.   16
ye became the servants of r.   18
your members servants to r.   19
of sin, ye were free from r.   20
that the r. of the law might be. 8:4*
but the spirit is life because of r. 10
who followed not after r., have attained to r., even the r.   9:30
followed after the law of r., hath not
  attained to the law of r.   31*
to establish their own r., have not
  submitted to the r. of God.   10:3
Moses describeth the r. which is. 5
the r. which is of faith speaketh. 6
the heart man believeth unto r.   10
not meat and drink, but r.   14:17
Christ is made unto us r. *1 Cor 1:30*
awake to r. and sin not, for. 15:34*
that we might be made the r. of God.
    2 Cor 3:9; 5:21
by the armour of r. on the right. 6:7
what fellowship hath r. with ?   14
increase the fruits of your r.   9:10
as the ministers of r.   11:15
if r. come by law, Christ. *Gal 2:21*
verily, r should have been.   3:21
we wait for the hope of r.   5:5
fruit of the Spirit is in all r. *Eph 5:9*
having on the breastplate of r. 6:14
the fruits of r. by Jesus. *Phil 1:11*
touching r. which is in the law. 3:6
r. which is of God by faith.
and follow after r.   *1 Tim 6:11*
    2 Tim 2:22
up for me a crown of r. *2 Tim 4:8*

not by works of r. which.   *Tit 3:5*
a sceptre of r. is sceptre.   *Heb 1:8*
is unskilful in the word of r.   5:13
by interpretation, king of r.   7:2
and became heir of the r. which. 11:7
subdued kingdoms, wrought r.   33
peaceable fruit of r.   12:11
worketh not r. of God.   *Jas 1:20*
the fruit of r. is sown in peace. 3:18
sin should live unto r.   *1 Pet 2:24*
faith through r. of God.   *2 Pet 1:1*
but saved Noah a preacher of r. 2:5
not to have known the way of r.   21
new earth, wherein dwelleth r. 3:13
every one that doeth r. *1 John 2:29*
he that doeth r. is righteous.   3:7
whosoever doeth not r. is not of. 10
for the fine linen is the r. *Rev 19:8*

for righteousness
counted it to him for r.   *Gen 15:6*
    Ps 106:31; Rom 4:3
for thy r.' sake bring.   *Ps 143:11*
he looked for r. but behold. *Isa 5:7*
which are persecuted for r. *Mat 5:10*
his faith is counted for r.   *Rom 4:5*
    Gal 3:6
imputed to him for r.   *Rom 4:22*
    Jas 2:23
end of the law for r.   *Rom 10:4*
if ye suffer for r.' sake. *1 Pet 3:14*

his righteousness
Lord render to every man his r.
    1 Sam 26:23
to give according to his r. *1 Ki 8:32*
    2 Chr 6:23
render unto man his r.   *Job 33:26*
Lord according to his r.   *Ps 7:17*
they shall declare his r. to a. 22:31
the heavens shall declare his r.
    50:6; 97:6
his r. hath he openly shewed. 98:2
and his r. unto children's.   103:17
and his r. endureth for ever. 111:3
    112:3, 9
that perisheth in his r.   *Eccl 7:15*
pleased for his r. sake. *Isa 42:21*
brought salvation, and his r. 59:16
when a righteous man doth turn from
  his r.   *Ezek 3:20; 18:24, 26*
in his r. that he hath done.   18:22
not be able to live for his r.   33:12
if he trust to his own r. and commit
  iniquity, his r.   13
and I shall behold his r.   *Mi 7:9*
kingdom of God and his r. *Mat 6:33*
his r. for remission of sins.
    Rom 3:25, 26
given to the poor, his r. *2 Cor 9:9*

in righteousness
in r. shalt thou judge.   *Lev 19:15*
before thee in truth and in r. *1 Ki 3:6*
judge the world in r.   *Ps 9:8*
I will behold thy face in r.   17:15
by terrible things in r. wilt thou. 65:5
words of my mouth are in r. *Pr 8:8*
throne shall be established in r. 25:5
shall be sanctified in r.   *Isa 5:16*
a king shall reign in r. and.   32:1
Lord have called thee in r.   45:13
have raised him in r. and will. 45:13
gone out of my mouth in r.   48:1
God of Israel, but not in r.   48:1
in r. shalt thou be established. 54:14
that speak in r., mighty to.   63:1
the Lord liveth, in r.   *Jer 4:2*
betroth thee unto me in r. *Hos 2:19*
sow to yourselves in r., reap. 10:12
God in truth and in r.   *Zech 8:8*
offer an offering in r.   *Mal 3:3*
judge the world in r.   *Acts 17:31*
and cut it short in r.   *Rom 9:28*
new man...is created in r. *Eph 4:24*
for instruction in r.   *2 Tim 3:16*
and in r. he doth judge. *Rev 19:11*

my righteousness
so my r. answer for me. *Gen 30:33*
saying, For my r. Lord.   *Deut 9:4*
Lord rewarded me according to my
  r. *2 Sam 22:21, 25; Ps 18:20, 24*
yea, return again, my r.   *Job 6:29*
my r. I hold fast, and will.   27:6
saidst, my r. is more than.   35:2
I call, O God of my r.   *Ps 4:1*

Lord, according to my r.   *Ps 7:8*
the right hand of my r.   *Isa 41:10*
I bring near my r.   46:13
my r. is near.   51:5
my r. shall not be abolished.   6
but my r. shall be for ever.   8
salvation is near to come, my r. 56:1
not having mine own r.   *Phil 3:9*

our righteousnesses
all our r. are as filthy.   *Isa 64:6*
not for our r. but for.   *Dan 9:18*

thy righteousness
nor for thy r. or.   *Deut 9:5, 6*
make the habitation of thy r. *Job 8:6*
and thy r. may profit the son. 35:8
lead me, O Lo d, in thy r. *Ps 5:8*
deliver me in thy r.   31:1; 71:2
Lord, according to thy r.   35:24
shall speak of thy r.   28; 71:24
thy r. is like the great.   36:6
O continue thy r. to the upright. 10
he shall bring forth thy r.   37:6
I have not hid thy r. within. 40:10
shall sing aloud of thy r.   51:14
let them not come into thy r. 69:27
shew forth thy r. all day.   71:15
I will make mention of thy r.   16
thy r. O God, is very high.   19
and give thy r. unto the king's. 72:1
thy r. be known in land of. 88:12
and in thy r. shall they be. 89:16
quicken me in thy r.   119:40
for word of thy r.   123*
thy r. is an everlasting.   142
answer me, and in thy r.   143:1
for thy r.' sake, bring my soul. 11
and they shall sing of thy r. 145:7
had thy r. been as waves. *Isa 48:18*
I will declare thy r. and.   57:12
thy r. shall go before thee. 58:8
and the Gentiles shall see thy r. 62:2
according to all thy r.   *Dan 9:16*

rightly
said, Is not he r. named ? *Gen 27:36*
Thou hast r. judged.   *Luke 7:43*
know that thou teachest r.   20:21
r. dividing the word of. *2 Tim 2:15*

rigour
Israel to serve with r.   *Ex 1:13, 14*
thou shalt not rule with r. *Lev 25:43*
    46, 53

Rimmon
Ain and R. cities of.   *Josh 15:32*
fled towards the wilderness, to the
  rock R.   *Judg 20:45, 47; 21:13*
Baanah and Rechab sons of R.
    2 Sam 4:2, 5, 9
goeth into the house of R. *2 Ki 5:18*
of Simeon were Ain, R. *1 Chr 4:32*
was given to Merari, R.   6:77
be turned as a plain to R. *Zech 14:10*

ring
*(The signet ring of a monarch
contained his seal, which was
affixed to a document instead of a
signature, as few people wrote in
those days, and fewer still read.
To give this ring to another was to
give him the right to sign in place
of the king. Rings of various sorts
were also worn as ornaments, either
by a monarch or others)*
Pharaoh took off his r. *Gen 41:42*
coupled unto one r. *Ex 26:24; 36:29*
king Ahasuerus took his r. *Esth 3:10*
with the king's r.   12; 8:8, 10
the king took off his r.   8:2
the father said, Put a r. *Luke 15:22*
a man with a gold r.   *Jas 2:2*

ringleader
and a r. of the sect of.   *Acts 24:5*

rings
four r. of gold for it.   *Ex 25:12*
put staves into the r.   14, 15; 27:7
    37:5; 38:7
their r. of gold.   26:29; 28:23, 26
    27; 30:4; 36:34; 37:3, 13; 39:16
    19, 20
upon net four brazen r.   27:4
the breastplate by the r.   28:28
jewels, bracelets, and r. *Num 31:50*

fastened to silver r. pillars. Esth 1:6
his hands are as gold r. S of S 5:14
will take away the r. and. Isa 3:21
their r. so high that they were dreadful, their r. were full. Ezek 1:18

ringstraked
(American Revision ring-streaked)
he goats that were r. Gen 30:35
if he said, The r. shall be. 31:8
rams were r., speckled. 10, 12

rinsed
pot be both scoured and r. Lev 6:28
and hath not r. his hands. 15:11
every vessel of wood shall be r. 12

riot, *substantive*
children not accused of r. Tit 1:6
to the same excess of r. 1 Pet 4:4

riot
count it pleasure to r. 2 Pet 2:13*

rioting
walk not in r. and. Rom 13:13*

riotous
not amongst r. eaters. Pr 23:20*
he that is a companion of r. 28:7*
substance with r. living. Luke 15:13

rip
wilt r. up their women. 2 Ki 8:12

ripe
brought forth r. grapes. Gen 40:10
first of thy r. fruits. Ex 22:29
of the first r. grapes. Num 13:20
whatsoever is first r. in the. 18:13
even like the figs that are first r.
Jer 24:2; Hos 9:10; Nah 3:12
sickle, for the harvest is r. Joel 3:13
desired the first r. fruit. Mi 7:1
for harvest of earth is r. Rev 14:15
for her grapes are fully r. 18

ripening
and the sour grape is r. Isa 18:5

ripped
all the women with child he r. up.
2 Ki 15:16
with child shall be r. up. Hos 13:16
because they have r. up. Amos 1:13

rise
if he r. again and walk. Ex 21:19
and a sceptre shall r. Num 24:17
r. that they r. not again. Deut 33:11
shall r. and go through. Josh 18:4
R. thou and fall upon us. Judg 9:21
thou shalt r. early, and set. 9:33
that he should r. to lie. 1 Sam 22:13
and suffered them not to r. 24:7
when child was dead, thou didst r.
2 Sam 12:21
all that r. against thee be. 18:32
upon my right hand r. Job 30:12
they were not able to r. Ps 18:38
though war should r. against. 27:3
down, shall not be able to r. 36:12
at midnight I will r. to give. 119:62
into deep pits, that they r. 140:10
calamity shall r. suddenly. Pr 24:22
when the wicked r. a man. 28:12, 28
I will r. now and go about the city.
S of S 3:2
prepare slaughter, that they do not r.
Isa 14:21
earth shall fall and not r. 24:20
deceased, they shall not r. 26:14
now will I r. saith the Lord. 33:10
down together, they shall not r. 43:17
every tongue that shall r. thou. 54:17
shall thy light r. in obscurity. 58:10
fall and r. no more. Jer 25:27
Babylon shall not r. from evil. 51:64
Israel shall no more r. Amos 5:2
I will r. against the house of. 7:9
he maketh sun to r. on. Mat 5:45
and third day he shall r. again. 20:19
Mark 9:31; 10:34; Luke 18:33
24:7
for nation shall r. against. Mat 24:7
Mark 13:8; Luke 21:10
many false prophets shall r.
Mat 24:11; Mark 13:22
r., let us be going. Mat 26:46
after three days I will r. again.
Mat 27:63; Mark 8:31

and should sleep, and r. Mark 4:27
be of good comfort, r.; he. 10:49
when they shall r. 12:23, 25
the dead, that they r. 26
trouble me not, I cannot r. Luke 11:7
though he will not r. because he. 8
when ye see a cloud r. out of. 12:54
Why sleep ye ? r. and pray. 22:46
to suffer and r. from. 24:46
Jesus saith, R. take up thy. John 5:8
thy brother shall r. again. 11:23
I know he shall r. 24
that he must r. again. 20:9
r. Peter, kill and eat. Acts 10:13
r. and stand upon thy feet. 26:16
should be the first that should r. 23
he that shall r. to reign. Rom 15:12
if so be the dead r. not. 1 Cor 15:15
16, 29, 32
in Christ shall r. first. 1 Thes 4:16
another priest should r. Heb 7:11
r. and measure the temple. Rev 11:1

rise up
ye shall r. up early and go. Gen 19:2
that I cannot r. up. 31:35
r. up and stand before Pharaoh.
Ex 8:20; 9:13
r. up and get you forth from. 12:31
thou shalt r. up before. Lev 19:32
r. up, Lord, let enemies. Num 10:35
call thee up, r. up and go. 22:20
r. up, Balak, and hear, thou. 23:18
behold, the people shall r. up. 24
Now, r. up, said I, and. Deut 2:13
r. ye up, and pass over the. 24
if a man r. up against his. 19:11
one witness shall not r. up: 15
if a false witness r. up against. 16
thine enemies that r. up. 28:7
the generation that shall r. up. 29:22
this people will r. up, and. 31:16
their gods, let them r. up. 32:38
then ye shall r. up from. Josh 8:7
a great flame r. up. Judg 20:38, 40
wherefore r. up early. 1 Sam 29:10
they said, Let us r. up. Neh 2:18
and the earth shall r. up. Job 20:27
many are they that r. up. Ps 3:1
save them from those that r. up. 17:7
me above those that r. up. 18:48
false witnesses did r. up, they. 35:11
he shall r. up no more. 41:8
them under that r. up against. 44:5
them that r. up against me. 59:1
the tumult of those that r. up. 74:23
desire of the wicked that r. up. 92:11
who will r. up for me against? 94:16
it is vain for you to r. up. 127:2
grieved with those that r. up ? 139:21
her children r. up, and call. Pr 31:28
the ruler r. up against. Eccl 10:4
he shall r. up at the voice. 12:4
unto me, R. up, my love. S of S 5:1
woe unto them that r. up. Isa 5:11
I will r. up against them. 14:22
Lord shall r. up as in mount. 28:21
r. up, ye women at ease. 32:9
should r. up every man. Jer 37:10
behold, waters r. up out of. 47:2
gather against her, and r. up. 49:14
against them that r. up against. 51:1
I am not able to r. up. Lam 1:14
it shall r. up wholly. Amos 8:8; 9:5
and never r. up again. 14
let us r. up against Edom. Ob 1
affliction shall not r. up. Nah 1:9
they not r. up suddenly ? Hab 2:7
until the day that I r. up. Zeph 3:8
his hand r. up against. Zech 14:13
children shall r. up against their.
Mat 10:21; Mark 13:12
the men of Nineveh shall r. up.
Mat 12:41; Luke 11:32
queen of the south shall r. up.
Mat 12:42; Luke 11:31
and if Satan r. up. Mark 3:26
r. up, lo, he that betrayeth me. 14:42
to say, R. up and walk. Luke 5:23
he said, R. up and stand forth. 6:8
in the name of Jesus r. up. Acts 3:6
I saw a beast r. up out. Rev 13:1

risen
the sun was r. when Lot. Gen 19:23

if sun be r. on him. Ex 22:3
ye are r. up in your. Num 32:14
ye are r. up against my. Judg 9:18
and when she was r. up. Ruth 2:15
a man is r. to pursue. 1 Sam 25:29
whole family is r. up. 2 Sam 14:7
I am r. up in room of David.
1 Ki 8:20; 2 Chr 6:10
of the man of God was r. 2 Ki 6:15
of Solomon is r. up. 2 Chr 13:6
when Jehoram was r. up to. 21:4
but we are r. and stand. Ps 20:8
for false witnesses are r. up. 27:12
for strangers are r. up against. 54:3
the proud are r. against. 86:14
glory of the Lord is r. Isa 60:1
violence is r. into a rod. Ezek 7:11
for the waters were r. waters. 47:5
even of late my people is r. Mi 2:8
hath not r. a greater. Mat 11:11
is John the Baptist, he is r. 14:2
Mark 6:14, 16; Luke 9:7
until the Son of man be r. again.
Mat 17:9; Mark 9:9
after I am r. I will go before.
Mat 26:32; Mark 14:28
disciples steal him away and say he
is r. Mat 27:64
he is not here: for he is r. as he said.
28:6; Mark 16:6
when Jesus was r. early. Mark 16:9
which had seen him after he was r.
14; John 21:14
that a great prophet is r. Luke 7:16
one of old prophets was r. 9:8, 19
master of the house is r. up. 13:25
the Lord is r. indeed, and. 24:34
when therefore he was r. John 2:22
must needs have r. again. Acts 17:3
yea rather that is r. again. Rom 8:34
then Christ is not r. 1 Cor 15:13
if Christ be not r. 14
but now is Christ r.
in baptism ye are also r. Col 2:12
if ye be r. with Christ, seek. 3:1
sun is no sooner r. Jas 1:11

risest
shalt talk of them. when thou r.
Deut 6:7; 11:19

riseth
as when a man r. against. Deut 22:26
cursed that r. up and. Josh 6:26
light when the sun r. 2 Sam 23:4
the sun and it r. not. Job 9:7
man lieth down, and r. not. 14:12
he r. up, and no man is sure. 24:22
he that r. up against me, as. 27:7
shall I do when God r. up ? 31:14
just man falleth, and r. Pr 24:16
r. also while it is yet night. 31:15
know from whence it r. Isa 47:11
Egypt r. up like a flood. Jer 46:8
the daughter r. up against. Mi 7:6
Jesus r. from supper, and. John 13:4

rising, *substantive*
if in skin of his flesh a r. Lev 13:2
see if the r. be white. 10; 19:43
if the spot stay, it is a r. of. 13:28
this is the law for a r. and. 14:56
held spears from the r. Neh 4:21
whom there is no r. Pr 30:31
to the brightness of thy r. Isa 60:3
what the r. from the dead should
mean. Mark 9:10
for the fall and r. of. Luke 2:34

sun-rising
toward r. of the sun. Num 2:3
before Moab, toward sun-r. 21:11
34:15; Deut 4:41, 47; Josh 12:1
13:5; 19:12, 27, 34
from the r. of the sun. Ps 50:1
from r. of sun, Lord's name. 113:3
from r. of sun shall he call. Isa 41:25
know from the r. of the sun. 45:6
glory from the r. of the sun. 59:19
from r. of sun my name. Mal 1:11
sepulchre at r. of the sun. Mark 16:2

rising
messengers, r. betimes. 2 Chr 36:15
my leanness in me. Job 16:8
wild asses go forth, r. betimes. 24:5
murderer r. with the light killeth. 14

his friend, r. early. *Pr* 27:14
I spake unto you, r. up early.
　　Jer 7:13; 25:3; 35:14
the prophets to you r. up early. 7:25
　　25:4; 26:5; 29:19; 35:15; 44:4
r. early, and protesting. 11:7
though I taught them, r. up. 32:33
sitting down and r. up. *Lam* 3:63
in the morning, r. before. *Mark* 1:35

rites
according to all the r. *Num* 9:3*

river
(Frequently this word is used where the Hebrew really means a valley; or where the stream is small and hardly deserves the name. When the river is referred to it usually means the Nile. Where the expression river of Egypt is used it may mean [1] the Nile, or [2] a small brook or desert stream which formed one of the boundaries of Egypt. The word is also used symbolically of a great abundance)
and passed over the r. *Gen* 31:21
Saul of Rehoboth by the r. 36:37
　　1 Chr 1:48
behold, he stood by the r. *Gen* 41:1
ye shall cast into the r. *Ex* 1:22
of Pharaoh came to wash at r. 2:5
the water of the r. shall become. 4:9
the r. shall die, and r. stink. 7:18
the r. shall bring forth frogs. 8:3
may remain in the r. only. 9, 11
journey, pass over the r. *Deut* 2:24*
Gilead even to the r. Arnon. 3:16
the city that is in the midst of the r.
　　Josh 13:9*; *2 Sam* 24:5*
draw to the r. Kishon. *Judg* 4:7
r. Kishon that ancient r. swept. 5:21
draw that city into the r. *2 Sam* 17:13
reigned over from the r. *1 Ki* 4:21
are on this side the r. *Ezra* 4:10
no portion on this side the r. 16
governor on this side the r. 5:3
to r. that runneth to Ahava. 8:15
behold he drinketh up a r. *Job* 40:23
make them drink of the r. *Ps* 36:8
a r. the streams shall make. 46:4
thou enrichest it with the r. 65:9
have dominion from the r. to. 72:8
her branches unto the r. 80:11
in the dry places like a r. 105:41
them the waters of the r. *Isa* 8:7
shake his hand over the r. 11:15
and the r. shall be wasted. 19:5
the harvest of the r. is her. 23:3*
pass through thy land as a r. 10*
off from channel of the r. 27:12
peace been as a r. O daughter. 48:18
extend peace to her like a r. 66:12
drink the waters of the r. *Jer* 2:18
out her roots by the r. 17:8
let tears run down like r. *Lam* 2:18
My r. is mine own. *Ezek* 29:3, 9
it was a r. that I could not. 47:5
live whither the r. cometh. 9
afflict you to the r. of. *Amos* 6:14*
from the fortress to the r. *Mi* 7:12
his dominion from the r. *Zech* 9:10
deeps of the r. shall dry up. 10:11*
were baptized in the r. *Mark* 1:5
we went by a r. side. *Acts* 16:13
pure r. of water of life. *Rev* 22:1
on either side of the r. was the. 2
see bank, beyond, brink, Chebar,
Euphrates

rivers
stretch out thine hand on the r.
　　Ex 7:19*; 8:5*
whatsoever hath fins in r. *Lev* 11:9
all that have not fins in the r. 10
to Jotbath, a land of r. *Deut* 10:7*
r. of Damascus better? *2 Ki* 5:12
I have dried up all the r. 19:24
　　Isa 37:25
not see the r. of honey. *Job* 20:17
he cutteth out the r. among. 28:10*
poureth me out r. of oil. 29:6†
planted by the r. of water. *Ps* 1:3*
thou driedst up mighty r. 74:15
waters to run down like r. 78:16
had turned their r. into blood. 44

set his right hand in the r. *Ps* 89:25
turneth r. into a wilderness. 107:33
r. of waters run down. 119:136
by the r. of Babylon there we. 137:1
and r. of waters in the. *Pr* 5:16†
in the hand of the Lord, as r. 21:1*
all r. run into the sea. *Eccl* 1:7
eyes of doves by the r. of waters.
　　S of S 5:12*
hiss for the fly in the r. *Isa* 7:18
a nation, whose land r. 18:2, 7
and they shall turn the r. far. 19:6
and on every high hill r. 30:25†
a man shall be as r. of water. 32:2†
be to us a place of broad r. 33:21
I will open r. in high places. 41:18
I will make the r. islands. 42:15
passest through the r. they. 43:2
and I will make r. in the. 19, 20
be dry, and will dry up thy r. 44:27
the thigh, pass over the r. 47:2
I make a r. wilderness, their. 50:2
them to walk by the r. *Jer* 31:9
are moved as the r. 46:7, 8
down with r. of waters. *Lam* 3:48†
Lord to the hills and r. *Ezek* 6:3*
that lieth in the midst of his r. 29:3
the fish of thy r. to stick to thy scales
　　. . . out of the midst of thy r. 4
and all the fish of thy r. 5
against thee, and against thy r. 10
I will make the r. dry, and. 30:12
him up on high with her r. 31:4
broken by the r. of the land. 12*
thou camest forth with thy r. 32:2
and the r. shall be full of thee. 6*
then will I cause their r. to run. 14
them on mountains by the r. 34:13*
in all thy r. shall they fall. 35:8*
say to the hills, to the r. and. 36:6*
whithersoever the r. shall. 47:9
for the r. of waters are. *Joel* 1:20*
all the r. of Judah shall flow. 3:18*
ten thousands of r. of oil. *Mi* 6:7
and drieth up the r. *Nah* 1:4
the gates of the r. shall be. 2:6
that was situate among the r. 3:8
displeased against the r.? *Hab* 3:8
didst cleave the earth with r. 9
flow r. of living water. *John* 7:38
on the third part of the r. *Rev* 8:10
poured out his vial on the r. 16:4

Rizpah
whose name was R. *2 Sam* 3:7
two sons of R. to Gibeonites. 21:8
R. spread sackcloth for her on. 10

road
ye made a r. to-day. *1 Sam* 27:10*

roar
let the sea r. *1 Chr* 16:32; *Ps* 96:11
　　98:7
though waters thereof r. *Ps* 46:3
thine enemies r. in thy. 74:4*
the young lions r. after their. 104:21
r. like young lions. *Isa* 5:29
in that day they shall r. against. 30
Lord shall r.; he shall prevail. 42:13*
we r. all like bears, and. 59:11
though they r. yet can. *Jer* 5:22
the Lord shall r. from on high. 25:30
when the waves thereof r. 31:35
their voice shall r. like the. 50:42
they shall r. together like lions. 51:38
when her waves do r. like great. 55
r. like a lion, when he shall r.
　　Hos 11:10
the Lord shall r. out of Zion.
　　Joel 3:16; *Amos* 1:2
will a lion r. if he hath? *Amos* 3:4

roared
lion r. against Samson. *Judg* 14:5
I have r. by reason of. *Ps* 38:8†
the sea, whose waves r. *Isa* 51:15
the young lions r. upon him. *Jer* 2:15
the lion hath r., who will? *Amos* 3:8

roareth
after it a voice r. he. *Job* 37:4
their voice r. like the sea. *Jer* 6:23
cried, as when a lion r. *Rev* 10:3

roaring, *substantive*
the r. of the lion. *Job* 4:10
from the words of my r.? *Ps* 22:1†

old through my r. all the. *Ps* 33:3†
king's wrath is as the r. *Pr* 19:12
the fear of a king is as the r. 20:2
their r. shall be like a lion. *Isa* 5:29
roar like the r. of the sea. 30
land was desolate by the noise of his
　　r. *Ezek* 19:7
a voice of the r. of young. *Zech* 11:3

roaring
upon me as a r. lion. *Ps* 22:13
as a r. lion, so is a wicked. *Pr* 28:15
as the young lion r. on. *Isa* 31:4*
conspiracy, like a r. lion. *Ezek* 22:25
within her are r. lions. *Zeph* 3:3
sea and the waves r. *Luke* 21:25
the devil, as a r. lion. *1 Pet* 5:8

roarings
my r. are poured out. *Job* 3:24†

roast, -ed
flesh that night, r. with fire. *Ex* 12:8
but r. with fire. 9; *Deut* 16:7
flesh to r. for the priest. *1 Sam* 2:15
they r. the passover. *2 Chr* 35:13
he roasteth r., is satisfied. *Isa* 44:16
yea, also I have r. flesh, and. 19
king of Babylon r. in fire. *Jer* 29:22

roasteth
the slothful man r. not. *Pr* 12:27

rob
not r. thy neighbour. *Lev* 19:13
beasts, which shall r. you. 26:22
they r. the threshing. *1 Sam* 23:1
r. not the poor, because. *Pr* 22:22
and that they may r. *Isa* 10:2*
the lot of them that r. us. 17:14
spoil, and r. those that. *Ezek* 39:10
will a man r. God? yet ye. *Mal* 3:8

robbed
and they r. all that came. *Judg* 9:25
in minds, as a bear r. *2 Sam* 17:8
wicked have r. me. *Ps* 119:61*
let a bear r. of her whelps. *Pr* 17:12
I have r. their treasures. *Isa* 10:13
but this is a people r. and. 42:22
treasures, they shall be r. *Jer* 50:37
give again that he had r. *Ezek* 33:15
rob those that r. them. 39:10
r. me, wherein have we r.? *Mal* 3:8
with a curse, for ye have r. me. 9
I r. other churches. *2 Cor* 11:8

robber
and the r. swalloweth up. *Job* 5:5*
and the r. shall prevail. 18:9*
beget a son that is a r. *Ezek* 18:10
is a thief and a r. *John* 10:1
Now Barabbas was a r. 18:40

robbers
tabernacles of r. prosper. *Job* 12:6
gave Israel to the r. *Isa* 42:24
house become a den of r.? *Jer* 7:11
the r. shall enter into it. *Ezek* 7:22
the r. of thy people. *Dan* 11:14*
troops of r. wait for a. *Hos* 6:9
and the troop of r. spoileth. 7:1
if r. by night, would they not? *Ob* 5
came before me are r. *John* 10:8
these men are not r. of. *Acts* 19:37
of waters, in perils of r. *2 Cor* 11:26

robbery
and become not vain in r. *Ps* 62:10
r. the r. of the wicked shall. *Pr* 21:7*
I hate r. for burnt offering. *Isa* 61:8
have exercised r. and. *Ezek* 22:29
who store up r. in their. *Amos* 3:10
city is full of lies and r. *Nah* 3:1
who thought it no r. to. *Phil* 2:6*

robbeth
whoso r. his father or. *Pr* 28:24

robe
make an ephod, and a r. *Ex* 28:4
shalt make the r. of the ephod. 31
on the hem of the r. 34; 39:25, 26
Aaron the coat and r. 29:5; *Lev* 8:7
stripped himself of his r. *1 Sam* 18:4
off the skirt of Saul's r. 24:4
see the skirt of thy r. in my hand . . .
　　the skirt of thy r. and killed. 11
was clothed with a r. *1 Chr* 15:27
judgement as a r. *Job* 29:14
clothe him with thy r. *Isa* 22:21
hath covered me with r. of. 61:10

laid his r. from him. *Jonah 3:6*
ye pull off the r. with the garment.
Mi 2:8
put on Jesus a scarlet r. *Mat 27:28*
after that, they took the r. off. 31
bring forth the best r. *Luke 15:22*
arrayed him in a gorgeous r. 23:11*
on Jesus a purple r. *John 19:2**
wearing the purple r. 5*

robes

with such r. were virgins apparelled.
2 Sam 13:18
having put on their r. *1 Ki 22:10*
put thou on thy r. 30; *2 Chr 18:9, 29*
shall lay away their r. *Ezek 26:16*
desire to walk in long r. *Luke 20:46*
and white r. were given. *Rev 6:11*
the Lamb, clothed with white r. 7:9
which are arrayed in white r.? 13
which have washed their r. 14

rock

before thee upon the r. *Ex 17:6*
thou shalt stand upon a r. 33:21
put thee in a cleft of the r. 22
speak to the r. before. *Num 20:8*
fetch you water out of this r.? 10
his rod smote the r. twice. 11
and thou puttest thy nest in a r. 24:21
thee water out of the r. *Deut 8:15*
he is the R., his work is perfect. 32:4
suck honey and oil out of the r. 13
he lightly esteemed the r. of. 15
of the R. that begat thee thou. 18
except their R. had sold them. 30
for their r. is not as our R. 31
where is their r. in whom they? 37
and lay them upon this r. *Judg 6:20*
there rose up fire out of the r. 21
altar to the Lord on this r. 26*
they slew Oreb on the r. Oreb. 7:25
Manoah offered it on a r. to. 13:19
in the top of the r. Etam. 15:8
turned to the r. of Rimmon. 20:45
neither is there any r. *1 Sam 2:2*
a sharp r. on one side, sharp r. 14:4
David came down into a r. 23:25
sackcloth on the r. *2 Sam 21:10*
he said, Lord is my r. *Ps 18:2; 92:15*
the God of my r. in him. *2 Sam 22:3*
and who is a r. save our God? 32
Ps 18:31
blessed be my r. . . . exalted be the
God of r. *2 Sam 22:47; Ps 18:46*
God of Israel said, The r. *2 Sam 23:3*
captains went to the r. *1 Chr 11:15*
from the top of the r. *2 Chr 25:12*
water for them out of the r. for their.
Neh 9:15; Ps 78:16; 105:41
the r. is removed out of. *Job 14:18*
and shall the r. be removed? 18:4
that they were graven in the r. 19:24
they embrace the r. for want of. 24:8
forth his hand upon the r. 28:9
and the r. poured out rivers. 29:6
time when wild goats of the r. 39:1
on the r. on the crag of the r. 28
set me up upon a r. *Ps 27:5; 40:2*
will I cry, O Lord, my r. 28:1
r. for an house of defence. 31:2
my r. and my fortress. 3; 71:3
I will say to God, My r. why? 42:9
lead me to the r. that is higher. 61:2
God only is my r. 62:2, 6
r. of my strength. 7
behold, he smote the r. 78:20
remembered that God was their r. 35
with honey out of the r. have. 81:16
r. of my salvation. 89:26
r. of my refuge. 94:22
make a joyful noise to the r. 95:1
which turned the r. into a. 114:8
way of a serpent upon a r. *Pr 30:19*
art in the clefts of the r. *S of S 2:14*
enter into the r. and hide. *Isa 2:10*
r. of offence to both houses. 8:14
slaughter of the r. of Oreb. 10:26
not mindful of the r. of thy. 17:10
an habitation for himself in a r. 22:16
as the shadow of a great r. 32:2
let inhabitants of the r. sing. 42:11*
caused waters to flow out of r. 48:21
look unto the r. whence ye. 51:1

faces harder than a r. *Jer 5:3*
girdle in a hole of the r. 13:4
which cometh from the r. 18:14
thee, O inhabitant of the r. 21:13
a hammer that breaketh the r. 23:29
cities, and dwell in the r. 48:28
dwellest in the clefts of the r. 49:16
it upon the top of a r. *Ezek 24:7*
blood upon the top of a r. 8
her like the top of a r. 26:4, 14
horses run upon the r.? *Amos 6:12*
in the clefts of the r. *Ob 3*
built his house upon a r. *Mat 7:24*
founded upon a r. 25; *Luke 6:48**
upon this r. I will build. *Mat 16:18*
own new tomb, which he had hewn
out in the r. 27:60; *Mark 15:46*
some fell upon a r. *Luke 8:6*
they on the r. 13
in Sion a stumbling stone, and r. of.
Rom 9:33; 1 Pet 2:8
spiritual r. that followed them, and
that r. was Christ. *1 Cor 10:4*

rocks

for from the top of the r. *Num 23:9*
the people hid themselves in r.
1 Sam 13:6
seek David upon the r. 24:2
brake in pieces the r. *1 Ki 19:11*
rivers among the r. *Job 28:10*
caves of the earth, and in r. 30:6
the r. in the wilderness. *Ps 78:15*
and the r. are a refuge for. 104:18
they their houses in the r. *Pr 30:26*
go into the holes of the r. *Isa 2:19*
the r. and tops of the ragged r. 21
rest in the holes of the r. 7:19
shall be the munitions of r. 33:16
under the clefts of the r. 57:5
city shall climb on the r. *Jer 4:29*
out of the holes of the r. 51:25
roll thee down from the r. 51:25
the r. are thrown down. *Nah 1:6*
quake, and the r. rent. *Mat 27:51*
have fallen upon the r. *Acts 27:29**
in the dens and in the r. *Rev 6:15*
and said to the r., Fall on us. 16

rod
(*This word is often used to mean
the shepherd's crook*)

became a r. in his hand. *Ex 4:4*
thou shalt take this r. in thine. 17
Moses took the r. of God in. 20; 17:9
to Aaron, Take thy r. 7:9, 19
down every man his r. 12
he lifted up the r. and. 20; 14:16
smite a servant with a r. 21:20
passeth under the r. *Lev 27:32*
man's name on his r. *Num 17:2*
the r. of Aaron for the house of. 8
with his r. he smote the rock. 20:11
forth the end of the r. *1 Sam 14:27*
him with the r. of men. *2 Sam 7:14*
let him take his r. away. *Job 9:34*
neither is the r. of God upon. 21:9
break them with a r. of iron. *Ps 2:9*
thy r. and thy staff they. 23:4
remember the r. of thine. 74:2*
transgression with a r. 89:32
the Lord shall send the r. 110:2
r. of wicked shall not rest on. 125:3*
a r. for the back of. *Pr 10:13; 26:3*
he that spareth his r. hateth. 13:24
the foolish is a r. of pride. 14:3
r. of his anger shall fail. 22:8
the r. of correction shall drive. 15
beat him with the r. 23:13, 14
the r. and reproof give. 29:15
thou hast broken the r. of. *Isa 9:4*
O Assyrian, the r. of mine. 10:5
as if the r. should shake itself. 15
he shall smite with a r. and lift. 24
as his r. was on the sea, so. 26
shall come forth a r. out of. 11:1*
shall smite the earth with the r. 4
the r. of him that smote thee. 14:29
is beaten out with a r. 28:27
which smote with a r. 30:31
and said, I see a r. of an. *Jer 1:11*
Israel the r. of his inheritance.
10:16*; 51:19*
how is the beautiful r. broken! 48:17
by the r. of his wrath. *Lam 3:1*

the r. hath blossomed. *Ezek 7:10*
violence is risen up into a r. 11
out of a r. of her branches, so that
she hath no strong r. to. 19:14
pass under the r. and bring. 20:37
the r. of my son. 21:10, 13
smite Judge of Israel with a r.
Mi 5:1
hear ye the r. and who hath. 6:9
feed thy people with thy r. 7:14
you with a r. or in love? *1 Cor 4:21*
wherein was Aaron's r. *Heb 9:4*
with a r. of iron. *Rev 2:27; 19:15*
given me a reed like to a r. 11:1
all nations with a r. of iron. 12:5

rode

Rebekah and her damsels r.
Gen 24:61
thirty sons that r. on. *Judg 10:4*
nephews that r. on ass colts. 12:14
Abigail r. on the ass. *1 Sam 25:20, 42*
four hundred which r. on camels.
30:17
Absalom r. upon a mule. *2 Sam 18:9*
he r. on a cherub, and did fly. 22:11
Ps 18:10
the old prophet r. on. *1 Ki 13:13*
and Ahab r. and went to. 18:45
Jehu r. in a chariot, and. *2 Ki 9:16*
remember when I and thou r. 25
save the beast that I r. *Neh 2:12*
the posts that r. on the. *Esth 8:14*

rods

Jacob took r. of green. *Gen 30:37*
might conceive among the r. 41
Aaron's rod swallowed up their r.
Ex 7:12
gave him twelve r. *Num 17:6*
and Moses laid up the r. before. 7
she had strong r. for the. *Ezek 19:11*
her strong r. were broken and. 12
was I beaten with r. *2 Cor 11:25*

roe, -s

as swift as the r. on. *1 Chr 12:8*
as the hind and pleasant r. *Pr 5:19**
deliver thyself as the r. from. 6:5
I charge you by the r. and hinds.
S of S 2:7; 3:5
is like a r. or a young hart. 9
be thou like a r. or hart. 2:17; 8:14
it shall be as the chased r. *Isa 13:14*

see **young**

wild roe

Asahel was as light of foot as a *wild
r.* *2 Sam 2:18*

roebuck, -s

ye may eat of the r. *Deut 12:15*, 22*
14:5*; 15:22*
besides harts and r. *1 Ki 4:23**

roll, verb

we cannot, till they r. *Gen 29:8*
and Joshua said, R. *Josh 10:18*
r. a great stone unto me this day.
1 Sam 14:33
and I will r. thee down. *Jer 51:25*
in Aphrah, r. thyself. *Mi 1:10*
who shall r. us away? *Mark 16:3*

roll, substantive

found at Achmetha a r. *Ezra 6:2*
take thee a great r. and. *Isa 8:1**
take thee a r. of a book. *Jer 36:2*
go and read in the r. 6
till after the r. was consumed. 23
take another r. 28
saith Lord, Thou hast burnt this r. 29
an hand was sent unto me, and lo,
a r. *Ezek 2:9*
eat this r. 3:1
he caused me to eat that r. 2
fill thy bowels with this r. that. 3
and behold a flying r. *Zech 5:1, 2*

rolled

they r. the stone from. *Gen 29:3*
that Jacob went near, and r. 10
I have r. away reproach of. *Josh 5:9*
in desolation they r. *Job 30:14*
with noise, and garments r. *Isa 9:5*
the heavens shall be r. together.
34:4; *Rev 6:14*
his own new tomb, he r. a great stone
to door. *Mat 27:60; Mark 15:46*

roller

angel came and r. back.	Mat 28:2
the stone was r. away.	16:4
found the stone r. away.	Luke 24:2

roller

bound up, to put a r. to.	Ezek 30:21

rolleth

he that r. a stone, it will.	Pr 26:27

rolling

nations shall flee like a r. thing.	
	Isa 17:13*

rolls

search was made in the house of the r.	
	Ezra 6:1*

Roman

a man that is a R.	Acts 22:25, 26
tell me, Art thou a R.?	27
that he was a R.	29; 23:27

Romans

the R. shall come and.	John 11:48
us to observe, being R.	Acts 16:21
beaten us, being R.	37
heard they were R.	38
prisoner into hands of the R.	28:17

Rome

strangers of R. we do.	Acts 2:10
all Jews to depart from R.	18:2
I must see R.	19:21
bear witness also at R.	23:11
we came to R., Paul dwelt.	28:16
to all that be in R., beloved.	Rom 1:7
preach gospel to you that are at R.	15
when he was in R. he.	2 Tim 1:17

roof

under the shadow of my r.	Gen 19:8
a battlement for thy r.	Deut 22:8
the r. and hid with flax which she had laid in order on r.	Josh 2:6
on the r. were 3000.	Judg 16:27
David walked on the r. . . . and from the r. he saw a woman.	2 Sam 11:2
watchman went up to the r.	18:24
booths on the r. of his.	Neh 8:16
gate from the r. of one.	Ezek 40:13
that thou shouldest come under my r.	Mat 8:8; Luke 7:6
they uncovered the r.	Mark 2:4

roof with **mouth**

tongue cleaved to r. of their mouth.	Job 29:10
cleave to r. of my mouth.	Ps 137:6
the r. of thy mouth like.	S of S 7:9
cleaveth to r. of his mouth.	Lam 4:4
tongue cleave to r. of thy mouth.	Ezek 3:26

roofs

on whose r. they burnt incense.	
	Jer 19:13; 32:29

room

is there r. in thy father's?	Gen 24:23
we have r. to lodge in.	25
r. for the camels.	31
Lord hath made r. for us.	26:22
captain in the r. of Joab.	2 Sam 19:13
in Joab's r. and he put Zadok the priest in the r. of.	1 Ki 2:35
had anointed him king in the r.	5:1
thy son whom I will set in thy r.	5
I am risen in the r. of David.	8:20
	2 Chr 6:10
thou anoint in thy r.	1 Ki 19:16
my feet in a large r.	Ps 31:8*
thou preparedst r. before it.	80:9
a man's gift maketh r.	Pr 18:16
shall not be r. enough.	Mal 3:10
Archelaus reigned in the r.	Mat 2:22
that there was no r. to.	Mark 2:2
he will shew you a large upper r.	14:15; Luke 22:12
because there was no r.	Luke 2:7
I have no r. to bestow my.	12:17
sit not down in the highest r.	14:8*
shame to take the lowest r.	9*
and sit down in the lowest r.	10*
it is done, and yet there is r.	22
went up to an upper r.	Acts 1:13
Festus came into Felix' r.	24:27*
that occupieth the r.	1 Cor 14:16*

rooms

r. shalt thou make in the.	Gen 6:14
captains in their r.	1 Ki 20:24
and dwelt in their r.	1 Chr 4:41*

uppermost r. at feasts.	Mat 23:6*
	Mark 12:39*; Luke 20:46*
chose out the chief r.	Luke 14:7*

root, *substantive*

a r. that beareth gall.	Deut 29:18
out of Ephraim was a r.	Judg 5:14
again take r. downward.	2 Ki 19:30
the foolish taking r.	Job 5:3
though the r. thereof wax old.	14:8
seeing the r. of the matter is.	19:28
my r. was spread out by the.	29:19
the vine to take deep r.	Ps 80:9
r. of the righteous shall.	Pr 12:3
the r. of the righteous yieldeth.	12
so their r. shall be rottenness, and.	
	Isa 5:24
there shall be a r. of Jesse.	11:10
	Rom 15:12
for out of the serpent's r.	Isa 14:29
I will kill thy r. with famine.	30
that come of Jacob to take r.	27:6
	37:31
their stock shall not take r.	40:24
as a r. out of a dry ground.	53:2
have taken r.: they grow.	Jer 12:2
r. was by great waters.	Ezek 31:7
out of a branch of her r.	Dan 11:7
smitten, their r. is dried.	Hos 9:16
neither r. nor branch.	Mal 4:1
axe is laid unto the r. of the trees.	
	Mat 3:10; Luke 3:9
because they had not r.	Mat 13:6
	21; Mark 4:6, 17; Luke 8:13
thou plucked up by the r.	Luke 17:6
if the r. be holy, so are.	Rom 11:16
with them partakest of the r.	17
thou bearest not the r. but the r.	18
love of money is the r.	1 Tim 6:10
lest any r. of bitterness.	Heb 12:15
r. of David hath prevailed.	Rev 5:5
I am the r. and offspring of.	22:16

root

he shall r. up Israel.	1 Ki 14:15
and would r. out all.	Job 31:12
and r. thee out of the land.	Ps 52:5
have set thee to r. out.	Jer 1:10*
lest ye r. up the wheat.	Mat 13:29

rooted

the Lord r. them out.	Deut 29:28
confidence shall be r. out.	Job 18:14
let my offspring be r. out.	31:8
transgressors shall be r. out of it.	
	Pr 2:22
Ekron shall be r. up.	Zeph 2:4
not planted, shall be r.	Mat 15:13
being r. and grounded.	Eph 3:17
r. and built up in him.	Col 2:7

roots

them up by the r.	2 Chr 7:20
his r. are wrapped about.	Job 8:17
his r. shall be dried up.	18:16
the mountains by the r.	28:9
juniper r. for their meat.	30:4
shall grow out of his r.	Isa 11:1
that spreadeth out her r.	Jer 17:8
and the r. thereof were.	Ezek 17:6
this vine did bend her r. toward.	7
not pull up the r. thereof?	9
the stump of his r.	Dan 4:15, 23, 26
first horns plucked up by the r.	7:8
he shall cast forth his r. as.	Hos 14:5
I destroyed his r. from.	Amos 2:9
tree dried up from the r.	Mark 11:20
dead, plucked up by the r.	Jude 12

ropes

bind me with new r.	Judg 16:11, 12
all Israel bring r. to.	2 Sam 17:13
let us put r. on our.	1 Ki 20:31, 32
the soldiers cut off the r.	Acts 27:32

rose, *substantive*

I am the r. of Sharon, and.	S of S 2:1
shall blossom as the r.	Isa 35:1

rose, *verb*

Cain r. up against Abel.	Gen 4:8
Lot r. up to meet them, and.	19:1
Abraham r. early, and went.	22:3
Esau did eat, and r. up, and.	25:34
the sun r. upon him as he.	32:31
his sons and daughters r. to.	37:35
nor r. any from his place.	Ex 10:23
Pharaoh r. up in the night.	12:30

overthrown them that r. up.	Ex 15:7
and all the people r. up and.	33:10
Phinehas r. up from.	Num 25:7
the Lord r. up from Seir.	Deut 33:2
the waters stood and r.	Josh 3:16
there r. up fire out of.	Judg 6:21
the men of Gibeah r. up.	20:5
she r. up before one.	Ruth 3:14
them that r. up against me, hast thou.	2 Sam 22:40; Ps 18:39
and the king r. up to.	1 Ki 2:19
the lepers r. in the.	2 Ki 7:5
the leprosy r. up in his.	2 Chr 26:19
expressed by name r. up.	28:15
our side when men r. up.	Ps 124:2
I r. up to open to my.	S of S 5:5
then r. up certain of the.	Jer 26:17
the lips of those that r. up.	Lam 3:62
then Nebuchadnezzar r.	Dan 3:24
I r. up and did the king's.	8:27
but Jonah r. up to flee.	Jonah 1:3
they r. early and corrupted.	Zeph 3:7
r. up, and thrust him out.	Luke 4:29
and he left all, r. up, and.	5:28
though one r. from the dead.	16:31
when he r. from prayer and.	22:45
they r. up the same hour, and.	24:33
Mary, that she r. up.	John 11:31
then high priest r. up, and.	Acts 5:17
these days r. up Theudas.	36
drink with him after he r.	10:41
king r. up, and the governor.	26:30
Christ both died and r.	Rom 14:9*
he was buried and r. again.	15:4
preached that he r. from the dead.	12
who died and r. again.	2 Cor 5:15
Jesus died and r. again.	1 Thes 4:14
her smoke r. up for ever.	Rev 19:3

***see* morning**

rot

the Lord make thy thigh to r.	
	Num 5:21*, 22*, 27*
name of the wicked shall r.	Pr 10:7
a tree that will not r.	Isa 40:20

rotten

and he. as a r. thing.	Job 13:28
esteemeth brass as r. wood.	41:27
so Ebed-melech took old r.	Jer 38:11
put now these r. rags under.	12
the seed is r. under their.	Joel 1:17

rottenness

maketh ashamed. is as r.	Pr 12:4
envy is the r. of the bones.	14:30
so their root shall be as r.	Isa 5:24
to the house of Judah as r.	Hos 5:12
when I heard r. entered.	Hab 3:16

rough

heifer to a r. valley.	Deut 21:4*
he stayeth his r. wind in.	Isa 27:8
and the r. places shall be.	40:4
horses to come as r.	Jer 51:27
the r. goat is the king.	Dan 8:21
shall they wear a r.	Zech 13:4*
and the r. ways shall be.	Luke 3:5

roughly

Joseph spake r.	Gen 42:7, 30
father answer thee r.?	1 Sam 20:10
answered the people r. and forsook.	
	1 Ki 12:13; 2 Chr 10:13
but the rich answereth r.	Pr 18:23

round, *verb*

ye shall not r. the corners.	Lev 19:27

round

compassed the house r.	Gen 19:4
there lay a small r. thing.	Ex 16:14
shall environ us r.	Josh 7:9
the molten sea was r.	1 Ki 7:23
a r. compass.	35
top of the throne was r.	10:19
Bashan have beset me r.	Ps 22:12
navel is like a r. goblet.	S of S 7:2
take away their r. tires.	Isa 3:18
shall compass thee r.	Luke 19:43

round *about*

God was on cities r. about.	Gen 35:5
digged r. about the river.	Ex 7:24
morning dew lay r. about.	16:13
bounds to the people r. about.	19:12
house to be scraped r. about.	
	Lev 14:41

Levites encamp *r. about* tabernacle.
  Num 1:50
Moses set the elders *r. about.* 11:24
all Israel, that were *r. about.* 16:34
up all that are *r. about* us. 22:4
people *r. about* you. *Deut* 6:14; 13:7
all your enemies *r. about.* 12:10
  25:19; *Josh* 21:44; *2 Chr* 15:15
measure the cities *r. about* him.
  Deut 21:2
and ye shall go *r. about.* *Josh* 6:3
house *r. about.* *Judg* 19:22; 20:5
Saul compassed David *r. about.*
  1 Sam 23:26
sent into the land of Philistines *r.*
  about. 31:9; *1 Chr* 10:9
he made darkness pavilions *r. about*
  him. *2 Sam* 22:12; *Ps* 18:11
had peace on all sides *r. about.*
  1 Ki 4:24
fame was in all nations *r. about.* 31
water ran *r. about* the altar. 18:35
of fire *r. about* Elisha. *2 Ki* 6:17
they lodged *r. about.* *1 Chr* 9:27
fashioned me *r. about.* *Job* 10:8
compass me *r. about.* 16:13
his troops encamp *r. about.* 19:12
snares are *r. about* thee. 22:10
it is turned *r. about* by his. 37:12
his teeth are terrible *r. about.* 41:14
against me *r. about.* *Ps* 3:6
above mine enemies *r. about.* 27:6
r. about them that fear him. 34:7
them that are *r. about.* 44:13; 79:4
Zion, and go *r. about* her. 48:12
go *r. about* the city. 59:6, 14
let all *r. about* him bring. 76:11
they came *r. about* me daily. 88:17
faithfulness *r. about* thee. 89:8
his enemies *r. about* him. 97:3
as the mountains are *r. about.* 125:2
olive plants *r. about* thy table. 128:3
I will camp against thee *r. about.*
  Isa 29:3
set him on fire *r. about.* 42:25
up thine eyes *r. about.* 49:18; 60:4
devour all things *r. about.* *Jer* 21:14
for fear was *r. about,* saith. 46:5*
against Babylon *r. about.* 50:29
shall be against her *r. about.* 51:2
full of eyes *r. about.* *Ezek* 10:12
will make places *r. about.* 34:26
gather yourselves together *r. about.*
  Joel 3:11
judge all the heathen *r. about.* 12
even *r. about* the land. *Amos* 3:11
me *r. about,* the weeds. *Jonah* 2:5
a wall of fire *r. about.* *Zech* 2:5
the vineyard *r. about.* *Mat* 21:33
all that dwelt *r. about.* *Luke* 1:65
the Lord shone *r. about* them. 2:9
shined *r. about* him a light. *Acts* 9:3
r. about to Illyricum, I. *Rom* 15:19
was a rainbow *r. about.* *Rev* 4:3
r. about the throne were four. 4
angels *r. about* the throne. 5:11
  see **camp**

rouse
lion; who shall *r.* him up? *Gen* 49:9

rovers
they helped David against the *r.*
  1 Chr 12:21

row, -s
four *r.* of stones. *Ex* 28:17; 39:10
the first *r.* 28:17; 39:10
the second *r.* 28:18; 39:11
the third *r.* 28:19; 39:12
the fourth *r.* 28:20; 39:13
cakes, six on a *r.* on the. *Lev* 24:6
pure frankincense on each *r.* 7
inner court with three *r.* *1 Ki* 6:36
four *r.* of cedar pillars. 7:2
fifteen in a *r.* 3
there were windows in three *r.* 4
round about was with three *r.* 12
two *r.* with pomegranates. 18, 42
  2 Chr 4:13
two *r.* of oxen cast. *2 Chr* 4:3
a *r.* of new timber, three *r.* of.
  Ezra 6:4
thy cheeks comely with *r.* of jewels.
  S of S 1:10
boiling places under *r.* *Ezek* 46:23

rowed
men *r.* hard to bring it. *Jonah* 1:13
when they had *r.* 25 or. *John* 6:19

rowers
thy *r.* brought thee. *Ezek* 27:26

rowing
he saw them toiling in *r.* *Mark* 6:48

royal
shall yield *r.* dainties. *Gen* 49:20
as one of the *r.* cities. *Josh* 10:2
why dwell in the *r.* city? *1 Sam* 27:5
and took the *r.* city. *2 Sam* 12:26
her of his *r.* bounty. *1 Ki* 10:13
mother of Ahaziah destroyed all the
  seed *r.* *2 Ki* 11:1; *2 Chr* 22:10
on Solomon *r.* majesty. *1 Chr* 29:25
they gave them *r.* wine. *Esth* 1:7
the queen with the crown *r.* 11
give her *r.* estate to another that. 19
was taken into his house *r.* 2:16
so that he set the crown *r.* on. 17
Esther put on her *r.* apparel, and king
  sat on his *r.* throne in his *r.* 5:1
let *r.* apparel be brought, and the
  crown *r.* 6:8
Mordecai went in *r.* apparel. 8:15
a *r.* diadem in the hand. *Isa* 62:3
spread his *r.* pavilion. *Jer* 43:10
to establish a *r.* statute. *Dan* 6:7
Herod arrayed in *r.* *Acts* 12:21
if ye fulfil the *r.* law, ye. *Jas* 2:8
ye are a *r.* priesthood. *1 Pet* 2:9

rubbing
and did eat, *r.* them in. *Luke* 6:1

rubbish
the stones out of the *r.* *Neh* 4:2
decayed and there is much *r.* 10

rubies
price of wisdom is above *r.*
  Job 28:18; *Pr* 8:11
is more precious than *r.* *Pr* 3:15
gold, and a multitude of *r.* 20:15
for her price is far above *r.* 31:10
were more ruddy than *r.* *Lam* 4:7

rudder bands
and loosed the *r. bands.* *Acts* 27:40

ruddy
David was *r.* and beautiful.
  1 Sam 16:12; 17:42
my beloved is white and *r.* chiefest.
  S of S 5:10
Nazarites were more *r.* *Lam* 4:7

rude
though I be *r.* in speech. *2 Cor* 11:6

rudiments
you after the *r.* of the. *Col* 2:8
if dead with Christ from the *r.* 20

rue
for ye tithe mint, and *r.* *Luke* 11:42

Rufus
Simon, father of Alexander and *R.*
  Mark 15:21
salute *R.* chosen in the. *Rom* 16:13

Ruhamah
say to your sisters, *R.* *Hos* 2:1

ruin
but they were the *r.* *2 Chr* 28:23
brought his holds to *r.* *Ps* 89:40
who knoweth the *r.* of? *Pr* 24:22*
a flattering mouth worketh *r.* 26:28
and let this *r.* be under. *Isa* 3:6
land of the Chaldeans to *r.* 23:13
of a defenced city a *r.* 25:2
shall not be your *r.* *Ezek* 18:30
shall fall in the day of thy *r.* 27:27
upon his *r.* shall all the fowls. 31:13
it fell, the *r.* of that house. *Luke* 6:49

ruined
Jerusalem is *r.* and Judah. *Isa* 3:8
and the *r.* cities are. *Ezek* 36:35
I the Lord build the *r.* places. 36

ruinous
be to lay waste fenced cities into *r.*
  heaps. *2 Ki* 19:25; *Isa* 37:26
it shall be a *r.* heap. *Isa* 17:1

ruins
that their *r.* may be. *Ezek* 21:15*
will I raise up his *r.* *Amos* 9:11
I will build again the *r.* *Acts* 15:16

rule, *substantive*
that had *r.* over Ahab's. *1 Ki* 22:31
Jews had *r.* over them. *Esth* 9:1
shall have *r.* over a son. *Pr* 17:2
for a servant to have *r.* over. 19:10
he that hath no *r.* over his. 25:28*
yet shall he have *r.* over. *Eccl* 2:19
stretcheth out his *r.* *Isa* 44:13*
never barest *r.* over them. 63:19
have put down all *r.* *1 Cor* 15:24
to the measure of the *r.* *2 Cor* 10:13*
be enlarged according to our *r.* 15*
walk according to this *r.* *Gal* 6:16
let us walk by the same *r.* *Phil* 3:16
remember them that have *r.* over.
  Heb 13:7
obey them that have the *r.* over. 17
salute all them that have the *r.* 24
  see **bare, bear**

rule
the greater light to *r.* the day, and
  lesser light to *r.* the. *Gen* 1:16
to *r.* over the day, and over. 18
and thy husband shall *r.* over. 3:16
desire, thou shalt *r.* over him. 4:7
not *r.* over him with rigour.
  Lev 25:43; 46:53
r. thou over us, thou. *Judg* 8:22
r. over you, nor shall my son *r.* 23
r. thou in the midst of thine enemies.
  Ps 110:2
sun to *r.* by day, for his mercy. 136:8
moon and stars to *r.* by night. 9
by me princes *r.* and. *Pr* 8:16
babes shall *r.* over them. *Isa* 3:4
as for my people, women *r.* 12
r. over their oppressors. 14:2
a fierce king shall *r.* over. 19:4
that *r.* this people that is in. 28:14
princes shall *r.* in judgement. 32:1
and his arm shall *r.* for him. 40:10
who made the righteous man *r.?* 41:2
they that *r.* over them make. 52:5
no strong rod to be a sceptre to *r.*
  Ezek 19:14
poured out, will I *r.* over you. 20:33
they shall no more *r.* over. 29:15
known that the heavens *r.* *Dan* 4:26
shall stand up, that shall *r.* 11:3
cause them to *r.* over many. 39
that the heathen should *r.* *Joel* 2:17
sit and *r.* on his throne. *Zech* 6:13
a governor that shall *r.* *Mat* 2:6*
who are accounted to *r.* *Mark* 10:42
let the peace of God *r.* *Col* 3:15
not how to *r.* his house. *1 Tim* 3:5
elders that *r.* well, worthy of. 5:17
r. with a rod. *Rev* 2:27; 12:5; 19:15

ruled
his eldest servant that *r.* *Gen* 24:2
word shall all my people be *r.* 41:40
three thousand *r.* over. *1 Ki* 5:16
have *r.* over all countries. *Ezra* 4:20
they that hated them *r.* *Ps* 106:41
he that *r.* nations in anger. *Isa* 14:6
servants have *r.* over us. *Lam* 5:8
with cruelty have ye *r.* *Ezek* 34:4
till he knew that God *r.* *Dan* 5:21

ruler
(*Revisions frequently translate*
this prince, or governor)
Pharaoh made Joseph *r.* over all
  Gen 41:43; 45:8; *Ps* 105:21
Joseph said to the *r.* of. *Gen* 43:16*
thou shalt not curse *r.* of. *Ex* 22:28
when a *r.* hath sinned. *Lev* 4:22
every one a *r.* among. *Num* 13:2
appointed thee *r.* *1 Sam* 25:30
  2 Sam 6:21; 7:8; *1 Chr* 11:2; 17:7
I took thee from following sheep to
  be *r.* *2 Sam* 7:8; *1 Chr* 17:7
appointed Solomon to be *r.* *1 Ki* 1:35
of Judah came the chief *r.* *1 Chr* 5:2
Azariah *r.* of house of God. 9:11
  2 Chr 31:13
fail thee a man to be *r.* *2 Chr* 7:18
he made Abijah *r.* among. 11:22
and Hananiah the *r.* of. *Neh* 7:2
Seraiah was *r.* of the house. 11:11
Benjamin with their *r.* *Ps* 68:27
even the *r.* of the people, let. 105:20
no guide, overseer, or *r.* *Pr* 6:7

sittest to eat with a r. *Pr 23:1*
so is a wicked r. over the. 28:15
if a r. hearken to lies, his. 29:12
many seek r.'s favour, but. 26
if the spirit of the r. rise. *Eccl 10:4*
which proceedeth from the r. 5
be thou our r. *Isa 3:6*
make me not a r. 7
send ye the lamb to the r. of. 16:1
in the land, r. against r. *Jer 51:46*
no king nor r. asked. *Dan 2:10*
and hath made thee r. over. 38, 48
shall be third r. in the. 5:7, 16, 29
he come that is to be r. *Mi 5:2*
things that have no r. *Hab 1:14*
there came a certain r. *Mat 9:18*
whom his Lord hath made r. 24:45
      Luke 12:42
make him r. over all. *Mat 24:47*
I will make thee r. over. 25:21, 23
there came from the r. of the synagogue's. *Mark 5:35; Luke 8:49*
the r. of the synagogue. *Luke 13:14*
when the r. of the feast. *John 2:9*
a man named Nicodemus, a r. 3:1
who made thee a r.? *Acts 7:27, 35*
the same did God send to be r. 35
beat Sosthenes the chief r. 18:17
shalt not speak evil of the r. 23:5

rulers
then make them r. over. *Gen 47:6*
r. of thousands, r. *Ex 18:21, 25*
Moses called the r. of the. 34:31
the r. brought onyx stones to. 35:27
and I will make them r. *Deut 1:13**
not the Philistines are r.? *Judg 15:11*
sons were chief r. *2 Sam 8:18**
were r. of his chariots. *1 Ki 9:22*
Jehu wrote to the r. *2 Ki 10:1*
Jehoiada set r. over. 11:4*, 19*
all there were r. of. *1 Chr 27:31*
r. of the house of God. *2 Chr 35:8*
the hand of the r. chief. *Ezra 9:2*
r. were behind the house. *Neh 4:16*
I rebuked the r. and said, Ye. 5:7
the r. of the people dwelt at. 11:1
and the half of the r. with me. 12:40
then contended I with the. 13:11
the r. of the provinces. *Esth 9:3*
the r. take counsel against. *Ps 2:2*
hear word of the Lord, ye r. *Isa 1:10*
broken the sceptre of the r. 14:5
all thy r. are fled together. 22:3
and your r. the seers hath. 29:10*
to a servant of r. kings shall. 49:7
any of his seed to be r. *Jer 33:26*
in pieces captains and r. 51:23*
prepare against her r. 28*
made drunk her r. 57*
were captains and r. *Ezek 23:6*
raise up those r. against thee. *Dan 3:3*
all the r. were gathered. *Dan 3:3*
her r. with shame do love. *Hos 4:18*
cometh one of the r. of. *Mark 5:22*
brought before r. 13:9*; *Luke 21:12*
called together the r. *Luke 23:13*
and r. also with the people. 35
how our priests and r. 24:20
do the r. know that ? *John 7:26*
have any of r. believed on him ? 48
many among the chief r. 12:42
ye did it, as also did r. *Acts 3:17*
the r. were gathered against. 4:5
the r. of the synagogue. 13:15
and their r. because they knew. 14:5
of the Jews, with their r. 14:5
masters drew them to the r. 16:19
they troubled the people and r. 17:8
r. not a terror to good. *Rom 13:3*
we wrestle against the r. *Eph 6:12*

rulest
and r. not thou over ? *2 Chr 20:6*
r. the raging of the sea. *Ps 89:9*

ruleth
he that r. over men. *2 Sam 23:3*
let them know that God r. *Ps 59:13*
he r. by his power for ever. 66:7
and his kingdom r. over all. 103:19
that r. his spirit is better. *Pr 16:32*
rich r. over the poor, and. 22:7
wherein one man r. over. *Eccl 8:9*
more than cry of him that r. 9:17
the most High r. *Dan 4:17, 25, 32*

Judah yet r. with God. *Hos 11:12*
he that r. with diligence. *Rom 12:8*
r. well his own house. *1 Tim 3:4*

ruling
must be just, r. in the. *2 Sam 23:3*
sit on throne, and r. *Jer 22:30*
r. their children and. *1 Tim 3:12*

rumbling
at r. of his wheels, fathers. *Jer 47:3*

rumour, -s
(*American Revision usually translates* tidings)
and he shall hear a r. *2 Ki 19:7*
      Isa 37:7
I have heard a r. from. *Jer 49:14*
r. in the land, a r. shall come one
year, in another year a r. 51:46
on mischief, r. shall be upon r.
      Ezek 7:26
we have heard a r. from. *Ob 1*
of wars and r. of wars. *Mat 24:6*
      Mark 13:7
r. of him went forth. *Luke 7:17**

rump
(*Revisions,* the fat tail)
ram and the fat and the r. *Ex 29:22*
      Lev 3:9; 7:3; 8:25; 9:19

run
whose branches r. over. *Gen 49:22*
whether his flesh r. with. *Lev 15:3*
if a woman's issue r. beyond. 25
lest angry fellows r. *Judg 18:25**
some shall r. before his. *1 Sam 8:11*
r. to the camp to thy brethren. 17:17*
asked me, that he might r. to. 20:6
r., find out now the arrows which. 36
horses, and fifty men to r. before.
      2 Sam 15:1; 1 Ki 1:5
let me now r. and bear tidings.
      2 Sam 18:19, 22, 23
I have r. through a troop. 22:30
      Ps 18:29
that I may r. to the man. *2 Ki 4:22*
r. now, I pray thee, to meet her. 26
as the Lord liveth, I will r. 5:20
eyes of Lord r. to and. *2 Chr 16:9*
as strong man to r. a race. *Ps 19:5*
them melt as waters, which r. 58:7
they r. and prepare themselves. 59:4
he caused waters to r. down. 78:16
the springs, which r. among. 104:10
I will r. the way of thy. 119:32
rivers of waters r. down mine. 136
for their feet r. to evil. *Pr 1:16*
      Isa 59:7
rivers r. into the sea. *Eccl 1:7*
draw me, we will r. *S of S 1:4*
of locusts shall he r. on. *Isa 33:4**
they shall r. and not be weary. 40:31
knew not thee shall r. to thee. 55:5
r. ye to and fro through. *Jer 5:1*
that your eyes may r. down. 9:18
hast r. with the footmen. 12:5
mine eyes shall r. down with tears,
because the Lord's. 13:17; 14:17
lament, and r. to and fro. 49:3
I will make him r. away. 19; 50:44
post shall r. to meet another. 51:31
let tears r. down like a. *Lam 2:18*
neither shall thy tears r. *Ezek 24:16*
cause their rivers to r. like oil. 32:14
many shall r. to and fro. *Dan 12:4*
horsemen, so shall they r. *Joel 2:4*
they shall r. like mighty men. 7
they shall r. in the city, shall r. on. 9*
judgement, r. down as. *Amos 5:24**
shall horses r. upon the rock ? 6:12
shall r. to and fro to seek word. 8:12
r. like the lightnings. *Nah 2:4*
write vision, that he may r. *Hab 2:2*
and ye r. every man to his. *Hag 1:9*
R., speak to this young man. *Zech 2:4*
eyes of the Lord r. to and fro. 4:10
they did r. to bring his. *Mat 28:8*
r. in a race r. all, but one receiveth
the prize, so r. that ye. *1 Cor 9:24*
I therefore so r. not as. 26
I should r. or had r. in. *Gal 2:2*
ye did r. well, who did ? 5:7
I have not r. in vain. *Phil 2:16*
let us r. with patience. *Heb 12:1*
that ye r. not to the same. *1 Pet 4:4*

runnest
when thou r. thou shalt. *Pr 4:12*

runneth
he r. upon him, even on. *Job 15:26*
he breaketh me, he r. upon me. 16:14
thou anointest my head, my cup r.
over. *Ps 23:5*
his word r. very swiftly. 147:15
the righteous r. into it. *Pr 18:10*
mine eyes r. down with water.
      Lam 1:16; 3:48
the bottles break, and the wine r.
      Mat 9:17*
then she r. and cometh. *John 20:2*
not of him that willeth, nor of him
that r. *Rom 9:16*

running
one bird be killed over r. water.
      Lev 14:5, 6, 50
dip them in r. water, and sprinkle. 51
cleanse the house with the r. 52
any man hath a r. issue. 15:2; 22:4
shall bathe his flesh in r. water. 13
unclean person take r. *Num 19:17*
and behold, a man r. alone.
      2 Sam 18:24, 26
the r. of the foremost is like r. 27
when Naaman saw him r. *2 Ki 5:21*
Athaliah heard the people r.
      2 Chr 23:12
and r. waters out of thine own well.
      Pr 5:15
feet that be swift in r. to. 6:18
the r. to and fro of locusts. *Isa 33:4**
with her rivers r. about. *Ezek 31:4*
the people r. to him. *Mark 9:15*
when Jesus saw the people r. 25
there came one r. and. 10:17
good measure and r. over. *Luke 6:38*
and r. under a certain island.
      Acts 27:16
as the sound of chariots r. *Rev 9:9*

rush, *substantive*
can the r. grow without mire ?
      Job 8:11
Lord will cut off branch and r. in one.
      Isa 9:14
any work which branch or r. 19:15

rush
nations shall r. like the rushing of
many waters. *Isa 17:13*

rushed
Abimelech and company r. *Judg 9:44*
the liers in wait hasted and r. 20:37
they r. with one accord. *Acts 19:29*

rushes
where dragons lay shall be reeds and
r. *Isa 35:7*

rusheth
every one turned, as horse r. *Jer 8:6*

rushing
and to the r. of nations, that make a
r. like the r. of many. *Isa 17:12*
nations shall rush like the r. 13
at r. of chariots fathers. *Jer 47:3*
voice of a great r. *Ezek 3:12, 13*
as of a r. mighty wind. *Acts 2:2*

rust
where moth and r. *Mat 6:19, 20*
r. of them shall be a witness. *Jas 5:3*

Ruth
name of the other was R. *Ruth 1:4*
R. clave to her. 14
who art thou ? I am R. 3:9
thou must buy it also of R. the. 4:5
moreover, R. have I purchased. 10
Booz begat Obed of R. *Mat 1:5*

S

Sabaoth
A Hebrew *word meaning* Hosts
or Armies. Jehovah Sabaoth, The
Lord of hosts, Rom 9:29.
except the Lord of S. *Rom 9:29*
the ears of the Lord of s. *Jas 5:4*

sabbath
*The Hebrew word means rest,
from the statement in* Gen 2:2, *that
God rested and hallowed the*

seventh day. By the Jewish law given at Sinai the seventh day was to be a day of rest, in which no secular work was to be done, and which was to be kept holy to God. At a later period the simple Jewish law of early days was added to by the traditions of the elders, until the sabbath rules became burdensome, and, in some cases, foolish. It was against this, and not against God's law of the sabbath that Jesus set himself in his teaching and healing.

The sabbath, one day out of each week, was kept by the Jews on the day now called Saturday. How early this was taken to be the seventh day is not known. After the ascension of Jesus the disciples met on the first day of each week for prayer and praise. The Jewish Christians for a long time kept both the seventh and the first ; but as Gentile Christians, having never kept any such day before, celebrated only the first day of the week as the Lord's Day, the celebration of the seventh by Christians was finally abandoned.

Because of the rule that a long journey should not be made on the sabbath, the short distance permitted, about a mile, received the name of a sabbath day's journey.

The word sabbath is often used in speaking of the rest of the fields from tillage, the rules for which are given in the Pentateuch.

is rest of the holy s.   *Ex* 16:23
eat that to-day, for to-day is a s.   25
Lord hath given you the s.   29
seventh day is the s.   20:10; 31:15
   35:2; *Lev* 23:3; *Deut* 5:14
ye shall keep the s.   *Ex* 31:14, 16
an atonement, it shall be a s. of rest.
   Lev 16:31; 23:3, 32
s. priest shall wave it.   23:11
from the morrow after the s.   15
after the seventh s. shall ye.   16
1st of the month shall ye have a s. 24
shall ye celebrate your s.   32
shall be a s. on the eighth a s.   39
every s. he shall set it in order. 24:8
shall the land keep a s.   25:2, 4, 6
burnt offering of every s. *Num* 28:10
neither new moon nor s.   *2 Ki* 4:23
you that enter in on the s.   11:5
you that go forth on the s., even they.
   7, 9; *2 Chr* 23:8
covert for the s. turned. *2 Ki* 16:18
shewbread every s.   *1 Chr* 9:32
desolate, she kept the s. *2 Chr* 36:21
known to them thy holy s.   *Neh* 9:14
buy it of them on the s.   10:31
winepresses on the s.   13:15
brought ware, and sold on the s. 16
Israel, by profaning the s.   18
began to be dark before the s.   19
came they no more on the s.   21
man that keepeth the s. *Isa* 56:2, 6
the s.; call the s. a delight.   58:13
from one s. to another shall.   66:23
but on the s. it shall be. *Ezek* 46:1
saying, When will the s.? *Amos* 8:5
in the end of the s. came. *Mat* 28:1
s. was made for man, not man for
   the s.   *Mark* 2:27
is Lord of the s.   28; *Luke* 6:5
when the s. was past.   *Mark* 16:1
on another s.   6
in the synagogue on the s.   13:10
doth not each on the s. loose?   15
and the s. drew on.   23:54
not only had broken the s. *John* 5:18
preached to them next s. *Acts* 13:42
on the s. we went out of city.   16:13
in the synagogue every s.   18:4
   see **day, days**

sabbaths
saying, My s. ye shall keep.
   Ex 31:13; *Lev* 19:3, 30; 26:2
seven s. shall be.   *Lev* 23:15

beside the s. of the Lord. *Lev* 23:38
and thou shalt number seven s. 25:8
enjoy her s., even then shall the land
   . . her s. 26:34, 43; *2 Chr* 36:21
did not rest in your s.   *Lev* 26:35
burnt sacrifices in the s. *1 Chr* 23:31
   2 Chr 2:4; 8:13; 31:3; *Neh* 10:33
new moons and s. I.   *Isa* 1:13
to eunuchs that keep my s.   56:4
did mock at her s.   *Lam* 1:7*
Lord caused s. to be forgotten.   2:6
also I gave them my s. *Ezek* 20:12
and my s. they greatly.   13, 16, 24
hast profaned my s.   22:8; 23:38
have hid their eyes from my s. 22:26
my laws and hallow my s.   44:24
part to give offerings for s.   45:17
worship at this gate in the s.   46:3
make to cease her s.   *Hos* 2:11

Sabeans
the S. fell on the oxen.   *Job* 1:15
merchandise of the S.   *Isa* 45:14
with the men of the common sort
   were brought S.   *Ezek* 23:42*
shall sell them to the S.   *Joel* 3:8

sack
to restore every man's money into
   his s. *Gen* 42:25, 35; 43:21; 44:1
put my silver cup in s.'s mouth. 44:2
they took down every man his s. 11
cup was found in Benjamin's s.   12
or s. of unclean must be. *Lev* 11:32

sackbut
sound of the s.   *Dan* 3:5, 7, 10, 15

sackcloth
(*A coarse cloth made of camel's and goat's hair. It was used for making the rough garments worn by mourners. It therefore became a symbol for sorrow and mourning*)
and Jacob put s. upon.   *Gen* 37:34
said, Gird you with s.   *2 Sam* 3:31
Rizpah took s. and spread it. 21:10
merciful kings, let us put s. on our
   loins, and ropes.   *1 Ki* 20:31, 32
s. on his flesh, and lay in s.   21:27
and he had s. within.   *2 Ki* 6:30
Hezekiah covered himself with s.
   19:1; *Isa* 37:1
elders of the priests covered with s.
   2 Ki 19:2; *Isa* 37:2
David and elders were clothed with
   s.   *1 Chr* 21:16
clothes, and put on s.   *Esth* 4:1
enter the gate clothed with s.   2
sewed s. upon my skin.   *Job* 16:15
hast put off my s. and.   *Ps* 30:11
sick, my clothing was s.   35:13
I made s. also my garment.   69:11
stomacher, a girding of s.   *Isa* 3:24
gird themselves with s.   15:3
go, and loose the s. from off.   20:2
Lord call to girding with s.   22:12
make you bare, and gird s.   32:11
   Jer 4:8; 6:26; 48:37; 49:3
I make s. the covering of the. 50:3
themselves with s. : virgins hang
   down heads. *Lam* 2:10; *Ezek* 7:18
   27:31
Lord with fasting and s.   *Dan* 9:3
virgin girded with s. for.   *Joel* 1:8
lie all night in s., ye ministers.   13
and I will bring up s.   *Amos* 8:10
of Nineveh put on s.   *Jonah* 3:5
the king covered him with s.   6
man and beast be covered with s. 8
became black as s. of hair. *Rev* 6:12
prophesy, clothed in s.   11:3

sackclothes
Israel assembled with s.   *Neh* 9:1

sacks
to fill their s. with corn. *Gen* 42:25*
   44:1
brought again in your s.   43:12
who put our money in our s.   22
given you treasure in your s.   23
the Gibeonites took old s. *Josh* 9:4

sacrifice
An offering of any sort to a deity, with the idea of procuring favour or avoiding disaster. The idea of sacrifice is deeply rooted in the

instincts of humanity ; for it is found among every race at the earliest known period of its history as a well-established and thoroughly understood custom. The sacrifices were, in general, of two sorts : [1] the offering of the first-fruits, or of incense, to show the dependence of man on his deity, and to thank him for his benefits ; [2] the burnt offering, to appease an angry god when displeased and ready to bring distress upon him.

Most probably the plan of sacrifices arranged by Moses was an adaptation of what had always been their customs, from the time of Abraham. One respect in which the Jews differed from the heathen nations around them was in the absence of human sacrifice.

The book of Hebrews shows how Jesus Christ, in becoming a sacrifice for man, made further sacrifices unnecessary.

The Jews ceased offering sacrifice when the Temple was destroyed, A.D. 70. The custom is now found only in savage tribes.

The word is also used symbolically, as the sacrifice of one's lips. Revisions very often translate it offering.

then Jacob offered s.   *Gen* 31:54
do s. to the Lord.   *Ex* 5:17; 8:8
say, It is the s. of the Lord's. 12:27
not offer blood of s.   23:18*; 34:25
and thou eat of his s.   34:15
nor shall s. of passover be left. 25
then he shall offer with s. *Lev* 7:12
leavened bread with s. of. 13; 22:29
if s. be a vow, it shall be eaten. 16
offereth a s. and bringeth.   17:8
which they do not offer a s.   27:11
or make a s. in performing a vow.
   Num 15:3, 8
it is for a sweet savour, a s.   28:6
   8, 13, 19, 24; 29:6, 13, 36
from them that offer s.   *Deut* 18:3
an altar, not for s.   *Josh* 22:26
for to offer a great s.   *Judg* 16:23
offer the yearly s. *1 Sam* 1:21; 2:19
wherefore kick ye at my s.   2:29
Eli's house not purged with s. 3:14
there is a s. of people to-day. 9:12
because he doth bless the s.   13
to obey is better than s.   15:22
call Jesse to the s. and I will. 16:3, 5
yearly s. for all the family.   20:6, 29
if this people do s. at.   *1 Ki* 12:27
till time of the evening s.   18:29
at the time of evening s. Elijah. 36
not offer s. to other gods. *2 Ki* 5:17
for I have a great s. to do to.   10:19
and to him shall ye do s.   17:36
save only to burn s. before. *2 Chr* 2:6
king Solomon offered a s. of.   7:5
myself for an house of s.   12
astonied until the evening s. *Ezra* 9:4
at the evening s. I arose up from. 5
s. thou didst not desire.   *Ps* 40:6
   51:16
made a covenant with me by s. 50:5
I will offer to thee the s.   116:17
bind the s. with cords to.   118:27
of my hands as evening s.   141:2
s. of the wicked is an.   *Pr* 15:8
more acceptable than s.   21:3
to hear than to give the s. *Eccl* 5:1
the Egyptians shall do s. *Isa* 19:21
for the Lord hath a s. in Bozrah. 34:6
wentest thou to offer s.   57:7
that bring the s. of praise. *Jer* 33:11
nor want a man to do s.   18
for God hath a s. in the north. 46:10
to my s., even a great s. *Ezek* 39:17
till ye be drunken of my s.   19
they shall slay the s. for.   44:11
where ministers boil the s.   46:24
daily s. was taken away. *Dan* 8:11
   9:27; 11:31
given him against the daily s.   8:12
be the vision of the daily s.?   13
from the time daily s. shall.   12:11

many days without a *s.* *Hos* 3:4
I desired mercy, and not *s.* 6:6
         Mat 9:13; 12:7
offer a *s.* of thanksgiving. *Amos* 4:5
then the men offered a *s.* *Jonah* 1:16
for the Lord hath prepared a *s.*
         Zeph 1:7, 8
if ye offer the blind for *s.* *Mal* 1:8
every *s.* shall be salted. *Mark* 9:49
and to offer a *s.* according. *Luke* 2:24
in those days they offered *s.* to.
         Acts 7:41
and would have done *s.* with. 14:13
that they had not done *s.* unto. 18
your bodies a living *s.* *Rom* 12:1
in *s.* to idols. *1 Cor* 8:4; 10:19, 28
a *s.* to God for a sweet. *Eph* 5:2
if I be offered on the *s.* *Phil* 2:17
a *s.* acceptable, wellpleasing. 4:18
needeth not daily, as those high
  priests, to offer up *s.* *Heb* 7:27
to put away sin by the *s.* 9:26
he saith, S. and offering. 10:5, 8
had offered one *s.* for sins, for. 12
there remaineth no more *s.* for. 26
to God a more excellent *s.* 11:4
let us offer the *s.* of praise. 13:15
  see **burnt, peace offering**

sacrifice, *verb*
let us go and *s.* to the Lord our God.
  Ex 3:18; 5:3, 8; 8:27; 10:25
Go ye, *s.* 8:25
shall we *s.* the abomination of ? 26
in not letting the people go to *s.* 29
I *s.* to Lord all that openeth. 13:15
thou shalt *s.* thereon thy. 20:24
thou shalt not *s.* it. *Deut* 15:21; 17:1
thou shalt therefore *s.* 16:2, 6
not *s.* the passover within any. 5
yearly to *s.* to the Lord. *1 Sam* 1:3
the people spared the best to *s.* 15:15
should have been destroyed to *s.* 21
come to *s.* to the Lord. 16:2, 5
went to Gibeon to *s.* there. *1 Ki* 3:4
as yet the people did *s.* and.
  2 Ki 14:4; *2 Chr* 33:17
nor shall *s.* to other gods. *2 Ki* 17:35
to Jerusalem to *s.* to. *2 Chr* 11:16
we seek your God, and do *s.* to.
         Ezra 4:2
will they *s.?* will they ? *Neh* 4:2
I will freely *s.* to thee. *Ps* 54:6
let them *s.* sacrifices of. 107:22
gather to my *s.* that I do *s.* for you.
         Ezek 39:17
they *s.* on the tops of. *Hos* 4:13
and they *s.* with harlots. 14
they *s.*, but the Lord accepteth. 8:13
are vanity, they *s.* bullocks. 12:11
men that *s.* kiss the calves. 13:2
I will *s.* to thee with. *Jonah* 2:9
therefore they *s.* unto. *Hab* 1:16
they that *s.* shall seethe. *Zech* 14:21
things Gentiles *s.*, they *s.* *1 Cor* 10:20

sacrificed
calf and *s.* thereunto. *Ex* 32:8
they *s.* unto devils, not. *Deut* 32:17
they *s.* thereon peace. *Josh* 8:31
and they *s.* there unto. *Judg* 2:5
said to the man that *s.* *1 Sam* 2:15
and *s.* sacrifices the same day. 6:15
went to Gilgal and *s.* 11:15
David *s.* oxen and. *2 Sam* 6:13
only the people *s.* in the high places.
  1 Ki 3:2, 3; *2 Ki* 12:3; 15:4, 35
    16:4; *2 Chr* 28:4
his strange wives, and *s.* *1 Ki* 11:8
lowest priests which *s.* *2 Ki* 17:32
then he *s.* there. *1 Chr* 21:28
assembled before ark *s.* *2 Chr* 5:6
Ahaz *s.* to the gods of. 28:23
Manasseh *s.* on the altar of. 33:16
for Amon *s.* to all the carved. 22
on graves of them that had *s.* 34:4
yea, they *s.* their sons. *Ps* 106:37
daughters, they *s.* to the idols. 38
these thou *s.* to them. *Ezek* 16:20
of my sacrifice which I have *s.* 39:19
s. to Baalim, and burnt. *Hos* 11:2
our Passover is *s.* for us. *1 Cor* 5:7
to eat things *s.* to idols. *Rev* 2:14, 20

sacrificedst
which thou *s.* the first day. *Deut* 16:4

---

sacrifices
Beer-sheba offered *s.* to. *Gen* 46:1
must give us also *s.* *Ex* 10:25
father in law, took *s.* for God. 18:12
of the *s.* of the Lord. *Lev* 10:13
the *s.* which they offer in the. 17:5
no more offer their *s.* to devils. 7
they called to the *s.* *Num* 25:2
my *s.* shall ye observe to offer. 28:2
bring your *s.* and tithes. *Deut* 12:6
which did eat the fat of their *s.* 32:38
there they shall offer the *s.* 33:19
s. of the Lord are their. *Josh* 13:14
the altar not for *s.*; but it. 22:28, 29
and sacrificed *s.* same. *1 Sam* 6:15
Lord as great delight in *s.?* 15:22
they sacrificed *s.* in. *1 Chr* 29:21
and consumed the *s.* *2 Chr* 7:1
bring *s.*; they brought in *s.* 29:31
where he offered *s.* be. *Ezra* 6:3
that they may offer *s.* to God. 10
day they offered great *s.* *Neh* 12:43
offer *s.* of righteousness. *Ps* 4:5
therefore I will offer *s.* of joy. 27:6
not reprove thee for thy *s.* 50:8
s. of God are a broken spirit. 51:17
then shalt thou be pleased with *s.* 19
Baal-peor, and eat *s.* of dead. 106:28
let them sacrifice the *s.* of. 107:22
than a house full of *s.* *Pr* 17:1
is the multitude of *s.?* *Isa* 1:11
year to year, let them kill *s.* 29:1
nor honoured me with thy *s.* 43:23
filled me with the fat of thy *s.* 24
their *s.* shall be accepted on. 56:7
nor are your *s.* sweet. *Jer* 6:20
burnt offerings to thy *s.* 7:21
commanded them concerning *s.* 22
bringing *s.* of praise to house. 17:26
high hill and offered *s.* *Ezek* 20:28
be ashamed, because of their *s.*
         Hos 4:19
their *s.* shall be as the bread. 9:4
and bring your *s.* every. *Amos* 4:4
have ye offered unto me *s.?* 5:25
Lord is more than all *s.* *Mark* 12:33
mingled with their *s.* *Luke* 13:1
have ye offered *s.* for ? *Acts* 7:42
that eat the *s.* partakers ? *1 Cor* 10:18
he may offer gifts and *s.* *Heb* 5:1
priest is ordained to offer *s.* 8:3
offered both gifts and *s.* 9:9
heavenly things with better *s.* 23
can never with those *s.* make. 10:1
but in those *s.* there is a. 3
in *s.* for sin thou hast had no. 6
offering oftentimes the same *s.* 11
for with such *s.* God is well. 13:16
to offer up spiritual *s.* *1 Pet* 2:5
  see **burnt**

sacrificeth
he that *s.* to any god, save. *Ex* 22:20
s. and to him that *s.* not. *Eccl* 9:2
people that *s.* in gardens. *Isa* 65:3
he that *s.* a lamb as if he cut. 66:3
and *s.* a corrupt thing. *Mal* 1:14

sacrificing
him *s.* sheep and oxen. *1 Ki* 8:5
s. to the calves that he had. 12:32

sacrilege
dost thou commit *s.?* *Rom* 2:22*

sad
them, behold they were *s. Gen* 40:6
was no more *s.* *1 Sam* 1:18
why is thy spirit so *s.?* *1 Ki* 21:5
I had not been before *s.* *Neh* 2:1
Why is thy countenance *s.?* 2
should not my countenance be *s.?* 3
the heart of righteous *s.* whom I have
  not made *s.* *Ezek* 13:22
not as hypocrites, of a *s. Mat* 6:16
was *s.* at that saying. *Mark* 10:22*
as ye walk, and are *s.* *Luke* 24:17

saddle
what *s.* he rideth upon. *Lev* 15:9

saddle, *verb*
I will *s.* me an ass. *2 Sam* 19:26
s. me the ass. *1 Ki* 13:13, 27

saddled
early, and *s.* his ass. *Gen* 22:3
Balaam *s.* his ass. *Num* 22:21
the Levite two asses *s.* *Judg* 19:10

---

met David with a couple of asses *s.*
         2 Sam 16:1
Ahithophel *s.* his ass, and gat. 17:23
Shimei *s.* and went after. *1 Ki* 2:40
so they *s.* him the ass. 13:13, 23, 27
she *s.* an ass. *2 Ki* 4:24

Sadducees
*A religious party or sect among
the Jews at the time of Christ. They
were probably disciples of a Zadok
—but authorities are uncertain who
he was or when he lived. The
sect was small but very wealthy,
and included the higher priests.
The chief distinction between these
and the Pharisees was the in-
sistence by the Sadducees that only
the written law was obligatory.
The special doctrines of the
Sadducees were [1] the denial of
a resurrection and a future life,
with all that includes ; [2] the denial
of the existence of angels or spirits.*
when he saw the S. come. *Mat* 3:7
the S. came tempting Jesus. 16:1
beware of the leaven of the S. 6, 11
beware of the doctrine of the S. 12
came to him the S. which say. 22:23
had heard that he had put the S. 34
the priests and the S. came. *Acts* 4:1
the S. laid their hands on. 5:17
the one part were S. 23:6
dissension between the Pharisees
  and S. 7
for the S. say, that there is no. 8

sadly
why look ye so *s.* to-day ? *Gen* 40:7

sadness
by *s.* of countenance the. *Eccl* 7:3

safe
and ye dwelled *s.* *1 Sam* 12:11*
man Absalom *s.?* *2 Sam* 18:29*, 32*
their houses are *s.* from. *Job* 21:9
up, and I shall be *s.* *Ps* 119:117
run into it, and are *s.* *Pr* 18:10
in the Lord shall be *s.* 29:25
carry the prey away *s.* *Isa* 5:29
they shall be *s.* in. *Ezek* 34:27*
had received him *s.* *Luke* 15:27
they may bring him *s.* *Acts* 23:24
they escaped all *s.* to land. 27:44
things, for you it is *s.* *Phil* 3:1

safeguard
me thou shalt be in *s.* *1 Sam* 22:23

safely
he led them on *s.* they. *Ps* 78:53
to me shall dwell *s.* *Pr* 1:33*
thou walk in thy way *s.* 3:23*
heart of her husband doth *s.* 31:11
them, and passed *s.* *Isa* 41:3
make them to lie down *s.* *Hos* 2:18
Jerusalem shall be *s.* *Zech* 14:11
and lead him away *s.* *Mark* 14:44
jailor to keep them *s.* *Acts* 16:23
  see **dwell**

safety
I was not in *s.* nor had I. *Job* 3:26*
his children are far from *s.* and. 5:4
mourn may be exalted to *s.* 11
thou shalt take thy rest in *s.* 11:18
be given him to be in *s.* 24:23*
I will set him in *s.* from. *Ps* 12:5
an horse is a vain thing for *s.* 33:17
of counsellors is *s.* *Pr* 11:14; 24:6
horse is for battle, but *s.* is. 21:31*
shall lie down in *s.* *Isa* 14:30
found we shut with all *s.* *Acts* 5:23
shall say, Peace and *s.* *1 Thes* 5:3
  see **dwell**

saffron
spikenard and *s.* *S of S* 4:14

said
Adam *s.* This is bone of. *Gen* 2:23
the serpent *s.* Hath God *s.* ye ? 3:1
Noah *s.* Blessed be the Lord. 9:26
Sarah hath *s.* hearken to her. 21:12
had *s.* It is my master. 24:65
began to come, as Joseph *s.* 41:54
returned to the Lord and *s.* *Ex* 5:22
serve the Lord as ye have *s.* 12:31
and herds, as ye have *s.* 32

Joshua did as Moses had s. *Ex* 17:10
out, as Moses had s. *Lev* 10:5
thou hast s. I will give. *Num* 11:21
ye s. should be a prey. 14:31
    Deut 1:39
did as Balaam had s. *Num* 23:50
sons of Joseph hath s. well. 36:5
God of thy fathers hath s. *Deut* 1:21
Hebron to Caleb, as Moses s.
    Judg 1:20
Israel, as thou hast s. 6:36, 37
thee, what Samuel s. *1 Sam* 10:15
who is he that s. Shall Saul? 11:12
to you in all ye s. to me. 12:1
David s. I shall now perish. 27:1
Lord, do as thou hast s. *2 Sam* 7:25
as thy servant s. so it is. 13:35
sweet psalmist of Israel s. 23:1
as my lord king hath s. *1 Ki* 2:38
thou hast s. My name shall be there.
    8:29; *2 Chr* 6:20
Jeroboam s. Now shall. *1 Ki* 12:26
s. to her, Go, do as thou hast s. 17:13
s. on this matter, another s. 22:20
the man of God had s. *2 Ki* 7:17
Lord, do as thou hast s. *1 Chr* 17:23
hast s. so must we do. *Ezra* 10:12
that s. We are many. *Neh* 5:2, 3
do as Esther hath s. *Esth* 5:5
to-morrow as the king hath s. 8
thou hast s., My doctrine. *Job* 11:4
if men of my tabernacle s. not. 31:31
when I s. Hitherto shalt thou. 38:11
who s. With our tongue. *Ps* 12:4
fool s. in his heart. 14:1; 53:1
my heart s. to thee, Thy face. 27:8
an impudent face, s. unto. *Pr* 7:13
thou hast s. I will ascend. *Isa* 14:13
s. We have made a covenant. 28:15
ye s. No, for we will flee. 30:16
thou hast s. None seeth me. 47:10
the priests s. not, Where? *Jer* 2:8
what the prophets s. 23:25
Jeremiah s. Amen. 28:6
because ye s. The Lord hath. 29:15
what thou hast s. to the king, also
    what the king s. unto thee. 38:25
of whom we s. Under his. *Lam* 4:20
and I s. Ah, Lord God. *Ezek* 9:8
not the rebellious house s.? 12:9
Tyrus hath s. against. 26:2; 36:2
O Tyrus, thou hast s. I am. 27:3
hast s. I am a god, I sit. 28:2
which hath s. My river is mine. 29:3
Nebuchadnezzar s. Blessed be God.
    Dan 3:28
another saint s. to that saint. 8:13
Jonah s. It is better for. *Jonah* 4:8
her who s. to me, Where? *Mi* 7:10
city that s. in her heart. *Zeph* 2:15
ye have s. it is vain to. *Mal* 3:14
behold, a voice which s. This is my
    beloved Son. *Mat* 17:5; *Luke* 3:22
also s. all the disciples. *Mat* 26:35
saith unto him, Thou hast s. 64
that that deceiver s. 27:63
he s. to Levi, Follow me. *Mark* 2:14
the angel s. to him. *Luke* 1:13, 30
s., Master, thou hast well s. 20:39
had seen angels, who s. that. 24:23
even so as the women had s. 24
straight the way, as s. *John* 1:23
but s. also, that God was his. 5:18
as the scripture hath s. out. 7:38
these things s. Esaias, when. 12:41
even as the Father s. unto me. 50
then Peter s., Repent and. *Acts* 2:38
all the chief priests hast s. 4:23
this is that Moses who s. 7:37
your own poets have s. 17:28
except law had s. Thou. *Rom* 7:7
as we s. before, so say. *Gal* 1:9
by him that s. to him. *Heb* 7:21
we know him that hath s. 10:30
the four beasts s. Amen. *Rev* 5:14
    see **Jesus**

said, *participle*
wherefore it is s. even. *Gen* 10:9
as it is s. to this day, in. 22:14
after it was s. Ye shall. *Ex* 5:19
it was s. by the word. *1 Ki* 13:17
perish, in which it was s. *Job* 3:3
surely it is meet to be s. to. 34:31

of Zion it shall be s. This. *Ps* 87:5
better it be s. to thee. *Pr* 25:7
thing whereof it may be s.? *Eccl* 1:10
it shall be s. in that day. *Isa* 25:9
it shall no more be s. The. *Jer* 16:14
shall it not be s. Where? *Ezek* 13:12
it was s. to them, Ye are. *Hos* 1:10
it was s. by them. *Mat* 5:21, 27, 33
heard it hath been s. 31, 38, 43
which is s. in law of Lord. *Luke* 2:24
having s. thus, he gave up. 23:46
it was s. The elder shall. *Rom* 9:12
that where it was s. Ye are not. 26
whilst it is s. To-day. *Heb* 3:15; 4:7
of whom it was s. In Isaac. 11:18
s. to them, They should. *Rev* 6:11

answered and **said**
all the people *answered and* s.
    Ex 24:3
one of the same place *answered and* s.
    1 Sam 10:12
Satan *answered and* s. Skin for skin.
    Job 2:4
Lord *answered* Job *and* s. 40:1
he *answered* one of them, *and* s.,
    Friend, I do thee no. *Mat* 20:13
John *answered and* s. *Luke* 9:49
    see **answered**

God **said**
yea, hath *God* s. ye.? *Gen* 3:1, 3
same day, as *God* had s. 17:23
whatsoever *God* hath s. 31:16
house of which *God* s. *2 Chr* 33:7
and the nation will I judge, s. *God*.
    Acts 7:7
living God, as *God* hath s. *2 Cor* 6:16

he **said**
he s. Escape for thy life. *Gen* 19:17
s. he not unto me, She is my? 20:5
if he s., The speckled shall. 31:8
he s. Lift up thine eyes and see. 12
he s. Let me go, for the day. 32:26
he s. What is thy name? and he s. 27
God, s. he, hath made me. 41:51
all that Jethro had s. *Ex* 18:24
stand before you, as he hath s.
    Deut 11:25; 18:2; 29:13
    Josh 13:14, 33
kept me alive, as he s. *Josh* 14:10
abated, when he had s. *Judg* 8:3
hide any thing he s. *1 Sam* 3:17
not fail thee, s. he, a man. *1 Ki* 2:4
do as he hath s., and fall upon him. 31
he s. by all his servants. *2 Ki* 17:23
build the house, as he s. *1 Chr* 22:11
he s. Lord, look on it. *2 Chr* 24:22
to man he s. Behold. *Job* 28:28
he hath s. in his heart. *Ps* 10:6
    11:13
he s. that he would destroy. 106:23
to whom he s. This is. *Isa* 28:12
the voice said, Cry, he s. What? 40:6
for he s. Surely they are my. 63:8
now the Lord hath done as he hath s.
    Jer 40:3
to the others he s. in. *Ezek* 9:5
because he hath s. The river. 29:9
of the evil he had s. *Jonah* 3:10
for he s. I am the Son. *Mat* 27:43
he has risen, as he s. 28:6
came and found as he s.
    Mark 14:16; *Luke* 22:13
there shall ye see him, as he s.
    Mark 16:7
not knowing what he s. *Luke* 9:33
when he s. these things. 13:17
remembered that he s. *John* 2:22
this he s. to prove him, for. 6:6
what sayest thou? he s. He is. 9:17
this he s., not that he cared. 12:6
this he s., signifying what death. 33
as soon as he s. to them, I am. 18:6
he s. It is finished, and bowed. 19:30
when he had so s. he shewed. 20:20
when he had s. this, he breathed. 22
when he had s. this, he fell. *Acts* 7:60
he s. Who art thou, Lord? 9:5
how he s. It is more blessed. 20:35
when he had so s. there arose. 23:7
he s. My grace is sufficient for thee,
    2 Cor 12:9
the angels s. he at any? *Heb* 1:5, 13

then s. he, Lo, I come to do. *Heb* 10:9
for he hath s. I will never. 13:5
he that s. Do not commit. *Jas* 2:11
he s. These things are. *Rev* 22:6

I **said**
I s. Lest I die for her. *Gen* 26:9
I have s. I will bring. *Ex* 3:17
in all things that I have s. 23:13
I s. I would scatter. *Deut* 32:26
that have I given, as I s. *Josh* 1:3
I s. unto you, I am the. *Judg* 6:10
I s. indeed, that thy. *1 Sam* 2:30
portion, of which I s. Set it by. 9:23
I s. Thou and Ziba. *2 Sam* 19:29
house of which I s. My. *2 Ki* 23:27
thing, therefore I s. it. *Job* 9:22
I s. I shall die in my nest. 29:18
I s. Days should speak, and. 32:7
in prosperity I s. I shall. *Ps* 30:6
I s. I will take heed to my. 39:1
then s. I, Lo, I come. 40:7
    Heb 10:7
I s. Lord, be merciful to. *Ps* 41:4
I have s. Ye are gods. 82:6
I s. My foot slippeth. 94:18
I s. O my God, take me not. 102:24
I s. Thou art my refuge and. 142:5
I s. in mine heart, Go to. *Eccl* 2:1, 15
    3:17, 18
s. I, Lord, how long? *Isa* 6:11
I s. not, Seek ye me in vain. 45:19
I s. Behold me, to a nation. 65:1
I s. when thou wast in. *Ezek* 16:6
he of whom I s. After. *John* 1:30
marvel not that I s. Ye must be. 3:7
the same that I s. from the. 8:25
I s. I am the Son of God. 10:36
s. I not to thee, If thou. 11:40
I s. it, that they may believe. 42
ye have heard how I s. to you. 14:28
these things I s. not at the. 16:4
in secret have I s. nothing. 18:20
heard me, what I have s. 21
I s. Not so, Lord, for. *Acts* 11:8
I have s. that ye are in our hearts.
    2 Cor 7:3
that as I s. ye may be ready. 9:3
    see **Jesus**

she **said**
for God, s. she, hath appointed me.
    Gen 4:25
she s. He is my brother. 20:5
this man? she s. I will. 24:58
then she s. A bloody. *Ex* 4:26
to say, and she s. Say on. *1 Ki* 2:14
she s. Truth, Lord, yet. *Mat* 15:27
she s. No man, Lord. *John* 8:11
she had so s. she went her. 11:28
she had thus s. she turned. 20:14
she s. Yea, for so much. *Acts* 5:8

they **said**
and they s. All that the Lord. *Ex* 24:7
they have well s. all. *Deut* 5:28
s. they, He is the son of. *2 Chr* 22:9
for they s. He is a leper. 26:23
they have s. Come, let us cut them.
    Ps 83:4
neither s. they, Where is? *Jer* 2:6
believe ye? they s. unto him, Yea.
    Mat 9:28
they all s. Let him be crucified. 27:22
for they s. He is beside. *Mark* 3:21
because they s. He hath an. 30
amazed, nor s. they any thing. 16:8
they s. The Lord hath. *Luke* 19:34
s. they, It is his angel. *Acts* 12:15

saidst
why s. thou, She is my? *Gen* 12:19
s. thou, She is my sister? 26:9
the Lord, which s. to me. 32:9
s. I will surely do thee good. 12
s. to them, I will multiply. *Ex* 32:13
mouth wherewith thou s. *Judg* 9:38
thou s. The word I have. *1 Ki* 2:42
thou s. my righteousness. *Job* 35:2
s. Seek ye my face. *Ps* 27:8
thou s. I shall be a lady. *Isa* 47:7
and thou s. I will not. *Jer* 2:20
but thou s. There is no hope. 25
I spake, but thou s. I will. 22:21
I called: thou s. Fear not. *Lam* 3:57
because thou s., Aha. *Ezek* 25:3

whom thou *s*. Give me. *Hos* 13:10
in that *s*. thou truly. *John* 4:18

sail. *substantive*
could not spread the *s*. *Isa* 33:23
thou spreadest forth to be thy *s*.
    Ezek 27:7
they strake *s*. and so. *Acts* 27:17*
and hoised up the main *s*. to. 40

sail
as he was about to *s*. *Acts* 20:3
Paul had determined to *s*. 16
we should *s*. into Italy. 27:1
all them that *s*. with thee. 24

sailed
as they *s*. he fell asleep. *Luke* 8:23
when we launched, we *s*. *Acts* 27:4
and when we had *s*. slowly. 7

sailing
finding a ship *s*. over. *Acts* 21:2*
centurion found a ship *s*. 27:6
when *s*. was now dangerous. 9*

sailors
all the company in ships, and *s*.
    stood afar off. *Rev* 18:17*

saint
*The Revisions translate this holy
one, and the plural holy ones,
where marked, except in Hos 11:12,
where it is Holy One, and Rev 15:3,
where the word is ages.*
then I heard one *s*. speak, another *s*.
    said to that *s*. which. *Dan* 8:13*
salute every *s*. in Christ. *Phil* 4:21*

saints
with ten thousands of *s*. *Deut* 33:2*
he loved the people; all his *s*. are. 3
keep the feet of his *s*. *1 Sam* 2:9*
s. rejoice in goodness. *2 Chr* 6:41
and to which of the *s*.? *Job* 5:1*
putteth no trust in his *s*. 15:15*
but to the *s*. that are in. *Ps* 16:3
sing to the Lord, O ye *s*. of. 30:4
O love the Lord, all ye his *s*. 31:23
fear the Lord, ye his *s*. 34:9
Lord forsaketh not his *s*. 37:28
gather my *s*. together to me. 50:5
for it is good before thy *s*. 52:9
the flesh of thy *s*. to beasts. 79:2
in the congregation of the *s*. 89:5*
in the assembly of the *s*. 7*
preserveth the souls of his *s*. 97:10
precious ... is death of his *s*. 116:15
and let thy *s*. shout for joy. 132:9
her *s*. shall shout aloud for joy. 16
all thy works praise, and *s*. 145:10
the praise of all his *s*. 148:14
praise in congregation of *s*. 149:1
let *s*. be joyful in glory, let them. 5
this honour have all his *s*. Praise. 9
the way of his *s*. *Pr* 2:8
but *s*. shall take. *Dan* 7:18, 22, 27
the horn made war with the *s*. 21
and shall wear out the *s*. of the. 25
is faithful with the *s*. *Hos* 11:12*
God shall come, and all the *s*. with
    thee. *Zech* 14:5*
many bodies of *s*. that. *Mat* 27:52
evil he hath done to my *s*. *Acts* 9:13
Peter came down also to the *s*. 32
called the *s*. and widows. 41
s. did I shut up in prison. 26:10
of God, called to be *s*. *Rom* 1:7
maketh intercession for the *s*. 8:27
to the necessity of the *s*. 12:13
Jerusalem to minister to the *s*. 15:25
contribution for the poor *s*. 26
may be accepted of the *s*. 31
in the Lord as becometh the *s*. 16:2
salute all the *s*. 15; *Heb* 13:24
sanctified, called to be *s*. *1 Cor* 1:2
law, and not before the *s*.? 6:1
do ye not know that the *s*. shall? 2
as in all the churches of the *s*. 14:33
the collection for the *s*. 16:1
themselves to the ministry of *s*. 15
with all the *s*. which are. *2 Cor* 1:1
upon us the ministering to the *s*. 8:4
the ministering to the *s*. 9:1
supplieth the want of the *s*. 12
the *s*. salute you. 13:13; *Phil* 4:22
to the *s*. at Ephesus, and. *Eph* 1:1

of your love to all the *s*. *Eph* 1:15
glory of his inheritance in the *s*. 18
fellow citizens with the *s*. 2:19
less than the least of all *s*. 3:8
able to comprehend with all *s*. 18
of the *s*. for the ministry. 4:12
once named, as becometh *s*. 5:3
and supplication for all *s*. 6:18
to all the *s*. in Christ. *Phil* 1:1
to all the *s*. and faithful. *Col* 1:2
of the love ye have to all the *s*. 4
inheritance of the *s*. in light. 12
now made manifest to his *s*. 26
our Lord with all his *s*. *1 Thes* 3:13
to be glorified in his *s*. *2 Thes* 1:10
washed the *s*.' feet. *1 Tim* 5:10
which thou hast to all *s*. *Philem* 5
the bowels of the *s*. are refreshed. 7
ministered to the *s*. *Heb* 6:10
once delivered to the *s*. *Jude* 3
with ten thousand of his *s*. 14*
prayers of the *s*. *Rev* 5:8; 8:3, 4
give reward to thy *s*. 11:18
to make war with the *s*. 13:7
patience and faith of the *s*. 10
here is the patience of the *s*. 14:12
thy ways, thou King of *s*. 15:3*
shed the blood of the *s*. 16:6
drunken with the blood of *s*. 17:6
found the blood of the *s*. 18:24
is the righteousness of the *s*. 19:8
the camp of the *s*. about. 20:9

saith
one *s*. This is my son that liveth, and
    the other *s*. Nay. *1 Ki* 3:23
thus *s*. Ben-hadad, Thy silver. 20:2
servant Ben-hadad *s*. I pray thee. 32
s. the king, Put this fellow in prison.
    22:27; *2 Chr* 18:26
thus *s*. the king, Is it peace?
    2 Ki 9:18, 19
thus *s*. the great king, the. 18:19
s. king, Let not Hezekiah deceive. 29
    31; *2 Chr* 32:10; *Isa* 36:14
thus *s*. Hezekiah, This day is a day
    of. *2 Ki* 19:3; *Isa* 37:3
thus *s*. Cyrus, king of Persia.
    2 Chr 36:23; *Ezra* 1:2
the depth *s*. and the sea *s*. *Job* 28:14
he *s*. Deliver him. 33:24
but none *s*. Where is God? 35:10
of the wicked *s*. *Ps* 36:1
understanding, she *s*. *Pr* 9:4, 16
naught, it is naught, *s*. the. 20:14
the slothful man *s*., There is a lion.
    22:13; 26:13
deceiveth, and *s*. Am not I? 26:19
who is he that *s*. and? *Lam* 3:37
not every one that *s*. to me. *Mat* 7:21
to him, Master *s*. My time. 26:18
Peter *s*. to him, Thou. *Mark* 8:29
fulfilled which *s*. 15:28; *Jas* 2:23
what the unjust judge *s*. *Luke* 18:6
who it is that *s*. Give. *John* 4:10
might be fulfilled, *s*. I thirst. 19:28
dwelleth not in temples made with
    hands, as *s*. *Acts* 7:48
thus *s*. the Holy Ghost, So. 21:11
the law *s*. it *s*. to them. *Rom* 3:19
for what *s*. the scripture? 4:3; 10:8
for scripture *s*. to Pharaoh. 9:17
for scripture *s*. Whosoever. 10:11
for Esaias *s*. 16, 20
first Moses *s*. 19
what the scripture *s*. of Elias? 11:2
but what *s*. the answer of God? 4
for while one *s*. I am of Paul.
    1 Cor 3:4
or *s*. not the law the same also? 9:8
be under obedience, as also *s*. 14:34
what *s*. the scripture? *Gal* 4:30
    1 Tim 5:18
as the Holy Ghost *s*. If. *Heb* 3:7
do ye think the scriptures *s*. *Jas* 4:5
the Spirit *s*. to the churches. *Rev* 2:7
    11, 17, 29; 3:6, 13, 22
s. the First and the Last. 2:8
s. the Son of God. 18
s. the Amen. 3:14
yea, *s*. the Spirit. 14:13
she *s*. I sit a queen, and am. 18:7
s. Surely I come quickly. 22:20

God *saith*
what my God *s*. that. *2 Chr* 18:13
thus *s*. God, Why transgress? 24:20
to wicked God *s*. What? *Ps* 50:16
thus *s*. God the Lord. *Isa* 42:5
wast refused, *s*. thy God. 54:6
There is no peace, *s*. my God. 57:21
shut the womb, *s*. thy God. 66:9
come to pass in the last days *s*. God.
    Acts 2:17

he saith
go to Joseph, what *he s*. *Gen* 41:55
all that *he s*. cometh. *1 Sam* 9:6
likewise what *he s*. *2 Sam* 17:5
when *he s*. to thee, Wash and be.
    2 Ki 5:13
for *he s*. to the snow, Be. *Job* 37:6
Eat and drink, *s. he* to. *Pr* 23:7
he that *s*. to wicked, Thou. 24:24
nor *s. he*, For whom do? *Eccl* 4:8
he s. to every one that he is. 10:3
he s. shall come to pass, he shall
    have whatsoever *he s*. *Mark* 11:23
whatsoever *he s*. to you. *John* 2:5
he s.? we cannot tell what *he s*.
    16:18
knoweth that *he s*. true. 19:35
he s. to Peter, Feed my. 21:15, 16
which, *s. he*, ye have. *Acts* 1:4
more silence, and *he s*. 22:2
to Israel *he s*. *Rom* 10:21
again *he s*. 15:10
for two, *s. he*, shall be. *1 Cor* 6:16
or *s. he* it altogether for our? 9:10
he s. I have heard thee. *2 Cor* 6:2
he s. not, And to seeds. *Gal* 3:16
See, *s. he*, that thou. *Heb* 8:5
in that *he s*. A new covenant. 13
see **Jesus, Lord**

sake
not curse the ground for man's *s*.
    Gen 8:21
Abram well for her *s*. 12:16
will not do it for forty's *s*. 18:29
not for twenty's *s*. 31
not for ten's *s*. 32
slay me for my wife's *s*. 20:11
thy seed for Abraham's *s*. 26:24
Egyptian's house for Joseph's *s*. 39:5
done to Egypt for Israel's *s*. *Ex* 18:8
let him go free for eye's *s*. 21:26
for his tooth's *s*. 27
enviest thou for my *s*.? *Num* 11:29
he was zealous for my *s*. 25:11
day of the plague for Peor's *s*. 18
people for his name's *s*. *1 Sam* 12:22
destroy the city for my *s*. 23:10
kingdom for Israel's *s*. *2 Sam* 5:12
for thy word's *s*. hast done all. 7:21
    1 Chr 17:19
kindness for Jonathan's *s*.
    2 Sam 9:1, 7
deal gently for my *s*. with. 18:5
out of a far country for thy name's *s*.
    1 Ki 8:41; *2 Chr* 6:32
David thy father's *s*. *1 Ki* 11:12
    13, 32, 34; 15:4; *2 Ki* 8:19; 19:34
    20:6; *Ps* 132:10
for Jerusalem's *s*. which I have.
    1 Ki 11:13
them for great mercies' *s*. *Neh* 9:31
entreated for children's *s*. *Job* 19:17
save me for thy mercies' *s*. *Ps* 6:4
    31:16
for his name's *s*. 23:3; 31:3
me for thy goodness' *s*. 25:7
for thy name's *s*. pardon mine. 11
us for thy mercies' *s*. 44:26
not be confounded for my *s*. 69:6
our sins for thy name's *s*. 79:9
saved them for his name's *s*. 106:8
me, for thy name's *s*. 109:21
for thy mercy and truth's *s*. 115:1
for thy name's *s*.: for thy righteous-
    ness' *s*. bring my soul. 143:11
own *s*. and David's *s*. *Isa* 37:35
for his righteousness' *s*. 42:21
for your *s*. I have sent to. 43:14
for Jacob's *s*. I have even. 45:4
for my name's *s*. will I defer. 48:9
even for mine own *s*. will I do it. 11
for Zion's *s*., for Jerusalem's *s*. 62:1

return for thy servant's *s*. *Isa* 63:17
out for my name's *s*. said.   66:5
thou it for thy name's *s*.   *Jer* 14:7
abhor us for thy name's *s*.   21
but I wrought for my name's *s*. that.
        Ezek 20:9, 14, 22, 44; 36:22
sanctuary, for the Lord's *s*. *Dan* 9:17
defer not for thine own *s*.   19
for my *s*. this great.   *Jonah* 1:12
shall Zion for your *s*. be. *Mi* 3:12
for righteousness' *s*.   *Mat* 5:10
against you falsely for my *s*.   11
before governors and kings, for my *s*.
        10:18; *Mark* 13:9; *Luke* 21:12
hated of all men, for my name's *s*.
        Mat 10:22; 24:9; *Mark* 13:13
                             Luke 21:17
loseth his life for my *s*.   *Mat* 10:39
        16:25; *Mark* 8:35; *Luke* 9:24
Herod bound John for Herodias' *s*.
        Mat 14:3; *Mark* 6:17
nevertheless, for the oath's *s*.
        Mat 14:9; *Mark* 6:26
kingdom of heaven's *s*.   *Mat* 19:12
left lands for my name's *s*. shall.
        29; *Mark* 10:29; *Luke* 18:29
no flesh be saved, but for elect's *s*.
        Mat 24:22; *Mark* 13:20
ariseth for the world's *s*. *Mark* 4:17
name for Son of man's *s*. *Luke* 6:22
not for Jesus' *s*. only.   *John* 12:9
lay down thy life for my *s*.?   13:38
for the very works' *s*.   14:11
do to you for my name's *s*.   15:21
suffer for my name's *s*.   *Acts* 9:16
for which hope's *s*. I am.   26:7
written for his *s*. alone.   *Rom* 4:23
are enemies for your *s*.   11:28
be subject for conscience *s*.   13:5
for Lord's *s*. strive with.   15:30
for Christ's *s*. ye are wise. *1 Cor* 4:10
this I do for the gospel's *s*.   9:23
question for conscience *s*. 10:25, 27
eat not, for his *s*. that shewed it, and
        for conscience *s*.   28
servants for Jesus' *s*.   *2 Cor* 4:5
delivered to death for Jesus' *s*. 11
in distresses for Christ's *s*.   12:10
as God for Christ's *s*.   *Eph* 4:32
also to suffer for his *s*.   *Phil* 1:29
for his body's *s*. which.   *Col* 1:24
for which thing's *s*. wrath of.   3:6
men we were for your *s*. *1 Thes* 1:5
highly for their work's *s*.   5:13
wine, for thy stomach's *s*. *1 Tim* 5:23
for filthy lucre's *s*.   *Tit* 1:11
yet for love's *s*. I rather. *Philem* 9
ordinance for Lord's *s*.   *1 Pet* 2:13
ye suffer for righteousness' *s*.   3:14
forgiven for name's *s*. *1 John* 2:12
for the truth's *s*. that.   *2 John* 2
because for his name's *s*.   *3 John* 7
and for my name's *s*. hast.   *Rev* 2:3

thy sake
the ground for *thy s*.   *Gen* 3:17
well with me for *thy s*.   12:13
hath blessed me for *thy s*.   30:27
for *thy s*. are we killed all day long.
        Ps 44:22; *Rom* 8:36
because for *thy s*. I have borne.
                              Ps 69:7
against thee, shall fall for *thy s*.
                             Isa 54:15
know that for *thy s*. I have. *Jer* 15:15
down my life for *thy s*.   *John* 13:37

sakes
the place for their *s*.   *Gen* 18:26
I will for their *s*. remember the.
                             Lev 26:45
the Lord was angry with me for your
        s. saying. *Deut* 1:37; 3:26; 4:21
to them for our *s*.   *Judg* 21:22
me much for your *s*.   *Ruth* 1:13
reproved kings for their *s*.
        1 Chr 16:21; *Ps* 105:14
for their *s*. therefore.   *Ps* 7:7
with Moses for their *s*.   106:32
and companions' *s*.   122:8
for my servant's *s*.   *Isa* 65:8
not this for your *s*.   *Ezek* 36:22, 32
but for their *s*. that.   *Dan* 2:30
and I will rebuke the devourer for
        your *s*., he shall not. *Mal* 3:11

for their *s*. which sat.   *Mark* 6:26
I am glad for your *s*. I.   *John* 11:15
not for me, but for your *s*.   12:30
and for their *s*. I sanctify.   17:19
for their fathers' *s*.   *Rom* 11:28
transferred for your *s*.   *1 Cor* 4:6
our *s*.? for our *s*. no doubt.   9:10
all things are for your *s*. *2 Cor* 4:15
though rich, yet for your *s*.   8:9
your *s*. before God.   *1 Thes* 3:9
things for the elect's *s*.   *2 Tim* 2:10

Salathiel
S. the son of Jechoniah.   *1 Chr* 3:17
                              Mat 1:12
which was the son of S.   *Luke* 3:27

sale
the years of the *s*. thereof. *Lev* 25:27
price of his *s*. shall be.   50
which cometh of the *s*.   *Deut* 18:8

Salem
Melchizedek king of S.   *Gen* 14:18
in S. also is his tabernacle.   *Ps* 76:2
Melchizedek king of S. who blessed.
                              Heb 7:1
king of S. is king of peace.   2

Salmon
Nahshon begat S.   *Ruth* 4:20
S. begat Boaz.   21; *1 Chr* 2:11
                            Mat 1:4, 5
white as snow in S.   *Ps* 68:14
which was the son of S.   *Luke* 3:32

Salmone
Crete, over against S.   *Acts* 27:7

Salome
Mary, mother of S.   *Mark* 15:40
                              16:1

salt
*This was even more indispensable
to the Hebrews than to us, as they
used it as an antidote to the effects
of the heat of the climate on
animal food, and it also was used
in the sacrifices. They had an
inexhaustible and ready supply of
it on the southern shores of the
Salt Sea, now called the Dead Sea.
Salt symbolized hospitality, dura-
bility and purity. To eat the salt
of the king was to owe him the
utmost fidelity. To eat bread and
salt together was to make an un-
breakable league of friendship.*
became a pillar of *s*.   *Gen* 19:26
offerings thou shalt offer *s*. *Lev* 2:13
whole land thereof is *s*.   *Deut* 29:23
Judah had the city of *s*.   *Josh* 15:62
city, and sowed it with *s*. *Judg* 9:45
in the valley of *s*.   *2 Sam* 8:13
cruse, put *s*. therein.   *2 Ki* 2:20
and cast the *s*. in there.   21
Edom in the valley of *s*. 10,000.
        14:7; *1 Chr* 18:12; 2 Chr 25:11
need of wheat, *s*., wine.   *Ezra* 6:9
and *s*. without prescribing.   7:22
he eaten without *s*.?   *Job* 6:6
inhabit places in a *s*. land. *Jer* 17:6
the priest shall cast *s*.   *Ezek* 43:24
thereof shall be given to *s*.   47:11
Moab shall be as *s*. pits.   *Zeph* 2:9
s. of the earth, but if the *s*. *Mat* 5:13
shall be salted with *s*.   *Mark* 9:49
s. have lost his saltness, wherewith
        will ye season it ? have *s*.   50
s. is good, but if *s*. have. *Luke* 14:34
speech be seasoned with *s*. *Col* 4:6
no fountain can yield *s*.   *Jas* 3:12

see covenant of salt

salt sea
(*Now called the Dead Sea*)
which is the *s*. sea.   *Gen* 14:3
shall be at the *s*. sea.   *Num* 34:12
coast even to the *s*. sea. *Deut* 3:17
came toward the *s*. sea.   *Josh* 3:16
even to *s*. sea. 12:3; 15:2, 5; 18:19

salted
thou wast not *s*. at all.   *Ezek* 16:4
wherewith shall it be *s*?   *Mat* 5:13
one shall be *s*. with fire and every
        sacrifice shall be *s*. *Mark* 9:49

saltness
if salt have lost his *s*.   *Mark* 9:50

salutation
what manner of *s*. this.   *Luke* 1:29
at *s*. of Mary, babe leaped. 41, 44
you, the *s*. of me, Paul. *1 Cor* 16:21
                        Col 4:18; *2 Thes* 3:17

salutations
scribes who love *s*. in.   *Mark* 12:38

salute
will *s*. thee and give.   *1 Sam* 10:4
that he might *s*. Samuel.   13:10
David sent to *s*. our master.   25:14
Joram his son to *s*.   *2 Sam* 8:10
s. him not, if any *s*. thee. *2 Ki* 4:29
we go to *s*. the children of.   10:13
and if ye *s*. your brethren. *Mat* 5:47
come into an house, *s*. it.   10:12
and began to *s*. him.   *Mark* 15:18
shoes, and *s*. no man.   *Luke* 10:4
Bernice came to *s*. Festus. *Acts* 25:13
s. my wellbeloved.   *Rom* 16:5
s. Andronicus.   7
s. Urbane our helper.   9
s. Apelles, *s*. them of Aristobulus'. 10
s. Herodian.   11
s. the beloved Persis.   12
s. Rufus chosen in the Lord.   13
s. with an holy kiss, churches *s*. 16
I Tertius, who wrote this, *s*. you. 22
the churches of Asia *s*. you. Aquila
        and Priscilla *s*. you. *1 Cor* 16:19
all the saints *s*. you.   *2 Cor* 13:13
                              Phil 4:22
s. every saint in Christ.   *Phil* 4:21
s. the brethren in Laodicea. *Col* 4:15
s. the household of.   *2 Tim* 4:19
all that are with me, *s*. thee. *Tit* 3:15
there *s*. thee Epaphras.   *Philem* 23
s. them that have the rule over you;
        they of Italy *s*. you. *Heb* 13:24
our friends *s*. thee, greet. *3 John* 14

saluted
the Danites came and *s*. *Judg* 18:15*
David came and *s*.   *1 Sam* 17:22
to the people and *s*. them.   30:21
Jehu *s*. Jehonadab.   *2 Ki* 10:15
running to Jesus, *s*. him. *Mark* 9:15
Mary entered, and *s*.   *Luke* 1:40
Paul, when he had *s*.   *Acts* 18:22
we came to Ptolemais, and *s*.   21:7
when Paul had *s*. James and.   19

saluteth
and Erastus *s*. you.   *Rom* 16:23
my fellow-prisoner *s*. you. *Col* 4:10
servant of Christ, *s*. you.   12
is at Babylon *s*. you.   *1 Pet* 5:13

salvation
[1] *Preservation from trouble or
danger.* [2] *Deliverance from sin
and its consequences.*
see the *s*. of the Lord.   *Ex* 14:13
                             2 Chr 20:17
the rock of his *s*.   *Deut* 32:15
the Lord wrought *s*.   *1 Sam* 11:13*
hath wrought this great *s*.   14:45
the Lord wrought a great *s*. 19:5*
he is the tower of *s*. for his king.
                            2 Sam 22:51*
from day to day his *s*.   *1 Chr* 16:23
save us, O God of our *s*. and.   35
be clothed with *s*.   *2 Chr* 6:41
s. belongeth to the Lord.   *Ps* 3:8
O that the *s*. of Israel.   14:7; 53:6
from the God of his *s*.   24:5
my soul shall rejoice in his *s*. 35:9
the *s*. of the righteous is of. 37:39
will I shew the *s*. of God.   50:23
answer us, O God of our *s*.?   65:5
Lord, even the God of our *s*. 68:19
our God, is the God of *s*.   20*
working *s*. in the midst of.   74:12
they trusted not in his *s*.   78:22
help us, O God of our *s*., for. 79:9
turn us, O God of our *s*.   85:4
surely his *s*. is nigh them that.   9
joyful noise to the rock of our *s*. 95:1
forth his *s*. from day to day. 96:2
hath made known his *s*.   98:2
have seen the *s*. of our God.   3
I will take the cup of *s*.   116:13
the voice of *s*. is in.   118:15
s. is far from the wicked.   119:155
clothe her priests with *s*.   132:16

that giveth s. unto kings. Ps 144:10
beautify the meek with s. 149:4
water out of the wells of s. Isa 12:3
glad and rejoice in his s. 25:9
s. will God appoint for walls. 26:1
be thou our s. in the time of. 33:2
knowledge, and strength of s. 6
and let them bring forth s. 45:8
saved with an everlasting s. 17
I will place s. in Zion for. 46:13
in a day of s. have I helped. 49:8
him that publisheth s. 52:7
shall see the s. of our God. 10
we look for s. but it is far. 59:11
therefore his arm brought s. 16
he put on an helmet of s. upon. 17
but shalt call thy walls s. 60:18
me with the garments of s. 61:10
and the s. thereof as a lamp. 62:1
own arm brought s. to me. 63:5
is s. hoped for from the hills and
mountains . . . s. of. Jer 3:23*
quietly wait for the s. Lam 3:26
S. is of the Lord. Jonah 2:9
ride on thy chariots of s. Hab 3:8
thou wentest forth for s. of thy
people, even for s. with thine. 13
he is just, and having s. Zech 9:9
up an horn of s. for us. Luke 1:69
knowledge of s. to his people. 77
all flesh shall see the s. of. 3:6
Jesus said, This day is s. 19:9
we know what we worship, for s. is
of the Jews. John 4:22
neither is there s. in any. Acts 4:12
the word of this s. sent. 13:26
thou shouldest be for s. unto the. 47
shew to us the way of s. 16:17
the s. of God is sent unto the. 28:28
the power of God unto s. Rom 1:16
confession is made unto s. 10:10
through their fall s. is come. 11:11
now is our s. nearer than. 13:11
comforted, it is for your s. 2 Cor 1:6
in the day of s. have I succoured thee;
behold now is the day of s. 6:2
worketh repentance to s. 7:10
the gospel of your s. Eph 1:13
take the helmet of s. and. 6:17
an evident token of s. Phil 1:28
work out your own s. with. 2:12
an helmet the hope of s. 1 Thes 5:8
hath appointed us to obtain s. 9
chosen you to s. 2 Thes 2:13
obtain the s. in Christ. 2 Tim 2:10
able to make thee wise unto s. 3:15
God that bringeth s. Tit 2:11
shall be heirs of s. Heb 1:14
if we neglect so great s.? 2:3
the Captain of their s. perfect. 10
the Author of eternal s. 5:9
things that accompany s. 6:9
second time without sin unto s. 9:28
through faith unto s. 1 Pet 1:5
receiving the end of your faith, s. 9
of which s. the prophets have. 10
the longsuffering of the Lord is s.
2 Pet 3:15
to you of the common s. Jude 3
saying; S. to our God. Rev 7:10
s. and glory, unto the Lord. 19:1
now is come s. and strength. 12:10

my salvation

song, he is become my s. Ex 15:2
shield, the horn of my. 2 Sam 22:3
the rock of my s. 47; Ps 18:46
for this is all my s. and. 2 Sam 23:5
he also shall be my s. Job 13:16
art the God of my s. Ps 25:5
the Lord is my light and my. 27:1
62:6; Isa 12:2
O God of my s. Ps 27:9; 51:14; 88:1
O Lord my s. 38:22
God, from him cometh my s. 62:1
he only is my s. 2, 6
in God is my s. 7
my God, rock of my s. 89:26
him, and shew him my s. 91:16
become my s. 118:14, 21; Isa 12:2
Lord, strength of my s. Ps 140:7
my s. he is become my s. Isa 12:2
far off, my s. shall not tarry. 46:13
thou mayest be my s. to end. 49:6

36

my s. is gone forth. Isa 51:5
my s. shall be for ever. 6
and my s. from generation to. 8
my s. is near to come, and my. 56:1
the God of my s. my God. Mi 7:7
joy in the God of my s. Hab 3:18
that this shall turn to my s. Phil 1:19

thy salvation

I have waited for thy s. Gen 49:18
because I rejoice in thy s. 1 Sam 2:1
also given me the shield of thy s.
2 Sam 22:36; Ps 18:35
I will rejoice in thy s. Ps 9:14
my heart shall rejoice in thy s. 13:5
we will rejoice in thy s. 20:5
in thy s. how greatly! 21:1
his glory is great in thy s. 5
say unto my soul, I am thy s. 35:3
thy faithfulness and thy s. 40:10
let such as love thy s. say, Lord. 16
me the joy of thy s. 51:12; 70:4
me in the truth of thy s. 69:13
I am poor, let thy s. set me up. 29
shall shew forth thy s. 71:15
O Lord, grant us thy s. 85:7
O visit me with thy s. 106:4
let thy s. come according. 119:41
my soul fainteth for thy s. 81
mine eyes fail for thy s. and. 123
Lord, I have hoped for thy s. 166
I have longed for thy s. O Lord. 174
forgotten the God of thy s. Isa 17:10
say to Zion, Behold, thy s. 62:11
eyes have seen thy s. Luke 2:30

Samaria

places which are in S. 1 Ki 13:32
Omri bought the hill S. of. 16:24
besieged S. 20:1; 2 Ki 6:24
if the dust of S. shall suffice.
1 Ki 20:10
there are men come out of S. 17
sat on their throne in the entrance of
the gate of S. 22:10; 2 Chr 18:9
chariot in the pool of S. 1 Ki 22:38
were in the midst of S. 2 Ki 6:20
shekel in the gate of S. 7:1, 18
king of Assyria took S. 17:6; 18:10
have they delivered S. out of mine
hand ? 18:34; Isa 36:19
Jerusalem the line of S. 2 Ki 21:13
prophet that came out of S. 23:18
upon the cities; from S. 2 Chr 25:13
Asnapper set in the cities of S.
Ezra 4:10
spake before army of S. Neh 4:2
Ephraim is S. and the head of S. is.
Isa 7:9
and the spoil of S. shall be. 8:4
Ephraim and inhabitants of S. 9:9
is not Hamath as Arpad ? S. 10:9
folly in the prophets of S. Jer 23:13
vines on the mountains of S. 31:5
certain from Shechem and S. 41:5
thine elder sister is S. Ezek 16:46
nor hath S. committed half. 51
S. is Aholah, and Jerusalem. 23:4
then the wickedness of S. Hos 7:1
thy calf, O S. hath cast thee. 8:5
but the calf of S. shall be broken. 6
inhabitants of S. shall fear. 10:5
as for S. her king is cut off as. 7
S. shall become desolate, she. 13:16
on mountains of S. Amos 3:9
Bashan, in mountain of S. 4:1
trust in the mountain of S. 6:1
swear by the sin of S. and. 8:14
possess the fields of S. Ob 19
which he saw concerning S. Mi 1:1
I will make S. as an heap of. 6
through the midst of S. Luke 17:11
must needs go through S. John 4:4
of me, who am a woman of S.? 9
through the regions of S. Acts 8:1
preached Christ to them of S. 5
the apostles heard that S. 14

in Samaria

Omri buried in S. 1 Ki 16:28
Ahab reigned in S. 29
was a sore famine in S. 18:2
as my father made in S. 20:34
king of Israel which is in S. 21:18
Ahab buried in S. 22:37
Ahaziah reigned in S. 51

Jehoram to reign in S. 2 Ki 3:1
were with the prophets in S. 5:3
was a great famine in S. 6:25
Jehu slew all that remained to Ahab
in S. 10:17
Jehoahaz reigned in S. 13:1
remained the grove also in S. 6
Jehoahaz buried in S. 9
Jehoash to reign in S. 10
Joash, buried in S. 13; 14:16
Jeroboam reigned in S. 14:23
Zechariah reigned in S. 15:8, 13
Menahem to reign in S. 17
Pekah to reign in S. 27
Hoshea to reign in S. 17:1
for Ahaziah was hid in S. 2 Chr 22:9
so Israel that dwell in S. Amos 3:12
be witnesses to me in S. Acts 1:8
had the churches rest in S. 9:31

to or unto Samaria

displeased came to S. 1 Ki 20:43
so king was brought to S. 22:37
from Carmel to S. 2 Ki 2:25
but Elisha led them to S. 6:19
Jehu sent letters to S. 10:1
Jehu came to S. 12, 17
Jehoash took hostages, and returned
to S. 14:14; 2 Chr 25:24
Menahem came to S. 2 Ki 15:14
king of Assyria went up to S. 17:5
Jehoshaphat went down to S.
2 Chr 18:2
brought the spoil of Judah to S. 28:8
as I have done unto S. Isa 10:11

Samaritan

but a certain S. came. Luke 10:33
gave thanks, and he was a S. 17:16
that thou art a S. and. John 8:48

Samaritans

places the S. had made. 2 Ki 17:29
into any city of the S. Mat 10:5
into a village of the S. Luke 9:52
no dealings with the S. John 4:9
many of the S. of that city. 39
the S. besought him to tarry. 40
many villages of the S. Acts 8:25

same

saying, This s. shall. Gen 5:29
the s. became mighty men. 6:4
Resen, the s. is a great city. 10:12
the s. is Zoar. 14:8
the s. is Hebron. 23:2, 19
let the s. be she that. 24:14, 44
appeared to Isaac the s. night. 26:24
spake them these s. words. 44:6
in the way of Ephrath, the s. 48:7
shall be of the s. Ex 25:31; 37:17
knops and branches shall be of the s.
25:36; 37:22
his horns shall be of the s. 27:2
37:25; 38:2
ephod shall be of the s. 28:8; 39:5
the s. goodness will we. Num 10:32
presumptuously, the s. 15:30
the Jebusite, the s. Josh 15:8
the s. shall go, the s. Judg 7:4
the s. shall reign over. 1 Sam 9:17
Zion, the s. is the city. 2 Sam 5:7
nor turn again by the s. way. 1 Ki 13:9
year ye shall eat that which springeth
of the s. 2 Ki 19:29; Isa 37:30
Abram, the s. is. 1 Chr 1:27
hath confirmed the s. to Jacob.
16:17; Ps 105:10
the s. may be a priest. 2 Chr 13:9
s. is Micaiah the son of Imla. 18:7
hath not the s. Hezekiah ? 32:12
Shimei, and Kelaiah, the s. is Kelita.
Ezra 10:23
the thirteenth day of s. Esth 9:1
wickedness reap the s. Job 4:8
what ye know, the s. do I. 13:2
of thy dogs in the s. Ps 68:23*
he poureth out of the s. 75:8
but thou art the s., and thy years shall
have no. 102:27; Heb 1:12
to the going down of the s.
Ps 113:3; Mal 1:11
the s. is the companion. Pr 28:24
remembered that s. poor. Eccl 9:15
prophet died the s. year. Jer 28:17
s. wicked man shall die. Ezek 3:18
this shall not be the s.: exalt. 21:26

go out by the way of the s. *Ezek* 44:3
the s. horn made war. *Dan* 7:21
go in to the s. maid. *Amos* 2:7
s. shall be called great. *Mat* 5:19
even the publicans the s.? 46
the s. is my brother and sister.
   12:50; *Mark* 3:35
s. is become the head of the corner.
Mat 21:42; *Luke* 20:17; *1 Pet* 2:7
shall endure, s. shall be saved.
   Mat 24:13; *Mark* 13:13
he that dippeth his hand with me...
   the s. shall betray me. *Mat* 26:23
that s. is he, hold. 48; *Mark* 14:44
thieves also cast the s. *Mat* 27:44
lose his life, the s. shall save it.
   Mark 8:35; *Luke* 9:24
desire to be first, the s. *Mark* 9:35
sinners also do even the s. *Luke* 6:33
for with the s. measure that ye. 38
is forgiven, the s. loveth little. 7:47
the s. shall be great. 9:48
the s. was accused that he. 16:1
the s. shall receive greater. 20:47
the s. had not consented to. 23:51
the s. was in the beginning. *John* 1:2
the s. came for a witness of. 7
the s. is he which baptizeth with. 33
the s. is true. 7:18
the s. I said to you from the. 8:25
the s. is a thief. 10:1
he abode two days still in the s. 11:6
high priest that s. year. 49; 18:13
the s. shall judge him in the. 12:48
abideth in me, the s. bringeth. 15:5
this s. Jesus shall so. *Acts* 1:11
God made that s. Jesus both. 2:36
the s. dealt subtilly with our. 7:19
the s. did God send to be. 35
began at the s. scripture and. 8:35
God hath fulfilled the s. to. 13:33
the s. heard Paul speak. 14:9
the s. followed Paul and us. 16:17
or else let these s. here say. 24:20
not only do the s. *Rom* 1:32
which do such, and doest the s. 2:3
who hath subjected the s. 8:20
the s. Lord over all is rich to. 10:12
members have not the s. 12:4
be of the s. mind one toward. 16
1 Cor 1:10; *Phil* 4:2; *1 Pet* 4:1
have praise of the s. *1 Cor* 1:10
ye all speak the s. thing. *1 Cor* 1:10
or saith not the law the s. also ? 9:8
did all eat the s. spiritual meat. 10:3
the s. drink. 4
but the s. Spirit. 12:4; *2 Cor* 4:13
   12:18
but the s. Lord. *1 Cor* 12:5
but it is the s. God. 6
all flesh is not the s. flesh. 15:39
but the s. which is made. *2 Cor* 2:2
I wrote this s. unto you, lest, 3
to the glory of the s. Lord. 8:19
s. might be ready as a matter. 9:5
the s. was mighty in me. *Gal* 2:8
the s. are the children of. 3:7
descended is the s. that. *Eph* 4:10
the s. shall he receive of Lord. 6:8
having the s. conflict. *Phil* 1:30
having s. love, being of one. 2:2
the s. rule, mind the s. things. 3:16
and watch in the s. with. *Col* 4:2
the s. commit thou to. *2 Tim* 2:2
likewise took part of the s. *Heb* 2:14
the heirs with him of the s. 11:9
Jesus Christ, the s. yesterday. 13:8
if any offend not, the s. is. *Jas* 3:2
even so minister the s. *1 Pet* 4:10
of the s. is he brought. *2 Pet* 2:19
by the s. word are kept in store. 3:7
denieth the Son, s. hath. *1 John* 2:23
as the s. anointing teacheth you. 27
overcometh, the s. shall. *Rev* 3:5
   see day, hour

Samson

called his name s. *Judg* 13:24
S. went to Timnath. 14:1
she pleased S. well. 7
S. made there a feast. 10
S.'s wife wept before him. 16
S. caught foxes. 15:4
to bind S. are we come. 10

S. is come hither. *Judg* 16:2
S. lay till midnight. 3
be upon thee, S. 9, 12, 14, 20
our god hath delivered S. into. 23
they said, Call for S. 25
S. called unto the Lord. 28
S. took hold of the pillars. 29
S. said, Let me die with. 30
fail me to tell of S. *Heb* 11:32

Samuel

son, and called him S. *1 Sam* 1:20
S. ministered before the Lord. 2:18
child S. grew before the Lord. 21
the Lord called S.: and he answered,
   Here am I. 3:4, 6, 8, 10
and S. feared to shew Eli the. 15
the Lord revealed himself to S. 21
and the word of S. came to all. 4:1
S. judged the children. 7:6, 15
S. cried to the Lord for Israel. 9
Philistines all the days of S. 13
displeased S. when they said. 8:6
refused to obey the voice of S. 19
and S. heard all the words of. 21
Lord told S. in his ear before. 9:15
so Saul did eat with S. that. 24
S. called Saul to the top of the. 26
S. took a vial of oil and. 10:1
we came to S. 14
tell me, I pray thee, what S. said. 15
then S. told the manner of the. 25
not forth after Saul and S. 11:7
the Lord sent S. 12:11
greatly feared the Lord and S. 18
he tarried the set time that S. 13:8
it grieved S. 15:11
S. turned about to go away, S.'s. 27
S. hewed Agag in pieces. 33
nevertheless, S. mourned for. 35
Jesse made seven of his sons to pass
   before S. 16:10
S. took the horn of oil and. 13
David fled and came to S. 19:18
said, Where are S. and David ? 22
S. died. 25:1
Saul said, Bring me up S. 28:11
Saul perceived that it was S. 14
sons of S. *1 Chr* 6:28
whom David and S. the seer. 9:22
word of the Lord by S. 11:3
all that S. had dedicated. 26:28
like that from S. *2 Chr* 35:18
S. among them that call. *Ps* 99:6
Moses and S. stood. *Jer* 15:1
the prophets from S. *Acts* 3:24
judges 450 years till S. 13:20
would fail me to tell of S. *Heb* 11:32

Sanballat

when S. heard of it. *Neh* 2:10, 19
when S. heard we builded. 4:1, 7
S. sent to me. 6:2, 5
for Tobiah and S. had hired. 12
my God, think upon S. 14
Joiada was son in law to S. 13:28

sanctification

of God is made unto us s. *1 Cor* 1:30
of God, even your s. *1 Thes* 4:3
to possess his vessel in s. 4
through s. of the Spirit. *2 Thes* 2:13
   1 Pet 1:2

sanctified

seventh day and s. it. *Gen* 2:3*
Moses s. the people. *Ex* 19:14
the tabernacle shall be s. for. 29:43
s. the tabernacle, and. *Lev* 8:10
s. the altar. 11
s. Aaron and his garments. 30
I will be s. in them that come. 10:3
if he that s. it will redeem. 27:15
and if he that s. the field will. 19
s. the tabernacle. *Num* 7:1
s. the firstborn of Israel. 8:17
because ye s. me not. *Deut* 32:51
s. Eleazar his son to. *1 Sam* 7:1
he s. Jesse and his sons to. 16:5
though it were s. this day in. 21:5
Levites s. themselves. *1 Chr* 15:14
priests present were s. *2 Chr* 5:11
I have chosen as s. 7:16*, 20*
and s. themselves. 29:15
they s. the house of the. 17
vessels have we prepared and s. 19

till other priests had s. *2 Chr* 29:34
the priests had not s. 30:3
sanctuary which he hath s. for ever. 8
were ashamed, and s. themselves. 15
congregation were not s. 17
a great number of the priests s. 24
in their set office they s. 31:18
and s. the sheep gate. *Neh* 3:1
they s. holy things to the Levites, and
   the Levites s. them to the. 12:47
Job sent and s. his sons. *Job* 1:5
holy God shall be s. in. *Isa* 5:16
I have commanded my s. ones. 13:3
I s. thee, and ordained. *Jer* 1:5
I will be s. in you. *Ezek* 20:41
   36:23
when I shall be s. in her. 28:22
I shall be s. in thee. 38:16
be s. in them in sight of. 25; 39:27
the priests that are s. 48:11
whom the Father s. *John* 10:36
that they also might be s. 17:19
an inheritance among them which
   are s. *Acts* 20:32; 26:18
s. by the Holy Ghost. *Rom* 15:16
them that are s. in Christ. *1 Cor* 1:2
but now ye are s. in the name. 6:11
husband is s. . . . wife is s. 7:14
it is s. by the word of. *1 Tim* 4:5
shall be a vessel s. for. *2 Tim* 2:21
and they who are s. are. *Heb* 2:11
by the which will we are s. 10:10
perfected them that are s. 14
covenant wherewith he was s. 29
to them that are s. by God. *Jude* 1*

sanctifieth

temple that s. the gold ? *Mat* 23:17
the altar that s. the gift ? 19
both he that s. and they. *Heb* 2:11
if blood of bulls s. to the. 9:13

sanctify

[1] *To dedicate.* [2] *To set aside
for holy uses.* [3] *To make holy.*
s. unto me all the firstborn. *Ex* 13:2
go and s. them to-day. 19:10
and let the priests also s. 22
about the mount, and s. it. 23
shalt anoint and s. 28:41; 29:33
   40:13; *Lev* 8:12; 21:8
thou shalt s. the breast. *Ex* 29:27
shalt s. the altar. 36, 37; 40:10
I will s. the tabernacle and. 29:44
and thou shalt s. the. 30:29; 40:10
   11; *Lev* 8:11
I am the Lord that doth s. *Ex* 31:13
   Lev 20:8; 21:8; *Ezek* 20:12
ye shall s. yourselves. *Lev* 11:44
20:7; *Num* 11:18; *Josh* 3:5; 7:13
   1 Sam 16:5
seed, I the Lord do s. *Lev* 21:15
I the Lord do s. them. 23; 22:9, 16
when a man shall s. his. 27:14
if a man shall s. his field. 16, 17
   18, 22
firstling, no man shall s. 26
ye believed me not, to s. me.
   Num 20:12; 27:14
keep the sabbath day to s. it.
   Deut 5:12*; *Neh* 13:22
firstling males thou shalt s. 15:19
up, s. the people, s. *Josh* 7:13
s. yourselves. *1 Chr* 15:12
   2 Chr 29:5; 35:6
he should s. the most. *1 Chr* 23:13
upright in heart to s. *2 Chr* 29:34
one that was not clean to s. 30:17
s. the Lord himself. *Isa* 8:13
they shall s. the Holy One. 29:23
they that s. themselves in. 66:17
I will s. my great name. *Ezek* 36:23
that the Lord do s. Israel. 37:28
magnify myself, and s. myself. 38:23
shall not s. people with garments.
   44:19; 46:20
s. ye a fast. *Joel* 1:14; 2:15
s. the congregation, assemble. 2:16
s. them through thy. *John* 17:17
and for their sakes I s. myself. 19
that he might s. and. *Eph* 5:26
very God of peace s. *1 Thes* 5:23
that he might s. people. *Heb* 13:12
but s. the Lord God in. *1 Pet* 3:15

sanctuaries
that he profane not my s. *Lev* 21:23
bring your s. to desolation. 26:31
strangers are come into s. *Jer* 51:51
hast defiled thy s. by. *Ezek* 28:18
the s. of Israel shall be. *Amos* 7:9

sanctuary
(*Generally a place set apart for the worship of God. Specifically the Temple at Jerusalem, most especially the Most Holy Place, or Holy of Holies. It is also used as meaning a refuge, or place of protection*)
plant them in the s. *Ex* 15:17
let them make me a s. 25:8
one after the shekel of the s. 30:13
shekels after the shekel of the s.
manner of work for the s. 36:1, 3, 4
more work for offering of the s. 6
the shekel of the s. 38:24, 25, 26
Lev 5:15; 27:3, 25; *Num* 3:47, 50
7:13, 19, 25, 31, 37; 18:16
cast the sockets of the s. *Ex* 28:27
before the vail of the s. *Lev* 4:6
brethren from before the s. 10:4
nor come into the s. till her. 12:4
atonement for the holy s. 16:33
shall reverence my s. 19:30; 26:2
go out of the s. nor profane the s. of
his God. 21:12
keeping charge of the s. *Num* 3:28
Aaron keeping charge of the s. 38
they minister in the s. 4:12
an end of covering the s. 15
the service of s. belonging. 7:9
Israel come nigh to the s. 8:19
set forward, bearing the s. 10:21
bear the iniquity of the s. 18:1
not come nigh the vessels of the s. 3
shall keep the charge of the s. 5
because he hath defiled the s. 19:20
a great stone by the s. *Josh* 24:26
instruments of the s. *1 Chr* 9:29
arise, and build ye the s. of. 22:19
for the governors of the s. 24:5
build an house for the s. 28:10
built thee a s. therein. *2 Chr* 20:8
go out of the s. for thou. 26:18
for a sin offering for the s. and. 29:21
to Lord, and enter into his s. 30:8
to the purification of the s. 19
Babylon slew men in the s. 36:17
the vessels of the s. *Neh* 10:39
send thee help from the s. *Ps* 20:2
as I have seen thee in the s. 63:2
seen thy goings in the s. 68:24
till I went into the s. of God. 73:17
enemy hath done wickedly in s. 74:3
they have cast fire into thy s. 7
thy way, O God, is in the s. 77:13
to the border of his s. 78:54
built his s. like high palaces. 69
strength and beauty are in his s. 96:6
from the height of his s. 102:19
Judah was his s., Israel his. 114:2
lift up your hands in the s. 134:2
Lord, praise God in his s. 150:1
hosts, he shall be for a s. *Isa* 8:14
that he shall come to his s. to. 16:12
profaned the princes of the s. 43:28
to beautify the place of my s. 60:13
trodden down thy s. 63:18
is the place of our s. *Jer* 17:12
entered into her s. *Lam* 1:10
the Lord hath abhorred his s. 2:7
prophet be slain in the s.? 20
stones of the s. are poured. 4:1
thou hast defiled my s. *Ezek* 5:11
will I be to them as a little s. 11:16
defiled my s. in the same day. 23:38
day into my s. to profane it. 39
between s. and the profane. 42:20*
with every going forth of the s. 44:5
day that he goeth into the s. 27
in it shall be the s. and most. 45:3
they issued out of the s. 47:12
s. shall be in the midst. 48:8, 10, 21
and the place of his s. *Dan* 8:11
to give the s. to be trodden. 13
he said to me, then shall the s. 14
face to shine upon thy s. 9:17
destroy the city and the s. 26
they shall pollute the s. 11:31

have polluted the s. *Zeph* 3:4
a minister of the s. and. *Heb* 8:2
covenant had a worldly s. 9:1
tabernacle which is called the s. 2*
blood is brought into the s. 13:11*

sand
(*The word is frequently used in the Bible as a symbol of uncounted multitudes, or a weight impossible to measure*)
seed as the s. *Gen* 22:17; 32:12
gathered corn as the s. of. 41:49
hid the Egyptian in the s. *Ex* 2:12
treasures hid in s. *Deut* 33:19
much people as the s. *Josh* 11:4
as the s. by the sea. *Judg* 7:12
gathered to fight as the s. *1 Sam* 13:5
all Israel be gathered as the s.
2 Sam 17:11
are many, as the s. *1 Ki* 4:20
largeness of heart as the s. 29
be heavier than the s. *Job* 6:3
multiply my days as the s. 29:18
fowls like as the s. *Ps* 78:27
in number than the s. 139:18
a stone is heavy, and the s. *Pr* 27:3
Israel be as the s. *Isa* 10:22
thy seed also had been as s. 48:19
which placed the s. for. *Jer* 5:22
increased to me above the s. 15:8
as the s. of the sea, cannot. 33:22
shall be as the s. of the sea.
Hos 1:10; *Rom* 9:27
the captivity as the s. *Hab* 1:9
built his house on s. *Mat* 7:26
of one, so many as the s. *Heb* 11:12
I stood upon the s. of the. *Rev* 13:1
the number of whom is as the s. 20:8

sandals
(*At first were only soles tied to the feet with strings or thongs; afterwards they were covered; and at last even shoes were called* Sandals)
but be shod with s. put. *Mark* 6:9
thyself, and bind thy s. *Acts* 12:8

sang
then s. Moses and Israel. *Ex* 15:1
Israel s. this song. *Num* 21:17
then s. Deborah and. *Judg* 5:1
David of whom they s.? *1 Sam* 29:5
the singers s. the. *2 Chr* 29:28
s. praises with gladness, and. 30
the singers s. aloud. *Neh* 12:42
when the morning stars s. *Job* 38:7
his word, s. his praise. *Ps* 106:12
Silas s. praises to God. *Acts* 16:25

sank
they s. into the bottom. *Ex* 15:5
they s. as lead in the mighty. 10

sap
the trees are full of s. *Ps* 104:16*

Saphir
thou inhabitant of S. *Mi* 1:11

Sapphira
Ananias, with S. his wife. *Acts* 5:1

sapphire
(*A precious stone of a bright blue colour. It is thought to mean lapis lazuli rather than our modern* sapphire)
paved work of s. stone. *Ex* 24:10
a s. a diamond. 28:18; 39:11
be valued with onyx or s. *Job* 28:16
their polishing was of s. *Lam* 4:7
as appearance of s. *Ezek* 1:26
over them as it were a s. 10:1
the s. and the emerald were. 28:13
of the wall was a s. *Rev* 21:19

sapphires
of it are the place of s. *Job* 28:6
ivory overlaid with s. *S of S* 5:14
foundations with s. *Isa* 54:11

Sarah
not Sarai, but S. shall. *Gen* 17:15
S. thy wife shall bear. 19; 18:14
where is S. thy wife? 18:9
it ceased to be with S. after. 11
S. laughed. 12
wherefore did S. laugh? 13

Abraham said of S. She. *Gen* 20:2
Abimelech restored S. 14
because of S. 18
the Lord did unto S. as he. 21:1
S. should have given children. 7
in all that S. said to thee. 12
years of the life of S. 127. 23:1
S. died. 2
Abraham buried S. his wife. 19
into his mother S.'s tent. 24:67
Abraham buried, and S.25:10; 49:31
daughter of Asher was S. *Num* 26:46
look to Abraham and to S. *Isa* 51:2
deadness of S.'s womb. *Rom* 4:19
at this time I will come, S. 9:9
through faith S. received strength.
Heb 11:11
as S. obeyed Abraham. *1 Pet* 3:6

Sarai
Abraham's wife was S. *Gen* 11:29
but S. was barren, she. 30; 16:1
Pharaoh because of S. 12:17
when S. dealt hardly with. 16:6
from the face of my mistress S. 8
thou shalt not call her name S. 17:15

sardine or **sardius**
(*Probably carnelian*)
shall be a s. *Ex* 28:17; 39:10
the s. and diamond. *Ezek* 28:13
he that sat was to look upon like a s.
stone. *Rev* 4:3
of the wall was a s. 21:20

Sardis
write and send it to S. and. *Rev* 1:11
of the church in S. write. 3:1
a few names in S. which have not. 4

sardonyx
(*A* Sardius *united to an* Onyx)
wall of the city was a s. *Rev* 21:20

Sarepta
save to S. a city of Sidon.
Luke 4:26; *1 Ki* 17:9

Saron
and all that dwelt at S. *Acts* 9:35

Saruch
Nachor, the son of S. *Luke* 3:35

sat
Rachel had taken and s. *Gen* 31:34
Tamar, covered with a vail. s. 38:14
that s. on his throne. *Ex* 12:29
when we s. by the flesh pots. 16:3
on the morrow Moses s. 18:13
they wept and s. before. *Judg* 20:26
now Eli s. on a seat by. *1 Sam* 1:9
Eli s. on a seat by the wayside. 4:13
as soon as he s. on his. *1 Ki* 16:11
the children of Belial s. before. 21:13
the two kings s. each on his. 22:10
but Elisha s. in his house, and elders
s. with him, and the. *2 Ki* 6:32
as David s. in his house. *1 Chr* 17:1
David s. before the Lord. 16
made booths, and s. *Neh* 8:17
their way, and s. chief. *Job* 29:25
I have not s. with vain. *Ps* 26:4
in the ways hast thou s. *Jer* 3:2
I s. not in the assembly of the
mockers nor rejoiced; I s. 15:17
s. in the winterhouse. 36:22
I s. where they s. *Ezek* 3:15
as I s. in my house, the elders s. 8:1
s. women weeping for Tammuz. 14
enquire of the Lord, and s. 20:1
but Daniel s. in the gate. *Dan* 2:49
people who s. in darkness saw great
light; to them that s. *Mat* 4:16
for them which s. with him. 14:9
Mark 6:26
I s. daily with you teaching in the.
Mat 26:55
Peter s. with the servants, to see. 58
blind Bartimaeus s. by. *Mark* 10:46
Luke 18:35; *John* 9:8
and he s. on the right. *Mark* 16:19
he that was dead s. up. *Luke* 7:15
Mary s. at Jesus' feet, and. 10:39
a colt whereon never man s. 19:30
Mark 11:2
Jesus, wearied, s. thus. *John* 4:6
cloven tongues s. upon. *Acts* 2:3
he who s. for alms at the. 3:10

he that *s*. on the throne. *Rev* 4:3
on the cloud one *s*. like the. 14:14
he that *s*. upon him was called. 19:11
make war against him that *s*. 19

sat *down*
the people *s. down* to. *Ex* 32:6
and they *s. down* at thy. *Deut* 33:3
and *s. down* astonied. *Ezra* 9:3
they *s. down* to examine the. 10:16
I *s. down* and mourned. *Neh* 1:4
king and Haman *s. down. Esth* 3:15
Job *s. down* among ashes. *Job* 2:8
there we *s. down*, yea. *Ps* 137:1
s. down under his shadow. *S of S* 2:3
and *s. down* with him. *Mat* 9:10
he *s. down* with the twelve. 20:20
                         Luke 22:14
minister, and *s. down*. *Luke* 14:10
s. down and taught the people. 5:3
people came, he *s. down. John* 8:2
synagogue and *s. down. Acts* 13:14
we *s. down* and spake to the. 16:13
s. down on right. *Heb* 1:3; 10:12

Satan
*A Hebrew word, signifying an
adversary, an enemy, an accuser.
Most commonly Satan is taken for
the Devil, or chief of the evil
spirits. It is also used for those
adversaries of Christianity who
seemed filled with some malignant
spirit in their persecution of the
Church,* Mat 12:26; Rev 20:2.
S. provoked David to. *1 Chr* 21:1
and *S*. came also. *Job* 1:6; 2:1
S., Whence comest thou? 1:7; 2:2
S., Hast thou considered? 1:8; 2:3
S. went out from the presence. 1:12
S., Behold, he is in thine. 2:6
so went *S*. forth from. 2:7
and let *S*. stand at his. *Ps* 109:6*
S. standing at his right. *Zech* 3:1
S., The Lord rebuke thee, O *S*. 2
him, Get thee hence, *S*. *Mat* 4:10
if *S*. cast out *S*. 12:26; *Mark* 3:23
             26; *Luke* 11:18
get thee behind me, *S*. *Mat* 16:23
             Mark 8:33; *Luke* 4:8
he was tempted of *S*. *Mark* 1:13
S. cometh and taketh. 4:15
I beheld *S*. as lightning. *Luke* 10:18
whom *S*. hath bound these. 13:16
entered *S*. into Judas Iscariot. 22:3
Simon, Simon, *S*. hath desired. 31
the sop, *S*. entered. *John* 13:27
why hath *S*. filled thine? *Acts* 5:3
from the power of *S*. to God. 26:18
God shall bruise *S*. under. *Rom* 16:20
one to *S*., that the spirit. *1 Cor* 5:5
that *S*. tempt you not for your. 7:5
lest *S*. should get an. *2 Cor* 2:11
S. himself is transformed. 11:14
given to me, the messenger of *S*. 12:7
come, but *S*. hindered. *1 Thes* 2:18
after the working of *S*. *2 Thes* 2:9
have delivered unto *S*. *1 Tim* 1:20
already turned aside after *S*. 5:15
but the synagogue of *S*. *Rev* 2:9
where Satan's seat is: where *S*. 13
not known the depths of *S*. 24
of the synagogue of *S*. 3:9
dragon was cast out, called *S*. 12:9
on the dragon, which is *S*. 20:2
S. shall be loosed out of his. 7

satest
thou *s*. in the throne. *Ps* 9:4
s. upon a stately bed. *Ezek* 23:41

satiate
I will *s*. soul of the priests. *Jer* 31:14
the sword shall be *s*. with. 46:10

satiated
I have *s*. the weary soul. *Jer* 31:25

satisfaction
shall take no *s*. for life. *Num* 35:31*
take no *s*. for him that is fled. 32*

satisfy
to *s*. the desolate and. *Job* 38:27
O *s*. us early with thy. *Ps* 90:14
with long life will I *s*. him. 91:16
I will *s*. her poor with bread. 132:15
let her breasts *s*. thee at. *Pr* 5:19
if he steal to *s*. his soul when. 6:30

if thou *s*. the afflicted. *Isa* 58:10
Lord shall guide and *s*. thy soul. 11
they shall not *s*. their. *Ezek* 7:19
whence can a man *s*.? *Mark* 8:4

satisfied
shall be *s*. upon them. *Ex* 15:9
shall eat and not be *s*. *Lev* 26:26
shall eat and be *s*. *Deut* 14:29
O Naphtali, *s*. with favour. 33:23
and why are ye not *s*.? *Job* 19:22
his offspring shall not be *s*. 27:14
of his flesh! we cannot be *s*. 31:31
I shall be *s*., when I awake. *Ps* 17:15
the meek shall eat and be *s*. 22:26
they shall be *s*. with the. 36:8
famine they shall be *s*. 37:19
grudge if they be not *s*. 59:15
my soul shall be *s*. as with. 63:5
we shall be *s*. with the. 65:4
of rock should I have *s*. thee. 81:16
the earth is *s*. with the fruit. 104:13
he *s*. them with the bread. 105:40
his land shall be *s*. *Pr* 12:11*
a man shall be *s*. with good by. 14
and a good man shall be *s*. 14:14
a man's belly be *s*. with. 18:20*
he that hath it shall abide *s*. 19:23
eyes, and thou shalt be *s*. 20:13
things that are never *s*. 30:15
the eye is not *s*. with. *Eccl* 1:8
neither is his eye *s*. with riches. 4:8
that loveth silver, shall not be *s*.5:10
eat and not be *s*. *Isa* 9:20; *Mi* 6:14
he roasteth roast and is *s*. *Isa* 44:16
of travail of his soul, and be *s*. 53:11
be *s*. with the breasts of her. 66:11
my people shall be *s*. *Jer* 31:14
spoil Chaldea shall be *s*. 50:10
his soul shall be *s*. on mount. 19
hand to Egyptians, to be *s*. *Lam* 5:6
couldest not be *s*. *Ezek* 16:28, 29
drink water, but were not *s*. *Amos* 4:8
death, and cannot be *s*. *Hab* 2:5

satisfiest
and thou *s*. the desire. *Ps* 145:16

satisfieth
who *s*. thy mouth with. *Ps* 103:5
for he *s*. the longing soul. 107:9
labour for that which *s*. not. *Isa* 55:2

satisfying
the righteous eateth to *s*. *Pr* 13:26
not in any honour to the *s*. *Col* 2:23*

satyr
and the *s*. shall cry to. *Isa* 34:14†

satyrs
dwell there, and *s*. dance. *Isa* 13:21†

Saul, *first king of Israel*
S. of Rehoboth reigned. *Gen* 36:37
S. died. 38
Kish had a son, whose name was *S*.
                  1 Sam 9:2; 14:51
Samuel a day before *S*. came. 9:15
when Samuel saw *S*. 17
S. drew near to Samuel. 18
set it before *S*., so *S*. did eat. 24
is *S*. also among the prophets?
                  10:11, 12; 19:24
S. was taken. 10:21
Spirit of God came upon *S*. 11:6
cometh not forth after *S*. and. 7
shall *S*. reign over us? 12
to Gilgal, there they made *S*. 15
S. blew the trumpet. 13:3
as for *S*. he was yet in Gilgal and. 7
S. went out to meet Samuel. 10
S. numbered the people. 15
for *S*. had adjured the people. 14:24
S. built an altar. 35
S. asked counsel of God. 37
S. went up from following the. 46
when *S*. saw any strong man, he. 52
me that I have set up *S*. 15:11
Samuel turned again after *S*. 31
Samuel came no more to see *S*. 35
long wilt thou mourn for *S*.? 16:1
if *S*. hear it. 2
Spirit of Lord departed from *S*. 14
the evil spirit from God was on *S*.
                  23; 18:10; 19:9
and you servants to *S*.? 17:8
for an old man in the days of *S*. 12
S. and all Israel were in the. 19

and *S*. armed David with his.
                  1 Sam 17:38
came out to meet king *S*. 18:6
S. eyed David from that day. 9
S. afraid; Lord departed from *S*. 12
when *S*. saw that he behaved. 15, 30
S. became David's enemy. 29
spake good of David to *S*. 19:4
Jonathan brought David to *S*. 7
S. sent messengers. 11, 14, 15, 20
Abner sat by *S*.'s side. 20:25
S. cast a javelin. 33
fled that day for fear of *S*. 21:10
saying, *S*. hath slain his. 11; 29:5
that he would surely tell *S*. 22:22
will *S*. come down as thy? 23:11
shall be king, and that *S*. my. 17
S. returned from pursuing after. 28
David cut off the skirt of *S*. 24:4
them not to rise against *S*. 7
David cried after *S*. 8
David sware to *S*. 22
David understood *S*. was. 26:4
beheld the place where *S*. lay. 5
behold, *S*. lay sleeping within. 7
S. knew David's voice. 17
S. returned. 25
one day by the hand of *S*. 27:1
behold, thou knowest what *S*. 28:9
S. sware to her by the Lord. 10
for thou art *S*. 12
S. fell straightway all along. 20
not this David servant of *S*? 29:3
Philistines followed hard upon *S*.
                  31:2; *1 Chr* 10:2
that *S*. and his sons were dead.
                  1 Sam 31:7; *1 Chr* 10:7
what the Philistines had done to *S*.
                  1 Sam 31:11; *1 Chr* 10:11
S. leaned on his spear. *2 Sam* 1:6
the shield of *S*. 21
of Israel, weep over *S*. 24
be ye valiant, for your master *S*. 2:7
the house of *S*. waxed weaker. 3:1
to translate the kingdom from house
  of *S*. and to set. 10; *1 Chr* 12:23
tidings saying, *S* is dead. *2 Sam* 4:10
when *S*. was king. 5:2; *1 Chr* 11:2
my mercy shall not depart, as I took
  it from *S*. *2 Sam* 7:15
any left of the house of *S*.? 9:1, 3
all the land of *S*. thy father. 7
out of the hand of *S*. 12:7; 22:1
blood of the house of *S*. 16:8
for *S*. and for his bloody. 21:1
will have no silver nor gold of *S*. 4
David took the bones of *S*. 12
in the days of *S*. they. *1 Chr* 5:10
S. died for his transgression. 10:13
himself close because of *S*. 12:1
enquired not at it in the days of *S*.13:3
all that Samuel and *S*. had. 26:28
Gibeah of *S*. is fled. *Isa* 10:29
God gave unto them *S*. *Acts* 13:21

see Jonathan

Saul (Paul)
feet, whose name was *S*. *Acts* 7:58
and *S*. was consenting unto. 8:1
as for *S*. he made havoc of the. 3
S. *S*. why persecutest thou me?
                  9:4; 22:7; 26:14
enquire for one called *S*. of. 9:11
brother *S*. the Lord hath. 17; 22:13
but *S*. increased more in. 9:22
laying wait was known of *S*. 24
S. was come to Jerusalem. 26
went to Tarsus to seek *S*. 11:25
the hands of Barnabas and *S*. 30
prophets brought up with *S*. 13:1
separate me Barnabas and *S*. 2
called for Barnabas and *S*. 7
S. set his eyes on him, and said. 9

save
[1] *To preserve from danger*. [2]
*To deliver from sin and its conse-
quences.*
God sent me before you to *s*.
                  Gen 45:7
goeth with you to *s*. you. *Deut* 20:4
there was none to *s*. her. 22:27
and no man shall *s*. thee. 28:29
thou shalt *s*. Israel. *Judg* 6:14
O my Lord, wherewith shall I *s*.? 15

for Baal ? will ye *s.* him ? *Judg* 6:31
thou wilt *s.* Israel by mine. 36
know that thou wilt *s.* Israel. 37
that lapped will I *s.* you. 7:7
anoint him, that he may *s.* my.
1 *Sam* 9:16
people shouted and said, God *s.* the
king. 10:24†; 2 *Sam* 16:16†
2 *Ki* 11:12†; 2 *Chr* 23:11
restraint, to *s.* by many. 1 *Sam* 14:6
if thou *s.* not thyself this. 19:11
David, go and *s.* Keilah. 23:2
of David I will *s.* Israel. 2 *Sam* 3:18
the afflicted people thou wilt *s.*
22:28; *Ps* 18:27
but there was none to *s.* them.
2 *Sam* 22:42; *Ps* 18:41
that thou mayest *s.* 1 *Ki* 1:12
behold they say, God *s.* king. 25†
God *s.* king Solomon. 34†, 39†
king, peradventure he will *s.* thy life.
20:31
for I will defend this city to *s.* it, for.
2 *Ki* 19:34; *Isa* 37:35
temple to *s.* his life. *Neh* 6:11
thine hand, but *s.* his life. *Job* 2:6
he shall not *s.* of that which. 20:20
and he shall *s.* the humble. 22:29
own right hand can *s.* thee. 40:14
s. Lord, let the king hear. *Ps* 20:9
s. thy people, feed them also. 28:9
Jer 31:7
he shall *s.* them, because. *Ps* 37:40
neither did their own arm *s.* 44:3
s. with thy right hand. 60:5; 108:6
for God will *s.* Zion, and. 69:35
he shall *s.* the children of the. 72:4
and he shall *s.* the souls of the. 13
when God arose to *s.* the meek. 76:9
O my God, *s.* thy servant that. 86:2
and *s.* the son of thine handmaid. 16
s. him from those that. 109:31
s. I beseech thee, O Lord. 118:25
hear their cry, and *s.* them. 145:19
and he shall *s.* thee. *Pr* 20:22
God will come and *s.* you. *Isa* 35:4
unto a god that cannot *s.* 45:20
he cannot answer, nor *s.* him. 46:7
astrologers stand up and *s.* 47:13
wander, none shall *s.* thee. 15
thus saith the Lord, I will *s.* 49:25
shortened, that it cannot *s.* 59:1
righteousness, mighty to *s.* 63:1
arise, if they can *s.* thee. *Jer* 2:28
but they shall not *s.* them at. 11:12
mighty man that cannot *s.* 14:9
for I am with thee to *s.* thee. 15:20
30:11; 42:11; 46:27
O Israel, I will *s.* thee from. 30:10
flee, *s.* your lives, be like the. 48:6
to warn the wicked, to *s. Ezek* 3:18
therefore will I *s.* my flock. 34:22
I will *s.* you. 36:29
I will *s.* them. 37:23
I will *s.* them by the Lord their God,
and will not *s.* them by. *Hos* 1:7
any other that may *s.* thee ? 13:10
of violence, and thou wilt not *s.*
Hab 1:2
he will *s.*, he will rejoice. *Zeph* 3:17
I will *s.* her that halteth, and. 19
I will *s.* my people from. *Zech* 8:7
Lord their God shall *s.* them. 9:16
will *s.* the house of Joseph. 10:6
the Lord also shall *s.* the tents. 12:7
Jesus, shall *s.* his people. *Mat* 1:21
for whosoever will *s.* his life. 16:25
Mark 8:35; *Luke* 9:24; 17:33
for the Son of man is come to *s.*
Mat 18:11; *Luke* 19:10
the temple, and buildest it in three
days, *s. Mat* 27:40; *Mark* 15:30
saved others, himself he cannot *s.*
Mat 27:42; *Mark* 15:31
Elias will come to *s.* *Mat* 27:49
is it lawful to *s.* life or to kill ?
Mark 3:4; *Luke* 6:9
Son of man is not come to destroy
men's lives, but to *s.* *Luke* 9:56
s. himself, if he be Christ. 23:35
s. thyself. 37
if Christ, *s.* thyself and us. 39
but to *s.* the world. *John* 12:47
s. yourselves from this. *Acts* 2:40

willing to *s.* Paul. *Acts* 27:43
if I might *s.* some of them.
Rom 11:14; 1 *Cor* 9:22
preaching to *s.* them. 1 *Cor* 1:21
s. thy husband, shalt *s.* thy. 7:16
the world to *s.* sinners. 1 *Tim* 1:15
in doing this thou shalt *s.* 4:16
to him that was able to *s. Heb* 5:7
he is able to *s.* them to the. 7:25
word, which is able to *s. Jas* 1:21
works, can faith *s.* him ? 2:14
one lawgiver, who is able to *s.* 4:12
the prayer of faith shall *s.* the. 5:15
shall *s.* a soul from death, and. 20
others *s.* with fear, pulling. *Jude* 23

see **alive**

save me

s. me out of the hand. 2 *Ki* 16:7
arise, O Lord, *s. me.* *Ps* 3:7
s. me for thy mercies' sake. 6:4
31:16; 109:26
s. me from all them that. 7:1
s. me from the lion's mouth. 22:21
house of defence to *s. me.* 31:2
nor shall my sword *s. me.* 44:6
s. me, O God, by thy name. 54:1
and the Lord shall *s. me.* 55:16
from heaven and, *s. me* from. 57:3
deliver me, and *s. me* from. 59:2
s. me, for waters are come in. 69:1
thine ear unto me, and *s. me.* 71:2
commandment to *s. me.* 3
s. me, for I have sought. 119:94
I cried unto thee, *s. me*, and. 146
thy right hand shall *s. me.* 138:7
Lord was ready to *s. me. Isa* 38:20
O Lord, *s. me*, and I shall. *Jer* 17:14
saying, Lord *s. me.* *Mat* 14:30
Father, *s. me* from this. *John* 12:27

save us

to us quickly, and *s. us. Josh* 10:6
if it be in rebellion, *s. us.* not. 22:22
the ark may *s. us* from. 1 *Sam* 4:3
to the Lord, that he will *s. us.* 7:8
how shall this man *s. us* ? 10:27
if there be no man to *s. us.* 11:3
s. thou us out of his hand.
2 *Ki* 19:19; *Isa* 37:20
s. us, O God of our. 1 *Chr* 16:35
stir up thy strength, and come and *s.*
us. *Ps* 80:2
s. us, O Lord our God. 106:47
for him, he will *s. us.* *Isa* 25:9
is our king, he will *s. us.* 33:22
trouble they will say, *s. us. Jer* 2:27
nation that could not *s. us. Lam* 4:17
Asher shall not *s. us.* *Hos* 14:3
saying, Lord *s. us.* *Mat* 8:25
doth also now *s. us.* 1 *Pet* 3:21

save, for except

s. what the young men. *Gen* 14:24
he knew not aught, *s.* the. 39:6
s. that which every man. *Ex* 12:16
any god, *s.* to the Lord. 22:20
s. Caleb. *Num* 14:30; 26:65
32:12; *Deut* 1:36
s. when there shall be no poor.
Deut 15:4
none, *s.* Hazor only. *Josh* 11:13
peace with Israel, *s.* the Hivite. 19
part to the Levites, *s.* cities. 14:4
there is nothing else, *s.* the sword of
Gideon. *Judg* 7:14
there is none other, *s.* 1 *Sam* 21:9
there escaped none, *s.* 400. 30:17
s. to every man his wife and. 22
poor man had nothing, *s.* one little
ewe lamb. 2 *Sam* 12:3
who is God, *s.* the Lord ? 22:32
Ps 18:31
in the house, *s.* we two. 1 *Ki* 3:18
in the ark *s.* the two tables. 8:9
s. in the matter of Uriah the. 15:5
fight not, *s.* with the king of. 22:31
anything, *s.* a pot of oil. 2 *Ki* 4:2
s. that the high places were. 2 *Chr* 5:2
s. only to burn sacrifice. 2 *Chr* 2:6
no son left, *s.* Jehoahaz the. 21:17
nor any with me, *s.* the. *Neh* 2:12
ask a petition, *s.* of thee, O king.
Dan 6:7, 12
any the Father, *s.* Son. *Mat* 11:27
not without honour, *s.* in his. 13:57

they saw no man, *s.* Jesus only.
Mat 17:8; *Mark* 9:8
cannot receive, *s.* they. *Mat* 19:11
no man to follow him, *s.* Peter,
James. *Mark* 5:37; *Luke* 8:51
s. that he laid his hands. *Mark* 6:5
take nothing, *s.* a staff only. 8
sent, *s.* unto Sarepta, a. *Luke* 4:26
returned, *s.* this stranger. 17:18
good *s.* one, that is God. 18:19
other boat, *s.* that one. *John* 6:22
hath seen the Father, *s.* he. 46
he needeth not, *s.* to. 13:10
s. that the Holy Ghost. *Acts* 20:23
s. to keep themselves from. 21:25
any thing, *s.* Jesus Christ. 1 *Cor* 2:2
s. the spirit of man which is in. 11
I forty stripes *s.* one. 2 *Cor* 11:24
I saw none, *s.* James. *Gal* 1:19
glory, *s.* in the cross. 6:14
buy or sell, *s.* he that. *Rev* 13:17

saved

they said, Thou hast *s.* *Gen* 47:25
midwives *s.* the men. *Ex* 1:17, 18
I had slain thee, and *s. Num* 22:33
Moses said, Have ye *s.* all? 31:15
Joshua *s.* Rahab the. *Josh* 6:25
mine own hand hath *s.* me. *Judg* 7:2
if he had *s.* them alive, I would. 8:19
wives which they had *s.* 21:14
David *s.* the inhabitants. 1 *Sam* 23:5
David *s.* neither man nor. 27:11
this day have *s.* thy life. 2 *Sam* 19:5
the king *s.* us, and now he is fled. 9
s. himself there, not. 2 *Ki* 6:10
saviours, who *s.* them. *Neh* 9:27
no king is *s.* by multitude. *Ps* 33:16
but thou hast *s.* us from our. 44:7
nevertheless, he *s.* them. 106:8
he *s.* them from that hated. 10
I have declared, and have *s.* and.
Isa 43:12
Look unto me, and be ye *s.* 45:22
that thou mayest be *s.* *Jer* 14:14
summer ended, and we are not *s.*8:20
Who then can be *s.*? *Mat* 19:25
Mark 10:26; *Luke* 18:26
no flesh should be *s.* *Mat* 24:22
Mark 13:20
he *s.* others. *Mat* 27:42
Mark 15:31; *Luke* 23:35
that we should be *s.* *Luke* 1:71
Thy faith hath *s.* thee. 7:50; 18:42
should believe and be *s.* 8:12
Lord, are there few that be *s.*? 13:23
through him, might be *s. John* 3:17
I say, that ye might be *s.* 5:34
added such as should be *s. Acts* 2:47
name whereby we must be *s.* 4:12
circumcised, ye cannot be *s.* 15:1
what must I do to be *s.*? 16:30
all hope we should be *s.* 27:20
in the ship, ye cannot be *s.* 31
we are *s.* by hope. *Rom* 8:24
that they may be *s.* 10:1
to us who are *s.* it is the. 1 *Cor* 1:18
that the spirit may be *s.* in day. 5:5
many, that they may be *s.* 10:33
by which also ye are *s.* if ye. 15:2
savour in them that are *s.* 2 *Cor* 2:15
with Christ, by grace are *s. Eph* 2:5
for by grace are ye *s.* through. 8
that they might be *s.* 1 *Thes* 2:16
received not the love of the truth, that
they might be *s.* 2 *Thes* 2:10
will have all men to be *s.* 1 *Tim* 2:4
to his mercy he *s.* us. *Tit* 3:5
wherein eight souls were *s.* by.
1 *Pet* 3:20
if the righteous scarcely be *s.* 4:18
s. Noah, the 8th person. 2 *Pet* 2:5
nations *s.* shall walk in. *Rev* 21:24

God or Lord saved

Lord *s.* Israel that day. *Ex* 14:30
1 *Sam* 14:23
O people, *s.* by Lord ? *Deut* 33:29
rejected your God, who *s.* you.
1 *Sam* 10:19
Lord *s.* them by hand. 2 *Ki* 14:27
Lord *s.* them by a great. 2 *Ki* 11:14
thus Lord *s.* Hezekiah. 2 *Chr* 32:22
Lord *s.* him out of all his. *Ps* 34:6
the Lord *s.* them out of their. 107:13

saved

angel of his presence s. *Isa* 63:9
God who hath s. us and. *2 Tim* 1:9
how that the *Lord*, having s. the.
 Jude 5

shall be **saved**

ye *shall* be s. from your enemies.
 Num 10:9
I *shall* be s. from mine enemies.
 2 Sam 22:4; *Ps* 18:3
cause thy face to shine, we *shall* be s.
 Ps 80:3, 7, 19
uprightly *shall* be s. *Pr* 28:18
and rest *shall* ye be s. *Isa* 30:15
but Israel *shall* be s. in Lord. 45:17
continuance, and we *shall* be s. 64:5
save me, and I *shall* be s. *Jer* 17:14
Judah *shall* be s. 23:6; 33:16
Jacob's trouble; but he *shall* be s.
 30:7
endureth to the end *shall* be s.
 Mat 10:22; 24:13; *Mark* 13:13
that believeth *shall* be s. *Mark* 16:16
man enter, he *shall* be s. *John* 10:9
call on name of the Lord, *shall* be s.
 Acts 2:21; *Rom* 10:13
thy house *shall* be s. *Acts* 11:14
through grace we *shall* be s. 15:11
Jesus, and thou *shalt* be s. 16:31
shall be s. from wrath. *Rom* 5:9
being reconciled, we *shall* be s. 10
sand, a remnant *shall* be s. 9:27
raised him, thou *shalt* be s. 10:9
so all Israel *shall* be s. as it is. 11:26
but he himself *shall* be s. *1 Cor* 3:15
shall be s. in childbearing, if.
 1 Tim 2:15

savest

my Saviour, thou s. *2 Sam* 22:3
how s. thou the arm that? *Job* 26:2
O thou that s. by thy right. *Ps* 17:7

saveth

liveth, who s. Israel. *1 Sam* 14:39
the Lord s. not with sword. 17:47
but he s. the poor from. *Job* 5:15
God, who s. the upright. *Ps* 7:10
now know I that the Lord s. 20:6
he s. such as be of a contrite. 34:18
they cry, he s. them out of. 107:19

saving

shewed me in s. my life. *Gen* 19:19
s. that every one put. *Neh* 4:23
with the s. strength of. *Ps* 20:6
he is the s. strength of his. 28:8
thy s. health among all nations. 67:2
s. the beholding of them. *Eccl* 5:11
s. that I will not utterly. *Amos* 9:8
s. for the cause of. *Mat* 5:32
cleansed, s. Naaman. *Luke* 4:27
believe to s. of the soul. *Heb* 10:39
Noah prepared an ark to the s. 11:7
no man knoweth, s. he. *Rev* 2:17

saviour

(*In general used for any one who
saves. In the New Testament
especially it refers nearly always to
our Lord and Saviour Jesus Christ*)
my refuge, my s. *2 Sam* 22:3
Lord gave Israel a s. *2 Ki* 13:5
they forgat God their s. *Ps* 106:21
he shall send them a s. *Isa* 19:20
Holy One of Israel thy s. 43:3
beside me there is no s. 11
O God of Israel, the s. 45:15
a just God and a s.; there is. 21
know that I am thy s. 49:26
that I the Lord am thy s. 60:16
people, so he was their s. 63:8
the s. of Israel in time. *Jer* 14:8
for there is no s. beside. *Hos* 13:4
rejoiced in God my s. *Luke* 1:47
in the city of David a s. 2:11
this is Christ the s. of. *John* 4:42
to be a prince and s. *Acts* 5:31
raised unto Israel a s., Jesus. 13:23
and Christ is the s. of the. *Eph* 5:23
whence we look for the s. *Phil* 3:20
by the commandment of God our s.
 1 Tim 1:1
in the sight of God our s. 2:3
God, who is the s. of all men. 4:10
the appearing of our s. *2 Tim* 1:10
to the commandment of God our s.
 Tit 1:3

the Lord Jesus Christ our s. *Tit* 1:4
the doctrine of God our s. 2:10
glorious appearing of our s. 13
after the kindness of God our s. 3:4
abundantly through Christ our s. 6
of God and our s. *2 Pet* 1:1
kingdom of our Lord and s. 11
knowledge of the Lord and s. 2:20
apostles of the Lord and s. 3:2
knowledge of our s. Christ. 18
sent the Son to be the s. *1 John* 4:14
to the only wise God our s. *Jude* 25

saviours

thou gavest them s. who. *Neh* 9:27
and s. shall come up on. *Ob* 21

savour

(*An odour or scent. Used frequently in a symbolic sense*)
ye have made our s. *Ex* 5:21
will not smell s. of. *Lev* 26:31
send forth a stinking s. *Eccl* 10:1*
because of the s. of thy. *S of S* 1:3
his stink and his ill s. *Joel* 2:20
if the salt have lost his s. *Mat* 5:13
 Luke 14:34
maketh manifest the s. *2 Cor* 2:14
the s. of death unto death, s. of. 16

sweet savour

Lord smelled a sweet s. *Gen* 8:21
it is a *sweet* s. an offering. *Ex* 29:18
Lev 1:9, 13, 17; 2:9; 3:5; 8:21
 Num 15:14; 18:17; 28:8
for a *sweet* s. an offering. *Ex* 29:25
 41; *Lev* 2:12; 3:16; 4:31; 6:15
 21; 8:28; 17:6; 23:13; *Num* 15:7
 24; 28:2, 6, 13, 27; 29:2, 6, 8
 Ezek 16:19
of *sweet* s. unto the Lord. *Lev* 23:18
 Num 28:24; 29:13, 36
to make a *sweet* s. *Num* 15:3
a burnt offering of a *sweet* s. 28:13
did offer *sweet* s. to their idols.
 Ezek 6:13
they made their *sweet* s. 20:28
accept you with your *sweet* s. 41
for we are to God a *sweet* s. of.
 2 Cor 2:15
for a *sweet*-smelling s. *Eph* 5:2*

savourest

thou s. not things of God.
 Mat 16:23*; *Mark* 8:33*

sweet savours

sacrifices of *sweet* s. *Ezra* 6:10

savoury

make me s. meat. *Gen* 27:4, 7, 14
Esau had made s. meat, and. 31

saw

the woman s. the tree was. *Gen* 3:6
sons of God s. the daughters. 6:2
Ham s. the nakedness of his. 9:22
they s. not their father's. 23
Abraham s. the place afar. 22:4
they said, We s. the Lord. 26:28
when he s. that he prevailed. 32:25
for she s. that Shelah was. 38:14
his master s. that the Lord. 39:3
in that we s. the anguish of. 42:21
when Joseph s. Benjamin. 43:16
when he s. the wagons which. 45:27
Issachar s. that rest was good. 49:15
his brethren s. that their. 50:15
Joseph s. Ephraim's children of. 23
when she s. that he was. *Ex* 2:2
when he s. that there was no. 12
they s. not one another for. 10:23
Israel s. that great work the. 14:31
they s. the God of Israel. 24:10, 11
all the people s. the cloudy. 33:10
we s. the children of. *Num* 13:28
ass s. the angel of Lord. 22:23, 27
and when Phinehas s. it he. 25:7
when they s. the land, they. 32:9
heard a voice, but s. no.*Deut* 4:12, 15
which thine eyes s. 7:19
all that s. it said, No. *Judg* 19:30
when she s. she was. *Ruth* 1:18
they s. the ark, and. *1 Sam* 6:13
when we s. they were no where.10:14
Israel, when they s. the man. 17:24
Saul s. that the Lord was. 18:28
David s. a woman. *2 Sam* 11:2

saw

s. that the wisdom of. *1 Ki* 3:28
when Zimri s. that the city. 16:18
when Ahab s. Elijah, he said. 18:17
when he s. that, he arose and. 19:3
Elisha s. it, and he s. *2 Ki* 2:12
s. the water on the other side. 3:22
man of God s. her afar off. 4:25
of the young man and he s. 6:17
he s. the oppression of Israel. 13:4
Ahaz s. an altar that was at. 16:10
they s. that the Lord. *2 Chr* 15:9
and they s. one another in. 25:21
when princes s. heaps, they. 31:8
when s. these things they. *Neh* 6:16
the princes which s. the. *Esth* 1:14
he s. that there was evil. 7:7
they s. that his grief was. *Job* 2:13
as infants which never s. light. 3:16
eye which s. him, shall see. 20:9
the young men s. me, and. 29:8
when the eye s. me, it gave. 11
they s. it, and so they. *Ps* 48:5
waters s. thee, O God, the waters s.
 77:16
your fathers proved me, and s. 95:9
the earth s. his lightnings and. 97:4
sea s. it and fled: Jordan. 114:3
s. ye him whom my soul loveth?
 S of S 3:3
isles s. it, and feared. *Isa* 41:5
sister Judah s. it. *Jer* 3:7
when Zedekiah s. them, and. 39:4
for then we were well, and s. 44:17
adversaries s. her and. *Lam* 1:7
I went in, and s. behold. *Ezek* 8:10
then they s. every high hill. 20:28
as soon as she s. them, she. 23:16
s. these men on whom. *Dan* 3:27
whereas the king s. a watcher. 4:23
the king s. part of the hand. 5:5
when Ephraim s. his sickness and
Judah s. his wound. *Hos* 5:13
who among you s. this house?
 Hag 2:3
the star which they s. *Mat* 2:9
s. the Spirit of God descending.
 3:16; *Mark* 1:10
dumb both spake and s. *Mat* 12:22
s. no man, save Jesus only. 17:8
husbandmen s. the son. 21:38
s. a man who had not on. 22:11
Lord, when s. we thee? 25:37, 44
when s. we thee a stranger? 38
when s. thee sick? 39
another maid s. him, and said. 26:71
 Mark 14:69; *Luke* 22:58
Judas, when he s. that he. *Mat* 27:3
they s. him they worshipped. 28:17
when Jesus s. their faith. *Mark* 2:5
he asked him, if he s. aught. 8:23
saying, Master, we s. one casting out
devils in thy. 9:38; *Luke* 9:49
when they s. what was. *Luke* 8:34
when the woman s. that she was. 47
when they were awake, they s. 9:32
his father s. him, and had. 15:20
one of them, when he s. he. 17:15
but him they s. not. 24:24
because ye s. miracles. *John* 6:26
Abraham s. my day, and was. 8:56
when he s. his glory. 12:41
that s. it, bare record. 19:35
disciples were glad when they s.
 20:20
when they s. the boldness. *Acts* 4:13
s. his face as it had been face. 6:15
Stephen s. the glory of God. 7:55
when Simon s. that Holy Ghost. 8:18
Philip, the eunuch s. him no more. 39
when his eyes were opened, he s. 9:8
all at Lydda s. him, and turned. 35
and when Tabitha s. Peter, she. 40
Cornelius s. a vision. 10:3
s. heaven opened. 11
and because he s. it pleased. 12:3
David s. corruption. 13:36
s. no corruption. 37
masters s. the hope of their. 16:19
he s. the city wholly given to. 17:16
they s. indeed the light and. 22:9
had looked, and s. no harm. 28:6
but when they s. that the gospel of the
uncircumcision. *Gal* 2:7
conflict which ye s. *Phil* 1:30

your fathers *s*. my works. *Heb* 3:9
s. he was a proper child.   11:23
record of all things he *s*. *Rev* 1:2
great fear fell on them who *s*. 11:11
when the dragon *s*. that he.   12:13
cried, when they *s*. smoke of. 18:18

saw, *substantive*
shall the *s*. magnify ?   *Isa* 10:15

saw joined with *Lord* or *God*
and *God s*. the light that. *Gen* 1:4
God called the dry land earth, and
   God s.   10, 12, 18, 21, 25, 31
God s. that the wickedness.   6:5
when the *Lord s*. that Leah. 29:31
when the *Lord s*. that he. *Ex* 3:4
when the *Lord s*. it, he. *Deut* 32:19
the *Lord s*. the affliction. *2 Ki* 14:26
when the *Lord s*. they. *2 Chr* 12:7
the *Lord s*. it, and it. *Isa* 59:15
Lord s. that there was no man. 16
God s. their works, that. *Jonah* 3:10
Lord s. her, he had compassion on.
              Luke 7:13

I saw
such as *I* never *s*. in Egypt for.
              Gen 41:19
one went out, and *I s*. him. 44:28
I s. among the spoils. *Josh* 7:21
I s. that he delivered. *Judg* 12:3
I s. the son of Jesse. *1 Sam* 22:9
I s. gods ascending out of the. 28:13
I s. Absalom hanged. *2 Sam* 18:10
I s. great tumult, but knew not. 29
I s. all Israel scattered. *1 Ki* 22:17
I s. the Lord on his throne.   19
              2 Chr 18:18
in those days *s*. *I* in Judah. *Neh* 13:15
I s. my help in the gate. *Job* 31:21
when *I s*. the prosperity. *Ps* 73:3
then *I s*. and considered. *Pr* 24:32
this also *I s*. from hand. *Eccl* 2:24
so *I s*. the wicked buried.   8:10
among whom *I s*. Jaazaniah son of.
              Ezek 11:1
took them away as *I s*. good. 16:50
then *I s*. that she was defiled. 23:13
I s. your fathers as the. .*Hos* 9:10
Ephraim, as *I s*. Tyrus, is.   13
I s. the Spirit descending. *John* 1:32
under the fig tree, *I s*. thee.   48
I s. in the way a light. *Acts* 26:13
the apostles *I s*. none. *Gal* 1:19
when *I s*. that they walked.   2:14
when *I s*. him, I fell at. *Rev* 1:17

sawed
costly stones *s*. with saws. *1 Ki* 7:9

sawest
what *s*. thou, that thou ? *Gen* 20:10
s. it and didst rejoice. *1 Sam* 19:5
afraid, for what *s*. thou ?   28:13
behold, thou *s*. him. *2 Sam* 18:11
when thou *s*. a thief. *Ps* 50:18
king, *s*. a great image. *Dan* 2:31
thou *s*. till that a stone grew. 34, 45
the tree thou *s*. which grew.   4:20
the ram which thou *s*. having. 8:20
seven stars thou *s*.; seven candlesticks thou *s*.   *Rev* 1:20
the beast that thou *s*. was.   17:8
the ten horns which thou *s*. 12, 16
waters thou *s*. where the whore.17:15
the woman which thou *s*. is that. 18

sawn
they were *s*. asunder. *Heb* 11:37

saws
he put Ammonites under *s*.
   2 Sam 12:31; *1 Chr* 20:3

say
lest thou shouldest *s*. *Gen* 14:23
what ye shall *s*. to me. 34:11, 12
for I heard them *s*. Let us. 37:17
we will *s*. Some evil beast hath. 20
I have heard *s*. that thou. 41:15
Judah said, What shall we *s*.? 44:16
so shall ye *s*. to Joseph, Forgive, I.
              50:17
thou *s*. unto the children of Israel, I
  AM hath. *Ex* 3:14,15; 19:3; 20:22
teach you what thou shalt *s*.   4:12
when your children shall *s*. 12:26
Pharaoh will *s*. of the children. 14:3
if the servant shall *s*. I love. 21:5

woman shall *s*. Amen.   *Num* 5:22
that thou shouldest *s*. to me. 11:12
know what the Lord will *s*. 22:19
have I now any power at all to *s*.? 38
the Lord our God shall *s*. *Deut* 5:27
then thou shalt *s*. to thy son. 6:21
of whom thou hast heard *s*. 9:2
thou shalt *s*., and at even *s*. 28:67
so that they will *s*. in that. 31:17
lest they should *s*. Our hand. 32:27
your children may not *s*. *Josh* 22:27
when they should *s*. to us in time. 28
shalt hear what they *s*. *Judg* 7:11
canst thou *s*. I love thee ? 16:15
is this ye *s*. to me, What ? 18:24
in all they *s*. unto thee. *1 Sam* 8:7
if they *s*. thus, Come up to us. 14:10
if he *s*. thus.   20:7
therefore thou shalt *s*. to my servant
  David.   *2 Sam* 7:8; *1 Chr* 7:21
he *s*. I have no delight. *2 Sam* 15:26
what you shall *s*. that will I. 21:4
of my lord *s*. so too. *1 Ki* 1:36
for he will not *s*. thee nay. 2:17
shall *s*. Why hath the Lord done thus
  to this land ? 9:8; *2 Ki* 7:21
Lord did *s*. Eat no bread. *1 Ki* 13:22
let not the king *s*. so.   22:8
              2 Chr 18:7
if we *s*. We will enter. *2 Ki* 7:4
so that they shall not *s*. this. 9:37
that thou *s*. nothing but truth to me.
              2 Chr 18:15
they should *s*. to Iddo. *Ezra* 8:17
O our God, what shall we *s*.? 9:10
who will *s*. to him, What dost thou ?
     Job 9:12; *Eccl* 8:4
they *s*. unto God, Depart. *Job* 21:14
then shalt thou *s*. There is. 22:29
what he would *s*. to me. 23:5
destruction and death *s*. We. 28:22
searched out what to *s*. 32:11
if any *s*. I have sinned. 33:27
teach us what we shall *s*. 37:19
many *s*. of my soul, There. *Ps* 3:2
there be that *s*. Who will shew ? 4:6
let them not *s*. We have. 35:25
so that a man shall *s*. There. 58:11
for who, *s*. they, doth hear ? 59:7
yet they *s*. Lord shall not see. 94:7
nor do they who go by *s*. 129:8
if they *s*. Come, let us lay. *Pr* 1:11
s. I have made my heart ? 20:9
when thou shalt *s*. I have. *Eccl* 12:1
people shall go and *s*. *Isa* 2:3
they *s*. Who seeth us ? and. 29:15
shall the work *s*. of him that made
  it ? or the thing framed *s*. of ? 16
who *s*. to the seers, See not. 30:10
the inhabitant shall not *s*. I. 33:24
one shall *s*. I am the Lord's. 44:5
surely shall one *s*. In the Lord. 45:24
lest thou shouldest *s*. My idol. 48:5
thou shouldest *s*. Behold, I knew. 7
Why have we fasted, *s*. they ? 58:3
cry, and he shall *s*. Here I am.   9
in trouble they will *s*. Arise. *Jer* 2:27
understandest what they *s*. 5:15
shall ye *s*. to them, The gods. 10:11
Therefore thou shalt *s*. this. 14:17
Report, *s*. they, and we will. 20:10
shall no more *s*. The Lord. 23:7
they shall *s*. no more, Fathers. 31:29
do to him even as he shall *s*. 39:12
all that the Lord shall *s*. 42:20
ye *s*. The Lord saith it. *Ezek* 13:7
wilt thou yet *s*. before him that ? 28:9
nor will we *s*. to the work. *Hos* 14:3
Ephraim shall *s*. What have I to ? 8
prophesy ye not, *s*. they to. *Mi* 2:6
they will *s*. Is not the Lord ? 3:11
see what he will *s*. to me. *Hab* 2:1
they that sell them *s*. I am.*Zech* 11:5
yet ye *s*., Wherein hast thou loved
  us ? *Mal* 1:2; 2:14, 17; 3:13
think not to *s*. within yourselves.
         Mat 3:9; *Luke* 3:8
shall *s*. all manner of evil. *Mat* 5:11
will *s*. to me in that day. 7:22
have ye understood ? they. 13:51
Jesus said, Whom do men *s*.? 16:13
   Mark 8:27; *Luke* 9:18
Whom *s*. ye that I am ? *Mat* 16:15
   Mark 8:29; *Luke* 9:20

s. aught to you, ye shall *s*. *Mat* 21:3
and *s*. to him, Hearest thou what
  these *s*.?   16
if we should *s*. From heaven, he will
  s. 25; *Mark* 11:31; *Luke* 20:5
if we shall *s*., Of men. *Mat* 21:26
      Mark 11:32; *Luke* 20:6
do not their works, for they *s*.
         Mat 23:3
and saith, See thou *s*. *Mark* 1:44
he wist not what to *s*. for they. 9:6
ye will surely *s*. this proverb,
  Physician, heal thyself. *Luke* 4:23
Simon, I have somewhat to *s*. 7:40
no thought what ye shall *s*. 12:11
shall teach what ye ought to *s*. 12
ye *s*. That Jerusalem is. *John* 4:20
he speaketh, and they *s*. 7:26
I have many things to *s*. of you.
          8:26; 16:12
S. we not well, that thou hast a ? 8:48
ye *s*. that he is your God. 54
ye call me master, ye *s*. well. 13:13
hear in all things ye shall *s*. *Acts* 3:22
they could *s*. nothing against it. 4:14
we heard him *s*. that Jesus. 6:14
do therefore this that we *s*. 21:33
who hath something to *s*. 23:18
or else let these same here *s*. 24:20
things but what Moses did *s*. 26:22
what shall we *s*. Is God ? *Rom* 3:5
as some affirm that we *s*. Let us. 8
what shall we then *s*.? 4:1; 6:1
   7:7; 8:31; 9:14, 30
shall thing formed *s*. to him ? 9:20
no man can *s*. that Jesus. *1 Cor* 12:3
how shall he *s*. Amen at thy ? 14:16
will they not *s*. that ye are mad ? 23
how *s*. some that there is ? 15:12
we, that we *s*. not. *2 Cor* 9:4
for his letters, *s*. they, are. 10:10
this we *s*. to you by word of the.
          1 Thes 4:15
neither what they *s*. *1 Tim* 1:7
having no evil thing to *s*. *Tit* 2:8
albeit I do not *s*. how. *Philem* 19
have many things to *s*. *Heb* 5:11
as I may so *s*. Levi paid tithes. 7:9
that is to *s*. not of this building. 9:11
that is to *s*. his flesh. 10:20
they that *s*. such things. 11:14
we may boldly *s*. The Lord. 13:6
let no man *s*. when he is. *Jas* 1:13
go to now ye that *s*. To-day. 4:13
that ye ought to *s*. If the Lord. 15
we *s*. we have fellowship. *1 John* 1:6
if we *s*. We have no sin, we.   8
if a man *s*. I love God, and. 4:20
I do not *s*. that he shall pray. 5:16
which *s*. they are apostles. *Rev* 2:2
which *s*. they are Jews. 9; 3:9
spirit and the bride *s*. Come. 22:17

      see **began**

say, *imperatively*
s. I pray thee, thou art. *Gen* 12:13
at every place, *s*. of the, He. 20:13
s. unto them, Go not. *Deut* 1:42
s., The sword of the. *Judg* 7:18
they said to him, S. now. 12:6
he said to him, S. on. *1 Sam* 15:16
  2 Sam 14:12; *1 Ki* 2:14, 16
    Luke 7:40; *Acts* 13:15
s. not, Go and come again. *Pr* 3:28
s. not, I will do so to him as. 24:29
lest I deny thee, and *s*. Who ? 30:9
s. not thou, What is the cause ?
         Eccl 7:10
s. ye to righteous, It. *Isa* 3:10
s. to them that are of fearful. 35:4
s. to cities of Judah, Behold. 40:9
hear, and *s*. It is truth. 43:9
neither let the eunuch *s*. I am. 56:3
s. ye to the daughter of Zion. 62:11
s. not, I am a child, for. *Jer* 1:7
s. ye, Stand fast, and prepare. 46:14
ask her that escapeth, and *s*. 48:19
s. Babylon is taken, Bel is. -50:2
thy foot, and *s*. Alas. *Ezek* 6:11
s. I am your sign, like as. 12:11
and *s*. What is thy mother ? 19:2
s. A sword is sharpened. 21:9
s. The sword is drawn for the. 28
s. unto him, Take away all. *Hos* 14:2

let them s. Spare thy people.
Joel 2:17
let the weak s. I am strong. 3:10
s. unto them, Turn ye. *Zech 1:3*
s. The Lord hath need of them.
Mat 21:3; Mark 11:3
s. in a word, and my. *Luke 7:7*
streets of the same, and s. 10:10
s. not ye, There are yet. *John 4:35*
s. ye ... Thou blasphemest ? 10:36
s. to Archippus, Take heed. *Col 4:17*

I say
his name, what shall I s.? *Ex 3:13*
I s. unto thee, Let my son. 4:23
speak all that I s. 6:29; *Ezek 44:5*
what shall I s. when Israel.*Josh 7:8*
of whom I s. This shall. *Judg 7:4*
if I s. expressly to the lad, Behold.
1 Sam 20:21
did not I s. Do not ? *2 Ki 4:28*
behold, I s. they are even as. 7:13
behold, I s. how they. *2 Chr 20:11*
did I s. Bring unto me ? *Job 6:22*
when I s. My bed shall. 7:13
if I s. I am perfect, it shall. 9:20
if I s. I will forget my complaint. 27
I will s. to God, Do not condemn.
10:2
good courage: wait, I s. *Ps 27:14*
if I s. I will speak thus, I. 73:15
I will s. He is my refuge. 91:2
I s. more than they that. 130:6
if I s. The darkness shall. 139:11
I s. an untimely birth is. *Eccl 6:3*
I s., sayest thou, but they. *Isa 36:5*
what shall I s.? he hath both. 38:15
I will s. to the north, Give up. 43:6
son of man, hear what I s. *Ezek 2:8*
I s. to the wicked. 3:18; 33:8, 14
I will s. the word, and will. 12:25
because I s. Ye are come to. 21:24
when I s. to the righteous. 33:13
I s. unto this man, Go. *Mat 8:9*
Luke 7:8
I s. not, Until seven. *Mat 18:22*
I s. to thee, Arise. *Mark 2:11; 5:41*
Luke 5:24; 7:14
the things which I s. *Luke 6:46*
these things I s. that ye. *John 5:34*
if I s. the truth, why do ye ? 8:46
if I should s. I know him not. 55
what shall I s. ? Father, save. 12:27
commandment, what I should s. 49
to declare, I s., his. *Rom 3:26*
I s. the truth in Christ, I lie not. 9:1
this I s. that every one. *1 Cor 1:12*
but this I s. brethren, the. 7:29
s. I these things as a man ? 9:8
I speak as to wise men, judge ye
what I s. *1 Cor 10:15*
what s. I then ? that the idol. 19
conscience, I s. not thy own. 29
what shall I s. to you ? 11:22
now this I s. brethren. 15:50
2 Cor 9:6; Gal 3:17; 5:16
Eph 4:17; Col 2:4
as we said before, so s. I. *Gal 1:9*
consider what I s. *2 Tim 2:7*
wilt do more than I s. *Philem 21*
what shall I more s.? *Heb 11:32*

I say unto you
when I s. unto you, Smite Amnon.
2 Sam 13:28
I not s. unto you, Go. *2 Ki 2:18*
I s. unto you, that Solomon in all.
Mat 6:29
I s. unto you, that publicans. 21:31
what I s. unto you, I. *Mark 13:37*
I s. not unto you, I. *John 16:26*
I Paul s. unto you, if ye. *Gal 5:2*
unto you I s. and to the rest in.
Rev 2:24

sayest
see, thou s. unto me, Bring.
whatsoever thou s. *Num 22:17*
all that thou s. unto me. *Ruth 3:5*
and now thou s. Go. *1 Ki 18:11, 14*
thou s. I have counsel and strength.
2 Ki 18:20; Isa 36:5
thou s. Lo, thou hast. *2 Chr 25:19*
will we do as thou s. *Neh 5:12*
no such things as thou s. 6:8
and thou s. How doth ? *Job 22:13*

and s. Return, ye children of men.
Ps 90:3
if thou s. Behold, we. *Pr 24:12*
why s. thou, O Jacob. *Isa 40:27*
that s. in thine heart, I am. 47:8
s. Because I am innocent, I will plead
. . . because thou s. *Jer 2:35*
s. Prophesy not against. *Amos 7:16*
know not what thou s. *Mat 26:70*
Jews ? Jesus said unto him, Thou s.
27:11; Mark 15:2; Luke 23:3
John 18:37
neither understand I what thou s.
Mark 14:68; Luke 22:60
that thou s. rightly. *Luke 20:21*
Who art thou ? What s.? *John 1:22*
stoned, but what s. thou ? 8:5
s. thou, ye shall be made free ? 33
12:34; 14:9
man, What s. thou of him ? 9:17
s. thou this of thyself or ? 18:34
thou that s. a man should not steal.
Rom 2:22
not what thou s. *1 Cor 14:16*
because thou s. I am rich. *Rev 3:17*

saying, substantive
his father observed s. *Gen 37:11*
and the s. pleased me. *Deut 1:23*
the s. displeased Saul. *1 Sam 18:8*
s. pleased Absalom. *2 Sam 17:4*
shall we do after his s.? if not. 6
David, according to the s. of. 24:19
and Shimei said, The s. *1 Ki 2:38*
that he might perform his s. 12:15
when Jeroboam heard the s. 13:4
the s. which he cried by the. 32
s. of the Lord. 15:29; *2 Ki 10:17*
according to the s. of Elijah.
1 Ki 17:15; 2 Ki 2:22
according to the s. of man of God.
2 Ki 5:14; 8:2
the s. pleased the king. *Esth 1:21*
I will open my dark s. *Ps 49:4*
was not this my s.? *Jonah 4:2*
after they heard this s. *Mat 15:12*
all men cannot receive this s. 19:11
young man heard this s. 22
this s. is commonly reported. 28:15
for this s. go thy way. *Mark 7:29*
and he spake that s. openly. 8:32
and they kept that s. with. 9:10
they understood not that s. 32
Luke 2:50; 9:45
he was sad at that s. *Mark 10:22*
she was troubled at his s. *Luke 1:29*
known abroad s. that was. 2:17
feared to ask him of that s. 9:45
this s. was hid from them. 18:34
herein is that s. true. *John 4:37*
many believed for the s. of the. 39
believe, not because of thy s. 42
this is an hard s.; who can ? 6:60
what manner of s. is this ? 7:36
they heard this s., said. 40
if a man keep my s. 8:51, 52
but I know him and keep his s. 55
that the s. of Esaias might. 12:38
if they have kept my s. they. 15:20
that the s. of Jesus might. 18:9, 32
when Pilate heard that s. he. 19:8
then went this s. abroad. 21:23
the s. pleased the whole. *Acts 6:5*
then fled Moses at this s. 7:29
told this s. to Paul. 16:36
comprehended in this s. *Rom 13:9*
brought to pass the s. *1 Cor 15:54*
this is a faithful s. that Christ Jesus.
1 Tim 1:15; 4:9; 2 Tim 2:11
Tit 3:8
this is a true s. if a man. *1 Tim 3:1*

saying
displeased in s. Why ? *1 Ki 1:6*
he prayed third time, s. *Mat 26:44*
s. I am Christ, and. *Mark 13:6*
Master, thus s. thou. *Luke 11:45*
a voice, s. Arise, Peter. *Acts 11:7*
s. none other things than those. 26:22

sayings
Moses told these s. to. *Num 14:39*
that when thy s. come. *Judg 13:17*
men told all those s. *1 Sam 25:12*
Abijah's s. are written. *2 Chr 13:22*
that are written among the s. 33:19

posterity approve their s. *Ps 49:13*
I will utter dark s. of old. 78:2
to understand the dark s. *Pr 1:6*
O my son, and receive my s. 4:10
incline thine ear to my s. 20
whoso heareth these s. *Mat 7:24, 26*
Luke 6:47
when Jesus had ended these s. the.
Mat 7:28; 19:1; 26:1; Luke 7:1
all these s. were noised. *Luke 1:65*
his mother kept all these s. 2:51
let these s. sink down into. 9:44
there was a division again for these
s. *John 10:19*
me not, keepeth not my s. 14:24
with these s. scarce. *Acts 14:18*
when they heard these s. they. 19:28
be justified in thy s. *Rom 3:4*
these are true s. of God. *Rev 19:9*
these s. are faithful and true. 22:6
blessed is he that keepeth the s. 7
and of them who keep the s. of. 9
seal not the s. of the prophecy of. 10

scab
in skin of his flesh a s. *Lev 13:2*
it is but a s. 6
if s. spread much in skin. 7, 8
this is the law for a s. 14:56
smite thee with a s. *Deut 28:27**
Lord will smite with a s. *Isa 3:17*

scabbard
put up thyself into thy s. *Jer 47:6*

scabbed
he that is scurvy or s. *Lev 21:20*
or scurvy, or s. ye shall. 22:22

scaffold
had made a brasen s. *2 Chr 6:13*

scales
these that have s. eat ye. *Lev 11:9*
Deut 14:9
that have no s. ye shall not eat.
Lev 11:10, 12; Deut 14:10
his s. are his pride. *Job 41:15*
mountains in s. and hills. *Isa 40:12*
fish to stick to thy s. *Ezek 29:4*
his eyes as it had been s. *Acts 9:18*

scaleth
a wise man s. the city. *Pr 21:22*

scall
it is a dry s. even a. *Lev 13:30*
s. be not deeper than the skin, shall
shut up him that hath the s. 31, 33
if the s. spread not. 32, 34
he shall be shaven, but the s. 33
but if the s. spread much. 35, 36
if the s. be at a stay, the s. 37
all manner of leprosy and s. 14:54

scalp
wound the hairy s. of such. *Ps 68:21*

scant
and the s. measure that. *Mi 6:10*

scapegoat, see goat

scarce
Jacob was s. gone out. *Gen 27:30*
with these sayings s. *Acts 14:18*

scarcely
for s. for a righteous man. *Rom 5:7*
if the righteous s. be. *1 Pet 4:18*

scarceness
eat bread without s. *Deut 8:9*

scarest
then thou s. me with dreams.
Job 7:14

scarlet
bound a s. thread. *Gen 38:28, 30*
blue and purple, and s. *Ex 25:4*
26:1, 31, 36; 27:16; 28:5, 6, 8, 15
35:6, 23, 25; 38:18, 23
wires, to work it in s. 39:3
cedar wood, s. and hyssop. *Lev 14:4*
6, 49, 51, 52; *Num 19:6*
on them a cloth of s. *Num 4:8*
shalt bind this line of s. *Josh 2:18*
and she bound the s. line in the. 21
who clothed you in s. *2 Sam 1:24*
are clothed with s. *Pr 31:21*
like a thread of s. *S of S 4:3*
though your sins be as s. *Isa 1:18*
brought up in s. *Lam 4:5*

shall be clothed with s. *Dan 5:7**
16*, 29*
valiant men are in s. *Nah 2:3*
put on Jesus a s. robe. *Mat 27:28*
took water, and s. wool. *Heb 9:19*
I saw a woman sit upon a s. coloured
beast. *Rev 17:3*
arrayed in purple and s. 4
buyeth the merchandise of s. 18:12
was clothed with s. 16

scatter
Lord s. them on earth. *Gen 11:9*
in Jacob, s. them in Israel. 49:7
and I will s. you. *Lev 26:33*
censers, and s. the fire. *Num 16:37*
and the Lord shall s. *Deut 4:27*
28:64; *Jer* 9:16; *Ezek* 22:15
I said, I would s. them. *Deut 32:26*
he shall s. them beyond. *1 Ki 14:15*
if ye transgress, I will s. *Neh 1:8*
s. them by thy power. *Ps 59:11*
s. thou the people that delight. 68:30
lifted up his hand to s. 106:27
cast forth lightning, and s. 144:6
abroad fitches, and s. *Isa 28:25*
whirlwind shall s. them. 41:16
therefore I will s. them. *Jer 13:24*
I will s. them as with an. 18:17
woe to the pastors that s. 23:1
I will s. into all winds them that are.
49:32, 36; *Ezek* 5:10, 12
shalt s. in the wind. *Ezek 5:2*
I will s. your bones round. 6:5
fill thine hand, and s. the. 10:2
I will s. toward every wind. 12:14
when I shall s. them among. 15
that I would s. them among. 20:23
I will s. the Egyptians. 29:12
30:23, 26
hew down the tree, and s. *Dan 4:14*
he shall s. among them the. 11:24
to s. the power of the holy. 12:7*
as a whirlwind to s. me. *Hab 3:14*
horn over Judah to s. it. *Zech 1:21*

scattered
lest we be s. abroad. *Gen 11:4*
so the Lord s. them abroad from. 8
the people were s. to. *Ex 5:12*
let thine enemies be s. *Num 10:35*
Ps 68:1
thy God hath s. thee. *Deut 30:3*
that remained were s. *1 Sam 11:11*
people were s. from Saul. 13:8
because I saw the people were s. 11
the battle was s. over. *2 Sam 18:8*
he sent out arrows and s. them.
22:15; *Ps* 18:14
I saw all Israel s. *1 Ki 22:17*
2 Chr 18:16
army were s. from him. *2 Ki 25:5*
Jer 52:8
there is a certain people s. *Esth 3:8*
the stout lions' whelps are s.
Job 4:11
brimstone shall be s. on his. 18:15
thou hast s. us among heathen.
Ps 44:11; 60:1
God hath s. the bones of him. 53:5
Almighty s. kings in it. 68:14
thou hast s. thine enemies. 89:10
of iniquity shall be s. 92:9
our bones are s. at the grave's. 141:7
to a nation s. and peeled. *Isa 18:2*
be brought of a people s. 7
of thyself the nations were s. 33:3
and hast s. thy ways to. *Jer 3:13*
their flocks shall be s. 10:21
ye have s. my flock, and. 23:2
nations whither I have s. thee. 30:11
he that s. Israel will gather. 31:10
that all Jews should be s.? 40:15
Israel is a s. sheep: the lions. 50:17
when ye shall be s. through. *Ezek 6:8*
though I s. them, I will be. 11:16
you out of countries where ye have
been s. 17; 20:34, 41; 28:25
they that remain shall be s. 17:21
whither they were s. 29:13
s. because there is no shepherd, they
. . . when they were s. 34:5
my flock was s. on the face of. 6
among his sheep that are s. where
they have been s. in the. 12

till ye have s. them. *Ezek 34:21*
s. them among the heathen. 36:19
that my people be not s. every. 46:18
people whom they have s. *Joel 3:2*
thy people is s. on the. *Nah 3:18*
mountains were s. *Hab 3:6*
horns which have s. *Zech 1:19, 21*
I s. them with whirlwind. 7:14
shepherd, and the sheep shall be s.
13:7; *Mat* 26:31; *Mark* 14:27
they were s. as sheep. *Mat 9:36*
he hath s. the proud. *Luke 1:51*
now, that ye shall be s. 16:32
obeyed Theudas were s. *Acts 5:36*
were s. abroad through the. 8:1
were s. went every where. 4, 11, 19
tribes that are s. abroad. *Jas 1:1*
Peter to the strangers s. *1 Pet 1:1**

scattereth
the thick cloud he s. his. *Job 37:11*
which s. the east wind upon. 38:24
he s. the hoarfrost like. *Ps 147:16*
there is that s. and yet. *Pr 11:24*
a king s. away all evil with. 20:8
a wise king s. the wicked. 26
the Lord s. the inhabitants. *Isa 24:1*
and he that gathereth not with me s.
Mat 12:30; *Luke* 11:23
the wolf catcheth and s. *John 10:12*

scattering
shew his anger with s. *Isa 30:30*

scent
yet through the s. of water. *Job 14:9*
therefore his s. is not. *Jer 48:11*
the s. thereof be the wine. *Hos 14:7*

sceptre
(*The word originally meant a rod
or a staff. Thence it came to
mean a shepherd's crook, and then
the wand or sceptre of a ruler.
The references to it, save in Esther,
are all metaphorical, expressing
supreme power*)
the s. shall not depart. *Gen 49:10*
and a s. shall rise out. *Num 24:17*
hold out the golden s. *Esth 4:11*
to Esther the golden s. 5:2; 8:4
the s. of thy kingdom is a right s.
Ps 45:6
Lord hath broken the s. *Isa 14:5*
rods for the s. of them. *Ezek 19:11*
no strong rod to be a s. to rule. 14
I will cut off him that holdeth the s.
Amos 1:5, 8
and the s. of Egypt. *Zech 10:11*
the s. of righteousness is the s. of.
Heb 1:8

Sceva
sons of one S. a Jew. *Acts 19:14*

schism
(*A division*)
should be no s. in the. *1 Cor 12:25*

scholar
they cast lots, the teacher as the s.
1 Chr 25:8
cut off master and the s. *Mal 2:12**

school
disputing in the s. of one. *Acts 19:9*

schoolmaster
(*The Roman pedagogue, who did
not teach, but was the slave whose
duty it was to take the child to the
school*)
the law was our s. to. *Gal 3:24**
are no longer under a s. 25

science
wisdom, understanding s. *Dan 1:4*
and oppositions of s. *1 Tim 6:20**

scoff
they shall s. at the kings. *Hab 1:10*

scoffers
in last days s. walking. *2 Pet 3:3*

scorch
given him to s. men. *Rev 16:8*

scorched
when sun was up they were s.
Mat 13:6; *Mark* 4:6
and men were s. with. *Rev 16:9*

scorn, verb
my friends s. me, mine. *Job 16:20*

scorn
he thought s. to lay hands. *Esth 3:6*
a reproach and s. *Ps* 44:13; 79:4
princes shall be a s. *Hab 1:10**
see laughed

scorner
(*A* Scorner, *as the word is used in
Scripture, is one who makes a mock
of sin, and of God's threatenings
and judgements against sinners;
one who derides all wholesome reproofs and counsels, and scoffs at
religion. Usually the revisions
change to* scoffer)
reproveth a s. getteth. *Pr 9:7*
reprove not a s., lest he hate thee. 8
but a s. heareth not rebuke. 13:1
a s. seeketh wisdom, and. 14:6
a s. loveth not one that. 15:12
smite a s. 19:25
when the s. is punished. 21:11
s. is his name, who dealeth in. 24
cast out the s. 22:10
and the s. is an abomination. 24:9
the s. is consumed, and. *Isa 29:20*

scorners
how long will s. delight? *Pr 1:12*
surely he scorneth the s. but. 3:34
judgements are prepared for s. and.
19:29
stretched out his hand with s. *Hos 7:5*

scornest
if thou s. thou alone. *Pr 9:12*
in that thou s. hire. *Ezek 16:31*

scorneth
s. the multitude of the city. *Job 39:7*
the ostrich, she s. the horse. 18
surely he s. the scorners. *Pr 3:34*
witness s. judgement, and. 19:28

scornful
in the seat of the s. *Ps 1:1*
s. men bring a city into. *Pr 29:8*
of the Lord, ye s. men. *Isa 28:14*

scorning
drinketh up s. like water? *Job 34:7*
is filled with s. of those. *Ps 123:4*
scorners delight in their s. *Pr 1:22*

scorpion
*A well-known venomous insect of
hot climates, shaped much like a
lobster, and closely akin to the
spider. It is usually about 2 or 3
inches long, but in tropical climates
grows much larger.
The word used in* 1 Ki 12:11 *is
metaphorical.*
will he offer him a s.? *Luke 11:12*
as the torment of a s. *Rev 9:5*

scorpions
wherein were s. *Deut 8:15*
I will chastise you with s.
1 Ki 12:11, 14; *2 Chr* 10:11, 14
among s. be not afraid. *Ezek 2:6*
tread on serpents and s. *Luke 10:19*
power, as s. have power. *Rev 9:3*
they had tails like to s. and. 10

scoured
a brasen pot, it shall be s. *Lev 6:28*

scourge
*A whip made of cords or leather
thongs fastened into a handle.
Usually there were three of these
thongs in each scourge, and they
were often reinforced with bits of
metal which tore the skin and flesh.
Notable scourgings mentioned in
the Bible are those of Christ, in the
Gospels, and of Paul, in 2 Cor
11:24. The scourge of small
cords used by Jesus in clearing the
Temple, was merely a symbol of
authority. Scourging differs from
beating, which was done with rods.
The word is also used to-day,
figuratively, for a cause of calamity
of any sort.*
hid from s. of the tongue. *Job 5:21*
if the s. slay suddenly, he. 9:23

scourge

shall stir up a s. for him.   Isa 10:26
when the overflowing s.   28:15, 18
when he had made a s.   John 2:15

scourge, verb

they will s. you in their.   Mat 10:17
they shall s. him.   20:19
    Mark 10:34; Luke 18:33
some of them ye shall s.   Mat 23:34
for you to s. a Roman?   Acts 22:25

scourged

maid, she shall be s.   Lev 19:20
they had s. Jesus, he.   Mat 27:26
    Mark 15:15; John 19:1

scourges

s. in your sides, and.   Josh 23:13

scourgeth

the Lord s. every son.   Heb 12:6

scourging

should be examined by s.   Acts 22:24

scourgings

others had trial of s., yea.   Heb 11:36

scrabbled

himself mad, and s.   1 Sam 21:13

scrape

dust that they s. off.   Lev 14:41
Job took a potsherd to s.   Job 2:8
I will also s. her dust.   Ezek 26:4

scraped

house to be s. within.   Lev 14:41
after he hath s. the house.   43

screech owl

s. also shall rest there.   Isa 34:14*

scribe

[1] In the Old Testament any government clerk or secretary. [2] The Sopherim (plur.) who copied, taught, and explained the law. Ezra was one of the most noted of those in Old Testament times. Before the Exile this work was done by the Levites, but later it was gradually put into the hands of a specially trained body of laymen. Not only did they copy the written law, but they formulated and wrote down the detailed rules made by later authorities, which made up what was called the oral law, or the traditions of the elders. They had much opportunity for the exercise of that hypocrisy for which our Lord denounced them in company with the Pharisees.

Seraiah was the s.   2 Sam 8:17
Sheva was s.   20:25
and Shebna the s.   2 Ki 18:18, 37
    19:2; Isa 36:3, 22; 37:2
Shaphan, the s.   2 Ki 22:3, 8, 9, 10
    12; 2 Chr 34:15, 18, 20; Jer 36:10
he took the principal s. of the host.
    2 Ki 25:19; Jer 52:25
and Shemaiah the s.   1 Chr 24:6
a wise man and a s.   27:32
Shimshai the s. wrote a letter.
    Ezra 4:8, 9, 17, 23
was a ready s. in the law.   7:6, 11
    12; Neh 8:4, 9, 13; 12:26, 36
Ezra the s. stood upon.   Neh 8:4
the priest, Zadok the s.   13:13
where is the s.? where?   Isa 33:18
sat there, even Elishama the s.
    Jer 36:12, 20, 21
Baruch the s.   26, 32
Jonathan the s.   37:15, 20
a s. said, Master, I will.   Mat 8:19
s. instructed unto the.   13:52
the s. said unto him.   Mark 12:32
where is the s.? where?   1 Cor 1:20

scribes

Ahiah, sons of Shisha, s.   1 Ki 4:3
the families of the s.   1 Chr 2:55
of Levites there were s.   2 Chr 34:13
then were the king's s. called.
    Esth 3:12; 8:9
the pen of the s. is in.   Jer 8:8
righteousness of the s.   Mat 5:20
having authority, and not as the s.
    7:29; Mark 1:22
many things of the s.   Mat 16:21
why say s. Elias.   17:10; Mark 9:11

Son of man shall be betrayed unto the chief priests and the s.   Mat 20:18
    Mark 10:33
when the s. saw, they.   Mat 21:15
s. and Pharisees sit in.   23:2
woe to you s.   13, 14, 15, 23, 25, 27
    29; Luke 11:44
priests and s. and elders.   Mat 26:3
    Mark 14:53; Luke 22:66
went certain s.   Mark 2:6
when the s. saw him eat with.   16
the s. said, he hath Beelzebub. 3:22
be rejected of s.   8:31; Luke 9:22
the s. questioning with.   Mark 9:14
the s. and chief priests heard it, and.
    11:18; Luke 19:47
s. say, By what authority?
    Mark 11:27
one of the s. asked, What is? 12:28
How say s. that Christ is the? 35
he said to them, Beware of s. 38
    Luke 20:46
s. sought how to take.   Mark 14:1
their s. and Pharisees murmured.
    Luke 5:30; 15:2
s. watched him.   6:7
the s. began to urge him.   11:53
the s. came upon him.   20:1
priests and s. sought to lay.   19
the chief priests and s. sought. 22:2
s. stood and vehemently.   23:10
the s. brought a woman.   John 8:3
the s. gathered against.   Acts 4:5
the s. brought Stephen to.   6:12
the s. of the Pharisees' part.   23:9

scrip

(Revisions, wallet. A sort of bag in which were carried a small amount of food and other necessary conveniences for a journey)
smooth stones in a s.   1 Sam 17:40
nor s. for your journey.   Mat 10:10
    Mark 6:8; Luke 9:3; 10:4
without s. lacked ye.   Luke 22:35
take his purse and his s.   36

scripture

(Literally from the Latin, a writing.
The word as used in the Bible refers almost invariably to the sacred writings, which at that time consisted of the Old Testament only. It is also used of a part of it, especially when that part is quoted in a later passage)
noted in the s. of truth.   Dan 10:21
read this s., The stone?   Mark 12:10
the s. was fulfilled, which.   15:28
said, This day is this s.   Luke 4:21
they believed the s. and.   John 2:22
on me, as the s. saith.   7:38
not the s. said, Christ cometh? 42
word came, and the s. cannot. 10:35
again another s. saith, They. 19:37
this s. must needs have.   Acts 1:16
the place of the s. which.   8:32
Philip began at the same s.   35
what saith the s.?   Rom 4:3; 11:2
    Gal 4:30
for the s. saith.   Rom 9:17; 10:11
    1 Tim 5:18
the s. foreseeing that God.   Gal 3:8
but the s. hath concluded all.   22
all s. is given by.   2 Tim 3:16
do ye think the s. saith?   Jas 4:5
the s., Behold I lay in Sion. 1 Pet 2:6
no prophecy is of s.   2 Pet 1:20

scriptures

read in the s. the stone?   Mat 21:42
ye do err, not knowing the s. 22:29
    Mark 12:24
how then shall the s. be? Mat 26:54
but the s. must be.   Mark 14:49
to them in all the s.   Luke 24:27
while he opened to us the s.? 32
that they might understand the s. 45
search the s.; for in them. John 5:39
with them out of the s.   Acts 17:2
and searched the s. daily.   11
Apollos, mighty in the s.   18:24
shewing by the s. that Jesus was. 28
prophets in the holy s.   Rom 1:2
that we through comfort of s. 15:4

and by the s. made known. Rom 16:26
Christ died according to s. 1 Cor 15:3
rose according to the s.   4
hast known the holy s.   2 Tim 3:15
as they do also other s.   2 Pet 3:16

scroll

rolled together as a s.   Isa 34:4
departed as a s. rolled.   Rev 6:14

scum

(Revisions, rust)
woe to the pot whose s.   Ezek 24:6
s. of it may be consumed.   11
her great s. went not forth of her, her
  s. shall be in the fire.   12

scurvy

none shall approach that is s. or.
    Lev 21:20
the s. or scabbed ye shall not. 22:22

Scythian

neither barbarian, S.   Col 3:11

sea

(The molten sea made for the Temple)
he made a molten s.   1 Ki 7:23
    2 Chr 4:2
were knops compassing s. 1 Ki 7:24
the s. was set above upon oxen. 25
    2 Chr 4:4
set the s. on right side of the. 39
took down the s. from.   2 Ki 16:17
the s. did Chaldeans break. 25:13, 16
s. was for the priests.   2 Chr 4:6
one s. and twelve oxen under. 15
concerning the pillars and s.
    Jer 27:19

sea

The Hebrews knew little, and most of them nothing, about the ocean as we understand this word, though the ocean is probably referred to in Gen 1. [1] The largest body of water really known to them was the Mediterranean Sea, which is probably referred to in Deut 11:24, and several other places. [2] The Red Sea was naturally a familiar name to them, Ex 15:4. [3] The Salt Sea, or Dead Sea, and other large inland waters are meant in such places as Deut 3:17; Joel 2:20. [4] Any great collections of waters, as the Nile, Isa 19:5, and the Euphrates, Jer 51:36, are in some places called Seas.

hand over the s.   Ex 14:16, 27
s. to go back, made the s. dry. 21
didst blow, the s. covered.   15:10
Lord made the s. and all.   20:11
    Ps 95:5; Jonah 1:9; Acts 4:24
    14:15
quails from the s.   Num 11:31
beyond s. that thou shouldest say,
  Who shall go over s.? Deut 30:13
you came unto the s.   Josh 24:6
he brought the s. upon them.   7
at s. a navy of Tharshish. 1 Ki 10:22
look toward the s.   18:43
coast to the s. of plain. 2 Ki 14:25
let the s. roar.   1 Chr 16:32
    Ps 96:11; 98:7
against thee beyond s. 2 Chr 20:2
divide the s., went through the s.
    Neh 9:11; Job 26:12; Ps 74:13
    78:13; Jer 31:35
am I a s. or a whale?   Job 7:12
is broader than the s.   11:9
as the waters fail from s.   14:11
s. saith, It is not with me.   28:14
or who shut up the s.?   38:8
he maketh the s. like a pot. 41:31
the s. into dry land.   Ps 66:6
dominion from s. to s.   72:8
but the s. overwhelmed their. 78:53
she sent out her boughs to s. 80:11
so is this great and wide s. 104:25
down to the s. in ships.   107:23
the s. saw it and fled.   114:3
O thou s., that thou?   5
gave to the s. his decree.   Pr 8:29
as the waters cover the s. Hab 2:14

stretched and gone over s. Isa 16:8
the waters shall fail from the s. 19:5
Zidon that pass over s. 23:2
be ashamed, O Zion, for the s. 4
stretched his hand over the s. 11
shall cry aloud from the s. 24:14
ye that go down to the s. 42:10
my rebuke, I dry up the s. 50:2
which hath dried the s.? 51:10
are like the troubled s. 57:20
their voice roareth like the s. Jer 6:23
thy plants are gone over s. 48:32
voice shall roar like the s. 50:42
I will dry up her s. and make. 51:36
the s. is come up upon. 42
breach is great like the s. Lam 2:13
as the s. causeth his waves to.
Ezek 26:3
came up from the s. Dan 7:3
wander from s. to s. Amos 8:12
shall we do, that the s.? Jonah 1:11
that day he shall come from s. to s.
Mi 7:12
he rebuketh the s. and. Nah 1:4
whose rampart was the s. 3:8
was thy wrath against s.? Hab 3:8
thou didst walk through the s. 15
heavens, earth, and s. Hag 2:6
shall be from s. to s. Zech 9:10
through the s. with affliction. 10:11
and rebuked the s. Mat 8:26
even winds and s. obey him.
8:27; Mark 4:39, 41
go thou to the s. and cast an.
Mat 17:27
for ye compass s. and land. 23:15
the s. and the waves. Luke 21:25
themselves to the s. Acts 27:40
he hath escaped the s. 28:4
passed through the s. 1 Cor 10:1
throne was a s. of glass. Rev 4:6
to hurt the earth and s. 7:2
Hurt not the earth nor the s. 3
who created the s. and the. 10:6
worship him that made the s. 14:7
I saw a s. of glass, mingled. 15:2
and the s. gave up the dead. 20:13
and there was no more s. 21:1
see coast, great, red, salt

by the sea
ye encamp by the s. Ex 14:2
encamping by the s. 9
be gathered as sand by the s.
2 Sam 17:11
Israel as sand by the s. 1 Ki 4:20
I will convey them by the s. 5:9
2 Chr 2:16
ambassadors by the s. Isa 18:2
as Carmel by the s. so. Jer 46:18
multitude was by the s. Mark 4:1
trade by the s. stood. Rev 18:17

in and into the sea
that came into the s. Ex 14:28
he thrown into the sea. 15:1, 21
host hath he cast into the s. 4
horsemen went into the s. 19
thy way is in the s. thy path. Ps 77:19
set his hand also in the s. 89:25
all rivers run into the s. Eccl 1:7
dragon that is in the s. Isa 27:1
maketh a way in the s. 43:16
was strong in the s. Ezek 26:17
the isles that are in the s. shall. 18
these waters go into the s. which
being brought forth into the s. 47:8
tempest in the s. Jonah 1:4
forth the wares into the s. 5
cast me into the s. 12, 15
smite her power into the s. Zech 9:4
smite the waves into the s. 10:11
casting a net into the s. Mat 4:18
Mark 1:16
great tempest in the s. Mat 8:24
swine ran into the s. 32; Mark 5:13
like a net cast into the s. Mat 13:47
be thou cast into the s. 21:21
Mark 11:23
and he were cast into the s.
Mark 9:42; Luke 17:2
be thou planted in the s. Luke 17:6
cast himself into the s. John 21:7
the wheat into the s. Acts 27:38
themselves first into the s. 43*

cloud, and in the s. 1 Cor 10:2
in perils in the s. 2 Cor 11:26
beast and things in the s. Jas 3:7
every creature in the s. Rev 5:13
burning was cast into the s. 8:8
living soul died in the s. 16:3
all that had ships in the s. 18:19
cast a millstone into the s. 21

of the sea
have dominion over fish of the s.
Gen 1:26, 28; Ps 8:8
upon all fishes of the s. Gen 9:2
seed as the sand of the s. 32:12
corn as the sand of the s. 41:49
dwell at the haven of the s. 49:13
in the heart of the s. Ex 15:8
the waters of the s. upon them. 19
all the fish of the s. be? Num 11:22
the channels of the s. 2 Sam 22:16
a cloud out of the s. 1 Ki 18:44
than the sand of the s. Job 6:3
upon the waves of the s. 9:8
the fishes of the s. shall. 12:8
covered the bottom of the s. 36:30
into the springs of the s.? 38:16
waters of the s. together. Ps 33:7
people from depths of the s. 68:22
like as the sand of the s. 78:27
rulest the raging of the s. 89:9
than the mighty waves of the s. 93:4
uttermost parts of the s. 139:9
the roaring of the s. Isa 5:30
her by the way of the s. 9:1
as the sand of the s. yet a remnant
shall. 10:22; Hos 1:10; Rom 9:27
even the strength of the s. Isa 23:4
as the waves of the s. 48:18
made the depths of the s. 51:10
abundance of the s. shall be. 60:5
them up out of the s. 63:11
for the bound of the s. Jer 5:22
neither the sand of the s. 33:22
the princes of the s. Ezek 26:16
situate at the entry of the s. 27:3
the ships of the s. were in thee. 9
all the pilots of the s. shall. 29
fishes of the s. shall shake. 38:20
the fishes of the s. shall be. Hos 4:3
calleth for the waters of the s.
Amos 5:8; 9:6
in the bottom of the s. 9:3
sins into depths of the s. Mi 7:19
men as the fishes of the s. Hab 1:14
consume the fishes of the s. Zeph 1:3
by way of the s. beyond. Mat 4:15
drowned in the depth of the s. 18:6
is like a wave of the s. Jas 1:6
raging waves of the s. Jude 13
the third part of the s. Rev 8:8
of earth and of the s. 12:12
a beast rise up out of the s. 13:1
is as the sand of the s. 20:8

see midst, sand

on or upon the sea
afar off upon the s. Ps 65:5
there is sorrow on the s. Jer 49:23
walking on the s. Mat 14:25
Mark 6:48; John 6:19
disciples saw him walking on the s.
Mat 14:26; Mark 6:49
should not blow on the s. Rev 7:1
his right foot upon the s. 10:2
which I saw stand upon the s. 5, 8
and I saw them stand on the s. 15:2
poured out his vial upon the s. 16:3

seafaring men
inhabited the s. men. Ezek 26:17

sea monsters
even the s. monsters draw out the.
Lam 4:3*

sea shore
as sand which is upon the s. shore.
Gen 22:17
saw the Egyptians dead upon s.
shore. Ex 14:30
as sand upon s. shore. Josh 11:4
Asher continued on the s. shore.
Judg 5:17
the Philistines as sand on the s.
shore. 1 Sam 13:5
heart as sand on s. shore. 1 Ki 4:29
given it a charge against the s. shore
Jer 47:7

sprang many, as sand by s. shore.
Heb 11:12

sea side
the way of the s. side. Deut 1:7
as sand by the s. side. Judg 7:12
Eloth at the s. side. 2 Chr 8:17
sat by the s. side. Mat 13:1
forth again by the s. side. Mark 2:13
to teach by the s. side. 4:1
Simon, whose house is by the s. side.
Acts 10:6, 32

seal
*Because of the fact that few could
read or write, the use of the seal
was far more common in olden
times than now. Each person had
his own private seal which it was
a capital crime to copy. This was
affixed to every sort of a document,
as we now sign our names.
The word is very frequently used
symbolically, as in Rom 4:11;
circumcision is said to be a seal
of the righteousness of faith.*
letters with Ahab's s. 1 Ki 21:8
as clay to the s. they. Job 38:14
shut up as with a close s. 41:15
s. on thy heart, as a s. on. S of S 8:6
hath set to his s. that God is true.
John 3:33*
circumcision a s. of. Rom 4:11
the s. of mine apostleship are ye.
1 Cor 9:2
having this s. the Lord 2 Tim 2:19
he opened the second s. Rev 6:3
the third s. 5
the fourth s. 7
the fifth s. 9
the sixth s. 12
another angel, having the s. 7:2
opened the seventh s. 8:1
that have not the s. of God. 9:4
and shut him up, and set a s. 20:3

seal, verb
our princes and priests s. unto it.
Neh 9:38; 10:1
s. the law among my. Isa 8:16
evidences, and s. them. Jer 32:44
seventy weeks to s. up. Dan 9:24
O Daniel, shut up the words, s. 12:4
s. those things the seven. Rev 10:4
s. not the sayings of the. 22:10

sealed
is not this s. up among? Deut 32:34
the letters were s. with. 1 Ki 21:8
written and s. with. Esth 3:12; 8:8
my transgression is s. Job 14:17
my spouse; a fountain s. S of S 4:12
the words of a book s. Isa 29:11
I subscribed and s. the. Jer 32:10
both that which was s. and. 11, 14
s. it with his own signet. Dan 6:17
and s. till the time. 12:9
God the Father s. John 6:27
when I have s. to them. Rom 15:28
who hath s. us and given. 2 Cor 1:22
ye were s. with that Holy. Eph 1:13
whereby ye are s. to-day. 4:30
book s. with seven seals. Rev 5:1
sea, till we have s. servants. 7:3
number of them which were s.; there
were s. 144,000 of all the. 4
of Juda were s. 12,000; of Reuben;
of Gad s. 5
of Nephthalim s.; of Manasses s. 6
of Levi; of Issachar were s. 7
of Joseph; of Benjamin were s. 8

sealest
thou s. up the sum full. Ezek 28:12

sealeth
commandeth the sun, and s. Job 9:7
he openeth their ears, and s. 33:16
he s. up hand of every man. 37:7

sealing
s. the stone and setting. Mat 27:66

seals
book sealed with seven s. Rev 5:1
who is worthy to loose the s.? 2
Juda prevailed to loose the s. 5
to take and open the s. 9
Lamb opened one of the s. 6:1

seam

was without s., woven. *John* 19:23

search

enquire and made s. *Deut* 13:14
that s. may be made in. *Ezra* 4:15
    5:17
s. hath been made, and it. 4:19; 6:1
prepare thyself to the s. *Job* 8:8
hast thou walked in the s.? 38:16*
accomplish a diligent s. *Ps* 64:6
my spirit made diligent s. 77:6
not found it by secret s. *Jer* 2:34

search, verb

he shall not s. whether. *Lev* 27:33
to s. out a resting place. *Num* 10:33
that they may s. the land. 13:2
which we have gone to s. it. 32
passed through to s. it, is. 14:7
of the men that went to s. 38
men, and they shall s. *Deut* 1:22
before to s. you out a place. 33
men to s. the country. *Josh* 2:2, 3
the Danites sent men to s. *Judg* 18:2
land, I will s. him out. *1 Sam* 23:23
servants unto thee to s. the city?
    2 Sam 10:3; *1 Chr* 19:3
servants, and they shall s. *1 Ki* 20:6
s. that none of the servants.
    2 Ki 10:23
is it good that he should s.? *Job* 13:9
shall not God s. this out? *Ps* 44:21
they s. and accomplish a. 64:6
s. me, O God, and know. 139:23
kings to s. out a matter. *Pr* 25:2
for men to s. their own glory. 27
I gave my heart to s. by wisdom.
    Eccl 1:13; 7:25
I the Lord s. the heart. *Jer* 17:10
when ye shall s. for me. 29:13
let us s. our ways, and. *Lam* 3:40
and none did s. or seek. *Ezek* 34:6
neither did my shepherds s. for. 8
I will both s. my sheep, and. 11
of seven months shall they s. 39:14
I will s. and take them out. *Amos* 9:3
I will s. Jerusalem with. *Zeph* 1:12
and s. diligently for the. *Mat* 2:8
s. the scriptures; for in. *John* 5:39
s. for out of Galilee ariseth. 7:52

searched

Laban s. the tent. *Gen* 31:34, 35
whereas thou hast s. all my. 37
the steward s. for the cup. 44:12
so they went up, and s. *Num* 13:21
evil report of the land, and s. 32
Caleb s. the land. 14:6, 38
of days ye s. the land. 34
valley of Eshcol, and s. *Deut* 1:24
we have s. it, and know. *Job* 5:27
he prepared it, yea, and s. 28:27
which I knew not, I s. out. 29:16
whilst ye s. out what to say. 32:11
his years be s. out. 36:26
O Lord, thou hast s. me. *Ps* 139:1
foundations of the earth s. *Jer* 31:37
though it cannot be s. 46:23
things of Esau s. out. *Ob* 6
s. the scriptures daily. *Acts* 17:11
prophets s. diligently. *1 Pet* 1:10

searchest

that thou s. after my sin. *Job* 10:6
if thou s. for her as for hid. *Pr* 2:4

searcheth

for the Lord s. all hearts. *1 Chr* 28:9
and he s. out all perfection. *Job* 28:3
and he s. after every green. 39:8
cometh and s. him. *Pr* 18:17
understanding s. him out. 28:11
that s. hearts, knows. *Rom* 8:27*
Spirit s. all things. *1 Cor* 2:10
that I am he which s. *Rev* 2:23

searching

they returned from s. *Num* 13:25
canst thou by s. find out God?
    Job 11:7
s. all the inward parts. *Pr* 20:27
there is no s. of his. *Isa* 40:28
s. what time the Spirit. *1 Pet* 1:11

searchings

of Reuben were great s. *Judg* 5:16

seared

having their conscience s. *1 Tim* 4:2*

seas

gathering of the waters called he s.
    Gen 1:10
and fill the waters in the s. 22
fins and scales in the s. eat. *Lev* 11:9
that have not fins in the s. be. 10
of abundance of the s. *Deut* 33:19
thou hast made the s. *Neh* 9:6
through paths of the s. *Ps* 8:8
founded it upon the s. 24:2
noise of the s., ... their waves. 65:7
let the s. praise him, and. 69:34
pleased, that did he in the s. 135:6
noise like noise of the s. *Isa* 17:12
increased above sand of s. *Jer* 15:8
thy borders in the midst of the s.
    Ezek 27:4
glorious in midst of the s. 25
hath broken thee in the midst of s.
    26, 27, 34
wares went forth out of the s. 33
seat of God, in midst of the s. 28:2
slain in the midst of the s. 8
art as a whale in the s. 32:2
palace between the s. *Dan* 11:45
me into midst of the s. *Jonah* 2:3
a place where two s. met. *Acts* 27:41

season

and they continued a s. *Gen* 40:4
this ordinance in his s. *Ex* 13:10
at the s. thou camest. *Deut* 16:6
unto thy land in his s. 28:12
the wilderness a long s. *Josh* 24:7*
about this s. thou shalt. *2 Ki* 4:16
woman bare a son at that s. 17
altar was at that s. *1 Chr* 21:29*
for long s. been without. *2 Chr* 15:3
corn cometh in his s. *Job* 5:26
pierced in the night s. 30:17
Mazzaroth in his s. 38:32
bringeth forth fruit in his s. *Ps* 1:3
I cry in the night s. and am. 22:2
a word spoken in due s. *Pr* 15:23
to every thing there is a s. *Eccl* 3:1
to speak a word in s. *Isa* 50:4*
latter rain in his s. *Jer* 5:24
day and night in their s. 33:20
shower come down in s. *Ezek* 34:26
prolonged for a s. *Dan* 7:12
wine in the s. thereof. *Hos* 2:9
at the s. he sent to the. *Mark* 12:2
be fulfilled in their s. *Luke* 1:20
departed from him for a s. 4:13
were present at that s. some. 13:1
at the s. he sent a servant. 20:10
to see him of a long s. 23:8*
went down at a certain s. *John* 5:4
ye were willing for a s. to. 35
seeing the sun for a s. *Acts* 13:11
stayed in Asia for a s. 19:22*
when I have a convenient s. 24:25
though it were but for a s. *2 Cor* 7:8
instant in s., out of s. *2 Tim* 4:2
departed for a s. *Philem* 15
pleasures of sin for a s. *Heb* 11:25
though for a s. if need be. *1 Pet* 1:6*
rest yet for a little s. *Rev* 6:11*
must be loosed a little s. 20:3*

see **appointed, due**

season, verb

shalt thou s. with salt. *Lev* 2:13
wherewith will ye s. it? *Mark* 9:50

seasoned

wherewith shall it be s.? *Luke* 14:34
be always with grace, s. *Col* 4:6

seasons

signs, and s. and days. *Gen* 1:14
the people at all s. *Ex* 18:22, 26
proclaim in their s. *Lev* 23:4
instruct me in the night s. *Ps* 16:7
he appointeth the moon for s. 104:19
the times and the s. *Dan* 2:21
the fruits in their s. *Mat* 21:41
know the times and the s. *Acts* 1:7
gave us rain and fruitful s. 14:17
been with you at all s. 20:18
of the s. ye have no. *1 Thes* 5:1

seat

Eglon rose out of his s. *Judg* 3:20
Eli sat upon a s. by a post.
    1 Sam 1:9; 4:13

he fell from off the s. *1 Sam* 4:18
be missed, because thy s. 20:18
the king sat on his s. on a s. by. 25
the Tachmonite that sat in the s.
    2 Sam 23:8*
caused a s. to be set. *1 Ki* 2:19*
set Haman's s. above all. *Esth* 3:1
come even to his s.! *Job* 23:3
prepared my s. in the street. 29:7
nor sitteth in the s. of the. *Ps* 1:1
sitteth on a s. in the city. *Pr* 9:14
where was the s. of the. *Ezek* 8:3
I sit in the s. of God, in midst. 28:2
and cause the s. of violence to come.
    Amos 6:3
Pharisees sit in Moses' s. *Mat* 23:2
where Satan's s. is. *Rev* 2:13*

see **judgement, mercy**

seated

the lawgiver was he s. *Deut* 33:21*

seats

moneychangers and the s. of them.
    Mat 21:12; *Mark* 11:15
love chief s. in the synagogues.
    Mat 23:6; *Mark* 12:39
the mighty from their s. *Luke* 1:52*
love the uppermost s. 11:43; 20:46
four-and-twenty s. upon. *Rev* 4:4*
sat before God on their s. 11:16*

Seba

the sons of Cush, S. *Gen* 10:7
the kings of Sheba and S. *Ps* 72:10
I gave Ethiopia and S. *Isa* 43:3

second

with s. and third stories. *Gen* 6:16
and so commanded he the s. 32:19
he made him to ride in the s. 41:43
the coupling of the s. *Ex* 26:4, 5
    10; 36:11, 12, 17
the s. row shall be an. 28:18; 39:11
he shall offer the s. for. *Lev* 5:10
set forth in the s. rank. *Num* 2:16
the s. lot came forth to. *Josh* 19:1
the s. bullock of seven. *Judg* 6:25
take s. bullock and offer. 26
the s. was offered. 28
then he sent out a s. *2 Ki* 9:19
brethren of s. degree. *1 Chr* 15:18
him in the s. chariot. *2 Chr* 35:24
silver basons of a s. sort. *Ezra* 1:10
to confirm this s. letter. *Esth* 9:29
alone, there is not a s. *Eccl* 4:8
with the s. child that shall. 15
the s. face was the. *Ezek* 10:14
behold, another beast, a s. like.
    Dan 7:5
howling from the s. *Zeph* 1:10*
in the s. chariot were. *Zech* 6:2
he came to the s. and. *Mat* 21:30
likewise the s. had her, and. 22:26
    Mark 12:21; *Luke* 20:30
s. commandment is like unto it.
    Mat 22:39; *Mark* 12:31
and it came to pass on s. *Luke* 6:1
if he shall come in s. watch. 12:38
the s. came saying, Lord thy. 19:18
this is the s. miracle that. *John* 4:54
were past the s. ward. *Acts* 12:10
as it is written in the s. psalm. 13:33
the s. man is the Lord. *1 Cor* 15:47
that ye might have a s. *2 Cor* 1:15
after the first and s. *Tit* 3:10
have been sought for the s. *Heb* 8:7
and after the s. veil, the. 9:3
into the s. went the high priest. 7
that he may establish the s. 10:9
this s. epistle I now write. *2 Pet* 3:1
hurt of the s. death. *Rev* 2:11; 20:6
the s. beast like a calf, the. 4:7
I heard the s. beast say, Come. 6:3
s. angel sounded, and as it. 8:8
the s. woe is past, the third. 11:14
the s. angel poured out his vial. 16:3
this is the s. death. 20:14; 21:8
the s. foundation of the wall. 21:19

see **day, month**

second time

called to Abraham the s. time.
    Gen 22:15
and dreamed the s. time. 41:5
had returned this s. time. 43:10
be washed the s. time. *Lev* 13:58

an alarm the *s. time.*   *Num* 10:6
circumcise Israel the *s. time.*
  Josh 5:2
smite him the *s. time.* *1 Sam* 26:8
sent to Joab the *s. time. 2 Sam* 14:29
Solomon the *s. time.*   *1 Ki* 9:2
s. time, they did it the *s. time.*
  18:34
again to Elijah the *s. time.* 19:7
a letter the *s. time.*   *2 Ki* 10:6
Solomon king *s. time.* *1 Chr* 29:22
gathered the *s. time.* *Esth* 2:19
his hand the *s. time.* *Isa* 11:11
came to me the *s. time* saying, What?
  Jer 1:13; 13:3; 33:1
came to Jonah the *s. time. Jonah* 3:1
not rise up the *s. time.* *Nah* 1:9
he went again the *s. time. Mat* 26:42
s. time the cock crew. *Mark* 14:72
can he enter the *s. time? John* 3:4
Jesus saith to Peter the *s. time.*
  21:16
at the *s. time* Joseph. *Acts* 7:13
to Peter again the *s. time.* 10:15
present the *s. time.* *2 Cor* 13:2
he shall appear the *s. time.*
  Heb 9:28

second year
they came the *s. year.* *Gen* 47:18
in the *s. year,* the first. *Ex* 40:17
in the *s. year* after. *Num* 1:1
in first month of *s. year.* 9:1
in the *s. year* the cloud was. 10:11
shall eat in the *s. year* that which.
  2 Ki 19:29; *Isa* 37:30
paid Jotham the *s. year. 2 Chr* 27:5
in the *s. year* of their. *Ezra* 3:8
it ceased to the *s. year* of. 4:24
in the *s. year* of reign. *Dan* 2:1
in *s. year* of Darius. *Hag* 1:1, 15
  2:10; *Zech* 1:7

secondarily
God set *s.* prophets. *1 Cor* 12:28

secret
not thou into their *s.* *Gen* 49:6*
heard the *s.* of God ? *Job* 15:8
when the *s.* of God was upon. 29:4
and bind their faces in *s.* 40:13*
the *s.* of the Lord is with. *Ps* 25:14
in *s.* of his tabernacle. 27:5*; 31:20
that they may shoot in *s.* 64:4*
when I was made in *s.* 139:15
but his *s.* is with the. *Pr* 3:32
stolen waters, bread eaten in *s.* 9:17
a gift in *s.* pacifieth anger. 21:14
discover not a *s.* to another. 25:9
I have not spoken in *s.* *Isa* 45:19
  48:16
no *s.* that they can hide. *Ezek* 28:3
God concerning this *s.* *Dan* 2:18
then was the *s.* revealed to. 19
the *s.* which the king hath. 27
this *s.* not revealed to me for. 30
thou couldest reveal this *s.* 47
because I know that no *s.* 4:9
he revealeth his *s.* to his. *Amos* 3:7
be in *s.:* and thy Father which seeth
  in *s.* shall reward. *Mat* 6:4, 6, 18
pray to thy Father which is in *s.* 6
to thy Father which is in *s.* 18
man doth any thing in *s. John* 7:4
feast as it were in *s.* 10
I speak openly, in *s.* have I. 18:20
are done of them in *s.* *Eph* 5:12

secret, *adjective*
idol in a *s.* place. *Deut* 27:15
s. things belong unto Lord. 29:29
I have a *s.* errand unto. *Judg* 3:19
my name, seeing it is *s.?* 13:18*
had emerods in their *s.* parts.
  1 Sam 5:9
take heed, abide in a *s.* place. *Job* 14:13
wouldest keep me *s.* *Job* 14:13
is there any *s.* with thee ? 15:11
shall be hid in his *s.* places. 20:26*
in *s.* places doth he. *Ps* 10:8*
lion lurking in *s.* places. 17:12
made darkness his *s.* place. 18:11*
cleanse thou me from *s.* faults.
  19:12*
hide me from the *s.* counsel. 64:2
I answered thee in the *s.* 81:7
our *s.* sins in the light of thy. 90:8

---

that dwelleth in the *s.* place. *Ps* 91:1
Open rebuke is better than *s.* love.
  Pr 27:5*
bring into judgement every *s.* thing.
  Eccl 12:14*
art in the *s.* places. *S of S* 2:14*
discover their *s.* parts. *Isa* 3:17
hidden riches of *s.* places. 45:3
found it by *s.* search. *Jer* 2:34
my soul shall weep in *s.* 13:17
can any hide himself in *s.?* 23:24
have uncovered his *s.* places. 49:10
he was to me as a lion in *s.* places.
  Lam 3:10
pollute my *s.* place. *Ezek* 7:22
deep and *s.* things. *Dan* 2:22
I will utter things which have been
  kept *s.* *Mat* 13:35; *Rom* 16:25
he is in *s.* chambers, believe it not.
  Mat 24:26*
was anything kept *s.* *Mark* 4:22*
  Luke 8:17
a candle in a *s.* place. *Luke* 11:33

secretly
thou flee away *s.?* *Gen* 31:27
if thy brother entice thee *s.*
  Deut 13:6
smiteth his neighbour *s.* 27:24
for want of all things *s.* 28:57
sent two men to spy *s. Josh* 2:1
commune with David *s.* and say.
  1 Sam 18:22
David knew that Saul *s.* 23:9
for thou didst it *s.* *2 Sam* 12:12
did *s.* those things that. *2 Ki* 17:9
now a thing was *s.* *Job* 4:12
will reprove you, if you *s.* 13:10
hath been *s.* enticed. 31:27
he lieth in wait *s.* as. *Ps* 10:9*
keep them *s.* in a pavilion. 31:20
Zedekiah asked *s.* Is ? *Jer* 37:17
Zedekiah the king sware *s.* 38:16
to Gedaliah in Mizpah *s.* 40:15
was to devour the poor *s. Hab* 3:14
went and called Mary her sister *s.*
  John 11:28
Joseph was a disciple, but *s.* 19:38

secrets
shew thee the *s.* of. *Job* 11:6
for he knoweth the *s.* of. *Ps* 44:21
a talebearer revealeth *s. Pr* 11:13
talebearer revealeth *s.* 20:19
God that revealeth *s. Dan* 2:28
he that revealeth *s.* maketh. 29
God is the revealer of *s.*
God shall judge the *s. Rom* 2:16
thus are the *s.* of his. *1 Cor* 14:25

secrets
taketh him by the *s.* *Deut* 25:11

sect
*This word is generally used to
mean a party in religion, differing
in belief from the main body. In
our old version it is frequently
translated heresy, which the Revisions change to sect. There
were several sects among the
Jews in the time of Christ, the
chief being :* [1] *the Pharisees or
formalists;* [2] *the Sadducees or
materialists ; and* [3] *the Essenes,
a sort of monastic body. Other
divisions, as the Herodians and
Zealots, were mainly political.
The religion preached by Christ
and his disciples was frequently
called a sect, for it was quite a
number of years before it was
extended to the Gentiles, and
the Jews who embraced it were
faithful to the major part of their
ancestral faith.*
which is the *s.* of the. *Acts* 5:17
the *s.* of the Pharisees. 15:5
a ringleader of the *s.* of the. 24:5
straitest *s.* of our religion. 26:5
this *s.* is every where spoken. 28:22

secure
the host, for it was *s. Judg* 8:11
manner of the Zidonians, *s.* 18:7
shall come to a people *s.* 10, 27

---

thou shalt be *s.* because. *Job* 11:18
they that provoke God are *s.* 12:6
will persuade him, and *s.* you.
  Mat 28:14*

securely
seeing he dwelleth, *s.* by. *Pr* 3:29
them that pass by *s.* *Mi* 2:8

security
when they had taken *s. Acts* 17:9

sedition
that they moved *s.* *Ezra* 4:15, 19
for a certain *s.* cast into prison.
  Luke 23:19*, 25*
this man a mover of *s. Acts* 24:5*

seditions
works of the flesh are *s. Gal* 5:20*

seduce
signs and wonders to *s. Mark* 13:22
written concerning them that *s.* you.
  1 John 2:26*
sufferest Jezebel to *s.* *Rev* 2:20

seduced
Manasseh *s.* them to. *2 Ki* 21:9
they have also *s.* Egypt. *Isa* 19:13*
have also *s.* my people. *Ezek* 13:10

seducers
but *s.* shall wax worse. *2 Tim* 3:13*

seduceth
the wicked *s.* them. *Pr* 12:26*

seducing
faith, giving heed to *s.* *1 Tim* 4:1

see
unto Adam, to *s.* what he. *Gen* 2:19
he sent a dove to *s.* if the. 8:8
and the Lord came down to *s.* 11:5
he said unto him, S. I have. 19:21
s. the smell of my son is as. 27:27
he said, I *s.* your father's. 31:5
Dinah went out to *s.* the. 34:1
but to *s.* the nakedness. 42:9, 12
thou saidst, You shall *s.* 44:23
your eyes *s.* and the eyes of. 45:12
he said, S. that ye fall not out. 24
s. Joseph before I die. 28
I had not thought to *s.* thy. 48:11
when ye *s.* them upon the stools.
  Ex 1:16
I will turn aside and *s.* this. 3:3, 4
s. whether my brethren be. 4:18
s. that thou do those wonders. 21
the officers did *s.* they were. 5:19
now shalt thou *s.* what I will. 6:1
that one cannot be able to *s.* 10:5
take heed to thyself, *s.* my face. 28
I will *s.* thy face no more. 29
when I *s.* the blood, I will. 12:13
repent when they *s.* war. 13:17
stand still and *s.* the. 14:13
s. for the Lord hath given. 16:29
they may *s.* the bread. 32
for there shall no man *s.* 33:20
and thou shalt *s.* my back parts. 23
the people shall *s.* the work. 34:10
priest shall *s.* him. *Lev* 13:10, 17
s. her nakedness and she *s.* 20:17
shall not go in to *s. Num* 4:20
shalt *s.* whether my word. 11:23
s. the land, what it is. 13:18
that provoked me *s.* it. 14:23
that thence he might *s.* the. 22:41
top of the rocks I *s.* him. 23:9
come to another place, whence thou
  mayest *s.* them, thou shalt *s.* 13
I shall *s.* him, but not now. 24:17
and *s.* the land, which I. 27:12
from Kadesh to *s.* land. 32:8
men that came up out of Egypt shall
  s. the land. 32:11; *Deut* 1:35
save Caleb, he shall *s.* *Deut* 1:36
I pray thee, let me *s.* the. 3:25
the land which thou shalt *s.* 28
that he *s.* no unclean thing. 23:14
all people shall *s.* that thou. 28:10
eyes which thou shalt *s.* 34, 67
thou shalt *s.* it no more again. 68
not given you eyes to *s.* 29:4
when they *s.* the plagues of. 22
s. I have set before thee life. 30:15
he said, I will *s.* what their. 32:20
s. now, I, even I, am he, there. 39
yet thou shalt *s.* land before. 52

I have caused thee to s. *Deut* 34:4
there a great altar to s. *Josh* 22:10
Samson turned aside to s. *Judg* 14:8
s. wherein his great strength. 16:5
shall s. an enemy in. *1 Sam* 2:32
ark, and rejoiced to s. it. 6:13
now s. this great thing. 12:16
ye may s. that your wickedness. 17
number now, and s. who. 14:17
and s. wherein this sin hath. 38
Samuel came no more to s. 15:35
thou mightest s. the battle. 17:28
and what I s. that I will tell. 19:3
messengers again to s. David. 15
me get away, I pray, and s. 20:29
Ye s. the man is mad. 21:14
know and s. his place, where. 23:22
my father s. yea, s. the skirt. 24:11
s. where king's spear is. 26:16
when thy father cometh to s. thee, let
Tamar . . . may s. it. *2 Sam* 13:5
now therefore, let me s. the. 14:32
S. thy matters are good and. 15:3
my lord the king may s. it. 24:3
s. what answer I shall return. 13
s. to thy house, David. *1 Ki* 12:16
2 *Chr* 10:16
Elijah said, S. thy son liveth.
1 *Ki* 17:23
and s. how this man seeketh. 20:7
mark and s. what thou doest, 22
thou shalt s. in that day. 2 *Chr* 18:24
if thou s. when I am. *2 Ki* 2:10
s. how he seeketh a. 5:7
open his eyes that he may s. 6:17
these men that they may s. 20
s. how this son of a murderer. 32
shalt s. it with thine eyes. 7:2, 19
let us send and s. 13
saying, Go and s. 14
went down to s. Joram. 8:29
9:16; 2 *Chr* 22:6
the watchman said, I s. a. *2 Ki* 9:17
go s. now this cursed woman. 34
come with me, and s. my. 10:16
thine eyes, and s. 19:16; *Isa* 37:17
title is this that I s.? *2 Ki* 23:17
he said, I did s. all Israel.
2 *Chr* 18:16
s. the salvation of the Lord. 20:17
go, and s. that ye hasten the. 24:5
come, let us s. one another. 25:17
was not meet to s. the. *Ezra* 4:14
didst s. affliction of our. *Neh* 9:9
to s. if Mordecai's. *Esth* 3:4
so long as I s. Mordecai the. 5:13
endure to s. the evil that shall come
upon my people ? to s. the. 8:6
neither let it s. the dawning. *Job* 3:9
mine eye shall no more s. 7:7
the eye that hath seen me shall s. 8
my days flee away, they s. no. 9:25
s. thou mine affliction. 10:15
as for my hope, who shall s.? 17:15
yet in my flesh shall I s. God. 19:26
whom I shall s. for myself. 27
the eye which saw him shall s. 20:9
eyes shall s. his destruction. 21:20
righteous s. it, and are glad. 22:19
know him not s. his days? 24:1
saith, No eye shall s. me. 15
did he s. it, and declare it. 28:27
doth not he s. my ways ? 31:4
shall pray, and he will s. his. 33:26
his life shall s. the light. 28
look unto the heavens, and s. 35:5
every man may s. it. 36:25
God will never s. it. *Ps* 10:11
God looked to s. if any. 14:2; 53:2
Holy One to s. corruption. 16:10
Acts 2:27, 31; 13:35
all they that s. laughed me. *Ps* 22:7
believed s. the goodness. 27:13
they that did s. me without. 31:11
O taste and s. that the Lord. 34:8
days, that he may s. good. 12
are cut off, thou shalt s. it. 37:34
many shall s. it and trust in. 40:3
if he come to s. me, he. 41:6
he shall go, they shall never s. 49:19
the righteous also shall s. and. 52:6
God shall let me s. my desire on my.
59:10; 92:11; 118:7

to s. thy power and glory. *Ps* 63:2
say, Who shall s. them ? 64:5
all that s. them shall flee away. 8
come and s. the works of God. 66:5
the humble shall s. this, and. 69:32
which hate me may s. it. 86:17
thou shalt s. the reward of. 91:8
and all the people s. his glory. 97:6
that I may s. the good of. 106:5
these s. the works of the. 107:24
righteous shall s. it and rejoice. 42
till he s. his desire upon his. 112:8
the wicked shall s. it and be. 10
glad when they s. me. 119:74
thou shalt s. the good of. 128:5
thou shalt s. thy children's. 6
thy eyes did s. my substance. 139:16
search, s. if there be any. 24
lest the Lord s. and. *Pr* 24:18
but the righteous shall s. 29:16
whereof it may be said, S. *Eccl* 1:10
till I might s. what was good. 2:3
men might s. that themselves. 3:18
bring him to s. what shall be. 22
there is profit to them that s. 7:11
to s. the business that is done. 8:16
O my dove, let me s. *S of S* 2:14
I went into the garden of nuts to s.
the fruits, and to s. 6:11; 7:12
his work, that we may s. *Isa* 5:19
lest they s. with their eyes. 6:10
that s. thee shall narrowly. 14:16
they shall s. and be ashamed. 26:11
eyes of the blind shall s. out. 29:18
eyes shall s. thy teachers. 30:20
the eyes of them that s. shall. 32:3
thine eyes shall s. the king. 33:17
thine eyes shall s. Jerusalem. 20
they shall s. the glory of the. 35:2
and all flesh shall s. it together. 40:5
that they may s. and know. 41:20
s. all this. 48:6
kings shall s. and arise. 49:7
for they shall s. eye to eye. 52:8
the earth shall s. salvation of our. 10
been told them shall they s. 15
when we shall s. him, there is. 53:2
he shall s. his seed, he shall. 10
he shall s. of travail of his soul. 11
then thou shalt s., and flow. 60:5
all that s. them shall. 61:9
the Gentiles shall s. thy. 62:2
behold, s. we beseech, we are. 64:9
and they shall come and s. 66:18
I s. a rod. *Jer* 1:11
s. a seething pot. 13
send to Kedar, s. if there be. 2:10
know and s. that it is an evil. 19
s. thy way in the valley, know. 23
and s. where thou hast not. 3:2
how long shall I s. the ? 4:21
s. now and know, and seek. 5:1
stand ye in the ways and s. 6:16
go to my place, and s. what. 7:12
me s. thy vengeance. 11:20; 20:12
out of the womb to s. labour. 20:18
he shall die and s. this land. 22:12
s. whether man doth travail ? why
do I s. every man with his? 30:6
and shalt s. and shalt read. 51:61
s. O Lord, consider, for. *Lam* 1:11
s. if there be any sorrow like. 12
thou shalt s. greater abominations.
Ezek 8:6, 13, 15
that s. vanity. 13:9
s. visions of peace for her. 16
may s. all thy nakedness. 16:37
all flesh shall s. that I. 20:48
whiles they s. vanity unto. 21:29
Pharaoh shall s. them. 32:31
the watchman s. the sword. 33:6
all the heathen shall s. my. 39:21
why should he s. your ? *Dan* 1:10
I s. four men loose, walking. 3:25
dream dreams, your young men shall
s. visions. *Joel* 2:23; *Acts* 2:17
might s. what would. *Jonah* 4:5
the man of wisdom shall s. *Mi* 6:9
mine enemy shall s. it. 7:10
the nations shall s. and be. 16
I will watch to s. what he. *Hab* 2:1
to s. what is the breadth. *Zech* 2:2
shall s. the plummet in hand. 4:10

I s. a flying roll. *Zech* 5:2
lift your eyes, s. what is this that. 5
s. it, and fear, Geza shall s. it. 9:5
yea, their children shall s. it. 10:7
and your eyes shall s. *Mal* 1:5
for they shall s. God. *Mat* 5:8
they may s. your good works. 16
and then shalt thou s. clearly. 7:5
Luke 6:42
s. thou tell no man, shew *Mat* 8:4
9:30; *Mark* 1:44; *Acts* 23:22
things you hear and s. *Mat* 11:4
out into wilderness to s.? a reed
shaken. 7, 8, 9, *Luke* 7:24, 25, 26
Master, we would s. a sign from.
Mat 12:38
seeing, ye shall s. 13:14; *Mark* 4:12
Acts 28:26
any time they should s. with their
eyes. *Mat* 13:15; *Acts* 28:27
your eyes, for they s. *Mat* 13:16
to s. those things which ye s. 17
the blind to s. 15:31; *Luke* 7:22
they s. the Son of man. *Mat* 16:28
when the king came in to s. 22:11
shall hear of wars, s. that ye. 24:6
they shall s. the Son of man coming.
30; *Mark* 13:26; *Luke* 21:27
Peter sat with the servants, to s. the
end. *Mat* 26:58
they said, S. thou to that. 27:4
s. ye to it. 24
let us s. whether Elias will. 49
come s. the place where the. 28:6
there shall they s. me. 10
they went out to s. what. *Mark* 5:14
he looked to s. her that had. 32
go and s. 6:38
I s. men as trees walking. 8:24
that we may s. and believe. 15:32
Bethlehem and s. this. *Luke* 2:15
flesh shall s. the salvation. 3:6
enter in may s. light. 8:16; 11:33
desiring to s. thee. 8:20
he desired to s. him. 9:9; 23:8
not taste of death till they s. 27
ground, I must go and s. it. 14:18
when ye shall desire to s. 17:22
s. here, or s. there, go not. 23
Zacchaeus sought to s. Jesus. 19:3
sycamore tree to s. him. 4
him when they s. him. 20:13
myself, handle me and s. 24:39
on whom thou shalt s. the Spirit.
John 1:33
come and s. 39, 46; 11:34; *Rev* 6:1
3, 5, 7
shalt s. greater things. *John* 1:50
s. a man who told me all. 4:29
shall never s. death. 8:51
rejoiced to s. my day. 56
how then doth he now s.? 19
I was blind, now I s. 25
that they who s. not might s. and that
they who s. might be. 39
if believe, thou shouldest s. 11:40
but that they might s. Lazarus. 12:9
Sir, we would s. Jesus. 21
ye have sorrow, but I will s. 16:22
except I s. in his hands. 20:25
and s. how they do. *Acts* 15:36
I must also s. Rome. 19:21
ye all shall s. my face. 20:25, 38
know his will, and s. that. 22:14
I called you, to s. you. 28:20
for I long to s. you. *Rom* 1:11
I s. another law in my. 7:23
spoken of, they shall s. 15:21
to s. you in my journey. 24
if any man s. thee that. *1 Cor* 8:10
s. that he may be with you. 16:10
s. that ye abound in. *2 Cor* 8:7
Jerusalem to s. Peter. *Gal* 1:18
make all men s. what is. *Eph* 3:9
s. that ye walk circumspectly. 5:15
the wife s. that she reverence. 33
whether I come and s. *Phil* 1:27
so soon as I s. how it will go. 2:23
to s. your face with. *1 Thes* 2:17
to s. us, as we also to s. you. 3:6
s. that none render evil for. 5:15
hath seen, nor can s. *1 Tim* 6:16
greatly desiring to s. *2 Tim* 1:4

s. thou make all according. *Heb* 8:5
no man s. the Lord. 12:14
s. that ye refuse not him that. 25
he come shortly, I will s. you. 13:23
s. that ye love one. *1 Pet* 1:22
he that will s. good days. 3:10
if any man s. his brother sin a sin
  not unto death. *1 John* 5:16
I shall shortly s. thee. *3 John* 14
every eye shall s. him. *Rev* 1:7
to s. the voice that spake. 12
eyesalve, that thou mayst s. 3:18
and s. thou hurt not the oil. 6:6
shall s. their dead bodies. 11:9
lest he walk naked, and they s. 16:15
I sit a queen, shall s. no sorrow. 18:7
when they shall s. the smoke. 9
he said to me, S. thou. 19:10; 22:9
and they shall s. his face. 22:4

see *not*, or *not* see

let me *not* s. the death. *Gen* 21:16
old, that he could *not* s. 27:1
ye shall *not* s. my face. 43:3, 5
for we may *not* s. the man's. 44:26
were dim, he could *not* s. 48:10
thou canst *not* s. my face. *Ex* 33:20
let me *not* s. my wretchedness.
  Num 11:15
they shall *not* s. the land. 14:23
utmost part, and shall *not* s. 23:13
thou shalt *not* s. thy. *Deut* 22:1
shalt *not* s. thy brother's ass. 4
Eli, his eyes dim, he could *not* s.
  1 Sam 3:2; 4:15
not s. my face, except. *2 Sam* 3:13
let *not* Absalom s. my face. 14:24
Ahijah could *not* s. *1 Ki* 14:4
not s. wind, nor shall ye s. *2 Ki* 3:17
thine eyes shall *not* s. all evil. 22:20
by me, and I s. him *not*. *Job* 9:11
he shall *not* s. the rivers of. 20:17
that thou canst *not* s. 22:11
himself that I *cannot* s. him. 23:9
that which I s. *not* teach. 34:32
sayest, thou shalt *not* s. him. 35:14
men s. *not* the bright light. 37:21
should still live, and *not* s. *Ps* 49:9
pass away, that they may *not* s. the
  sun. 58:8
be darkened, that they s. *not*. 69:23
we s. *not* our signs, there. 74:9
and shall *not* s. death. 89:48
the Lord shall *not* s. 94:7
the eye, shall he *not* s.? 9
eyes have they, but they s. *not*.
  115:5; 135:16; *Jer* 5:21
is lifted up, they will *not* s. *Isa* 26:11
say to the seers, S. *not*. 30:10
thou shalt *not* s. a fierce. 33:19
I shall *not* s. the Lord, even. 38:11
they s. *not*, that they may be. 44:9
eyes, that they *cannot* s. 18
they said, He shall *not* s. *Jer* 12:4
prophets say, Ye shall *not* s. 14:13
like heath, he shall *not* s. 17:6
he shall *not* s. when heat. 8
that I shall *not* s. him? 23:24
cover thy face, that thou s. *not* the
  ground. *Ezek* 12:6, 12
yet shall he *not* s. it, though he. 13
gods of gold, which s. *not*. *Dan* 5:23
thou shalt *not* s. evil. *Zeph* 3:15
because they seeing s. *not*; and hearing they hear not. *Mat* 13:13
ye shall *not* s. me henceforth. 23:39
  Luke 13:35
Jesus said, S. ye *not* all? *Mat* 24:2
having eyes, s. ye *not*? *Mark* 8:18
not s. death, before. *Luke* 2:26
seeing, they might *not* s. 8:10
to s. and ye shall *not* s. it. 17:22
cannot s. the kingdom. *John* 3:3
shall *not* s. life, but wrath. 36
they who s. *not* might see. 9:39
that they should *not* s. with. 12:40
shall *not* s. me. 16:16, 17, 19
I *not* s. thee in the garden? 18:26
when I could *not* s. for. *Acts* 22:11
that they should *not* s. *Rom* 11:10
darkened that they may *not* s. 10
for I will *not* s. you. *1 Cor* 16:7
but we s. *not* yet all things. *Heb* 2:8
he should *not* s. death. 11:5

now ye s. him *not*, yet. *1 Pet* 1:8
he is blind, and *cannot* s. *2 Pet* 1:9

we see

we shall s. what will. *Gen* 37:20
light shall we s. light. *Ps* 36:9
neither shall we s. sword. *Jer* 5:12
where we shall s. no war. 42:14
that we may s. and believe.
  Mark 15:32; *John* 6:30
now we say, We s. your. *John* 9:41
for that we s. not. *Rom* 8:25
now we s. through a. *1 Cor* 13:12
we might s. your face. *1 Thes* 3:10
but we s. Jesus, who was. *Heb* 2:9
so we s. that they could not. 3:19
for we shall s. him as. *1 John* 3:2

ye see, or see ye

ye shall s. them again. *Ex* 14:13
then ye shall s. the glory of. 16:7
when ye s. the ark of. *Josh* 3:3
s. ye him whom the? *1 Sam* 10:24
to hissing, as ye s. *2 Chr* 29:8
to desolation, as ye s. 30:7
I said, Ye s. the distress. *Neh* 2:17
s. ye my casting down. *Job* 6:21
what will ye s. in the? *S of S* 6:13
and s. ye indeed, but. *Isa* 6:9
s. ye, when he lifteth up an. 18:3
ye blind, that ye may s. 42:18
when ye s. your hearts shall. 66:14
O generation, s. ye the word of the.
  Jer 2:31
ye shall s. this place no more. 42:18
therefore ye shall s. no. *Ezek* 13:23
ye shall s. their way and. 14:22
they shall comfort you when ye s. 23
because ye s. the thing. *Dan* 2:8
to s. those things which ye s. and.
  Mat 13:17
Jesus said, S. ye not all? *Mat* 24:2
when ye shall s. all these. 33
  Mark 13:29; *Luke* 21:31
hereafter shall ye s. the Son of.
  Mat 26:64; *Mark* 14:62
I am innocent, s. ye to it.
  Mat 27:24; *Mark* 15:36
into Galilee; there shall ye s. him
  Mat 28:7; *Mark* 16:7
when ye s. a cloud rise. *Luke* 12:54
and when ye s. the south wind. 55
when ye shall s. Abraham. 13:28
when ye shall s. Jerusalem. 21:20
ye s. and know of yourselves. 30
and bones, as ye s. me. 24:39
ye shall s. heaven open. *John* 1:51
except ye s. signs ye will not. 4:48
what if ye shall s. the Son of. 6:62
but ye s. me. 14:19
and ye s. me no more. 16:10
while ye shall s. me. 16, 17, 19
shed this which ye now s. *Acts* 2:33
whom ye s. and know. 3:16
ye s. and hear, that not alone. 19:26
ye s. this man, about whom. 25:24
for ye s. your calling. *1 Cor* 1:26
ye s. how large a letter. *Gal* 6:11
when ye s. him again. *Phil* 2:28
much more, as ye s. day. *Heb* 10:25
ye s. how that by works. *Jas* 2:24
though now ye s. him not. *1 Pet* 1:8

seed

[1] *The seed of plants.* [2] *The
posterity of any particular man, as
the seed of Abraham, referring to
all his descendants.*

herbs yielding s. *Gen* 1:11, 12, 29
give us s. that we may live. 47:19
lo, here is s. for you. 23
shall be your own for s. 24
was like coriander s. *Ex* 16:31
fall on any sowing s. *Lev* 11:37
water be put upon the s. 38
sow thy field with mingled s. 19:19
shall sow your s. in vain. 26:16
according to the s. an homer of
  barley s. valued at 50. 27:16
s. of the land is the Lord's.
it is no place of s. or of figs. *Num* 20:5
where thou sowedst s. *Deut* 11:10
all the increase of thy s. 14:22
thy s. sown be defiled s. 22:9*
thou shalt carry much s. into. 28:38

the king will take the tenth of s.
  1 Sam 8:15
two measures of s. *1 Ki* 18:32
unicorn bring home thy s.? *Job* 39:12
forth bearing precious s. *Ps* 126:6
in the morning sow thy s. *Eccl* 11:6
the s. of an homer shall. *Isa* 5:10
in the morning make thy s. 17:11
great waters the s. of Sihor. 23:3
that it may give s. to the. 55:10
nor shall sow s. nor plant. *Jer* 35:7
have we vineyard, field, nor s. 9
he took also of the s. *Ezek* 17:5
the s. is rotten under. *Joel* 1:17
him that soweth s. *Amos* 9:13
is the s. yet in the barn? *Hag* 2:19
s. shall be prosperous. *Zech* 8:12
I will corrupt your s. *Mal* 2:3
which receive s. by the. *Mat* 13:19
s. into stony places. 20
s. among the thorns. 22
but he that received s. into good. 23
a man which sowed good s. 24
didst not thou sow good s.? 27
he that soweth the good s. is. 37
the good s. are the children of. 38
if a man should cast s. *Mark* 4:26
and the s. should spring and. 27
to sow his s.: some fell by. *Luke* 8:5
parable is this; the s. is word. 11
every s. his own body. *1 Cor* 15:38
that ministereth s. to. *2 Cor* 9:10
not of corruptible s. *1 Pet* 1:23
for his s. remaineth in. *1 John* 3:9

seed for *posterity*

appointed me another s. *Gen* 4:25
to keep s. alive upon the face. 7:3
to me thou hast given no s. 15:3
preserve s. of our father. 19:32, 34
marry her, and raise up s. to. 38:8
  Mat 22:24; *Mark* 12:19
  Luke 20:28
Onan knew that the s. *Gen* 38:9
conceived s. and born. *Lev* 12:2
hath a blemish of the s. 21:21
what man of the s. of Aaron. 22:4
woman shall conceive s. *Num* 5:28
which is not of s. of Aaron. 16:40
their s. after them. *Deut* 1:8; 11:9
he chose their s. after them. 4:37
  10:15
the mouths of their s. 31:21
s. the Lord shall give. *Ruth* 4:12
the Lord give thee s. *1 Sam* 2:20
thou wilt not cut off my s. 24:21
king's s. in Edom. *1 Ki* 11:14
will for this afflict the s. of David. 39
of Ahaziah, arose and destroyed all
  the s. *2 Ki* 11:1; *2 Chr* 22:10
the Lord rejected all the s. of.
  2 Ki 17:20
Ishmael of the s. royal came. 25:25
  Jer 41:1
O ye s. of Israel his. *1 Chr* 16:13
they could not shew their s.
  Ezra 2:59; *Neh* 7:61
the holy s. have mingled. *Ezra* 9:2
the s. of Israel separated. *Neh* 9:2
if Mordecai be of the s. *Esth* 6:13
took upon them and their s. 9:27, 31
of them perish from their s. 28
their s. is established in. *Job* 21:8
their s. shalt thou destroy. *Ps* 21:10
ye the s. of Jacob, glorify him; and
  fear him, all ye the s. of. 22:23
a s. shall serve him, it shall be. 30
but the s. of the wicked shall. 37:28
the s. also of his servants. 69:36
their s. shall be established. 102:28
to overthrow their s. 106:27
the s. of righteous shall. *Pr* 11:21
ah, sinful nation, a s. of. *Isa* 1:4
the holy s. shall be the. 6:13
the s. of evildoers shall. 14:20
I said not unto s. of Jacob. 45:19
in the Lord shall all s. of Israel. 25
the s. of the adulterer and. 57:3
of transgression, a s. of falsehood. 4
their s. shall be known among the
  Gentiles; that they are s. 61:9
bring forth a s. out of Jacob. 65:9
they are the s. of the blessed. 23
thee wholly a right s. *Jer* 2:21

I will cast out the whole s. of. Jer 7:15
which led the s. of the house. 23:8
sow with s. of man and s. of. 31:27
then s. of Israel also shall cease. 36
off all the s. of Israel. 37; 33:26
so will I multiply the s. of. 33:22
taken of the king's s. Ezek 17:13
I lifted up my hand to the s. 20:5
that be of the s. of Zadok. 43:19
maidens of the s. of Israel. 44:22
children of the king's s. Dan 1:3
themselves with the s. of. 2:43
Darius of the s. of the Medes. 9:1
might seek a godly s. Mal 2:15
dying left no s. Mark 12:20, 21, 22
that Christ cometh of s. John 7:42
this man's s. hath God. Acts 13:23
was made of the s. of David.
　　　　　　Rom 1:3; 2 Tim 2:8
be sure to all his s. Rom 4:16
the promise counted for s. 9:8
of sabaoth had left us a s. 29
it was added, till the s. Gal 3:19
strength to conceive s. Heb 11:11
the remnant of her s. Rev 12:17

see Abraham

his seed
with Isaac and his s. Gen 17:19
Jacob came, and all his s. 46:6, 7
and his s. shall become a. 48:19
a statute of his s. after him.
　　　　　　Ex 28:43; 30:21
giveth any of his s. to Molech.
　　　　　　Lev 20:2, 3, 4
nor shall ye profane his s. 21:15
servant Caleb and his s. Num 14:24
and his s. shall be in many. 24:7
he shall have it, and his s. 25:13
I multiplied his s. and. Josh 24:3
thee of Saul and his s. 2 Sam 4:8
to David and his s. for evermore.
　　　　　2 Sam 22:51; Ps 18:50
on head of Joab and his s. for ever,
upon David and his s. 1 Ki 2:33
covenant to give it to his s. Neh 9:8
peace to all his s. Esth 10:3
his s. shall inherit the. Ps 25:13
nor have I seen his s. begging. 37:25
he is merciful, and his s. is. 26
his s. also will I make to endure.
　　　　　　89:29, 36
his s. shall be mighty. 112:2
he shall see his s. Isa 53:10
cast out, he and his s.? Jer 22:28
for no man of his s. shall prosper. 30
punish Shemaiah and his s. 29:32
I will not take any of his s. 33:26
Jehoiachim and his s. 36:31
Esau, his s. is spoiled. 49:10
him and his s. after him. Acts 7:5
that his s. should sojourn in a. 6

thy seed
between thy s. and her s. Gen 3:15
to thy s. will I give this land. 12:7
13:15; 15:18; 17:8; 24:7; 26:3
28:4, 13; 35:12; 48:4; Ex 33:1
　　　　　　Deut 34:4
I will make thy s. as dust.
　　　Gen 13:16; 16:10; 28:14
he said to him, So shall thy s. be.
　　　15:5; Rom 4:18
that thy s. shall be a stranger in a.
　　　　　　Gen 15:13
between me and thy s. after thee;
. . . to thee and thy s. 17:7, 10
thou and thy s. after thee in. 9
a stranger not of thy s. shall. 12
in Isaac shall thy s. be called. 21:12
　　　　　　Heb 11:18
Ishmael a nation, because he is thy s.
　　　　　　Gen 21:13
thy s. possess the gate of enemies.
　　　22:17; 24:60
in thy s. all the nations of the. 22:18
26:4; 28:14; Acts 3:25
and multiply thy s. for. Gen 26:24
will make thy s. as the sand. 32:12
shewed me also thy s. 48:11
not any of thy s. pass. Lev 18:21
whosoever of thy s. hath any. 21:17
I give thee and thy s. Num 18:19
sign on thy s. for ever. Deut 28:46
Lord will make plagues of thy s. 59

circumcise heart of thy s. Deut 30:6
choose life, that thou and thy s. 19
be between my s. and thy s.
　　　　　　1 Sam 20:42
I will set up thy s. 2 Sam 7:12
　　　　　　1 Chr 17:11
cleave to thee and thy s. 2 Ki 5:27
thy s. shall be great. Job 5:25
thy s. will I establish. Ps 89:4
I will bring thy s. from. Isa 43:5
I will pour my spirit upon thy s.
　　　　　　44:3
thy s. also had been as the. 48:19
and thy s. shall inherit the. 54:3
depart out of the mouth of thy s. nor
thy seed's s. 59:21
thy s. from the land of captivity.
　　　Jer 30:10; 46:27
thy s. which is Christ. Gal 3:16

your seed
will I give to your s. Ex 32:13
whosoever of your s. goeth. Lev 22:3
so shall your s. and your. Isa 66:22

seeds
vineyard with divers s. Deut 22:9
when he sowed, some s. Mat 13:4
which is the least of all s. 32
　　　　　　Mark 4:31
he saith not, and to s. as. Gal 3:16

seedtime
s. and harvest shall not. Gen 8:22

seeing, substantive
or who maketh the s.? Ex 4:11

seeing
driven away, no man s. Ex 22:10
s. him not, cast it upon him, that he
die. Num 35:23
mine eyes even s. it. 1 Ki 1:48
maketh the s. eye. Pr 20:12
eye is not satisfied with s. Eccl 1:8
dismayed at the s. of it. Isa 21:3
shutteth his eyes from s. evil. 33:15
s. many things, but thou. 42:20
s. vanity, and divining. Ezek 22:28
because they s. see not. Mat 13:13
s. ye shall see and shall not perceive. 14; Mark 4:12; Acts 28:26
washed and came s. John 9:7
he s. this, spake of the. Acts 2:31
s. Peter and John about to go. 3:3
s. one of them suffer wrong. 7:24
the people s. the miracles. 8:6
speechless, hearing a voice, but s. 9:7
be blind, not s. the sun for. 13:11
he endured as s. him. Heb 11:27
in s. and hearing, vexed. 2 Pet 2:8

seeing, adverb
what wilt thou give me, s. Gen 15:2
s. thou hast not withheld. 22:12
s. the Lord hath prospered. 24:56
come ye to me, s. ye hate me? 26:27
s. his life is bound up in. 44:30
s. all the congregation. Num 16:3
my name, s. it is secret. Judg 13:18
s. I have a Levite. 17:13
s. women are destroyed out. 21:16
the Lord hath testified. Ruth 1:21
s. I have rejected him. 1 Sam 16:1
s. the Lord is departed from. 28:16
s. there is no wrong in. 1 Chr 12:17
s. the root of the matter. Job 19:28
s. he judgeth those that are. 21:22
s. times are not hidden from. 24:1
s. thou hatest instruction. Ps 50:17
s. he dwelleth securely. Pr 3:29
s. I have lost my. Isa 49:21
s. the Lord hath given. Jer 47:7
s. thou couldest reveal. Dan 2:47
s. I know not a man. Luke 1:34
s. thou art in the same condemnation. 23:40
s. he is Lord of heaven. Acts 17:24
s. he giveth to all life and. 25
s. it is one God who shall. Rom 3:30
s. then that we have. 2 Cor 3:12
s. that ye have put off. Col 3:9
s. it remaineth some must. Heb 4:6
s. then that we have a great. 14
hard to be uttered, s. ye are dull.
　　　　　　5:11
s. they crucify the Son of God. 6:6
s. he ever liveth to make. 7:25

s. we are compassed about. Heb 12:1
s. ye have purified your. 1 Pet 1:22
s. ye look for such things, be diligent.
　　　　　　2 Pet 3:14
s. ye know these things before. 17

seek
I s. my brethren, tell. Gen 37:16
s. me, s. my occasion. 43:18
and s. ye the priesthood also?
　　　　　　Num 16:10
Balaam went not to s. for. 24:1
if thou s. him with all. Deut 4:29
to his habitation shall ye s. 12:5
till thy brother s. after it. 22:2
Saul his son, Go s. the asses.
　　　　　　1 Sam 9:3
ye ? he said, To s. the asses. 10:14
to s. out a cunning player. 16:16
Saul come to s. his life. 23:15, 25
　　　　　24:2; 26:2
they that s. evil to my Lord. 25:26
is risen to pursue and s. thy soul. 29
Israel is come out to s. a flea. 26:20
s. me a woman that hath a. 28:7
came up to s. David. 2 Sam 5:17
Shimei went to s. his. 1 Ki 2:40
Lord hath not sent to s. the. 18:10
they s. my life to take. 19:10, 14
let them go and s. thy. 2 Ki 2:16
to the man whom ye s. 6:19
s. the commandments. 1 Chr 28:8
if thou s. him, he. 9; 2 Chr 15:2
thine heart to s. God. 2 Chr 19:3
that prepareth his heart to s. 30:19
to s. his God, he did it with. 31:21
Josiah began to s. after the. 34:3
build, for we s. your God. Ezra 4:2
prepared his heart to s. the. 7:10
to s. him a right way for us. 8:21
them for good that s. him. 22
to s. the welfare of. Neh 2:10
I would s. unto God. Job 5:8
shalt s. me in morning, but. 7:21
if thou wouldest s. unto God. 8:5
his children shall s. to please. 20:10
will ye s. after leasing ? Ps 4:2
forsaken them that s. thee. 9:10
s. out his wickedness till thou. 10:15
any that did s. God. 14:2; 53:2
of them that s. him. 24:6
that will I s. after. 27:4
s. ye my face, thy face, Lord, will I s.
　　　　　　8
s. peace, and pursue it. 34:14
　　　　　　1 Pet 3:11
let them be put to shame that s.
　　　　　　Ps 35:4
s. my life, they that s. 38:12
confounded that s. after my soul.
　　　　　40:14; 70:2
oppressors s. after my soul. 54:3
God, early will I s. thee. 63:1
those that s. my soul go into the. 9
let not those that s. thee be. 69:6
heart shall live that s. God. 32
let all those that s. thee rejoice. 70:4
dishonour that s. my hurt. 71:13
unto shame that s. my hurt. 24
that they may s. thy name. 83:16
the young lions s. their meat. 104:21
his children s. their bread. 109:10
blessed, that s. him with. 119:2
I will walk at liberty, for I s. 45
as a sheep, s. thy servant. 176
I will s. thy good. 122:9
they shall s. me, but. Pr 1:28
and those that s. me early. 8:17
and fro of them that s. death. 21:6
sorrow ? they that tarry long at
wine, they that go to s. 23:30
when I shall awake, I will s. it. 35
upright: the just s. his soul. 29:10
many s. the ruler's favour. 26
I gave my heart to s. Eccl 1:13
I applied mine heart to s. out. 7:25
though a man labour to s. it. 8:17
I will s. him whom my. S of S 3:2
thy beloved, that we may s. 6:1
learn to do well, s. Isa 1:17
s. unto them that have familiar
spirits; should not a people s.? 8:19
to it shall the Gentiles s. 11:10

they shall *s*. to the charmers. *Isa* 19:3
my spirit within me will I *s*.   26:9
s. ye out of book of the Lord. 34:16
thou shalt *s*. them, and not.   41:12
when the needy *s*. water, and.   17
I said not to Jacob, *S*. ye.   45:19
yet they *s*. me daily, and.   58:2
that *s*. her, in her month. *Jer* 2:24
thou thy way to *s*. love ?   33
thee, they will *s*. thy life.   4:30
the men of Anathoth, that *s*.   11:21
to fall by them that *s*.   19:7; 21:7
they that *s*. their lives shall.   9
them that *s*. thy life.   22:25; 38:16
s. the peace of the city.   29:7
ye shall *s*. me, and find me.   13
them that *s*. their life.   34:20, 21
give Pharaoh into the hand of them
   that *s*. his life.   44:30
Egyptians to those that *s*.   46:26
them that *s*. their life.   49:37
all her people sigh, they *s*. *Lam* 1:11
they shall *s*. peace there. *Ezek* 7:25
then shall they *s*. a vision.   26
flock was scattered, none did *s*. 34:6
I will search my sheep, and *s*.   11
as a shepherd so will I *s*. out.   12
I will *s*. that which was lost.   16
I set my face unto God, to *s*. by
   prayer.   *Dan* 9:3
he shall *s*. them, but not. *Hos* 2:7
saith the Lord, *S*. me. *Amos* 5:4
s. him that maketh the seven.   8
s. good and not evil, that ye.   14
to *s*. the word of the Lord.   8:12
shall I *s*. comforters for ? *Nah* 3:7
thou shalt be hid, thou shalt *s*.   11
s. ye the Lord, ye meek. *Zeph* 2:3
a shepherd shall not *s*. *Zech* 11:16
in that day I will *s*. to destroy. 12:9
they should *s*. the law at. *Mal* 2:7
that he might *s*. a godly seed.   15
Herod will *s*. young child. *Mat* 2:13
things do the Gentiles *s*.   6:32
s. ye first the kingdom of God.   33
   Luke 12:31
s. and ye shall find, knock.
   Mat 7:7; *Luke* 11:9
for I know that ye *s*. Jesus.
   Mat 28:5; *Mark* 16:6
they said to him, All men *s*.
   Mark 1:37
thy mother and thy brethren *s*. 3:32
generation *s*. after a sign. 8:12; 11:29
do the nations *s*. after. *Luke* 12:30
many, I say unto you, will *s*.   13:24
doth she not *s*. diligently till ?   15:8
whosoever shall *s*. to save.   17:33
the Son of man is come to *s*.   19:10
why *s*. ye the living among ?   24:5
unto them, What *s*. ye ? *John* 1:38
ye *s*. me, not because ye saw.   6:26
he whom they *s*. to kill ?   7:25
ye shall *s*. me, and shall not. 34, 36
ye shall *s*. me, and shall die.   8:21
but ye *s*. to kill me.   37, 40
ye shall *s*. me, and whither I. 13:33
unto them, Whom *s*. ye ?   18:4, 7
if ye *s*. me, let these go their way. 8
three men *s*. thee.   *Acts* 10:19
I am he whom ye *s*.   21
to Tarsus, to *s*. Saul.   11:25
to them who *s*. for glory. *Rom* 2:7
and they *s*. my life.   11:3
and the Greeks *s*.   1 *Cor* 1:22
let no man *s*. his own, but.   10:24
s. that ye may excel to.   14:12
since ye *s*. a proof of. 2 *Cor* 13:3
do I persuade, or *s*. to ? *Gal* 1:10
if, while we *s*. to be justified.   2:17
for all *s*. their own. *Phil* 2:21
if ye be risen, *s*. those things. *Col* 3:1
of them that *s*. him. *Heb* 11:6
they declare plainly that they *s*.   14
no city, but we *s*. one to come. 13:14
in those days shall men *s*. *Rev* 9:6
   see face, Lord

   not seek, or seek *not*
the priest shall *not s*. *Lev* 13:36
neither s. after wizards.   19:31
that ye *s*. *not* after. *Num* 15:39
thou shalt *not s*. their peace.
   Deut 23:6; *Ezra* 9:12

daughter, shall I *not s*.? *Ruth* 3:1
the wicked will *not s*.   *Ps* 10:4
they *s*. *not* thy statutes.   119:155
lovers, they *s*. thee *not*. *Jer* 30:14
great things ? *s*. them *not*.   45:5
but *s*. *not* Beth-el.   *Amos* 5:5
a shepherd shall *not s*. *Zech* 11:16
s. *not* what ye shall eat. *Luke* 12:29
because I *s*. *not* mine. *John* 5:30
s. *not* the honour that cometh.   44
I *s*. *not* mine own glory.   8:50
s. *not* to be loosed. Art thou loosed?
   s. *not* a wife.   1 *Cor* 7:27
for I *s*. *not* yours, but.   2 *Cor* 12:14

   seekest
him, what *s*. thou ?   *Gen* 37:15
the man whom thou *s*.   *Judg* 4:22
the man thou *s*. is as.   2 *Sam* 17:3
thou *s*. to destroy a mother.   20:19
that thou *s*. to go to.   1 *Ki* 11:22
if thou *s*. her as silver.   *Pr* 2:4
s. thou great things ? seek. *Jer* 45:5
yet no man said, What *s*.? *John* 4:27
woman, whom *s*. thou ?   20:15

   seeketh
Saul my father *s*. to.   1 *Sam* 19:2
that he *s*. my life ?   20:1
that *s*. my life, *s*. thy life.   22:23
Saul *s*. to destroy the city.   23:10
saying, David *s*. thy hurt ?   24:9
who came forth of my bowels *s*. my
   life.   2 *Sam* 16:11
and see how this man *s*.   1 *Ki* 20:7
see how he *s*. a quarrel.   2 *Ki* 5:7
thence she *s*. the prey.   *Job* 39:29
watcheth righteous, and *s*. *Ps* 37:32
he that diligently *s*. good procureth
   favour, but he that *s*.   *Pr* 11:27
a scorner *s*. wisdom and.   14:6
he that hath understanding *s*.   15:14
a transgression, *s*. love.   17:9
an evil man *s*. only rebellion.   11
he that exalteth his gate *s*.   18:1
having separated himself, *s*.   19
ear of the wise *s*. knowledge.   15
the virtuous woman *s*. wool.   31:13
which yet my soul *s*. but. *Eccl* 7:28
he *s*. unto him a cunning. *Isa* 40:20
any that *s*. the truth, I.   *Jer* 5:1
Zion, whom no man *s*. after.   30:17
this man *s*. not the welfare.   38:4
the soul that *s*. him.   *Lam* 3:25
him that *s*. unto him.   *Ezek* 14:10
as a shepherd *s*. out his.   34:12
and he that *s*. findeth.   *Mat* 7:8
   Luke 11:10
an adulterous generation *s*. a sign.
   Mat 12:39; 16:4
leaveth the 99, and *s*. that.   18:12
Father *s*. such to worship him.
   John 4:23
doeth in secret, and *s*. to be.   7:4
s. his own glory; *s*. the glory.   18
is one that *s*. and judgeth.   8:50
there is none that *s*.   *Rom* 3:11
not obtained that which he *s*.   11:7
charity *s*. not her own.   1 *Cor* 13:5

   seeking
Mordecai *s*. the wealth.   *Esth* 10:3
s. judgement, and hasting. *Isa* 16:5
s. rest, and findeth none.
   Mat 12:43; *Luke* 11:24
like to a merchantman *s*. goodly.
   Mat 13:45
s. of him a sign from.   *Mark* 8:11
to Jerusalem, *s*. him.   *Luke* 2:45
s. something out of his mouth.   11:54
come *s*. fruit, and find none.   13:7
and came to Capernaum, *s*. for
   Jesus.   *John* 6:24
s. to turn away the deputy from.
   Acts 13:8
went about *s*. some to lead him.   11
not *s*. mine own profit. 1 *Cor* 10:33
s. whom he may devour.   1 *Pet* 5:8

   seem
s. to him a deceiver.   *Gen* 27:12
not *s*. hard, when.   *Deut* 15:18
then thy brother should *s*. vile. 25:3
if it *s*. evil unto you to.   *Josh* 24:15
let not all the trouble *s*.   *Neh* 9:32
if the thing *s*. right.   *Esth* 8:5

the chariot shall *s*. like.   *Nah* 2:4*
but if any man *s*. to.   1 *Cor* 11:16
those members which *s*. to be. 12:22
I may not *s*. as if I would terrify.
   2 *Cor* 10:9
lest any of you should *s*.   *Heb* 4:1
if any among you *s*. to be religious.
   Jas 1:26*

   see good
   seemed
but he *s*. as one that.   *Gen* 19:14
and they *s*. unto him but a.   29:20
this wisdom *s*. great unto. *Eccl* 9:13
given earth unto whom it *s*. meet.
   Jer 27:5
their words *s*. to them. *Luke* 24:11*
but these who *s*. to be.   *Gal* 2:6*
James, Cephas, and John, who *s*. 9*

   seemeth
it *s*. there is a plague in. *Lev* 14:35
s. it but a small thing ?   *Num* 16:9
s. it light to be a king's son in law ?
   1 *Sam* 18:23
there is a way which *s*. right.
   Pr 14:12; 16:25
in his own cause *s*. just.   18:17
s. it a small thing to ? *Ezek* 34:18
taken what he *s*. to.   *Luke* 8:18*
he *s*. a setter forth of.   *Acts* 17:18
it *s*. unreasonable to send.   25:27
if any *s*. wise, let him.   1 *Cor* 3:18*
now no chastening *s*. to. *Heb* 12:11
   see good

   seemly
delight is not *s*. for a fool. *Pr* 19:10
honour is not *s*. for a fool.   26:1

   seen
God hath *s*. mine affliction and.
   Gen 31:42
fathers have not *s*.   *Ex* 10:6
whether he hath *s*. or known.
   Lev 5:1
those men which have *s*. *Num* 14:22
nor hath he *s*. perverseness.   23:21
thou hast *s*. it, thou shalt.   27:13
we have *s*. the sons of.   *Deut* 1:28
thou hast *s*. how the Lord bare.   31
thine eyes have *s*. all the Lord. 3:21
s. what the Lord did because.   4:3
the things thine eyes have *s*.   9
we have *s*. that God doth talk. 5:24
things thine eyes have *s*.   10:21
have not *s*. the chastisement.   11:2
but your eyes have *s*. all the.   7
nor have our eyes *s*. it.   21:7
temptations thine eyes have *s*. 29:3
his mother, I have not *s*. him.   33:9
eyes have *s*. what I have. *Josh* 24:7
the elders who had *s*. the. *Judg* 2:7
because we have *s*. God.   13:22
five lords had *s*. it.   1 *Sam* 6:16
see his place, and who hath *s*. 23:22
day thine eyes have *s*. how.   24:10
king what thou hast *s*. 2 *Sam* 18:21
queen of Sheba had *s*.   1 *Ki* 10:4
mine eyes had *s*.   7; 2 *Chr* 9:3, 6
had *s*. what way man.   1 *Ki* 13:12
hast thou *s*. all this great ?   20:13
s.? Hezekiah said. All things in mine
   house . . . *s*. 2 *Ki* 20:15; *Isa* 39:4
when he had *s*. him.   2 *Ki* 23:29
many that had *s*. the first house.
   Ezra 3:12
of that which they had *s*. *Esth* 9:26
eye that hath *s*. me shall.   *Job* 7:8
say, I have not *s*. thee.   8:18
died, and no eye had *s*. me.   10:18
mine eye had *s*. all this, mine. 13:1
they that have *s*. him shall.   20:7
vulture's eye hath not *s*.   28:7
s. doors of the shadow ?   38:17
or hast thou *s*. the treasures ?   22
thou hast *s*. it, for.   *Ps* 10:14
our eye hath *s*.   35:21
this thou hast *s*.   22
so have we *s*. in city of Lord.   48:8
mine eye hath *s*. his desire.   54:7
have *s*. thy goings, O God.   68:24
years wherein we have *s*. evil. 90:15
ends of earth have *s*. salvation. 98:3
whom thine eyes have *s*.   *Pr* 25:7

who hath not *s*. the evil. *Eccl* 4:3
not *s*. the sun, nor known. 6:5
yea, though he live, yet hath he *s*. 6
eyes have *s*. the Lord. *Isa* 6:5
walked in darkness have *s*. 9:2
nor hath eye *s*. what he hath. 64:4
who hath heard, who hath *s*.? 66:8
isles afar off that have not *s*. 19
Lord, thou hast well *s*. *Jer* 1:12
hast thou *s*. what backsliding? 3:6
thou hast *s*. me, and tried my. 12:3
because they have *s*. her. *Lam* 1:8
she hath *s*. heathen entered. 10
thy prophets have *s*. vain and foolish
 things for thee, they have *s*. 2:14
have found, we have *s*. it. 16
O Lord, thou hast *s*. my wrong. 3:59
thou hast *s*. all their vengeance. 60
thou hast *s*. what the. *Ezek* 8:12
then said he, Hast thou *s*. this? 15
 17; 47:6
and have *s*. nothing. 13:3
they have *s*. vanity.
have ye not *s*. a vain vision? 7
Gabriel whom I had *s*. *Dan* 9:21
and the diviners have *s*. a lie.
 Zech 10:2
s. his star in the east. *Mat* 2:2
to see those things which ye see, and
 have not *s*. 13:17; *Luke* 10:24
and ye, when ye had *s*. *Mat* 21:32
they have *s*. the kingdom. *Mark* 9:1
what things they had *s*. 9
them which had *s*. him. 16:14
that he had *s*. a vision. *Luke* 1:22
for all things they had *s*. 2:20
not see death before he had *s*. 26
mine eyes have *s*. thy salvation. 30
saying, We have *s*. strange. 5:26
things which they had *s*. 9:36
works that they had *s*. 19:37
he hoped to have *s*. some. 23:8
saying, that they had *s*. a. 24:23
that they had *s*. a spirit. 37
no man hath *s*. God at any time, the.
 John 1:18; *1 John* 4:12
we testify that we have *s*. *John* 3:11
what he hath *s*. and heard.
the Galileans had *s*. all he did. 4:45
ye have not at any time *s*. 5:37
those men, when they had *s*. 6:14
not any man hath *s*. the Father. 46
hast thou *s*. Abraham? 8:57
which before had *s*. him. 9:8
that thou hast both *s*. and. 37
had *s*. what Jesus did. 11:45
he that hath *s*. me, hath *s*. 14:9
have *s*. and hated both me. 15:24
she had *s*. the Lord. 20:18
have *s*. the Lord. 25
because thou hast *s*. me. 29
speak things we have *s*. *Acts* 4:20
fashion that he had *s*. 7:44
he hath *s*. in a vision a man. 9:12
declared to them how he had *s*.
what this vision he had *s*. 10:17
how he had *s*. an angel. 11:13
when he had *s*. the grace of God. 23
after he had *s*. the vision. 16:10
they had *s*. the brethren, they. 40
they had *s*. before with him. 21:29
of what thou hast *s*. 22:15; 26:16
eye hath not *s*. nor ear. *1 Cor* 2:9
s. Jesus Christ our Lord? 9:1
things ye have heard and *s*. *Phil* 4:9
as have not *s*. my face. *Col* 2:1
those things he hath not *s*. 18
whom no man hath *s*. *1 Tim* 6:16
that which we have *s*. *1 John* 1:1
and we have *s*. it. 2
that which we have *s*. declare. 3
whosoever sinneth hath not *s*. 3:6
we have *s*. and do testify. 4:14
not his brother whom he hath *s*., how
 can he love God . . . not *s*.? 20
evil, hath not *s*. God. *3 John* 11
things which thou hast *s*. *Rev* 1:19
when I had heard and *s*. I fell. 22:8

have I **seen**
thee *have I s*. righteous. *Gen* 7:1
now *have I s*. thy people to offer.
 1 Chr 29:17
yet *have I* not *s*. righteous. *Ps* 37:25

all things *have I s*. in. *Eccl* 7:15
all this *have I s*. and applied. 8:9
this wisdom *have I s*. under. 9:13
wherefore *have I s*. them? *Jer* 46:5
for now *have I s*. with. *Zech* 9:3

I have **seen**
I have s. all that Laban. *Gen* 31:12
I have s. God face to face. 32:30
for therefore *I have s*. thy face.
 33:10; 46:30
I have s. the affliction. *Ex* 3:7
I have also *s*. the oppression. 9, 16
I have s. this people. *Deut* 9:13
alas, for because *I have s*. an angel.
 Judg 6:22
I have s. a woman in Timnah. 14:2
I have s. a son of Jesse, cunning.
 1 Sam 16:18
surely *I have s*. yesterday the blood
 of Naboth. *2 Ki* 9:26
I have s. thy tears. 20:5; *Isa* 38:5
as *I have s*., they that plow. *Job* 4:8
I have s. the foolish taking. 5:3
that which *I have s*. I declare. 15:17
if *I have s*. any perish for want. 31:19
I have s. the wicked in. *Ps* 37:35
I have s. violence and strife. 55:9
glory, so as *I have s*. thee in. 63:2
I have s. an end of all. 119:96
I have s. all the works. *Eccl* 1:14
I have s. the travail which. 3:10
is a sore evil which *I have s*. 5:13
I have s. it is good to eat. 18
evil which *I have s*. 6:1; 10:5
I have s. servants upon horses. 10:7
I am warm, *I have s*. *Isa* 44:16
I have s. his ways, and will. 57:18
behold, *I have s*. it, saith. *Jer* 7:11
I have s. thine adulteries. 13:27
I have s. folly in prophets. 23:13, 14
I have s. affliction by rod. *Lam* 3:1
known unto me the dream *I have s*.
 Dan 2:26
dream that *I have s*. 4:9, 18
I have s. an horrible. *Hos* 6:10
I speak that *I have s*. *John* 8:38
I have s. the affliction. *Acts* 7:34

ye have **seen**
of all that *ye have s*. *Gen* 45:13
Egyptians whom *ye have s*. *Ex* 14:13
ye have s. what I did unto. 19:4
ye have s. that I have talked. 20:22
ye have s. all that the Lord did.
 Deut 29:2; *Josh* 23:3
ye have s. their abominations.
 Deut 29:17
what *ye have s*. we do. *Judg* 9:48
have ye s. this man? *1 Sam* 17:25
ye yourselves *have s*. it. *Job* 27:12
ye have s. the breaches. *Isa* 22:9
ye have s. all the evil. *Jer* 44:2
ye have s. lies, therefore I am.
 Ezek 13:8
what things *ye have s*. *Luke* 7:22
ye also *have s*. me, and. *John* 6:36
ye do that which *ye have s*. 8:38
ye know him, and *have s*. him. 14:7
as *ye have s*. him go. *Acts* 1:11
and *ye have s*. the end. *Jas* 5:11

seen, *passive*
tops of the mountains *s*. *Gen* 8:5
shall be *s*. in the cloud. 9:14
of the Lord it shall be *s*. 22:14
no leavened bread be *s*. *Ex* 13:7
 Deut 16:4
but my face shall not be *s*. *Ex* 33:23
neither let any man be *s*. 34:3
Lord, art *s*. face to face. *Num* 14:14
a shield or spear *s*. *Judg* 5:8
no such deed done nor *s*. 19:30
they might not be *s*. *2 Sam* 17:17
he was *s*. upon the wings. 22:11
there was no stone *s*. *1 Ki* 6:18
ends of the staves were not *s*. 8:8
no such almug trees were *s*. 10:12
consumed, it cannot be *s*. *Job* 33:21
channels of water were *s*. *Ps* 18:15
s. that Moab is weary. *Isa* 16:12
thy shame shall be *s*. 47:3
and his glory shall be *s*. 60:2
and the Lord shall be *s*. *Zech* 9:14
alms to be *s*. of men. *Mat* 6:1, 5

saying, It was never so *s*. *Mat* 9:33
all their works they do to be *s*. 23:5
he had been *s*. of her. *Mark* 16:11
being *s*. of them forty days.
 Acts 1:3; 13:31
things of him clearly *s*. *Rom* 1:20
but hope that is *s*. is not hope. 8:24
he was *s*. of Cephas. *1 Cor* 15:5
after that he was *s*. of above 500. 6
s. of James. 7
last of all he was *s*. of me also. 8
we look not at things *s*., but at things
 not *s*.: for things *s*. *2 Cor* 4:18
in flesh, *s*. of angels. *1 Tim* 3:16
evidence of things not *s*. *Heb* 11:1
so that things which are *s*. were. 3
warned of God of things not *s*. 7
having *s*. them afar off, were. 13
whom having not *s*. ye love. *1 Pet* 1:8
there was *s*. in his temple the ark.
 Rev 11:19

seer
(*Another word for Prophet. Seer
one who sees, inferring that he sees
visions*)

s. he that is a prophet was beforetime called a *s*. *1 Sam* 9:9
is the *s*. here? 11
where the *s*.'s house is. 18
Saul, and said, I am the *s*. 19
art not thou a *s*.? *2 Sam* 15:27
word came to Gad, David's *s*.
 24:11; *1 Chr* 21:9
Samuel the *s*. did ordain in their set
 office. *1 Chr* 9:22
Heman the king's *s*. in the. 25:5
all that Samuel the *s*. had. 26:28
in the book of Samuel the *s*. and in
 the book of Gad the *s*. 29:29
visions of Iddo the *s*. *2 Chr* 9:29
acts of . . . book of Iddo the *s*. 12:15
Hanani the *s*. came to Asa. 16:7
then Asa was wroth with the *s*. 10
Jehu son of Hanani the *s*. went. 19:2
of Gad the king's *s*. 29:25
David and Asaph the *s*. 30
Jeduthun the king's *s*. 35:15
said unto Amos, O thou *s*. flee.
 Amos 7:12

seers
Israel and Judah by a *s*. *2 Ki* 17:13
words of the *s*. that spake.
 2 Chr 33:18
among the sayings of the *s*. 19*
your rulers, the *s*. hath. *Isa* 29:10
who say to the *s*. see not, and. 30:10
shall the *s*. be ashamed. *Mi* 3:7

seest
the land thou *s*. to thee. *Gen* 13:15
that spake, Thou God *s*. me. 16:13
Laban said, All that thou *s*. is. 31:43
that day thou *s*. my face. *Ex* 10:28
lest when thou *s*. the sun. *Deut* 4:19
every place that thou *s*. 12:13
goest to battle and *s*. horses. 20:1
and *s*. among captives a. 21:11
thou *s*. the shadow of. *Judg* 9:36
s. thou how Ahab. *1 Ki* 21:29
hast thou eyes, *s*. thou? *Job* 10:4
s. thou a man diligent? *Pr* 22:29
s. thou a man wise in his? 26:12
s. thou a man that is hasty? 29:20
if thou *s*. the oppression. *Eccl* 5:8
fasted, and thou *s*. not? *Isa* 58:3
when thou *s*. the naked, that. 7
to Jeremiah, What *s*. thou? *Jer* 1:11
 13; 24:3; *Amos* 7:8; 8:2
 Zech 4:2; 5:2
s. thou not what they do in cities?
 Jer 7:17
O Lord, that *s*. the reins. 20:12
and behold, thou *s*. it. 32:24
son of man, *s*. thou? *Ezek* 8:6
declare all thou *s*. to the house. 40:4
and as thou *s*. deal. *Dan* 1:13
thou *s*. the multitude. *Mark* 5:31
Jesus said, *S*. thou these? 13:2
he said to Simon, *S*.? *Luke* 7:44
thou *s*. how many. *Acts* 21:20
s. thou how faith? *Jas* 2:22
what thou *s*. write in a book and.
 Rev 1:11

seeth

after him that s. me ? *Gen 16:13*
when he s. lad is not with us. *44:31*
and when he s. thee he. *Ex 4:14*
and when he s. the blood. *12:23*
priest s. the plague in. *Lev 13:20*
when he s. that their power is. *Deut 32:36*
Lord s. not as man s. *1 Sam 16:7*
pleasant, as my lord s. *2 Ki 2:19*
and s. the place of stones. *Job 8:17*
he s. wickedness also. *11:11*
covering to him that he s. not. *22:14*
and his eye s. every precious. *28:10*
s. under the whole heaven. *24*
his eyes are on man, he s. *34:21*
but now mine eye s. thee. *42:5*
for he s. that his day. *Ps 37:13*
he s. that wise men die. *49:10*
shall rejoice, when he s. *58:10*
neither day nor night s. *Eccl 8:16*
watchman declare what he s. *Isa 21:6*
looketh upon it, s. it. *28:4*
and they say, Who s. us.? *29:15*
none s. me. *47:10*
Lord s. us not. *Ezek 8:12; 9:9*
the vision that he s. is for. *12:27*
if he beget a son that s. *18:14*
if when he s. the sword come. *33:3*
when any s. a man's bone. *39:15*
thy father who s. *Mat 6:4, 6, 18*
he s. tumult, and. *Mark 5:38*
he s. Abraham afar off. *Luke 16:23*
next day John s. Jesus. *John 1:29*
do nothing but what he s. *5:19*
who s. the Son, and believeth. *6:40*
by what means he now s. *9:21*
but an hireling s. the wolf. *10:12*
he stumbleth not, because he s. *11:9*
s. me, s. him that sent me. *12:45*
because it s. him not, nor. *14:17*
a little while, and the world s. *19*
s. the stone taken away. *20:1*
Peter went in and s. the linen. *6*
and s. two angels in white. *12*
s. the disciple whom Jesus. *21:20*
what a man s. why doth ? *Rom 8:24*
what he s. me to be. *2 Cor 12:6*
s. brother have need. *1 John 3:17*

seethe

(*American Revision*, boil)
and s. that ye will s. *Ex 16:23*
thou shalt not s. a kid in his mother's milk. *23:19; 34:26; Deut 14:21*
thou shalt s. his flesh. *Ex 29:31*
s. pottage for the sons. *2 Ki 4:38*
let them s. the bones. *Ezek 24:5*
come and s. therein. *Zech 14:21*

seething

came, while flesh was s. *1 Sam 2:13*
goeth smoke as out of a s. pot. *Job 41:20*
I said, I see a s. pot. *Jer 1:13*

Seir

to the land of S. the. *Gen 32:3*
till I come to my lord to S. *33:14*
these are the sons of S. *36:20, 21*
1 Chr 1:38
S. shall be a possession. *Num 24:18*
destroyed you in S. *Deut 1:44*
from Sinai and rose up from S. *33:2*
thou wentest out of S. *Judg 5:4*
of the inhabitants of S. *2 Chr 20:23*
of children of S. 10,000. *25:11*
gods of the children of S. *14*
he calleth to me out of S. *Isa 21:11*
that Moab and S. do say. *Ezek 25:8*

mount Seir

Horites in their *mount* S. *Gen 14:6*
dwelt Esau in *mount* S. *36:8, 9*
we compassed *mount* S. *Deut 2:1*
have given *mount* S. to Esau. *5*
Josh 24:4
sons of Simeon, 500 men went to *mount* S. *1 Chr 4:42*
mount S. whom thou wouldest not let Israel invade. *2 Chr 20:10*
ambushments against *mount* S. *22*
Moab stood up against *mount* S. *23*
face against *mount* S. *Ezek 35:2*
say to it, Behold, O *mount* S. *3*
thus will I make *mount* S. *7, 15*

seize

ye shall rise up and s. *Josh 8:7*
night, let darkness s. *Job 3:6*
let death s. upon them. *Ps 55:15**
let us kill him, and s. *Mat 21:38*

seized

feeble, fear hath s. on. *Jer 49:24*

selah

This Hebrew word is found seventy one times in the book of Psalms, and three times in Habakkuk. It is very probably a musical or liturgical sign.
The older view was that it indicated a pause, but it is now believed to be derived from a word signifying Up! This may have been intended for the players, for the singers, or for the congregation, or for all of them.

help for him in God, s. *Ps 3:2*
heard me out of his holy hill, s. *4*
blessing is upon thy people, s. *8*
forgavest iniquity of my sin, s. *32:5*
See *Ps* 4:2, 4; 7:5; 9:16, 20; 20:3
21:2; 24:6, 10; 32:4, 7; 39:5, 11
44:8; 46:3, 7, 11; 47:4; 48:8
49:13, 15; 50:6; 52:3, 5; 54:3
55:7, 19; 57:3, 6; 59:5, 13; 60:4
61:4; 62:4, 8; 66:4, 7, 15; 67:1
4; 68:7, 19, 32; 75:3; 76:3, 9
77:3, 9, 15; 81:7; 82:2; 83:8
84:4, 8; 85:2; 87:3, 6; 88:7, 10
89:4, 37, 45, 48; 140:3, 5, 8; 143:6
Hab 3:3, 9, 13

Seleucia

they departed unto S. *Acts 13:4*

own self

swarest by thine *own* s. *Ex 32:13*
I can of mine *own* s. *John 5:30*
thou me with thine *own* s. *17:5*
I judge not mine *own* s. *1 Cor 4:3*
even thine *own* s. *Philem 19*
who his *own* s. bare our. *1 Pet 2:24*

selfsame

healed the s. hour. *Mat 8:13*
that one and s. Spirit. *1 Cor 12:11*
wrought us for s. thing. *2 Cor 5:5*
this s. thing that ye. *7:11*

see same **day**

selfwill

in their s., they digged. *Gen 49:6*

selfwilled

bishop must not be s. *Tit 1:7*
presumptuous are they, s. *2 Pet 2:10*

sell

(In case of extreme necessity the Hebrews were allowed to sell themselves and their children into temporary servitude. This was closely regulated, however, in the law)

Jacob said, S. me this. *Gen 25:31*
come, let us s. him to the. *37:27*
if a man s. his daughter. *Ex 21:7*
to s. her to strange nation, shall. *8*
they shall s. the live ox and. *35*
an ox, and kill it, or s. it. *22:1*
if thou s. aught unto. *Lev 25:14*
if a man s. a dwelling house. *29*
if thy brother s. himself unto. *47*
thou shalt s. me meat. *Deut 2:28*
s. that which dieth of itself. *14:21*
thou shalt not s. her at all. *21:14*
s. Sisera into the hand. *Judg 4:9*
Ahab did s. himself to. *1 Ki 21:25*
go s. the oil, and pay. *2 Ki 4:7*
and will ye even s. your ? *Neh 5:8*
on the sabbath day to s. *10:31*
buy truth, and s. it not. *Pr 23:23*
s. land into the hand. *Ezek 30:12*
they shall not s. the firstfruits. *48:14*
I will s. your sons and daughters into hand of Judah, they shall s. *Joel 3:8*
that we may s. corn. *Amos 8:5*
yea, and s. the refuse of the. *6*
and they that s. them. *Zech 11:5*
go and s. that thou hast. *Mat 19:21*
Mark 10:21; *Luke* 12:33; 18:22
go ye rather to them that s. *Mat 25:9*
let him s. his garment. *Luke 22:36*

send

we will buy and s. and. *Jas 4:13*
no man might buy or s. *Rev 13:17*

seller

buyer, so with the s. *Isa 24:2*
rejoice, nor the s. mourn. *Ezek 7:12*
the s. shall not return to that. *13*
woman named Lydia, a s. *Acts 16:14*

sellers

merchants and s. *Neh 13:20*

sellest

thou s. thy people for. *Ps 44:12*

selleth

a man and s. him, he shall surely. *Ex 21:16; Deut 24:7*
Naomi s. a part of land. *Deut 4:3*
head of him that s. corn. *Pr 11:26*
maketh fine linen and s. it. *31:24*
that s. nations through. *Nah 3:4*
he s. all, and buyeth. *Mat 13:44*

selvedge

from the s. in the coupling. *Ex 26:4; 36:11*

selves

also of your own s. *Acts 20:30*
but first gave their own s. to the. *2 Cor 8:5*
own s. Know ye not your own s.? *13:5*
lovers of their own s. *2 Tim 3:2*
deceiving your own s. *Jas 1:22*

Semei

which was the son of S. *Luke 3:26*

senate

they called all the s. *Acts 5:21*

senators

and teach his s. wisdom. *Ps 105:22*

send

God shall s. his angel. *Gen 24:7, 40*
I pray thee, s. me good speed. *12*
he said, S. me away unto. *54, 56*
a pledge, till thou s. it ? *38:17*
wilt s. our brother with us. *43:4*
God did s. me before you, to. *45:5*
s. by hand of him whom. *Ex 4:13*
that he s. children of Israel. *7:2**
s. therefore now, and gather. *9:19*
that they might s. them out. *12:33*
whom thou wilt s. with me. *33:12*
s. him away by the hand. *Lev 16:21*
s. thou men to search land, of every tribe shall ye s. a man. *Num 13:2*
of every tribe s. a thousand. *31:4*
we will s. men before us. *Deut 1:22*
thy God will s. the hornet. *7:20*
the elders shall s. and fetch. *19:12*
give her a bill of divorce, and s. *24:1*
Lord shall s. upon thee. *28:20*
Lord shall s. against thee. *48*
thou didst s. come again. *Judg 13:8*
s. away the ark of God. *1 Sam 5:11*
6:8
tell us wherewith we shall s. it. *6:2*
if ye s. away the ark of God, s. *3*
saying, Up, that I may s. thee. *9:26*
give us respite, that we may s. *11:3*
the Lord shall s. thunder. *12:17*
Samuel said to Jesse. S. *16:11*
Saul sent, and said, S. me David. *19*
young men thou didst s. *25:25*
David sent saying, S. me. *2 Sam 11:6*
come hither, that I may s. *14:32*
by them ye shall s. unto me. *15:36*
now therefore s. quickly. *17:16*
all thou didst s. for. *1 Ki 20:9*
ye shall not s. *2 Ki 2:16*
he said, S. *17*
doth s. to me to recover a man. *5:7*
that I may s. and fetch him. *6:13*
let us s. and seek. *7:13*
s. to meet Jehu. *9:17*
the Lord began to s. against. *15:37*
let us s. abroad our. *1 Chr 13:2*
s. me therefore a man. *2 Chr 2:7*
s. me also cedar trees, fir trees. *8*
then hear thou, and s. rain. *6:27*
Ahaz did s. to king of Assyria. *28:16*
Sennacherib did s. servants. *32:9*
let king s. his pleasure. *Ezra 5:17*
that thou wouldest s. me. *Neh 2:5*
so it pleased the king to s. me. *6*
eat, drink, and s. portions. *8:10, 12*
s. forth their little ones. *Job 21:11*

canst thou s. lightnings ? *Job* 38:35
s. thee help from sanctuary. *Ps* 20:2
O s. out thy light and truth.   43:3
he shall s. from heaven, and . . .
   reproach; God shall s. forth. 57:3
God didst s. a plentiful rain.   68:9
he doth s. out his voice, a.   33*
shall s. rod of thy strength. 110:2
O Lord, I beseech thee, s. 118:25
s. thine hand from above, rid. 144:7*
sluggard to them that s.   *Pr* 10:26
truth to them that s. to thee. 22:21
faithful messenger to them that s.
   him.   25:13
ointment to s. forth a.   *Eccl* 10:1
whom shall I s.? I said, Here am I, s.
   Isa 6:8
Lord shall s. among his fat ones.10:16
s. ye the lamb to the ruler of. 16:1
he shall s. them a Saviour.   19:20
that s. forth thither the feet. 32:20
didst s. thy messengers far off. 57:9
to all that I shall s. thee.   *Jer* 1:7
s. unto Kedar.   2:10
s. for cunning women.   9:17
s. the yokes to king of Edom. 27:3
s. of them of the captivity.   29:31
for the which the Lord shall s. 42:5
the Lord, to whom we s. free.   6
pray ye the Lord that he will s. forth
   labourers.   *Mat* 9:38; *Luke* 10:2
that I am come to s. peace.   10:34
till he s. forth judgement.   12:20
Son of man shall s. forth his angels.
   13:41; 24:31; *Mark* 13:27
s. her away, for she crieth. *Mat* 15:23
straightway he will s. them.   21:3
   Mark 11:3
that he might s. them to preach.
   Mark 3:14; 6:7
would not s. them away out.   5:10
besought him, saying, S. us.   12
s. Lazarus.   *Luke* 16:24
s. to my father's house.   27
whom the Father will s. *John* 14:26
believed that thou didst s. me. 17:8
shall s. Jesus Christ who. *Acts* 3:20
same that God s. to be ruler.   7:35
and now s. men to Joppa.   10:5, 32
   11:13
disciples determined to s.   15:25
to s. chosen men of.   15:22, 25
that he would s. for him to.   25:3
it seemeth unreasonable to s.   27
Lord to s. Timotheus. *Phil* 2:19, 23
I supposed it necessary to s.   25
God shall s. delusion. *2 Thes* 2:11
when I shall s. Artemas. *Tit* 3:12
doth fountain s. sweet ? *Jas* 3:11
write and s. it to seven. *Rev* 1:11
and they shall s. gifts one.   11:10

I send

behold I s. an angel.   *Ex* 23:20
did I not earnestly s.? *Num* 22:37
and I s. not to thee.   *1 Sam* 20:12
business whereabout I s. thee. 21:2
if I s. pestilence.   *2 Chr* 7:13
   Ezek 14:19
say, Whom shall I s.?   *Isa* 6:8
nations to whom I s. thee. *Jer* 25:15
I s. thee to the children of Israel.
   Ezek 2:3, 4
I s. my four sore judgements. 14:21
behold I s. you forth.   *Mat* 10:16
behold I s. my messenger before.
   11:10; *Mark* 1:2; *Luke* 7:27
behold I s. you prophets. *Mat* 23:34
if I s. them away fasting. *Mark* 8:3
I s. you forth as lambs. *Luke* 10:3
I s. the promise of my Father. 24:49
receiveth whom I s.   *John* 13:20
sent me, even so I s. you.   20:21
to be kept till I s. him. *Acts* 25:21
unto whom now I s. thee.   26:17

I will send

I will s. and fetch thee. *Gen* 27:45
come, and I will s. thee unto. 37:13
he said, I will s. thee a.   38:17
I will s. thee unto Pharaoh. *Ex* 3:10
   Acts 7:34
I will s. swarms of flies. *Ex* 8:21
I will s. all my plagues upon. 9:14
I will s. my fear.   23:27

I will s. hornets.   *Ex* 23:28
I will s. an angel before thee. 33:2
I will s. wild beasts.   *Lev* 26:22
I will s. pestilence.   25
I will s. faintness.   36
I will s. grass in thy.   *Deut* 11:15
I will s. the teeth of beasts. 32:24
I will s. thee a man.   *1 Sam* 9:16
I will s. thee to Jesse the.   16:1
I will shew it thee, and s. thee. 20:13
and I will s. rain upon.   *1 Ki* 18:1
yet I will s. my servants.   20:6
I will s. thee away with this.   34
I will s. a blast upon him. *2 Ki* 19:7
   Isa 37:7
I will s. him against.   *Isa* 10:6
I will s. those that escape.   66:19
behold I will s. serpents. *Jer* 8:17
I will s. a sword after them.   9:16
   24:10; 25:16, 27; 29:17; 49:37
I will s. for many fishers.   16:16
I will s. and take the families. 25:9
I will s. Nebuchadnezzar my. 43:10
behold, I will s. unto him.   48:12
and I will s. unto Babylon.   51:2
I will s. famine.   *Ezek* 5:16, 17
   14:13; *Amos* 8:11
I will s. mine anger upon. *Ezek* 7:3
I will s. into her pestilence.   28:23
I will s. you corn, and.   *Joel* 2:19
I will s. a curse.   *Mal* 2:2
I will s. my messenger, and he. 3:1
I will s. Elijah.   4:5
I will not s. them away. *Mat* 15:32
I will s. them prophets. *Luke* 11:49
what shall I do ? I will s.   20:13
the Comforter whom I will s.
   John 15:26; 16:7
I will s. thee far hence. *Acts* 22:21
approve, them I will s.   *1 Cor* 16:3
    see fire

sendest

when thou s. him. *Deut* 15:13*, 18*
whithersoever thou s. *Josh* 1:16
that thou s. to enquire.   *2 Ki* 1:6
and s. him away.   *Job* 14:20
thou s. thy Spirit, they.   *Ps* 104:30

sendeth

latter husband s. her out. *Deut* 24:3
that the Lord s. rain.   *1 Ki* 17:14
and who s. waters upon.   *Job* 5:10
he s. them out, they overturn. 12:15
he s. the springs into.   *Ps* 104:10
he s. forth his.   147:15, 18
that s. a message by the.   *Pr* 26:6
my spikenard s. forth. *S of S* 1:12
that s. ambassadors by.   *Isa* 18:2
and s. rain on the just.   *Mat* 5:45
he s. forth two of his disciples.
   Mark 11:1; 14:13
s. and desireth conditions of peace.
   Luke 14:32
Claudius Lysias to Felix s.
   Acts 23:26

sending

evil in s: me away. *2 Sam* 13:16*
his s. messengers.   *2 Chr* 36:15
   Jer 7:25; 25:4; 26:5; 29:19
and of s. portions.   *Esth* 9:19, 22
by s. evil angels.   *Ps* 78:49*
it shall be for the s.   *Isa* 7:25
rebelled in s. ambassadors unto.
   Ezek 17:15
God s. his own Son in the likeness
   of sinful flesh.   *Rom* 8:3

Sennacherib

S. came up against Judah.
   2 Ki 18:13; *Isa* 36:1
see and hear the words of S.
   2 Ki 19:16; *Isa* 37:17
thou hast prayed to me against S.
   2 Ki 19:20; *Isa* 37:21
S. departed and dwelt at Nineveh.
   2 Ki 19:36; *Isa* 37:37
the Lord saved Hezekiah from S.
   2 Chr 32:22

senses

have their s. exercised. *Heb* 5:14

sensual

is earthly, s., devilish. *Jas* 3:15
be s. having not the Spirit. *Jude* 19

---

sent

s. coat of many colours. *Gen* 37:22
Judah s. the kid by hand.   38:20
Tamar s. to her father in law.   25
then Pharaoh s. and called. 41:14
but Benjamin, Jacob s. not.   42:4
it was not you that s. me.   45:8
s. messengers unto Joseph. 50:16
I AM hath s. me to you.   *Ex* 3:14
why is it that thou hast s. me ? 5:22
the names of the men Moses s.
   Num 13:16; 14:36
Balak king of Moab hath s. 22:10
hid the messengers we s. *Josh* 6:17
old was I when Moses s. me. 14:7
I cut her in pieces and s. *Judg* 20:6
s. into the land of the.   *1 Sam* 31:9
return to him that s.   *2 Sam* 24:13
my lord hath not s.   *1 Ki* 18:10
elders did as Jezebel had s.   21:11
return unto king that s.   *2 Ki* 1:6
king of Israel s. to the place.   6:10
thistle s. to the cedar in.   14:9
according as Ahaz had s.   16:11
Rab-shakeh said to them, Hath my
   master s. me ?   18:27; *Isa* 36:12
his master s. to reproach. *2 Ki* 19:4
Lord God of Israel, Tell the man that
   s.   22:15, 18; *2 Chr* 34:23
copy of the letter they s. *Ezra* 4:11
they s. unto me four times. *Neh* 6:4
king s. and loosed him.   *Ps* 105:20
his Spirit hath s. me.   *Isa* 48:16
their nobles have s. their. *Jer* 14:3
I have not s. these prophets. 23:21
because thou hast s. letters. 29:25
say unto the king that s. you. 37:7
whom ye s. to present.   42:9, 20
ye have s. for men.   *Ezek* 23:40
who hath s. his angel.   *Dan* 3:28
Ephraim went and s.   *Hos* 5:13
when they had s. unto.   *Zech* 7:2
receiveth him that s. me. *Mat* 10:40
   Mark 9:37; *Luke* 9:48
   John 13:20
s. Jesus two disciples.   *Mat* 21:1
Pilate's wife s. unto him.   27:19
immediately the king s. *Mark* 6:27
John Baptist hath s. us. *Luke* 7:20
Jesus s. them two and two.   10:1
he s. his servant at supper.   14:17
they s. a message after him. 19:14
mocked him, and s. him.   23:11
to them that s. us.   *John* 1:22
do the will of him that s. me. 4:34
the Father who hath s. me.   5:23
believeth on him that s. me.   24
   12:44
but the will of the Father which hath
   s. me.   5:30; 6:38, 39, 40
ye s. unto John, and he.   5:33
bear witness that the Father hath s.
   5:36, 37; 6:57; 8:16, 18
except the Father which s. me. 6:44
but his that s. me.   7:16
seeketh his glory that s. him.   18
Pharisees and priests s. officers. 32
the works of him that s. me.   9:4
whom the Father hath s.   10:36
believe thou hast s. me.   11:42
seeth him that s. me.   12:45
Father who s. me gave me a.   49
mine, but Father's who s. me. 14:24
know not him that s. me.   15:21
go my way to him that s. me. 16:5
know Jesus whom thou hast s. 17:3
s. me into the world, so have I s. 18
believe that thou hast s. me.   21
know thou hast s. me.   23
that thou hast s. me.   25
as my Father hath s. me.   20:21
s. to the prison to have. *Acts* 5:21
I ask for what intent ye have s.10:29
s. it to elders by Barnabas.   11:30
the rulers of the synagogue s. 13:15
we have therefore s. Judas. 15:27
the magistrates have s. to.   16:35
Paul's friends s. unto him.   19:31
Christ s. me not to.   *1 Cor* 1:17
we have s. with him.   *2 Cor* 8:18
in Thessalonica ye s. once. *Phil* 4:16
testify that the Father s. the Son.
   1 John 4:14

sent away

Pharaoh s. away Abraham and his.
    Gen 12:20
s. Ishmael and Hagar away.   21:14
they s. away Rebekah their.   24:59
s. Keturah's children away.   25:6
me and have s. me away.   26:27
as we have s. thee away in peace. 29
Isaac s. away Jacob to.   28:5
blessed Jacob and s. him away.   6
I might have s. thee away.   31:27
surely thou hadst s. me away.   42
s. he his brethren away.   45:24
s. her away, may not.   *Deut* 24:4
Rahab s. spies away.   *Josh* 2:21
s. Reubenites and Gadites away.
       22:6, 7
s. his daughter away.   *Judg* 11:38
s. all the people away. *1 Sam* 10:25
thou s. away my enemy ?   19:17
David s. Abner away.   *2 Sam* 3:21
is it that thou hast s. him away ? 24
cut garments, and s. them away.
     10:4; *1 Chr* 19:4
lords of Philistines s. David away.
      1 Chr 12:19
s. widows away empty.   *Job* 22:9
and beat him, and s. him away.
    Mark 12:3, 4; *Luke* 20:10, 11
he hath s. empty away.   *Luke* 1:53
but Jesus s. him away.   8:38
them, they s. them away. *Acts* 13:3
s. away Paul and Silas.   17:10, 24

God sent

God s. me before you.   *Gen* 45:7
God of your fathers hath s. me.
      Ex 3:13
the God of Jacob hath s. me.   15
God s. an evil spirit between Abime-
   lech and.   *Judg* 9:23
God s. an angel unto. *1 Chr* 21:15
that God had not s. him. *Neh* 6:12
Lord their God s. him.   *Jer* 43:1
God hath not s. to thee to say.   2
God hath s. his angel.   *Dan* 6:22
God s. not his Son to.   *John* 3:17
he whom God hath s. speaketh.   34
raised up his Son Jesus, s. *Acts* 3:26
word of God s. unto the.   10:36
God s. forth his Son.   *Gal* 4:4
God hath s. forth the Spirit of.   6
God s. his only begotten. *1 John* 4:9
God s. his Son to be a propitiation.
      10
God s. his angel to shew. *Rev* 22:6

he sent

to his father he s. after. *Gen* 45:23
he s. Judah before him unto. 46:28
he had s. her back.   *Ex* 18:2
hearkened not to words he s.
      Judg 11:28
and he s. for David.   *1 Sam* 17:31
he s. of the spoil unto the.   30:26
he s. to meet them.   *2 Sam* 10:5
      1 Chr 19:5
when he s. again, he would.   14:29
he s. from above, he took me.
     22:17; *Ps* 18:16
for he s. unto me for my. *1 Ki* 20:7
therefore he s. lions.   *2 Ki* 17:26
yet he s. prophets.   *2 Chr* 24:19
he s. unto Amaziah a prophet. 25:15
he s. and called for his. *Esth* 5:10
he s. them meat to the. *Ps* 78:25
he s. a man before them.   105:17
he s. Moses his servant and.   26
he s. darkness, and made it dark. 28
but he s. leanness into.   106:15
he s. his word and healed. 107:20
he s. redemption unto his.   111:9
he hath s. me to bind up the brokenhearted.   *Isa* 61:1; *Luke* 4:18
he s. unto us in Babylon. *Jer* 29:28
for the which he hath s. me. 42:21
from above he s. fire.   *Lam* 1:13
after the glory hath he s. *Zech* 2:8
he s. other servants.   *Mat* 21:36
last of all he s. unto them his Son.
     37; *Mark* 12:4
he s. forth his armies.   *Mat* 22:7
he that s. me to baptize. *John* 1:33
for whom he hath s., him.   5:38
on him whom he hath s.   6:29

he that s. me is true. *John* 7:28; 8:26
and he hath s. me.   7:29
and he that s. me is with me.   8:29
I of myself, but he s. me.   42
wherefore he s. for Paul. *Acts* 24:26
he s. and signified it by.   *Rev* 1:1

I sent

I have s. to tell my lord. *Gen* 32:5
I s. this kid, and thou hast.   38:23
token that I have s. thee. *Ex* 3:12
fathers when I s. them. *Num* 32:8
I s. Moses also and Aaron.
    Josh 24:5; *Mi* 6:4
have not I s. thee ?   *Judg* 6:14
I have s. Naaman my.   *2 Ki* 5:6
the law which I s. to you by. 17:13
my messenger that I s.?   *Isa* 42:19
for your sake I have s. to Babylon.
      43:14
in the thing whereto I s. it.   55:11
I s. unto you all my servants the.
   Jer 7:25; 26:5; 35:15; 44:4
I s. them not, nor commanded.
   14:14, 15; 23:21, 32; 27:15; 29:9
I s. him not, he caused you. 29:31
surely had I s. thee.   *Ezek* 3:6
to thee am I now s.   *Dan* 10:11
my great army which I s. *Joel* 2:25
I have s. among you.   *Amos* 4:10
I have s. forth thy prisoners out.
      Zech 9:11
know that I have s. this.   *Mal* 2:4
for therefore am I s.   *Luke* 4:43
when I s. you without.   22:35
so have I s. them into.   *John* 17:18
for I have s. them.   *Acts* 10:20
immediately therefore I s. to thee. 33
for this cause have I s. *1 Cor* 4:17
yet have I s. brethren.   *2 Cor* 9:3
gain of you by any whom I s.? 12:17
desired Titus, and with him I s.   18
whom I have s. for the same purpose.
     Eph 6:22; *Col* 4:8
I s. him therefore.   *Phil* 2:28
for this cause I s. to know.*1 Thes* 3:5
whom I have s. again.   *Philem* 12

see **Lord**

sent forth

Noah s. forth a raven.   *Gen* 8:7
s. forth a dove.   10
hath s. forth her maidens. *Pr* 9:3
Herod s. forth and slew. *Mat* 2:16
these twelve Jesus s. forth.   10:5
and s. forth his servants to.   22:3
Herod s. forth and laid. *Mark* 6:17
scribes s. forth spies. *Luke* 20:20
the brethren s. him forth. *Acts* 9:30
they s. forth Barnabas as far. 11:22

sent out

God s. Lot out of midst. *Gen* 19:29
David therefore s. out. *1 Sam* 26:4
and he s. out arrows.   *2 Sam* 22:15
      Ps 18:14
who hath s. out the wild ? *Job* 39:5
poured out, skies s. out. *Ps* 77:17
she s. out her boughs to sea. 80:11
whom I have s. out of this place.
      Jer 24:5
she hath s. out her little. *Ezek* 31:4
Jacob s. out our fathers. *Acts* 7:12
Rahab had s. them out.   *Jas* 2:25

sent, passive

it is a present s. to my. *Gen* 32:18
I am s. to thee with.   *1 Ki* 14:6
forasmuch as thou art s. *Ezra* 7:14
shall be s. against him.   *Pr* 17:11
an ambassador is s. unto. *Jer* 49:14
behold, a hand was s.   *Ezek* 2:9
not s. to a people of a strange. 3:5
whom a messenger was s.   23:40
then was part of hand s. *Dan* 5:24
an ambassador is s. among.   Ob 1
s. but unto lost sheep. *Mat* 15:24
and stonest them who are s. 23:37
      Luke 13:34
I am Gabriel, and am s. *Luke* 1:19
angel Gabriel was s. from God.   26
a man s. from God.   *John* 1:6
John was s. to bear witness.   8*
they who were s. were of the.   24
I said, I am not Christ, but s.   3:28

which is by interpretation, S.*John* 9:7
is s. greater than he that s.   13:16
men that were s. had.   *Acts* 10:17
to the men who were s.   21; 11:11
as soon as I was s. for.   10:29
so they being s. forth by.   13:4
word of this salvation s.   26
the salvation of God is s.   28:28
except they be s.?   *Rom* 10:15
which were s. from you. *Phil* 4:18
spirits s. forth to minister for them.
      Heb 1:14
with the Holy Ghost s. *1 Pet* 1:12
as them that are s. by him.   2:14
the seven spirits s. forth. *Rev* 5:6

sentence

shall shew thee the s.   *Deut* 17:9
do according to the s.   10*, 11*
let my s. come forth.   *Ps* 17:2
a divine s. is in the lips. *Pr* 16:10
s. is not executed speedily. *Eccl* 8:11
now also will I give s.   *Jer* 4:12*
Pilate gave s. that it. *Luke* 23:24
s. is that we trouble.   *Acts* 15:19*
we had the s. of death.   *2 Cor* 1:9

sentences

shewing of hard s. found. *Dan* 5:12
a king understanding dark s.   8:23

sentest

s. forth thy wrath which.   *Ex* 15:7
land whither thou s. us. *Num* 13:27
the messengers thou s. us.   24:12
things thou s. to me for.   *1 Ki* 5:8

separate, verb

[1] *To part or divide*, Gen 30:40.
[2] *To consecrate and set apart for
some special ministry or service*,
Acts 13:2. [3] *To forsake the
communion of the church*, Jude 19.
[4] *To excommunicate*, Luke 6:22.

Abram said, S. thyself.   *Gen* 13:9
Jacob did s. the lambs.   30:40
shall ye s. the children.   *Lev* 15:31
and his sons that they s.   22:2
shall s. themselves to vow a vow, to
   s. themselves unto.   *Num* 6:2
the Nazarite shall s. himself.   3
thus shalt thou s. the Levites. 8:14
s. yourselves from among.   16:21
shalt s. three cities.   *Deut* 19:2, 7
Lord shall s. him unto evil.   29:21
didst s. them to be thine. *1 Ki* 8:53
s. yourselves from people of the.
      Ezra 10:11
Jeremiah went to s. himself thence.
      Jer 37:12*
he shall s. them, as a. *Mat* 25:32
when men shall s. you. *Luke* 6:22
s. me Barnabas and Saul. *Acts* 13:2
who shall s. us from the love of
   Christ ?   *Rom* 8:35
nor any other ... able to s. us from. 39
they who s. themselves. *Jude* 19

separate

head of Joseph and of him that was s.
    Gen 49:26; *Deut* 33:16
the s. cities of Ephraim. *Josh* 16:9
was before the s. place. *Ezek* 41:12
the house and the s. places.   13
the breadth of the s. place.   14
chamber over against the s. place.
      42:1, 10, 13
come out from among them, and be
   ye s.   *2 Cor* 6:17
undefiled, s. from sinners. *Heb* 7:26

separated

then Abram and Lot s.   *Gen* 13:11
Lord said, after that Lot was s.   14
two manner of people be s.   35:23
so shall we be s.   *Ex* 33:16
I am the Lord who have s. you.
      Lev 20:24
which I have s. from you as.   25
of Israel hath s. you.   *Num* 16:9
the Lord s. the tribe of. *Deut* 10:8
when he s. sons of Adam.   32:8
there s. unto David.   *1 Chr* 12:8
Aaron was s. that he should. 23:13
David s. to the service of sons. 25:1
then Amaziah s. them, *2 Chr* 25:10
all that had s. themselves. *Ezra* 6:21
then I s. twelve of the chief.   8:24

priests and Levites have not s.
                Ezra 9:1
who would not come, be s.   10:8
by their names were s.   16
we are s. upon the wall. *Neh* 4:19
Israel s. themselves from.   9:2
they that had s. clave to the. 10:28
they s. from Israel the mixed. 13:3
man having s. himself.   *Pr* 18:1
but the poor is s. from his.   19:4
the Lord hath s. me from. *Isa* 56:3
iniquities have s. between. 59:2
for themselves are s.   *Hos* 4:14
they went and s. themselves. 9:10
Paul departed and s.   *Acts* 19:9
Paul an apostle, s. unto the. *Rom* 1:1
God who s. me from my. *Gal* 1:15
Peter withdrew and s. himself. 2:12

separateth
fulfilled in which he s.   *Num* 6:5
the days he s. himself.   5
and a whisperer s. chief. *Pr* 16:28
he that repeateth a matter s. 17:9
of the stranger which s. *Ezek* 14:7

separation
the days of the s. for her. *Lev* 12:2
two weeks, as in her s.   5
out of the time of her s.   15:25
days of s. shall he eat. *Num* 6:4
all days of his s. no razor shall. 5
all the days of his s. he is holy. 8
to Lord the days of his s. and bring a
  lamb, because his s. was.   12
when the days of his s. are. 13
Nazarite shall shave the head of his
  s. and take the hair of his s. 18
after the hair of the Nazarite's s. 19
his s. after the law of s.   21
kept for a water of s.   19:9
the water of s. hath not. 13, 20
he that sprinkleth the water of s. . . .
  that toucheth water of s. 19:21
purified with the water of s. 31:23
wall round to make a s. *Ezek* 42:20

separating
weep in the fifth month, s. *Zech* 7:3

Sepharvaim
brought men from S. *2 Ki* 17:24
where are the gods of S.? 18:34
               Isa 36:19
where is the king of S.? *2 Ki* 19:13
               Isa 37:13

sepulchre
*Or grave. The Hebrews have al-
ways taken great care about the
burial of their dead. Most of
their sepulchres were hollow places
dug into rocks, as was that bought
by Abraham, for the burying of
Sarah, Gen 23:6, those of the
kings of Judah and Israel; and that
wherein our Saviour was laid.*
  *Our Saviour in Mat 23:7, com-
pares the hypocritical Pharisees to
whited sepulchres which appeared
fine without, but inwardly were full
of rottenness and corruption. It
is said, that every year, on the
fifteenth of February, the Jews
took care to whiten their sepulchres
anew.*
  *The Revisions usually change this
to tomb.*

withhold from thee his s. *Gen* 23:6
no man knoweth of his s. *Deut* 34:6
buried in his father's s. *Judg* 8:32
two men by Rachel's s. *1 Sam* 10:2
Asahel in his father's s. *2 Sam* 2:32
Ish-bosheth buried in Abner's s. 4:12
Ahithophel buried in the s. of. 17:23
bones of Saul in the s. of Kish. 21:14
shall not come to the s. *1 Ki* 13:22
bury me in the s. wherein the man. 31
Ahaziah in the s. with. *2 Ki* 9:28
they cast the man into the s. 13:21
Amon was buried in his s. in. 21:26
they told him. It is the s. of the. 23:17
Josiah buried in his own s. 30
           2 Chr 35:24
their throat is an open s. *Ps* 5:9
             Rom 3:13

hewed thee out a s. here as he that
  heweth out a s. on. *Isa* 22:16
stone to the door of s. *Mat* 27:60
Mary, sitting over against the s. 61
command that the s. be. 64, 66
Mary came to see the s. 28:1
depart quickly from the s. 8
and laid him in a s. . . . door of the s.
   Mark 15:46; *Luke* 23:53
            Acts 13:29
the s. at rising of sun. *Mark* 16:2
the stone from the door of the s. 3
entering into the s.   5
they fled from the s.   8
women also beheld the s. *Luke* 23:55
morning they came to the s. 24:1
found the stone rolled from s. 2
            John 20:1
returned from the s. *Luke* 24:9
Peter ran to the s.   12
which were early at the s. 22
with us went to the s.   24
in the garden there was a new s.
           John 19:41
for the s. was nigh at hand. 42
Mary when it was dark to the s. 20:1
taken away the Lord out of the s. 2
disciple came to the s. 3, 4, 8
Peter, and went into the s. 6
at the s. weeping . . . she stooped
  down and looked into the s. 11
and his s. is with us. *Acts* 2:29
Jacob laid in the s. that. 7:16

sepulchres
in the choice of our s. bury. *Gen* 23:6
Josiah spied the s. and took the
  bones out of the s. *2 Ki* 23:16
Jehoram not buried in s. *2 Chr* 21:20
Joash not buried in s. of. 24:25
Ahaz not in s. of kings. 28:27
buried in the chiefest of the s. 32:33
place of my fathers' s. *Neh* 2:3
me to the city of my fathers' s. 5
repaired to place over against s. 3:16
are like unto whited s. *Mat* 23:27
because ye garnish the s. of the. 29
ye build the s. of the prophets.
       Luke 11:47, 48

Seraiah
Zadok the priest, and S. *2 Sam* 8:17
the captain of the guard took S. the
  chief. *2 Ki* 25:18; *Jer* 52:24
to Gedaliah, S. *2 Ki* 25:23
             Jer 40:8
S. begat Joab. *1 Chr* 4:14
Josibiah son of S.   35
Azariah begat S. and S. begat. 6:14
Ezra the son of S. *Ezra* 7:1
S. sealed.   *Neh* 10:2
S. was ruler of the house. 11:11
S. the priest went up with. 12:1
the fathers: of S., Meraiah. 12
king commanded S. to. *Jer* 36:26
Jeremiah commanded S. the son of
  Neriah, this S. was a. 51:59
Jeremiah said to S., When thou. 61

seraphims
above it stood the s. each. *Isa* 6:2
then flew one of the s. having. 6

sergeants
sent the s. saying, Let. *Acts* 16:35
the s. told these words unto. 38

Sergius Paulus
S. Paulus a prudent man. *Acts* 13:7

serpent
*There are several words in the
Bible for various sorts of serpents.
It is not always certain which of the
many sorts is referred to. The
Hebrew word nachash is a general
term for any sort of serpent.
Satan is called a serpent partly
because of various qualities of the
serpent which seem similar to his;
partly because he assumed the form
of a serpent in Eden; and partly
because the serpent was a common
symbol for evil.*
  *In the wilderness the Israelites
were plagued with fiery serpents.
They were probably so called from
the intense burning pain of their*

bite. *The brazen serpent was made
by Moses at the command of God
to heal those who were so troubled.
This was preserved till the time of
Hezekiah, when it was destroyed
because it had become an object of
worship.*

the s. was more subtle. *Gen* 3:1
woman said, The s. beguiled me. 13
          2 Cor 11:3
Dan shall be a s. by the. *Gen* 49:17
the rod became a s. *Ex* 4:3, 7, 9
           10, 15
make thee a fiery s. *Num* 21:8
Moses made a s. of brass . . . if a s.
  had bitten any man . . . s. of. 9
in pieces the brasen s. *2 Ki* 18:4
formed the crooked s. *Job* 26:13
like the poison of a s. *Ps* 58:4
their tongues like a s. 140:3
at the last it biteth like a s. *Pr* 23:32
the way of a s. upon a rock. 30:19
s. shall bite him. *Eccl* 10:8
surely the s. will bite without. 11
s.'s root shall come forth a cockatrice;
  his fruit . . . flying s. *Isa* 14:29
punish the s., that crooked s. 27:1
viper and fiery flying s. 30:6
shall be the s.'s meat. 65:25
thereof shall go like a s. *Jer* 46:22
and a s. bit him. *Amos* 5:19
I will command the s. and. 9:3
lick the dust like a s. *Mi* 7:17
will he give him a s.? *Mat* 7:10
          Luke 11:11
as Moses lifted up the s. *John* 3:14
that old s. called. *Rev* 12:9; 20:2
nourished, from face of the s. 12:14
the s. cast out of his mouth. 15

serpents
rods, they became s. *Ex* 7:12
the Lord sent fiery s. *Num* 21:6
take away the s. from us. 7
wherein were fiery s. *Deut* 8:15
also send the poison of s. 32:24*
I will send s. among you. *Jer* 8:17
be ye therefore wise as s. *Mat* 10:16
ye s. how can ye escape ? 23:33
they shall take up s. *Mark* 16:18
power to tread on s. *Luke* 10:19
and were destroyed of s. *1 Cor* 10:9
beasts and of s. is tamed. *Jas* 3:7
tails were like unto s. *Rev* 9:19

servant
*This word in the Bible usually
means bond-servant, or slave, as
there were rarely any others who
acted as servants. See slave. It
also means any one who serves
another, as Joshua was the servant
of Moses. Here the Revisions
frequently change it to minister.
Servant is put for the subject of a
prince. The servant of Pharaoh,
the servants of Saul and those of
David, are their subjects in general, and their domestics in particular, 2 Sam 11:11; 12:19; 1 Chr 21:3.
In like manner also the Philistines,
the Syrians, and several other
nations, were servants of David;
they obeyed him, they were his
subjects, they paid him tribute,
2 Sam 8:6.
Moses is often called the servant
of the Lord, Deut 34:5, Josh 1:2.
Servant is also taken for a person
of a servile ignoble condition and
spirit, who is altogether unfit for
places of dignity, Eccl 10:7.*

Canaan, a s. of servants. *Gen* 9:25
I am Abraham's s. 24:34
became a s. to tribute. 49:15
if the s. plainly say. *Ex* 21:5
wast a s. in Egypt. *Deut* 5:15
thou shalt not deliver the s. 23:15
priest's s. came. *1 Sam* 2:13, 15
Samuel said, Bid the s. pass. 9:27
let thy handmaid be a s. 25:41
is not this David the s. of? 29:3
I am a young man s. to an. 30:13
s. named Ziba. *2 Sam* 9:2; 19:17

Ziba the *s.* of Mephibosheth.
   2 Sam 16:1
king's *s.* and me thy *s.*   18:29
Jeroboam Solomon's *s.* *1 Ki* 11:26
if thou wilt be a *s.* to this.   12:7
she said to her *s.,* Drive. *2 Ki* 4:24
when the *s.* of the man of.   6:15
Tobiah the *s.* the. *Neh* 2:10, 19
there; and the *s.* is free. *Job* 3:19
as a *s.* earnestly desireth the.   7:2
leviathan for a *s.* for ever ?   41:4
who was sold for a *s.* *Ps* 105:17
the fool shall be *s.* to. *Pr* 11:29
is despised and hath a *s.*   12:9
favour is toward a wise *s.*   14:35
a wise *s.* shall have rule over. 17:2
much less for a *s.* to rule.   19:10
and the borrower is *s.* to the.   22:7
a *s.* will not be corrected.   29:19
accuse not *s.* to his master.   30:10
the earth cannot bear a *s.* when. 22
as with the *s.* so with. *Isa* 24:2
to a *s.* of rulers.   49:7
is Israel a *s.?*   *Jer* 2:14
s. of the living God. *Dan* 6:20
can *s.* of my lord talk?   10:17
s. honoureth his master. *Mal* 1:6
nor the *s.* above his lord. *Mat* 10:24
it is enough for the *s.* to be.   25
s. fell down and worshipped. 18:26
the lord of that *s.* was moved.   27
O thou wicked *s.* I forgave.   32
chief among you, let him be your *s.*
   20:27; 23:11; *Mark* 10:44
wise *s.* whom lord. *Mat* 24:45
blessed is that *s.* whom his lord. 46
   Luke 12:43
but if that evil *s.* shall say.
   Mat 24:48; *Luke* 12:45
the lord of that *s.* shall come.
   Mat 24:50; *Luke* 12:46
good and faithful *s.* enter thou into
  joy. *Mat* 25:21, 23; *Luke* 19:17
thou wicked and slothful *s.*
   Mat 25:26; *Luke* 19:22
cast the unprofitable *s.* *Mat* 25:30
Peter struck a *s.* of the high priest,
  and smote off his ear.   26:51
   Mark 14:47; *John* 18:10
and he sent to the husbandmen a *s.*
   Mark 12:2
that *s.* which knew his. *Luke* 12:47
so that *s.* came and shewed.   14:21
but which of you having a *s.*   17:7
he thank that *s.?* I trow not.   9
at the season he sent a *s.* 20:10, 11
sin, is the *s.* of sin. *John* 8:34
the *s.* abideth not in the house.   35
the *s.* is not greater than his lord.
    13:16; 15:20
the *s.* knoweth not what.   15:15
Paul a *s.* of Jesus Christ. *Rom* 1:1
judgest another man's *s.?*   14:4
I commend to you Phebe, our *s.* 16:1
thou called being a *s.?* *1 Cor* 7:21*
called, being a *s.* is the Lord's. 22*
yet I have made myself a *s.*   9:19*
I should not be the *s.* *Gal* 1:10
differeth nothing from a *s.*   4:1*
wherefore thou art no more a *s.* 7*
him the form of a *s.* *Phil* 2:7
Epaphras, a *s.* of Christ. *Col* 4:12
s. of Lord must not strive. *2 Tim* 2:24
as a *s.* but above a *s.* a brother.
   Philem 16
in his house as a *s.* *Heb* 3:5
Simon Peter, a *s.* of. *2 Pet* 1:1
Jude the *s.* of Jesus Christ. *Jude* 1

see David, hired, maid

servant, and servants *of God*
forgive the *s.* of the God of thy.
   Gen 50:17
as Moses the *s.* of God. *1 Chr* 6:49
Moses the *s.* of God said. *2 Chr* 24:9
law, which was given by Moses the *s.*
  of God to observe. *Neh* 10:29
he said, O Daniel, *s.* of the living
  God.   *Dan* 6:20
law of Moses the *s.* of God. *Ps* 9:11
a *s.* of God.   *Tit* 1:1
James a *s.* of God. *Jas* 1:1
not using liberty, but as a *s.* of God.
   1 Pet 2:16

sealed the *s. of* our God. *Rev* 7:3
song of Moses the *s. of* God.   15:3

his servant
and Canaan shall be *his s.* *Gen* 9:26
    27
Lord and *his s.* Moses. *Ex* 14:31
if a man smite *his s.* and die. 21:20
if he smite the eye of *his s.* that. 26
but *his s.* Joshua departed. 33:11*
saith my Lord to *his s.?* *Josh* 5:14
God commanded *his s.* Moses. 9:24
down with Phurah *his s.* *Judg* 7:11
the Levite went, having *his s.* 19:3
rose to depart, he and *his s.*   9
king sin against *his s.* *1 Sam* 19:4
impute any thing to *his s.*   22:15
the Lord hath kept *his s.*   25:39
thus pursue after *his s.?*   26:18
king hear the words of *his s.*   19
hath commanded *his s.* *2 Sam* 9:11
fulfilled the request of *his s.* 14:22
my lord come to *his s.?*   24:21
he will not slay *his s.* *1 Ki* 1:51
by the hand of Moses *his s.*   8:56
cause of *his s.* and Israel.   59
hand of *his s.* Ahijah. 14:18; 15:29
Elijah came and left *his s.*   19:3
he spake by *his s.* Elijah. *2 Ki* 9:36
he spake by *his s.* Jonah.   14:25
Hoshea became *his s.* and.   17:3
and Jehoiakim became *his s.*   24:1
seed of Israel *his s.* *1 Chr* 16:13
spake against *his s.* Hezekiah.
   2 Chr 32:16
let every one with *his s.* *Neh* 4:22
in prosperity of *his s.* *Ps* 35:27
O ye seed of Abraham *his s.* 105:6
he sent Moses *his s.* and Aaron. 26
remembered Abraham *his s.*   42
heritage unto Israel *his s.* 136:22
that delicately bringeth up *his s.*
   Pr 29:21
that confirmeth the word of *his s.*
   Isa 44:26
redeemed *his s.* Jacob.   48:20
from the womb to be *his s.*   49:5
obeyeth the voice of *his s.*   50:10
caused every man *his s.* *Jer* 34:16
his s. was healed in the. *Mat* 8:13
he hath holpen *his s.* *Luke* 1:54
would come and heal *his s.*   7:3
and sent *his s.* at supper time. 14:17
his angel unto *his s.* John. *Rev* 1:1

see Lord

man-servant
shalt not do any work, thou, nor
  thy *man-s.* *Ex* 20:10; *Deut* 5:14
not covet thy neighbour's *man-s.*
   Ex 20:17; *Deut* 5:21
if he smite out his *man-s.'s* tooth.
   Ex 21:27
if the ox shall push a *man-s.*   32
eat them, thou, and thy *man-s.*
   Deut 12:18
Lord, thou and thy *man-s.*   16:11
feast, thou, and thy *man-s.*   14
the cause of my *man-s.* *Job* 31:13
should let his *man-s.* go free.
   Jer 34:9, 10

my servant
I will multiply thy seed for *my s.'s*
  sake.   *Gen* 26:24
he with whom it is found shall be *my*
  s.   44:10*, 17*
my s. Moses is not so. *Num* 12:7
why were ye not afraid to speak
  against *my s.?*   8
but *my s.* Caleb had another. 14:24
Moses *my s.* is dead. *Josh* 1:2
that my son had stirred up *my s.*
   1 Sam 22:8
therefore he shall be *my s.*   27:12
my lord, O king, *my s.* *2 Sam* 19:26
sent Naaman *my s.* *2 Ki* 5:6
according to the law *my s.*   21:8
considered *my s.* Job? *Job* 1:8; 2:3
I called *my s.* and he gave.   19:16
right, as *my s.* Job hath.   42:7
go to *my s.* Job, he shall pray.   8
like as *my s.* Isaiah. *Isa* 20:3
I will call *my s.* Eliakim.   22:20

Israel, art *my s.,* fear not. *Isa* 41:8, 9
behold *my s.* whom I uphold.   42:1
blind but *my s.* that I sent ?   19
ye are witnesses, and *my s.*   43:10
hear, O Jacob, *my s.*   44:1
fear not, O Jacob, *my s.*   2
for thou art *my s.*   21; 49:3
for Jacob *my s.'s* sake, and.   45:4
thou shouldest be *my s.*   49:6
behold, *my s.* shall deal.   52:13
so will I do for *my s.'s* sake. 65:8
Nebuchadnezzar *my s.* *Jer* 25:9
    27:6; 43:10
fear thou not, O *my s.* Jacob. 30:10
    46:27, 28
land I have given to *my s.* Jacob.
   Ezek 28:25; 37:25
thee, O Zerubbabel *my s.* *Hag* 2:23
bring forth *my s.* the BRANCH.
   Zech 3:8
the law of Moses *my s.* *Mal* 4:4
my s. lieth at home sick. *Mat* 8:6
speak, and *my s.* shall be healed.   8
   Luke 7:7
and to *my s.,* Do this, and he doeth it.
   Mat 8:9; *Luke* 7:8
behold, *my s.* whom I. *Mat* 12:18
there shall also *my s.* be. *John* 12:26

thy servant
I pray thee, from *thy s.* *Gen* 18:3
behold, *thy s.* hath found grace.
    19:19; *Neh* 2:5
hast appointed for *thy s.* *Gen* 24:14
the mercies shewed to *thy s.* 32:10
shalt say, They be *thy s.* Jacob's. 18
which God hath given *thy s.*   33:5
grey hairs of *thy s.* our father. 44:31
thy s. became surety for the lad. 32
hast spoken unto *thy s.* *Ex* 4:10
for thee, and for *thy s.* *Lev* 25:6
thou afflicted *thy s.?* *Num* 11:11
hast begun to shew *thy s.*
   Deut 3:24
and he shall be *thy s.* for ever. 15:17
down with Phurah *thy s.* *Judg* 7:10
deliverance into hand of *thy s.* 15:18
speak, Lord, for *thy s.* heareth.
   1 Sam 3:9, 10
thy s. slew both the lion.   17:36
if he say thus, *thy s.* shall.   20:7
for *thy s.* knew nothing of all. 22:15
I beseech thee, tell *thy s.*   23:11
know what *thy s.* can do.   28:2
hast spoken of *thy s.'s* house.
   2 Sam 7:19
thou, Lord God, knowest *thy s.*   20
to bless the house of *thy s.*   29
answered, Behold *thy s.*   9:6
the king's sons came as *thy s.* 13:35
even there will *thy s.* be.   15:21
he hath slandered *thy s.*   19:27
away the iniquity of *thy s.*   24:10
but me, even me *thy s.* and Zadok
  the priest, and. *1 Ki* 1:26
king said, so will *thy s.* do.   2:38
and *thy s.* is in the midst of.   3:8
give *thy s.* understanding heart.   9
to the prayer of *thy s.*   8:28
but I *thy s.* fear the Lord.   18:12
this day that I am *thy s.*   36
thy s. Ben-hadad saith, I pray. 20:32
as *thy s.* was busy here and there. 40
thy s. my husband is dead, and thou
  knowest *thy s.* did fear. *2 Ki* 4:1
pardon *thy s.* in this thing.   5:18
Gehazi said, Thy *s.* went no.   25
but what, is *thy s.* a dog ?   8:13
I am *thy s.*   16:7
prosper, I pray thee, *thy s.* this day.
   Neh 1:11
by them is *thy s.* warned. *Ps* 19:11
thy s. from presumptuous sins.   13
put not *thy s.* away in anger.   27:9
shine upon *thy s.:* save me.   31:16
hide not thy face from *thy s.* 69:17
O my God, save *thy s.* that.   86:2
give *thy s.* strength unto *thy s.*   16
void the covenant of *thy s.*   89:39
truly I am *thy s.* 116:16; 119:125
    143:12
lest thou hear *thy s.* *Eccl* 7:21
hear the prayer of *thy s.* *Dan* 9:17
now lettest thou *thy s.* *Luke* 2:29

servants

Canaan, a servant of s.	Gen 9:25
have I given him for s.	27:37
children of Israel are s.	Lev 25:55
and say, We are your s.	Josh 9:11
that ye be not s. unto.	1 Sam 4:9
Philistine, and you s. to Saul ?	17:8
will we be your s.: but if I kill him,	
then shall ye be our s.	9
but the s. of the king would.	22:17
many s. break away from.	25:10
to wash the feet of the s. of.	41
became David's s.	2 Sam 8:2
Edom became David's s.	14
fifteen sons and twenty s.	9:10
all in the house of Ziba s.	12
Hanun took David's s. and shaved.	
	10:4; 1 Chr 19:4
the s. of my Lord are.	2 Sam 11:11
two of the s. of Shimei.	1 Ki 2:39
the s. of Amon.	2 Ki 21:23
not all my lord's s.?	1 Chr 21:3
children of Israel Solomon made no	
s.	2 Chr 8:9
Babylon, where they were s.	36:20
we are the s. of the God.	Ezra 5:11
their s. bare rule over.	Neh 5:15
behold, we are s. this day, s.	9:36
they have slain the s.	Job 1:15, 17
as the eyes of s. look.	Ps 123:2
I got me s. and had s. born.	Eccl 2:7
I have seen s. upon horses, and	
princes walking as s.	10:7
shall possess them for s.	Isa 14:2
s. whom they had let go free, to re-	
turn... subjection for s.	Jer 34:11
s. have ruled over us.	Lam 5:8
ye s. of the most high God.	Dan 3:26
upon the s. will I pour.	Joel 2:29
be a spoil to their s.	Zech 2:9
then said the king to the s.	Mat 22:13
the lord of those s. cometh.	25:19
the s. did strike Jesus.	Mark 14:65*
blessed are those s.	Luke 12:37, 38
say, We are unprofitable s.	17:10
I call you not s., for.	John 15:15
these men are s. of the.	Acts 16:17
ye yield yourselves s. to obey.	
	Rom 6:16
that ye were the s. of sin.	17
made free, ye became the s.	18
your members s. to sin.	19
s. of sin, ye were free from.	20
and become s. to God.	22
be not ye the s. of men.	1 Cor 7:23
and ourselves your s.	2 Cor 4:5
s. be obedient to your.	Eph 6:5
Col 3:22; Tit 2:9; 1 Pet 2:18	
eye service, but as the s. of.	Eph 6:6
Paul and Timotheus the s.	Phil 1:1
masters, give unto your s.	Col 4:1
let as many s. as are.	1 Tim 6:1
but as the s. of God.	1 Pet 2:16
they themselves are the s. of.	
	2 Pet 2:19
till we have sealed the s.	Rev 7:3
see **hired, Lord, maid, men,**	
women	

his servants

feast unto all his s.	Gen 40:20
Pharaoh made his s.	Ex 9:20
in the night, he and his s.	12:30
his two s. with him.	Num 22:22
repent himself for his s.	Deut 32:36
the blood of his s.	43
and give to his s.	1 Sam 8:14, 15
tenth, ye shall be his s.	17
Saul spake to all his s. to kill.	19:1
and all his s. were standing.	22:6
his s. came near.	2 Ki 5:13
are not his s. come to ?	1 Chr 19:3
they shall be his s.	2 Chr 12:8
his s. spake yet more against.	32:16
therefore we his s. will.	Neh 2:20
put no trust in his s.	Job 4:18
the seed also of his s.	Ps 69:36
to deal subtilly with his s.	105:25
himself concerning his s.	135:14
if hearken to lies, all his s.	Pr 29:12
of the Lord, to be his s.	Isa 56:6
the Lord shall call his s. by.	65:15
be known toward his s.	66:14
on horses, he and his s.	Jer 22:4
punish him, his seed and his s.	36:31

prince give a gift to his s.	Ezek 46:17
and delivered his s. that.	Dan 3:28
take account of his s.	Mat 18:23
he sent his s. to husbandmen.	21:34
he called his ten s.	Luke 19:13
his s. ye are to whom.	Rom 6:16
to shew his s. things.	Rev 1:1; 22:6
hath avenged blood of his s.	19:2
praise God, all ye his s. and.	5
throne shall be in it, and his s.	22:3

my servants

they are my s. whom I brought.	
	Lev 25:42, 55
I have appointed my s.	1 Sam 21:2
my s. shall be with thy servants.	
	1 Ki 5:6; 2 Chr 2:8
yet I will send my s.	1 Ki 20:6
let my s. go with thy servants.	22:49
the blood of my s.	2 Ki 9:7
the half of my s. wrought.	Neh 4:16
neither I nor my s. put off our.	23
I and my s. might exact of.	5:10
all my s. were gathered thither.	16
and some of my s. sat.	13:19
mine elect and my s. shall.	Isa 65:9
my s. shall eat.	13
my s. shall sing for joy.	14
I have even sent to you all my s.	
	Jer 7:25; 44:4
world, then would my s. fight.	
	John 18:36
on my s. I will pour out.	Acts 2:18
prophetess, to seduce my s.	Rev 2:20

see **prophets**

thy servants

thy s. are no spies.	Gen 42:11
out the iniquity of thy s.	44:16*
thy s. are shepherds, both we.	47:3
said, Behold, we be thy s.	50:18
wherefore dealest thou thus with thy	
s.?	Ex 5:15
these thy s. shall bow down.	11:8
Abraham and Israel thy s.	32:13
	Deut 9:27
thy s. will do as my lord.	
	Num 32:25, 31
to Joshua, We are thy s.	Josh 9:8
slack not thy hand from thy s.	10:6
pray for thy s. to the.	1 Sam 12:19
faithful among all thy s.?	22:14
comfortably to thy s.	2 Sam 19:7
word, return thou and all thy s.	14
they told Shimei, thy s.	1 Ki 2:39
my servants shall be with thy s.	5:6
	2 Chr 2:8
and mercy with thy s.	1 Ki 8:23
	32
hear thou and judge thy s.	1 Ki 10:8
	2 Chr 6:23
happy are these thy s.	1 Ki 10:8
	2 Chr 9:7
they will be thy s. for ever.	
	1 Ki 12:7; 2 Chr 10:7
content, and go with thy s.	2 Ki 6:3
now these are thy s. and.	Neh 1:10
attentive to prayer of thy s.	11
the bodies of thy s. have.	Ps 79:2
of the blood of thy s. shed.	10
Lord, the reproach of thy s.	89:50
repent thee concerning thy s.	90:13
let thy work appear unto thy s.	16
for thy s. take pleasure in.	102:14
children of thy s. shall continue.	28
this day, for all are thy s.	119:91
by thy s. hast thou.	Isa 37:24
return, for thy s.' sake.	63:17
prove thy s. I beseech.	Dan 1:12
as thou seest, deal with thy s.	13
grant unto thy s. that.	Acts 4:29

serve

shall s. them 400 years.	Gen 15:13
that nation whom they shall s.	14
elder shall s. the younger.	25:23
let people s. thee, nations.	27:29
by thy sword shalt thou live, and s.	40
therefore s. me for nought ?	29:15
I will s. thee seven years for.	18
thou shalt s. with me seven.	27
they made Israel to s.	Ex 1:13
ye shall s. God upon this mountain.	
	3:12
my son go, that he may s. me.	4:23
let my people go, that they may s.	
	7:16; 8:1, 20; 9:1, 13; 10:3

that we may s. Egyptians, for it had	
been better for us to s.	Ex 14:12
not bow down to them, nor s. them.	
	20:5; Deut 5:9
Hebrew servant, six years he shall s.	
	Ex 21:2
ear, and he shall s. him for ever.	6
him to s. as bondservant.	Lev 25:39
s. thee unto the year of jubile.	40
the family of the Gershonites to s.	
	Num 4:24
made for them, so shall they s.	26
of fifty they shall s. no more.	8:25
Levi, for their service they s.	18:21
be driven to s. them.	Deut 4:19
the Lord thy God, and s. him.	6:13
10:12, 20; 11:13; 13:4; Josh 22:5	
24:14, 15; 1 Sam 7:3; 12:14, 20	
	24
sold to thee, and s. six years.	
	Deut 15:12
to thee, and shall s. thee.	20:11
shalt thou s. thine enemies.	28:48
this day whom ye will s.	Josh 24:15
should s. Shechem, should s. Hamor.	
	Judg 9:28
that we should s. him ?	38
occasion shall s. thee.	1 Sam 10:7
with us, and we will s. thee.	11:1
deliver us, and we will s.	12:10
be our servants, and s. us.	17:9
whom should I s.? should I not s.?	
	2 Sam 16:19
a people I knew not shall s. me.	
	22:44; Ps 18:43
heavy yoke lighter, and we will s.	
	1 Ki 12:4; 2 Chr 10:4
Jehu shall s. Baal.	2 Ki 10:18
the land, and s. the king of.	25:24
Jer 27:11, 12, 17; 28:14; 40:9	
and s. him with a perfect heart.	
	1 Chr 28:9
chosen you to s. him.	2 Chr 29:11*
Josiah made all present to s.	34:33
that we should s. him ?.	Job 21:15
if they obey and s. him, they.	36:11
unicorn be willing to s. thee ?	39:9
a seed shall s. him and.	Ps 22:30
kings, all nations shall s. him.	72:11
all they that s. graven images.	97:7
perfect way, he shall s. me.	101:6*
wherein thou wast made to s.	Isa 14:3
the Egyptians shall s. with.	19:23*
I have not caused thee to s.	43:23
but thou hast made me to s.	24†
themselves to the Lord, to s.	56:6*
the nation that will not s. thee.	60:12
so shall ye s. strangers.	Jer 5:19
cause thee to s. thine enemies.	17:4
these nations shall s. the king.	25:11
many nations shall s. themselves.	
	14; 27:7
of field have I given to s. him.	27:6
the nation which will not s. the king.	8
that say, Ye shall not s.	9, 14
no more s. themselves of him.	30:8
that none should s. himself.	34:9, 10
fear not to s. the Chaldeans.	40:9
I will s. the Chaldeans.	10
the countries to s. wood.	Ezek 20:32
O house of Israel, go s. ye.	39
all of them in the land shall s. me.	40
his army s. a great service.	29:18
food to them that s. the city.	48:18*
that s. the city, shall s. it out of.	19*
God whom we s. is able.	Dan 3:17
they might not s. any, except.	28
languages should s. him.	7:14
all dominions shall s. and obey.	27
s. him with one consent.	Zeph 3:9
it is in vain to s. God.	Mal 3:14
him only shalt thou s.	Mat 4:10
	Luke 4:8
no man can s. two masters; ye can-	
not s. God.	Mat 6:24; Luke 16:13
delivered, might s. him.	Luke 1:74
sister hath left me to s. alone.	10:40
he will come forth and s. them.	12:37
lo, these many years do I s. thee.	
	15:29
say, Gird thyself and s. me ?	17:8
is chief, as he that doth s.	22:27
if any man s. me, let him follow.	
	John 12:26

serve

word of God, and s.   Acts 6:2
shall they come forth and s.   7:7
angel of God, whom I s.   27:23
whom I s. with my spirit in the gospel
   of his Son.   Rom 1:9
we should not s. sin.   6:6
we should s. in newness of.   7:6
so then, with the mind I s. the. 25
it was said, the elder shall s.   9:12
they that are such s. not our. 16:18
but by love s. one another. Gal 5:13
for ye s. the Lord Christ. Col 3:24
turned from idols to s.   1 Thes 1:9
I thank God whom I s.   2 Tim 1:3
who s. unto the example and shadow
   of heavenly.   Heb 8:5
purge from dead works to s.? 9:14
whereby ye may s. God.   12:28
no right to eat, which s. the. 13:10
they s. him day and night. Rev 7:15
and his servants shall s. him. 22:3
      see Lord

serve joined with gods

thou shalt not s. their gods. Ex 23:24
   Deut 6:14; 28:14; Josh 23:7
   2 Ki 17:35; Jer 25:6; 35:15
if thou s. their gods it will. Ex 23:33
s. gods, the work of men's hands.
   Deut 4:28; 28:36, 64; Jer 16:13
that they may s. other gods.
            Deut 7:4; 31:20
s. other gods and worship.   8:19
   11:16; 30:17; Josh 24:20
            2 Chr 7:19
nations s. their gods? Deut 12:30
and s. other gods.   13:2, 6, 13
from God to s. other gods.   29:18
we should s. other gods. Josh 24:16
more than their fathers to s. other
   gods. Judg 2:19; Jer 11:10; 13:10
saying, Go s. other goas.
            1 Sam 26:19
to anger, to s. other gods. Jer 44:3
they s. not thy gods.   Dan 3:12
do ye not s. my gods?   14
we will not s. thy gods.   18

served

twelve years they s.   Gen 14:4
Jacob s. seven years.   29:20, 30
children for whom I s. thee. 30:26
knowest how I have s. thee.   29
with all my power I have s.   31:6
I s. thee 14 years for thy two.   41
wherein the nations s.   Deut 12:2
hath gone and s. other gods.   17:3
         29:26; Josh 23:16
fathers s. other gods. Josh 24:2, 15
gods which your fathers s.   14
and Israel s. the Lord all the days
   of Joshua.   31; Judg 2:7
Israel s. Baalim.   Judg 2:11, 13
         3:7; 10:6, 10
to sons, and s. their gods.   3:6
Israel s. Chushan-rishathaim.
so Israel s. Eglon king of Moab. 14
Why hast thou s. us thus?   8:1
ye have forsaken me, and s. 10:13
they put away gods, s. 16; 1 Sam 7:4
peace and s. Israel.   2 Sam 10:19
s. in thy father's presence. 16:19
presents and s. Solomon. 1 Ki 4:21
because they s. other gods.   9:9
            2 Chr 7:22
Ahab s. Baal.   1 Ki 16:31
Ahazian s. Baal.   22:53
Ahab s. Baal a little.   2 Ki 10:18
Hezekiah s. not the king of.   18:7
Manasseh s. host of heaven. 21:3
            2 Chr 33:3
Amon s. the idols that his father s.
   2 Ki 21:21; 2 Chr 33:22
Judah s. groves and.   2 Chr 24:18
they have not s. thee in. Neh 9:35
and they s. their idols. Ps 106:36
thee as thou hast s. us.   137:8
the king himself is s.   Eccl 5:9
as ye have s. strange gods. Jer 5:19
and moon, whom they have s. 8:2
after other gods and s. them. 16:11
worshipped other gods and s. 22:9
he hath s. thee six years. 34:14
for the service which he had s.
            Ezek 29:18, 20

the hands of those that s. Ezek 34:27
Israel s. for a wite; he.   Hos 12:12
Anna s. God night and. Luke 2:37*
a supper and Martha s. John 12:2
after David had s. his. Acts 13:36
who worshipped and s.   Rom 1:25
he hath s. with me in.   Phil 2:22

servedst

thou s. not the Lord.   Deut 28:47

servest

thy God whom thou s.   Dan 6:16
is thy God whom thou s. able? 20

serveth

of Merari all that s.   Num 3:36
his son that s. him   Mal 3:17
s. God, and him that s. not.   18
sitteth at meat or he that s.? but I
   am among . . . s.   Luke 22:27
he that in these things s. Christ is.
            Rom 14:18
prophecy s. not them.   1 Cor 14:22*
wherefore then s. the law? Gal 3:19

service

for the s. that thou.   Gen 29:27
thou knowest the s. which.   30:26
s. in field; all their s. wherein they.
            Ex 1:14
come to land, ye shall keep this s.
            12:25; 13:5
say, What mean ye by this s.? 12:26
all vessels in all the s.   27:19
make the clothes of the s.   31:10
            35:19
more than enough for the s.   36:5
tribe of Levi to do s.   Num 3:7, 8
charge of Gershonites for the s. 26
s. of sanctuary the charge. 31; 4:4
shall appoint them to the s. 4:19
in to perform the s. to do work. 23
the s. of the Gershonites. 24, 27, 28
s. of the sons of Merari. 30, 33, 43
that they may do the s. of the. 7:5
Levites may execute the s. of. 8:11
they shall go in to wait upon s. 24
shall cease waiting on the s.   25
thing to bring you to the s. 16:9
joined to thee for all the s. 18:4
given as a gift to do the s.   6
tenth in Israel for their s. 21, 31
that we might do the s. Josh 22:27
thou the grievous s. lighter. 1 Ki 12:4
David set over the s.   1 Chr 6:31
very able men for the work of the s.
            9:13; 26:8
distributed them in their s. 24:3
for all the work of the s.   28:13
be with thee for all the s.   21
to consecrate his s. to the Lord.? 29:5
and gave for the s. of house.   7
of the priests to their s. 2 Chr 8:14
they may know my s. and s. 12:8
money to such as did the s. 24:12
so the s. of the house was set. 29:35
every man according to his s. 31:2
work that he began in the s.   21
encouraged them to the s. of. 35:2
so the s. of the Lord was. 10, 16
in their courses, for the s. of God.
            Ezra 6:18; 7:19
part of a shekel for s. Neh 10:32
to grow for the s.   Ps 104:14
useth neighbour's s. without wages.
            Jer 22:13
army to serve a great s. Ezek 29:18
charge of house for all the s. 44:14
who killeth you will think he doeth
   s. unto God.   John 16:2
pertaineth the s. of God. Rom 9:4
which is your reasonable s. 12:1
that my s. may be accepted. 15:31*
administration of this s. 2 Cor 9:12
wages of them to do you s. 11:8*
did s. to them who by nature. Gal 4:8
with good will doing s.   Eph 6:7
if I be offered upon the s. Phil 2:17
supply your lack of s. toward. 30
rather do s. because they. 1 Tim 6:2
had ordinances of divine s. Heb 9:1
the priests accomplishing the s. 6
make him that did the s. perfect. 9
works, and charity, and s. Rev 2:19*

bond-service

Solomon did levy a tribute of bond-s.
            1 Ki 9:21

eye service

eye s. as men pleasers.   Eph 6:6

servile

ye shall do no s. work.   Lev 23:7
   8, 21, 25, 35, 36; Num 28:18, 25
            26; 29:1, 12, 35

serving

let Israel go from s. us.   Ex 14:5
hired servant in s. thee. Deut 15:18
cumbered about much s. Luke 10:40
s. the Lord with all humility.
            Acts 20:19
tribes instantly s. God day. 26:7
fervent in spirit, s. Lord. Rom 12:11
foolish, s. divers lusts.   Tit 3:3

servitor

s. said, Should I set this? 2 Ki 4:43*

servitude

ease somewhat grievous s. of thy.
            2 Chr 10:4*
gone because of great s.   Lam 1:3

set

s. the stars in firmament. Gen 1:17
Lord s. a mark upon Cain. 4:15*
door of the ark shalt s. in the. 6:16
I do s. my bow in the cloud. 9:13
Abraham s. calf before them. 18:8
the angel s. Lot without the. 19:16
s. it before my brethren and. 31:37
Pharaoh s. him over the land. 41:33
I have s. thee over all the land. 41
if I bring him not, and s. him. 43:9
Jacob s. Ephraim before.   48:20
nor did he s. his heart.   Ex 7:23*
s. apart to Lord all that open. 13:12
thou shalt s. bounds.   19:12, 23
which thou shalt s. before.   21:1
I will s. thy bounds from the. 23:31
thou shalt s. on table shew. 25:30
s. the table without.   26:35
s. in order things that are to be s. in.
            40:4
thou shalt s. the altar of gold.   5
s. altar of burnt offering.   6
s. the laver between.   7
he s. the staves on the ark.   20
s. the bread in order.   23
sabbath he shall s. it in. Lev 24:8
I will s. my tabernacle among. 26:11
Judah, these shall first s. forth.
            Num 2:9
as the camp is to s. forward. 4:15
the priest shall s. her before. 5:16
thou shalt s. the Levites.   8:13
s. forward bearing the.   10:17
Lord said, S. the fiery serpent. 21:8
let the Lord s. a man over. 27:16*
I have s. the land before you.
            Deut 1:8, 21
as all this law which I s.   4:8, 44
Lord did not s. his love on.   7:7
I s. before you a blessing.   11:26
judgements which I s. before. 14:24
choose to s. his name there. 14:24
            Neh 1:9
shalt say, I will s. a king. Deut 17:14
in any wise shalt s. him the. 15
which they of old time have s. 19:14
s. down the basket.   26:4, 10*
the Lord thy God will s. thee. 28:1
would not s. sole of her foot. 56
I have s. before you life. 30:15, 19
he s. bounds of the people by. 32:8
s. your hearts unto all the.   46
he s. them a statute in. Josh 24:25
till I bring and s. my.   Judg 6:18
that lappeth, him shalt thou s. 7:5
but newly s. the watch.   19
Lord s. every man's sword.   22
out of the dust, to s. them among
   princes; he hath s.   1 Sam 2:8
the Philistines s. the ark of. 5:2
as for thine asses, s. not thy. 9:20
ye have said, Nay, but s. a. 10:19
the Lord hath s. a king over. 12:13
Israel s. the battle in array. 17:2, 8
   2 Sam 10:17; 1 Ki 20:12
            1 Chr 19:17

they s. the ark of God.   2 Sam 6:3
s. Uriah in forefront of the.   11:15
yet didst thou s. thy servant.   19:28
that all Israel s. their.   1 Ki 2:15
son, whom I will s. on throne.   5:5
he s. the one in Beth-el, the.   12:29
and s. Naboth on high among.   21:9
thou shalt s. aside that.   2 Ki 4:4
let us s. for him there a bed.   10
s. on the great pot, and seethe.   38
what, should I s. this before an ?   43
s. bread and water before.   6:22
s. thine house in order.   20:1
           Isa 38:1
they s. the ark in midst. 1 Chr 16:1
s. your heart to seek.   22:19
because I s. my affection to.   29:3
s. their hearts to seek. 2 Chr 11:16
he feared, and s. himself to.   20:3
they s. the house of God.   24:13
Josiah s. the priests in their.   35:2
they s. the priests in.   Ezra 6:18
pleased the king, and I s.   Neh 2:6
we s. a watch against them.   4:9
increase to kings s. over us.   9:37
I gathered and s. them.   13:11
the terrors of God s.   Job 6:4
thou shouldest s. thine heart.   7:17
why hast thou s. me as a mark ?   20
shall s. me a time to plead ?   9:19
and he hath s. darkness in.   19:8
have disdained to s. with.   30:1
they s. forward my calamity.   13
s. thy words in order before.   33:5
if he s. his heart upon man.   34:14
and s. others in their stead.   24
canst thou s. dominion ?   38:33
the kings of the earth s.   Ps 2:2
yet have I s. my king on my holy.   6
I will not be afraid if 10,000 s.   3:6
the Lord hath s. apart him that.   4:3
who hast s. thy glory above.   8:1
I will s. him in safety from.   12:5
I have s. the Lord always.   16:8
in them hath he s. a tabernacle. 19:4
thou hast s. my feet in a large room.
           31:8
brought me up, and s. my feet. 40:2
I will s. them in order.   50:21
they have not s. God before.   54:3
if riches, s. not your heart.   62:10
surely thou didst s. them in.   73:18
thou hast s. all the borders of. 74:17
that they might s. their hope.   78:7
a generation that s. not their.   8
and shall s. us in the way.   85:13
violent men have not s. thee.   86:14
thou hast s. our iniquities.   90:8
s. his love upon me, therefore will I
   deliver him and s.   91:14
I will s. no wicked thing.   101:3
thou hast s. a bound that they. 104:9
s. thou a wicked man over.   109:6
that he may s. him with.   113:8
Lord answered, and s. me in. 118:5
fruit of thy body will I s.   132:11
proud have s. gins for me.   140:5
s. a watch, O Lord, before.   141:3
ye have s. at nought all.   Pr 1:25
landmark which thy fathers have s.
           22:28
wilt thou s. thine eyes on ?   23:5
also he hath s. the world.   Eccl 3:11
God hath s. the one against.   7:14
he sought out, and s. in order. 12:9
s. me as a seal upon thine heart.
       S of S 8:6
let us s. a king in midst of it. Isa 7:6
the Lord will s. them in their.   14:1
s. it with strange slips.   17:10
I will s. Egyptians against.   19:2
go s. a watchman, let him.   21:6
shall s. themselves in array.   22:7
who would s. briers and ?   27:4
I will s. in the desert the fir.   41:19
till he have s. judgement.   42:4
who as I, shall s. it in order ?   44:7
they carry him, and s. him.   46:7
mountain hast thou s. thy bed. 57:7
I have s. watchmen on thy walls.
       62:6; Jer 6:17
I will s. a sign among.   Isa 66:19
see, I have s. thee over.   Jer 1:10
lay wait, they s. a trap.   5:26

I have s. thee for a tower. Jer 6:27
the place where I s. my.   7:12*
they s. their abominations in.   30
law which I s. before them.   9:13
I s. before you the way of life. 21:8
for I will s. mine eyes on.   24:6
to walk in my law, which I s.   26:4
his servant, whom he had s.   34:16
I s. pots of wine before sons.   35:5
my friends have s. thee on.   38:22
statutes which I s. before.   44:10
hath s. me in dark places. Lam 3:6
he hath s. me as a mark for.   12
I have s. it in the midst.   Ezek 5:5
I s. it far from thee.   7:20
s. a mark on the foreheads.   9:4
for I have s. thee for a sign.   12:6
thou hast s. my oil before. 16:18, 19
off highest branch, I will s. it. 17:22
then nations s. against him on. 19:8
in thee have they s. light.   22:7
king of Babylon s. himself.   24:2
s. on a pot, s. it on, and also.   3
her blood, she s. it upon the.   7, 8
whereon they s. their minds.   25
I shall s. glory in the land.   26:20
they of Persia s. forth thy.   27:10
though thou s. thy heart.   28:2
cherub, and I have s. thee so.   14
they s. her a bed in the midst. 32:25
I will s. my sanctuary in.   37:26
I will s. my glory among.   39:21
s. thy heart upon all that I.   40:4
have s. keepers of my charge. 44:8
king thought to s. him.   Dan 6:3
he s. his heart on Daniel to.   14
to walk in his laws which he s. 9:10
thou didst s. thine heart to.   10:12
lest I s. her as in the day.   Hos 2:3
s. their heart on their iniquity.   4:8
Judah, he hath s. an harvest.   6:11
how shall I s. thee as Zeboim ? 11:8
we may s. forth wheat.   Amos 8:5
I will s. mine eyes upon them.   9:4
though thou s. thy nest.   Ob 4
that he may s. his nest.   Hab 2:9
I said, Let them s. a fair. Zech 3:5
it shall be s. there upon her.   5:11
make crowns, and s. them.   6:11
I s. all men, every one against. 8:10
I am come to s. a man.   Mat 10:35
he shall s. the sheep on his. 25:33
and s. an hedge about it. Mark 12:1
to s. at liberty them.   Luke 4:18
and s. him on his own beast. 10:34
I have nothing to s. before.   11:6
Herod with men of war s.   23:11
every man doth s. forth. John 2:10
he hath s. to his seal, that.   3:33
no, not so much as to s.   Acts 7:5
then Paul s. his eyes on him. 13:9
I have s. thee to be a light to.   47
no man shall s. on thee to.   18:10
whom God s. forth to be. Rom 3:25
why dost thou s. at nought ? 14:10
God hath s. forth us.   1 Cor 4:9
s. them to judge who are least. 6:4
now God hath s. the members. 12:18
God hath s. some in the church. 28
when he s. him at his own. Eph 1:20
s. your affection on things. Col 3:2
thou didst s. him over work. Heb 2:7
I have s. before thee an open door.
       Rev 3:8
shut him up, and s. a seal.   20:3*

set up

stone and s. it up for a pillar, and.
       Gen 28:18, 22; 31:45; 35:14
shalt s. up the tabernacle.   Ex 40:2
thou shalt s. up the court. 8, 18, 21
he s. up hanging at door of tabernacle.   28*, 33
nor shall ye s. up any.   Lev 26:1*
when the tabernacle is pitched, the
   Levites shall s. it up. Num 1:51
that Moses had fully s. up the. 7:1
and other did s. it up against. 10:21
s. up these stones.   Deut 27:2, 4
Joshua s. up twelve stones. Josh 4:9
shall he s. up gates of it.   6:26
       1 Ki 16:34
children of Dan s. up.   Judg 18:30
they s. them up Micah's graven. 31

it repenteth me I have s. up Saul.
       1 Sam 15:11
behold, Saul hath s. him up a.   12
to s. up throne of David. 2 Sam 3:10
I will s. up thy seed after thee. 7:12
to s. up his son after.   1 Ki 15:4
they s. them up images. 2 Ki 17:10
s. them up an altar in. 1 Chr 21:18*
Amaziah s. them up to. 2 Chr 25:14
Manasseh s. up groves and.   33:19
offered freely to s. up.   Ezra 2:68
Jews have s. up the walls thereof.
       4:12, 13, 16
a great king of Israel, s. up.   5:11*
being s. up, let him be hanged. 6:11
to give us a reviving, to s. up.   9:9
they sanctified it, and s. up.
       Neh 3:1, 3, 6, 13, 14, 15; 7:1
time I had not s. up the doors.   6:1
to s. up on high those.   Job 5:11
hath shaken me, and s. me up. 16:12
name of God we will s. up. Ps 20:5
he shall hide me, and s. me up. 27:5
O God, s. me up on high.   69:29
s. up their ensigns for signs.   74:4
thou hast s. up right hand of. 89:42*
I was s. up from everlasting, from.
       Pr 8:23
Lord shall s. up the.   Isa 9:11
he shall s. up an ensign for.   11:12
they s. up towers thereof.   23:13
that s. up wood of their.   45:20*
I will s. up my standard.   49:22
s. up thy remembrance.   57:8
s. up the standard toward.   Jer 4:6
none to s. up my curtains.   10:20
have ye s. up altars to that.   11:13
and I will s. up shepherds.   23:4
s. thee up way marks, make. 31:21
s. up a standard, publish.   50:2
       51:12, 27
s. up the watchmen, prepare. 51:12
he hath s. up horn of thy. Lam 2:17*
these men have s. up.   Ezek 14:3*
the deep s. him up on high.   31:4
I will s. up one shepherd.   34:23
God of heaven shall s. up. Dan 2:44
golden image I have s. up.   3:14
whom he would he s. up and. 5:19
that maketh desolate s. up.   12:11
they have s. up kings.   Hos 8:4
work wickedness are s. up. Mal 3:15
and s. up over his head. Mat 27:37
and s. up false witnesses. Acts 6:13
again the ruins, and s. it up.   15:16

set, passive

there was s. meat before. Gen 24:33
because the sun was s.   28:11
a ladder was s. upon earth.   12
stones s. in ephod.   Ex 25:7; 28:11
       35:9, 27
two tenons s. in order.   26:17
they are s. on mischief.   32:22
the rings to be s.   37:3
the lamps s. in order.   39:37
name was much s. by. 1 Sam 18:30
as thy life was much s. by.   26:24
crown was s. on David's head.
       2 Sam 12:30; 1 Chr 20:2
a seat to be s. for the.   1 Ki 2:19
could not see, for his eyes were s.
       14:4
that every man is s. at. 2 Ki 12:4*
appointed in their s.   1 Chr 9:22
Joab saw that battle was s.   19:10
onyx stones and stones to be s. 29:2
I am s. on the throne.   2 Chr 6:10
house of Lord was s. in.   29:35
in their s. office to give.   31:15
in their s. office they sanctified. 18
and what should be s. on. Job 36:16
eyes are privily s. against. Ps 10:8
s. thrones of judgement.   122:5
let my prayer be s. forth.   141:2
heart is fully s. in them. Eccl 8:11
folly s. in great dignity; rich. 10:6
are as the eyes of doves fitly s.
       S of S 5:12
his hands are as gold rings s.   14
s. upon sockets of fine gold.   15
thy belly as a heap of wheat s. 7:2
and instead of well s. hair. Isa 3:24
s. in my ward whole nights.   21:8

s. in array, as men for war.
     Jer 6:23; *Joel* 2:5
children's teeth are *s.* on edge.
     Jer 31:29; *Ezek* 18:2
teeth shall be *s.* on edge. *Jer* 31:30
her that was *s.* apart. *Ezek* 22:10
judgement was *s.*, books. *Dan* 7:10
thy land shall be *s.* open. *Nah* 3:13
a city *s.* on a hill cannot. *Mat* 5:14
he was *s.* on judgement seat. 27:19
sun did *s.*, they brought. *Mark* 1:32
a candle, and not to be *s.* on a. 4:21
things, and be *s.* at nought.   9:12
this child is *s.* for the. *Luke* 2:34
for I also am a man *s.* under.   7:8
eat such things as are *s.*   10:8
were *s.* six water pots. *John* 2:6
stone *s.* at nought of. *Acts* 4:11
in danger to be for *s.* at nought. 19:27
this man might have been *s.* 26:32
whatsoever is *s.* before. *1 Cor* 10:27
Christ had been evidently *s. Gal* 3:1
I am *s.* for the defence. *Phil* 1:17
to lay hold on the hope *s. Heb* 6:18
who is *s.* on the right hand of the
    throne.   8:1; 12:2
let us run the race that is *s.*   12:1
joy that was *s.* before him.   2
Timothy is *s.* at liberty.   13:23
cities are *s.* forth for an. *Jude* 7
s. down with my Father. *Rev* 3:21
a throne was *s.* in heaven, one.   4:2
    see face, faces, feasts

set day
on a *s. day* Herod. *Acts* 12:21

set time
shall bear to thee at this *s. time.*
     Gen 17:21
at the *s. time* of which God.   21:2
appointed a *s. time*, saying. *Ex* 9:5
according to the *s. time* Samuel.
     1 Sam 13:8
longer than the *s. time. 2 Sam* 20:5
appoint me a *s. time. Job* 14:13
s. time to favour her. *Ps* 102:13

Seth
after his image, and called him S.
     Gen 5:3
S. begat Enos.   6; *1 Chr* 1:1
     Luke 3:38

setter
s. forth of strange gods. *Acts* 17:18

settest
in all thou *s.* thy hand to.
    Deut 23:20*; 28:8*, 20*
am I a sea, that thou *s.* a watch?
     Job 7:12
thou *s.* a print upon the heels. 13:27†
thou *s.* a crown of gold. *Ps* 21:3
thou *s.* me before thy face.   41:12

setteth
when the tabernacle *s. Num* 1:51
when camp *s.* forward, Aaron.   4:5
poor, and *s.* his heart. *Deut* 24:15
cursed be he that *s.* light.   27:16
s. me on high places. *2 Sam* 22:34
     Ps 18:33
he *s.* an end to darkness. *Job* 28:3
he *s.* himself in a way. *Ps* 36:4
which by his strength *s.* fast.   65:6
God *s.* the solitary in families. 68:6
he putteth down one, and *s.* 75:7*
as a flame *s.* the mountains. 83:14
yet *s.* poor on high from. 107:41
wait as he that *s.* his snares. *Jer* 5:26
Baruch *s.* thee on against us.   43:3
that *s.* up his idol in his heart.
     Ezek 14:4*, 7*
removeth kings and *s. Dan* 2:21
s. up over it the basest of men. 4:17
and *s.* him on a pinnacle. *Mat* 4:5
s. it on a candlestick. *Luke* 8:16*
tongue *s.* on fire the course. *Jas* 3:6

setting
in their *s.* of their threshold by.
     Ezek 43:8
stone, and *s.* a watch. *Mat* 27:66*
when sun was *s.* they. *Luke* 4:40

settings
set in it *s.* of stones. *Ex* 28:17

settle
(*American Revision*, ledge)
ground even to lower *s. Ezek* 43:14
s. shall be fourteen cubits long.   17
blood on the four corners of the *s.*
    20; 45:19

settle, *verb*
I will *s.* him in mine. *1 Chr* 17:14
I will *s.* you after your. *Ezek* 36:11*
s. it in your hearts, not. *Luke* 21:14
God stablish, strengthen, *s.* you.
     1 Pet 5:10

settled
built a *s.* place for thee. *1 Ki* 8:13
he *s.* his countenance. *2 Ki* 8:11
Lord, thy word is *s.* in. *Ps* 119:89
before mountains were *s. Pr* 8:25
he hath *s.* on his lees. *Jer* 48:11
punish men that are *s. Zeph* 1:12
in faith grounded and *s. Col* 1:23

settlest
thou *s.* the furrows thereof. *Ps* 65:10

seven
(*A sacred number among the Jews, also indicating perfection or completion. It was used very often in a symbolic manner for the whole of a thing.*
The number seven entered very largely into the religious life and observances of the Jews)
up *s.* well favoured kine. *Gen* 41:2
s. other kine came up. 3, 4, 18, 19
    20, 27
s. ears of corn, came up, rank.   5
s. thin ears, and blasted. 6, 7, 23
    24, 27
Bilhah, all the souls were *s.* 46:25
the priest of Midian had *s. Ex* 2:16
s. sabbaths shall be. *Lev* 23:15
number *s.* sabbaths of years. 25:8
build me here *s.* altars, and prepare
   s. oxen and *s. Num* 23:1, 29
I have prepared *s.* altars. 4, 14
s. nations greater and. *Deut* 7:1
s. weeks thou shalt number. 16:9
to flee before thee *s.* ways. 28:7
shalt flee *s.* ways before them. 25
s. priests bearing *s.* trumpets.
     Josh 6:4, 6, 8, 13
of Israel *s.* tribes not received. 18:2
shall divide it into *s.* parts.   5
by cities into *s.* parts in a book.   9
if they bind me with *s. Judg* 16:7
if thou weavest *s.* locks.   13
shave off *s.* locks.   19
barren hath borne *s. 1 Sam* 2:5
with the Philistines *s.* months. 6:1
Jesse made *s.* of his sons to. 16:10
they fell all *s.* together. *2 Sam* 21:9
sons of Elioenai were *s. 1 Chr* 3:24
house of their fathers were *s.* 5:13
s. bullocks, *s.* rams. *2 Chr* 29:21
sent of king and of his *s. Ezra* 7:14
s. chamberlains that. *Esth* 1:10
the *s.* princes which saw the.   14
he gave her *s.* maidens meet. 2:9
in *s.* troubles no evil shall. *Job* 5:19
yea, *s.* are an abomination. *Pr* 6:16
wisdom hath hewn out her *s.*   9:1
for there are *s.* abominations. 26:25
give a portion to *s.* also. *Eccl* 11:2
in that day *s.* women take. *Isa* 4:1
smite it in the *s.* streams. 11:15
hath borne *s.* languisheth. *Jer* 15:9
s. months shall they be. *Ezek* 39:12
after the end of *s.* months shall. 14
up unto it by *s.* steps. 40:22, 26
breadth of the door *s.* cubits. 41:3
Messiah, shall be *s.* weeks.
     Dan 9:25
we shall raise against him *s. Mi* 5:5
one stone shall be *s.* eyes. *Zech* 3:9
his *s.* lamps thereon, and *s.* pipes to
   s. lamps.   4:2
of Zerubbabel with those *s.*   10
they said, S. loaves. *Mat* 15:34, 36
     Mark 8:5
they took up *s.* baskets full.
    Mat 15:37; *Mark* 8:8
nor the *s.* loaves. *Mat* 16:10
s. brethren, and the first deceased.
   22:25; *Mark* 12:20; *Luke* 20:29

in the resurrection whose wife shall
   she be of the *s.?*   *Mat* 22:28
and *s.* had her. *Mark* 12:22, 23
     Luke 20:31, 33
out of whom he cast *s.* devils.
    Mark 16:9; *Luke* 8:2
when he destroyed *s. Acts* 13:19
who was one of the *s.* deacons. 21:8
s. churches in Asia. *Rev* 1:4
send it to the *s.* churches in Asia. 11
I saw *s.* golden candlesticks.   12
in midst of *s.* candlesticks one.   13
s. stars are angels of the churches.
   the *s.* candlesticks ... are the *s.* 20
who walketh in midst of the *s.* 2:1
Lamb as slain, having *s.* horns, and
   s. eyes, which are the *s.*   5:6
I saw the *s.* angels which.   8:2
s. angels prepared themselves.   6
when he cried, *s.* thunders. 10:3
seal up what the *s.* thunders.   4
having *s.* heads, and *s.* crowns.
    12:3; 13:1; 17:3, 7
I saw *s.* angels having the *s.* 15:1, 6
gave to *s.* angels *s.* golden vials.   7
to enter into the temple, till the *s.*
   plagues of the *s.* angels were.   8
voice, saying to the *s.* angels. 16:1
one of the *s.* angels which had the *s.*
   vials, and talked.   17:1; 21:9
the *s.* heads are *s.* mountains. 17:9
there are *s.* kings, five are fallen. 10
the beast is of *s.* and. *Rev* 17:11
   see days, hundred, lambs, lamps,
    seals, thousand

seven bullocks
here *s. bullocks, s.* rams. *Num* 23:29
on the seventh day *s. bullocks.* 29:32
offered *s. bullocks, s.* rams.
     1 Chr 15:26
brought *s. bullocks, s.* rams.
     2 Chr 29:21
now, *s. bullocks, s.* rams. *Job* 42:8
prepare a burnt offering, *s. bullocks.*
     Ezek 45:23

seven men
let *s. men* of his sons. *2 Sam* 21:6
s. men that can render. *Pr* 26:16
took *s. men* that were near the.
     Jer 52:25
look out *s. men* of honest report.
     Acts 6:3

seven rams, *see* **seven bullocks**

seven sons
daughter is better than *s. sons.*
     Ruth 4:15
were born unto him *s. sons. Job* 1:2
he had also *s. sons*, and.   42:13
there were *s. sons* of one Sceva.
     Acts 19:14

seven spirits
taketh with himself *s.* other *spirits.*
   Mat 12:45; *Luke* 11:26
from *s. spirits* before the. *Rev* 1:4
hath the *s. spirits* of God.   3:1
lamps, which are the *s. spirits.* 4:5
eyes, which are the *s. spirits.* 5:6

seven stars
that maketh the *s. stars. Amos* 5:8*
had in his right hand *s. stars.*
     Rev 1:16; 2:1; 3:1
mystery of *s. stars* ... *s. stars* are
   the angels of the *s.* churches. 1:20

seven and thirty, *see* **thirty**

seven times
Jacob bowed before Esau *s. times.*
     Gen 33:3
priest shall sprinkle of the blood *s.*
   times. Lev 4:6, 17; 8:11; 14:7
   16:14, 19; *Num* 19:4
oil with his fingers *s. times.*
     Lev 14:16, 27
sprinkle the house *s. times.*   51
number *s. times* seven years. 25:8
punish you *s. times* more. 26:18, 21
    24, 28
compass city *s. times. Josh* 6:4, 15
and he said, Go again *s. times.*
     1 Ki 18:43
child sneezed *s. times. 2 Ki* 4:35
wash in Jordan *s. times.* 5:10, 14

silver purified s. times. *Ps* 12:6
s. times a day do I praise. 119:164
falleth s. times, and riseth. *Pr* 24:16
heat the furnace one s. times more.
Dan 3:19
let s. times pass over him. 4:16
23, 25, 32
shall I forgive ? till s. times.
Mat 18:21
I say not, till s. times, but until
seventy times s. 22
trespass against thee s. times a day,
and s. times a day. *Luke* 17:4
seven and twenty, see **twenty**

seven years
I will serve thee s. years. *Gen* 29:18
served s. years. 20
serve s. other years. 27, 30
good kine are s. years, and the seven
good ears are s. years. 41:26
kine are s. years, seven empty ears
shall be s. years of famine. 27
come s. years of plenty. 29, 34, 47, 48
arise s. years of famine. 30, 36, 54
the s. years of plenteousness. 53
seven times s. years. *Lev* 25:8
was built s. years before Zoan.
Num 13:22
end of every s. years a release.
Deut 15:1; 31:10
Israel to Midian s. years. *Judg* 6:1
second bullock of s. years old. 25
Ibzan of Bethlehem judged Israel
s. years. 12:9
David was king in Hebron s. years.
2 Sam 2:11; 5:5; *1 Ki* 2:11
1 Chr 29:27
shall s. years of famine come ?
2 Sam 24:13
Solomon was s. years in building.
1 Ki 6:38
famine shall come upon land s.
years. *2 Ki* 8:1
with the Philistines s. years. 2
s. years old was Jehoash when he.
11:21; *2 Chr* 24:1
at end of s. years let ye. *Jer* 34:14
burn weapons with fire s. years.
Ezek 39:9
an husband s. years. *Luke* 2:36

sevenfold
shall be taken on him s. *Gen* 4:15
avenged s. Lamech 70 and s. 24
render s. into their bosom. *Ps* 79:12
found he shall restore s. *Pr* 6:31
of the sun shall be s. *Isa* 30:26

sevens
beast shalt thou take by s. *Gen* 7:2
air by s. the male and female. 3

seventeen
Joseph being s. years old. *Gen* 37:2
in the land of Egypt s. years. 47:28
reigned s. years in Jerusalem.
1 Ki 14:21
son of Jehu reigned s. years.
2 Ki 13:1
bought field, weighed s. *Jer* 32:9

seventeenth
on s. day the fountains. *Gen* 7:11
ark rested on the s. day in. 8:4
to reign the s. year. *1 Ki* 22:51
in s. year of Pekah son. *2 Ki* 16:1
the s. lot came to Hezir. *1 Chr* 24:15
s. lot came to Joshbekashah. 25:24

seventh
in s. he shall go out free. *Ex* 21:2
but in the s. is the sabbath. 31:15
after the s. sabbath. *Lev* 23:16
at the s. time when the. *Josh* 6:16
s. lot came out for the tribe. 19:40
at the s. time there arose a cloud.
1 Ki 18:44
David was the s. son. *1 Chr* 2:15
s. lot came forth to Hakkoz. 24:10
Elioenai the s. son of. 26:3
Issachar was the s. son of. 5
s. captain for the s. month. 27:10
and the third, to the s. *Mat* 22:26
yesterday at s. hour the. *John* 4:52
Enoch the s. from Adam. *Jude* 14
he had opened the s. seal. *Rev* 8:1
of the voice of the s. angel. 10:7

the s. angel sounded, there.*Rev* 11:15
s. angel poured out his vial. 16:17
the s. foundation was a. 21:20
see **day**

seventh month
ark rested in s. month on. *Gen* 8:4
in s. month afflict your souls.
Lev 16:29; 23:27; 25:9
in the s. month shall ye. 23:24
in s. month an holy. *Num* 29:1, 12
at feast of the s. month. *1 Ki* 8:2
in the s. month Ishmael smote
Gedaliah. *2 Ki* 25:25; *Jer* 41:1
in s. month Solomon. *2 Chr* 7:10
the heaps in the s. month. 31:7
when s. month was come, and the.
Ezra 3:1; *Neh* 7:73
the first day of s. month. *Ezra* 3:6
the s. month Ezra read. *Neh* 8:2
in feasts of s. month Israel. 14
died in the s. month. *Jer* 28:17
in the s. month shall he. *Ezek* 45:25
in the s. month the word. *Hag* 2:1
in fifth and s. month. *Zech* 7:5
the fast of the s. month shall. 8:19

seventh year
the s. year thou shalt let. *Ex* 23:11
in the s. year shall be a. *Lev* 25:4
shall we eat in the s. year ? 20
saying, The s. year, year of release.
Deut 15:9
in the s. year thou shalt let. 12
in the s. year Jehoiada sent and.
2 Ki 11:4; *2 Chr* 23:1
in s. year of Jehu. *2 Ki* 12:1
in s. year of Hoshea king of. 18:9
went up unto Jerusalem in the s.
year of the king. *Ezra* 7:7, 8
leave s.year, and exaction.*Neh* 10:31
taken to king in s. year. *Esth* 2:16
away captive in s. year. *Jer* 52:28
the s. year elders came to enquire.
Ezek 20:1

seventy
truly Lamech s. and sevenfold.
Gen 4:24
and Cainan lived s. years. 5:12
Terah lived s. years and. 11:26
Abram was s.-five years old. 12:4
of Jacob were s. souls. *Ex* 1:5
and s. elders of Israel. 24:1, 9
the offering was s. talents. 38:29
was one silver bowl of s. shekels.
Num 7:13, 19, 25, 31, 37, 43, 49
55, 61, 67, 73, 79
each bowl weighing s. shekels. 85
gather unto me s. men of. 11:16, 24
of the spirit unto the s. elders. 25
slaying his s. brethren. *Judg* 9:56
had s. sons in Samaria. *2 Ki* 10:1, 6
took king's sons, and slew s. 7
children of Hodaviah s.-four.
Ezra 2:40; *Neh* 7:43
with Jeshaiah s. males. *Ezra* 8:7
Zabbud, with them s. males. 14
Tyre shall be forgotten s. years.
Isa 23:15
after end of s. years, the Lord. 17
king of Babylon s. years. *Jer* 25:11
when s. years are accomplished. 12
29:10
there stood before them s. men.
Ezek 8:11
accomplish s. years in. *Dan* 9:2
s. weeks are determined upon. 24
even those s. years, did. *Zech* 7:5
till seven times, but until s. times.
Mat 18:22
Lord appointed other s. *Luke* 10:1
the s. returned again with joy. 17

sever
will s. in that day the land. *Ex* 8:22
Lord shall s. between cattle. 9:4
shall s. out men of continual employment. *Ezek* 39:14
and s. the wicked from. *Mat* 13:49

several
and a s. tenth deal of flour mingled.
Num 28:13, 21, 29; 29:10, 15
Azariah ... his death, and dwelt in a s.
house. *2 Ki* 15:5†; *2 Chr* 26:21†
in every s. city put. *2 Chr* 11:12

in every s. city of Judah. *2 Chr* 28:25
sons of Aaron in every s. city. 31:19
according to his s. ability. *Mat* 25:15
every s. gate was one of. *Rev* 21:21

severally
dividing to every man s. *1 Cor* 12:11

severed
I have s. you from other people.
Lev 20:26*
Moses s. three cities. *Deut* 4:41*
Heber had s. himself. *Judg* 4:11

severity
the goodness and s. of God: on them
which fell, s.; but. *Rom* 11:22

sew
time to rend and a time to s. *Eccl* 3:7
woe to the women that s. pillows to
all armholes. *Ezek* 13:18

sewed
they s. fig leaves together. *Gen* 3:7
I have s. sackcloth upon. *Job* 16:15

sewest
in a bag, and thou s. up mine iniquity.
Job 14:17*

seweth
no man s. a piece of new cloth on.
Mark 2:21

shade
the Lord is thy s. upon. *Ps* 121:5

shadow
(*This word has often the rare
meaning of a shelter. It also means
at times, as in Col 2:17, a repre-
sentation, a sample which gives an
idea of what the real thing is to be.
In many cases the American Revision changes to shade*)
they came under the s. of my roof.
Gen 19:8
put your trust in my s. *Judg* 9:15
seest the s. of the mountains. 36
s. go forward ten degrees ? *2 Ki* 20:9
it is a light thing for the s. to go. 10
s. ten degrees backward. 11
our days on earth are as a s.
1 Chr 29:15; *Job* 8:9
earnestly desireth the s. *Job* 7:2
he fleeth also as a s. and. 14:2
all my members are as a s. 17:7
trees cover him with their s. 40:22
hide me under the s. *Ps* 17:8
their trust under the s. 36:7; 57:1
in the s. of thy wings will. 63:7
covered with the s. of it. 80:10
shall abide under the s. of the. 91:1
my days are like a s. that. 102:11
I am gone like a s. when. 109:23
man is like to vanity: his days are
as a s. 144:4; *Eccl* 8:13
he spendeth as a s. *Eccl* 6:12
I sat under his s. with. *S of S* 2:3
a tabernacle for a s. in daytime.
Isa 4:6
make thy s. as the night in. 16:3
thou hast been a s. from the. 25:4
down the heat with s. of a cloud. 5
trust in the s. of Egypt. 30:2
and the trust in the s. of Egypt. 3
as the s. of a great rock in. 32:2
and gather under her s. 34:15
I will bring again the s. of the. 38:8
in s. of his hand hath he hid me.
49:2; 51:16
they stood under the s. *Jer* 48:45
under his s. we shall live. *Lam* 4:20
in the s. thereof shall. *Ezek* 17:23
and under his s. dwelt all. 31:6
are gone down from his s. 12
that dwelt under his s. in midst. 17
field had s. under it. *Dan* 4:12
under elms, because s. *Hos* 4:13
they that dwell under his s. 14:7
and sat under it in the s. *Jonah* 4:5
might be s. over his head. 6
lodge under the s. of it. *Mark* 4:32
that s. of Peter might. *Acts* 5:15
which are a s. of things. *Col* 2:17
who serve unto the s. of. *Heb* 8:5
the law having a s. of good. 10:1
with whom is no s. of. *Jas* 1:17
see **death**

shadowing
woe to the land s. with wings.
Isa 18:1*
cedar with a s. shroud.   Ezek 31:3
over cherubims of glory s. the.
Heb 9:5*

shadows
until the day break, and the s. flee
away.   S of S 2:17; 4:6
for s. of the evening are.   Jer 6:4

Shadrach, see Abed-nego

shady
he lieth under the s. trees.Job 40:21*
the s. trees cover him with.   22*

shaft
his s. and branches, his bowls and.
Ex 25:31*; 31:17*; Num 8:4*
make me a polished s.   Isa 49:2

shake
I will go out and s. myself.Judg 16:20
lap, and said, So God s.   Neh 5:13
which made my bones to s. Job 4:14
he shall s. off his unripe grape. 15:33
could heap up words, and s.   16:4
out the lip, they s. head.   Ps 22:7
though the mountains s.   46:3
their loins continually to s.   69:23
the fruit thereof shall s. like. 72:16
ariseth to s. the earth. Isa 2:19, 21
as if the rod should s. itself. 10:15†
he shall s. his hand against.   32
the Lord shall s. his hand.   11:15†
exalt the voice unto them, s.   13:2*
I will s. heavens.   13*; Joel 3:16
Hag 2:6, 21
foundations of the earth do s.
Isa 24:18
Bashan and Carmel s. off.   33:9
s. thyself from the dust, O.   52:2
is broken, all my bones s. Jer 23:9
thy walls shall s. at noise of.
Ezek 26:10
not the isles s. at the sound ?   15
the suburbs shall s. at the.   27:28
I made nations s. at the sound. 31:16
all men of the earth shall s. at. 38:20
s. off his leaves, and.   Dan 4:14
lintel that the posts may s. Amos 9:1
I will s. all nations, desire. Hag 2:7
I will s. my hand on them. Zech 2:9
s. off the dust of your feet. Mat 10:14
Mark 6:11; Luke 9:5
fear of him the keepers did s.
Mat 28:4*
house, and could not s. it. Luke 6:48
once more I s. not the earth only.
Heb 12:26

shaked
they looked on me, they s. their.
Ps 109:25

shaken
the sound of a s. leaf shall chase.
Lev 26:36*
Israel as a reed is s. in water.
1 Ki 14:15
the daughter of Jerusalem hath s.
2 Ki 19:21; Isa 37:22
even thus be he s. out.   Neh 5:13
taken me by my neck, s. Job 16:12*
that the wicked might be s.   38:13
of the hills were s.   Ps 18:7
fir trees shall be terribly s. Nah 2:3
if s. they fall into the mouth.   3:12
a reed s. with the wind.   Mat 11:7
Luke 7:24
and powers of heaven shall be s.
Mat 24:29; Mark 13:25
Luke 21:26
good measure, pressed, s. together.
Luke 6:38
prayed, the place was s. Acts 4:31
of the prison were s.   16:26
be not soon s. in mind. 2 Thes 2:2
that are s., that those things which
cannot be s. may.   Heb 12:27
as a fig tree when s. of.   Rev 6:13

shaketh
which s. the earth out of.   Job 9:6
the voice of the Lord s.   Ps 29:8
breaches thereof, for it s.   60:2
magnify against him that s. it ?
Isa 10:15†

---

the Lord which he s. over it. Isa 19:16
that s. hand from holding of.   33:15

shaking
laugheth at the s. of.   Job 41:29*
the s. of the head among. Ps 44:14
as the s. of an olive tree. Isa 17:6
24:13
shall fear, because of the s. of. 19:16
battles of s. shall he fight.   30:32
s. and bones came.   Ezek 37:7*
shall be a great s. in Israel.   38:19

Shalim
they passed through the land of S.
1 Sam 9:4

Shalisha
through the land of S.   1 Sam 9:4

Shallum
S. son of Jabesh killed. 2 Ki 15:10
Menahem slew S. son of Jabesh. 14
to Huldah the prophetess, the wife of
S.   22:14; 2 Chr 34:22
of Judah, S.   1 Chr 2:40
of Simeon, S.   4:25
of Levi, S.   6:12
S. the son of Naphtali.   7:13
S. a porter.   9:17, 19
S. the Korahite.   31
Jehizkiah the son of S. 2 Chr 28:12
porters, the children of S. Ezra 2:42
10:24; Neh 7:45; Jer 35:4
S. the son of Zadok, the.   Ezra 7:2
S. and Amariah had taken.   10:42
unto him repaired S. Neh 3:12, 15
thus saith the Lord touching S. son
of.   Jer 22:11
Hanameel the son of S. thine.   32:7

Shalmanezer
S. came up against Samaria.
2 Ki 17:3; 18:9

shambles
sold in the s. that eat. 1 Cor 10:25

shame
them naked unto their s.   Ex 32:25
put them to s. in any.   Judg 18:7
father had done him s. 1 Sam 20:34
I cause my s. to go ? 2 Sam 13:13
returned with s. of face. 2 Chr 32:21
shall be clothed with s.   Job 8:22
ye turn my glory into s.?   Ps 4:2
put them to s. that seek after. 35:4*
let them be clothed with s.   26
let them be put to s. that wish me
evil.   40:14*; 83:17
desolate for reward of their s. 40:15
to s. that hated us.   44:7; 53:5
hast cast off and put us to s. 44:9*
the s. of my face hath.   15; 69:7
known my reproach and s.   69:19
back for reward of their s.   70:3
let them be brought unto s.   71:24
fill their faces with s. O Lord. 83:16*
thou hast covered him with s. 89:45
mine adversaries be clothed with s.
109:29*
testimonies; O Lord, put me not to s.
119:31
enemies will I clothe with s. 132:18
but s. shall be the promotion of.
Pr 3:35
a scorner, getteth s.   9:7†
is a son that causeth s.   10:5
pride cometh, then cometh s.   11:2
but a prudent man covereth s. 12:16
loathsome and cometh to s.   13:5
s. shall be to him that refuseth.   18
is against him that causeth s. 14:35
over a son that causeth s.   17:2
heareth, it is folly and s. to him.18:13
mother, is a son causeth s.   19:26
neighbour hath put thee to s.   25:8
heareth it put thee to s.   10
himself brings his mother to s. 29:15
uncovered, to s. of Egypt. Isa 20:4
chariots shall be the s. of.   22:18
Pharaoh shall be your s.   30:3, 5
be uncovered, yea, thy s. shall. 47:3
I hid not my face from s.   50:6
not be put to s. nor confounded; for
thou shalt forget s. of.   54:4
for your s. ye shall have double. 61:7
s. devoured the labour. Jer 3:24*
we lie down in s. and our.   25

I will discover, that thy s. Jer 13:26
days may be consumed with s. 20:18
a perpetual s., which shall.   23:40
nations have heard of thy s.   46:12
Moab turned back with s.!   48:39
s. hath covered our faces, for. 51:51*
s. shall be on all faces.   Ezek 7:18
thine own s. for thy sins.   16:52, 54
thy mouth because of thy s.   63
have they borne their s.   32:24, 25
bear their s. with them that go.   30
nor bear the s. of the heathen. 34:29
because ye have borne the s.   36:6
they shall bear their s.   7; 44:13
nor cause to hear in thee the s. 36:15
they have borne their s.   39:26
shall awake, some to s.   Dan 12:2
change their glory into s.   Hos 4:7
her rulers with s. do love.   18
separated themselves unto that s.
9:10
Ephraim shall receive s.   10:6
for thy violence s. shall.   Ob 10
pass ye away, having thy s. Mi 1:11
prophesy, they shall not take s.   2:6
s. shall cover her which said.   7:10
shew the kingdoms thy s.   Nah 3:5
consulted s. to thy house. Hab 2:10
thou art filled with s. for glory.   16
the unjust knoweth no s. Zeph 3:5
where they have been put to s.   19
thou begin with s. to take. Luke 14:9
were counted worthy to suffer s.
Acts 5:41*
these things to s. you.   1 Cor 4:14
I speak to your s.   6:5; 15:34
if a man have long hair, it is a s. 11:6
church of God, and s. them ?   22
it is a s. for a woman to speak. 14:35
a s. to speak of things.   Eph 5:12
whose glory is in their s. Phil 3:19
and put him to an open s.   Heb 6:6
the cross, despising the s.   12:2
foaming out their own s.   Jude 13
that s. of thy nakedness.   Rev 3:18
naked, and they see his s.   16:15

shamed
thou hast s. the faces.   2 Sam 19:5
ye have s. the counsel.   Ps 14:6

shamefacedness
adorn themselves with s. 1 Tim 2:9*

shameful
up altars to that s. thing. Jer 11:13
and s. spewing be on thy glory.
Hab 2:16*

shamefully
conceived them, hath done s. Hos 2:5
sent him away s. handled.
Mark 12:4; Luke 20:11
and were s. entreated.   1 Thes 2:2

shamelessly
vain fellows, s. uncovereth.
2 Sam 6:20

shameth
of riotous men s. his father. Pr 28:7

Shamgar
after him was S. the son. Judg 3:31
the days of S. highways.   5:6

Shammah
the son of Reuel, S.   Gen 36:13
17; 1 Chr 1:37
S. the son of Jesse.   1 Sam 16:9
17:13; 1 Chr 2:13
after him was S. the Hararite.
2 Sam 23:11, 33
25
S. the Harodite.
son of Zophah, S.   1 Chr 7:37

Shammuah
to spy the land, S. son of Zacur.
Num 13:4
S. the son of David.   2 Sam 5:14
1 Chr 14:4
Abda son of S. dwelt at. Neh 11:17

shape
descended in bodily s. Luke 3:22*
his voice, nor seen his s. John 5:37*

shapen
I was s. in iniquity.   Ps 51:5

shapes
s. of the locusts were like. *Rev 9:7*

Shaphan
Josiah sent S. the scribe to repair.
　　　2 Ki 22:3; 2 Chr 34:8
Hilkiah gave the book to S.
　　　2 Ki 22:8; 2 Chr 34:15
Ahikam the son of S. and S. the
　scribe.　　　　　*2 Ki 22:12*
Ahikam the son of S.　　　25:22
　　　Jer 39:14; 40:11
the hand of son of S. *Jer 26:24*
sent by Elasah son of S.　　29:3
chamber of Gemariah son of S. 36:10
stood Jaazaniah son of S. *Ezek 8:11*

Shaphat
of the tribe of Simeon, S. *Num 13:5*
anoint Elisha son of S.　*1 Ki 19:16*
if the head of Elisha the son of S.
　shall stand on him.　　*2 Ki 6:31*
Shemaiah, Neariah, S. *1 Chr 3:22*
of the Gadites, S. in Bashan.　5:12
in valleys was S. son of Adlai. 27:29

share
went down to sharpen every man his
　s.　　　　　　　*1 Sam 13:20*

Sharezer
S. his son smote him.　*2 Ki 19:37*
　　　　　　　　　Isa 37:38

Sharon
in all the suburbs of S. *1 Chr 5:16*
over the herds that fed in S. 27:29
I am the rose of S. the. *S of S 2:1*
S. is like a wilderness.　*Isa 33:9*
of Carmel and S. given thee.　35:2
S. shall be a fold of flocks.　65:10

sharp
Zipporah took a s. stone.　*Ex 4:25*
make thee s. knives.　　*Josh 5:2**
Joshua made s. knives and.　　3*
between passages a s. *1 Sam 14:4**
s. stones are under him, he spread-
　eth s. pointed things. *Job 41:30**
arrows s. in the heart.　　*Ps 45:5*
thy tongue like a s. razor.　　52:2
their tongue is a s. sword.　　57:4
s. arrows of mighty with.　　120:4
her end is s. as a twoedged. *Pr 5:4*
bears false witness is s. arrow. 25:18
whose arrows are s.　　*Isa 5:28*
I will make thee a s. threshing. 41:15
my mouth like a s. sword.　　49:2
take thee a s. knife.　　*Ezek 5:1*
the contention was so s. *Acts 15:39*
went a s. twoedged sword.
　　　　Rev 1:16; 19:15
he that hath the s. sword.　　2:12
in his hand a s. sickle.　14:14, 17
to him that had the s. sickle.　18

sharpen
went down to s. every. *1 Sam 13:20*
a file for axes, and to s.　　21*

sharpened
they s. their tongues.　　*Ps 140:3*
a sword is s. and furbished.
　　　　　Ezek 21:9, 10, 11

sharpeneth
mine enemy s. his eyes.　*Job 16:9*
iron s. iron, so a man s. *Pr 27:17*

sharper
the most upright is s.　　*Mi 7:4**
the word of God is s.　　*Heb 4:12*

sharply
did chide with Gideon s.　*Judg 8:1*
rebuke them s. that they.　*Tit 1:13*

sharpness
present I should use s. *2 Cor 13:10*

Shaul
S. (sixth king of Edom). *1 Chr 1:48*

shave
but scall shall he not s.　*Lev 13:33*
person shall s. off his hair.　14:8, 9
nor shall they s. the corner of. 21:5
shall s. his head in the day of his
　cleansing . . . shall he s. *Num 6:9*
Nazarite shall s. the head of his. 18
let them s. their flesh, and.　8:7*
captive shall s. her head. *Deut 21:12*
caused him to s. off seven locks.
　　　　　　　　　Judg 16:19

Lord shall s. with a razor. *Isa 7:20*
neither shall they s.　*Ezek 44:20*
be at charges, that they s. their.
　　　　　　　　　Acts 21:24

shaved
Joseph s. and changed. *Gen 41:14*
s. off half their beards. *2 Sam 10:4*
　　　　　　　　　1 Chr 19:4
Job rent his mantle and s. *Job 1:20*

shaven
be s. but the scall shall. *Lev 13:33*
hair of his separation is s. *Num 6:19*
if I be s. my strength.　*Judg 16:17*
to grow again after he was s.　22
men having their beards s. *Jer 41:5*
all one as if she were s. *1 Cor 11:5*
if it be a shame to be s. let her.　6

sheaf
s. arose, and also stood upright . . .
　obeisance to my s.　　*Gen 37:7*
a s. of the firstfruits.　*Lev 23:10*
wave the s. before the Lord. 11, 12
hast forgot a s. shalt not go to fetch
　it.　　　　　　*Deut 24:19*
they take away the s.　*Job 24:10*
Judah like a torch in a s. *Zech 12:6*

Shealtiel, *see* Zerubbabel

shear
and Laban went to s.　*Gen 31:19*
Judah goeth to Timnah to s.　38:13
nor shalt s. the firstling. *Deut 15:19*
Nabal did s. his sheep. *1 Sam 25:4*

shearer
a lamb dumb before his s. *Acts 8:32*

shearers
went up unto his sheep s. *Gen 38:12*
heard that thou hast s. *1 Sam 25:7*
my flesh I have killed for my s.　11
Absalom had s. in Baal-hazor.
　　　　　　　2 Sam 13:23, 24
sheep before her s. is.　*Isa 53:7*

shearing
and Nabal was a sheep. *1 Sam 25:2*

shearing house
of Ahaziah at s. house.　*2 Ki 10:12*
slew them at the pit of s. house. 14

Shear-jashub
meet Ahaz, thou and S.　*Isa 7:3*

sheath
the sword out of his s. *1 Sam 17:51*
with a sword fastened in the s.
　　　　　　　　2 Sam 20:8
the angel put the sword into his s.
　　　　　　　　1 Chr 21:27
will draw his sword out of the s.
　　　　　　　Ezek 21:3, 4, 5
cause it to return into his s.? will. 30
put up thy sword into s. *John 18:11*

sheaves
behold, we were binding s. *Gen 37:7*
let me glean and gather among the s.
　　　　　　　　　Ruth 2:7, 15
sabbath bringing in s.　*Neh 13:15*
he shall come bringing s. *Ps 126:6*
that bindeth s. his bosom.　129:7
a cart pressed full of s. *Amos 2:13*
shall gather them as the s. *Mi 4:12*

Sheba, Shebah
son of Raamah S.　　*Gen 10:7*
S. son of Joktan.　　　　28
Jokshan begat S. and Dedan. 25:3
　　　　　　　　　1 Chr 1:32
Isaac called the well S. *Gen 26:33*
in their inheritance S. *Josh 19:2*
queen of S. heard of the fame of.
　　　　　1 Ki 10:1; 2 Chr 9:1
the son of Raamah, S. *1 Chr 1:9*
son of Joktan, S.　　　　　9
children of Gad, S. and Jorai. 5:13
companies of S. waited. *Job 6:19*
kings of S. and Seba.　*Ps 72:10*
to him shall be given of gold of S.
　　　　　　　　15; *Isc 60:6*
is incense from S.?　　*Jer 6:20*
merchants of S. thy merchants.
　　　　　　　　Ezr 27:22, 23
S. shall say, Art thou come? 38:13
see **Bichri**

Shebna
to the king, there came out to them
　S.　　*2 Ki 18:18, 37; Isa 36:3*
Hezekiah sent S. to Isaiah. *2 Ki 19:2*
　　　　　　　　　Isa 37:2
thee to this treasurer, S. *Isa 22:15*

Shechem
to Salem a city of S.　*Gen 33:18*
at the hand of Hamor, S.'s father. 19
S. lay with Dinah.　　　34:2
they slew S.　　　　　26
under an oak that was by S.　35:4
their father's flock in S.　37:12
the vale of Hebron to S.　14
of S. the family of the. *Num 26:31*
lot for the children of S.　*Josh 17:2*
S. in mount Ephraim a city of.
　　　　20:7; 21:21; *1 Chr 6:67*
the tribes of Israel to S. *Josh 24:1*
bones of Joseph buried they in S. 32
Gideon's concubine in S. *Judg 8:31*
son of Jerubbaal went to S.　9:1
hearken to me, ye men of S.　7
come out from the men of S.　20
who is S.?　　　　　28
Gaal and brethren come to S.　31
they should not dwell in S.　41
the evil of the men of S. did God. 57
Rehoboam went to S.　　*1 Ki 12:1*
　　　　　　　　　2 Chr 10:1
Jeroboam built S. in mount Ephraim.
　　　　　　　　　1 Ki 12:25
Shemida, Ahian and S. *1 Chr 7:19*
I will rejoice, I will divide S.
　　　　　　　Ps 60:6; 108:7
came certain from S.　　*Jer 41:5*

shed
Joab s. Amasa's bowels to the.
　　　　　　　　2 Sam 20:10
is s. for many for the.　*Mat 26:28*
promise of Holy Ghost, he hath s.
　　　　　　　　　Acts 2:33*
love of God is s. abroad in. *Rom 5:5*
he s. on us abundantly.　*Tit 3:6**
　　　　　　see **blood**

shedder
beget a son that is a s. *Ezek 18:10*

sheddeth
whosoever s. man's blood, his.
　　　　　　　　　Gen 9:6
the city s. blood in the. *Ezek 22:3*

shedding
and without s. of blood. *Heb 9:22*

sheep
Abel was a keeper of s.　*Gen 4:2*
daughter cometh with the s. 29:6, 9
hand of Lord is upon the s. *Ex 9:3**
ye shall take it out from the s.　12:5
sacrifice thereon thy s. and.　20:24
if a man steal a s. and kill it or sell.
　　　　　　　　22:1, 4, 9
to his neighbour a s. to keep.　10
with the firstling of s.　30; 34:19
if his offering be of the s. *Lev 1:10*
shall eat no manner of fat of s. 7:23
ye shall offer a male of the s. 22:19
sanctify the firstling of a s.　27:26
the firstling of the s.　*Num 18:17*
cities and folds for your s. 32:24, 36
bless the flocks of thy s. *Deut 7:13**
thou shalt not sacrifice s.　17:1
from them that offer s.　18:3, 4
thy brother's s. go astray.　22:1
blessed shall be the flocks of thy s.
　　　　　　　　　28:4
cursed shall be the flocks of thy s.
　　　　　　　　18; 31:51
butter of kine, milk of s.　32:14
at Jericho ox and s.　*Josh 6:21*
Joshua took Achan's s. and.　7:24
left neither s. nor oxen.　*Judg 6:4*
take tenth of your s. *1 Sam 8:17**
upon the spoil and took s.　14:32
every man his ox and his s.　34
slay both ox and s.　　　15:3
Saul spread the s.　　　9
this bleating of s. in my ears?　14
the people took of the spoil, s.　21
behold, he keepeth the s.　16:11
my son, who is with the s.　20
returned to feed his father's s. 17:15
he rose early and left the s. with. 20

sheep (continued)

kept his father's s.   *1 Sam* 17:34
3000 s.: he was shearing his s. 25:2
Abigail hasted, and took five s.   18
David took away the s.   27:9
thee from following thy s. *2 Sam* 7:8
brought David butter and s.   17:29
Lo, I have sinned, but these s. what?
    24:17; *1 Chr* 21:17
Adonijah hath slain s. *1 Ki* 1:19, 25
Solomon's provision for one day
   hundred s.   4:23
all the congregation sacrificing s. 8:5
Solomon offered s.   63; *2 Chr* 5:6
    7:5
is it a time to receive s.? *2 Ki* 5:26
from Hagarites 250,000 s. *1 Chr* 5:21
oxen and s. abundantly.   12:40
Asa carried from the Ethiopians s.
    2 Chr 14:15
offered of the spoil 7000 s.   15:11
Ahab killed s. and oxen for.   18:2
consecrated things were 3000 s. 29:33
give 7000 s. and the princes gave to
   the congregation 10,000 s.   30:24
in the tithes of oxen and s.   31:6
daily one ox, six choice s. *Neh* 5:18
substance also was 7000 s., 3000
   camels.   *Job* 1:3
fallen, and hath burnt up the s.   16
warmed with fleece of my s.   31:20
for he had 14,000 s. and 6000. 42:12
given him all s. and oxen.   *Ps* 8:7
thou hast given us like s. for. 44:11
like s. are laid in the grave.   49:14
anger smoke against thy s.?   74:1
own people go forth like s.   78:52
people and s. of thy pasture. 79:13
the s. of his hand.   95:7; 100:3
gone astray like a lost s.   119:176
that our s. may bring forth. 144:13
thy teeth are like a flock of s.
    S of S 4:2*; 6:6*
a man shall nourish two s. *Isa* 7:21
gladness, and killing of s.   22:13
all we like s. have gone astray. 53:6
pull them out like s. for. *Jer* 12:3
pastors that scatter the s.   23:1
my people hath been lost s.   50:6
Israel is a scattered s.; the lions. 17
my s. wander through. *Ezek* 34:6
I will search my s. and seek, 11, 12
and for a wife he kept s. *Hos* 12:12
the flocks of s. are made. *Joel* 1:18
as a young lion among the flocks of s.
    Mi 5:8
shepherd, and s. shall be scattered.
    Zech 13:7; *Mat* 26:31
    Mark 14:27
false prophets in s.'s clothing.
    Mat 7:15
go rather to the lost s. of the. 10:6
if one s. fall into a pit on the. 12:11
is a man better than a s.?   12
unto the lost s. of Israel.   15:24
if a man have a 100 s. and. 18:12
he rejoiceth more of that s.   13
    Luke 15:4, 6
as a shepherd divideth his s.
    Mat 25:32
he shall set s. on his right hand. 33
temple those that sold s. *John* 2:14
out of the temple, and the s.   15
by the door is shepherd of the s. 10:2
the s. hear his voice.   3, 27
the s. follow him.   4*
verily I am the door of the s.   7
were robbers, but the s. did not. 8
shepherd giveth his life for his s. 11
hireling leaveth the s. and fleeth. 12*
hireling careth not for the s.   13
good shepherd, I know my s.   14*
I lay down my life for the s.   15
other s. I have.   16
because ye are not of my s.   26
Peter, Feed my s.   21:16, 17
great Shepherd of s. *Heb* 13:20
none buyeth s., horses. *Rev* 18:13

as sheep

be not as s. which have. *Num* 27:17
Israel scattered on the hills as s.
    1 Ki 22:17; *2 Chr* 18:16
the day long; we are counted as s.
    Ps 44:22; *Rom* 8:36

---

it shall be as a s. that no. *Isa* 13:14
and as a s. before his shearers. 53:7
together as s. of Bozra.   *Mi* 2:12
fainted and were scattered as s.
    Mat 9:36; *Mark* 6:34
I send you forth as s.   *Mat* 10:16
led as s. to the slaughter. *Acts* 8:32
were as s. going astray. *1 Pet* 2:25

sheepcote

took thee from the s.   *2 Sam* 7:8
    1 Chr 17:7

sheepcotes

Saul came to the s.   *1 Sam* 24:3

sheepfold

he that entereth not the s. *John* 10:1

sheepfolds

build s. for our cattle. *Num* 32:16
thou among the s.?   *Judg* 5:16
David, took him from the s. *Ps* 78:70

sheep gate

brethren built the s. *gate*. *Neh* 3:1
up of the corner to the s. *gate*.   32
they went on to the s. *gate*.   12:39

sheep market

Jerusalem by the s. *market* a pool.
    John 5:2

sheepmaster

Mesha king of Moab was a s.
    2 Ki 3:4

see shearers

sheepskins

in the s. and goatskins. *Heb* 11:37

sheet

a vessel descending as a great s.
    Acts 10:11; 11:5

sheets

I will give you thirty s. *Judg* 14:12*
thirty s. and thirty change.   13*

shekel

*(The unit of weight and of money
among the Jews. It weighed about
½ ounce, and as coined in silver was
worth about two shillings and nine-
pence, or 65 cents. In gold one or
two pounds, or 4.85 to 9.69 dollars
according to period)*
took an earring of half a s. *Gen* 24:22
a s. after the s. of the sanctuary, a s.
   Ex 30:13; *Num* 3:47; *Ezek* 45:12
give less than half a s.   *Ex* 30:15
the fourth part of a s.   *1 Sam* 9:8
of fine flour for a s. *2 Ki* 7:1, 16, 18
charged yearly with the third of a s.
    Neh 10:32
small, and the s. great.   *Amos* 8:5

shekels

land is worth 400 s. *Gen* 23:15, 16
her hands of ten s. weight.   24:22
give her master thirty s. *Ex* 21:32
s. of sweet cinnamon 250 s., of sweet
   calamus 250 s.   30:23
the estimation by s.   *Lev* 5:15
    27:3, 4, 5, 6, 7, 16
one spoon of ten s. of gold, full of
   incense.   *Num* 7:14, 20, 26, 32
   38, 44, 50, 56, 62, 68, 74, 80
amerce him in 100 s.   *Deut* 22:19
to the damsel's father fifty s.   29
saw in the spoils 200 s. *Josh* 7:21
earrings was 1700 s.   *Judg* 8:26
the 1100 s. of silver were taken. 17:2
had restored the s.   3
I will give thee ten s. of silver.   10
Absalom weighed his hair, 200 s.
    2 Sam 14:26
I would have given thee ten s. 18:11
David bought oxen for fifty s. 24:24
six hundred s. of gold to. *1 Ki* 10:16
each man fifty s. of silver. *2 Ki* 15:20
gave to Ornan 600 s.   *1 Chr* 21:25
governors had taken 40 s. by year.
    Neh 5:15
I bought the field for 17 s. *Jer* 32:9
by weight twenty s. a day. *Ezek* 4:10

see sanctuary

Shelah

Judah's son S.   *Gen* 38:5
gave her not to S. my son.   26
Judah, Er, Onan and S.   46:12
   Num 26:20; *1 Chr* 2:3; 4:21

Arphaxad begat S. and S. Eber.
    1 Chr 1:18, 24

Shelemiah

lot eastward fell to S. *1 Chr* 26:14
S. and Nathan had taken strange.
    Ezra 10:39
I made S. the priest.   *Neh* 13:13
S. son of Cushi.   *Jer* 36:14
S. son of Abdeel.   26

shelter

the rock for want of a s. *Job* 24:8
for thou hast been s. for. *Ps* 61:3*

Shelumiel

the prince of Simeon, S. the son of.
    Num 1:6; 2:12; 7:36; 10:19

Shem

Noah begat S.   *Gen* 5:32; 6:10
    10:1; *1 Chr* 1:4
S. took a garment and.   *Gen* 9:23
blessed be the Lord God of S.   26
dwell in the tents of S.   27
the children of S.   10:21, 22, 31
    11:10; *1 Chr* 1:17
which was the son of S. *Luke* 3:36

Shemaiah

word of God came to S. the man.
   1 Ki 12:22; *2 Chr* 11:2; 12:7
Shimri the son of S.   *1 Chr* 4:37
of Reuben, S. the son of Joel.   5:4
of the Levites, S.   9:14, 16; 15:8
   11; 24:6; 26:4, 6, 7; *2 Chr* 17:8
   29:14; 31:15; 35:9; *Ezra* 8:16
    10:21, 31
S. (the son of Adonikam). *Ezra* 8:13
S. keeper of the east gate. *Neh* 3:29
I came to the house of S. son.   6:10
S. a priest sealed.   10:8
of the Levites, S.   11:15; 12:6, 18
    35, 36
S. the priest.   12:34, 42
Urijah the son of S.   *Jer* 26:20
say to S. the Nehelamite.   29:24
    31, 32
and Delaiah the son of S.   36:12

Sheminith

with harps on the S.   *1 Chr* 15:21

Shenir

the Amorites call S.   *Deut* 3:9
look from the top of S.   *S of S* 4:8

Shephatiah

S. the fifth son of David. *2 Sam* 3:4
    1 Chr 3:3
Meshullam son of S.   *1 Chr* 9:8
the Haruphite came to David. 12:5
the ruler of the Simeonites was S.
    27:16
the children of S., 372.   *Ezra* 2:4
    Neh 7:9
S. heard the words of.   *Jer* 38:1

shepherd

every s. is abomination. *Gen* 46:34
from thence is the s., the stone. 49:24
he put the stones into a s.'s bag.
    1 Sam 17:40
the Lord is my s. I shall. *Ps* 23:1
give ear, O s. of Israel, thou. 80:1
words which are given from one s.
    Eccl 12:11
departed from me as a s. *Isa* 38:12
he shall feed his flock like a s. 40:11
saith of Cyrus, He is my s.   44:28
that brought them up with the s. 63:11
and keep him as a s.   *Jer* 31:10
array himself as a s. putteth. 43:12
who is that s. that will stand? 49:19
    50:44
I will also break in pieces s. 51:23
because there is no s. *Ezek* 34:5
prey, because there was no s.   8
as a s. seeketh out his flock.   12
s. over them, my servant David shall
   feed . . . be their s.   23; 37:24
s. taketh out of mouth. *Amos* 3:12
because there was no s. *Zech* 10:2
instruments of a foolish s.   11:15
raise up a s. in the land.   16
woe to the idle s. that leaveth. 17
O sword, against my s. and.   13:7
is an hireling, and not s. *John* 10:12
I am the good s., know my sheep. 14
shall be one fold and one s.   16

that great s. of the sheep. *Heb* 13:20
returned unto the s. *1 Pet* 2:25
when the chief s. shall appear. 5:4
    see **sheep**

shepherds

and the men are s. *Gen* 46:32
thy servants are s. 47:3
and the s. came and drove. *Ex* 2:17
delivered us out of the hand of s. 19
thy s. which were with. *1 Sam* 25:7
kids beside the s.' tents. *S of S* 1:8
shall the s. make their. *Isa* 13:20
when multitude of s. is called. 31:4
and they are s. that cannot. 56:11
the s. with their flocks shall come.
    Jer 6:3
I will set up s. over them. 23:4
howl, ye s. and cry. 25:34
the s. have no way to flee. 35
a voice of the cry of the s. and. 36
shall be an habitation of s. 33:12
their s. have caused them to go. 56
the s. of Israel, woe to the s. of Israel
  ... should not s. feed ? *Ezek* 34:2
nor did my s. search for my flock, but
  s. fed themselves and fed. 8
I am against the s. neither shall the s.
  feed themselves any more. 10
habitations of the s. shall. *Amos* 1:2
raise against him seven s. *Mi* 5:5
thy s. slumber, O king of Assyria.
  Nah 3:18
shall be cottages for s. *Zeph* 2:6
kindled against the s. *Zech* 10:3
voice of the howling of the s. 11:3
and their own s. pity them not. 5
three s. also I cut off in one. 8
same country s. in field. *Luke* 2:8
were told them by the s. 18
the s. returned, glorifying and. 20

sherd

shall not be found a s. *Isa* 30:14

sherds

thou shalt break the s. *Ezek* 23:34

sheriffs

sent to gather the s. *Dan* 3:2
then the s. and rulers were. 3

Sheshach

the king of S. shall drink. *Jer* 25:26
how is S. taken! how is the! 51:41

Sheshbazzar

he numbered them to S. *Ezra* 1:8
did S. bring up from Babylon. 11
delivered to S. whom he had. 5:14
S. laid the foundation of the. 16

shew, *substantive*

*(In all places the American Revision
uses the modern spelling* show,
when the word is retained)
walketh in a vain s. *Ps* 39:6
the s. of their countenance. *Isa* 3:9
and for a s. make long. *Luke* 20:47*
to make a fair s. in flesh. *Gal* 6:12
spoiled powers made a s. *Col* 2:15
which things have a s. of wisdom. 23

shew

speak, saying, S. a miracle. *Ex* 7:9
I raised up for to s. in thee. 9:16
that I might s. my signs. 10:1
and thou shalt s. thy son in. 13:8*
the salvation Lord will s. to. 14:13*
shalt s. way they must walk. 18:20
  Deut 1:33
it according to all that I s. *Ex* 25:9
s. me now thy way. 33:13
s. me thy glory. 18
I stood to s. you the word of the.
  Deut 5:5
no covenant, nor s. mercy. 7:2
Lord may s. thee mercy. 13:17
they shall s. thee the sentence. 17:9
thou shalt do as they shall s. 10, 11
not regard old, nor s. favour. 28:50
ask thy father, and he will s. 32:7
he would not s. the land. *Josh* 5:6
s. us, we pray thee, the entrance into
  the city, and we will s. *Judg* 1:24
then s. me a sign that thou. 6:17
Samuel feared to s. Eli the vision.
  1 Sam 3:15
s. them the manner of the. 8:9

man of God peradventure can s.
  1 Sam 9:6*
stand, that I may s. thee the. 27*
I will come and s. thee what. 10:8
come up to us, and we will s. 14:12
do nothing, he will s. it me. 20:2*
not unto thee, and s. it thee. 12*
he fled, and did not s. it. 22:17*
men, and they will s. thee. 25:8*
he will s. me, both it. *2 Sam* 15:25
if he will s. himself a. *1 Ki* 1:52
therefore, and s. thyself a man. 2:2
to Elijah, Go s. thyself. 18:1, 2
will ye not s. me which ? *2 Ki* 6:11
to s. himself strong. *2 Chr* 16:9
s. their father's house whether they.
  Ezra 2:59; *Neh* 7:61
the pillar of fire to s. *Neh* 9:19
to s. the people and. *Esth* 1:11
Mordecai charged her not to s. 2:10
of the writing to s. Esther. 4:8
s. me wherefore thou. *Job* 10:2
he would s. thee the secrets of. 11:6
I was afraid, durst not s. you. 32:6
if a messenger to s. to man. 33:23
many will say, Who will s.? *Ps* 4:6
may s. forth all thy praise. 9:14
wilt s. me the path of life. 16:11
s. me thy ways, O Lord, teach. 25:4
the Lord will s. them his. 14
mouth shall s. forth thy praise. 51:15
my mouth shall s. forth thy. 71:15*
we thy people will s. forth. 79:13
s. us mercy, O Lord, grant. 85:7
s. me a token of good, that. 86:17
wilt thou s. wonders to the? 88:10
to s. that Lord is upright, he. 92:15
O God,to whom vengeance belongeth,
  s. thyself. 94:1*
can s. forth all his praise ? 106:2
a man must s. himself. *Pr* 18:24*
formed them with s. no. *Isa* 27:11
the Lord shall s. lightning. 30:30
them forth and s. us what shall happen, let them s. the. 41:22*
s. the things that are to come. 23*
who among them can s. us ? 43:9
people have I formed, shall s. 21*
coming, let them s. to them. 44:7*
and s. yourselves men. 46:8
say to them in darkness, s. 49:9
s. my people their transgression.
  58:1
they shall s. forth the praises. 60:6*
thou shalt s. them all. *Jer* 16:10
into a land, where I will not s. 13
thy God may s. us the way. 42:3
to s. the king of Babylon. 51:31
thou shalt s. her all her. *Ezek* 22:2*
for with their mouth they s. 33:31
wilt thou not s. us what thou ? 37:18
upon all that I shall s. thee. 40:4
son of man, s. the house to. 43:10
s. them the form of the house. 11*
the sorcerers for to s. king his.
  Dan 2:2*
will s. the interpretation. 4, 7
if ye s. the dream and interpretation,
  therefore s. the dream and. 6
not a man that can s. the king's. 10
s. the king the interpretation. 16
cannot the wise men s. to the. 27
I thought it good to s. the signs. 4:2
shall s. me the interpretation. 5:7
and I am come to s. thee. 9:23*
dost thou s. me iniquity ? *Hab* 1:3
s. thyself to the priest. *Mat* 8:4
  Mark 1:44; *Luke* 5:14; 17:14
go and s. John these. *Mat* 11:4*
he shall s. judgement to the. 12:18
therefore mighty works do s. forth.
  Mat 14:2*; *Mark* 6:14*
desired he would s. a sign. *Mat* 16:1
s. me the tribute money. 22:19
  Luke 20:24
came to s. him the buildings of the.
  Mat 24:1
arise false Christs, and shall s. great.
  Mat 24:24; *Mark* 13:22
s. you a large upper room furnished.
  Mark 14:15; *Luke* 22:12
I am sent to s. thee these glad.
  Luke 1:19*
s. how great things God hath. 8:39*

he will s. him greater works.
  John 5:20
if thou do these things s. thyself. 7:4*
where he were, he should s. it. 11:57
s. us the Father and it. 14:8, 9
he will s. you things to come. 16:13*
he shall receive of mine, and s. it.
  14*, 15*
but I shall s. you plainly of the. 25*
Lord s. whether of these. *Acts* 1:24
the land which I shall s. thee. 7:3
Go, s. these things to James. 12:17*
the men who s. to us the way. 16:17*
Felix willing to s. the Jews. 24:27
that he should s. light to. 26:23*
who s. work of the law. *Rom* 2:15
thee, that I might s. my power. 9:17
willing to s. his wrath, endured. 22
ye do s. the Lord's death till he
  come. *1 Cor* 11:26*
yet s. I you a more excellent. 12:31
I s. you a mystery, we shall. 15:51*
s. ye to them the proof. *2 Cor* 8:24
s. the exceeding riches. *Eph* 2:7
for they themselves s. *1 Thes* 1:9*
that Christ might s. all. *1 Tim* 1:16
let them learn first to s. piety. 5:4
which in his times he shall s. 6:15
study to s. thyself approved unto
  God. *2 Tim* 2:15*
that every one of you s. *Heb* 6:11
God willing to s. to the heirs. 17
s. me thy faith without. *Jas* 2:18
let him s. his works out of. 3:13
ye should s. forth the praises of.
  1 Pet 2:9
and s. unto you that eternal life.
  1 John 1:2*
he sent his angel to s. his servants.
  Rev 1:1; 22:6

I will shew

a land that I will s. thee. *Gen* 12:1
I will be gracious, I will s. mercy on
  whom I will s. mercy. *Ex* 33:19
I will s. thee the man. *Judg* 4:22
I will s. thee what thou. *1 Sam* 16:3
evil, then I will s. it thee. 20:13*
I will surely s. myself. *1 Ki* 18:15
I will s. you what Syrians. *2 Ki* 7:12
I will s. thee that which. *Job* 15:17
I also will s. mine opinion. 32:10
  17; 36:2
I will s. forth all thy marvellous.
  Ps 9:1
I will s. the salvation. 50:23; 91:16
I will s. them the back. *Jer* 18:17
I will s. thee great and mighty. 33:3
I will s. mercies unto you. 42:12*
I will s. the king the interpretation.
  Dan 2:24
I will s. thee what is noted. 10:21*
and now I will s. thee the truth. 11:2
I will s. wonders in heaven.
  Joel 2:30; *Acts* 2:19
I will s. to him marvellous things.
  Mi 7:15
I will s. the nations thy. *Nah* 3:5
angel said, I will s. thee. *Zech* 1:9
I will s. you to whom he. *Luke* 6:47
I will s. him how great things he.
  Acts 9:16
I will s. thee my faith by. *Jas* 2:18
I will s. thee things which. *Rev* 4:1
I will s. thee the judgement of. 17:1
I will s. thee the bride, the. 21:9
  see **kindness**

shewbread

shall set upon a table s. *Ex* 25:30
make the table, and the s. 35:13
  39:36
on table of s. shall. *Num* 4:7
was no bread but the s. *1 Sam* 21:6
table of gold whereon the s. was.
  1 Ki 7:48
Kohathites to prepare s. *1 Chr* 9:32
service both for the s. and. 23:29
gave gold for the tables of s. 28:16
house for the continual s. *2 Chr* 2:4
tables whereon the s. was set. 4:19
s. also they set in order. 13:11
have cleansed the s. table. 29:18
ourselves for the s. *Neh* 10:33

into the house of God, and did eat *s.*
    Mat 12:4; *Mark* 2:26; *Luke* 6:4
wherein was the *s.*   *Heb* 9:2

shewed (showed)
a white spot, and it be *s.* to priest.
    Lev 13:19, 49
and *s.* them the fruit of the land.
    Num 13:26
which Moses *s.* in the sight of.
    Deut 34:12*
and when he *s.* them the entrance.
    Judg 1:25
s. Sisera, that Barak was gone up.
    4:12*
haste, and *s.* her husband.   13:10*
come up, for he hath *s.* me. 16:18*
it hath been *s.* me all.   *Ruth* 2:11
came and *s.* to the men. *1 Sam* 11:9
Jonathan *s.* him all those.   19:7
Abiathar *s.* David that Saul. 22:21*
Thou hast *s.* this day how.   24:18*
messenger *s.* David. *2 Sam* 11:22
thou hast not *s.* it to.   *1 Ki* 1:27
his might that he *s.* 16:27; 22:45
where fell it ? he *s.* him.   *2 Ki* 6:6
took an oath, and *s.* them.   11:4
and *s.* them all the house of his.
    20:13; *Isa* 39:2
there is nothing I have not *s.*
    2 Ki 20:15; *Isa* 39:4
s. riches of his glorious. *Esth* 1:4
Esther had not *s.* her.   2:10, 20
for they had *s.* him the people.   3:6
pity should be *s.* from.   *Job* 6:14
s. thy strength to this. *Ps* 71:18*
they *s.* his signs among them.
    105:27*; *Acts* 7:36*
my complaint, I *s.* before him my.
    Ps 142:2*
his wickedness shall be *s.* *Pr* 26:26
labour, wherein I have *s.* *Eccl* 2:19
who *s.* to him the way ? *Isa* 40:14
they *s.* no difference. *Ezek* 22:26*
and *s.* to chief priests. *Mat* 28:11
devil *s.* him all kingdoms. *Luke* 4:5
the disciples of John *s.* him. 7:18
and he said, He that *s.* mercy. 10:37
that servant came and *s.*   14:21
are raised, Moses *s.* at bush. 20:37
good works have I *s.* you. *John* 10:32
he *s.* unto them his hands.   20:20
Jesus *s.* himself again.   21:1, 14*
    Acts 1:3
miracle of healing was *s.* *Acts* 4:22
Moses *s.* himself to them. 7:26*
had *s.* wonders and signs.   36
which *s.* before of the coming.   52
he *s.* how he had seen an. 11:13
confessed, *s.* their deeds.   19:18
but have *s.* and have taught. 20:20
I have *s.* you all things, how.   35*
tell no man thou hast *s.*   23:22
but first Paul *s.* to them of. 26:20
the barbarous people *s.* no.   28:2
none of brethren *s.* or spake.   21*
for his sake that *s.* it. *1 Cor* 10:28
love which ye have *s.*   *Heb* 6:10
judgement, that hath *s.* no. *Jas* 2:13
angel *s.* me the city of. *Rev* 21:10
he *s.* me a pure river of water. 22:1
worship the angel who *s.* me.   8

God, or Lord shewed, *expressly,*
  or implicitly
thy mercy *s.* to me in. *Gen* 19:19
that thou hast *s.* kindness. 24:14
least of the mercies thou hast *s.* 32:10
the *Lord s.* Joseph mercy, and. 39:21
God s. Pharaoh what he is. 41:25*
forasmuch as *God* hath *s.* thee. 39
and lo, *God* hath *s.* me also. 48:11*
the *Lord s.* him a tree. *Ex* 15:25
make them after the pattern *s.* 25:40
    26:30; 27:8; *Heb* 8:5
of the *Lord* might be *s.* *Lev* 24:12
the *Lord* had *s.* Moses. *Num* 8:4
all signs I have *s.* among them.
    14:11*; *Deut* 6:22
and upon earth he *s.* *Deut* 4:36
behold, the *Lord* our *God s.*   5:24
the *Lord s.* him all the land.   34:1
nor would he have *s.* *Judg* 13:23
hast *s.* to thy servant David my.
    1 Ki 3:6; *2 Chr* 1:8

38

Lord hath *s.* me, he.   *2 Ki* 8:10
the *Lord* hath *s.* me that thou. 13
the *Lord* had *s.* David. *2 Chr* 7:10
s. from *Lord* our *God.*   *Ezra* 9:8
he hath *s.* me his marvellous.
    Ps 31:21
thou hast *s.* thy people hard.   60:3
thou hast *s.* me great and.   71:20
wonders he had *s.* them.   78:11
his righteousness hath *s.* in. 98:2
he *s.* his people the power of. 111:6
God is the *Lord* who hath *s.* 118:27*
I have *s.* when there was no. 43:12
s. them; I did them suddenly. 48:3
before it came to pass I *s.* it thee. 5
Lord s. me two baskets. *Jer* 24:1
the word the *Lord* hath *s.* me. 38:21
the *Lord* hath *s.* me. *Ezek* 11:25
gave statutes and *s.* them. 20:11
thus hath the *Lord s.* me. *Amos* 7:1
    4:7; 8:1
he hath *s.* thee, O man.   *Mi* 6:8
and the *Lord s.* me four. *Zech* 1:20
s. me Joshua standing before the
  angel of the *Lord.*   3:1
he hath *s.* strength with. *Luke* 1:51
heard how *Lord* had *s.* great. 58*
which *God* before had *s.* *Acts* 3:18*
God s. I should not call any. 10:28
God raised him third day and *s.* 40*
God hath *s.* it to them. *Rom* 1:19*
Lord Jesus hath *s.* me. *2 Pet* 1:14*

shewedst
and *s.* signs and wonders. *Neh* 9:10
I know it; then thou *s.* *Jer* 11:18

shewest
s. thyself marvellous. *Job* 10:16
thou *s.* lovingkindness. *Jer* 32:18
Jews said, What sign *s.* thou to us ?
    John 2:18; 6:30*

sheweth
to do, he *s.* to Pharaoh. *Gen* 41:28
whatsoever he *s.* me. *Num* 23:3
none *s.* me that my. *1 Sam* 22:8*
he *s.* mercy to his anointed, to.
    2 Sam 22:51; *Ps* 18:50
he *s.* them their work. *Job* 36:9
noise thereof *s.* concerning it. 33*
firmament *s.* his handywork. *Ps* 19:1
night unto night *s.* knowledge. 2
good man *s.* favour, and. 112:5*
he *s.* his word unto Jacob. 147:19
he that speaketh truth, *s.* *Pr* 12:17
the tender grass *s.* itself.   27:25
yea, there is none that *s.* *Isa* 41:26
and *s.* him all kingdoms. *Mat* 4:8
Father loveth, and *s.* the. *John* 5:20

shewing, *verb*
and *s.* mercy unto thousands.
    Ex 20:6; *Deut* 5:10
s. to generation to come. *Ps* 78:4*
my beloved *s.* himself. *S of S* 2:9
thine iniquities by *s.* *Dan* 4:27
s. of hard sentences found.   5:12
s. glad tidings of kingdom. *Luke* 8:1*
and *s.* the coats which. *Acts* 9:39
s. by scripture that Jesus. 18:28
of God, *s.* himself that. *2 Thes* 2:4*
in all things *s.* thyself. *Tit* 2:7
not purloining, but *s.* all good.   10
but be gentle, *s.* all meekness. 3:2

shewing
deserts till day of his *s.* to Israel.
    Luke 1:80

Shibboleth
say now S. and he said. *Judg* 12:6

shield
A piece of defensive armour, com-
monly of wood, covered with
leather, plates of gold, or brass.
Sometimes shields were made all of
gold, or brass. Those that Solo-
mon made were of beaten gold,
1 Ki 10:17. *Shishak king of Egypt*
took these away, and Rehoboam
made others of brass to serve in
their stead, 1 Ki 14:26, 27.
In scripture God is often called the
shield of his people, Gen 15:1, Ps
5:12. *Faith in scripture is like-*
wise called a shield, Eph 6:16.

Shields *were hung up upon towers*
for ornaments, or as trophies of
victory. The tower of David was
adorned with a thousand shields,
S of S 4:4.
I am thy *s.*, and thy exceeding great
  reward.   *Gen* 15:1
saved by the Lord, the *s.* of thy.
    Deut 33:29
was there a *s.* or spear seen in
  Israel ?   *Judg* 5:8
one bearing a *s.* *1 Sam* 17:7, 41
me with a spear and a *s.*   45*
s. of the mighty is vilely cast away, *s.*
    2 Sam 1:21
he is my *s.* 22:3; *Ps* 3:3; 28:7
    119:114; 144:2
given me the *s.* of thy salvation.
    2 Sam 22:36; *Ps* 18:35
of gold went to one *s.* *1 Ki* 10:17
come before it with a *s.* nor cast a.
    2 Ki 19:32; *Isa* 37:33
that could handle *s.* *1 Chr* 12:8
children of Judah that bare *s.*   24
of Naphtali with *s.* and spear.   34
could handle spear and *s. 2 Chr* 25:5
spear and *s.* rattleth. *Job* 39:23*
compass him as with a *s.* *Ps* 5:12
the Lord is our *s.* 33:20; 59:11
    84:9
take hold of the *s.* and buckler. 35:2
the arrows of bow, the *s.*   76:3
the Lord God is a sun and *s.* 84:11
be thy *s.* and buckler.   91:4
help and their *s.* 115:9, 10, 11
he is a *s.* to them that. *Pr* 30:5
princes, and anoint the *s.* *Isa* 21:5
quiver, Kir uncovered the *s.* 22:6
order buckler and *s.* *Jer* 46:3
Libyans, that handle the *s.*   9
the buckler and *s.* *Ezek* 23:24
hanged the *s.* and helmet. 27:10, 11
the *s.* of his mighty men. *Nah* 2:3
taking the *s.* of faith. *Eph* 6:16

shields
David took the *s.* of gold that were
  on. *2 Sam* 8:7; *1 Chr* 18:7
Solomon made 300 *s.* of beaten.
    1 Ki 10:17; *2 Chr* 9:16
all, even all *s.* of gold, which Solomon. *1 Ki* 14:26; *2 Chr* 12:9
Rehoboam made in their stead brazen *s.* *1 Ki* 14:27; *2 Chr* 12:10
priest gave king David *s. 2 Ki* 11:10
    2 Chr 23:9
every several city put *s. 2 Chr* 11:12
out of Benjamin that bare *s.* 14:8
    17:17
Uzziah prepared for them *s.* 26:14
darts and *s.* in abundance. 32:5, 27
half of them held spears and *s.*
    Neh 4:16
the *s.* of the earth belong. *Ps* 47:9
bucklers, all *s.* of mighty men.
    S of S 4:4
the arrows, gather the *s.* *Jer* 51:11
great company with bucklers and *s.*
    Ezek 38:4, 5
they shall burn the *s.* and.   39:9

Shiggaion
(*This word is found in the title of*
Ps 7. *The meaning is not cer-*
tainly known. It was perhaps a
wild, mournful ode)

Shiloah
refuseth the waters of S. *Isa* 8:6

Shiloh
(*It has long been supposed to refer*
directly to Christ, the Messiah; but
as there is no reference to it in the
New Testament many are now
doubtful. Some consider it as
referring to the city of Shiloh)
the sceptre shall not depart from
  Judah, nor a lawgiver from between his feet, until S. come.
    Gen 49:10

Shiloh
assembled together at S. *Josh* 18:1
cast lots for you in S.   8, 10
departed from Israel out of S. 22:9
house of God was in S. *Judg* 18:31

the young virgins to S.   Judg 21:12
feast of the Lord in S. yearly.   19
if the daughters of S. come out.   21
up to worship in S.   1 Sam 1:3
to house of the Lord in S.   24
so did the priests in S. to all.   2:14
the Lord appeared again in S.   3:21
ark of the Lord out of S.   4:3
man came to S. with his clothes.   12
Ahitub the Lord's priest in S.   14:3
the house of Eli in S.   1 Ki 2:27
get thee to S. to Ahijah the.   14:2
wife arose and went to S.   4
the tabernacle of S.   Ps 78:60
my place which was in S.   Jer 7:12
house as I have done to S.   14
I make this house like S.   26:6, 9
there came certain from S.   41:5

Shilonite, see Ahijah

Shimeah
friend, Jonadab son of S. 2 Sam 13:3
32; 21:21; 1 Chr 20:7
S. was born to David in.   1 Chr 3:5
Berachiah, the son of S.   6:39

Shimei
S. son of Gera of Bahurim.
2 Sam 16:5; 19:16
S. went along on the hill's side. 16:13
thou hast with thee S.   1 Ki 2:8
that two of the servants of S.   39
S. the son of Elah, officer in.   4:18
S. son of Pedaiah.   1 Chr 3:19
S. son of Joel.   5:4
Mishma, Hamuel, Zaccur, S.   4:26
S. had sixteen sons and six.   27
S. son of Gershom.   6:17, 42, 23:7
S. son of Merari.   6:29
sons of S.   23:9, 10
the tenth lot to S.   25:17
over vineyards was S.   27:27
Heman, Jehiel and S.   2 Chr 29:14
dedicated things was S.   31:12, 13
S. had taken a strange wife.
Ezra 10:23, 33, 38
of Jair, the son of S.   Esth 2:5
the family of S. shall.   Zech 12:13

Shimshai
S. the scribe wrote a.   Ezra 4:8, 9
the king sent an answer to S.   17

Shinar
Calneh in the land of S.   Gen 10:10
a plain in the land of S.   11:2
Amraphel king of S.   14:1
recover remnant from S.   Isa 11:11
into the land of S.   Dan 1:2
house in the land of S.   Zech 5:11

shine
Lord make his face s.   Num 6:25
neither let light s. on it.   Job 3:4
s. on counsel of the wicked.   10:3
thou shalt s. forth, thou.   11:17*
spark of his fire shall not s.   18:5
and the light shall s. upon.   22:28
light he commandeth not to s. 36:32*
the light of his cloud to s.   37:15
light doth s. and his eyes.   41:18*
he maketh a path to s. after him. 32
make thy face to s.   Ps 31:16
face to s. upon us. 67:1; 80:3, 7, 19
between cherubims, s. forth.   80:1
oil to make his face to s.   104:15
make thy face to s. upon.   119:135
maketh his face to s.   Eccl 8:1
not cause her light to s.   Isa 13:10
arise, s. for thy light is come.   60:1
are waxen fat, they s.   Jer 5:28
cause thy face to s.   Dan 9:17
wise shall s. as the brightness. 12:3
let your light so s.   Mat 5:16
shall the righteous s. forth.   13:43
his face did s. as sun, and his. 17:2
gospel of Christ should s. 2 Cor 4:4*
God who commanded light to s.   6
ye s. as lights in world.   Phil 2:15
light of a candle shall s. Rev 18:23
sun nor moon to s. in it.   21:23

shined
the Lord s. forth from.   Deut 33:2
when his candle s. upon.   Job 29:3
if I beheld the sun when it s.   31:26
of beauty God hath s.   Ps 50:2

---

upon them hath the light s.   Isa 9:2
earth s. with his glory.   Ezek 43:2
suddenly there s. about.   Acts 9:3
the angel came, and a light s.   12:7
for God hath s. in our.   2 Cor 4:6

shineth
moon, and it s. not.   Job 25:5*
the night s. as the day.   Ps 139:12
shining light that s. more.   Pr 4:18
as lightning s. even to.   Mat 24:27*
and s. to other part.   Luke 17:24
the light s. in darkness.   John 1:5
as to a light that s. in.   2 Pet 1:19
the true light now s.   1 John 2:8
was as the sun s.   Rev 1:16

shining
by clear s. after rain.   2 Sam 23:4
path of just is as the s. light. Pr 4:18
will create the s. of a.   Isa 4:5
withdraw their s.   Joel 2:10; 3:15
they went at the s.   Hab 3:11
raiment became s. white.   Mark 9:3
when the s. of a candle. Luke 11:36
two men stood by them in s.   24:4
a burning and a s. light.   John 5:35
the brightness of sun s.   Acts 26:13

ship
*(In the Gospels the Revisions
change this word to boat)*
the way of a s. in the midst. Pr 30:19
no gallant s. shall pass.   Isa 33:21
Jonah found a s. going.   Jonah 1:3
a tempest, so that the s. was.   5
forth the wares into the s.   5
in a s. with Zebedee.   Mat 4:21
and they left the s. and followed. 22
that the s. was covered with.   8:24
the s. was tossed with waves. 14:24
Mark 4:37
in the s. mending their.   Mark 1:19
father Zebedee in the s.   20
hinder part of the s. asleep.   4:38
neither had they in the s.   8:14
immediately the s. was.   John 6:21
net on right side of the s.   21:6
accompanied him to the s. Acts 20:38
finding a s. sailing over unto.   21:2
into a s. of Adramyttium.   27:2

ship boards
all thy s. boards of fir trees.
Ezek 27:5

shipmaster
s. said, What meanest?   Jonah 1:6
every s. and sailors afar.   Rev 18:17

shipmen
Hiram sent s. that had.   1 Ki 9:27
the s. were about to flee out of.
Acts 27:30*

shipping
they took s. and came.   John 6:24

ships
shall be an haven for s.   Gen 49:13
and s. shall come from Chittim.
Num 24:24
thee into Egypt with s.   Deut 28:68
did Dan remain in s.?   Judg 5:17
king Solomon made a navy of s.
1 Ki 9:26
s. of Tarshish to go to Ophir, the s.
22:48; 2 Chr 20:37
my servants go with thine in the s.
1 Ki 22:49
sent him s. and servants. 2 Chr 8:18
king's s. went to Tarshish.   9:21
passed away as the swift s. Job 9:26
thou breakest the s. of.   Ps 48:7
there go the s.: there is that. 104:26
down to the sea in s. that.   107:23
merchant s. she brings.   Pr 31:14
Lord on the s. of Tarshish. Isa 2:16
howl, ye s. of Tarshish, no. 23:1, 14
whose cry is in the s.   43:14
the s. of Tarshish first, to.   60:9
all s. of the sea with.   Ezek 27:9
s. of Tarshish did sing of thee.   25
come down from their s.   29
go forth from me in s.   30:9
for s. of Chittim shall.   Dan 11:30
north shall come with many s.   40
they filled both the s.   Luke 5:7
behold also the s. though.   Jas 3:4
the third part of the s.   Rev 8:9

---

the company in s. stood. Rev 18:17*
made rich all that had s.   19

shipwreck
stoned, thrice I suffered s.
2 Cor 11:25
faith have made s.   1 Tim 1:19

Shishak
in fifth year of Rehoboam, S. king.
1 Ki 14:25; 2 Chr 12:2
together because of S. I left you in
the hand of S.   2 Chr 12:5
be poured out on Jerusalem by S. 7
S. took away the treasures of.   9

shittah tree
in wilderness the s. tree.   Isa 41:19

Shittim
Israel abode in S.   Num 25:1
sent out of S. two men.   Josh 2:1
they removed from S. and.   3:1
water the valley of S.   Joel 3:18
him from S. to Gilgal.   Mi 6:5

shittim wood
(Acacia, as in Revisions)
skins and s. wood.   Ex 25:5; 35:7
shall make an ark of s. wood.
25:10; 37:1; Deut 10:3
make staves of s. wood.   Ex 25:13
28; 27:6; 37:4, 15, 28; 38:6
thou shalt make a table of s. wood.
25:23; 37:10
make boards for tabernacle of s.
wood.   26:15; 36:20
thou shalt make bars of s. wood.
26:26; 36:31
pillars of s. wood. 26:32, 37; 36:36
make an altar of s. wood.   27:1
30:1
with whom was found s. wood. 35:24

shivers
potter shall be broken to s. Rev 2:27

shock
like as a s. of corn cometh. Job 5:26

shocks
Samson burnt up the s.   Judg 15:5

shod
captives and s. them.   2 Chr 28:15
I s. thee with badgers'. Ezek 16:10
be s. with sandals, put not on.
Mark 6:9
s. with the preparation.   Eph 6:15

shoe
To take off shoe was, [1] A sign of
reverence, Ex 3:5; [2] Of disgrace, Deut 25:10; [3] Of a contract, Ruth 4:7; [4] Of mourning,
Ezek 24:17.
wife shall loose his s.   Deut 25:9
the house of him that hath his s.   10
thy s. is not waxen old upon.   29:5
thy s. from off thy foot.   Josh 5:15
man plucked off his s.   Ruth 4:7
it for thee, so he drew off his s.   8
over Edom will I cast out my s.
Ps 60:8; 108:9
and put off thy s.   Isa 20:2

shoelatchet
take from thread to a s.   Gen 14:23
whose s. I am not worthy. John 1:27

shoes
put off thy s. from thy feet.
Ex 3:5; Acts 7:33
with your s. on your feet.   12:11
s. shall be iron and.   Deut 33:25*
old s. and clouted upon.   Josh 9:5
our s. are become old with.   13
put the blood in his s.   1 Ki 2:5
are thy feet with s.!   S of S 7:1*
nor the latchet of their s.   Isa 5:27
put on thy s. upon.   Ezek 24:17, 23
they sold the poor for a pair of s.
Amos 2:6
buy the needy for a pair of s.   8:6
whose s. I am not worthy. Mat 3:11
carry neither s. nor staves.
Luke 10:4
s. I am not worthy to.   Mark 1:7
Luke 3:16; Acts 13:25
ring on his hand, and s. Luke 15:22
you without purse and s.   22:35

shone

that the skin of his face s. *Ex* 34:29
the skin of his face s. they. 30, 35
rose up early, sun s. 2 *Ki* 3:22
glory of the Lord s. round. *Luke* 2:9
suddenly there s. from. *Acts* 22:6
the day s. not for a third. *Rev* 8:12

shook

for oxen s. the ark. 2 *Sam* 6:6*
the earth s. 22:8; *Ps* 18:7; 68:8*
77:18
I s. my lap, and said. *Neh* 5:13
out and s. the kingdoms. *Isa* 23:11
but they s. off the dust. *Acts* 13:51
he s. his raiment, and said. 18:6
he s. off the beast into the fire. 28:5
voice then s. the earth. *Heb* 12:26

shoot

middle bar to s. through. *Ex* 36:33*
I will s. three arrows. 1 *Sam* 20:20
the arrows which I s. 36
not that they would s.? 2 *Sam* 11:20
then Elisha said, S. 2 *Ki* 13:17
he shall not s. an arrow there.
19:32; *Isa* 37:33
valiant men able to s. 1 *Chr* 5:18
engines to s. arrows. 2 *Chr* 26:15
they may privily s. at. *Ps* 11:2
they s. out the lip, they shake. 22:7
when he bendeth his bow to s. 58:7*
to s. their arrows, even bitter. 64:3
that they may s. in secret. 4
God shall s. at them with an. 7
s. out thine arrows, and. 144:6*
bend the bow, s. at her. *Jer* 50:14
neither s. up their top. *Ezek* 31:14*
ye shall s. forth your branches. 36:8
when they now s. forth. *Luke* 21:30

shooters

s. shot from off the. 2 *Sam* 11:24

shooteth

and his branch s. forth. *Job* 8:16
measure-when it s. forth. *Isa* 27:8*
mustard seed s. out. *Mark* 4:32*

shooting

right hand and left in s. 1 *Chr* 12:2
in the s. up of the latter. *Amos* 7:1

shore

(*Revisions*, beach)
multitude stood on the s. *Mat* 13:2
it was full, they drew to s. 48
Jesus stood on the s. *John* 21:4
we kneeled down on the s. *Acts* 21:5
a certain creek with a s. 27:39
mainsail and made toward s. 40
see sea

shorn

like a flock of sheep that are even s.
S of S 4:2
s. his head in Cenchrea. *Acts* 18:18
let her also be s.: but if it be a shame
for a woman to be s. 1 *Cor* 11:6

short

Lord's hand waxed s.? *Num* 11:23
the light is s. because. *Job* 17:12*
triumphing of the wicked is s. 20:5
how s. my time is. *Ps* 89:47
come s. of glory of God. *Rom* 3:23
because a s. work will Lord. 9:28*
brethren, the time is s. 1 *Cor* 7:29*
from you for a s. time. 1 *Thes* 2:17
he hath but a s. time. *Rev* 12:12
he must continue a s. space. 17:10*
see come, cut

shortened

days of his youth hast thou s.
Ps 89:45
my strength, he s. my days. 102:23
years of wicked shall be s. *Pr* 10:27
is my hand s. at all, that? *Isa* 50:2
the Lord's hand is not s. 59:1
should be s. no flesh be saved, but
for the elect's sake s. *Mat* 24:22
Mark 13:20

shorter

bed is s. than that a man. *Isa* 28:20

shortly

is established, and God will s. bring
it to pass. *Gen* 41:32
vessels shall s. be brought again.
Jer 27:16

now will I s. pour out. *Ezek* 7:8
would depart s. thither. *Acts* 25:4
bruise Satan under your feet s.
Rom 16:20
I will come to you s. 1 *Cor* 4:19
I trust to send Timotheus s. unto.
Phil 2:19
I also myself shall come s. 24
hoping to come unto thee s.
1 *Tim* 3:14
thy diligence to come s. 2 *Tim* 4:9
come s. I will see you. *Heb* 13:23
s. I must put off this. 2 *Pet* 1:14*
I trust I shall s. see. 3 *John* 14
things that must s. come. *Rev* 1:1
22:6

shot, *verb*

her blossoms s. forth. *Gen* 40:10
the archers s. at him, and. 49:23
shall surely be stoned, or s. through.
Ex 19:13
we have s. at them. *Num* 21:30
the arrow which Jonathan had s.
1 *Sam* 20:37
the shooters s. from. 2 *Sam* 11:24
said, Shoot, and he s. 2 *Ki* 13:17
archers s. at king Josiah. 2 *Chr* 35:23
s. out lightnings, and. *Ps* 18:14
tongue is an arrow s. out. *Jer* 9:8*
it became a vine, and s. *Ezek* 17:6
this vine s. forth her branches. 7
waters when he s. forth. 31:5
he hath s. up his top among. 10*

shot

down as it were a bow s. *Gen* 21:16

shoulder

bread on Hagar's s. *Gen* 21:14
her pitcher upon her s. 24:15, 45
Issachar bowed his s. to. 49:15
the ephod shall have two s. *Ex* 28:7
the chains on the s. pieces. 25
the s. of the heave offering. 29:27*
they made s. pieces for it to. 39:4
priest shall take sodden s. of the
ram. *Num* 6:19; *Deut* 18:3
man a stone upon his s. *Josh* 4:5
laid a bow on his s. *Judg* 9:48
cook took up the s. 1 *Sam* 9:24*
withdrew the s. and. *Neh* 9:29
I would take it upon my s. *Job* 31:36
I removed his s. from. *Ps* 81:6
broken the staff of his s. *Isa* 9:4
government shall be upon his s. 6
shall be taken from off thy s. 10:27
of David will I lay upon his s. 22:22
they bear him upon the s. 46:7
I bare it on my s. *Ezek* 12:7
prince shall bear upon his s. 12
even the thigh and s. 24:4
and rent all their s. 29:7, 18
thrust with side and with s. 34:21
and pulled away the s. *Zech* 7:11

shoulder *blade*

fall from my s. blade. *Job* 31:22

heave shoulder

the heave s. have I taken.
Lev 7:34*; *Num* 6:20*
the heave s. shall ye eat. *Lev* 10:14*
the heave s. and weave breast. 15*

right shoulder

the ram the *right* s. *Ex* 29:22*
the *right* s. shall ye give. *Lev* 7:32*
offereth, shall have the *right* s. 33*
took the fat and the *right* s. 8:25*
fat, and upon the *right* s. 26*
the *right* s. waved is thine. 9:21*
Num 18:18*

shoulders

laid the garment upon both their s.
Gen 9:23
bound upon their s. *Ex* 12:34
two stones on s. of ephod. 28:12
39:7
of Kohath should bear on their s.
Num 7:9
dwell between his s. *Deut* 33:12
took bar and all, and put them upon
his s. *Judg* 16:3
from his s. and upward higher.
1 *Sam* 9:2; 10:23
target of brass between his s. 17:6
bare the ark on their s. 1 *Chr* 15:15

a burden upon your s. 2 *Chr* 35:3
they shall fly on the s. of. *Isa* 11:14
burden depart from off their s. 14:25
will carry riches upon the s. 30:6
shall be carried upon their s. 49:22
shall bear it upon thy s. *Ezek* 12:6
lay them on men's s. *Mat* 23:4
it on his s. rejoicing. *Luke* 15:5

shout, *substantive*

and the s. of a king. *Num* 23:21
shouted with a great s. *Josh* 6:5, 20
with a great s. so that. 1 *Sam* 4:5
the noise of this great s.? 6
men of Judah gave a s. 2 *Chr* 13:15
with a great s. when they praised.
Ezra 3:11
could not discern the s. of joy. 13
God is gone up with a s. *Ps* 47:5
Lord shall give a s. as. *Jer* 25:30
shall lift a s. against Babylon. 51:14
people gave a s. saying. *Acts* 12:22
shall descend from heaven with a s.
1 *Thes* 4:16

shout

them that s. for mastery. *Ex* 32:18
trumpet, all people shall s. *Josh* 6:5
not s. till I bid you s.; then s. 10
s.; for the Lord hath given you. 16
s. unto God with the voice. *Ps* 47:1
s. thou inhabitants of Zion. *Isa* 12:6
let them s. from the top of. 42:11
s. ye lower parts of the earth. 44:23
sing and s. among chief. *Jer* 31:7
Babylon hath sinned. S. against. 50:14
when I s. he shutteth. *Lam* 3:8*
s. O Israel, be glad with. *Zeph* 3:14
s. O daughter of Jerusalem. *Zech* 9:9

shouted

as they s. he said, There. *Ex* 32:17
consumed, they s. and fell. *Lev* 9:24
so the people s. when. *Josh* 6:20
the Philistines s. against Samson.
Judg 15:14
all Israel s. with a great. 1 *Sam* 4:5
people s. and said, God save. 10:24
going forth and s. for battle. 17:20
the men of Israel and Judah s. 52
as Judah s. God smote. 2 *Chr* 13:15
praised the Lord, they s. *Ezra* 3:11
people s. aloud for joy. 12, 13
see joy

shouteth

like a mighty man that s. because
of wine. *Ps* 78:65

shouting

brought up ark with s. 2 *Sam* 6:15
1 *Chr* 15:28
they sware to the Lord with s.
2 *Chr* 15:14
he smelleth the battle and s. afar off.
Job 39:25
wicked perish, there is s. *Pr* 11:10
the s. for summer fruits is fallen.
Isa 16:9, 10*
let them hear the s. at. *Jer* 20:16
with s.; their s. shall be no s. 48:33
lift up the voice with s. *Ezek* 21:22
devour Rabbah with s. *Amos* 1:14
Moab shall die with tumult, s. 2:2

shoutings

forth the headstone with s. *Zech* 4:7

shovel

winnowed with the s. *Isa* 30:24

shovels

make his pans and his s. *Ex* 27:3
he made the pots, and the s. 38:3
on the purple cloth s. *Num* 4:14
lavers, the s. and the basons of brass.
1 *Ki* 7:40, 45; 2 *Chr* 4:11, 16
pots and s. he took away.
2 *Ki* 25:14; *Jer* 52:18

shower

there shall be an overflowing s.
Ezek 13:11, 13
I will cause s. to come down. 34:26
say, There cometh a s. *Luke* 12:54

showers

distil as s. on the grass. *Deut* 32:2
the poor are wet with s. *Job* 24:8
the earth soft with s. *Ps* 65:10

shrank

he shall come down as s. Ps 72:6
therefore the s. have been. Jer 3:3
can the heavens give s.? 14:22
shall be s. of blessing. Ezek 34:26
shall be as s. on grass. Mi 5:7
the Lord shall give them s. of rain.
Zech 10:1

shrank
Israel eat not of sinew that s.
Gen 32:32*

shred
came and s. wild gourds. 2 Ki 4:39

shrines
made silver s. for Diana. Acts 19:24

shroud
was a cedar with a shadowing s.
Ezek 31:3

shrubs
child under one of the s. Gen 21:15

Shuah
Keturah bare Ishbak, S. Gen 25:2
1 Chr 1:32
daughter of a Canaanite named S.
Gen 38:2, 12; 1 Chr 2:3

Shual
turned to the land of S. 1 Sam 13:17

Shuhite, see Bildad

Shulamite
return, O S. What will ye see in the
S.? S of S 6:13

shun
but s. profane and vain. 2 Tim 2:16

Shunammite
a fair damsel Abishag a S. 1 Ki 1:3
Abishag the S. to wife. 2:17
why dost thou ask Abishag the S.? 22
call this S. 2 Ki 4:12, 36
yonder is that S. 25

shunned
I have not s. the whole. Acts 20:27*

Shushan
to pass as I was in S. Neh 1:1
were gathered to S. Esth 2:8
but the city S. was perplexed. 3:15
gather all the Jews in S. and. 4:16
the city of S. rejoiced and. 8:15
number slain in S. was brought. 9:11
Jews slew in S. three hundred. 15
see palace

shut
the Lord s. him in. Gen 7:16
wilderness hath s. them in. Ex 14:3
let her be s. out from camp.
Num 12:14
Miriam was s. out from the camp. 15
nor s. thy hand from. Deut 15:7
s. the gate of Jericho. Josh 2:7
they s. the tower to them. Judg 9:51
for he is s. in, by entering into.
1 Sam 23:7
gates to be s. till after. Neh 13:19
not the pit s. her mouth. Ps 69:15
s. their eyes, lest they. Isa 6:10
so he shall open and none shall s.; he
shall s. and none shall. 22:22
for he hath s. their eyes. 44:18
and gates shall not be s. 45:1
kings shall s. their mouths. 52:15
thy gates shall not be s. day. 60:11
shall I s. the womb? saith. 66:9
Spirit said, Go s. thyself. Ezek 3:24
looked toward the east was s. 44:1
this gate shall be s., it shall not be
opened, God . . . it shall be s. 2
the gate shall be s. the six. 46:1
the gate shall not be s. till the. 2
after his going forth, one shall s. 12
my God hath s. the lions'. Dan 6:22
prison truly found we s. Acts 5:23
power to s. heaven. Rev 11:6
gates shall not be s. by day. 21:25
see door

shut up
priest shall s. him up that hath.
Lev 13:4, 5, 21, 26, 31, 33, 50, 54
the priest shall not s. him up. 11
priest shall s. up the house. 14:38
goeth in while the house is s. up. 46
the Lord's wrath be kindled, and he
s. up the heaven. Deut 11:17

their rock the Lord had s. them up.
Deut 32:30*
there is none s. up nor left. 36
Jericho was straitly s. up. Josh 6:1
Lord had s. up Hannah's womb.
1 Sam 1:5
because the Lord had s. up her. 6
hid them and s. up their calves. 6:10
concubines were s. up to day of.
2 Sam 20:3
when heaven is s. up. 1 Ki 8:35
2 Chr 6:26; 7:13
from Jeroboam him that is s. up and.
1 Ki 14:10; 21:21; 2 Ki 9:8
was not any s. up. 2 Ki 14:26
king of Assyria s. him up. 17:4
Ahaz s. up doors of house.
2 Chr 28:24; 29:7
Shemaiah who was s. up. Neh 6:10
because it s. not up my. Job 3:10
if he cut off, and s. up, who? 11:10
or who hath s. up the sea? 38:8
his scales are s. up together. 41:15
hast not s. me up into. Ps 31:8
he in anger s. up his tender? 77:9
I am s. up, and I cannot come. 88:8
spring s. up, a fountain. S of S 4:12
every house is s. up, no. Isa 24:10
shall be s. up in the prison. 22
the south shall be s. up. Jer 13:19
as fire s. up in my bones. 20:9
the prophet was s. up by Zedekiah.
32:2, 3
word of Lord came, while he was s.
up. 33:1; 39:15
I am s. up, I cannot go to the. 36:5
s. up the vision. Dan 8:26
s. up the words. 12:4
ye s. up kingdom of. Mat 23:13
he s. up John in prison. Luke 3:20
heaven was s. up three years. 4:25
many saints did I s. up. Acts 26:10
s. up unto the faith that. Gal 3:23
s. up the devil, and set. Rev 20:3

shutteth
he s. up a man, there. Job 12:14
he s. his eyes to devise. Pr 16:30
he that s. his lips. is a man. 17:28
s. his eyes from seeing. Isa 33:15
also when I cry, he s. Lam 3:8
and s. up his bowels. 1 John 3:17
no man s.; and s., and no man
openeth. Rev 3:7

shutting
about time of s. the gate. Josh 2:5

shuttle
swifter than a weaver's s. Job 7:6

sick
behold thy father is s. Gen 48:1
the law of her that is s. Lev 15:33
sent, she said, He is s. 1 Sam 19:14
three days ago I fell s. 30:13
the child, and it was s. 2 Sam 12:15
vexed, he fell s. for Tamar. 13:2
make thyself s. 5
Amnon made himself s. 6
son of Jeroboam fell s. 1 Ki 14:1
cometh to ask for son, for he is s. 5
son of the woman fell s. 17:17
down in Samaria, was s. 2 Ki 1:2
the king of Syria was s. 8:7
went to see Joram son of Ahab, because he was s. 29; 2 Chr 22:6
Elisha was fallen s. of. 2 Ki 13:14
was Hezekiah s. unto death. 20:1
2 Chr 32:24; Isa 38:1
heard that Hezekiah had been s.
2 Ki 20:12; Isa 39:1
sad, seeing thou art not s.? Neh 2:2
when they were s., my clothing was
sackcloth. Ps 35:13
maketh the heart s. Pr 13:12
stricken me, and I was not s. 23:35*
me with apples, I am s. of love.
S of S 2:5
tell him that I am s. of love. 5:8
whole head is s. and the whole heart
faint. Isa 1:5
shall not say, I am s. 33:24
when Hezekiah had been s. 38:9
behold them that are s. Jer 14:18
healed that which was s. Ezek 34:4
strengthen that which was s. 16

and was s. certain days. Dan 8:27
princes made him s. with. Hos 7:5
will I make thee s. in. Mi 6:13*
if ye offer the lame and s.? Mal 1:8
ye brought the lame, and the s. 13
brought to him all s. people.
Mat 4:24
saw his wife's mother laid, and s. of
a fever. 8:14; Mark 1:30
and healed all that were s.
Mat 8:16; 14:14
not a physician, but they that are s.
9:12; Mark 2:17; Luke 5:31
heal the s., cleanse the lepers.
Mat 10:8; Luke 9:2; 10:9
I was s. and ye visited. Mat 25:36
saw we thee s.? in prison? 39, 44
hands on a few s. folk. Mark 6:5
they laid the s. in the streets. 56
Acts 5:15
lay hands on the s. and. Mark 16:18
centurion's servant was s. Luke 7:2
whole that had been s. 10
nobleman's son was s. John 4:46
Lazarus of Bethany was s. 11:1, 2
he whom thou lovest is s. 3
he had heard he was s. he abode. 6
in those days Dorcas was s. and.
Acts 9:37
unto the s. handkerchiefs. 19:12
father of Publius lay s. of a. 28:8
heard that he had been s. Phil 2:26
he was s. nigh unto death. 27
have I left at Miletum s. 2 Tim 4:20
is any s. let him call elders. Jas 5:14
prayer of faith shall save the s. 15
see palsy

sickle
as thou beginnest to put s. to.
Deut 16:9
s. unto thy neighbour's corn. 23:25
cut off him that handleth s. Jer 50:16
put ye in the s. for the. Joel 3:13
he putteth in the s. Mark 4:29
and in his hand a sharp s. Rev 14:14
an angel crying, Thrust in thy s. 15
16, 18, 19
he also having a sharp s. 17

sickly
for this cause many are s. among.
1 Cor 11:30

sickness
I will take s. away from. Ex 23:25
man lie with a woman having her s.
Lev 20:18
will take from thee all s. Deut 7:15
every s. that is not written. 28:61
whatsoever s. there be. 1 Ki 8:37
2 Chr 6:28
his s. was so sore, there. 1 Ki 17:17
Elisha sick of the s. 2 Ki 13:14
great s. by disease of thy bowels, by
reason of the s. 2 Chr 21:15
by reason of his s. so he died. 19
all his bed in his s. Ps 41:3
and wrath with his s. Eccl 5:17
was recovered of his s. Isa 38:9
will cut me off with pining s. 12
Ephraim saw his s., and Judah saw
his wound. Hos 5:13
healing all manner of s. Mat 4:23
preaching and healing every s. 9:35
power to heal all manner of s. 10:1
Mark 3:15
this s. is not unto death. John 11:4

sicknesses
the sore s. and of long. Deut 28:59
when they see the s. Lord laid. 29:22
saying, Himself bare our s. Mat 8:17

side
shall set in the s. thereof. Gen 6:16
walked along by river s. Ex 2:5
blood on the two s. posts. 12:7, 22
blood on the lintel and s. posts. 23
Moses' hands, the one on the one s.
and the other on the other s. 17:12
who is on Lord's s.? let him. 32:26
sword by his s. go in and out. 27*
he shall kill it on s. of. Lev 1:11
blood shall be wrung out at the s. 15
sin offering sprinkled on s. of. 5:9
s. and a wall on that s. Num 22:24

as gardens by the river's *s. Num* 24:6
inherit on yonder *s.* Jordan. 32:19
ask from one *s.* of heaven to the.
Deut 4:32*
put the book of the law in the *s.* 31:26
a Levite sojourned on *s.* of Ephraim
Judg 19:1, 18
fell backward by the *s.* *1 Sam* 4:18
put the mice in a coffer by the *s.* 6:8
I will shoot three arrows on the *s.*
20:20
and Abner sat by Saul's *s.* 25
sword into his fellow's *s. 2 Sam* 2:16
came by way of the hill *s.* 13:34
on the hill *s.* over against. 16:13
Who is on my *s.?* who ? *2 Ki* 9:32
David, and on thy *s.* *1 Chr* 12:18
Benjamin on his *s.* *2 Chr* 11:12*
his sword girded by his *s. Neh* 4:18
shall be ready at his *s.* *Job* 18:12
thousand shall fall at thy *s. Ps* 91:7
the Lord is on my *s.* I will. 118:6
the Lord who was on our *s.* 124:1, 2
the *s.* of their oppressors. *Eccl* 4:1
shall be nursed at thy *s.* *Isa* 60:4*
not turn from one *s.* to another.
Ezek 4:8
days that thou shalt lie upon thy *s.* 9
writer's inkhorn by his *s.* 9:2, 3, 11
I will open the *s.* of Moab. 25:9
because ye have thrust with *s.* 34:21
it raised itself on one *s.* *Dan* 7:5
shall not stand on his *s.* 11:17
thieves, on either *s.* one. *John* 19:18
soldiers with a spear pierced his *s.* 34
them his hands and his *s.* 20:20
except I thrust my hand into his *s.* 25
and thrust it into my *s.* 27
the angel smote Peter on the *s.,* and
raised him up. *Acts* 12:7
we went out by the river *s.* 16:13
on either *s.* of river was. *Rev* 22:2
see **chambers, left, sea, south,
way, west**

every **side**
of Abiram on *every s.* *Num* 16:27
the trumpets on *every s. Judg* 7:18
delivered them from their enemies
on *every s.* 8:34; *1 Sam* 12:11
enemies on *every s.* *1 Sam* 14:47
about him on *every s.* *1 Ki* 5:3
given me rest on *every s.* 4
hath he not given you rest on *every s.?*
1 Chr 22:18
he hath given us rest on *every s.*
2 Chr 14:7
Lord guided them on *every s.* 32:22
about all he hath on *every s. Job* 1:10
make him afraid on *every s.* 18:11
destroyed me on *every s.* I. 19:10
wicked walk on *every s.* *Ps* 12:8
fear was on *every s.* while. 31:13
little hills rejoice on *every s.* 65:12*
comfort me on *every s.* 71:21*
fear is on *every s.* *Jer* 6:25; 20:10
49:29
that they may come to thee on *every*
s. *Ezek* 16:33
set against him on *every s.* 19:8
them against thee on *every s.* 23:22
sword upon her on *every s.* 28:23
swallowed you up on *every s.* 36:3
I will gather them on *every s.* 37:21
to my sacrifice on *every s.* 39:17
keep thee in on *every s. Luke* 19:43
we are troubled on *every s.*
2 Cor 4:8; 7:5

farther **side**
farther s. of Jordan. *Mark* 10:1*

on this **side**
one cherub *on this s.,* other on that
side. *Ex* 37:8
quails a day's journey *on this s.*
Num 11:31
on this s. and on that side. 22:24
inheritance *on this s.* Jordan. 32:19
32*; 34:15*
refuge *on this s.* Jordan. 35:14*
some *on this s.* of Ai, and some on
that side. *Josh* 8:22
Israel and judges stood *on this s.* 33
arrows are *on this s.* *1 Sam* 20:21
Saul went *on this s.* of the. 23:26

no portion *on this s.* the river.
governor *on this s.* the river. 5:3*
Ezra 4:16*
6*, 6:13*; 8:36*
throne of the governor *on this s.* the
river. *Neh* 3:7*
two wings, *on this s.* *Ezek* 1:23
two tables *on this s.* and two on that
side. 40:39
on this s., four tables on that side. 41
on bank of river *on this s.* 47:12
stood other two, the one *on this s.*
Dan 12:5
stealeth shall be cut off as *on this s.*
... sweareth *on that side. Zech* 5:3

on other **side**
your fathers dwelt *on the other s.* of
the flood. *Josh* 24:2*
I and Jonathan will be *on the other s.*
1 Sam 14:40
saw water *on other s.* *2 Ki* 3:22*
stood *on* one and *other s. 2 Chr* 9:19
stoodest *on the other s.* *Ob* 11
found him *on the other s.* of the sea.
John 6:25

right **side**
chamber was *on right s.* *1 Ki* 6:8
the *right s.* the house; set the sea
on right s. 7:39; *2 Chr* 4:10
five candlesticks on the *right s.*
1 Ki 7:49; *2 Chr* 4:8
of a lion on the *right s. Ezek* 1:10
lie again *on* thy *right s.* and shalt. 4:6
from under *right s.* of house. 47:1, 2
on right s. the bowl. *Zech* 4:3, 11
they saw a young man sitting *on right*
s. of sepulchre. *Mark* 16:5
angel standing *on right s. Luke* 1:11
cast the net *on* the *right s. John* 21:6

sides
were written on both *s.* *Ex* 32:15
shall be thorns in your *s.*
Num 33:55; *Judg* 2:3
be scourges in your *s.* *Josh* 23:13
needlework on both *s.* *Judg* 5:30
David and his men in *s.* of the cave.
1 Sam 24:3*
peace on all *s.* round. *1 Ki* 4:24
beautiful is Zion on the *s.* *Ps* 48:2
wife as a fruitful vine by *s.* 128:3*
I will sit also in the *s.* *Isa* 14:13*
thou shalt be brought down to *s.* 15*
ye shall be borne upon her *s.* 66:12
nation raised from *s.* of the earth.
Jer 6:22*
maketh her nest in the *s.* 48:28†
their calamity from all *s.* 49:32
upon their four *s. Ezek* 1:17; 10:11
whose graves are set in the *s.* 32:23*
these are his *s.* east and west. 48:1
say unto him that is by *s. Amos* 6:10*
Jonah was gone down into the *s.* of
the ship. *Jonah* 1:5*

Sidon, called **Zidon,** *1 Chr* 1:13
Canaan begat **S.** his. *Gen* 10:15
Canaanites was from S. 19
Laish was far from S. *Judg* 18:28
done in Tyre and S. *Mat* 11:21
it shall be more tolerable for
22; *Luke* 10:13, 14
into the coasts of Tyre and S. behold,
a woman. *Mat* 15:21; *Mark* 7:24
they about Tyre and S. came.
Mark 3:8; *Luke* 6:17
the coasts of Tyre and S. *Mark* 7:31
sent, save to Sarepta a city of S.
Luke 4:26
was displeased with them of S.
Acts 12:20
next day we touched at S. 27:3

siege
cut to employ them in *s. Deut* 20:19
eat thy children in the *s.* 28:53
nothing left him in the *s.* 55, 57
whereon do ye trust, that ye abide in
the *s.?* *2 Chr* 32:10
I will lay *s.* against thee. *Isa* 29:3
flesh of his friend in the *s. Jer* 19:9
lay *s.* against it and build a fort.
Ezek 4:2, 3
days of the *s.* are fulfilled. 5:2

he hath laid *s.* against us. *Mi* 5:1
waters for the *s.,* fortify. *Nah* 3:14
trembling, when in the *s. Zech* 12:2

sieve
sift the nations with the *s.* of vanity.
Isa 30:28
I will sift, like as corn is sifted in a *s.*
Amos 9:9

sift
to *s.* the nations with. *Isa* 30:28
I will *s.* Israel as corn is. *Amos* 9:9
Satan hath desired to have you, that
he may. *Luke* 22:31

sigh
all merry-hearted do *s.* *Isa* 24:7
her priests *s.* *Lam* 1:4
all her people *s.* 11
they have heard that I *s.* 21
foreheads of men that *s. Ezek* 9:4
breaking of thy loins, and with bitterness *s.* before their eyes. 21:6

sighed
Israel *s.* by reason of. *Ex* 2:23
up to heaven, he *s.* *Mark* 7:34
s. deeply in his spirit, and. 8:12

sighest
to thee, Wherefore *s.?* *Ezek* 21:7

sigheth
yea, she *s.* and turneth. *Lam* 1:8

sighing
my *s.* cometh before I eat. *Job* 3:24
for the *s.* of the needy. *Ps* 12:5
with grief, my years with *s.* 31:10
let the *s.* of the prisoner. 79:11
all the *s.* thereof have. *Isa* 21:2
sorrow and *s.* shall flee away. 35:10
I fainted in my *s.* and I. *Jer* 45:3

sighs
for my *s.* are many. *Lam* 1:22

sight
(*Revisions frequently change to
eyes*)
that is pleasant to the *s.* *Gen* 2:9
turn and see this great *s.* *Ex* 3:3
s. of glory of Lord was like. 24:17*
the plague in *s.* be deeper.
Lev 13:3*, 20*, 25*, 30*
in *s.* be not deeper. 4*, 31*, 32*, 34
if the plague in *s.* be lower. 14:37
in our own *s.* as grasshoppers, and so
we were in their *s.* *Num* 13:33
give him charge in their *s.* 27:19
shalt be mad for *s. Deut* 28:34, 67
them from out of your *s. Josh* 23:5
did those great signs in our *s.* 24:17
reputed vile in your *s.?* *Job* 18:3
I am an alien in their *s.* 19:15
seed is established in their *s.* 21:8
them in the open *s.* of others. 34:26
be cast down at the *s.* of him ? 41:9
the heathen in our *s.* *Ps* 79:10
better is the *s.* of the eyes. *Eccl* 6:9
prudent in their own *s.* *Isa* 5:21
he shall not judge after the *s.* 11:3
evil done in Zion in your *s. Jer* 51:24
shalt bake it with dung in their *s.*
Ezek 4:12
remove by day in their *s.* 12:3
dig thou through the wall in their *s.* 5
in whose *s.* I made myself. 20:9
heathen in whose *s.* I brought. 14, 22
yourselves in your own *s.* 43; 36:31
a false divination in their *s.* 21:23
thereof, and write in their *s.* 43:11
s. thereof to end of. *Dan* 4:11, 20
whoredoms out of her *s. Hos* 2:2*
the blind receive their *s.,* the lame.
Mat 11:5; 20:34; *Luke* 7:21
the recovering of *s.* to the blind.
Luke 4:18
that came to that *s.* smote. 23:48
he vanished out of their *s.* 24:31
washed, and I received *s. John* 9:11
cloud received him out of their *s.*
Acts 1:9
saw it, he wondered at the *s.* 7:31
was three days without *s.* 9:9
he received *s.* forthwith, arose. 18
walk by faith, not by *s.* *2 Cor* 5:7
so terrible was the *s.* *Heb* 12:21*

sight *of God*
good understanding in the *s. of God.*
     Pr 3:4
is abomination in the *s. of God.*
     Luke 16:15
right in the *s. of God* to. *Acts 4:19*
not right in the *s. of God.*   8:21
had in remembrance in the *s. of God.*
     10:31
in the *s. of God* speak we. *2 Cor 2:17*
conscience in the *s. of God.*   4:2
our care for you in *s. of God.*   7:12
by the law in *s. of God.*   *Gal 3:11*
remembering work of faith in *s. of God.*   *1 Thes 1:3*
this is good and acceptable in the *s. of God.*   *1 Tim 2:3*
thee charge in the *s. of God.*   6:13
which is in the *s. of God* of. *1 Pet 3:4*
     see **Lord**

his sight
if thou wilt do that which is right in
his *s.*   *Ex 15:26*
if the plague is in his *s.* be. *Lev 13:5*
scall be in his *s.* at a stay.   37
burn the heifer in his *s.* *Num 19:5*
he brought thee out in his *s.*
     Deut 4:37*
Lord departed out of his *s. Judg 6:21*
Lord, to do evil in his *s.? 2 Sam 12:9*
went and made cakes in his *s.* 13:8
remove them out of his *s.*
    2 Ki 17:18, 20, 23; 24:3
do what is right in his *s. 1 Chr 19:13**
are not clean in his *s.*   *Job 15:15*
stars are not pure in his *s.*   25:5
are far above out of his *s.*   *Ps 10:5*
shall their blood be in his *s.*   72:14
to a man that is good in his *s.*
     Eccl 2:26
be not hasty to go out of his *s. 8:3**
and we shall live in his *s.*   *Hos 6:2*
immediately received his *s.* and.
    Mark 10:52; Luke 18:43
he had received his *s. John 9:15, 18*
he might receive his *s.*   *Acts 9:12*
no flesh be justified in his *s.*
     Rom 3:20
present you holy in his *s.*   *Col 1:22*
is manifest in his *s.*   *Heb 4:13*
is well pleasing in his *s.*   13:21
things that are pleasing in his *s.*
     1 John 3:22

in the **sight**
grievous in Abraham's *s. Gen 21:11*
aught left *in the s.* of my lord.   47:18
signs *in the s.* of the people. *Ex 4:30*
he smote the waters *in the s.*   7:20
Moses sprinkled the ashes *in the s.*
     9:8
great *in the s.* of Pharaoh's.   11:3
Moses did so *in the s.* of the.   17:6
come down *in the s.* of people. 19:11
fire by night *in the s.* of Israel. 40:38
shall be cut off *in the s.*   *Lev 20:17*
out of Egypt *in the s.* of the.   26:45
ministered *in the s.* of Aaron.
     Num 3:4*
Eleazar went *in the s.* of.   20:27
woman *in the s.* of Moses.   25:6
went with high hand *in the s.* 33:3
is your wisdom *in the s.* of nations.
     Deut 4:6
Joshua *in the s.* of all Israel. 31:7
terror Moses shewed *in the s.* 34:12
to magnify thee *in the s.* of Israel.
     Josh 3:7; 4:14
he said, *In the s.* of Israel.   10:12
David accepted *in the s.* of the.
     1 Sam 18:5
lie with thy wives *in the s.* of this sun.
     2 Sam 12:11
in the *s.* of all Israel. *1 Chr 28:8*
Solomon *in the s.* of Israel. 29:25
Hezekiah magnified *in the s.* of nations.
     2 Chr 32:23
in the *s.* of kings of Persia. *Ezra 9:9*
grant him mercy *in the s.* of. *Neh 1:11*
opened the book *in the s.* of all. 8:5
things did he *in the s.* of their fathers.
     Ps 78:12
he openly shewed *in the s.* of. 98:2
in vain net is spread *in the s. Pr 1:17*

beloved *in the s.* of my mother.
     Pr 4:3
walk *in the s.* of thine.   *Eccl 11:9*
break the bottle *in the s. Jer 19:10*
I gave the evidence *in the s. 32:12**
hid stones *in the s.* of the men. 43:9
execute judgements *in the s.* of the.
     Ezek 5:8
Jerusalem a reproach *in s.* of.   14
judgement on thee *in the s.* 16:41
name not polluted *in s.* of.   20:22
thee to ashes *in the s.* of all. 28:18
sanctified in them *in s.* of heathen.
     25; 39:27
lay desolate *in the s.* of all. 36:34
I will discover lewdness *in s.* of.
     Hos 2:10
gave him wisdom *in the s. Acts 7:10*
provide things honest *in the s.* of all.
     Rom 12:17
come down *in s.* of men.   *Rev 13:13*
miracles he had power to do *in s.* 14

my **sight**
bury my dead out of my *s.*
     Gen 23:4, 8
found grace in my *s.*   *Ex 33:12, 17*
coming is good in my *s. 1 Sam 29:6*
thou art good in my *s.* as an.   9
be base in mine own *s.*   *2 Sam 6:22*
and dress the meat in my *s.*   13:5
me a couple of cakes in my *s.*   6
not fail thee a man in my *s.*
    1 Ki 8:25; 2 Chr 6:16
hallowed for my name will I cast out
of my *s.*   *1 Ki 9:7; 2 Chr 7:20*
do that is right in my *s. 1 Ki 11:38*
which was evil in my *s. 2 Ki 21:15*
Judah also out of my *s.*   23:27
shed much blood in my *s. 1 Chr 22:8*
shall not tarry in my *s.*   *Ps 101:7*
wast precious in my *s.*   *Isa 43:4*
abominations out of my *s.*   *Jer 4:1*
I will cast you of my *s.* as.   7:15
of Judah have done evil in my *s.* 30
cast them out of my *s.* and.   15:1
if it do evil in my *s.* that it.   18:10
and had done right in my *s.* 34:15
he went in my *s.* to fill. *Ezek 10:2*
up from the earth in my *s.*   19
be hid from my *s.* in the bottom.
     Amos 9:3
thee ? Lord, that I might receive my
s.   *Mark 10:51; Luke 18:41*

thy **sight**
hath found grace in thy *s. Gen 19:19*
let it not be grievous in thy *s.* 21:12
If I have found grace in thy *s.* 33:10
    47:29; *Ex 33:13, 16; 34:9*
     Judg 6:17
rule with rigour in thy *s. Lev 25:53*
little in thine own *s. 1 Sam 15:17*
cut off thine enemies out of thy *s.*
     2 Sam 7:9*
yet a small thing in thy *s.*   9
I have found grace in thy *s.* 14:22
let my life be precious in thy *s.*
     2 Ki 1:13, 14
I have done that which is good in thy
s.   20:3; *Isa 38:3*
shall not stand in thy *s.*   *Ps 5:5*
let heathen be judged in thy *s.* 9:19
heart be acceptable in thy *s.* 19:14
and done this evil in thy *s.*   51:4
who may stand in thy *s.* ?   76:7
a thousand years in thy *s.*   90:4
for in thy *s.* shall no man.   143:2
been in thy *s.* O Lord.   *Isa 26:17*
forgive not iniquity, neither blot out
their sin from thy *s.*   *Jer 18:23*
I am cast out of thy *s.*   *Jonah 2:4*
so it seemed good in thy *s.*
    Mat 11:26; Luke 10:21
sinned against heaven and in thy *s.*
     Luke 15:21
unto him, Receive thy *s.*   18:42
that thou mightest receive thy *s.*
     Acts 9:17
Brother Saul, receive thy *s.*   22:13
    see **favour, find**

sights
shall be fearful *s.* signs from.
     Luke 21:11*

sign
This word is used [1] *as we use
the word sign or token,* Gen 9:12,
13. [2] *For a miracle,* Ex 4:17.
[3] *The phenomena of the heavens,*
Jer 10:2.
if they believe not nor hearken to
voice of first *s.* they.   *Ex 4:8*
to-morrow shall this *s.* be.   8:23
it shall be a *s.* to thee upon.   13:9
for it is a *s.* between me and you.
    31:13, 17; *Ezek 20:12, 20*
and they shall be a *s.*   *Num 16:38*
and they became a *s.*   26:10
bind them for a *s.*   *Deut 6:8; 11:18*
a prophet, and giveth thee a *s.* 13:1
and *s.* come to pass whereof.   2
they shall be on thee for a *s.* 28:46
that this may be a *s.*   *Josh 4:6*
shew me a *s.* that thou.   *Judg 6:17*
appointed *s.* between Israel.   20:38
a *s.* to thee, in one day they shall.
    1 Sam 2:34; 2 Ki 19:29
we will go up: and this shall be a *s.*
     1 Sam 14:10
gave a *s.* the same day, saying, This
is the *s.* the Lord hath. *1 Ki 13:3*
according to the *s.* the man of.   5
shall be the *s.* that the ?   *2 Ki 20:8*
this *s.* shalt thou have of the Lord. 9
    Isa 37:30; 38:7, 22
him, he gave him a *s.*   *2 Chr 32:24*
ask thee a *s.* of the Lord. *Isa 7:11*
give you a *s.*; Behold a virgin shall. 14
be for a *s.* unto the Lord.   19:20
walked barefoot for a *s.*   20:3
a name, for an everlasting *s.* 55:13
I will set a *s.* among them.   66:19
set up a *s.* of fire in Beth-haccerem.
     Jer 6:1*
and this shall be a *s.* unto you. 44:29
this shall be a *s.* to the house of.
     Ezek 4:3
I have set thee for a *s.* to.   12:6, 11
I will make him a *s.* a proverb. 14:8
thus Ezekiel is a *s.*   24:24
thou shalt be a *s.*   27
then shall he set up a *s.* by it. 39:15
we would see a *s.* from.   *Mat 12:38*
    16:1; *Mark 8:11; Luke 11:16*
evil and adulterous generation seeketh after a *s.*   *Mat 12:39; 16:4*
    Mark 8:12; Luke 11:29
no *s.* be given to it, but the *s.* of the
prophet Jonas.   *Mat 12:39*
    Mark 8:12; Luke 11:29, 30
be the *s.* of thy coming ? *Mat 24:3*
shall appear the *s.* of the Son.   30
betrayed him gave them a *s.* 26:48
what *s.* when all these. *Mark 13:4*
for a *s.* which shall be. *Luke 2:34*
what *s.* shewest thou unto us ?
    John 2:18; 6:30
a ship, whose *s.* was Castor and
Pollux.   *Acts 28:11*
s. of circumcision, a seal. *Rom 4:11*
for the Jews require a *s.*, and the
Greeks seek.   *1 Cor 1:22*
tongues are for a *s.*, not.   14:22
I saw another *s.* in heaven. *Rev 15:1*

sign, *verb*
decree, *s.* the writing.   *Dan 6:8*

signed
king Darius *s.* the writing. *Dan 6:9*
knew that the writing was *s.*   10
hast thou not *s.* a decree ?   12

signet
give me thy *s.* and.   *Gen 38:18, 25*
engraver on stone, like engravings of
a *s.*   *Ex 28:11, 21, 36; 39:14, 30*
though Coniah were *s.* on. *Jer 22:24*
sealed it with his own *s.*   *Dan 6:17*
and make thee as a *s.*   *Hag 2:23*

signets
onyx stones graven as *s.*   *Ex 39:6*

signification
none of them without *s. 1 Cor 14:10*

signified
Agabus *s.* there should. *Acts 11:28*
s. it by his angel to his.   *Rev 1:1*

signifieth
s. removing of those things shaken.
    Heb 12:27

signify
to *s.* the accomplishment of the.
    Acts 21:26*
s. thee to chief captain that.   23:15
and not to *s.* the crimes laid.   25:27
searching what the Spirit of Christ in
   them did *s.*   *1 Pet* 1:11

signifying
said, *s.* by what death he should die.
    John 12:33; 18:32; 21:19
the Holy Ghost this *s.*   *Heb* 9:8

signs
for *s.* and for seasons.   *Gen* 1:14
not believe these two *s.*   *Ex* 4:9
in thy hand thou shalt do *s.*   17
all words of Lord and all *s.* which he.
    Ex 4:28, 30; *Josh* 24:17
I will multiply my *s.* in.   *Ex* 7:3
mayest tell thy son my *s.*   10:2
for all the *s.* which I.   *Num* 14:11
to take him a nation by *s. Deut* 4:34
    26:8
Lord shewed *s.* on Egypt, on.   6:22
the great *s.* which thine.
    Deut 7:19; 29:3
in all *s.* which the Lord sent.   34:11
when these *s.* are come.   *1 Sam* 10:7
and all those *s.* came to pass.   9
set up their ensigns for *s.*   *Ps* 74:4
we see not our *s.*, there is no more. 9
shewed his *s.* among them.   105:27
I and the children are for *s. Isa* 8:18
be not dismayed at the *s.*   *Jer* 10:2
which hast set *s.* and wonders. 32:20
Israel out of Egypt with *s.*   21
I thought it good to shew *s. Dan* 4:2
how great are his *s.*! how mighty! 3
he worketh *s.* in heaven and.   6:27
can ye not discern the *s.? Mat* 16:3
and false prophets, and shall shew
   great *s.*   24:24; *Mark* 13:22
these *s.* follow them.   *Mark* 16:17
confirming the word with *s.*   20
made *s.* to his father.   *Luke* 1:62
and great *s.* shall there be.   21:11
there shall be *s.* in the sun.   25
except ye see *s.* ye will. *John* 4:48
and many other *s.* truly did.   20:30
I will shew *s.* in the earth. *Acts* 2:19
a man approved of God by *s.*   22
many *s.* were done by the apostles.
    43; 5:12
that *s.* may be done by the.   4:30
after he had shewed *s.* and.   7:36
beholding the *s.* done.   8:13
granted *s.* and wonders to be.   14:3
not wrought by me through mighty *s.*
    Rom 15:19; *2 Cor* 12:12
working of Satan, with *s.*   *2 Thes* 2:9
bearing them witness with *s.* and.
    Heb 2:4

Sihon
S. would not suffer Israel to pass.
    Num 21:23; *Judg* 11:20
let the city of *S.* be.   *Num* 21:27
gone out from the city of *S.*   28
do to him as thou didst to *S.*   34
    Deut 3:2, 6
S. king of Heshbon would. *Deut* 2:30
behold, I have begun to give *S.*   31
S. came out against us.   32; 29:7
    Judg 11:20
do to them as he did to *S. Deut* 31:4
all that he did to *S.*   *Josh* 9:10
God delivered *S.* into. *Judg* 11:21
possessed the land of *S. Neh* 9:22
shall come from the midst of *S.*
    Jer 48:45

Sihon *king of the Amorites*
Israel sent messengers unto *S.* king
   of the Amorites.   *Num* 21:21
    Deut 2:26; *Judg* 11:19
Hesbon was a city of *S. king of Amo-*
  rites.   *Num* 21:26; *Josh* 12:2
his daughters into captivity to *S.*
  king of Amorites.   *Num* 21:29
as thou didst to *S. king of Amorites.*
    34; *Deut* 3:2

slain *S. king of the Amorites* and.
    Deut 1:4; *Ps* 135:11; 136:19
cities of *S. king of Amorites.*
    Josh 13:10
kingdom of *S. king of Amorites.* 21
officer in country of *S. king of Amo-*
  rites.   *1 Ki* 4:19

Sihor
from *S.* which is before. *Josh* 13:3
to drink the waters of *S. Jer* 2:18

Silas
sent *S.* chief among the brethren.
    Acts 15:22, 27
it pleased *S.* to abide there.   34
Paul chose *S.*   40
caught Paul and *S.*   16:19
at midnight Paul and *S.* prayed.   25
fell down before Paul and *S.*   29
consorted with Paul and *S.*   17:4
sent away *S.* by night.   10
receiving a commandment to *S.*   15
when *S.* was come.   18:5

silence
This word signifies not only the or-
dinary silence, or refraining from
speaking; but also an entire ruin
or destruction, a total subjection,
Isa 15:1; Jer 8:14; *death and the*
grave, Ps 94:17; 115:17.
before me, there was *s.*   *Job* 4:16
men gave ear, and kept *s.* at. 29:21
lying lips be put to *s.*   *Ps* 31:18*
I was dumb with *s.*, I held.   39:2
my soul had almost dwelt in *s.* 94:17
any that go down into *s.*   115:17
to *s.*; Kir brought to *s.*   *Isa* 15:1*
God hath put us to *s.*   *Jer* 8:14
alone and keepeth *s.*   *Lam* 3:28
cast them forth with *s.*   *Amos* 8:3
had put Sadducees to *s. Mat* 22:34
was made a great *s.* he. *Acts* 21:40
in Hebrew, they kept more *s.* 22:2*
let woman learn in *s.*   *1 Tim* 2:11*
nor to usurp authority over the man,
   but to be in *s.*   12*
put to *s.* the ignorance. *1 Pet* 2:15
there was *s.* in heaven.   *Rev* 8:1
    see **keep, kept**

silent
the wicked shall be *s.*   *1 Sam* 2:9
night season, and am not *s. Ps* 22:2
s. to me, lest if thou be *s.*   28:1*
sing praise to thee, not be *s.* 30:12
wicked be *s.* in the grave.   31:17
sit thou *s.* and get thee. *Isa* 47:5
cities, let us be *s.* there. *Jer* 8:14
be *s.* O all flesh, before. *Zech* 2:13

silk
her clothing is *s.* and.   *Pr* 31:22
I covered thee with *s. Ezek* 16:10
thy raiment was of *s.* and.   13
their merchandise of *s. Rev* 18:12

silly
and envy slayeth the *s.*   *Job* 5:2
Ephraim also is like a *s. Hos* 7:11
captive *s.* women laden. *2 Tim* 3:6

Siloah, Siloam
the wall of pool of *S.*   *Neh* 3:15
wash in the pool of *S. John* 9:7, 11

Silvanus
among you by me and *S. 2 Cor* 1:19
Paul, *S.* and Timotheus to.
    1 Thes 1:1; *2 Thes* 1:1
by *S.* a faithful brother. *1 Pet* 5:12

silver
is worth 400 shekels of *s. Gen* 23:15
weighed 400 shekels of *s.*   16
make gods of *s.* or gold. *Ex* 20:23
sockets of *s.*   26:19, 21, 25, 32
    36:24, 26, 30, 36
hooks shall be of *s.*   27:17; 38:19
they did offer an offering of *s.* 35:24
s. of them that were numbered of.
    38:25
estimation by shekels of *s. Lev* 5:15
of male 50 shekels of *s.*   27:3
female three shekels of *s.*   6
barley seed at fifty shekels of *s.* 16
was one *s.* charger, one *s.* bowl of
   70 shekels.   *Num* 7:13, 19, 25
    31, 37, 43, 49, 55, 61, 67, 73, 79

chargers of *s.*, twelve *s.*   *Num* 7:84
each charger of *s.* weighing.   85
make thee two trumpets of *s.*   10:2
him in 100 shekels of *s. Deut* 22:19
damsel's father 50 shekels of *s.*   29
I saw 200 shekels of *s.*   *Josh* 7:21
and the *s.* under it.   22, 24
1100 shekels of *s.* that were taken
   from thee, behold, *s.*   *Judg* 17:2
when he had restored the *s.*   3
gave *s.* to the founder.   4
I will give thee ten shekels of *s.* 10
fourth part of a shekel of *s.*
    1 Sam 9:8
given 10 shekels of *s. 2 Sam* 18:11
receive 1000 shekels of *s.*   12
oxen for 50 shekels of *s.*   24:24
none were of *s.*   *1 Ki* 10:21
    2 Chr 9:20
s. to be in Jerusalem.   *1 Ki* 10:27
shalt pay a talent of *s.*   20:39
I pray thee, a talent of *s. 2 Ki* 5:22
each man fifty shekels of *s.*   15:20
Hezekiah gave him all the *s.* 18:15
that Hilkiah may sum the *s.* 22:4*
s. also for all instruments of *s.*
    1 Chr 28:14; 29:2, 5
for candlesticks of *s.*   28:15
for every bason of *s.*   17
brought Jehoshaphat presents of *s.*
    2 Chr 17:11
had taken 40 shekels of *s. Neh* 5:15
who filled houses with *s.*   *Job* 3:15
thou shalt have plenty of *s.*   22:25
though he heap up *s.* as the.   27:16
innocent shall divide the *s.*   17
shall *s.* be weighed for price. 28:15
words are pure, as *s.* tried. *Ps* 12:6
O God, hast tried us, as *s.*   66:10
if thou seekest her as *s.* and. *Pr* 2:4
wisdom is better than . . . of *s.* 3:14
receive instruction, and not *s.* 8:10
and my revenue than choice *s.* 19
of the just is as choice *s.*   10:20
chosen rather than *s.*   16:16
fining pot is for *s.*, and the.   17:3
away the dross from the *s.*   25:4
he that loveth *s.* shall not be satisfied
   with *s.*   *Eccl* 5:10
on her a palace of *s.*   *S of S* 8:9
thy *s.* is become dross.   *Isa* 1:22
covering of thy images of *s.*   30:22
refined thee, but not with *s.*   48:10
for iron I will bring *s.* and for. 60:17
reprobate *s.* shall men.   *Jer* 6:30
s. spread into plates is brought. 10:9
even seventeen shekels of *s.*   32:9
are even the dross of *s. Ezek* 22:18
as they gather *s.*, brass, and iron. 20
as *s.* is melted in the midst.   22
with *s.* Tarshish traded in.   27:12
breast and arms were of *s. Dan* 2:32
pleasant places for *s.*   *Hos* 9:6
molten images of their *s.*   13:2
sold the righteous for *s.*   *Amos* 2:6
that we may buy poor for *s.*   8:6
howl, all they that bear *s. Zeph* 1:11
Tyrus heaped up *s.* as dust. *Zech* 9:3
refine them as *s.* is refined.   13:9
as a refiner and purifier of *s. Mal* 3:3
    see **fillets, gold, pieces**

silver, *adjective*
put my *s.* cup in sack's mouth.
    Gen 44:2
covered with *s.* dross.   *Pr* 26:23
or ever *s.* cord be loosed or the
   golden bowl be broken. *Eccl* 12:6
the goldsmith casteth *s.*   *Isa* 40:19
chief priests took the *s. Mat* 27:6
Demetrius made *s.* shrines.
    Acts 19:24

talents of **silver**
for two *talents of s.*   *1 Ki* 16:24
with him ten *talents of s. 2 Ki* 5:5
and bound two *talents of s.*   23
gave Pul 1000 *talents of s.*   15:19
sent 1000 *talents of s.*   *1 Chr* 19:6
thousand thousand *talents of s.* 22:14
7000 *talents of* refined *s.*   29:4
mighty men for 100 *talents of s.*
    2 Chr 25:6
gave Jotham 100 *talents of s.*   27:5
land in 100 *talents of s.*   36:3

decree it be done to 100 *talents of s.*
Ezra 7:22
to their hand 650 *talents of s.* 8:26
ten thousand *talents of s. Esth 3*:9

vessels of silver

all the *s. vessels* weighed 2400
shekels. *Num 7*:85
with him *vessels of s. 2 Sam 8*:10
his present, *vessels of s. 1 Ki 10*:25
not made *vessels of s. 2 Ki 12*:13
all manner of *vessels of s.,* gold and
brass. *1 Chr 18*:10; *2 Chr 24*:14
hands with *vessels of s. Ezra 1*:6, 11
vessels of gold and *s.* of the. 5:14
let the golden and *s. vessels.* 6:5
I weighed *s. vessels.* 8:26
bring golden and *s. vessels. Dan 5*:2
precious *vessels of s.* and gold. 11:8
see **vessels**

silverlings

thousand vines at a thousand *s.*
Isa 7:23

silversmith

Demetrius a *s.* made. *Acts 19*:24

Simeon

called his name *S. Gen 29*:33
S. and Levi took each man. 34:25
S. son of Leah. 35:23
Joseph took from them *S.* 42:24
S. is not. 36
and he brought *S.* out unto. 43:23
the sons of *S.* 46:10; *Ex 6*:15
Num 1:22; 26:12; *1 Chr 4*:24, 42
12:25
Reuben and *S.* they shall. *Gen 48*:5
S. and Levi are brethren. 49:5
S. son of Israel. *Ex 1*:2
prince of *S.* was Shelumiel.
Num 1:6; 2:12; 7:36
S. Levi and Judah stand to bless.
Deut 27:12
lot came forth to *S. Josh 19*:1
S. had their inheritance within. 9
S. went with Judah. *Judg 1*:3
Judah with *S.* 17
the strangers out of *S. 2 Chr 15*:9
so did Josiah in the cities of *S.* 34:6
S. have a portion. *Ezek 48*:24
one gate of *S.* 33
whose name was *S. Luke 2*:25
S. blessed Joseph and Mary. 34
which was the son of *S.* 3:30
at Antioch, *S.* that was. *Acts 13*:1
S. hath declared how God. 15:14

tribe of Simeon

tribe of S. numbered. *Num 1*:23
the *tribe of S.* shall pitch. 2:12
over the host of the *tribe of S.* 10:19
of the *tribe of S.* Shaphat. 13:5
of *tribe of S.* Shemuel to. 34:20
second lot came out for the *tribe of
S. Josh 19*:1
inheritance of the *tribe of S.* 8
Levites had out of *tribe of S.* 21:4
9; *1 Chr 6*:65
of the *tribe of S.* were. *Rev 7*:7

similitude

the *s.* of the Lord shall. *Num 12*:8*
heard voice of words, but saw no *s.*
Deut 4:12* 15*
lest ye make the *s.* of any figure. 16*
under it was *s.* of oxen. *2 Chr 4*:3
glory into *s.* of an ox. *Ps 106*:20*
corner stones polished after *s.* 144:12
one like the *s.* of the. *Dan 10*:16
after the *s.* of Adam's. *Rom 5*:14*
after *s.* of Melchizedek ariseth.
Heb 7:15*
made after the *s.* of God. *Jas 3*:9*

similitudes

I have used *s.* by ministry of.
Hos 12:10

Simon

S. the Canaanite. *Mat 10*:4
Mark 3:18
his brethren James, Joses, and *S.*
Mat 13:55; *Mark 6*:3
blessed art thou, *S.* Bar-jona.
Mat 16:17
what thinkest thou, *S.* of ? 17:25

in the house of *S.* the leper. *Mat 26*:6
Mark 14:3
man of Cyrene, *S.* by. *Mat 27*:32
Mark 15:21; *Luke 23*:26
they entered into the house of *S.*
Mark 1:29; *Luke 4*:38
S. sleepest thou ? *Mark 14*:37
the ships, which was *S.'s. Luke 5*:3
he said unto *S.* Launch out into. 4
John who were partners with *S.* 10
S. called Zelotes. 6:15; *Acts 1*:13
S. I have somewhat to. *Luke 7*:40
S. S. Satan hath desired to. 22:31
and hath appeared to *S.* 24:34
his own brother *S. John 1*:41
Jesus said, Thou art *S.* the son. 42
Judas Iscariot the son of *S.* 6:71
12:4; 13:2, 26
S. son of Jonas, lovest thou me ?
21:15, 16, 17
a man, *S.* who before. *Acts 8*:9
then *S.* himself believed also. 13
Peter tarried many days at Joppa
with one *S.* 9:43; 10:6, 17, 32
see **Peter**

simple

[1] *Undesigning, straightforward,*
Rom 16:19. [2] *Ignorant, yet sincere*
and willing to be taught, Prov 9:4.
[3] *Silly, foolish, credulous, easily*
deceived with the smooth words and
fair pretences of false and deceitful
men, Pr 14:15; 22:3.

law . . . making wise the *s. Ps 19*:7
Lord preserveth the *s.*: I was. 116:6
understanding to the *s.* 119:130
give subtilty to *s.,* to young. *Pr 1*:4
how long, ye *s.* ones, will ye ? 22
the turning away of the *s.* shall. 32
among the *s.* ones a young. 7:7
O ye *s.* understand wisdom. 8:5
whoso is *s.* let him turn. 9:4, 16
a foolish woman is *s.* and. 13
s. believeth every word. 14:15
the *s.* inherit folly. 18
the *s.* will beware. 19:25
the scorner is punished, the *s.* 21:11
the *s.* pass on and are. 22:3; 27:12
do for him that is *s. Ezek 45*:20
deceive the hearts of *s. Rom 16*:18*
have you wise unto good, and *s.* 19

simplicity

they went in their *s. 2 Sam 15*:11
simple ones, will ye love *s.? Pr 1*:22
let him do it with *s. Rom 12*:8*
in *s.* we had our. *2 Cor 1*:12*
be corrupted from the *s.* that. 11:3

sin

Any thought, word, action, omis-
sion, or desire, contrary to the law
of God. Sin is taken both for the
guilt and punishment of sin, Ps
32:1; Mat 9:2.

doest not well, *s.* lieth. *Gen 4*:7
forgiving iniquity, transgression, and
s. Ex 34:7
if priest *s.* according to *s. Lev 4*:3
when *s.* is known, congregation. 14
offereth it for *s.* 6:26; 9:15
and not suffer *s.* upon thy. 19:17
the *s.* which he hath done shall. 22
or woman shall commit a *s. Num 5*:6
thee lay not the *s.* upon us. 12:11
it is a purification for *s.* 19:9, 17
our father died in his own *s.* 27:3
he cry unto the Lord . . . and it be *s.*
unto thee. *Deut 15*:9; 24:15
shall not rise up for any *s.* 19:15
committed *s.* worthy of death. 21:22
there is in damsel no *s.* 22:26
it, and it would be *s.* in thee. 23:21
to vow, it shall be no *s.* 22
be put to death for his own *s.* 24:16
2 Ki 14:6; *2 Chr 25*:4
for rebellion is as the *s. 1 Sam 15*:23
forgive *s.* of thy people. *1 Ki 8*:34
forgive the *s.* of thy servants. 36
2 Chr 6:25, 27
this thing became a *s.* 12:30; 13:34
the *s.* money was not. *2 Ki 12*:16
his bones are full of *s. Job 20*:11
blessed is he whose *s. Ps 32*:1

and in *s.* did my mother. *Ps 51*:5
s. of their mouth let them. 59:12
and let his prayer become *s.* 109:7
let not the *s.* of his mother. 14
the wicked tendeth to *s. Pr 10*:16
of words there wanteth not *s.* 19
fools make a mock at *s.* but. 14:9
s. is a reproach to any people. 34
plowing of the wicked is *s.* 21:4
thought of foolishness is *s.* 24:9
woe to them that draw *s. Isa 5*:18
that they may add *s.* to *s.* 30:1
your hands have made for *s.* 31:7
make his soul an offering for *s.* 53:10
he bare the *s.* of many, and. 12
s. of Judah written with. *Jer 17*:1
I will give thy high places for *s.* 3
their land was filled with *s.* 51:5
punishment of the *s.* of. *Lam 4*:6
eat up *s.* of my people. *Hos 4*:8
the *s.* of Israel shall be. 10:8
none iniquity in me that were *s.* 12:8
that swear by the *s.* of. *Amos 8*:14
she is the beginning of *s. Mi 1*:13
fruit of my body for *s.* of my. 6:7
a fountain opened for *s. Zech 13*:1
all manner of *s.* shall be. *Mat 12*:31
which taketh away the *s. John 1*:29
he that is without *s.* among. 8:7
committeth *s.* is the servant of *s.* 34
blind, he should have no *s.* 9:41
they had not had *s.* 15:22, 24
will reprove the world of *s.* 16:8
of *s.* because they believe not. 9
me unto thee hath greater *s.* 19:11
Lord, lay not this *s.* to. *Acts 7*:60
Gentiles are all under *s. Rom 3*:9
by the law is the knowledge of *s.* 20
blessed are they whose *s.* is. 4:7
the world, and death by *s.* 5:12
the law *s.* was in the world. 13
s. abounded, grace much more. 20
that as *s.* reigned unto death. 21
say ? shall we continue in *s.?* 6:1
how shall we that are dead to *s.?* 2
the body of *s.* might be destroyed
. . . we should not serve *s.* 6
that is dead is freed from *s.* 7
that he died, he died unto *s.* once. 10
to be dead indeed unto *s.* 11
let not *s.* therefore reign in your. 12
members as instruments to *s.* 13
for *s.* shall not have dominion. 14
servants ye are . . . whether of *s.* 16
ye were the servants of *s.* 17
being then made free from *s.* 18, 22
when ye were the servants of *s.* 20
for wages of *s.* is death, but the. 23
is the law *s.?* God forbid. Nay, I had
not known *s.* 7:7
s. taking occasion wrought in me . . .
for without the law *s.* was. 8
commandment came, *s.* revived. 9
for *s.* by the commandment. 11
s., that it might appear *s.,* that *s.* 13
but I am carnal, sold under *s.* 14
but *s.* that dwelleth in me. 17, 20
me into captivity to the law of *s.* 23
but with the flesh, the law of *s.* 25
and for *s.,* condemned *s.* in. 8:3
body is dead because of *s.* 10
is not of faith, is *s.* 14:23
every *s.* a man doth is. *1 Cor 6*:18
the sting of death is *s.* and the
strength of *s.* is the law. 15:56
made him to be *s.* for us, who knew
no *s.* *2 Cor 5*:21
Christ the minister of *s.? Gal 2*:17
hath concluded all under *s.* 3:22
man of *s.* be revealed. *2 Thes 2*:3
through the deceitfulness of *s.*
Heb 3:13
like as we are, yet without *s.* 4:15
he appeared to put away *s.* 9:26
he shall appear without *s.* unto. 28
in sacrifices for *s.* thou hast. 10:6
offering for *s.* thou wouldest not. 8
is no more offering for *s.* 18
than to enjoy pleasures of *s.* 11:25
let us lay aside the *s.* that doth. 12:1
not yet resisted, striving against *s.* 4
those beasts, for *s.* are burned. 13:11
lust conceived, it bringeth forth *s.*:
and *s.,* when finished. *Jas 1*:15

to persons, ye commit *s*. *Jas* 2:9
doeth not good, to him it is *s*. 4:17
did no *s*. neither was. *1 Pet* 2:22
flesh hath ceased from *s*. 4:1
cannot cease from *s*. *2 Pet* 2:14
the blood of Jesus Christ cleanseth us
　from all *s*. *1 John* 1:7
if we say we have no *s*. we. 8
committteth *s*. transgresseth also the
　law, for *s*. is the. 3:4
and in him is no *s*. 5
committeth *s*. is of the devil. 8
born of God doth not commit *s*. 9
his brother. a *s*. which is not to
　death. There is a *s*. unto. 5:16
all unrighteousness is *s*. and there is
　a *s*. not unto death. 17

see bear, offering

sin, *verb*

how can I do this great wickedness
　and *s*. against God? *Gen* 39:9
Reuben said, Do not *s*. 42:22
before you, that ye *s*. not. *Ex* 20:20
make thee *s*. against me. 23:33
s. through ignorance against com-
　mandments. *Lev* 4:2
if the priest *s*. 3
if congregation *s*. 13
if any one of the common people *s*. 27
if a soul *s*. and hear the voice. 5:1
if a soul commit a trespass and *s*.
　 15, 17; *Num* 15:27
if a soul *s*. and lie unto. *Lev* 6:2
shall one man *s*. and wilt thou be?
　 Num 16:22
so should you *s*. against Lord.
　 Deut 20:18
shalt not cause the land to *s*. 24:4
s. against another; if a man *s*. against
　the Lord, who shall? *1 Sam* 2:25
God forbid I should *s*. in. 12:23
behold, the people *s*. against. 14:33
slay them, and *s*. not in eating. 34
let not the king *s*. against. 19:4
wherefore wilt thou *s*. against? 5
if they *s*. against thee. *1 Ki* 8:46
　 2 Chr 6:36
made Judah to *s*. with idols.
　 2 Ki 21:11
if a man *s*. against his. *2 Chr* 6:22
afraid, and do so, and *s*. *Neh* 6:13
did not Solomon *s*. by these? 13:26
in all this did not Job *s*. *Job* 2:10
thy habitation and not *s*. 5:24
if I *s*., then thou markest me. 10:14
I suffered my mouth to *s*. 31:30
stand in awe, and *s*. not. *Ps* 4:4
I will take heed, that I *s*. not. 39:1
I might not *s*. against thee. 119:11
not thy mouth to cause thy flesh to *s*.
　 Eccl 5:6
to cause Judah to *s*. *Jer* 32:35
righteous *s*. not, and he doth not *s*.
　 Ezek 3:21
made many altars to *s*., altars shall
　be unto him to *s*. *Hos* 8:11
and now they *s*. more and. 13:2
oft shall my brother *s*.? *Mat* 18:21
s. no more, lest a worse. *John* 5:14
do I condemn thee, *s*. no. 8:11
who did *s*., this man, or his? 9:2
shall we *s*. because we are not?
　 Rom 6:15
s. so against the brethren and wound
　their conscience, ye *s*. *1 Cor* 8:12
righteousness, and *s*. not. 15:34
be ye angry, and *s*. not. *Eph* 4:26
them that *s*. rebuke. *1 Tim* 5:20
if we *s*. wilfully after. *Heb* 10:26
that ye *s*. not, and if any man *s*. we.
　 1 John 2:1
cannot *s*. because he is born of. 3:9
if . . . *s*. not unto death, he shall
　give him life for them that *s*. 5:16

see Israel

great sin

and my kingdom *great s*. *Gen* 20:9
brought this *great s*. on them.
　 Ex 32:21
said, Ye have sinned a *great s*. 30
this people have sinned a *great s*. 31
s. of the young men was very *great*.
　 1 Sam 2:17

Jeroboam made them sin a *great s*.
　 2 Ki 17:21

his sin

bring for *his s*. he sinned. *Lev* 4:3
or if *his s*. come to his knowledge.
　 23, 28
atonement for *his s*. and it shall be
　forgiven. 4:26, 35; 5:6, 10, 13
a kid of the goats for *his s*. 28
his trespass offering for *his s*. 5:6
Nadab walked in the way of *his s*.
　 1 Ki 15:26
in the way of Jeroboam and *his s*. 34
Zimri in *his s*. which he did. 16:19
Omri walked in *his s*. 26
beside *his s*. wherewith. *2 Ki* 21:16
acts of Manasseh, and *his s*. 17
all *his s*. before he was humbled.
　 2 Chr 33:19
addeth rebellion to *his s*. *Job* 34:37
fruit to take away *his s*. *Isa* 27:9
he shall die in *his s*. *Ezek* 3:20
　 18:24
if he turn from *his s*. and. 33:14
bound up; *his s*. is hid. *Hos* 13:12
to declare to Israel *his s*. *Mi* 3:8

my sin

what is *my s*. that thou hast?
　 Gen 31:36
therefore forgive *my s*. *Ex* 10:17
I pray thee, pardon *my s*., and turn
　again. *1 Sam* 15:25
what is *my s*. before thy father?
　 20:1
come to call *my s*. to? *1 Ki* 17:18
thou searchest after *my s*. *Job* 10:6
know transgression and *my s*. 13:23
thou not watch over *my s*.? 14:16
if I be cleansed from *my s*.? 35:3
my s. and iniquity to thee, and thou
　. . . iniquity of *my s*. *Ps* 32:5
in my bones because of *my s*. 38:3
for I will be sorry for *my s*. 18
cleanse me from *my s*. 51:2
my s. is ever before me. 3
not for *my s*. O Lord. 59:3
I am pure from *my s*.? *Pr* 20:9
I was confessing *my s*. *Dan* 9:20

see offering

our sin

our iniquity and *our s*. *Ex* 34:9
what is *our s*. we have? *Jer* 16:10

their sin

Lord said, Because *their s*. is very.
　 Gen 18:20
forgive, I pray thee, *their s*. 50:17
　 2 Chr 7:14
if thou wilt forgive *their s*. *Ex* 32:32
when I visit, I will visit *their s*. 34
they shall confess *their s*. *Num* 5:7
look not unto the stubbornness, nor
　to *their s*. *Deut* 9:27
if they turn from *their s*. *1 Ki* 8:35
　 2 Chr 6:26
let not *their s*. be blotted. *Neh* 4:5
hast covered all *their s*. 85:2
declare *their s*. as Sodom. *Isa* 3:9
I will recompense *their s*. double.
　 Jer 16:18
neither blot out *their s*. from. 18:23
and I will remember *their s*. 31:34
may forgive their iniquity and *their s*.
　 36:3
no cloke for *their s*. *John* 15:22

thy sin

hath put away *thy s*. *2 Sam* 12:13
is taken away, *thy s*. is purged.
　 Isa 6:7

your sin

atonement for *your s*. *Ex* 32:30
be sure *your s*. will find you out.
　 Num 32:23
I took *your s*., the calf which ye.
　 Deut 9:21
ye say, We see; therefore *your s*.
　remaineth. *John* 9:41

see Israel

Sin

into the wilderness of *S*. *Ex* 16:1
Israel journeyed from *S*. 17:1
　 Num 33:12

pour my fury upon *S*. *Ezek* 30:15
S. shall have great pain, No shall. 16

Sinai

Lord came from *S*. unto. *Deut* 33:2
melted, even that *S*. *Judg* 5:5
S. was moved at the. *Ps* 68:8
the Lord is among them as in *S*. 17

see mount

since

the Lord hath blessed thee *s*. my
　coming. *Gen* 30:30
and I saw him not *s*. 44:28
let me die, *s*. I have seen. 46:30
s. I came to Pharaoh. *Ex* 5:23
hail, such as not in Egypt *s*. the. 9:18
Egypt, *s*. it became a nation. 24
ridden ever *s*. I was thine.
　 Num 22:30
arose not a prophet *s*. *Deut* 34:10
swear, *s*. I have shewed. *Josh* 2:12
Lord kept me alive, even *s*. 14:10
all that thou hast done . . . *s*. death
　of thy husband. *Ruth* 2:11
s. I said, I have invited. *1 Sam* 9:24
three days *s*. I came out. 21:5
I found no fault in him *s*. he. 29:3
s. the time that I brought. *2 Sam* 7:6
and *s*. I commanded judges. 11
　 1 Chr 17:10
s. the time of Solomon. *2 Chr* 30:26
s. the people began to bring. 31:10
s. the days of Esar-haddon king.
　 Ezra 4:2
s. that time till now hath it. 5:16
s. days of our fathers have we. 9:7
s. man was placed upon. *Job* 20:4
commanded morning *s*. thy days?
　 38:12
s. thou art laid down. *Isa* 14:8
concerning Moab *s*. that time. 16:13
s. thou wast precious in my. 43:4
s. I appointed the ancient. 44:7
s. the beginning men have not. 64:4
s. they return not from. *Jer* 15:7
for *s*. I spake, I cried out, I. 20:8
but *s*. ye say, the burden of. 23:38
s. I spake against him, I. 31:20
s. we left off to burn incense. 44:18
s. thou speakest of him. 48:27
as never was *s*. there. *Dan* 12:1
s. those days were when one came.
　 Hag 2:16
not *s*. the beginning. *Mat* 24:21
long is it ago *s*. this came to him?
　 Mark 9:21
been *s*. the world began. *Luke* 1:70
　 John 9:32
s. the time I came in, she hath not.
　 Luke 7:45
s. that time kingdom of God. 16:16
is the third day *s*. these things. 24:21
s. the world began. *Acts* 3:21
　 Rom 16:25
received the Holy Ghost *s*. ye be-
　lieved? *Acts* 19:2
yet but twelve days *s*. I went. 24:11
for *s*. by man came death, by man.
　 1 Cor 15:21
s. ye seek a proof of Christ in me.
　 2 Cor 13:3
s. we heard of your faith. *Col* 1:4
word of oath which was *s*. the law.
　 Heb 7:28
for *s*. the fathers fell asleep, all.
　 2 Pet 3:4
as was not *s*. men were. *Rev* 16:18

see day

sincere

The Latin word, sincerus, *is derived from* sine *and* cera, *without
wax, honey separated from the
wax, or pure honey. In the scripture* sincere *signifies pure, or without mixture,* Phil 1:10; 1 Pet 2:1.
*Sincerity is opposed to double-
mindedness or deceit, when the
sentiments of the heart are contrary
to the language of the mouth,* 1 Cor
5:8.

ye may be *s*. till day. *Phil* 1:10
as babes, desire *s*. milk. *1 Pet* 2:2

sincerely
now if ye have done truly and s.
Judg 9:16*, 19*
one preach Christ, not s. Phil 1:16*

sincerity
serve the Lord in s. and. Josh 24:14
unleavened bread of s. 1 Cor 5:8
in godly s. we have had. 2 Cor 1:12
but as of s. in the sight of God. 2:17
to prove s. of your love. 8:8
them that love our Lord Jesus in s.
Eph 6:24
doctrine shewing gravity, s. Tit 2:7

sinew
Israel eat not of the s. that shrank
... Jacob in the s. Gen 32:32*
thy neck is an iron s. Isa 48:4

sinews
hast fenced me with bones and s.
Job 10:11
pierced, and my s. take no. 30:17*
the s. of his stones are. 40:17
I will lay s. upon you. Ezek 37:6
the s. and the flesh came up. 8

sinful
an increase of s. men. Num 32:14
ah s. nation, a people. Isa 1:4
eyes of the Lord are on the s. kingdom. Amos 9:8
be ashamed in this s. generation.
Mark 8:38
for I am a s. man, O Lord. Luke 5:8
into the hands of s. men. 24:7
that sin might become exceeding s.
Rom 7:13
Son in the likeness of s. flesh. 8:3

sing
s. to the Lord. Ex 15:21
1 Chr 16:23; Ps 30:4; 95:1; 96:1
2; 98:1; 147:7; 149:1; Isa 12:5
noise of them that s. Ex 32:18
spring up, O well, s. ye. Num 21:17
did they not s. one ? 1 Sam 21:11
unto him, s. psalms. 1 Chr 16:9
trees of the wood s. out. 33
when they began to s. 2 Chr 20:22
commanded the Levites to s. 29:30
widow's heart to s. for. Job 29:13
so will we s. and praise. Ps 21:13
praise the Lord, s. unto him. 33:2
s. unto him a new song. 3; Isa 42:10
my tongue s. of thy righteousness.
Ps 51:14; 145:7
shout for joy, they also s. 65:13
s. forth the honour of his name. 66:2
the earth s. to thee, they shall s. 4
nations be glad and s. for. 67:4
s. to God, ye kingdoms of. 68:32
to thee will I s. with the harp. 71:22
98:5
s. aloud unto God our strength. 81:1
the fowls which s. among the. 104:12
s. unto him, s. psalms unto. 105:2
saying, S. us one of the songs. 137:3
how shall we s. Lord's song in a ? 4
yea, they shall s. in the ways. 138:5
let the saints s. aloud upon. 149:5
but the righteous doth s. Pr 29:6
seventy years shall Tyre s. Isa 23:15
they shall s. for the majesty. 24:14
awake and s. ye that dwell. 26:19
in that day s. ye unto her. 27:2
the tongue of the dumb s. 35:6
therefore we will s. my songs. 38:20
inhabitants of the rock s. 42:11
s. for Lord hath done it. 44:23
49:13
voice together shall they s. 52:8
s. to the Lord, ye waste places. 9
s. O barren, thou that didst. 54:1
my servants shall s. for joy. 65:14
s. with gladness for Jacob. Jer 31:7
they shall come and s. in the. 12
all that is therein shall s. 51:48
ships of Tarshish did s. Ezek 27:25
shall s. as in the days. Hos 2:15
their voice shall s. in. Zeph 2:14
s. O daughter. 3:14; Zech 2:10
merry ? let him s. psalms. Jas 5:13
they s. the song of Moses. Rev 15:3

I will sing
I will s. to the Lord. Ex 15:1
Judg 5:3; Ps 13:6
my heart is fixed, I will s. Ps 57:7
I will s. unto thee among the. 9
I will s. of thy power, of. 59:16; 89:1
O my strength, will I s. for God. 17
I will s. of mercy and judgement.
101:1
I will s. unto the Lord as. 104:33
I will s. a new song unto. 144:9
will I s. to my wellbeloved a song.
Isa 5:1
for this cause will I s. Rom 15:9
I will s. with the spirit, and I will s.
with understanding. 1 Cor 14:15
see praise, praises

singed
nor an hair of their head s. Dan 3:27

singer
Heman a s. the son. 1 Chr 6:33
to chief s. on my stringed instruments. Hab 3:19*

singers
king made psalteries for s.
1 Ki 10:12; 2 Chr 9:11
these are the s., chief of the Levites.
1 Chr 9:33; 15:16
s. were appointed to sound. 15:19
and the s. had fine linen. 27
the trumpeters and s. 2 Chr 5:13
Jehoshaphat appointed s. unto. 20:21
rejoiced and also the s. 23:13; 29:28
the s. the sons of Asaph. 35:15
the s. an hundred twenty. Ezra 2:41
s. dwelt in their. 70; Neh 7:73
some of the s. went up. Ezra 7:7
not lawful to impose toll upon s. 24
the s. gave their hands to. 10:24
the porters and the s. Neh 7:1
the s. clave to their brethren. 10:29
the s. were over the business. 11:22
a portion shall be for the s. 23
12:47; 13:5
sons of s. gathered themselves. 12:28
s. had builded them villages. 29
s. sang aloud. 42
s. kept ward of their God. 45
David, there were chief of s. 46
for the Levites and the s. 13:10
s. went before, players. Ps 68:25
as well the s. as the players. 87:7
the chambers of the s. Ezek 40:44

men singers, women singers
I gat me men s. and women s.
Eccl 2:8

singeth
so is he that s. songs to. Pr 25:20

singing
women came out of cities of Israel s.
1 Sam 18:6
they ministered with s. 1 Chr 6:32*
played before God with s. 13:8*
burnt offerings with s. 2 Chr 23:18
s. with loud instruments unto. 30:21
dedication of the wall with s.
Neh 12:27
his presence with s. Ps 100:2
our tongue filled with s. 126:2
time of the s. of birds. S of S 2:12
break forth into s. Isa 14:7
there shall be no s. 16:10
rejoice even with joy and s. 35:2
break forth into s. ye. 44:23
Chaldeans with a voice of s. 48:20
earth, and break forth into s. 49:13
shall come with s. to Zion. 51:11
break forth into s. O barren. 54:1
shall break forth into s. 55:12
will joy over thee with s. Zeph 3:17
s. in your heart to the Lord.
Eph 5:19; Col 3:16

singing men, singing women
can I hear any more the voice of s.
men, s. women ? 2 Sam 19:35
all the s. men spake. 2 Chr 35:25
s. men, 200 s. women. Ezra 2:65
245 s. men and s. women. Neh 7:67

single
thine eye be s. thy whole body shall.
Mat 6:22; Luke 11:34

singleness
with gladness and s. of heart.
Acts 2:46
servants, be obedient, in s. of your
heart. Eph 6:5; Col 3:22

singular
shall make a s. vow. Lev 27:2*

sink
I s. in deep mire where. Ps 69:2
out of the mire, and let me not s. 14
thus shall Babylon s. and. Jer 51:64
beginning to s. he cried. Mat 14:30
so that they began to s. Luke 5:7
let these sayings s. down. 9:44

sinned
Pharaoh s. yet more. Ex 9:34
Ye have s. a great sin. 32:30, 31
whosoever hath s. against me, him
will I blot out of my book. 33
bring for the sin he hath s. Lev 4:3
sin the congregation have s. 14
when a ruler hath s. 22, 23
one of common people s. 28
he shall confess he hath s. 5:5
for sin which he hath s. shall. 6
atonement for the sin he hath s. and.
10, 11, 13; Num 6:11
he hath s., he shall restore. Lev 6:4
lay not sin on us wherein we have s.
Num 12:11
ye have s. against the Lord. 32:23
and, behold, ye had s. against the
Lord. Deut 9:16
your sins which ye s. in doing. 18
Israel hath s. and transgressed.
Josh 7:11
wherefore I have not s. Judg 11:27
because he hath not s. 1 Sam 19:4
know that I have not s. 24:11
they have s. against thee, and shall.
1 Ki 8:33, 35; 2 Chr 6:24, 26
forgive thy people that s. 1 Ki 8:50
2 Chr 6:39
sins of Jeroboam which he s.
1 Ki 15:30; 16:13, 19
What have I s. that thou ? 18:9
Israel had s. against. 2 Ki 17:7
sin that Manasseh had s. 21:17
s. against thy judgements. Neh 9:29
may be that my sons have s. Job 1:5
in all this Job s. not, nor charged. 22
if children have s. against him. 8:4
the grave those which have s. 24:19
they s. yet more. Ps 78:17, 32
thy first father hath s. Isa 43:27
sayest, I have not s. Jer 2:35
they have s. against me. 33:8
because ye have s. and not obeyed.
40:3; 44:23
because they have s. against the.
50:7; Zeph 1:17
Babylon hath s. against. Jer 50:14
Jerusalem hath grievously s.
Lam 1:8
our fathers have s. and are not. 5:7
in sin that he hath s., in. Ezek 18:24
with violence, and thou hast s. 28:16
places wherein they s. 37:23
they increased so they s. Hos 4:7
O Israel, thou hast s. from. 10:9
hast s. against thy soul. Hab 2:10
neither this man s. nor. John 9:3
for as many as have s. without law;
as have s. in the law. Rom 2:12
for all have s. and come short.
3:23; 5:12
over them that had not s. 5:14
not as it was by one that s. so. 16
marry, thou hast not s. and if a virgin ... hath not s. 1 Cor 7:28
bewail many that have s. 2 Cor 12:21
which heretofore have s. 13:2
with them that had s. ? Heb 3:17
spared not the angels that s. 2 Pet 2:4
if we say we have not s. 1 John 1:10

I have sinned
Pharaoh said, I have s. this time.
Ex 9:27; 10:16
Balaam said to angel of Lord, I have
s. Num 22:34
indeed I have s. against the Lord
God. Josh 7:20

Saul said, *I have s.*   *1 Sam* 15:24
               30; 26:21
to Nathan, *I have s.*   *2 Sam* 12:13
      24:10, 17; *1 Chr* 21:8, 17
doth know that *I have s.* 2 *Sam* 19:20
I have s.; what shall I do ? *Job* 7:20
if any say, *I have s.*   33:27
heal my soul; for *I have s.* Ps 41:4
against thee, thee only *have I s.* 51:4
I have s. against him.   *Mi* 7:9
I have s. in betraying.   *Mat* 27:4
Father, *I have s.* against heaven, and
   before thee.   *Luke* 15:18, 21
          we have sinned
not sin on us, wherein *we have s.*
                Num 12:11
we will go up, for *we have s.* 14:40
                Deut 1:41
we have s., we have spoken.
                Num 21:7
we have s. because we have.
   Judg 10:10; *1 Sam* 12:10
we have s.: do to us.   *Judg* 10:15
that day, and said, *We have s.*
                1 Sam 7:6
we have s. and have done perversely.   *1 Ki* 8:47
saying, *We have s.*   *2 Chr* 6:37
the sins which *we have s.*   *Neh* 1:6
we have s. with our fathers. *Ps* 106:6
against whom *we have s.* *Isa* 42:24
art wroth, for *we have s.*   64:5
in our shame, for *we have s.* *Jer* 3:25
us water of gall, for *we have s.* 8:14
backslidings are many, *we have s.*
                   14:7
our wickedness, for *we have s.*   20
woe to us that *we have s.* *Lam* 5:16
we have s. and have committed.
                 Dan 9:5
confusion, because *we have s.*   8
poured on us, because *we have s.* 11
O Lord, *we have s.* we have.   15

            sinner
the wicked and the *s.*   *Pr* 11:31
overthroweth the *s.*   13:6
the wealth of the *s.* is laid up.   22
to the *s.* he giveth travail. *Eccl* 2:26
but the *s.* shall be taken by her. 7:26
though *s.* do evil an hundred. 8:12
as is the good, so is the *s.* and. 9:2
but one *s.* destroyeth much good. 18
s. being 100 years old. *Isa* 65:20
in the city who was a *s.* *Luke* 7:37
what woman this is: for she is a *s.* 39
joy in heaven over one *s.*   15:7, 10
God be merciful to me a *s.*   18:13
guest with a man that is a *s.*   19:7
how can a man a *s.* do ? *John* 9:16
we know this man is a *s.*   24
whether he be a *s.* I know not.   25
am I also judged as a *s.*? *Rom* 3:7
he that converteth a *s.* *Jas* 5:20
shall the ungodly and *s.* appear ?
                 1 Pet 4:18

           sinners
the men of Sodom were *s.* *Gen* 13:13
the censers of these *s.* *Num* 16:38
utterly destroy the *s.*   *1 Sam* 15:18
standeth not in the way of *s.* Ps 1:1
nor *s.* in the congregation of sinners
therefore will he teach *s.* in.   25:8
gather not my soul with *s.* nor. 26:9
and *s.* shall be converted.   51:13
let the *s.* be consumed out. 104:35
if *s.* entice thee, consent not. *Pr* 1:10
evil pursueth *s.* but to the.   13:21
let not thine heart envy *s.*   23:17
the destruction of the *s.* *Isa* 1:28
he shall destroy the *s.* thereof. 13:9
the *s.* in Zion are afraid.   33:14
s. of my people shall die. *Amos* 9:10
many *s.* sat at meat with Jesus.
          Mat 9:10; *Mark* 2:15
why eateth your master with publicans and *s.?* *Mat* 9:11; *Mark* 2:16
         Luke 5:30; 15:2
to call the righteous, but *s.* to.
   Mat 9:13; *Mark* 2:17; *Luke* 5:32
a friend of publicans and *s.*
      Mat 11:19; *Luke* 7:34
Son of man is betrayed into the hands
   of *s.*   *Mat* 26:45; *Mark* 14:41

for *s.* also love those.   *Luke* 6:32
what thank have ye ? for *s.* also. 33
for *s.* also lend to *s.* to receive.   34
these were *s.* above all.   13:2, 4*
the publicans and *s.* for to.   15:1
that God heareth not *s.* *John* 9:31
while we were yet *s.*, Christ. *Rom* 5:8
disobedience many were made *s.* 19
we Jews by nature, not *s.* *Gal* 2:15
we ourselves also are found *s.*   17
the law is made for *s.*   *1 Tim* 1:9
that Christ Jesus came to save *s.* 15
holy, separate from *s.*   *Heb* 7:26
endured such contradiction of *s.* 12:3
cleanse your hands, ye *s.*, purify.
                 Jas 4:8
speeches which ungodly *s.* *Jude* 15

           sinnest
if thou *s.* what doest ?   *Job* 35:6

           sinneth
make atonement for soul that *s.*
              Num 15:28*
have one law for him that *s.*   29*
not rise, in any sin he *s.* *Deut* 19:15
if they sin against thee, for there is no
   man that *s.* not.   *1 Ki* 8:46
      2 Chr 6:36; *Eccl* 7:20
he that *s.* against me.   *Pr* 8:36
despiseth his neighbour *s.*   14:21
he that hasteth with his feet *s.* 19:2
whoso provoketh a king, *s.*   20:2
when the land *s.* then. *Ezek* 14:13
the soul that *s.* it shall die. 18:4, 20
righteousness in the day he *s.* 33:12
but fornicator *s.* against. *1 Cor* 6:18
let him do what he will, he *s.* not. 7:36
he is subverted, and *s.*   *Tit* 3:11
whosoever abideth in him *s.* not,
   whosoever *s.* hath.   *1 John* 3:6
is of the devil, for devil *s.* from.   8
whosoever is born of God *s.* not. 5:18

           sinning
I withheld thee from *s.*   *Gen* 20:6
that a man doth, *s.* therein. *Lev* 6:3

            sins
He shall give Israel up, because of *s.*
   of Jeroboam.   *1 Ki* 14:16
Abijam walked in the *s.* of.   15:3
smote Nadab because of the *s.* 16:13
s. of Baasha, and the *s.* of.   16:13
for his *s.* which Zimri sinned.   19
a light thing to walk in the *s.*   31
Jehoram cleaved to the *s.* 2 *Ki* 3:3
from the *s.* of Jeroboam Jehu. 10:29
not from the *s.* of Jeroboam. 13:6, 11
departed not from the *s.*   14:24
departed from *s.*   15:9, 18, 24, 28
Israel walked in all the *s.*   17:22
Judah for the *s.* of Manasseh. 24:3
not even with you *s.?* *2 Chr* 28:10
and confess the *s.* of the children.
                 Neh 1:6
mine iniquities and *s.?* *Job* 13:23
from presumptuous *s.*   *Ps* 19:13
remember not the *s.* of my.   25:7
holden with cords of his *s.* *Pr* 5:22
up strifes, love covereth all *s.* 10:12
he that covereth his *s.* shall. 28:13
double for all her *s.*   *Isa* 40:2
made me to serve with thy *s.* 43:24
I will not remember thy *s.*   25
blotted out as a cloud thy *s.* 44:22
I give to spoil for all thy *s.* *Jer* 15:13
thy *s.* were increased.   30:14, 15
the *s.* of Judah sought for.   50:20
the punishment of his *s.* *Lam* 3:39
for the *s.* of her prophets and. 4:13
Edom, he will discover thy *s.*   22
neither hath Samaria committed half
   thy *s.*   *Ezek* 16:51
thine own shame for thy *s.*   52
beget son that seeth all his father's *s.*
                 18:14
will turn from all his *s.*   21
and he shall bear the *s.* of. 23:49
none of his *s.* that he hath. 33:16
break off thy *s.* by.   *Dan* 4:27
determined to make an end of *s.* 9:24
the *s.* of the house of Israel. *Mi* 1:5
desolate because of thy *s.*   6:13
for the remission of *s.* *Mat* 26:28
of repentance for the remission of *s.*
         Mark 1:4; *Luke* 3:3

that remission of *s.* should be.
                Luke 24:47
Thou wast altogether born in *s.*
                 John 9:34
s. ye remit, whose soever *s.* ye. 20:23
baptized for remission of *s.* *Acts* 2:38
repentance and remission of *s.* 5:31
shall receive remission of *s.*   10:43
wash away thy *s.* calling on. 22:16
for the remission of *s.*   *Rom* 3:25
the motions of *s.* did work in.   7:5
who were dead in *s.*   *Eph* 2:1, 5
in putting off the body of *s.* *Col* 2:11
of other men's *s.*   *1 Tim* 5:22
some men's *s.* open beforehand. 24
silly women laden with *s.* 2 *Tim* 3:6
make reconciliation for *s.* *Heb* 2:17
offer gifts and sacrifices for *s.*   5:1
also for himself, to offer for *s.*   3
first for his own *s.* then for.   7:27
offered to bear *s.* of many.   9:28
no more conscience of *s.*   10:2
a remembrance again made of *s.*   3
blood of bulls not take away *s.*   4
can never take away *s.*   11
one sacrifice for *s.* for ever.   12
no more sacrifice for *s.*   26
shall hide multitude of *s.* *Jas* 5:20
we being dead to *s.*   *1 Pet* 2:24
hath once suffered for *s.*   3:18
cover the multitude of *s.*   4:8
purged from his old *s.* 2 *Pet* 1:9
but also for *s.* of the whole world.
               1 John 2:2
be not partakers of her *s.* *Rev* 18:4
s. have reached unto heaven.   5
   see **forgive, forgiven**
        my **sins**
hide thy face from *my s.*   *Ps* 51:9
O God, *my s.* are not hid.   69:5
thou hast cast *my s.*   *Isa* 38:17
       our **sins**
for we have added to all *our s.* this.
               1 Sam 12:19
add more to *our s.*   *2 Chr* 28:13
kings set over us because of *our s.*
                 Neh 9:37
purge away *our s.* for thy name's.
                 Ps 79:9
our secret *s.* in the light of.   90:8
with us according to *our s.*   103:10
our s. testify against us. *Isa* 59:12
if *our s.* be upon us. *Ezek* 33:10
because of *our s.* thy people are.
                 Dan 9:16
Christ died for *our s.*   *1 Cor* 15:3
who gave himself for *our s.* *Gal* 1:4
when he had by himself purged *our s.*
                 Heb 1:3
who his own self bare *our s.* in his.
               1 Pet 2:24
confess *our s.* he is faithful and just
   to forgive us *our s.*   *1 John* 1:9
propitiation for *our s.*   2:2; 4:10
manifested to take away *our s.*   3:5
washed us from *our s.*   *Rev* 1:5
       their **sins**
transgressions in *their s.* *Lev* 16:16
over the live goat all *their s.*   21
to make atonement for *their s.*   34
consumed in all *their s.* *Num* 16:26
they provoked him with *their s.*
               1 Ki 14:22
me to anger with *their s.*   16:2
and confessed *their s.*   *Neh* 9:2
house of Jacob *their s.* *Isa* 58:1
and visit *their s.*   *Jer* 14:10
            Hos 8:13; 9:9
cast all *their s.* into the.   *Mi* 7:19
his people from *their s.* *Mat* 1:21
were baptized, confessing *their s.*
             3:6; *Mark* 1:5
and *their s.* should be. *Mark* 4:12
the remission of *their s.* *Luke* 1:77
shall take away *their s.* *Rom* 11:27
to fill up *their s.*   *1 Thes* 2:16
will be merciful to *their s.* *Heb* 8:12
their s. and iniquities I will. 10:17
       your **sins**
clean from all *your s.* *Lev* 16:30
seven times for *your s.* 26:18, 24, 28
plagues on you according to *your s.*
                 21

water, because of *your s. Deut* 9:18
will not forgive *your s. Josh* 24:19
though *your s.* be as scarlet, they shall
be as white as snow. *Isa* 1:18
and *your s.* have hid his face. 59:2
your s. have withholden. *Jer* 5:25
in all your doings *your s.* appear.
Ezek 21:24
know *your* transgressions and mighty
s. Amos 5:12
and die in *your s. John* 8:21, 24
repent, that *your s.* may. *Acts* 3:19
not raised, ye are yet in *your s.*
1 Cor 15:17
you being dead in *your s. Col* 2:13
your s. are forgiven. *1 John* 2:12

sir

s. we came at first time. *Gen* 43:20*
s. didst thou not sow ? *Mat* 13:27
said, I go *s.* and went not. 21:30
s. we remember that that. 27:63
s. thou hast nothing to. *John* 4:11
s. give me this water that I. 15
s. I perceive that thou art a. 19
the nobleman saith, *S.* come ere. 49
s. I have no man to put me. 5:7
certain Greeks saying, *S.* we. 12:21
s. if thou have borne him. 20:15
I said unto him, *S.* thou. *Rev* 7:14*

Sirion

the Sidonians call *S. Deut* 3:9
Lebanon and *S.* like a. *Ps* 29:6

sirs

s. ye are brethren, why ? *Acts* 7:26
crying out, *S.* why do ye ? 14:15
he said, *S.* what must I do ? 16:30
s. ye know that by this craft. 19:25
s. I perceive this voyage will. 27:10
Paul said, *S.* ye should have. 21
wherefore, *s.* be of good cheer. 25

Sisera

of Jabin's host was *S. Judg* 4:2
S. fled away on his feet. 17
S. lay dead. 22
the stars fought against *S.* 5:20
with the hammer she smote *S.* 26
the mother of *S.* looked out. 28
into the hand of *S. 1 Sam* 12:9
children of *S.* went up. *Ezra* 2:53
Neh 7:55
do unto them, as to *S. Ps* 83:9

sister

*This name has much the same
latitude as that of brother. As
Christian men were used to salute
one another by the name of brothers
or brethren, so they called Christian
women, who professed the same
faith in Christ, by the name of
sisters, Jas 2:15, 16.*
Rebekah their *s. Gen* 24:59
thou art our *s.,* be thou mother. 60
heard of Jacob his *s.'s* son. 29:13
Rachel envied her *s.* and said. 30:1
defiled Dinah their *s.* 34:13
we cannot give our *s.* to one. 14
should he deal with our *s.* 31
his *s.* stood afar off to wit. *Ex* 2:4
Jochebed his father's *s.* to wife. 6:20
Miriam *s.* of Aaron took a. 15:20
not uncover the nakedness of thy *s.*
Lev 18:9
she is thy *s.* 11
not nakedness of father's *s.* 13
mother's *s.* 13
not take a wife to her *s.* 18
if a man take his *s.* and see. 20:17
of thy father's *s.,* mother's *s.* 19
for his *s.* a virgin; for her he. 21:3
not be defiled for his *s. Num* 6:7
he that lieth with his *s. Deut* 27:22
younger *s.* fairer than she ? *Judg* 15:2
Absalom had a fair *s. 2 Sam* 13:1
he fell sick for his *s.* Tamar. 2
I love my brother Absalom's *s.* 4
had forced his *s.* Tamar. 22, 32
Jehosheba *s.* of Ahaziah took Joash.
2 Ki 11:2; *2 Chr* 22:11
a little *s.* and she hath no breasts . . .
do for our *s.* in the ? *S of S* 8:8
her treacherous *s.* Judah. *Jer* 3:7
her *s.* feared not. 8

her *s.* hath not turned. *Jer* 3:10
him, saying, Ah, my *s.* 22:18
thou art the *s.* of thy sisters who.
Ezek 16:45
thy elder *s.* is Samaria, thy younger
s. Sodom. 46
Sodom thy *s.* hath not done as. 48
this was the iniquity of thy *s.* 49
for thy *s.* Sodom was not. 56
in thee hath humbled his *s.* 22:11
elder, and Aholibah her *s.* 23:4
and when her *s.* Aholibah saw. 11
was alienated from her *s.* 18
walked in the way of thy *s.* 31
thy *s.'s* cup deep and large. 32, 33
for *s.* that hath no husband. 44:25
the same is my brother, *s. Mat* 12:50
she had a *s.* called Mary.
Luke 10:39; *John* 11:1, 5
therefore his *s.* sent. *John* 11:3
by the cross his mother's *s.* 19:25
Paul's *s.'s* son heard of. *Acts* 23:16
commend to you Phœbe our *s.* a servant. *Rom* 16:1
a brother or a *s.* is not. *1 Cor* 7:15
power to lead about a *s.* a wife ? 9:5*
Marcus *s.'s* son toBarnabas.*Col*4:10*
if a brother or *s.* be naked. *Jas* 2:15
children of thy elect *s.* 2 John 13

my sister

pray thee, thou art my *s. Gen* 12:13
why saidst, She is my *s* ? 19; 20:2
5, 12; 26:7, 9
I have wrestled with my *s.* 30:8
Let my *s.* Tamar come. *2 Sam* 13:5, 6
Come lie with me, my *s.* 11
Hold now thy peace, my *s.* 20
said to the worm, Thou art my *s.*
Job 17:14
Thou art my *s.*; and call. *Pr* 7:4
hast ravished my heart, my *s.* my.
S of S 4:9
how fair is thy love, my *s.* my. 10
a garden inclosed is my *s.* my. 12
I am come into my garden, my *s.* 5:1
open to me, my *s.* my love, my. 2
same is my brother, my *s. Mark* 3:35
that my *s.* hath left me ? *Luke* 10:40

sister in law

s. in law is gone back to her people
. . . after thy *s. in law. Ruth* 1:15

sisters

will save alive my father, and my *s.*
Josh 2:13
whose *s.* were Zeruiah. *1 Chr* 2:16
they called for their three *s. Job* 1:4
his brethren and all his *s.* 42:11
the sister of thy *s. Ezek* 16:45
thou hast justified thy *s.* in. 51, 52
when thy *s.* and daughters. 55
when thou shalt receive thy *s.* 61
unto your *s.* Ruhamah. *Hos* 2:1
are not his *s.* with us ? *Mat* 13:56
Mark 6:3
s. or father, or mother. *Mat* 19:29
Mark 10:29; *Luke* 14:26
100 fold, houses, brethren, *s.*
Mark 10:30
women, as *s.* with purity. *1 Tim* 5:2

sit

war, and shall ye *s.* here ? *Num* 32:6
ye that *s.* in judgement. *Judg* 5:10
s. still, my daughter. *Ruth* 3:18
turn aside, *s.* down here. 4:1, 2
and make them *s.* in. *1 Sam* 9:22
we will not *s.* down till he. 16:11
I should not fail to *s.* with. 20:5
behold, the king doth *s.* 2 Sam 19:8
Solomon shall *s. 1 Ki* 1:13, 17
who hath given one to *s.* 48; 3:6
not fail thee a man to *s.* on the throne.
8:25; *2 Chr* 6:16; *Jer* 33:17
why *s.* we here ? *2 Ki* 7:3, 4
thy sons shall *s.* on. 10:30; 15:12
men who *s.* on wall. 18:27; *Isa* 36:12
and will not *s.* with the. *Ps* 26:5
they that *s.* in the gate speak. 69:12
such as *s.* in darkness and. 107:10
said to my Lord, *S.* thou at. 110:1
princes also did *s.* and speak. 119:23
to rise early and *s.* up late. 127:2*
their children shall *s.* upon. 132:12

folly in dignity, and rich *s. Eccl* 10:6
being desolate, shall *s. Isa* 3:26
I will *s.* upon mount of the. 14:13
he shall *s.* upon the throne in. 16:5
their strength is to *s.* still. 30:7
bring them that *s.* in darkness. 42:7
s. in the dust, *s.* on. 47:1; 52:2
s. thou silent, get thee into. 47:5
thou that sayest, I shall not *s.* 8
nor a fire to *s.* before it. 14
why do we *s.* still ? *Jer* 8:14
that *s.* on David's throne. 13:13
s. down now. 18; 36:15
he shall have none to *s.* 36:30
and *s.* in thirst. 48:18
how doth city *s.* solitary ! *Lam* 1:1
elders of Zion *s.* on ground. 2:10
they shall *s.* upon the. *Ezek* 26:16
because thou hast said, I *s.* in. 28:2
and they *s.* before thee as. 33:31
prince shall *s.* in it to eat. 44:3
the ancient of days did *s. Dan* 7:9
but the judgement shall *s.* they. 26
there will I *s.* to judge. *Joel* 3:12
they shall *s.* every man. *Mi* 4:4
when I *s.* in darkness, Lord. 7:8
and thy fellows that *s. Zech* 3:8
he shall *s.* and rule upon. 6:13
s. as a refiner and purifier of silver.
Mal 3:3
many shall *s.* down with. *Mat* 8:11
s. in the throne of his glory, ye also
shall *s.* 19:28; 25:31; *Luke* 22:30
my two sons may *s.* on. *Mat* 20:21
but to *s.* on my right hand. 23
Mark 10:37, 40
s. thou on my right hand till I make.
Mat 22:44; *Mark* 12:36
Luke 20:42; *Heb* 1:13
the scribes and Pharisees *s.* in.
Mat 23:2
s. ye here while I pray yonder.
26:36; *Mark* 14:32
make them *s.* by fifties. *Luke* 9:14
make them to *s.* down, and. 12:37
shall *s.* down in the kingdom. 13:29
bidden, *s.* not down in highest. 14:8
take thy bill, *s.* down quickly. 16:6
will say to him, Go, and *s.* 17:7
Make the men *s.* down. *John* 6:10
would raise up Christ to *s.* on.
Acts 2:30*
that he would come up and *s.* 8:31
to see thee *s.* at meat in. *1 Cor* 8:10
hath made us *s.* in heavenly. *Eph* 2:6
and say, *S.* thou here in a. *Jas* 2:3
will I grant to *s.* with me. *Rev* 3:21
a woman *s.* on a scarlet beast. 17:3
for she saith in her heart, I *s.* 18:7

sith

s. thou hast not hated blood, even.
Ezek 35:6†

sittest

why *s.* thou thyself alone ? *Ex* 18:14
talk of them when thou *s.* in thine
house. *Deut* 6:7; 11:19
thou *s.* and speakest against thy.
Ps 50:20
thou *s.* to eat with a ruler. *Pr* 23:1
hear, O king of Judah, that *s.* on.
Jer 22:2
s. thou to judge me after ? *Acts* 23:3

sitteth

from the firstborn that *s. Ex* 11:5
every thing whereon he *s. Lev* 15:4
whereon he or she *s.* be unclean.
6, 20, 23, 26
when he *s.* on the throne. *Deut* 17:18
Solomon *s.* on throne of. *1 Ki* 1:46
do so to Mordecai that *s. Esth* 6:10
nor *s.* in the seat of the. *Ps* 1:1
s. in the heavens shall laugh. 2:4
he *s.* in the lurking places. 10:8
s. on the flood; yea, the Lord *s.* king
for ever, the Lord will. 29:10
God *s.* on the throne of his. 47:8
Lord reigneth, he *s.* between. 99:1
for she *s.* at the door of. *Pr* 9:14
a king that *s.* in the throne. 20:8
when he *s.* among the elders. 31:23
while king *s.* at his table. *S of S* 1:12
spirit of judgement to him that *s.*
Isa 28:6

it is he that s. on the circle. *Isa* 40:22
partridge s. on eggs. *Jer* 17:11
saith of the king that s. upon. 29:16
he s. alone and keepeth. *Lam* 3:28
behold, all the earth s. *Zech* 1:11
a woman that s. in the midst. 5:7
sweareth by him that s. *Mat* 23:22
s. not down first and. *Luke* 14:28, 31
he that s. at meat or he that serveth ?
is not he that s. at meat ? 22:27
revealed to another that s. by.
1 Cor 14:30
where Christ s. on the right hand.
Col 3:1
he, as God, s. in the. *2 Thes* 2:4
power to him that s. *Rev* 5:13
from the face of him that s. 6:16
salvation to our God which s. 7:10
he that s. on throne shall dwell. 15
the whore that s. upon. 17:1, 15
mountains, on which the woman s. 9

sitting

dam s. on the young. *Deut* 22:6
s. in a summer parlour. *Judg* 3:20
seen the s. of his servants.
1 Ki 10:5; *2 Chr* 9:4
found the man of God s. *1 Ki* 13:14
I saw the Lord s. on his throne.
22:19; *2 Chr* 18:18; *Isa* 6:1
of the prophets were s. *2 Ki* 4:38
captains of the host were s. 9:5
the queen also s. by him. *Neh* 2:6
see Mordecai the Jew s. *Esth* 5:13
my down-s. and up-rising. *Ps* 139:2
kings and princes s. upon the throne
of David. *Jer* 17:25; 22:4, 30
the king then s. in the gate. 38:7
behold their s. down. *Lam* 3:63
s. at receipt of. *Mat* 9:9; *Mark* 2:14
Luke 5:27
like children s. in the markets.
Mat 11:16; *Luke* 7:32
behold, two blind men s. *Mat* 20:30
thy king cometh, s. on an ass.
21:5*; *John* 12:15
ye shall see the Son of man s. on the.
Mat 26:64; *Mark* 14:62
and s. down, they watched him there.
Mat 27:36
the other Mary s. over against. 61
that was possessed s. *Mark* 5:15
they saw a young man s. on. 16:5
found him s. in midst of. *Luke* 2:46
doctors of the law s. by. 5:17
found him s. clothed, and in. 8:35
s. in sackcloth and ashes. 10:13
changers of money s. *John* 2:14
two angels in white s. 20:12
house where they were s. *Acts* 2:2
eunuch was returning, and s. 8:28
saw twenty-four elders s. *Rev* 4:4

sitting place

each side of s. *place*. *2 Chr* 9:18*

situate

Tyrus, O thou that art s. at entry.
Ezek 27:3*
populous No that was s. *Nah* 3:8

situation

s. of the city is pleasant. *2 Ki* 2:19
beautiful for s., the joy of. *Ps* 48:2*

Sivan

that is the month S. *Esth* 8:9

six

s. cakes on a row on the. *Lev* 24:6
s. covered waggons, and. *Num* 7:3
on every hand s. fingers, every foot s.
2 Sam 21:20; *1 Chr* 20:6
sixteen sons and s. *1 Chr* 4:27
eastward were s. Levites. 26:17
prince shall offer to Lord, shall be s.
lambs without blemish. *Ezek* 46:4
new moon shall be s. lambs. 6
see **branches, days, hundreds**

six boards

thou shalt make s. *boards*. *Ex* 26:22
tabernacle he made s. *boards*. 36:27

six brethren

moreover these s. *brethren*.
Acts 11:12

six cities

shall be s. *cities* for refuge.
Num 35:6, 13, 15

six cubits

Goliath's height was s. *cubits*.
1 Sam 17:4
chamber was s. *cubits*. *1 Ki* 6:6
reed of s. *cubits* long. *Ezek* 40:5
the little chambers were s. *cubits*. 12
he measured posts s. *cubits*. 41:1
doors s. *cubits*. 3
wall of the house s. *cubits*. 5
a full reed of s. great cubits. 8
of the image of gold s. *cubits*.
Dan 3:1

six curtains

couple s. *curtains* by themselves.
Ex 26:9; 36:16

six measures

gave Ruth of barley s. *measures*.
Ruth 3:15
she said, These s. *measures*. 17

six men

s. *men* came from the way. *Ezek* 9:2

six months

king . . . seven years, s. *months*.
2 Sam 2:11; 5:5; *1 Chr* 3:4
s. *months* Joab remained in Edom.
1 Ki 11:16
Zachariah reigned s. *months* over.
2 Ki 15:8
s. *months* with oil of myrrh and s.
months with sweet. *Esth* 2:12
heaven was shut up three years and
s. *months*. *Luke* 4:25; *Jas* 5:17
at Corinth a year and s. *months*.
Acts 18:11

six names

s. of their *names* on one stone, and
the other s. *names* of. *Ex* 28:10

six paces

when the Levites had gone s. *paces*
he. *2 Sam* 6:13

six sheep

for me daily s. *choice sheep*.
Neh 5:18

six sons

me, I have borne s. *sons*. *Gen* 30:20
sons of Shechaniah, s. *1 Chr* 3:22
and Azel had s. *sons*, whose names.
8:38; 9:44

six steps

the throne had s. *steps*. *1 Ki* 10:19
twelve lions on the s. *steps*. 20
2 Chr 9:18

six things

these s. *things* doth. *Pr* 6:16

six times

smitten five or s. *times*. *2 Ki* 13:19

six troubles

deliver thee in s. *troubles*, in seven.
Job 5:19

six waterpots

set there s. *waterpots* of stone.
John 2:6

six wings

each one had s. *wings*. *Isa* 6:2
beasts had each s. *wings*. *Rev* 4:8

six years

I served thee s. *years*. *Gen* 31:41
s. *years* he shall serve. *Ex* 21:2
Deut 15:12; *Jer* 34:14
s. *years* thou shalt sow. *Ex* 23:10
s. *years* thou shalt prune. *Lev* 25:3
hired servant in serving s. *years*.
Deut 15:18
judged Israel s. *years*. *Judg* 12:7
Omri reigned s. *years*. *1 Ki* 16:23
nurse in the house of the Lord s.
years. *2 Ki* 11:3; *2 Chr* 22:12

sixscore

Hiram sent Solomon s. *1 Ki* 9:14

sixth

bare Jacob the s. son. *Gen* 30:19
thou shalt couple s. curtain. *Ex* 26:9
my blessing on you s. year. *Lev* 25:21
the s. lot came out for. *Josh* 19:32
Ithream, David's s. son. *2 Sam* 3:5
1 Chr 3:3
in s. year of Hezekiah. *2 Ki* 18:10
house was finished in s. *Ezra* 6:15

drink also water by measure, the s.
part of an hin. *Ezek* 4:11
in the s. year the hand of. 8:1
I will leave but the s. part of. 39:2
the oblation of the s. part of an. 45:13
a meat offering the s. part. 46:14
went out about the s. *Mat* 20:5
all the land from the s. to ninth hour.
27:45; *Mark* 15:33; *Luke* 23:44
about the s. hour Jesus. *John* 4:6
it was about the s. hour. 19:14
pray about the s. hour. *Acts* 10:9
when he opened s. seal. *Rev* 6:12
s. angel sounded, and I heard. 9:13
saying to the s. angel, Loose. 14
s. angel poured out vial on. 16:12
the s. foundation of the wall. 21:20
see **day, month**

sixteen

Zilpah bare to Jacob s. *Gen* 46:18
sockets of silver, s. sockets.
Ex 26:25; 36:30
Jehoash reigned s. years. *2 Ki* 13:10
Azariah, when s. years old. 14:21
over Judah s. years in Jerusalem.
15:33; *2 Chr* 27:1, 8; 28:1
Shimei had s. sons. *1 Chr* 4:27
among sons of Eleazar were s. 24:4
sons and s. daughters. *2 Chr* 13:21

sixteenth

s. lot came forth to. *1 Chr* 24:14
the s. lot came forth to. 25:23

sixty

Mahalaleel lived s. years. *Gen* 5:15
Enoch lived s.five years and begat. 21
the male from twenty to s. *Lev* 27:3
if it be from s. years old above. 7
s. rams, s. he goats, s. lambs.
Num 7:88
brought forth s. fold. *Mat* 13:8, 23
Mark 4:8, 20

size

the curtains were all of one s.
Ex 36:9, 15
of one measure and s. *1 Ki* 6:25*
one measure, and of one s. 7:37*
for all manner of s. David left.
1 Chr 23:29

skies

of the s. his pavilions round about.
2 Sam 22:12; *Ps* 18:11
the s. sent out a sound. *Ps* 77:17
and let the s. pour down. *Isa* 45:8
is lifted up even to the s. *Jer* 51:9

skilful

Reuben and Gadites s. *1 Chr* 5:18
instructed, because he was s. 15:22
with thee every willing s. man. 28:21
deliver thee into the hand of men s.
to destroy. *Ezek* 21:31
children s. in all wisdom. *Dan* 1:4
such are s. of lamentation to.
Amos 5:16

skilfully

sing a new song, play s. *Ps* 33:3

skilfulness

and guided them by s. *Ps* 78:72

skill, verb

not any that can s. to hew timber.
1 Ki 5:6†; *2 Chr* 2:8
a man that can s. to grave. *2 Chr* 2:7†
that could s. of instruments. 34:12†

skill

nor yet favour to men of s. but.
Eccl 9:11
God gave them knowledge and s.
Dan 1:17
I am now come forth to give thee s.
9:22

skin

it is his raiment for s. *Ex* 22:27
flesh of the bullock, and his s. and
dung burn. 29:14; *Lev* 4:11
Moses wist not that the s. of his face.
Ex 34:29, 30, 35
offereth shall have the s. *Lev* 7:8
if dead fall on s. or sack it. 11:32
shall have in the s. a rising. 13:2
look on the plague in the s. of the
flesh, and if deeper than the s. 3
if bright spot be white in the s. 4

if the plague spread not in the s.
    Lev 13:5, 6, 22, 28
if scab spread abroad in the s.
    7, 8, 27, 35, 36
if the rising be white in the s.   10
it is an old leprosy in the s. of.   11
rend it out of garment or s.   56
s. wherein is seed washed.   15:17
burn heifer, her s. and.   *Num* 19:5
s. for s. all that a man hath. *Job* 2:4
my s. is broken, and become.   7:5
thou hast clothed me with s.   10:11
I sewed sackcloth on my s.   16:15
devour the strength of his s.   18:13*
to my s. and to my flesh, and I am
  escaped with the s. of my.   19:20
after my s. worms destroy.   26
my s. is black upon me.   30:30
canst thou fill his s. with barbed?
    41:7
my bones cleave to my s. *Ps* 102:5*
Ethiopian change his s.?   *Jer* 13:23
my flesh and s. hath he.   *Lam* 3:4
their s. cleaveth to their bones. 4:8
our s. was black like an oven. 5:10
I will cover you with s., and put
  breath in you.   *Ezek* 37:6, 8
who pluck off their s.   *Mi* 3:2
who eat flesh, and flay their s.   3
John had a girdle of s.   *Mark* 1:6*

skins

Lord made coats of s.   *Gen* 3:21
she put s. of kids of goats.   27:16
were found red s. of rams and badgers' s., brought them.   *Ex* 35:23
law of the plague of s.   *Lev* 13:59
shall burn in fire their s.   16:27
raiment, all made of s.   *Num* 31:20
in sheep s. and goat s.   *Heb* 11:37

skip

maketh them also to s.   *Ps* 29:6

skipped

mountains s. like rams. *Ps* 114:4, 6

skippedst

since thou spakest of him, thou s.
  for joy.   *Jer* 48:27*

skipping

behold, he cometh s. upon. *S of S* 2:8

skirt

(*The lower part of the long mantle
worn by the Jews*)

uncover his father's s.   *Deut* 22:30
uncovereth his father's s.   27:20
spread therefore thy s.   *Ruth* 3:9
he laid hold on the s.   *1 Sam* 15:27
David cut off the s. of Saul's. 24:4
because he cut off Saul's s.   5
my father, see the s. of thy robe. 11
behold, I spread my s.   *Ezek* 16:8
if one bear holy flesh in the s. and
  with his s. do touch.   *Hag* 2:12
shall take hold of s. of.   *Zech* 8:23

skirts

that went down to the s. of. *Ps* 133:2
in s. is found blood of poor. *Jer* 2:34
for thy iniquity are thy s.   13:22
will I discover thy s.   26; *Nah* 3:5
her filthiness is in her s.   *Lam* 1:9
bind a few hairs in thy s. *Ezek* 5:3

skull

millstone to break his s. *Judg* 9:53
more of Jezebel than s.   *2 Ki* 9:35
to say, the place of a s. *Mat* 27:33
    Mark 15:22; *John* 19:17

sky

in his excellency on the s. *Deut* 33:26
him spread out the s.?   *Job* 37:18
it will be fair weather: for the s. is
  red.   *Mat* 16:2*, 3
discern face of the s.   *Luke* 12:56*
many as the stars of the s. *Heb* 11:12*

slack

(*Sluggish, loosened, slowed down*)

he will not be s. to him. *Deut* 7:10
How long are ye s. to go? *Josh* 18:3
dealeth with a s. hand.   *Pr* 10:4
said to Zion, Let not thine hands be s.
    Zeph 3:16
Lord is not s. concerning. *2 Pet* 3:9

slack, *verb*

vow a vow, thou shalt not s. to pay it.
    Deut 23:21
saying, S. not thy hand. *Josh* 10:6
s. not riding for me.   *2 Ki* 4:24*

slacked

the law is s., and judgement. *Hab* 1:4

slackness

slack, as some men count s.
    2 Pet 3:9

slain, *verb*

for I have s. a man to.   *Gen* 4:23
therefore he hath s. them in.
    Num 14:16
surely now I had s. thee.   22:33
after he had s. Sihon.   *Deut* 1:4*
be not known who hath s. him. 21:1
and have s. his sons.   *Judg* 9:18
jaw bone of an ass have I s. 15:16*
thought to have s. me.   20:5
Saul hath s. his. *1 Sam* 18:7; 21:11
shewed David that Saul had s. 22:21
saying, I have s. the.   *2 Sam* 1:16
Abner, because he had s.   3:30
men have s. a righteous person. 4:11
hast s. Uriah with the sword. 12:9
Absalom hath s. all king's sons. 13:30
they have not s. all, for Amnon. 32
when the Philistines had s. 21:12
Ishbi-benob thought to have s. 16
Adonijah hath s. oxen. *1 Ki* 1:19, 25
Pharaoh had gone up and s. 9:16
lion hath torn and s. him. 13:26
Zimri hath s. the king.   16:16*
Ahab told how he had s. all. 19:1
for Israel have s. thy.   10, 14
servants who had s. king. *2 Ki* 14:5
hast s. thy brethren. *2 Chr* 21:13
for the band of men had s. 22:1
when they had s. Ahaziah, they. 9
quiet after they had s.   23:21
s. them in rage that reacheth. 28:9
Jews have s. 500 men. *Esth* 9:12
the Sabeans have s. *Job* 1:15, 17
men have been s. by her. *Pr* 7:26
destroyed and s. people. *Isa* 14:20
bodies of men whom I have s. in my
  anger.   *Jer* 33:5
he had s. Gedaliah. 41:4, 9, 16, 18
hast s. them in day. *Lam* 2:21; 3:43
hast s. my children.   *Ezek* 16:21
s. their children to idols.   23:39
I have s. them by words. *Hos* 6:5
your young men have I s. *Amos* 4:10
by wicked hands have s. *Acts* 2:23
have s. them that shewed. 7:52
nothing till we have s. Paul. 23:14

slain

Jacob came upon the s. *Gen* 34:27
the blood of the s. bird. *Lev* 14:51
and ye shall be s. before. 26:17*
shall the flocks and the herds be s.?
    Num 11:22
toucheth any s. 19:16, 18; 31:19
drink the blood of the s.   23:24
name of the Israelite that was s. was
  Zimri.   25:14
woman that was s. was Cozbi. 15, 18
rest of them that were s.   31:8
if one be found s. in land giveth.
    Deut 21:1*
the city next to the s. man.
thine ox shall be s. before. 28:31
arrows drunk with blood of s. 32:42
will I deliver them up all s. *Josh* 11:6
among them that were s.   13:22
the woman that was s. *Judg* 20:4*
Hophni and Phinehas were s.
    1 Sam 4:11
as Lord liveth, he shall not be s. 19:6
to-morrow thou shalt be s.   11
shall he be s.? what hath?   20:32
Philistines, and fell down s. in
  mount Gilboa. 31:1; *1 Chr* 10:1
when the Philistines came to strip
  the s.   *1 Sam* 31:8
beauty of Israel is s. *2 Sam* 1:19
from the blood of the s. from fat. 22
O Jonathan, thou wast s. in. 25
Israel were s. before David's. 18:7*
was gone to bury the s. *1 Ki* 11:15
the kings are surely s. *2 Ki* 3:23*
from among them that were s. 11:2

within ranges let him be s. *2 Ki* 11:8
on her, and there was she s. 16
there fell down many s., because the
  war was of God.   *1 Chr* 5:22
fell s. of Israel 500,000. *2 Chr* 13:17
I and my people, to be s. *Esth* 7:4
number of the s. in Shushan. 9:11
and where the s. are.   *Job* 39:30
ye shall be s. all of you.   *Ps* 62:3
like the s. that lie in the grave. 88:5
Rahab in pieces as one s.   89:10
man saith, I shall be s.   *Pr* 22:13
those that are ready to be s. 24:11
shall fall under the s.   *Isa* 10:4
raiment of those that are s. 14:19
thy s. men were not s. with. 22:2
shall no more cover her s. 26:21
s. according to slaughter, or s. 27:7
their s. also shall be cast out. 34:3
and the s. of the Lord shall. 66:16
that I might weep for s.   *Jer* 9:1
behold the s. with the sword. 14:18
men be s. by sword in battle. 18:21*
s. of the Lord be from one. 25:33
filled the pit with the s.   41:9
thus the s. shall fall in land. 51:4
her s. shall fall in the midst. 47
caused s. of Israel to fall, so at Babylon shall fall the s. of all.   49
priest and prophet be s. *Lam* 2:20
be s. with sword, are better than they
  that be s. with hunger.   4:9
and the s. shall fall in.   *Ezek* 6:7
when the s. men shall be among. 13
and fill the courts with s.   9:7
your s. in the city, ye have filled the
  streets with the s.   11:6
your s., they are the flesh, and this. 7
s. it is the sword of great men s.
    21:14*
upon necks of them that are s. 26:6
daughters in field shall be s. 26:8
deaths of them that are s.   28:8
great pain when the s. shall. 30:4
shall fill the land with the s.   11
with him unto them that be s. 31:17
with them s. with sword. 18; 32:29
fall in the midst of the s. 32:20, 25
lie s. by the sword. 21, 22, 23, 24
circumcised, s. by sword. 25, 26, 30
all his army s. by sword. 31, 32
mountains with his s. men.   35:8
breathe upon these s.   37:9
wise men to be s.; they sought Daniel
  and his fellows to be s. *Dan* 2:13
was Belshazzar the king s.   5:30
I beheld, even till beast was s. 7:11
and many shall fall down s. 11:26
there is multitude of s.   *Nah* 3:3
ye Ethiopians shall be s. *Zeph* 2:12
Son of man must be s. *Luke* 9:22
Theudas was s.; and all. *Acts* 5:36
ye offered to me s. beasts?   7:42
Pilate that he should be s. 13:28
by the cross, having s. *Eph* 2:16
they were stoned, were s. *Heb* 11:37
who was s. among you. *Rev* 2:13
stood a Lamb, as it had been s. 5:6
thou wast s.   9
the Lamb that was s.   12; 13:8
souls of them that were s. for. 6:9
in the earthquake were s.   11:13
the blood of all that were s. 18:24
remnant s. with sword of. 19:21

slander

bringing up a s. on land. *Num* 14:36*
for I have heard the s. *Ps* 31:13*
he that uttereth a s.   *Pr* 10:18

slandered

he hath s. thy servant. *2 Sam* 19:27

slanderers

must be grave, not s. *1 Tim* 3:11

slanderest

s. thine own mother's son. *Ps* 50:20

slandereth

whoso s. his neighbour, him. *Ps* 101:5

• slanderously

as we be s. reported.   *Rom* 3:8

slanders

revolters walking with s. *Jer* 6:28
neighbour will walk with s. 9:4

slang
from his bag a stone and s. it.
1 Sam 17:49

slaughter
that first s. which. *1 Sam* 14:14
not been now much greater s.? 30
as David returned from s. of Philistine. 17:57; 18:6; *2 Sam* 1:1
is s. among people who. *2 Sam* 17:9
was come from the s. *2 Chr* 25:14
as sheep for the s. *Ps* 44:22
after her, as an ox to the s. *Pr* 7:22
the s. of Midian at Oreb. *Isa* 10:26
prepare s. for his children. 14:21
according to s. of them that. 27:7
and delivered them to s. 34:2
he is brought as a lamb to the s. 53:7
Jer 11:19
shall all bow down to the s. *Isa* 65:12
Tophet, but valley of. *Jer* 7:32
19:6
pull them out like sheep for s., prepare them for day of s. 12:3
for the days of your s. are. 25:34
young men are gone down to s. 48:15
let them go down to the s. 50:27
them down like lambs to the s. 51:40
and every man a s. weapon in his.
Ezek 9:2
is sharpened to make sore s. 21:10
it is wrapped up for the s. 15
to open the mouth in the s. 22
the sword is drawn: for the s. 28
when the s. is made in the. 26:15
are profound to make s. *Hos* 5:2
Esau may be cut off by s. *Ob* 9
Lord, Feed the flock of s. *Zech* 11:4
I will feed the flock of s. O poor. 7
he was laid as a sheep to s. *Acts* 8:32
Saul yet breathing out s. against. 9:1
we are accounted as sheep for the s.
Rom 8:36
Abraham returning from the s. of the
kings. *Heb* 7:1
your hearts, as in day of s. *Jas* 5:5
see great

slave, -s
(*Slavery under the Hebrews was as mild as was possible in that age. No Hebrew could become permanently the slave of another Hebrew, but must be freed when he had paid the debt for which he was sold; in the seventh year of his service whether the debt was paid or not; and in the year of Jubilee, whatever the time he had served. Gentile slaves were mostly war captives, or purchased from regular slave-dealers. These could be freed at the will of the master, but there was no law requiring it*)
is he a homeborn s.? *Jer* 2:14
the merchandise of s. *Rev* 18:13

slay
that findeth me shall s. *Gen* 4:14
Lord, wilt thou s. also a? 20:4
and they will s. me for my. 11
will I s. my brother Jacob. 27:41
gather together against me and s.
34:30*
therefore and let us s. him. 37:20
What profit is it if we s. brother? 26
s. my two sons if I bring him. 42:37
bring these men home. s. 43:16
behold, I will s. thy son. *Ex* 4:23
the innocent and righteous s. 23:7
shalt s. ram and sprinkle. 29:16
bring them out to s. them. 32:12
s. every man his brother. 27
s. sin offering. *Lev* 4:29, 33
s. the lamb. 14:13
with a beast, ye shall s. beast. 20:15
one shall s. red heifer. *Num* 19:3
s. ye every one his men joined. 25:5
revenger of blood shall s. 35:19, 21
of blood pursue and s. *Deut* 19:6
Israel did s. Balaam. *Josh* 13:22
alive, would not s. you. *Judg* 8:19
his firstborn. Up and s. them. 20
s. me, that men say not. 9:54
Lord would s. them. *1 Sam* 2:25
ark of God that it s. us not. 5:11

any man his ox, and s. *1 Sam* 14:34
spare them not, but s. both. 15:3
up to me, that I may s. him. 19:15
if there be in me iniquity, s. 20:8
said, Turn and s. the priests. 22:17
me, stand upon me and s. *2 Sam* 1:9
let king swear to me he will not s.
1 Ki 1:51
child, in no wise s. it. 3:26, 27
did Baasha s. and reigned. 15:28
find thee, he shall s. me. 18:12
shall Jehu s.: him that escapeth from
sword of Jehu shall Elisha s. 19:17
art departed, a lion shall s. 20:36
young men wilt thou s. *2 Ki* 8:12
go in and s. them, let none. 10:25
sent lions, and they s. them. 17:26
s. her not in the house. *2 Chr* 23:14
priests too few to s. all the. 29:34
we will s. them and cause. *Neh* 4:11
if the scourge s. suddenly. *Job* 9:23
though he s. me, yet will I. 13:15
viper's tongue shall s. him. 20:16
evil shall s. wicked that. *Ps* 34:21
s. them not, lest my people. 59:11
they s. the widow and the. 94:6
that he might s. the broken. 109:16
thou wilt s. the wicked. 139:19
of the simple shall s. them. *Pr* 1:32
his lips shall he s. wicked. *Isa* 11:4
with famine, and he shall s. 14:30
Lord shall s. the dragon that. 27:1
for Lord God shall s. thee. 65:15
the forest shall s. them. *Jer* 5:6
Judah captive and s. them. 20:4
shall s. Ahab and Zedekiah. 29:21
I will s. Ishmael, son of Nathaniah;
wherefore should he s.? 40:15
found that said, S. us not. 41:8
s. all her bullocks; woe unto. 50:27
s. utterly old and young. *Ezek* 9:6
they shall s. their sons and. 23:47
he shall s. with sword thy. 26:8
he shall s. thy people by. 11
they shall s. the burnt. 44:11
set her like a dry land and s. *Hos* 2:3
yet will I s. the fruit. 9:16
s. all princes thereof. *Amos* 2:3
I will s. the last of them with. 9:1
sword, and it shall s. them. 4
whose possessors s. them. *Zech* 11:5
some of them they shall s. and.
Luke 11:49
bring hither, and s. them. 19:27

to slay
be far from thee to s. *Gen* 18:25
stretched his hand to s. his. 22:10
they conspired against him to s. him.
37:18
Pharaoh sought to s. Moses. *Ex* 2:15
sword in their hand to s. us. 5:21
man come on neighbour to s. 21:14
brought them out to s. *Deut* 9:28
cursed that taketh reward to s. 27:25
brought the ark to s. us. *1 Sam* 5:10
why then sin, to s. David? 19:5
Saul went to watch him and s. 11
of his father to s. David. 20:33
the king to s. Abner. *2 Sam* 3:37
Saul sought to s. them in his. 21:2
thou come to s. my son? *1 Ki* 17:18
the hand of Ahab to s. me. 18:9
utterly to s. and. *2 Chr* 20:23
to s. thee, in night to s. *Neh* 6:10
to s. the power that would assault.
Esth 8:11
to s. such as be of upright. *Ps* 37:14
and seeketh to s. him. 32
sword to s. dogs, to tear. *Jer* 15:3
all their counsel to s. me. 18:23
sent Ishmael to s. thee? 40:14
to s. the souls that. *Ezek* 13:19
two tables to s. thereon. 40:39
gone forth to s. wise men. *Dan* 2:14
continually to s. nations. *Hab* 1:17
Jesus, and sought to s. *John* 5:16
they took counsel to s. *Acts* 5:33
but they went about to s. him. 9:29
angels prepared to s. third. *Rev* 9:15

slayer
refuge that the s. may flee thither.
Num 35:11; *Deut* 4:42; 19:3, 4
Josh 20:3

shall judge between s. *Num* 35:24
congregation shall deliver s. 25
if the s. shall at any time come. 26
of blood find and kill the s. 27
s. shall return into the land of his. 28
Josh 20:6
of blood pursue the s. *Deut* 20:6
not deliver the s. up. *Josh* 20:5
Hebron to be a city of refuge for s.
21:13
gave Shechem for the s. 21, 27, 32
to be a city of refuge for s. 38
sword is furbished to be given to s.
Ezek 21:11

slayeth
to him, whosoever s. Cain. *Gen* 4:15
neighbour and s. him. *Deut* 22:26
wrath killeth and envy s. *Job* 5:2
that s. thee, I am God? . . . man in
hand of them that s. *Ezek* 28:9*

slaying
when Israel made an end of s.
Josh 8:24; 10:20
rendered wickedness in s. *Judg* 9:56
on widow by s. her son. *1 Ki* 17:20
s. oxen, killing sheep. *Isa* 22:13
s. the children in the valleys. 57:5
while they were s. them. *Ezek* 9:8*

sleep
(*Sleep is used in the Bible for natural sleep; for the indolence and dullness of the soul; or figuratively for death*)
God caused a deep s. to. *Gen* 2:21
sun going down, a deep s. 15:12
Jacob awaked out of his s. 28:16
thus I was, my s. departed. 31:40
awaked out of his s. *Judg* 16:14, 20
a deep s. from God. *1 Sam* 26:12
when deep s. falleth on men.
Job 4:13; 33:15
nor be raised out of their s. 14:12
lest I s. the s. of death. *Ps* 13:3
stouthearted slept their s. 76:5
horse are cast into a deep s. 6
awaked as one out of s. 78:65
them away, they are as a s. 90:5
for so he giveth his beloved s. 127:2
I will not give s. to mine eyes. 132:4
shalt lie down, and thy s. *Pr* 3:24
their s. is taken away, unless. 4:16
not s. to thine eyes, nor slumber. 6:4
wilt thou arise out of thy s.? 9
a little s. a little slumber. 10; 24:33
casteth into a deep s. 19:15
love not s. lest thou come. 20:13
the s. of a labouring man. *Eccl* 5:12
neither day nor night seeth s. 8:16
on you spirit of deep s. *Isa* 29:10
I awaked, and my s. *Jer* 31:26
sleep a perpetual s. 51:39, 57
spirit troubled, and his s. *Dan* 2:1
passed the night and his s. 6:18
I was in a deep s. on my. 8:18; 10:9
as a man that is wakened out of s.
Zech 4:1
being raised from s. did. *Mat* 1:24
were heavy with s. *Luke* 9:32
may awake him out of s. *John* 11:11
spoken of taking of rest in s. 13
awaking out of his s. *Acts* 16:27
Eutychus being fallen into a deep s.
20:9
time to awake out of s. *Rom* 13:11

sleep, verb
down in that place to s. *Gen* 28:11
raiment, wherein shall he s.? *Ex* 22:27
thou shalt not s. with. *Deut* 24:12
he may s. in his own raiment. 13
thou shalt s. with thy fathers. 31:16
2 Sam 7:12
and she made him s. *Judg* 16:19
was laid down to s. *1 Sam* 3:3
my lord the king shall s. *1 Ki* 1:21
on that night could not the king s.
Esth 6:1
shall I s. in the dust. *Job* 7:21
lay me down in peace and s. *Ps* 4:8
lighten mine eyes, lest I s. the. 13:3
shall neither slumber nor s. 121:4
s. not, except they have. *Pr* 4:16
how long wilt thou s. O? 6:9
folding of the hands to s. 10; 24:33

the s. of a labouring man is sweet ...
not suffer him to s.   *Eccl* 5:12
I s. but my heart waketh. *S of S* 5:2
none shall slumber nor s.   *Isa* 5:27
s. a perpetual sleep.   *Jer* 51:39, 57
and they shall s. in.   *Ezek* 34:25
many that s. in the dust.   *Dan* 12:2
s. on now, and take your rest.
     Mat 26:45; *Mark* 14:41
and should s. and the seed should.
     Mark 4:27
he said, Why s. ye ?   *Luke* 22:46
Lord, if he s. he shall.   *John* 11:12
many among you s.   *1 Cor* 11:30
we shall not all s., but we.   15:51
them who s. in Jesus.   *1 Thes* 4:14
let us not s. as do others.   5:6
they that s. sleep in the night.   7
that whether we wake or s.   10

sleeper
what meanest thou, O s.? *Jonah* 1:6

sleepest
awake, why s. thou ?   *Ps* 44:23
when thou s. it shall.   *Pr* 6:22
Simon, s. thou ?
awake, thou that s. and.   *Mark* 14:37
     Eph 5:14

sleepeth
Peradventure he s.   *1 Ki* 18:27
he that s. in harvest is a son that
causeth shame.   *Pr* 10:5
their baker s. all night.   *Hos* 7:6
place, for the maid is not dead but s.
   Mat 9:24; *Mark* 5:39; *Luke* 8:52
our friend Lazarus s.   *John* 11:11

sleeping
behold, Saul lay s.   *1 Sam* 26:7
watchmen blind: s.   *Isa* 56:10*
suddenly he find you s. *Mark* 13:36
he cometh and findeth them s. 14:37
Peter was s. between.   *Acts* 12:6

sleight
about by the s. of men.   *Eph* 4:14

slept
Adam s.   *Gen* 2:21
Pharaoh s. and dreamed.   41:5
Uriah s. at door of the. *2 Sam* 11:9
while thine handmaid s.   *1 Ki* 3:20
as he lay and s. an angel.   19:5
I have been quiet and have s.
     Job 3:13
I laid me down and s.   *Ps* 3:5
the stouthearted have s.   76:5
while men s. his enemy. *Mat* 13:25
tarried, they slumbered and s. 25:5
of saints which s. arose.   27:52
stole him away while we s.   28:13
the firstfruits of them that s.
     1 Cor 15:20

     see **fathers**

slew
seed instead of Abel, whom Cain s.
     Gen 4:25
they s. all the males.   34:25
they s. Hamor.   26
for in their anger they s. a man. 49:6
Moses s. the Egyptian.   *Ex* 2:12*
the Lord s. all the firstborn.   13:15
he s. the bullock and took the blood.
     Lev 8:15, 23
Aaron s. the calf of the.   9:8, 15
s. the burnt offering, presented. 12
they s. all the males.   *Num* 31:7
s. kings of Midian, Balaam also they
s.   8
and s. the men of Ai.   *Josh* 8:21
Gibeonites, they s. them not.   9:26
Joshua s. the five kings and. 10:26
they s. of them in Bezek. *Judg* 1:4*
they s. Sheshai.   10*
they s. the Canaanites.   17*
they s. of Moab 10,000 men. 3:29*
Shamgar s. of the Philistines.   31*
they s. Oreb and Zeeb the.   7:25
he s. men of Penuel.   8:17
men were they whom ye s.?   18
s. Zebah, Zalmunna.   21
Abimelech s. his brethren.   9:5
Samson s. thirty men of.   14:19*
jawbone Samson s. 1,000.   15:15*
delivered our enemy, which s. 16:24
the dead which he s. at his.   30
Hannah s. a bullock.   *1 Sam* 1:25

the Philistines s. of Israel. *1 Sam* 4:2
Israel s. the Ammonites.   11:11*
and his armourbearer s.   14:13
the people s. oxen and calves.   32
every man brought his ox and s.   34
thy servant s. both the lion.   17:36*
put his life in his hand, and s. 19:5*
Doeg s. 85 persons that did.   22:18
sang, Saul s. his thousands.   29:5
the Amalekites s. not any.   30:2
the Philistines s. Jonathan.   31:2
Abishai his brother s.   *2 Sam* 3:30
David s. them and cut off.   4:12
David s. of the Syrians.   8:5*
David s. the men of 700.   10:18
for Saul, because he s.   21:1
he s. two lion-like men of Moab, he
s. lion in.   23:20; *1 Chr* 11:22
he s. an Egyptian, a goodly man.
   2 Sam 23:21; *1 Chr* 11:23
and Amasa, whom he s.   *1 Ki* 2:5
Zimri on the throne s. all.   16:11*
what I did when Jezebel s.   18:13
they took them, and Elijah s.   40
Had Zimri peace, who s. his ?
     2 Ki 9:31
behold, I s. him, but who s.? 10:9*
he s. all that remained to.   17*
people s. Mattan the priest.   11:18
they s. Athaliah. 20; *2 Chr* 23:15, 17
was confirmed Amaziah s. servants.
   2 Ki 14:5; *2 Chr* 25:3
but their children s. not.
   2 Ki 14:6; *2 Chr* 25:4
he s. of Edom in valley of salt.
   2 Ki 14:7; *1 Chr* 18:12*
took Damascus and s.   *2 Ki* 16:9
lions which s. some of them.   17:25
Amon conspired and s. him.   21:23
people of the land s. them.   24
     2 Chr 33:25
Josiah s. all the priests.   *2 Ki* 23:20
Nebuchadnezzar s. sons of Zedekiah.
   25:7; *Jer* 39:6; 52:10
of Gath in that land s.   *1 Chr* 7:21
Jehoram s. all his brethren with.
     2 Chr 21:4
Jehu found, and s. the princes. 22:8
Pekah s. in Judah in one day.   28:6
they s. thy prophets.   *Neh* 9:26
the Jews s. of their.   *Esth* 9:16
God s. the fattest of.   *Ps* 78:31
when he s. them, then they.   34
waters into blood, and s.   105:29
who s. great kings.   135:10
s. famous kings.   136:18
killeth an ox is as if he s. *Isa* 66:3
because he s. me not.   *Jer* 20:17
Ishmael s. all the Jews that.   41:3
he forbare, and s. them not.   8
s. all that were pleasant. *Lam* 2:4
fire s. the men that took. *Dan* 3:22
whom he would he s.   5:19
Herod sent, and s. all the children.
     Mat 2:16
took his servants and s. them. 22:6
ye s. between the temple.   23:35
tower in Siloam fell, and s. *Luke* 13:4
raised up Jesus, whom ye s. *Acts* 5:30
Jesus whom they s. and.   10:39
the commandment s. me. *Rom* 7:11
Cain who s. his brother. *1 John* 3:12

slew him
against Abel and s. him.   *Gen* 4:8
wicked, and the Lord s. him.   38:7
displeased the Lord, and he s. him.
     10
of me, A woman s. him. *Judg* 9:54
took and s. him at passages.   12:6
by beard and s. him. *1 Sam* 17:35
the Philistine and s. him.   50
so I stood upon him and s. him.
     2 Sam 1:10
Ish-bosheth and s. him.   4:7
I took hold of him, and s. him.   10
compassed Absalom and s. him.
     18:15
the son of Shimeah and s. him. 21:21
he went down and s. him.   23:21
upon Joab and s. him.   *1 Ki* 2:34
a lion met him by the way and s.
him.   13:24; 20:36
my master and s. him.   *2 Ki* 10:9

they sent after him to Lachish, and
s. him.   *2 Ki* 14:19; *2 Chr* 25:27
against him and s. him.   *2 Ki* 15:10
smote Shallum and s. him.   14
against Pekah and s. him.   30
Pharaoh-necho s. him at.   23:29
therefore he s. him.   *1 Chr* 10:14
so that Athaliah s. him not.
     2 Chr 22:11
his own servants s. him on.   24:25
forth of his own bowels s. him. 32:21
his servants s. him in his.   33:24
Jehoiakim who s. him.   *Jer* 26:23
Ishmael s. him whom the king. 41:2
cast him out of vineyard and s. him.
     Mat 21:39
raiment of them that s. him.
     Acts 22:20

slewest
Goliath whom thou s.   *1 Sam* 21:9

slide
their foot shall s. in.   *Deut* 32:35
in the Lord, I shall not s. *Ps* 26:1*
his heart, none of steps shall s. 37:31

slidden
this people of Jerusalem s. back ?
     Jer 8:5

slideth
Israel s. back as a.   *Hos* 4:16*

slightly
hurt of my people s. *Jer* 6:14; 8:11

slime
had brick for stone, s.   *Gen* 11:3
she daubed the ark with s.   *Ex* 2:3

slimepits
Siddim was full of s.   *Gen* 14:10

sling, *verb*
every one could s. stones at an hair
breadth.   *Judg* 20:16
them shall he s. out.   *1 Sam* 25:29
I will s. out inhabitants. *Jer* 10:18

sling
(*A common weapon among the
Jews, especially among the shepherds, who could sling a stone to a
long distance with great accuracy,
and thus drive away wild beasts
when other weapons would be use-
less*)
his s. in his hand.   *1 Sam* 17:40
over the Philistine with a s.   50
as out of the middle of a s.   25:29
bindeth a stone in a s. so is. *Pr* 26:8

slingers
the s. went about it.   *2 Ki* 3:25

slings
Uzziah prepared s. to. *2 Chr* 26:14*

slingstones
s. are turned with him.   *Job* 41:28

slip
that my feet did not s. *2 Sam* 22:37
     Ps 18:36
he that is ready to s.   *Job* 12:5
that my footsteps s. not.   *Ps* 17:5
we should let them s.   *Heb* 2:1

slippery
their way be dark and s.   *Ps* 35:6
didst set them in s. places.   73:18
be to them as s. ways.   *Jer* 23:12

slippeth
and the head s. from.   *Deut* 19:5
when my foot s. they.   *Ps* 38:16
when I said, My foot s.; thy.   94:18

slips
shalt set it with strange s. *Isa* 17:10

slipt
David s. out of Saul's. *1 Sam* 19:10
my steps had well nigh s. *Ps* 73:2

slothful
be not s. to go to possess. *Judg* 18:9
the s. shall be under.   *Pr* 12:24
s. roasteth not that he took in.   27
the way of the s. is a hedge. 15:19*
the s. hideth his hand in. 19:24*; 26:15*
the desire of s. killeth him.   21:25
the s. man saith.   22:13*; 26:13*
I went by field of the s.   24:30

Thou wicked and s. servant.
Mat 25:26
not s. in business, fervent in spirit.
Rom 12:11
that ye be not s. but followers of.
Heb 6:12

slothfulness
s. casteth into a deep. Pr 19:15
by much s. the building. Eccl 10:18

slow
s. of speech, and of a s. tongue.
Ex 4:10
art a God s. to anger. Neh 9:17
is s. to wrath, is of great. Pr 14:29
O fools and s. of heart. Luke 24:25
the Cretians are liars, s. Tit 1:12*
every man be s. to speak, s. Jas 1:19
see **anger**

slowly
when we had sailed s. Acts 27:7

sluggard
go to the ant, thou s. Pr 6:6
how long wilt thou sleep, O s.? 9
eyes,.so is the s. to them. 10:26
the soul of the s. desireth. 13:4
s. will not plow, therefore. 20:4*
s. is wiser in his own conceit. 26:16

sluices
that make s. and ponds. Isa 19:10*

slumber, substantive
I will not give s. to mine. Ps 132:4
give not sleep to thine eyes, nor s.
Pr 6:4
yet a little sleep, a little s. 10; 24:33
given them the spirit of s. Rom 11:8*

slumber
keepeth thee will not s. Ps 121:3
Israel, shall neither s. nor sleep. 4
none shall s. nor sleep. Isa 5:27
lying down, loving to s. 56:10
thy shepherds s. O king. Nah 3:18

slumbered
while the bridegroom tarried they
all s. Mat 25:5

slumbereth
their damnation s. not. 2 Pet 2:3

slumberings
God speaketh in s. upon. Job 33:15

small
it is a s. matter thou hast. Gen 30:15
it shall become s. dust in all. Ex 9:9
as round thing, as s. as the. 16:14
every s. matter they shall. 18:22, 26
beat some of it very s. 30:36
sweet incense beaten s. Lev 16:12
a s. thing that the God of? Num 16:9
is it a s. thing that thou hast? 13
Jair went and took the s. 32:41
calf s. even as s. as dust. Deut 9:21*
doctrine shall distil as s. rain. 32:2
a s. thing in thy sight, O Lord God.
2 Sam 7:19; 1 Chr 17:17
till there be not one s. stone found.
2 Sam 17:13
I beat them as s. as the dust. 22:43
Ps 18:42
I desire one s. petition. 1 Ki 2:20
after the fire, a still s. voice. 19:12
inhabitants were of s. power, they.
2 Ki 19:26; Isa 37:27
he brought out the grove and stamped
it s. to powder. 2 Ki 23:6, 15
Syrians came with a s. 2 Chr 24:24
passover offerings 2600 s. 35:8
chief of Levites gave 500 s. cattle. 9
though thy beginning was s. Job 8:7
are the consolations of God s.? 15:11
for he maketh s. the drops. 36:27*
I am s. yet do not I. Ps 119:141
adversity, thy strength is s. Pr 24:10
had left to us a s. remnant. Isa 1:9
it a s. thing for you to weary? 7:13
the remnant shall be very s. 16:14
him all vessels of s. quantity. 22:24
strangers shall be like s. dust. 29:5
are counted as the s. dust. 40:15
mountains, and beat them s. 41:15
brought me the s. cattle. 43:23
for a s. moment have I. 54:7
a s. one shall become a strong. 60:22
and they shall not be s. Jer 30:19
yet a s. number shall return. 44:28

39

I will make thee s. among. Jer 49:15
whoredoms a s. matter? Ezek 16:20
seemeth it s. to have eaten? 34:18
strong with a s. people. Dan 11:23
Jacob arise? he is s. Amos 7:2, 5
I have made thee s. among. Ob 2
hath despised day of s. things?
Zech 4:10
they had a few s. fishes. Mark 8:7
had made a scourge of s. cords.
John 2:15
barley.loaves and two s. fishes. 6:9
there was no s. stir. Acts 12:18
Paul and Barnabas had no s. 15:2
there arose no s. stir about. 19:23
Demetrius brought no s. gain. 24
and no s. tempest lay on us. 27:20
very s. thing that I should. 1 Cor 4:3
turned with a very s. helm. Jas 3:4
see **great**

smallest
Benjamite, of s. of tribes?
1 Sam 9:21
to judge the s. matters? 1 Cor 6:2

smart
for a stranger shall s. for it. Pr 11:15

smell
smelled the s. of his raiment, said,
See, s. of my son is as. Gen 27:27
spikenard sendeth forth the s.
S of S 1:12*
tender grape give a good s. 2:13*
the s. of thy ointment better. 4:10
s. of thy garments is like the. 11
s. of thy nose like apples. 7:8
mandrakes give a s. and at. 13*
instead of sweet s. there. Isa 3:24*
s. of the fire had passed. Dan 3:27
olive, his s. as Lebanon. Hos 14:6
sent an odour of sweet. Phil 4:18

smell, verb
like unto that to s. thereto. Ex 30:38
I will not s. the savour. Lev 26:31
which neither see nor s. Deut 4:28
all thy garments s. of myrrh. Ps 45:8
noses have they, they s. not. 115:6
not s. in your solemn. Amos 5:21

smelled
Lord s. a sweet savour. Gen 8:21
Isaac s. smell of his raiment. 27:27

smelleth
he s. the battle afar off. Job 39:25

smelling
fingers with sweet s. myrrh on.
S of S 5:5*
lilies dropping sweet s. myrrh. 13*
where were the s.? 1 Cor 12:17
sacrifice to God for sweet s. Eph 5:2

smite
The word smite ordinarily meaning
simply strike, is very often used in
the Bible with the meaning of killing,
or putting to death, 1 Sam 17:49;
2 Sam 6:7. To smite with the
tongue is to utter such reproaches
as shall hurt as do blows the
physical body, Jer 18:18.
to one company and s. it. Gen 32:8
lest he will come and s. me. 11
I will s. upon the waters. Ex 7:17
say to Aaron, S. the dust. 8:16
suffer the destroyer to s. you. 12:23
behold, thou shalt s. the rock. 17:6
together, and one s. another. 21:18
if a man s. his servant and he. 20
if a man s. the eye of his servant. 26
if he s. out his man servant's or. 27
that we may s. them. Num 22:6
sceptre out of Israel shall s. 24:17
vex the Midianites and s. 25:17
s. him with an instrument. 35:16
and if he s. him with throwing. 17
with a hand weapon of wood. 18
or in enemity s. him with his. 21
thou shalt s. Canaanites. Deut 7:2
shalt surely s. inhabitants. 13:15
if any s. his neighbour. 19:11
thou shalt s. every male. 20:13
or three thousand s. Ai. Josh 7:3
help that we may s. Gibeon. 10:4
pursue after, and s. the. 19
did Moses and Israel s. 12:6; 13:12

thou shalt s. the Midianites as one.
Judg 6:16
then Benjamin began to s. 20:31, 39
go and s. the inhabitants of. 21:10
go and s. Amalek, and. 1 Sam 15:3
I will s. thee, and take. 17:46
Saul said, I will s. David. 18:11
Saul sought to s. David to. 19:10
javelin at him to s. him. 20:33
shall I go and s. the Philistines? Go,
s. Philistines. 23:2
let me s. him to the earth at once. I
pray thee, and I will not s. the. 26:8
why should I s. thee? 2 Sam 2:22
I say, S. Amnon, then kill. 13:28
lest he s. city with the edge. 15:14
people shall flee, and I will s. 17:2
Joab said, Why didst thou not s. him
there? 18:11
s. me, I pray thee, and the men refused to s. him. 1 Ki 20:35, 37
s. every fenced city. 2 Ki 3:19
I s. them? shall I s. them? 6:21
s. them, wouldest thou s. those? 22
shalt s. the house of Ahab 9:7
Jehu, said, S. him also in. 27
shall s. Syrians, till thou. 13:17
he said to the king, S. upon. 18
now thou shalt s. Syria. 19
sun shall not s. thee. Ps 121:6
let righteous s. me, it shall. 141:5
s. a scorner, the simple. Pr 19:25
the heat nor sun s. them. Isa 10:24
ye fast to s. with the fist of. 58:4
come, let us s. him with. Jer 18:18
king of Babylon shall s. Judah. 21:7
he shall s. the land of. 43:11; 46:13
Nebuchadrezzar shall s. 49:28
part of hair, and s. about it. Ezek 5:2
s. with thy hand, and stamp. 6:11
him through the city and s. 9:5
son of man, s. therefore. 21:12
prophesy, and s. thine hands. 14
he said, S. the lintel. Amos 9:1
shall s. judge of Israel. Mi 5:1
melteth, the knees. Nah 2:10
and shall s. the waves. Zech 10:11
the men, and they shall s. 11:6
whoso shall s. thee on. Mat 5:39
to s. his fellow-servants. 24:49
Lord, shall we s. with? Luke 22:49
commanded to s. Paul. Acts 23:2
ye suffer, if a man s. 2 Cor 11:20
witnesses have power to s. the earth.
Rev 11:6

smite, referred to God, expressly
or implicitly
nor will I s. any more. Gen 8:21
out my hand and s. Egypt. Ex 3:20
behold, I will s. all thy borders. 8:2
that I may s. thee and thy. 9:15
I will s. all the firstborn in. 12:12
when I s. the land of Egypt. 13, 23
I will s. them with the. Num 14:12
Lord shall s. with consumption.
Deut 28:22
Lord shall s. with the botch. 27
s. with madness. 28
Lord shall s. thee in the knees. 35
s. through the loins of them. 33:11
The Lord shall s. him. 1 Sam 26:10
for then shall the Lord go out to s.
2 Sam 5:24; 1 Chr 14:15
Lord shall s. Israel as a. 1 Ki 14:15
Elisha said, S. this people with.
6:18
plague will the Lord s. 2 Chr 21:14
s. with a scab daughters. Isa 3:17
he shall s. the earth with rod. 11:4
s. Egypt in the seven streams. 15
19:22
I will s. the inhabitants of this city.
Jer 21:6
will also s. mine hands. Ezek 21:17
I shall s. them that dwell in. 32:15
I will s. thy bow out of thy. 39:3
will s. the winter house. Amos 3:15
Lord will s. her power. Zech 9:4
that day I will s. every horse. 12:4
awake, O sword, s. the shepherd.13:7
Mat 26:31; Mark 14:27

plague wherewith the Lord will s.
　　　　　　　　Zech 14:12, 18
lest I come and s. the.　　*Mal* 4:6
that with it he should s.　*Rev* 19:15

smiters
I gave my back to the s.　*Isa* 50:6

smitest
he said, Wherefore s.?　　*Ex* 2:13
if I have spoken well, why s. thou
me?　　　　　　　　　*John* 18:23

smiteth
he that s. a man so he die. *Ex* 21:12
he s. father and mother, surely. 15
to deliver her husband out of the hand
of him that s. him.　　*Deut* 25:11
cursed be he that s. his.　　27:24
he that s. Kirjath-sepher.
　　　　　　　Josh 15:16; *Judg* 1:12
that s. the Jebusites.　*2 Sam* 5:8*
　　　　　　　　　　1 Chr 11:6
by understanding he s.　*Job* 26:12
turn not to him that s.　*Isa* 9:13
cheek to him that s. him. *Lam* 3:30
that I am the Lord that s. *Ezek* 7:9
that s. thee on one cheek. *Luke* 6:29

smith
there was no s. found. *1 Sam* 13:19
the s. with tongs worketh. *Isa* 44:12
I have created the s. that.　54:16
Demetrius a silver s.　*Acts* 19:24
Alexander the copper s. *2 Tim* 4:14

smiths
away all princes, craftsmen and s.
　　　　　2 Ki 24:14, 16; *Jer* 24:1
the s. were departed.　　*Jer* 29:2

smiting
Moses spied an Egyptian s. *Ex* 2:11
when he returned from s. the.
　　　　　　　　　　2 Sam 8:13
smote him, so that in s. *1 Ki* 20:37
they went forward s.　　*2 Ki* 3:24
make the sick in s. thee.　*Mi* 6:13

smitten
Lord had s. the river.　　*Ex* 7:25
flax and the barley was s.　9:31
wheat and the rye were not s.　32
if a thief be found, and be s.　22:2
go not up, that ye be not s.
　　　　　　Num 14:42; *Deut* 1:42
that thou hast s. me?　*Num* 22:28
wherefore hast thou s. thine ass? 32
their firstborn the Lord had s. 33:4
thine enemies to be s.　*Deut* 28:7
Lord shall cause thee to be s.　25
Judah had s. Jerusalem.　*Judg* 1:8
Benjamin said, They are s. 20:32
saw they were s.　　　　36
surely they are s. down.　　39
Israel was s. before. *1 Sam* 4:2, 10
why hath Lord s. us to-day?　3
the men that died, not, were s. 5:12
because the Lord had s. many. 6:19
the Philistines were s.　　7:10
Saul had a s. garrison of.　13:4
Amalekites had s. Ziklag.　30:1
had s. of Abner's men. *2 Sam* 2:31
Toi heard that David had s. the.
　　　　　8:9, 10; *1 Chr* 18:9, 10
Syrians saw that they were s.
　　　　　　　2 Sam 10:15*, 19*
that he may be s. and die.　11:15
people Israel be s. down. *1 Ki* 8:33
after he had s. every male.　11:15
and when he also had s. *2 Ki* 2:14
have surely s. one another.　3:23
have s. five or six times, then hadst
thou s. Syria till thou.　　13:19
indeed s. Edom. 14:10; *2 Chr* 25:19
mount Seir were s.　*2 Chr* 20:22
why shouldest thou be s.?　25:16
because the Lord hath s. him. 26:20
Edomites had come and s.　28:17
they have s. me upon.　*Job* 16:10
save me, for thou hast s.　*Ps* 3:7
him whom thou hast s.　69:26
my heart is s. and withered. 102:4
he hath s. my life down to.　143:3
therefore the Lord hath s. *Isa* 5:25
gate is s. with destruction.　24:12
hath he s. him, as he smote? 27:7
did esteem him stricken, s.　53:4
in vain have I s. your.　　*Jer* 2:30

why hast thou s. us, and? *Jer* 14:19
though ye had s. whole army. 37:10
I have s. my hand at.　*Ezek* 22:13
me, saying, The city is s.　33:21
year after the city was s.　40:1
he hath s. and he will bind. *Hos* 6:1
Ephraim is s., their root is.　9:16
I have s. you, yet have.　*Amos* 4:9
commandest me to be s.? *Acts* 23:3
part of the sun was s.　*Rev* 8:12

smoke
Sodom, and lo, the s. of the country
went up as s. of a.　　*Gen* 19:28
was altogether on a s.　*Ex* 19:18
the s. of Ai ascended up to heaven.
　　　　　　　　　Josh 8:20, 21
should make s. rise.　*Judg* 20:38
when pillar of s. began to rise.　40
a s. out of his nostrils, and fire out.
　　　　　　　2 Sam 22:9; *Ps* 18:8
out of his nostrils goeth s. *Job* 41:20
shall consume into s.　*Ps* 37:20
s. is driven away, so drive.　68:2
my days are consumed like s. 102:3
become like a bottle in the s. 119:83
as s. to the eyes, so is a.　*Pr* 10:26
out of wilderness like pillars of s.
　　　　　　　　　　S of S 3:6
her assemblies a s. by day. *Isa* 4:5
the house was filled with s.　6:4
mount up like the lifting up of s. 9:18
come from the north a s.　14:31
the s. thereof shall go up.　34:10
shall vanish away like s.　51:6
these are a s. in my nose, a.　65:5
they shall be as the s. out. *Hos* 13:3
and fire and pillars of s. *Joel* 2:30
burn her chariots in the s. *Nah* 2:13
blood, fire, and vapour of s. *Acts* 2:19
s. of the incense ascended. *Rev* 8:4
there arose a s. out of the.　9:2
there came out of the s. locusts.　3
their mouths issued fire and s.　17
of men killed by the fire and s.　18
s. of their torment ascended. 14:11
temple was filled with s. from. 15:8
lament for her when they see s. 18:9
cried when they saw the s. of.　18
and her s. rose up for ever.　19:3

smoke, *verb*
anger of Lord shall s.　*Deut* 29:20
why doth thine anger s.?　*Ps* 74:1
the hills, and they s.　104:32
mountains, and they shall s.　144:5

smoking
behold a s. furnace.　　*Gen* 15:7
saw the mountain s.　　*Ex* 20:18
for the two tails of these s. *Isa* 7:4
the s. flax shall he not quench. 42:3
　　　　　　　　　　Mat 12:20

smooth
man, and I am a s. man. *Gen* 27:11
put the skins of kids on the s.　16
chose him five s. stones. *1 Sam* 17:40
speak unto us s. things.　*Isa* 30:10
among s. stones of the stream. 57:6
the rough ways shall be made s.
　　　　　　　　　　Luke 3:5

smoother
words of his mouth were s. *Ps* 55:21
her mouth is s. than oil.　*Pr* 5:3

smootheth
he that s. with hammer.　*Isa* 41:7

smote
they s. the men at door.　*Gen* 19:11
s. Midian in field of Moab.　36:35
　　　　　　　　　　1 Chr 1:46
he lift up the rod, and s.　*Ex* 7:20
he s. the dust.　　　　8:17
the hail s. every herb.　　9:25
who passed over, when he s. 12:27
the Lord s. all the firstborn in.　29
　　　Num 3:13; 8:17; *Ps* 78:51
　　　　　　105:36; 135:8
Lord s. the people with. *Num* 11:33
came down and s. them.　14:45
Moses s. the rock. 20:11; *Ps* 78:20
Balaam s. the ass to turn her.
　　　　　　Num 22:23, 25, 27
Balak s. his hands together.　24:10
the country the Lord s. is a.　32:4
Amalek s. the hindmost. *Deut* 25:18
Og came against us, and we s. 29:7

the men of Ai s. of them.　*Josh* 7:5
s. them not, because princes.　9:18
they s. all the souls that.　11:11
and s. all the kings with.　12, 17
because he s. his neighbour.　20:5
Jael s. the nail into.　*Judg* 4:21
hammer she s. Sisera, she s.　5:26
came into a tent, and s. it.　7:13
Samson s. them hip and thigh. 15:8
Lord s. Benjamin before.　20:35
these are the gods that s. *1 Sam* 4:8
it is not his hand that s. us.　6:9
s. the men of Beth-shemesh, s.　19
David s. the Philistine in.　17:49
Saul s. the javelin into the.　19:10
that the Lord s. Nabal.　25:38
David s. them from twilight. 30:17
deliver him that s. his. *2 Sam* 14:7
Zedekiah s. Micaiah.　*1 Ki* 22:24
　　　　　　　　　　2 Chr 18:23
Elijah s. the waters.　*2 Ki* 2:8
Elisha s. the waters.　　14
and he s. them with blindness. 6:18
the Lord s. the king, so that he. 15:5
to Menahem, therefore he s. it.　16
angel of the Lord s. 185,000.　19:35
　　　　　　　　　　Isa 37:36
God s. Jeroboam.　　*2 Chr* 13:15
the Lord s. the Ethiopians.　14:12
and cursed them, and s. *Neh* 13:25
and s. down the chosen.　*Ps* 78:31
he s. his enemies in the.　66
found me, they s. me.　*S of S* 5:7
stay on him that s. them. *Isa* 10:20
he who s. the people is.　14:6
because the rod of him that s.　29
be beaten down which s.　30:31
him that s. the anvil.　41:7
in my wrath I s. thee, but.　60:10
then Pashur s. Jeremiah. *Jer* 20:2
after I was instructed, I s.　31:19
then arose Ishmael and s.　41:2
which Nebuchadrezzar s.　46:2
a stone cut out, which s. the.
　　　　　　　　　　Dan 2:34, 35
Belshazzar's knees s. one.　5:6
moved with choler s. the ram.　8:7
a worm s. the gourd.　*Jonah* 4:7
I s. you with blasting.　*Hag* 2:17
Peter drew his sword, s. *Mat* 26:51
prophesy, who is he that s. thee. 68
　　　　　　　　　　Luke 22:64
but the publican s. upon. *Luke* 18:13
many beholding Jesus, s.　23:48
angel s. Peter on the side. *Acts* 12:7

smote him
he that s. him be quit.　*Ex* 21:19
he that s. him shall.　*Num* 35:21
David's heart s. him.　*1 Sam* 24:5
s. him under the fifth rib.
　　　　　　　2 Sam 2:23; 3:27; 4:6
s. him there for his error.　6:7
　　　　　　　　　　1 Chr 13:10
man s. him, so that he. *1 Ki* 20:37
his sons s. him with sword.
　　　　　　2 Ki 19:37; *Isa* 37:38
Syria s. him, king of Israel s. him.
　　　　　　　　　　2 Chr 28:5
hath he smitten him as he smote
those that s. him?　*Isa* 27:7
of his covetousness I s. him.　57:17
princes were wroth with Jeremiah,
and s. him.　　*Jer* 37:15
others s. him with palms. *Mat* 26:67
they took the reed and s. him. 27:30
　　　　Mark 15:19; *Luke* 22:63
　　　　　　　　　　John 19:3
angel of the Lord s. him. *Acts* 12:23

smotest
rod wherewith thou s.　*Ex* 17:5

Smyrna
send to the church in S.　*Rev* 1:11
the church in S. write.　2:8

snail
lizard, the s. and mole. *Lev* 11:30*
as a s. let every one of.　*Ps* 58:8

snare
this man be a s. unto us? *Ex* 10:7
gods, it will surely be a s. unto thee.
　　　23:33; *Deut* 7:16; *Judg* 2:3
the inhabitants of the land, lest it be
a s. in the midst of thee. *Ex* 34:12
thing became a s. unto. *Judg* 8:27

her, that she may be a s. *1 Sam* 18:21
wherefore then layest thou a s.? 28:9
a net, he walketh on a s. *Job* 18:8*
s. is laid for him in the ground. 10*
table become a s. unto them, and.
Ps 69:22; *Rom* 11:9
shall deliver thee from s. *Ps* 91:3
their idols: which were a s. 106:36
wicked have laid s. for me. 119:110
escaped as a bird out of the s. of the
fowlers; the s. is broken. 124:7
proud have hid a s. for me. 140:5
keep me from the s. which. 141:9
have they privily laid s. for. 142:3
as a bird hasteth to the s. *Pr* 7:23
a fool's lips are the s. of his. 18:7
s. to man who devoureth. 20:25
lest learn his ways, and get a s. 22:25
of an evil man is a s. 29:6
bring a city into s. but wise. 8*
the fear of man bringeth a s. 25
birds that are caught in s. *Eccl* 9:12
for a s. to the inhabitants. *Isa* 8:14
fear, and the pit, and the s. are upon.
24:17, 18; *Jer* 48:43, 44
that lay a s. for him. *Eccl* 29:21
I have laid a s. for thee. *Jer* 50:24
s. is come upon us. *Lam* 3:47*
he shall be taken in my s.
Ezek 12:13; 17:20
because ye have been a s. *Hos* 5:1
prophet is a s. of a fowler. 9:8
a s. upon the earth where no gin is
for him ? . . . up a s.? *Amos* 3:5
for as a s. shall it come. *Luke* 21:35*
not that I may cast a s. *1 Cor* 7:35
lest he fall into the s. *1 Tim* 3:7
will be rich, fall into a s. 6:9
may recover out of the s. *2 Tim* 2:26

snared
silver, lest thou be s. *Deut* 7:25
take heed that thou be not s. 12:30
wicked is s. in the work of. *Ps* 9:16
art s. with the words of thy mouth.
Pr 6:2; 12:13
so are the sons of men s. *Eccl* 9:12
stumble and fall and be s. *Isa* 8:15
might fall. and be s. and. 28:13
are all of them s. in holes. 42:22

snares
shall be s. and traps. *Josh* 23:13
s. of death prevented me.
2 Sam 22:6; *Ps* 18:5
therefore s. are round. *Job* 22:10
nose pierceth through s. 40:24
on wicked he shall rain s. *Ps* 11:6
after my life lay s. for me. 38:12
commune of laying the s. privily. 64:5
to depart from the s. of death.
Pr 13:14; 14:27
thorns and s. are in the. 22:5
woman whose heart is s. *Eccl* 7:26
they lay wait as he that setteth s.
Jer 5:26*
they have digged and hid s. 18:22

snatch
he shall s. on right hand. *Isa* 9:20

snorting
s. of his horses was heard. *Jer* 8:16

snout
jewel of gold in a swine's s. *Pr* 11:22

snow
hand was leprous as s. *Ex* 4:6*
leprous, white as s. *Num* 12:10
slew a lion in the midst of a pit, in the
time of s. *2 Sam* 23:30
out a leper white as s. *2 Ki* 5:27
and wherein the s. is hid. *Job* 6:16
if I wash myself in s. water. 9:30
heat consumeth s. waters. 24:19
he saith to the s., Be thou on. 37:6
into treasures of the s.? 38:22
I shall be whiter than s. *Ps* 51:7
it was white as s. in Salmon. 68:14*
he giveth s. like wool. 147:16
fire, hail s. and vapour. 148:8
as the cold of s. in time. *Pr* 25:13
as s. in summer, so honour. 26:1
she is not afraid of the s. for. 31:21
scarlet shall be white as s. *Isa* 1:18
as the s. from heaven. 55:10
will a man leave the s.? *Jer* 18:14

her Nazarites purer than s. *Lam* 4:7
garment was white as s. *Dan* 7:9
his raiment white as s. *Mat* 28:3
Mark 9:3*
his hairs as white as s. *Rev* 1:14

snowy
lion in a pit in a s. day. *1 Chr* 11:22*

snuffed
wild asses s. up the wind. *Jer* 14:6*
ye have s. at it, saith the. *Mal* 1:13

snuffdishes
s. shall be of pure gold. *Ex* 25:38
37:23
cloth, and cover his s. *Num* 4:9

snuffers
s. of pure gold. *Ex* 37:23; *1 Ki* 7:50
2 Chr 4:22
s. made of money that. *2 Ki* 12:13
pots and s. took they away. 25:14
Jer 52:18

snuffeth
a wild ass that s. up the. *Jer* 2:24

so
so Abraham departed. *Gen* 12:4
as the stars, so. 15:5; *Rom* 4:18
Rebekah said, If it be so. *Gen* 25:22
done foolishly in so doing. 31:28
if it must be so now do this. 43:11
Moses spake so to the. *Ex* 6:9
let Lord be so with you, as. 10:10
even so shall ye make it. 25:9
as the Lord commanded, so. 39:43
as the sin offering, so is. *Lev* 7:7
so I am commanded. 8:35; 10:13
as he hath done, so shall. 24:19, 20
bear all that is made, so. *Num* 4:26
as ye are, so shall stranger. 15:15
so the plague was stayed. 25:8
Ps 106:30
so shall the Lord do to. *Deut* 7:19
as nations Lord destroyeth, so. 8:20
so thou shalt put the evil away. 17:7
19:19; 21:21; 22:21, 22, 24
as when man riseth, even so. 22:26
and as thy days, so shall. 33:25
as strength then, even so. *Josh* 14:11
as I have done, so God hath.*Judg*1:7
so let all thine enemies perish. 5:31
As thou art, so were they. 8:18
man is, so is his strength. 21
as they did to me, so have I. 15:11
then speakest thou so to me ?
1 Sam 9:21
so shall it be done unto his. 11:7
so shall thy mother be childless.
15:33
hast thou deceived me so ? 19:17
as his name is, so is he. 25:25
so shall his part be that. 30:24
so shalt thou say to my. *2 Sam* 7:8
as thy servant said, so it is. 13:35
so let him curse. Who shall then
. . . done so ? 16:10; *1 Ki* 1:6
so shall I be saved from mine.
2 Sam 22:4; *Ps* 18:3
so the Lord was entreated for.
2 Sam 24:25
even so will I certainly. *1 Ki* 1:30
my lord the king say so too. 36
the king said, So shall thy. 20:40
not king say so. 22:8; *2 Chr* 18:7
so it fell out to him. *2 Ki* 7:20
so be established, so. *2 Chr* 20:20
so kill the passover and. 35:6
so it ceased to the second year of.
Ezra 4:24
so I prayed. *Neh* 2:4
so God shake out. 5:13
not children of Israel done so. 8:17
so didst thou get thee a name. 9:10
and so will I go in unto. *Esth* 4:16
so it is, hear it. *Job* 5:27
I know it is so of truth: but ? 9:2
and if it were so, why ? 21:4
so should I be delivered for. 23:7
in so doing, my Maker. 32:22
so will we sing and. *Ps* 21:13
let them not say, So would. 35:25
do good, so shalt thou dwell. 37:3
so panteth my soul after thee. 42:1
so shall the King desire thy. 45:11
as we have heard, so have we. 48:8

so is thy praise to the ends. *Ps* 48:10
thy glory, so as I have seen. 63:2
so foolish was I, and ignorant. 73:22
so he fed them. 78:72
so we thy people. 79:13
so will we not go back from. 80:18
so I gave them up. 81:12
so is thy wrath. 90:11
so the Lord pitieth them. 103:13
so let it come, so let it be. 109:17
so is every one that. 115:8; 135:18
he hath not dealt so with. 147:20
so shalt thou find favour and. *Pr* 3:4
so shall they be life to thy soul 22
so shall thy poverty. 6:11; 24:34
whirlwind, so is the wicked. 10:25
in his heart, so is he. 23:7
as the one dieth, so dieth. *Eccl* 3:19
all points as he came, so shall. 5:16
as is the good, so is the sinner. 9:2
so shall it come to pass, so. *Isa* 14:24
for so Lord said to me, I will. 18:4
as with the people, so with. 24:2
so have we been in thy sight. 26:17
so is Pharaoh king of Egypt to. 30:6
hast laboured, if so be thou shalt be
able to profit; if so thou. 47:12
as a lamb, so he openeth not. 53:7
so shall thy sons; so shall God. 62:5
they are my people, so he was. 63:8
so will I comfort you, ye shall. 66:13
saith the Lord so shall your seed. 22
people love to have it so. *Jer* 5:31
that they may find it so. 10:18
so shall ye be my people, I your God.
11:4; *Ezek* 37:23
saith Lord, so will I break. *Jer* 19:11
Come, and let us go, so we. 35:11
obey the Lord, so shall it be. 38:20
so he dwelt among the people. 39:14
so shall be with all men that. 42:17
mouth in dust, if so be. *Lam* 3:29
as I have done, so shall. *Ezek* 12:11
saying, As is the mother, so is. 16:44
repent, so iniquity shall not. 18:30
covereth, I have set thee so. 28:14
so thou shalt do, so shall ye. 45:20
if it be so, our God is. *Dan* 3:17
shalt abide for me; so will. *Hos* 3:3
so were they filled. 13:6
so shall they run. *Joel* 2:4
so the Lord of hosts shall. *Amos* 5:14
so their dwelling should. *Zeph* 3:7
so my Spirit remaineth. *Hag* 2:5
so is this people, so is this. 14
to our doings, so hath. *Zech* 1:6
so will I save you, and ye. 8:13
so shall be plague of horse. 14:15
Suffer it to be so now. *Mat* 3:15
for so persecuted they. 5:12
let your light so shine. 16
shall teach men so. 19
if God so clothe the grass. 6:30
as thou hast believed, so be. 8:13
it was never so seen in. 9:33
even so, Father: for so it seemed
good in thy. 11:26; *Luke* 10:21
so shall the Son of man be. *Mat* 12:40
Luke 11:30; 17:24
if case of the man be so. *Mat* 19:10
when cometh shall find so doing.
24:46; *Luke* 12:43
are ye so without ? *Mark* 7:18
so shall it not be among you. 10:43
watch, and find them so. *Luke* 12:38
and so it is. 54
found it so as the women said. 24:24
God so loved the world. *John* 3:16
Father said to me, so I speak. 12:50
ye say well, for so I am. 13:13
even so I do. 14:31
ye bear much fruit, so shall. 15:8
as the Father hath loved me, so. 9
so have I also sent them into world.
17:18; 20:21
thou the high priest so ? 18:22
this Jesus shall so come. *Acts* 1:11
he hath so fulfilled. 3:18
are these things so ? 7:1
as a lamb dumb, so opened he. 8:32
for so hath the Lord. 13:47
they so spake, that a great. 14:1
so were the churches. 16:5
so mightily grew the word of. 19:20

for *so* had he appointed. *Acts* 20:13
so worship I the God. 24:14
so came to pass they escaped. 27:44
not as the offence, *so* also. *Rom* 5:15
so they that are in the flesh. 8:8
so then it is not of him that. 9:16
so all Israel shall be saved. 11:26
so doing shalt heap coals of. 12:20
so every one shall give. 14:12
saved, yet *so* as by fire. *1 Cor* 3:15
let man *so* account of us. 4:1
concerning him that hath *so*. 5:3
is it *so*, that there is not a wise? 6:5
so let him walk, *so* ordain I. 7:17
good for a man *so* to be. 26
but she is happier if she *so* abide. 40
when ye sin *so* against the. 8:12
even *so* hath Lord ordained. 9:14
so run. 24, 26
so let him eat that bread. 11:28
one body, *so* also is Christ. 12:12
so we preach, and *so* ye. 15:11
as he is Christ's, *so*. *2 Cor* 10:7
so will I keep myself from. 11:9
so am I; Israelites? is not a wise? 22
so, I did not burden you. 12:16
then persecuted, even *so* it is now.
Gal 4:29
bear burdens, and *so* fulfil the. 6:2
new man, *so* making peace. *Eph* 2:15
mark them which walk *so*. *Phil* 3:17
my brethren, *so* stand fast in. 4:1
received Christ Jesus, *so*. *Col* 2:6
even *so* we speak, not. *1 Thes* 2:4
and *so* shall we ever be with. 4:17
so I sware in my wrath. *Heb* 3:11
as I may *so* say, Levi paid. 7:9
so be ye holy. *1 Pet* 1:15
so is the will of God. 2:15
if the will of God be *so*. 3:17
he ought himself *so* to walk.
1 John 2:6
God *so* loved us, we ought. 4:11
because as he is, *so* are we. 17
even *so*, amen. *Rev* 1:7
even *so*, come, Lord Jesus. 22:20
see **did, do, great, long, much**

so be it

said, According to your words, *so be it*. *Josh* 2:21
I answered and said, So be it, O.
Jer 11:5

not so

do *not so* wickedly. *Gen* 19:7
oh *not so*, my Lord. 18
it must *not be so* done in. 29:26
not so, my father, this is. 48:18
not so, go ye that are. *Ex* 10:11
servant Moses is *not so*. *Num* 12:7
Lord, but they did *not so*. *Judg* 2:17
is it *not so*? 14:15
it is *not so*. *1 Sam* 20:2
the matter is *not so*. *2 Sam* 20:21
house be *not so* with God. 23:5
but it is *not so* with me. *Job* 9:35
if it be *not so*, who will? 24:25
but now because it is *not so*. 35:15
ungodly are *not so*, but are. *Ps* 1:4
the foolish doeth *not so*. *Pr* 15:7
not so, nor heart think so. *Isa* 10:7
but his lies shall *not be so*. 16:6
it shall *not be so*; his lies shall *not so* affect it. *Jer* 48:30
beginning it was *not so*. *Mat* 19:8
but it shall *not be so* among. 20:26
not so, lest there be not. 25:9
not so, but he shall be. *Luke* 1:60
over them, but shall *not be so*. 22:26
if it were *not so*, I would. *John* 14:2
Not so, Lord. *Acts* 10:14; 11:8
not only so, but we glory. *Rom* 5:3
not only so, but we also joy in. 11
ye have *not so* learned. *Eph* 4:20
things ought *not so* to be. *Jas* 3:10

so that

so that all that hear. *Gen* 21:6
so that I come again to my. 28:21
so that land of Egypt and. 47:13
so that he would not let Israel go.
Ex 10:20; 11:10
smiteth a man, *so that*. 21:12
so that thou shalt be mad for.
Deut 28:34

so that they could not. *Judg* 2:14
shouted, *so that* the. *1 Sam* 4:5
so that his name was. 18:30
so that thy children take heed.
1 Ki 8:25; *2 Chr* 6:16
his face, *so that* he died. *2 Ki* 8:15
so that they shall not say. 9:37
so that after him was none. 18:5
so that there should be. *Ezra* 9:14
so that this man was. *Job* 1:3
set me as a mark, *so that* I am. 7:20
so that I am not able. *Ps* 40:12
so that a man shall say. 58:11
he led them safely, *so that*. 78:53
so that it went ill with. 106:32
so that he wanted nothing. *Eccl* 6:2
so that thou didst not lay. *Isa* 47:7
been forsaken, *so that* no. 60:15
so that I will not take. *Jer* 33:26
so that the Lord could no. 44:22
so that in all your doings your sins.
Ezek 21:24
so that all the trees in Eden. 31:9
so that no beast might. *Dan* 8:4
so that no man did lift. *Zech* 1:21
answered not, *so that*. *Mark* 15:5
so that they which would pass to.
Luke 16:26
so that they are without. *Rom* 1:20
so that from Jerusalem I. 15:19
so that contrariwise. *2 Cor* 2:7
so that I rejoiced the more. 7:7
so that ye cannot do the. *Gal* 5:17
so that ye were ensamples to all.
1 Thes 1:7
so that we may boldly say, the Lord
is my helper. *Heb* 13:6

was so, or so was

and it *was so*. *Gen* 1:7, 9, 11, 15
24, 30
interpreted to us, *so it was*. 41:13
so it was always, cloud. *Num* 9:16
so it was when cloud was on. 20
so it was when the cloud abode. 21
fleece only, and it *was so*. *Judg* 6:38
it *was so* that all who saw it. 19:30
men of Ashdod saw that it *was so*.
1 Sam 5:7
it *was so* that when he turned. 10:9
it *was so* from that day. 30:25
it *was so* when any came to the king.
2 Sam 15:2
it *was so* that when any man. 5
so was all the counsel of. 16:23
so was it charged me. *1 Ki* 13:9
so it was that Israel. *2 Ki* 17:7
so was Israel carried away to. 23
so was the commandment of the
Lord. *2 Chr* 29:25
and *so it was* that while. *Luke* 2:6
Jesus, who *was so* named of. 21
and *so was* also James and. 4:6
affirmed it *was even so*. *Acts* 12:15

So

he sent messengers to S. *2 Ki* 17:4

soaked

their land shall be *s*. with. *Isa* 34:7*

sober

whether we be *s*. it is. *2 Cor* 5:13*
but let us watc.. and be *s*. *1 Thes* 5:6
are of the day be *s*., putting on. 8
a bishop then must be *s*. *1 Tim* 3:2*
Tit 1:8*
deacons' wives must be *s*. faithful.
1 Tim 3:11*
that aged men be *s*. grave. *Tit* 2:2*
teach the young women to be *s*. 4
loins of your mind, be *s*. *1 Pet* 1:13
be ye therefore *s*. and watch. 4:7*
be *s*., be vigilant, because your. 5:8

soberly

but to think *s*. according. *Rom* 12:3
that we should live *s*. *Tit* 2:12

sober minded

exhort young men to be *s. minded*.
Tit 2:6

soberness

the words of truth and *s*. *Acts* 26:25

sobriety

adorn themselves with *s*. *1 Tim* 2:9
in faith and holiness with *s*. 15

socket

talents, a talent for a *s*. *Ex* 38:27

sockets

make forty *s*. of silver... two *s*.
under one board for two tenons,
two *s*. *Ex* 26:19, 21, 25; 36:24, 26
their *s*. of silver, sixteen *s*. 26:25
36; 30:36
thou shalt cast five *s*. of brass. 26:37
36:38
their twenty *s*. shall be of brass.
27:10; 38:10, 11
pillars ten, their *s*. ten. 27:12; 38:12
one side, their *s*. three. 27:14
side shall be three *s*. 15; 38:14, 15
be four, their *s*. four. 27:16
of silver and their *s*. brass. 17, 18
make bars, pillars, *s*. of. 35:11
court, pillars, and their *s*. 17
s. of the sanctuary, *s*. of the veil,
hundred *s*. 38:27
brass of the offerings he made *s*. 30
s. of the court, and the *s*. of. 31
tabernacle and fastened his *s*. 40:18
charge of the sons of Merari shall be
the *s*. *Num* 3:26, 37; 4:31, 32
marble set on *s*. of gold. *S of S* 5:15

sod

(*American Revision, everywhere
in the Old Testament, boiled*)
Jacob *s*. pottage, Esau. *Gen* 25:29
offerings *s*. they in pots. *2 Chr* 35:13

sodden

(*American Revision, everywhere
in the Old Testament, boiled*)
eat not of it raw, nor *s*. *Ex* 12:9
wherein it is *s*. shall be broken, if it
be *s*. in a brasen pot. *Lev* 6:28
priest shall take the *s*. *Num* 6:19
he will not have *s*. flesh. *1 Sam* 2:15
the women have *s*. their. *Lam* 4:10

sodering

it is ready for *s*.; he fastened. *Isa* 41:7

Sodom

destroyed S. and Gomorrah.
Gen 13:10
the men of S. were wicked. 13
goods of S. and Gomorrah. 14:11
they took Lot who dwelt in S. 12
king of S. went out to meet. 17
because the cry of S. is great. 18:20
if I find in S. fifty righteous. 26
Lord rained upon S. fire out. 19:24
like the overthrow of S. *Deut* 29:23
Isa 13:19; *Jer* 49:18; 50:40
vine is of the vine of S. *Deut* 32:32
we should have been as S. *Isa* 1:9
word of the Lord, ye rulers of S. 10
declare their sin as S. 3:9
of them unto me as S. *Jer* 23:14
punishment of sin of S. *Lam* 4:6
thy younger sister is S. *Ezek* 16:46
48, 49, 55
again the captivity of S. 53
as God overthrew S. *Amos* 4:11
Moab shall be as S. *Zeph* 2:9
tolerable for land of S. *Mat* 10:15
11:24; *Mark* 6:11; *Luke* 10:12
Lot went out of S. *Luke* 17:29
seed, we had been as S. *Rom* 9:29
turning cities of S. and. *2 Pet* 2:6
even as S. and Gomorrah. *Jude* 7
city spiritually called S. *Rev* 11:8

sodomite

there shall be no *s*. of. *Deut* 23:17

sodomites

there were also *s*. in. *1 Ki* 14:24
Asa took away the *s*. 15:12
Jehoshaphat took the remnant of the
s. 22:46
down the houses of the *s*. *2 Ki* 23:7

soft

God maketh my heart *s*. *Job* 23:16*
speak *s*. words unto thee? 41:3
makest it *s*. with showers. *Ps* 65:10
a *s*. answer turneth. *Pr* 15:1
and a *s*. tongue breaketh. 25:15
s. raiment; they that wear *s*. clothing.
Mat 11:8; *Luke* 7:25

softer

words were *s*. than oil. *Ps* 55:21

softly

I will lead on s., as the children be
able to endure. *Gen* 33:14
Jael went s. to him and. *Judg* 4:21
came s. and uncovered. *Ruth* 3:7
lay in sackcloth, went s. *1 Ki* 21:27
waters of Shiloah that go s. *Isa* 8:6
I shall go s. all my years in. 38:15
when south wind blew s. *Acts* 27:13

soil

it was planted in a good s. *Ezek* 17:8

sojourn

down into Egypt to s. *Gen* 12:10
This one fellow came in to s. 19:9
s. in this land, and I will be. 26:3
they said, For to s. in the land. 47:4
will s. with thee and keep. *Ex* 12:48
Lev 19:33; *Num* 9:14; 15:14
which s. that offereth sacrifice.
Lev 17:8
of strangers that s. that eateth. 10
s. among you, that hunteth. 13
of strangers that s., that giveth. 20:2
of strangers that s., of them. 25:45
a Levite went to s. *Judg* 17:8
said to Micah, I go to s. where. 9
Elimelech went to s. *Ruth* 1:1
widow with whom I s. *1 Ki* 17:20
s. wheresoever thou canst s. *2 Ki* 8:1
woe is me, that I s. in Meshech.
Ps 120:5
carry her afar off to s. *Isa* 23:7
went down into Egypt to s. 52:4
faces to enter into Egypt and go to s.
Jer 42:15, 17; 44:12, 14, 28
place whither ye desire to s. 42:22
shall no more s. there. *Lam* 4:15
them from where they s. *Ezek* 20:38
and strangers who s. among. 47:22
that his seed should s. *Acts* 7:6

sojourned

from thence Abraham s. *Gen* 20:1
and s. in the Philistines' land. 21:34
I s. with Laban, and stayed. 32:4
Abraham and Isaac s. 35:27
come from where he s. *Deut* 18:6
s. in Egypt with a few, and. 26:5
s. in Bethlehem-judah. *Judg* 17:7
an old man of Ephraim s. in. 19:16
she s. in the land of the. *2 Ki* 8:2
Jacob s. in the land. *Ps* 105:23
by faith he s. in the land. *Heb* 11:9

sojourner

I am a s. with you, give. *Gen* 23:4
a s. of the priest shall not. *Lev* 22:10
relieve him: though he be a s. 25:35
shall be as a s. with thee. 40
s. wax rich by thee and brother sell
himself to s. 47
six cities a refuge for Israel and s.
Num 35:15
I am a stranger, a s., as. *Ps* 39:12

sojourners

strangers and s. with me. *Lev* 25:23
the Beerothites were s. *2 Sam* 4:3
we are s. as were all. *1 Chr* 29:15

sojourneth

borrow of her that s. *Ex* 3:22
be to him that is homeborn, and to
stranger that s. 12:49; *Lev* 16:29
stranger that s. eat blood. *Lev* 17:12
that s. among you shall keep. 18:26
meat for stranger that s. 25:6
be for you and for the stranger that s.
Num 15:15; 16:29; 19:10
forgiven the stranger that s. 15:26
refuge for stranger that s. *Josh* 20:9
in any place where he s. *Ezra* 1:4
every one that s. in Israel. *Ezek* 14:7
in whatever tribe stranger s. 47:23

sojourning

the s. of Israel in Egypt. *Ex* 12:40
a certain Levite s. on. *Judg* 19:1
pass the time of your s. *1 Pet* 1:17

solace

come, let us s. ourselves. *Pr* 7:18

sold

Esau s. his birthright. *Gen* 25:33
father hath s. us, devoured. 31:15
s. Joseph to the Ishmaelites. 37:28
the Midianites s. him into. 36

Joseph s. corn unto the. *Gen* 41:56
was that s. to all the people. 42:6
Joseph your brother whom ye s. 45:4
angry with yourselves that ye s. 5
the Egyptians s. every man. 47:20
the priests s. not their lands. 22
nothing then shall be s. *Ex* 22:3
the land shall not be s. *Lev* 25:23
redeem that which his brother s. 25
house that was s. shall go out. 33
of the suburbs may not be s. 34
shall not be s. as bondmen. 42
no devoted thing shall be s. 27:28
and if thy brother be s. *Deut* 15:12
there shall ye be s. unto your. 28:68
except their Rock had s. them. 32:30
he s. them into the hands. *Judg* 2:14
s. them to Cushan-rishathaim. 3:8
s. to Jabin. 4:2
s. them into the hands of the. 10:7
s. them into the hand of Sisera.
1 Sam 12:9
thou hast s. thyself to. *1 Ki* 21:20
ass's head was s. for 80. *2 Ki* 6:25
fine flour s. for a shekel. 7:1, 16
Israel s. themselves to do. 17:17
our brethren who were s. to the . . .
they be s. unto us? *Neh* 5:8
in day wherein they s. victuals. 13:15
who brought ware and s. on. 16
are s. I and my people to be slain and
perish; but . . . been s. *Esth* 7:4
Joseph who was s. for. *Ps* 105:17
creditors is it to whom I s. you ? for
your iniquities have ye s. *Isa* 50:1
ye have s. yourselves for. 52:3
brother who hath been s. *Jer* 34:14
our wood is s. unto us. *Lam* 5:4
return to that which is s. *Ezek* 7:13
and they have s. a girl. *Joel* 3:3
children of Judah have ye s. 7
out of place whither ye s. them. 7
s. the righteous for silver. *Amos* 2:6
are not two sparrows s.? *Mat* 10:29
went and s. all that he had. 13:46
commanded him to be s. 18:25
s. and bought, overthrew . . . that s.
21:12; *Mark* 11:15; *Luke* 19:45
might have been s. for much and.
Mat 26:9; *Mark* 14:5; *John* 12:5
are not five sparrows s.? *Luke* 12:6
bought, they s. they planted. 17:28
the temple those that s. *John* 2:14
said to them that s. doves, Take. 16
and s. their possessions and goods.
Acts 2:45; 4:34
Joses having land s. it and. 4:37
Ananias s. a possession. 5:1
after it was s. was it not in thine ? 4
ye s. the land for so much ? 8
I am carnal, s. under sin. *Rom* 7:14
is s. in shambles, that. *1 Cor* 10:25
one morsel of meat s. *Heb* 12:16

soldier

parts, to every s. a part. *John* 19:23
Cornelius called a devout s. that
waited on. *Acts* 10:7
to dwell by himself, with a s. 28:16
hardness as a good s. *2 Tim* 2:3
who hath chosen him to be a s. 4

soldiers

the s. fell upon the. *2 Chr* 25:13*
to require of the king s. *Ezra* 8:22
the armed s. of Moab. *Isa* 15:4*
having s. under me. *Mat* 8:9
Luke 7:8
s. took Jesus, and gathered unto him
the whole band of s. *Mat* 27:27
gave large money unto the s. 28:12
s. demanded, saying. *Luke* 3:14
the s. mocked him, offered. 23:36
s. platted a crown of. *John* 19:2
the s. took his garments, and. 23
these things the s. did. 24
s. brake the legs. 32
but one of the s. with a spear. 34
Peter to four quaternions of s.
Acts 12:4
Peter was sleeping between two s. 6
no small stir among the s. 18
saw the chief captain and s. 21:32
that he was borne of the s. 35
make ready 200 s. to go to. 23:23

Paul said to the s. Except. *Acts* 27:31
then the s. cut off the ropes. 32
the s.' counsel was to kill. 42

sole

but the dove found no rest for the s.
of her foot. *Gen* 8:9
a sore botch from the s. *Deut* 28:35
would not set the s. of her foot. 56
neither shall the s. of thy foot. 65
every place s. of your foot. *Josh* 1:3
from the s. of his foot to the crown
of his head was no. *2 Sam* 14:25
Satan smote Job from s. *Job* 2:7
from s. of foot to head. *Isa* 1:6
s. of their feet like the s. *Ezek* 1:7
see **feet**

solemn

in your s. days ye. *Num* 10:10*
sing praise with a s. sound. *Ps* 92:3
it is iniquity, even the s. *Lam* 1:13
called as in a s. day. *Lam* 2:22
what will ye do in s. day ? *Hos* 9:5
see **assembly, feast, feasts**

solemnities

Zion, the city of our s. *Isa* 33:20
offerings in s. of Israel. *Ezek* 45:17*
in the s. meat offering shall. 46:11

solemnity

in the s. of the year of. *Deut* 31:10*
shall have song as when a holy s. is.
Isa 30:29*

solemnly

the man did s. protest. *Gen* 43:3
yet protest s. to them. *1 Sam* 8:9

solitarily

people which dwell s. in. *Mi* 7:14

solitary

that night be s., let no. *Job* 3:7*
and famine they were s. 30:3*
setteth the s. in families. *Ps* 68:6
in the wilderness in a s. 107:4*
wilderness and s. place. *Isa* 35:1
how doth city sit s. that. *Lam* 1:1
Jesus departed into a s. *Mark* 1:35*

Solomon

born to David in Jerusalem, S.
2 Sam 5:14; *1 Chr* 3:5; 14:4
he called his name S. *2 Sam* 12:24
S. his brother he called not.
1 Ki 1:10, 19, 26
S. thy son shall reign after. 13, 17, 30
I and my son S. shall be. 1:21
God save king S. 34, 39
David even so be he with S. 37
hath made S. king. 43
God make the name of S. 47
let S. swear to me that he will. 51
David charged S. his son. 2:1
king S. sware. 23
established in the hand of S. 46
S. made affinity with Pharaoh. 3:1
S. loved the Lord. 3
the Lord appeared to S. 5; 9:2
2 Chr 1:7; 7:12
S. had asked this thing. *1 Ki* 3:10
S.'s provision for one day. 4:22
God gave S. wisdom. 29; 5:12
came to hear the wisdom of S. 4:34
Mat 12:42; *Luke* 11:31
Tyre sent his servants to S. *1 Ki* 5:1
king S. raised a levy out of. 13
so S. built the house and. 6:14
2 Chr 7:11; *Acts* 7:47
the work that S. made. *1 Ki* 7:51
S. assembled the elders of Israel.
8:1; *2 Chr* 5:2
S. spread forth his hands. *1 Ki* 8:22
when S. made an end of praying.
54; *2 Chr* 7:1
S. held a feast. *1 Ki* 8:65
S. made a navy of ships. 9:26
when the queen of Sheba heard of
the fame of S. 10:1; *2 Chr* 9:1
all the earth sought to S. *1 Ki* 10:24
2 Chr 9:23
but king S. loved many. *1 Ki* 11:1
S. clave to these in love. 2
when S. was old. 4
S. went after Ashtoreth and. 5
S. did evil. 6
S. built for Chemosh and Molech. 7

the Lord was angry with S. *1 Ki* 11:9
Edomite, an adversary to S. 14
S. built Millo. 27
S. made Jeroboam ruler over. 28
S. sought therefore to kill. 40
S. slept with his fathers. 43
fled from the presence of S. 12:2
shields of gold which S. made.
    14:26; *2 Chr* 12:9
of which the Lord said to David and
    to S. *2 Ki* 21:7; *2 Chr* 33:7
S. my son is young. *1 Chr* 22:5
for his name shall be S. 9
to help S. 17
S. thy son, he shall build. 28:6
thou S. my son, know the God. 9
David gave to S. the pattern. 11
S. my son, whom God alone. 29:1
give to S. my son a perfect. 19
S. sat on the throne of the. 23
Lord magnified S. exceedingly. 25
S. numbered all the. *2 Chr* 2:17
are the things wherein S. 3:3
since time of S. not such joy. 30:26
children of S.'s servants. *Ezra* 2:55
    58; *Neh* 7:57, 60; 11:3
the commandment of S. *Neh* 12:45
did not king S. sin by ? 13:26
proverbs of S. *Pr* 1:1; 10:1; 25:1
of songs which is S.'s. *S of S* 1:1
but comely, as the curtains of S. 5
behold, his bed which is S.'s. 3:7
behold king S. 11
S. had a vineyard at. 8:11
S. must have a thousand. 12
the sea S. made was. *Jer* 52:20
David begat S. *Mat* 1:6
S. begat Roboam. 7
S. in all his glory. 6:29; *Luke* 12:27
a greater than S. is here.
    Mat 12:42; *Luke* 11:31
Jesus walked in S.'s. *John* 10:23
people ran to them to S.'s. *Acts* 3:11
with one accord in S.'s porch. 5:12

some

Lot said, lest s. evil. *Gen* 19:19
let me now leave with thee s. 33:15
cast him into s. pit, and we will say,
    S. evil beast hath. 37:20
took s. of his brethren and. *Ex* 16:17
gathered s. more, s. less. 16:17
but s. of them left of it till. 20
s. went out on seventh day. 27
shall put s. of the blood. *Lev* 4:7, 18
the priest shall dip his finger in s. 17
Arad took s. of them. *Num* 21:1
thou shalt put s. of thine. 27:20
because he hath found s. *Deut* 24:1
let fall s. of the handfuls. *Ruth* 2:16
s. bade me kill thee. *1 Sam* 24:10
hid in s. pit, or in s. *2 Sam* 17:9
in him there is found s. *1 Ki* 14:13
s. mischief will come. *2 Ki* 7:9
but I will grant s. deliverance.
    2 Chr 12:7
Asa oppressed s. of the people.16:10
s. had wives by whom. *Ezra* 10:44
s. said, We have mortgaged our.
    Neh 5:3
saw I s. treading winepresses. 13:15
and s. of my servants set. 19
s. remove landmarks. *Job* 24:2
s. trust in chariots, s. *Ps* 20:7
I looked for s. to take pity. 69:20
unless they cause s. to fall. *Pr* 4:16
not leave s. gleaning ? *Jer* 49:9
and it cast down s. of the. *Dan* 8:10
s. of them of understanding. 11:35
s. to everlasting life, and s. to. 12:2
overthrown s., as God. *Amos* 4:11
they not leave s. grapes ? *Ob* 5
s. fell by the way side. *Mark* 4:4; *Luke* 8:5
s. fell on stony places, where they had
    not much. *Mat* 13:5; *Mark* 4:5
and s. fell among thorns. *Mat* 13:7
    Mark 4:7; *Luke* 8:7
S. say thou art John the Baptist, s.
    Mat 16:14; *Mark* 8:28; *Luke* 9:19
be s. standing here, which shall not.
    Mat 16:28; *Mark* 9:1; *Luke* 9:27
s. eunuchs which were so born, s.
    made. *Mat* 19:12

s. ye shall kill and crucify, s.
    Mat 23:34
they worshipped him, but s. 28:17
s. fell upon a rock, and. *Luke* 8:6
and s. of you shall cause to. 21:16
there are s. of you that. *John* 6:64
Peter overshadow s. of. *Acts* 5:15
giving out that himself was s. 8:9
how can I except s. man should ? 31
seeking s. to lead him by. 13:11
s. of them believed. 17:4
hear s. new thing. 21
s. mocked. 32
s. cried one thing, s. 19:32; 21:34
I pray you take s. meat. 27:34
s. on boards, s. on broken. 44
s. believed and s. believed not. 28:24
that I may impart to you s.
    Rom 1:11
that I might have s. fruit. 13
for what if s. did not believe ? 3:3
as s. affirm that we say, Let us. 8
for a good man s. would even. 5:7
any means I might save s. of. 11:14
and if s. of the branches be. 17
now s. are puffed up. *1 Cor* 4:18
such were s. of you, but ye. 6:11
for s. with conscience of the. 8:7
might by all means save s. 9:22
neither be idolaters as were s. 10:7
commit fornication, as s. of them. 8
as s. tempted Christ and were. 9
nor murmur ye as s. of them. 10
and God hath set s. in the. 12:28
greater part remain, but s. 15:6
how say s. that there is no ? 12
for s. have not the knowledge. 34
I think to be bold against s. which
    think of us as if. *2 Cor* 10:2
not compare ourselves with s. 12
be s. that trouble you. *Gal* 1:7
s. prophets, s. evangelists. *Eph* 4:11
s. indeed preach Christ. *Phil* 1:15
there are s. among you. *2 Thes* 3:11
charge s. that they teach. *1 Tim* 1:3
from which s. having swerved. 6
s. having put away, have made. 19
in latter times s. shall depart. 4:1
s. are already turned aside. 5:15
s. men's sins open beforehand, s. 24
the good works of s. are. 25
which while s. coveted after. 6:10
overthrow the faith of s. *2 Tim* 2:18
s. vessels to honour and s. 20
house is builded by s. man. *Heb* 3:4
for s. when they heard, did. 16
it remaineth, that s. must. 4:6
as the manner of s. is. 10:25
having provided s. better. 11:40
thereby s. entertained angels. 13:2
Lord is not slack, as s. *2 Pet* 3:9
in which are s. things hard to be. 16
of s. have compassion. *Jude* 22
devil shall cast s. of you. *Rev* 2:10

somebody

Jesus said, S. hath touched me.
    Luke 8:46*
boasting himself to be s. *Acts* 5:36

something

for he thought, s. hath. *1 Sam* 20:26
that s. should be given. *Mark* 5:43
and seeking to catch s. *Luke* 11:54
should give s. to poor. *John* 13:29
to receive s. of them. *Acts* 3:5
as though ye would enquire s. 23:15*
man who hath s. to say to thee. 18
a man think himself to be s. *Gal* 6:3

sometime, -s

ye when were s. afar off. *Eph* 2:13*
for ye were s. darkness, but. 5:8*
you that were s. alienated. *Col* 1:21*
in which ye walked s. when. 3:7
also were s. foolish. *Tit* 3:3*
who s. were disobedient . . . in days
    of Noah. *1 Pet* 3:20*

somewhat

have done s. against commandments.
    Lev 4:13*, 27*
ruler hath done s. through. 22*
if the plague be s. dark. 13:6, 21
    26, 28, 56
bright spot, and s. reddish. 19, 24
he said, I have s. to say. *1 Ki* 2:14

him, and take s. of him. *2 Ki* 5:20
ease s. grievous servitude of.
    2 Chr 10:4*
ease s. the yoke. 9*
make it s. lighter for us. 10
Simon, I have s. to say. *Luke* 7:40
as to enquire s. of him. *Acts* 23:20
if first I be s. filled with. *Rom* 15:24*
that you may have s. to. *2 Cor* 5:12
though I should boast s. more. 10:8
those who seemed to be s. *Gal* 2:6
necessity this man have s. *Heb* 8:3
nevertheless, I have s. *Rev* 2:4

son

*This word is used as now, and also
for a grandson, 2 Sam 9:6, and even
for more remote descendants, Isa
19:11. The word is also used for a
pupil, much as one uses it now, as a
term of affection, 1 Tim 1:2. It
is also used in such expressions as
son of Belial, 1 Sam 25:17*

I will give thee s. of Sarah.
    Gen 17:16, 19; 18:10, 14
Sarah bare Abraham a s. 21:2, 7
cast this bondwoman and her s. 10
my master's wife bare a s. 24:36
appointed for my master's s. 44
let her be thy master's s.'s wife. 51
therefore given me this s. 29:33
heard me, and given me a s. 30:6
shall add to me another s. 24
shalt have this s. also. 35:17
because he was the s. of his. 17
if it be a s. then ye. *Ex* 1:16
every s. that is born ye shall. 22
grew, and he became her s. 2:10
cut off the foreskin of her s. 4:25
have gored a s. or a daughter. 21:31
the s. of thy handmaid may. 23:12
that s. that is priest in stead. 29:30
her purifying for a s. *Lev* 12:6
the s. of an Israelitish. 24:10
the Israelitish woman's s. 11
his uncle, or his uncle's s. may. 25:49
me, thou s. of Zippor. *Num* 23:18
because he hath no s. 27:4
if a man die and have no s. 8
if s. of thy mother entice. *Deut* 13:6
the s. of the beloved, firstborn, be-
    fore the s. of the hated. 21:16, 17
a stubborn and rebellious s. 18
this our s. is stubborn and. 20
eye shall be evil towards her s. 28:56
in his youngest s. set up. *Josh* 6:26
border went by the valley of s. 15:8
arise, Barak, lead captivity captive,
    thou s. of. *Judg* 5:12
have made thee the s. of his. 9:18
Is not he the s. of Jerubbaal ? 28
the s. of a strange woman. 11:2
besides her he had neither s. 34
conceive and bear a s. 13:3, 5, 7
the woman bare a s. and called. 24
Ruth bare a s. *Ruth* 4:13
a s. born to Naomi. 17
Hannah gave her s. suck until.
    1 Sam 1:23
Fear not, for thou hast born a s. 4:20
Kish had a s. whose name was. 9:2
that is come to s. of Kish ? 10:11
I have seen a s. of Jesse. 16:18
whose s. is this ? 17:55
whose s. art thou ? 58
cometh not the s. of Jesse ? 20:27
s. of the perverse rebellious. 30
as long as the s. of Jesse liveth. 31
will s. of Jesse give you fields. 22:7
Doeg said, I saw the s. of Jesse. 9
Hear now, thou s. of Ahitub. 12
who is the s. of Jesse ? 25:10
he is such a s. of Belial. 17
am the s. of a stranger. *2 Sam* 1:13
Jonathan hath yet a s. lame. 9:3
given thy master's s. all that. 9
master's s. may have food to eat;
    Mephibosheth thy master's s. 10
I will shew kindness to the s. 10:2
where is thy master's s.? 16:3
my hand against the king's s. 18:12
I have no s. to keep my name in. 18
tidings, because king's s. is dead. 20

inheritance in the s. of Jesse.
2 Sam 20:1
thou hast given him a s. *1 Ki* 3:6
bowels yearned upon her s. 26
David a wise s. over this. 5:7
Hiram was a widow's s. of. 7:14
neither inheritance in the s. of Jesse.
12:16; *2 Chr* 10:16
Abijah the s. of Jeroboam. *1 Ki* 14:1
to ask a thing of thee for her s. 5
the s. of the mistress of the. 17:17
on the widow, by slaying her s. 20
carry him back to Joash the king's s.
22:26; *2 Chr* 18:25
reigned, because he had no s.
2 Ki 1:17
she said unto her s., Bring me. 4:6
season thou shalt embrace a s. 16
and the woman bare a s. at. 17
did I desire a s. of my lord ? 28
took up her s. 37
thy s. that we may eat him: and she
hath hid her s. 6:29
see ye how this s. of a murderer. 32
the woman, whose s. he had. 8:1
her s. whom Elisha restored to. 5
Athaliah saw her s. was dead. 11:1
2 Chr 22:10
shewed them the king's s. *2 Ki* 11:4
he brought forth the king's s. and. 12
side, thou s. of Jesse. *1 Chr* 12:18
also was the s. of the giant. 20:6
behold, a s. shall be born to. 22:9
there was never a s. left him.
2 Chr 21:17
buried him, because he is s. of. 22:9
he said, Behold, the king's s. 23:3
Zabdiel their overseer, s. *Neh* 11:14
he shall neither have s. *Job* 18:19
kiss the S. lest he be angry. *Ps* 2:12
thine own mother's s. 50:20
righteousness unto the king's s. 72:1
the s. of thine handmaid. 86:16
nor shall the s. of wickedness. 89:22
I am the s. of thine. 116:16
as a father the s. in whom he. *Pr* 3:12
I was my father's s., only. 4:3
a wise s. maketh a glad father. 10:1
15:20
a wise s.: he that sleepeth in harvest
is a s. causeth. 10:5; 17:2; 19:26
a wise s. heareth his father's. 13:1
foolish s. is a grief to his. 17:25
a foolish s. is the calamity. 19:13
keepeth the law, is a wise s. 28:7
what, the s. of my womb, s. of ? 31:2
he begetteth a s., nothing. *Eccl* 5:14
blessed land, when king is s. 10:17
not afraid of anger of the s. *Isa* 7:4
let us set a king in it, even the s. 6
Samaria is Remaliah's s. 9
virgin shall conceive and bear a s. 14
us a child is born, unto us a s. 9:6
fallen, O Lucifer, s. of. 14:12
I will cut off from Babylon s. 22
I am s. of the wise, the s. of. 19:11
not have compassion on the s. 49:15
the s. of the stranger speak. 56:3
mourning, as for an only s. *Jer* 6:26
should not have a s. to reign. 33:21
deliver neither s. nor daughter.
Ezek 14:20
also the soul of the s. is mine. 18:4
if he beget s. that is a robber. 10
a s. that seeth his father's sins. 14
why, doth not s. bear iniquity of the
father ? when the s. hath done. 19
s. shall not bear the iniquity of the
father, nor the father of the s. 20
for s. or daughter they may. 44:25
which bare him a s. *Hos* 1:3, 8
he is an unwise s. for he. 13:13
nor was I a prophet's s. *Amos* 7:14
as mourning of an only s. 8:10
for the s. dishonoureth. *Mi* 7:6
a s. honoureth his father. *Mal* 1:6
she shall bring forth a s. *Mat* 1:21
Luke 1:31
Jesus said, S. be of good cheer.
Mat 9:2; *Mark* 2:5
he that loveth s. or. *Mat* 10:37
the S., but the Father; nor any the
Father, save the S., and he to whom
the S. 11:27; *Luke* 10:22

the carpenter's s. *Mat* 13:55
Mark 6:3; *Luke* 4:22
Christ the s. of the living. *Mat* 16:16
S. go work to-day in my. 21:28
but when husbandmen saw the s. 38
of Christ ? whose s. is he ? 22:42
having yet one s. his. *Mark* 12:6
and the father betray the s. 13:12
knoweth not the s., but Father. 32
art thou the Christ, the s. of ? 14:61
Elisabeth shall bear thee a s.
Luke 1:13
be called the S. of the Highest. 32
Elisabeth conceived a s. 36
she brought forth a s. 57
mother said, S. why hast thou ? 2:48
30 years, being, as was supposed,
the s. of Joseph, who was s. 3:23
dead man carried out, only s. 7:12
if s. of peace be there, your. 10:6
if a s. shall ask bread of any. 11:11
shall be divided against the s. 12:53
the younger s. gathered all. 15:13
s. thou art ever with me, and all. 31
s. remember, that thou in. 16:25
forasmuch as he also is the s. 19:9
only begotten s. which is in the bosom
of. *John* 1:18
Jesus of Nazareth, s. of Joseph. 45
the Father loveth the s., and hath
given all things. 3:35; 5:20
on the s.: he that believeth not s. 3:36
nobleman whose s. was sick. 4:46
s. can do nothing of himself, what
things Father . . . the s. 5:19
even so the s. quickeneth whom. 21
committed all judgement to the s. 22
honour the s. He that honoureth not
the s. honoureth not the Father. 23
so hath he given to the s. to have. 26
every one who seeth s. and. 6:40
said, Is not this Jesus the s.? 42
but the S. abideth ever. 8:35
if s. therefore shall make you free. 36
is this your s.? 9:19
We know that this is our s. 20
Father may be glorified in s. 14:13
none of them is lost, but the s. 17:12
Simon, s. of Jonas, lovest ? 21:15
Barnabas, the s. of consolation, a
Levite. *Acts* 4:36
and nourished for her own s. 7:21
David the s. of Jesse, a man. 13:22
Pharisee, the s. of a Pharisee. 23:6
Paul's sister's s. heard of their. 16
Sarah shall have a s. *Rom* 9:9
shall s. also himself. *1 Cor* 15:28
but s. and if s. then an heir. *Gal* 4:7
and her s.: for the s. of the bondwoman shall not be heir with s. 30
s. with father, he served. *Phil* 2:22
Marcus, sister's s. to. *Col* 4:10
man of sin, s. of perdition. *2 Thes* 2:3
I commit unto thee, s. Timothy.
1 Tim 1:18
and he shall be to me a s. *Heb* 1:5
unto the s. he saith, Thy throne is. 8
but Christ as a s. over his. 3:6
though he were a s. yet learned. 5:8
of the oath maketh the s. 7:28
s. of Pharaoh's daughter. 11:24
and scourgeth every s. 12:6
for what s. is he whom father ? 7
of Balaam, s. of Bosor. *2 Pet* 2:15
denieth Father and s. *1 John* 2:22
s. the same hath not the Father, but
he that acknowledgeth the s. 23
ye also shall continue in the s. 24
sent the s. to be the Saviour. 4:14
he that hath the s. hath life, and he
that hath not the s. of God. 5:12
from Lord Jesus Christ, s. *2 John* 3
hath both the Father and the s. 9

see David

son of God
fourth is like s. of God. *Dan* 3:25
if thou be the s. of God, command.
Mat 4:3; 27:40; *Luke* 4:3, 9
do with thee, Jesus thou s. of God ?
Mat 8:29; *Luke* 8:28
truth thou art s. of God. *Mat* 14:33
thou be Christ the s. of God. 26:63
I am the s. of God. 27:43

truly this was the s. of God.
Mat 27:54; *Mark* 15:39
Jesus Christ the s. of God. *Mark* 1:1
saying, Thou art the s. of God.
3:11; *John* 1:49
shall be called s. of God. *Luke* 1:35
son of Adam, which was the s. of
God. 3:38
crying out, thou art Christ the s. of
God. 4:41; *John* 6:69; 11:27
then the s. of God ? *Luke* 22:70
this is the s. of God. *John* 1:34
the only begotten s. of God. 3:18
hear the voice of the s. of God. 5:25
thou believe on the s. of God ? 9:35
I said, I am the s. of God. 10:36
s. of God might be glorified. 11:4
made himself the s. of God. 19:7
Jesus is Christ, the s. of God. 20:31
he said, I believe that Jesus Christ is
the s. of God. *Acts* 8:37
that he is the s. of God. 9:20
declared to be the s. of God with.
Rom 1:4
for the s. of God was not yea and
nay. *2 Cor* 1:19
faith of the s. of God. *Gal* 2:20
of knowledge of s. of God. *Eph* 4:13
high priest, Jesus the s. of God.
Heb 4:14
themselves the s. of God afresh. 6:6
like to the s. of God abideth. 7:3
trodden under foot s. of God. 10:29
for this purpose the s. of God was.
1 John 3:8
confess Jesus is the s. of God. 4:15
believeth Jesus is the s. of God. 5:5
he that believeth on the s. of God. 10
believe on the name of s. of God. 13
we know that the s. of God is. 20
things saith the s. of God. *Rev* 2:18

his son
after name of *his* s. Enoch. *Gen* 4:17
what *his* younger s. had done. 9:24
grievous because of *his* s. 21:11
the knife to slay *his* s. 22:10
burnt offering instead of *his* s. 13
brother's daughter to *his* s. 24:48
sent from Isaac *his* s. while. 25:6
Abraham, God blessed *his* s. 11
Shechem *his* s. came to gate. 34:20
Hamor and Shechem *his* s. 26
Jacob mourned for *his* s. 37:34
betrothed her to *his* s. *Ex* 21:9
every man upon *his* s. 32:29
but for *his* s. he may. *Lev* 21:2
on Eleazar *his* s. *Num* 20:26, 28
as a man doth bear *his* s. *Deut* 1:31
thou shalt not give to *his* s. 7:3
as a man chasteneth *his* s. so the. 8:5
not any maketh *his* s. to pass. 18:10
mourned for *his* s. *2 Sam* 13:37
serve in presence of *his* s.? 16:19
king was grieved for *his* s. 19:2
out of *his* s.'s hand. *1 Ki* 11:35
and to *his* s. will I give one tribe. 36
give him a lamp, to set up *his* s. 15:4
for all the sins of Elah *his* s. 16:13
in *his* s.'s days will I bring. 21:29
took *his* eldest s., offered. *2 Ki* 3:27
Ahaz made *his* s. to pass. 16:3
Manasseh made *his* s. to pass. 21:6
said to David and to Solomon *his* s.
7; *2 Chr* 33:7
no man might make *his* s. pass.
2 Ki 23:10
the king slew *his* s. *2 Chr* 24:22
his rod, hateth *his* s. *Pr* 13:24
shall have him become *his* s. 29:21
what is *his* s.'s name, if thou. 30:4
all nations shall serve *his* s. and *his*
son's s. *Jer* 27:7
thou *his* s. O Belshazzar. *Dan* 5:22
as a man spareth *his* s. *Mal* 3:17
what man, whom if *his* s.? *Mat* 7:9
he sent unto them *his* s. 21:37
made a marriage for the s. 22:2
how is he then *his* s.? 45
Mark 12:37; *Luke* 20:44
gave *his* only begotten s. *John* 3:16
God sent not *his* s. to condemn. 17
Jacob gave to *his* s. Joseph. 4:5
come down and heal *his* s. 47

glorified *his s.* Jesus.   *Acts* 3:13
God having raised up *his s.*   26
serve in the gospel of *his s. Rom* 1:9
reconciled to God by the death of *his*
  s.   5:10
God sending *his* own *s.* in.   8:3
to the image of *his s.*   29
he that spared not *his* own *s.* 32
fellowship of *his s.* Jesus. *1 Cor* 1:9
God to reveal *his s.* in me. *Gal* 1:16
God sent forth *his s.* made.   4:4
God sent the spirit of *his s.* into. 6
into kingdom of *his* dear *s. Col* 1:13
and to wait for *his s.   1 Thes* 1:10
hath in these last days spoken unto
  us by *his s.*   *Heb* 1:2
offered up *his* only begotten *s.* 11:17
offered Isaac *his s.* on altar. *Jas* 2:21
is with Father and *his s.* Jesus.
                            1 John 1:3
blood of Jesus Christ *his s.*   7
on the name of *his s.* Jesus.   3:23
God sent *his* only begotten *s.* 4:9
sent *his s.* to be the propitiation. 10
which he hath testified of *his s.* 5:9
hath made him a liar; he believeth
  not record God gave of *his s.* 10
this life is in *his s.*   11
we are in *his s.* Jesus.   20
    see **beloved**

son *in law*
any besides ? *s. in law.   Gen* 19:12
Samson the *s. in law* of. *Judg* 15:6
father said unto his *s. in law.* 19:5
s. in law to the king. *1 Sam* 18:18, 23
shalt this day be my *s. in law.* 21
be the king's *s. in law.*   22
David well to be king's *s. in law.* 26
might be the king's *s. in law.*   27
faithful as the king's *s. in law* ? 22:14
Jehoram was *s. in law.   2 Ki* 8:27
Tobiah was *s. in law* to. *Neh* 6:18
was *s. in law* to Sanballat the. 13:28

my son
not be heir with *my s.   Gen* 21:10
wilt not deal falsely with *my s.* 23
he said, Here am I, *my s.*   22:7
my s. God will provide himself.   8
wife to *my s.* of Canaanites. 24:3, 37
and take a wife unto *my s.* 4, 7, 38
that thou bring not *my s.*   6, 8
my s. obey my voice.   27:8, 43
Upon me be thy curse. *my s.*   13
here am I; who art thou, *my s.*? 18
thou be *my* very *s.* Esau or not. 21, 24
see, the smell of *my s.* is as.   27
I do now unto thee, *my s.*?   37
the soul of *my s.* longeth for. 34:8
and said, It is *my s.'s* coat. 37:33
I will go into the grave to *my s.* 35
remain, till Shelah *my s.*   38:11
I gave her not to Shelah *my s.*   26
he said, *My s.* shall not go.   42:38
God be gracious to thee, *my s.* 43:29
it is enough, Joseph *my s.*   45:28
Jacob said, I know it, *my s.*   48:19
from the prey, *my s.* thou.   49:9
Israel is *my s.* even my.   *Ex* 4:22
let *my s.* go, that he may serve. 23
my s. give glory to the.   *Josh* 7:19
neither shall *my s.* rule. *Judg* 8:23
Blessed be thou of Lord, *my s.* 17:2
dedicated for *my s.* to make a.   3
I called not, *my s.*; lie.   *1 Sam* 3:6
What is there done, *my s* ?   4:16
What shall I do for *my s.*?   10:2
though it be in Jonathan *my s.* 14:39
and Jonathan *my s.* will be.   40
between me and Jonathan *my s.*   42
that *my s.* hath made a league with
  the son of Jesse, or that *my s.* 22:8
is this thy voice, *my s.* David ?
                            24:16; 26:17
I have sinned, return, *my s.* 26:21
Blessed be thou, *my s.* David.   25
father, he shall be *my s. 2 Sam* 7:14
king said, Nay, *my s.* let us. 13:25
lest they destroy *my s.*   14:11
destroy me and *my s.* out of the. 16
behold *my s.* who came forth. 16:11
wherefore wilt thou run, *my s.*? 18:22
thus he said, *My s.* Absalom. *my s.*
  my s. Absalom.   33; 19:4

I and *my s.* be counted.   *1 Ki* 1:21
she arose and took *my s.*   3:20
behold, it was not *my s.* which.   21
Nay; but the living is *my s.*   22
thy son is the dead, and *my s.*   23
dress it for me and *my s.*   17:12
thou come to me to slay *my s.*   18
and we will eat *my s.*   *2 Ki* 6:28
my s. and did eat him: give thy s. 29
give thy daughter to *my s.*   14:9
                            2 Chr 25:18
shall be *my s.   1 Chr* 17:13; 22:10
now, *my s.* Lord will be with. 22:11
I have chosen him to be *my s.* 28:6
thou, Solomon *my s.* know God.   9
Solomon *my s.* whom God.   29:1
give to Solomon *my s.* a perfect. 19
Thou art *my s.*; this day.   *Ps* 2:7
  Acts 13:33; *Heb* 1:5; 5:5
my s. despise not the chastening of.
  Pr 3:11; *Heb* 12:5
do this now, *my s.* and.   *Pr* 6:3
my s. give me thine heart.   23:26
my s. fear thou the Lord.   24:21
my s. be wise, and make.   27:11
what, *my s.*? and what, the *s.*? 31:2
further by these, *my s.   Eccl* 12:12
is Ephraim *my* dear *s.*?   *Jer* 31:20
it contemneth the rod of *my s.*, as
  every tree.   *Ezek* 21:10
I called *my s.* out of Egypt.
  Hos 11:1; *Mat* 2:15
This is *my* beloved *s. Mat* 3:17; 17:5
have mercy on *my s.*: for he. 17:15
they will reverence *my s.*   21:37
  Mark 12:6
brought to thee *my s.*   *Mark* 9:17
thee, look upon *my s.   Luke* 9:38
for this *my s.* was dead and. 15:24
to Timothy *my* own *s.   1 Tim* 1:2
my s. be strong in grace. *2 Tim* 2:1
to Titus *mine* own *s.*   *Tit* 1:4
I beseech thee for *my s. Philem* 10
his God, he shall be *my s. Rev* 21:7

thy son
thy s. thine only *s.* Isaac. *Gen* 22:2
thou hast not withheld *thy s.* 12, 16
must I needs bring *thy s.*?   24:5
I am *thy s.* thy firstborn.   27:32
whether it be *thy s.'s* coat.   37:32
behold, *thy s.* Joseph cometh. 48:2
I will slay *thy s.* even.   *Ex* 4:23
ears of *thy s.* and son's s.   10:2
thou shalt shew *thy s.* in that. 13:8
when *thy s.* asketh thee, what is
  this ?   14; *Deut* 6:20
not do any work, thou, nor *thy s.*
  Ex 20:10; *Deut* 5:14
shalt say unto *thy s.   Deut* 6:21
shalt thou take unto *thy s.*   7:3
they will turn away *thy s.* from. 4
thou must eat them before the Lord,
  thou, and *thy s.* 12:18; 16:11, 14
if *thy s.* entice thee secretly. 13:6
bring out *thy s.* that.   *Judg* 6:30
thou, *thy s.* and *thy* son's *s.* 8:22
send me David *thy s.   1 Sam* 16:19
servants, and to *thy s.* David. 25:8
one hair of *thy s.* fall. *2 Sam* 14:11
and life of *thy s.* Solomon. *1 Ki* 1:12
thy s. Solomon shall reign. 13, 17, 30
the dead is *thy s.*   3:22
and *thy s.* is the dead.   23
thy s. whom I will set upon.   5:5
out of the hand of *thy s.*   11:12
I will give one tribe to *thy s.*   13
for thee and for *thy s.*   17:13
give me *thy s.*   19
Elisha said, See, *thy s.* liveth. 23
he said, Take up *thy s.   2 Ki* 4:36
give *thy s.* that we may eat. 6:28, 29
I am thy servant, and *thy s.*   16:7
thy s. shall build my house . . .
  to be my *s. 1 Chr* 28:6; *2 Chr* 6:9
chasten *thy s.* while.   *Pr* 19:18
correct *thy s.* and he shall.   29:17
Jesus said, Bring *thy s.   Luke* 9:41
worthy to be called *thy s.* 15:19, 21
as soon as this *thy s.* was come. 30
go thy way, *thy s.* liveth.
  John 4:50, 51, 53
glorify *thy s.* that *thy s.* also. 17:1
mother, Woman, behold *thy s.* 19:26

son *of man*
he said, S. *of man,* stand.   *Ezek* 2:1
s. of man, I send thee to the.   3
and thou, *s. of man,* be not.   6
thou *s. of man,* hear what I say.   8
s. of man, eat that thou findest. 3:1
s. of man, cause thy belly to eat. 3
s. of man, go get thee to the house. 4
s. of man, all the words that I. 10
s. of man, I have made thee a.   17
O *s. of man,* they shall put.   25
thou also *s. of man,* take thee. 4:1
s. of man, I will break staff of. 16
thou *s. of man,* take thee a.   5:1
s. of man, set thy face toward
  the mountains.   6:2
thou *s. of man,* thus saith the. 7:2
s. of man, lift up thine eyes.   8:5
he said, S. *of man,* seest thou ?   6
S. *of man,* dig now in the wall.   8
s. of man, hast thou seen what ? 12
thou seen this, O *s. of man* ? 15, 17
s. of man, these are the men.   11:2
prophesy, O *s. of man.*   4
s. of man, thy brethren are.   15
s. of man, thou dwellest in a. 12:2
thou *s. of man,* prepare thee.   3
s. of man, hath not the house of ? 9
s. of man, eat thy bread with.   18
s. of man, what is that proverb ? 22
s. of man, behold, they of house. 27
s. of man, prophesy against the
  prophets.   13:2
s. of man, set thy face against thy
  people.   17
s. of man, these men have set. 14:3
s. of man, when the land sinneth. 13
s. of man, What is the vine tree ? 15:2
s. of man, cause Jerusalem.   16:2
s. of man, put forth a riddle. 17:2
s. of man, speak to the elders. 20:3
s. of man, wilt thou judge them ? 4
therefore *s. of man,* speak to.   27
s. of man, set thy face toward the
  south.   46
s. of man, set thy face toward
  Jerusalem.   21:2
sigh therefore, thou *s. of man.*   6
s. of man, prophesy and say, a. 9, 28
cry and howl *s. of man,* for it.   12
s. of man, prophesy and smite.   14
also thou *s. of man,* appoint.   19
s. of man, wilt thou judge ?   22:2
s. of man, house of Israel is to. 18
s. of man, say to her, Thou art. 24
s. of man, there were two women of.
                                  23:2
s. of man, wilt thou judge Aholah? 36
s. of man, write thee the name. 24:2
s. of man, I take away the desire. 16
s. of man, shall it not be in day ? 25
s. of man, set thy face against
  the Ammonites.   25:2
s. of man, because that Tyrus. 26:2
s. of man, take up a lamentation.
                             27:2; 28:12
s. of man, say unto the prince. 28:2
s. of man, set thy face against Zidon.
                                    21
s. of man, set thy face against
  Pharaoh.   29:2
s. of man, Nebuchadrezzar.   18
s. of man, prophesy, and say, Thus
  saith the Lord.   30:2
s. of man, I have broken the.   21
s. of man, speak to Pharaoh.   31:2
s. of man, take up a lamentation for
  Pharaoh.   32:2
s. of man, wail for the multitude. 18
s. of man, speak to children.   33:2
thou, O *s. of man,* I have set.   7
O *s. of man,* speak to the house. 10
s. of man, say to the children.   12
s. of man, they that inhabit.   24
s. of man, thy people still are. 30
s. of man, prophesy against the
  shepherds.   34:2
s. of man, set thy face against mount
  Seir.   35:2
thou *s. of man,* prophesy to.   36:1
s. of man, when the house of.   17
he said, S. *of man,* can these ? 37:3
prophesy, *s. of man,* and say.   9
s. of man, these bones are the.   11

song

s. of man, take thee one stick. *Ezek* 37:16
s. of man, set thy face against Gog. 38:2
s. of man, prophesy and say unto Gog. 14
s. of man, prophesy against Gog. 39:1
s. of man, thus saith the Lord. 17
43:18
s. of man, behold with thine. 40:4
he said, S. of man, the place. 43:7
s. of man, shew the house to. 10
s. of man, mark well, behold. 44:5
he said, S. of man, hast thou? 47:6
see **man**

song

We find in Scripture several songs composed upon important occasions; for example, Moses made one after the passage through the Red Sea, to thank God for the deliverance of his people, Ex 15:1, 2, etc. David composed a song in mourning for the death of Saul and Jonathan, and another for the death of Abner, 2 Sam 1:18, 19; 3:33. Jeremiah wrote his Lamentations, which are a song, wherein he deplores the calamities and ruin of Jerusalem; and he made another upon the death of Josiah king of Judah, 2 Chr 35:25. Deborah and Barak made a triumphant hymn after the defeat of Sisera, Judg 5:1, 2, 3, etc. The Canticles, or the Song of Songs, and the 45th Psalm, are songs to celebrate weddings, and are considered by many to be allegorical. Hannah the mother of Samuel, and king Hezekiah, returned thanks to God in songs, for the favours they had received, 1 Sam 2:1, 2, etc.; Isa 38:10, 11, etc. The songs of the Virgin Mary, Zacharias the father of John the Baptist, and old Simeon are of the same nature. They are thanksgivings to God for blessings received from him, Luke 1:46, 68; 2:29 30.

the children of Israel sang this s. unto. *Ex* 15:1; *Num* 21:17
the Lord is my strength and s. and. *Ex* 15:2; *Ps* 118:14; *Isa* 12:2
write this s.: that this s. *Deut* 31:19
this s. shall testify. 21
Moses wrote this s. 22
the words of this s. 30; 32:44
awake, Deborah, utter a s. *Judg* 5:12
to Lord words of this s. *2 Sam* 22:1
whom David set over the service of s. *1 Chr* 6:31
chief of Levites was for a s. 15:22, 27
under their father for s. in. 25:6
s. of the Lord began. *2 Chr* 29:27
now I am their s., yea, I am. *Job* 30:9
and with my s. will I. *Ps* 28:7
unto him a new s. 33:3; *Isa* 42:10
and he hath put a new s. *Ps* 40:3
night his s. shall be with me. 42:8
the s. of the drunkards. 69:12
the name of God with a s. 30
remembrance my s. in night. 77:6
O sing a new s. 96:1; 98:1; 149:1
there they required of us a s. 137:3
how shall we sing the Lord's s. in? 4
I will sing a new s. unto. 144:9
man to hear the s. of fools. *Eccl* 7:5
the s. of songs which is. *S of S* 1:1
I sing a s. of my beloved. *Isa* 5:1
not drink wine with a s. 24:9
in that day shall this s. be sung. 26:1
shall have a s. as in the night. 30:29
a derision and their s. *Lam* 3:14
them as a very lovely s. *Ezek* 33:32
they sung a new s., saying, Thou art worthy. *Rev* 5:9; 14:3
learn that s. but the 144,000. 14:3
s. of Moses and s. of the Lamb. 15:3

songs

sent thee away with s. *Gen* 31:27
his s. were a thousand. *1 Ki* 4:32
were instructed in the s. *1 Chr* 25:7*

of David there were s. *Neh* 12:46
maker who giveth s. in. *Job* 35:10
shall compass about with s. *Ps* 32:7
have been my s. in house. 119:54
Sing us one of the s. of Zion. 137:3
so is he that singeth s. *Pr* 25:20
the song of s. which is. *S of S* 1:1
sweet melody, sing s. *Isa* 23:16
part of earth have we heard s. 24:16
shall come to Zion with s. 35:10
will sing my s. to the stringed. 38:20
noise of thy s. to cease. *Ezek* 26:13
away from me the noise of thy s.
Amos 5:23
s. of temple shall be howlings. 8:3
I will turn all your s. into. 10
in psalms and spiritual s. *Eph* 5:19
one another in hymns and spiritual s.
Col 3:16

sons

(In Revisions very frequently, children)
the s. of Noah entered. *Gen* 7:13
the s. of Noah that went forth. 9:18
there are the three s. of Noah. 19
were s. born after the flood. 10:1
and spake to his s. in law. 19:14
in the presence of the s. of. 23:11
and let thy mother's s. bow. 27:29
s. of Jacob came upon slain. 34:27
lad was with the s. of Bilhah. 37:2
s. of Israel came to buy corn. 42:5
one man's s. we are no spies. 11, 32
the s. of Israel carried Jacob. 46:5
earrings in ears of your s. *Ex* 32:2
eat the flesh of your s. *Lev* 26:29
ye take too much upon you, ye s. of Levi. *Num* 16:7
of their tents, their wives and s. 27:3
in his own sin, and had no s. 27:3
if they be married to s. of. 36:3
a sodomite of the s. *Deut* 23:17
separated the s. of Adam. 32:8
Caleb drove three s. of Anak.
Josh 15:14; *Judg* 1:20
they were even the s. *Judg* 8:19
Gideon had 70 s. 30
Jair had thirty s. 10:4
Abdon had forty s. and thirty. 12:14
s. of Belial beset house. 19:22
are there yet any more s.? *Ruth* 1:11
better to thee than ten s.? *1 Sam* 1:8
s. of Eli were s. of Belial. 2:12
will take your s. and appoint. 8:11
there were three s. of. *2 Sam* 2:18
these men s. of Zeruiah be too. 3:39
eat as one of the king's s. 9:11
invited all the king's s. 13:23
hath slain all the king's s. 30
what to do with you, ye s. of Zeruiah? 16:10; 19:22
but s. of Belial shall be as. 23:6
all the king's s. *1 Ki* 1:9, 19, 25
kindness to s. of Barzillai. 2:7
for he was wiser than the s. 4:31
a certain man of the s. of. 20:35
set two men, s. of Belial. 21:10
she shut the door upon her and upon her s. *2 Ki* 4:5
meetest of your master's s. 10:3
the heads of the king's s. 8
stole him from the king's s. 11:2
they slew s. of Zedekiah before his.
2 Ki 25:7; *Jer* 39:6; 52:10
birthright was given to s. *1 Chr* 5:1
Ornan and his four s. with. 21:20
Eleazar, who had no s. 24:28
among the s. of my fathers. 28:4
as the Lord said of the s. *2 Chr* 23:3
for blood of the s. of Jehoiada. 24:25
one of the s. of Joiada. *Neh* 13:28
the ten s. of Haman. *Esth* 9:10
let Haman's ten s. be hanged. 13, 14
who among s. of mighty can? *Ps* 89:6
our s. may be as plants. 144:12
as apple tree so is my beloved among s. *S of S* 2:3
guide her among all the s. *Isa* 51:18
s. of the stranger that join. 56:6
draw near hither, ye s. of. 57:3
the s. of the stranger shall. 60:10
the s. of them that afflicted thee. 14
the s. of the alien shall be. 61:5

s. of the stranger shall not. *Isa* 62:8
the fathers and s. shall. *Jer* 6:21
even fathers and s. together. 13:14
high places to burn their s. 19:5
beget s., take wives for your s. 29:6
I set before s. of Rechabites. 35:5
no wine, ye, nor your s. for ever. 6
Israel no s.? hath he no heir? 49:1
precious s. of Zion. *Lam* 4:2
fathers shall eat the s., s. *Ezek* 5:10
when ye make your s. pass. 20:31
they caused their s. to pass. 23:37
s. of the living God. *Hos* 1:10
I raised up of your s. *Amos* 2:11
he shall purify s. of Levi. *Mal* 3:3
therefore ye s. of Jacob are. 6
is, The s. of thunder. *Mark* 3:17
whom do your s. cast? *Luke* 11:19
but as my beloved s. *1 Cor* 4:14
receive the adoption of s. *Gal* 4:5
because ye are s., God hath sent. 6
bringing many s. to glory. *Heb* 2:10
blessed both s. of Joseph. 11:21
dealeth with you as with s. 12:7
then are ye bastards, and not s. 8

sons *of God*

the s. of God saw the. *Gen* 6:2
the s. of God came in to the. 4
s. of God came to present. *Job* 1:6
2:1
all the s. of God shouted for. 38:7
are s. of the living God. *Hos* 1:10
them power to become s. of God.
John 1:12
led by the Spirit of God, they are the s. of God. *Rom* 8:14
the manifestation of s. of God. 19
be harmless, the s. of God. *Phil* 2:15
be called the s. of God. *1 John* 3:1
beloved, now are we the s. of God. 2

his sons

Noah and his s. went into the ark.
Gen 7:7
Noah went forth, and his s. 8:18
God blessed Noah and his s. 9:1
his s. Isaac and Ishmael buried. 25:9
them into the hands of his s. 30:35
his s. Esau and Jacob buried. 35:29
end of commanding his s. 49:33
his s. did unto him as he. 50:12
his s. carried him into the land. 13
Jethro came with his s. and. *Ex* 18:5
Aaron and his s. to minister. 28:1
put the garments on his s. 41; 29:8
tip of the right ear of his s. 29:20
sprinkle the blood upon his s. 21
sanctify that which is for his s. 27
Lev 8:30
priest of his s. that is anointed.
Lev 6:22
smote Og and his s. *Num* 21:35
we smote Sihon, his s. *Deut* 2:33
Lord hath chosen him and his s. 18:5
when he maketh his s. to. 21:16
have slain his s. 70 persons on.
Judg 9:18
Micah consecrated one of his s. 17:5
was to him as one of his s. 11
his s. were priests to tribe of. 18:30
now Eli heard all that his s. did.
1 Sam 2:22
his s. made themselves vile. 3:13
Samuel when old made his s. 8:1
his s. walked not in his ways. 3
me a king among his s. 16:1
grieved, every man for his s. 30:6
upon Saul and upon his s. and slew.
31:2; *1 Chr* 10:2
let seven men of his s. *2 Sam* 21:6
his s. came and told. *1 Ki* 13:11
his s. had seen what way the. 12
blood of Naboth and his s. *2 Ki* 9:26
his s. smote him with the sword.
19:37; *Isa* 37:38
Jeroboam and his s. *2 Chr* 11:14
and his s. by a covenant of salt. 13:5
light to him, and to his s. for. 21:7
his s. save the youngest of his s. 17
were servants to him and his s. 36:20
life of the king and his s. *Ezra* 6:10
he and his s. be hanged. *Esth* 9:25
and his s. went and feasted. *Job* 1:4
his s. come to honour, he. 14:21

guide Arcturus with *his s.?* *Job* 38:32
Job saw *his s.* and *his s.*' sons. 42:16
Jonadab commanded *his s.* not to.
                     Jer 35:14
give a gift to any of *his s. Ezek* 40:16
his s. shall be stirred up. *Dan* 11:10

my sons

his father, They are *my s. Gen* 48:9
nay, *my s.* for it is no good report I
  hear.   *1 Sam* 2:24
Samuel said, Behold, *my s.*   12:2
of all *my s.* he hath chosen.
              1 Chr 28:5
Hezekiah said, *My s.* *2 Chr* 29:11
Job said, It may be that *my s.*
                   Job 1:5
to come concerning *my s. Isa* 45:11
but as *my* beloved *s.* I. *1 Cor* 4:14
    see seven

thy sons

into ark, thou and *thy s.* *Gen* 6:18
ark, thou, thy wife, and *thy s.* 8:16
ordinance to thee and *thy s.*
     Ex 12:24; *Num* 18:8
firstborn of *thy s.* shalt. *Ex* 22:29
make *thy s.* go a whoring. 34:16
all the firstborn of *thy s.* thou. 20
not drink wine, nor *thy s. Lev* 10:9
it is thy due, and *thy s.*' due.   14
thou and *thy s.* shall bear. *Num* 18:1
but thou and *thy s.* with thee.   2
thou and *thy s.* shall keep your. 7
holy for thee and for *thy s.*   9
given them to thee and to *thy s.* 11
teach them *thy s.* and *thy s.*' sons.
                 Deut 4:9
and honourest *thy s.* *1 Sam* 2:29
thou art old, and *thy s.* walk not. 8:5
to-morrow shalt thou and *thy s.*
                   28:19
and *thy s.* shall till. *2 Sam* 9:10
door upon thee and *thy s.* *2 Ki* 4:4
said to Jehu, *Thy s.* shall sit on.
      15:12; *1 Chr* 17:11
thy s. shall be eunuchs in Babylon.
    2 Ki 20:18; *Isa* 39:7
bring *thy s.* in their arms. *Isa* 49:22
thy s. have fainted, they lie. 51:20
come to thee, *thy s.* shall. 60:4, 9
marrieth virgin, so shall *thy s.* 62:5
thy s. and daughters are. *Jer* 48:46
raised up *thy s.* O Zion, against *thy*
  s.   *Zech* 9:13

two sons

to Eber were born *two s. Gen* 10:25
             1 Chr 1:19
two of the *s.* of Jacob. *Gen* 34:25
unto Joseph were born *two s.* 41:50
slay my *two s.* if I bring him. 42:37
that my wife bare me *two s.* 44:27
took with him his *two s.* 48:1, 5
Zipporah and her *two s.* *Ex* 18:3
the death of the *two s.* *Lev* 16:1
two s. Mahlon and. *Ruth* 1:1, 2
she was left and her *two s.*   3
left of her *two s.*   5
come upon thy *two s.* *1 Sam* 2:34
the *two s.* of Eli were there. 4:4
thy two s. Hophni and Phinehas. 17
thy handmaid had *two s.* *2 Sam* 14:6
there with them their *two s.* 15:36
but the king took the *two s.* 21:8
creditor to take *two s.* *2 Ki* 4:1
grant that these my *two s.* may sit
  in thy kingdom. *Mat* 20:21
a certain man had *two s.* 21:28
              Luke 15:11
took with him Peter and the *two s.*
  of Zebedee. *Mat* 26:37
Midian, where he begat *two s.*
             Acts 7:29
that Abraham had *two s. Gal* 4:22

soon

ye are come so *s.* to-day ? *Ex* 2:18
ye shall *s.* utterly perish. *Deut* 4:26
my maker would *s.* take me.
              Job 32:22
they shall *s.* be cut down. *Ps* 37:2
shall *s.* stretch out her hands. 68:31
I should *s.* have subdued. 81:14
for it is *s.* cut off, and we. 90:10
they *s.* forgat his works. 106:13
that is *s.* angry dealeth. *Pr* 14:17

how *s.* is the fig tree ! *Mat* 21:20
I marvel that ye are so *s.* *Gal* 1:6
ye be not *s.* shaken in. *2 Thes* 2:2
not selfwilled, not *s.* angry. *Tit* 1:7

as soon *as*

as *s. as* he came nigh. *Ex* 32:19
ran *as s. as* he had stretched.
             Josh 8:19
as s. as they hear they shall be obedient to me. *2 Sam* 22:45; *Ps* 18:44
they go astray *as s. as.* *Ps* 58:3
as s. as his ministration. *Luke* 1:23
as s. as I see how it will. *Phil* 2:23

sooner

be restored to you the *s. Heb* 13:19
sun is no *s.* risen, but it. *Jas* 1:11

soothsayer

Diviner or Magician. *These were*
very common among Eastern
nations, magicians and sooth-
sayers being referred to at various
times, from the mention in Ex 7:11
of the magicians of Pharaoh, to the
time of the Apostles, when the trade
was still very lucrative, Acts 8:9;
13:6; 19:19.
  The law of Moses forbade the
consultation of magicians and sooth-
sayers, upon pain of death, Lev
20:6. Saul *did what he could to*
drive them out of the country of
Israel, 1 Sam 28:3. *But, for all*
this, many were still to be found ;
and the Israelites were always
much addicted to these sorts of
superstitions. And the same king
who had been so eager in driving
them out of his dominions, at last
went to consult one himself, 1 Sam
28:7, 8, etc.
  see divinations, exorcists
Balaam the son of Beor the *s.,* did
  Israel slay. *Josh* 13:22

soothsayers

people, because they are *s. Isa* 2:6
the secret cannot the *s.* *Dan* 2:27
to bring Chaldeans and *s.* 5:7
king made master of the *s.* 11
shalt have no more *s.* *Mi* 5:12

soothsaying

masters much gain by *s. Acts* 16:16

sop

I shall give a *s.,* when he had dipped
  the *s.,* he gave it to. *John* 13:26
after the *s.* Satan entered. 27, 30

sope (soap)

wash and take thee much *s. Jer* 2:22
who may abide his coming ? for he
  is like fuller's *s.* *Mal* 3:2

sorcerer

found a certain *s.* a false. *Acts* 13:6
Elymas the *s.* withstood them. 8

sorcerers

also called wise men and *s. Ex* 7:11
hearken not to your *s.* *Jer* 27:9
commanded to call *s.* *Dan* 2:2
swift witness against the *s. Mal* 3:5
s. shall have their part. *Rev* 21:8
for without are dogs and *s.* 22:15

sorceress

hither, ye sons of the *s.* *Isa* 57:3

sorceries

come on thee for thy *s.* *Isa* 47:9
with the multitude of thy *s.* 12
bewitched them with *s.* *Acts* 8:11
repented they of their *s. Rev* 9:21
for by thy *s.* were all nations. 18:23

sorcery

which beforetime used *s. Acts* 8:9

sore

they pressed *s.* upon the. *Gen* 19:9
because thou *s.* longest after. 31:30
day, when they were *s.* 34:25
the famine waxed *s.* in land. 41:56
s. in all lands. 57
s. in Canaan. 43:1; 47:4, 13
they mourned with a *s.* 50:10
Lord shewed signs great and *s.* on.
              Deut 6:22
smite thee with a *s.* botch. 28:35

s. sicknesses, and of long.*Deut* 28:59
so that Israel was *s.* *Judg* 10:9
because she lay *s.* upon him. 14:17
Samson was *s.* athirst, and. 15:18
against Gibeah, the battle was *s.*
  20:34; *1 Sam* 31:3*; *2 Sam* 2:17
             2 Ki 3:26
lifted up their voices and wept *s.*
             Judg 21:2
also provoked her *s.* *1 Sam* 1:6
prayed to the Lord, and wept *s.* 10
hand is *s.* on us, and on Dagon. 5:7
there was *s.* war against the. 14:52
I am *s.* distressed. 28:15, 21
his servants wept *s.* *2 Sam* 13:36
sickness so *s.* no breath. *1 Ki* 17:17
and there was a *s.* famine in. 18:2
Syria was *s.* troubled. *2 Ki* 6:11
Hezekiah wept *s.* 20:3; *Isa* 38:3
know his own *s.* grief. *2 Chr* 6:29*
so Jehoram died of *s.* 21:19
Ahaz transgressed *s.* against. 28:19
have me away, for I am *s.* 35:23
people wept very *s.* *Ezra* 10:1
it grieved me *s.* therefore. *Neh* 13:8
smote Job with *s.* boils. *Job* 2:7
he maketh *s.* and bindeth. 5:18
and vex in his *s.* displeasure. *Ps* 2:5
soul is *s.* vexed, but thou, O Lord.6:3
enemies be ashamed, and *s.* 10
fast, thy hand presseth me *s.* 38:2
I am feeble and *s.* broken, I. 8
thou hast *s.* broken us in. 44:19
my heart is *s.* pained within. 55:4
shewed me great and *s.* 71:30
thou hast thrust *s.* at me. 118:13
chastened me *s.* but not given. 18
s. travail hath God. *Eccl* 1:13; 4:8
there is *s.* evil I have seen. 5:13, 16
with *s.* and great sword. *Isa* 27:1
we roar like bears, mourn *s.* 59:11
be not wroth very *s.* O Lord. 64:9
thy peace, afflict us very *s.?* 12
mine eye shall weep *s.* *Jer* 13:17
weep *s.* for him that goeth. 22:10
famine was *s.* in city, there. 52:6
she weepeth *s.* in the. *Lam* 1:2
mine enemies chased me *s.* 3:52
when I send my four *s. Ezek* 14:21
it is sharpened to make a *s.* 21:10
king was *s.* displeased. *Dan* 6:14
destroy you even with *s.* *Mi* 2:10
the Lord hath been *s.* *Zech* 1:2, 15
for he is lunatick, and *s.* vexed.
             Mat 17:15*
Hosanna, they were *s.* 21:15*
they were *s.* amazed in. *Mark* 6:51
spirit cried, rent him *s.* and. 9:26
Jesus began to be *s.* amazed. 14:33
wept *s.* and kissed Paul. *Acts* 20:37
    see afraid

sore, *substantive*

if a white reddish *s.* it. *Lev* 13:42*
if rising of *s.* be white reddish. 43*
s. or sickness there be. *2 Chr* 6:28*
stand aloof from my *s.* *Ps* 38:11*
my *s.* ran in the night and. 77:2*
there fell a grievous *s.* *Rev* 16:2

Sorek

a woman in valley of *S. Judg* 16:4

sorely

archers *s.* grieved him. *Gen* 49:23
so shall they be *s.* pained at. *Isa* 23:5

sorer

how much *s.* punishment. *Heb* 10:29

sores

bruises, and putrifying *s.* *Isa* 1:6
at his gate full of *s. Luke* 16:20, 21
blasphemed God because of their
  pains and *s.* *Rev* 16:11

sorrow

I will greatly multiply thy *s.* and conception, in *s.* thou shalt. *Gen* 3:16
in *s.* shalt thou eat of it all days. 17*
ye bring down my gray hairs with *s.*
  to the grave. 42:38; 44:29, 31
s. take hold of inhabitants. *Ex* 15:14*
terror shall cause *s.* of. *Lev* 26:16
shall give *s.* of mine. *Deut* 28:65*
I bare him with *s.* *1 Chr* 4:9
this is nothing else but *s. Neh* 2:2

was turned from s. to joy. *Esth* 9:22
because it hid not s. from mine eyes.
Job 3:10*
I would harden myself in s. 6:10*
mine eye is dim by reason of s. 17:7
and s. is turned into joy. 41:22
having s. in my heart. *Ps* 13:2
and my s. is continually. 38:17
I held my peace, and my s. 39:2
mischief also and s. are in. 55:10
their strength labour and s. 90:10
brought low through s. 107:39
I found trouble and s. 116:3
that winketh eye, causeth s. *Pr* 10:10
rich, he addeth no s. with it. 22
but by s. of heart the spirit. 15:13
a fool, doeth it to his s. 17:21
who hath woe ? who hath s.? 23:29
he that increaseth knowledge.
Eccl 1:18
he hath much s. and wrath. 5:17
s. is better than laughter, heart. 7:3
therefore remove s. from thy. 11:10
unto the land, behold s. *Isa* 5:30
shall give thee rest from thy s. 14:3
heap in the day of desperate s. 17:11
Ariel, and there shall be s. 29:2
s. and sighing shall flee away. 35:10
have, ye shall lie down in s. 50:11
and s. and mourning shall. 51:11
sing, but ye shall cry for s. 65:14
comfort myself against s. *Jer* 8:18
to see labour and s.? 20:18
why criest thou ? thy s. is. 30:15
rejoice from their s. 31:13
hath added grief to my s. 45:3
there is s. on the sea, it cannot. 49:23
any s. like unto my s. *Lam* 1:12
behold my s. 18
give them s. of heart. 3:65
filled with drunkenness and s.
Ezek 23:33
them sleeping for s. *Luke* 22:45
said these things, s. filled. *John* 16:6
sorrowful, but your s. shall be. 20
when she is in travail, hath s. 21
therefore have s. but I will see you
again, and your heart shall. 22
that I have continual s. *Rom* 9:2
when I came, I should have s.
2 *Cor* 2:3
swallowed up with overmuch s. 7
godly s. worketh repentance to salvation, but the s. of the world. 7:10
also, lest I have s. upon s. *Phil* 2:27
s. give her: for she saith, I . . .
shall see no s. *Rev* 18:7
no more death, neither sorrow. 21:4

sorrow, verb
and they shall not s. any. *Jer* 31:12
land shall tremble and s. 51:29
they shall s. a little for. *Hos* 8:10
that ye s. not as others. *1 Thes* 4:13

sorrowed
now I rejoice that ye s. to. *2 Cor* 7:9
selfsame thing, that ye s. after a. 11

sorroweth
thy father s. for you. *1 Sam* 10:2

sorrowful
a woman of a s. spirit. *1 Sam* 1:15
things my soul refused to touch are
as my s. meat. *Job* 6:7
poor and s.: let salvation. *Ps* 69:29
laughter the heart is s. *Pr* 14:13
replenished every s. soul. *Jer* 31:25
gather then that are s. *Zeph* 3:18
shall see it, and be very s. *Zech* 9:5
he went away s. *Mat* 19:22
Luke 18:23, 24
they were exceeding s. *Mat* 26:22
Mark 14:19
and he began to be s. *Mat* 26:37
my soul is exceeding s. even unto
death. 38; *Mark* 14:34
ye shall be s. but sorrow. *John* 16:20
as s. yet always rejoicing. *2 Cor* 6:10
and I may be the less s. *Phil* 2:28

sorrowing
father and I sought thee s. *Luke* 2:48
s. they should see his face no more.
Acts 20:38

sorrows
their cry, for I know their s. *Ex* 3:7
s. of hell compassed me about.
2 *Sam* 22:6; *Ps* 18:4, 5; 116:3
I am afraid of all my s., . . . thou wilt
not hold me innocent. *Job* 9:28
distributeth s. in his anger. 21:17
they cast out their s. 39:3
s. shall be multiplied that. *Ps* 16:4
many s. shall be to wicked. 32:10
rise up, to eat the bread of s. 127:2
for all his days are s. and. *Eccl* 2:23
pangs and s. shall take. *Isa* 13:8
a man of s. and acquainted. 53:3
borne our griefs and carried our s. 4
not s. take as a woman. *Jer* 13:21
s. have taken her as a woman. 49:24
by vision my s. are. *Dan* 10:16
s. of travailing woman. *Hos* 13:13
these are beginning of s. *Mat* 24:8
Mark 13:8
they pierced themselves through with
many s. *1 Tim* 6:10

sorry
of you that is s. for me. *1 Sam* 22:8
holy to Lord, neither be ye s.
Neh 8:10
I will be s. for my sin. *Ps* 38:18
who shall be s. for thee ? *Isa* 51:19
and the king was s. *Mat* 14:9
Mark 6:26
they were exceeding s. *Mat* 17:23
if I make you s., . . . glad, but the
same which is made s.? *2 Cor* 2:2
you s., same epistle made you s. 7:8
ye were made s., for ye were s. 9

sort
two of every s. shalt bring into ark.
Gen 6:19, 20
every bird of every s. into. 7:14
they divided one s. *1 Chr* 24:5
be able to offer after this s. 29:14
silver basons of second s. *Ezra* 1:10
Artaxerxes king after this s. 4:8
four times after this s. *Neh* 6:4
men of the common s. *Ezek* 23:42
to ravenous birds of every s. 39:4
every oblation of every s. 44:30
than children of your s. *Dan* 1:10
no God can deliver after this s. 3:29
fellows of the baser s. *Acts* 17:5
more boldly in some s. *Rom* 15:15
work, of what s. it is. *1 Cor* 3:13
sorrowed after a godly s. *2 Cor* 7:11
of this s. are they who creep into.
2 *Tim* 3:6
journey after a godly s. 3 *John* 6

sorts
a garment of divers s. *Deut* 22:11
days store of all s. of wine. *Neh* 5:18
he sent divers s. of flies. *Ps* 78:45
105:31
instruments and that of all s. *Eccl* 2:8
merchants in all s. of things.
Ezek 27:24
clothed with all s. of armour. 38:4

Sosipater
and S. my kinsmen. *Rom* 16:21

Sosthenes
the Greeks took S. and. *Acts* 18:17
Paul and S. to the church. *1 Cor* 1:1

sottish
foolish, they are s. children. *Jer* 4:22

sought
he s. where to weep, entered his
chamber. *Gen* 43:30
when Pharaoh heard, he s. *Ex* 2:15
men are dead which s. thy life. 4:19
that the Lord met him and s. 24
every one that s. the Lord went. 33:7
Moses diligently s. goat. *Lev* 10:16
was not his enemy, nor s. *Num* 35:23
because he s. to thrust. *Deut* 13:10
pursuers s. the spies. *Josh* 2:22
Samson s. occasion against.
Judg 14:4
Danites s. them an inheritance. 18:1
Saul s. to smite David. *1 Sam* 19:10
Saul s. no more again for him. 27:4
ye s. for David in times past to be
king. 2 *Sam* 3:17

head of thine enemy that s. thy life.
2 *Sam* 4:8
Saul s. to slay them in his zeal. 21:2
they s. for a fair damsel. *1 Ki* 1:3
all the earth s. to Solomon. 10:24
Solomon s. therefore to kill. 11:40
s. three days for Elijah. 2 *Ki* 2:17
Hebronites were s. for. *1 Chr* 26:31
have s. the Lord our God. 2 *Chr* 14:7
disease he s. not to the Lord. 16:12
Jehoshaphat s. not unto. 17:3
s. to the Lord God of his father. 4
he s. Ahaziah, and they caught him;
because Jehoshaphat s. the. 22:9
s. after gods of Edom ? 25:15, 20
he s. God in the days of Zechariah,
as long as he s. the Lord. 26:5
these s. their register. *Ezra* 2:62
Neh 7:64
they s. the Levites out. *Neh* 12:27
s. to lay hand on. *Esth* 2:21; 6:2
wherefore Haman s. to destroy. 3:6
to lay hand on such as s. 9:2
I s. the Lord, and he heard me.
Ps 34:4; 77:2
assemblies of violent men s. 86:14
s. out of all that have. 111:2
whole heart have I s. thee. 119:10
for I have s. thy precepts. 94
s. out many inventions. *Eccl* 7:29
preacher s. out and set in order. 12:9
the preacher s. to find. 10
shalt be called, s. out, city. *Isa* 62:12
s. of them that asked not for me; I
am . . . s. not. 65:1; *Rom* 10:20
for my people that have s. me.
Isa 65:10
moon, whom they have s. *Jer* 8:2
for the pastors have not s. 10:21
king s. to put him to death. 26:21
to Nebuchadrezzar that s. his. 44:30
iniquity of Israel shall be s. 50:20
they s. meat to relieve. *Lam* 1:19
and I s. for a man. *Ezek* 22:30
tho' s. for, yet shalt thou never. 26:21
neither have ye s. that which. 34:4
they s. Daniel and his. *Dan* 2:13
and my lords s. unto me. 4:36
s. occasion against Daniel. 6:4
even I, had s. for the meaning. 8:15
Esau's hidden things s. up. *Ob* 6
that have not s. the Lord. *Zeph* 1:6
bay went forth and s. to go. *Zech* 6:7
they are dead which s. *Mat* 2:20
s. to lay hands on him. 21:46
Mark 12:12; *Luke* 20:19
from that time he s. opportunity to
betray him. *Mat* 26:16; *Luke* 22:6
they s. false witness against Jesus.
Mat 26:59; *Mark* 14:55
s. how they might destroy him.
Mark 11:18; 14:1; *Luke* 19:47
22:2
thy father and I s. thee. *Luke* 2:48
how is it that ye s. me ? wist ? 49
and they s. means to bring. 5:18
multitude s. to touch him. 6:19
others s. of him a sign from. 11:16
he s. fruit thereon, and. 13:6
Zacchaeus s. to see Jesus. 19:3
s. to slay him. *John* 5:16, 18; 7:1
then the Jews s. him. 7:11; 11:56
s. to take him. 7:30; 10:39
Master, the Jews of late s. 11:8
from thenceforth Pilate s. to. 19:12
and when Herod had s. *Acts* 12:19
they s. to bring them out to. 17:5
because s. it not by faith. *Rom* 9:32
nor of men s. we glory. *1 Thes* 2:6
in Rome he s. me out. *2 Tim* 1:17
no place should have been s. for.
Heb 8:7
though he s. it carefully with. 12:17

sought *him*
he s. *him* he could not. *1 Sam* 10:21
the Lord hath s. *him* a man. 13:14
Saul s. *him* every day, God. 23:14
we s. *him* not after the. *1 Chr* 15:13
have s. *him*, he hath. 2 *Chr* 14:7
when they s. *him*, he was. 15:4
for they s. *him* with their whole. 15
I s. *him*, but he could not. *Ps* 37:36
slew them, then they s. *him*. 78:34

on my bed I s. him whom my soul
loveth; I s. him. S of S 3:1, 2; 5:6
and they s. him among. Luke 2:44
people s. him, and came. 4:42

soul

(This word is used in the Bible in
much the same variety of senses as
it is used to-day. The Hebrews
used the word rather more generally, and the renderings of
Hebrew expressions given in the
margins of many editions of the
Bible frequently contain the word
when it does not appear in the
text, but some other word, as
mind, life, or persons, is used.
Frequently, where the word soul
is used in the Authorised or " King
James " Version the revisions have
changed it to life)

man became a living s. Gen 2:7
the s. of my son longeth for. 34:8
as her s. was in departing. 35:18
if a s. shall sin through. Lev 4:2*
if a s. sin, and hear the voice. 5:1*
or if s. touch any unclean thing. 2*
if a s. swear. 4*
if a s. commit a trespass. 15
if a s. sin and commit any. 17*
if a s. lie. 6:2*
an atonement for the s. 17:11*
no s. of you shall eat blood. 12
if the priest buy any s. with. 22:11
whatsoever s. doth any work. 23:30
or if your s. abhor my. 26:15
because their s. abhorred my. 43
even the same s. shall. Num 9:13
the s. of the people was. 21:4
she hath bound her s. 30:4, 5, 6, 7
8, 9, 10, 11, 12, 13
one s. of five hundred for. 31:28
serve him with all your s. Deut 11:13
lay up these my words in your s. 18
love the Lord God with all your s.
13:3; Josh 22:5; 1 Ki 2:4
s. of Jonathan was knit to s. of.
1 Sam 18:1
s. of my lord bound up in. 25:29
because the s. of all the people. 30:6
are hated of David's s. 2 Sam 5:8
the s. of David longed to go. 13:39
to thee with all their s. 1 Ki 8:48
let this child's s. come into. 17:21
let her alone for her s. is. 2 Ki 4:27
commandments with all their s. 23:3
your s. to seek the Lord. 1 Chr 22:19
to thee with all their s. 2 Chr 6:38
Lord God with all their s. 15:12
given to the bitter in s.? Job 3:20
in whose hand is the s. of. 12:10
if your s. were in my s.'s stead. 16:4
s. of the wounded crieth out. 24:12
is perfect, converting the s. Ps 19:7
to deliver their s. from death. 33:19
the Lord redeemeth the s. of. 34:22
the redemption of their s. is. 49:8†
redeem their s. from deceit. 72:14
O deliver not the s. of thy. 74:19
not their s. from death. 78:50
rejoice the s. of thy servant. 86:4
they gather against the s. of. 94:21
sent leanness into their s. 106:15
thirsty, their s. fainted in them. 107:5
longing s. and filleth hungry s. 9
s. abhorreth all manner of meat. 18
s. is melted because of trouble. 26
suffer the s. of righteous. Pr 10:3
liberal s. shall be made fat. 11:25
but the s. of transgressors. 13:2
the s. of the sluggard desireth. 4
accomplished is sweet to the s. 19
words are sweet to the s. 16:24
the s. be without knowledge. 19:2
and an idle s. shall suffer hunger. 15
s. of the wicked desireth evil. 21:10
Lord will spoil s. of those. 22:23*
he refresheth the s. of his masters.
25:13
as cold waters to a thirsty s. so is. 25
the full s. loatheth an honeycomb;
but to the hungry s. every. 27:7
woe to their s.! they have. Isa 3:9
empty the s. of the hungry. 32:6

s. delight itself in fatness. Isa 55:2
hear, and your s. shall live. 3
thou satisfy the afflicted s. 58:10
their s. delighteth in their. 66:3
sword reacheth to the s. Jer 4:10†
delivered the s. of the poor. 20:13
their s. shall be as a watered. 31:12
satiate the s. of the priests. 14
satiated the weary s. and I have replenished every sorrowful s. 25
liveth, that made us this s. 38:16
meat to relieve the s. Lam 1:11
when their s. was poured out. 2:12
the Lord is good to the s. that. 3:25
as s. of father, so s. of son is mine,
the s. that sinneth. Ezek 18:4, 20
what your s. pitieth shall. 24:21
their s. shall not come. Hos 9:4*
me about, even to the s. Jonah 2:5
able to kill the s.: fear him that can
destroy both s. and. Mat 10:28
with all the heart and s. Mark 12:33
fear came upon every s.: and many
wonders. Acts 2:43
every s. which will not hear. 3:23
believed of one heart and s. 4:32
anguish on every s. of man that.
Rom 2:9
let every s. be subject to the. 13:1
that your s. and body. 1 Thes 5:23
piercing to dividing of s. Heb 4:12
we have as an anchor of the s. 6:19
believe to saving of the s. 10:39
shall save a s. from death. Jas 5:20
which war against the s. 1 Pet 2:11
Lot vexed his righteous s. 2 Pet 2:8
and every living s. died. Rev 16:3

see **afflicted, bitterness**

his soul

his s. clave to Dinah. Gen 34:3
we saw anguish of his s. 42:21
ransom for his s. to Lord. Ex 30:12
to bind his s. to Lord. Num 30:2
his s. was grieved for. Judg 10:16
she urged him, so that his s. 16:16
Josiah who turned to the Lord with
all his s. 2 Ki 23:25; 2 Chr 34:31
and his s. within him. Job 14:22
in the bitterness of his s. 21:25
what his s. desireth, even. 23:13
when God taketh away his s. 27:8
by wishing a curse to his s. 31:30*
he keepeth back his s. from. 33:18
his s. abhorreth dainty meat. 20
yea, his s. draweth near unto. 22
he will deliver his s. from. 28, 30
loveth violence, his s. hateth. Ps 11:5
who hath not lifted up his s. 24:4
his s. shall dwell at ease. 25:13
he lived he blessed his s. 49:18
shall he deliver his s. from? 89:48
those that condemn his s. 109:31
if he steal to satisfy his s. Pr 6:30
eateth to satisfying of his s. 13:25
his way, preserveth his s. 16:17
lips are the snare of his s. 18:7
his mouth, keepeth his s. 21:23
that doth keep his s. shall be. 22:5
deliver his s. from hell. 23:14
but the just seek his s. 29:10*
that he should make his s. Eccl 2:24
wanteth nothing for his s. 6:2
and his s. be not filled with good. 3
his s. is empty; behold he is faint and
his s. hath appetite. Isa 29:8
that he cannot deliver his s. 44:20
shalt make his s. an offering. 53:10
he shall see of the travail of his s. 11
because he poured out his s. 12
his s. shall be satisfied. Jer 50:19
deliver every man his s. 51:6*, 45
right, he shall save his s. Ezek 18:27
warning, shall deliver his s. 33:5
his s. that is lifted up, is not. Hab 2:4
lose his own s.? what can man . . .
for s.? Mat 16:26*; Mark 8:37*
his s. was not left in hell. Acts 2:31*

my soul

and my s. shall live. Gen 12:13
thither, and my s. shall live. 19:20
that my s. may bless thee. 27:4, 25
O my s. come not thou into. 49:6
and my s. shall not. Lev 26:11, 30

O my s. thou hast trodden down.
Judg 5:21
poured out my s. 1 Sam 1:15
yet thou huntest my s. to. 24:11†
because my s. was precious. 26:21*
who hath redeemed my s. 2 Sam 4:9
1 Ki 1:29
the things my s. refused. Job 6:7
my s. chooseth strangling. 7:15
yet would I not know my s. 9:21*
my s. is weary of life, I will speak in
bitterness of my s. 10:1
ye vex my s. with words ? 19:2
who hath vexed my s. 27:2
pursue my s. as the wind. 30:15*
and now my s. is poured out. 16
my s. grieved for the poor ? 25
which say of my s., There is. Ps 3:2
my s. is sore vexed. 6:3
deliver my s. 4; 17:13; 22:20
116:4; 120:2
lest he tear my s. like a lion. 7:2
let the enemy persecute my s. 5
how say ye to my s. Flee as a ? 11:1
I take counsel in my s.? 13:2
not leave my s. in hell. 16:10
Acts 2:27
he restoreth my s. Ps 23:3
to thee I lift my s. 25:1
O keep my s. and deliver me. 20
gather not my s. with sinners. 26:9
thou hast brought up my s. 30:3
thou hast known my s. in. 31:7
yea, my s. and my belly are. 9
my s. shall make her boast in. 34:2
my s. I am thy salvation. 35:3
put to shame that seek after my s. 4
they have digged a pit for my s. 7
and my s. shall be joyful in. 9
me to the spoiling of my s. 12
as for me, I humbled my s. 13
rescue my s. from their. 17
let them be confounded that seek
after my s. 40:14
heal my s. for I have sinned. 41:4
as the hart, so panteth my s. 42:1
my s. thirsteth for the. 2; 143:6
I remember, I pour out my s. 42:4
cast down, O my s.? 5, 11; 43:5
O my God, my s. is cast down. 42:6
God will redeem my s. from. 49:15
oppressors seek after my s. 54:3
with them that uphold my s. 4
hath delivered my s. in peace. 55:18
steps, when they wait for my s. 56:6
for thou hast delivered my s. 13
be merciful, O God: for my s. 57:1
my s. is among lions. 4
my s. is bowed down. 6
for lo, they lie in wait for my s. 59:3
truly my s. waiteth upon God. 62:1
my s. wait thou only upon God. 5
O God, my s. thirsteth for. 63:1
my s. shall be satisfied as with. 5
my s. followeth hard after thee. 8
but those that seek my s. to. 9
what God hath done for my s. 66:16
waters are come in unto my s. 69:1
when I wept and chastened my s. 10
draw nigh to my s. and redeem it. 18
that seek after my s. 70:2; 71:13
my s. shall rejoice which. 71:23
my sore ran, my s. refused to. 77:2
my s. longeth for the courts. 84:2
preserve my s. 86:2
O Lord, do I lift up my s. 4; 143:8
thou hast delivered my s. 86:13
violent men sought after my s. 14
my s. is full of troubles, my life. 88:3
Lord, why castest thou off my s.? 14
my s. had almost dwelt in. 94:17
thy comforts delight my s. 19
bless the Lord, O my s. 103:1, 2, 22
104:1, 35
that speak against my s. 109:20
return unto thy rest, O my s. 116:7
for thou hast delivered my s. 8
my s. breaketh for the. 119:20
my s. cleaveth to the dust. 25
my s. melteth for heaviness. 28
my s. fainteth for thy salvation. 81
my s. is continually in my hand. 109
therefore doth my s. keep them. 129
my s. hath kept thy testimonies. 167

let *my s.* live, and it.   *Ps* 119:175
deliver *my s.* O Lord, from.   120:2
my s. hath dwelt with him that.   6
I wait for the Lord, *my s.*   130:5, 6
my s. is even as a weaned.   131:2
me with strength in *my s.*   138:3
my s. knoweth right well.   139:14
leave not *my s.* destitute.   141:8
no man cared for *my s.*   142:4
bring *my s.* out of prison, that I.   7
enemy hath persecuted *my s.*   143:3
O Lord, bring *my s.* out of.   11
praise the Lord, O *my s.*   146:1
I bereave *my s.* of good ?   *Eccl* 4:8
which yet *my s.* seeketh, but.   7:28
O thou whom *my s.* loveth.
     S of S 1:7; 3:1, 2, 3, 4
my s. failed when he spake.   5:6
my s. made me like chariots.   6:12
and feasts *my s.* hateth.   *Isa* 1:14
with *my s.* have I desired thee.   26:9
thou hast in love to *my s.*   38:17
mine elect, in whom *my s.* delighteth.
     42:1
my s. shall be joyful in.   61:10
hast heard, O *my s.*   *Jer* 4:19
my s. is wearied because of.   31
my s. be avenged ?   5:9, 29; 9:9
O Jerusalem, lest *my s.* depart.   6:8
beloved of *my s.* into the.   12:7
my s. shall weep in secret.   13:17
have digged a pit for *my s.*   18:20
over them with *my* whole *s.*   32:41
that should relieve *my s. Lam* 1:16
thou hast removed *my s.* far.   3:17
my s. hath them still in.   20
Lord is my portion, saith *my s.*   24
pleaded the causes of *my s.*   58
behold, *my s.* hath not.   *Ezek* 4:14
my s. fainted within me.   *Jonah* 2:7
my body for the sin of *my s. Mi* 6:7
my s. desired the first ripe fruit. 7:1
cut off, *my s.* loathed.   *Zech* 11:8
beloved, in whom *my s.*   *Mat* 12:18
my s. is exceeding sorrowful. 26:38
     Mark 14:34
my s. doth magnify.   *Luke* 1:46
I will say to *my s.,* Soul, eat. 12:19
my s. is troubled, and.   *John* 12:27
for a record upon *my s.*   *2 Cor* 1:23
my s. shall have no pleasure in.
     Heb 10:38

our **soul**
our s. is dried away.   *Num* 11:6
no bread, *our s.* loatheth this.   21:5
our s. waiteth for Lord.   *Ps* 33:20
for *our s.* is bowed down.   44:25
who holdeth *our s.* in life.   66:9
our s. is exceedingly filled.   123:4
gone over *our s.*   124:4, 5
our s. is escaped as a bird out.   7
the desire of *our s.* is to.   *Isa* 26:8

own **soul**
if a friend is as thine *own s.*
     Deut 13:6
knit to David, and he loved him as
   his *own s.*   *1 Sam* 18:1, 3; 20:17
keep alive his *own s.*   *Ps* 22:29
destroyeth his *own s.*   *Pr* 6:32
sinneth, wrongeth his *own s.*   8:36
doeth good to his *own s.*   11:17
he that refuseth instruction despiseth
   his *own s.*   15:32
wisdom, loveth his *own s.*   19:8
commandments keepeth his *own s.*
     16
king, sinneth against his *own s.* 20:2
with thief, hateth his *own s.*   29:24
gain whole world and lose his *own s.?*
     Mat 16:26; *Mark* 8:36
pierce through thy *own s. Luke* 2:35

that **soul**
that s. shall be cut off from his.
   Gen 17:14; *Ex* 31:14; *Lev* 7:20
   21, 25, 27; 19:8; *Num* 15:30
that s. shall be cut off from Israel.
   Ex 12:15; *Num* 19:13
whoso eateth leavened bread, *that s.*
   shall be cut. *Ex* 12:19; *N m* 19:20
face against *that s. Lev* 17:10; 20:6
that s. shall be cut off.   22:3
that s. will I destroy from.   23:30
that s. shall utterly be.   *Num* 15:31

thy **soul**
eat, that *thy s.* may.   *Gen* 27:19, 31
take heed, and keep *thy s. Deut* 4:9
if thou seek him with all *thy s.*   29
thy God with all *thy s.*   6:5; 30:6
Lord thy God. with all *thy s.*   10:12
thy s. lusteth after.   12:15; 14:26
do them with all *thy s.*   26:16
with all thine heart and *thy s.*   30:2
unto the Lord with all *thy s.*   10
take as much as *thy s.* desireth.
     1 Sam 2:16
whatsoever *thy s.* desireth, I.   20:4
to all the desire of *thy s.*   23:20
risen to pursue and seek *thy s.* 25:29
reign according to all *thy s.* desireth.
     1 Ki 11:37
Lord shall preserve *thy s. Ps* 121:7
is pleasant to *thy s.*   *Pr* 2:10
shall they be life to *thy s.* and. 3:22
and let not *thy s.* spare for.   19:18*
and get a snare to *thy s.*   22:25
he that keepeth *thy s.,* doth ? 24:12
knowledge of wisdom be to *thy s.* 14
give delight to *thy s.*   29:17
which have said to *thy s. Isa* 51:23
if thou draw out *thy s.* to.   58:10
the Lord shall satisfy *thy s.*   11
hath *thy s.* loathed Zion ? *Jer* 14:19
then *thy s.* shall live.   38:17, 20
hast delivered *thy s. Ezek* 3:19; 21
     33:9
sinned against *thy s.*   *Hab* 2:10
heart and with all *thy s. Mat* 22:27
   Mark 12:30; *Luke* 10:27
this night *thy s.* shall be. *Luke* 12:20
prosper, even as *thy s.* prospereth.
     3 John 2
the fruits *thy s.* lusted.   *Rev* 18:14

see **liveth**

souls
Abraham took *s.* they.   *Gen* 12:5
the *s.* by Leah were thirty.   46:15
by Zilpah sixteen *s.*   18
by Rachel fourteen *s.*   22
all the *s.* Jacob had by Bilhah.   25
all the *s.* that came into Egypt.   26
Egypt, were two *s.*: all *s.* of house of
   Jacob were seventy *s.* 27; *Ex* 1:5
according to number of *s. Ex* 12:4
an atonement for your *s.*   30:15, 16
     Lev 17:11; *Num* 31:50
even *s.* that commit.   *Lev* 18:29
make your *s.* abominable.   20:25
against their own *s.*   *Num* 16:38*
wherewith have bound their *s.* 30:9
destroyed them and all the *s.* that.
     Josh 10:28, 30, 32; 11:11
your hearts and in all your *s.* 23:14
s. of thine enemies.   *1 Sam* 25:29
and shall save the *s.* of.   *Ps* 72:13
preserveth the *s.* of his saints. 97:10
he that winneth *s.* is wise. *Pr* 11:30
a true witness delivereth *s.*   14:25
spirit should fail, and *s. Isa* 57:16
is found the blood of *s.*   *Jer* 2:34
ye shall find rest for your *s.*   6:16
     Mat 11:29
procure great evil against our *s.*
     Jer 26:19
great evil against your *s.?*   44:7
meat to relieve their *s.*   *Lam* 1:11
not satisfy their *s.*   *Ezek* 7:19
to hunt *s.* will ye hunt *s.* . . . will ye
   save the *s.* alive.?   13:18, 20
to slay the *s.* that should not die. 19
deliver but their own *s.*   14:14
all *s.* are mine.   18:4
they have devoured *s.*   22:25
are like wolves to destroy *s.*   27
patience possess your *s. Luke* 21:19
added to them 3000 *s.*   *Acts* 2:41
Jacob and his kindred 75 *s.*   7:14
confirming *s.* of the disciples. 14:22
troubled you, subverting your *s.* 15:24
in all in the ship 276 *s.*   27:37
imparted our own *s.*   *1 Thes* 2:8
for they watch for your *s. Heb* 13:17
is able to save your *s.*   *Jam* 1:21
the salvation of your *s. 1 Pet* 1:9
purified your *s.* in obeying truth. 22
to the Shepherd of your *s.*   2:25
wherein few, that is, eight *s.*   3:20

keeping of their *s.* to him. *1 Pet* 4:19
sin; beguiling unstable *s. 2 Pet* 2:14
I saw under the altar the *s. Rev* 6:9
no man buyeth slaves and *s.*   18:13
I saw the *s.* of them that were. 20:4

see **afflict**

sound, *substantive*
his *s.* shall be heard.   *Ex* 28:35
the *s.* of a shaken leaf.   *Lev* 26:36
as soon as ye hear the *s.* of the
   trumpet.   *Josh* 6:5, 20
hearest the *s.* of a going in the tops.
     2 Sam 5:24; *1 Chr* 14:15
ark with shouting and the *s.* of the.
     2 Sam 6:15; *1 Chr* 15:28
when ye hear the *s.* say. *2 Sam* 15:10
rent with the *s.* of them. *1 Ki* 1:40
when Joab heard the *s.* of the.   41
when Ahijah heard the *s.* of.   14:6
there is a *s.* of abundance of. 18:41
is not the *s.* of his master's feet
   behind him ?   *2 Ki* 6:32
but Asaph made a *s.*   *1 Chr* 16:5
those that should make a *s.*   42
as one, to make one *s. 2 Chr* 5:13
in what place ye hear *s. Neh* 4:20
a dreadful *s.* in his ears. *Job* 15:21
at the *s.* of the organ.   21:12
hear the *s.* that goeth out.   37:2
nor believeth he it is the *s.* 39:24*
the Lord gone up with *s. Ps* 47:5
water, skies sent out a *s.*   77:17
people that know the joyful *s.* 89:15
the harp with a solemn *s.*   92:3
trumpets and *s.* of cornet.   98:6
praise him with the *s.* of.   150:3
s. of the grinding is low. *Eccl* 12:4
O my soul, the *s.* of.   *Jer* 4:19
I hear the *s.* of the trumpet ?   21
Hearken to the *s.* of trumpet. 6:17
trembled at *s.* of the neighing. 8:16
I will take from them *s.* of. 25:10
where we shall hear no *s.*   42:14
s. of battle is in the land. 50:22
a *s.* of a cry cometh from. 51:54
s. of the cherubim's.   *Ezek* 10:5
the *s.* of thy harps shall be. 26:13
shall not the isles shake at the *s.?* 15
suburbs shall shake at *s.* of. 27:28
I made nations to shake at *s.* 31:16
heareth the *s.* and taketh.   33:4
he heard *s.* of trumpet and took. 5
when ye hear the *s. Dan* 3:5, 7, 10, 15
Moab shall die with *s.*   *Amos* 2:2
that chant to the *s.* of the viol. 6:5
his angels with a great *s. Mat* 24:31
hearest thy *s.* but canst. *John* 3:8*
suddenly there came a *s.*   *Acts* 2:2
verily their *s.* went into. *Rom* 10:18
without life giving *s. 1 Cor* 14:7*
trumpet give an uncertain *s.*   8*
ye are not come to the *s. Heb* 12:19
s. of many waters.   *Rev* 1:15*
s. of their wings was as the *s.* 9:9
the *s.* of a millstone shall be. 18:22*

sound, *adjective*
let my heart be *s.* in.   *Ps* 119:80*
he layeth up *s.* wisdom.   *Pr* 2:7
my son, keep *s.* wisdom and. 3:21
counsel is mine and *s.* wisdom. 8:14
s. heart is the life of the flesh. 14:30
received him safe and *s. Luke* 15:27
contrary to *s.* doctrine. *1 Tim* 1:10
but hath given us the spirit of a *s.*
   mind.   *2 Tim* 1:7*
hold fast the form of *s.* words.   13
will not endure *s.* doctrine.   4:3
may be able by *s.* doctrine. *Tit* 1:9
rebuke them, that they may be *s.* 13
the things which become *s.*   2:1
that the aged men be *s.* in faith.   2
s. speech that cannot be.   8

sound, *verb*
of jubile to *s.* in day of atonement
   make the trumpet *s. Lev* 25:9*
ye shall not *s.* an alarm. *Num* 10:7
and Asaph were appointed to *s.*
     1 Chr 15:19
bowels shall *s.* for Moab. *Isa* 16:11
heart shall *s.* for Moab. *Jer* 48:36
and *s.* an alarm in my.   *Joel* 2:1
therefore do not *s.* a.   *Mat* 6:2
for the trumpet shall *s. 1 Cor* 15:52

angels prepared themselves to s.
Rev 8:6
three angels who are yet to s. 13
seventh angel shall begin to s. 10:7

sounded
the trumpet s. long. Ex 19:19
I have s. my father. 1 Sam 20:12
priests s. trumpets. 2 Chr 7:6, 13, 14
the people rejoiced, and s. 23:13
sang and the trumpeters s. 29:28
he that s. the trumpet. Neh 4:18
as soon as voice of salutation s.
L.ke 1:44
from you s. out the word. 1 Thes 1:8
the first angel s. and there. Rev 8:7
the second s. 8, 10, 12
the fifth s. 9:1, 13
seventh s. 11:15

sounded (of the sea)
they s. and found it twenty fathoms;
they s. again and. Acts 27:28

soundeth
when the trumpet s. long. Ex 19:13

sounding
instruments of music s. 1 Chr 15:16
them 120 priests s. 2 Chr 5:12
his priests with s. trumpets. 13:12*
upon the high s. cymbals. Ps 150:5
where is thy zeal, the s.? Isa 63:15*
the s. again of mountains. Ezek 7:7*
charity, I am as s. brass. 1 Cor 13:1

soundness
there is no s. in my flesh. Ps 38:3, 7
no s. in it, but wounds. Isa 1:6
this perfect s. in presence. Acts 3:16

sounds
give a distinction in the s. 1 Cor 14:7

sour
when the s. grape is. Isa 18:5*
fathers have eaten a s. grape, and.
Jer 31:29; Ezek 18:2
man that eateth s. grape. Jer 31:30
their drink is s. they have. Hos 4:18

south
journeyed towards the s. Gen 12:9
Abram went up into the s. 13:1
spread abroad to north and s. 28:14
tabernacle toward the s. Ex 26:35
dwell in the land of the s. Num 13:29
possess thou west and s. Deut 33:23
smote country of the s. Josh 10:40
abide in their coast on the s. 18:5
the Canaanites in the s. Judg 1:9
out of a place toward s. 1 Sam 20:41
against the s. of Judah, s. 27:10
had invaded the s. 30:1, 14
they went out to the s. 2 Sam 24:7
three looking towards s. 1 Ki 7:25
2 Chr 4:4
porters were toward s. 1 Chr 9:24
Philistines invaded s. 2 Chr 28:18
the chambers of the s. Job 9:9
out of s. cometh the whirlwind. 37:9
her wings toward the s. 39:26
neither from east nor s. Ps 75:6
the north and s. thou hast. 89:12
them from the north and s. 107:3
captivity as the streams in s. 126:4
goeth toward the s. Eccl 1:6
tree fall toward the s. or the. 11:3
as whirlwinds in the s. Isa 21:1
of the beasts of the s. 30:6
and I will say to the s., Keep. 43:6
the cities of the s. shall. Jer 13:19
from the s. bringing burnt. 17:26
buy fields in the cities of the s. 32:44
in the cities of the s. shall the. 33:13
toward the s. and drop thy word toward s. . . . s. field. Ezek 20:46
forest of s. . . . faces from s. to. 47
against all flesh from s. to. 21:4
as the frame of a city on s. 40:2
he brought me toward the s. 24
prospect was toward the s. 44
another door was toward the s. 41:11
by way of the s. gate; and he that entereth by the way of s. go. 46:9
waxed great toward the s. Dan 8:9
and the king of the s. shall. 11:5
king's daughter of the s. shall. 6
king of the s. shall come into his. 9
king of the s. shall be moved. 11

arms of the s. shall not. Dan 11:15
and the king of the s. shall be. 25
return, and come toward the s. 29
the king of the s. shall push at. 40
they of s. shall possess. Ob 19
shall possess the cities of the s. 20
when men inhabited the s. Zech 7:7
go with whirlwinds of the s. 9:14
mountain remove toward the s. 14:4
queen of the s. shall rise. Mat 12:42
come from s. to sit down. Luke 13:29
and go toward the s. Acts 8:26
on the s. three gates, on. Rev 21:13

south border
s. border the outmost coast of the
salt sea. Num 34:3
the s. border of Judah. Josh 15:2

south country
sojourned toward the s. country.
Gen 20:1
dwelt in the s. country. 24:62
Joshua took all the s. country.
Josh 11:16; 12:8
go forth toward s. country. Zech 6:6

south field
the forest of the s. field. Ezek 20:46

south land
thou hast given me a s. land.
Josh 15:19; Judg 1:15

south quarter
s. quarter from Zin by. Num 34:3
s. quarter from end of. Josh 18:15

south side
twenty boards on the s. side.
Ex 26:18; 36:23
on s. side shall be standard of.
Num 2:10
camps which lie on the s. side. 10:6
he measured the s. side. Ezek 42:18
the waters came at the s. side. 47:1
and the s. side 4500. 48:16, 33

southward
to Abraham, Look s. Gen 13:14
pitch on side of tabernacle s.
Num 3:29
Get ye up this way s. 13:17
I saw the ram pushing s. Dan 8:4

south west
lying towards the s. west. Acts 27:12

south wind
earth by the s. wind. Job 37:17
he brought in the s. wind. Ps 78:26
come, thou s. wind. S of S 4:16
when see s. wind blow. Luke 12:55
the s. wind blew softly. Acts 27:13

sow
the s. washed, to her. 2 Pet 2:22

sow, verb
and ye shall s. the land. Gen 47:23
six years s. the land. Ex 23:10
Lev 25:3
shall not s. with mingled seed.
Lev 19:19; Deut 22:9
7th year thou shalt not s. Lev 25:4, 11
we shall not s. nor gather. 20
ye shall s. the eighth year. 22
ye shall s. your seed in vain. 26:16
in the third year s. ye. 2 Ki 19:29
Isa 37:30
they that s. wickedness. Job 4:8
then let me s. and let another. 31:8
s. fields, and plant. Ps 107:37
they that s. in tears shall. 126:5
he that observeth the wind shall not
s. Eccl 11:4
in the morning s. thy seed, and. 6
plow all day to s.? Isa 28:24
give rain of seed, thou shalt s. 30:23
blessed are ye that s. beside. 32:20
break fallow ground, s. not. Jer 4:3
I will s. the house of Israel. 31:27
ye build house nor s. seed. 35:7
and I will s. her unto me. Hos 2:23
s. to yourselves in righteousness. 10:12

thou shalt s. but thou. Mi 6:15
I will s. them among. Zech 10:9
fowls of the air s. not. Mat 6:26
a sower went forth to s.; and when
he. 13:3; Mark 4:3; Luke 8:5

didst not thou s. good seed?
Mat 13:27
ravens: they neither s. Luke 12:24
that thou didst not s. 19:21, 22

sowed
Isaac s. in that land. Gen 26:12
Abimelech s. Shechem. Judg 9:45
when he s. some fell by the way.
Mat 13:4; Mark 4:4; Luke 8:5
which s. good seed. Mat 13:24
the enemy s. tares. 25, 39

sowedst
Egypt, where thou s. Deut 11:10

sower
give seed to s. and bread. Isa 55:10
cut off s. from Babylon. Jer 50:16
behold, a s. went forth to sow.
Mat 13:3; Mark 4:3; Luke 8:5
the parable of the s. Mat 13:18
s. soweth the word. Mark 4:14
ministereth seed to the s. 2 Cor 9:10

sowest
that which thou s. is. 1 Cor 15:36
thou s. not that body that shall. 37

soweth
he s. discord. Pr 6:14
he that s. discord. 19
to him that s. righteousness. 11:18
a froward man s. strife. 16:28*
he that s. iniquity shall. 22:8
overtake him that s. seed. Amos 9:13
he that s. good seed is. Mat 13:37
sower s. the word. Mark 4:14
both he that s. and reapeth.
John 4:36
one s. and another reapeth. 37
s. sparingly; he who s. bountifully.
2 Cor 9:6
for whatsoever a man s. Gal 6:7
that s. to his flesh, shall reap corruption; but he that s. to the. 8

sowing
fall upon any s. seed. Lev 11:37
shall reach to the s. time. 26:5

sown
fall on sowing seed to be s. Lev 11:37
valley neither eared nor s. Deut 21:4
lest the fruit of thy seed s. 22:9
that land is not s. nor beareth. 29:23
when Israel had s. the. Judg 6:3
light is s. for the righteous. Ps 97:11
every thing s. by the brooks. Isa 19:7
planted, yea, shall not be s. 40:24
garden causeth the things s. 61:11
after me in a land not s. Jer 2:2
they have s. wheat, but shall. 12:13
shall be tilled and s. Ezek 36:9
have s. the wind, shall. Hos 8:7
more of thy name be s. Nah 1:14
ye have s. much, and. Hag 1:6
catcheth away that which was s.
Mat 13:19; Mark 4:15
reaping where thou hast not s.
Mat 25:24
these are they which s. Mark 4:16
s. among thorns. 18
are s. in good ground. 20
which when it is s. is less than. 31
if we have s. to you. 1 Cor 9:11
it is s. in corruption. 15:42
is s. in dishonour. 43
it is s. a natural body, it is raised. 44
multiply your seed s. and increase.
2 Cor 9:10
righteousness is s. in peace. Jas 3:18

space
abode with him the s. of. Gen 29:14
and put a s. betwixt drove. 32:16
the s. of seven sabbaths. Lev 25:8*
if it be not redeemed in the s. of. 30
there shall be a s. between. Josh 3:4
s. between David's company and.
1 Sam 26:13
for a little s. grace. Ezra 9:8*
s. of two full years. Jer 28:11
s. of one hour after. Luke 22:59
about s. of three hours. Acts 5:7
the apostles forth a little s. 34*
beasts by the s. of forty years. 13:20
gave judges about the s. 13:20
God gave them Saul for the s. 21
he spake boldly the s. of three. 19:8

continued by the s. of two years.
　　　　　　　　　　Acts 19:10
all with one voice about s. of.　34
by the s. of three years I.　20:31
it rained not by the s. of. Jas 5:17*
I gave her s. to repent of her.
　　　　　　　　　　Rev 2:21*
there was silence about the s.　8:1
blood came by the s. of 1600. 14:20*
he must continue a short s.　17:10*

Spain
take my journey into S. Rom 15:24
I will come by you into S.　28

spake
(Revisions frequently change to
said)
Lot went out, and s. to. Gen 19:14
saying, Thus s. the man.　24:30
while he yet s. with them.　29:9
it came to pass as she s. to.　39:10
that is it that I s. unto you.　42:14
for he s. unto them by an.　23
old man of whom ye s. is.　43:27
younger brother of whom ye s.?　29
and Joseph wept when they s. 50:17
Miriam and Aaron s.　Num 12:1
the people s. against God.　21:5
so I s. to you, and ye.　Deut 1:43
bring thee by way whereof I s. 28:68
they s. to the master.　Judg 19:22
kinsman of whom Boaz s. Ruth 4:1
now Hannah s. in her heart.
　　　　　　　　　　1 Sam 1:13
On this manner s. David.　18:24
nevertheless Saul s. not any. 20:26
for the people s. of stoning him. 30:6
was alive, we s. to him. 2 Sam 12:18
while he yet s., behold.　1 Ki 1:42
s. before king Solomon.　3:22
saying which Elisha s.　2 Ki 2:22
Thus and thus s. he to me.　9:12
went up at saying which Gad s.
　　　　　　　　　　1 Chr 21:19
one s. saying after.　2 Chr 18:19
Hezekiah s. comfortably to them.
　　　　　　　　30:22; 32:6
servant s. yet more against.　32:16
s. against the God of Jerusalem.　19
that s. to Manasseh in the.　33:18
children s. half in speech. Neh 13:24
to pass, when they s.　Esth 3:4
they sat down, and none s. Job 2:13
and they s. against me.　19:18
after my words they s. not.　29:22
for they s. not, but stood still. 32:16
fire burned, then s. I with.　Ps 39:3
yea, they s. against God.　78:19
so that he s. unadvisedly.　106:33
man s. to Ithiel and Ucal. Pr 30:1
my beloved s. and said. S of S 2:10
my soul failed when he s.　5:6
I hearkened and heard, they s.
　　　　　　　　　　Jer 8:6
for since I s. I cried out, I cried. 20:8
so I s. to the people in. Ezek 24:18
words which the horn s.　Dan 7:11
Ephraim s. trembling.　Hos 13:1
that feared Lord s. often. Mal 3:16
while he s. these things. Mat 9:18
17:5; 26:47; Mark 5:35; 14:43
　　　　Luke 8:49; 22:47, 60
devil was cast out, dumb s.
　　Mat 9:33; 12:22; Luke 11:14
they perceived that he s. of them.
　　　　　　　　　　Mat 21:45
as he s. to our fathers. Luke 1:55
not the saying which he s.　2:50
he s. unto them of the kingdom. 9:11
who s. of his decease which he.　31
other things blasphemously s. 22:65
remember how he s. to you.　24:6
as they s. Jesus stood in midst.　36
was he of whom I s.　John 1:15
no man s. openly of him for.　7:13
Never man s. like this man.　46
not that he s. of the Father.　8:27
they were which he s. to them. 10:6
all things that John s. of this.　41
howbeit Jesus s. of his death. 11:13
this s. he not of himself.　51
others said, An angel s. to.　12:29
fulfilled which he s.　38; 18:9, 32
when he saw his glory, and s. 12:41

doubting of whom he s. John 13:22
who it should be of whom he s.　24
for what intent he s. this.　28
this s. he, signifying by what. 21:19
resist spirit by which he s. Acts 6:10
those things which Philip s.　8:6
while Peter yet s. these.　10:44
Jews s. against those things.　13:45
so s. that a great multitude.　14:1
but s. evil of that way before. 19:9
for the words which he s.　20:38
voice of him that s. to me.　22:9
as he thus s. for himself.　26:24
Well s. the Holy Ghost by.　28:25
child, I s. as child.　1 Cor 13:11
that ye all s. with tongues.　14:5
the blessedness ye s. of ? Gal 4:15
of which tribe Moses s.　Heb 7:14
him that s. on earth.　12:25
holy men of God s. as.　2 Pet 1:21
voice that s. with me.　Rev 1:12
another beast s. as a dragon. 13:11

God spake
Jacob called the place where God s.
　Beth-el.　Gen 35:15
God s. all these words.　Ex 20:1
the Lord our God s. to us. Deut 1:6
not one thing failed of good things
　God s.　Josh 23:14
how in the bush God s. Mark 12:26
we know that God s.　John 9:29
and God s. on this wise.　Acts 7:6
God who s. in time past.　Heb 1:1

see **Lord**

Lord or **God spake**, implicitly
who s. to me, and sware. Gen 24:7
behold the man whom I s. to thee of.
　　　　　　　　　　1 Sam 9:17
Lord hath done to him as he s. 28:17
s. I a word with any of ? 2 Sam 7:7
God said, The rock of Israel s. 23:3
word which I s. unto.　1 Ki 6:12
fulfilled that which he s.　2 Chr 6:4
he s. to him, and gave him.　32:24
he s. and it was done.　Ps 33:9
he s. unto them in the cloudy.　99:7
he s. and there came flies. 105:31
he s. and the locusts came.　34
when I s. ye did not hear. Isa 65:12
　　　　　　　　　　64:4
I s. to you, rising up.　Jer 7:13
I s. not to your fathers, I.　22
I sent them not, neither s.　14:14
commanded not, nor s. it.　19:5
I s. unto thee in thy prosperity. 22:21
for since I s. against him.　31:20
a voice of one that s. Ezek 1:28; 2:2
he s. unto the man clothed.　10:2
his words which he s.　Dan 9:21
in Beth-el, there he s. with. Hos 12:4
as he s. by mouth of his. Luke 1:70
words which I s. to you.　24:44
he s. in a certain place.　Heb 4:4

spakest
art thou the man that s.? Judg 13:11
the silver thou s. of also.　17:2
words which thou s.　1 Sam 28:21
thou s. also with thy mouth, and hast.
　　　　1 Ki 8:24; 2 Chr 6:15
be verified which thou s.　1 Ki 8:26
separate them, as thou s. by.　53
s. with them from heaven. Neh 9:13
then thou s. in vision to.　Ps 89:19
since thou s. of him.　Jer 48:27

span
a s. shall be the length, and a s. the.
　　　　　　　Ex 28:16; 39:9
height six cubits and a s. 1 Sam 17:4
out heaven with the s.?　Isa 40:12
eat their children of a s. Lam 2:20*
of the altar shall be a s. Ezek 43:13

spanned
hath s. the heavens.　Isa 48:13*

spare
not s. the place for the fifty righteous.
　　　　　　　　　　Gen 18:24
then I will s. all the place.　26
thou shalt not s. nor.　Deut 13:8
Lord will not s. him, but.　29:20*
Amalek, s. them not.　1 Sam 15:3
and s. me according to.　Neh 13:22
let him not s.; I have not. Job 6:10

reins asunder, doth not s. Job 16:13
though he s. it and forsake.　20:13
cast upon him, and not s.　27:22
they s. not to spit in my face. 30:10
O s. me that I may.　Ps 39:13
shall s. the poor and needy.　72:13*
he will not s. in the day.　Pr 6:34
thy soul s. for his crying.　19:18*
no man shall s. his brother. Isa 9:19
eye shall not s. children.　13:18
break it, he shall not s.　30:14
s. not, lengthen cords.　54:2
cry aloud, s. not, lift up voice. 58:1
I will not s. them.　Jer 13:14
　　　　　　　　　　Ezek 24:14
he shall not s. them.　Jer 21:7
s. no arrows.　50:14
s. ye not her young men.　51:3
nor shall mine eye s. nor will I have.
　Ezek 5:11; 7:4, 9; 8:18; 9:10
let not your eye s. neither.　9:5
let them say, S. thy people. Joel 2:17
should not I s. Nineveh ? Jonah 4:11*
and not s. continually to.　Hab 1:17
I will s. them as a man.　Mal 3:17
have bread enough to s. Luke 15:17
lest he also s. not thee.　Rom 11:21
trouble, but I s. you.　1 Cor 7:28
that to s. you I came not. 2 Cor 1:23
come again, I will not s.　13:2

spared
the people s. Agag.　1 Sam 15:9
for the people s. the best of the.　15
kill thee, but mine eye s.　24:10
s. to take of his own flock, and.
　　　　　　　　　　2 Sam 12:4
king s. Mephibosheth son of.　21:7
master hath s. Naaman.　2 Ki 5:20
he s. not their soul.　Ps 78:50
mine eye s. them from. Ezek 20:17
he that s. not his own Son. Rom 8:32
if God s. not the natural.　11:21
if God s. not the angels.　2 Pet 2:4
and s. not the old world, but.　5

spareth
he that s. his rod.　Pr 13:24
he that hath knowledge, s.　17:27
righteous giveth, and s. not.　21:26
them, as a man s. his son. Mal 3:17

sparing
enter in, not s. the flock. Acts 20:29

sparingly
who soweth s. shall reap s. 2 Cor 9:6

spark
and the s. of his fire shall. Job 18:5
maker of it shall be as a s. Isa 1:31

sparkled
s. like the colour of.　Ezek 1:7

sparks
trouble, as s. fly upward. Job 5:7
go burning lamps, s. of fire.　41:19
yourselves about with s. Isa 50:11*

sparrow
s. hath found an house.　Ps 84:3
I am as a s. alone upon the.　102:7

sparrows
are not two s. sold for ? Mat 10:29
are of more value than many s.　31
　　　　　　　　　　Luke 12:7
are not five s. sold for ? Luke 12:6

spat
spoken, he s. on ground.　John 9:6

speak
(Revisions frequently, say or talk)
on me to s. to God. Gen 18:27, 31
we cannot s. unto thee bad.　24:50
take heed thou s. not to.　31:24
s. to my lord Esau.　32:4, 19
say ? what shall we s.?　44:16
I know that he can s. well. Ex 4:14
since I came to s. to Pharaoh. 5:23
thou shalt s. all that I command. 7:2
shalt not s. in a cause to decline. 23:2
where I will meet you, to s.　29:42
wherefore should Egyptians s.? 32:12
until he went in to s. with.　34:35
were ye not afraid to s.? Num 12:8
the fame of thee will s.　14:15
why they that s. in proverbs. 21:27
as the Lord shall s. to me.　22:8
I s. to thee, that thou shalt s.　35

Balak, and thus thou shalt s.
                 Num 23:5
must I not take heed to s. that ? 12
of Zelophehad s. right.   27:7
words which he shall s. *Deut* 18:19
which shall presume to s. a word. 20
and thou shalt s. and say.   26:5
your children might s. to. *Josh* 22:24
that a man cannot s. to. *1 Sam* 25:17
went also to s. to David. *2 Sam* 3:19
Joab took him aside to s. with.   27
so did Nathan s. to David.   7:17
why s. ye not one word of ?   19:10
near hither that I may s. with. 20:16
they were wont to s. in old time. 18
she went to s. to him.   *1 Ki* 2:19
wilt s. good words to them.   12:7
               2 Chr 10:7
saying, Thus shalt thou s. *1 Ki* 12:10
spirit from me to s. to thee.   22:24
               2 Chr 18:23
sent me to thy master and to thee to
s.?   *2 Ki* 18:27; *Isa* 36:12
what can David s.?   *1 Chr* 17:18
rail and s. against God. *2 Chr* 32:17
could not s. in the Jews' language.
               Neh 13:24
to s. to the king to hang. *Esth* 6:4
wilt thou s. these things ? *Job* 8:2
but, oh that God would s.   11:5
ye s. wickedly for God and ?   13:7
and afterwards we will s.   18:2
my lips shall not s. wickedness. 27:4
I said, Days should s. and.   32:7
I have yet to s. on God's.   36:2
man s. he shall be swallowed. 37:20
will he s. soft words unto thee ? 41:3
then shall he s. to them.   *Ps* 2:5
destroy them that s. leasing.   5:6
they s. vanity, they s. with a.   12:2
their mouth they s. proudly.   17:10
which s. peace to their.   28:3
in his temple doth every one s. 29:9
s. grievous things proudly.   31:18
for they s. not peace, but.   35:20
my tongue shall s. of thy.   28
they s. mischievous things.   38:12
would declare and s. of them. 40:5
enemies s. evil of me, when ? 41:5
my mouth shall s. of wisdom. 49:3
lovest lying rather than to s.   52:3
and lying which they s.   59:12
mouth of them that s. lies.   63:11
they that sit in the gate s.   69:12
for mine enemies s. against. 71:10
they s. wickedly, s. loftily.   73:8
what God the Lord will s.: for he will
   s. peace unto his people.   85:8
they utter and s. hard things ? 94:4
reward of them that s. evil. 109:20
have mouths, but they s. not. 115:5
               135:16
princes also did sit and s.   119:23
my tongue shall s. of thy word. 172
shall s. with the enemies.   127:5
for they s. against thee.   139:20
men shall s. of might of thy. 145:6
they shall s. of the glory of thy. 11
my mouth shall s. the praise.   21
my mouth shall s. truth.   *Pr* 8:7
when lips s. right things.   23:16
silent, and a time to s.   *Eccl* 3:7
those that are asleep to s. *S of S* 7:9
if they s. not according. *Isa* 8:20
shall s. and say unto thee.   14:10
five cities in Egypt shall s.   19:18
with another tongue shall he s. to
   this people.   28:11
shalt s. out of the ground.   29:4
stammerers shall s. plainly.   32:4
vile person will s. villany.   6
that I should know how to s. 50:4
that I am he that doth s.   52:6
trust in vanity, and s. lies.   59:4
whatsoever I command thee thou
   shalt s.   *Jer* 1:7
because ye s. this word.   5:14
thou shalt s. all these words.   7:27
s. the truth, taught to s. lies.   9:5
as palm tree, but s. not.   10:5
believe not, though they s. fair. 12:6
shalt s. this word to them.   13:12
I shall s. about a nation.   18:7, 9
I stood before thee to s. good.   20

I said, I will not s. any more. *Jer* 20:9
s. a vision of their own heart. 23:16
s. all the words I commanded thee
   to s.   26:2, 8
the Lord hath sent me to s.   15
thus shalt thou also s. to.   29:24
and shall s. with him mouth.   32:4
he shall s. with thee mouth.   34:3
thou shalt s. my words. *Ezek* 2:7
words that I shall s. receive.   3:10
they say of me, Doth he not s.? 20:49
and thou shalt s. and be no.   24:27
mighty shall s. to him.   32:21
if dost not s. to warn wicked. 33:8
thus ye s.   10
and s. one to another.   30
children of thy people shall s. 37:18
prepared corrupt words to s. *Dan* 2:9
s. any thing amiss against the. 3:29
he shall s. great words.   7:25
shall s. lies at one table, but. 11:27
but at the end it shall s. *Hab* 2:3
how or what ye shall s. *Mat* 10:19
               Mark 13:11
for it is not ye that s. *Mat* 10:20
               Mark 13:11
how can ye being evil s.? *Mat* 12:34
every idle word that men shall s. 36
without, desiring to s. with.   46
why doth this man thus s.? *Mark* 2:7
do a miracle, that can lightly s. 9:39
not this man of whom ye s. 14:71
in my name they shall s. with. 16:17
I am sent to s. to thee. *Luke* 1:19
not able to s. till these shall.   20
when he came out he could not s. 22
suffered them not to s.   4:41
all men shall s. well of you.   6:26
and to provoke him to s. of. 11:53
s. a word against Son of man. 12:10
verily we s. that we do know, and.
               John 3:11
of age, ask him, he shall s.   9:21
s. of himself; that shall he s. 16:13
when I shall no more s. to you in. 25
are not all these which s.? *Acts* 2:7
we do hear them s. in tongues. 11
that they s. to no man in this. 4:17
not to s. at all in the name. 18; 5:40
we cannot but s.   4:20
boldness they may s. thy word. 29
him s. blasphemous words.   6:11
ceaseth not to s. blasphemous. 13
cometh shall s. unto thee.   10:32
as I began to s.   11:15
same heard Paul s.   14:9
I beseech thee suffer me to s. 21:39
thou shalt not s. evil of ruler. 23:5
permitted to s. for thyself.   26:1
I s. forth the words of truth and.   25
I will not dare to s. of. *Rom* 15:18
that ye all s. same thing. *1 Cor* 1:10
things also we s., not man's.   2:13
not s. to you as to spiritual.   3:1
do all s. with tongues ?   12:30
if all s.   14:23
for women to s. in church.   35
and forbid not to s. with tongues. 39
in the sight of God s. we. *2 Cor* 2:17
we also believe and therefore s. 4:13
we s. before God in Christ.   12:19
it is a shame to s. of.   *Eph* 5:12
manifest, as I ought to s. *Col* 4:4
so that we need not to s. *1 Thes* 1:8
so we s. not as pleasing men.   2:4
forbidding us to s. to Gentiles.   16
put them in mind to s. evil. *Tit* 3:2
to come, whereof we s. *Heb* 2:5
though we thus s.   6:9
of which we cannot s.   9:5
let every man be slow to s. *Jas* 1:19
they s. against you as evil doers.
               1 Pet 2:12
his lips that they s. no guile.   3:10
whereas they s. evil of you, as.   16
not afraid to s. evil of dignities.
               2 Pet 2:10
s. evil of the things that they.   12
they s. great swelling words.   18
of world, therefore s. *1 John* 4:5
these filthy dreamers s. evil. *Jude* 8
but these s. evil of those things. 10
depths of Satan, as they s. *Rev* 2:24
of the beast should both s.   13:15

speak, *imperatively*
s. thou with us, and we.   *Ex* 20:19
s. ye to the rock before. *Num* 20:8
Lord said, S. no more to. *Deut* 3:26
s. thou unto us all that the Lord shall
   s. to thee.   5:27
s. ye that ride on white. *Judg* 5:10
consider, take advice, and s. 19:30
S. Lord, for thy.   *1 Sam* 3:9, 10
saying ? if not; s. thou. *2 Sam* 17:6
s. that which is good.   *1 Ki* 22:13
               2 Chr 18:12
s. in Syrian language.   *2 Ki* 18:26
               Isa 36:11
and to morrow s. thou. *Esth* 5:14
or s. to the earth, and it. *Job* 12:8
or let me s. and answer thou. 13:22
s. for I desire to justify thee. 33:32
s. what thou knowest.   34:33
lift not your horn: s. not. *Ps* 75:5
s. not in the ears of.   *Pr* 23:9
s. word, it shall not stand. *Isa* 8:10
s. unto us smooth things.   30:10
s. ye comfortably to Jerusalem. 40:2
come near, then let them s.   41:1
son of a stranger s. saying.   56:3
s. to them all that I.   *Jer* 1:17
hath my word, let him s. word. 23:28
I said, Let my lord s. *Dan* 10:19
s. every man the truth. *Zech* 8:16
               Eph 4:25
s. word only, my servant. *Mat* 8:8
what I tell in darkness, that s. 10:27
shall be given you in that hour, s. ye.
               Mark 13:11
s. to my brother that he. *Luke* 12:13
let me freely s. to you of. *Acts* 2:29
go, stand and s. in the temple. 5:20
be not afraid, but s., hold not. 18:9
let him s. to himself. *1 Cor* 14:28
let prophets s. two or three.   29
s. the things that become. *Tit* 2:1
these things s. and exhort.   15
so s. ye and do, as they. *Jas* 2:12
s. not evil one of another.   4:11
let them s. as the oracles. *1 Pet* 4:11

I speak
people may hear when I s. *Ex* 19:9
shalt obey and do all that I s. 23:22
God putteth in my mouth that shall I
   s.   *Num* 22:38
which I s. in your ears. *Deut* 5:1
I s. not with your children.   11:2
Lord saith, that will I s. *1 Ki* 22:14
if I s. of strength, lo, he. *Job* 9:19
would I s. and not fear him.   35
I would s. to the Almighty.   13:3
let me alone, that I may s.   13
I also could s. as ye do, I.   16:4
though I s., my grief is not.   6
told him that I s. if a man s. 37:20
I s. of things which I.   *Ps* 45:1
troubled that I cannot s.   77:4
when I s. they are for war. 120:7
I the Lord s. righteousness. *Isa* 45:19
I that s. in righteousness.   63:1
ah, Lord God, I cannot s. for. *Jer* 1:6
to whom shall I s. and give ? 6:10
hear this word that I s. in.   28:7
voice of the Lord which I s. 38:20
when I s. with thee, I. *Ezek* 3:27
O Daniel, understand words that I s.
               Dan 10:11
therefore s. I to them. *Mat* 13:13
Jesus saith, I that s. to. *John* 4:26
the words that I s. to you.   6:63
of God or whether I s. of myself. 7:17
I s. to the world those things. 8:26
as my Father hath taught me I s. 28
I s. that which I have seen with. 38
gave commandment what I should s.
               12:49
whatsoever I s. therefore, as the
   Father said unto me, so I s.   50
I s. not of all, I know whom. 13:18
the words that I s. I s. not.   14:10
things I s. in the world.   17:13
may I s. unto thee ? *Acts* 21:37
I also s. freely.   26:26
unrighteous ? I s. as a man. *Rom* 3:5
I s. after the manner of men. 6:19
               Gal 3:15
I s. to them that know the. *Rom* 7:1

I s. to you Gentiles, I am. *Rom* 11:13
I s. to your shame. *1 Cor* 6:5; 15:34
I s. this by permission, not of. 7:6
but to the rest *s. I,* not the Lord. 12
and this *I s.* for your own profit. 35
I s. as to wise men, judge ye. 10:15
though *I s.* with tongues of men. 13:1
except *I* shall *s.* to you by. 14:6
I s. with tongues more than you. 18
I had rather *s.* five words with. 19
I s. as to my children. *2 Cor* 6:13
I s. not this to condemn you. 7:3
that which *I s., I s.* it not after. 11:17
I s. as concerning reproach, *I s.* 21
are they ministers ? *I s.* as a fool. 23
but *I s.* concerning Christ. *Eph* 5:32
I may *s.* boldly, as I ought to *s.* 6:20
not that *I s.* in respect. *Phil* 4:11
I s. the truth in Christ, I. *1 Tim* 2:7

I will **speak,** or *will I* **speak**
let not Lord be angry, and *I will s.*
    Gen 18:30, 32
and *I will s.* to him in a dream.
    Num 12:6
with him *will I s.* mouth to mouth. 8
what the Lord saith, that *will I s.*
  24:13; *1 Ki* 22:14; *2 Chr* 18:13
O ye heavens, and *I will s. Deut* 32:1
Gideon said, *I will s.* but. *Judg* 6:39
I will s. to the king. *2 Sam* 14:15
I will s. for thee to king. *1 Ki* 2:18
I will s. in the anguish. *Job* 7:11
I will s. in the bitterness of. 10:1
I will s. that I may be. 32:20
hold thy peace, and *I will s.* 33:31
I beseech thee, and *I will s.* 42:4
O my people, and *I will s. Ps* 50:7
if I say, *I will s.* thus, I. 73:15
I will s. of thy testimonies. 119:46
I will s. of the honour. 145:5
hear, for *I will s.* of excellent things.
    Pr 8:6
me to great men, and *I will s. Jer* 5:5
feet, and *I will s.* to thee. *Ezek* 2:1
I will s. and the word I *s.* shall. 12:25
I will allure her, and *s. Hos* 2:14
with other lips *will I s. 1 Cor* 14:21

speaker
s. be established in earth. *Ps* 140:11
he was the chief *s.* *Acts* 14:12

speakest
wherefore then *s.* thou so to me ?
    1 Sam 9:21
why *s.* thou any more ? *2 Sam* 19:29
the words thou *s.* in thy. *2 Ki* 6:12
thou *s.* as one of the foolish women.
    Job 2:10
thou sittest and *s.* against. *Ps* 50:20
be justified when thou *s.* 51:4
why *s.* thou, O Israel, My. *Isa* 40:27
thou *s.* falsely of Ishmael. *Jer* 40:16
thou *s.* falsely, the Lord hath. 43:2
him not warning, nor *s. Ezek* 3:18
for thou *s.* lies in the name of.
    Zech 13:3
why *s.* thou to them in ? *Mat* 13:10
Lord, *s.* thou this parable to us or to?
    Luke 12:41
now *s.* thou plainly, and *s.* no.
    John 16:29
Pilate saith to him, *S.* thou ? 19:10
this whereof thou *s.? Acts* 17:19

speaketh
mouth that *s.* to you. *Gen* 45:12
as a man *s.* unto his friend. *Ex* 33:11
all that the Lord *s. Num* 23:26
when a prophet *s.* in the. *Deut* 18:22
s. flattery to his friends. *Job* 17:5
for God *s.* once, yea, twice. 33:14
tongue that *s.* proud things. *Ps* 12:3
s. the truth in his heart. 15:2
the mouth of the righteous *s.* 37:30
to see me, he *s.* vanity. 41:6
whose mouth *s.* vanity. 144:8, 11
from the man that *s.* froward things.
    Pr 2:12
he *s.* with his feet, he teacheth. 6:13
a false witness that *s.* lies and. 19
the wicked *s.* frowardness. 10:32
he that *s.* truth, sheweth. 12:17
there is that *s.* like the piercings. 18
deceitful witness *s.* lies. 14:25
they love him that *s.* right. 16:13

that *s.* lies shall not escape. *Pr* 19:5
and he that *s.* lies shall perish. 9
the man that heareth *s.* constantly.
    21:28
he *s.* fair, believe him not. 26:25
and every mouth *s.* folly. *Isa* 9:17
even when the needy *s.* right. 32:7
he that *s.* uprightly shall dwell. 33:15
their tongue *s.* deceit; one *s. Jer* 9:8
which the Lord *s.* to you. 10:1
thus *s.* the Lord the God of. 28:2
29:25; 30:2; *Hag* 1:2; *Zech* 6:12
    7:9
voice of Almighty God when he *s.*
    Ezek 10:5
they abhor him that *s.* uprightly.
    Amos 5:10
Spirit of your Father who *s.* in you.
    Mat 10:20
whoso *s.* a word against the Son of
  man; but whosoever *s.* 12:32
for out of the abundance of the heart
  the mouth *s.* 34; *Luke* 6:45
he that is of the earth, *s. John* 3:31
he whom God sent, *s.* the words. 34
he that *s.* of himself, seeketh. 7:18
but lo, he *s.* boldly, they say. 26
s. a lie, he *s.* of his own. 8:44
who maketh himself a king, *s.* 19:12
pray, of whom *s.* the prophet this ?
    Acts 8:34
righteousness of faith *s. Rom* 10:6
s. in an unknown tongue; howbeit in
  the Spirit he *s.* *1 Cor* 14:2
he that prophesieth, *s.* unto men. 3
s. in an unknown tongue edifieth. 4
prophesieth, than he that *s.* 5
unto him that *s.* a barbarian. 11
that *s.* in an unknown tongue. 13
now Spirit *s.* expressly. *1 Tim* 4:1
he being dead yet *s. Heb* 11:4
exhortation which *s.* to you. 12:5
that *s.* better things than that. 24
refuse not him that *s. . . . .* from him
  that *s.* from heaven. 25
he that *s.* evil of his brother and
  judgeth his brother, *s. Jas* 4:11
and their mouth *s.* great. *Jude* 16

speaking
done *s.,* Rebekah came. *Gen* 24:15
before I had done *s.* in mine. 45
God *s.* out of the midst. *Deut* 5:26
s. of them when thou sittest. 11:19
then she left *s.* unto her. *Ruth* 1:18
s. peace to all his seed. *Esth* 10:3
yet *s.* another came. *Job* 1:16, 17, 18
can withhold himself from *s.?* 4:2
no more, they left off *s.* 32:15
thy lips from *s.* guile. *Ps* 34:13
as soon as they be born, *s.* lies. 58:3
away from thee *s.* vanity. *Isa* 58:9
nor *s.* thine own words. 13
in lying, and *s.* oppression. 59:13
they are yet *s.* I will hear. 65:24
rising up early and *s. Jer* 7:13
    25:3; 35:14
he weakeneth the hands in *s.* 38:4
they left off *s.*; the matter was. 27
and a mouth *s.* great things.
    Dan 7:8; *Rev* 13:5
I heard one saint *s.* and. *Dan* 8:13
whiles I was *s.* praying. 9:20, 21
they abode, *s.* boldly. *Acts* 14:3
s. perverse things, to draw. 20:30
no man *s.* by the Spirit. *1 Cor* 12:3
proof of Christ in me. *2 Cor* 13:3
but *s.* the truth in love. *Eph* 4:15
s. to yourselves in psalms. 5:19
shall depart from faith, *s.* lies.
    1 Tim 4:2
busybodies *s.* things which. 5:13
same excess of riot, *s.* evil of you.
    1 Pet 4:4

see **end**

speaking, *substantive*
be heard for much *s. Mat* 6:7
let all evil *s.* be put away. *Eph* 4:31

speakings
all guile, envies, and evil *s. 1 Pet* 2:1

spear
Stretch out thy *s. Josh* 8:18*, 26*
was there a *s.* seen ? *Judg* 5:8
s. with any, but with. *1 Sam* 13:22

s. was like a weaver's beam.
  1 Sam 17:7; *2 Sam* 21:19
    1 Chr 20:5
a sword, and with a *s. 1 Sam* 17:45
saveth not with sword and *s.* 47
under thy hand *s.* or sword ? 21:8
and Saul's *s.* stuck in the. 26:7, 11
I pray thee, with the *s.* 8
now see where the king's *s.* is. 16
Saul leaned upon his *s. 2 Sam* 1:6
Abner with the end of the *s.* 2:23
with iron and staff of a *s.* 23:7
he lift up his *s.* against 800. 8
he lifted up his *s.* against 300 and
  slew them. 18; *1 Chr* 11:11, 20
he slew Egyptian with his own *s.*
    2 Sam 23:21; *1 Chr* 11:23
quiver rattleth, glittering *s.* and.
    Job 39:23
s. of him that layeth at him. 41:26
laugheth at the shaking of a *s.* 29*
draw out also the *s.,* stop. *Ps* 35:3
and cutteth *s.* in sunder. 46:9
lay hold on bow and *s. Jer* 6:23
lifteth up the sword and *s. Nah* 3:3
shining of the glittering *s. Hab* 3:11
soldier with a *s.* pierced. *John* 19:34

spearmen
rebuke the company of *s. Ps* 68:30*
ready two hundred *s. Acts* 23:23

spears
Hebrews make them swords or *s.*
    1 Sam 13:19
to captains did priest give king
  David's *s. 2 Ki* 11:10; *2 Chr* 23:9
city he put shields and *s. 2 Chr* 11:12
for them shields and *s.* 26:14
the people with their *s. Neh* 4:13
half of them held the *s.* 16, 21
whose teeth are *s.* and. *Ps* 57:4
shall beat *s.* into pruning hooks.
    Isa 2:4; *Mi* 4:3
furbish the *s.* and put on. *Jer* 46:4
they shall burn *s.* with. *Ezek* 39:9
pruning hooks into *s. Joel* 3:10

special
chosen thee to be a *s. Deut* 7:6*
God wrought *s.* miracles. *Acts* 19:11
see **especially**

speckled
from thence the *s.* cattle. *Gen* 30:32
the *s.* shall be thy wages; then the
  cattle bare *s.* 31:8
is to me as a *s.* bird. *Jer* 12:9
behind were red horses, *s. Zech* 1:8*

spectacle
made a *s.* to the world. *1 Cor* 4:9

sped
have they not *s.?* have. *Judg* 5:30*

speech
hearken to my *s. Gen* 4:23
earth was of one *s.* 11:1
Lord, I am slow of *s. Ex* 4:10
and give occasion of *s. Deut* 22:14*
my *s.* shall distil as dew, as. 32:2
about this form of *s. 2 Sam* 14:20*
seeing the *s.* of all Israel. 19:11
s. pleased the Lord. *1 Ki* 3:10
children spake half in *s.* of Ashdod.
    Neh 13:24
he removeth away the *s. Job* 12:20
hear diligently my *s.* and. 13:17
  21:2; *Ps* 17:6; *Isa* 28:23; 32:9
my *s.* nothing worth ? *Job* 24:25
my *s.* dropped upon them. 29:22
order our *s.* by reason of. 37:19
day unto day uttereth *s. Ps* 19:2
there is no *s.* where their voice. 3
with her fair *s.* she caused. *Pr* 7:21
excellent *s.* becometh not a. 17:7
scarlet, thy *s.* is comely. *S of S* 4:3
thy *s.* shall be low out of the dust;
  thy *s.* shall whisper. *Isa* 29:4
of a deeper *s.* than thou canst. 33:19
shall use this *s.* in Judah. *Jer* 31:23
voice of *s.* as the noise. *Ezek* 1:24*
sent to a people of a strange *s.* 3:5, 6
O Lord, I have heard thy *s. Hab* 3:2*
art one of them, thy *s. Mat* 26:73
impediment in his *s. Mark* 7:32
art a Galilean, and thy *s.* 14:70
not understand my *s.? John* 8:43

40

saying in the s. of Lycaonia.
　　　　　　　　　Acts 14:11
continued his s. till midnight. 20:7
excellency of s. or wisdom. *1 Cor* 2:1
s. was not with enticing words. 4
and will know, not the s. but. 4:19
use great plainness of s. *2 Cor* 3:12
great is my boldness of s. 7:4
bodily presence weak, his s. 10:10
though I be rude in s. yet not in. 11:6
your s. be always with grace. *Col* 4:6
sound s. that cannot be. *Tit* 2:8

speeches
with him not in dark s. *Num* 12:8
and the s. of one that is. *Job* 6:26
or with s. wherewith he can ? 15:3
I answer him with your s. 32:14
by fair s. deceive the. *Rom* 16:18
them of all their hard s. *Jude* 15

speechless
garment, and he was s. *Mat* 22:12
beckoned unto them and remained s.
　　　　　　　　　Luke 1:22*
journeyed with him stood s. *Acts* 9:7

speed
Lord, I pray thee, send me good s.
　　　　　　　　　Gen 24:12
a decree, let it be done with s.
　　　　　　　　　Ezra 6:12*
shall come with s. swiftly. *Isa* 5:26
come to him with all s. *Acts* 17:15
nor bid him God s. *2 John* 10*
biddeth him God s. is partaker. 11*
see **make, made**

speedily
that I should s. escape. *1 Sam* 27:1
not in plains, but s. *2 Sam* 17:16*
offerings divided they s. *2 Chr* 35:13
the king had sent, so they did s.
　　　　　　　　　Ezra 6:13*
that thou mayest buy s. with. 7:17*
shall require, it be done s. 21*
let judgement be executed s. 26*
he s. gave her her things. *Esth* 2:9
deliver me s. *Ps* 31:2
hear me s. 69:17; 143:7
tender mercies s. prevent us. 79:8
when I call, answer me s. 102:2
sentence is not executed s. *Eccl* 8:11
shall spring forth s. *Isa* 58:8
and if ye recompense me, s. *Joel* 3:4
let us go s. and pray. *Zech* 8:21
he will avenge them s. *Luke* 18:8

speedy
make even a s. riddance. *Zeph* 1:18*

spend
I will s. mine arrows. *Deut* 32:23
they s. their days in wealth, and.
　　　　　　　　　Job 21:13
s. their days in prosperity. 36:11
we s. our years as a tale. *Ps* 90:9*
why s. money for that which is not ?
　　　　　　　　　Isa 55:2
because he would not s. *Acts* 20:16
I will very gladly s. *2 Cor* 12:15

spendest
whatsoever thou s. more, I will.
　　　　　　　　　Luke 10:35

spendeth
foolish man s. it up. *Pr* 21:20*
with harlots s. substance. 29:3*
which he s. as a shadow. *Eccl* 6:12

spent
and the water was s. in. *Gen* 21:15
not hide it how that our money is s.
　　　　　　　　　47:18
strength shall be s. in vain. *Lev* 26:20
by Jebus, day was far s. *Judg* 19:11
for the bread is s. in. *1 Sam* 9:7
days are s. without hope. *Job* 7:6
for my life is s. with grief. *Ps* 31:10
s. my strength for naught. *Isa* 49:4
bread in the city was s. *Jer* 37:21
and had s. all that she had.
　　　　　　　　　Mark 5:26; *Luke* 8:43
when the day was now far s.
　　　　　　　　　Mark 6:35; *Luke* 24:29
the prodigal had s. all. *Luke* 15:14
s. their time to tell. *Acts* 17:21
the night is far s., the day. *Rom* 13:12
spend and be s. for you. *2 Cor* 12:15

spewing
and shameful s. shall be on thy glory.
　　　　　　　　　Hab 2:16*

spice
rulers brought s. and oil. *Ex* 35:28
my myrrh with my s. *S of S* 5:1

spice
flesh and s. it well. *Ezek* 24:10

spice *merchants*
of the traffic of the s. merchants.
　　　　　　　　　1 Ki 10:15

spiced
thee to drink of s. wine. *S of S* 8:2

spicery
Ishmaelites bearing s. balm and.
　　　　　　　　　Gen 37:25

spices
a present, balm and s. *Gen* 43:11
s. for anointing oil. *Ex* 25:6; 35:8
thee principal s. of myrrh. 30:23, 34
the pure incense of sweet s. 37:29
camels that bare s. *1 Ki* 10:2, 10
　　　　　　　　　2 Chr 9:1
they brought to Solomon s.
　　　　　　　　　1 Ki 10:25; *2 Chr* 9:24
shewed them s. ointment and all that
was. *2 Ki* 20:13; *Isa* 39:2
appointed to oversee s. *1 Chr* 9:29
priests made the ointment of s. 30
Sheba gave Solomon s. *2 Chr* 9:9
divers s. prepared for the. 16:14
treasures for s. and gold. 32:27
thine ointments than all s. *S of S* 4:10
aloes, with all the chief s. 14
blow upon my garden, that s. 16
his cheeks are as a bed of s. 5:13
gone down to the beds of s. 6:2
hart upon the mountains of s. 8:14
fairs with chief of all s. *Ezek* 27:22
Mary had bought sweet s.
　　　　　　　　　Mark 16:1; *Luke* 24:1
returned and prepared s. *Luke* 23:56
it in linen with the s. *John* 19:40

spider
trust shall be a s.'s web. *Job* 8:14
the s. taketh hold with. *Pr* 30:28
eggs and weave s.'s web. *Isa* 59:5

spied
he s. an Egyptian smiting. *Ex* 2:11
s. the company of Jehu. *2 Ki* 9:17
they s. a band of men. 13:21
he s. sepulchres that were. 23:16
see **espy, espied**

spies
them, Ye are s. *Gen* 42:9, 14, 16
we are no s. 11, 31
the man took us for s. 30
then shall I know ye are no s. 34
by the way of the s. *Num* 21:1
men that were s. went in. *Josh* 6:23
the s. saw a man come. *Judg* 1:24
David therefore sent out s. and.
　　　　　　　　　1 Sam 26:4
Absalom sent s. throughout all the
tribes of Israel. *2 Sam* 15:10
him and sent forth s. *Luke* 20:20
received s. with peace. *Heb* 11:31

spikenard
my s. sendeth forth. *S of S* 1:12
fruits, camphire with s. 4:13, 14
having an alabaster box of ointment of s. *Mark* 14:3; *John* 12:3

spilled
Onan s. it on the. *Gen* 38:9
bottles burst, and wine is s.
　　　　　　　　　Mark 2:22; *Luke* 5:37

spilt
we are as water s. on. *2 Sam* 14:14

spin
were wise hearted, did s. *Ex* 35:25
they toil not, neither do they s.
　　　　　　　　　Mat 6:28; *Luke* 12:27

spindle
her hands to the s. *Pr* 31:19*

spirit
In Hebrew, Ruach, in Greek,
Pneuma, *wind, air. In scripture
the word Spirit is taken,* [1] *For
the Holy Ghost, the third person
of the Trinity.* [2] *For the renewed nature, or spiritual part in*

man. *Mat* 26:41. [3] *Signifies
the soul, which continues in being
even after the death of the body.*
Acts 7:59. [4] *Good angels are
called spirits,* *Heb* 1:14. [5] *The
devils are often called unclean
spirits, evil spirits,* *Mark* 5:13;
Luke 7:21. *So in* 1 *Sam* 18:10.
[6] *Spirit signifies an apparition or
ghost,* *Mat* 14:26, *Luke* 24:37, 39.
[7] *For the breath, the respiration,
the animal life that is in beasts,*
Eccl 3:21. [8] *Spirit is also taken
for the wind,* *Amos* 4:13, *He that
createth the wind, or spirit. These
are the four spirits of the heavens,
in Hebrew, winds,* *Zech* 6:5. *And
in* *John* 3:8, *The wind bloweth where
it listeth, in Greek, pneuma, the
spirit.*
Pharaoh's s. was troubled. *Gen* 41:8
the s. of Jacob their father. 45:27
to Moses for anguish of s. *Ex* 6:9
every one whom his s. made. 35:21
I will take of the s. *Num* 11:17, 25
the s. rested upon them and. 26
that the Lord would put his s. 29
he had another s. with him. 14:24
a man in whom is the s. 27:18
thy God hardened his s. *Deut* 2:30
nor was there s. in them. *Josh* 5:1
when he had drunk, his s. *Judg* 15:19
when he had eaten, his s. came again
to him. *1 Sam* 30:12
there was no s. in her. *1 Ki* 10:5
　　　　　　　　　2 Chr 9:4
Why is thy s. so sad ? *1 Ki* 21:5
came forth a s. 22:21; *2 Chr* 18:20
portion of thy s. be on me. *2 Ki* 2:9
s. of Elijah doth rest on Elisha. 15
the Lord stirred up the s. *1 Chr* 5:26
the s. came upon Amasai. 12:18
all that he had by the s. 28:12
against Jehoram s. of. *2 Chr* 21:16
whose s. God raised to go up.
　　　　　　　　　Ezra 1:5
testifiedst by the s. in. *Neh* 9:30
s. passed before my face. *Job* 4:15
thou turnest thy s. against. 15:13
s. of my understanding causeth. 20:3
whose s. came from thee ? 26:4
by his s. he garnished the. 13
a s. in man, inspiration of. 32:8
s. within me constraineth me. 18
if he gather to himself his s. 34:14
in whose s. there is no guile. *Ps* 32:2
clean heart, renew a right s. 51:10
and uphold me with thy free s. 12
cut off the s. of princes. 76:12
and whose s. was not stedfast. 78:8
thou sendest forth thy s. 104:30
they provoked his s., so. 106:33
whither shall I go from thy s.? 139:7
s. is good, lead me to land. 143:10
he that is hasty of s. *Pr* 14:29
therein is a breach in the s. 15:4
an haughty s. before a fall. 16:18
he that ruleth his s. than he that. 32
the s. of a man will sustain. 18:14
the s. of a man is the candle. 20:27
that hath no rule over his s. 25:28
the s. of man, s. of beast. *Eccl* 3:21
hasty in thy s. to be angry. 7:9
power over s. to retain the s. 8:8
s. of the ruler rise against. 10:4
not what is the way of the s. 11:5*
and the s. shall return to God. 12:7
the s. of Egypt shall fail. *Isa* 19:3
poured on you the s. of deep. 29:10
they that erred in s. shall come. 24
their horses flesh, and not s. 31:3
till the s. be poured upon us. 32:15
his s. it hath gathered them. 34:16
he that giveth s. to them that. 42:5
the Lord God and his s. hath. 48:16
forsaken and grieved in s. 54:6
the s. shall fail before me, and the
souls. 57:16
the s. of the Lord God is upon me.
　　　　　　　　　61:1; *Luke* 4:18
the garment of praise for the s. of.
　　　　　　　　　Isa 61:3
Lord raised the s. of king. *Jer* 51:11
whither s. was to go. *Ezek* 1:12, 20

s. was in wheels. *Ezek* 1:21; 10:17
s. entered into me when. 2:2; 3:24
then the *s.* took me up. 3:12; 11:24
so *s.* lifted me up, and took me away
  . . . heat of my *s.* 3:14; 8:3; 11:1
that follow their own *s.*   13:3
every *s.* shall faint, all knees. 21:7
Nebuchadnezzar's *s.* was. *Dan* 2:1
the *s.* of the holy gods: and before
  him I told. 4:8, 9, 18; 5:11, 14
excellent *s.* . . . were found. 5:12; 6:3
if a man walking in the *s. Mi* 2:11
Lord stirred up the *s.* of Zerubbabel.
                     Hag 1:14
hath sent in his *s.* by. *Zech* 7:12
formeth *s.* of man within.   12:1
the residue of the *s.* Therefore take
  heed to your *s. Mal* 2:15, 16
Jesus was led up of the *s. Mat* 4:1
                    Luke 4:1
were troubled; saying, It is a *s.*
       Mat 14:26*; *Mark* 6:49*
how doth David in *s.* call ? *Mat* 22:43
the *s.* indeed is willing.   26:41
                Mark 14:38
s. descending on him.   *Mark* 1:10
                John 1:32
s. driveth him into the. *Mark* 1:12
and he sighed deeply in his *s.* 8:12
straightway the *s.* tare him. 9:20
the *s.* cried and rent him.   26*
go before him in the *s.* of Elias.
                Luke 1:17
child waxed strong in *s.* 80; 2:40
and he came by the *s.* into the. 2:27
in power of the *s.* into Galilee. 4:14
her *s.* came again, and she. 8:55
what manner of *s.* ye are of. 9:55
Jesus rejoiced in *s.* and said. 10:21
a woman who had a *s.* of. 13:11
that they had seen a *s.* 24:37
for a *s.* hath not flesh and. 39
shalt see *s.* descending. *John* 1:33
the *s.* by measure to him. 3:34
worship the Father in *s.* 4:23
s.: they must worship him in *s.* 24
it is the *s.* that quickeneth; words
  . . . they are *s.* and they. 6:63
this spake he of the *s.* 7:39
he groaned in *s.* 11:33
troubled in *s.* and testified. 13:21
spake as the *s.* gave them. *Acts* 2:4
were not able to resist the *s.* 6:10
then the *s.* said unto Philip. 8:29
the *s.* said unto Peter. 10:19; 11:12
Agabus signified by the *s.* 11:28
assayed, but the *s.* suffered. 16:7
his *s.* was stirred within him. 17:16
Paul was pressed in *s.* 18:5*
being fervent in *s.* 25
now I go bound in the *s.* to. 20:22
said to Saul through the *s.* 21:4
that there is no angel nor *s.* 23:8
if a *s.* or an angel hath spoken. 9
Son of God according to the *s.*
                Rom 1:4
is that of the heart, in the *s.* 2:29
not after the flesh, but after *s.* 8:1, 4
the law of the *s.* of life hath. 2
after the *s.* the things of the *s.* 5
in the flesh, but *s.* if so be that *s.* 9
but the *s.* is life because of. 10
s. of him that raised up Jesus from
  the dead . . . bodies by his *s.* 11
but if ye through the *s.* do mortify. 13
the *s.* itself beareth witness with our
  s. 16
who have firstfruits of the *s.* 23
s. also helpeth our infirmities; the
  s. itself maketh intercession. 26
what is the mind of the *s.* 27
fervent in *s.* 12:11
for the love of the *s.* 15:30
but in demonstration of *s. 1 Cor* 2:4
revealed them to us by his *s.*: for *s.*
searcheth all things, yea, the deep.10
save the *s.* of a man which is. 11
not *s.* of the world, but the *s.* 12
absent in body, but present in *s.* 5:3
that *s.* may be saved in day of the. 5
joined to the Lord is one *s.* 6:17
God in your body and in your *s.* 20
holy both in body and *s.* 7:34
of gifts, but same *s.* 12:4, 8, 9, 11

is given by *s.* the word. *1 Cor* 12:8
s. are we all baptized into one body;
  and have been all . . . into one *s.* 13
in the *s.* he speaketh. 14:2
I will sing with the *s.* 15
shalt bless with the *s.* 16
was made a quickening *s.* 15:45
new testament, not of letter but of
  the *s.* . . . but the *s. 2 Cor* 3:6
shall not ministration of the *s.?* 8
the Lord is that *s.*: where the *s.* 17
the same *s.* of faith, we. 4:13
all filthiness of the flesh and *s.* 7:1
because his *s.* was refreshed. 13
another *s.* which ye have not. 11:4
walked we not in the same *s.?* 12:18
received ye the *s.* by the ? *Gal* 3:2
having begun in the *s.* 3
ministereth to you the *s.* 5
promise of the *s.* through faith. 14
sent forth the *s.* of his Son. 4:6
for we through *s.* wait for hope. 5:5
walk in the *s.* 16
lusteth against the *s.* and the *s.* 17
but if ye be led by the *s.* 18
the *s.*, let us walk in the *s.* 25
soweth to *s.* shall of the *s.* reap. 6:8
grace of our Lord be with your *s.* 18
                Philem 25
the *s.* that now worketh in. *Eph* 2:2
access by one *s.* unto the Father. 18
of God through the *s.* 22
to the apostles by the *s.* 3:5
might by his *s.* in inner man. 16
to keep unity of the *s.* in the. 4:3
there is one body, and one *s.* 4
and be renewed in the *s.* of. 23
with wine, but be filled with *s.* 5:18
take sword of the *s.* which is. 6:17
with all prayer in the *s.* 18
the supply of the *s.* of. *Phil* 1:19
that ye stand fast in one *s.* 27
if any fellowship of the *s.* 2:1
which worship God in the *s.* 3:3
to us your love in the *s. Col* 1:8
flesh, yet am I with you in *s.* 2:5
quench not *s.*, despise. *1 Thes* 5:19
pray your *s.* soul, and body be. 23
neither by *s.* nor by word. *2 Thes* 2:2
Lord shall consume with the *s.* 8*
sanctification of the *s.* and belief. 13
justified in *s.* seen of angels.
                1 Tim 3:16
now the *s.* speaketh expressly. 4:1
an example in *s.*, in faith. 12
Christ be with thy *s. 2 Tim* 4:22
asunder of soul and *s. Heb* 4:12
who through the eternal *s.* 9:14
without the *s.* is dead. *Jas* 2:26
the *s.* that dwelleth in us. 4:5
through sanctification of the *s.* to.
                1 Pet 1:2
in obeying truth through the *s.* 22
of a meek and quiet *s.* 3:4
death in flesh, but quickened by *s.* 18
according to God in the *s.* 4:6
by the *s.* which he hath. *1 John* 3:24
beloved, believe not every *s.* 4:1
every *s.* that confesseth Jesus. 2
every *s.* that confesseth not that. 3
because he hath given us of his *s.* 13
s. that beareth witness. 5:6
witness in earth, the *s.* the water. 8
sensual, not having the *s. Jude* 19
in the *s.* on the Lord's. *Rev* 1:10
hear what the *s.* saith unto the
  churches. 2:7, 11, 17, 29; 3:6, 13, 22
and immediately I was in the. 4:2
the *s.* of life from God. 11:11*
blessed dead: Yea, saith the *s.* 14:13
carried me away in the *s.* 17:3; 21:10
the *s.* and the bride say. 22:17
see **evil, holy, Lord, lying,
vexation**

spirit *of adoption*
have received the *s.* of adoption.
                Rom 8:15

spirit *of antichrist*
this is that *s.* of antichrist ye heard.
                1 John 4:3

spirit *of bondage*
not received the *s.* of bondage.
                Rom 8:15

born of the **spirit**
except a man be *born of the s.* he.
                John 3:5
is *born of the s.* is spirit. 6
one that is *born of the s.* 8
that was *born after the s. Gal* 4:29

broken spirit
of God are a *broken s. Ps* 51:17
sorrow of the heart the *s.* is *broken.*
                Pr 15:13
a *broken s.* drieth the bones. 17:22
  see **contrite**

spirit *of burning*
of Jerusalem by the *s.* of burning.
                Isa 4:4

spirit *of Christ*
have not the *s.* of Christ. *Rom* 8:9
what the *s.* of Christ in. *1 Pet* 1:11

spirit *of counsel*
the *s.* of counsel shall rest. *Isa* 11:2

spirit *of divination*
possessed with a *s.* of divination.
                Acts 16:16

dumb **spirit**
my son, who hath a *dumb s.*
                Mark 9:17
thou *dumb s.* I charge thee. 25

earnest of the **spirit**
hath given us the *earnest of the s.*
           2 Cor 1:22; 5:5

spirit *of error*
the *s.* of truth and error. *1 John* 4:6

faithful **spirit**
he that is of *faithful s.*   *Pr* 11:13
  see **familiar**

spirit *of fear*
given us the *s.* of fear. *2 Tim* 1:7

foul **spirit**
he rebuked the *foul s. Mark* 9:25
the hold of every *foul s. Rev* 18:2

fruit of the **spirit**
the *fruit of the s.* is love. *Gal* 5:22
for the *fruit of the s.* is in. *Eph* 5:9*

good **spirit**
thou gavest thy *good s. Neh* 9:20
thy *s.* is *good,* lead me. *Ps* 143:10

spirit *of God*
s. of God moved on the. *Gen* 1:2
man in whom the *s.* of God. 41:38
filled Bezaleel with the *s.* of God.
           Ex 31:3; 35:31
and the *s.* of God came. *Num* 24:2
the *s.* of God came on Saul, and.
      1 Sam 10:10; 11:6; 19:23
s. of God came on the messengers.
                19:20
the *s.* of God came upon Azariah.
                2 Chr 15:1
s. of God is in my nostrils. *Job* 27:3
the *s.* of God hath made me. 33:4
in vision by the *s.* of God into
  Chaldea. *Ezek* 11:24
s. of God descending. *Mat* 3:16
out devils by the *s.* of God. 12:28
if so be that the *s.* of God. *Rom* 8:9
as are led by the *s.* of God. 14
by the power of the *s.* of God. 15:19
man, but the *s.* of God. *1 Cor* 2:11
the things of the *s.* of God. 14
s. of God dwelleth in you. 3:16
sanctified by the *s.* of our God. 6:11
also that I have the *s.* of God. 7:40
by the *s.* of God, calleth. 12:3
the *s.* of the living God. *2 Cor* 3:3
not the holy *s.* of God. *Eph* 4:30
s. of God resteth on. *1 Pet* 4:14
know ye the *s.* of God. *1 John* 4:2

spirit *of glory*
s. of glory resteth on. *1 Pet* 4:14

spirit *of grace*
I will pour upon the house of David
  the *s.* of grace. *Zech* 12:10
done despite to the *s.* of grace.
                Heb 10:29

humble **spirit**
is to be of an *humble s. Pr* 16:19
shall uphold the *humble* in *s.* 29:23
that is of an *humble s. Isa* 57:15

spirit of jealousy
and s. of jealousy. Num 5:14, 30
spirit of judgement
blood of Jerusalem by s. of judgement. Isa 4:4
be for a s. of judgement to him. 28:6
spirit of knowledge
s. of knowledge shall rest. Isa 11:2
spirit of meekness
come to you in the s. of meekness? 1 Cor 4:21
restore such a one in the s. of meekness. Gal 6:1
my spirit
my s. shall not always strive with. Gen 6:3
whereof drinketh up my s. Job 6:4
in the anguish of my s. 7:11
visitation hath preserved my s. 10:12
if so, why should not my s.? 21:4
thine hand I commit my s. Ps 31:5
I complained, and my s. was. 77:3
and my s. made diligent search. 6
my s. was overwhelmed in me. 142:3
is my s. overwhelmed in me. 143:4
hear me speedily, O Lord, my s. 7
pour out my s. unto you. Pr 1:23
yea, with my s. will I seek thee. Isa 26:9
a covering, but not of my s. 30:1
things is the life of my s. 38:16
I have put my s. upon him. 42:1
pour my s. upon thy seed. 44:3
my s. that is upon thee shall. 59:21
in the heat of my s. Ezek 3:14
and I will put my s. within you. 36:27; 37:14
for I have poured out my s. on. 39:29
my s. was troubled. Dan 2:3
grieved in my s. 7:15
I will pour out my s. upon all flesh. Joel 2:28, 29; Acts 2:17, 18
so my s. remaineth among you: fear. Hag 2:5
nor by power, but by my s. Zech 4:6
these have quieted my s. in the. 6:8
I will put my s. upon. Mat 12:18
my s. hath rejoiced in God my. Luke 1:47
hands I commend my s. 23:46
Lord Jesus, receive my s. Acts 7:59
whom I serve with my s. Rom 1:9
are gathered together and my s. 1 Cor 5:4
my s. prayeth, but my. 14:14
they have refreshed my s. 16:18
I had no rest in my s. 2 Cor 2:13
new spirit
I will put a new s. within you. Ezek 11:19; 36:26
a new heart and a new s. 18:31
newness of spirit
serve in newness of the s. Rom 7:6
patient spirit
patient in s. is better. Eccl 7:8
perverse spirit
mingled a perverse s. Isa 19:14
poor in spirit
blessed are the poor in s. Mat 5:3
spirit of promise
sealed with that holy s. of promise. Eph 1:13
spirit of prophecy
testimony of Jesus is the s. of prophecy. Rev 19:10
spirit of slumber
them the s. of slumber. Rom 11:8
sorrowful spirit
woman of a sorrowful s. 1 Sam 1:15
spirit of truth
S. of truth whom world. John 14:17
even the S. of truth which. 15:26
when S. of truth is come. 16:13
we S. of truth and error. 1 John 4:6
unclean spirit
I will cause unclean s. to pass out. Zech 13:2
when the unclean s. is gone out of a man. Mat 12:43; Luke 11:24

their synagogue a man with an unclean s. Mark 1:23
and when the unclean s. had. 26
said, He hath an unclean s. 3:30
him a man with an unclean s. 5:2
come out of the man, thou unclean s. 8; Luke 8:29
young daughter had an unclean s. Mark 7:25
Jesus rebuked unclean s. Luke 9:42
spirit of understanding
the s. of understanding. Isa 11:2
spirit of whoredoms
s. of whoredoms caused. Hos 4:12
for the s. of whoredoms is in. 5:4
spirit of wisdom
filled with s. of wisdom. Ex 28:3
full of the s. of wisdom. Deut 34:9
s. of wisdom shall rest. Isa 11:2
give to you s. of wisdom. Eph 1:17
wounded spirit
but a wounded s. who? Pr 18:14
spirits
O God, the God of s. of all flesh. Num 16:22; 27:16
who maketh his angels s. Ps 104:4*; Heb 1:7
the Lord weigheth the s. Pr 16:2
these are the four s. of. Zech 6:5
and he cast out the s. Mat 8:16
he gave them power against unclean s. 10:1; Mark 6:7
authority commandeth he the unclean s. Mark 1:27; Luke 4:36
unclean s. fell down. Mark 3:11
the unclean s. entered into. 5:13
rejoice not that s. are. Luke 10:20
were vexed with unclean s. Acts 5:16
for unclean s. crying, came. 8:7
another discerning of. 1 Cor 12:10
s. of the prophets are. 14:32
depart from faith, giving heed to seducing s. 1 Tim 4:1
not all ministering s.? Heb 1:14
be in subjection to Father of s. 12:9
s. of just men made perfect. 23
and preached to the s. in prison. 1 Pet 3:19
try the s. whether they. 1 John 4:1
I saw three unclean s. Rev 16:13
s. of devils, working miracles. 14
see **evil, familiar, seven**
spiritual
the prophet is a fool, the s. Hos 9:7
impart to you some s. Rom 1:11
we know that the law is s. 7:14
partakers of their s. things. 15:27
speak, comparing s. things with s. 1 Cor 2:13
but he that is s. judgeth all things. 15
not speak to you as unto s. 3:1
sown unto you s. things. 9:11
all eat the same s. meat. 10:3
s. drink, drank of that s. rock. 4
now concerning s. gifts. 12:1
desire s. gifts. 14:1
ye are zealous of s. gifts. 12
himself to be a prophet, or s. 37
s. body, there is a s. body. 15:44
which is s. but that which is natural; and afterwards that which is s. 46
ye which are s. restore. Gal 6:1
blessed us with all s. Eph 1:3
in psalms and s. songs. 5:19
wrestle against s. wickedness. 6:12
be filled with all s. understanding. Col 1:9
another in psalms and s. songs. 3:16
ye are built up a s. house, to offer up s. sacrifices. 1 Pet 2:5
spiritually
but to be s. minded is. Rom 8:6
because are s. discerned. 1 Cor 2:14
which s. is called Sodom. Rev 11:8
spit
that hath the issue, s. on. Lev 15:8
if her father had but s. Num 12:14
she shall s. in his face. Deut 25:9
and they spare not to s. Job 30:10
they did s. in his face. Mat 26:67
and they s. upon him and. 27:30
and he s. and touched. Mark 7:33

he had s. on his eyes. Mark 8:23
they shall s. upon him and. 10:34
began to s. on him. 14:65; 15:19
spite
for thou beholdest s. Ps 10:14
spitefully
they entreated them s. Mat 22:6*
shall be s. entreated. Luke 18:32*
spitted
spitefully entreated and s. on. Luke 18:32
spitting
face from shame and s. Isa 50:6
spittle
he let his s. fall down. 1 Sam 21:13
till I swallow down my s. Job 7:19
he made clay of s. and. John 9:6
spoil, substantive
he shall divide the s. Gen 49:27
said, I will divide the s. Ex 15:9
Israel took the s. Num 31:9, 11
brought the prey and s. to Moses. 12
cattle we took for prey and the s. Deut 2:35; 3:7; Josh 8:27; 11:14
thou shalt gather all s. Deut 13:16
s. thou shalt take. 20:14; Josh 8:2
necks of them that take s. Judg 5:30
thirty men and took their s. 14:19
freely to-day of the s. 1 Sam 14:30
the people flew upon the s. and. 32
but didst fly upon the s. and. 15:19
but the people took of the s. 21
because the great s. that. 30:16
neither s. nor any thing. 19
and said, This is David's s. 20
not give them aught of the s. 22
s. to the elders of Judah and his friends; behold, a . . . the s. 26
brought in a great s. 2 Sam 3:22
he brought forth of the s. 12:30
Moab, to the s. 2 Ki 3:23
they shall become a s. to. 21:14
be brought much s. 1 Chr 20:2
they carried away s. 2 Chr 14:13, 14
Lord at same time of the s. 15:11
take the s.: they were three days in gathering the s. it was. 20:25
the Syrians sent s. to the king. 24:23
of them, and took much s. 25:13
took much s. and brought s. 28:8
men left the captives and the s. 14
with the s. clothed all that were. 15
been delivered to a s. Ezra 9:7
to take the s. of them for a prey. Esth 3:13; 8:11
but on the s. laid they not. 9:10
I plucked the s. out of. Job 29:17
at home, divided the s. Ps 68:12
word, as one findeth great s. 119:162
fill our houses with s. Pr 1:13
than to divide the s. with. 16:19
he shall have no need of s. 31:11
the s. of the poor is in. Isa 3:14
the s. of Samaria shall be. 8:4
rejoice when they divide the s. 9:3
him a charge to take the s. 10:6
your s. shall be gathered, like. 33:4
prey of a great s. divided. 23
they are for a s. and none. 42:22
who gave Jacob for a s.? 24
he shall divide the s. with. 53:12
violence and s. is heard in. Jer 6:7
and treasures will I give to s. 15:13
substance and treasures to s. 17:3
I cried violence and s. 20:8
that s. thee shall be a s. 30:16
their cattle shall be a s. 49:32
and Chaldea shall be a s. 50:10
it to the wicked for a s. Ezek 7:21
he shall scatter among them the s. Dan 11:24
they shall fall by s. many days. 33
s. of silver, take s. of gold. Nah 2:9
the s. of beasts shall. Hab 2:17
they shall be a s. to their. Zech 2:9
thy s. shall be divided in the. 14:1

spoil, verb
ye shall s. the Egyptians. Ex 3:22
s. them until morning. 1 Sam 14:36
returned after him only to s.
　　　　　　　　　2 Sam 23:10
they who hate us s. for. Ps 44:10
pass by the way s. him. 89:41
and let the stranger s. his labour.
　　　　　　　　　109:11
will s. soul of those that. Pr 22:23
s. not his resting place. 24:15
take us the foxes that s. S of S 2:15
they shall s. them of the. Isa 11:14
portion of them that s. us. 17:14
when shalt cease to s. thou. 33:1
the evenings shall s. them. Jer 5:6
I will give Jerusalem to them that
　shall s. it. 20:5
they that s. thee shall be a s. 30:16
the day that cometh to s. the. 47:4
go up to Kedar and s. the men. 49:28
that s. her shall be satisfied. 50:10
and they s. it, so that it. Ezek 14:15
and they shall s. the pomp. 32:12
s. those that spoiled them. 39:10
shall break their altars, shall s.
　　　　　　　　　Hos 10:2
he shall s. the treasure of all. 13:15
of the people shall s. thee. Hab 2:8
my people shall s. the.n. Zeph 2:9
into a strong man's house, and s.?
　　　　　Mat 12:29; Mark 3:27
beware lest any man s. Col 2:8

spoiled
sons of Jacob came and s. the city.
　　　　　　　　　Gen 34:27
they s. all that was in Hamor's. 29
they s. the Egyptians. Ex 12:36
only oppressed and s. Deut 28:29
hand of spoilers that s. Judg 2:14
hand of those that s. them. 16
delivered Israel from them that s.
　　　　　　　　　1 Sam 14:48
they s. the Philistines' tents. 17:53
Israel s. the tents of. 2 Ki 7:16
Asa s. all the cities. 2 Chr 14:14
he leadeth counsellors away s.
　　　　　　　　　Job 12:17
away s., overthroweth the mighty. 19
the stouthearted are s. Ps 76:5
soul of those that s. them. Pr 22:23
shall be s., their wives. Isa 13:16
land the rivers have s. 18:2, 7
be utterly emptied and s. 24:3
spoilest, and wast not s. 33:1
is a people robbed and s. 42:22
servant? why is he s.? Jer 2:14
woe unto us, for we are s. 4:13
is s.: suddenly are my tents s. 20
and when thou art s. what wilt? 30
how are we s.! 9:19
my tabernacle is s. 10:20
deliver him that is s. 21:12; 22:3
for the Lord hath s. their. 25:36
Nebo is s. 48:1
Moab is s. and gone. 15, 20
howl, for Ai is s. 49:3
Esau, his seed is s. 10
the Lord hath s. Babylon. 51:55
and hath s. none by violence.
　　　　　　　　　Ezek 18:7, 16
hath s. by violence. 12, 18
them to be removed and s. 23:46
spoil those that s. them. 39:10
fortresses shall be s. Hos 10:14
thy palaces shall be s. Amos 3:11
strengtheneth the s. against. 5:9
say, We be utterly s. Mi 2:4
hast s. many nations. Hab 2:8
the nations which s. you. Zech 2:8
howl, because the mighty are s. 11:2
is s.: for the pride of Jordan is s. 3
and having s. principalities. Col 2:15

spoiler
covert from face of s. the s. Isa 16:4
s. spoileth, go up, O Elam. 21:2
for the s. shall suddenly. Jer 6:26
I have brought upon them a s. 15:8
the s. shall come upon every. 48:8
the s. of Moab shall come upon. 18
s. is fallen upon thy summer. 32
because the s. is come upon. 51:56

spoilers
delivered them into the hand of s.
　　　　　Judg 2:14; 2 Ki 17:20
s. came out of camp. 1 Sam 13:17
the garrison and the s. they. 14:15
the s. are come upon all. Jer 12:12
for the s. shall come to her. 51:48
yet from me shall s. come to her. 53

spoilest
woe to thee that s. and thou. Isa 33:1

spoileth
needy from him that s. Ps 35:10
the spoiler s. Isa 21:2
troop of robbers s. Hos 7:1
the cankerworm s. Nah 3:16

spoiling
me evil for good, to the s. Ps 35:12
of the s. of the daughter. Isa 22:4
a voice from Horonaim s. Jer 48:3
for s. and violence are. Hab 1:3
for ye took joyfully the s. Heb 10:34

spoils
I saw among the s. a goodly garment.
　　　　　　　　　Josh 7:21
out of s. in battle did. 1 Chr 26:27
their pride with the s. Isa 25:11
and divideth his s. Luke 11:22
gave the tenth of the s. Heb 7:4

spoken
what he hath s. of him. Gen 18:19
have s. in mine ears. Num 14:28
we have s. against the Lord. 21:7
hath he s. and shall he not? 23:19
words they have s. to thee. they have
　well said ... have s. Deut 5:28
because he hath s. to turn. 13:5
s. that which they have s. 18:17
done all he hath s. 1 Sam 25:30
unless thou hadst s., the people had
　gone up. 2 Sam 2:27
my lord the king hath s. 14:19
Ahithophel hath s. after this. 17:6
have not s. this word. 1 Ki 2:23
answer this people who have s. to?
　　　　　12:9; 2 Chr 10:9
people said, It is well s. 1 Ki 18:24
wouldest thou be s. for to? 2 Ki 4:13
tongue hath s. in my. Job 33:2
Job hath s. without knowledge. 34:35
ye have not s. of me as. 42:7, 8
my mouth hath s. when. Ps 66:14
glorious things are s. of thee. 87:3
they have s. against me with. 109:2
a word s. in due season. Pr 15:23
a word fitly s. is like apples. 25:11
to all words that are s. Eccl 7:21
when she shall be s. for. S of S 8:8
for the sea hath s. Isa 23:4
he hath s. 38:15
defiled, your lips have s. lies. 59:3
hath s. to us in the name. Jer 26:16
and have s. lying words in. 29:23
not what this people have s.? 33:24
ye and your wives have s. 44:25
have ye not s. a lying? Ezek 13:7
because ye have s. vanity, and. 8
to thee it is s. Dan 4:31
yet they have s. lies. Hos 7:13
they have s. words, swearing. 10:4
with you, as ye have s. Amos 5:14
nor shouldest thou have s. Ob 12
thereof have s. lies. Mi 6:12
the idols have s. vanity. Zech 10:2
what have we s. so? Mal 3:13
he hath s. blasphemy. Mat 26:65
s. of for a memorial. Mark 14:9
things which were s. Luke 2:33
and for a sign which shall be s. 34
s. in darkness, what s. in ear. 12:3
they the things which were s. 18:34
if I had not come and s. John 15:22
as many as have s. Acts 3:24
none of these things ye have s. 8:24
lest that come upon you s. of. 13:40
the word first have been s. to you. 46
to the things that were s. 16:14
things cannot be s. against. 19:36
if a spirit or angel hath s. 23:9
things that were s. by Paul. 27:11
when he had thus s., took bread. 35
every where it is s. against. 28:22
your faith is s. of through. Rom 1:8

according to that which was s.
　　　　　　　　　Rom 4:18
your good be evil s. of. 14:16
to whom he was not s. of. 15:21
why am I evil s. of for? 1 Cor 10:30
it be known what is s.? 14:9
hath in these last days s. Heb 1:2
if the word s. by angels was. 2:2
of those things to be s. after. 3:5
he would not afterward have s. 4:8
ue of whom these things are s. 7:13
of things which we have s. 8:1
the word should not be s. any. 12:19
have s. unto you the word. 13:7
their part he is evil s. of. 1 Pet 4:14
truth shall be evil s. of. 2 Pet 2:2
of words which were s. before. 3:2
ungodly sinners have s. Jude 15
the words which were s. before. 17

spoken with God, expressly
of which God had s. to him. Gen 21:2
an holy people to thy God as he hath
　s. Deut 26:19
God hath s. in his. Ps 60:6; 108:7
God hath s. once; twice. 62:11
was s. unto you by God. Mat 22:31
which God hath s. by. Acts 3:21
　　　　　　　　　see Lord

I have, or have I spoken
which I have s. to thee. Gen 28:15
this is the thing I have s. 41:28
all this land I have s. Ex 32:13
the place of which I have s. 34
out of my grief have I s. 1 Sam 1:16
Eli all things which I have s. 3:12
the matter which I have s. 20:23
and after that I have s. Job 21:3
once have I s. but I will not. 40:5
I believed, therefore have I s.
　　　　　Ps 116:10; 2 Cor 4:13
I have not s. in secret. Isa 45:19
　　　　　　　　　48:16
I have s. it, I will also bring. 46:11
I, even I, have s.; yea, I have. 48:15
I have s. it, I have proposed it.
　　　　　　　　　Jer 4:28
I have not s. to them yet. 23:21
I have s. unto you, rising early and.
　　　　　　　　　25:3; 35:14
words I have s. to thee. 30:2; 36:2
because I have s. but they. 35:17
word which I have s. Ezek 12:28
saith it, albeit I have not s. 13:7
for I have s. it, saith the. 26:5; 28:10
fire of my jealousy have I s. 36:5, 6
art thou he of whom I have s.? 38:17
fire of my wrath have I s. 19
is the day whereof I have s. 39:8
I have also s. by the. Hos 12:10
the word that I have s. John 12:48
for I have not s. of myself but. 49
these things have I s. 14:25; 15:11
　　　　　　　　　16:1, 25, 33
the word I have s. to you. 15:3
if I have s. evil, bear witness. 18:23

had spoken
the word Joseph had s. Gen 44:2
did as Balaam had s. Num 23:2
words he had s. to king. 1 Ki 13:11
the Jezreelite had s. to him. 21:4
word which Elijah had s. 2 Ki 1:17
as the man of God had s. 7:18
because we had s. unto. Ezra 8:22
king's words that he had s. Neh 2:18
Mordecai, who had s. good. Esth 7:9
had waited till Job had s. Job 32:4
wrote words the Lord had s. Jer 36:4
and when he had s. this. Dan 10:11
when he had s. such words. 15
when he had s. unto me, I was. 19
he had s., the leprosy. Mark 1:42
they knew that he had s. the parable.
　　　　　12:12; Luke 20:19
when he had thus s. Luke 19:28
　　　24:40; John 9:6; 11:43; 18:22
　　　　　Acts 19:41; 20:36; 26:30
the man believed the word that Jesus
　had s. John 4:50
they thought he had s. 11:13
when he had s. this, he saith. 11:19
that he had s. unto him. Acts 9:27
departed, after Paul had s. 28:25
when Moses had s. every. Heb 9:19

spoken with prophet

but *prophet* hath *s.* it. *Deut* 18:22
if *prophet* be deceived when he hath
s. *Ezek* 14:9
that which was *s.* by Jeremy the
prophet. *Mat* 2:17; 27:9
might be fulfilled which was *s.* by
the *prophet.* 2:23; 13:35; 27:35
s. of by the *prophet* Esaias. 3:3
which was *s.* by Esaias the *prophet.*
4:14; 8:17; 12:17; 21:4
of desolation *s.* of by Daniel the
prophet. 24:15; *Mark* 13:14
believe all that the *prophets* have *s.*
Luke 24:25
s. of by the *prophet* Joel. *Acts* 2:16
take *prophets*, who have *s.* *Jas* 5:10

thou hast spoken

this city for the which *thou hast s.*
Gen 19:21
nor since *thou hast s.* to. *Ex* 4:10
Moses said, *Thou hast s.* well. 10:29
this thing that *thou hast s.* 33:17
be great, as *thou hast s.* *Num* 14:17
the thing which *thou hast s.* is good.
Deut 1:14
thou hast s. friendly to. *Ruth* 2:13
maid servants which *thou hast s.* of.
2 Sam 6:22
but *thou hast s.* also of thy servant's.
7:19, 25; *1 Chr* 17:17, 23
good is the word of the Lord which
thou hast s. *2 Ki* 20:19; *Isa* 39:8
fail of all that *thou hast s.* *Esth* 6:10
surely *thou hast s.* in my. *Job* 33:8
behold, *thou hast s.* and done evil.
Jer 3:5
and that which *thou hast s.* is. 32:24
the words which *thou hast s.* 44:16
O Lord, *thou hast s.* against. 51:62
I have heard all thy blasphemies
which *thou hast s.* *Ezek* 35:12

spokes

their felloes and *s.* *1 Ki* 7:33

spokesman

thy *s.* unto the people. *Ex* 4:16

spoon

one *s.* of ten shekels of gold, full of.
Num 7:14, 20, 26, 32, 38, 44, 50
56, 62

spoons

dishes thereof and *s.* *Ex* 25:29
he made his dishes and his *s.* 37:16
and put thereon the dishes and the *s.*
Num 4:7
bowls, twelve *s.* of gold. 7:84, 86
the *s.* were of pure gold. 7:50
2 Chr 4:22
the *s.* took he away. *2 Ki* 25:14
Jer 52:18, 19
of rest of the money *s.* *2 Chr* 24:14

sport

make *s.* And he made *s.* *Judg* 16:25
beheld while Samson made *s.* 27
it is a *s.* to a fool to do. *Pr* 10:23
and saith, Am not I in *s.*? 26:19

sport

against whom do ye *s.*? *Isa* 57:4

sporting

Isaac was *s.* with. *Gen* 26:8
s. themselves with their. *2 Pet* 2:13*

spot

a red heifer without *s.* *Num* 19:2
two lambs without *s.* 28:3*
9*, 11*; 29:17*, 26*
their *s.* is not the *s.* *Deut* 32:5
lift up thy face without *s.* *Job* 11:15
fair, there is no *s.* in thee. *S of S* 4:7
church, not having *s.* *Eph* 5:27
keep this commandment without *s.*
1 Tim 6:14
who offered himself without *s.* to
God. *Heb* 9:14*
as of a lamb without *s.* *1 Pet* 1:19
may be found without *s.* *2 Pet* 3:14

see bright

spots

can leopard change his *s.*? *Jer* 13:23
s. they are and blemishes, sporting
themselves with their. *2 Pet* 2:13
these are *s.* in your feasts. *Jude* 12

spotted

thence all the *s.* cattle. *Gen* 30:32
every one that is not *s.* shall be. 33
forth cattle speckled and *s.* 39
the garment *s.* by the flesh. *Jude* 23

spouse

(*Revisions*, bride)
from Lebanon, my *s.* *S of S* 4:8
my heart, my sister, my *s.* 9
fair is thy love, my sister, my *s.* 10
thy lips, O my *s.* drop as the. 11
inclosed is my sister, my *s.* 12
into my garden, my sister, my *s.* 5:1

spouses

(*Revisions*, brides)
and your *s.* shall commit. *Hos* 4:13
I will not punish your *s.* when. 14

spouts, see waterspouts

sprang

and did yield fruit that *s.* up.
Mark 4:8*; *Luke* 8:8*
for a light and *s.* in. *Acts* 16:29
it is evident our Lord *s.* *Heb* 7:14
s. of one so many as the stars. 11:12

see sprung

spread

field where Jacob had *s.* his tent.
Gen 33:19; 35:21
and the plague *s.* *Lev* 13:5, 6, 23, 28
if the scall *s.* not. 32, 34
but if the scall *s.* much. 35, 36
if the plague be *s.* 51; 14:39, 44
and if the plague be not *s.* 13:53
55; 14:18
shall *s.* cloth of blue. *Num* 4:7, 11
they shall *s.* a scarlet cloth. 8
s. a purple cloth. 13
they shall *s.* on it a covering of. 14
s. the cloth before the. *Deut* 22:17
they *s.* a garment. *Judg* 8:25
Philistines *s.* themselves. 15:9
came and *s.* themselves in valley of.
2 Sam 5:18, 22; *1 Chr* 14:9*, 13*
they *s.* Absalom a tent. *2 Sam* 16:22
woman *s.* a covering on the. 17:19
Rizpah *s.* sackcloth for her. 21:10
carvings of cherubims, and *s.* gold.
1 Ki 6:32
he arose, with his hands *s.* 8:54
Hazael *s.* a thick cloth. *2 Ki* 8:15
s. the letter before the Lord. 19:14
Isa 37:14
he *s.* a cloud for a. *Ps* 105:39
they have *s.* a net by the way. 140:5
in vain net is *s.* in sight. *Pr* 1:17
worm *s.* is under thee. *Isa* 14:11
they that *s.* nets on the waters. 19:8
they could not *s.* the sail. 33:23
to *s.* sackcloth and ashes. 58:5
and they shall *s.* them. *Jer* 8:2
silver *s.* into plates is brought. 10:9
he hath *s.* net for my feet. *Lam* 1:13
s. the roll before me. *Ezek* 2:10
my net also will I *s.* 12:13; 17:20
thou shalt be a place to *s.* 26:14
because ye have been a net *s.* upon
Tabor. *Hos* 5:1
when they shall go, I will *s.* 7:12
branches shall *s.*, his beauty. 14:6
as the morning *s.* upon. *Joel* 2:2
their horsemen shall *s.* *Hab* 1:8
behold, I will *s.* dung upon. *Mal* 2:3
s. their garments in the. *Mat* 21:8
Mark 11:8; *Luke* 19:36
but that it *s.* no further. *Acts* 4:17

spread abroad

families of the Canaanites were *s.*
abroad. *Gen* 10:18
thou shalt *s.* abroad to west. 28:14
I will *s.* abroad my hands. *Ex* 9:29
Moses *s.* abroad his hands to. 33
he *s.* abroad the tent over. 40:19
but if the scab *s.* much abroad.
Lev 13:7, 22, 27
they *s.* abroad the quails round the.
Num 11:32
they were *s.* abroad on the earth.
1 Sam 30:16
I did stamp and *s.* abroad mine
enemies. *2 Sam* 22:43
the Philistines *s.* themselves abroad.
1 Chr 14:13*

Uzziah's name *s.* abroad.
2 Chr 26:8, 15
prosperity be *s.* abroad *Zech* 1:17
I have *s.* you abroad as the. 2:6
departed, *s.* abroad his fame in all.
Mat 9:31; *Mark* 1:28; 6:14
God-ward is *s.* abroad. *1 Thes* 1:8

spread forth

valleys are they *s.* forth. *Num* 24:6
the cherubims *s.* forth. *1 Ki* 8:7
Solomon *s.* forth. 22; *2 Chr* 6:12, 13
plague of his own heart, and *s.* forth
his hands. *1 Ki* 8:38; *2 Chr* 6:29
when ye *s.* forth your hands. *Isa* 1:15
he shall *s.* forth hands, as he. 25:11
saith God, he that *s.* forth 42:5
a place to *s.* forth nets. *Ezek* 47:10

spread over

they shall *s.* over it a cloth. *Num* 4:6
s. therefore thy skirt over. *Ruth* 3:9
that is *s.* over all nations. *Isa* 25:7
s. his royal pavilion over. *Jer* 43:10
shall *s.* his wings over Moab. 48:40
s. his wings over Bozrah. 49:22
I *s.* my skirt over thee. *Ezek* 16:8
nations *s.* their net over him. 19:8

spread out

cherubims *s.* out wings. *Ex* 37:9
1 Chr 28:18
I *s.* out my hands to the. *Ezra* 9:5
my root was *s.* out by. *Job* 29:19
hast thou with him *s.* out the sky?
37:18
have *s.* out my hands. *Isa* 65:2
hath *s.* out his hand. *Lam* 1:10
I will therefore *s.* out my net over.
Ezek 32:3

spreadest

fine linen which thou *s.* *Ezek* 27:7

spreadeth

if the priest see that scab *s.* *Lev* 13:8
as an eagle *s.* abroad. *Deut* 32:11
God who alone *s.* out. *Job* 9:8
and he *s.* his cloud upon it. 26:9
behold, he *s.* his light upon it. 36:30
he *s.* sharp pointed things. 41:30
flattereth his neighbour *s.* a net.
Pr 29:5
as he that swimmeth *s.* *Isa* 25:11
and the goldsmith *s.* it over. 40:19
that *s.* the heavens as a tent. 22
I the Lord that *s.* abroad the. 44:24
the daughter of Zion *s.* *Jer* 4:31
a tree that *s.* out her roots. 17:8
Zion *s.* forth her hands. *Lam* 1:17

spreading

appears, it is a *s.* plague. *Lev* 13:57
the wicked *s.* himself. *Ps* 37:35
and became a *s.* vine. *Ezek* 17:6
place for the *s.* of nets. 26:5

spreadings

can any understand the *s.*? *Job* 36:29

sprigs

he shall cut off the *s.* with pruning
hooks. *Isa* 18:5
a vine, and shot forth *s.* *Ezek* 17:6

spring, substantive

about *s.* of the day Samuel called.
1 Sam 9:26
he went forth to the *s.* *2 Ki* 2:21
fountain and corrupt *s.* *Pr* 25:26
spouse, is a *s.* shut up. *S of S* 4:12
shalt be like *s.* of water. *Isa* 58:11
all the leaves of her *s.* *Ezek* 17:9*
his *s.* shall become dry. *Hos* 13:15

see day spring

spring

Israel sang, *S.* up, O. *Num* 21:17
depths that *s.* out of valleys and.
Deut 8:7
day began to *s.* they. *Judg* 19:25
neither doth trouble *s.* *Job* 5:6
of the tender herb to *s.* forth. 38:27
truth shall *s.* out of the. *Ps* 85:11
wicked *s.* as the grass. 92:7
before they *s.* forth, I tell. *Isa* 42:9
new thing, now it shall *s.* 43:19
shall *s.* up as among the grass. 44:4
and let righteousness *s.* 45:8
and thine health shall *s.* forth. 58:8

causeth things that are sown to s.:
Lord will cause praise to s.*Isa* 61:11
for the pastures do s. *Joel* 2:22
the seed should s., he. *Mark* 4:27

springeth
even to hyssop that s. *1 Ki* 4:33
the second year that which s. of.
2 Ki 19:29; *Isa* 37:30
thus judgement s. up as. *Hos* 10:4

springing
there a well of s. water. *Gen* 26:19
as the tender grass s. *2 Sam* 23:4
thou blessedst the s. *Ps* 65:10
him a well of water s. up. *John* 4:14
any root of bitterness s. *Heb* 12:15

springs
to the plain under the s. of Pisgah.
Deut 4:49*
all the country of the s. *Josh* 10:40*
in the plains and in the s. 12:8*
give me s. of water. And he gave
her the upper s. 15:19; *Judg* 1:15
hast thou entered into the s. of the
sea? *Job* 38:16
all my s. are in thee. *Ps* 87:7
s. into the valleys. 104:10
he turneth the water s. into. 107:33
dry ground into water s. 35
land become s. of water. *Isa* 35:7
I will make the dry land s. 41:18
even by the s. of water shall. 49:10
dry up her sea and make her s. dry.
Jer 51:36

sprinkle
let Moses s. the ashes. *Ex* 9:8
he shall s. on him that. *Lev* 14:7
the priest shall s. of the oil. 16
priest shall s. of the oil with. 27
s. the house seven times. 51
shall s. on the mercy seat. 16:14, 15
s. water of purifying. *Num* 8:7
shall s. it upon the tent, and. 19:18
the clean person shall s. it on. 19
shall he s. many nations. *Isa* 52:15
will I s. clean water. *Ezek* 36:25

sprinkled
Moses s. the ashes up. *Ex* 9:10
was not s. on him. *Num* 19:13, 20
and s. dust on their heads. *Job* 2:12
he s. both the book and. *Heb* 9:19
having our hearts s. from an. 10:22
see **blood**

sprinkleth
priest's that s. the blood. *Lev* 7:14
he that s. the water. *Num* 19:21

sprinkling
the ashes of a heifer s. *Heb* 9:13
through faith he kept the s. 11:28
to Jesus, and to the blood of s. 12:24
and the s. of the blood. *1 Pet* 1:2

sprout
a tree that it will s. again. *Job* 14:7

sprung
seven thin ears s. up. *Gen* 41:6, 23
it is a leprosy s. up in. *Lev* 13:42
sat in shadow of death, light is s. up.
Mat 4:16
forthwith they s. up. 13:5; *Mark* 4:5
the thorns s. up and choked them.
Mat 13:7; *Luke* 8:7
but when blade was s. up. *Mat* 13:26
as soon as it was s. up. *Luke* 8:6

spue
that the land s. you not out also.
Lev 18:28*; 20:22*
drink, s. and fall. *Jer* 25:27
so then I will s. thee out. *Rev* 3:16

spued
as it s. out nations. *Lev* 18:28*

spun
that which they had s. *Ex* 35:25
the women s. goats' hair. 26

spunge
(*Revisions*, sponge)
took a s. and filled it with vinegar.
Mat 27:48; *Mark* 15:36
John 19:29

spy
men which Moses sent to s. land.
Num 13:16, 17
Moses sent to s. out Jaazer. 21:32

Joshua sent two men to s. secretly.
Josh 2:1; 6:23, 25
sent to s. the land. *Judg* 18:2, 14, 17
his servants to s. out the city.
2 Sam 10:3; *1 Chr* 19:3
he said, Go and s. *2 Ki* 6:13
came in privily to s. out. *Gal* 2:4

square
all doors and posts were s. *1 Ki* 7:5
s. round about, and 50. *Ezek* 45:2
see **four-square**

squared
of the temple were s. *Ezek* 41:21

squares
in four s. thereof. *Ezek* 43:16*
fourteen broad in the four s. 17*

stability
knowledge shall be the s. *Isa* 33:6
I will make Rabbah a s. *Ezek* 25:5

stable, *substantive*
world also shall be s. *1 Chr* 16:30

stablish, -ed, -eth, *see* **establish, -ed, -eth**

Stachys
salute Urbane, and S. *Rom* 16:9

stacks
so that the s. of corn. *Ex* 22:6*

stacte
(*This Greek word signifies the
gum that distils from the myrrh
trees. Moses speaks of stacte
in the enumeration of the drugs
that were to enter into the composition of the perfume, which was
to be offered in the holy place upon
the golden altar*)
take to thee sweet spices, s. and.
Ex 30:34

staff
with my s. I passed. *Gen* 32:10
Thy signet and thy s. 38:18, 25
eat it, with your s. in. *Ex* 12:11
and walk abroad on his s. 21:19
bare one cluster of grapes between
two upon a s. *Num* 13:23
smote the ass with a s. 22:27
put forth the end of his s. *Judg* 6:21
s. of his spear was like a weaver's.
1 Sam 17:7; *2 Sam* 21:19
David took his s. in his hand, and.
1 Sam 17:40
one that leaneth on a s. *2 Sam* 3:29
he must be fenced with the s. 23:7
to him with a s. 21; *1 Chr* 11:23
take my s.: lay my s. on. *2 Ki* 4:29
Gehazi laid the s. on the face. 31
on s. of this reed. 18:21; *Isa* 36:6
thy rod and thy s. *Ps* 23:4
take from Judah the s. *Isa* 3:1
for thou hast broken the s. 9:4
and the s. in their hand is. 10:5
or as if the s. should lift up. 15
and shall lift up his s. 10:24
the Lord hath broken the s. 14:5
are beaten out with a s. 28:27
where grounded s. shall pass. 30:32
say, How is the strong s.! *Jer* 48:17
have been a s. of reed. *Ezek* 29:6
and their s. declareth. *Hos* 4:12
every man with his s. in. *Zech* 8:4
and I took my s. even Beauty. 11:10
then I cut asunder my other s. 14
journey, save a s. only. *Mark* 6:8
leaning on the top of his s. *Heb* 11:21
see **bread**

stagger
to s. like a drunken man. *Job* 12:25
Ps 107:27
they s. but not with strong drink.
Isa 29:9

staggered
he s. not at the promise of God.
Rom 4:20*

staggereth
as a drunken man s. *Isa* 19:14

stain
the shadow of death s. it. *Job* 3:5*
Lord purposed to s. the pride of.
Isa 23:9
their blood sprinkled, I will s. 63:3

stairs
up with winding s. *1 Ki* 6:8
him on the top of the s. *2 Ki* 9:13
stood on the s. Joshua. *Neh* 9:4
secret places of the s. *S of S* 2:14*
and his s. shall look. *Ezek* 43:17*
Paul stood on the s. *Acts* 21:40

stakes
not one of the s. shall. *Isa* 33:20
cords and strengthen thy s. 54:2

stalk
seven rank ears came up on one s.
Gen 41:5, 22
it hath no s.: the bud. *Hos* 8:7*

stalks
and she hid them with the s. of flax.
Josh 2:6

stall
eat the calves out of the midst of the
s. *Amos* 6:4
grow up as calves of the s. *Mal* 4:2
loose his ox from the s. *Luke* 13:15

stalled
than a s. ox and hatred. *Pr* 15:17

stalls
Solomon had forty thousand s. of.
1 Ki 4:26; *2 Chr* 9:25
Hezekiah had s. for all manner of
beasts. *2 Chr* 32:28
shall be no herd in the s. *Hab* 3:17

stammerers
the tongue of the s. shall. *Isa* 32:4

stammering
s. lips and another tongue. *Isa* 28:11*
see a people of a s. tongue. 33:19*

stamp
I did s. them as the mire of the street.
2 Sam 22:43
hand, s. with thy foot. *Ezek* 6:11

stamped
I s. the calf and ground. *Deut* 9:21
Josiah s. the grove. *2 Ki* 23:6
s. high places small to powder. 15
her idol and s. it. *2 Chr* 15:16*
hast s. with the feet. *Ezek* 25:6
fourth beast s. residue. *Dan* 7:7, 19
the he goat cast down and s. 8:7*
cast down some of stars, and s. 10*

stamping
at noise of s. of hoofs. *Jer* 47:3

stanched
her issue of blood s. *Luke* 8:44

stand
cloudy pillar s. at door. *Ex* 33:10
priest shall estimate it, so shall it s.
Lev 27:14, 17
her vows shall s. *Num* 30:4, 5, 7, 11
her vows or her bond shall not s. 12
hath chosen him to s. *Deut* 18:5
if he s. to it and say, I like. 25:8
when he shall s. at entering gate.
Josh 20:4
now s. and see this great thing.
1 Sam 12:16
I will go out and s. before my. 19:3
the house, priests could s. to minister. *1 Ki* 8:11; *2 Chr* 5:14
as the Lord liveth, before whom I s.
1 Ki 17:1; 18:15; *2 Ki* 3:14; 5:16
will come out and s. *2 Ki* 5:11
how then shall we s.? 10:4
the angel of the Lord s. *1 Chr* 21:16
to s. every morning to thank. 23:30
all present to s. to it. *2 Chr* 34:32
rulers of congregation s. *Ezra* 10:14*
see if Mordecai's matters would s.
Esth 3:4
to gather themselves, and to s. 8:11
lean on his house, it shall not s.
Job 8:15
he shall s. at the latter day. 19:25
and they s. as a garment. 38:14
and my kinsmen s. afar off. *Ps* 38:11
on right hand did s. queen. 45:9
and he made the waters to s. 78:13
Satan at his right hand. 109:6
he shall s. at the right hand. 31
our feet shall s. within thy. 122:2
if thou shouldest mark iniquities, O
Lord, who shall s.? 130:3
house of righteous shall s. *Pr* 12:7

counsel of the Lord shall s. Pr 19:21
and s. not in the place of.   25:6
s. not in an evil thing.   Eccl 8:3*
thus saith Lord God, It shall not s.
                              Isa 7:7; 8:10
a root of Jesse, which shall s. 11:10
purposed, so it shall s.   14:24
my Lord, I s. continually on.   21:8
your agreement with hell shall not s.
                                 28:18
liberal things shall he s.   32:8*
word of our God shall s. for.   40:8
counsel shall s. and I will do. 46:10
s. now with thine enchantments.
                                 47:12
and strangers shall s. and feed. 61:5
s. ye in the ways and see. Jer 6:16
know whose word shall s.   44:28
did not s. because day was.   46:21
keeping of his covenant it might s.
                              Ezek 17:14
their loins to be at a s.   29:7
and the kingdom shall s. Dan 2:44
king of the north shall not s.   11:6
king of the south shall not s.   25
nor shall he s. that handleth the.
                              Amos 2:15
he shall s. and feed in.   Mi 5:4
S., s., shall they cry.   Nah 2:8
and who shall s. when he ? Mal 3:2
kingdom divided against itself shall
not s. Mat 12:25, 26; Mark 3:24
                         25; Luke 11:18
when ye s. praying.   Mark 11:25
why s. ye gazing up ?   Acts 1:11
go, s. and speak in the temple.   5:20
Paul said, I s. at Caesar's.   25:10
I s. and am judged for hope.   26:6
this grace wherein we s.   Rom 5:2
according to election might s.   9:11
God is able to make him s.   14:4
the gospel wherein ye s. 1 Cor 15:1
and why s. we in jeopardy ?   30
joy, for by faith ye s.   2 Cor 1:24
having done all to s.   Eph 6:13
s. having your loins girt about.   14
grace of God wherein ye s.
                              1 Pet 5:12
behold, I s. at the door.   Rev 3:20
who shall be able to s.?   6:17
merchants s. afar off for fear. 18:15

stand abroad
s. abroad, man shall.   Deut 24:11

stand against
neither shalt thou s. against the blood
of thy neighbour.   Lev 19:16
widow shall s. against.   Num 30:9
that my words shall s. against you.
                              Jer 44:29
to s. against wiles of devil. Eph 6:11

stand aloof
and my friends s. aloof.   Ps 38:11

stand back
said, S. back. This fellow. Gen 19:9

stand before
rise up early, s. before Pharaoh.
                         Ex 8:20; 9:13
could not s. before Moses.   9:11
I will s. before thee on the rock. 17:6
woman s. before a beast. Lev 18:23
no power to s. before your enemies.
         26:37; Josh 7:12, 13; Judg 2:14
s. before the congregation to minister.   Num 16:9
and he shall s. before Eleazar. 27:21
till he s. before congregation. 35:12
                              Josh 20:6
shall no man be able to s. before
thee. Deut 7:24; 11:25; Josh 1:5
                         10:8; 23:9
can s. before the children ? Deut 9:2
tribe of Levi to s. before the. 10:8
    2 Chr 29:11; Ezek 44:11, 15
the men shall s. before. Deut 19:17
s. this day all of you before. 29:10
who is able to s. before ? 1 Sam 6:20
I pray thee, s. before me.   16:22
virgin s. before the king.   1 Ki 1:2
happy are these thy servants who s.
before thee.   10:8; 2 Chr 9:7
s. on the mount before.   1 Ki 9:11
we s. before this house. 2 Chr 20:9

we cannot s. before thee. Ezra 9:15
is able to s. before me ?   Job 41:10
can s. before his cold ?   Ps 147:17
in business ? he shall s. before kings,
he shall not s. before.   Pr 22:29
who is able to s. before envy ? 27:4
come and s. before me.   Jer 7:10
thou shalt s. before me.   15:19
want a man to s. before me. 35:19
appoint ? who is that shepherd that
will s. before me ? 49:19; 50:44
might s. before king.   Dan 1:5
beasts might s. before him.   8:4
in the ram, to s. before him.   7
none shall s. before him, he. 11:16
s. before his indignation ? Nah 1:6
s. before the Son of man. Luke 21:36
we shall all s. before judgement seat
of Christ.   Rom 14:10
I saw the dead, small and great, s.
before God.   Rev 20:12

stand by
behold I s. by the well. Gen 24:43
s. by the river's brink.   Ex 7:15
and all the people s. by thee. 18:14
s. by the burnt offering. Num 23:3
while they s. by let them. Neh 7:3
who say, S. by thyself, I. Isa 65:5
s. by the way and ask.   Jer 48:19
prince shall s. by the.   Ezek 46:2
give places to walk among these that
s. by.   Zech 3:7
ones that s. by the Lord.   4:14
the people which s. by. John 11:42

stand fast
shall s. fast with him.   Ps 89:28
all his commandments s. fast. 111:8*
say ye, S. fast, and.   Jer 46:14
watch ye, s. fast in.   1 Cor 16:13
s. fast therefore in liberty. Gal 5:1
s. fast in one spirit.   Phil 1:27
so s. fast in the Lord.   4:1
live, if ye s. fast in Lord. 1 Thes 3:8
s. fast and hold.   2 Thes 2:15

stand forth
get up, and s. forth with. Jer 46:4
he saith to the man, S. forth.
              Mark 3:3; Luke 6:8

stand here
s. here by well of water. Gen 24:13
he said, S. here by the burnt offering.
                        Num 23:15
thee, s. thou here by me. Deut 5:31
turn aside, and s. here. 2 Sam 18:30
s. ye here all day idle ? Mat 20:6
some s. here who shall not. Mark 9:1
even by him doth this man s. here
whole.   Acts 4:10

stand in
s. in the door of the tent. Judg 4:20
s. in holy place according. 2 Chr 35:5
the ungodly shall not s. in. Ps 1:5
s. in awe, sin not, commune.   4:4
foolish shall not s. in thy sight. 5:5
who shall s. in his holy place ? 24:3
of the world s. in awe.   33:8
who may s. in thy sight when ? 76:7
hast not made him to s. in. 89:43
s. in house of Lord. 134:1; 135:2
s. in gate of Lord's house. Jer 7:2
the wild asses did s. in the. 14:6
s. in the gate of the children. 17:19
s. in the court of the Lord's. 26:2
have not gone up to s. in the battle.
                         Ezek 13:5
that should s. in gap before. 22:30
they shall s. in judgement. 44:24
had ability in them to s. in. Dan 1:4
s. in the glorious land.   11:16
shall s. in thy lot at the end. 12:13
feet s. in that day on.   Zech 14:4
when ye see abomination s. in holy
place.   Mat 24:15
Gabriel, that s. in presence of God.
                         Luke 1:19
not s. in wisdom of men. 1 Cor 2:5
to change my voice, for I s. in.
                         Gal 4:20*

stand on
to-morrow I will s. on top. Ex 17:9
of Elisha shall s. on him. 2 Ki 6:31
shall not s. on his side. Dan 11:17

arms shall s. on his part, and they
shall pollute.   Dan 11:31
s. on sea of glass, having. Rev 15:2

stand out
eyes s. out with fatness.   Ps 73:7

stand perfect
may s. perfect and complete in will.
                         Col 4:12

stand still
Fear ye not, s. still and see the.
    Ex 14:13; 2 Chr 20:17
s. still, I will hear what. Num 9:8*
ye shall s. still in Jordan. Josh 3:8
sun s. still upon Gibeon, and. 10:12
s. thou still a while.   1 Sam 9:27
now s. still that I may reason. 12:7
we will s. still in our place. 14:9
s. still and consider the. Job 37:14
escaped sword s. not still. Jer 51:50
the chariot to s. still.   Acts 8:38

stand strong
mountain to s. strong.   Ps 30:7

stand there
that they may s. there. Num 11:16
as Levites who s. there. Deut 18:7
to the poor, S. thou there. Jas 2:3

stand together
let us s. together: who ? Isa 50:8

stand up
s. up and bless the Lord. Neh 9:5
I s. up, and thou regardest me not.
                         Job 30:20
in order before me, s. up.   33:5
take hold of shield, s. up. Ps 35:2
who will s. up for me against ? 94:16
with child that shall s. up. Eccl 4:15
images shall not s. up.   Isa 27:9*
let them s. up yet they shall. 44:11
prognosticators s. up.   47:13
them, they s. up together.   48:13
awake, s. up, O Jerusalem. 51:17
nor their trees s. up in. Ezek 31:14
four kingdoms shall s. up. Dan 8:22
of fierce countenance shall s. up. 23
he shall also s. up against prince. 25
there shall s. up three kings. 11:2
and a mighty king shall s. up. 3, 4
her roots shall one s. up.   7
many shall s. up against king. 14
s. up in his estate a raiser of taxes. 20
estate shall s. up a vile person. 21
time shall Michael s. up.   12:1
Peter said, S. up; I.   Acts 10:26

stand upon
thou shalt s. upon a rock. Ex 33:21
s. upon mount Gerizim. Deut 27:12
these shall s. upon mount Ebal. 13
and they shall s. upon.   Josh 3:13
Saul said, S. upon me.   2 Sam 1:9
s. upon the mount.   1 Ki 19:11
son of man, s. upon thy feet.
              Ezek 2:1; Acts 26:16
pilots of the sea shall s. upon the
land.   Ezek 27:29
ye s. upon sword, ye work. 33:26
fishes shall s. upon it from. 47:10
made s. upon the feet.   Dan 7:4
I will s. upon my watch.   Hab 2:1
while they s. upon feet. Zech 14:12
angel I saw s. upon sea. Rev 10:5

stand upright
risen and s. upright.   Ps 20:8
understand words, s. upright.
                         Dan 10:11
said, S. upright on thy feet. And he
leaped and walked.   Acts 14:10

stand with
men that shall s. with you. Num 1:5

stand without
not able to s. without.   Ezra 10:13
s. without, desiring to speak.
    Mat 12:47; Luke 8:20
ye begin to s. without. Luke 13:25

standard
and every man by his own s.
              Num 1:52; 2:2, 17
east side shall the s. of Judah. 2:3
south side shall be the s. of.   10
west side shall be the s. of.   18
north side shall be the s. of Dan. 25
in the first place went the s. 10:14

I will set up my s. to the people.
Isa 49:22*
Lord shall lift up a s. against. 59:19*
lift up a s. for the people. 62:10*
set up s. toward Zion. *Jer* 4:6
how long shall I see the s. and ? 21
set ye up a s. in the land. 50:2
51:12, 27

standardbearer
they shall be as when a s. *Isa* 10:18

standards
hindmost with their s. *Num* 2:31
so they pitched by their s. and. 34

standest
come in; wherefore s. thou without ?
Gen 24:31
the place whereon thou s. is holy.
Ex 3:5; *Josh* 5:15; *Acts* 7:33
why s. thou afar off ? *Ps* 10:1
were broken off, thou s. by faith.
Rom 11:20

standeth
and that thy cloud s. *Num* 14:14
son of Nun, which s. before thee.
Deut 1:38
hearken to the priest that s. 17:12
but with him that s. with us. 29:15
to feel pillars whereon the house s.
Judg 16:26*
Haman s. in the court. *Esth* 6:5
the gallows s. in the house of. 7:9
nor s. in the way of sinners. *Ps* 1:1
my foot s. in an even place. 26:12
the counsel of the Lord s. 33:11
God s. in the congregation. 82:1
but my heart s. in awe. 119:161
wisdom s. in the top of. *Pr* 8:2
behold, he s. behind. *S of S* 2:9
Lord s. up to plead, s. to. *Isa* 3:13
in his place, and he s. 46:7
justice s. afar off, truth is. 59:14
the great prince who s. for. *Dan* 12:1
feed that that s. still. *Zech* 11:16*
s. one among you, whom. *John* 1:26
the friend of the bridegroom s. 3:29
to his own master he s. *Rom* 14:4
that s. stedfast in heart. *1 Cor* 7:37
no flesh while the world s. 8:13
thinketh he s. take heed. 10:12
the foundation of God s. *2 Tim* 2:19
every priest s. daily. *Heb* 10:11
behold, the judge s. *Jas* 5:9
angel who s. on the sea. *Rev* 10:8

standing, *substantive*
mire where there is no s. *Ps* 69:2
receive of you his s. *Mi* 1:11*

standing
nor rear ye up a s. image. *Lev* 26:1*
angel of the Lord s. *Num* 22:23, 31
Samuel s. as appointed. *1 Sam* 19:20
servants were s. about him. 22:6
and the lion s. by. *1 Ki* 13:25, 28
host of heaven s. 22:19; *2 Chr* 18:18
and two lions s. by. *2 Chr* 9:18
Esther the queen s. in. *Esth* 5:2
turneth wilderness into a s. water.
Ps 107:35*
the rock into a s. water. 114:8*
I saw the Lord s. upon. *Amos* 9:1
I will cut off thy s. images. *Mi* 5:13*
Satan s. at his right hand. *Zech* 3:1
which go forth from s. before. 6:5
they love to pray s. in. *Mat* 6:5
be some s. here. 16:28; *Luke* 9:27
s. idle in the market. *Mat* 20:3, 6
his mother s. without. *Mark* 3:31
the abomination s. where it. 13:14
an angel s. on the right. *Luke* 1:11
the publican s. afar off smote. 18:13
and woman s. in midst. *John* 8:9*
she turned and saw Jesus s. 20:14
but Peter s. up with. *Acts* 2:14
beholding the man healed s. 4:14
found the keepers s. without. 5:23
the men are s. in the temple. 25
s. on the right hand of God. 7:55, 56
I was s. by and consenting. 22:20
first tabernacle was yet s. *Heb* 9:8
earth s. out of the water. *2 Pet* 3:5*
four angels s. on four. *Rev* 7:1
two candlesticks s. before. 11:4

s. afar off for the fear of. *Rev* 18:10
I saw an angel s. in the sun. 19:17
see **corn**

stank
died, and the river s. *Ex* 7:21
frogs on heaps, and land s. 8:14
manna bred worms and s. 16:20
Ammon saw they s. *2 Sam* 10:6*

star
This word included, for the Hebrew, all heavenly bodies except the sun and the moon. The stars and the grouping into constellations early attracted man's attention, and they are alluded to in the earliest-written of the books of the Bible. Among idolaters the stars soon became objects of worship. They were supposed to foretell events, and a whole science was built up around them.
Several stars spoken of especially in the New Testament have a figurative rather than a literal use.
[1] The day star is given as a sign of Christ's coming, or as a symbol of the spirit's illumination of the heart of one who has accepted Christ, 2 Pet 1:19.
[2] The morning star, which precedes the coming of day, is given as a designation of Christ as bringing the day of gospel light, Rev 2:28.
[3] The star of the wise men, which is the subject of much discussion, Mat 2:2.
The number of the stars was looked upon as infinite. When the scripture would express a very extraordinary increase and multiplication, it uses the symbol of the stars of heaven, or of the sand of the sea, Gen 15:5; 22:17; 26:4.
there shall come a s. out. *Num* 24:17
but ye have borne the s. *Amos* 5:26
for we have seen his s. *Mat* 2:2
of them what time s. appeared. 7
lo, the s. which they saw in east. 9
when they saw s. they rejoiced. 10
s. of your god Remphan. *Acts* 7:43
s. differeth from another s. in glory.
1 Cor 15:41
there fell a great s. *Rev* 8:10, 11
a s. fell from heaven unto. 9:1
day **star**
till the *day* s. arise in. *2 Pet* 1:19
morning **star**
give him the *morning* s. *Rev* 2:28
the bright and *morning* s. 22:16

stare
may tell all my bones: they look and
s. upon me. *Ps* 22:17

stargazers
let the s. stand up and. *Isa* 47:13

stars
lights, he made s. also. *Gen* 1:16
tell the s. if thou be able to. 15:5
sun, moon, and eleven s. made. 37:9
when thou seest s. should. *Deut* 4:19
the s. in their courses. *Judg* 5:20
the morning till the s. *Neh* 4:21
let the s. of the twilight. *Job* 3:9
sun, and sealeth up the s. 9:7
behold height of the s. how. 22:12
s. are not pure in his sight. 25:5
when the morning s. sang. 38:7
moon and s. which thou. *Ps* 8:3
moon and s. to rule by night. 136:9
he telleth number of the s. 147:4
sun, moon, all ye s. of light. 148:3
while the sun or s. be. *Eccl* 12:2
throne above s. of God. *Isa* 14:13
giveth the s. for a light. *Jer* 31:35
I will make the s. *Ezek* 32:7
it cast down some of the s. *Dan* 8:10
shall shine as the s. for ever. 12:3
s. shall withdraw. *Joel* 2:10; 3:15
set thy nest among the s. *Ob* 4
be signs in sun, moon, and s.
Luke 21:25
when neither sun nor s. *Acts* 27:20
glory of s. for one star. *1 Cor* 15:41

so many as s. of the sky. *Heb* 11:12
raging waves, wandering s. *Jude* 13
the third part of the s. *Rev* 8:12
head a crown of twelve s. 12:1
see **heaven, seven**

state
every man at his best s. is. *Ps* 39:5*
the last s. of that man is worse than.
Mat 12:45; *Luke* 11:26
see **estate**

stately
satest upon a s. bed. *Ezek* 23:41

station
from thy s. and state. *Isa* 22:19*

stature
saw are men of great s. *Num* 13:32
on the height of his s. *1 Sam* 16:7
s. with six fingers and with six toes.
2 Sam 21:20; *1 Chr* 11:23; 20:6
this thy s. is like a palm tree and.
S of S 7:7
the high ones of s. shall. *Isa* 10:33
men of s. shall come over. 45:14
upon head of every s. *Ezek* 13:18
a spreading vine of low s. 17:6
her s. was exalted among. 19:11
was a cedar of an high s. 31:3
not add one cubit to his s.
Mat 6:27†; *Luke* 12:25
Jesus increased in wisdom and s.
Luke 2:52
Zaccheus little of s. climbed. 19:3
measure of the s. of fulness of Christ.
Eph 4:13

statute
there he made a s. and. *Ex* 15:25
shall be theirs for perpetual s. 29:9
a perpetual s. *Lev* 3:17; 16:34
24:9; *Num* 19:21
it shall be for a s. of judgement.
Num 27:11; 35:29
and he set them a s. *Josh* 24:25
David made it a s. for. *1 Sam* 30:25
was a s. for Israel and. *Ps* 81:4
to establish a royal s. *Dan* 6:7
that no s. king establisheth may. 15

statutes
know the s. of God. *Ex* 18:16
teach Israel all the s. *Lev* 10:11
these are the s. the Lord. *Num* 30:16
shall hear all these s. *Deut* 4:6
Lord commanded us to do all these
s. 6:24
shalt obeerve and do these s. 16:12
to keep these s. to do them. 17:19
walking in s. of David. *1 Ki* 3:3
and walked in s. of the heathen.
2 Ki 17:8, 19
neither do they after their s. 34
the s. he wrote, ye shall. 37
take heed to do the s. *2 Chr* 33:8
them s. and laws. *Neh* 9:14
s. of Lord are right. *Ps* 19:8
I gave them s. that. *Ezek* 20:25
walk in the s. of life. 33:15
for s. of Omri are kept. *Mi* 6:16
see **statute for ever**

his statutes
ear to his commandments and keep
all his s. *Ex* 15:26; *Deut* 6:17
10:13; 11:1
shalt do his s. which I. *Deut* 27:10
not observe to do his s. 28:15
his s., I did not depart. *2 Sam* 22:23
hearts be perfect to walk in his s.
1 Ki 8:61
they rejected his s. *2 Ki* 17:15
made a covenant to keep his s.
23:3; *2 Chr* 34:31
even a scribe of his s. *Ezra* 7:11
put away his s. from me. *Ps* 18:22
observe his s. and laws. 105:45
in his law, nor in his s. *Jer* 44:23
see **judgements**

my statutes
kept my s. and laws. *Gen* 26:5
ye shall therefore keep my s.
Lev 18:5, 26; 19:19
ye shall do my s. 25:18
if ye walk in my s. 26:3
if ye despise my s. 15
they abhorred my s. 43

if thou wilt keep my s. *1 Ki* 3:14
will not keep my s. 9:6
hast not kept my s. 11:11
he kept my s. 34
keep my s. *2 Ki* 17:13
turn away, and forsake my s.
　　　　2 Chr 7:19
to do to declare my s.? *Ps* 50:16
if they break my s., keep not. 89:31
they walked in my s. *Jer* 44:10
hath changed my s. more. *Ezek* 5:6
ye have not walked in my s. 7
they may walk in my s. and. 11:20
son hath kept all my s. 18:19
cause you to walk in my s. 36:27
my s. did take hold of. *Zech* 1:6

thy statutes
him a perfect heart to keep thy s.
　　　　1 Chr 29:19
O Lord, teach me thy s. *Ps* 119:12
　　26, 33, 64, 68, 124, 135
I will delight myself in thy s. 119:16
servant did meditate in thy s. 23
and I will meditate in thy s. 48
thy s. have been my songs in. 54
that I might learn thy s. 71
let my heart be sound in thy s. 80
bottle, yet do I not forget thy s. 83
heart to perform thy s. alway. 112
I will have respect to thy s. 117
them that err from thy s. 118
for the wicked seek not thy s. 155
when thou hast taught thy s. 171

staves
thou shalt make s. of shittim wood.
　Ex 25:13, 28; 27:6; 30:5; 37:4
put s. into rings. 25:14, 15; 27:7
　　　　37:5; 38:7
s. of shittim wood. 37:15, 28; 38:5
he set s. on the ark and put. 40:20
they shall put in s. thereof.
　　　　Num 4:6, 8, 11, 14
people digged with their s. 21:18
am I a dog, that thou comest to me
　with s.? *1 Sam* 17:43
carried the ark with s. *1 Chr* 15:15
strike through with his s. *Hab* 3:14
I took unto me two s. I. *Zech* 11:7
nor take two coats nor s. *Mat* 10:10
　　　　Luke 9:3
great multitude with s. from chief
　priests. *Mat* 26:47; *Mark* 14:43
thief with sword and s.? *Mat* 26:55
　Mark 14:48; *Luke* 22:52

stay, *substantive*
plague in his sight be at a s. *Lev* 13:5
scall in his sight be at a s. 37
but the Lord was my s. *2 Sam* 22:19
　　　　Ps 18:18
away the s. and staff, the whole s. of
　bread, and the whole s. *Isa* 3:1
even they that are the s. 19:13*

stay
neither s. thou in all the. *Gen* 19:17
ye shall s. no longer. *Ex* 9:28
if bright spot s. *Lev* 13:23, 28
s. not, but pursue after. *Josh* 10:19
would ye s. for them from. *Ruth* 1:13
s. and I will tell thee. *1 Sam* 15:16
make speed, haste, s. not. 20:38
s. now thine hand. *2 Sam* 24:16
　　　　1 Chr 21:15
he will not s. them when. *Job* 37:4
or who can s. the bottles of ? 38:37*
let no man s. him. *Pr* 28:17
s. me with flagons. *S of S* 2:5
shall no more s. on him. *Isa* 10:20†
s. yourselves and wonder, cry. 29:9
and s. on oppression. 30:12†
woe to them that s. on horses. 31:1†
for they s. themselves on the. 48:2
let him trust in Lord, and s. 50:10†
s. not, for I will bring evil. *Jer* 4:6
forbearing, I could not s. 20:9
none can s. his hand, or. *Dan* 4:35
not s. in the place of. *Hos* 13:13*

stayed
and Noah s. yet other seven days.
　　　　Gen 8:10, 12
with Laban, and I have s. 32:4
flocks and herds be s. *Ex* 10:24
and Hur s. up Moses' hands. 17:12

---

dead and living, plague was s.
　Num 16:48, 50; 25:8; *2 Sam* 24:25
　　　　Ps 106:30
I s. in mount forty days. *Deut* 10:10
still, and the moon s. *Josh* 10:13
hast s. three days. *1 Sam* 20:19
David s. his servants with. 24:7*
that were left behind s. 30:9
now Jonathan s. by. *2 Sam* 17:17
that the plague may be s. 24:21
　　　　1 Chr 21:22
king was s. up in his chariot, and
　died. *1 Ki* 22:35; *2 Chr* 18:34
a vessel more, and oil s. *2 Ki* 4:6
and he smote thrice, and s. 13:18
the king of Assyria s. not in. 15:20
thy proud waves be s. *Job* 38:11
whose mind is s. on thee. *Isa* 26:3
no hands s. on her. *Lam* 4:6*
great waters were s. *Ezek* 31:15
heaven is s., the earth is s. *Hag* 1:10
came to him and s. him. *Luke* 4:42
but he himself s. in Asia. *Acts* 19:22

stayeth
he s. his rough wind in the day of.
　　　　Isa 27:8*

stays
were s. on either side throne; two
　lions stood beside the s.
　　1 Ki 10:19; *2 Chr* 9:18

stead
he closed up the flesh in s. *Gen* 2:21
me another seed in s. of Abel. 4:25
Abraham offered the ram in s. 22:13
am I in God's s. 30:2
abide in s. of the lad. 44:33
he shall be to thee in s. of a mouth,
　thou shalt be to him in s. *Ex* 4:16
to gather stubble in s. of straw. 5:12
that son that is priest in his s. 29:30
　　　　Lev 16:32
I have taken the Levites in s. of all
　firstborn. *Num* 3:12, 41, 45; 8:16
cattle of the Levites in s. 3:41, 45
in s. of thy husband. 5:19, 20, 29
mayest be to us in s. of eyes. 10:31
risen up in your father's s. 32:14
Esau dwelt in their s. *Deut* 2:12
dwelt in their s. 21, 22, 23
son ministered in his s. 10:6
whom he raised in their s. *Josh* 5:7
I pray, her sister in s. *Judg* 15:2
Saul, in whose s. thou. *2 Sam* 16:8
he made Amasa captain in s. 17:25
sit on my throne in my s. *1 Ki* 1:30
for he shall be king in my s. 35
made me king in s. of David. 3:7
Rehoboam made in their s. 14:27
placed in cities of Samaria in s. of
　Israel. *2 Ki* 17:24
queen in s. of Vashti. *Esth* 2:4, 17
were in my soul's s. *Job* 16:4
let thistles grow in s. of wheat, and
　cockle in s. of barley. 31:40
to thy wish in God's s. 33:6*
shall set others in their s. 34:24
in s. of thy fathers shall. *Ps* 45:16
wicked cometh in his s. *Pr* 11:8
shall stand up in his s. *Eccl* 4:15
in s. of sweet smell there shall be
　stink, in s. of. *Isa* 3:24
in s. of the thorn shall come up fir
　tree, and in s. of the brier. 55:13
who taketh strangers in s. of her.
　　　　Ezek 16:32
pray you in Christ's s. *2 Cor* 5:20*
in thy s. might have. *Philem* 13*

see reigned

steads
they dwelt in their s. till. *1 Chr* 5:22

steady
Moses' hands were s. *Ex* 17:12

steal
(*Theft was made the subject of one
of the ten commandments. There
was no penalty attached to theft of
property but restitution, double or
more, as the case might be. If
restitution was not made it was
treated as a case of debt, the
property or even the person of the
debt being sold to cover it. The*

---

man-stealer, *who reduced his prey
to slavery, was to be put to death*)
wherefore didst thou s.? *Gen* 31:27
how then should we s. silver ? 44:8
thou shalt not s. *Ex* 20:15; *Lev* 19:11
　Deut 5:19; *Mat* 19:18; *Rom* 13:9
if a man s. an ox, he shall. *Ex* 22:1
as people s. away. *2 Sam* 19:3
if he s. to satisfy his soul. *Pr* 6:30
or lest I be poor and s. and. 30:9
will ye s., murder, and ? *Jer* 7:9
prophets that s. my words. 23:30
and where thieves break through
　and s. *Mat* 6:19
do not break through nor s. 20
come and s. him away. 27:64
do not kill, do not s. *Mark* 10:19
　　　　Luke 18:20
cometh not, but for to s. *John* 10:10
preachest a man should not s., dost
　thou s.? *Rom* 2:21
him that stole s. no more. *Eph* 4:28

stealers
law was made for men-s. *1 Tim* 1:10

stealeth
he that s. a man and. *Ex* 21:16
a tempest s. him away in. *Job* 27:20
that s. shall be cut off. *Zech* 5:3

stealing
if a man be found s. any. *Deut* 24:7
by swearing and s. they. *Hos* 4:2

stealth
the people gat them by s. *2 Sam* 19:3

stedfast
yea, thou shalt be s. *Job* 11:15
whose spirit was not s. *Ps* 78:8
neither were they s. in his. 37*
living God, and s. for ever. *Dan* 6:26
he that standeth s. in his heart doeth
　well. *1 Cor* 7:37
my beloved brethren, be ye s. 15:58
our hope of you is s. *2 Cor* 1:7
for if the word spoken by angels was
　s. *Heb* 2:2
have as an anchor sure and s. 6:19
whom resist s. in faith. *1 Pet* 5:9

stedfastly
that she was s. minded. *Ruth* 1:18
settled his countenance s. *2 Ki* 8:11
he s. set his face to go. *Luke* 9:51
looked s., behold, two men. *Acts* 1:10
s. in the apostles' doctrine. 2:42
they all looking s. on him. 6:15*
up s. into heaven, saw glory. 7:55
who s. beholding him and. 14:9
Israel could not s. behold. *2 Cor* 3:7
could not s. look to the end of. 13

stedfastness
beholding the s. of your faith in
　Christ. *Col* 2:5
ye fall from your own s. *2 Pet* 3:17

steel
(*Revisions*, brass)
a bow of s. is broken. *2 Sam* 22:35
　　　　Ps 18:34
bow of s. shall strike. *Job* 20:24
iron break northern iron and s.?
　　　　Jer 15:12

steep
the s. places shall fall. *Ezek* 38:20
are poured down a s. place. *Mi* 1:4
swine ran violently down a s. place.
　Mat 8:32; *Mark* 5:13; *Luke* 8:33

stem
a rod out of the s. of. *Isa* 11:1*

step
there is but a s. between. *1 Sam* 20:3
if my s. hath turned out. *Job* 31:7

Stephanas
the household of S. *1 Cor* 1:16
the house of S., the firstfruits. 16:15
I am glad of the coming of S. 17

Stephen
they chose S. a man. *Acts* 6:5, 8
they stoned S., calling upon God. 7:59
devout men carried S. to his. 8:2
on the persecution about S. 11:19
of thy martyr S. was shed. 22:20

stepped
whosoever first s. in was. *John* 5:4

steppeth
while I am coming, another s. down.
John 5:7

steps
neither go up by s. to. *Ex* 20:26
thou hast enlarged my s.
2 Sam 22:37; *Ps* 18:36
the throne had six s. *1 Ki* 10:19
2 Chr 9:18
twelve lions stood on the s.
1 Ki 10:20; *2 Chr* 9:19
thou numberest my s. *Job* 14:16
the s. of his strength shall be. 18:7
my foot hath held his s. 23:11
I washed my s. with butter. 29:6
my ways and count my s. 31:4
to him the number of my s. 37
compassed us in our s. *Ps* 17:11
s. of a good man are ordered. 37:23*
the law in his heart, none of his s. 31
nor have our s. declined from. 44:18
mark my s. when they wait. 56:6
prepared a net for my s. 57:6
as for me, my s. had well. 73:2
set us in the way of his s. 85:13
order my s. in thy word. 119:133
when goest thy s. shall not. *Pr* 4:12
her s. take hold on hell. 5:5
but the Lord directeth his s. 16:9
the s. of the needy shall. *Isa* 26:6
it is not in man that walketh to direct
his s. *Jer* 10:23
they hunt our s., we cannot.*Lam* 4:18
up to it by seven s. *Ezek* 40:22, 26
up to it had eight s. 31, 34, 37
he brought me by s. whereby. 49
the Ethiopians shall be at his s.
Dan 11:43
but walk in s. of that faith. *Rom* 4:12
not in the same s.? *2 Cor* 12:18
ye should follow his s. *1 Pet* 2:21

stern
four anchors out of the s. *Acts* 27:29

steward
and the s. of my house. *Gen* 15:2*
near to the s. of Joseph's. 43:19
drinking himself drunk in the house
of his s. *1 Ki* 16:9
the lord saith unto his s. *Mat* 20:8
wife of Chuza, Herod's s. *Luke* 8:3
is that faithful and wise s. 12:42
certain rich man who had a s. 16:1
thou mayest be no longer s. 8
Lord commended the unjust s. 8
blameless, as the s. of God. *Tit* 1:7

stewards
and David assembled captains and s.
1 Chr 28:1*
as ministers and s. of. *1 Cor* 4:1
it is required in s. that a man. 2
as good s. of manifold. *1 Pet* 4:10

stewardship
give an account of thy s. *Luke* 16:2
taketh away from me the s. 3, 4

stick, *verb*
his bones, not seen, s. out. *Job* 33:21
his scales are joined, they s. 41:17
for thine arrows s. fast. *Ps* 38:2
I will cause the fish to s. *Ezek* 29:4

stick
cut down a s. and cast. *2 Ki* 6:6
withered and become like a s.
Lam 4:8
s. write upon it: then take another s.
Ezek 37:16
one to another into one s. 17, 19

sticketh
there is a friend s. closer. *Pr* 18:24

sticks
a man that gathered s. *Num* 15:32
they found him gathering s. 33
woman was gathering s. *1 Ki* 17:10
gathering two s. to go in. 12
and the s. whereon. *Ezek* 37:20
gathered a bundle of s. *Acts* 28:3

stiff
rebellion and thy s. neck. *Deut* 31:27
speak not with a s. neck. *Ps* 75:5
but made their neck s. *Jer* 17:23

stiffened
he s. his neck and. *2 Chr* 36:13

stiffhearted
impudent children and s. *Ezek* 2:4

stiffnecked
people is a s. people. *Ex* 32:9
thou art a s. people. 33:3; *Deut* 9:6
Ye are a s. people. *Ex* 33:5
it is a s. people. 34:9; *Deut* 9:13
circumcise your heart, be no more s.
Deut 10:16
be not s. as your fathers. *2 Chr* 30:8
ye s. ye do always resist. *Acts* 7:51

still, *adjectve*
shall be as s. as a stone. *Ex* 15:16
good, and are ye s.? *Judg* 18:9
after fire a s. small voice. *1 Ki* 19:12
Gilead is ours, and we be s. 22:3
and if we sit s. here. *2 Ki* 7:4
for now should I have lain s. *Job* 3:13
your heart and be s. *Ps* 4:4
beside the s. waters. 23:2
be s. and know that I am. 46:10
the earth feared, and was s. 76:8
peace, and be not s. O God. 83:1
that waves thereof are s. 107:29
be s. ye inhabitants of. *Isa* 23:2
cried, their strength is to sit s. 30:7
I have been s. and refrained. 42:14
why do we sit s.? *Jer* 8:14
of the Lord, rest and be s. 47:6
feed that that standeth s. *Zech* 11:16
to the sea, Peace, be s. *Mark* 4:39

still, *adverb*
were s. ill favoured, as at. *Gen* 41:21
and wilt hold them s. *Ex* 9:2
and if it appear s. in. *Lev* 13:57
and Caleb lived s. *Num* 14:38
Balaam blessed you s. *Josh* 24:10
but if ye shall s. do. *1 Sam* 12:25
Saul said, Thou also shalt s. 26:25
good to have beenthere s.*2 Sam*14:32
and cursed s. as he came. 16:5
the people sacrificed s. and burnt.
2 Ki 12:3; 15:4, 35; *2 Chr* 33:17
had no power to keep s. *2 Chr* 22:9
and s. he holdeth fast. *Job* 2:3
his wife said, Dost thou s. retain? 9
though he keep it s. within. 20:13
he should s. live for ever. *Ps* 49:9
such a one as goeth on s. 68:21
for all this they sinned s. 78:32
in thy house: they will be s. 84:4
they shall s. bring forth fruit. 92:14
when I awake, I am s. 139:18
he s. taught the people. *Eccl* 12:9
but his hand is stretched out s.
Isa 5:25; 9:12, 17, 21; 10:4
they say s. unto them that. *Jer* 23:17
those will I let remain s. in. 27:11
I earnestly remember him s. 31:20
if ye will s. abide in this. 42:10
my soul hath them s. in. *Lam* 3:20
thy people s. are talking. *Ezek* 33:30
winding about s. upward. 41:7
when he had said these words, he
abode s. in Galilee. *John* 7:9; 11:6
it pleased Silas to abide s.
Acts 15:34; 17:14
s. in unbelief, be graffed. *Rom* 11:23
abide s. at Ephesus. *1 Tim* 1:3
unjust s.: filthy s.: holy s. *Rev* 22:11
see stand, stood

still, *verb*
that thou mightest s. enemy. *Ps* 8:2

stilled
Caleb s. the people. *Num* 13:30
so the Levites s. all. *Neh* 8:11

stillest
waves arise thou s. them. *Ps* 89:9

stilleth
s. the noise of the seas. *Ps* 65:7

sting
O death, where is thy s.? *1 Cor* 15:55
the s. of death is sin. 56

stingeth
it s. like an adder. *Pr* 23:32

stings
were s. in their tails. *Rev* 9:10

stink, *substantive*
smell, there shall be s. *Isa* 3:24*

their s. shall come out of. *Isa* 34:3†
s. shall come up, and ill. *Joel* 2:20†
made s. of your camps. *Amos* 4:10†

stink
ye have made me to s. *Gen* 34:30*
die, and the river shall s. *Ex* 7:18
that was laid up did not s. 16:24
my wounds s. and are. *Ps* 38:5

stinketh
their fish s. because there. *Isa* 50:2
Lord, by this time he s. *John* 11:39

stinking
to send forth a s. savour. *Eccl* 10:1†

stir, *verb*
he lay down as a lion, who shall s.
him up ? *Num* 24:9
innocent s. up himself. *Job* 17:8
is so fierce that dare s. him. 41:10
s. up thyself, and awake. *Ps* 35:23
and he did not s. up all his. 78:38
s. up thy strength, and come. 80:2
but grievous words s. *Pr* 15:1
that ye s. not up my love. *S of S* 2:7
3:5; 8:4
the Lord shall s. up a. *Isa* 10:26
behold, I will s. up the Medes. 13:17
he shall s. up jealousy like. 42:13
he shall s. up all against. *Dan* 11:2
shall s. up his power against. 25
that thou s. up the gift. *2 Tim* 1:6
meet to s. you up. *2 Pet* 1:13; 3:1

stir
was no small s. among the soldiers.
Acts 12:18
small s. about that way. 19:23

stirred
whose heart s. him up. *Ex* 35:21
26; 36:2
that my son hath s. up. *1 Sam* 22:8
if the Lord have s. thee up. 26:19
Lord s. up an adversary. *1 Ki* 11:14
God s. him up another adversary. 23*
whom Jezebel his wife s. up. 21:25
God s. up the spirit. *1 Chr* 5:26
Lord s. up against Jehoram the
2 Chr 21:16
Lord s. up the spirit of Cyrus. 36:22
Ezra 1:1
and my sorrow was s. *Ps* 39:2
but his sons shall be s. *Dan* 11:10*
king of the south shall be s. up. 25*
the Lord s. up the spirit. *Hag* 1:14
they s. up the people. *Acts* 6:12
17:13; 21:27
Jews s. up devout women. 13:50*
the unbelieving Jews s. up. 14:2
his spirit was s. in him. 17:16*

stirreth
an eagle s. up her nest. *Deut* 32:11
hatred s. up strifes, but. *Pr* 10:12
man s. up strife. 15:18; 29:22
that is of a proud heart s. 28:25
hell from beneath s. up. *Isa* 14:9
none s. up himself to take hold. 64:7
he s. up people teaching. *Luke* 23:5

stirs
full of s. a tumultuous city. *Isa* 22:2*

stock
or to the s. of the stranger's family.
Lev 25:47
though the s. thereof die. *Job* 14:8
yea, their s. shall not take. *Isa* 40:24
down to the s. of a tree ? 44:19
saying to a s., Thou art my father.
Jer 2:27
are brutish, the s. is a doctrine. 10:8
of the s. of Abraham. *Acts* 13:26
of the s. of Israel, an. *Phil* 3:5

stocks
my feet also in the s. *Job* 13:27
he putteth my feet in s. 33:11
the correction of the s. *Pr* 7:22
adultery with stones and s. *Jer* 3:9
put Jeremiah in the s. 20:2, 3
put him in prison and s. 29:26*
ask counsel at their s. *Hos* 4:12
their feet fast in the s. *Acts* 16:24

Stoics
Were a school of Grecian philoso-
phers, who took their name from
the Greek word stoa, meaning

stole   636   stoned

portico, *because Zeno, the head of the Stoics, taught in a portico in the city of Athens. They held, that a wise man ought to be free from all passions; never to be moved either with joy or grief, esteeming all things to be ordered by an inevitable necessity and fate. Josephus says, that the Pharisees approach very near to the sentiments of the Stoics. They affected the same stiffness, patience, apathy, austerity, and insensibility. The sect of the Stoics was still considerable at Athens when St. Paul visited that city,* Acts 17:18.

stole
Jacob s. away unawares. Gen 31:20
so Absalom s. the hearts of Israel.
                                2 Sam 15:6
Jehosheba s. Joash from among
king's.   2 Ki 11:2; 2 Chr 22:11
his disciples s. him.   Mat 28:13
let him that s. steal no more, but.
                                Eph 4:28

stolen
that shall be counted s. Gen 30:33
Rachel had s. her father's images.
                                31:19, 32
thou hast s. away unawares to.   26
hast thou s. my gods ?   30
whether s. by day, or s. by.   39
indeed I was s. away out.   40:15
if the stuff be s. out of.   Ex 22:7
if it be s. from him, he shall. 12
s. and dissembled also. Josh 7:11
men of Judah s. thee ? 2 Sam 19:41
Jabesh had s. the bones of.   21:12
s. waters are sweet.   Pr 9:17
would they not have s. till ?   Ob 5

stomach
little wine for thy s.'s sake.1 Tim 5:23

stomacher
instead of a s. a girding.   Isa 3:24*

stone
*Precious stones as named in the Bible are difficult to identify, as no sufficient description is given of them.
The corner stone, or the head stone of the corner,* Ps 118:22, *is that put as the angle of a building, whether at the foundation, or at the top of the wall, and is of fundamental importance. It is often used metaphorically. Jesus Christ is the corner stone rejected by the Jews, but become the corner stone of the church, and the stone that binds and unites the Jews and Gentiles in the union of the same faith,* Mat 21:42; Eph 2:20.
As Christ the Head is called the corner stone, so also his members, true believers, who are built upon, and derive spiritual life from the foundation, Christ, *are called stones,* 1 Pet 2:5. *As the law was engraven on two tables of stones, so believers have the law written in their hearts. They are stones for their constancy, strength, and unmovableness in all the storms of life.
The white stone,* Rev 2:17, *has been variously regarded. Some think it is an allusion to an ancient custom of delivering a white stone to those who were acquitted in judgement, or of giving a white stone as a reward to such as conquered in their games.
Great heaps of stones, raised up for a witness of any memorable event, and to preserve the remembrance of some matter of great importance are the most ancient monuments among the Hebrews. Jacob and Laban raised such a monument upon mount Gilead, in memory of their covenant,* Gen 31:46. Joshua *erected one at Gilgal made of stones taken out of*

the Jordan, *to preserve the memorial of his miraculous passage over this river,* Josh 4:5, 6, 7. *The Israelites that dwelt beyond Jordan, also raised one upon the banks of the river, as a testimony that they constituted but one nation with their brethren on the other side,* Josh 22:10.
had brick for s. and slime. Gen 11:3
up a s. for a pillar. 28:18, 22; 31:45
they rolled s. from the well's mouth.
                                29:3, 8, 10
Jacob set up a pillar of s.   35:14
the shepherd, the s. of Israel. 49:24
Zipporah took a sharp s.   Ex 4:25*
sank into the bottom as a s.   15:5
arm they shall be as still as s.   16
and they took a s. and put it. 17:12
wilt make an altar of s.   20:25
smite another with a s.   21:18
names on one s., six on other s. 28:10
work of an engraver in s.   11
neither shall ye set up any image of
s. in your land.   Lev 26:1
with throwing a s.   Num 35:17, 23
take you up every man of you a s.
upon his shoulder.   Josh 4:5
the border went up to the s.   15:6
descended to the s. of Bohan. 18:17
s. shall be a witness unto us. 24:27
slew seventy persons on one s.
                             Judg 9:5, 18
which s. remaineth.   1 Sam 6:18
Samuel set up a s. and called. 7:12
from his bag a s. and slang it, the s.
sunk into the Philistine's.   17:49
over the Philistine with a s.   50
shalt remain by the s. Ezel. 20:19
died in him, he became as a s. 25:37
there be not one small s. 2 Sam 17:13
house was built of s.   1 Ki 6:7
cedar, there was no s. seen.   10
cast every man his s.   2 Ki 3:25
with thee hewers of s. 1 Chr 22:15
skilful to work in gold, silver, and s.
                             2 Chr 2:14
thou threwest as a s.   Neh 9:11
is molten out of the s.   Job 28:2
waters are hid as with a s.   38:30
his heart is as firm as a s.   41:24
lest thou dash thy foot against a s.
                     Ps 91:12; Mat 4:6; Luke 4:11
s. which builders refused . . . s. of.
Ps 118:22; Mat 21:42; Mark 12:10
as he that bindeth a s.   Pr 26:8
and he that rolleth a s. it will. 27
s. is heavy, a fool's wrath.   27:3
and to a s. thou hast.   Jer 2:27
they shall not take of thee a s. for a
corner, nor a s. for.   51:26
cast a s. upon me.   Lam 3:53
a s. was cut out of the mountain.
                             Dan 2:34, 45
s. was laid upon the mouth.   6:17
for the s. shall cry out.   Hab 2:11
saith to the dumb s., Arise.   19
s. was laid upon a s. in.   Hag 2:15
s. that I have laid before Joshua, upon
one s. shall be seven.   Zech 3:9
shall bring forth the head s.   4:7
their hearts as an adamant s.   7:12
if his son ask bread, will he give him
a s.?   Mat 7:9; Luke 11:11
whosoever shall fall on this s. shall
be broken. Mat 21:44; Luke 20:18
not left here one s. upon. Mat 24:2
Mark 13:2; Luke 19:44; 21:6
sealing the s.   Mat 27:66
the angel rolled back the s.   28:2
saw that the s. was rolled away.
Mark 16:4; Luke 24:2; John 20:1
command this s. that it be. Luke 4:3
s. which the builders rejected.
              20:17; Acts 4:11; 1 Pet 2:7
he was withdrawn from them about
a s.'s cast.   Luke 22:41
is by interpretation a s. John 1:42*
set there six waterpots of s.   2:6
let him first cast s. at her.   8:7
it was a cave, and a s. lay.   11:38
take ye away the s.   39
they took away the s.   41
is like to a s. graven.   Acts 17:29

fell a great hail, every s. Rev 16:21
an angel took up a s. like a.   18:21
see **corner, great, hewed, stumbling, wall**

stone, *verb*
and will they not s. us ?   Ex 8:26
they be almost ready to s. me. 17:4
people of land shall s.   Lev 20:2
shall s. the wizards with stones. 27
let congregation s. him. 24:14, 16, 23
congregation bade s.   Num 14:10
s. him with stones.   15:35, 36
shalt s. him with stones. Deut 13:10
shalt s. idolaters.   17:5
s. rebellious son.   21:21
they shall s. her that playeth. 22:21
ye shall s. adulterers with stones. 24
carry Naboth out, s. him. 1 Ki 21:10
and they shall s. thee.   Ezek 16:40
the company shall s. them.   23:47
men, the people will s. us. Luke 20:6
stones again to s. him.   John 10:31
for which works do ye s. me ?   32
saying, For a good work we s.   33
Jews of late sought to s. thee. 11:8
assault made to s. them. Acts 14:5
burdensome **stone**
make Jerusalem a burdensome s.
                             Zech 12:3
hewn **stone**
not build altar of hewn s. Ex 20:25
masons, to buy timber and hewn s.
                     2 Ki 12:6; 2 Chr 34:11
my ways with hewn s.   Lam 3:9
tables were of hewn s.   Ezek 40:42
built houses of hewn s.   Amos 5:11
sepulchre hewn in s.   Luke 23:53
living **stone**
to whom coming, as unto a living s.
chosen of God.   1 Pet 2:4
precious **stone**
a gift is a precious s. to him. Pr 17:8
I lay in Zion a precious corner s.
                     Isa 28:16; 1 Pet 2:6
every precious s. was.   Ezek 28:13
decked with gold and precious s.
                             Rev 17:4
like to a s. most precious.   21:11
tables of **stone**
I will give thee tables of s. Ex 24:12
                                31:18
Lord said, Hew thee two tables of s.
                     34:1; Deut 10:1
he hewed two tables of s.   Ex 34:4
                             Deut 10:3
he wrote on the two tables of s.
                     Deut 4:13; 5:22
up to receive the tables of s.   9:9
delivered to me two tables of s. 10
gave me the two tables of s.   11
in ark save two tables of s. 1 Ki 8:9
not in tables of s. but in fleshly.
                             2 Cor 3:3
tried **stone**
Zion a stone, a tried s.   Isa 28:16
white **stone**
I will give him a white s. Rev 2:17
stone joined with **wood**
vessels of wood and s.   Ex 7:19
gods the work of men's hands, wood
and s.   Deut 4:28; 28:36, 64
          29:17; 2 Ki 19:18; Isa 37:19
                             Ezek 20:32
praised the gods of gold, wood, and
s.   Dan 5:4, 23
not worship idols of wood and s.
                             Rev 9:20

stone of Zoheleth
sheep by s. of Zoheleth.   1 Ki 1:9

stoned
be s. or shot through.   Ex 19:13
ox shall be surely s. 21:28, 29, 32
all Israel s. Achan.   Josh 7:25
all Israel s. Adoram.   1 Ki 12:18
                             2 Chr 10:18
they s. Naboth.   1 Ki 21:13, 14, 15
they s. Zechariah in.   2 Chr 24:21
beat one, s. another.   Mat 21:35
that such should be s.   John 8:5
they should have been s. Acts 5:26
they s. Stephen, calling.   7:58, 59
having s. Paul, drew him out. 14:19

beaten, once was I s.   *2 Cor* 11:25
they were s. they were.   *Heb* 11:37
the mount it shall be s.   12:20

stones
his brethren, gather s.   *Gen* 31:46
engrave the two s.   *Ex* 28:11, 12
settings of s., even four rows of s. 17
the s. shall be with the names of. 21
s. for a memorial to Israel.   39:7
they take away the s.   *Lev* 14:40
other s. in the place of those s.   42
down the house, the s. of it.   45
or hath his s. broken.   21:20
a land whose s. are iron.   *Deut* 8:9
that is wounded in the s.   23:1
these s. in mount Ebal.   27:4
build an altar of s.   5
write on the s. all the words.
you hence twelve s.   *Josh* 4:3, 9
What mean ye by these s.?   6, 21
twelve s. out of the midst.
twelve s. did Joshua pitch.   20
on the s. a copy of the law.   8:32
every one could sling s. at an hair-
breadth.   *Judg* 20:16
him five smooth s.   *1 Sam* 17:40
Shimei cast s. at David and.
     2 Sam 16:6, 13
prepared timber and s.   *1 Ki* 5:18
s. of eight and s. of ten cubits. 7:10
silver to be in Jerusalem as s. and.
   10:27; *2 Chr* 1:15; 9:27
took away the s. of Ramah.
    1 Ki 15:22; *2 Chr* 16:6
Elijah took twelve s.   *1 Ki* 18:31
with the s. he built an altar.   32
good piece of land with s. *2 Ki* 3:19
Kir-haraseth left they the s.   25
it upon a pavement of s.   16:17
in hurling of s. and.   *1 Chr* 12:2
Uzziah prepared slings to cast s.
    2 Chr 26:14
will they revive the s. out of the
heaps?   *Neh* 4:2
in league with s. of field.   *Job* 5:23
strength the strength of s.?   6:12
and seeth the place of s.   8:17
the waters wear the s.   14:19
the gold of Ophir as the s. of. 22:24
the s. of it are the place of.   28:6
the sinews of his s. are.   40:17*
take pleasure in her s.   *Ps* 102:14
thy little ones against the s.   137:9
away s., a time to gather s. *Eccl* 3:5
whoso removeth s. shall be.   10:9
and gathered out the s.   *Isa* 5:2
down to the s. of the pit.   14:19
s. of the altar as chalk s.   27:9
behold, I will lay thy s. with. 54:11
thy borders of pleasant s.   12
smooth s. of the stream.   57:6
bring for s., iron.   60:17
gather out the s.   62:10
adultery with s. and stocks. *Jer* 3:9
set his throne on these s.   43:10
the s. of the sanctuary.   *Lam* 4:1
lay thy s. in the water. *Ezek* 26:12
in the midst of the s. of fire. 28:14
from the midst of the s. of fire. 16
I will pour down the s.   *Mi* 1:6
consume it with the s.   *Zech* 5:4
as s. of a crown lifted up.   9:16
of these s. to raise up children.
    Mat 3:9; *Luke* 3:8
these s. be made bread.   *Mat* 4:3
cutting himself with s.   *Mark* 5:5
and at him they cast s. and.   12:4
Master, see what manner of s. 13:1
s. would immediately.   *Luke* 19:40
took up s. to cast. *John* 8:59; 10:31
engraven in s. was glorious.*2 Cor* 3:7
ye as lively s. are built.   *1 Pet* 2:5
see **costly, great, stone, verb**

corner stones
our daughters may be as *corner* s.
    Ps 144:12

stones *of darkness*
he searcheth out the s. *of darkness.*
    Job 28:3

stones *of emptiness*
stretch out upon it s. *of emptiness.*
    Isa 34:11

glistering **stones**
I have prepared *glistering* s. for
house.   *1 Chr* 29:2

gravel **stones**
hath broken my teeth with *gravel* s.
    Lam 3:16

heap of **stones**
raised a great *heap of* s. *Josh* 7:26
and raise a great *heap of* s.   8:29
they laid a *heap of* s. on Absalom.
    2 Sam 18:17

hewed **stones**
they brought *hewed* s. to.*1 Ki* 5:17*
the measures of *hewed* s.   7:9, 11

hewn **stones**
will build with *hewn* s.   *Isa* 9:10

marble **stones**
I have prepared *marble* s. in.
    1 Chr 29:2

precious **stones**
gold with *precious* s.   *2 Sam* 12:30
queen of Sheba came with *precious* s.
    1 Ki 10:2
navy of Hiram brought *precious* s.
   11; *2 Chr* 9:10
I prepared all manner of *precious* s.
    1 Chr 29:2
whom *precious* s. were found.   8
the house with *precious* s. *2 C r* 3:6
treasuries for *precious* s.   32:27
occupied in thy fairs with *precious* s.
    Ezek 27:22
honour with *precious* s. *Dan* 11:38
build on this foundation *precious* s.
    1 Cor 3:12
no man buyeth *precious* s. *Rev* 18:12
decked with gold and *precious* s. 16
garnished with *precious* s.   21:19

whole **stones**
shalt build the altar of *whole* s.
   Deut 27:6; *Josh* 8:31

wrought **stones**
masons to hew *wrought* s. *1 Chr* 22:2

stonesquarers
builders and s. did hew.   *1 Ki* 5:18*

stonest
s. them that are sent to thee.
    Mat 23:37; *Luke* 13:34

stoning
people spake of s. David. *1 Sam* 30:6

stony
overthrown in s. places.   *Ps* 141:6*
I will take the s. heart. *Ezek* 11:19
    36:26
some fell on s. places. *Mat* 13:5*, 20*
    Mark 4:5*, 16*

stood
but Abraham s. yet.   *Gen* 18:22
pillar of cloud s. behind.   *Ex* 14:19
he s. between the dead. *Num* 16:48
ye came near and s.   *Deut* 4:11
I s. between the Lord and you.   5:5
the waters s. and rose up. *Josh* 3:16
twelve stones where the priests' feet
s.   4:3, 9
Joash said to all that s.   *Judg* 6:31
pillars on which the house s. 16:29
Lord s. and called Samuel.
    1 Sam 3:10
when he s. among the people. 10:23
Goliath s. and cried to the.   17:8
servants that s. about him.   22:7
king said to footmen that s.   17
and all the congregation of Israel s.
   1 Ki 8:14; *2 Chr* 6:3; 7:6
Solomon s. and blessed.   *1 Ki* 8:55
sons of prophets s. to view. *2 Ki* 2:7
the people s. to the covenant. 23:3
on scaffold Solomon s.   *2 Chr* 6:13
they s. and confessed.   *Neh* 9:2
the other Jews s. for.   *Esth* 9:16
commanded and it s. fast. *Ps* 33:9
above it s. the seraphims.   *Isa* 6:2
they s. not because Lord. *Jer* 46:15
they s. under the shadow.   48:45
those s., these s.   *Ezek* 1:21; 10:17
when they s. they let down.   1:24
was a voice when they s.   25
came near where I s.   *Dan* 8:17
when he had spoken this, I s. 10:11
s. to confirm and to strengthen. 11:1

I looked, and behold, there s.
    Dan 12:5
s. and measured the earth. *Hab* 3:6
he s. among the myrtle trees.
    Zech 1:8, 10, 11
brethren s. without.   *Mat* 12:46
withered hand s. forth.   *Luke* 6:8
the Pharisee s. and prayed.   18:11
Simon Peter s. and.   *John* 18:25
but Mary s. without at.   20:11
the lame man leaping up s. *Acts* 3:8
the men that were with him s.   9:7
s. a man of Macedonia and.   16:9
Paul s. forth in the midst.   27:21
s. only in meats, and.   *Heb* 9:10

stood *above*
Lord s. *above* the ladder. *Gen* 28:13
Zechariah s. *above* the people.
    2 Chr 24:20
the waters s. *above* the.   *Ps* 104:6

stood *afar*
his sister s. *afar* off.   *Ex* 2:4
removed and s. *afar* off.   20:18, 21
lepers who s. *afar* off.   *Luke* 17:12
s. *afar* off beholding.   23:49
trade by sea s. *afar* off. *Rev* 18:17

stood *at*
they s. *at* nether part.   *Ex* 19:17
they s. every man at his tent. 33:8
the cloudy pillar s. *at* door of.   9
Naaman s. *at* door of.   *2 Ki* 5:9
singers s. *at* the east.   *2 Chr* 5:12
the king s. *at* his pillar, at.   23:13
cherubims s. *at* door. *Ezek* 10:19
the king s. *at* the parting.   21:21
woman s. *at* his feet.   *Luke* 7:38
but Peter s. *at* the door. *John* 18:16
another angel came and s. *at* the
altar.   *Rev* 8:3

stood *before*
to the place where he s. *before* the
Lord.   *Gen* 19:27
Egypt, and s. *before* Joseph. 43:15
ashes and s. *before* Pharaoh. *Ex* 9:10
the congregation s. *before*. *Lev* 9:5
Zelophehad s. *before* Moses.
    Num 27:2
s. *before* the congregation. *Josh* 20:9
Phinehas s. *before* ark. *Judg* 20:28
and s. *before* Saul.   *1 Sam* 16:21
Bath-sheba s. *before*.   *1 Ki* 1:28
Solomon s. *before* the ark.   3:15
were harlots s. *before* him.   16
Solomon s. *before* the altar.   8:22
    2 Chr 6:12
old men that s. *before* Solomon.
   1 Ki 12:6; *2 Chr* 10:6
young men that s. *before* him.
   1 Ki 12:8; *2 Chr* 10:8
spirit s. *before* the Lord. *1 Ki* 22:21
    2 Chr 18:20
the Shunammite s. *before* Elisha.
    2 Ki 4:12
returned and s. *before* Elisha. 5:15
Gehazi went in and s. *before*.   25
Hazael came and s. *before*.   8:9
two kings s. not *before* him.   10:4
arose, and s. *before* king. *Esth* 8:4
Moses his chosen s. *before* him.
    Ps 106:23
Samuel s. *before* me.   *Jer* 15:1
I s. *before* thee to speak.   15:20
s. *before* them seventy. *Ezek* 8:11
therefore they s. *before* the king.
    Dan 1:19; 2:2
great image s. *before* thee.   2:31
they s. *before* the image.   3:3
times ten thousand s. *before*.   7:10
s. *before* the river a ram.   8:3
s. *before* me as the appearance. 15
Joshua s. *before* the angel. *Zech* 3:3
spake to those that s. *before* him. 4
and Jesus s. *before* the. *Mat* 27:11
three men s. *before* the. *Acts* 10:17
a man s. *before* me in bright.   30
Peter s. *before* the gate.   12:14
while I s. *before* the council. 24:20
multitude s. *before* throne. *Rev* 7:9
angels which s. *before* God.   8:2
dragon s. *before* the woman. 12:4

stood *beside*
Absalom s. *beside* the.   *2 Sam* 15:2
lions s. *beside* the stays. *1 Ki* 10:19

which *s. beside* the king. *Jer* 36:21
the six men *s. beside*. *Ezek* 9:2
then he went in and *s. beside*. 10:6

stood by
lo, three men *s. by* him. *Gen* 18:2
behold, he *s. by* the camels. 24:30
and lo, he *s. by* the river. 41:1
not refrain himself before all that *s. by* him. 45:1
the people *s. by* Moses. *Ex* 18:13
Balak *s. by* his. *Num* 23:6, 17
all that *s. by* him went. *Judg* 3:19
the men *s. by* the entering of. 18:16
that *s. by* thee, praying. *1 Sam* 1:26
servants *s. by* with. *2 Sam* 13:31
and Jeroboam *s. by* the. *1 Ki* 13:1
ass *s. by* it, the lion also *s. by*. 24
two *s. by* Jordan. *2 Ki* 2:7, 13
king *s. by* a pillar. 11:14; 23:3
they came and *s. by* the conduit of the upper pool. 18:17; *Isa* 36:2
the angel *s. by* the. *1 Chr* 21:15
the women that *s. by*. *Jer* 44:15
and the man *s. by* me. *Ezek* 43:6
to one of them that *s. by*. *Dan* 7:16
angel of the Lord *s. by*. *Zech* 3:5
one of them that *s. by*. *Mark* 14:47
some of them that *s. by*. 15:35
he *s. by* the lake of. *Luke* 5:1
he said to them that *s. by*. 19:24
two men *s. by* them in shining. 24:4
an officer that *s. by*. *John* 18:22
there *s. by* the cross of Jesus. 19:25
two men *s. by* them in. *Acts* 1:10
and all the widows *s. by* him. 9:39
to the centurion that *s. by*. 22:25
commanded them that *s. by*. 23:2
they that *s. by* said, Revilest? 4
night following the Lord *s. by* him. 11
there *s. by* me this night the. 27:23

stood in
Aaron, who *s. in* the way. *Ex* 5:20
then Moses *s. in* the gate. 32:26
Lord *s. in* the door of. *Num* 12:5
thereon, and *s. in* the door. 16:18
Dathan and Abiram *s. in* door. 27
the angel *s. in* the way. 22:22, 24
angel went further and *s. in* a. 26
the priests *s. in* midst of Jordan. *Josh* 3:17; 4:10
Jotham *s. in* the top of. *Judg* 9:7
Gaal *s. in* the entering of the. 35
Abimelech *s. in* the entering of. 44
the priests *s. in* the entering. 18:17
he *s. in* the midst of. *2 Sam* 23:12
and he *s. in* the entering. *1 Ki* 19:13
and *s. in* the border. *2 Ki* 3:21
the Shunammite *s. in* the door. 4:15
and they *s. in* their place. *2 Chr* 30:16; 35:10
king *s. in* his place, and. 34:31
and all the people *s. in*. *Neh* 8:7
Esther *s. in* the inner court. *Esth* 5:1
Jeremiah *s. in* court of. *Jer* 19:14
for who hath *s. in* counsel. 23:18
but if they had *s. in* my counsel. 22
Jaazaniah *s. in* the midst. *Ezek* 8:11
neither have *s. in* crossway. *Ob* 14
Jesus himself *s. in* the midst of them. *Luke* 24:36; *John* 20:19, 26
then Paul *s. in* the. *Acts* 17:22
in the midst of the elders *s. Rev* 5:6

stood on
Philistines *s. on* a mountain on the one side. Israel *s. on. 1 Sam* 17:3
then David *s. on* the top. 26:13
Benjamin *s. on* the top. *2 Sam* 2:25
Asaph, who *s. on* his. *1 Chr* 6:39
sons of Merari *s. on* the left. 44
the cherubims *s. on*. *2 Chr* 3:13
cherubims *s. on* the. *Ezek* 10:3
whole multitude *s. on*. *Mat* 13:2
Jesus *s. on* the shore. *John* 21:4
Paul *s. on* the stairs. *Acts* 21:40
and lo, a lamb *s. on* the. *Rev* 14:1

stood over
pillar of cloud *s. over*. *Deut* 31:15
man *s. over* against him. *Josh* 5:13
glory of the Lord *s. over* the threshold of the house. *Ezek* 10:4
glory of the Lord *s. over* cherubims. 18

star *s. over* where young. *Mat* 2:9
s. over her and rebuked. *Luke* 4:39

stood round
sheaves *s. round* about. *Gen* 37:7
disciples *s. round* about. *Acts* 14:20
Jews *s. round* about Paul, and. 25:7
angels *s. round* about the. *Rev* 7:11

stood still
the sun *s. still*, and. *Josh* 10:13*
as for cities that *s. still* in. 11:13
came to the place *s. still. 2 Sam* 2:23
trumpet and all the people *s. still*. 28
saw that all people *s. still*. 20:12
and they *s. still* in the. *Neh* 12:39
it *s. still*, but I could not. *Job* 4:16
they spake not, but *s. still*. 32:16
sun and moon *s. still* in. *Hab* 3:11
and Jesus *s. still* and. *Mat* 20:32
Jesus *s. still* and commanded him. *Mark* 10:49
that bare him *s. still*. *Luke* 7:14

stood there
and *s. with* him there. *Ex* 34:5
the field and *s. there*. *1 Sam* 6:14
twelve lions *s. there*. *1 Ki* 10:20
2 Chr 9:19
glory of the Lord *s. there. Ezek* 3:23
from the days of Gibeah *there* they *s.* *Hos* 10:9
some of them that *s. there*. *Mat* 27:47; *Mark* 11:5
and officers *s. there*. *John* 18:18

stood up
Abraham *s. up* from. *Gen* 23:3
Abraham *s. up* and bowed. 7
but Moses *s. up* and. *Ex* 2:17
the people *s. up* all that. *Num* 11:32
Satan *s. up* gainst Israel. *1 Chr* 21:1
then David the king *s. up* upon. 28:2
Abijah *s. up* and said. *2 Chr* 13:4
the Levites *s. up* to praise. 20:19
Ammon and Moab *s. up* against. 23
s. up against them that came. 28:12
till there *s. up* a priest with Urim and. *Ezra* 2:63; *Neh* 7:65
when he opened the book the people *s. up*. *Neh* 8:5
they *s. up* in their place and. 9:3
then *s. up* upon the stairs, of. 4
that Mordecai *s. up* not *up*. *Esth* 5:9
Haman *s. up* to make request. 7:7
the hair of my flesh *s. up. Job* 4:15
and the aged arose and *s. up*. 29:8
I *s. up* and cried in the. 30:28
then *s. up* Phinehas and. *Ps* 106:30
they lived, and *s. up. Ezek* 37:10
whereas four *s. up* for it. *Dan* 8:22
Jesus *s. up* to read in. *Luke* 4:16
a certain lawyer *s. up* and. 10:25
in those days Peter *s. up. Acts* 1:15
the kings of the earth *s. up*. 4:26
s. up one Gamaliel, a doctor. 5:34
Agabus *s. up*, and signified. 11:28
Paul *s. up*, and beckoning. 13:16
whom when the accusers *s. up*. 25:18

stood upon
behold I *s. upon* the bank. *Gen* 41:17
David ran and *s. upon. 1 Sam* 17:51
so I *s. upon* Saul and. *2 Sam* 1:10
the sea *s. upon* twelve oxen. *1 Ki* 7:25; *2 Chr* 4:4
he revived and *s. upon. 2 Ki* 13:21
Ezra the scribe *s. upon*. *Neh* 8:4
glory of the Lord *s. upon. Ezek* 11:23
the Lord *s. upon* a wall. *Amos* 7:7
the two prophets *s. upon. Rev* 11:11
I *s. upon* the sand of the sea. 13:1

stood with
there *s. with* him no man. *Gen* 45:1
every man *s. with* his. *1 Ki* 11:11
the Levites *s. with*. *2 Chr* 29:26
then Joshua *s. with* his. *Ezra* 3:9
he *s. with* his right hand. *Lam* 2:4
two men that *s. with* him. *Luke* 9:32
Judas also *s. with* them. *John* 18:5
Peter *s. with* them and warmed. 18
no man *s. with* me. *2 Tim* 4:16
Lord *s. with* me. 17

stoodest
that thou *s.* in the way. *Num* 22:34
day that thou *s.* before. *Deut* 4:10
in the day that thou *s.* on. *Ob* 11

stool
a bed, table, and a *s.* *2 Ki* 4:10

stools
ye see them upon the *s.* *Ex* 1:16*

stoop
the proud helpers do *s.* *Job* 9:13
maketh the heart of man *s. Pr* 12:25
they *s.*, they bow down. *Isa* 46:2
I am not worthy to *s.* *Mark* 1:7

stooped
Judah *s.* down, he couched. *Gen* 49:9
David *s.* to the earth. *1 Sam* 24:8*
Saul *s.* to the ground. 28:14*
had no compassion on him that *s.* *2 Chr* 36:17
Jesus *s.* down and wrote. *John* 8:6, 8
and as she wept, she *s.* down. 20:11

stoopeth
Bel boweth down, Nebo *s. Isa* 46:1

stooping
s. down saw the linen clothes. *Luke* 24:12; *John* 20:5

stop
that the rain *s.* thee not. *1 Ki* 18:44
s. all wells of water. *2 Ki* 3:19, 25
he took counsel to *s.* *2 Chr* 32:3
s. the way against them. *Ps* 35:3
and all iniquity shall *s.* her. 107:42
it shall *s.* the noses of. *Ezek* 39:11
no man shall *s.* me of. *2 Cor* 11:10

stopped
windows of heaven were *s. Gen* 8:2
Philistines had *s.* the wells. 26:15, 18
or his flesh be *s.* from. *Lev* 15:3
s. all the fountains and the brook. *2 Chr* 32:4
Hezekiah *s.* the watercourse. 30
breaches began to be *s.* *Neh* 4:7
speaketh lies shall be *s.* *Ps* 63:11
that the passages are *s. Jer* 51:32*
refused, and *s.* their ears. *Zech* 7:11
they *s.* their ears and ran. *Acts* 7:57
every mouth may be *s.* *Rom* 3:19
whose mouths must be *s.* *Tit* 1:11
through faith *s.* the mouths of lions. *Heb* 11:33

stoppeth
the poor hath hope, and iniquity *s.* her mouth. *Job* 5:16
adder that *s.* her ear. *Ps* 58:4
whoso *s.* his ears at the. *Pr* 21:13
s. his ears from hearing. *Isa* 33:15

store
saith the Lord, who *s.* up violence and robbery in their. *Amos* 3:10

store, substantive
and great *s.* of servants. *Gen* 26:14*
that food shall be for *s.* to. 41:36
eat of the old *s.* *Lev* 25:22; 26:10
blessed shall be thy basket and thy *s.* *Deut* 28:5*, 17*
is not this laid up in *s.* with? 32:34
of spices very great *s.* *1 Ki* 10:10
fathers have laid up in *s. 2 Ki* 20:17
all this *s.* cometh of. *1 Chr* 29:16
he put *s.* of victuals. *2 Chr* 11:11
is left is this great *s.* 31:10
s. of all sorts of wine. *Neh* 5:18
affording all manner of *s. Ps* 144:13
fathers have laid up in *s. Isa* 39:6
there is none end of the *s. Nah* 2:9
of you lay by him in *s. 1 Cor* 16:2
laying up in *s.* a good. *1 Tim* 6:19
same word are kept in *s. 2 Pet* 3:7

store cities
cities of *s.* Solomon had. *1 Ki* 9:19
2 Chr 8:6
and all the *s. cities* which he built. *2 Chr* 8:4
all the *s. cities* of Naphtali. 16:4
Jehoshaphat built *s. cities*. 17:12

storehouse
the tithes into the *s.* *Mal* 3:10
neither have *s.* nor barn. *Luke* 12:24

storehouses
Joseph opened all the *s. Gen* 41:56
blessing on thee in thy *s. Deut* 28:8*
over the *s.* was Jehonathan. *1 Chr* 27:25*
Hezekiah made *s.* also. *2 Chr* 32:28

layeth up the depth in s.   *Ps* 33:7
open her s., cast her up.   *Jer* 50:26

stories
with second and third s.   *Gen* 6:16
galleries three s. over.   *Ezek* 41:16
against gallery in three s.   42:3*, 6
he that buildeth his s.   *Amos* 9:6*

stork
(*A bird of the heron family, white, with black wings and bright red beak, or entirely black. Both species were found in Palestine. They are migratory birds, and very regular in their coming and going. They feed upon offal, and were therefore not permitted to be used by the Israelites as food*)
the s. thou shalt not eat.   *Lev* 11:19
      Deut 14:18
as for the s., the fir trees. *Ps* 104:17
s. knoweth her appointed.   *Jer* 8:7
like the wings of a s.   *Zech* 5:9

storm
and as chaff that the s.   *Job* 21:18
and as s. hurleth him out of.   27:21
I would hasten my escape from
   the windy s.   *Ps* 55:8
make them afraid with thy s. 83:15
he maketh the s. a calm.   107:29
and for a covert from s.   *Isa* 4:6
hast been a refuge from the s. 25:4
which as destroying s. shall.   28:2
thou shalt be visited with s.   29:6*
ascend and come like a s. *Ezek* 38:9
in the whirlwind and s.   *Nah* 1:3
there arose a great s.   *Mark* 4:37
there came down a s. of wind.
      Luke 8:23

stormy
raiseth the s. wind.   *Ps* 107:25
snow and vapour, s. wind.   148:8
s. wind shall rend.   *Ezek* 13:11
I will rend it with a s. wind.   13

story
Abijah in the s. of Iddo. *2 Chr* 13:22*
written in the s. of the book.   24:27*

stout
the s. lion's whelps are.   *Job* 4:11*
the fruit of the s. heart.   *Isa* 10:12
whose look was more s.   *Dan* 7:20
your words have been s.   *Mal* 3:13

stouthearted
s. are spoiled, they slept.   *Ps* 76:5
hearken unto me, ye s.   *Isa* 46:12

stoutness
that say in the pride and s. *Isa* 9:9

straight
shall ascend every man s. *Josh* 6:5
the kine took s. the way. *1 Sam* 6:12
make thy way s. before.   *Ps* 5:8
let thine eyelids look s.   *Pr* 4:25
crooked cannot be made s. *Eccl* 1:15
make that s. he made crooked ? 7:13
make s. in desert a highway. *Isa* 40:3
the crooked shall be made s.   4
   42:16; 45:2*; *Luke* 3:5
to walk in a s. way.   *Jer* 31:9
and their feet were s. feet. *Ezek* 1:7
every one s. forward.   9, 12; 10:22
firmament were their wings s. 1:23
of Lord, make his paths s. *Mat* 3:3
   Mark 1:3; *Luke* 3:4; *John* 1:23
made s. and glorified.   *Luke* 13:13
street which is called S.   *Acts* 9:11
and make s. paths for.   *Heb* 12:13

straightway
shall s. find him before. *1 Sam* 9:13
then Saul fell s. all along.   28:20
he goeth after her s. as.   *Pr* 7:22
s. there remained no.   *Dan* 10:17
Jesus went up s. out of water.
      Mat 3:16; *Mark* 1:10
and they s. left their nets.
      Mat 4:20; *Mark* 1:18
Lord hath need of them, and s. 17
      Mat 21:3; *Mark* 11:3
s. one of them ran and. *Mat* 27:48
s. the fountain of her. *Mark* 5:29
s. they knew him.   6:54
s. desireth new.   *Luke* 5:39
will not s. pull him out ?   14:5

God shall s. glorify him. *John* 13:32
then fell she down s. at.   *Acts* 5:10
and s. he preached Christ.   9:20
was baptized, he and all his, s. 16:33
then s. they departed from.   22:29
told me, I sent s. to thee.   23:30
s. forgetteth what manner. *Jas* 1:24

strain
guides s. at a gnat and. *Mat* 23:24

strait, *substantive*
saw that they were in a s. *1 Sam* 13:6
I am in a great s.   *2 Sam* 24:14
      1 Chr 21:13
would have removed thee out of the
   s.   *Job* 36:16*
for I am in a s. betwixt.   *Phil* 1:23

strait
we dwell is too s. for us.   *2 Ki* 6:1
the place is too s. for.   *Isa* 49:20
enter ye in at s. gate.   *Mat* 7:13*
because s. is the gate and narrow is
   the way.   14*; *Luke* 13:24*

straiten
their lives, shall s. them. *Jer* 19:9†

straitened
his strength shall be s.   *Job* 18:7
breadth of the waters is s.   37:10
thy steps shall not be s.   *Pr* 4:12
therefore the building was s. more.
      Ezek 42:6
is the spirit of the Lord s.?   *Mi* 2:7
how am I s. till it be accomplished!
      Luke 12:50
ye are not s. in us, but ye are s. in
   your.   *2 Cor* 6:12

straiteneth
enlargeth nations and s. *Job* 12:23*

straitest
after the most s. sect.   *Acts* 26:5

straitly
man asked us s. of our state and.
      Gen 43:7
for Joseph had s. sworn.   *Ex* 13:19
Jericho was s. shut up.   *Josh* 6:1
thy father s. charged people with
   oath.   *1 Sam* 14:28
he s. charged them, saying, See that,
   Mat 9:30*; *Mark* 3:12*; 5:43*
      Luke 9:21*
he s. charged him and. *Mark* 1:43*
but let us s. threaten them.*Acts* 4:17
did not we s. command you ?   5:28

straitness
shalt eat flesh of thy children in s.
   Deut 28:53†, 55†, 57†
place where there is no s. *Job* 36:16
eat flesh of his friend in the s.
      Jer 19:9†

straits
sufficiency he shall be in s. *Job* 20:22
overtook her between the s. *Lam* 1:3

strake
they fearing, s. sail.   *Acts* 27:17*
see **struck**

strakes
Jacob piled white s. in. *Gen* 30:37†
the walls with hollow s. *Lev* 14:37†

strange
but Joseph made himself s. *Gen* 42:7
not ashamed that ye make yourselves s. to me.   *Job* 19:3*
my breath is s. to my wife.   17
man is froward and s.   *Pr* 21:8*
wherein they think it s.   *1 Pet* 4:4
s. concerning trial, as though s.   12
   see **children, god, gods**

strange act
pass his act, his s. act.   *Isa* 28:21

strange apparel
clothed with s. apparel. *Zeph* 1:8*

strange cities
even to s. cities.   *Acts* 26:11*

strange country
as in a s. country.   *Heb* 11:9*

strange doctrines
be not carried about with s. doctrines.
      Heb 13:9

strange fire
Abihu offered s. fire before the.
   Lev 10:1; *Num* 3:4; 26:61

---

strange flesh
Gomorrah, going after s. flesh.
      Jude 7

strange incense
shall offer no s. incense.   *Ex* 30:9

strange land
have been a stranger in a s. land.
      Ex 2:22; 18:3
shall we sing Lord's song in a s. land?
      Ps 137:4
his seed should sojourn in a s. land.
      Acts 7:6

strange language
a people of s. language.   *Ps* 114:1

strange lips
shalt set it with s. lips.   *Isa* 17:10

strange nation
to sell her to a s. nation.   *Ex* 21:8

strange punishment
a s. punishment to the.   *Job* 31:3*

strange speech
not sent to a people of s. speech.
      Ezek 3:5, 6

strange thing
counted as a s. thing.   *Hos* 8:12
as though some s. thing. *1 Pet* 4:12

strange things
seen s. things to-day.   *Luke* 5:26
thou bringest certain s. things to.
      Acts 17:20

strange vanities
me to anger with s. vanities? *Jer* 8:19

strange vine
plant of a s. vine.   *Jer* 2:21

strange waters
and drunk s. waters.   *2 Ki* 19:24

strange wives
he for all his s. wives.   *1 Ki* 11:8
we have taken s. wives. *Ezra* 10:2
      10, 14, 17, 44
yourselves from the s. wives.   11
were found to have taken s. wives. 18
in marrying s. wives.   *Neh* 13:27

strange woman
the son of a s. woman.   *Judg* 11:2
from the s. woman.   *Pr* 2:16
the lips of a s. woman drop.   5:3
ravished with a s. woman ?   20
flattery of s. woman.   6:24*; 7:5
take a pledge of him for a s. woman.
      20:16*; 27:13
and a s. woman is a narrow. 23:27

strange women
loved many s. women.   *1 Ki* 11:1
the mouth of s. women is. *Pr* 22:14
eyes shall behold s. women.   23:33

strange work
do his work, his s. work. *Isa* 28:21

strangely
lest adversaries should behave themselves s.   *Deut* 32:27

stranger
[1] *One that is in a strange land*,
Gen 23:4. [2] *One that is not a Jew, but of some other nation*, Isa 14:1. [3] *One who is not of the king's stock and family*, Mat 17:25, 26. [4] *A woman that is not a man's own wife*, Pr 5:20. *The Revisions usually change this word to alien, or foreigner; occasionally to sojourner.*
thy seed shall be a s. in a land.
      Gen 15:13
give land wherein thou art a s.
   17:8; 28:4; 37:1
bought with money of any s.   17:12
bought with money of the s.   27
I am a s. with you.   23:4; *Ps* 39:12
      119:19
I have been a s. in a.   *Ex* 2:22
shall be cut off, whether a s. 12:19
   Lev 16:29; 17:15; *Num* 15:30
no s. eat thereof. *Ex* 12:43; 29:33
when a s. will keep the passover.
      12:48; *Num* 9:14
shall be to him that is homeborn and
   the s.   *Ex* 12:49; *Lev* 24:22
      Num 9:14; 15:15, 16, 2†

nor s. that is within thy gates.
  Ex 20:10; Deut 5:14
vex or oppress a s. Ex 22:21
ye know heart of a s. seeing. 23:9
shalt rest, that the s. may be. 12
putteth any of it upon a s. 30:33
neither shall any s. among. Lev 17:12
thou shalt leave them for s. 19:10
  23:22; 25:6
if a s. sojourn in the land ye. 19:33
the s. be as one born among you.
  34; Num 15:15
there shall no s. eat. Lev 22:10, 13
if she be married to a s. she. 12
neither from a s.'s hand shall ye. 25
as well s. when blasphemeth. 24:16
yea, though he be a s. thou. 25:35
if a s. wax rich by thee, and thy poor
 brother sell himself to the s. 47
Levites set up tabernacle, the s. that.
  Num 1:51; 3:10, 38
and if a s. sojourn and will. 15:14
that no s. come near to offer. 16:40
and a s. shall not come nigh. 18:4
the s. that cometh nigh shall. 7
it shall be unto Israel and the s. 19:10
six cities of refuge for the s. 35:15
  Josh 20:9
judge righteously between the s.
  Deut 1:16
Lord loveth the s. in giving. 10:18
love the s., for ye were strangers. 19
that dieth of itself: give to s. 14:21
not set a s. over thee who is. 17:15
thou wast a s. in his land. 23:7
unto a s. thou mayest lend. 20
not marry without to a s. 25:5
shalt rejoice, thou, and the s. 26:11
the s. shall get up above thee. 28:43
thy s. to enter into covenant. 29:11
s. that shall come from afar. 22
gather the people, and thy s. 31:12
as well the s. as he. Josh 8:33
aside to city of a s. Judg 19:12
grace, seeing I am a s.? Ruth 2:10
I am the son of a s. an Amalekite.
  2 Sam 1:13
for thou art a s. and also an. 15:19
there was no s. with us. 1 Ki 3:18
moreover concerning a s. 8:41
  2 Chr 6:32
do according to all that the s. calleth.
  1 Ki 8:43; 2 Chr 6:33
and no s. passed among. Job 15:19
my maids count me for a s. 19:15
the s. did not lodge in street. 31:32
I am become a s. to my. Ps 69:8
they slay the widow and the s. 94:6
let the s. spoil his labour. 109:11
to deliver thee even from the s.
  Pr 2:16
labours be in the house of a s. 5:10
embrace the bosom of a s.? 20
stricken thine hand with a s. 6:1
they may keep thee from the s. 7:5
he that is surety for a s. shall. 11:15
and a s. doth not intermeddle. 14:10
take his garment that is surety for a
 s. 20:16; 27:13
let a s. praise thee, and not. 27:2
eat thereof, but a s. eateth. Eccl
neither let the son of a s. Isa 56:3
the sons of the s. that join. 6
the sons of the s. shall not. 62:8
why shouldest thou be as a s. in ?
  Jer 14:8
every s. that setteth up. Ezek 14:7
oppression with the s. 22:7, 29
no s. uncircumcised shall enter. 44:9
what tribe the s. sojourneth. 47:23
day that he became a s. Ob 12*
and that turn aside the s. Mal 3:5
I was a s. and ye. Mat 25:35, 43
when saw we thee a s.? 38, 44
returned, save this s. Luke 17:18
art thou only a s. in Jerusalem?24:18
s. will they not follow, but. John 10:5
Moses was a s. in land. Acts 7:29
 see **fatherless, proselyte**

strangers
not counted of him s.? Gen 31:15
the land wherein they were s. 36:7
  Ex 6:4

for ye were s. in the land of Egypt.
  Ex 22:21; 23:9; Lev 19:34; 25:23
s. that offer an. Lev 17:8; 22:18
whatsoever of the s. that. 17:10
the s. that hunteth shall pour. 13
the s. that giveth of his seed. 20:2
children of the s. shall. 25:45
not oppress a servant though of s.
  Deut 24:14
after gods of the s. of land. 31:16*
s. that were conversant. Josh 8:35
s. shall submit themselves unto me.
  2 Sam 22:45
s. shall fade away and be afraid.
  46; Ps 18:44, 45
when ye were s. in it. 1 Chr 16:19
  Ps 105:12
to gather the s. in Israel. 1 Chr 22:2
for we are s. as were all. 29:15
numbered all the s. 2 Chr 2:17
all Judah and the s. 15:9
the s. of Israel and all Judah. 30:25
seed of Israel separated themselves
 from all s. Neh 9:2
cleansed I them from all s. 13:30
for s. are risen up against me and.
  Ps 54:3
the Lord preserveth the s. 146:9
lest s. be filled with thy. Pr 5:10
let them be only thine own, not s. 17
s. devour it in your presence, it is
 desolate as . . . by s. Isa 1:7
themselves in the children of s. 2:6
of the fat ones shall s. eat. 5:17*
and the s. shall be joined. 14:1
thou hast made a palace of s. 25:2
bring down the noise of s. 5
multitude of thy s. shall be. 29:5*
the sons of s. shall build up. 60:10
and s. shall stand and feed. 61:5
I have loved s. and after. Jer 2:25
scattered thy ways to the s. 3:13
so shall ye serve s. in a land. 5:19
s. shall no more serve. 30:8
live in the land where ye be s. 35:7
for s. are come into the. 51:51
our inheritance is turned to s.
  Lam 5:2
give it into hand of s. Ezek 7:21
you into the hands of s. 11:9
a wife who taketh s. instead. 16:32
therefore I will bring s. upon. 28:7
the deaths by the hand of s. 10
land waste by the hand of s. 30:12
s. have cut him off. 31:12
brought into my sanctuary s. 44:7
inheritance to you and to the s. 47:22
s. have devoured his. Hos 7:9
if so be it yield, the s. shall. 8:7
there shall no s. pass. Joel 3:17
in the day that s. carried. Ob 11
take tribute ? of children or of s.?
  Mat 17:25
Peter saith to him, Of s. 26
to bury s. in. 27:7
know not the voice of s. John 10:5
and s. of Rome, Jews. Acts 2:10
when they dwelt as s. in the. 13:17
s. from the covenants of. Eph 2:12
no more s. but fellow-citizens. 19
if she have lodged s., if. 1 Tim 5:10
confessed they were s. Heb 11:13
be not forgetful to entertain s. 13:2
so the s. scattered through Persia.
  1 Pet 1:1
I beseech you as s. and pilgrims. 2:11
whatsoever thou dost to s. 3 John 5

strangled
the lion did tear and s. for. Nah 2:12
that they abstain from things s.
  Acts 15:20, 29; 21:25

strangling
so that my soul chooseth s. Job 7:15

straw
we have both s. and. Gen 24:25
he gave s. and provender for. 32
ye shall no more give s. Ex 5:7
  10, 16, 18
go ye, get you s. where you. 11
yet there is both s. and. Judg 19:19
brought barley also and s. 1 Ki 4:28
he esteemeth iron as s. Job 41:27

and the lion shall eat s. like the ox.
  Isa 11:7; 65:25
be trodden down, even as s. 25:10

strawed
*(Revisions change to strewed or
  to scattered)*
he ground the calf, s. it. Ex 32:20
he s. upon the graves. 2 Chr 34:4
cut down branches and s. them.
  Mat 21:8; Mark 11:8
and gathering where thou hast not s.
  Mat 25:24
and gather where I have not s. 26

stream
what he did at the s. Num 21:15*
and as the s. of brooks. Job 6:15*
then the s. had gone over. Ps 124:4
beat off to the s. of Egypt. Isa 27:12
breath as an overflowing s. 30:28
like a s. of brimstone, doth. 33
among smooth stones of the s. 57:6*
the Gentiles like a flowing s. 66:12
fiery s. issued and came. Dan 7:10
and righteousness as a mighty s.
  Amos 5:24
s. beat vehemently. Luke 6:48, 49

streams
thine hand on their s. Ex 7:19; 8:5
s. whereof shall make glad. Ps 46:4
he brought s. also out of rock. 78:16
gushed out, the s. overflowed. 20
turn again our captivity as s. 126:4
well of living waters, s. S of S 4:15
smite it in the seven s. Isa 11:15
on every high hill shall be s. 30:25
place of broad rivers and s. 33:21
the s. thereof shall be turned. 34:9
break out, and s. in the desert. 35:6

street
we will abide in the s. Gen 19:2
shalt gather all the spoil into the
 midst of the s. Deut 13:16
of thy house into the s. Josh 2:19
he sat down in a s. of the city.
  Judg 19:15, 17
only lodge not in the s. 20
had stolen from the s. 2 Sam 21:12
them as the mire of the s. 22:43
and gathered them in the east s.
  2 Chr 29:4*; 32:6*
in s. of house of God. Ezra 10:9*
people gathered as one man into the
 s. Neh 8:1*
he read therein before the s. 3*
so people made booths in the s. 16*
bring him on horseback through the
 s. Esth 6:9, 11
have no name in the s. Job 18:17
prepared my seat in the s. 29:7
stranger did not lodge in the s. 31:32
passing through the s. Pr 7:8
nor cause his voice to be heard in
 the s. Isa 42:2; Mat 12:19
laid thy body as the s. Isa 51:23
for truth is fallen in the s. 59:14
bread out of bakers' s. Jer 37:21
hunger in top of every s. Lam 2:19
out in the top of every s. 4:1
made thee an high place in every s.
  Ezek 16:24, 31
the s. shall be built again. Dan 9:25
into the s. called Straight. Acts 9:11
and passed through one s. 12:10
shall lie in the s. of city. Rev 11:8
s. of the city was pure gold. 21:21
in the midst of the s. was. 22:2

streets
not in the s. of Askelon. 2 Sam 1:20
make s. in Damascus. 1 Ki 20:34
out as dirt in the s. Ps 18:42
guile depart not from her s. 55:11
sheep may bring forth ten thousands
 in our s. 144:13*
no complaining in our s. 14
uttereth her voice in the s. Pr 1:20*
and rivers of water in the s. 5:16
is she without, now in the s. 7:12*
a lion without, I shall be slain in the
 s. 22:13
man saith, A lion is in the s. 26:13
the doors shall be shut in the s.
  Eccl 12:4*

mourners go about the *s.* *Eccl* 12:5
go about the city in *s.* *S of S* 3:2
carcases were torn in midst of *s.*
Isa 5:25
down like the mire of the *s.* 10:6
in their *s.* they shall gird. 15:3*
a crying for wine in the *s.* 24:11
sons lie at the head of all the *s.* 51:20
run ye to and fro through *s.* *Jer* 5:1
seest thou not what they do in *s.*77:17
cease from the *s.* of Jerusalem. 34
cut off young men from the *s.* 9:21
proclaim these words in the *s.* 11:6
according to the number of the *s.* 13
people shall be cast out in *s.* 14:16
mirth shall be heard in *s.* of. 33:10
my anger was kindled in the *s.* 44:6
wickedness they have committed in
s. of Jerusalem. 9
the incense that ye burn in *s.* 21
lamentations in the *s.* of Moab. 48:38
her young men shall fall in her *s.*
49:26; 50:30
are thrust through in her *s.* 51:4
sucklings swoon in the *s.* of the city.
Lam 2:11, 12
the old lie on the ground in the *s.* 21
feed delicately, are desolate in *s.* 4:5
Nazarites are not known in the *s.* 8
wandered as blind men in the *s.* 14
steps, that we cannot go in our *s.* 18
cast their silver in the *s.* *Ezek* 7:19
ye have filled the *s.* thereof. 11:6
of his horses tread down thy *s.* 26:11
pestilence and blood into her *s.* 28:23
wailing be in all *s.* and. *Amos* 5:16*
down as mire of the *s.*, *Mi* 7:10
rage in the *s.*, shall justle. *Nah* 2:4
in pieces at the top of the *s.* 3:10
I made their *s.* waste. *Zeph* 3:6
old women shall dwell in *s.* *Zech* 8:4
s. of the city shall be full of boys. 5
up fine gold as mire in the *s.* 9:3
down their enemies in the *s.* 10:5
a trumpet before thee in *s.* *Mat* 6:2
to pray standing in corners of *s.* 5
they laid the sick in the *s.*
Mark 6:56*; *Acts* 5:15
go out into the *s.* of. *Luke* 10:10
Thou hast taught in our *s.* 13:26
go out quickly into the *s.* and. 14:21

strength

not henceforth yield her *s.* *Gen* 4:12
by *s.* the Lord brought you out.
Ex 13:3, 14, 16
he hath the *s.* of an unicorn.
Num 23:22; 24:8
thou hast trodden down *s.* *Judg* 5:21
they are girded with *s.* *1 Sam* 2:4
wicked be silent, for by *s.* shall. 9
he shall give *s.* unto his king. 10
the *s.* of Israel shall not lie. 15:29
eat, that thou mayest have *s.* 28:22
girded me with *s.* to battle, hast.
2 Sam 22:40; *Ps* 18:32, 39
I have counsel and *s.* for war.
2 Ki 18:20; *Isa* 36:5
and there is not *s.* to bring forth.
2 Ki 19:3; *Isa* 37:3
s. and gladness are in. *1 Chr* 16:27
give to the Lord glory and *s.* 28
Ps 29:1; 96:7
brethren, able men for *s.* *1 Chr* 26:8
in thine hand it is to give *s.* 29:12
neither did Jeroboam recover *s.*
2 Chr 13:20
s. of the bearers is. *Neh* 4:10
if I speak of *s.* lo, he. *Job* 9:19
with him is wisdom and *s.* 12:13*, 16
weakened the *s.* of the mighty. 21*
devour the *s.* of his skin. 18:13*
no; but he would put *s.* in me. 23:6*
whereto might *s.* of their hands. 30:2
not esteem all the forces of *s.* 36:19
hast thou given the horse *s.*? 39:19*
in his neck remaineth *s.* 41:22
of babes hast ordained *s.* *Ps* 8:2
saving *s.* of his right hand. 20:6
the Lord is the *s.* of my life. 27:1
and he is the saving *s.* of his. 28:8*
the Lord will give *s.* to his. 29:11
not delivered by much *s.* 33:16
that I may recover *s.* 39:13
41

God is our refuge and *s.* *Ps* 46:1
81:1
Ephraim is the *s.* 60:7*; 108:8*
ascribe ye *s.* unto God, his *s.* 68:34
God of Israel is he that giveth *s.* 35
but God is the *s.* of my heart. 73:26
sing aloud unto God our *s.* 81:1
blessed is the man whose *s.* 84:5
they go from *s.* to *s.*, every one. 7
and if by reason of *s.* they. 90:10
is clothed with majesty and *s.* 93:1
the *s.* of the hills is his also. 95:4*
s. and beauty are in his. 96:6
king's *s.* also loveth judgement. 99:4
thou strengthenedst me with *s.* 138:3
O God the Lord, the *s.* of my. 140:7
I have *s.* *Pr* 8:14*
the way of the Lord is *s.* 10:29*
increase is by the *s.* of ox. 14:4
casteth down the *s.* thereof. 21:22
of knowledge increaseth *s.* 24:5*
she girdeth her loins with *s.* 31:17
s. and honour are her clothing. 25
Wisdom is better than *s.* *Eccl* 9:16
then must he put to more *s.* 10:10
princes eat for *s.* and not for. 17
and men of *s.* to mingle. *Isa* 5:22
by the *s.* of my hand I have. 10:13
sea hath spoken, even the *s.* 23:4*
been a *s.* to the poor, a *s.* to. 25:4*
in Jehovah is everlasting *s.* 26:4*
for *s.* to them that turn the. 28:6
the *s.* of Pharaoh shall be. 30:3
shall be stability and *s.* of. 33:6*
lift up thy voice with *s.* 40:9
no might, he increaseth *s.* 29
he hath poured on him the *s.* 42:25
he worketh it with the *s.* 44:12*
have I righteousness and *s.* 45:24
awake, awake, put on thy *s.* 51:9
moreover I will deliver all the *s.* of
this city. *Jer* 20:5*
fortify the height of her *s.* 51:53
they are gone without *s.* *Lam* 1:6
pour my fury on sin, *s.* *Ezek* 30:15*
the pomp of her *s.* shall. 18*; 33:28*
given thee power, *s.* glory. *Dan* 2:37
but there shall be in it of the *s.* 41
neither shall there be any *s.* 11:15
to enter with the *s.* of his whole. 17
pollute the sanctuary of *s.* 31*
the Lord the *s.* of. *Joel* 3:16*
horns by our own *s.*? *Amos* 6:13
Ethiopia and Egypt were her *s.*
Nah 3:9
thou also shalt seek *s.* because. 11*
destroy *s.* of kingdoms. *Hag* 2:22
he hath shewed *s.* with. *Luke* 1:51
ancle bones received *s.* *Acts* 3:7
without *s.*, Christ died. *Rom* 5:6
the sting of death is sin; the *s.* of sin
is the law. *1 Cor* 15:56*
out of measure, above *s.* *2 Cor* 1:8*
Sara herself received *s.* *Heb* 11:11
for thou hast a little *s.* *Rev* 3:8*
worthy is Lamb to receive *s.* 5:12*
Now is come salvation and *s.* 12:10*
their power and *s.* to beast. 17:13*

see no

his strength

sea returned to *his s.* *Ex* 14:27
is the beginning of *his s.* *Deut* 21:17
as the man is. so is *his s.* *Judg* 8:21
see wherein *his* great *s.* lieth. 16:5
his s. was not known. 9
his s. went from him. 19
a bow with *his* full *s.* *2 Ki* 9:24
seek the Lord and *his s.* *1 Chr* 16:11
Ps 105:4
the steps of *his s.* shall. *Job* 18:7
his s. shall be hunger bitten. 12
of death shall devour *his s.* 13
one dieth in *his* full *s.* being. 21:23
to the great rain of *his s.* 37:6*
trust him because *his s.* is? 39:11
rejoiceth in *his s.* 21
his s. is in his loins. 40:16
deliver any by *his* great *s. Ps* 33:17*
that made not God *his s.* 52:7
because of *his s.* will I wait. 59:9
who by *his s.* setteth fast the. 65:6
ascribe *s.* to God, *his s.* is. 68:34
the generation to come *his s.* 78:4

delivered *his s.* into captivity.
Ps 78:61
hungry, and *his s.* faileth. *Isa* 44:12
sworn by the arm of *his s.* 62:8
in the greatness of *his s.* 63:1
by *his s.* shall stir up all. *Dan* 11:2*
strangers devoured *his s.* *Hos* 7:9
and by *his s.* he had power. 12:3*
was as the sun in *his s.* *Rev* 1:16

in strength

but his bow abode *in s.* *Gen* 49:24
went *in* the *s.* of that. *1 Ki* 19:8
he is wise in heart, and mighty *in s.*
Job 9:4; 36:5
I will go in the *s.* of the. *Ps* 71:16*
his angels that excel *in s.* 103:20
he delighteth not *in* the *s.* 147:10
themselves *in s.* of Pharaoh. *Isa* 30:2
and he shall feed *in* the *s.* *Mi* 5:4
increased the more *in s.* *Acts* 9:22

my strength

the beginning of *my s.* *Gen* 49:3
Lord is *my s.* and song. *Ex* 15:2
2 Sam 22:33; *Ps* 18:2*; 28:7
118:14; *Isa* 12:2
as *my s.* was then, even so is *my s.*
Josh 14:11
if I be shaven, *my s.* *Judg* 16:17
what is *my s.* that I should hope?
Job 6:11
is *my s.* of stones? or is my? 12
love thee, O Lord, *my s.* *Ps* 18:1
O Lord, *my s.* 19:14*; 22:19*
my s. is dried up. 22:15
the net, for thou art *my s.* 31:4*
my s. fails because of mine iniquity.
10; 38:10; 71:9
art the God of *my s.* why go? 43:2
to thee, O *my s.* will I sing. 59:17
art rock of *my s.* 62:7
he weakened *my s.* 102:23
blessed be Lord *my s.* who. 144:1*
let him take hold of *my s.* *Isa* 27:5
I have spent *my s.* for nought. 49:4
my God shall be *my s.* 5
O Lord, *my s.* *Jer* 16:19
he made *my s.* to fall. *Lam* 1:14
I said, *My s.* and hope is. 3:18
the Lord God is *my s.* *Hab* 3:19
my s. in Lord of hosts. *Zech* 12:5
my s. is made perfect. *2 Cor* 12:9*

their strength

as for cities that stood still in *their s.*
Josh 11:13*
he is *their s.* in the time. *Ps* 37:39*
their death, *their s.* is firm. 73:4
he smote the chief of *their s.* 78:51
105:36
art the glory of *their s.* 89:17
yet is *their s.* labour and. 90:10*
the glory of young men is *their s.*
Pr 20:29
I have cried, *their s.* is. *Isa* 30:7*
on Lord shall renew *their s.* 40:31
let the people renew *their s.* 41:1
I will bring down *their s.* 63:6*
take from them *their s.* *Ezek* 24:25
and vine do yield *their s.* *Joel* 2:22

thy strength

guided them in *thy s.* *Ex* 15:13
days, so shall *thy s.* be. *Deut* 33:25
wherein *thy s.* lieth. *Judg* 16:6, 15
thou, and the ark of *thy s.* *2 Chr* 6:41
Ps 132:8
the king shall joy in *thy s.* *Ps* 21:1
O Lord, in *thine* own *s.* 13
thy name, judge me by *thy s.* 54:1
hath commanded *thy s.* 68:28
until I have shewed *thy s.* 71:18
divide the sea by *thy s.* 74:13
thou hast declared *thy s.* 77:14
stir up *thy s.* and come. 80:2*
O turn to me, give *thy s.* to. 86:16
Lord shall send rod of *thy s.* 110:2
if thou faint in day of adversity, *thy*
s. *Pr* 24:10
give not *thy s.* unto women. 31:3
mindful of rock of *thy s.* *Isa* 17:10
awake, awake, put on *thy s.* 52:1
where is thy zeal and *thy s.*? 63:15
he shall bring down *thy s. Amos* 3:11

thy God with all thy heart and all *thy*
s. Mat k 12:30, 33; Luke 10:27

your strength
and *your s.* shall be spent in vain.
Lev 26:20
joy of the Lord is *your s.* Neh 8:10
howl, ye ships, *your s.* Isa 23:14
in confidence will be *your s.* 30:15
excellency of *your s.* Ezek 24:21

strengthen
charge Joshua, and encourage him
and *s.* him. Deut 3:28
s. me, I pray thee. Judg 16:28
go, *s.* thyself, and mark. 1 Ki 20:22
to *s.* their hands in the. Ezra 6:22
now therefore, O God, *s.* Neh 6:9
but I would *s.* you with. Job 16:5
Lord send thee help, *s.* thee. Ps 20:2
wait on Lord, he shall *s.* thy heart.
27:14*; 31:24*
Lord will *s.* him upon the bed. 41:3*
s. that which thou hast. 68:28
mine arm also shall *s.* him. 89:21
s. thou me according to. 119:28
and I will *s.* him with. Isa 22:21
to *s.* themselves in the strength. 30:2
not well *s.* their mast. 33:23
s. ye the weak hands. 35:3
I will *s.* thee. 41:10
lengthen thy cords, and *s.* 54:2
s. also the hands of evil. Jer 23:14
nor shall any *s.* himself. Ezek 7:13
neither did she *s.* hand of poor. 16:49
I will *s.* arms of the king. 30:24, 25*
I will *s.* that which was sick. 34:16
to confirm and to *s.* him. Dan 11:1
strong shall not *s.* his. Amos 2:14
and I will *s.* the house. Zech 10:6
I will *s.* them in the Lord, they. 12
thou art converted, *s.* Luke 22:32*
you perfect, stablish, *s.* 1 Pet 5:10
be watchful and *s.* things. Rev 3:2*

strengthened
Israel *s.* himself, and sat. Gen 48:2
the Lord *s.* Eglon against. Judg 3:12
shall thine hands be *s.* 7:11
and *s.* his hand in God. 1 Sam 23:16
let your hands be *s.* 2 Sam 2:7
who *s.* themselves. 1 Chr 11:10
and Solomon was *s.* 2 Chr 1:1
s. the kingdom of Judah. 11:17
when Rehoboam had *s.* himself. 12:1
have *s.* themselves against. 13:7
Jehoshaphat *s.* himself against. 17:1
Jehoram *s.* himself and slew. 21:4
Jehoiada *s.* himself and took. 23:1
house in his state, and *s.* it. 24:13
Amaziah *s.* himself, and led. 25:11*
Uzziah *s.* himself exceedingly. 26:8
and distressed Ahaz, but *s.* 28:20
Hezekiah *s.* himself, and built. 32:5*
all that were about them. Ezra 1:6
I was *s.* as hand of my God. 7:28
they *s.* their hands for. Neh 2:18
hast *s.* the weak hands. Job 4:3
hast *s.* the feeble knees. 4*
and *s.* himself in his. Ps 52:7
for he hath *s.* the bars of. 147:13
when he *s.* the fountains of. Pr 8:28
ye have *s.* the hands of. Ezek 13:22
diseased have ye not *s.* nor. 34:4
one touched me, and *s.* me.
Dan 10:18, 19
he that begat her and *s.* her. 11:6
many, but he shall not be *s.* by. 12*
though I have bound and *s.* Hos 7:15
Saul was *s.* Acts 9:19
to be *s.* with might by Spirit.Eph 3:16
s. with all might according. Col 1:11
stood with me and *s.* me. 2 Tim 4:17

strengthenedst
s. me with strength in. Ps 138:3*

strengtheneth
he *s.* himself against. Job 15:25*
and bread which *s.* Ps 104:15
girdeth her loins, and *s.* Pr 31:17
wisdom *s.* the wise more. Eccl 7:19
the cypress and oak he *s.* Isa 44:14
s. the spoiled against. Amos 5:9*
I can do all things through Christ
which *s.* me. Phil 4:13

strengthening
appeared an angel *s.* Luke 22:43
Paul went to Galatia, *s.* Acts 18:23*

stretch
s. out thy hand upon. Ex 7:19
s. forth thine hand over streams. 8:5
s. out thy rod and smite dust. 16
cherubims shall *s.* forth their. 25:20
s. out spear that is in. Josh 8:18
I will *s.* over Jerusalem. 2 Ki 21:13
if thou *s.* thine hands. Job 11:13
doth the hawk *s.* her wings ? 39:26
shall soon *s.* out her hands. Ps 68:31
that a man can *s.* himself. Isa 28:20
he shall *s.* upon it the line. 34:11
s. forth the curtains of thy. 54:2
there is none to *s.* forth. Jer 10:20
king of Babylon shall *s.* Ezek 30:25
and *s.* themselves upon. Amos 6:4
man, *S.* forth thy hand. Mat 12:13
thou shalt *s.* forth thy. John 21:18
for we *s.* not ourselves. 2 Cor 10:14

stretched
Abraham *s.* forth hand. Gen 22:10
Israel *s.* out right hand, laid. 48:14
Aaron *s.* out his hand. Ex 8:6, 17
Moses *s.* forth his rod. 9:23; 10:13
Moses *s.* forth his hand to heaven.
10:22; 14:21, 27
and Joshua *s.* out the spear.
Josh 8:18, 26
they ran as soon as he had *s.* 19
the cherubims *s.* forth. 1 Ki 6:27
he *s.* himself upon the child. 17:21
2 Ki 4:34, 35
angel with a sword *s.* 1 Chr 21:16
who hath *s.* the line upon ? Job 38:5
or *s.* our hands to a. Ps 44:20
I have *s.* out my hands unto. 88:9
to him that *s.* out the earth. 136:6
because I have *s.* out. Pr 1:24
because they walk with *s.* Isa 3:16
s. forth his hand against them; his
hand is *s.* 5:25; 9:12, 17, 21; 10:4
this is the hand that is *s.* out. 14:26
hand is *s.* out, and who shall ? 27
her branches are *s.* out. 16:8
he *s.* out his hand over sea. 23:11
that *s.* out the heavens. 42:5; 45:12
51:13
the shadows are *s.* out. Jer 6:4
he *s.* out the heavens. 10:12
he *s.* out heaven by his. 51:15
Lord hath *s.* out a line. Lam 2:8
and their wings were *s.* Ezek 1:11
one cherub *s.* forth his hand. 10:7
behold, I have *s.* out my hand. 16:27
he *s.* out his hand with. Hos 7:5
that *s.* themselves shall. Amos 6:7
a line shall be *s.* forth. Zech 1:16
and he *s.* forth his hand. Mat 12:13
Mark 3:5
ye *s.* forth no hands. Luke 22:53
Herod *s.* forth his hands. Acts 12:1
all day long I have *s.* Rom 10:21
see arm

stretchedst
thou *s.* out thy right hand. Ex 15:12

stretchest
who *s.* out the heavens. Ps 104:2

stretcheth
for he *s.* out his hand. Job 15:25
he *s.* out the north over the. 26:7
she *s.* out her hand to. Pr 31:20
that *s.* out the heavens. Isa 40:22
the carpenter *s.* out his rule. 44:13
that *s.* forth the heavens alone. 24
Zech 12:1

stretching
s. of his wings shall fill. Isa 8:8
by *s.* forth thy hand. Acts 4:30

stricken
Abram and Sarah well *s.* in age.
Gen 18:11; 24:1
now Joshua was *s.* in years.
Josh 13:1; 23:1, 2
when Jael had *s.* Judg 5:26
old and *s.* in years. 1 Ki 1:1
if thou hast *s.* thy hand. Pr 6:1
they have *s.* me and I was. 23:35
why should ye be *s.* any more ?
Isa 1:5

surely they are *s.* Isa 16:7
did esteem him *s.* 53:4
of my people was he *s.* 8
thou hast *s.* them, they. Jer 5:3
s. through for want of the. Lam 4:9
Elisabeth well *s.* in. Luke 1:7, 18

strife
there was a *s.* between. Gen 13:7
Abram said, Let there be no *s.* 8
ye rebelled in the *s.* of. Num 27:14
myself alone bear your *s.*? Deut 1:12
I and my people were at great *s.* with.
Judg 12:2
all the people were at *s.* 2 Sam 19:9
shalt keep them from *s.* Ps 31:20
for I have seen violence and *s.* 55:9
thou makest us a *s.* to our. 80:6
him at the waters of *s.* 106:32*
man stirreth up *s.* . . . . slow to anger
appeaseth *s.* Pr 15:18; 29:22
a froward man soweth *s.* 16:28
house full of sacrifices with *s.* 17:1
beginning of *s.* is as when one. 14
loveth transgression, that loveth *s.* 19
for a man to cease from *s.* 20:3
cast out the scorner, and *s.* 22:10
he that meddleth with *s.* 26:17
is no talebearer, the *s.* ceaseth. 20
so is a contentious man to kindle *s.* 21
a proud heart stirreth up *s.* 28:25
of wrath bringeth forth *s.* 30:33
behold, ye fast for *s.* and. Isa 58:4
hast borne me a man of *s.* Jer 15:10
even to the waters of *s.*
Ezek 47:19*; 48:28*
there are that raise up *s.* Hab 1:3
there was a *s.* among. Luke 22:24
walk honestly, not in *s.* Rom 13:13
there is among you *s.* 1 Cor 3:3
of the flesh are wrath, *s.* Gal 5:20*
preach Christ even of *s.* Phil 1:15
let nothing be done through *s.* 2:3*
whereof cometh envy, *s.* 1 Tim 6:4
to them an end of all *s.* Heb 6:16*
bitter envying and *s.* Jas 3:14*
where *s.* is, there is confusion. 16*

strifes
hatred stirreth up *s.*: love. Pr 10:12
envyings, wraths, *s.* 2 Cor 12:20*
doting about questions and *s.* of
words. 1 Tim 6:4*
that they do gender *s.* 2 Tim 2:23

strike
and *s.* blood on the two side posts.
Ex 12:7*, 22
shall *s.* off the heifer's. Deut 21:4
come and *s.* his hand. 2 Ki 5:11*
who is he that will *s.* hands with ?
Job 17:3
and the bow of steel shall *s.* 20:24
shall *s.* through kings in. Ps 110:5
till a dart *s.* through. Pr 7:23
it is not good to *s.* princes. 17:26
one of them that *s.* hands. 22:26
thou didst *s.* through. Hab 3:14
s. him with palms of. Mark 14:65*

striker
a bishop must be sober, no *s.*
1 Tim 3:3; Tit 1:7

striketh
he *s.* them as wicked men. Job 34:26
of understanding *s.* hands. Pr 17:18
scorpion, when he *s.* a man. Rev 9:5

string
ready their arrow upon *s.* Ps 11:2
s. of his tongue was loosed, he.
Mark 7:35*

stringed
him with *s.* instruments. Ps 150:4
will sing my songs to *s.* Isa 38:20
to chief singer on my *s.* Hab 3:19

strings
make ready their arrows upon *s.*
Ps 21:12*
with the psaltery, and an instrument
of ten *s.* 33:2; 92:3; 144:9

strip
and *s.* Aaron of his. Num 20:26
Philistines came to *s.* slain.
1 Sam 31:8; 1 Chr 10:8
s. ye, make ye bare, gird. Isa 32:11

they shall s. thee of thy clothes.
    Ezek 16:39; 23:26
lest I s. her naked, and. *Hos* 2:3

stripe
wound for wound, s. for s. *Ex* 21:25

stripes
(*Strokes given by a scourge or rod. The law forbade giving more than 40 and the Jews stopped at 39 for fear of wrong count*)
forty s. he may give him . . . above
    these with many s. *Deut* 25:3
and with s. of the children of men.
    2 Sam 7:14
visit their iniquity with s. *Ps* 89:32
than an hundred s. into. *Pr* 17:10
and s. prepared for the back. 19:29
so do s. the inward parts. 20:30
with his s. we are healed. *Isa* 53:5
    1 Pet 2:24
be beaten with many s. *Luke* 12:47
not, shall be beaten with few s. 48
had laid many s. upon. *Acts* 16:23
same hour and washed their s. 33
in s., in imprisonments. *2 Cor* 6:5
s. above measure, in prisons. 11:23
received I forty s. save one. 24

stripling
Inquire whose son the s. *1 Sam* 17:56

stripped
that they s. Joseph out. *Gen* 37:23
Israel s. themselves of. *Ex* 33:6
Moses s. Aaron of his. *Num* 20:28
Jonathan s. himself of. *1 Sam* 18:4
Saul s. off his clothes also. 19:24
the Philistines s. Saul of his. 31:9
jewels which they s. off. *2 Chr* 20:25
he s. me of my glory. *Job* 19:9
for thou hast s. the naked of. 22:6
therefore I will go s. *Mi* 1:8
they s. Jesus, put on. *Mat* 27:28
thieves, which s. him. *Luke* 10:30

strive
spirit shall not always s. *Gen* 6:3
the herdmen of Gerar did s. 26:20
if men s. together, and. *Ex* 21:18
if man s. and hurt a woman with
    child, he shall. 22; *Deut* 25:11
with whom thou didst s. *Deut* 33:8
did he ever s. against Israel or?
    Judg 11:25
why dost thou s. against? *Job* 33:13
with them that s. with me. *Ps* 35:1
s. not with a man. *Pr* 3:30
go not forth hastily to s., lest. 25:8
and they that s. with thee. *Isa* 41:11
potsherd s. with potsherds. 45:9*
let no man s.; thy people are as they
    that s. *Hos* 4:4
he shall not s., nor cry. *Mat* 12:19
s. to enter in at the strait gate.
    Luke 13:24
s. with me in your prayers to.
    Rom 15:30
and if a man also s. *2 Tim* 2:5*
that they s. not about words. 14
of the Lord must not s. 24

strived
so have I s. to preach. *Rom* 15:20*

striven
because thou hast s. *Jer* 50:24

striveth
woe to him that s. with. *Isa* 45:9
every man that s. for mastery.
    1 Cor 9:25

striving
with one mind s. for faith. *Phil* 1:27
s. according to his working. *Col* 1:29
ye have not resisted to blood, s.
    against sin. *Heb* 12:4

strivings
delivered me from the s. of the people,
    and. *2 Sam* 22:44; *Ps* 18:43
avoid contentions and s. *Tit* 3:9*

stroke
hard between s. and s. *Deut* 17:8
and his hand fetcheth a s. 19:5
by their word shall every s. 21:5
their enemies with the s. *Esth* 9:5
my s. is heavier than. *Job* 23:2
take thee away with his s. 36:18

remove thy s. away from. *Ps* 39:10
people with a continual s. *Isa* 14:6
the Lord healeth the s. of. 30:26
of thine eyes with a s. *Ezek* 24:16

strokes
a fool's mouth calleth for s. *Pr* 18:6*

strong
Issachar is a s. ass. *Gen* 49:14
arms of his hands were made s. 24
with a s. hand shall he let them go.
    Ex 6:1; 13:9
the Lord turned a mighty s. 10:19
sea to go back by a s. east. 14:21
Edom came against him with a s.
    Num 20:20
children of Ammon was s. 21:24
Balaam said, S. is thy. 24:21
the s. wine to be poured out. 28:7
one city too s. for us. *Deut* 2:36*
as yet I am as s. this. *Josh* 14:11
were waxen s. 17:13; *Judg* 1:28
Lord hath driven out great nations
    and s. *Josh* 23:9
but there was a s. tower. *Judg* 9:51
out of the s. came forth. 14:14
that they were too s. for him. 18:26
Saul saw any s. man. *1 Sam* 14:52*
Abner made himself s. for the house
    of Saul. *2 Sam* 3:6
Syrians be too s. for me, if Ammon
    be too s. for. 10:11; *1 Chr* 19:12
make thy battle more s. *2 Sam* 11:25
the conspiracy was s. 15:12
from my s. enemy; . . . for they were
    too s. for me. 22:18*; *Ps* 18:17
shall hear of thy name and s. hand.
    1 Ki 8:42
a great and s. wind rent the. 19:11
cities exceeding s. *2 Chr* 11:12
so they made Rehoboam s. 17
eyes run to shew himself s. 16:9
when Uzziah was s. he. 26:16
redeemed by thy s. hand. *Neh* 1:10
and they took s. cities and. 9:25*
mouth be like as a s. wind. *Job* 8:2*
speak of strength, lo, he is s. 9:19*
with thy s. hand thou. 30:21*
spread out the sky, which is s.? 37:18
bones are as s. pieces of. 40:18*
and rejoiceth as a s. man. *Ps* 19:5
Lord s. and mighty, the Lord. 24:8
my mountain to stand s. 30:7
be thou my s. rock, and house. 31:2
me his kindness in a s. city. 21
poor from him that is too s. 35:10
are lively and they are s. 38:19
bring me into s. city? 60:9; 108:10
thou hast been a s. tower from. 61:3
be my s. habitation. 71:3*
thou art my s. refuge. 7
the branch thou madest s. 80:15, 17
O Lord, who is a s. Lord? 89:8*
s. is thy hand, and high is thy. 13
with a s. hand, and a stretched out
    arm. 136:12; *Jer* 32:21
yea, many s. men have. *Pr* 7:26*
rich man's wealth is his s. city.
    10:15; 18:11
s. men retain riches. 11:16*
fear of the Lord is a s. tower. 14:26
name of the Lord is a s. tower. 18:10
is harder to be won than a s. city. 19
the bosom pacifieth s. wrath. 21:14
a wise man is s. 24:5
ants are a people not s. 30:25
the battle is not to the s. *Eccl* 9:11
and the s. men shall bow. 12:3
as a seal, for love is s. *S of S* 8:6
the s. shall be as tow. *Isa* 1:31
Lord bringeth on them waters, s. 8:7
spake thus to me with a s. 11
his s. cities shall be as a. 17:9
therefore shall the s. people. 25:3
be sung: We have a s. city. 26:1
with his s. sword shall punish. 27:1
Lord hath a mighty and s. one. 28:2
lest your bands be made s. 22
horsemen, because they are s. 31:1
will come with a s. hand. 40:10*
for that he is s. in power, not. 26
bring forth your s. reasons. 41:21
divide the spoil with the s. 53:12
a small one shall become a s. 60:22

against you with a s. arm. *Jer* 21:5
say ye, We are mighty, s.? 48:14*
How is the s. staff broken! 17
against habitation of the s. 49:19
Redeemer is s.; the Lord of. 50:34
up to the habitation of the s. 44
make the watch s., set up. 51:12
thy face s. thy forehead s. *Ezek* 3:8*
but the hand of the Lord was s. 14
the pomp of the s. to cease. 7:24
had s. rods for sceptres of. 19:11
her s. rods were broken. 12
so she hath no s. rod to be a. 14
thy s. garrisons shall go. 26:11*
the renowned city which wast s. 17
bind it, to make it s. to hold. 30:21
and I will break the s. arms. 22
s. shall speak to him out of. 32:21
destroy the fat and the s. 34:16
tree grew, and was s. *Dan* 4:11, 20
O king, art grown and become s. 22
the fourth beast terrible, s. 7:7
when he was s. the great horn. 8:8
he shall become s. with a. 11:23
nation is come up on my land, s.
    Joel 1:6; 2:2
as the noise of a s. people set. 2:5
for he is s. that executeth his. 11
let the weak say, I am s. 3:10
the Amorite was s. as. *Amos* 2:9
and the s. shall not strengthen. 14
the spoiled against the s. 5:9
he shall rebuke s. nations. *Mi* 4:3
was cast far off, s. nation. 7
hear, ye s. foundations of the. 6:2*
make thy loins s., fortify. *Nah* 2:1
s. nations shall come to. *Zech* 8:22
enter into a s. man's house . . . the s.
    man? *Mat* 12:29; *Mark* 3:27
grew and waxed s. *Luke* 1:80; 2:40
when a s. man armed keepeth. 11:21
through faith hath made this man s.
    Acts 3:16
was s. in faith, giving. *Rom* 4:20
we that are s. ought to bear. 15:1
weak, but ye are s. *1 Cor* 4:10
am weak, then am I s. *2 Cor* 12:10
we are weak, and ye are s. 13:9
God shall send them s. *2 Thes* 2:11*
up prayers with s. crying. *Heb* 5:7
of milk, and not of s. meat. 12*
s. meat belongeth to them that. 14*
we might have a s. consolation. 6:18
weakness were made s. 11:34
ye are s., word of God. *1 John* 2:14
I saw a s. angel proclaiming. *Rev* 5:2
s. voice, Babylon is fallen. 18:2*
for s. is the Lord God who. 8

see **drink**

be **strong**
see whether they be s. *Num* 13:18
the people be s. that dwell. 28
keep commandments, that ye may
    be s. *Deut* 11:8
drive out Canaanites, though they
    be s. *Josh* 17:18
be s. and quit yourselves. *1 Sam* 4:9
hands of all with these shall be s.
    2 Sam 16:21
be thou s. and shew. *1 Ki* 2:2
be too s. for me, if Ammon be too s.
    for thee. *1 Chr* 19:12
Lord hath chosen thee, be s. 28:10
be s., your work shall. *2 Chr* 15:7
if thou wilt go, do it, be s. for. 25:8
that ye may be s. and eat. *Ezra* 9:12
that our oxen may be s. *Ps* 144:14*
fearful heart, Be s., fear not. *Isa* 35:4
can thy hands be s., in? *Ezek* 22:14
fourth kingdom shall be s. *Dan* 2:40
kingdom shall be partly s. 42
Peace be unto thee, be s., yea, be s.
    10:19
the south shall be s. and he shall be
    s. above him and have. 11:5
that know their God shall be s. 32
be s. O Zerubbabel, be s. O Joshua,
    be s. all ye people of. *Hag* 2:4
let your hands be s. ye that hear in
    these days. *Zech* 8:9
but let your hands be s. 13
quit you like men, be s. *1 Cor* 16:13
finally, brethren, be s. in. *Eph* 6:10

my son, *be s.* in grace. *2 Tim* 2:1
see **courage**

strong hold and holds
tents or in *s. holds.* *Num* 13:19
them caves and *s. holds.* *Judg* 6:2
abode in wilderness in *s. holds.*
    1 Sam 23:14
hide himself with us in *s. holds?* 19
and David dwelt in *s. holds.* 29
took the *s. hold* of Zion. *2 Sam* 5:7
and came to the *s. hold* of. 24:7
their *s. holds* wilt thou. *2 Ki* 8:12
fortified the *s. holds.* *2 Chr* 11:11
brought his *s. holds* to ruin. *Ps* 89:40
to destroy the *s. holds.* *Isa* 23:11
over to his *s. holds* for fear. 31:9
destroy thy *s. holds.* *Jer* 48:18
Kerioth is taken, the *s. holds.* 41
down *s. holds* of Judah. *Lam* 2:2
hath destroyed his *s. holds.* 5
forecast his devices against the *s.*
  holds. *Dan* 11:24
he do in the most *s. holds.* 39*
the *s. hold* of the daughter. *Mi* 4:8*
Lord is a *s. hold* in the day. *Nah* 1:7
for siege, fortify thy *s. holds.* 3:14*
deride every *s. hold.* *Hab* 1:10
did build herself a *s. hold. Zech* 9:3
s. hold, ye prisoners of hope. 12
to pulling down of *s. holds.2 Cor* 10:4

strong ones
poor may fall by his *s. ones. Ps* 10:10
the neighing of his *s. ones. Jer* 8:16

stronger
one people shall be *s.* *Gen* 25:23
whensoever the *s.* cattle did. 30:41
were Laban's, and *s.* Jacob's. 42
be not able, they are *s.* *Num* 13:31
the men said, What is *s.? Judg* 14:18
Saul and Jonathan were *s.* than lions.
    2 Sam 1:23
but David waxed *s.* and *s.* and. 3:1
but Ammon being *s.* than she. 13:14
gods of hills, therefore *s.,* surely we
  shall be *s.* than. *1 Ki* 20:23, 25
hath clean hands shall be *s.* and *s.*
    Job 17:9
he made them *s.* than. *Ps* 105:24
deliver me, for they are *s.* 142:6
thou art *s.* than I, and. *Jer* 20:7
him that was *s.* than he. 31:11
when a *s.* than he shall. *Luke* 11:22
weakness of God is *s.* *1 Cor* 1:25
provoke Lord? are we *s.?* 10:22

strongest
a lion which is *s.* among. *Pr* 30:30*

strongly
foundation thereof be *s.* *Ezra* 6:3

strove
they *s.* with him. *Gen* 26:20, 21
well, and for that they *s.* not. 22
two men of the Hebrews *s. Ex* 2:13
and a man of Israel *s. Lev* 24:10
the children of Israel *s. Num* 20:13
Dathan, who *s.* against Moses. 26:9
they two *s.* together in. *2 Sam* 14:6
four winds *s.* upon the. *Dan* 7:2*
the Jews *s.* among. *John* 6:52
himself with them as they *s. Acts* 7:26
and *s.* saying, We find no evil. 23:9

struck
he *s.* it into the pan or. *1 Sam* 2:14
the Lord *s.* the child. *2 Sam* 12:15
Joab *s.* him not again, and. 20:10
the Lord *s.* Jeroboam. *2 Chr* 13:20
one of them *s.* a servant. *Mat* 26:51
s. Jesus on the face. *Luke* 22:64
    John 18:22

struggled
children *s.* together. *Gen* 25:22

stubble
scattered to gather *s.* *Ex* 5:12
which consumed them as *s.* 15:7
thou pursue the dry *s.? Job* 13:25
they are as *s.* before the wind. 21:18
are turned with him into *s.* 41:28
darts are counted as *s.* 29
as *s.* before the wind. *Ps* 83:13
as fire devoureth the *s.* so. *Isa* 5:24
chaff and bring forth *s.* 33:11
take them away as *s.* 40:24
he gave them as driven *s.* 41:2

---

they shall be as *s.* the fire. *Isa* 47:14
will I scatter them as *s. Jer* 13:24
flame, that devoureth the *s. Joel* 2:5
house of Esau shall be for *s. Ob* 18
devoured as *s.* fully dry. *Nah* 1:10
wickedly and proud be *s.* *Mal* 4:1
gold, wood, hay, *s.* *1 Cor* 3:12

stubborn
if a man have a *s.* *Deut* 21:18
say to elders, This our son is *s.* 20
not from their *s.* way. *Judg* 2:19
might not be as fathers, a *s. Ps* 78:8
she is loud and *s.;* her feet. *Pr* 7:11*

stubbornness
look not to *s.* of this. *Deut* 9:27
and *s.* is as iniquity. *1 Sam* 15:23

stuck
spear *s.* in the ground. *1 Sam* 26:7
I have *s.* unto thy. *Ps* 119:31
for part of the ship *s. Acts* 27:41*

studieth
heart of the righteous *s.* *Pr* 15:28
for their heart *s.* destruction. 24:2

studs
of gold with *s.* of silver. *S of S* 1:11

study
and much *s.* is a weariness of the.
    Eccl 12:12
that ye *s.* to be quiet. *1 Thes* 4:11
s. to shew thyself approved unto.
    2 Tim 2:15*

stuff
hast searched all my *s. Gen* 31:37
regard not your *s.;* the good of. 45:20
money or *s.* to keep. *Ex* 22:7
the *s.* they had was sufficient. 36:7
even among their own *s. Josh* 7:11
himself among the *s. 1 Sam* 10:22†
two hundred abode by the *s.* 25:13†
part be that tarrieth by *s.* 30:24†
prepare thee *s.* for removing and.
    Ezek 12:3
shalt thou bring forth thy *s.* 4, 7
and his *s.* in the house. *Luke* 17:31*

stumble
and thy foot not *s.* *Pr* 3:23; 4:12
know not at what they *s.* 4:19
none shall be weary, nor *s. Isa* 5:27
many among them shall *s.* 8:15
they err in vision, they *s.* 28:7
we grope, we *s.* at noon day. 59:10
that they should not *s.* 63:13
before your feet *s.* on dark mountains. *Jer* 13:16
they have caused them to *s.* 18:15
my persecutors shall *s.* 20:11
way wherein they shall not *s.* 31:9
they shall *s.* and fall toward. 46:6
and the most proud shall *s.* 50:32
he shall *s.* and fall. *Dan* 11:19
shall *s.* in their walk. *Nah* 2:5
multitude of slain, they *s.* upon. 3:3
caused many to *s.* at. *Mal* 2:8
offence to them that *s.* *1 Pet* 2:8

stumbled
and they that *s.* are girt. *1 Sam* 2:4
ark, for the oxen *s.* *1 Chr* 13:9
to eat up my flesh, they *s. Ps* 27:2
the mighty man hath *s. Jer* 46:12
for they *s.* at that stumblingstone.
    Rom 9:32
I say then, Have they *s.* that? 11:11

stumbleth
let not thy heart be glad when he *s.*
    Pr 24:17*
walk in the day, he *s.* not. *John* 11:9
walk in the night, he *s.* 10
any thing whereby thy brother *s.*
    Rom 14:21

stumbling
there is none occasion of *s.* in him.
    1 John 2:10

stumblingblock
a *s.* before the blind. *Lev* 19:14
take up the *s.* out of the way of my.
    Isa 57:14
and I lay a *s.* before him. *Ezek* 3:20
it is the *s.* of their iniquity. 7:19
put the *s.* of their iniquity. 14:3, 4, 7
table be made a trap, a *s. Rom* 11:9
that no man put a *s.* in his. 14:13

Christ crucified, to Jews a *s.*
    1 Cor 1:23
this liberty of yours become a *s.* 8:9
Balak to cast a *s.* before. *Rev* 2:14

stumblingblocks
behold, I will lay *s.* before. *Jer* 6:21
I will consume the *s.* *Zeph* 1:3

stumblingstone
shall be for a *stone* of *s.* *Isa* 8:14
stumbled at that *s.* *Rom* 9:32*
in Sion a *s.* and rock of offence. 33*
a *stone* of *s.* to them. *1 Pet* 2:8

stump
only the *s.* of Dagon. *1 Sam* 5:4
s. in the earth. *Dan* 4:15, 23, 26

subdue
God said, Replenish the earth and *s.*
  it. *Gen* 1:28
s. all thine enemies. *1 Chr* 17:10
he shall *s.* the people. *Ps* 47:3
have holden, to *s.* nations. *Isa* 45:1
another rise, and he shall *s.* three.
    Dan 7:24
turn again, he will *s.* *Mi* 7:19*
they shall devour and *s. Zech* 9:15*
able to *s.* all things. *Phil* 3:21

subdued
and the land be *s.* before. *Num* 32:22
land shall be *s.* before you. 29
bulwarks, until it be *s. Deut* 20:20*
and the land was *s.* *Josh* 18:1
so Moab was *s.* *Judg* 3:30
God *s.* Jabin. 4:23
thus Midian was *s.* 8:28
Ammon was *s.* 11:33
Philistines were *s.* *1 Sam* 7:13
  2 Sam 8:1; *1 Chr* 18:1; 20:4
all nations which he *s.* *2 Sam* 8:11
them that rose up against me hast
  thou *s.* under. 22:40; *Ps* 18:39
and the land is *s.* *1 Chr* 22:18
I should soon have *s.* *Ps* 81:14
things shall be *s.* unto. *1 Cor* 15:28*
who through faith *s.* *Heb* 11:33

subduedst
thou *s.* the inhabitants. *Neh* 9:24

subdueth
it is God that *s.* the people under me.
    Ps 18:47; 144:2
iron breaks and *s.* all. *Dan* 2:40

subject
and was *s.* to them. *Luke* 2:51
even the devils are *s.* to us. 10:17
that the spirits are *s.* to you. 20
is not *s.* to the law of. *Rom* 8:7
creature was made *s.* to vanity. 20
let every soul be *s.* to the. 13:1
wherefore ye must needs be *s.* 5
spirits of prophets are *s. 1 Cor* 14:32
Son also himself be *s.* to him. 15:28
church is *s.* to Christ. *Eph* 5:24
as though living in the world, are ye
  s.? *Col* 2:20
put them in mind to be *s.* *Tit* 3:1
lifetime *s.* to bondage. *Heb* 2:15
Elias was *s.* to like. *Jas* 5:17
servants, be *s.* to your. *1 Pet* 2:18
and powers being made *s.* 3:22
all of you be *s.* one to another. 5:5*

subjected
of him who hath *s.* the. *Rom* 8:20

subjection
were brought into *s.* *Ps* 106:42
brought them into *s. Jer* 34:11, 16
bring my body into *s.* *1 Cor* 9:27*
they glorify God for your professed *s.*
    2 Cor 9:13*
to whom we give place by *s. Gal* 2:5
learn in silence with all *s. 1 Tim* 2:11
having his children in *s.* with. 3:4
put in *s.* the world to come. *Heb* 2:5
put all things in *s.* under his feet. 8
rather be in *s.* to the Father of. 12:9
wives, be in *s.* to your. *1 Pet* 3:1, 5

submit
return, and *s.* thyself. *Gen* 16:9
strangers shall *s.* themselves to me.
    2 Sam 22:45; *Ps* 18:44
enemies shall *s.* themselves. *Ps* 66:3
till every one *s.* himself with. 68:30
that ye *s.* yourselves. *1 Cor* 16:16

wives, *s.* yourselves to your own
husbands. *Eph* 5:22; *Col* 3:18
s. yourselves: for they. *Heb* 13:17
s. yourselves therefore to God.
Jas 4:7
s. yourselves to every. *1 Pet* 2:13
ye younger, *s.* yourselves to. 5:5

submitted
the sons of David *s.* *1 Chr* 29:24
the Lord should have *s.* *Ps* 81:15
s. to the righteousness. *Rom* 10:3

submitting
s. yourselves one to another in fear.
Eph 5:21

suborned
then they *s.* men who said. *Acts* 6:11

subscribe
another shall with his hand *s. Isa* 44:5
men shall *s.* evidences. *Jer* 32:44

subscribed
I *s.* the evidence, and. *Jer* 32:10
the witnesses that *s.* the book. 12

substance
destroy every living *s.* *Gen* 7:4*
every living *s.* was destroyed. 23*
Abram took all the *s.* they. 12:5
their *s.* was great, so that they. 13:6
shall come out with great *s.* 15:14
cattle and their *s.* be ours ? 34:23
his cattle and all his *s.* 36:6*
how the earth swallowed them up,
and all the *s.* *Deut* 11:6*
bless, Lord, his *s.* and accept. 33:11
Levites cities for their *s. Josh* 14:4
were the rulers of the *s.* *1 Chr* 27:31
the stewards over all the *s.* of. 28:1
they carried away all *s.* *2 Chr* 21:17
the king's portion of his *s.* 31:3
God had given Hezekiah *s.* 32:29
bullocks, these were of king's *s.* 35:7
a right way for our *s.* *Ezra* 8:21
not come, all his *s.* should. 10:8
Job's *s.* also was seven. *Job* 1:3
his *s.* is increased in the land. 10
robber swalloweth up their *s.* 5:5
give a reward for me of your *s.*? 6:22
rich, nor shall his *s.* continue. 15:29
according to his *s.* shall the. 20:18
our *s.* is not cut down, but. 22:20*
me up and dissolvest my *s.* 30:22*
their *s.* to their babes. *Ps* 17:14
Joseph ruler over all his *s.* 105:21
my *s.* was not hid from thee. 139:15*
eyes did see my *s.* yet being. 16
we shall find all precious *s. Pr* 1:13
honour the Lord with thy *s.* and. 3:9
he shall give all the *s.* of his. 6:31
those that love me inherit *s.* 8:21
but he casteth away the *s.* 10:3*
but the *s.* of a diligent man is. 12:27
by usury increaseth his *s.* 28:8
with harlots, spendeth his *s.* 29:3
give all his *s.* for love. *S of S* 8:7
as an oak, whose *s.* is in them, so the
holy seed shall be *s.* *Isa* 6:13*
thy *s.* will I give to the spoil.
Jer 15:13; 17:3
I am become rich, I have found me
out *s.* *Hos* 12:8*
nor laid hands on their *s.* *Ob* 13
I will consecrate their *s.* *Mi* 4:13
to him of their *s.* *Luke* 8:3
wasted his *s.* with riotous. 15:13
knowing that ye have in heaven a
better and enduring *s. Heb* 10:34*
now faith is the *s.* of things. 11:1*

subtil
the serpent was more *s.* *Gen* 3:1*
was a very *s.* man. *2 Sam* 13:3*
an harlot, and *s.* of heart. *Pr* 7:10*

subtilly
that he dealeth very *s. 1 Sam* 23:22
to deal *s.* with his. *Ps* 105:25
the same dealt *s.* with. *Acts* 7:19

subtilty
thy brother came with *s. Gen* 27:35*
Jehu did it in *s.* that. *2 Ki* 10:19
to give *s.* to the simple. *Pr* 1:4
might take Jesus by *s.* *Mat* 26:4
said, O full of all *s.* *Acts* 13:10*
beguiled Eve through *s.* *2 Cor* 11:3

suburbs
but the field of the *s.* may. *Lev* 25:34
the *s.* of them shall be. *Num* 35:3
cities shall ye give with their *s.* 7
save cities with *s.* for their cattle.
Josh 14:4; 21:2
horses by chamber in *s. 2 Ki* 23:11*
Levites left their *s.* and came to
Judah. *2 Chr* 11:14
the *s.* shall shake at the. *Ezek* 27:28
round about for the *s.* thereof. 45:2
place for dwelling and for *s.* 48:15
the *s.* of the city shall be. 17
see **cities**

subvert
to *s.* a man in his cause. *Lam* 3:36
who *s.* whole houses. *Tit* 1:11*

subverted
such is *s.* and sinneth. *Tit* 3:11*

subverting
with words, *s.* souls. *Acts* 15:24
words to no profit, but to *s.* of.
2 Tim 2:14

succeed
the firstborn shall *s.* his. *Deut* 25:6

succeeded
but the children of Esau *s.* them.
Deut 2:12, 22
the Ammonites *s.* them, and. 21

succeedest
when thou *s.* them in their land.
Deut 12:29*; 19:1

success
then thou shalt have good *s.*
Josh 1:8

Succoth
to S. and made booths for his cattle,
therefore it is called S. *Gen* 33:17
from Rameses to S. *Ex* 12:37
they took their journey from S.
13:20; *Num* 33:5, 6
Gad had in the valley, S. *Josh* 13:27
the men of S. give bread. *Judg* 8:5
answered as the men of S. 8
he taught the men of S. 16
king cast them in the clay ground
between S. *1 Ki* 7:46; *2 Chr* 4:17
I will mete out the valley of S.
Ps 60:6; 108:7

Succoth-benoth
men of Babylon made S. *2 Ki* 17:30

succour
when the Syrians came to *s.* Hadadezer. *2 Sam* 8:5
it is better that thou *s.* us out. 18:3
he is able to *s.* them. *Heb* 2:18

succoured
Abishai *s.* him, and. *2 Sam* 21:17
of salvation have I *s.* *2 Cor* 6:2

succourer
she hath been a *s.* of. *Rom* 16:2

such
Jabal was the father of *s. Gen* 4:20
Jubal was the father of *s.* as. 21
savoury meat, *s.* as I love. 27:4, 9, 14
wife of daughters of Heth, *s.* as. 46
speckled and spotted, of *s.* 30:32
s. as I never saw in Egypt. 41:19
wot ye not that *s.* a man as? 44:15
s. hail as hath not. *Ex* 9:18, 24
no *s.* locusts as they, nor shall be *s.*
10:14
shall be a great cry, *s.* as there. 11:6
thou shalt provide able men, *s.* 18:21
s. as have not been done in all. 34:10
s. water cometh be unclean . . . be
drunk in every *s.* *Lev* 11:34
two pigeons *s.* as he is. 14:22, 30, 31
the soul that turneth after *s.* 20:6
soul that hath touched any *s.* 22:6
giveth of *s.* to the Lord, shall. 27:9
instead of *s.* as open. *Num* 8:16
hath been any *s.* thing. *Deut* 4:32
O that there were *s.* an heart. 5:29
shalt do no more any *s.* 13:11; 19:20
s. abomination is wrought. 14; 17:4
s. time as thou beginnest. 16:9
at least *s.* as before knew. 29:2
was no *s.* deed done or seen. 19:30
hath not been *s.* a thing. *1 Sam* 4:7

he is *s.* a son of Belial. *1 Sam* 25:17
look on *s.* a dead dog as I. *2 Sam* 9:8
with *s.* robes were the virgins. 13:18
hast thou thought *s.* a thing ? 14:13
s. as faint in wilderness. 16:2
recompense me with *s.?* 19:36
came no more *s.* abundance of
spices. *1 Ki* 10:10
no *s.* almug trees. 12; *2 Chr* 9:11
thou pass not *s.* a place. *2 Ki* 6:9
windows, might *s.* a thing be ? 7:19
bringing *s.* evil on Jerusalem. 21:12
surely there was not holden *s.* 23:22
s. as went forth to. *1 Chr* 12:33, 36
the Lord bestowed on him *s.* 29:25
s. as none of the kings. *2 Chr* 1:12
nor was any *s.* spice as the. 9:9
s. as set their hearts to seek. 11:16
people rejoiced, and *s.* taught. 23:13
gave it to *s.* as did the work. 24:12
done it of a long time in *s.* sort. 30:5
and at *s.* a time. *Ezra* 4:10, 11, 17
7:12
all *s.* as had separated. 6:21
all *s.* as know the laws of. 7:25
which hath put *s.* a thing in. 27
and of *s.* as lay in wait by. 8:31
and hast given *s.* deliverance. 9:13
put away the wives, and *s.* are. 10:3
I said, Should *s.* a man ? *Neh* 6:11
except *s.* to whom the king shall.
Esth 4:11
the kingdom for *s.* a time. 14
to lay hand on *s.* as sought. 9:2
and upon all *s.* as joined 27
and lettest *s.* words go. *Job* 15:13
surely *s.* are the dwellings. 18:21
to *s.* as keep his covenant. *Ps* 25:10
103:18
and *s.* as breathe out cruelty. 27:12
to slay *s.* as be of upright. 37:14
s. as be blessed of him shall. 22
respecteth not proud nor *s.* 40:4
let *s.* as love thy salvation. 16; 70:4
his hands against *s.* as be at. 55:20
God is good to *s.* as are of. 73:1
s. as sit in darkness, and. 107:10
as for *s.* as turn aside to. 125:5
s. knowledge is too. 139:6
people that is in *s.* a case. 144:15
but *s.* as are upright. *Pr* 11:20
but *s.* as keep the law contend. 28:4
in cause of *s.* as are appointed. 31:8
behold, the tears of *s.* as. *Eccl* 4:1
dimness shall not be *s.* as. *Isa* 9:1
s. as are escaped of the. 10:20
behold, *s.* is our expectation. 20:6
eat this year *s.* as groweth. 37:30
is it *s.* a fast that I have ? 58:5
s. a thing ? who hath seen *s.?* 66:8
see if there be *s.* a thing. *Jer* 2:10
my soul be avenged on *s.* a nation.
5:9, 29; 9:9
s. as are for death, to death, *s.* as are
for sword, *s.* as are for famine, *s.*
as are for captivity. 15:2; 43:11
I will deliver *s.* as are left in. 21:7
in speaking *s.* words unto them. 38:4
for none shall return, but *s.* as. 44:14
s. as had ability in them. *Dan* 1:4
had spoken *s.* words to me. 10:15
s. as do wickedly shall be. 11:32
shall be a time of trouble, *s.* 12:1
shall call *s.* as are skilful. *Amos* 5:16
in anger and fury, *s.* they. *Mi* 5:15
s. as are clothed with. *Zeph* 1:8
glorified God who had given *s.* power
to men. *Mat* 9:8
receive one *s.* little child in my name.
18:5; *Mark* 9:37
suffer little children to come unto me,
for of *s.* *Mat* 19:14; *Mark* 10:14
Luke 18:16
then shall be great tribulation, *s.* as.
Mat 24:21; *Mark* 13:19
in *s.* an hour as ye think. *Mat* 24:44
he said, Go into the city to *s.* a man.
26:18
sown among thorns, *s.* as. *Mark* 4:18
ground, are *s.* as hear the word. 20
with many *s.* parables spake he. 33
for the Father seeketh *s.* *John* 4:23
Moses commanded that *s.* 8:5
is a sinner do *s.* miracles ? 9:16

the Lord added daily *s.* as should be
  saved.   *Acts* 2:47
s. as I have give I thee, rise.   3:6
to whom we gave no *s.*   15:24
who having received *s.* a   16:24
will be no judge of *s.* matters. 18:15
that they observe no *s.* thing. 21:25
Away with *s.* a fellow from.   22:22
I doubted of *s.* manner of.   25:20
and altogether *s.* as I am.   26:29
that are *s.* serve not.   *Rom* 16:18
s. fornication as is not.   *1 Cor* 5:1
and *s.* were some of you, but.   6:11
is not under bondage in *s.* cases. 7:15
s. shall have trouble in the flesh. 28
no temptation, but *s.* as is.   10:13
we have no *s.* custom.   11:16
s. are they that are earthy, *s.* 15:48
that ye submit yourselves to *s.* 16:16
acknowledge ye them that are *s.*   18
sufficient to *s.* a man is.   *2 Cor* 2:6
s. trust we have through Christ. 3:4
seeing then that we have *s.* hope. 12
let *s.* an one think, *s.* as we are in
  word by letters, *s.* will we. 10:11
for *s.* are false apostles.   11:13
not find you *s.* as I would; and that I
  shall be found to you *s.* as. 12:20
meekness, against *s.*   *Gal* 5:23
spot or wrinkle, or any *s.* *Eph* 5:27
receive him, and hold *s.*   *Phil* 2:29
is the avenger of all *s.*   *1 Thes* 4:6
now them that are *s.*   *2 Thes* 3:12
corrupt men, from *s.*   *1 Tim* 6:5
traitors, heady, from *s.*   *2 Tim* 3:5
he that is *s.* is subverted.   *Tit* 3:11
ye are become *s.* as have. *Heb* 5:12
s. an high priest became us.   7:26
have *s.* an high priest, who is.   8:1
endured *s.* contradiction of.   12:3
for with *s.* sacrifices God is.   13:16
we will go into *s.* a city.   *Jas* 4:13
all *s.* rejoicing is evil.   16
came *s.* a voice to him.   *2 Pet* 1:17
we ought to receive *s.*   *3 John* 8
s. as are in the sea.   *Rev* 5:13
s. as was not since men were. 16:18
on *s.* the second death hath.   20:6

such *like*

and doeth not *s.* *like.*   *Ezek* 18:14
revellings and *s.* *like.*   *Gal* 5:21

such *a one*

find *s.* *a* one as this is.   *Gen* 41:38
ho, *s.* *a* one, turn aside.   *Ruth* 4:1
open thine eyes on *s.* *a one*? *Job* 14:3
I was *s.* *a* one as thyself.   *Ps* 50:21
hairy scalp of *s.* *a* one as.   68:21
to deliver *s.* *an one.*   *1 Cor* 5:5
if a drunkard, with *s.* *an one.*   11
s. *a* one be swallowed up. *2 Cor* 2:7
let *s.* *an one* think this, that. 10:11
s. *an one* caught up to the.   12:2
of *s.* *an one* will I glory, yet.   5
restore *s.* *an one* in the.   *Gal* 6:1
I beseech thee, being *s.* *an one* as
  Paul.   *Philem* 9

such *and* such

appointed my servants to *s.* *and s.*
  place.   *1 Sam* 21:2
given *s.* *and s.* things.   *2 Sam* 12:8
in *s.* *and s.* a place shall.   *2 Ki* 6:8

such *things*

they lent *s.* *things* as.   *Ex* 12:36
s. *things* have befallen.   *Lev* 10:19
they that do *s.* *things.*   *Deut* 25:16
nor have told us *s.* *things* as these.
            Judg 13:23
Why do ye *s.* *things* ? *1 Sam* 2:23
shall eat *s.* *things* as.   *2 Ki* 19:29
the captain took *s.* *things* as. 25:15
there are no *s.* *things* done as thou.
            Neh 6:8
with *s.* *things* as belonged. *Esth* 2:9
yea, who knoweth not *s.* *things* as ?
            Job 12:3
I have heard many *s.* *things.*   16:2
and many *s.* *things* are with. 23:14
who hath heard *s.* *things.* *Jer* 18:13
shall he escape that doth *s.* *things* ?
            Ezek 17:15
no king asked *s.* *things.* *Dan* 2:10
many other *s.* *like things* ye do.
            Mark 7:8, 13

troubled, *s.* *things* must. *Mark* 13:7
of whom I hear *s.* things ? *Luke* 9:9
remain, eating *s.* *things* as. 10:7, 8
but give alms of *s.* *things.*   11:41
because they suffered *s.* *things.* 13:2
the people murmured *s.* *things.*
            John 7:32
no accusation of *s.* *things.* *Acts* 25:18
they laded us with *s.* *things* as. 28:10
who commit *s.* *things* are. *Rom* 1:32
them who commit *s.* *things.*   2:2
judgest them which do *s.* *things.*   3
that do *s.* *things* shall not inherit.
            Gal 5:21
they that say *s.* *things.* *Heb* 11:14
be content with *s.* *things* as.   13:5
that ye look for *s.* *things.* *2 Pet* 3:14

suck

made him to *s.* honey. *Deut* 32:13
shall *s.* of the abundance of.   33:19
breast that I should *s.*?   *Job* 3:12
he shall *s.* the poison of asps. 20:16
young ones also *s.* up blood.   39:30
shalt *s.* the milk of the Gentiles, and
  shalt *s.* the breast of.   *Isa* 60:16
that ye may *s.* and be satisfied. 66:11
then shall ye *s.*, ye shall be borne. 12
drink it and *s.* it out.   *Ezek* 23:34*
and those that *s.* breasts. *Joel* 2:16

suck, *give*

that Sarah should have given children *s.*   *Gen* 21:7
Hannah abode and gave her son *s.*
            1 Sam 1:23
to give my child *s.*   *1 Ki* 3:21
the sea monsters give *s.* *Lam* 4:3
and to them that give *s.* *Mat* 24:19
      Mark 13:17; *Luke* 21:23
paps that never gave *s.* *Luke* 23:29

sucked

that *s.* the breasts of.   *S of S* 8:1
paps that thou hast *s.* *Luke* 11:27

sucking

nursing father beareth the *s.* child.
            Num 11:12
Samuel took a *s.* lamb. *1 Sam* 7:9
s. child shall play on the. *Isa* 11:8
woman forget her *s.* child ?   49:15
tongue of the *s.* child.   *Lam* 4:4

suckling

the *s.* also with the man. *Deut* 32:25
slay both man and woman, infant and
  s.   *1 Sam* 15:3
off from you child and *s.* *Jer* 44:7

sucklings

children and *s.* of Nob. *1 Sam* 22:19
out of the mouth of babes and *s.*
        Ps 8:2; *Mat* 21:16
s. swoon in the streets. *Lam* 2:11

sudden

s. fear troubleth thee.   *Job* 22:10
be not afraid of *s.* fear.   *Pr* 3:25
s. destruction cometh.   *1 Thes* 5:3

suddenly

man die very *s.* by him.   *Num* 6:9
the Lord spake *s.* unto Moses. 12:4
but if he thrust him *s.* without. 35:22
Lord will destroy you *s.* *Deut* 7:4*
Joshua came unto them *s.*
         Josh 10:9; 11:7
lest he overtake us *s.* *2 Sam* 15:14*
the thing was done *s.* *2 Chr* 29:36
taking root, but *s.* I cursed. *Job* 5:3
scourge slay *s.* he will laugh.   9:23
return and be ashamed *s.* *Ps* 6:10
s. do they shoot at him and.   64:4
with an arrow *s.* shall they be.   7
therefore his calamity shall come *s.*;
  he shall be broken *s.* *Pr* 6:15
calamity shall rise *s.*   24:22
shall *s.* be destroyed, and.   29:1
it falleth *s.* upon them. *Eccl* 9:12
it shall be at an instant *s.* *Isa* 29:5
whose breaking cometh *s.*   30:13
shall come upon these *s.*   47:11
I did them *s.* and they came. 48:3
s. are my tents spoiled. *Jer* 4:20
spoiler shall *s.* come upon us.   6:26
caused him to fall upon it *s.* 15:8
bring a troop *s.* on them.   18:22
s. make him run away. 49:19; 50:44

Babylon is *s.* fallen and.   *Jer* 51:8
shall they not rise up *s.*   *Hab* 2:7
the Lord shall *s.* come.   *Mal* 3:1
s. saw no man any more. *Mark* 9:8
lest coming *s.* he find you.   13:36
s. there was with angel. *Luke* 2:13
a spirit taketh him, and he *s.*   9:39
and *s.* there came a sound. *Acts* 2:2
s. there shined a light.   9:3; 22:6
and *s.* there was a great.   16:26
should have fallen down dead *s.* 28:6
lay hands *s.* on no man. *1 Tim* 5:22*

sue

if any man will *s.* thee.   *Mat* 5:40*

suffer

This word frequently means [1]
bear, Pr 19:19; [2] bear with, Mat
17:17; [3] permit, 1 Tim 2:12.

s. the destroyer to come.   *Ex* 12:23
thou shalt not *s.* a witch to.   22:18
nor shalt *s.* salt of the covenant to.
            Lev 2:13
shalt rebuke him, and not *s.* 19:17
or *s.* them to bear the iniquity. 22:16*
not *s.* Israel to pass.   *Num* 21:23
s. them not to enter.   *Josh* 10:19
not *s.* them to come down to the valley.   *Judg* 1:34
would not *s.* him to go in.   15:1
Samson said, *S.* me that I.   16:26
not *s.* the revengers of blood any.
          2 Sam 14:11*
that he might not *s.*   *1 Ki* 15:17
king's profit to *s.* them.   *Esth* 3:8
he will not *s.* me to take.   *Job* 9:18
s. me that I may speak, after. 21:3
winepresses, and *s.* thirst.   24:11
s. me a little, and I will shew. 32:2
trouble which I *s.* of them. *Ps* 9:13
neither *s.* thine Holy One to see corruption. 16:10; *Acts* 2:27; 13:35
young lions do lack and *s.* *Ps* 34:10
he will never *s.* the righteous. 55:22
while I *s.* thy terrors, I am.   88:15
nor *s.* my faithfulness to.   89:33
a proud heart will not I *s.*   101:5
he will not *s.* thy foot to be.   121:3
s. the soul of righteous to. *Pr* 10:3
an idle soul shall *s.* hunger.   19:15
man of wrath shall *s.* punishment. 19*
s. not thy mouth to cause. *Eccl* 5:6
rich not *s.* him to sleep.   12
nor *s.* their locks to.   *Ezek* 44:20
S. it to be so now.   *Mat* 3:15
s. me first to bury my father.   8:21
          Luke 9:59
s. us to go away into the swine.
       Mat 8:31; *Luke* 8:32
that he must *s.* many things of the
  elders.   *Mat* 16:21; 17:12
  Mark 8:31; 9:12; *Luke* 9:22; 17:25
how long shall I *s.* you ? *Mat* 17:17*
      Mark 9:19*; *Luke* 9:41*
s. little children to come. *Mat* 19:14
     Mark 10:14; *Luke* 18:16
neither *s.* ye them that. *Mat* 23:13
ye *s.* him no more to do. *Mark* 7:12
Jesus would not *s.* any man to. 11:16
desired to eat this passover before I
  s.   *Luke* 22:15
s. ye thus far, and he touched his. 51
it behoved Christ to *s.*   24:46
       Acts 3:18; 26:23
that Christ should *s.*   *Acts* 3:18
counted worthy to *s.* shame.   5:41
seeing one of them *s.* wrong.   7:26
how great things he must *s.* for. 9:16
beseech thee, *s.* me to speak. 21:39*
if so be that we *s.* with. *Rom* 8:17
if any man's work be burnt, he shall
  s. loss.   *1 Cor* 3:15
bless; being persecuted, we *s.* 4:12*
why not rather *s.* yourselves ?   6:7
not used this power but *s.*   9:12*
will not *s.* you to be tempted. 10:13
one member *s.* all members *s.* 12:26
sufferings which we also *s.* *2 Cor* 1:6
for ye *s.* fools gladly, seeing. 11:19*
for ye *s.* if a man bring you.   20*
if I preach, why do I yet *s.*? *Gal* 5:11*
lest they should *s.* persecution. 6:12
to believe and to *s.* for.   *Phil* 1:29
to abound and to *s.* need.   4:12*

suffered

before, that we should s. 1 Thes 3:4
God for which ye also s. 2 Thes 1:5
I s. not a woman to teach nor to.
               1 Tim 2:12*
we both labour and s.   4:10*
I also s. these things.   2 Tim 1:12
wherein I s. trouble as an evil.   2:9
if we s. we shall also reign.   12*
all that live godly shall s.   3:12
rather to s. affliction.   Heb 11:25*
remember them which s.   13:3*
s. the word of exhortation.   22*
ye do well, and s. for it. 1 Pet 2:20
but if ye s. for righteousness.   3:14
it is better that ye s. for well.   17
none of you s. as a murderer.   4:15
yet if any man s. as a Christian.   16
let them that s. according to the.   19
those things thou shalt s.   Rev 2:10
not s. dead bodies to be put.   11:9

suffered

s. I thee not to touch her.   Gen 20:6
God s. him not to hurt me.   31:7
and hast not s. me to kiss my.   28
and s. thee to hunger.   Deut 8:3
God hath not s. thee so to do. 18:14
s. not a man to pass over. Judg 3:28
David s. them not to rise. 1 Sam 24:7
and s. not the birds.   2 Sam 21:10
he s. no man to do them wrong.
    1 Chr 16:21; Ps 105:14
neither have I s. my.   Job 31:30
for thy sake I s. rebuke.   Jer 15:15
it to be so; then he s. him. Mat 3:15
Moses s. you to put away your. 19:8
nor s. his house to be broken. 24:43
             Luke 12:39
I have s. many things.   Mat 27:19
he s. not the devils to speak.
      Mark 1:34; Luke 4:41
howbeit, Jesus s. him not. Mark 5:19
s. many things of many.   26
and he s. no man to follow him.   37
Moses to write a bill of.   10:4
he s. them to enter.   Luke 8:32*
he s. no man to go in, save.   51
were sinners, because they s.   13:2
Christ have s. these things ?   24:26
about forty years s. he.   Acts 13:18†
who s. all nations to walk in.   14:16
but the Spirit s. them not.   16:7
Christ must needs have s.   17:3
disciples s. him not to enter.   19:30
Paul was s. to dwell by.   28:16
his cause that s. wrong.   2 Cor 7:12
thrice I s. shipwreck.   11:25
s. so many things in vain ?   Gal 3:4
for whom I have s. the loss. Phil 3:8
that we had s. before.   1 Thes 2:2
ye have s. like things of your.   14
himself hath s. being tempted.
               Heb 2:18
obedience by things which he s. 5:8
they were not s. to continue.   7:23*
for then must he often have s.   9:26
Jesus also s. without the gate. 13:12
Christ s. for us, leaving. 1 Pet 2:21
when he s. he threatened not.   23
for Christ hath once s. for sins. 3:18
as Christ hath s. for us in the flesh:
he that hath s. in the flesh.   4:1
after ye have s. a while.   5:10

sufferest

s. that woman Jezebel.   Rev 2:20

suffereth

bless God who s. not our.   Ps 66:9
and s. not their cattle to.   107:38
of heaven s. violence.   Mat 11:12
yet vengeance s. him.   Acts 28:4
charity s. long and is kind, envieth
not.   1 Cor 13:4

suffering

wind not s. us, we sailed. Acts 27:7
s. of death, crowned.   Heb 2:9
for an example of s. affliction, and of
patience.   Jas 5:10
if a man endure grief, s. 1 Pet 2:19
an example, s. the vengeance, Jude 7

sufferings

I reckon that the s. of.   Rom 8:18
for as the s. of Christ.   2 Cor 1:5
enduring the same s. which we.   6

ye are partakers of the s. 2 Cor 1:7
the fellowship of his s.   Phil 3:10
who now rejoice in my s.   Col 1:24
make the captain of their salvation
perfect through s.   Heb 2:10
the s. of Christ, and the. 1 Pet 1:11
ye are partakers of Christ's s.   4:13
am a witness of the s. of Christ. 5:1

suffice

to s. them? or shall fish of the sea be
gathered together to s.? Num 11:22
let it s. thee; speak no. Deut 3:26
if dust of Samaria shall s. for.
               1 Ki 20:10
let it s. you of all. Ezek 44:6; 45:9
may s. to have wrought.   1 Pet 4:3

sufficed

yet so they s. them not. Judg 21:14
she did eat, and was s.   Ruth 2:14
she had reserved, after she was s. 18

sufficeth

us the Father and it s. us. John 14:8

sufficiency

in fulness of his s. he shall. Job 20:22
sufficient, but our s. is of. 2 Cor 3:5
s. in all things ye may abound.   9:8

sufficient

had was s. for work.   Ex 36:7
thou shalt lend him s.   Deut 15:8
let his hand be s. for him, thou. 33:7
honey as is s. for thee.   Pr 25:16
Lebanon is not s. to burn, nor the
beasts thereof s. for.   Isa 40:16
s. unto the day is the evil. Mat 6:34
whether he have s. to.   Luke 14:28
200 penny-worth of bread is not s.
               John 6:7
s. to such a man is this.   2 Cor 2:6
who is s. for these things ?   2:16
not that we are s. of ourselves.   3:5
he said to me, My grace is s.   12:9

sufficiently

sanctified themselves s. 2 Chr 30:3
before the Lord to eat s. Isa 23:18

suit

give thee a s. of apparel. Judg 17:10
man who hath any s.   2 Sam 15:4
yea, many shall make s.   Job 11:19

suits

changeable s. of apparel. Isa 3:22*

sum

there be laid on him a s. Ex 21:30*
takest the s. of the children of. 30:12
this is the s. of the tabernacle. 38:21
take the s. of all the. Num 1:2; 26:2
not take the s. of the Levites.   49
s. of the sons of Kohath.   4:2
the s. of the sons of Gershon.   22
s. of people from twenty years. 26:4
take the s. of the prey that.   31:26
have taken the s. of the men.   49
Joab gave up the s. unto the king.
       2 Sam 24:9; 1 Chr 21:5
may s. the silver brought. 2 Ki 22:4
the s. of money that.   Esth 4:7*
how great is the s. of!   Ps 139:17
thou sealest up the s. full of wisdom.
              Ezek 28:12
Daniel told the s. of the.   Dan 7:1
Abraham bought for a s. Acts 7:16*
with a great s. obtained I.   22:28
we have spoken this is the s. Heb 8:1

summer

s. and winter, day and.   Gen 8:22
turned into drought of s.   Ps 32:4
hast made s. and winter.   74:17
her meat in s.   Pr 6:8; 30:25
he that gathereth in s. is a.   10:5
as snow in s. and as rain in.   26:1
the fowls shall s. upon.   Isa 18:6
hasty fruit before the s.   28:4
the harvest is past, the s.   Jer 8:20
as the chaff of the s.   Dan 2:35
in s. and in winter shall.   Zech 14:8
leaves, ye know that s. is. Mat 24:32
        Mark 13:28; Luke 21:30

summer chamber

surely he covereth his feet in his s.
chamber.   Judg 3:24†

summer fruit

bread and s. fruit for.   2 Sam 16:2
a basket of s. fruit.   Amos 8:1, 2

summer fruits

Ziba brought 100 bunches of s. fruits.
               2 Sam 16:1
shouting for thy s. fruits.   Isa 16:9
wine and s. fruits.   Jer 40:10, 12
fallen on s. fruits and vintage. 48:32
have gathered s. fruits.   Mi 7:1

summer house

I will smite winter house with s.
house.   Amos 3:15

summer parlour

sitting in a s. parlour.   Judg 3:20†

sumptuously

fared s. every day.   Luke 16:19

sun

(*The sun has been the object of
worship and adoration to the
greatest part of the people of the
East. It is thought to be the sun
that the Phenicians worshipped
under the name of Baal, the
Moabites under the name of
Chemosh, the Ammonites by that
of Moloch, and the Israelites by
the name of Baal and by the king
of the host of heaven. They did
not separate his worship from that
of the moon, whom they called
Astarte, and the queen of heaven*)
when the s. went down. Gen 15:17
the s. was risen when Lot.   19:23
all night, because the s. was. 28:11
passed over Penuel, s. rose. 32:31
the s. moon, and stars made.   37:9
and when the s. waxed.   Ex 16:21
if s. be risen, blood shall be.   22:3
and when the s. is down, he shall.
        Lev 22:7; Deut 23:11
before the Lord against the s.
               Num 25:4
seest the s. and moon.   Deut 4:19
worshipped either the s. or.   17:3
shall the s. go down upon it.   24:15
fruits brought forth by s.   33:14
the going down of the s.   Josh 1:4
as soon as the s. was down.   8:29
S. stand thou still upon.   10:12
and the s. stood still, and the.   13
as the s. when he goeth.   Judg 5:31
Gideon returned before the s. 8:13*
as soon as the s. is up, thou.   9:33
they said to him before the s. 14:18
s. went down when they were. 19:14
by time the s. be hot.   1 Sam 11:9
the s. went down, they.   2 Sam 2:24
if taste bread or aught till the s. 3:35
thy wives in sight of this s.   12:11
this thing before Israel and the s. 12
morning when the s. riseth.   23:4
they rose, and s. shone.   2 Ki 3:22
also that burn incense to s.   23:5
burnt the chariot of the s. with fire. 11
opened till the s. be hot.   Neh 7:3
is green before the s.   Job 8:16
which commandeth the s.   9:7
I went mourning without the s. 30:28
if I beheld s. when it shined.   31:26
he set a tabernacle for s.   Ps 19:4
they may not see the s.   58:8
shall fear thee as long as s.   72:5
be continued as long as the s.   17
prepared the light and the s.   74:16
for the Lord God is a s.   84:11
throne shall endure as the s.   89:36
the s. ariseth, they gather. 104:22
s. shall not smite thee by day. 121:6
made the s. to rule by day.   136:8
praise ye him, s. and moon.   148:3
s. also ariseth, and the s.   Eccl 1:5
he hath not seen the s. nor.   6:5
profit from that see the s.   7:11
for the eyes to behold the s.   11:7
while the s. or the stars be.   12:2
s. hath looked upon me.   S of S 1:6
fair as moon, clear as the s.   6:10
the s. shall be ashamed.   Isa 24:23
moon shall be as the light of the s.
and the light of the s.   30:26
gone down in s. dial, so the s.   38:8

nor shall the heat, nor s. *Isa* 49:10
s. shall be no more thy light. 60:19
s. shall no more go down, nor. 20
spread them before the s. *Jer* 8:2
her s. is gone down while it. 15:9
which giveth the s. for a light. 31:35
they worshipped the s. *Ezek* 8:16
cover the s. with a cloud. 32:7
s. and the moon shall be darkened.
    Joel 2:10; 3:15; *Mat* 24:29
    Mark 13:24; *Luke* 23:45
s. shall be turned into. *Joel* 2:31
I will cause the s. to go. *Amos* 8:9
s. did arise, and the s. beat on the
  head of Jonah. *Jonah* 4:8
the s. shall go down. *Mi* 3:6
but when the s. ariseth. *Nah* 3:17
s. and moon stood still. *Hab* 3:11
s. of righteousness arise. *Mal* 4:2
he maketh his s. to rise. *Mat* 5:45
when s. was up they were scorched.
    13:6; *Mark* 4:6
righteous shine as the s. *Mat* 13:43
his face did shine as the s. 17:2
    Rev 1:16; 10:1
when the s. did set they. *Mark* 1:32
when the s. was setting. *Luke* 4:40
shall be signs in the s. and. 21:25
the s. into darkness. *Acts* 2:20
blind, not seeing the s. for. 13:11
above the brightness of the s. 26:13
neither s. nor stars appeared. 27:20
is one glory of the s. *1 Cor* 15:41
let not the s. go down. *Eph* 4:26
s. is no sooner risen. *Jas* 1:11
the s. became black as. *Rev* 6:12
nor shall the s. light on them. 7:16
third part of the s. was. 8:12
s. and the air were darkened. 9:2
a woman clothed with the s. 12:1
poured out his vial on the s. 16:8
angel standing in the s.; and he. 19:17
had no need of the s. 21:23; 22:5

see **goeth, going, rising**

under the **sun**
labour which he taketh *under the s.*?
Eccl 1:3; 2:18, 19, 20, 22; 5:18; 9:9
no new thing *under the s.* 1:9
all the works done *under s.*; all is
  vanity. 14; 2:17; 4:3; 8:17; 9:3
was no profit *under the s.* 2:11
I saw *under the s.* the place. 3:16
that are done *under the s.* 4:1
and I saw vanity *under the s.* 7
a sore evil I have seen *under the s.*
    5:13; 6:1; 10:5
shall be after him *under the s.* 6:12
heart to every work *under the s.* 8:9
hath no better thing *under the s.* 15
in any thing *under the s.* 9:6
he hath given thee *under the s.* 9
I saw *under the s.* that race. 11
wisdom have I seen also *under s.* 13

sunder
cutteth the spear in s. *Ps* 46:9
he brake their bands in s. 107:14
cut the bars of iron in s. 16
stones that are beaten in s. *Isa* 27:9
I will cut in s. the bars of iron. 45:2
I will burst thy bonds in s. *Nah* 1:13
come and cut him in s. *Luke* 12:46

sundered
scales stick together, they cannot be
  s. *Job* 41:17

sundry
God who at s. times. *Heb* 1:1*

sung
they s. together by course. *Ezra* 3:11
day shall this song be s. *Isa* 26:1
when they had s. an hymn, they went.
  Mat 26:30; *Mark* 14:26
they s. a new song, saying. *Rev* 5:9
they s. as it were a new song. 14:3

sunk
that the stone s. into. *1 Sam* 17:49
and Jehoram s. down. *2 Ki* 9:24
heathen are s. down in. *Ps* 9:15
no water, but mire: so Jeremiah s.
    Jer 38:6
thy feet are s. in the mire, they. 2
her gates are s. into the. *Lam* 2:9
Eutychus s. down with. *Acts* 20:9*

sup
their faces shall s. up. *Hab* 1:9*
ready wherewith I may s. *Luke* 17:8
I will s. with him, and he. *Rev* 3:20

superfluity
lay apart all filthiness, s. *Jas* 1:21*

superfluous
man hath any thing s. *Lev* 21:18
lamb that hath any thing s. 22:23
the ministering, it is s. *2 Cor* 9:1

superscription
(*It was a custom among the
Romans to write on a board the
crime for which any man suffered
death and to carry the board before
him to execution*)
is this image and s.? *Mat* 22:20
    Mark 12:16; *Luke* 20:24
the s. of his accusation. *Mark* 15:26
    Luke 23:38

superstition
questions against him of their own s.
    Acts 25:19*

superstitious
in all things ye are too s. *Acts* 17:22*

supped
cup, when he had s. *1 Cor* 11:25

supper
made a s. to his lords. *Mark* 6:21
makest a dinner or s. *Luke* 14:12
a certain man made a great s. 16
and sent his servant at s. time. 17
none bidden shall taste of my s. 24
likewise also the cup after s. 22:20
there they made Jesus a s.; Martha
  served. *John* 12:2
and s. being ended. 13:2
Jesus riseth from s. 4
leaned on his breast at s. 21:20
not to eat the Lord's s. *1 Cor* 11:20
taketh before other his own s. 21
called to the marriage s. *Rev* 19:9
come to the s. of the great God. 17

supplant
brother will utterly s. *Jer* 9:4

supplanted
for he hath s. me these. *Gen* 27:36

supple
washed in water to s. *Ezek* 16:4*

suppliants
my s. shall bring mine. *Zeph* 3:10

supplication
and I have not made s. *1 Sam* 13:12*
have respect to his s. *1 Ki* 8:28
    2 Chr 6:19
hearken thou to the s. *1 Ki* 8:30
    45:49; *2 Chr* 6:35
and make s. to thee. *1 Ki* 8:33, 47
    2 Chr 6:24
eyes may be open to s. *1 Ki* 8:52
praying all this prayer and s. 54
wherewith I have made s. 59
I have heard thy s. that thou. 9:3
what s. shall be made. *2 Chr* 6:29
heard Manasseh's s. then. 33:13
and should make s. to. *Esth* 4:8
make thy s. to the Almighty. *Job* 8:5
make my s. to my judge. 9:15
heard my s.: receive my. *Ps* 6:9
Lord I made my s. 30:8; 142:1
hide not thyself from my s. 55:1
let my s. come before thee. 119:170
they shall make s. to thee. *Isa* 45:14
will present their s. to Lord. *Jer* 36:7
O king, let my s. be accepted. 37:20
I presented my s. before the. 38:26
let our s. be accepted before. 42:2
me to present your s. before. 9
and Daniel making s. *Dan* 6:11
while I was presenting my s. 9:20
he wept and made s. unto. *Hos* 12:4
accord in prayer and s. *Acts* 1:14*
with all prayer and s. in spirit for.
    Eph 6:18
by prayer and s. let *Phil* 4:6

supplications
hearken to s. of thy. *2 Chr* 6:21
their prayer and their s. 39
leviathan make many s.? *Job* 41:3

hear voice of my s. when I cry.
    Ps 28:2; 140:6
because he hath heard the voice of
  my s. 28:6; 31:22; 116:1
attend to the voice of my s. 86:6
be attentive to my s. 130:2; 143:1
weeping and s. of Israel. *Jer* 3:21
come with weeping and with s. 31:9
to seek by prayer and s. *Dan* 9:3
prayer of thy servant and his s. 17
we do not present our s. for. 18
at the beginning of thy s. the. 23
the Spirit of grace and s. *Zech* 12:10
the first of all s. be made. *1 Tim* 2:1
she continueth in s. and prayers. 5:5
offered up prayers and s. *Heb* 5:7

supplied
your part, they have s. *1 Cor* 16:17
what was lacking to me, the brethren
  s. *2 Cor* 11:9

supplieth
not only s. the want of. *2 Cor* 9:12*
that which every joint s. *Eph* 4:16

supply, substantive
a s. for their want, that their abundance be a s. for your. *2 Cor* 8:14
through prayer and the s. *Phil* 1:19

supply, verb
his life to s. lack of service. *Phil* 2:30
but my God shall s. all your. 4:19

support
ye ought to s. the weak. *Acts* 20:35*
    1 Thes 5:14

suppose
let not my lord s. that. *2 Sam* 13:32
I s. that he to whom. *Luke* 7:43
s. ye that I am come to give? 12:51
s. ye that these Galileans? 13:2
I s. the world could not. *John* 21:25
not drunken, as ye s. *Acts* 2:15
I s. that this is good. *1 Cor* 7:26
I s. I was not behind. *2 Cor* 11:5
sorer punishment s. ye? *Heb* 10:29
a faithful brother, as I s. *1 Pet* 5:12

supposed
they s. they should have. *Mat* 20:10
s. it had been a spirit. *Mark* 6:49
Jesus being, as was s. *Luke* 3:23
terrified and s. that they. 24:37
for he s. his brethren. *Acts* 7:25
whom they s. that Paul had. 21:29
acusation of such things as I s. 25:18
I s. it necessary to send. *Phil* 2:25

supposing
they s. him to have been. *Luke* 2:44
she s. him to be the gardener, saith.
    John 20:15
who drew Paul out, s. *Acts* 14:19
jailor s. that the prisoners. 16:27
s. that they had obtained. 27:13
s. to add affliction to my. *Phil* 1:16
men of corrupt minds, s. *1 Tim* 6:5

supreme
it be to the king as s. *1 Pet* 2:13

sure
cave, were made s. *Gen* 23:17, 20
I am s. the king will. *Ex* 3:19
and be s. your sin. *Num* 32:23
only be s. that thou eat. *Deut* 12:23
build him a s. house. *1 Sam* 2:35
s. that evil is determined by. 20
will make my Lord a s. house. 25:28
because I was s. that. *2 Sam* 1:10
ordered in all things and s. 23:5
build thee a s. house. *1 Ki* 11:38
we make a s. covenant. *Neh* 9:38
no man is s. of life. *Job* 24:22
testimony of the Lord is s. *Ps* 19:7
thy testimonies are very s. 93:5
all his commandments are s. 111:7
and make s. thy friend. *Pr* 6:3
that hateth suretiship, is s. 11:15
righteousness shall be s. reward. 18
as a nail in a s. place. *Isa* 22:23, 25
I lay in Zion for a s. 28:16
my people shall dwell in s. 32:18
given him; waters shall be s. 33:16
even the s. mercies of David. 55:3
    Acts 13:34
interpretation thereof is s. *Dan* 2:45
thy kingdom shall be s. unto. 4:26

sepulchre be made s. *Mat* 27:64, 66
your way, make it as s. as you.　65
be s. of this, that the kingdom of God
　is come nigh.　*Luke* 10:11
believe and are s. that.　*John* 6:69
we are s. that thou knowest.　16:30
s. that the judgement of.　*Rom* 2:2
to end the promise might be s. 4:16
I am s. that when I come.　15:29
of God standeth s.　*2 Tim* 2:19
hope we have as anchor s. *Heb* 6:19
to make your calling s.　*2 Pet* 1:10
we have also a more s. word.　19

surely

eatest thereof, thou shalt s. die.
　Gen 2:17
the woman, Ye shall not s. die.　3:4
and s. your blood of your lives. 9:5
Abraham shall s. become a.　18:18
her not, thou shalt s. die.　20:7
s. the fear of God is not in.　11
Jacob said, S. Lord is in this. 28:16
I will s. give the tenth unto.　22
Laban said, S. thou art my.　29:14
s. the Lord hath looked upon.
come in unto me, for s. I.　30:16
s. thou hadst sent me away.　31:42
and thou saidst, I will s. do.　32:12
s. ye are spies.　42:16
s. now we had returned this.　43:10
s. he is torn in pieces.　44:28
and I will also s. bring thee.　46:4
I die, God will s. visit you.　50:24
　25; *Ex* 13:19
S. this thing is known.　*Ex* 2:14
I have s. seen the affliction. 3:7, 16
she said, S. a bloody husband. 4:25
he shall s. thrust you out hence. 11:1
thou wilt s. wear away, thou.　18:18
but he shall s. be stoned.　19:13
he shall be s. punished.　21:20, 22
then the ox shall be s. stoned.　28
he shall s. pay ox for ox, dead.　36
he that kindleth fire shall s.　22:6
if it be hurt or die, he shall s.　14
if lie with her, he shall s. endow. 16
to me, I will s. hear their cry.　23
thou shalt s. bring it back to.　23:4
if thou see, thou shalt s. help.　5
if thou serve their gods, it will s. be
　a snare.　33; *1 Ki* 11:2
anointing shall s. be an.　*Ex* 40:15
s. it floweth with milk.　*Num* 13:27
s. they shall not see the land. 14:23
I will s. do it to all this evil.　35
of man shalt thou s. redeem.　18:15
s. now I had slain thee, and.　22:33
s. there is no enchantment.　23:23
had said, They shall s. die.　26:65
s. give them a possession of.　27:7
s. none from twenty years old and.
　32:11; *Deut* 1:35
s. this great nation is.　*Deut* 4:6
testify this day that ye shall s. perish.
　8:19; 30:18
shalt s. kill the idolater.　13:9
shalt s. smite the inhabitants.　15
shalt s. lend him sufficient.　15:8
shalt s. give thy poor brother.　10
shalt s. rejoice in the feast.　16:15
shalt s. help him to lift them.　22:4
the Lord will s. require thy.　23:21
and I will s. hide my face.　31:18
s. the land shall be thine. *Josh* 14:9
they said, S. he covereth. *Judg* 3:24
and Deborah said, I will s. go.　4:9
the Lord said to Gideon, S. I.　6:16
forth to meet me, shall s. be.　11:31
we will bind, but s. we will.　15:13
s. they are smitten down.　20:39
he saith cometh s. to.　*1 Sam* 9:6
Agag said, S. the bitterness.　15:32
they said, S. to defy Israel.　17:25
for Saul thought, s. he is.　20:26
I knew it that Doeg would s. 22:22
I know well that thou shalt s. 24:20
s. in vain have I kept all.　25:21
s. there had not been left to.　34
s. thou shalt know what thy.　28:2
s. as the Lord liveth, thou.　29:6
pursue, for thou shalt s.　30:8
s. the people had gone up. *2 Sam* 2:27
I will s. shew thee kindness for. 9:7

he said, S. the men prevailed.
　2 Sam 11:23
s. where the king shall be.　15:21
I will s. go forth with you.　18:2
she spake, They shall s. ask.　20:18
nay, but I will s. buy it of.　24:24
I have s. built thee house. *1 Ki* 8:13
I will s. rend the kingdom.　11:11
against the altar shall s.　13:32
I will s. shew myself unto.　18:15
s. we shall be stronger.　20:23, 25
they said, S. it is the king of. 22:32
s. were it not I regard.　*2 Ki* 3:14
is blood, the kings are s. slain.　23
I thought, he will s. come out.　5:11
told me that thou shouldest s.　8:14
s. I have seen yesterday the.　9:26
the Lord will s. deliver us.　18:30
　Isa 36:15
s. there was not holden.　*2 Ki* 23:22
s. at command of the Lord.　24:3
not prevail, but shalt s.　*Esth* 6:13
s. now he would awake for. *Job* 8:6
s. I would speak to the.　13:3
he will s. reprove you, if ye.　10
s. the mountain falling cometh. 14:18
s. such as are the dwellings.　18:21
s. he shall not feel quietness.　20:20
s. there is a vein for the silver. 28:1
s. take it upon my shoulder.　31:36
s. thou hast spoken in.　33:8
s. God will not do wickedly.　34:12
s. God will not hear vanity.　35:13
s. in the floods they.　*Ps* 32:6
s. every man walketh in vain.　39:6
his beauty consumes, s. every.　11
s. thou didst set them in.　73:18
s. the wrath of man shall.　76:10
s. I will remember thy.　77:11
s. his salvation is nigh them.　85:9
s. he shall deliver thee from.　91:3
s. he shall not be moved.　112:6
s. I have behaved and quieted. 131:2
s. I will not come into my.　132:3
s. thou wilt slay the wicked. 139:19
s. the righteous shall give.　140:13
s. in vain the net is spread. *Pr* 1:17
s. he scorneth the scorners, but. 3:34
walketh uprightly, walketh s.　10:9
that giveth to the rich, shall s. 22:16
s. there is an end.　23:18
s. I am more brutish.　30:2
s. the churning of milk.　33
s. this also is vanity.　*Eccl* 4:16
s. oppression maketh a wise.　7:7
s. it shall be well with them.　8:12
s. the serpent will bite.　10:11
will not believe, s. ye shall not be.
　Isa 7:9
s. as I have thought so shall.　14:24
shall mourn, s. are stricken.　16:7
s. the princes of Zoan are.　19:11
s. this iniquity shall not be.　22:14
behold, the Lord will s. cover.　17
he will s. violently turn and toss. 18
s. your turning of things.　29:16
grass withereth, s. the people. 40:7
s. God is in thee, and there.　45:14
s. in Lord have I righteousness.　24
yet s. my judgement is with.　49:4
s. he hath borne our griefs.　53:4
they shall s. gather together.　54:15
s. the isles shall wait for me.　60:9
s. I will no more give thy corn. 62:8
he said S. they are my people. 63:8
s. his anger shall turn from. *Jer* 2:35
s. as a wife treacherously.　3:20
s. thou hast greatly deceived.　4:10
s. they swear falsely.　5:2
I said, S. these are poor.　4
I will s. consume them, saith.　8:13
s. our fathers have inherited. 16:19
yet s. I will make thee a.　22:6
s. thou shalt be ashamed for.　22
s. thus saith the Lord, so will. 24:8
ye shall s. bring innocent.　26:15
have s. heard Ephraim.　31:18
s. after that I was turned.　19
therefore I will s. have mercy.　20
but thou shalt s. be taken.　34:3
we will s. tell the king of all. 36:16
the Chaldeans shall s. depart.　37:9
this city shall s. be given.　38:3
I will s. deliver thee, thou.　39:18

we will perform our vows. *Jer* 44:25
my words shall s. stand against.　29
s. as Carmel by the sea, so.　46:18
unpunished, but s. drink it.　49:12
s. the least of the flock shall draw.
　20; 50:45
saying, S. I will fill thee.　51:14
of recompences shall s. requite.　56
he shall s. live, because. *Ezek* 3:21
　18:9, 17, 19, 21, 28; 33:13, 15, 16
s. because thou hast defiled my. 5:11
s. in the place where the king. 17:16
s. with a mighty hand will I.　20:33
he shall s. deal with him.　31:11
s. they in the wastes shall fall. 33:27
as I live, s. because my flock.　34:8
s. in the fire of my jealousy.　36:5
s. the heathen, they shall bear.　7
s. in that day there shall be a. 38:19
known that which shall s.　*Hos* 5:9
s. they are vanity, they.　12:11
s. the Lord will do nothing. *Amos* 3:1
Gilgal shall s. go into captivity.　5:5
Israel shall s. be led away. 7:11, 17
s. I will never forget any of.　8:7
I will s. assemble, O Jacob, all of
　thee, I will s. gather.　*Mi* 2:12
because it will s. come.　*Hab* 2:3
as I live, s. Moab shall.　*Zeph* 2:9
s. thou wilt fear me, and.　3:7
s. thou also art one of them.
　Mat 26:73; *Mark* 14:70
things which are most s.　*Luke* 1:1
ye will s. say unto me this.　4:23
known s. that I came.　*John* 17:8
saying, S. blessing, I will. *Heb* 6:14
S. I come quickly, even. *Rev* 22:20
see die

surely be put to death

toucheth this man, shall s. be put to
　d.　*Gen* 26:11
whosoever toucheth the mount, shall
　be s. put to d.　*Ex* 19:12
killeth a man, shall be s. put to d.
　21:12
smiteth his father, shall be s. put to
　d.　15
stealeth a man shall s. be put to d. 16
that curseth his father shall s. be put
　to d.　17; *Lev* 20:9
lieth with a beast, shall s. be put to d.
　Ex 22:19; *Lev* 20:15, 16
defileth the sabbath shall s. be put to
　d.　*Ex* 31:14, 15
to Moloch, s. be put to d. *Lev* 20:2
adulteress shall s. be put to d.　10
wife, both shall s. be put to d.　11
daughter in law, both shall s. be put
　to d.　12
with mankind, both s. be put to d. 13
blasphemeth, shall s. be put to d.
　24:16
killeth any man, shall s. be put to d.
　17; *Num* 35:16, 17, 18, 21, 31
redeemed, but shall s. be put to d.
　Lev 27:29
came not up, shall s. be put to d.
　Judg 21:5
not s. put me to d.?　*Jer* 38:15

sureties

them that are s. for debts. *Pr* 22:26

suretiship

he that hateth s. is sure.　*Pr* 11:15

surety

*One who undertakes to pay
another man's debt, in case the
principal debtor, either through
unfaithfulness or poverty, should
prove insolent. It was an ancient
custom in suretyship for the surety
to give his hand to, or strike hands
with the creditor,* Job 17:3, Pr 6:1, 2.

I will be s. for him.　*Gen* 43:9
for thy servant became s. for. 44:32
put me in a s. with thee.　*Job* 17:3
be s. for thy servant.　*Ps* 119:122
my son, if thou be s. for.　*Pr* 6:1
he that is s. for a stranger.　11:15
and becometh s. in presence.　17:18
his garment that is s. for a stranger.
　20:16; 27:13
Jesus made s. of a better. *Heb* 7:22

of a surety
know *of a s.* thy seed. *Gen* 15:13
shall I *of a s.* bear a child? 18:13
Abimelech said, Behold, *of a s.* 26:9
I know *of a s.* the Lord. *Acts* 12:11*

surfeiting
be overcharged with *s.* *Luke* 21:34

surmisings
cometh envy, strife, evil *s.* *1 Tim* 6:4

surname
and *s.* himself by the name of Israel.
　　　　　Isa 44:5
Lebbaeus, whose *s.* was. *Mat* 10:3
Simon, whose *s.* is Peter. *Acts* 10:5
　　　　　32; 11:13
John, whose *s.* was Mark. 12:12
　　　　　25; 15:37*

surnamed
I have *s.* thee, though. *Isa* 45:4
and Simon he *s.* Peter. *Mark* 3:16
　　　　　Acts 10:18
he *s.* them Boanerges. *Mark* 3:17
Satan entered into Judas, *s.* Iscariot.
　　　　　Luke 22:3*
Barsabas, who was *s.* *Acts* 1:23
Joses, who by the apostles was *s.*
　　Barnabas. 4:36
to send Judas, *s.* Barsabas. 15:22*

surprised
sinners afraid, fearfulness *s.*
　　　　　Isa 33:14†
the strong holds are *s.* *Jer* 48:41
praise of the whole earth *s.*! 51:41

Susanna
Joanna and *S.* ministered. *Luke* 8:3

sustain
widow woman to *s.* thee. *1 Ki* 17:9
years didst thou *s.* them. *Neh* 9:21
the Lord, he shall *s.* thee. *Ps* 55:22
the spirit of a man will *s.* *Pr* 18:14

sustained
and wine have I *s.* him. *Gen* 27:37
for the Lord *s.* me. *Ps* 3:5
righteousness, it *s.* him. *Isa* 59:16

sustenance
left no *s.* for Israel. *Judg* 6:4
provided the king of *s.* *2 Sam* 19:32
our fathers found no *s.* *Acts* 7:11

swaddled
those that I have *s.* hath. *Lam* 2:22*
salted at all nor *s.* at all. *Ezek* 16:4

swaddling
darkness a *s.* band for. *Job* 38:9
wrapped him in *s.* *Luke* 2:7, 12

swallow
(*The words swallow and crane are
frequently interchanged in the old
version of the Bible, so that the
Revisions merely substitute the
word swallow for crane and crane
for swallow and the sense of the
verse is not really changed.
There are many varieties of this
common bird found in Palestine*)
the *s.* hath found a nest. *Ps* 84:3
as the *s.* by flying, so the. *Pr* 26:2
like a crane or a *s.* so. *Isa* 38:14
crane and *s.* observe. *Jer* 8:7

swallow, *verb*
earth open and *s.* them. *Num* 16:30
for they said, Lest the earth *s.* 34
why wilt thou *s.* up? *2 Sam* 20:19
far be it from me, that I should *s.* 20
let me alone till I *s.* down. *Job* 7:19
he shall restore, and not *s.* 20:18
the Lord shall *s.* them up. *Ps* 21:9
O God, man would *s.* me up. 56:1
would daily *s.* me up. 2
of him that would *s.* me up. 57:3
neither let the deep *s.* me up. 69:15
let us *s.* them up alive. *Pr* 1:12
lips of a fool will *s.* up. *Eccl* 10:12
will *s.* up death in victory. *Isa* 25:8
the strangers shall *s.* it up. *Hos* 8:7
hear this, O ye that *s.* up. *Amos* 8:4
drink, and they shall *s.* down. *Ob* 16
Lord prepared a fish to *s.* *Jonah* 1:17
at a gnat, and *s.* a camel. *Mat* 23:24

swallowed
but Aaron's rod *s.* up. *Ex* 7:12
right hand, the earth *s.* them. 15:12
earth opened and *s.* *Num* 16:32
　　　　　26:10; *Deut* 11:6
lest the king be *s.* up. *2 Sam* 17:16
heavier than sand: therefore my
　words are *s.* up. *Job* 6:3*
he hath *s.* down riches, he. 20:15
surely he shall be *s.* up. 37:20
say, We have *s.* him up. *Ps* 35:25
the earth opened and *s.* up. 106:17
they had *s.* us up quick. 124:3
the priest and the prophet are *s.* up.
　　　　　Isa 28:7
they that *s.* thee up shall. 49:19
s. me up like a dragon. *Jer* 51:34
out of his mouth that which hath *s.* 44
hath *s.* up all the habitation of Jacob.
　　　　　Lam 2:2
he hath *s.* up Israel, he hath *s.* up. 5
they hiss and say, We have *s.* 16
because they have *s.* *Ezek* 36:3
Israel is *s.* up among the. *Hos* 8:8
death is *s.* up in victory. *1 Cor* 15:54
lest such one should be *s.* *2 Cor* 2:7
that mortality might be *s.* up. 5:4
the earth opened and *s.* *Rev* 12:16

swalloweth
and the robber *s.* up. *Job* 5:5*
he *s.* the ground with. 39:24*

swan
the *s.*, the pelican, unclean.
　　　Lev 11:18*; *Deut* 14:16*

sware
(*The old form of the past tense of
swear*)
Beersheba, because they *s.* both of
　them. *Gen* 21:31
the Lord God of heaven that *s.* 24:7
the servant *s.* to him concerning. 9
Swear to me, and he *s.* to him. 25:33
perform the oath which I *s.* 26:3
Abimelech and Isaac *s.* to one. 31
and Jacob *s.* by the fear of his. 31:53
Joseph *s.* to Jacob his father. 47:31
to this land he *s.* to Abraham. 50:24
the land which the Lord *s.* *Ex* 13:5
　11; 33:1; *Num* 14:16, 30; 32:11
　Deut 1:8, 35; 6:10, 18, 23; 7:13
　8:1; 11:9, 21; 26:3; 28:11; 30:20
　31:21, 23; 34:4; *Josh* 1:6; 5:6
　　　　　21:43
anger was kindled, and he *s.* saying.
　　　Num 32:10; *Deut* 1:34
were wasted, as Lord *s.* *Deut* 2:14
Lord *s.* that I should not go. 4:21
not forget the covenant which he *s.* 31
which he *s.* to thy salvation. 7:12
covenant which he *s.* 8:18; 9:5
bring out Rahab, as ye *s.* *Josh* 6:22
princes of congregation *s.* to. 9:15
because of the oath which we *s.* 20
Moses *s.* on that day, saying. 14:9
rest according to all that he *s.* 21:44
brought to land which I *s.* *Judg* 2:1
Saul *s.* that David shall. *1 Sam* 19:6
David *s.* moreover to Jonathan. 20:3
David *s.* to Saul, and Saul. 24:22
Saul *s.* to her by the Lord, . . . no
　punishment. 28:10
David *s.* he would not eat till sun.
　　　　　2 Sam 3:35
king David *s.* to Shimei. 19:23
　　　　　1 Ki 2:8
king David *s.* to. *1 Ki* 1:29, 30
Solomon *s.* that Adonijah. 2:23
Gedaliah *s.* to them. *2 Ki* 25:24
　　　　　Jer 40:9
they *s.* to the Lord with. *2 Chr* 15:14
they *s.* to put away. *Ezra* 10:5
to whom I *s.* in my wrath. *Ps* 95:11
　　　　　Heb 3:11
how he *s.* to Lord and vowed. 132:2
so the king *s.* secretly. *Jer* 38:16
I *s.* and entered into. *Ezek* 16:8
s. by him that liveth for ever.
　　　　　Dan 12:7; *Rev* 10:6
Herod *s.* to the daughter. *Mark* 6:23
remember oath which he *s.* to Abra-
　ham. *Luke* 1:73
to whom *s.* he that they. *Heb* 3:18

swear
swear by no greater, he *s.* *Heb* 6:13
that said, The Lord *s.* and will. 7:21
　see their **fathers**

swarest
to whom thou *s.* by thine. *Ex* 32:13
land thou *s.* to fathers. *Num* 11:12
land given us, as thou *s.* *Deut* 26:15
thou *s.* that Solomon. *1 Ki* 1:17
kindnesses thou *s.* to. *Ps* 89:49

swarm
there came a grievous *s.* *Ex* 8:24
a *s.* of bees and honey in. *Judg* 14:8

swarms
s. of flies upon thee, houses of the
　. . . be full of *s.* of flies. *Ex* 8:21
no *s.* of flies shall be in Goshen. 22
that the *s.* of flies may depart. 29
he removed the *s.* of flies from. 31

swear
*In the Bible this has either the
meaning of profanity, which is forbidden, or of a solemn asseveration,
which is allowed,* Lev 19:12; Ex
20:7; Deut 6:13; Jer 4:2.

to Abraham, *S.* to me. *Gen* 21:23
and Abraham said, I will *s.* 24
and I will make thee *s.* by. 24:3
my master made me *s.* saying. 37
Jacob said, *S.* to me, and he. 25:33
Jacob said unto Joseph, *S.* 47:31
my father made me *s.*, saying 50:5
concerning which I did *s.* *Ex* 6:8*
if a soul *s.* *Lev* 5:4
and ye shall not *s.* by my. 19:12
if man *s.* an oath to bind. *Num* 30:2
and thou shalt *s.* by his name.
　　　Deut 6:13; 10:20
Rahab said to spies, *S.* to me.
　　　　　Josh 2:12
which thou hast made us *s.* 17, 20
nor cause to *s.* by their gods. 23:7
s. to me that ye will. *Judg* 15:12
Jonathan caused David to *s.* again.
　　　　　1 Sam 20:17
s. that thou wilt not cut off my. 24:21
s. by God that thou wilt. 30:15
I *s.* by the Lord. *2 Sam* 19:7
didst not thou *s.* unto thine? *1 Ki* 1:13
saying, Let king Solomon *s.* 51
did I not make thee to *s.*? 2:42
an oath be laid on him to cause him
　to *s.* 8:31; *2 Chr* 6:22
made him *s.* by God. *2 Chr* 36:13
then Ezra made Levites and all
　Israel to *s.* *Ezra* 10:5
I made them *s.* by God. *Neh* 13:25
in that day shall he *s.* I. *Isa* 3:7*
five cities in Egypt shall *s.* 19:18
to me every tongue shall *s.* 45:23
which *s.* by the Lord, but not. 48:1
that *s.* by his name, *S.* Jer 4:2
Lord liveth, they *s.* falsely. 5:2
will ye *s.* falsely? 7:9
ways of my people, to *s.* by my name,
　as they taught people to *s.* 12:16
I *s.* by myself, saith the Lord. 22:5
them this land thou didst *s.* 32:22
up to Beth-aven nor *s.* *Hos* 4:15
they that *s.* by the sin. *Amos* 8:14
that *s.* by the Lord, that *s.* *Zeph* 1:5
s. not at all. *Mat* 5:34
s. not by thy head. 36
shall *s.* by the temple; *s.* by. 23:16
whoso shall *s.* by the altar. 18
shall *s.* by the altar, sweareth. 20
shall *s.* by the temple. 21
shall *s.* by heaven. 22
then began he to curse and *s.* 26:74
　　　　　Mark 14:71
could *s.* by no greater, he *s.* *Heb* 6:13
for men verily *s.* by the greater. 16
my brethren, *s.* not. *Jas* 5:12

swearers
be a swift witness against false *s.*
　　　　　Mal 3:5

sweareth
what was lost, and *s.* *Lev* 6:3*
that *s.* to his hurt, and. *Ps* 15:4
every one that *s.* by him shall. 63:11
s. as he that feareth an oath. *Eccl* 9:2
he that *s.* shall swear by. *Isa* 65:16

and every one that s. shall. *Zech* 5:3
enter into the house of him s.   4
whosoever s. by the gift. *Mat* 23:18
s. by the altar.   20
s. by temple, and by him.   21
s. by throne of God, and by him.   22

swearing
and hear the voice of s.   *Lev* 5:1*
because of s. the land.   *Jer* 23:10
s. and lying, and stealing.   *Hos* 4:2
have spoken words, s. falsely.   10:4

sweat
in the s. of thy face.   *Gen* 3:19
any thing that causeth s. *Ezek* 44:18
his s. was as it were great drops of
blood.   *Luke* 22:44

sweep
I will s. it with the besom. *Isa* 14:23
the hail shall s. away the.   28:17
doth not s. the house.   *Luke* 15:8

sweeping
is like a s. rain which.   *Pr* 28:3

sweet
waters were made s.   *Ex* 15:25
take of myrrh and s.   30:23
David the s. psalmist.   *2 Sam* 23:1
eat the fat, and drink the s. *Neh* 8:10
wickedness be s. in   *Job* 20:12
valley shall be s. to him.   21:33
thou bind the s. influences ? 38:31*
took s. counsel together and walked.
  Ps 55:14
meditation of him shall be s. 104:34
how s. are thy words unto! 119:103
my words, for they are s.   141:6
and thy sleep shall be s.   *Pr* 3:24
stolen waters are s., and bread. 9:17
the desire accomplished is s. 13:19
pleasant words are s. to the. 16:24
bread of deceit is s. to a man. 20:17
and lose thy s. words.   23:8
the honeycomb, which is s.   24:13
soul every bitter thing is s.   27:7
of a labouring man is s.   *Eccl* 5:12
truly the light is s., and.   11:7
his fruit was s.   *S of S* 2:3
for s. is thy voice.   14
dropped with s. smelling myrrh. 5:5*
cheeks as a bed of spices, as s.
flowers: his lips like lilies, dropping s.   13*
his mouth is most s. yea, he is. 16
instead of s. smell, there.   *Isa* 3:24
put bitter for s. and s. for bitter. 5:20
make s. melody, sing songs to. 23:16
your sacrifices s. unto me. *Jer* 6:20*
awaked, and my sleep was s. 31:26
same place s. water.   *Jas* 3:11
thy mouth s. as honey. *Rev* 10:9, 10
see incense, odours, savour

sweet *calamus*
take of s. *calamus* 250.   *Ex* 30:23

sweet *cane*
hast brought me no s. *cane* with
money.   *Isa* 43:24
the s. *cane* came from a.   *Jer* 6:20

sweet *spices*
take to thee s. *spices*.   *Ex* 30:34
pure incense of s. *spices*.   37:29
bought s. *spices* that they. *Mark* 16:1

sweet *wine*
blood as with s. *wine*.   *Isa* 49:26
mount shall drop s. *wine*. *Amos* 9:13
and s. *wine*, but shalt not. *Mi* 6:15*

sweeter
men of city said, What is s. than ?
  Judg 14:18
s. also than honey.   *Ps* 19:10
thy words are s. than honey. 119:103

sweetly
worm shall feed s. on him. *Job* 24:20
wine, that goeth down s. *S of S* 7:9*

sweetness
should I forsake my s.? *Judg* 9:11
of the strong came forth s.   14:14
s. of the lips increaseth.   *Pr* 16:21
so doth s. of a man's friend.   27:9
roll was in my mouth as honey for s.
  Ezek 3:3

swell
and thy belly to s.   *Num* 5:21, 22
her belly shall s. and her thigh.   27
nor did thy foot s. these.   *Deut* 8:4

swelled
40 years their feet s. not. *Neh* 9:21

swelling
shake with s. thereof.   *Ps* 46:3
as a breach s. out in a. *Isa* 30:13
do in the s. of Jordan ? *Jer* 12:5*
from the s. of Jordan. 49:19*; 50:44*
speak great s. words.   *2 Pet* 2:18
speaking great s. words. *Jude* 16

swellings
I fear lest there be s.   *2 Cor* 12:20

swept
the river of Kishon s.   *Judg* 5:21
valiant men s. away ? *Jer* 46:15
house, when come, he findeth it
empty, s. *Mat* 12:44; *Luke* 11:25

swerved
which some having s.   *1 Tim* 1:6

swift
shall bring a nation as s. *Deut* 28:49
were as s. as roes on.   *1 Chr* 12:8
passed away as the s. ships. *Job* 9:26
he is s. as the waters, he.   24:18
feet that be s. in running. *Pr* 6:18
race is not to the s.   *Eccl* 9:11
go, ye s. messengers.   *Isa* 18:2
Lord rideth upon a s. cloud.   19:1
we will ride on the s.: therefore shall
they that pursue you be s. 30:16
your brethren on s. beasts.   66:20
s. dromedary traversing her ways.
  Jer 2:23
let not s. flee away, nor mighty. 46:6
flight shall perish from s. *Amos* 2:14
he that is s. of foot shall not.   15
bind the chariot to s. beast. *Mi* 1:13
I will be a s. witness.   *Mal* 3:5
their feet are s. to shed. *Rom* 3:15
let every man be s. to hear. *Jas* 1:19
themselves s. destruction. *2 Pet* 2:1

swifter
s. than eagles, stronger. *2 Sam* 1:23
s. than a weaver's shuttle. *Job* 7:6
now my days are s. than a post. 9:25
horses are s. than eagles. *Jer* 4:13
our persecutors are s.   *Lam* 4:19
their horses are s. than.   *Hab* 1:8

swiftly
his word runneth very s. *Ps* 147:15
shall come with speed s. *Isa* 5:26
Gabriel being caused to fly s.
  Dan 9:21
if ye recompense me s.   *Joel* 3:4

swim
stick, and the iron did s.   *2 Ki* 6:6
make I my bed to s.   *Ps* 6:6
spreadeth forth hands to s. *Isa* 25:11
risen, waters to s. in.   *Ezek* 47:5
lest any of them should s. out and.
  Acts 27:42
that they who could s.   43

swimmest
the land wherein thou s. *Ezek* 32:6

swimmeth
as he that s. spreadeth.   *Isa* 25:11

swine
the s. is unclean to you.   *Lev* 11:7
  Deut 14:8
as a jewel of gold in a s.'s. *Pr* 11:22
eat s.'s flesh, and broth of. *Isa* 65:4
oblation, as if he offered s.'s. 66:3
eating s.'s flesh, and abomination. 17
cast ye your pearls before s. *Mat* 7:6
an herd of s. feeding.   8:30
  Mark 5:11; *Luke* 8:32
suffer us to go into the herd of s.
  Mat 8:31; *Mark* 5:12
they went into the s. . . . the whole
herd of s. ran.   *Mat* 8:32
  Mark 5:13; *Luke* 8:33
they that fed the s. fled. *Mark* 5:14
them also concerning the s.   16
into his field to feed s. *Luke* 15:15
belly with husks the s. did eat. 16

swollen
when he should have s. *Acts* 28:6

swoon
because the children s.   *Lam* 2:11

swooned
they s. as the wounded.   *Lam* 2:12

sword
*The sword in scripture is often used
for war,* Gen 27:40; Lev 26:2.
*By sword is understood the judge-
ments which God inflicts upon
sinners,* Deut 3:41, 42; *also the
instrument which God uses to
execute his judgements,* Ps 17:13.
Sword *is figuratively put for power
and authority,* Rom 13:4. *The
word of God is called the* sword of
the Spirit, Eph 6:17. *Moses calls
God the* sword of *Israel's excellency,* Deut 33:29. *He is their
strength, the author of all their
past or approaching victories, by
whose assistance they did excel,
and gloriously conquer, and triumph
over their enemies.*
cherubims, and flaming s. *Gen* 3:24
took each man his s. and.   34:25
put a s. in their hands.   *Ex* 5:21
he said, Put every man his s. 32:27
nor shall the s. go through. *Lev* 26:6
bring a s. upon you.   25; *Ezek* 5:17
  6:3; 14:17; 29:8, 33:2
I will draw out a s. after. *Lev* 26:33
fall as it were before a s.   37
the angel's s. drawn. *Num* 22:23, 31
I would there were a s. in mine. 29
s. without, and terror.   *Deut* 32:25
and who is the s. of thy!   33:29
stood with his s. drawn.   *Josh* 5:13
not with thy s. nor with thy. 24:12
this is nothing save the s. *Judg* 7:14
say, The s. of the Lord, and. 18, 20
and the Lord set every man's s.
  7:22; *1 Sam* 14:20
120,000 men that drew s. *Judg* 8:10
the youth drew not his s. for.   20
he said unto him, Draw thy s. 9:54
400,000 that drew s.   20:2, 17
26,000 men that drew s.   15
all these drew the s.   25
25,100 men that drew the s.   35
25,000 that drew the s.   46
neither s. nor spear.   *1 Sam* 13:22
as thy s. hath made women. 15:33
his s. on his armour.   17:39; 25:13
but there was no s. in the.   17:50
David ran and took his s.   51
even to his s. and to his bow. 18:4
under thy hand a spear or s.   21:8
the s. of Goliath is here wrapt.   9
and he gave him the s. of.   22:10
given him bread, and a s.   13
Gird ye on every man his s. and they
girded on every man his s. 25:13
draw thy s. and thrust me through
therewith. . . . Saul took a s. and
fell upon it.   31:4; *1 Chr* 10:4
armourbearer fell likewise upon his
s. and died with him. *1 Sam* 31:5
  1 Chr 10:5
the s. of Saul returned. *2 Sam* 1:22
and thrust his s. through.   2:16
Abner said, Shall the s. devour ? 26
fail one that falleth on the s.   3:29
the s. devoureth one as well. 11:25
the s. shall never depart from. 12:10
wood devoured more than s.   18:8
Amasa took no heed to the s. 20:10
his hand clave unto the s.   23:10
800,000 men that drew the s. 24:9
a s. and they brought a s. *1 Ki* 3:24
him that escapeth the s. of.   19:17
to bear buckler and s.   *1 Chr* 5:18
men that drew s. and Judah was
470,000 that drew s.   21:5
that the s. of thine enemies overtake, or else three days the s.   12
the angel having a s. drawn.   16
and he put up his s. again into. 27
he was afraid, because of the s.   30
s. of judgement cometh. *2 Chr* 20:9
our kings are delivered to the s.
  Ezra 7:3
one had his s. girded.   *Neh* 4:18
their enemies with the s.   *Esth* 9:5

sword

in war to deliver from power of the s.
Job 5:20
and he is waited for of the s. 15:22
s.: for wrath bringeth the punishments of the s. 19:29
the glittering s. cometh. 20:25*
multiplied, it is for the s. 27:14
make his s. to approach. 40:19
the s. of him that layeth at. 41:26
turn not, he will whet his s. *Ps* 7:12
the wicked, which is thy s. 17:13
wicked have drawn out the s. 37:14
their s. shall enter into their. 15
gird thy s. on thy thigh. 45:3
and their tongue a sharp s. 57:4
who whet their tongue like a s. 64:3
brake he the shield and the s. 76:3
his people over unto the s. 78:62
twoedged s. in their hand. 149:6
is sharp as a twoedged s. *Pr* 5:4
like the piercings of a s. 12:18
beareth false witness is a s. 25:18
every man hath his s. upon his thigh.
S of S 3:8
nation shall not lift up s. *Isa* 2:4
s., not of a mean man, shall. 31:8
the s. of the Lord is filled. 34:6
them as the dust to his s. 41:2
my mouth like a sharp s. 49:2
the famine and the s. are. 51:19
will I number you to the s. 65:12
by his s. will the Lord plead. 66:16
your own s. devoured. *Jer* 2:30
whereas the s. reacheth unto. 4:10
neither shall we see s. 5:12; 14:13
for the s. of the enemy is. 6:25
will send a s. after them. 9:16; 24:10
25:27; 29:17; 49:37
for the s. of the Lord shall. 14:12
Ye shall not see the s. 14:13
say, S. and famine shall not be. 15
in the streets because of the s. 16
are for the s., to the s. 15:2; 43:11
I will appoint the s. to slay. 15:3
them will I deliver to the s. 9
blood by the force of the s. 18:21
be mad because of the s. 25
I will call for a s. 29; *Ezek* 38:21
that are wicked to the s. *Jer* 25:31
the people left of the s. found. 31:2
city is given because of the s. 32:24
a liberty for you, to the s. 34:17
the s. ye feared shall overtake. 42:16
number which escape the s. 44:28
the s. shall devour and. 46:10, 14
O thou s. of the Lord, how? 47:6
O madmen, the s. shall pursue. 48:2
cursed that kepeeth back his s. 10
for fear of the oppressing s. 50:16
a s. is on the Chaldeans, saith. 35
a s. is on the liars, a s. is on. 36
a s. is on their horses, a s. on. 37
ye that have escaped the s. 51:50
by peril because of the s. *Lam* 5:9
I will draw out a s. *Ezek* 5:2, 12
I bring the s. upon thee. 17; 6:3
some that shall escape the s. 6:8
the s. is without, the pestilence. 7:15
the s. and I will bring a s. 11:8
if I bring a s. and say, S. go. 14:17
four sore judgements, the s. 21
prophesy and say, A s. a s. 21:9, 11
terrors, by reason of the s. on. 12
and what if the s. contemn? 13
s. be doubled, the s. of the great men
slain, it is the s. of great men. 14
set the point of the s. against. 15
appoint two ways, that the s. 19
appoint a way, that s. may come. 20
the s. the s. is drawn for the. 28
s. shall come upon Egypt. 30:4
make it strong to hold the s. 21
I will cause the s. to fall out. 22
the s. of the king of Babylon. 32:11
if when he seeth the s. come. 33:3
if the s. come and take him. 4, 6
watchman see the s. come; if the s.
come and take any person. 6
ye stand upon your s. and ye. 26
blood by the force of the s. 35:5
break the bow and the s. *Hos* 2:18
and the s. shall abide on. 11:6
will I command the s. *Amos* 9:4
nation shall not lift up s. *Mi* 4:3

will I give up to the s. *Mi* 6:14
the s. shall devour the. *Nah* 2:13
lifteth up both the bright s. 3:3
there the s. shall cut thee off. 15
made thee as the s. of. *Zech* 9:13
the s. shall be upon his arm. 11:17
O s. against my shepherd. 13:7
to send peace, but a s. *Mat* 10:34
one of them drew his s. and. 26:51
Mark 14:47; *John* 18:10
put up again thy s. *Mat* 26:52
John 18:11
a s. shall pierce through. *Luke* 2:35
he that hath no s. let him buy. 22:36
he drew his s. and. *Acts* 16:27
separate us? shall s.? *Rom* 8:35
for he beareth not the s. in. 13:4
s. of the Spirit, which is. *Eph* 6:17
than any twoedged s. *Heb* 4:12
went a twoedged s. *Rev* 1:16
which hath the sharp s. with. 2:12
given to him a great s. 6:4
mouth goeth a sharp s. 19:15, 21

by the sword

by the s. thou shalt live. *Gen* 27:40
shall fall before you by the s.
Lev 26:7, 8
were fallen by the s. *2 Sam* 1:12
have fallen by the s. *2 Chr* 29:9
from perishing by the s. *Job* 33:18
they shall perish by the s. 36:12
got not the land by their s. *Ps* 44:3
their priests fell by the s. 78:64
Lord, Their young men shall die by
the s. *Jer* 11:22; 18:21; *Lam* 2:21
consume them by the s. *Jer* 14:12
by s. and famine shall those. 15
shall be consumed by the s. 16:4
44:12, 18, 27
cause them to fall by the s. 19:7
abideth, shall die by the s. 21:9
38:2; 42:17, 22
why will ye die by the s.? 27:13
shall be delivered to the s. 32:36
are thrown down by the s. 33:4
thou shalt not die by the s. 34:4
punished Jerusalem by the s. 44:13
shall be slain by the s. *Ezek* 26:6
he shall slay thy people by the s. 11
be judged in her by the s. 28:23
them that be slain by the s. 31:18
32:20, 21, 22, 25, 30; 33:27
so they fell all by the s. 39:23
not save them by bow, nor by s.
Hos 1:7
Jeroboam shall die by the s.
Amos 7:11
people shall die by the s. 9:10
every one by the s. *Hag* 2:22
had the wound by a s. *Rev* 13:14

see edge, fall

from the sword

delivered me from the s. of. *Ex* 18:4
as fleeing from a s. *Lev* 26:36
him that escapeth from the s of
Jehu. *1 Ki* 19:17
that escaped from the s. *2 Chr* 36:20
saveth poor from the s. *Job* 5:15
turneth he back from the s. 39:22
deliver my soul from the s.; my darling from the power. *Ps* 22:20
David from the hurtful s. 144:10
fled from the drawn s. *Isa* 21:15
but he shall flee from the s. 31:8
such as are left from the s. *Jer* 21:7
let us go from the oppressing s. 46:16
few men of them from s. *Ezek* 12:16
is brought back from the s. 38:8

my sword

from Amorite with my s. *Gen* 48:22
I will draw my s. my. *Ex* 15:9
I whet my glittering s. *Deut* 32:41
and my s. shall devour flesh. 42
neither brought my s. *1 Sam* 21:8
neither shall my s. save me. *Ps* 44:6
for my s. shall be bathed. *Isa* 34:5
I will draw my s. out. *Ezek* 21:3
therefore my s. shall go out of. 4
I the Lord have drawn my s. out. 5
I have put my s. in his. 30:24, 25
when I shall brandish my s. 32:10
shall be slain by my s. *Zeph* 2:12

with the sword

captives taken with the s. *Gen* 31:26
lest he fall on us with the s. *Ex* 5:3
I will kill you with the s. 22:24
toucheth one slain with the s.
Num 19:16
out against thee with the s. 20:18
Balaam also they slew with the s.
31:8
the Lord shall smite thee with the s.
Deut 28:22
whom Israel slew with the s.
Josh 10:11; 13:22
king of Hazor with the s. 11:10
comest to me with a s. *1 Sam* 17:45
the Lord saveth not with a. and. 47
killed Uriah with the s. *2 Sam* 12:9
a girdle with a s. fastened. 20:8
being girded with a s. 21:16
will not slay his servant with the s.
1 Ki 1:51
not put thee to death with the s. 2:8
and slew them with the s. 32
slain all the prophets with the s. 19:1
slain thy prophets with the s. 10, 14
young men wilt thou slay with the s.
2 Ki 8:12
and him that followeth her, kill with
the s. 11:15; *2 Chr* 23:14
they slew Athaliah with the s.
2 Ki 11:20; *2 Chr* 23:21
Sennacherib king of Assyria with the
s. *2 Ki* 19:37; *2 Chr* 32:21
Isa 37:38
his brethren with the s. *2 Chr* 21:4
their young men with the s. 36:17
as with a s. in my bones. *Ps* 42:10
be devoured with the s. *Isa* 1:20
slain, thrust through with a s. 14:19
men are not slain with the s. 22:2
the Lord with his strong s. 27:1
thy cities with the s. *Jer* 5:17
behold the slain with the s. 14:18
shall slay Judah with the s. 20:4
who slew Urijah with the s. 26:23
nation will I punish with the s. 27:8
persecute them with the s. 29:18
smote Gedaliah with the s. 41:2
that be slain with the s. *Lam* 4:9
shall die with the s. *Ezek* 7:15
slew her with the s. 23:10
daughters of Tyrus with the s. 26:8
with them that be slain with the s.
31:17; 32:28, 32; 35:8
his brother with the s. *Amos* 1:11
men have I slain with the s. 4:10
house of Jeroboam with the s. 7:9
slay the last of them with the s. 9:1
the land of Assyria with the s. *Mi* 5:6
s. shall perish with the s. *Mat* 26:52
we smite with the s.? *Luke* 22:49
killed James with the s. *Acts* 12:2
were tempted, were slain with the s.
Heb 11:37
against them with the s. *Rev* 2:16
and power to kill with s. and. 6:8
with s. must be killed with s. 13:10
remnant were slain with the s. 19:21

swords

Hebrews make them s. *1 Sam* 13:19
700 men that drew s. *2 Ki* 3:26
the people with their s. *Neh* 4:13
his words were drawn s. *Ps* 55:21
behold, they belch out, s. are. 59:7
whose teeth are as s. *Pr* 30:14
they all hold, s., being. *S of S* 3:8
beat their s. into plowshares and
their spears. *Isa* 2:4; *Mi* 4:3
they fled from the s. and. *Isa* 21:15
thrust thee through with their s.
Ezek 16:40
dispatch them with their s. 23:47
strangers shall draw their s. 28:7
they shall draw their s. 30:11
by the s. of the mighty will. 32:12
they have laid their s. under. 27
your plowshares into s. *Joel* 3:10
a great multitude with s. from the
chief. *Mat* 26:47; *Mark* 14:43
as against a thief with s. and staves
to take me? *Mat* 26:55
Mark 14:48; *Luke* 22:52
behold, here are two s. *Luke* 22:38

sworn

by myself have I s. saith the Lord.
   Gen 22:16; Isa 45:23; Jer 49:13
              51:14; Amos 6:8
had straitly s. Israel.   Ex 13:19
the Lord hath s. that he will. 17:16
about which he hath s.   Lev 6:5
would keep the oath he had s.
           Deut 7:8; Jer 11:5
multiply thee, as he hath s. to thy
   fathers.   Deut 13:17
thy coast, as he hath s.   19:8
shall establish thee, as he hath s.
            28:9; 29:13
to land Lord hath s. 31:7; Neh 9:15
because the princes had s. Josh 9:18
we have s. to them by the Lord. 19
            2 Sam 21:2
for evil, as Lord had s. Judg 2:15
now the men of Israel had s. 21:1
we have s. not to give them. 7, 18
I have s. unto the house of Eli.
           1 Sam 3:14
forasmuch as we have s.   20:42
Lord hath s. to David. 2 Sam 3:9
children of Israel had s. to. 21:2
they had s. with all. 2 Chr 15:15
many in Judah s. to.   Neh 6:18
the land which thou hadst s. 9:15*
who hath not s. deceitfully. Ps 24:4
I have s. unto David my.   89:3
s. by my holiness that. 35; Amos 4:2
are mad against me, are s. Ps 102:8
the Lord hath s. and will. 110:4
I have s. and I will. 119:106
the Lord hath s. in truth to. 132:11
the Lord of hosts hath s. Isa 14:24
I have s. by myself, the word. 45:23
I have s. that waters of Noah no more
   go over the earth, so have I s. 54:9
Lord hath s. by his right hand. 62:8
they have s. by them.   Jer 5:7
have s. by my great name. 44:26
them that have s. oaths. Ezek 21:23
hath s. by the excellency. Amos 8:7
the mercy thou hast s.   Mi 7:20
knowing God hath s. by. Acts 2:30
drew nigh which God had s. 7:17*
I have s. in my wrath.   Heb 4:3

sycamine

say to this s. tree, Be. Luke 17:6

sycamore, see sycomore

sycomore

This tree is not the sycamore
of England and America but
an entirely different tree, the
Egyptian fig tree, or fig-mul-
berry. It spreads its branches
widely, making a delightful shade,
for which reason it was often
planted by the roadside, Luke 19:4.
Its fruit was much like a fig, but
to make it eatable it used to be
thought necessary to puncture it
three or four days before it was
ripe, Amos 7:14. But this is not
done now, the fruit ripening in the
ordinary manner. The value of the
tree was mainly in its timber.

sycomore fruit

a gatherer of s. fruit. Amos 7:14

sycomore tree

climbed up into a s. tree. Luke 19:4

sycomore trees

Solomon made cedars to be as s.
  trees. 1 Ki 10:27; 2 Chr 1:15; 9:27
over the s. trees was Baal-hanan.
           1 Chr 27:28
destroyed their s. trees. Ps 78:47

sycomores

the s. are cut down, but. Isa 9:10

synagogue

This word is found only once in
the Old Testament in Ps 74:8,
and there is no indication that synagogues existed before the Exile,
although there are some reasons
to think that they were in existence
centuries earlier. As to Ps 74:8,
They have burned up all the
synagogues of God in the land; the

original is, all the assemblies of
God, by which must be understood
the places where the people assembled to worship God. But this
does not infer that those places
were what we now mean by synagogues. After the Maccabaean
period there were synagogues in
every settlement where there were
enough Jews to erect one. It is
said that there were in the city of
Jerusalem alone no less than four
hundred and sixty, or even four
hundred and eighty; but this is
most probably an exaggeration.
Every trading fraternity had a
synagogue of their own, and even
strangers built some for those of
their own nation. Hence it is, that
in Acts 6:9, mention is made of
the synagogues of the Libertines,
Cyrenians, Alexandrians, Cilicians,
and Asiatics; which were appointed
for the use of such of the inhabitants
of these cities, or of these nations,
as should at any time be at Jerusalem. The synagogue worship became the regular worship of the
people outside of Jerusalem, the
temple being visited at one or more
of the great feasts.
In Palestine the synagogue was so
built that the worshipper would
face Jerusalem. At the upper end
was the chest which contained the
Book of the Law. Here were the
chief seats so desired by the Pharisees, Mat 23:6; Jas 2:2, 3. In
later times the congregation was
divided, men on one side and
women on the other, with a lattice
partition between.
The word is used in the New
Testament [1] for the building,
Luke 7:5. [2] For the organization which worshipped there, Acts
6:9. The ruler of the synagogue
was the one who had the responsi-
bility of maintaining order, deciding
on the order of public worship, etc.,
Luke 8:41; Acts 18:8. The minister had duties of a lower kind,
more like those of a modern deacon,
or of a sacristan.
Worship was held in the synagogue every sabbath, and every
feast day, the main part of the service being the reading of the law,
with an exposition of what was
read, Acts 15:21; 13:15.
The ordinary school for Jewish
children was in the synagogue of
each village. Every boy was supposed to attend, and the teaching
was mostly in the Law and other
Scriptures.
The organization of the synagogue, where possible, included a
council of the elders; and in these
cases they had a certain amount of
judicial power, Mat 10:17.
The synagogue of the Libertines,
or freedmen, Acts 6:9, was, according to most interpreters, that of
those Jews, who having been led
away captive by Pompey and
others, had afterwards recovered
their liberty, and returned to
Jerusalem, when Tiberias drove the
Jews out of Italy.
he went into their s.   Mat 12:9
he taught them in their s. 13:54
            Mark 6:2
and there was in their s. a man with.
     Mark 1:23; Luke 4:33
when they were come out of the s.
     Mark 1:29; Luke 4:38
one of the rulers of the s. besought.
  Mat 5:22, 36, 38; Luke 8:41; 4:16
he went into the s. on the sabbath.
            Luke 4:16
the eyes of all in the s. were. 20
nation and hath built us a s. 7:5
things said he in the s. John 6:59

he should be put out of the s.
            John 9:22
they should be put out of s. 12:42
I ever taught in the s. and. 18:20
certain of the s. which is called the s.
  of the Libertines.   . Acts 6:9
the s. on the sabbath day. 13:14
the rulers of the s. sent to them. 15
the Jews were gone out of the s. 42
Barnabas went both into the s. 14:1
to Thessalonica where was a s. 17:1
therefore he disputed in the s. 17
and he reasoned in the s. 18:4
house joined hard to the s.   7
Crispus the chief ruler of the s. 8
Sosthenes chief ruler of the s. 17
to speak boldy in the s.   26:11
beat in every s. such. 22:19; 26:11
but are the s. of Satan.   Rev 2:9
I will make them of the s. of. 3:9

synagogues

burned up all the s. of God. Ps 74:8
Jesus went teaching in their s. and.
  Mat 4:23; 9:35; Mark 1:39
           Luke 13:10
the hypocrites do in the s. Mat 6:2
love to pray standing in the s. 5
they will scourge you in their s.
        10:17; 23:34
for they love the chief seats in the s.
  23:6; Mark 12:39; Luke 11:43
           20:46
and in the s. ye shall be. Mark 13:9
he taught in the s. being. Luke 4:15
and he preached in the s. of. 44
they bring you unto the s. 12:11
delivering you up to the s. 21:12
put you out of the s.   John 16:2
of him letters to the s. Acts 9:2
he preached Christ in the s. 20
Barnabas preached in the s. 13:5
being read in the s. every. 15:21
up the people in the s. 24:12

Syria

served the gods of S. Judg 10:6
David put garrisons in S.
     2 Sam 8:6; 1 Chr 18:6
I abode at Geshur in S. 2 Sam 15:8
for the kings of S. did. 1 Ki 10:29
Rezon abhorred Israel and reigned
  over S.   11:25
anoint Hazael to be king of S. 19:15
           2 Ki 13:3
war between S. and Israel.1 Ki 22:1
by Naaman deliverance given to S.
           2 Ki 5:1
the bands of S. came no. 6:23
was no man in the camp of S. 7:5
that thou shalt be king of S. 8:13
the king of S. had destroyed. 13:7
arrow of deliverance from S. 17
but now thou shalt smite S. 19
S. recovered Elath to S. 16:6
thou shalt push S. 2 Chr 18:10
the host of S. came up. 24:23
the gods of kings of S. help. 28:23
S. is confederate with. Isa 7:2
for head of S. is Damascus, and. 8
of the daughters of S. Ezek 16:57
S. was thy merchant for thy. 27:16
into the country of S. Hos 12:12
the people of S. shall go. Amos 1:5
went throughout all S. Mat 4:24
was governor of S.   Luke 2:2
to the brethren in S. Acts 15:23
went through S. and Cilicia. 41
sailed thence into S. 18:18; 21:3
           Gal 1:21

see king

Syriac

spake to the king in S. Dan 2:4

Syrian

daughter of Bethuel the S., Laban
  the S. Gen 25:20; 28:5; 31:20, 24
a S. ready to perish. Deut 26:5
spared Naaman this S. 2 Ki 5:20
speak in the S. language. 18:26
           Isa 36:11
letter was written in the S. tongue
  and interpreted in the S. Ezra 4:7
saving Naaman the S. Luke 4:27

Syrians

S. of Damascus came to succour
Hadadezer ... of S. *2 Sam 8:5*
the S. became David's servants. 6
 1 Chr 18:5, 6
from smiting of the S. *2 Sam 8:13*
sent and hired the S. 10:6
if the S. be too strong for me. 11
 1 Chr 19:12
so the S. feared to help the children
 of. *2 Sam 10:19; 1 Chr 19:19*
the S. fled and Israel. *1 Ki 20:20*
Israel's little flocks, but S. 27
Israel slew of the S. 100,000. 29
these shall thou push the S. 22:11
the S. had taken a maid. *2 Ki 5:2*
beware, for thither the S. are. 6:9
fall into the host of the S. 7:4
the Lord made the host of the S. 6
we came to camp of the S. 10
S. wounded Joram. 8:28, 29; 9:15
 2 Chr 22:5
from under the hand of S. *2 Ki 13:5*
for thou shalt smite the S. in. 17
the S. came to Elath and. 16:6
the S. before, and the. *Isa 9:12*
fear of the army of S. *Jer 35:11*
have not I brought the S.? *Amos 9:7*

Syrophenician

Greek, a S. by nation. *Mark 7:26*

T

Tabeal

midst of it, even the son of T. *Isa 7:6*

Taberah

name of the place T. *Num 11:3*
at T. he provoked the. *Deut 9:22*

tabering

the voice of doves t. *Nah 2:7*

tabernacle

This word literally means tent, and is used of any sort of temporary tent or booth, as well as for the tabernacle erected for the worship of God. Where the word is plural, except in the expression feast of tabernacles, it has the meaning of dwelling, or dwelling-place.

The Tabernacle erected for worship in the wilderness was thirty cubits in length, and ten in breadth and in height. It was divided into two partitions: the first was called The Holy Place, which was twenty cubits long, and ten wide: here were placed the table of shewbread, the golden candlestick, and the golden altar of incense. The second was called The most Holy Place, whose length was ten cubits, and breadth ien cubits. Here the ark of the covenant was kept, which was a symbol of God's gracious presence with the Jewish church. The most Holy was divided from the Holy Place by a curtain, or veil of very rich cloth, which hung upon four pillars of shittim wood, that were covered with plates of gold, Ex 26:1; Heb 9:2, 3. St. Paul refers to our natural body as a tabernacle, 2 Cor 5:1; 2 Pet 1:13.

The feast of tabernacles, Lev 23:34, was so called, because the Israelites kept it under booths of branches in memory of their dwelling in tents in their passage through the wilderness. It was one of the three great yearly feasts, when all the males were obliged to present themselves before the Lord. It was celebrated after harvest, on the 15th day of the month Tisri, which answers to our month of October. The feast continued eight days; but the first day and the last were the most solemn.

The Revised Versions most frequently use the word tent, in place of tabernacle.

the manner of the t. *Ex 25:9*
thou shalt make the t. with. 26:1
curtains, and it shall be one t.
 6; 36:13
of goats' hair to be a covering upon
 the t. 26:7; 35:11; 36:14
for the t. of shittim wood. 26:15, 17
 20, 26; 36:20, 22, 23, 28, 31, 32
make bars for the t. 26:26, 27
rear up the t. 30
vessels of t. of brass. 27:19; 39:40
the t. shall be sanctified. 29:43
all the furniture of the t. 31:7
Moses pitched the t. without. 33:7
departed not out of the t. 11
the pins of the t. 35:18; 38:20, 31
wrought the work of the t. 36:8
thus was the work of the t. 39:32
they brought the t. to Moses. 33
thou shalt set up the t. 40:2
anoint the t. 9
on the first day, the t. was reared up.
 17, 18; *Num 7:1*
the tent over the t. *Ex 40:19*
he brought the ark into the t. 21
court round about the t. 33
glory of the Lord filled the t. 34, 35
cloud taken up from over the t. 36
 Num 9:17; 10:11; 12:10
cloud was on the t. by day, and fire.
 Ex 40:38; Num 9:18, 19, 22
Moses anointed the t. *Lev 8:10*
not when they defile my t. 15:31
not an offering before the t. 17:4
I will set my t. among you. 26:11
Levites over the t.; bear the t.; encamp round the t. *Num 1:50, 53*
the t. setteth forward, and when t. 51
keep the charge of the t. 53; 3:7
 25; 18:3; 31:30, 47
t. to do the service of the t. 3:7
shall pitch behind the t. 23
pitch northward of the t. 35
those that encamp before the t. 38
oversight of the t. pertaineth. 4:16
bear the curtains of the t. 25
shall bear the boards of the t. 31
take of the dust of the t. 5:17
their offering before the t. 7:3
on the day that the t. was reared up,
 the cloud covered the t. 9:15
Kohathites did set up the t. 10:21
elders round about the t. 11:24
went not out unto the t. 26
small to do the service of the t. 16:9
get you up from about the t. 24, 27
whoso cometh near to the t. 17:13
Lord appeared in t. in. *Deut 31:15*
wherein the Lord's t. *Josh 22:19*
set the ark in the midst of the t.
 2 Sam 6:17
walked in a tent and in a t. 7:6
Zadok took a horn of oil out of the t.
 1 Ki 1:39
Joab fled to the t. of the Lord. 2:28
vessels in the t. were brought up.
 8:1; *2 Chr 5:5*
the service of the t. *1 Chr 6:48*
keepers of the gates of the t. 9:19
oversight of the house of the t. 23
the priests, before t. of the. 16:39
but have gone from one t. 17:5
for the t. which Moses made. 21:29
no more carry the t. 23:26
brazen altar before the t. *2 Chr 1:5*
shalt know that thy t. *Job 5:24*
the light shall be dark in his t. 18:6
shall be rooted out of his t. 14
destruction shall dwell in his t. 15
encamp round about my t. 19:12
with him that is left in his t. 20:26
secret of God was upon my t. 29:4
if the men of my t. said not. 31:31
understand the noise of his t.?
 36:29*
who shall abide in thy t.? *Ps 15:1*
in them hath he set a t. for. 19:4
in the secret of his t. shall. 27:5
I will offer in his t. sacrifices. 6
I will abide in thy t. for ever. 61:4
in Salem is his t., his dwelling. 76:2
so that he forsook the t. of. 78:60
moreover he refused the t. of. 67
I will not come into the t. 132:3, 7

the t. of the upright shall. *Pr 14:11*
there shall be a t. for a. *Isa 4:6**
he shall sit upon it in the t. 16:5
a t. that shall not be taken. 33:20
my t. is spoiled, and all my. *Jer 10:20*
were pleasant in the t. *Lam 2:4*
violently taken away his t. 6
my t. also shall be. *Ezek 37:27*
was the breadth of the t. 41:1
but ye have borne the t. *Amos 5:26**
day will I raise up the t. of. 9:11
took up the t. of Moloch. *Acts 7:43*
desired to find a t. for the God. 46
and will build again the t. 15:16
if our house of this t. *2 Cor 5:1*
we that are in this t. do groan. 4
true t. which the Lord. *Heb 8:2*
Moses was about to make the t. 5
there was a t. made, called. 9:2
t. which is called the holiest. 3
went always into the first t. 6
while as the first t. was yet. 8
by a greater and more perfect t. 11
he sprinkled with blood the t. 21
no right to eat which serve t. 13:10
as long as I am in this t. *2 Pet 1:13*
shortly I must put off my t. 14
to blaspheme his name and his t.
 Rev 13:6
behold the temple of the t. 15:5

see **congregation, door**

tabernacle *of witness*

laid up the rods in the t. *of witness.*
 Num 17:7
Moses went into the t. *of witness.* 8
before the t. *of witness.* 18:2
bring the collection for t. *of witness.*
 2 Chr 24:6
fathers had the t. *of witness.*
 Acts 7:44

tabernacles

how goodly are thy t. O. *Num 24:5*
wickedness dwell in thy t. *Job 11:14*
the t. of robbers prosper, and. 12:6
and fire shall consume the t. 15:34
away iniquity far from thy t. 22:23
bring me unto thy t. *Ps 43:3*
make glad the holy place of t. 46:4
their strength in t. of Ham. 78:51
t. of Edom have consulted. 83:6
how amiable are thy t. O Lord. 84:1
salvation is in the t. of the. 118:15
we will go into his t. and. 132:7
he shall plant the t. of. *Dan 11:45*
thorns shall be in their t. *Hos 9:6*
make thee to dwell in t. 12:9
cut off the man out of the t. *Mal 2:12*
let us make here three t. *Mat 17:4*
 Mark 9:5; Luke 9:33
Abraham dwelling in t. *Heb 11:9*

see **feast**

Tabitha

a disciple named T. *Acts 9:36*
to the body, said, T. arise. 40

table

shalt also make a t. of. *Ex 25:23*
places of staves to bear the t. 27, 28
 37:14
thou shalt set the t. without. 26:35
thou shalt anoint the t. and. 30:27
Bezaleel shall make the t. 31:8
he made the t. 37:10
the vessels on the t. 16
brought the t. unto Moses. 39:33
thou shalt bring in the t. and. 40:4
put the t. in the tent of the. 22
on a row on the pure t. *Lev 24:6*
charge shall be the t. *Num 3:31*
their meat under my t. *Judg 1:7*
not to the king's t. *1 Sam 20:29*
Jonathan arose from the t. in. 34
Mephibosheth shall eat bread at my
 t. *2 Sam 9:7, 10, 11, 13; 19:28*
those that eat at thy t. *1 Ki 2:7*
came to king Solomon's t. 4:27
when the queen of Sheba saw the
 meat of his t. 10:5; *2 Chr 9:4*
as they sat at t. word of. *1 Ki 13:20*
which eat at Jezebel's t. 18:19
let us set for him a t. *2 Ki 4:10*
at my t. 150 Jews. *Neh 5:17*
should be set on thy t. *Job 36:16*
thou preparest a t. *Ps 23:5*

table 655 take

let their *t.* become a snare. *Ps* 69:22
can God furnish a *t.* in the? 78:19
olive plants about thy *t.* 128:3
on the *t.* of thy heart. *Pr* 3:3; 7:3
hath also furnished her *t.* 9:2
the king sitteth at his *t.* *S of S* 1:12
prepare the *t.*, watch, eat. *Isa* 21:5
write it before them in a *t.* 30:8*
prepare a *t.* for that troop. 65:11
it is graven on the *t.* of. *Jer* 17:1
and a *t.* prepared before. *Ezek* 23:41
ye shall be filled at my *t.* 39:20
this is the *t.* that is before. 41:22
shall come near to my *t.* 44:16
speak lies at one *t.* *Dan* 11:27
the *t.* of the Lord is. *Mal* 1:7
ye say, The *t.* of the Lord is. 12
crumbs which fall from their master's *t.* *Mat* 15:27; *Mark* 7:28
fell from rich man's *t.* *Luke* 16:21
the hand of him that betrayeth me
is with me on the *t.* 22:21
ye may eat and drink at my *t.* 30
one of them that sat at *t.* *John* 12:2*
no man at the *t.* knew for. 13:28
their *t.* be made a snare. *Rom* 11:9
devils, ye cannot be partakers of the
Lord's *t.* and of the. *1 Cor* 10:21
see shewbread

writing **table**
Zacharias asked for a *writing t.*
Luke 1:63

tables
Frequently meaning tablets, *Ex*
32:15; Isa 30:8. *To serve tables
was to oversee the caring for the
poor,* Acts 6:2.
the *t.* were written on. *Ex* 32:15
t. were the work of God, graven on
the *t.* 16
he cast the *t.* out of his hands. 19
on these *t.* the words in first *t.* 34:1
he wrote on the *t.* *Deut* 10:4
put the *t.* in the ark. 5; *Heb* 9:4
David gave gold for *t.* *1 Chr* 28:16
Solomon also made ten *t.* *2 Chr* 4:8
the *t.* whereon the shewbread. 19
all *t.* are full of vomit. *Isa* 28:8
eight *t.* whereupon they. *Ezek* 40:41
four *t.* were of hewn stone for. 42
and make it plain on *t.* *Hab* 2:2
he overthrew the *t.* of the money
changers. *Mat* 21:12; *Mark* 11:15
cups, pots, and of *t.* *Mark* 7:4
and overthrew the *t.* *John* 2:15
leave the word of God, and serve *t.*
Acts 6:2
t. of stone, but fleshly *t.* *2 Cor* 3:3
see stone, two

tablets
they brought *t.*, all jewels. *Ex* 35:22*
we brought *t.* to make. *Num* 31:50*
I will take away the *t.* *Isa* 3:20*

Tabor
and draw toward mount *T.* *Judg* 4:6
Barak was gone up to mount *T.* 12
they whom ye slew at *T.*? 8:18
come to the plain of *T.* *1 Sam* 10:3
T. and Hermon shall rejoice in thy
name. *Ps* 89:12
surely, as *T.* is among. *Jer* 46:18
been a net spread upon *T.* *Hos* 5:1

tabret
away with *t.* and harp. *Gen* 31:27
high place with a *t.* *1 Sam* 10:5*
aforetime I was as a *t.* *Job* 17:6*
the *t.*, pipe, and wine are. *Isa* 5:12

tabrets
to meet Saul with *t.* *1 Sam* 18:6*
the mirth of *t.* ceaseth. *Isa* 24:8
shall be with *t.* and harps. 30:32
be adorned with thy *t.* *Jer* 31:4
workmanship of thy *t.* *Ezek* 28:13

taches
(*Revisions substitute the word
clasps*)
thou shalt make fifty *t.* *Ex* 26:6
make fifty *t.* of brass. 11; 35:11
hang up the vail under the *t.* 26:33
he made fifty *t.* of gold. 36:13, 18
brought his *t.*, his boards. 39:33

tackling
we cast out the *t.* of. *Acts* 27:19

tacklings
thy *t.* are loosed, could. *Isa* 33:23

Tadmor
Solomon built *T.* in the. *2 Chr* 8:4

Tahapanes, *or* **Tehaphnehes**
children of *T.* have broken. *Jer* 2:16
thus came they even to *T.* 43:7
publish in Noph and *T.* 46:14
at *T.* also the day. *Ezek* 30:18

Tahpenes
sister of *T.* the queen. *1 Ki* 11:19

tail
hand, take it by the *t.* *Ex* 4:4
head, not the *t.* *Deut* 28:13, 44
foxes and turned *t.* to *t.* *Judg* 15:4
behemoth moveth his *t.* *Job* 40:17
off from Israel head and *t.* *Isa* 9:14
teacheth lies, he is the *t.* 15
the head or *t.* may do. 19:15
his *t.* drew the third. *Rev* 12:4

tails
firebrand between two *t.* *Judg* 15:4
two *t.* of these smoking firebrands.
Isa 7:4
t. like to scorpions, stings in their *t.*
Rev 9:10
power in their *t.*: their *t.* were. 19

take
wilt *t.* the left hand. *Gen* 13:9
the persons, *t.* the goods to. 14:21
arise, *t.* thy wife and thy. 19:15
t. now thy son, thine only son. 22:2
thou shalt not *t.* a wife to. 24:3, 37
to *t.* my master's brother's. 48
what is thine with me, *t.* it. 31:32
if thou *t.* other wives besides. 50
t. our daughters unto you. 34:9
will *t.* your daughters to us. 16
let her *t.* it to her, lest we be. 38:23
I will *t.* you to me for a. *Ex* 6:7
for thereof must we *t.* to. 10:26
and thy rod *t.* in thine hand. 17:5
shalt not *t.* the name of the Lord thy
God. 20:7; *Deut* 5:11
t. him from mine altar. *Ex* 21:14
and thou shalt *t.* no gift. 23:8
Deut 16:19
pardon and *t.* us for. *Ex* 34:9
lest thou *t.* of their daughters. 16
Deut 7:3
neither *t.* her son's. *Lev* 18:17
neither shalt thou *t.* a wife to. 18
and if a man *t.* a wife, and. 20:14
not *t.* a wife that is a whore, nor *t.* a.
21:7; *Ezek* 44:22
t. a wife in her virginity. *Lev* 21:13
t. thou no usury of him, or. 25:36
ye shall *t.* them as an inheritance. 46
t. the Levites from among. *Num* 8:6
I will *t.* of the spirit that is on. 11:17
Korah said, Ye *t.* too much. 16:3, 7
ye shall *t.* no satisfaction. 35:31, 32
t. ye wise men and. *Deut* 1:13
and *t.* him a nation, from. 4:34
then thou shalt *t.* an awl and. 15:17
elders of that city shall *t.* 22:18
shall not *t.* his father's wife. 30
may not *t.* her again to be his. 24:4
no man shall *t.* a millstone to. 6
t. a widow's raiment to pledge. 17
if he say, I like not to *t.* her. 25:8
when ye *t.* of the accursed thing.
Josh 6:18
family which the Lord shall *t.*; household which the Lord shall *t.* 7:14
they should *t.* his carcase. 8:29
their land did Joshua *t.* at. 10:42
they shall *t.* him into the city. 20:4
t. ye possession among us. 22:19
for the necks of them that *t.* spoil.
Judg 5:30
that thou goest to *t.* a wife. 14:3
have ye called us to *t.* that? 15*
consider, *t.* advice, and speak. 19:30
t. knowledge of me. *Ruth* 2:10
t. as much as thy soul desireth, and
if not I will *t.* it by. *1 Sam* 2:16
he will *t.* your sons for himself. 8:11
he will *t.* your daughters. 13
he will *t.* your fields. 14

t. the tenth of your seed. *1 Sam* 8:15
he will *t.* your menservants. 16
how thy brethren fare, and *t.* 17:18
and *t.* thine head from thee. 46
messengers to *t.* David. 19:14, 20
if thou wilt *t.* that, *t.* it, there. 21:9
huntest my soul to *t.* it. 24:11
shall I then *t.* my bread, and? 25:11
t. now the spear that is at his. 26:11
he spared to *t.* of his. *2 Sam* 12:4
I will *t.* thy wives before thine. 11
t. it, lest I *t.* the city, and it be. 28
t. the thing to his heart. 13:33; 19:10
me go over, and *t.* off his head. 16:9
said, Yea, let him *t.* all. 19:30
Jeroboam, *T.* ten pieces. *1 Ki* 11:31
will not *t.* the whole kingdom. 34
t. with thee ten loaves. 14:3
t. the prophets of Baal. 18:40
war or peace, *t.* them alive. 20:18
arise, *t.* possession of. 21:15, 16
t. Micaiah, carry him back. 22:26
2 Chr 18:25
creditor is come to *t.* *2 Ki* 4:1
t. my staff and go. 29
t. a blessing of thy servant. 5:15
urged him to *t.* it. 16
I will *t.* somewhat. 20
be content, *t.* two talents. 23
t. a present and go. 8:8
t. this box of oil in thine. 9:1, 3
t. ye the heads of your. 10:6
he said, *T.* them alive. 14
let the priests *t.* it. 12:5
said, *T.* bow and arrows. 13:15, 18
shall yet *t.* root downward. 19:30
Isa 37:31
I will not *t.* that which. *1 Chr* 21:24
those did Cyrus *t.* *Ezra* 5:14
t. these vessels. 15
not *t.* their daughters. 9:12
Neh 10:30; 13:25
t. the apparel, and do. *Esth* 6:10
knoweth the way that I *t.* *Job* 23:10
they *t.* the widow's ox for a. 24:3
and they *t.* a pledge of the poor. 9
and my sinews *t.* no rest. 30:17
surely I would *t.* it upon. 31:36
thou *t.* him for a servant for? 41:4
therefore *t.* to you now seven. 42:8
the rulers *t.* counsel. *Ps* 2:2
persecute my soul, and *t.* it. 7:5*
I will *t.* no bullock out of thy. 50:9
shouldest *t.* my covenant in. 16
and *t.* not thy Holy Spirit. 51:11
t. him, for there is none to. 71:11
t. a psalm, and bring. 81:2
t. the houses of God. 83:12
will I not utterly *t.* from him. 89:33
and let another *t.* his office. 109:8
t. the cup of salvation, and. 116:13
t. not the word of truth. 119:43
if I *t.* the wings of the. 139:9
and thine enemies *t.* thy name. 20
his own iniquities shall *t.* *Pr* 5:22
neither let her *t.* thee with her. 6:25
can a man *t.* fire in his bosom? 27
let us *t.* our fill of love until. 7:18
t. his garment that is surety for
stranger, *t.* a pledge. 20:16; 27:13
and *t.* the name of my God. 30:9*
and shall *t.* nothing of. *Eccl* 5:15
and to *t.* his portion and rejoice. 19
t. us the foxes. *S of S* 2:15
them of Jacob to *t.* root. *Isa* 27:6
time it goeth, it shall *t.* you. 28:19
not a sherd to *t.* fire from. 30:14
is divided, the lame *t.* the. 33:23
their stock shall not *t.* root. 40:24
will *t.* thereof and warm. 44:15
t. the millstones, and grind. 47:2
I will *t.* vengeance, I will not. 3
vanity shall *t.* them, wind. 57:13*
t. delight in approaching to. 58:2
also *t.* of them for priests. 66:21
t. thee much sope [soap]. *Jer* 2:22
I will *t.* you one of a city. 3:14
t. the girdle that thou. 13:4, 6
shall not sorrows *t.* thee as a. 21
if thou *t.* forth the precious. 15:19
thou shalt not *t.* thee a wife. 16:2
have digged a pit to *t.* me. 18:22
t. of the ancients of the people. 19:1
we shall *t.* our revenge. 20:10

I will t. all the families. *Jer 25:*9
I will t. from them the voice. 10
if they refuse to t. the cup at. 28
t. ye wives, and beget sons. 29:6
come to the city to t. it. 32:24
money, and t. witnesses. 25, 44
king of Babylon shall t. it. 28
t. Jeremiah, and look well to. 39:12
Gilead, and t. balm. 46:11; 51:8
t. vengeance upon her; as she. 50:15
shall not t. of thee a stone. 51:26
behold I will t. vengeance for the. 36
what thing shall I t. to witness? *Lam 2:*13
t. thee a tile and lay it. *Ezek 4:*1
t. thou an iron pan. 3
t. unto thee wheat, barley, and. 9
t. a sharp knife, t. a razor, 5:1
t. fire from between the wheels. 10:6
I will t. the stony heart out. 11:19
that I may t. the house. 14:5
will men t. a pin of it to hang? 15:3
remove the diadem, t. off the. 21:26
thou shalt t. thine inheritance. 22:16*
t. the choice of the flock, and. 24:5
fury to come up to t. vengeance. 8
I t. from them their strength. 25
t. a multitude, t. her spoil, t. 29:19
if people of the land t. a man. 33:2
I will t. you from among the. 36:24
t. thee one stick, t. another. 37:16
I will t. the stick of Joseph. 19
to t. a spoil, and to t. a prey. 38:12
art thou come to t. prey, to t. a? 13
the prince not t. the people's. 46:18
but the saints shall t. the. *Dan 7:*18
the king shall t. the most. 11:15
to the isles, and shall t. many. 18
go t. unto thee a wife of. *Hos 1:*2
I was as they that t. off the. 11:4
t. with you words, and turn. 14:2
ye t. from him burdens. *Amos 5:*11
afflict the just, they t. a bribe. 12
shall mine hand t. them. 9:2, 3
t. I beseech thee, my life. *Jonah 4:*3
they covet fields and t. *Mi 2:*2
that they shall not t. shame. 6*
the Lord will t. vengeance. *Nah 1:*2
t. ye the spoil of silver, t. the. 2:9
heap dust and t. it. *Hab 1:*10
build the house; and I will t. *Hag 1:*8
I t. thee, O Zerubbabel my. 2:23
t. of them of the captivity. *Zech 6:*10
t. yet instruments of a foolish. 11:15
fear not to t. unto thee. *Mat 1:*20
and t. the young child and. 2:13
t. no thought for your life. 6:25*
28*, 31*, 34*; 10:19*; *Mark 13:*11*
*Luke 12:*11*, 22*, 26*
and the violent t. the. *Mat 11:*12
t. my yoke upon you, and learn. 29
It is not meet to t. the children's bread. 15:26; *Mark 7:*27
they had forgotten to t. bread. *Mat 16:*5; *Mark 8:*14
kings of earth t. custom. *Mat 17:*25
then t. with thee one or two. 18:16
t. that thine is and go thy. 20:14
on the house top not come down to t. any. 24:17; *Mark 13:*15
t. therefore the talent. *Mat 25:*28
that they might t. Jesus. *Mark 14:*1, 44
took bread and said, T. *Mat 26:*26
*Mark 14:*22; *1 Cor 11:*24
sleep on now, and t. your rest. *Mat 26:*45; *Mark 14:*41
they that t. sword shall. *Mat 26:*52
with swords and staves to t. me. 55
*Mark 14:*48
t. nothing for their journey. *Mark 6:*8; *Luke 9:*3
his brother should t. his wife. *Mark 12:*19; *Luke 20:*28
casting lots what every man should t. *Mark 15:*24
whether Elias will come to t. 36
David did t. and eat the. *Luke 6:*4
forbid him not to t. thy coat. 29
said, T. care of him. 10:35
soul, t. thine ease. 12:19
then begin with shame to t. the. 14:9
t. thy bill and write. 16:6, 7
t. from him the pound. 19:24

t. this and divide it. *Luke 22:*17
hath a purse, let him t. it. 36
Jesus said to them, T. *John 2:*16
of them may t. a little. 6:7
that they would come and t. him. 15
they sought to t. him. 7:30, 32
10:39; 11:57
loveth me, because I lay down my life, that I might t. it. 10:17, 18
he shall t. of mine, and shew. 16:15
thou shouldest t. them out. 17:15
t. ye him, and judge him. 18:31
Pilate saith, T. ye him, and. 19:6
bishoprick let another t. *Acts 1:*20
further to t. Peter also. 12:3
to t. out of them a people. 15:14
Barnabas determined to t. with. 37
Paul thought not good to t. him. 38
there intending to t. in Paul. 20:13
I t. you to record this day. 26*
them t. and purify thyself. 21:24
besought them to t. meat. 27:33, 34
why not rather t. wrong? *1 Cor 6:*7
shall I then t. the members of? 15
doth God t. care for oxen? 9:9
t. upon us the ministering. *2 Cor 8:*4
ye suffer, if a man t. of you. 11:20*
therefore I t. pleasure in. 12:10
t. to you the whole. *Eph 6:*13
and t. the helmet of salvation. 17
how shall he t. care of? *1 Tim 3:*5
t. Mark, and bring him. *2 Tim 4:*11
a commandment to t. tithes. *Heb 7:*5
t. my brethren, the prophets, for a. *Jas 5:*10
if ye t. it patiently, it. *1 Pet 2:*20
hold fast, that no man t. *Rev 3:*11
thou art worthy to t. the book. 5:9
power given him to t. peace from. 6:4
t. the little book. 10:8
t. it and eat it. 9
let him t. the water of life. 22:17

see counsel

take away
wouldest thou t. *away* my son's mandrakes? *Gen 30:*15
ye will t. Benjamin *away*. 42:36
t. this child *away*, and. *Ex 2:*9
that he may t. *away* the frogs. 8:8
that he may t. *away* from me. 10:17
and I will t. sickness *away*. 23:25
*Deut 7:*15
I will t. *away* mine hand. *Ex 33:*23
it shall he t. *away*. *Lev 3:*4; 4:9; 7:4
t. *away* all the fat thereof. 4:31, 35
that they t. *away* the stones. 14:40
shalt t. *away* the ashes. *Num 4:*13
thou shalt quite t. *away* their. 17:10
t. *away* the serpents from us. 21:7
until ye t. a. the accursed. *Josh 7:*13
shall I not t. you *away*? *2 Sam 4:*11
except thou t. *away* the blind. 5:6
t. *away* the iniquity of thy. 24:10
mayest t. *away* the innocent blood. *1 Ki 2:*31
t. *away* the remnant of the. 14:10*
t. *away* the posterity. 16:3*; 21:21*
now, O Lord, t. *away* my life. 19:4
seek my life to t. it *away*. 10, 14
shall my servants t. *away*. 20:6
t. the kings *away* and put. 24
the Lord will t. *away*. *2 Ki 2:*3, 5
sent to t. *away* mine head. 6:32
till I come and t. you *away*. 18:32
*Isa 36:*17
I will not t. my mercy *away* from him. *1 Chr 17:*13
to t. *away* his sackcloth. *Esth 4:*4
why dost thou not t. *away*? *Job 7:*21
t. his rod *away* from me. 9:34
they violently t. *away* flocks. 24:2
they t. *away* the sheaf from the. 10
my maker would soon t. me a. 32:22
lest he t. thee *away* with. 36:18*
devised to t. *away* my life. *Ps 31:*13
he shall t. thee *away* and. 52:5
he shall t. them *away* with. 58:9
t. me not *away* in the midst. 102:24
why should he t. *away* thy bed? *Pr 22:*27
t. *away* the dross from the. 25:4
t. *away* the wicked from before. 5

I will t. *away* all thy tin. *Isa 1:*25
t. *away* the stay and staff. 3:1
t. *away* bravery. 18
to t. *away* our reproach. 4:1
I will t. *away* the hedge. 5:5
t. *away* the righteousness of. 23
to t. *away* the right from. 10:2
of his people shall he t. *away*. 25:8
all the fruit, to t. *away* his sin. 27:9
thy sons shall they t. *away*. 39:7
whirlwind shall t. them *away*. 40:24
if thou t. *away* from the midst. 58:9
destroy and t. *away* her. 5:10
t. me not *away* in thy long. 15:15
shall t. *away* the detestable things. *Ezek 11:*18
they shall t. *away* thy nose. 23:25
t. *away* thy fair jewels. 26
t. *away* thy labour. 29
behold, I t. *away* the desire. 24:16
come and t. him *away*. 33:4, 6
and I will t. *away* the stony. 36:26
t. *away* your exactions from. 45:9
and they shall t. *away*. *Dan 7:*26
they shall t. *away* the daily. 11:31
utterly t. them *away*. *Hos 1:*6
and t. *away* my corn in the. 2:9
for I will t. *away* the names. 17
and new wine t. *away* the heart. 4:11
I will t. *away* and none shall. 5:14
unto him, T. *away* all iniquity. 14:2
that he will t. you *away*. *Amos 4:*2
t. *away* from me the noise of. 5:23
they covet houses, and t. them *away*. *Mi 2:*2
I will t. *away* out of the midst of. *Zeph 3:*11
t. *away* the filthy garments. *Zech 3:*4
I will t. *away* his blood out. 9:7
one shall t. you *away*. *Mal 2:*3
and t. *away* thy coat, let. *Mat 5:*40
t. *away* and cast him into. 22:13
Father, t. *away* this cup. *Mark 14:*36
to t. *away* my reproach. *Luke 1:*25
not come down to t. it *away*. 17:31
said, T. *away* the stone. *John 11:*39
the Romans shall t. *away* our. 48
when I shall t. *away*. *Rom 11:*27
blood should t. *away* sins. *Heb 10:*4
manifested to t. *away*. *1 John 3:*5
t. *away* from the words of the book, God shall t. *away* his. *Rev 22:*19

take heed
t. *heed* that thou speak not to Jacob. *Gen 31:*24, 29
t. *heed* to thyself. *Ex 10:*28; 34:12
*Deut 4:*9; 12:13, 19, 30
*1 Sam 19:*2; *1 Tim 4:*16
t. *heed* to yourselves. *Ex 19:*12
*Deut 2:*4; 4:15, 23; 11:16
*Josh 23:*11; *Jer 17:*21
must I not t. *heed* to? *Num 23:*12
t. *heed* in the plague of. *Deut 24:*8
t. *heed* and hearken, O. 27:9
t. diligent *heed* to do. *Josh 22:*5
if thy children t. *heed*. *1 Ki 2:*4
8:25; *2 Chr 6:*16
t. *heed* now; for the Lord. *1 Chr 28:*10
t. *heed* what ye do, for ye judge not for man. *2 Chr 19:*6
fear of the Lord be on you, t. *heed*. 7
so that they will t. *heed* to do. 33:8
*Ezra 4:*22
t. *heed*, regard not. *Job 36:*21
I said, I will t. *heed* to. *Ps 39:*1
t. no *heed* to all words. *Eccl 7:*21
T. *heed* and be quiet, fear. *Isa 7:*4
t. *heed* every one of his. *Jer 9:*4
have left off to t. *heed* to. *Hos 4:*10
t. *heed* to your spirit. *Mal 2:*15, 16
t. *heed* that ye do not your alms before men. *Mat 6:*1
t. *heed* of the leaven of the Pharisees. 16:6; *Mark 8:*15
t. *heed* that no man deceive you. 24:4; *Mark 13:*5
he said to them, T. *heed*. *Mark 4:*24
t. *heed* to yourselves. 13:9
*Luke 17:*3; 21:34; *Acts 5:*35; 20:28
t. *heed*: behold, I have foretold you all things. *Mark 13:*23

t. ye *heed,* watch, pray. *Mark* 13:33
t. heed therefore how ye hear.
　　　　　　　　　　Luke 8:18
t. heed that the light in thee. 11:35
t. heed and beware of. 12:15
he said, *T. heed* that ye be. 21:8
saying, *T. heed* what thou doest.
　　　　　　　　　　Acts 22:26*
t. heed lest he also spare not thee.
　　　　　　　　　　Rom 11:21*
let every man *t. heed.* *1 Cor* 3:10
t. heed lest this liberty of. 8:9
that standeth *t. heed* lest he. 10:12
t. heed that ye be not consumed one
　of another. *Gal* 5:15
t. heed to the ministry. *Col* 4:17
t. heed lest an evil heart. *Heb* 3:12
ye do well that ye *t. heed.* *2 Pet* 1:19

take *hold*
sorrow shall *t. hold* on. *Ex* 15:14
trembling shall *t. hold* upon. 15
that the loops *t. hold* one of. 26:5*
and if mine hand *t. hold. Deut* 32:41
terrors *t. hold* on him. *Job* 27:20
justice *t. hold* on thee. 36:17
it might *t. hold* on the ends. 38:13
t. hold of shield and. *Ps* 35:2
wrathful anger *t. hold* of. 69:24*
neither *t.* they *hold* of the paths of
　life. *Pr* 2:19*
t. fast *hold* of instruction, let. 4:13
her steps *t. hold* on hell. 5:5
it is good that thou *t. hold* of this.
　　　　　　　　　　Eccl 7:18
will *t. hold* of the boughs. *S of S* 7:8
when a man shall *t. hold* of. *Isa* 3:6
seven women shall *t. hold* of. 4:1
sorrows shall *t. hold* of them. 13:8
let him *t. hold* of my strength. 27:5
to the eunuchs that *t. hold* of. 56:4
himself to *t. hold* of thee. 64:7
thou shalt *t. hold* but. *Mi* 6:14*
did they not *t. hold* of your fathers ?
　　　　　　　　　　Zech 1:6*
ten men shall *t. hold* of him. 8:23
that they might *t. hold. Luke* 20:20
could not *t. hold* of his words. 26

take *up*
t. up the fifth part of the. *Gen* 41:34
and the priest shall *t. up.* *Lev* 6:10
t. up the censers out of. *Num* 16:37
t. up the ark of the. *Josh* 3:6; 6:6
t. up every man a stone out. 4:5
the Lord would *t. up* Elijah. *2 Ki* 2:1
he said, *T. up* thy son. 4:36
t. up the iron. 6:7
t. up and cast him into the. 9:25
we *t. up* corn for them. *Neh* 5:2*
nor *t. up* their names. *Ps* 16:4
then the Lord will *t.* me *up.* 27:10
that thou shalt *t. up* this. *Isa* 14:4
t. up the stumblingblock out. 57:14
t. up a lamentation on the. *Jer* 7:29
for the mountains will I *t. up.* 9:10
t. up wailing for us. 18
t. up Jeremiah, before he die. 38:10
t. up a lamentation for the princes.
　　　　　　　　　　Ezek 19:1
t. up a lamentation for Tyrus.
　　　　　　　26:17; 27:2, 32
t. up a lamentation upon king of
　Tyrus. 28:12
t. up a lamentation for Pharaoh. 32:2
shall one *t. up* a snare. *Amos* 3:5*
hear his word which I *t. up.* 5:1
a man's uncle shall *t.* him *up.* 6:10
t. me *up* and cast me. *Jonah* 1:12
shall one *t. up* a parable. *Mi* 2:4
they *t. up* all of them. *Hab* 1:15
not all these *t. up* a parable ? 2:6
Jesus saith, Arise, *t. up* thy bed.
Mat 9:6; *Mark* 2:9, 11; *Luke* 5:24
　　　　　　　John 5:8, 11, 12
let him *t. up* his cross and follow me.
　　Mat 16:24; *Mark* 8:34; 10:21
　　　　　　　　　　Luke 9:23
and *t. up* the fish that. *Mat* 17:27
shall *t. up* serpents. *Mark* 16:18

taken
Lord God had *t.* from man. *Gen* 2:22
because she was *t.* out of man. 23
of the ground wast thou *t.* 3:19, 23
vengeance shall be *t.* on him. 4:15

42

the woman was *t.* into. *Gen* 12:15
so I might have *t.* her to me. 19
heard that his brother was *t.* 14:14
I have *t.* upon me to speak. 18:27
which thou hast *t.* is a wife. 20:3
is he that hath *t.* venison ? 27:33
the riches God hath *t.* from. 31:16
now Rachel had *t.* the images. 34
staves shall not be *t.* *Ex* 25:15
shoulder have I *t.* of Israel. *Lev* 7:34
t. the Levites for the firstborn of.
　　　　　　　　Num 3:12; 8:16, 18; 18:6
neither she be *t.* with the. 5:13
and the tabernacle was *t.* 10:17
I have not *t.* one ass from. 16:15
we have *t.* the sum of the. 31:49
their inheritance be *t.* 36:3
Lord hath *t.* you out of. *Deut* 4:20
wife, and hath not *t.* her. 20:7
when a man hath *t.* a wife. 24:1
t. a new wife, he shall be free at . . .
　his wife which he hath *t.* 5
they have *t.* of the. *Josh* 7:11
he that is *t.* shall be burnt. 15
and the tribe of Judah was *t.* 17
and Zabdi was *t.* 17
and Achan was *t.* 18
Lord hath *t.* vengeance. *Judg* 11:36
he told not them that he had *t.* 14:9
because he had *t.* his wife. 15:6
the 1100 shekels that were *t.* 17:2
the ark of God was *t.* *1 Sam* 4:11
　　　　　　　　17, 19, 21, 22
which the Philistines had *t.* 7:14
and Saul was *t.* 10:21
whose ox have I *t.?* 12:3
nor hast thou *t.* aught of any. 4
Saul and Jonathan were *t.* 14:41
Cast lots, and Jonathan was *t.* 42
and David's two wives were *t.* 30:5
that they had *t.* to them. 19
hast *t.* his wife to. *2 Sam* 12:9, 10
and I have *t.* the city of waters. 27
thou art *t.* in thy mischief. 16:8
because they cannot be *t.* 23:6
saw that the city was *t.* *1 Ki* 16:18
killed and also *t.* possession ? 21:19
when I am *t.* from thee *2 Ki* 2:10
of Hosea, Samaria was *t.* 18:10
household being *t.* for Eleazar, and
　one *t.* for Ithamar. *1 Chr* 24:6
captives you have *t.* *2 Chr* 28:11
king had *t.* counsel to keep. *Ezra* 9:2
for they have *t.* of their. 9:2*
and we have *t.* strange wives. 10:2*
　　　　　　　　14*, 17*, 18*
all these had *t.* strange wives. 44
had *t.* of them bread. *Esth* 2:15
who had *t.* Esther for his. 2:15
so Esther was *t.* unto king. 16
king took off his ring he had *t.* 8:2
also *t.* me by my neck. *Job* 16:12
he hath *t.* the crown from. 19:9
thou hast *t.* a pledge from thy. 22:6
they are *t.* out of the way. 24:24
iron is *t.* out of the earth. 28:2
in net is their own foot *t.* *Ps* 9:15
let them be *t.* in the devices. 10:2
even be *t.* in their pride. 59:12
have *t.* crafty counsel against. 83:3
I *t.* as an heritage for ever. 119:111
thy foot from being *t.* *Pr* 3:26
thou art *t.* with the words of. 6:2
he hath *t.* a bag of money. 7:20
transgressors shall be *t.* in. 11
my labour which I had *t.* *Eccl* 2:18
nor any thing *t.* from it. 3:14
the sinner shall be *t.* by her. 7:26
as the fishes that are *t.* in. 9:12
t. evil counsel against thee. *Isa* 7:5
shall be broken, and snared, and *t.*
　　　　　　　　　　　8:15
who hath *t.* this counsel ? 24:18
shall be *t.* in the snare. 24:18
might be broken, snared, and *t.*
　　　　　　　　　　Isa 28:13
that shall not be *t.* down. 33:20*
thou whom I have *t.* from ends. 41:9
shall the prey be *t.* from the ? 49:24
I have *t.* the cup of trembling. 51:22
he was *t.* from prison and. 53:8
the wife shall be *t.* *Jer* 6:11
ashamed, dismayed, and *t.* 8:9

planted, they have *t.* root. *Jer* 12:2
shalt surely be *t.* 34:3; 38:23
day that Jerusalem was *t.* 38:28
when they had *t.* him, they. 39:5
he had *t.* him, being bound. 40:1
dwell in your cities, that ye have *t.* 10
Kiriathaim is *t.* 48:1
thy treasures, thou also shalt be *t.* 7
joy and gladness is *t.* from the. 33
Kirioth is *t.* 41
thy sons are *t.* captives. 46
hear the counsel he hath *t.* 49:20
sorrows have *t.* Damascus. 24
Nebuchadnezzar hath *t.* counsel. 30
publish and say, Babylon is *t.* 50:2
　　　　　　　　24; 51:31, 41
anointed of the Lord was *t.* *Lam* 4:20
the prince of Israel is *t. Ezek* 12:13
shall wood be *t.* thereof to do ? 15:3
also *t.* thy fair jewels of gold. 16:17
thou hast *t.* thy sons and thy. 20
and hath *t.* the king thereof. 17:12
t. of the king's seed, hath *t.* 13
and he shall be *t.* in my snare. 20
neither hath *t.* any increase. 18:8
usury, and hath *t.* increase. 13
that hath *t.* off his hand from. 17*
he was *t.* in their pit. 19:4, 8
call to remembrance, that they may
　be *t.* 21:23
they *t.* gifts; thou hast *t.* usury. 22:12
have *t.* vengeance with a. 25:15
his father had *t.* out. *Dan* 5:2, 3
ye have *t.* my silver. *Joel* 3:5
if he have *t.* nothing ? *Amos* 3:4, 5
so shall Israel be *t.* that dwell. 12*
have we not *t.* to us horns by ? 6:13
the city shall be *t.* and. *Zech* 14:2
bridegroom shall be *t.* *Mat* 9:15
we have *t.* no bread. 16:7
the kingdom of God shall be *t.* 21:43
one shall be *t.* 24:40; *Luke* 17:34
　　　　　　　　　　35, 36
had *t.* counsel, they gave. *Mat* 28:12
from him *t.* even that. *Mark* 4:25
when he had *t.* the five loaves. 6:41
t. him in his arms, he said. 9:36
night, and have *t.* nothing. *Luke* 5:5
of fishes which they had *t.* 9
if I have *t.* any thing from. 19:8*
some would have *t.* him. *John* 7:44
a woman *t.* in adultery. 8:3, 4
ye have *t.* and by wicked. *Acts* 2:23
for his life is *t.* from the. 8:33
this man was *t.* of the Jews. 23:27*
fasting, having *t.* nothing. 27:33
not as though the word hath *t.* none
　effect. *Rom* 9:6*
no temptation *t.* you. *1 Cor* 10:13
being *t.* from you for. *1 Thes* 2:17*
will let, until he be *t.* *2 Thes* 2:7
let not a widow be *t.* *1 Tim* 5:9*
who are *t.* captive by him at his will.
　　　　　　　　　　2 Tim 2:26
every high priest *t.* from. *Heb* 5:1
made to be *t.* and destroyed.
　　　　　　　　　　2 Pet 2:12
when he had *t.* the book. *Rev* 5:8
hast *t.* to thee thy great. 11:17
beast was *t.* and with him. 19:20

taken *away*
servants hath *t. away.* *Gen* 21:25
Jacob came and hath *t. away.* 27:35
he hath *t. away* my blessing. 36
God hath *t. away* my reproach. 30:23
Jacob hath *t. away* all that is. 31:1
thus God hath *t. away* the cattle. 9
hast thou *t.* us *away* to die ? *Ex* 14:11
as the fat is *t. away* from the sacri-
　fice. *Lev* 4:31, 35
trespass in a thing *t. away* by. 6:2
after that he hath *t. away.* 14:43
nor *t. away* aught for. *Deut* 26:14
be violently *t. away* from. 28:31
have *t. away* my gods. *Judg* 18:24
day when it was *t. away.* *1 Sam* 21:6
the high places were not *t. away.*
　　　1 Ki 22:43; *2 Ki* 12:3; 14:4
　　　　　　2 Chr 15:17; 20:33
before I be *t. away* from thee. *2 Ki* 2:9
altars Hezekiah had *t. away.* 18:22
　　　　　2 Chr 32:12; *Isa* 36:7
t. away the groves. *2 Chr* 19:3

taken

the Lord hath *t. away.* *Job* 1:21
hath violently *t. away* an. 20:19
God liveth, who hath *t. away.* 27:2
hath *t. away* my judgement. 34:5
and the mighty shall be *t. away.* 20
t. away all thy wrath. *Ps* 85:3
their sleep is *t. away.* *Pr* 4:16
thine iniquity is *t. away.* *Isa* 6:7
of Samaria shall be *t. away.* 8:4
the burden shall be *t. away.* 10:27
the gladness is *t. away.* 16:10
Damascus is *t. away.* 17:1
the mighty shall be *t* away. 49:25
that my people is *t. away* for. 52:5
t. away, righteous is *t. away.* 57:1
like the wind have *t.* us *away.* 64:6
I have *t. away* my peace. *Jer* 16:5
hath violently *t. away.* *Lam* 2:6
t. away in his iniquity. *Ezek* 33:6
their dominion *t. away.* *Dan* 7:12
by him the daily sacrifice was *t.*
away. 8:11; 12:11
fishes shall be *t. away.* *Hos* 4:3
and I have *t. away* your horses.
Amos 4:10
t. away my glory for ever. *Mi* 2:9
the Lord hath *t. away* thy judgements. *Zeph* 3:15
from him shall be *t. away.* *Mat* 13:12
25:29; *Luke* 8:18; 19:26
the bridegroom shall be *t. away.*
Mark 2:20; *Luke* 5:35
that good part which shall not be *t.*
away. *Luke* 10:42
ye have *t. away* the key of. 11:52
they might be *t. away.* *John* 19:31
seeth the stone *t. away* from. 20:1
they have *t. away* the Lord. 2
they have *t. away* my Lord. 13
judgement was *t. away.* *Acts* 8:33
should be saved was *t. away.* 27:20
this, might be *t. away.* *1 Cor* 5:2
vail shall be *t. away.* *2 Cor* 3:16

taken hold

and have *t. hold* upon. *1 Ki* 9:9
days of affliction have *t. hold* upon.
Job 30:16
iniquities have *t. hold.* *Ps* 40:12*
anguish have *t. hold* on me. 119:143
pangs have *t. hold* on me. *Isa* 21:3
anguish hath *t. hold* on us. *Jer* 6:24

taken up

cloud was *t. up* from. *Ex* 40:36
not *t. up,* till the day it was *t. up.* 37
the cloud was *t. up.* *Num* 9:17, 21
but when it was *t. up.* 22; 10:11
Absalom was *t. up.* *2 Sam* 18:9
they have *t. up* a curse. *Isa* 10:29
shall be *t. up* a curse. *Jer* 29:22
ye are *t. up* in the lips. *Ezek* 36:3
so Daniel was *t. up* out. *Dan* 6:23
there was *t. up* of the. *Luke* 9:17
day in which he was *t. up.* *Acts* 1:2
while they beheld, he was *t. up.* 9
this same Jesus which is *t. up.* 11*
day he was *t. up* from us. 22
and was *t. up* dead. 20:9
when they had *t. up* they. 27:17*
had *t. up* the anchors. 40*

takest

the water thou *t.* out of the. *Ex* 4:9
when thou *t.* the sum of. 30:12
journey thou *t.* not be. *Judg* 4:9
thou *t.* away their breath. *Ps* 104:29
what is man that thou *t.?* 144:3
and thou *t.* no knowledge. *Isa* 58:3
t. up that thou layedst. *Luke* 19:21

takest heed

if thou *t. heed* to fulfil. *1 Chr* 22:13*

taketh

that *t.* his name in vain. *Ex* 20:7
Deut 5:11
persons nor *t.* reward. *Deut* 10:17
t. a man's life to pledge. 24:6
putteth her hand and *t.* him. 25:11
cursed be he that *t.* reward. 27:25
as an eagle *t.* them, beareth. 32:11
tribe which the Lord *t.* *Josh* 7:14
smiteth Kirjath-sepher and *t.* it.
15:16; *Judg* 1:12
and *t.* away reproach. *1 Sam* 17:26
as a man *t.* away dung. *1 Ki* 14:10*

t. it even out of the thorns. *Job* 5:5
he *t.* the wise in their craftiness. 13
1 Cor 3:19
he *t.* away, who can? *Job* 9:12*
and *t.* away the understanding. 12:20
he *t.* away the heart of the chief. 24
what is the hope, when God *t.?* 27:8
he *t.* it with his eyes, his nose. 40:24
nor *t.* up reproach against. *Ps* 15:3
nor *t.* reward against the innocent. 5
Lord *t.* my part with them. 118:7*
happy shall he be that *t.* 137:9
he *t.* not pleasure in the legs. 147:10
the Lord *t.* pleasure in them. 11
for the Lord *t.* pleasure in his. 149:4
which *t.* away the life. *Pr* 1:19
better than he that *t.* a city. 16:32
a wicked man *t.* a gift out of. 17:23
as he that *t.* away a garment. 25:20
is like one that *t.* a dog by. 26:17
of all his labour which he *t.* *Eccl* 1:3*
heart *t.* not rest in the night. 2:23
sheep that no man *t.* up. *Isa* 13:14
he *t.* up the isles as a very. 40:15
the carpenter *t.* the cypress. 44:14
nor is there any that *t.* her by. 51:18
who *t.* strangers instead. *Ezek* 16:32
and *t.* not warning. 33:4
but he that *t.* warning. 5
as the shepherd *t.* out of. *Amos* 3:12*
the devil *t.* him up into. *Mat* 4:5
t. him up into an exceeding high. 8
t. from garment, and rent is made
worse. 9:16; *Mark* 2:21
and *t.* not his cross and. *Mat* 10:38
he goeth, *t.* seven other spirits.
12:45; *Luke* 11:26
Jesus *t.* Peter, James. *Mat* 17:1
Mark 9:2; 14:33
Satan cometh and *t.* away the word.
Mark 4:15; *Luke* 8:12
he *t.* the father and. *Mark* 5:40
he *t.* him, he teareth him. 9:18
that *t.* away thy cloak. *Luke* 6:29
and of him that *t.* thy goods. 30
spirit *t.* him, and he suddenly. 9:39
a stronger *t.* from him all his. 11:22
my lord *t.* away from me the. 16:3
the Lamb of God which *t.* *John* 1:29
no man *t.* it from me, I lay it. 10:18
beareth not fruit, he *t.* away. 15:2
your joy no man *t.* from you. 16:22
Jesus then cometh, *t.* bread. 21:13
is God unrighteous, who *t.?*
Rom 3:5*
in eating every one *t.* *1 Cor* 11:21
no man *t.* this honour. *Heb* 5:4
he *t.* away the first that he may. 10:9

taketh hold

I am afraid, and trembling *t. hold* on
my flesh. *Job* 21:6
the spider *t. hold* with. *Pr* 30:28
every one that *t. hold* of. *Isa* 56:5

taking

with God there is no *t.* of. *2 Chr* 19:7
I have seen the foolish *t.* root.*Job* 5:3
by *t.* heed thereto. *Ps* 119:9
at noise of *t.* of Babylon. *Jer* 50:46
dealt against Judah by *t.* *Ezek* 25:12
I taught Ephraim also to go, *t.* them
by their arms. *Hos* 11:3
which of you by *t.* thought?
Mat 6:27*; *Luke* 12:25*
Son of man is as a man *t.* a far.
Mark 13:34*
the devil *t.* him up into. *Luke* 4:5
t. up that I laid not down. 19:22
he had spoken of *t.* rest. *John* 11:13
sin *t.* occasion by the. *Rom* 7:8, 11
t. my leave of them, I. *2 Cor* 2:13
t. wages of them to do you. 11:8
above all *t.* the shield of. *Eph* 6:16
in flaming fire *t.* vengeance on them.
2 Thes 1:8*
t. the oversight thereof. *1 Pet* 5:2*
they went forth *t.* nothing. *3 John* 7

tale (quantity)

the *t.* of bricks which. *Ex* 5:8
he deliver the *t.* of bricks. 18
they gave the foreskins in full *t.* to
the king. *1 Sam* 18:27
bring vessels in and out by *t.*
1 Chr 9:28

tale

years as a *t.* that is told. *Ps* 90:9

talebearer

up and down as a *t.* *Lev* 19:16
a *t.* revealeth. *Pr* 11:13; 20:19
the words of a *t.* are. 18:8*; 26:22*
where there is no *t..* the strife. 26:20*

talent

[1] *A weight among the Jews, of* 50
to 100 *pounds, according to the*
standard in use at the time. The
value of the gold talent would be as
as much as 29,000 *dollars, or nearly*
£6000, *that of the silver talent up*
to 1940 *dollars, or nearly* £400.
In the times of the New Testament
the talent was reckoned only in
silver, and was worth about 1150
dollars, or £240. *These amounts*
are not intended to be absolutely
exact, but give values in round
numbers. There is great diversity
in estimates given, Ex 25:39; 38:25.
[2] *The gifts of God bestowed on*
men, Mat 25:15.

of a *t.* of pure gold make it.
Ex 25:39; 37:24
sockets, a *t.* for a socket. 38:27
the weight of the crown was a *t.*
2 Sam 12:30
pay a *t.* of silver. *1 Ki* 20:39
give them a *t.* of silver. *2 Ki* 5:22
a tribute of a *t.* of gold. 23:33
2 Chr 36:3
lifted up a *t.* of lead. *Zech* 5:7
hid thy *t.* in the earth. *Mat* 25:25
take therefore the *t.* from him. 28
about the weight of a *t.* *Rev* 16:21

talents

of the offering, was 29 *t.* *Ex* 38:24
of 100 *t.* of silver were cast. 27
hill of Samaria for two *t.* *1 Ki* 16:24
Naaman took ten *t.* *2 Ki* 5:5
be content, take two *t.* 23
Menahem gave Pul 1000 *t.* 15:19
Hezekiah 300 *t.* and 30 of gold. 18:14
land to a tribute of 100 *t.* 23:33
2 Chr 36:3
Ammonites sent 1000 *t.* *1 Chr* 19:6
David gave 3000 *t.* of gold. 29:4
gold, 5000 *t.* and of silver 10,000 *t.* 7
we do for the 100 *t.?* *2 Chr* 25:9
of Ammon gave him 100 *t.* 27:5
owed him 10,000 *t.* *Mat* 18:24
gave five *t.,* to another two. 25:15
see gold, silver

tales

men that carry *t.* to. *Ezek* 22:9*
their words seemed to them as idle
t. *Luke* 24:11*

Talitha cumi

(*An Aramaic expression meaning*
Damsel, arise. Used by Jesus
when raising Jairus's daughter)
he said unto her, *T.,* damsel, arise.
Mark 5:41

talk

should a man full of *t.?* *Job* 11:2
reason with unprofitable *t.?* 15:3
the *t.* of the lips is mischievous.
Pr 14:23
end of his *t.* is mischievous.
Eccl 10:13
entangle him in his *t.* *Mat* 22:15

talk, verb

I will come down and *t.* *Num* 11:17
God doth *t.* with man. *Deut* 5:24
t. of them when thou sittest. 6:7
t. no more so exceeding proudly.
1 Sam 2:3
t. not with us in the Jews' language.
2 Ki 18:26
sing psalms, *t.* ye of all his wondrous. *1 Chr* 16:9; *Ps* 105:2
and will ye *t.* deceitfully? *Job* 13:7
they *t.* to the grief of. *Ps* 69:26
my tongue shall *t.* of thy. 71:24
meditate and *t.* of thy doings. 77:12
I *t.* of thy wondrous works. 119:27
kingdom and *t.* of thy power. 145:11
awakest it shall *t.* with thee. *Pr* 6:22
and their lips *t.* of mischief. 24:2
let me *t.* with thee of. *Jer* 12:1

arise and I will there *t.*   *Ezek* 3:22
servant *t.* with my lord ? *Dan* 10:17
I will not *t.* much with.   *John* 14:30

talked
brethren *t.* with him.   *Gen* 45:15
ye have seen that I have *t.* with you.
    Ex 20:22; *Deut* 5:4
and the Lord *t.* with Moses. *Ex* 33:9
of his face shone while he *t.*   34:29
Saul *t.* unto the priest. *1 Sam* 14:19
to pass as he *t.* with. *2 Chr* 25:16
princes hear that I have *t.*   *Jer* 38:25
t. with him two men, Moses and.
    Luke 9:30
heart burn, while he *t.* with us? 24:32
marvelled that he *t.* with. *John* 4:27
Peter *t.* with Cornelius. *Acts* 10:27
and *t.* long, even till break of.   20:11
they *t.* between themselves.   26:31
he that *t.* with me had a. *Rev* 21:15

talkers
up in the lips of *t.*   *Ezek* 36:3
unruly and vain *t.*   *Tit* 1:10

talkest
sign that thou *t.* with me. *Judg* 6:17
yet *t.* with the king.   *1 Ki* 1:14
no man said, Why *t.* thou with her ?
    John 4:27

talketh
tongue *t.* of judgement.   *Ps* 37:30
seen him, and it is he that *t.* with.
    John 9:37

talking
he left off *t.* with him.   *Gen* 17:22
he is a god, he is *t.* or.   *1 Ki* 18:27
they were *t.* with him.   *Esth* 6:14
the princes refrained *t.* and. *Job* 29:9
thy people are still *t.*   *Ezek* 33:30
Moses and Elias *t.* with him.
    Mat 17:3; *Mark* 9:4
neither filthiness, nor foolish *t.*
    Eph 5:4
a trumpet *t.* with me.   *Rev* 4:1

tall
a people *t.* as the Anakims.
    Deut 2:10, 21; 9:2
cut down the *t.* cedar trees and the
choice fir.   *2 Ki* 19:23; *Isa* 37:24

taller
people is greater and *t.*   *Deut* 1:28

Tamar
Er, whose name was *T.*   *Gen* 38:6
was told Judah, *T.* hath played.   24
house of Pharez, whom *T.* bare to.
    Ruth 4:12; *1 Chr* 2:4; *Mat* 1:3
a fair sister, named *T.*   *2 Sam* 13:1
Ammon fell sick for *T.*   2'
he forced *T.*   22, 32
daughter, whose name was *T.* 14:27
side southward from *T.* *Ezek* 47:19

tame
nor could any man *t.* him. *Mark* 5:4
but the tongue can no man *t.*; it is
an unruly evil.   *Jas* 3:8

tamed
in sea, is *t.*, and hath been *t.* *Jas* 3:7

Tammuz
there sat women weeping for *T.*
    Ezek 8:14

tanner
Peter tarried with one Simon a *t.*
    Acts 9:43
lodged with one Simon a *t.* 10:6, 32

tapestry, *see* **coverings**

tare
the king arose and *t.* *2 Sam* 13:31*
two she bears *t.* forty.   *2 Ki* 2:24
straightway the spirit *t.* him.
    Mark 9:20; *Luke* 9:42

tares
Darnel, *a weed of which some
varieties are poisonous. It looks
much like wheat until near harvest
time, when the two can be readily
distinguished,* Mat 13:29.
his enemy sowed *t.*   *Mat* 13:25
up, then appeared the *t.* also.   26
from whence then hath it *t.*?   27
lest while ye gather up the *t.*   29
declare to us the parable of the *t.* 36

target
(A large, heavy shield)
Goliath had a *t.* of.   *1 Sam* 17:6*
six hundred shekels of gold went to
one *t.*   *1 Ki* 10:16†; *2 Chr* 9:15†

targets
made two hundred *t.*   *1 Ki* 10:16†
Asa had an army that bare *t.* and.
    2 Chr 14:8*

tarried
Abraham's servant *t.* all. *Gen* 24:54
Jacob *t.* there all night and.   28:11
Jacob and Laban *t.* all night in. 31:54
when the cloud *t.*   *Num* 9:19, 22
t. till they were ashamed. *Judg* 3:25
Ehud escaped while they *t.* and.   26
they *t.* till afternoon and did.   19:8
save that she *t.* a little.   *Ruth* 2:7
t. seven days according. *1 Sam* 13:8
but David *t.* still at.   *2 Sam* 11:1
the king *t.* in a place that.   15:17
Zadok and Abiathar *t.* at.   29
but he *t.* longer than the set.   20:5
they came, for he *t.* at.   *2 Ki* 2:18
and she that *t.* at home.   *Ps* 68:12
while the bridegroom *t.*   *Mat* 25:5
marvelled that he *t.*   *Luke* 1:21
the child Jesus *t.* behind in.   2:43
then he *t.* with them.   *John* 3:22
Peter *t.* many days in Joppa.
    Acts 9:43
Judas and Silas . . . *t.* a space. 15:33
Paul *t.* a good while at Corinth and.
    18:18
these going before *t.* for us at.   20:5
finding the disciples, we *t.*   21:4
as we *t.* many days at Caesarea. 21:10
Festus *t.* at Jerusalem more.   25:6
fourteenth day ye have *t.* fasting.
    27:33
landing at Syracuse, we *t.*   28:12

tarriest
now why *t.* thou ? arise. *Acts* 22:16

tarrieth
shall his part be that *t.* *1 Sam* 30:24
that *t.* not for a man, nor.   *Mi* 5:7

tarry
[1] *To remain,* Gen 27:41. [2]
To wait for, Ex 24:14. [3] *To delay,* Gen 45:9.
and *t.* all night, and.   *Gen* 19:2
and *t.* with Laban a few days. 27:44
found favour in thine eyes, *t.* 30:27
Come down to me, *t.* not.   45:9
thrust out, and could not *t.* *Ex* 12:39
t. ye here for us till we come. 24:14
leper shall *t.* out of his tent. *Lev* 14:8
I pray you *t.* here also. *Num* 22:19
why *t.* the wheels of ?   *Judg* 5:28
he said, I will *t.* until thou.   6:18
and *t.* all night.   19:6, 9
the man would not *t.*   10
would ye *t.* for them till they were
grown ?   *Ruth* 1:13
t. this night, and it shall be.   3:13
t. until thou have weaned him.
    1 Sam 1:23
seven days shalt thou *t.* till I. 10:8
if they say, *T.* till we come.   14:9
t. at Jericho till your beards be.
    2 Sam 10:5; *1 Chr* 19:5
t. here to-day.   *2 Sam* 11:12
I will *t.* in the plain.   15:28
Joab said, I may not *t.* thus.   18:14
will not *t.* one with thee.   19:7
t. here, I pray thee; for the Lord hath
sent me.   *2 Ki* 2:2, 4, 6
the lepers said, If we *t.* till the. 7:9
open door and flee, and *t.* not.   9:3
glory of this, and *t.* at home.   14:10
a liar shall not *t.* in my.   *Ps* 101:7
that *t.* long at the wine.   *Pr* 23:30
my salvation shall not *t.* *Isa* 46:13
that turneth aside to *t.*   *Jer* 14:8
t., wait for it; for it will not *t.* *Hab* 2:3
t. ye here and watch.   *Mat* 26:38
    Mark 14:34
and he went in to *t.*   *Luke* 24:29
but *t.* ye in the city of Jerusalem. 49
besought that he would *t.* *John* 4:40
if I will that he *t.* till.   21:22, 23
they prayed Peter to *t.* *Acts* 10:48

desired Paul to *t.* longer. *Acts* 18:20
were desired to *t.* with them. 28:14
wherefore *t.* one for.   *1 Cor* 11:33
I trust to *t.* a while with you.   16:7
but I will *t.* at Ephesus until.   8
but if I *t.* long, that.   *1 Tim* 3:15
he that shall come, will come and
not *t.*   *Heb* 10:37

tarrying
make no *t.* O my God.   *Ps* 40:17
    70:5

Tarshish
the sons of Javan; Elishah, and *T.*
    Gen 10:4; *1 Chr* 1:7
king had at sea a navy of *T.* with a.
    1 Ki 10:22; *2 Chr* 9:21
make ships to go to *T.* *2 Chr* 20:36
broken and not able to go to *T.* 37
thou breakest ships of *T.* *Ps* 48:7
the kings of *T.* shall bring.   72:10
Lord on all the ships of *T.* *Isa* 2:16
howl, ye ships of *T.* it is.   23:1, 14
over to *T.* howl, ye inhabitants.   6
thy land, O daughter of *T.*   10
the ships of *T.* shall wait for.   60:9
send those that escape to *T.* 66:19
silver is brought from *T.*   *Jer* 10:9
T. was thy merchant.   *Ezek* 27:12
the ships of *T.* did sing of thee. 25
the merchants of *T.* shall say. 38:13
rose up to flee unto *T.*   *Jonah* 1:3
therefore I fled before unto *T.*   4:2

Tarsus
enquire for one Saul of *T.* *Acts* 9:11
brethren sent him forth to *T.*   30
Barnabas departed to *T.* to.   11:25
I am a man who am a Jew of *T.*
    21:39; 22:3

Tartak
the Avites made *T.*   *2 Ki* 17:31

task, -s
your works, your daily *t.*   *Ex* 5:13
why not fulfilled your *t.* in ?   14
minish from your daily *t.*   19

taskmasters
set over them *t.* to afflict. *Ex* 1:11
cry by reason of their *t.*   3:7
and Pharaoh commanded *t.*   5:6
t. told them.   10
t. hasted them.   13
officers which the *t.* had set.   14

taste
the *t.* of manna like.   *Ex* 16:31
the *t.* of it was as the *t.* of fresh oil.
    Num 11:8
is there any *t.* in the white of an egg ?
    Job 6:6
cannot my *t.* discern perverse ?   30
are thy words to my *t.*! *Ps* 119:103
honeycomb is sweet to *t.*   *Pr* 24:13
fruit was sweet to my *t.* *S of S* 2:3
his *t.* remained in him.   *Jer* 48:11

taste, *verb*
[1] *To try the relish of any thing
by the tongue,* Job 34:3. [2]
Figuratively, to prove, Ps 34:8.
[3] *To eat a little,* 1 Sam 14:29, 43.
did but *t.* a little honey. *1 Sam* 14:43
if I *t.* bread or aught else. *2 Sam* 3:35
can thy servant *t.* what I eat ? 19:35
the mouth *t.* his meat ?   *Job* 12:11
O *t.* and see that the Lord. *Ps* 34:8
neither herd nor flock *t.* *Jonah* 3:7
standing here which shall not *t.* of.
    Mat 16:28; *Mark* 9:1; *Luke* 9:27
none bidden shall *t.* of. *Luke* 14:24
he shall never *t.* death. *John* 8:52
touch not, *t.* not, handle. *Col* 2:21
that he should *t.* death.   *Heb* 2:9

tasted
so none *t.* any food.   *1 Sam* 14:24
I *t.* a little of this honey.   29
Belshazzar, whiles he *t.* wine.
    Dan 5:2
when he had *t.* thereof. *Mat* 27:34
the ruler had *t.* the water. *John* 2:9
t. of the heavenly gift.   *Heb* 6:4
have *t.* the good word of God.   5
have *t.* that the Lord.   *1 Pet* 2:3

tasteth
words as the mouth *t*.   *Job* 34:3

tattlers
not only idle but *t*. and.   *1 Tim* 5:13

taught
I have *t*. you what.   *Deut* 4:5
Moses *t*. the children of Israel. 31:22
with them he *t*. the men.   *Judg* 8:16
and *t*. them how to fear.   *2 Ki* 17:28
thou hast *t*. them the.   *2 Chr* 6:27
Levites *t*. the people in Judah. 17:9
people rejoiced, such as *t*.   23:13
that *t*. the good knowledge of. 30:22*
said to the Levites that *t*. all.   35:3
that *t*. the people said.   *Neh* 8:9
O God, thou hast *t*. me.   *Ps* 71:17
                 119:102
when thou hast *t*. me.   119:171
he *t*. me also, and said.   *Pr* 4:4
t. thee in the way of wisdom.   11
prophecy that his mother *t*. him. 31:1
he still *t*. the people.   *Eccl* 12:9
their fear is *t*. by the.   *Isa* 29:13
counsellor hath *t*. him.   40:13, 14
all thy children shall be *t*.   54:13
hast thou *t*. the wicked.   *Jer* 2:33
t. their tongues to speak lies.   9:5
which their fathers *t*. them.   14
t. my people to swear by.   12:16
for thou hast *t*. them to be.   13:21
thou hast *t*. rebellion against. 28:16
he hath *t*. rebellion against.   29:32
though I have *t*. them. rising. 32:33
women *t*. not to do after. *Ezek* 23:48
as a heifer that is *t*.   *Hos* 10:11
I *t*. Ephraim to go, taking them. 11:3
man *t*. me to keep cattle. *Zech* 13:5*
he *t*. them as one having authority.
     Mat 7:29; *Mark* 1:22
and did as they were *t*.   *Mat* 28:15
told him all things they had done and
        t.   *Mark* 6:30
as he was wont he *t*. them.   10:1
while he *t*. in the temple.   12:35
Luke 19:47; 20:1; *John* 7:14, 28
teach us to pray, as John *t*. his.
        Luke 11:1
thou hast *t*. in our streets.   13:26
shall be all *t*. of God.   *John* 6:45
he sat down and *t*. them.   8:2
as my father hath *t*. me, I.   28
I ever *t*. in the synagogue and. 18:20
being grieved that they *t*. the people.
        Acts 4:2
into the temple early and *t*.   5:21
Paul and Barnabas *t*. much people.
        11:26; 14:21
certain men *t*. the brethren.   15:1
t. diligently the things of the. 18:25
I have shewed you, and *t*.   20:20
t. according to the perfect.   22:3
nor was I *t*. it but by.   *Gal* 1:12
let him that is *t*. in the word.   6:6
been *t*. by him as truth.   *Eph* 4:21
the faith, as ye have been *t*. *Col* 2:7
ye are *t*. of God to love. *1 Thes* 4:9
hold the traditions ye have been *t*.
        2 Thes 2:15
the word, as he hath been *t*. *Tit* 1:9
anointing hath *t*. you.   *1 John* 2:27
who *t*. Balak to cast a.   *Rev* 2:14

taunt
will deliver them to be a *t*. *Jer* 24:9
a reproach and a *t*.   *Ezek* 5:15

taunting
all these take up a *t*. proverb.
        Hab 2:6

taverns
meet us as far as the three *t*.
        Acts 28:15*

taxation
every one according to *t*. *2 Ki* 23:35

taxed
but Jehoiakim *t*. the.   *2 Ki* 23:35
a decree that all the world should be
        t.   *Luke* 2:1*
all went to be *t*.   3*
Joseph went to be *t*.   5*

taxes
stand up a raiser of *t*.   *Dan* 11:20

taxing
and this *t*. was first made. *Luke* 2:2*
in the days of the *t*.   *Acts* 5:37*

teach
and I will *t*. you what.   *Ex* 4:15
in his heart that he may *t*.   35:34
that ye may *t*. Israel.   *Lev* 10:11
to *t*. when it is unclean.   14:57
judgements which I *t*. you. *Deut* 4:1
and that they may *t*. their children. 10
Lord commanded me to *t*.   14; 6:1
t. you not to do after their.   20:18
priests the Levites shall *t*. you. 24:8
write and *t*. the children of.   31:19
shall *t*. Jacob thy judgements. 33:10
t. us what we shall do.   *Judg* 13:8
I will *t*. you the good.   *1 Sam* 12:23
bade them *t*. the use.   *2 Sam* 1:18
to *t*. in the cities of.   *2 Chr* 17:7
to *t*. in Israel statutes.   *Ezra* 7:10
any *t*. God knowledge?   *Job* 21:22
t. you by the hand of God.   27:11
of years should *t*. wisdom.   32:7
t. us what we shall say unto. 37:19
will *t*. sinners in the way.   *Ps* 25:8
will he guide and *t*. his way.   9
him that feareth Lord shall he *t*. 12
t. you the fear of the Lord.   34:11
then will I *t*. trangressors.   51:13
so *t*. us to number our days. 90:12
and *t*. his senators wisdom. 105:22
t. a just man, and he will.   *Pr* 9:9
and he will *t*. us of his ways. *Isa* 2:3
        Mi 4:2
whom shall he *t*. knowledge? *Isa* 28:9
for his God doth instruct and *t*.   26
and *t*. your daughters.   *Jer* 9:20
they shall *t*. no more every man his.
        31:34; *Heb* 8:11
t. my people the difference between.
        Ezek 44:23
whom they might *t*. learning of.
        Dan 1:4*
priests thereof *t*. for hire.   *Mi* 3:11
stone, Arise, it shall *t*.!   *Hab* 2:19
shall *t*. men so.   *Mat* 5:19
t. all nations.   28:19
Lord, *t*. us to pray, as.   *Luke* 11:1
Holy Ghost shall *t*. you what. 12:12
t. the Gentiles.   *John* 7:35
dost thou *t*. us?   9:34
Holy Ghost shall *t*. you all.   14:26
Jesus began to do and *t*.   *Acts* 1:1
speak nor *t*. in the name of Jesus.
        4:18; 5:28
to *t*. and preach Jesus Christ.   5:42
t. customs which are not.   16:21
as I *t*. every where in.   *1 Cor* 4:17
even nature itself *t*. you?   11:14
that by my voice I might *t*.   14:19
charge some they *t*. no.   *1 Tim* 1:3
but I suffer not a woman to *t*.   2:12
bishop must be apt to *t*.   3:2
        2 Tim 2:24
things command and *t*.   *1 Tim* 4:11
these things *t*. and exhort.   6:2
if any man *t*. otherwise, he.   3
shall be able to *t*. others. *2 Tim* 2:2
that they *t*. young women.   *Tit* 2:4
ye have need that one *t*.   *Heb* 5:12
not that any man *t*. you.   *1 John* 2:27
that woman Jezebel to *t*.   *Rev* 2:20

see began

teach *me*
t. me and I will hold my.   *Job* 6:24
I see not, *t*. thou me.   34:32
t. me thy paths   *Ps* 25:4
lead me and *t*. me.   5
t. me thy way, O Lord. 27:11; 86:11
t. me thy statutes.   119:12. 26, 33
        64, 68, 124, 135
t. me good judgements.   119:66
t. me thy judgements.   108
t. me to do thy will, for.   143:10

teach *thee*
I will *t*. thee what thou.   *Ex* 4:12
which they shall *t*. thee. *Deut* 17:11
shall not they *t*. thee?   *Job* 8:10
beasts, and they shall *t*. thee. 12:7
earth. and it shall *t*. thee.   8
I shall *t*. thee wisdom.   33:33
I will *t*. thee in the way.   *Ps* 32:8
thy right hand shall *t*. thee.   45:4

teach *them*
t. them ordinances and.   *Ex* 18:20
that thou mayest *t*. them.   24:12
t. them thy sons, and.   *Deut* 4:9
which thou shalt *t*. them.   5:31
t. them diligently to thy. 6:7; 11:19
know to *t*. them war.   *Judg* 3:2
that thou *t*. them the good way.
        1 Ki 8:36
t. them the manner of.   *2 Ki* 17:27
t. ye *them* that know.   *Ezra* 7:25
keep my testimony that I shall *t*.
        them.   *Ps* 132:12
do and *t*. them shall be.   *Mat* 5:19
he began to *t*. them.   *Mark* 6:34
to *t*. them that the son of.   8:31

teacher
cast lots, as well the *t*.   *1 Chr* 25:8
the image, a *t*. of lies.   *Hab* 2:18
we know thou art a *t*.   *John* 3:2
thou art a *t*. of babes.   *Rom* 2:20
I am a *t*.   *1 Tim* 2:7; *2 Tim* 1:11

teachers
more understanding than all my *t*.
        Ps 119:99
obeyed the voice of my *t*.   *Pr* 5:13
t. be removed into a corner any
     more . . . shall see thy *t*. *Isa* 30:20
thy *t*. have transgressed.   43:27*
certain prophets and *t*.   *Acts* 13:1
hath set prophets, *t*.   *1 Cor* 12:28
are all *t*.?   29
evangelists, pastors, and *t*. *Eph* 4:11
desiring to be *t*. of law.   *1 Tim* 1:7
to themselves *t*. having.   *2 Tim* 4:3
that the aged women be *t*.   *Tit* 2:3
time ye ought to be *t*.   *Heb* 5:12
as there shall be false *t*.   *2 Pet* 2:1

teachest
the man whom thou *t*.   *Ps* 94:12
thou art true, and *t*. the way of God.
   Mat 22:16; *Mark* 12:14; *Luke* 20:21
thou *t*. the Jews to.   *Acts* 21:21
thou that *t*. another, *t*.?   *Rom* 2:21

teacheth
he *t*. my hands to war. *2 Sam* 22:35
        Ps 18:34
t. us more than the beasts. *Job* 35:11
God exalteth, who *t*. like?   36:22
that *t*. man knowledge.   *Ps* 94:10
which *t*. my hands to war.   144:1
a wicked man *t*. with.   *Pr* 6:13*
of the wise *t*. his mouth.   16:23*
the prophet that *t*. lies.   *Isa* 9:15
I am thy God which *t*. thee.   48:17
the man that *t*. all men.   *Acts* 21:28
or he that *t*., on teaching. *Rom* 12:7
man's wisdom *t*. but which the Holy
     Ghost *t*.   *1 Cor* 2:13
let him communicate to him that *t*.
        Gal 6:6
as the same anointing *t*. *1 John* 2:27

teaching
been without a *t*. priest. *2 Chr* 15:3
rising up early and *t*. them.
        Jer 32:33
Jesus went about Galilee, *t*.
   Mat 4:23; 9:35; *Luke* 13:10
worship me, *t*. for doctrines the.
       Mat 15:9; *Mark* 7:7
unto him as he was *t*.   *Mat* 21:23
I sat daily with you *t*. in.   26:55
t. them to observe all things. 28:20
t. throughout all Jewry. *Luke* 23:5
the apostles *t*. the people. *Acts* 5:25
Barnabas continued in Antioch, *t*.
     and preaching.   15:35
Paul *t*. the word of God at.   18:11
Paul *t*. at Rome with all.   28:31
or he that teacheth, on *t*. *Rom* 12:7
warning and *t*. every man. *Col* 1:28
t. and admonishing one another. 3:16
t. things which they.   *Tit* 1:11
t. us, that denying ungodliness. 2:12

tear
then will I *t*. your flesh.   *Judg* 8:7
lest he *t*. my soul like a lion. *Ps* 7:2
did *t*. me and ceased not.   35:15
lest I *t*. you in pieces.   50:22
over them the dogs to *t*.   *Jer* 15:3
nor shall men *t*. themselves.   16:7*

pillows I will *t.* from.   *Ezek* 13:20
kerchiefs will I *t.* and deliver.   21
I, even I, will *t.* and go.   *Hos* 5:14
the wild beast shall *t.* them.   13:8
off pity, his anger did *t.*   *Amos* 1:11
the lion did *t.* enough.   *Nah* 2:12
the shepherd shall *t.*   *Zech* 11:16

teareth

lion, and *t.* the arm.   *Deut* 33:20
he *t.* me in his wrath.   *Job* 16:9
he *t.* himself in his anger.   18:4
as a young lion *t.* in pieces.   *Mi* 5:8
taketh him, he *t.* him and he foameth.
  Mark 9:18*; *Luke* 9:39

tears

I have seen thy *t.*   2 *Ki* 20:5
  Isa 38:5
but mine eye poureth out *t.* unto.
  Job 16:20
I water my couch with my *t. Ps* 6:6
hold not thy peace at my *t.*   39:12
my *t.* have been my meat day. 42:3
put thou my *t.* in thy bottle.   56:8
feedest them with the bread of *t.* and
givest them *t.* to drink in.   80:5
delivered mine eyes from *t.*   116:8
that sow in *t.* shall reap in joy. 126:5
behold the *t.* of such as.   *Eccl* 4:1
I will water thee with *t.*   *Isa* 16:9
wipe away *t.* from all faces.   25:8
eyes were a fountain of *t. Jer* 9:1
our eyes may run down with *t.·*   18
mine eyes shall run down with *t.*
  13:17
let mine eyes run with *t.*   14:17
weeping, thine eyes from *t.*   31:16
she weepeth, and her *t.* are. *Lam* 1:2
mine eyes do fail with *t.*   2:11
let *t.* run down like a river.   18
neither shall thy *t.*   *Ezek* 24:16
altar of the Lord with *t.*   *Mal* 2:13
the father said with *t. Mark* 9:24
wash his feet with her *t. Luke* 7:38
she hath washed my feet with *t.*   44
serving the Lord with many *t.*
  Acts 20:19
to warn every one with *t.*   31
wrote to you with many *t.*   2 *Cor* 2:4
being mindful of thy *t.*   2 *Tim* 1:4
up supplications with *t.*   *Heb* 5:7
sought it carefully with *t.*   12:17
shall wipe away all *t. Rev* 7:17; 21:4

teats

shall lament for the *t.*   *Isa* 32:12*
they bruised the *t. Ezek* 23:3†, 21†

Tebeth

tenth month, which is *T. Esth* 2:16

tedious

that I be not further *t.*   *Acts* 24:4

teeth

and his *t.* shall be white.   *Gen* 49:12
flesh was yet between their *t.*
  Num 11:33
t. of beasts upon them. *Deut* 32:24
fleshhook of three *t.*   1 *Sam* 2:13
the *t.* of the young lions. *Job* 4:10
I take my flesh in my *t.?*   13:14
with the skin of my *t.*   19:20
plucked the spoil out of his *t.* 29:17
Leviathan's *t.* are terrible.   41:14
thou hast broken the *t.* of. *Ps* 3:7
whose *t.* are spears and arrows. 57:4
break their *t.*, O God, in.   58:6
given us as a prey to their *t.*   124:6
as vinegar to the *t.* so.   *Pr* 10:26
whose *t.* are swords, jaw-*t.*   30:14
thy *t.* are like a flock. *S of S* 4:2; 6:6
an instrument having *t.*   *Isa* 41:15
children's *t.* are set on edge.
  Jer 31:29; *Ezek* 18:2
eateth sour grapes, his *t. Jer* 31:30
hath broken my *t.* with.   *Lam* 3:16
ribs between the *t.* of it. *Dan* 7:5
beast had great iron *t.*   7, 19
hath the cheek *t.* of a lion. *Joel* 1:6
you cleanness of *t.*   *Amos* 4:6
that bite with their *t.*   *Mi* 3:5
from between his *t.*   *Zech* 9:7
cast the same in his *t. Mat* 27:44*
t. were as the *t.* of lions.   *Rev* 9:8

see gnash

tell *tree*
as a *t. tree* and as an oak.   *Isa* 6:13

Tekel

written, Mene, Mene, T.   *Dan* 5:25
T. thou art weighed in the.   27

Tekoah, *or* **Tekoa**
Joab sent to *T.* to fetch.   2 *Sam* 14:2
when the woman of *T.* spake to.   4
Abiah bare Ashur the father of *T.*
  1 *Chr* 2:24
Ashur the father of *T.* had two. 4:5
built Etam and *T.*   2 *Chr* 11:6
went into the wilderness of *T.* 20:20
blow the trumpet in *T.*   *Jer* 6:1
was among herdmen of *T. Amos* 1:1

tell

[1] *To count, number, or reckon,*
Gen 15:5. [2] *To declare or make*
known, Gen 12:18; 21:26.
t. the stars if thou be.   *Gen* 15:5
and I have sent to *t.* my Lord. 32:5
as to *t.* the man whether ye.   43:6
we cannot *t.* who put our money. 22
t. my father of all my glory. 45:13
mayest in the ears.   *Ex* 10:2
t. the priest, saying, It.   *Lev* 14:35
they will *t.* it to the.   *Num* 14:14
t. us wherewith we shall *1 Sam* 6:2
give to the man of God, to *t.*   9:8
liveth, O king, I cannot *t.*   17:55
he would surely *t.* Saul.   22:22
I beseech thee *t.* thy servant. 23:11
should *t.* on us, saying, So.   27:11
t. it not in Gath.   2 *Sam* 1:20
go *t.* my servant.   7:5; 1 *Chr* 17:4
feared to *t.* him that.   2 *Sam* 12:18
was alive, I said, Who can *t.?*   22
thou shalt *t.* to Zadok and.   15:35
go *t.* the king what thou hast. 18:21
that thou shouldest *t.*   1 *Ki* 1:20
go, *t.* thy lord, Elijah is. 18:8, 11, 14
when I come and *t.* Ahab, he.   12
t. my lord the king, all thou.   20:9
t. him, let not him that girdeth.   11
that we may *t.* the king's. 2 *Ki* 7:9
It is false; *t.* us now.   9:12
to go to *t.* it in Jezreel.   15
t. the man that sent you.   22:15
  2 *Chr* 34:23
I may *t.* all my bones.   *Ps* 22:17
publish and *t.* of all thy.   26:7
go round about her, *t.* the.   48:12
that ye may *t.* the generation.   13
son's name, if thou canst *t. Pr* 30:4
who can *t.* a man what shall be
after?   *Eccl* 6:12; 10:14
for who can *t.* him when it?   8:7
hath wings shall *t.* the matter. 10:20
t. him that I am sick of. *S of S* 5:8
go and *t.* this people.   *Isa* 6:9
t. this.   48:20
t. such as are for death. *Jer* 15:2
dreams which they *t.* 23:27; 28:32
we will *t.* the king of all.   36:16
t. us now how thou didst write.   17
t. it in Arnon, that Moab is.   48:20
wilt thou not *t.* us what? *Ezek* 24:19
O king, *t.* thy servants the dream.
  Dan 2:4, 7, 9
t. the king the interpretation.   36
t. ye your children, and let your
children *t.* their children. *Joel* 1:3
who can *t.* if God will? *Jonah* 3:9
see thou *t.* no man.   *Mat* 8:4
  Mark 8:26, 30; 9:9; *Luke* 5:14
  8:56; *Acts* 23:22
disciples that they should *t.* no man.
  Mat 16:20; *Mark* 7:36; *Luke* 9:21
t. the vision to no man.   *Mat* 17:9
t. him his fault.   18:15
t. it unto the church.   17
t. ye the daughter of Sion.   21:5
t. us, when shall these things be?
  24:3; *Mark* 13:4
that thou *t.* us, whether. *Mat* 26:63
  Luke 22:67; *John* 10:24
go and *t.* his disciples that. *Mat* 28:7
as they went to *t.* his disciples.   9
  Mark 16:7
anon they *t.* him of her. *Mark* 1:30
t. them how great things the.   5:19
said, We cannot *t.* 11:33; *Luke* 20:7

t. John what things ye.   *Luke* 7:22
go ye, and *t.* that fox, I cast. 13:32
but canst not *t.* whence.   *John* 3:8
when he is come, he will *t.*   4:25
but ye cannot *t.* whence I come. 8:14
we cannot *t.* what he saith.   16:18
or did other *t.* thee of me?   18:34
who shall *t.* you the.   *Acts* 15:7‡
but either to *t.* or hear some. 17:21
certain thing to *t.* him.   23:17
the body I cannot *t.*   2 *Cor* 12:2, 3
fail to *t.* of Gideon.   *Heb* 11:32

tell *me*

why didst not *t. me* she? *Gen* 12:18
t. me nor heard I of it.   21:26
t. me whose daughter art?   24:23
t. me, and if not, *t. me* that I.   49
t. me what shall thy wages be? 29:15
from me, and didst not *t. me.*   31:27
t. me thy name.   32:29
t. me where they feed.   37:16
t. me now what thou hast done, hide.
  Josh 7:19
t. me wherein thy great. *Judg* 16:6
wilt not redeem it, *t. me. Ruth* 4:4
t. me where the seer's. *1 Sam* 9:18
t. me I pray thee what Samuel. 10:15
Saul said, *T. me* what thou.   14:43
Jonathan, who shall *t. me?*   20:10
how went the matter? *t. me,* I.
  2 *Sam* 1:4
lean, wilt thou not *t. me?*   13:4
that thou *t. me* nothing   1 *Ki* 22:16
shall I do for thee? *t. me.* 2 *Ki* 4:2
t. me the great things that.   8:4
of understanding. *t. me. Job* 34:34
t. me, O thou whom.   *S of S* 1:7
which if ye *t. me. Mat* 21:24
t. me which of them.   *Luke* 7:42
t. me where thou hast. *John* 20:15
t. me whether ye sold the. *Acts* 5:8
t. me, art thou a Roman?   22:27
is that thou hast to *t. me?*   23:19
t. me, ye that desire to. *Gal* 4:21

tell *thee*

one of the mountains I will *t. thee*
of.   *Gen* 22:2
land which I will *t. thee* of.   26:2
word we did *t. thee* in.   *Ex* 14:12
sheweth me, I will *t. thee. Num* 23:3
the judgement which they shall *t.*
thee.   *Deut* 17:11
elders, and they will *t. thee.* 32:7
not told it and shall I *t.* it thee?
  Judg 14:16
he will *t. thee* what thou. *Ruth* 3:4
I will *t. thee* all that is. 1 *Sam* 9:19
I will *t. thee* what the Lord. 15:16
I see, that I will *t. thee.*   19:3
then would not I *t.* it thee?   20:9
t. thee what shall become of the
child.   1 *Ki* 14:3
did I not *t. thee* that he would prophesy no good? 22:18; 2 *Chr* 18:17
t. thee that the Lord. 1 *Chr* 17:10
I am escaped alone to *t. thee.*
  Job 1:15, 16, 17, 19
teach thee and *t. thee.*   8:10
the air, and they shall *t. thee.* 12:7
if I were hungry I would not *t. thee.*
  Ps 50:12
let thy wise men *t. thee. Isa* 19:12
words that I shall *t. thee. Jer* 19:2
I *t. thee* thou shalt not. *Luke* 12:59
t. thee, the cock shall not.   22:34
he shall *t. thee* what thou oughtest
to do.   *Acts* 10:6; 11:14
I will *t. thee* the mystery. *Rev* 17:7

I tell *you,* **or** **tell** *I you*
that I may *t.* you what. *Gen* 49:1
I will *t. you* what I will do. *Isa* 5:5
they spring forth, I *t. you.*   42:9
I *t. you* in darkness.   *Mat* 10:27
neither *t. I you* by what authority.
  21:27; *Mark* 11:33; *Luke* 20:8
I will *t. you* by what. *Mark* 11:29
but I *t. you* of a truth. *Luke* 4:25
  9:27
I *t. you* that many prophets.   10:24
I *t. you* nay, but rather.   12:51
I *t. you* nay, but except.   13:3, 5
I *t. you* I know not whence.   27
I *t. you* there shall be two.   17:34

I t. *you* that he will avenge. *Luke* 18:8
I t. *you* this man went to his. 14
I t. *you* that if these should. 19:40
he said, If I t. *you* ye will not. 22:67
shall ye believe if I t. *you* ? *John* 3:12
because I t. *you* the truth. 8:45
Gal 4:16
I t. *you* before it come. *John* 13:19
I t. *you* the truth, it is. 16:7
of which I t. *you* before. *Gal* 5:21
of whom I now t. *you*. *Phil* 3:18

tellest
thou t. my wanderings. *Ps* 56:8

telleth
the Lord t. thee that he. *2 Sam* 7:11
Elisha t. the king of. *2 Ki* 6:12
goeth abroad he t. it. *Ps* 41:6
he that t. lies shall not tarry. 101:7
he t. the number of the stars. 147:4
under hands of him that t. *Jer* 33:13
Philip cometh and t. *John* 12:22

telling
when Gideon heard the t. *Judg* 7:15
hast made an end of t. *2 Sam* 11:19
as he was t. the king how. *2 Ki* 8:5

Tema
sons of Ishmael, Hadar, T. *Gen* 25:15
1 Chr 1:30
the troops of T. looked. *Job* 6:19
the inhabitants of T. *Isa* 21:14
I made Dedan and T. *Jer* 25:23

Teman
Eliphaz were T. Omar. *Gen* 36:11
duke T., duke Kenaz. 15, 42
1 Chr 1:53
is wisdom no more in T.? *Jer* 49:7
Lord hath purposed against T. 20
make it desolate from T. *Ezek* 25:13
will send a fire upon T. *Amos* 1:12
thy mighty men, O T., shall. *Ob* 9
God came from T. *Hab* 3:3

Temanite, *see* Eliphaz

temper
an hin of oil to t. with. *Ezek* 46:14*

temperance
as he reasoned of t. *Acts* 24:25
meekness, t.: against such. *Gal* 5:23
to knowledge t. and to t. *2 Pet* 1:6

temperate
for the mastery, is t. *1 Cor* 9:25
a bishop must be t. *Tit* 1:8
aged men t. 2:2

tempered
unleavened t. with oil. *Ex* 29:2*
a perfume t. together, pure. 30:35*
but God hath t. the body together.
1 Cor 12:24

tempest
[1] *A most violent commotion of the air, either with or without rain, hail, or snow, Acts 27:18, 20.* [2] *Grievous, and unexpected affliction, Job 9:17.*

breaketh me with a t. *Job* 9:17
a t. stealeth him away in. 27:20
on wicked shall he rain a t. *Ps* 11:6*
from the windy storm and t. 55:8
so persecute them with thy t. 83:15
one, which as a t. of hail. *Isa* 28:2
visited with storm and t. 29:6
shall be beaten with a t. 30:30
shall be a covert from the t. 32:2
afflicted, tossed with t. 54:11
with a t. in the day of his. *Amos* 1:14
there was a mighty t. in. *Jonah* 1:4
for my sake this great t. is come. 12
there arose a great t. *Mat* 8:24
tossed with a t. *Acts* 27:18*
no small t. lay on us, hope was. 20
come to darkness and t. *Heb* 12:18
are carried with a t. *2 Pet* 2:17*

tempestuous
it shall be very t. round. *Ps* 50:3
wrought and was t. *Jonah* 1:11, 13
against it a t. wind. *Acts* 27:14

temple
A house or dwelling of God, a building erected and set apart for the worship of the true God. The

---

word is used in the Bible, [1] *Of the tabernacle,* 1 Sam 1:9. [2] *Of Solomon's temple, the wonder of the whole world. This is referred to in all parts of the Bible written before the captivity, when this temple was destroyed. It is also referred to at the time of the building of the second temple, after the Return.* [3] *The temple as rebuilt in the times of Ezra and Nehemiah. This was larger than that of Solomon, but not so rich and beautiful.* [4] *All references in the New Testament to the existing temple are to Herod's temple, built by Herod the Great to win the allegiance of the Jews.* [5] *Of Christ's body or human nature, in which the fulness of the Godhead dwelt,* John 2:19, 21; Col 2:9. [6] *Of the human body,* 1 Cor 3:16.

a seat by a post of the t. *1 Sam* 1:9
he did hear my voice out of his t.,
and my cry. *2 Sam* 22:7; *Ps* 18:6
the t. before it was 40. *1 Ki* 6:17
had prepared the t. *2 Chr* 35:20
and put the vessels in his t. 36:7
that they builded the t. *Ezra* 4:1
out of the t. brought to t. 5:14; 6:5
the t., shut doors of the t. *Neh* 6:10
and to enquire in his t. *Ps* 27:4
in his t. doth every one speak. 29:9
thy lovingkindness, O God, in the
midst of thy t. 48:9
because of thy t. at Jerusalem. 68:29
and his train filled the t. *Isa* 6:1
and to the t. thy foundation. 44:28
a voice from the t., a voice. 66:6
declare the vengeance of his t.
Jer 50:28; 51:11
he brought me to the t. *Ezek* 41:1
vessels taken out of the t. *Dan* 5:2, 3
the songs of the t. shall. *Amos* 8:3
that the t. might be built. *Zech* 8:9
come suddenly to his t. *Mal* 3:1
set him on a pinnacle of the t.
Mat 4:5; *Luke* 4:9
is one greater than the t. *Mat* 12:6
Whosoever shall swear by the t. or by
the gold of the t. 23:16, 17, 21
whom ye slew between the t. 35*
to shew him the buildings of the t.
24:1; *Luke* 21:5
I am able to destroy the t. *Mat* 26:61
thou that destroyest the t. 27:40
Mark 15:29
behold the vail of the t. *Mat* 27:51
Mark 15:38; *Luke* 23:45
any vessel through the t. *Mark* 11:16
I will destroy this t. made. 14:58
departed not from the t. *Luke* 2:37
drove them all out of the t. *John* 2:15
destroy this t. 19
forty and six years was this t. 20
he spake of t. of his body. 21
gate of the t. to ask alms of them
that entered the t. *Acts* 3:2, 10
the t. of goddess Diana. 19:27
and drew him out of the t. 21:30
gone about to profane the t. 24:6
neither against the t. nor. 25:8
that ye are the t. of God ? *1 Cor* 3:16
t. of God, him shall God destroy, for
the t. of God is holy, which t. 17
your body is the t. of the Holy ? 6:19
sit at meat in an idol's t. 8:10
live of the things of the t. 9:13
hath the t. of God with idols ? for ye
are the t. of the. *2 Cor* 6:16
day and night in his t. *Rev* 7:15
saying, Rise and measure the t. 11:1
t. of God was opened in heaven, and
the . . . was seen in his t. 19
angel came out of the t. 14:15, 17
the t. of the tabernacle was. 15:5
seven angels came out of the t. 6
t. was filled with smoke from the. 8
a great voice out of the t. 16:1, 17
no t. therein, for the Lord God
almighty and Lamb are t. 21:22

see holy, Lord

---

in, or *into the* **temple**
spears that were *in the t.* *2 Ki* 11:10
priest's office *in the t.* *1 Chr* 6:10
head *in the t.* of Dagon. 10:10
candlesticks *in the t.* *2 Chr* 4:7, 8
these vessels *into the t.* *Ezra* 5:15
would go *into the t.* to save his life.
Neh 6:11
priests *in the t.* profane. *Mat* 12:5
into the t., cast out all them that sold
and bought *in the t.* 21:12
Mark 11:15; *Luke* 19:45
blind and lame came to see him *in
the t.* *Mat* 21:14
children crying *in the t.* and. 15
I sat daily teaching *in the t.* 26:55
Luke 21:37
pieces of silver *in the t.* *Mat* 27:5*
I was daily teaching *in the t.*
Mark 14:49; *Luke* 22:53
tarried so long *in the t.* *Luke* 1:21
he had seen a vision *in the t.* 22
by the spirit *into the t.* 2:27
they found him *in the t.* sitting. 46
two men went up *into the t.* 18:10
and were continually *in the t.* 24:53
one accord *in the t.* *Acts* 2:46
went up together *into the t.* 3:1
about to go *into the t.* 3
stand and speak *in the t.* 5:20
the men are standing *in the t.* 25
Paul entered *into the t.* 21:26
saw him *in the t.* 27
Greeks also *into the t.* 28, 29
even while I prayed *in the t.* I. 22:17
found me *in the t.* disputing. 24:12
found me purified *in the t.* 18
the Jews caught me *in the t.* 26:21
he as God sitteth *in the t.* of God.
2 Thes 2:4
will I make a pillar *in the t.* of my
God. *Rev* 3:12
no man was able to enter *into t.* 15:8

temples
Maker, and buildeth t. *Hos* 8:14*
ye carried into your t. *Joel* 3:5
Most High dwelleth not in t. made
with hands. *Acts* 7:48; 17:24

temples, *of the head*
Jael smote the nail into his t.
Judg 4:21, 22
she had stricken through his t. 5:26
thy t. like a piece of pomegranate.
S of S 4:3; 6:7

temporal
which are seen are t. *2 Cor* 4:18

tempt
[1] *When spoken of God it means to try or test, with the idea of proving man's faith and obedience, and the desire and certainty that man will not fail,* Gen 22:1. [2] *Man tempts God when he puts him to the proof simply to see if he will keep his promises,* Isa 7:12; Mat 4:7. [3] *The endeavour of the evil one or of evil men to cause a man to commit sin. It is nearly always in this sense that the word* temptation *is used.*

God did t. Abraham. *Gen* 22:1
do ye t. the Lord ? *Ex* 17:2
ye shall not t. the Lord. *Deut* 6:16
I will not ask, nor will I t. *Isa* 7:12
yea, they that t. God are. *Mal* 3:15
is written again, Thou shalt not t.
the. *Mat* 4:7; *Luke* 4:12
why t. ye me ? *Mat* 22:18
Mark 12:15; *Luke* 20:23
together to t. the Spirit. *Acts* 5:9
now therefore why t. ye God ? 15:10
that Satan t. you not for. *1 Cor* 7:5
neither let us t. Christ as. 10:9

temptation
harden not your hearts, as in the day
of t. *Ps* 95:8*; *Heb* 3:3
and lead us not into t. *Mat* 6:13
Luke 11:4
that ye enter not into t. *Mat* 26:41
Mark 14:38; *Luke* 22:40, 46
devil had ended all his t. *Luke* 4:13
and in time of t. fall away. 8:13

hath no *t.* taken you; but will with
  the *t.*   *1 Cor* 10:13
and my *t.* in my flesh ye.   *Gal* 4:14
will be rich fall into *t.*   *1 Tim* 6:9
man that endureth *t.*   *Jas* 1:12
also from the hour of *t.*   *Rev* 3:10

temptations
out of a nation by *t.*   *Deut* 4:34
great *t.* thine eyes saw.   7:19; 29:3
with me in my *t.*   *Luke* 22:28
with many tears and *t.*   *Acts* 20:19
when ye fall into divers *t.*   *Jas* 1:2
in heaviness through manifold *t.*
             1 Pet 1:6
deliver the godly out of *t.* *2 Pet* 2:9

tempted
and because they *t.* the.   *Ex* 17:7
and have *t.* me now.   *Num* 14:22
not tempt God as ye *t.*   *Deut* 6:16
and they *t.* God in.   *Ps* 78:18, 41
yet they *t.* and provoked he.   56
when your fathers *t.* me.   95:9
             Heb 3:9
but lusted, and *t.* God in. *Ps* 106:14
to be *t.* of the devil.   *Mat* 4:1
       Mark 1:13; *Luke* 4:2
a lawyer *t.* him, saying. *Luke* 10:25
as some of them *t.* and. *1 Cor* 10:9
who will not suffer you to be *t.*   13
lest thou also be *t.*   *Gal* 6:1
means the tempter *t.* you. *1 Thes* 3:5
he hath suffered being *t.* *Heb* 2:18
but was in all points *t.* like as. 4:15
were sawn asunder, were *t.*   11:37
when he is *t.*, I am *t.* of God; for God
  cannot be *t.* with evil.   *Jas* 1:13
but every man is *t.* when he is.   14

tempter
when the *t.* came to him.   *Mat* 4:3
lest by means the *t.* have. *1 Thes* 3:5

tempteth
cannot be tempted, neither *t.* he any.
             Jas 1:13

tempting
the Pharisees *t.* Christ.   *Mat* 16:1
     Mark 8:11; *Luke* 11:16
also came to him, *t.* him. *Mat* 19:3
him a question, *t.* him.   22:35
put away his wife, *t.* him. *Mark* 10:2
this they said *t.* him, that. *John* 8:6

ten
Abraham dwelt *t.* years.   *Gen* 16:3
t. shall be found there: he said, I will
  not destroy it for *t.*'s sake. 18:32
the servant took *t.* camels of. 24:10
bracelets for her hands of *t.*   22
Jacob took *t.* bulls and *t.*   32:15
Joseph's *t.* brethren went to.   42:3
Joseph's sent *t.* asses and *t.*   45:23
tabernacle with *t.* curtains. *Ex* 26:1
pillars *t.* and their sockets *t.*   27:12
wrote *t.* commandments.   34:28
          Deut 4:13; 10:4
t. women shall bake.   *Lev* 26:26
for the female *t.* shekels.   27:5, 7
one spoon of *t.* shekels. *Num* 7:14
             20, 26
least gathered *t.* homers.   11:32
the fourth day *t.* bullocks.   29:23
there fell *t.* portions to. *Josh* 17:5
lot out of Ephraim, Manasseh, and
  Dan, *t.* cities.   21:5; *1 Chr* 6:61
with Phinehas *t.* princes. *Josh* 22:14
Gideon took *t.* men of.   *Judg* 6:27
judged Israel *t.* years.
I will give thee *t.* shekels of. 17:10
we will take *t.* men of an.   20:10
Moab about *t.* years.   *Ruth* 1:4
Boaz took *t.* men of the elders. 4:2
am not I better to thee than *t.* sons?
           1 Sam 1:8
take these *t.* loaves and run. 17:17
carry these *t.* cheeses to the.   18
David sent out *t.* young men. 25:5
David left *t.* concubines to keep.
          2 Sam 15:16
have given thee *t.* shekels.   18:11
t. young men smote Absalom.   15
they said, We have *t.* parts.   19:43
the king took his *t.* concubines. 20:3
t. fat oxen in one day.   *1 Ki* 4:23
t. knots in a cubit compassing. 7:24

made *t.* bases of brass. *1 Ki* 7:27, 37
he made *t.* lavers of brass.   38, 43
          2 Chr 4:6
t. pieces; I will give *t.* *1 Ki* 11:31, 35
with thee *t.* loaves to Ahijah.   14:3
t. talents, *t.* changes.   *2 Ki* 5:5
fifty horsemen and *t.* chariots. 13:7
Menahem reigned *t.* years.   15:17
Ishmael came and *t.* men with him.
      25:25; *Jer* 41:1, 2
he made *t.* candlesticks. *2 Chr* 4:7
t. tables.   8
and *t.* brethren were.   *Ezra* 8:24
bring one of *t.* to dwell.   *Neh* 11:1
the *t.* sons of Haman. *Esth* 9:10, 12
and let Haman's *t.* sons be.   13, 14
instrument of *t.* strings.   *Ps* 33:2
         92:3; 144:9
more than *t.* mighty men. *Eccl* 7:19
t. acres of vineyard shall. *Isa* 5:10
an homer of *t.* baths, *t.* *Ezek* 45:14
the fourth beast had *t.* horns.
       Dan 7:7, 20, 24
shall leave *t.* to the house. *Amos* 5:3
if *t.* men remain in one house.   6:9
came to an heap of twenty measures,
  there were but *t.*   *Hag* 2:16
of the roll is *t.* cubits.   *Zech* 5:2
t. men shall take hold of him.   8:23
and when the *t.* heard it. *Mat* 20:24
         Mark 10:41
be likened to *t.* virgins.   *Mat* 25:1
to him that hath *t.* talents.   25:28
woman having *t.* pieces. *Luke* 15:8
there met him *t.* men that.   17:12
Were there not *t.* cleansed?   17
delivered them *t.* pounds.   19:13
thy pound hath gained *t.* pounds. 16
have thou authority over *t.* cities. 17
to him that hath *t.* pounds.   24
Lord, he hath *t.* pounds.   25
a dragon having *t.* horns. *Rev* 12:3
         13:1; 17:3
of seven heads and *t.* horns.   17:7
t. horns thou sawest are the *t.*   12
the *t.* horns thou sawest shall.   16

see **cubits, days, degrees, thousand, thousands**

ten *times*
and hath changed my wages *t.* times.
       Gen 31:7, 41
tempted me now these *t.* times.
         Num 14:22
they said unto us *t.* times. *Neh* 4:12
these *t.* times have ye.   *Job* 19:3
he found them *t.* times.   *Dan* 1:20

tend
thoughts of diligent *t.* to.   *Pr* 21:5

tendeth
of the righteous *t.* to life. *Pr* 10:16
as righteousness *t.* to life, so. 11:19
is that withholdeth, but it *t.* to.   24
the talk of the lips *t.* only to. 14:23
the fear of the Lord *t.* to life. 19:23

tender
[1] *Weak and feeble,* Gen 33:13.
[2] *Of a compassionate and forgiving temper,* Eph 4:32.
ran and fetched a calf *t.* and good.
       Gen 18:7
that the children are *t.*   33:13
so the man that is *t.*   *Deut* 28:54
the *t.* and delicate woman.   56
the small rain on the *t.* herb.   32:2
as the *t.* grass springing. *2 Sam* 23:4
because thy heart was *t.* *2 Chr* 34:27
       2 Chr 34:27
is young and *t.*   *1 Chr* 22:5; 29:1
that the *t.* branch will not. *Job* 14:7
to cause the bud of the *t.* herb. 38:27
t. and beloved in sight.   *Pr* 4:3
hay appears, and the *t.* grass. 27:25
the vines with *t.* grape. *S of S* 2:13
for our vines have *t.* grapes.   15*
see whether the *t.* grape.   7:12
thou shalt no more be called *t.* and.
       Isa 47:1
up before him as a *t.* plant.   53:2
I will crop off a *t.* one. *Ezek* 17:22
brought Daniel into *t.* love. *Dan* 1:9*
in earth, in the *t.* grass.   4:15, 23

when his branch is *t.*   *Mat* 24:32
         Mark 13:28
through the *t.* mercy.   *Luke* 1:78
pitiful, and of *t.* mercy.   *Jas* 5:11*
     see **mercies**

tenderhearted
when Rehoboam was young and *t.*
       2 Chr 13:7
be kind and *t.* one to.   *Eph* 4:32

tenderness
foot on the ground for *t.* *Deut* 28:56

tenons
two *t.* in one board.   *Ex* 26:17, 19
         36:22, 24

tenor
according to the *t.* of.   *Gen* 43:7
after *t.* of these words.   *Ex* 34:27

tens
such over them to be rulers of *t.*
       Ex 8:21, 25
heads, captains over *t.*   *Deut* 1:15

tent
(*This word is often used of the
tabernacle. Tents were the only
homes of the early patriarchs.
Their use was common through all
Bible times, as it is now among the
desert tribes*)
was uncovered in his *t.*   *Gen* 9:21
and pitched his *t.*   12:8; 13:3
Lot pitched his *t.* towards.   13:12
Abraham removed his *t.* and.   18
he sat in *t.* door.   18:1
he hastened into the *t.*   6
thy wife? he said, In the *t.*   9
her into his mother Sarah's *t.* 24:67
and Isaac pitched his *t.* in.   26:17
built an altar, and pitched his *t.* 25
Jacob had pitched his *t.* in.   31:25
Jacob's *t.*, Leah's *t.*, Rachel's *t.*   33
Jacob pitched his *t.* before. 33:18, 19
Israel spread his *t.* beyond.   35:21
Jethro came into the *t.*   *Ex* 18:7
couple the *t.* together that it.   26:11
stood every man at his *t.* door. 33:8
every man in his *t.* door.   10
make the tabernacle, his *t.*   35:11
he made taches to couple the *t.* 36:18
he made a covering for the *t.*   19
brought the *t.* to Moses.   39:33
the *t.* over the tabernacle, and put
  the covering of the *t.*   40:19
leper shall tarry out of his *t.* seven.
       Lev 14:8
Gershon shall be the *t.* *Num* 3:25
the cloud covered the *t.* of.   9:15
weep every man in his *t.*   11:10
a man dieth in a *t.*: all that come into
  the *t.* and is in the *t.*   19:14
clean person shall sprinkle the *t.* 18
the man of Israel into the *t.*   25:8
earth in the midst of my *t.* *Josh* 7:21
the *t.*; and it was hid in his *t.*   22
out of the midst of the *t.*   23
all Israel burnt his *t.* and all.   24
Sisera fled on his feet to the *t.* of.
       Judg 4:17
stand in the door of the *t.*   20
Jael took a nail of the *t.* and.   21
be above women in the *t.*   5:24
of Israel every man to his *t.*   7:8
barley bread came unto a *t.*   13
will not any of us go to his *t.* 20:8
and they fled every man into his *t.*
  1 Sam 4:10; *2 Sam* 18:17; 19:8
sent every man to his *t.* *1 Sam* 13:2
Goliath's armour into his *t.*   17:54
but I have walked in a *t.* *2 Sam* 7:6
       1 Chr 17:5
spread Absalom a *t.* on. *2 Sam* 16:22
retired every man to his *t.*   20:22
went into one *t.*, another *t.* *2 Ki* 7:8
David pitched a *t.* for.   *1 Chr* 15:1
they set it in midst of the *t.*   16:1
       2 Chr 1:4
fled every man to his *t.* *2 Chr* 25:22
the *t.* which he placed.   *Ps* 78:60
nor Arabian pitch *t.* there. *Isa* 13:20
is removed as a shepherd's *t.* 38:12
spreadeth them out as a *t.*   40:22
enlarge the place of thy *t.*   54:2
to stretch forth my *t.*   *Jer* 10:20
rise up every man in his *t.*   37:10

tenth

I will surely give the *t.*   *Gen* 28:22
the *t.* shall be holy.   *Lev* 27:32
children of Levi the *t.*   *Num* 18:21*
enter to *t.* generation.   *Deut* 23:2, 3
king will take the *t.* of.   *1 Sam* 8:15
he will take the *t.* of your sheep. 17
t. captain of sons of.   *1 Chr* 12:13
the *t.* lot came forth to.   24:11
t. lot came forth to Shimei.   25:17
the *t.* captain for the *t.* month. 27:13
but yet in it shall be a *t.*   *Isa* 6:13
in the *t.* year of Zedekiah. *Jer* 32:1
it was about the *t.* hour. *John* 1:39
t. foundation a chrysoprasus.
                                     Rev 21:20

see **day, deal, month, part**

tentmakers

occupation they were *t.*   *Acts* 18:3

tents

father of such as dwell in *t. Gen* 4:20
Japheth shall dwell in the *t.*   9:27
flocks, and herds, and *t.*   13:5
plain man, dwelling in *t.*   25:27
into the maid servants' *t.*   31:33
for them that are in *t.*   *Ex* 16:16
Israel shall pitch their *t.* *Num* 1:52
cloud abode, they pitched *t.*   9:17
cloud abode, they rested in their *t.*
                                18, 20, 22, 23
whether they dwell in *t.* or.   13:19
depart from the *t.* of these.   16:26
stood in the door of their *t.*   27
Israel abiding in his *t.*   24:2
how goodly are thy *t.* O Jacob.   5
in your *t.* and said.   *Deut* 1:27
a place to pitch your *t.* in.   33
Get ye into your *t.* again.   5:30
swallowed them up and their *t.* 11:6
turn and go unto thy *t.*   16:7
rejoice, Issachar, in thy *t.*   33:18
and get you into your *t. Josh* 22:4, 6
with much riches unto your *t.*   8
came with their *t.*   *Judg* 6:5
of them that dwelt in *t.*   8:11
the Philistines' *t.*   *1 Sam* 17:53
and Judah abide in *t.*   *2 Sam* 11:11
every man to his *t.*   20:1
                       1 Ki 12:16; *2 Chr* 10:16
Israel went to their *t.*   *1 Ki* 8:66
                                     2 Chr 7:10
Syrians left their *t.*   *2 Ki* 7:7, 10
Israel spoiled the *t.* of the.   16
people fled into their *t.*   8:21; 14:12
of Israel dwelt in their *t.*   13:5
smote the *t.* of Ham.   *1 Chr* 4:41
dwelt in the Hagarites' *t.*   5:10
also the *t.* of cattle.   *2 Chr* 14:15
to praise in the gates of the *t.* 31:2
at Ahava we abode in *t.*   *Ezra* 8:15
none dwell in their *t.*   *Ps* 69:25
Israel to dwell in their *t.*   78:55
than to dwell in the *t.* of.   84:10
murmured in their *t.* and.   106:25
woe is me, that I dwell in the *t.* 120:5
but comely, as the *t.* of Kedar.
                                   S of S 1:5
kids beside the shepherds' *t.*   8
suddenly are my *t.* spoiled. *Jer* 4:20
they shall pitch their *t.* against. 6:3
the captivity of Jacob's *t.*   30:18
days ye shall dwell in *t.*   35:7
but we have dwelt in *t.* and.   10
their *t.* and flocks shall they. 49:29
I saw the *t.* of Cushan in. *Hab* 3:7
the Lord shall save the *t.* *Zech* 12:7
plague shall be in these *t.*   14:15

Terah

Nahor begat *T.*   *Gen* 11:24
                                     1 Chr 1:26
T. begat Abram.   *Gen* 11:26, 27
                                     Josh 24:2
T. took Abram his son.   *Gen* 11:31

teraphim

made an ephod and *t.*   *Judg* 17:5
in these houses is *t.*   18:14
took the *t.*   20
abide many days without *t. Hos* 3:4

termed

be *t.* forsaken, neither shall thy land
any more be *t.* desolate. *Isa* 62:4

terraces

made of algum trees *t.*   *2 Chr* 9:11

terrestrial

there are bodies *t.*: the glory of the *t.*
                                  1 Cor 15:40

terrible

for it is a *t.* thing.   *Ex* 34:10
went through that *t.* wilderness.
                                Deut 1:19; 8:15
a mighty God and *t.*   7:21; 10:17
                          Neh 1:5; 4:14; 9:32
hath done for thee *t.* things.
                           Deut 10:21; *2 Sam* 7:23
angel of God, very *t.*   *Judg* 13:6
with God is *t.* majesty.   *Job* 37:22
the glory of his nostrils is *t.*   39:20
his teeth are *t.* round about.   41:14
shall teach thee *t.* things. *Ps* 45:4
for the Lord Most High is *t.*   47:2
by *t.* things in righteousness.   65:5
say unto God, How *t.* art thou | 66:3
t. in his doing towards the children. 5
t. out of thy holy places.   68:35
t. to the kings of the earth.   76:12
praise thy great and *t.* name.   99:3
who had done *t.* things by. |06:22
of the might of thy *t.* acts.   145:6
thou art *t.* as an army.   *S of S* 6:4*
lay low the haughtiness of the *t.*
                                     Isa 13:11
go to a people *t.* hitherto.   18:2
from a people *t.* hitherto.   7
from the desert, from a *t.* land. 21:1
the city of the *t.* nations shall. 25:3
when the blast of the *t.* ones is.   4
the branch of the *t.* ones shall be. 5
multitude of the *t.* ones shall.   29:5
for the *t.* one is brought to naught. 20
and the prey of the *t.* shall be. 49:25
when thou didst *t.* things.   64:3
out of the hand of the *t.*   *Jer* 15:21
with me as a mighty *t.* one.   20:11
skin was black, because of *t.* famine.
                                    Lam 5:10*
colour of the *t.* crystal.   *Ezek* 1:22
behold therefore I will bring the *t.* of.
                          28:7; 30:11; 31:12
I will cause to fall the *t.* of.   32:12
form of the image was *t. Dan* 2:31
fourth beast dreadful and *t.*   7:7*
day of Lord is very *t.*   *Joel* 2:11
t. day of the Lord come.   31
the Chaldeans are *t.* and.   *Hab* 1:7
the Lord will be *t.* unto.   *Zeph* 2:11
so *t.* was the sight that.   *Heb* 12:21

terribleness

Lord brought us out with great *t.*
                                    Deut 26:8
thee a name of greatness and *t.*
                                   1 Chr 17:21*
thy *t.* hath deceived thee. *Jer* 49:16

terribly

shake *t.* the earth.   *Isa* 2:19*, 21*
fir trees shall be *t.* shaken. *Nah* 2:3

terrified

fear not nor be *t.*   *Deut* 20:3
hear of wars, be not *t.*   *Luke* 21:9
but they were *t.* and.   24:37
and in nothing *t.* by your. *Phil* 1:28

terrifiest

then thou *t.* me through.   *Job* 7:14

terrify

blackness of the day *t.* it. *Job* 3:5
rod, and let not his fear *t.*   9:34
contempt of families *t.* me ?   31:34
seem as if I would *t.*   *2 Cor* 10:9

terror

and the *t.* of God was.   *Gen* 35:5
even appoint over you *t.*   *Lev* 26:16
the sword without and *t. Deut* 32:25
in all the great *t.* which Moses. 34:12
and that your *t.* is fallen. *Josh* 2:9
from God was a *t.* to me.   *Job* 31:23
behold, my *t.* shall not make.   33:7
not be afraid for the *t.*   *Ps* 91:5
lop the bough with *t.*   *Isa* 10:33
land of Judah shall be a *t.*   19:17
thine heart shall meditate *t.*   33:18
thou shalt be far from *t.*   54:14
be not a *t.* to me.   *Jer* 17:17
a *t.* to thyself.   20:4

terrors

forth Israel with great *t.*   *Jer* 32:21
cause *t.* to be on all.   *Ezek* 26:17
I will make thee a *t.*   21; 27:36
                                     28:19
which caused *t.* in the land.   32:23
                                  24, 25, 26, 27
with their *t.* they are ashamed.   30
I have caused my *t.* in the land.   32
for rulers are not a *t.*   *Rom* 13:3
knowing therefore the *t.*   *2 Cor* 5:11
be not afraid of their *t.*   *1 Pet* 3:14

terrors

a nation by great *t.*   *Deut* 4:34
t. of God do set themselves. *Job* 6:4
t. shall make him afraid on.   18:11
bring him to the king of *t.*   14
the sword cometh, *t.* are.   20:25
are in the *t.* of the shadow.   24:17
t. take hold on him as waters. 27:20
t. are turned upon me.   30:15
the *t.* of death are fallen. *Ps* 55:4
utterly consumed with *t.*   73:19
while I suffer thy *t.* I am.   88:15
wrath goeth over me, thy *t.*   16
I caused *t.* to fall upon.   *Jer* 15:8
thou hast called my *t.*   *Lam* 2:22
t. by reason of the sword shall be.
                                    Ezek 21:12

Tertius

I *T.* who wrote this epistle salute.
                                     Rom 16:22

Tertullus

certain orator named *T.*   *Acts* 24:1
T. began to accuse Paul, saying.   2

testament

(*The usual meaning of this word,
as in Old Testament and New
Testament, is covenant, that is, the
old and the new Dispensation, or
relations between God and man.
In a few cases it seems to mean the
same as it does now in law, in the
phrase* last will and testament,
Heb 9:16, 17. *But the Revisions
render the term in each case by the
word* covenant)
this is my blood in new *t.*
                         Mat 26:28; *Mark* 14:24
this cup is the new *t.*   *Luke* 22:20
                                     1 Cor 11:25
ministers of the new *t.*   *2 Cor* 3:6
vail, in reading the old *t.*   14
a surety of a better *t.*   *Heb* 7:22
of the new *t.* for the redemption of
transgressions under first *t.*   9:15
where a *t.* is there must also.   16
for a *t.* is of force after men.   17
the blood of the *t.* which God.   20
the ark of his *t.*   *Rev* 11:19

testator

be the death of the *t.*   *Heb* 9:16*
no strength while the *t.* liveth.   17*

testified

and it hath been *t.* to his. *Ex* 21:29
hath *t.* falsely against.   *Deut* 19:18
seeing the Lord hath *t.*   *Ruth* 1:21
thy mouth hath *t.*   *2 Sam* 1:16
yet the Lord *t.* against.   *2 Ki* 17:13
his testimonies which he *t.*   15
prophets *t.* against them. *2 Chr* 24:19
                                     Neh 9:26
I *t.* against them.   *Neh* 13:15, 21
which the woman *t.*   *John* 4:39
Jesus himself *t.* that a prophet.   44
                                     13:21
when they had *t.* and.   *Acts* 8:25
Paul *t.* to the Jews, that Jesus. 18:5
for as thou hast *t.* of me.   23:11
to whom he *t.* the kingdom.   28:23
are false, because we have *t.* of God,
                                    1 Cor 15:15
forewarned you and *t.*   *1 Thes* 4:6
gave himself, to be *t.*   *1 Tim* 2:6
in a certain place *t.* saying. *Heb* 2:6
when it *t.* beforehand.   *1 Pet* 1:11
God hath *t.* of his Son.   *1 John* 5:9
and *t.* of the truth that.   *3 John* 3

testifiedst

and *t.* against them.   *Neh* 9:29, 30

testifieth

the pride of Israel *t.* to.   *Hos* 7:10
seen and heard, that he *t. John* 3:32

testify

disciple which t. of these. *John* 21:24
t. thou art a priest for. *Heb* 7:17
he which t. these things. *Rev* 22:20

testify
one witness not t. against any.
Num 35:30
I t. against you that ye. *Deut* 8:19
if a false witness t. against. 19:16
this song shall t. against. 31:21
hearts to the words which I t. 32:46
didst t. against them. *Neh* 9:34
yea, thine own lips t. *Job* 15:6
O Israel, I will t. against thee.
Ps 50:7; 81:8
before thee, and our sins t. *Isa* 59:12
though our iniquities t. *Jer* 14:7
the pride of Israel doth t. *Hos* 5:5
t. in the house of Jacob. *Amos* 3:13
have I done ? t. against me. *Mi* 6:3
that he may t. to them. *Luke* 16:28
any should t. of man. *John* 2:25
and t. that we have seen. 3:11
they t. of me. 5:39
because I t. of it. 7:7
he shall t. of me. 15:26
other words did he t. *Acts* 2:40
t. that it is he who was ordained.
10:42
to t. the gospel of the grace. 20:24
life know they, if they would t. 26:5
I t. to every man that. *Gal* 5:3
t. in the Lord, that ye. *Eph* 4:17
seen, and do t., that. *1 John* 4:14
have sent my angel to t. *Rev* 22:16
I t. to every man that heareth. 18

testifying
t. both to the Jews and. *Acts* 20:21
obtained witness, God t. *Heb* 11:4
t. that this is the true. *1 Pet* 5:12

testimonies
these are the t. which. *Deut* 4:45
ye shall diligently keep the t. 6:17
what mean the t. which God ? 20
keep his statutes and his t. *1 Ki* 2:3
2 Ki 23:3; *1 Chr* 29:19; *2 Chr* 34:31
rejected his t. and. *2 Ki* 17:15
kings hearkened to thy t. *Neh* 9:34
his covenant and his t. *Ps* 25:10
and keep not his t. 78:56
thy t. are sure. 93:5
kept his t. and the ordinance. 99:7
Blessed are they that keep his t. and
seek him. 119:2
rejoiced in the way of thy t. 14
for I have kept thy t. 22, 167, 168
thy t. are my delight. 24
I stuck to thy t. 31
incline my heart to thy t., not to. 36
I will speak of thy t. also. 46
and I turned my feet to thy t. 59
let those that have known thy t. 79
but I will consider thy t. 95
for thy t. are my meditation. 99
t. have I taken as an heritage. 111
I love thy t. 119
that I may know thy t. 125
thy t. are wonderful, therefore. 129
thy t. are righteous and very. 138
the righteousness of thy t. is. 144
and I shall keep thy t. 146
concerning thy t., I have known. 152
yet do I not decline from thy t. 157
not walked in his t. *Jer* 44:23

testimony
[1] *A witnessing evidence, or
proof, Acts 14:3. [2] The whole
scripture, or word of God, which
declares what is to be believed and
practised, Ps 19:7. [3] The two
tables of stone, whereon the law, or
ten commandments, were written,
which were witnesses of that covenant made between God and his
people, Ex 25:16, 21; 31:18. [4]
The book of the law which testifies
of God's will and man's duty, 2 Ki
11:12. [5] The ark in which the
law was deposited, Ex 16:34.*
of manna before the t. *Ex* 16:34
put into the ark the t. 25:16, 21
vail which is before the t. 27:21

mercy seat that is over the t. *Ex* 30:6
Lev 16:13
and put it before the t. *Ex* 30:36
gave to Moses two tables of t. 31:18
the two tables of t. 32:15; 34:29
sum of the tabernacle of t. 38:21
over the tabernacle of t. *Num* 1:50
pitch about the tabernacle of t. 53
covered the tent of the t. 9:15
taken off the tabernacle of t. 10:11
up the rods before the t. 17:4
Aaron's rod again before the t. 10
shoe, and this was a t. in. *Ruth* 4:7
gave the king the t. *2 Ki* 11:12
2 Chr 23:11
for he established a t. *Ps* 78:5
ordained in Joseph for a t. 81:5
so shall I keep the t. of. 119:88
the tribes go up to the t. of. 122:4
children will keep my t. 132:12
bind up the t. *Isa* 8:16
to the law and to the t. 20
the gift Moses commanded for a t.
Mat 8:4; *Mark* 1:44; *Luke* 5:14
for a t. against them. *Mat* 10:18
Mark 13:9
shake off the dust for a t.
Mark 6:11; *Luke* 9:5
shall turn to you for a t. *Luke* 21:13
no man receiveth his t. *John* 3:32
he that receiveth his t. hath. 33
it is written, the t. of two men. 8:17
and we know that his t. is. 21:24
to whom also he gave t. *Acts* 13:22
who gave t. to the word of. 14:3
not receive thy t. of me. 22:18
as the t. of Christ was. *1 Cor* 1:6
unto you the t. of God. 2:1
the t. of our conscience. *2 Cor* 1:12
because our t. among. *2 Thes* 1:10
be not ashamed of the t. *2 Tim* 1:8
for a t. of those things. *Heb* 3:5
Enoch had this t. that he. 11:5
who bare record of the t. *Rev* 1:2
in the isle of Patmos for the t. 9
them that were slain for the t. 6:9
shall have finished their t. 11:7
by the word of their t. 12:11
them which have t. of Jesus. 17
tabernacle of the t. in heaven. 15:5
that have the t. of Jesus; for the t. of
Jesus is the spirit of. 19:10
see ark

Tetrarch, see Herod

thank
that love you, what t. have you ?
Luke 6:32, 33, 34

thank, verb
Levites to t. the Lord. *1 Chr* 16:4
David delivered this psalm to t. 7
to stand every morning to t. 23:30
we t. thee and praise thy. 29:13
I t. thee and praise thee. *Dan* 2:23
I t. thee, O Father, Lord of heaven
and. *Mat* 11:25; *Luke* 10:21
doth he t. that servant ? *Luke* 17:9
God, I t. thee, that I am not. 18:11
Father, I t. thee, that. *John* 11:41
I t. my God through Jesus Christ.
Rom 1:8; 7:25
I t. my God always on. *1 Cor* 1:4
I t. God that I baptized none. 14
I t. my God I speak with. 14:18
I t. my God on every remembrance
of you. *Phil* 1:3
for this cause also I t. *1 Thes* 2:13
we are bound to t. God. *2 Thes* 1:3
I t. Jesus Christ who hath enabled.
1 Tim 1:12
I t. God, whom I serve with pure.
2 Tim 1:3
I t. my God, making. *Philem* 4
see offering

thanked
bowed himself and t. *2 Sam* 14:22*
Paul t. God and took. *Acts* 28:15
but God be t. that ye were the servants. *Rom* 6:17

thankful
be t. to him, bless his name.
Ps 100:4*; *Col* 3:15
him not, neither were t. *Rom* 1:21*

thankfulness
noble Felix, with all t. *Acts* 24:3
were as one in t. the Lord. *2 Chr* 5:13

thanks
companies that gave t. *Neh* 12:31
two companies that gave t. 40
he prayed and gave t. *Dan* 6:10
he took the cup and gave t.
Mat 26:27; *Luke* 22:17
seven loaves and gave t. *Mark* 8:6
when he had given t. he gave. 14:23
Anna gave t. to the Lord. *Luke* 2:38
he took bread, and gave t. 22:19
when he had given t. *John* 6:11
after the Lord had given t. 23
and gave t. to God. *Acts* 27:35
Lord, for he giveth God t.; he eateth
not, and giveth God t. *Rom* 14:6
when he had given t. *1 Cor* 11:24
for thou verily givest t. well. 14:17
t. be to God, who giveth us. 15:57
t. may be given to many. *2 Cor* 1:11
t. be to God who causeth us. 2:14
t. to God, who put the same. 8:16
t. be to God for his unspeakable
gift. 9:15
giving t. always for all. *Eph* 5:20
what t. can we render ? *1 Thes* 3:9
of praise, giving t. *Heb* 13:15
give t. to him that sat. *Rev* 4:9
see give, giving

thanksgiving
[1] *An acknowledging and confessing with gladness, the benefits and
mercies, which God bestows either
upon ourselves or others, Phil 4:6;
1 Tim 2:1. [2] The sacrifice of
thanksgiving, Lev 7:12, 15. [3]
Psalms of thanksgiving, Neh 12:8.*
if he offer it for a t. *Lev* 7:12, 13
15; 22:29
principal to begin the t. *Neh* 11:17
which was over the t., he and. 12:8
of praise and t. to God. 46
publish with the voice of t. *Ps* 26:7
offer unto God t. and pay thy. 50:14
I will magnify him with t. 69:30
come before his face with t. 95:2
enter into his gates with t. 100:4
sacrifice sacrifices of t. 107:22
offer to thee sacrifices of t. 116:17
sing unto the Lord with t.; sing. 147:7
t. and melody shall be. *Isa* 51:3
of them shall proceed t. *Jer* 30:19
offer a sacrifice of t. *Amos* 4:5
to thee with the voice of t. *Jonah* 2:9
grace might through the t. *2 Cor* 4:15
which causeth through us t. 9:11
with t. let your requests. *Phil* 4:6
abounding therein with t. *Col* 2:7
watch in the same with t. 4:2
to be received with t. *1 Tim* 4:3
good, if it be received with t. 4
t. and honour be to our. *Rev* 7:12

thanksgivings
the dedication with t. *Neh* 12:27
abundant by many t. to. *2 Cor* 9:12

thankworthy
this is t. if a man. *1 Pet* 2:19*

that
t. is it which compasseth. *Gen* 2:11
what Adam called, t. was the. 19
t. be far from thee, to slay. 18:25
t. shalt be accounted stolen. 30:33
shall make like unto t. *Ex* 30:38
when Moses heard t. he. *Lev* 10:20
yet for all I will not cast. 26:44
besides t. his hand. *Num* 6:21
the word which I say, t. 22:20
t. will I speak. 24:13; *1 Ki* 22:14
anger was abated, when he had said
t. *Judg* 8:3
do according to t. which. 11:36
behold, t. which is left. *1 Sam* 9:24
if thou wilt take t. take it. 21:9
for t. thou hast done to me. 24:19
with t. which the Lord hath. 30:23
if t. had been too little. *2 Sam* 12:8
in t. thou lovest thine enemies. 19:6
offer of t. which doth cost. 24:24

according to *t.* which was written.
  2 Ki 14:6; *2 Chr* 35:26
t. which thou hast prayed. *2 Ki* 19:20
t. which thou hast promised.
  2 Chr 6:15, 16
t. which they have need. *Ezra* 6:9
t. do after the will of your. 7:18
t. which I was afraid of is. *Job* 3:25
t. which I have seen I will. 15:17
he shall not save of *t.* which. 20:20
what his soul desireth even *t.* 23:13
t. which I see not, teach. 34:32
t. will I seek after, that. *Ps* 27:4
then I restored *t.* which I took. 69:4
when I wept, *t.* was to my. 10
the thing hath been, it is *t.* which shall
  be; *t.* which is done, is *t. Eccl* 1:9
t. which is wanting cannot be. 15
what was *t.* good for the sons of. 2:3
what profit in *t.* wherein he ? 3:9
and God requireth *t.* which is. 15
when thou vowest, pay *t.* thou. 5:4
knowest not whether this or *t.* 11:6
t. which I have heard. *Isa* 21:10
for *t.* which had not been told them
  shall they see, *t.* they had. 52:15
for *t.* which Manasseh. *Jer* 15:4
t. which I have built, *t.* which. 45:4
t. Daniel regardeth not thee, O king.
  Dan 6:13
for *t. t.* is determined shall. 11:36
t. t. dieth, let it die, *t. t. Zech* 11:9
for *t.* which is conceived. *Mat* 1:20
whole from *t.* hour. 9:22; 15:28
for Sodom than for *t.* city. 10:15
  Mark 6:11
taken away *t.* he hath. *Mat* 13:12
  25:29; *Mark* 4:25
t. shall ye receive. *Mat* 20:7
t. observe and do. 23:3
is *t.* to us ? see thou to *t.* 27:4
t. which cometh out, *t. Mark* 7:20
given in *t.* hour, *t.* speak. 13:11
all will I give, for *t.* is. *Luke* 4:6
even *t.* he seemeth to have. 8:18
he *t.* made *t.* which is without make
  t. which is within also ? 11:40
not faithful in *t.* which is. 16:12
t. which is highly esteemed. 15
we have done *t.* which was. 17:10
t. which was come to pass. 24:12
he was not *t.* light. *John* 1:8
t. was the light. 9
t. which is born of flesh, *t.* born. 3:6
we speak *t.* we know, testify *t.* 11
is not thy husband, in *t.* saidst. 4:18
is *t.* saying true, one soweth. 37
what man is *t.* which said to ? 5:12
labour for *t.* meat which. 6:27
Moses gave you not *t.* bread. 32
I am *t.* bread of life. 48
this is *t.* bread. 58
I speak *t.* I have seen with my
  Father; ye do *t.* which ye. 8:38
t. thou doest, do quickly. 13:27
t. will I do. 14:13
what he shall hear, *t.* shall. 16:13
what is *t.* to thee, follow. 21:22, 24
went abroad, that *t.* disciple. 23
this is *t.* which was spoken. *Acts* 2:16
all glorified God for *t.* which. 4:21
heard *t.* they lifted up. 24; 5:21, 33
this is *t.* Moses which said. 7:37
t. word you know, which. 10:37
because *t.* which may be. *Rom* 1:19
according to *t.* which was. 4:18
in *t.* he died, in *t.* he liveth. 6:10
t. being dead wherein we were held,
  t. we. 7:6
was then *t.* which is good made ? 13
t. I do, I allow not. 15
t. I would not, *t.* I do. 19
put away from you *t. 1 Cor* 5:13
nay, you defraud, and *t.* your. 6:8
t. spiritual rock, and *t.* rock. 10:4
spoken of, for *t.* which I. 30
t. which also I delivered unto. 11:23
eat of *t.* bread, and drink of *t.* cup. 28
t. which is perfect, *t.* which. 13:10
and yet for all *t.* they will not. 14:21
and *t.* which thou sowest thou sowest
  not *t.* body that shall be. 15:37
t. was not first which is spiritual, but
  t. which. 46

if *t.* which is done away. *2 Cor* 3:11
it is accepted according to *t.* 8:12
what I do, *t.* I will do, *t.* I may. 11:2
what a man soweth, *t. Gal* 6:7
that I may apprehend *t. Phil* 3:12
might perfect *t.* which. *1 Thes* 3:10
all things; hold fast *t.* is good. 5:21
life *t.* now is, and of *t. 1 Tim* 4:8
keep *t.* which is committed. 6:20
if he oweth, put *t.* on. *Philem* 18
and was heard in *t.* he. *Heb* 5:7
which entereth into *t.* within. 6:19
could not endure *t.* which. 12:20
for *t.* is unprofitable for you. 13:17
shall live, and do this or *t. Jas* 4:15
he *t.* will harm you, if ye be followers
  of *t.? 1 Pet* 3:13; *3 John* 11
t. which was from the. *1 John* 1:1
t. which we have seen. 3; 2:24
let *t.* abide in you which ye. 2:24
t. which ye have, hold. *Rev* 2:25
see **after, day, man, place, so,**
  soul, thing, time

theatre
with one accord into the *t. Acts* 19:29
not adventure himself into the *t.* 31

Thebez
went Abimelech to *T.* and took *T.*
  Judg 9:50
that he died in *T.* *2 Sam* 11:21

thee
t. have I seen righteous. *Gen* 7:1
multiply *t.* exceedingly. 17:2
in blessing I will bless *t.* 22:17
I *t.*, and the cave I give it *t.* 23:11
back any thing from me but *t.* 39:9
the stranger shall get above *t.*
  Deut 28:43
have not rejected *t.* but. *1 Sam* 8:7
arrows are beyond *t.* 20:22, 37
the king charged *t. 2 Sam* 18:12
they have not set *t. Ps* 86:14
enemy to entreat *t.* well. *Jer* 15:11
I will recompense *t. Ezek* 7:9
I will leave *t.* and all the fish. 29:5
when saw we *t.* an hungered, and fed
  t.? Mat 25:37
when saw we *t.* a stranger ? 38
when saw we *t.* sick ? 39
he that bade *t.* and him. *Luke* 14:9
but the root bearest *t. Rom* 11:18
lest he also spare not *t.* 21

see **teach, tell**

about **thee**
thou shalt dig *about t. Job* 11:18
shut thy doors *about t. Isa* 26:20
sword devour round *about t.*
  Jer 46:14; *Ezek* 5:12
all those that be *about t. Jer* 49:5
among nations that are round *about*
  t. Ezek 5:14
to the nations round *about t.* 15
cast a trench *about t. Luke* 19:43
cast thy garment *about t. Acts* 12:8

after **thee**
to thy seed *after t. Gen* 17:7, 8, 9
  10; 35:12; 48:4
with thy children *after t. Deut* 4:40
  12:25, 28
after t. Benjamin among. *Judg* 5:14
set up thy seed *after t. 2 Sam* 7:12
will come in *after t.* and. *1 Ki* 1:14
nor *after t.* shall any arise like thee.
  3:12; *2 Chr* 1:12
panteth my soul *after t. Ps* 42:1
my soul followeth hard *after t.* 63:8
my soul thirsteth *after t.* 143:6
we will run *after t. S of S* 1:4
they shall come *after t. Isa* 45:14
called a multitude *after t. Jer* 12:6
after t. shall rise another. *Dan* 2:39
cry at Beth-aven, *after t. Hos* 5:8

against **thee**
that rose *against t. Ex* 15:7
of the field multiply *against t.* 23:29
sinned, for we have spoken *against t.*
  Num 21:7
Lord be kindled *against t. Deut* 6:15
and he cry to the Lord *against t.*
  15:9; 24:15
they hired Balaam *against t.* 23:4
against t. one way, and flee. 28:7

the Lord shall send *against t.*
  Deut 28:48, 49
there for a witness *against t.* 31:26
fortify the city *against t. Judg* 9:31
we have sinned *against t.* 10:10
  Neh 1:6; *Jer* 14:7, 20
I have not sinned *against t.*
  Judg 11:27; *1 Sam* 24:11
he hath not sinned *against t.*
  1 Sam 19:4
hath testified *against t. 2 Sam* 1:16
I will raise up evil *against t.* 12:11
that rose up *against t.* 18:31, 32
because they have sinned *against t.*
  1 Ki 8:33, 35; *2 Chr* 6:24, 26
if they sin *against t.* and repent.
  1 Ki 8:46; *2 Chr* 6:36
people that have sinned *against t.*
  and all their. *1 Ki* 8:50; *2 Chr* 6:39
king of Syria will come up *against t.*
  1 Ki 20:22
out to fight *against t. 2 Ki* 19:9
man prevail *against t. 2 Chr* 14:11
hath spoken evil *against t.* 18:22
a great multitude *against t.* 20:2
I come not *against t.* this day. 35:21
very corruptly *against t. Neh* 1:7
they rebelled *against t.* 9:26
why hast thou set me as a mark
  against t.? Job 7:20
would open his lips *against t.* 11:5
own lips testify *against t.* 15:6
my wrath is kindled *against t.* 42:7
have rebelled *against t. Ps* 5:10
they intended evil *against t.* 21:11
Lord, heal my soul, for I have sinned
  against t. 41:4
and I will testify *against t.* 50:7
against t. have I sinned, and done
  this evil. 51:4
that rise up *against t.* 74:23
  139:21; *Eccl* 10:4
that I might not sin *against t.*
  Ps 119:11
for they speak *against t.* 139:20
evil counsel *against t. Isa* 7:5
shall lift up his staff *against t.* 10:24
fight *against t.* but they shall not prevail *against t. Jer* 1:19; 15:20
behold I am *against t.* 21:13; 50:31
  51:25; *Ezek* 5:8; 21:3; 26:3
  28:22; 29:3, 10; 35:3; 38:3
  39:1; *Nah* 2:13; 3:5
thy enemies opened their mouth
  against t. Lam 2:16
still are talking *against t. Ezek* 33:30
hath conspired *against t. Amos* 7:10
spoken so much *against t. Mal* 3:13
that thy brother hath aught *against t.*
  Mat 5:23
if thy brother trespass *against t.*
  18:15; *Luke* 17:3, 4
which these witness *against t.?*
  Mat 26:62; *Mark* 14:60; 15:4
I have somewhat *against t. Rev* 2:4
a few things *against t.* 14, 20

at **thee**
hath shaken her head *at t. 2 Ki* 19:21
  Isa 37:22
fir trees rejoice at *t. Isa* 14:8
as many were astonied *at t.* 52:14
  Ezek 26:16; 27:35; 28:19
by clap their hands *at t. Lam* 2:15
shall hiss *at t. Ezek* 27:36
many people amazed *at t.* 32:10

before **thee**
is not whole land *before t.? Gen* 13:9
Ishmael might live *before t.* 17:18
behold my land is *before t.* 20:15
  47:6
heaven shall send his angel *before t.*
  24:7; *Ex* 23:20, 23; 32:34; 33:2
Rebekah is *before t. Gen* 24:51
I cannot rise up *before t.* 31:35
I will go *before t.* 33:12; *Isa* 45:2
set him *before t. Gen* 43:9
will stand *before t.* there. *Ex* 17:6
I will send my fear *before t.* 23:27
before t. which shall drive out the
  Canaanites *before t.* 28, 29, 30, 31
  34:11; *Deut* 4:38; 9:4, 5; 18:12
goodness pass *before t.* and I will
  proclaim . . . *before t. Ex* 33:19

I will cast out before t. Ex 34:24
 Deut 6:19; 7:1; 9:4
hate thee flee before t. Num 10:35
no man able to stand before t.
 Deut 7:24; Josh 1:5; 10:8
they shall flee before t. Deut 28:7
I have set before t. this day. 30:15
he shall go over before t. 31:3, 8
shalt see the land before t. 32:52
shall put incense before t. 33:10
Lord gone out before t.? Judg 4:14
bring forth, and set it before t. 6:18
 1 Sam 9:24
let me set a morsel of bread before
 t. 1 Sam 28:22
Lord go out before t. 2 Sam 5:24
Saul, whom I put away before t. 7:15
be established for ever before t.
 16, 26; 1 Chr 17:24
as he walked before t. 1 Ki 3:6
none like thee before t. 12
thy servants that walk before t.
 8:23; 2 Chr 6:14
which stand continually before t.
 1 Ki 10:8; 2 Chr 9:7
done evil above all that were before
 t. 1 Ki 14:9
how I have walked before
 t. 2 Ki 20:3; Isa 38:3
for God is gone forth before t.
 1 Chr 14:15
from him that was before t. 17:13
before t. in our trespasses, we cannot stand before t. Ezra 9:15
sin be blotted out before t. Neh 4:5
his heart faithful before t. 9:8
trouble seem little before t. 32
Lord, all my desire is before t. and.
 Ps 38:9
age is as nothing before t. 39:5
adversaries are all before t. 69:19
I was as a beast before t. 73:22
the prisoner come before t. 79:11
let my prayer come before t.: incline
 thine ear unto my cry. 88:2; 141:2
hast set our iniquities before t. 90:8
my ways are before t. 119:168
let my cry come before t. 169
diligently what is before t. Pr 23:1
they joy before t. as men. Isa 9:3
righteousness shall go before t. 58:8
lips, was right before t. Jer 17:16
I stood before t. to turn. 18:20
the prophets that have been before t.
 of old. 28:8
all the land is before t.: go. 40:4
wickedness come before t. Lam 1:22
and they sit before t. Ezek 33:31
also before t. O king. Dan 6:22
I sent before t. Moses. Mi 6:4
fellows that sit before t. Zech 3:8
a trumpet before t. Mat 6:2
which shall prepare thy way before t.
 11:10; Mark 1:2; Luke 7:27
I have sinned before t. Luke 15:18
to say before t. what. Acts 23:30
been here before t. to object. 24:19
before t. O king Agrippa. 25:26
set before t. an open door. Rev 3:8

behind thee
life, look not behind t. Gen 19:17
Amalek smote the feeble behind t.
 Deut 25:18
castest my words behind t. Ps 50:17
hear a word behind t. Isa 30:21

beside thee
to redeem it beside t. Ruth 4:4
there is none beside t. 1 Sam 2:2
 2 Sam 7:22; 1 Chr 17:20
that I desire beside t. Ps 73:25
other lords beside t. have. Isa 26:13
eye seen, O God, beside t. 64:4

between thee
I will put enmity between t. Gen 3:15
my covenant between me and t.
 17:2, 7
witness between me and t. 31:44
 48:50
Lord watch between me and t. 49
the Lord be between t. and me for.
 1 Sam 20:23, 42
set it for a wall of iron between t.
 Ezek 4:3

been witness between t. Mal 2:14
fault between t. and. Mat 18:15

by thee
the people stand by t. Ex 18:14
woman that stood by t. 1 Sam 1:26
I said to thee, Set it by t. 9:23
by t. I ran through a troop.
 2 Sam 22:30; Ps 18:29
by t. have I been holpen. Ps 71:6
when thou hast it by t. Pr 3:28
dwell securely by t. 29
but by t. only will we make mention
 of thy name. Isa 26:13
when I passed by t. Ezek 16:6, 8
seeing that by t. we enjoy quietness.
 Acts 24:2
saints are refreshed by t. Philem 7

concerning thee
Lord said con. t. and me. Josh 14:6
he hath spoken con. t. 1 Sam 25:30
I will give charge con. t. 2 Sam 14:8
spoken evil con. t. 1 Ki 22:23
hath given commandment con. t.
 Nah 1:14
angels charge con. t. Mat 4:6
neither we letters con. t. Acts 28:21

for thee
food for t. and them. Gen 6:21
shall pray for t. 20:7
but as for t. and thy servants, I.
 Ex 9:30
sabbath shall be meat for t. and.
 Lev 25:6
shall be most holy for t. Num 18:9
as for t. stand by me. Deut 5:31
 18:14; 2 Sam 13:13
I will try them for t. Judg 7:4
have made ready a kid for t. 13:15
better for t. to be a priest to. 18:19
shall I not seek rest for t.? Ruth 3:1
buy it for t. 4:8
hath it been kept for t. 1 Sam 9:24
soul desireth, I will do it for t. 20:4
I am distressed for t. 2 Sam 1:26
be too strong for t., help thee. 10:11
would God I had died for t. 18:33
requirest, that I will do for t. 19:38
I will speak for t. unto. 1 Ki 2:18
and after make for t. and. 17:13
thou shalt make streets for t. 20:34
what I shall do for t. 2 Ki 2:9
what is to be done for t.? 4:13
and as for t. 2 Chr 7:17; Dan 2:29
 Zech 9:11
surely now he would awake for t.
 Job 8:6
earth be forsaken for t.? 18:4
my soul thirsteth for t., my. Ps 63:1
praise waiteth for t. O God. 65:1
it is time for t. O Lord. 119:126
fruits I have laid up for t. S of S 7:13
beneath is moved for t. Isa 14:9
have waited for t. 26:8; 33:2
Ethiopia and Seba for t. 43:3
therefore will I give men for t. 4
for my praise will I refrain for t. 48:9
who shall he sorry for t. 51:19
is nothing too hard for t. Jer 32:17
so shall they burn odours for t. 34:5
I will weep for t. 48:32
I laid a snare for t. 50:24
I take vengeance for t. 51:36
I take to witness for t. Lam 2:13
thy prophets have seen for t. 14
it watcheth for t.; behold. Ezek 7:6
be horribly afraid for t. 32:10
another, so will I be for t. Hos 3:3
he hath set a harvest for t. 6:11
I seek comfort for t. Nah 3:7
is profitable for t. Mat 5:29, 30
for Sodom than for t. 11:24
it is not lawful for t. to have her.
 14:4; Mark 6:18
one for t.. and one for Moses.
 Mat 17:4; Mark 9:5; Luke 9:33
better for t. to enter into life.
 Mat 18:8, 9; Mark 9:43, 45
him, All men seek for t. Mark 1:37
thy brethren seek for t. 3:32
the Lord hath done for t. 5:19
but I have prayed for t. Luke 22:32
come, and calleth for t. John 11:28

hard for t. to kick against the pricks.
 Acts 9:5; 26:14
to send for t. into his house. 10:22
season, I will call for t. 24:25
grace is sufficient for t. 2 Cor 12:9

from thee
be far°from t. to slay. Gen 18:25
anger turn away from t. 27:45
hath withheld from t. the fruit. 30:2
behold, I go out from t. Ex 8:29
put off thy ornaments from t. 33:5
be too far from t. Deut 12:21; 14:24
him go free from t. 15:12, 13, 18
I will not go away from t. 16
cities far from t. 20:15
it is not hidden from t. neither. 30:11
shekels taken from t. Judg 17:2
Eli said unto her, Put away thy wine
 from t. 1 Sam 1:14
hath rent the kingdom from t. 15:28
 1 Ki 11:11
take thine head from t. 1 Sam 17:46
far be it from t. 20:9; Mat 16:22
not withhold me from t. 2 Sam 13:13
before I be taken from t. 2 Ki 2:9
shall issue from t. 20:18; Isa 39:7
came up from t. to us. Ezra 4:12
be withholden from t. Job 42:2
groaning is not hid from t. Ps 38:9
sins are not hid from t. 69:5
they that are far from t. shall. 73:27
so will we not go back from t. 80:18
darkness hideth not from t. 139:12
my substance was not hid from t. 15
wrath I hid my face from t. Isa 54:8
shall not depart from t. 10
my soul depart from t. Jer 6:8
I will cut off from t. Ezek 21:3, 4
those that be far from t. shall. 22:5
I take away from t. the desire. 24:16
secret that they can hide from t. 28:3
gone into captivity from t. Mi 1:16
iniquity to pass from t. Zech 3:4
pluck it out and cast it from t.
 Mat 5:29, 30; 18:8, 9
I came out from t. John 17:8
for a promise from t. Acts 23:21
see departed

in thee
in t. shall all families be blessed.
 Gen 12:3; 28:14
in t. shall Israel bless. 48:20
to shew in t. my power. Ex 9:16
no unclean thing in t. Deut 23:14
it would be sin in t. 21
shall be no sin in t. 22
king hath delight in t. 1 Sam 18:22
evil hath not been found in t. 25:28
 29:6
I have no delight in t. 2 Sam 15:26
good things found in t. 2 Chr 19:3
put trust in t . . . love thy name be
 joyful in t. Ps 5:11; 7:1; 9:10
 16:1; 17:7; 25:2, 20; 31:1, 19
 55:23
rejoice in t. 9:2; 40:16; 70:4; 85:6
 S of S 1:4
our fathers trusted in t. Ps 22:4, 5
I trusted in t. 31:14
hope in t. 33:22; 38:15; 39:7
trust in t. 56:3; 57:1; 84:12; 86:2
 141:8; 143:8
there shall no strange god be in t.
 81:9
man whose strength is in t. 84:5
all my springs are in t. 87:7
there is no spot in t. S of S 4:7
because he trusteth in t. Isa 26:3
surely God is in t.; and there. 45:14
for the Lord delighteth in t. 62:4
that my fear is not in t. Jer 2:19
I will do in t. what I. Ezek 5:9
will execute judgements in t. 10, 15
the contrary is in t. from. 16:34
I will kindle a fire in t., and it. 20:47
were in t. to their power to. 22:6
in t. have they set light by father. 7
in t. are men that carry tales. 9
in t. have they taken gifts. 12
set palaces in t., dwellings in t. 25:4
O Tyrus, that were in t. 27:8, 9
till iniquity was found in t. 28:15
be sanctified in t. O Gog. 38:16

spirit of the holy gods is in t.
Dan 4:9, 18; 5:14
for in t. the fatherless. Hos 14:3
Israel were found in t. Mi 1:13
cry ? is there no king in t.? 4:9
if the light that is in t. Mat 6:23
which have been done in t. 11:23
my beloved Son; in t. I. Luke 3:22
the light which is in t. be not. 11:35
not leave in t. one stone. 19:44
art in me, and I in t. John 17:21
shew my power in t. Rom 9:17
in t. shall all nations. Gal 3:8
the gift that is in t. 1 Tim 4:14
faith that is in t. first in Lois and
Eunice, and . . . in t. 2 Tim 1:5
stir up the gift of God which is in t. 6
of the truth that is in t. 3 John 3
heard no more at all in t. Rev 18:22
shall shine no more at all in t. 23

into thee
no more into t. the. Isa 52:1

of thee
of t. a great nation. Gen 12:2
17:6; 35:11; 46:3; 48:4; Ex 32:10
and my soul shall live because of t.
Gen 12:13
I have heard say of t. that. 41:15
heard the fame of t. Num 14:15
I will put the dread of t. and the fear
of t. . . . because of t. Deut 2:25
Lord require of t. 10:12; Mi 6:8
take knowledge of t. Ruth 2:19
with my father of t. 1 Sam 19:3
and the Lord avenge me of t. 24:12
I will require of t. 2 Sam 3:13
but I will surely buy it of t. 24:24
one petition of t. 1 Ki 2:16, 20
as this is done of t. 11:11
house as he said of t. 1 Chr 22:11
and honour come of t. 29:12
all things come of t., and of thine. 14
God exacteth of t. less. Job 11:6
for I will demand of t. 38:3; 40:7
42:4
heard of t. by the hearing. 42:5
my praise shall be of t. Ps 22:25
71:6
glorious things are spoken of t. 87:3
lest he be weary of t. Pr 25:17
two things have I required of t. 30:7
they that shall be of t. Isa 58:12
up himself to take hold of t. 64:7
I will not make a full end of t.
Jer 30:11; 46:28
thus saith the Lord of t., Thou. 34:4
shall not take of t. a stone. 51:26
man and beast out of t. Ezek 29:8
rivers shall be full of t. 32:6
made known what we desired of t.
Dan 2:23
petition, save of t. O king. 6:7, 12
assemble all of t. Mi 2:12
yet out of t. shall come forth. 5:2
shall fear because of t. 7:17
come out of t. a wicked. Nah 1:11
who are of t. to whom. Zeph 3:18
for out of t. shall come. Mat 2:6
need to be baptized of t. 3:14
him that would borrow of t. 5:42
no man eat fruit of t. Mark 11:14
which shall be born of t. Luke 1:35
every man that asketh of t. 6:30
soul shall be required of t. 12:20
how is it that I hear this of t.? 16:2
hast given me are of t. John 17:7
and to hear words of t. Acts 10:22
nor spake any harm of t. 28:21
we desire to hear of t. what. 22
I have no need of t. 1 Cor 12:21
let me have joy of t. Philem 20

see, in the midst

off thee
head from off t. and birds shall eat
thy flesh from off t. Gen 40:19
break his yoke from off t. Nah 1:13

on or upon thee
my wrong be upon t. Gen 16:5
this breach be upon t. 38:29
of these diseases upon t. Ex 15:26
woollen come upon t. Lev 19:19
his face shine upon t. Num 6:25

up his countenance upon t. Num 6:26
of the spirit which is upon t. 11:17
all these things are come upon t.
Deut 4:30; 30:1
the Lord may have compassion upon
t. 13:17; 30:3
so blood be upon t. 19:10
blessings come on t. 28:2
all these curses shall come upon t.
28:15, 20, 45
the Philistines be upon t., Samson.
Judg 15:9, 12, 14, 20
is it not upon t. and thy. 1 Sam 9:20
hand shall not be upon t. 24:12, 13
all Israel are upon t. 1 Ki 1:20
upon t. shall he offer the priests, and
. . . shall be burnt upon t. 13:2
bring evil upon t. and take. 21:21
shalt shut door upon t. 2 Ki 4:4
Lord, for we rest upon t. 2 Chr 14:11
wrath upon t. from the Lord. 19:2
to do: but our eyes are upon t. 20:12
but now it is come upon t. Job 4:5
I have called upon t. Ps 17:6
31:17; 86:5, 7; 88:9; Lam 3:57
I was cast upon t. Ps 22:10
wait upon t. 25:3, 5, 21; 59:9
meditate on t. 63:6
these wait upon t. 104:27; 145:15
that we may look upon t. S of S 6:13
I will turn my hand upon t. Isa 1:25
pit, and the snare are upon t. 24:17
whose mind is stayed upon t. 26:3
they shall come upon t. in. 47:9
desolation shall come upon t. 11, 13
and bind them on t. as a. 49:18
will I have mercy on t. 54:8, 10
my spirit that is upon t. 59:21
glory of Lord is risen upon t. 60:1, 2
will wait upon t. for thou. Jer 14:22
for who shall have pity upon t.? 15:5
all that prey upon t. will I. 30:16
they shall put bands upon t.
Ezek 3:25; 4:8
and I will bring the sword upon t.
5:17; 29:8
when they leaned upon t. 29:7
as I had pity upon t. Mat 18:33
let no fruit grow on t. 21:19
the Holy Ghost shall come upon t.
Luke 1:35
days shall come upon t. that. 19:43
hand of Lord is upon t. Acts 13:11
no man shall set on t. to. 18:10
beat them that believed on t. 22:19
which went before on t. 1 Tim 1:18
on t. as a thief, and thou shalt not
know . . . come upon t. Rev 3:3

over thee
and he shall rule over t. Gen 3:16
shall not reign over t. Deut 15:6
him king over t.: thou mayest not set
a stranger over t. 17:15; 28:36
Lord will again rejoice over t. 30:9
give his angels charge over t.
Ps 91:11; Luke 4:10
God rejoice over t. Isa 62:5
them to be chief over t. Jer 13:21
enemy to rejoice over t. Lam 2:17
I spread my skirt over t. Ezek 16:8
spread out my net over t. 32:3
and seven times shall pass over t.
Dan 4:25, 32
shall clap the hands over t. Nah 3:19
will rejoice over t., he will joy over t.
Zeph 3:17

through thee
through t. will we push. Ps 44:5

to or unto thee
unto t. shall be his desire. Gen 4:7
to t. will I give it. 13:15, 17; 17:8
26:3; 28:4, 13; 35:12
certainly return unto t. 18:10, 14
to t. a covering of the eyes. 20:16
nations bow down to t. 27:29
which I have spoken to t. of. 28:15
give the tenth of all unto t. 22
better I give her to t. than to. 29:19
all that Laban doth unto t. 31:12
God hath said unto t. do. 16
thine with me, and take to t. 32
torn I brought not unto t. 39
not pass over this heap to t. 52

let me come in unto t. Gen 38:16
if I bring him not to t. 42:37; 43:9
44:32
money we brought again unto t. 44:8
for they did unto t. evil. 50:17
shall be a token unto t. Ex 3:12
to t. instead of a mouth. 4:16
be unto t. for a sign. 13:9
2 Ki 19:29; Isa 38:7
they shall bring unto t. Ex 18:22
take unto t. Aaron thy brother. 28:1
unto t. principal spices. 30:23
know what to do unto t. 33:5
shall be holy unto t. for. Lev 21:8
that they bring unto t. pure. 24:2
Lord be gracious unto t. Num 6:25
word shall come to pass unto t. 11:23
Levi may be joined unto t. 18:2, 4
it is a covenant of salt unto t. 19
Balak, lo, I am come unto t. 22:38
unto t. it was shewed. Deut 4:35
gold of their gods unto t. 7:25
and it be sin unto t. 15:9, 24:15
Lord will raise up unto t. 18:15
up a prophet like unto t. 18
and take the young to t. 22:7
from his master unto t. 23:15
who is like unto t., O people. 33:29
1 Sam 26:15; Ps 35:10; 71:19
will we hearken unto t. Josh 1:17
household home unto t. 2:18
of whom I say unto t. Judg 7:4
I will restore it unto t. 17:3
perform unto t. the part. Ruth 3:13
he shall be unto t. a restorer of thy
life: for thy daughter in law,
better to t. than seven sons. 4:15
am not I better to t. than ? 1 Sam 1:8
in all that they say unto t. 8:7
so do they unto t. 8
man I speak to t. of shall. 9:17
we will come out to t. 11:3
him whom I name unto t. 16:3
but I come to t. in the name. 17:45
for there is peace to t. 20:21
peace be to t. 25:6
whom I shall name unto t. 28:8
no punishment happen to t. 10
about all Israel unto t. 2 Sam 3:12
child that is born unto t. shall. 12:14
bring back all the people unto t. 17:3
that will be worse unto t. 19:7
his head shall be thrown to t. 20:21
I will give thanks unto t. 22:50
Ps 18:49; 30:12; 75:1; 119:62
that I may do it unto t. 2 Sam 24:12
any arise like unto t. 1 Ki 3:12
that they call for unto t. 8:52
will give ten tribes unto t. 11:31
and will give Israel unto t. 38
sent to t. with heavy tidings. 14:6
for what have I done to t.? 19:20
send my servants unto t. 20:6
inheritance of my fathers unto t. 21:3
from me to speak unto t.? 22:24
it shall be so unto t. 2 Ki 2:10
this letter is come unto t. 5:6
Naaman shall cleave unto t. 27
take it up to t. 6:7
what said Elisha to t.? 8:14
he said, I have an errand to t. 9:5
came this mad fellow to t.? 11
from whence came they unto t.?
20:14; Isa 39:3
peace be unto t. and. 1 Chr 12:18
unto t. will I-give the land. 16:18
Ps 105:11
appertaineth not unto t. 2 Chr 26:18
matter belongeth unto t. Ezra 10:4
them to turn them to t. Neh 9:26
the silver is given to t. Esth 3:11
what shall I do unto t.? Job 7:20
for unto t. will I pray. Ps 5:2, 3
committeth himself unto t. 10:14
goodness extendeth not to t. 16:2
they cried unto t. and were. 22:5
unto t., O Lord, do I lift up my soul.
25:1; 86:4; 143:8
my heart said unto t., Thy face. 27:8
unto t. will I cry. 28:1, 2; 30:8
31:22; 56:9; 61:2; 86:3; 88:13
130:1; 141:1
may sing praise to t. 30:12; 56:12
59:17; 66:4; 71:22, 23

acknowledged my sin *unto t. Ps* 32:5
unto t. O Lord, belongeth. 62:12
and *unto t.* shall the vow be. 65:1
O thou that hearest prayer, *unto t.* 2
my prayer is *unto t.* in an. 69:13
gods there is none like *unto t.* 86:8
a strong Lord like *unto t.?* 89:8
unto t. O Lord, will I. 101:1; 108:3
138:1; 144:9; *Heb* 2:12
let my cry come *unto t. Ps* 102:1
what shall be given *unto t.?* 120:3
unto t. will I lift up. 123:1; 141:8
light are both alike to *t.* 139:12
made known *to t.* this day, even *to t.*
Pr 22:19
Eat and drink, saith he *to t.* 23:7
better it be said *unto t.* Come. 25:7
speak and say *unto t. Isa* 14:10
be very gracious *unto t.* 30:19
hath my master sent me *to t.?* 36:12
two things shall come *to t.* 47:9
thus shall they be *unto t.* with. 15
together and come *to t.* 49:18
two things are come *unto t.* 51:19
knew not thee shall run *unto t.* 55:5
moon give light *unto t.*: the Lord shall
be *unto t.* an everlasting. 60:19
come no more *unto t. Jer* 2:31
come *unto t.* for thou art our. 3:22
as there is none like *unto t.* 10:6
who would not fear, for *to t.* doth ? 7
for *unto t.* have I revealed my.
11:20; 20:12
let them return *unto t.* but. 15:19
a man child is born *unto t.* 20:15
unto t. in thy prosperity. 22:21
done these things *unto t.* 30:15
I speak *unto t.*: so it shall be well
unto t. 38:20
I will look well *unto t.* 40:4
we will not hearken *unto t.* 44:16
but thy life will I give *unto t.* 45:5
Israel a derision *unto t.?* 48:27
I liken *to t.*, O Jerusalem ? what shall
I equal *to t.*, that I ? *Lam* 2:13
shall pass through *unto t.* 4:21
turn thou us *unto t.* and we. 5:21
hearkened *unto t. Ezek* 3:6
Israel will not hearken *unto t.* 7
to do any of these *unto t.* 16:5
I said *unto t.* when thou wast in. 6
no reward is given *unto t.* 34
establish *unto t.* an everlasting. 60
and I will give them *unto t.* for. 61
shall be sure *unto t. Dan* 4:26
to t. it is spoken, the kingdom is. 31
righteousness belongeth *unto t.* 9:7
what shall I do *unto t.? Hos* 6:4
to t. will I cry. *Joel* 1:19
the beasts cry *unto t.* 20
thus will I do *unto t.*: and because
I will do this *unto t. Amos* 4:12
shall we do *unto t.? Jonah* 1:11
my prayer came in *unto t.* 2:7
saying, I will prophesy *unto t.* of
wine. *Mi* 2:11
unto t. shall it come. 4:8
what have I done *unto t.?* 6:3
he shall come *to t.* even from. 7:12
I even cry out *unto t. Hab* 1:2
right hand be turned *unto t.* 2:16
Lord hath sent me *unto t. Zech* 2:11
behold, thy king cometh *unto t.* 9:9
Mat 21:5
hast believed, so be it done *unto t.*
Mat 8:13
hath not revealed it *unto t.* 16:17
and I say also *unto t.* that thou. 18
I will give *unto t.* the keys of. 19
this shall not be *unto t.* 22
him be *unto t.* as an heathen. 18:17
Jesus saith, I say not *unto t.* Until. 22
this last even as *unto t.* 20:14
thou stonest them sent *unto t.* 23:37
Luke 13:34
did not minister *unto t.? Mat* 25:44
I say *unto t.* Arise. *Mark* 5:41
Luke 5:24; 7:14
What wilt thou that I do *unto t.?*
Mark 10:51; *Luke* 18:41
I am sent to speak *unto t. Luke* 1:19
myself worthy to come *unto t.* 7:7
I have somewhat to say *unto t.* 40
God hath done *unto t.* 8:39

saith, I that speak *unto t.* am he.
John 4:26
a worse thing come *unto t.* 5:14
what did he *to t.?* 9:26
said I not *unto t.?* 11:40
world, and I am come *to t.* 17:11, 13
have delivered him *unto t.* 18:30
he that delivered me *unto t.* 19:11
what is that *to t.?* follow. 21:22, 23
appeared *unto t.* sent me. *Acts* 9:17
cometh, shall speak *unto t.* 10:32
therefore I sent *to t.* 33
captain, May I speak *unto t.?* 21:37
for I have appeared *unto t.* 26:16
will I confess *to t. Rom* 15:9
committed *unto t.* keep. 2 *Tim* 1:14
but now profitable *to t. Philem* 11
but how much more *to t.?* 16
thou hast taken *to t.* thy. *Rev* 11:17

towards thee
his works have been very good *towards t.* 1 *Sam* 19:4
I would not look *towards t.* nor.
2 *Ki* 3:14
mine heart *towards t. Jer* 12:3
so will I make my fury *towards t.* to
rest. *Ezek* 16:42
when I am pacified *towards t.* 63
but *towards t.* goodness. *Rom* 11:22

under thee
the earth that is *under t. Deut* 28:23
the people fall *under t. Ps* 45:5
take thy bed from *under t.? Pr* 22:27
worm is spread *under t. Isa* 14:11
laid a wound *under t.* *Ob* 7

with thee
with t. will I establish. *Gen* 6:18
my covenant is *with t.* 17:4
now will we deal worse *with t.* than.
Gen 19:9
saying, God is *with t.* in all. 21:22
will send his angel *with t.* 24:40
I will be *with t.* 26:3
I am *with t.* 24; 28:15; 31:3; 46:4
Ex 3:12; *Deut* 31:23; *Josh* 1:5
3:7; 1 *Ki* 11:38; *Isa* 43:2
the Lord was *with t. Gen* 26:28
God shall be *with t.* *Ex* 18:19
I will meet *with t.* 25:22; 30:6, 36
my presence shall go *with t.* 33:14
Deut 31:6, 8; *Judg* 6:16
not abide *with t.* all night. *Lev* 19:13
if no man hath lien *with t.* be thou.
Num 5:19
some man hath lien *with t.* 20
What men are these *with t.?* 20
God hath been *with t. Deut* 2:7
go well *with t.* 4:40; 5:16; 6:3, 18
12:25, 28; 19:13; 22:7
go because he is well *with t.* 15:16
the Lord thy God is *with t.* 20:1
Josh 1:9; *Judg* 6:12; 2 *Sam* 7:3
against the city that maketh war
with t. *Deut* 20:20
he shall dwell *with t.* even. 23:16
I will surely go *with t. Judg* 4:9
the people that are *with t.* 7:2
this shall go *with t.* 4
peace be *with t.* 19:20
that it may be well *with t. Ruth* 3:1
for God is *with t.* 1 *Sam* 10:7
Luke 1:28
I am *with t.* according to. 1 *Sam* 14:7
the Lord be *with t.* 17:37; 20:13
1 *Chr* 22:11, 16
and no man *with t.?* 1 *Sam* 21:1
I will deliver Israel *with t.* 28:19
so long as I have been *with t.* 29:8
my hand shall be *with t.* 2 *Sam* 3:12
I was *with t.* 7:9; 1 *Chr* 17:8
Amnon been *with t.* 2 *Sam* 13:20
Why should be go *with t.?* 26
Lord thy God will be *with t.* 14:17
1 *Chr* 28:20
and truth be *with t.* 2 *Sam* 15:20
I may not tarry thus *with t.* 18:14
there will not tarry one *with t.* 19:7
thou hast *with t.* Shimei. 1 *Ki* 2:8
uprightness of heart *with t.* 3:6
perform my word *with t.* 6:12
I will not go in *with t.* 13:8, 16

what have I to do *with t.?* 1 *Ki* 17:18
2 *Ki* 3:13; 2 *Chr* 35:21; *Mark* 5:7
Luke 8:28; *John* 2:4
is it well *with t.?* 2 *Ki* 4:26
went not mine heart *with t.?* 5:26
ever thou and Judah *with t.* 14:10
2 *Chr* 25:19
nothing *with t.* to help. 2 *Chr* 14:11
we will be *with t.* 18:3; *Ezra* 10:4
let not the army of Israel go *with t.*
2 *Chr* 25:7
be at peace *with t.* *Job* 5:23
I know that this is *with t.* 10:13
me into judgement *with t.* 14:3
number of his months are *with t.* 5
of God small *with t.?* is there any
secret thing *with t.?* 15:11
perfect in knowledge *with t.* 36:4
behemoth, which I made *with t.*
40:15
nor shall evil dwell *with t. Ps* 5:4
with t. is the fountain of life. 36:9
I am a stranger *with t.* and. 39:12
I am continually *with t.* 73:23
have fellowship *with t.?* 94:20
dealt bountifully *with t.* 116:7
it shall be well *with t.* 128:2
but there is forgiveness *with t.* 130:4
awake, I am still *with t.* 139:18
my commandments *with t. Pr* 2:1
and not strangers *with t.* 5:17
it shall talk *with t.* 6:22
his heart is not *with t.* 23:7
may seek him *with t. S of S* 6:1
outcast dwell *with t.* Moab. *Isa* 16:4
I am *with t.* 41:10; 43:5; *Jer* 1:8
19; 15:20; 30:11; 46:28
Acts 18:10
they that strive *with t. Isa* 41:11, 12
that contendeth *with t.* 49:25
I would not be wroth *with t.* 54:9
I will plead *with t. Jer* 2:35
when I plead *with t.* 12:1
and he shall speak *with t.* 34:3
with t. will I break in pieces the
nations. 51:20
with t. will I break in pieces horse
and rider. 21
with t. will I break in pieces old and
young. 22
with t. will I break shepherd. 23
and thorns be *with t. Ezek* 2:6
I will there talk *with t.* 3:22
into a covenant *with t.* 16:8
I will even deal *with t.* as thou. 59
establish my covenant *with t.* 62
that I shall deal *with t.* 22:14
they occupied *with t.* in lambs. 27:21
beasts of the earth *with t.* 32:4
his bands and many people *with t.*
38:6, 9, 15; 39:4
the prophet shall fall *with t. Hos* 4:5
Is there yet any *with t.? Amos* 6:10
were at peace *with t.* *Ob* 7
all the saints *with t. Zech* 14:5
will he be pleased *with t.? Mal* 1:8
What have we to do *with t.?*
Mat 8:29; *Mark* 1:24; *Luke* 4:34
desiring to speak *with t. Mat* 12:47
then take *with t.* one or two. 18:16
Peter said, Though I should die *with
t.* 26:35; *Mark* 14:31
I am ready to go *with t. Luke* 22:33
is he that talketh *with t.* 9:37
glory which I had *with t.* 17:5
him, We also go *with t.* 21:3
Thy money perish *with t. Acts* 8:20
that it may be well *with t.*, and that
thou mayest live long. *Eph* 6:3
grace be *with t.* 1 *Tim* 6:21
bring *with t.* 2 *Tim* 4:11, 13

within thee
the stranger *within t. Deut* 28:43
say, Peace be *within t. Ps* 122:8
thy children *within t.* 147:13
if thou keep them *within t. Pr* 22:18
thoughts lodge *within t. Jer* 4:14
thy children *within t. Luke* 19:44

without thee
without t. shall no man lift up his.
Gen 41:44

theft, -s

be sold for his *t.*   *Ex* 22:3
if the *t.* be certainly found in.   4
out of the heart proceed *t.*
    Mat 15:19; *Mark* 7:22
repented they of their *t.*   *Rev* 9:21

their's

be a stranger in a land that is not *t.'s.*
    Gen 15:13
every beast of *t.'s,* be our's ? *34:23
times as much as any of *t.'s.* *43:34
priests' office shall be *t.'s.* *Ex* 29:9
for *t.'s* is thine own nakedness.
    Lev 18:10
and touch nothing of *t.'s. Num* 16:26
t.'s, every meat offering of *t.'s.* 18:9
for *t.'s* was the first lot. *Josh* 21:10
    1 Chr 6:54
let thy word be like one of *t.'s.*
    2 Chr 18:12
shall stand, mine, or *t.'s. Jer* 44:28
remain, nor any of *t.'s. Ezek* 7:11
thing in Israel shall be *t.'s.* 44:29
dwelling places that are not *t.'s.*
    Hab 1:6
for *t.'s* is the kingdom. *Mat* 5:3, 10
call on our Lord, both *t.'s. 1 Cor* 1:2
manifest, as *t 's* was.   *2 Tim* 3:9

them

male, female created he *t. Gen* 1:27
your little ones, *t.* will. *Num* 14:31
t. will the Lord bring. *Deut* 28:61
t. that honour me, I.   *1 Sam* 2:30
t. shall he sling out, as out. 25:29
t. they hold also to.   *1 Ki* 13:11
t. that burnt incense.   *2 Ki* 23:5
t. hath the Lord chosen. *1 Chr* 15:2
t. did Solomon make to. *2 Chr* 8:8
let *t.* shout for joy, let *t. Ps* 5:11
nor let *t.* wink with eye that. 35:19
let *t.* also that hate him flee. 68:1
even *t.* that contended. *Isa* 41:12
even *t.* will I bring to my. 56:7
they cast *t.* into the den. *Dan* 6:24
t. that worship the host. *Zeph* 1:5
take away *t.* that rejoice in thy. 3:11
shall gather out *t.* which. *Mal* 3:41
then let *t.* which be in Judea flee.
    24:16; *Mark* 13:14; *Luke* 21:21
neither believed they *t. Mark* 16:13
to set at liberty *t.* that.   *Luke* 4:18
and *t.* that were entering in. 11:52
cast out *t.* that sold and *t.* 19:45
and *t.* that were with *t.* 24:33
other sheep I have, *t.*   *John* 10:16
that we trouble not *t.*   *Acts* 15:19
t. take and purify thyself with *t.* 21:24
that I beat *t.* that believed. 22:19
t. he also called: *t.* he also justified:
and *t.* he also glorified. *Rom* 8:30
provoke to emulation *t.* which. 11:14
to judge *t.* also that.   *1 Cor* 5:12
but *t.* that are without God. 13
acknowledge ye *t.* that are. 16:18
even so *t.* also that.   *1 Thes* 4:14
now *t.* that are such, we. *2 Thes* 3:12
shalt save thyself and *t. 1 Tim* 4:16
t. that sin rebuke before all. 5:20
hath perfected *t.* that.   *Heb* 10:14
remember *t.* that are in bonds. 13:3
let *t.* that suffer according to will of
God.   *1 Pet* 4:19
horses and *t.* that sat on *t. Rev* 9:17
and measure *t.* that worship. 11:1
to blaspheme *t.* that dwell in. 13:6
beast was taken, and *t.* 19:20
    see teach

above them

proudly, he was *above t. Ex* 18:11
were over and *above t.*   *Num* 3:49
lifted *above t.* that rose against me.
    2 Sam 22:49
images that were *above t.* he cut.
    2 Chr 34:4

about them

cities round *about t.*   *Gen* 35:5
city was moved *about t. Ruth* 1:19
the heathen that were *about t.*
    2 Ki 17:15
make *about t.* walls. *2 Chr* 14:7
all *about t.* strengthened. *Ezra* 1:6
eyes round *about t.* four. *Ezek* 1:18
despise them round *about t.* 28:26

---

great multitude *about t. Mark* 9:14
fear came on all that dwelt round
about t.   *Luke* 1:65
of the Lord shone round *about t.* 2:9
and the cities *about t.* in.   *Jude* 7

after them

seven other kine came up *after t.*
    Gen 41:3, 19, 27
withered sprung up *after t.* 23
shall arise *after t.* seven years. 30
which thou begettest *after t.* 48:6
neither *after t.* shall be. *Ex* 10:14
he shall follow *after t.* and I. 14:4
go a whoring *after t.* *Lev* 20:6
and their seed *after t.* *Deut* 1:8
chose their seed *after t.* 4:37; 10:15
pursue *after t.* quickly. *Josh* 2:5
the men pursued *after t.* 7; 8:16
    Judg 8:12; 20:45
generation *after t.* *Judg* 2:10
reap, go thou *after t.* *Ruth* 2:9
Philistines went *after t. 1 Sam* 6:12
they followed hard *after t.* in. 14:22
upon their children that were left
after t.   *1 Ki* 9:21; *2 Chr* 8:8
went *after t.* to Jordan. *2 Ki* 7:15
not from *after t.* to wit. 10:29
go not up *after t.* *1 Chr* 14:14
and I *after t.*   *Neh* 12:33
cried *after t.* as after. *Job* 30:5
strangers, and *after t.* *Jer* 2:25
send a sword *after t.* 9:16; 49:37
    Ezek 5:2, 12; 12:14
Sheshach shall drink *after t.*
    Jer 25:26
iniquity of the fathers into the bosom
of their children *after t.* 32:18
good of their children *after t.* 39
army pursued *after t.* 39:5
and utterly destroy *after t.* 50:21
shall look *after t.* *Ezek* 29:16
did search or seek *after t.* 34:6
king shall rise *after t.* *Dan* 7:24
horses go forth *after t.* *Zech* 6:6
land was desolate *after t.* 7:14
see here; or, see there: go not *after*
t.   *Luke* 17:23; 21:8
away disciples *after t.* *Acts* 20:30

against them

against t. by night.   *Gen* 14:15
my wrath may wax hot *against t.*
    Ex 32:10; *Num* 12:9; *Deut* 2:15
    31:17; *Judg* 2:15
congregation *against t. Num* 16:19
Bashan went out *against t.* 21:33
forcing an axe *against t. Deut* 20:19
go out one way *against t.* 28:25
song shall testify *against t.* 31:21
and earth to record *against t.* 28
and the other issued out of the city
against t.   *Josh* 8:22
intend to go up *against t.* in. 22:33
strive or fight *against t.? Judg* 11:25
he moved David *against t.* to say.
    2 Sam 24:1
he testified *against t.* *2 Ki* 17:15
dwelt over *against t.* *1 Chr* 5:11
they were helped *against t.* for. 20
ye down *against t.* *2 Chr* 20:16, 17
prophets testified *against t.* 24:19
    Neh 9:26, 29, 30, 34
stood up *against t.* that came. 28:12
hired counsellors *against t. Ezra* 4:5
but his wrath is *against t.* 8:22
we set a watch *against t.* *Neh* 4:9
set a great assembly *against t.* 5:7
dealt proudly *against t.* 9:10
brethren were over *against t.* 12:9
hired Balaam *against t.* 13:2
I testified *against t.* 15, 21
those that rise up *against t. Ps* 17:7
face of the Lord is *against t.* that do
evil.   34:16; *1 Pet* 3:12
doth witness *against t.* *Isa* 3:9
forth his hand *against t.* 5:25
stir up the Medes *against t.* 13:17
I will rise up *against t.* 14:22
I will utter my judgements *against*
t.   *Jer* 1:16
I will give sentence *against t.* 4:12
I am *against t.* 23:32

---

prophesy *against t.*   *Jer* 25:30
    Ezek 6:2; 13:17; 25:2
evil he pronounced *against t.*
    Jer 26:19; 35:17; 36:31
it prevaileth *against t.*   *Lam* 1:13
set my face *against t.* *Ezek* 15:7
my anger *against t.* in Egypt. 20:8
out of thy hatred *against t.* 35:11
bring thee *against t.* 38:17
horn prevailed *against t.* *Dan* 7:21
is kindled *against t.* *Hos* 8:5
shall be gathered *against t.* 10:10
for a testimony *against t. Mat* 10:18
    Mark 6:11; 13:9; *Luke* 9:5
spoken that parable *against t.*
    Mark 12:12; *Luke* 20:19
off the dust of their feet *against t.*
    Acts 13:51
rose up together *against t.* 16:22
spirit was prevailed *against t.* 19:16
I gave my voice *against t.* 26:10
being mad *against t.* 11
judgement of God is *against t.* that.
    Rom 2:2
and be not bitter *against t. Col* 3:19
accusation *against t.* *2 Pet* 2:11
shall make war *against t. Rev* 11:7
    see fight, over

among or amongst them

men of activity among *t. Gen* 47:6
of Israel from among *t.* *Ex* 7:5
which I have done *amongst t.* 10:2
that I may dwell among *t.* 25:8
    29:46; *Ps* 68:18
be no plague among *t.* *Ex* 30:12
defile my tabernacle that is among *t.*
    Lev 15:31
not numbered among *t.* *Num* 1:47
fire of Lord burnt among *t.* 11:1, 3
the mixt multitude among *t.* 4
the Lord is among *t.* 16:3; *Ps* 68:17
Aaron shall have no part among *t.*
    Num 18:20; *Josh* 14:3
shout of a king is among *t.*
    Num 23:21
the hornet among *t.* *Deut* 7:20
that was born among *t.* *Josh* 8:33
were conversant among *t.* 35
that they dwelt among *t.* 9:16
that he may dwell among *t.* 20:4
that which I did *amongst t.* 24:5
the Canaanites dwelt among *t.*
    Judg 1:30
strange gods from among *t.* 10:16
he wrought among *t.* *1 Sam* 6:6
    Neh 9:17
chiefest place among *t.* *1 Sam* 9:22
and he prophesied among *t.* 10:10
thy servant among *t.* *2 Sam* 19:28
the Lord sent lions among *t.*
    2 Ki 17:25
Levi and Benjamin not counted
among *t.*   *1 Chr* 21:6
found mighty men among *t.* 26:31
found among *t.* abundance of spoil.
    2 Chr 20:25
that were naked among *t.* 28:15
were among *t.* 200 singing men.
    Ezra 2:65
midst among *t.* and slay. *Neh* 4:11
establish the Purim among *t.*
    Esth 9:21
and Satan came also among *t.*
    Job 1:6; 2:1
no stranger passed among *t.* 15:19
garments among *t.,* and cast lots upon.
    Ps 22:18; *Mat* 27:35; *John* 19:24
seize upon them; for wickedness is
among *t.*   *Ps* 55:15
and I lie even among *t.* that. 57:4
among *t.* were damsels. 68:25
sorts of flies among *t.* 78:45
sending evil angels among *t.* 49
and Samuel among *t.* that call. 99:6
shewed his signs among *t.* 105:27
out Israel from among *t.* 136:11
barren among *t. S of S* 4:2; 6:6
weary or stumble among *t. Isa* 5:27
many among *t.* shall stumble. 51
there was no man among *t.* 41:28
who among *t.* can declare this? 43:9
which among *t.* hath declared. 48:14
I will set a sign among *t.* 66:19

they shall fall among t. that fall.
    Jer 6:15; 8:12
O congregation, what is among t. 18
house of Judah from among t. 12:14
and pestilence among t.   24:10
3word that I will send among t. 25:16
but wounded men among t.   37:10
ten men found among t. that.   41:8
as a menstruous woman among t.
    Lam 1:17
there hath been a prophet among t.
    Ezek 2:5; 33:33
and remained there among t.   3:15
shalt not go out among t.   25
one man among t. had a writer's. 9:2
Israel that are among t.   12:10
and the prince that is among t.   12
I am prophet among t.   22:26
I sought a man among t.   30
a prophet hath been among t. 33:33
David a prince among t.   34:24
myself known among t.   35:11
among t. was found none. Dan 1:19
came up among t. another.   7:8
shall scatter among t. the prey. 11:24
there is none among t.   Hos 7:7
that is feeble among t.   Zech 12:8
tumult shall be among t.   14:13
I say, Among t. that are born of.
    Mat 11:11
two fishes divided he among t.
    Mark 6:41
a reasoning among t.   Luke 9:46
was also a strife among t.   22:24
Peter sat down among t. in.   55
was a division among t.   John 9:16
if I had not done among t.   15:24
among t. that lacked.   Acts 4:34
Paul departed from among t. 17:33
the word of God among t.   18:11
inheritance among t. that are. 20:32
    26:18
were grafted in among t. Rom 11:17
we speak wisdom among t. that.
    1 Cor 2:6
come out from among t. 2 Cor 6:17
man dwelling amongst t. 2 Pet 2:8
preeminence among t.   3 John 9
that are ungodly among t.   Jude 15
on the throne shall dwell among t.
    Rev 7:15

at them

we have shot at t.: Heshbon is
perished.   Num 21:30
not be affrighted at t.   Deut 7:21
his enemies, he puffeth at t. Ps 10:5
O Lord, shalt laugh at t.   59:8
but God shall shoot at t.   64:7
heathen are dismayed at t. Jer 10:2

before them

and set it before t.   Gen 18:8
he passed over before t.   33:3
before t. there were no such locusts.
    Ex 10:14
the Lord went before t. by day.
    13:21; Num 14:14
thou shalt set before t.   Ex 21:1
ark of the Lord went before t.
    Num 10:33
to go out and in before t.   27:17
    1 Sam 18:16
destroyed them from before t.
    Deut 2:12, 21, 22; 1 Chr 5:25
    Neh 9:24
shalt flee seven ways before t.
    Deut 28:25
armed men went before t. Josh 6:13
land was subdued before t.   18:1
man of their enemies before t. 21:44
Ehud before t.   Judg 3:27
take before t. waters.   7:24
tabret, a pipe and harp, before t.
    1 Sam 10:5
and Shobach went before t.
    2 Sam 10:16; 1 Chr 19:16
Amasa went before t.   2 Sam 20:8
give them compassion before t.
    1 Ki 8:50; 2 Chr 30:9
prophets prophesied before t.
    1 Ki 22:10; 2 Chr 18:19
Moabites fled before t.   2 Ki 3:24
Gehazi passed on before t.   4:31
so he set it before t.   44

bread and water before t. 2 Ki 6:22
Lord carried away before t.   17:11
priest sounded trumpets before t.
    2 Chr 7:6
Ezra the scribe before t. Neh 12:36
will pay my vows before t. Ps 22:25
not set God before t.   54:3; 86:14
the heathen also before t.   78:55
he sent a man before t.   105:17
all that have been before t. Eccl 4:16
hatred by all that is before t.   9:1
now go write it before t.   Isa 30:8
darkness light before t.   42:16
dividing the water before t.   63:12
lest I confound thee before t.
    Jer 1:17
my law which I set before t.   9:13
charged Baruch before t.   32:13
more be a nation before t.   33:24
to be dismayed before t.   49:37
before t. seventy men.   Ezek 8:11
oil and incense before t.   16:18, 19
I will set judgement before t. 23:24
brandish my sword before t.   32:10
stand before t. to minister.   44:11
a fire devoureth before t. . . . garden
of Eden before t.   Joel 2:3
the earth shall quake before t.   10
the Amorite before t.   Amos 2:9
breaker is come up before t. and
    their king . . . before t.   Mi 2:13
angel of Lord before t.   Zech 12:8
the star went before t.   Mat 2:9
she danced before t.   14:6
and was transfigured before t. 17:2
    Mark 9:2
but he denied before t.   Mat 26:70
gave to his disciples to set before t.
    Mark 6:41; 8:6, 7
Jesus went before t. and they. 10:32
Judas went before t.   Luke 22:47
he did eat before t.   24:43
shepherd goeth before t. John 10:4
so many miracles before t.   12:37
he set meat before t.   Acts 16:34
set Paul before t.   22:30
I said to Peter before t. all. Gal 2:14

behind them

and stood behind t.   Ex 14:19
of Ai looked behind t.   Josh 8:20
the Benjamites looked behind t.
    Judg 20:40
a compass behind t.   2 Sam 5:23
to come about behind t. 2 Chr 13:13
behind t. a flame burneth, behind t.
    Joel 2:3

beside them

the asses were feeding beside t.
    Job 1:14
wheels turned not from beside t.
    Ezek 10:16, 19; 11:22
I have gained beside t. five talents.
    Mat 25:20, 22

between them

oath of the Lord shall be between t.
    Ex 22:11
and bells of gold between t.   28:33
valley between t. and Ai. Josh 8:11
a valley between t. and the Philis-
    tines.   1 Sam 17:3
great space being between t. 26:13
Lord's oath between t. 2 Sam 21:7
they divided the land between t.
    1 Ki 18:6
can come between t.   Job 41:16
shall be between t. both. Zech 6:13
was so sharp between t. Acts 15:39

by them

neither seek after wizards, to be
defiled by t.   Lev 19:31
nor cause to swear by t. Josh 23:7
to prove Israel by t.   Judg 3:1, 4
by t. ye shall send to. 2 Sam 15:36
was perfected by t.   2 Chr 24:13
for by t. judgeth he the. Job 36:31
by t. is thy servant.   Ps 19:11
by t. beyond the river.   Isa 7:20
and have sworn by t. that. Jer 5:7
the wheels went by t.   Ezek 1:19
I be enquired of at all by t.?   14:3
by t. their portion is fat.   Hab 1:16

that it was said by t. of old.
    Mat 5:21, 27, 33
would have passed by t. Mark 6:48
two men stood by t. in white.
    Luke 24:4; Acts 1:10
miracle has been done by t. Acts 4:16
God hath wrought by t.   15:12
things shall live by t.   Rom 10:5
provoke you to jealousy by t.   19
by t. which are of the house of.
    1 Cor 1:11
thou by t. mightest war. 1 Tim 1:18
confirmed to us by t.   Heb 2:3
reported to you by t.   1 Pet 1:12

concerning them

so con. t. Moses.   Num 32:28
Samson said con. t., Now I. Judg 15:3
commandment con. t.   Neh 11:23
to be ignorant con. t.   1 Thes 4:13
have I written con. t.   1 John 2:26

for them

food for thee and for t.   Gen 6:21
is large enough for t.   34:21
and they set on bread for t.   43:32
the Lord fighteth for t.   Ex 14:25
make an atonement for t. Lev 4:20
    9:7; 10:17; Num 8:21; 16:46
there is one law for t. the. Lev 7:7
a resting place for t.   Num 10:33
for t., fishes gathered for t.   11:22
fail with longing for t. Deut 28:32
hand went a fiery law for t.   33:2
Joshua cast lots for t.   Josh 18:10
Judah was too much for t.   19:9
Dan went out too little for t.   47
do for wives for t.?   Judg 21:16
inheritance for t. escaped.   17
would ye tarry for t. till? Ruth 1:13
prayed for t. saying.   2 Chr 30:18
of the Lord for me and for t. 34:21
God keepeth mercy for t. Neh 1:5
we take up corn for t. that we. 5:2
broughtest forth water for t.   9:15
banquet I shall prepare for t.
    Esth 5:8
of Sheba waited for t.   Job 6:19
the Almighty do for t.?   22:17
wilderness yieldeth food for t. 24:5
laid up for t. that fear thee, for t.
    that trust in thee.   Ps 31:19
thou hast founded for t.   104:8
and he remembered for t. 106:45
hath done great things for t. 126:2
Assyrian founded it for t. Isa 23:13
for her merchandise shall be for t. 18
he hath cast the lot for t., and. 34:17
places shall be glad for t.   35:1
in the ways hast thou sat for t. as.
    Jer 3:2
lift up cry nor prayer for t.   7:16
nor shall men lament for t.   16:6
neither men tear themselves for t. 7
thee to speak good for t.   18:20
shalt make for t. yokes.   28:13
there be wailing for t.   Ezek 7:11
but as for t. whose heart.   11:21
to pass through the fire for t.   16:21
a land I had espied for t.   20:6
flock may not be meat for t.   34:10
I will raise up for t. a plant.   29
enquired of to do for t.   36:37
make reconciliation for t.   45:15
his inheritance shall be his sons' for t.
    46:17
for t. even for the priests.   48:10
no place was found for t. Dan 2:35
    Rev 20:11
make a covenant for t.   Hos 2:18
I will hiss for t. and.   Zech 10:8
place shall not be found for t.   10
pray for t. which despitefully use.
    Mat 5:44; Luke 6:28
nor lawful for t. that.   Mat 12:4
it shall be done for t. of my.   18:19
hard for t. that trust.   Mark 10:24
there was no room for t.   Luke 2:7
is not sufficient for t.   John 6:7
I pray for t.: . . . but for them. 17:9, 20
and John prayed for t.   Acts 8:15
Cornelius waited for t. and.   10:24
now while Paul waited for t.   17:16
God hath prepared for t. 1 Cor 2:9
it is good for t. if they abide.   7:8

but prophesying serveth *for t.*
       1 Cor 14:22
him which died *for t.*   *2 Cor* 5:15
what conflict I have *for t.*   *Col* 2:1
hath a great zeal *for t.* that.   4:13
to minister *for t.* who shall ? *Heb* 1:14
make intercession *for t.*   7:25
he hath prepared *for t.* a city.   11:16
it had been better *for t.*   *2 Pet* 2:21
give life *for t.* that sin. *1 John* 5:16

from **them**
will be restrained *from t. Gen* 11:6
he took *from t.* Simeon and.   42:24
not taken one ass *from t. Num* 16:15
I have given you *from t.*   18:26
from t. that have many ye shall give
   many, but *from t.* that have. 35:8
and hide thyself *from t. Deut* 22:1, 4
hide my face *from t.*   31:17
    Ezek 7:22; *Mi* 3:4
their calves home *from t. 1 Sam* 6:7
them, turn away *from t. 1 Chr* 14:14
but they turned *from t. 2 Chr* 20:10
deliver me *from t.* that.   *Ps* 31:15
defend me *from t.* that rise up. 59:1
will he withhold *from t.*   84:11
withhold not good *from t.*   *Pr* 3:27
his soul shall be far *from t.*   22:5
desired I kept not *from t. Eccl* 2:10
little that I passed *from t. S of S* 3:4
given shall pass *from t. Jer* 8:13
leave my people and go *from t.* 9:2
turn away thy wrath *from t.*   18:20
I will take *from t.* the voice.   25:10
I will not turn away *from t.*   32:40
I have set it far *from t. Ezek* 7:20
mind was alienated *from t.*   23:17
the day when I take *from t.*   24:25
hid I my face *from t.*   39:23, 24
hide my face any more *from t.*   29
withdrawn himself *from t. Hos* 5:6
them, so they went *from t.*   11:2
with the garment *from t.*   *Mi* 2:8
the bridegroom shall be taken *from t.*
Mat 9:15; *Mark* 2:20; *Luke* 5:35
and fled *from t.* naked. *Mark* 14:52
understood not, it was hid *from t.*
    Luke 9:45; 18:34
parted *from t.* and carried.   24:51
did hide himself *from t. John* 12:36
but thrust him *from t.*   *Acts* 7:39
delivered *from t.* that.   *Rom* 15:31
sorrow *from t.* of whom. *2 Cor* 2:3
I may cut off occasion *from t.* 11:12
is not counted *from t.*   *Heb* 7:6
clean escaped *from t.*   *2 Pet* 2:18
death shall flee *from t.*   *Rev* 9:6

see **depart, -ed**

in **them**
heaven and earth, the sea, and all
   that *in t.* is. *Ex* 20:11; *Acts* 4:24
and be consecrated *in t.*   *Ex* 29:29
I will be sanctified *in t.*   *Lev* 10:3
he shall live *in t.*   18:5; *Neh* 9:29
  Ezek 20:11, 13, 21; *Gal* 3:12
was sanctified *in t.*   *Num* 20:13
such an heart *in t.*   *Deut* 5:29
any understanding *in t.*   32:28
nor was there spirit *in t. Josh* 5:1
built not, and ye dwell *in t.*   24:13
wash *in t.* and be clean ? *2 Ki* 5:12
how much less *in t.* that ? *Job* 4:19
excellency *in t.* go away ?   21
in t. hath he set a tabernacle. *Ps* 19:4
their soul fainteth *in t.*   107:5
so is every one that trusteth *in t.*
    115:8; 135:18
pleasure *in t.* that fear.   147:11
froward or perverse *in t.*   *Pr* 8:8
there is no good *in t.*   *Eccl* 3:12
their heart is fully set *in t.*   8:11
I have no pleasure *in t.*   12:1
whose substance is *in t. Isa* 6:13
there is no light *in t.*   8:20
shalt not prosper *in t. Jer* 2:37
the word is not *in t.*   5:13
what wisdom is *in t.?*   8:9
cannot do evil nor is it *in t.*   10:5
there is no breath *in t.*   14; 51:17
houses, and dwell *in t.*   29:5, 28
have not walked *in t. Ezek* 5:6
accomplished my fury *in t.*   13
of the living creature was *in t.* 10:17

sin, *in t.* shall he die. *Ezek* 18:24, 26
be sanctified *in t.* in sight.   28:25
pine away *in t.*   33:10
was no breath *in t.*   37:8
concubines drank *in t. Dan* 5:3, 23
the just shall walk *in t. Hos* 14:9
ye shall not walk *in t. Amos* 5:11
they shall kindle *in t.* and.   *Ob* 18
evil, he delighteth *in t. Mal* 2:17
in t. is fulfilled the.   *Mat* 13:14
in t. therefore come and. *Luke* 13:14
in t. ye think ye have. *John* 5:39
and I am glorified *in t.*   17:10
I *in t.*, and thou in me.   23
may be *in t.* and I *in t.*   26
God, is manifest *in t.*   *Rom* 1:19
but have pleasure *in t.* that do.   32
in t. that are saved, *in t. 2 Cor* 2:15
will dwell *in t.* and walk *in t.*   6:16
that we should walk *in t. Eph* 2:10
the ignorance that is *in t.*   4:18
walked, when ye lived *in t. Col* 3:7
all deceivableness *in t. 2 Thes* 2:10
continue *in t.*: for in.   *1 Tim* 4:16
with faith *in t.* that.   *Heb* 4:2
Christ which was *in t.*   *1 Pet* 1:11
speaking *in t.* of these. *2 Pet* 3:16
and all that are *in t.*   *Rev* 5:13
and ye that dwell *in t.*   12:12
for *in t.* is filled up the.   15:1
dead which were *in t.*   20:13
in t. the names of the.   21:14

into **them**
the breath came *into t. Ezek* 37:10
into the swine, that we may enter
   into t. Mark 5:12; *Luke* 8:32
from God entered *into t. Rev* 11:11

of **them**
the eyes of *t.* both were. *Gen* 3:7
cry of *t.* is waxen great.   19:13
generation *of t.* that hate me.
    Ex 20:5; *Deut* 5:9
to thousands *of t.* that love me.
    Ex 20:6; *Deut* 20:10
of t. that do any work. *Ex* 35:35
do against any *of t.*   *Lev* 4:2
of t. ye shall not eat.   11:4
of t. eat.   22; *Deut* 20:19
an offering by fire *of t. Lev* 22:22
of t. buy bondmen and.   25:44, 45
land also shall be left *of t.*   26:43
were numbered *of t.*   *Num* 1:21
    23, 25; 2:4, 13; 3:22, 34
took money *of t.* that.   3:49
take it *of t.*   7:5
were *of t.* that were written. 11:26
nor shall any *of t.* that.   14:23
fled at the cry *of t.*   16:34
not a man *of t.*   26:64
which ye let remain *of t.*   33:55
neither be afraid *of t. Deut* 1:29
 7:18; 20:1, 3; *Josh* 11:6; *Neh* 4:14
buy meat *of t.*, buy water *of t.*
    Deut 2:6
loins *of t.* that rise, and *of t.* 33:11
there shall not a man *of t. Josh* 10:8
and *of t.* shall I be had. *2 Sam* 6:22
nor left he any *of t.*   *2 Ki* 10:14
he was intreated *of t. 1 Chr* 5:20
of t. were expressed by. *Ezra* 8:20
would not buy it *of t.*   *Neh* 10:31
he perceiveth it not *of t. Job* 14:21
in keeping *of t.* there is. *Ps* 19:11
arrows against the face *of t.* 21:12
this is the generation *of t.*   24:6
delivered him out *of t.* all.   34:19
none *of t.* that trust in him shall. 22
if I would speak *of t.* they are. 40:5
and *of t.* that are afar off.   65:5
heart are the ways of *t.*   84:5
all *of t.* shall wax old like. 102:26
tossed to and fro *of t.* that. *Pr* 21:6
God shall come forth *of t. Eccl* 7:18
they that are led *of t. Isa* 9:16
portion *of t.* that spoil us.   17:14
he shall be intreated *of t.*   19:22
Hezekiah was glad *of t.* and.   39:2
that when I asked *of t.*   41:28
spring forth I tell you *of t.*   42:9
spoiled, they are all *of t.* snared. 22
image, are all *of t.* vanity.   44:9
of t. that asked not for me, I am
   found *of t.*   65:1; *Rom* 10:20

those that escape *of t.*   *Isa* 66:19
I will take *of t.* for priests.   21
because *of t.* that dwell in. *Jer* 8:19
be not afraid *of t.*   10:5; *Ezek* 2:6
    Luke 12:4
of t. unto me as Sodom. *Jer* 23:14
shall serve themselves *of t.*   25:14
and *of t.* shall be taken up.   29:22
and out *of t.* shall proceed.   30:19
should serve himself *of t.*   34:9, 10
and none *of t.* shall remain.   42:17
    Ezek 7:11
all *of t.* mourning every. *Ezek* 7:16
all *of t.* in the land shall.   20:40
all *of t.* desirable young men.   23:6
    12, 23
in dyed attire, all *of t.* princes.   15
of t. clothed with all sorts.   38:4
and gates all *of t.* dwelling.   11
they say *of t.* Let the men. *Hos* 13:2
all *of t.*; he that fleeth *of t. Amos* 9:1
off their skin from *off t. Mi* 3:2, 3
land desolate because *of t.*   7:13
a goodly price that I was prized at
   of *t.*   *Zech* 11:13
whether *of t.* twain did. *Mat* 21:31
perceived that he spake *of t.*   45
whose wife shall she be *of t.?*
  Mark 12:23; *Luke* 20:33
of t. he chose twelve. *Luke* 6:13
tell me, which *of t.* will love ?   7:42
which *of t.* should be greatest.
    9:46; 22:24
which *of t.* it was that.   22:23
and said, Thou art also *of t.*   58
then enquired he *of t. John* 4:52
remember that I told you *of t.* 16:4
of t. which thou gavest me.   18:9
to take out *of t.* a people. *Acts* 15:14
there lie in wait *of t.* more.   23:21
if the fall *of t.* be the riches of world,
   and diminishing *of t. Rom* 11:12
if the casting away *of t.* be the.   15
out *of t.* all the Lord.   *2 Tim* 3:11
are not *of t.* who draw back, but *of t.*
    Heb 10:39
is sown in peace *of t.*   *Jas* 3:18
of t. which keep sayings. *Rev* 22:9

see **both, one, some**

on or upon **them**
images and sat *upon t.*   *Gen* 31:34
my name be named *on t.*   48:16
shall be satisfied *upon t.*   *Ex* 15:9
Lord break forth *upon t.*   19:22, 24
so great a sin *upon t.*   32:21
will visit their sin *upon t.*   34
their blood shall be *upon t.*
    Lev 20:11, 12, 13, 16, 27
upon t. that are left will I.   26:36
of the spirit *upon t. Num* 11:17, 29
the earth closed *upon t.* and. 16:33
have no pity *upon t.*   *Deut* 7:16
silver or gold that is *on t.*   25
on t. was written according.   9:10
not lift up any iron tool *upon t.* 27:5
I will heap mischiefs *upon t.* 32:23
shall come *upon t.* make haste. 35
down great stones *upon t. Josh* 10:11
upon t. came the curse. *Judg* 9:57
blood gushed out *upon t. 1 Ki* 18:28
if able to set riders *upon t.*
    2 Ki 18:23; *Isa* 36:8
burnt men's bones *upon t. 2 Ki* 23:20
charge was *upon t.*   *1 Chr* 9:27
laid their hands *on t. 2 Chr* 29:23
    Acts 6:6; 8:17; 13:3
Lord came not *upon t. 2 Chr* 32:26
Lord brought *upon t.* king.   33:11
he brought *upon t.* the king. 36:17
for fear was *upon t.*   *Ezra* 3:3
of the Jews fell *upon t. Esth* 8:17
fear of Mordecai fell *upon t.*   9:3
Jews took *upon t.* to keep the. 27
nor is the rod of God *upon t.*
    Job 21:9
eye of the Lord is *upon t. Ps* 33:18
fear took hold *upon t.* there. 48:6
set not your heart *upon t.*   62:10
thine indignation *upon t.*   69:24
down manna *upon t.* to eat. 78:24
he rained flesh also *upon t.* as. 27
he cast *upon t.* the fierceness.   49
he shall bring *upon t.* their. 94:23

to everlasting upon t.   Ps 103:17
plague brake in upon t.   106:29
I see my desire upon t.   118:7
upon t. hath the light.   Isa 9:2
thy chastening was upon t.   26:16
will not have mercy on t.   27:11
he that hath mercy on t. shall.   49:10
evil shall come upon t.   Jer 2:3
I will bring upon t.   11:8, 11; 23:12
  36:31; 49:37
have compassion on t.   12:15
I will set mine eyes upon t.   24:6
  32:42
I will have mercy upon t.   33:26
calamity was come upon t.   46:21
she doted upon t.   Ezek 23:16
flesh came upon t.   37:8
no wool shall come upon t.   44:17
of fire had passed on t.   Dan 3:27
pour out my wrath upon t.   Hos 5:10
go, I will spread my net upon t.   7:12
mine eyes upon t. for evil.   Amos 9:4
lookest thou upon t. that.   Hab 1:13
I will bring them again: for I have
  mercy upon t.   Zech 10:6
who will not come up upon t.   14:17
should put his hands upon t.
  Mat 19:13; Mark 10:16
and his mercy is on t.   Luke 1:50
angel of the Lord came upon t.   2:9
this, he breathed on t.   John 20:22
Sadducees came upon t.   Acts 4:1
they laid hands on t.   3
great grace was upon t.   33
fear came on all t. that heard.   5:5
the Holy Ghost fell on t. as on us.
  11:15; 19:6
took upon t. to call over.   19:13
and the man leapt on t. and.   16
men which have a vow on t.   21:23
on t. which fell, severity.   Rom 11:22
peace be on t. and mercy   Gal 6:16
wrath is come upon t.   1 Thes 2:16
destruction cometh upon t.   5:3
taking vengeance on t.   2 Thes 1:8
and on t. that are out of.   Heb 5:2
avenge our blood on t.   Rev 6:10
nor shall the sun light on t.   7:16
and great fear fell upon t.   11:11
and upon t. which worshipped.   16:2

over them

set over t. taskmasters.   Ex 1:11
taskmasters had set over t.   5:14
place such over t. to be rulers.   18:21
were over t. that were numbered.
  Num 7:2
thy cloud standeth over t.   14:14
to anoint a king over t.   Judg 9:8
Jephthah captain over t.   11:11
rejected me that I should not reign
  over t.   1 Sam 8:7
the manner of the king that shall
  reign over t.   9
standing as appointed over t.   19:20
became a captain over t.   22:2
anointed me king over t.   2 Sam 2:7
was the ruler over t.   1 Chr 9:20
over t. that did the work was. 27:26
he that made thee king over t.
  2 Chr 2:11; 9:8
had the dominion over t.   Neh 9:28
the enemies of the Jews hoped to
  have power over t.   Esth 9:1
have dominion over t.   Ps 49:14
hated them ruled over t.   106:41
bringeth the wheel over t.   Pr 20:26
babes shall rule over t.   Isa 3:4
women rule over t.   12
a fierce king shall rule over t.   19:4
they that rule over t. make.   52:5
I will appoint over t.   Jer 15:3
I will set shepherds over t.   23:4
watched over t., to pluck up, so will I
  watch over t. to build.   31:28
yea, I will rejoice over t. to.   32:41
I will watch over t. for evil.   44:27
there appeared over t. as it were a
  sapphire stone.   Ezek 10:1
of Israel was over t.   19; 11:22
set up one shepherd over t.   34:23
servant shall be king over t.   37:24
thee ruler over t. all.   Dan 2:38
heathen should rule over t.   Joel 2:17
43

shall be dark over t.   Mi 3:6
the Lord shall reign over t. in.   4:7
that have no ruler over t.   Hab 1:14
and the Lord shall be seen over t.
  Zech 9:14
exercise dominion over t.   Mat 20:25
  Mark 10:42; Luke 22:25
men that walk over t.   Luke 11:44
I should reign over t.   19:27
to call over t. that had.   Acts 19:13
even over t. that had not sinned.
  Rom 5:14
triumphing over t. in it.   Col 2:15
they had a king over t.   Rev 9:11
earth shall rejoice over t.   11:10

through them

that through t. I may prove Israel.
  Judg 2:22
none can pass through t.   Jer 9:10

to or unto them

will send thee unto t.   Gen 37:13
unto t. and spake roughly unto t.
  42:7
provision, thus did Joseph unto t. 25
spake kindly unto t.   50:21
and God had respect unto t.
  Ex 2:25; 1 Ki 13:23
what shall I say unto t.?   Ex 3:13
darkness to t.   14:20
the waters were a wall unto t.   22
not bow down thyself to t. nor serve.
  20:5; Josh 23:7; 2 Ki 17:35
shall be a statute for ever to t.
  Ex 30:21; Lev 17:7
I have given it unto t.   Lev 6:17
but thus do unto t.   Num 4:19
all that appertain unto t.   16:30
as I thought to do unto t.   33:56
and to t. ye shall add forty.   35:6
Lord sware to give unto t.   Deut 1:8
  31:23
hath God so nigh unto t.?   4:7
this we will do unto t.   Josh 9:20
so did he unto t.   26
bowed themselves unto t.   Judg 2:17
mayest do to t. as thou shalt.   9:33
unto me, so have I done unto t. 15:11
nothing lacking to t.   1 Sam 30:19
sent spoil to t.   27, 28, 29, 30, 31
but went not in unto t.   2 Sam 20:3
speak good words to t.   1 Ki 12:7
messenger came to t.   2 Ki 9:18, 20
let the priests take it to t.   12:5
thereof pertained to t.   1 Chr 9:27
spake comfortably to t.   2 Chr 32:6
custom was paid unto t.   Ezra 4:20
separated themselves unto t.   6:21
restore to t. this day their.   Neh 5:11
month was turned unto t.   Esth 9:22
layeth not folly to t.   Job 24:12
morning is to t. even as the.   17
give them, render to t.   Ps 28:4
for there is no want to t. that.   34:9
thou hadst a favour unto t.   44:3
do unto t. as to the Midianites.   83:9
them are like unto t.   115:8; 135:18
do good to t. that are upright.   125:4
a buckler to t. that walk.   Pr 2:7
a tree of life to t. that lay.   3:18
they are right to t. that find.   8:9
so is the sluggard to t. that.   10:26
mercy and truth be to t. that.   14:22
so is a faithful messenger to t. 25:13
a shield unto t. that put their.   30:5
wisdom giveth life to t.   Eccl 7:12
to t. that have familiar.   Isa 19:3
the word was unto t. precept. 28:13
to t. that have no might he.   40:29
hath given spirit to t. that walk. 42:5
these things will I do unto t.   16
to t. that are in darkness.   49:9
  Mat 4:16; Luke 1:79
to t. will I give in mine.   Isa 56:5
to t. hast thou poured a.   57:6
to t. that turn from transgression in
  Jacob.   59:20
everlasting joy shall be unto t.   61:7
thus shall it be done unto t.   Jer 5:13
word of the Lord is unto t.   6:10
but return not thou unto t.   15:19
evil I thought to do unto t.   18:8
though I was husband unto t.   31:32
and do unto t. as thou.   Lam 1:22

the Lord is good unto t. that.
  Lam 3:25
of heart, thy curse unto t.   65
I do send thee unto t.   Ezek 2:4
had I sent thee unto t. they.   3:6
and thou shalt not be to t. a.   26
yet will I be to t. as a little.   11:16
so shall it be done unto t.   12:11
I made myself known unto t.   20:9
lo, thou art unto t. as a very.   33:32
shall be to t. a renown.   39:13
because they ministered unto t. before idols.   44:12
oblation shall be unto t.   48:12
shall be for food unto t.   18
the dream be to t. that.   Dan 4:19
might give account unto t.   6:2
and keeping mercy to t. that.   9:4
but many shall cleave to t.   11:34
staff declareth unto t.   Hos 4:12
destruction unto t. because.   7:13
I was to t. as they that take off. 11:4
said, he would do unto t.   Jonah 3:10
say they to t. that prophesy, they
  shall not prophesy to t.   Mi 2:6
be ye not like unto t.   Mat 6:8
do ye so to t.   7:12
he spake unto t. of John the.   17:13
servants, they did unto t.   21:36
but go ye rather to t. that sell.   25:9
but to t. that are without in parables.
  Mark 4:11
shall be given to t. for whom.   10:40
and was subject unto t.   Luke 2:51
do ye also to t. likewise.   6:31
if ye do good to t. that do good.   33
if ye lend to t. of whom ye hope. 34
give the Holy Spirit to t. that.   11:13
that he may testify unto t.   16:28
of the vineyard do unto t.?   20:15
Jesus turning unto t. said.   23:28
their words seemed unto t. as. 24:11
he expounded unto t. in all the.   27
to t. gave he power to become the
  sons of God, even to t.   John 1:12
we may give an answer to t. that. 22
not commit himself unto t.   2:24
spake to t. of the Father.   8:27
they are remitted unto t.   20:23
who was guide to t. that.   Acts 1:16
unto t. cloven tongues, as of.   2:3
added unto t. about 3000 souls.   41
durst no man join himself to t. 5:13
whom God hath given to t. that.   32
not done sacrifice unto t.   14:18
preach the gospel unto t.   16:10
my necessities, and to t. that. 20:34
no man may deliver me unto t. 25:11
God hath shewed it unto t.   Rom 1:19
to t. who by patient continuance. 2:7
for good to t. that love God.   8:28
made manifest unto t. that.   10:20
unto t. that are sanctified.   1 Cor 1:2
unto t. that are called, both.   24
my answer to t. that do examine. 9:3
not permitted unto t. to speak. 14:34
if gospel hid, it is hid to t.   2 Cor 4:3
to t. which were apostles.   Gal 1:17
unto t. who are of the household of
  faith.   6:10
preached peace to t. that.   Eph 2:17
is to t. an evident token.   Phil 1:28
tribulation to t. that trouble you.
  2 Thes 1:6
meditate, give thyself wholly to t.
  1 Tim 4:15
but unto all t. that love.   2 Tim 4:8
nothing wanting to t.   Tit 3:13
not enter, but to t. that believed not.
  Heb 3:18
preached as well as unto t.   4:2
I will be to t. a God.   8:10
yieldeth unto t. that are.   12:11
word should not be spoken to t.   19
Lord promised to t. that love him.
  Jas 1:12; 2:5
gospel preached also to t.   1 Pet 4:6
to t. that obtained like.   2 Pet 1:1
happened unto t. according to.   2:22
unto t. was given power, as.   Rev 9:3
to t. it was given that they should. 5
they sat, and judgement was given
  unto t.   20:4

see **say, woe**

toward **them**

so great is his mercy *toward t.* that
fear him. *Ps 103:11*
Jesus was moved with compassion
toward t. Mat 14:14; Mark 6:34
walk in wisdom *toward t. Col 4:5*
honestly *toward t.* that. *1 Thes 4:12*

under **them**

clave asunder that was *under t.*
Num 16:31
and the cloud is not *under t. Job 26:8*

with **them**

deal worse with thee than *with t.*
Gen 19:9
Hamor communed *with t.* 34:8
Joseph saw Benjamin *with t.* 43:16
established my covenant *with t.Ex 6:4*
thou shalt make no covenant *with t.*
23:32; *Deut 7:2*
shall pine away *with t. Lev 26:39*
to break my covenant *with t.* 44
thou shalt not go *with t. Num 22:12*
arise, go *with t.* 20
we will not inherit *with t.* on. 32:19
meddle not *with t. Deut 2:5, 19*
that it might be well *with t.* 5:29
neither make marriages *with t.* 7:3
Josh 23:12
thus shall ye deal *with t. Deut 7:5*
who keepeth covenant *with t.* 9
and Joshua made peace *with t.*
Josh 9:15, 16
and the Lord was *with t. Judg 1:22*
and do *with t.* what seemeth. 19:24
shalt prophesy *with t. 1 Sam 10:6*
lest I destroy you *with t.* 15:6
nor did he eat *with t. 2 Sam 12:17*
they have there *with t.* their. 15:36
and thou be angry *with t. 1 Ki 8:46*
2 Chr 6:36
they that be *with t. 2 Ki 6:16*
with t. that should go out on the sabbath and came. 11:9; *2 Chr 23:8*
no reckoning made *with t. 2 Ki 22:7*
brethren were to come *with t.*
1 Chr 9:25
and *with t.* 120 priests. *2 Chr 5:12*
with many, or *with t.* that. 14:11
with t. he sent Levites, and *with t.*
17:8
book of the law of the Lord *with t.* 9
and he was *with t.* hid in the. 22:12
with t. were the prophets. *Ezra 5:2*
thou spakest *with t. Neh 9:13*
that they might do *with t.* as. 24
and I contended *with t.* and. 13:25
to do *with t.* as it seemeth. *Esth 3:11*
seed is established in their sight
with t. Job 21:8
is perished *with t. Ps 9:6*
secret of the Lord is *with t.* 25:14
plead my cause *with t.* that. 35:1
with t. to the house of God. 42:4
the Lord is *with t.* that. 54:4; 118:7
I am counted *with t.* that go. 88:4
for *with t.* thou hast. 119:93
not thou in the way *with t. Pr 1:15*
desire to be *with t.* 24:1
keep the law contend *with t.* 28:4
it shall be well *with t. Eccl 8:12*
shall be joined *with t. Isa 14:11*
thou shalt not be joined *with t.* 20
shall come down *with t.* 34:7
and made covenant *with t.* 57:8
this is my covenant *with t.* 59:21
silver and their gold *with t.* 60:9
everlasting covenant *with t.* 61:8
and their offspring *with t.* 65:23
deal thus *with t.* in time. *Jer 18:23*
word of the Lord be *with t.* 27:18
I will gather *with t.* the blind. 31:8
an everlasting covenant *with t.* 32:40
and didst commit whoredom *with t.*
Ezek 16:17, 28; 23:7, 43
bring thee down *with t.* that. 26:20
with t. that go down to the pit. 31:14
32:18, 24, 25, 29
I will **make** *with t.* covenant of
peace. 34:25; 37:26
I the Lord their God am *with t.* 34:30
Zech 10:5
my tabernacle also shall be *with t.*
Ezek 37:27

also shall fall *with t. Hos 5:5*
as long as the bridegroom is *with t.?*
Mat 9:15; Mark 2:19; Luke 5:34
also the wheat *with t. Mat 13:29*
have been partakers *with t.* 23:30
and took no oil *with t.* 25:3
the Lord working *with t. Mark 16:20*
he eateth *with t. Luke 15:2*
though he bear *with t.* 18:7
found the eleven and them that were
with t. 24:33
while I was *with t.* in the world.
John 17:12
betrayed him stood *with t.* 18:5
but Thomas was not *with t.* 20:24
he was *with t.* coming. *Acts 9:28*
made while she was *with t.* 39
arise, and go *with t.* 10:20
didst eat *with t.* 11:3
spirit bade me go *with t.* 12
hand of the Lord was *with t.* 21
they took *with t.* John. 12:25
all that God had done *with t.* 14:27
15:4
not good to take him *with t.* 15:38
down and prayed *with t.* all. 20:36
be at charges *with t.* that. 21:24
and *with t.* partakest of. *Rom 11:17*
rejoice *with t.* that do rejoice, and
weep *with t.* that weep. 12:15
therefore partakers *with t. Eph 5:7*
grace be *with t.* that love our. 6:24
shall be caught up together *with t.*
1 Thes 4:17
peace, *with t.* that call. *2 Tim 2:22*
was it not *with t.* that had sinned ?
Heb 3:17
for finding fault *with t.* he. 8:8
covenant I will make *with t.* 10:16
Rahab perished not *with t.* 11:31
in bonds, as bound *with t.* 13:3
ye husbands, dwell *with t. 1 Pet 3:7*
that ye run not *with t.* to the. 4:4
latter end is worse *with t. 2 Pet 2:20*
had heads, and *with t. Rev 9:19*
with men, he will dwell *with t.* 21:3

without **them**

while she lieth desolate *without t.*
Lev 26:43

themselves

they wearied *t.* to find. *Gen 19:11*
t. for the Egyptians by *t.* 43:32
go and gather straw for *t. Ex 5:7*
prepared for *t.* victual. 12:39
people have corrupted *t.* 32:7
Deut 9:12; 32:5; Judg 2:19
wash, and so make *t. Num 8:7*
even our enemies *t. Deut 32:31*
sons made *t.* vile and. *1 Sam 3:13*
both of them discovered *t.* to. 14:11
if they shall bethink *t. 1 Ki 8:47*
2 Chr 6:37
choose one bullock for *t. 1 Ki 18:23*
Edom made a king over *t.*
2 Ki 8:20; 2 Chr 21:8
sold *t.* to do evil in the. *2 Ki 17:17*
made to *t.* of the lowest of them. 32
eat such things as grow of *t.* 19:29
had made *t.* odious to. *1 Chr 19:6*
people shall humble *t. 2 Chr 7:14*
princes and king humbled *t.* 12:6, 7
which they stript off for *t.* 20:25
they made ready for *t.* and. 35:14
of their daughters for *t. Ezra 9:2*
decreed for *t.* and seed. *Esth 9:31*
they had marked for *t. Job 24:16*
they rolled *t.* upon me. 30:14
they are firm in *t.* 41:23
the kings of the earth set *t. Ps 2:2*
the nations may know *t.* to be. 9:20
which hate us spoil for *t.* 44:10
whereof they are fallen *t.* 57:6
they joined *t.* also to Baal. 106:28
desires, lest they exalt *t.* 140:8
riches make *t.* wings. *Pr 23:5*
might see that they *t. Eccl 3:18*
and they please *t.* in children. *Isa 2:6*
they have rewarded evil to *t.* 3:9
but *t.* are gone into captivity. 46:2
they shall not deliver *t.* from. 47:14
call *t.* of the holy city, and. 48:2
sons of the stranger that join *t.* 56:6

seek her will not weary *t. Jer 2:24*
and the nations shall bless *t.* 4:2
do they not provoke *t.* to the ? 7:19
they weary *t.* 9:5
they had done against *t.* 11:17
have put *t.* to pain, but shall. 12:13
nor cut *t.* nor make *t.* bald for. 16:6
great kings shall serve *t.* of. 27:7
and their nobies shall be of *t.* 30:21
that none should serve *t.* of. 34:10
lifted up, these lift up *t. Ezek 10:17*
their appearance and *t.* 22
shall only be delivered *t.* 14:18
of Israel did feed *t.* 32:2
nor shall the shepherds feed *t.* 10
Levites of the house have for *t.* 45:5
for *t.* are separated which. *Hos 4:14*
they assembled *t.* for corn. 7:14
but they separated *t.* to that. 9:10
shall proceed of *t. Hab 1:7*
the people shall weary *t.* for. 2:13
the golden oil out of *t. Zech 4:12*
who slay them, and hold *t.* 11:5
mighty works do shew forth *t.*
Mat 14:2; Mark 6:14
reasoned among *t. Mat 16:7*
Mark 8:16; Luke 20:14
there be eunuchs, who made *t.*
Mat 19:12
reasoned with *t.* 21:25; *Mark 11:31*
Luke 20:5
but they *t.* will not move. *Mat 23:4*
have no root in *t. Mark 4:17*
kept that saying with *t.* 9:10
counsel of God against *t. Luke 7:30*
certain which trusted in *t.* 18:9
spies which should feign *t.* 20:20
were at enmity between *t.* 23:12
my joy fulfilled in *t. John 17:13*
they *t.* went not into the. 18:28
Judas and Silas being prophets also
t. Acts 15:32
but let them come *t.* and fetch. 16:37
and when they opposed *t.* and. 18:6
that they kept *t.* from things. 21:25
certain Jews bound *t.* 23:12, 21
hope toward God which they *t.* 24:15
they agreed not among *t.* 28:25
had great reasoning among *t.* 29
professing *t.* to be wise. *Rom 1:22*
their own bodies between *t.* 24
receiving in *t.* that recompence. 27
the law, are a law unto *t.* 2:14
have not submitted *t.* to 10:3
shall receive to *t.* damnation. 13:2
nor abusers of *t.* with. *1 Cor 6:9*
not henceforth live unto *t. 2 Cor 5:15*
power they were willing of *t.* 8:3
measuring *t.* by *t.* comparing *t.* with
t. 10:12
t. into the apostles of Christ. 11:13
neither do they *t.* keep. *Gal 6:13*
who have given *t.* over to. *Eph 4:19*
esteem other better than *t. Phil 2:3*
for they *t.* shew of us. *1 Thes 1:9*
them that defile *t.* with. *1 Tim 1:10*
t. in modest apparel. 2:9; *1 Pet 3:5*
purchased to *t.* a good. *1 Tim 3:13*
laying up in store for *t.* a good. 6:19
those that oppose *t. 2 Tim 2:25*
may recover *t.* out of the snare. 26
heap to *t.* teachers, having. 4:3
one of *t.* even a prophet. *Tit 1:12*
seeing they crucify to *t. Heb 6:6*
that not to *t.* but us. *1 Pet 1:12*
bring upon *t.* swift. *2 Pet 2:1*
sporting *t.* with their own. 13
they *t.* are the servants of. 19
giving *t.* over to fornication. *Jude 7*
they corrupt *t.* 10
feeding *t.* without fear. 12
who separate *t.*, sensual, having. 19
see **gather, hide, spread**

then

t. began men to call. *Gen 4:26*
the Canaanite dwelt *t.* in. 13:7
t. shall thy seed also be. 16
t. will I slay my brother. 27:41
t. shall the Lord be my God. 28:21
if our brother be with us, *t.* we. 44:26
t. defiledst thou it; he went up. 49:4
if *t.* their hearts be humbled, and
they *t.* accept of the. *Lev 26:41*

t. I will remember my covenant.
        Lev 26:42
as my strength was *t*.   *Josh* 14:11
if the Lord be with me, *t*. I.   12
they choose new gods, *t*.   *Judg* 5:8
what meaneth *t*. this bleating of the
   sheep ?   *1 Sam* 15:14
t. remember thine handmaid. 25:31
t. hear thou in heaven. *1 Ki* 8:32, 34
         36, 39, 45, 49
there was *t*. no king in.   22:47
t. let fire come down.   *2 Ki* 1:10
Jehoshaphat being *t*. king.   8:16
t. open the door and flee and. 9:3
and David was *t*. in.   *1 Chr* 11:16
t. Manasseh knew the. *2 Chr* 33:13
t. the prophets prophesied. *Ezra* 5:1
t. rose up Zerubbabel to build the. 2
t. went Haman forth that. *Esth* 5:9
t. said Zeresh his wife, and his. 14
t. was the king's wrath.   7:10
I should have slept, *t*.   *Job* 3:13
he seeth also, will he not *t*.? 11:11
t. shalt thou have delight in. 22:26
t. thou shalt say, There is lifting up. 29
because thou wast *t*. born. 38:21
t. the Lord will take me. *Ps* 27:10
t. will I teach transgressors. 51:13
was not an enemy, *t*. I could. 55:12
t. I restored that which I took not
   away.   69:4
t. believed they his words. 106:12
t. shall I not be ashamed. 119:6
t. shalt thou understand the fear of
   the Lord.   *Pr* 2:5
t. shalt thou understand righteousness.   9
t. there shall be a reward. 24:14
t. judgement shall dwell. *Isa* 32:16
t. shall thy light break forth. 58:8
t. shalt thou call, and the Lord. 9
t. shalt thou not remove. *Jer* 4:1
when thou doest evil, *t*. thou. 11:15
t. thou shewedst me their doings. 18
t. they should have turned. 23:22
t. will I cast away the seed. 33:26
t. shall they know that. *Ezek* 39:28
t. was part of the hand. *Dan* 5:24
t. they that feared the Lord spake
   often.   *Mal* 3:16
and *t*. come and offer.   *Mat* 5:24
t. shall they fast. 9:15; *Mark* 2:20
           Luke 5:35
t. will he spoil his house. *Mat* 12:29
           Mark 3:27
and *t*. he shall reward. *Mat* 16:27
Jesus saith, *T*. are the.   17:26
saying, Who *t*. can be saved ? 19:25
   Mark 10:26; *Luke* 18:26
for a witness to all, *t*. *Mat* 24:14
for *t*. shall be great tribulation. 21
t. all the disciples forsook. 26:56
and whence is he *t*. his son ?
         Mark 12:37
t. let them that be in Judaea flee to.
   13:14; *Luke* 21:21
t. shalt thou see clearly. *Luke* 6:42
asked What *t*.? Art thou Elias ?
         John 1:21
Why baptizest thou *t*.?   1:25
t. I go unto him that sent me. 7:33
t. shall ye know that I am he. 8:28
t. Peter said to them. *Acts* 2:38
t. they that gladly received his word.
          41
t. hath God to the Gentiles granted.
   11:18; 26:20
what fruit had ye *t*. in ? *Rom* 6:21
what shall we say *t*.? Is the law sin ?
     7:7; 9:14
if children, *t*. heirs, heirs of. 8:17
so *t*. at this present time there. 11:5
t. shall every man have. *1 Cor* 4:5
what say I *t*.? that the idol is. 10:19
but *t*. face to face: now I know in
   part; *t*. shall I know even. 13:12
what is it *t*.?   14:15
t. am I strong.   *2 Cor* 12:10
come by the law, *t*. Christ. *Gal* 2:21
if ye be Christ's, *t*. are ye. 3:29
but as *t*. he that was born. 4:29
t. shall have rejoicing in. 6:4
t. sudden destruction. *1 Thes* 5:3
t. shall that Wicked be. *2 Thes* 2:8

first for his own sins, *t*. *Heb* 7:27
t. are ye bastards, and not. 12:8
t. have we confidence. *1 John* 3:21

thence

wife to my son from *t*. *Gen* 24:7
send and fetch thee from *t*. 27:45
from *t*. is the shepherd. 49:24
cut down from *t*. *Num* 13:23, 24
Curse me them from *t*. 23:13, 27
if from *t*. thou shalt seek. *Deut* 4:29
the Lord brought thee out *t*. 5:15
     6:23; 24:18
send and fetch him *t*.   19:12
from *t*. will the Lord gather thee, and
   from *t*.   30:4; *Neh* 1:9
t. am I.   *Judg* 19:18
bring from *t*. the ark of. *1 Sam* 4:4
   2 Sam 6:2; *1 Chr* 13:6
go not forth from *t*. *1 Ki* 2:36
shall not be from *t*. any more death.
       2 Ki 2:21
went up from *t*. to Beth-el. 23
from *t*. to Carmel, and from *t*. to. 25
the lepers carried *t*. silver and. 7:8
out Uzziah from *t*. *2 Chr* 26:20
therefore, be ye far from *t*. *Ezra* 6:6
depart, go ye out from *t*. *Isa* 52:11
no more *t*. an infant of days. 65:20
every one that goeth *t*. shall. *Jer* 5:6
signet, yet would I pluck thee *t*. 22:24
cause to cease from *t*. man. 36:29
forth, to separate himself *t*. 37:12
and he shall go forth from *t*. 43:12
I will bring thee down from *t*. 49:16
all abominations from *t*. *Ezek* 11:18
her vineyards from *t*. *Hos* 2:15
from *t*. go ye to Hamath. *Amos* 6:2
dig into hell, *t*. shall my hand. 9:2, 3
t. will I command the sword, in. 4
among stars, *t*. will I bring. *Ob* 4
by no means come out *t*. *Mat* 5:26
there abide, till ye go *t*. 10:11
when ye depart *t*. shake. *Mark* 6:11
that would come from *t*. *Luke* 16:26

thenceforth

t. it shall be accepted. *Lev* 22:27
was magnified from *t*. *2 Chr* 32:23
is *t*. good for nothing. *Mat* 5:13
from *t*. Pilate sought. *John* 19:12*

Theophilus

thee, most excellent *T*. *Luke* 1:3
treatise have I made, O *T*. *Acts* 1:1

there

t. he put the man whom. *Gen* 2:8
if I find forty-five *t*. I will. 18:28
he blessed him *t*.   32:29
t. God appeared.   35:7
t. they buried Abraham and Sarah, *t*.
   they buried Isaac and. 49:31
no swarms of flies shall be *t*. *Ex* 8:22
t. he made a statute, *t*. he. 15:25
behold, I will stand before thee *t*.17:6
the mount, and be *t*. 24:12; 34:2
and he was *t*. with the Lord. 34:28
t. eat it.   *Lev* 8:31
shall leave them *t*.   16:23
and talk with thee *t*. *Num* 11:17
we saw the children of Anak *t*. 13:28
   33; *Deut* 1:28; *Josh* 14:12
died *t*. and was buried *t*. *Num* 20:1
Aaron shall die *t*. 26, 28; *Deut* 10:6
t. ye shall serve gods, work of.
   Deut 4:28; 28:36, 64; *Jer* 16:13
and *t*. they be unto this day.
     Deut 10:5; *Josh* 4:9
choose to put his name *t*. *Deut* 12:5
   14:23; 16:2, 11; *1 Ki* 8:29; 9:3
it may be *t*. for a witness. *Deut* 31:26
where he bowed, *t*. he. *Judg* 5:27
I will try them for thee *t*. 7:4
inhabitants of Jabesh-gilead *t*. 21:9
where thou diest, *t*. will. *Ruth* 1:17
the priests of the Lord were *t*.
     1 Sam 1:3; 4:4
worshipped the Lord *t*.   1:28
and renew the kingdom *t*. 11:14
t. they made Saul king before the
   Lord, *t*. they sacrificed, and *t*. 15
of the servants of Saul *t*. 21:7
Doeg the Edomite was *t*. 22:22
Joab smote Abner *t*. *2 Sam* 3:27

God smote Uzzah *t*. and *t*. he died.
      2 Sam 6:7
even *t*. also will thy servant. 15:21
hast thou not *t*. Zadok and ? 35
staves, and *t*. they are. *1 Ki* 8:8
chosen to put my name *t*. 11:36
   2 Ki 23:27; *2 Chr* 6:5, 6; 7:16
the ravens to feed thee *t*. *1 Ki* 17:4
when they said, He is not *t*.; he. 18:10
and left his servant *t*.   19:3
and cast the salt in *t*. *2 Ki* 2:21
he came and lay *t*.   4:11
and we shall die *t*.   7:4
come, there was no man *t*. 5, 10
they left their gods, *t*. *1 Chr* 14:12
prophet of the Lord was *t*. *2 Chr* 28:9
they slew Sennacherib *t*. with. 32:21
God hath caused his name to dwell *t*.
      Ezra 6:12
t. the wicked cease from troubling,
   and *t*. the weary be at. *Job* 3:17
t. the prisoners rest together. 18
small and great are *t*.; the servant. 19
t. the righteous might dispute. 23:7
t. they cry, but none giveth. 35:12
and where the slain are, *t*. 39:30
t. were they in great fear. *Ps* 14:5
        53:5
daughter of Tyre shall be *t*. 45:12
fear took hold upon them *t*. 48:6
went through flood, *t*. did we. 66:6
cities that they may dwell *t*. 69:35
Tyre, this man was born *t*. 87:4, 6
players on instruments shall be *t*. 7
t. go the ships, *t*. is that. 104:26
t. the Lord commanded the. 133:3
behold, thou art *t*. 139:8
t. shall thy hand lead me.   10
I was *t*.: when he set. *Pr* 8:27
that the dead are *t*.   9:18
where no wood is, *t*. the fire. 26:20
was *t*., iniquity was *t*. *Eccl* 3:16
for *t*. is a time *t*. for every. 17
tree falleth, *t*. it shall be. 11:3
t. thy mother brought. *S of S* 8:5
nor shall shepherds make their fold *t*.
      Isa 13:20
beasts of the desert shall lie *t*. 21
t. shalt thou die, and *t*. the. 22:18
to Chittim, *t*. also shalt thou. 23:12
here a little, and *t*. a little. 28:10
t. glorious Lord will be a. 33:21
and an highway shall be *t*. 35:8
but the redeemed shall walk *t*. 9
from the beginning; *t*. am I. 48:16
my servant shall dwell *t*. 65:9
is *t*. no balm in Gilead, no physician
   t.?   *Jer* 8:22
t. will I cause thee to hear. 18:2
t. thou shalt die, and shalt be buried
   t.   20:6
country: *t*. shall ye die. 22:26; 42:16
and *t*. shall they be till I. 27:22
he was *t*. when Jerusalem. 38:28
will go into Egypt, and *t*. will. 42:14
against Ashkelon, *t*. hath he. 47:7
go to the plain, I will *t*. *Ezek* 3:22
see it, though he shall die *t*. 12:13
I will plead with him *t*. for. 17:20
and they offered *t*. their sacrifices, *t*.
   they presented the. 20:28
and *t*. will I plead with you face. 35
t. will I accept them, *t*. 40
and I will leave you *t*. and. 22:20
t. were their breasts pressed, *t*. 23:3
and they shall be *t*. a base. 29:14
Ashur is *t*. and all her. 32:32
whereas the Lord was *t*. 35:10
name shall be, The Lord is *t*. 48:35
and she shall sing *t*. as. *Hos* 2:15
yea, grey hairs are here and *t*. 7:9
t. I hated them.   9:15
t. he spake with us. 12:4
I will plead with them *t*. *Joel* 3:2
one plow *t*. with oxen ? *Amos* 6:12
t. eat bread and prophesy *t*. 7:12
t. be delivered, *t*. Lord shall.
      Mi 4:10
shall cry *t*. bitterly. *Zeph* 1:14
be thou *t*. till I bring. *Mat* 2:13
t. rememberest that thy brother. 5:23
leave *t*. thy gift before the altar. 24
where your treasure is, *t*. will. 6:21

t. shall be gnashing of teeth.
Mat 8:12; 22:13; 24:51
they enter in, and dwell t. 12:45
Luke 11:26
in my name, t. am I in. Mat 18:20
lo, here is Christ, or t. 24:23
Mark 13:21
I hid thy talent, t. thou. Mat 25:25
down, they watched him t. 27:36
in Galilee, t. shall ye see him. 28:7
Mark 16:7
I may preach t. also. Mark 1:38
and he could t. do no mighty. 6:5
and if the son of peace be t.
Luke 10:6
t. will I bestow all my fruits. 12:18
where I am, t. shall my. John 12:26
that where I am, t. ye may be. 14:3
that shall befall me t. Acts 20:22
t. it shall be told thee of all. 22:10
t. be called the children. Rom 9:26
for there shall be no night t.
Rev 21:25; 22:5
see **abode, is, none, one, stand, stood, was**

thereabout
were much perplexed t. Luke 24:4

thereat
their hands and feet t. Ex 30:19
40:31
there be which go in t. Mat 7:13*

thereby
t. shall I know thou hast. Gen 24:14
should be defiled t. Lev 11:43
with God, t. good will. Job 22:21
whoso is deceived t. is. Pr 20:1
shall be endangered t. Eccl 10:9
gallant ships pass t. Isa 33:21
passeth t. shall be astonished.
Jer 18:16; 19:8
any son of man pass t. 51:43
wall and carry on t. Ezek 12:5, 12
he shall not fall t. 33:12
he shall die t. 18*
do what is lawful, he shall live t. 19
also shall border t. Zech 9:2
God might be glorified t. John 11:4
having slain the enmity t. Eph 2:16
who are exercised t. Heb 12:11
root springing up, and t. many. 15
t. some have entertained. 13:2
word that ye may grow t. 1 Pet 2:2*

therefore
t. shall a man leave his. Gen 2:24
shall keep my covenant t. 17:9
guilty, t. is this distress. 42:21
t. God dealt well with. Ex 1:20
i. go. 4:12
they be idle, t. they cry. 5:8, 17
t. shall ye observe. 12:17; 13:10
t. he giveth you on the sixth. 16:29
ye shall keep the sabbath t. 31:14
ye shall t. sanctify yourselves, be holy;
for I am holy. Lev 11:44, 45; 21:6
t. I do visit the iniquity. 18:25
ye shall t. keep my statutes and. 26
t. keep my ordinances. 30; 19:37
20:22; 22:9
ye shall not t. oppress one. 25:17
t. the Levites shall be. Num 3:12
t. the Lord thy God commanded.
Deut 5:15; 15:11, 15; 24:18, 22
t. thou shalt serve thine. 28:48
t. we turn again to. Judg 11:8
t. also I have lent him. 1 Sam 1:28
t. hath the Lord done this. 28:18
t. Michal had no child. 2 Sam 6:23
be strong t. and shew. 1 Ki 2:2
t. thy life shall go for his life. 20:42
t. thou shalt not. 2 Ki 1:6, 16
t. they have destroyed them. 19:18
t. he slew Saul, and. 1 Chr 10:14
t. hath he brought all. 2 Chr 7:22
t. gave them up to desolation. 30:7
t. we his servants will arise and.
Neh 2:20
t. I chased him from me. 13:28
t. they say to God. Job 21:14
judgement is before him, t. 35:14
t. take unto you seven bullocks. 42:8
t. my heart is glad. Ps 16:9
t. lead me. 31:3

t. the children of men put. Ps 36:7
t. God hath blessed thee for. 45:2
t. God hath anointed thee with oil. 7
t. shall the people praise. 17
have no changes, t. they fear. 55:19*
t. in the shadow of thy wings. 63:7
t. his people return hither. 73:10
set his love upon me, t. will I. 91:14
t. he said that he would. 106:23
t. have I spoken. 116:10; 2 Cor 4:13
t. I hate every false way. Ps 119:104
are wonderful: t. doth my soul. 129
depart from me t. ye. 139:19
t. leave off contention. Pr 17:14
God is in heaven, t. let. Eccl 5:2
t. the misery of man is great. 8:6
t. the heart of men is set in them. 11
t. the Lord will smite. Isa 3:17
t. the Lord of hosts shall. 10:16
t. hath the curse devoured. 24:6
t. he hath poured the fury of. 42:25
t. his arm brought salvation. 59:16
t. they shall fall among. Jer 6:15
ye obeyed not, t. this thing is. 40:3
Lord is my portion, t. will. Lam 3:24
t. I fled before unto. Jonah 4:2
t. I am returned to Jerusalem with.
Zech 1:16
t. came a great wrath from. 7:12
t. ye sons of Jacob are. Mal 3:6
be ye t. perfect. Mat 5:48
fear ye not t. 10:31
what t. God hath joined. 19:6
what shall we have t.? 20
watch t. 24:42, 44; 25:13
Mark 13:35
go ye t. teach all nations. Mat 28:19
t. came I forth. Mark 1:38
do ye not t. err? 12:24
David t. himself calleth him Lord. 37
for t. am I sent. Luke 4:43
be ye t. merciful. 6:36
t. shall they be your judges. 11:19
t. also said the wisdom of God. 49
have married a wife, and t. I. 14:20
what t. shall the Lord of the vineyard do? 20:15; Mark 12:9
t. in the resurrection? Mat 20:33
this my joy t. is fulfilled. John 3:29
ye t. hear them not, because. 8:47
but ye say, We see; t. your sin. 9:41
t. doth my Father love me. 10:17
whatsoever I speak t., even as. 12:50
chosen you, t. the world. 15:19
repent ye t. and be converted.
Acts 3:19
t. it was imputed to. Rom 4:22
t. if thine enemy hunger. 12:20
t. glorify God in your body and.
1 Cor 6:20
not the hand, is it t. not of? 12:15, 16
t. be ye stedfast, unmoveable. 15:58
t. as ye abound in every. 2 Cor 8:7
be not ye t. partakers. Eph 5:7
t. as the church is subject to. 24
be not t. ashamed of the. 2 Tim 1:8
see **now**

therefrom
that ye turn not aside t. Josh 23:6
sins of Jeroboam, he departed not t.
2 Ki 3:3; 13:2

therein
multiply t. Gen 9:7
for fifty righteous t. 18:24
the cave that is t. I give. 23:11, 17, 20
you, dwell and trade t. 34:10, 21
was there any worm t. Ex 16:24
doeth any work t. be cut. 31:14; 35:2
shalt thou put t. the ark of. 40:3
tabernacle and all t. 9; Lev 8:10
sinning t. Lev 6:3
done in trespassing t. 7
no white hairs t. 13:21
black hairs t. 37
ordinances to walk t. 18:4
Judg 2:22; Isa 42:5
shall be no blemish t. Lev 22:21
ye shall do no work t.: it is. 23:3
Deut 16:8; Num 29:7; Jer 17:24
do no servile work t. Lev 23:7, 8, 21
25, 35, 36; Num 28:18; 29:35
eat your fill and dwell t. Lev 25:19
be wood t. or not. Num 13:20

put fire t. and put incense.
Num 16:7, 46
lest thou be snared t. Deut 7:25
destroy all that is t. 13:15
Josh 10:28, 39
if there be any blemish t. Deut 15:21
he shall read t. all the days. 17:19
people that is found t. shall. 20:11
nor any grass groweth t. 29:23
thou shalt meditate t. day. Josh 1:8
the city and all t. shall. 6:17, 24
my name might be t. 1 Ki 8:16
new cruse, and put salt t. 2 Ki 2:20
let the fields rejoice, and all that is t.
1 Chr 16:32; Ps 96:12
sedition been made t. Ezra 4:19
there was no breach left t. Neh 6:1
but the people were few t. 7:4
found it written t. 5, 13:1
he read t. 8:3
made the earth, the seas, and all that
is t. 9:6; Ps 24:1; 69:34; 98:7
let no joyful voice come t. Job 3:7
he shall not rejoice t. 20:18
shall dwell t. for ever. Ps 37:29
love his name shall dwell t. 69:36
for wickedness of them that dwell t.
107:34; Jer 12:4
that have pleasure t. Ps 111:2
thy commandments, t. do. 119:35
made the sea and all t. is. 146:6
Acts 14:15; 17:24; Rev 10:6
shall fall t. Pr 22:14; 26:27
Jer 23:12; Hos 14:9
make a breach t. for us. Isa 7:6
the people that dwell t. shall. 33:24
though fools, shall not err t. 35:8
gladness shall be found t. 51:3
they that dwell t. shall die in. 6
whosoever goeth t. shall not. 59:8
walk t.; we will not walk t. Jer 6:16
my voice, neither walked t. 9:13
and no man dwelleth t. 44:2
48:9; 50:3, 40
and all that is t. shall sing. 51:48
behold, t. shall be left. Ezek 14:22
city, to the pot whose scum is t. 24:6
mourn that dwelleth t. Hos 4:3
Amos 8:8; 9:5
t. shall be cut off and die, but the
third part shall be left t. Zech 13:8
he shall not enter t. Mark 10:15
Luke 18:17
and let no man dwell t. Acts 1:20
t. is the righteousness of God.
Rom 1:17
dead to sin, live any longer t.? 6:2
wherein he is called, t. 1 Cor 7:24
that t. I may speak boldly. Eph 6:20
that t. I do rejoice, and. Phil 1:18
taught, abounding t. with. Col 2:7
that some must enter t. Heb 4:6
not, nor hadst pleasure t. 10:8
of liberty, and continueth t. Jas 1:25
the earth and works t. 2 Pet 3:10
rise and measure them that worship
t. Rev 11:1
causeth them that dwell t. to. 13:12
and I saw no temple t. 21:22
see **dwelt**

thereinto
in the countries enter t. Luke 21:21

thereof
eatest t. surely die. Gen 2:17; 3:5
I will do in midst t. Ex 3:20
for t. must we take to serve. 10:26
no stranger shall eat t. 12:43
45:48; 2 Ki 7:2
then shall he eat t. Ex 12:44
I have not eaten t. in. Deut 26:14
shall eat and leave t. 2 Ki 4:43, 44
know not the ways t. Job 24:13
the humble shall hear t. Ps 34:2
the whole disposing t. Pr 16:33
not power to eat t. Eccl 6:2

thereon
shalt sacrifice t. the. Ex 20:24
cloud abode t. 40:35; Num 9:22
spread ground corn t. 2 Sam 17:19
an ass that I may ride t. 19:26
God of our fathers look t. 1 Chr 12:17
let him be hanged t. Ezra 6:11
said, Hang Haman t. Esth 7:9

perverseness, and stay *t.*   *Isa* 30:12
it to hang a vessel *t.*   *Ezek* 15:3
they set him *t.*   *Mat* 21:7
   Luke 19:35; *John* 12:14
and found nothing *t.*   *Mat* 21:19
   Mark 11:13; *Luke* 13:6
thought *t.* he wept.   *Mark* 14:72
another buildeth *t.*   *1 Cor* 3:10
open the book or look *t. Rev* 5:3, 4
was given to him that sat *t.*   6:4
gates, and names written *t.* 21:12

thereout
he shall take *t.* his handful of flour.
   Lev 2:2
there came water *t.*   *Judg* 15:19

thereto
unto that to smell *t.*   *Ex* 30:38
add the fifth part *t. Lev* 5:16; 6:5
   27:13, 31
before a beast to lie down *t.* 18:23
shall be put *t.* in a vessel. *Num* 19:17
thou shalt not add *t.*   *Deut* 12:32
king of Edom would not hearken *t.*
   Judg 11:17
thou mayest add *t.*   *1 Chr* 22:14
heavy, but I will add *t. 2 Chr* 10:14
Jehoram compelled Judah *t.* 21:11*
by taking heed *t.* according to thy.
   Ps 119:9
and falleth down *t.*   *Isa* 44:15
thy speech agreeth *t. Mark* 14:70
no man disannulleth or addeth *t.*
   Gal 3:15

thereunto
made a molten calf, and sacrificed *t.*
   Ex 32:8
all the places nigh *t.*   *Deut* 1:7
and watching *t.* with all. *Eph* 6:18
that we are appointed *t. 1 Thes* 3:3
the comers *t.* perfect.   *Heb* 10:1
ye are *t.* called, that ye. *1 Pet* 3:9

thereupon
playedst the harlot *t.* *Ezek* 16:16
of Judah shall feed *t.*   *Zeph* 2:7
heed how he buildeth *t. 1 Cor* 3:10
work abide which he hath built *t.* 14

therewith
to blind mine eyes *t.*   *1 Sam* 12:3
and cut off his head *t.*   17:51
and thrust me through *t.*   31:4
   1 Chr 10:4
I have *t.* sent Naaman. *2 Ki* 5:6
and repaired *t.* the house of. 12:14
treasure and trouble *t. Pr* 15:16
a stalled ox, and hatred *t.*   17
quietness *t.*   17:1
lest thou be filled *t.* and.   25:16
travail to be exercised *t. Eccl* 1:13
stones shall be hurt *t.*   10:9
prepare thy bread *t.*   *Ezek* 4:15
oil, wine, ye shall be satisfied *t.*
   Joel 2:19
state, I have learned *t. Phil* 4:11
food and raiment, let us be *t.* content.
   1 Tim 6:8
t. bless we God, and *t.*   *Jas* 3:9
and not content *t.*   *3 John* 10

these
by *t.* were the isles of. *Gen* 10:5, 32
Jacob take a wife of such as *t.* 27:46
t. daughters, *t.* children, *t.* 31:43
asketh, saying, Whose are *t.?* 32:17
Joseph said, Bring *t.* men home,
  make ready, for *t.* men.   43:16
gave light by night to *t. Ex* 14:20
and if he do not *t.* three unto. 21:11
t. be thy gods, O Israel. 32:4, 8
hath sinned in one of *t. Lev* 5:13
t. shall ye not eat.   11:4
t. shall ye eat. 9, 21, 22; *Deut* 14:9
for *t.* ye shall be unclean. *Lev* 11:24
t. shall be unclean.   29
ye shall not offer *t.* fo.   22:22, 25
unto *t.* the land shall. *Num* 26:53
but among *t.* there was not a.   64
t. stand on mount.   *Deut* 27:12
and *t.* shall stand upon mount.   13
Lord hath not chosen *t. 1 Sam* 16:10
Saul, I cannot go with *t.*   17:39
meanest thou by *t.? 2 Sam* 16:2
as *t.* which the queen of. *1 Ki* 10:10
Solomon clave to *t.* strange. 11:2

be dew nor rain *t.* years. *1 Ki* 17:1
Lord, With *t.* shalt thou push the
  Syrians. 22:11; *2 Chr* 18:10
Lord said, *T.* have no master.
  1 Ki 22:17; *2 Chr* 18:16
Nebuzar-adan took *t.* *2 Ki* 25:20
t. were of the king's. *2 Chr* 35:7
t. sought their register. *Ezra* 2:62
t. went and could not shew. *Neh* 7:61
now *t.* that sealed the covenant. 10:1
who knoweth not such things as *t.?*
   Job 12:3
t. wait all upon thee, that. *Ps* 104:27
days were better than *t. Eccl* 7:10
further, by *t.* my son, be.   12:12
no one of *t.* shall fail. *Isa* 34:16
what said *t.* men?   39:3
remember *t.* O Jacob.   44:21
t. shall come from far, *t.* from north,
  and from the west, and *t.* 49:12
begotten me *t.?* who that brought up
  t.? I was left alone; *t.* where? 21
I receive comfort in *t.?*   57:6
but *t.* have altogether. *Jer* 5:5
t. men have done evil in all. 38:9
I give *t.* thee into hand of *t.* 16
pomegranates were like to *t.* 52:22
for *t.* pine away, stricken. *Lam* 4:9
when those went, *t.* went, and when
  those stood, *t. Ezek* 1:21; 10:17
greater abominations than *t.* 8:15
t. men have set up their idols. 14:3
thee, to do any of *t.* to thee. 16:5
and *t.* hast thou sacrificed unto. 20
t. discovered her nakedness. 23:10
in *t.* were they thy merchants. 27:21
what thou meanest by *t.*   37:18
they brought *t.* men.   *Dan* 3:13
t. men were bound.   21
princes saw *t.* men.   27
over *t.* Darius set three.   6:2
then *t.* men assembled, and. 11, 15
t. great beasts, which are four. 7:17
by a dead body touch *t. Hag* 2:13
I will shew thee what *t.* be.
   Zech 1:9; 4:5, 13
I said to the angel, What be *t.? 1:19*
   21; 4:12
what is more than *t.* cometh of evil.
   Mat 5:37
not arrayed like one of *t.*   6:29
Hearest thou what *t.* say? 21:16
on *t.* commandments hang. 22:40
t. ought ye to have done. 23:23
done it unto one of the least of *t.* 25:40
did it not to one of the least of *t.* 45
and *t.* shall go into everlasting. 46
what is it which *t.* witness? 26:62
   Mark 14:60
no other commandment greater than
  t.   *Mark* 12:31
t. shall receive greater.   40
Seest thou *t.* great buildings? 13:2
am sent to shew thee *t. Luke* 1:19
God is able of *t.* stones to.   3:8
let *t.* sayings sink down into. 9:44
see greater things than *t. John* 1:50
in *t.* lay a great multitude of. 5:3
what he doeth, *t.* doeth the Son. 19
shew him greater works than *t.* 20
shall we buy bread that *t.?*   6:5
he do more miracles than *t.?* 7:31
neither pray I for *t.* alone. 17:20
and *t.* have known that thou.   25
seek me, let *t.* go their way. 18:8
lovest thou me more than *t.?* 21:15
of *t.* which companied. *Acts* 1:21
shew whether of *t.* two thou.   24
others said, *T.* men are full of. 2:13
likewise foretold of *t.* days. 3:24
What shall we do to *t.* men? 4:16
before *t.* days rose up.   5:36
refrain from *t.* men, and let.   38
can any forbid that *t.* should? 10:47
t. that have turned the world. 17:6
t. were more noble than those. 11
t. having not the law, are. *Rom* 2:14
more shall *t.* be graffed. 11:24
even so have *t.* also now not. 31
upon *t.* we bestow. *1 Cor* 12:23
t. three, but the greatest of *t.* 13:13
having *t.* promises, let us cleanse.
   2 Cor 7:1
but of *t.* who seemed to. *Gal* 2:6

t. only are my fellow-workers to.
   Col 4:11
let *t.* also first be proved. *1 Tim* 3:10
himself from *t.* he shall. *2 Tim* 2:21
with *t.*, but heavenly things with better sacrifices than *t.* *Heb* 9:23
now where remission of *t.* is. 10:18
by *t.* might be partakers. *2 Pet* 1:4
but *t.* as brute beasts made. 2:12
Enoch also prophesied of *t. Jude* 14
t. be they who separate.   19
t. have power to shut heaven.
   Rev 11:6
t. were redeemed.   14:4
t. have one mind.   17:13
he said, *T.* sayings are faithful. 22:6
see **abominations, things, words**

these *are,* or *are* **these**
by the man whose *t.* are. *Gen* 38:25
whose *t.* are.   48:8
t. are that Aaron and Moses. *Ex* 6:26
t. are the judgements.   21:1
   Lev 26:46; *Deut* 6:1
t. are unclean.   *Lev* 11:31
t. are my feasts.   23:2, 4
God said, What men *are* *t.* with
  thee?   *Num* 22:9
t. are tokens of her. *Deut* 22:17
what cities *are t.* thou? *1 Ki* 9:13
happy *are t.* thy servants. 10:8
her sons *are t.* *1 Chr* 2:18
t. are ancient things.   4:22
now *t.* are thy servants. *Neh* 1:10
t. are part of his ways. *Job* 26:14
behold, *t.* are the ungodly. *Ps* 73:12
who are *t.* that flee as a cloud, as ?
   Isa 60:8
t. are a smoke in my nose. 65:5
surely *t.* are poor, they. *Jer* 5:4
The temple of the Lord *are t.* 7:4
t. are the men that. *Ezek* 11:2
they said, *T. are* the people. 36:20
visions of thy head *are t. Dan* 2:28
spirit straitened ? *are t.* his doings ?
   Mi 2:7
then said I, O my lord, what *are t.?*
   Zech 1:9; 4:4; 6:4
and *t. are* they by the way side.
   Mark 4:15, 16, 18, 20
famines, *t. are* the beginnings. 13:8
and brethren *are t.* which. *Luke* 8:21
t. are not the words of. *John* 10:21
but *t. are* in the world, and I. 17:11
but *t. are* written that ye. 20:31
t. are not drunken, as. *Acts* 2:15
t. are not the children of. *Rom* 9:8
t. are contrary the one to. *Gal* 5:17
flesh are manifest, which *are t.* 19
t. are wells without water. *2 Pet* 2:17
t. are murmurers, walking. *Jude* 16
what *are t.* which are arrayed in ?
   Rev 7:13
t. are they which came out of. 14
t. are they which were not defiled with
  women. *T. are* they which. 14:4
t. are the true sayings. 19:9; 22:6

Thessalonica
at *T.* was a synagogue. *Acts* 17:1
more noble than those of *T.*   11
one Aristarchus of *T.* being. 27:2
even in *T.* ye sent once. *Phil* 4:16
for Demas is departed into *T.*
   2 Tim 4:10

Theudas
days rose up *T.* boasting. *Acts* 5:36

they
of thee a nation mightier than *t.*
   Num 14:12
t. and all theirs went down. 16:33
not come nigh. that neither *t.* 18:3
more honourable than *t.* 22:15
be stronger than *t. 1 Ki* 20:23, 25
are more than *t.* that. *2 Ki* 6:16
t. that hate me, *t.* would. *Ps* 69:4
there be higher than *t. Eccl* 5:8
and *t.* together shall be against.
   Isa 9:21
but *t.* also have erred through. 28:7
therefore *t.* that pursue you. 30:16
t. are thy lot. to them thou. 57:6
t. that shall be of thee shall. 58:12
t., their kings and priests. *Jer* 2:26

Column 1 — thick

whom neither *t*. nor their fathers.
 Jer 9:16; 19:4; 44:3
t. whose judgement was not. 49:12
t. and their fathers have. *Ezek* 2:3
wast corrupted more than *t*. in ways.
 16:47
abominations more than *t*. 51, 52
know that *t*. are my people. 34:30
when an hungered, and *t*. that were.
 Mat 12:3; *Mark* 2:25; *Luke* 6:3
receive this, save *t*. to. *Mat* 19:11
t. that are great exercise. 20:25
t. that are whole have no need.
 Mark 2:17; *Luke* 5:31
and *t*. that had eaten were.
 Mark 8:9
hardly shall *t*. which have riches.
 10:23
t. that went before and *t*. that. 11:9
and *t*. that were sent. *Luke* 7:10
t. on the rock are *t*. which. 8:13
t. which have continued. 22:28
for *t*. also went unto the feast.
 John 4:45
dead shall hear, and *t*. that. 5:25
t. that have done good, *t*. that. 29
scriptures: and *t*. are *t*. which. 39
what are *t*. amongst so many? 6:9
I am come, that *t*. which see not
 might see, and that *t*. which. 9:39
t. are not of the world, even. 17:16
that *t*. all may be one, as thou. 21
that *t*. may be made perfect. 23
Father, I will that *t*. whom thou hast
 given me be with me, that *t*. 24
t. went not in, lest *t*. 18:28
t. of circumcision contended with.
 Acts 11:2
now *t*. that were scattered. 19
t. that dwell at Jerusalem because *t*.
 13:27
through grace we shall be saved even
 as *t*. 15:11
we and *t*. of that place. 21:12
are we better than *t*.? *Rom* 3:9
for if *t*. which are of the law. 4:14
t. that are in the flesh cannot. 8:8
not only *t*. but ourselves also. 23
t. which are the children of the. 9:8
t. also, if *t*. abide not still. 11:23
for *t*. that are such serve not. 16:18
t. that have wives, as though *t*. had
 none. *1 Cor* 7:29
t. that weep, *t*. that rejoice, *t*. 30
t. that use this world, as not. 31
that *t*. who run in a race run. 9:24
that *t*. which are approved. 11:19
whether it were I or *t*. so we. 15:11
then *t*. also which are fallen. 18
afterwards *t*. that are Christ's. 23
 Gal 5:24
as is earthy, such are *t*. *1 Cor* 15:48
t. who seemed somewhat. *Gal* 2:6
t. gave the right hand of. 9
know ye, that *t*. which are. 3:7, 9
I would *t*. were cut off which. 5:12
t. who do such things shall not. 21
nor *t*. who are circumcised. 6:13
t. shew of us what entering in we
 had. *1 Thes* 1:9
for *t*. that sleep; *t*. that be. 5:7
t. that used the office. *1 Tim* 3:13
t. who labour in the word. 5:17
and *t*. that are otherwise cannot. 25
t. that will be rich fall into. 6:9
of this sort are *t*. which. *2 Tim* 3:6
that *t*. which have believed. *Tit* 3:8
more excellent name than *t*. *Heb* 1:4
seeing *t*. to whom it was first. 4:6
that *t*. without us should. 11:40
t. watch, as *t*. that must. 13:17
salute all the saints, *t*. of Italy. 24
as *t*. that shall be judged. *Jas* 2:12
t. went out that *t*. might be made
 manifest, that *t*. were. *1 John* 2:19
t. are of the world, *t*. speak. 4:5
these are *t*. who separate. *Jude* 19
t. who pierced him. *Rev* 1:7
for *t*. are worthy. 3:4; 16:6
whence came *t*.? 7:13
these are *t*. who came out of. 14
for *t*. are virgins. These are *t*. 14:4
here are *t*. that keep the. 12
but *t*. that are written in. 21:27

thick

art waxen fat, thou art grown *t*.
 Deut 32:15
the mule went under the *t*. boughs.
 2 Sam 18:9
he took a *t*. cloth and. *2 Ki* 8:15*
fetch branches of *t*. trees to make
 booths. *Neh* 8:15
runneth on the *t*. bosses. *Job* 15:26
axes on the *t*. trees. *Ps* 74:5*
be under every *t*. oak. *Ezek* 6:13
exalted among *t*. branches. 19:11
his top was among the *t*. boughs.
 31:3, 10, 14
ladeth himself with *t*. clay. *Hab* 2:6
people were gathered *t*. together.
 Luke 11:29*

see clouds, darkness

thicker

little finger shall be *t*.than my father's
 loins. *1 Ki* 12:10; *2 Chr* 10:10

thicket

a ram caught in a *t*. by. *Gen* 22:13
the lion is come up from his *t*. *Jer* 4:7

thickets

themselves in *t*. in rocks. *1 Sam* 13:6
kindle in the *t*. of forest. *Isa* 9:18
he shall cut down the *t*. of. 10:34
shall flee and go into *t*. *Jer* 4:29

thickness

the *t*. of the sea was an. *2 Chr* 4:5
the *t*. of the pillars was. *Jer* 52:21
t. of the wall was five. *Ezek* 41:9
the chambers were in the *t*. 42:10

thief

(*The Revisions usually change*
thief and thieves to robber and
robbers, as having a little more
exactly the meaning)
if a *t*. be found breaking. *Ex* 22:2, 7
if the *t*. be not found, then the. 8
then that *t*. shall die. *Deut* 24:7
in the night is as a *t*. *Job* 24:14
after them as after a *t*. 30:5
when thou sawest a *t*. *Ps* 50:18
men do not despise *t*. if. *Pr* 6:30
whoso is partner with a *t*. 29:24
as a *t*. is ashamed when. *Jer* 2:26
the *t*. cometh in, and. *Hos* 7:1
enter at windows like a *t*. *Joel* 2:9
into the house of the *t*. *Zech* 5:4
in what watch the *t*. would come.
 Mat 24:43; *Luke* 12:39
ye come as against a *t*.? *Mat* 26:55
 Mark 14:48; *Luke* 22:52
in heaven, where no *t*. *Luke* 12:33
door, the same is a *t*. *John* 10:1
the *t*. cometh not but to steal. 10
but because he was a *t*. and. 12:6
day of the Lord cometh as a *t*.
 1 Thes 5:2; *2 Pet* 3:10
overtake you as a *t*. *1 Thes* 5:4
none of you suffer as a *t*. *1 Pet* 4:15
I will come on thee as a *t*. *Rev* 3:3
 16:15

thieves

thy princes are companions of *t*.
 Isa 1:23
not Israel found among *t*.? *Jer* 48:27
if *t*. by night, they will. 49:9; *Ob* 5
and where *t*. break. *Mat* 6:19
and where *t*. do not break. 20
made it a den of *t*. 21:13
 Mark 11:17; *Luke* 19:46
two *t*. crucified with him. *Mat* 27:38
 Mark 15:27
t. also cast the same in. *Mat* 27:44
Jericho and fell among *t*. *Luke* 10:30
to him that fell among *t*.? 36
came before me are *t*. *John* 10:8
nor *t*., shall inherit the kingdom of
 God. *1 Cor* 6:10

thigh

put thy hand under my *t*. *Gen* 24:2
 9; 47:29
the hollow of Jacob's *t*. 32:25
he halted upon his *t*. 31
the Lord maketh thy *t*. to rot.
 Num 5:21, 22, 27
dagger on his right *t*. *Judg* 3:16
dagger from his right *t*. 21
smote them hip and *t*. 15:8

gird thy sword on thy *t*. *Ps* 45:3
hath his sword on his *t*. *S of S* 3:8
uncover the *t*., pass over. *Isa* 47:2*
I smote upon my *t*. *Jer* 31:19
smite therefore upon *t*. *Ezek* 21:12
gather the *t*. and shoulder. 24:4
he hath on his *t*. a name. *Rev* 19:16

thighs

breeches shall reach from loins to the
 t. *Ex* 28:42
the joints of thy *t*. are. *S of S* 7:1
his belly and his *t*. were. *Dan* 2:32

thin

and behold seven *t*. ears. *Gen* 41:6
 7, 23, 24
the seven *t*. kine are seven. 27
gold into *t*. plates. *Ex* 39:3
in it a yellow *t*. hair. *Lev* 13:30
additions made of *t*. work. *1 Ki* 7:29*
Jacob shall be made *t*. *Isa* 17:4

thine

any thing that is *t*. *Gen* 14:23
thou and all that are *t*. 20:7
discern what is *t*. with me. 31:32
issue after them shall be *t*. 48:6
it shall be *t*. and thy sons. *Lev* 10:15
 Num 18:9, 11, 13, 14, 15, 18
ridden ever since I was *t*. *Num* 22:30
that which is *t*. with thy. *Deut* 15:3
if any of *t*. be driven into. 30:4
mountains shall be *t*. and the outgoings of it shall be *t*. *Josh* 17:18
the man of whom I. *1 Sam* 2:33
given it to a neighbour of *t*. 15:28
t. are all that pertained to Mephibosheth. *2 Sam* 16:4
mine nor *t*. but divide. *1 Ki* 3:26
O king, I am *t*. and all that. 20:4
shall lick thy blood, even *t*. 21:19
t. are we, David, and. *1 Chr* 12:18
not take that which is *t*. 21:24
t. O Lord, is the greatness, power,
 and glory: the earth is *t*..*t*. is.29:11
righteousness even *t*. *Ps* 71:16
day is *t*., the night also is *t*. 74:16
are *t*., the earth also is *t*. 89:11
I am *t*., save me; I sought. 119:94
of Egypt shall be *t*. *Isa* 45:14
we are *t*.: thou never barest. 63:19
of inheritance is *t*. *Jer* 32:8
t. is the kingdom. *Mat* 6:13
take that is *t*. 20:14
there thou hast that is *t*. 25:25
worship me, all shall be *t*. *Luke* 4:7
but *t*. eat and drink? 15:30
all I have is *t*. 15:31
my will but *t*. be done. 22:42
t. they were. *John* 17:6
for they are *t*. 9
all mine are *t*. and *t*. are mine. 10

thing

the *t*. was very grievous. *Gen* 21:11
t. proceedeth from the Lord. 24:50
which *t*. ought not to be done. 34:7
 2 Sam 13:12
young man deferred not to do the *t*.
 Gen 34:19
and the *t*. which he did displeased.
 38:10; *2 Sam* 11:27
because the *t*. is established by.
 Gen 41:32
not any green *t*. in the. *Ex* 10:15
in the *t*. wherein they dealt. 18:11
Jethro said, The *t*. that thou. 17
for any manner of lost *t*. 22:9
if it be an hired *t*. it came for. 15
a terrible *t*. that I will do. 34:10
a *t*. most holy of your offerings.
 Lev 2:3, 10
and the *t*. be hid from the eyes. 4:13
trespass in a *t*. taken away. 6:2
t. deceitfully gotten, or the lost *t*. 4
she shall touch no hallowed *t*. 12:4
it is a wicked *t*.; they shall be. 20:17
but if the Lord make a new *t*., and
 the earth. *Num* 16:30
the *t*. which thou hast spoken is.
 Deut 1:14
what *t*. soever I command. 12:32
and the *t*. certain. 13:14; 17:4
if the *t*. follow not, nor. 18:22
it is not a vain *t*. for you; it is. 32:47

from the accursed *t.*   *Josh* 6:18
the *t.* pleased the children of. 22:33
which *t.* became a snare. *Judg* 8:27
do not so vile a *t.*   19:24
finished the *t.* to-day.   *Ruth* 3:18
I will do a *t.* in Israel. *1 Sam* 3:11
what is the *t.* that the Lord hath? 17
there hath not been such a *t.*   4:7
the *t.* displeased Samuel, when. 8:6
and we will shew you a *t.*   14:12
Saul, and the *t.* pleased him. 18:20
not take the *t.* to heart. *2 Sam* 13:33
hast thou thought such a *t.?*   14:13
hide not the *t.* that I shall ask.   18
what *t.* thou shalt hear, tell. 15:35
she spread corn, and the *t.*   17:19
the wife of Jeroboam cometh to ask
   a *t.* of thee.   *1 Ki* 14:5
Thou hast asked a hard *t.* *2 Ki* 2:10
in heaven, might such a *t.* be. 7:19
that the Lord will do the *t.*   20:9
t. was right in the eyes. *1 Chr* 13:4
let the *t.* thou hast spoken. 17:23
for the *t.* was done. *2 Chr* 29:36
the *t.* pleased the king and congregation.   30:4
hath put such a *t.* in. *Ezra* 7:27
the *t.* pleased the king and he did
   so.   *Esth* 2:4
the *t.* was known to Mordecai.   22
the *t.* pleased Haman, and he. 5:14
and if the *t.* seem right before.   8:5
the *t.* I greatly feared is. *Job* 3:25
now a *t.* was secretly brought. 4:12
God would grant me the *t.*   6:8
he as a rotten *t.* consumeth. 13:28
who can bring a clean *t.* out? 14:4
thou shalt decree a *t..* it shall. 22:28
he performeth the *t.* that is. 23:14
plentifully declared the.*t.?*   26:3
of me the *t.* that is right.   42:7, 8
people imagine a vain *t.?*   *Ps* 2:1
horse is a vain *t.* for safety. 33:17
because I follow the *t.* that. 38:20
nor alter the *t.* that is gone out. 89:34
I will set no wicked *t.* before. 101:3
wisdom is the principal *t.*   *Pr* 4:7
for it is a pleasant *t.* if thou. 22:18
glory of God to conceal a *t.*   ,25:2
t. that hath been, it is that which shall
   be, and there is no new *t. Eccl* 1:9
better is the end of a *t.* than.   7:8
the interpretation of a *t.?*   8:1
a man hath no better *t.* than to.   15
pleasant *t.* it is for the eyes to. 11:7
is it a small *t.* for you to? *Isa* 7:13
there is no green *t.*   15:6
rolling *t.* before the whirlwind. 17:13
shall the *t.* framed say of him? 29:16
that turn aside the just for a *t.*   21
the isles as a very little *t.*   40:15
and they shall be as a *t.* of. 41:12
I will do a new *t.*; now it shall. 43:19
prosper in the *t.* whereto. 55:11
who hath heard such a *t.?*   66:8
see if there be such a *t.*   *Jer* 2:10
a horrible *t.* is committed.   5:30
altars to that shameful *t.* 11:13
they prophesy unto you a *t.* 14:14
Israel hath done a horrible *t.* 18:13
in the prophets a horrible *t.* 23:14
Lord hath created a new *t.* in. 31:22
king said, I will ask thee a *t.* 38:14
that God may shew us the *t.*   42:3
that whatsoever *t.* the Lord.   4
we will do what *t.* goeth out. 44:17
what *t.* shall I take to witness for
   thee, what *t.* shall I?   *Lam* 2:13
he hath spoken a *t.*   *Ezek* 14:9
as if that were a very little *t.* 16:47
the king said, The *t.* is. *Dan* 2:5, 8
and it is a rare *t.* that the king.   11
Arioch made the *t.* known to.   15
Daniel made the *t.* known to.   17
the same hour was the *t.*   4:33
could not shew the interpretation of
   the *t.*   5:15
the interpretation of the *t.*: Mene. 26
t. is true, according to the law. 6:12
t. was revealed to Daniel; and *t.* was
   true: and he understood the *t.* 10:1
I have seen an horrible *t.*   *Hos* 6:10
were counted as a strange *t.*   8:12
ye which rejoice in a *t.*   *Amos* 6:13

to the Lord, a corrupt *t.*   *Mal* 1:14
what *t.* is this? what?   *Mark* 1:27
how or what *t.* ye shall. *Luke* 12:11
sin no more, lest a worse *t.* come.
          John 5:14
Herein is a marvellous *t.*   9:30
it is unlawful *t.* for man. *Acts* 10:28
tell or hear some new *t.*   17:21
they observe no such *t.*   21:25
for he hath a certain *t.* to tell. 23:17
of whom I have no certain *t.* 25:26
why should it be thought a *t.?* 26:8
which *t.* I also did in Jerusalem. 10
shall *t.* formed say to?   *Rom* 9:20
I beseech you that ye all speak the
   same *t.*   *1 Cor* 1:10
with me it is a very small *t.*   4:3
some eat it as a *t.* offered.   8:7
wrought us for the selfsame *t.* is
   God.   *2 Cor* 5:5
this selfsame *t.* that ye.   7:11
let us mind the same *t.*   *Phil* 3:16
seeing it is a righteous *t. 2 Thes* 1:6
covenant an unholy *t.*   *Heb* 10:29
a fearful *t.* to fall into the hands. 31
as though some strange *t.* *1 Pet* 4:12
which *t.* is true in him. *1 John* 2:8
doctrine of Nicolaitanes, which *t.* I
   hate.   *Rev* 2:15
see **accursed, great, holy, light,**
   one, small

any thing

I will not take *any t.* that. *Gen* 14:23
is *any t.* too hard for the?   18:14
cannot do *any t.* till thou be. 19:22
neither do thou *any t.* unto. 22:12
Thou shalt not give me *any t.* 30:31
nor hath he kept back *any t.* 39:9
he looked not to *any t.* under.   23
unto thee any likeness of *any t.*
   Ex 20:4; *Deut* 4:18, 23, 25; 5:8
nor *any t.* that is thy neighbour's.
     Ex 20:17; *Deut* 5:21
forgiven him for *any t.*   *Lev* 6:7
in *any t.* made of skin.   13:48, 49
         52, 53, 57, 59
that sitteth on *any t.*   15:6, 23
who toucheth *any t.* that was. 10, 22
ye shall not eat *any t.* with. 19:26
or that hath *any t.* superfluous.
        21:18, 22, 23
without doing *any t.* else. *Num* 20:19
any power at all to say *any t.?* 22:38
cast upon him *any t.*   35:22
hath been *any such t.*   *Deut* 4:32
thou shalt not lack *any t.* in.   8:9
not eat *any abominable t.*   14:3
ye shall not eat *any t.* that dieth. 21
nor shall there *any t.* of the. 16:4
usury of *any t.* that is lent. 23:19
lend thy brother *any t.*   24:10
have not known *any t.*   31:13
failed not aught of *any t. Josh* 21:45
art thou *any t.* better? *Judg* 11:25
put them to shame in *any t.* 18:7
a place where there is no want of *any
   t.*   10; 19:19
thee, if thou hide *any t. 1 Sam* 3:17
but Saul spake not *any t.*   20:26
but the lad knew not *any t.*   39
let no man know *any t.* of the. 21:2
let not the king impute *any t.* 22:15
neither missed we *any t.*   25:15
there was not lacking *any t.* 30:19
hard to do *any t.* to her. *2 Sam* 13:2
went in simplicity, they knew not *any
   t.*   15:11
there was not *any t.* hid. *1 Ki* 10:3
turned not aside from *any t.* 15:5
whether *any t.* would come. 20:33
hath not *any t.* save a.   *2 Ki* 4:2
hath dedicated *any t. 1 Chr* 26:28
silver was not *any t.*   *2 Chr* 9:20
that none unclean in *any t.* 23:19
is there *any secret t.?*   *Job* 15:11
if thou hast *any t.* to say. 33:32
shall not want *any good t. Ps* 34:10
my heart to *any evil t.*   141:4
any t. whereof it may be said.
        Eccl 1:10
nothing be put to it, nor *any t.* 3:14
heart not be hasty to utter *any t.* 5:2
dead know not *any t.* nor have. 9:5

is there *any t.* too hard? *Jer* 32:27
is not he that can do *any t.*   38:5
nor *any t.* for which he hath. 42:21
which speak *any t.* amiss. *Dan* 3:29
man nor beast taste *any t. Jonah* 3:7
agree touching *any t.*   *Mat* 18:19
to take *any t.* out of his house.
     24:17; *Mark* 13:15
nor was *any t.* kept secret.
     Mark 4:22; *Luke* 8:17
thou canst do *any t.* have. *Mark* 9:22
if haply he might find *any t.* 11:13
neither said they *any t.* to.   16:8
if I have taken *any t.*   *Luke* 19:8
lacked ye *any t.?* and they. 22:35
was not *any t.* made.   *John* 1:3
can there *any good t.* come?   46
no man that doeth *any t.* in.   7:4
if ye ask *any t.* in my name. 14:14
I have never eaten *any t. Acts* 10:14
as though he needed *any t.* 17:25
Caesar, have I offended *any t.* 25:8
committed *any t.* worthy of.   11
lay *any t.* to the charge? *Rom* 8:33
owe no man *any t.* but to love. 13:8
any t. whereby thy brother. 14:21
nor to know *any t.* save. *1 Cor* 2:2
neither is he that planteth *any t.* 3:7
think that he knoweth *any t.*   8:2
that the idol is *any t.*   10:19
if they will learn *any t.* let. 14:35
to whom ye forgive *any t.* I forgive,
   for if I forgive *any t.*   *2 Cor* 2:10
not sufficient to think *any t.* as. 3:5
giving no offence in *any t.* that. 6:3
for if I have boasted *any t.* to. 7:14
neither circumcision availeth *any t.*
         Gal 5:6
wrinkle, or *any such t.*   *Eph* 5:27
if in *any t.* ye be.   *Phil* 3:15
need not to speak *any t.* *1 Thes* 1:8
if there be *any other t.* *1 Tim* 1:10
that he shall receive *any t.* *Jas* 1:7
if we ask *any t.* according to his will.
       1 John 5:14
not hurt *any green t.*   *Rev* 9:4
in no wise enter *any t.* that. 21:27

every thing

every t. that is in the.   *Gen* 6:17
Noah and *every* living *t.*   8:1
every moving *t.* that liveth.   9:3
every t. whereon he sitteth, unclean.
        Lev 15:4
every t. she sitteth on shall.   20
ye shall offer *every t.* upon. 23:37
every devoted *t.* is most holy. 27:28
every t. devoted in Israel shall be.
     Num 18:14; *Ezek* 44:29
every t. that openeth the matrix be.
       Num 18:15
every t. that may abide fire. 31:23
from *every* wicked *t.*   *Deut* 23:9
the priests stood till *every t.* was.
       Josh 4:10
every t. that was vile. *1 Sam* 15:9
send unto me *every t. 2 Sam* 15:36
told *every t.* that had.   *Esth* 6:13
eye seeth *every* precious *t. Job* 28:10
searcheth after *every* green *t.* 39:8
that thou canst do *every t.*   42:2
let *every t.* that hath breath praise.
        Ps 150:6
every bitter *t.* is sweet.   *Pr* 27:7
to *every t.* there is a season. *Eccl* 3:1
hath made *every t.* beautiful in.   11
judgement with *every* secret *t.* 12:14
every t. sown by the brooks. *Isa* 19:7
every t. shall live where. *Ezek* 47:9
told *every t.* and what was befallen.
        Mat 8:33
in *every t.* ye are enriched. *1 Cor* 1:5
        2 Cor 9:11
as ye are bound in *every t.* in faith.
        2 Cor 8:7
and *every* high *t.* that exalteth. 10:5
their husbands in *every t. Eph* 5:24
in *every t.* by prayer and. *Phil* 4:6
in *every t.* give thanks. *1 Thes* 5:18
see **creepeth, creeping, evil,**
   good, living

that thing

hide from Abraham *that t. Gen* 18:17
and the Lord did *that t.*   *Ex* 9:6

he hath sinned in *that t.*   *Lev* 5:5
committed *that* wicked *t. Deut* 17:5
to tell no man *that t.*   *Luke* 9:21
if ye be not able to do *that t.* 12:26
not himself in *that t.*   *Rom* 14:22

this **thing**
thee concerning *this t.*   *Gen* 19:21
thou hast done *this t.*   20:10
hath done *this t.*; neither.   21:26
done *this t.* and not withhold. 22:16
if wilt do *this t.* I will again. 30:31
we cannot do *this t.* to give. 34:14
this is the *t.* I have spoken. 41:28
should do according to *this t.* 44:7
why have ye done *this t.*? *Ex* 1:18
Moses said, Surely *this t.*   2:14
Pharaoh heard *this t.*, he sought. 15
Lord shall do *this t.* in land.   9:5
observe *this t.* for an.   12:24
this is the *t.* which the Lord. 16:16
   32; 35:4; *Lev* 8:5; 9:6; 17:2
   Num 30:1; 36:6; *Deut* 15:15
              24:18, 22
what is *this t.* thou doest ? *Ex* 18:14
this t. is too heavy for thee.   18
if thou shalt do *this t.* and God.   23
this is the *t.* that thou shalt.   29:1
I will do *this t.* that thou.   33:17
if ye will do *this t.*, if ye. *Num* 32:20
this t. Lord doth command.   36:6
yet in *this t.* ye did not. *Deut* 1:32
for *this t.* the Lord thy God. 15:10
if *this t.* be true, and tokens. 22:20
through *this t.* ye shall prolong. 32:47
and have done *this t.*   *Josh* 9:24
done it for fear of *this t.*   22:24
Who hath done *this t.*? Gideon hath
   done *this t.*   *Judg* 6:29
let *this t.* be done for me, let. 11:37
this shall be the *t.* which we.   20:9
and *this* is the *t.* that ye.   21:11
my father hide *this t.* from me?
               1 Sam 20:2
that I should do *this t.*   24:6
this t. is not good that.   26:16
happen to thee for *this t.*   28:10
Lord hath done *this t.* unto thee. 18
ye have done *this t.*   *2 Sam* 2:6
liveth, I will not do *this t.*   11:11
say to Joab, Let not *this t.*   25
man that hath done *this t.*   12:5
because he did *this t.* and had.   6
but I will do *this t.* before all.   12
brother; regard not *this t.*   13:20
the king doth speak *this t.* as. 14:13
I am come to speak of *this t.*   15
thy servant Joab hath done *this t.* 20
why doth my lord the king delight in
   this t.?   24:3
is *this t.* done by my ?   *1 Ki* 1:27
Solomon had asked *this t.* 3:10, 11
him concerning *this t.*   11:10
return every man, for *this t.* 12:24
made two calves, and *this t.*   30
after *this t.* Jeroboam.   13:33
this t. became sin to the house.   34
tell my lord the king *this t.*   20:9
do *this t.*, take the kings away.   24
the Lord pardon in *this t.* 2 *Ki* 5:18
Syria was troubled for *this t.*   6:11
windows, might *this t.* be.   7:2
this is the *t.* that ye shall do. 11:5
              2 *Chr* 23:4
Ye shall not do *this t.*   *2 Ki* 17:12
God forbid that I should do *this t.*
              1 *Chr* 11:19
my lord require *this t.*?   21:3
was displeased with *this t.*   7
because I have done *this t.*   8
return every man, *this t.* 2 *Chr* 11:4
with him, because of *this t.*   16:10
when I heard *this t.* I rent. *Ezra* 9:3
Israel concerning *this t.*   10:2
have transgressed in *this t.*   13
what is *this t.* that ye do ? *Neh* 2:19
Lord will do *this t.* that.   *Isa* 38:7
but *this* is the *t.* that I command.
              Jer 7:23
if ye do *this t.* indeed, then.   22:4
therefore *this t.* is come upon. 40:3
Thou shalt not do *this t.*   16
oh do not *this* abominable *t.* 44:4
her that had done *this t.* *Mark* 5:32

and see *this t.* which is.   *Luke* 2:15
it was that should do *this t.*   22:23
sayest thou *this t.* of ? *John* 18:34
why hast thou conceived *this t.* in
   thine heart ?   *Acts* 5:4
for *this t.* was not done in a. 26:26
continually upon *this* very *t.*
              Rom 13:6
if I do *this t.* willingly, I. *1 Cor* 9:17
for *this t.* I besought.   2 *Cor* 12:8
being confident in *this* very *t.* that.
              Phil 1:6
but *this* one *t.* I do, I press.   3:13

unclean **thing**
if a soul touch any *unclean t.*
        Lev 5:2; 7:21
flesh that toucheth *unclean t.*   7:19
wife, it is an *unclean t.*   20:21
no *unclean t.* in thee.   *Deut* 23:14
and eat not any *unclean t.* *Judg* 13:4
              7, 14
touch no *unclean t.*   *Isa* 52:11
           2 *Cor* 6:17
we are all as an *unclean t. Isa* 64:6
any *t.* that is *unclean.*   *Acts* 10:14

things
with the good *t.* of Egypt. *Gen* 45:23
if a soul sin through ignorance concerning *t.*   *Lev* 4:2, 13, 22, 27
lest thou forget *t.* thine.   *Deut* 4:9
with all lost *t.* of thy brother's. 22:3
the secret *t.* belong unto the. 29:29
t. that shall come on them.   32:35
for the chief *t.* of the ancient. 33:15
took the *t.* which Micah. *Judg* 18:27
ye go after vain *t.*   *1 Sam* 12:21
people took the chief of the *t.* 15:21
I offer thee three *t.*   2 *Sam* 24:12
           1 *Chr* 21:10
Solomon brought in the *t. 1 Ki* 7:51
Asa brought in the *t.*   15:15
          2 *Chr* 15:18
wicked *t.* to provoke   2 *Ki* 17:11
and these are ancient *t. 1 Chr* 4:22
the office over *t.* that were.   9:31
t. of gold, silver for *t.* of silver, brass
   for *t.* of brass, iron for *t.*   29:2
and also in Judah *t.*   2 *Chr* 12:12
let *t.* for purification.   *Esth* 2:3, 12
who doth marvellous *t.*   *Job* 5:9
the *t.* that my soul refuseth.   6:7
my taste discern perverse *t.*?   30
he discovereth deep *t.* out of. 12:22
only do not two *t.* to me: then. 13:20
writest bitter *t.* against me.   26
he beholdeth all high *t.*   41:34
I have uttered *t.* too wonderful. 42:3
that speaketh proud *t.*   *Ps* 12:3
thine eyes behold the *t.*   17:2
speak grievous *t.* proudly.   31:18
they laid to my charge *t.* I.   35:11
hurt, speak mischievous *t.*   38:12
I speak of the *t.* which I.   45:1
hand shall teach thee terrible *t.*   4
shewed thy people hard *t.*   60:3
by terrible *t.* wilt thou answer. 65:5
who only doeth wondrous *t.* 72:18
marvellous *t.* did he in. 78:12; 98:1
and dost wondrous *t.*   86:10
glorious *t.* are spoken of thee. 87:3
utter and speak hard *t.*?   94:4
terrible *t.* by the Red sea. 106:22
himself to behold the *t.* that. 113:6
I may behold wondrous *t.* 119:18
great matters, or in *t.* too high. 131:1
that speaketh froward *t.*   *Pr* 2:12
of excellent *t.* . . . . shall be right. 8:6
eyes to devise froward *t.*   16:30
written to thee excellent *t.*   22:20
when thy lips speak right *t.*   23:16
heart shall utter perverse *t.*   33
two *t.* have I required of thee. 30:7
there are three *t.* that are never. 15
there be three *t.* that be too.   18
for three *t.* the earth is.   21
four *t.* which are little on the.   24
there be three *t.* which go well.   29
any remembrance of *t.*   *Eccl* 1:11
wisdom, and the reason of *t.*   7:25
he hath done excellent *t.*   *Isa* 12:5
thou hast done wonderful *t.*   25:1
unto all people a feast of fat *t.*   6
surely your turning of *t.*   29:16

prophesy not to us right *t. Isa* 30:10
liberal deviseth liberal *t.* and by
   liberal *t.* shall he stand.   32:8
shew the *t.* that are to come. 41:23
t. come to pass, and new *t.*   42:9
I will make crooked *t.* straight.   16
the *t.* that are coming and.   44:7
of *t.* to come concerning my. 45:11
I the Lord speak, I declare *t.*   19
thee new *t.*, even hidden *t.*   48:6
the eunuchs that choose the *t.* 56:4
when thou didst terrible *t.*   64:3
and all our pleasant *t.* are laid.   11
broth of abominable *t.* is in.   65:4
walked after *t.* that do not profit.
          Jer 2:8; 16:19
the *t.* I have given them shall. 8:13
shall eat them as common *t.*   31:5
Jerusalem remembered her pleasant
   t.   *Lam* 1:7
they have given her pleasant *t.*   11
prophets have seen foolish *t.*   2:14
I know the *t.* that come. *Ezek* 11:5
like *t.* shall not come, neither. 16:10
at the same time shall *t.*   38:10
the deep and secret *t.*   *Dan* 2:22
shall speak marvellous *t.*   11:36
your temples my goodly *t. Joel* 3:5
t. of Esau searched out! how are
   his hidden *t.* sought up!   *Ob* 6
unto him marvellous *t.*   *Mi* 7:15
who hath despised the day of small
   t.?   *Zech* 4:10
thought for *t.* of itself.   *Mat* 6:34
bringeth out of his treasure *t.* 13:52
savourest not *t.* that be of God.
         16:23; *Mark* 8:33
to Caesar the *t.* that are Caesar's, and
   to God the *t.* that are God's.
Mat 22:21; *Mark* 12:17; *Luke* 20:25
lusts of other *t.*   *Mark* 4:19
but the *t.* which come out of.   7:15
seen strange *t.* to-day.   *Luke* 5:26
call me Lord, and do not the *t.* 6:46
the eyes which see the *t.*   10:23
in the abundance of the *t.* he. 12:15
and did commit *t.* worthy of.   48
the *t.* which are impossible. 18:27
hadst known the *t.* which.   19:42
for the *t.* concerning me   22:37
all people beholding the *t.*   23:48
hast not known the *t.* which. 24:18
he expounded the *t.* concerning. 27
thou shalt see greater *t.*   *John* 1:50
told you earthly *t.*, heavenly *t.*? 3:12
the Spirit will shew you *t.*   16:13
speaking of *t.* pertaining.   *Acts* 1:3
we cannot but speak the *t.*   4:20
the people imagine vain *t.*?   25
that aught of the *t.* he possessed. 32
preaching the *t.* concerning.   8:12
abstain from *t.* strangled. 15:20, 29
she attended to the *t.* spoken. 16:14
Apollos taught diligently the *t.* 18:25
persuading *t.* concerning the.   19:8
not knowing the *t.* that shall. 20:22
arise, speaking perverse *t.* to.   30
that they keep from *t.* offered. 21:25
neither can they prove the *t.* 24:13
saying none other *t.* than the. 26:22
some believed the *t.* that were. 28:24
invisible *t.* of him are clearly seen,
   being understood by *t. Rom* 1:20
judgest, doest the same *t.*   2:1
Gentiles do by nature *t.* contained. 14
and approvest the *t.* that are.   18
mind the *t.* of the flesh, mind *t.* 8:5
nor *t.* present, nor *t.* to come.   38
           1 *Cor* 3:22
mind not high *t.*   *Rom* 12:16
provide *t.* honest.   17
follow after *t.* that make for. 14:19
whatsoever *t.* were written.   15:4
partakers of spiritual *t.*, their duty is
   to minister to them in carnal *t.* 27
foolish *t.* of the world, weak *t.* to confound *t.* which are.   *1 Cor* 1:27
base *t.* and *t.* despised hath.   28
the *t.* which God hath prepared. 2:9
the Spirit searcheth the deep *t.*   10
knoweth the *t.* of a man, even so the
   t. of God knoweth no man.   11
we might know the *t.* that are.   12
t. we speak, comparing spiritual *t.* 13

man receiveth not the *t.* of. *1 Cor* 2:14
will bring to light the hidden *t.* 4:5
much more *t.* shall pertain to. 6:3, 4
careth for the *t.* of the Lord. 7:32, 34
married careth for the *t.* that are. 33
as touching *t.* offered to idols. 8:1
sown spiritual *t.* if reap carnal *t.* 9:11
the *t.* which the Gentiles. 10:20
a man, I put away childish *t.* 13:11
and even *t.* without life giving. 14:7
acknowledge that the *t.* that. 37
let all your *t.* be done with. 16:14
write none other *t.* unto. *2 Cor* 1:13
or the *t.* that I purpose, do I. 17
but have renounced the hidden *t.* 4:2
the *t.* which are seen, *t.* seen are
temporal, *t.* not seen are. 18
every one may receive the *t.* 5:10
old *t.* are passed away, all *t.* are. 17
providing for honest *t.*, not only. 8:21
do ye look on *t.* after the? 10:7
we will not boast of *t.* without. 13, 15
boast in another man's line of *t.* 16
I will glory of the *t.* which. 11:30
if I build again the *t.* *Gal* 2:18
which *t.* are an allegory, for. 4:24
so that ye cannot do the *t.* 5:17
and, ye masters, do the same *t.* unto.
Eph 6:9
that ye may approve *t.* that. *Phil* 1:10
the *t.* which happened unto me. 12
look not on his own *t.*, but every man
also on the *t.* of others. 2:4
of *t.* in heaven, *t.* in earth, *t.* 10
not the *t.* which are Jesus Christ's. 21
to write the same *t.* 3:1
who mind earthly *t.* 19
whatsoever *t.* are true, honest. 4:8
having received the *t.* sent from. 18
t. in earth, or *t.* in heaven. *Col* 1:20
which are a shadow of *t.* unto.
2:17; *Heb* 10:1
t. have indeed a shew of. *Col* 2:23
affection on *t.* above, not on *t.* 3:2
for which *t.'s* sake the wrath of. 6
suffered like *t.* of your. *1 Thes* 2:14
and will do the *t.* which. *2 Thes* 3:4
speaking *t.* which they. *1 Tim* 5:13
the *t.* which thou hast. *2 Tim* 2:2
continue in *t.* which thou. 3:14
set in order the *t.* wanting. *Tit* 1:5
teaching *t.* they ought not for. 11
speak thou the *t.* which become. 2:1
give heed to the *t.* which. *Heb* 2:1
be faithful high priest in *t.* pertaining
to God. 17; 5:1
learned he obedience by the *t.* 5:8
persuaded better *t.* of you, and *t.*
that accompany salvation. 6:9
that by two immutable *t.*, in which. 18
of the *t.* we have spoken this. 8:1
shadow of heavenly *t.* 5
patterns of *t.* in the heavens be purified, but heavenly *t.* with. 9:23
now faith is the substance of *t.* hoped
for, the evidence of *t.* not. 11:1
t. seen were not made of *t.* which. 3
Noah being warned of God of *t.* 7
Esau concerning *t.* to come. 20
that speaketh better *t.* than. 12:24
and *t.* in the sea are tamed. *Jas* 3:7
minister *t.* which are now reported;
which *t.* the angels. *1 Pet* 1:12
redeemed with corruptible *t.* 18
speak evil of the *t.* they. *2 Pet* 2:12
neither the *t.* that are. *1 John* 2:15
Jesus Christ to shew to his servants
t. which must shortly. *Rev* 1:1; 22:6
t. which thou hast seen, the *t.* which
are, and *t.* which shall be. 1:19
a few *t.* against thee, . . . to eat *t.*
sacrificed unto idols. 2:14, 20
strengthen the *t.* which remain. 3:2
I will shew thee *t.* which must. 4:1
who created heaven, earth, sea, and
all *t.* that therein are. 10:6
former *t.* are passed away. 21:4
take his part from *t.* written. 22:19
see **creeping, dedicate, detestable, evil, former, holy, many,
precious, such**

all **things**
herb have I given you *all t. Gen* 9:3

blessed Abraham in *all t. Gen* 24:1
the servant told Isaac *all t.* that. 66
in *all t.* I have said. *Ex* 23:13
do according to *all t.* which I. 29:35
Aaron and his sons did *all t. Lev* 8:36
the Levites over *all t. Num* 1:50
and purify *all t.* made of. 31:20
I commanded you *all t. Deut* 1:18
as the Lord our God is in *all t.* 4:7
ye shall not do after *all t.* that. 12:8
for the abundance of *all t.* 28:47
thine enemies in want of *all t.* 48
want of *all t.* secretly in siege. 57
we hearkened to Moses in *all t.*
Josh 1:17
the spies told him *all t.* that. 2:23
manner, to confirm *all t. Ruth* 4:7
perform *all t.* concerning. *1 Sam* 3:12
if thou hide any of *all t.* he said. 18
shewed David *all* those *t.* 19:7
told David *all* the *t.* *2 Sam* 11:18
to know *all t.* that are in. 14:20
covenant ordered in *all t.* 23:5
he did *all t.* as did the. *1 Ki* 21:26
captains did according to *all t.* that
Jehoiada. *2 Ki* 11:9; *2 Chr* 23:8
Amaziah, according to *all t.* that.
2 Ki 14:3
they have seen *all t.* that are. 20:15
all t. come of thee. *1 Chr* 29:14
Solomon brought *all t.* *2 Chr* 5:1
tithe of *all t.* brought they in. 31:5
the Lord made *all t.* *Neh* 9:6
Acts 14:15; 17:24, 25; *Col* 1:16
Rev 4:11
he beholdeth *all* high *t.* *Job* 41:34
thou hast put *all t.* under his feet.
Ps 8:6; *1 Cor* 15:27; *Eph* 1:22
that performeth *all t.* for me. *Ps* 57:2
precepts concerning *all t.* to. 119:128
precious than *all t.* *Pr* 3:15; 8:11
the Lord hath made *all t.* for. 16:4
great God that formed *all t.* 26:10
seek the Lord understand *all t.* 28:5
all t. are full of labour. *Eccl* 1:8
all t. have I seen in days. 7:15
all t. come alike to all, there. 9:2
this is an evil among *all t.* done. 3
but money answereth *all t.* 10:19
I am the Lord that maketh *all t.*
Isa 44:24; 66:2
for he is the former of *all t.*
Jer 10:16; 51:19
heart is deceitful above *all t.* 17:9
do not even according to *all t.* 42:5
we wanted *all t.* and have. 44:18
I spake *all t.* the Lord. *Ezek* 11:25
all creeping *t.* shall shake. 38:20
the first of *all t.* shall be. 44:30
as iron subdueth *all t.* *Dan* 2:40
I will consume *all t.* *Zeph* 1:2
all t. ye would that men. *Mat* 7:12
all t. are delivered unto me of my
Father. 11:27; *Luke* 10:22
they shall gather *all t.* *Mat* 13:41
Elias shall restore *all t.* 17:11
Mark 9:12
is impossible, but with God *all t.* are.
Mat 19:26; *Mark* 10:27; 14:36
all t. whatsoever ye shall. *Mat* 21:22
behold *all t.* are ready, come unto the
marriage. · *Mat* 22:4; *Luke* 14:17
sweareth by it, and by *all t.* thereon.
Mat 23:20
teaching them to observe *all t.* 28:20
he expounded *all t.* to. *Mark* 4:34
told him *all t.*, both what they. 6:30
He hath done *all t.* well. 7:37
all t. are possible to him. 10:27
I have foretold you *all t.* 13:23
praising God for *all t.* *Luke* 2:20
performed *all t.* according to. 39
they wondered at *all t.* which. 9:43
and behold, *all t.* are clean. 11:41
all t. written concerning Son. 18:31
21:22; *Acts* 24:14
all t. were made by him. *John* 1:3
and hath given *all t.* 3:35; 13:3
is come, he will tell us *all t.* 4:25
see a man who told me *all t.* 29
Father sheweth the Son *all t.* 5:20
all t. that John spake of him. 10:41
Holy Ghost, he shall teach you *all t.*
and bring *all t.* to your. 14:26

all t. I have heard, I have. *John* 15:15
all t. that the Father hath. 16:15
sure that thou knowest *all t.* 30
that *all t.* thou hast given me. 17:7
Jesus therefore knowing *all t.*
18:4; 19:28
Lord, thou knowest *all t.* 21:17
had *all t.* common. *Acts* 2:44; 4:32
of restitution of *all t.* 3:21
him shall ye hear in *all t.* he shall. 22
to hear *all t.* commanded. 10:33
we are witnesses of *all t.* 39
are justified from *all t.* 13:39
heaven, earth, sea, and *all t.* 14:15
you *all t.* how ye ought. 20:35
it shall be told thee of *all t.* 22:10
believing *all t.* which are. 24:14
touching *all* the *t.* whereof. 26:2
and we know that *all t.* *Rom* 8:28
also freely give us *all t.*? 32
him, and to him, are *all t.* 11:36
that he may eat *all t.* 14:2
all t. indeed are pure, but it is. 20
Spirit searcheth *all t.* *1 Cor* 2:10
he that is spiritual judgeth *all t.* 15
no man glory in men, for *all t.* 3:21
are the offscouring of *all t.* 4:13
all t. are lawful unto me, but *all t.* are
. . . *all t.* are lawful. 6:12; 10:23
of whom are *all t.*; and one Lord
Jesus Christ, by whom are *all t.* 8:6
suffer *all t.* 9:12
I am made *all t.* to all men. 22
that striveth is temperate in *all t.* 25
as I please all men in *all t.* 10:33
that ye remember me in *all t.* 11:2
but *all t.* are of God. 12; *2 Cor* 5:18
charity beareth *all t.*, believeth *all t.*,
hopeth *all t.*, endureth *all t.*
1 Cor 13:7
let *all t.* be done unto edifying. 14:26
let *all t.* be done decently. 40
all t. shall be subdued, then shall the
Son be subject . . . *all t.* 15:28
ye be obedient in *all t.* *2 Cor* 2:9
for *all t.* are for your sakes. 4:15
old things are passed away; behold
all t. are. 5:17
in *all t.* approving ourselves. 6:4
nothing, yet possessing *all t.* 10
in *all t.* ye have approved. · 7:11
but as we speak *all t.* to you. 14
confidence in you in *all t.* 16
all sufficiency in *all t.* 9:8
made manifest to you in *all t.* 11:6
in *all t.* I kept myself from being. 9
but we do *all t.* for your. 12:19
continueth not in *all t.* *Gal* 3:10
in one *all t.* in Christ. *Eph* 1:10
worketh *all t.* after the counsel. 11
gave him to be head over *all t.* 22
in God, who created *all t.* by. 3:9
up, that he might fill *all t.* 4:10
grow up into him in *all t.* which. 15
all t. that are reproved are. 5:13
giving thanks always for *all t.* 20
shall make known to you *all t.* 6:21
Col 4:9
do *all t.* without murmurings.
Phil 2:14
I count *all t.* but loss for knowledge
of Christ . . . loss of *all t.* 3:8
he is able even to subdue *all t.* to. 21
and in *all t.* I am instructed. 4:12
I can do *all t.* through Christ. 13
is before *all t.*, by him *all t.* *Col* 1:17
in *all t.* he might have the. 18
and by him to reconcile *all t.* 20
obey your parents in *all t.* 3:20
obey in *all t.* your masters. 22
prove *all t.*; hold fast. *1 Thes* 5:21
must be faithful in *all t.* *1 Tim* 3:11
is profitable unto *all t.* 4:8
of God who quickeneth *all t.* 6:13
who giveth us richly *all t.* to enjoy. 17
understanding in *all t.* *2 Tim* 2:7
endure *all t.* for the elect's sake. 10
but watch thou in *all t.*, endure. 4:5
unto pure *all t.* are pure. *Tit* 1:15
all t. shewing thyself a pattern. 2:7
and please them well in *all t.* 9
the doctrine of God in *all t.* 10
appointed heir of *all t.* *Heb* 1:2
upholding *all t.* by the word of. 3

put *all t.* in subjection under his feet;
but now we see not yet *all t. Heb* 2:8
are *all t.* and by whom are *all t.* 10
in *all t.* it behoved him to be like. 17
he that built *all t.* is God. 3:4
all t. are naked and opened. 4:13
make *all t.* according to the. 8:5
almost *all t.* are by the law. 9:22
in *all t.* willing to live. 13:18
above *all t.* my brethren. *Jas* 5:12
the end of *all t.* is at hand. *1 Pet* 4:7
above *all t.* have fervent charity. 8
God in *all t.* may be glorified. 11
hath given us *all t.* that. *2 Pet* 1:3
all t. continue as they were. 3:4
ye have an unction, and ye know *all t.*
1 John 2:20
anointing teacheth you *all t.* 27
heart, and knoweth *all t.* 3:20
I wish above *all t.* that. *3 John* 2
who bare record of *all t. Rev* 1:2
thou hast created *all t.* and. 4:11
I make *all t.* new. 21:5
he shall inherit *all t.* 7

these things
them of her mother's house *these t.*
Gen 24:28
Jacob said, All *these t.* are. 42:36
he shall be guilty in one of *these t.*
Lev 5:5, 17
yourselves in any of *these t.* 18:24
committed all *these t.* 20:23
not be reformed by *these t.* 26:23
these t. are the burden of sons of.
Num 4:15
of the country shall do *these t.* 15:13
these t. ye shall do to Lord. 29:39
these t. shall be for a statute. 35:29
when all *these t.* are. *Deut* 4:30
all that do *these t.* are an. 18:12
when all *these t.* are come. 30:1
as we heard *these t.*, our. *Josh* 2:11
have shewed us *these t. Judg* 13:23
had told him *these t.* *1 Sam* 25:37
these t. did these three mighty.
2 Sam 23:17; *1 Chr* 11:19
these t. did Benaiah. *2 Sam* 23:22
1 Chr 11:24
these t. did Araunah. *2 Sam* 24:23
I have done all *these t.* *1 Ki* 18:36
proclaimed *these t.* *2 Ki* 23:17
in *these t.* was Solomon. *2 Chr* 3:3
Solomon sin by *these t.? Neh* 13:26
wilt thou speak *these t.? Job* 8:2
these t. hast thou hid in. 10:13
lo, all *these t.* worketh God. 33:29
he that doeth *these t. Ps* 15:5
I remember *these t.*, I pour. 42:4
these t. hast thou done and. 50:21
these six *t.* doth the Lord. *Pr* 6:16
these t. also belong to wise. 24:23
for *these t.* God will bring. *Eccl* 11:9
O Lord, by *these t.* men live, and in
all *these t.* is the life. *Isa* 38:16
who hath created *these t.?* 40:26
these t. will I do, and not. 42:16
I the Lord do all *these t.* 45:7
not lay *these t.* to heart. 47:7
these two *t.* shall come to thee. 9
save thee from *these t.* 13
them hath declared *these t.* 48:14
these two *t.* are come unto. 51:19
refrain thyself for *these t.?* 64:12
she had done all *these t. Jer* 3:7
procured *these t.* unto thee. 4:18
shall I not visit for *these t.?* 5:9
29; 9:9
have turned away *these t.* 5:25
for in *these t.* do I delight. 9:24
come *these t.* on me? 13:22
thou hast made all *these t.* 14:22
thy sins I have done *these t.* 30:15
for *these t.* I weep, mine. *Lam* 1:16
our heart is faint; for *these t.* 5:17
seeing thou doest all *these t.*
Ezek 16:30; 17:18
hast fretted me in all *these t.* 16:43
know ye not what *these t.?* 17:12
like to any one of *these t.* 18:10
I will do *these t.* unto thee. 23:30
thou not tell what *these t.?* 24:19
none that holdeth with me in *these t.*
Dan 10:21

all *these t.* shall be finished. *Dan* 12:7
what shall be the end of *these t.?* 8
shall understand *these t. Hos* 14:9
these are the *t.* which ye shall do.
Zech 8:16
for all *these* are *t.* that I hate. 17
he thought on *these t. Mat* 1:20
when Herod heard *these t.* 2:3
these t. do the Gentiles seek . . . all
these t. 6:32; *Luke* 12:30
all *these t.* shall be added unto you.
Mat 6:33; *Luke* 12:31
hast hid *these t.* from the wise.
Mat 11:25; *Luke* 10:21
ye understood *these t.? Mat* 13:51
hath this man *these t.?* 56; *Mark* 6:2
these are the *t.* which defile a man.
Mat 15:20
all *these t.* have I kept from. 19:20
by what authority doest thou *these t.?*
21:23; *Mark* 11:28; *Luke* 20:2
authority I do *these t. Mat* 21:24
27; *Mark* 11:29, 33; *Luke* 20:8
all *these t.* shall come on. *Mat* 23:36
See ye not all *these t.?* 24:2
when shall *these t.* be? 3
Mark 13:4; *Luke* 21:7
all *these t.* must come to pass.
Mat 24:6; *Luke* 21:9, 28
ye shall see all *these t. Mat* 24:33
Mark 13:29; *Luke* 21:31
till all *these t.* be fulfilled.
Mat 24:34; *Mark* 13:30
till the day that *these t. Luke* 1:20
but Mary kept all *these t.* and. 2:19
not answer him to *these t.* 14:6
asked what *these t.* meant. 15:26
understood none of *these t.* 18:34
to escape all *these t.* that. 21:36
do *these t.* in a green tree. 23:31
is third day since *these t.* 24:21
Christ to have suffered *these t.?* 26
and ye are witnesses of *these t.* 48
Take *these t.* hence. *John* 2:16
seeing that thou doest *these t.* 18
to him, How can *these t.* be? 3:9
Israel, and knowest not *these t.?* 10
he had done *these t.* on the. 5:16
if thou do *these t.* shew thyself. 7:4
these t. understood not his disciples,
they . . . had *these t.* were. 12:16
these t. said Esaias, when he. 41
if ye know *these t.* happy. 13:17
all *these t.* will they do. 15:21; 16:3
these t. therefore the soldiers. 19:24
these t. were done, that the. 36
his witnesses of *these t. Acts* 5:32
are *these t.* so? 7:1
my hand made all *these t.?* 50
when they heard *these t.* they. 54
pray for me, that none of *these t.*
8:24
sirs, why do ye *these t.?* 14:15
Lord, who doeth all *these t.* 15:17
know what *these t.* mean. 17:20
seeing *these t.* cannot be. 19:36
none of *these t.* move me. 20:24
saying that *these t.* were so. 24:9
and there be judged of *these t.* 25:9
thee a witness of *these t.* 26:16
the king knoweth of *these t.* 26
then say to *these t.? Rom* 8:31
for he that in *these t.* serveth. 14:18
say I *these t.* as a man. *1 Cor* 9:8
I used none of *these t.* nor have. 15
these t. were our examples. 10:6
sufficient for *these t.? 2 Cor* 2:16
because of *these t.* cometh. *Eph* 5:6
praise, think on *these t. Phil* 4:8
and above all *these t.* put. *Col* 3:14
in remembrance of *these t.1 Tim* 4:6
these t. command. 11
meditate on *these t.* 15
these t. give in charge. 5:7
observe *these t.* 21
these t. exhort. 6:2; *Tit* 2:15
flee *these t.* *1 Tim* 6:11
of *these t.* put them. *2 Tim* 2:14
these t. I will that thou affirm constantly. *These t.* are good. *Tit* 3:8
for he of whom *these t.* are spoken.
Heb 7:13
brethren, *these t.* ought not. *Jas* 3:10
for if *these t.* be in you. *2 Pet* 1:8

he that lacketh *these t.* is. *2 Pet* 1:9
for if ye do *these t.* ye shall. 10
in remembrance of *these t.* 12
to have *these t.* always in. 15
seeing all *these t.* shall be. 3:11
speaking in them of *these t.* 16
seeing ye know *these t.* before. 17
angel who shewed me *these t.*
Rev 22:8
to testify to you *these t.* in the. 16
he which testifieth *these t.* 20

those **things**
eat *those t.* wherewith. *Ex* 29:33
in *those t.* which they. *Lev* 22:2
those t. which are revealed.
Deut 29:29
did secretly *those t.* *2 Ki* 17:9
will observe *those t.* *Ps* 107:43
for all *those t.* hath mine hand made,
and all *those t.* have. *Isa* 66:2
approach to *those t. Ezek* 42:14
those t. which ye see, and hear *those
t.* *Mat* 13:17; *Luke* 10:24
offer *those t.* which Moses commanded. *Mark* 1:44
a performance of *those t. Luke* 1:45
wondered at *those t.* told them. 2:18
then whose shall *those t.* be, which
thou hast provided? 12:20
I do always *those t.* *John* 8:29
but *those t.* he hath so fulfilled.
Acts 3:18
gave heed to *those t.* which. 8:6
spake against *those t.* which. 13:45
searched whether *those t.* 17:11
cared for none of *those t.* 18:17
of *those t.* in which I will appear.
26:16
those t. spoken by Paul. 27:11
to do *those t.* which are. *Rom* 1:28
calleth *those t.* which be not. 4:17
in *those t.* whereof ye are now
ashamed, for end of *those t.* 6:21
the man that doeth *those t.* 10:5
I may glory in *those t.* which. 15:17
to speak of any of *those t.* 18
eating of *those t.* *1 Cor* 8:4, 10
besides *those t.* which. *2 Cor* 11:28
even to speak of *those t. Eph* 5:12
forgetting *those t.* which are behind,
and reaching to *those t. Phil* 3:13
those t. which ye have learned. 4:9
intruding into *those t.* he. *Col* 2:18
seek *those t.* which are above. 3:1
for a testimony of *those t. Heb* 3:5
the removing of *those t.* which are
shaken, that *those t.* which. 12:27
ye give not *those t.* which. *Jas* 2:16
do *those t.* that are pleasing in his.
1 John 3:22
we lose not *those t.* we. *2 John* 8
but speak evil of *those t.* *Jude* 10
they that keep *those t.* *Rev* 1:3
fear none of *those t.* which. 2:10
those t. the seven thunders. 10:4
were judged out of *those t.* 20:12

unclean **things**
and they shall eat *unclean t. Hos* 9:3

what **things**
tell thy son *what t.* I have. *Ex* 10:2
Father knoweth *what t.* ye. *Mat* 6:8
should tell no man *what t. Mark* 9:9
began to tell them *what t.* 10:32
what t. soever ye desire. 11:24
go, tell John *what t.* ye. *Luke* 7:22
what t. they said to him. 24:19
and they told *what t.* were done. 35
what t. soever he doeth. *John* 5:19
they understood not *what t.* 10:6
some told them *what t.* Jesus. 11:46
what t. God wrought. *Acts* 21:19
what t. were gain to me. *Phil* 3:7

think
but *t.* on me, when it be. *Gen* 40:14
let them marry to whom they *t.* best.
Num 36:6
to *t.* that all the king's. *2 Sam* 13:33
ye *t.* to withstand kingdom of Lord.
2 Chr 13:8
t. on me, my God, for. *Neh* 5:19
thou and the Jews *t.* to rebel. 6:6
my God, *t.* thou on Tobiah and. 14
t. not thou shalt escape. *Esth* 4:13

why then should I *t*. upon ? *Job* 31:1
t. the deep to be hoary. 41:32
wise man *t*. to know it. *Eccl* 8:17
nor doth his heart *t*. so. *Isa* 10:7
t. to cause my people. *Jer* 23:27
I know the thoughts that I *t*. 29:11
and thou shalt *t*. an evil. *Ezek* 38:10
he shall *t*. to change times. *Dan* 7:25
if so be that God will *t*. *Jonah* 1:6
if ye *t*. good, give me. *Zech* 11:12
and *t*. not to say within. *Mat* 3:9
t. not that I am come to destroy. 5:17
t. they shall be heard for much. 6:7
why *t*. ye evil in your hearts ? 9:4
t. not I am come to send. 10:34
how *t*. ye ? if a man have. 18:12
what *t*. ye ? a certain man had. 21:28
what *t*. ye of Christ ? 22:42; 26:66
Mark 14:64
in such an hour as ye *t*. not.
Mat 24:44; *Luke* 12:40
t. ye that they were sinners above.
Luke 13:4
them ye *t*. ye have eternal. *John* 5:39
do not *t*. I will accuse you to. 45
what *t*. ye, that he will not ? 11:56
killeth you will *t*. that he doeth. 16:2
whom *t*. ye that I am ? *Acts* 13:25
not to *t*. that the Godhead. 17:29
t. myself happy, king Agrippa. 26:2
not to *t*. of himself more highly than
he ought to *t*., but to *t*. *Rom* 12:3
in us not to *t*. of men. *1 Cor* 4:6
I *t*. that God hath set forth us. 9
if any man *t*. that he behaveth. 7:36
I *t*. also that I have the Spirit. 40
if any man *t*. that he knoweth. 8:2
of body, which we *t*. to be less. 12:23
if any man *t*. himself to be a. 14:37
ourselves to *t*. any thing. *2 Cor* 3:5
I *t*. to be bold against some, which *t*.
of us as if we walked. 10:2
that he is Christ, let him *t*. 7, 11
I say again, Let no man *t*. me. 11:16
lest any *t*. of me above what. 12:6
if a man *t*. himself to be. *Gal* 6:3
above all that we ask or *t*. *Eph* 3:20
if there be any praise, *t*. *Phil* 4:8
let not that man *t*. he shall. *Jas* 1:7
do ye *t*. that the scripture ? 4:5
wherein they *t*. strange. *1 Pet* 4:4
t. it not strange concerning the. 12
I *t*. it meet as long as I am in this.
2 Pet 1:13

thinkest
t. thou that David doth honour thy ?
2 Sam 10:3; *1 Chr* 19:3
t. thou this right, that ? *Job* 35:2
Jesus said, What *t*. thou ?
Mat 17:25; 22:17
t. thou that I cannot pray ? 26:53
which *t*. thou was neighbour to ?
Luke 10:36
hear of thee what thou *t*. *Acts* 28:22
t. thou this, O man, that ? *Rom* 2:3

thinketh
me *t*. the running of the. *2 Sam* 18:27
yet the Lord *t*. on me. *Ps* 40:17
for as he *t*. in his heart. *Pr* 23:7
let him that *t*. he standeth, take heed.
1 Cor 10:12
seeketh not her own, *t*. no evil. 13:5
man *t*. he hath whereof. *Phil* 3:4

thinking
t. to have brought good. *2 Sam* 4:10
t., David cannot come in hither. 5:6

third
he the second and the *t*. *Gen* 32:19
saw Ephraim's children of *t*. 50:23
to *t*. and fourth generation. *Ex* 20:5
34:7; *Num* 14:18; *Deut* 5:9
and the *t*. row a ligure, an agate.
Ex 28:19; 39:12
Ephraim in the *t*. rank. *Num* 2:24
Edomite shall enter in *t*. *Deut* 23:8
the *t*. lot came up for. *Josh* 19:10
a captain of the *t*. fifty. *2 Ki* 1:13
the *t*. lot came forth to. *1 Chr* 24:8
t. lot came forth for Zaccur. 25:10
t. captain of the host for the *t*. 27:5
shall Israel be the *t*. with. *Isa* 19:24
t. was the face of a lion. *Ezek* 10:14
and another *t*. kingdom. *Dan* 2:39

t. ruler in kingdom. *Dan* 5:7; 16:29
t. chariot white horses. *Zech* 6:3
out about the *t*. hour. *Mat* 20:3
likewise the second also, and the *t*.
22:26; *Mark* 12:21; *Luke* 20:31
it was *t*. hour, and they. *Mark* 15:25
come in the *t*. watch. *Luke* 12:38
he sent a *t*. and they. 20:12
it is but the *t*. hour of the. *Acts* 2:15
fell down from the *t*. loft. 20:9
be ready at the *t*. hour of. 23:23
up to the *t*. heaven. *2 Cor* 12:2
the *t*. beast had a face as a. *Rev* 4:7
the *t*. seal, I heard the *t*. beast. 6:5
the *t*. angel sounded, there fell. 8:10
and behold, the *t*. woe cometh. 11:14
and the *t*. angel followed them. 14:9
the *t*. angel poured out his vial. 16:4
the *t*. foundation was a. 21:19
see **day, month, part**

third *time*
Samuel the *t*. time. *1 Sam* 3:8
messengers again the *t*. time. 19:21
do it the *t*. time. And they did it
the *t*. time. *1 Ki* 18:34
be doubled the *t*. time. *Ezek* 21:14
and he prayed the *t*. time.
Mat 26:44; *Mark* 14:41
t. time Jesus shewed. *John* 21:14
t. time, Lovest thou me ? Peter was
grieved . . . to him *t*. time. 17
the *t*. time I am ready to come.
2 Cor 12:14; 13:1

third *year*
t. year, which is the year. *Deut* 16:12
in *t*. year of Asa, did Baasha slay.
1 Ki 15:28, 33
Lord came to Elijah in *t*. year. 18:1
in *t*. year, Jehoshaphat came to. 22:2
in the *t*. year of Hoshea. *2 Ki* 18:1
in the *t*. year sow ye and reap.
19:29; *Isa* 37:30
in *t*. year of Jehoshaphat's reign.
2 Chr 17:7
paid the second and *t*. year. 27:5
t. year of the reign of Ahasuerus.
Esth 1:3
t. year of the reign of Jehoiakim.
Dan 1:1
t. year of the reign of Belshazzar. 8:1
t. year of Cyrus king of Persia. 10:1

thirdly
t. teachers, after that. *1 Cor* 12:28

thirst, *substantive*
our children with *t*. *Ex* 17:3
serve thine enemies in *t*. *Deut* 28:48
to add drunkenness to *t*. 29:19*
shall die for *t*. and fall. *Judg* 15:18
you to die by *t*. *2 Chr* 32:11
water for their *t*. *Neh* 9:15, 20
winepresses and suffer *t*. *Job* 24:11
in my *t*. they gave me. *Ps* 69:21
wild asses quench their *t*. 104:11
multitude dried up with *t*. *Isa* 5:13
their tongue faileth for *t*. 41:17
fish stinketh, and dieth for *t*. 50:2
thy throat from *t*. *Jer* 2:25
from thy glory, and sit in *t*. 48:18
roof of his mouth for *t*. *Lam* 4:4
naked, and slay her with *t*. *Hos* 2:3
not a *t*. for water, but of. *Amos* 8:11
young men shall faint for *t*. 13
in hunger and *t*. *2 Cor* 11:27

thirst, *verb*
they shall not hunger nor *t*. *Isa* 49:10
which hunger and *t*. after. *Mat* 5:6
this water, shall *t*. again. *John* 4:13
drinketh, shall never *t*. 14; 6:35
this water, that I *t*. not. 15
if any man *t*. let him come unto. 7:37
after this Jesus saith, I *t*. 19:28
if thine enemy *t*. give. *Rom* 12:20
this present hour we *t*. *1 Cor* 4:11
and they shall not *t*. *Rev* 7:16

thirsted
people *t*. there for water. *Ex* 17:3
they *t*. not when he led. *Isa* 48:21

thirsteth
my soul *t*. for God. *Ps* 42:2; 63:1*
143:6*
ho, every one that *t*., come. *Isa* 55:1

thirsty
little water, for I am *t*. *Judg* 4:19
the people is *t*. in the. *2 Sam* 17:29
my flesh longeth in a *t*. land.
Ps 63:1; 143:6
hungry and *t*., their soul. 107:5
if thine enemy be *t*. give. *Pr* 25:21
as cold water to a *t*. soul, so is. 25
water to him that was *t*. *Isa* 21:14
it shall be as when a *t*. man. 29:8
the drink of the *t*. to fail. 32:6
t. land shall become springs. 35:7
pour water upon him that is *t*. 44:3
shall drink, but ye shall be *t*. 65:13
in a dry and *t*. ground. *Ezek* 19:13
for I was *t*. and ye gave. *Mat* 25:35
when saw we thee *t*. and gave ? 37
for I was *t*. and ye gave me no. 42

thirteen
Ishmael his son was *t*. *Gen* 17:25
ye shall offer *t*. young bullocks.
Num 29:13, 14
his own house *t*. years. *1 Ki* 7:1
brethren of Hosah *t*. *1 Chr* 26:11
of the gate *t*. cubits. *Ezek* 40:11

thirteenth
t. year they rebelled. *Gen* 14:4
the *t*. lot came forth. *1 Chr* 24:13
t. lot came forth to Shubael. 25:20
in the *t*. year of the reign. *Jer* 1:2
from the *t*. year of Josiah the. 25:3
see **day**

thirtieth
Shallum to reign in nine and *t*. year.
2 Ki 15:13
in the nine and *t*. year of king. 17
seven and *t*. year of the captivity of.
25:27; *Jer* 52:31
five and *t*. year of Asa. *2 Chr* 15:19
in the six and *t*. year of the. 16:1
the two and *t*. year of Artaxerxes.
Nah 5:14; 13:6

thirty
height of the ark was *t*. *Gen* 6:15
Salah lived *t*. years, and. 11:14
Peleg lived *t*. years, and. 18
Serug lived *t*. years, and. 22
shall be *t*. found, he said, I will not
do it if I *t*nd *t*. there. 18:30
t. milch camels with their. 32:15
Joseph was *t*. years old. 41:46
their master *t*. shekels. *Ex* 21:32
the length of one curtain *t*. cubits.
26:8; 36:15
thy estimation shall be *t*. *Lev* 27:4
from *t*. years old and upwards.
Num 4:3, 23, 30, 35, 39, 43, 47
1 Chr 23:3
Jair had *t*. sons, and they had *t*.
Judg 10:4
t. sons and *t*. daughters he sent
abroad, took in *t*. daughters. 12:9
forty sons and *t*. nephews. 14
they brought *t*. companions. 14:11
give you *t*. sheets, *t*. change. 12
ye shall give *t*. sheets, *t*. change. 13
Samson slew *t*. men, and took. 19
to smite about *t*. men of. 20:31, 39
them, about *t*. persons. *1 Sam* 9:22
David was *t*. years old. *2 Sam* 5:4
and three of the *t*. chief. 23:13
Benaiah was more honourable than
the *t*. 23; *1 Chr* 11:15, 25; 27:6
Asahel, brother of Joab, was one of
the *t*. *2 Sam* 23:24
provision for one day was *t*.
1 Ki 4:22
house of the Lord was *t*. cubits. 6:2
house of the forest was *t*. cubits. 7:2
of the porch was *t*. cubits. 6
a line of *t*. cubits did compass. 23
to Hezekiah *t*. talents. *2 Ki* 18:14
captain, and *t*. with him. *1 Chr* 11:42
of them was *t*. chargers. *Ezra* 1:9
t. basons of gold, silver basons. 10
take from hence *t*. men. *Jer* 38:10
t. chambers were on. *Ezek* 40:17
and the side chambers were *t*. 41:6
there were courts joined of *t*. 46:22
for my price *t*. pieces. *Zech* 11:12
and I took the *t*. pieces of silver. 13
Mat 27:9

brought some t. fold. *Mat 13:8, 23*
 Mark 4:8, 20
with him for t. pieces. *Mat 26:15*
again the t. pieces of silver. *27:3*
Jesus began to be about t. *Luke 3:23*
about 25 or t. furlongs. *John 6:19*
 see **days, thousand**

thirty one
the kings Joshua subdued t. and one.
 Josh 12:24
in the t. and *first* year. *1 Ki 16:23*
Josiah eight years old, and reigned t.
and one. *2 Ki 22:1; 2 Chr 34:1*

thirty *two*
Reu lived t. *two* years. *Gen 11:20*
Lord's tribute was t. *two* persons.
 Num 31:40
t. *two* kings were with Ben-hadad.
 1 Ki 20:1, 16
king commanded his t. *two* captains.
 22:31
Jehoram was t. *two* years. *2 Ki 8:17*
 2 Chr 21:5, 20

thirty three
all the souls of sons and daughters t.
three. *Gen 46:15*
purifying t. *three* days. *Lev 12:4*
in Jerusalem t. and *three. 2 Sam 5:5*
1 Ki 2:11; 1 Chr 3:4; 29:27

thirty four
Eber lived t. *four* years. *Gen 11:16*

thirty five
lived *five* and t. years. *Gen 11:12*
Jehoshaphat was t. *five* years old.
 1 Ki 22:42; 2 Chr 20:31
made two pillars t. *five. 2 Chr 3:15*

thirty six
Ai smote t. *six* men. *Josh 7:5*

thirty seven
Hittite, t. *seven* in all. *2 Sam 23:39*
in the t. and *seventh. 2 Ki 13:10*

thirty eight
brook Zered, *t.eight* years.*Deut2:14*
in the t. and *eighth* year of Asa.
 1 Ki 16:29
the t. and *eighth* year of Azariah.
 2 Ki 15:8
an infirmity t. *eight* years. *John 5:5*

thirty nine
Asa in the t. and *ninth. 2 Chr 16:12*

this
t. same shall comfort us. *Gen 5:29*
T. shall not be thine heir. *15:4*
and I will speak but t. once. *18:32*
they said, T. one fellow came. *19:9*
we will give thee t. also for. *29:27*
but in t. will we consent. *34:15*
sent the coat, and said, T. *37:32*
bound a thread, saying, T. *38:28*
is not t. it in which my lord? *44:5*
if ye take t. from me,and mischief.
t. shall be a token that I. *Ex 3:12*
in t. thou shalt know that I. *7:17*
neither did he set his heart to t. *23*
t. they shall give, each half. *30:13*
t. shall be thine of the most holy.
 Num 18:9; Deut 18:3
live when God doth t.? *Num 24:23*
O that they were wise, that they
understood t. *Deut 32:29*
is not t. laid up in store with me? *34*
t. shall go with thee, t. *Judg 7:4*
come up t. once, for he hath. *16:18*
the Lord chosen t. *1 Sam 16:8, 9*
Let not Jonathan know t. *20:3*
that t. be no grief unto thee. *25:31*
t. was a small thing in. *2 Sam 7:19*
Shimei be put to death for t.? *19:21*
is not t. the blood of the men? *23:17*
to judge t. thy so great. *1 Ki 3:9*
and t. was the cause that he. *11:27*
I will for t. afflict the seed of. *39*
by t. I know that thou art a. *17:24*
should I set t. before an. *2 Ki 4:43*
glory of t. and tarry at home. *14:10*
commandment of Lord came t. *24:3*
because t. was in thine heart, not.
 2 Chr 1:11
able to give thee more than t. *25:9*
his pleasure concerning t. *Ezra 5:17*

be made a dunghill for t. *Ezra 6:11*
put such a thing as t. in the. *7:27*
besought our God for t. *8:23*
given us such deliverance as t. *9:13*
stand before thee because of t. *15*
remember me concerning t.
 Neh 13:14, 22
to kingdom for such a time as t.
 Esth 4:14
lo, t. we have searched it. *Job 5:27*
of the Lord hath wrought t. *12:9*
men shall be astonied at t. *17:8*
for t. I make haste. *20:2*
knowest thou not t. of old? *4*
hear and let t. be your. *21:2*
in t. thou art not just, I will. *33:12*
thinkest thou t. to be right? *35:2*
t. shall be the portion. *Ps 11:6*
though war rise, in t. will I. *27:3*
for t. shall every one that is. *32:6*
t. thou hast seen, keep not. *35:22*
by t. I know that thou. *41:11*
for t. God is our God for ever. *48:14*
t. their way is their folly. *49:13*
now consider t. ye that forget. *50:22*
shall turn back, t. I know for. *56:9*
twice have I heard t. that. *62:11*
t. also shall please the Lord. *69:31**
the humble shall see t. and be. *32*
when I thought to know t. it. *73:16*
the Lord heard t. and was. *78:21, 59*
for t. was a statute for Israel. *81:4*
t. he ordained in Joseph for a. *5*
neither doth a fool understand t. *92:6*
let t. be the reward of mine. *109:20*
t. I had, because I kept. *119:56*
t. honour have all his saints. *149:9*
for t. a man is envied of. *Eccl 4:4*
t. hath more rest than the other. *6:5*
enquire wisely concerning t. *7:10*
thou shouldest take hold of t.; yea
also from t. withdraw not. *18*
t. have I found. *27*
lo, t. only have I found. *29*
whether shall prosper, either t. *11:6*
who hath required t.? *Isa 1:12*
and he said. Lo t. hath touched. *6:7*
Lord of hosts will perform t. *9:7*
surely t. iniquity shall not be. *22:14*
by t. shall the iniquity of Jacob. *27:9*
t. also cometh forth from. *28:29*
Read t. I pray thee. *29:11, 12*
have I cried concerning t. *30:7*
them can declare t.? *43:9; 45:21*
remember t. *46:8*
hear now t. *47:8; 48:1, 16; 51:21*
declare ye, tell t. *48:20*
t. shall ye have of mine hand. *50:11*
blessed is the man that doeth t. *56:2*
wilt thou call t. a fast? *58:5*
is not t. the fast that I have? *6*
when ye see t. your hearts. *66:14*
O ye heavens, at t. *Jer 2:12*
procured t. unto thyself? *17*
for t. gird you with sackcloth. *4:8*
for t. shall the earth mourn. *28*
shall I pardon thee for t.? *5:7*
shall not my soul be avenged on such
a nation as t.? *9, 29; 9:9*
that glorieth, glory in t. *9:24*
I will t. once cause them to. *16:21*
was not t. to know me? saith. *22:16*
t. hath been thy manner from thy. *21*
long shall t. be in the heart? *23:26*
t. shall be the covenant that I. *31:33*
I knew that t. was the word. *32:8*
t. I call to mind, therefore I hope.
 Lam 3:21
for t. our heart is faint; our. *5:17*
he said, Hast thou seen t.?
 Ezek 8:15, 17; 47:6
t. was the iniquity of thy. *16:49*
in t. your fathers have. *20:27*
saith the Lord. t. shall not be. *21:26*
her sister Aholibah saw t. *23:11*
t. cometh, ye shall know. *24:24*
 33:33
I will set for t. be enquired. *36:37*
t. gate shall be shut, no man. *44:2*
not find occasion against t. Daniel
 Dan 6:5, 28
t. shall be their derision. *Hos 7:16*
t. liketh you, O children. *Amos 4:5*

the Lord repented for t. *Amos 7:3, 6*
the land tremble for t.? *8:8*
saith the Lord that doeth t. *9:12*
was not t. my saying? *Jonah 4:2*
t. shall they have for their pride.
 Zeph 2:10
t. shall come to pass if ye will obey
Lord. *Zech 6:15*
t. shall be the plague. *14:12, 15*
t. shall be the punishment of. *19*
t. hath been by your means. *Mal 1:9*
should I accept t. of your hands? *13*
will cut off the man that doeth t. *2:12*
known what t. meaneth. *Mat 12:7*
is not t. the carpenter's son? *13:55*
Mark 6:3; Luke 4:22; John 6:42
saying, Lord, t. shall not. *Mat 16:22*
know t. that if the good man of the
house. *24:43; Luke 12:39*
shall also t. that t. woman. *Mat 26:13*
saying, Truly t. was the Son. *27:54*
if t. come to the governor's. *28:14*
the second is like, namely, t.
 Mark 12:31
I know t.? for I am old. *Luke 1:18*
how shall t. be, seeing I know? *34*
manner of child shall t. be? *66*
added yet t. above all, that. *3:20*
have ye not read so much as t.? *6:3*
be sure of t. *10:11*
in t. rejoice not. *20*
t. my son was dead and is. *15:24*
take t. and divide it among. *22:17*
t. must yet be accomplished. *37*
certainly t. was a righteous. *23:47*
saying, T. was he of. *John 1:15*
remembered he had said t. *2:22*
on t. came his disciples. *4:27*
is not t. the Christ? *29*
marvel not at t. *5:28*
he said t. to prove him, for. *6:6*
is not t. he whom they seek? *7:25*
t. did not Abraham. *8:40*
believest thou t.? *11:26*
t. spake he not of himself. *51*
t. he said, not that he cared. *12:6*
for what intent he spake t. *13:28*
by t. shall all men know ye are. *35*
love hath no man than t. *15:13*
by t. we believe that thou. *16:30*
t. Jesus shall so come in. *Acts 1:11*
what meaneth t.? *2:12*
he seeing t. before. *31*
t. Jesus hath God raised up. *32*
he hath shed forth t. which ye. *33*
when they heard t. they were. *37*
Israel, why marvel ye at t.? *3:12*
whereunto t. would grow. *5:24*
that t. Jesus of Nazareth shall
destroy t. place. *6:14*
t. Moses whom they refused. *7:35*
as for t. Moses, we wot not. *40*
repent therefore of t. thy. *8:22*
scripture which he read was t. *32*
is not t. he that destroyed? *9:21*
when the Gentiles heard t. *13:48*
to t. agree the words of the. *15:15*
t. did she many days, but. *16:18*
when they heard t. they were. *19:5*
but t. I confess to thee, that. *24:14*
thinkest thou t. O man. *Rom 2:3*
knowing t. that our old man is. *6:6*
not only t. but when Rebecca. *9:10*
therefore I have performed t. *15:28*
t. I say, every one saith. *1 Cor 1:12*
to them that examine me is t. *9:3*
in t. that I declare to you. *11:17*
shall I praise you in t.? *22*
not knowledge, I speak t. to. *15:34*
in t. we groan, earnestly. *2 Cor 5:2*
I speak not t. to condemn you. *7:3*
t. they did, not as we hoped. *8:5*
of himself think t. again. *10:7, 11*
and t. also we wish, even your. *13:9*
t. would I learn of you. *Gal 3:2*
fulfilled in one word, even in t. *5:14*
t. I say therefore, and. *Eph 4:17*
for t. ye know, that no whoremonger.
 5:5
t. I pray, that your love. *Phil 1:9*
I know that t. shall turn to my. *19*
when with you, t. we. *2 Thes 3:10*
knowing t. *1 Tim 1:9; Jas 1:3*
 2 Pet 1:20; 3:3

doing *t*. thou shalt both. *1 Tim* 4:16
but *t*. with an oath.   *Heb* 7:21
t. did he once.   27
t. the children of God. *1 John* 3:10
in *t*. was manifested the love.   4:9
by *t*. we know that we love.   5:2
remembrance, though ye once knew
   t.   *Jude* 5
t. thou hast, that thou hatest. *Rev* 2:6
see **after, all, book, cause, child,
city, day, do, doctrine, done,
evil, house, land, law, life,
man, month, people, thing,
word, world**

is this
the woman, What *is t*. that thou ?
  Gen 3:13; 12:18; 26:10; 29:25
what man *is t*. that walketh in the ?
  24:65
what *is t*. that God hath ?   42:28
is t. your younger brother ?   43:29
what deed *is t*. that ye have ? 44:15
saying, What *is t.*?   *Ex* 13:14
  Judg 18:24
is t. that thou hast brought ? *Ex* 17:3
what trespass *is t*. ye ? *Josh* 22:16
what *is t*. thou hast done ?
  Judg 15:11; *2 Sam* 12:21
what wickedness *is t*.? *Judg* 20:12
what *is t*. come to the son of Kish ?
  1 Sam 10:11
Saul said, *Is t*. thy voice ?   24:16
is t. the manner of man ? *2 Sam* 7:19
is t. thy kindness to thy friend ? 16:17
what confidence *is t.*?   *2 Ki* 18:19
is t. a work of one day.   *Ezra* 10:13
who *is t*. that darkeneth ? *Job* 38:2
who *is t*. cometh out of ? *S of S* 3:6
who *is t*. that cometh up from ? 8:5
is t. your joyous city ?   *Isa* 23:7
who *is t*. that cometh from ?   63:1
who *is t*. that engaged ? *Jer* 30:21
who *is t*. that cometh up as ?   46:7
is t. of thy whoredoms a small matter ?   *Ezek* 16:20
is not *t*. a brand plucked ? *Zech* 3:2
see what *is t*. that goeth forth.   5:5
manner of man *is t*. that the winds ?
  Mat 8:27; *Mark* 4:41; *Luke* 8:25
said, *Is* not *t*. the son ? *Mat* 12:23
who *is t.*?   21:10
what thing *is t.*? *Mark* 1:27
whence *is t*. to me, that ? *Luke* 1:43
a word *is t*.! with authority he. 4:36
who *is t*. which speaketh ?   5:21
who *is t*. that forgiveth sins ? 7:49
but who *is t*. of whom I hear ?   9:9
he said, What *is t*. then that ? 20:17
of saying *is t*. he said ? *John* 7:36
is t. your son, who ye say was ? 9:19
what *is t*. that he saith ?   16:17, 18
for our rejoicing *is t*.   *2 Cor* 1:12
unto me *is t*. grace given, that I
  should preach.   *Eph* 3:8
religion and undefiled *is t*. *Jas* 1:27

this *is*
Adam said, *T*. is now bone. *Gen* 2:23
t. is thy kindness which thou. 20:13
T. is none other but the house of
  God, and *t*. is the gate of. 28:17
Jacob saw them, he said, *T*. is. 32:2
Can we find such a one as *t*. is ? 41:38
for *t*. is the firstborn.   48:18
t is my name for ever.   *Ex* 3:15
tne magicians said, *T*. is the.   8:19
t. is that which the Lord.   16:23
t. is that the Lord spake. *Lev* 10:3
t. is it that belongeth.   *Num* 8:24
and *t*. is thine, the heave.   18:11
such wickedness as *t*. is. *Deut* 13:11
and *t*. is the manner of the.   15:2
anoint him, for *t*. is he. *1 Sam* 16:12
t. is done of thee.   *1 Ki* 11:11
t. is the sign which the Lord. 13:3
t. is but a light thing in. *2 Ki* 3:18
t. is not the way, neither is.   6:19
t. is the woman. and *t*. is her.   8:5
so that they shall not say, *T*. is
t. is that king Ahaz. *2 Chr* 28:22
t. is nothing but sorrow. *Neh* 2:2
t. is thy God that brought thee. 9:18
behold, *t*. is the joy of.   *Job* 8:19

I know that *t*. is with thee. *Job* 10:13
t. is the place of him that.   18:21
t. is the portion of a wicked man.
  20:29; 27:13
t. is the generation of.   *Ps* 24:6
t. is the hill God desireth to. 68:16
t. is my infirmity, but I will.   77:10
know that *t*. is thy hand.   109:27
t. is the Lord's.   118:23; *Mat* 21:42
t. is my comfort in mine. *Ps* 119:50
t. is my rest for ever, here. 132:14
may be said, See, *t*. is new. *Eccl* 1:10
to rejoice in labour, *t*. is the.   5:19
t. is the whole duty of man.   12:13
t. is my beloved, and *t*. is. *S of S* 5:16
sing to the Lord; *t*. is known. *Isa* 12:5
lo, *t*. is our God, we have.   25:9
t. is all the fruit, to take away. 27:9
t. is the rest, and *t*. is the.   28:12
saying, *T*. is the way, walk.   30:21
for *t*. is as the waters of Noah. 54:9
t. is the heritage of the servants. 17
as for me, *t*. is my covenant. 59:21
t. is thy wickedness, it.   *Jer* 4:18
t. is a nation that obeyeth not. 7:28
t. is a grief.   10:19
t. is thy lot.   13:25
t. is the name whereby . . . The Lord
  our Righteousness.   23:6; 33:16
t. is Zion, whom no man.   30:17
t. is Jerusalem, I set it.   *Ezek* 5:5
t. is a lamentation, and shall. 19:14
t. is Pharaoh and all his.   31:18
t. is the writing that.   *Dan* 5:25
arise, depart, for *t*. is not. *Mi* 2:10
t. is the rejoicing city. *Zeph* 2:15
t. is the curse that.   *Zech* 5:3
he said, *T*. is an ephah that.   6
t. is wickedness.
for *t*. is he that was spoken. *Mat* 3:3
t. is my beloved Son.   17; 17:5
  Mark 9:7; *Luke* 9:35
for *t*. is the law and.   *Mat* 7:12
t. is he of whom it is written. 11:10
  Luke 7:27
t. is Elias which was for. *Mat* 11:14
t. is he which received seed. 13:19
Jesus said, With men *t*. is.   19:26
t. is the heir.   21:38; *Mark* 12:7
  Luke 20:14
t. is the first commandment.
  Mat 22:38; *Mark* 12:30
Take, eat, *t*. is my body. *Mat* 26:26
t. is my blood. 28; *Mark* 14:22, 24
  Luke 22:19, 20; *1 Cor* 11:24, 25
t. is one of them, and. *Mark* 14:69
manner of woman *t*. is.   *Luke* 7:39
t. is your hour and the power. 22:53
t. is the record of John. *John* 1:19
I bare record that *t*. is the Son. 34
t. is the condemnation, that.   3:19
that *t*. is indeed the Christ.   4:42
  7:26, 41
t. is the work of God, that.   6:29
t. is the Father's will.   39, 40
t. is the bread which cometh.   50
t. is that bread which came.   58
t. is an hard saying, who can ?   60
some said, *T*. is he.   9:9
we know *t*. is our son.   20
t. is my commandment, that. 15:12
t. is life eternal, that they.   17:3
t. is that which was spoken by the
  prophet Joel.   *Acts* 2:16
t. is that Moses which said.   7:37
t. is he that was in the church.   38
Saul increased, proving that *t*. is
  very Christ.   9:22
t. is my covenant.   *Rom* 11:27
  Heb 8:10; 10:16
t. is not to eat the.   *1 Cor* 11:20
obey your parents, for *t*. is. *Eph* 6:1
if I live, *t*. is the fruit.   *Phil* 1:22
for *t*. is well pleasing.   *Col* 3:20
for *t*. is the will of God. *1 Thes* 4:3
  5:18
t. is a faithful saying. *1 Tim* 1:15
  3:1; 4:9; *Tit* 3:8
for *t*. is acceptable in the. *1 Tim* 2:3
for *t*. is thankworthy, if. *1 Pet* 2:19
take it patiently, *t*. is acceptable. 20
t. is the message. *1 John* 1:5; 3:11
and *t*. is the promise, even.   2:25

t. is his commandment that we.
  1 John 3:23
t. is that spirit of antichrist.   4:3
t. is the love of God, that we.   5:3
and *t*. is the victory, even our.   4
t. is he that came by water.   6
t. is the witness cf God which.   9
t. is the record, that God hath.   11
t. is the confidence that we have. 14
t. is the true God, and eternal.   20
t. is love, that we walk.   *2 John* 6
t. is a deceiver and an antichrist. 7
years were finished, *t*. is. *Rev* 20:5
into lake of fire, *t*. is the second. 14

thistle
t. that was in Lebanon, a wild . . . the
  t.   *2 Ki* 14:9; *2 Chr* 25:18
thorn and *t*. shall come.   *Hos* 10:8

thistles
thorns and *t*. shall it.   *Gen* 3:18
let *t*. grow instead of.   *Job* 31:40
do men gather figs of *t*.?   *Mat* 7:16

thither
near, oh let me escape *t*. *Gen* 19:20
escape *t*. till thou be come *t*.   22
bring not my son *t*.   24:6, 8
bring in *t*. the ark.   *Ex* 26:33
that the slayer may flee *t*. *Num* 35:6
  11, 15; *Deut* 4:42; 19:3, 4
  Josh 20:3, 9
saying, Thou shalt not go in *t*.
  Deut 1:37, 38, 39
unto his habitation, *t*. thou.   12:5
t. ye shall bring your burnt.   6, 11
Israel went *t*. a whoring. *Judg* 8:27
and *t*. fled all the men and.   9:51
to Israelites that came *t*. *1 Sam* 2:14
the ark of God about *t*.   5:8
if the man should come *t*.   10:22
before it was brought *t*.   *1 Ki* 6:7
waters were divided hither and *t*.
  2 Ki 2:8, 14
turned in *t*. to eat bread.   4:8, 11
t. the Syrians are come down. 6:9
saying, Carry *t*. one of the.   17:27
resort ye *t*. to us: our God. *Neh* 4:20
t. brought I again the vessels. 13:9
they came *t*. and were.   *Job* 6:20
the rain returneth not *t*. *Isa* 55:10
he shall not return *t*.   *Jer* 22:11
but to the land. *t*. shall they not. 27
t. was their spirit to go. *Ezek* 1:20
Israel shall come *t*. and shall. 11:18
these waters shall come *t*.   47:9
t. cause thy mighty ones. *Joel* 3:11
he was afraid to go *t*.   *Mat* 2:22
t. will the eagles be. *Luke* 17:37
where I am, *t*. ye.   *John* 7:34, 36
and goest thou *t*. again ?   11:8
Jesus ofttimes resorted *t*.   18:2
Judas cometh *t*. with lanterns.   3
Philip ran *t*. to him, and. *Acts* 8:30
women which resorted *t*.   16:13

thitherward
t. and came to Micah's. *Judg* 18:15
Zion, with their faces *t*.   *Jer* 50:5

Thomas
T. and Matthew the.   *Mat* 10:3
  Mark 3:18; *Luke* 6:15; *Acts* 1:13
T. said, Let us go and. *John* 11:16
T. was not with them when. 20:24
T. was with them.   26
T. Reach hither thy finger.   27
Simon Peter and *T*.   21:2

thongs
as they bound him with *t*. *Acts* 22:25

thorn
(*There are some* 18 *or* 20 *Hebrew
words which point to different
kinds of prickly shrubs, which
are variously rendered in the
Authorized Version. Probably
there is no other country where so
many plants of this sort exist.
There are at least* 200 *different
species of thorny plants found there*)
bore his jaw through with a *t*.?
  Job 41:2*
as a *t*. goeth into the hand. *Pr* 26:9
instead of the *t*. shall. *Isa* 55:13
no more any grieving *t*. *Ezek* 28:24
the *t*. shall come up on. *Hos* 10:8

is sharper than a *t.* hedge. *Mi* 7:4
there was given me a *t.* 2 *Cor* 12:7

thorns

t. and thistles shall it. *Gen* 3:18
break out and catch in *t.* *Ex* 22:6
they shall be *t.* in your sides.
    Num 33:55; *Judg* 2:3
but they shall be *t.* in your eyes.
    Josh 23:13
of Belial shall be as *t.* 2 *Sam* 23:6
Manasseh among the *t.* 2 *Chr* 33:11*
pots can feel the *t.*, he shall. *Ps* 58:9
quenched as the fire of *t.* 118:12
man is an hedge of *t.* *Pr* 15:19
t. and snares are in the way. 22:5
was all grown over with *t.* 24:31
as the crackling of *t.* under. *Eccl* 7:6
as the lily among. so is. *S of S* 2:2
they shall rest upon all *t.* *Isa* 7:19
as *t.* cut up shall they be. 33:12
and *t.* shall come up in her. 34:13
and sow not among *t.* *Jer* 4:3
sown wheat, but shall reap *t.* 12:13
hedge up thy way with *t.* *Hos* 2:6
t. shall be in their tabernacles. 9:6
be folden together as *t.* *Nah* 1:10
do men gather grapes of *t.*?
    Mat 7:16; *Luke* 6:44
fell among *t.* *Mat* 13:7, 22
    Mark 4:7, 18; *Luke* 8:7, 14
platted a crown of *t.* *Mat* 27:29
    Mark 15:17; *John* 19:2
    see **briers**

those

Esau said, Who are *t.*? *Gen* 33:5
let them be of *t.* that. 1 *Ki* 2:7
upon *t.* did Solomon levy a. 9:21
t. did Cyrus king of Persia. *Ezra* 1:8
did what they would to *t.* *Esth* 9:5
to set up on high *t.* *Job* 5:11
seeing he judgeth *t.* that. 21:22
are of *t.* that rebel. 24:13
so doth the grave *t.* which. 19
t. that remain of him shall. 27:15
t. that wait on the Lord. *Ps* 37:9
t. that have made a covenant. 50:5
t. planted in house of Lord. 92:13
t. that fear thee turn unto me, and *t.*
    that have known thy. 119:79
to do to *t.* that love thy name. 132
am not I grieved with *t.* that ? 139:21
t. that seek me early shall. *Pr* 8:17
with *t.* that shall come. *Eccl* 1:11
but it shall be for *t.* *Isa* 35:8
t. that remember thee in thy ways,
    in those is continuance. 64:5
t. will I let remain in. *Jer* 27:11
t. that walk in pride he. *Dan* 4:37
t. that have not sought. *Zeph* 1:6
thou savourest *t.* things. *Mat* 16:23
among *t.* that are born. *Luke* 7:28
but *t.* mine enemies bring. 19:27
woman, where are *t.*? *John* 8:10
keep through thy name *t.* thou. 17:11
t. that thou gavest me I have. 12
from Samuel and *t.* that. *Acts* 3:24
there come in *t.* that. 1 *Cor* 14:23
what things were gain. *t.* I. *Phil* 3:7
Saviour, especially of *t.* 1 *Tim* 4:10
belongeth to *t.* who by. *Heb* 5:14
an ensample to *t.* that. 2 *Pet* 2:6
allure *t.* that were clean escaped. 18
    see **days, things**

thou

the woman whom *t.* gavest. *Gen* 3:12
know thou, that *t.* shalt surely die, *t.*
    20:7; 1 *Sam* 22:16
t. art our sister, be *t.* *Gen* 24:60
t. art now the blessed of the. 26:29
discreet and wise as *t.* art. 41:39
throne will I be greater than *t.* 40
t. shalt be near to me, *t.* and. 45:10
t. art he whom thy brethren. 49:8
t. shalt come up, *t.* and. *Ex* 19:24
t. and all the company. *Num* 16:11
be *t.* and they, and Aaron before. 16
may rest as well as *t.* *Deut* 5:14
nations mightier than *t.* 7:1; 20:1
t. hast not known, *t.* nor. 13:6; 28:64
that both *t.* and thy seed. 30:19
that is better than *t.* 1 *Sam* 15:28
T. are more righteous than I. 24:17
blessed be *t.* that kept me. 25:33

Nathan said to David *T.* 2 *Sam* 12:7
said, Of what city art *t.*? 15:2
T. and Ziba divide the land. 19:29
t. even *t.* knowest the. 1 *Ki* 8:39
t. and thy father's house. 18:18
order the battle ? he said *T.* 20:14
that when I and *t.* rode. 2 *Ki* 9:25
that *t.* shouldest fall, even *t.* and.
    14:10; 2 *Chr* 25:19
t. art the God, even *t.* 2 *Ki* 19:15
    19; *Neh* 9:6; *Isa* 37:20
but *t.* art a God, ready to. *Neh* 9:17
t. and thy father's house shall be
    . . . whether *t.* art. *Esth* 4:14
which are higher than *t.* *Job* 35:5
I will fear no evil, for *t.* *Ps* 23:4
it was *t.*, a man mine equal. 55:13
t. art he that took me out of. 71:6
t. even *t.* art to be feared, and who
    may stand . . . once *t.* art ? 76:7
t. whose name is Jehovah. 83:18
t. art the same, thy years. 102:27
they may know, that *t.* Lord. 109:27
t. art my God, and I will. 118:28
t. art my hiding place. 119:114
arise into thy rest, *t.* and ark. 132:8
up into heaven. *t.* art there. 139:8
tell me, O *t.* whom my. *S of S* 1:7
t. art my servant, I have. *Isa* 41:9
and saith, Deliver me, for *t.* 44:17
verily *t.* art a God that hidest. 45:15
who art *t.*, that *t.* shouldest be ? 51:12
t. art our father *t.* O Lord. 63:16
to me, I am holier than *t.* 65:5
t. shalt continue from. *Jer* 17:4
there *t.* shalt die, *t.* and all thy. 20:6
will ye die, *t.* and thy people ? 27:13
t. O Lord, remainest for. *Lam* 5:19
O *t.* that dwellest in the. *Ezek* 7:7
more righteous than *t.* 16:52
it is *t.* O king, that art. *Dan* 4:22
t. his son hast not humbled. 5:32
whence comest *t.*? of what people art
    t.? *Jonah* 1:8
O *t.* that art named the. *Mi* 2:7
t. O tower of the flock, to thee. 4:8
art *t.* not from everlasting? *Hab* 1:12
art *t.* O great mountain ? *Zech* 4:7
but *t.* when *t.* prayest. *Mat* 6:6
but *t.* when *t.* fastest, anoint. 17
t. art the Christ, the Son of the. 16:16
    Mark 8:29; *Luke* 4:41; *John* 11:27
not as I will, but as *t.* wilt. *Mat* 26:39
saying, *T.* also wast with Jesus. 69
    Mark 14:67
hail, *t.* that art highly. *Luke* 1:28
saying, Art *t.* he that ? 7:19, 20
lest a more honourable than *t.* 14:8
owest *t.* unto my lord ? 16:5, 7
t. in thy lifetime receivedst thy
    good things . . . and *t.* art. 25
if thou hadst known, even *t.* 19:42
to ask him, Who art *t.*? *John* 1:19
    22; 8:25; 21:12
they asked, art *t.* Elias ? art *t.* ? 1:21
t. art Simon thou shalt be called. 42
t. art a master in Israel ? 3:10
that *t.* being a Jew, askest. 4:9
to him, Art *t.* also of Galilee ? 7:52
but what sayest *t.*? 8:5
t. art his disciple. 9:28
t. hast seen him, and he. 37
I in them, and *t.* in me, that. 17:23
art not *t.* one of this man's ? 18:17
t. Lord, who knowest. *Acts* 1:24
t. art in the gall of bitterness. 8:23
whereby *t.* and thy house. 11:14
t. child of the devil, *t.* enemy, wilt *t.*
    not cease to pervert the ? 13:10
t. art my son, this day have I. 33
art not *t.* that Egyptian which ? 21:38
tell me, art *t.* a Roman ? he. 22:27
I would, that not only *t.* but. 26:29
t. therefore which teachest another.
    Rom 2:21
but be *t.* an example. 1 *Tim* 4:12
t. O man of God, flee these. 6:11
be not *t.* ashamed of the. 2 *Tim* 1:8
t. therefore, my son, be strong. 2:1
t. therefore receive him. *Philem* 12
t., Lord, hast laid the foundation of
    the earth. *Heb* 1:10
they shall be changed, but *t.* art. 12
who art *t.* that judgest ? *Jas* 4:12

t. art worthy, O Lord, to. *Rev* 4:11
t. art worthy to take the book. 5:9
    see **alone**

though

vine was as *t.* it budded. *Gen* 40:10
t. he wist it not, yet is. *Lev* 5:17
thou shalt relieve him, *t.* he be. 25:35
t. I walk in the imagination of.
    Deut 29:19
drive out Canaanites, *t.* they have
    iron chariots and *t.* *Josh* 17:18
t. thou detain me, I will. *Judg* 13:16
t. ye have done this, yet will. 15:7
t. I be not like one of thy hand-
    maidens. *Ruth* 2:13
t. it be in Jonathan. 1 *Sam* 14:39
I will shoot arrows, as *t.* I. 20:20
t. it were sanctified this day. 21:5
t. I am this day weak, *t.* 2 *Sam* 3:39
t. I should receive a thousand. 18:12
t. there were of you cast. *Neh* 1:9
t. he slay me, yet will I. *Job* 13:15
t. wickedness be sweet in. 20:12
what the hypocrite's hope, *t.* 27:8
t. he heap up silver as the dust. 16
as *t.* he had been my friend or.
    Ps 35:14
t. he fall, he shall not utterly. 37:24
t. the Lord be high, yet hath. 138:6
t. hand join in hand. *Pr* 11:21; 16:5
than he that is perverse, *t.* 28:6
t. he understand, he will not. 29:19
the wayfaring men *t.* fools. *Isa* 35:8
surnamed thee, *t.* thou hast not.
    45:4, 5
he cause grief, yet will he. *Lam* 3:32
t. briers and thorns be with thee, *t.*
    Ezek 2:6; 3:9; 12:3
t. these three men. 14:14, 16, 18, 20
t. he be sought for, yet. 26:21
not humbled, *t.* thou. *Dan* 5:22
t. thou be little among. *Mi* 5:2
t. they be quiet, and. *Nah* 1:12
ye will not believe, *t.* it. *Hab* 1:5
t. it tarry. wait for it, it will. 2:3
t. I should die with thee. *Mat* 26:35
face was as *t.* he would. *Luke* 9:53
avenge his elect, *t.* he bear. 18:7
he made as *t.* he would have. 24:28
wrote on the ground, as *t.* *John* 8:6
t. ye believe not me. believe. 10:38
t. he were dead, yet shall. 11:25
as *t.* by our own power we. *Acts* 3:12
ye shall not believe, *t.* a man. 13:41
as *t.* he needed any thing. 17:25
t. he be not far from every one. 27
as *t.* ye would enquire. 23:15, 20
t. he hath escaped the sea. 28:4
things which be not, as *t.* *Rom* 4:17
no adulteress, *t.* she be married. 7:3
that have wives, be as *t.* 1 *Cor* 7:29
as *t.* they wept not, as *t.* they. 30
but *t.* our outward man. 2 *Cor* 4:16
t. he was rich. yet for our sakes. 8:9
for *t.* we walk in the flesh, we. 10:3
in nothing am I behind, *t.* I. 12:11
do what is honest, *t.* we be. 13:7
t. we or an angel preach. *Gal* 1:8
heir differeth nothing *t.* he be. 4:1
t. I might also have confidence in.
    Phil 3:4
not as *t.* I had attained or were. 12
t. I be absent in the flesh. *Col* 2:5
why, as *t.* living, are ye subject. 20
t. he were a son, yet learned.
    Heb 5:8
better things, *t.* we thus speak. 6:9
t. he sought it carefully with. 12:17
t. a man say he hath faith. *Jas* 2:14
as *t.* some strange thing. 1 *Pet* 4:12
put you in remembrance, *t.* ye know.
    2 *Pet* 1:12
put you in remembrance, *t.* ye once
    knew this. *Jude* 5

thought

I *t.* the fear of God is not. *Gen* 20:11
Judah saw her, he *t.* her to. 38:15
Israel said, I had not I *t.* to. 48:11
but as for you, ye *t.* evil. 50:20*
of the evil he *t.* to do. *Ex* 32:14*
t. to promote thee to. *Num* 24:11
I shall do unto you, as I *t.* 33:56
ye do to him, as ye *t.* *Deut* 19:19

I verily *t.* that thou hadst hated her.
Judg 15:2
the men of Gibeah *t.* to have. 20:5
therefore Eli *t.* she had. *1 Sam* 1:13
Saul *t.* to make David fall. 18:25
who *t.* that I would have given him
a reward. *2 Sam* 4:10*
Amnon *t.* it hard to do any. 13:2
ishbi-benob *t.* to have slain. 21:16
I *t.* he will surely come. *2 Ki* 5:11
Rehoboam *t.* to make. *2 Chr* 11:22*
Sennacherib *t.* to win them. 32:1
t. to do me mischief. *Neh* 6:2
he *t.* scorn to lay hands. *Esth* 3:6
Haman *t.* in his heart, to. 6:6*
we have *t.* of thy loving. *Ps* 48:9
when I *t.* to know this, it was 73:16
I *t.* on my ways, and turned. 119:59
if thou hast *t.* evil, lay. *Pr* 30:32
as I have *t.* so shall it. *Isa* 14:24
of the evil I *t.* to do. *Jer* 18:8
Lord of hosts *t.* to do to us. *Zech* 1:6
as I *t.* to punish you. 8:14
I *t.* to do well. 15
a book for them that *t.* *Mal* 3:16
but while he *t.* on these. *Mat* 1:20
and when he *t.* thereon. *Mark* 14:72
nor *t.* I myself worthy. *Luke* 7:7
he *t.* within himself, what. 12:17*
they *t.* the kingdom of God. 19:11*
they *t.* he had spoken. *John* 11:13
t. the gift of God may. *Acts* 8:20
while Peter *t.* on the vision. 10:19
wist not it was true, but *t.* he. 12:9
Paul *t.* not good to take him. 15:38
why should it be *t.* a thing ? 26:8*
I *t.* that I ought to do many things. 9
when I was a child, I *t.* *1 Cor* 13:11
t. it not robbery to be. *Phil* 2:6*
punishment he be *t.* *Heb* 10:29*

thought, *substantive*
that there be not a *t.* in. *Deut* 15:9
my father take *t.* for us. *1 Sam* 9:5†
is despised in the *t.* of him. *Job* 12:5
that no *t.* can be withholden. 42:2*
their *t.* is, their houses. *Ps* 49:11
the inward *t.* of every one of. 64:6
thou understandest my *t.* 139:2
t. of foolishness is sin. *Pr* 24:9
king, no not in thy *t.* *Eccl* 10:20
shalt think an evil *t.* *Ezek* 38:10*
to man what is his *t.* *Amos* 4:13
I say to you, Take no *t.* *Mat* 6:25*
31, 34*; 10:19*; *Mark* 13:11*
Luke 12:11*. 22*
which of you by taking *t.* can add one
cubit ? *Mat* 6:27*; *Luke* 12:25*
why take *ye t.* for raiment ?
Mat 6:28*; *Luke* 12:26*
if the *t.* of thy heart. *Acts* 8:22
bringing into captivity every *t.* to
the obedience of Christ. *2 Cor* 10:5

thoughtest
thou *t.* I was such a one. *Ps* 50:21

thoughts
imagination of the *t.* of his. *Gen* 6:5
for Reuben there were great *t.* of
heart. *Judg* 5:15*
understandeth the *t.* *1 Chr* 28:9
the imagination of the *t.* 29:18
in *t.* from the visions. *Job* 4:13
are broken off, even my *t.* 17:11
therefore do my *t.* cause me. 20:2
I know your *t.* and devices. 21:27
God is not in all his *t.* *Ps* 10:4
and the *t.* of his heart to all. 33:11
thy *t.* cannot be reckoned. 40:5
all their *t.* are against me. 56:5
thy works! thy *t.* are very deep. 92:5
Lord knoweth the *t.* of man. 94:11
in the multitude of my *t.* 19
I hate vain *t.* but thy law. 119:113*
how precious are thy *t.* 139:17
O God, try me, and know my *t.* 23
in that very day his *t.* perish. 146:4
the *t.* of the righteous. *Pr* 12:5
the *t.* of the wicked are an. 15:26*
and thy *t.* shall be established. 16:3
the *t.* of the diligent tend to. 21:5
man forsake his *t.* *Isa* 55:7
for my *t.* are not your *t.* saith. 8
so are my *t.* higher than your *t.* 9
evil, their *t.* are *t.* of iniquity. 59:7

walketh after their own *t.* *Isa* 65:2
their works and their *t.* 66:18
vain *t.* lodge in thee ? *Jer* 4:14
even the fruit of their *t.* 6:19
till he have performed the *t.* 23:20*
I know the *t.* that I think towards
you, *t.* of peace and not. 29:11
mightest know the *t.* of. *Dan* 2:30
Nebuchadnezzar's *t.* upon bed. 4:5
Daniel was astonished, and his *t.* 19
Belshazzar's *t.* troubled him. 5:6
Let not thy *t.* trouble thine. 10
but they know not the *t.* *Mi* 4:12
Jesus, knowing their *t.* said. *Mat* 9:4
12:25; *Luke* 5:22*; 6:8; 9:47
11:17
out of the heart proceed evil *t.*
Mat 15:19; *Mark* 7:21
the *t.* of many hearts. *Luke* 2:35
and why do *t.* arise in your ? 24:38*
their *t.* accusing, or else. *Rom* 2:15
the Lord knoweth the *t.* *1 Cor* 3:20*
God is a discerner of the *t.* *Heb* 4:12
become judges of evil *t.* *Jas* 2:4

thousand
thy brother a *t.* pieces. *Gen* 20:16
of every tribe a *t.* shall ye send to
the war. *Num* 31:4, 5, 6
suburbs of cities are *t.* cubits. 35:4
you a *t.* times so many. *Deut* 1:11
covenant to a *t.* generations. 7:9
how should one chase a *t.*? 32:30
Josh 23:10
died, about a *t.* men. *Judg* 9:49
Samson slew a *t.* men. 15:15, 16
an hundred of a *t.*, a *t.* out of. 20:10
the captain of their *t.* *1 Sam* 17:18
David his captain over a *t.* 18:13
three *t.* sheep and a *t.* goats. 25:2
from him a *t.* chariots and seven.
2 Sam 8:4; *1 Chr* 18:4
though I should receive a *t.* 18:12
t. men of Benjamin with him. 19:17
a *t.* burnt offerings did Solomon.
1 Ki 3:4; *2 Chr* 1:6
gave Pul a *t.* talents. *2 Ki* 15:19
craftsmen and smiths a *t.* 24:16
greatest was over a *t.* *1 Chr* 12:14
of Naphtali a *t.* captains, and. 34
word he commanded to a *t.* 16:15
Ammon sent a *t.* talents. 19:6
sacrifices unto the Lord a *t.* bullocks,
a *t.* rams, and a *t.* lambs. 29:21
did give a *t.* bullocks. *2 Chr* 30:24
bring forth a *t.* chargers. *Ezra* 1:9
gold, and other vessels a *t.* 10
answer him one of a *t.* *Job* 9:3
interpreter, one of a *t.* 33:23
t. yoke of oxen, a *t.* she asses. 42:12
cattle on a *t.* hills are. *Ps* 50:10
day in courts is better than a *t.* 84:10
a *t.* years in thy sight are but. 90:4
a *t.* shall fall at thy side, and. 91:7
yea, though he live a *t.* *Eccl* 6:6
one man among a *t.* have I. 7:28
whereon there hang a *t.* *S of S* 4:4
fruit was to bring a *t.* pieces. 8:11
thou, O Solomon, must have a *t.* 12
a *t.* vines, at a *t.* silverlings. *Isa* 7:23
one *t.* shall flee at the rebuke. 30:17
a little one shall become a *t.* 60:22
measured a *t.* cubits. *Ezek* 47:3
again he measured a *t.* and. 4, 5
feast to a *t.* of his lords, and drank
wine before the *t.* *Dan* 5:1
out by a *t.* shall leave. *Amos* 5:3
day is with the Lord as a *t.* years, and
a *t.* years as one day. *2 Pet* 3:8
bound Satan a *t.* years. *Rev* 20:2
deceive nations no more, till *t.* 3
reigned with Christ a *t.* years. 4
and when the *t.* years are expired. 7

one thousand two hundred sixty
prophesy one *t.* 260 days. *Rev* 11:3
feed her one *t.* 260 days. 12:6

one thousand two hundred ninety
be one *t.* 290 days. *Dan* 12:11

one thousand three hundred
thirty-five
to the *t.* 335 days. *Dan* 12:12

one thousand six hundred
of one *t.* 600 furlongs. *Rev* 14:20

two thousand
two *t.* cubits, on the west side two *t.*,
south side two *t.* *Num* 35:5
you and the ark two *t.* *Josh* 3:4
sea contained two *t.* baths. *1 Ki* 7:26
deliver thee two *t.* horses if thou be
able. *2 Ki* 18:23; *Isa* 36:8
gave two *t.* pounds of. *Neh* 7:72
about two *t.* swine were. *Mark* 5:13

two thousand two hundred
two *t.* 200 pounds of silver. *Neh* 7:71

two thousand three hundred
two *t.* 300 days, sanctuary. *Dan* 8:14

two hundred thousand
captive of brethren 200 *t.* *2 Chr* 28:8

two hundred eighty thousand
out of Benjamin two hundred eighty
t. *2 Chr* 14:8

two hundred thousand thousand
of horsemen were two hundred thousand thousand. *Rev* 9:16*

three thousand
of the people three *t.* *Ex* 32:28
to Ai about three *t.* men. *Josh* 7:4
three *t.* went to bind. *Judg* 15:11
upon the roof three *t.* men. 16:27
Saul chose three *t.* men. *2 Sam* 13:2
took three *t.* chosen men. 24:2; 26:2
three *t.* sheep and a *t.* goats. 25:2
spake three *t.* proverbs. *1 Ki* 4:32
sea held three *t.* baths. *2 Chr* 4:5
his substance was three *t.* *Job* 1:3
captive three *t.* Jews. *Jer* 52:28
to them three *t.* souls. *Acts* 2:41

four thousand
Israel about four *t.* men. *1 Sam* 4:2
four *t.* porters, four *t.* *1 Chr* 23:5
Solomon had four *t.* stalls for horses.
2 Chr 9:25
they that did eat were four *t.*
Mat 15:38; *Mark* 8:9
seven loaves among four *t.*
Mat 16:10; *Mark* 8:20
wilderness four *t.* men. *Acts* 21:38

four thousand five hundred
of the city four *t.* 500 measures, east
side . . . four *t.* 500 measures.
Ezek 48:16, 30, 32, 33, 34

five thousand
about five *t.* men. *Josh* 8:12
of them five *t.* men. *Judg* 20:45
of gold five *t.* talents. *1 Chr* 29:7
for offerings five *t.* *2 Chr* 35:9
they gave five *t.* pounds. *Ezra* 2:69
eaten were about five *t.* *Mat* 14:21
neither remember the five loaves of
the five *t.* 16:9; *Mark* 6:44; 8:19
Luke 9:14; *John* 6:10
number that believed were about
five *t.* *Acts* 4:4

five thousand four hundred
and silver five *t.* 400. *Ezra* 1:11

six thousand
with six *t.* horsemen. *1 Sam* 13:5
six *t.* pieces of gold. *2 Ki* 5:5
and six *t.* were officers. *1 Chr* 23:4
for Job had six *t.* camels. *Job* 42:12

six thousand seven hunderd and
twenty
asses, six *t.* seven hundred and
twenty. *Ezra* 2:67; *Neh* 7:69

seven thousand
seven *t.* in Israel who have not.
1 Ki 19:18; *Rom* 11:4
Israel, being seven *t.* *1 Ki* 20:15
men of might, seven *t.* *2 Ki* 24:16
mighty men, seven *t.* *1 Chr* 12:25
from him seven *t.* horsemen. 18:4
the Syrians seven *t.* men. 19:18
I prepared seven *t.* talents of. 29:4
they offered seven *t.* *2 Chr* 15:11
congregation seven *t.* sheep. 30:24
also was slain seven *t.* sheep. *Job* 1:3
were slain seven *t.* men. *Rev* 11:13

seven thousand seven hundred
brought Jehoshaphat seven *t.* 700
rams, seven *t.* 700. *2 Chr* 17:11

ten thousand
an hundred shall put ten *t.* *Lev* 26:8
two put ten *t.* to flight ? *Deut* 32:20

them in Bezek *ten t.* men. *Judg* 1:4
they slew of Moab *ten t.* men. 3:29
Barak, go, and take *ten t.* men. 4:6
he went up with *ten t.* men. 10, 14
remained to Gideon *ten t.* 7:3
against Gibeah *ten t.* men. 20:34
art worth *ten t.* of us. *2 Sam* 18:3
Lebanon, *ten t.* a month. *1 Ki* 5:14
Jehoahaz *ten t.* footmen. *2 Ki* 13:7
Edom in the valley *ten t.* 14:7
away even *ten t.* captives. 24:14
children of Seir *ten t.* *2 Chr* 25:11
other *ten t.* left alive, did Judah. 12
gave Jotham the same year *ten t.* . . .
ten t. of barley. 27:5
congregation *ten t.* sheep 30:24
I will pay *ten t.* talents. *Esth* 3:9
ten t. shall fall at thy. *Ps* 91:7
chiefest among *ten t.* *S of S* 5:10
the breadth of the land shall be *ten t.*
Ezek 45:1, 3, 5; 48:9, 10, 13, 18
ten t. times *ten t.* stood. *Dan* 7:10
him *ten t.* talents. *Mat* 18:24
able with *ten t.* to meet. *Luke* 14:31
though ye have *ten t.* *1 Cor* 4:15
than *ten t.* words in an. 14:19
was *ten t.* times *ten t.* *Rev* 5:11

twelve **thousand**
fell of Ai were *twelve t.* *Josh* 8:25
sent *twelve t.* men to. *Judg* 21:10
Solomon had *twelve t.* *1 Ki* 4:26
10:26; *2 Chr* 1:14; 9:25
of tribe of Juda, Reuben, Gad,
sealed *twelve t.* *Rev* 7:5
of Aser, Naphthalim, Manasses,
sealed *twelve t.* 6
of Simeon, Levi, Issachar, were
sealed *twelve t.* 7
of Zabulon, Joseph, Benjamin,
sealed *twelve t.* 8
city *twelve t.* furlongs. 21:16

fourteen **thousand**
Job had *fourteen t.* sheep. *Job* 42:12
fourteen **thousand** *seven hundred*
plague *fourteen t.* 700. *Num* 16:49

sixteen **thousand**
were *sixteen t.* *Num* 31:40, 46
sixteen **thousand** *seven hundred*
fifty
gold of offering *sixteen t.* *seven hundred and fifty.* *Num* 31:52
seventeen **thousand** *two hundred*
sons of Jediael *seven t. two hundred.*
1 Chr 7:11

eighteen **thousand**
Israel *eighteen t.* men. *Judg* 20:25
of Benjamin *eighteen t.* men. 44
Manasseh *eighteen t.* *1 Chr* 12:31
of the Edomites *eighteen t.* 18:12
they gave of brass *eighteen t.* 29:7

twenty **thousand**
Hadadezer king of Zobah, *twenty t.*
2 Sam 8:4; *1 Chr* 18:4
of Ammon hired Syrians, *twenty t.*
2 Sam 10:6
Absalom's company *twenty t.* 18:7
Hiram *twenty t.* measures of wheat.
1 Ki 5:11; *2 Chr* 2:10
work *twenty t.* drams. *Neh* 7:71, 72
chariots of God *twenty t.* *Ps* 68:17
cometh, with *twenty t.* *Luke* 14:31

twenty two **thousand**
Levites *twenty two t.* *Num* 3:39
males were *twenty two t.* 43
Simeonites *twenty two t.* 26:14
returned of Gideon's army *twenty two t.* *Judg* 7:3
of Israel *twenty two t.* 20:21
David slew of the Syrians *twenty two t.* *2 Sam* 8:5; *1 Chr* 18:5
Solomon offered *twenty two t.* oxen.
1 Ki 8:63; *2 Chr* 7:5
of Tola *twenty two t.* *1 Chr* 7:2
of Bela *twenty two t.* 7

twenty three **thousand**
Levites *twenty three t.* *Num* 26:62
day *three* and *twenty t.* *1 Cor* 10:8

twenty four **thousand**
plague *twenty four t.* *Num* 25:9
twenty four t. Levites to forward.
1 Chr 23:4
served were *twenty four t.* 27:1

twenty five **thousand**
destroyed of Benjamites *twenty five t.* *Judg* 20:35, 46
of land *twenty five t.* *Ezek* 45:1
3, 5, 6; 48:8, 9, 10, 13

twenty six **thousand**
numbered *twenty six t.* *Judg* 20:15
apt to war, *twenty six t.* *1 Chr* 7:40

twenty seven **thousand**
twenty seven t. men. *1 Ki* 20:30

twenty eight **thousand**
expert in war, *twenty eight t.*
1 Chr 12:35

thirty **thousand**
and the asses were *thirty t.*
Num 31:39, 45
Joshua chose *thirty t.* *Josh* 8:3
Israel *thirty t.* footmen. *1 Sam* 4:10
men of Judah were *thirty t.* 11:8
Philistines gathered *thirty t.* 13:5
David gathered *thirty t.* *2 Sam* 6:1
levy was *thirty t.* men. *1 Ki* 5:43

thirty two **thousand**
thirty two t. women. *Num* 31:35
Ammon hired *thirty two t.* chariots.
1 Chr 19:7

thirty two **thousand** *two hundred*
number of Manasseh *thirty two t.
two hundred.* *Num* 1:35; 2:21
thirty two **thousand** *five hundred*
of Ephraim were numbered *thirty two t. five hundred.* *Num* 26:37

thirty three **thousand**
gave *thirty three t.* *2 Chr* 35:7
thirty five **thousand**
of Benjamin were *thirty five t.*
Num 1:37
thirty six **thousand**
were *thirty* and *six t.* *Num* 31:38
congregation *thirty six t.* beeves. 44
soldiers were *thirty six t.* *1 Chr* 7:4
thirty seven **thousand**
Naphtali *thirty* and *seven t.*
1 Chr 12:34
thirty eight **thousand**
Levites from *thirty* years, *thirty eight t.* *1 Chr* 23:3

forty **thousand**
about *forty t.* prepared. *Josh* 4:13
was there a shield seen among *forty t.?* *Judg* 5:8
David slew *forty t.* *2 Sam* 10:18
Solomon had *forty t.* *1 Ki* 4:26
expert in war, *forty t.* *1 Chr* 12:36
slew of Assyrians *forty t.* 19:18
forty **thousand** *five hundred*
of Ephraim were *forty t. five hundred.* *Num* 1:33; 2:19
Gad were numbered *forty t.* and *five hundred.* 26:18
forty one **thousand** *five hundred*
of Asher numbered *forty one t. five hundred.* *Num* 1:41; 2:28
forty two **thousand**
Ephraimites *forty two t.* *Judg* 12:6
whole congregation *forty two t.*
Ezra 2:64; *Neh* 7:66
forty three **thousand** *seven hundred thirty*
of Reubenites *forty three t.* *seven hundred thirty.* *Num* 26:7
forty four **thousand** *seven hundred sixty*
of Reubenites to war *forty four t. seven hundred sixty.* *1 Chr* 5:18
forty five **thousand** *four hundred*
of Naphtali were *forty five t.* four hundred.* *Num* 26:50
forty five **thousand** *six hundred*
of Benjamin *forty five t. six hundred.*
Num 26:41
forty five **thousand** *six hundred fifty*
numbered of Gad *forty five t. six hundred fifty.* *Num* 1:25; 2:15
forty six **thousand** *five hundred*
of Reuben *forty six t.* and *five hundred.* *Num* 1:21; 2:11

fifty **thousand**
the Lord smote *fifty t.* *1 Sam* 6:19
Hagarites' sheep *fifty t.* *1 Chr* 5:21
of Zebulun *fifty t.* could keep. 12:33
the book *fifty t.* pieces. *Acts* 19:19
fifty two **thousand** *seven hundred*
of Manasseh *fifty two t.* and *seven hundred.* *Num* 26:34
fifty three **thousand** *four hundred*
of Naphtali *fifty three t.* four hundred.* *Num* 1:43; 2:30
fifty four **thousand** *four hundred*
of Issachar *fifty four t. four hundred.*
Num 1:29; 2:6
fifty seven **thousand** *four hundred*
of Zebulun *fifty seven t. four hundred.* *Num* 1:31; 2:8
fifty nine **thousand** *three hundred*
of Simeon *fifty nine t. three hundred.* *Num* 1:23; 2:13

sixty **thousand**
sixty t. horsemen. *2 Chr* 12:3
sixty **thousand** *five hundred*
of Zebulunites, *sixty t.* and *five hundred.* *Num* 26:27
sixty one **thousand**
was *sixty one t.* asses. *Num* 31:34
they gave *sixty one t.* *Ezra* 2:69
sixty two **thousand** *seven hundred*
of tribe of Dan *sixty two t. seven hundred.* *Num* 1:39; 2:26
sixty four **thousand** *three hundred*
of Issachar *sixty four t.* and *three hundred.* *Num* 26:25
sixty four **thousand** *four hundred*
of the Shuhamites *sixty four t. four hundred.* *Num* 26:43

seventy **thousand**
the people *seventy t.* *2 Sam* 24:15
Solomon had *seventy t.* that bare.
1 Ki 5:15; *2 Chr* 2:2, 18
fell of Israel *seventy t.* *1 Chr* 21:14
seventy two **thousand**
booty of beeves was *seventy two t.*
Num 31:33
seventy four **thousand** *six hundred*
number of Judah *seventy four t.* and *six hundred.* *Num* 1:27; 2:4
seventy five **thousand**
seventy five t. sheep. *Num* 31:32
their foes *seventy five t.* *Esth* 9:16
seventy six **thousand** *five hundred*
numbered of Judah *seventy six t. five hundred.* *Num* 26:22
eighty **thousand**
Solomon had *eighty t.* hewers in the.
1 Ki 5:15; *2 Chr* 2:2, 18
eighty seven **thousand**
of Issachar, reckoned *eighty seven t.*
1 Chr 7:5
thousand **thousand**
of Israel were a *t. t.* *1 Chr* 21:5
have prepared a *t. t.* talents. 22:14
came with a host of a *t. t.* 2 *Chr* 14:9
two hundred **thousand** **thousand**
army of horsemen *two hundred t. t.*
Rev 9:16

thousands
be thou the mother of *t.* *Gen* 24:60
over them rulers of *t.* *Ex* 18:21, 25
shewing mercy to *t.* of them. 20:6
Deut 5:10
keeping mercy for *t.* *Ex* 34:7
heads of *t.* in Israel. *Num* 1:16
10:4; *Josh* 22:14, 21, 30
to the many *t.* of Israel. *Num* 10:36
were delivered out of the *t.* 31:5
them captains over *t.* *Deut* 1:15
the Lord came with ten *t.* of saints.
33:2; *Jude* 14
are the *t.* of Manasseh. *Deut* 33:17
him captains over *t.* *1 Sam* 8:12
yourselves by your *t.* 10:19
they have ascribed but *t.* 18:8
make you all captains of *t.?* 22:7
search him out throughout *t.* 23:23
Philistines passed on by *t.* 29:2

people came out by *t.* *2 Sam* 18:4
thy law is better than *t.* *Ps* 119:72
lovingkindness unto *t.* *Jer* 32:18
thousand *t.* ministered. *Dan* 7:10
thou be little among the *t.* *Mi* 5:2
Lord be pleased with *t.* of rams ? 6:7
how many *t.* of Jews. *Acts* 21:20
number of them was *t.* of *t. Rev* 5:11
see **captains**

ten thousands
the *ten t.* of Ephraim. *Deut* 33:17
David slain his *ten t.* *1 Sam* 18:7
8; 21:11; 29:5
I will not be afraid of *ten t. Ps* 3:6
sheep may bring forth *ten t.* 144:13
cast down many *ten t. Dan* 11:12
ten t. of rivers of oil. *Mi* 6:7

thread
take from a *t.* to a latchet. *Gen* 14:23
his hand a scarlet *t.* 38:28, 30
shalt bind this scarlet *t. Josh* 2:18
withs as a *t.* of tow. *Judg* 16:9*
ropes from his arms as a *t.* 12
thy lips are like a *t.* of. *S of S* 4:3

threaten, -ed
but let us straitly *t.* them not to.
Acts 4:17, 21
when he suffered he *t.* not. *1 Pet* 2:23

threatening, -s
Lord, behold their *t.* and. *Acts* 4:29
Saul yet breathing out *t.* and. 9:1
same things unto them, forbearing *t.*
Eph 6:9

three
he looked, and lo, *t.* men. *Gen* 18:2
not these *t.* unto her. *Ex* 21:11
t. branches of the candlestick.
25:32; 37:18
t. bowls made like unto. 33; 37:19
altar shall be *t.* cubits. 27:1; 38:1
pillars *t.,* their sockets *t.* 14, 15
38:14, 15
t. tenth deals of fine flour for a meat.
Lev 14:10; *Num* 15:9; 28:12
for the female estimation *t. Lev* 27:6
come out ye *t.* And they *t.* came out.
Num 12:4
t. tenth deals for a bullock. 28:20
28; 29:3, 9, 14
ye shall give *t.* cities on this. 35:14
Moses severed *t.* cities. *Deut* 4:41
19:2; 3, 7, 9
at the mouth of *t.* 17:6; 19:15
and Caleb drove thence the *t.* sons.
Josh 15:14; *Judg* 1:20
t. men for each tribe. *Josh* 18:4
the *t.* companies blew. *Judg* 7:20
he divided the people into *t.* 9:43
Hannah took with her *t. 1 Sam* 1:24
with fleshhook of *t.* teeth. 2:13
Hannah bare *t.* sons and two. 21
t. men, one carrying *t.* kids, another
carrying *t.* loaves of bread. 10:3
people in *t.* companies. 11:11
the *t.* eldest of Jesse's. 17:13, 14
I will shoot *t.* arrows on the. 20:20
Saul died, and his *t.* sons. 31:6
1 Chr 10:6
Saul and his *t.* sons. *1 Sam* 31:8
there were born *t.* sons. *2 Sam* 14:27
Joab thrust *t.* darts through. 18:14
Eleazar, one of the *t.* mighty. 23:9
1 Chr 11:12
t. of the thirty chief. *2 Sam* 23:13
t. mighty brake through. 16, 17
Abishai brother of Joab chief among
t. 23:18, 19
attained not to the first *t.* 19, 23
Benaiah had the name among *t.* 22
I offer thee *t.* things. 24:12
1 Chr 21:10
inner court with *t.* rows. *1 Ki* 6:36
were windows in *t.* rows. 7:4
t. oxen looking toward the north *t.* to
the west, *t.* to the south, *t.* to. 25
t. pound of gold went to one. 10:17
Alas ! that the Lord hath called
these *t.* kings. *2 Ki* 3:10, 13
sons of Zeruiah were *t. 1 Chr* 2:16
sons of Neariah *t.* 3:23
sons of Mushi *t.* 23:23
fourteen sons and *t.* daughters. 25:5
be laid with *t.* rows. *Ezra* 6:4
44

to Job *t.* daughters. *Job* 1:2; 42:13
the Chaldeans made out *t.* 1:17
Job's *t.* friends heard of all. 2:11
t. things which are never. *Pr* 30:15
there be *t.* things too wonderful. 18
t. things the earth is disquieted. 21
there be *t.* things which go well. 29
two or *t.* berries in the top. *Isa* 17:6
though these *t.* men were in it.
Ezek 14:14, 16, 18
the little chambers were *t.* 40:10, 21
the side chambers were *t.* 41:6
t. gates, after names of tribes. 48:31
32, 33, 34
did not we cast *t.* men ? *Dan* 3:24
set over these *t.* presidents. 6:2
it had *t.* ribs in the mouth. 7:5
were *t.* of the first horns. 8, 20, 24
mourning *t.* full weeks. 10:2, 3
there shall stand up *t.* kings. 11:2
for *t.* transgressions. *Amos* 1:3, 6, 9
11, 13
t. transgressions of. 2:1, 4, 6
so two or *t.* cities wandered. 4:8
t. shepherds I cut off. *Zech* 11:8
hid in *t.* measures of meal.
Mat 13:33; *Luke* 13:21
let us make here *t.* tabernacles.
Mat 17:4; *Mark* 9:5; *Luke* 9:33
in the mouth of two or *t.* witnesses.
Mat 18:16; *2 Cor* 13:1
where two or *t.* are gathered together
in my name. *Mat* 18:20
t. was neighbour to ? *Luke* 10:36
Friend, lend me *t.* loaves. 11:5
divided, *t.* against two, and two
against *t.* 12:52
t. hours after, when his. *Acts* 5:7
t. men seek thee. 10:19; 11:11
us as far as The *t.* taverns. 28:15
faith, hope, charity . . . *t. 1 Cor* 13:13
by two, or at most by *t.* and. 14:27
let the prophets speak two or *t.* 29
but before two or *t. 1 Tim* 5:19
two or *t.* witnesses. *Heb* 10:28
there are *t.* that bear record in heaven:
these *t.* are one. *1 John* 5:7
t. bear witness in earth, and these *t.* 8
and *t.* measures of barley. *Rev* 6:6
trumpet of *t.* angels who are. 8:13
by these *t.* was the third part. 9:18
I saw *t.* unclean spirits like. 16:13
city was divided into *t.* parts. 19
on the east *t.* gates, on the north *t.*
gates, on south *t.* . . . . west *t.* 21:13
see **days, hundred**

three months
about *t.* months after. *Gen* 38:24
she hid him *t.* months. *Ex* 2:2
in house of Obed-edom, *t.* months.
2 Sam 6:11; *1 Chr* 13:14
wilt thou flee *t.* months before ?
2 Sam 24:13; *1 Chr* 21:12
son of Josiah reigned *t.* months.
2 Ki 23:31; *2 Chr* 36:2
Jehoiachin reigned *t.* months.
2 Ki 24:8; *2 Chr* 36:9
there were yet *t.* months. *Amos* 4:7
nourished up *t.* months. *Acts* 7:20
boldly the space of *t.* months. 19:8
Paul abode in Greece *t.* months. 20:3
Moses was hid *t.* months. *Heb* 11:23

three times
t. times thou shalt keep. *Ex* 23:14
t. times in the year all thy males. 17
Deut 16:16
thou hast smitten me these *t. times.*
Num 22:28, 32
turned from me these *t. times.* 33
blessed them these *t. times.* 24:10
hast mocked me these *t. times.*
Judg 16:15
and bowed *t. times.* *1 Sam* 20:41
offered *t. times* a year. *1 Ki* 9:25
himself on the child *t. times.* 17:21
t. times did Joash beat. *2 Ki* 13:25
offering *t. times* in the. *2 Chr* 8:13
his knees *t. times* a day. *Dan* 6:10
his petition *t. times* a day. 13
this was done *t. times.* *Acts* 11:10

three years
heifer of *t. years* old, a she goat *t.*
years old . . . *t. years.* *Gen* 15:9

uncircumcised *t. years.* *Lev* 19:23
bring forth fruit for *t. years.* 25:21
at the end of *t. years.* *Deut* 14:28
had reigned *t. years.* *Judg* 9:22
in Geshur *t. years.* *2 Sam* 13:38
in the days of David *t. years.* 21:1
at end of *t. years* Shimei's servant.
1 Ki 2:39
once in *t. years* came the navy.
10:22; *2 Chr* 9:21
Abijam reigned *t. years* in Jerusalem. *1 Ki* 15:2; *2 Chr* 13:2
they continued *t. years.* *1 Ki* 22:1
besieged Samaria *t. years.* *2 Ki* 17:5
and at the end of *t. years.* 18:10
became his servant *t. years.* 24:1
either *t. years'* famine, or three
months to be. *1 Chr* 21:12
strong *t. years, t. years* they walked
in way of David. *2 Chr* 11:17
Abijah reigned *t. years.* 13:2
males, from *t. years* old. 31:16
an heifer of *t. years* old. *Isa* 15:5*
Jer 48:34*
within *t. years,* as years of. *Isa* 16:14
walked barefoot *t. years.* 20:3
nourishing them *t. years.* *Dan* 1:5
your tithes after *t. years.* *Amos* 4:4
heaven shut up *t. years.* *Luke* 4:25
Jas 5:17
t. years I come seeking. *Luke* 13:7
t. years I ceased not to. *Acts* 20:31
after *t. years* I went up. *Gal* 1:18

threefold
t. cord is not quickly. *Eccl* 4:12

threescore
Isaac *t.* years old when. *Gen* 25:26
took from them *t.* cities. *Deut* 3:4
Josh 13:30
so that three hundred and *t.* died.
2 Sam 2:31
pertained *t.* great cities. *1 Ki* 4:13
his provision was *t.* measures. 22
The house . . . built for the Lord,
the length thereof was *t.* cubits.
6:2; *2 Chr* 3:3
and he took *t.* men. *2 Ki* 25:19
married when *t.* years. *1 Chr* 2:21
Rehoboam took *t.* *2 Chr* 11:21
temple *t.* cubits, breadth *t.* *Ezra* 6:3
t. valiant men are. *S of S* 3:7
there are *t.* queens, fourscore. 6:8
put to death *t.* men of the. *Jer* 52:25
whose height was *t.* cubits. *Dan* 3:1
from Jerusalem about *t.* *Luke* 24:13
widow be taken under *t.* *1 Tim* 5:9
see **sixty**

threescore and one
Lord's tribute of asses, *t.* and one.
Num 31:39

threescore and two
able men *t.* and two. *1 Chr* 26:8
t. and two years old. *Dan* 5:31
in *t.* and two weeks the street. 9:25
after *t.* and two weeks Messiah. 26

threescore and five
within *t.* and five years. *Isa* 7:8

threescore and six
souls which came with Jacob *t.* and
six. *Gen* 46:26
of her purifying *t.* and six days.
Lev 12:5

threescore and seven
t. and seven priests'. *Neh* 7:72

threescore and eight
brethren *t.* and eight. *1 Chr* 16:38

threescore and ten
which came into Egypt, were *t.* and
ten. *Gen* 46:27; *Deut* 10:22
for Israel *t.* and ten days. *Gen* 50:3
twelve wells of water, and *t.* and ten
palm trees. *Ex* 15:27; *Num* 33:9
t. and ten kings, their. *Judg* 1:7
had *t.* and ten sons. 8:30; 9:2
they gave him *t.* and ten pieces. 9:4
he slew *t.* and ten persons. 5, 18, 24
rode on *t.* and ten ass colts. 12:14
brought *t.* and ten bullocks.
2 Chr 29:32
sabbath, to fulfil *t.* and ten. 36:21
of our years are *t.* and ten. *Ps* 90:10

threescore

thou hast had indignation these *t. and ten years?* Zech 1:12
t. and ten horsemen. Acts 23:23
see seventy

threescore *and twelve*
t. and twelve beeves. Num 31:38

threescore *and fifteen*
kindred *t. and fifteen.* Acts 7:14

threescore *and seventeen*
Succoth *t. and seventeen.* Judg 8:14

thresh

thou shalt *t.* the mountains. *Isa* 41:15
it is time to *t.* her. *Jer* 51:33*
arise, and *t.* O daughter. *Mi* 4:13
thou didst *t.* the heathen. *Hab* 3:12

threshed

Gideon *t.* wheat by the. *Judg* 6:11*
fitches not *t.* with a threshing.
Isa 28:27
because they *t.* Gilead. *Amos* 1:3

thresheth

t. in hope, be partaker. *1 Cor* 9:10

threshing

your *t.* shall reach unto. *Lev* 26:5
here be *t.* instruments. *2 Sam* 24:22
1 Chr 21:23
like the dust by *t.* *2 Ki* 13:7
Ornan was *t.* wheat. *1 Chr* 21:20
O my *t.* and the corn of my floor.
Isa 21:10
he will not ever be *t.* it. 28:28
will make thee a new sharp *t.* 41:15
see floor, floors

threshold

hands were upon the *t.* *Judg* 19:27
hands cut off upon the *t.* *1 Sam* 5:4
tread not on the *t.* of Dagon. 5
to *t.* the child died. *1 Ki* 14:17
the glory of God was gone up to the *t.* of the house. *Ezek* 9:3; 10:4
God departed from the *t.* 10:18
in their setting of their *t.* by. 43:8
prince shall worship at the *t.* 46:2
out from under the *t.* eastward. 47:1
all that leap on the *t.* *Zeph* 1:9

thresholds

keeping ward at the *t.* *Neh* 12:25*
of their threshold by my *t.* *Ezek* 43:8
desolation shall be in the *t.*
Zeph 2:14

threw

Shimei *t.* stones at David and cast dust. *2 Sam* 16:13
they *t.* Jezebel down. *2 Ki* 9:33
and they *t.* down the. *2 Chr* 31:1*
a certain poor widow and she *t.* in two mites, which. *Mark* 12:42
the devil *t.* him down. *Luke* 9:42
as they cried, and *t.* *Acts* 22:23

threwest

their persecutors thou *t.* *Neh* 9:11

thrice

t. in the year shall. *Ex* 34:23, 24
and Joash smote *t.* *2 Ki* 13:18
thou shalt smite Syria but *t.* 19
thou shalt deny me *t.* *Mat* 26:34
75; *Mark* 14:30, 72; *Luke* 22:34
61; *John* 13:38
this was done *t.* *Acts* 10:16
t. was I beaten with rods, once was I stoned, *t.* I suffered. *2 Cor* 11:25
I besought the Lord *t.* 12:8

throat

their *t.* is an open sepulchre.
Ps 5:9; *Rom* 3:13
crying, my *t.* is dried. *Ps* 69:3
nor speak they through their *t.* 115:7
put a knife to thy *t.* if. *Pr* 23:2
and withhold thy *t.* from. *Jer* 2:25
servant took him by the *t. Mat* 18:28

throne

The seat in which a king sits on ceremonial occasions. The scripture describes the throne of Solomon as the finest and richest throne in the world, 1 Ki 10:20. It was all of ivory, and plated with pure gold. The ascent was six steps; the back was round, and two arms supported the seat. Twelve

golden lions, one on each side of every step, made a principal part of its ornament.
Throne is also used as a symbol of sovereign power and dignity; thus Pharaoh tells Joseph, Gen 41:40, Only in the throne will I be greater than thou.
Heaven is the throne of God, Isa 66:1. Justice and judgement are the habitation of the throne of the Lord, Ps 89:14. Christ Jesus is set down at the right hand of the throne of God, Heb 12:2.

only in the *t.* will I be. *Gen* 41:40
when he sitteth on *t.* of. *Deut* 17:18
make them inherit the *t.* *1 Sam* 2:8
to set up the *t.* of David. *2 Sam* 3:10
stablish *t.* of his kingdom. 7:13, 16
Solomon shall sit on my *t.*
1 Ki 1:13, 17, 24, 30, 35
given one to sit on my *t.* this day. 48
not fail thee a man on the *t.* 2:4; 8:25
9:5; *2 Chr* 6:16; *Jer* 33:17
Solomon sat on *t.* of. *1 Ki* 2:12, 24
8:20; 10:9; *1 Chr* 29:23
the king made a great *t.* *1 Ki* 10:18
2 Chr 9:17
set him on his father's *t.* *2 Ki* 10:3
fourth generation shall sit on the *t.*
30; 15:12
Joash sat on *t.* 11:19; *2 Chr* 23:20
repaired unto the *t.* of the. *Neh* 3:7
kings are they on the *t.* *Job* 36:7
thou satest in the *t.* *Ps* 9:4
the Lord's *t.* is in heaven, his. 11:4
thy *t.* O God, is for ever. 45:6
Lam 5:19; *Heb* 1:8
God sitteth on the *t.* of. *Ps* 47:8
I will build thy *t.* to all. 89:4
judgement are habitation of thy *t.* 14
t. of iniquity have fellowship? 94:20
thy body will I set on thy *t.* 132:11
children shall sit on thy *t.* 12
a king that sitteth in the *t.* *Pr* 20:8
the Lord sitting upon a *t.* *Isa* 6:1
on *t.* of David and his kingdom. 9:7
I will exalt my *t.* above the. 14:13
shall be for a glorious *t.* 22:23
there is no *t.* O daughter. 47:1
the heaven is my *t.* and earth. 66:1
Acts 7:49
shall call Jerusalem the *t.* *Jer* 3:17
kings that sit on David's *t.* 13:13
disgrace the *t.* of thy glory. 14:21
a glorious high *t.* from the. 17:12
kings sitting on the *t.* 25; 22:4, 30
O king, that sittest upon the *t.* 22:2
29:16
none to sit on the *t.* of David. 36:30
I will set my *t.* in Elam. 49:38
was the likeness of a *t.* *Ezek* 1:26
10:1
the place of my *t.* shall Israel. 43:7
I will overthrow the *t.* of. *Hag* 2:22
by heaven, for it is God's *t.*
Mat 5:34; 23:22
the Son of man shall sit in the *t.*
19:28; 25:31
give him the *t.* of David. *Luke* 1:32
let us come boldly to the *t.* *Heb* 4:16
right hand the *t.* of God. 8:1; 12:2
I grant to sit in my *t.* *Rev* 3:21
a *t.* was set in heaven, and one. 4:2
a rainbow round about the *t.* 3
about the *t.* were four and. 4
t. proceeded lightnings and thunderings ... seven lamps before *t.* 5
before the *t.* there was a sea of glass, in *t.* and round about the *t.* were. 6
thanks to him that sat on the *t.* 9
fall down before him that sat on the *t.* 10; 7:11
him that sat on the *t.* a book. 5:1
midst of the *t.* stood a Lamb. 6
right hand of him that sat on the *t.* 7
many angels about the *t.* 11
be unto him that sitteth upon the *t.* 13
6:16
multitude stood before the *t.* 7:9
our God which sitteth on the *t.* 10
are they before the *t.* of God and serve him: he that sitteth on *t.* 15

the Lamb in midst of the *t.* shall.
Rev 7:17
altar which was before the *t.* 8:3
a new song before the *t.* 14:3
without fault before the *t.* of God. 5
a voice from the *t.* 16:17; 19:5
God that sat on the *t.* 19:4
I saw a great white *t.* and. 20:11
he that sat on *t.* said, Behold. 21:5
river, proceeding out of the *t.* 22:1
the *t.* of God and of the Lamb. 3

his throne

from firstborn of Pharaoh that sitteth on his *t.* *Ex* 11:5; 12:29
and the king and his *t.* *2 Sam* 14:9
the Lord make his *t.* greater.
1 Ki 1:37, 47
and sat down on his *t.* 2:19
upon his seed, and on his *t.* shall. 33
Zimri sat on his *t.*, he slew. 16:11
and Jehoshaphat king of Judah, sat each on his *t.* 22:10; *2 Chr* 18:9
I saw the Lord sitting on his *t.*
1 Ki 22:19; *2 Chr* 18:18
and Jeroboam sat upon his *t.*
2 Ki 13:13
set his *t.* above it. 25:28; *Jer* 52:32
back the face of his *t.* *Job* 26:9
he hath prepared his *t.* *Ps* 9:7
his *t.* to endure as the days. 89:29
shall endure, and his *t.* as the sun. 36
thou hast cast his *t.* down to. 44
the habitation of his *t.* 97:2
the Lord hath prepared his *t.* 103:19
and his *t.* is upholden. *Pr* 20:28
set each his *t.* at the gates. *Jer* 1:15
should not have a son on his *t.* 33:21
and I will set his *t.* upon these. 43:10
deposed from his kingly *t.* *Dan* 5:20
his *t.* was like the fiery flame. 7:9
Nineveh rose from his *t.* *Jonah* 3:6
rule upon his *t.* and he shall be a priest on his *t.* and. *Zech* 6:13
Christ to sit on his *t.* *Acts* 2:30
from seven spirits which are before his *t.* *Rev* 1:4
sit down with my Father in his *t.* 3:21
caught up to God, to his *t.* 12:5
see establish, established

thrones

for there are set *t.* of. *Ps* 122:5
raised up from their *t.* *Isa* 14:9
come down from their *t.* *Ezek* 26:16
till the *t.* were cast down. *Dan* 7:9
upon twelve *t.* judging the twelve.
Mat 19:28; *Luke* 22:30
him, whether they be *t.* *Col* 1:16
I saw *t.* and they sat upon. *Rev* 20:4

throng

lest they should *t.* him. *Mark* 3:9
the multitude *t.* thee. *Luke* 8:45*

thronged

and much people *t.* him. *Mark* 5:24
Luke 8:42

thronging

thou seest the multitude *t.* the.
Mark 5:31

through

thrust both of them *t.* *Num* 25:8
Ahaziah fell *t.* a lattice. *2 Ki* 1:2
yet *t.* the scent of water. *Job* 14:9
their tongue walketh *t.* *Ps* 73:9
t. idleness the house droppeth.
Eccl 10:18
shewing himself *t.* the. *S of S* 2:9
I would go *t.* them, I would burn.
Isa 27:4
thou passest *t.* the waters, and *t.* 43:2
go *t.* go *t.* the gates, prepare. 62:10
after he brought me *t.* *Ezek* 46:19
and brought me *t.* the waters. 47:4
the third part *t.* fire. *Zech* 13:9
he walketh *t.* dry places. *Mat* 12:4
they let him down *t.* the. *Luke* 5:19
ye are clean *t.* the word I. *John* 15:3
keep *t.* thine own name those. 17:11
sanctify them *t.* thy truth, thy. 17
believing ye might have life *t.* 20:31
peace with God *t.* our Lord Jesus.
Rom 5:1
is eternal life *t.* Jesus Christ. 6:23
if ye *t.* the spirit do mortify the. 8:13

of him, *t*. him, to him, are. *Rom* 11:36
to God be glory *t*. Jesus Christ. 16:27
t. the thanksgiving of.   *2 Cor* 4:15
for I *t*. the law am dead to. *Gal* 2:19
kindness towards us *t*. Christ Jesus.
         Eph 2:7
habitation of God *t*. the Spirit.   22
is above all, and *t*. all, in you all. 4:6
t. the ignorance that is in them.   18
pierced themselves *t*.   *1 Tim* 6:10
who *t*. the eternal Spirit. *Heb* 9:14
t. the vail, that is to say.   10:20
t. the blood of the everlasting. 13:20

throughly
(*American Revision changes to
thoroughly*)
cause him to be *t*. healed. *Ex* 21:19
his images brake they in pieces *t*.
         2 Ki 11:18
my grief were *t*. weighed. *Job* 6:2*
wash me *t*. from mine.   *Ps* 51:2
shall *t*. glean the remnant. *Jer* 6:9
if ye *t*. amend your ways and your
doings, if ye *t*. execute.   7:5
he shall *t*. plead their cause. 50:34
I *t*. washed away thy. *Ezek* 16:9
he will *t*. purge his floor. *Mat* 3:12
         Luke 3:17
been *t*. made manifest. *2 Cor* 11:6
man of God *t*. furnished unto.
         2 Tim 3:17*

throughout
I led Abraham *t*. the land. *Josh* 24:3
search him *t*. thousands of Judah.
         1 Sam 23:23
Hezekiah *t*. all Judah. *2 Chr* 31:20
be preached *t*. the world. *Mark* 14:9
woven from the top *t*.   *John* 19:23
is spoken of *t*. the world. *Rom* 1:8
see generations

throw
ye shall *t*. down their altars.
         Judg 2:2*
t. down the altar of Baal thy.   6:25
t. her down. So they.   *2 Ki* 9:33
the nations to *t*. down.   *Jer* 1:10
as I have watched over them, to *t*.
down.   31:28
they shall *t*. down thine. *Ezek* 16:39
I will *t*. down all thy strong. *Mi* 5:11
build, but I will *t*. down.   *Mal* 1:4

throwing
him with *t*. a stone.   *Num* 35:17*

thrown
the horse and his rider hath he *t*.
         Ex 15:1, 21
because he hath *t*. down. *Judg* 6:32
his head be *t*. to thee. *2 Sam* 20:21
Israel have *t*. down thine altars.
         1 Ki 19:10, 14
it shall not be *t*. down. *Jer* 31:40
her walls are *t*. down.   50:15
the Lord hath *t*. down. *Lam* 2:2
he hath *t*. down, and hath not.   17
I will leave thee *t*. into. *Ezek* 29:5
mountains shall be *t*. down. 38:20
and the rocks are *t*. down. *Nah* 1:6
upon another, that shall not be *t*.
   Mat 24:2; *Mark* 13:2; *Luke* 21:6
when the devil had *t*. him. *Luke* 4:35
Babylon shall be *t*. down. *Rev* 18:21

thrust
he shall surely *t*. you.   *Ex* 11:1
because they were *t*. out of. 12:39
Balaam's ass *t*. herself. *Num* 22:25
Phinehas *t*. both of them.   25:8
but if he *t*. him of hatred.   35:20
but if he *t*. him suddenly without. 22
hath spoken . . . to *t*. thee. *Deut* 13:5
because he sought to *t*. thee from. 10
t. the awl through his ear.   15:17
he shall *t*. out the enemy.   33:27
Ehud *t*. the dagger into. *Judg* 3:21
he *t*. the fleece together, and.   6:38
and Zebul *t*. out Gaal and.   9:41
his young men *t*. Abimelech.   54
wives' eyes grew up, and they *t*. 11:2
t. out all your right eyes. *1 Sam* 11:2
T. me through therewith . . . come
and *t*. me.   31:4; *1 Chr* 10:4
and *t*. his sword in his. *2 Sam* 2:16
Joab *t*. 3 darts through heart. 18:14

shall be as thorns *t*. away. *2 Sam* 23:6
Solomon *t*. out Abiathar.   *1 Ki* 2:27
came near to *t*. her away. *2 Ki* 4:27
they *t*. Uzziah out.   *2 Chr* 26:20
thou hast *t*. at me, that. *Ps* 118:13
found shall be *t*. through. *Isa* 13:15
of those that are *t*. through.   14:19
they that are *t*. through. *Jer* 51:4
shall *t*. thee through with swords.
         Ezek 16:40
t. with side and shoulder.   34:21
to *t*. them out of their.   46:18
neither one *t*. another. *Joel* 2:8
shall *t*. him through. *Zech* 13:3
they rose and *t*. him. *Luke* 4:29
and prayed him he would *t*. out. 5:3
shalt be *t*. down to hell.   10:15
and you yourselves *t*. out.   13:28
and *t*. my hand into his side.
         John 20:25, 27
he that did the wrong *t*. *Acts* 7:27
but our fathers *t*. him from them. 39
t. them into the inner prison. 16:24
and now do they *t*. us out privily ? 37
if it were possible, to *t*. in.   27:39
stoned or *t*. through with. *Heb* 12:20
t. in thy sickle, for the. *Rev* 14:15
he sat on the cloud, *t*. in his sickle. 16
t. in thy sharp sickle and gather. 18
the angel *t*. in his sickle into.   19

thrusteth
God *t*. him down, not man. *Job* 32:13

thumb
thou put it on the *t*. of their right
hand.   *Ex* 29:20; *Lev* 8:23, 24
         14:14, 17, 25, 28

thumbs
him and cut off his *t*.   *Judg* 1:6
their *t*. and toes cut off.   7

Thummim
Urim *and* Thummim; *According to
the Hebrew,* Ex 28:30, *the literal
signification of these two words is,*
lights *and* perfections, *or the shining
and the perfect. According to St.
Jerome,* doctrine *and* judgement.
According to the LXX, declaration
or manifestation, *and* truth. *They
were worn in or attached to the
breastplate of the high priest when
inquiring of God.*
breastplate of judgement, the Urim
and the *T*.   *Ex* 28:30; *Lev* 8:8
let thy *T*. and Urim be with thy Holy
One.   *Deut* 33:8
stood up priest with Urim and *T*.
         Ezra 2:63; *Neh* 7:65

thunder
the Lord sent *t*. and hail. *Ex* 9:23
the *t*. shall cease, nor shall.   29
thundered with great *t*. *1 Sam* 7:10
he shall send *t*.   12:17
the Lord sent *t*.   18
the *t*. of his power who ? *Job* 26:14
a way for the lightning of the *t*.
       28:26; 38:25
clothed his neck with *t*.?   39:19*
smelleth the *t*. of the captains.   25
the voice of thy *t*. was in. *Ps* 77:18
in the secret place of *t*.   81:7
at the voice of thy *t*. they.   104:7
visited of the Lord with *t*. *Isa* 29:6
which is, The sons of *t*. *Mark* 3:17
as it were the noise of *t*. *Rev* 6:1
as the voice of a great *t*.   14:2

thunder, *verb*
shall he *t*. upon them.   *1 Sam* 2:10
or canst thou *t*. with a voice ?
         Job 40:9

thunderbolts
their flocks to hot *t*.   *Ps* 78:48

thundered
the Lord *t*. with a great. *1 Sam* 7:10
the Lord *t*. from heaven.
     2 Sam 22:14; *Ps* 18:13
heard it, said that it *t*. *John* 12:29

thundereth
he *t*. with the voice of his. *Job* 37:4
God *t*. marvellously with his.   5
the God of glory *t*.   *Ps* 29:3

thunderings
be no more mighty *t*.   *Ex* 9:28
and all the people saw the *t*.   20:18
out of the throne proceeded *t*.
         Rev 4:5; 19:6
there were voices and *t*. 8:5; 11:19

thunders
the *t*. and hail ceased. *Ex* 9:33, 34
there were *t*. and lightnings.   19:16
         Rev 16:18
see seven

thus
t. did Noah, according as God.
         Gen 6:22
t. she was reproved.   20:16
why am I *t*.?   25:22
dealest thou *t*. with us ? *Ex* 5:15
t. shall ye eat it, with your.   12:11
hast thou dealt *t*. with us ?   14:11
t. separate the children. *Lev* 15:31
t. shall Aaron come into the.   16:3
t. shalt thou separate the. *Num* 8:14
deal *t*. with me, kill me.   11:15
hath the Lord done *t*.? *Deut* 29:24
wherefore liest thou *t*. on ? *Josh* 7:10
hast thou served us *t*.? *Judg* 8:1
why askest thou *t*. after my ? 13:18
if they say *t*. to us, Tarry. *1 Sam* 14:9
but if they say *t*., Come up to us. 10
if he say *t*., It is well.   20:7
         2 Sam 15:26
be more vile than *t*.   *2 Sam* 6:22
I may not tarry *t*. with thee.   18:14
t. he said, O my son Absalom.   33
t. they spake before.   *1 Ki* 3:22
t. the Lord saved Hezekiah.
         2 Chr 32:22
and *t*. they returned.   *Ezra* 5:11
and therein was a record *t*.   6:2
even *t*. be he shaken out. *Neh* 5:13
t. shall it be done to. *Esth* 6:9, 11
why then are ye *t*.?   *Job* 27:12
if I say I will speak *t*.   *Ps* 73:15
t. my heart was grieved, and.   21
t. shall the man be blessed. 128:4
when *t*. it shall be in the. *Isa* 24:13
t. shall they be unto thee with. 47:15
for *t*. hath the Lord. *Jer* 4:27; 6:6
t. shall it be done unto them.   5:13
deal *t*. with them in time of. 18:23
why hath the Lord done *t*. to ? 22:8
t. might we procure evil.   26:19
to whom art thou *t*. like ? *Ezek* 31:18
is it not even *t*. O children of Israel ?
         Amos 2:11
t. ye brought an offering. *Mal* 1:13
t. it is written of the prophet.
     Mat 2:5; *Luke* 24:46
t. it becomes us to fulfil. *Mat* 3:15
scriptures be fulfilled, that *t*. 26:54
t. hath Lord dealt with. *Luke* 1:25
hast thou *t*. dealt with us ?   2:48
master, *t*. saying, thou reproachest.
         11:45
t. shall it be when Son of man. 17:30
Pharisee prayed *t*., God, I.   18:11
said, Suffer ye *t*. far.   22:51
having said *t*. he gave up.   23:46
t. spake, Jesus himself stood in. 24:36
when he had *t*. spoken, he.   40
it is written, *t*. it behoved Christ. 46
journey, sat *t*. on well. *John* 4:6
when he *t*. had spoken, he cried.11:43
if we let him *t*. alone, all will.   48
he said, *T*. saith the Holy. *Acts* 21:11
Why hast made me *t*.? *Rom* 9:20
t. are the secrets of his heart made
manifest.   *1 Cor* 14:25
love of Christ constraineth us, because we *t*. judge, that if.*2 Cor* 5:14
be perfect, be *t*. minded. *Phil* 3:15
though we *t*. speak.   *Heb* 6:9
t. I saw horses in vision. *Rev* 9:17
because thou hast judged *t*.   16:5
see did, do, Lord

thus *and* thus
Achan said *t*. and *t*.   *Josh* 7:20
t. and *t*. dealeth Micah. *Judg* 18:4
t. and *t*. did Ahithophel counsel
Absalom, and *t*. and *t*. have I.
         2 Sam 17:15
t. and *t*. shalt thou say to. *1 Ki* 14:5

T. *and* t. said the maid. *2 Ki* 5:4
he said, *T. and* t. spake he to. 9:12

Thyatira
Lydia, of the city of *T.* *Acts* 16:14
send it to *T.* *Rev* 1:11
of the church in *T.* write. 2:18
unto you and unto the rest in *T.* 24

thyine
merchandise of *t.* wood. *Rev* 18:12

thyself
separate *t.* I pray thee. *Gen* 13:9
persons, and take goods to *t.* 14:21
return, and submit *t.* under. 16:9
that thou hast unto *t.* 33:9
as yet exaltest *t.* *Ex* 9:17
wilt thou refuse to humble *t.?* 10:3
take heed to *t.*, see my face.28; 34:12
Deut 4:9; 12:13, 19, 30
why sittest thou *t.* alone ? *Ex* 18:14
so shall it be easier for *t.* and. 22
come and present *t.* there. 34:2
an atonement for *t.* *Lev* 9:7
neighbour's wife to defile *t.* 18:20
lie with any beast to defile *t.* 23
love thy neighbour as *t.* 19:18
Mat 19:19; 22:39; *Mark* 12:31
thou shalt love him as *t.* *Lev* 19:34
bear it not *t.* alone. *Num* 11:17
except thou make *t.* a prince. 16:13
nations greater than *t.* *Deut* 9:1
spoil shalt thou take to *t.* 20:14
wherewith thou coverest *t.* 22:12
redeem thou my right to *t. Ruth* 4:6
if iniquity be in me, slay me *t.*
1 Sam 20:8
thee from avenging *t.* 25:26
thou shalt bestir *t.* *2 Sam* 5:24
has confirmed to *t.* thy people. 7:24
thy bed and make *t.* sick. 13:5
feign *t.* a mourner and put. 14:2
t. wouldest have set *t.* against. 18:13
thou wilt shew *t.* merciful. 22:26
Ps 18:25
with the pure thou wilt shew *t.* pure.
2 Sam 22:27; *Ps* 18:26
and shew *t.* a man. *1 Ki* 2:2
thou hast not asked for *t.* long life.
3:11; *2 Chr* 1:11
with me and refresh *t.* *1 Ki* 13:7
pray thee, and disguise *t.* 14:2
why feignest thou *t.* to be ? 6
go shew *t.* to Ahab, and I. 18:1
strengthen *t.* and see what. 20:22
so shall thy judgement be, *t.* hast. 40
because thou hast sold *t.* to. 21:20
hast humbled *t.* *2 Ki* 22:19
2 Chr 34:27
advise with *t.* what. *1 Chr* 21:12
thou hast joined *t.* with Ahaziah.
2 Chr 20:37
thy brethren, better than *t.* 21:13
think not with *t.* that thou. *Esth* 4:13
dost restrain wisdom to *t.? Job* 15:8
acquaint *t.* with him, and. 22:21
thou opposest *t.* against me. 30:21
thine anger, lift up *t.* *Ps* 7:6
why hidest thou *t.* in times ? 10:1
stir up *t.* and awake to my. 35:23
delight *t.* also in the Lord. 37:4
when thou doest well to *t.* 49:18
altogether such an one as *t.* 50:21
boastest thou *t.* in mischief ? 52:1
displeased, O turn *t.* to us. 60:1
madest strong for *t.* 80:15, 17
shew *t.* 94:1
lift up *t.* thou judge. 2
do this, my son, and deliver *t.*
Pr 6:3, 5
thou shalt be wise for *t.* 9:12
fret not *t.* because of evil men. 24:19
and make it fit for *t.* in the. 27
put not forth *t.* in presence of. 25:6
boast not *t.* of to-morrow. 27:1
foolishly in lifting up *t.* 30:32
make *t.* over wise; why shouldest
thou destroy *t* ? *Eccl* 7:16
that thou *t.* also hast cursed. 22
hide *t.* as for a little. *Isa* 26:20
lifting up *t.* the nations were. 45:15
art a God that hidest *t.* 45:15
shake *t.* from the dust, loose *t.* 52:2
thou hast discovered *t.* to. 57:8

thou didst debase *t.* even. *Isa* 57:9
thou delight *t.* in the Lord. 58:14
make *t.* a glorious name. 63:14
wilt thou refrain *t.* for these ? 64:12
which say, Stand by *t.*, come. 65:5
procured this unto *t.* *Jer* 2:17
clothest *t.* with crimson, in vain shalt
thou make *t.* fair; thy lovers. 4:30
sackcloth, wallow *t.* in ashes. 6:26
t. shall discontinue from. 17:4
I will make thee a terror to *t.* 20:4
because thou clothest *t.* in. 22:15
redemption is thine, buy it for *t.* 32:8
seekest thou great things for *t.* 45:5
furnish *t.* to go into captivity. 46:19
how long wilt thou cut *t.?* 47:5
O sword, put up *t.* into thy. 6
give *t.* no rest, let not. *Lam* 2:18
thou hast covered *t.* with. 3:44
be drunken, make *t.* naked. 4:21
go shut *t.* within thine. *Ezek* 3:24
thou madest to *t.* images. 16:17
and thou hast defiled *t.* in. 22:4
for whom thou didst wash *t.* 23:40
hast lifted up *t.* in height. 31:10
prepare for *t.* and all thy. 38:7
said, Let thy gifts be to *t. Dan* 5:17
but hast lifted up *t.* against. 23
and to chasten *t.* before thy. 10:12
thou hast destroyed *t.* *Hos* 13:9
though thou exalt *t.* as the. *Ob* 4
Aphrah roll *t.* in dust. *Mi* 1:10
now gather *t.* in troops, O. 5:1
make *t.* many as the. *Nah* 3:15
deliver *t.* O Zion, that. *Zech* 2:7
If thou be the Son of God, cast *t.*
down. *Mat* 4:6; *Luke* 4:9
shalt not forswear *t.* *Mat* 5:33
shew *t.* to priest. 8:4; *Mark* 1:44
Luke 5:14
save *t.* *Mat* 27:40; *Mark* 15:30
Luke 23:39
Physician, heal *t.* *Luke* 4:23
when thou *t.* beholdest not. 6:42
Lord, trouble not *t.* for I am. 7:6
love thy neighbour as *t.* 10:27
Rom 13:9; *Gal* 5:14; *Jas* 2:8
will not rather say, Make ready and
gird *t.* *Luke* 17:8
what sayest thou of *t.?* *John* 1:22
if thou do these things, shew *t.* 7:4
thou bearest record of *t.* it. 8:13
whom makest thou *t.?* 53
a man, makest *t.* God. 10:33
thou wilt manifest *t.* unto us ? 14:22
sayest thou this of *t.?* or did ? 18:34
young, thou girdest *t.* 21:18
join *t.* to this chariot. *Acts* 8:29
gird *t.* 12:8
do *t.* no harm. 16:28
purify *t.* with them, that all may
know that thou *t.* walkest. 21:24
t. mayest take knowledge. 24:8
permitted to speak for *t.* . . . *Festus
said, Paul, thou art beside *t.* 26:1
thou condemnest *t.* *Rom* 2:1
that thou *t.* art guide of the blind. 19
teachest thou not *t.?* 21
hast thou faith ? have it to *t.* 14:22
considering *t.* lest thou. *Gal* 6:1
oughtest to behave *t.* *1 Tim* 3:15
and exercise *t.* rather unto. 4:7
these things, give *t.* wholly to. 15
take heed to *t.* and to the doctrine;
in doing this thou shalt save *t.* 16
other men's sins: keep *t.* pure. 5:22
minds, from such withdraw *t.* 6:5
to shew *t.* approved. *2 Tim* 2:15
shewing *t.* a pattern of. *Tit* 2:7

Tiberias
which is the sea of *T.* *John* 6:1
there came other boats from *T.* 23

Tibni
half of the people followed *T.*
1 Ki 16:21
against those that followed *T.* 22

tidings
heard these evil *t.* *Ex* 33:4
wife heard the *t.* *1 Sam* 4:19
they told the *t.* of the men of Jabesh.
11:4*, 5*
alive to bring *t.* to Gath. 27:11*

when *t.* came of Saul. *2 Sam* 4:4
t. came, saying, Absalom. 13:30
run and bear the king *t.* 18:19
shalt not bear *t.* this day. 20
thou hast no *t.* ready. 22
Cushi came, Cushi said, *T.* my. 31
then *t.* came to Joab. *1 Ki* 2:28
sent to thee with heavy *t.* 14:6
and sent to carry *t.* to. *1 Chr* 10:9
not be afraid of evil *t.* *Ps* 112:7
man that brought *t.* *Jer* 20:15
for they have heard evil *t.* 49:23
shalt answer for the *t.* *Ezek* 21:7
t. out of the east shall. *Dan* 11:44
I am sent to shew thee these glad *t.*
Luke 1:19; 2:10
shewing the glad *t.* of the. 8:1
t. of these things came. *Acts* 11:22*
we declare unto you glad *t.* 13:32
t. came to the chief captain. 21:31
that bring glad *t.* of good. *Rom* 10:15
see **good**

tie
and *t.* the kine. *1 Sam* 6:7, 10
bind on thy heart and *t.* *Pr* 6:21

tied
they *t.* to it a lace of blue. *Ex* 39:31
but horses *t.*, and asses *t. 2 Ki* 7:10
ye shall find an ass *t.* *Mat* 21:2
Mark 11:2, 4; *Luke* 19:30

Tiglath-pileser
T. came and took Ijon. *2 Ki* 15:29
Ahaz sent messengers to *T.* 16:7
carried away Beerah. *1 Chr* 5:6
stirred up the spirit of *T.* 26
T. came and distressed Ahaz.
2 Chr 28:20

tile
son of man, take thee a *t.* *Ezek* 4:1

tiling
they let him down through the *t.*
Luke 5:19*

till
do any thing *t.* thou be. *Gen* 19:22
t. I know what God will. *1 Sam* 22:3
if I taste bread *t.* the. *2 Sam* 3:35
he was helped *t.* he. *2 Chr* 26:15
the wrath arose, *t.* there. 36:16
t. there stood up a priest. *Ezra* 2:63
Neh 7:65
be angry with us *t.* thou. *Ezra* 9:14
all the days will I wait *t.* *Job* 14:14
t. I die. 27:5
not purged, *t.* ye die. *Isa* 22:14
wickedness *t.* thou find. *Ps* 10:15
a wise man keepeth it in *t.* *Pr* 29:11*
t. I might see what was. *Eccl* 2:3
stir not up my love *t.* he please.
S of S 2:7; 3:5
that lay field to field, *t.* *Isa* 5:8
no rest, *t.* he establish, and *t.* he
make Jerusalem a praise. 62:7
destroy *t.* they. *Jer* 49:9; *Ob* 5
t. he had cast them out. *Jer* 52:3
t. the Lord look down. *Lam* 3:50
wast perfect, *t.* iniquity. *Ezek* 28:15
t. seven times pass over. *Dan* 4:23
but go thou thy way *t.* the. 12:13
t. they acknowledge their. *Hos* 5:15
t. he rain righteousness upon. 10:12
t. she had brought forth. *Mat* 1:25*
t. heaven and earth pass, one. 5:18
I am straitened *t.* it be. *Luke* 12:50
doth not seek diligently *t.* she. 15:8
he said unto them, Occupy *t.* 19:13
if I will that he tarry *t.* I come.
John 21:22, 23
t. another king arose. *Acts* 7:18
not eat, *t.* they had killed Paul.
23:12, 14, 21
t. we all come in the. *Eph* 4:13
without offence, *t.* the day. *Phil* 1:10
t. I come, give attendance to reading. *1 Tim* 4:13
which ye have, hold fast *t.* I come.
Rev 2:25
t. we have sealed the servants. 7:3
t. the seven plagues were. 15:8
t. the thousand years should. 20:3
see **consumed, morning, until**

till, *verb*
was not a man to *t.* the ground.
Gen 2:5; 3:23

thy servants shall *t.*   *2 Sam* 9:10
they shall *t.* it, and dwell therein.
         Jer 27:11

tillage
was over them that were for *t.*
         1 Chr 27:26
have the tithes of *t.*   *Neh* 10:37
much food is in the *t.*   *Pr* 13:23

tilled
ye shall be *t.* and sown.   *Ezek* 36:9
the desolate land shall be *t.*   34

tiller
but Cain was a *t.* of.   *Gen* 4:2

tillest
when thou *t.* ground, it.   *Gen* 4:12

tilleth
he that *t.* land shall.   *Pr* 12:11
he that *t.* his land shall have.   28:19

timber
break down the *t.* thereof. *Lev* 14:45
prepared *t.* and stones to build.
   1 Ki 5:18; *1 Chr* 22:14; *2 Chr* 2:9
away the *t.* of Ramah.   *1 Ki* 15:22
t. is laid in the walls.   *Ezra* 5:8
let *t.* be pulled down from.   6:11*
that he may give me *t.*   *Neh* 2:8
they shall lay thy *t.* in. *Ezek* 26:12
the beam out of the *t.*   *Hab* 2:11
consume it with the *t.*   *Zech* 5:4

timbrel
and Miriam took a *t.* in.   *Ex* 15:20
they take the *t.* and harp. *Job* 21:12
bring hither the *t.*   *Ps* 81:2
praises to him with the *t.*   149:3
praise him with the *t.* and.   150:4

timbrels
went out after her with *t.*   *Ex* 15:20
his daughter came out with *t.*
         Judg 11:34
of Israel played before the Lord on *t.*
     2 Sam 6:5; *1 Chr* 13:8
damsels playing with *t.*   *Ps* 68:25

time
(*This word is frequently used with
the meaning of* season)
return according to the *t.* of life.
         Gen 18:10, 14
the *t.* that women go out to.   24:11
from the *t.* he had made him.   39:5
the *t.* drew nigh that Israel.   47:29
pay for loss of his *t.*   *Ex* 21:19
if beyond the *t.* of her.   *Lev* 15:25
a wife besides the other in her life *t.*
         18:18
the *t.* was the *t.* of first. *Num* 13:20
what *t.* the fire devoured.   26:10
t. thou put the sickle.   *Deut* 16:9
at the *t.* of the going down of the sun.
     Josh 10:27; *2 Chr* 18:34
did Joshua take at one *t.* *Josh* 10:42
all the *t.* the house of.   *Judg* 18:31
the *t.* I commanded   *2 Sam* 7:11
at the *t.* when kings go forth.   11:1
eight hundred he slew at one *t.* 23:8
is it *t.* to receive money ? *2 Ki* 5:26
were to come from *t.* to *t.* *1 Chr* 9:25
on this side the river, and at such a *t.*
     Ezra 4:10, 17; 7:12
and it is a *t.* of rain.   10:13
return ? and I set him a *t.* *Neh* 2:6
what *t.* they wax warm.   *Job* 6:17
who shall set me a *t.* to plead? 9:19
accomplished before his *t.*   15:32
which were cut down out of *t.* 22:16
which I reserved against the *t.* 38:23
knowest thou the *t.* they bring forth ?
         39:1, 2
in a *t.* when thou mayest. *Ps* 32:6
not be ashamed in the evil *t.*   37:19
the Lord will deliver him in *t.* 41:1
what *t.* I am afraid, I will.   56:3
to thee in an acceptable *t.*   69:13
their *t.* should have endured. 81:15
remember how short my *t.* is. 89:47
until the *t.* that his word.   105:19
there is a *t.* to every purpose.
       Eccl 3:1, 17; 8:6
a *t.* to be born, and a *t.* to die; a *t.*
         3:2
thou die before thy *t.?*
         7:17
a wise man's heart discerneth *t.* 8:5
but *t.* and chance happeneth.   9:11

of men snared in an evil *t. Eccl* 9:12
that draweth near the *t.*   *Isa* 26:17
from the *t.* it goeth forth it.   28:19
declared this from ancient *t.?* 45:21*
from the *t.* that it was.   48:16
in an acceptable *t.* have I heard thee.
     49:8; *2 Cor* 6:2
Lord will hasten it in his *t. Isa* 60:22
at the *t.* I visit, they shall. *Jer* 6:15
crane and swallow observe the *t.* 8:7
looked for a *t.* of health, and.   15
the Saviour thereof in *t.*   14:8
and for the *t.* of healing, and.   19
it is even the *t.* of Jacob's.   30:7
and the *t.* of their visitation.   46:21
         50:27
the *t.* that I will visit him.   49:8
         50:31
will appoint me the *t.?* 49:19; 50:44
floor, it is *t.* to thresh her.   51:33
from *t.* to *t.* shalt thou.   *Ezek* 4:10
thy *t.* was the *t.* of love, I.   16:8
as at the *t.* of thy reproach of.   57
day is near, it shall be the *t.*   30:3
ye would gain the *t.*   *Dan* 2:8
to speak before me, till the *t.*   9
that he would give him *t.*   16
at what *t.* ye hear the sound of cornet.   3:5, 15
were prolonged for a *t.*   7:12
t. came that the saints possessed. 22
t. and the dividing of *t.*   25; 12:7
at the *t.* of the end shall be.   8:17
about the *t.* of evening.   9:21
forecast his devices for a *t.* 11:24
to make them white, even to the *t.* 35
at the *t.* of the end shall be the king.   45
shall be a *t.* of trouble.   12:1
even to the *t.* of the end.   4, 9
from the *t.* the daily sacrifice.   11
it is *t.* to seek the Lord. *Hos* 10:12
till the *t.* that she which travaileth.
         Mi 5:3
is it *t.* to dwell in your ?   *Hag* 1:4
that at evening *t.* it.   *Zech* 14:7
her fruit before the *t.*   *Mal* 3:11
the *t.* they were carried. *Mat* 1:11
Herod enquired what *t.* the star. 2:7
to torment us before the *t.?* 8:29
and when the *t.* of the fruit.   21:34
master saith, My *t.* is.   26:18
the *t.* is fulfilled, repent. *Mark* 1:15
and so endure but for a *t.*   4:17
this is a desert, and now the *t.* 6:35
for the *t.* of figs was not yet. 11:13
ye know not when the *t.* is.   13:33
Elisabeth's full *t.* came. *Luke* 1:57
all kingdoms in a moment of *t.* 4:5
but this woman, since the *t.*   7:45
which in *t.* of temptation fall. 8:13
ye shall not see me, till the *t.* 13:35
thou knewest not the *t.* of thy. 19:44
t. is not come, your *t.*   *John* 7:6
the *t.* cometh that whosoever. 16:2
the *t.* cometh when I shall no.   25
all the *t.* the Lord went.   *Acts* 1:21
but when the *t.* of the promise. 7:17
in which *t.* Moses was born.   20
spent their *t.* in nothing else. 17:21
it is high *t.* to awake. *Rom* 13:11
judge nothing before the *t.* *1 Cor* 4:5
except with consent for a *t.*   7:5
but this I say, brethren, the *t.*   29
redeeming the *t.*   *Eph* 5:16
       Col 4:5
from you for a short *t. 1 Thes* 2:17
that he might be revealed in his *t.*
       2 Thes 2:6
t. come, when they will. *2 Tim* 4:3
and the *t.* of my departure is.   6
grace to help in *t.* of need.
         Heb 4:16
when for the *t.* ye ought to.   5:12
which was a figure for the *t.*   9:9
imposed on them till the *t.*   10
the *t.* would fail me to tell of. 11:32
appeareth a little *t.*   *Jas* 4:14
what manner of *t.* the.   *1 Pet* 1:11
pass the *t.* of your sojourning.   17
should live the rest of his *t.*   4:2
for the *t.* is at hand. *Rev* 1:3; 22:10
sware, that there should be *t.* 10:6
t. of the dead, that they.   11:18
that he hath but a short *t.*   12:12

she is nourished for a *t.* and times,
and half a *t.*   *Rev* 12:14
see **appointed, before, come,
day, due, last, long, many,
old, past, process, second, set,
third**

any time
may redeem at *any t.*   *Lev* 25:32
if the slayer at *any t.*   *Num* 35:26
sounded my father to-morrow at *any*
t.   *1 Sam* 20:12
displeased him at *any t.*   *1 Ki* 1:6
bear thee up, lest at *any t.* thou dash.
     Mat 4:6; *Luke* 4:11
lest at *any t.* the adversary deliver.
         Mat 5:25
lest at *any t.* they should see. 13:15
         Mark 4:12
transgressed I at *any t. Luke* 15:29
lest at *any t.* your hearts be. 21:34
hath seen God at *any t.*   *John* 1:18
ye heard his voice at *any t.*   5:37
unclean hath at *any t.* entered.
         Acts 11:8
who goeth a warfare *any t.* at his
own charges ?   *1 Cor* 9:7
nor at *any t.* used we. *1 Thes* 2:5
to which of the angels said he at *any*
t.?   *Heb* 1:5, 13
lest at *any t.* we should let.   2:1
hath seen God at *any t. 1 John* 4:12

in the time
came to pass in *the t.* of. *Gen* 38:27
commanded in *the t.* of. *Ex* 34:18
them deliver in *the t.*   *Judg* 10:14
in *the t.* of wheat harvest.   15:1
in *the t.* of old age he.   *1 Ki* 15:23
in *the t.* of distress.   *2 Chr* 28:22
in *the t.* of their trouble. *Neh* 9:27
more than in *the t.* when corn. *Ps* 4:7
as a fiery oven in *the t.*   21:9
in *the t.* of trouble he shall.   27:5
he is their strength in *the t.*   37:39
cast me not off in *the t.* of.   71:9
as the cold of snow in *the t.* of
harvest.   *Pr* 25:13
unfaithful man in *the t.* of.   19
salvation in *the t.* of trouble. *Isa* 33:2
in *the t.* of trouble they. *Jer* 2:27
if they can save thee in *the t.*   28
in *the t.* of visitation they shall be
cast down.   8:12
in *the t.* of visitation they shall perish.
     10:15; 51:18
shall not save them at all in *the t.* of
trouble.   11:12
I will not hear them in *the t.* that. 14
enemy to entreat thee well in *the t.*
of evil, and *in the t.*   15:11
deal thus with them in *the t.* 18:23
handleth the sickle in *the t.*   50:16
in *the t.* when thou shalt. *Ezek* 27:34
a perpetual hatred, in *the t.* of their
calamity, in *the t.* that their. 35:5
I will take away my corn in *the t.*
thereof.   *Hos* 2:9
ask rain in *the t.* of the. *Zech* 10:1
in *the t.* of harvest I. *Mat* 13:30
many lepers in *the t.* of. *Luke* 4:27

same time
Lord's anger was kindled the *same t.*
         Num 32:10
for Aaron also the *same t. Deut* 9:20
then Libnah revolted at the *same t.*
     2 Ki 8:22; *2 Chr* 21:10
the *same t.* 700 oxen.   *2 Chr* 15:11
the people at the *same t.*   16:10
at the *same t.* came to. *Ezra* 5:3
vineyards at the *same t. Jer* 39:10
at the *same t.* shalt thou think evil.
         Ezek 38:10
at the *same t.* my reason. *Dan* 4:36
as never was to that *same t.*   12:1
the *same t.* there arose. *Acts* 19:23

that time
not recover in that *t.?* *Judg* 11:26
to-morrow by *that t.* the sun be hot.
         1 Sam 11:9
since *that t.* hath it been. *Ezra* 5:16
to pass from *that t.* forth.
       Neh 4:16; 13:21
spoken concerning Moab since *that t.*
         Isa 16:13

in *that t.* shall the present be. *Isa* 18:7
I not told thee from *that t.?*   44:8
hath told it from *that t.?*   45:21
from *that t.* that thine ear.   48:8
that t. Israel shall come.   *Jer* 50:4
in *that t.* the iniquity of Israel.   20
keep silence in *that t.*   *Amos* 5:13
from *that t.* Jesus began.   *Mat* 4:17
from *that t.* began to shew.   16:21
from *that t.* Judas sought.   26:16
since *that t.* the kingdom of God is
   preached.   *Luke* 16:16
that t. many disciples.   *John* 6:66
about *that t.* Herod.   *Acts* 12:1

at that time
king of Moab at *that t.*   *Num* 22:4
and I spake to you *at that t.* saying.
   Deut 1:9
judges *at that t.* saying.   16
I commanded you *at that t.* 18; 3:18
Joshua *at that t.* saying.   3:21
I besought the Lord *at that t.*   23
the Lord and you *at that t.*   5:5
the Lord hearkened to me *at that t.*
   9:19; 10:10
the ark was *at that t.*   *1 Sam* 14:18
Israel brought under *at that t.*
   2 Chr 13:18
not keep the passover *at that t.* 30:3
kept the passover *at that t.*   35:17
at that t. they shall call.   *Jer* 3:17
at that t. shall they bring out.   8:1
at that t. cause the branch of. 33:15
at that t. shall Michael.   *Dan* 12:1
face from them *at that t.*   *Mi* 3:4
at that t. I will search.   *Zeph* 1:12
at that t. I will undo all that.   3:19
at that t. will I bring you again.   20
at Jerusalem *at that t.*   *Luke* 23:7
at that t. there was a great. *Acts* 8:1
at that t. ye were without Christ.
   Eph 2:12

this time
this t. will my husband.   *Gen* 29:34
Pharaoh hardened his heart at *this t.*
   Ex 8:32
I will at *this t.* send all my.   9:14
to-morrow about *this t.* I will.   18
said, I have sinned *this t.*   27
according to *this t.* it.   *Num* 23:23
nor would as at *this t.*   *Judg* 13:23
not give unto them at *this t.*   21:22
for about *this t.* ye shall find him.
   1 Sam 9:13
the counsel is not good at *this t.*
   2 Sam 17:7
I will not at *this t.* put.   *1 Ki* 2:26
by to-morrow about *this t.* 19:2; 20:6
   2 Ki 7:1, 18; 10:6
in all *this t.* was not I at.   *Neh* 13:6
thy peace at *this t.*: art come to the
   kingdom . . . t. as *this* ? *Esth* 4:14
blessed be the Lord from *this t.* forth.
   Ps 113:2
bless the Lord from *this t.* forth.
   115:18
will preserve thee from *this t.* 121:8
new things from *this t.*   *Isa* 48:6
wilt thou not from *this t.?*   *Jer* 3:4
this is *t.* of the Lord's.   51:6
haughtily; for *this t.* is evil. *Mi* 2:3
since the beginning of the world to
   this t.   *Mat* 24:21; *Mark* 13:19
receive an hundred-fold now in *this
   t.*   *Mark* 10:30; *Luke* 18:30
do not discern *this t.?*   *Luke* 12:56
by *this t.* he stinketh.   *John* 11:39
wilt thou at *this t.* restore ? *Acts* 1:6
go thy way for *this t.*   24:25
to declare at *this t.*   *Rom* 3:26
sufferings of *this* present t.   8:18
at *this t.* will I come, and Sarah. 9:9
so at *this* present t. there is.   11:5
not to come at *this t.*   *1 Cor* 16:12
that now at *this t.* your. *2 Cor* 8:14

times
he hath supplanted me these two t.
   Gen 27:36
ye shall not observe t.   *Lev* 19:26*
   Deut 18:10*, 14*
hated him not in t. past. *Deut* 4:42
the Spirit of the Lord began to move
   him at t.   *Judg* 13:25

---

as at other t. and shake. *Judg* 16:20
in array as at other t.   20:30
began to kill as at other t.   31
as at other t., Samuel.   *1 Sam* 3:10
with his hand as at other t.   18:10*
on his seat as at other t.   20:25
not heard of ancient t. that I have
   formed it ? *2 Ki* 19:25; *Isa* 37:26
Manasseh observed t.   *2 Ki* 21:6*
   2 Chr 33:6*
understanding of the t. *1 Chr* 12:32
the t. that went over him and. 29:30
in those t. there was no. *2 Chr* 15:5
men which knew the t.   *Esth* 1:13
t. are not hidden from.   *Job* 24:1
Lord will be a refuge in t.   *Ps* 9:9
thyself in t. of trouble ?   10:1
my t. are in thy hand, deliver. 31:15
thou didst in the t. of old.   44:1
the years of ancient t.   77:5
be the stability of thy t.   *Isa* 33:6
from ancient t. things not.   46:10
of the t. far off.   *Ezek* 12:27
he changeth the t. and.   *Dan* 2:21
he shall think to change t.   7:25
shall be built in troublous t.   9:25
in those t. there shall many.   11:14
t. and an half.   12:7; *Rev* 12:14
not discern the signs of the t.?
   Mat 16:3
the t. of the Gentiles. *Luke* 21:24
for you to know the t.   *Acts* 1:7
when the t. of refreshing.   3:19
till the t. of restitution of all.   21
who in t. past suffered all.   14:16*
hath determined the t.   17:26*
the t. of this ignorance God.   30
as ye in t. past have not. *Rom* 11:30
of Jews five t. received I forty
   stripes.   *2 Cor* 11:24
persecuted us in t. past.   *Gal* 1:23
and months, t. and years.   4:10
of the fulness of t.   *Eph* 1:10
the t. ye have no need. *1 Thes* 5:1
in latter t. some shall.   *1 Tim* 4:1
in his t. he shall shew, who is. 6:15
perilous t. shall come.   *2 Tim* 3:1
hath in due t. manifested.   *Tit* 1:3
God who at sundry t. spake to the.
   Heb 1:1*

see **appointed, many, seven, ten,
three**

all times
that he come not at *all t.*   *Lev* 16:2
of his people at *all t.*   *1 Ki* 8:59
I will bless the Lord at *all t.*: his
   praise.   *Ps* 34:1
trust in him at *all t.* ye people. 62:8
doeth righteousness at *all t.* 106:3
to thy judgements at *all t.*   119:20
satisfy thee at *all t.*   *Pr* 5:19
a friend loveth at *all t.*   17:17

Timnath
to his shearers in T.   *Gen* 38:12
Samson went down to T. *Judg* 14:1

Timotheus
a certain disciple named T. *Acts* 16:1
T. my workfellow saluteth you.
   Rom 16:21
if T. come.   *1 Cor* 16:10
T. our brother.   *2 Cor* 1:1
was preached even by me and T. 19
Lord to send T. to you.   *Phil* 2:19
we sent T. to establish. *1 Thes* 3:2
to T. my own son.   *1 Tim* 1:2, 18
   2 Tim 1:2
T. is set at liberty.   *Heb* 13:23

tin
t. that may abide fire.   *Num* 31:22
take away all thy t.   *Isa* 1:25
brass, and t. and iron. *Ezek* 22:18
lead and t. into the furnace.   20
thy merchant in t. and lead.   27:12

tingle
ears of every one that heareth it
   shall t. *1 Sam* 3:11; *2 Ki* 21:12
   Jer 19:3

tinkling
mincing and making a t.   *Isa* 3:16
bravery of their t. ornaments.   18*
as a t. cymbal.   *1 Cor* 13:1*

---

tip
may dip the t. of his finger in water.
   Luke 16:24
see right **ear**

tire
bind the t. of thy head. *Ezek* 24:17

tired
Jezebel t. her head.   *2 Ki* 9:30

tires
Lord will take away their t. *Isa* 3:18*
and your t. shall be on. *Ezek* 24:23

Tirshatha
(*This word is not strictly a proper
name, but the title of the Governor
of Judaea, under the Persians. In
some places it is rendered governor*)
T. said that they should not eat of the
   holy things. *Ezra* 2:63; *Neh* 7:65
the T. gave gold to the.   *Neh* 7:70
sealed were Nehemiah the T.   10:1

Tirzah
Hoglah, Milcah, and T. *Num* 26:33
   27:1; 36:11; *Josh* 17:3
smote the king of T.   *Josh* 12:24
wife came to T.   *1 Ki* 14:17
dwelt and reigned in T.   15:21, 33
Elah reigned in T.   16:8
Zimri reigned in T.   15
Omri besieged T.   17
Omri reigned in T.   23
smote coasts from T.   *2 Ki* 15:16
O my love, as T.   *S of S* 6:4

Tishbite, *see* **Elijah**

tithe
The practice of paying tithes *is very
ancient; for we find,* Gen 14:20,
that Abraham gave tithes *to Melchizedek, king of Salem, at his
return from his expedition against
Chedorlaomer, and the four kings
in confederacy with him. Abraham
gave him the* tithe *of all the booty
taken from the enemy. Jacob
imitated this piety of his grand-
father when he vowed to the Lord
the* tithe *of all the substance he
might acquire in Mesopotamia,*
Gen 28:22. *Under the law, Moses
ordained,* Lev 27:30, 31, 32, All
the *tithe* of the land, whether of the
seed of the land, or of the fruit of the
tree, is the Lord's; it is holy unto the
Lord, etc.

*There were three sorts of tithes
to be paid from the people (besides
those from the Levites to the
priests),* Num 28:26, 27, etc. (1)
*To the Levites, for their main-
tenance,* Num 18:21, 24. (2) *For
the Lord's feasts and sacrifices, to
be eaten in the place which the
Lord should choose to put his name
there; to wit, where the ark should
be, the tabernacle or temple.
This tenth part was either sent
to Jerusalem in kind, or, if it was
too far, they sent the value in
money, which was to be laid out for
oxen, sheep, wine, or what else they
pleased,* Deut 14:22, 23, 24, etc.
(3) *Besides these two, there was
to be, every third year, a tithe for
the poor, to be eaten in their own
dwellings,* Deut 14:28, 29.

*In the New Testament, neither our
Saviour, nor his apostles have commanded any thing in this affair of
tithes.*

all the t. of the land is.   *Lev* 27:30
concerning the t. of the herd.   32
a tenth part of the t.   *Num* 18:26
thy gates the t. of corn. *Deut* 12:17
eat t. in the place the Lord.   14:23
three years bring forth the t.   28
firstfruits of corn and the t. of all.
   2 Chr 31:5, 6, 12; *Neh* 13:12
shall bring up t. of tithes. *Neh* 10:38
ye pay t. of mint, anise. *Mat* 23:23

tithe, *verb*
t. increase of thy seed. *Deut* 14:22
for ye t. mint, and rue. *Luke* 11:42

tithes

Melchizedek *t.* of all. *Gen* 14:20
redeem aught of his *t.* *Lev* 27:31
the *t.* I have given to. *Num* 18:24
take of the children of Israel *t.* 26
unto the Lord of all your *t.* 28
shall bring your *t.* *Deut* 12:6, 11
made an end of tithing the *t.* 26:12
Levites might have the *t.* *Neh* 10:37
were appointed for the *t.* 12:44
they laid the *t.* of corn. 13:5
bring your *t.* after three years.
Amos 4:4; *Mal* 3:10
ve have robbed me. In *t.* *Mal* 3:8
I give *t.* of all that I. *Luke* 18:12
priesthood have commandment to
take *t.* *Heb* 7:5
he received *t.* of Abraham, and. 6
and here men that die receive *t.* 8
Levi who receiveth *t.* payed *t.* in. 9

tithing

hast made an end of *t.*, third year
which is the year of *t.* *Deut* 26:12

title

he said, What *t.* is that ? *2 Ki* 23:17*
Pilate wrote a *t.* and put it on the
cross. *John* 19:19
t. then read many of the Jews. 20

titles

give flattering *t.* to man. *Job* 32:21
for I know not to give flattering *t.* 22

tittle

one *t.* shall in no wise pass. *Mat* 5:18
than for one *t.* of the law. *Luke* 16:17

Titus

because I found not *T.* *2 Cor* 2:13
us by the coming of *T.* 7:6
joyed we for the joy of *T.* 13
boasting which I made before *T.* 14
we desired *T.* 8:6
care into the heart of *T.* 16
whether any enquire of *T.* he is. 23
I desired *T.* Did *T.* make a ? 12:18
I took *T.* with me. *Gal* 2:1
neither *T.* was compelled to. 3
T. is departed to. *2 Tim* 4:10

to *and* **fro, see fro**

Tobiah

children of *T.* not shew. *Ezra* 2:60
Sanballat and *T.* heard. *Neh* 2:10
19; 4:7; 6:1
T. had hired him. 6:12
my God, think thou upon *T.* 14
and *T.* sent letters to put me. 19
Eliashib was allied to *T.* 13:4
all the household stuff of *T.* 8

to-day, see day

toe

great *t.* of their right foot. *Ex* 29:20
Lev 8:23, 24; 14:14, 17, 25, 28

toes

thumbs and his great *t.* *Judg* 1:6
having thumbs and *t.* cut off. 7
fingers and *t.* were. *1 Chr* 20:6, 24
the *t.* part of iron. *Dan* 2:41, 42

Togarmah

sons of Gomer, Riphath, *T.*
Gen 10:3; *1 Chr* 1:6
they of the house of *T.* *Ezek* 27:14

together

plow with ox and ass *t.* *Deut* 22:10
he divided her, *t.* with. *Judg* 19:29
died that same day *t.* *1 Sam* 31:6
we were *t.*, there was no. *1 Ki* 3:18
women, *t.* with the daughter. 11:1
when thou and I rode *t.* *2 Ki* 9:25
we ourselves *t.* will build. *Ezra* 4:3
let us take counsel *t.* *Neh* 6:7
let us meet *t.* 10
there the prisoners rest *t.* *Job* 3:18
have fashioned me *t.* round. 10:8
go down, when our rest *t.* is. 17:16
the poor hide themselves *t.* 24:4
all flesh shall perish *t.* 34:15
counsel *t.* against the Lord. *Ps* 2:2
all *t.* become filthy. 14:3; *Rom* 3:12
and let us exalt his name *t.* *Ps* 34:3
the transgressors be destroyed *t.*
37:38; *Isa* 1:28
the rich and poor meet *t.* *Pr* 22:2
and the deceitful man meet *t.* 29:13

if two lie *t.* then they. *Eccl* 4:11
t. shall be against Judah. *Isa* 9:21
t. with my dead body shall. 26:19
that we may behold it *t.* 41:23
with the voice *t.* shall they. 52:8, 9
and the lamb shall feed *t.* 65:25
the bones came *t.*, bone. *Ezek* 37:7
he and his princes *t.* *Amos* 1:15
can two walk *t.* except they ? 3:3
or three are gathered *t.* *Mat* 18:20
what God hath joined *t.* 19:6
Mark 10:9
he calleth *t.* his friends. *Luke* 15:6
that believed were *t.* *Acts* 2:44
ye have agreed *t.* to tempt. 5:9
all things work *t.* for good. *Rom* 8:28
hath quickened us *t.* *Eph* 2:5
hath raised us *t.* 6
building fitly framed *t.* 21, 22
striving *t.* for the faith. *Phil* 1:27
brethren, be followers of *t.* me. 3:17
being knit *t.* in love. *Col* 2:2, 19
dead in sins, hath he quickened *t.* 13
shall be caught up *t.* *1 Thes* 4:17
we should live *t.* with him. 5:10
you by our gathering *t.* *2 Thes* 2:1
as being heirs *t.* of the. *1 Pet* 3:7
see **dwell**

toil

concerning our work and *t.* *Gen* 5:29
hath made me forget my *t.* 41:51

toil, *verb*

they *t.* not, neither do they spin.
Mat 6:28; *Luke* 12:27

toiled

Master, we have *t.* all. *Luke* 5:5

toiling

and he saw them *t.* *Mark* 6:48*

token

this is the *t.* of the covenant.
Gen 9:12, 13, 17
and it shall be a *t.* of the. 17:11
this shall be a *t.* that I. *Ex* 3:12
the blood shall be for a *t.* on. 12:13
it shall be for a *t.* upon. 13:16*
to be kept for a *t.* *Num* 17:10
and give me a true *t.* *Josh* 2:12
shew me a *t.* for good. *Ps* 86:17
given them a *t.* saying. *Mark* 14:44
is to them an evident *t.* *Phil* 1:28
a manifest *t.* of righteous. *2 Thes* 1:5
of Paul, which is the *t.* in. 3:17

tokens

being *t.* of damsel's virginity.
Deut 22:15, 17, 20
and do ye not know their *t.*?*Job* 21:29
they are afraid at thy *t.* *Ps* 65:8
who sent *t.* in the midst of. 135:9*
that frustrateth the *t.* of. *Isa* 44:25

Tola

T. the son of Issachar. *Gen* 46:13
1 Chr 7:1
T. son of Puah arose to. *Judg* 10:1

told

who *t.* thee that thou wast naked ?
Gen 3:11
and Ham *t.* his two brethren. 9:22
till I have *t.* mine errand. 24:33
Joseph *t.* his brethren. 37:5, 9
he *t.* it to his father and his. 10
T. not I thee, All that ? *Num* 23:26
it be *t.* thee, and behold. *Deut* 17:4
which our fathers *t.* of. *Judg* 6:13
was a man that *t.* a dream. 7:13
I asked not, neither *t.* he me. 13:6
nor would as at this time have *t.* 23
he came up, and *t.* his father. 14:2
but he *t.* not his father. 6, 9, 16
1 Sam 3:11
day he *t.* her, she *t.* the riddle.
Judg 14:17
she urged him, he *t.* her. 16:17, 18
he *t.* us that the asses were found.
1 Sam 10:16
Abigail *t.* not her husband. 25:19
and the woman sent and *t.* David.
2 Sam 17:17
and *t.* them, they *t.* David. 17:17
t. her all her questions, not any.
he *t.* not. *1 Ki* 10:3; *2 Chr* 9:2
the words they *t.* also to. *1 Ki* 13:11
came and *t.* it in the city where. 25

hast *t.* thou wilt build. *1 Chr* 17:25
I *t.* them what they should say to.
Ezra 8:17
Haman *t.* of the glory of. *Esth* 5:11
for Esther had *t.* what he was. 8:1
which wise men have *t.* *Job* 15:18
fathers have *t.* us. *Ps* 44:1; 78:3
have not I *t.* thee from ? *Isa* 44:8
who hath *t.* it from that time ? 45:21
what had not been *t.* them. 52:15
because he had *t.* them. *Jonah* 1:10
the city and *t.* every thing. *Mat* 8:33
body, and went and *t.* Jesus. 14:12
they went and *t.* it to. *Mark* 16:13
when he saw the Jews it. *John* 5:15
it shall be *t.* thee what thou must do.
Acts 9:6; 22:10
into the castle and *t.* Paul. 23:16
he *t.* us your earnest. *2 Cor* 7:7

told, *participle*

it was certainly *t.* thy. *Josh* 9:24
oxen could not be *t.* *1 Ki* 8:5
was it not *t.* my lord what ? 18:13
gave money, being *t.* *2 Ki* 12:11
years as a tale that is *t.* *Ps* 90:9
it was *t.* the house of David. *Isa* 7:2
and the vision which is *t.* *Dan* 8:26
there shall this be *t.* for. *Mat* 26:13
a performance of things which were *t.*
Luke 1:45
those things *t.* by shepherds. 2:18

told *him*

which God had *t.* him. *Gen* 22:3, 9
I have *t.* him, I will judge his.
1 Sam 3:13
Samuel *t.* him every whit and. 18
the kingdom he *t.* him not. 10:16
she *t.* him nothing till morning. 25:36
the man of God *t.* him. *2 Ki* 6:10
be *t.* him that I speak. *Job* 37:20
but the woman *t.* him. *Mark* 5:33

told *me*

thou hast mocked me and *t.* me lies.
Judg 16:10, 13
hast not *t.* me wherein thy. 15
for it is *t.* me that he dealeth very
subtilly. *1 Sam* 23:22
when one *t.* me, saying, Saul is dead.
2 Sam 4:10
the half was not *t.* me. *1 Ki* 10:7
2 Chr 9:6
t. me I should be king. *1 Ki* 14:2
me and hath not *t.* me. *2 Ki* 4:27
he *t.* me that thou shouldest. 8:14
see a man which *t.* me all things.
John 4:29, 39
even as it was *t.* me. *Acts* 27:25

told *you*

hath it not been *t.* you ? *Isa* 40:21
believe, though it be *t.* you. *Hab* 1:5
I have *t.* you before. *Mat* 24:25
see him, lo, I have *t.* you. 28:7
if I have *t.* you earthly. *John* 3:12
a man that hath *t.* you truth. 8:40
he said, I have *t.* you already. 9:27
10:25
I would have *t.* you. 14:2
now I have *t.* you before it. 29
have I *t.* you, that when time shall
come . . . *t.* you of them. 16:4
Jesus said, I have *t.* you that. 18:8
I *t.* you before, and. *2 Cor* 13:2
as I have also *t.* you in. *Gal* 5:21
of whom I have *t.* you. *Phil* 3:18
we *t.* you that we should suffer.
1 Thes 3:4
when with you, I *t.* you. *2 Thes* 2:5
they *t.* you there should. *Jude* 18

tolerable

it shall be more *t.* for Sodom and.
Mat 10:15; 11:24; *Mark* 6:11
Luke 10:12
more *t.* for Tyre and Sidon
Mat 11:22; *Luke* 10:14

toll

then will they not pay *t.* *Ezra* 4:13*
t., tribute, and custom, was paid. 20*
lawful to impose *t.* on them. 7:24*

tomb

shall remain in the *t.* *Job* 21:32
Joseph laid the body in his own new *t.*
Mat 27:60

disciples laid John's corpse in a *t.*
    Mark 6:29

tombs
met him two possessed with devils,
  coming out of the *t.*   *Mat* 8:28
    Mark 5:2, 3, 5; *Luke* 8:27
because ye build the *t.* *Mat* 23:29*

to-morrow, see morrow

tongs
(*American Revision changes this
  word to* snuffers)
shalt make thee *t.* thereof. *Ex* 25:38
they shall cover his *t.*   *Num* 4:9
lamps and *t.* of gold.   *1 Ki* 7:49
    2 Chr 4:21
a coal which he had taken with the *t.*
    Isa 6:6
smith with the *t.* worketh. 44:12*

tongue
*This word is taken in three differ-
ent senses.* (1) *For the material
tongue, or organ of speech,* Jas 3:5.
(2) *For the* tongue *or language that
is spoken in any country,* Deut
28:49. (3) *For good or bad dis-
course,* Pr 12:18; 17:20.
  To gnaw one's *tongue, is a token
of fury, despair, and torment. The
men that worship the beast are
said to gnaw their tongues for* pain,
Rev 16:10. The scourge of the
tongue, Job 5:21, *is malicious
scandal, calumny, insulting, and
offensive speeches.*
  The gift of *tongues, which God
granted to the Apostles and disciples assembled at Jerusalem,
on the day of Pentecost,* Acts 2:3,
4, *etc., is not fully understood.
St. Paul speaks of it as still existing,*
1 Cor 12:10; 14:2.

not a dog move his *t.*   *Ex* 11:7
none moved his *t.* against. *Josh* 10:21
the water with his *t.*   *Judg* 7:5
from the scourge of the *t. Job* 5:21
and thou choosest the *t.* of.   15:5
hide wickedness under his *t.* 20:12
poison of asps, the viper's *t.* shall. 16
their *t.* cleaved to roof of.   29:10
they flatter with their *t.*   *Ps* 5:9
under his *t.* is mischief and. 10:7
shall cut off the *t.* that speaketh. 12:3
who have said, With our *t.* will.   4
that backbiteth not with his *t.* 15:3
keep thy *t.* from evil.   34:13
    1 Pet 3:10
and his *t.* talketh of.   *Ps* 37:30
and thy *t.* frameth deceit. 50:19
thy *t.* deviseth mischiefs like. 52:2
and their *t.* is a sharp sword. 57:4
who whet their *t.* like a sword. 64:3
shall make their *t.* to fall on.   8
t. of thy dogs shall be dipped. 68:23
and their *t.* walketh through. 73:9
ag*a*inst me with a lying *t.* 109:2
*.*one to thee, thou false *t.?* 120:3
our *t.* filled with singing. 126:2
a proud look, a lying *t.*   *Pr* 6:17
from the flattery of the *t.* of a.   24
the *t.* of the just is as choice. 10:20
the froward *t.* shall be cut out. 31
t. of the wise is health. 12:18
but a lying *t.* is but for a.   19
t. of the wise useth knowledge. 15:2
a wholesome *t.* is a tree of life. 4
and the answer of the *t.* is. 16:1
giveth heed to a naughty *t.* 17:4
he that hath a perverse *t.* falleth. 20
life are in the power of the *t.* 18:21
treasures by a lying *t.* is vanity. 21:6
whoso keepeth his *t.* keepeth. 23
soft *t.* breaketh the bone. 25:15
angry countenance a backbiting *t.* 23
lying *t.* hateth those afflicted. 26:28
that flattereth with the *t.* 28:23
and in her *t.* is the law of. 31:26
milk are under thy *t.* *S of S* 4:11
because their *t.* is against. *Isa* 3:8
Lord shall destroy the *t.* 11:15
t. is as a devouring fire. 30:27
the *t.* of the stammerers shall. 32:4
a people of a stammering *t.* 33:19
shall the *t.* of the dumb sing. 35:6

and when their *t.* faileth for. *Isa* 41:17
that unto me every *t.* shall. 45:23
the Lord hath given me the *t.* 50:4
t. that shall rise against thee. 54:17
whom draw ye out the *t.?* 57:4
t. hath muttered perverseness. 59:3
their *t.* like their bow. *Jer* 9:3
taught their *t.* to speak lies. 5
their *t.* is as an arrow shot out. 8
let us smite him with the *t.* 18:18
the *t.* of the sucking child cleaveth.
    Lam 4:4
I will make thy *t.* cleave. *Ezek* 3:26
princes shall fall for the rage of their
  t.   *Hos* 7:16
holdest thy *t.* when the wicked
  devoureth.   *Hab* 1:13*
their *t.* shall consume. *Zech* 14:12
spit, and touched his *t.* *Mark* 7:33
and straightway his *t.* was loosed.
    35; *Luke* 1:64
and bridleth not his *t.* *Jas* 1:26
so the *t.* is a little member. 3:5
the *t.* is a fire.   6
the *t.* can no man tame.   8
nor let us love in *t.* but. *1 John* 3:18

see **deceitful, hold**

my tongue
his word was in my *t.* *2 Sam* 23:2
sold, I had held my *t.* *Esth* 7:4
is there iniquity in my *t.? Job* 6:30
nor shall my *t.* utter deceit. 27:4
my *t.* hath spoken in my mouth. 33:2
and my *t.* cleaveth to my. *Ps* 22:15
my *t.* shall speak of thy righteousness.   35:28; 51:14; 71:24
that I sin not with my *t.*   39:1
was hot, then spake I with my *t.* 3
my *t.* is the pen of a ready. 45:1
God was extolled with my *t.* 66:17
my *t.* shall speak of thy. 119:172
let my *t.* cleave to the roof. 137:6
not a word in my *t.* but thou. 139:4
finger, and cool my *t.* *Luke* 16:24
rejoice, my *t.* was glad. *Acts* 2:26

tongue *for language, speech*
isles were divided every one after
  his *t.*   *Gen* 10:5
of speech, and of a slow *t. Ex* 4:10
a nation whose *t.* shall. *Deut* 28:49
letter was written in the Syrian *t.* and
  interpreted in Syrian *t. Ezra* 4:7*
for with another *t.* will. *Isa* 28:11
they might teach the *t.* of. *Dan* 1:4
called in the Hebrew *t.* Bethesda.
    John 5:2
field called in their proper *t.* Aceldama.   *Acts* 1:19*
every man in our own *t.?* 2:8*
in the Hebrew *t.* Saul, Saul. 26:14*
every *t.* shall confess. *Rom* 14:11
he that speaketh in an unknown *t.*
  1 Cor 14:2, 4, 13, 14, 19, 27
except ye utter by the *t.* words. 9
hath a psalm, hath a *t.*   26
that every *t.* confess that. *Phil* 2:11
hast redeemed us out of every *t.*
    Rev 5:9
in the Hebrew *t.* is Abaddon. 9:11
the gospel to preach to every *t.* 14:6
the Hebrew *t.* Armageddon. 16:16

tongued
be grave, not double-*t.* *1 Tim* 3:8

tongues
of Ham, after their *t. Gen* 10:20
sons of Shem, after their *t.* 31
them from the strife of *t. Ps* 31:20
O Lord, and divide their *t.* 55:9
lied to him with their *t.* 78:36
they sharpened their *t.* like. 140:3
gather all nations and *t. Isa* 66:18
that use their *t.* and say. *Jer* 23:31
shall speak with new *t. Mark* 16:17
there appeared to them cloven *t.*
    Acts 2:3
began to speak with other *t.*   4
we hear in our *t.* the wonderful. 11
heard them speak with *t.* 10:46
and they spake with *t.* and. 19:6
with their *t.* they have used deceit.
    Rom 3:13

to another divers kinds of *t.*
    1 Cor 12:10, 28
do all speak with *t.?* do all ? 30
though I speak with the *t.* of. 13:1
there be *t.*, they shall cease.   8
I would ye all spake with *t.* 14:5
if I come to you speaking with *t.* 6
I thank God, I speak with *t.* 18
with men of other *t.* will I speak. 21
t. are for a sign.   22
if all speak with *t.*   23
forbid not to speak with *t.* 39
people and *t.* stood before. *Rev* 7:9
again before nations and *t.* 10:11
t. and nations shall see their. 11:9
power was given him over all *t.* 13:7
and they gnawed their *t.* for. 16:10
sawest are nations and *t.* 17:15

took
Enoch was not, for God *t.* him.
    Gen 5:24
his mother *t.* him a wife out. 21:21
God, which *t.* me from my. 24:7
the lord of the land *t.* us for. 42:30
Moses *t.* the redemption money.
    Num 3:49, 50
the Lord *t.* of the Spirit that. 11:25
king Arad *t.* some of them. 21:1
I *t.* thee to curse mine. 23:11
so I *t.* the chief of your. *Deut* 1:15
only the cattle we *t.* for a prey. 2:35
there was not a city we *t.* not. 3:4
I *t.* your sin, the calf which. 9:21
I *t.* this woman and found. 22:14
I coveted them, and *t.* *Josh* 7:21
the men *t.* of their victuals. 9:14
I *t.* your father Abraham. 24:3
Philistines *t.* Samson. *Judg* 16:21
silver is with me, I *t.* it. 17:2
no man *t.* them into his house. 19:15
the man *t.* his concubine, and. 25
I *t.* my concubine, and cut. 20:6
brought up, the priest *t. 1 Sam* 2:14
Philistines *t.* the ark of God. 5:1, 2
Samuel *t.* a vial of oil and. 10:1
so Saul *t.* the kingdom over. 14:47
people *t.* of the spoil, sheep. 15:21
Samuel *t.* horn of oil and. 16:13
Saul *t.* him, would not let him. 18:2
David *t.* the spear from. 26:12
I *t.* the crown and. *2 Sam* 1:10
Uzzah *t.* hold of it for the. 6:6
I *t.* thee from the sheepcote. 7:8
not depart, as I *t.* it from Saul. 15
but *t.* the poor man's lamb. 12:4
Zadok the priest *t.* an. *1 Ki* 1:39
she arose and *t.* my son from. 3:20
the cities my father *t.* I will. 20:34
but Jehu *t.* no heed to. *2 Ki* 10:31
yet David *t.* the castle. *1 Chr* 11:5
which *t.* Manasseh among thorns.
    2 Chr 33:11
vessels which Nebuchadnezzar *t.*
    Ezra 5:14; 6:5
whom Mordecai *t.* for his. *Esth* 2:7
then *t.* Haman the apparel and. 6:11
t. upon them, that they would. 9:27
he that *t.* me out of the womb.
    Ps 22:9; 71:6
fear *t.* hold upon them there. 48:6
we *t.* sweet counsel together. 55:14
he chose David, and *t.* from. 78:70
I *t.* me faithful witnesses. *Isa* 8:2
with whom *t.* he counsel ? 40:14
then *t.* I the cup at the. *Jer* 25:17
in the day I *t.* them by the hand.
    31:32; *Heb* 8:9
even they *t.* Jeremiah out. *Jer* 39:14
and he *t.* me by a lock. *Ezek* 8:3
he *t.* fire from between the. 10:7
he heard the trumpet, and *t.* 33:5
the Lord *t.* me as I followed the.
    Amos 7:15
I *t.* me two staves, Beauty and
  Bands.   *Zech* 11:7
I *t.* the thirty pieces and cast. 13
himself *t.* our infirmities. *Mat* 8:17
like leaven which a woman *t.* 13:33
    Luke 13:21
the foolish virgins *t.* no oil. *Mat* 25:3
ye *t.* me in.   35
I was a stranger and ye *t.* me not. 43
the first *t.* a wife, and. *Mark* 12:20

second *t.* her and died. *Mark* 12:21
         Luke 20:29, 30
in the temple teaching, and ye *t.* me
    not.   *Mark* 14:49
that disciple *t.* her to his. *John* 19:27
to them who *t.* Jesus.   *Acts* 1:16
but Barnabas *t.* him, and.   9:27
t. with them John whose.   12:25
t. on them to call over them.   19:13
whom we *t.* and would have judged
    according to our law.   24:6
Paul thanked God and *t.*   28:15
I went up, and *t.* Titus.   *Gal* 2:1
and *t.* upon him the form.   *Phil* 2:7
t. it out of the way.   *Col* 2:14
he also himself *t.* part.   *Heb* 2:14
ye *t.* joyfully the spoiling of.   10:34
he *t.* the book.   *Rev* 5:7
angel *t.* the censer.   8:5
I *t.* the little book out of the.   10:10

took away

he *t. away* my birthright. *Gen* 27:36
a west wind *t. away* the.   *Ex* 10:19
he *t.* not *away* the pillar of.   13:22
shall restore that which he *t. away.*
           Lev 6:4
Gideon *t. away* their.   *Judg* 8:21
Israel *t. away* my land when. 11:13
Israel *t.* not *away* the land.   15
David *t. away* the.   *1 Sam* 27:9
Shishak *t. away* the treasures.
           1 Ki 14:26
Asa *t. away* the sodomites.   15:12
and they *t. away* the stones of.   22
Josiah *t. away* the horses. *2 Ki* 23:11
all the vessels wherewith they min-
    istered the Chaldeans *t. away.*
    25:14, 15; *Jer* 52:18, 19
Asa *t. away* the altars. *2 Chr* 14:3, 5
Jehoshaphat *t. away* the high.   17:6
Hezekiah *t. away* the altars.   30:14
Manasseh *t. away* the strange. 33:15
I restored that which I *t.* not *away.*
           Ps 69:4
keepers *t. away* my vail. *S of S* 5:7
I *t.* them *away* as I saw good.
           Ezek 16:50
and I *t.* the king *away* in my wrath.
           Hos 13:11
flood came and *t.* them all *away.*
           Mat 24:39
then they *t. away* the stone from.
           John 11:41

he took

Shechem saw her, he *t.*   *Gen* 34:2
when he *t.* it out, his hand.   *Ex* 4:6
he *t.* the book of the covenant. 24:7
and he *t.* the calf which they. 32:20
he *t.* the vail off, until he.   34:34
he *t.* all the fat on the inwards.
         Lev 8:16, 25
he *t.* the elders of the city. *Judg* 8:16
he *t.* men of the elders.   *Ruth* 4:2
he *t.* a yoke of oxen.   *1 Sam* 11:7
when Saul saw any valiant man, he *t.*
    him unto him.   14:52
he *t.* Agag king of the.   15:8
he *t.* his staff in his hand.   17:40
he *t.* hold of her, and. *2 Sam* 13:11
he *t.* three darts, and thrust.   18:14
above, he *t.* me.   22:17; *Ps* 18:16
he *t.* her son out of.   *1 Ki* 17:19
he *t.* the mantle of.   *2 Ki* 2:14
he *t.* his eldest son and.   3:27
he *t.* them from their hand.   5:24
he *t.* a thick cloth and dipped. 8:15
and he *t.* unto him bow and.   13:15
he *t.* him a potsherd to.   *Job* 2:8
slothful roasteth not that which he *t.*
           Pr 12:27
he *t.* his brother by the.   *Hos* 12:3
he *t.* the seven loaves.   *Mat* 15:36
           Mark 8:6
he *t.* the cup.   *Mat* 26:27
    Luke 22:17; *1 Cor* 11:25
he *t.* with him Peter, James, John.
    Mat 26:37; *Luke* 9:28
he *t.* water and washed. *Mat* 27:24
and he *t.* the blind man. *Mark* 8:23
he *t.* a child and set him in.   9:36
he *t.* the five loaves.   *Luke* 9:16
he *t.* out two pence and gave. 10:35
he *t.* bread. 22:19; 24:30 *Acts* 27:35

---

he *t.* them the same hour. *Acts* 16:33
he *t.* Paul's girdle and bound. 21:11
he *t.* not on him the.   *Heb* 2:16
he *t.* the blood of calves.   9:19

they took

they *t.* them wives.   *Gen* 6:2
and they *t.* all the goods of.   14:11
they *t.* Lot, Abram's brother's son. 12
and they *t.* every man. *Num* 16:18
and they *t.* of the fruit. *Deut* 1:25
people went up and they *t.* the city.
           Josh 6:20
the king of Ai they *t.* alive.   8:23
save Hivites, all other they *t.* 11:19
they *t.* their daughters.   *Judg* 3:6
they *t.* them alive and.   *2 Ki* 10:14
they *t.* the young men.   *Lam* 5:13
I saw that they *t.* both. *Ezek* 23:13
and they *t.* his glory.   *Dan* 5:20
because they *t.* him for a prophet.
           Mat 21:46
so they *t.* the money, and did. 28:15
they *t.* him, and killed him, and cast.
           Mark 12:8
they *t.* him and led him. *Luke* 22:54
           John 19:16
and they *t.* knowledge.   *Acts* 4:13
they *t.* him down from the tree and
    laid.   13:29
they *t.* him, and expounded. 18:26

took up

Balaam *t. up* his parable. *Num* 23:7
    18; 24:3, 15, 20, 21, 23
the priests *t. up* the ark. *Josh* 3:6
    6:12; *1 Ki* 8:3
then the man *t. up* his. *Judg* 19:28
cook *t. up* the shoulder. *1 Sam* 9:24
they *t. up* Asahel and. *2 Sam* 2:32
Mephibosheth's nurse *t.* him *up.* 4:4
prophet *t. up* the carcase. *1 Ki* 13:29
he *t. up* also the mantle. *2 Ki* 2:13
the Shunammite *t. up* her son. 4:37
and he *t.* him *up* to him into. 10:15
I *t. up* the wine and gave. *Neh* 2:1
they *t.* Jeremiah *up* out of. *Jer* 38:13
then the Spirit *t.* me *up.* *Ezek* 3:12
        11:24; 43:5
flame slew men that *t. up* Shadrach,
    Meshach and Abed-nego. *Dan* 3:22
so they *t. up* Jonah.   *Jonah* 1:15
they *t. up* the body of John.
     Mat 14:12; *Mark* 6:29
t. up of the fragments. *Mat* 14:20
    15:37; *Mark* 6:43; 8:8, 20
many baskets ye *t. up.* *Mat* 16:9, 10
he *t.* them *up* in the bed and. *Mark* 2:12
t. him *up* in his arms. *Luke* 2:28
t. up stones to cast at him.
     John 8:59; 10:31
daughter *t.* Moses *up.*   *Acts* 7:21
yea, ye *t. up* the tabernacle of.   43
but Peter *t.* him *up,* saying.   10:26
we *t. up* our carriages and.   21:15
angel *t. up* a stone.   *Rev* 18:21

tookest

though thou *t.* vengeance. *Ps* 99:8
and *t.* thy broidered.   *Ezek* 16:18

tool

if thou lift up thy *t.* upon it. *Ex* 20:25
fashioned it with a graving *t.*   32:4
lift up any iron *t.* on them. *Deut* 27:5
nor any *t.* of iron heard.   *1 Ki* 6:7

tooth

give *t.* for *t.*   *Ex* 21:24; *Lev* 24:20
    Deut 19:21; *Mat* 5:38
or his maidservant's *t.* he shall let
    him go free for his *t.'s.* *Ex* 21:27
is like a broken *t.,* a foot. *Pr* 25:19

top

tower whose *t.* may reach. *Gen* 11:4
the *t.* of the ladder reached to. 28:12
Jacob poured oil on the *t.* of.   18
on the *t.* of the mount: and called
    Moses to the.   *Ex* 19:20; 34:2
like devouring fire on the *t.* 24:17
be an hole in the *t.* of it.   28:32*
the *t.* with pure gold.   30:3; 37:26
they gat up into the *t.*   *Num* 14:40
Aaron died there in the *t.* of. 20:28
for from the *t.* of the rocks.   23:9
the *t.* of Pisgah.   *Deut* 3:27; 34:1

---

from sole of foot to the *t. Deut* 28:35*
on *t.* of the head of him that. 33:16*
build an altar on the *t.*   *Judg* 6:26
the people gat up to the *t.* of. 9:51*
Samson dwelt in the *t.* of the. 15:8*
communed on the *t.* of the house.
        1 Sam 9:25, 26
spread a tent on the *t.* of the house.
        2 Sam 16:22
the *t.* of the throne.   *1 Ki* 10:19
him on the *t.* of the stairs. *2 Ki* 9:13
from the *t.* of the rock. *2 Chr* 25:12
the *t.* of the sceptre.   *Esth* 5:2
of corn on *t.* of mountains. *Ps* 72:16
a sparrow alone on the house-*t.* 102:7
she standeth in the *t.* of.   *Pr* 8:2
It is better to dwell in a corner of the
    house-*t.*   21:9; 25:24
lieth on the *t.* of a mast.   23:34
t. of Amana, from the. *S of S* 4:8
Lord's house shall be established in
    the *t.*   *Isa* 2:2; *Mi* 4:1
two or three berries in the *t. Isa* 17:6
beacon on the *t.* of a mountain. 30:17
let them shout from the *t.* of. 42:11
faint for hunger in *t.* of every street.
        Lam 2:19†
poured out in *t.* of every street. 4:1†
he cropped off the *t.* of. *Ezek* 17:4*
from the *t.* of his young twigs.   22*
she set it on the *t.* of a rock.   24:7*
blood on the *t.* of a rock.   8*
her like the *t.* of a rock. 26:4*, 14*
his *t.* was among the thick boughs.
        31:3, 10, 14
law of the house: on the *t.* of. 43:12
her children were dashed at the *t.* of
    all the streets.   *Nah* 3:10†
on the house-*t.* not come. *Mat* 24:17
    Mark 13:15; *Luke* 17:31
vail rent from *t.* to the bottom.
     Mat 27:51; *Mark* 15:38
house-*t.* and let down.   *Luke* 5:19
was woven from the *t.*   *John* 19:23
leaning on *t.* of his staff. *Heb* 11:21

    see Carmel, hill

topaz

(*A green gem of golden hue, one of
the stones in the high priest's
breastplate*)
the first row a sardius, a *t. Ex* 28:17
        39:10
the *t.* of Ethiopia shall. *Job* 28:19
the sardius, the *t.*   *Ezek* 28:13
beryl, the ninth a *t.*   *Rev* 21:20

Tophet

Tophet, "place of burning," *was
at Jerusalem, lying to the south of
the city, in the valley of the children
of Hinnom. There they burned
the carcases and other filthiness
from the city. It was in the same
place that they cast away the ashes
and remains of the images of false
gods, when they demolished their
altars, and broke down their
statues. Isaiah seems to allude to
this custom of burning dead carcases
in Tophet, when speaking of the
defeat of the army of Sennacherib,
Isa* 30:33.

Josiah defiled *T.* in the. *2 Ki* 23:10
for *T.* is ordained of old. *Isa* 30:33
built the high places of *T. Jer* 7:31
no more be called *T.*   32; 19:6
they shall bury in *T.,* till. 7:32; 19:11
and even make this city as *T.* 19:12
Jerusalem shall be defiled as *T.* 13
then came Jeremiah from *T.*   14

tops

the *t.* of the mountains.   *Gen* 8:5
sound of a going in the *t.* of the.
     2 Sam 5:24; *1 Chr* 14:15
as the grass upon the house-*t.*
    2 Ki 19:26; *Ps* 129:6; *Isa* 37:27
and cut off as the *t.* of. *Job* 24:24
t. of the ragged rocks. *Isa* 2:21*
on the *t.* of houses every one. 15:3
wholly gone up to the house-*t.* 22:1
be lamentation on all house-*t.*
        Jer 48:38

their slain men shall be in all the *t*. of
the mountains.   *Ezek* 6:13
they sacrifice on the *t*. of. *Hos* 4:13
worship the host of heaven on house-
t.   *Zeph* 1:5
that preach ye upon the house-*t*.
    Mat 10:27
proclaimed on the house-*t*. *Luke* 12:3

torch
make the governors of Judah like a
t.   *Zech* 12:6

torches
shall be with flaming *t*.   *Nah* 2:3*
the chariots shall seem like *t*.   4
with lanterns and *t*.   *John* 18:3

torment
into this place of *t*.   *Luke* 16:28
because fear hath *t*.   *1 John* 4:18*
their *t*. was as the *t*. of.   *Rev* 9:5
smoke of their *t*. ascendeth.   14:11
so much *t*. and sorrow give her. 18:7
afar off for the fear of her *t*.   10, 15

torment, *verb*
art thou come to *t*. us?   *Mat* 8:29
that thou *t*. me not.   *Mark* 5:7
    Luke 8:28

tormented
lieth grievously *t*.   *Mat* 8:6
send Lazarus, for I am *t*. in this
flame.   *Luke* 16:24*
comforted, and thou art *t*.   25*
destitute, afflicted, *t*.   *Heb* 11:37*
but that they should be *t*.   *Rev* 9:5
two prophets *t*. them that.   11:10
he shall be *t*. with fire and.   14:10
and shall be *t*. day and night. 20:10

tormentors
delivered him to the *t*.   *Mat* 18:34

torments
taken with divers diseases and *t*.
    Mat 4:24
in hell he lift up his eyes, being in *t*.
    Luke 16:23

torn
that which was *t*. of beasts I brought
not.   *Gen* 31:39
Surely he is *t*. in pieces.   44:28
if *t*. in pieces, let him bring it for witness . . . what was *t*.   *Ex* 22:13
shall eat any flesh *t*. of beasts.   31
fat of that which is *t*. may. *Lev* 7:24
if any eat that which was *t*.   17:15
dieth of itself, or *t*. of beasts. 22:8
lion, which hath *t*. him.   *1 Ki* 13:26
not eaten carcase nor *t*. the ass. 28
carcases *t*. in the midst of. *Isa* 5:25*
goeth out shall be *t*.   *Jer* 5:6
not eaten of that which is *t*. *Ezek* 4:14
not eat any thing that is *t*.   44:31
for he hath *t*. and he will. *Hos* 6:1
brought that which was *t*. *Mal* 1:13*
when the unclean spirit hath *t*. him.
    Mark 1:26

tortoise
*This is probably a sort of lizard.
It is numbered among the unclean
animals, Lev* 11:29.
the *t*. shall be unclean. *Lev* 11:29*

tortured
others were *t*. not accepting deliverance.   *Heb* 11:35

toss
he will turn and *t*. thee. *Isa* 22:18
though the waves thereof *t*. *Jer* 5:22

tossed
I am *t*. up and down.   *Ps* 109:23
is a vanity, *t*. to and fro. *Pr* 21:6
O thou afflicted, *t*. with. *Isa* 54:11
was now *t*. with waves. *Mat* 14:24*
t. with a tempest.   *Acts* 27:18*
children, *t*. to and fro.   *Eph* 4:14
wavereth is like a wave *t*. *Jas* 1:6

tossings
I am full of *t*. to and fro.   *Job* 7:4

tottering
all of you as a *t*. fence.   *Ps* 62:3

touch
not eat of it, nor shall ye *t*. *Gen* 3:3
suffered I thee not to *t*. her.   20:6
that ye *t*. not the border. *Ex* 19:12

there shall not an hand *t*. it. *Ex* 19:13
if a soul *t*. any unclean.   *Lev* 5:2
or if he *t*. the uncleanness of man.
    5:3; 7:21
whatsoever shall *t*. the flesh.   6:27
their carcase ye shall not *t*.   11:8
    Deut 14:8
whosoever doth *t*. them when dead.
    Lev 11:31
he shall *t*. no hallowed thing.   12:4
they shall not *t*. any holy. *Num* 4:15
depart and *t*. nothing of theirs. 16:26
we may not *t*. them.   *Josh* 9:19
they should not *t*. thee.   *Ruth* 2:9
and he shall not *t*. thee any more.
    2 Sam 14:10
t. the young man Absalom.   18:12
the man that shall *t*. them.   23:7
t. not mine anointed.   *1 Chr* 16:22
    Ps 105:15
but *t*. all he hath and he will curse.
    Job 1:11
t. his bone and his flesh, he will. 2:5
there shall no evil *t*. thee.   5:19
that my soul refused to *t*.   6:7
t. the mountains and they. *Ps* 144:5
t. no unclean thing.   *Isa* 52:11
    2 Cor 6:17
that *t*. the inheritance of. *Jer* 12:14
so that men could not *t*. *Lam* 4:14
it is unclean, depart, *t*. not.   15
if one with his skirt do *t*. *Hag* 2:12
if one that is unclean *t*. any of.   13
if I may but *t*. his garment.
   Mat 9:21; *Mark* 5:28
they might *t*. the hem.   *Mat* 14:36
   Mark 5:28; 6:56; 8:22
they pressed on him to *t*. him.
   Mark 3:10; *Luke* 6:19
they besought him to *t*. the blind.
    Mark 8:22
ye yourselves *t*. not the. *Luke* 11:46
that he would *t*. them.   18:15
unto her, *T*. me not.   *John* 20:17
a man not to *t*. a woman. *1 Cor* 7:1
t. not, taste not, handle not. *Col* 2:21
firstborn, should *t*. them. *Heb* 11:28
if so much as a beast *t*. the.   12:20

touched
as we have not *t*. thee. *Gen* 26:29
t. the hollow of Jacob's.   32:25, 32
the soul which hath *t*.   *Lev* 22:6
and whosoever hath *t*. *Num* 31:19
the angel of the Lord *t*. *Judg* 6:21
hearts God had *t*.   *1 Sam* 10:26
the wings of cherubims *t*. *1 Ki* 6:27
an angel *t*. him and said.   19:5, 7
when the man *t*. the bones of Elisha.
    2 Ki 13:21
so Esther *t*. the top of.   *Esth* 5:2
the hand of God hath *t*. *Job* 19:21
lo, this hath *t*. thy lips.   *Isa* 6:7
Lord *t*. my mouth.   *Jer* 1:9
and the he goat *t*. not.   *Dan* 8:5
but he *t*. me. 18; 9:21; 10:10, 16, 18
and Jesus *t*. him.   *Mat* 8:3
   Mark 1:41; *Luke* 5:13
t. her hand, and the fever. *Mat* 8:15
with an issue of blood *t*. the hem.
   9:20; *Mark* 5:27; *Luke* 8:44
then *t*. he their eyes, saying.
    Mat 9:29; 20:34
as many as *t*. him were made perfectly whole.   14:36; *Mark* 6:56
who *t*. my clothes? *Mark* 5:30, 31
    Luke 8:45, 47
into his ears, and he spit, and *t*. his
tongue.   *Mark* 7:33
he came and *t*. the bier. *Luke* 7:14
what cause she had *t*. him.   8:47
and Jesus *t*. his ear and.   22:51
next day we *t*. at Sidon. *Acts* 27:3
priest which cannot be *t*. *Heb* 4:15
mount that might be *t*.   12:18

toucheth
he that *t*. this man shall. *Gen* 26:11
whosoever *t*. the mount. *Ex* 19:12
whatsoever *t*. the altar shall. 29:37
that *t*. them, shall be holy.   30:29
    Lev 6:18
the flesh that *t*. any.   *Lev* 7:19
whosoever *t*. their carcase.   11:24
    27, 36, 39

every one that *t*. them shall.
    Lev 11:26
whoso *t*. his bed, shall wash.   15:5
t. his flesh.   7
t. any thing under him.   10
whomsoever he *t*. that hath the. 11
the vessel of earth that he *t*. shall. 12
whoso *t*. her.   19
whosoever *t*. her bed.   21
whosoever *t*. any thing that she. 22
if on her bed, when he *t*. it, he shall.
   15:23, 27; 22:4, 5; *Num* 19:22
he that *t*. the dead body. *Num* 19:11
    13, 16
t. a bone.   18
t. the water of separation.   21
broken when it *t*. fire.   *Judg* 16:9
it *t*. thee and thou art.   *Job* 4:5
he *t*. the hills and they.   *Ps* 104:32
whosoever *t*. her, shall not. *Pr* 6:29
when the east wind *t*. it. *Ezek* 17:10
out, and blood *t*. blood.   *Hos* 4:2
Lord is he that *t*. the land. *Amos* 9:5
he that *t*. you, *t*. the apple. *Zech* 2:8
what woman this is that *t*. him.
    Luke 7:39
and that wicked one *t*. *1 John* 5:18

touching
Esau, as *t*. thee, doth. *Gen* 27:42
for him, as *t*. his sin that. *Lev* 5:13
thus do to the Levites *t*. *Num* 8:26
t. matter thou and I.   *1 Sam* 20:23
t. the words which thou. *2 Ki* 22:18
t. the Almighty, we cannot find him.
    Job 37:23
I have made *t*. the king.   *Ps* 45:1
a song of my beloved, *t*.   *Isa* 5:1
utter judgements *t*. all.   *Jer* 1:16
t. the house of the king of.   21:11
thus saith the Lord *t*. Shallum. 22:11
the vision is *t*. the whole. *Ezek* 7:13
as *t*. any thing that they. *Mat* 18:19
as *t*. the resurrection of the. 22:31
   Mark 12:26; *Acts* 24:21
t. those things whereof. *Luke* 23:14
to do as *t*. these men.   *Acts* 5:35
as *t*. the Gentiles who believe. 21:25
as *t*. the election, they. *Rom* 11:28
now as *t*. things offered. *1 Cor* 8:1
t. our brother Apollos.   16:12
as *t*. the ministering to. *2 Cor* 9:1
of the Hebrews, as *t*. the. *Phil* 3:5
t. the righteousness in the law.   6
t. whom ye received.   *Col* 4:10
t. brotherly love, ye.   *1 Thes* 4:9
in the Lord *t*. you.   *2 Thes* 3:4

tow
a thread of *t*. is broken. *Judg* 16:9
and the strong shall be as *t*. *Isa* 1:31
they are quenched as *t*.   43:17*

toward, *or* towards
Ephraim *t*. Israel's left hand, Manasseh *t*. Israel's right.   *Gen* 48:13
face *t*. the wilderness.   *Num* 24:1
his eye shall be evil *t*. *Deut* 28:54
shall be evil *t*. her husband.   56
heart is *t*. the governors. *Judg* 5:9
behold, if there be good *t*. David.
    1 Sam 20:12
prayer thy servant shall make *t*.
   1 Ki 8:29, 30, 35; *2 Chr* 6:21
done good in Israel, both *t*. God, and
t. his house.   *2 Chr* 24:16
endureth for ever *t*. Israel. *Ezra* 3:11
I will worship *t*. thy holy temple.
    Ps 5:7; 138:2
eyes are ever *t*. the Lord.   25:15
hands *t*. thy holy oracle.   28:2
favour is *t*. a wise servant. *Pr* 14:35
the great goodness *t*. house. *Isa* 63:7
my mind could not be *t*. *Jer* 15:1
being open *t*. Jerusalem. *Dan* 6:10
horn waxed great *t*. the south.   8:9
look *t*. thy holy temple. *Jonah* 2:4
as it began to dawn *t*. the first day.
    Mat 28:1
peace, good will *t*. men. *Luke* 2:14
treasure, and not rich *t*. God. 12:21
with us, for it is *t*. evening. 24:29
Greeks, repentance *t*. God, and faith
t. our Lord Jesus.   *Acts* 20:21
of offence *t*. God and *t*. men. 24:16

faith which thou hast *t.* the Lord
Jesus Christ, and *t.* all. *Philem* 5
see **heaven, him, me, thee,**
them, us, you

towel

he riseth, and took a *t.* *John* 13:4
wipe their feet with the *t.* 5

tower

[1] Watch-towers *or fortified posts*
in frontier or exposed places are
mentioned in Scripture, as the tower
of Edar, etc., Gen 35:21; Isa 21:5,
8, 11; Mi 4:8.
[2] *Besides these military towers*
we read of towers built in vine-
yards as an almost necessary ad-
dition to them, Isa 5:2; Mat 21:33.
[3] *God is often alluded to as a*
tower, with the idea of protection,
Ps 61:3; Pr 18:10.

let us build us a city and *t.* *Gen* 11:4
came down to see the city and *t.* 5
tent beyond the *t.* of Edar. 35:21
I will break down this *t.* *Judg* 8:9
he beat down the *t.* of Penuel. 17
men of the *t.* of Shechem. 9:46
but there was a strong *t.* within. 51
is the *t.* of salvation. *2 Sam* 22:51*
when he came to the *t.* he. *2 Ki* 5:24*
hast been a strong *t.* *Ps* 61:3
the Lord is a strong *t.* *Pr* 18:10
like the *t.* of David. *S of S* 4:4
neck is as a *t.* of ivory, thy nose is as
the *t.* of Lebanon, looking. 7:4
he built a *t.* in the midst. *Isa* 5:2
I have set thee for a *t.* *Jer* 6:27†
city shall be built from *t.* of. 31:38
Egypt desolate, from the *t.* of Syene.
Ezek 29:10
from the *t.* of Syene shall they fall
in it. 30:6
O *t.* of the flock, to thee. *Mi* 4:8
set me upon the *t.* and. *Hab* 2:1
be inhabited from *t.* of. *Zech* 14:10
built a *t.* and let it out to husbandmen. *Mat* 21:33; *Mark* 12:1
those 18 on whom the *t.* *Luke* 13:4
you intending to build a *t.* 14:28

high tower

God is my *high t.* *2 Sam* 22:3
Ps 18:2; 144:2
day of Lord on every *high t.* *Isa* 2:15

towers

build cities and make *t.* *2 Chr* 14:7
moreover Uzziah built *t.* in. 26:9
he built *t.* in the desert and. 10
Jotham built castles and *t.* 27:4
raised up the wall to the *t.* 32:5
Zion and tell her *t.* *Ps* 48:12
and my breasts like *t.* *S of S* 8:10
the Assyrian set up the *t.* *Isa* 23:13
hill rivers, when the *t.* fall. 30:25
the forts and *t.* shall be for. 32:14
he that counted the *t.?* 33:18
they shall break down her *t.*
Ezek 26:4, 9
Gammadims were in thy *t.* 27:11
their *t.* are desolate. *Zeph* 3:6

to wit

to wit whether the Lord had made
his journey. *Gen* 24:21
to wit what would be done. *Ex* 2:4
to wit, that God was in Christ reconciling. *2 Cor* 5:19
you *to wit* of the grace of God. 8:1

town

(*The Revised Versions frequently*
change this reading either to city
or to village *according as either is*
appropriate)
house was on the *t.* wall. *Josh* 2:15
and the elders of *t.* *1 Sam* 16:4
shut in, by entering into a *t.* 23:7
give me a place in some *t.* 27:5
woe to him that builds a *t.* *Hab* 2:12
t. ye shall enter. *Mat* 10:11
blind man out of the *t.* *Mark* 8:23
nor go into the *t.* nor tell it to. 26
Christ cometh out of the *t.* of.
John 7:42
the *t.* of Mary and her sister. 11:1
Jesus was not yet come into the *t.* 30

townclerk
the *t.* had appeased the. *Acts* 19:35.

towns
dwelt in unwalled *t.* *Esth* 9:19
on all her *t.* the evil. *Jer* 19:15
Jerusalem be inhabited as *t.* without
walls. *Zech* 2:4
went through the *t.* *Luke* 9:6
that they may go into the *t.* 12

trade
their *t.* hath been about cattle.
Gen 46:32*, 34*

trade, *verb*
dwell and *t.* ye. *Gen* 34:10, 21
as many as *t.* by sea. *Rev* 18:17*

traded
Tarshish *t.* in thy fairs. *Ezek* 27:12
Javan, Tubal, Meshech, *t.* the. 13
Togarmah *t.* with horses. 14
Judah and Israel *t.* in thy market. 17
five talents, went and *t.* *Mat* 25:16

trading
how much every man had gained by
t. *Luke* 19:15

tradition
(*Usually this word means laws and*
regulations handed down orally
from one generation to another, and
forming the Oral Law of the Jews,
which Jesus frequently denounced
when it was against the real law
of God)
why do thy disciples transgress the
t. of ? *Mat* 15:2; *Mark* 7:5
transgress the commandment of God
by your *t.?* *Mat* 15:3; *Mark* 7:9
commandment of God of none effect
by your *t.* *Mat* 15:6; *Mark* 7:13
t. of the elders. *Mark* 7:3, 8, 9
after the *t.* of men. *Col* 2:8
not after the *t.* which he. *2 Thes* 3:6
received by *t.* from. *1 Pet* 1:18*

traditions
being zealous of the *t.* *Gal* 1:14
hold the *t.* ye have. *2 Thes* 2:15

traffick
ye shall *t.* in the land. *Gen* 42:34

traffick, *substantive*
of *t.* of merchants. *1 Ki* 10:15
it into a land of *t.* *Ezek* 17:4
by thy *t.* hast thou increased. 28:5
sanctuaries by iniquity of *t.* 18

traffickers
whose *t.* are the honourable. *Isa* 23:8

train
Jerusalem with a great *t.* *1 Ki* 10:2
his *t.* filled the temple. *Isa* 6:1

train, *verb*
t. up a child in the way. *Pr.* 22:6

trained
his *t.* servants, 318. *Gen* 14:14

traitor
Iscariot, which was the *t.* *Luke* 6:16

traitors
men shall be *t.,* heady. *2 Tim* 3:4

trample
the dragon shalt thou *t.* *Ps* 91:13
will *t.* them in my fury. *Isa* 63:3
pearls, lest they *t.* them. *Mat* 7:6

trance
vision falling into a *t.* *Num* 24:4*, 16*
he fell into a *t.* and saw. *Acts* 10:10
and in a *t.* I saw a vision. 11:5
in the temple, I was in a *t.* 22:17

tranquillity
lengthening of thy *t.* *Dan* 4:27

transferred
have in figure *t.* to myself. *1 Cor* 4:6

transfigured
(*The history of Christ's* transfiguration *is recorded in each of the first*
three Gospels. All three agree
that this transfiguration was cele-
brated upon a mountain, which
modern commentators think was
Mount Hermon*)
and he was *t.* before them.
Mat 17:2; *Mark* 9:2

transformed
but be ye *t.* by renewing. *Rom* 12:2
for Satan is *t.* into an. *2 Cor* 11:14*
if his ministers also be *t.* 15*

transforming
t. themselves into. *2 Cor* 11:13*

transgress
wherefore now do ye *t.* the commandment ? *Num* 14:41; *2 Chr* 24:20
the Lord's people to *t.* *1 Sam* 2:24
if ye *t.* I will scatter you. *Neh* 1:8
shall we hearken to you to *t.?* 13:27
my mouth shall not *t.* *Ps* 17:3
let them be ashamed who *t.* 25:3
bread that man will *t.* *Pr* 28:21
thou saidst, I will not *t.* *Jer* 2:20
purge out them that *t.* *Ezek* 20:38
come to Beth-el and *t.* *Amos* 4:4
why do thy disciples *t.?* *Mat* 15:2
t. the commandment of God ? 3
who by circumcision dost *t.* the law.
Rom 2:27

transgressed
I have not *t.* thy commandments.
Deut 26:13
Israel hath sinned, and they have
also *t.* my covenant. *Josh* 7:11, 15
t. covenant of Lord your God. 23:16
he said, Ye have *t.* *1 Sam* 14:33
I have *t.* the commandment. 15:24
wherein they have *t.* *1 Ki* 8:50
Achar, who *t.* in the. *1 Chr* 2:7*
they *t.* against the God of. 5:25*
because they *t.* against. *2 Chr* 12:2*
Uzziah *t.* against the Lord. 26:16*
and Ahaz *t.* sore against. 28:19*
the priests and the people *t.* 36:14*
ye have *t.* and taken. *Ezra* 10:10*
we are many that have *t.* in. 13
they have *t.* the laws. *Isa* 24:5
teachers have *t.* against me. 43:27
carcases of men that have *t.* 66:24
the pastors *t.* against me. *Jer* 2:8
why will ye plead ? ye all have *t.* 29
acknowledge that thou hast *t.* 3:13
iniquities whereby they *t.* 33:8
I will give the men that *t.* 34:18
we have *t.* and have rebelled.
Lam 3:42
they and their fathers have *t.*
Ezek 2:3
transgressions whereby ye *t.* 18:31
yea, all Israel have *t.* *Dan* 9:11
because they have *t.* *Hos* 7:13
not ashamed for doings wherein thou
t. *Zeph* 3:11
nor *t.* I at any time thy. *Luke* 15:29
see **covenants**

transgressest
why *t.* thou the king's ? *Esth* 3:3

transgresseth
his mouth *t.* not in judgement.
Pr 16:10
because he *t.* by wine. *Hab* 2:5*
committeth sin, *t.* law. *1 John* 3:4*
whoso *t.* and abideth not. *2 John* 9*

transgressing
wrought wickedness in *t.* *Deut* 17:2
in *t.* and lying against. *Isa* 59:13

transgression
forgiving *t.* and sin. *Ex* 34:7
Num 14:18
or if it be in *t.* against. *Josh* 22:22*
that there is no *t.* in. *1 Sam* 24:11
carried to Babylon for their *t.*
1 Chr 9:1
so Saul died for his *t.* which. 10:13*
Ahaz cast away in *t.* *2 Chr* 29:19*
because of *t.* of those carried away.
Ezra 9:4*
mourned because of their *t.* 10:6*
thou not pardon my *t.?* *Job* 7:21
cast them away for their *t.* 8:4
make me to know my *t.* and. 13:23
my *t.* is sealed up in a bag. 14:17
I am clean without *t.* 33:9
is incurable without *t.* 34:6
innocent from the great *t.* *Ps* 19:13
is he whose *t.* is forgiven. 32:1
the *t.* of the wicked saith. 36:1
against me; not for my *t.* 59:3
visit their *t.* with a rod. 89:32

fools because of their *t.* are.
   Ps 107:17
the wicked is snared by *t. Pr* 12:13
covereth a *t.* seeketh love.   17:9
he loveth *t.* that loveth strife.   19
glory to pass over a *t.*   19:11
for the *t.* of a land many are.   28:2
and saith, It is no *t.*   24
in the *t.* of an evil man there.   29:6
when the wicked are multiplied, *t.* 16
and a furious man aboundeth in.   22
the *t.* thereof shall be.   *Isa* 24:20
for the *t.* of my people was he. 53:8
ye not children of *t.*, a seed of ? 57:4
shew my people their *t.*   58:1
and to them that turn from *t.*   59:20
him in the day of his *t.*   *Ezek* 33:12
against the daily sacrifice by reason
of *t.*   *Dan* 8:12
concerning sacrifice, and the *t.*   13
determined to finish the *t.*   9:24
at Gilgal multiply *t.*, bring. *Amos* 4:4
t. of Jacob is all this, and for the sins
   . . . what is the *t.*?   *Mi* 1:5
power to declare to Jacob his *t.* 3:8
firstborn for my *t.*?   6:7
that passeth by the *t.* of the.   7:18
which Judas by *t.* fell.   *Acts* 1:25*
no law is, there is no *t.*   *Rom* 4:15
after similitude of Adam's *t.*   5:14
the woman being deceived was in the
  t.   *1 Tim* 2:14
every *t.* received just recompence of.
    Heb 2:2
for sin is the *t.* of the.   *1 John* 3:4*

transgressions

pardon your *t.* for my.   *Ex* 23:21
atonement because of their *t.*
    Lev 16:16
confess over the goat all their *t.*   21
will not forgive your *t.*   *Josh* 24:19
thy people all their *t.*   *1 Ki* 8:50
if I covered my *t.* as Adam, by
  hiding.   *Job* 31:33
if thy *t.* be multiplied, what ? 35:6
them their work and *t.*   36:9
in the multitude of their *t. Ps* 5:10
sins of my youth, nor my *t.*   25:7
I said I will confess my *t.*   32:5
deliver me from all my *t.* and. 39:8
blot out all my *t.*   51:1
for I acknowledge my *t.*: my sin.   3
as for our *t.* thou shalt purge.   65:3
so far hath he removed our *t.* 103:12
he that blotteth out thy *t. Isa* 43:25
out as a thick cloud thy *t.*   44:22
for your *t.* is your mother put. 50:1
but he was wounded for our *t.* 53:5
t. are multiplied before thee, and our
  sins testify . . . for our *t.*   59:12
because their *t.* are many. *Jer* 5:6
for the multitude of her *t. Lam* 1:5
the yoke of my *t.* is bound by.   14
as hast done to me for all my *t.*   22
any more with their *t.*   *Ezek* 14:11
all his *t.* shall not be.   18:22
turneth away from all his *t.*   28
turn yourselves from your *t.*   30
cast away all your *t.* whereby.   31
in that your *t.* are discovered. 21:24
if our *t.* be upon us and we pine.
    33:10
themselves any more with *t.* 37:23
according to their *t.* have I. 39:24
for three *t.* of Damascus. *Amos* 1:3
for three *t.* of Gaza.   6
for three *t.* of Ammon.   13
I will visit the *t.* of Israel.   3:14
I know your manifold *t.* and.   5:12
for the *t.* of Israel were.   *Mi* 1:13
the law was added because of *t.*, till
  the seed.   *Gal* 3:19
for the redemption of the *t. Heb* 9:15

transgressor

the *t.* shall be a ransom. *Pr* 21:18*
the words of the *t.*   22:12*
thou wast called a *t.*   *Isa* 48:8
I make myself a *t.*   *Gal* 2:18
kill, thou art become a *t. Jas* 2:11

transgressors

the *t.* shall be destroyed. *Ps* 37:38
then will I teach *t.* thy ways.   51:13
be not merciful to any wicked *t.* 59:5

t. shall be rooted out.   *Pr* 2:22*
the perverseness of *t.* shall.   11:3*
t. shall be taken in their own naughtiness.   6*
but the soul of the *t.* shall eat. 13:2*
but the way of *t.* is hard.   15*
and she increaseth the *t.*   23:28*
rewardeth the fool and the *t.* 26:10*
the destruction of *t.* shall. *Isa* 1:28
bring it again to mind, O ye *t.* 46:8
numbered with the *t.* and bare the
  sin of many, . . . for the *t.*   53:12
when the *t.* are come to.   *Dan* 8:23
but the *t.* shall fall therein. *Hos* 14:9
he was numbered with *t. Mark* 15:28
    Luke 22:37
convinced of the law as *t.*   *Jas* 2:9

translate

to *t.* the kingdom from. *2 Sam* 3:10

translated

t. us into the kingdom of. *Col* 1:13
Enoch was *t.* that he should not see
  death.   *Heb* 11:5

translation

before his *t.* he had this. *Heb* 11:5

transparent

was as it were *t.* glass. *Rev* 21:21

trap, -s

but they shall be *t.*   *Josh* 23:13
and a *t.* is laid for him. *Job* 18:10
let it become a *t.*   *Ps* 69:22
they lay wait, set a *t.*   *Jer* 5:26
be made a snare, a *t.*   *Rom* 11:9

travail

time of her *t.* behold.   *Gen* 38:27
Moses told Jethro, all the *t. Ex* 18:8
them as of a woman in *t.*   *Ps* 48:6
    Jer 6:24; 13:21; 22:23; 49:24
    50:43; *Mi* 4:9, 10
this sore *t.* hath God.   *Eccl* 1:13
are sorrows, his *t.* is grief.   2:23
to the sinner he giveth *t.*   26
I have seen the *t.* God hath.   3:10
again I considered all *t.* and.   4:4
than both the hands full with *t.*   6
vanity, yea it is a sore *t.*   8
riches perish by evil *t.*   5:14
I *t.* not.   *Isa* 23:4
see of the *t.* of his soul.   53:11
sing, thou that didst not *t.*   54:1
voice as of a woman in *t.*   *Jer* 4:31
whether a man doth *t.*? . . . as a
  woman in *t.*?   30:6
compassed me with gall and *t.*
    Lam 3:5
a woman when she is in *t.* hath sorrow.   *John* 16:21
my children, of whom I *t.* in birth.
    Gal 4:19
for ye remember our labour and *t.*
    1 Thes 2:9
destruction cometh, as *t.*   5:3
but wrought with *t.* night and day.
    2 Thes 3:8

travailed

Rachel *t.*   *Gen* 35:16
Tamar *t.*   38:28
Phinehas' wife bowed herself, and *t.*
    1 Sam 4:19
she *t.* she brought forth. *Isa* 66:7
as soon as Zion *t.* she brought.   8

travailest

cry, thou that *t.* not.   *Gal* 4:27

travaileth

behold, he *t.* with iniquity. *Ps* 7:14
they shall be in pain as a woman that
  t.   *Isa* 13:8
as the pangs of a woman that *t.* 21:3
and with them her that *t. Jer* 31:8
till she who *t.* hath brought. *Mi* 5:3
the whole creation *t.* in pain until
  now.   *Rom* 8:22

travailing

I cry like a *t.* woman.   *Isa* 42:14
sorrows of a *t.* woman. *Hos* 13:13
a woman cried, *t.* in birth. *Rev* 12:2

travel

thou knowest the *t.* that. *Num* 20:14
Paul's companion in *t.* *Acts* 19:29
chosen of the churches to *t.* with us.
    2 Cor 8:19

travelled

t. as far as Phenice and. *Acts* 11:19

traveller

there came a *t.* to the. *2 Sam* 12:4
opened my doors to the *t. Job* 31:32

travellers

the *t.* walked through. *Judg* 5:6

travelleth

wicked man *t.* with pain. *Josh* 15:20
poverty come as one that *t.*
    Pr 6:11*; 24:34*

travelling

in Arabia lodge, O ye *t. Isa* 21:13†
who is this *t.* in the greatness ? 63:1
heaven is as a man *t.* *Mat* 25:14

traversing

thou art a swift dromedary *t.* her
  ways.   *Jer* 2:23

treacherous

t. dealer dealeth treacherously.
    Isa 21:2; 24:16
turned not, and her *t.* sister Judah.
    Jer 3:7
her *t.* sister Judah feared not.   8
her *t.* sister Judah hath not.   10
Israel hath justified herself more
  than *t.* Judah.   11
be an assembly of *t.* men.   9:2
are light and *t.* persons. *Zeph* 3:4

treacherously

men of Shechem dealt *t. Judg* 9:23
and dealest *t.*, and they deait not *t.*
  with thee.   *Isa* 33:1
thou wouldest deal very *t.*   48:8
as a wife *t.* departeth.   *Jer* 3:20
the house of Judah hath dealt *t.*
    5:11; *Mal* 2:11
happy that deal very *t.*?   *Jer* 12:1
even they have dealt *t.* with thee.   6
all her friends have dealt *t. Lam* 1:2
they have dealt *t.* against. *Hos* 5:7
there have they dealt *t.* against. 6:7
why do we deal *t.* every ? *Mal* 2:10
against whom thou hast dealt *t.*   14
let none deal *t.* against the wife.   15
your spirit, that ye deal not *t.*   16

treachery

Joram said, There is *t.*   *2 Ki* 9:23

tread

soles of your feet *t.*   *Deut* 11:24
you on all the land that ye *t.*   25
thou shalt *t.* upon their high. 33:29
none *t.* on the threshold. *1 Sam* 5:5
t. their winepresses, and. *Job* 24:11
and *t.* down the wicked in.   40:12
let him *t.* down my life.   *Ps* 7:5
name will we *t.* them under.   44:5
t. down our enemies. 60:12; 108:13
thou shalt *t.* upon the lion.   91:13
who hath required this at your hand,
  to *t.* my courts ?   *Isa* 1:12*
to *t.* them down, like the mire. 10:6
upon my mountains *t.* him.   14:25
treaders shall *t.* out no wine. 16:10
the foot shall *t.* it down.   20
t. them in mine anger.   63:3, 6
a shout, as they that *t.*   *Jer* 25:30
wine to fail, none shall *t.*   48:33
with his hoofs shall he *t. Ezek* 26:11
but ye must *t.* the residue.   34:18
fourth beast shall *t.* it.   *Dan* 7:23
Ephraim loveth to *t.*   *Hos* 10:11
the Lord will *t.* on the.   *Mi* 1:3
when the Assyrian shall *t.*   5:5
thou shalt *t.* the olives, but.   6:15
t. the mortar, make.   *Nah* 3:14
as mighty men which *t. Zech* 10:5
and ye shall *t.* down the. *Mal* 4:3
I will give you power to *t.* on scorpions.   *Luke* 10:19
holy city shall they *t.*   *Rev* 11:2

treader, -s

t. shall tread out no wine. *Isa* 16:10
the *t.* of grapes shall overtake the
  sower.   *Amos* 9:13

treadeth

not muzzle ox when he *t. Deut* 25:4
    1 Cor 9:9; *1 Tim* 5:18
which *t.* upon the waves. *Job* 9:8
come as the potter *t.* clay. *Isa* 41:25
thy garments like him that *t.*   63:2

he that *t.* on the high places of the
   earth.   *Amos* 4:13
and when he *t.* within.   *Mi* 5:6
if he go through, he both *t.* down. 8
he *t.* the winepress of.   *Rev* 19:15

treading
in those days saw I some *t.* winepresses on the sabbath. *Neh* 13:15
it shall be for the *t.* of.   *Isa* 7:25
of trouble and of *t.* down.   22:5
forasmuch as your *t.*   *Amos* 5:11*

treason
acts of Zimri and his *t.*   *1 Ki* 16:20
Athaliah cried, *T. T.*   *2 Ki* 11:14
           2 Chr 23:13

treasure
The word treasure, *among the*
Hebrews, signifies anything col-
lected together; provisions, stores.
So they say, a treasure of corn, of
wine, of oil, of honey, Jer 41:8. *So*
also treasures of gold, silver, brass,
Ezek 28:4; Dan 11:43. *Snow,*
winds, hail, rain, waters, are in the
treasuries *of God,* Job 38:22;
Ps 135:7. *The wise men opened*
their treasures, that is, their boxes
or bundles, to offer presents to our
Saviour, Mat 2:11.

God hath given you *t.*   *Gen* 43:23
ye shall be a peculiar *t.* to me.
       Ex 19:5†; *Ps* 135:4
open to thee his good *t. Deut* 28:12
gave them to the *t.* of.   *1 Chr* 29:8
after their ability to *t.* of work.
           Ezra 2:69*
the Tirshatha gave to *t.*   *Neh* 7:70*
the fathers gave to the *t.* of.   71*
thou fillest with hid *t.*   *Ps* 17:14
Israel for his peculiar *t.*   135:4†
of the righteous is much *t. Pr* 15:6
a little, than great *t.* and trouble. 16
there is a *t.* to be desired.   21:20
I gathered the peculiar *t. Eccl* 2:8
fear of the Lord is his *t. Isa* 33:6
have taken the *t.* and. *Ezek* 22:25
he shall spoil *t.* of all.   *Hos* 13:15
for where your *t.* is, there. *Mat* 6:21
           Luke 12:34
t. of his heart, an evil man out of the
  evil *t.*   *Mat* 12:35; *Luke* 6:45
heaven is like to a *t.* hid. *Mat* 13:44
who bringeth out of his *t.* things. 52
shalt have *t.* in heaven.   19:21
      Mark 10:21; *Luke* 18:22
so is he that layeth up *t. Luke* 12:21
provide a *t.* in the heavens.   33
had charge of all her *t.*   *Acts* 8:27
we have this *t.* in earthen. *2 Cor* 4:7
ye have heaped *t.* for the.   *Jas* 5:3

treasure *cities*
for Pharaoh *t. cities.*   *Ex* 1:11

treasure *house*
let search be made in the king's *t.*
  house.   *Ezra* 5:17
out of the king's *t. house.*   7:20
Levites shall bring up the tithe into
  the *t. house.*   *Neh* 10:38
brought vessels into *t. house* of his
  god.   *Dan* 1:2

treasured
Tyre, it shall not be *t.*   *Isa* 23:18

treasurer
forth the vessels by the *t. Ezra* 1:8
get thee unto this *t.*, even. *Isa* 22:15

treasurers
make a decree to all *t.*   *Ezra* 7:21
and I made *t.* over the. *Neh* 13:13
gathered the *t.*   *Dan* 3:2, 3

treasures
sealed up among my *t. Deut* 32:34
suck of *t.* hid in the sand.   33:19
he put dedicated things among the *t.*
           1 Ki 7:51*
Shishak took away the *t.* of.   14:26
Asa took gold left in the *t.*   15:18
           2 Chr 16:2
Jehoash took gold found in *t.*
      2 Ki 12:18; 14:14
gold that was found in the *t.*   16:8
gave him silver found in the *t.* 18:15

and gold and all that was found in his
  t.   *2 Ki* 20:13, 15; *Isa* 39:2, 4
thence all the *t.* of the house of the
  Lord, and the *t.* of the king's.
      2 Ki 24:13; *2 Chr* 36:18
Ahijah was over *t.* of. *1 Chr* 26:20*
Shebuel was ruler of the *t.*   24*
his brethren were over the *t.*   26
and over the king's *t.* was.   27:25*
concerning the *t.*   *2 Chr* 8:15
appointed for the *t.*   *Neh* 12:44
it more than for hid *t.*   *Job* 3:21
into the *t.* of the snow ? or hast thou
  seen the *t.* of the hail ?   38:22*
if thou searchest for her as for hid *t.*
           Pr 2:4
I will fill the *t.* of those that. 8:21*
t. of wickedness profit.   10:2
the getting of *t.* by a lying.   21:6
neither any end of their *t. Isa* 2:7
I have robbed their *t.*   10:13
their *t.* on bunches of camels. 30:6
and I will give thee the *t.*   45:3
he bringeth wind out of his *t.*
      Jer 10:13*; 51:16*
thy *t.* I will give to the spoil. 15:13
          17:3; 20:5
slay us not: for we have *t.* 41:8*
thou hast trusted in thy *t.*   48:7
daughter, that trusted in her *t.* 49:4
a sword is on her *t.*; they shall. 50:37
many waters, abundant in *t.* 51:13
silver and gold into thy *t. Ezek* 28:4
power over the *t.* of gold. *Dan* 11:43
are there yet the *t.* of wickedness in
  the house of ?   *Mi* 6:10
they had opened their *t. Mat* 2:11
lay not up for yourselves *t.* 6:19
but lay up for yourselves *t.*   20
in whom are hid all the *t. Col* 2:3
than the *t.* in Egypt.   *Heb* 11:26

treasurest
t. up wrath against the.   *Rom* 2:5

treasuries
Levites were over the *t. 1 Chr* 9:26
Solomon pattern of the *t.* 28:11, 12
Hezekiah made *t.* for. *2 Chr* 32:27
the tithe unto the *t.*   *Neh* 13:12
I made treasurers over the *t.*   13
to bring it into the king's *t. Esth* 3:9
promised to pay to the king's *t.* 4:7
the wind out of his *t.*   *Ps* 135:7

treasury
they shall come into the *t.* of the Lord.
      Josh 6:19, 24
the house under the *t.*   *Jer* 38:11
it is not lawful to put them into the *t.*
           Mat 27:6
the *t.*, and beheld how the people cast
  money into the *t.*   *Mark* 12:41
rich men casting their gifts into the *t.*
           Luke 21:1
spake Jesus in the *t.*   *John* 8:20

treatise
former *t.* have I made.   *Acts* 1:1

tree
you every *t.* for meat.   *Gen* 1:29
God made every *t.* to grow, the *t.* of
  life also, and the *t.*   2:9
of every *t.* of the garden thou. 16
but of the *t.* of knowledge. 17; 3:3
when the woman saw that the *t.* 3:6
hast thou eaten of the *t.?*   11, 17
the woman gave me of the *t.*   12
lest he take also of the *t.* of life. 22
keep the way of the *t.* of life.   24
rest yourselves under the *t.*   18:4
he stood by them under the *t.*   8
Pharaoh shall hang thee on a *t.* 40:19
the hail brake every *t.*   *Ex* 9:25
the locusts shall eat every *t.* 10:5
and the Lord shewed him a *t.* 15:25
seed or fruit of *t.* is Lord's. *Lev* 27:30
a stroke to cut down the *t. Deut* 19:5
t. of the field is man's life.   20:19
and if thou hang him on a *t.* 21:22
not remain all night on the *t.*   23
bird's nest in the way in any *t.* 22:6
take the king of Ai down from the *t.*
           Josh 8:29
now Saul abode under a *t.* in Ramah.
          1 Sam 22:6*

buried them under a *t.* at Jabesh.
         1 Sam 31:13*
shall fell every good *t.*   *2 Ki* 3:19
were both hanged on a *t. Esth* 2:23
there is hope of a *t.* if it. *Job* 14:7
hath he removed like a *t.*   19:10
shall be broken as a *t.*   24:20
like a *t.* planted by the rivers. *Ps* 1:3
she is a *t.* of life to them. *Pr* 3:18
the fruit of the righteous is a *t.* 11:30
desire cometh, it is a *t.* of life. 13:12
tongue is a *t.* of life.   15:4
if the *t.* fall toward the south or the
  north; where the *t.*   *Eccl* 11:3
a *t.* that will not rot.   *Isa* 40:20
down to the stock of a *t.?*   44:19
eunuch say, I am a dry *t.*   56:3
as days of a *t.* are the days. 65:22
themselves behind one *t.*   66:17
for one cutteth a *t.* out. *Jer* 10:3
destroy the *t.* with the fruit. 11:19
he shall be as a *t.* planted by. 17:8
vine *t.* more than any *t.? Ezek* 15:2
the high *t.*, exalted the low *t.*, dried up
  the green *t.*, made dry *t.* to. 17:24
rod of my son, as every *t.*   21:10
nor any *t.* in the garden of.   31:8
the *t.* of the field shall yield. 34:27
multiply the fruit of the *t.*   36:30
and behold a *t.*   *Dan* 4:10
the *t.* grew.   11, 20
said thus, Hew down the *t.* 4:14, 23
fear not for the *t.* beareth. *Joel* 2:22
every *t.* that bringeth not forth good
  fruit. *Mat* 3:10; 7:19; *Luke* 3:9
good *t.* bringeth forth good fruit, but
  a corrupt *t. Mat* 7:17; *Luke* 6:43
good *t.* cannot bring forth. *Mat* 7:18
the *t.* good and his fruit good; for the
  t. is known.   12:33; *Luke* 6:44
mustard seed becometh a *t.*
      Mat 13:32; *Luke* 13:19
say to the sycamine *t.*   *Luke* 17:6
ye slew and hanged on a *t. Acts* 5:30
they slew, and hanged on a *t.* 10:39
took him down from the *t.*   13:29
one that hangeth on a *t. Gal* 3:13
in his own body on the *t. 1 Pet* 2:24
I give to eat of the *t.* of life. *Rev* 2:7
should not blow on any *t.*   7:1
hurt any green thing, nor *t.*   9:4
was there the *t.* of life.   22:2
have right to the *t.* of life.   14
      see **green**

trees
amongst the *t.* of garden. *Gen* 3:8
all the *t.* were made sure.   23:17
did eat the fruit of the *t. Ex* 10:15
planted all manner of *t. Lev* 19:23
the boughs of goodly *t.*   23:40
and the *t.* of the field shall.   26:4
neither shall the *t.* of the land. 20
as *t.* of lign aloes which the Lord . . .
  as cedar *t.* beside.   *Num* 24:6
not plant a grove of any *t. Deut* 16:21
not destroy *t.* thereof by axe. 20:19
t. thou knowest not to be *t.* for. 20
all thy *t.* and fruit shall the. 28:42
hanged them on five *t.*   *Josh* 10:26
took them down off the *t.*   27
the *t.* went forth to anoint. *Judg* 9:8
be promoted over the *t.*   9, 11, 13
the *t.* said to the fig tree, reign. 10
t. said to the vine.   12
t. said to the bramble.   14
cut down a bough from the *t.*   48
spake of *t.* from cedar. *1 Ki* 4:33
felled all the good *t.* *2 Ki* 3:25
then shall the *t.* of the wood sing.
      1 Chr 16:33; *Ps* 96:12
firstfruits of all *t. Neh* 10:35, 37
under the shady *t.* *Job* 40:21, 22
lifted up axes on thick *t. Ps* 74:5
their sycamore *t.* with frost. 78:47
the *t.* of the Lord are full of. 104:16
and brake the *t.* of their. 105:33
fruitful *t.* and cedars praise. 148:9
I planted *t.* of all kinds. *Eccl* 2:5
apple tree among the *t. S of S* 2:3
with all *t.* of frankincense.   4:14
heart was moved as the *t. Isa* 7:2
the rest of the *t.* of his forest. 10:19
strengtheneth among the *t.*   44:14

t. of fields shall clap their. *Isa* 55:12
called *t.* of righteousness.   61:3
Lord said, Hew down *t.*   *Jer* 6:6
be poured out upon the *t.*   7:20
all the *t.* of the field.   *Ezek* 17:24
they saw all the thick *t.*   20:28
was exalted above all the *t.*   31:5
so that all the *t.* of Eden.   9
many *t.* on the one side and.   47:7
by the rivers shall grow all *t.*   12
all the *t.* of the field are.   *Joel* 1:12
the flame hath burnt all the *t.*   19
the axe is laid unto the root of the *t.*
                Mat 3:10; *Luke* 3:9
others cut down branches from the *t.*
                Mat 21:8; *Mark* 11:8*
I see men as *t.* walking.   *Mark* 8:24
fig tree and all the *t.*   *Luke* 21:29
t. whose fruit withereth.   *Jude* 12
hurt not the *t.* till we have. *Rev* 7:3
and the third part of the *t.*   8:7
see **palm**

tremble

nations shall *t.* because.   *Deut* 2:25
fear not and do not *t.*   20:3
of those that *t.* at the.   *Ezra* 10:3
earth, the pillars thereof *t.* *Job* 9:6
the pillars of heaven *t.* and.   26:11
hast made the earth to *t.*   *Ps* 60:2
Lord trembleth, let the people *t.* 99:1
t. thou earth at the presence. 114:7
of the house shall *t.*   *Eccl* 12:3
hills did *t.*, their carcases. *Isa* 5:25
man that made the earth to *t.* 14:16
t. ye women that are at ease. 32:11
that the nations may *t.* at thy. 64:2
hear word of Lord, ye that *t.*   66:5
will ye not *t.* at my presence?
                         Jer 5:22
at his wrath the earth shall *t.* 10:10
and they shall *t.* for all the.   33:9
the land of Babylon shall *t.*   51:29
they shall *t.* at every moment.
                  Ezek 26:16; 32:10
now shall isles *t.* in the day.   26:18
men *t.* before the God.   *Dan* 6:26
then the children shall *t.* *Hos* 11:10
t. as a bird out of Egypt.   11
inhabitants of the land *t.*   *Joel* 2:1
quake, the heavens shall *t.*   10
shall not the land *t.* for.   *Amos* 8:8
the land of Midian did *t.*   *Hab* 3:7
devils also believe and *t.* *Jas* 2:19*

trembled

Isaac *t.* very exceedingly. *Gen* 27:33
that was in the camp *t.*   *Ex* 19:16
earth *t.* and the heavens. *Judg* 5:4
2 *Sam* 22:8; *Ps* 18:7; 77:18; 97:4
Eli's heart *t.* for the.   *1 Sam* 4:13
the spoilers *t.*   14:15
the elders of the town *t.*   16:4
and his heart greatly *t.*   28:5
to me every one that *t.*   *Ezra* 9:4
and lo the mountains *t.*   *Jer* 4:24
                          Hab 3:10*
whole land *t.* at neighing. *Jer* 8:16
all people and nations *t.*   *Dan* 5:19
when I heard, my belly *t.* and I *t.* in.
                         Hab 3:16
sepulchre, for they *t.*   *Mark* 16:8
then Moses *t.*   *Acts* 7:32
Felix *t.*   24:25*

trembleth

at this also my heart *t.*   *Job* 37:1
looketh on earth and it *t.* *Ps* 104:32
my flesh *t.* for fear of thee. 119:120
I will look, to him that *t.* *Isa* 66:2

trembling

t. take hold on the mighty. *Ex* 15:15
shall give thee a *t.* heart. *Deut* 28:65
people followed him *t.*   *1 Sam* 13:7
there was a very great *t.*   14:15
all people sat *t.* because. *Ezra* 10:9
fear came upon me and *t.*   *Job* 4:14
I am afraid and *t.* taketh.   21:6*
fear and rejoice with *t.*   *Ps* 2:11
fearfulness and *t.* are come.   55:5
the dregs of the cup of *t. Isa* 51:17*
out of thy hand the cup of *t.*   22*
have heard a voice of *t.*   *Jer* 30:5
drink thy water with *t.*   *Ezek* 12:18
clothe themselves with *t.*   26:16

spoken this, I stood *t.*   *Dan* 10:11
when Ephraim spake *t.*   *Hos* 13:1
Jerusalem a cup of *t.*   *Zech* 12:2*
the woman fearing and *t. Mark* 5:33
                         Luke 8:47
Saul *t.* said, Lord, what wilt thou
have me to do?   *Acts* 9:6
gaoler came *t.* and fell down. 16:29
you in fear and much *t.*   *1 Cor* 2:3
how with fear and *t.* ye. *2 Cor* 7:15
obedient with fear and *t.*   *Eph* 6:5
salvation with fear and *t.* *Phil* 2:12

trench

David came to the *t.*   *1 Sam* 17:20*
lay sleeping within the *t.* 26:5*, 7*
Elijah made a *t.* about.   *1 Ki* 18:32
and he filled the *t.* also.   35, 38
enemies shall cast a *t. Luke* 19:43*

trespass

*(American Revision usually, and
English sometimes, substitutes the
word guilt for this word)*
what is my *t.* that thou?   *Gen* 31:36
we pray thee, forgive the *t.*   50:17*
of *t.* whether for ox.   *Ex* 22:9
he shall bring for his *t.*   *Lev* 5:15
if they shall confess their *t.*   26:40
when any do a *t.* against.   *Num* 5:6
he shall recompense his *t.* with.   7
no kinsman to recompense the *t.*   8
if she have done *t.* against her.   27
forgive the *t.* of thine. *1 Sam* 25:28
why will he be a cause of *t.* to?
                         1 Chr 21:3
on Judah for their *t.*   *2 Chr* 24:18
add more to our sins and *t.*   28:13
Manasseh's prayer and *t.* are. 33:19
have been chief in this *t.*   *Ezra* 9:2
and our *t.* is grown up unto the.   6
we have been in a great *t.*   7, 13
wives, to increase *t.* of Israel. 10:10
a ram of the flock for their *t.*   19
with him there for his *t. Ezek* 17:20
in his *t.* he hath trespassed.   18:24
because of their *t.* they.   *Dan* 9:7
see **commit, committed, offering**

trespass, *verb*

if any man *t.* against his. *1 Ki* 8:31
warn that they *t.* not.   *2 Chr* 19:10
Ahaz did *t.* yet more against.   28:22
if brother *t.*, tell him his. *Mat* 18:15
if thy brother *t.* against. *Luke* 17:3*
if he *t.* against thee seven times.   4

trespass *money*

the *t. money* was not.   *2 Ki* 12:16

trespassed

he hath certainly *t.* against. *Lev* 5:19
their trespass which they *t.* 26:40
him against whom he *t.*   *Num* 5:7
because ye *t.* against me. *Deut* 32:51
go out of sanctuary, for thou hast *t.*
                         2 Chr 26:18
for our fathers have *t.* and.   29:6
be not like your fathers who *t.* 30:7
but Amon *t.* more and more.   33:23
who have *t.* against our God.
                         Ezra 10:2
his trespass that he *t.*   *Ezek* 17:20
they *t.* against me.   39:23, 26
their trespass that they *t.* *Dan* 9:7
because they have *t.*   *Hos* 8:1

trespasses

are before thee in our *t.*   *Ezra* 9:15
as goeth on still in his *t.*   *Ps* 68:21
they have borne their shame and *t.*
                         Ezek 39:26
if ye forgive men their *t. Mat* 6:14
not men their *t.* neither will your
Father forgive your *t.*   15; 18:35
may forgive you your *t. Mark* 11:25
your Father forgive your *t.*   26
not imputing their *t.*   *2 Cor* 5:19
were dead in *t.* and sins.   *Eph* 2:1
having forgiven you all *t.* *Col* 2:13

trespassing

that he hath done in *t.*   *Lev* 6:7
sinneth against me by *t. Ezek* 14:13

trial

he will laugh at the *t.* of.   *Job* 9:23
because it is a *t.*   *Ezek* 21:13

how that in a great *t.*   *2 Cor* 8:2
others had *t.* of cruel.   *Heb* 11:36
that the *t.* of your faith. *1 Pet* 1:7*
strange concerning the fiery *t.* 4:12

tribe

Jacob had twelve sons, who were
the heads of so many great families,
which altogether formed a great
nation; every one of these families
was called a tribe. But Jacob on
his death bed adopted Ephraim
and Manasseh, the sons of Joseph,
as two tribes of Israel, Gen 48:5.
Instead of twelve tribes, there were
now thirteen, that of Joseph being
divided into two. However, in
the distribution of lands to the
people made by Joshua, by the
command of God, they counted but
twelve tribes, and made but twelve
lots. For the tribe of Levi, which
was appointed to the service of the
tabernacle of the Lord, had no
share in the distribution of the land,
but only some cities to dwell in,
and the firstfruits, tithes and oblations of the people, Num 35:2;
Josh 13:7, 8, 14, 33.
   The twelve tribes, while they were
in the desert, encamped round
about the tabernacle of the covenant, every one according to its
order. The Levites were distributed around the tabernacle,
nearer the holy place than the other
tribes, Num 2:2, 3, etc.
   In the marches of the army of
Israel, the twelve tribes were divided into four great bodies, as
bodies of troops, each composed of
three tribes. Between the second
and third there came the Levites
and priests, with the ark of the
Lord, the curtain, the planks, the
pillars, and all the other furniture
of the tabernacle.
   The twelve tribes continued united
under one head, making but one
state, one people, and one mon-
archy, till after the death of Solomon. Then ten of the tribes of
Israel revolted from the house of
David, and received for their king
Jeroboam, the son of Nebat; and
only the tribes of Judah and Benjamin continued under the government of Rehoboam, 1 Ki 12:16, 20.
After a separate existence of a
little over 200 years, Shalmaneser,
king of Assyria, took the city of
Samaria, destroyed it, took away
the rest of the inhabitants of
Israel, carried them beyond the
Euphrates, and sent other inhabitants into the country to cultivate
and possess it, 2 Ki 17:6, 24; 18:10,
11. This ended the kingdom of
the ten tribes of Israel.
   As to the tribes of Judah and
Benjamin, who remained under the
government of the kings of the
family of David, they continued a
much longer time in their own
country. But at last Nebuchadnezzar took the city of Jerusalem, entirely
ruined it, and burnt the temple, and
took away all the inhabitants of
Judah and Benjamin to Babylon, and
to the other provinces of his empire.
This captivity continued for seventy
years, as the prophet had foretold
them, Jer 25:11, 12; 29:10.
   Then came the Return under Ezra
and Nehemiah, the rebuilding of
Jerusalem and the temple. But
the people never entirely regained
their independence. There has
been much discussion of the
identity of the ten tribes after the
destruction of their kingdom, on the
understanding that they were
destroyed as a race as well as a
nation. But the Jews are always

spoken of in the New Testament
as the twelve tribes, never as the
two, and Ezra 6:17 certainly indicates that they were thus considered at the time of the Return.

shall be a man of every t. head of
house of. Num 1:4; 13:2; 34:18
cut ye not off the t. of the. 4:18
the t. of thy father bring thou. 18:2
of every t, a thousand. 31:4, 5, 6
the t. of the sons of Joseph. 36:5
they shall marry only to the family of
the t. 6, 8
neither shall the inheritance remove
from one t. to another t.; but. 9
I took one of a t. Deut 1:23
Josh 3:12; 4:2, 4
family or t. whose heart. Deut 29:18
t. which the Lord taketh. Josh 7:14
from you three men for each t. 18:4
thou be a priest to a t. Judg 18:19
should be one t. lacking. 21:3, 6
but will give one t. to thy son.
1 Ki 11:13, 32, 36
of the family of that t. 1 Chr 6:61
in what t. the stranger. Ezek 47:23
pertaineth to another t. Heb 7:13
of Judah; of which t. Moses. 14
see Reuben, Simeon and the rest

tribes
according to the twelve t. Ex 28:21
39:14
tents according to their t. Num 24:2
according to t. of your fathers. 33:54
to give to the nine t. 34:13
Josh 13:7; 14:2
the two t. and the half have received.
Num 34:15; Josh 14:3
wise men, known among your t.
Deut 1:13
the place where the Lord shall choose
out of all your t. to. 12:5, 14
chosen him out of all thy t. 18:5
ye shall be brought according to your
t. Josh 7:14
before Lord by your t. 1 Sam 10:19
and I will give ten t. 1 Ki 11:31
according to number of the t. 18:31
feeble among their t. Ps 105:37
whither the t. go up, the t. 122:4
that are the stay of t. Isa 19:13
be my servant to raise up the t. 49:6
return for the t. of thine. 63:17
according to their t. Ezek 45:8
to the oaths of the t. Hab 3:9
then shall all the t. of the earth.
Mat 24:30
which promise our 12 t. Acts 26:7
to the twelve t. which are. Jas 1:1
144,000 of all the t. Rev 7:4
see Israel

tribulation
when thou art in t. if thou. Deut 4:30
let them deliver you in the time of t.
Judg 10:14*
deliver me out of all t. 1 Sam 26:24
when t. ariseth, he is. Mat 13:21
then shall be great t., such. 24:21
immediately after the t. 29
Mark 13:24
ye shall have t.: but be. John 16:33
we must through much t. enter the
kingdom. Acts 14:22
t. and anguish on every soul. Rom 2:9
knowing that t. worketh. 5:3
shall t. separate us from the ? 8:35
rejoicing in hope, patient in t. 12:12
comforteth us in all our t. 2 Cor 1:4*
exceeding joyful in all our t. 7:4*
we told you, that we should suffer t.
1 Thes 3:4*
recompense t. to them. 2 Thes 1:6*
am your companion in t. Rev 1:9
I know thy works, and t. and. 2:9
ye shall have t. ten days. 10
I will cast them into great t. 22
which came out of great t. 7:14

tribulations
you out of all your t. 1 Sam 10:19*
but we glory in t. also. Rom 5:3
ye faint not at my t. Eph 3:13
for your faith in all t. 2 Thes 1:4*

tributaries
found therein shall be t. Deut 20:11
the Canaanites became t. Judg 1:30
33, 35

tributary
how is she become t.! Lam 1:1

tribute
[1] Tribute was exacted at all
times from conquered nations.
The Jews paid it when dependent
and received it when powerful.
[2] The tribute money mentioned
in Mat 17:24, 25 was the half
shekel paid by every Israelite
toward the general expenses of the
temple. [3] The tribute named
in Mat 22:17 was the tax paid to
Rome.
became a servant to t. Gen 49:15*
levy a t. to the Lord. Num 31:28
the Lord's t. of the sheep was. 37
beeves, the Lord's t. was 72. 38
asses, the Lord's t. was 61. 39
16,000, the Lord's t. 32 persons. 40
with a t. of a freewill. Deut 16:10
Canaanites serve under t.
Josh 16:10*; 17:13*
was over the t. 2 Sam 20:24
1 Ki 4:6*; 12:18*; 2 Chr 10:18*
did Solomon levy a t. 1 Ki 9:21*
put the land to a t. 2 Ki 23:33
Solomon make to pay t. 2 Chr 8:8*
Philistines brought t. silver. 17:11
then will they not pay t. Ezra 4:13
and toll, t. and custom was. 20
of the t. expences be given 6:8
not lawful to impose t. on. 7:24
money for king's t. Neh 5:4
slothful shall be under t. Pr 12:24*
t. money came to Peter and said,
Doth not . . . pay t.? Mat 17:24*
kings of the earth take t.? 25
is it lawful to give t. to ? 22:17
Mark 12:14; Luke 20:22
shew me the t. money. Mat 22:19
to give t. to Caesar. Luke 23:2
cause pay ye t. also. Rom 13:6
therefore t. to whom t. is due. 7

trickleth
mine eye t. down. Lam 3:49*

tried
shall every stroke be t. Deut 21:5
the word of the Lord is t.
2 Sam 22:31; Ps 18:30
when he hath t. me, I. Job 23:10
desire is that Job may be t. 34:36
silver is t. in a furnace. Ps 12:6
thou hast t. me and shalt find. 17:3
hast t. us, as silver is t. 66:10
the word of the Lord is t. 105:19
I lay in Zion a t. stone. Isa 28:16
thou hast t. mine heart. Jer 12:3
shall be purified and t. Dan 12:10*
try them as gold is t. Zech 13:9
Abraham when he was t. Heb 11:17
when t. he shall receive. Jas 1:12*
gold, though it be t. 1 Pet 1:7*
hast t. them which say. Rev 2:2
into prison, that ye may be t. 3:18*
thee to buy of me gold t.

triest
I know that thou t. 1 Chr 29:17
O Lord, that t. the reins. Jer 11:20
but, O Lord of hosts, that t. 20:12

trieth
ear t. words, as the mouth. Job 34:3
the righteous God t. the. Ps 7:9
the Lord t. the righteous. 11:5
but the Lord t. the hearts. Pr 17:3
God who t. our nearts. 1 Thes 2:4*

trimmed
Mephibosheth had not t. his beard.
2 Sam 19:24
all those virgins arose and t. their
lamps. Mat 25:7

trimmest
why t. thou thy way to ? Jer 2:33

triumph, verb
of the uncircumcised t. 2 Sam 1:20
let not mine enemies t. Ps 25:2
enemy doth not t. over me. 41:11

Philistia, t. thou because of. Ps 60:8*
t. in the works of thy hands. 92:4
how long shall the wicked t.? 94:3
us to give thanks and t. 106:47
over Philistia will I t. 108:9*
causeth us to t. in Christ. 2 Cor 2:14

triumph
with the voice of t. Ps 47:1

triumphed
hath t. gloriously. Ex 15:1, 21

triumphing
that the t. of the wicked. Job 20:5
made a show of them, t. Col 2:15

Troas
by Mysia they came to T. Acts 16:8
loosing from T. 11
tarried for us at T. 20:5
when I came to T. to. 2 Cor 2:12
the cloke I left at T. 2 Tim 4:13

trodden
I give the land that he hath t. upon.
Deut 1:36; Josh 14:9
O my soul, thou hast t. Judg 5:21*
which wicked men have t. Job 22:15
the lion's whelps have not t. it. 28:8
thou hast t. down all. Ps 119:118*
vineyard shall be t. down. Isa 5:5
art cast out, as carcase t. 14:19
meted out and t. down. 18:2, 7
t. under him as straw is t. 25:10
Ephraim shall be t. under. 28:3
then ye shall be t. down. 18
I have t. the winepress alone 63:3
our adversaries have t. down. 18
they have t. my portion. Jer 12:10
the Lord hath t. under foot the
mighty men, he hath t. Lam 1:15*
my flock eat what ye have t. under
feet. Ezek 34:19
sanctuary and host to be t. Dan 8:13
now shall she be t. as mire. Mi 7:10
salt unsavoury to be t. Mat 5:13
way side and was t. down. Luke 8:5
Jerusalem shall be t. down of. 21:24
who hath t. under foot. Heb 10:29
the winepress was t. Rev 14:20

trode
t. the grapes and cursed. Judg 9:27
Israel t. the Benjamites. 20:43
the people t. upon him in the gate.
2 Ki 7:17, 20
Jehu t. Jezebel under foot. 9:33
a beast t. down the thistle. 14:9
2 Chr 25:18
insomuch that they t. Luke 12:1

troop
a t. cometh. Gen 30:11
Gad, a t. shall overcome him. 49:19
I pursue after this t.? 1 Sam 30:8
Benjamin became one t. 2 Sam 2:25*
Joab came from pursuing a t. 3:22
by thee have I run through a t.
22:30; Ps 18:29
Philistines were gathered into a t.
2 Sam 23:11
the t. pitched in the valley of. 13
ye are they that prepare a table for
that t. Isa 65:11*
when thou shalt bring a t. Jer 18:22
the t. of robbers spoileth. Hos 7:1
he hath founded his t. Amos 9:6*

troops
t. of Tema looked. Job 6:19*
his t. come together and raise. 19:12
they assembled by t. in Jer 5:7
and as t. of robbers wait. Hos 6:9
in t. O daughter of t. Mi 5:1
invade them with his t. Heb 3:16

trouble
in my t. I prepared for. 1 Chr 22:14*
when they in their t. did turn unto the
Lord. 2 Chr 15:4*; Neh 9:27
let not all the t. seem. Neh 9:32*
I quiet, yet t. came. Job 3:26
neither doth t. spring out of. 5:6
yet man is born to t. as the sparks. 7
few days and full of t. 14:1
t. and anguish shall make. 15:24*
will God hear his cry when t.? 27:9
weep for him that was in t.? 30:25
quietness, who can make t.? 34:29*

reserved against time of *t*. *Job* 38:23
be a refuge in times of *t*. *Ps* 9:9
O Lord, consider my *t*. which. 13*
thou thyself in times of *t*.? 10:1
be not far from me, for *t*. is. 22:11
for in time of *t*. he shall hide. 27:5
thou hast considered my *t*. 31:7*
upon me, O Lord, for I am in *t*. 9*
thou shalt preserve me from *t*. 32:7
strength in the time of *t*. 37:39
deliver him in time of *t*. 41:1*
refuge, a present help in *t*. 46:1
hath delivered me out of *t*. 54:7
give us help from *t*.: for vain. 60:11*
spoken when I was in *t*. 66:14*
face from me, for I am in *t*. 69:17*
not in *t*. as other men. 73:5
years did he consume in *t*. 78:33*
upon them indignation and *t*. 49
thou calledst in *t*. and I. 81:7
I will be with him in *t*.; I will. 91:15
face from me when I am in *t*. 102:2*
they cried unto the Lord in their *t*.
107:6, 13, 19
their soul is melted because of *t*. 26
cry unto the Lord in their *t*. 28
hell gat hold on me, I found *t*. 116:3
t. and anguish have taken. 119:143
though I walk in the midst of *t*. 138:7
out my complaint before him, I
shewed before him my *t*. 142:2
bring my soul out of *t*. 143:11
righteous is delivered out of *t*.
Pr 11:8; 12:13
revenues of the wicked is *t*. 15:6
little, than great treasure and *t*. 16
unfaithful man in *t*. is like. 25:19
they are a *t*. to me. *Isa* 1:14
look to the earth and behold *t*. 8:22*
and behold, at eveningtide *t*. 17:14
Lord, in *t*. have they visited. 26:16
into the land of *t*. they will. 30:6
salvation also in time of *t*. 33:2
not save him out of his *t*. 46:7
nor bring forth for *t*. 65:23*
in time of *t*. they will say. *Jer* 2:27
save thee in the time of thy *t*. 28
for health, and behold *t*. 8:15*
save them at all in time of *t*. 11:12
they cry to me for their *t*. 14
Saviour of Israel in time of *t*. 14:8
time of healing, and behold *t*. 19*
it is the time of Jacob's *t*. 30:7
have heard of my *t*. *Lam* 1:21
be a time of *t*. such as. 1 *Cor* 7:28*
have *t*. in the flesh. 1 *Cor* 7:28*
be able to comfort them which are
in *t*. 2 *Cor* 1:4*
not have you ignorant of our *t*. 8*
wherein I suffer *t*. as. 2 *Tim* 2:9*
see day

trouble, verb

lest ye *t*. the camp. *Josh* 6:18
Joshua said, The Lord shall *t*. 7:25
one of them that *t*. me. *Judg* 11:35
they cried in the Jews' speech unto
the people to *t*. them. 2 *Chr* 32:18
increased that *t*. me ! *Ps* 3:1*
those that *t*. me, rejoice when. 13:4*
the foot of man *t*. them any more, nor
the hoofs of beasts *t*. *Ezek* 32:13
the interpretation *t*. thee. *Dan* 4:19
let not thy thoughts *t*. thee. 5:10
out of the north shall *t*. him. 11:44
why *t*. ye the woman ? *Mat* 26:10
Mark 14:6
Lord, *t*. not thyself, for. *Luke* 7:6
he shall say, *T*. me not, the. 11:7
that we *t*. not Gentiles. *Acts* 15:19
these men do exceedingly *t*. 16:20
t. not yourselves, for his life. 20:10*
but there be some that *t*. *Gal* 1:7
were cut off who *t*. you. 5:12*
henceforth let no man *t*. me. 6:17
tribulation to them that *t*. you.
2 *Thes* 1:6*
lest any root of bitterness *t*. you.
Heb 12:15

troubled

ye have *t*. me, to make. *Gen* 34:30
Pharaoh's spirit was *t*. 41:8
his brethren were *t*. at his. 45:3
the Lord *t*. the host of. *Ex* 14:24*

Why hast thou *t*. us ? *Josh* 7:25
Jonathan said, My father hath *t*. the
land. 1 *Sam* 14:29
evil spirit from the Lord *t*. him. 16:14
saw that Saul was sore *t*. 28:21
all the Israelites were *t*. 2 *Sam* 4:1
I have not *t*. Israel. 1 *Ki* 18:18
Syria was sore *t*. for this. 2 *Ki* 6:11
then the people *t*. them in. *Ezra* 4:4
thee and thou art *t*. *Job* 4:5
why should not my spirit be *t*.? 21:4*
am I *t*. at his presence. 23:15
shall be *t*. at midnight. 34:20*
hide thy face and I was *t*. *Ps* 30:7
I am *t*. 38:6*
waters thereof roar and be *t*. 46:3
the kings were *t*., and hasted. 48:5*
I remembered God, and was *t*. 77:3*
I am so *t*. that I cannot speak. 4
afraid, the depths also were *t*. 16*
let them be confounded and *t*. 83:17*
by thy wrath are we *t*. 90:7
hidest thy face, they are *t*. 104:29
is as a *t*. fountain and. *Pr* 25:26
and years shall ye be *t*. *Isa* 32:10
tremble, ye women, be *t*. ye. 11
wicked are like the *t*. sea. 57:20
my bowels are *t*. for him. *Jer* 31:20†
I am in distress, my bowels are *t*.
Lam 1:20; 2:11
of the people shall be *t*. *Ezek* 7:27
are in the sea shall be *t*. 26:18*
their kings shall be *t*. in. 27:35
Nebuchadnezzar's spirit was *t*.
Dan 2:1, 3
and the visions of my head *t*. me.
4:5; 7:15
Daniel astonied, his thoughts *t*. 4:19
Belshazzar's thoughts *t*. him. 5:6, 9
my cogitations much *t*. me. 7:28
were *t*. because there. *Zech* 10:2*
Herod was *t*. and all Jerusalem.
Mat 2:3
saw him on sea, they were *t*. 14:26
Mark 6:50
see that ye be not *t*. for all. *Mat* 24:6
Mark 13:7; *John* 14:1, 27
Zacharias was *t*. *Luke* 1:12
Mary was *t*. 29
Martha, thou art *t*. about. 10:41
why are ye *t*. and why do ? 24:38
down and *t*. the water. *John* 5:4
I have no man when water is *t*. 7
Jesus groaned and was *t*. 11:33
12:27; 13:21
from us have *t*. you. *Acts* 15:24
and they *t*. the people and. 17:8
we are *t*. on every side. 2 *Cor* 4:8*
7:5*
and to you that are *t*. 2 *Thes* 1:7*
ye be not *t*. neither by spirit. 2:2
of their terror, nor be *t*. 1 *Pet* 3:14

troubledst

and thou *t*. the waters. *Ezek* 32:2

troubler

Achar, the *t*. of Israel. 1 *Chr* 2:7

troubles

many evils and *t*. *Deut* 31:17, 21
he shall deliver thee in six *t*.: yea.
Job 5:19
the *t*. of mine heart. *Ps* 25:17
O God, out of all his *t*. 22
saved him out of all his *t*. 34:6
thou hast shewed me sore *t*. 71:20
for my soul is full of *t*. 88:3
keepeth his soul from *t*. *Pr* 21:23
former *t*. are forgotten. *Isa* 65:16
shall be famine and. *Mark* 13:8

troublest

why *t*. thou the Master ? *Mark* 5:35

troubleth

spirit from God *t*. 1 *Sam* 16:15
Art thou he that *t*. Israel? 1 *Ki* 18:17
sudden fear *t*. thee. *Job* 22:10
my heart soft, Almighty *t*. me. 23:16
he that is cruel *t*. his. *Pr* 11:17
he that *t*. his own house shall. 29
he that is greedy of gain *t*. 15:27
I know that no secret *t*. *Dan* 4:9
because this widow *t*. me. *Luke* 18:5
he that *t*. you shall bear. *Gal* 5:10

troubling

there the wicked cease from *t*. and
there the weary. *Job* 3:17
stepped in first after the *t*. *John* 5:4

troublous

be built again in *t*. times. *Dan* 9:25

trough, -s

her pitcher into the *t*. *Gen* 24:20
rods in the watering *t*. 30:38
filled the *t*. to water. *Ex* 2:16
see kneadingtroughs

that servant ? I *t*. not. *Luke* 17:9

trucebreakers

last days men shall be *t*. 2 *Tim* 3:3*

true

see comment on truth
we are *t*. men. *Gen* 42:11, 31
if ye be *t*. men. 19
I know that ye are *t*. men. 33, 34
if ye be *t*. and thing certain.
Deut 17:4; 22:20
and give me a *t*. token. *Josh* 2:12
it is *t*. that I am thy. *Ruth* 3:12
God, and thy words be *t*. 2 *Sam* 7:28
it was a *t*. report I heard. 1 *Ki* 10:6
2 *Chr* 9:5
but that which is *t*. 1 *Ki* 22:16
thou gavest them *t*. laws. *Neh* 9:13
of the Lord are *t*. *Ps* 19:9
thy word is *t*. from the. 119:160
a *t*. witness delivereth. *Pr* 14:25
the Lord be a *t*. witness. *Jer* 42:5
he that hath executed *t*. *Ezek* 18:8
is it *t*. O Shadrach, do ? *Dan* 3:14*
t. O king. 24
king said, The thing is *t*. 6:12
vision which is told is *t*. 8:26
revealed and the thing was *t*. 10:1
execute *t*. judgement and. *Zech* 7:9
we know that thou art *t*. *Mat* 22:16
Mark 12:14
your trust the *t*. riches. *Luke* 16:11
that was the *t*. light. *John* 1:9
when the *t*. worshippers shall. 4:23
is that saying *t*., One soweth. 37
myself, my witness is not *t*. 5:31
he witnesseth of me is *t*. 32
giveth you the *t*. bread. 6:32
the same is *t*. 7:18
he that sent me is *t*. 28; 8:26
thy record is not *t*. 8:13
yet my record is *t*. 14
my judgement is *t*. 16
the testimony of two men is *t*. 17
John spake of this man were *t*. 10:41
I am the *t*. vine, my Father. 15:1
and his record is *t*. 19:35; 21:24
wist not that it was *t*. *Acts* 12:9
but as God is *t*., our. 2 *Cor* 1:18*
as deceivers, and yet *t*. 6:8
after God is created in *t*. holiness.
Eph 4:24
also, *t*. yokefellow, help. *Phil* 4:3
things are *t*., think on these. 8
this is a *t*. saying. If. 1 *Tim* 3:1*
this witness is *t*. Wherefore. *Tit* 1:13
t. tabernacle which the Lord pitched.
Heb 8:2
which are the figures of the *t*. 9:24
let us draw near with a *t*. 10:22
t. grace of God wherein. 1 *Pet* 5:12
according to the *t*. proverb, The dog
is. 2 *Pet* 2:22
which thing is *t*. in him and in you:
because . . . *t*. light. 1 *John* 2:8
that we may know him that is *t*. and
we are in him that is *t*., even. 5:20
that our record is *t*. 3 *John* 12
that is holy, he that is *t*. *Rev* 3:7
the faithful and *t*. witness. 14
How long, O Lord, holy and *t*.? 6:10
just and *t*. are thy ways, thou. 15:3
t. and righteous are. 16:7; 19:2
the *t*. sayings of God. 19:9; 22:6
was called Faithful and *T*. 19:11
write, for these words are *t*. 21:5

true God

without the *t*. God. 2 *Chr* 15:3
the Lord is the *t*. God. *Jer* 10:10
to know the only *t*. God. *John* 17:3

idols to serve the *t. God. 1 Thes* 1:9
this is the *t. God* and.   *1 John* 5:20

truly
and now if ye will deal *t.*
     Gen 24:49; 47:29
t. his younger brother shall.   48:19
as *t.* as I live, saith. *Num* 14:21, 28
thou shalt *t.* tithe the. *Deut* 14:22
that we will deal *t.* and. *Josh* 2:14
t. the Lord hath delivered all.   24
if ye have done *t.*   *Judg* 9:16, 19
t. there is but a step between me and
death.   *1 Sam* 20:3
for *t.* my words shall not. *Job* 36:4
t. my soul waiteth upon. *Ps* 62:1
t. God is good to Israel, even. 73:1
t. I am thy servant, I am.   116:16
they that deal *t.* are his. *Pr* 12:22
t. the light is sweet. *Eccl* 11:7
t. in vain is salvation hoped for from
hills, *t.* in the Lord. *Jer* 3:23
t. this is a grief and I.   10:19
known that the Lord hath *t.*   28:9
judgements to deal *t.* *Ezek* 18:9
but *t.* I am full of power. *Mi* 3:8
the harvest *t.* is plenteous.
     Mat 9:37; *Luke* 10:2
Elias *t.* shall first come. *Mat* 17:11
saying, *T.* this was the Son.   27:54
the spirit *t.* is ready. *Mark* 14:38
the way of God *t.* *Luke* 20:21
t. Son of man goeth, as it.   22:22
I have no husband: in that saidst
thou *t.*   *John* 4:18
for John *t.* baptized with. *Acts* 1:5
Moses *t.* said to the fathers.   3:22
the prison *t.* found we shut.   5:23
t. signs of an apostle. *2 Cor* 12:12
and they *t.* were many. *Heb* 7:23
t. if they had been mindful.   11:15
t. our fellowship is with. *1 John* 1:3

trump
at the last *t.*: the dead. *1 Cor* 15:52
descend with the *t.* of God.
     1 Thes 4:16

trumpet
the voice of the *t.* exceeding loud.
     Ex 19:16
heard the noise of the *t.*   20:18
blow but with one *t.* *Num* 10:4
and he put a *t.* in every. *Judg* 7:16
when I blow with a *t.* then.   18
blow up the *t.* in the. *Ps* 81:3
and when he bloweth a *t.* *Isa* 18:3
great *t.* shall be blown and. 27:13
lift up thy voice like a *t.*   58:1
blow ye the *t.* in the land. *Jer* 4:5
blow the *t.* in Tekoah and set.   6:1
blow the *t.* among the. 51:27
they have blown the *t.* *Ezek* 7:14
if he blow the *t.* and warn. 33:3
watchman blow not the *t.*   6
blow ye the *t.* in Ramah. *Hos* 5:8
set the *t.* to thy mouth. 8:1
blow the *t.* in Zion. *Joel* 2:1, 15
shall a *t.* be blown? *Amos* 3:6
a day of the *t.* against. *Zeph* 1:16
God shall blow the *t.* *Zech* 9:14
I heard a great voice, as of a *t.*
     Rev 1:10; 4:1
the other voices of the *t.*   8:13
sixth angel which had the *t.*   9:14
see **blew, sound,** *subst. verb*

trumpeters
princes and *t.* stood. *2 Ki* 11:14
as the *t.* and singers. *2 Chr* 5:13
the singers sang, and the *t.* 29:28
the voice of *t.* shall be. *Rev* 18:22

trumpets
a memorial of blowing *t. Lev* 23:24
     Num 29:1
make two *t.* of silver of. *Num* 10:2
sons of Aaron shall blow with the *t.* 8
blow an alarm with the *t.*   9
shall blow with *t.* over your.   10
and with the *t.* to blow in his. 31:6
shall blow with the *t.* *Josh* 6:4
priests bearing the seven *t.* of.   8
that blew with the *t.*   9, 13, 16, 20
the two hundred men took *t.*
     Judg 7:8, 16
when I blow, then blow ye the *t.* 18
45

---

they blew the *t.*, brake the.
     Judg 7:19, 20, 22
they blew with *t.* saying. *2 Ki* 9:13
and trumpeters blew with *t.* 11:14
made for house of the Lord *t.* 12:13
cymbals and with *t.* *1 Chr* 13:8
priests did blow with *t.* 15:24
     16:6, 42; *2 Chr* 5:12; 7:6
     13:12, 14
all Israel brought up the ark with *t.*
     1 Chr 15:28
lift up their voice with *t. 2 Chr* 5:13
the song began with the *t.* 29:27
saith among the *t.* Ha, ha. *Job* 39:25
with *t.* make a joyful noise. *Ps* 98:6
see **feast, seven**

trust
and whose *t.* shall be. *Job* 8:14
putteth no *t.* in his saints. 15:15
that maketh the Lord his *t. Ps* 40:4
O Lord God, thou art my *t.* 71:5
in thee is my *t.*; leave not. 141:8
that thy *t.* may be in. *Pr* 22:19
that putteth his *t.* in the Lord. 28:25
who putteth his *t.* in the Lord. 29:25
the *t.* in Egypt shall be. *Isa* 30:3
that putteth *t.* in me shall. 57:13†
commit to your *t.* the. *Luke* 16:11
such *t.* have we through Christ to.
     2 Cor 3:4
was committed to my *t. 1 Tim* 1:11
which is committed to thy *t.*   6:20*
see **put**

trust, *verb*
wings thou art come to *t. Ruth* 2:12
in him will I *t.*   *2 Sam* 22:3†
     Ps 18:2; 91:2
a buckler to all that *t.* in him.
     2 Sam 22:31; *Ps* 18:30
now on whom dost thou *t.? 2 Ki* 18:20
     2 Chr 32:10; *Isa* 36:5
so is Pharaoh to all that *t.* in him.
     2 Ki 18:21; *Isa* 36:6
if ye say, We *t.* in the Lord our God.
     2 Ki 18:22; *Isa* 36:7
make you *t.* in the Lord, saying,
The Lord. *2 Ki* 18:30; *Isa* 36:15
yet will I *t.* in him. *Job* 13:15†
that is deceived *t.* in vanity. 15:31
judgement is before him, therefore
t. in him. 35:14*
wilt thou *t.* him because he? 39:11
some *t.* in chariots, and. *Ps* 20:7
I *t.* in thee. 25:2; 31:6; 55:23
     56:3; 143:8
for them that *t.* in thee. 31:19†
none that *t.* in him shall be. 34:22†
t. in the Lord. 37:3, 5; 40:3; 62:8
   115:9, 10, 11; *Pr* 3:5; *Isa* 26:4
because they *t.* in him. *Ps* 37:40*
I will not *t.* in my bow, nor. 44:6
they that *t.* in their wealth. 49:6
I *t.* in the mercy of God for. 52:8
I will *t.* in the covert of. 61:4*
t. not in oppression, become. 62:10
be glad, and *t.* in him. 64:10†
under his wings shalt thou *t.* 91:4*
better to *t.* in the Lord. 118:8, 9
I shall have to answer, for I *t.* 119:42
that *t.* in the Lord shall be as. 125:1
shield, and he in whom I *t.* 144:2†
her husband doth *t.* in her. *Pr* 31:11
God my salvation, I will *t. Isa* 12:2
poor of his people shall *t.* in it. 14:32*
and to *t.* in the shadow of. 30:2
because ye *t.* in oppression and.   12
and *t.* in chariots, because. 31:1
be ashamed that *t.* in graven. 42:17
let him *t.* in the name of the. 50:10
and on mine arm shall they *t.* 51:5
they *t.* in vanity and speak lies. 59:4
t. ye not in lying words. *Jer* 7:4
ye *t.* in lying words that cannot.   8
by my name, wherein ye *t.*   14
take ye heed, and *t.* ye not in. 9:4
makest this people to *t.* in a lie.
     28:15; 29:31
Pharaoh and all that *t.* in him. 46:25
and let thy widows *t.* in me. 49:11
but thou didst *t.* in thy beauty.
     Ezek 16:15
t. to his own righteousness. 33:13
because thou didst *t.* in. *Hos* 10:13

---

them that *t.* in the mountain of.
     Amos 6:1*
t. ye not in a friend, put. *Mi* 7:5
them that *t.* in him. *Nah* 1:7†
they shall *t.* in the name of the Lord.
     Zeph 3:12†
and in his name shall the Gentiles *t.*
     Mat 12:21*; *Rom* 15:12*
them that *t.* in riches. *Mark* 10:24
Moses, in whom ye *t.* *John* 5:45
for I *t.* to see you in. *Rom* 15:24*
but I *t.* to tarry a while. *1 Cor* 16:7
that we should not *t.* in. *2 Cor* 1:9
in whom we *t.* that he will yet. 10*
I *t.* ye shall acknowledge even. 13*
I *t.* are made manifest in. 5:11*
if any man *t.* to himself, that he. 10:7
I *t.* ye shall know we are not. 13:6*
thinketh he hath whereof to *t.*
     Phil 3:4*
because we *t.* in the living God.
     1 Tim 4:10*
that they *t.* not in uncertain. 6:17*
for we *t.* we have a good. *Heb* 13:18*
but I *t.* to come unto you. *2 John* 12*
but I *t.* I shall shortly see. *3 John* 14

trusted
rock in whom they *t.? Deut* 32:37†
Sihon *t.* not Israel to. *Judg* 11:20
because they *t.* to the liers. 20:36
he *t.* in the Lord God of. *2 Ki* 18:5
but I have *t.* in thy mercy. *Ps* 13:5
fathers *t.* in thee; they have *t.* 22:4, 5
he *t.* on the Lord that he would.   8*
I have *t.* also in the Lord. 26:1
     28:7; 31:14
have *t.* in his holy name. 33:21
familiar friend in whom I *t.* 41:9
but *t.* in the abundance of his. 52:7
they *t.* not in his salvation. 78:22
t. in thy wickedness. *Isa* 47:10
thou hast *t.* in falsehood. *Jer* 13:25
thou hast *t.* in thy works. 48:7
daughter that *t.* in her treasures.
     49:4
servants that *t.* in him. *Dan* 3:28
she *t.* not in the Lord. *Zeph* 3:2
he *t.* in God, let him. *Mat* 27:43
armour wherein he *t.* *Luke* 11:22
he spake to certain which *t.* 18:9
we *t.* it had been he which should
     have redeemed Israel. 24:21*
who first *t.* in Christ. *Eph* 1:12*
in whom ye also *t.* after ye heard. 13
women who *t.* in God. *1 Pet* 3:5*

trustedst
down wherein thou *t.* *Deut* 28:52
shall impoverish thy fenced cities
     wherein thou *t.* *Jer* 5:17
land of peace wherein thou *t.* 12:5*

trustest
what confidence is this wherein thou
     t.? 2 Ki 18:19; *Isa* 36:4
thou *t.* on staff of this bruised reed.
     2 Ki 18:21; *Isa* 36:6
let not thy God in whom thou *t.*
     2 Ki 19:10; *Isa* 37:10

trusteth
he *t.* that he can draw up. *Job* 40:23*
for the king *t.* in the Lord. *Ps* 21:7
t. in the Lord, mercy shall. 32:10
the man that *t.* in him. 34:8†; 84:12
     Pr 16:20; *Jer* 17:7
for my soul *t.* in thee. *Ps* 57:1*
save thy servant that *t.* 86:2
so is every one that *t.* in them.
     115:8; 135:18
he that *t.* in his riches. *Pr* 11:28
he that *t.* in his own heart. 28:26
thou wilt keep him in perfect peace,
     because he *t.* in thee. *Isa* 26:3
cursed be the man that *t. Jer* 17:5
the maker of his work *t. Hab* 2:18
widow indeed, *t.* in God. *1 Tim* 5:5*

trusting
his heart is fixed, *t.* in. *Ps* 112:7

trusty
removeth away the speech of the *t.*
     Job 12:20

truth
[1] *What is opposed to a false-*
hood, lie, or deceit, Pr 12:17. [2]

Fidelity, sincerity, and punctuality in keeping promises. Generally to truth, taken in this sense, if referred to God, is joined mercy or kindness, as in Gen 24:27. [3] Truth is put for the true doctrine of the gospel, Gal 3:1. [4] Truth is opposed to hypocrisy, dissimulation or formality, Heb 10:22.

not left destitute of his *t. Gen* 24:27
of the least of all the *t.* 32:10
whether there be any *t.* in. 42:16
men of *t.* *Ex* 18:21
Lord abundant in *t.* 34:6
behold, if it be *t.* *Deut* 13:14
a God of *t.* 32:4
kindness and *t.* to you. *2 Sam* 2:6
return thou, mercy and *t.* be. 15:20
of Lord in thy mouth is *t. 1 Ki* 17:24
if peace and *t.* be in my days.
2 Ki 20:19; *Isa* 39:8
say nothing but the *t.* *2 Chr* 18:15
wrought that which was *t.* 31:20*
with words of peace and *t. Esth* 9:30
he that speaketh the *t.* in. *Ps* 15:2
of the Lord are mercy and *t.* 25:10
redeemed me, O Lord God of *t.* 31:5
prosperously, because of *t.* 45:4
desirest *t.* in the inward parts. 51:6
send forth his mercy and his *t.* 57:3
be displayed because of the *t.* 60:4
O prepare mercy and *t.,* which. 61:7
mercy and *t.* are met together. 85:10
t. shall spring out of the earth. 11
plenteous in mercy and *t.* 86:15
mercy and *t.* shall go before. 89:14
his *t.* shall be thy shield and. 91:4
judge the people with his *t.* 96:13
remembered his mercy and his *t.*
98:3*
his *t.* endureth to all. 100:5*; 117:2
I have chosen the way of *t.* 119:30*
and thy law is the *t.* 142, 151
God who keepeth *t.* for ever. 146:6
let not mercy and *t.* *Pr* 3:3
for my mouth shall speak *t.* 8:7
he that speaketh *t.* sheweth. 12:17
lip of *t.* shall be established. 19
mercy and *t.* be to them that. 14:22
mercy and *t.* iniquity is purged. 16:6
mercy and *t.* preserve the. 20:28
of the words of *t.;* thou mightest
answer the words of *t.* 22:21
buy the *t.* and sell it not. 23:23
written were words of *t. Eccl* 12:10
are faithfulness and *t.* *Isa* 25:1
the nation which keepeth *t.* 26:2†
forth judgement unto *t.* 42:3
them hear, and say, It is *t.* 43:9
nor any pleadeth for *t.:* they. 59:4
for *t.* is fallen in the street and. 14
yea *t.* faileth, and he that. 15
any that seeketh the *t.* *Jer* 5:1
are not thine eyes upon the *t.?* 3
t. is perished and cut off from. 7:28
they are not valiant for the *t.* 9:3
and will not speak the *t.* 5
abundance of peace and *t.* 33:6
the king of heaven, all whose works
are *t.* *Dan* 4:37
I asked him the *t.* of all. 7:16, 19
and it cast down the *t.* to the. 10:21
noted in the scripture of *t.* 10:21
now will I shew thee the *t.* 11:2
there is no *t.* nor mercy. *Hos* 4:1
thou wilt perform the *t.* *Mi* 7:20
be called a city of *t.* *Zech* 8:3
speak ye every man the *t.*
16
Eph 4:25
execute the judgement of *t.* and
peace. *Zech* 8:16
love the *t.* and peace. 19
the law of *t.* was in his. *Mal* 2:6
she said, T. Lord, yet dogs eat the.
Mat 15:27*
fearing told him all the *t. Mark* 5:33
Master, thou hast said the *t.* 12:32*
full of grace and *t.* *John* 1:14
but grace and *t.* came by Jesus. 17
he bare witness unto the *t.* 5:33
ye shall know the *t.,* the *t.* shall. 8:32
a man that told you the *t.* 40
t. because there is no *t.* in him. 44
because I tell you the *t.* ye. 45

if I say the *t.* why do ye ? *John* 8:46
I am the way, and the *t.* and. 14:6
I tell you the *t.;* It is expedient. 16:7
of *t.* will guide you into all *t.* 13
sanctified through the *t.* 17:19
should bear witness to the *t.* Every
one that is of the *t.* heareth. 18:37
Pilate saith unto him What is *t.?* 38
forth the words of *t.* *Acts* 26:25
who hold the *t.* in. *Rom* 1:18
who changed the *t.* of God into. 25
of God is according to *t.* 2:2
that do not obey the *t.* 8
which hast the form of the *t.* in. 20
for if the *t.* of God hath more. 3:7
I say the *t.* in Christ, I lie not. 9:1
circumcision for *t.* of God. 15:8
unleavened bread of *t.* *1 Cor* 5:8
but by manifestation of the *t.*
2 Cor 4:2
boasting, I made, is found a *t.* 7:14
as the *t.* of Christ is in me. 11:10
a fool, for I will say the *t.* 12:6
nothing against *t.,* but for the *t.* 13:8
the *t.* of the gospel might. *Gal* 2:5
they walked not according to *t.* 14
that ye should not obey the *t.* 3:1
5:7
because I tell you the *t.?* 4:16
but speaking the *t.* in love. *Eph* 4:15
have been taught by him as the *t.* 21
fruit of the Spirit is in all *t.* 5:9
your loins girt about with *t.* 6:14
not the love of the *t.* *2 Thes* 2:10
damned who believed not the *t.* 12
salvation, through belief of the *t.* 13
knowledge of the *t.* *1 Tim* 2:4
I speak the *t.* in Christ and. 7
pillar and ground of the *t.* 3:15
of them which know the *t.* 4:3
and destitute of the *t.* 6:5
who concerning the *t.* *2 Tim* 2:18
to acknowledging of the *t.* 25
to the knowledge of the *t.* 3:7
so do these resist the *t.* 8
turn away their ears from the *t.* 4:4
the acknowledging of *t.* *Tit* 1:1
of men that turn from the *t.* 14
after we received knowledge of the *t.*
Heb 10:26
and lie not against the *t.* *Jas* 3:14
if any of you err from the *t.* 5:19
your souls in obeying *t. 1 Pet* 1:22
the way of *t.* shall be evil. *2 Pet* 2:2
we lie and do not the *t.* *1 John* 1:6
we deceive ourselves, the *t.* is. 8
the *t.* is not in him. 2:4
ye know not the *t.,* but because ye
know it, and no lie is of the *t.* 21
is *t.* and is no lie. 27
know that we are of the *t.* 3:19
because the Spirit is *t.* 5:6
that have known the *t.* *2 John* 1
for the *t.'s* sake which dwelleth in. 2
came and testified of the *t. 3 John* 3
be fellow-helpers to the *t.* 8
of all men and of the *t.* 12
see spirit

in truth

serve him *in t.* *Josh* 24:14
1 Sam 12:24
if *in t.* ye anoint me king. *Judg* 9:15
walk *in t.* *1 Ki* 2:4
as he walked *in t.* *2 Ki* 20:3
I have walked *in t.* 2 Ki 20:3
all his works are done *in t.*
Ps 33:4*; 111:8
the Lord hath sworn *in t.* 132:11
to all that call upon him *in t.* 145:18
the Holy One of Israel *in t. Isa* 10:20
he shall sit upon it *in t.* judging. 16:5
God of Israel, but not *in t.* 48:1
I will direct their work *in t.* and.
61:8
the Lord liveth *in t.* *Jer* 4:2
I will be their God *in t.* *Zech* 8:8
teachest the way of God *in t.*
Mat 22:16; *Mark* 12:14
shall worship the Father *in* spirit and
t. *John* 4:23, 24
all things to you *in t.* *2 Cor* 7:14
in pretence or *in t.* Christ is. *Phil* 1:18
the grace of God *in t.* *Col* 1:6

but as it is *in t.* the word of God.
1 Thes 2:13
love in tongue, but *in t. 1 John* 3:18
the Son of the Father, *in t. 2 John* 3
rejoiced that I found of thy children
walking *in t.* 4; *3 John* 4

in the truth

hear me *in the t.* of. *Ps* 69:13
he was a murderer and abode not *in
the t.* *John* 8:44
charity rejoiceth not in iniquity, bu;
in the t. *1 Cor* 13:6
established *in the* present *t.*
2 Pet 1:12
elect lady, whom I love *in the t.*
2 John 1; *3 John* 1
thou walkest *in the t.* *3 John* 3

of a truth

of *a t.* women have been. *1 Sam* 21:5
of *a t.* Lord, the kings of Assyria.
2 Ki 19:17; *Isa* 37:18
I know it is so of *a t.* *Job* 9:2
of *a t.* many houses shall. *Isa* 5:9
for of *a t.* the Lord hath. *Jer* 26:15
of *a t.* it is, your God. *Dan* 2:47
of *a t.* thou art the Son. *Mat* 14:33
I tell you of *a t.* *Luke* 4:25; 9:27
of *a t.* I say unto you. 12:44; 21:3
of *a t.* this fellow also was. 22:59
this is of *a t.* that prophet.
John 6:14; 7:40
of *a t.* against thy holy. *Acts* 4:27
of *a t.* I perceive that God is. 10:34
God is in you of *a t.* *1 Cor* 14:25

thy truth

lead me in *thy t.* and. *Ps* 25:5
and I have walked in *thy t.* 26:3
praise and declare *thy t.?* 30:9
and *thy t.* from the great. 40:10
let *thy t.* continually preserve. 11
send out thy light and *thy t.* 43:3
cut them off in *thy t.* 54:5
thy t. unto the clouds. 57:10; 108:4
I will praise *thy t.* 71:22
will walk in *thy t.* 86:11
swarest to David in *thy t.* 89:49*
glory for *thy t.'s* sake. 115:1; 138:2
that go into the pit cannot hope for
thy t. *Isa* 38:18
children shall make known *thy t.* 19
might understand *thy t.* *Dan* 9:13
thy t.: thy word is truth. *John* 17:17

word of truth

take not *word of t.* out. *Ps* 119:43
approving ourselves by the *word of t.*
2 Cor 6:7
ye heard the *word of t.* *Eph* 1:13
whereof ye heard before in the *word
of t.* *Col* 1:5
dividing the *word of t.* *2 Tim* 2:15
begat he us by *word of t.* *Jas* 1:18

try

and I will *t.* them for thee. *Judg* 7:4
God left him to *t.* him. *2 Chr* 32:31
that thou shouldest *t.* *Job* 7:18
doth not the ear *t.* words ? 12:11
his eyelids *t.* the. *Ps* 11:4
t. my reins and my heart. 26:2
t. me. 139:23
thou mayest know and *t.* *Jer* 6:27
I will melt them and *t.* them. 9:7
Zech 13:9
I *t.* the reins. *Jer* 17:10
search and *t.* our ways. *Lam* 3:40
shall fall to *t.* them. *Dan* 11:35*
the fire shall *t.* every. *1 Cor* 3:13*
fiery trial which is to *t.* you.
1 Pet 4:12*
t. the spirits whether. *1 John* 4:1*
hour of temptation to *t.* *Rev* 3:10

trying

the *t.* of your faith worketh. *Jas* 1:3

Tryphena, Tryphosa

salute T. and T. *Rom* 16:12

Tubal

sons of Japheth, Javan, T. *Gen* 10:2
1 Chr 1:5
those that escape to T. *Isa* 66:19
Javan, T. they were. *Ezek* 27:13
there is Meshech, T. and her. 32:26
the chief prince of Meshech and T.
38:2, 3; 39:1

tumbled
a cake of barley bread *t. Judg* 7:13

tumult
the noise of this *t.?*   *1 Sam* 4:14
I saw a *t.* but knew not. *2 Sam* 18:29
rage against me and thy *t.* is come.
  2 Ki 19:28*; *Isa* 37:29*
which stilleth the *t.* of.   *Ps* 65:7
the *t.* of those that rise up.   74:23
thine enemies make a *t.*   83:2
at the noise of the *t.* the.   *Isa* 33:3
with noise of a great *t.*   *Jer* 11:16
t. rise among thy people. *Hos* 10:14
and Moab shall die with *t. Amos* 2:2
a great *t.* from the Lord. *Zech* 14:13
but rather a *t.* was made. *Mat* 27:24
he seeth the *t.* and them. *Mark* 5:38
know the certainty for *t. Acts* 21:34*
multitude, nor with *t.*   24:18

tumults
behold the great *t.* in the. *Amos* 3:9
as ministers in *t.*   *2 Cor* 6:5
whisperings, swellings, *t.*   12:20

tumultuous
a *t.* noise of the kingdoms gathered.
  Isa 13:4
thou that art a *t.* city.   22:2
the head of the *t.* ones. *Jer* 48:45

turn
when every maid's *t.* was come to.
  Esth 2:12
now when the *t.* of Esther was.   15

turn, *verb*
that I may *t.* to the right. *Gen* 24:49
make thine enemies *t.*   *Ex* 23:27
t. from thy fierce wrath and.   32:12
t. ye not unto idols, nor. *Lev* 19:4
to-morrow *t.* you, get. *Num* 14:25
we will not *t.* to the right.   20:17
we will not *t.* into the fields.   21:22
he smote the ass to *t.* her.   22:23
was no way to *t.* to the right or.   26
t. you, and go to the mount. *Deut* 1:7
and *t.* ye, take your journey.   40
that the Lord may *t.* from.   13:17
then shall *t.* it into money.   14:25
then the Lord will *t.*   30:3
then will they *t.* to other gods. 31:20
t. not from it to the right. *Josh* 1:7
an altar to *t.* from following. 22:23, 29
then he will *t.* and do you hurt. 24:20
nor will any of us *t.*   *Judg* 20:8
t. thee, behold, I am.   *1 Sam* 14:7
t. and slay the priests of.   22:17, 18
none can *t.* to the right. *2 Sam* 14:19
the king said, Let him *t.* to his.   24
Lord, *t.* Ahithophel's counsel. 15:31
t. from their sin.   *1 Ki* 8:35
  2 Chr 6:26, 37; 7:14
if ye shall at all *t.* from. *1 Ki* 9:6
get hence, *t.* thee eastward.   17:3
he said, *T.* thine hand.   22:34
  2 Chr 18:33
and Jehu said, *T.* thee behind me.
  2 Ki 9:18, 19
t. ye from your evil ways.   17:13
  Jer 18:8; 26:3; *Zech* 1:3, 4
to *t.* the kingdom of. *1 Chr* 12:23
but Josiah would not *t.* his face.
  2 Chr 35:22
if ye *t.* and keep my.   *Neh* 1:9
Ezek 3:20; 18:21; 33:11, 14, 19
and *t.* their reproach on. *Neh* 4:4
prophets which testified to *t.*   9:26
of the saints wilt thou *t.?*   *Job* 5:1
t. from him that he may rest. 14:6
mind, and who can *t.* him?   23:13
t. the needy out of the way.   24:4
how long will ye *t.* my glory? *Ps* 4:2
if he *t.* not, he will whet his.   7:12
thou shalt make them *t.* their. 21:12
t. thee unto me.   25:16; 69:16
  86:16
t. us, O God of our salvation. 85:4
let those that fear thee *t.* 119:79
to David, he will not *t.* 132:11
t. you at my reproof, I. *Pr* 1:23
pass not by it, *t.* from it.   4:15
t. not to the right hand nor to.   27
all are of dust, and all *t. Eccl* 3:20
t. my beloved, and be. *S of S* 2:17

I will *t.* my hand on thee. *Isa* 1:25
they shall every man *t.* to his. 13:14
and they shall *t.* the rivers.   19:6
he will violently *t.* and toss. 22:18
she shall *t.* to her hire, and. 23:17
for strength to them that *t.*   28:6
when ye *t.* to the right hand. 30:21
t. ye to him from whom Israel. 31:6
t. from transgression.   59:20
surely his anger shall *t. Jer* 2:35
and I said, *T.* unto me.   3:7, 14
t. it into the shadow of death. 13:16
for I will *t.* their mourning.   31:13
t. thou me, and I shall be turned. 18
hearkened not to *t.* from.   44:5
they shall *t.* every one to. 50:16
t. us unto thee, O Lord. *Lam* 5:21
he *t.* not from his wickedness.
  Ezek 3:19; 33:9
shall not *t.* thee from one side. 4:8
my face will I *t.* also from.   7:22
repent and *t.* yourselves from your
  idols.   14:6; 18:30, 32; 33:9, 11
  Hos 12:6; *Joel* 2:12
I will *t.* unto you, and ye. *Ezek* 36:9
to *t.* thine hand upon the.   38:12
that we might *t.* from. *Dan* 9:13
t. his face unto the isles, and take
  many; shall cause ... *t.*   11:18
then he shall *t.* his face toward. 19
and they that *t.* many to.   12:3
not frame their doings to *t. Hos* 5:4
therefore *t.* thou to thy God.   12:6
and I will *t.* mine hand. *Amos* 1:8
ye who *t.* judgement.   5:7
and I will *t.* your feasts.   8:10
let them *t.* every one from his evil
  way.   *Jonah* 3:8
then will I *t.* to people. *Zeph* 3:9
t. ye to the strong hold, ye. *Zech* 9:12
I will *t.* mine hand upon the. 13:7
t. the heart of fathers. *Mal* 4:6
on thy right cheek, *t. Mat* 5:39
to *t.* the hearts of the fathers to.
  Luke 1:17
and it shall *t.* to you for a.   21:13
of life, lo we *t.* to. *Acts* 13:46
that ye should *t.* from these. 14:15
and to *t.* them from darkness. 26:18
that they should repent and *t.*   20
I know this shall *t.* to. *Phil* 1:19
commandments of men that *t.*
  Tit 1:14
and we *t.* about their. *Jas* 3:3
to *t.* from the holy. *2 Pet* 2:21
and have power to *t. Rev* 11:6

turn *again*
if the raw flesh *t. again. Lev* 13:16
therefore we *t. again. Judg* 11:8
she said, *T. again,* my daughters.
  Ruth 1:11, 12
I pray thee, *t. again* with me.
  1 Sam 15:25, 30
shall *t. again* to thee. *1 Ki* 8:33
heart of this people *t. again.* 12:27
eat not, nor *t. again* by the. 13:9, 17
go *t. again* to the king *2 Ki* 1:6
t. again and tell Hezekiah. 20:5
t. again to the Lord. *2 Chr* 30:6
if ye *t. again.*   9
and man shall *t. again. Job* 34:15
nor did I *t. again* till. *Ps* 18:37
O *t.* thyself to us *again.*   60:1
t. us *again,* O Lord God. 80:3, 7, 19
them not *t. again* to folly.   85:8
they *t.* not *again* to cover. 104:9
t. again our captivity, as. 126:4
t. ye *again* every one from. *Jer* 25:5
t. again, O virgin of Israel, *t. again.*
  31:21
try our ways and *t. again* to the
  Lord.   *Lam* 3:40
t. again and thou shalt see.
  Ezek 8:6, 13, 15
he will *t. again,* he will. *Mi* 7:19
children and *t. again. Zech* 10:9
lest they *t. again* and rend. *Mat* 7:6
shall *t.* to you *again. Luke* 10:6
times in a day *t. again* to thee. 17:4
how *t.* ye *again* to the weak elements?   *Gal* 4:9

turn *aside*
I will now *t. aside* and.   *Ex* 3:3

shall not *t. aside* to the. *Deut* 5:32
and ye *t. aside* and serve. 11:16, 28
that he *t.* not *aside* from.   17:20
my death ye will *t. aside.*   31:29
that ye *t.* not *aside* therefrom to the.
  Josh 23:6; *1 Sam* 12:20, 21
ho, such a one, *t. aside. Ruth* 4:1
Asahel, *t. aside* and. *2 Sam* 2:21
howbeit he refused to *t. aside.*   23
the king said, *T. aside* and.   18:30
such as *t. aside* to lies. *Ps* 40:4
of them that *t. aside.*   101:3
as for such as *t. aside* to.   125:5
to *t. aside* the needy from. *Isa* 10:2
t. aside the just for a thing.   29:21
get out of the way, *t. aside.*   30:11
to *t. aside* the right of a. *Lam* 3:35
and that *t. aside* the way. *Amos* 2:7
and they *t. aside* the poor in.   5:12
that *t. aside* the stranger. *Mal* 3:5

turn *away*
brother's fury *t. away. Gen* 27:44
till thy brother's anger *t. away.*   45
for if ye *t. away* from after him.
  Num 32:15; *Deut* 30:17
they will *t. away* thy son. *Deut* 7:4
he hath spoken to *t.* you *away.* 13:5
that his heart *t.* not *away.*   17:17
no unclean thing and *t. away.* 23:14
surely they will *t. away* your heart.
  1 Ki 11:2
how wilt thou *t. away* the face of one
  captain?   *2 Ki* 18:24; *Isa* 36:9
go not up; *t. away.*   *1 Chr* 14:14
O Lord God, *t.* not *away* the face of.
  2 Chr 6:42; *Ps* 132:10
Amaziah did *t. away* from following.
  2 Chr 25:27
that his wrath may *t. away.*   29:10
  30:8; *Ps* 106:23; *Pr* 24:18
Lord will not *t. away* his face.
  2 Chr 30:9
t. away mine eyes from. *Ps* 119:37
t. away my reproach which I fear. 39
infamy *t.* not *away.* *Pr* 25:10
but wise men *t. away* wrath.   29:8
t. away thine eyes from. *S of S* 6:5
thou *t. away* thy foot from. *Isa* 58:13
who can *t.* her *away?* *Jer* 2:24
and thou shalt not *t. away.*   3:19
saith Lord, Shall he *t. away?*   8:4
I stood to *t. away* thy wrath. 18:20
I will *t. away* your captivity. 29:14
  Zeph 2:7
I will not *t. away* from. *Jer* 32:40
to *t. away* captivity. *Lam* 2:14
t. away your faces from. *Ezek* 14:6
and for four I will not *t. away* the.
  Amos 1:3, 6, 9, 11, 13; 2:1, 4, 6
God will *t. away* from. *Jonah* 3:9
and did *t. many away* from iniquity.
  Mal 2:6
of thee, *t.* not thou *away. Mat* 5:42
seeking to *t. away* the. *Acts* 13:8
t. away ungodliness. *Rom* 11:26
heady, from such *t. away. 2 Tim* 3:5
they shall *t. away* their ears.   4:4
how escape, if we *t. away* from him?
  Heb 12:25

turn *back*
t. back and cover that. *Deut* 23:13
a hook in thy nose and *t.* thee *back.*
  2 Ki 19:28; *Isa* 37:29
makest us to *t. back.* *Ps* 44:10
shall mine enemies *t. back.*   56:9
who shall *t.* it *back?* *Isa* 14:27
neither will I *t. back.* *Jer* 4:28
t. back thine hand as a.   6:9
behold, I will *t. back* the.   21:4
flee ye, *t. back,* dwell deep.   49:8
I will *t.* thee *back.* *Ezek* 38:4; 39:2
when I *t. back* your. *Zeph* 3:20
not *t. back* to take up. *Mark* 13:16

turn *in*
now, my lords, *t. in,* I. *Gen* 19:2
t. in, my lord, *t. in* to. *Judg* 4:18
let us *t. in* to this city of.   19:11
of God shall *t. in* thither. *2 Ki* 4:10
let him *t. in* hither. *Pr* 9:4, 16

turn *to the Lord*
if thou *t. to the Lord* thy God.
  Deut 4:30; 30:10

trouble did *t. to the Lord.* 2 Chr 15:4
world shall *t. to the Lord.* Ps 22:27
let us try our ways and *t. to the Lord.*
    Lam 3:40
take with you words and *t. to the*
    Lord. Hos 14:2
heart and *t. to the Lord.* Joel 2:13
many of Israel shall he *t. to the*
    Lord. Luke 1:16
nevertheless, when it shall *t. to the*
    Lord. 2 Cor 3:16

turned

sword which *t.* every way. Gen 3:24
Joseph *t.* about from them. 42:24
the rod which was *t.* Ex 7:15
in the river shall be *t.* to blood. 17, 20
    Ps 78:44; 105:29
heart of Pharaoh was *t.* Ex 14:5
when the hair is *t.* white. Lev 13:3
    10, 17, 20, 25
they *t.* and went by way. Num 21:33
ass saw me and *t.* from me. 22:33
t. the curse into a blessing.
    Deut 23:5; Neh 13:2
in that they are *t.* unto. Deut 31:18
so the Lord *t.* from the fierceness of
his anger. Josh 7:26
they *t.* quickly out of. Judg 2:17
Samson took firebrands and *t.* 15:4
therefore they *t.* their backs. 20:42
and thou shalt be *t.* into another man.
    1 Sam 10:6
even they also *t.* to be with. 14:21
whithersoever he *t.* himself he. 47
as Samuel *t.* about to go. 15:27
David *t.* from him towards. 17:30
Asahel *t.* not from. 2 Sam 2:19
the victory that day was *t.* 19:2
the kingdom is *t.* about. 1 Ki 2:15
Joab *t.* after Adonijah, though. 28
the king *t.* his face about. 8:14
because his heart was *t.* from. 11:9
so Naaman *t.* and went. 2 Ki 5:12
Ahaz *t.* the covert from the. 16:18
t. his face to the wall, and prayed.
    20:2; Isa 38:2
Josiah *t.* himself he spied. 2 Ki 23:16
was no king that *t.* to the Lord. 25
Lord *t.* not from the fierceness. 26
he *t.* the kingdom unto. 1 Chr 10:14
the wrath of the Lord *t.* 2 Chr 12:12
t. from them and destroyed. 20:10
for our fathers have *t.* their. 29:6
t. the heart of the king of. Ezra 6:22
wrath of our God be *t.* from. 10:14
neither *t.* they from their. Neh 9:35
though it was *t.* to the contrary.
    Esth 9:1
the mouth which was *t.* to them. 22
God *t.* me into the hands. Job 16:11
and they whom I loved are *t.* 19:19
yet his meat in his bowels is *t.* 20:14
under it is *t.* up as it were fire. 28:5
terrors are *t.* upon me. 30:15
my harp is *t.* to mourning, and. 31
if my step hath *t.* out of the. 31:7
it is *t.* as clay to the seal. 38:14
and sorrow is *t.* into joy. 41:22
and the Lord *t.* the captivity. 42:10
the wicked shall be *t.* Ps 9:17
thou hast *t.* my mourning. 30:11
he *t.* the sea into dry land. 66:6
and *t.* my hand against their. 81:14
he *t.* their heart to hate. 105:25
which *t.* the rock into a. 114:8
I *t.* my feet unto thy. 119:59
and I *t.* myself to behold. Eccl 2:12
night of my pleasure he *t.* Isa 21:4
Lebanon shall be *t.* into a. 29:17
the streams thereof shall be *t.* 34:9
we have *t.* every one to his. 53:6
therefore he was *t.* to be their. 63:10
how then art thou *t.* into a degenerate
plant? Jer 2:21
they have *t.* their back to me. 27
Judah hath not *t.* to me with. 3:10
their houses shall be *t.* unto. 6:12
no man repented, every one *t.* 8:6
should have *t.* them from. 23:22
and I shall be *t.* 31:18
after that I was *t.* 19
they *t.* unto me the back. 32:33
now *t.* and had done right. 34:15
but ye *t.* and polluted my. 16

how hath Moab *t.* the? Jer 48:39
Lord, mine heart is *t.* Lam 1:20
surely against me is he *t.* 3:3
our inheritance is *t.* to strangers. 5:2
our dance is *t.* into mourning. 15
O Lord, and we shall be *t.* 21
they *t.* not when they went.
    Ezek 1:9, 12; 10:11
a vine, whose branches *t.* 17:6
she is *t.* unto me, I shall be. 26:2
my comeliness was *t.* Dan 10:8
vision my sorrows are *t.* upon me. 16
Ephraim is a cake not *t.* Hos 7:8
Ephraim, mine heart is *t.* 11:8
sun shall be *t.* into darkness.
    Joel 2:31; Acts 2:20
ye have *t.* judgement. Amos 6:12
they *t.* from their evil. Jonah 3:10
cup shall be *t.* unto thee. Hab 2:16
all the land shall be *t.* Zech 14:10
Jesus *t.* about in press. Mark 5:30
the Lord *t.* and looked. Luke 22:61
but your sorrow shall be *t.* into joy.
    John 16:20
God *t.* and gave them up. Acts 7:42
all at Lydda saw him and *t.* 9:35
believed and *t.* to the Lord. 11:21
Gentiles are *t.* to God. 15:19
t. the world upside down. 17:6
shew how ye *t.* to God. 1 Thes 1:9
and they shall be *t.* unto. 2 Tim 4:4
t. to flight the armies. Heb 11:34
lest that which is lame be *t.* 12:13
t. with a very small helm. Jas 3:4
let your laughter be *t.* to. 4:9
the dog is *t.* to his own. 2 Pet 2:22

turned again

behold it was *t. again* as. Ex 4:7
Ehud *t. again* from the. Judg 3:19
Israel *t. again*, went a whoring. 8:33
t. again, Benjamites amazed. 20:41
Samuel *t. again* after. 1 Sam 15:31
I *t.* not *again* till I. 2 Sam 22:38
when the man *t. again* from his
chariot. 2 Ki 5:26
Lord *t. again* the captivity. Ps 126:1

turned aside

that he *t. aside* to see. Ex 3:4
they have *t. aside* quickly. 32:8
    Deut 9:12, 16
he *t. aside* to see the. Judg 14:8
the kine *t.* not *aside.* 1 Sam 6:12
but *t. aside* after lucre. and. 8:3
David *t.* not *aside* from. 1 Ki 15:5
a man *t. aside* and brought. 20:39
Josiah *t.* not *aside* to. 2 Ki 22:32
of their way are *t. aside.* Job 6:18
they were *t. aside* like. Ps 78:57
is thy beloved *t. aside*? S of S 6:1
heart hath *t.* him *aside.* Isa 44:20
he hath *t. aside* my ways. Lam 3:11
have *t. aside* unto vain. 1 Tim 1:6
for some are already *t. aside.* 5:15

turned away

because ye are *t. away.* Num 14:43
wherefore Israel *t. away.* 20:21
of the Lord may be *t. away.* 25:4
t. my wrath *away* from Israel. 11
wives *t. away* his heart. 1 Ki 11:3, 4
Ahab *t. away* and would eat. 21:4
our fathers *t. away* their. 2 Chr 29:6
which hath not *t. away.* Ps 66:20
time *t.* he his anger *away.* 78:38
his anger is not *t. away*, but his hand.
    Isa 5:25; 9:12, 17, 21; 10:4
thy anger is *t. away.* 12:1
nor *t.* I *away.* 50:5
and judgement is *t. away.* 59:14
your iniquities have *t. away* these.
    Jer 5:25
sunk, they are *t. away* back. 38:22
have seen them *t. away* back? 46:5
shepherds have *t.* them *away.* 50:6
let thy fury be *t. away.* Dan 9:16
for mine anger is *t. away.* Hos 14:4
the Lord hath *t. away* excellency of
Jacob. Nah 2:2
this Paul hath *t. away.* Acts 19:26
Asia be *t. away* from me. 2 Tim 1:15

turned back

the people *t. back* upon. Josh 8:20
Joshua at that time *t. back.* 11:10

Saul is *t. back* from. 1 Sam 15:11
of Jonathan *t.* not *back.* 2 Sam 1:22
t. their heart *back.* 1 Ki 18:37
not king of Israel, they *t. back.* 22:33
when the messengers *t. back*, Why
are ye now *t. back*? 2 Ki 1:5
he *t. back* and looked on them. 2:24
so the king of Assyria *t. back.* 15:20
Ornan *t. back*, and. 1 Chr 21:20
because they *t. back.* Job 34:27
enemies are *t. back.* Ps 9:3
let them be *t. back* that devise.
    35:4; 70:2, 3
our heart is *t. back* from. 44:18
children of Ephraim *t. back* in. 78:9
yea, they *t. back* and tempted. 41, 57
and let them be *t. back* that. 129:5
they shall be *t. back* that. Isa 42:17
the anger of the Lord is not *t. back.*
    Jer 4:8
they are *t. back* to iniquities. 11:10
they also are *t. back*, and. 46:21
he hath *t.* me *back*, and. Lam 1:13
them that are *t. back* from the Lord.
    Zeph 1:6
t. back again to Jerusalem seeking.
    Luke 2:45
out of the lepers *t. back*, and. 17:15
she *t.* herself *back* and. John 20:14
in their hearts *t. back.* Acts 7:39

turned in

the two angels *t. in.* Gen 19:1
Judah *t. in* to Hirah the. 38:1
when Sisera had *t. in.* Judg 4:18
the Danites *t. in* thither and. 18:3
Elisha *t. in* thither to. 2 Ki 4:8
he *t. into* the chamber and lay. 11

turnest

whithersoever thou *t.* 1 Ki 2:3
that thou *t.* thy spirit. Job 15:13
thou *t.* man to destruction. Ps 90:3

turneth

soul that *t.* after wizards. Lev 20:6
whose heart *t.* away this. Deut 29:18
shall I say, when Israel *t.*? Josh 7:8
the horse *t.* not back. Job 39:22
he *t.* rivers into a. Ps 107:33
he *t.* the wilderness into a. 35
the way of the wicked he *t.* 146:9
a soft answer *t.* away. Pr 15:1
a gift, whithersoever it *t.* 17:8
he *t.* the king's heart. 21:1
as the door *t.* upon his hinges. 26:14
that *t.* away his ear from. 28:9
a lion that *t.* not away for. 30:30
the wind *t.* about unto. Eccl 1:6
be as one that *t.* aside? S of S 1:7
the people *t.* not to him. Isa 9:13
the Lord *t.* the earth upside. 24:1
that *t.* wise men backward. 44:25
that *t.* aside to tarry. Jer 14:8
Damascus is feeble, and *t.* 49:24
yea, she sigheth and *t.* Lam 1:8
he *t.* his hand against me all. 3:3
when righteous *t.* away. Ezek 18:24
    26; 33:18
when the wicked man *t.* away.
    18:27, 28; 33:12
t. the shadow of death. Amos 5:8

turning

Jerusalem as a dish, *t.* it. 2 Ki 21:13
he hardened his heart from *t.* unto
the Lord. 2 Chr 36:13
the *t.* away of the simple. Pr 1:32
your *t.* of things upside. Isa 29:16
t. away he hath divided. Mi 2:4
to bless you in *t.* you. Acts 3:26
whom is no shadow of *t.* Jas 1:17
t. Sodom and Gomorrah. 2 Pet 2:6
t. the grace of God into. Jude 4

turtle, -s, turtledove, -s
(*Turtle means* turtledove)

take a *t.* and a young pigeon.
    Gen 15:9
his offering of *t.* Lev 1:14
for his trespass two *t.* or two pigeons.
    5:7; 12:8; 14:22, 30; 15:14, 29
be not able to bring two *t.* 5:11
she shall bring a *t.* for. 12:6
day he shall bring two *t.* Num 6:10
O deliver not the soul of thy *t.* unto
the wicked. Ps 74:19

the voice of the t. is. S of S 2:12
t. and crane observe the. Jer 8:7
to offer a sacrifice, A pair of t. or
two young pigeons. Luke 2:24

tutors
the heir while a child is under t. and
governors. Gal 4:2*

twain
thou shalt be my son in law in the
one of the t. 1 Sam 18:21*
shut the door on them t. and prayed.
2 Ki 4:33
with t. he covered his face, with t. he
covered his feet, with t. Isa 6:2
they cut the calf in t. Jer 34:18
both t. shall come out. Ezek 21:19
go a mile, go with him t. Mat 5:41
cleave to his wife, and they t. 19:5
wherefore they are no more t. 6
Mark 10:8
whether of t. did the ? Mat 21:31
whether of the t. will ye ? 27:21
the vail of the temple was rent in t. 51
Mark 15:38
to make in himself of t. Eph 2:15

twelfth
oxen, he with the t. 1 Ki 19:19
the t. lot came forth to Jakim.
1 Chr 24:12
the t. lot came forth to Hashabiah.
25:19
t. captain for the t. month. 27:15
in the t. year of Josiah's reign.
2 Chr 34:3
in the t. year of king. Esth 3:7
in the t. year, in the t. Ezek 32:1
in the t. year and fifteenth day. 17
in the t. year of our captivity. 33:21
the t. foundation was an. Rev 21:20
see **day, month**

twelve
t. years they served. Gen 14:4
t. princes shall Ishmael beget.
17:20; 25:16
now the sons of Jacob were t. 35:22
they said, Thy servants are t.
brethren. 42:13, 32
all these are the t. tribes. 49:28
they came to Elim, where were t.
wells. Ex 15:27
t. pillars according to the t. 24:4
t. precious stones. 28:21; 39:14
thou shalt bake t. cakes. Lev 24:5
t. princes. Num 1:44
they brought t. oxen. 7:3
t. chargers, t. silver bowls, t. 84
t. bullocks, rams t., lambs of the
first year t. 87
t. rods, according to house. 17:2, 6
on second day offer t. young. 29:17
I took t. men of you. Deut 1:23
take ye t. men out of the tribes.
Josh 3:12; 4:2
take ye t. stones out of Jordan.
4:3, 8, 9, 20
went over by number t. of Benjamin,
and t. of the servants. 2 Sam 2:15
Solomon had t. officers. 1 Ki 4:7
the sea stood on t. oxen. 7:25, 44
2 Chr 4:15
t. lions on the one side. 1 Ki 10:20
2 Chr 9:19
Jeroboam's garment in t. pieces.
1 Ki 11:30
Elijah took t. stones and built. 18:31
found Elisha plowing with t. 19:19
with brethren and sons t. So to the
end. 1 Chr 25:9
for a sin offering t. he goats.
Ezra 6:17; 8:35
I separated t. of the chief. 8:24
t. years not eaten bread. Neh 5:14
t. brazen bulls, Nebuzar-adan took.
Jer 52:20
the altar shall be t. cubits long, t.
broad. Ezek 43:16
land according to the t. tribes. 47:13
at end of t. months he. Dan 4:29
diseased with an issue of blood t.
Mat 9:20; Mark 5:25; Luke 8:43
the names of the t. apostles.
Mat 10:2; Luke 6:13

they took up of fragments t. baskets.
Mat 14:20; Mark 6:43; 8:19
Luke 9:17; John 6:13
sit upon t. thrones, judging the t.
tribes. Mat 19:28; Luke 22:30
he sat down with the t. Mat 26:20
Mark 14:17; Luke 22:14
yet spake, Judas one of the t. came.
Mat 26:47; Mark 14:10, 43
Luke 22:47; John 6:71
than t. legions of angels. Mat 26:53
she was of the age of t. years.
Mark 5:42; Luke 8:42
of the t., that dippeth. Mark 14:20
and when Jesus was t. Luke 2:42
have I not chosen you t.? John 6:70
not t. hours in the day ? 11:9
Thomas one of the t. was. 20:24
and Jacob begat the t. Acts 7:8
all the men were about t. 19:7
but t. days since I went up. 24:11
to which promise our t. tribes. 26:7
of Cephas, then of the t. 1 Cor 15:5
to the t. tribes which are. Jas 1:1
head a crown of t. stars. Rev 12:1
t. gates, at the gates t. angels. 21:12
city had t. foundations, and in them
the names of the t. apostles. 14
the t. gates were t. pearls. 21
tree of life bare t. manner of. 22:2
see **hundred, thousand**

twenty
shall be t. found there. He said, I will
not destroy it for t.'s. Gen 18:31
this t. years have I been. 31:38, 41
for Esau, t. he goats, t. rams. 32:14
and ten bulls, t. she asses. 15
they sold Joseph for t. pieces. 37:28
a shekel is t. gerahs. Ex 30:13
Lev 27:25; Num 3:47; 18:16
Ezek 45:12
t. years old and above. Ex 30:14
38:26; Num 1:3, 18, 20; 14:29
26:2; 32:11; 1 Chr 23:24, 27
2 Chr 25:5; 31:17; Ezra 3:8
of the male from t. years. Lev 27:3
5 years old to t. years, t. shekels. 5
shall not eat neither ten days, nor t.
days. Num 11:19
the shekel is t. gerahs. 18:16
oppressed Israel t. years. Judg 4:3
from Aroer even t. cities. 11:33
judged Israel t. years. 15:20; 16:31
in Kirjath-jearim t. years. 1 Sam 7:2
armourbearer slew t. men. 14:14
to David with t. men. 2 Sam 3:20
Ziba had fifteen sons and t. servants.
9:10; 19:17
provision daily, t. oxen. 1 Ki 4:23
at the end of t. years, when Solomon.
9:10; 2 Chr 8:1
Solomon gave Hiram t. 1 Ki 9:11
man of God t. loaves. 2 Ki 4:42
I even weighed t. basons. Ezra 8:27
weight, t. shekels a day. Ezek 4:10
of the porch was t. cubits. 40:49
the breadth of the door was t. 41:2
heap of t. measures. to draw out
fifty vessels . . . but t. Hag 2:16
the flying roll t. cubits. Zech 5:2
and found it t. fathoms. Acts 27:28

twenty two
judged Israel t. two years. Judg 10:3
Jeroboam reigned t. two years.
1 Ki 14:20
Ahab reigned over Israel t. two
years. 16:29
t. and two years old was Ahaziah.
2 Ki 8:26
Amon t. two years old when. 21:19
of his father's house t. two captains.
1 Chr 12:28
but Abijah begat t. and two sons.
2 Chr 13:21

twenty three
Tola judged Israel t. three years.
Judg 10:2
Jehoahaz was t. three years old.
2 Ki 23:31
Jair had t. three cities. 1 Chr 2:22
of Josiah to t. third year. Jer 25:3
in the t. third year of. 52:30

twenty four
were t. and four bullocks. Num 7:88
fingers and toes t. four. 2 Sam 21:20
reigned t. and four years. 1 Ki 15:33
consider from t. fourth day and.
Hag 2:18
the throne were t. four seats, and on
the seats I saw t. four. Rev 4:4
the t. four elders fell down. 5:8
11:16; 19:4

twenty five
from t. five years old. Num 8:24
reigned t. and five years in Jerusalem. 1 Ki 22:42; 2 Chr 20:31
t. five years old when he began to.
2 Ki 14:2; 2 Chr 25:1
Jotham t. five years old. 2 Ki 15:33
2 Chr 27:1, 8
Hezekiah t. five years old. 2 Ki 18:2
2 Chr 29:1
Jehoiakim t. five years. 2 Ki 23:36
2 Chr 36:5
the wall finished in t. fifth day.
Neh 6:15
t. fifth day Evil-merodach lifted.
Jer 52:31

twenty six
in the t. sixth year of Asa. 1 Ki 16:8

twenty seven
t. seventh day of second month.
Gen 8:14
27th year of Asa. 1 Ki 16:10, 15
on t. seventh day of twelfth month.
2 Ki 25:27

twenty eight
length of curtain t. eight cubits.
Ex 26:2; 36:9
reigned t. and eight years. 2 Ki 10:36
Rehoboam begat t. eight sons.
2 Chr 11:21

twenty nine
Nahor lived t. nine years. Gen 11:24
Amaziah reigned t. nine years.
2 Ki 14:2
Hezekiah reigned t. nine years. 18:2
2 Chr 25:1; 29:1
see **thousand**

twice
dream was doubled t. Gen 41:32
shall be t. as much. Ex 16:5, 22
rod he smote the rock t. Num 20:11
out of his presence t. 1 Sam 18:11
appeared unto him t. 1 Ki 11:9
there, not once nor t. 2 Ki 6:10
Jerusalem once or t. Neh 13:20
speaketh once, yea t. Job 33:14
yea t.; but I will proceed no. 40:5
Lord gave Job t. as much as. 42:10
t. have I heard, power. Ps 62:11
a thousand years t. told. Eccl 6:6
before cock crow t. thou shalt deny
me. Mark 14:30, 72
I fast t. in the week. Luke 18:12
t. dead, plucked up by. Jude 12

twigs
the top of his young t. Ezek 17:4
off from the top of his young t. 22

twilight
smote them from the t. 1 Sam 30:17
the lepers rose in the t. to go to the.
2 Ki 7:5
they arose and fled in the t. 7
let the stars of the t. thereof be dark.
Job 3:9
adulterer waiteth for the t. 24:15
way to her house in the t. Pr 7:9
shalt carry it forth in the t.
Ezek 12:6*
and brought it forth in the t. 7*
the prince shall bear it in the t. 12*

twined, *see* **fine**

twinkling
all be changed, in the t. 1 Cor 15:52

twins
Rebekah had t. Gen 25:24
Tamar had t. 38:27
every one bear t. S of S 4:2
like two roes that are t. 4:5; 7:3

two
took unto him t. wives. Gen 4:19
t. of every sort shalt thou bring. 6:19

of beasts that are not clean by *t.*
Gen 7:2; 9:15
t. nations are in thy womb, and *t.*
manner of people shall be. 25:23
he hath supplanted me these *t.* 27:36
and now I am become *t.* bands. 32:10
Issachar is an ass couching between
t. burdens. 49:14
they gathered *t.* omers. *Ex* 16:22
if he continue a day or *t.* 21:21
t. turtledoves or *t.* pigeons. *Lev* 5:7
12:8; 14:22; 15:14, 29; *Num* 6:10
not able to bring *t.* turtledoves.
Lev 5:11
she shall be unclean *t.* weeks. 12:5
Aaron shall take *t.* goats. 16:7
cast lots upon *t.* 8
shalt set the cakes in *t.* rows. 24:6
brought a waggon for *t.* *Num* 7:3
t. oxen. 17, 23, 29, 35, 41, 47, 53
59, 65, 71
make thee *t.* trumpets of silver. 10:2
his ass, Balaam's *t.* servants. 22:22
t. rams. 29:14, 17, 20, 23, 26, 29, 32
and divide the prey into *t.* 31:27
t. kings. *Deut* 3:8, 21; 4:47
Josh 2:10; 9:10
at the mouth of *t.* or three witnesses,
be put to death. *Deut* 17:6; 19:15
Mat 18:16; *2 Cor* 13:1
if a man have *t.* wives. *Deut* 21:15
should *t.* put ten thousand to ? 32:30
t. tribes. *Josh* 14:3, 4; 21:16
t. cities. 21:25
man a damsel or *t.* *Judg* 5:30
let me alone *t.* months, that. 11:37
be avenged for my *t.* eyes. 16:28
t. went till they came to. *Ruth* 1:19
which *t.* did build the house. 4:11
t. wives. *1 Sam* 1:2; 27:3; 30:5
18; *2 Sam* 2:2
with *t.* lines measured. *2 Sam* 8:2
he did to the *t.* captains. *1 Ki* 2:5
there was none save we *t.* in. 3:18
Hiram and Solomon, *t.* made. 5:12
t. months they were at. home. 14
and they *t.* were alone in. 11:29
Jeroboam made *t.* calves. 12:28
2 Ki 17:16
I am gathering *t.* sticks. *1 Ki* 17:12
how long halt ye between *t.*? 18:21
Israel pitched like *t.* little. 20:27
fire burnt up the *t.* *2 Ki* 1:14
they *t.* went on. 2:6
came forth *t.* she bears. 24
give, I pray thee, *t.* changes. 5:22
be content, take *t.* talents, and. 23
t. measures of barley for. 7:1, 16, 18
behold, *t.* kings stood not. 10:4
of Tekoah, had *t.* wives. *1 Chr* 4:5
more honourable than the *t.* 11:21
Jehoiada took for Joash *t.* wives.
2 Chr 24:3
only do not *t.* things unto. *Job* 13:20
kindled against thy *t.* friends. 42:7
t. things have I required. *Pr* 30:7
t. are better than one. *Eccl* 4:9
if *t.* lie together. 11
t. shall withstand him. 12
thy *t.* breasts are like *t.* young roes.
S of S 4:5; 7:3
it were company of *t.* armies. 6:13
t. or three berries in top of. *Isa* 17:6
but these *t.* things shall come. 47:9
these *t.* things are come unto. 51:19
have committed *t.* evils. *Jer* 2:13
I will take one of a city, and *t.* 3:14
son of man, appoint thee *t.* ways.
Ezek 21:19
were *t.* women, daughters of. 23:2
hast said, These *t.* nations. 35:10
shall be no more *t.* nations. 37:22
Joseph shall have *t.* portions. 47:13
behold, there stood other *t.* *Dan* 12:5
can *t.* walk together ? *Amos* 3:3
so *t.* or three cities wandered. 4:8
t. olive trees by it. *Zech* 4:3, 11, 12
these are the *t.* anointed ones. 4:14
there came out *t.* women who. 5:9
four chariots from between *t.* 6:1
I took unto me *t.* staves and. 11:7
t. parts therein shall be cut off. 13:8
no man can serve *t.* masters.
Mat 6:24; *Luke* 16:13

than having *t.* hands or *t.* feet.
Mat 18:8; *Mark* 9:43
rather than having *t.* eyes.
Mat 18:9; *Mark* 9:47
with thee one or *t.* more. *Mat* 18:16
that if *t.* of you shall agree on. 19
where *t.* or three are gathered. 20
on these *t.* hang all the law. 22:40
then shall *t.* be in the field. 24:40
received *t.* he gained other *t.* 25:17
send them forth by *t.* and *t.* *Mark* 6:7
he sendeth *t.* disciples. 11:1; 14:13
Luke 19:29
she threw in *t.* mites. *Mark* 12:42
after that Jesus appeared to *t.* 16:12
he that hath *t.* coats, let. *Luke* 3:11
certain creditor which had *t.* 7:41
neither take money, nor have *t.* 9:3
took out *t.* pence and gave. 10:35
shew whether of these *t.* *Acts* 1:24
for *t.* shall be one flesh. *1 Cor* 6:16
Eph 5:31
let it be by *t.* or at the. *1 Cor* 14:27
let the prophets speak *t.* or three. 29
these are the *t.* covenants. *Gal* 4:24
a strait betwixt *t.*, a desire. *Phil* 1:23
but before *t.* or three. *1 Tim* 5:19
that by *t.* immutable things . . . we.
Heb 6:18
died without mercy under *t.* 10:28
there come *t.* woes more. *Rev* 9:12
I will give power to my *t.* 11:3
these are *t.* olive trees and *t.* 4
because these *t.* prophets. 10
woman were given *t.* wings. 12:14
he had *t.* horns like a lamb. 13:11
see **daughters, days, fifty, forty,**
hundred, kidneys, lambs,
sons, thirty, thousand, twenty
two *men*
t. men of the Hebrews. *Ex* 2:13
there remained *t.* men. *Num* 11:26
out *t.* men to spy secretly. *Josh* 2:1
Rahab hid the *t.* men. 4
the *t.* men returned. 23
find *t.* men by Rachel's. *1 Sam* 10:2
there were *t.* men in one city, one
rich. *2 Sam* 12:1
fell on *t.* men more. *1 Ki* 2:32
set *t.* men, sons of Belial. 21:10, 13
t. blind men followed. *Mat* 9:27
talked with him *t.* men. *Luke* 9:30
t. men in one bed. 17:34
t. men in the field. 36
t. men went up to the temple. 18:10
perplexed, behold, *t.* men stood.
Luke 24:4; *Acts* 1:10
testimony of *t.* men is true.
John 8:17
they sent *t.* men to Peter. *Acts* 9:38
two *tables*
gave to Moses *t.* tables. *Ex* 31:18
the *t.* tables were in his hands.
32:15; 34:29
hew thee *t.* tables of stone. 34:1
Deut 10:1
he hewed *t.* tables of stone.
Ex 34:4; *Deut* 10:3
he wrote upon *t.* tables. *Deut* 4:13
5:22
the Lord delivered unto me *t.* tables.
9:10, 11
nothing in the ark save the *t.* tables.
1 Ki 8:9; *2 Chr* 5:10
t. tables on this side. *Ezek* 40:39
t. tables on that. 40
two *years*
begat Arphaxad *t.* years. *Gen* 11:10
these *t.* years hath the famine. 45:6
when Saul had reigned *t.* years.
1 Sam 13:1
Ish-bosheth Saul's son reigned *t.*
years. *2 Sam* 2:10
after *t.* years, Absalom had. 13:23
Absalom dwelt *t.* years in. 14:28
Nadab reigned over Israel *t.* years.
1 Ki 15:25
Elah reigned *t.* years. 16:8
Ahaziah reigned *t.* years. 22:51
2 Ki 15:23; 21:19
after *t.* years his bowels. *2 Ki* 21:19
within *t.* full years will I bring again
the vessels. *Jer* 28:3, 11

words of Amos, *t.* years. *Amos* 1:1
slew children from *t.* years. *Mat* 2:16
t. years they in Asia. *Acts* 19:10
Paul dwelt *t.* years in his. 28:30
twofold
ye make him *t.* more the child of hell,
Mat 23:15
Tychicus
T. of Asia accompanied. *Acts* 20:4
T. shall make known to. *Eph* 6:21
all my state shall *T.* *Col* 4:7
and *T.* have I sent to. *2 Tim* 4:12
when I shall send *T.* *Tit* 3:12
Tyrannus
disputing in the school of one *T.*
Acts 19:9
Tyre
coast turneth to the strong city *T.*
Josh 19:29
the strong hold of *T.* *2 Sam* 24:7
fetched Hiram out of *T.* *1 Ki* 7:13
his father was a man of *T.* 14
2 Chr 2:14
Hiram came out from *T.* to.
1 Ki 9:12
and drink to them of *T.* *Ezra* 3:7
there dwelt men of *T.* *Neh* 13:16
the daughter of *T.* shall. *Ps* 45:12
with the inhabitants of *T.* 83:7
Philistia and *T.* 87:4
the burden of *T.* *Isa* 23:1
pained at the report of *T.* 5
this counsel against *T.*? 8
T. shall be forgotten. 15
Lord will visit *T.* 17
what have ye to do with me, O
T.? *Joel* 3:4
if the mighty works had been done
in *T.* *Mat* 11:21; *Luke* 10:13
Herod was displeased with them of
T. *Acts* 12:20
see **king, Sidon**
Tyrus
made all the kings of *T.* *Jer* 25:22
send yokes to the kings of *T.* 27:3
to cut off from *T.* and Zidon. 47:4
because *T.* said against. *Ezek* 26:2
behold, I am against thee, O *T.* 3
take up a lamentation for *T.* 27:2
what city is like *T.*, like the ? 32
say to the prince of *T.* 28:2
lamentation on the king of *T.* 12
great service against *T.* 29:18
Ephraim, as I saw *T.* *Hos* 9:13
transgressions of *T.* *Amos* 1:9
a fire on the wall of *T.* 10
T. and Zidon, though it. *Zech* 9:2
T. build herself a strong hold. 3

U

Ucal
spake to Ithiel and *U.* *Pr* 30:1
unaccustomed
Ephraim, as a bullock *u.* *Jer* 31:18
unadvisedly
so that he spake *u.* with. *Ps* 106:33
unawares
Jacob stole away *u.* to Laban.
Gen 31:20, 26
slayer may flee thither, who killeth
any person *u.* *Num* 35:11*, 15*
Deut 4:42; *Josh* 20:3*, 9*
let destruction come on him at *u.*
Ps 35:8
day come upon you *u.* *Luke* 21:34*
because of false brethren *u.* *Gal* 2:4*
have entertained angels *u.* *Heb* 13:2
certain men crept in *u.* *Jude* 4*
unbelief
did not many mighty works there
because of their *u.* *Mat* 13:58
could not cast him out, because of
your *u.* 17:20*
because of their *u.* *Mark* 6:6
help thou mine *u.* 9:24
upbraided them with their *u.* 16:14
shall their *u.* make faith ? *Rom* 3:3*
not at the promise through *u.* 4:20

because of *u.* they were. *Rom* 11:20
if they abide not still in *u.* shall.   23
obtained mercy through their *u.* 30*
concluded them all in *u.*   32*
did it ignorantly in *u.*   *1 Tim* 1:13
you an evil heart of *u.*   *Heb* 3:12
not enter in because of *u.*   19; 4:6*
lest any fall after the same example
of *u.*   4:11*

unbelievers
him his portion with *u.* *Luke* 12:46*
goeth to law before *u.*   *1 Cor* 6:6
come in those that are *u.*   14:23
unequally yoked with *u. 2 Cor* 6:14

unbelieving
the *u.* Jews stirred up.   *Acts* 14:2
for the *u.* husband is sanctified by the
wife, the *u.* wife is.   *1 Cor* 7:14
u. depart, let him depart.   15
unto them that are *u.*   *Tit* 1:15
the *u.* shall have their part. *Rev* 21:8

unblameable
to present you holy, *u.*   *Col* 1:22*
stablish your hearts in *1 Thes* 3:13

unblameably
how *u.* we have behaved ourselves.
1 Thes 2:10

uncertain
trumpet give an *u.*   *1 Cor* 14:8
nor trust in *u.* riches.   *1 Tim* 6:17

uncertainly
I therefore so run, not as *u.*; so fight I.
1 Cor 9:26

unchangeable
but this man hath an *u.*   *Heb* 7:24

uncircumcised
the *u.* man child shall.   *Gen* 17:14
sister to one that is *u.*   34:14
then shall Pharaoh hear me, who am
of *u.* lips ?   *Ex* 6:12, 30
for no *u.* person shall eat of.   12:48
shall count the fruit *u.*   *Lev* 19:23
if then their *u.* hearts be.   26:41
for they were *u.*   *Josh* 5:7
to take a wife of the *u.*   *Judg* 14:3
fall into the hands of these *u.* 15:18
let us go over unto the garrison of
these *u.*   *1 Sam* 14:6
who is this *u.* Philistine ? 17:26, 36
lest these *u.* come and abuse me.
31:4; *1 Chr* 10:4
the daughters of the *u. 2 Sam* 1:20
come into thee the *u.*   *Isa* 52:1
their ear is *u.*, they cannot. *Jer* 6:10
the circumcised with the *u.*   9:25
are *u.*, all house of Israel are *u.* 26
die the death of the *u.*   *Ezek* 28:10
thou shalt lie in the midst of the *u.*
31:18; 32:19, 21, 24, 25, 26, 27, 28
29, 30, 32
ye have brought strangers *u.* in heart
and *u.* in flesh into my.   44:7, 9
stiffnecked and *u.* in heart and ears.
Acts 7:51
thou wentest in to men *u.* and. 11:3
faith which he had yet being *u.*
Rom 4:11, 12
let him not become *u.*   *1 Cor* 7:18

uncircumcision
thy circumcision is made *u.*
Rom 2:25
u. keep the righteousness of the law,
shall not his *u.* be counted ?   26
shall not *u.* which is by nature ?   27
justify the *u.* through faith.   3:30
cometh this blessedness then upon
the circumcision or the *u.?*   4:9
when he was in circumcision or in
u.? not in circumcision but *u.*   10
is any man called in *u.?*   *1 Cor* 7:18
circumcision is nothing, and *u.*   19
gospel of *u.* was committed. *Gal* 2:7
neither circumcision availeth nor *u.*
5:6; 6:15
who are called *u.* by that. *Eph* 2:11
you being dead in the *u.*   *Col* 2:13
neither circumcision nor *u.* but. 3:11

uncle
Uzziel, the *u.* of Aaron.   *Lev* 10:4
if a man lie with his *u.'s* wife, he hath
uncovered his *u.'s.*   20:20

either his *u.* or *u.'s* son.   *Lev* 25:49
and Saul's *u.* said.   *1 Sam* 10:14, 15
Abner, son of Ner, Saul's *u.*   14:50
Jonathan David's *u.* a.   *1 Chr* 27:32
Mordecai brought up Hadassah his
u.'s daughter.   *Esth* 2:7, 15
son of Shallum thine *u.*   *Jer* 32:7
Hanameel my *u.'s* son came. 8, 9, 12
and a man's *u.* shall.   *Amos* 6:10

unclean
any *u.* thing, the carcase of *u.* cattle or
u. things . . . be *u. Lev* 5:2; 11:26
put difference between *u.* and clean.
10:10; 11:47
it is *u.* to you.   11:4, 5, 6, 7, 29
Deut 14:19
they are *u.* unto you.   *Lev* 11:8
26, 27, 28, 31; *Deut* 14:7
ye shall be *u.*; *u.* until the evening.
Lev 11:24, 25, 28, 31, 32, 33, 39
40; 14:46; 15:5, 6, 7, 8, 10, 11
16, 17, 18, 19, 21, 22, 23, 27; 17:15
22:6; *Num* 19:7, 8, 10, 21, 22
it shall be *u Lev* 11:32, 33, 34, 35
36, 38; 15:4, 9, 20, 24, 26
then she shall be *u.* seven days. 12:2
5; 15:25
priest shall look on him and pronounce him *u.* 13:3, 8, 11, 15, 20
22, 25, 27, 30, 44, 59
he is *u.* 13:11, 14, 36, 44, 46; 15:2, 24
plague is, shall cry, *U. u.*   13:45
cast them into an *u.* place.   14:40
41, 45
to teach when it is *u.* and.   57
whereby he may be made *u.*   22:5
not make himself *u.* for.   *Num* 6:7
u. and clean eat thereof. *Deut* 12:15
22; 15:22
of your possession be *u. Josh* 22:19
to possess is an *u.* land.   *Ezra* 9:11
hypocrites is among the *u. Job* 36:14
event to the clean and *u.*   *Eccl* 9:2
man of *u.* lips, I dwell in the midst of
a people of *u.* lips.   *Isa* 6:5
the *u.* shall not pass over it.   35:8
no more come into thee the *u.* 52:1
depart ye, it is *u.*; depart. *Lam* 4:15
put no difference between clean and
u.   *Ezek* 22:26
discern between the clean and *u.*
44:23
they shall eat *u.* things in.   *Hos* 9:3
one that is *u.* touch any of these,
shall it be *u.?*   *Hag* 2:13
they offer there is *u.*   14
had a spirit of an *u.* devil. *Luke* 4:33
not call any man common or *u.*
Acts 10:28; 11:8
u. of itself . . . any thing to be *u.*, to
him it is *u.*   *Rom* 14:14
else were your children *u. 1 Cor* 7:14
touch not the *u.* thing.   *2 Cor* 6:17
that no *u.* person hath any. *Eph* 5:5
of heifer sprinkling the *u. Heb* 9:13
Babylon is become a cage of every *u.*
bird.   *Rev* 18:2
see beast, spirit, thing

unclean *spirits*
he gave power against *u. spirits.*
Mat 10:1; *Mark* 6:7
he commandeth *u. spirits.*
Mark 1:27; *Luke* 4:36
u. spirits, when they saw. *Mark* 3:11
u. spirits went out and entered. 5:13
were vexed with *u. spirits. Acts* 5:16
for *u. spirits* came out of many.   8:7
I saw three *u. spirits.*   *Rev* 16:13

uncleanness
if he touch the *u.* of man, whatsoever
u. it be.   *Lev* 5:3; 7:21; 22:5
having his *u.* on him.   7:20; 22:3
is to be cleansed from his *u.*   14:19
separate Israel from their *u.*   15:31
she is put apart for her *u.*   18:19
not gone aside to *u.*   *Num* 5:19
he shall be unclean, his *u.* is. 19:13
by reason of *u.* that.   *Deut* 23:10
he hath found some *u.* in her. 24:1*
was purified from her *u. 2 Sam* 11:4
brought out all the *u. 2 Chr* 29:16
have filled the land with their *u.*
Ezra 9:11

as the *u.* of a removed.   *Ezek* 36:17
according to their *u.* have I.   39:24
shall be a fountain opened for sin and
u.   *Zech* 13:1
full of bones, and all *u.*   *Mat* 23:27
also gave them up to *u.*   *Rom* 1:24
your members servants to *u.*   6:19
not repented of the *u.*   *2 Cor* 12:21
flesh are these, *u.*, strife. *Gal* 5:19
to work all *u.* with.   *Eph* 4:19
all *u.*, let it not be once named.   5:3
fornication, *u.* and covetousness.
Col 3:5
for our exhortation was not of *u.*
1 Thes 2:3
God hath not called us to *u.*   4:7
walk in the lust of *u.*   *2 Pet* 2:10*

uncleannesses
I will save you from all your *u.*
Ezek 36:29

unclothed
not for that we would be *u. 2 Cor* 5:4

uncomely
he behaveth *u.* toward.   *1 Cor* 7:36*
u. parts have more abundant. 12:23

uncondemned
they have beaten us openly *u.*, being
Romans.   *Acts* 16:37
a man that is a Roman and *u.* 22:25

uncorruptness
doctrine shewing *u.*, gravity. *Tit* 2:7

uncover
u. not your heads neither. *Lev* 10:6
not *u.* nakedness of one that.   18:6
thy father shalt thou not *u.*   7
of thy father's wife shalt not *u.*   8
son's daughter shalt not *u.*   10
nakedness of thy father's . . . not *u.* 11
not *u.* . . of father's sister.   12, 13
u. the nakedness of thy father's.   14
not *u.* . . . of thy daughter in law. 15
not *u.* the nakedness of a woman. 17
not *u.* the nakedness of thy wife's. 18
not *u.* nakedness of a woman put
apart.   19; 20:18
the high priest shall not *u.*   21:10
the priest shall *u.* the.   *Num* 5:18
go in and *u.* his feet.   *Ruth* 3:4
u. thy locks, lay the thigh. *Isa* 47:2*

uncovered
and Noah was *u.* within.   *Gen* 9:21
he hath *u.* his father's.   *Lev* 20:11
u. his sister's nakedness.   17
she hath *u.* the fountain of her.   18
u. his uncle's nakedness.   20
she came softly and *u.*   *Ruth* 3:7
who *u.* himself as the.   *2 Sam* 6:20
with their buttocks *u.*   *Isa* 20:4
quiver, and Kir *u.* the shield.   22:6
thy nakedness shall be *u.*, thy. 47:3
but I have *u.* his secret.   *Jer* 49:10
and thine arm shall be *u. Ezek* 4:7
let thy foreskin be *u.*   *Hab* 2:16*
they *u.* the roof where.   *Mark* 2:4
with her head *u.*   *1 Cor* 11:5*
a woman pray unto God *u.?*   13*

uncovereth
for he *u.* his near kin.   *Lev* 20:19
he *u.* his father's skirt.   *Deut* 27:20
vain fellows *u.* himself.   *2 Sam* 6:20

unction
but ye have an *u.* from. *1 John* 2:20*

undefiled
blessed are the *u.* in.   *Ps* 119:1*
my love, my dove, my *u. S of S* 5:2
my dove, my *u.* is one; she is.   6:9
who is holy, harmless, *u. Heb* 7:26
in all, and the bed *u.*   13:4
pure religion and *u.*   *Jas* 1:27
to an inheritance incorruptible, *u.*
1 Pet 1:4

under
the deep that lieth *u.* *Gen* 49:25
I will bring you out from *u. Ex* 6:6
of my tent, and silver *u.* it. *Josh* 7:21
u. whose wings thou art. *Ruth* 2:12
what is *u.* thy hand give. *1 Sam* 21:3
and put no fire *u.*   *1 Ki* 18:23
revolted from *u.* the hand. *2 Ki* 8:20
Israel went out from *u.* the.   13:5

purpose to keep *u*. Judah for.
    2 Chr 28:10
name will we tread them *u*. *Ps* 44:5
should be *u*. my head. *S of S* 8:3
with idols *u*. every green tree.
    Isa 57:5; *Jer* 2:20
perish from the earth, and from *u*.
    Jer 10:11; *Lam* 3:66
get away from *u*. it. *Dan* 4:14
u. the whole heaven hath not. 9:12
gone a whoring from *u*. *Hos* 4:12
from two years old and *u*. *Mat* 2:16
u. authority, having soldiers *u*. 8:9
enter *u*. my roof. *Luke* 7:6
when thou wast *u*. the fig tree.
    John 1:48
have proved that they are all *u*. sin.
    Rom 3:9
not *u*. the law, but *u*. grace. 6:15
but I am carnal, sold *u*. sin. 7:14
brought *u*. power of any. *1 Cor* 6:12
u. the law, as *u*. the law. 9:20
I keep *u*. my body and bring it. 27
our fathers were *u*. the cloud. 10:1
u. the curse. *Gal* 3:10
hath concluded all *u*. sin. 22
we were kept *u*. the law. 23
faith is come, we are no longer *u*. 25
and things *u*. the earth. *Phil* 2:10
as are *u*. the yoke. *1 Tim* 6:1
for *u*. it the people. *Heb* 7:11
in chains *u*. darkness. *Jude* 6
see **feet, him, law, me, sun, thee, them, us**

undergirding
used helps, *u*. the ship. *Acts* 27:17

underneath
u. are the everlasting. *Deut* 33:27

undersetters
the four corners thereof had *u*.
    1 Ki 7:30, 34

understand
they may not *u*. one. *Gen* 11:7
thou canst *u*. a dream. 41:15
ye shall *u*. that these. *Num* 16:30
tongue thou shalt not *u*. *Deut* 28:49
servants in the Syrian language, for
 we *u*. it. *2 Ki* 18:26; *Isa* 36:11
the Lord made me *u*. *1 Chr* 28:19
before those that could *u*. *Neh* 8:3
the people to *u*. the law. 7, 8, 13
cause me to *u*. wherein. *Job* 6:24
I would *u*. what he would say. 23:5
of his power who can *u*.? 26:14
nor do the aged *u*. judgement. 32:9
can any *u*. the spreadings? 36:29
if there were any that did *u*.
    Ps 14:2; 53:2
who can *u*. his errors? cleanse. 19:12
know not, neither will they *u*. 82:5
neither doth a fool *u*. this. 92:6
u. ye brutish among the people. 94:8
u. the lovingkindness of. 107:43
make me to *u*. the way of. 119:27
I *u*. more than the ancients. 100
then shalt thou *u*. the fear. *Pr* 2:5
then shalt thou *u*. righteousness. 9
u. wisdom, and, ye fools, be of. 8:5
prudent is to *u*. his way. 14:8
reprove one, and he will *u*. 19:25
how can a man then *u*. his? 20:24
evil men *u*. not judgement, but they
 that seek the Lord *u*. all. 28:5
for though he *u*. he will not. 29:19
Hear ye indeed, but *u*. not. *Isa* 6:9
lest they *u*. with their heart.
    John 12:40
whom shall he make to *u*.? *Isa* 28:9
it shall be a vexation only to *u*. 19
the heart of the rash shall *u*. 32:4
tongue that thou canst not *u*. 33:19
u. together that the Lord. 41:20
that ye may know and *u*. 43:10
hearts, that they cannot *u*. 44:18
shepherds that cannot *u*. 56:11
who is the wise man that may *u*.
 this? *Jer* 9:12
words thou canst not *u*. *Ezek* 3:6
make this man to *u*. the. *Dan* 8:16
but he said unto me, *U*. O son. 17
and *u*. thy truth. 9:13
u. the matter. 23, 25
didst set thy heart to *u*. 10:12

I am come to make thee *u*.*Dan* 10:14
and they that *u*. shall instruct. 11:33
none . . . *u*., but the wise shall *u*. 12:10
people that doth not *u*. *Hos* 4:14
and he shall *u*. these things? 14:9
neither *u*. they the counsel. *Mi* 4:12
neither do they *u*. *Mat* 13:13
hear and not *u*. 14
hear and *u*. 15:10; *Mark* 7:14
do not ye yet *u*.? *Mat* 15:17; 16:9, 11
    Mark 8:17, 21
whoso readeth, let him *u*. *Mat* 24:15
    Mark 13:14
and not perceive, that hearing they
 may hear and not *u*. *Mark* 4:12
    Luke 8:10; *Acts* 28:26
I know not nor *u*. I what. *Mark* 14:68
that they might *u*. the. *Luke* 24:45
ye not *u*. my speech? *John* 8:43
have not heard shall *u*. *Rom* 15:21
and though I *u*. all mysteries . . . I
 am nothing. *1 Cor* 13:2
through faith we *u*. worlds. *Heb* 11:3
evil of things they *u*. not. *2 Pet* 2:12*

understandest
what *u*. thou, which is not? *Job* 15:9
thou *u*. my thoughts. *Ps* 139:2
neither *u*. thou what they. *Jer* 5:15
Philip said, *U*. thou what? *Acts* 8:30

understandeth
Lord *u*. the imaginations. *1 Chr* 28:9
God *u*. the way thereof. *Job* 28:23
is in honour and *u*. not. *Ps* 49:20
all plain to him that *u*. *Pr* 8:9
easy unto him that *u*. 14:6
in this, that he *u*. me. *Jer* 9:24
the word and *u*. it not. *Mat* 13:19
heareth the word and *u*. it. 23
there is none that *u*. *Rom* 3:11
men, for no man *u*. *1 Cor* 14:2
say Amen, seeing he *u*. not what? 16

understanding
Bezaleel with wisdom and *u*. and in.
    Ex 31:3; 35:31; 36:1
wisdom and your *u*. *Deut* 4:6
neither is there any *u*. in. 32:28
hast asked for thyself *u*. *1 Ki* 3:11
Solomon wisdom and *u*. 4:29
was filled with wisdom and *u*. 7:14
were men that had *u*. *1 Chr* 12:32
give thee wisdom and *u*. 22:12
a wise son endued with *u*. *2 Chr* 2:12
Zechariah had *u*. in the visions. 26:5
for Elnathan, men of *u*. *Ezra* 8:16*
could hear with *u*. *Neh* 8:2
knowledge and having *u*. 10:28
but I have *u*. as well as you. *Job* 12:3
in length of days is *u*. 12
he hath *u*. 13
away the *u*. of the aged. 20
hid their heart from *u*. 17:4
the spirit of my *u*. causeth me. 20:3
and by his *u*. he smiteth. 26:12
where is the place of *u*.? 28:12, 20
to depart from evil is *u*. 28
Almighty giveth them *u*. 32:8
hearken to me, ye men of *u*. 34:10
if now thou hast *u*. hear this. 16
let men of *u*. tell me, let a wise. 34
declare, if thou hast *u*. 38:4
who hath given *u*. to the heart? 36
he imparted to her *u*. 39:17
mule that hath no *u*. *Ps* 32:9
sing ye praises with *u*. 47:7
of my heart shall be of *u*. 49:3
give me *u*. 119:34, 73, 125, 144, 169
I have more *u*. 99
through thy precepts I get *u*. 104
thy word giveth *u*. 130
our Lord, his *u*. is infinite. 147:5
to perceive words of *u*. *Pr* 1:2
that thou apply thine heart to *u*. 2:2
liftest up thy voice for *u*. 3
cometh knowledge and *u*. 6
thee, *u*. shall keep thee. 11
and lean not unto thine own *u*. 3:5
happy is the man that getteth *u*. 13
by *u*. hath he established the. 19
ye children, attend to know *u*. 5, 7
get *u*. 5, 7
my son, bow thine ear to my *u*. 5:1
committeth adultery, lacketh *u*. 6:32
and call *u*. thy kinswoman. 7:4

not *u*. put forth her voice? *Pr* 8:1
I am *u*. 14
as for him that wanteth *u*. 9:4, 16
and go in the way of *u*. 6
knowledge of the holy is *u*. 10
that hath *u*. wisdom is found. 10:13
slow to wrath is of great *u*. 14:29
in the heart of him that hath *u*. 33
hath *u*. seeketh knowledge. 15:14
heareth reproof getteth *u*. 32
to get *u*. rather to be chosen. 16:16
u. is a wellspring of life to him. 22
before him that hath *u*. 17:24
a fool hath no delight in *u*. but. 18:2
he that keepeth *u*. shall find. 19:8
reprove one that hath *u*. he will. 25
wandereth out of the way of *u*. 21:16
there is no *u*. nor counsel against. 30
and instruction, and *u*. 23:23
by *u*. an house is established. 24:3
poor that hath *u*. searcheth. 28:11
the prince that wanteth *u*. is an. 16
and have not the *u*. of a man. 30:2
yet riches to men of *u*. *Eccl* 9:11
the spirit of *u*. shall rest. *Isa* 11:2
make him of quick *u*. in the fear. 3*
for it is a people of no *u*. 27:11
the *u*. of their prudent men. 29:14
framed it, He had no *u*.? 16
erred in spirit shall come to *u*. 24
shewed to him the way of *u*.? 40:14
there is no searching of his *u*. 28
is there knowledge nor *u*. 44:19
which shall feed you with *u*. *Jer* 3:15
is foolish, they have no *u*. 4:22
people and without *u*. 5:21
out the heaven by his *u*. 51:15
with thy *u*. thou hast got. *Ezek* 28:4
u. science. *Dan* 1:4
Daniel had *u*. in visions. 17
in all matters of *u*. he found. 20
knowledge to them that know *u*. 2:21
u. returned to me, I blessed. 4:34
light and *u*. was found. 5:11, 12, 14
u. dark sentences. 8:23
came forth to give thee *u*. 9:22
had *u*. of the vision. 10:1
some of them of *u*. shall fall. 11:35
according to their own *u*. *Hos* 13:2
there is no *u*. in him. *Ob* 7
shall I not destroy *u*. out of the? 8
are ye also yet without *u*.?
    Mat 15:16; *Mark* 7:18
and to love him with all the *u*.
    Mark 12:33
to me, having had perfect *u*. of.
    Luke 1:3*
were astonished at his *u*. 2:47
then opened he their *u*. that. 24:45
without *u*., unmerciful. *Rom* 1:31
bring to nothing the *u*. of. *1 Cor* 1:19
my spirit prayeth, but my *u*. is. 14:14
pray with the *u*., sing with the *u*. 15
speak five words with my *u*. 19
be not children in *u*., but in *u*. 20
the eyes of your *u*. being. *Eph* 1:18
having the *u*. darkened, being. 4:18
but *u*. what the will of the Lord. 5:17
God which passeth all *u*. *Phil* 4:7
filled with all spiritual *u*. *Col* 1:9
the full assurance of *u*. 2
u. neither what they say. *1 Tim* 1:7
the Lord give thee *u*. in. *2 Tim* 2:7
Son hath given us an *u*. *1 John* 5:20
him that hath *u*. count. *Rev* 13:18
  see **good**

understanding, adjective
take ye wise men and *u*. *Deut* 1:13
great nation is an *u*. people. 4:6
give thy servant an *u*. *1 Ki* 3:9
thee a wise and an *u*. heart. 12
be ye of an *u*. heart. *Pr* 8:5

man of understanding
brought us a *man of u*. *Ezra* 8:18
a *man of u*. shall attain. *Pr* 1:5
but a *man of u*. hath wisdom. 10:23
man of u. holdeth his peace. 11:12
man of u. walketh uprightly. 15:21
a *man of u*. is of an excellent. 17:27
lips, is esteemed a *man of u*. 28
but a *man of u*. will draw out. 20:5
but by a *man of u*. and. 28:2

void of understanding

young man void of u.   Pr 7:7
a rod for back of him that is void of
u.   10:13
vain persons is void of u.   12:11
a man void of u. striketh.   17:18
vineyard of the man void of u. 24:30

understood

not that Joseph u. them. Gen 42:23
were wise, that they u. Deut 32:29
they u. that ark of Lord. 1 Sam 4:6
David u. that Saul was come. 26:4
people u. it was not of David to.
  2 Sam 3:37
they had u. the words.   Neh 8:12
I u. of the evil Eliashib did.   13:7
ear hath heard and u. it.   Job 13:1
have I uttered that I u. not.   42:3
went to sanctuary, then u. Ps 73:17*
a language that I u. not.   81:5
fathers u. not thy wonders.   106:7
u. from foundations of.   Isa 40:21
not known nor u.: for he shut. 44:18
at the vision, but none u.   Dan 8:27
I Daniel u. by books.   9:2
he u. the vision.   10:1
I heard, but I u. not: then.   12:8
have ye u. all these things?
  Mat 13:51
u. they how he bade them.   16:12
u. that he spake of John.   17:13
they u. not that saying. Mark 9:32
  Luke 2:50; 9:45; John 8:27; 10:6
and they u. none of.   Luke 18:34
these things u. not his.   John 12:16
have u. that God by his hand would
  ... but they u. not.   Acts 7:25
I rescued him, having u. he.   23:27
I u. that he was of Cilicia.   34
being u. by the things that. Rom 1:20
child, I u. as a child.   1 Cor 13:11
by tongue words easy to be u.   14:9
some things hard to be u. 2 Pet 3:16

undertake

oppressed, u. for me.   Isa 38:14*

undertook

Jews u. to do as they.   Esth 9:23

undo

to u. heavy burdens.   Isa 58:6
at that time I will u. all. Zeph 3:19*

undone

thou art u. O people.   Num 21:29
Joshua left nothing u.   Josh 11:15
woe is me, for I am u.   Isa 6:5
not to leave the other u. Mat 23:23
  Luke 11:42

undressed

grapes of thy vine u.   Lev 25:5, 11

unequal

are not your ways u.? Ezek 18:25, 29

unequally

be ye not u. yoked with. 2 Cor 6:14

unfaithful

confidence in an u. man.   Pr 25:19

unfaithfully

they dealt u. like their.   Ps 78:57*

unfeigned

Holy Ghost, by love u.   2 Cor 6:6
a pure heart and faith u. 1 Tim 1:5
remembrance the u. faith. 2 Tim 1:5
through the Spirit unto u. love of the
brethren.   1 Pet 1:22

unfruitful

riches, choke word, and he becometh
u.   Mat 13:22; Mark 4:19
my understanding is u. 1 Cor 14:14
no fellowship with the u. works.
  Eph 5:11
works, that they be not u. Tit 3:14
be barren nor u. in the. 2 Pet 1:8

ungirded

the man u. the camels.   Gen 24:32

ungodliness

the wrath of God revealed against
all u.   Rom 1:18
and he shall turn away u.   11:26
increase unto more u.   2 Tim 2:16
that, denying u. and worldly. Tit 2:12

ungodly

death compassed me, the floods of u.
men.   2 Sam 22:5; Ps 18:4
Shouldest thou help u.? 2 Chr 19:2*
delivered me to the u.   Job 16:11
say to princes, Ye are u.?   34:18*
in the counsel of the u.   Ps 1:1*
the u. are not so.   4*
u. not stand in judgement.   5*
but the way of the u. shall perish. 6*
broken the teeth of the u.   3:7*
cause against an u. nation.   43:1
these are the u. who prosper. 73:12*
an u. man diggeth up evil. Pr 16:27*
an u. witness scorneth.   19:28*
that justifieth the u.   Rom 4:5
Christ died for the u.   5:6
the law is for the u. and. 1 Tim 1:9
where shall the u. and sinner?
  1 Pet 4:18
flood on world of the u.   2 Pet 2:5
those who after should live u.   3:7
and perdition of u. men.   3:7
u. men turning the grace.   Jude 4
that are u. of their u. deeds.   15
walk after their own u. lusts.   18

unholy

may put difference between holy and
u.   Lev 10:10*
law was made for the u. 1 Tim 1:9
shall be unthankful, u.   2 Tim 3:2
of covenant an u. thing. Heb 10:29

unicorn

(This animal is mythical. The
word as used in the Bible probably
means the wild ox, as the Revised
Versions render it)
as it were the strength of an u.
  Num 23:22; 24:8
will the u. be willing to? Job 39:9
canst thou bind the u. in the?   10
Sirion like a young u.   Ps 29:6
exalt like the horn of an u.   92:10

unicorns

like the horns of u.   Deut 33:17
from the horns of the u. Ps 22:21
and the u. shall come.   Isa 34:7

unite

u. my heart to fear thy.   Ps 86:11

united

mine honour, be not thou u.Gen 49:6

unity

to dwell together in u.   Ps 133:1
endeavouring to keep the u. Eph 4:3
till we come in the u. of the faith. 13

unjust

deliver me from the u.   Ps 43:1
and the hope of u. men.   Pr 11:7*
who by u. gain increaseth his. 28:8
an u. man is an abomination. 29:27
u. knoweth no shame.   Zeph 3:5
rain on the just and u.   Mat 5:45
the Lord commended the u. steward.
  Luke 16:8*
he that is u. in the least, is u.   10*
hear what the u. judge saith. 18:6*
I am not as other men are, u.   11*
both of the just and u.   Acts 24:15
go to law before the u.? 1 Cor 6:1*
the just for the u.   1 Pet 3:18*
reserve the u. to the day of judgement.   2 Pet 2:9*
he that is u. let him be u. still.
  Rev 22:11*

unjustly

how long will ye judge u.? Ps 82:2
in land of uprightness will he deal u.
  Isa 26:10*

unknown

To the u. God.   Acts 17:23
that speaketh in an u. tongue.
  1 Cor 14:2, 4, 13, 27
if I pray in an u. tongue, my.   14
than ten thousand words in an u. 19
as u. and yet well known. 2 Cor 6:9
I was u. by face unto the churches
of Judaea which were. Gal 1:22

unlade

there the ship was to u.   Acts 21:3

unlawful

an u. thing for a man.   Acts 10:28
with their u. deeds.   2 Pet 2:8*

unlearned

that they were u.   Acts 4:13
occupieth the room of the u.
  1 Cor 14:16
come in those that are u.   23, 24
but foolish and u. questions avoid.
  2 Tim 2:23*
which they that are u.   2 Pet 3:16

unleavened

they baked u. cakes of.   Ex 12:39
it shall be an u. cake of fine flour
mingled with oil, or u. Lev 2:4, 5
he shall offer u. cakes mingled. 7:12
and Moses took one u. cake.   8:26
priest shall take one u. cake, one u.
wafer, and put them.   Num 6:19
old corn of the land u.   Josh 5:11
ready a kid and u. cakes. Judg 6:19
take the flesh and the u. cakes.   20
and u. cakes; fire out of the rock
consumed the flesh and u.   21
for flour and u. cakes. 1 Chr 23:29
a new lump, as ye are u. 1 Cor 5:7
see bread

unless

unclean u. he wash his.   Lev 22:6
u. she had turned from me, I had.
  Num 22:33
u. thou hadst spoken. 2 Sam 2:27
I had fainted, u. I had.   Ps 27:13
u. the Lord had been my help. 94:17
u. thy law had been my.   119:92
sleep not, u. they cause.   Pr 4:16
ye are saved, u. ye have. 1 Cor 15:2

unloose

not worthy to stoop down and u.
  Mark 1:7; Luke 3:16; John 1:27

unmarried

I say to the u.   1 Cor 7:8
let her remain u.   11
he that is u.   32
the u. woman careth for.   34

unmerciful

implacable, u.   Rom 1:31

unmindful

begat thee thou art u.   Deut 32:18

unmoveable

of the ship remained u. Acts 27:41
be ye stedfast, u.   1 Cor 15:58

unoccupied

Shamgar, highways were u. Judg 5:6

unperfect

substance, yet being u.   Ps 139:16

unprepared

with me, and find you u. 2 Cor 9:4

unprofitable

reason with u. talk?   Job 15:3
cast the u. servant into. Mat 25:30
We are u. servants.   Luke 17:10
altogether become u.   Rom 3:12
genealogies, for they are u. Tit 3:9
time past was to thee u. Philem 11
for that is u. for you.   Heb 13:17

unprofitableness

weakness and u. thereof. Heb 7:18

unpunished

wicked shall not be u.   Pr 11:21
the proud shall not be u.   16:5
at calamities, shall not be u.   17:5
false witness shall not be u. 19:5, 9
utterly u.? ye shall not be u. Jer 25:29
not leave thee altogether u.   30:11
not leave thee wholly u.   46:28
go u.? thou shalt not go u.   49:12

unquenchable

garner, but burn up the chaff with u.
fire.   Mat 3:12; Luke 3:17

unreasonable

it seemeth to me u. to send a.
  Acts 25:27
delivered from u. men. 2 Thes 3:2

unrebukeable

this commandment u. 1 Tim 6:14*

unreproveable

to present you holy, u. in. Col 1:22

unrighteous
hand to be an u. witness. Ex 23:1
against me, be as the u. Job 27:7
out of the hand of the u. Ps 71:4
woe unto them that decree u.
　Isa 10:1
let the u. man forsake his. 55:7
not been faithful in the u. Luke 16:11
is God u. who taketh ? Rom 3:5
the u. shall not inherit. 1 Cor 6:9
for God is not u. to forget. Heb 6:10

unrighteously
all that do u. are an. Deut 25:16

unrighteousness
ye shall do no u. in judgement.
　Lev 19:15, 35
there is no u. in him. Ps 92:15
buildeth his house by u. Jer 22:13
the mammon of u. Luke 16:9
and no u. is in him. John 7:18
all u. of men who hold the truth in u.
　Rom 1:18
filled with all u., fornication. 29
them that obey u., indignation. 2:8
if our u. commend the. 3:5
members as instruments of u. 6:13
is there u. with God ? 9:14
righteousness with u.? 2 Cor 6:14
deceiveableness of u. 2 Thes 2:10
not, but had pleasure in u. 12
be merciful to their u. Heb 8:12*
receive the reward of u. 2 Pet 2:13*
who loved the wages of u. 15*
to cleanse us from all u. 1 John 1:9
all u. is sin: there is a sin not. 5:17

unripe
shake off his u. grape. Job 15:33

unruly
warn them that are u. 1 Thes 5:14
not accused of riot, or u. Tit 1:6
for there are many u. and vain. 10
the tongue is an u. evil. Jas 3:8*

unsatiable
because thou wast u. Ezek 16:28

unsavoury
can what is u. be eaten ? Job 6:6

unsearchable
great things and u. Job 5:9
Lord, his greatness is u. Ps 145:3
heart of kings is u. Pr 25:3
how u. are his judgements, and his
ways! Rom 11:33
the u. riches of Christ. Eph 3:8

unseemly
working that which is u. Rom 1:27
not behave itself u. 1 Cor 13:5

unshod
thy foot from being u. Jer 2:25

unskilful
babe is u. in the word. Heb 5:13*

unspeakable
be to God for his u. gift. 2 Cor 9:15
paradise and heard u. words. 12:4
in whom ye rejoice with joy u. and
full of glory. 1 Pet 1:8

unspotted
to keep himself u. from. Jas 1:27

unstable
u. as water, thou shalt. Gen 49:4†
a double minded man is u. in all.
　Jas 1:8
from sin, beguiling u. 2 Pet 2:14
are unlearned and u. wrest. 3:16

unstopped
ears of the deaf shall be u. Isa 35:5

untaken
the same vail u. away. 2 Cor 3:14

untempered
and lo others daubed it with u.
　Ezek 13:10, 11, 14, 15; 22:28

unthankful
for he is kind to the u. Luke 6:35
blasphemers, u., unholy. 2 Tim 3:2

until
u. I have done that I. Gen 28:15
and stayed there u. now. 32:4
our youth, even u. now. 46:34
nor a lawgiver depart, u. 49:10
this people u. now. Num 14:19

to Dan u. the captivity. Judg 18:30
will not eat u. he come. 1 Sam 9:13
to see Saul u. his death. 15:35
from thy youth u. now. 2 Sam 19:7
nor trimmed, u. the day he. 24
with bread and water of affliction, u.
I come. 1 Ki 22:27; 2 Chr 18:26
she left the land, u. now. 2 Ki 8:6
city be not built, u. Ezra 4:21
since then u. now hath it. 5:16
u. the fierce wrath of God. 10:14
keep me secret u. thy. Job 14:13
u. his iniquity be found. Ps 36:2
u. I went into the sanctuary. 73:17
u. I find a place for the Lord. 132:5
u. the day break. S of S 2:17; 4:6
u. the spirit be poured. Isa 32:15
u. I come and take you away. 36:17
u. the righteousness thereof. 62:1
and there shall he be u. Jer 32:5
be consumed u. there be an. 44:27
overturn, u. he come. Ezek 21:27
bear indignation, u. he. Mi 7:9
be thou there u. I bring. Mat 2:13
the prophets and the law prophesied
u. John. 11:13; Luke 16:16
trodden down u. the times of the
Gentiles. Luke 21:24; Rom 11:25
u. ye be endued with power from on
high. Luke 24:49
u. the day in which he. Acts 1:2
for u. the law, sin was. Rom 5:13
judge nothing u. the. 1 Cor 4:5
will perform it u. the day of Jesus
Christ. Phil 1:6
will let, u. he be taken out. 2 Thes 2:7
u. the appearing of our Lord Jesus.
　1 Tim 6:14
u. the words of God. Rev 17:17
lived not u. the 1000 years. 20:5

untimely
or as an hidden u. birth. Job 3:16
pass away like the u. birth. Ps 58:8
I say that an u. birth is. Eccl 6:3
fig tree casteth her u. figs. Rev 6:13

untoward
save yourselves from this u.
　Acts 2:40*

unwalled
took sixty cities, beside u. towns.
　Deut 3:5
dwelt in the u. towns. Esth 9:19
land of u. villages. Ezek 38:11

unwashen
but to eat with u. hands defileth not.
　Mat 15:20; Mark 7:2, 5*

unweighed
left all the vessels u. 1 Ki 7:47

unwise
do you thus requite the Lord, O u.
people ? Deut 32:6
he is an u. son, he should not stay.
　Hos 13:13
to the wise and to the u. Rom 1:14*
not u. but understanding. Eph 5:17*

unwittingly
if a man eat of the holy thing u.
　Lev 22:14
killeth any person u. Josh 20:3*, 5*

unworthily
this cup of the Lord u. 1 Cor 11:27
and drinketh u. eateth. 29

unworthy
ourselves u. of life. Acts 13:46
are ye u. to judge the ? 1 Cor 6:2

up ! exclamation
Lot said, U., get you out. Gen 19:14
Joseph said, U. follow after. 44:4
u. make us gods that. Ex 32:1
u. sanctify the people. Josh 7:13
u. for this is the day in. Judg 4:14
he said to his firstborn, U., slay. 8:20
u. thou and the people that. 9:32
u. and let us be going, but. 19:28
saying, U. that I may. 1 Sam 9:26

up
rose u. early and gat them u. saying,
We . . . will go u. Num 14:40
go not u. for the Lord is not. 42
they presumed to go u. unto. 44
from battle before sun u. Judg 8:13

as soon as sun is u. thou. Judg 9:33
as soon as ye be u. early, depart.
　1 Sam 29:10
when David was u. 2 Sam 24:11
to die from my youth u. Ps 88:15
from the ground u. to. Ezek 41:16
when the sun was u. they were.
　Mat 13:6; Mark 4:6
kept from my youth u. Mat 19:20
　Luke 18:21
and they filled them u. John 2:7
　see down

upbraid
with whom ye did u. me. Judg 8:15*
then began he to u. the. Mat 11:20

upbraided
he u. them with their. Mark 16:14

upbraideth
all men liberally and u. not. Jas 1:5

Upharsin
MENE, MENE, TEKEL, U.
　Dan 5:25

Uphaz
gold is brought from U. Jer 10:9
girded with gold of U. Dan 10:5

upheld
salvation and my fury it u. me.
　Isa 63:5

uphold
and u. me with thy free. Ps 51:12
the Lord is with them that u. 54:4
u. me according to thy word. 119:116
honour shall u. the humble in spirit.
　Pr 29:23*
I will u. thee with the right hand.
　Isa 41:10
behold my servant whom I u. 42:1
that there was none to u. 63:5
they also that u. Egypt. Ezek 30:6

upholden
thy words have u. him. Job 4:4
the king's throne is u. Pr 20:28

upholdest
as for me, thou u. me in mine.
　Ps 41:12

upholdeth
but the Lord u. the. Ps 37:17
for the Lord u. him with his. 24
thy right hand u. me. 63:8
the Lord u. all that fall. 145:14

upholding
u. all things by the word. Heb 1:3

upper
shall strike blood on the u. Ex 12:7*
covering on his u. lip. Lev 13:45
no man take the u. millstone to.
　Deut 24:6
he gave her the u. springs.
　Josh 15:19; Judg 1:15
they stood by the conduit of the u.
pool. 2 Ki 18:17; Isa 7:3; 36:2
shall lodge in u. lintels. Zeph 2:14*
he will shew you a large u. room.
　Mark 14:15; Luke 22:12
up into an u. room. Acts 1:13
passed through the u. coasts. 19:1
　see chamber

uppermost
in the u. basket were all. Gen 40:17
in the top of the u. bough. Isa 17:6
cities shall be as an u. branch. 9
they love the u. rooms at. Mat 23:6*
　Mark 12:39*; Luke 11:43*

upright
my sheaf arose and also stood u.
　Gen 37:7
yoke and made you go u. Lev 26:13
Surely as Lord liveth, thou hast been
u. 1 Sam 29:6; 2 Chr 29:34
I was also u. before him.
　2 Sam 22:24*; Ps 18:23*
with the u. man thou wilt shew thyself u. 2 Sam 22:26*; Ps 18:25*
were more u. in heart. 2 Chr 29:34
Job was a perfect and u. man.
　Job 1:1, 8; 2:3
if thou wert u. he would awake. 8:6
the just u. man is laughed. 12:4*
u. men shall be astonished. 17:8

doth behold the *u*.   *Ps* 11:7
then shall I be *u*., I shall be. 19:13
the Lord is good and *u*. 25:8; 92:15
praise is comely for the *u*.   33:1
to slay such as be of *u*.   37:14
knoweth the days of the *u*.   18
perfect man and behold the *u*.   37
the *u*. shall have dominion.   49:14
Lord in the assembly of the *u*. 111:1
the generation of the *u*.   112:2
unto the *u*. there ariseth light.   4
righteous art thou, and *u*. are. 119:137
do good to them that are *u*. 125:4
the *u*. shall dwell in thy.   140:13
for the *u*. shall dwell in. *Pr* 2:21
of Lord is strength to the *u*. 10:29
integrity of the *u*. shall guide. 11:3
the righteousness of the *u*. shall. 6
by the blessings of the *u*. the city. 11
such as are *u*. in their way are. 20*
mouth of the *u*. shall deliver. 12:6
righteousness keepeth the *u*. 13:6
the tabernacle of the *u*. shall. 14:11
but the prayer of the *u*. is his. 15:8
highway of the *u*. is to depart. 16:17
shall be a ransom for the *u*. 21:18
but as for the *u*. he directeth. 29
the *u*. shall have good things. 28:10*
the bloodthirsty hate the *u*. 29:10*
he that is *u*. is an abomination to. 27
God hath made man *u*. *Eccl* 7:29
was written in *u*. words. 12:10*
remember thy love, the *u*. love.
    S of S 1:4*
thou most *u*. dost weigh. *Isa* 26:7
they are *u*. as palm tree. *Jer* 10:5
touched me and set me *u*. *Dan* 8:18
enter and *u*. ones with him. 11:17
is none *u*. among men. *Mi* 7:2
the most *u*. is sharper than a. 4
soul lifted up is not *u*. *Hab* 2:4
see **heart, stand, stood**

uprightly
walketh *u*. shall abide in. *Ps* 15:2
do ye judge *u*.?   58:1
I will judge *u*.   75:2
from them that walk *u*. 84:11
buckler to them that walk *u*. *Pr* 2:7*
he that walketh *u*. walketh. 10:9
of understanding walketh *u*. 15:21
walketh *u*. shall be saved. 28:18
he that speaketh *u*. shall. *Isa* 33:15
him that speaketh *u*. *Amos* 5:10
my words do good to him that
    walketh *u*.   *Mi* 2:7
that they walked not *u*. *Gal* 2:14

uprightness
before thee in *u*. of heart. *1 Ki* 3:6
thou hast pleasure in *u*. *1 Chr* 29:17
is not this thy hope and the *u*. of thy
    ways ?   *Job* 4:6*
to shew unto man his *u*.   33:23*
minister judgement to the people in
    u.   *Ps* 9:8
let integrity and *u*. preserve. 25:21
for ever and are done in *u*. 111:8
lead me into the land of *u*. 143:10
paths of *u*. to walk. *Pr* 2:13
he that walketh in *u*. feareth. 14:2
poor that walketh in his *u*. 28:6*
the way of the just is *u*. *Isa* 26:7
in the land of *u*. will he deal. 10
each one walking in his *u*. 57:2
see **heart**

uprising
my downsitting and *u*. *Ps* 139:2

uproar
city being in an *u*. *1 Ki* 1:41
lest there be an *u*. *Mat* 26:5
    Mark 14:2
all the city on an *u*. *Acts* 17:5
in question for this day's *u*. 19:40*
after the *u*. was ceased, Paul. 20:1
that all Jerusalem was in an *u*. 21:31
Egyptian who madest an *u*.? 38

upside *down*
Jerusalem as a man wipeth a dish,
    turning it *u. down*. *2 Ki* 21:13
wicked he turneth *u. down*. *Ps* 146:9
turneth the earth *u. down*. *Isa* 24:1
turning of things *u. down*. 29:16
have turned the world *u. down*.
    Acts 17:6

upward
twenty years old and *u*. *Ex* 38:26
Num 1:3, 20, 22, 24, 26, 28; 14:29
1 Chr 23:24; *2 Chr* 31:17; *Ezra* 3:8
shalt number every male from a
    month old and *u*. *Num* 3:15, 22
    28, 34, 39, 40, 43; 26:62
u. even to fifty. 4:3, 23, 30, 35
    39, 43, 47; *1 Chr* 23:3
five years old and *u*. *Num* 8:24
Saul was higher from shoulders *u*.
    1 Sam 9:2; 10:23
remnant shall bear fruit *u*.
    2 Ki 19:30; *Isa* 37:31
males from three years old and *u*.
    2 Chr 31:16
to trouble as sparks fly *u*. *Job* 5:7
spirit of man that goeth *u*. *Eccl* 3:21
king and God, and look *u*. *Isa* 8:21
mine eyes fail with looking *u*. 38:14
from appearance of his loins *u*.
    Ezek 1:27; 8:2
was a winding about still *u*. 41:7*
from this day and *u*. *Hag* 2:15, 18

Ur
before his father in *U*. *Gen* 11:28
brought thee out of *U*. of the Chal-
    dees. 15:7; *Neh* 9:7
Eliphal the son of *U*. *1 Chr* 11:35

urge
scribes and pharisees began to *u*.
    Luke 11:53*

urged
Jacob *u*. Esau, and he. *Gen* 33:11
Delilah *u*. Samson. *Judg* 16:16
his father in law *u*. him. 19:7
when they *u*. him till. *2 Ki* 2:17
Naaman *u*. Elisha. 5:16
he *u*. Gehazi. 23

urgent
the Egyptians were *u*. *Ex* 12:33
king's commandment was *u*.
    Dan 3:22

Uri
Bezaleel the son of *U*. *Ex* 31:2
    35:30; 38:22; *1 Chr* 2:20
    2 Chr 1:5
Geber the son of *U*. *1 Ki* 4:19
Shallum, Telem, and *U*. *Ezra* 10:24

Uriah, *called* **Urijah**
is not this Bath-sheba the wife of *U*.?
    2 Sam 11:3
send me *U*. 6
sent it by *U*. 14
U. is dead. 17
thou hast killed *U*. the Hittite. 12:9
U. one of David's worthies.
    1 Chr 11:41
in the matter of *U*. *1 Ki* 15:5
by Meremoth son of *U*. *Ezra* 8:33
next repaired Meremoth son of
    U. *Neh* 3:4, 21
Ezra and beside him stood *U*. 8:4
I took faithful witnesses, *U*. *Isa* 8:2
Solomon of the wife of *U*. *Mat* 1:6

Urijah
Ahaz sent *U*. the fashion. *2 Ki* 16:10
thus did *U*. as king Ahaz. 16
U. prophesied. *Jer* 26:20
U. fled into Egypt. 21

Urim
breastplate of judgement, the *U*.
    Ex 28:30; *Lev* 8:8
counsel after the judgement of *U*.
    Num 27:21
let thy *U*. be with thy. *Deut* 33:8
neither by dreams, by *U*. *1 Sam* 28:6
stood up a priest with *U*. and.
    Ezra 2:63; *Neh* 7:65
see **Thummim**

us
with *u*. even *u*. who are all of *u*.
    Deut 5:3
save thyself and *u*. *Luke* 23:39
even *u*. whom he hath. *Rom* 9:24
God hath set forth *u*. *1 Cor* 4:9
and will also raise up *u*. by. 6:14
acknowledged *u*. in part. *2 Cor* 1:14
he which establisheth *u*. with. 21
who hath reconciled *u*. to. 5:18
brethren, as ye have *u*. *Phil* 3:17
let *u*. who are of the. *1 Thes* 5:8

for God hath not appointed *u*.
    1 Thes 5:9
of his own will begat he *u*. *Jas* 1:18
about **us**
lick up all that are round *about u*.
    Num 22:4
heathen that are *about u*. *Neh* 5:17
the heathen *about u*. saw. 6:16
a reproach to all *about u*. *Dan* 9:16
after **us**
will come out *after u*. *Josh* 8:6
to our generations *after u*. 22:27
away, for she crieth *after u*.
    Mat 15:23
against **us**
seek occasion *against u*. *Gen* 43:18
enemies and fight *against u*. *Ex* 1:10
that ye murmur *against u*.? 16:7
are not *against u*. but God. 8
Sihon came out *against u*.
    Deut 2:32; 29:7
Og came out *against u*. 3:1
of Ai came out *against u*. *Josh* 8:5
Amorites gathered *against u*. 10:6
rebel not against the Lord, nor
    against u. 22:19
ye come up *against u*.? *Judg* 15:10
delivered company that came *against*
    u. *1 Sam* 30:23
surely the men prevailed *against u*.
    2 Sam 11:23
man that devised *against u*. 21:5
wrath of Lord *against u*. *2 Ki* 22:13
great company that cometh *against*
    u. *2 Chr* 20:12
under that rise *against u*. *Ps* 44:5
remember not *against u*. 79:8
when men rose up *against u*. 124:2
wrath was kindled *against u*. 3
feller is come up *against u*. *Isa* 14:8
and our sins testify *against u*.
    59:12; *Jer* 14:7
all this evil *against u*. *Jer* 16:10
maketh war *against u*. 21:2
shall come down *against u*.? 13
setteth thee on *against u*. 43:3
their mouth *against u*. *Lam* 3:46
art very wroth *against u*. 5:22
words he spake *against u*. *Dan* 9:12
Forbid him not. For he that is not
    against u. *Mark* 9:40; *Luke* 9:50
who can be *against u*.? *Rom* 8:31
blotting out the handwriting that was
    against u. *Col* 2:14
prating *against u*. with. *3 John* 10
among or *amongst* **us**
mighty prince *among u*. *Gen* 23:6
the Lord *among u*. or not ? *Ex* 17:7
I pray thee, go *among u*. 34:9
God is not *among u*. *Deut* 31:17
ye dwell *among u*. *Josh* 9:7, 22
take possession *among u*. 22:19
perceive the Lord is *among u*. 31
voice be heard *among u*. *Judg* 18:25
among u. it may save us. *1 Sam* 4:3
not *among u*. any that can skill to
    hew. *1 Ki* 5:6
his hands *amongst u*. *Job* 34:37
not *among u*. any that knoweth.
    Ps 74:9
cast in thy lot *among u*. *Pr* 1:14
who *among u*. shall dwell with the
    devouring fire ? *Isa* 33:14
Is not the Lord *among u*.? *Mi* 3:11
a great prophet is risen up *among u*.
    Luke 7:16
Word was made flesh and dwelt
    among u. *John* 1:14
Lord Jesus went in and out *among u*.
    Acts 1:21
God made choice *among u*. 15:7
at **us**
if it first begin *at u*. *1 Pet* 4:17
before **us**
make us gods which shall go *before*
    u. *Ex* 32:23; *Acts* 7:40
will send men *before u*. *Deut* 1:22
God delivered *before u*. 2:33
dried up from *before u*. *Josh* 4:23
they flee *before u*. 8:6
drave out *before u*. 24:18
the Lord shall **drive out** *before u*.
    Judg 11:24

down *before u.* as.   *Judg* 20:32, 39
king may judge us and go out *before*
u.   *1 Sam* 8:20
thy servant pass on *before u.*   9:27
land is yet *before u.*   *2 Chr* 14:7
cause the Holy One of Israel to cease
from *before u.*   *Isa* 30:11
laws which he set *before u. Dan* 9:10
to lay hold on the hope set *before u.*
                    Heb 6:18
the race that is set *before u.*   12:1

behind us
also he is *behind u.   Gen* 32:18, 20

between or *betwixt* us
now an oath *betwixt u.   Gen* 26:28
may judge *betwixt u.* both.   31:27
God of Abraham judge *betwixt u.* 53
Jordan a border *between u.*
                    Josh 22:25
be a witness *between u.*   27, 28, 34
the Lord be witness *between u.*
                    Judg 11:10; *Jer* 42:5
neither is there any daysman *betwixt*
u.   *Job* 9:33
between u. and you.   *Luke* 16:26
put no difference *between u.* and.
                    Acts 15:9
the middle wall of partition *between*
u.   *Eph* 2:14

by us
hath not the Lord spoken also *by u.?*
                    Num 12:2
man of God passeth *by u. 2 Ki* 4:9
Jesus was preached among you *by u.*
                    2 Cor 1:19
to the glory of God *by u.*   20
savour of his knowledge *by u.* 2:14
of Christ, ministered *by u.*   3:3
God did beseech you *by u.*   5:20
ye might receive damage *by u.* 7:9
which is administered *by u.* 8:19, 20

concerning us
do according to all which is written
concerning u.   2 Ki 22:13

for us
hath made room *for u. Gen* 26:22
yet any inheritance *for u.?*   31:14
better *for u.* to serve.   *Ex* 14:12
tarry ye here *for u.* until.   24:14
better *for u.* to return.   *Num* 14:3
people, for they are bread *for u.*   9
one city too strong *for u. Deut* 2:36
say, Who shall go up *for u.?* 30:12
Who shall go over the sea *for u.?* 13
art thou *for u.* or for our ? *Josh* 5:13
of Peor too little *for u.?*   22:17
who go up *for u.* against ? *Judg* 1:1
cry unto the Lord *for u.   1 Sam* 7:8
lest father take thought *for u.*   9:5
the Lord will work *for u.*   14:6
they will not care *for u.   2 Sam* 18:3
neither *for u.* shalt thou kill.   21:4
hast been careful *for u.   2 Ki* 4:13
we dwell is too strait *for u.*   6:1
as *for u.* the Lord is.   *2 Chr* 13:10
him a right way *for u.   Ezra* 8:21
our God shall fight *for u.   Neh* 4:20
he shall choose our inheritance *for u.*
                    Ps 47:4
God is a refuge *for u.*   62:8
that thou hast wrought *for u.* 68:28
hath done great things *for u.* 126:3
send, and who will go *for u.? Isa* 6:8
thou wilt ordain peace *for u.* 26:12
take up a wailing *for u.   Jer* 9:18
there is no healing *for u.*   14:19
I pray thee, of the Lord *for u.* 21:2
pray to the Lord our God *for u.* 37:3
                    42:2, 20
as *for u.* our eyes as.   *Lam* 4:17
Lord, it is good *for u.* to be here.
          Mat 17:4; *Mark* 9:5; *Luke* 9:33
there be not enough *for u. Mark* 6:36
there make ready *for u. Mark* 14:15
hast raised up an horn of salvation
for u.   *Luke* 1:69
is not against us is *for u.*   9:50
for u. to whom it shall.   *Rom* 4:24
sinners, Christ died *for u.*   5:8
maketh intercession *for u.*   8:26
if God be *for u.* who can be ?   31
but delivered him up *for u.* all.   32
maketh intercession *for u.*   34

Christ is sacrificed *for u.   1 Cor* 5:7
together by prayer *for u.   2 Cor* 1:11
light affliction worketh *for u.*   4:17
made him to be sin *for u.*   5:21
us, made a curse *for u.   Gal* 3:13
us, and given himself *for u. Eph* 5:2
praying *for u.* that God.   *Col* 4:3
who died *for u.*, that we should live.
          1 Thes 5:10; *1 John* 3:16
pray *for u. 1 Thes* 5:25; *2 Thes* 3:1
                    Heb 13:18
who gave himself *for u.*   *Tit* 2:14
the forerunner is *for u.* entered.
                    Heb 6:20
eternal redemption *for u.*   9:12
in the presence of God *for u.*   24
he hath consecrated *for u.*   10:20
provided some better thing *for u.*
                    11:40
because Christ hath suffered *for u.*
                    1 Pet 2:21; 4:1

from us
said to Isaac, Go *from u. Gen* 26:16
shall he go up *from u.? 1 Sam* 6:20
and see who is gone *from u.*   14:17
his wrath turn *from u.   2 Chr* 29:10
                    Ezra 10:14
away their cords *from u.   Ps* 2:3
our transgressions *from u.* 103:12
judgement far *from u.   Isa* 59:9
salvation but it is far off *from u.* 11
hast hid thy face *from u.*   64:7
the anger of the Lord is not turned
from u.   *Jer* 4:8
Nebuchadrezzar may go up *from u.*
                    21:2
hide it not *from u.*, we will not. 38:25
he was taken up *from u.   Acts* 1:22
certain who went out *from u.* 15:24
nor by letter as *from u. 2 Thes* 2:2
they went out *from u.*, but they were
not of us.   *1 John* 2:19

see depart

in us
if the Lord delight *in u.   Num* 14:8
thou, which is not *in u.   Job* 15:9
thou hast wrought all our works *in u.*
                    Isa 26:12
also may be one *in u.   John* 17:21
law might be fulfilled *in u. Rom* 8:4
which shall be revealed *in u.*   18
ye might learn *in u.* not. *1 Cor* 4:6
of Christ abound *in u.   2 Cor* 1:5
so death worketh *in u.* but.   4:12
ye are not straitened *in u.* but. 6:12
power that worketh *in u. Eph* 3:20
by Holy Ghost which dwelleth *in u.*
                    2 Tim 1:14
that dwelleth *in u.* lusteth. *Jas* 4:5
truth is not *in u.   1 John* 1:8
his word is not *in u.*   10
we know that he abideth *in u.* 3:24
God dwelleth *in u.*   4:12, 13
for the truth's sake which dwelleth *in*
u.   *2 John* 2

of us
the man is become as one *of u.*
                    Gen 3:22
lacketh not a man *of u. Num* 31:49
faint because *of u.*   *Josh* 2:24
which slew many *of u. Judg* 16:24
which *of u.* shall go up first ? 20:18
which *of u.* is for the king of Israel ?
                    2 Ki 6:11
he was entreated *of u. Ezra* 8:23
hath been mindful *of u. Ps* 115:12
laid on him the iniquity *of u.* all.
                    Isa 53:6
Abraham be ignorant *of u.*   63:16
hath taken hold *of u.   Jer* 6:24
O Lord, art in the midst *of u.* 14:9
he be not far from every one *of u.*
                    Acts 17:27
who is the father *of u.* all. *Rom* 4:16
account *of u.* as ministers. *1 Cor* 4:1
advantage *of u.* for we.   *2 Cor* 2:11
be of God and not *of u.*   4:7
some who think *of u.* as if we. 10:2
is the mother *of u.* all.   *Gal* 4:26
but to every one *of u.* is.   *Eph* 4:7
became followers *of u. 1 Thes* 1:6
they themselves shew *of u.* what.   9
the word which ye heard *of u.* 2:13

remembrance *of u.* always.*1 Thes* 3:6
that as ye have received *of u.*   4:1
tradition he received *of u. 2 Thes* 3:6
the commandment *of u.*   *2 Pet* 3:2
of u., for if they had been *of u.* they
might shew . . . *of u. 1 John* 2:19

on us, or *upon* us
brought guiltiness *upon u. Gen* 26:10
this distress come *upon u.*   42:21
fall *upon u.* and take us for.   43:18
upon u. with pestilence.   *Ex* 5:3
lay not the sin *upon u.   Num* 12:11
evils come *upon u.?   Deut* 31:17
lest wrath be *upon u.*   *Josh* 9:20
Rise thou and fall *upon u. Judg* 8:21
his hand is sore *upon u.   1 Sam* 5:7
heavy yoke which he put *upon u.*
          1 Ki 12:4, 9; *2 Chr* 10:4, 9
some mischief will come *upon u.*
                    2 Ki 7:9
made a breach *upon u. 1 Chr* 15:13
cometh *upon u.* as sword. *2 Chr* 20:9
the wrath poured *upon u.*   34:21
by the good hand of our God *upon u.*
                    Ezra 8:18, 31
after all that is come *upon u.*   9:13
let not all the trouble seem little that
hath come *upon u.*   *Neh* 9:32
all that is brought *upon u.*   33
bring all this evil *upon u.?*   13:18
his hand *upon u.* both.   *Job* 9:33
thy countenance *upon u.*   *Ps* 4:6
mercy, O Lord, be *upon u.*   33:22
all this is come *upon u.*; yet. 44:17
cause his face to shine *upon u.* 67:1
beauty of the Lord be *upon u.* 90:17
till he have mercy *upon u.*   123:2
upon u. O Lord, have mercy *upon u.*3
          Mat 9:27; 20:30, 31; *Luke* 17:13
Spirit be poured *upon u. Isa* 32:15
snare is come *upon u.*   *Lam* 3:47
O Lord, what is come *upon u.*   5:1
and sins be *upon u.   Ezek* 33:10
curse is poured *upon u.   Dan* 9:11
by bringing *upon u.* a great evil.
                    12, 13, 14
and to the hills, Fall *on u. Hos* 10:8
                    Luke 23:30; *Rev* 6:16
cause this evil is *on u. Jonah* 1:7, 8
None evil can come *upon u. Mi* 3:11
have compassion *upon u.*   7:19
his blood be *on u.* and.   *Mat* 27:25
Peter, said, Look *on u.*   *Acts* 3:4
so earnestly *on u.* as though ?   12
bring this man's blood *upon u.* 5:28
Holy Ghost on them, as *on u.* 11:15
Mary, who bestowed much labour *on*
u.   *Rom* 16:6
shed *on u.* abundantly.   *Tit* 3:6
love the Father hath bestowed *on u.*
                    1 John 3:1

over us
indeed reign *over u.?   Gen* 37:8
who made thee a prince and a judge
over u.?   Ex 2:14; *Acts* 7:27
thyself a prince *over u. Num* 16:13
Gideon, Rule *over u.*   *Judg* 8:22
to the olive tree, Reign *over u.*   9:8
                    10, 12, 14
but we will have a king *over u.*
                    1 Sam 8:19; 10:19
Shall Saul reign *over u.?*   11:12
Saul was king *over u.   2 Sam* 5:2
whom we anointed *over u.*   19:10
thou hast set *over u.*   *Neh* 9:37
own: who is lord *over u.?   Ps* 12:4
had dominion *over u.   Isa* 26:13
servants have ruled *over u.*: there is
none.   *Lam* 5:8
this man to reign *over u. Luke* 19:14

through us
through u. thanksgiving to God.
                    2 Cor 9:11

to or *unto* us
a man to come in *unto u. Gen* 19:31
hast thou done *unto u.?* 20:9; 26:10
their daughters *to u.* for wives. 34:21
Hebrew *unto u.* to mock us.   39:14
What is this that God hath done *unto*
u.?   42:28; *Jer* 5:19
thou mayest be *to u.   Num* 10:31
Lord shall do *unto u.*, the same.   32
speak thou *unto u.* and.   *Deut* 5:27

revealed belong unto u. Deut 29:29
heaven and bring it unto u. 30:12
the sea and bring it unto u. 13
seemeth good and right to thee to do
  unto u. Josh 9:25; Judg 10:15
of God come again unto u. Judg 13:8
to him, as he hath done to u. 15:10
with us, and be to u. a father. 18:19
woe unto u. 1 Sam 4:8; Jer 4:13
  6:4; Lam 5:16
if they say thus unto u. 1 Sam 14:9
were very good unto u. 25:15
they were a wall unto u. by. 16
the ark of God to u. 1 Chr 13:3
came from thee to u. Ezra 4:12
brethren be sold unto u.? Neh 5:8
let us choose to u. judgement.
  Job 34:4
O turn thyself to u. again. Ps 60:1
not unto u. O Lord, not unto u. 115:1
except had left unto u. a. Isa 1:9
unto u. a child is born, unto u. 9:6
Art thou become like unto u.? 14:10
shall not come unto u. 28:15
prophesy not unto u. right things,
  speak unto u. smooth. 30:10
Lord will be unto u. a place. 33:21
speak not to u. in the Jews'. 36:11
to u. the appointed weeks. Jer 5:24
hath spoken to u. in the name. 26:16
the Lord shall send thee to u. 42:5
thou hast spoken unto u. 44:16
our wood is sold unto u. Lam 5:4
unto u. is this land given. Ezek 11:15
what these things are to u.? 24:19
but unto u. confusion. Dan 9:7, 8
he shall come unto u. Hos 6:3
what should a king do to u.? 10:3
may be calm unto u. Jonah 1:11
Lord thought to do unto u. Zech 1:6
made them equal unto u. Mat 20:12
saying, Lord, Lord, open to u. 25:11
  Luke 13:25
what is that to u.? see. Mat 27:4
delivered them unto u. Luke 1:2
hath made known unto u. 2:15
devils are subject unto u. 10:17
this parable unto u.? 12:41
neither can they pass to u. 16:26
shewest thou unto u.? John 2:18
manifest thyself unto u.? 14:22
that he sayeth unto u.? 16:17
oracles to give unto u. Acts 7:38
to u. who did eat and drink. 10:41
the like after as unto u. 11:17
fulfilled the same unto u. 13:33
Holy Ghost which is given unto u.
  Rom 5:5
but unto u. it is the power. 1 Cor 1:18
of God is made unto u. wisdom. 30
God revealed them unto u. 2:10
but to u. there is but one God. 8:6
committed to u. word of. 2 Cor 5:19
gave themselves unto u. by. 8:5
as ye abound in your love to u. 7
who declared unto u. Col 1:8
that God would open unto u. 4:3
for unto u. was the gospel. Heb 4:2
unto u. they did minister. 1 Pet 1:12

toward us
thine anger toward u. to cease.
  Ps 85:4
kindness is great toward u. 117:2
his love toward u. Rom 5:8
hath abounded toward u. Eph 1:8
in his kindness toward u. 2:7
love of God toward u. 1 John 4:9

under us
subdue the people under u. Ps 47:3

with us
no man is with u. Gen 31:50
make ye marriages with u. 34:9
ye shall dwell with u. 10
they dwell with u. 23
send our brother with u. 43:4; 44:26
lad is not with u. 44:30, 31
the God of the Hebrews with u.
  Ex 3:18; 5:3
hast thou dealt thus with u.? 14:11
speak thou with u.: but let not God
  speak with u. 20:19
not in that thou goest with u.? 33:16
come thou with u., we. Num 10:29

it shall be, if thou go with u.
  Num 10:32
was well with u. in Egypt. 11:18
and the Lord is with u. 14:9
refuseth to come with u. 22:14
made a covenant with u. Deut 5:2, 3
standeth here with u., also with him
  that is not here with u. 29:15
make a league with u. Josh 9:6, 11
if the Lord be with u. Judg 6:13
thou mayest go with u. 11:8
Hold thy peace and go with u. 18:19
the ark of God shall not abide with
  u. 1 Sam 5:7
Amnon go with u. 2 Sam 13:26
no more out with u. to battle. 21:17
stranger with u. in house. 1 Ki 3:18
the Lord our God be with u. 8:57
be with u. are more than they that.
  2 Ki 6:16; 2 Chr 32:7
God is with u. 2 Chr 13:12; 32:8
you have nothing to do with u. to
  build. Ezra 4:3
be angry with u. till thou? 9:14
with u. are the gray-headed and.
  Job 15:10
Lord of hosts is with us. Ps 46:7, 11
wilt thou be angry with u. for? 85:5
he hath not dealt with u. 103:10
come with u. Pr 1:11
God is with u. Isa 8:10
transgressions are with u. 59:12
law of the Lord is with u. Jer 8:8
break not thy covenant with u. 14:21
that it may be well with u. 42:6
Bethel, there he spake with u.
  Hos 12:4
so hath he dealt with u. Zech 1:6
interpreted, is, God with u. Mat 1:23
his sisters are all with u. 13:56
  Mark 6:3
there were with u. seven. Mat 22:25
thou thus dealt with u.? Luke 2:48
he followeth not with u. 9:49
abide with u. 24:29
while he talked with u. 32
numbered with u. and had. Acts 1:17
his sepulchre is with u. unto. 2:29
one that helpeth with u. 1 Cor 16:16
chosen to travel with u. 2 Cor 8:19
are troubled, rest with u. 2 Thes 1:7
like precious faith with u. 2 Pet 1:1
have fellowship with u. 1 John 1:3
have continued with u. 2:19
the truth shall be with u. 2 John 2

within us
our hearts burn within u. while he
  opened to us the? Luke 24:32

without us
reigned as kings without u. 1 Cor 4:8
that they without u. should not be
  made perfect. Heb 11:40

use
be used in any other u. Lev 7:24
aught for any unclean u. Deut 26:14
teach Judah the u. of bow.2 Sam 1:18
according to the u. of. 1 Chr 28:15
did change the natural u. Rom 1:26
the men leaving the natural u. 27
which is good to the u. Eph 4:29
shall be a vessel meet for the
  master's u. 2 Tim 2:21
by u. have their senses. Heb 5:14

use, verb
ye u. enchantment. Lev 19:26
u. trumpets for calling. Num 10:2
after which ye u. to go a. 15:39
could u. both right. 1 Chr 12:2
that u. their tongues, and. Jer 23:31
as yet they shall u. this speech. 31:23
in vain shalt thou u. many. 46:11
they shall no more u. it as a proverb.
  Ezek 12:23
shall u. this proverb against. 16:44
what mean ye, that ye u.? 18:2
ye shall not have occasion to u. 3
Babylon stood to u. divination. 21:21
you, pray for them that despitefully
  u. you. Mat 5:44; Luke 6:28
when ye pray, u. not vain. Mat 6:7
an assault made, to u. them despitefully. Acts 14:5
be made free, u. it rather. 1 Cor 7:21

they that u. this world as. 1 Cor 7:31
did I u. lightness? 2 Cor 1:17
we u. great plainness. 3:12
lest being present, I should u. 13:10
u. not liberty for an occasion to the.
  Gal 5:13
the law is good if a man u. 1 Tim 1:8
then let them u. the office of. 3:10
u. a little wine for thy. 5:23
u. hospitality one to another.
  1 Pet 4:9

used
if the ox hath u. to push. Ex 21:36*
the fat may be u. in any. Lev 7:24
for so u. the young. Judg 14:10
whom Samson had u. as his. 20
u. enchantments. 2 Ki 17:17; 21:6
  2 Chr 33:6*
a wild ass u. to the. Jer 2:24
people of land have u. Ezek 22:29
thy envy which thou hast u. 35:11
and u. similitudes by. Hos 12:10
the disciples of John u. Mark 2:18*
man, called Simon, which beforetime
  u. Acts 8:9
them which u. curious arts. 19:19*
tongues they u. deceit. Rom 3:13
not u. this power. 1 Cor 9:12
u. none of these things. 15
nor at any time u. we. 1 Thes 2:5
they that have u. the office of a.
  1 Tim 3:13
of them that were so u. Heb 10:33

uses
to maintain good works for necessary
  u. Tit 3:14

usest
as thou u. to those that. Ps 119:132

useth
any that u. divination. Deut 18:10
apparel which the king u. Esth 6:8
the tongue of the wise u. Pr 15:2*
the poor u. entreaties, but rich. 18:23
u. his neighbour's service. Jer 22:13
u. proverbs, shall use. Ezek 16:44
every one that u. milk. Heb 5:13*

using
to perish with the u. Col 2:22
and not u. your liberty. 1 Pet 2:16

usurer
not be to him as an u. Ex 22:25*

usurp
woman to u. authority. 1 Tim 2:12*

usury
By usury is generally understood
in the Bible any interest on a loan,
whether in money or in wheat or
other commodities. Modern usage
has confined the meaning of the
word to an unlawful interest.
The law of God prohibits rigorous
imposing of interest or exacting it,
or a return of a loan without regard
to the condition of the borrower;
whether poverty occasioned his
borrowing, or a visible prospect of
gain by employing the borrowed
goods.
The Hebrews were plainly commanded in Ex 22:25, etc., not to
receive interest for money from
any that borrowed for necessity, as
in the case in Neh 5:5, 7.
thou lay upon him u. Ex 22:25
take thou no u. of him. Lev 25:36, 37
shalt not lend on u. Deut 23:19
thou mayest lend upon u. 20
ye exact u. Neh 5:7
let us leave off this u. 10
not his money to u. Ps 15:5
he that by u. increaseth. Pr 28:8
as with the taker of u., so with the
  giver of u. Isa 24:2
I have neither lent on u. nor men
  have lent to me on u. Jer 15:10
not given forth on u. Ezek 18:8, 17
given forth on u. 13
thou hast taken u. 22:12
received mine own with u.
  Mat 25:27*; Luke 19:23

us-ward
thy thoughts which are to u. Ps 40:5

the greatness of his power to *u.*
Eph 1:19
but his longsuffering to *u.* *2 Pet* 3:9

utmost, outmost
to the *u.* bound of the. *Gen* 49:26
might see the *u.* of the people.
Num 22:41; 23:13
be driven out to *o.* parts. *Deut* 30:4
Edom and all that are in the *u.*
corners. *Jer* 9:26*; 25:23*; 49:32*
she came from *u.* parts. *Luke* 11:31

utter
if he do not *u.* it, then he. *Lev* 5:1
our life if ye *u.* it not this. *Josh* 2:14
if thou *u.* it, we will quit. 20
awake, Deborah, *u.* song. *Judg* 5:12
shall not they *u.* words ? *Job* 8:10
should a wise man *u.* vain ? 15:2*
nor shall my tongue *u.* deceit. 27:4
lips shall *u.* knowledge. 33:3*
I will *u.* dark sayings. *Ps* 78:2
how long shall they *u.* hard ? 94:4*
who can *u.* the mighty acts ? 106:2
my lips shall *u.* praise. 119:171
they shall *u.* the memory. 145:7
false witness will *u.* lies. *Pr* 14:5
thine heart shall *u.* use. 23:33
of labour, man cannot *u.* it. *Eccl* 1:8
let not thine heart be hasty to *u.* 5:2
a vile person will *u.* error. *Isa* 32:6
tell this, *u.* it even to the end. 48:20
I will *u.* my judgements. *Jer* 1:16
u. his voice from his holy. 25:30
u. a parable unto the. *Ezek* 24:3
the Lord shall *u.* his voice. *Joel* 2:11
u. his voice from Jerusalem. 3:16
Amos 1:2
I will *u.* things kept. *Mat* 13:35
except *u.* words easy to. *1 Cor* 14:9
not lawful for a man to *u.* *2 Cor* 12:4

utter, outer
a man I appointed to *u.* *1 Ki* 20:42
heard to the *o.* court. *Ezek* 10:5
me forth into the *u.* court. 42:1*
he will make an *u.* end of. *Nah* 1:8*
there shall be no more *u.* destruction. *Zech* 14:11*

utterance
as the Spirit gave them *u.* *Acts* 2:4
enriched by him in all *u.* *1 Cor* 1:5
in *u.* and knowledge. *2 Cor* 8:7
that *u.* may be given. *Eph* 6:19
open to us a door of *u.* *Col* 4:3*

uttered
if she had a husband when she *u.*
Num 30:6*, 8*
Jephthah *u.* all his words before
the Lord. *Judg* 11:11*
the most High *u.* his voice.
2 Sam 22:14; *Ps* 46:6
whom hast thou *u.* words ? *Job* 26:4
therefore have I *u.* that I. 42:3
which my lips *u.* when. *Ps* 66:14
deep *u.* his voice and. *Hab* 3:10
groanings which cannot be *u.*
Rom 8:26
to say, and hard to be *u.* *Heb* 5:11*
had cried, seven thunders *u.* their
voices. *Rev* 10:3
when the seven thunders had *u.* 4

uttereth
for thy mouth *u.* thine. *Job* 15:5*
day unto day *u.* speech. *Ps* 19:2
wisdom *u.* her voice in. *Pr* 1:20
in the city she *u.* her words. 21
and he that *u.* a slander is. 10:18
a fool *u.* all his mind, but *u.* 29:11
when he *u.* his voice. *Jer* 10:13
51:16
the great man *u.* his. *Mi* 7:3

uttering
u. from the heart words. *Isa* 59:13

utterly
u. put out remembrance. *Ex* 17:14
if her father *u.* refuse to give. 22:17
thou shalt *u.* overthrow their. 23:24
pronounce him *u.* unclean.*Lev* 13:44
enemies I will not destroy *u.* 26:44
that soul shall *u.* be cast. *Num* 15:31
I will *u.* destroy their cities. 21:2
if her husband hath *u.* made. 30:12

u. destroying men, women. *Deut* 3:6
yourselves, ye shall *u.* perish. 4:26
thou shalt *u.* destroy the Canaanites.
7:2; 20:17
shalt *u.* detest the silver and. 7:26
ye shall *u.* destroy the. 12:2
destroying *u.* city of idolaters. 13:15
after my death ye will *u.* 31:29
that he might *u.* destroy. *Josh* 11:20
put Canaanites to tribute, but did
not *u.* drive. 17:13; *Judg* 1:28
I thought thou hadst *u.* *Judg* 15:2
shall *u.* destroy every male. 21:11
smite, *u.* destroy. *1 Sam* 15:3, 18
he hath made Israel *u.* to. 27:12
valiant shall *u.* melt. *2 Sam* 17:10
the sons of Belial . . . shall be *u.*
burned with fire. 23:7
Israel could not *u.* destroy. *1 Ki* 9:21
lands, by destroying them *u.*
2 Ki 19:11; *Isa* 37:11
u. to slay them of. *2 Chr* 20:23
thou didst not *u.* consume. *Neh* 9:31
though he fall shall not *u.* *Ps* 37:24
the wicked are *u.* consumed. 73:19
my lovingkindness not *u.* 89:33
statutes, O forsake me not *u.* 119:8
take not the word of truth *u.* out. 43
substance for love, it would *u.* be.
S of S 8:7
and the idols he shall *u.* *Isa* 2:18
answered, until the land be *u.* 6:11
Lord *u.* destroy the tongue of. 11:15
land be *u.* emptied. 24:3
earth is *u.* broken. 19
done by destroying them *u.* 37:11
young men shall *u.* fall. 40:30
Lord hath *u.* separated me. 56:3
nations shall be *u.* wasted. 60:12
for every brother will *u.* *Jer* 9:4
if they will not obey, I will *u.* 12:17
hast thou *u.* rejected Judah ? 14:19
behold, I, even I will *u.* 23:39
I will *u.* destroy them. 25:9; 50:21
26; 51:3, 58
should ye be *u.* unpunished ? 25:29
but thou hast *u.* rejected. *Lam* 5:22
slay *u.* old and young. *Ezek* 9:6
being planted, shall it not *u.* ? 17:10
make themselves *u.* bald. 27:31
the land of Egypt *u.* waste. 29:10
shall go forth *u.* to make. *Dan* 11:44
but I will *u.* take them. *Hos* 1:6
the king of Israel be *u.* cut off. 10:15
I will *u.* destroy the house. *Amos* 9:8
one say, We be *u.* spoiled. *Mi* 2:4
for the wicked: . . . he is *u.* *Nah* 1:15
I will *u.* consume all. *Zeph* 1:2
right eye shall be *u.* *Zech* 11:17
now there is *u.* a fault. *1 Cor* 6:7
shall *u.* perish in their. *2 Pet* 2:12
Babylon shall be *u.* burnt. *Rev* 18:8
see **destroyed**

uttermost
when lepers came to *u.* part of camp.
2 Ki 7:5*, 8*
you cast out to *u.* part. *Neh* 1:9
I shall give thee *u.* parts for. *Ps* 2:8
till thou hast paid the *u.* *Mat* 5:26*
she came from the *u.* parts to. 12:42*
elect from the *u.* part. *Mark* 13:27
I will know the *u.* of. *Acts* 24:22
wrath is come upon them to the *u.*
1 Thes 2:16
able to save them to the *u.* *Heb* 7:25
see **utmost**

Uz
children of Aram; *U.,* Hul.
Gen 10:23
children of Dishan; *U.,* Aran. 36:28
1 Chr 1:42
Shem; Lud, Aram, and *U. 1 Chr* 1:17
a man in the land of *U.* *Job* 1:1
I made the king of *U.* *Jer* 25:20
daughter of Edom, in *U.* *Lam* 4:21

Uzza, Uzzah
U. and Ahio drave the cart.
2 Sam 6:3; *1 Chr* 13:7
U. put forth his hand to the ark.
2 Sam 6:6; *1 Chr* 13:9
because the Lord had made a breach
upon *U.* *2 Sam* 6:8

buried in the garden of *U. 2 Ki* 21:18
Amon buried in the garden of *U.* 26
sons of Merari, Mahli, *U. 1 Chr* 6:29
removed them, and begat *U.* 8:7
the children of *U.* *Ezra* 2:49
Neh 7:51

Uzziah, *called* **Azariah, Ozias**
A. made king. *2 Ki* 14:21; *2 Chr* 26:1
to reign in 39th year of *U. 2 Ki* 15:13
Jotham did all that his father *U.* 34
a son of Kohath, *U.* *1 Chr* 6:24
U. the Ashterathite, a valiant. 11:44
storehouses, was the son of *U.* 27:25
the Ammonites gave gifts to *U.*
2 Chr 26:8
U. prepared shields and slings. 14
it pertaineth not unto thee, *U.* to. 18
U. the king was a leper to the day. 21
U. son of Harim had taken a strange
wife. *Ezra* 10:21
dwelt Athaiah son of *U.* *Neh* 11:4
vision in the days of *U.* *Isa* 1:1
Hos 1:1 ; *Amos* 1:1
in the year *U.* died, I saw. *Isa* 6:1
earthquake in days of *U.* *Zech* 14:5
Joram begat *Ozias.* *Mat* 1:8
Ozias begat Joatham. 9

Uzziel
Kohath, Amram, Izhar, *U.* *Ex* 6:18
Num 3:19; *1 Chr* 6:2, 18; 23:12
sons of *U.* *Ex* 6:22; *Lev* 10:4
Num 3:30; *1 Chr* 15:10; 23:20
24:24
of Simeon had *U.* for. *1 Chr* 4:42
U. son of Bela. 7:7
U. the son of Heman. 25:4
Jeduthun; Shemaiah, *U. 2 Chr* 29:14
U. of the goldsmiths. *Neh* 3:8

V

vagabond
a fugitive and *v.* shalt. *Gen* 4:12*
I shall be a fugitive and *v.* 14*
then certain *v.* Jews. *Acts* 19:13*

vagabonds
let his children be *v.* *Ps* 109:10

vail, or veil
*The use of the vail in the East
was not so general in ancient as in
modern times, as much of the
present custom dates from the time
of Mohammed only. The vail
was worn only as an article of
ornamental dress; by betrothed
maidens in the presence of their
future husbands and at the wedding; or by loose women for purposes of concealment.*
*The vail of the temple was that
separating the Holy Place from the
Holy of Holies. This signified
separation, since none but the high
priest could pass beyond into the
most sacred place, and he only on
the Day of Atonement. It was
rent at the time of the crucifixion
to show that now all men could
freely come to God.*
*The Apostle speaks of the vail of
ignorance, blindness, and hardness
of heart, which kept the Jews from
understanding the scriptures of the
Old Testament, the spiritual sense
and meaning of the law, and from
seeing that Christ is the end of the
law for righteousness, John 9:39;
2 Cor 3:14, 15.*

Rebekah took a *v.* and. *Gen* 24:65
covered herself with a *v.* 38:14
shalt make a *v.* of blue. *Ex* 26:31
Moses put a *v.* on his face. 34:33, 35
made a *v.* of blue. 36:35; *2 Chr* 3:14
cover the ark with the *v.* *Ex* 40:3
holy place within the *v.* *Lev* 16:2
bring his blood within the *v.* 15
not go unto the *v.* nor come. 21:23
without the *v.* shall Aaron. 24:3
v. that thou hast upon. *Ruth* 3:15*
keepers took away my *v. S of S* 5:7*
destroy the *v.* spread. *Isa* 25:7

v. of the temple was rent. *Mat* 27:51
    Mark 15:38; *Luke* 23:45
Moses, which put a v.   *2 Cor* 3:13
for until this day remaineth the same
  v. untaken away; which v. is. 30
even to this day the v. is upon. 15
v. shall be taken away.   16
into that within the v.   *Heb* 6:19
the second v., the tabernacle. 9:3
through the v., that is to say. 10:20

vails

Lord will take away the v. *Isa* 3:23

vain

(Vain *and* vanity *are used in the*
Bible entirely with the idea of
emptiness, fruitlessness, or worth-
lessness, not in the sense of con-
ceited or conceit. Vain *is often used*
of an idol, as an empty worthless
substitute for God)

not regard v. words.   *Ex* 5:9*
for it is not a v. thing. *Deut* 32:47
Abimelech hired v. persons. *Judg* 9:4
there were gathered v. men. 11:3
after v. things, which cannot profit
  nor deliver . . . are v. *1 Sam* 12:21
as one of the v. fellows. *2 Sam* 6:20
became v. and went after heathen.
                  2 Ki 17:15
but they are but v. words. 18:20
                  Isa 36:5
to Jeroboam v. men. *2 Chr* 13:7†
he knoweth v. men, he. *Job* 11:11
for v. man would be wise, though. 12
wise man utter v. knowledge ? 15:2
Job said, Shall v. words ?   16:3
are ye thus altogether v.? 27:12
the people imagine a v. thing ?
          Ps 2:1; *Acts* 4:25
I have not sat with v. *Ps* 26:4†
an horse is a v. thing for. 33:17
man walketh in a v. shew. 39:6
for v. is the help of man. 60:11
                  108:12
become not v. in robbery. 62:10
I hate v. thoughts, but. 119:113*
it is v. for you to rise up. 127:2
followeth v. persons is. *Pr* 12:11
that followeth v. persons shall. 28:19
deceitful and beauty is v. 31:30
all days of his v. life which. *Eccl* 6:12
bring no more v. oblations; incense
  is an abomination.   *Isa* 1:13
they are but v. words, I have. 36:5
vanity, and are become v. *Jer* 2:5
how long thy v. thoughts ? 4:14*
customs of the people are v. 10:3
the prophets make you v. 23:16
have seen v. things. *Lam* 2:14
our eyes failed for our v. help. 4:17
no more any v. vision. *Ezek* 12:24
have ye not seen a v. vision ? 13:7
ye have said, It is v. *Mal* 3:14
when ye pray, use not v. *Mat* 6:7
but became v. in their. *Rom* 1:21
thoughts of wise are v. *1 Cor* 3:20
then is our preaching v. and your
  faith is also v.   15:14, 17
let no man deceive you with v. words.
                Eph 5:6*
lest any spoil you through philosophy
  and v. deceit.   *Col* 2:8
have turned aside to v. *1 Tim* 1:6
avoiding profane and v. babblings.
       6:20; *2 Tim* 2:16
unruly and v. talkers. *Tit* 1:10
for they are unprofitable and v. 3:9
this man's religion is v. *Jas* 1:26
wilt thou know, O v. man ? 2:20
your v. conversation. *1 Pet* 1:18

in vain

not take the name of the Lord in v.
      Ex 20:7; *Deut* 5:11
sow your seed in v. *Lev* 26:16
strength shall be spent in v. 20
in v. have I kept it. *1 Sam* 25:21
why then labour I in v.? *Job* 9:29
comfort ye me in v. seeing ? 21:34
Job open his mouth in v. 35:16
her labour is in v. without. 39:16
the hope of him is in v. 41:9
they are disquieted in v. *Ps* 39:6
cleansed my heart in v. 73:13

thou made all men in v.? *Ps* 89:47
in v.: watchman waketh in v. 127:1
enemies take thy name in v. 139:20
surely in v. the net is. *Pr* 1:17
the name of my God in v. 30:9*
Egyptians shall help in v. *Isa* 30:7
it not in v., he formed it. 45:18*
seed of Jacob, Seek ye me in v. 19
have laboured in v., I have spent my
  strength for nought and in v. 49:4
they shall not labour in v. 65:23
in v. have I smitten your. *Jer* 2:30
in v. is salvation hoped for. 3:23
in v. shalt thou make thyself. 4:30
the founder melteth in v. 6:29
lo, certainly in v. made he it, the pen
  of the scribes is in v. 8:8*
in v. shalt thou use many. 46:11
arrows, none shall return in v. 50:9
people shall labour in v. 51:58
that I have not said in v. *Ezek* 6:10
diviners comfort in v. *Zech* 10:2
but in v. they do worship me.
       Mat 15:9; *Mark* 7:7
for he beareth not the sword in v.
                  Rom 13:4
ye have believed in v. *1 Cor* 15:2
his grace bestowed upon me was not
  in v.   10
your labour is not in v. in the Lord. 58
the grace of God in v. *2 Cor* 6:1
boasting of you should be in v. 9:3*
means I should run in v. *Gal* 2:2
law, then Christ is dead in v. 21
have ye suffered so many things in
  v.? if it be yet in v.   3:4
bestowed on you labour in v. 4:11
that I may rejoice that I have not run
  in v. nor laboured in v. *Phil* 2:16
that it was not in v. *1 Thes* 2:1
and our labour be in v. 3:5
the scripture saith in v.? *Jas* 4:5

vainglory

not be desirous of v. *Gal* 5:26
nothing be done through v. *Phil* 2:3

vainly

v. puffed up by his fleshly. *Col* 2:18

vale

kings were joined in the v. of Siddim.
                Gen 14:3, 8
the v. of Siddim was full of. 37:14
out of the v. of Hebron. 37:14
in the hills and in the v. *Deut* 1:7*
the country of the v. *Josh* 10:40*
and cedars as sycamore trees in the
  v.   *1 Ki* 10:27*; *2 Chr* 1:15*
in the cities of the v. *Jer* 33:13*

valiant

when Saul saw any v. *1 Sam* 14:52
son of Jesse, a mighty v. man. 16:18
be v. for me, and fight the. 18:17
Art not thou a v. man ? 26:15
all the v. men took the body. 31:12
ye be v.   *2 Sam* 2:7; 13:28
he knew that v. men were. 11:16
he that is v.   17:10
of Jehoiada, the son of a v. man of
  Kabzeel. 23:20; *1 Chr* 11:22
for thou art a v. man. *1 Ki* 1:42*
of Tola were v. men. *1 Chr* 7:2
the v. men of the armies. 11:26*
eighty priests, men. *2 Chr* 26:17
Solomon's; threescore v. men are
  about it, of the v. of. *S of S* 3:7*
inhabitants like a v. man. *Isa* 10:13
v. ones shall cry without. 33:7
are not v. for the truth. *Jer* 9:3*
are thy v. men swept away ? 46:15*
the v. men are in scarlet. *Nah* 2:3
waxed v. in fight. *Heb* 11:34*

valiantest

12,000 men of the v. *Judg* 21:10

valiantly

Edom a possession, Israel shall do v.
          Num 24:18
behave ourselves v. *1 Chr* 19:13*
through God we shall do v.
      Ps 60:12; 108:13
the right hand of the Lord doeth v.
            118:15, 16

valley

Sometimes meaning gorge or
ravine.

The valleys most referred to in
Scripture, or best known in Jewish
history, are :

[1] The vale of Siddim, *or the*
slime pits, in which were the cities
of Sodom and Gomorrah, Gen 14:3.

[2] The valley of Eshcol, *where*
were famous vineyards, Num 32:9.

[3] The valley of Achor, *where*
Achan was punished, Josh 7:24.

[4] The valley of Elah, *where*
David killed Goliath, 1 Sam 17:2, 19.

[5] The valley of Jezreel, *the city*
where Ahab's palace was built, and
where Naboth's vineyard was,
Josh 19:18; 1 Ki 21:1, 23.

[6] The valley of Jehoshaphat,
which Joel prophesied should be
the place of final judgement,
Joel 3:2. *It is not certain where*
this was, as the name was applied
to the ravine between Jerusalem
and the Mt. of Olives only in the
middle of the fourth century.

[7] The valley of Hinnom, *or*
Gehenna, near Jerusalem. See
Tophet.

of Sodom met him at v. *Gen* 14:17
they went up to v. of. *Num* 32:9
they came to v. of Eshcol. *Deut* 1:24
heifer to a rough v. and strike off the
  heifer's neck in the v. 21:4
the plain of v. of Jericho, a. 34:3
he buried Moses in a v. in the. 6
brought them to the v. of. *Josh* 7:24
moon, in the v. of Ajalon. 10:12
which is at the end of the v. 15:8
out inhabitants of the v. *Judg* 1:19
was sent on foot into the v. 5:15
Midian was beneath in the v. 7:8, 12
a woman in the v. of Sorek. 16:4
wheat harvest in the v. *1 Sam* 6:13
slewest in the v. of Elah. 21:9
spread themselves in the v. of
  Rephaim. *2 Sam* 5:18, 22; 23:13
the Syrians in the v. of salt. 8:13
cast him into some v. *2 Ki* 2:16
make this v. full of ditches. 3:16
he slew of Edom in the v. of salt
  ten thousand. 14:7; *1 Chr* 18:12
in v. of Berachah. *2 Chr* 20:26
in the v. of Hinnom. 28:3
to fight in v. of Megiddo. 35:22
the clods of the v. shall. *Job* 21:33
he paweth in the v. and. 39:21
through the v. of death. *Ps* 23:4
out the v. of Succoth. 60:6; 108:7
who passing through v. of Baca. 84:6
the ravens of the v. shall. *Pr* 30:17
see the fruits of the v. *S of S* 6:11
ears in the v. of Rephaim. *Isa* 17:5
the burden of the v. of vision. 22:1
trouble in the v. of vision. 5
is on the head of the fat v. 28:4
wroth as in the v. of Gibeon. 21
every v. shall be exalted. 40:4
v. of Achor a place for herds. 65:10
see thy way in the v. *Jer* 2:23
v. of Hinnom, but v. 7:32; 19:6
thee, O inhabitant of the v. 21:13
the v. also shall perish, and. 48:8
thou in thy flowing v.? 49:4
in the v. which was full. *Ezek* 37:1
break the bow of Israel in the v. of.
                Hos 1:5
give the v. of Achor for a. 2:15
bring them into the v. of. *Joel* 3:2
multitudes, multitudes in the v. 14
shall water the v. of Shittim. 18
as the mourning in the v. *Zech* 12:11
and there shall be a great v. 14:4
flee to the v. of the mountains. 5
every v. be filled every. *Luke* 3:5
see gate

valleys

as the v. are they spread. *Num* 24:6
depths that spring out of the v. and.
               Deut 8:7
land is a land of hills and v. 11:11

valour

but he is not God of the *v.* *1 Ki* 20:28
clifts of *v.* in caves of earth. *Job* 30:6
or will he harrow the *v.* after? 39:10
the *v.* are covered over. *Ps* 65:13
they go down by the *v.* unto. 104:8
he sendeth the springs into the *v.* 10
the lily of the *v.* *S of S* 2:1
thy choicest *v.* shall be full. *Isa* 22:7
are on the head of the fat *v.* 28:1
fountains in midst of the *v.* 41:18
slaying the children in the *v.* 57:5
gloriest thou in the *v.*? *Jer* 49:4
Lord to the *v.* *Ezek* 6:3; 36:4, 6
mountains like doves of the *v.* 7:16

valour

Moab 10,000 men of *v.* *Judg* 3:29
thou mighty man of *v.* 6:12
Gileadite, a mighty man of *v.* 11:1
was a mighty man of *v.* *1 Ki* 11:28
Naaman, a mighty man in *v.* *2 Ki* 5:1
Zadok, man of *v.* *1 Chr* 12:28
a mighty man of *v.* *2 Chr* 17:17
see mighty **men**

value

lies, ye are all physicians of no *v.*
Job 13:4
ye are of more *v.* than many sparrows. *Mat* 10:31; *Luke* 12:7

value, *verb*

the priest shall *v.* him. *Lev* 27:8
priest shall *v.* it, whether it be. 12
children of Israel did *v.* *Mat* 27:9*

valued

of barley seed *v.* at 50. *Lev* 27:16
wisdom cannot be *v.* with. *Job* 28:16
neither shall it be *v.* with pure. 19
price of him that was *v.* *Mat* 27:9*

valuest

as thou *v.* it who art the priest, so
shall it be. *Lev* 27:12

vanish

wax warm, they *v.* *Job* 6:17
the heavens shall *v.* away. *Isa* 51:6
knowledge, it shall *v.* *1 Cor* 13:8*
old, is ready to *v.* away. *Heb* 8:13

vanished

hosts; is their wisdom *v.*? *Jer* 49:7
he *v.* out of their sight. *Luke* 24:31

vanisheth

consumed and *v.* away. *Job* 7:9
a vapour that *v.* away. *Jas* 4:14

vanities

me to anger with their *v.* *Deut* 32:21
1 Ki 16:13, 26; *Jer* 8:19
them that regard lying *v.* *Ps* 31:6
vanity of *v.* saith the preacher.
Eccl 1:2; 12:8
of dreams there are also *v.* 5:7
the stock is a doctrine of *v.* *Jer* 10:8*
are there any among the *v.* of the
Gentiles that can cause rain? 14:22
they that observe lying *v.* *Jonah* 2:8
turn from these *v.* *Acts* 14:15*

vanity

see meaning of **vain**

they followed *v.* and. *2 Ki* 17:15
so am I made to possess months of *v.*
Job 7:3
let me alone, for my days are *v.* 16
let not him that is deceived trust in
v., for *v.* shall be his. 15:31
mischief and bring forth *v.* 35*
if I have walked with *v.* or. 31:5
surely God will not hear *v.* 35:13
how long will ye love *v.*? *Ps* 4:2
his tongue is mischief and *v.* 10:7*
they speak *v.* every one to his. 12:2†
not lifted up his soul unto *v.* 24:4
his best estate is altogether *v.* 39:5
every man is *v.* 11
come to see me, he speaketh *v.*
41:6†; 144:8†, 11†
low degree are *v.*, lighter than *v.* 62:9
days did he consume in *v.* 78:33
thoughts of man, they are *v.* 94:11
mine eyes from beholding *v.* 119:37
man is like to *v.*: his days are. 144:4
wealth gotten by *v.* shall. *Pr* 13:11
by a lying tongue is *v.* 21:6
soweth iniquity shall reap *v.* 22:8*
remove from me *v.* and lies. 30:8

v. of vanities, saith the preacher, all
is *v.* *Eccl* 1:2, 14; 3:19; 11:8
12:8
this is also *v.* 2:1, 15, 19, 21, 23
4:8, 16; 5:10; 6:2, 9; 7:6; 8:10, 14
behold, all was *v.* and vexation.
2:11, 17, 26; 4:4
I saw *v.* 4:7
for he cometh in with *v.* 6:4
many things that increase *v.* 11
I seen in the days of my *v.* 7:15
there is a *v.* that is done on. 8:14
with wife all the days of thy *v.* 9:9
childhood and youth are *v.* 11:10
that draw iniquity with cords of *v.*
Isa 5:18
nations with the sieve of *v.* 30:28
to him are counted *v.* 40:17
the judges of the earth as *v.* 23
behold, they are all *v.* 41:29; 44:9
v. shall take them: but he that. 57:13
if thou take away, speaking *v.* 58:9
they trust in *v.* 59:4
they have walked after *v.* *Jer* 2:5
they are *v.* and the work of errors.
10:15; 51:18
fathers have inherited *v.* 16:19
have burnt incense to *v.* 18:15
they have seen *v.* and divination.
Ezek 13:6; 22:28
because ye have spoken *v.* 13:8
prophets see *v.* 9; 21:29
shall see no more *v.* 13:23
surely they are *v.* *Hos* 12:11
people shall weary themselves for
very *v.* *Hab* 2:13
the idols have spoken *v.* *Zech* 10:2
was made subject to *v.* *Rom* 8:20
not as Gentiles walk in *v.* *Eph* 4:17
they speak great swelling words of *v.*
2 Pet 2:18

vapour

pour down rain according to the *v.*
Job 36:27
cattle also concerning the *v.* 33
and *v.* fulfilling his word. *Ps* 148:8
shew signs in the earth, *v.* of smoke.
Acts 2:19
your life? it is even a *v.* *Jas* 4:14

vapours

v. to ascend from the ends of the.
Ps 135:7; *Jer* 10:13; 51:16

variableness

lights, with whom is no *v.* *Jas* 1:17

variance

set a man at *v.* against. *Mat* 10:35
of the flesh are hatred, *v.* *Gal* 5:20*

Vashti

V. the queen made a feast. *Esth* 1:9
queen *V.* refused to come at. 12
that *V.* come no more before. 19
Esther queen instead of *V.* 2:17

vaunt

lest Israel *v.* themselves. *Judg* 7:2

vaunteth

charity *v.* not itself. *1 Cor* 13:4

vehement

fire that hath a *v.* flame. *S of S* 8:6*
prepared a *v.* east wind. *Jonah* 4:8*
what *v.* desire it wrought in you!
2 Cor 7:11

vehemently

he spake the more *v.* *Mark* 14:31
the stream beat *v.* on that house.
Luke 6:48*, 49*
began to urge him *v.* 11:53
stood and *v.* accused him. 23:10

veil, *see* **vail**

vein

there is a *v.* for the silver. *Job* 28:1*

vengeance

v. shall be taken on him. *Gen* 4:15
to me belongeth *v.* and recompence.
Deut 32:35; *Ps* 94:1; *Heb* 10:30
I will render *v.* to mine enemies.
Deut 32:41
for he will render *v.* to his. 43
the Lord hath taken *v.* *Judg* 11:36
when he seeth the *v.* *Ps* 58:10
tookest *v.* of their inventions. 99:8
to execute *v.* upon the heathen. 149:7

not spare in the day of *v.* *Pr* 6:34
it is the day of the Lord's *v.* and.
Isa 34:8; 61:2; *Jer* 51:6
God will come with *v.* *Isa* 35:4
I will take *v.* 47:3; *Jer* 51:36
garments of *v.* for clothing. *Isa* 59:17
day of *v.* is in mine heart. 63:4
let me see thy *v.* on them. *Jer* 11:20
20:12
a day of *v.* 46:10
the *v.* of the Lord, take *v.* 50:15, 28
the *v.* of Lord, the *v.* of his temple.
28; 51:11
thou hast seen all their *v.* *Lam* 3:60
fury come up to take *v.* *Ezek* 24:8
Edom by taking *v.* hath. 25:12
I will lay my *v.* on Edom. 14
Philistines have taken *v.* 15
when I shall lay my *v.* on the. 17
I will execute great *v.* *Ezek* 25:17
Mi 5:15
Lord will take *v.* on his. *Nah* 1:2
these be the days of *v.* *Luke* 21:22
whom *v.* suffereth not to live.
Acts 28:4*
unrighteous who taketh *v.*? *Rom* 3:5
v. is mine, I will repay, saith. 12:19
flaming fire, taking *v.* *2 Thes* 1:8
an example, suffering the *v.* *Jude* 7*

venison

because he did eat of his *v.* *Gen* 25:28
field and take me some *v.* 27:3, 7
thee, and eat of my *v.* 19, 31
I will eat of my son's *v.* 25
where is he that hath taken *v.*? 35

venom

is the cruel *v.* of asps. *Deut* 32:33

venomous

saw the *v.* beast hang. *Acts* 28:4

vent

wine which hath no *v.* *Job* 32:19

venture

drew a bow at *v.* and smote the
king. *1 Ki* 22:34; *2 Chr* 18:33

verified

so shall your words be *v.* *Gen* 42:20
let thy word be *v.* *1 Ki* 8:26
2 Chr 6:17

verily

are *v.* guilty concerning. *Gen* 42:21
saying, *V.* my sabbaths. *Ex* 31:13
I *v.* thought thou hadst hated her.
Judg 15:2
v. our Lord hath made. *1 Ki* 1:43
v. she hath no child, her. *2 Ki* 4:14
I will *v.* buy it for the. *1 Chr* 21:24
my acquaintance are *v.* *Job* 19:13
do good, and *v.* thou. *Ps* 37:3
v. every man at his best state. 39:5
v. there is a reward for the righteous,
v. he is a God that. 58:11
but *v.* God hath heard me. 66:19
I have cleansed my heart. 73:13
v. thou art a God that hidest thyself.
Isa 45:15
v. it shall be well with thy remnant.
v. I will cause the. *Jer* 15:11
v. I say unto you. *Mat* 5:18; 6:2, 5
16; 8:10; 10:15, 23, 42; 11:11
13:17; 16:28; 17:20; 18:3, 13, 18
19:23, 28; 21:21, 31; 23:36; 24:2
34, 47; 25:12, 40, 45; 26:13
Mark 3:28; 6:11; 8:12; 9:1, 41
10:15, 29; 11:23; 12:43; 13:30
14:9, 18, 25; *Luke* 4:24; 11:51
12:37; 13:35; 18:17, 29; 21:32
v. I say unto thee. *Mat* 5:26; 26:34
Mark 14:30; *Luke* 23:43
Elias *v.* cometh first. *Mark* 9:12
nay *v.* let them come. *Acts* 16:37
John *v.* baptized with baptism. 19:4
or *v.* a man which am a Jew. 22:3
I *v.* thought I ought to do. 26:9
for circumcision *v.* profiteth if thou.
Rom 2:25
v. their sound went into all. 10:18
pleased them *v.*; debtors they. 15:27
I *v.* as absent in body. *1 Cor* 5:3
v. righteousness had been. *Gal* 3:21
for *v.* he took not on him the nature
of angels. *Heb* 2:16
for men *v.* swear by the greater. 6:16

for they *v*. for a few days. *Heb* 12:10
who *v*. was foreordained. *1 Pet* 1:20
in him *v*. is the love of. *1 John* 2:5

verily, verily

v. v. I say unto you. *John* 1:51
  5:19, 24, 25; 6:26, 32, 47, 53
  8:34, 51, 58; 10:1, 7; 12:24
  13:16, 20, 21; 14:12; 16:20, 23
v. v. I say unto thee. 3:3, 11
  13:38; 21:18

verity

works of his hands are *v*. *Ps* 111:7*
Gentiles in faith and *v*. *1 Tim* 2:7*

vermilion

cedar and painted with *v*. *Jer* 22:14
pourtrayed with *v*. *Ezek* 23:14

very

thou be my *v*. son Esau. *Gen* 27:21
in *v*. deed for this I. *Ex* 9:16
Moses was *v*. meek. *Num* 12:3
but the word is *v*. nigh. *Deut* 30:14
in *v*. deed except thou. *1 Sam* 25:34
Saul was come in *v*. deed. 26:4
have done *v*. foolishly. *2 Sam* 24:10
king Ahaziah did *v*. *2 Chr* 20:35
we have dealt *v*. corruptly. *Neh* 1:7
inward part is *v*. wickedness. *Ps* 5:9
into that *v*. destruction let. 35:8
also, O God, is *v*. high. 71:19
establish in the *v*. heavens. 89:2
thy thoughts are *v*. deep. 92:5
thy testimonies are *v*. sure. 93:5
testimonies are *v*. faithful. 119:138
thy word is *v*. pure, therefore. 140
in that *v*. day his thoughts. 146:4
word runneth *v*. swiftly. 147:15
he separateth *v*. friends. *Pr* 17:9
for yet a *v*. little while. *Isa* 10:25
  29:17
the land that is *v*. far off. 33:17
he taketh up the isles as a *v*. 40:15
be ye *v*. desolate, saith. *Jer* 2:12
I am pained at my *v*. heart. 4:19
transgressed to this *v*. day. *Ezek* 2:3
that were a *v*. little thing. 16:47
labour in the *v*. fire, and the people
weary themselves for *v*. *Hab* 2:13
the *v*. hairs of your head. *Mat* 10:30
shall deceive the *v*. elect. 24:24
that this is the *v*. Christ. *John* 7:26
  Acts 9:22
taken in adultery, in *v*. act. *John* 8:4
me for the *v*. works' sake. 14:11
the *v*. God of peace. *1 Thes* 5:23
and not the *v*. image of. *Heb* 10:1
the Lord is *v*. pitiful, of. *Jas* 5:11

see **great, much**

vessel

not put any in thy *v*. *Deut* 23:24
though sanctified this day in the *v*.
  1 Sam 21:5
a little water in a *v*. *1 Ki* 17:10
v. There is not a *v*. more. *2 Ki* 4:6
pieces like a potter's *v*. *Ps* 2:9
I am like a broken *v*. 31:12
forth a *v*. for the finer. *Pr* 25:4
an offering in a clean *v*. *Isa* 66:20
the *v*. was marred in the hand of the
potter. *Jer* 18:4
v. wherein is no pleasure? 22:28
shall fall like a pleasant *v*. 25:34
been emptied from *v*. to *v*. 48:11
have broken Moab like a *v*. 38
hath made me an empty *v*. 51:34
put them in one *v*. and. *Ezek* 4:9
a pin of it to hang any *v*.? 15:3
shall be as a *v*. wherein is. *Hos* 8:8
carry any *v*. through the temple.
  Mark 11:16
no man covereth a candle with a *v*.
  Luke 8:16
for he is a chosen *v*. *Acts* 9:15
Peter saw a certain *v*. 10:11; 11:5
hath power to make one *v*. *Rom* 9:21
know to possess his *v*. in. *1 Thes* 4:4
he shall be a *v*. to honour. *2 Tim* 2:21
giving honour unto the wife as unto
the weaker *v*. *1 Pet* 3:7

vessels

best fruits in your *v*. *Gen* 43:11
anoint the altar and *v*. *Ex* 40:10
  Lev 8:11
Levites not come nigh *v*. *Num* 18:3
46

bread is spent in our *v*. *1 Sam* 9:7
and the *v*. of the young men. 21:5
borrow thee *v*. abroad of all thy
neighbours, even empty *v*. *2 Ki* 4:3
the *v*. king Ahaz did. *2 Chr* 29:19
king brought forth the *v*. *Ezra* 1:7
take these *v*. 5:15
v. are given to thee. 7:19
he weighed the silver and the *v*.
  8:25, 33
thither brought I again the *v*. of
the house of God. *Neh* 13:9
even in *v*. of bulrushes. *Isa* 18:2
v. of small quantity, the *v*. 22:24
be ye clean that bear the *v*. 52:11
abominable things is in their *v*. 65:4
returned with their *v*. *Jer* 14:3
v. of the Lord's house. 27:16; 28:3
they have brought the *v*. *Dan* 5:23
he shall spoil treasure of all pleasant
v. *Hos* 13:15
to draw out fifty *v*. out. *Hag* 2:16
gathered the good into *v*. *Mat* 13:48
the wise took oil in their *v*. 25:4
the *v*. of wrath. *Rom* 9:22
of mercy. 23
as *v*. of a potter shall. *Rev* 2:27

see **brass, earthen, gold, silver**

vestments

bring forth *v*. for the. *2 Ki* 10:22

vestry

him that was over the *v*. *2 Ki* 10:22

vesture, -s

Joseph in *v*. of fine linen. *Gen* 41:42
the quarters of thy *v*. *Deut* 22:12
they cast lots upon my *v*. *Ps* 22:18
  Mat 27:35; *John* 19:24
as a *v*. shalt thou change. *Ps* 102:26
and as a *v*. shalt thou fold. *Heb* 1:12*
he was clothed with a *v*. dipped in
blood. *Rev* 19:13*
his *v*. and on his thigh a name. 16*

vex

thou shalt not *v*. a stranger.
  Ex 22:21*; *Lev* 19:33*
not take a wife to her sister to *v*.
  Lev 18:18*
v. the Midianites and. *Num* 25:17
for they *v*. you with their wiles. 18
ye let remain shall *v*. you. 33:55
how will he *v*. himself? *2 Sam* 12:18
God did *v*. them with. *2 Chr* 15:6
how long will ye *v*. my soul?
  Job 19:2
and *v*. them in his sore. *Ps* 2:5
let us go up against Judah and *v*. it.
  Isa 7:6
Judah shall not *v*. Ephraim. 11:13
I will *v*. the hearts of. *Ezek* 32:9
shall they not awake that shall *v*.
thee? *Hab* 2:7
Herod did *v*. certain of. *Acts* 12:1*

vexation

(*Where this word occurs in
Ecclesiastes the Revised Versions
change it to* striving)

shall send on thee *v*. *Deut* 28:20*
is vanity and *v*. of spirit. *Eccl* 1:14
  2:11, 17
this also is *v*. of spirit. 1:17; 2:26
  4:4, 16; 6:9
man of the *v*. of his heart? 2:22
both the hands full with *v*. 4:6
such as was in her *v*. *Isa* 9:1*
be a *v*. only to understand. 28:19*
shall howl for *v*. of spirit. 65:14

vexations

great *v*. were on all the. *2 Chr* 15:5

vexed

the Egyptians *v*. us. *Num* 20:15*
reason of them that *v*. *Judg* 2:18
the Ammonites *v*. Israel. 10:8
so that his soul was *v*. unto. 16:16
Saul *v*. his enemies on. *1 Sam* 14:47†
Amnon was so *v*. that. *2 Sam* 13:2
alone, for her soul is *v*. *2 Ki* 4:27
to enemies who *v*. them. *Neh* 9:27*
the Almighty, who hath *v*. *Job* 27:2
my bones are *v*. *Ps* 6:2
my soul is sore *v*. 3
be ashamed and sore *v*. 10

they rebelled and *v*. his. *Isa* 63:10*
infamous and much *v*. *Ezek* 22:5*
in thee they *v*. the fatherless. 7*
v. the poor. 29
my daughter is grievously *v*. with
a devil. *Mat* 15:22
he is lunatic and sore *v*. 17:15*
they that were *v*. with unclean spirits.
  Luke 6:18*; *Acts* 5:16
delivered just Lot, *v*. *2 Pet* 2:7*
v. his righteous soul from day. 8

vial

(*Where this word or the plural
occurs in Revelation the Revised
Versions change it to* bowl)

Samuel took a *v*. of oil. *1 Sam* 10:1
first angel poured his *v*. *Rev* 16:2
second *v*. upon the sea. 3
third *v*. upon the rivers. 4
fourth *v*. upon the sun. 8
fifth *v*. upon the seat of the beast. 10
sixth *v*. upon the Euphrates. 12
seventh *v*. into the air. 17

vials

golden *v*. full of odours. *Rev* 5:8
seven angels seven golden *v*. 15:7
pour out the *v*. of the wrath. 16:1
angels which had seven *v*. 17:1; 21:9

victory

v. that day was turned. *2 Sam* 19:2
the Lord wrought a great *v*. that day.
  23:10, 12
thine, O Lord, is the *v*. *1 Chr* 29:11
hath gotten him the *v*. *Ps* 98:1*
swallow up death in *v*. and wipe away
tears. *Isa* 25:8*; *1 Cor* 15:54
forth judgement unto *v*. *Mat* 12:20
O grave, where is thy *v*.? *1 Cor* 15:55
to God, who giveth us the *v*. 57
and this is the *v*., even. *1 John* 5:4
the *v*. over the beast. *Rev* 15:2

victual, -s

goods of Sodom, and *v*. *Gen* 14:11
they prepared any *v*. *Ex* 12:39
him thy *v*. for increase. *Lev* 25:37
usury of *v*. of any thing. *Deut* 23:19
prepare *v*. *Josh* 1:11
take *v*. with you. 9:11*
the men took of their *v*. and. 14*
suit of apparel and *v*. *Judg* 17:10
he gave him *v*. and sword of Goliath.
  1 Sam 22:10
which provided *v*. for the king.
  1 Ki 4:7, 27
Pharaoh appointed him *v*. 11:18
if the people bring *v*. *Neh* 10:31
in the day they sold *v*. 13:15
so captain gave Jeremiah *v*. *Jer* 40:5
for then had we plenty of *v*. 44:17
went into villages to buy *v*.
  Mat 14:15*; *Luke* 9:12†

view

go *v*. the land. *Josh* 2:1
v. the country. 7:2*
of prophets stood to *v*. *2 Ki* 2:7*, 15

viewed

the men *v*. Ai. *Josh* 7:2
I *v*. the people. *Ezra* 8:15
and I *v*. the walls of. *Neh* 2:13, 15

vigilant

a bishop must be *v*. *1 Tim* 3:2*
be sober, be *v*. because. *1 Pet* 5:8

vile

lest thy brother should seem *v*. to
thee. *Deut* 25:3
man do not so *v*. a thing. *Judg* 19:24*
because his sons made themselves
v. *1 Sam* 3:13*
every thing that was *v*. they destroyed. 15:9
yet be more *v*. than. *2 Sam* 6:22
why are we reputed *v*. in? *Job* 18:3*
I am *v*.; what shall I answer? 40:4*
in whose eyes a *v*. person. *Ps* 15:4*
the *v*. person be no more. *Isa* 32:5†
for the *v*. person will speak. 6†
the precious from the *v*. *Jer* 15:19
make them like *v*. figs. 29:17
Lord, for I am become *v*. *Lam* 1:11
in his estate shall stand up a *v*. person. *Dan* 11:21

image, and will make thy grave, for
thou art *v*.   *Nah* 1:14
filth on thee and make thee *v*.   3:6
God gave them up to *v*.   *Rom* 1:26
change our *v*. body.   *Phil* 3:21*
come in a poor man in *v*. raiment.
    Jas 2:2

vilely
mighty is *v*. cast away.   *2 Sam* 1:21

viler
of base men, they were *v*. *Job* 30:8*

vilest
wicked when the *v*. men.   *Ps* 12:8

village
go into the *v*. over against. *Mat* 21:2
    Mark 11:2; *Luke* 19:30
two of them went that same day to a
v.   *Luke* 24:13
they drew nigh unto the *v*.   28

villages
frogs died out of the *v*.   *Ex* 8:13*
houses of the *v*. counted. *Lev* 25:31
the inhabitants of the *v*. *Judg* 5:7*
together in one of the *v*.   *Neh* 6:2
Jews of *v*. made the 14th day of.
    Esth 9:19
let us lodge in the *v*.   *S of S* 7:11
I will go up to the land of unwalled *v*.
    Ezek 38:11
strike the head of his *v*. *Hab* 3:14*
they may go into the *v*. and buy.
    Mat 14:15; *Mark* 6:36
   see cities

villany
vile person will speak *v*. *Isa* 32:6*
they have committed *v*. *Jer* 29:23*

vine
*God compares his people to a vine,
which he had brought out of
Egypt, and planted in Palestine, as
a good soil, but which, instead of
bringing forth good fruit, brought
forth only bitter fruit, and wild
grapes, Ps 80:8; Isa 5:1, etc. In
John 15:1, Christ says, I am the
true vine, and my Father is the
husbandman.*
   *The vine of Sodom, Deut 32:32,
is probably what is known as the
apples of Sodom, which appear as
edible fruit, but on being plucked
turn at once to dust, like a puff-
ball. The phrase is perhaps figurative, no real fruit being intended.
Noah planted the vine after the
deluge, and was the first that
cultivated it, Gen 9:20. Many are
of opinion, that wine was not unknown before the deluge, and that
this Patriarch only continued to
cultivate the vine after this great
catastrophe, as he had done before. But others think that he
knew not the force of wine, having
never used it before, nor having
ever seen any one use it. He is
supposed to be the first that pressed
out the juice of the grape, and to
have reduced it to a liquor. Before
him, men only ate the grapes, like
other fruit.*

in my dream, behold, a *v*. *Gen* 40:9
v. were three branches.   10
binding his foal to the *v*. and his ass's
colt to the choice *v*.   49:11
nor gather grapes of thy *v*. undressed.   *Lev* 25:5, 11
nothing made of the *v*. tree. *Num* 6:4
for their *v*. is of the *v*. *Deut* 32:32
said to *v*., Reign over us. *Judg* 9:12
thing that cometh of the *v*.   13:14
every man under his *v*.   *1 Ki* 4:25
found a wild *v*. and.   *2 Ki* 4:39
eat ye every man of his own *v*.
    18:31; *Isa* 36:16
his unripe grape as the *v*. *Job* 15:33
thou hast brought a *v*.   *Ps* 80:8
behold, and visit this *v*.   14
thy wife shall be as a fruitful *v*. 128:3
to see whether the *v*. flourished.
    S of S 6:11; 7:12
shall be as clusters of the *v*.   7:8

it with the choicest *v*.   *Isa* 5:2
for the *v*. of Sibmah.   16:8
I will bewail the *v*. of Sibmah.   9
    Jer 48:32
the *v*. languisheth.   *Isa* 24:7
lament for the fruitful *v*.   32:12
falleth off from the *v*. as a fig.   34:4
a noble *v*.: how then turned into degenerate plant of . . . *v*.? *Jer* 2:21
the remnant of Israel as a *v*.   6:9
grapes on the *v*. nor figs.   8:13
what is the *v*. tree more? *Ezek* 15:2
as the *v*. tree which I have given.   6
spreading *v*. of low stature.   17:6
this *v*. did bend her roots.   7
thy mother is like a *v*. in.   19:10
Israel is an empty *v*.   *Hos* 10:1
revive as corn, grow as the *v*.   14:7
he laid my *v*. waste.   *Joel* 1:7
the *v*. is dried up, the fig tree.   12
the fig tree and the *v*. yield.   2:22
every man under his *v*.   *Mi* 4:4
as yet the *v*. hath not brought forth.
    Hag 2:19
every man under the *v*. *Zech* 3:10
the *v*. shall give her fruit.   8:12
neither shall your *v*. cast. *Mal* 3:11
v., until in my Father's. *Mat* 26:29
    Mark 14:25; *Luke* 22:18
true *v*., my Father is. *John* 15:1, 5
bear fruit, except it abide in *v*.   4
can a *v*. bear figs?   *Jas* 3:12
gather clusters of the *v*. *Rev* 14:18
the angel gathered the *v*. of.   19*

vinedressers
captain of guard left the poor of the
land to be *v*. *2 Ki* 25:12; *Jer* 52:16
had husbandmen and *v*. *2 Chr* 26:10
of alien shall be your *v*. *Isa* 61:5
howl, O ye *v*.   *Joel* 1:11

vinegar
*(The Hebrew word translated
vinegar was applied to a beverage
turned sour, or made artificially.
It was not pleasant to take but was
used by labourers. The vinegar
of the Romans was much the same,
and was probably that given to
Jesus while on the cross)*
shall drink no *v*. of wine.   *Num* 6:3
dip thy morsel in the *v*.   *Ruth* 2:14
gall for my meat, in my thirst they
gave me *v*. *Ps* 69:21; *Mat* 27:34*
as *v*. to the teeth, so is.   *Pr* 10:26
as *v*. upon nitre, so is he.   25:20
they took a spunge and filled it with
v.   *Mat* 27:48; *Mark* 15:36
    Luke 23:36; *John* 19:29, 30

vines
of *v*. or pomegranates.   *Num* 20:5
a land of wheat, and barley, and *v*.
    Deut 8:8
their *v*. with hail.   *Ps* 78:47
their *v*. also and fig trees.   105:33
v. give a good smell.   *S of S* 2:13
little foxes, that spoil the *v*.; for our
v. have tender grapes.   15*
were a thousand *v*.   *Isa* 7:23
they shall eat up thy *v*.   *Jer* 5:17
thou shalt yet plant *v*. on.   31:5*
I will destroy her *v*. and. *Hos* 2:12
nor shall fruit be in the *v*. *Hab* 3:17

vineyard
Noah planted a *v*. and.   *Gen* 9:20
if a man shall cause a *v*. *Ex* 22:5
thou shalt deal with thy *v*.   23:11
shalt not glean thy *v*.   *Lev* 19:10
thou shalt prune thy *v*.   25:3
thy field, nor prune thy *v*.   4
he that hath planted a *v*.? *Deut* 20:6
not sow thy *v*. with divers seeds, lest
the fruit of thy seed and *v*.   22:9
into thy neighbour's *v*.   23:24
gatherest the grapes of thy *v*. 24:21
thou shalt plant a *v*. and not. 28:30
Naboth had a *v*. hard by. *1 Ki* 21:1
v., I will give thee a better *v*.   2, 6
eat bread, I will give thee the *v*.   7
the *v*. thy right hand.   *Ps* 80:15*
I went to the *v*. of the man void of.
    Pr 24:30
of her hand she planted a *v*.   31:16

mine own *v*. have I not.   *S of S* 1:6
Solomon had a *v*.; he let the *v*. 8:11
my *v*. which is mine.   12
daughter of Zion is left as a cottage
in a *v*.   *Isa* 1:8
for ye have eaten up the *v*.   3:14
my beloved touching his *v*.   5:1
for the *v*. of the Lord of hosts is.   7
yea, ten acres of *v*. shall yield.   10
sing ye to her, A *v*. of red wine. 27:2
have destroyed my *v*.   *Jer* 12:10
Rechabites shall not plant *v*. 35:7, 9
I will make Samaria as plantings of
a *v*.   *Mi* 1:6
hire labourers into his *v*. *Mat* 20:1
them, Go ye also into the *v*.   4, 7
go work to-day in my *v*.   21:28
a certain householder planted a *v*.
    33; *Mark* 12:1; *Luke* 20:9
fig tree planted in his *v*. *Luke* 13:6
to the dresser of the *v*., Behold.   7
who planteth a *v*. and?   *1 Cor* 9:7

vineyards
given us inheritance of *v*. *Num* 16:14
not pass through the *v*. 20:17; 21:22
Lord stood in a path of the *v*. 22:24
give thee *v*. and olive trees which
thou plantedst not.   *Deut* 6:11
    Josh 24:13; *Neh* 9:25
thou shalt plant *v*. and. *Deut* 28:39
burnt up the corn, with *v*. *Judg* 15:5
Go and lie in wait in the *v*.   21:20
your fields and your *v*.   *1 Sam* 8:14
give every one of you *v*.?   22:7
to receive *v*. and sheep? *2 Ki* 5:26
to a land of bread and *v*.   18:32
in the third year . . . plant *v*. 19:29
over the *v*. was Shimei, over the increase of the *v*. for.   *1 Chr* 27:27
we have mortgaged our *v*. *Neh* 5:3
restore to them their *v*. and.   11
not the way of the *v*.   *Job* 24:18
and plant *v*. to yield.   *Ps* 107:37
houses, I planted me *v*.   *Eccl* 2:4
me the keeper of the *v*. *S of S* 1:6
as a cluster of camphire in the *v*. 14
let us get up early to the *v*.   7:12
in the *v*. there shall be no singing.
    Isa 16:10
houses and inhabit; shall plant *v*. and
eat the fruit.   65:21; *Amos* 9:14
houses and *v*. shall be.   *Jer* 32:15
gave the poor *v*. and fields.   39:10
build houses and plant *v*. *Ezek* 28:26
I will give her her *v*.   *Hos* 2:15
worm devoured your *v*.   *Amos* 4:9
ye have planted *v*. but ye shall. 5:11
and in all *v*. shall be wailing.   17
they shall plant *v*. but not. *Zeph* 1:13

vintage
shall reach to the *v*. and the *v*. shall
reach to the.   *Lev* 26:5
than the *v*. of Abiezer?   *Judg* 8:2
the *v*. of the wicked.   *Job* 24:6
I have made their *v*. shouting to
cease.   *Isa* 16:10
grapes when *v*. is done.   24:13
the *v*. shall fail, gathering.   32:10
the spoiler is fallen upon thy *v*.
    Jer 48:32
grapegleanings of the *v*.   *Mi* 7:1
the forest of the *v*. is.   *Zech* 11:2*

viol
harp and *v*. and wine.   *Isa* 5:12*
that chant to the sound of the *v*.
    Amos 6:5

violated
her priests have *v*. my. *Ezek* 22:26

violence
earth was filled with *v*. *Gen* 6:11, 13
thing taken away by *v*.   *Lev* 6:2*
thou savest me from *v*. *2 Sam* 22:3
him that loveth *v*. his.   *Ps* 11:5
v. and strife in the city.   55:9
weigh the *v*. of your hands.   58:2
redeem their soul from *v*.   72:14
therefore *v*. covereth them as. 73:6
they drink the wine of *v*.   *Pr* 4:17
v. covereth the mouth of. 10:6, 11
transgressors shall eat *v*.   13:2
a man that doeth *v*. to the. 28:17*
done no *v*. nor was deceit. *Isa* 53:5*
and the act of *v*. is in their.   59:6

v. shall no more be heard. *Isa* 60:18
v. and spoil is heard in. *Jer* 6:7
I cried v. and spoil. 20:8
do no v. to the stranger. 22:3
thine eyes, thine heart are for v. 17
v. done to me and my flesh. 51:35
a rumour, v. in the land. 46
v. is risen up into a rod. *Ezek* 7:11
for the city is full of v. 23
filled the land with v. 8:17; 28:16
because of the v. of them. 12:19
hath spoiled none by v. 18:7, 16
spoiled and oppressed by v. 12, 18
O princes of Israel, remove v. 45:9
be a wilderness, for the v. *Joel* 3:19
who store up v. in their. *Amos* 3:10
ye that cause the seat of v. to. 6:3
for thy v. shame shall. *Ob* 10
every one from the v. *Jonah* 3:8
fields, and take them by v. *Mi* 2:2*
rich men thereof are full of v. 6:12
how long shall I cry unto thee of v.!
　　　　　Hab 1:2
v. is before me. 3
they shall come all for v. 9
and for the v. of the land. 2:8
v. of Lebanon cover thee, v. of. 17
houses with v. and deceit. *Zeph* 1:9
have done v. to the law. 3:4
for one covereth v. with. *Mal* 2:16
of heaven suffereth v. *Mat* 11:12
do v. to no man, nor accuse any.
　　　　　Luke 3:14
captain brought them without v.
　　　　　Acts 5:26
Paul borne of soldiers for v. 21:35
hinder part was broken with v. 27:41
quenched the v. of fire. *Heb* 11:34*
with v. shall Babylon. *Rev* 18:21*

violent

thou hast delivered me from the v.
　man. 2 *Sam* 22:49; *Ps* 18:48
his v. dealing come on his. *Ps* 7:16
the assemblies of v. men. 86:14
preserve me from the v. 140:1, 4
evil shall hunt the v. man to. 11
a v. man enticeth his. *Pr* 16:29
if thou seest v. perverting. *Eccl* 5:8
the v. take it by force. *Mat* 11:12

violently

servants had v. taken. *Gen* 21:25
shall restore that which he took v.
　　　　　Lev 6:4*
thine ass shall be v. *Deut* 28:31
he hath v. taken away. *Job* 20:19
they v. take away flocks, and. 24:2
he will surely v. turn. *Isa* 22:18
he hath v. taken away. *Lam* 2:6
swine ran v. into the sea. *Mat* 8:32*
　　　Mark 5:13*; *Luke* 8:33*

viols

the noise of thy v. is. *Isa* 14:11
hear the melody of thy v. *Amos* 5:23

viper

(*The viper is one of the most
poisonous serpents, but the word
is used in the New Testament for
any poisonous serpent*)
of asps, the v.'s tongue. *Job* 20:16
from whence come the v. *Isa* 30:6
crushed breaketh out into a v. 59:5
came a v. and fastened. *Acts* 28:3

vipers

O generation of v. *Mat* 3:7; 12:34
　　　　　23:33; *Luke* 3:7

virgin

*In Greek, parthenos; in Hebrew,
almah. These words properly
signify an unmarried young woman,
who has preserved the purity of her
body. But sometimes virgin is
made use of to express a young
woman whether she has kept her
virginity or no, Joel 1:8.*

fair to look upon, a v. *Gen* 24:16
when the v. cometh forth to. 43
for his sister, a v. he. *Lev* 21:3
take a v. of his own people. 14
an evil name upon a v. *Deut* 22:19
a v. betrothed. 23
a v. not betrothed. 28
the young man and the v. 32:25

fell sick for Tamar; for she was a v.
　　　　　2 *Sam* 13:2
sought for king a young v. 1 *Ki* 1:2
the v. daughter of Zion hath despised
　thee. 2 *Ki* 19:21; *Isa* 37:22
behold a v. shall conceive. *Isa* 7:14
　　　　　Mat 1:23
O thou oppressed v. *Isa* 23:12
in the dust, O v. of Babylon. 47:1
marrieth a v. so thy sons. 62:5
the v. daughter of my. *Jer* 14:17
v. of Israel hath done a. 18:13
be built, O v. of Israel. 31:4
the v. rejoice in the dance. 13
turn again, O v. of Israel, to. 21
take balm, O v. the daughter. 46:11
trodden the v. daughter of. *Lam* 1:15
thee, O v. daughter of Zion. 2:13
lament like a v. girded. *Joel* 1:8
the v. of Israel is fallen. *Amos* 5:2
sent from God to a v. *Luke* 1:27
if a v. marry, she hath. 1 *Cor* 7:28
between a wife and a v. 34
I may present you as a chaste v.
　　　　　2 *Cor* 11:2

virginity

take a wife in her v. *Lev* 21:13
tokens of her v. *Deut* 22:15, 17, 20
bewail my v. *Judg* 11:37, 38
the teats of their v. *Ezek* 23:3, 8
Anna lived seven years from her v.
　　　　　Luke 2:36

virgins

pay according to the dowry of v.
　　　　　Ex 22:17
daughters that were v. 2 *Sam* 13:18
favour above all the v. *Esth* 2:17
the v. her companions. *Ps* 45:14
as ointment, therefore do the v. love
　thee. *S of S* 1:3
threescore queens and v. 6:8
nor do I bring up v. *Isa* 23:4
her priests sigh, her v. *Lam* 1:4
my v. and young men are gone. 18
the v. of Jerusalem hang. 2:10
v. and young men are fallen. 21
shall the fair v. faint. *Amos* 8:13
heaven be likened to ten v. *Mat* 25:1
Philip had four daughters, v.
　　　　　Acts 21:9
concerning v. I have no. 1 *Cor* 7:25
not defiled, for they are v. *Rev* 14:4

young virgins

Jabesh-gilead were four hundred
　young v. *Judg* 21:12
there be fair young v. sought for
　king. *Esth* 2:2
together all the fair young v. 3

virtue

v. had gone out of him. *Mark* 5:30
　　　　　Luke 6:19*; 8:46*
if there be any v. think. *Phil* 4:8
hath called us to glory and v.
　　　　　2 *Pet* 1:3
add to your faith v. and to v. 5

virtuous

thou art a v. woman. *Ruth* 3:11†
a v. woman is a crown. *Pr* 12:4†
who can find a v. woman? 31:10†

virtuously

have done v. but thou. *Pr* 31:29†

visage

his v. was marred more. *Isa* 52:14
their v. is blacker than. *Lam* 4:8
and the form of his v. *Dan* 3:19

visible

were all things created, v. and in-
　visible. *Col* 1:16

vision

the v. of the Almighty. *Num* 24:4, 16
there was no open v. 1 *Sam* 3:1
feared to shew Eli the v. 15
according to all these words and this
　v. 2 *Sam* 7:17; 1 *Chr* 17:15
they are written in the v. 2 *Chr* 32:32
as a v. of the night. *Job* 20:8
thou spakest in v. to thy. *Ps* 89:19
no v. the people perish. *Pr* 29:18
the v. of Isaiah. *Isa* 1:1
a grievous v. is declared. 21:2

burden of the valley of v. *Isa* 22:1, 5
they err in v., they stumble. 28:7
as a dream of a night v. 29:7
the v. is become as a book. 11
unto you a false v. *Jer* 14:14
they speak a v. of their own. 23:16
prophets find no v. from. *Lam* 2:9
v. is touching the whole. *Ezek* 7:13
then shall they seek a v. of. 26
according to the v. that I saw. 8:4
　　　　　11:24; 43:3
prolonged and every v. 12:22
say to them, the effect of every v. 23
no more any vain v. nor. 24
the v. that he seeth is for many. 27
have ye not seen a vain v.? 13:7
to Daniel in a night v. *Dan* 2:19
I saw in my v. by night, the. 7:2
a v. appeared unto me, even. 8:1
how long shall be the v. concerning
　sacrifice? 13
man to understand the v. 16
time of the end shall be the v. 17
shut up the v. 26
I was astonished at the v. 27
whom I had seen in the v. at. 9:21
consider the v. 23
and to seal up the v. 24
had understanding of the v. 10:1
the v.: men with me saw not v. 7, 8
for yet the v. is for many days. 14
by v. my sorrows are turned. 16
themselves to establish the v. 11:14
v. of Obadiah. *Ob* 1
that ye shall not have a v. *Mi* 3:6
the book of the v. of. *Nah* 1:1
write the v. and make it. *Hab* 2:2
for the v. is yet for an appointed. 3
the prophets shall be ashamed every
　one of his v. *Zech* 13:4
charged, saying, Tell the v. to no
　man. *Mat* 17:9
that he had seen a v. *Luke* 1:22
they had seen a v. of angels. 24:23
doubted of the v. *Acts* 10:17, 19
in a trance I saw a v., A vessel. 11:5
true, but thought he saw a v. 12:9
a v. appeared to Paul. 16:9; 18:9
disobedient to the heavenly v. 26:19
I saw the horses in the v. *Rev* 9:17
see oracle, prophet, Thummim

in a vision

came to Abram *in a* v. *Gen* 15:1
make myself known to him *in a* v.
　　　　　Num 12:6
brought me *in a* v. by. *Ezek* 11:24
I saw *in a* v. and I was. *Dan* 8:2
said the Lord *in a* v. *Acts* 9:10
Saul hath seen *in a* v. a man. 12
Cornelius saw *in a* v. an angel. 10:3

visions

God spake to Israel in v. *Gen* 46:2
written in the v. of Iddo. 2 *Chr* 9:29
understanding in v. of God. 26:5
in thoughts from the v. *Job* 4:13
terrifiest me through v. 7:14
and I saw the v. of God. *Ezek* 1:1
he brought me in the v. of God. 8:3
in v. of peace for her. 13:16
in v. he brought me to the land. 40:2
understanding in all v. *Dan* 1:17
the v. of thy head on thy bed. 2:28
Daniel had v. of his head. 4:5
the v. of my head troubled. 4:5
I saw in the v. by and. 7, 13
v. of my head troubled me. 15
I have multiplied v. *Hos* 12:10
your young men shall see v.
　　　　　Joel 2:28; *Acts* 2:17
I will come to v. and. 2 *Cor* 12:1

visit

(*To come with a special purpose,
either of blessing or punishment*)
God will surely v. you. *Gen* 50:24
　　　　　25; *Ex* 13:19
when I v. I will v. their. *Ex* 32:34
I do v. the iniquity. *Lev* 18:25
thou shalt v. thy habitation and not
　sin. *Job* 5:24
v. him every morning. 7:18
O Lord, awake to v. all. *Ps* 59:5
from heaven and v. this vine. 80:14
I v. their transgression with. 89:32

remember me, O v. me with.Ps 106:4
the Lord will v. Tyre. Isa 23:17
neither shall they v. the ark of the.
Jer 3:16
v. for these things ? 5:9, 29; 9:9
at time I v. them, they shall. 6:15
will remember iniquity and v. 14:10
knowest, remember and v. 15:15
I will v. on you the evil of. 23:2
shall they be till I v. them. 27:22
I will v. you and perform. 29:10
there shall he be till I v. him. 32:5
the time I will v. Esau. 49:8
v. Babylon. 50:31
he will v. thine iniquity. Lam 4:22
I will v. on her the days. Hos 2:13
now will he v. their sins. 8:13; 9:9
I will also v. the altars. Amos 3:14
Lord shall v. and turn. Zeph 2:7
which shall not v. those. Zech 11:16
it came into his heart to v. Acts 7:23
hath declared how God did v. 15:14
go again and v. our brethren in. 36
is this, to v. the fatherless. Jas 1:27

visitation
after the v. of all men. Num 16:29
thy v. hath preserved. Job 10:12
ye do in the day of v.? Isa 10:3
in the time of their v. shall. Jer 8:12
in the time of v. they shall perish.
10:15; 51:18
of Anathoth, even in the year of their
v. 11:23; 23:12; 48:44
the time of their v. 46:21; 50:27
the days of v. are come. Hos 9:7
thy v. cometh, now shall be. Mi 7:4
not the time of thy v. Luke 19:44
they may glorify God in the day of
v. 1 Pet 2:12

visited
and the Lord v. Sarah as. Gen 21:1
I have surely v. you. Ex 3:16
that the Lord had v. Israel. 4:31
if they be v. after visitation of all
men. Num 16:29
that Samson v. his wife. Judg 15:1
she heard how the Lord had v. his.
Ruth 1:6
the Lord v. Hannah. 1 Sam 2:21
now it is not so, he hath v. in his
anger. Job 35:15
thou hast v. me, thou. Ps 17:3
he shall not be v. with evil. Pr 19:23
days shall they be v. Isa 24:22
therefore hast thou v. and. 26:14
Lord, in trouble have they v. 26
thou shalt be v. of the Lord. 29:6
Jerusalem is the city to be v. Jer 6:6
flock and have not v. them. 23:2
days thou shalt be v. Ezek 38:8
the Lord of hosts hath v. Zech 10:3
I was sick, and ye v. me. Mat 25:36
ye v. me not. 43
he hath v. and redeemed. Luke 1:68
dayspring from on high hath v. us. 78
saying, That God hath v. his. 7:16

visitest
and the son of man, that thou v.
him ? Ps 8:4; Heb 2:6
thou v. the earth and waterest it.
Ps 65:9

visiteth
when he v. what shall I ? Job 31:14

visiting
v. the iniquity of the fathers. Ex 20:5
34:7; Num 14:18; Deut 5:9

vocation
ye walk worthy of the v. Eph 4:1*

voice
By this word is not only understood the voice of a man or beast,
but all other sorts of sounds, noises,
or cries. And even thunder is also
called the voice of God. To hear
or to hearken to any one's voice is to
obey him, Ex 15:26.
the v. of thy brother's. Gen 4:10
v. is Jacob's v. but the hands. 27:22
and Jacob lifted up his v. and. 29:11
heard that I lifted up my v. 39:15
believe the v. of latter sign. Ex 4:8
God answered him by a v. 19:19

beware of him, obey his v. Ex 23:21
people answered with one v. 24:3
it is not the v. of them that. 32:18
if a soul hear the v. of. Lev 5:1
the congregation lifted up their v.
Num 14:1
be obedient to his v. Deut 4:30
not be obedient to his v. 8:20
any noise with your v. Josh 6:10
they knew the v. of the. Judg 18:3
is this thy v. my son David ?
1 Sam 24:16; 26:17
and the most High uttered his v.
2 Sam 22:14
*was no v. nor any that answered.
1 Ki 18:26, 29
after the fire a still small v. 19:12
there was neither v. nor. 2 Ki 4:31
there was no v. of man, but. 7:10
hast thou exalted thy v. and lifted up
thine eyes ? 19:22; Isa 37:23
by lifting up the v. with. 1 Chr 15:16
Job's friends lifted up their v. and.
Job 2:12
to be solitary, let no joyful v. 3:7
my organ into the v. of them. 30:31
a v. roareth, he thundereth with the
v. 37:4
marvellously with his v. 5
thunder with a v. like him ? 40:9
the Highest gave his v. Ps 18:13
I may publish with the v. of. 26:7
thou heardest the v. of my. 31:22
house of God with the v. of. 42:4
for the v. of him that. 44:16
he uttered his v., the earth. 46:6
shout unto God with the v. 47:1
he hath attended to the v. of. 66:19
his v. and that a mighty v. 68:33
forget not the v. of thine. 74:23
I cried unto the Lord with my v.
77:1; 142:1
the v. of thy thunder was in. 77:18
attend to the v. of my. 86:6
floods have lifted up their v. 93:3
sing unto the Lord with the v. 98:5
by reason of the v. of my. 102:5
hearkening to the v. of his. 103:20
at v. of thy thunder they. 104:7
v. of rejoicing in tabernacles. 118:15
give ear to my v. when I cry. 141:1
her v. in the streets. Pr 1:20
if thou liftest up thy v. 2:3
I have not obeyed the v. of. 5:13
understanding put forth her v.? 8:1
to you, O men, I call, my v. is. 4
a fool's v. is known by. Eccl 5:3
God be angry at thy v.? 6
bird of the air shall carry the v. 10:20
he shall rise up at the v. of. 12:4
the v. of my beloved. S of S 2:8
the v. of the turtle is heard in. 12
it is the v. of my beloved. 5:2
posts moved at the v. of. Isa 6:4
exalt the v. unto them, shake. 13:2
thy v. be as one that hath a. 29:4
be gracious to thee at the v. 30:19
will not be afraid of their v. 31:4
the v. of him that crieth in. 40:3
Mat 3:3; Mark 1:3; Luke 3:4
v. said, Cry. Isa 40:6
with the v. of singing. 48:20
that obeyeth the v. of his. 50:10
joy, thanksgiving, and the v. 51:3
with the v. together shall they. 52:8
v. of weeping shall be no more heard
in her, nor v. of crying. 65:19
a v. of noise, a v. from temple, a v.
66:6
a v. declareth from Dan. Jer 4:15
give out their v. against the cities. 16
their v. roareth like the sea. 6:23
50:42
v. of mirth, v. of gladness, v. of the
bridegroom, v. of bride. 7:34
16:9; 25:10; 33:11
v. of the cry of the daughter. 8:19
uttereth his v., there is a multitude
of waters. 10:13; 51:16
a v. of the cry of shepherds. 25:36
and the v. of them that make. 30:19
a v. was heard in Ramah. 31:15
saith the Lord, refrain thy v. 16
the v. thereof shall go like. 46:22*

a v. of crying shall be from. Jer 48:3*
the v. of them that flee. 50:28
hath destroyed out of her the great
v. 51:55
I heard as the v. of the Almighty.
Ezek 1:24*
as the v. of the Almighty God. 10:5
and a v. of a multitude. 23:42
of one that hath a pleasant v. 33:32
his v. was like a noise of many
waters. 43:2; Rev 1:15; 19:6
fell a v. from heaven. Dan 4:31
lamentable v. to Daniel. 6:20
v. of his words like the v. of. 10:6
Lord shall utter his v. Joel 2:11
shall utter his v. from Jerusalem.
3:16; Amos 1:2
I will sacrifice with v. Jonah 2:9
as with the v. of doves. Nah 2:7
a v. from heaven, This is my beloved
Son, in. Mat 3:17; Mark 1:11
Luke 3:22
a v. out of the cloud, This is.
Mat 17:5; Mark 9:7; Luke 9:35, 36
as soon as the v. of thy. Luke 1:44
the v. of one crying in. John 1:23
of the bridegroom's v. 3:29
him, for they know his v. 10:4
for they know not the v. of. 5
a v. saying, I have glorified it. 12:28
this v. came not because of me. 30
is of the truth heareth my v. 18:37
hearing a v., but seeing no. Acts 9:7
came a v. saying, Rise, Peter. 10:13
and the v. spake unto him. 15; 11:9
when she knew Peter's v. she. 12:14
it is the v. of a god, and not. 22
all with one v. cried, Great is. 19:34
except it be for this one v. 24:21
I gave my v. against them. 26:10*
the meaning of the v. 1 Cor 14:11
that by my v. I might teach. 19
now to change my v. Gal 4:20
with v. of the archangel. 1 Thes 4:16
v. then shook the earth. Heb 12:26
came a v. from the excellent glory.
2 Pet 1:17
ass speaking with man's v. 2:16
I turned to see the v. Rev 1:12
there came a great v. saying. 16:17

voice joined with hear
hear my v. ye wives of. Gen 4:23
did ever people hear v.? Deut 4:33
he made thee to hear his v. 36
if we hear the v. of God. 5:25
he said, Hear, Lord, the v. 33:7
can I hear the v. of ? 2 Sam 19:35
and he did hear my v. out of. 22:7
they hear not the v. of the. Job 3:18
hear attentively the noise of his v.
37:2
my v. shalt thou hear in. Ps 5:3
hear, O Lord, when I cry with my v.
27:7; 28:2; 64:1; 119:149; 130:2
140:6
hear me, because of the v. of. 55:3
aloud and he shall hear my v. 17
to-day if ye will hear his v., harden
not. 95:7; Heb 3:7, 15; 4:7
hear thy v., for sweet is thy v.
S of S 2:14
hear my v. ye careless. Isa 32:9
nor can men hear the v. Jer 9:10
any man hear his v. Mat 12:19
the dead shall hear the v. of the Son
of God. John 5:25, 28
and sheep hear his v. 10:3, 16, 27
and shouldest hear the v. Acts 22:14
if any man hear my v. Rev 3:20
see heard, lift, Lord, loud, obey,
obeyed

voice with hearken, hearkened
because thou hast hearkened unto
the v. of thy wife. Gen 3:17
Abram hearkened to the v. 16:2
hath said hearken to her v. 21:12
shall hearken to thy v. Ex 3:18
will not hearken unto my v. 4:1
nor hearken to the v. of the first. 8
neither hearken unto thy v. 9
if diligently hearken to the v. 15:26
hearken unto my v., I will give. 18:19
hearkened to the v. of Jethro. 24

and not *hearkened* to my *v.*
  Num 14:22; *Deut* 9:23; 28:45
Lord *hearkened* to the *v. Num* 21:3
the Lord would not *hearken* to your
  v.   *Deut* 1:45
hearken to the *v.* of the Lord. 13:18
only if thou carefully *hearken* to the
  v. 15:5; 26:17; 28:1, 2; 30:10
not *hearken* to the *v.* of Lord. 28:15
hearkened to the *v.* of a man.
  Josh 10:14
this people have not *hearkened* to
  my *v.*   *Judg* 2:20
and God *hearkened* to the *v.* 13:9
not *hearken* to the *v.* of Israel. 20:13
they *hearkened* not unto the *v.* of
  their father.   *1 Sam* 2:25
hearken to the *v.* of the people. 8:7
  9:22
I have *hearkened* to your *v.* 12:1
Saul *hearkened* to the *v.* 19:6
I have *hearkened* to thy *v.* 25:35
hearken thou to the *v.* of thy. 28:22
he would not *hearken* to our *v.*
  2 Sam 12:18
not *hearken* to her *v.* 13:14
Ben-hadad *hearkened* to their *v.*
  1 Ki 20:25
will *hearken* to my *v.* *2 Ki* 10:6
not believe he had *hearkened* to my
  v.   *Job* 9:16
hearken to *v.* of my words. 34:16
hearken to the *v.* of my cry. *Ps* 5:2
will not *hearken* to the *v.* of. 58:5
would not *hearken* to my *v.* 81:11
the companions *hearken* to thy *v.*
  S of S 8:13
hearken to the *v.* of them. *Jer* 18:19

voices

lepers lifted up their *v. Luke* 17:13
instant with loud *v.* that he might be
  crucified, the *v.* of them. 23:23
knew him not for our *v. Acts* 13:27
they lift up their *v.* and said. 22:22
so many *v.* in the world. *1 Cor* 14:10
out of the throne proceeded *v.*
  Rev 4:5; 16:18
into the earth: and there were *v.* 8:5
woe, by reason of the other *v.* 13
thunders uttered their *v.* 10:3, 4
there were great *v.* in heaven. 11:15
was opened, and there were *v.* 19

void

the earth was without form and *v.*
  Gen 1:2; *Jer* 4:23
but if her husband made them *v.*
  Num 30:12, 15
they are a people *v.* of. *Deut* 32:28
kings sat in a *v.* place. *1 Ki* 22:10*
  2 Chr 18:9*
made *v.* the covenant of. *Ps* 89:39*
have made *v.* thy law. 119:126
v. of wisdom despiseth. *Pr* 11:12
my word shall not return to me *v.*
  Isa 55:11
I will make *v.* the counsel. *Jer* 19:7
Nineveh is empty, *v.* *Nah* 2:10
conscience *v.* of offence. *Acts* 24:16
then make *v.* the law ? *Rom* 3:31*
law be heirs, faith is made *v.* 4:14
make my glorying *v.* *1 Cor* 9:15

see **understanding**

volume

Lo, I come: in the *v.* of the book it
is written. *Ps* 40:7*; *Heb* 10:7*

voluntarily

prepare offerings *v.* to. *Ezek* 46:12*

voluntary

it of his own *v.* will. *Lev* 1:3*
a *v.* offering shall be eaten. 7:16*
princes shall prepare a *v.* burnt.
  Ezek 46:12*
in a *v.* humility and. *Col* 2:18

vomit

riches and shall *v.* them. *Job* 20:15
eaten shall thou *v.* up. *Pr* 23:8
filled with honey and *v.* it. 25:16

vomit, *substantive*
dog returneth to his *v.* *Pr* 26:11
man staggereth in his *v.* *Isa* 19:14
for all tables are full of *v.* 28:8

shall wallow in his *v.* *Jer* 48:26
turned to his own *v.* *2 Pet* 2:22

vomited

the fish *v.* out Jonah on dry land.
  Jonah 2:10

vomiteth

the land *v.* out her inhabitants.
  Lev 18:25

vow

*Is a promise made to God, of doing
some good thing hereafter. The use
of vows was common in Bible times.
When Jacob went into Mesopotamia he vowed to God the tenth
of his estate, and promised to offer
it at Beth-el to the honour and service of God, Gen 28:20, 22. There
are several laws for the regulation
and due execution of vows. A
man might devote himself, or his
children, to the Lord. Samuel was
vowed and consecrated to the service of the Lord, and was offered
to him, to serve in the tabernacle,
1 Sam 1:22, 28. If a man or
woman vowed themselves, or their
children to the Lord, they were
obliged to adhere strictly to his
service, according to the conditions
of the vow; if not, they were to be
redeemed. The price for redeeming persons of such and such an
age is particularly limited, Lev 27:2,
3, etc. Only if the person was
poor, and could not procure the
sum limited, the priest imposed a
ransom upon him according to his
abilities.
If any one had vowed an animal
that was clean, he had not the liberty
of redeeming it, or of exchanging
it, but was obliged to sacrifice it to
the Lord, or give it to the priest,
according to the manner of his
vow. If it was an unclean animal,
and such as was not allowed to be
sacrificed, the priest made valua-
tion of it; and if the proprietor would
redeem it, he added a fifth part to
the value, by way of forfeit. The
same was done in proportion, when
the thing vowed was a house or a
field. See Lev 27:9, 10, etc. They
could not devote the firstlings of
beasts, because they belonged to
the Lord, Lev 27:26. Whatsoever
was solemnly devoted to the Lord
could not be redeemed, of whatever nature or quality it was, Lev
27:28. Concerning the vows of the
Nazarites, see* **Nazarite.**
*The vows and promises of children
were void, except they were ratified,
either by the express or tacit consent of their parents. And it was
the same with the vows of married
women; they were of no validity,
unless they were confirmed by the
express or tacit consent of their
husbands,* Num 30:1, 2, 3, etc.
*Under the New Testament, a vow
is either general to all Christians,
as that which is made at
baptism; or particular and special,
as when we bind ourselves to a
greater endeavour, to leave some
sin, or perform some duty. A
vow, as one observes, must be
made deliberately and devoutly,
for a sudden passion makes not a
vow; and we ought to vow nothing
but what is in our power to perform.
Some vows are of evil things to an
evil end; such vows ought neither
to be made nor kept; of this kind
was the vow or curse which the
Jews bound themselves under, who
conspired to murder Paul,* Acts
23:12.
*The performance of solemn vows
is strictly enjoined upon us in
scripture,* Eccl 5:4.

Jacob vowed a *v. Gen* 28:20; 31:13
if the sacrifice be a *v.* *Lev* 7:16
  22:18, 21
but for a *v.* it shall not. 22:23
shall make a singular *v.* 27:2
vow a *v.* of a Nazarite. *Num* 6:2
the days of the *v.* 5
according to the *v.* 21
sacrifice in performing a *v.* 15:3, 8
Israel vowed a *v.* to the Lord. 21:2
if a man vow a *v.* 30:2
if a woman vow a *v.* 3
and her father hear her *v.* and. 4
every *v.* of a widow shall stand. 9
every *v.* her husband may. 13
price of a dog for a *v.* *Deut* 23:18
when thou shalt vow a *v.* unto. 21
Jephthah vowed a *v.* *Judg* 11:30
with her according to his *v.* 39
Hannah vowed a *v.* and. *1 Sam* 1:11
up to offer to the Lord his *v.* 21
let me go and pay my *v.* *2 Sam* 15:7
servant vowed a *v.* at Geshur. 8
to thee shall the *v.* be. *Ps* 65:1
when thou vowest a *v.* *Eccl* 5:4
they shall vow a *v.* unto. *Isa* 19:21
head, for he had a *v.* *Acts* 18:18
men which have a *v.* on them. 21:23

vow, *verb*

themselves to *v.* a vow. *Num* 6:2
if forbear to *v.*, it shall. *Deut* 23:22
and *v.* and pay to the Lord your God.
  Ps 76:11
that thou shouldest not *v.* *Eccl* 5:5

vowed

Jacob *v.* a vow. *Gen* 28:20; 31:13
ability that *v.* shall priest. *Lev* 27:8
Nazarites who hath *v.* *Num* 6:21
Israel *v.* a vow to the Lord. 21:2
if all an husband when she *v.* 30:6
and if she *v.* in her husband's. 10
shalt keep according as thou hast *v.*
  Deut 23:23
Jephthah *v.* a vow unto. *Judg* 11:30
and *v.* to the mighty God. *Ps* 132:2
pay that which thou hast *v.* *Eccl* 5:4
pay that that I have *v.* *Jonah* 2:9

vowest

when thou *v.* a vow, defer. *Eccl* 5:4

voweth

who *v.* to the Lord a. *Mal* 1:14

vows

his oblation for all his *v.* *Lev* 22:18
gifts and beside all your *v.* 23:38
shall do beside your *v.* *Num* 29:39
then all her *v.* shall stand. 30:4
  7, 9, 11
not any of her *v.* or bonds. 5, 8, 12
then he established all her *v.* 14
thither bring your *v.* *Deut* 12:6, 11
  17, 26
thou shalt pay thy *v.* *Job* 22:27
I will pay my *v.* unto the Lord.
  Ps 22:25; 66:13; 116:14, 18
pay thy *v.* 50:14
thy *v.* are upon me, O God. 56:12
O God, hast heard my *v.* 61:5
I may daily perform my *v.* 8
this day have I paid my *v.* *Pr* 7:14
it is a snare after *v.* to make. 20:25
and what, the son of my *v.* ? 31:2
surely perform our *v.* *Jer* 44:25
feared the Lord and made *v.*
  Jonah 1:16
O Judah, keep thy solemn feasts,
  perform thy *v.* *Nah* 1:15

voyage

I perceive this *v.* will be. *Acts* 27:10

vulture

(*A bird of prey, which was declared unclean,* Lev 11:14. *Probably the word means the kite as
the Revised Versions give it
usually, or the falcon as in Job*)
v. and the kite after his kind shall.
  Lev 11:14; *Deut* 14:13
a path which the *v.* eye. *Job* 28:7*
there shall the *v.* also be. *Isa* 34:15

W

wafer

one w. out of the basket of the unleavened. *Ex* 29:23; *Lev* 8:26
one cake, one w. on. *Num* 6:19

wafers

taste of it was like w. *Ex* 16:31
and w. unleavened anointed. *Ex* 29:2
w. anointed with oil. *Lev* 2:4; 7:12
Num 6:15

wag

passeth by shall w. his. *Jer* 18:16*
w. their heads at daughter. *Lam* 2:15
passeth shall w. his hand. *Zeph* 2:15

wages

what shall thy w. be? *Gen* 29:15
appoint me thy w. and I will. 30:28
changed my w. ten times. 31:7, 41
the speckled shall be thy w. 8
this child, I will give thee w. *Ex* 2:9
w. of hired not abide. *Lev* 19:13
service without w. *Jer* 22:13
yet had he no w. nor. *Ezek* 29:18
her spoil shall be the w. for. 19
earneth w. to put into a. *Hag* 1:6
the hireling in his w. *Mal* 3:5
be content with your w. *Luke* 3:14
reapeth receiveth w. *John* 4:36
for the w. of sin is death. *Rom* 6:23
taking w. of them to do. *2 Cor* 11:8
Balaam loved the w. *2 Pet* 2:15

wagging

passed by reviled him, w. their heads. *Mat* 27:39; *Mark* 15:29

waggon

brought a w. for two of the princes. *Num* 7:3

waggons

w. out of Egypt. *Gen* 45:19, 21
when Jacob saw the w. Joseph. 27
two w., four oxen to sons. *Num* 7:7
four w. and eight oxen to the. 8
against thee with w. *Ezek* 23:34

wail

w. for the multitude of. *Ezek* 32:18
I will w. and howl. *Mi* 1:8
earth shall w. for him. *Rev* 1:7*

wailed

them that wept and w. greatly. *Mark* 5:38

wailing

decree came there was w. *Esth* 4:3
for the mountains will I take up w *Jer* 9:10
let them take up a w. for us. 18
for a voice of w. is heard out of. 19
teach your daughters w. 20
neither shall there be w. *Ezek* 7:11
weep for thee with bitter w. 27:31*
w. shall be in all streets and they shall say . . . to w. *Amos* 5:16
and in all vineyards shall be w. 17
I will make a w. like the. *Mi* 1:8
there shall be w. and gnashing of teeth. *Mat* 13:42*, 50*
the merchants stand afar off, w. *Rev* 18:15*, 19*

wait

him by laying of w. *Num* 35:20
any thing without laying w. 22
in his heart he layeth his w. *Jer* 9:8*
see laid, lay

wait

Aaron and sons shall w. on their priest's office. *Num* 3:10; 8:24
1 Chr 23:28; *2 Chr* 5:11; 13:10
should I w. for the Lord? *2 Ki* 6:33
of my time I will w. till. *Job* 14:14
if I w. the grave is my house. 17:13
let none that w. on thee be ashamed. *Ps* 25:3; 69:6
God of salvation, on thee do I w. 25:5
preserve me, for I w. on thee. 21
w. on the Lord. 27:14; 37:34
Pr 20:22
w. patiently for him. *Ps* 37:7
that w. on the Lord shall inherit. 9
Lord, what w. I for? 39:7
I will w. on thy name. 52:9

mark my steps when they w. *Ps* 56:6
because of his strength will I w. 59:9
w. only on God. 62:5
mine eyes fail while I w. for. 69:3
these all w. upon thee. 104:27
145:15
so our eyes w. on the Lord. 123:2
I w. for the Lord, my soul doth w. 130:5
I will w. upon the Lord. *Isa* 8:17
Lord w. to be gracious to you, blessed are all they that w. 30:18
but they that w. on the Lord shall renew their strength. 40:31
the isles shall w. for his law. 42:4
shall not be ashamed that w. 49:23
isles shall w. upon me. 51:5
we w. for light, but behold. 59:9
the isles shall w. for me. 60:9
we will w. upon thee. *Jer* 14:22
Lord is good to them that w. for him. *Lam* 3:25
a man hope and quietly w. 26
as troops of robbers w. *Hos* 6:9
keep mercy and w. on thy God. 12:6
I will w. for the God of. *Mi* 7:7
though vision tarry, w. for. *Hab* 2:3
therefore w. ye upon me. *Zeph* 3:8
ship should w. on him. *Mark* 3:9
like unto men that w. *Luke* 12:36
but w. for the promise. *Acts* 1:4
with patience w. for it. *Rom* 8:25
or ministry, let us w. on. 12:7*
which w. at the altar. *1 Cor* 9:13
we through the Spirit w. *Gal* 5:5
and to w. for his Son. *1 Thes* 1:10
see liars

waited

w. for thy salvation. *Gen* 49:18
the prophet w. for king. *1 Ki* 20:38
w. on Naaman's wife. *2 Ki* 5:2
and then they w. on their office. *1 Chr* 6:32, 33
porters that w. in king's gate. 9:18
2 Chr 35:15
and the priests w. on. *2 Chr* 7:6
and Levites that w. *Neh* 12:44
the companies of Sheba w. *Job* 6:19
he is w for of the sword. 15:22
to me men gave ear, w. and. 29:21
w. for me as for the rain. 23
when I w. for light, there came. 30:26
now Elihu had w. till Job had. 32:4
I w. patiently for the Lord. *Ps* 40:1
they w. not for counsel. 106:13
wicked have w. for me to. 119:95
God, we have w. for him. *Isa* 25:9
judgements have we w. for. 26:8
us, we have w. for thee. 33:2
she saw that she had w. *Ezek* 19:5
of Maroth w. carefully. *Mi* 1:12
flock that w. upon me. *Zech* 11:11
Joseph of Arimathaea, who also w. *Mark* 15:43; *Luke* 23:51
the people w. for Zacharias. *Luke* 1:21
a soldier that w. on him. *Acts* 10:7
Cornelius w. for Peter and. 24
Paul w. for them, his spirit. 17:16
longsuffering of God w. in days of Noah. *1 Pet* 3:20

waiteth

eye of the adulterer w. *Job* 24:15
our soul w. for the Lord. *Ps* 33:20
truly my soul w. upon. 62:1; 130:6
praise w. for thee, O God. 65:1
he that w. on his master. *Pr* 27:18
prepared for him that w. *Isa* 64:4
blessed is he that w. and cometh to the 1335 days. *Dan* 12:12
as showers that w. not. *Mi* 5:7
w. for the manifestation of. *Rom* 8:19
the husbandman w. for. *Jas* 5:7

waiting

from the age of 50 years they shall cease w. upon the. *Num* 8:25
w. at the posts of my doors. *Pr* 8:34
Simeon w. for the consolation of. *Luke* 2:25
folk w. for the moving. *John* 5:3
groan, w. for the adoption. *Rom* 8:23
w. for the coming of our Lord Jesus Christ. *1 Cor* 1:7

into the patient w. for Christ. *2 Thes* 3:5

wake, awake

when I a., I am still with. *Ps* 139:18
perpetual sleep and not w. *Jer* 51:39
prepare war, w. up the mighty men. *Joel* 3:9*
whether we w. or sleep. *1 Thes* 5:10

waked

angel came again and w. *Zech* 4:1

wakened

let heathen be w. and. *Joel* 3:12*
as a man that is w. out. *Zech* 4:1

wakeneth

he w. morning by morning, he w. mine ear. *Isa* 50:4

waketh

city, watchman w. in vain. *Ps* 127:1
I sleep but my heart w. *S of S* 5:2

waking

thou holdest mine eyes w. *Ps* 77:4

walk

the Lord, before whom I w. *Gen* 24:40
my fathers did w. bless. 48:15
whether they will w. in. *Exod* 16:4
way wherein they must w. 18:20
if he w. abroad, he that smote. 21:19
neither shall ye w. in their ordinances. *Lev* 18:3; 20:23
if ye w. in my statutes and. 26:3
1 Ki 6:12; *Ezek* 33:15; *Zech* 3:7
I will w. among you. *Lev* 26:12
if ye w. contrary to me. 21, 23, 27
then will I w. contrary to you. 24, 28
shall w. in all the ways. *Deut* 5:33
13:4; 28:9; *Ezek* 37:24
if ye w. after other gods. *Deut* 8:19
though I w. in the imagination. 29:19
take diligent heed to w. *Josh* 22:5
speak, ye that w. by the. *Judg* 5:10
thy house should w. before me for ever. *1 Sam* 2:30
he shall w. before mine anointed. 35
thou art old, thy sons w. not in. 8:5
w. to keep my commandments as . . . David did w. *1 Ki* 3:14; 8:25
9:4; 11:38; *2 Chr* 7:17
with thy servants that w. before thee with all. *1 Ki* 8:23; *2 Chr* 6:14
the good way wherein they should w. *1 Ki* 8:36; *2 Chr* 6:27
the wicked w. on every. *Ps* 12:8
though I w. through the valley. 23:4
but as for me, I will w. in mine. 26:11
that I may w. before God in. 56:13
they know not; they w. on in. 82:5
from them that w. uprightly. 84:11
teach me, O Lord, I will w. 86:11
shall w. in the light of thy. 89:15
if his children w. not in my. 30
I will w. in my house with a. 101:2
have they, but they w. not. 115:7
I will w. before the Lord in. 116:9
they do no iniquity, they w. 119:3
I will w. at liberty, for I seek. 45
I w. in the midst of trouble. 138:7
way wherein I should w. 143:8
he is a buckler to them that w. uprightly. *Pr* 2:7
that thou mayest w. in the way. 20
then shalt thou w. in thy way. 3:23
we will w. in his paths. *Isa* 2:5
Mi 4:2
Jacob, let us w. in the light. *Isa* 2:5
they w. with stretched forth. 3:16
that I should not w. in the way. 8:11
redeemed shall w. there. 35:9
they that wait on Lord shall w. 40:31
spirit to them that w. therein. 42:5
for they would not w. in his ways. 24
wait for brightness, but we w. 59:9
nor w. after imagination. *Jer* 3:17
the house of Judah shall w. with. 18
but they said, We will not w. 6:16
if ye w. not after other gods to. 7:6
will ye w. after other gods whom? 9:4
every neighbour will w. with. 9:4
w. in imagination of their heart, and w. after. 13:10; 16:12; 18:12
adultery, and w. in lies. 23:14
way wherein we may w. 42:3

the foxes _w._ upon it. _Lam_ 5:18
_w._ in my statutes. _Ezek_ 11:20
shall _w._ in my judgements. 37:24
those that _w._ in pride. _Dan_ 4:37
they shall _w._ after the Lord: he shall
  roar like a. _Hos_ 11:10
the just shall _w._ in them. 14:9
they shall _w._ every one. _Joel_ 2:8
two _w._ together except ? _Amos_ 3:3
_w._ every one in name of his god, and
  we will _w._ in the name. _Mi_ 4:5
and ye _w._ in the counsels of. 6:16
thou didst _w._ through the sea.
  Hab 3:15*
that they shall _w._ like blind men.
  Zeph 1:17
they might _w._ to and fro through
  the earth. _Zech_ 6:7
they shall _w._ up and down. 10:12
the lame _w._, the lepers are cleansed.
  Mat 11:5; _Luke_ 7:22
why _w._ not thy disciples ? _Mark_ 7:5
men that _w._ over them. _Luke_ 11:44
I must _w._ to-day and. 13:33
communications as ye _w._? 24:17
for Jesus would not _w._ _John_ 7:1
shall not _w._ in darkness but. 8:12
if any man _w._ in the day. 11:9
if a man _w._ in the night, he. 10
who also _w._ in the steps of that faith
  of. _Rom_ 4:12
so we should _w._ in newness of. 6:4
who _w._ not after flesh, but. 8:1, 4
for we _w._ by faith, not. _2 Cor_ 5:7
I will dwell in them and _w._ 6:16
we _w._ in the flesh, not war. 10:3
as many as _w._ according. _Gal_ 6:16
ordained we should _w._ _Eph_ 2:10
ye _w._ worthy of the vocation. 4:1
that ye _w._ not as other Gentiles. 17
then that ye _w._ circumspectly. 5:15
mark them which _w._ so. _Phil_ 3:17
many _w._ of whom I told you. 18
that ye might _w._ worthy of the Lord.
  Col 1:10; _1 Thes_ 2:12
ye may _w._ honestly. _1 Thes_ 4:12
some which _w._ among you disorderly. _2 Thes_ 3:11
but chiefly them that _w._ _2 Pet_ 2:10
have fellowship, and _w._ in darkness.
  1 John 1:6
but if we _w._ in the light as he. 7
_w._ after his commandments, as ye
  . . . ye should _w._ _2 John_ 6
to hear that my children _w._ _3 John_ 4
mockers should _w._ after. _Jude_ 18
shall _w._ with me in white. _Rev_ 3:4
see, nor hear, nor _w._ 9:20
watcheth, lest he _w._ naked. 16:15
the nations shall _w._ in the light. 21:24

walk, _imperatively_
arise, _w._ through the land.
  Gen 13:17; _Josh_ 18:8
Almighty God, _w._ before me.
  Gen 17:1
_w._ about Zion and go. _Ps_ 48:12
my son, _w._ not in the way. _Pr_ 1:15
_w._ in the ways of thy heart and eyes.
  Eccl 11:9
O Jacob, let us _w._ in the. _Isa_ 2:5
This·is the way, _w._ ye in it. 30:21
_w._ in the light of your fire and. 50:11
the good way, _w._ therein. _Jer_ 6:16
go not forth into fields, nor _w._ 25
_w._ ye in all the ways I. 7:23
_w._ ye not in statutes. _Ezek_ 20:18
they might _w._ to and fro. _Zech_ 6:7
or to say, Arise and _w._ _Mat_ 9:5
  Mark 2:9; _Luke_ 5:23; _John_ 5:8
  11, 12; _Acts_ 3:6
_w._ while ye have the light, lest darkness. _John_ 12:35
let us _w._ honestly as in the day.
  Rom 13:13
as the Lord hath called every one, so
  let him _w._ _1 Cor_ 7:17
_w._ in the Spirit, and not fulfil the
  lusts. _Gal_ 5:16, 25
_w._ in love. _Eph_ 5:2
_w._ as children of light.
let us _w._ by the same rule. _Phil_ 3:16
Christ, so _w._ ye in him. _Col_ 2:6
_w._ in wisdom toward them. 4:5

to walk
to _w._ in my ordinances. _Lev_ 18:4
to _w._ in his ways, and fear him.
  Deut 8:6; 10:12; 11:22; 13:5
  19:9; 26:17; 30:16; _Josh_ 22:5
  Judg 2:22; _1 Ki_ 2:3; 8:58
  2 Chr 6:31
take heed _to w._ before. _1 Ki_ 2:4
heart perfect, _to w._ in his statutes.
  8:61; _Ezek_ 36:27
a light thing _to w._ in sins. _1 Ki_ 16:31
Jehu took no heed _to w._ _2 Ki_ 10:31
Josiah made a covenant _to w._ after.
  23:3; _2 Chr_ 34:31
take heed _to w._ in my law. _2 Chr_ 6:16
ought ye not _to w._ in the fear of
  God ? _Neh_ 5:9
they entered into an oath _to w._ 10:29
they refused _to w._ in his. _Ps_ 78:10
leave right _to w._ in ways. _Pr_ 2:13
poor that knoweth _to w._ _Eccl_ 6:8
_to w._ in paths, in a way. _Jer_ 18:15
if ye will not hearken _to w._ 26:4
I will cause them _to w._ in a. 31:9
I will cause men _to w._ _Ezek_ 36:12
nor have we obeyed _to w._ _Dan_ 9:10
_to w._ humbly with thy God. _Mi_ 6:8
he will make me _to w._ _Hab_ 3:19
whom Lord hath sent _to w._ _Zech_ 1:10
will give places _to w._ among. 3:7
they saw the lame _to w._ _Mat_ 15:31
the scribes desire _to w._ _Luke_ 20:46
had made this man _to w._ _Acts_ 3:12
suffered all nations _to w._ 14:16
to circumcise, nor _to w._ after. 21:21
how ye ought _to w._ and. _1 Thes_ 4:1
ought himself so _to w._ _1 John_ 2:6

walked
Enoch _w._ with God. _Gen_ 5:22, 24
Noah was a just man, and _w._ 6:9
Israel _w._ upon the dry. _Ex_ 14:29
that also they have _w._ _Lev_ 26:40
Israel _w._ forty years in. _Josh_ 5:6
of the way their fathers _w._ in.
  Judg 2:17
travellers _w._ through byways. 5:6
when Israel _w._ through the. 11:16
Samuel's sons _w._ not. _1 Sam_ 8:3
Abner and his men _w._ _2 Sam_ 2:29
David _w._ on the roof·of the. 11:2
that they walk before me as thou
  hast _w._ _1 Ki_ 8:25
as David thy father _w._ 9:4
  2 Chr 6:16; 7:17
have not _w._ in my ways. _1 Ki_ 11:33
Ezek 5:6, 7; 11:12; 20:13, 16, 21
he _w._ in the way of his father.
  _1 Ki_ 15:26; 22:52
in the sight of the Lord and _w._ in.
  15:34; 16:2; _2 Ki_ 13:6; 17:22
returned, and _w._ in house. _2 Ki_ 4:35
Hoshea _w._ in the statutes of. 17:8
Judah kept not commandments of the
  Lord, but _w._ in. 19; _2 Chr_ 21:13
forsook the Lord, and _w._ not in the
  way of the Lord. _2 Ki_ 21:22
  Jer 9:13; 32:23; 44:10, 23
Josiah _w._ in ways of David.
  _2 Ki_ 22:2; _2 Chr_ 34:2
for three years they _w._ in the way
  of David. _2 Chr_ 11:17
Jehoshaphat _w._ in God's. 17:4
hast not _w._ in the ways of. 21:12
when by his light I _w._ _Job_ 29:3
if mine heart _w._ after mine. 31:7
we _w._ to the house of. _Ps_ 55:14
to hearts' lust: they _w._ in. 81:12
O that Israel had _w._ in my ways! 13
in the way I _w._ have they. 142:3
people that _w._ in darkness. _Isa_ 9:2
as my servant Isaiah hath _w._ 20:3
that they have _w._ after vanity.
  Jer 2:5, 8
but _w._ in counsels of their evil heart.
  7:24; 11:8
after whom they have _w._ 8:2; 9:14
  16:11
yet hast not thou _w._ _Ezek_ 16:47
hath _w._ in my statutes. 18:9, 17
thou hast _w._ in the way of. 23:31
hast _w._ in the midst of the. 28:14
way which their fathers _w._ _Amos_ 2:4
even the old lion, _w._ _Nah_ 2:11

we have _w._ to and fro through the
  earth. _Zech_ 1:11; 6:7
what profit that we have _w._ mournfully ? _Mal_ 3:14
damsel arose and _w._ _Mark_ 5:42
to two of them as they _w._ 16:12
many disciples _w._ no more with him.
  John 6:66
Jesus _w._ no more openly. 11:54
and he leaping up, stood and _w._
  Acts 3:8; 14:10
a cripple, who never had _w._ 14:8
who think as if we _w._ _2 Cor_ 10:2
gain of you ? _w._ we not in the same
  spirit ? _w._ we not in ? 12:18
but when I saw they _w._ not. _Gal_ 2:14
wherein in time past ye _w._ _Eph_ 2:2
  Col 3:7
_w._ in lasciviousness. _1 Pet_ 4:3

he walked
to David, as _he w._ before. _1 Ki_ 3:6
Abijam _w._ in all the sins of his father.
  15:3; _2 Ki_ 21:21
he _w._ in all the ways. _1 Ki_ 16:26
he _w._ in all the ways of Asa. 22:43
  2 Chr 20:32
and _he w._ in the way of the kings of.
  _2 Ki_ 8:18, 27; 16:3; _2 Chr_ 21:6
  22:3, 5; 28:2
he _w._ in the first ways. _2 Chr_ 17:3
Nebuchadnezzar _w._ in the palace of.
  Dan 4:29
he willingly _w._ after the. _Hos_ 5:11
he _w._ with me in peace. _Mal_ 2:6
Peter _w._ on the water. _Mat_ 14:29
to walk even as _he w._ _1 John_ 2:6

I have walked
and that _I have w._ _Lev_ 26:41
I have w. before you from childhood.
  1 Sam 12:2
I have w. in a tent and tabernacle.
  2 Sam 7:6
in all places wherein _I have w._ 7
remember how _I have w._ _2 Ki_ 20:3
if _I have w._ with vanity. _Job_ 31:5
judge me, for _I have w._ _Ps_ 26:1
I have w. in thy truth. 3; _Isa_ 38:3

walkedst
when young, _w._ whither. _John_ 21:18

walkest
shalt talk of them when thou _w._
  Deut 6:7; 11:19
day thou _w._ abroad. _1 Ki_ 2:42
thou _w._ through the fire. _Isa_ 43:2
thou thyself _w._ orderly. _Acts_ 21:24
brother grieved, now _w._ _Rom_ 14:15
truth in thee even as thou _w._ _3 John_ 3

walketh
what man is this that _w._? _Gen_ 24:65
thy God _w._ in midst of. _Deut_ 23:14
behold, the king _w._ _1 Sam_ 12:2
he is cast into a net, and he _w._
  Job 18:8
he _w._ in the circuit of heaven. 22:14
goeth in company, and _w._ with. 34:8
blessed the man that _w._ not in. _Ps_ 1:1
he that _w._ uprightly shall dwell. 15:2
man _w._ in a vain shew. 39:6
and their tongue _w._ through. 73:9
nor for the pestilence that _w._ 91:6
he that _w._ in a perfect way. 101:6
who _w._ upon the wings of. 104:3
blessed is every one that _w._ 128:1
a wicked man _w._ with a. _Pr_ 6:12
_w._ uprightly _w._ surely. 10:9; 28:18
he that _w._ with wise men. 13:20
he that _w._ in uprightness. 14:2
a man of understanding _w._ 15:21*
better is the poor that _w._ 19:1; 28:6
just man _w._ in his integrity. 20:7
whoso _w._ wisely, he shall. 28:26
the fool _w._ in darkness. _Eccl_ 2:14
when he that is a fool _w._ by. 10:3
he that _w._ righteously. _Isa_ 33:15
that _w._ in darkness and hath. 50:10
which _w._ in a way that was. 65:2
it is not in man that _w._ _Jer_ 10:23
that _w._ after the imagination. 23:17
whose heart _w._ after the heart of
  their detestable things. _Ezek_ 11:21
my words do good to him that _w._
  uprightly. _Mi_ 2:7

spirit is gone out, he *w.* through dry.
    Mat 12:43; *Luke* 11:24
he that *w.* in darkness. *John* 12:35
from brother that *w.* 2 *Thes* 3:6
devil *w.* about seeking. 1 *Pet* 5:8
hateth his brother, *w.* 1 *John* 2:11
w. in midst of the seven. *Rev* 2:1

walking
voice of Lord *w.* in garden. *Gen* 3:8
Lord knoweth thy *w.* through this
    great wilderness. *Deut* 2:7
Solomon, *w.* as David. 1 *Ki* 3:3
Zimri *w.* in the way of. 16:19
from *w.* up and down in the earth.
    Job 1:7; 2:2
or beheld the moon *w.* in. 31:26
I have seen princes *w.* *Eccl* 10:7
haughty, *w.* and mincing. *Isa* 3:16
and he did so, *w.* naked. 20:2
each one *w.* in his uprightness. 57:2
all grievous revolters, *w.* *Jer* 6:28
I see four men loose, *w.* *Dan* 3:25
if a man *w.* in the spirit and. *Mat* 2:11
Jesus went to them *w.* *Mat* 14:25
saw him *w.* on the sea, they were
    troubled. 26; *Mark* 6:48
I see men as trees *w.* *Mark* 8:24
w. in all the commandments blame-
    less. *Luke* 1:6
lame man *w.* and leaping. *Acts* 3:8,9
were edified, *w.* in the fear. 9:31
not *w.* in craftiness, nor. 2 *Cor* 4:2
scoffers, *w.* after their own lusts.
    2 *Pet* 3:3; *Jude* 16
thy children *w.* in truth. 2 *John* 4

wall
in their selfwill they digged down a
    w. *Gen* 49:6*
branches run over the *w.* 22
waters were a *w.* to them. *Ex* 14:22
sight lower than the *w.* *Lev* 14:37
a *w.* being on this side, a *w.* on.
    Num 22:24*
Balaam's foot against the *w.* 25
house upon the town *w.* *Josh* 2:15
the *w.* of the city shall fall down flat.
    6:5, 20
I will smite David to the *w.*
    1 *Sam* 18:11; 19:10
sat upon his seat by the *w.* 20:25
they were a *w.* to us both. 25:16
morning light any that pisseth against
    the *w.* 22*; 34*; 1 *Ki* 14:10*
    16:11*; 21:21*; 2 *Ki* 9:8*
they fastened Saul's body to the *w.*
    1 *Sam* 31:10
knew ye not that they would shoot
    from the *w.*? 2 *Sam* 11:20
the *w.*, why went ye nigh the *w.*? 21
the people battered the *w.* 20:15
head shall be thrown over the *w.* 21
by my God have I leaped over a *w.*
    22:30; *Ps* 18:29
that springs out of the *w.* 1 *Ki* 4:33
a *w.* fell upon 27,000 of the. 20:30
dogs shall eat Jezebel by *w.* 21:23*
a burnt offering upon the *w.* 2 *Ki* 3:27
a little chamber on the *w.* 4:10
king was passing by upon the *w.* 6:26
was sprinkled on the *w.* 9:33
language in the ears of the people
    that are on the *w.* 18:26; *Isa* 36:11
then Hezekiah turned his face to the
    w. 2 *Ki* 20:2; *Isa* 38:2
Joash brake down the *w.* of Jerusa-
    lem. 2 *Chr* 25:23
Nebuchadnezzar brake down the *w.*
    36:19
who hath commanded you to make
    this *w.*? *Ezra* 5:3
to give us a *w.* in Judah. 9:9
the *w.* of Jerusalem is. *Neh* 1:3
I viewed the *w.* 2:15
let us build the *w.* 17
break down their stone *w.* 4:3
so built we the *w.*; all the *w.* was. 6
all of us to the *w.*, every one. 15
thou buildest the *w.*, that thou. 6:6
so the *w.* was finished in the. 15
at the dedication of the *w.* of. 12:27
Why lodge ye about the *w.*? 13:21
as a bowing *w.* shall ye be. *Ps* 62:3
as an high *w.* in his. *Pr* 18:11

the stone *w.* thereof was. *Pr* 24:31
standeth behind our *w.* *S of S* 2:9
if she be a *w'.*, we will build. 8:9
I am a *w.* 10
of Lord on every fenced *w.* *Isa* 2:15
I will break down the *w.* of. 5:5*
is as a storm against the *w.* 25:4
swelling out in an high *w.* 30:13
we grope for the *w.* like the. 59:10
thee a fenced brasen *w.* *Jer* 15:20
I will kindle a fire in the *w.* of. 49:27
yea, the *w.* of Babylon shall. 51:44
to destroy the *w.* of the. *Lam* 2:8
their heart cried, O *w.* of the. 18
for a *w.* of iron between. *Ezek* 4:3
a hole in the *w.* 8:7
dig in the *w.* 8; 12:5
Israel pourtrayed upon the *w.* 8:10
lo, when the *w.* is fallen. 13:12, 15
accomplish my wrath upon the *w.* 15
every *w.* shall fall. 38:20
after he measured the *w.* of. 41:5
in setting the *w.* between me. 43:8
on the plaster of the *w.* *Dan* 5:5
street shall be built, and the *w.* 9:25*
I will make a *w.* that she shall not
    find. *Hos* 2:6*
they shall climb the *w.* *Joel* 2:7
they shall run upon the *w.* and. 9
a fire on the *w.* of Gaza. *Amos* 1:7
on the *w.* of Tyrus. 10
in the *w.* of Rabbah. 14
hand on the *w.*, a serpent bit. 5:19
behold, the Lord stood upon a *w.* 7:7
haste to the *w.* thereof. *Nah* 2:5
shall cry out of the *w.* *Hab* 2:11
disciples by night let him down by
    the *w.* *Acts* 9:25; 2 *Cor* 11:33
smite thee, thou whited *w.* *Acts* 23:3
broken down the middle *w.* *Eph* 2:14
the *w.* of the city had twelve founda-
    tions. *Rev* 21:14
the building of the *w.* of it was. 18
    see **built**

walled
if a man sell a dwelling house in a *w.*
    city. *Lev* 25:29
the house in the *w.* city shall. 30
the cities *w.* and very great.
    Num 13:28*; *Deut* 1:28*

wallow
gird thee with sackcloth, *w.* *Jer* 6:26
cry, *w.* yourselves in ashes. 25:34
Moab shall *w.* in his vomit. 48:26
they shall *w.* themselves. *Ezek* 27:30

wallowed
Amasa *w.* in blood in. 2 *Sam* 20:12
fell on the ground and *w.* *Mark* 9:20

wallowing
and the sow washed to *w.* 2 *Pet* 2:22

walls
if plague be in the *w.* *Lev* 14:37, 39
having no *w.* counted as fields. 25:31
were fenced with high *w.* *Deut* 3:5
till thy high fenced *w.* come. 28:52
men fled between two *w.* 2 *Ki* 25:4
Chaldees brake down the *w.* of Jeru-
    salem round. 10; *Jer* 39:8
if this city be built and *w.* set up.
    Ezra 4:13, 16
timber is laid in the *w.* 5:8
heard that the *w.* of Jerusalem.
    Neh 4:7
oil within their *w.* *Job* 24:11
build thou the *w.* of. *Ps* 51:18
they go about it on *w.* thereof. 55:10
peace be within thy *w.* 122:7
broken down, without *w.* *Pr* 25:28
keepers of the *w.* took. *S of S* 5:7
of breaking down the *w.* *Isa* 22:5
the fortress of thy *w.* 25:12
salvation will God appoint for *w.* and
    bulwarks. 26:1
w. are continually before me. 49:16
w. a place and a name better. 56:5
strangers shall build up thy *w.* 60:10
thou shalt call thy *w.* salvation. 18
I have set watchmen on thy *w.* 62:6
against the *w.* of Jerusalem. *Jer* 1:15
go ye up upon her *w.* and. 5:10
Babylon's *w.* are. 50:15; 51:58

they shall destroy the *w.* of Tyrus.
    Ezek 26:4, 12
of Arvad were upon thy *w.* 27:11
talking against thee by the *w.* 33:30
dwelling without *w.* or gates. 38:11
in the day that thy *w.* *Mi* 7:11
as towns without *w.* *Zech* 2:4
by faith the *w.* of Jericho fell down.
    Heb 11:30

wander
caused me to *w.* from. *Gen* 20:13
children shall *w.* in the wilderness.
    Num 14:33; 32:13; *Ps* 107:40
that causeth blind to *w.* *Deut* 27:18
he causeth them to *w.* in. *Job* 12:24
when his young ravens *w.* for. 38:41
then would I *w.* far off. *Ps* 55:7
let them *w.* up and down. 59:15
O let me not *w.* from thy. 119:10
they shall *w.* every one. *Isa* 47:15
Thus have they loved to *w.* *Jer* 14:10
that shall cause him to *w.* 48:12
shall *w.* from sea to sea. *Amos* 8:12

wandered
Hagar *w.* in the wilderness of Beer-
    sheba. *Gen* 21:14
they *w.* in the wilderness. *Ps* 107:4
    Isa 16:8
have *w.* as blind men. *Lam* 4:14
my sheep *w.* through. *Ezek* 34:6
two or three cities *w.* to. *Amos* 4:8
w. about in sheepskins. *Heb* 11:37
they *w.* in deserts, in mountains. 38

wanderers
I will send to him *w.* *Jer* 48:12
they shall be *w.* among. *Hos* 9:17

wanderest
every green tree thou *w.* *Jer* 2:20

wandereth
he *w.* abroad for bread. *Job* 15:23
that *w.* out of the way. *Pr* 21:16
as a bird that *w.* from her nest, so is
    a man that *w.* from his. 27:8
bewray not him that *w.* *Isa* 16:3
none shall gather up him that *w.*
    Jer 49:5

wandering
was *w.* in the field. *Gen* 37:15
bird by *w.*, as the swallow. *Pr* 26:2
sight of the eyes than the *w.* *Eccl* 6:9
it shall be as a *w.* bird. *Isa* 16:2
to be idle, *w.* about. 1 *Tim* 5:13
w. stars to whom is reserved dark-
    ness. *Jude* 13

wanderings
thou tellest my *w.* *Ps* 56:8

want
serve thy enemies in *w.* *Deut* 28:48
she shall eat them for *w.* of all. 57
a place where is no *w.* *Judg* 18:10
    19:19
they embrace the rock for *w.* of.
    Job 24:8
for *w.* and famine they were. 30:3
if I have seen any perish for *w.* 31:19
there is no *w.* to them. *Ps* 34:9
and thy *w.* as an armed man.
    Pr 6:11; 24:34
fools die for *w.* of wisdom. 10:21*
there is that is destroyed for *w.* of
    judgement. 13:23*
in *w.* of people is destruction. 14:28
that is hasty only to *w.* 21:5
to rich shall surely come to *w.* 22:16
stricken through for *w.* of. *Lam* 4:9
I have given you *w.* of bread in.
    Amos 4:6
she of her *w.* cast in. *Mark* 12:44
he began to be in *w.* *Luke* 15:14
be a supply for their *w.* 2 *Cor* 8:14
not only supplieth the *w.* of. 9:12
not speak in respect of *w.* *Phil* 4:11

want, verb
my shepherd, I shall not *w.* *Ps* 23:1
Lord shall not *w.* any good. 34:10
of the wicked shall *w.* *Pr* 13:25
none shall *w.* her mate. *Isa* 34:16
David not *w.* a man to sit. *Jer* 33:17
Levites not *w.* a man. 18
Jonadab shall not *w.* a man. 35:19
that they may *w.* bread. *Ezek* 4:17

wanted

we have w. all things.   *Jer* 44:18
when they w. wine.   *John* 2:3*
I w. I was chargeable.   *2 Cor* 11:9

wanteth

shall lend him for his need in that he
   w.   *Deut* 15:8
that w. understanding.   *Pr* 9:4, 16
in multitude of words there w. 10:19
prince that w. understanding. 28:16
so that he w. nothing for his soul.
   Eccl 6:2
goblet that w. not liquor. *S of S* 7:2

wanting

and all his priests, let none be w.:
   whoso be w. shall not. *2 Ki* 10:19
words, yet they are w. to. *Pr* 19:7*
that which is w. cannot. *Eccl* 1:15
thou art weighed in the balances, and
   art found w.   *Dan* 5:27
the things that are w.   *Tit* 1:5
that nothing be w. unto them. 3:13
ye may be perfect and entire, w.
   nothing.   *Jas* 1:4*

wanton

Zion walk with w. eyes.   *Isa* 3:16
to wax w. against Christ. *1 Tim* 5:11
ye have lived in pleasure and been w.
   Jas 5:5*

wantonness

walk honestly, not in chambering
   and w.   *Rom* 13:13
they allure through lusts and much
   w.   *2 Pet* 2:18*

wants

let all thy w. lie on me. *Judg* 19:20
that ministered to my w. *Phil* 2:25*

war

*We may distinguish two kinds of
wars among the Hebrews. Some
were of obligation as being expressly commanded by the Lord;
but others were free and voluntary.
The first were such as God commanded them to undertake. For
example, against the Amalekites
and the Canaanites, which were
nations devoted to destruction for
their sins. The others were under-
taken by the captains of the people,
to revenge some injuries offered to
the nation, to punish some insults
or offences. Such was that which
the Hebrews made against the city
of Gibeah, and against the tribe of
Benjamin, which would uphold them
in their fault,* Judg 20:8. *And such
was that which David made against
the Ammonites, whose king had
affronted his ambassadors,* 2 Sam
10:1–14. *Or to maintain and defend their allies ; as that of Joshua
against the kings of the Canaanites,
to protect the Gibeonites,* Josh 10:6–
11.
The common meaning of war, *in
scripture, is a state of hostility
between nations, states, provinces,
or parties, as in* 1 Ki 14:30; Luke
14:31, *and many other places :
but it is taken in a spiritual sense
in* 2 Cor 10:3, *where the apostle
says,* We do not *war after the flesh.*

when there is w. they join. *Ex* 1:10
repent when they see w.   13:17
will have w. with Amalek.   17:16
a noise of w. in the camp.   32:17
all that are able to go forth to w.
   Num 1:3; 20:22; 26:2; *Deut* 3:18
ye go to w. ye shall blow. *Num* 10:9
Arm some of yourselves to w. 31:3
1000 shall ye send to w.   4
shall your brethren go to w.?   32:6
armed before the Lord to w. 20, 27
hath God assayed to take him a
   nation by w.?   *Deut* 4:34
but will make w. against thee.
   20:12, 19, 20
when thou goest forth to w. 21:10*
taken a wife, he shall not go to w. 24:5
and the land rested from w.
   Josh 11:23; 14:15
so is my strength now, for w. 14:11

that Israel might know to teach them
   w.   *Judg* 3:2
chose new gods, then was w. in. 5:8
not to each his wife in the w.   21:22
was sore w. against Philistines.
   1 Sam 14:52; 19:8
for the Philistines make w.   28:15
long w. between the house of Saul
   and the house of David. *2 Sam* 3:1
David demanded how the w.   11:7
shed the blood of w. in peace, and put
   the blood of w.   *1 Ki* 2:5
w. between Rehoboam and Jeroboam.   14:30; 15:6
there was w. between Abijam. 15:7
there was w. between Asa and. 16, 32
or be come out for w., take.   20:18
three years without w.   22:1
counsel and strength for w.
   2 Ki 18:20
they made w. with the Hagarites.
   1 Chr 5:10, 19
many slain, because the w. was. 22
if thy people go to w. *2 Chr* 6:34*
no w. to the 35th year.   15:19
house wherewith I have w.   35:21
redeem in w. from power. *Job* 5:20
changes and w. are against. 10:17*
reserved against the day of w. 38:23
though w. should rise.   *Ps* 27:3
words smooth, but w. was in. 55:21
the people that delight in w. 68:30
I speak, they are for w.   120:7
are gathered together for w. 140:2
good advice make w.   *Pr* 20:18
counsel thou shalt make thy w. 24:6
a time of w., and a time. *Eccl* 3:8
there is no discharge in that w. 8:8
nor shall they learn w. any more.
   Isa 2:4; *Mi* 4:3
thy mighty shall fall in w. *Isa* 3:25
from the grievousness of w. 21:15
counsel and strength for w. 36:5
hast heard the alarm of w. *Jer* 4:19
prepare ye w. against her, arise. 6:4
in array as men for w. against. 23*
Nebuchadnezzar maketh w.   21:2
where we shall see no w.   42:14
We are mighty men for w.?   48:14
an alarm of w. to be heard in. 49:2
nor Pharaoh make for him in w.
   Ezek 17:17
the same horn made w. *Dan* 7:21
to the end of the w. are.   9:26
prepare w., wake up the. *Joel* 3:9
as men averse from w.   *Mi* 2:8
they even prepare w. against. 3:5
king going to make w.? *Luke* 14:31
the beast shall make w.   *Rev* 11:7
there was w. in heaven against. 12:7
to make w. with the remnant of. 17
who is able to make w. with ? 13:4
to make w. with saints. 7; 17:14
righteousness doth he make w. 19:11
kings gathered to make w.   19
   see **expert, man, men**

war, *verb*

doest me wrong to w. *Judg* 11:27
he teacheth my hands to w.
   2 Sam 22:35; *Ps* 18:34; 144:1
Rezin and Pekah came up to Jerusalem to w. *2 Ki* 16:5; *Isa* 7:1
they that w. against thee. *Isa* 41:12
walk in flesh, we do not w. *2 Cor* 10:3
that thou mightest w. a. *1 Tim* 1:18
of your lusts that w. in.   *Jas* 4:1
ye fight and w. yet ye have not. 2
from lusts which w.   *1 Pet* 2:11

weapons of war

girded on *weapons of w. Deut* 1:41
six hundred with *weapons of w.*
   Judg 18:11, 16, 17
how are the *weapons of w.* perished !
   2 Sam 1:27
better than *weapons of w. Eccl* 9:18
back the *weapons of w. Jer* 21:4
battle axe and *weapons of w.* 51:20
hell with *weapons of w. Ezek* 32:27

ward

put them in w.   *Gen* 40:3, 4, 7
wroth and put me in w.   41:10
Joseph put his brethren in w. 42:17
the blasphemer in w.   *Lev* 24:12

gatherer of sticks in w. *Num* 15:34
ten concubines in w. *2 Sam* 20:3
had kept the w. of the house of Saul.
   1 Chr 12:29*
they cast lots, w. against w. 25:8⁴
lot came by causeway of going up, w.
   against w.   26:16
to give thanks w. over against w.
   Neh 12:24
were porters keeping the w. at. 25
kept w. of their God and w. of. 45
set in my w. whole nights. *Isa* 21:8
Irijah a captain of the w. *Jer* 37:13
they put Zedekiah in w. *Ezek* 19:9*
they were past first and second w.
   Acts 12:10

wardrobe

the wife of Shallum, the keeper of
   the w. *2 Ki* 22:14; *2 Chr* 34:22

wards

of the tabernacle by w. *1 Chr* 9:23
having w. one against another to
   minister.   26:12*
I appointed the w. of. *Neh* 13:30

ware

w. no clothes nor abode. *Luke* 8:27

ware

Lord shall come in an hour he is not
   w. of.   *Mat* 24:50
they were w. of it and fled to Lystra.
   Acts 14:6
coppersmith be thou w. *2 Tim* 4:15

ware, *substantive*

if people bring w. on. *Neh* 10:31
brought all manner of w.   13:16
sellers of all kind of w. lodged. 20

wares

gather up thy w. out of. *Jer* 10:17
by reason of the multitude of w.
   Ezek 27:16*, 18*, 33
the mariners cast forth w. *Jonah* 1:5

warfare

gathered armies for w. *1 Sam* 28:1
cry to her that her w. is. *Isa* 40:2
goeth a w. any time at ? *1 Cor* 9:7*
the weapons of our w. *2 Cor* 10:4
mightest war a good w. *1 Tim* 1:18

warm

and the flesh of the child waxed w.
   2 Ki 4:34
what time they wax w. *Job* 6:17
how thy garments are w.   37:17
how can one be w. alone ? *Eccl* 4:11
he will take thereof and w. *Isa* 44:15
and saith, Aha, I am w.   16
not be a coal to w. at nor fire. 47:14
ye clothe you, but there is none w.
   Hag 1:6

warmed

he were not w. with fleece. *Job* 31:20
Peter w. himself.   *Mark* 14:54
   John 18:18, 25
depart in peace, be ye w. *Jas* 2:16

warmeth

ostrich that w. her eggs. *Job* 39:14
w. himself and saith, Aha. *Isa* 44:16

warming

when she saw Peter w. *Mark* 14:67

warn

shall w. them that they trespass not.
   2 Chr 19:10
nor speakest to w. *Ezek* 3:18; 33:8
yet if thou w. wicked. 3:19; 33:9
if thou w. the righteous.   3:21
w. the people   33:3, 7
I ceased not to w. every. *Acts* 20:31
beloved sons I w. you. *1 Cor* 4:14
w. them that are unruly. *1 Thes* 5:14

warned

place man of God w. him. *2 Ki* 6:10
by them is thy servant w. *Ps* 19:11
live, because he is w. *Ezek* 3:21
see and the people be not w.   33:6
Joseph being w. of God departed.
   Mat 2:12, 22
of vipers, who hath w. you to flee
   from the wrath ? 3:7; *Luke* 3:7
Cornelius w. from God. *Acts* 10:22
by faith Noah being w. *Heb* 11:7

warning

I speak and give w.? *Jer 6:10*
word and give them w. *Ezek 3:17*
thou givest him not w. nor. 18, 20
taketh not w. 33:4
he heard and took not w. 5
w. every man, and teaching. *Col 1:28*

warp

plague in the w. or woof. *Lev 13:48*
49, 51, 57, 59
burn w. 52
rend w. 56
wash the w. 58

warred

and they w. against the Midianites.
Num 31:7
Balak king of Moab w. *Josh 24:9**
Jeroboam, how he w. *1 Ki 14:19*
acts of Jehoshaphat, how he w. 22:45
the king of Syria w. *2 Ki 6:8*
Uzziah w. against the. *2 Chr 26:6*

warreth

no man that w. entangleth.*2 Tim 2:4**

warring

found the king of Assyria w. against.
2 Ki 19:8; Isa 37:8
law in my members w. *Rom 7:23*

warrior, -s

chosen men who were w. *1 Ki 12:21*
2 Chr 11:1
battle of the w. is with. *Isa 9:5**

wars

It is said in the book of the w. of the.
Num 21:14
had not known all the w. of Canaan.
Judg 3:1
David, for Hadadezer had w. with
Toi. *2 Sam 8:10; 1 Chr 18:10*
hast made great w. *1 Chr 22:8*
thou shalt have w. *2 Chr 16:9*
he maketh w. to cease. *Ps 46:9*
ye shall hear of w. and rumours of w.
Mat 24:6; Mark 13:7; Luke 21:9
from whence come w.? *Jas 4:1*

was

with God and w. not. *Gen 5:24*
God w. with the lad, he grew. 21:20
that the Lord w. with thee. 26:28
Jacob told Rachel, he w. her. 29:12
thus I w. in the day, drought. 31:40
and behold, Joseph w. not. 37:29
Lord w. with Joseph, he. 39:2, 22
drew near where God w. *Ex 20:21*
w. not in the company. *Num 27:3*
as I w. with Moses, so I. *Josh 1:5*
God be with thee as he w. 17
the Lord w. with Joshua, and. 6:27
as yet I am as strong as I w. 14:11
how w. this wickedness? *Judg 20:3*
they ewe where the man of God w.
1 Sam 9:10
the ewe lamb w. unto. *2 Sam 12:3*
the counsel of Ahithophel w. 16:23
whose the living child w. *1 Ki 3:26*
God be with us as he w. with. 8:57
the Lord w. not in the wind, the Lord
w. not in the earthquake. 19:11
w. not in the fire. 12
king discerned him that he w. 20:41
to Ahab all that w. in my. *2 Ki 10:30*
told what he w. to her. *Esth 8:1*
I w. not in safety, neither. *Job 3:26*
as I w. in the days of my youth. 29:4
away and lo he w. not. *Ps 37:36*
I w. as a man that heareth not. 38:14
fear, where no fear w. 53:5
not be such as w. in her. *Isa 9:1*
people w. not till Assyrian. 23:13
w. not Israel a derision unto thee?
w. he found among? *Jer 48:27*
I w. no prophet, neither w. I a
prophet's son, but I w. *Amos 7:14*
I pray thee, Lord, w. not? *Jonah 4:2*
w. not Esau Jacob's brother? *Mal 1:2*
such as w. not since the beginning of.
Mat 24:21; Mark 13:19
the roof where he w. *Mark 2:4*
always night and day he w. 5:5
baptism of John, w. it from heaven,
or of men? 11:30; *Luke 20:4*

and the Word w. with God, and
the Word w. God. *John 1:1*
w. the true light, that lighteth. 9
saying, He w. before me. 15, 30
he that w. with thee beyond. 3:26
ascend up where he w. before. 6:62
before Abraham w., I am. 8:58
I am glad for your sakes I w. 11:15
I said, because I w. with you. 16:4
with thee before the world w. 17:5
one of twelve w. not with them. 20:24
full of fishes, yet w. not the. 21:11
after sold, w. it not in thy? *Acts 5:4*
sold Joseph, but God w. with him.7:9
what w. I that I could withstand
God? 11:17
near, demanded who he w. 21:33
our word w. not yea. *2 Cor 1:18, 19*
I w. not a whit behind chiefest. 11:5
our entrance unto you w. *I Thes 2:1*
our exhortation w. not in deceit. 3
manifest as theirs also w. *2 Tim 3:9*
how great this man w. *Heb 7:4*
the world w. not worthy. 11:38
what manner of man he w. *Jas 1:24*
from him which is and which w.
Rev 1:4, 8; 4:8
the beast thou sawest w. 17:8, 11

see **so**

it was

came to pass as he interpreted, so it
w. *Gen 41:13*
he it w. sold to all the people. 42:6
now it w. not you that sent me. 45:8
they wist not what it w. *Ex 16:15*
it w. of the Lord to harden their
hearts. *Josh 11:20*
I brought Moses word as it w. 14:7
so it w. when Israel had sown.
Judg 6:3
it w. not of the king to. *2 Sam 3:37*
but I knew not what it w. 18:29
is my brother's: for it w. *1 Ki 2:15*
his hand became as it w. 13:6
perceived that it w. not the. 22:33
left the camp as it w. *2 Ki 7:7*
command to Mordecai to know what
it w. and why it w. *Esth 4:5*
return to earth as it w. *Eccl 12:7*
it w. but a little that I. *S of S 3:4*
as it w. to Israel in the. *Isa 11:16*
from the time that it w. 48:16
his it w. *Ezek 16:15*
thus it w. saith the Lord. 19
went to see what it w. *Mark 5:14*
not tell whence it w. *Luke 20:7*
enquire which of them it w. 22:23
knew not whence it w. *John 2:9*
was healed wist not who it w. 5:13
and knew not that it w. Jesus. 20:14
21:4
knowing that it w. the Lord. 21:12
not as it w. by one that. *Rom 5:16*

behold it was

God saw every thing, behold it w.
Gen 1:31
looked on earth, behold it w. 6:12
morning, behold, it w. Leah. 29:25
behold it w. not toward Jacob. 31:2
Pharaoh awoke and behold it w.41:7
for behold it w. in the sack's. 42:27
and behold it w. burnt. *Lev 10:16*
1 Sam 30:3
behold it w. dead, behold it w. my.
1 Ki 3:21

there was

light, and there w. light. *Gen 1:3*
and there w. not a man to till. 2:5
there w. not found an help meet. 20
there w. a great cry in Egypt, for
there w. not ... there w. *Ex 12:30*
there w. not a man. *Num 26:64*
there w. not one city too strong.
Deut 2:36; 3:4
there w. no strange god with. 32:12
there w. not a man left. *Josh 8:17*
there w. not a word Joshua read. 35
there w. not any left to. 11:11
there w. not a city that made. 19
host of Sisera fell; there w. not a
man left. *Judg 4:16*
for there w. his house, there he
judged. *1 Sam 7:17*

there w. not a man that came not.
2 Ki 10:21
and there w. she slain. 11:16
there w. not one of them left.
Ps 106:11
and there w. the hiding. *Hab 3:4*
there w. a readiness. *2 Cor 8:11*
see **none**

behold there was

behold there w. not one of cattle.
Ex 9:7
behold there w. a man told a dream.
Judg 7:13
behold there w. a swarm of. 14:8
behold there w. an image in the bed.
1 Sam 19:16
behold there w. a cake. *1 Ki 19:6*
behold there w. no man there.
2 Ki 7:5, 10
behold there w. lifted up a talent of.
Zech 5:7
behold there w. a great earthquake.
Mat 28:2

wash

*Since the common foot-coverings
of the East were sandals, and the
roads were hot and dusty during the
dry season and muddy during the
rains, it was a necessary custom to
see that the feet were washed on
entering a house. The common
utensils made it hard to wash one's
own feet, and as a rule it was the
task of a menial, but when one
wished to honour his visitor ex-
tremely, or to indicate his own
humility, he would himself perform
the service.
At the Lord's Supper the feet of
the Apostles had to be washed; no
disciple would acknowledge himself
the lowest among them; and it
was our Saviour himself who, to
give them an example of humility, washed their feet, John
13:5.
Ceremonial washing, as distinct
from washing for cleanliness, was
one of the traditions of the Jews,
Heb 9:10. To wash one's feet in
butter, etc., Job 29:6; Ps 58:10,
was a figurative expression to indicate a great quantity of these
things. To wash one's hands was
a sign of innocence, Mat 27:4.*

I pray you w. your feet. *Gen 18:4*
19:2; 24:2
Pharaoh came to w. *Ex 2:5*
sons thou shalt bring and w. them.
29:4; 30:19, 20, 21; 40:12
shalt w. that whereon it. *Lev 6:27*
w. the thing wherein the plague is.
13:54
of skin it be, which thou shalt w. 58
shave and w. himself in water. 14:8
Deut 23:11
w. his flesh in water. *Lev 14:9; 15:16*
16:4, 24; 22:6
if he w. not, he shall bear. 17:16
shall w. their hands. *Deut 21:6*
w. thyself therefore and anoint.
Ruth 3:3
let thy handmaid be a servant to w.
feet. *1 Sam 25:41*
Go down and w. thy feet. *2 Sam 11:8*
Elisha said, Go w. in Jordan seven.
2 Ki 5:10
may I not w. in them and be? 12
when he saith to thee, W. and? 13
lavers to w. in, sea for priests to w.
in. *2 Chr 4:6*
if I w. myself with snow water.
Job 9:30
I will w. my hands in. *Ps 26:6*
w. me throughly from mine. 51:2
w. me and I shall be whiter. 7
shall w. his feet in the blood. 58:10
w. you, make you clean. *Isa 1:16*
w. thee with nitre and. *Jer 2:22*
O Jerusalem, w. thy heart. 4:14
for whom thou didst w. *Ezek 23:40*
but when thou fastest, w. *Mat 6:17*
they w. not their hands when. 15:2

except they *w.* oft they. *Mark* 7:3, 4
a woman began to *w.* his feet with
tears.   *Luke* 7:38
Jesus said, Go *w.* in the. *John* 9:7, 11
began to *w.* the disciples' feet. 13:5
Lord, dost thou *w.* my feet ?   6
never *w.* my feet. If I *w.* thee not. 8
ye also ought to *w.* one another's. 14
be baptized, and *w.* away thy sins.
     Acts 22:16
see clothes, feet

washed
gave them water, they *w. Gen* 43:24
Joseph *w.* his face and went out. 31
Judah *w.* his garments in.   49:11
w. as the Lord commanded Moses.
     Ex 40:32
on plague after it is *w. Lev* 13:55
be *w.* the second time and.   58
concubine *w.* their feet. *Judg* 19:21
arose and *w.* himself. *2 Sam* 12:20
w. the chariot in pool. *1 Ki* 22:38
I *w.* my steps with butter. *Job* 29:6
I have *w.* my hands in. *Ps* 73:13
a generation not *w. Pr* 30:12
I have *w.* my feet, how ? *S of S* 5:3
his eyes are *w.* with milk and.   12
w. away the filth of the. *Isa* 4:4
nor wast *w.* in water to. *Ezek* 16:4
I throughly *w.* away thy blood.   9
Pilate took water and *w. Mat* 27:24
she hath *w.* my feet. *Luke* 7:44*
marvelled he had not first *w.* 11:38
he went and *w.* and came seeing.
     John 9:7, 11, 15
is *w.* needeth not save to. 13:10
Lord and Master have *w.*   14
whom when they had *w. Acts* 9:37
took them, *w.* their stripes. 16:33
but ye are *w.,* but ye are sanctified.
     1 Cor 6:11
have *w.* the saints' feet. *1 Tim* 5:10
having our bodies *w. Heb* 10:22
sow that was *w.* to her wallowing.
     2 Pet 2:22
that *w.* us from our sins. *Rev* 1:5*
have *w.* their robes and made. 7:14
see clothes

washest
thou *w.* away the things. *Job* 14:19

washing
David saw a woman *w. 2 Sam* 11:2
but the fisherman were *w. Luke* 5:2

washing, -s
somewhat dark after in. *Lev* 13:56
that every one put them off for *w.*
     Neh 4:23*
like sheep which came up from the
w.   *S of S* 4:2; 6:6
as the *w.* of cups, pots. *Mark* 7:4, 8
cleanse it with *w.* of water. *Eph* 5:26
he saved us, by the *w.* of. *Tit* 3:5
in meats and divers *w. Heb* 9:10

washpot
Moab is my *w. Ps* 60:8; 108:9

wast
thou *w.* a servant in land. *Deut* 5:15
thou *w.* a bondman in the land of
Egypt. 15:15; 16:12; 24:18, 22
because thou *w.* a stranger.   23:7
thou *w.* he that leddest. *2 Sam* 5:2
where *w.* thou when I laid the foundations of the earth ? *Job* 38:4
thou art taken and *w.* not. *Jer* 50:24
I said to thee, when thou *w.* in thy
blood.   *Ezek* 16:6
even thou *w.* as one of them. *Ob* 11
Peter, saying, Thou also *w.* with
Jesus. *Mat* 26:69; *Mark* 14:67
when thou *w.* under the fig tree, I saw
thee.   *John* 1:48
which art, and *w.* and art to come.
     Rev 11:17; 16:5

waste, *adjective*
the desolate *w.* ground and. *Job* 38:27
young lions yelled and made his land
w.   *Jer* 2:15
for Noph shall be *w.* and. 46:19*
Bozrah shall become a *w.* 49:13
will make Jerusalem *w. Ezek* 5:14*
the land of Egypt shall be *w.* 29:9
     10; 30:12

which have been always *w. Ezek* 38:8
empty, and void and *w. Nah* 2:10
have made their streets *w. Zeph* 3:6
mine house that is *w. Hag* 1:9
see **cities, lay, laid, places**

waste, *substantive*
he found him in the *w. Deut* 32:10
solitary, fleeing into the *w. Job* 30:3
Lord maketh the earth *w. Isa* 24:1
I will make *w.* mountains. 42:15
they that made the *w.* shall. 49:17
to what purpose is this *w.?*
     Mat 26:8; *Mark* 14:4

waste, *verb*
meal shall not *w.*   *1 Ki* 17:14
of wickedness *w.* them. *1 Chr* 17:9
of the wood doth *w.* it. *Ps* 80:13*
w. inhabitants of Pekod. *Jer* 50:21*
shall *w.* the land of Assyria. *Mi* 5:6

wasted
till your carcases be *w. Num* 14:33*
the Kenite shall be *w.* 24:22
of men of war were *w. Deut* 2:14*
barrel of meal *w.* not. *1 Ki* 17:16
Joab *w.* the country of. *1 Chr* 20:1
that *w.* us required of us. *Ps* 137:3
till the cities be *w. Isa* 6:11
and the river shall be *w.* and. 19:5
nations shall be utterly *w.* 60:12
are *w.* and desolate as. *Jer* 44:6
field is *w.,* the corn is. *Joel* 1:10
the younger son *w.* his. *Luke* 15:13
was accused that he had *w.* his. 16:1
the church and *w.* it. *Gal* 1:13*

wasteness
a day of *w.,* desolation. *Zeph* 1:15

waster
him that is a great *w. Pr* 18:9*
I have created the *w. Isa* 54:16

wastes
they shall build the old *w. Isa* 61:4
cities shall be perpetual *w. Jer* 49:13
that inhabit those *w.* of. *Ezek* 33:24
surely they in the *w.* shall fall. 27
the Lord to the desolate *w.* 36:4
and the *w.* shall be builded. 10, 33

wasteth
man dieth and *w.* away. *Job* 14:10†
nor for destruction that *w. Ps* 91:6
he that *w.* father and. *Pr* 19:26*

wasting
w. and destruction are in. *Isa* 59:7
not heard *w.* nor destruction. 60:18*

watch
Watch *is used in three senses :*
[1] *to watch in order to guard,*
[2] *to watch, meaning to look for,*
[3] *a watch in the night. The
night was divided, not into hours,
but into watches. In the Old
Testament, three are named : the
First Watch, till midnight ; the
Middle Watch, till 3 a.m.; and the
Morning Watch, till 6 a.m. In
the New Testament there were
four watches of three hours each,
from 6 p.m. to 6 a.m. See* **watches.**
morning *w.* Lord looked. *Ex* 14:24
middle *w.;* and they had but newly
set the *w. Judg* 7:19
Saul came in the morning *w.*
     1 Sam 11:11
so shall ye keep the *w.* of the house.
   2 Ki 11:6, 7; *2 Chr* 23:6
prayed to God and set a *w. Neh* 4:9
one in his *w.* and over against. 7:3
that thou settest a *w.? Job* 7:12
a thousand years as a *w. Ps* 90:4
set a *w.* O Lord, before my. 141:3
the *w.* strong, set up. *Jer* 51:12
I will stand upon my *w.* **Hab** 2:1
in the fourth *w.* of the night Jesus.
     Mat 14:25; *Mark* 6:48
had known what *w.* the thief would.
     Mat 24:43
ye have a *w.* 27:65
sealing the stone, setting a *w.* 66
behold, some of the *w.* came. 28:11
the shepherds keeping *w. Luke* 2:8
in the second *w.* or third. 12:38

watch, *verb*
the Lord *w.* between me. *Gen* 31:49
Saul sent to *w.* David. *1 Sam* 19:11
w. ye, keep the vessels. *Ezra* 8:29
thou not *w.* over my sin ? *Job* 14:16
I *w.* and am as a sparrow. *Ps* 102:7
more than they that *w.* for. 130:6
w. in the watchtower. *Isa* 21:5
and all that *w.* for iniquity. 29:20
a leopard shall *w.* over. *Jer* 5:6
will I *w.* over them to build. 31:28
I will *w.* over them for evil. 44:27
the munition, *w.* the way. *Nah* 2:1
I will *w.* to see what he. *Hab* 2:1
w. therefore, ye know not the hour.
     Mat 24:42; 25:13; *Mark* 13:35
     Luke 21:36; *Acts* 20:31
Jesus said, Tarry ye here, and *w.*
with me.   *Mat* 26:38
could ye not *w.* with me ?   40
     Mark 14:34, 37
w. and pray.   *Mat* 26:41
   Mark 13:33; 14:38; *Col* 4:2
who commanded the porter to *w.*
     Mark 13:34
unto you, I say unto all, W.   37
w. ye, stand fast in faith. *1 Cor* 16:13
let us *w.* and be sober. *1 Thes* 5:6
     1 Pet 4:7
w. thou in all things. *2 Tim* 4:5
obey them, for they *w. Heb* 13:17

watched
all my familiars *w.* for. *Jer* 20:10
like as I have *w.* over them. 31:28
w. for a nation that could. *Lam* 4:17
Lord *w.* upon evil, and. *Dan* 9:14
good man would have *w. Mat* 24:43
     Luke 12:39
and sitting down they *w. Mat* 27:36
they *w.* him whether he would heal.
   Mark 3:2; *Luke* 6:7; 14:1
they *w.* him and sent forth spies.
     Luke 20:20
w. the gates day and. *Acts* 9:24

watcher, -s
published that *w.* come. *Jer* 4:16
a *w.* and an holy one. *Dan* 4:13
by decree of the *w.*   17
the king saw a *w.*   23

watches
brethren over against them in *w.*
     Neh 12:9
on thee in the night *w. Ps* 63:6
eyes prevent the night *w.* 119:148
in beginning of the *w.* pour. *Lam* 2:19

watcheth
wicked *w.* the righteous. *Ps* 37:32
end is come, it *w.* for thee. *Ezek* 7:6
blessed is he that *w.* and. *Rev* 16:15

watchful
be *w.,* strengthen the things. *Rev* 3:2

watching
Eli sat on a seat by the wayside *w.*
     1 Sam 4:13
blessed heareth me, *w.* daily. *Pr* 8:34
our *w.* we have watched. *Lam* 4:17
centurion *w.* Jesus, saw. *Mat* 27:54
the lord when he cometh shall find *w.*
     Luke 12:37
praying and *w.* with all. *Eph* 6:18

watchings
in tumults, in labours, in *w.* in fastings.   *2 Cor* 6:5
in *w.* often, in hunger, thirst. 11:27

watchman
the *w.* cried and told. *2 Sam* 18:25
the *w.* saw another man running. 26
the *w.* told, he cometh not again.
     2 Ki 9:18, 20
keepeth city, *w.* waketh. *Ps* 127:1
go set a *w. Isa* 21:6
w., what of the night ?   11
set up the *w.,* prepare the ambushes.
     Jer 51:12
Son of man, I have made thee a *w.*
     Ezek 3:17; 33:7
set him up for their *w.* 33:2
the *w.* of Ephraim was. *Hos* 9:8

watchmen
w. that go about the city found me.
     S of S 3:3; 5:7
w. shall lift up the voice. *Isa* 52:8

his w. are blind, they are. *Isa* 56:10
I have set w. on thy walls. 62:6
also I set w. over you. *Jer* 6:17
w. on mount Ephraim shall. 31:6
the day of thy w. and. *Mi* 7:4

watch tower
when Judah came toward the w.
tower. *2 Chr* 20:24
watch in the w. tower. *Isa* 21:5
I stand continually on the w. tower. 8

water
Hagar by a fountain of w. *Gen* 16:7
let a little w. I pray you, be. 18:4
Abraham took a bottle of w. 21:14
Laban gave the man w. to. 24:32
I pray thee, a little w. to drink. 43
the w. is ours. 26:20
we have found w. 32
Joseph's house gave them w. 43:24
unstable as w., thou shalt not. 49:4
raw, nor sodden with w. *Ex* 12:9
shall come w. out of the rock. 17:6
any likeness that is in the w. 20:4
bless thy bread and thy w. 23:25
sons shall wash them with w. 29:4
30:20; 40:12; *Lev* 8:6; 16:4, 24
strawed it on the w. *Ex* 32:20
shall be scoured and rinsed in w.
Lev 6:28; 15:12
vessel, it must be put into w. 11:32
but if any w. be upon the seed. 38
w. that causeth the curse. *Num* 5:22
sprinkle w. of purification upon. 8:7
for a w. of separation. 19:9, 13, 20
21; 31:23
thou shalt bring forth to them w. out
of the rock. 20:8, 10, 11; *Neh* 9:15
Ps 114:8
this is the w. of Meribah. *Num* 20:13
24; 27:14
nor is there any w. 21:5
people, and I will give them w. 16
he shall pour the w. out of. 24:7
shall make go through the w. 31:23
to a land of brooks of w. *Deut* 8:7
the land drinketh w. of rain. 11:11
shalt pour it on earth as w.
24; 15:23
met you not with w. in way. 23:4
Neh 13:2
melted and became as w. *Josh* 7:5
he asked w. and she gave. *Judg* 5:25
bring them down to the w. 7:4, 5
w. came out of the jaw and. 15:19
to Mizpeh and drew w. *1 Sam* 7:6
take my bread and my w.? 25:11
take now the cruse of w. 26:11
nor drunk any w. three days. 30:12
we are as w. spilt on. *2 Sam* 14:14
pass quickly over the w. 17:21
till w. dropped on them out. 21:10
bread and drank w. *1 Ki* 13:19
hast eaten bread and drunk w. 22
as a reed is shaken in the w. 14:15
I pray thee, a little w. 17:10
them with bread and w. 18:4, 13
w. ran about the altar, filled trench
with w. 35
fire of the Lord . . . licked up the w. 38
feed him with bread and w. of affliction till I. 22:27; *2 Chr* 18:26
the w. is naught, and. *2 Ki* 2:19
Elisha, who poured w. on. 3:11
valley shall be filled with w. 17
and the sun shone on the w. 22
the axe head fell into the w. 6:5
set bread and w. before them. 22
he dipped a thick cloth in w.,and.8:15
made a conduit, brought w. 20:20
of Assyria find much w. *2 Chr* 32:4
can flag grow without w.? *Job* 8:11
the scent of w. it will bud. 14:9
drinketh iniquity like w. 15:16
thou hast not given w. to the. 22:7
who drinketh scorning like w. 34:7
I am poured out like w. *Ps* 22:14
river of God that is full of w. 65:9
through fire and through w. 66:12
have they shed like w. 79:3
round about me daily like w. 88:17
into his bowels like w. 109:18
as when one letteth out w. *Pr* 17:14
heart of man is like deep w. 20:5

in w. face answereth to face.*Pr* 27:19
earth that is not filled with w. 30:16
thy wine mixed with w. *Isa* 1:22
take away the whole stay of w. 3:1
land of Tema brought w. to him
that was thirsty. 21:14
not found a sherd to take w. 30:14
though the Lord gave you the w. 20
when the poor seek w. and. 41:17
I will pour w. on him that is. 44:3
dividing the w. before them. 63:12
girdle and put it not in w. *Jer* 13:1
them drink the w. of gall. 23:15
mine eyes run down with w.
Lam 1:16; 3:48
pour out thy heart like w. 2:19
we have drunken our w. for. 5:4
may want bread and w. *Ezek* 4:17
all knees shall be weak as w. 7:17
21:7
nor wast thou washed in w. to. 16:4
then washed I thee with w. and. 9
then will I sprinkle clean w. 36:25
lovers that give me my w. *Hos* 2:5
my wrath upon them like w. 5:10
king is cut off as foam upon w. 10:7
of bread nor thirst for w. *Amos* 8:11
but Nineveh is of old like a pool of w.
Nah 2:8
the overflowing of the w. *Hab* 3:10
with w. unto repentance. *Mat* 3:11
Mark 1:8; *Luke* 3:16; *John* 1:26
Jesus went up out of the w.
Mat 3:16; *Mark* 1:10
whoso giveth a cup of cold w.
Mat 10:42; *Mark* 9:41
bid me come unto thee on the w.
Mat 14:28
oft into the fire and w. 17:15
Pilate took w. and washed. 27:24
a man bearing a pitcher of w.: follow.
Mark 14:13; *Luke* 22:10
ship was filled with w. *Luke* 8:23
rebuked the w. 24
the w. obeyed him. 25
dip the tip of his finger in w. 16:24
Fill the waterpots with w. *John* 2:7
except a man be born of w. and. 3:5
because there was much w. there. 23
given thee living w. 4:10, 11
give me this w. 15
again where he made w. wine. 46
waiting for the moving of the w. 5:3
down and troubled the w. 4
of his belly shall flow living w. 7:38
after that he poureth w. into a. 13:5
came thereout blood and w. 19:34
for John truly baptized with w.
Acts 1:5; 11:16
here is w. 8:36
they went down both into the w. 38
can any forbid w., these be ? 10:47
it with the washing of w. *Eph* 5:26
blood of calves with w. *Heb* 9:19
bodies washed with pure w. 10:22
yield salt w. and fresh. *Jas* 3:12
eight souls were saved by w.
1 Pet 3:20
are wells without w. *2 Pet* 2:17
overflowed with w., perished. 3:6
he that came by w. and. *1 John* 5:6
witness, Spirit, w. and blood. 8
clouds they are without w. *Jude* 12
cast out of his mouth w. *Rev* 12:15
Euphrates, and w. dried up. 16:12
of the fountain of the w. of life. 21:6
me a pure river of w. of life. 22:1
let him take the w. of life freely. 17
see **bathe, bitter, draw, drew,
drink, well**

water, verb
a river went out of Eden to w. the
garden. *Gen* 2:10
w. ye the sheep and go and. 29:7, 8
I w. my couch with my. *Ps* 6:6
come down as showers that w. 72:6
pools of water to w. the. *Eccl* 2:6
w. thee with my tears. *Isa* 16:9
I will w. it every moment, lest. 27:3
he might w. it by furrows. *Ezek* 17:7
I will w. with my blood the land. 32:6
a fountain shall w. the valley of
Shittim. *Joel* 3:18

no water
there was no w. in it. *Gen* 37:24
they went three days and found no
w. *Ex* 15:22; 17:1; *Num* 20:2
33:14; *Deut* 8:15
Lord said, Eat no bread and drink
no w. *1 Ki* 13:22
was no w. for the host, and.*2 Ki* 3:9
thirsty land where no w. is. *Ps* 63:1
as a garden that hath no w. *Isa* 1:30
the smith drinketh no w. 44:12
fish stinketh because there is no w.
50:2
cisterns that can hold no w. *Jer* 2:13
to the pits and found no w. 14:3
there was no w. but mire. 38:6
sent prisoners out of pit wherein is
no w. *Zech* 9:11
thou gavest me no w. for my feet.
Luke 7:44

waterbrooks
the hart panteth after the w. *Ps* 42:1

watercourse
stopped the upper w. *2 Chr* 32:30
who hath divided a w.? *Job* 38:25

watercourses
they shall spring as willows by the w.
Isa 44:4

watered
a mist that w. the face. *Gen* 2:6
Jordan, that it was well w. 13:10
of that well they w. flocks. 29:2, 3
Jacob w. the flock of Laban. 10
Moses helped and w. their flocks.
Ex 2:17, 19
he that watereth shall be w. himself.
Pr 11:25
shalt be like a w. garden. *Isa* 58:11
shall be as a w. garden. *Jer* 31:12
I have planted, Apollos w. *1 Cor* 3:6

wateredst
w. it with thy foot as a. *Deut* 11:10

waterest
the earth and w. it. *Ps* 65:9
thou w. the ridges thereof. 10

watereth
he w. the hills from his. *Ps* 104:13
that w. shall be watered. *Pr* 11:25
rain returneth not, but w. *Isa* 55:10
neither he that planteth any thing, nor
he that w. *1 Cor* 3:7, 8

waterflood
let not the w. overflow me. *Ps* 69:15

watering
rods in the w. troughs. *Gen* 30:38
by w. he wearieth the thick cloud.
Job 37:11*
doth not each of you lead his ass to
w.? *Luke* 13:15

waterpot, -s
set there six w. of stone. *John* 2:6
Jesus saith, Fill the w. with water. 7
the woman then left her w. 4:28

waters
God moved upon face of w. *Gen* 1:2
divide the w. from the w. 6, 7
let the w. be gathered. 9
w. bring forth. 20
do bring a flood of w. on earth. 6:17
w. increased. 7:17
w. prevailed. 18, 19, 20, 24
w. decreased. 8:1, 3, 5
w. were dried up. 13
not be cut off any more by w. 9:11
behold, I will smite the w. *Ex* 7:17
w. were turned to blood. 20
out his hand over the w. 8:6
by a strong east wind the w. 14:21
w. were a wall. 22, 29
w. returned. 28; 15:19
the w. were gathered together. 15:8
they could not drink of the w. of. 23
they encamped there by the w. 27
as cedar trees beside w. *Num* 24:6
to Jotbath, land of rivers of w.
Deut 10:7
ye trespassed at the w. of. 32:51
strive at the w. of Meribah. 33:8
the w. which came down. *Josh* 3:16
the w. of Jordan were cut off. 4:7
dried up the w. of Jordan. 23; 5:1
pitched at the w. of Merom. 11:5

Canaan by w. of Megiddo. *Judg* 5:19
and take the w. before them. 7:24
Lord hath broken forth as a breach
of w. *2 Sam* 5:20; *1 Chr* 14:11
Joab said, I have taken the city of w.
2 Sam 12:27
Elijah smote the w. *2 Ki* 2:8, 14
the spring of the w., thus saith the
Lord, I have healed these w. 21
are not . . . rivers of Damascus, better
than all the w. of Israel? 5:12
counsel to stop the w. *2 Chr* 32:3
are poured out like the w. *Job* 3:24
sendeth w. upon the fields. 5:10
remember thy misery as w. 11:16
he withholdeth the w. and. 12:15
as the w. fail from the sea. 14:11
the w. wear the stones: thou. 19
and abundance of w. cover thee.
22:11; 38:34
he is swift as the w.; their. 24:18
formed from under the w. 26:5
he bindeth up the w. in his thick. 8
he hath compassed the w. with. 10
terrors take hold on him as w. 27:20
the w. forgotten of the foot. 28:4
weighed the w. by measure. 25
was spread out by the w. 29:19
as a wide breaking in of w. 30:14
and the breadth of the w. is. 37:10
the w. are hid as with a stone. 38:30
he leadeth me beside the still w.
Ps 23:2
gathered the w. of the seas. 33:7
though the w. thereof roar. 46:3
let them melt away as w. 58:7
for the w. are come in unto. 69:1
w. of a full cup are wrung. 73:10
w. saw thee, O God, the w. 77:16
he made the w. to stand as. 78:13
and caused w. to run down like. 16
he smote the rock, that the w. gushed
out. 20; 105:41; 114:8; *Isa* 48:21
I proved them at the w. of Meribah.
Ps 81:7; 106:32
w. stood above the mountains. 104:6
turned their w. into blood. 105:29
the w. covered their enemies.
106:11
rivers of w. run down. 119:136
the w. had overwhelmed us. 124:4
then the proud w. had gone. 5
him that stretched the earth above
the w. 136:6
wind to blow and w. flow. 147:18
ye w. above the heavens. 148:4
drink w. out of thine own. *Pr* 5:15
let rivers of w. be dispersed. 16
that the w. should not pass. 8:29
stolen w. are sweet, and bread. 9:17
as cold w. to a thirsty soul. 25:25
who hath bound the w. in a ? 30:4
cast thy bread upon the w. *Eccl* 11:1
a well of living w. and. *S of S* 4:15
people refuseth the w. of. *Isa* 8:6
the Lord bringeth on them w. 7
as the w. cover the seas.
Hab 2:14
for the w. of Nimrim. *Isa* 15:6
for the w. of Dimon shall be. 9
like the rushing of mighty w. 17:12
and the w. shall fail from. 19:5
and ye gathered the w. of the. 22:9
w. shall overflow the hiding. 28:17
ye that sow beside all w. 32:20
bread be given him, his w. 33:16
for in the wilderness shall w. 35:6
who hath measured the w. in. 40:12
when thou passest through w. I. 43:2
a path in the mighty w. 16
I give w. in the wilderness and. 20
forth out of the w. of Judah. 48:1
he caused the w. to flow out. 21
which hath dried the w. of. 51:10
is as w. of Noah unto me, w. 54:9
thirsteth, come ye to the w. 55:1
like the sea, whose w. cast up. 57:20
of water, whose w. fail not. 58:11
me the fountain of living w. *Jer* 2:13
to drink the w. of Sihor ? 18
as a fountain casteth out her w. 6:7
God hath given us w. of gall. 8:14
O that my head were w. and. 9:1
eyelids gush out with w. 18

is a multitude of w. in the heavens.
Jer 10:13; 51:16
nobles sent little ones to the w. 14:3
as a liar, and as w. that fail ? 15:18
as a tree planted by the w. 17:8
the Lord, fountain of living w. 13
shall the cold flowing w. be ? 18:14
whose w. are moved as the rivers.
46:7, 8
behold, w. rise up out of the. 47:2
for the w. of Nimrim shall. 48:34
a drought is upon her w. and. 50:38
w. flowed over mine head. *Lam* 3:54
is like a vine by the w. *Ezek* 19:10
w. made him great, the deep. 31:4
that none of the trees by w. exalt. 14
and troublest the w. with thy. 32:2
behold, w. issued from under. 47:1
brought me through w.; the w. 3, 4
for the w. were risen, w. to. 5
these w. issue out toward the. 8, 12
even to the w. of strife. 19; 48:28
to the man upon the w. *Dan* 12:6, 7
calleth for w. of sea. *Amos* 5:8; 9:6
let judgement run down as w. 5:24
w. compassed me about. *Jonah* 2:5
as w. that are poured down. *Mi* 1:4
No, that had the w. round ? *Nah* 3:8
draw the w. for the siege. 14
living w. shall go from. *Zech* 14:8
in perils of w., in perils of. *2 Cor* 11:26
lead them unto living fountains of w.
Rev 7:17
the w. became wormwood, and many
died of the w. because. 8:11
have power over w. to turn. 11:6
made the fountain of w. 14:7
angel poured his vial on the w. 16:4
I heard the angel of the w. say. 5
the w. where the whore sits. 17:15

see **deep, great**

in, or *into* **waters**
as lead in the mighty w. *Ex* 15:10
a tree, which when cast *into* the w. 25
ye eat of all that are *in* the w.: whatsoever hath fins and scales in the w.
Lev 11:9; 10:46; *Deut* 14:9
hath no fins nor scales *in* the w. unclean. *Lev* 11:12
the likeness of any fish *in* the w.
Deut 4:18; 5:8
of priests rest *in* the w. *Josh* 3:13
stone *into* the mighty w. *Neh* 9:11
heads of dragons *in* w. *Ps* 74:13
beams of his chambers *in* w. 104:3
and perished *in* the w. *Mat* 8:32
him *into* fire and *into* w. *Mark* 9:22

many **waters**
seed shall be in *many* w. *Num* 24:7
he drew me out of *many* w.
2 Sam 22:17; *Ps* 18:16
the Lord is upon *many* w. *Ps* 29:3
than the noise of *many* w. 93:4
many w. cannot quench love, neither
can floods. *S of S* 8:7
the rushing of *many* w. *Isa* 17:13
dwellest upon *many* w. *Jer* 51:13
by reason of *many* w. *Ezek* 19:10
like a noise of *many* w.: and the earth
shined. 43:2; *Rev* 1:15; 14:2; 19:6
that sitteth on *many* w. *Rev* 17:1

waterspouts
deep at noise of thy w. *Ps* 42:7

watersprings
he turneth the w. irto. *Ps* 107:33
turneth dry ground into w. 35

wave
is like a w. of the sea. *Jas* 1:6*

wave, *verb*
shalt w. them for a wave offering.
Ex 29:24; *Lev* 23:20; *Num* 6:20
thou shalt w. the breast. *Ex* 29:26
w. the shoulder. 27; *Lev* 7:30
8:29; 9:21; 10:15
he shall w. the sheaf. *Lev* 23:11, 12
the priest shall w. the. *Num* 5:25

waved
w. them for a wave. *Lev* 8:27, 29
take one lamb to be w. 14:21

see **breast, loaves, offering**

wavereth
he that w. is like a wave. *Jas* 1:6*

wavering
hold fast profession of faith without
w. *Heb* 10:23
ask in faith, nothing w. *Jas* 1:6*

waves
all thy w. are gone over me.
Ps 42:7; *Jonah* 2:3
stilleth the noise of their w. *Ps* 65:7
89:9; 107:29
afflicted me with all thy w. 88:7
voice, floods lift up their w. 93:3
is mightier than mighty w. 4*
wind which lifteth up the w. 107:25
righteousness as the w. *Isa* 48:18
I am the Lord, that divided the sea,
whose w. roared. 51:15; *Jer* 31:35
though the w. toss, yet can. *Jer* 5:22
with the multitude of the w. 51:42
when her w. do roar like great. 55
as the sea causeth his w. *Ezek* 26:3
and shall smite the w. *Zech* 10:11
was covered with the w. *Mat* 8:24
but the ship was tossed with w.
14:24; *Mark* 4:37
signs, the sea and w. *Luke* 21:25*
was broken with the w. *Acts* 27:41
raging w. of sea, foaming. *Jude* 13

wax, *substantive*
my heart is like w. *Ps* 22:14
as w. melteth, so the wicked. 68:2
the hills melted like w. at the. 97:5
the valleys cleft as w. *Mi* 1:4

wax
my wrath shall w. hot. *Ex* 22:24
32:10
Lord, why doth thy wrath w.? 32:11
the anger of my lord w. hot. 22
or a stranger w. rich by thee, and thy
brother by him w. *Lev* 25:47
his eyes began to w. dim. *1 Sam* 3:2
what time they w. warm. *Job* 6:17
though the root thereof w. old. 14:8
all of them shall w. old. *Ps* 102:26
Isa 50:9; 51:6; *Heb* 1:11
his flesh shall w. lean. *Isa* 17:4
shall his face now w. pale. 29:22
our hands w. feeble, anguish hath.
Jer 6:24
the love of many shall w. cold.
Mat 24:12
provide bags which w. *Luke* 12:33
began to w. wanton. *1 Tim* 5:11
seducers shall w. worse. *2 Tim* 3:13

waxed
(*grew, increased*)
Isaac w. great. *Gen* 26:13
famine w. sore. 41:56
Israel w. exceeding. *Ex* 1:7, 20
and when the sun w. hot. 16:21
when the trumpet w. louder. 19:19
Moses' anger w. hot, and he. 32:19
is the Lord's hand w.? *Num* 11:23
raiment w. not old. *Deut* 8:4; 29:5
Neh 9:21
w. fat, and kicked. *Deut* 32:15
that Joshua w. old and. *Josh* 23:1
she that hath many children is w.
feeble. *1 Sam* 2:5
but David w. stronger. *2 Sam* 3:1
1 Chr 11:9
and David went down, fought, and w.
faint. *2 Sam* 21:15
of the child w. warm. *2 Ki* 4:34
Abijah w. mighty and. *2 Chr* 13:21
Jehoshaphat w. great. 17:12
Jehoiada w. old. 24:15
Mordecai w. greater. *Esth* 9:4
silence, my bones w. old. *Ps* 32:3
Damascus is w. feeble. *Jer* 49:24
Babylon's hands w. feeble. 50:43
the he goat w. great *Dan* 8:8, 9, 10
this people's heart is w. gross.
Mat 13:15; *Acts* 28:27
the child w. strong in spirit.
Luke 1:80; 2:40
a grain of mustard seed w. 13:19*
Paul and Barnabas w. *Acts* 13:46
w. valiant in fight. *Heb* 11:34
of the earth are w. rich. *Rev* 18:3

waxen, waxed
after I am w. old shall ? *Gen* 18:12
cry of Sodom was w. great. 19:13
brother be w. poor. *Lev* 25:25, 35, 39

w. fat, then will they turn to other
gods.   Deut 31:20
of Israel were w. strong. Josh 17:13
become great and w. rich. Jer 5:27
they are w. fat, they shine, they. 28
increased and w. great. Ezek 16:7

waxeth
mine eye w. old because.   Ps 6:7
what w. old, is ready.   Heb 8:13

waxing
brethren w. confident by. Phil 1:14

way
Is taken in a moral sense, [1] For
conduct, Ps 1:6. [2] Ways are put
for the laws of the Lord, Gen 18:19;
Ps 18:21. [3] Way is put for custom, manners, and way of life, Gen
6:12; Jer 10:2. [4] The method of
salvation, or doctrine of the gospel,
Acts 19:9.
To go the way of all the earth,
means dying and the grave, Josh
23:14.
Jesus Christ is called the way,
John 14:6, because it is by him
alone that believers obtain eternal
life.
if thou do prosper my w. Gen 24:42
to give them provision for the w.
        42:25; 45:21
led not through the w. of. Ex 13:17
led the people through the w.   18
of cloud to lead them the w.   21
shew them the w. 18:20; Neh 9:19
        Ps 107:4
discouraged because of w. Num 21:4
there was no w. to turn to.   22:26
by what w. we must go. Deut 1:22
        Josh 3:4
remember the w. which. Deut 8:2
if the w. be too long for thee. 14:24
return no more that w.   17:16
thou shalt prepare thee a w. 19:3
the w. is long.   6
thou shalt go out one w.   28:25
ye will turn aside from the w.31:29
behold I am going w. of. Josh 23:14
Lord preserved us in all the w. 24:17
from their stubborn w.   Judg 2:19
all that came along that w.   9:25
whether our w. which we go. 18:5
before the Lord is your w.   6
get you early on your w.   19:9
kine took straight w.   1 Sam 6:12
can shew us our w. to go.   9:6*
the man of God to tell us our w.   8
the good and the right w.   12:23
I have gone the w. the Lord. 15:20
thy servant will go a little w. over
Jordan.   2 Sam 19:36
I go the w. of all the earth. 1 Ki 2:2
them the good w. to walk.   8:36
nor turn again by the same w. 13:9
he went another w.   12
what w. went he ?   13
one w., Obadiah another w. 18:6
which w. went the Spirit of the Lord
from me ?   22:24; 2 Chr 18:23
which w. shall we go ? w. 2 Ki 3:8
departed from him a little w. 5:19
all the w. full of garments.   7:15
taught them the good w. 2 Chr 5:27
to seek of him a right w. Ezra 8:21
to a man whose w. is hid. Job 3:23
to wander where there is no w.
        12:24; Ps 107:40
I shall go the w. whence. Job 16:22
hast thou marked the old w.? 22:15
but he knoweth the w.   28:23
God understandeth the w.   28:23
where is the w. where light ? 38:19
Lord knoweth the w. of.   Ps 1:6
lest ye perish from the w.   2:12
he setteth himself in a w.   36:4
he made a w. to his anger. 78:50
wisely in a perfect w.   101:2, 6
make me understand the w. 119:27
remove from me the w. of lying. 29
I have chosen the w. of truth.   30
I will run the w. of thy.   32
teach me, O Lord, the w. 33; 143:8
I hate every false w. 119:104, 128

be any wicked w. in me. Ps 139:24
the w. of the wicked he turneth.146:9
he preserveth the w. of.   Pr 2:8
to deliver thee from the w.   12
the w. of the wicked is as.   4:19
reproofs of instruction are the w. of
life.   6:23; 15:24; Jer 21:8
her corner, he went the w.   Pr 7:8
her house is the w. to hell, going. 27
the w. of a fool is right in.   12:15
the w. of the wicked seduceth.   26
but the w. of transgressors. 13:15
there is a w. which seemeth right.
        14:12; 16:25
the w. of the wicked is an.   15:9
to him that forsaketh the w.   10
the w. of the slothful man is as an
hedge of thorns, but the w.   19
leadeth him into the w. that. 16:29
the w. of man is froward and. 21:8
w. of an eagle, of a serpent. 30:19
such is the w. of an adulterous. 20
knowest not what is the w. of the
Spirit.   Eccl 11:5
to err and destroy the w. Isa 3:12
w. of the just is uprightness. 26:7
an highway and a w., called w. 35:8
who shewed him the w. of ? 40:14
maketh a w. in the sea. 43:16; 51:10
I will even make a w. in the. 43:19
all my mountains a w.   49:11
prepare a w.   57:14
the w. of peace they know not.
        59:8; Rom 3:17
cast up the high w.   Isa 62:10
where is the good w.   Jer 6:16
learn not the w. of heathen. 10:2
I know that the w. of man is not. 23
wherefore doth the w. of the ? 12:1
to walk in paths, in a w. not. 18:15
them one heart and one w. 32:39
thy God may shew us the w. 42:3
they shall ask the w. to Zion. 50:5
appoint a w. that the sword may
come.   Ezek 21:20
saw that they took both one w. 23:13
glory of God came from the w. 43:2
and turn aside the w.   Amos 2:7
munition, watch the w.   Nah 2:1
he shall prepare the w.   Mal 3:1
broad is the w. that leadeth. Mat 7:13
narrow is the w. which leadeth. 14
no man might pass by that w. 8:28
not into the w. of the Gentiles. 10:5
art true, and teachest the w. of God.
        22:16; Mark 12:14; Luke 20:21
by what w. they might. Luke 5:19
a certain priest that w.   10:31
he was yet a great w. off.   15:20
for he was to pass that w.   19:4
some other w. is a thief. John 10:1
the w. ye know.   14:4
Lord, how can we know the w.?   5
I am the w., the truth, and the life. 6
which shew to us the w. Acts 16:17
expounded to him w. of God. 18:26
but spake evil of that w.   19:9
no small stir about that w.   23
after the w. which they call. 24:14
to fall in brother's w.   Rom 14:13
with the temptation also make a w. to
escape.   1 Cor 10:13
unto you a more excellent w. 12:31
our Lord Jesus direct our w. unto.
        1 Thes 3:11
the w. into the holiest not. Heb 9:8
by a living w. which he hath. 10:20
she had sent them out another w.
        Jas 2:25
the w. of truth shall be. 2 Pet 2:2
forsaken the right w. and are gone
astray, following the w. of.   15
known the w. of righteousness. 21
that the w. of kings of the. Rev 16:12

by the **way**
befall him by the w. ye go. Gen 42:38
Joseph said, See that ye fall not out
by the w.   45:24
a serpent by the w., an adder. 49:17
by the w. in the inn, the.   Ex 4:24
you into the wilderness, by the w. of
the Red sea.   Num 14:25; 21:4
        Deut 1:2, 40; 2:1

talk of them, when thou walkest by
the w.   Deut 6:7; 11:19
Amalek did to thee by the w. 25:17
met thee by the w. 18; 1 Sam 15:2
bring thee by the w. I spake. 28:68
men of war died by the w. Josh 5:4
not circumcised them by the w.   7
nor turn again by the same w. that
thou camest.   1 Ki 13:9, 17
a lion met him by the w. and.   24
waited for the king by the w. 20:38
water by the w. of Edom. 2 Ki 3:20
bridle in lips, I will turn thee back by
the w.   19:28; Isa 37:29, 34
as lay in wait by the w. Ezra 8:31
have ye not asked them that go by
the w.?   Job 21:29
pass by the w. plucked her. Ps 80:12
all that pass by the w. spoil. 89:41
when fools walk by the w. Eccl 10:3
bring blind by the w. they. Isa 42:16
that leadeth thee by the w. 48:17
forsaken God when he led thee by
the w.   Jer 2:17
walk not by the w. for the sword of
the enemy.   6:25
came by the w. of gate. Ezek 43:4
prince shall enter by the w. of porch.
        44:3; 46:2, 8
he that entereth by the w.   46:9
as a leopard by the w.   Hos 13:7
if I send them away fasting, they will
faint by the w.   Mark 8:3
by the w. he asked his disciples. 27
ye disputed by the w.? 9:33, 34
salute no man by the w. Luke 10:4
he talked with us by the w. 24:32
for I will not see you now by the w.
        1 Cor 16:7

every **way**
a flaming sword which turned every
w.   Gen 3:24
refrained my feet from every evil w.
        Ps 119:101
I hate every false w.   104, 128
every w. of man right in.   Pr 21:2
buildest thine eminent place in the
head of every w.   Ezek 16:31
much every w. because to. Rom 3:2
every w., whether in.   Phil 1:18
        see evil

his **way**
all flesh had corrupted his w. on
earth.   Gen 6:12
as for God, his w. is perfect.
        2 Sam 22:31; Ps 18:30
condemning the wicked, to bring his
w.   1 Ki 8:32; 2 Chr 6:23
this is the joy of his w.   Job 8:19
also shall hold on his w.   17:9
who shall declare his w. to ? 21:31
his w. have I kept and not. 23:11
hath enjoined him his w.? 36:23
meek will he teach his w. Ps 25:9
who prospereth in his w.   37:7
and he delighteth in his w.   23
wait on the Lord and keep his w. 34
a young man cleanse his w.? 119:9
me in beginning of his w. Pr 8:22
righteousness of the perfect direct
his w.   11:5
prudent is to understand his w. 14:8
a man's heart deviseth his w. 16:9
he that keepeth his w. preserveth. 17
of man perverteth his w.   19:3
when he is gone his w., then. 20:14
upright, he directeth his w. 21:29
make his w. prosperous. Isa 48:15
let the wicked forsake his w. 55:7
the destroyer of the Gentiles is on
his w.   Jer 4:7
to warn the wicked from his wicked
w.   Ezek 3:18
and he turn not from his wicked w.
        3:19; 33:8, 9
not return from his wicked w. 13:22
the Lord hath his w. in. Nah 1:3
himself and goeth his w. Jas 1:24
sinner from the error of his w. 5:20
        see went

in the **way**
I being in the w. the Lord. Gen 24:27
Lord who led me in the right w. 48

Lord was with me *in the w.* Gen 35:3
Rachel buried *in the w.* 19; 48:7
Aaron stood *in the w.* Ex 5:20
send angel before thee to keep thee *in the w.* 23:20
who went *in the w.* Deut 1:33
you not with bread *in the w.* 23:4
Jeroboam *in the w.* 1 Ki 11:29
his carcase was cast *in the w.* 13:24
25, 28
he walked *in the w.* of his father. 15:26; 22:52
and walked *in the w.* of Jeroboam. 15:34; 16:2, 19, 26; 22:52
as Obadiah was *in the w.* 18:7
he walked *in the w.* of the kings of. 2 Ki 8:18; 16:3; 2 Chr 21:6, 13
he walked *in the w.* of the house of Ahab. 2 Ki 8:27
and walked not *in the w.* 21:22
three years they walked *in the w.* of David. 2 Chr 11:17
he walked *in the w.* of Asa. 20:32
help us against the enemy *in the w.* Ezra 8:22
to give them light *in the w.* Neh 9:12
by day to lead *in the w.* 19
a trap for him *in the w.* Job 18:10
nor standeth *in the w.* Ps 1:1
will he teach sinners *in the w.* 25:8
shall he teach *in the w.* 12; 32:8
and shalt set us *in the w.* 85:13
my strength *in the w.* 102:23
drink of the brook *in the w.* 110:7
the undefiled *in the w.* 119:1
I have rejoiced *in the w.* 14
and lead me *in the w.* 139:24
in the w. have they privily. 142:3
walk not thou *in the w.* Pr 1:15
that thou mayest walk *in the w.* 2:20
I have taught thee *in the w.* 4:11
go not *in the w.* of evil men. 14
lead *in the w.* of righteousness. 8:20
go *in the w.* of understanding. 9:6
he is *in the w.* of life that. 10:17
in the w. of righteousness is. 12:28
him that is upright *in the w.* 13:6
if it be found *in the w.* of righteousness. 16:31
thorns and snares are *in the w.* 22:5
train up a child *in the w.* he. 6
guide thy heart *in the w.* 23:19
saith, There is a lion *in the w.* 26:13
upright *in the w.* is. 29:27
fears shall be *in the w.* Eccl 12:5
should not walk *in the w.* Isa 8:11
in the w. of thy judgements. 26:8
went on frowardly *in the w.* 57:17
which walked *in the w.* that. 65:2
to do *in the w.* of Egypt ? or what hast thou to do *in the w.?* Jer 2:18
in the w. of thy sister. Ezek 23:31
so priests murder *in the w.* Hos 6:9
agree quickly whiles thou art *in the w.* Mat 5:25
garments *in the w.*; others strewed branches *in the w.* 21:8
Mark 11:8; Luke 19:36
John came *in the w.* Mat 21:32
to guide our feet *into the w.* of peace. Luke 1:79
as thou art *in the w.* give. 12:58
appeared to thee *in the w.* Acts 9:17
he had seen the Lord *in the w.* 27
they have gone *in the w.* Jude 11

see Lord

my way
the Lord hath prospered *my w.* Gen 24:56
he maketh *my w.* perfect. 2 Sam 22:33; Ps 18:32
fenced up *my w.* that I. Job 19:8
why sayest thou, *My w.?* Isa 40:27
hear, O Israel, is not *my w.* equal ? Ezek 18:25
I go *my w.* John 8:21
brought on *my w.* Rom 15:24
to be brought on *my w.* 2 Cor 1:16*

out of the way
turned aside quickly *out of the w.* I commanded them. Ex 32:8
Deut 9:12, 16; Judg 2:17

the ass turned aside *out of the w.* Num 22:23
turn aside *out of the w.* Deut 11:28
thrust thee *out of the w.* 13:5
blind to wander *out of the w.* 27:18
the needy *out of the w.* Job 24:4
they are taken *out of the w.* 24
step hath turned *out of the w.* 31:7
wandereth *out of the w.* Pr 21:16
and through strong drink are *out of the w.* Isa 28:7*
get you *out of the w.* 30:11
stumblingblock *out of the w.* 57:14
are departed *out of the w.* Mal 2:8
are all gone *out of the w.* Rom 3:12
he took the handwriting *out of the w.* Col 2:14
he be taken *out of the w.* 2 Thes 2:7
compassion on them that are *out of the w.* Heb 5:2*
is lame be turned *out of the w.* 12:13

own way
the fruit of their *own w.* Pr 1:31
a man understand his *own w.?* 20:24
every one to his *own w.* Isa 53:6
they all look to their *own w.* 56:11
their *own w.* have I. Ezek 22:31
they defiled Israel by their *own w.* 36:17

their way
take heed to *their w.* to walk before. 1 Ki 2:4; 8:25; 2 Chr 6:16
the paths of *their w.* are. Job 6:18
his troops raise up *their w.* 19:12
I chose out *their w.*, sat chief. 29:25
let *their w.* be dark. Ps 35:6
this *their w.* is their folly. 49:13
perverted *their w.* and. Jer 3:21
know and try *their w.* 6:27
their w. shall be to them as. 23:12
do to them after *their w.* and judge. Ezek 7:27; 9:10; 11:21
ye shall see *their w.* and. 14:22
as for them *their w.* is not. 33:17
their w. was before me as. 36:17
according to *their w.* and doings. 19
being brought on *their w.* Acts 15:3

see went

this way
me in *this w.* that I go. Gen 28:20
Moses looked *this w.* and. Ex 2:12
to flee *this w.* or that. Josh 8:20
Elisha said, *This* is not the *w.*; follow me. 2 Ki 6:19
saying, *This* is the *w.*, walk ye in it. Isa 30:21
if he found any of *this w.* Acts 9:2
I persecuted *this w.* unto the. 22:4

thy way
Lord will prosper *thy w.* Gen 24:40
I pray, shew me *thy w.* Ex 33:13
thy w. is perverse. Num 22:32
make *thy w.* prosperous. Josh 1:8
return on *thy w.* to the wilderness. 1 Ki 19:15
make *thy w.* straight. Ps 5:8
teach me *thy w.* O Lord, lead me. 27:11; 86:11
commit *thy w.* unto the Lord. 37:5
our steps declined from *thy w.* 44:18
that *thy w.* may be known. 67:2
thy w. O God, is in the. 77:13
thy w. is in the sea, thy path in. 19
quicken thou me in *thy w.* 119:37
thou walk in *thy w.* safely. Pr 3:23
remove *thy w.* far from her. 5:8
in the greatness of *thy w.* Isa 57:10
see *thy w.* in the valley. Jer 2:23
why trimmest thou *thy w.* to ? 33
thou about to change *thy w.?* 36
thy w. have procured these. 4:18
will recompense *thy w.* Ezek 16:43
I will hedge up *thy w.* Hos 2:6
thou didst trust in *thy w.* 10:13
messenger, who shall prepare *thy w.* Mat 11:10; Mark 1:2; Luke 7:27

wayfaring
he saw a *w.* man in the. Judg 19:17
his own flock, to dress for the *w.* man. 2 Sam 12:4
highways lie waste, the *w.* Isa 33:8
w. men, though fools, shall. 35:8

a lodging place of *w.* men. Jer 9:2
thou be as a *w.* man ? 14:8

waymarks
set thee up *w.*, make thee. Jer 31:21

ways
shall rise early and go on your *w.* Gen 19:2
walk in all the *w.* Lord. Deut 5:33
walked in the *w.* of Asa. 1 Ki 22:43
he walked in all the *w.* of Manasseh. 2 Ki 21:21
he walked in all the *w.* of David. 22:2
not walked in the *w.* of. 2 Chr 17:3; 34:2
walked in the *w.* of the house. 22:3
he walked in the *w.* of the kings. 28:2
they know not the *w.* of. Job 24:13
they raise up the *w.* of their. 30:12
eyes are upon the *w.* of men. 34:21
the chief of the *w.* of God. 40:19
heart are the *w.* of them. Ps 84:5
so are the *w.* of every one greedy. Pr 1:19
to walk in the *w.* of darkness. 2:13
whose *w.* are crooked, and they. 15
wisdom's *w.* are *w.* of. 3:17
paths . . . her *w.* are moveable. 5:6
w. of man are before the eyes. 21
go to the ant, consider her *w.* 6:6
heart decline to her *w.* 7:25
the end thereof are the *w.* of death. 14:12; 16:25
the *w.* of man are clean in his. 16:2
when a man's *w.* please the Lord. 7
taketh a gift to pervert the *w.* 17:23
she looketh well to the *w.* of. 31:27
O young man, walk in the *w.* of thy heart. Eccl 11:9
they shall feed in the *w.* Isa 49:9
traversing her *w.* Jer 2:23
in the *w.* hast thou sat for. 3:2
stand in the *w.* and see, ask. 6:16
amend your *w.* and your doings. 7:3, 5; 26:13
walk in all the *w.* I have. 7:23
if they diligently learn the *w.* 12:16
make your *w.* and your doings. 18:11
thine eyes are open on the *w.* of. 32:19
the *w.* of Zion do mourn. Lam 1:4
let us search and try our *w.* 3:40
are not your *w.* unequal ? Ezek 18:25, 29
shall ye remember your *w.* 20:43
your wicked *w.* or doings. 44
son of man, appoint these two *w.*, that the sword may. 21:19
stood at head of the two *w.* to use. 21
consider your *w.* Hag 1:5, 7
do to us according to our *w.* and. Zech 1:6
and the rough *w.* shall. Luke 3:5
known to me the *w.* of life. Acts 2:28

see by-ways, evil, high, seven

any ways
do *any w.* hide their eyes. Lev 20:4
if ye shall *any w.* make. Num 30:15
any w. able to deliver. 2 Chr 32:13

his ways
of Lord, to walk in *his w.* and fear him. Deut 8:6; 26:17; 28:9
30:16; 1 Ki 2:3
to walk in all *his w.* Deut 10:12
11:22; Josh 22:5; 1 Ki 8:58
and walk ever in *his w.* Deut 19:9
all *his w.* are judgement. 32:4
Dan 4:37
walked not in *his w.* 1 Sam 8:3
David behaved wisely in *his w.* 18:14
and give to every man according to *his w.* 1 Ki 8:39; 2 Chr 6:30
and *his w.* are written. 2 Chr 13:22
Jotham prepared *his w.* before. 27:6
his w. are written in book. 7; 28:26
these are parts of *his w.* Job 26:14
man find according to *his w.* 34:11
not consider any of *his w.* 27
his w. are always grievous. Ps 10:5
he made known *his w.* unto Moses. 103:7
iniquity, they walk in *his w.* 119:3
one that walketh in *his w.* 128:1
is righteous in all *his w.* 145:17

choose none of *his w.*   *Pr* 3:31
he that perverteth *his w.*   10:9
he that is perverse in *his w.*   14:2
he that despiseth *his w.* shall. 19:16
lest thou learn *his w.* and.   22:25
that is perverse in *his w.*   28:6
he that is perverse in *his w.* shall. 18
he will teach us of *his w.*   *Isa* 2:3
                    Mi 4:2
they would not walk in *his w.Isa*42:24
I will direct all *his w.* saith. 45:13
seen *his w.* and will heal.   57:18
give every man according to *his w.*
             Jer 17:10; 32:19
that he should return from *his w.*
               Ezek 18:23
I will judge Israel according to *his w.*   30; 33:20
of a fowler in all *his w.*   *Hos* 9:8
punish Jacob according to *his w.*12:2
march on every one in *his w. Joel* 2:7
the hills did bow, *his w.*   *Hab* 3:6
thou shalt go before the Lord to prepare *his w.*   *Luke* 1:76
his w. are past finding. *Rom* 11:33
man is unstable in all *his w. Jas* 1:8
rich man fade away in *his w.*   11
     see **Lord**

my ways
if thou wilt walk in *my w.* as thy
  father. *1 Ki* 3:14; 11:38; *Zech* 3:7
and not walked in *my w.* *1 Ki* 11:33
doth not he see *my w.?*   *Job* 31:4
I will take heed to *my w.* *Ps* 39:1
Israel had walked in *my w.*   81:13
they have not known *my w.* 95:10
                  Heb 3:10
O that *my w.* were directed.*Ps* 119:5
I have declared *my w.* and thou. 26
I thought on *my w.* and turned. 59
all *my w.* are before *inee.*   168
acquainted with all *my w.*   139:3
blessed are they that keep *my w.*
                  Pr 8:32
let thine eyes observe *my w.* 23:26
neither are your ways *my w. Isa* 55:8
so are *my w.* higher than your. 9
and delight to know *my w.*   58:2
he hath inclosed *my w.*   *Lam* 3:9
he turned aside *my w.* and.   11
my w. equal, your *w.? Ezek* 18:29
if thou wilt walk in *my w. Zech* 3:7
ye have not kept *my w.*   *Mal* 2:9
remembrance of *my w.* *1 Cor* 4:17

own ways
I will maintain my *own w. Job* 13:15
be filled with his *own w.* *Pr* 14:14
not doing thine *own w.*   *Isa* 58:13
have chosen their *own w.*   66:3
then remember your *own* evil *w.*
             Ezek 36:31
be ashamed for your *own w.*   32
nations to walk in *own w. Acts* 14:16

their ways
pray and turn from *their* wicked *w.*
              2 Chr 7:14
eyes are upon *their w.* *Job* 24:23
turn to *their* crooked *w.* *Ps* 125:5
who go right on *their w.*   *Pr* 9:15
return not from *their w.* *Jer* 15:7
mine eyes are upon all *their w.* 16:17
them to stumble in *their w.*   18:15
comfort you when ye see *their w.*
             Ezek 14:23
not walked after *their w.*   16:47
punish them for *their w.* *Hos* 4:9
misery are in *their w.* *Rom* 3:16
follow *their* pernicious *w. 2 Pet* 2:2

thy ways
not prosper in *thy w.* *Deut* 28:29
sons walk not in *thy w.* *1 Sam* 8:5
may fear thee to walk in *thy w.*
              2 Chr 6:31
uprightness of *thy w.*   *Job* 4:6
the knowledge of *thy w.*   21:14
thou makest *thy w.* perfect? 22:3
light shall shine upon *thy w.* 28
shew me *thy w.* O Lord. *Ps* 25:4
I teach transgressors *thy w.* 51:13
to keep thee in all *thy w.*   91:11
have respect unto *thy w.*   119:15
in all *thy w.* acknowledge him. *Pr* 3:6

---

let *thy w.* be established. *Pr* 4:26
nor *thy w.* to that which destroyeth
  kings.   31:3
made us err from *thy w.* *Isa* 63:17
remember thee in *thy w.*   64:5
taught the wicked *thy w.* *Jer* 2:33
thou hast scattered *thy w.*   3:13
judge thee according to *thy w.*
          Ezek 7:3, 4, 8, 9
corrupted more than they in all *thy*
  w.   16:47
then remember *thy w.* and be.   61
according to *thy w.* shall they. 24:14
thou wast perfect in *thy w.* 28:15
whose hand are all *thy w. Dan* 5:23
just and true are *thy w.* *Rev* 15:3

way side
where is harlot that was by the *w.*
  side?   *Gen* 38:21
Eli sat on a seat by the *w.* side
  watching.   *1 Sam* 4:13
the proud have spread a net by the
  w. side.   *Ps* 140:5
seeds fell by the *w.* side. *Mat* 13:4
  19; *Mark* 4:4, 15; *Luke* 8:5, 12
two blind men sitting by the *w.* side.
              Mat 20:30
blind Bartimaeus sat by the high *w.*
  side.   *Mark* 10:46; *Luke* 18:35

we
been about cattle, *w.* and. *Gen* 46:34
the men said, We be not able; for they
  are stronger than *w.* *Num* 13:31
greater and taller than *w. Deut* 1:28
that *w.* may be like all. *1 Sam* 8:20
w. will be with thee, be. *Ezra* 10:4
w. his servants will arise. *Neh* 2:20
w., our sons and our daughters. 5:2
w. after our ability have.   8
w. are but of yesterday. *Job* 8:9
w. are his people, sheep. *Ps* 100:3
become weak as *w.* are? *Isa* 14:10
w. are thine.   63:19
for *w.* are many.   *Mark* 5:9
why could not *w.* cast him out? 9:28
that *w.* being delivered. *Luke* 1:74
w. be Abraham's seed. *John* 8:33
thou art his disciple, *w.* are. 9:28
are *w.* blind also?   40
they may be one as *w.* 17:11, 22
and *w.* are his witnesses. *Acts* 5:32
              10:39
the Holy Ghost as well as *w.* 10:47
w. are men of like passions. 14:15
w., or ever he come, are ready. 23:15
w., being many, are one body in
  Christ.   *Rom* 12:5
w. that are strong ought to bear. 15:1
w. are labourers together. *1 Cor* 3:9
w. are fools, but ye are wise, *w.* 4:10
w. bless, persecuted, *w.* suffer it. 12
w. in him; one Lord and *w.* by. 8:6
are not *w.* rather?   9:12
w. being many are one bread. 10:17
do *w.* provoke Lord, are *w.?* 22
w. are your rejoicing. *2 Cor* 1:14
w., that ye say not, ye, should. 9:4
Christ's, so are *w.* Christ's. 10:7
they may be found even as *w.* 11:12
though *w.* or an angel. *Gal* 1:8
so *w.,* when *w.* were children. 4:3
now *w.,* as Isaac, are the children. 28
w. are his workmanship. *Eph* 2:10
w. which are alive shall be caught in
  ... so shall *w.* ever. *1 Thes* 4:17
w. are not of the night nor of. 5:5
whose house are *w.* if *w.* hold fast.
               Heb 3:6
w. are not of them who draw. 10:39
w. are of God. Hereby. *1 John* 4:6
w. know that *w.* are of God. 5:19

weak
they be strong or *w.* *Num* 13:18
then shall I be *w.* as other men.
           Judg 16:7, 11, 17
I am this day *w.* though. *2 Sam* 3:39
let not your hands be *w. 2 Chr* 15:7*
strengthened the *w.* hands. *Job* 4:3
I am *w.*   *Ps* 6:2*
my knees are *w.*   109:24
also become *w.* as we? *Isa* 14:10
strengthen ye the *w.* hands. 35:3
shall be *w.* as water. *Ezek* 7:17; 21:7

---

how *w.* is thy heart? *Ezek* 16:30
the *w.* say, I am strong. *Joel* 3:10
but the flesh is *w.*   *Mat* 26:41
             Mark 14:38
ought to support the *w.* *Acts* 20:35
being not *w.* in faith, he. *Rom* 4:19
for the law was *w.* through the. 8:3
him that is *w.* in the faith. 14:1
another who is *w.* eateth herbs. 2
brother stumbleth or is made *w.* 21
bear the infirmities of the *w.* 15:1
w. things to confound the. *1 Cor* 1:27
we are *w.*   4:10
conscience being *w.*   8:7, 10
wound their *w.* conscience. 12
to the *w.* became I as *w.,* that I might
  gain the *w.*: I am made. 9:22
for this cause many are *w.* 11:30
bodily presence is *w.* *2 Cor* 10:10
I speak as though we had been *w.*
                11:21
who is *w.* and I am not *w.?* 29
for when I am *w.* then am I. 12:10
which to you-ward is not *w.* but. 13:3
for we are *w.* in him, but shall live. 4
are glad when we are *w.*   9
how turn ye again to the *w.? Gal* 4:9
support the *w.,* be patient toward
  all.   *1 Thes* 5:14

weaken
which didst *w.* nations. *Isa* 14:12*

weakened
of the land *w.* Judah. *Ezra* 4:4
their hands shall be *w.* *Neh* 6:9
he *w.* my strength in. *Ps* 102:23

weakeneth
he *w.* the strength of. *Job* 12:21*
he *w.* the hands of the men of war.
              Jer 38:4

weaker
Saul's house *w.* and. *2 Sam* 3:1
to the wife as the *w.* vessel. *1 Pet* 3:7

weak handed
while he is *w.* handed. *2 Sam* 17:2

weakness
the *w.* of God is stronger. *1 Cor* 1:25
I was with you in *w.* and.   2:3
it is sown in *w.;* it is raised. 15:43
made perfect in *w.* *2 Cor* 12:9
though crucified through *w.*   13:4
going before for the *w.* *Heb* 7:18
out of *w.* were made strong. 11:34

wealth
of Jacob took all their *w. Gen* 34:29
my hand got me this *w. Deut* 8:17
giveth thee power to get *w.*   18
kinsman, a man of *w.* *Ruth* 2:1
thou shalt see an enemy in all the *w.*
             1 Sam 2:32
Menahem exacted money of men of
  w.   *2 Ki* 15:20
thou hast not asked *w. 2 Chr* 1:11
I will give thee riches, and *w.* 12
nor seek their peace or *w.* for ever.
             Ezra 9:12*
Mordecai seeking the *w. Esth* 10:3*
spend their days in *w.* *Job* 21:13*
if I rejoiced because my *w.* was
  great.   31:25
and dost not increase *w. Ps* 44:12
they that trust in *w.* and boast. 49:6
die and leave their *w.* to others. 10
w. and riches shall be in his. 112:3
lest strangers be filled with thy *w.*
             Pr 5:10*
rich man's *w.* is his. 10:15; 18:11
w. gotten by vanity shall be. 13:11
the *w.* of the sinner is laid up. 22
w. maketh many friends, the. 19:4
God hath given *w.* *Eccl* 5:19; 6:2
w. of all the heathen shall be.
             Zech 14:14
this craft we have *w.* *Acts* 19:25
but seek every man another's *w.*
           1 Cor 10:24*

common wealth
being aliens from the *common w.* of
  Israel.   *Eph* 2:12

wealthy
us out into a *w.* place. *Ps* 66:12
up into the *w.* nation. *Jer* 49:31*

weaned

Isaac grew and was *w.*   *Gen* 21:8
not go till the child be *w.*   *1 Sam* 1:22
whom Tahpenes *w.* in.   *1 Ki* 11:20
as a child that is *w.* of his mother, my
  soul is as a *w.* child.   *Ps* 131:2
the *w.* child put his hand.   *Isa* 11:8
that are *w.* from the milk.   28:9
when she *w.* Lo-ruhama.   *Hos* 1:8

weapon

a paddle upon thy *w.*   *Deut* 23:13
other hand held a *w.*   *Neh* 4:17
flee from the iron *w.*   *Job* 20:24
no *w.* formed against thee. *Isa* 54:17
with his destroying *w.*   *Ezek* 9:1, 2

weapons

take, I pray thee, thy *w.*   *Gen* 27:3
neither my sword nor *w. 1 Sam* 21:8
round about, every man with his *w.*
  in.   *2 Ki* 11:8, 11; *2 Chr* 23:7, 10
even the Lord and the *w.* of his indignation.   *Isa* 13:5; *Jer* 50:25
every one with his *w.*   *Jer* 22:7
on fire and burn *w.*   *Ezek* 39:9, 10
with lanterns and *w.*   *John* 18:3
the *w.* of our warfare.   *2 Cor* 10:4
  see war

wear

thou wilt surely *w.* away. *Ex* 18:18
woman not *w.* what.   *Deut* 22:5
thou shalt not *w.* garment of.   11
to burn incense, to *w.* an. *1 Sam* 2:28
85 persons that did *w.* an.   22:18
royal apparel the king useth to *w.*
  Esth 6:8
the waters *w.* the stones. *Job* 14:19
we eat our own bread and *w Isa* 4:1
shall *w.* out the saints of. *Dan* 7:25
nor shall they *w.* a rough garment.
  Zech 13:4
that *w.* soft clothing are. *Mat* 11:8
day began to *w.* away.   *Luke* 9:12

weareth

ye respect him that *w.* the.   *Jas* 2:3

wearied

they *w.* themselves to.   *Gen* 19:11
nor have I *w.* thee with. *Isa* 43:23
thou hast *w.* me with thine.   24
thou art *w.* in the multitude of. 47:13
thou art *w.* in the greatness of. 57:10
my soul is *w.* because of. *Jer* 4:31*
w. thee? If in land of peace, wherein thou trustedst, they *w.* thee. 12:5
she hath *w.* herself with lies.
  Ezek 24:12
wherein have I *w.* thee?   *Mi* 6:3
w. the Lord. Yet ye say, Wherein
  have we *w.* him?   *Mal* 2:17
Jesus being *w.* sat thus.   *John* 4:6
lest ye be *w.* and faint in. *Heb* 12:3

wearieth

by watering he *w.* the.   *Job* 37:11*
labour of the foolish *w. Eccl* 10:15

weariness

much study is a *w.* of.   *Eccl* 12:12
he said, What a *w.* is it!   *Mal* 1:13
in *w.* and painfulness. *2 Cor* 11:27*

wearing

in Shiloh *w.* an ephod.   *1 Sam* 14:3
Jesus came forth in *w.* the. *John* 19:5
let it not be *w.* of gold.   *1 Pet* 3:3

wearisome

and *w.* nights are appointed. *Job* 7:3

weary

Rebekah said, I am *w.*   *Gen* 27:46
Amalek smote thee, when thou wast
  w.   *Deut* 25:18
Sisera was fast asleep and *w.*
  Judg 4:21*
bread unto thy men that are *w.?* 8:15
all the people came *w. 2 Sam* 16:14
upon him while he is *w.*   17:2
Philistines till his hand was *w.* 23:10
wicked cease, and the *w.*   *Job* 3:17
my soul is *w.* of my life, leave. 10:1
now he hath made me *w.*   16:7
not given water to *w.* to drink. 22:7
I am *w.* with my groaning. I. *Ps* 6:6
confirm thy inheritance when *w.* 68:9
w. of my crying, my throat.   69:3
47

my son, be not *w.* of Lord's. *Pr* 3:11
lest he be *w.* of thee, and so.   25:17
feasts are trouble, I am *w.*   *Isa* 1:14
none shall be *w.* nor stumble.   5:27
to *w.* men, but will ye *w.?*   7:13
it is seen that Moab is *w.* in.   16:12
ye may cause the *w.* to rest.   28:12
of a great rock in a *w.* land.   32:2
fainteth not, neither is *w.*   40:28
the youths shall faint and be *w.*   30
they shall run, and not be *w.*   31
but thou hast been *w.* of me. 43:22
a burden to the *w.* beast.   46:1
in season to him that is *w.*   50:4
all that seek her will not *w. Jer* 2:24
I am *w.* with holding in, I will. 6:11
they *w.* themselves to commit. 9:5
will destroy thee, I am *w.*   15:6
I was *w.* with forbearing, I.   20:9
I have satiated the *w.* soul.   31:25
labour in the fire and be *w.*   51:58
Babylon sink: and they shall be *w.* 64
w. themselves for vanity. *Hab* 2:13
lest by her continual coming she *w.*
  me.   *Luke* 18:5*
let us not be *w.* in well doing.
  Gal 6:9; *2 Thes* 3:13

weasel

the *w.* and the mouse.   *Lev* 11:29

weather

fair *w.* cometh out of.   *Job* 37:22*
a garment in cold of.   *Pr* 25:20
it will be fair *w.:* for the. *Mat* 16:2
it will be foul *w.* to day.   3

weave

they that *w.* networks.   *Isa* 19:9
cockatrice' eggs and *w.* spider's.59:5

weaver

to work the work of *w.*   *Ex* 35:35
Goliath's spear was like a *w.'s* beam.
  1 Sam 17:7; *2 Sam* 21:19
  1 Chr 11:23; 20:5
swifter than a *w.'s* shuttle. *Job* 7:6
I have cut off like a *w.*   *Isa* 38:12

weavest

if thou *w.* seven locks.   *Judg* 16:13

web

seven locks with the *w.*   *Judg* 16:13
with pin of beam and the *w.*   14
trust shall be a spider's *w. Job* 8:14
weave the spider's *w.*   *Isa* 59:5

webs

their *w.* shall not become. *Isa* 59:6

wedding

that were bidden to *w.*   *Mat* 22:3*
the *w.* is ready.   8
the *w.* is furnished.   10
that had not on a *w.* garment. 11
will return from the *w. Luke* 12:36*
bidden of any man to a *w.*   14:8*

wedge

Achan saw a *w.* of gold. *Josh* 7:21
Joshua took Achan and the *w.*   24
precious than golden *w. Isa* 13:12*

wedlock

as women that break *w. Ezek* 16:38

weeds

the *w.* were wrapped.   *Jonah* 2:5

week

The Hebrews had three sorts of
weeks. [1] Weeks of days, *which
were reckoned from one sabbath
to another.* [2] Weeks of years,
*which were reckoned from one
sabbatical year to another, and
which consisted of seven years.*
[3] Weeks of *seven times seven
years, or of forty nine years, which
are reckoned from one jubilee to
another.*
fulfil her *w.*   *Gen* 29:27
and fulfilled her *w.*   28
covenant with many for one *w.:* and
  in the midst of the *w. Dan* 9:27
to dawn toward the first day of the *w.*
  Mat 28:1; *Mark* 16:2, 9
  Luke 24:1; *John* 20:1, 19
I fast twice in the *w.*   *Luke* 18:12

the first day of the *w.*   Paul
  preached.   *Acts* 20:7
on the first day of the *w. 1 Cor* 16:2

weeks

shall be unclean two *w.*   *Lev* 12:5
bring a meat offering after your *w.*
  Num 28:26
appointed *w.* of harvest. *Jer* 5:24
seventy *w.* are determined on thy
  people.   *Dan* 9:24
threescore and two *w.*   25, 26
mourning three full *w.*   10:2
till three *w.* were fulfilled.   3
  see feast, seven

weep

(*Weeping and other open expressions of emotion, whether of joy
or sorrow, were common among
the people of the East, contrary to
the repression common in the
West. The louder the wail the
greater the grief. For that reason
men and women were hired to
weep and wail at funerals*)
mourn and *w.* for Sarah.   *Gen* 23:2
did yearn, sought where to *w.* 43:30
Moses heard the people *w.* throughout their families.   *Num* 11:10
they *w.* unto me, saying, Give.   13
what aileth the people that they *w.?*
  1 Sam 11:5
they had no more power to *w.*   34
Israel, *w.* over Saul.   *2 Sam* 1:24
thou didst *w.* for the child.   12:21
and didst rend thy clothes, and *w.*
  2 Chr 34:27
mourn not, nor *w.*   *Neh* 8:9
widows shall not *w.*   *Job* 27:15*
did not I *w.* for him that?   30:25
into the voice of them that *w.*   31
a time to *w.* and a time.   *Eccl* 3:4
to the high places to *w.*   *Isa* 15:2
I will *w.* bitterly, labour not to. 22:4
thou shalt *w.* no more, he will. 30:19
of peace shall *w.* bitterly.   33:7
that I might *w.* day and.   *Jer* 9:1
not hear it, my soul shall *w.* in secret
  places . . . shall *w.* sore.   13:17
w. ye not for the dead, nor bemoan
  him: but *w.* sore for him that.22:10
Sibmah, I will *w.* for thee.   48:32
for these things I *w.*   *Lam* 1:16
nor shalt thou mourn nor *w.*
  Ezek 24:16, 23
w. for thee with bitterness.   27:31
awake, ye drunkards, *w.*   *Joel* 1:5
let the priests *w.* between the. 2:17
declare it not in Gath, *w.*   *Mi* 1:10
should I *w.* in fifth month. *Zech* 7:3
ye this ado, and *w.?*   *Mark* 5:39
blessed are ye that *w.*   *Luke* 6:21
to you that laugh now, ye shall *w.* 25
Lord saw her and said, *W.* not.
  7:13; 8:52; *Rev* 5:5
w. not for me, but *w.* for. *Luke* 23:28
the grave to *w.* there.   *John* 11:31
ye shall *w.* and lament, but.   16:20
what mean ye to *w.* and break my
  heart?   *Acts* 21:13
w. with them that *w.*   *Rom* 12:15
they that *w.* as though they wept not.
  1 Cor 7:30
and mourn, and *w.*   *Jas* 4:9
go to now, ye rich men, *w.* and.   5:1
merchants of earth shall *w.* and.
  Rev 18:11

weepest

Hannah, why *w.* thou?   *1 Sam* 1:8
and they say unto her, Woman, why
  w. thou?   *John* 20:13, 15

weepeth

Joab, behold the king *w. 2 Sam* 19:1
Hazael said, Why *w.?*   *2 Ki* 8:12
he that goeth forth and *w. Ps* 126:6
she *w.* sore in night, her. *Lam* 1:2

weeping

w. before the door of.   *Num* 25:6
days of *w.* for Moses.   *Deut* 34:8
her husband went along with her *w.*
  2 Sam 3:16
they went up, *w.* as they.   15:30
noise of joy from *w.*   *Ezra* 3:13

prayed and confessed, w. *Ezra* 10:1
province was fasting and w. *Esth* 4:3
my face is foul with w. *Job* 16:16
heard the voice of my w. *Ps* 6:8
w. may endure for a night. 30:5
mingled my drink with w. 102:9
in their streets howl, w. *Isa* 15:3
bewail with the w. of Jazer the vine
of Sibmah. 16:9; *Jer* 48:32
Lord of hosts call to w. *Isa* 22:12
the voice of w. shall be no. 65:19
the w. of Israel heard. *Jer* 3:21
mountains will I take up a w. 9:10
they shall come with w. and. 31:9
lamentation and bitter w.; Rachel w.
for her children. 15; *Mat* 2:18
restrain thy voice from w. *Jer* 31:16
went forth to meet them w. 41:6
continual-w. shall go up, a cry. 48:5
Judah going and w. to seek. 50:4
there sat women w. for. *Ezek* 8:14
with fasting and with w. *Joel* 2:12
altar of the Lord with w. *Mal* 2:13
there shall be w. and. *Mat* 8:12
22:13; 24:51; 25:30; *Luke* 13:28
at his feet behind him w. *Luke* 7:38
when Jesus saw her w. and the Jews
also w. which came. *John* 11:33
without at the sepulchre, w. 20:11
widows stood by him w. *Acts* 9:39
often, now tell you even w. *Phil* 3:18
shall stand afar off w. *Rev* 18:15
shipmaster and sailors cried, w. 19

weigh

crown to w. a talent. *1 Chr* 20:2
keep them until ye w. *Ezra* 8:29
ye w. the violence of your. *Ps* 58:2
thou dost w. the path of. *Isa* 26:7

weighed

Abraham w. to Ephraim. *Gen* 23:16
by the Lord actions are w. *1 Sam* 2:3
his spear's head w. 600 shekels.
17:7; *2 Sam* 21:16
Absalom w. the hair of. *2 Sam* 14:26
priests w. to them the silver and
gold. *Ezra* 8:25
w. into their hands the silver. 26, 33
my grief were throughly w.! *Job* 6:2
nor shall silver be w. for the. 28:15
let me be w. in an even balance. 31:6
hath w. the mountains. *Isa* 40:12
Jeremiah w. him the money. *Jer* 32:9
Tekel, thou art w. in. *Dan* 5:27
so they w. for my price. *Zech* 11:12

weigheth

and he w. the waters. *Job* 28:25
but the Lord w. the spirits. *Pr* 16:2

weighing

each charger w. *Num* 7:85
golden spoons w. 86

weight

As the Hebrews had not the use
of coined money, which was of a
certain determined weight, they
weighed all the gold and silver they
used in trade. The shekel, the
half shekel, and the talents, are
not only denominations of money
of a certain value, of gold and
silver, but also of a certain weight.
When Moses named the drugs
which were to compose the perfume
to be burnt upon the golden altar,
he says, that they were to take
five hundred shekels of myrrh, etc.,
Ex 30:23. And in *2 Sam* 14:26,
it is said, that Absalom's hair
weighed two hundred shekels.
The shekel of the sanctuary,
according to several interpreters,
was double the common shekel;
but others think it was the same
as the common shekel, and the
words of the sanctuary, are added,
to express a just and exact weight,
according to the standards that
were kept in the temple, or tabernacle.

mouth of sack, in full w. *Gen* 43:21
shall there be a like w. *Ex* 30:34
unrighteousness in w. *Lev* 19:35
you your bread by w. 26:26

a perfect and just w. *Deut* 25:15
w. of golden earrings. *Judg* 8:26
w. of king's crown a. *2 Sam* 12:30
neither was the w. of the brass found
out. *1 Ki* 7:47; *2 Ki* 25:16
gave gold by w. for things of gold,
silver also by w. *1 Chr* 28:14
the w. for the winds. *Job* 28:25
just w. is his delight. *Pr* 11:1
a just w. and balance are. 16:11
thy meat shall be by w. *Ezek* 4:10
and they shall eat bread by w. 16
he cast the w. of lead. *Zech* 5:8
us a more exceeding. *2 Cor* 4:17
let us lay aside every w. *Heb* 12:1
every stone of hail the w. of a talent.
Rev 16:21

weightier

ye have omitted the w. *Mat* 23:23

weights

just w. shall ye have. *Lev* 19:36
in thy bag divers w. *Deut* 25:13
all the w. of the bag. *Pr* 16:11
divers w. and measures. 20:10, 23
the bag of deceitful w. *Mi* 6:11

weighty

heavy and the sand w. *Pr* 27:3
for his letters, say they, are w.
2 Cor 10:10

welfare

of their w. and said. *Gen* 43:27
each other of their w. *Ex* 18:7
Tou sent to David to enquire of his w.
1 Chr 18:10
was come a man to seek the w. of
Neh 2:10
and my w. passeth away. *Job* 30:15
have been for their w. *Ps* 69:22
this man seeketh not the w. of his
people. *Jer* 38:4

well, *substantive*

she saw a w. of water. *Gen* 21:19
witness I have digged this w. 30
here by w. of water. 24:13, 43
a fruitful bough by a w. 49:22
is the w. whereof the. *Num* 21:16
spring up, O w. 17
princes digged the w. 18
man that had a w. in. *2 Sam* 17:18
drink of the water of the w. of Beth-
lehem. 23:15; *1 Chr* 11:17, 18
who passing ... make it a w. *Ps* 84:6
drink waters out of thine own w.
Pr 5:15
righteous man is a w. of life. 10:11
a w. of living waters. *S of S* 4:15
w. was there. Jesus being wearied
... sat thus on the w. *John* 4:6
the w. is deep. 11
Jacob gave us the w. 12
shall be in him a w. of water. 14

well, *adverb*

if thou doest not w., sin. *Gen* 4:7
that it may be w. with me. 12:13
he entreated Abram w. for her. 16
Jordan was w. watered. 13:10
Abraham and Sarah w. stricken in
age. 18:11; 24:1
Jacob said, Is he w.? and they said,
He is w. 29:6
when it shall be w. with thee. 40:14
father w.? is he yet alive ? 43:27
dealt w. with the midwives. *Ex* 1:20
I know that he can speak w. 4:14
for it was w. with us. *Num* 11:18
Caleb said, We are w. able. 13:30
of sons of Joseph hath said w. 36:5
saying pleased me w. *Deut* 1:23
brethren, as w. as you. 3:20
that it may go w. with thee. 4:40
5:16; 6:3, 18; 12:25, 28; 19:13
22:7; *Ruth* 3:1; *Eph* 6:3
may rest as w. as thou. *Deut* 5:14
I heard the words of this people;
they have w. said. 28; 18:17
that it might be w. with them. 5:29
that it may be w. with you. 33
Jer 7:23
but shalt w. remember. *Deut* 7:18
because he is w. with thee. 15:16
if thou hast dealt w. with. *Judg* 9:16
me, for she pleaseth me w. 14:3, 7

as w. men of every city. *Judg* 20:48
w. let him do the kinsman's part.
Ruth 3:13
he shall play and thou shalt be w.
1 Sam 16:16
if he say thus, It is w. 20:7
I know w. thou shalt surely. 24:20
he dealt bread as w. *2 Sam* 6:19
called, and said, All is w. 18:28
David, Thou didst w. that it was in
thine heart to. *1 Ki* 8:18; *2 Chr* 6:8
answered, It is w. spoken. *1 Ki* 18:24
Is it w. with thee ? is it w. with thy
husband ? is it w. with the child ?
It is w. *2 Ki* 4:26
Is all w.? 5:21; 9:11
we do not w. 7:9
of Babylon; and it shall be w. with.
25:24; *Ps* 128:2; *Jer* 40:9
Judah things went w. *2 Chr* 12:12
thou doest w. to thyself. *Ps* 49:18
thou hast dealt w. with thy. 119:65
when it goeth w. with. *Pr* 11:10
the prudent man looketh w. 14:15
I saw and considered it w. 24:32
things which go w., yea, four. 30:29
she looketh w. to the ways of. 31:27
it shall be w. with them. *Eccl* 8:12
but it shall not be w. with the. 13
it shall be w. with him. *Isa* 3:10
me, Thou hast w. seen. *Jer* 1:12
Lord said, It shall be w. with. 15:11
It was w. with him, he. 22:15, 16
take him, look w. to him, do. 39:12
come, and I will look w. to. 40:4
that it may be w. with us. 42:6
for then we were w. and. 44:17
make it boil w. and seethe. *Ezek* 24:5
spice it w. 10
mark w., behold, and hear. 44:5
of one that can play w. on. 33:32
said the Lord, Doest thou w. to be
angry ? *Jonah* 4:4
I do w. to be angry, even unto. 9
hypocrites, w. did Esaias prophesy.
Mat 15:7; *Mark* 7:6; *Acts* 28:25
w. done, thou good and faithful servant. *Mat* 25:21, 23; *Luke* 19:17
he hath done all things w. *Mark* 7:37
he had answered them w. 12:28
Zacharias and Elisabeth w. *Luke* 1:7
when all men speak w. of you. 6:26
if it bear fruit, w.; and if not. 13:9
Master, thou hast w. said. 20:39
John 4:17
say we not w. thou hast a devil.
John 8:48
ye call me Lord, ye say w. 13:13
if w. why smitest thou me ? 18:23
keep his virgin, doeth w. *1 Cor* 7:37
giveth her in marriage, doeth w. 38
affect you, but not w. *Gal* 4:17
run w.; who did hinder you ? 5:7
ye have w. done, ye did. *Phil* 4:14
one that ruleth w. his. *1 Tim* 3:4
let the elders that rule w. be. 5:17
and to please them w. *Tit* 2:9
is one God; thou doest w. *Jas* 2:19
see as, do, doing, favoured
pleased

very well

as thou very w. knowest. *Acts* 25:10
he ministered to me, tou knowest
very w. *2 Tim* 1:18

wellbeloved

myrrh is my w. unto. *S of S* 1:13
now will I sing to my w. *Isa* 5:1
he sent his w. son. *Mark* 12:6
salute w. Epenetus. *Rom* 16:5
the elder to the w. Gaius. *3 John* 1

well nigh

as for me, my steps had w. nigh
slipped. *Ps* 73:2

wells

w. Abraham's servants. *Gen* 26:15
and Isaac digged again the w. 18
where were twelve w. *Ex* 15:27
drink of the water of w. *Num* 20:17
and w. digged which thou. *Deut* 6:11
and ye shall stop all w. *2 Ki* 3:19
they stopped all the w. of water. 25
towers and digged w. *2 Chr* 26:10
shall draw water out of w. *Isa* 12:3

these are *w*. without water, clouds
that are. *2 Pet 2:17*

wellspring
understanding is a *w*. of. *Pr 16:22*
the *w*. of wisdom as a. 18:4

wen
maimed, or having a *w*. *Lev 22:22*

wench
a *w*. told Jonathan. *2 Sam 17:17**

went
with me in the way I *w*. *Gen 35:3*
in the first place *w*. standard of
Judah. *Num 10:14*
into the land whereto he *w*. 14:24
kindled because Balaam *w*. 22:22
Balaam *w*. not to seek for. 24:1
Phinehas *w*. after the man. 25:8
in all the way ye *w*. *Deut 1:31*
he preserved us in all the way we *w*.
Josh 24:17
so Simeon *w*. with Judah. *Judg 1:3*
and Judah *w*. with Simeon. 17
strength *w*. from him. 16:19
said, Whither *w*. ye ? *1 Sam 10:14*
there *w*. with Saul a band. 26
the man *w*. for an old man. 17:12
but David *w*. to feed his father's. 15
David and his men *w*. wherever they
could go. 23:13
because they *w*. not with us. 30:22
how *w*. the matter ? *2 Sam 1:4*
as he *w*. to recover his border.
8:3; *1 Chr 18:3*
Lord preserved David whithersoever
he *w*.*2 Sam* 8:6, 14; *1 Chr* 18:6, 13
w. in their simplicity. *2 Sam 15:11*
as he *w*., thus he said, O my. 18:33
Solomon *w*. not fully. *1 Ki 1:6*
said, What way *w*. he ? 13:12
he *w*. after the man of God. 14
he said, Which way *w*. the Spirit of
the Lord ? 22:24; *2 Chr 18:23*
but they *w*. not. *1 Ki 22:48*
they two *w*. on. *2 Ki 2:6*
he said, W. not my heart with
thee ? 5:26
for he *w*. with them, and they. 6:4
when he *w*. in to his wife. *1 Chr 7:23*
when they *w*. from nation to nation.
16:20; *Ps 105:13*
so all Israel *w*. to their. *2 Chr 10:16*
in Judah things *w*. well. 12:12
people *w*. to house of Baal. 23:17
knew not whither I *w*. *Neh 2:16*
in the evening she *w*., and on the
morrow returned. *Esth 2:14*
I *w*. with them to the house of God.
Ps 42:4
it *w*. ill with Moses for their. 106:32
a young man *w*. the way to. *Pr 7:8*
he *w*. on frowardly in the way of his
heart. *Isa 57:17*
they *w*. every one straight forward.
Ezek 1:9
turned not when they *w*. 12; 10:11
they *w*. on their four sides. 1:17
when those *w*., these *w*. 21
for their heart *w*. after their. 20:16
she *w*. after her lovers. *Hos 2:13*
then *w*. Ephraim to the. 5:13
they *w*. to Baal-peor and. 9:10
as they called them, so they *w*. 11:2
before him *w*. the pestilence, burning
coals. *Hab 3:5*
of thine arrows, they *w*. 11
he repented and *w*. *Mat 21:29*
said, I go, sir, but *w*. not. 30
while they *w*. to buy, the. 25:10
they left their father and *w*. after.
Mark 1:20
all *w*. to be taxed, every. *Luke 2:3*
one *w*. to them from the dead. 16:30
as they *w*. they were cleansed. 17:14
Joseph *w*. to Pilate and. 23:52
the Galileans also *w*. to. *John 4:45*
every man *w*. to his own house. 7:53
I *w*. and washed and I. 9:11
from Goa and *w*. to God. 13:3
they *w*. backward and fell to. 18:6
then *w*. this saying abroad. 21:23
they *w*. every where preaching the.
Acts 8:4
Saul . . . threatenings *w*. unto the. 9:1

as they *w*. on their journey, Peter *w*.
to pray. *Acts 10:9*
they *w*. both into synagogue. 14:1
w. not with them to the work. 15:38
as we *w*. to prayer, a damsel. 16:16
as I *w*. to Damascus with. 26:12
he *w*. and preached to. *1 Pet 3:19*

see **along**

went *about*
the people *w*. about. *Num 11:8*
the slingers *w*. about it. *2 Ki 3:25*
they *w*. about and taught. *2 Chr 17:9*
I *w*. about to cause my. *Eccl 2:20*
the watchmen that *w*. about found
me. *S of S 5:7*
Jesus *w*. about teaching. *Mat 4:23*
9:35; *Mark 6:6*
they *w*. about to slay him.
Acts 9:29; 21:31; 26:21
Jesus *w*. about doing good. 10:38
he *w*. about seeking some to. 13:11

see **arose**

went *aside*
Jesus took them and *w*. aside
privately. *Luke 9:10*
chief captain *w*. aside. *Acts 23:19*

went *astray*
afflicted I *w*. astray. *Ps 119:67*
when Israel *w*. astray after idols.
Ezek 44:10, 15
priests which *w*. not astray when
Israel *w*. astray as Levites *w*.
astray. 48:11
than of the ninety and nine which *w*.
not astray. *Mat 18:13*

went *away*
Samson *w*. away with doors of the
gates. *Judg 16:3*
and *w*. away with the pin of. 14
and his concubine *w*. away. 19:2
the mule that was under him *w*.
away. *2 Sam 18:9*
was wroth, and *w*. away. *2 Ki 5:11*
queen of Sheba *w*. away. *2 Chr 9:12*
he *w*. away sorrowful. *Mat 19:22*
Mark 10:22
he *w*. away second time. *Mat 26:42*
he *w*. away the third time. 44
Mark 14:39
of him many *w*. away. *John 12:11*
the disciples *w*. away to their. 20:10
morrow Peter *w*. away. *Acts 10:23*

went *back*
so he *w*. back and did. *1 Ki 13:19*
king Joram *w*. back to. *2 Ki 8:29*
many disciples *w*. back. *John 6:66*

went *before*
the Lord *w*. before. *Ex 13:21*
the angel of God which *w*. before the
camp. 14:19
the ark of the covenant *w*. before
them. *Num 10:33; Josh 3:6*
the armed men *w*. before the priests.
Josh 6:9, 13
one bearing a shield *w*. before him.
1 Sam 17:7, 41
Ahio *w*. before the ark. *2 Sam 6:4*
and Shobach *w*. before them. 10:16
1 Chr 19:16
Amasa *w*. before them. *2 Sam 20:8*
they that *w*. before were affrighted.
Job 18:20
the singers *w*. before. *Ps 68:25*
they saw *w*. before them. *Mat 2:9*
multitudes that *w*. before them
cried. 21:9; *Mark 11:9*
they which *w*. before rebuked him.
Luke 18:39
he *w*. before, to Jerusalem. 19:28
Judas *w*. before, drew near. 22:47
prophecies which *w*. before.
1 Tim 1:18

went *behind*
the angel removed and *w*. behind.
Ex 14:19

went *down*
Abram *w*. down into Egypt to
sojourn. *Gen 12:10*
sun *w*. down, a smoking furnace and.
15:17; *Judg* 19:14; *2 Sam 2:24*
Joseph's brethren *w*. down. *Gen 42:3*
Benjamin *w*. down. 43:15

Moses *w*. down from the mount to
the people. *Ex* 19:14, 25; 32:15
w. down alive into pit. *Num 16:33*
how our fathers *w*. down into. 20:15
Deut 10:22; 26:5; *Josh 24:4*
Israel *w*. down after. *Judg* 3:27, 28
Barak *w*. down from mount. 4:14
Gideon *w*. down with Phurah. 7:11
Samson *w*. down to Timnath and
saw a woman. 14:1, 5, 7
him before the sun *w*. down. 18
Samson *w*. down to Ashkelon. 19
Ruth *w*. down unto the. *Ruth 3:6*
the Israelites *w*. down. *1 Sam* 13:20
his father's house *w*. down to him.
22:1
David heard, and *w*. down to the
hold. *2 Sam 5:17*
but Uriah *w*. not down. 11:9, 10, 13
court, whither they *w*. down. 17:18
David *w*. down against the. 21:15
three of the thirty chief *w*. down and.
23:13; *1 Chr 11:5*
Benaiah *w*. down and slew a lion in.
2 Sam 23:20
Benaiah *w*. down to the Egyptian,
and slew. 21; *1 Chr* 11:22, 23
Elijah *w*. down with him. *2 Ki 1:15*
Elijah and Elisha *w*. down. 2:2
Naaman *w*. down and dipped. 5:14
Ahaziah *w*. down to see Joram.
8:29; *2 Chr 22:6*
Jehoshaphat *w*. down. *2 Chr 18:2*
ointment that *w*. down. *Ps 133:2*
w. down into the garden. *S of S* 6:11
people *w*. down aforetime. *Isa 52:4*
I *w*. down to the potter's. *Jer 18:3*
in the day when he *w*. down to the
grave. *Ezek 31:15*
they also *w*. down to hell. 17
Jonah *w*. down to Joppa. *Jonah 1:3*
I *w*. down to the bottoms of. 2:6
man *w*. down justified. *Luke 18:14*
angel *w*. down and troubled the
water. *John 5:4*
Jacob *w*. down into. *Acts 7:15*
Philip *w*. down to Samaria. 8:5
and they both *w*. down into the. 38
then Peter *w*. down to the. 10:21
Herod *w*. down from Judaea. 12:19
Paul *w*. down and embracing. 20:10

went *forth*
a raven *w*. forth. *Gen 8:7*
w. forth from Ur. 11:31
Noah *w*. forth, his sons and. 18, 19
out of that land *w*. forth. 10:11
they *w*. forth to go into land. 12:5
there *w*. forth a wind. *Num 11:31*
the princes *w*. forth to. 31:13; 33:1
trees *w*. forth to anoint. *Judg 9:8*
as he *w*. forth it fell out. *2 Sam 20:8*
Elisha *w*. forth unto the spring of the
waters. *2 Ki 2:21*
whithersoever he *w*. forth. 18:7
then *w*. Haman forth. *Esth 5:9*
Satan *w*. forth from. *Job* 1:12; 2:7
angel of the Lord *w*. forth. *Isa 37:36*
the former things *w*. forth, I. 48:3
Shallum who *w*. forth. *Jer 22:11*
thy renown *w*. forth among the
heathen. *Ezek 16:14*
her great scum *w*. not forth. 24:12
that which *w*. forth by an. *Amos 5:3*
burning coals *w*. forth. *Hab 3:5*
behold, a sower *w*. forth. *Mat 13:3*
ten virgins *w*. forth to meet. 25:1
took up bed and *w*. forth. *Mark 2:12*
name's sake they *w*. forth. *3 John 7*
he *w*. forth conquering. *Rev 6:2*

went *her way*
woman *w*. her way. *1 Sam 1:18*
the woman *w*. her way. *John 4:28*
so said, she *w*. her way. 11:28

went *his way*
and the Lord *w*. his way. *Gen 18:33*
Rebekah and *w*. his way. 24:61
and drink and *w*. his way. 25:34
Jethro *w*. his way into. *Ex 18:27*
Saul *w*. his way. *1 Sam 24:7*
David *w*. on *his way*. 26:25
of Adonijah *w*. his way. *1 Ki 1:49*
so Mordecai *w*. his way. *Esth 4:17*
Jeremiah *w*. his way. *Jer 28:11*

his enemy sowed tares and w. his
  way.   *Mat* 13:25
he passing through midst of them,
  w. his way.   *Luke* 4:30
he w. his way and published.   8:39
Judas w. his way and communed
  with priests.   22:4
man believed, and w. his way.
    John 4:50
eunuch w. on his way.   *Acts* 8:39
Ananias w. his way and.   9:17
    see Jesus, went

went in, or into
Noah w. into the ark and. *Gen* 7:7
w. in two and two.   9
w. in male and female.   16
Joseph w. into the house to. 39:11
Moses and Aaron w. in to Pharaoh.
    Ex 5:1; 7:10
Israel w. into the midst of the. 14:22
the Egyptians w. in.   23; 15:19
until Moses w. in to speak. 34:35
when Aaron w. into the. *Lev* 16:23
that were spies w. in. *Josh* 6:23
the haft also w. in after. *Judg* 3:22
so the Levite w. in and dwelt. 17:10
when the Levite w. in to lodge. 19:15
Saul w. in to cover.   *1 Sam* 24:3
then w. David in before. *2 Sam* 7:18
Bath-sheba w. in unto.   *1 Ki* 1:15
disguised w. into the battle. 22:30
Elisha w. in, shut the. *2 Ki* 4:33
then she w. in, fell at his feet. 37
and one w. in and told his lord. 5:4
Gehazi w. in and stood before. 25
when they w. in to offer.   10:24
Uzziah w. into the temple of the
  Lord.   *2 Chr* 26:16
Azariah the priest w. in after. 17
so the children w. in.   *Neh* 9:24
the king w. into the palace garden.
    Esth 7:7
until I w. into the sanctuary of God.
    Ps 73:17
Urijah fled and w. into. *Jer* 26:21
so I w. in.   *Ezek* 8:10
six men w. in.   9:2
clothed with linen w. in. 10:2, 3, 6
when they w. into captivity. 25:3
Israel w. into captivity for. 39:23
Daniel w. in and desired of the king.
    Dan 2:16
w. in unto Arioch.   24
he w. into his house to pray. 6:10
the devils w. into the herd of swine.
    Mat 8:32
certain householder w. into. 21:33
  Mark 12:1; *Luke* 19:12; 20:9
they that were ready w. in to the
  marriage.   *Mat* 25:10
w. into the holy city, and. 27:53
how David w. into the house of God.
    Mark 2:26; *Luke* 6:4
Joseph w. in boldly to Pilate.
    Mark 15:43
burn incense when he w. in. *Luke* 1:9
Mary w. into the hill country. 39
and he w. in to tarry with. 24:29
that disciple w. in with. *John* 18:15
clothes lying, yet w. he not in. 20:5
then w. in also that other disciple. 8
all the time the Lord w. in. *Acts* 1:21
as Peter talked he w. in and. 10:27
he departed and w. into. 12:17
they w. into the synagogue on. 13:14
Paul w. into the synagogue. 17:2
    10; 19:8
their sound w. into all. *Rom* 10:18

went in, as to a woman
Abram w. in unto Hagar. *Gen* 16:4
the firstborn w. in and lay. 19:33
Leah; and he w. in unto her. 29:23
he w. in also unto Rachel. 30
Jacob w. in unto Bilhah. 30:4
saw Shuah and w. in to her. 38:2
Onan w. in to his brother's wife. 9
harlot and w. in unto her. *Judg* 16:1
Boaz w. in unto Ruth. *Ruth* 4:13
David comforted Bath-sheba his
  wife, and w. in. *2 Sam* 12:24
Absalom w. in to his father's. 16:22
Ithra w. in to Abigail the daughter
  of Nahash.   17:25

David w. not in to them. *2 Sam* 20:3
Hezron w. in to.   *1 Chr* 2:21
when Ephraim w. in to his wife. 7:23
yet they w. in unto her. *Ezek* 23:44

went over
there arose and w. over. *2 Sam* 2:15
and they w. over Jordan. 19:17
Barzillai w. over Jordan with. 31
so they two w. over on. *2 Ki* 2:8
smote the waters and w. over. 14
these w. over Jordan. *1 Chr* 12:15
and times that w. over him. 29:30
other company w. over. *Neh* 12:38
street, to them that w. over. *Isa* 51:23

went out
Cain w. out from the presence of the
  Lord.   *Gen* 4:16
Isaac w. out to meditate in. 24:63
Dinah w. out to see the daughters of
  the land.   34:1
washed his face and w. out. 43:31
and the one w. out from me. 44:28
Moses w. out to his brethren.
    Ex 2:11, 13
Aaron w. out from Pharaoh. 8:12, 30
    9:33
hosts of the Lord w. out. 12:41; 14:8
all the women w. out after. 15:20
there w. out some people on. 16:27
Moses w. out to meet his. 18:7
every one w. out unto the. 33:7
there w. out fire from. *Lev* 10:2
them when they w. out. *Num* 10:34
two men w. out into the. 11:26
Sihon w. out against Israel. 21:23
Og, the king of Bashan, w. out. 33
behold, I w. out to withstand. 22:32
none w. out, and none. *Josh* 6:1
the men of Ai w. out. 8:14, 17
the Canaanite w. out and all. 11:4
they w. out, the Lord was. *Judg* 2:15
all that stood by him w. out. 3:19
master of the house w. out. 19:23
I w. out full, and came. *Ruth* 1:21
ere the lamp of God w. out in the
  temple.   *1 Sam* 3:3
I w. out after the bear, and. 17:35
David w. out where Saul sent him.
    18:5, 13, 16; 19:8
even he w. out to lie on. *2 Sam* 11:13
they w. out every man from. 13:9
the day the king w. out of. 19:19
they w. out at noon. *1 Ki* 20:16
w. out first.   17
the king of Israel w. out and. 21
the child w. out to his father to
  the reapers.   *2 Ki* 4:18
took up her son, and w. out. 37
Gehazi w. out from his presence a
  leper.   5:27
they w. out each in his chariot. 9:21
arrow w. out of Jehoram's. 24
David w. out to meet. *1 Chr* 12:17
David heard of it, and w. out. 14:8
Azariah w. out to meet. *2 Chr* 15:2
was no peace to him that w. out. 5
Jehu w. out to meet. 19:2
to praise as they w. out. 20:21
Josiah w. out against Pharaoh-
  necho.   35:20
as the word w. out of the king's
  mouth.   *Esth* 7:8
when I w. out to the gate through the
  city.   *Job* 29:7
that I w. not out of the door? 31:34
when he w. out through the land of
  Egypt.   *Ps* 81:5
Jeremiah came in and w. out among
  people.   *Jer* 37:4
the cherub and w. out. *Ezek* 10:7
the city that w. out by. *Amos* 5:3
neither any peace to him that w. out.
    Zech 8:10
Jesus said, What w. ye out into the?
  Mat 11:7, 8, 9; *Luke* 7:24, 25, 26
a man who w. out early to. *Mat* 20:1
he w. out about third hour. 3, 5, 6
those servants w. out into. 22:10
his friends w. out to lay hold on him:
  He is beside himself. *Mark* 3:21
unclean spirits w. out and entered.
    5:13; *Luke* 8:33; *Acts* 19:12

they w. out to see what it was that
  was done. *Mark* 5:14; *Luke* 8:35
for there w. virtue out. *Luke* 6:19
Peter w. out and wept. 22:62
they which heard it, w. out. *John* 8:9
Jesus hid himself and w. out. 59
rose up hastily, and w. out. 11:31
received the sop w. out. 13:30
w. out that other disciple. 18:16
the Lord w. in and out. *Acts* 1:21
certain w. out from us have. 15:24
Abraham w. out, not. *Heb* 11:8
they w. out from us, but were not of
  us, they w. out. *1 John* 2:19

went their way
of Dan w. their way. *Judg* 18:26
Amalekites burnt Ziklag and w.
  their way.   *1 Sam* 30:2
all the people w. their way to eat.
    Neh 8:12
w. their way as a flock. *Zech* 10:2
that kept swine fled and w. their
  way.   *Mat* 8:33
whatsoever is right I will give you.
  And they w. their way. 20:4
light of it and w. their ways. 22:5
these words, they w. their way. 22:22
w. their way and found the colt.
  Mark 11:4; *Luke* 19:32
but some w. their ways. *John* 11:46
as they w. on their way. *Acts* 8:36

went through
thou didst divide the sea, they w.
  through. *Neh* 9:11; *Ps* 66:6
we w. through fire and. *Ps* 66:12
forsaken, so that no man w. through
  thee.   *Isa* 60:15
he w. through the corn fields on the.
  Mark 2:23; *Luke* 6:1

went up
God w. up from Abraham. *Gen* 17:22
God w. up from Jacob in. 35:13
w. up to father's bed, he w. up. 49:4
Moses, Aaron and Hur w. up.
    Ex 17:10
Moses w. up unto God. 19:3, 20
  24:13, 15; 34:4; *Deut* 10:3
w. up, and searched the. *Num* 13:21
but the men that w. up with. 31
they w. up into mount Hor. 20:27
    33:38
w. presumptuously up. *Deut* 1:43
so that the people w. up. *Josh* 6:20
brethren that w. up with me. 14:8
Judah w. up and the Lord. *Judg* 1:4
the house of Joseph also w. up. 22
Barak and Deborah w. up with. 4:10
Gideon w. up thence to. 8:8, 11
Elkanah w. up out of his city.
    1 Sam 1:3, 7, 21
Hannah w. not up; until child. 22
the cry of the city w. up to. 5:12
as he w. up barefoot. *2 Sam* 15:30
David, according to the saying of
  Gad, w. up. 24:19; *1 Chr* 21:19
Elijah w. up by a whirlwind to
  heaven.   *2 Ki* 2:11
Elisha w. up and lay upon. 4:34, 35
Hezekiah w. up. 19:14; *Isa* 37:14
Josiah w. up into the house of the
  Lord. *2 Ki* 23:2; *2 Chr* 34:30
Joab w. up first and was. *1 Chr* 11:6
children of the province that w. up.
  Ezra 2:1, 59; *Neh* 7:6, 61
they w. up in haste to Jerusalem to
  the Jews.   *Ezra* 4:23
Ezra w. up.   7:6
genealogy of them that w. up. 8:1
the priest that w. up. *Neh* 12:1
it w. up and down among. *Ezek* 1:13
cloud of incense w. up. 8:11
the glory of the Lord w. up. 10:4
    11:23, 24
he w. up and down among the lions.
    19:6
Jesus w. up straightway. *Mat* 3:16
and seeing the multitudes w.
  5:1; 14:23; 15:29; *Luke* 9:28
two men w. up into the. *Luke* 18:10
then w. he also up unto. *John* 7:10
as he w. up, two men. *Acts* 1:10
Peter and John w. up into the. 3:1
Peter w. up upon the housetop. 10:9

went

Paul w. up to Jerusalem. *Acts 24:11*
   Gal 1:18; 2:1, 2
w. I up to Jerusalem. *Gal 1:17*
they w. up on the breadth. *Rev 20:9*

went a whoring
Israel w. a whoring after other gods.
   Judg 2:17; 8:33
w. a whoring with her. *Ps 106:39*

wentest
Reuben, thou w. up to. *Gen 49:4*
Lord, when thou w. out of. *Judg 5:4*
whithersoever thou w. *2 Sam 7:9*
w. thou not with thy friend? *16:17*
w. thou not with me? *19:25*
O God, when thou w. *Ps 68:7*
even thither w. thou up. *Isa 57:7*
thou w. to the king with ointment. *9*
when thou w. after me in. *Jer 2:2*
heart toward the way thou w. *31:21*
thou w. forth for salvation. *Hab 3:13*
thou w. in to men uncircumcised.
   Acts 11:3

wept
Hagar sat and w. *Gen 21:16*
Esau w. *27:38*
Jacob w. *29:11; 33:4; 37:35*
   Hos 12:4
from his brethren and w. *Gen 42:24*
43:30; 45:2, 14, 15; 46:29; 50:1, 17
and, behold, the babe w. *Ex 2:6*
and the children of Israel also w.
   Num 11:4, 18, 20; 14:1; Deut 1:45
34:8; Judg 2:4; 20:23, 26; 21:2
Samson's wife w. before. *Judg 14:16*
daughters and w. *Ruth 1:9, 14*
Hannah w. and did. *1 Sam 1:7, 10*
all people w. *11:4; 2 Sam 3:32, 34*
Jonathan and David w. *1 Sam 20:41*
Saul w. *24:16*
David w. *30:4; 2 Sam 1:12*
David w. at the grave. *2 Sam 3:32*
was yet alive I fasted and w. *12:22*
the king and servants w. sore. *13:36*
all the country w. *15:23*
w. as he went. *30*
king was much moved and w. *18:33*
the man of God w. *2 Ki 8:11*
Joash w. over Elisha and. *13:14*
remember how I have walked.
Hezekiah w. sore. *20:3; Isa 38:3*
king of Judah hath w. *2 Ki 22:19*
seen the first house w. *Ezra 3:12*
people w. very sore. *10:1; Neh 8:9*
I heard these words, I w. *Neh 1:4*
lifted up their voice and w. *Job 2:12*
when I w. and chastened. *Ps 69:10*
Babylon, we sat down and w. *137:1*
Peter w. *Mat 26:75; Mark 14:72*
   Luke 22:62
he seeth them that w. *Mark 5:38*
   Luke 8:52
as they mourned and w. *Mark 16:10*
you, and ye have not w. *Luke 7:32*
he beheld the city and w. *19:41*
Jesus w. *John 11:35*
at the sepulchre: as she w. *20:11*
they w. sore and fell on. *Acts 20:37*
as though they w. not. *1 Cor 7:30*
I w. because no man. *Rev 5:4*

were
cannot do this, for that w. *Gen 34:14*
third day when they w. sore. *25*
Jacob said to all that w. with. *35:2*
gave all the strange gods that w. *4*
Israel saw they w. in evil. *Ex 5:19*
since day they w. upon earth. *10:6*
w. ye not afraid to speak? *Num 12:8*
we w. in our own sight as grasshoppers, and so we w. in. *13:33*
w. it not better for us to? *14:3*
O that there w. such an. *Deut 5:29*
for ye w. strangers in the. *10:19*
whereas ye w. as the stars. *28:62*
w. it not that I feared the. *32:27*
O that they w. wise, that they. *29*
I wist not whence they w. *Josh 2:4*
thou seest mountains as if they w.
   men. *Judg 9:36*
and there they w. not. *1 Sam 9:4*
that valiant men w. *2 Sam 11:16*
we w. together; there. *1 Ki 3:18*
place where the officers w. *4:28*
did evil above all that w. *16:30, 33*

w. it not that I regard. *2 Ki 3:14*
and the tents as they w. *7:10*
as many as w. of a free heart.
   2 Chr 29:31
though there w. of you cast. *Neh 1:9*
for there w. that said, We. *5:2, 3, 4*
seed, whether they w. *Job 7:61*
Oh that I w. as in months. *29:2*
a sojourner, as all my fathers w.
   Ps 39:12
whose captives they w. *Isa 14:2*
they w. no gods, but work of. *37:19*
because they w. not. *Jer 31:15*
though Noah, Daniel, and Job w. in.
   Ezek 14:14, 16, 18, 20
heathen among whom they w. *20:9*
there w. but ten, there w. *Hag 2:16*
persecuted prophets which w. before.
   Mat 5:12
David did and they that w.? *12:3, 4*
   Mark 2:25, 26; Luke 6:3, 4
whether he w. the Christ. *Luke 3:15*
this man, if he w. a prophet. *7:39*
w. not ten cleansed? where? *17:17*
if this man w. not of God. *John 9:33*
if any man knew where he w. *11:57*
if ye w. of the world, world. *15:19*
thine they w., and thou gavest. *17:6*
they said, If he w. not a. *18:30*
w. not a little comforted. *Acts 20:12*
saying that these things w. so. *24:9*
calleth things that be not as though
   they w. *Rom 4:17*
them my people that w. not. *9:25*
if whole body w. an eye, where w.
hearing? if whole w. hearing, where
w. smelling? *1 Cor 12:17*
whatsoever they w. maketh. *Gal 2:6*
w. by nature children of. *Eph 2:3*
for even when we w. *2 Thes 3:10*
things continue as they w. *2 Pet 3:4*
until their brethren, be killed as they
w., should be fulfilled. *Rev 6:11*

as it were
it seemeth, there is as if w. a plague.
   Lev 14:35
as it w. the company. *S of S 6:13*
that draw sin as it w. *Isa 5:18*
as if staff lift up itself as it w. *10:15*
hide thyself as it w. for a. *26:20*
and we hid as it w. our faces. *53:3*
his sweat as it w. great. *Luke 22:44*
up not openly, but as it w. *John 7:10*
sought it as it w. by works. *Rom 9:32*
apostles, as it w. to death. *1 Cor 4:9*
and his face was as it w. *Rev 10:1*
I saw one of his heads as it w. *13:3*
they sung as it w. a new song. *14:3*
I saw as it w. a sea of glass. *15:2*

if it were
if it w. so, why should not my spirit
be troubled? *Job 21:4*
if it w. possible to deceive the very
elect. *Mat 24:24*
they might touch if it w. the border.
   Mark 6:56
if it w. not so, I would. *John 14:2*
if it w. a matter of wrong. *Acts 18:14*

wert
O that thou w. as my. *S of S 8:1*
I would thou w. cold or. *Rev 3:15*

west
spread abroad to the w. *Gen 28:14*
the w. and the south. *Deut 33:23*
looking toward the w. *1 Ki 7:25*
on quarters were porters, toward the
   east, w. *1 Chr 9:24; 2 Chr 4:4*
they put to flight them toward east
   and w. *1 Chr 12:15*
cometh not from the w. *Ps 75:6*
as east is from the w., so far. *103:12*
them from the east and w. *107:3*
Philistines toward the w. *Isa 11:14*
and gather thee from the w. *43:5*
they may know from the w. *45:6*
come from the north and w. *49:12*
fear the Lord from the w. *59:19*
are his sides east and w. *Ezek 48:1*
he goat came from the w. *Dan 8:5*
tremble from the w. *Hos 11:10*
I will save my people from the w.
   Zech 8:7
of Olives shall cleave toward w. *14:4*

from east and w. and sit down with.
   Mat 8:11; Luke 13:29
east and shineth to w. *Mat 24:27*
cloud rise out of the w. *Luke 12:54*
on south three gates, and w. three
   gates. *Rev 21:13*

west border
great sea for border, this shall be
   w. border. *Num 34:6*
w. border was to the great sea.
   Josh 15:12
w. border a portion. *Ezek 45:7*

west quarter
this was the w. quarter. *Josh 18:14*

west side
on w. side hanging 50 cubits.
   Ex 27:12; 38:12
the w. side the standard. *Num 2:18*
measure on the w. side of the. *35:5*
even to the w. side a portion.
   Ezek 48:3, 4, 5, 6, 7, 8, 23, 24

western
as for the w. border. *Num 34:6*

westward
looked eastward and w. *Gen 13:14*
behind the tabernacle w. *Num 3:23*
lift up thine eyes w. *Deut 3:27*
shall be 10,000 w. *Ezek 48:18*
I saw the ram pushing w. *Dan 8:4*

west wind
a strong w. wind took. *Ex 10:19*

wet
they are w. with showers. *Job 24:8*
let it be w. with the dew of heaven.
   Dan 4:15, 23, 25, 33; 5:21

whale
(*The word sometimes translated
whale in the Old Testament is
at other times translated dragon, serpent, or sea-monster. The whale of
Jonah is called in that book merely a
great fish. In the New Testament
the word used in the original may
mean almost any large sea-animal,
whale, seal, shark, or tunny*)
am I a sea, or a w. that? *Job 7:12**
Pharaoh, thou art as a w. in the.
   *Ezek 32:2**
days in the w.'s belly. *Mat 12:40*

whales
God created great w. *Gen 1:21**

what
w. shall I do now to? *Gen 27:37*
my master wotteth not w. is. *39:8*
w. shall we say to my lord? w. shall
   we speak? *44:16*
know not with w. we. *Ex 10:26*
when son asketh, W. is this? *13:14*
w. are we? *16:7*
for they wist not w. it was. *15*
say, W. shall we eat? *Lev 25:20*
and see the land w. it. *Num 13:18*
w. the land is, and w. cities. *19, 20*
it was not declared w. *15:34*
w. is Aaron? *16:11*
w. hath the Lord spoken? *23:17*
but w. the Lord saith, that. *24:13*
   1 Ki 22:14; 2 Chr 18:13
w. the Lord did because. *Deut 4:3*
w. Lord did to Pharaoh. *7:18; 11:6*
Israel, w. doth the Lord require of
   thee? *10:12; Mi 6:8*
w. man is there? *Deut 20:5, 6, 7, 8*
O Lord, w. shall I say? *Josh 7:8*
and Caleb said to her, W.? *15:18*
   Judg 1:14; 1 Ki 1:16; Mat 20:21
w. have ye to do with the Lord God
   of Israel? *Josh 22:24*
thou shalt hear w. they. *Judg 7:11*
w. hast thou to do with me? *11:12*
w. say ye? *18:8*
the priest said, W. do ye? *18*
w. have I more? w. is this? w. aileth
   thee? *24*
and he will tell thee w. thou shalt.
   Ruth 3:4; 1 Sam 10:8
w. is the thing the Lord? *1 Sam 3:17*
and he said, W. is there done? *4:16*
w. have I to do with you?
   2 Sam 16:10; 19:22
let us hear likewise w. he saith. *17:5*

a tumult, but I knew not w.
2 Sam 18:29
their father said, W.? 1 Ki 13:12
cut off house of Jeroboam w.? 14:14
w. have I to do with thee? 17:18
2 Ki 3:13; 2 Chr 35:21; John 2:4
said, Ask w. I shall do for thee?
2 Ki 2:9; 4:2
Jehu said, W. hast thou? 9:18, 19
w. said these men, and from
whence? 20:14; Isa 39:3
w. have they seen in thine house?
2 Ki 20:15; Isa 39:4
Jehoshaphat said, Take heed w. ye
do. 2 Chr 19:6
nor know w. to do, but our. 20:12
w. shall we do for the hundred? 25:9
w. shall we say after this?
Ezra 9:10; Job 37:19
king said, For w. dost? Neh 2:4
W. thing is this ye do? 19; 13:17
to know w. it was, and why. Esth 4:5
w. wilt thou, queen Esther? w. is thy
request? 5:3, 6; 7:2; 9:12
w. is man, that thou? Job 7:17
15:14; Ps 8:4; 144:3; Heb 2:6
w. shall I do unto thee? Job 7:20
who will say unto him, W.? 9:12
Eccl 8:4; Ezek 12:9; Dan 4:35
let come on me w. will. Job 13:13
w. then shall I do? w. shall? 31:14
Luke 10:25; 12:17; 16:3
let us know w. is good. Job 34:4
Mi 6:8
w. doest thou against him? w. doest
to him? Job 35:6
if thou be righteous, w. givest? 7
w. man is he that feareth the Lord?
Ps 25:12; 34:12; 89:48
I will hear w. God the Lord. 85:8
w. shall be given unto thee? w.? 120:3
consider diligently w. is. Pr 23:1
lest thou know not w. to do. 25:8
w. is his name? w. is his? 30:4
w. my son? and w. the son? 31:2
I said of mirth, W. doeth? Eccl 2:2
Watchman, w. of the night?
Isa 21:11
w. hast thou here? 22:16
w. shall I say? 38:15; John 12:27
therefore w. have I here? Isa 52:5
w. wilt thou do? Jer 4:30
saying, W. have I done? 8:6
w. wilt thou say? 13:21
and say, W. is done? 48:19
O Ephraim, w. shall I? Hos 6:4
give them, O Lord, w. wilt.? 9:14
w. have I do any more with idols?
14:8
yea, and w. have ye to do with me?
Joel 3:4
and declare unto man w. Amos 4:13
O my Lord, w. are these? Zech 1:9
4:4; 6:4
I said, W. be these? 1:19; 4:5, 13
w. is it? 5:6
w. do ye more than? Mat 5:47
no thought w. ye shall eat, or w.
6:25, 31; Luke 12:22, 29
w. have we to do with thee, Jesus?
Mat 8:29; Mark 1:24; 5:7
Luke 4:34; 8:28
dave ye not read w. David did?
Mat 12:3; Mark 2:25; Luke 6:3
have forsaken all; w.? Mat 19:27
they said, W. is that to us? 27:4
told w. they had done, and w. they.
Mark 6:30
for he wist not w. to say. 9:6
this cup, not w. I will, but w. 14:36
people asked, W. shall we do then?
Luke 3:10; 12:17
the Lord said, to w. are they? 7:31
w. will I, if it be already? 12:49
they know not w. they do. 23:34
w. then? John 1:21
w. did he to thee? 9:26
w. I should say, and w. I. 12:49
w. is this that he saith? 16:18
w. is that to thee? follow. 21:22, 23
w. shall we do? Acts 2:37; 4:16
Lord, W. wilt thou have me to do?
9:6; 22:10
w. is it, Lord? 10:4

w. was I, that I could? Acts 11:17
w. must I do? 16:30
Unto w. then were ye baptized? 19:3
w. is it therefore? 21:22
w. shall we say? Rom 3:5; 4:1
6:1; 7:7
w. then? 3:9; 6:15; 8:31; 9:14, 30
11:7; 1 Cor 10:19; 14:15
w. I would that do I not, but w. I
hate, that do I. Rom 7:15
w. will ye? shall I come? 1 Cor 4:21
w. I do, that I will do. 2 Cor 11:12
yet w. I shall choose I. Phil 1:22
understanding neither w. 1 Tim 1:7
consider w. I say; and the Lord give
thee. 2 Tim 2:7
w. shall I more say? Heb 11:32
ye know not w. shall be on the morrow. For w. is your life? Jas 4:14
searching w. or w. manner. 1 Pet 1:11
it doth not yet appear w. 1 John 3:2
see **things**

whatsoever
now w. God hath said. Gen 31:16
even of w. passeth under. Lev 27:32
I will do w. thou sayest. Num 22:17
nor w. the Lord our God. Deut 2:37
w. I command you, observe. 12:32
do thou to us w. Judg 10:15
1 Sam 14:36
w. plague, w. sickness. 1 Ki 8:37
w. supplication be made. 38
2 Chr 6:28
w. is under the whole. Job 41:11
leaf not wither; w. he doeth. Ps 1:3
w. passeth through the paths. 8:8
God is in the heavens, he hath done
w. he. 115:3. 135:6; Eccl 8:3
w. God doeth, it shall. Eccl 3:14
w. I command thee, thou. Jer 1:7
we will do w. goeth out of. 44:17
w. is more than these. Mat 5:37
w. ye would that men should. 7:12
Herod promised with an oath to give
her w. she. 14:7; Mark 6:22
have done unto him w. they listed.
Mat 17:12; Mark 9:13
and w. is right I will give you.
Mat 20:4, 7
all things w. ye shall ask in prayer,
believing, ye shall. 21:22
Mark 11:23, 24; John 14:13
w. they bid you observe. Mat 23:3
observe all things w. I have. 28:20
his mother saith, W. he saith to you.
John 2:5
ye are my friends, if ye do w. 15:14
w. ye shall ask in my name. 16
16:23
him hear in all things w. Acts 3:22
for w. is not of faith. Rom 14:23
w. is sold in the shambles, that eat.
1 Cor 10:25
w. is set before you, eat. 27
or w. ye do, do all to the glory. 31
w. they were, it maketh. Gal 2:6
w. a man soweth, that shall. 6:7
w. things are true, w. Phil 4:8
I have learned in w. state I am. 11
w. ye do in word . . . do all in the
name of the Lord Jesus. Col 3:17
w. ye do, do it heartily as to. 23
w. we ask we receive of him.
1 John 3:22; 5:15
thou doest faithfully w. 3 John 5

wheat
Reuben found mandrakes in w.
Gen 30:14
but the w. and rye were. Ex 9:32
the firstfruits of w. harvest. 34:22
Num 18:12
goats, with the fat of kidneys of w.
Deut 32:14
and Gideon threshed w. Judg 6:11
time of w. harvest, Samson. 15:1
to glean unto the end of w. harvest.
Ruth 2:23
they of Beth-shemesh reaping w.
1 Sam 6:13
is it not w. harvest day? 12
would have fetched w. 2 Sam 4:6
Solomon gave Hiram w. 1 Ki 5:11

I give the w. for the meat offering.
1 Chr 21:23
have need of, w. salt, wine. Ezra 6:9
to an hundred measures of w. 7:22
let thistles grow instead of w.
Job 31:40
fed them with finest of w. Ps 81:16
thee with the finest of w. 147:14
fool in a mortar among w. Pr 27:22
thy belly is like a heap of w. set.
S of S 7:2
they have sown w. but. Jer 12:13
what is the chaff to the w.? 23:28
flow together, for w., for wine. 31:12
Judah traded in w. of. Ezek 27:17
floors shall be full of w. Joel 2:24
from him burdens of w. Amos 5:11
that we may set forth w. 8:5
poor, and sell refuse of w. 6
gather his w. into the garner.
Mat 3:12; Luke 3:17
sowed tares among the w. Mat 13:25
lest ye root up also the w. 29
to burn them, but gather the w. 30
said 100 measures of w. Luke 16:7
that he may sift you as w. 22:31
except a corn of w. fall. John 12:24
and cast out the w. Acts 27:38
it may chance of w. or. 1 Cor 15:37
I heard a voice, a measure of w.
Rev 6:6
merchandise of w. is departed. 18:13
see **barley**

wheaten
cakes and wafers; of w. flour shalt
thou make them. Ex 29:2*

wheel
make them like a w. Ps 83:13
a wise king bringeth the w. Pr 20:26*
w. broken at the cistern. Eccl 12:6
nor break it with the w. Isa 28:28
one w. upon the earth. Ezek 1:15
w. in the midst of a w. 16; 10:10
wheels, in my hearing, O w. 10:13

wheels
took off their chariot w. Ex 14:25
why tarry the w. of his? Judg 5:28
their w. like a whirlwind. Isa 5:28
a work on the w. Jer 18:3
the rumbling of his w. 47:3
the appearance of the w. Ezek 1:16
of w. over against them. 3:13
the w. also were beside them.
10:19; 11:22
come against thee with w. 23:24
at the noise of the w. 26:10
and his w. a burning fire. Dan 7:9
of the rattling of the w. Nah 3:2

whelp, -s
a bear robbed of her w. 2 Sam 17:8
let a bear robbed of her w. Pr 17:12
she nourished her w. Ezek 19:2
one of her w. . . . a young lion. 3
she took another of her w. and. 5
bear bereaved of her w. Hos 13:8
the lion did tear enough for his w.
Nah 2:12
see **lions**

when
w. it is unclean and w. Lev 14:57
w. thou sittest and w. thou walkest,
w. thou liest down, and w. thou
risest up. Deut 6:7; 11:19
w. I begin, I will also. 1 Sam 3:12
hear thou in heaven thy dwelling
place: w. thou hearest. 1 Ki 8:30
the king said, W. wilt? Neh 2:6
ye fools, w. will ye be wise? Ps 94:8
for who can tell him w.? Eccl 8:7
clean? w. shall it once be? Jer 13:27
w. ve fasted. Zech 7:5
w. ye did eat, and w. ye did drink. 6
w. shall these things be? and what?
Mat 24:3; Mark 13:4; Luke 21:7
w. he is come, he will tell us all
things. John 4:25; 16:8
w. he had so said, he shewed. 20:20
w. they heard this, they. Acts 2:37
w. we were with you. 2 Thes 3:10
w. he shall appear, we. 1 John 2:28

whence

the angel said, Hagar, *w.* camest
thou ? *Gen* 16:8
Joseph said to them, *W.* come ye ?
42:7; *Josh* 9:8
is not like Egypt, from *w.* ye came
out. *Deut* 11:10
I wist not *w.* they were. *Josh* 2:4
I asked him not *w.* he. *Judg* 13:6
Micah said, *W.* comest thou ? 17:9
19:17; *2 Sam* 1:3; *2 Ki* 5:25
Job 1:7; 2:2; *Jonah* 1:8
men ? from *w.* came these men unto
thee ? *2 Ki* 20:14; *Isa* 39:3
before I go *w.* I shall not return.
Job 10:21; 16:22
not know from *w.* it riseth. *Isa* 47:11
look to the rock *w.* ye are. 51:1
I will return to my house, *w.* I came.
Mat 12:44; *Luke* 11:24
w. hath this man this wisdom ?
Mat 13:54
w. hath this man all these things ?
56; *Mark* 6:2
calleth him Lord, *w.* is ? *Mark* 12:37
w. is this to me, that the mother of
my Lord ? *Luke* 1:43
I know you not *w.* ye are. 13:25, 27
W. knowest thou me ? *John* 1:48
and ye know *w.* I am. 7:28
ye cannot tell *w.* I come. 8:14
we know not from *w.* he is. 9:29, 30
from *w.* we look for the. *Phil* 3:20
from *w.* he received him. *Heb* 11:19
w. come wars and fightings ? *Jas* 4:1
remember from *w.* thou. *Rev* 2:5
in white robes ? *w.* came they ? 7:13

whensoever

w. ye will ye may do. *Mark* 14:7

where

w. art thou ? *Gen* 3:9
w. is he ? *Ex* 2:20; *2 Sam* 9:4
Job 14:10
in all places *w.* I record. *Ex* 20:24
w. I will meet you to speak. 29:42
30:6, 36
shall say, *W.* are their gods ?
Deut 32:37
if not, *w.* and who is he ? *Job* 9:24
W. is God my maker who ? 35:10
w. wast thou ? 38:4
to me, *W.* is thy God ? *Ps* 42:3, 10
wherefore should heathen say, *W.* is
their God ? 79:10; 115:2; *Joel* 2:17
these, *w.* had they been ? *Isa* 49:21
said they, *W.* is the Lord ? *Jer* 2:6, 8
let no man know *w.* ye be. 36:19
w. it was said to them. *Hos* 1:10
fathers, *w.* are they ? *Zech* 1:5
they said, *W.* Lord ? *Luke* 17:37
Jews said, *W.* is he ? *John* 7:11
9:12
w. I am. 7:34; 12:26; 14:3; 17:24

whereabout

know *w.* I send thee. *1 Sam* 21:2

whereas

w. I rewarded thee evil. *1 Sam* 24:17
w. it was in thine heart. *1 Ki* 8:18
w. ye say, The Lord. *Ezek* 13:7
will possess it, *w.* the Lord. 35:10
w. ye know not what will. *Jas* 4:14

whereby

iniquity *w.* they have sinned. *Jer* 33:8
transgressions *w.* ye have transgressed. *Ezek* 18:31
trespasses *w.* they have trespassed.
39:26
w. shall I know this ? *Luke* 1:18
no other name *w.* we must. *Acts* 4:12
the Spirit, *w.* we cry. *Rom* 8:15
w. ye are sealed to the day. *Eph* 4:30

wherefore

w. should I fast ? can I bring him ?
2 Sam 12:23
who shall then say, *W.* hast ? 16:10
w. one ? That he might seek a godly
seed. *Mal* 2:15
O thou of little faith, *w.*? *Mat* 14:31
Jesus said, Friend, *w.* art ? 26:50
what is the cause *w.* ye ? *Acts* 10:21

whereto

in the thing *w.* I sent it. *Isa* 55:11

---

w. we have already attained, let us
walk. *Phil* 3:16

wherewith

O my Lord, *w.* shall I ? *Judg* 6:15
the Lord said to him, *W.*?
1 Ki 22:22; *2 Chr* 18:20
but against the house *w.* I have war.
2 Chr 35:21
so shall I have *w.* to. *Ps* 119:42
w. shall I come before ? *Mi* 6:6
if salt lose its savour, *w.* shall it be?
Mat 5:13; *Mark* 9:5; *Luke* 14:34
the love *w.* thou hast. *John* 17:26
for this great love *w.* he. *Eph* 2:4

wherewithal

what shall we eat ? or *w.*? *Mat* 6:31

whet

if I *w.* my glittering sword I will
reward. *Deut* 32:41
if he turn not, he will *w.* *Ps* 7:12
who *w.* their tongue like a. 64:3
iron blunt and he do not *w.* *Eccl* 10:10

whether

w. they be for peace, or *w.* *1 Ki* 20:18
w. they were of Israel. *Ezra* 2:59
Neh 7:61
w. they will hear or forbear.
Ezek 2:5, 7; 3:11
w. of them twain did the will of his
father ? *Mat* 21:31
w. is greater, the gold or ? 23:17
doctrine, *w.* it be of God. *John* 7:17
w. we live or die, we are. *Rom* 14:8
w. it were I or they, so. *1 Cor* 15:11
w. in the body, or *w.* out of the body.
2 Cor 12:2, 3
but try the spirits *w.* *1 John* 4:1

which

of the tree *w.* I commanded thee,
saying. *Gen* 3:17
in *w.* there shall be neither. 45:6
a heifer upon *w.* never. *Num* 19:2
in *w.* there shall not be. *Luke* 21:6
w. of you convinceth me ? *John* 8:46
for *w.* of those works do ye ? 10:32
in the *w.* I will appear. *Acts* 26:16
in the *w.* ye also walked. *Col* 3:7
a better hope; by *w.* we. *Heb* 7:19
of *w.* we cannot now speak. 9:5
follow peace with all men, and holiness, without *w.* no man. 12:14
that worthy name, by *w.* *Jas* 2:7
by *w.* he preached to. *1 Pet* 3:19

while, whiles

w. I am yet alive with. *Deut* 31:27
thou shalt not only *w.* yet I live shew
me the kindness. *1 Sam* 20:14
w. the child was yet alive.
2 Sam 12:18, 21, 22
Lord is with you *w.* ye. *2 Chr* 15:2
w. Josiah was yet young, he. 34:3
God shall rain it on him *w.* *Job* 20:23
tear my soul, *w.* there is none. *Ps* 7:2
though *w.* he lived he blessed. 49:18
thus will I bless thee *w.* I live.
63:4; 146:2
will praise God *w.* I have my being.
104:33; 146:2
w. he may be found. *Isa* 55:6
her sun is gone down *w.* it was yet
day. *Jer* 15:9
w. he was not yet gone back. 40:5
agree *w.* thou art in the. *Mat* 5:25
that deceiver said, *w.* he. 27:63
of bride-chamber fast *w.* the bridegroom ? *Mark* 2:19; *Luke* 5:34
I spake *w.* I was yet. *Luke* 24:44
do work of him that sent me *w.* it is
day. *John* 9:4
that liveth in pleasure is dead *w.*
she liveth. *1 Tim* 5:6
w. it is said, To-day if. *Heb* 3:15
see little

a while

Joseph wept on his neck *a* good *w.*
Gen 46:29
Samuel said to Saul, Stand thou
still *a w.* *1 Sam* 9:27
spoken for *a* great *w.* *2 Sam* 7:19
root, but dureth for *a w.* *Mat* 13:21
which for *a w.* believe, and in time
of temptation fall away. *Luke* 8:13

---

he would not for *a w.*: but. *Luke* 18:4
after have suffered *a w.* *1 Pet* 5:10

all the while

all the *w.* David was in. *1 Sam* 22:4
none missing all the *w.* they were in
Carmel. 25:7, 16
will be his manner all the *w.* 27:11
all the *w.* my breath is in me and
Spirit of God. *Job* 27:3

long while

had talked a long *w.* even till break
of day. *Acts* 20:11

whip

a *w.* for the horse, a rod. *Pr* 26:3
the noise of a *w.*, the noise. *Nah* 3:2

whips

father chastised you with *w.*, I will.
1 Ki 12:11, 14; *2 Chr* 10:11, 14

whirleth

wind *w.* continually and. *Eccl* 1:6*

whirlwind

Lord would take up Elijah by a *w.*
2 Ki 2:1, 11
cometh the *w.* and cold. *Job* 37:9*
the Lord answered Job out of the *w.*
38:1; 40:6
as with a *w.*, both living and. *Ps* 58:9
Pr 10:25; *Hos* 13:3
destruction cometh as a *w.* *Pr* 1:27
counted it like flint and their wheels
like a *w.* *Isa* 5:28
a rolling thing before the *w.* 17:13*
the *w.* shall take them away. 40:24
shalt fan them, the *w.* shall. 41:16
Lord come with chariots like a *w.*
66:15; *Jer* 4:13
a *w.* of the Lord is gone. *Jer* 23:19*
a great *w.* shall be raised up. 25:32*
a continuing *w.* shall fall on. 30:23*
behold, a *w.* came out of. *Ezek* 1:4*
king shall come against him like a *w.*
Dan 11:40
they shall reap the *w.* *Hos* 8:7
devour palaces in the day of the *w.*
Amos 1:14
the Lord hath his way in the *w.*
Nah 1:3
out as a *w.* to scatter. *Hab* 3:14
but I scattered them with a *w.*
Zech 7:14

whirlwinds

as *w.* in the south pass. *Isa* 21:1
Lord shall go forth with *w.* *Zech* 9:14

whisper

all that hate me *w.* together. *Ps* 41:7
thy speech shall *w.* out. *Isa* 29:4

whispered

when David saw that his servants *w.*
2 Sam 12:19

whisperer

a *w.* separateth chief. *Pr* 16:28

whisperers

full of envy, murder, debate, deceit,
w. *Rom* 1:29

whisperings

be *w.* swellings, tumults. *2 Cor* 12:20

whit

Samuel told Eli every *w.* *1 Sam* 3:18
a man every *w.* whole. *John* 7:23
feet, but is clean every *w.* 13:10
I was not a *w.* behind. *2 Cor* 11:5

white

Jacob made the *w.* appear in the
rods. *Gen* 30:37
and his teeth shall be. 49:12
like coriander seed, *w.* *Ex* 16:31
if the hair be turned *w.* *Lev* 13:3
4, 20, 25
if the bright spot be *w.* 4, 19, 24*
rising be *w.* in the skin. 10, 19, 43*
be no *w.* hairs therein. 21, 26
Miriam became leprous, *w.* as snow.
Num 12:10
ye that ride on *w.* asses. *Judg* 5:10
Gehazi went out a leper *w.* as snow.
2 Ki 5:27
the Levites being arrayed in *w.*
2 Chr 5:12*
Mordecai went out in *w.* apparel.
Esth 8:15
taste in the *w.* of an egg ? *Job* 6:6

white

w. as snow in Salmon. *Ps* 68:14*
garments be always *w.* *Eccl* 9:8
my beloved is *w.* and ruddy, the.
  S of S 5:10
be as scarlet, they shall be as *w.* as
 snow. *Isa* 1:18
Damascus traded in *w.* wool.
  Ezek 27:18
garment was *w.* as snow. *Dan* 7:9
shall fall to make them *w.* 11:35
be purified and made *w.* 12:10
thereof are made *w.* *Joel* 1:7
horses, speckled and *w.* *Zech* 1:8
not make one hair *w.* or black.
  Mat 5:36
his raiment was *w.* as the light.
  17:2; *Luke* 9:29
the angel's raiment was *w.*
  Mat 28:3; *Acts* 1:10
a man clothed in a long *w.* garment.
  Mark 16:5
fields are *w.* already. *John* 4:35
and his hairs were *w.* *Rev* 1:14
will give him a *w.* stone and. 2:17
they shall walk with me in *w.* 3:4
shall be clothed in *w.* raiment. 5
  4:4; 7:9, 13; 15:6; 19:8, 14
buy *w.* raiment, that thou. 3:18
behold a *w.* horse. 6:2; 19:11
made them *w.* in the blood. 7:14
a *w.* cloud. 14:14
I saw a *w.* throne. 20:11

white, *verb*
no fuller on earth can *w.* *Mark* 9:3

whited
like to *w.* sepulchres. *Mat* 23:27
smite thee, thou *w.* wall. *Acts* 23:3

whiter
I shall be *w.* than snow. *Ps* 51:7
her Nazarites are *w.* than milk.
  Lam 4:7

whither
maid, *w.* wilt thou go? *Gen* 16:8
keep thee in all places *w.* 28:15
Saul's uncle said, *W.* went ye?
  1 Sam 10:14
Thy servant went no *w.* *2 Ki* 5:25
w. is thy beloved gone? *S of S* 6:1
I said, *W.* do these bear the ephah?
  Zech 5:10
went, not knowing *w.* *Heb* 11:8
 see **go, goest, goeth**

whithersoever
the Lord preserved David *w.* he.
  2 Sam 8:6, 14; *2 Ki* 18:7
  1 Chr 18:6, 13
w. it turneth it prospereth. *Pr* 17:8
he turneth the king's heart *w.* 21:1
I will follow thee *w.* thou goest.
  Mat 8:19; *Luke* 9:57
these follow the Lamb *w. Rev* 14:4

who
w. art thou, my son? *Gen* 27:18, 32
  Ruth 3:9, 16; *John* 1:19, 22
  8:25; 21:12
Esau said, *W.* are those? *Gen* 33:5
  48:8
w. am I? *Ex* 3:11; *1 Sam* 18:18
  2 Sam 7:18
w. is the Lord? *Ex* 5:2; *Pr* 30:9
  John 9:36
w. is like thee, O Lord, among the
 gods? *Ex* 15:11; *Deut* 33:29
  1 Sam 26:15; *Ps* 35:10
Moses stood and said, *W.? Ex* 32:26
w. is David? and *w.* is? *1 Sam* 25:10
w. is on my side, *w.?* *2 Ki* 9:32
but *w.* slew all these? 10:9
Jehu said, *W.* are ye? 13
w. would go into the temple to save
 his life? *Neh* 6:11
w. is he? and where is he?
 Esth 7:5; *Job* 17:3; 42:3; *Jer* 9:12
W. will shew us any good? *Ps* 4:6
for *w.*, say they, doth hear? 59:7
w. hath woe? *w.* hath sorrow? *w.*
 hath . . . ? *w.* hath? *Pr.* 23:29
w. will go for us? *Isa* 6:8
W. seeth us? 29:15
w. shall come down? *Jer* 21:13
saying, *W.* shall come unto? 49:4
w. is like me? *w.* will? 19; 50:44

of Zion: *w.* can heal thee? *Lam* 2:13
w. is he that saith, and it? 3:37
saying, *W.* is this? *Mat* 21:10
  Luke 5:21; 7:49; 9:9
W. is he that smote thee? *Mat* 26:68
to see Jesus *w.* he was. *Luke* 19:3
healed, wist not *w.* it. *John* 5:13
Lord, *w.* is it? 13:25
he said, *W.* art thou, Lord?
  Acts 9:5; 22:8; 26:15
but *w.* are ye? 19:15
captain demanded *w.* he was. 21:33
w. then is Paul? and *w.? 1 Cor* 3:5
and *w.* is sufficient? *2 Cor* 2:16
w. is weak? *w.* is offended? 11:29
w. art thou that judgest? *Jas* 4:12
w. is a liar, but he that? *1 John* 2:22
w. shall be able to stand? *Rev* 6:17
saying, *W.* is like unto the beast? *w.*
 is able to? 13:4
w. shall not fear thee, O Lord? 15:4

whole
shalt burn *w.* ram on altar.
  Ex 29:18; *Lev* 8:21
even the *w.* bullock shall. *Lev* 4:12
w. house of Israel bewail. 10:6
Joshua took the *w.* land. *Josh* 11:23
because my life is yet *w. 2 Sam* 1:9
him with their *w.* desire. *2 Chr* 15:15
shalt be pleased with *w.* *Ps* 51:19
them up alive, and *w.* *Pr* 1:12
the *w.* disposing thereof is. 16:33
for this is the *w.* duty. *Eccl* 12:13
thy Redeemer, the Holy One, the
 God of *w.* earth shall he be called.
 Isa 54:5; *Mi* 4:13; *Zech* 4:14
a vessel that cannot be made *w.*
  Jer 19:11
pluck up, even this *w.* land. 45:4
when *w.* it was meet. *Ezek* 15:5
ye have robbed me, even this *w.*
 nation. *Mal* 3:9
not that thy *w.* body. *Mat* 5:29, 30
the *w.* herd of swine ran. 8:32
till the *w.* was leavened. 13:33
  Luke 13:21
profited if he shall gain the *w.* world
 and lose his own soul? *Mat* 16:26
  Mark 8:36; *Luke* 9:25
w. multitude of them arose and led
 him. *Luke* 23:1
and himself believed, and his *w.*
 house. *John* 4:53
expedient that the *w.* nation. 11:50
came almost the *w.* city. *Acts* 13:44
if *w.* body were an eye. *1 Cor* 12:17
I pray your *w.* spirit. *1 Thes* 5:23
shall keep the *w.* law. *Jas* 2:10
end of the *w.* world. *1 John* 2:2
and the *w.* world lieth in. 5:19
 see **congregation, heart**

whole for *sound*
they abide in the camp till they were
 w. *Josh* 5:8
and his hands make *w.* *Job* 5:18
w. need not a physician. *Mat* 9:12
  Mark 2:17; *Luke* 5:31
touch his garment, I shall be *w.*
  Mat 9:21; *Mark* 5:28
woman was made *w.* *Mat* 9:22
his hand was made *w.* 12:13
  Mark 3:5; *Luke* 6:10
daughter was made *w.* *Mat* 15:28
saw the maimed to be *w.* 31
thee *w.*; go in peace and be *w.* of.
 Mark 5:34; *Luke* 8:48; 17:19
found the servant *w.* *Luke* 7:10
Wilt thou be made *w.? John* 5:6
thou art made *w.*: sin no more. 14
made a man every whit *w.* 7:23
what means he is made *w. Acts* 4:9
Jesus Christ maketh thee *w.* 9:34

wholesome
a *w.* tongue is a tree of. *Pr* 15:4
consent not to *w.* words. *1 Tim* 6:3*

wholly
it shall be *w.* burnt. *Lev* 6:22, 23
thou shalt not *w.* reap corners. 19:9
for they are *w.* given to. *Num* 3:9
a cloth *w.* of blue. 4:6
are *w.* given me. 8:16
because they have not *w.* 32:11

give the land, because he hath *w.*
 Deut 1:36; *Josh* 14:8, 9, 14
I had *w.* dedicated the. *Judg* 17:3
a sucking lamb *w.* *1 Sam* 7:9
all the people *w.* at thy. *1 Chr* 28:21
one dieth, being *w.* at ease. *Job* 21:23
thou art *w.* gone up to the. *Isa* 22:1
planted thee *w.* a right seed. *Jer* 2:21
she is *w.* oppression in the. 6:6
Judah shall be *w.* carried. 13:19
if ye *w.* set your faces to. 42:15
yet will I not leave thee *w.* 46:28
Babylon not be inhabited, but *w.*
 desolate. 50:13
of Israel *w.*, are they. *Ezek* 11:15
and it shall rise up *w.* as a flood.
  Amos 8:8; 9:5
he saw the city *w.* given. *Acts* 17:16
of peace sanctify you *w. 1 Thes* 5:23
give thyself *w.* to them. *1 Tim* 4:15

whom
take thy only son Isaac *w. Gen* 22:2
wives, for *w.* I served thee. 30:26
the old man of *w.* ye spake, is he
 alive? 43:27, 29
will be gracious to *w.* I. *Ex* 33:19
after *w.* they have gone. *Lev* 17:7
people, amongst *w.* I am. *Num* 11:21
they are children in *w.* *Deut* 32:20
where their gods? their rock in *w.* 37
choose you this day *w.* *Josh* 24:15
that of *w.* I say, this shall. *Judg* 7:4
and to *w.* shall he go up from us?
  1 Sam 6:20
and on *w.* is all the desire of? 9:20
David, of *w.* they sang one. 29:5
David said unto me, To *w.?* 30:13
and again, *w.* should I serve?
  2 Sam 16:19
Ahab said, By *w.? 1 Ki* 20:14; 22:8
 Ezra 10:44; *Rom* 1:5; 5:2, 11
  Gal 6:14
thy God in *w.* thou trustest.
  2 Ki 19:10; *Isa* 37:10
but to the saints, in *w.* *Ps* 16:3
my God, my strength, in *w.* I. 18:2
w. have I in heaven but thee? 73:25
not trust in son of man, in *w.* 146:3
as a father the son, in *w.* *Pr* 3:12
good from them to *w.* it is due. 27
a king against *w.* there is no. 30:31
he, For *w.* do I labour? *Eccl* 4:8
w. my soul loveth. *S of S* 3:1, 2, 3
I heard a voice saying, *W.* shall I
 send? *Isa* 6:8
in day of visitation? to *w.* 10:3
what hast thou here? *w.?* 22:16
turn to him from *w.* Israel. 31:6
to *w.* then will ye liken God?
  40:18, 25; 46:5
behold mine elect, in *w.* my. 42:1
art my servant, O Israel, in *w.* 49:3
famine and sword; by *w.* shall? 51:19
against *w.* do ye sport? 57:4
of *w.* hast thou been afraid? 11
w. they have loved, *w.* they have
 served, after *w.* they have walked,
 and *w.* they sought. *Jer* 8:2
from *w.* I am not able to rise up.
  Lam 1:14
w. we said, Under his shadow. 4:20
Son of man, speak unto Pharaoh, . . .
 W. art thou like? *Ezek* 31:2
to *w.* art thou like in glory? 18
w. he would he slew, *w.* he . . . and
 w. he would he. *Dan* 5:19
O Lord, by *w.* shall Jacob arise?
  Amos 7:2, 5
on *w.* hath not thy wickedness
 passed? *Nah* 3:19
in *w.* I am well pleased. *Mat* 3:17
  17:5; *Mark* 1:11; *2 Pet* 2:17
this is *w.* of *w.* it is written.
  Mat 11:10; *John* 1:15, 16
w. say ye that I am? *Mat* 16:15
  Mark 8:29; *Luke* 9:20
quickeneth *w.* he will. *John* 5:21
Moses, in *w.* ye trust. 45
Lord, to *w.* shall we go? 6:68
w. thou hast sent. 17:3
of *w.* speaketh the? *Acts* 8:34
whose I am, and *w.* I serve. 27:23
to *w.* he was not spoken. *Rom* 15:21

God is faithful, by _w._ ye. _1 Cor_ 1:9
but ministers by _w._ ye believed? 3:5
liberty to be married to _w._   7:39
one God, of _w._ are all things.   8:6
            Heb 2:10
in _w._ we trust that he.   _2 Cor_ 1:10
in _w._ we have redemption through.
          Eph 1:7; _Col_ 1:14
in _w._ also we have obtained.
             Eph 1:11
in _w._ ye also trusted: in _w._ also. 13
among _w._ also we all had our.   2:3
in _w._ the building groweth to a.   21
in _w._ ye also are builded.   22
in _w._ ye have boldness and.   3:12
among _w._ ye shine as.   _Phil_ 2:15
for _w._ I have suffered the loss.   3:8
_w._ we preach.   _Col_ 1:28
in _w._ are hid all the treasures.   2:3
in _w._ ye are circumcised.   11
that wicked, _w._ the Lord. _2 Thes_ 2:8
to save sinners, of _w._ I. _1 Tim_ 1:15
of _w._ is Hymenaeus and Alexander.
        20; _2 Tim_ 2:17
of _w._ are Phygellus.   _2 Tim_ 1:15
the coppersmith, of _w._ be.   4:15
to _w._ be glory for ever.   18
  Gal 1:5; _Heb_ 13:21; _1 Pet_ 4:11
with _w._ was he grieved ? _Heb_ 3:17
to _w._ sware he they should not? 18
to the eyes of him with _w._   4:13
to _w._ Abraham gave the tenth.   7:2
of _w._ the world was not.   11:38
father of lights, with _w._   _Jas_ 1:17
unto _w._ it was revealed. _1 Pet_ 1:12
to _w._ coming, as unto a living.   2:4
to _w._ darkness is reserved.
       2 Pet 2:17; _Jude_ 13
for of _w._ a man is overcome, . . .
   brought in bondage. _2 Pet_ 2:19
to _w._ it was given to hurt. _Rev_ 7:2
with _w._ kings of earth.   17:2
       see **before**

whomsoever

_w._ thou findest thy gods. _Gen_ 31:32
_w._ the Lord our God.   _Judg_ 11:24
he giveth it to _w._ he will. _Dan_ 4:17
       25:32; 5:21
he to _w._ the Son will.   _Mat_ 11:27
but on _w._ it shall fall.   21:44
           Luke 20:18
the devil said, To _w._ I.   _Luke_ 4:6
to _w._ much is given, much.   12:48
on _w._ I lay hands, may.   _Acts_ 8:19
_w._ ye shall approve by.   _1 Cor_ 16:3

whore

(_Revised Versions change this to_
harlot, _and often make same change
in its derivatives_)
do not cause her to be a _w._ lest the
   land.   _Lev_ 19:29
not take a wife that is a _w._   21:7
profane herself by playing the _w._   9
to play the _w._ in her. _Deut_ 22:21
no _w._ of the daughters of.   23:17
bring the hire of a _w._ or price.   18
his concubine played the _w._ _Judg_ 19:2
a _w._ is a deep ditch.   _Pr_ 23:27
adulterer and the _w._   _Isa_ 57:3
thou hadst a _w.'s_ forehead. _Jer_ 3:3
thou hast played the _w._ _Ezek_ 16:28
judgement of the great _w._ _Rev_ 17:1
            19:2
waters where the _w._ sitteth.   17:15
these shall hate the _w._ and make. 16

whoredom

she is with child by _w._   _Gen_ 38:24
lest the land fall to _w._   _Lev_ 19:29
the lightness of her _w._ she. _Jer_ 3:9
the lewdness of thy _w._   13:27
come to thee for thy _w._ _Ezek_ 16:33
they poured their _w._ upon her. 23:8
defiled her with their _w._   17
defile my holy name by their _w._ 43:7
let them put away their _w._ far.   9
_w._ and wine take away. _Hos_ 4:11
O Ephraim, thou committest _w._ 5:3
is the _w._ of Ephraim, Israel.   6:10

whoredoms

shall wander and bear _w._ _Num_ 14:33
_w._ of thy mother Jezebel. _2 Ki_ 9:22

---

like to the _w._ of the house of Ahab.
         2 Chr 21:13
thou hast polluted the land with thy
   _w._   _Jer_ 3:2
is this of thy _w._ a small ? _Ezek_ 16:20
all thy _w._ hast not remembered. 22
hast multiplied thy _w._   25
hast increased thy _w._   26
from other women in thy _w._   34
also thy lewdness and thy _w._ 23:35
a wife and children of _w._ _Hos_ 1:2
let her put away her _w._ out of. 2:2
for they be the children of _w._   4
the spirit of _w._ hath.   4:12; 5:4
of _w.,_ that selleth nations through her
   _w._ and families.   _Nah_ 3:4
       see **commit**

whoremonger

no _w._ hath any inheritance in the
   kingdom of Christ.   _Eph_ 5:5

whoremongers

(_Revised Versions change this to_
fornicators)
the law made for _w._   _1 Tim_ 1:10*
but _w._ and adulterers God. _Heb_ 13:4
_w._ shall have their part. _Rev_ 21:8
for without are _w._ and.   22:15

whores

they give gifts to all _w._ _Ezek_ 16:33
are separated with _w._   _Hos_ 4:14

whoring, _see_ go, gone, went

whorish

by means of a _w._ woman. _Pr_ 6:26
broken with their _w._ heart. _Ezek_ 6:9
an imperious _w._ woman.   16:30

whose

_w._ art thou ? _w._ are ?   _Gen_ 32:17
_w._ ox, or _w._ ass have ? _1 Sam_ 12:3
_w._ is the land ? make.   _2 Sam_ 3:12
a remnant shall know _w._ _Jer_ 44:28
_w._ name is the Lord.   48:15; 51:57
the God in _w._ hands thy. _Dan_ 5:23
saith Lord, _w._ name is. _Amos_ 5:27
he saith to them, _W._ is ? _Mat_ 22:20
     Mark 12:16; _Luke_ 20:24
_w._ son is he ?   _Mat_ 22:42
then _w._ shall those ? _Luke_ 12:20
_w._ it shall be.   _John_ 19:24
angel of God, _w._ I am. _Acts_ 27:23
Christ over his house, _w._ _Heb_ 3:6
       see **heart**

who-, whosesoever

_w._ would, he consecrated. _1 Ki_ 13:33
blessed _w._ shall not be. _Mat_ 11:6
_w._ hath, to him shall be given:
   hath not, from. 13:12; _Luke_ 8:18
_w._ sins ye remit, _w._   _John_ 20:23
O man, _w._ thou art that. _Rom_ 2:1
_w._ shall eat this bread. _1 Cor_ 11:27
his judgement, _w._ he be. _Gal_ 5:10
_w._ will, let him take of. _Rev_ 22:17

why

it be so, _w._ am I thus ? _Gen_ 25:22
_w._ are ye come to me ? _Judg_ 11:7
Judah said, _W._ are ye come ? 15:10
turn again, _w._ will ye ? _Ruth_ 1:11
Eli said, _W._ do ye such things ?
           1 Sam 2:23
_w._ art thou alone, and no man ? 21:1
king said, _W._ should he go with thee?
         2 Sam 13:26
in saying, _W._ hast thou done so ?
          _1 Ki_ 1:6
forbear, _w._ shouldest thou be smitten ?   _2 Chr_ 25:16
what it was and _w._ it was. _Esth_ 4:5
_w._ sayest thou, O Jacob, My way is
   hid ?   _Isa_ 40:27
_w._ do ye sit still ? assemble yourselves.   _Jer_ 8:14
_w._ will ye die ?   27:13; _Ezek_ 18:31
            33:11
us, _W._ did ye not then ? _Mat_ 21:25
   Mark 11:31; _Luke_ 20:5
he saith, _W._ make ye this ado, and
   weep ?   _Mark_ 5:39
_w._ hast thou thus dealt ? _Luke_ 2:48
they said, _W._ have ye ? _John_ 7:45
He is mad, _w._ hear ye him ? 10:20
and heard a voice, Saul, _w._
   persecutest thou me ? _Acts_ 9:4
       22:7; 26:14

Sirs, _w._ do ye these things ?
         Acts 14:15
_W._ doth he yet find fault? _Rom_ 9:19
thing formed say, _W._ hast thou ? 20
_w._ am I evil spoken of ? _1 Cor_ 10:30

wicked

wilt thou also destroy the righteous
   with the _w._?   _Gen_ 18:23, 25
Er was _w._   38:7
I and my people are _w._   _Ex_ 9:27
for I will not justify the _w._   23:7
it is a _w._ thing, they. _Lev_ 20:17*
thought in thy _w._ heart. _Deut_ 15:9
committed that _w._ thing.   17:5
keep thee from every _w._ thing. 23:9
condemn the _w._   25:1; _1 Ki_ 8:32
the _w._ shall be silent. _1 Sam_ 2:9
proceedeth from the _w._   24:13
Israel wrought _w._ things. _2 Ki_ 17:11
servants, by requiting _w._ _2 Chr_ 6:23
themselves and turn from their _w._
   7:14; _Ezek_ 18:21; 33:11, 19
Athaliah that _w._ woman. _2 Chr_ 24:7
nor turned they from their _w._ ways.
      Neh 9:35; _Ezek_ 3:19; 13:22
the adversary is this _w._ _Esth_ 7:6
Haman's _w._ device shall return. 9:25
there the _w._ cease from. _Job_ 3:17
the perfect and the _w._   9:22
if I be _w._ why then labour I in vain ?
       29; 10:15
thou knowest that I am not _w._ 10:7
wherefore do the _w._ live ?   21:7
the _w._ is reserved to the day.   30
let mine enemy be as the _w._   27:7
say to a king, Thou art _w._ ?   34:18
that the _w._ might be shaken. 38:13
from the _w._ their light is.   15
and tread down the _w._ in.   40:12
God is angry with the _w._ _Ps_ 7:11
thou hast destroyed the _w._ for. 9:5
the _w._ is snared in the work of his. 16
_w._ shall be turned into hell.   17
the _w._ in pride doth persecute. 10:2
the _w._ boasteth.   3
the _w._ will not seek God.   4
wherefore doth the _w._ contemn ? 13
lo, the _w._ bend their bow.   11:2
but the _w._ and him that.   5
upon the _w._ he shall rain snares. 6
the _w._ walk on every side.   12:8
keep me from the _w._ that.   17:9
deliver my soul from the _w._   13
and I will not sit with the _w._ 26:5
when the _w._ came upon me.   27:2
draw me not away with the _w._ 28:3
let the _w._ be ashamed and silent in
   the grave.   31:17
evil shall slay the _w._: and they. 34:21
man who bringeth _w._ devices. 37:7
yet a little, the _w._ shall not be.   10
          _Pr_ 10:25
the _w._ plotteth.   _Ps_ 37:12
the _w._ have drawn out the sword. 14
the riches of many _w._   16
the _w._ shall perish.   20
the _w._ borroweth, and payeth not. 21
the _w._ watcheth the righteous.   32
when the _w._ are cut off, thou.   34
I have seen the _w._ in great power. 35
deliver them from the _w._   40
keep my mouth, while the _w._ 39:1
the _w._ are estranged from the. 58:3
be not merciful to any _w._   59:5
so let the _w._ perish at the.   68:2
the _w._ of the earth shall wring. 75:8
when the _w._ spring as the grass. 92:7
Lord, how long shall the _w._? 94:3
the pit be digged for the _w._   13
I will set no _w._ thing before. 101:3
I will not know a _w._ person.   4
I will early destroy all the _w._   8
consumed and let the _w._ be. 104:35
the flame burnt up the _w._ 106:18
the _w._ shall see it and be. 112:10
the _w._ have waited for me. 119:95
thou puttest away all the _w._   119
salvation is far from the _w._   155
surely thou wilt slay the _w._ 139:19
if there be any _w._ way in me.   24
further not his _w._ device lest. 140:8
to practise _w._ works with.   141:4

w. fall into their own nets. Ps 141:10
all the w. will he destroy. 145:20
he casteth the w. down to. 147:6
the w. shall be cut off. Pr 2:22
iniquities shall take the w. 5:22
a heart that deviseth w. 6:18
but the w. shall not inhabit. 10:30
the w. shall fall by his own. 11:5
when a w. man dieth, his. 7
righteous delivered, the w. cometh. 8
and when the w. perish there. 10
w. worketh a deceitful work. 18
w. shall not be unpunished. 21, 31
but a man of w. devices. 12:2
the w. are overthrown. 7; 21:12
the w. desireth the net of evil. 12:12
w. is snared by the transgression. 13
but the w. shall be filled with. 21
a w. messenger falleth into. 13:17
and a man of w. devices is. 14:17
the w. bow at the gates of the. 19
the w. is driven away in his. 32
the Lord is far from the w. 15:29
yea, even the w. for the day. 16:4
a w. doer giveth heed to. 17:4
he that justifieth the w. and he. 15
when the w. cometh, then. 18:3
a wise king scattereth the w. 20:26
the w. shall be ransom for. 21:18
when he bringeth it with a w. mind. 27
but the w. shall fall into. 24:16
neither be thou envious at the w. 19
take away the w. from before. 25:5
man falling down before the w. 26
a w. heart is like a potsherd. 26:23
the w. flee when no man. 28:1
forsake the law praise the w. 4
when the w. rise. 12, 28
so is a w. ruler.
when the w. beareth rule. 29:2
w. regardeth not to know it. 7
his servants are w. 12
the w. are multiplied. 16
judge the righteous and w. Eccl 3:17
be not overmuch w. neither. 7:17
I saw the w. buried, they. 8:10
not be well with the w. 13
which justify the w. for. Isa 5:23
of his lips shall he slay the w. 11:4
I will punish the w. for. 13:11
he deviseth w. devices to. 32:7
he made his grave with the w. 53:9
let the w. forsake his way. 55:7
w. are like the troubled sea. 57:20
thou hast taught the w. Jer 2:33
for the w. are not plucked. 6:29
deceitful and desperately w. 17:9*
he will give the w. to the. 25:31
to warn the w. Ezek 3:18, 19; 33:8, 9
behold the w. abominations. 8:9
these men give w. counsel in. 11:2
I any pleasure that the w.? 18:23
not according to your w. 20:44
the righteous and the w. 21:3, 4
profane w. prince of Israel whose.25
if the w. restore the pledge. 33:15
but the w. shall do. Dan 12:10
pure with w. balances? Mi 6:11
not at all acquit the w. Nah 1:3
out of thee a w. counsellor. 11
for the w. shall no more pass. 15
w. doth compass about the righteous. Hab 1:4
the w. devoureth the man. 13
stumblingblocks with the w. Zeph 1:3
between righteous and w. Mal 3:18
and ye shall tread down the w. 4:3
w. than himself. Even so shall it be to this w. Mat 12:45; Luke 11:26
angels shall sever the w. Mat 13:49
a w. generation seeketh after. 16:4
thou w. servant. 18:32; 25:26 Luke 19:22
and by w. hands have. Acts 2:23*
were a matter of w. lewdness. 18:14
put away that w. person. 1 Cor 5:13
in your mind by w. works. Col 1:21
and then shall that w. be. 2 Thes 2:8*
see man, men

of the wicked
the place of the w. shall come to naught. Job 8:22
given into the hand of the w. 9:24

shine upon the counsel of w. Job 10:3
but the eye of the w. shall. 11:20
me into the hands of the w. 16:11
the light of the w. shall be. 18:5
are the dwellings of the w. 21
the triumphing of the w. 20:5
every hand of the w. shall. 22*
the counsel of the w. is far from me. 21:16; 22:18
how oft is candle of the w. put out? 21:17; Pr 13:9; 24:20
dwelling places of the w.? Job 21:28
gathered the vintage of the w. 24:6
and I brake the jaws of the w. 29:17
preserveth not the life of the w. 36:6
fulfilled the judgement of the w. 17
let the wickedness of the w. Ps 7:9
the arm of the w. man. 10:15
the assembly of the w. have. 22:16
the transgression of the w. 36:1
let not the hand of the w. 11
the arms of the w. shall be. 37:17
but the seed of the w. shall be. 28
end of the w. shall be cut off. 38
of the oppression of the w. 55:3
his feet in the blood of the w. 58:10
me from the counsel of the w. 64:2
deliver me out of the hand of the w. 71:4; 74:19; 82:4; 97:10
saw the prosperity of the w. 73:3
all the horns of the w. also. 75:10
ye accept the persons of the w.? 82:2
and see the reward of the w. 91:8
shall hear my desire of the w. 92:11
the mouth of the w. is opened. 109:2
desire of the w. shall perish. 112:10 Pr 10:28
because of the w. that forsake thy law. Ps 119:53
the hands of the w. have robbed. 61
the rod of the w. shall not. 125:3
asunder the cords of the w. 129:4
Lord, from the hands of the w. 140:4
O Lord, the desires of the w. 8
the way of the w. he turneth. 146:9
in frowardness of the w. Pr 2:14
of the desolation of the w. 3:25
curse is in the house of the w. 33
not into the path of the w. 4:14
the way of the w. is as darkness. 19
away the substance of the w. 10:3
covereth the mouth of the w. 6, 11
but the name of the w. 10:7
fruit of the w. tendeth to sin. 16
heart of the w. is little worth. 20
the fear of the w. it shall come. 24
but the years of the w. shall be. 27
the mouth of the w. speaketh. 32
overthrown by mouth of the w. 11:11
expectation of the w. is wrath. 23
but the counsels of the w. 12:5
the words of the w. are to lie in. 6
but the tender mercies of the w. 10
but the way of the w. seduceth. 26
belly of the w. shall want. 13:25
the house of the w. shall be. 14:11
but in the revenues of the w. 15:6
sacrifice of the w. is an abomination. 8; 21:27
the way of the w. is an abomination to the Lord. 15:9
the thoughts of the w. are an. 26
the mouth of the w. poureth out. 28
to accept the person of the w. 18:5
mouth of the w. devoureth. 19:28
plowing of the w. is sin. 21:4
robbery of the w. shall destroy. 7
the soul of the w. desireth evil. 10
considereth the house of the w. 12
broken the staff of the w. Isa 14:5
the deeds of the w. Jer 5:28
the way of the w. prosper? 12:1
thee out of the hand of the w. 15:21
whirlwind shall fall upon the head of the w. 23:19; 30:23
have strengthened the hands of the w. Ezek 13:22
wickedness of the w. shall. 18:20
upon the necks of the w. 21:29
land into the hand of the w. 30:12
I have no pleasure in the death of the w. 33:11
as for the wickedness of the w. 12
none of the w. shall. Dan 12:10

treasures of wickedness in house of the w. Mi 6:10
woundedst the head out of the house of the w. Hab 3:13
able to quench all the fiery darts of the w. Eph 6:16
conversation of the w. 2 Pet 2:7
away with the error of the w. 3:17
see one

to or unto the wicked
destruction to the w.? Job 31:3
shall be to the w. Ps 32:10
unto the w. God saith, What? 50:16
he that saith unto the w. Pr 24:24
is abomination to the w. 29:27
the righteous and to the w. Eccl 9:2
woe unto the w.! it shall be. Isa 3:11
let favour be shewed to w. 26:10
no peace, saith the Lord, unto the w. 48:22; 57:21
when I say unto the w. Ezek 3:18 33:8, 14
give it to the w. of the earth. 7:21

wickedly
Lot said, Do not so w. Gen 19:7 Judg 19:23
ye sinned in doing w. Deut 9:18
but if ye shall still do w. 1 Sam 12:25
kept the ways of the Lord and have not w. 2 Sam 22:22; Ps 18:21
I have sinned and have done w. 2 Sam 24:17*
Manasseh hath done w. 2 Ki 21:11
have done amiss, dealt w. 2 Chr 6:37
Neh 9:33; Ps 106:6; Dan 9:5, 15
of Israel, did very w. 2 Chr 20:35
his counsellor to do w. 22:3
you speak w. for God? Job 13:7
surely God will not do w. 34:12
they speak w. concerning. Ps 73:8
the enemy hath done w. in. 74:3
they speak against thee w. 139:20
such as do w. against. Dan 11:32
but the wicked shall do w. 12:10
all that do w. shall be. Mal 4:1

wickedness
God saw that the w. of. Gen 6:5
how can I do this great w? 39:9
it is w. Lev 18:17; 20:14
land full of w. 19:29
be no w. among you. 20:14
w. of these nations. Deut 9:4, 5
shall do no more any such w. 13:11
be any that hath wrought w. 17:2
of the w. of thy doings. 28:20
thus God rendered the w. Judg 9:56
Tell us, how was this w.? 20:3
what w. is this that is done? 12
you may see that your w. is great. 1 Sam 12:17
ye have done all this w.: yet. 20
w. proceedeth from the. 24:13
returned the w. of Nabal on. 25:39
evil according to his w. 2 Sam 3:39
neither shall the children of w. afflict them any. 7:10; Ps 89:22
but if w. be found in. 1 Ki 1:52
knowest all the w. thy heart. 2:44
We have committed w. 8:47
Ahab sold himself to work w. 21:25
Manasseh wrought much w. 2 Ki 21:6
nor the children of w. 1 Chr 17:9
sow w., reap the same. Job 4:8*
he seeth w. 11:11
not w. dwell in thy tabernacles. 14
w. be sweet in his mouth. 20:12
w. shall be broken. 24:20
my lips shall not speak w. 27:4
God that he should do w. 34:10
not God hath pleasure in w. Ps 5:4
their inward part is very w. 9
let the w. of the wicked come. 7:9
seek out his w. 10:15
according to the w. of their. 28:4
thou hatest w. 45:7
strengthened himself in his w. 52:7
w. is in the midst thereof. 55:11
w. is in their dwellings and. 15
ye work w.; ye weigh violence. 58:2
dwell in the tents of w. 84:10
fruitful land into barrenness for the w. of them. 107:34; Jer 12:4
eat the bread of w. Pr 4:17

and w. is an abomination to. *Pr* 8:7
treasures of w. profit nothing. 10:2
wicked shall fall by his own w. 11:5
not be established by w. 12:3
w. overthroweth the sinner. 13:6
driven away in his w. 14:32
to kings to commit w. 16:12
the wicked for their w. 21:12
his w. shall be shewed before. 26:26
saith, I have done no w. 30:20
place of judgement, that w. *Eccl* 3:16
prolongeth his life in w. 7:15
heart to know the w. of folly. 25
nor shall w. deliver those that. 8:8
for w. burneth as the fire. *Isa* 9:18
ye smite with the fist of w. 58:4
chosen, to loose the bands of w. 6
thine own w. shall correct. *Jer* 2:19
wash thine heart from w. 4:14
so she casteth out her w. 6:7
see what I did for the w. of. 7:12
no man repented of his w. 8:6
we acknowledge, O Lord, our w. and
iniquity. 14:20
doth return from his w. 23:14
city whose w. I hid my face. 33:5
w. of your kings, their wives, your
own w. and the w. of ? 44:9
if he turn not from his w. *Ezek* 3:19
changed my judgement into w. 5:6
is risen up into a rod of w. 7:11
the w. of the wicked shall. 18:20
turneth from the w. he hath. 27
driven him out for his w. 31:11
he turneth from his w. 33:12, 19
the w. of Samaria was. *Hos* 7:1
for the w. of their doings I. 9:15
ye have plowed w. and. 10:13
do to you because of your w. 15
fats overflow; for their w. is great.
Joel 3:13
are there treasures of w. in the
house of the wicked ? *Mi* 6:10
and he said, This is w. And he cast
it into the. *Zech* 5:8
them the border of w. *Mal* 1:4
yea, they that work w. are. 3:15
out of the heart proceedeth w., deceit. *Mark* 7:22
inward part is full of w. *Luke* 11:39
this man, if any w. in him. *Acts* 25:5
being filled with all w. *Rom* 1:29
leaven of malice and w. *1 Cor* 5:8
against spiritual w. in. *Eph* 6:12
whole world lieth in w. *1 John* 5:19

their wickedness

took not to their w. *Deut* 9:27
them off in their own w. *Ps* 94:23
the wicked for their w. *Pr* 21:12
touching all their w. *Jer* 1:16
for I will pour their w. upon. 14:16
house have I found their w. 23:11
desolation, because of their w. 44:3
their ear to turn from their w. 5
let all their w. come before.*Lam* 1:22
consider not that I remember all
their w. *Hos* 7:2
they make king glad with their w. 3
all their w. is in Gilgal, there. 9:15
Nineveh, for their w. is come up.
Jonah 1:2
but Jesus perceived their w. and
said. *Mat* 22:18

thy wickedness

Lord shall return thy w. *1 Ki* 2:44
is not thy w. great ? *Job* 22:5
thy w. may hurt a man as. 35:8
nast trusted in thy w. *Isa* 47:10
polluted the land with thy w. *Jer* 3:2
this is thy w. for it is bitter. 4:18
confounded for all thy w. 22:22
to pass after all thy w. *Ezek* 16:23
before thy w. was discovered. 57
upon whom hath not thy w.?*Nah* 3:19
therefore of this thy w. *Acts* 8:22

wide

but thou shalt open thy hand w.
Deut 15:8*; 11*
the land was w. *1 Chr* 4:40
opened their mouth w. as for rain.
Job 29:23
same os rue as a w. breaking. 30:14

opened their mouth w. against me.
Ps 35:21
open thy mouth w. and I. 81:10
so is this great and w. sea. 104:25
he that openeth w. his lips shall have
destruction. *Pr* 13:3
than to dwell with a brawling woman
in a w. house. 21:9; 25:24
make ye a w. mouth ? *Isa* 57:4
will build me a w. house. *Jer* 22:14
thy gates be set w. open. *Nah* 3:13
w. is the gate that leadeth. *Mal* 7:13

wideness

between chambers the w. of 20
cubits. *Ezek* 41:10*

widow

Among the Hebrews, even before
the law, a widow who had no children
by her husband, was allowed to
marry the brother of her deceased
husband, in order to raise up
children who might enjoy his
inheritance, and perpetuate his
name and family, Gen 38:6, 8, 9, 11.
The law that appoints these marriages is delivered in Deut 25:5, 6,
etc.
It was looked upon as a great un-
happiness for a man to die without
an heir, and to see his inheritance
pass into another family. This law
was not confined to brothers in
law only, but was extended to more
distant relatives of the same line,
as may be seen in the example
of Ruth, who married Boaz, after
she had been refused by a nearer
kinsman. Widowhood, as well as
barrenness, was a kind of shame
and reproach in Israel, Isa 54:4.
It was presumed, that a woman of
merit and reputation might have
found a husband, either in the
family of her deceased husband,
if he died without children or in
some other family, if he had left
children.
God frequently recommends to his
people to be very careful in affording
relief to the widow and orphan,
Ex 22:22; Deut 10:18. St. Paul
would have us honour widows that
are widows indeed, and desolate,
that is, destitute of such as ought to
help and relieve them, such as their
husbands and children, 1 Tim 5:3,
4, 5. There were widows in the
Christian church, who, because
of their poverty, were maintained
at the charge of the faithful, and
who were to attend upon the poor
and sick.
remain a w. in thy. *Gen* 38:11
she put her w.'s garments off. 14
ye shall not afflict any w. *Ex* 22:22
a w. or an harlot shall. *Lev* 21:14
if the priest's daughter be a w. 22:13
every vow of a w. shall. *Num* 30:9
execute the judgement of a w.
Deut 10:18
the stranger, fatherless, and w.
14:29; 16:11, 14; 26:12
a w.'s raiment to pledge. 24:17
shall be for the stranger, for the
fatherless and w. 19, 20, 21; 26:13
the judgement of the w. 27:19
I am a w. woman. *2 Sam* 14:5
he was a w.'s son of tribe. *1 Ki* 7:14
Zeruah was a w. woman. 11:26
I have commanded a w. to. 17:9
they take the w.'s ox for. *Job* 24:3
and doeth not good to the w. 21
I caused the w.'s heart to sing. 29:13
caused the eyes of the w. to. 31:16
they slay the w. and the. *Ps* 94:6
be fatherless, his wife a w. 109:9
the fatherless and the w. 146:9
the border of the w. *Pr* 15:25
plead for the w. *Isa* 1:17
neither doth the cause of the w. 23
I shall not sit as a w. nor. 47:8
if ye oppress not the w. *Jer* 7:6
22:3; *Zech* 7:10

how is she become as a w.! *Lam* 1:1
they vexed the w. *Ezek* 22:7
but take a w. that had a. 44:22
those that oppress the w. *Mal* 3:5
certain poor w. threw. *Mark* 12:42
w. cast in more than all. 43
Luke 21:3
Anna was a w. about. *Luke* 2:37
his mother, and she was a w. 7:12
there was a w. in that city. 18:3
because this w. troubleth me, I. 5
if any w. have children. *1 Tim* 5:4
she that is a w. indeed trusteth. 5
let not a w. be taken into the. 9
as queen, and am no w. *Rev* 18:7

widowhood

the garments of her w. *Gen* 38:19
David's concubines shut up, living in
w. *2 Sam* 20:3
loss of children, and w. *Isa* 47:9
the reproach of thy w. 54:4

widows

wives shall be w. *Ex* 22:24
thou hast sent w. away. *Job* 22:9
be buried in death, and w. 27:15
and a judge of the w., is God. *Ps* 68:5
w. made no lamentation. 78:64
he have mercy on their w. *Isa* 9:17
w. may be their prey, that. 10:2
their w. are increased. *Jer* 15:8
let their wives be w. and. 18:21
leave thy children, let thy w. 49:11
our mothers are as w. *Lam* 5:3
have made her many w. *Ezek* 22:25
ye devour w.³ houses, for pretence
make long prayers. *Mat* 23:14
Mark 12:40; *Luke* 20:47
were many w. in Israel. *Luke* 4:25
murmuring because their w. were
neglected. *Acts* 6:1
all the w. stood by him. 9:39
called the saints and w. 41
I said to the w., It is good. *1 Cor* 7:8
honour w. that are w. *1 Tim* 5:3
but the younger w. refuse, they. 11
if any have w., let them relieve. 16
pure religion is to visit the fatherless
and w. in affliction. *Jas* 1:27

wife

Abraham's w. was Sarai. *Gen* 11:29
31; 12:17, 20; 20:18; 24:36
hast taken a man's w. 20:3
Hagar took a w. for Ishmael. 21:21
a w. to my son Isaac. 24:4, 38
Abraham took a w., her name. 25:1
Jacob take a w. of the daughters of
Heth, what good ? 27:46; 28:1, 6
Judah took a w. for Er his. 38:6
go in unto thy brother's w. and. 8
his master's w. cast her eyes. 39:7
covet thy neighbour's w. nor any
thing. *Ex* 20:17; *Deut* 5:21
if his master have given him a w.
Ex 21:4
if he take him another w. her food. 10
nakedness of thy father's w. shalt.
Lev 18:8; 20:11; *Deut* 27:20
of thy son's w. *Lev* 18:15
thy brother's w. 16, 20, 21
neither shalt thou take a w. 18
lie with thy neighbour's w. 20; 20:10
if a man take a w. and her. 20:14
if a man lie with his uncle's w. 20
priests shall not take a w. 21:7*
the high priest shall take a w. 13
if any man's w. go aside. *Num* 5:12
29
be a w. to one of the family. 36:8
or if the w. of thy bosom. *Deut* 13:6
what man hath betrothed a w.? 20:7
if any man take a w. and. 22:13
humbleth his neighbour's w. 24
not take his father's w. 30
a man hath taken a w. and. 24:1
and be another man's w. 2
hath taken a new w. he shall not. 5
w. of the dead shall not marry. 25:5
like not to take his brother's w. 7
then shall his brother's w. come. 9
the w. of the one draweth near. 11
betroth a w. and another lie. 28:30
his eye be evil toward the w. 54
Deborah, w. of Lapidoth. *Judg* 4:4

Jael the w. of Heber the Kenite.
    Judg 4:17, 21; 5:24
thou goest to take a w. of the. 14:3
Samson's w. wept before him. 16
but his w. was given to his. 20
cursed be he that giveth a w. 21:18
buy it of Ruth, the w. of. Ruth 4:5
thou hast taken the w. 2 Sam 12:10
be not known to be the w. 1 Ki 14:2
Ahijah said, Come in, thou w. 6
waited on Naaman's w. 2 Ki 5:2
w. of Jehoiada hid him. 2 Chr 22:11
with the w. of thy youth. Pr 5:18
in to his neighbour's w. 6:29
whoso findeth a w. findeth. 18:22
contentions of a w. a. 19:13
and a prudent w. is from the. 14
live joyfully with the w. Eccl 9:9
children of the married w. Isa 54:1
hath called thee as a w. of youth. 6
surely as a w. treacherously de-
    parteth. Jer 3:20
neighed after his neighbour's w. 5:8
the husband and the w. shall. 6:11
shalt not take thee a w. in. 16:2
as a w. that committeth. Ezek 16:32
nor hath defiled his neighbour's w.
    18:6, 15
and defiled his neighbour's w. 11
    22:11; 33:26
take unto thee a w. of. Hos 1:2
Israel served for a w. and. 12:12
between thee and the w. of thy
    youth, the w. of thy. Mal 2:14
treacherously against his w. 15
of her that had been the w. Mat 1:6
for sake of Philip's w. 14:3
hath forsaken w. or children for my.
    19:29; Mark 10:29; Luke 18:29
the first, when he had married a w.,
    deceased. Mat 22:25
    Mark 12:20; Luke 20:29
I have married a w. Luke 14:20
remember Lot's w. 17:32
should have his father's w. 1 Cor 5:1
render to the w. due benevolence,
    and likewise also the w. 7:3
the w. hath not power over her. 4
let not the w. depart from her. 10
if any brother hath a w. that. 12
unbelieving w. is sanctified by. 14
what knowest thou, O w.? 16
loosed from a w.? seek not a w. 27
between a w. and a virgin. 34
the w. is bound as long as her. 39
is the head of the w. Eph 5:23
his w. even as himself, and the w.
    see that she reverence her. 33
the husband of one w. 1 Tim 3:2
    12; Tit 1:6
a widow, having been the w. of one
    man. 1 Tim 5:9
giving honour to w. as. 1 Pet 3:7*
the bride, the Lamb's w. Rev 21:9

his wife
mother, and shall cleave unto his w.
Gen 2:24; Mat 19:5; Mark 10:7
naked, the man and his w. Gen 2:25
they shall say, This is his w. 12:12
hold on the hand of his w. 19:16
but his w. looked back from. 26
restore the man his w. 20:7
became his w. 24:67; 1 Sam 25:42
the Lord for his w. Gen 25:21
place asked him of his w. 26:7
toucheth this man or his w. shall. 11
because thou art his w. 39:9
then his w. shall go out. Ex 21:3
endow her to be his w. 22:16
not approach to his w. Lev 18:14
he be jealous of his w. Num 5:14, 30
the man shall bring his w. 15
between a man and his w. 30:16
she shall be his w. Deut 22:19, 29
he shall cheer up his w. that. 24:5
Manoah arose and went after his w.
    Judg 13:11
Samson visited his w. with. 15:1
catch you every man his w. 21:21
save to every man his w. and chil-
    dren. 1 Sam 30:22
thou hast taken his w. 2 Sam 12:9
whom Jezebel his w. 1 Ki 21:25

of Ahab was his w. 2 Ki 8:18
called his friends and his w.
    Esth 5:10
and let his w. be a widow. Ps 109:9
if a man put away his w. Jer 3:1
Mat 5:31, 32; 19:9; Mark 10:11
    Luke 16:18
he saw his w.'s mother sick of a
    fever. Mat 8:14
Is it lawful for a man to put away his
    w.? 19:3; Mark 10:2
of a man be so with his w. Mat 19:10
seven brethren, the first deceased,
    and left his w. to. 22:25
    Mark 12:19; Luke 20:28
and hate not his w. Luke 14:26
his w. also being privy to it. Acts 5:2
his w. not knowing what was. 7
Paul found Aquila with his w. 18:2
came with his w. Drusilla. 24:24
man have his own w. 1 Cor 7:2
the husband put away his w. 11
how he may please his w. 33
he that loveth his w. Eph 5:28
shall be joined to his w. 31
so love his w. 33
and his w. hath made. Rev 19:7

my wife
slay me for my w.'s sake. Gen 20:11
she became my w. 12
she is my w. 26:7
give me my w. 29:21
I love my w. Ex 21:5
I will go in to my w. Judg 15:1
saying, Deliver me my w. Michal.
    2 Sam 3:14
my house to lie with my w.? 11:11
is strange to my w. Job 19:17
then let my w. grind unto. 31:10
so I spake, and at even my w. died.
    Ezek 24:18
she is not my w. nor. Hos 2:2
my w. is well stricken. Luke 1:18

thy wife
to the voice of thy w. Gen 3:17
not tell me she was thy w. 12:18
behold thy w., take her, and go. 19
Sarah, thy w. shall bear thee a son.
    17:19; 18:10
arise, take thy w. and thy. 19:15
Of a surety she is thy w. 26:9
might lightly have lien with thy w. 10
unto thee, and thy w. Ex 18:6
wouldest have her to thy w.
    Deut 21:11
to her, and she shall be thy w. 13
taken the wife of Uriah to be thy w.
    2 Sam 12:10
thy w. shall be as a. Ps 128:3
thy w. shall be an harlot. Amos 7:17
thou shalt save thy w. 1 Cor 7:16

to wife
taken her to me to w. Gen 12:19
Get me this damsel to w. 34:4
give him her to w. 8, 12
not given to Shelah to w. 38:14
gave Joseph to w. Asenath. 41:45
of his own people to w. Lev 21:14
I gave my daughter to this man to
    w. Deut 22:16
will I give Achsah my daughter to w.
    Josh 15:16, 17; Judg 1:12, 13
get her for me to w. Judg 14:2
Merab, her will I give thee to w.
    1 Sam 18:17
the Shunammite, to w. 1 Ki 2:17
cedar, give thy daughter to my son
    to w. 2 Ki 14:9; 2 Chr 25:18
daughter of Ahab to w. 2 Chr 21:6
the seven had her to w. Mark 12:23
    Luke 20:33
the second took her to w. and died.
    Luke 20:30

wild
Ishmael will be a w. man. Gen 16:12*
which is w. by nature. Rom 11:24
    see ass, beast, beasts

wilderness
A wilderness, or desert place, in
the Bible means simply a place that
is not inhabited and usually not
cultivated. Much could be used
as pasture.

The desert of Arabia, wherein the
Israelites sojourned forty years
after the Exodus, is called wilderness, Neh 9:19, 21; Ps 78:40, 52,
107:4; Jer 2:2.
The wilderness of Shur lies towards the Red Sea. This was
the place of Hagar's wandering,
Gen 16:7; and the Israelites passed
through it after the Exodus, Ex
15:22.
The wilderness of Paran was in
Arabia Petrea. Ishmael, the son
of Abraham, dwelt in the borders
of this wilderness, Gen 21:21. It
was from hence that Moses sent
out spies to bring intelligence concerning the land of promise, Num
13:3.
The wilderness of Sin, between
Elim and Sinai, Ex 16:1.
The desert of Sinai, is that which
lies about, and is adjacent to,
mount Sinai. The people encamped there a long time, and
received the greater part of those
laws which are written in the books
of Moses, Ex 19:2.
are entangled, in the. Ex 14:3
we had died in this w. Num 14:2
shall fall in this w. 29, 32, 35
went through all that terrible w.
    Deut 1:19; 8:15
in the waste howling w. 32:10
way to w. of Damascus. 1 Ki 19:15
the w. yieldeth food for. Job 24:5
through the depths as through the w.
    Ps 106:9; 136:16; Amos 2:10
he turneth the w. into. Ps 107:35
cometh out of w.? S of S 3:6; 8:5
that made world as a w.? Isa 14:17
w. and solitary place shall be. 35:1
I will make the w. a pool. 41:18
let the w. and cities lift up. 42:11
I make the cities a w. 50:2
and he will make her w. like. 51:3
cities are a w., Zion is a w. 64:10
a w. unto Israel? Jer 2:31
lo, the fruitful place was a w. 4:26
pleasant portion a desolate w. 12:10
will make thee a w. 22:6; Hos 2:3
more desolate than the w.
    Ezek 6:14
behind them a desolate w. Joel 2:3
shall be a desolate w. 3:19
Nineveh dry like a w. Zeph 2:13

in the wilderness
which I did in the w. Num 14:22
leave them in the w. and ye shall.
    32:15; Ezek 29:5
Lord led thee forty years in the w.
    Deut 8:2; 29:5; Josh 5:6; 14:10
who fed thee in the w. Deut 8:16
thou sustain them in w. Neh 9:21
of temptation in the w. Ps 95:8
better dwell in the w. Pr 21:19
shall dwell in the w. Isa 32:16
for in the w. shall waters. 35:6
the voice of him that crieth in the w.
    40:3; Mat 3:3; Mark 1:3
    Luke 3:4; John 1:23
I will plant in the w. the. Isa 41:19
make a way in the w. 43:19
wentest after me in the w. Jer 2:2
in the w. a lodging place. 9:2
left found grace in the w. 31:2
like the heath in the w. 48:6
laid wait for us in the w. Lam 4:19
she is planted in the w. Ezek 19:13
Israel rebelled against me in the w.
    20:13
hand to them in the w. 15, 23
shall dwell safely in the w. 34:25
like grapes in the w. Hos 9:10
in the w. in the dry land. 13:5
John came preaching in the w. of
    Judaea. Mat 3:1
we have so much bread in the w., as
    to fill? Mat 15:33; Mark 8:4
ninety and nine in the w. Luke 15:4
an angel appeared to him in the w.
    Acts 7:30, 38
in perils in the w. 2 Cor 11:26

into the wilderness

by a fit man *into the w.*   *Lev* 16:21
let go the goat *into the w.*   22
brought them *into the w. Ezek* 20:10
I will bring you *into the w.*   35
and bring her *into the w. Hos* 2:14
what went ye out *into the w.* to see ?
   a reed ?   *Mat* 11:7; *Luke* 7:24
of the devil *into the w.*   *Luke* 8:29
which leddest *into the w. Acts* 21:38
woman fled *into the w. Rev* 12:6, 14
me in the spirit *into the w.*   17:3

wiles

vex you with their *w.*   *Num* 25:18
against the *w.* of the devil. *Eph* 6:11

wilfully

if we sin *w.* after we have. *Heb* 10:26

wilily

work *w.* and took old sacks. *Josh* 9:4

will

for good *w.* of him that. *Deut* 33:16
deliver me not to *w.* of.   *Ps* 27:12
wilt not deliver him to *w.* of.   41:2
delivered thee to *w.* of. *Ezek* 16:27
or receiveth it with good *w.* at your
   hand.   *Mal* 2:13
that doeth the *w.* of my Father.
   Mat 7:21; 12:50
it is not the *w.* of your Father. 18:14
whether of them did the *w.* of ? 21:31
on earth peace, good *w. Luke* 2:14
delivered Jesus to their *w.*   23:25
were born, not of the *w. John* 1:13
meat is to do the *w.* of him that. 4:34
I seek the *w.* of my Father.   5:30
and this is the Father's *w.*   6:39, 40
saying, The *w.* of the Lord be done.
   Acts 21:14
understanding what the *w. Eph* 5:17
with good *w.* doing service, as.   6:7
some also preach Christ of good *w.*
   Phil 1:15
by the which *w.* we are. *Heb* 10:10
have wrought the *w.* of.   *1 Pet* 4:3
came not by the *w.* of. *2 Pet* 1:21

see self

will

*(The word will as a verb is some-
times the future auxiliary, but it often
means to wish, to exercise will, to
be willing)*

her go whither she *w. Deut* 21:14
let come on me what *w. Job* 13:13
king's heart whither he *w. Pr* 21:1
and giveth it to whomsoever he *w.*
   Dan 4:17, 25, 32; 5:21
I *w.*, be thou clean.   *Mat* 8:3
   Mark 1:41; *Luke* 5:13
what I *w.* with mine ?   *Mat* 20:15
what *w.* ye that I shall do ?   32
not as I *w.* but as thou wilt.   26:39
   Mark 14:36
whom *w.* ye that I ?   *Mat* 27:17, 21
   Mark 15:9; *John* 18:39
I *w.* that thou give me.   *Mark* 6:25
whensoever ye *w.* ye may do.   14:7
what *w.* ye then that I should ? 15:12
to whomsoever I *w.* I.   *Luke* 4:6
and what *w.* I, if it be ?   12:49
even so the Son quickeneth whom he
   w.   *John* 5:21
wherefore hear it again ? *w.* ye ? 9:27
what ye *w.* it shall be done.   15:7
I *w.* that they be with me.   17:24
if I *w.* that he tarry till.   21:22, 23
I *w.* return again to you. *Acts* 18:21
to *w.* is present with me. *Rom* 7:18
hath he mercy on whom he *w.* have
   mercy, and whom he *w.* he.   9:18
shortly, if the Lord *w.*   *1 Cor* 4:19
what *w.* ye ? shall I come to you ? 21
let him do what he *w.*   7:36
be married to whom she *w.*   39
every man severally as he *w.* 12:11
was a readiness to *w.*   *2 Cor* 8:11
worketh in you, both to *w. Phil* 2:13
I *w.* that men pray.   *1 Tim* 2:8
I *w.* that the younger women.   5:14
these things I *w.* that thou. *Tit* 3:8
if the Lord *w.* we shall do. *Jas* 4:15
as often as they *w.*   *Rev* 11:6
whosoever *w.* let him take.   22:17

his will

doeth according to *his w. Dan* 4:35
he did according to *his w.*   8:4
do *his w.*   11:3, 16, 36
neither did according to *his w.*
   Luke 12:47
if any man will do *his w. John* 7:17
shouldest know *his w. Acts* 22:14
knowest *his w.*   *Rom* 2:18
who hath resisted *his w.?*   9:19
power over *his* own *w.*   *1 Cor* 7:37
his w. was not at all to come. 16:12
good pleasure of *his w.*   *Eph* 1:5
known to us the mystery of *his w.* 9
with knowledge of *his w.*   *Col* 1:9
captive by him at *his w. 2 Tim* 2:26
good work to do *his w. Heb* 13:21
according to *his w.* he hears.
   1 John 5:14
hearts to fulfil *his w.*   *Rev* 17:17

my will

nevertheless, not *my w. Luke* 22:42
who shall fulfil all *my w. Acts* 13:22
this thing against *my w.*   *1 Cor* 9:17

will not

so *w. not* we go back.   *Ps* 80:18
I *w. not* be enquired.   *Ezek* 20:3
I *w. not* again pass by them any
   more.   *Amos* 7:8; 8:2
and said, I *w. not.*   *Mat* 21:29
yet *w.* I *not* deny thee.   26:35
though all shall be offended, yet
   w. not I.   *Mark* 14:29
ye *w. not* come to me that ye may
   have life.   *John* 5:40

will of God

after the *w.* of your *God. Ezra* 7:18
who shall do the *w.* of *God* is my
   brother.   *Mark* 3:35
w. of man, but of *God.*   *John* 1:13
generation by *w.* of *God. Acts* 13:36
journey by *w.* of *God. Rom* 1:10
maketh intercession according to the
   w. of *God.*   8:27
and perfect *w.* of *God.*   12:2
with joy, by the *w.* of *God.* 15:32
an apostle of Jesus Christ by the *w.*
   of *God.*   *1 Cor* 1:1; *2 Cor* 1:1
   Eph 1:1; *Col* 1:1; *2 Tim* 1:1
to us by the *w.* of *God.*   *2 Cor* 8:5
according to the *w.* of *God. Gal* 1:4
doing the *w.* of *God* from.   *Eph* 6:6
may stand complete in all the *w.* of
   God.   *Col* 4:12
for this is the *w.* of *God. 1 Thes* 4:3
   5:18
done the *w.* of *God.*   *Heb* 10:36
so is the *w.* of *God* that. *1 Pet* 2:15
if the *w.* of *God* be so.   3:17
lusts of men, but to *w.* of *God.* 4:2
suffer according to the *w.* of *God.* 19
he that doeth the *w.* of *God* abideth.
   1 John 2:17

own will

it of his *own* voluntary *w. Lev* 1:3
ye shall offer it at your *own w.*
   19:5; 22:19, 29
according to his *own w. Dan* 11:16
I seek not mine *own w. John* 5:30
not to do mine *own w.*   6:38
after counsel of his *own w. Eph* 1:11
gifts of Holy Ghost, according to his
   own w.   *Heb* 2:4
of his *own w.* begat he us. *Jas* 1:18

thy will

I delight to do *thy w.*   *Ps* 40:8
teach me to do *thy w.*; thou. 143:10
thy w. be done in earth.   *Mat* 6:10
   Luke 11:2
not pass, *thy w.* be done. *Mat* 26:42
lo, I come to do *thy w. Heb* 10:7, 9

willeth

so then it is not of him that *w.* nor
   of him that runneth.   *Rom* 9:16

willing

the woman will not be *w. Gen* 24:5
if the woman will not be *w.*   8
whosoever is of a *w.* heart. *Ex* 35:5
   21, 22, 29*
God with a *w.* mind.   *1 Chr* 28:9
who is a *w.* to consecrate his ?   29:5
will the unicorn be *w.?*   *Job* 39:9*

thy people shall be *w.* in.   *Ps* 110:3
if ye be *w.* ye shall eat good. *Isa* 1:19
not *w.* to make her public. *Mat* 1:19
the spirit is *w.* but the flesh.   26:41
Pilate *w.* to content.   *Mark* 15:15*
but he, *w.* to justify.   *Luke* 10:29*
if thou be *w.* remove this.   22:42
Pilate therefore *w.* to.   23:20*
ye were *w.* for a season. *John* 5:35
Felix *w.* to shew the Jews a pleasure.
   Acts 24:27*
but Festus *w.* to do the Jews. 25:9*
and the centurion, *w.* to save. 27:43*
what if God, *w.* to shew ? *Rom* 9:22
w. rather to be absent.   *2 Cor* 5:8
they were *w.* of themselves.   8:3*
if there be first a *w.* mind.   12*
w. to have imparted.   *1 Thes* 2:8*
ready to distribute, *w.*   *1 Tim* 6:18
God, *w.* to shew to the heirs of.
   Heb 6:17*
w. to live honestly in all.   13:18*
not *w.* that any should perish, but.
   2 Pet 3:9*

willingly

every man that giveth *w.*   *Ex* 25:2
the people *w.* offered.   *Judg* 5:2, 9
we will *w.* give the earrings.   8:25
and rulers offered *w. 1 Chr* 29:6, 9
   14, 17; *2 Chr* 35:8; *Ezra* 1:6; 3:5
Amasiah *w.* offered.   *2 Chr* 17:16
blessed the men that *w. Neh* 11:2
she worketh *w.* with.   *Pr* 31:13
he doth not afflict *w.*   *Lam* 3:33
Ephraim *w.* walked.   *Hos* 5:11
they *w.* received him.   *John* 6:21
the creature made subject to vanity
   not *w.*   *Rom* 8:20
if I do this thing *w.*   *1 Cor* 9:17
not as of necessity, but *w.*
   Philem 14; *1 Pet* 5:2
for this they *w.* are.   *2 Pet* 3:5

willows

ye shall take *w.* of the.   *Lev* 23:40
the *w.* of the brook compass him.
   Job 40:22
our harps upon the *w.*   *Ps* 137:2
away to the brook of *w.*   *Isa* 15:7
they shall spring up as *w.* by.   44:4

willow tree

he set it as a *w.* tree.   *Ezek* 17:5

will worship

of wisdom in *w. worship.*   *Col* 2:23

wilt

Caleb said to her, What *w.* thou ?
   Judg 1:14; *Esth* 5:3; *Mat* 20:21
   Mark 10:51; *Luke* 18:41
if thou *w.* look on thine. *1 Sam* 1:11
w. not thou, O God ?   *Ps* 60:10
   108:11
w. thou be angry with us ?   85:5
w. thou not revive us again to ?   6
why *w.* thou, my son, be ravished ?
   Pr 5:20
w. thou not from this time cry unto
   me ?   *Jer* 3:4
O Jerusalem, *w.* thou not be ? 13:27
w. thou judge them, son of man ?
   Ezek 20:4; 22:2
w. thou not tell us what ?   24:19
w. thou yet say before him ?   28:9
Lord, if thou *w.* thou canst make.
   Mat 8:2; *Mark* 1:40; *Luke* 5:12
w. thou then that we go and gather
   them up ?   *Mat* 13:28
unto thee even as thou *w.*   15:28
if thou *w.* let us make three.   17:4
the disciples said, Where *w.* thou ?
   26:17; *Mark* 14:12; *Luke* 22:9
not as I will, but as thou *w.*
   Mat 26:39; *Mark* 14:36
king said, Ask of me whatsoever
   thou *w.*   *Mark* 6:22
w. thou that we command fire to ?
   Luke 9:54
Jesus said, *W.* thou be made whole ?
   John 5:6
w. thou at this time restore the
   kingdom ?   *Acts* 1:6

wimples

away mantles and *w.*   *Isa* 3:22*

win

he thought to w. them. *2 Chr 32:1*
that I may w. Christ. *Phil 3:8*

wind

The powerful operations of God's Spirit, quickening or reviving the heart toward God, are compared to the blowing of the wind, John 3:8. For as with the wind, man perceives, by the effects of it, that there is such a thing, and that it does blow, yet his power cannot restrain it, neither can his reason reach to know whence it rises, or from how far it comes, or how far it reaches; so is the spiritual change wrought in the soul, freely, where, in whom, when, and in what measure the Spirit pleases; and also powerfully, so as to make an evident sensible change, though the manner thereof be incomprehensible.

God made a w. to pass. *Gen 8:1*
blow with thy w. *Ex 15:10*
the w. brought quails. *Num 11:31*
he was seen upon the wings of the
  w. *2 Sam 22:11; Ps 18:10; 104:3*
black with cloud and w. *1 Ki 18:45*
strong w. rent the mountains, but the
  Lord was not in the w. *19:11*
ye shall not see a w. nor. *2 Ki 3:17*
there came a w. from. *Job 1:19*
speeches which are as w. *6:26*
O remember that my life is w. *7:7†*
mouth be like a strong w. *8:2*
as stubble before the w. *21:18*
pursue my soul as the w. *30:15*
thou liftest me up to the w. *22*
not light in the clouds, but the w.
  37:21; Ps 103:16
like chaff which the w. *Ps 1:4*
w. that passeth away and. *78:39*
he bringeth the w. out of. *135:7*
he causeth his w. to blow. *147:18*
he shall inherit the w. *Pr 11:29*
clouds and w. without rain. *25:14*
north w. driveth away rain. *23*
hideth her, hideth the w. *27:16*
gathered the w. in his fists. *30:4*
w. goeth toward the south, and
  turneth . . . and the w. *Eccl 1:6*
brings the w. out of his treasuries.
  5:16
the w. shall eat up all thy. *22:22*
thou shalt scatter in the w. *Ezek 5:2*
I will scatter toward every w. *12:14*
w. son of man, say to the w. *37:9*
and the w. carried them. *Dan 2:35*
the w. hath bound her up. *Hos 4:19*
they have sown w. and shall reap. *8:7*
on w. and followeth the east w. *12:1*
he that createth the w. *Amos 4:13*
Lord sent out a great w. *Jonah 1:4*
and the w. was in their. *Zech 5:9*
a reed shaken with the w.? *Mat 11:7*
  Luke 7:24
w. was contrary. *Mat 14:24*
  Mark 6:48; Acts 27:4
the w. ceased. *Mat 14:32*
  Mark 4:39; 6:51
w. bloweth where it. *John 3:8*
sound as of a mighty w. *Acts 2:2*
carried about with every w. *Eph 4:14*
like a wave driven with the w. and.
  Jas 1:6
shaken of a mighty w. *Rev 6:13*
that the w. should not blow. *7:1*

window

a w. shalt thou make. *Gen 6:16**
Noah opened the w. of the ark. *8:6*
Gerar looked out at a w. *26:8*
spies down through a w. *Josh 2:15*
bound the scarlet line in the w. *21*
Sisera's mother looked out at a w.
  Judg 5:28
Michal looked through a w., and saw
  David. *2 Sam 6:16*
Jezebel painted her face, and looked
  out at a w. *2 Ki 9:30*
Open the w. eastward. *13:17*
at the w. of my house. *Pr 7:6*
there sat in a w. a certain young
  man. *Acts 20:9*
through a w. was I let. *2 Cor 11:33*

windows

and the w. of heaven. *Gen 7:11*
w. of heaven were stopped. *8:2*
if the Lord make w. in heaven.
  2 Ki 7:2, 19
those that look out of the w. be
  darkened. *Eccl 12:3*
looked forth at the w. *S of S 2:9*
w. from on high are. *Isa 24:18*
I will make thy w. of agates. *54:12**
flee as the doves to their w. *60:8*
come up into our w. *Jer 9:21*
that cutteth him out w. *22:14*
his w. being open in his. *Dan 6:10*
they shall enter in at the w. like a
  thief. *Joel 2:9*
shall sing in the w. *Zeph 2:14*
if I will not open the w. *Mal 3:10*

winds

weight for the w. *Job 28:25*
come from the four w. *Ezek 37:9*
the w. blew, and beat. *Mat 7:25, 27*
rebuked the w. *8:26; Luke 8:24*
even the w. and the sea obey him?
  Mat 8:27; Mark 4:41; Luke 8:25
are driven of fierce w. *Jas 3:4*
clouds carried about of w. *Jude 12*
see east, four, scatter, stormy

windy

hasten from the w. storm. *Ps 55:8*

wine

There were many excellent vineyards in Palestine, and wine was made for common use. Water was scanty, especially at some seasons, and likely to be infected. Wine and milk were therefore the common beverages. The use of wine was forbidden to the priests during all the time they were in the tabernacle, and employed in the service of the altar, Lev 10:9. This liquor was also forbidden to the Nazarites Num 6:3.

In Gen 27:28, 37, corn and wine denote all sorts of temporal good things. In the style of the sacred writers, the wine, or the cup, often represents the anger of God, Ps 60:3; Jer 25:15. There were certain charitable women at Jerusalem, as they tell us, who used to mix certain drugs with wine, to make it stronger, and more capable of easing pain. Some think it was such a mixture that was offered to our Saviour to drink, before he was fastened to the cross, Mark 15:23.

Noah awoke from his w. *Gen 9:24*
brought forth bread and w. *14:18*
garments in w. and clothes in. *49:11*
his eyes were red with w. *12*
part of an hin of w. for a drink.
  Ex 29:40; Lev 23:13; Num 15:5
separate himself from w. *Num 6:3*
half an hin of w. *15:10; 28:14*
shalt cause the strong w. *28:7**
their w. is the poison. *Deut 32:33*
leave w. which cheereth. *Judg 9:13*
there is also bread and w. for. *19:19*
away thy w. from thee. *1 Sam 1:14*
when the w. was gone out of. *25:37*
piece of flesh, and a flagon of w.
  2 Sam 6:19*; 1 Chr 16:3*

when Amnon's heart is merry with
  w. *2 Sam 13:28*
the w. that such as be faint. *16:2*
w. was before him, I took up the w.
  Neh 2:1
had taken bread and w. *5:15*
ten days store of all sorts of w. *18*
lading asses with w. and. *13:15*
they gave them royal w. *Esth 1:7*
king was merry with w. *10*
Esther at the banquet of w. 5:6; 7:2
from the banquet of w. *7:7*
drinking w. in eldest brother's house.
  Job 1:13, 18
behold, my belly is as w. that. *32:19*
the w. is red, it is full of. *Ps 75:8*
shouteth by reason of w. *78:65*
w. that maketh glad the. *104:15*
she hath mingled her w. *Pr 9:2*
w. is a mocker, strong drink. *20:1*
sorrow? they that tarry long at the w.;
  they that go to seek mixt w. *23:30*
look not thou upon the w. when. *31*
give w. to those. that be of. *31:6*
heart to give myself to w. *Eccl 2:3*
w. maketh merry, but money. *10:19*
for thy love is better than w.
  S of S 1:2; 4:10
I have drunk my w. with my. *5:1*
of thy mouth like the best w. *7:9*
thy silver dross, thy w. *Isa 1:22*
that continue till night, till w. *5:11*
pipe and w. are in their feasts. *12*
eating flesh and drinking w. *22:13*
there is a crying for w. in the. *24:11*
a vineyard of red w. *27:2*
that are overcome with w.! *28:1*
w., and through strong drink are out
  of the way; they are . . . of w. *7*
drunken, but not with w. *29:9; 51:21*
yea, come, buy w. and milk. *55:1*
say they. I will fetch w. *56:12*
whom w. hath overcome. *Jer 23:9*
take the w. cup of this fury. *25:15*
pots full of w. *35:5*
Jews gathered w. *40:12*
I have caused w. to tail from. *48:33*
drunken of her w. are mad. *51:7*
Damascus merchant in w. *Ezek 27:18*
the king gave of the w. *Dan 1:5*
not to defile himself with the w. *8*
Belshazzar drank w. before. *5:1, 4*
whiles he tasted w. *2*
concubines drunk w. *23*
neither came w. nor flesh. *10:3*
take away my w. in the. *Hos 2:9*
gods and love flagons of w. *3:1**
the scent shall be as the w. *14:7*
all ye drinkers of w. *Joel 1:5*
prophesy to thee of w. *Mi 2:11*
he transgresseth by w. *Hab 2:5*
make a noise, as through w. *Zech 9:15*
shall rejoice, as through w. *10:7*
neither drinking w. *Luke 7:33*
wanted w., the mother of Jesus saith
  unto him, They have no w. *John 2:3*
water that was made w. *9; 4:46*
doth set forth good w., but thou hast
  kept good w. till now. *2:10*
be not drunk with w. *Eph 5:18*
not given to w. *1 Tim 3:3*, 8*
  Tit 1:7*; 2:3
use a little w. for thy stomach's sake.
  1 Tim 5:23
walked in excess of w. *1 Pet 4:3**
give her the cup of the w. *Rev 16:19*
made drunk with the w. of her fornication.
  17:2; 18:3
*see bottle, corn, drink, new,
offerings, oil, sweet*

winebibber, -s

be not among w. *Pr 23:20*
behold a man gluttonous, and a w.
  Mat 11:19; Luke 7:34

wine bottles

Gibeonites took w. bottles old and
  rent. *Josh 9:4**
bottles of w. which we filled. *13**

wine cellars

over the w. cellars was. *1 Chr 27:27*

winefat

him that treadeth in the w.? *Isa 63:2†*
a place for the w. *Mark 12:1**

wisdom

winepress
fulness of the w.   *Num* 18:27, 30
furnish him out of thy w. *Deut* 15:14
wheat by the w.   *Judg* 6:11
slew at the w. of Zeeb.   7:25
help thee out of the w.?   *2 Ki* 6:27
he also made a w. therein. *Isa* 5:2
I have trodden the w. alone.   63:3
of Judah as in a w.   *Lam* 1:15
the floor and w. shall not. *Hos* 9:2
digged a w. in it, and   *Mat* 21:33
the angel cast it into the great w.
   Rev 14:19
the w. was trodden without the city,
blood came out of the w.   20
he treadeth the w. of the wrath. 19:15

winepresses
treading w. on sabbath.   *Neh* 13:15
tread their w. and.   *Job* 24:11
wine to fail from the w.   *Jer* 48:33
upon the king's w.   *Zech* 14:10

wines
a feast, of w. on the lees. *Isa* 25:6

wing
w. of the cherub, five cubits the other
  w.   *1 Ki* 6:24, 27; *2 Chr* 3:11, 12
none that moved the w.   *Isa* 10:14
dwell fowl of every w.   *Ezek* 17:23

winged
God created every w.   *Gen* 1:21
likeness of any w. fowl.   *Deut* 4:17
eagle with great wings, long-w. of
divers colours, full of.   *Ezek* 17:3

wings
I bare you on eagles' w.   *Ex* 19:4
w. covering the mercy seat with
  their w.   25:20; 37:9; *1 Ki* 8:7
cleave it with w. thereof. *Lev* 1:17
abroad her w., taketh them, beareth
  them on her w.   *Deut* 32:11*
under whose w. thou art. *Ruth* 2:12
was seen upon the w. *2 Sam* 22:11
goodly w. to the peacock? or w. and
  feathers to the ostrich? *Job* 39:13*
the shadow of thy w.   *Ps* 17:8
fly on the w. of the wind.   18:10
   104:3
their trust under the shadow of thy
  w.   36:7; 57:1; 61:4; 91:4
Oh that I had w. like a dove!   55:6
in the shadow of thy w. will.   63:7
yet shall ye be as the w.   68:13
take the w. of the morning.   139:9
riches make themselves w. *Pr* 23:5
that which hath w. shall. *Eccl* 10:20
stood the seraphims: each one had
  six w.   *Isa* 6:2
the stretching out of his w.   8:8
the land shadowing with w.   18:1
mount up with w. as eagles.   40:31
give w. to Moab, it may fly. *Jer* 48:9
spread his w. over Moab.   40
spread his w. over Bozrah.   49:22
four faces and four w.   *Ezek* 1:6
their w. were joined.
I heard the noise of their w. . . . let
  down their w.   24, 25; 3:13; 10:5
w. full of eyes.   10:12
a great eagle with great w.   17:3
another great eagle with great w.   7
lion and had eagle's w.: I beheld till
  the w. thereof were.   *Dan* 7:4
upon the back of it four w. of a fowl 6
bound her up in her w.   *Hos* 4:19
the wind was in their w.   *Zech* 5:9
arise with healing in his w. *Mal* 4:2
as a hen gathereth her chickens under
  her w.   *Mat* 23:37; *Luke* 13:34
the sound of their w. as of *Rev* 9:9
to the woman were given two w.12:14

wink
what do thy eyes w. at? *Job* 15:12†
nor let them w. with the eye. *Ps* 35:19

winked
this ignorance God w. at. *Acts* 17:30*

winketh
a wicked man w. with.   *Pr* 6:13
he that w. with the eye.   10:10

winneth
he that w. souls is wise. *Pr* 11:30

winnowed
which hath been w. with. *Isa* 30:24

winnoweth
behold, Boaz w. barley.   *Ruth* 3:2

winter
summer and w. shall not. *Gen* 8:22
made summer and w.   *Ps* 74:17
for lo, the w. is past, the. *S of S* 2:11
in summer and in w.   *Zech* 14:8
flight be not in the w. nor on the.
   Mat 24:20; *Mark* 13:18
dedication was in w.   *John* 10:22
do thy diligence to come before w.
   2 Tim 4:21

winter, verb
beasts shall w. on them.   *Isa* 18:6
haven was not commodious to w. in,
  the more . . . to w.   *Acts* 27:12
abide and w. with you.   *1 Cor* 16:6
determined there to w.   *Tit* 3:12

wintered
in a ship which had w.   *Acts* 28:11

winterhouse
king sat in the w.   *Jer* 36:22
I will smite the w. with the summer
  house.   *Amos* 3:15

wipe
I will w. Jerusalem as.   *2 Ki* 21:13
w. not out my good deeds I have
  done.   *Neh* 13:14
swallow up death in victory; Lord
  will w.   *Isa* 25:8; *Rev* 7:17; 21:4
a woman did w. them with hairs of.
  Luke 7:38, 44; *John* 11:2; 12:3
he began to w. them.   *John* 13:5

wiped
shall not be w. away.   *Pr* 6:33

wipeth
as a man w. a dish.   *2 Ki* 21:13
she eateth, and w. her mouth. *Pr* 30:20

wiping
w. it, and turning it.   *2 Ki* 21:13

wires
they cut gold plates into w. to work
  it.   *Ex* 39:3

wisdom
*(This word is used in the Scriptures
not only for learning, but for skill
in the arts; the instinct of birds or
beasts; discretion; and spiritual
insight)*
filled him with the Spirit of God in w.
   Ex 31:3, 6; 35:31, 35
whose heart stirred them up in w.
   35:26; 36:1, 2
for this is your w. and.   *Deut* 4:6
according to the w. of an angel of
  God.   *2 Sam* 14:20
to all the people in her w.   20:22
saw that the w. of God.   *1 Ki* 3:28
God gave Solomon w.   4:29; 5:12
   2 Chr 1:12
Solomon's w. excelled w. of Egypt.
  1 Ki 4:30, 34; 7:14; 10:4, 23, 24
   2 Chr 9:3, 22, 23
only Lord give thee w. *1 Chr* 22:12*
give me w.   *2 Chr* 1:10
but hast asked w.   11
thou Ezra, after the w.   *Ezra* 7:25
they die, even without w. *Job* 4:21
the people, w. shall die with you. 12:2
and it should be your w.   13:5
dost thou restrain w. to thyself? 15:8
counselled him that hath no w.? 26:3
but where shall w. be found? 28:12
cometh w. and where place?   20
of years should teach w.   32:7
say, We have found out w.   13
me and I shall teach thee w.   33:33
Job's words were without w.   34:35
mighty in strength and w.   36:5*
number the clouds in w.?   38:37
hath deprived her of w.   39:17
of the righteous speaketh w.*Ps* 37:30
shalt make me to know w.   51:6
apply our hearts unto w.   90:12
in w. hast thou made all.   104:24
and teach his senators w.   105:22
to him that by w. made.   136:5*
to know w.   *Pr* 1:2
fools despise w. and instruction   7

w. crieth.   *Pr* 1:20; 8:1
incline thine ear unto w.   2:2
the Lord giveth w.   6
he layeth up sound w. for the.   7
w. entereth into thine heart.   10
happy is the man that findeth w. 3:13
the Lord by w. hath founded.   19
keep sound w.   21
get w.   4:5, 7
my son, attend unto my w.   5:1
say to w., Thou art my sister.   7:4
understand w.   8:5*
I w. dwell with prudence, and.   12
counsel is mine, and sound w.   14
w. builded her house.   9:1
man of understanding hath w. 10:23
the just bringeth forth w.   31
commended according to his w. 12:8
a scorner seeketh w. and.   14:6
the w. of the prudent is to.   8
w. resteth in heart of him that.   33
better is it to get w. than gold! 16:16
in hand of a fool to get w.?   17:16
man intermeddleth with all w. 18:1
he that getteth w. loveth   19:8
is no w. against the Lord.   21:30
cease from thine own w.   23:4
for a fool will despise the w.   9
buy w.   23
through w. is an house built.   24:3
whoso loveth w. rejoiceth his. 29:3
the rod and reproof give w.   15
I neither learned w. nor have. 30:3
openeth her mouth with w.   31:26
heart to search out by w. *Eccl* 1:13
I have gotten more w. than all.   16
I gave my heart to know w. and.   17
for in much w. is much grief.   18
acquainting mine heart with w. 2:3
so I was great, and my w.   9
I turned myself to behold w.   12
w. excelleth folly.   13
whose labour is in w.   21
God giveth to a man w.   26
w. giveth life.   7:12
w. strengtheneth the wise.   19
all this have I proved by w.   23
heart to know and seek out w.   25
a man's w. maketh his face.   8:1
applied my heart to know w.   16
there is no w. in the grave.   9:10
this w. have I seen also under. 13
a poor man by his w. delivered. 15
that is in reputation for w.   10:1
his w. faileth him, and he saith he. 3*
by my w. I have done it.   *Isa* 10:13
for the w. of their wise men. 29:14
w. shall be the stability of.   33:6
wise man glory in his w.   *Jer* 9:23
the world by his w.   10:12; 51:15
were skilful in all w.   *Dan* 1:4, 17
with counsel and w.   2:14*
for w. and might are his.   20
he giveth w. to the wise, and.   21
O God, who hast given me w.   23
not revealed for any w. I have.   30
w. like the w. of the gods was. 5:11
came from utmost parts to hear the
  w. of.   *Mat* 12:42; *Luke* 11:31
hath this man this w.?   *Mat* 13:54
turn the disobedient to the w. of.
   Luke 1:17
Jesus filled with w.   2:40
increased in w.   52
said the w. of God, I will send. 11:49
give you a mouth and w.   21:15
look out seven men full of the Holy
  Ghost and w.   *Acts* 6:3
were not able to resist the w.   10
gave Joseph w. in the sight of. 7:10
was learned in all the w. of the. 22
to preach the gospel: not with w. of
  words.   *1 Cor* 1:17
I will destroy the w. of the wise. 19
foolish the w. of this world.   20
after that in the w. of God the world
  by w. knew not God.   21
sign, and Greeks seek after w.   22
power of God and the w. of.   24
who of God is made unto us w. 2:4
not with words of man's w.   2:4
not stand in the w. of men.   5
we speak w.   6
but we speak the w. of God   7

which man's *w.* teacheth. *1 Cor* 2:13
w. of this world is foolishness. 3:19
not with fleshly *w.*   *2 Cor* 1:12
toward us in all *w.*   *Eph* 1:8
known the manifold *w.* of God. 3:10
might be filled with all *w. Col* 1:9
teaching every man in all *w.* 28
words dwell in you in all *w.* 3:16
walk in *w.* toward them that are. 4:5
if any lack *w.* let him ask. *Jas* 1:5
this *w.* descendeth not from. 3:15
according to the *w.* given. *2 Pet* 3:15
the Lamb to receive *w. Rev* 5:12
blessing, and glory, and *w.* 7:12
the mind which hath *w.* 17:9

wisdom, joined with *is*
and *is w.* driven quite ? *Job* 6:13
with the ancient *is w.* 12:12, 13, 16
the price of *w. is* above rubies.
     28:18; *Pr* 8:11
fear of the Lord that *is w. Job* 28:28
w. is the principal thing, get *w. Pr* 4:7
understanding *w. is* found. 10:13
but with the lowly *is w.* 11:2
but with the well advised *is w.* 13:10
w. of prudent *is* to understand. 14:8
w. is before him that hath. 17:24
w. is too high for a fool, he. 24:7
for in much *w. is* much grief.
     Eccl 1:18
w. is good with an inheritance. 7:11
for *w. is* a defence, and money. 12
w. is better than strength; never-the-
less, the poor man's *w. is.* 9:16
w. is better than weapons of. 18
but *w. is* profitable to direct. 10:10
word what *w. is* in them ? *Jer* 8:9
Is w. no more in Teman ? *is* their *w.*
   vanished ? 49:7
that excellent *w. is* found. *Dan* 5:14
sinners, but *w. is* justified of her
   children. *Mat* 11:19; *Luke* 7:35
what *w. is* this which is given to him ?
     Mark 6:2
the *w.* that *is* from above. *Jas* 3:17
here *is w.* Let him that. *Rev* 13:18

of wisdom
shew thee the secrets *of w. Job* 11:6
price *of w.* is above rubies. 28:18
my mouth shall speak *of w. Ps* 49:3
the fear of the Lord is the beginning
   of w. 111:10; *Pr* 9:10
to receive the instruction *of w. Pr* 1:3
taught thee in the way *of w.* 4:11
but fools die for want *of w.* 10:21*
that is void *of w.* despiseth. 11:12
to him that is destitute *of w.* 15:21
of the Lord is the instruction *of w.* 33
the wellspring *of w.* as a. 18:4
so shall the knowledge *of w.* 24:14
great experience *of w. Eccl* 1:16
thou sealest up the sum, full *of w.*
     Ezek 28:12
in all matters *of w.* he found them
   better. *Dan* 1:20
the man *of w.* shall see. *Mi* 6:9
O the depth of the *w.* of God!
     Rom 11:33
of speech or *of w.*   *1 Cor* 2:1
by the Spirit the word *of w.* 12:8
hid all the treasures *of w. Col* 2:3
have indeed a shew *of w.* 23
works with meekness *of w. Jas* 3:13

see **spirit**

thy wisdom
according to *thy w.*   *1 Ki* 2:6
report that I heard of *thy w.* 10:6
thy w. and prosperity exceedeth. 7
that stand before thee continually
   and hear *thy w.* 8; *2 Chr* 9:5, 7
the half of *thy w.* was. *2 Chr* 9:6
the hawk fly by *thy w.? Job* 39:26
thy w., it hath perverted. *Isa* 47:10
with *thy w.* hast gotten. *Ezek* 28:4, 5
thou hast corrupted *thy w.* by. 17

wise
be desired to make one *w. Gen* 3:6
is none so discreet and *w.* 41:39
the gift blindeth the *w.*   *Ex* 23:8
     Deut 16:19
great nation is a *w.* people. *Deut* 4:6
O that they were *w.,* that they. 32:29
her *w.* ladies answered. *Judg* 5:29

my lord is *w.* according. *2 Sam* 14:20
I have given thee a *w.*   *1 Ki* 3:12
given David a *w.* son over this great
   people. 5:7; *2 Chr* 2:12
for Zachariah his son, a *w.* counsellor.
     1 Chr 26:14*
he taketh the *w.* in their own craftiness. *Job* 5:13
he is *w.* in heart and mighty. 9:4
for vain man would be *w.* 11:12*
he that is *w.* may be profitable. 22:2
great men are not always *w.* 32:9
not any that are *w.* of heart. 37:24
be *w.* now, O ye kings. *Ps* 2:10
is sure, making *w.* the simple. 19:7
he hath left off to be *w.* and. 36:3
fools, when will ye be *w.?* 94:8
whoso is *w.* and will observe. 107:43
a *w.* man shall attain to *w. Pr* 1:5*
to understand the words of the *w.* 6
be not *w.* in thine own eyes. 3:7
the *w.* shall inherit glory: but. 35
be *w.* 6:6; 8:33; 23:19; 27:11
if thou be *w.* thou shalt be *w.* 9:12
a *w.* son maketh a glad father. 10:1
     15:20
gathereth in summer is a *w.* son. 10:5
the *w.* in heart will receive. 8
he that refraineth his lips is *w.* 19
servant to the *w.* in heart. 11:29
he that winneth souls is *w.* 30
hearkeneth to counsel is *w.* 12:15
tongue of the *w.* is health. 18
a *w.* son heareth his father's. 13:1
the law of the *w.* is a fountain. 14
with *w.* men shall be *w.* 20
but the lips of the *w.* shall. 14:3
crown of the *w.* is their riches. 24
is toward a wise servant. 35
tongue of *w.* useth knowledge. 15:2
the lips of the *w.* disperse. 7
a scorner will not go to the *w.* 12
the way of life is above to the *w.* 24
reproof abideth among the *w.* 31
the *w.* in heart shall be called prudent. 16:21
the heart of the *w.* teacheth his. 23
a *w.* servant shall have rule. 17:2
holdeth his peace is counted *w.* 28
the ear of the *w.* seeketh. 18:15
that thou mayest be *w.* in thy latter
   end. 19:20
is deceived thereby, is not *w.* 20:1
a *w.* king scattereth the wicked. 26
simple is made *w.:* when the *w.* is
   instructed he receiveth. 21:11
oil in the dwelling of the *w.* 20
ear, hear the words of the *w.* 22:17
thy heart be *w.* my heart shall. 23:15
he that begetteth a *w.* son shall. 24
for by *w.* counsel thou shalt. 24:6
also belong to the *w.* 23
so is a *w.* reprover upon an. 25:12
answer a fool lest he be *w.* 26:5
seest thou a man *w.* in his own. 12
keepeth the law is a *w.* son. 28:7
rich man is *w.* in his own conceit. 11
four things that are exceeding *w.*
     30:24
and why was I more *w.? Eccl* 2:15
no remembrance of the *w.* 16
I have shewed myself *w.* 19
better is a *w.* child than a. 4:13
for what hath the *w.* more than ? 6:8
heart of the *w.* is in the house. 7:4
hear the rebuke of the *w.* 5
neither make thyself over *w.* 16
wisdom strengtheneth *w.* more. 19
I said, I will be *w.* but it was. 23
the *w.* and their works are in the. 9:1
I saw that bread is not to the *w.* 11
preacher was *w.,* he taught. 12:9
the words of the *w.* are as goads. 11
woe to them that are *w. Isa* 5:21
I am the son of the *w.?* 19:11
is *w.* and will bring evil. 31:2
they are *w.* to do evil. *Jer* 4:22
We are *w.,* and the law of. 8:8
counsel perish from the *w.* 18:18
God giveth wisdom to *w. Dan* 2:21
they that be *w.* shall shine as. 12:3
none of the wicked; but the *w.* 10
the *w.* shall understand. *Hos* 14:9
and Zidon be very *w. Zech* 9:2

therefore *w.* as serpents. *Mat* 10:16
hast hid these things from *w.* and
   prudent, and. 11:25; *Luke* 10:21
then is a faithful and *w.? Mat* 24:45
five virgins were *w.* and. 25:2
the *w.* took oil in their vessels. 4
faithful and *w.* steward ? *Luke* 12:42
I am debtor to the *w.*   *Rom* 1:14
professing themselves *w.,* they. 22
lest ye should be *w.* in your. 11:25
be not *w.* in your own. 12:16
I would have you *w.* to. 16:19
to God only *w.,* be glory. 27
     1 Tim 1:17; *Jude* 25
I will destroy the wisdom of the *w.*
     1 Cor 1:19
where is the *w.?* 20
to confound the *w.* 27
as a *w.* masterbuilder, I. 3:10
to be *w.* in this world, let him become
   a fool, that he may be *w.* 18
he taketh the *w.* in their own. 19
knoweth the thoughts of the *w.* 20
but ye are *w.* in Christ. 4:10
themselves, are not *w. 2 Cor* 10:12*
seeing ye yourselves are *w.* 11:19
not as fools, but as *w.*   *Eph* 5:15
are able to make thee *w. 2 Tim* 3:15

see **man, men**

any wise
afflict them in *any w.*   *Ex* 22:23
shall in *any w.* rebuke. *Lev* 19:17*
if he will in *any w.* redeem. 27:19*
in *any w.* set him king. *Deut* 17:15†
thou shalt in *any w.* bury. 21:23*
shalt in *any w.* let the dam. 22:7†
in *any w.* keep from the. *Josh* 6:18
if ye do in *any w.* go back. 23:12
in *any w.* send a trespass. *1 Sam* 6:3
let me go in *any w.*   *1 Ki* 11:22
fret not thyself in *any w. Ps* 37:8*
not deny thee in *any w. Mark* 14:31

in no wise
the fat of beasts torn, *in no w.* eat of
   it. *Lev* 7:24
give the child, and *in no w.* slay it.
     1 Ki 3:26, 27
one tittle shall *in no w.* pass from the
   law. *Mat* 5:18
he shall *in no w.* lose his. 10:42
a woman could *in no w. Luke* 13:11
shall *in no w.* enter therein. 18:17
     Rev 21:27
I will *in no w.* cast out. *John* 6:37
ye shall *in no w.* believe. *Acts* 13:41
than they ? *in no w.*   *Rom* 3:9

on this wise
on this w. ye shall bless. *Num* 6:23
the birth of Jesus Christ was *on this*
   w. *Mat* 1:18
and *on this w.* shewed. *John* 21:1
God spake *on this w.*   *Acts* 7:6
he said *on this w.,* I will give. 13:34
speaketh *on this w.*   *Rom* 10:6
the seventh day *on this w. Heb* 4:4

wise hearted
to all that are *w. hearted. Ex* 28:3
I have put wisdom in all that are
   w. hearted. 31:6
every *w. hearted* among you. 35:10
that were *w. hearted* did spin. 25
wrought every *w. hearted* man. 36:1
Aholiab and every *w. hearted* man. 2
every *w. hearted* man made ten. 8

wise men
all the magicians of Egypt, and all
   the *w. men. Gen* 41:8; *Ex* 7:11

wise woman
and Joab fetched thence a *w. woman.*
     2 Sam 14:2
then cried a *w. woman* out. 20:16
every *w. woman* buildeth. *Pr* 14:1

wisely
come on, let us deal *w.*   *Ex* 1:10
David behaved himself *w.*
     1 Sam 18:5, 14, 15, 30
Rehoboam dealt *w.*   *2 Chr* 11:23
charming never so *w. Ps* 58:5
for they shall *w.* consider of. 64:9
I will behave myself *w.* in a. 101:2
handleth a matter *w.*   *Pr* 16:20
w. considereth the house. 21:12

whoso walketh *w.* shall be. *Pr 28:26*
thou dost not enquire *w. Eccl 7:10*
because he had done *w. Luke 16:8*

wiser
'or Solomon was *w.*   *1 Ki 4:31*
who maketh us *w.* than the fowls of
   heaven ?   *Job 35:11*
thou hast made me *w. Ps 119:98*
and he will be yet *w. Pr 9:9*
the sluggard is *w.* in his own. *26:16*
behold, thou art *w.* than. *Ezek 28:3*
are in their generation is *w. Luke 16:8*
foolishness of God is *w. 1 Cor 1:25*

wish
I am according to thy *w. Job 33:6**
put to shame that *w.* evil. *Ps 40:14**
more than heart could *w.*   *73:7*
I could *w.* myself accursed. *Rom 9:3*
this also we *w.*, even. *2 Cor 13:9**
I *w.* above all things.   *3 John 2**

wished
Jonah fainted, and *w. Jonah 4:8**
they cast anchor, and *w. Acts 27:29*

wishing
my mouth to sin, by *w. Job 31:30**

wist
(American Revision substitutes the
more modern word knew)
it is manna : for they *w.* not. *Ex 16:15*
Moses *w.* not that his face.   *34:29*
though he *w.* not, yet is he guilty.
   Lev 5:17, 18
but I *w.* not whence.   *Josh 2:4*
w. not that there were liers.   *8:14*
he *w.* not that the Lord. *Judg 16:20*
he *w.* not what to say.   *Mark 9:6*
neither *w.* they what to.   *14:40*
w. ye not I must be about ? *Luke 2:49*
he that was healed *w.* not. *John 5:13*
w. not that it was true.   *Acts 12:9*
said Paul, I *w.* not he was.   *23:5*

witch
not suffer a *w.* to live.   *Ex 22:18**
not be among you a *w. Deut 18:10**

witchcraft
is as the sin of *w.*   *1 Sam 15:23*
Manasseh used *w.* and. *2 Chr 33:6**
the works of the flesh are idolatry,
   w.   *Gal 5:20**

witchcrafts
so long as Jezebel's *w. 2 Ki 9:22*
I will cut off *w.* out of. *Mi 5:12*
w. that selleth nations through her
   . . . through her *w. Nah 3:4*

withal
w. how Elijah had slain. *1 Ki 19:1*
whilst that I *w.* escape. *Ps 141:10*
and not *w.* to signify. *Acts 25:27*

withdraw
priest, *W.* thine hand. *1 Sam 14:19*
will not *w.* his anger. *Job 9:13*
w. thine hand far from me : let. *13:21*
that he may *w.* man from.   *33:17*
w. thy foot from thy neighbour's
   house.   *Pr 25:17**
from this *w.* not thine hand. *Eccl 7:18*
shall thy moon *w.* itself. *Isa 60:20*
the stars shall *w.* their shining.
   Joel 2:10; 3:15
w. yourselves from every brother.
   2 Thes 3:6
corrupt minds *w.* thyself. *1 Tim 6:5*

withdrawest
why *w.* thou thy right ? *Ps 74:11**

withdraweth
he *w.* not his eyes from. *Job 36:7*

withdrawn
have *w.* the inhabitants. *Deut 13:13*
but my beloved had *w. S of S 5:6*
he hath not *w.* his hand. *Lam 2:8*
that hath *w.* his hand. *Ezek 18:8*
the Lord hath *w.* himself. *Hos 5:6*
w. from them about a. *Luke 22:41**

withdrew
they *w.* the shoulder and. *Neh 9:29*
I *w.* mine hand. *Ezek 20:22*
knew it, he *w.* himself. *Mat 12:15*
Jesus *w.* himself from thence.
   Mark 3:7; Luke 5:16

48

---

but when they were come, he *w.*
   *Gal 2:12**

wither
his leaf also shall not *w. Ps 1:3*
and they shall *w.* as the green. *37:2*
reeds and flags shall *w. Isa 19:6*
by the brooks shall *w.*   *7**
upon them, and they shall *w.* 40:24
the herbs of the field *w.? Jer 12:4*
cut off the fruit thereof that it *w.?* it
   shall *w.* in all the. *Ezek 17:9*
utterly *w.?* it shall *w.* in furrows. 10
top of Carmel shall *w. Amos 1:2*

withered
behold seven ears *w.* thin. *Gen 41:23*
my heart is smitten and *w. Ps 102:4*
I am *w.*   *11*
hay is *w.* away, the grass. *Isa 15:6*
thereof are *w.*, be broken off. *27:11*
the Nazarite's skin is *w. Lam 4:8*
her strong rods were *w. Ezek 19:12*
of the field are *w.* joy is so. *Joel 1:12*
broken down, for the corn is *w.*   17
whereupon it rained not *w. Amos 4:7*
the gourd that it *w. Jonah 4:7*
and behold there was a man which
   had his hand *w. Mat 12:10*
   Mark 3:1, 3; Luke 6:6, 8
were scorched, because having no
   root, they *w. Mat 13:6; Mark 4:6*
presently the fig tree *w. Mat 21:19*
   20; *Mark 11:21*
it *w.* away because it. *Luke 8:6*
of *w.* folk, waiting for. *John 5:3*
forth as a branch and is *w.*   15:6

withereth
the flag *w.* before any. *Job 8:12*
it is cut down and *w. Ps 90:6*
as the grass which *w.* before it. *129:6*
the grass *w.*, the flower fadeth.
   Isa 40:7, 8; 1 Pet 1:24
risen, but it *w.* the grass. *Jas 1:11*
trees whose fruit *w.* without fruit.
   *Jude 12**

withheld
for I *w.* thee from sinning. *Gen 20:6*
seeing thou hast not *w.* thy.   *22:12*
who *w.* from thee the fruit ?   *30:2*
if I have *w.* the poor. *Job 31:16*
I *w.* not my heart from. *Eccl 2:10*

withheldest
w. not thy manna from. *Neh 9:20*

withhold
none of us shall *w.* from. *Gen 23:6*
for he will not *w.* me. *2 Sam 13:13*
but who can *w.* himself ? *Job 4:2*
w. not thy tender mercies. *Ps 40:11*
no good thing will he *w.* from. *84:11*
w. not good from them to. *Pr 3:27*
w. not correction from the.   *23:13*
in the evening *w.* not thy. *Eccl 11:6*
w. thy foot from being unshod.
   Jer 2:25

withholden
Lord hath *w.* thee from. *1 Sam 25:26*
thou hast *w.* bread from. *Job 22:7*
from the wicked their light is *w.* 38:15
that no thought can be *w.*   *42:2**
hast not *w.* the request. *Ps 21:2*
showers have been *w. Jer 3:3*
your sins have *w.* good things. *5:25*
hath not *w.* the pledge. *Ezek 18:16**
the drink offering is *w. Joel 1:13*
also I have *w.* the rain. *Amos 4:7*

withholdeth
behold, he *w.* the waters. *Job 12:15*
there is that *w.* more. *Pr 11:24*
he that *w.* corn, the people.   *26*
and now ye know what *w.* that he
   might be revealed. *2 Thes 2:6**

within
none of men was *w. Gen 39:11*
w. a full year he may. *Lev 25:29**
of Simeon was *w.* Judah. *Josh 19:1**
why not recover them *w.* that time ?
   Judg 11:26
thou camest not *w.* the. *1 Sam 13:11*
w. the oracle he made. *1 Ki 6:23*
to the king's house *w.*   *2 Ki 7:11*
whoso would not come *w. Ezra 10:8*
daughter is all glorious *w. Ps 45:13**
will walk *w.* my house with a. *101:2*

---

little city, few men *w.* it. *Eccl 9:14*
shut thyself *w.* thy house. *Ezek 3:24*
any vain vision *w.* Israel.   *12:24*
minister in the gates and *w.*   *44:17*
her princes *w.* are roaring. *Zeph 3:3**
think not to say *w.* yourselves.
   Mat 3:9; Luke 3:8
w. herself, If I but touch. *Mat 9:21*
w. they are full of extortion. *23:25*
cleanse first what is *w.* the cup.   26
are *w.* full of dead men's bones.   27
w. ye are full of hypocrisy.   28
for from *w.* proceed. *Mark 7:21*
all these evil things come from *w.* 23
from *w.* shall answer. *Luke 11:7*
he thought *w.* himself. *12:17 16:3*
   18:4
his disciples were *w. John 20:26*
we found no man *w. Acts 5:23*
judge them that are *w.? 1 Cor 5:12*
fightings, *w.* were fears. *2 Cor 7:5*
full of eyes *w.* : rest not. *Rev 4:8**
a book written *w.* and on the back. *5:1*
see **gates, him, me, thee, them,**
   us, without, you

without
wherefore standest thou *w.?*
   Gen 24:31
the wife of the dead shall not marry
   w. unto a stranger. *Deut 25:5*
appointed eighty men *w. 2 Ki 10:24*
Have her forth *w.* the ranges. *11:15**
I now come up *w.* the Lord against
   this place ?   *18:25; Isa 36:10*
Israel hath been long *w. 2 Chr 15:3*
Jehoram departed *w.*   *21:20*
they that did see me *w. Ps 31:11*
wisdom crieth *w.*; she. *Pr 1:20**
now she is *w.*   *7:12**
there is a lion *w.*   *22:13*
prepare thy work *w.*, and.   *24:27*
valiant ones shall cry *w. Isa 33:7*
be redeemed *w.* money.   *52:3*
milk *w.* money and *w.* price.   *55:1*
cut off the children from *w. Jer 9:21*
w. man, *w.* beast, and *w.* 33:10, 12
w. a king, *w.* a prince, *w.* a sacrifice,
   w. an image, *w.* an ephod, and *w.*
   a teraphim.   *Hos 3:4*
not fall *w.* your father. *Mat 10:29*
to them that are *w.* all. *Mark 4:11*
whatsoever from *w.* entereth.   *7:18*
whole multitude were praying *w.*
   Luke 1:10
to judge them that are *w.? 1 Cor 5:12*
them that are *w.* God judgeth.   13
having no hope, and *w. Eph 2:12*
walk in wisdom toward them that
   are *w. Col 4:5*
walk honestly toward them that are
   w.   *1 Thes 4:12*
report of them that are *w. 1 Tim 3:7*
w. father, *w.* mother, *w. Heb 7:3*
also suffered *w.* the gate.   *13:12*
that they also may *w. 1 Pet 3:1*
w. are dogs and sorcerers. *Rev 22:15*

without, joined with **within**
pitch the ark *within* and *w. Gen 6:14*
overlay the ark *within* and *w.*
   Ex 25:11; 37:2
be bare *within* or *w. Lev 13:55*
the sword *w.* and terror *within.*
   Deut 32:25
written *within* and *w. Ezek 2:10*
is *w.* and famine *within.*   *7:15*
made that which is *w.* make that
   which is *within* also ? *Luke 11:40*
w. were fightings, *within. 2 Cor 7:5*
see **blemish, camp, cause, city,**
   fail, fear, him, knowledge,
   law, me, stand, stood, us. you

withs
(withes)
if they bind me with seven green *w.*
   Judg 16:7
the lords brought *w.*   8
he brake the *w.*   9

withstand
went out to *w.* Balaam. *Num 22:32**
young, could not *w.* them. *2 Chr 13:7*
now ye think to *w.* the kingdom.   8
none is able to *w.* thee.   *20:6*
no man could *w.* the Jews. *Esth 9:2*

prevail, two shall *w.* him. *Eccl* 4:12
arms of the south shall not *w.*, neither
  any strength to *w.*   *Dan* 11:15
I that I could *w.* God ?   *Acts* 11:17
able to *w.* in the evil day. *Eph* 6:13

withstood

they *w.* Uzziah the king. *2 Chr* 26:18
prince of Persia *w.* me. *Dan* 10:13
Elymas the sorcerer *w.*   *Acts* 13:8
at Antioch I *w.* Peter.   *Gal* 2:11*
and Jambres *w.* Moses. *2 Tim* 3:8
hath greatly *w.* our words.   4:15

witness

Since there was little writing
among most of the people in
olden times the evidence of a
transaction was most often given
by some tangible memorial, as in
Gen 21:30; Josh 22:10, or some
significant ceremony.
  Witness in Greek is Martūs, or
Martūr, and signifies one that
gives testimony to the truth at
the expense of his life. It is in this
sense that the word is mainly used
in the New Testament, and our
word martyr has come from this
also.
  The law appoints, that in case of a
capital charge one witness only
was not sufficient, Deut 17:6.
When any one was condemned to
die the witnesses were the first
that began the execution. They
threw the first stone, for example,
if the party was to be stoned,
Deut 17:7. The law condemned
a false witness to the same punishment that he would have subjected
his neighbour to, Deut 19:16, 17,
18, 19. On the whole the law was
very careful to provide evidence in
all cases, and to punish both false
swearing and one who kept back
a part of the truth.
  The disciples who had been
with Jesus, were to be witnesses
for him, Luke 24:48, and when they
chose another apostle in place of
Judas, they thought fit to appoint
one who had been a witness of the
resurrection along with them,
Acts 1:22.
  The apostle Paul, in Rom 8:16
says, that the Spirit itself beareth
witness with our spirit, that we are
the children of God.

they may be a *w.* that I digged this
  well.   *Gen* 21:30
let this covenant be a *w.*   31:44
this heap is a *w.*; this pillar. 48, 52
God is *w.* between me and thee. 50
    1 Thes 2:5
let him bring it for a *w.* *Ex* 22:13
hand to be an unrighteous *w.* 23:1
if a soul sin, and is a *w.*   *Lev* 5:1
be no *w.* against her. *Num* 5:13
one *w.* shall not testify against. 35:30
    Deut 17:6; 19:15
that this song may be a *w.* for me
  against. *Deut* 31:19, 21, 26
the altar is a *w.* between us.
    Josh 22:27, 28, 34
this stone shall be a *w.* to us. 24:27
Lord be *w.* between us. *Judg* 11:10
    Jer 42:5
the Lord is *w.* against you this day.
    1 Sam 12:5
wrinkles, which is a *w.* *Job* 16:8
behold, my *w.* is in heaven, my. 19
when the eye saw me, it gave *w.* to
  me.   29:11
established as a faithful *w.* *Ps* 89:37
a faithful *w.* will not lie, but a false *w.*
    Pr 14:5
a true *w.* delivereth souls, but a deceitful *w.*   25*
an ungodly *w.* scorneth. 19:28
not *w.* against thy neighbour. 24:28
it shall be for a *w.* to the Lord of
  hosts.   *Isa* 19:20
I have given him for a *w.* to. 55:4

I know, and am a *w.*   *Jer* 29:23
Lord be a true and faithful *w.* 42:5
let the Lord God be *w.*   *Mi* 1:2
Lord be *w.* between thee. *Mal* 2:14
I will be a swift *w.* against the. 3:5
be preached for a *w.* to. *Mat* 24:14*
the council sought for *w. Mark* 14:55
w. agreed not together. 56, 59
need we further *w.?* *Luke* 22:71
for a *w.* to bear *w.*   *John* 1:7
and ye receive not our *w.* 3:11
to whom thou bearest *w.* 26
if I bear *w.* of myself, my *w.* 5:31
I know the *w.* he witnesseth of. 32
but I have greater *w.* than. 36
sent me hath borne *w.* of me. 37
ordained to be a *w.* with us. *Acts* 1:22
gave *w.* of the resurrection. 4:33
to him give all the prophets *w.* 10:43
he left not himself without *w.* 14:17
for thou shalt be his *w.* to all. 22:15
a minister and a *w.* of these. 26:16
God is my *w.* whom I serve. *Rom* 1:9
conscience also bearing *w.* 2:15; 9:1
this *w.* is true. Rebuke. *Tit* 1:13*
God also bearing them *w.* *Heb* 2:4
the Holy Ghost is a *w.* to us. 10:15
by which Abel obtained *w.* 11:4
shall be *w.* against you. *Jas* 5:3*
Peter a *w.* of the sufferings of Christ.
    1 Pet 5:1
w. of men, the *w.* of God is greater,
  for this is the *w.* of. *1 John* 5:9
he that believeth hath the *w.* 10
borne *w.* of thy charity. *3 John* 6
who is the faithful *w.*   *Rev* 1:5
these things saith the true *w.* 3:14
were beheaded for the *w.* 20:4*
see **bare, bear, beareth, false,
tabernacle**

witness, *verb*

I call heaven and earth to *w.* against.
    Deut 4:26
behold, here I am, *w.* *1 Sam* 12:3
their countenance doth *w.* *Isa* 3:9
I take *w.* for thee ? *Lam* 2:13*
what is it which these *w.* against ?
    Mat 26:62; *Mark* 14:60
thou not how many things they *w.*
  against ? *Mat* 27:13; *Mark* 15:4*

witnessed

the men of Belial *w.* against Naboth.
    1 Ki 21:13
being *w.* by the law and. *Rom* 3:21
who before Pontius Pilate *w.* a good
  confession. *1 Tim* 6:13
it is *w.* that he liveth. *Heb* 7:8

witnesses

to death by mouth of *w. Num* 35:30
at the mouth of two or three *w.*
  Deut 17:6; 19:15; *2 Cor* 13:1
the hands of the *w.* shall be first upon
  him.   *Deut* 17:7
are *w.* against yourselves that ye
  . . . We are *w.* *Josh* 24:22
ye are *w.* that I have bought.
    Ruth 4:9, 10
and the elders said, We are *w.* 11
thou renewest thy *w.* *Job* 10:17
I took to me faithful *w.* *Isa* 8:2
nations bring forth their *w.* 43:9
ye are my *w.* saith the Lord. 10, 12
    44:8
they are their own *w.*; they see. 44:9
evidence and took *w. Jer* 32:10, 12
field for money, and take *w.* 25, 44
mouth of two or three *w. Mat* 18:16
be *w.* to yourselves that ye. 23:31
what further need of *w.?* 26:65
    Mark 14:63
and ye are *w.* of these. *Luke* 24:48
ye shall be *w.* to me in. *Acts* 1:8
this Jesus hath God raised up,
  whereof we all are *w.* 2:32; 3:15
we are his *w.* of these things. 5:32
    10:39
w. laid down their clothes at. 7:58
but unto *w.* chosen before of. 10:41
his *w.* unto the people. 13:31
ye are *w.* and God also. *1 Thes* 2:10
receive no accusation but before two
  or three. *1 Tim* 5:19
good profession before many *w.* 6:12

things heard of me among many *w.*
    2 Tim 2:2
died without mercy under two or
  three *w.*   *Heb* 10:28
with so great a cloud of *w.* 12:1
give power to my two *w.* *Rev* 11:3
  see **false**

witnesseth

the witness that he *w.* *John* 5:32
save that Holy Ghost *w. Acts* 20:23*

witnessing

w. both to small and. *Acts* 26:22*

wits'

and are at their *w.* end. *Ps* 107:27

wittingly

guided his hands *w.* for. *Gen* 48:14

witty

I find out knowledge of *w.* inventions.
    Pr 8:12*

wives

took unto him two *w.* *Gen* 4:19
they took them *w.* of all which. 6:2
give me my *w.* and children. 30:26
if thou take other *w.* besides. 31:50
that our *w.* and children. *Num* 14:3
nor shall he multiply *w. Deut* 17:17
if a man have two *w.*, one. 21:15
sons: for he had many *w. Judg* 8:30
how shall we do for *w.?* 21:7, 16
we may not give them *w.* of. 18
Elkanah. He had two *w.*; Hannah
  and Peninnah. *1 Sam* 1:2
also both of them David's *w.* 25:43
David took more *w.* out. *2 Sam* 5:13
I gave thee thy master's *w.* 12:8
Solomon had 700 *w.* *1 Ki* 11:3
his *w.* turned away his heart. 4
he sent unto me for my *w.* 20:7
Ashur had two *w.* *1 Chr* 4:5
the sons of Uzzi had many *w.* 7:4
Shaharaim had two *w.* 8:8
Rehoboam loved Maachah above all
  his *w.*   *2 Chr* 11:21
and he desired many *w.* 23
Jehoiada took for him two *w.* 24:3
and our *w.* are in captivity for. 29:9
to put away all the *w. Ezra* 10:3, 44
the *w.* also and children. *Neh* 12:43*
I saw Jews that had married *w.*13:23
the *w.* shall give to husbands honour.
    Esth 1:20
take ye *w.*, and take *w.* *Jer* 29:6
wine, we, nor our *w.* nor sons. 35:8
his *w.* and concubines. *Dan* 5:2, 3
drank, they married *w.* *Luke* 17:27
us on our way, with *w.* *Acts* 21:5
they that have *w.* be as though they
  had none. *1 Cor* 7:29
w. submit yourselves to. *Eph* 5:22
    Col 3:18; *1 Pet* 3:1
so let the *w.* be to their. *Eph* 5:24
refuse profane and old *w.' 1 Tim* 4:7
by the conversation of the. *1 Pet* 3:1
  see **strange**

their wives

little ones, and *their w.* took they.
    Gen 34:29; *1 Sam* 30:3
they took their daughters to be *their
w.*   *Judg* 3:6
all Judah with *their w.* *2 Chr* 20:13
would put away *their w. Ezra* 10:19
a great cry of the people and of *their
w.*   *Neh* 5:1
their w. and daughters entered into
  an oath. 10:28
and *their w.* ravished. *Isa* 13:16
houses shall be turned to others, with
  their fields and *w. Jer* 6:12; 8:10
have none to bury *their w.* 14:16
let *their w.* be bereaved of. 18:21
the wickedness of *their w.* 44:9
men who knew *their w.* had. 15
nor take for *their w.* a. *Ezek* 44:22
cast them and *their w.* *Dan* 6:24
their w. shall mourn apart.
    Zech 12:12, 13, 14
to love *their w.* as their. *Eph* 5:28
even so must *their w.* be grave,
  sober.   *1 Tim* 3:11*

thy wives

I will take *thy w.* before thine eyes,
  . . . lie with *thy w. 2 Sam* 12:11

saved the lives of *thy w.* 2 Sam 19:5
gold is mine, and *thy w.* 1 Ki 20:3
deliver me *thy w.* and children. 5
Lord will smite thy people and *thy*
w. 2 Chr 21:14
bring *thy w.* and children. Jer 38:23
thy w. and concubines. Dan 5:23

your wives
take waggons for *your w.* Gen 45:19
come not at *your w.* Ex 19:15*
your w. shall be widows. 22:24
golden earrings of *your w.* 32:2
your w. and your little ones and your
cattle. Deut 3:19; Josh 1:14
your w.: shouldest enter into covenant with the Lord. Deut 29:11
fight for *your w.* and. Neh 4:14
wickedness of *your w.* Jer 44:9
Lord, saying; Ye and *your w.* 25
you to put away *your w.* Mat 19:8
husbands, love *your w.* Eph 5:25
Col 3:19

wizard
a *w.* shall surely be put. Lev 20:27
be found among you a *w.* Deut 18:11

wizards
nor seek after *w.* to be. Lev 19:31
the soul that turneth after *w.* 20:6
Saul had put *w.* out of the land.
1 Sam 28:3, 9
Manasseh dealt with *w.* 2 Ki 21:6
2 Chr 33:6
Josiah put the *w.* and. 2 Ki 23:24
Seek unto *w.* that peep. Isa 8:19
shall seek to idols and *w.* 19:3

woe
w. to thee, Moab ! Num 21:29
Jer 48:46
w. unto us, for there hath. 1 Sam 4:7
8; Jer 4:13; 6:4; Lam 5:16
who hath *w.*? who hath ? Pr 23:29
w. to him that is alone. Eccl 4:10
w. to thee, O land, when. 10:16
w. to their soul, for they. Isa 3:9
w. unto the wicked ! it shall be. 11
w. to the multitude of. 17:12
w. to the land shadowing. 18:1
w. to the crown of pride, to. 28:1
w. to Ariel. 29:1
w. to the rebellious children. 30:1
w. to thee that spoilest. 33:1
w. to him that striveth with. 45:9
w. to him that saith to fatherless. 10
w. unto thee, O Jerusalem. Jer 13:27
w. to him that buildeth by. 22:13
w. to the pastors that destroy. 23:1
w. to Nebo. 48:1
written, mourning and *w.* Ezek 2:10
w. to foolish prophets, that. 13:3
w. to women that sew pillows. 18
w. w. to thee. 16:23
w. to bloody city. 24:6, 9; Nah 3:1
Howl, *W.* worth the day! Ezek 30:2
w. be to the shepherds that. 34:2
w. to you that desire the. Amos 5:18
w. to him that increaseth. Hab 2:6
w. to him that coveteth an evil. 9
w. to him that buildeth a town. 12
w. to him that giveth his. 15
w. to him that saith to the wood. 19
w. to the inhabitants of. Zeph 2:5
w. to her that is filthy. 3:1
w. to the idol shepherd. Zech 11:17
w. unto thee, Chorazin ! *w.* unto thee.
Mat 11:21; Luke 10:13
w. unto the world because of
offences, *w.* Mat 18:7; Luke 17:1
w. unto you scribes and. Mat 23:13
14, 15 23, 25, 27, 29; Luke 11:44
w. unto you, ye blind guides, which
say. Mat 23:16
but *w.* unto that man by. 26:24
Mark 14:21; Luke 22:22
w. unto you that are rich. Luke 6:24
w. to you that are full, *w.* to you. 25
w. unto you when all men speak. 26
but *w.* unto you Pharisees. 11:42, 43
he said, *W.* to you also. 46, 47, 52
I heard an angel flying, saying, *W. w.*
w. Rev 8:13; 12:12
one *w.* is past. 9:12
the second *w.* is past. 11:14

---

woe is me
w. is me, that I sojourn. Ps 120:5
w. is me! for I am undone. Isa 6:5
w. is me now, for my soul. Jer 4:31
w. is me for my hurt. 10:19
w. is me, my mother. 15:10
w. is me, for the Lord hath. 45:3
w. is me! for I am as when. Mi 7:1

woe unto me
if I be wicked, *w. unto me.* Job 10:15
My leanness, *w. unto me.* Isa 24:16
w. unto me if I preach. 1 Cor 9:16

woe to them
w. to them that join house to house.
Isa 5:8
w. to them that rise up early in. 11
w. to them that draw iniquity. 18
w. to them that call evil good. 20
w. to them that are wise in their. 21
w. to them that are mighty to. 22
w. to them that decree. 10:1
w. to them that seek deep to. 29:15
w. to them that go down into. 31:1
w. to them, for their day. Jer 50:27
w. to them, for they have. Hos 7:13
w. to them when I depart from. 9:12
w. to them that are at. Amos 6:1
w. to them that devise. Mi 2:1
w. to them which are with child, and
to them that give. Mat 24:19
Mark 13:17; Luke 21:23
w. unto them! for they have gone in
the way of Cain. Jude 11

woeful
neither I desired the *w.* day.
Jer 17:16

woes
behold, there come two *w.* Rev 9:12

wolf
In a country where a large part
of wealth consisted of flocks of
sheep the habits of wolves became
thoroughly well known, and were
often used as symbols of such
habits and actions of mankind as
might bear a resemblance to them,
as Gen 49:27.
Isaiah describing the tranquillity of
the reign of the Messiah, says, The
wolf shall dwell with the lamb, and
the leopard shall lie down with the
kid, *etc.,* Isa 11:6. *Persecutors are*
elsewhere compared to wolves,
Mat 10:16, Behold, I send you
forth as sheep in the midst of
wolves.
shall ravin as a *w.* Gen 49:27
the *w.* shall dwell with. Isa 11:6
the *w.* and the lamb shall. 65:25
a *w.* of the evenings shall. Jer 5:6
but he that is an hireling, seeth the
w. coming: and the *w.* John 10:12

wolves
her princes are like *w.* Ezek 22:27
fiercer than evening *w.* Hab 1:8
her judges evening *w.* Zeph 3:3
they are ravening *w.* Mat 7:15
as sheep in the midst of *w.* 10:16
as lambs among *w.* Luke 10:3
grievous *w.* shall enter in. Acts 20:29

woman
Woman *was created to be a com-*
panion and helper to man. She
was equal to him in that authority
and jurisdiction that God gave
them over all other animals. But
after the fall, God made her subject
to the government of man, Gen
3:16.
Weak and ineffectual men are
sometimes spoken of as women,
Isa 3:12; 19:16.
and the rib, taken from man, made
he a *w.* Gen 2:22
she shall be called *W.,* she was. 23
between thee and the *w.* 3:15
the *w.* will not come. 24:5, 39
let the same be the *w.* the Lord. 44
and hurt a *w.* with child. Ex 21:22
nor shall a *w.* stand. Lev 18:23
with mankind as with a *w.* 20:13*

---

he shall set the *w.* Num 5:18, 30
the *w.* shall be a curse among. 27
brought a Midianitish *w.* in. 25:6
Phinehas thrust the *w.* through. 8
if a *w.* vow a vow unto the Lord. 30:3
now kill every *w.* that hath. 31:17
I took this *w.* and found. Deut 22:14
the *w.* took the two men. Josh 2:4
bring out thence the *w.* 6:22
Sisera into the hand of a *w.* Judg 4:9
a certain *w.* cast a piece of a millstone. 9:53; 2 Sam 11:21
men say not of me, a *w.* Judg 9:54
man that spakest to the *w.*? 13:11
is there never a *w.* among ? 14:3
Samson loved a *w.* in the. 16:4
the *w.* in the dawning of the. 19:26
the *w.* was left of her sons. Ruth 1:5
know thou art a virtuous *w.* 3:11
w. like Rachel and Leah. 4:11
Hannah said, I am a *w.* of a sorrowful
spirit. 1 Sam 1:15
I am the *w.* that stood by thee. 26
Lord give thee seed of this *w.* 2:20
seek me a *w.* that hath a. 28:7
me concerning this *w.* 2 Sam 3:8
from the roof David saw a *w.* 11:2
put now this *w.* out from me. 13:17
the *w.* spread a covering over. 17:19
then *w.* went unto all people. 20:22
I and this *w.* dwell in. 1 Ki 3:17
herself to be another *w.* 14:5
the son of the *w.* fell sick. 17:17
where was a great *w.* 2 Ki 4:8
there cried a *w.* saying, Help. 6:26
this is the *w.* 8:5
see this cursed *w.* 9:34
Athaliah that wicked *w.* 2 Chr 24:7
if my heart have been deceived by a
w. Job 31:9
pain as of a *w.* in travail. Ps 48:6
Isa 13:8; 21:3; 26:17; Jer 4:31
6:24; 13:21; 22:23; 30:6; 31:8
48:41; 49:22, 24; 50:43
thee from the evil *w.* Pr 6:24
met him a *w.* subtile of heart. 7:10
a foolish *w.* is clamorous. 9:13
a virtuous *w.* is a crown. 12:4; 31:10
every wise *w.* buildeth her. 14:1
than with a brawling *w.* in. 21:9, 19
who can find a virtuous *w.*? 31:10
a *w.* that feareth the Lord shall. 30
the *w.* whose heart is snares and
nets. Eccl 7:26
but a *w.* among all those have I. 28
cry like a travailing *w.* Isa 42:14
or to the *w.,* What hast thou ? 45:10
can a *w.* forget her sucking ? 49:15
Lord hath called thee as a *w.* 54:6*
of Zion to a delicate *w.* Jer 6:2
created a new thing, a *w.* 31:22
Jerusalem is a menstruous *w.*
Lam 1:17
imperious whorish *w.* Ezek 16:30
unto her, as they go in to a *w.* 23:44
uncleanness of a removed *w.* 36:17
go yet, love a *w.* beloved. Hos 3:1
the sorrows of a travailing *w.* shall
come upon. 13:13; Mi 4:9, 10
this is a *w.* that sitteth in. Zech 5:7
whoso looketh on a *w.* to lust after
her. Mat 5:28
a *w.* which was diseased with an
issue. 9:20; Mark 5:25; Luke 8:43
leaven, which a *w.* took. Mat 13:33
O *w.,* great is thy faith, be it. 15:28
and last of all the *w.* died also. 22:27
Mark 12:22; Luke 20:32
Why trouble ye the *w.*? Mat 26:10
this that this *w.* hath done shall. 13
if a *w.* shall put away. Mark 10:12
manner of *w.* this is ? Luke 7:39
Simon, Seest thou this *w.*? 44
ought not this *w.,* being a daughter of
Abraham ? 13:16
w. what have I to do with thee ?
John 2:4
askest drink of me who am a *w.*? 4:9
on him for the saying of the *w.* 39
brought to him a *w.* taken in. 8:3, 4
when Jesus saw none but the *w.* 10
he saith to his mother, *W.* 19:26
Dorcas: this *w.* was full. Acts 9:36
and a *w.* named Damaris. 17:34

the natural use of the *w. Rom* 1:27
the *w.* which hath an husband is. 7:2
for a man not to touch a *w. I Cor* 7:1
every *w.* have her own husband. 2
but every *w.* that prayeth. 11:5
if the *w.* be not covered, let her. 6
the *w.* is the glory of the man. 7
man is not of the *w.*; but the *w.* 8
neither man for the *w.*; but the *w.* 9
the *w.* ought to have power on. 10
nevertheless, neither is the man
without the *w.*, nor the *w.* 11
as the *w.* is of the man, even so is the
man also by the *w.* 12
comely that a *w.* pray uncovered? 13
if a *w.* have long hair, it is a glory. 15
forth his Son, made of a *w. Gal* 4:4
then destruction cometh as travail on
a *w.* 1 *Thes* 5:3
I suffer not a *w.* to teach. 1 *Tim* 2:12
the *w.* being deceived, was in the. 14
sufferest that *w.* Jezebel. *Rev* 2:20
there appeared *w.* clothed with. 12:1
the *w.* fled. 6
the earth helped the *w.* 16
dragon was wroth with the *w.* 17
I saw a *w.* sit on a scarlet. 17:3
a *w.* drunken. 6
I will tell the mystery of the *w.* 7
see **born, man, strange**

young **woman**

the seed which Lord shall give thee
of this *young w. Ruth* 4:12

womankind

with mankind as with *w. Lev* 18:22

womb

two nations are in thy *w. Gen* 25:23
there were twins in her *w.* 24; 38:27
Lord opened Leah's *w.* 29:31
God opened Rachel's *w.* 30:22
of breasts, and of *w.* 49:25
openeth the *w.* is mine. *Ex* 13:2
are given me, instead of such as
open every *w.*, even. *Num* 8:16
bless the fruit of thy *w. Deut* 7:13
Nazarite from the *w. Judg* 13:5, 7
any more sons in my *w.? Ruth* 1:11
had shut up her *w.* 1 *Sam* 1:5, 6
why died I not from the *w.? Job* 3:11
brought me forth of the *w.?* 10:18
the *w.* shall forget him, he. 24:20
that made me in the *w.* make him?
fashion us in the *w.?* 31:15
if it had issued out of the *w.* 38:8
out of whose *w.* came the ice? 29
who took me out of the *w. Ps* 22:9
I was cast upon thee from the *w.* 10
are estranged from the *w.* 58:3
I been holden up from the *w.* 71:6
from the *w.* of the morning. 110:3
the barren *w.* saith not, It. *Pr* 30:16
what, the son of my *w.?* 31:2
nor how bones grow in *w. Eccl* 11:5
Lord formed thee from the *w.*

Isa 44:2, 24; 49:5
which are carried from the *w.* 46:3
a transgressor from the *w.* 48:8
called me from the *w.* 49:1
compassion on the son of her *w.?* 15
bring forth, and shut the *w.?* 66:9
camest forth out of the *w. Jer* 1:5
because he slew me not from the *w.*;
or my mother's *w.* to be. 20:17
why came I forth of the *w.?* 18
pass through the fire all that openeth
the *w. Ezek* 20:26
their glory shall fly away from the
birth and *w. Hos* 9:11*
give them a miscarrying *w.* 14
brother by the heel in the *w.* 12:3
shalt conceive in thy *w. Luke* 1:31
leaped in her *w.* for joy. 41, 44
he was conceived in the *w.* 2:21
every male that openeth the *w.* 23

see **fruit, mother**

wombs

fast closed up all the *w. Gen* 20:18
blessed are the *w.* that. *Luke* 23:29

women

the time that *w.* go out to. *Gen* 24:11
all the *w.* went out after. *Ex* 15:20
w. that were wise hearted. 35:25
all the *w.* whose heart stirred. 26

ten *w.* shall bake your bread in one
oven. *Lev* 26:26
Moses said, Have ye saved all the
w. alive? *Num* 31:15
the *w.* and little ones. *Deut* 20:14
the law before the *w. Josh* 8:35
blessed above *w.* shall Jael wife of.
Judg 5:24
they saved alive of the *w.* of. 21:14
they lay with the *w.* 1 *Sam* 2:22
as thy sword hath made *w.* 15:33
the *w.* came out of the cities. 18:6
the *w.* answered one another as. 7
kept themselves from *w.* 21:4
of a truth *w.* have been kept. 5
Amalekites had taken the *w.* 30:2
passing the love of *w.* 2 *Sam* 1:26
the king left ten *w.* to keep. 15:16
then came two *w.* that. 1 *Ki* 3:16
and rip up their *w.* with child.
2 *Ki* 8:12, 15, 16
where the *w.* wove hangings. 23:7
even him did outlandish *w.* cause to
sin. *Neh* 13:26
made a feast for the *w. Esth* 1:9
loved Esther above all the *w.* 2:17
little children and *w.* 3:13; 8:11
no *w.* found so fair as. *Job* 42:15
among the honourable *w. Ps* 45:9
give not thy strength to *w. Pr* 31:3
O thou fairest among *w. S of S* 1:8
5:9; 6:1
as for my people, *w.* rule. *Isa* 3:12
in that day seven *w.* shall take. 4:1
day Egypt shall be like to *w.* 19:16
the *w.* come, and set them. 27:11
rise up, ye *w.* that are at ease. 32:9
careless *w.* 10
tremble, ye *w.* that are at ease. 11
the *w.* knead their dough. *Jer* 7:18
mourning and cunning *w.* 9:17
word of the Lord, O ye *w.* 20
w. left, shall be brought to. 38:22
Jeremiah said to all the *w.* 44:24
they shall become as *w.* and. 50:37
men of Babylon became as *w.* 51:30
shall the *w.* eat children? *Lam* 2:20
the pitiful *w.* have sodden. 4:10
they ravished *w.* in Zion, and. 5:11
there sat *w.* weeping. *Ezek* 8:14
maids, little children, and *w.* 9:6
woe to *w.* that sew pillows to. 13:18
is in thee from other *w.* 16:34
I will judge these as *w.* that. 38
there were two *w.*, daughters. 23:2
judge after the manner of *w.* 45
w. may be taught not to do after. 48
he shall give him the daughter of *w.*
Dan 11:17
nor shall regard the desire of *w.* 37
their *w.* with child shall. *Hos* 13:16
because they have ripped up *w.* with
child. *Amos* 1:13
the *w.* of my people have. *Mi* 2:9
in the midst of thee are *w. Nah* 3:13
two *w.* and had wings. *Zech* 5:9
old *w.* shall dwell in the streets. 8:4
the houses rifled, the *w.* shall. 14:2
that are born of *w.* there hath not risen
a greater. *Mat* 11:11; *Luke* 7:28
they that had eaten were 5000 men,
besides *w. Mat* 14:21; 15:38
two *w.* grinding at the mill. 24:41
Luke 17:35
and many *w.* were then. *Mat* 27:55
blessed art thou among *w.*
Luke 1:28, 42
certain *w.* also made us. 24:22
and found it even so as the *w.* 24
in prayer with the *w. Acts* 1:14
stirred up the devout *w.* 13:50
we spake to the *w.* which. 16:13
of the chief *w.* not a few. 17:4, 12
their *w.* did change the. *Rom* 1:26
let your *w.* keep silence. 1 *Cor* 14:34
shame for *w.* to speak in churches. 35
help those *w.* which laboured with
me. *Phil* 4:3
w. adorn themselves in. 1 *Tim* 2:9
which becometh *w.* professing. 10
let the *w.* learn in silence with. 11
intreat the elder *w.* as mothers. 5:2
that the younger *w.* marry. 14*
captive silly *w.* laden. 2 *Tim* 3:6

aged *w.* behave as becometh. *Tit* 2:3
they may teach the younger *w.* 4
w. received their dead. *Heb* 11:35
the holy *w.* adorned. 1 *Pet* 3:5
they had hair as hair of *w. Rev* 9:8
that are not defiled with *w.* 14:4
see **children, men, singing,
strange**

womenservants

gave *w.* to Abraham. *Gen* 20:14
had menservants and *w.* 32:5*

won

out of the spoils *w.* in. 1 *Chr* 26:27
a brother offended is harder to be *w.*
5
w. by the conversation. 1 *Pet* 3:1*

wonder

give thee a sign or a *w. Deut* 13:1
and the sign or the *w.* come. 2
upon thee for a sign and a *w.* 28:46
him to enquire of the *w.* 2 *Chr* 32:31
I am as a *w.* to many. *Ps* 71:7
walked barefoot for a *w. Isa* 20:3
marvellous work and a *w.* 29:14
they were filled with *w. Acts* 3:10
a great *w.* in heaven. *Rev* 12:1*, 3*

wonder, *verb*

stay yourselves, and *w.*; cry. *Isa* 29:9
the prophets shall *w.* *Jer* 4:9
behold ye, regard and *w. Hab* 1:5
behold, ye despisers, *w. Acts* 13:41
dwell on the earth shall *w. Rev* 17:8

wondered

he *w.* there was no. *Isa* 59:16
I *w.* that there was none. 63:5
for they are men *w.* at. *Zech* 3:8*
all they that heard it *w. Luke* 2:18
they all *w.* at the gracious. 4:22
believed not for joy, and *w.* 24:41
Moses *w.* *Acts* 7:31
Simon [Magus] *w.* 8:13*
all the world *w.* after. *Rev* 13:3
I saw her, I *w.* with great. 17:6

wonderful

make thy plagues *w. Deut* 28:59
thy love to me was *w.* 2 *Sam* 1:26
house . . . shall be *w.* great. 2 *Chr* 2:9
things too *w.* for me. *Job* 42:3
thy testimonies are *w. Ps* 119:129
knowledge is too *w.* for me. 139:6
there be three things that are too *w.*
Pr 30:18
his name shall be called W. *Isa* 9:6
for thou hast done *w.* things. 25:1
of hosts who is *w.* in counsel. 28:29
a *w.* thing is committed. *Jer* 5:30
when they saw the *w.* *Mat* 21:15

see **works**

wonderfully

when he had wrought *w.* 1 *Sam* 6:6
thee for I am *w.* made. *Ps* 139:14
Jerusalem came down *w. Lam* 1:9
he shall destroy *w.* and. *Dan* 8:24

wondering

the man *w.* at her, held. *Gen* 24:21*
Peter *w.* at that which was come to
pass. *Luke* 24:12
ran together greatly *w. Acts* 3:11

wonderously, wondrously

angel did *w.*: Manoah. *Judg* 13:19*
the Lord hath dealt *w. Joel* 2:26

wonders

my hand and smite Egypt with all my
w. *Ex* 3:20; 7:3; 11:9
Deut 6:22; 7:19; 26:8; 34:11
see thou do those *w.* *Ex* 4:21
did these *w.* 11:10
fearful in praises, doing *w.?* 15:11
hath God assayed to go and take a
nation by *w.?* *Deut* 4:34
to-morrow the Lord will do *w.*
among you. *Josh* 3:5
remember his *w.* 1 *Chr* 16:12
Ps 105:5
thou shewedst *w.* upon. *Neh* 9:10
nor were mindful of thy *w.* 17
Ps 78:11, 43
doeth *w.* without number. *Job* 9:10
remember thy *w.* of old. *Ps* 77:11
thou art the God that doest *w.* 14
shew *w.* to the dead? 88:10

shall thy *w*. be known in the? *Ps* 88:12
shall praise thy *w*. O Lord. 89:5
his *w*. among all people. 96:3*
they shewed his *w*. in the. 105:27
our fathers understood not thy *w*. in
Egypt. 106:7
see his works and his *w*. 107:24
who sent *w*. into the midst of. 135:9
who alone doeth great *w*. 136:4
I and the children are for *w*. in
Israel. *Isa* 8:18
who hath set signs and *w*. *Jer* 32:20
brought forth thy people with *w*. 21
to shew the signs and *w*. *Dan* 4:2
signs! how mighty his *w*.! 3
he worketh *w*. in heaven. 6:27
it be to the end of these *w*.? 12:6
I will shew *w*. in heaven. *Joel* 2:30
Acts 2:19
false prophets, and shall shew great
w. *Mat* 24:24; *Mark* 13:22
Except ye see signs and *w*. *John* 4:48
approved of God by *w*. *Acts* 2:22
fear on every soul, many signs and *w*.
were. 43; 5:12; 14:3; 15:12
that *w*. may be done by the. 4:30
Stephen did great *w*. among. 6:8
after he had shewed *w*. in the land of
Egypt. 7:36
obedient through *w*. *Rom* 15:19
an apostle wrought in *w*. *2 Cor* 12:12
is with signs and lying *w*. *2 Thes* 2:9
witness with signs and *w*. *Heb* 2:4
he doeth great *w*., so that he maketh
fire come down. *Rev* 13:13*

wondrous

sing psalms, talk ye of all his *w*.
1 Chr 16:9; *Ps* 26:7; 105:2
119:27; 145:5
consider the *w*. works. *Job* 37:14
dost thou know the *w*. works ? 16
I declared thy *w*. works. *Ps* 71:17
the God of Israel, who only doeth *w*.
things. 72:18; 86:10
that thy name is near, thy *w*. 75:1
they believed not for his *w*. 78:32
who had done *w*. works in. 106:22
that I may behold *w*. things. 119:18
according to his *w*. works. *Jer* 21:2

wont

if the ox were *w*. to push. *Ex* 21:29
was I ever *w*. to do so to thee ?
Num 22:30
where David and his men were *w*. to
haunt. *1 Sam* 30:31
were *w*. to speak in. *2 Sam* 20:18
seven times more than *w*. *Dan* 3:19
the governor was *w*. to. *Mat* 27:15
as he was *w*., he taught. *Mark* 10:1
he went as he was *w*. to. *Luke* 22:39*
where prayer was *w*. to. *Acts* 16:13

wood

Abraham took *w*. and put. *Gen* 22:6
Behold the fire and the *w*. 7
whether there be *w*. *Num* 13:20
things that are made of *w*. 31:20
make thee an ark of *w*. *Deut* 10:1
goeth into a *w*. to hew *w*. 19:5*
from the hewer of thy *w*. 29:11
Josh 9:21, 23, 27; *Jer* 46:22
the mountain is a *w*. *Josh* 17:18*
and they clave the *w*. *1 Sam* 6:14
they of the land came to a *w*. 14:25
went to David into the *w*. 23:16
the *w*. devoured more. *2 Sam* 18:8*
lay the bullock on *w*. *1 Ki* 18:23
she bears out of the *w*. *2 Ki* 2:24
I have prepared *w*. for things of.
1 Chr 29:2
the boar out of the *w*. *Ps* 80:13
it in the fields of the *w*. 132:6
as when one cleaveth *w*. 141:7
where no *w*. is, there the. *Pr* 26:20
as *w*. to fire, so is a contentious. 21
he that cleaveth *w*. shall. *Eccl* 10:9
itself as if it were no *w*. *Isa* 10:15
thereof is fire and much *w*. 30:33
they that set up the *w*. of. 45:20
will bring silver, for *w*. brass. 60:17
I will make my words fire, this
people *w*. *Jer* 5:14
the children gather *w*., the. 7:18
the yokes of *w*. but shalt. 28:13

shall *w*. be taken thereof to do any
work ? *Ezek* 15:3
heap on *w*. 24:10
no *w*. out of the field. 39:10
dwell solitary in the *w*. *Mi* 7:14*
that saith to the *w*. Awake. *Hab* 2:19
go up, bring *w*. and build. *Hag* 1:8
hearth of fire among the *w*. *Zech* 12:6
on this foundation, *w*., hay. *1 Cor* 3:12
but also vessels of *w*. *2 Tim* 2:20

see **offering**, **stone**

woods

sleep safely in the *w*. *Ezek* 34:25

woof

be in the warp or *w*. *Lev* 13:48
be spread in the warp or the *w*. 51
whether warp or *w*. 52
be not spread, wash the *w*. 53, 58
rend it out of the warp or *w*. 56
of leprosy in the warp or *w*. 59

wool

I will put a fleece of *w*. *Judg* 6:37
100,000 rams with *w*. *2 Ki* 3:4
giveth snow like *w*. *Ps* 147:16
she seeketh *w*. and flax. *Pr* 31:13
like crimson, shall be as *w*. *Isa* 1:18
like *w*.: but my righteousness. 51:8
was thy merchant in *w*. *Ezek* 27:18
ye clothe you with the *w*. 34:3
and no *w*. shall come upon. 44:17
the hair of his head like *w*. *Dan* 7:9
Rev 1:14
lovers that give me my *w*. *Hos* 2:5
I will recover my *w*. and my flax. 9

woollen

whether *w*. or linen. *Lev* 13:47, 59
the warp or woof of *w*. 48, 52
mingled of linen and *w*. come upon
thee. 19:19*; *Deut* 22:11

word

(Word, *the Greek* logos, *is sometimes used of Jesus Christ*, John 1.
The word of God *is a name often
given to the scriptures, and the law
of God*)
go and bring me *w*. again. *Gen* 37:14
Mat 2:8
O my lord, let me speak a *w*.
Gen 44:18; *2 Sam* 14:12
according to *w*. of Moses. *Ex* 8:13
Israel did according to the *w*. 12:35
Levi did according to the *w*. 32:28
Lev 10:7
they brought back *w*. *Num* 13:26
lodge here, I will bring you *w*. 22:8
Deut 1:22
yet the *w*. I shall say to. *Num* 22:20
the *w*. I shall speak. 35
the *w*. God putteth. 38
the Lord put a *w*. in Balaam's. 23:5
they brought us *w*. again. *Deut* 1:25
ye shall not add unto the *w*. I. 4:2
but by every *w*. that proceedeth out.
8:3*; *Mat* 4:4
presume to speak a *w*. *Deut* 18:20
how shall we know the *w*.? 21
Jer 28:9
by their *w*. shall every controversy be
tried. *Deut* 21:5
the *w*. is nigh thee. 30:14; *Rom* 10:8
remember the *w*. Moses. *Josh* 1:13
not a *w*. which Joshua read not. 8:35
I brought him *w*. 14:7
brought them *w*. 22:32
the *w*. of Samuel came. *1 Sam* 4:1
not answer Abner a *w*. *2 Sam* 3:11
in all places spake I a *w*. *1 Chr* 17:6
the *w*. thou hast spoken concerning
thy servant. *2 Sam* 7:25
till there come *w*. from you. 15:28
speak ye not a *w*. of bringing. 19:10
the king's *w*. prevailed. 24:4
1 Chr 21:4
brought the king *w*. again. *1 Ki* 2:30
2 Ki 22:9, 20; *2 Chr* 34:16, 28
w. that I have heard is good.
1 Ki 2:42*
hath not failed one *w*. of all. 8:56
the people answered not a *w*. 18:21
Isa 36:21

he smote according to the *w*. of
Elisha. *2 Ki* 6:18
hear the *w*. of the great king. 18:28
mindful of the *w*. which he commanded. *1 Chr* 16:15; *Ps* 105:8
advise what *w*. I shall. *1 Chr* 21:12*
remember, the *w*. that thou. *Neh* 1:8
he did according to the *w*. *Esth* 1:21
as the *w*. went out of the king's. 7:8
none spake a *w*. to Job. *Job* 2:13
by the *w*. of thy lips, I have. *Ps* 17:4
the Lord gave the *w*. 68:11
remember the *w*. unto thy. 119:49
mine eyes fail for the *w*. of thy. 123
not a *w*. in my tongue. 139:4
a good *w*. maketh the. *Pr* 12:25
whoso despiseth the *w*. shall. 13:13
simple believe the *w*. but. 14:15
a *w*. spoken in due season, how ! 15:23
a *w*. fitly spoken is like apples. 25:11
where the *w*. of a king is. *Eccl* 8:4
despised *w*. of the Holy. *Isa* 5:24
speak *w*. and it shall not stand. 8:10
the Lord sent a *w*. to Jacob, it. 9:8
man an offender for a *w*. 29:21
thine ears shall hear a *w*. 30:21
counsellor could answer a *w*. 41:28
that confirmeth the *w*. of. 44:26
w. is gone out of my mouth. 45:23
should know how to speak a *w*. 50:4
become wind, and the *w*. *Jer* 5:13
let your ear receive *w*. 9:20; 10:1
nor shall the *w*. perish from. 18:18
for every man's *w*. shall be. 23:36
them, diminish not a *w*. 26:2
for I have pronounced the *w*. 34:5
king said, Is there any *w*.? 37:17
for the *w*. thou hast spoken. 44:16
therefore hear the *w*. at my mouth.
Ezek 3:17; 33:7
the *w*. that I shall speak. 12:25
the *w*. that I have spoken shall. 28
would confirm the *w*. 13:6
hear what is *w*. that cometh. 33:30
changed the king's *w*. *Dan* 3:28
the demand is by the *w*. of. 4:17
while the *w*. was in the king's. 31
for *w*. came to the king. *Jonah* 3:6
to the *w*. I covenanted. *Hag* 2:5
speak the *w*. only, he shall. *Mat* 8:8
whoso speaketh a *w*. against the Son
of man. 12:32; *Luke* 12:10
every idle *w*. men. *Mat* 12:36
when any one heareth the *w*. of the
kingdom. 13:19, 20, 22, 23
Mark 4:16, 18, 20; *Luke* 8:15
or persecution ariseth because of the
w., he. *Mat* 13:21; *Mark* 4:17
he answered her not a *w*.
Mat 15:23
that every *w*. may be established.
18:16; *2 Cor* 13:1
able to answer him a *w*. *Mat* 22:46
he answered him to never a *w*. 27:14
to bring his disciples *w*. 28:8
sower soweth the *w*. *Mark* 4:14
Peter called to mind the *w*. 14:72
the Lord confirming the *w*. 16:20
saying, What a *w*. is this! *Luke* 4:36
say in a *w*. and my servant shall. 7:7
Jesus, a prophet mighty in *w*. 24:19
the *W*. and the *W*. was with God, and
the *W*. was God. *John* 1:1
the *W*. was made flesh, and. 14
they believed the *w*. that Jesus said.
2:22; 4:50
w. I have spoken shall judge. 12:48
w. which ye hear is not mine. 14:24
ye are clean through the *w*. I. 15:3
remember the *w*. that I said. 20
that *w*. might be fulfilled, written. 25
believe on me through their *w*. 17:20
the *w*. which God sent to. *Acts* 10:36
if ye have any *w*. of exhortation, say
on. 13:15
to you is the *w*. of this salvation. 26
by my mouth, should hear *w*. 15:7
they received the *w*. with all. 17:11
I commend you to the *w*. of. 20:32
Paul had spoken one *w*. 28:25
of no effect, *w*. of faith. *Rom* 10:8
make Gentiles obedient by *w*. 15:18
kingdom of God is not in *w*.
1 Cor 4:20

word (continued)

w. of wisdom, to another the w. of
knowledge. *1 Cor 12:8*
w. toward you was not. *2 Cor 1:18*
God committed to us the w. of. 5:19
such as we are in w. by letters. 10:11
law is fulfilled in one w. *Gal 5:14*
let him that is taught in the w. 6:6
washing of water by the w. *Eph 5:26*
are bold to speak the w. *Phil 1:14*
holding forth the w. of life to. 2:16
heard in the w. of the truth. *Col 1:5*
let the w. of Christ dwell in. 3:16
whatsoever ye do in w. or deed. 17
our gospel came not to you in w.
only. *1 Thes 1:5*
having received the w. in much. 6
w. . . , ye receive it not as w. of men,
but as it is in truth, w. of God. 2:13
not by Spirit, nor by w. *2 Thes 2:2*
have been taught, whether by w. 15
and stablish you in every good w. 17
if any man obey not our w. by. 3:14
be thou an example of believers in
w. *1 Tim 4:12*
they who labour in the w. 5:17
their w. will eat as doth. *2 Tim 2:17*
preach w.; be instant in season. 4:2
holding fast the faithful w. *Tit 1:9*
upholding all things by the w. of his
power. *Heb 1:3*
if the w. spoken by angels was. 2:2
but the w. preached did not. 4:2
is unskilful in the w. of. 5:13
but the w. of the oath, which. 7:28
intreated w. should not be. 12:19
brethren, suffer the w. of. 13:22
meekness the ingrafted w. *Jas 1:21*
be ye doers of the w. and not. 22
if any be a hearer of the w. and. 23
if any man offend not in w., the. 3:2
the sincere milk of the w. *1 Pet 2:2*
who stumble at the w. being. 8
not the w., may without the w. 3:1
we have a more sure w. of prophecy.
2 Pet 1:19
the heavens by the same w. are. 3:7
handled, of the w. of life. *1 John 1:1*
let us not love in w. but in. 3:18
the Father, the W. and. 5:7
because thou hast kept w. *Rev 3:10*
they overcame by the w. of. 12:11

word of God

that I may shew thee the w. of God.
1 Sam 9:27
the w. of God came to Shemaiah,
1 Ki 12:22
the w. of God came to Nathan.
1 Chr 17:3
every w. of God is pure. *Pr 30:5*
the w. of our God shall. *Isa 40:8*
making the w. of God. *Mark 7:13*
w. of God came unto John. *Luke 3:2*
alone, but by every w. of God. 4:4
on him to hear the w. of God. 5:1
the seed is the w. of God. 8:11
these that hear the w. of God. 21
they that hear the w. of God. 11:28
gods to whom w. of God. *John 10:35*
they spake the w. of God. *Acts 4:31*
should leave the w. of God. 6:2
the w. of God increased. 7; 12:24
Samaria had received the w. of God.
8:14
Gentiles had received the w. of God.
11:1
desired to hear the w. of God. 13:7
city came to hear the w. of God. 44
w. of God should have been first. 46
mightily grew the w. of God. 19:20
not as though the w. of God hath
taken none effect. *Rom 9:6*
hearing by the w. of God. 10:17
came the w. of God out from you ?
1 Cor 14:36
corrupt the w. of God. *2 Cor 2:17*
not handling the w. of God. 4:2
and the sword of the Spirit, which is
the w. of God. *Eph 6:17*
which is given me to fulfil the w. of
God. *Col 1:25*
received the w. of God. *1 Thes 2:13*
it is sanctified by the w. of God and
prayer. *1 Tim 4:5*

but the w. of God is not bound.
2 Tim 2:9
the w. of God be not blasphemed.
Tit 2:5
the w. of God is quick. *Heb 4:12*
tasted the good w. of God. 6:5
framed by the w. of God. 11:3
spoken to you the w. of God. 13:7
being born again by the w. of God.
1 Pet 1:23
by the w. of God the heavens were of
old. *2 Pet 3:5*
are strong, and the w. of God abideth
in you. *1 John 2:14*
record of the w. of God. *Rev 1:2*
isle of Patmos, for the w. of God. 9
that were slain for w. of God. 6:9
name is called the w. of God. 19:13
beheaded for the w. of God. 20:4

see heard

his word

at his w. shall they go out, and at
his w. they shall come. *Num 27:21*
he shall not break his w. 30:2
the Lord stablish his w. *1 Sam 1:23*
his w. was in my tongue. *2 Sam 23:2*
may continue his w. *1 Ki 2:4*
the Lord hath performed his w. that
he spake. 8:20; *2 Chr 6:10*
to enquire of his w. *2 Ki 1:16*
might perform his w. *2 Chr 10:15*
in God I will praise his w., in God I
have put my trust. *Ps 56:4, 10*
unto the voice of his w. 103:20
the time that his w. came. 105:19
rebelled not against his w. 28
they believed not his w. but. 106:24
he sent his w. and healed. 107:20
I wait for the Lord and in his w. do I
hope. 130:5
his w. runneth very swiftly. 147:15
sendeth out his w. and melteth. 18
he sheweth his w. unto Jacob. 19
wind fulfilling his w. 148:8
that tremble at his w. *Isa 66:5*
but his w. was in my heart as a fire.
Jer 20:9
he hath fulfilled his w. *Lam 2:17*
that executeth his w. *Joel 2:11*
out the spirits with his w. *Mat 8:16*
for his w. was with power. *Luke 4:32*
many believed because of his own w.
John 4:41
ye have not his w. abiding. 5:38
gladly received his w. *Acts 2:41*
but hath in due times manifested
his w. *Tit 1:3*
whoso keepeth his w. *1 John 2:5*

see Lord

my word

whether my w. shall come to pass.
Num 11:23
ye rebelled against my w. 20:24
will I perform my w. *1 Ki 6:12*
rain, but according to my w. 17:1
so shall my w. be that goeth forth
out of my mouth. *Isa 55:11*
him that trembleth at my w. 66:2
hasten my w. to perform. *Jer 1:12*
my w., let him speak my w. 23:28
is not my w. like as a fire ? 29
the prophets that steal my w. 30
I will perform my good w. 29:10
but my w. shall not pass. *Mat 24:35*
he that heareth my w. *John 5:24*
continue in my w., then are ye. 8:31
kill me because my w. hath. 37
ye cannot hear my w. 43
thou hast kept my w., and hast not
denied my name. *Rev 3:8*

this word

is not this the w. that ? *Ex 14:12*
since the Lord spake this w. to
Moses. *Josh 14:10*
they sent this w. to the king.
2 Sam 19:14*
hast not spoken this w. *1 Ki 2:23*
this is the w. that the Lord hath
spoken of him. *2 Ki 19:21*
Isa 16:13; 24:3; 37:22
shall alter this w. *Ezra 6:11*
should do according to this w. 10:5
not according to this w. *Isa 8:20*

because ye despise this w. *Isa 30:12*
ye speak this w. *Jer 5:14; 23:38*
proclaim there this w. and say. 7:2
speak unto them this w. 13:12
thou say this w. to them. 14:17
down, and speak there this w. 22:1
in the reign of Jehoiakim this w.
came. 26:1; 27:1; 34:8; 36:1
hear now this w. 28:7; *Amos 3:1*
4:1; 5:1
spoken this w. to me. *Dan 10:11*
this is the w. of the Lord. *Zech 4:6*
him audience to this w. *Acts 22:22*
for this is w. of promise. *Rom 9:9*
this w., Yet once more. *Heb 12:27*
this is the w. which is. *1 Pet 1:25*

thy word

be according to thy w. *Gen 30:34*
according to thy w. shall my. 41:40
Be it according to thy w. *Ex 8:10*
I have pardoned, according to thy w.
Num 14:20
have observed thy w. *Deut 33:9*
done according to thy w. *1 Ki 3:12*
let thy w. I pray thee, be. 8:26
done all these things at thy w. 18:36
let thy w. I pray thee, be like the
word of one of. 22:13; *2 Chr 18:12*
heed according to thy w. *Ps 119:9*
thy w. have I hid in mine heart. 11
statutes, I will not forget thy w 16
live, and keep thy w. 17, 101
quicken me according to thy w.
25, 107, 154
strengthen thou me according to thy
w. 28, 116
stablish thy w. 38
salvation according to thy w. 41
I trust in thy w. 42
comfort in affliction, for thy w. 50
be merciful to me according to thy w.
58, 65, 76
but now have I kept thy w. 67
I have hoped in thy w. 74, 147
I hope in thy w. 81, 114
mine eyes fail for thy w. 82
ever, O Lord, thy w. is settled. 89
thy w. is a lamp. 105
order my steps in thy w., let not. 133
thy w. is pure. 140
that I might meditate in thy w. 148
because they kept not thy w. 158
thy w. is true. 160
standeth in awe of thy w. 161
I rejoice at thy w. 162
give me understanding according to
thy w. 169
deliver me according to thy w. 170
my tongue shall speak of thy w. 172
thou hast magnified thy w. 138:2
thy w. was to me the joy. *Jer 15:16*
drop thy w. toward the south.
Ezek 20:46
drop thy w. toward the holy. 21:2
drop not thy w. against. *Amos 7:16*
made naked, even thy w. *Hab 3:9*
according to thy w. *Luke 1:38*
in peace, according to thy w. 2:29
nevertheless at thy w. I will let. 5:5
and they have kept thy w. *John 17:6*
I have given them thy w. 14
thy w. is truth. 17
with all boldness they may speak thy
w. *Acts 4:29*

see truth

words

shalt put w. in his mouth. *Ex 4:15*
let them not regard vain w. 5:9
returned the w. of the people. 19:8
the gift perverteth the w. of the
righteous. 23:8; *Deut 16:19*
the w. which were in the first tables.
Ex 34:1
Moses wrote the w. of the covenant.
28; *Deut 10:2*
I sent to Sihon with w. *Deut 2:26*
go aside from any of the w. 28:14
keep the w. of his covenant. 29:9
2 Ki 23:3, 24; 2 Chr 34:31
hear, O earth, the w. of. *Deut 32:1*
Ps 54:2; 78:1; Pr 7:24
Saul was afraid of the w. of Samuel.
1 Sam 28:20

the w. of men of Judah were fiercer.
2 Sam 19:43
w. of prophets declare good to the
king.   1 Ki 22:13; 2 Chr 18:12
Elisha telleth the w.   2 Ki 6:12
but they are but vain w.   18:20
Isa 36:5
sing praises with the w. 2 Chr 29:30
the people rested on the w.   32:8
he sent letters with w. of peace and
truth.   Esth 9:30
ye imagine to reprove w.? Job 6:26
shall w. of thy mouth be like ? 8:2
not the ear try w.?   12:11; 34:3
thou lettest such w. go out.   15:13
shall vain w. have an end ?   16:3
I could heap up w. against you.   4
ere ye make an end of w.?   18:2
ye break me in pieces with w.? 19:2
I would know the w. he would. 23:5
I have esteemed the w. of his.   12
he multiplieth w. without.   35:16
darkeneth counsel by w.?   38:2
let the w. of my mouth.   Ps 19:14
why so far from the w. of ?   22:1
the w. of his mouth are iniquity.
36:3
thou lovest all devouring w.   52:4
w. of his mouth were smoother than
butter.   55:21
for w. of their lips, let them. 59:12
to understand the w. of.   Pr 1:6
decline not from the w.   4:5; 5:7
thou art snared with the w. of.   6:2
in multitude of w. there wanteth not
sin.   10:19
w. of the wicked are to lie in wait for
blood.   12:6
w. of the pure are pleasant w. 15:26
the w. of a man's mouth are as. 18:4
w. of a talebearer are as wounds.
8; 26:22
he pursueth them with w.   19:7
he causeth thee to err from w.   27
he overthroweth the w. of the. 22:12
bow down thine ear, hear the w.   17
certainty of the w. of truth; that thou
mightest answer the w. of.   21
thou shalt lose thy sweet w.   23:8
will not be corrected by w.   29:19
a fool's voice is known by multitude
of w.   Eccl 5:3; 10:14
the w. of a wise man's mouth. 10:12
find out acceptable w.: that which was
written, even w. of truth.   12:10
the w. of the wise are as goads. 11
become as the w. of a book sealed.
Isa 29:11
it may be God will hear the w. 37:4
uttering from the heart w. of. 59:13
w. of this covenant.   Jer 11:2, 6
because of the Lord, and the w. 23:9
w. of Jonadab son of Rechab. 35:14
remnant shall know whose w. 44:28
whose w. thou canst not.   Ezek 3:6
shall speak great w. against most
High.   Dan 7:25
shut up the w.   12:4
the w. are closed up.   9
I have slain them by the w. of my
mouth.   Hos 6:5
take with you w. and turn to.   14:2
good and comfortable w. Zech 1:13
should ye not hear the w.?   7:7
saying the same w.   Mat 26:44
Mark 14:39
wondered at gracious w. Luke 4:22
the w. that I speak unto you, they are
spirit.   John 6:63
to whom we go ? thou hast the w. 68
I have given to them the w.   17:8
with many other w. did. Acts 2:40
Moses was mighty in w. and. 7:22
was warned to hear w. of thee. 10:22
Peter, who shall tell thee w. 11:14
to this agree the w. of the prophets.
15:15
have troubled you with w.   24
but if it be a question of w.   18:15
to remember the w. of the.   20:35
most of all for the w. he spake. 38
but I speak forth w. of truth. 26:25
by good w. deceive hearts of the
simple.   Rom 16:18*

not with wisdom of w.   1 Cor 1:17
2:4, 13
except ye utter w. easy to.   14:9*
I had rather speak five w. with. 19
deceive you with vain w.   Eph 5:6
nourished up in w. of faith and doctrine.   1 Tim 4:6
that they strive not about w. to no
profit.   2 Tim 2:14
greatly withstood our w.   4:15
be mindful of the w. spoken by prophets.   2 Pet 3:2
hear the w. of this prophecy.
Rev 1:3; 22:18
take away from the w. of this. 22:19

all the words

all the w. of Joseph.   Gen 45:27
Moses told Aaron all the w. of the
Lord.   Ex 4:28
Moses told the people all the w.
24:3; Num 11:24
Moses wrote all the w. of the Lord.
Ex 24:4
on the tables were written all the w.
Deut 9:10
keep all the w.
write on stones all the w.   27:3, 8
that confirmeth not all the w.   26
not observe to do all the w.   28:58
may do all the w. of this law. 29:29
and observe to do all the w.   31:12
Moses spake all the w. of.   32:44
set your hearts to all the w.   46
he read all the w. of the law, the
blessings and.   Josh 8:34
Samuel told all the w. of the Lord.
1 Sam 8:10
Lord will hear all the w. of Rab-
shakeh.   2 Ki 19:4; Isa 37:17
Josiah read all the w. of the covenant.   2 Ki 23:2; 2 Chr 34:30
all the w. of my mouth.   Pr 8:8
unto all the w. spoken.   Eccl 7:21
bring on them all the w.   Jer 11:8
speak all the w. that I command
thee.   26:2
to all the w. of Jeremiah.   20
write all the w. I have spoken.
30:2; 36:2
Baruch wrote all the w. of the Lord.
36:4, 32
had ended all the w. of Lord. 43:1
speak to the people all the w. of this
life.   Acts 5:20

words of God

hath said, which heard the w. of
God.   Num 24:4, 16
Heman the king's seer in the w. of
God.   1 Chr 25:5
every one that trembleth at the w. of
God.   Ezra 9:4
they rebelled against the w. of God.
Ps 107:11
he whom God sent, speaketh w. of
God.   John 3:34
of God, heareth the w. of God. 8:47
until the w. of God be fulfilled.
Rev 17:17

see heard

his words

they hated him yet the more for his
w.   Gen 37:8
thou heardest his w. out of the fire.
Deut 4:36
Jephthah uttered all his w. before
the Lord.   Judg 11:11
he let none of his w. fall to the
ground.   1 Sam 3:19
but they despised his w. 2 Chr 36:16
and lay up his w. in thine. Job 22:22
he hath not directed his w.   32:14
his w. were without wisdom. 34:35
for he multiplieth his w. against. 37
his w. softer than oil.   Ps 55:21
then believed they his w.   106:12
knowledge spareth his w. Pr 17:27
seest thou a man that is hasty in his
w.?   29:20
add thou not unto his w., lest. 30:6
will not call back his w.   Isa 31:2
heed to any of his w.   Jer 18:18
he hath confirmed his w. Dan 9:12

the land is not able to bear all his w.
Amos 7:10
the disciples were astonished at his
w.   Mark 10:24
to catch him in his w.   12:13
Luke 20:20
not take hold of his w. Luke 20:26*
they remembered his w.   24:8
see lord

my words

he said, Hear now my w. Num 12:6
Job 34:2
make them hear my w.   Deut 4:10
therefore lay up my w. in.   11:18
and I will put my w. in his.   18:18
whosoever will not hearken to my w.
19; Jer 29:19; 35:13
and they uttered my w.   Neh 6:19
therefore my w. are swallowed up.
Job 6:3
Oh that my w. were now written!
19:23
after my w. they spake not.   29:22
hearken to all my w.   33:1; 34:16
Acts 2:14
my w. shall be of the uprightness of
my heart.   Job 33:3; 36:4
give ear to my w. O Lord.   Ps 5:1
seeing thou castest my w.   50:17
every day they wrest my w.   56:5
they shall hear my w.: for they.141:6
known my w. unto you.   Pr 1:23
if thou wilt receive my w.   2:1
let thine heart retain my w.   4:4
attend to my w.   4:20
keep my w.   7:1
I have put my w. in thy mouth, and
say unto Zion. Isa 51:16; Jer 1:9
my w. which I have put. Isa 59:21
I will make my w. in thy mouth fire.
Jer 5:14
have not hearkened to my w.   6:19
refused to hear my w. 11:10; 13:10
will cause thee to hear my w.   18:2
they might not hear my w.   19:15
my people to hear my w.   23:22
ye have not heard my w.   25:8
bring upon that land all my w.   13
I will bring my w. on this city. 39:16
you may know my w. shall.   44:29
thou shalt speak my w. unto them
Ezek 2:7; 3:4, 10
there shall none of my w.   12:28
do not my w. do good to ?   Mi 2:7
my w. did they not take hold of your
fathers ?   Zech 1:6
whosoever shall be ashamed of me
and my w. Mark 8:38; Luke 9:26
but my w. shall not pass away.
Mark 13:31; Luke 21:33
thou believest not my w. Luke 1:20
shall ye believe my w.?   John 5:47
if any man hear my w. and.   12:47
he that receiveth not my w.   48
will keep my w.   14:23
my w. abide in you.   15:7

their words

their w. pleased Hamor. Gen 34:18
I believed not their w.   2 Chr 9:6
through all the earth, their w. to end
of the world. Ps 19:4; Rom 10:18
be not afraid of their w. Ezek 2:6
their w. seemed to them as idle
tales.   Luke 24:11

these words

according to these w.   Gen 39:17
to the tenor of these w.   43:7
these are the w. thou shalt speak.
Ex 19:6, 7
God spake all these w.   20:1
Deut 5:22
Lord said, Write thou these w.
Ex 34:27; Jer 36:17
these are the w. which the Lord.
Ex 35:1; Deut 6:6; 29:1
as he had made an end of speaking
all these w.   Num 16:31
Deut 32:45; 1 Sam 24:16
observe, hear all these w.
Deut 12:28; Zech 8:9
David laid up these w. 1 Sam 21:12
his servants with these w.   24:7

to all *these w.*, and this vision, so
did.   *2 Sam* 7:17; *1 Chr* 17:15
thy master and to thee to speak
these w.?   2 Ki 18:27; *Isa* 36:12
the man of God proclaimed *these w.*
        2 Ki 23:16
go proclaim *these w.*   *Jer* 3:12
speak all *these w.* unto. 7:27; 26:15
all *these w.*   16:10
ye will not hear *these w.*   22:5
prophesy thou all *these w.*   25:30
Let no man know of *these w.* 38:24
when he had written *these w.*   45:1
                     51:60
thou shalt read all *these w.*   51:61
these are the *w.* I spake. *Luke* 24:44
these w. spake his parents, because
they feared Jews.   *John* 9:22
these are not *w.* of him that. 10:21*
hear *these w.*; Jesus of. *Acts* 2:22
while Peter yet spake *these w.* 10:44
besought *these w.* might be preached
to them.   13:42
when he had said *these w.*   28:29
comfort one another with *these w.*
               1 Thes 4:18
for *these w.* are true.   *Rev* 21:5

thy words

shall receive of *thy w.*   *Deut* 33:3
will not hearken to *thy w. Josh* 1:18
do not according to *thy w. Judg* 11:10
Manoah said, Now let *thy w.* 13:12
transgressed *thy w.*   *1 Sam* 15:24
hearkened to *thy w.*   28:21
thy w.' sake hast thou done all these
great things.   *2 Sam* 7:21
that God, and *thy w.* be true.   28
in and confirm *thy w.*   *1 Ki* 1:14
hast performed *thy w.*   *Neh* 9:8
thy w. upheld him that was falling.
                   Job 4:4
said I would keep *thy w. Ps* 119:57
how sweet are *thy w.* to my!   103
entrance of *thy w.* giveth light.   130
enemies have forgotten *thy w.*   139
shalt lose *thy* sweet *w.*   *Pr* 23:8
despise the wisdom of *thy w.*   9
therefore let *thy w.* be few. *Eccl* 5:2
thy w. were found, and I did eat
them.   *Jer* 15:16
hear *thy w.* but do them not.
          Ezek 33:31, 32
the first day *thy w.* were heard, and
I am come for *thy w. Dan* 10:12
for by *thy w.* thou shalt be justified,
and by *thy w.* thou.   *Mat* 12:37

your words

that *your w.* be proved. *Gen* 42:16
bring Benjamin, so shall *your w.* 20
let it be according unto *your w.*
         44:10; *Josh* 2:21
the voice of *your w. Deut* 1:34; 5:28
I waited for *your w.*; I gave ear.
             Job 32:11
that heareth *your w.*   *Isa* 41:26
to God according to *your w. Jer* 42:4
multiplied *your w.* against me.
             Ezek 35:13
ye have wearied the Lord with *your
w.*   *Mal* 2:17
your w. have been stout.   3:13
you nor hear *your w.*   *Mat* 10:14

work

Is taken, [1] *For such business as
is proper to every man's calling,
which may be done in six days.*
Ex 20:9, Six days shalt thou labour
and do all thy *work.* [2] *For any
thought, word, or outward action,
whether good or evil,* Eccl 12:14,
God shall bring every *work* into
judgement. [3] Work *is put for
miracle,* John 7:21.
  The *works* of God, denote, [1] *His*
work *of creation.* [2] *His* works
*of providence in preserving and
governing the world.* [3] *His* work
*of redemption, and particularly
the faith of true believers is called
the work of God.*
  *By good works are to be under-
stood all manner of duties inward
and outward, thoughts as well as*

*words and actions, toward God or
man, which are commanded in the
law of God, and proceed from a
pure heart and faith unfeigned.*
let there more *w.* be laid on the men.
              Ex 5:9
no manner of *w.* shall be done.
   12:16; 20:10; *Lev* 16:29; 23:3, 28
          31; *Num* 29:7
shew them *w.* that they.   *Ex* 18:20
whoso doeth any *w.* therein shall be
cut off.   31:14, 15; *Lev* 23:30
six days shall *w.* be. *Ex* 35:2; 20:9
sufficient for all the *w.* and.   36:7
convocation, ye shall do no servile *w.*
    Lev 23:7, 8, 21, 25, 35, 36
   Num 28:18. 25, 26; 29:1, 12, 35
the *w.* of men's hands.   *Deut* 4:28
   27:15; *2 Ki* 19:18; *2 Chr* 32:19
        Ps 115:4; 135:15
in it thou shalt not do any *w.*
   Deut 5:14; 16:8; *Jer* 17:22, 24
that the Lord may bless thee in all *w.*
   Deut 14:29; 24:19; 28:12; 30:9
do no *w.* with the firstling of. 15:19
anger through the *w.* of your hands.
   31:29; *1 Ki* 16:7; *Jer* 32:30
bless the Lord and accept *w.* 33:11
officers which were over the *w.*
   1 Ki 5:16; 9:23; *1 Chr* 29:6
           2 Chr 2:18
another court of the like *w. 1 Ki* 7:8
into the hands of them that did the *w.*
   2 Ki 12:11; 22:5*, 9
employed in that *w.* day. *1 Chr* 9:33
to minister as every day's *w.* 16:37
Solomon young, and the *w.* is great.
        29:1; *Neh* 4:19
every *w.* that he began. *2 Chr* 31:21
the men did the *w.* faithfully. 34:12
then ceased the *w.* of.   *Ezra* 4:24
this *w.* goeth fast on, prospereth. 5:8
let the *w.* of this house of God. 6:7
hands in the *w.* of house of God. 22
neither is it a *w.* of one day.   10:13
put not their necks to *w. Neh* 3:5
slay them, and cause the *w.*   4:11
why should the *w.* cease whilst ? 6:3
they perceived this *w.* was.   7:70
fathers gave to the *w.*   *Job* 1:10
thou hast blessed the *w.*   1:10
thou shouldest despise the *w.*   10:3
thou wilt have a desire to *w.*   14:15
go they forth to their *w.*   24:5
for the *w.* of a man shall he render
unto him.   34:11; *1 Pet* 1:17
are all the *w.* of his hands. *Job* 34:19
he sheweth them their *w.* and. 36:9
when I consider the *w.* of thy fingers.
           Ps 8:3, 6
the wicked is snared in the *w.* 9:16
firmament sheweth his handy *w.* 19:1
after the *w.* of their hands.   28:4
we heard what *w.* thou didst.   44:1
establish thou the *w.* of our.   90:17
proved me and saw my *w.*   95:9
I hate the *w.* of them that.   101:3
the heavens are the *w.* of thy. 102:25
on the *w.* of thy hands.   143:5
worketh a deceitful *w.*   *Pr* 11:18
time there for every *w.*   *Eccl* 3:17
why should God destroy the *w.*? 5:6
I applied mine heart to every *w.* 8:9
according to *w.* of the wicked, according to the *w.* of the.   14
there is no *w.* in the grave.   9:10
God will bring every *w.* into. 12:14
w. of the hands of a cunning workman.   *S of S* 7:1
they worship the *w.* of their own
hands. *Isa* 2:8; 37:19; *Jer* 1:16
      10:3, 9, 15; 51:18
he shall not look to the *w. Isa* 17:8
neither shall there be any *w.* 19:15
blessed be Assyria the *w.* of.   25
do his *w.*, his strange *w.*   28:21
shall the *w.* say of him that ? 29:16*
he seeth his children, and the *w.* 23
the *w.* of righteousness shall. 32:17
concerning the *w.* of my hands command me.   45:11
my *w.* is with my God.   49:4*
they shall inherit the *w* of my. 60:21
will direct their *w.* in truth.   61:8*

all are the *w.* of thy hands. *Isa* 64:8
mine elect shall long enjoy *w.* 65:22
great in counsel and mighty in *w.*
                Jer 32:19
recompense her according to her *w.*
       50:29; *Lam* 3:64
be taken to do any *w.? Ezek* 15:3
is it meet for any *w.?*   4
it was meet for no *w.*   5
w. of an imperious whorish.   16:30
w. of the craftsman.   *Hos* 13:2
we will say no more to the *w.*   14:3
shalt no more worship *w.*   *Mi* 5:13
for I will work a *w.* in.   *Hab* 1:5
and so is every *w.* of.   *Hag* 2:14
there do no mighty *w.*   *Mark* 6:5
I have done one *w.* and. *John* 7:21
finished the *w.* thou gavest me. 17:4
if this *w.* be of men it will. *Acts* 5:38
for the *w.* whereunto I have.   13:2
wonder, for I work a *w.* in your days,
a *w.* which ye will not believe. 41
the *w.* which they fulfilled.   14:26
not with them to the *w.*   15:38
which shew *w.* of the law. *Rom* 2:15
a short *w.* will the Lord make. 9:28
otherwise *w.* is no more *w.*   11:6*
every man's *w.* shall be. *1 Cor* 3:13
if any man's *w.* abide.   14
if *w.* be burnt.   15
are not ye my *w.* in the Lord ?   9:1
he gave some for the *w.*   *Eph* 4:12
for the *w.* of Christ he.   *Phil* 2:30
that God may fulfil the *w.* of faith.
            2 Thes 1:11
every good word and *w.*   2:17
do the *w.* of an evangelist. *2 Tim* 4:5
patience have her perfect *w. Jas* 1:4
but a doer of the *w.* shall be.   25

see evil, needle

work, *verb*

go and *w.*   *Ex* 5:18
six days thou shalt *w.*   34:21
whoso doeth *w.* therein shall.   35:2
they did *w.* wilily and went. *Josh* 9:4
the Lord will *w.* for us. *1 Sam* 14:6
sold thyself to *w.* evil. *1 Ki* 21:20, 25
people had a mind to *w.*   *Neh* 4:6
left hand, where he doth *w. Job* 23:9
in heart ye *w.* wickedness. *Ps* 58:2
time for thee, Lord, to *w.*   119:126
w. a deceitful work.   *Pr* 11:18
they that *w.* in flax, shall. *Isa* 19:9
I will *w.* and who shall let it ? 43:13
ye *w.* abomination and. *Ezek* 33:26
he shall *w.* deceitfully. *Dan* 11:23
woe to them that *w.* evil.   *Mi* 2:1
I will *w.* a work in your days, which.
        Hab 1:5; *Acts* 13:41
w. for I am with you.   *Hag* 2:4
they that *w.* wickedness. *Mal* 3:15
son, go *w.* to-day in.   *Mat* 21:28
six days in which men ought to *w.*
            Luke 13:14
my Father worketh hitherto, and I
w.   *John* 5:17
that we might *w.* the works?   6:28
What dost thou *w.?*   30
w. the works of him that sent me . . .
cometh when no man can *w.*   9:4
sin by the law did *w.* in.   *Rom* 7:5
we know that all things *w.*   8:28
to *w.* all uncleanness.   *Eph* 4:19
w. out your own salvation. *Phil* 2:12
study to *w.* with your own hands.
            1 Thes 4:11
of iniquity doth *w.*   *2 Thes* 2:7
if any would not *w.*, neither.   3:10
that with quietness they *w.*   12

see iniquity

work of God, works of God

tables were the *w.* of God. *Ex* 32:16
wondrous *w.* of God.   *Job* 37:14
declare the *w.* of God.   *Ps* 64:9
come and see the *w.* of God.   66:5
not forget the *w.* of God.   78:7
consider the *w.* of God.   *Eccl* 7:13
beheld all the *w.* of God.   8:17
knowest not the *w.* of God.   11:5
work the *w.* of God.   *John* 6:28
this is the *w.* of God that ye.   29
the *w.* of God should be made manifest in him.   9:3

speak the *w. of God.* *Acts* 2:11
destroy not *w. of God.* *Rom* 14:20

see **good, great**

his work

God ended *his w.* *Gen* 2:2
rested from *his w.* 3
every man from *his w.* *Ex* 36:4
he is the rock, *his w.* *Deut* 32:4
an old man came from *his w.* at even.
Judg 19:16
asses and put to *his w.* *1 Sam* 8:16
and wrought all *his w.* *1 Ki* 7:14
with the king for *his w.* *1 Chr* 4:23
of Israel he made no servants for *his
w.* *2 Chr* 8:9
Baasha let *his w.* cease, he. 16:5
every man to *his w.* *Neh* 4:15
for the reward of *his w.* *Job* 7:2*
that thou magnify *his w.* 36:24
that all men may know *his w.* 37:7
renderest to every man according to
his w. *Ps* 62:12; *Pr* 24:29
man goeth forth to *his w. Ps* 104:23
his w. is honourable and. 111:3
all the weights of the bag are *his w.*
Pr 16:11
whether *his w.* be pure or. 20:11
but as for the pure *his w.* is. 21:8
let him hasten *his w.* that. *Isa* 5:19
performed *his whole w.* 10:12
may do *his w., his strange w.* 28:21
behold, *his w.* is before him. 40:10*
62:11*
an instrument for *his w.* 54:16
giveth him not for *his w. Jer* 22:13*
the maker of *his w.* *Hab* 2:18
to every man *his w.* *Mark* 13:34
my meat is to finish *his w.John* 4:34
every man prove *his own w. Gal* 6:4
give every man as *his w. Rev* 22:12

see **Lord**

our work

this shall comfort us concerning *our
w.* *Gen* 5:29

thy work

six days do all *thy w.* *Ex* 20:9
23:12; *Deut* 5:13
Lord recompense *thy w. Ruth* 2:12
meditate also of all *thy w. Ps* 77:12
let *thy w.* appear unto thy. 90:16
made me glad through *thy w.* 92:4
prepare *thy w.* without. *Pr* 24:27
or *thy w.,* He hath no hands ?
Isa 45:9
for *thy w.* shall be rewarded, saith
the Lord. *Jer* 31:16
revive *thy w.* in the midst. *Hab* 3:2

your work

not aught of *your w.* *Ex* 5:11
for *your w.* shall be rewarded.
2 Chr 15:7
ye are of nothing, *your w.* is of
nought. *Isa* 41:24
remembering *your w.* of faith, and
labour of love. *1 Thes* 1:3
God is not unrighteous to forget
your w. *Heb* 6:10

worker

was a *w.* in brass. *1 Ki* 7:14

workers

w. with familiar spirits. *2 Ki* 23:24
we then as *w.* together. *2 Cor* 6:1
false apostles, deceitful *w.* 11:13
beware of evil *w.* *Phil* 3:2

see **iniquity**

worketh

lo, all these things *w.* God. *Job* 33:29
he that walketh uprightly, and *w.*
righteousness. *Ps* 15:2
he that *w.* deceit shall not. 101:7
w. a deceitful work. *Pr* 11:18*
a flattering mouth *w.* ruin. 26:28
w. willingly with her hands. 31:13
what profit hath he that *w.? Eccl* 3:9
the smith with his tongs *w.* in the
coals, and he *w.* it. *Isa* 44:12
thou meetest him that *w.* 64:5
he *w.* signs and wonders. *Dan* 6:27
my Father *w.* hitherto. *John* 5:17
he that *w.* righteousness. *Acts* 10:35
glory and peace to every one that *w.*
good. *Rom* 2:10

to him that *w.* is the reward. *Rom* 4:4
to him that *w.* not, but believeth. 5
because the law *w.* wrath, for. 15
knowing that tribulation *w.* 5:3
love *w.* no ill to his neighbour. 13:10
God that *w.* all in all. *1 Cor* 12:6
all these *w.* that one and the. 11
for he *w.* the work of the. 16:10
so then death *w.* in us. *2 Cor* 4:12
w. for us a more exceeding. 17
w. repentance to salvation, but the
sorrow of the world *w.* death. 7:10
w. miracles among you. *Gal* 3:5
but faith, which *w.* by love. 5:6
who *w.* all things after. *Eph* 1:11
the spirit that now *w.* in the. 2:2
the power that *w.* in us. 3:20
for it is God that *w.* in you. *Phil* 2:13
his working, which *w.* in. *Col* 1:29
effectually *w.* in you. *1 Thes* 2:13
of your faith *w.* patience. *Jas* 1:3
the wrath of man *w.* not. 20
nor whatsoever *w.* abomination.
Rev 21:27

workfellow

Timothy my *w.* saluteth. *Rom* 16:21*

working

like a sharp razor, *w.* *Ps* 52:2
w. salvation in the midst of. 74:12
who is excellent in *w.* *Isa* 28:29*
be shut the six *w.* days. *Ezek* 46:1
the Lord *w.* with them. *Mark* 16:20
men with men *w.* that. *Rom* 1:27
sin *w.* death in me by that. 7:13
and labour, *w.* with our. *1 Cor* 4:12
not we power to forbear *w.?* 9:6
to another the *w.* of miracles. 12:10
according to the *w.* of. *Eph* 1:19
given me by the effectual *w.* 3:7
according to the effectual *w.* 4:16
w. with his hands the. 28
according to the *w.* whereby he is
able. *Phil* 3:21
his *w.* which worketh in. *Col* 1:29
is after the *w.* of Satan. *2 Thes* 2:9
w. not at all, but are. 3:11
w. in you that which is. *Heb* 13:21
spirits of devils *w.* miracles.
Rev 16:14

workman

wisdom to work all manner of work
of the cunning *w. Ex* 35:35; 38:23
the work of a cunning *w. S of S* 7:1
the *w.* melteth a graven. *Isa* 40:19
he seeketh to him a cunning *w.* 20
work of the *w.* with the axe. *Jer* 10:3
the *w.* made it therefore. *Hos* 8:6
w. is worthy of his meat. *Mat* 10:10*
a *w.* that needeth not be. *2 Tim* 2:15

workmanship

and in all manner of *w.* *Ex* 31:3, 5
35:31
to all the *w.* thereof. *2 Ki* 16:10
the *w.* of tabrets was. *Ezek* 28:13
for we are his *w.* created in Christ
Jesus. *Eph* 2:10

workmen

they gave that to the *w.* to repair.
2 Ki 12:14, 15; *2 Chr* 34:10, 17
there are *w.* with thee. *1 Chr* 22:15
number of *w.* 4
w. wrought. *2 Chr* 24:13
to set forward the *w.* in. *Ezra* 3:9
the *w.,* they are of men. *Isa* 44:11
called with the *w.* of like occupation.
Acts 19:25

works

fulfil your *w.* and your. *Ex* 5:13
the Lord hath sent me to do all these
w. *Num* 16:28
the Lord blessed thee in all the *w.*
Deut 2:7; 16:15
which knew not the *w.* *Judg* 2:10
according to all the *w.* they have
done. *1 Sam* 8:8
w. the man of God did. *1 Ki* 13:11
me to anger with all the *w.* of their
hands. *2 Ki* 22:17; *2 Chr* 34:25
from their wicked *w.* *Neh* 9:35
have done abominable *w.* *Ps* 14:1
concerning the *w.* of men, by the
word of thy lips. 17:4
I will triumph in the *w.* of. 92:4

the *w.* of the Lord are great. *Ps* 111:2
of his *w.* his hands are verity. 7
forsake not the *w.* of. 138:8
to practise wicked *w.* with. 141:4
let her own *w.* praise her. *Pr* 31:31
I have seen the *w. Eccl* 1:14; 2:11
wrought all our *w.* in us. *Isa* 26:12
have done all these *w.* *Jer* 7:13
to anger with the *w.* of your hands to.
25:6, 7; 44:8
according to their deeds and the *w.*
25:14; *Rev* 2:23
w. may be abolished. *Ezek* 6:6
honour him whose *w.* *Dan* 4:37
the *w.* of the house of. *Mi* 6:16
John heard in prison the *w. Mat* 11:2
shew him greater *w.* *John* 5:20
the *w.* which the Father hath given
me, the same *w.* that I do. 36
thy disciples may see the *w.* 7:3
because I testify that the *w.* 7
if children, ye would do the *w.* 8:39
I must work the *w.* of him. 9:4
w. that I do in my Father's. 10:25
of these *w.* do ye stone me ? 32
if I do not the *w.* 37
believe the *w.* 38
he doeth the *w.* 14:10
believe me for the very *w.'* 11
the *w.* that I do, shall he do; ... *w.* 12
not done among them the *w.* 15:24
they rejoiced in the *w.* *Acts* 7:41
Gentiles should do *w.* meet. 26:20
by what law ? of *w.? Rom* 3:27
if Abraham were justified by *w.* 4:2
imputeth righteousness without *w.* 6
not of *w.* but of him that. 9:11
but as it were by the *w.* of. 32
is it no more of *w.:* ... but if it be
of *w.,* is it no more of grace. 11:6
let us therefore cast off the *w.* 13:12
is not justified by the *w.* of the law,
for by the *w.* of the law. *Gal* 2:16
Spirit by the *w.* of the law ? 3:2
doeth he it by the *w.* of the law ? 5
as many as are of *w.* of the law. 10
the *w.* of the flesh are manifest. 5:19
not of *w.* lest any man. *Eph* 2:9
unfruitful *w.* of darkness. 5:11
in your mind by wicked *w. Col* 1:21
to esteem them in love for their *w.'s*
sake. *1 Thes* 5:13
saved us, not according to our *w.*
2 Tim 1:9; *Tit* 3:5
but in *w.* they deny God. *Tit* 1:16
the heavens are the *w.* *Heb* 1:10
thou didst set him over the *w.* 2:7
your fathers ... saw my *w.* forty.3:9
although the *w.* were finished. 4:3
of repentance from dead *w.* 6:1
purge conscience from dead *w.* 9:14
if he have not *w.* can ? *Jas* 2:14
faith without *w.* is dead. 17, 20, 26
w.: shew me thy faith without *w.* 18
Abraham justified by *w.?* 2:21
by *w.* was faith made perfect. 22
ye see then that by *w.* a man. 24
was not the harlot justified by *w.?* 25
the earth and the *w.* *2 Pet* 3:10
that he might destroy *w.* *1 John* 3:8
keepeth my *w.* to the end. *Rev* 2:26
yet repented not of the *w.* of. 9:20
double according to her *w.* 18:6

see **evil, good, work** *of God*

his works

his w. have been to thee very good.
1 Sam 19:4
Hezekiah prospered in all *his w.*
2 Chr 32:30
and all *his w.* are done. *Ps* 33:4
forgat *his w.* and. his wonders.
78:11; 106:13
bless the Lord, all *his w.* 103:22
Lord shall rejoice in *his w.* 104:31
let them declare *his w.* with. 107:22
people the power of *his w.* 111:6
mercies are over all *his w.* 145:9
the Lord is holy in all *his w.* 17
possessed me before *his w. Pr* 8:22
to every man according to *his w.*
24:12; *Mat* 16:27; *2 Tim* 4:14
rejoice in *his own w.* *Eccl* 3:22
righteous in all *his w.* *Dan* 9:14

to God are all *his* w.   *Acts* 15:18
seventh day from all *his* w. *Heb* 4:4
ceased from *his* own *w*.?   10
faith wrought with *his* w.? *Jas* 2:22
of a good conversation *his* w.   3:13
   see **Lord, marvellous, mighty**

their **works**

let the people from *their* w.? *Ex* 5:4
shalt not do after *their* w.   23:24
according to these *their* w. *Neh* 6:14
he knoweth *their* w.   *Job* 34:25
considereth all *their* w. *Ps* 33:15
and they learned *their* w.   106:35
defiled with *their* own w.   39
and *their* w. are in the hand of God.
     Eccl 9:1
their w. are in the dark. *Isa* 29:15
they are vanity, *their* w.   41:29
nor shall they cover themselves with
   their w.: *their* w. are works. 59:6
their w. and their thoughts.   66:18
forget any of *their* w.   *Amos* 8:7
God saw *their* w. that. *Jonah* 3:10
not ye after *their* w.   *Mat* 23:3
all *their* w. they do to be seen.   5
be according to *their* w. *2 Cor* 11:15
and *their* w. do follow. *Rev* 14:13
the dead judged according to *their*
  w.   20:12. 13

thy **works**

according to *thy* w.?   *Deut* 3:24
bless thee in all *thy* w.   15:10
Lord hath broken *thy* w. *2 Chr* 20:37
tell of all *thy* wondrous w. *Ps* 26:7
     145:4
How terrible art thou in *thy* w.! 66:3
that I may declare all *thy* w. 73:28
nor any works like unto *thy* w. 86:8
O Lord, how great are *thy* w.! 92:5
satisfied with fruit of *thy* w. 104:13
how manifold are *thy* w.!   24
I meditate on all *thy* w.   143:5
all *thy* w. shall praise thee. 145:10
commit *thy* w. unto the.   *Pr* 16:3
now God accepteth *thy* w. *Eccl* 9:7
I will declare *thy* w.   *Isa* 57:12
hast trusted in *thy* w.   *Jer* 48:7
faith without *thy* w.   *Jas* 2:18
I know *thy* w.   *Rev* 2:2, 9, 13, 19
     3:1, 8, 15
I have not found *thy* w. perfect. 3:2

wonderful **works**

Lord, are *thy* *wonderful* w. *Ps* 40:5
his *wonderful* w. that he.   78:4
Lord for his *wonderful* w. to the
  children of men! 107:8, 15, 21, 31
made his *wonderful* w. to be. 111:4
in thy name have done many *wonder-*
  ful w.   *Mat* 7:22
do hear them speak in our tongues
  the *wonderful* w. of.   *Acts* 2:11
   see **wondrous**

world

*To the Eastern people of earliest
times the world was very small,
including little except Mesopotamia,
Canaan, Arabia, and parts of
Egypt. During Old Testament
times it remained much the same,
extending a little to the East, as the
nations there grew to power;
and other parts of Asia and Africa
became somewhat known to the
adventurous. Few knew more than
rumours of Italy and even Greece.
In the time of Christ the world
really meant the Roman Empire,
with parts of Asia and Africa which
were more or less under its sway.
All outside of this was vague. In
Bible language world is frequently
used for the inhabitants of the
world, and, in the New Testament,
of mortal existence in distinction
from spiritual life.
The Revised Versions often substitute the word earth.*

he hath set the w.   *1 Sam* 2:8
the foundations of the w. were discovered. *2 Sam* 22:16; *Ps* 18:15
the w. also shall not.   *1 Chr* 16:30
chased out of the w.   *Job* 18:18

disposed the whole w.?   *Job* 34:13
do on the face of the w.   37:12
he shall judge the w. in righteousness.   *Ps* 9:8; 96:13; 98:9
soul from the men of the w.   17:14
their words to end of the w.   19:4
     Rom 10:18
all the ends of the w.   *Ps* 22:27
the earth and the w. is the Lord's.
    24:1; 98:7; *Nah* 1:5
let the inhabitants of the w. *Ps* 33:8
all ye inhabitants of the w.   49:1
for the w. is mine.   50:12
the lightnings lightened the w. 77:18
     97:4
thou hast founded the w.   89:11
formed the earth and the w.   90:2
the w. also is established, it.   93:1
w. also shall be established.   96:10
not made the dust of the w. *Pr* 8:26
also he hath set the w.   *Eccl* 3:11†
I will punish the w. for.   *Isa* 13:11
is this he that made the w.?   14:17
the face of the w. with cities.   21
w. languisheth and fadeth.   24:4
the face of the w. with fruit.   27:6
let the w. hear, and all that.   34:1
ye shall not be confounded, w. 45:17
the devil sheweth him all the kingdoms of w.   *Mat* 4:8; *Luke* 4:5
ye are the light of the w. *Mat* 5:14
the field is the w.; good seed. 13:38
it be in the end of this w.   40, 49
gain the whole w. and lose his own ?
  16:26; *Mark* 8:36; *Luke* 9:25
woe to the w. because of. *Mat* 18:7
gospel of kingdom shall be preached
  in all the w.   24:14; *Mark* 14:9
which have been since the w. began.
    Luke 1:70†; *Acts* 3:21†
a decree that all the w.   *Luke* 2:1
worthy to obtain that w.   20:35
in the w., the w. was made by him,
  and w.   *John* 1:10; *Acts* 17:24
taketh away the sin of w. *John* 1:29
God so loved the w. that he.   3:16
that the w. through him might.   17
Christ, the Saviour of the w.
    4:42; *1 John* 4:14
that giveth life unto the w. *John* 6:33
I give for the life of the w.   51
things, shew thyself to the w.   7:4
the w. cannot hate you, but me.   7
I am the light of the w.   8:12; 9:5
the w. is gone after him.   12:19
not to judge, but to save the w.   47
the Spirit, whom the w.   14:17
a little while and the w. seeth.   19
thou wilt manifest thyself unto us
  and not unto the w.?   22
I give, not as the w. giveth.   27
that the w. may know I love.   14:31
if w. hate you.   15:18; *1 John* 3:13
if ye were of the w., the w. *John* 15:19
but the w. shall rejoice.   16:20
the w. and go to the Father.   28
I have overcome the w.   33
with thee before the w. was.   17:5
men thou gavest me out of the w.   6
I pray not for the w. but for them. 9
w. hated them, because they are not
  of the w.   14
not take them out of the w.   15
the w., even as I am not of w.   16
that the w. may believe thou. 21, 23
O Father, the w. hath not known. 25
I spake openly to the w.   18:20
suppose w. could not contain. 21:25
turned the w. upside down. *Acts* 17:6
Diana, whom Asia and the w. worshippeth.   19:27
a mover of sedition among all the
  Jews throughout the w.   24:5
your faith is spoken of through the
  whole w.   *Rom* 1:8
how shall God judge the w.?   3:6
that all the w. may become guilty. 19
should be heir of the w.   4:13
of them be the riches of the w. 11:12
of them be the reconciling of.   15
the w. by wisdom knew. *1 Cor* 1:21
God ordained before the w.   2:7
received not the spirit of the w.   12
or the w., or life, or death.   3:22

are made a spectacle to w. *1 Cor* 4:9
we are made as the filth of w.   13
must ye needs go out of the w. 5:10
saints shall judge the w.?   6:2
things that are in the w.   7:33, 34
I will eat no flesh while the w. 8:13*
not be condemned with the w. 11:32
God reconciling the w.   *2 Cor* 5:19
Jesus, by whom the w. is crucified to
  me, and I to the w.   *Gal* 6:14
in Christ before the w. began.
    2 Tim 1:9*; *Tit* 1:2*
subjection the w. to come. *Heb* 2:5
have tasted the powers of the w. 6:5*
the w. was not worthy.   11:38
unspotted from the w.   *Jas* 1:27
the tongue is a fire, a w. of.   3:6
the friendship of the w. is enmity
  with God? A friend of the w. is. 4:4
spared not the old w., bringing in the
  flood upon the w.   *2 Pet* 2:5
whereby the w. that then was.   3:6
propitiation for sins of w. *1 John* 2:2
love not the w.   15
but is of the w.   16
the w. passeth away, and the.   17
the w. knoweth us not, because. 3:1
w.: therefore speak they of the w.4:5
of God, overcometh the w.   5:4, 5
we are of God, and whole w. lieth. 19
shall come upon all the w. *Rev* 3:10
deceiveth the whole w.   12:9
and all the w. wondered after. 13:3
   see **foundation**

in, or *into the* **world**

who prosper *in the* w.   *Ps* 73:12*
preached *in the* whole w. *Mat* 26:13
hundred-fold, and *in the* w. to come
  eternal. *Mark* 10:30; *Luke* 18:30
lighteth every man that cometh *into*
  the w.   *John* 1:9
he was *in the* w. and the world.   10
God sent not his Son *into the* w. to
  condemn the world.   3:17
light is come *into the* w. and men. 19
prophet that should come *into the* w.
    6:14; 11:27
in the w., I am the light of world. 9:5
I am come a light *into the* w. 12:46
in w. ye shall have tribulation. 16:33
I am no more *in the* w., but these are
  in the w.   17:11
while I was with them *in the* w.   12
cause came I *into the* w.   18:37
as by one man sin entered *into the* w.
    Rom 5:12
until the law, sin was *in the* w.   13
an idol is nothing *in the* w. *1 Cor* 8:4
having no hope, without God *in the*
  w.   *Eph* 2:12
gospel is come to you as it is in all
  the w.   *Col* 1:6
Christ Jesus came *into the* w. to save
  sinners.   *1 Tim* 1:15
and believed on *in the* w.   3:16
he cometh *into the* w.   *Heb* 10:5
afflictions that are *in the* w. *1 Pet* 5:9
things that are *in the* w. *1 John* 2:15
false prophets are gone out *into the*
  w.   4:1
even now already is it *in the* w.   3
greater than he that is *in the* w.   4
Son *into the* w. that we might live. 9
many deceivers are entered *into*
  w.   *2 John* 7

this **world**

forgiven him in *this* w.   *Mat* 12:32
the care of *this* w. choke the word.
    13:22; *Mark* 4:19
for the children of *this* w. are wiser
  than.   *Luke* 16:8
The children of *this* w. marry. 20:34
ye are of *this* w.; I am not of *this* w.
    John 8:23
I am come into *this* w.   9:39
he that hateth life in *this* w. 12:25
is the judgement of *this* w.; now shall
  the prince of *this* w. be cast.   31
he should depart out of *this* w. 13:1
for prince of *this* w. cometh. 14:30
because the prince of *this* w. 16:11
My kingdom is not of *this* w.: if my
  kingdom were of *this* w.   18:36

be not conformed to *this w.*: but be
ye. *Rom* 12:2
of *this w.?* hath not God made foolish
the wisdom of *this w.? 1 Cor* 1:20
not the wisdom of *this w.* 2:6
seemeth to be wise in *this w.* 3:18
wisdom of *this w.* is foolishness. 19
the fornicators of *this w.* 5:10
they that use *this w.* as not. 7:31
the god of *this w.* hath blinded the
minds. *2 Cor* 4:4
he might deliver us from *this* present
evil *w. Gal* 1:4
not only in *this w.,* but in. *Eph* 1:21
to the course of *this w.* 2:2
the rulers of the darkness of *this w.*
6:12
nothing into *this w. 1 Tim* 6:7
that are rich in *this w.* 17
loved *this* present *w. 2 Tim* 4:10
godly in *this* present *w. Tit* 2:12
chosen the poor of *this w. Jas* 2:5
but whoso hath *this w.'s. 1 John* 3:17
is, so are we in *this w.* 4:17

worldly

denying ungodliness and *w. Tit* 2:12
the first covenant had a *w. Heb* 9:1

worlds

by whom also he made the *w.Heb* 1:2
the *w.* were framed by the. 11:3

worm

was there any *w.* therein. *Ex* 16:20
I have said to the *w.,*Thou.*Job* 17:14
the *w.* shall feed sweetly on. 24:20
much less man that is a *w.* 25:6
but I am a *w.* and no man. *Ps* 22:6
the *w.* is spread under. *Isa* 14:11
fear not, thou *w.* Jacob, and. 41:14
w. shall eat them like wool. 51:8
for their *w.* shall not die, nor their
fire. 66:24; *Mark* 9:44, 46, 48
God prepared a *w.,* it smote the
gourd. *Jonah* 4:7

worms

their manna bred *w. Ex* 16:20
grapes, for the *w.* shall. *Deut* 28:39
my flesh is clothed with *w. Job* 7:5
though *w.* destroy this body. 19:26
they shall lie down, and *w.* 21:26
worm under thee, and the *w.* cover.
Isa 14:11
out of their holes like *w. Mi* 7:17
Herod was eaten of *w. Acts* 12:23

wormwood

a root that beareth *w. Deut* 29:18
her end is bitter as *w.,* sharp as a
sword. *Pr* 5:4
I will feed them with *w. Jer* 9:15
23:15
made me drunken with *w. Lam* 3:15
remembering my misery, the *w.* 19
who turn judgement to *w. Amos* 5:7
star is called *w.* and the third part of
the waters became *w. Rev* 8:11

worse

we will deal *w.* with thee. *Gen* 19:9
be *w.* than all that befell. *2 Sam* 19:7
Omri did *w.* than all. *1 Ki* 16:25*
Judah was put to the *w.* before.
2 Ki 14:12; *2 Chr* 25:22
the Syrians were put to the *w.*
1 Chr 19:16, 19
people be put to the *w. 2 Chr* 6:24*
Manasseh made Jerusalem do *w.*
33:9*
they did *w.* than their fathers.
Jer 7:26; 16:12
see your faces *w.* liking? *Dan* 1:10
the rent is made *w. Mat* 9:16
Mark 2:21
the last state of that man is *w.* than
first. *Mat* 12:45; *Luke* 11:26
last error shall be *w. Mat* 27:64
bettered, but grew *w. Mark* 5:26
then that which is *w. John* 2:10
sin no more, lest a *w.* thing. 5:14
eat not, are we the *w. 1 Cor* 8:8
for the better, but for the *w.* 11:17
denied the faith, and is *w. 1 Tim* 5:8
shall wax *w.* and *w. 2 Tim* 3:13
the latter end is *w. 2 Pet* 2:20

worship

lad will go yonder and *w. Gen* 22:5
to Lord, and *w.* ye afar off. *Ex* 24:1
for thou shalt *w.* no other god. 34:14
be driven to *w.* them. *Deut* 4:19
if thou *w.* other gods. 8:19; 11:16
30:17
before Lord, and *w.* before the Lord.
26:10; *Ps* 22:27, 29; 86:9
man went up early to *w. 1 Sam* 1:3
turn again, that I may *w.* 15:25, 30
the people went to *w. 1 Ki* 12:30
to *w.* in house of Rimmon. *2 Ki* 5:18
ye fear, and him shall ye *w.* 17:36*
hath said to Judah, Ye shall *w.* 18:22
2 Chr 32:12; *Isa* 36:7
w. the Lord in the beauty of holiness.
1 Chr 16:29; *Ps* 29:2; 66:4; 96:9
Mat 4:10; *Luke* 4:8
I will *w.* toward thy holy temple.
Ps 5:7; 138:2
he is thy Lord, and *w.* thou. 45:11
neither shalt thou *w.* any. 81:9
O come let us *w.* and bow. 95:6
w. him, all ye gods. 97:7
w. at his footstool, for. 99:5; 132:7
exalt the Lord, and *w.* at his. 99:9
they *w.* the work of their hands.
Isa 2:8, 20; 46:6
w. the Lord in the holy mount. 27:13
princes also shall *w.* because. 49:7
all flesh shall come to *w.* 66:23
that enter in at these gates to *w.*
Jer 7:2; 26:2
they that *w.* other gods, be. 13:10
go not after other gods to *w.* 25:6
we *w.* her without our men? 44:19
he shall *w.* at threshold. *Ezek* 46:2
the people of the land shall *w.* 3
he that entereth to *w.* by the. 9
w. the golden image. *Dan* 3:5, 10, 15
not *w.* the image. 12, 18, 28
do not ye *w.* the golden image? 3:14
if ye *w.* 15
no more *w.* the work of. *Mi* 5:13
them that *w.* the host. *Zeph* 1:5
men shall *w.* him, every one. 2:11
to *w.* the King the Lord of hosts.
Zech 14:16, 17
star, and come to *w.* him. *Mat* 2:2
that I may come and *w.* him also. 8
if thou wilt fall down and *w.* me.
4:9; *Luke* 4:7
in vain do they *w.* me. *Mat* 15:9
Mark 7:7
Jerusalem is the place where men
ought to *w. John* 4:20
ye *w.* ye know not what: we know
what we *w.*: for salvation. 4:22
they shall *w.* the Father in. 23, 24
certain Greeks came up to *w.* 12:20
God gave up to *w. Acts* 7:42*, 43
came to Jerusalem to *w.* 8:27
whom ye ignorantly *w.* 17:23
persuaded men to *w.* God. 18:13
to Jerusalem to *w.* God. 24:11
they call heresy, so *w.* I the. 14*
down, he will *w.* God. *1 Cor* 14:25
which *w.* God in spirit. *Phil* 3:3
the angels of God *w.* him. *Heb* 1:6
make them come and *w. Rev* 3:9
and *w.* him that liveth for ever. 4:10
that they should not *w.* devils. 9:20
of God, and them *w.* therein. 11:1
all on the earth shall *w.* 13:8, 12
they that would not *w.* the image. 15
w. him that made heaven, earth. 14:7
if any man *w.* the beast and. 9
who *w.* the beast, have no rest. 11
all nations shall come and *w.* 15:4
I fell at his feet to *w.* 19:10; 22:8
w. God. 22:9

worshipped

Abraham bowed and *w.* the Lord.
Gen 24:26, 48
Abraham's servant *w.* the Lord. 52
Israel bowed and *w. Ex* 4:31
12:27; 33:10
a calf, and *w.* it. 32:8; *Ps* 106:19
Moses *w. Ex* 34:8
other gods, and *w. Deut* 17:3; 29:26
1 Ki 9:9; *2 Ki* 21:21; *2 Chr* 7:22
Jer 1:16; 8:2; 16:11; 22:9
Gideon *w.* *Judg* 7:15

Hannah *w.* before Lord. *1 Sam* 1:19
Samuel *w.* 28
Saul *w.* the Lord. 15:31
then David arose and *w.*
2 Sam 12:20; 15:32
and *w.* Ashtaroth. *1 Ki* 11:33
Baal and *w.* him. 16:31; 22:53
w. all the host of heaven and served.
2 Ki 17:16; 21:3; *2 Chr* 33:3
congregation bowed down and *w.*
the Lord. *1 Chr* 29:20; *2 Chr* 7:3
29:28, 29, 30
all people *w.* the Lord. *Neh* 8:6; 9:3
Job *w.* *Job* 1:20
w. the sun. *Ezek* 8:16
king *w.* Daniel. *Dan* 2:46
w. the golden image. 3:7
fell down and *w.* Christ. *Mat* 2:11
a leper came and *w.* him. 8:2
a certain ruler *w.* him. 9:18
were in the ship *w.* him. 14:33
woman came and *w.* him. 15:25
fell down and *w.* his lord. 18:26
by the feet and *w.* him. 28:9
his disciples *w.* him. 17; *Luke* 24:52
out of the tombs and *w. Mark* 5:6
and bowing knees, *w.* him. 15:19
our fathers *w.* in this. *John* 4:20
blind man believed, and *w.* him. 9:38
fell down and *w.* Peter. *Acts* 10:25
Lydia *w.* God. 16:14
neither is *w.* with men's. 17:25*
Justus *w.* God. 18:7
w. the creature more. *Rom* 1:25
above all that is *w. 2 Thes* 2:4
Jacob *w. Heb* 11:21
the twenty-four elders *w. Rev* 5:14
11:16; 19:4
the angels *w.* God. 7:11
they *w.* the dragon, they *w.* 13:4
a sore fell on them which *w.* 16:2
them that *w.* his image. 19:20
souls that had not *w.* the beast. 20:4

worshipper

if any man be a *w.* of God. *John* 9:31
the city of Ephesus is a *w.* of Diana.
Acts 19:35*

worshippers

destroy the *w.* of Baal. *2 Ki* 10:19
all the *w.* of Baal came. 21
that there be none but the *w.* 23
then the true *w.* shall. *John* 4:23
the *w.* once purged. *Heb* 10:2

worshippeth

host of heaven *w.* thee. *Neh* 9:6
yea, he maketh a god, and *w.* it.
Isa 44:15, 17
falleth not down and *w. Dan* 3:6, 11
Asia and the world *w. Acts* 19:27

worshipping

as he was *w.* in the house of Nisroch.
2 Ki 19:37; *Isa* 37:38
fell before the Lord, *w. 2 Chr* 20:18
mother of Zebedee's children came
w. Mat 20:20
beguile you in *w.* of angels. *Col* 2:18

worst

I will bring the *w.* of the. *Ezek* 7:24

worth

as much money as it is *w. Gen* 23:9
the land is *w.* four hundred. 15
priest shall reckon the *w. Lev* 27:23
hath been *w.* a double. *Deut* 15:18
but thou art *w.* ten thousand of us.
2 Sam 18:3
give ye *w.* of thy vineyard. *1 Ki* 21:2
thy speech nothing *w. Job* 24:25
heart of wicked is little *w. Pr* 10:20
howl ye, Woe *w.* the day! *Ezek* 30:2

worthies

he shall recount his *w. Nah* 2:5

worthily

do thou *w.* in Ephratah. *Ruth* 4:11

worthy

I am not *w.* of the least. *Gen* 32:10
if the wicked man be *w. Deut* 25:2
he gave a *w.* portion. *1 Sam* 1:5*
Lord liveth, ye are *w.* to die. 26:16
who is *w.* to be praised. *2 Sam* 22:4
Ps 18:3

shew himself a *w*. man. *1 Ki* 1:52
this man is *w*. to die. *Jer* 26:11
he is not *w*. 16
whose shoes I am not *w*. *Mat* 3:11
Lord, I am not *w*. that thou shouldest
come under. 8:8; *Luke* 7:6
for the workman is *w*. of his meat.
Mat 10:10
enquire who in it is *w*. and. 11
be *w*. . . . but if it be not *w*. 13
me, he is not *w*. of me. 37, 38
which were bidden were not *w*. 22:8
I am not *w*. to unloose. *Mark* 1:7
Luke 3:16; *John* 1:27; *Acts* 13:25
bring forth fruits *w*. of. *Luke* 3:8
that he was *w*. for whom. 7:4
nor thought I myself *w*. to come. 7
for the labourer is *w*. of his. 10:7
commit things *w*. of stripes. 12:48
I am no more *w*. to be. 15:19, 21
shall be accounted *w*. to. 20:35
be accounted *w*. to escape. 21:36*
very *w*. deeds are done. *Acts* 24:2
are not *w*. to be compared with the
glory. *Rom* 8:18
that ye walk *w*. of the. *Eph* 4:1
that ye might walk *w*. of. *Col* 1:10
would walk *w*. of God. *1 Thes* 2:12
w. of all acceptation. *1 Tim* 1:15; 4:9
the labourer is *w*. of his reward. 5:18
sorer punishment, suppose ye, shall
he be thought *w*.? *Heb* 10:29
of whom the world was not *w*. 11:38
blaspheme that *w*. name? *Jas* 2:7*
in white, for they are *w*. *Rev* 3:4
thou art *w*. to receive glory. 4:11
5:12
Who is *w*. to open the book? 5:2
found *w*. to open the book. 4
thou art *w*. to take the book and. 9
to drink, for they are *w*. 16:6
 see **count, counted, death**

wot, -teth

(*The American Revision everywhere, and the English Revision
usually, put here the modern word
know, which has the same meaning*)
I *w*. not who hath done. *Gen* 21:26
my master *w*. not what is with. 39:8
w. ye not that such a man? 44:15
as for this Moses, we *w*. *Ex* 32:1
23; *Acts* 7:40
I *w*. he whom thou blessest is
blessed. *Num* 22:6
the men went I *w*. not. *Josh* 2:5
I *w*. that through ignorance ye did it.
Acts 3:17
w. ye not what the scripture saith?
Rom 11:2
I shall choose I *w*. not. *Phil* 1:22

would
I *w*. it might be according. *Gen* 30:34
I *w*. there were a sword. *Num* 22:29
whosoever *w*., he consecrated him.
1 Ki 13:33
do with them as they *w*. *Neh* 9:24
Jews did what they *w*. to. *Esth* 9:5
not hearken, and Israel *w*. *Ps* 81:11
but ye *w*. none of my. *Pr* 1:25
they *w*. none of my counsel. 30
whom he *w*. he slew, and whom he
w. he kept alive, and whom he *w*.
he set up, and *w*. *Dan* 5:19
whatsoever ye *w*. that men should.
Mat 7:12; *Luke* 6:31
to release a prisoner whom they *w*.
Mat 27:15
calleth to him whom he *w*., and they
came unto him. *Mark* 3:13
we *w*. thou shouldest do for us. 10:35
what *w*. ye that I should do? 36
fishes as much as they *w*. *John* 6:11
reason *w*. that I should. *Acts* 18:14
what I *w*. that I do not. *Rom* 7:15
for the good that I *w*. I do not. 19
I *w*. that all men were. *1 Cor* 7:7
I *w*. that ye all spake with. 14:5
not find you such as I *w*. *2 Cor* 12:20
w. that we should remember. *Gal* 2:10
I *w*. they were cut off, which. 5:12
do the things that ye *w*. 17
I *w*. ye knew what great. *Col* 2:1

forbiddeth them that *w*. *3 John* 10
I know thy works, I *w*. *Rev* 3:15

would God
w. God we had died in Egypt, when.
Ex 16:3; *Num* 14:2
w. God that all the Lord's people
were prophets! *Num* 11:29
w. God we had died when our. 20:3
w. God it were even, *w*. God it were
morning! *Deut* 28:67
w. to God we had dwelt on the other
side Jordan! *Josh* 7:7
w. God this people were. *Judg* 9:29
w. God I had died for. *2 Sam* 18:33
w. God my lord were. *2 Ki* 5:3
w. God that all were such as I am.
Acts 26:29
I *w*. to God ye did reign. *1 Cor* 4:8
w. to God ye could bear with me.
2 Cor 11:1

would not
if I knew, then *w*. not I tell it thee?
1 Sam 20:9
his armourbearer *w*. not. 31:4
1 Chr 10:4
he *w*. not, nor did he eat with them.
2 Sam 12:17
but Amnon *w*. not hearken. 13:16
howbeit David *w*. not go, but. 25
but Joab *w*. not come to. 14:23
but Jehoshaphat *w*. not. *1 Ki* 22:49
which Lord *w*. not pardon. *2 Ki* 24:4
yet *w*. they *not* give ear. *Neh* 9:30
yet *w*. I not believe he. *Job* 9:16
and ye *w*. not. *Isa* 30:15
Mat 23:37; *Luke* 13:34
besought him to have patience, he *w*.
not. *Mat* 18:30
were bidden: they *w*. not come. 22:3
we *w*. not have been partakers with
them. 23:30
w. not have suffered his house. 24:43
tasted, he *w*. not drink. 27:34
he *w*. not that any man. *Mark* 9:30
angry, and *w*. not go in. *Luke* 15:28
he *w*. not for a while, but. 18:4
he *w*. not lift so much as his. 13
who *w*. not that I should reign. 19:27
he *w*. not walk in Jewry. *John* 7:1
that he *w*. *not* delay to. *Acts* 9:38
when he *w*. not be persuaded. 21:14
I do that which I *w*. not. *Rom* 7:16
I *w*. not, brethren, that ye should be.
11:25; *1 Cor* 10:1
I *w*. not ye should have fellowship.
1 Cor 10:20
you, such as ye *w*. not. *2 Cor* 12:20
because we *w*. not be chargeable to
you. *1 Thes* 2:9
then *w*. he not afterward. *Heb* 4:8

wouldest
Caleb said, What *w*. thou?
Josh 15:18; *1 Ki* 1:16
walkedst whither thou *w*. *John* 21:18

wouldest not
whither thou *w*. not. *John* 21:18
offering thou *w*. not. *Heb* 10:5, 8

wound, *substantive*
give *w*. for *w*., stripe for. *Ex* 21:25
blood ran out of the *w*. *1 Ki* 22:35
my *w*. is incurable without transgression. *Job* 34:6
a *w*. and dishonour. *Pr* 6:33
the blueness of a *w*. cleanseth. 20:30
the stroke of their *w*. *Isa* 30:26
woe is me, for my *w*. is. *Jer* 10:19
and why is my *w*. incurable? 15:18
w. is grievous. 30:12; *Nah* 3:19
thee with *w*. of an enemy. *Jer* 30:14
Judah saw his *w*. . . . yet could he not
cure your *w*. *Hos* 5:13
they that eat have laid a *w*. *Ob* 7*
her *w*. is incurable, it is. *Mi* 1:9
and his deadly *w*. was healed.
Rev 13:3*, 12*, 14*

wound
alive; I *w*. and I heal. *Deut* 32:39
God shall *w*. the head. *Ps* 68:21*
he shall *w*. the heads over. 110:6*
when ye *w*. their weak. *1 Cor* 8:12

wound, *verb*
they *w*. body of Jesus. *John* 19:40*
young men *w*. up Ananias. *Acts* 5:6*

wounded
is *w*. in the stones. *Deut* 23:1
w. of the Philistines. *1 Sam* 17:52
Saul was *w*. of the archers. 31:3*
1 Chr 10:3*
I have *w*. mine enemies.
2 Sam 22:39*; *Ps* 18:38*
in smiting he *w*. him. *1 Ki* 20:37
carry me out, for I am *w*. 22:34
2 Chr 18:33
the Syrians *w*. Joram. *2 Ki* 8:28
for I am sore *w*. *2 Chr* 35:23
soul of the *w*. crieth out. *Job* 24:12
suddenly shall they be *w*. *Ps* 64:7
of those whom thou hast *w*. 69:26
my heart is *w*. within me. 109:22
cast down many *w*. *Pr* 7:26
a *w*. spirit who can bear? 18:14*
found me, they *w*. me. *S of S* 5:7
art thou not it that *w*.? *Isa* 51:9*
but he was *w*. for our. 53:5
I *w*. thee with the wound. *Jer* 30:14
but *w*. men among them. 37:10
through all the land the. 51:52
when they swooned as *w*. *Lam* 2:12
when the *w*. cry, shall? *Ezek* 26:15
the *w*. shall be judged in the. 28:23
groanings of a deadly *w*. 30:24
when they fall on the sword, shall not
be *w*. *Joel* 2:8*
I was *w*. in the house. *Zech* 13:6
cast stones and they *w*. him in the
head. *Mark* 12:4; *Luke* 20:12
thieves, which *w*. him. *Luke* 10:30
they fled out of that house naked and
w. *Acts* 19:16
heads, as it were *w*. *Rev* 13:3*

woundedst
thou *w*. the head out of. *Hab* 3:13

woundeth
he *w*., and his hands make. *Job* 5:18

wounding
slain a man to my *w*. *Gen* 4:23

wounds, *substantive*
went back to be healed of the *w*.
2 Ki 8:29; 9:15; *2 Chr* 22:6
he multiplied my *w*. *Job* 9:17
my *w*. stink, are corrupt. *Ps* 38:5
and bindeth up their *w*. 147:3
words of a talebearer are as *w*.
Pr 18:8*; 26:22
who hath woe? who hath *w*.? 23:29
faithful are *w*. of friend, but. 27:6
in it, but *w*., bruises, and. *Isa* 1:6
continually is grief and *w*. *Jer* 6:7
I will heal thee of thy *w*. saith. 30:17
what are these *w*. in thy hands?
Zech 13:6
bound up his *w*. *Luke* 10:34

wove
the women *w*. hangings. *2 Ki* 23:7

woven
ephod have binding of *w*. work.
Ex 28:32; 39:22
made coats of fine linen *w*. 39:27
the coat was without seam, *w*.
John 19:23

wrap
he can *w*. himself in it. *Isa* 28:20
a reward; so they *w*. it up. *Mi* 7:3*

wrapped
Tamar *w*. herself and sat. *Gen* 38:14
Goliath's sword is *w*. *1 Sam* 21:9
Elijah *w*. his face in. *1 Ki* 19:13
mantle and *w*. it together. *2 Ki* 2:8
roots are *w*. about the heap. *Job* 8:17
sinews of his stones are *w*. 40:17*
the sword is *w*. up for. *Ezek* 21:15*
the weeds were *w*. about. *Jonah* 2:5
Joseph the body in a clean linen
cloth. *Mat* 27:59; *Mark* 15:46*
Luke 23:53
Mary *w*. him in swaddling clothes.
Luke 2:7
babe *w*. in swaddling clothes. 12
napkin *w*. together in a. *John* 20:7*

wrath

(*Generally the Revised Versions use the more modern terms* anger, vexation, indignation, fury)

cursed be their w. for it. *Gen* 49:7
lest w. come upon all. *Lev* 10:6
that no w. be on the congregation.
   Num 1:53; 18:5
for there is w. gone out from. 16:46
remember, how thou provokedst the
   Lord thy God to w. *Deut* 9:7, 22
the Lord rooted them out in anger
   and w. 29:28
were it not I feared the w. 32:27
let them live, lest w. *Josh* 9:20
and w. fell on all the. 22:20
if the king's w. arise. *2 Sam* 11:20
turned not from great w. *2 Ki* 23:26
because there fell w. *1 Chr* 27:24
therefore is w. upon thee. *2 Chr* 19:2
they trespass not, and so w. 10
w. came upon Judah for. 24:18
and there is fierce w. 28:13
that his fierce w. may turn. 29:10
therefore there was w. upon. 32:25
provoked God to w. *Ezra* 5:12
should there be w. against ? 7:23
yet ye bring more w. *Neh* 13:18
shall arise too much w. *Esth* 1:18
when the w. of the king was. 2:1
not, then Haman full of w. 3:5
was the king's w. pacified. 7:10
for w. killeth the foolish man. *Job* 5:2
w. bringeth the punishments. 19:29
he shall drink of the w. of. 21:20
hypocrites in heart heap up w. 36:13
because there is w., beware. 18
forsake w. *Ps* 37:8
in w. they hate me. 55:3
surely the w. of man shall praise
   thee, the remainder of w. 76:10
stretch thy hand against w. of. 138:7
of the wicked is w. *Pr* 11:23
a fool's w. presently known. 12:16
that is slow to w. is of great. 14:29
a soft answer turneth away w. 15:1
w. of a king as messengers. 16:14
king's w. is as the roaring. 19:12
a man of great w. shall suffer. 19
bosom pacifieth strong w. 21:14
who dealeth in proud w. 24
but a fool's w. is heavier. 27:3
w. is cruel, and anger is. 4
but wise men turn away w. 29:8
forcing of w. bringeth forth. 30:33
much w. with his sickness. *Eccl* 5:17
day of Lord cometh with w. *Isa* 9:19
he who smote the people in w. 14:6
in a little w. I hid my face. 54:8
fight against you in w. *Jer* 21:5
driven them in great w. 32:37
in that ye provoke me to w. 44:8
w. is on all the multitude. *Ezek* 7:12
and he reserveth w. for. *Nah* 1:2
O Lord, in w. remember. *Hab* 3:2
not deliver in day of w. *Zeph* 1:18
therefore came a great w. *Zech* 7:12
fathers provoked me to w. 8:14
to flee from w. to come. *Mat* 3:7
   Luke 3:7
they were filled with w. *Luke* 4:28
   Acts 19:28
be w. on this people. *Luke* 21:23
but treasurest up w. against the day
   of w. *Rom* 2:5
that obey unrighteousness, w. 8
because the law worketh w. 4:15
we shall be saved from w. 5:9
endured the vessels of w. fitted. 9:22
but rather give place unto w. 12:19
minister of God to execute w. 13:4
be subject, not only for w. 5
works of flesh are w., strife. *Gal* 5:20
by nature the children of w. *Eph* 2:3
not sun go down upon your w. 4:26
let all w., anger, and clamour. 31
provoke not your children to w. 6:4
put off all these; w., malice. *Col* 3:8
who delivered us from the w. to
   come. *1 Thes* 1:10
for w. is come on them to. 2:16
hath not appointed us to w. 5:9
holy hands, without w. *1 Tim* 2:8

Moses not fearing the w. of the king.
   Heb 11:27
slow to speak, slow to w. *Jas* 1:19
w. of man worketh not. 20
and hide us from the w. *Rev* 6:16
come down, having great w. 12:12
she made all nations drink wine of w.
   14:8; 18:3

day of wrath

his goods flow away in the *day of* his
   w. *Job* 20:28
the wicked brought forth to the *day
   of* w. 21:30
Lord strike through kings in *day of*
   w. *Ps* 110:5
profit not in the *day of* w. *Pr* 11:4
that day is a *day of* w. *Zeph* 1:15
w. against the *day of* w. *Rom* 2:5
the great *day of* his w. is. *Rev* 6:17

wrath of God

the fierce w. of God is. *2 Chr* 28:11
till the w. of God be turned from us.
   Ezra 10:14
the w. of God came. *John* 3:36
but the w. of God abideth. *John* 3:36
the w. of God is revealed. *Rom* 1:18
things, w. of God cometh on the
   children. *Eph* 5:6; *Col* 3:6
shall drink of the wine of the w. of
   God. *Rev* 14:10
into winepress of the w. of God. 19
is filled up the w. of God. 15:1
golden vials full of the w. of God. 7
vials of the w. of God on earth. 16:1
winepress of the w. of God. 19:15

his wrath

Lord overthrew in his w. *Deut* 29:23
nor executedst his w. *1 Sam* 28:18
turned not from his w. *2 Ki* 23:26
his fierce w. may turn away.
   2 Chr 29:10; 30:8
his w. is against them. *Ezra* 8:22
from the banquet in his w. *Esth* 7:7
he teareth me in his w. *Job* 16:9
the fury of his w. on him. 20:23
he speak to them in his w. *Ps* 2:5
swallow them up in his w. 21:9
take them away in his w. 58:9
did not stir up all his w. 78:38
the fierceness of his w. 49
stood to turn away his w. 106:23
his w. against him that. *Pr* 14:35
turn away his w. from him. 24:18
Moab's pride and his w. *Isa* 16:6
the Lord hath forsaken the generation of his w. *Jer* 7:29
at his w. the earth shall. 10:10
I know his w., saith the Lord. 48:30
hath thrown down in his w. *Lam* 2:2
affliction by the rod of his w. 3:1
because he kept his w. *Amos* 1:11
God willing to shew his w. *Rom* 9:22
of fierceness of his w. *Rev* 16:19
see **kindled**, **wrath of the Lord**

my wrath

my w. shall wax hot. *Ex* 22:24
let me alone, that my w. 32:10
hath turned my w. away. *Num* 25:11
my w. shall not be poured out on
   Jerusalem. *2 Chr* 12:7
to whom I sware in my w. *Ps* 95:11
against the people of my w. *Isa* 10:6
for in my w. I smote thee. 60:10
for my w. is on all the multitude.
   Ezek 7:14
thus will I accomplish my w. 13:15
thee in fire of my w. 21:31; 22:21
them with the fire of my w. 22:31
of my w. have I spoken. 38:19
I will pour out my w. on. *Hos* 5:10
I took him away in my w. 13:11
so sware in my w. they. *Heb* 3:11
as I have sworn in my w., if they. 4:3

thy wrath

thou sentest thy w. which. *Ex* 15:7
doth thy w. wax hot against ? 32:11
turn from thy fierce w. and. 12
keep me secret until thy w. be past.
   Job 14:13
cast abroad the rage of thy w. 40:11
rebuke me not in thy w. *Ps* 38:1
pour out thy w. on the heathen. 79:6

taken away all thy w. *Ps* 85:3
thy w. lieth hard on me. 88:7
thy fierce w. goeth over me. 16
how long shall thy w. burn ? 89:46
and by thy w. are we troubled. 90:7
days are passed away in thy w. 9
according to thy fear, so is thy w. 11
thine indignation and thy w. 102:10
I stood to turn away thy w. *Jer* 18:20
was thy w. against the sea. *Hab* 3:8
thy w. is come, and time. *Rev* 11:18

wrathful

let thy w. anger take. *Ps* 69:24
a w. man stirreth up. *Pr* 15:18

wraths

be envyings, w., strifes. *2 Cor* 12:20

wreath

two rows of pomegranates on each
   w. *2 Chr* 4:13*

wreathed

my transgressions are w. *Lam* 1:14*

wreathen

two chains at the ends, of w. work.
   Ex 28:14, 22, 24, 25; 39:15, 17, 18
pillar of w. work he carried away.
   2 Ki 25:17*

wreaths

w. of chain work for. *1 Ki* 7:17
two w. to cover the. *2 Chr* 4:12*
pomegranates on the two w. 13*

wrest

many, to w. judgement. *Ex* 23:2
thou shalt not w. the judgement of
   thy poor. 6
thou shalt not w. judgement; neither
   take a gift. *Deut* 16:19
day they w. my words. *Ps* 56:5
they that are unstable w. *2 Pet* 3:16

wrestle

we w. not against flesh. *Eph* 6:12

wrestled

wrestlings have I w. with. *Gen* 30:8
there w. a man with him. 32:24
thigh was out of joint as he w. 25

wrestlings

with great w. have I wrestled with
   my sister. *Gen* 30:8

wretched

O w. man that I am ! *Rom* 7:24
knowest not thou art w. *Rev* 3:17

wretchedness

let me not see my w. *Num* 11:15

wring

the priest shall w. off his head.
   Lev 1:15; 5:8
all the wicked shall w. *Ps* 75:8†

wringed

Gideon w. the dew out. *Judg* 6:38

wringing

the w. of the nose bringeth forth
   blood. *Pr* 30:33

wrinkle

a glorious church not having spot or
   w. *Eph* 5:27

wrinkles

hast filled me with w. *Job* 16:8*

write

I will w. on these tables. *Ex* 34:1
   Deut 10:2
W. thou these words. *Ex* 34:27
w. thou every man's. *Num* 17:2
thou shalt w. Aaron's name on. 3
w. them on posts. *Deut* 6:9; 11:20
then let him w. her a bill of divorcement, and. 24:1, 3; *Mark* 10:4
w. on the stones the. *Deut* 27:3, 8
now therefore w. ye this. 31:19
Uzziah did Isaiah w. *2 Chr* 26:22
we might w. the names. *Ezra* 5:10
sure covenant and w. it. *Neh* 9:38
w. ye also for the Jews. *Esth* 8:8
w. them on the table. *Pr* 3:3; 7:3
w. in the great roll with. *Isa* 8:1
that w. grievousness which. 10:1
few, that a child may w. them. 19
now go, w. it before them. 30:8
saith the Lord, W. ye. *Jer* 22:30
w. the words I have spoken. 30:2
   36:2, 17, 28

I will *w*. it in their hearts. *Jer* 31:33
   Heb 8:10
son of man, *w*. the name. *Ezek* 24:2
w. upon the sticks for. 37:16
w. it in their sight, that they. 43:11
w. the vision and make it. *Hab* 2:2
it seemed good to me to *w*. to thee
 in order. *Luke* 1:3
take thy bill and *w*. fifty. 16:6
w. fourscore. 7
and the prophets did *w*. *John* 1:45
w. not, King of the Jews, but. 19:21
that we *w*. to them that. *Acts* 15:20
thing to *w*. unto my lord, that I might
 have somewhat to *w*. 25:26
I *w*. not these things to. *1 Cor* 4:14
things I *w*. are the. 14:37
for we *w*. none other things to you.
   2 Cor 1:13
to this end also did I *w*., that. 2:9
it is superfluous for me to *w*. to. 9:1
I *w*. to them which heretofore. 13:2
therefore I *w*. these things, being. 10
now the things I *w*. unto. *Gal* 1:20
to *w*. the same things. *Phil* 3:1
not that I *w*. to you. *1 Thes* 4:9; 5:1
so I *w*. *2 Thes* 3:17
these things I *w*. *1 Tim* 3:14
minds will I *w*. them. *Heb* 10:16
I now *w*. unto you. *2 Pet* 3:1
   1 John 2:1
these things *w*. we to. *1 John* 1:4
brethren, I *w*. no new. 2:7
again, a new commandment I *w*. 8
I *w*. to you, little children. 12, 13
I *w*. to you, fathers, I *w*. to you. 13
having many things to *w*. *2 John* 12
ink and pen *w*. to you. *3 John* 13
diligence to *w*. of common salvation,
 it was needful for me to *w*. *Jude* 3
what thou seest, *w*. *Rev* 1:11, 19
unto the angel of the church of . . . *w*.
 2:1, 8, 12, 18; 3:1, 7, 14
I will *w*. on him the name of my God
 . . . I will *w*. upon him my new.3:12
to *w*.: a voice saying, *w*. not. 10:4
W., Blessed are the dead which.14:13
W., Blessed are they which. 19:9
w.: for these words are true. 21:5
  ***see* book**

writer
handle the pen of the *w*. *Judg* 5:14*
the pen of a ready *w*. *Ps* 45:1
a man with a *w*.'s inkhorn by his
 side. *Ezek* 9:2, 3

writest
for thou *w*. bitter things. *Job* 13:26
sticks whereon thou *w*. *Ezek* 37:20

writeth
count, when he *w*. up. *Ps* 87:6

writing
and the *w*. was the *w*. of. *Ex* 32:16
plate of the holy crown a *w*. 39:30
according to the first *w*. *Deut* 10:4
made an end of *w*. the law. 31:24
the Lord made me understand in *w*.
   1 Chr 28:19
Huram answered in *w*. *2 Chr* 2:11
came a *w*. from Jehoram. 21:12
prepare according to the *w*. of. 35:4
Cyrus put the proclamation in *w*.
  36:22; *Ezra* 1:1
the *w*. of the letter was in. *Ezra* 4:7
unto all provinces according to the *w*.
 Esth 1:22; 3:12; 8:9; 9:27
copy of the *w*. was published. 3:14
to Hatach a copy of the *w*. 4:8
the *w*. in the king's name may. 8:8
the *w*. of Hezekiah, when. *Isa* 38:9
not written in the *w*. of. *Ezek* 13:9
whosoever shall read this *w*. *Dan* 5:7
could not read the *w*. 8
should read this *w*. 15
if thou canst read the *w*. thou. 16
yet I will read the *w*. to the king. 17
this is the *w*. that was. 24, 25
sign the *w*. 6:8
king Darius signed the *w*. 9
when Daniel knew that the *w*. 10
give her a *w*. of divorcement.
  Mat 5:31; 19:7
the *w*. was, Jesus of. *John* 19:19

hand-writing
blotting out the *hand-w*. *Col* 2:14

writings
if ye believe not his *w*. *John* 5:47

writing table
asked for a *w*. table. *Luke* 1:63

written
w. with the finger of God. *Ex* 31:18
   Deut 9:10
elders did as it was *w*. *1 Ki* 21:11
these *w*. by name smote. *1 Chr* 4:41
the passover as it was *w*. *2 Chr* 30:5
a letter wherein was *w*. *Ezra* 5:7
therein was a record thus *w*. 6:2
weight of the vessels was *w*. 8:34
sent an open letter, wherein was *w*.
   Neh 6:6
they found *w*. in the law. 8:14
and therein was found *w*. 13:1
it be *w*. among the laws. *Esth* 1:19
let it be *w*. that they may be. 3:9
of king Ahasuerus was it *w*. 12
found *w*. that Mordecai told of. 6:2
let it be *w*. to reverse Haman's. 8:5
let them not be *w*. with. *Ps* 69:28
be *w*. for the generation to. 102:18
on them the judgement *w*. 149:9
have not I *w*. to thee excellent
 things ? *Pr* 22:20
that which was *w*. was. *Eccl* 12:10
shall be *w*. in the earth. *Jer* 17:13
hast *w*., saying, The king ? 36:29
the roll was *w*. within. *Ezek* 2:10
nor *w*. in the writing of house. 13:9
writing that was *w*. *Dan* 5:24, 25
set up his accusation *w*. *Mat* 27:37
is it not *w*., My house ? *Mark* 11:17
of his accusation was *w*. 15:26
 Luke 23:38; *John* 19:20
place where it was *w*. *Luke* 4:17
rejoice that your names are *w*. 10:20
all things *w*. shall be accomplished.
  18:31; 21:22
disciples remembered that it was *w*.
   John 2:17
Is it not *w*. in your law, I said? 10:34
but these are *w*. that ye might. 20:31
w. every one, the world could not
 contain the books . . . be *w*. 21:25
fulfilled all that was *w*. *Acts* 13:29
the Gentiles, we have *w*. 21:25
the work of the law *w*. *Rom* 2:15
now it was not *w*. for his sake. 4:23
they are *w*. for our admonition.
   1 Cor 10:11
ye are our epistle *w*. in our. *2 Cor* 3:2
w. not with ink, but with the. 3
if the ministration of death *w*. in. 7
I Paul have *w*. with. *Philem* 19
firstborn *w*. in heaven. *Heb* 12:23*
things which are *w*. therein. *Rev* 1:3
and in the stone a new name *w*. 2:17
not *w*. in the book of life. 13:8
having his Father's name *w*. 14:1
upon her head was a name *w*. 17:5
name *w*. on his thigh. 19:12, 16
names of the twelve tribes *w*. 21:12

is written
observe to do all that *is w*. *Josh* 1:8
that which *is w*. concerning us.
   2 Ki 22:13
for writing which *is w*. in. *Esth* 8:8
every one that *is w*. among. *Isa* 4:3
sin of Judah *is w*. with. *Jer* 17:1
oath that *is w*. in the law. *Dan* 9:11
what *is w*. in the law ? *Luke* 10:26
What is this then that *is w*.? 20:17
this that *is w*. must be. 22:37
be fulfilled that *is w*. *John* 15:25
to think of men above that which *is
w*. *1 Cor* 4:6
for our sakes, no doubt, this *is w*.9:10
the saying that *is w*., Death. 15:54

it is written
as *it is w*. in the law of. *Josh* 8:31
1 Ki 2:3; *2 Chr* 23:18; 25:4; 31:3
 35:12; *Ezra* 3:2, 4; 6:18
 Neh 8:15; 10:34, 36; *Dan* 9:13
it is w. of me. *Ps* 40:7; *Heb* 10:7
it is w. before me. *Isa* 65:6
thus *it is w*. by the prophet.
  Mat 2:5; *Luke* 24:46

this is he of whom *it is w*.
  Mat 11:10; *Luke* 7:27
as *it is w*. of him. *Mat* 26:24
  Mark 9:13; 14:21
it is w. *Mat* 26:31; *Mark* 14:27
  Luke 4:8; *Acts* 23:5
and how *it is w*. of the. *Mark* 9:12
as *it is w*. in the law. *Luke* 2:23
according as *it is w*. *Rom* 11:8
 1 Cor 1:31; *2 Cor* 4:13
for *it is w*. *Rom* 12:19; 14:11
   Gal 3:10
not himself, but as *it is w*. *Rom* 15:3
so *it is w*., The first man. *1 Cor* 15:45
because *it is w*., Be ye holy; for I am
 holy. *1 Pet* 1:16

I have, or *have I* **written**
commandment, *I have w*. *Ex* 24:12
I have w. to him great. *Hos* 8:12
Pilate said, What *I have w*. *I have*
 w. *John* 19:22
I have w. to you fathers. *1 John* 2:14
these things *have I w*. 26; 5:13

were **written**
of them that *were w*. *Num* 11:26
words *were* now *w*. *Job* 19:23
fulfilled which *were w*. *Luke* 24:44
things *were w*. of him. *John* 12:16
were w. aforetime *were w*. for our
 learning. *Rom* 15:4
 ***see* book, chronicle**

wrong
Sarai said, My *w*. be. *Gen* 16:5
to him that did the *w*. *Ex* 2:13
against him what is *w*. *Deut* 19:16
thou doest me *w*. to war. *Judg* 11:27
seeing there is no *w*. in. *1 Chr* 12:17
no man to do them *w*.: yea, he reproved kings for. 16:21; *Ps* 105:14
not done *w*. to the king. *Esth* 1:16
behold, I cry out of *w*. *Job* 19:7
do no *w*., do no violence. *Jer* 22:3
buildeth his chambers by *w*. 13*
seen my *w*.: judge thou. *Lam* 3:59
therefore to *w*. judgement. *Hab* 1:4*
Friend, I do thee no *w*. *Mat* 20:13
one of them suffer *w*. *Acts* 7:24
why do ye *w*. one to another ? 26
neighbour *w*. thrust him away. 27
if it were a matter of *w*. 18:14
the Jews have I done no *w*. 25:10
do ye not rather take *w*.? *1 Cor* 6:7
nay, ye do *w*. and defraud your. 8
that had done the *w*. nor for his
 cause that suffered *w*. *2 Cor* 7:12
I was not burdensome to you ? forgive me this *w*. 12:13
w. shall receive for the *w*. *Col* 3:25

wronged
receive us, we have *w*. *2 Cor* 7:2
if he hath *w*. thee, or. *Philem* 18

wrongeth
he that sinneth against me *w*. his own
 soul. *Pr* 8:36

wrongfully
the devices ye *w*. *Job* 21:27
let not mine enemies *w*. *Ps* 35:19
they that hate me *w*. are. 38:19
being mine enemies *w*. 69:4
me *w*., help thou me. 119:86
they have oppressed the stranger *w*.
   Ezek 22:29
endure grief, suffering *w*. *1 Pet* 2:19

wrote
Moses *w*. all the words of the Lord
 and rose. *Ex* 24:4; *Deut* 31:9
Lord *w*. upon the tables words of.
 Ex 34:28; *Deut* 4:13; 5:22; 10:4
and Moses *w*. their. *Num* 33:2
Moses *w*. this song the. *Deut* 31:22
Joshua *w*. upon the. *Josh* 8:32
Samuel *w*. the manner of the king-
 dom. *1 Sam* 10:25
David *w*. a letter to Joab.
  2 Sam 11:14, 15
Jezebel *w*. letters in. *1 Ki* 21:8, 9
Jehu *w*. *2 Ki* 10:1, 6
Shemaiah *w*. *1 Chr* 24:6
Hezekiah *w*. letters to. *2 Chr* 30:1
Sennacherib *w*. to rail on the. 32:17
they *w*. an accusation. *Ezra* 4:6
Rehum *w*. 8, 9

letters which Haman w. *Esth* 8:5
Mordecai w. letters. 10; 9:20, 29
Baruch w. from Jeremiah. *Jer* 36:4
    18, 27, 32
so Jeremiah w. in a book. 51:60
fingers of a man's hand w. *Dan* 5:5
then king Darius w. unto all. 6:25
Daniel had a dream; then he w. 7:1
your hardness Moses w. *Mark* 10:5
Master, Moses w. to us. 12:19
    Luke 20:28
Zacharias w. saying. *Luke* 1:63
for Moses w. of me. *John* 5:46
Jesus with his finger w. 8:6, 8
Pilate w. a title and put. 19:19
John w. and testified of. 21:24
the apostles w. letters. *Acts* 15:23
the brethren w. exhorting. 18:27
Lysias w. a letter after. 23:25
who w. this epistle. *Rom* 16:22
I w. unto you. *1 Cor* 5:9; *2 Cor* 2:3, 4
    7:12; *Eph* 3:3; *Philem* 21
things whereof ye w. to me. *1 Cor* 7:1
not as though I w. a new. *2 John* 5
I w. to the church. *3 John* 9

wroth

Cain was very w. *Gen* 4:5
why art thou w.? 6
Jacob was w. 31:36
Jacob's sons were w. 34:7
w. with two officers. 40:2; 41:10
Moses was w. *Ex* 16:20
    Num 16:15; 31:14
wilt thou be w. with all? *Num* 16:22
your words and was w. *Deut* 1:34
3:26; 9:19; *2 Sam* 22:8; *2 Chr* 28:9
    Ps 18:7; 78:21, 59, 62
Saul was very w. *1 Sam* 18:8; 20:7
Philistines were w. with him. 29:4
Abner was w. *2 Sam* 3:8
David was w. 13:21
but Naaman was w. *2 Ki* 5:11
and the man of God was w. 13:19
Asa was w. *2 Chr* 16:10
Uzziah was w. 26:19
Sanballat was w. *Neh* 4:1, 7
Ahasuerus was very w. *Esth* 1:12
Bigthan and Teresh were w. 2:21
thou hast been w. with. *Ps* 89:38
shall be w. as in the. *Isa* 28:21
I was w. with my people. 47:6
I would not be w. with thee. 54:9
nor will I be always w. 57:16
of his covetousness was I w. and
    smote him: I hid me ... was w. 17
behold, thou art w.; for we. 64:5
be not w. very sore, O Lord; we. 9
princes were w. *Jer* 37:15
rejected us, thou art very w. against
    us. *Lam* 5:22
Herod was w. *Mat* 2:16
his lord was w., and. 18:34
king was w. 22:7
dragon was w. *Rev* 12:17

wrought

Shechem had w. folly in. *Gen* 34:7
what things I have w. in. *Ex* 10:2
then w. Bezaleel and Aholiab. 36:1
all the wise men w. the. 4, 8; 39:6
they have w. confusion. *Lev* 20:12
What hath God w.? *Num* 23:23
of them all w. jewels. 31:51
that such abomination is w.
    Deut 13:14; 17:4
that hath w. wickedness. 17:2
heifer which hath not been w. 21:3
w. folly in Israel. 22:21; *Josh* 7:15
    Judg 20:10
for the evils which they shall have w.
    Deut 31:18
she had w., The man's name with
    whom I w. to-day. *Ruth* 2:19
Lord had w. wonderfully. *1 Sam* 6:6
w. salvation in Israel. 11:13; 19:5
for Jonathan hath w. with. 14:45
otherwise I should have w. false-
    hood. *2 Sam* 18:13
the Lord w. a great victory. 23:10, 12
who ruled over the people that w.
    1 Ki 5:16; 9:23
of the sea w. like. 16:20
and the treason he w. 16:20
but Omri w. evil in the eyes. 25

Jehoram w. evil. *2 Ki* 3:2; *2 Chr* 21:6
Israel w. wicked things. *2 Ki* 17:11
    Neh 9:18
Manasseh w. much wickedness.
    2 Ki 21:6; *2 Chr* 33:6
families that w. fine. *1 Chr* 4:21
masons to hew w. stones. 22:2
and he w. cherubims. *2 Chr* 3:14
they hired such as w. iron. 24:12
so the workman w. 13; 34:10, 13
half of my servants w. *Neh* 4:16
every one with one of his hands w. 17
this work was w. of our. 6:16
the Lord hath w. this. *Job* 12:9
thou hast w. iniquity? 36:23
hast w. for them that trust. *Ps* 31:19
clothing is of w. gold. 45:13
which thou hast w. for us. 68:28
how he had w. his signs in. 78:43
made in secret, curiously w. 139:15
all works my hands had w. *Eccl* 2:11
works w. under the sun. 17
for thou hast w. all our works in us.
    Isa 26:12
we have not w. any deliverance. 18
who hath w. and done it? 41:4
she hath w. lewdness. *Jer* 11:15
and behold, he w. a work. 18:3
I w. for my name's sake. *Ezek* 20:9
    14, 22, 44
because they w. for me. 29:20
wonders that God hath w. *Dan* 4:2
the sea w. and was. *Jonah* 1:11, 13
meek of earth who have w. *Zeph* 2:3
these last have w. but. *Mat* 20:12*
she hath w. a good work on me.
    26:10; *Mark* 14:6
that they are w. of God. *John* 3:21
wonders were w. among. *Acts* 5:12
God hath w. 15:12; 21:19
abode with Aquila and w. 18:3
God w. special miracles by. 19:11
w. in me all manner of. *Rom* 7:8
Christ hath not w. by me. 15:18
he that hath w. us for. *2 Cor* 5:5
what carefulness it w. in you? 7:11
the signs of an apostle were w.
    12:12
for he that w. effectually. *Gal* 2:8
which he w. in Christ. *Eph* 1:20
but we w. with labour. *2 Thes* 3:8
who, through faith, w. *Heb* 11:33
seest thou how faith w.? *Jas* 2:22
to have w. the will of. *1 Pet* 4:3
lose not those things which we have
    w. *2 John* 8
the false prophet that w. *Rev* 19:20

wroughtest

to her, Where w. thou? *Ruth* 2:19

wrung

the blood shall be w. out. *Lev* 1:15*
    5:9*
waters are w. to them. *Ps* 73:10†
thou hast w. out of the dregs of the
    cup. *Isa* 51:17*

Y

yarn

y. out of Egypt, the king's merchants
    ... y. *1 Ki* 10:28*; *2 Chr* 1:16*

ye

ye shall be as gods. *Gen* 3:5
but ye have no portion in. *Neh* 2:20
ye are they which justify. *Luke* 16:15
but ye are washed, ye are sanctified.
ye are justified in. *1 Cor* 6:11
ye are bought with a price. 20
ye also helping by prayer. *2 Cor* 1:11
ye are our epistle, written. 3:2
ye are not straitened in us. 6:12
not that other men be eased, ye. 8:13
as I am, for I am as ye are. *Gal* 4:12
ye which are spiritual, restore. 6:1
ye who sometimes were. *Eph* 2:13
in whom ye also are builded. 22
joy, are not even ye? *1 Thes* 2:19
ye are our glory. 20
if ye stand fast in the Lord. 3:8
but ye, brethren, are not in. 5:4
ye are all children of light and. 5

but ye, brethren, be. *2 Thes* 3:13
but ye are a chosen. *1 Pet* 2:9

yea

y., hath God said, Ye. *Gen* 3:1
but let your communication be Y., y.;
    Nay, nay. *Mat* 5:37; *Jas* 5:12
said unto him, Y. *Mat* 9:28; 13:51
Sapphira said, Y. for so. *Acts* 5:8
thou a Roman? he said, Y. 22:27
y. y. and nay, nay. *2 Cor* 1:17
toward you was not y. and nay. 18
Son of God was not y. and nay. 19
God in him are y. and amen. 20
I do rejoice, y. and will. *Phil* 1:18
y. and I count all things but loss. 3:8
y. and all that live godly. *2 Tim* 3:12
y. brother, let me have. *Philem* 20

year

shall bear the next y. *Gen* 17:21
Isaac received the same y. 26:12
with bread that y. 47:17
first month of the y. *Ex* 12:2
keep it a feast unto the Lord in the
    y. 23:14; *Lev* 23:41
three times in the y. all thy males.
    Ex 23:17; 34:23, 24; *Deut* 16:16
out from thee in one y. *Ex* 23:29
ingathering at the y.'s end. 34:22
atonement once a y. *Lev* 16:34
it is a y. of rest. 25:5
redeem it within a y. 29
if it were a y. that the. *Num* 9:22
each day for a y. shall ye. 14:34
saying, The y. of release. *Deut* 15:9
the third y., which is the y. of. 26:12
fruit of Canaan that y. *Josh* 5:12
that y. the Ammonites. *Judg* 10:8
to lament four days in a y. 11:40
thee ten shekels by the y. 17:10
David dwelt a y. and. *1 Sam* 27:7
that after the y. was. *2 Sam* 11:1
it was at every y.'s end that. 14:26
three times in a y. did. *1 Ki* 9:25
gold that came to Solomon in one y.
    10:14; *2 Chr* 9:13
this y. such things as grow of them-
    selves in second and third y.
    2 Ki 19:29; *Isa* 37:30
gave him the same y. *2 Chr* 27:5
keep two days every y. *Esth* 9:27
thou crownest the y. with. *Ps* 65:11
in the y. that king Uzziah. *Isa* 6:1
in the y. that king Ahaz died. 14:28
in a y. all the glory of Kedar. 21:16
to proclaim the acceptable y. of the
    Lord, and the. 61:2; *Luke* 4:19
and the y. of my redeemed. *Isa* 63:4
bring evil on the men of Anathoth,
    even the y. *Jer* 11:23; 23:12; 48:44
shall not be careful in the y. 17:8
thus saith the Lord; this y. 28:16
prophet died the same y. 17
shall both come in one y. *Ezek* 4:6
each day for a y. 4:6
it shall be his to the y. of. 46:17
with calves of a y. old? *Mi* 6:6
his parents went to Jerusalem every
    y. *Luke* 2:41
let it alone this y. also. 13:8
high priest that same y., said, Ye
    know. *John* 11:49, 51; 18:13
whole y. they assembled. *Acts* 11:26
Paul continued a y. at Corinth. 18:11
to be forward a y. ago. *2 Cor* 8:10
was ready a y. ago; your zeal. 9:2
went in once a y. *Heb* 9:7, 25
made of sins every y. 10:3
continue there a y. and buy. *Jas* 4:13
who were prepared for a month and
    a y. *Rev* 9:15
see **first, second, third, fifth,**
seventh

year after year

there was a famine three years y.
    after y. *2 Sam* 21:1

year by year

increase of thy seed that the field
    bringeth forth y. by y. *Deut* 14:22
eat it before the Lord y. by y. 15:20
as he did so y. by y., so. *1 Sam* 1:7
gave to Hiram y. by y. *1 Ki* 5:11

they brought a rate *v. by v.*
   1 Ki 10:25; *2 Chr* 9:24
as he had done *v. by v.*   *2 Ki* 17:4
wood offering *v. by v.*   *Neh* 10:34
firstfruits of all trees *v. by v.*   35
which they offered *v. by v. Heb* 10:1

year to year
ordinance from *v. to v.*   *Ex* 13:10
coat to him from *v. to v. 1 Sam* 2:19
Samuel went from *v. to v.* in. 7:16
your God from *v. to v. 2 Chr* 24:5
add *v. to v.*; let them. *Isa* 29:1
from *v. to v.* to worship. *Zech* 14:16

yearly
as a *v.* hired servant. *Lev* 25:53
daughters of Israel went *v.* to
  lament.   *Judg* 11:40
of the Lord in Shiloh *v.* 21:19
Elkanah went up *v.* to. *1 Sam* 1:3
to offer the *v.* sacrifice. 21; 2:19
there is a *v.* sacrifice there. 20:6
keep 14th day of month Adar, and
  fifteenth of same *v.* *Esth* 9:21

yearn
for his bowels did *v.* *Gen* 43:30

yearned
for her bowels *v.* upon. *1 Ki* 3:26

years
for seasons, days, and *v. Gen* 1:14
these are the days of the *v.* 25:7
an old man and full of *v.* 8
an hundred thirty seven *v.* 17
few and evil have the *v.* of. 47:9
according to the number of *v.*
  Lev 25:15, 16, 50, 52
the money according to the *v.* 27:18
consider the *v.* of many. *Deut* 32:7
Joshua was old and stricken in *v.*
  Josh 13:1
been with me these *v. 1 Sam* 29:3
David was old and stricken in *v.*
  1 Ki 1:1
not be dew nor rain these *v.* 17:1
Asa had no war in those *v. 2 Chr* 14:6
after certain *v.* he went down. 18:2
are thy *v.* as man's days ? *Job* 10:5
the number of *v.* is hidden to. 15:20
when a few *v.* are come, I. 16:22
and multitude of *v.* should. 32:7
they shall spend their *v.* in. 36:11
nor can number of his *v.* be. 26
and my *v.* are spent. *Ps* 31:10
wilt prolong his *v.* as many. 61:6
I considered the *v.* of ancient. 77:5
I will remember the *v.* of the. 10
their *v.* did he consume in. 78:33
for a thousand *v.* in thy sight are but.
  90:4; *2 Pet* 3:8
we spend our *v.* as a tale. *Ps* 90:9
our *v.* are threescore *v.* and ten. 10
according to the *v.* wherein we. 15
thy *v.* are throughout all. 102:24
thou art the same, thy *v.* shall. 27
the *v.* of thy life shall be many.
  Pr 4:10; 9:11
lest thou give thy *v.* unto. 5:9
the *v.* of the wicked shall be. 10:27
evil days come not, nor *v. Eccl* 12:1
the *v.* of an hireling. *Isa* 21:16
of the residue of my *v.* 38:10
I shall go softly all my *v.* 15
I have laid on thee the *v. Ezek* 4:5
art come even unto thy *v.* 22:4
in latter *v.* thou shalt come. 38:8
by books the number of the *v.Dan*9:2
in the end of *v.* they shall join. 11:6
continue more *v.* than the king. 8
shall come after certain *v.* 13
even to the *v.* of many. *Joel* 2:2
I will restore the *v.* the locusts. 25
in the midst of the *v.* *Hab* 3:2
the offering be pleasant as in the
  former *v.* *Mal* 3:4
well stricken in *v.* *Luke* 1:7, 18
days and months, and *v. Gal* 4:10
thy *v.* shall not fail. *Heb* 1:12
by faith Moses, when he was come
  to *v.*, refused. 11:24
bound Satan a thousand *v. Rev* 20:2
till the thousand *v.* should be. 3
reigned with Christ a thousand *v.* 4
when the thousand *v.* are expired. 7

see numeral words in their places,
as hundred, two, three. *Also*
many, old, sin

yell
like lions, they shall *v.* *Jer* 51:38*

yelled
roared and *v.* on him. *Jer* 2:15

yellow
behold, if there be in it a *v.* thin hair.
  Lev 13:30
if there be in it no *v.* hair. 32
priests shall not seek for *v.* hair. 36
covered with *v.* gold. *Ps* 68:13

yesterday
fulfilled your task *v.?* *Ex* 5:14
why came not the son of Jesse to
  meat *v.?* *1 Sam* 20:27
thou camest but *v.* *2 Sam* 15:20
I have seen *v.* the blood. *2 Ki* 9:26
we are but of *v.* and know. *Job* 8:9
a thousand years in thy sight are but
  as *v.* *Ps* 90:4
v. at the seventh hour. *John* 4:52
didst the Egyptian *v.?* *Acts* 7:28
Jesus Christ, the same *v. Heb* 13:8

yesternight
behold, I lay *v.* with my. *Gen* 19:34
your fathers spake to me *v.* 31:29
affliction, and rebuked thee *v.* 42

yet
v. did not the butler. *Gen* 40:23
as *v.* exaltest thyself. *Ex* 9:17
knowest thou not *v.* that Egypt ? 10:7
if ye will not *v.* hearken. *Lev* 26:18
v. for all that, when they be. 44
v. in this thing ye did. *Deut* 1:32
v. they are thy people and. 9:29
ye are not as *v.* come to the. 12:9
v. the Lord hath not given you. 29:4
as *v.* I am as strong. *Josh* 14:11
Lord said, The people are *v.* too
  many. *Judg* 7:4
v. ye have forsaken me and. 10:13
v. honour me now before the elders.
  1 Sam 15:30
v. he hath made with me an everlasting covenant. *2 Sam* 23:5
v. hast not been as my. *1 Ki* 14:8
v. I have left me 7000. 19:18
there is *v.* one by whom we. 22:8
as *v.* the people did sacrifice. 43
  2 Ki 14:4
v. the Lord would not destroy
  Judah. *2 Ki* 8:19
them from his presence as *v.* 13:23
as *v.* the people had not prepared.
  2 Chr 20:33
people did *v.* corruptly. 27:2
not cleansed, *v.* did they eat. 30:18
temple was not *v.* laid. *Ezra* 3:6
v. our God hath not forsaken us.
  9:9; *Neh* 9:19
v. required not I bread. *Neh* 5:18
v. ye bring more wrath upon. 13:18
v. all this availeth me. *Esth* 5:13
while he was *v.* *Job* 1:16, 17, 18
then should I *v.* have comfort. 6:10
though he slay me, *v.* will I. 13:15
v. he shall perish for ever. 20:7
when the Almighty was *v.* 29:5
v. he knoweth it not in great. 35:15
v. have I set my king on my. *Ps* 2:6
v. have I not seen the righteous forsaken. 37:25
I shall *v.* praise him. 42:5, 11
  43:5; 71:14
this is come, *v.* have we. 44:17
v. have I not declined. 119:51, 157
v. do I not forget thy statutes. 83
  109, 141
v. will not his foolishness. *Pr* 27:22
v. is not washed from their. 30:12
better is he which hath not *v.* been.
  Eccl 4:3
kiss thee, *v.* I should. *S of S* 8:1
v. a remnant of them. *Isa* 10:22
for the Lord will *v.* choose. 14:1
v. gleaning grapes shall be. 17:6
while it is *v.* in his hand, he. 28:4
this is the rest, *v.* they would. 12
v. he also is wise, and will. 31:2
Israel be not gathered, *v.* shall. 49:5

they may forget, *v.* will I not.
  Isa 49:15
he was oppressed, *v.* he. 53:7
I will *v.* plead with you. *Jer* 2:9
v. return to me. 3:1
v. they prosper. 5:28
v. my mind could not be. 15:1
prophets, *v.* they ran: *v.* they. 23:21
v. they were not afraid, nor. 36:24
though they cry, *v.* will. *Ezek* 8:18
v. will I be to them as a little. 11:16
said, I am a god, *v.* thou art a. 28:2
v. thou art not the enquired. 36:37
v. made we not our prayer before
  God. *Dan* 9:13
because it is *v.* for a time. 11:35
v. he shall come to his end. 45
grey hairs are upon him, *v. Hos* 7:9
v. I am the Lord thy God from. 13:4
given you want of bread, *v.* have ye
  not returned to me. *Amos* 4:6
  8, 9, 10, 11; *Hag* 2:17
he shall say, Is there *v.? Amos* 6:10
v. I will look toward thy. *Jonah* 2:4
v. forty days and Nineveh. 3:4
was my saying, when I was *v.* 4:2
are there *v.* the treasures ? *Mi* 6:10
v. was she carried away. *Nah* 3:10
v. I will rejoice in the Lord, I will
  joy. *Hab* 3:18
v. is she thy companion. *Mal* 2:14
do not ye *v.* understand, that ?
  Mat 15:17; 16:9; *Mark* 8:17
I kept, what lack I *v.?* *Mat* 19:20
but the end is not *v.* 24:6
  Mark 13:7
time of figs was not *v.* *Mark* 11:13
words I spake while *v.* *Luke* 24:44
unto her, Mine hour is not *v.* come.
  John 2:4; 7:6, 30; 8:20
for the Holy Ghost was not *v.* 7:39
though he were dead *v.* shall. 11:25
for as *v.* they knew not the. 20:9
as *v.* the Holy Ghost was fallen upon
  none of them. *Acts* 8:16
he had *v.* being uncircumcised.
  Rom 4:11, 12
we were *v.* without strength. 5:6
while we were *v.* sinners. 8
why doth he *v.* hope for ? 8:24
Why doth he *v.* find fault ? 9:19
ye are *v.* carnal. *1 Cor* 3:3
v. so as by fire. 15
to the married I command, *v.* not I,
  but the Lord. 7:10
v. for all that will they not. 14:21
v. not I, but the grace of God. 15:10
your faith is vain, ye are *v.* 17
that he will *v.* deliver. *2 Cor* 1:10
to spare you I came not as *v.* 23
v. true, as unknown, *v.* known. 6:8
v. not I, but Christ. *Gal* 2:20
in vain ? if it be *v.* in vain. 3:4
I, brethren, if I *v.* preach. 5:11
when I was *v.* with you. *2 Thes* 2:5
v. is he not crowned. *2 Tim* 2:5
we see not *v.* all things. *Heb* 2:8
like as we are, *v.* without sin. 4:15
for he was *v.* in the loins of. 7:10
and by it he being dead *v.* 11:4
warned of things not seen as *v.* 7
keep the whole law, *v.* *Jas* 2:10
v. if thou kill. 4:2
v. ye have not. 4:2
it doth not *v.* appear. *1 John* 3:2
and is not, and *v.* is. *Rev* 17:8
and the other is not *v.* come. 10
received no kingdom as *v.* 12
  see alive

yield
the ground, it shall not henceforth *v.*
  her strength. *Gen* 4:12
fat, shall *v.* royal dainties. 49:20
that it may *v.* to you the increase.
  Lev 19:25
v. her increase, trees *v.* fruit. 26:4
for your land shall not *v.* her. 20
but *v.* yourselves to the Lord.
  2 Chr 30:8
the land shall *v.* her increase.
  Ps 67:6; 85:12
plant vineyards, which may *v.* 107:37
speech she caused him to *v. Pr* 7:21

vineyard shall *y.* one bath, and the
seed of an homer shall *y. Isa* 5:10
the bud shall *y.* no meal: if so be it *y.*
the stranger shall. *Hos* 8:7
the fig tree and vine *y. Joel* 2:22
fields shall *y.* no meat. *Hab* 3:17
but do not thou *y.* unto. *Acts* 23:21
nor *y.* ye your members as instruments of . . . sin, *y. Rom* 6:13*
that to whom ye *y.* yourselves servants. 16*
y. your members servants to. 19*
no fountain *y.* salt water. *Jas* 3:12

yielded

his sons, *y.* up the ghost. *Gen* 49:33
rod of Aaron *y.* almonds. *Num* 17:8
y. their bodies that they. *Dan* 3:28
Jesus cried again, and *y. Mat* 27:50
then Sapphira *y.* up the. *Acts* 5:10
ye have *y.* your members. *Rom* 6:19

yieldeth

it *y.* much increase. *Neh* 9:37
wilderness *y.* food for. *Job* 24:5
y. the peaceable fruit of. *Heb* 12:11

yielding

bring forth herb *y.* seed, tree *y.*
fruit. *Gen* 1:11, 12
given you every tree *y.* seed. 29
for *y.* pacifieth great. *Eccl* 10:4
see **fruit**

yoke

*This term is used both literally and
figuratively in the Bible. Figuratively it is used* [1] *Of the yoke of
bondage, or slavery,* Lev 26:13;
Deut 28:48. [2] *Of the yoke of
afflictions and crosses,* Lam 3:27.
[3] *Of the yoke of punishment for
sin,* Lam 1:14. [4] *Of the yoke
of Christ's service,* Mat 11:29, 30.

that thou shalt break his *y.*
Gen 27:40; *Jer* 30:8
I have broken the bands of your *y.*
Lev 26:13; *Ezek* 34:27
a red heifer without blemish, on
which never came *y. Num* 19:2
Deut 21:3; *1 Sam* 6:7
he shall put a *y.* of iron upon thy
neck. *Deut* 28:48; *Jer* 28:14
Saul took a *y.* of oxen. *1 Sam* 11:7
an half acre, which a *y.* of. 14:14
y. grievous, make his heavy *y.*
1 Ki 12:4, 10, 11, 14; *2 Chr* 10:4
with twelve *y.* of oxen. *1 Ki* 19:19
he took a *y.* of oxen, and slew. 21
Job had five hundred *y. Job* 1:3
he had a thousand *y.* of oxen. 42:12
thou hast broken the *y.* of his burden.
Isa 9:4; 10:27; 14:25
hast very heavily laid thy *y.* 47:6
and that ye break every *y.* 58:6
I have broken thy *y. Jer* 2:20
altogether broken the *y.* 5:5
not put their neck under the *y.* 27:8
bring their neck under the *y.* 11, 12
broken the *y.* of the king. 28:2; 4, 11
Hananiah had broken the *y.* 12*
unaccustomed to the *y.* 31:18
husbandman and his *y.* 51:23
the *y.* of my transgressions.*Lam* 1:14
good for a man to bear the *y.* 3:27
they that take off the *y. Hos* 11:4
now will I break his *y. Nah* 1:13
take my *y.* upon you. *Mat* 11:29
my *y.* is easy. 30
bought five *y.* of oxen. *Luke* 14:19
to put a *y.* on the disciples' neck.
Acts 15:10
be not entangled with the *y. Gal* 5:1
as are under the *y.* *1 Tim* 6:1

yoked

be not unequally *y.* with. *2 Cor* 6:14

yokefellow

I intreat thee also, true *y. Phil* 4:3

yokes

make thee bonds and *y. Jer* 27:2*
y. of wood; but make *y.* of iron. 28:13
break the *y.* of Egypt. *Ezek* 30:18

49

yonder

I and the lad will go *y. Gen* 22:5
scatter thou the fire *y. Num* 16:37
while I meet the Lord *y.* 23:15
y. is that Shunammite. *2 Ki* 4:25
Remove hence to *y.* place.*Mat* 17:20
here, while I go and pray *y.* 26:36

you

a space between *y.* and ark. *Josh* 3:4
and shake my head at *y. Job* 16:4
your iniquities have separated between *y.* and your God. *Isa* 59:2
and I will put a new spirit within *y.*
Ezek 11:19; 36:26, 27
are about *y.,* bear shame. 36:7, 36
I am pressed under *y. Amos* 2:13
y. only have I known of all. 3:2
he that heareth *y.* heareth me; and
he that despiseth *y. Luke* 10:16
and *y.* yourselves thrust out. 13:28
the name of God is blasphemed
through *y. Rom* 2:24
lest they come and find *y.* unprepared. *2 Cor* 9:4
gospel in the regions beyond *y.* 10:16
for I seek not yours but *y.* 12:14
y. hath he quickened. *Eph* 2:1
y. that were sometime alienated and
enemies. *Col* 1:21
y., being dead in your sins, hath he
quickened. 2:13

see **tell**

after you

with you, and seed *after y. Gen* 9:9
inheritance for your children *after y.*
Lev 25:46; *1 Chr* 28:8
draw out a sword *after y. Lev* 26:33
as they pursued *after y. Deut* 11:4
that shall rise up *after y.* 29:22
behold, I come *after y. 1 Sam* 25:19
shall follow close *after y. Jer* 42:16
which long a*fter y. 2 Cor* 9:14
Phil 1:8
longed *after y. Phil* 2:26

against you

I have sinned *against y. Ex* 10:16
I will set my face *against y.*
Lev 26:17; *Jer* 44:11
they murmur *against y. Num* 17:5
came out *against y. Deut* 1:44
earth to witness *against y.* this day,
that ye shall soon. 4:26; 30:19
I testify *against y.* that ye. 8:19
the Lord was wroth *against y.* 9:19
11:17; *Josh* 23:16
Jericho fought *against y. Josh* 24:11
the Lord is witness *against y.*
1 Sam 12:5; *Mi* 1:2
Ammonites came *against y.*
1 Sam 12:12
hand of Lord shall be *against y.* 15
counselled *against y. 2 Sam* 17:21
to cry alarm *against y. 2 Chr* 13:12
heap up words *against y. Job* 16:4
I devise a device *against y.*
Jer 18:11
will fight *against y.* in anger. 21:5
of evil pronounced *against y.* 26:13
Chaldeans that fight *against y.* 37:10
the king of Babylon shall not come
against y. 19
cannot do any thing *against y.* 35:5
words shall stand *against y.* 44:29
conceived a purpose *against y.* 49:30
I am *against y. Ezek* 13:8
enemy said *against y.* 36:2
Lord hath spoken *against y.*
Amos 3:1; 5:1; *Zeph* 2:5
I will raise up *against y.* a nation.
Amos 6:14
take up a parable *against y. Mi* 2:4
manner of evil *against y. Mat* 5:11
go into the village over against *y.*
21:2; *Mark* 11:2; *Luke* 19:30
the very dust of your city we do
wipe off *against y. Luke* 10:11
be a witness *against y. Jas* 5:3
whereas they speak *against y.* as
evil doers. *1 Pet* 2:12

among or amongst you

strange gods that are *among y.*
Gen 35:2; *Josh* 24:23; *1 Sam* 7:3

tabernacle *amongst y. Lev* 26:11
I will walk *among y.* and will. 12
I will send wild beasts *among y.* 22
I will send pestilence *among y.* 25
despised the Lord who is *among y.*
Num 11:20; 14:42; *Deut* 6:15
7:21; *Josh* 3:10
who is there a*mong y.? 2 Chr* 36:23
Ezra 1:3
who *among y.* will give ? *Isa* 42:23
who is *among y.* that feareth ? 50:10
purge out from *among y. Ezek* 20:38
who is left *among y.* that ? *Hag* 2:3
who is there *among y.?* *Mal* 1:10
it shall not be so *among y.*
Mat 20:26; *Mark* 10:43
among y. let him be your servant.
Mat 20:27; 23:11; *Luke* 22:26
he that is least *among y. Luke* 9:48
but I am *among y.* as he. 22:27
standeth one among *y. John* 1:26
he that is without sin *among y.* 8:7
brethren, look ye out among *y.* seven
men. *Acts* 6:3
and whosoever *among y.* 13:26
let them who *among y.* are. 25:5
some fruit *among y. Rom* 1:13
every man that is *among y.* 12:3
no divisions *among y. 1 Cor* 1:10
contentions *among y.* 11; 11:18
to know any thing *among y.* 2:2
is *among y.* envying, strife. 3:3
if any man *among y.* seemeth. 18
there is fornication *among y.* 5:1
taken away from *among y.* 2
how say some *among y.* that ? 15:12
Christ who was preached *among y.*
2 Cor 1:19
in presence am base *among y.* 10:1
will humble me *among y.* 12:21
not be once named *among y.Eph* 5:3
what manner of men were *among*
y. 1 Thes 1:5
if any man *among y. Jas* 1:26
is any *among y.* afflicted ? 5:13
is any sick *among y.?* 14
feed the flock of God which is *among*
y. 1 Pet 5:2
false teachers *among y. 2 Pet* 2:1
who was slain *among y. Rev* 2:13

see **sojourneth**

before you

the land shall be *before y. Gen* 34:10
God did send me *before y.* 45:5, 7
for evil is *before y. Ex* 10:10
these the nations are defiled which
I cast out *before y. Lev* 18:24
20:23; *Num* 33:52, 55; *Deut* 11:23
Josh 3:10; 9:24; 23:5, 9; 24:8
12; *Judg* 6:9
men of the land done which were
before y. Lev 18:27, 28, 30
shall fall *before y.* 26:7, 8
are there *before y. Num* 14:43
shall be subdued *before y.* 32:29
set the land *before y. Deut* 1:8
Lord who goeth *before y.* shall. 30
set *before y.* this day. 4:8; 11:32
I set *before y.* a blessing and a curse.
11:26; 30:19
dried up Jordan *before y. Josh* 4:23
I sent the hornet *before y.* 24:12
behold, he is *before y. 1 Sam* 9:12
the king walketh *before y.* 12:2
my statutes which I have set *before*
y. 2 Chr 7:19; *Jer* 26:4; 44:10
Lord will go *before y. Isa* 52:12
behold, I set *before y.* the. *Jer* 21:8
so persecuted they the prophets
which were *before y. Mat* 5:12
kingdom of God *before y.* 21:31
risen again, I will go *before y.* 26:32
28:7; *Mark* 14:28; 16:7
eat such things as are set *before y.*
Luke 10:8; *1 Cor* 10:27
doth this man stand here *before y.*
whole. *Acts* 4:10

by you

I will not be enquired of *by y.*
Ezek 20:3, **31**
I trust to be brought on my way *by y.*
Rom 15:24
if the world shall be judged *by y.*
1 Cor 6:2

was refreshed by y. all. *2 Cor 7:13*
shall be enlarged by y. *10:15*

concerning you

what Lord will command *concerning
y. Num 9:8*
which the Lord spake *concerning y.
Josh 23:14*
hath said *concerning y. Jer 42:19*
this is the will of God *concerning y.
1 Thes 5:18*

for you

as *for y. Gen 44:17; 50:20
Num 14:32; Deut 1:40; Josh 23:9
Job 17:10*
one ordinance shall be *for y.
Num 15:15, 16*
all that he did *for y. Deut 1:30
4:34; 1 Sam 12:24*
as *for y.* O house of Israel.
Ezek 20:39; 34:17
behold I am *for y.* and I will. *36:9*
but one decree *for y. Dan 2:9*
to what end is it *for y.? Amos 5:18*
is it not *for y.* to know judgement ?
Mi 3:1
is it time *for y.,* to dwell ? *Hag 1:4*
commandment is *for y. Mal 2:1*
more tolerable for Tyre and Sidon,
than *for y. Mat 11:22; Luke 10:14*
kingdom prepared *for y. Mat 25:34*
that I should do *for y. Mark 10:36*
this is my body which is given *for y.
Luke 22:19*
blood shed *for y. 20; 1 Cor 11:24*
prepare a place *for y. John 14:2, 3*
I will pray the Father *for y. 16:26*
is not *for y.* to know the times or
the seasons. *Acts 1:7*
therefore have I called *for y. 28:20*
God through Christ *for y. Rom 1:8*
was Paul crucified *for y.? 1 Cor 1:13*
care *for y.* appear. *2 Cor 7:12; 8:16*
by their prayer *for y. 9:14; Phil 1:4
Col 1:3, 9; 4:12; 2 Thes 1:11*
and be spent *for y. 2 Cor 12:15*
I cease not to give thanks *for y.
Eph 1:16; 1 Thes 1:2; 3:9
2 Thes 1:3; 2:13*
at my tribulations *for y. Eph 3:13
Col 1:24*
is not grievous, but *for y. Phil 3:1*
which is laid up *for y. Col 1:5*
which is given to me *for y. 25*
great conflict I have *for y. 2:1*
that he hath a great zeal *for y. 4:13*
is unprofitable *for y. Heb 13:17*
reserved in heaven *for y. 1 Pet 1:4*
on him, for he careth *for y. 5:7*

from you

sent me away *from y. Gen 26:27*
we are very far *from y. Josh 9:22*
not removed *from y. 1 Sam 6:3*
come word *from y. 2 Sam 15:28*
wrath turn away *from y. 2 Chr 30:8*
turn away his face *from y. 9*
will hide mine eyes *from y. Isa 1:15*
have hid his face *from y. 59:2*
good things *from y. Jer 5:25*
which are gone *from y. 34:21*
keep nothing back *from y. 42:4*
cast away *from y.* your. *Ezek 18:31*
remove far *from y.* the. *Joel 2:20*
I have withholden the rain *from y.
Amos 4:7*
kingdom of God shall be taken *from
y. Mat 21:43*
no man taketh *from y. John 16:22*
who is taken up *from y. Acts 1:11*
but seeing ye put it *from y. 13:46*
word of God out *from y. 1 Cor 14:36*
of commendation *from y. 2 Cor 3:1*
let evil speaking be put away *from y.
Eph 4:31*
for *from y.* sounded out. *1 Thes 1:8*
but we being taken *from y. 2:17*
and he will flee *from y. Jas 4:7*

in you

be any truth *in y. Gen 42:16*
let him also rejoice *in y. Judg 9:19*
sanctified *in y. Ezek 20:41; 36:23*
will put breath *in y. 37:6, 14*
I have no pleasure *in y.* saith the
Lord. *Mal 1:10*

---

but the Spirit which speaketh *in y.
Mat 10:20*
works which were done *in y. 11:21*
not his word abiding *in y. John 5:38*
not the love of God *in y. 42*
the flesh, ye have no life *in y. 6:53*
he shall be *in y. 14:17*
and I *in y. 20; 15:4*
if my words abide *in y. 15:7
1 John 2:14, 24*
the Spirit dwelleth *in y. Rom 8:9
1 John 2:27*
and if Christ be *in y. Rom 8:10*
as much as lieth *in y.,* live. *12:18*
Christ is confirmed *in y. 1 Cor 1:6*
Holy Ghost which is *in y. 6:19*
God is *in y.* of a truth. *14:25*
having confidence *in y.* all. *2 Cor 2:3
7:16; 8:22; Gal 5:10*
but life *in y. 2 Cor 4:12*
he was comforted *in y. 7:7*
he would finish *in y.* the same. *8:6*
exceeding grace of God *in y. 9:14*
is not weak, but mighty *in y. 13:3*
that Jesus Christ is *in y.? 5*
I travail, till Christ be formed *in y.
Gal 4:19*
one God ... who is above all, and
through all, and *in y.* all. *Eph 4:6*
let this mind be *in y.* which. *Phil 2:5*
it is God which worketh *in y. 13*
which bringeth forth fruit, as it doth
also *in y. Col 1:6*
which is Christ *in y.,* the hope. *27*
Christ dwell *in y.* richly. *3:16*
worketh *in y. 1 Thes 2:13*
so that we glory *in y. 2 Thes 1:4*
Christ may be glorified *in y. 12*
every good thing *in y. Philem 6*
working *in y.* that which is well-
pleasing. *Heb 13:21*
the hope that is *in y. 1 Pet 3:15*
if these things be *in y. 2 Pet 1:8*
which thing is true in him and *in y.
1 John 2:8*
greater is he that is *in y.* than. *4:4*

of you

why should I be deprived *of y.* both ?
Gen 27:45
may be done *of y. Ex 12:16*
unto me every one *of y. Deut 1:22*
faint because *of y. Josh 2:9*
to these nations because *of y. 23:3*
that all *of y.* have conspired against
me. *1 Sam 22:8*
O people, every one *of y. 1 Ki 22:28*
what Ezra requires *of y. Ezra 7:21*
though there were *of y.* cast out unto
uttermost part of heaven. *Neh 1:9*
ye shall be slain all *of y. Ps 62:3*
that escape *of y.* shall. *Ezek 6:9*
he shall receive *of y. Mi 1:11*
which *of y.* by taking thought can add
one cubit ? *Mat 6:27; Luke 12:25*
doth not each one *of y.? Luke 13:15*
of y. convinceth me of ? *John 8:46*
I speak not *of y.* all, I know. *13:18*
which God did by him in the midst
of y. Acts 2:22
in turning every one *of y. 3:26*
which was set at nought *of y. 4:11*
faith both *of y.* and me. *Rom 1:12*
declared to me *of y. 1 Cor 1:11*
such were some *of y.* but ye. *6:11*
the feet, I have no need *of y. 12:21*
every one *of y.* hath a psalm. *14:26*
let every one *of y.* lay by him. *16:2*
and our hope *of y.* is. *2 Cor 1:7*
boasted any thing to him *of y. 7:14*
suffer, if a man take *of y. 11:20*
did I make a gain *of y.? 12:17*
Did Titus make a gain *of y.? 18*
this only would I learn *of y. Gal 3:2*
for as many *of y.* as have been. *27*
voice, for I stand in doubt *of y. 4:20*
brother, who is one *of y. Col 4:9, 12*
neither *of y.* sought we. *1 Thes 2:6*
every one *of y.* should know. *4:4*
no evil thing to say *of y. Tit 2:8*
the hire which is *of y.* kept. *Jas 5:4*
they speak evil *of y. 1 Pet 3:16; 4:4*

on, or upon you

plague shall not be *upon y. Ex 12:13*

---

bestow *upon y.* a blessing. *Ex 32:29*
oil of the Lord is *upon y. Lev 10:7*
they said, Ye take too much *upon y.
Num 16:3, 7*
not set his love *upon y. Deut 7:7*
things are come *upon y. Josh 23:15*
they will be *upon y. Neh 4:12*
of the Lord be *upon y. Ps 129:8*
he may have mercy *upon y. 30:18
Jer 42:12*
I will visit *upon y.* the. *Jer 23:2*
this thing is come *upon y. 40:3*
I will blow *upon y.* in. *Ezek 22:21*
days shall come *upon y. Amos 4:2*
before the fierce anger of the Lord
come *upon y. Zeph 2:2*
upon y. may come the. *Mat 23:35*
of God is come *upon y. Luke 11:20*
and so that day come *upon y. 21:34*
I send the promise of my Father
upon y. 24:49
darkness come *upon y. John 12:35*
Holy Ghost is come *upon y. Acts 1:8*
not cast a snare *upon y. 1 Cor 7:35*
upon y. labour in vain. *Gal 4:11*
howl for your miseries that shall
come *upon y. Jas 5:1*
of God resteth *upon y. 1 Pet 4:14*
I will put *upon y.* none. *Rev 2:24*

over you

I will even appoint *over y. Lev 26:16*
hate you shall reign *over y. 17*
rejoiced *over y.* to do you good, he
will rejoice *over y. Deut 28:63*
rule *over y.* nor my son rule *over y.:
Lord shall rule *over y. Judg 8:23*
seventy reign *over y.* or one ? *9:2*
ye anoint me king *over y. 15*
that shall reign *over y. 1 Sam 8:11*
I have made a king *over y. 12:1*
the Lord hath set a king *over y. 13*
David to be king *over y. 2 Sam 3:17*
chief priest is *over y. 2 Chr 19:11*
watchmen *over y.* saying. *Jer 6:17*
fury poured out will I rule *over y.
Ezek 20:33*
heaven *over y.* is stayed. *Hag 1:10*
me a divider *over y.? Luke 12:14*
not have dominion *over y. Rom 6:14*
of this power *over y. 1 Cor 9:12*
over y. with godly zeal. *2 Cor 11:2*
we were comforted *over y.* in affliction. *1 Thes 3:7*
know them which are *over y. 5:12*
remember them which have the rule
over y. Heb 13:7
obey them that have the rule *over y.
17*
salute them that have the rule *over
y. 24*

to or unto you

every herb *to y.* it shall. *Gen 1:29*
and take our daughters *unto y. 34:9*
and will be *to y.* a God. *Ex 6:7*
children shall say *unto y. 12:26*
not make *unto y.* gods of gold. *20:23*
it shall be *unto y.* most holy. *30:36*
I will also do this *unto y. Lev 26:16*
they shall be *to y.* for an. *Num 10:8*
be *to y.* a memorial. *10*
unto y. for a fringe. *15:39*
I shall do *unto y.* as I thought. *33:56*
to them, and they *to y. Josh 23:12*
as they have been *to y. 1 Sam 4:9*
unto y. O men, I call. *Pr 8:4*
this iniquity shall be *to y. Isa 30:13*
to y. it is commanded. *Dan 3:4*
unto y. that fear my name. *Mal 4:2*
that men should do *to y. Mat 7:12
Luke 6:31*
to your faith be it *unto y. Mat 9:29*
because it is given *unto y.* to know.
13:11; Mark 4:11; Luke 8:10
unto y. that hear shall. *Mark 4:24*
unto y. is born this day a Saviour.
Luke 2:11
to them which do good *to y. 6:33*
I appoint *unto y.* a kingdom. *22:29*
for the promise is *unto y. Acts 2:39*
unto y. first, God having raised. *3:26*
therefore came I *unto y. 10:29*
to y. is the word of this. *13:26*

doubtless I am to y.   *1 Cor 9*:2
word of God *unto y.* only ?   14:36
to reach even *unto y.*   *2 Cor* 10:13
we are come as far as *to y.*   14
but *to y.* of salvation.   *Phil* 1:28
unto y. it is given not only to.   29
our gospel came not *unto y.* in word.
  1 Thes 1:5
to y. who are troubled.   *2 Thes* 1:7
unto y. that believe.   *1 Pet* 2:7
but *unto y.* I say, and.   *Rev* 2:24
  see **say, told**

toward **you**
good work *toward y.*   *Jer* 29:10
thoughts I think *toward y.*   11
judgement is *toward y.*   *Hos* 5:1
our word *toward y.* was.   *2 Cor* 1:18
is more abundant *toward y.*   7:15
all grace abound *toward y.*   9:8
being absent am bold *toward y.* 10:1
by the power of God *toward y.* 13:4
abound in love one toward another,
as we do *toward y.*   *1 Thes* 3:12

with **you**
then we will dwell *with y. Gen* 34:16
but God shall be *with y.*   48:21
my bones hence *with y.*   *Ex* 13:19
that I have talked *with y.*   20:22
Aaron and Hur are *with y.*   24:14
with y. shall be a man.   *Num* 1:4
where I will meet *with y.*   17:4
it may be well *with y. Deut* 5:33
no part *with y.*   12:12
God goeth *with y.*   20:4
nor *with y.* only do I make.   29:14
neither will I be *with y.*   *Josh* 7:12
said, The Lord be *with y.*   *Ruth* 2:4
and mother be *with y.*   *1 Sam* 22:3
me, and I will go *with y.*   23:23
what have I to do *with y.?*
  2 Sam 16:10; 19:22
go forth *with y.* myself.   18:2
master's sons are *with y. 2 Ki* 10:2
see there be *with y.* none of.   23
and it shall be well *with y.*   25:24
  Jer 40:9
Lord your God *with y.? 1 Chr* 22:18
there are *with y.* golden calves.
  2 Chr 13:8
the Lord is *with y.* while ye.   15:2
for the Lord, who is *with y.* in. 19:6
the Lord will be *with y.*   20:17
with y., even *with y.,* sins ?   28:10
let us build *with y.:* for we. *Ezra* 4:2
lest I deal *with y.* after.   *Job* 42:8
do *with y.* as this potter ? *Jer* 18:6
I am *with y.* 42:11; *Hag* 1:13; 2:4
will I plead *with y. Ezek* 20:35, 36
when I have wrought *with y.*   44
the Lord shall be *with y. Amos* 5:14
with y., for God is *with y. Zech* 8:23
how long shall I be *with y.? Mat* 17:17
  Mark 9:19; *Luke* 9:41
the poor always *with y.,* but me ye.
  Mat 26:11; *John* 12:8
I drink it new *with y.* in. *Mat* 26:29
I am *with y.* alway, unto the.   28:20
you, while I was *with y. Luke* 24:44
yet a little while am I *with y.,* then I
go to.   *John* 7:33; 12:35; 13:33
Have I been so long *with y.?*   14:9
that he may abide *with y.*   16
he dwelleth *with y.*   17
being present *with y.*   25
peace I leave *with y.*   27
because I was *with y.*   16:4
I should bear *with y.*   *Acts* 18:14
I have been *with y.* at all.   20:18
comforted together *with y. Rom* 1:12
I may *with y.* be refreshed.   15:32
now the God of peace be *with y.* all.
  33; *2 Cor* 13:11; *Phil* 4:9
the grace of our Lord Jesus Christ
be *with y.*   *Rom* 16:20, 24
  1 Cor 16:23; *Phil* 4:23; *Col* 4:18
  1 Thes 5:28; 2 *Thes* 3:18
  2 Tim 1:2; 4:22; *Tit* 3:15
  Heb 13:25; *2 John* 3; *Rev* 22:21
was *with y.* in weakness. *1 Cor* 2:3
that we also might reign *with y.* 4:8
see that he may be *with y.*   16:10
my love be *with y.* all in Christ. 24
establisheth us *with y.*   *2 Cor* 1:21

and present us *with y.*   *2 Cor* 4:14
hearts to die and live *with y.*   7:3
when I was present *with y.*   11:9
  Gal 1:18, 20
I joy and rejoice *with y.*   *Phil* 2:17
am I *with y.* in the spirit.   *Col* 2:5
glorified, as it is *with y. 2 Thes* 3:1
the Lord be *with y.* all.   16
God dealeth *with y.* as.   *Heb* 12:7
peace be *with y.* all.   *1 Pet* 5:14
spots and blemishes, while they
feast *with y.*   *2 Pet* 2:13

young
have not cast their *y.*   *Gen* 31:38
the flocks and herds with *y.*   33:13
nothing cast their *y.*   *Ex* 23:26
not kill it and her *y.*   *Lev* 22:28
take the dam with the *y. Deut* 22:6
let the dam go and take the *y.*   7
shew favour to the *y.*   28:50
eagle fluttereth over her *y.*   32:11
had a *y.* son Micha.   *2 Sam* 9:12
my son is *y.*   *1 Chr* 22:5; 29:1
when Rehoboam was *y. 2 Chr* 13:7
Josiah, while he was yet *y.*   34:3
ewes great with *y.*   *Ps* 78:71
where she may lay her *y.*   84:3
those that are with *y.*   *Isa* 40:11
for the *y.* of the flock.   *Jer* 31:12
cropped off the top of his *y.* twigs.
  Ezek 17:4, 22
whose *y.* daughter had. *Mark* 7:25*
when *y.* thou girdedst. *John* 21:18
see **child, children, man, men,
old**

young *ass,* or *asses*
the shoulders of *y. asses.*   *Isa* 30:6
the *y. asses* shall eat clean.   24
he found a *y. ass,* sat. *John* 12:14
  see **bullock**

young *bullocks*
shall offer two *y. bullocks.*
  Num 28:11, 19, 27
need, both *y. bullocks.*   *Ezra* 6:9

young *calf*
take thee a *y. calf* for.   *Lev* 9:2*

young *cow*
man shall nourish a *y. cow. Isa* 7:21

young *dromedaries*
he sent letters by riders on *y. dromedaries.*   *Esth* 8:10*

young *eagles*
y. eagles shall eat it.   *Pr* 30:17

young *hart*
my beloved is like a *y. hart.*
  S of S 2:9, 17; 8:14
see **lion, lions**

young *one*
her eye shall be evil toward her *y.
one.*   *Deut* 28:57
neither shall seek the *y. one,* nor
heal.   *Zech* 11:16*

young *ones*
whether they be *y. ones Deut* 22:6
when his *y. ones* cry to.   *Job* 38:41
bring forth their *y. ones.*   39:3
their *y. ones* are in good liking.   4
is hardened against her *y. ones.*   16
the eagles' *y. ones* also suck.   30
their *y. ones* shall lie.   *Isa* 11:7
give suck to their *y. ones.* *Lam* 4:3

young *pigeon*
dove, and a *y. pigeon.*   *Gen* 15:9
bring a *y. pigeon* for a.   *Lev* 12:6

young *pigeons*
offering of *y. pigeons.*   *Lev* 1:14
a lamb, he shall bring two *y. pigeons.*
  5:7; 12:8; 14:22, 30; 15:14, 29
  Num 6:10; *Luke* 2:24
if he be not able to bring two *y.
pigeons.*   *Lev* 5:11

young *ravens*
food to *y. ravens* which cry. *Ps* 147:9

young *roes*
thy breasts are like two *y. roes.*
  S of S 4:5; 7:3

young *unicorn*
Sirion like a *y. unicorn.*   *Ps* 29:6

young *virgin*
for my lord a *y. virgin.*   *1 Ki* 1:2

young *virgins*
found 400 *y. virgins.*   *Judg* 21:12
let fair *y. virgins* be sought. *Esth* 2:2
together all the *y. virgins.*   3

young *woman*
thee of this *y. woman.*   *Ruth* 4:12

young *women*
they may teach *y. women.*   *Tit* 2:4

younger
Noah knew what his *y.* son.*Gen* 9:24*
firstborn said to the *y.*   19:31, 34
and the *y.* she also bare a son.   38
the elder shall serve the *y.*   25:23
  Rom 9:12
on Jacob her *y.* son.   *Gen* 27:15
called Jacob her *y.* son.   42
the name of the *y.* daughter.   29:16
seven years for the *y.*   18
to give the *y.* before firstborn.   26
is this your *y.* brother ?   43:29*
his right hand on the *y.*   48:14
his *y.* brother shall be greater.   19
Caleb's *y.* brother. *Judg* 1:13; 3:9
is not her *y.* sister fairer ?   15:2
Saul's *y.* daughter. *1 Sam* 14:49
cast lots over against their *y.*
brethren.   *1 Chr* 24:31
that are *y.* than I, have me in derision.   *Job* 30:1
y. sister is Sodom.   *Ezek* 16:46
sisters, thine elder and *y.*   61
y. said, Father, give me. *Luke* 15:12
the *y.* son gathered all, and took. 13
let him be as the *y.*   22:26
intreat the *y.* men as. *1 Tim* 5:1
the *y.* women as sisters, with all.   2
the *y.* widows refuse, for when.   11
that the *y.* women marry.   14
likewise, ye *y.* submit.   *1 Pet* 5:5

youngest
the *y.* is this day with our father.
  Gen 42:13, 32
except your *y.* brother come.   15, 20
  34; 44:23, 26
they sat, the *y.* according.   43:33
in the sack's mouth of the *y.*   44:2
eldest, and left off at the *y.*   12
in his *y.* son shall he set up gates of
it.   *Josh* 6:26; *1 Ki* 16:34
yet Jotham the *y.* son.   *Judg* 9:5
remaineth yet the *y.*   *1 Sam* 16:11
David was the *y.:* the eldest. 17:14
save Jehoahaz the *y.*   *2 Chr* 21:17
his *y.* son king in his stead.   22:1

yours
the land of Egypt is *y.*   *Gen* 45:20
feet tread shall be *y.*   *Deut* 11:24
answered, Our life for *y. Josh* 2:14
the battle is not *y.* but. *2 Chr* 20:15
in land that is not *y.*   *Jer* 5:19
y. is the kingdom of God. *Luke* 6:20
they will keep *y.* also. *John* 15:20
for all things are *y.*   *1 Cor* 3:21, 22
lest this liberty of *y.* become.   8:9
refreshed my spirit and *y.*   16:18
for I seek not *y.* but you. *2 Cor* 12:14

yourselves
wash, and rest *y.* under.   *Gen* 18:4
be not angry with *y.* that ye.   45:5
gather *y.* together. 49:1, 2; *Jer* 6:1
  Ezek 39:17; *Joel* 3:11; *Zeph* 2:1
  Rev 19:17
take heed unto *y.*   *Ex* 19:12
  Deut 2:4; 4:15, 23; 11:16
  Josh 23:11; *Jer* 17:21
as for the perfume, ye shall not make
to *y.*   *Ex* 30:37
consecrate *y.* to-day to the.   32:29
ye shall not make *y.* abominable,
neither shall ye make *y. Lev* 11:43
sanctify *y.* 11:44; 20:7; *Num* 11:18
  Josh 3:5; 7:13; *1 Sam* 16:5
  1 Chr 15:12; *2 Chr* 29:5; 35:6
ye defile *y.*   *Lev* 11:44; 18:24, 30
nor make to *y.* molten gods.   19:4
lift you up *y.?*   *Num* 16:3
separate *y.* from this.   21
Moses saying, Arm some of *y.* 31:3
women-children keep for *y.*   18
purify both *y.* and your.   19

lest ye corrupt y.   *Deut* 4:16, 25
mightier nations than y.   11:23
not cut y. for the dead.   14:1
present y. in the tabernacle.   31:14
ye will utterly corrupt y.   29
hide y. there three days.   *Josh* 2:16
keep y. from the accursed thing, lest
    ye make y. accursed.   6:18
take for a prey unto y.
nor serve them, nor bow y. unto. 23:7
and bowed y. to them.   16
ye are witnesses against y. that ye
    have chosen.   24:22
not fall upon me y.   *Judg* 15:12
quit y. like men, O ye. *1 Sam* 4:9
present y. before the Lord.   10:19
Saul said, Disperse y.   14:34
you one bullock for y.   *1 Ki* 18:25
set y. in array, and they set.   20:12
    2 Chr 20:17; *Jer* 50:14
have consecrated y.   *2 Chr* 29:31
but yield y. unto the Lord.   30:8
to give over y. to die by.   32:11
prepare y. by the houses of.   35:4
separate y. from the.   *Ezra* 10:11
their daughters for y.   *Neh* 13:25
that ye make y. strange.   *Job* 19:3
if ye will indeed magnify y.   5
all ye y. have seen it.   27:12
and offer up for y. a burnt.   42:8
associate y., O ye people: gird y.
    Isa 8:9; *Joel* 1:13
stay y.   *Isa* 29:9
shew y. .nen.   46:8
are in darkness, shew y.   49:9
for iniquities have ye sold y.   50:1
that compass y. about with.   11
ye have sold y. for nought.   52:3
against whom do ye sport y.   57:4
by inflaming y. with idols under.   5
in their glory shall ye boast y.   61:6
circumcise y. to the Lord.   *Jer* 4:4
humble y. 13:18; *Jas* 4:10; *1 Pet* 5:6
wallow y. in ashes, ye.   *Jer* 25:34
innocent blood upon y.   26:15
saith the Lord, deceive not y.   37:9
that ye might cut y. off and.   44:8
repent and turn y.   *Ezek* 14:6
    18:30, 32
defile not y. with the idols. 20:7, 18
ye pollute y. with all your idols.   31
then shall ye lothe y.   43; 36:31
keepers of my charge for y.   44:8
to y. in righteousness.   *Hos* 10:12
your God ye made to y.   *Amos* 5:26
eat for y. and drink for.   *Zech* 7:6
think not to say within y.   *Mat* 3:9
    Luke 3:8
lay not up for y.   *Mat* 6:19
lay up for y.   20
Why reason ye among y.?   16:8
neither go in y.   23:13; *Luke* 11:52
child of hell than y.   *Mat* 23:15
ye be witnesses unto y.   31
go ye rather, and buy for y.   25:9
come ye y. apart into.   *Mark* 6:31
that ye disputed among y.?   9:33
have salt in y. and peace one.   50
but take heed to y.: they shall deliver
    you up.   13:9; *Luke* 17:3; 21:34
    Acts 5:35; 20:28
ye y. touch not the.   *Luke* 11:46
provide y. bags which wax.   12:33
ye y. like unto men that wait for. 36
why even of y. judge ye not?   57
kingdom, ye y. thrust out.   13:28
make to y. friends of the.   16:9
ye are they which justify y.   15
he said, Go shew y. unto the. 17:14
know of y. that summer is.   21:30
and divide it among y.   22:17
but weep for y. and for.   23:28
ye y. bear me witness.   *John* 3:28
said, Murmur not among y.   6:43
do ye enquire among y. of? 16:19
signs God did, as you y.   *Acts* 2:22
save y. from this untoward.   40
seeing ye judge y. unworthy. 13:46
from which if ye keep y. ye.   15:29
trouble not y. for his life.   20:10
you y. know, that these hands.   34
reckon ye also y. to be.   *Rom* 6:11
but yield y. unto God, as those.   13
whom ye yield y. servants to.   16

dearly beloved, avenge not y., but
    rather give place.   *Rom* 12:19
put from y. that wicked. *1 Cor* 5:13
ye not rather suffer y. to be?   6:7
ye may give y. to fasting and.   7:5
judge in y.: is it comely that? 11:13
I beseech, that ye submit y.   16:16
yea, what clearing of y., in all things
    ye have approved y.   *2 Cor* 7:11
seeing ye y. are wise.   11:19
examine y. whether ye be in.   13:5
faith, and that not of y.   *Eph* 2:8
speaking to y. in psalms.   5:19
submitting y. one to another.   21
wives, submit y. unto your. *Col* 3:18
y., brethren, know our entrance in
    unto you.   *1 Thes* 2:1
y. know that we are appointed.   3:3
ye y. are taught of God, to.   4:9
y. know that the day of the Lord. 5:2
wherefore comfort y. together.   11
and be at peace among y.   13, 15
that ye withdraw y.   *2 Thes* 3:6
y. know how ye ought to follow us. 7
knowing in y. ye have.   *Heb* 10:34
remember, as being y. also.   13:3
and submit y.: for they watch for. 17
ye not then partial in y.?   *Jas* 2:4
submit y. to God.   4:7
not fashioning y. to.   *1 Pet* 1:14
submit y. to every ordinance. 2:13
arm y. likewise with the same. 4:1
fervent charity among y.   8
ye younger, submit y. unto.   5:5
keep y. from idols.   *1 John* 5:21
look to y. that we lose not. *2 John* 8
building up y. on your most. *Jude* 20
keep y. in the love of God, looking. 21

youth

is evil from his y.   *Gen* 8:21
youngest according to his y.   43:33
about cattle, from our y.   46:34
father's house, as in her y. *Lev* 22:13
being in her father's house in her y.
    Num 30:3, 16
the y. drew not a sword, because yet
    a y.   *Judg* 8:20
thou art but a y., and he a man of
    war from his y.   *1 Sam* 17:33
for he was but a y.   42
whose son is this y.?   55
befell thee from my y.   *2 Sam* 19:7
fear the Lord from my y. *1 Ki* 18:12
the iniquities of my y.   *Job* 13:26
are full of the sin of his y.   20:11
as I was in the days of my y. 29:4*
on my right hand rise the y. 30:12*
from my y. he was brought up. 31:18
return to the days of his y.   33:25
hypocrites die in y. and.   36:14
not the sins of my y.   *Ps* 25:7
thou art my trust from my y.   71:5
hast taught me from my y.   17
and ready to die from my y.   88:15
the days of his y. hast thou.   89:45
so that thy y. is renewed.   103:5
thou hast the dew of thy y.   110:3
so are the children of thy y.   127:4
afflicted me from my y.   129:1
as plants grown up in y.   144:12
the guide of her y.   *Pr* 2:17
with the wife of thy y.   5:18
O young man in thy y.   *Eccl* 11:9
for childhood and y. are vanity. 10*
Creator in the days of thy y.   12:1
hast laboured from thy y. *Isa* 47:12
thy merchants from thy y.   15
forget the shame of thy y.   54:4
hath called thee as a wife of y.   6
the kindness of thy y.   *Jer* 2:2
thou art the guide of my y.   3:4
of our fathers from our y.   24
we and our fathers from our y.   25
been thy manner from thy y.   22:21
bear the reproach of my y.   31:19
evil before me from their y.   32:30
been at ease from his y.   48:11
bear the yoke in his y.   *Lam* 3:27
been polluted from my y. *Ezek* 4:14
remembered days of thy y. 16:22, 43
my covenant in days of thy y.   60
whoredoms in their y.   23:3
her y. they lay with her and.   8

the days of her y.   *Ezek* 23:19, 21
as in the days of her y.   *Hos* 2:15
for the husband of her y.   *Joel* 1:8
to keep cattle from my y. *Zech* 13:5
and the wife of thy y.   *Mal* 2:14
let none deal treacherously against
    the wife of his y.   15
all these have I kept from my y.
    up; what lack I yet? *Mat* 19:20
    Mark 10:20; *Luke* 18:21
life from my y. know all. *Acts* 26:4
let no man despise thy y. *1 Tim* 4:12

youthful

flee also y. lusts, but.   *2 Tim* 2:22

youths

I discerned among the y.   *Pr* 7:7
even the y. shall faint.   *Isa* 40:30

you-ward

which to y.-ward is not. *2 Cor* 13:3
grace given me to y.-ward. *Eph* 3:2

Z

Zacchaeus

Z. make haste and.   *Luke* 19:5

Zachariah, Zechariah

Z. son of Jeroboam reigned.
    2 Ki 14:29; 15:8, 11
Abi daughter of Z. 18:2; *2 Chr* 29:1
chief of the Reubenites; Jeiel, Z.
    1 Chr 5:7
Z. porter of the door.   9:21; 15:18
    20, 24; 26:2
Geder, Ahio, Z. and Mickloth. 9:37
next to Asaph, Z.   16:5
Z. son of Isshiah.   24:25
Z. the fourth son of Hosah. 26:11
Z. the son of Shelemiah, a wise. 14
was Iddo the son of Z.   27:21
Jehoshaphat sent to Z.   *2 Chr* 17:7
on Jahaziel son of Z.   20:14
Jehiel and Z. the sons of.   21:2
Spirit of God came upon Z.   24:20
sought God in the days of Z.   26:5
of the sons of Asaph, Z.   29:13
Z. of the Kohathites was.   34:12
Hilkiah, Z. rulers of the house. 35:8
Z. the son of Iddo prophesied.
    Ezra 5:1; 6:14; *Neh* 12:16
sons of Pharosh, Z.   *Ezra* 8:3
Z. the son of Bebai.   11
Elam, Z.   10:26
on Ezra's left hand stood Z. *Neh* 8:4
Z. the son of Amariah.   11:4
Z. the son of Shiloni.   5
Z., the son of Pashur.   12
Z. the son of Jonathan.   12:35
Z. with trumpets.   41
Z. the son of Jeberechiah. *Isa* 8:2
Z. the son of Barachiah. *Zech* 1:1
    7:1; *Mat* 23:35; *Luke* 11:51
see also Zacharias, p. 783

Zadok

Z. and Abimelech.   *2 Sam* 8:17
Z. and Abiathar carried the.   15:29
hast thou not with thee Z. and? 35
Z. and Abiathar were priests.
    1 Ki 4:4
but Z. was not with Adonijah.
    1 Ki 1:8, 26
Z. and Nathan have anointed.   45
and Z. the priest. 2:35; *1 Chr* 29:22
Azariah the son of Z.   *1 Ki* 4:2
Jerusha the daughter of Z. was.
    2 Ki 15:33; *2 Chr* 27:1
Ahitub begat Z.   *1 Chr* 6:8; 12:53
    9:11; 18:16
Z. a young man, mighty man. 12:28
both Z. of the sons of Eleazar. 24:3
of the Aaronites, Z. was.   27:17
priest of the house of Z. *2 Chr* 31:10
Shallum, the son of Z.   *Ezra* 7:2
Z. repaired.   *Neh* 3:4, 29
Z. sealed.   10:21
of the priests, the son of Z.   11:11
made Z. the scribe treasurer.   13:13

these are the sons of Z. *Ezek 40:46*
43:19; 44:15
priests sanctified of sons of Z. *48:11*

Zalmunna
after Zebah and Z. *Judg 8:5*
Zebah and Z. in thy hand. *6, 15*
arose and slew Zebah and Z. *21*
princes as Zebah and Z. *Ps 83:11*

Zarah, see also Zerah
Judah's son was called Z.
Gen 38:30; 46:12
Tamar bare Pharez and Z.
1 Chr 2:4; Mat 1:3
the sons of Z., Zimri, and. *1 Chr 2:6*

Zarephath
get thee to Z. *1 Ki 17:9*
he went to Z. *10*
Israel shall possess to Z. *Ob 20*

zeal
to slay them in his z. *2 Sam 21:2*
come and see my z. for. *2 Ki 10:16*
the z. of the Lord shall do this. *19:31*
Isa 37:32
the z. of thy house hath eaten me up
and. *Ps 69:9; John 2:17*
my z. hath consumed. *Ps 119:139*
the z. of the Lord will. *Isa 9:7*
and he was clad with z. as. *59:17*
where is thy z. and thy? *63:15*
have spoken it in my z. *Ezek 5:13*
that they have z. of God. *Rom 10:2*
yea, what z.! *2 Cor 7:11*
your z. provoked many. *9:2*
concerning z., persecuting. *Phil 3:6*
hath a great z. for you. *Col 4:13**

zealous
was z. for my sake. *Num 25:11**
he was z. for his God and made. *13**
are all z. of the law. *Acts 21:20*
Paul was z. towards God. *22:3*
Gal 1:14
are z. of spiritual gifts. *1 Cor 14:2*
purify a peculiar people, z. *Tit 2:14*
I rebuke and chasten: be z. *Rev 3:19*

zealously
they z. affect you, but. *Gal 4:17*
it is good to be z. affected in a. *18*

Zebah, see Zalmunna

Zebedee
ship with Z. their father. *Mat 4:21*
apostles, James and John the sons of
Z. *10:2; 26:37; Mark 1:19; 3:17*
10:35; Luke 5:10; John 21:2
mother of Z.'s children. *Mat 20:20*
27:56
they left their father Z. *Mark 1:20*

Zeboim
king of Z. *Gen 14:2*
overthrow of Z. *Deut 29:23*
the valley of Z. to the. *1 Sam 13:18*
Benjamin dwelt at Z. *Neh 11:34*
how shall I set thee at Z.? *Hos 11:8*

Zebul
the son of Jerubbaal, and Z. his
officer. *Judg 9:28*
Z. thrust out Gaal and his. *41*

Zebulun
Leah called his name Z. *Gen 30:20*
Reuben, Simeon, Judah, Z. *35:23*
the sons of Z. *46:14; Num 1:30*
26:26
Z. shall dwell at the. *Gen 49:13*
of Z.: Eliab the son of Helon.
Num 1:9; 2:7; 7:24; 10:16
mount Ebal to curse; Reuben, Gad,
Asher, Z. *Deut 27:13*
of Z. he said, Rejoice, Z. in. *33:18*
third lot came up for Z. *Josh 19:10*
nor did Z. drive out the. *Judg 1:30*
Barak called Z. and Naphtali. *4:10*
out of Z. they that handle. *5:14*
Z. and Naphtali were a people that
jeoparded their lives. *18*
he sent messengers to Z. *6:35*
buried in the country of Z. *12:12*
of Z. Ishmaiah was the. *1 Chr 27:19*
divers of Z. humbled. *2 Chr 30:11*
the princes of Z. and. *Ps 68:27*
afflicted the land of Z. *Isa 9:1*
Z. a portion. *Ezek 48:26*
one gate of Z. *33*

in the borders of Z. *Mat 4:13*
the land of Z. and Nephthalim. *15*

tribe of Zebulun
the tribe of Z. 57,400. *Num 1:31*
then the tribe of Z.: Eliab.*2:7; 10:16*
tribe of Z., Gaddiel to spy. *13:10*
prince of the tribe of Z. to. *34:25*
out of the tribe of Z. twelve cities.
Josh 21:7, 34; 1 Chr 6:63, 77
of the tribe of Z. were sealed 12,000.
Rev 7:8

Zedekiah
Z. made horns of iron. *1 Ki 22:11*
2 Chr 18:10
Z. smote Micaiah on the cheek.
1 Ki 22:24; 2 Chr 18:23
changed his name to. *2 Ki 24:17*
sons of Z. and put out the eyes of Z.
25:7; Jer 39:6, 7; 52:10, 11
son of Josiah, Z. *1 Chr 3:15*
sons of Jehoiakim: Z. *16*
Z. his brother king. *2 Chr 36:10*
I will deliver Z. and his. *Jer 21:7*
Lord make thee like Z. and. *29:22*
Z. shall not escape from the. *32:4*
he shall lead Z. to Babylon. *5*
the army overtook Z. *39:5; 52:8*

Zeeb, see Oreb

Zelophehad
Z. had no sons, but daughters.
Num 26:33; Josh 17:3
the daughters of Z. speak. *Num 27:7*
daughters of Z. were married. *36:11*

Zelotes, see Simon

Zelzah
Rachel's sepulchre at Z. *1 Sam 10:2*

Zenas
bring Z. the lawyer and. *Tit 3:13*

Zephaniah
the captain took Z. second priest.
2 Ki 25:18; Jer 52:24
Z. of the sons of the. *1 Chr 6:36*
Zedekiah sent Z. to. *Jer 21:1*
letters in thy name to Z. *29:25*
Z. read this letter in the ears. *29*
Z. the son of Maaseiah. *37:3*
the word came to Z. *Zeph 1:1*
house of Josiah son of Z. *Zech 6:10*
be to Hen the son of Z. *14*

Zerah, see also Zarah
the son of Reuel, Z. *Gen 36:13, 17*
1 Chr 1:37
Jobab the son of Z. reigned.
Gen 36:33; 1 Chr 1:44
of Z. the family. *Num 26:13, 20*
of Zabdi, the son of Z. *Josh 7:1*
did not Achan the son of Z.? *22:20*
sons of Simeon were Z. *1 Chr 4:24*
Z. son of Iddo. *6:21*
Ethni the son of Z. *41*
of the sons of Z. Jeuel dwelt in. *9:6*
Z. the Ethiopian came. *2 Chr 14:9*
of the children of Z. *Neh 11:24*

Zeresh
Haman called for Z. his. *Esth 5:10*

Zerubbabel
of Pedaiah, Z., sons of Z. *1 Chr 3:19*
which came up with Z. *Ezra 2:2*
Neh 12:1
Z. the son of. *Ezra 3:2, 8; 5:2*
Israel in the days of Z. *Neh 12:47*
Lord by Haggai to Z. *Hag 1:1*
then Z. obeyed the voice of. *12*
stirred up the spirit of Z. *14*
yet now be strong, O Z. *2:4*
speak to Z. of Judah. *21*
word of the Lord unto Z. *Zech 4:6*
before Z. thou shalt become. *7*
the hands of Z. have laid. *9*

Zeruiah
three sons of Z. there. *2 Sam 2:18*
the sons of Z. be too hard. *3:39*
Joab son of Z. *8:16; 1 Chr 18:15*
What have I do with you, ye sons of
Z.? *2 Sam 16:10; 19:22*
whose sisters were Z. *1 Chr 2:16*

Ziba
art thou Z.? *2 Sam 9:2*
Z. had fifteen sons. *16:4*
the king said to Z., Thine are. *16:4*
I said, Thou and Z. divide. *19:29*

Zibeon
Anah the daughter of Z. the Hivite.
Gen 36:2, 14
these are the children of Z. *24*
1 Chr 1:40
duke Z. *Gen 36:29*

Zidon
border shall be to Z. *Gen 49:13*
chased them to great Z. *Josh 11:8*
Kanah, even unto great Z. *19:28*
and served the gods of Z. *Judg 10:6*
because it was far from Z. *18:28*
which belongeth to Z. *1 Ki 17:9*
drink unto them of Z. *Ezra 3:7*
whom the merchants of Z. *Isa 23:2*
be thou ashamed, O Z.: the sea. *4*
O thou virgin, daughter of Z. *12*
all the kings of Z. *Jer 25:22*
yokes to the king of Z. *27:3*
to cut off from Tyre and Z. *47:4*
the inhabitants of Z. *Ezek 27:8*
set thy face against Z. and. *28:21*
I am against thee, O Z. *22*
what have ye to do with me, O Tyre,
and Z.? *Joel 3:4*
Z. though it be very wise. *Zech 9:2*

Zidonians
Z. and Amalekites did. *Judg 10:12*
after the manner of the Z. *18:7*
but king Solomon loved women of Z.
1 Ki 11:1
Ashtoreth, goddess of the Z. *33*
Z. that are gone down. *Ezek 32:30*

Zif
the month of Z. which is. *1 Ki 6:1*
was laid in the month Z. *37*

Ziklag
Achish gave Z. to. *1 Sam 27:6*
we burnt Z. *30:14*
abode two days in Z. *2 Sam 1:1*
I slew them in Z. *4:10*
they dwelt at Z. *1 Chr 4:30*
Neh 11:28
came to David to Z. *12:1, 20*

Zilpah
Laban gave to Leah, Z. *Gen 29:24*
Leah gave Z. her maid. *30:9*
Z. Leah's maid bare Jacob. *10, 12*
the sons of Z., Gad. *35:26; 46:18*
was with the sons of Z. *37:2*

Zimri
that was slain was Z. *Num 25:14*
Z. conspired against. *1 Ki 16:9, 16*
Z. reigned seven days in Tirzah. *15*
had Z. peace, who slew? *2 Ki 9:31*
the sons of Zorah, Z. *1 Chr 2:6*
Z. the son of Jehoadah. *8:36*
Jarah begat Z. *9:42*
I made all the kings of Z. *Jer 25:25*

Zin
from wilderness of Z. *Num 13:21*
to the desert of Z. *20:1; 33:36*
ye rebelled in the desert of Z.
27:14; Deut 32:51

Zion, Sion
David took strong hold of Z. the.
2 Sam 5:7; 1 Chr 11:5
the city of David, which is Z.
1 Ki 8:1; 2 Chr 5:2
king on my holy hill of Z. *Ps 2:6*
walk about Z. and go round. *48:12*
thy good pleasure unto Z. *51:18*
for God will save Z. and. *69:35*
the Lord loveth the gates of Z. *87:2*
he said of Z., This and that man. *5*
Z. heard and was glad. *97:8*
arise and have mercy on Z. *102:13*
Lord shall build up Z. *16*
turned the captivity of Z. *126:1*
turned back that hate Z. *129:5*
the Lord hath chosen. *132:13*
dew on the mountains of Z. *133:3*
when we remembered Z. *137:1*
Sing us one of the songs of Z. *3*
reign, even thy God, O Z. *146:10*
praise the Lord, O Jerusalem, praise
thy God, O Z. *147:12*
let the children of Z. be. *149:2*
Z. shall be redeemed. *Isa 1:27*
shout, thou inhabitant of Z. *12:6*
that the Lord hath founded Z. *14:32*
the Lord hath filled Z. with. *33:5*

look on Z.   Isa 33:20
for controversy of Z.   34:8
come to Z. with songs.   35:10
O Z. that bringest good tidings. 40:9
the first shall say to Z.   41:27
but Z. said, The Lord hath.   49:14
for the Lord shall comfort Z.   51:3
come with singing unto Z.   11
and say unto Z., Thou art my.   16
put on thy strength, O Z.   52:1
saith unto Z., Thy God reigneth !   7
Lord shall bring again Z.   8
Redeemer shall come to Z.   59:20
call thee the Z. of the holy.   60:14
for Z.'s sake will I not hold.   62:1
Z. is a wilderness, Jerusalem. 64:10
as soon as Z. travailed, she.   66:8
I will bring you to Z.   Jer 3:14
set up the standard toward Z.   4:6
Judah ? thy soul lothed Z.   14:19
Z. shall be plowed like a field.
                               26:18; Mi 3:12
this is Z. whom no man.   Jer 30:17
arise ye, and let us go up to Z. 31:6
and sing in the height of Z.   12
they shall ask the way to Z.   50:5
shall the inhabitant of Z. say.   51:35
the ways of Z. do mourn.   Lam 1:4
Z. spreadeth forth her hands, and. 17
the precious sons of Z.   4:2
because the mountain of Z.   5:18
be glad, ye children of Z.   Joel 2:23
Lord will roar from Z.   Amos 1:2
they build up Z. with.   Mi 3:10
for the law shall go forth of Z.   4:2
say, Let our eye look upon Z.   11
I am jealous for Z.   Zech 1:14
The Lord shall yet comfort Z.   17
deliver thyself, O Z.   2:7
jealous for Z.   8:2
Lord, I am returned to Z.   3
raised up thy sons, O Z.   9:13

see daughter, daughters

in Zion

praises to the Lord, who dwelleth in
Z.   Ps 9:11; 76:2; Joel 3:21
praise waiteth for thee, O God, in
Z.   Ps 65:1
every one in Z. appeareth.   84:7
Lord is great in Z.; he is high. 99:2
name of the Lord in Z.   102:21

that is left in Z. shall be.   Isa 4:3
my people that dwellest in Z.   10:24
I lay in Z. for a foundation a stone,
a tried stone.   28:16; I Pet 2:6
people shall dwell in Z.   Isa 30:19
the Lord, whose fire is in Z.   31:9
the sinners in Z. are afraid.   33:14
I will place salvation in Z.   46:13
unto them that mourn in Z.   61:3
is not Lord in Z.? is not ?   Jer 8:19
declare in Z. the vengeance.   50:28
let us declare in Z. the work.   51:10
that they have done in Z.   24
sabbaths be forgotten in Z.   Lam 2:6
hath kindled a fire in Z.   4:11
they ravished the women in Z.   5:11
blow ye the trumpet in Z. and sound.
                                   Joel 2:1, 15
your God dwelling in Z.   3:17
that are at ease in Z.   Amos 6:1
behold, I lay in Z. a.   Rom 9:33

mount Zion

a remnant, they that escape out of
mount Z.   2 Ki 19:31; Isa 37:32
joy of whole earth mount Z. Ps 48:2
let mount Z. rejoice.   11
this mount Z. wherein thou.   74:2
the mount Z. which he loved.   78:68
as mount Z. which cannot be.   125:1
of mount Z. a cloud.   Isa 4:5
dwelleth in mount Z.   8:18; 18:7
his work upon mount Z.   10:12
shall reign in mount Z.   24:23
fight against mount Z.   29:8
fight for mount Z.   31:4
in mount Z. shall be deliverance.
                                Joel 2:32; Ob 17
come up on mount Z.   Ob 21
reign over them in mount Z. Mi 4:7
are come unto mount Z. Heb 12:22
lo, a Lamb stood on the mount Z.
                                   Rev 14:1

out of Zion

Oh that the salvation of Israel were
come out of Z.!   Ps 14:7; 53:6
the Lord strengthen thee out of Z.
                               20:2; 110:2
bless thee out of Z.   128:5; 134:3
blessed be the Lord out of Z.   135:21
for out of Z. shall go.   Isa 2:3
wailing is heard out of Z.   Jer 9:19

shall roar out of Z.   Joel 3:16
shall come out of Z.   Rom 11:26

Zippor, *see* Balak

Zipporah

Jethro gave Moses Z.   Ex 2:21
Z. took a sharp stone.   4:25
Jethro took Z.   18:2

Zoan

seven years before Z.   Num 13:22
things did he in Z.   Ps 78:12, 43
princes of Z. are fools. Isa 19:11, 13
for his princes were at Z.   30:4
I will set fire in Z. and.   Ezek 30:14

Zoar

of Bela, which is Z.   Gen 14:2, 8
the city was called Z.   19:22
city of palm trees to Z.   Deut 34:3
fugitives shall flee unto Z. Isa 15:5
their voice from Z.   Jer 48:34

Zobah

against the kings of Z.   1 Sam 14:47
Hadadezer the king of Z. 2 Sam 8:3
                          1 Ki 11:24; 1 Chr 18:3, 9
Igal son of Nathan of Z. 2 Sam 23:36
fled from the king of Z. 1 Ki 11:23

Zophar

Z. the Naamathite.   Job 2:11; 11:1
                                   20:1; 42:9

Zorah

coast of inheritance of Dan, was Z.
                                  Josh 19:41
man of Z. named Manoah. Judg 13:2
Spirit moved Samson between Z. 25
buried Samson between Z.   16:31
the Danites sent from Z.   18:2
unto their brethren to Z.   8
Rehoboam built Z. and. 2 Chr 11:10

Zorobabel

Salathiel begat Z.   Mat 1:12
Z. begat Abiud.   13
Rhesa the son of Z.   Luke 3:27

Zuar, *see* Nathanael

Zur

Cozbi the daughter of Z. Num 25:15
Z. a prince of Midian slain.
                                  Josh 13:21
Z. the son of.   1 Chr 8:30; 9:36

Zurishaddai, *see* Shelumiel

Zuzims

the kings smote the Z.   Gen 14:5

APPENDIX

A List of Proper Names, seldom mentioned in Scripture, and not included in the body of the Concordance

---

ABDIEL. *1 Chr* 5:15
Abelshittim. *Num* 33:49
Abez. *Josh* 19:20
Abi. *2 Ki* 18:2
Abiasaph. *Ex* 6:24
Abida. *Gen* 25:4; *1 Chr* 1:33
Abiel. (1) *1 Sam* 9:1; 14:51. (2) *1 Chr* 11:32
Abihud. *1 Chr* 8:3
Abilene. *Luke* 3:1
Abimael. *Gen* 10:26-28; *1 Chr* 1:20-22
Abishalom. *1 Ki* 15:2, 10
Abishua. (1) *1 Chr* 6:4, 5, 50; *Ezra* 7:5. (2) *1 Chr* 8:4
Abishur. *1 Chr* 2:28, 29
Abital. *2 Sam* 3:4; *1 Chr* 3:3
Abitub. *1 Chr* 8:11
Accad. *Gen* 10:10
Achaz (Ahaz). *Mat* 1:9
Achbor. (1) *Gen* 36:38, 39; *1 Chr* 1:49. (2) *2 Ki* 22:12, 14. (3) *Jer* 26:22; 36:12
Adadah. *Josh* 15:21, 22
Adah. (1) *Gen* 4:19, 20, 23. (2) *Gen* 36:2, 4, 10, 12, 16
Adaiah. (1) *2 Ki* 22:1. (2) *1 Chr* 6:41. (3) *1 Chr* 8:12-21. (4) *1 Chr* 9:10-12; *Neh* 11:12. (5) *2 Chr* 23:1. (6) *Ezra* 10:29. (7) *Ezra* 10:34-39. (8) *Neh* 11:5
Adalia. *Esth* 9:8
Adamah. *Josh* 19:35, 36
Adami. *Josh* 19:33
Adbeel. *Gen* 25:13; *1 Chr* 1:29
Addan (Addon). *Ezra* 2:59; *Neh* 7:61
Addar. (1) *Josh* 15:3. (2) *1 Chr* 8:3
Ader. *1 Chr* 8:15
Adiel. (1) *1 Chr* 4:36. (2) *1 Chr* 9:12. (3) *1 Chr* 27:25
Adin. (1) *Ezra* 2:15; *Neh* 7:20. (2) *Ezra* 8:6. (3) *Neh* 10:14-16
Adina. *1 Chr* 11:42
Adino. *2 Sam* 23:8
Adithaim. *Josh* 15:33-36
Adlai. *1 Chr* 27:29
Admatha. *Esth* 1:14
Adna. (1) *Ezra* 10:30. (2) *Neh* 12:12-15
Adnah. (1) *1 Chr* 12:20. (2) *2 Chr* 17:14
Adoniram. *1 Ki* 4:6; 5:14
Adonizedek. *Josh* 10:1, 3
Adoraim. *2 Chr* 11:5-9
Adoram. (1) *2 Sam* 20:24. (2) *1 Ki* 12:18
Aeneas. *Acts* 9:33, 34
Aenon. *John* 3:23
Aharah. *1 Chr* 8:1
Aharhel. *1 Chr* 4:8
Ahasai. *Neh* 11:13
Ahasbai. *2 Sam* 23:34
Ahban. *1 Chr* 2:29
Aher. *1 Chr* 7:12
Ahi. (1) *1 Chr* 5:15. (2) *1 Chr* 7:34
Ahiam. *2 Sam* 23:33; *1 Chr* 11:35

Ahian. *1 Chr* 7:19
Ahiezer. (1) *Num* 1:12; 2:25; 7:66, 71; 10:25. (2) *1 Chr* 12:3
Ahihud. (1) *Num* 34:27. (2) *1 Chr* 8:7
Ahilud. *2 Sam* 8:16; 20:24; *1 Ki* 4:3, 12; *1 Chr* 18:15
Ahimoth. *1 Chr* 6:25
Ahinadab. *1 Ki* 4:14
Ahira. *Num* 1:15; 2:29; 7:78, 83; 10:27
Ahiram. *Num* 26:38
Ahishahar. *1 Chr* 7:10
Ahishar. *1 Ki* 4:6
Ahlab. *Judg* 1:31
Ahlai. (1) *1 Chr* 2:31. (2) *1 Chr* 11:41
Ahoah. *1 Chr* 8:4
Ahumai. *1 Chr* 4:2
Ahuzam. *1 Chr* 4:6
Ahuzzath. *Gen* 26:26
Aiah, Ajah. (1) *Gen* 36:24; *1 Chr* 1:40. (2) *2 Sam* 3:7; 21:8, 10, 11
Aija. *Neh* 11:31
Aijalon, Ajalon. (1) *Josh* 19:42; 21:24; *Judg* 1:35. (2) *Judg* 12:12. (3) *1 Sam* 14:31; *1 Chr* 8:13; 2 Chr 11:10; 28:18. (4) *1 Chr* 6:69
Aijeleth Shahar. *Ps* 22 title
Akan (Jakan). *Gen* 36:27; *1 Chr* 1:42
Akkub. (1) *1 Chr* 3:24. (2) *1 Chr* 9:17; *Neh* 11:19; 12:25. (3) *Ezra* 2:42; *Neh* 7:45. (4) *Ezra* 2:45. (5) *Neh* 8:7
Akrabbim. *Num* 34:4; *Josh* 15:3
Alameth. *1 Chr* 7:8
Alammelech. *Josh* 19:26
Alamoth. *1 Chr* 15:20; *Ps* 46 title
Alemeth. (1) *1 Chr* 6:60. (2) *1 Chr* 8:36; 9:42
Aliah (Alva). *Gen* 36:40; *1 Chr* 1:51
Alian (Alvan). *Gen* 36:23; *1 Chr* 1:40
Allon. (1) *Josh* 19:33. (2) *1 Chr* 4:37
Allon Bachuth. *Gen* 35:8
Almodad. *Gen* 10:26; *1 Chr* 1:20
Almon. *Josh* 21:18
Almon-Diblathaim. *Num* 33:46, 47
Aloth. *1 Ki* 4:16
Altaschith. *Ps* 57 title; 58 title; 59 title; 75 title
Alvan. See Alian
Amad. *Josh* 19:26
Amal. *1 Chr* 7:35
Amam. *Josh* 15:26
Amariah. (1) *1 Chr* 6:7, 52; *Ezra* 7:3. (2) *1 Chr* 6:11. (3) *1 Chr* 23:19; 24:23. (4) *2 Chr* 19:11. (5) *2 Chr* 31:15. (6) *Ezra* 10:42. (7) *Neh* 10:3; 12:2, 13. (8) *Neh* 11:4. (9) *Zeph* 1:1
Amasai. (1) *1 Chr* 6:25, 35; *2 Chr* 29:12. (2) *1 Chr* 12:18. (3) *1 Chr* 15:24

Amashai. *Neh* 11:13
Amasiah. *2 Chr* 17:16
Ami. *Ezra* 2:57
Amittai. *2 Ki* 14:25; *Jonah* 1:1
Ammiel. (1) *Num* 13:12. (2) *2 Sam* 9:4, 5; 17:27. (3) *1 Chr* 3:5. (4) *1 Chr* 26:5
Ammihud. (1) *Num* 1:10; 2:18; 7:48, 53; 10:22; *1 Chr* 7:26. (2) *Num* 34:20. (3) *Num* 34:28. (4) *2 Sam* 13:37. (5) *1 Chr* 9:4
Ammihur. *2 Sam* 13:37
Ammishaddai. *Num* 1:12; 2:25; 7:66, 71; 10:25
Ammizabad. *1 Chr* 27:6
Amok. *Neh* 12:7, 20
Amraphel. *Gen* 14:1, 9
Amzi. (1) *1 Chr* 6:46. (2) *Neh* 11:12
Anab. *Josh* 11:21; 15:50
Anaharath. *Josh* 19:19
Anaiah. (1) *Neh* 8:4. (2) *Neh* 10:22
Anamim. *Gen* 10:13; *1 Chr* 1:11
Anan. *Neh* 10:26
Anani. *1 Chr* 3:24
Ananiah. *Neh* 3:23
Anath. *Judg* 3:31; 5:6
Anem. *1 Chr* 6:73
Aniam. *1 Chr* 7:19
Anim. *Josh* 15:50
Antothijah. *1 Chr* 8:24
Anub. *1 Chr* 4:8
Aphekah. *Josh* 15:53
Aphiah. *1 Sam* 9:1
Aphik. *Josh* 13:4; 19:30; *Judg* 1:31
Aphrah. *Mi* 1:10
Aphses. *1 Chr* 24:15
Appaim. *1 Chr* 2:30, 31
Apphia. *Philem* 2
Ara. *1 Chr* 7:38
Arabah. *Josh* 18:18
Arad. (1) *Num* 21:1; 33:40. (2) *1 Chr* 8:15. (3) *Josh* 12:14. *Judg* 1:16
Arah. (1) *1 Chr* 7:39. (2) *Ezra* 2:5; *Neh* 7:10. (3) *Neh* 6:18
Aramnaharaim. *Ps* 60 title
Aramzobah. *Ps* 60 title
Aran. *Gen* 36:28; *1 Chr* 1:42
Archi. *Josh* 16:2
Ard. (1) *Gen* 46:21. (2) *Num* 26:40
Ardon. *1 Chr* 2:18
Areli. *Gen* 46:16; *Num* 26:17
Aridai. *Esth* 9:9
Aridatha. *Esth* 9:8
Arieh. *2 Ki* 15:25
Arisai. *Esth* 9:9
Armoni. *2 Sam* 21:8
Arnan. *1 Chr* 3:21
Arod. *Num* 26:17
Arodi. *Gen* 46:16
Aruboth. *1 Ki* 4:10
Arumah. *Judg* 9:41
Arvad. *Ezek* 27:8, 11
Arza. *1 Ki* 16:9
Asareel. *1 Chr* 4:16
Asarelah. *1 Chr* 25:2
Aser. *Luke* 2:36; *Rev* 7:6

775

Ashan. *Josh* 15:42; 19:7; *1 Chr* 4:32; 6:59
Ashbea. *1 Chr* 4:21
Ashbel. *Gen* 46:21; *Num* 26:38; *1 Chr* 8:1
Ashdoth Pisgah. *Deut* 3:17; 4:49; *Josh* 12:3; 13:20
Ashima. *2 Ki* 17:30
Ashkenaz. (1) *Gen* 10:3; *1 Chr* 1:6. (2) *Jer* 51:27
Ashnah. (1) *Josh* 15:33. (2) *Josh* 15:43
Ashpenaz. *Dan* 1:3
Ashteroth Karnaim. *Gen* 14:5
Ashvath. *1 Chr* 7:33
Asiel. *1 Chr* 4:35
Asnah. *Ezra* 2:50
Aspatha. *Esth* 9:7
Asriel. (1) *Num* 26:31; *Josh* 17:2. (2) *1 Chr* 7:14
Asshurim. *Gen* 25:3
Assir. (1) *Ex* 6:24; *1 Chr* 6:22. (2) *1 Chr* 6:23, 37. (3) *1 Chr* 3:17
Assos. *Acts* 20:13, 14
Asuppim. *1 Chr* 26:15, 17
Atarah. *1 Chr* 2:26
Ataroth. (1) *Num* 32:3, 34. (2) *Josh* 16:5. (3) *Josh* 16:2, 7. (4) *1 Chr* 2:54. (5) *Num* 32:35
Ater. (1) *Ezra* 2:16; *Neh* 7:21. (2) *Ezra* 2:42; *Neh* 7:45. (3) *Neh* 10:17
Athaiah. *Neh* 11:4
Athlai. *Ezra* 10:28
Attai. (1) *1 Chr* 2:35, 36. (2) *1 Chr* 12:11. (3) *2 Chr* 11:20
Ava. *2 Ki* 17:24
Avim. (1) *Deut* 2:23; *Josh* 13:3. (2) *Josh* 18:23
Avith. *Gen* 36:35; *1 Chr* 1:46
Azal. *Zech* 14:5
Azaliah. *2 Ki* 22:3; *2 Chr* 34:8
Azaniah. *Neh* 10:9
Azareel. (1) *1 Chr* 12:6. (2) *1 Chr* 25:18. (3) *1 Chr* 27:22. (4) *Ezra* 10:41. (5) *Neh* 11:13; 12:36
Azaz. *1 Chr* 5:8
Azaziah. (1) *1 Chr* 15:21. (2) *1 Chr* 27:20. (3) *2 Chr* 31:13
Azbuk. *Neh* 3:16
Azel. *1 Chr* 8:37, 38; 9:43, 44
Azem. *Josh* 15:29; 19:3; *1 Chr* 4:29
Azgad. (1) *Ezra* 2:12; *Neh* 7:17. (2) *Ezra* 8:12. (3) *Neh* 10:15
Aziel. *1 Chr* 15:20
Aziza. *Ezra* 10:27
Azmaveth. (1) *2 Sam* 23:31; *1 Chr* 11:33. (2) *1 Chr* 8:36; 9:42. (3) *1 Chr* 12:3. (4) *Ezra* 2:24; *Neh* 12:29. (5) *1 Chr* 27:25
Azmon. *Num* 34:4, 5; *Josh* 15:4
Aznoth Tabor. *Josh* 19:34
Azor. *Mat* 1:13, 14
Azotus. *Acts* 8:40
Azriel. (1) *1 Chr* 5:24. (2) *1 Chr* 27:19. (3) *Jer* 36:26
Azrikam. (1) *1 Chr* 3:23. (2) *1 Chr* 8:38; 9:44. (3) *1 Chr* 9:14; *Neh* 11:15. (4) *2 Chr* 28:7
Azubah. (1) *1 Ki* 22:42; *2 Chr* 20:31. (2) *1 Chr* 2:18, 19
Azur (Azzur). (1) *Neh* 10:17. (2) *Jer* 28:1. (3) *Ezek* 11:1
Azzah. *Deut* 2:23; *1 Ki* 4:24; *Jer* 25:20
Azzan. *Num* 34:26

BAALAH. *Josh* 15:9
Baalath. *Josh* 19:44; *1 Ki* 9:18; *2 Chr* 8:6
Baalath-beer. *Josh* 19:8
Baale. *2 Sam* 6:2
Baal-gad. *Josh* 11:17; 12:7; 13:5
Baal-hanan. (1) *Gen* 36:38, 39; *1 Chr* 1:49, 50. (2) *1 Chr* 27:28
Baal-hazor. *2 Sam* 13:23
Baal-hermon. *Judg* 3:3; *1 Chr* 5:23
Baara. *1 Chr* 8:8
Baaseiah. *1 Chr* 6:40
Bakbakkar. *1 Chr* 9:15
Bakbuk. *Ezra* 2:51; *Neh* 7:53
Bakbukiah. *Neh* 11:17; 12:9, 25

Bamoth. *Num* 21:19, 20
Bamoth-baal. *Josh* 13:17
Bani. (1) *2 Sam* 23:36. (2) *1 Chr* 6:46. (3) *1 Chr* 9:4. (4) *Ezra* 2:10; 10:29. (5) *Ezra* 10:34. (6) *Ezra* 10:38. (7) *Neh* 3:17; 8:7; 9:4, 5. (8) *Neh* 9:4; 10:13. (9) *Neh* 10:14. (10) *Neh* 11:22
Barachiah. *Zech* 1:1, 7
Bariah. *1 Chr* 3:22
Barkos. *Ezra* 2:53; *Neh* 7:55
Bashan-havoth-jair. *Deut* 3:14
Basmath. *1 Ki* 4:15
Bath-rabbim. *S of S* 7:4
Bathshua. *1 Chr* 3:5
Bavai. *Neh* 3:18
Bazlith. *Ezra* 2:52; *Neh* 7:54
Bealiah. *1 Chr* 12:5
Bealoth. *Josh* 15:24
Bebai. (1) *Ezra* 2:11; *Neh* 7:16. (2) *Ezra* 8:11; 10:28. (3) *Neh* 10:15
Bechorath. *1 Sam* 9:1
Bedad. *Gen* 36:35; *1 Chr* 1:46
Bedeiah. *Ezra* 10:35
Beeliada. *1 Chr* 14:7
Beer. (1) *Num* 21:16. (2) *Judg* 9:21
Beera. *1 Chr* 7:37
Beerah. *1 Chr* 5:6
Beer-elim. *Isa* 15:8
Beeri. (1) *Gen* 26:34. (2) *Hos* 1:1
Beer-lahai-roi. *Gen* 16:14; 24:62; 25:11
Beeroth. (1) *Deut* 10:6. (2) *Josh* 9:17; 18:25; *2 Sam* 4:2; *Ezra* 2:25; *Neh* 7:29
Beeshterah. *Josh* 21:27
Bela. (1) *Gen* 14:2, 8. (2) *Gen* 36:32, 33; *1 Chr* 1:43, 44. (3) *Gen* 46:21; *Num* 26:38, 40; *1 Chr* 7:6, 7; 8:1, 3. (4) *1 Chr* 5:8
Ben. *1 Chr* 15:18
Beneberak. *Josh* 19:45
Benejaakan. *Num* 33:31, 32
Benhail. *2 Chr* 17:7
Benhanan. *1 Chr* 4:20
Beninu. *Neh* 10:13
Beno. *1 Chr* 24:26, 27
Benzoheth. *1 Chr* 4:20
Beon. *Num* 32:3
Bera. *Gen* 14:2
Beraiah. *1 Chr* 8:21
Berechiah. (1) *1 Chr* 3:20. (2) *1 Chr* 6:39; 15:17. (3) *1 Chr* 9:16. (4) *1 Chr* 15:23. (5) *2 Chr* 28:12. (6) *Neh* 3:4, 30; 6:18
Bered. (1) *Gen* 16:14. (2) *1 Chr* 7:20
Beri. *1 Chr* 7:36
Beriah. (1) *Gen* 46:17; *Num* 26:44, 45; *1 Chr* 7:30, 31. (2) *1 Chr* 7:23. (3) *1 Chr* 8:13, 16. (4) *1 Chr* 23:10, 11
Berodach-baladan. See Merodach-baladan
Berothah. *Ezek* 47:16
Besai. *Ezra* 2:49; *Neh* 7:52
Besodeiah. *Neh* 3:6
Betah. *2 Sam* 8:8
Beten. *Josh* 19:25
Bethanath. *Josh* 19:38; *Judg* 1:33
Bethanoth. *Josh* 15:59
Betharabah. *Josh* 15:6, 61; 18:22
Betharam. *Josh* 13:27
Betharbel. *Hos* 10:14
Bethazmaveth. *Neh* 7:28
Bethbaalmeon. *Josh* 13:17
Bethbarah. *Judg* 7:24
Bethbirei. *1 Chr* 4:31
Bethcar. *1 Sam* 7:11
Bethdagon. (1) *Josh* 15:41. (2) *Josh* 19:27
Bethemek. *Josh* 19:27
Bethgader. *1 Chr* 2:51
Bethharan. *Num* 32:36
Bethhoglah. *Josh* 15:6; 18:19, 21
Bethjeshimoth. *Num* 33:49; *Josh* 12:3; 13:20; *Ezek* 25:9
Bethlebaoth. *Josh* 19:6
Bethmaachah. *2 Sam* 20:14, 15, 18; *2 Ki* 15:29

Bethmarcaboth. *Josh* 19:5; *1 Chr* 4:31
Bethmeon. *Jer* 48:23
Bethnimrah. *Num* 32:36; *Josh* 13:27
Bethpalet. *Josh* 15:27; *Neh* 11:26
Bethpazzez. *Josh* 19:21
Bethrapha. *1 Chr* 4:12
Bethrehob. *Judg* 18:28; *2 Sam* 10:6
Bethshean. *Josh* 17:11, 16; *Judg* 1:27; *1 Ki* 4:12; *1 Chr* 7:29
Bethshittah. *Judg* 7:22
Bethtappuah. *Josh* 15:53
Bethul. *Josh* 19:4
Bethzur. (1) *Josh* 15:58; *2 Chr* 11:7; *Neh* 3:16. (2) *1 Chr* 2:45
Betonim. *Josh* 13:26
Bezai. (1) *Ezra* 2:17; *Neh* 7:23. (2) *Neh* 10:18
Bezer. (1) *Deut* 4:43; *Josh* 20:8; 21:36; *1 Chr* 6:78. (2) *1 Chr* 7:37
Bigtha. *Esth* 1:10
Bigvai. (1) *Ezra* 2:2; *Neh* 7:7. (2) *Ezra* 2:14; *Neh* 7:19. (3) *Ezra* 8:14. (4) *Neh* 10:16
Bileam. *1 Chr* 6:70
Bilgah. (1) *1 Chr* 24:14. (2) *Neh* 12:5, 18
Bilgai. *Neh* 10:8
Bilhan. (1) *Gen* 36:27; *1 Chr* 1:42. (2) *1 Chr* 7:10
Bilshan. *Ezra* 2:2; *Neh* 7:7
Bimhal. *1 Chr* 7:33
Binea. *1 Chr* 8:37; 9:43
Binnui. (1) *Ezra* 8:33. (2) *Ezra* 10:30. (3) *Ezra* 10:38. (4) *Neh* 3:24; 10:9. (5) *Neh* 7:15. (6) *Neh* 12:8
Birsha. *Gen* 14:2
Birzavith. *1 Chr* 7:31
Bishlam. *Ezra* 4:7
Bithiah. *1 Chr* 4:18
Bithron. *2 Sam* 2:29
Bizjothjah. *Josh* 15:28
Biztha. *Esth* 1:10
Bocheru. *1 Chr* 8:38; 9:44
Bohan. *Josh* 15:6; 18:17
Bozez. *1 Sam* 14:4
Bozkath. *Josh* 15:39; *2 Ki* 22:1
Bunah. *1 Chr* 2:25
Bunni. (1) *Neh* 9:4. (2) *Neh* 11:15. (3) *Neh* 10:15

CALAH. *Gen* 10:11, 12
Calcol. *1 Chr* 2:6
Canneh. *Ezek* 27:23
Caphtorim. *Gen* 10:14; *Deut* 2:23; *1 Chr* 1:12
Carcas. *Esth* 1:10
Careah. *2 Ki* 25:23
Carshena. *Esth* 1:14
Casluhim. *Gen* 10:14; *1 Chr* 1:12
Chanaan (see Canaan). *Acts* 7:11; 13:19
Chedorlaomer. *Gen* 14:1, 4, 5, 9, 17
Chelal. *Ezra* 10:30
Chellub. (1) *1 Chr* 4:11. (2) *1 Chr* 27:26
Chelluh. *Ezra* 10:35
Chelubai. *1 Chr* 2:9
Chenaanah. (1) *1 Ki* 22:11, 24; *2 Chr* 18:10, 23. (2) *1 Chr* 7:10
Chenani. *Neh* 9:4
Chephar-haammonia. *Josh* 18:24
Chephirah. *Josh* 9:17; 18:26; *Ezra* 2:25; *Neh* 7:29
Cheran. *Gen* 36:26; *1 Chr* 1:41
Chesalon. *Josh* 15:10
Chesed. *Gen* 22:22
Chesil. *Josh* 15:30
Chesulloth. *Josh* 19:18
Chezib. *Gen* 38:5
Chidon. *1 Chr* 13:9
Chinnereth. *Num* 34:11; *Deut* 3:17; *Josh* 11:2; 12:3; 13:27; 19:35; *1 Ki* 15:20
Chislon. *Num* 34:21
Chisloth-tabor. *Josh* 19:12
Chorashan. *1 Sam* 30:30
Chozeba. *1 Chr* 4:22
Chub. *Ezek* 30:5
Chun. *1 Chr* 18:8

Cinneroth. *1 Ki* 15:20
Clauda. *Acts* 27:16
Claudia. *2 Tim* 4:21
Claudius. (1) *Acts* 11:28; 18:2.
(2) *Acts* 23:26
Clement. *Phil* 4:3
Cnidus. *Acts* 27:7
Colhozeh. (1) *Neh* 3:15. (2) *Neh* 11:5
Conaniah (Cononiah). (1) *2 Chr* 31:12; 31:13. (2) *2 Chr* 35:9
Coos. *Acts* 21:1
Core. *Jude* 11
Cosam. *Luke* 3:28
Coz. *1 Chr* 4:8
Cuthah or Cuth. *2 Ki* 17:24, 30

DABAREH. *Josh* 21:28
Dalaiah. *1 Chr* 3:24
Dalphon. *Esth* 9:7
Danjaan. *2 Sam* 24:6
Dannah. *Josh* 15:49
Dara. *1 Chr* 2:6
Darda. *1 Ki* 4:31
Debir. (1) *Josh* 10:3. (2) *Josh* 10:38, 39; 11:21; 12:13; 15:7, 15, 49; 21:15; *Judg* 1:11; *1 Chr* 6:58. (3) *Josh* 13:26
Dekar. *1 Ki* 4:9
Delaiah. (1) *1 Chr* 24:18. (2) *Ezra* 2:60; *Neh* 7:62. (3) *Neh* 6:10. (4) *Jer* 36:12, 25
Derbe. *Acts* 14:6, 20; 16:1; 20:4
Deuel. *Num* 1:14; 2:14; 7:42, 47; *Deut* 10:20
Diblaim. *Hos* 1:3
Diblath. *Ezek* 6:14
Dibri. *Lev* 24:11
Diklah. *Gen* 10:27; *1 Chr* 1:21
Dilean. *Josh* 15:38
Dimnah. *Josh* 21:35
Dimonah. *Josh* 15:22
Dinhabah. *Gen* 36:32; *1 Chr* 1:43
Dishan. *Gen* 36:21, 28, 30; *1 Chr* 1:38, 42
Dishon. (1) *Gen* 36:21, 26, 30; *1 Chr* 1:38. (2) *Gen* 36:25; *1 Chr* 1:38, 41
Dizahab. *Deut* 1:1
Dodai. *1 Chr* 27:4
Dodanim. *Gen* 10:4; *1 Chr* 1:7
Dodavah. *2 Chr* 20:37
Dodo. (1) *Judg* 10:1. (2) *2 Sam* 23:9; *1 Chr* 11:12. (3) *2 Sam* 23:24; *1 Chr* 11:26
Dophkah. *Num* 33:12, 13

EBIASAPH. *1 Chr* 6:23, 37; 9:19
Ebronah. *Num* 33:34
Eder. (1) *Gen* 35:21. (2) *Josh* 15:21. (3) *1 Chr* 23:23; 24:30
Edrei. (1) *Num* 21:33; *Deut* 1:4; 3:1, 10; *Josh* 12:4; 13:12, 31. (2) *Josh* 19:37
Ehi. *Gen* 46:21
Eker. *1 Chr* 2:27
Eladah. *1 Chr* 7:20
Elasah. (1) *Ezra* 10:22. (2) *Jer* 29:3
Eldaah. *Gen* 25:4; *1 Chr* 1:33
Elead. *1 Chr* 7:21
Eleph. *Josh* 18:28
Eliadah. *1 Ki* 11:23
Eliah. (1) *1 Chr* 8:27. (2) *Ezra* 10:26
Eliahba. *2 Sam* 23:32; *1 Chr* 11:33
Eliasaph. (1) *Num* 1:14; 2:14; 7:42, 47; 10:20. (2) *Num* 3:24
Eliathah. *1 Chr* 25:4, 27
Elidad. *Num* 34:21
Eliel. (1) *1 Chr* 6:34. (2) *1 Chr* 5:24. (3) *1 Chr* 8:20. (4) *1 Chr* 8:22. (5) *1 Chr* 11:46. (6) *1 Chr* 11:47. (7) *1 Chr* 12:11. (8) *1 Chr* 15:9. (9) *1 Chr* 15:11. (10) *2 Chr* 31:13
Elienai. *1 Chr* 8:20
Elika. *2 Sam* 23:25
Elioenai. (1) *1 Chr* 3:23, 24. (2) *1 Chr* 4:36. (3) *1 Chr* 7:8. (4) *Ezra* 10:22. (5) *Ezra* 10:27. (6) *Neh* 12:41. (7) *1 Chr* 26:3. (8) *Ezra* 8:4
Eliphal. *1 Chr* 11:35

Elipheleh. *1 Chr* 15:18, 21
Elishaphat. *2 Chr* 23:1
Elizaphan. (1) *Num* 3:30; *1 Chr* 15:8. (2) *Num* 34:25 (3) *2 Chr* 29:13
Elizur. *Num* 1:5; 2:10; 7:30, 35; 10:18
Ellasar. *Gen* 14:1, 9
Elnaam. *1 Chr* 11:46
Eloi. *Mark* 15:34
Elon-beth-hanan. *1 Ki* 4:9
Eloth. *1 Ki* 9:26; *2 Chr* 8:17; 26:2
Elpaal. *1 Chr* 8:11, 12, 18
Elpalet. *1 Chr* 14:5
Elparan. *Gen* 14:6
Eltekeh. *Josh* 19:44; 21:23
Eltekon. *Josh* 15:59
Eltolad. *Josh* 15:30; 19:4
Eluzai. *1 Chr* 12:5
Elzabad. (1) *1 Chr* 12:12. (2) *1 Chr* 26:7
Elzaphan. (1) *Ex* 6:22; *Lev* 10:4. (2) *Num* 34:25
Enam. *Josh* 15:34
Enan. *Num* 1:15; 2:29; 7:78, 83; 10:27
Engannim. (1) *Josh* 15:34. (2) *Josh* 19:21; 21:29
Enhaddah. *Josh* 19:21
Enhakkore. *Judg* 15:19
Enhazor. *Josh* 19:37
Enmishpat. *Gen* 14:7
Enrimmon. *Neh* 11:29
Enshemesh. *Josh* 15:7; 18:17
Entappuah. *Josh* 17:7
Ephai. *Jer* 40:8
Epher. (1) *Gen* 25:4; *1 Chr* 1:33. (2) *1 Chr* 4:17. (3) *1 Chr* 5:24
Ephlal. *1 Chr* 2:37
Ephod. *Num* 34:23
Eran. *Num* 26:36
Erech. *Gen* 10:10
Eri. *Gen* 46:16; *Num* 26:16
Eshbaal. *1 Chr* 8:33; 9:39
Eshban. *Gen* 36:26; *1 Chr* 1:41
Eshean. *Josh* 15:52
Eshek. *1 Chr* 8:39
Eshtaol. *Josh* 15:33; 19:41; *Judg* 13:25; 16:31; 18:2, 8, 11
Eshtemoa. (1) *Josh* 15:50; 21:14; *1 Sam* 30:28; *1 Chr* 6:57. (2) *1 Chr* 4:17, 19
Eshton. *1 Chr* 4:11, 12
Ethbaal. *1 Ki* 16:31
Ether. *Josh* 15:42; 19:7
Ethnan. *1 Chr* 4:7
Ethni. *1 Chr* 6:41
Evi. *Num* 31:8; *Josh* 13:21
Ezar. *1 Chr* 1:38
Ezbai. *1 Chr* 11:37
Ezbon. (1) *Gen* 46:16. (2) *1 Chr* 7:7
Ezekias. *Mat* 1:9, 10
Ezem. *1 Chr* 4:29
Ezer. (1) *1 Chr* 7:21. (2) *Neh* 12:42. (3) *1 Chr* 4:4. (4) *1 Chr* 12:9. (5) *Neh* 3:19. (6) *Gen* 36:21, 27, 30; *1 Chr* 1:38, 42
Ezion-gaber (Ezion-geber). *Num* 33:35, 36; *Deut* 2:8; *1 Ki* 9:26; 22:48; *2 Chr* 8:17; 20:36
Ezri. *1 Chr* 27:26

GAASH. *Josh* 24:30; *Judg* 2:9; *2 Sam* 23:30; *1 Chr* 11:32
Gaba. *Josh* 18:24; *Ezra* 2:26; *Neh* 7:30
Gabbai. *Neh* 11:8
Gaddi. *Num* 13:11
Gaddiel. *Num* 13:10
Gadi. *2 Ki* 15:14, 17
Gaham. *Gen* 22:24
Gahar. *Ezra* 2:47; *Neh* 7:49
Galal. (1) *1 Chr* 9:15. (2) *1 Chr* 9:16; *Neh* 11:17
Gamul. *1 Chr* 24:17
Gareb. (1) *2 Sam* 23:38; *1 Chr* 11:40. (2) *Jer* 31:39.
Gashmu. *Neh* 6:6
Gatam. *Gen* 36:11, 16; *1 Chr* 1:36
Gath-hepher. *2 Ki* 14:25
Gath-rimmon. (1) *Josh* 19:45. (2) *Josh* 21:25; *1 Chr* 6:69

Gazez. (1) *1 Chr* 2:46. (2) *1 Chr* 2:46
Gazzam. *Ezra* 2:48; *Neh* 7:51
Geber. (1) *1 Ki* 4:13. (2) *1 Ki* 4:19
Geder. *Josh* 12:13
Gederah. *Josh* 15:36
Gederoth. *Josh* 15:41; *2 Chr* 28:18
Gederothaim. *Josh* 15:36
Gedor. (1) *Josh* 15:58. (2) *1 Chr* 12:7. (3) *1 Chr* 8:31; 9:37. (4) *1 Chr* 4:4, 18. (5) *1 Chr* 4:39
Geliloth. *Josh* 18:17
Gemalli. *Num* 13:12
Genubath. *1 Ki* 11:20
Gesham. *1 Chr* 2:47
Geshem. *Neh* 2:19; 6:1, 2
Gether. *Gen* 10:23; *1 Chr* 1:17
Geuel. *Num* 13:15
Gezer. *Josh* 10:33; 12:12; 16:3, 10; 21:21; *Judg* 1:29; *1 Ki* 9:15, 16, 17; *1 Chr* 6:67; 7:28; 20:4
Gibbar. *Ezra* 2:20
Gibethon. *Josh* 19:44; 21:23; *1 Ki* 15:27; 16:15, 17
Gibea. *1 Chr* 2:49
Giddalti. *1 Chr* 25:4, 29
Giddel. (1) *Ezra* 2:47; *Neh* 7:49. (2) *Ezra* 2:56; *Neh* 7:58.
Gidom. *Judg* 20:45
Gilalia. *Neh* 12:36
Giloh. *Josh* 15:51; *2 Sam* 15:12
Gimzo. *2 Chr* 28:18
Ginath. *1 Ki* 16:21, 22
Ginnethon. *Neh* 10:6; 12:4, 16
Gispa. *Neh* 11:21
Gittah-hepher. *Josh* 19:13
Gittaim. (1) *2 Sam* 4:3. (2) *Neh* 11:33
Goath. *Jer* 31:39
Gudgodah. *Deut* 10:7
Guni. (1) *Gen* 46:24; *Num* 26:48; *1 Chr* 7:13. (2) *1 Chr* 5:15
Gurbaal. *2 Chr* 26:7

HAAHASHTARI. *1 Chr* 4:6
Habaiah. *Ezra* 2:61; *Neh* 7:63
Habakkuk. *Hab* 1:1; 3:1
Habaziniah. *Jer* 35:3
Habor. *2 Ki* 17:6; 18:11; *1 Chr* 5:26
Hachaliah. *Neh* 1:1; 10:1
Hachmoni. *1 Chr* 27:32
Hadad. (1) *Gen* 36:35, 36; *1 Chr* 1:46, 47. (2) *1 Ki* 11:14, 17, 19, 21, 25. (3) *1 Chr* 1:30. (4) *1 Chr* 1:50, 51
Hadar. (1) *Gen* 25:15. (2) *Gen* 36:39
Hadashah. *Josh* 15:37
Hadattah. *Josh* 15:25
Hadid. (1) *Ezra* 2:33; *Neh* 7:37; 11:34
Hadlai. *2 Chr* 28:12
Hagab. *Ezra* 2:46
Hagabah. *Ezra* 2:45; *Neh* 7:48
Haggeri. *1 Chr* 11:38
Haggi. *Gen* 46:16; *Num* 26:15
Haggiah. *1 Chr* 6:30
Hai. *Gen* 12:8; 13:3
Hakkatan. *Ezra* 8:12
Hakkoz. *1 Chr* 24:10
Hakupha. *Ezra* 2:51; *Neh* 7:53
Halah. *2 Ki* 17:6; 18:11; *1 Chr* 5:26
Halak. *Josh* 11:17; 12:7
Halhul. *Josh* 15:58
Hali. *Josh* 19:25
Halohesh. (1) *Neh* 3:12. (2) *Neh* 10:24
Hamath-zobah. *2 Chr* 8:3
Hammath. *Josh* 19:35
Hammelech. *Jer* 36:26; 38:6
Hammoleketh. *1 Chr* 7:18
Hammon. (1) *Josh* 19:28. (2) *1 Chr* 6:76
Hammoth-dor. *Josh* 21:32
Hamonah. *Ezek* 39:16
Hamuel. *1 Chr* 4:26
Hamul. *Gen* 46:12; *Num* 26:21; *1 Chr* 2:5
Hamutal. *2 Ki* 23:31; 24:18; *Jer* 52:1

Hanan. (1) *1 Chr* 8:23. (2) *1 Chr*
8:38; 9:44. (3) *1 Chr* 11:43.
(4) *Ezra* 2:46; *Neh* 7:49. (5)
Neh 8:7. (6) *Neh* 10:10; 13:13.
(7) *Neh* 10:22. (8) *Neh* 10:26.
(9) *Jer* 35:4
Hanes. *Isa* 30:4
Hannathon. *Josh* 19:14
Hanniel. (1) *Num* 34:23. (2) *1 Chr*
7:39
Haphraim. *Josh* 19:19
Haradah. *Num* 33:24, 25
Hareph. *1 Chr* 2:51
Hareth. *1 Sam* 22:5
Harhaiah. *Neh* 3:8
Harhas. *2 Ki* 22:14
Harhur. *Ezra* 2:51; *Neh* 7:53
Harim. (1) *1 Chr* 24:8; *Ezra* 2:39;
10:21; *Neh* 3:11; 7:42. (2)
Ezra 2:32; *Neh* 7:35. (3) *Ezra*
10:31. (4) *Neh* 10:5. (5) *Neh*
10:27. (6) *Neh* 12:15
Hariph. (1) *Neh* 7:24. (2) *Neh*
10:19
Harnepher. *1 Chr* 7:36
Haroeh. *1 Chr* 2:52
Harsha. *Ezra* 2:52; *Neh* 7:54
Harum. *1 Chr* 4:8
Harumaph. *Neh* 3:10
Haruz. *2 Ki* 21:19
Hasadiah. *1 Chr* 3:20
Hasenuah. *1 Chr* 9:7
Hashabiah. (1) *1 Chr* 6:45. (2)
1 Chr 9:14. (3) *1 Chr* 25:3.
(4) *1 Chr* 26:30. (5) *1 Chr*
27:17. (6) *2 Chr* 35:9. (7)
Ezra 8:19. (8) *Ezra* 8:24. (9)
Neh 3:17. (10) *Neh* 10:11. (11)
Neh 11:15. (12) *Neh* 11:22.
(13) *Neh* 12:21. (14) *Neh* 12:24
Hashbadana. *Neh* 8:4
Hashem. *1 Chr* 11:34
Hashmonah. *Num* 33:29, 30
Hashub. (1) *1 Chr* 9:14; *Neh*
11:15. (2) *Neh* 3:11. (3) *Neh*
3:23. (4) *Neh* 10:23
Hashubah. *1 Chr* 3:20
Hashum. (1) *Ezra* 2:19; 10:33;
Neh 7:22. (2) *Neh* 8:4. (3)
Neh 10:18
Hasrah. *2 Chr* 34:22
Hassenaah. *Neh* 3:3
Hasupha. *Ezra* 2:43; *Neh* 7:46
Hatach. *Esth* 4:5, 6, 9, 10
Hathath. *1 Chr* 4:13
Hatipha. *Ezra* 2:54; *Neh* 7:56
Hatita. *Ezra* 2:42; *Neh* 7:45
Hattil. *Ezra* 2:57; *Neh* 7:59
Hattush. (1) *1 Chr* 3:22. (2) *Ezra*
8:2; *Neh* 3:10; 10:4. (3) *Neh*
12:2
Hauran. *Ezek* 47:16, 18
Havilah. (1) *Gen* 10:7; *1 Chr* 1:9.
(2) *Gen* 10:29; *1 Chr* 1:23.
(3) *Gen* 2:11. (4) *Gen* 25:18;
1 Sam 15:7
Havoth-jair. *Num* 32:41; *Deut*
3:14; *Judg* 10:4
Hazaiah. *Neh* 11:5
Hazar-addar. *Num* 34:4
Hazar-enan. *Num* 34:9, 10; *Ezek*
47:17; 48:1
Hazar-gaddah. *Josh* 15:27
Hazar-hatticon. *Ezek* 47:16
Hazarmaveth. *Gen* 10:26; *1 Chr*
1:20
Hazarshual. *Josh* 15:28; 19:3;
1 Chr 4:28; *Neh* 11:27
Hazarsusah. *Josh* 19:5
Hazerim. *Deut* 2:23
Hazezon-tamar. *Gen* 14:7; *2 Chr*
20:2
Haziel. *1 Chr* 23:9
Hazo. *Gen* 22:22
Heber. (1) *1 Chr* 4:18. (2) *1 Chr*
5:13. (3) *1 Chr* 8:17. (4) *1 Chr*
8:22. (See also p. 296)
Helah. *1 Chr* 4:5, 7
Helbah. *Judg* 1:31
Heleb. *2 Sam* 23:29
Heled. *1 Chr* 11:30
Helek. *Num* 26:30; *Josh* 17:2
Helem. (1) *1 Chr* 7:35. (2) *Zech*
6:14

Heleph. *Josh* 19:33
Helez. (1) *2 Sam* 23:26; *1 Chr*
11:27; 27:10. (2) *1 Chr* 2:39
Helkai. *Neh* 12:15
Helkath. *Josh* 19:25; 21:31
Helon. *Num* 1:9; 2:7; 7:24, 29;
10:16
Hemam (Homam). *Gen* 36:22;
1 Chr 1:39
Hemath. (1) *Amos* 6:14. (2) *1 Chr*
2:55
Hemdan. *Gen* 36:26
Hena. *2 Ki* 18:34; 19:13; *Isa* 37:13
Henadad. *Ezra* 3:9; *Neh* 3:18, 24;
10:9
Hepher. (1) *Num* 26:32; 27:1;
Josh 17:2, 3. (2) *1 Chr* 4:6.
(3) *1 Chr* 11:36. (4) *Josh* 12:17;
1 Ki 4:10
Heres. *Judg* 1:35
Heresh. *1 Chr* 9:15
Hesed. *1 Ki* 4:10
Heshmon. *Josh* 15:27
Hethlon. *Ezek* 47:15; 48:
Hezeki. *1 Chr* 8:17
Hezion. *1 Ki* 15:18
Hezir. (1) *1 Chr* 24:15. (2) *Neh*
10:20
Hezrai. *2 Sam* 23:35
Hezro. *1 Chr* 11:37
Hiddai. *2 Sam* 23:30
Hierapolis. *Col.* 4:13
Hilen. *1 Chr* 6:58
Hillel. *Judg* 12:13, 15
Hirah. *Gen* 38:1, 12
Hizkiah. *Zeph* 1:1
Hizkijah. *Neh* 10:17
Hobah. *Gen* 14:15
Hod. *1 Chr* 7:37
Hodaiah. *1 Chr* 3:24
Hodaviah. (1) *1 Chr* 5:24. (2)
1 Chr 9:7. (3) *Ezra* 2:40
Hodesh. *1 Chr* 8:9
Hodevah. *Neh* 7:43
Hodiah. (1) *1 Chr* 4:19. (2) *Neh*
8:7; 9:5; 10:10, 13. (3) *Neh*
10:18
Hoglah. *Num* 26:33; 27:1; 36:11;
Josh 17:3
Hoham. *Josh* 10:3
Holon. (1) *Josh* 15:51; 21:15 (2)
Jer 48:21
Homam. *1 Chr* 1:39
Horam. *Josh* 10:33
Horem. *Josh* 19:38
Hori. (1) *Gen* 36:22, 30; *1 Chr*
1:39. (2) *Num* 13:5
Horim. *Gen* 14:6; 36:20, 21, 29;
Deut 2:12, 22
Hosah. (1) *Josh* 19:29. (2) *1 Chr*
16:38; 26:10, 11, 16
Hoshaiah. (1) *Neh* 12:32. (2) *Jer*
42:1; 43:2
Hoshama. *1 Chr* 3:18
Hotham. (1) *1 Chr* 7:32. (2) *1 Chr*
11:44
Hothir. *1 Chr* 25:4, 28
Hukkok. *Josh* 19:34
Hukok. *1 Chr* 6:75
Hul. *Gen* 10:23; *1 Chr* 1:17
Huldah. *2 Ki* 22:14; *2 Chr* 34:22
Humtah. *Josh* 15:54
Hupham. *Num* 26:39
Huppah. *1 Chr* 24:13
Huppim. *Gen* 46:21; *1 Chr* 7:12, 15
Huram. (1) *1 Chr* 8:5. (2) *2 Chr*
2:3, 11, 12. (3) *2 Chr* 4:11, 16
Hushah. *1 Chr* 4:4
Husham. *Gen* 36:34, 35; *1 Chr*
1:45, 46
Hushim. (1) *Gen* 46:23. (2) *1 Chr*
7:12. (3) *1 Chr* 8:8, 11
Huz. *Gen* 22:21

IBLEAM. *Josh* 17:11; *Judg* 1:27;
2 Ki 9:27
Ibneiah. *1 Chr* 9:8
Ibnijah. *1 Chr* 9:8
Ibri. *1 Chr* 24:27
Ibzan. *Judg* 12:8, 10
Idalah. *Josh* 19:15
Idbash. *1 Chr* 4:3
Igal. (1) *Num* 13:7. (2) *2 Sam*
23:36

Igeal. *1 Chr* 3:22
Iim. (1) *Num* 33:45. (2) *Josh*
15:29
Ijeabarim. *Num* 21:11; 33:44
Ijon. *1 Ki* 15:20; *2 Ki* 15:29;
2 Chr 16:4
Ikkesh. *2 Sam* 23:26; *1 Chr* 11:28;
27:9
Ilai. *1 Chr* 11:29
Imla. *1 Ki* 22:8, 9; *2 Chr* 18:7, 8
Immer. (1) *1 Chr* 9:12; *Ezra* 2:37;
10:20; *Neh* 7:40; 11:13. (2)
1 Chr 24:14. (3) *Ezra* 2:59;
Neh 7:61. (4) *Neh* 3:29. (5)
Jer 20:1
Imna. *1 Chr* 7:35
Imnah. (1) *1 Chr* 7:30. (2) *2 Chr*
31:14
Imrah. *1 Chr* 7:36
Imri. (1) *1 Chr* 9:4. (2) *Neh* 3:2
Ir. *1 Chr* 7:12
Iram. *Gen* 36:43; *1 Chr* 1:54
Iri. *1 Chr* 7:7
Irnahash. *1 Chr* 4:12
Irpeel. *Josh* 18:27
Irshemesh. *Josh* 19:41
Iru. *1 Chr* 4:15
Iscah. *Gen* 11:29
Ishbah. *1 Chr* 4:17
Ishbak. *Gen* 25:2; *1 Chr* 1:32
Ishbibenoh. *2 Sam* 21:16
Ishi. (1) *1 Chr* 2:31. (2) *1 Chr*
4:20. (3) *1 Chr* 4:42. (4) *1 Chr*
5:24. (5) *Hos* 2:16
Ishiah. (1) *1 Chr* 7:3. (2) *1 Chr*
24:21. (3) *1 Chr* 24:25. (4)
Ezra 10:31
Ishma. *1 Chr* 4:3
Ishmaiah. *1 Chr* 27:19
Ishmerai. *1 Chr* 8:18
Ishod. *1 Chr* 7:18
Ishpan. *1 Chr* 8:22
Ishtob. *2 Sam* 10:6, 8
Ishuah. *Gen* 46:17; *1 Chr* 7:30
Ishui. (1) *Gen* 46:17; *Num* 26:44;
1 Chr 7:30. (2) *1 Sam* 14:49
Ismachiah. *2 Chr* 31:13
Ismaiah. *1 Chr* 12:4
Ispah. *1 Chr* 8:16
Ithai. *1 Chr* 11:31
Ithmah. *1 Chr* 11:46
Ithnan. *Josh* 15:23
Ithra. *2 Sam* 17:25
Ithran. (1) *Gen* 36:26; *1 Chr* 1:41.
(2) *1 Chr* 7:37
Ithream. *2 Sam* 3:5; *1 Chr* 3:3
Ittah-kazin. *Josh* 19:13
Ittai. *2 Sam* 15:19, 21, 22; 18:2, 5, 12
Izhar. *Ex* 6:18. 21; *Num* 3:19;
16:1; *1 Chr* 6:2, 18, 38; 23:12, 18
Izrahiah. *1 Chr* 7:3
Izri. *1 Chr* 25:11

JAAKAN. *Deut* 10:6; *1 Chr* 1:42
Jaakobah. *1 Chr* 4:36
Jaala. *Ezra* 2:56; *Neh* 7:58
Jaanai. *1 Chr* 5:12
Jaareoregim. *2 Sam* 21:19
Jaasau. *Ezra* 10:37
Jaasiel. (1) *1 Chr* 11:47. (2) *1 Chr*
27:21
Jaazer. *Num* 21:32; 32:35; *Josh*
13:25; 21:39; *2 Sam* 24:5;
1 Chr 6:81; 26:31; *Jer* 48:32
Jaaziah. *1 Chr* 24:26, 27
Jaaziel. *1 Chr* 15:18
Jabneel. (1) *Josh* 15:11. (2) *Josh*
19:33
Jabneh. *2 Chr* 26:6
Jachan. *1 Chr* 5:13
Jada. *1 Chr* 2:28, 32
Jadau. *Ezra* 10:43
Jaddua. (1) *Neh* 10:21. (2) *Neh*
12:11, 22
Jadon. *Neh* 3:7
Jagur. *Josh* 15:21
Jahath. (1) *1 Chr* 4:2. (2) *1 Chr*
6:20, 43. (3) *1 Chr* 23:10, 11.
(4) *1 Chr* 24:22. (5) *2 Chr* 32:12
Jahaziah. *Ezra* 10:15
Jahaziel. (1) *1 Chr* 12:4. (2) *1 Chr*
16:6. (3) *1 Chr* 23:19; 24:23.
(4) *2 Chr* 20:14. (5) *Ezra* 8:5
Jahdai. *1 Chr* 2:47

Jahdiel. *1 Chr* 5:24
Jahdo. *1 Chr* 5:14
Jahleel. *Gen* 46:14; *Num* 26:26
Jahmai. *1 Chr* 7:2
Jahzah. *1 Chr* 6:78
Jahzeel. *Gen* 46:24; *Num* 26:48; *1 Chr* 7:13
Jahzerah. *1 Chr* 9:12
Jakim. (1) *1 Chr* 8:19. (2) *1 Chr* 24:12
Jalon. *1 Chr* 4:17
Jamin. (1) *Gen* 46:10; *Ex* 6:15; *Num* 26:12; *1 Chr* 4:24. (2) *1 Chr* 2:27. (3) *Neh* 8:7
Jamlech. *1 Chr* 4:34
Janoah. *2 Ki* 15:29
Janohah. *Josh* 16:6, 7
Janum. *Josh* 15:53
Japhia. (1) *Josh* 10:3. (2) *Josh* 19:12. (3) *2 Sam* 5:15; *1 Chr* 3:7; 14:6
Japhlet. *1 Chr* 7:32, 33
Japhleti. *Josh* 16:3
Japho. *Josh* 19:46
Jarah. *1 Chr* 9:42
Jaresiah. *1 Chr* 8:27
Jarha. *1 Chr* 2:34, 35
Jarib. (1) *1 Chr* 4:24. (2) *Ezra* 8:16. (3) *Ezra* 10:18
Jarmuth. (1) *Josh* 10:3, 5, 23; 12:11; 15:35; *Neh* 11:29. (2) *Josh* 21:29
Jaroah. *1 Chr* 5:14
Jashen. *2 Sam* 23:32
Jashobeam. (1) *1 Chr* 11:11; 27:2. (2) *1 Chr* 12:6
Jashub. (1) *Num* 26:24; *1 Chr* 7:1. (2) *Ezra* 10:29
Jashubilehem. *1 Chr* 4:22
Jathniel. *1 Chr* 26:2
Jattir. *Josh* 15:48; 21:14; *1 Sam* 30:27; *1 Chr* 6:57
Jaziz. *1 Chr* 27:31
Jearim. *Josh* 15:10
Jeaterai. *1 Chr* 6:21
Jeberechiah. *Isa* 8:2
Jebus. *Josh* 18:16, 28; *Judg* 19:10, 11; *1 Chr* 11:4, 5
Jecamiah. *1 Chr* 3:18
Jecholiah. *2 Ki* 15:2; *2 Chr* 26:3
Jechonias. *Mat* 1:11, 12
Jedaiah. (1) *1 Chr* 4:37. (2) *Neh* 3:10
Jedaiah. (1) *1 Chr* 9:10; 24:7; *Ezra* 2:36; *Neh* 7:39. (2) *Neh* 11:10; 12:6, 19; *Zech* 6:10, 14. (3) *Neh* 12:7, 21
Jediael. (1) *1 Chr* 7:6, 10, 11. (2) *1 Chr* 11:45. (3) *1 Chr* 12:20. (4) *1 Chr* 26:2
Jedidah. *2 Ki* 22:1
Jeezer. *Num* 26:30
Jehaleleel. (1) *1 Chr* 4:16. (2) *2 Chr* 29:12
Jehdeiah. (1) *1 Chr* 4:20. (2) *1 Chr* 27:30
Jehezekel. *1 Chr* 24:16
Jehiah. *1 Chr* 15:24
Jehiel. (1) *1 Chr* 15:18, 20; 16:5. (2) *1 Chr* 23:8; 29:8. (3) *1 Chr* 27:32. (4) *2 Chr* 21:2. (5) *2 Chr* 29:14. (6) *2 Chr* 31:13. (7) *2 Chr* 35:8. (8) *Ezra* 8:9. (9) *Ezra* 10:2. (10) *Ezra* 10:21. (11) *Ezra* 10:26
Jehieli. *1 Chr* 26:21, 22
Jehizkiah. *2 Chr* 28:12
Jehoadah. *1 Chr* 8:36
Jehoaddan. *2 Ki* 14:2; *2 Chr* 25:1
Jehohanan. (1) *1 Chr* 26:3. (2) *2 Chr* 17:15. (3) *2 Chr* 23:1. (4) *Ezra* 10:28. (5) *Neh* 12:13. (6) *Neh* 12:42.
Jehoiarib. (1) *1 Chr* 9:10. (2) *1 Chr* 24:7
Jehonathan. (1) *1 Chr* 27:25. (2) *2 Chr* 17:8. (3) *Neh* 12:18
Jehoshabeath. *2 Chr* 22:11
Jehosheba. *2 Ki* 11:2
Jehozabad. (1) *2 Ki* 12:21; *2 Chr* 24:26. (2) *1 Chr* 26:4. (3) *2 Chr* 17:18
Jehozadak. *1 Chr* 6:14, 15
Jehubbah. *1 Chr* 7:34

Jehucal. *Jer* 37:3; 38:1
Jehud. *Josh* 19:45
Jehudi. *Jer* 36:14, 21, 23
Jehudijah. *1 Chr* 4:18
Jehush. *1 Chr* 8:39
Jeiel. (1) *1 Chr* 5:7. (2) *1 Chr* 9:35. (3) *1 Chr* 11:44. (4) *1 Chr* 15:18, 21; 16:5. (5) *2 Chr* 20:14. (6) *2 Chr* 26:11. (7) *2 Chr* 29:13. (8) *2 Chr* 35:9. (9) *Ezra* 8:13. (10) *Ezra* 10:43
Jekabzeel. *Neh* 11:25
Jekameam. *1 Chr* 23:19; 24:23
Jekamiah. *1 Chr* 2:41
Jekuthiel. *1 Chr* 4:18
Jemima. *Job* 42:14
Jemuel. *Gen* 46:10; *Ex* 6:15
Jerah. *Gen* 10:26; *1 Chr* 1:20
Jered. *1 Chr* 4:18
Jeremai. *Ezra* 10:33
Jeremoth. (1) *1 Chr* 8:14. (2) *Ezra* 10:26. (3) *Ezra* 10:27. (4) *1 Chr* 23:23. (5) *1 Chr* 25:22
Jeriah. *1 Chr* 23:19; 24:23; 26:31
Jeribai. *1 Chr* 11:46
Jeriel. *1 Chr* 7:2
Jerioth. *1 Chr* 2:18
Jeroham. (1) *1 Sam* 1:1; *1 Chr* 6:27, 34. (2) *1 Chr* 8:27. (3) *1 Chr* 9:8. (4) *1 Chr* 9:12; *Neh* 11:12. (5) *1 Chr* 12:7. (6) *1 Chr* 27:22. (7) *2 Chr* 23:1
Jeruel. *2 Chr* 20:16
Jerusha. *2 Ki* 15:33; *2 Chr* 27:1
Jesaiah. (1) *1 Chr* 3:21. (2) *1 Chr* 25:3, 15. (3) *1 Chr* 26:25. (4) *Ezra* 8:7. (5) *Ezra* 8:19. (6) *Neh* 11:7
Jeshanah. *2 Chr* 13:19
Jesharelah. *1 Chr* 25:14
Jeshebeah. *1 Chr* 24:13
Jesher. *1 Chr* 2:18
Jeshimon. (1) *Num* 21:20; 23:28. (2) *1 Sam* 23:24; 26:1
Jeshishai. *1 Chr* 5:14
Jeshohaiah. *1 Chr* 4:36
Jesiah. (1) *1 Chr* 12:6. (2) *1 Chr* 23:20
Jesimiel. *1 Chr* 4:36
Jesui. *Num* 26:44
Jether. (1) *Judg* 8:20. (2) *1 Ki* 2:5, 32; *1 Chr* 2:17. (3) *1 Chr* 2:32. (4) *1 Chr* 4:17. (5) *1 Chr* 7:38
Jetheth. *Gen* 36:40; *1 Chr* 1:51
Jethlah. *Josh* 19:42
Jetur. (1) *Gen* 25:15; *1 Chr* 1:31. (2) *1 Chr* 5:19
Jeuel. *1 Chr* 9:6
Jeush. (1) *Gen* 36:5, 14, 18; *1 Chr* 1:35. (2) *1 Chr* 7:10. (3) *1 Chr* 23:10, 11. (4) *2 Chr* 11:19
Jeuz. *1 Chr* 8:10
Jezaniah. *Jer* 40:8; 42:1
Jezer. *Gen* 46:24; *Num* 26:49; *1 Chr* 7:13
Jeziah. *Ezra* 10:25
Jeziel. *1 Chr* 12:3
Jezliah. *1 Chr* 8:18
Jezoar. *1 Chr* 4:7
Jezrahiah. *Neh* 12:42
Jibsam. *1 Chr* 7:2
Jidlaph. *Gen* 22:22
Jimnah. *Gen* 46:17; *Num* 26:44
Jiphtah. *Josh* 15:43
Jiphthahel. *Josh* 19:14, 27
Joahaz. *2 Chr* 34:8
Joatham. *Mat* 1:9
Joad. (1) *Gen* 10:29; *1 Chr* 1:23. (2) *Gen* 36:33, 34; *1 Chr* 1:44, 45. (3) *Josh* 11:1. (4) *1 Chr* 8:9. (5) *1 Chr* 8:18
Jochebed. *Ex* 6:20; *Num* 26:59
Joed. *Neh* 11:7
Joelah. *1 Chr* 12:7
Joezer. *1 Chr* 12:6
Jogbehah. *Num* 32:35; *Judg* 8:11
Jogli. *Num* 34:22
Joha. (1) *1 Chr* 8:16. (2) *1 Chr* 11:45
Joiada. *Neh* 12:10, 11, 22; 13:28
Joiakim. *Neh* 12:10, 12, 26
Joiarib. (1) *Ezra* 8:16. (2) *Neh* 11:5. (3) *Neh* 11:10; 12:6, 19
Jokdeam. *Josh* 15:56

Jokim. *1 Chr* 4:22
Jokmeam. *1 Chr* 6:68
Jokneam. (1) *Josh* 12:22; 19:11; 21:34. (2) *1 Ki* 4:12
Jokshan. *Gen* 25:2, 3; *1 Chr* 1:32
Joktan. *Gen* 10:25, 26, 29; *1 Chr* 1:19, 20, 23
Joktheel. (1) *Josh* 15:38. (2) *2 Ki* 14:7
Jonan. *Luke* 3:30
Jonath-elem-rechokim. *Ps* 56 title
Jorah. *Ezra* 2:18
Jorai. *1 Chr* 5:13
Jorkoam. *1 Chr* 2:44
Josaphat. *Mat* 1:8
Joshah. *1 Chr* 4:34
Joshaphat. *1 Chr* 11:43
Joshaviah. *1 Chr* 11:46
Joshbekashah. *1 Chr* 25:4, 24
Josibiah. *1 Chr* 4:35
Josiphiah. *Ezra* 8:10
Jotbah. *2 Ki* 21:19
Jotbathah. *Num* 33:33, 34; *Deut* 10:7
Jozabad. (1) *1 Chr* 12:4. (2) *1 Chr* 12:20. (3) *2 Chr* 31:13. (4) *2 Chr* 35:9. (5) *Ezra* 8:33. (6) *Ezra* 10:22. (7) *Ezra* 10:23. (8) *Neh* 8:7. (9) *Neh* 11:16
Jozachar. *2 Ki* 12:21
Jozadak. *Ezra* 3:2, 8; 5:2; 10:18; *Neh* 12:26
Jubal. *Gen* 4:21
Jucal. *Jer* 38:1
Judith. *Gen* 26:34
Julia. *Rom* 16:15
Julius *Acts* 27:1, 3
Junia. *Rom* 16:7
Jushab-hesed. *1 Chr* 3:20

KABZEEL. *Josh* 15:21; *2 Sam* 23:20; *1 Chr* 11:22
Kadmiel. (1) *Ezra* 2:40; *Neh* 7:43. (2) *Ezra* 3:9. (3) *Neh* 9:4, 5; 10:9; 12:8, 24
Kallai. *Neh* 12:20
Kanah. (1) *Josh* 16:8; 17:9. (2) *Josh* 19:28
Karkaa. *Josh* 15:3
Karkor. *Judg* 8:10
Kartah. *Josh* 21:34
Kartan. *Josh* 21:32
Kattath. *Josh* 19:15
Kedemah. *Gen* 25:15; *1 Chr* 1:31, 33.
Kedemoth. (1) *Deut* 2:26. (2) *Josh* 13:18; 21:37; *1 Chr* 6:79
Kedesh. (1) *Josh* 12:22; 19:37. (2) *Josh* 20:7; 21:32; *Judg* 4:6; 9:10, 11; *2 Ki* 15:29; *1 Chr* 6:76. (3) *1 Chr* 6:72. (4) *Josh* 15:23
Kehelathah. *Num* 33:22, 23
Kelaiah. *Ezra* 10:23
Kelita. (1) *Ezra* 10:23. (2) *Neh* 8:7. (3) *Neh* 10:10
Kemuel. (1) *Gen* 22:21. (2) *Num* 34:24. (3) *1 Chr* 27:17
Kenan. *1 Chr* 1:2
Kenath. *Num* 32:42; *1 Chr* 2:23
Keren-happuch. *Job* 42:14
Keros. *Ezra* 2:44; *Neh* 7:47
Kezia. *Job* 42:14
Keziz. *Josh* 18:21
Kibroth-hattaavah. *Num* 11:34, 35; 33:16, 17; *Deut* 9:22
Kibzaim. *Josh* 21:22
Kinah. *Josh* 15:22
Kirjath. *Josh* 18:28
Kirjath-arim. *Ezra* 2:25
Kirjath-baal. *Josh* 15:60; 18:14
Kirjath-huzoth. *Num* 22:39
Kirjath-sannah. *Josh* 15:49
Kirjath-sepher. *Josh* 15:15, 16; *Judg* 1:11, 12
Kishi. *1 Chr* 6:44
Kishion. *Josh* 19:20; 21:28
Kishon. *Judg* 4:7, 13; 5:21; *1 Ki* 18:40; *Ps* 83:9
Kithlish. *Josh* 15:40
Kitron. *Judg* 1:30
Koa. *Ezek* 23:23
Kolaiah. (1) *Neh* 11:7. (2) *Jer* 29:21
Kore. (1) *1 Chr* 9:19; 26:1, 19. (2) *2 Chr* 31:14
Koz. *Ezra* 2:61; *Neh* 7:63
Kushaiah. *1 Chr* 15:17

LAADAH. *1 Chr* 4:21
Laadan. (1) *1 Chr* 7:26. (2) *1 Chr* 23:7, 8, 9; 26:21
Lael. *Num* 3:24
Lahad. *1 Chr* 4:2
Lahairoi. *Gen* 24:62; 25:11
Lahmam. *Josh* 15:40
Lahmi. *1 Chr* 20:5
Lakum. *Josh* 19:33
Lapidoth. *Judg* 4:4
Lasea. *Acts* 27:8
Lasha. *Gen* 10:19
Lasharon. *Josh* 12:18
Lebanah. *Ezra* 2:45; *Neh* 7:48
Lebaoth. *Josh* 15:32
Lebonah. *Judg* 21:19
Lecah. *1 Chr* 4:21
Lehabim. *Gen* 10:13; *1 Chr* 1:11
Lehi. *Judg* 15:9, 14, 19
Leshem. *Josh* 19:47
Letushim. *Gen* 25:3
Leummim. *Gen* 25:3
Libni. (1) *Ex* 6:17; *Num* 3:18; *1 Chr* 6:17, 20. (2) *1 Chr* 6:29.
Likhi. *1 Chr* 7:19
Linus. *2 Tim* 4:21
Lod. *1 Chr* 8:12; *Ezra* 2:33; *Neh* 7:37; 11:35
Lodebar. *2 Sam* 9:4, 5; 17:27
Lotan. *Gen* 36:20, 22, 29; *1 Chr* 1:38, 39
Lubims. *2 Chr* 12:3; 16:8; *Nah* 3:9
Lud. (1) *Gen* 10:22; *1 Chr* 1:17. (2) *Isa* 66:19; *Ezek* 27:10
Ludim. *Gen* 10:13; *1 Chr* 1:11
Luhith. *Isa* 15:5; *Jer* 48:5
Lycia. *Acts* 27:5

MAADAI. *Ezra* 10:34
Maadiah. *Neh* 12:5
Maai. *Neh* 12:36
Maaleh-acrabbim. *Josh* 15:3
Maarath. *Josh* 15:59
Maasiai. *1 Chr* 9:12
Maaz. *1 Chr* 2:27
Maaziah. (1) *1 Chr* 24:18. (2) *Neh* 10:8
Machbanai. *1 Chr* 12:13
Machbenah. *1 Chr* 2:49
Machi. *Num* 13:15
Machnadebai. *Ezra* 10:40
Madai. *Gen* 10:2; *1 Chr* 1:5
Madmannah. (1) *Josh* 15:31. (2) *1 Chr* 2:49
Madmenah. *Isa* 10:31
Madon. *Josh* 11:1; 12:19
Magbish. *Ezra* 2:30
Magdalene. *Mat* 27:56, 61; 28:1; *Mark* 15:40, 47; 16:1, 9; *Luke* 8:2; 24:10; *John* 19:25; 20:1, 18
Magdiel. *Gen* 36:43; *1 Chr* 1:54
Magor-missabib. *Jer* 20:3
Magpiash. *Neh* 10:20
Mahalah. *1 Chr* 7:18
Mahalath. (1) *Gen* 28:9. (2) *2 Chr* 11:8. (3) *Ps* 53 title; *Ps* 88 title
Mahanehdan. *Judg* 18:12
Maharai. *2 Sam* 23:28; *1 Chr* 11:30; 27:13
Mahath. (1) *1 Chr* 6:35; *2 Chr* 29:12. (2) *2 Chr* 31:13
Mahazioth. *1 Chr* 25:4, 30
Mahlah. *Num* 26:33; 27:1; 36:11; *Josh* 17:3
Mahli. (1) *Ex* 6:19; *Num* 3:20; *1 Chr* 6:19, 29; 23:21; 24:26, 28; *Ezra* 8:18. (2) *1 Chr* 6:47; 23:23; 24:30
Mahol. *1 Ki* 4:31
Makaz. *1 Ki* 4:9
Makheloth. *Num* 33:25, 26
Makkedah. *Josh* 10:10, 16, 17, 21, 28, 29; 12:16; 15:41
Maktesh. *Zeph* 1:11
Malachi. *Mal* 1:1
Malchiah. (1) *1 Chr* 6:40. (2) *1 Chr* 9:12; *Neh* 11:12. (3) *1 Chr* 24:9. (4) *Ezra* 10:25. (5) *Ezra* 10:25. (6) *Ezra* 10:31. (7) *Neh* 3:11. (8) *Neh* 3:14. (9) *Neh* 3:31. (10) *Neh* 8:4. (11) *Neh* 10:3; 12:42. (12) *Jer* 21:1; 38:1
Malchiel. *Gen* 46:17; *Num* 26:45; *1 Chr* 7:31

Malchiram. *1 Chr* 3:18
Maleleel. *Luke* 3:37
Malothi. *1 Chr* 25:4, 26
Malluch. (1) *1 Chr* 6:44. (2) *Ezra* 10:29. (3) *Ezra* 10:32. (4) *Neh* 10:4; 12:2. (5) *Neh* 10:27
Manahath. (1) *Gen* 36:23; *1 Chr* 1:40. (2) *1 Chr* 8:6
Maoch. *1 Sam* 27:2
Maon. (1) *Josh* 15:55; *1 Sam* 25:2. (2) *1 Chr* 2:45
Maralah. *Josh* 19:11
Mareshah. (1) *Josh* 15:44; *2 Chr* 11:8; 14:9, 10; 20:37; *Mi* 1:15. (2) *1 Chr* 2:42. (3) *1 Chr* 4:21
Maroth. *Mi* 1:12
Marsena. *Esth* 1:14
Maschil. *Ps* 32 title, and 42, 44, 45, 52, 53, 54, 55, 74, 78, 88, 89, 142
Mash. *Gen* 10:23
Mashal. *1 Chr* 6:74
Masrekah. *Gen* 36:36; *1 Chr* 1:47
Massa. *Gen* 25:14; *1 Chr* 1:30
Matred. *Gen* 36:39; *1 Chr* 1:50
Matri. *1 Sam* 10:21
Mattanah. *Num* 21:18, 19
Mattaniah. (1) *2 Ki* 24:17. (2) *1 Chr* 9:15; *2 Chr* 20:14; *Neh* 11:17, 22; 12:8, 25, 35. (3) *1 Chr* 25:4, 16. (4) *2 Chr* 29:13. (5) *Ezra* 10:26. (6) *Ezra* 10:27. (7) *Ezra* 10:30. (8) *Ezra* 10:37. (9) *Neh* 13:13
Mattatha. *Luke* 3:31
Mattathah. *Ezra* 10:33
Mattenai. (1) *Ezra* 10:33. (2) *Ezra* 10:37. (3) *Neh* 12:19
Matthan. *Mat* 1:15.
Matthat. (1) *Luke* 3:24. (2) *Luke* 3:29
Mattithiah. (1) *1 Chr* 9:31. (2) *1 Chr* 15:18, 21; 16:5. (3) *1 Chr* 25:3, 21. (4) *Ezra* 10:43. (5) *Neh* 8:4
Meah. *Neh* 3:1; 12:39
Mearah. *Josh* 13:4
Mebunnai. *2 Sam* 23:27
Medan. *Gen* 25:2; *1 Chr* 1:32
Medeba. *Num* 21:30; *Josh* 13:9, 16; *1 Chr* 19:7; *Isa* 15:2
Mehetabel. (1) *Gen* 36:39; *1 Chr* 1:50. (2) *Neh* 6:10
Mehida. *Ezra* 2:52; *Neh* 7:54
Mehir. *1 Chr* 4:11
Mehujael. *Gen* 4:18
Mehuman. *Esth* 1:10
Mehunim. *Ezra* 2:50; *Neh* 7:52
Mejarkon. *Josh* 19:46
Mekonah. *Neh* 11:28
Melatiah. *Neh* 3:7
Melchishua. *1 Sam* 14:49; 31:2; *1 Chr* 8:33; 9:39; 10:2
Melea. *Luke* 3:31
Melech. *1 Chr* 8:35; 9:41
Melicu. *Neh* 12:14
Melita. *Acts* 28:1
Melzar. *Dan* 1:11, 16
Menan. *Luke* 3:31
Meonenim. *Judg* 9:37
Meonothai. *1 Chr* 4:14
Mephaath. *Josh* 13:18; 21:37; *1 Chr* 6:79; *Jer* 48:21
Meraiah. *Neh* 12:12
Meraioth. (1) *1 Chr* 6:6, 7, 52; *Ezra* 7:3. (2) *1 Chr* 9:11; *Neh* 11:11. (3) *Neh* 12:15
Merathaim. *Jer* 50:21
Mered. *1 Chr* 4:17, 18
Meremoth. (1) *Ezra* 8:33; *Neh* 3:4, 21. (2) *Ezra* 10:36. (3) *Neh* 10:5; 12:3
Meres. *Esth* 1:14
Meribbaal. *1 Chr* 8:34; 9:40
Merodach-baladan. *2 Ki* 20:12; *Isa* 39:1
Mesha. (1) *Gen* 10:30. (2) *2 Ki* 3:4. (3) *1 Chr* 2:42. (4) *1 Chr* 8:9
Meshelemiah. *1 Chr* 9:21; 26:1, 2, 9
Meshezabeel. (1) *Neh* 3:4. (2) *Neh* 10:21; 11:24
Meshillemith. *1 Chr* 9:12
Meshillemoth. (1) *2 Chr* 28:12. (2) *Neh* 11:13
Meshobab. *1 Chr* 4:34

Meshullam. (1) *2 Ki* 22:3. (2) *1 Chr* 3:19. (3) *1 Chr* 5:13. (4) *1 Chr* 8:17. (5) *1 Chr* 9:7. (6) *1 Chr* 9:8. (7) *1 Chr* 9:11; *Neh* 11:11. (8) *1 Chr* 9:12. (9) *2 Chr* 34:12. (10) *Ezra* 8:16. (11) *Ezra* 10:15. (12) *Ezra* 10:29. (13) *Neh* 3:4, 30; 6:18. (14) *Neh* 3:6. (15) *Neh* 8:4. (16) *Neh* 10:7. (17) *Neh* 10:20. (18) *Neh* 11:7. (19) *Neh* 12:13, 33. (20) *Neh* 12:16. (21) *Neh* 12:25
Meshullemeth. *2 Ki* 21:19
Mezahab. *Gen* 36:39; *1 Chr* 1:50
Miamin. (1) *Ezra* 10:25. (2) *Neh* 12:5
Mibhar. *1 Chr* 11:38
Mibsam. (1) *Gen* 25:13; *1 Chr* 1:29. (2) *1 Chr* 4:25
Mibzar. *Gen* 36:42; *1 Chr* 1:53
Micha. (1) *2 Sam* 9:12. (2) *Neh* 10:11. (3) *Neh* 11:17, 22
Michmas. *Ezra* 2:27; *Neh* 7:31
Michmash. *1 Sam* 13:2, 5, 11, 16, 23; 14:5, 31; *Neh* 11:31; *Isa* 10:28
Michmethah. *Josh* 16:6; 17:7
Michri. *1 Chr* 9:8
Michtam. *Ps* 16 title, and 56, 57, 58, 59, 60
Middin. *Josh* 15:61
Migdalel. *Josh* 19:38
Migdalgad. *Josh* 15:37
Migdol. (1) *Ex* 14:2; *Num* 33:7. (2) *Jer* 44:1; 46:14
Migron. *1 Sam* 14:2; *Isa* 10:28
Mijamin. (1) *1 Chr* 24:9. (2) *Neh* 10:7
Mikloth. (1) *1 Chr* 8:32; 9:37, 38. (2) *1 Chr* 27:4
Mikneiah. *1 Chr* 15:18, 21
Milalai. *Neh* 12:36
Miniamin. (1) *2 Chr* 31:15. (2) *Neh* 12:17, 41
Minni. *Jer* 51:27
Minnith. *Judg* 11:33; *Ezek* 27:17
Miphkad. *Neh* 3:31
Mirma. *1 Chr* 8:10
Misgab. *Jer* 48:1
Misham. *1 Chr* 8:12
Misheal. *Josh* 19:26; 21:30
Mishma. *Gen* 25:14; *1 Chr* 1:30; 4:25, 26
Mishmannah. *1 Chr* 12:10
Mispereth. *Neh* 7:7
Misrephothmaim. *Josh* 11:8; 13:6
Mithcah. *Num* 33:28, 29
Mithredath. (1) *Ezra* 1:8. (2) *Ezra* 4:7
Mitylene. *Acts* 20:14
Mizpar. *Ezra* 2:2
Mizraim. *Gen* 10:6, 13; *1 Chr* 1:8, 11
Mizzah. *Gen* 36:13, 17; *1 Chr* 1:37
Moadiah. *Neh* 12:17
Moladah. *Josh* 15:26; 19:2; *1 Chr* 4:28; *Neh* 11:26
Molid. *1 Chr* 2:29
Moreh. (1) *Gen* 12:6; *Deut* 11:30. (2) *Judg* 7:1
Moreshethgath. *Mi* 1:14
Mosera. *Deut* 10:6
Moseroth. *Num* 33:30, 31
Moza. (1) *1 Chr* 2:46. (2) *1 Chr* 8:36, 37; 9:42, 43
Mozah. *Josh* 18:26
Muppim. *Gen* 46:21
Mushi. *Ex* 6:19; *Num* 3:20; *1 Chr* 6:19, 47; 23:21, 23; 24:26, 30
Muthlabben. *Ps* 9 title

NAAM. *1 Chr* 4:15
Naamah. (1) *Gen* 4:22. (2) *1 Ki* 14:21, 31; *2 Chr* 12:13. (3) *Josh* 15:41
Naarah. *1 Chr* 4:5, 6
Naarai. *1 Chr* 11:37
Naaran. *1 Chr* 7:28
Naarath. *Josh* 16:7
Nachon. *2 Sam* 6:6
Nachor. *Luke* 3:34
Nahaliel. *Num* 21:19
Nahallal. *Josh* 19:15; 21:35; *Judg* 1:30

Naham. *1 Chr* 4:19
Nahamani. *Neh* 7:7
Naharai. *2 Sam* 23:37; *1 Chr* 11:...
Nahath. (1) *Gen* 36:13, 17; *1 C...*
  1:37. (2) *1 Chr* 6:26. (3) *2 C...*
  31:13
Nahbi. *Num* 13:14
Nahshon, *see* Naashon, p. 447
Nahum. *Nah* 1:1
Naphish. (1) *Gen* 25:15; *1 Chr*
  1:31. (2) *1 Chr* 5:19
Naphtuhim. *Gen* 10:13; *1 Chr* 1:11
Narcissus. *Rom* 16:11
Nathan-melech. *2 Ki* 23:11
Neah. *Josh* 19:13
Neariah. (1) *1 Chr* 3:22, 23. (2)
  1 Chr 4:42
Nebajoth. (1) *Gen* 25:13; 28:9;
  36:3; *1 Chr* 1:29. (2) *Isa* 60:7
Neballat. *Neh* 11:34
Nebushasban. *Jer* 39:13
Necho. *2 Chr* 35:20, 22; 36:4
Nedabiah. *1 Chr* 3:18
Neginah. *Ps* 4 title
Nehiloth. *Ps* 5 title
Nehum. *Neh* 7:7
Nehushta. *2 Ki* 24:8
Neiel. *Josh* 19:27
Nekeb. *Josh* 19:33
Nekoda. (1) *Ezra* 2:48; *Neh* 7:50.
  (2) *Ezra* 2:60; *Neh* 7:62
Nemuel. (1) *Num* 26:9. (2) *Num*
  26:12; *1 Chr* 4:24
Nepheg. (1) *Ex* 6:21. (2) *2 Sam*
  5:15; *1 Chr* 3:7; 14:6
Nephishesim. *Neh* 7:52
Nephthalim. *Mat* 4:13, 15; *Rev* 7:6
Nephtoah. *Josh* 15:9; 18:15
Nephusim. *Ezra* 2:50
Nergal-sharezer. *Jer* 39:3, 13
Neri. *Luke* 3:27
Netophah. *Ezra* 2:22; *Neh* 7:26
Netophathi. *Neh* 12:28
Neziah. *Ezra* 2:54; *Neh* 7:56
Nezib. *Josh* 15:43
Nibhaz. *2 Ki* 17:31
Nibshan. *Josh* 15:62
Nicolas. *Acts* 6:5
Nimrah. *Num* 32:3
Nimrim. *Isa* 15:6; *Jer* 48:34
Nobah. (1) *Num* 32:42. (2. Name
  of place) *Num* 32:42; *Judg* 8:1
Nod. *Gen* 4:16
Nodab. *1 Chr* 5:19
Nogah. *1 Chr* 3:7; **14:6**
Nohah. *1 Chr* 8:2
Non. *1 Chr* 7:27
Nophah. *Num* 21:30

OBAL. *Gen* 10:28
Oboth. *Num* 21:10, 11; 33:43, 44
Ohad. *Gen* 46:10; *Ex* 6:15
Ohel. *1 Chr* 3:20
Omar. *Gen* 36:11, 15; *1 Chr* 1:36
Omega. *Rev* 1:8, 11; 21:6; 22:13
Omer. *Ex* 16:16, 18, 22, 32, 33, 36
Onam. (1) *Gen* 36:23; *1 Chr* 1:40.
  (2) *1 Chr* 2:26, 28
Ono. (1) *1 Chr* 8:12; *Ezra* 2:33;
  Neh 7:37; 11:35. (2) *Neh* 6:2
Ophni. *Josh* 18:24
Ophrah. (1) *Josh* 18:23; *1 Sam*
  13:17. (2) *Judg* 6:11, 24; 8:27,
  32; 9:5. (3) *1 Chr* 4:14
Oren. *1 Chr* 2:25
Osee (Hosea). *Rom* 9:25
Othni. *1 Chr* 26:7
Ozni. *Num* 26:16

PADAN. *Gen* 48:7
Padon. *Ezra* 2:44; *Neh* 7:47
Pahath-moab. (1) *Ezra* 2:6; 10:30;
  Neh 3:11; 7:11. (2) *Ezra* 8:4.
  (3) *Neh* 10:14
Pai. *1 Chr* 1:50
Palal. *Neh* 3:25
Pallu. *Gen* 46:9; *Ex* 6:14; *Num*
  26:5, 8; *1 Chr* 5:3
Palti. *Num* 13:9
Paltiel. (1) *Num* 34:26; (2) *2 Sam*
  3:15
Parah. *Josh* 18:23
Parmashta. *Esth* 9:9
Parnach. *Num* 34:25

Pa...
  2:... 7:8.
Pahru...0:25.
Patrobas. 4...
Pedahel. *N...*
Pedahzur. *N...*
  59; 10:23
Pedaiah. (1) *2 K...*
  3:18, 19. (3) 1...
  Neh 3:25. (5) Ne...
  Neh 11:7...
Pekod. *Jer* 50:21; *Ezek...*
Pelaiah. (1) *1 Chr* 3:24.
  8:7. (3) *Neh* 10:10
Pelaliah. *Neh* 11:12
Peleg. *Gen* 10:25; 11:16, 17, 18;
  19; *1 Chr* 1:19, 25
Pelet. (1) *1 Chr* 2:47. (2) *1 Chr*
  12:3
Peleth. (1) *Num* 16:1. (2) *1 Chr*
  2:33
Peninnah. *1 Sam* 1:2, 4
Peresh. *1 Chr* 7:16
Perezuzzah. *2 Sam* 6:8; *1 Chr*
  13:11
Perida. *Neh* 7:57
Peruda. *Ezra* 2:55
Pethahiah. (1) *1 Chr* 24:16. (2)
  Ezra 10:23. (3) *Neh* 9:5. (4)
  Neh 11:24
Pethor. *Num* 22:5; *Deut* 23:4
Pethuel. *Joel* 1:1
Peulthai. *1 Chr* 26:5
Phalti. *1 Sam* 25:44
Phanuel. *Luke* 2:36
Phibeseth. *Ezek* 30:17
Phichol. *Gen* 21:22, 32; 26:26
Philemon. *Philem* 1
Phut. (1) *Gen* 10:6; *1 Chr* 1:8.
  (2) *Ezek* 27:10. (3) *Nah* 3:9
Phuvah. (1) *Gen* 46:13; *Num*
  26:23; *1 Chr* 7:1. (2) *Judg*
  10:1
Pildash. *Gen* 22:22
Pileha. *Neh* 10:24
Piltai. *Neh* 12:17
Pinon. *Gen* 36:41; *1 Chr* 1:52
Piram. *Josh* 10:3
Pirathon. *Judg* 12:15
Pison. *Gen* 2:11
Pithom. *Ex* 1:11
Pithon. *1 Chr* 8:35; 9:41
Pochereth. *Ezra* 2:57; *Neh* 7:59
Poratha. *Esth* 9:8
Prisca. *See* Priscilla
Prochorus. *Acts* 6:5
Ptolemais. *Acts* 21:7
Punon. *Num* 33:42, 43
Putiel. *Ex* 6:25

RAAMAH. (1) *Gen* 10:7; *1 Chr*
  1:9. (2) *Ezek* 27:22
Raamiah. *Neh* 7:7
Raamses. *Ex* 1:11
Rabbith. *Josh* 19:20
Rabmag. *Jer* 39:3, 13
Rabsaris. (1) *Jer* 39:3, 13. (2)
  2 Ki 18:17
Rachal. *1 Sam* 30:29
Raddai. *1 Chr* 2:14
Raguel. *Num* 10:29
Raham. *1 Chr* 2:44
Rakem. *1 Chr* 7:16
Rakkath. *Josh* 19:35
Rakkon. *Josh* 19:46
Ramath. *Josh* 19:8
Ramathaim-zophim. *1 Sam* 1:1
Ramathlehi. *Judg* 15:17
Ramathmizpeh. *Josh* 13:26
Rameses. *Gen* 47:11; *Ex* 12:37;
  Num 33:3, 5
Ramiah. *Ezra* 10:25
Reaiah. (1) *1 Chr* 4:2. (2) *1 Chr*
  5:5. (3) *Ezra* 2:47; *Neh* 7:50
Reba. *Num* 31:8; *Josh* 1~:21
Rechah. *1 Chr* 4:12

Reelaiah. *Ezra* 2:2
Regem. *1 Chr* 2:47
Regemmelech. *Zech* 7:2
Rehabiah. *1 Chr* 23:17; ...
Rehob. (1) *Num* 13:21; *Josh* 19:28.
  26:25 ... *Judg* 1:31; *2 Sam*
  30; 21:31; *1 Chr* 6:75. (2) *2 Sam*
  10:8; 12 ... *Neh* 10:11
  8:3... *1 Ki* 1:8 ... 13:21
Rei. *1 Ki* ... *Num* 31:8; (3) *Josh*
Rekem ... *Chr* 2:43, 44.
  Josh 19:21
...meth. *Josh* 19:7
...mon-methoar. *Josh* 19:13
...mon ... 26:7
...el. *1 Chr* 7:25 ... 3:21. (2)
...1 *Chr* ... (3) *1 Chr* 7:2.
...4:42 ... (5) *Neh* 3:9
...en 10:12
...1 *Chr* 7:25 ... 19, 20, 21; 1 *Chr*
...1:18, 19 ... 10, 13, 17;
...Gen 36:4, 10 (2) *1 Chr* 9:8
...en 37 (4) *1 Chr* 9:8
Reumah ...
Rezeph. 2... *Isa* 37:12
Rezia. *1 Chr...*
Rezon. *1 Ki* 11...
Ribai. *2 Sam* 23:29; *1 Chr* 11:31;
Riblah. *Num* 34:11; *2 Ki* 23:33;
  25:6, 21; *Jer* 39:5, 6; 52:9, 10,
  26, 27
Rimmon-parez. *Num* 33:19, 20
Rinnah. *1 Chr* 4:20
Riphath. *Gen* 10:3; *1 Chr* 1:6
Rissah. *Num* 33:21, 22
Rithmah. *Num* 33:18, 19
Rogelim. *2 Sam* 17:27; 19:31
Rohgah. *1 Chr* 7:34
Romanti-ezer. *1 Chr* 25:4, 31
Rumah. *2 Ki* 23:36

SABTAH. *Gen* 10:7; *1 Chr* 1:9
Sabtecha. *Gen* 10:7; *1 Chr* 1:9
Sacar. (1) *1 Chr* 11:35. (2) *1 Chr*
  26:4
Sadoc. *Mat* 1:14
Sala, Salah. *Gen* 10:24; 11:12, 13,
  14, 15; *Luke* 3:35
Salamis. *Acts* 13:5
Salchah. *Deut* 3:10; *Josh* 12:5;
  13:11; *1 Chr* 5:11
Salim. *Josh* 3:23
Sallai. (1) *Neh* 11:8. (2) *Neh* 12:20
Sallu. (1) *Neh* 12:7. (2) *1 Chr*
  9:7; *Neh* 11:7
Salma. *1 Chr* 2:51, 54
Samgar-nebo. *Jer* 39:3
Samlah. *Gen* 36:36, 37; *1 Chr*
  1:47, 48
Samos. *Acts* 20:15
Samothracia. *Acts* 16:11
Sansannah. *Josh* 15:31
Saph. *2 Sam* 21:8
Saraph. *1 Chr* 4:22
Sargon. *Isa* 20:1
Sarid. *Josh* 19:10, 12
Sarsechim. *Jer* 39:3
Sebat. *Zech* 1:7
Secacah. *Josh* 15:61
Sechu. *1 Sam* 19:22
Secundus. *Acts* 20:4
Segub. (1) *1 Ki* 16:34. (2) *1 Chr*
  2:21, 22
Seirath. *Judg* 3:26
Sela. *2 Ki* 14:7; *Isa* 16:1
Sela-hammahlekoth. *1 Sam* 23:28
Seled. *1 Chr* 2:30
Sem. *Luke* 3:36
Semachiah. *1 Chr* 26:7
Senaah. *Ezra* 2:35; *Neh* 7:38
Seneh. *1 Sam* 14:4
Senir. *1 Chr* 5:23; *Ezek* 27:5
Senuah. *Neh* 11:9
Seorim. *1 Chr* 24:8
Sephar. *Gen* 10:30
Sepharad. *Ob* 20
Serah (Sarah). *Gen* 46:17; *Num*
  26:46; *1 Chr* 7:30
Sered. *Gen* 46:14; *Num* 26:26

Serug. *Gen* 11:20, 21.
1 Chr 1:26
Sethur. *Num* 13:13
Shaalabbin. *Josh* 19:42
Shaalbim. *Judg* 1:35;
2:49
Shaaph. (1) *1 Chr* 2:
47. (2) *1 Chr* 2:49
Shaaraim. (1) *Josh*
15:36. (2) *1 Chr* 4:31
Shaashgaz. *Esth* 2:14
Shabbethai. *Ezra* 10:15;
Neh 8:7; 11:16
Shachia. *1 Chr* 8:10
Shaharaim. *1 Chr* 8:8
Shahazimah. *Josh* 19:22
Shalem. *Gen* 33:18
Shalisha. *1 Sam* 9:4
Shallecheth. *1 Chr* 26:16
Shallum. *Ezra* ...
Shalman. *Hos* 10:14
Shama. *1 Chr* 11:44
Shamariah. *2 Chr* 11:19
Shamir. (1) *Josh* 15:48;
Judg 10:1. (2) *1 Chr*
24:24
Shamma. *1 Chr* 7:37
Shammah. (1) *Gen* ...
Shammai. ...
Shammoth. *1 Chr* 11:27
Shamsherai. *1 Chr* 8:26
Shapham. *1 Chr* 5:12
Shaphan. ...
Sharai. *Ezra* 10:40
Sharar. *2 Sam* 23:33
Sharuhen. *Josh* 19:6
Shashai. *Ezra* 10:40
Shashak. *1 Chr* 8:14, 25
Shaul. (1) *Gen* 46:10;
Num 26: ...
... 13; *1 Chr* 4:24. (2)
1 Chr 6:24
Shaveh. *Gen* 14:17
Shavehkiriathaim. *Gen* 14:5
Shavsha. *1 Chr* 18:16
Sheal. *Ezra* 10:29
Sheariah. *1 Chr* 8:38; 9:44
Shebam. *Num* 32:3
Shebaniah. (1) *1 Chr* 15:24. (2)
Neh 9:4, 5; 10:10. (3) *Neh*
10:4; 12:14. (4) *Neh* 10:12
Shebarim. *Josh* 7:5
Sheber. *1 Chr* 2:48
Shebna. (1) *2 Ki* 18:18, 26, 37;
19:2; *Isa* 36:3, 11, 22; 37:2.
(2) *Isa* 22:15
Shebuel. (1) *1 Chr* 23:16; 26:24.
(2) *1 Chr* 25:4
Shecaniah. (1) *1 Chr* 24:11. (2)
2 Chr 31:15
Shechaniah. (1) *1 Chr* 3:21, 22.
(2) *Ezra* 8:3. (3) *Ezra* 8:5. (4)
Ezra 10:2. (5) *Neh* 3:29. (6)
Neh 6:18. (7) *Neh* 12:3
Shedeur. *Num* 1:5; 2:10; 7:30,
35; 10:18
Shehariah. *1 Chr* 8:26
Sheleph. *Gen* 10:26; *1 Chr* 1:20
Shelesh. *1 Chr* 7:35
Shelomi. *Num* 34:27
Shelomith. (1) *Lev* 24:11. (2) *1 Chr*
3:19. (3) *1 Chr* 23:9. (4) *1 Chr*
23:18. (5) *1 Chr* 26:25, 26,
28. (6) *2 Chr* 11:20. (7) *Ezra*
8:10
Shelomoth. *1 Chr* 24:22
Shema. (1) *Josh* 15:26. (2) *1 Chr*
2:43, 44. (3) *1 Chr* 5:8. (4)
1 Chr 8:13. (5) *Neh* 8:4
Shemaah. *1 Chr* 12:3
Shemariah. (1) *1 Chr* 12:5. (2)
2 Chr 11:19. (3) *Ezra* 10:32.
(4) *Ezra* 10:41
Shemeber. *Gen* 14:2
Shemer. *1 Ki* 16:24
Shemidah. *Num* 26:32; *Josh* 17:2;
1 Chr 7:19
Shemiramoth. (1) *1 Chr* 15:18, 20;
16:5. (2) *2 Chr* 17:8
Shemuel. (1) *Num* 34:20. (2) *1 Chr*
6:33. (3) *1 Chr* 7:2
Shen. *1 Sam* 7:12
Shenazar. *1 Chr* 3:18
Shepham. *Num* 34:10, 11
Shepho. *Gen* 36:23; *1 Chr* 1:40
Shephuphan. *1 Chr* 8:5
Sherah. *1 Chr* 7:24

... 24; *Neh*
... *Neh* 10:12;
...

... 2; *Josh* 15:14;
... 2:31, 34, 35
... 2:17
... 1:14
... ai. *Ezra* 5:3, 6; 6:6,
... (2) *2 Sam* 20:25. (2) *1 Chr*
...
...h. *Num* 32:38
...on. *Josh* 15:11
...lon. *Josh* 19:19
Shihorlibnath. *Josh* 19:26
Shilhi. *1 Ki* 22:42; *2 Chr* 20:31
Shilhim. *Josh* 15:32
Shillem. *Gen* 46:24; *Num* 26:49
Shiloni (Shilonite). *Neh* 11:5
Shilshah. *1 Chr* 7:37
Shimea. (1) *1 Chr* 20:7. (2) *1 Chr*
3:5. (3) *1 Chr* 6:30. (4) *1 Chr*
6:39
Shimeam. *1 Chr* 9:38
Shimeath. *2 Ki* 12:21; *2 Chr* 24:26
Shimeon. *Ezra* 10:31
Shimma. *1 Chr* 2:13
Shimon. *1 Chr* 4:20
Shimrath. *1 Chr* 8:21
Shimri. (1) *1 Chr* 4:37. (2) *1 Chr*
11:45. (3) *1 Chr* 26:10. (4)
2 Chr 29:13
Shimrith. *2 Chr* 24:26
Shimron. (1) *Gen* 46:13; *Num*
26:24; *1 Chr* 7:1. (2) *Josh*
11:1; 19:15
Shimron-meron. *Josh* 12:20
Shinab. *Gen* 14:2
Shiphi. *1 Chr* 4:37
Shiphrah. *Ex* 1:15
Shiphtan. *Num* 34:24
Shisha. *1 Ki* 4:3
Shitrai. *1 Chr* 27:29
Shiza. *1 Chr* 11:42
Shoa. *Ezek* 23:23
Shobab. (1) *2 Sam* 5:14; *1 Chr*
3:5; 14:4. (2) *1 Chr* 2:18
Shobach. *2 Sam* 10:16, 18
Shobai. *Ezra* 2:42; *Neh* 7:45
Shobal. (1) *Gen* 36:20, 23, 29;
1 Chr 1:38, 40. (2) *1 Chr* 2:50,
52. (3) *1 Chr* 4:1, 2
Shobek. *Neh* 10:24
Shobi. *2 Sam* 17:27
Shoham. *1 Chr* 24:27
Shomer. (1) *2 Ki* 12:21. (2) *1 Chr*
7:32
Shophach. *1 Chr* 19:16, 18
Shophan. *Num* 32:35
Shoshannim. *Ps* 45 title; 69 title;
80 title
Shua. *1 Chr* 7:32
Shual. *1 Chr* 7:36
Shubael. (1) *1 Chr* 24:20. (2) *1 Chr*
25:20
Shuham. *Num* 26:42
Shunem. *Josh* 19:18; *1 Sam* 28:4;
2 Ki 4:8
Shuni. *Gen* 46:16; *Num* 26:15
Shupham. *Num* 26:39
Shuppim. (1) *1 Chr* 7:12, 15. (2)
1 Chr 26:16
Shur. *Gen* 16:7; 20:1; 25:18; *Ex*
15:22; *1 Sam* 15:7; 27:8
Shushaneduth. *Ps* 60 title
Shuthelah. (1) *Num* 26:35, 36;
1 Chr 7:20. (2) *1 Chr* 7:21
Siaha. *Ezra* 2:44; *Neh* 7:47
Sibbechai. *2 Sam* 21:18; *1 Chr*
11:29; 20:4; 27:11
Sibmah. *Josh* 13:19; *Isa* 16:8, 9;
Jer 48:32
Sibraim. *Ezek* 47:16
Sichem (Shechem). *Gen* 12:6
Siddim. *Gen* 14:3, 8, 10
Silla. *2 Ki* 12:20
Sinim. *Isa* 49:12
Siphmoth. *1 Sam* 30:28
Sippai. *1 Chr* 20:4
Sirah. *2 Sam* 3:26
Sisamai. *1 Chr* 2:40
Sitnah. *Gen* 26:21

Socho. (1) *1 Chr* 4:18. (2) *2 Chr*
11:7; 28:18
Socoh. (1) *Josh* 15:35; *1 Sam* 17:1;
1 Ki 4:10. (2) *Josh* 15:48
Sodi. *Num* 13:10
Sopater. *Acts* 20:4
Sophereth. *Ezra* 2:55; *Neh* 7:57
Sotai. *Ezra* 2:55; *Neh* 7:57
Suah. *1 Chr* 7:36
Sur. *2 Ki* 11:6
Susi. *Num* 13:11
Sychar. *John* 4:5
Sychem. *See* Shechem
Syene. *Ezek* 29:10; 30:6
Syntyche. *Phil* 4:2
Syracuse. *Acts* 28:12

TAANACH. *Josh* 12:21; 17:11;
21:25; *Judg* 1:27; 5:19; *1 Ki*
4:12; *1 Chr* 7:29
Taanath. *Josh* 16:6
Tabbaoth. *Ezra* 2:43; *Neh* 7:46
Tabbath. *Judg* 7:22
Tabeel. *Ezra* 4:7
Tabrimon. *1 Ki* 15:18
Tahan. (1) *Num* 26:35. (2) *1 Chr*
7:25
Tahath. (1) *Num* 33:26, 27. (2)
1 Chr 6:24, 37. (3) *1 Chr* 7:20.
(4) *1 Chr* 7:20
Tahrea. *1 Chr* 9:41
Tahtimhodshi. *2 Sam* 24:6
Talmai. (1) *Num* 13:22; *Josh*
15:14; *Judg* 1:10. (2) *2 Sam*
3:3; 13:37; *1 Chr* 3:2
Talmon. *1 Chr* 9:17; *Ezra* 2:42;
Neh 7:45; 11:19; 12:25
Tanhumeth. *2 Ki* 25:23; *Jer* 40:8
Taphath. *1 Ki* 4:11
Tappuah. (1) *Josh* 12:17; 15:34.
(2) *Josh* 16:8; 17:8. (3) *1 Chr*
2:43
Tarah. *Num* 33:27, 28
Taralah. *Josh* 18:27
Tarea. *1 Chr* 8:35
Tartan. *2 Ki* 18:17; *Isa* 20:1
Tatnai. *Ezra* 5:3, 6; 6:6, 13
Tebah. *Gen* 22:24
Tebaliah. *1 Chr* 26:11
Tehaphnehes. *Ezek* 30:18
Tehinnah. *1 Chr* 4:12
Tel-abib. *Ezek* 3:15
Telah. *1 Chr* 7:25
Telaim. *1 Sam* 15:4
Telem. (1) *Josh* 15:24. (2) *Ezra*
10:24
Tel-melah. *Ezra* 2:59; *Neh* 7:61
Temeni. *1 Chr* 4:6
Teresh. *Esth* 2:21; 6:2
Thaddaeus. *Mat* 10:3; *Mark* 3:18
Thahash. *Gen* 22:24
Thamah. *Ezra* 2:53; *Neh* 7:55
Thamar. *Mat* 1:3
Thara. *Luke* 3:34
Thelasar. *2 Ki* 19:12; *Isa* 37:12
Tiberius Caesar. *Luke* 3:1
Tibhath. *1 Chr* 18:8
Tidal. *Gen* 14:1, 9
Tikvah. (1) *2 Ki* 22:14; *2 Chr*
34:22. (2) *Ezra* 10:15
Tilon. *1 Chr* 4:20
Timaeus. *Mark* 10:46
Timna. (1) *Gen* 36:12. (2) *Gen*
36:22; *1 Chr* 1:39. (3) *1 Chr*
1:36
Timnah, Thimnathah. (1) *Gen*
36:40; *1 Chr* 1:51. (2) *Josh*
15:10, 57; 19:43; *2 Chr* 28:18
Timnath-heres. *Judg* 2:9
Timnath-serah. *Josh* 19:50; 24:30
Timon. *Acts* 6:5
Tiphsah. (1) *1 Ki* 4:24. (2) *1 Ki*
15:16
Tiras. *Gen* 10:2; *1 Chr* 1:5
Tirhakah. *2 Ki* 19:9; *Isa* 37:9
Tirhanah. *1 Chr* 2:48
Tiria. *1 Chr* 4:16
Toah. *1 Chr* 6:34
Tob. *Judg* 11:3, 5
Tobadonijah. *2 Chr* 17:8
Tochen. *1 Chr* 4:32
Tohu. *1 Sam* 1:1
Toi. *2 Sam* 8:9, 10; *1 Chr* 18:9, 10
Tolad. *1 Chr* 4:29

.....el. *Deut* 1:1
..achonitis. *Luke* 3:1
.rogyllium. *Acts* 20:15
Trophimus. *Acts* 20:4; 21:29; *2 Tim* 4:20
Tubal-cain. *Gen* 4:22

UEL. *Ezra* 10:34
Ulai. *Dan* 8:2, 16
Ulam. (1) *1 Chr* 7:16, 17. (2) *1 Chr* 8:39, 40
Ulla. *1 Chr* 7:39
Ummah. *Josh* 19:30
Unni. (1) *1 Chr* 15:18, 20. (2) *Neh* 12:9
Uriel. (1) *1 Chr* 6:24; 15:5, 11. (2) *2 Chr* 13:2
Uthai. (1) *1 Chr* 9:4. (2) *Ezra* 8:14
Uzai. *Neh* 3:25
Uzal. *Gen* 10:27; *1 Chr* 1:21
Uzzensherah. *1 Chr* 7:24
Uzzi. (1) *1 Chr* 6:5, 6, 51; *Ezra* 7:4. (2) *1 Chr* 7:2, 3. (3) *1 Chr* 7:7. (4) *1 Chr* 9:8. (5) *Neh* 11:22. (6) *Neh* 12:19, 42

VAJEZATHA. *Esth* 9:9
Vaniah. *Ezra* 10:36
Vashni. *1 Chr* 6:28
Vophsi. *Num* 13:14

ZAANAIM. *Judg* 4:11
Zaanan. *Mi* 1:11
Zaanannim. *Josh* 19:33
Zaavan. *Gen* 36:27; *1 Chr* 1:42
Zabad. (1) *1 Chr* 2:36, 37. (2) *1 Chr* 7:21. (3) *1 Chr* 11:41. (4) *2 Chr* 24:26. (5) *Ezra* 10:27. (6) *Ezra* 10:33. (7) *Ezra* 10:43
Zabbai. (1) *Ezra* 10:28. (2) *Neh* 3:20
Zabbud. *Ezra* 8:14
Zabdi. (1) *Josh* 7:1, 17, 18. (2) *1 Chr* 8:19. (3) *1 Chr* 27:27. (4) *Neh* 11:17
Zabdiel. (1) *1 Chr* 27:2. (2) *Neh* 11:14
Zabud. *1 Ki* 4:5
Zaccai. *Ezra* 2:9; *Neh* 7:14

Zaccur. (1) *Num* 13:4. (2) *1 Chr* 4:26. (3) *1 Chr* 24:27. (4) *1 Chr* 25:2, 10; *Neh* 12:35. (5) *Neh* 3:2. (6) *Neh* 10:12. (7) *Neh* 13:13
Zacharias. *Luke* 1:5, 12, 13, 18, 21, 40, 67; 3:2
Zacher. *1 Chr* 8:31
Zaham. *2 Chr* 11:19
Zair. *2 Ki* 8:21
Zalaph. *Neh* 3:30
Zalmon. (1) *Judg* 9:48; *Ps* 68:14. (2) *2 Sam* 23:28
Zalmonah. *Num* 33:41, 42
Zamzummim. *Deut* 2:20
Zanoah. (1) *Josh* 15:34; *Neh* 3:13; 11:30. (2) *Josh* 15:56. (3) *1 Chr* 4:18
Zaphnath-paaneah. *Gen* 41:45
Zareah. *Neh* 11:29
Zared. *Num* 21:12; *Deut* 2:13, 14
Zaretan. *Josh* 3:16; *1 Ki* 4:12; 7:46
Zareth-shahar. *Josh* 13:19
Zattu. (1) *Ezra* 2:8; 10:27; *Neh* 7:13. (2) *Neh* 10:14
Zaza. *1 Chr* 2:33
Zebadiah. (1) *1 Chr* 8:15. (2) *1 Chr* 8:17. (3) *1 Chr* 12:7. (4) *1 Chr* 26:2. (5) *1 Chr* 27:7. (6) *2 Chr* 17:8. (7) *2 Chr* 19:11. (8) *Ezra* 8:8. (9) *Ezra* 10:20
Zebaim. *Ezra* 2:57; *Neh* 7:59
Zebina. *Ezra* 10:43
Zedad. *Num* 34:8; *Ezek* 47:15
Zelah. *Josh* 18:28; *2 Sam* 21:14
Zelek. *2 Sam* 23:37; *1 Chr* 11:39
Zemaraim. (1) *Josh* 18:22. (2) *2 Chr* 13:4
Zemira. *1 Chr* 7:8
Zenan. *Josh* 15:37
Zephath. *Judg* 1:17
Zephathah. *2 Chr* 14:10
Zepho. *Gen* 36:11, 15; *1 Chr* 1:36
Zephon. *Num* 26:15
Zerahiah. (1) *1 Chr* 6:6, 51; *Ezra* 7:4. (2) *Ezra* 8:4
Zereda. *1 Ki* 11:26
Zeredathah. *2 Chr* 4:17

Zer.....
Zere.....
Zeri. ...
Zeror. ...
Zeruah. ...
Zetham. ...
Zethan. *1 C...*
Zethar. *Est*....
Zia. *1 Chr* 5:...
Zibia. *1 Chr* 8:...
Zibiah. *2 Ki* 12:...
Zichri. (1) *Ex* 6:2...
(3) *1 Chr* 8:23.
(5) *1 Chr* 9:15. (...
(7) *1 Chr* 27:16. (8..
(9) *2 Chr* 23:1. (10..
(11) *Neh* 11:9. (12)
Ziddim. *Josh* 19:35
Zidkijah. *Neh* 10:1
Ziha. (1) *Ezra* 2:43; *Net...*
(2) *Neh* 11:21
Zillah. *Gen* 4:19, 22, 23
Zilthai. (1) *1 Chr* 8:20. (2) *1...* 12:20
Zimmah. (1) *1 Chr* 6:20. (2) *1 Ch...* 6:42. (3) *2 Chr* 29:12
Zimran. *Gen* 25:2; *1 Chr* 1:32
Zina. *1 Chr* 23:10
Zior. *Josh* 15:54
Ziph. (1) *Josh* 15:24; *1 Sam* 23:14, 15, 24; 26:2; *2 Chr* 11:8. (2) *Josh* 15:55. (3) *1 Chr* 2:42. (4) *1 Chr* 4:16
Ziphah. *1 Chr* 4:16
Ziphion. *Gen* 46:16
Ziphron. *Num* 34:9
Zithri. *Ex* 6:22
Ziz. *2 Chr* 20:16
Ziza. (1) *1 Chr* 4:37. (2) *1 Chr* 23:11. (3) *2 Chr* 11:20
Zobebah. *1 Chr* 4:8
Zoheleth. *1 Ki* 1:9
Zoheth. *1 Chr* 4:20
Zophah. *1 Chr* 7:35, 36
Zophai. *1 Chr* 6:26
Zophim. (1) *Num* 23:14. (2) *1 Sam* 1:1
Zuph. (1) *1 Sam* 1:1; *1 Chr* 6:35. (2) *1 Sam* 9:5
Zuriel. *Num* 3:35

A LIST OF

THE PROPER NAMES

IN THE

OLD AND NEW TESTAMENTS

With the Meaning or Signification of the
Words in Their Original Languages

BY REV. ALFRED JONES, M.A.

Author of "The Proper Names of the Old Testament Scriptures,
Expounded and Illustrated," etc., etc.

NOTE—Some few PROPER NAMES which rarely occur in Scripture appear in this
List only, and not in the following part of the Concordance; to these the
Scripture References are here annexed.

A LIST OF

THE PROPER NAMES

IN THE

OLD AND NEW TESTAMENTS

FOREWORD

THE STUDY of the Word of God can best be facilitated by a wise and constant use of this Concordance. Here you will find almost every word of the whole Bible arranged alphabetically, so that at any time the student may find the location of any passage that he may desire. By this means also, the student will discover that many statements are incorrectly quoted from the Bible. Sometimes quotations are made which are not found in the Bible in any form. This may be discovered by consulting your Concordance and looking for any of the prominent words used in that quotation.

By means of this Concordance the student may study any subject desired. For instance, you might wish to study the subject of trees. Find the word "tree" in the Concordance, and then notice every place where the word occurs, and what is the subject under consideration. You will find that the "oak tree" is usually mentioned in connection with death. The "fig tree" is usually connected with political Israel, etc.

If you wish to study the subject of "grace," or "horses," or of the "blood," or of the "coming of Christ," or of the "judgments," or any other subject, just find that word in your Concordance and look up the various Scriptures in which that word occurs. By this means you will become well acquainted with your Bible, and with God's Truth.

If you hear a verse of Scripture quoted, and you do not know where it is found, seek the prominent word in the Concordance, follow down the Scriptures that are listed there, and you will find the verse that you desire to locate.

This Concordance is a library of instruction. It is a lexicon of explanation. It is a source of inspiration and knowledge which is indispensable to the Bible student. Permit me to encourage every student of the Word of God to own a copy of this wonderful and valuable book.

WALTER L. WILSON, M.D., L.H.D.

Kansas City, Missouri

A LIST OF

THE PROPER NAMES

IN THE

OLD AND NEW TESTAMENTS

AARON, *signifies* mountain of strength to the Jewish people, even as Christ is everlasting strength to His Church; *or*, a teacher, *or* teaching. *The first high priest of the Jews, the son of Amram, brother to Moses. He was, with his sons, anointed and consecrated to the priest's office,* Lev. 8.

AARONITES.

ABADDON, the destroyer, total destruction.

ABAGTHA, father of the wine-press, given by fortune.

ABANA, stone, *or* a building.

ABARIM, passages, *or* passengers, plur. of the appell. *ébher,* beyond.

ABDA, a servant, *or* servitude.

ABDI, servant of the Lord.

ABDIEL, the servant of God.

ABDON, servile.

ABED-NEGO, servant of the sun, *Dan.* 3. 23.

ABEL, vanity, *or* breath, *or* transitoriness; *second son of Adam,* Gen. 4. 4.

ABEL, *a city.*

ABEL-BETH-MAACHAH, mourning to the house of Maachah.

ABEL K'RAMIVM, plain of the vineyards. (See Judg. 11. 33.)

ABEL-MAIM, the mourning of the waters; *or,* the valley of waters.

ABEL-MEHOLAH, meadow of dancing.

ABEL-MIZRAIM, the mourning of the Egyptians, *Gen.* 50, 11.

ABEL-SHITTIM, meadows of acacias. *It was a city near the river Jordan in the wilderness,* Num. 33. 49.

ABEZ, white, perhaps tin was found there. *A city in the tribe of Issachar,* Josh. 19. 20.

ABI, my father. *The mother of Hezekiah,* 2 Kings 18. 2.

ABIA. *See* ABIAH.

ABIAH, the Lord is my father, *or* the father of the Lord.

ABI-ALBON, father of strength.

ABIASAPH, father of gathering, *Ex.* 6. 24.

ABIATHAR, father of plenty, *or* father of him that survived, 1 Sam. 22. 20.

ABIB, green fruits, *or* ears of corn.

ABIDAH, the father of knowledge, *or* the knowledge of the father. *One of the sons of Midian,* Gen. 25. 4.

ABIDAN, father of judgment, *or* my father is judge.

ABIEL, father of strength. *He was the father of Kish,* 1 Sam. 9. 1.

ABIEZER, father of help, *or* help of the father, *or* my father is my help.

ABI-EZRITE.

ABIGAIL, father of joy, *or* the joy of the father, 1 Sam. 25. 3.

ABIHAIL, father of strength, *or* father of firmness.

ABIHU, [whose] father is He, *i.e.,* God.

ABIHUD, father of praise, *or* glory of my father; the same as Hodaiah.

ABIJAH, the will of the Lord, *or* the Lord is my father.

ABIJAM, father of the sea, a maritime person.

ABILENE, grassy place, near the city Abila.

A province between Libanus and Antilibanus, whereof Lysanias was tetrarch, Luke 3. 1.

ABIMAEL, a father sent from God, *or* my father comes from God. *He was the son of Joktan,* Gen. 10. 28.

ABIMELECH, father of the king, *or* my father the king.

ABINADAB, father of willingness; *or,* my father is a prince.

ABINOAM, father of pleasantness, the father of Barak.

ABIRAM, father of loftiness, *or* one who lifts up himself. *A son of Eliab.*

ABISHAG, father of error.

ABISHAI, father of gifts, *or* father of the present.

ABISHALOM, the father of peace, *or* the peace of the father; *or,* the recompence of the father. 1 Kings 15. 2.

ABISHUA, father of salvation, *or* of magnificence, *or* the salvation of my father, 1 Chron. 6. 4.

ABISHUR, the father of a wall, *or* of uprightness; *or,* my father is upright, 1 Chron. 2. 28.

ABITAL, the father of dew. *One of David's wives,* 2 Sam. 3. 4.

ABITUB, father of goodness, *or* my father is good, 1 Chron. 8. 11.

ABNER, father of light, *or* the lamp of the father, *or* the son of the father.

ABRAM, a high father; father of a multitude.

ABRAHAM, father of a multitude. *A son of Terah, and founder through the promise of God of the Jewish nation. He was an inhabitant of the city of Ur, whose people were ignicolists, or worshippers of fire; there are reasons for concluding that Abraham was at one time an idolater as well as his father and brethren.* (Josh. 24. 3.) *These descendants of Shem were examples of the proneness of man to wander: "all we like sheep have gone astray;" for they were all on forbidden ground—among the rebellious sons of Ham—united under the idolatrous and tyrannical Nimrod; instead of being in their own country, and among their own kin. The Messiah was promised to be of his family,* Gen. 12. 3; Acts 3. 25; Gal. 3. 8. *The spiritual children of faithful Abraham, are those that believe in Jesus Christ, and do the works of Abraham,* John 8. 39; Rom. 4. 16; 9. 7; Gal. 3. 7, 29.

ABSALOM, father of peace, *or* the peace of the father.

ACCAD, band or chain. *The city where Nimrod reigned,* Gen. 10. 10.

ACCHO, sand made warm by heat of the sun.

ACELDAMA, the field of blood, *Acts* 1. 19.

ACHAIA, grief, *or* trouble.

ACHAICUS, a native of Achaia, gracious.

ACHAN, *or* ACHAR, he that troubles and bruises.

ACHBOR, a mouse. *He was father of Baalhanan, the seventh king of Edom,* Gen. 36. 38.

ACHIM, He (*i.e.,* God) will establish.

ACHISH, fear.

ACHMETHA, a city.

ACHOR, trouble.

ACHSAH, anklet or adorned.

ACHSHAPH, enchantment tricks; *or,* one that breaks: *or* the lip *or* brim of any thing.

ACHZIB, lying; deceptive as a fishing hook.

ADADAH, ornament. *The name of a city,* Josh. 15. 22.

ADAH, an ornament. *The wife of Lamech,* Gen. 4. 19. *Also the wife of Esau,* Gen. 36. 2.

ADAIAH, ornament of the Lord. *The father of Jedidah, mother of Josiah,* 2 Kings 22. 1.

ADALIAH, strong mind. *One of Haman's sons,* Esth. 9. 8.

ADAM, red earth. *He was called ADAM, not because he would return to dust; but because he was created out of the ground, and probably with a prophetic reference to the fact that he would return to the dust, if at any time he transgressed. He was not called Enosh, miserable, for he was perfect and happy; nor Ish, husband, because he had no female and was solitary, for that term was not used till Ishah was taken out of Ish, wife of her husband. He was called Adam with reference to his origin, the earth. Also he was called Ish, husband, when associated with his wife in the garden of Eden; and Enosh, miserable, after his fall. The name of the first man, who was made after the image of God, in a holy and happy estate, but by his fall and disobedience broke covenant with God, and thereby brought himself and all his posterity into an estate of sin and misery,* Rom. 5. 12. *But our Lord Jesus Christ, the second Adam, is the Saviour and Redeemer of all that truly believe in Him.* Mark 16. 16; Acts 4. 12; 16. 31.

ADAMAH, red earth. *A city,* Josh. 19. 36.

ADAMI, my man, red, earthy, human. *A city,* Josh. 19. 33.

ADAR, wide.

ADBEEL, sorrow of God: *otherwise,* a vexer of God. *One of Ishmael's sons,* Gen. 25. 13.

ADDI, my witness, adorned, passage, prey.

ADDON, basis, foundation, the Lord. *The name of a place,* Neh. 7. 61.

ADIEL, ornament of the Lord, 1 Chron. 4. 36.

ADIN, soft, adorned, *or* voluptuous, dainty. *Ezra* 8. 6.

ADINA, pliant, 1 Chron. 11. 42.

ADINO, whose pleasure is the spear, 2 Sam. 23. 8.

ADITHAIM, two-fold ornament, Josh. 15. 36.

ADLAI, justice of the Lord, 1 Chron. 27. 29.

ADMAH, earthy, red earth.

ADMATHA, a cloud of death, a mortal vapour, *Esth.* 1. 14.

ADNAH, rest, *or* testimony eternal. 1 Chron. 12. 20.

ADONI-BEZEK the lightning of the Lord, *or* the Lord of lightning; *or,* the Lord of Bezek; *for he was king of this city.*

ADONIJAH, the Lord is my Lord.

ADONIKAM, the Lord of enemies.

ADONIRAM, my Lord is most high; or the Lord of might and elevation, 1 Kings 4. 6.
ADONI-ZEDEK, justice of the Lord, or the Lord of justice. He was king of Jerusalem, Josh. 10. 1.
ADORAIM, twofold habitation, 2 Chron. 11. 9.
ADORAM, vide Adoniram. 2 Sam. 20. 24.
ADRAMMELECH, the cloke, glory, grandeur, or power of the king.
ADRAMMYTTIUM, ensign of elevation, now called Adrampt.
ADRIA, restless, the Adriatic sea, now the gulf of Venice.
ADRIEL, flock of God, 1 Sam. 18. 19.
ADULLAM, the justice of the people.
ÆNON, fountain of the sun, John 3. 23.
AGABUS, a locust.
AGAG, fire.
AGAGITE, of the race of Agag.
AGAR, see HAGAR.
AGRIPPA, this word is Latin, and signifies one who at his birth causes great pain, who is born with his feet foremost, ægre partus, Acts 12. 1.
AGUR, or gathering, or gathered together.
AHAB, the brother of the father, uncle, or father of the brother.
AHARAH, after a brother, 1 Chron. 8. 1.
AHARHEL, behind the breastwork, 1 Chron. 4. 8.
AHASAI, possessor of God, Neh. 11. 13.
AHASBAI, I flee to the Lord, 2 Sam. 23. 34.
AHASUERUS, prince, head, or chief.
AHAVA, essence, or generation.
AHAZ, one that takes and possesses.
AHAZIAH, possession of the Lord.
AHBAN, brother of the prudent, 1 Chron. 2. 29.
AHER, coming slowly, 1 Chron. 7. 12.
AHI, brother, 1 Chron. 5. 15; 7. 34.
AHIAH, brother of the Lord.
AHIAM, brother's mother, 2 Sam. 23. 33; 1 Chron. 11. 35.
AHIAN, brotherly.
AHIEZER, brother of assistance. A prince of the tribe of Dan, Num. 1. 12.
AHIHUD, brother of praise. The prince of the tribe of Asher, Num. 34. 27.
AHIJAH, brother of the Lord.
AHIJAH, the same as AHIAH.
AHIKAM, brother of rising up.
AHIKAM, a brother that raises up.
AHILUD, a brother born. He was secretary to David, 2 Sam. 8. 16.
AHIMAAZ, brother of anger. Three bore this name.
AHIMAN, who is my brother?
AHIMELECH, my brother is a king, or the brother of my king. Three bore this name.
AHIMOTH, brother of death, or my brother is dead, 1 Chron. 6. 25.
AHINADAB, brother of nobility, 1 Kings 4. 14.
AHINOAM, the beauty and comeliness of the brother, or brother of grace.
AHIO, brotherly.
AHIRA, brother of iniquity; otherwise brother or companion of the shepherd. He was chief of the tribe of Naphtali, Num. 1. 15.
AHIRAM, brother of height, Num. 6. 38.
AHISAMACH, brother of strength or support, or my brother supports me.
AHISHAR, or AHISHAHAR, brother of the dawn, or brother of a song. He was steward of Solomon's household, 1 Kings 4. 6; 1 Chron. 7. 10.
AHITHOPHEL, brother of folly.
AHITUB, brother of goodness, or my brother is good.
AHLAB, which is of milk, or which is fat; otherwise, brother of the heart. The name of a city, Judg. 1. 31.
AHOLAH, she has her own tent.
AHOLIAB, the tent, or tabernacle of the father.
AHOLIBAH, my tent and my tabernacle in her.
AHOLIBAMAH, my tabernacle is exalted.
AHUMAI, brother of waters, 1 Chron. 4. 2.
AHUZZAM, their possession, 1 Chron. 4. 6.
AHUZZATH, a passion, Gen. 26. 26.
AI, or HAI, mass or heap of ruins.
AIATH, the same as AI.
AIN, a fountain, Num. 34. 11; Josh. 15. 32; 19. 7; 21. 16; 1 Chron. 4. 32.
AJALON, a large stag.
AKAN, or JAKAN, to twist, Gen. 36. 27; 1 Chron. 1. 42.

AKKUB, insidious, 1 Chron. 3. 24; 9. 17; Ezra 2. 42, 45; Neh. 7. 45; 8. 7; 11. 19; 12. 25.
ALAMETH, covering, 1 Chron. 7. 8.
ALAMMELECH, oak of the king. A city, Josh. 19. 26.
ALEMETH, a hiding-place, 1 Chron. 6. 60; 8. 36; 9. 42.
ALEXANDER, defender of men.
ALEXANDER, a Greek word, and signifies one that assists men, or one that helps stoutly; or, one that turns away evil.
ALEXANDRIA, a city in Egypt.
ALLON, an oak, or strong, 1 Chron. 4. 37.
ALLON-BACHUTH, the oak of weeping. The place where Rebekah's nurse was buried, Gen. 35. 8.
ALMODAD, measure of God, Gen. 10. 26.
ALMODAD, immeasurable.
ALMON, hidden.
ALMON DIBLATHAIM, Almon towards Diblathaim, Num. 33. 46, 47.
ALPHA, the first letter of the Greek alphabet, marked A, Rev. 1. 8, 11; 21. 6; 22. 13.
ALPHEUS, first, or chief, or an ox.
ALUSH, a crowd of men, Num. 33. 13, 14.
ALVAH, iniquity, Gen. 36. 40; 1 Chron. 1. 51.
ALVAN, unrighteous, Gen. 36. 23; 1 Chron. 1. 40.
AMAD, eternal people, Josh. 19. 26.
AMAL, troublesome, 1 Chron. 7. 35.
AMALEK, a people that licks up, or that takes away all; otherwise, a people that strikes, or that uses ill.
AMALEKITES, people descended from Amalek
AMAM, people, Josh. 15. 26.
AMANA, a confirmation; integrity and truth.
AMARIAH, promised of the Lord, 1 Chron. 6. 7, 11, 52; 23. 19; 24. 23; 2 Chron. 19. 11; 31. 15; Ezra 7. 3; 10. 42; Neh. 10. 3; 11. 4; 12. 2, 13; Zeph. 1. 1.
AMASA, burden of the people.
AMASAI, burden of the Lord, 1 Chron. 6. 25, 35; 12. 18; 15. 24; 2 Chron. 29. 12.
AMASIAH, carried of the Lord, 2 Chron. 17. 16.
AMAZIAH, the strength of the Lord.
AMITTAI, truth of the Lord, 2 Kings 14. 25; Jon. 1. 1.
AMMAH, beginning.
AMMI, the same with AMMAH.
AMMIEL, one of the people of God, Num. 13. 12; 2 Sam. 9. 4, 5; 17. 27; 1 Chron. 3. 5; 26. 5.
AMMIHUD, people of praise, or praise is with me. Num. 1. 10.
AMMINADAB, people of liberality.
AMMI-NADIB, my people is liberal, or prince of the people, or a people that vows.
AMMISHADDAI, the people of the Almighty, or the Almighty is with me, Num. 1. 12.
AMMIZABAD, people of the bountiful giver, 1 Chron. 27. 6.
AMMON, great people.
AMMONITES. A people that descended of Ben-ammi, son of Lot by his youngest daughter.
AMNON, a nourisher, faithful and true; otherwise, foster-father, or tutor; or, son of the mother.
AMOK, deep. Neh. 12. 7.
AMON, faithful, true.
AMORITE, bitter, a rebel; otherwise, a babbler, a mountaineer, or prater.
AMOS, weighty, burden.
AMOZ, strong, robust.
AMPHIPOLIS, a city encompassed by the sea on both sides of the city, or a double-sided city.
AMPLIAS, enlargement. A Latin word.
AMRAM, an exalted people; or, their sheaves, or handfuls of corn.
AMRAPHEL, one that speaks of hidden things; one that speaks of judgment, or ruin, Gen. 14. 1, 9.
AMZI, strong, 1 Chron. 6. 46; Neh. 11. 12.
ANAH, one who answers, or who sings; otherwise poor or afflicted.
ANAK, a collar, or ornament.
ANAKIMS.
ANAMIM, responding waters, Gen. 10. 13; 1 Chron. 1. 11.
ANAMMELECH, answer, or song of the king.
ANAN, a cloud.
ANANI, a cloud of the Lord, 1 Chron. 3. 24.
ANANIAH, cloud of the Lord, Neh. 3. 23.

ANANIAS, graciously given of the Lord.
ANATH, answer to prayer, Judg. 3. 31; 5. 6.
ANATHOTH, answer to prayers.
ANDREW, a stout and strong man. Greek.
ANDRONICUS, victor of men. Greek.
ANEM, two fountains, 1 Chron. 6. 73.
ANER, exile.
ANNA, gracious, merciful.
ANNAS, graciously given. A high priest who sent Christ bound to Caiaphas his father-in-law.
ANTICHRIST, an adversary to Christ.
ANTIOCH, resistance. A Greek word. A city on the Orontes, one hundred miles north of Jerusalem, Acts 11. 19.
ANTIPAS, likeness of his father. One of the martyrs slain by the people of Pergamos, Rev. 2. 13.
ANTIPATRIS, likeness of his father.
APELLES, a Greek word, from the verb ἀπελλω, I exclude, I separate.
APHEK, a stream, a rapid torrent; or, strength, vigour.
APOLLONIA, perdition, destruction.
APOLLOS, one that destroys and lays waste.
APOLLYON, one that exterminates or destroys.
APPHIA, that produces, or is fruitful, Philem. 2.
APPII-FORUM, a town so called from Appius Claudius, whose statue was erected there.
APPII-FORUM, market of Appius.
AQUILA, an eagle. Latin.
AR, city.
ARABIA, sterile, or a place wild and desert; or, hostages, ravens; and also, mixtures; because this country was inhabited by different kinds of people.
ARABIAN.
ARAD, wild ass, Num. 21. 1; 33. 40; Josh. 12. 14; Judg. 1. 16; 1 Chron. 8. 15.
ARAH, wandering, 1 Chron. 7. 39; Ezra 2. 5; Neh. 6. 18; 7. 10.
ARAM, highness, magnificence; otherwise, one that deceives, or their curse. ARAM signifies Syria in Gen. 22. 21, and elsewhere.
ARARAT, mount of descent.
ARAUNAH, a large ash.
ARBA, quadrangular.
ARCHELAUS, prince of the people. Greek.
ARCHIPPUS, a governor of horses, or master of the horse. Greek.
ARCTURUS, a gathering together.
ARD, fugitive. A son of Benjamin, Gen. 46. 21.
ARELI, lion of God. Gen. 46. 16.
AREOPAGITE, belonging to the council called Areopagus.
AREOPAGUS, the hill of Mars; a place where the magistrates of Athens held their supreme council; from ἄρειος, Mars; and πάγος, a hill.
ARETAS, one that is agreeable, that pleases, that is virtuous.
ARGOB, a turf of earth, a heap of stones, or curse of the well.
ARIDAI, donum Ario, Esther 9. 9.
ARIDATHA, great birth, Esther 9. 8.
ARIEH, lion, 2 Kings 15. 25.
ARIEL, the altar, light, or lion of God.
ARIMATHEA, a lion dead to the Lord; or, the light of the death of the Lord; or simply, Ramath, or Ramah, a city where Samuel dwelt, 1 Sam. 1. 19.
ARIOCH, "the mighty lion."
ARISTARCHUS, a good prince, the best prince. Greek.
ARISTOBULUS, a good counsellor, good advice. Greek.
ARMAGEDDON, the mountain of Megiddo, or the mountain of the gospel; otherwise, the mountain of fruits, or of apples.
ARMENIA, a province which is supposed to take its name from Aram.
ARNON, rejoicing, or leaping for joy.
AROER, heath, tamarisk; or, the nakedness of the skin; or, nakedness of the watch, or of the enemy.
ARPAD, prop.: or, that lie down, that makes his bed.
ARPHAXAD, boundary of the Chaldeans; or, one that releases.
ARTAXERXES, in Hebrew, Artachsasta, the silence of light, or light that imposes silence; otherwise, joy that is in haste. A Persian name.
ARTEMAS, gift of Diana.
ARUBOTH, flood-gates, 1 Kings 4. 10.

ARUMAH, elevated, *Judg.* 9. 41.
ARVAD, place of future, *Ezek.* 27. 8, 11.
ARZA, earth, 1 *Kings* 16. 9.
ASA, physician, or cure.
ASAHEL, the work, or creature of God.
ASAHEL, made of God.
ASAHIAH, made of Jehovah, 2 *Kings* 22. 12, 14.
ASAIAH, the L·rd hath wrought; or, a creature of the Lord.
ASAPH, one that assembles together; or, one that finishes and completes.
ASAREEL, bound of God, 1 *Chron.* 4. 16.
ASARELAH, upright of God, 1 *Chron.* 25. 2.
ASENATH, who belongs to Nuth.
ASHAN, smoke, *Josh.* 15. 42; 19. 7; 1 *Chron.* 43. 2; 6. 59.
ASHBEA, I adjure, 1 *Chron.* 4. 21.
ASHBEL, fire of Bel, *Gen.* 46. 21; *Num.* 26. 38; 1 *Chron.* 8. 1.
ASHDOD, inclination, leaning; or, a wild open place; or, pillage, theft.
ASHER, blessedness, or happiness.
ASHIMA, crime; or, position; or, fire of the sea. *The name of an idol,* 2 *Kings* 17. 30.
ASHKENAZ, a fire that distils or spreads. *One of the sons of Gomer,* Gen. 10. 3.
ASHNAH, strong, *Josh.* 15. 33, 43.
ASHTAROTH, Astartes, *i.e.,* statue of Astarte, *Deut.* 1. 4; *Josh.* 9. 10; 12. 4; 13. 12, 31; *Judg.* 2. 13; 10. 6; 1 *Sam.* 7. 3, 4; 12. 10; 31. 10; 1 *Chron.* 6. 71.
ASHTEROTH KARNAIM, Ashtaroth of horns, *i.e.,* the crescent moons, Gen. 14. 5.
ASHTORETH, Queen of Heaven, *i.e.,* the new moon, 1 *Kings* 11. 5, 33; 2 *Kings* 23. 13.
ASHUR, blackness, one that is happy, that walks on prosperingly.
ASIA, land of fire.
ASKELON, migration.
ASNAPPER, bull or calf; or, fruitfulness, or increase of danger.
ASSIR, prisoner, fettered, 1 *Chron.* 3. 17.
ASSOS, approaching, coming near to, *Acts* 20. 13.
ASSYRIA.
ASSYRIAN.
ASYNCRITUS, incomparable.
ATAD, a thorn.
ATHALIAH, taken away of the Lord.
ATHENIANS, inhabitants of Athens.
ATHENS, *so called from Athene; or Athenaia, Minerva.* Fountain of fire, *i.e,* the sun. *It was called from Athene. The discoveries of Schliemann on the site of Ilium, or Troy, have thrown light on Biblical archæology. The tutelary goddess of Troy, whom Homer calls* θέα γλαυκῶπις Ἀθήνη, *"the goddess Athens with the owl's face," does not express the true meaning or idea of the goddess, for there can be no reasonable doubt that the sun was the object of worship under this name, and which was always with cruel rites.*
ATTALIA, mild, *Acts* 14. 25.
AVEN, vanity.
AUGUSTUS, increased, augmented; or, royal, majestic.
AZARIAH, assistance, or help of the Lord; or, he that hears the Lord, or whom the Lord hears.
AZEKAH, strength of walls.
AZGAD, strong in fortune; a strong army, or the strength of a troop; *otherwise,* a gang of rubbers, or a troop of soldiers. *Ezra* 2. 12.
AZIEL, comforted of God, 1 *Chron.* 15. 20.
AZIZA, strong, *Ezra* 10. 27.
AZMAVETH, strong in death, 2 *Sam.* 23. 31; 1 *Chron.* 8. 36; 9. 42; 11, 33; 12. 3; 27. 25; *Ezra* 2. 24; *Neh.* 12. 29.
AZMON, strong, *Num.* 34. 4, 5; *Josh.* 15. 4.
AZNOTH-TABOR, the ears of Tabor; or, the ears of choice, purity, contrition, *Josh.* 19. 34.
AZOTUS, *the same as* ASHDOD, pillage, theft, *Acts* 8. 40.
AZRIEL, help of God, 1 *Chron.* 5. 24; 27. 19; *Jer.* 36. 26.
AZRIKAM, help against an enemy, 1 *Chron.* 3. 23; 8. 38; 9. 14, 44; 2 *Chron.* 28. 7; *Neh.* 11. 15.
AZUBAH, deserted, 1 *Kings* 22. 42; 1 *Chron.* 2. 18, 19; 2 *Chron.* 20. 31.
AZUR, helper, *Ezek.* 11. 1; *Jer.* 28. 1.
AZZAH, strong, *Deut.* 2. 23; 1 *Kings* 4. 24; *Jer.* 25. 20.
AZZAN, very strong, *Num.* 34, 26.
AZZUR, he that assists, or he that is assisted, *Neh.* 10. 17.

B.

BAAL, lord, *i.e.,* possessor of anything. *The sun was chiefly called by this name.*
BAALAH, her lord; or, she that is governed or subdued, a spouse. *A city,* Josh. 15. 9.
BAALATH BEER, lady of the well, *Josh.* 19. 8.
BAAL-BERITH, lord of the covenant; or, he that possesses, or subdues the covenant.
BAAL-GAD, the lord of the troop, of the army, or of felicity; *otherwise,* the Lord is master of the troop, Josh. 11. 17.
BAAL-HAMON, one that possesses or rules a multitude, a populous place.
BAAL-HERMON, the posse·sor of destruction; or, of a thing cursed, devoted, or consecrated to God. *It is a mountain,* Judg. 3. 3.
BAALI, lord, master, or lord over me.
BAALIM, masters, false gods.
BAALIM, idols of Baal.
BAALIS, a rejoicing, or proud lord.
BAAL-MEON, the master of the house.
BAAL-PEOR, l·rd of the opening.
BAAL-PERAZIM, lord of divisions; or, he that possesses and enjoys divisions and dissipations.
BAAL SHALISHA, lord over three, the third idol, the third husband; or, that governs or presides over three.
BAAL-TAMAR, lord of the palm-tree.
BAAL ZEBUB, lord of flies.
BAAL-ZEPHON, lord of the north; or, hidden, secret.
BAANAH, in the answer, in affliction.
BAASHAH, evil.
BABEL, confusion.
BABYLON, *the same with* BABEL.
BABYLONIANS.
BABYLONISH.
BACA, weeping.
BAHURIM, village of choice youths.
BAJITH, a house, or temple.
BAKBAKKAR, diligent, searching, 1 *Chron.* 9. 15.
BAKBUK, emptied, *Ezra* 2. 51; *Neh.* 7. 53.
BAKBUKIAH, emptied of the Lord, *Neh.* 11. 17; 12. 9, 25.
BALAAM, destruction of the people. He was probably one of the *Moshelim* of the ancient Asiatics, who added to his poetic gift of sorcery and divination.
BALAK, who lays waste and destroys; or, who licks and laps.
BAMAH, an eminence, or high place.
BAMOTH, high places, *Num.* 21. 19, 20.
BAMOTH BAAL, high place of Baal, *Josh.* 13. 17.
BANI, built, 2 *Sam.* 23. 36; 1 *Chron.* 6. 46; 9. 4; *Ezra* 2. 10; 10. 29, 34, 38; *Neh.* 3. 17; 8. 7; 9. 4, 5; 10. 13, 14; 11. 22.
BARABBAS, son of the father, or of the master, or the son of confusion and shame.
BARACHEL, who blesses God, who bends the knee before God. *The father of Elihu,* Job 32. 2.
BARACHIAS, *the same with* BARACHEL.
BARAK, thunder, or in vain.
BARIAH, fugitive, 1 *Chron.* 3. 22.
BAR-JESUS, son of Jesus, or Joshua.
BAR-JONA, the son of Jona, or of a dove.
BARKOS, son of his father, *Ezra* 2. 53; *Neh.* 7. 55.
BARNABAS, the son of consolation.
BARSABAS, promised with an oath, or son of swearing.
BARTHOLOMEW, a son of Tholmai.
BARTIMEUS, the son of Timeus.
BARUCH, who is blessed, who bends the knee.
BARZILLAI, made of iron, most firm and true.
BASHAN, soft, sandy soil.
BASHEMATH, perfumed.
BATHRABBIM, daughter of many, *Cant.* 7. 4.
BATH-SHEBA, the seventh daughter, or the daughter of an oath.
BATHSHUA, daughter of an oath, 1 *Chron.* 3. 5.
BAVAI, by the mercy of the Lord, *Neh.* 3. 18.
BEDAD, alone, solitary; or, in friendship, in the bosom, or the nipple. *He was father of Hadad,* Gen. 36. 35.
BEDAD, separation.
BEDAN, fat.
BEEL-ZEBUB, *the same with* BAAL-ZEBUB.

BEER, a well. *The name of a city,* Num. 21. 16.
BEER-ELIM, well of the mighty ones, *Isa.* 15. 8.
BEER-LAHAI-ROI, the well of him that liveth an·t seeth me, Gen. 16. 14.
BEEROTH, wells, *Deut.* 10. 6; *Josh.* 9. 17; 18. 25; 2 *Sam.* 4. 2; *Ezra* 2. 25; *Neh.* 7. 29.
BEER-SHEBA, the fountain of an oath; *otherwise,* the seventh well, or the well of satiety.
BEKAH, *half a shekel.*
BEL, Lord.
BELIAL, wicked, worthless.
BELSHAZZAR, master of the treasure, or who lays up treasures in secret.
BELTESHAZZAR, who lays up treasures in secret; or, he that secretly endures pain and pressure.
BENAIAH built up of the Lord.
BENAIAH, son of the Lord; or, the understanding of the Lord; or, the Lord's building.
BEN-AMMI, the son of my people.
BENE-BERAK, sons of thunder, *Josh.* 19. 45.
BEN-HADAD, the son of Hadad, son of most high.
BENJAMIN, the son of the right hand.
BENJAMITE.
BENONI, son of my sorrow.
BEN-ZOHETH, son of most violent transportation, 1 *Chron.* 4. 20.
BEOR, burning; *otherwise,* torch.
BERA, son of evil, *Gen.* 14. 2.
BERACHAH, blessing, or bending of knee.
BEREA, heavy, weighty; *from* βάρος, weight.
BEREA, weighty, important.
BERIAH, in calamity, *Gen.* 46. 17; *Num.* 26. 44, 45; 1 *Chron.* 7. 23, 30, 31; 8. 13, 16; 23. 10, 11.
BERITH, covenant.
BERNICE, one that brings victory.
BESOR, glad news, or incarnation.
BETAH, confidence. *A city,* 2 *Sam.* 8. 8.
BETHABARA, the house of passage, or house of the ferry boat.
BETHANY, the house of palms; of the grave of the Lord.
BETH-AVEN, the house of vanity, of iniquity, of trouble, of strength.
BETH-BARAH, place of the ford, *Judg.* 7. 24.
BETH-BIREI, the house of my Creator; or, the temple of my Creator, 1 *Chron.* 4. 31.
BETH-CAR, the house of the battering rams. *A city,* 1 *Sam.* 7. 11.
BETH-DAGON, the house of corn; or, the habitation of the fish; or, the temple of the god Dagon. Josh. 15. 41; 19. 27.
BETH-DIBLATHAIM, the house of two cakes of figs.
BETHEL, the house of God.
BETHELITE.
BETHER, division; *otherwise,* in the turtle, or in the trial, or perquisition.
BETHESDA, the house of effusion; or, the house of pity, or mercy.
BETH-EZEL, a neighbour's house.
BETH-GAMUL, the house of recompence, or, of the weaned; or, the house of the camel.
BETH-HACCEREM, house of the vineyard.
BETH-HORON, house of wrath; or, house of the hole, or of the cave, or of liberty.
BETH-LEHEM, the house of bread.
BETH-LEHEM-EPHRAIM, house of bread of fruitfulness.
BETH-LEHEM-JUDAH, house of bread of praise.
BETH-LEHEMITE.
BETH-PEOR, the house of opening.
BETH-PHAGE, the house of figs.
BETHSAIDA, the house of fishing, or of hunters, or of snares.
BETH-SHAN, the house of rest; or, the dwelling of sleep.
BETH-SHEMESH, the house of the sun; or, the house of service, or of ministry.
BETHUEL, virgin of God.
BEULAH, married.
BEZALEEL, in the shadow of God.
BEZEK, lightning; or, in chains or fetters.
BICHRI, first-born, or first-fruits; *otherwise,* in the ram, or the sheep.
BIDKAR, son of thrusting through.
BIGTHA, given by fortune, *Esther* 1. 10.
BIGTHANA, given by fortune, *Esther* 6. 2.

BIGTHAN, gift of fortune, *i.e.*, the sun. *Esth.* 2. 21, called also Bigthana, chap. 6. 2.

BIGVAI, happy, *Ezra* 2. 2, 14; 8. 14; *Neh.* 7. 7, 19; 10. 16.

BILDAD, son of contrition.

BILGAH, consolation, 1 *Chron.* 24. 14; *Neh.* 12. 5, 18.

BILGAI, consolation of the Lord, *Neh.* 10. 8.

BILHAH, who is old, troubled, or confused; or, which spreads itself.

BILSHAN, son of tongue, *i.e.*, eloquent, *Ezra* 2. 2; *Neh.* 7. 7. The Hebrews called a talkative man, *Ish shepayim*, a man of lips.

BIMHAL, son of corruption, 1 *Chron.* 7. 33.

BINEA, gushing forth, 1 *Chron.* 8. 37; 9. 43.

BIRSHA, son of wickedness. *Gen.* 14. 2.

BITHIAH, daughter of the Lord, 1 *Chron.* 4. 18.

BITHRON, division; or, in his examination; or, daughter of the song; or, the habitation of the song, or of anger, or of liberty, 2 *Sam.* 2. 29.

BITHYNIA, violent precipitation; *from the Greek word βία, violence, and the verb θύνω, I make haste.*

BIZTHA, eunuch, *Esther* 1. 10.

BLASTUS, one that sprouts and brings forth.

BOANERGES, the sons of thunder, James and John, the sons of Zebedee.

BOAZ or BOOZ, in a strength, or in the goat.

BOCHIM, the place of weeping, or of mourners, or of mulberry trees.

BOZEZ, mud, bog; or, in him the flower. *The name of a rock,* 1 *Sam.* 14. 4.

BOZRAH, fortification.

BUL, changeable, perishing. *The name of a month.*

BUZ, despised, or plundered.

BUZI, my contempt.

BUZITE, a descendant from Buz.

C.

CABBON, cake, *Josh.* 15. 40.

CABUL, fetter.

CAIAPHAS, a searcher; or, he that seeks with diligence.

CAIN, possession, or possessed.

CAINAN, possessor, or purchaser; or, one that laments; or, the builder of a nest.

CALAH, old age, completion. *A city, Gen.* 10. 12.

CALEB, a dog, or crow, or a basket; or, as the heart.

CALEB-EPHRATAH, *a place so called by a conjunction of the names of Caleb and his wife Ephratah.* See EPHRATAH.

CALNEH, fortified dwellings.

CALNO, fortified dwellings.

CALVARY, the place of a skull. *So called because it was a place of executions, where criminals expiated their crimes, and so rolled away their sin from the nation; but it was. chiefly in reference to the death of Christ, who there rolled away the sins of the world.*

CAMON, his resurrection.

CANA, "place of reeds," *i.e.*, full of reeds.

CANAAN. a merchant, a trader. *He was the son of Ham, and gave name to the land of Canaan. The Canaanites were a wicked people, for they descended from a wicked father, Gen.* 13. 7.

CANAANITE.

CANDACE, queen or ruler of children.

CAPERNAUM, village of consolation. It was on the western side of the Lake of Gennesereth.

CAPHTOR, a sphere, a crown, a palm.

CAPPADOCIA, *in Hebrew,* CAPHTOR, *which see.*

CARCAS, eagle, *Esther* 1. 10.

CARCHEMISH, fortress of Chemosh.

CARMEL, fruitful field, the same as the Hebrew appellation.

CARMELITE.

CARMI, vine-dresser.

CARPUS, fruit, or fruitful. *Greek.*

CASIPHIA, silver of the Lord, or covetousness.

CASTOR and POLLUX, sons of Zeus, *Acts* 28. 11.

CEDRON, black, or sad; turbid.

CENCHREA, millet, small pulse.

CEPHAS, a rock, or stone.

CESAR. *a Latin name, from the word cædo,*

cut, because he was out out of his mother's womb; or from the word Cæsaries, a head of hair, which he is said to have been born with.

CESAREA, a bush of hair.

CHALCOL, who nourishes, consumes, and sustains the whole.

CHALDEA, as it were demons, or fields.

CHALDEAN.

CHALDEES.

CHANAAN, merchant, low, *Acts* 7. 11; 13. 19.

CHARASHIM, craftsman, 1 *Chron.* 4. 14; *Neh.* 11. 35.

CHARRAN, very dry, parched.

CHEBAR, abundant, *Ezek.* 10. 15, 20.

CHEDORLAOMER, handful of sheaves; otherwise, the roughness of the sheaf, *Gen.* 14. 4.

CHELAL, completion, *Ezra* 10. 30.

CHELUB, binding together, 1 *Chron.* 4. 11; 27. 26.

CHELUBAI, binding together of the Lord, 1 *Chron.* 2. 9.

CHEMARIMS, *the name of Baal's priests.*

CHEMOSH, of the swift, *i.e.*, the sun.

CHENANIA, preparation, or disposition, or strength, or rectitude of the Lord.

CHEREETHIMS, who cuts, who tears away and exterminates.

CHEREETHITES, see CHERETHIMS.

CHERITH, cutting, piercing, slaying.

CHESED, increase, *Gen.* 22. 22.

CHESIL, orion, constellations, *Josh.* 15. 30.

CHESULLOTH, confidences, *Josh.* 19. 18.

CHIDON, great distinction, 1 *Chron.* 13. 9.

CHILEAB, totality of the father, or the perfection of the father, 2 *Sam.* 3. 3.

CHILION, pining, consuming.

CHILMAD, as teaching or learning.

CHIMHAM, great desire.

CHINNERETH, harp, *Num.* 34. 11; *Deut.* 3. 17; *Josh.* 13. 27; 19. 35.

CHINNEROTH, harps, *Josh.* 11. 2; 12. 3; 1 *Kings* 15. 20.

CHIOS, snow.

CHISLEU, rashness, confidence, the flanks.

CHITTIM, those that bruise; or, gold; or, staining or dyeing.

CHIUN, an Egyptian god, supposed to be the wife of Saturn.

CHLOE, green herb.

CHORAZIN, proclamations.

CHUN, firm, 1 *Chron.* 18. 8.

CHUSHAN-RISHATHAIM, Ethiopian; or, blackness of iniquities.

CHUZA, the seer, or prophet; or Ethiopian. *The husband of Joanna.*

CILICIA, rough.

CIS, snaring, *Acts* 13. 21.

CLAUDA, a broken voice, a lamentable voice. *It is an island, Acts* 27. 16.

CLAUDIA, lame, 2 *Tim.* 4. 21.

CLEMENT, mild, good, modest, merciful, *Phil.* 4. 3.

CLEOPHAS, the whole glory; or, glory altogether.

CNIDUS, nettle or desire, *Acts* 27. 7.

COLOSSE, punishment, correction; *from the word κολάζω, I punish.*

CONIAH, the strength or stability of the Lord.

CONIAH, established of the Lord.

CONONIAH, established of the Lord.

COOS, woolly fleece, *Acts* 21. 1.

CORINTH, horn, *i.e.*, strong.

CORINTHIANS.

CORNELIUS, of a horn. *Or κορήλιος, as if it were κέρας τοῦ ἡλίς.* the beam of the sun.

COSAM, most abundant, snaring of birds, *Luke* 3. 28.

COZ, a thorn, 1 *Chron.* 4. 8.

COZBI, lying.

COZBI, a liar; or, as sliding away.

CRESCENS, growing, increasing.

CRETE, belonging to the sun, *denominated from the Curetes, the ancient priests of the Isle, who were sun worshippers.*

CRETES.

CRETIANS.

CRISPUS, curled.

CUSH, Ethiopians, or black.

CUSHAN, Ethiopia, black, blackness, heat.

CUSHI, the same.

CYPRUS, fair, or fairness.

CYRENE, κυρήνη, the fountain of the sun, a corrup. of *kure*, Ceres, the God of fire, and called by the Cnidians, *kura*, *i.e.*, the sun; and the Heb. *en*, fountain.

CYRENIANS, *people of Cyrene.*

CYRENIUS, who governs.

CYRUS, the sun. *Ctesias says, He was denominated Cyrus from the sun, which was so called.*

D.

DABAREH, a sheep walk.

DABBASHETH, "bunch" of acorns.

DABERATH, word, thing; or, a bee; or, submissive and obedient.

DAGON, corn; or, a fish.

DALMANUTHA, widowhood, exhaustion, leanness, branch. *A country, Mark* 8. 10.

DALMATIA, deceitful lamps, or vain brightness.

DAMARIS, a little wife.

DAMASCUS, 1. activity; 2. silent habitation; 3. blood drawn out; 4. blood mingled, *i.e.*, a place made up of different races of men; or, 5. pearl of possession. *The derivation of this word is very uncertain, as it is differently spelt in the original in various places of Scripture; but the above are literal interpretations of the name according to the five Hebrew forms of the name.*

DAN, judgment, or he that judges.

DANIEL, judgment of God; or, God is my judge. *A prophet descended from the royal family of David, who was carried captive to Babylon when he was very young. He was favoured with the vision of the four beasts, and of the ram and he-goat; Gabriel informed him of the seventy weeks, which is a famous prophecy of the time of the coming of the Messiah.*

DANJAAN, judge of woodland.

DANNAH, low branch.

DARA, of the companion; or, race of wickedness, 1 *Chron.* 2. 6.

DARDA, pearl of wisdom.

DARIUS, a restrainer. *The king of the Medes,* Dan. 5. 31.

DARKON, thrusting through.

DATHAN, belonging to a fountain.

DAVID, beloved, dear. *The son of Jesse, the king of Judah and Israel, who was a great type of the Messiah, the King and spiritual head of his church. It is taken for Christ himself, who was descended of the family of David,* Jer. 30. 9; Ezek. 34. 23; 37. 24, 25.

DEBIR, an oracle.

DEBORAH, eloquent, or a bee.

DECAPOLIS, *a Greek word compounded of two others, of δεκά, ten, and πόλις, a city, because this country contained ten cities.*

DEDAN, leading forward.

DEDANIM, the descendants of Dedan.

DELILAH, drawn up of the Lord.

DELILAH, delicate.

DEMAS, popular, ruler of people.

DEMETRIUS, belonging to Ceres, or to corn.

DERBE, juniper. *The name of a city,* Acts 14. 6.

DEUEL, invocation of God, *Num.* 1. 14.

DIANA, or Artemis, 1. the moon; 2. great mother; 3. nourisher. *The Latin word may signify luminous; the Greek word ἄρτεμις signifies perfect.*

DIBON, weeping.

DIBON-GAD, abundance of sons, happy and powerful; or, happy, or great understanding, or edifice.

DIBRI, promise of the Lord.

DIDYMUS, a twin.

DIKLAH, a palm tree.

DIMON, where it is red, or dunghill.

DINAH, judgment, or who judges.

DINHABAH, his judgment in her, or she gives judgment; or, who gives judgment, *Gen.* 36. 32.

DIONYSIUS, the bright god, *i.e.*, the sun.

DIONYSIUS, divinely touched, *from διος, divine, and νύω, I strike.*

DIOTREPHES, nourished by Jupiter, or Jupiter's foster-child; *from διος, of Jupiter, and τρεφος, a foster-child.*

DODAI, beloved of the Lord.

DODANIM, leaders.

DODAVAH, love of the Lord.

DOEG, who acts with uneasiness, or fearful.

DOPHKAH, knocking.

DOR, generation, or habitation.

DORCAS, the female of a roebuck. *Greek.*

DOTHAN, two customs.

DRUSILLA, watered by the dew, *from δροσός, the dew.*

DUMAH, silence, or resemblance.

DURAH, generation, or habitation.

E.

EASTER, the passover, *a feast of the Jews. This word is not properly translated, for in the original, Acts 12. 4, it is* το πάχα, *which signifies the pass-over; which was a yearly feast among the Jews, established in commemoration of the coming forth out of Egypt, and of the angel's passing by and sparing the houses of the Israelites sprinkled with blood, when the first-born of the Egyptians were slain. Easter was a goddess of the Saxons, in honour of whom sacrifices were offered about that time of the year. The word Easter seems not to have been properly used in the English Bible or English Liturgy.*

EBAL, stone, heap of barrenness.

EBED, servant, *i.e.,* of God.

EBED-MELECH, servant of the king.

EBENEZER, stone of help.

EBER, he who passed over.

EBIASAPH, father of increase, 1 Chron. 6. 23, 37; 9. 19.

EBRONAH, passage of the sea, Num. 33. 34, 35.

ED, witness.

EDAR, EDER, flock, Gen. 35. 21; Josh. 15. 21; 1 Chron. 23. 23; 24. 30.

EDÆN, Paradise, a place of delight.

EDEN, pleasure, *or* delight.

EDOM, red.

EDOMITE.

EDREI, strong arm. *The city of Og,* Num. 21. 33; Deut. 1. 4; 3. 1, 10; Josh. 12. 4; 13. 12, 31.

EGLAH, a girl, heifer, chariot, round.

EGLAIM, drops of the sea.

EGLON, *the same as* EGLAH.

EGYPT, *in Hebrew,* Mizraim, land of Egypt, *or* Koft *or* Coft: and may be interpreted hollow land, or land of depression, or hidden land. The Copts called it Elkibit, inundated land; and this idea is in all the kindred roots. It was also called Mizraim, two-fold depression, and also the land of Ham, and Khemi, black land.

EGYPTIAN.

EHUD, joining togethe

EKRON. barrenness, tore away.

EKRONITES.

ELAH, an oak, a curse, oath, imprecation.

ELAM, a virgin; *or,* hidden.

ELAMITES.

ELATH, a hind, *or* strength, *or* an oak.

ELBETHEL, the God of Bethel.

ELDAD, loved of God, *or* favoured of God.

ELEALEH, ascension of God, *or* burnt-offering of God.

ELEAZAR, the help of God, *or* court of God.

EL-ELOHE, Israel, God the God of Israel.

ELHANAN, grace, gift *or* mercy of God.

ELI, ELI, my God, my God.

ELI, a foster son.

ELIAB, God my father, *or* my God father.

ELIADA, whom God knows.

ELIAKIM, God will set up.

ELIAM, the people of God, *or* the God of the people.

ELIAS. *See* ELIJAH. God Lord, *or* strength of the Lord.

ELIASHIB, whom God will bring back.

ELIATHAH, thou art my God; *or,* my God comes. *The son of Haman,* 1 Chron. 25. 4, 27.

ELIENAI, God of my eyes, 1 Chron. 8. 20.

ELIEZER, God of help.

ELIHOREPH, the God of reward, *i.e.,* gathering fruits.

ELIHU, he is my God himself.

ELIHUD, God is my praise, *or* the praise of my God.

ELIJAH, God the Lord; *or* the strong Lord.

ELIKA, God of the congregation, 2 Sam. 23. 25.

ELIM, strong oaks, perhaps a grove of oaks was there.

ELIMELECH, my God is king.

ELIOENAI, God the Lord of my eyes, to whom my eyes are directed, 1 Chron. 3. 23, 24; 4. 36; 7. 8; 26. 3; Ezra 8. 4; 10. 22, 27; Neh. 12. 41.

ELIPHALET, the God of deliverance; *or,* my God who puts to flight.

ELIPHAZ, my God is gold.

ELISABETH, God is the oath of her, *i.e.,* she worships the Lord God; God hath sworn the oath of God, *or* the fulness of God.

ELISHA, God the Saviour, salvation of God, *or* God that saves. *The name of a prophet whom Elijah anointed in his room,* 1 Kings 19. 16.

ELISHAH, God the Saviour, son of Javan, Gen. 10. 4. *Or the isles of* Elishah, Ezek. 27. 7.

ELISHAMAH, God hearing, *or* my God will hear.

ELISHAPHAT, God the judge.

ELISHEBA. *See* ELISABETH.

ELISHEBA, God of the seven, *or* oath of my God.

ELISHUA, God the rich.

ELIZUR, God is my strength, my rock; *or,* stone, *or* rock of God. *Num.* 1. 5; 2. 10; 7. 30, 35; 10. 18.

ELKANAH, God has redeemed.

ELMODAM, the God of measure; *or,* Immeasurable.

ELNAAM, God of pleasantness, 1 Chron. 11. 46.

ELNATHAN, God has given, *or* the gift of God.

ELON, oak, *or* grove, *or* strong.

ELPAAL, God the maker, 1 Chron. 8. 11, 12, 18.

ELTEKEH, God-fearing, Josh. 19. 44; 21. 23.

ELTEKON, God the foundation, Josh. 15. 59.

ELUL, cry, outcry. *The sixth month of the Hebrew year.*

ELUZAI, God of my congregation, *i.e.,* of my family, 1 Chron. 12. 5.

ELYMAS, *this name in Arabic signifies a magician.*

ELZABAD, God gave, 1 Chron. 12. 12; 26.7.

EMIMS, fears of terrors; *or,* formidable, *or* people.

EMMANUEL, God with us, a mysterious name of our blessed Lord.

EMMAUS, people despised, *or* obscure.

EMMOR, an ass.

ENDOR, fountain of habitation.

ENEAS, laudable, *from the Greek verb* αἰνέω, I praise.

EN-EGLAIM, the fountain of the two calves.

EN-GANNIM, fountain of the gardens, Josh. 15. 34; 19. 21; 21. 29.

EN-GEDI, fountain of the goat, *or* of happiness.

EN-HADDAH, fountain of celerity, *i.e.,* flowing quickly, Josh. 19. 21.

EN-HAKKORE, fountain of calling, *or* of prayer, Judg. 15. 19.

EN-HAZOR, fountain of Hazor, Josh. 19. 37.

EN-MISHPAT, fountain of judgment, Gen. 14. 7.

ENOCH, dedicated, *or* disciplined and well regulated.

ENON, cloud *or* mass of darkness; *or,* his fountain; *or,* his eye.

ENOS, frail, fallen man, subject to all kind of evil in soul and body.

EN-RIMMON, fountain of the pomegranate, Neh. 11. 29.

EN-ROGEL, fountain of the fuller.

EN-SHEMESH, fountain of the sun, *or* sacred to the sun, Josh. 15. 7; 18. 17.

EN-TAPPUAH, fountain of the apple tree, Josh. 17. 7.

EPAPHRAS, favoured by Venus, *i.e.,* handsome, syncopated form of Epaphroditus.

EPAPHRODITUS, agreeable, handsome. *One whom Paul sent to the Philippians.*

EPENETUS, laudable, worthy of praise. *One of the first who embraced the gospel in Asia.*

EPHAH, darkness.

EPHER, a young hart, Gen. 25. 4; 1 Chron. 1. 33; 4. 17; 5. 24.

EPHES-DAMMIM, the portion *or* effusion of blood, *or* drop of blood, of grapes.

EPHESIANS, *the people of Ephesus.*

EPHESUS, city of the moon, *i.e.,* sacred to Artemis, *or* the moon. *The derivation is obscure, but it is most probably the true meaning, from the fact that it was sacred to the moon, and, moreover, its modern Turkish name, Asalook, has that meaning.*

EPHPHATHA, be opened.

EPHRAIM, twofold increase, *or* that brings fruit, *or* that grows.

EPHRAIMITE.

EPHRATAH, abundance, *or* bearing fruit, *or* increasing. *It is believed that the city* Ephratah, *otherwise called* Beth-lehem, *took its name from* Ephratah, *Caleb's wife.*

EPHRATH, *see* EPHRATAH.

EPHRATHITE, *an inhabitant of* Ephratah, *or a descendant from* Ephraim.

EPHRON, a great and choice fawn.

EPICUREANS, who give assistance; *from the Greek word* ἐπικουρέω, I help, I assist. *A sect of heathen philosophers. This sect of philosophers was founded by Epicurus, a most voluminous writer. Diogenes Laertes says he left three hundred volumes of writings, but they are almost all lost. St. Paul, while at Athens, encountered the followers of this absurd egotist, and in his sublime, wonderful, and unanswerable speech, he overturned all the schools of Gentile ethics, and more especially that of the Epicureans and Stoics, because they were most opposed to Christianity, and whose ethical systems Tertullian sums up in two words, "Zenois vigor et Zenonis stupor."*

ER, watcher, watch, *or* enemy.

ERAN, watchful, Num. 26. 36.

ERASTUS, lovely, *or* amiable.

ERECH, length, *or* which lengthens: *otherwise,* health, physic. *A city,* Gen. 10. 10.

ESAIAS, salvation of the Lord. ISAIAH.

ESAR-HADDON, gift of fire.

ESAU, covered with hair, hairy.

ESEK, contention.

ESH-BAAL, the fire of the Baal, 1 Chron. 8. 33.

ESHBAN, very red, Gen. 36. 26; 1 Chron. 1. 41.

ESHCOL, a bunch of grapes.

ESHEAN, support, Josh. 15. 52.

ESHEK, oppression, 1 Chron. 8. 39.

ESHTAOL, stout, strong woman. Josh. 15. 33; 19. 41; Judg. 13. 25; 16. 31; 18. 2, 8, 11.

ESHTEMOA, woman of fame. Josh. 15. 50; 21. 14; 1 Sam. 30. 28; 1 Chron. 4. 17, 19; 6. 57.

ESHTON, womanly, 1 Chron. 4. 11, 12.

ESLI, near me; *otherwise,* he that separates.

ESROM, the dart of joy; *or,* division of the song.

ESTHER, a star, a Jewish maiden. *When King Ahasuerus divorced his queen, he caused all the beautiful women in his dominions to be brought before him, among whom was the Jewish maiden, Hodassah, who being so beautiful, he made her his queen, and called her Sitarah, a star, which in the Greek is* Aster, *and Heb.* Ester.

ETAM, ravenous bird. 1 Chron. 4. 3.

ETHAM, boundary of the sea, an Egyptian name.

ETHAN, strong; *or,* the gift of the island

ETHANIM, strong, *or* valiant. *The seventh month of the ecclesiastical year of the Hebrews.*

ETHBAAL, with Baal; *or,* he that rules and possesses. 1 Kings 16. 31.

ETHER, abundance, Josh. 15. 42; 19. 7.

ETHIOPIA, *in Hebrew* Cush, blackness; *in Greek it signifies* heat, burning : *from* αἴθω, I burn, *and* ὄψις, face.

ETHIOPIAN, ETHIOPIANS.

ETHNAN, gift, 1 Chron. 4. 7.

EUBULUS, a prudent and good counsellor. *Greek.*

EUNICE, good victory.

EUODIAS, sweet scent, *or* that smells sweet.

EUPHRATES, fertilizing, fruitful.

EUROCLYDON, a tempestuous wind, Acts 27. 14.

EUTYCHUS, happy, fortunate; *from* εὐ, good, *and* τύχη, fortune.

EVE, life.

EVIL MERODACH, the fool of Merodach.

EZBAI, spoils, 1 Chron. 11. 37.

EZBON, great beauty, Gen. 46. 16; 1 Chron. 7. 7.

EZEKIAS, strength of the Lord, Matt. 1. 9, 10.

EZEKIEL, the strength of God, *or* supported of God, *or* God is my strength.

EZEL, going abroad.

EZION-GEBER, the backbone of a man, *or* of the strong; *or,* counsel of the man. *A city,* 1 Kings 9. 26.

EZRA, a helper. *He wrote the book of Ezra, wherein we have the history of the return from Babylon to Jerusalem, after the seventy years' captivity. Zerubbabel restored the temple; Ezra, the worship of God; Nehemiah, the city of Jerusalem.*

F.

FAIR-HAVENS, good ports. *The Greek name is* Καλοὶ λιμένες, *Acts* 27. 8.

FELIX, happy, or prosperous.
FESTUS, festival, or joyful.
FORTUNATUS, fortunate, prosperous.

G.

GAAL, loathing.
GAASH, shaking, earthquake, commotion, tumult, or overthrow. A mountain, Josh. 24. 30; Judg. 2. 9; 2 Sam. 23. 30; 1 Chron. 11. 32.
GABA, hill, Josh. 18. 24; Ezra 2. 26; Neh. 7. 30.
GABBAI, an exactor of tribute. Syrian word, Neh. 11. 8.
GABBATHA, pavement. In Greek lithostrotus, paved with stones; from λίθος, a stone, and στρωτός, paved.
GABRIEL, man of God, or strength of God, or my strong God.
GAD, a band, or happy, or armed and prepared.
GADARENES, surrounded, walled.
GADDI, troop of God; otherwise, a kid. The son of Susi, Num. 13. 11.
GADDIEL, troop of God; or, the Lord is my happiness, or my army. Num. 13. 10.
GADITES.
GAIUS, joy, gladness.
GALATIA, Gallo Græcia.
GALATIANS.
GALBANUM, a sort of gum or sweet spice.
GALEED, the heap of witness.
GALILEE, wheel, revolution, or revolution of the wheel.
GALILEANS.
GALLIM, who heap up, who cover, who roll.
GALLIO, revel; an imitator of the Galli or priests of Cybele.
GAMALIEL, recompence of God, or camel of God, or weaned of God.
GAMMADIMS, soldiers placed in the towers of Turus. The word in Hebrew signifies a cubit, whence some call them pigmies, or dwarfs. Others think that the word is Syriac, and signifies bold and courageous men. Others say they were men who came from Gammade, a town of Phenicia.
GATAM, great fatigue; or, their touch; or, the lowing of the perfect. Grandson of Esau, Gen. 36. 11, 16; 1 Chron. 1. 36.
GATH, wine-press.
GATH-RIMMON, wine-press of the pomegranate.
GAZA, strong, fortified. It was also called Azzah, heat, fire, i.e., the sun, and its people were sun worshippers.
GAZEZ, shearer, 1 Chron. 2. 46.
GAZZAM, violently torn off, Ezra 2. 48; Neh. 7. 51.
GEBA, a hill, or cup.
GEBAL, bound, or limit.
GEBIM, pits, Isa. 10. 31.
GEDALIAH, God is my greatness; or, magnified of the Lord.
GEDER, a wall, Josh. 12. 13.
GEDEROTH, fortifications, folds, Josh. 15. 41; 2 Chron. 28. 18.
GEHAZI, valley of sight.
GEMALLI, camel possessor, Num. 13. 12.
GEMARIAH, completion, or accomplishment of the Lord.
GENNESARET, harp, or the garden of the prince; otherwise, protection of the prince, or of him that governs.
GENUBATH, theft, robbery; or, garden, or, protection of the daughter, 1 Kings 11. 20.
GERA, termination.
GERAH, the twentieth part of a shekel.
GERAR. See GERA.
GERGESENES, those who come from pilgrimage, or from fight. A people beyond Galilee.
GERIZIM, cutters-down.
GERSHOM, a stranger there; or, a traveller of reputation.
GERSHON, his banishment; or, the change of pilgrimage.
GESHUR, exile, expulsion.
GESHURITES.
GETHER, fear, the vale of trial; or of searching; or, the press of inquiry, or of contemplation. The son of Aram, Gen. 10. 23; 1 Chron. 1. 17.
GETHSEMANE, a very fat valley; or, the valley of oil.
GIAH, to guide, draw out, produce; breaking forth, of a fountain.

GIBBAR, hero, Ezra 2. 20.
GIBBETHON, a lofty place, Josh. 19. 44; 21. 23; 1 Kings 15. 27; 16. 15, 17.
GIBEAH, a hill.
GIBEONITES, people of Gibeon.
GIDDALTI, I have trained up, 1 Chron. 25. 4, 29.
GIDEON, he that bruises and breaks; or, cutting off iniquity.
GIDEONI. See GIDEON.
GIHON, great eruption of waters, valley of grace; or, breast, or impetuous.
GILBOA, bubbling water of a fountain.
GILEAD, perpetual fountain.
GILEADITES.
GILGAL, rolling away, so called from the circumcision of the Israelites, for it was the rolling away of the reproach of Egypt from off them; from galal, to call away.
GILOH, exodus of a great multitude; that overturns, that passes, that reveals, or discovers. A city, Josh. 15. 51; 2 Sam. 15. 12.
GILONITE.
GIMZO, sycamores, 2 Chron. 28. 18.
GINATH, similitude, 1 Kings 16. 21, 22.
GINNETHON, gardener, Neh. 10. 6; 12. 4, 16.
GIRGASHITE, who arrives from pilgrimage, dwellers on a clayey soil.
GISPA, soothing, Neh. 11. 21.
GITTAIM, two wine-presses, 2 Sam. 4. 3; Neh. 11. 33.
GITTITE, a wine-press.
GIZONITE, stone quarrier, 1 Chron. 11. 34.
GOB, snare, pit.
GOG, roof, covering, extension.
GOLAN, passage, or revolution, great exodus.
GOLGOTHA, place of skulls, as it was the spot where criminals were executed, and where they expiated their crimes, and so rolled away their sin from the nation.
GOLIATH, exile. A giant slain by David.
GOMER, complete, accomplish; otherwise, consuming, a consumer.
GOMORRAH, a rebellious people; or, the people that fear.
GOSHEN, the peace or temple of the sun, for Gozan; drawing near.
GOZAN, fleece, or pasture; or, who nourishes the body; cut through.
GRECIA, the country of the Greeks.
GRECIANS.
GREECE, beyond.
GREEK.
GREEKS.
GUNI, my garden, Gen. 46. 24; Num. 26. 48; 1 Chron. 5. 15; 7. 13.
GUR, sojourning, dwelling, assembly, or fear.

H.

HABAIAH, hidden of the Lord, Ezra 2. 61; Neh. 7. 63.
HABAKKUK, he that embraces, or a wrestler, Hab. 1. 1; 3. 1.
HABOR, uniting together, 2 Kings 17. 6; 18. 11; 1 Chron. 5. 26.
HACHALIAH, dark-flashing of the Lord, Neh. 1. 1; 10. 1.
HACHILAH, my hope is in her; or, hook in her.
HACHMONI, very wise, 1 Chron. 27. 32.
HADAD, chief, most eminent, a title of the kings of Syria. The god of Rimmon was styled Adad. It was originally a title of the sun. It signified THE FIRST. Gen. 36. 35, 36; 1 Kings 11. 14, 17, 19, 21, 25; 1 Chron. 1. 30, 46, 47, 50. 51.
HADADEZER, whose help is Hadad.
HADADRIMMON, bursting of the pomegranate. Rimmon was a god of the Syrians; the invocation of the god Rimmon.
HADAR, ornament; chamberer, Gen. 25. 15; 36. 39.
HADAREZER, majesty of help.
HADASSAH, a myrtle, or joy.
HADORAM, their beauty, their noble generation, their power, their cloke; or, praise, or a cry lifted up.
HADRACH, point, spherical.
HAGAB, grasshopper, Ezra 2. 46.
HAGABAH, grasshopper, Ezra 2. 45; Neh. 7. 48.
HAGAR, a stranger, or, that fears; flight.
HAGARENES, of the family of Hagar.
HAGARITES, the same.
HAGGAI, festival of the Lord.

HAGGITH, rejoicing.
HALLELUIAH, praise the Lord or praise to the Lord.
HAM, hot, heat, or black.
HAMAN, noise, tumult; or, he that prepares.
HAMATH, a wall, or a defence.
HAMMATH, warm baths, Josh. 19. 35.
HAMMEDATHA, twin.
HAMMOLEKETH, queen, 1 Chron. 7. 18.
HAMON-GOG, the multitude of Gog.
HAMOR, an ass, or clay, or wine.
HAMUEL, heat of God, 1 Chron. 4. 26.
HAMUTAL, akin to the dew, 2 Kings 23. 31; 24. 18; Jer. 52. 1.
HANAMEEL, gift of God.
HANANEEL, grace, mercy, gift of God.
HANANI, graciously given of the Lord.
HANANIAH, grace, or gift of the Lord.
HANNAH. gracious, merciful; or, taking rests. The wife of Elkanah, and mother of Samuel.
HANOCH, dedicated, initiated.
HANUM, gracious, merciful; or, he that rests.
HARA, mountainous, 1 Chron. 5. 26.
HARADAH, fear (of an host), Num. 33. 24, 25.
HARAN, mountaineer, or mountainous country. The son of Terah.
HARAN, a place. See CHARRAN.
HARARITE, mountaineer, 2 Sam. 23. 11, 33; 1 Chron. 11. 34, 35.
HARBONAH, his destruction, or his sword, or his dryness; or, the anger of him that builds, or that understandeth.
HAREPH, maturity, i.e., the flower of life, 1 Chron. 2. 51.
HARETH, a cutting, 1 Sam. 22. 5.
HAROD, astonishment, fear, trembling.
HAROEH, a seer, 1 Chron. 2. 52.
HAROSHETH, manufactures, i.e., cutting and carving. Or, vessel of earth, or forest.
HARSHA, enchanter, Ezra 2. 52; Neh. 7. 54.
HARUM, high, i.e., illustrious, 1 Chron. 4. 8.
HARUMAPH, flat-nosed, Neh. 3. 10.
HARUPHITE, matured, 1 Chron. 12. 5.
HASADIAH, love of the Lord, 1 Chron. 3. 20.
HASHABIAH, esteemed of the Lord, 1 Chron. 6. 45; 9. 14; 25. 3; 26. 30; 27. 17; 2 Chron. 35. 9; Ezra 8. 19, 24; Neh. 3. 17; 10. 11; 11. 15, 22; 12. 21, 24.
HASHABNIAH, esteemed of the Lord, Neh. 3. 10; 9. 5.
HASHBADANA, reason, thought, Neh. 8. 4.
HASHEM, dull, 1 Chron. 11. 34.
HASHMONAH, very fat, Num. 33. 29.
HASHUM, great, wealthy, Ezra 2. 19; 10. 33; Neh. 7. 22; 8. 4; 10. 18.
HATACH, gift, Esther 4. 5, 6, 9, 10.
HATATH, terror.
HATIPHA, seized, Ezra 2. 54; Neh. 7. 56.
HATITA, digging, exploring, Ezra 2. 42; Neh. 7. 45.
HATTIL, ingratitude, Ezra 2. 57; Neh. 7. 59.
HAURAN, very white, Ezek. 47. 16, 18.
HAVILAH, that suffers pain; that brings forth; or, that speaks, or declares to her, Gen. 2. 11; 10. 7, 29; 25. 18; 1 Sam. 15. 7; 1 Chron. 1. 9, 23.
HAVOTH-JAIR, the villages that enlighten, or that show forth light, Num. 32. 41; Deut. 3. 14; Judg. 10. 4.
HAZAEL, he who sees God.
HAZAIAH, sun of the Lord, Neh. 11. 5.
HAZAR ADDAR, villages of greatness, Num. 34. 4.
HAZAR ENAN, villages of fountains, Num. 34. 9, 10; Ezek. 47. 17; 48. 1.
HAZAR GADDAH, village of fortune, Josh. 15. 27.
HAZARMAVETH, court, or dwelling of death. The son of Joktan. Gen. 10. 26; 1 Chron. 1. 20.
HAZAR SHUAL, village of the fox, Josh. 15. 28; 19. 3; 1 Chron. 4. 28; Neh. 11. 27.
HAZELELPONI, the shadow looking at me, shade, and sorrow of countenance; or submersion of the face.
HAZEROTH, villages, hamlets; court, or porch.
HAZIEL, vision of God, 1 Chron. 23. 9.
HAZOR, court, or fence.
HAZOR HADATTAH, new castle, Josh. 15. 25.
HEBER, fellowship.
HEBREWS, descended from Eber.
HEBRON, society, confederation.

HEGAI, or HEGE, venerable, Esth. 2. 3, 8, 15.

HELAH, scum, 1 Chron. 4. 5, 7.

HELAM an army.

HELBON, milk, or fatness.

HELDAI, life.

HELEB, fat, i.e., fertile, 2 Sam. 23. 29.

HELED, life, duration, 1 Chron. 11. 30.

HELEG, justice.

HELEM, robust, Zech. 6 14.

HELEPH, exchange, Josh. 19. 33.

HELEZ, liberation, 2 Sam. 23. 26; 1 Chron. 2. 39; 11. 27; 27. 10.

HELI, ascending, or climbing up.

HELI, strength of the Lord, Luke 3. 23.

HELKAI, portion of the Lord, Neh. 12. 15.

HELKATH, field of swords, Josh. 19. 25; 21. 31.

HELKATH-HAZZURIM, the field of strong men, of swords.

HEMAM, faithful, son of Lotan, Gen. 36. 22.

HEMDAN, desire, delight, Gen. 36. 26.

HEN, grace; or quiet, or rest.

HENA, a city of Mesopotamia; derivation unknown, 2 Kings 18. 34; 19. 13; Isa. 37. 13.

HENADAD, the favour of Hadad, Ezra 3. 9; Neh. 3. 18, 24; 10. 9.

HEPHER, a well, or pit, Num. 26. 32; 27. 1; Josh. 17. 2, 3; 1 Chron. 4. 6.

HEPHZI-BAH, my pleasure, or delight in her.

HERMAS, Mercury, a Greek name for 'Ερμῆς, Mercurius, in the N. T., Rom. 16. 14.

HERMES, Mercury, or grain, or the projector, as probably derived from the Heb. root haram, from the root ramah, to throw, to deceive, to beguile.

HERMOGENES, begotten of Mercury, or generation of lucre. Greek.

HERMON, anathema, destruction.

HERMONITES.

HEROD, a hero, or like a hero.

HERODIANS.

HERODIAS, the wife of Herod.

HERODION, song of Juno; from 'Ηρα, Juno, and ᾠδή, a song; or, the conqueror of heroes.

HESED, mercy, 1 Kings 4. 10.

HESHBON, reason, device.

HESHMON, very fat, Josh. 15. 27.

HETH, trembling, or fear.

HETHLON, hidden place, to wrap up. The name of a city, Ezek. 47. 15; 48. 1.

HEZEKI, strength, 1 Chron. 8. 17.

HEZEKIAH, strong in the Lord; or, taken and supported by the Lord.

HEZION, vision, 1 Kings 15. 18.

HEZIR, swine, 1 Chron. 24. 15; Neh. 10. 20.

HEZRAI, bulwark of the Lord, 2 Sam. 23. 35.

HEZRON, the dart of joy, or division of the song.

HIDDEKEL, sharp voice, or sound. Swift.

HIEL, God lives, or the life of God.

HIERAPOLIS, holy city; from ἱερὸν, holy, and πόλις, a city. Col. 4. 13.

HIGGAION, meditation, consideration.

HILKIAH, God is my portion; according to others, the Lord's gentleness.

HILLEL, he that praises. The father of Abdon, Judg. 12. 13, 15.

HINNOM, lamentation.

HIRAH, nobility, Gen. 38. 1, 12.

HIRAM, exaltation of life; or, their whiteness, or their liberty; or, he that destroys, or anathematizes.

HITTITES, who is broken, or fears. Descendants of Heth, the son of Canaan, Gen. 10. 15.

HIVITES, wicked, bad, or wickedness, Gen. 10. 17: 34. 2: 36. 2; Ex d. 3. 8; 13. 5; 23. 23, 28; 33. 2; 34. 11; Deut. 7. 1; 20. 17; Josh. 3. 10; 9. 1, 7; 11. 3, 19; 12. 8; 24. 11; Judg. 3. 3, 5; 2 Sam. 24. 7; 1 Kings 9. 20; 1 Chron. 1. 15; 2 Chron. 8. 7.

HOBAB, beloved, Num. 10. 29; Judg. 4. 11.

HOBAH, hiding-place, secrecy, Gen. 14. 15.

HOD, glory, 1 Chron. 7. 37.

HODAIAH, praise the Lord, 1 Chron. 3. 24

HODAVIAH, praise the Lord, 1 Chron. 5. 24; 9. 7; Ezra 2. 40.

HODESH, the new moon, i.e., beautiful as the new moon, 1 Chron. 8. 9.

HODIJAH, praise of the Lord, 1 Chron. 4. 19; Neh. 8. 7; 9. 5; 10. 10, 13, 18.

HOGLAH, partridge, boxer, Num. 26. 33; 27. 1; 36. 11; Josh. 17. 3.

HOHAM, a multitude of a multitude, Josh. 10. 3.

HOLAN, sandy.

HOPHNI, he that covers; or, my fist.

HOR, mountain, Num. 20. 22, 23, 25, 27; 21. 4; Deut. 32. 50.

HOREB, desert, solitude, destruction, dryness.

HOR-HAGIDGAD, the hill of thunder.

HORMAH, devoted or consecrated to God; utter destruction; anathema.

HORONAIM, two caverns.

HORONITE, anger, fury, or liberty.

HOSAH, a place of refuge, Josh. 19. 29; 1 Chron. 16. 38; 26. 10, 11, 16.

HOSEA and HOSHEA, saviour, or salvation.

HOSHAIAH, set free of the Lord, Neh. 12. 32; Jer. 42. 1; 43. 2.

HOTHAM, signet ring, 1 Chron. 7. 32; 11. 44.

HOTHIR, whom God let remain, 1 Chron. 25. 4, 28.

HUKKUK, appointed portion.

HULDAH, weasel, 2 Kings 22. 14; 2 Chron. 34. 22.

HUL, pain, infirmity, bringing forth children, sand, or expectation. The son of Aram, Gen. 10. 23; 1 Chron. 1. 17.

HUMTAH, a place of lizards, Josh. 15. 54.

HUR, hole, cavern.

HURAM, most noble, 1 Chron. 8. 5; 2 Chron. 2. 3, 12; 4. 11, 16.

HUSHAI, hasting of the Lord.

HUZZAB, molten.

HYMENEUS, nuptial, or marriage.

I.

IBHAR, whom He (scil. God) elects, 2 Sam. 5. 15; 1 Chron. 3. 6; 14. 5

IBLEAM, devouring the people, Josh. 17. 11; Judg. 1. 27; 2 Kings 9. 27.

IBNEIAH, he will be built up of the Lord, 1 Chron. 9. 8.

IBRI, beyond the river, 1 Chron. 24. 27.

IBZAN, great fatigue, Judg. 12. 8, 10.

ICHABOD, inglorious, or the glory is departed.

IDALAH, place of execution, Josh. 19. 15.

IDBASH, he will be as agreeable as honey, 1 Chron. 4. 3.

IDDO, great calamity, 1 Kings 4. 14; 1 Chron. 6. 21; 27. 21: 2 Chron. 9. 29: 12. 15; 13. 22; Ezra 5. 1; 6. 14; 8. 17; Neh. 12. 4, 16; Zech. 1. 1, 7.

IGDALIAH, the Lord will make great, Jer. 35. 4.

IGEAL, he will redeem, 1 Chron. 3 22

IIM, ruinous heaps, Num. 33. 45; Josh. 15. 29.

IJE-'ABARIM, ruins of Abarim, Num. 21. 11; 33. 44.

IJON. a great heap, 1 Kings 15. 20; 2 Kings 15. 29: 2 Chron. 16. 4.

IKKESH, perverse, 2 Sam. 23. 26; 1 Chron. 11. 28; 27. 9.

IMLA, he will fill up, 1 Kings 22. 8, 9; 2 Chron. 18. 7, 8.

IMMANUEL, God with us, Isa. 7. 14; 8. 8.

IMMER. He promised. i.e., the Lord, 1 Chron. 9. 12; 24. 14; Ezra 2. 37, 59; 10. 20; Neh. 3. 29; 7. 40, 61; 11. 13; Jer. 20. 1.

IMNAH, prosperity, 1 Chron. 7. 30; 2 Chron. 31. 14.

IMNA, God will restrain, 1 Chron. 7. 35.

IMRAH, he will extol himself, 1 Chron. 7. 36.

IPHEDEIAH, the Lord will redeem, 1 Chron. 8. 25.

IR, citizen, 1 Chron. 7. 12.

IR-NAHASH, city of serpents, 1 Chron. 4. 12.

IR-SHEMESH, city of the sun. Josh. 19. 41.

IRA, watchful, 2 Sam. 20. 26; 23. 26, 38; 1, Chron. 11. 28, 40; 27. 9.

IRAD, city of witness, Gen. 4. 18.

IRAM, belonging to a city, Gen. 36. 43; 1 Chron. 1. 54.

IRIJAH, he will see the Lord, Jer. 37. 13, 14.

IRON, pious, Josh. 19. 38.

IRPEEL, God will restore, Josh. 18. 27.

IRU, belonging to a city, 1 Chron. 4. 15.

ISAAC, he will laugh.

ISAIAH, salvation of the Lord.

ISCAH, she will look out, Gen. 11. 29.

ISHBAH, he will praise, 1 Chron. 4. 17.

ISHBAK, he will remain, Gen. 25. 2; 1 Chron. 1. 32.

ISHBI-BENOB, his seat is in the high place, 2 Sam. 21. 16.

ISH-BOSHETH, man of shame, 2 Sam. 2. 8, 10, 12, 15; 3. 8, 14, 15; 4. 5, 8, 12.

ISHI, salvation, 1 Chron. 2. 31; 4. 20, 42; 5. 24.

ISHIAH, ISSHIAH, ISHIJAH, gift of the Lord, 1 Chron. 7. 3; 24. 21, 25; Ezra 10. 31.

ISHMA, desolateness, i.e., unfortunate, 1 Chron. 4. 3.

ISHMAEL, he will hear God.

ISHMAIAH, he will hear the Lord, 1 Chron. 27. 19.

ISHMERAI, he will be kept of the Lord, 1 Chron. 8. 18.

ISHOD, man of beauty, 1 Chron. 7. 18.

ISHPAN, he will hide, 1 Chron. 8. 22.

ISHTOB, man of Tob, 2 Sam. 10. 6, 8.

ISHUAH, he will be equal, Gen. 46. 17; 1 Chron. 7. 30.

ISHUI, JESUI, ISHUAI, ISUI, equal, Gen. 46. 17; Num. 26. 44; 1 Sam. 14. 49; 1 Chron. 7. 30.

ISMACHIAH, supported of the Lord, 2 Chron. 31. 13.

ISPAH, he will be eminent, 1 Chron. 8. 16.

ISRAEL, he will be prince with God.

ISSACHAR, he is wages.

ITHAMAR, land of palm.

ITHIEL, God is with me, Neh. 11. 7; Prov. 30. 1.

ITHMAH, bereavedness, 1 Chron. 11. 46.

ITHNAN, stable, Josh. 15. 23.

ITHRAN, exalted, Gen. 36. 26; 1 Chron. 7. 41; 7. 37.

ITHREAM, exalted of the people, 2 Sam. 3. 5; 1 Chron. 3. 3.

ITTAH KAZIN, time of the judge, Josh. 19. 13.

ITTAI, nearness of the Lord, 2 Sam. 15. 19, 21, 22; 18. 2, 5, 12; 23. 29.

IVAH, overturned, 2 Kings 18. 34; 19. 13; Isa. 37. 13.

IZHAR, anointed, oil, Exod. 6. 18, 21; Num. 3. 19; 16. 1; 1 Chron. 6. 2, 18, 38; 23. 12, 18.

IZRAHIAH, brought to light of the Lord, 1 Chron. 7. 3.

IZRAHITE, he will be bright, 1 Chron. 27. 8.

J.

JAAKAN, twister, Deut. 10. 6; 1 Chron. 1. 42.

JAAKOBAH, a healer, a supplanter, 1 Chron. 4. 36.

JAALAM, he will be hid, or he will hide, Gen. 36. 5, 14, 18; 1 Chron. 1. 35.

JAANAI, the Lord hears, 1 Chron. 5. 12.

JAARE-OREGIM, tapestry of the weavers, 2 Sam. 21. 19.

JAASAU, made of the Lord, Ezra 10. 37

JAASIEL, made of God, 1 Chron. 11 47; 27. 21.

JAAZANIAH, he will be heard of the Lord.

JAAZER, JAZER, whom the Lord helps, Num. 21. 32; 32. 1, 3, 35; Josh. 13. 25; 21. 39; 2 Sam. 24. 5; 1 Chron. 6. 81; 26. 31; Isa. 16. 8, 9; Jer. 48. 32.

JAAZIAH, he is comforted of the Lord, 1 Chron. 24. 26, 27.

JAAZIEL, he is comforted of God, 1 Chron. 15. 18.

JABAL, leading, flowing.

JABBOK, emptying, pouring out.

JABESH, dry, arid.

JABEZ, he will cause pain, i.e., to his mother.

JABIN, he will understand.

JABNEEL, caused to be built of God, Josh. 15. 11; 19. 33.

JABNEH, will be built, i.e., he will be prospered, 2 Chron. 26. 6.

JACHAN, he will stir up, 1 Chron. 5. 13.

JACHIN, he will establish.

JACOB, he will trip up the heels; one who supplants; or trip up the heels as racers do; and as Jacob was named a supplanter, he fulfilled the prophecy in his nomination, for although he was the younger, yet he obtained the birthright, and from him descended He, in whom all the nations of the earth are blessed.

JADA, he knows, 1 Chron. 2. 28, 32.

JADDUA, celebrated, known, Neh. 10. 21; 12. 11, 22.

JADON, whom God will judge, Neh. 3. 7.

JAEL, ibex, or chamois.

JAGUE, lodging.

JAHATH, he will carry away.

JAHAZ, a round depressed place.

JAHAZIAH, he will see the Lord, Ezra 10. 15.

JAHAZIEL, he will be seen of God, 1 *Chron.* 12. 4; 16. 6; 23. 19; 24. 23; 2 *Chron.* 20. 14; *Ezra* 8. 5.

JAHDAI, he will be directed of the Lord, 1 *Chron.* 2. 47.

JAHDIEL, he will be made glad of God, 1 *Chron.* 5. 24.

JAHDO, his union, 1 *Chron.* 14. 5.

JAHLEEL, hope of God, *Gen.* 46. 14; *Num.* 26. 26.

JAHMAI, he will be guarded of the Lord, 1 *Chron.* 7. 2.

JAHZEEL, he will allot of God, *Gen.* 46. 24; *Num.* 26. 48; 1 *Chron.* 7. 13.

JAHZERAH, he will cause to return, 1 *Chron.* 9. 12.

JAIR (1), he will enlighten.

JAIR (2), he will embroider.

JAIRUS, he will enlighten, or he will diffuse light.

JAKEH, pious, fearing God, *Prov.* 30. 1.

JAKIM, He (*i.e.*, God) will set him up, 1 *Chron.* 8. 19; 24. 12.

JALON, abiding, 1 *Chron.* 4. 17.

JAMBRES, magician.

JAMES, supplanter, *from the Greek form of the Hebrew name Jacob. There were three persons in the New Testament who bore this name.*

JAMIN, right hand, *Gen.* 46. 10; *Ex.* 6. 15; *Num.* 26. 12; 1 *Chron.* 2. 27; 4. 24; *Neh.* 8. 7.

JAMLECH, He (*i.e.*, God) will be made to reign, 1 *Chron.* 4. 34.

JANNA, he will answer.

JANNES, full of pleasure, *or* full of favour, 2 *Tim.* 3. 8.

JANOAH, rest, 2 *Kings* 15. 29.

JANUM, sleep, *Josh.* 15. 53.

JAPHETH, enlargement.

JAPHIA, illustrious, *Josh.* 10. 3; 19. 12; 2 *Sam.* 5. 15; 1 *Chron.* 3. 7; 14. 6.

JAPHLET, whom God will free, 1 *Chron.* 7. 32, 33.

JAPHLETI, will be liberated of the Lord, *Josh.* 16. 3.

JAPHO, beautiful city, *Josh.* 19. 46.

JAREB, he will plead.

JARED, descent.

JARESIAH, he will be nourished of the Lord, 1 *Chron.* 8. 27.

JARHA, increasing moon, 1 *Chron.* 2. 34, 35.

JARIB, he will plead the cause, *Ezra* 8. 16; 10. 18; called Jachin, *Gen.* 46. 10, and *Ex.* 6. 15.

JARMUTH, high, *Josh.* 10. 3, 5, 23; 12. 11; 15. 35; 21. 29; *Neh.* 11. 29.

JAROAH, moon, 1 *Chron.* 5. 14.

JASHEN, sleeping, 2 *Sam.* 23. 32.

JASHER, vid. JESHER.

JASIEL, made of God; *same as* Jaasiel.

JASHOBEAM, he will return among the people, 1 *Chron.* 11. 11; 12. 6; 27. 2.

JASHUB, he will return, *Num.* 26. 24; 1 *Chron.* 7. 1; *Ezra* 10. 29.

JASHUBI-LEHEM, he is restored by bread.

JASON, healed.

JATHNIEL, he will be given of God, 1 *Chron.* 26. 2.

JATTIR, pre-eminent, lofty, *Josh.* 15. 48; 21. 14; 1 *Sam.* 30. 27; 1 *Chron.* 6. 57.

JAVAN, supple, clay, *Gen.* 10. 2, 4; 1 *Chron.* 1. 7; *Isa.* 66. 19; *Ezek.* 27. 13, 19

JAZIZ, he will bring abundance, 1 *Chron.* 27. 31.

JEARIM, forests.

JEATERAI, he will abound of the Lord, 1 *Chron.* 6. 21.

JEBERECHIAH, he will be blessed of the Lord, *Isa.* 8. 2.

JEBUS, treading down, *or* a place trodden down, *Josh.* 18. 16, 28; *Judg.* 19. 10, 11; 1 *Chron.* 11. 4, 5.

JECHOLIAH, made strong of the Lord, 2 *Kings* 15. 2; 2 *Chron.* 26. 3.

JECONIAH, he will be established of the Lord.

JEDAIAH (1), praise of the Lord; (2), known of the Lord, 1 *Chron.* 4. 37; 9. 10; 24. 7; *Ezra* 2. 36; *Neh.* 3. 10; 7. 39; 11. 10; 12. 6, 7, 19, 21; *Zech.* 6. 10, 14.

JEDIAEL, beloved, 2 *Kings* 22. 1.

JEDIDAH, beloved of the Lord.

JEDUTHUN, praising, celebrating.

JEGAR SAHADUTHA, the heap of witness. *The Syrian name which Laban gave*

to the heap of stones, *which Jacob called* Galeed, *or* hill of witness.

JEHALELEEL, he will praise God, 1 *Chron.* 4. 16; 2 *Chron.* 29. 12.

JEHDEIAH, he will be gladdened of the Lord, 1 *Chron.* 24. 20; 27. 30.

JEHIAH, he lives of the Lord, *i.e.*, by the mercy of the Lord, 1 *Chron.* 15. 24.

JEHIEL, he lives of God, *i.e.*, by the mercy of God he lives, 1 *Chron.* 15. 18, 20; 16. 5; 23. 8; 27. 32; 29. 8; 2 *Chron.* 21. 2; 29. 14; 31. 13; 35. 8; *Ezra* 8. 9; 10. 2; 21. 26.

JEHOADAH, the Lord will adorn him, 1 *Chron.* 8. 36.

JEHOADDAN, Lord of pleasure, 2 *Kings* 14. 2; 2 *Chron.* 25. 1.

JEHOAHAZ, whom the Lord holds fast.

JEHOASH, the Lord gave.

JEHOHANAN, the Lord graciously gave, 1 *Chron.* 26. 3; 2 *Chron.* 17. 15; 23. 1; *Ezra* 10. 28; *Neh.* 12. 13, 42.

JEHOIACHIN, the Lord will establish.

JEHOIADA, the Lord knows.

JEHOIAKIM, the Lord will set up.

JEHOIARIB, the Lord will contend, *i.e.*, will defend him.

JEHONADAB, the Lord gave spontaneously, *i.e.*, gave him freely to his parents.

JEHORAM, the Lord exalts, *i.e.*, he is lifted up, and made magnificent of the Lord.

JEHOSHAPHAT, the Lord judges, *i.e.*, he will plead for him.

JEHOSHEBA, the Lord's oath, the Lord (is her) oath, *i.e.*, she is a worshipper of the Lord, 2 *Kings* 11. 2.

JEHOVAH, He will be, *i.e.*, the Eternal, who always is. *From the words in which God revealed His nature and nomination,* I am that I am; I will be that I will be; and Jehovah Elohim.

JEHOVAH-JIREH, the Lord will see, the Lord will provide, *i.e.*, will give a means of deliverance.

JEHOVAH-NISSI, the Lord is my ensign. *The name which Moses gave the altar he erected on Mount Horeb.*

JEHOVAH-SHALOM, the Lord is peace, the peace of the Lord.

JEHOZABAD, whom the Lord gave, 2 *Kings* 12. 21; 1 *Chron.* 26. 4; 2 *Chron.* 17. 18; 24. 26.

JEHOZADAK, the Lord has made just.

JEHU, the Lord (is) He. *Several persons bore this name, but the son of Nimshi was the most eminent of them.*

JEHUBBAH, he will be hidden, 1 *Chron.* 7. 34.

JEHUCAL, he will be made able, *i.e.*, strengthened of the Lord, *Jer.* 37. 3; 38. 1.

JEHUD, praise, a city of Dan, *Josh.* 19. 45.

JEHUDI, praise the Lord, *Jer.* 36. 14, 21, 23.

JEHUDIJAH, Jewish, 1 *Chron.* 4. 18.

JEHUSH, he will gather together, 1 *Chron.* 8. 39.

JEIEL, hidden of God, 1 *Chron.* 5. 7; 9. 35; 11. 44; 15. 18, 21; 16. 5; 2 *Chron.* 20. 14; 26. 11; 29. 13; 35. 9; *Ezra* 8. 13; 10. 43.

JEKABZEEL, God will assemble together, *i.e.*, the people, *Neh.* 11. 25.

JEKAMEAM, he will gather together the people, a camp, 1 *Chron.* 23. 19; 24. 23.

JEKAMIAH, he will be gathered of the Lord, 1 *Chron.* 2. 41.

JEKUTHIEL, the fear of God; *a son of Ezra,* 1 *Chron.* 4. 18.

JEMIMA, dove. *But it is a word of doubtful meaning, both in Hebrew and Arabic.* Job 42. 14.

JEMUEL, the day of God, *Gen.* 46. 10; *Ex.* 6. 15.

JEPHTHAH, he will open, *i.e.*, he will liberate.

JEPHUNNEH, he will be beheld, *i.e.*, cared for of God.

JERAH, the moon, *Gen.* 10. 26; 1 *Chron.* 1. 20.

JERAHMEEL, he will obtain mercy.

JEREMAI, he will be exalted of the Lord, *Ezra* 10. 33.

JEREMIAH, elevated of the Lord, *or* exalted of the Lord. *He was called to the extraordinary office of a prophet in his younger years, and continued in that office for at least forty years together. In his time iniquity did exceedingly abound in the land of Judah. He earnestly and frequently calls the people to repentance, both by his reproofs and threatenings for their sins. He denounced*

the captivity of the people by the Babylonians, for which he was put in prison; he lived to see this prophecy fulfilled. But for the comfort and support of the faithful, he foretells their return after seventy years, and the enlargement of the church by Christ. His style is generally the most plain of any of the prophets.

JEREMOTH, high places. *Eleven persons bore this name in the Hebrew Bible, but no place was so named.* 1 *Chron.* 8. 14; *Ezra* 10. 26, 27.

JEREMY, elevated of the Lord. *Shortened form for Jeremiah.*

JERIAH, fear of the Lord, 1 *Chron.* 23. 19; 24. 23; 26. 31.

JERIBAI, he will contend, 1 *Chron.* 11. 46.

JERICHO, the moon, *i.e.*, city of the moon. *Jericho is situated about eighteen miles east of Jerusalem, and about five miles from the Jordan. It was called the City of the Moon by the Canaanites, who, together with all Eastern nations, worshipped that planet from the first ages after the flood. Job knew how much this idolatrous worship prevailed among his own people when he declared himself innocent of it.* (Job 31. 26.)

JERIEL, founded of God, 1 *Chron.* 7. 2.

JERIOTH, curtains, 1 *Chron.* 2. 18.

JEROBOAM, whose people are countless. *But although he is so denominated, yet he will be for ever known as he who made Israel to sin.*

JERUBBAAL, he will contend with Baal; *a cognomen of Gideon.*

JERUEL, founded of God, vid. JERIEL, 2 *Chron.* 20. 16.

JERUSALEM, foundations of peace, *or* He will provide peace, *or* He will pour peace on thee in floods; *i.e.*, God shall flood thee with prosperity. (1) *A composition of the Heb.* y'ru, *from the root* yarah, *to lay* foundations, *and* Shalaim, peace; *and it was so called with prophetic reference to the sacrifice of Jesus Christ, whose voluntary death is the only foundation of peace between heaven and earth, God and man; or we may regard it as a composition of the Hebrew words,* Yirêh, he will provide, *or* he will see, *and* Shalêm, peace. *The capital of the kingdom of Judah; mean geographical position, Lat.* 31° 46' 43" N. *and Long.* 35° 13' E. *from Greenwich. The ancients believed that it stood in the centre of the earth, and in the maps of mediæval times it is so represented. This idea arose, probably from the literal interpretation of the Psalmist,* "For God is my king of old, working salvation in the midst of the earth." *But it is worthy of remark that the ancient opinion is not far from the truth, both geographically and ethnologically.* (2) *The Church of Christ on earth is called by St. Paul, in his allegory in the Epistle to the Galatians,* "Jerusalem which is above." *He had been speaking of the earthly Jerusalem under the law, which is Hagar, and is in bondage with her children; that is to say, she was not delivered from the law, sin, and death.* (3) *The new Jerusalem of the Church triumphant, which our blessed Lord calls in* Rev. iii. 12, "the city of my God."

JERUSHA, possessed, named by her husband, 2 *Kings* 15. 33; 2 *Chron.* 27. 1.

JESHANAH, old, ancient, 2 *Chron.* 13. 19.

JESHARELAH, upright towards God, 1 *Chron.* 25. 14.

JESHEDEAR, habitation of the father.

JESHER, upright, just. *A son of Caleb. There was a book called by this name, on account of its subject,* "the book of the upright." *Josh.* 10. 13; 2 *Sam.* 1. 18; 1 *Chron.* 2. 18.

JESHISHAI, ancient of the Lord, *i.e.*, a good old man, 1 *Chron.* 5. 14.

JESHOHAIAH, depression of the Lord, 1 *Chron.* 4. 36.

JESHUA, salvation of the Lord.

JESHURUN, upright.

JESIMIEL, made of God, *i.e.*, created, 1 *Chron.* 4. 36.

JESSE, wealth of the Lord.

JESUI, salvation of the Lord, vid. JESHUA, *Num.* 26. 44.

JESUS (CHRIST), the Lord will save, the Lord of salvation, the Lord the saviour; *a Greek form of the Hebrew name* Y'hoshúa, *which is a compound of the Hebrew* Y' *for* Yah, the Lord, *and the Hebrew* shua, *to* be freed, or y'shua, salvation, aid, deliverance. (See Matt. i. 21.) *The name of the eternal Son of God, of one substance and equal with the Father, the mediator of the covenant of grace, who in the fulness of time became man, and so was and continues to be God and man in two distinct natures and one person for ever. The word Jesus is taken for the doctrine of Jesus, Acts 8. 35, and for Joshua, who brought God's people into the land of Canaan, and was therein an eminent type of our Lord Jesus.*

JETHER, excellence, Judg. 8. 20; 1 Kings 2. 5, 32; 1 Chron. 2. 17, 32; 4. 17; 7. 38.

JETHETH, strengthener, a nail, Gen. 36. 40; 1 Chron. 1. 51.

JETHLAH, He (i.e., God) will exalt, Josh. 19. 42.

JETHRO, the same as JETHER.

JETUR, defence, or enclosure, Gen. 25. 15; 1 Chron. 1. 31; 5. 19.

JEUZ, counsellor, 1 Chron. 8. 10.

JEW, confessor, or one who praises the Lord.

JEZEBEL, without cohabitation, or isle of the dunghill. *The wife of Ahab, whose carcase became as the dung upon the face of the field, because of her wickedness.*

JEZER, frame, form, i.e., of his parents, Gen. 46. 24; Num. 26, 49; 1 Chron. 7. 13.

JEZIAH, he will be sprinkled of the Lord, i.e., purified, or forgiven of the Lord, Ezra 10. 25.

JEZIEL, assembly of God, 1 Chron. 12. 3.

JEZLIAH, he will be drawn out of the Lord, i.e., preserved, 1 Chron. 8. 18.

JEZREEL, he will be sown of God, i.e., have a numerous progeny.

JIBSAM, he will smell sweetly, 1 Chron. 7. 2.

JIDLAPH, he will weep, Gen. 22. 22.

JIPHTHAH-EL, he will be opened of God, Josh. 19. 14, 27.

JOAB, Lord, father, or whose father is the Lord.

JOAH, Lord brother, 2 Kings 18. 18, 26; 1 Chron. 6. 21; 26. 4; 2 Chron. 29. 12; 34. 8; Isa. 36. 3, 11, 22.

JOANNA, the Lord is grace, or the Lord gives graciously.

JOATHAN, lord of integrity, or the Lord is upright, Matt. 1. 9.

JOB, the persecuted, or he will not cry out.

JOBAB, crying out, i.e., a desert, Gen. 10. 29; 36. 33, 34; Josh. 11. 1; 1 Chron. 1. 23, 44, 45; 8. 9, 18.

JOCHEBED, Lord of glory, or glory of the Lord, Ex. 6. 20; Num. 26. 59.

JOED, Lord of witness, Neh. 11. 7.

JOEL, Lord of God, or the Lord (is) God.

JOELAH, removing of oaks, 1 Chron. 12. 7.

JOEZER, Lord of help, or help of the Lord, 1 Chron. 12. 6.

JOGBEHAH, exalted, Num. 32. 35; Judg. 8. 11.

JOGLI, led into exile, Num. 34. 22.

JOHA, haste, 1 Chron. 8. 16; 11. 45.

JOHN, Lord of grace, or whom the Lord graciously gave; or it may be interpreted, the Lord hath begun to speak.

JOKDEAM, possessed of the people, Josh. 15. 56.

JOKMEAM, gathered of the people, 1 Chron. 6. 68.

JOKSHAN, sportsman, Gen. 25. 2, 3; 1 Chron. 1. 32.

JOKTAN, he will be small, Gen. 10. 25, 26, 29; 1 Chron. 1. 19, 20, 23.

JOKTHEEL, subdued of God, Josh. 15. 38; 2 Kings 14. 7.

JONADAB, vid. JEHONADAB.

JONAH, dove.

JONAN, the Lord of grace, Luke 3. 30.

JONATHAN, the Lord gave.

JOPPA, beautiful city.

JORAH, autumnal rain, Ezra 2. 18.

JORAI, he will be built up of the Lord, 1 Chron. 5. 13.

JORAM, the Lord exalts.

JORDAN, descending; a river; so called from descending, flowing down.

JORIM, the Lord will exalt.

JORKOAM, paleness of the people, 1 Chron. 2. 44.

JOSAPHAT, the Lord judges, i.e., pleads for him, Matt. 1. 8.

JOSE, vid. JOSES, Luke 3. 29.

JOSEPH, he shall add. *There were seven persons in the Bible who bore this name.*

JOSES, aid.

JOSHAH, aid, 1 Chron. 4. 34.

JOSHAVIAH, sit upright of the Lord, 1 Chron. 11. 46.

JOSHBEKASHAH, a seat in a hard place, 1 Chron. 25. 4, 24.

JOSHIAH, given of the Lord.

JOSIAS, given of the Lord; a Greek form of JOSIAH.

JOSIBIAH, he will be made to sit down of the Lord, i.e., to live in tranquillity and peace, 1 Chron. 4. 35.

JOSIPHIAH, added of the Lord, Ezra 8. 10.

JOTBAH, pleasant, 2 Kings 21. 19.

JOTBATHAH, goodness, Num. 33. 33, 34; Deut. 10. 7.

JOTHAM, the Lord is upright, or Lord of integrity.

JOZACHAR, the Lord is remembered, or Lord of remembrance, 2 Kings 12. 21.

JUBAL, jubilee, music, a son of Lamech, and probably the inventor of music, of the harp and organ, Gen. 4. 21.

JUDA, praised; a Greek form of the Hebrew name. *There were seven persons who bore this name.*

JUDÆA, the land of Judah. It was the most important of all the portions into which Palestine was divided in the time of our blessed Lord.

JUDAH, praised.

JUDAS, a man of the city of Kerioth, and therefore called Ish-Kerioth, or Iscariot.

JUDITH, praised, Gen. 26. 34.

JULIA, having curly hair, Rom. 16. 15.

JULIUS, curly-headed, as from the Greek, having curly hair, Acts 27. 1, 3.

JUNIA, belonging to Juno; a contraction of Juvino, fem. of Jove. *It originally signified the goddess. Rom. 16. 7.*

JUPITER, zeus, God. *It is the same as θεός, deus, i.e., the sun; and is cognate with the Persian Deev or Dew (bright, shining, hence heaven), and the Sanscrit Deva and Devata. Perhaps it is akin to dies, day (as in Diespiter, i.e., Dies Pater, or Father Day), and hence Zeus is the Heaven, the god who gives light from heaven, and fertility to the earth.*

JUSTUS, just. *There were three men who bore this name.*

JUTTAH, it will be stretched out, Josh. 15. 55; 21. 16.

K.

KADESH BARNEA, sacred desert of wandering.

KADMIEL, going before God, i.e., walking religiously, Ezra 2. 40; 3. 9; Neh. 7. 43; 9. 4, 5; 10. 9; 12. 8, 24.

KADMONITES, Orientals, Easterlings, ancients, Gen. 15. 19.

KALLAI, lightly esteemed of God, Neh. 12. 20.

KANAH, place of reeds, i.e., full of reeds, Josh. 16. 8; 17. 9; 19. 28.

KARKAA, the ground, i.e., pavement, Josh. 15. 3.

KARKOR, soft and level ground, from Arabic Zebah and Zalmunna encamped here when attacked by Gideon, Judg. 8. 10.

KARTAH, city, Josh. 21. 34.

KARTAN, two cities, Josh. 21. 32.

KATTATH, very small; a city; also called Kitron, Josh. 19. 15.

KEDAR, dark-skinned man.

KEDEMAH, eastward, Gen. 25. 15; 1 Chron. 1. 31.

KEDEMOTH, beginnings, Deut. 2. 26; Josh. 13. 18; 21. 37; 1 Chron. 6. 79.

KEDESH, sanctuary; a Levitical city of refuge in Galilee, Josh. 15. 23; 20. 7; 21. 32; Judg. 4. 6, 9, 10, 11; 2 Kings 15. 29; 1 Chron. 6. 72, 76.

KEHELATHAH, towards the place of assembly, as it was the nineteenth station of the Israelites in the desert, Num. 33. 22, 23.

KEILAH, fortress, refuge; a fortified town of Judah.

KELELAH, congregation of the Lord.

KEMUEL, congregation of God, Gen. 22. 21; Num. 34. 24; 1 Chron. 27. 17.

KENATH, possession, Num. 32. 42; 1 Chron. 2. 23.

KENAZ, hunting.

KENITE, a nest.

KEREN-HAPPUCH, splendour of colour, Job 42. 14.

KERIOTH, cities.

KEROS, a tack, a hook, Ezra 2. 44; Neh. 7. 47.

KETURAH, incense, perfume; the name of the second wife of Abraham, and many Jews regard her as the same as Hagar, as also the Targums of Jerusalem and Jonathan Ben Uzziel.

KEZIA, Cassia, i.e., equally as precious. A daughter of Job. Job 42. 14.

KEZIZ, cuttings off, Josh. 18. 21.

KIBROTH-HATTAAVAH, graves of lust, i.e., the graves of the people who lusted, Num. 11. 34, 35; 33. 16, 17; Deut. 9. 22.

KIBZAIM, two heaps, Josh. 21. 22.

KIDRON, very black, or full of darkness. *A torrent which flowed between Jerusalem and Mount Olivet; from the steep sides of the heights on each side, and the thickness of the trees, the valley had a black appearance.*

KINAH, lamentation, Josh. 15. 22.

KIR, a wall, a fortress.

KIRIATHAIM, vid. KIRJATHAIM.

KIRIOTH, cities.

KIRJATH ARBA, city of Arba.

KIRJATH-HUZOTH, a city of streets, Num. 22. 39.

KIRJATH-JEARIM, a city of woods, Josh. 9. 17; 15. 9, 60; 18. 14, 15; Judg. 18. 12; 1 Sam. 6. 21; 7. 1, 2; 1 Chron. 2. 50, 52, 53; 13. 5, 6; 2 Chron. 1. 4; Neh. 7. 29; Jer. 26. 20.

KIRJATH-SANNAH, a city of learning, i.e., a university, Josh. 15. 49.

KIRJATH-SEPHER, a city of books; perhaps it was a university, or city of learning, among the early settlers after the deluge, and where were kept their ancient records, Josh. 15. 15, 16; Judg. 1. 11, 12.

KIRJATHAIM, double city, or twofold.

KISH, snaring, bird-catching.

KISHI, snaring of the Lord, 1 Chron. 6. 44.

KISHION, very hard, Josh. 19. 20.

KISHON, tortuous, winding about; a river which rises in Mount Tabor, and flows into the Mediterranean Sea, Josh. 21. 28; Judg. 4. 7, 13; 5. 21; 1 Kings 18. 40; Ps. 83. 9.

KITHLISH, wall of man, Josh. 15. 40.

KITRON, knotty, Judg. 1. 30.

KOHATH, congregation.

KOHATHITES.

KOLAIAH, the voice of the Lord, Neh. 11, 7; Jer. 29. 21.

KORAH, ice, hail.

KORE, partridge, 1 Chron. 9. 19; 26. 1, 19; 2 Chron. 31. 14.

L.

LAADAH, order, 1 Chron. 4. 21.

LAADAN, put into order, 1 Chron. 7. 26; 23. 7, 8, 9; 26. 21.

LABAN, white. Son of Bethuel, and brother of Rebekah; and uncle of Jacob and Esau.

LACHISH, obstinate.

LAEL, by God, i.e., he swears or worships God, Num. 3. 24.

LAHAD, in triumph or joy, 1 Chron. 4. 2.

LAHMAM, because of violence, Josh. 15. 40.

LAHMI, a warrior, 1 Chron. 20. 5.

LAISH, lion. *The Greeks and Romans also named their children after the king of the forest.*

LAKUM, stopping up the way, Josh. 19. 33.

LAMECH, powerful.

LAODICEA, just people. *The capital of Phrygia, situated about forty miles from Ephesus. It is now called Esky-Hissa.*

LAPIDOTH, torches, Judg. 4. 4.

LASEA, rough, hairy; from the Greek Λασιος, hairy. A city on the southern coast of Crete, and about five miles east of the Fair Havens. Acts 27. 8.

LASHA, fissure; a city of Sodom, Gen. 10. 19.

LAZARUS, helpless, destitute of help. *This name is a contraction of Ἐλεάζαρος, and the same as the Heb. Elazar, whom God helps.*

LEAH, married.

LEBANAH, moon, Ezra 2. 45; Neh. 7. 48.

LEBANON, very white. *The name of a mountain consisting of two ridges, on the borders of Syria and Palestine, and so called because the eastern ridge was covered with perpetual snow.*

LEBONAH, frankincense, *Judg.* 21. 19.

LECAH, progress, 1 *Chron.* 4. 21.

LEHABIM, flames, scorching heat. *Descendants of Mizraim, and called* Lehabæi, *Gen.* 10. 13; 1 *Chron.* 1. 11.

LEHI, jawbone; a place on the borders of the land of the Philistines, so called because Samson made there a slaughter of the Philistines with the jawbone of an ass, *Judg.* 15. 9, 14, 19.

LEMUEL, by God. *It is probable that this is a name of Solomon.*

LESHEM, precious stone. *A town, which was also called* Laish *and* Dan, *Josh.* 19. 47.

LETUSHIM, artificers, hammerers, whetter. *Tubal-Cain was the first of this craft. He is said to be father, but, literally, the whetter, the sharpener, Gen.* 25. 3.

LEUMMIM, peoples, nations, *Gen.* 25. 3.

LEVI, adhesive, joined. *A third son of Jacob by Leah.*

LIBNAH, whiteness; seventeenth station of the Israelites in the wilderness.

LIBNI, white, *Ex.* 6. 17; *Num.* 3. 18; 1 *Chron.* 6. 17, 20, 29.

LIBYA, heat, *i.e.,* of the sun; hence said to be so called from a daughter of Jove. *A region in Africa, going along the Mediterranean Sea, to the west of Egypt.*

LIKHI, learned, 1 *Chron.* 7. 19.

LO-AMMI, not of my people; a mystical name of a son of the Prophet Hosea.

LO-DEBAR, without pasture; a city of Gilead, 2 *Sam.* 9. 4, 5; 17. 27.

LO-RUHAMAH, without mercy; a mystical name of a daughter of Hosea.

LOD, contention; the name of a town of Judea, the same as Lydda of the New Testament, on the Mediterranean Sea, 1 *Chron.* 8. 12; *Ezra* 2. 33; *Neh.* 7. 37; 11. 35.

LOIS, better; the grandmother of Timothy, 2 *Tim.* 1. 5.

LOT, covering; a son of Haran.

LOTAN, covering up, *Gen.* 36. 20, 22, 29; 1 *Chron.* 1. 38, 39.

LUBIM, dwellers in a thirsty land, 2 *Chron.* 12. 3; 16. 8; *Nah.* 3. 9.

LUCIUS, light, *i.e.,* of the sun; from lux, light.

LUD, bending. *Gen.* 10. 22; 1 *Chron.* 1. 17; *Isa.* 66. 19; *Ezek.* 27. 10.

LUHITH, tables, slabs of stone; a town of Moab, *Isa.* 15. 5; *Jer.* 48. 5.

LUKE, light, *i.e.,* of the sun.

LUZ, an almond tree, and the name of a town in the tribe of Benjamin.

LYCAONIA, a country sacred to the sun, or country of the god of light, *i.e.,* the sun.

LYCIA, light, *i.e.,* of the sun.

LYDDA, perverted, binding; a city of the tribe of Benjamin, and anciently called Lod.

LYDIA, bending.

LYSANIAS, set free; a tetrach of Abilene.

LYSIAS, he who has the power to set free; a Roman tribune commanding in Jerusalem.

LYSTRA, unbinding; a city of the province of Lycaonia.

M.

MAACHAH, oppression. *Eleven persons bore this name.*

MAADAI, ornament of the Lord, *Ezra* 10. 34.

MAAI, compassion, *Neh.* 12. 36.

MAALEH-ACRABBIM, the going up of scorpions, *Josh.* 15. 3.

MAARATH, a place naked of trees, *Josh.* 15. 59.

MAASEIAH (1) refuge of the Lord; (2) work of the Lord. *There were twenty persons who bore this name in the Old Testament.*

MAASIAI, a contraction of the preceding name.

MAAZ, anger, 1 *Chron.* 2. 27.

MAAZIAH, consolation of the Lord, 1 *Chron.* 24. 18; *Neh.* 10. 8.

MACEDONIA, mother of the Cetims or Ketims, or mother-land of Juno or the Moon, *being a composition of the Greek* Mc and κc, *for* ma *and* γα, *mother-earth or land; and* Diona, *for* μα *and* Iona, *Juno the moon, to which it was consecrated. The name of a province of Greece.*

MACHBANAI, bond of the Lord, 1 *Chron.* 12. 13.

MACHBENAH, bond, 1 *Chron.* 2. 49.

MACHI, decrease, *Num.* 13. 15.

MACHIR, sold.

MACHNADEBAI, what is like the liberality of the Lord? A son of Bani, who married contrary to the law, *Ezra* 10. 40.

MACHPELAH, double, a double cave; or a cave within a cave, wherein Abraham buried his dead.

MADAI, extended of the Lord, *Gen.* 10. 2; 1 *Chron.* 1. 5.

MADIAN, strip; a region on the coast of the Red Sea, *Acts* 7. 29.

MADMEN, dunghill, *Jer.* 48. 2.

MADON, contention, strife; a Cannanitish city subdued by Joshua, *Josh.* 11. 1; 12 19.

MAGBISH, congregation, *Ezra* 2. 30.

MAGDALA, tower, castle; a country on the east coast of the Red Sea.

MAGDIEL, prince of God, *Gen.* 36. 43; 1 *Chron.* 1. 54.

MAGOG, place of Gog or expansion, *i.e.,* increase of family, *Gen.* 10. 2; 1 *Chron.* 1. 5; *Ezek.* 38. 2; 39. 6; *Rev.* 20. 8.

MAGOR-MISSABIB, fear round about, *Jer.* 20. 3.

MAGPIASH, killer of moths, *Neh.* 10. 20.

MAHALALEEL, praise of God, *Gen.* 5. 12, 13, 15, 16; 17; 1 *Chron.* 1. 2; *Neh.* 11. 4.

MAHALATH, harp, wind instrument, *Gen.* 28. 9; 2 *Chron.* 11. 18; *Ps.* 53, *title.*

MAHALI, infirmity.

MAHANAIM, two hosts, two camps.

MAHANEH-DAN, camp of Dan, *Judg.* 18. 12.

MAHARAI, impetuosity of the Lord, 2 *Sam.* 23. 28; 1 *Chron.* 11. 30; 27. 13.

MAHATH, seizing, 1 *Chron.* 6. 35; 2 *Chron.* 29. 12; 31. 13.

MAHAVITE, places of assembly, 1 *Chron.* 11. 46.

MAHAZIOTH, visions, 1 *Chron.* 25. 4, 30.

MAHER-SHALAL-HASH-BAZ, haste to the spoil! quick to the prey! *This name was given to a son of the prophet Isaiah, at the command of God.*

MAHLAH, disease, *Num.* 26. 33; 27. 1; 36. 11; *Josh.* 17. 3.

MAHLON, great infirmity.

MAHOL, exultation, 1 *Kings* 4. 31.

MAKAZ, end, extremity, 1 *Kings* 4. 9.

MAKHELOTH, congregations; one of the stations of the Israelites in the wilderness, *Num.* 33. 25, 26.

MAKKEDAH, a place of shepherds; a place in the plains of the tribe of Judah, *Josh.* 10. 10, 16, 21, 28, 29; 12. 16; 15. 41.

MAKTESH, mortar, a hollow place; a place near Jerusalem like a mortar, *Zeph.* 1. 11.

MALACHI, angel of the Lord. *The last of the Old Testament prophets.* *Mal.* 1. 1.

MALCHAM, most high king.

MALCHI-SHUA, king of help; one of Saul's sons, who was slain on Mount Gilboa.

MALCHIAH, MALCHIJAH, king of the Lord. *There were nine of this name in the Old Testament.* 1 *Chron.* 6. 40; 9. 12; 24. 9; *Neh.* 3. 11, 14, 31; 8. 4; 10. 3; 11. 12; 12. 42; *Ezra* 10. 25, 31; *Jer.* 21. 1; 38. 1.

MALCHIEL, king of God.

MALCHIRAM, king of height, 1 *Chron.* 3. 18.

MALCHUS, king; the same as the Chaldean and Syriac. A servant of the High Priest, leader of the band of men which came to take Jesus.

MALELEEL, praise of God, *Luke* 3. 37.

MALLOTHI, I speak, 1 *Chron.* 25. 4, 26.

MALLUCH, reigning, 1 *Chron.* 6. 44; *Ezra* 10. 29, 32; *Neh.* 10. 4, 27; 12. 2.

MAMRE, from seeing, from the vision.

MANAHATH, gift, *Gen.* 36. 23; 1 *Chron.* 1. 40; 8. 6.

MANASSES, forgetfulness; the firstborn of Joseph, *Matt.* 1. 10; *Rev.* 7. 6.

MANOAH, rest, *i.e.,* recreation, consolation.

MAON, place of habitation, *Josh.* 15. 55; 1 *Sam.* 25. 2; 1 *Chron.* 2. 45.

MARA, MARAH, bitterness.

MARALAH, place of concussions, *i.e.,* a place subject to earthquakes, *Josh.* 19. 11.

MARESHAH, that which is at the head, *Josh.* 15. 44; 1 *Chron.* 2. 42; 4. 21; 2 *Chron.* 11. 8; 14. 9, 10; 20. 37; *Micah* 1. 15.

MARK, indolent; *the same as the Latin* Marcus, *from* marceo, *to be languid, to be lazy. He was the son of Mary, the sister of Barnabas, and one of the four Evangelists. He founded the Church of Alexandria.*

MAROTH, bitterness, bitter fountains, *Micah* 1. 12.

MARSEANA, lofty.

MARSENA, lofty; a Persian prince, *Esth.* 1. 14.

MARTHA, lady, mistress.

MARY, exalted of the Lord. *A compound of the Heb. words* Mara, *to lift up oneself, and* Yah, *the abbreviated form of the name of Jehovah.*

MASH, drawn out. *The LXX. translate it* Meshech, *and the Samaritan Pentateuch has* Mosok. *Gen.* 10. 23.

MASREKAH, vineyards. *A city of Edom, Gen.* 36. 36; 1 *Chron.* 1. 47.

MASSA, bearing patiently. A son of Ishmael. *Gen.* 25. 14; 1 *Chron.* 1. 30.

MASSAH, temptation.

MATHUSALA, when he is dead it shall be sent, *i.e.,* the deluge of waters, *Luke* 3. 37.

MATRED, thrusting forward, *Gen.* 36. 39; 1 *Chron.* 1. 50.

MATRI, rainy, 1 *Sam.* 10. 21.

MATTAN, gift.

MATTANAH, gift, *Num.* 21. 18, 19.

MATTANIAH, gift of the Lord. *Nine persons bore this name in the Old Testament.* 2 *Kings* 24. 17; 1 *Chron.* 9. 15; 25. 4, 16; 2 *Chron.* 20. 14; 29. 13; *Neh.* 11. 17, 22; 12. 8, 25, 35; 13. 13; *Ezra* 10. 26, 27, 30, 37.

MATTATHA, gift, *Luke* 3. 31.

MATTHIAS, gift of the Lord.

MATTHAN, gift, *Matt.* 1. 15.

MATTHAT, gift, *Luke* 3. 24, 29.

MATTHEW, gift of the Lord.

MATTENAI, gift of the Lord, *Ezra* 10. 33, 37; *Neh.* 12. 19.

MATHIAS, gift of the Lord.

MATTITHIAH, gift of the Lord, 1 *Chron.* 9. 31; 15. 18, 21; 16. 5; 25. 3, 21; *Ezra* 10. 43; *Neh.* 8. 4.

MEAH, a hundred, *Neh.* 3. 1; 12. 39.

MEARAH, a cave, *Josh.* 13. 4.

MEBUNNAI, building of the Lord, 2 *Sam.* 23. 27.

MECHERATHITE, Swordite, *i.e.,* a soldier, and a proper name for a soldier. *He was one of the heroes of David.* 1 *Chron.* 11. 36.

MEDAD, love; one of the two elders included in seventy elders who remained in the camp *Num.* 11. 26, 27.

MEDAN, strife, *Gen.* 25. 2; 1 *Chron.* 1. 32.

MEDE, a Median.

MEDEBA, water of rest, *Num.* 21. 30; *Josh.* 13. 9, 16; 1 *Chron.* 19. 7; *Isa.* 15. 2.

MEGIDDO, place of multitudes; and it has been the scene of many battles.

MEHETABEL, benefit of God, *Gen.* 36. 39; 1 *Chron.* 1. 50; *Neh.* 6. 10.

MEHIDA, a joining together, *Ezra* 2. 52; *Neh.* 7. 54.

MEHIR, price, wages, 1 *Chron.* 4. 11.

MEHUJAEL, destroyed of God, *Gen.* 4. 18.

MEHUMAN, faithful, *Esth.* 1. 10.

ME-JARKON, water of great greenness, *Josh.* 19. 46.

MEKONAH, base, *i.e.,* foundation, *Neh.* 11. 28.

MELATIAH, delivered of the Lord, *Neh.* 3. 7.

MELCHIZEDEK, king of righteousness. *The name of a king of Salem. He was also priest of the Most High God; and all true Christians are dignified like Him, for they are, as St. Peter says, a royal priesthood,* 1 *Pet.* 2. 9. *The Jews generally say he was the same as* Shem.

MELEA, fulness; father of Eliakim, *Luke* 3. 31.

MELECH, king, 1 *Chron.* 8. 35; 9. 41.

MELITA, kindness, goddess of generation, refuge. *It was called by the Arabians* Alitta, *and the Assyrians* Mylitta, *and by the Romans* Venus. *Acts* 28. 1.

MEMPHIS, haven of good men, gate of the blessed.

MEMUCAN, dignity, *Esth.* 1. 14, 16, 21.

MENAHEM, consoling, comforter.

MEONOTHAI, habitation of the Lord, 1 *Chron.* 4. 14.

MEPHAATH, beauty, *Josh.* 13. 18; 21. 37; 1 *Chron.* 6. 79; *Jer.* 48. 21.

MEPHIBOSHETH, exterminating the idol.

MERAB, multiplication.
MERAIAH, lifted up of the Lord. Neh. 12. 12.
MERAIOTH, rebellious, 1 Chron. 6. 7, 52; 9. 11; Ezra 7. 3; Neh. 11. 11; 12. 15.
MERARI, bitterness.
MERATHAIM, two-fold rebellion, Jer. 50. 21.
MERCURIUS, Hermes, interpreter.
MERED, rebellion, 1 Chron. 4. 17, 18.
MEREMOTH, e'evation, Ezra 8. 33; 10. 36; Neh. 3. 4, 21; 10. 5; 12. 3.
MERES, lofty, Esth. 1. 14.
MERIB-BAAL, contender against Baal, 1 Chron. 8. 34; 9. 40.
MERIBAH, chiding.
MERODACH, the great lord, the illuminator of the gods; and may be the same with Nimrod.
MERODACH-BALADAN, the great lord is lord. Merodach is the same god as Marduk, which is Jupiter, the most brilliant, Isa. 33. 1.
MEROM, a high place.
MEROZ, refuge.
MESHA ile retreat; (2) salvation, Gen. 10. 30; 1 Chron. 8. 9.
MESHACH, agile, expeditious.
MESHECH, drawing out.
MESHELEMIAH, whom the Lord repays, 1 Chron. 9. 21; 26. 1, 2, 9.
MESHEZABEEL, liberated of God, Neh. 3. 4; 10. 21; 11. 24.
MESHILLEMOTH, MESHILLEMITH, those who repay, 1 Chron. 9. 12; 2 Chron. 28. 12; Neh. 11. 13.
MESHOBAB, returning, 1 Chron. 4. 34.
MESHULLAM, repaying. The name of sixteen persons in the Bible. 2 Kings 22. 3; 1 Chron. 3. 19; 5. 13; 8. 17; 9. 7, 8, 11, 12; 2 Chron. 34. 12; Ezra 8. 16; 10. 15, 29; Neh. 3. 4, 6, 30; 6. 18; 8. 4; 10. 7, 20; 11. 7, 11; 12. 13, 16, 25, 33.
MESHULLEMETH, repaying, 2 Kings 21. 19.
MEZOBAITE, congregation of the Lord, 1 Chron. 11. 47.
MESOPOTAMIA, region between the two rivers, and the Greek name for Aram Naharaim, or Syria of the two rivers.
METHEG-AMMAH, the bridle of the Metropolis. A city of Gath.
METHUSAEL, man of God, Gen 4. 18.
METHUSELAH, when he is dead it shall be sent, i.e., the deluge.
MEZAHAB, waters of gold, Gen. 36. 39; 1 Chron. 1. 50.
MIAMIN, from the right hand, Ezra 10 25; Neh. 12. 5.
MIBHAR, most choice, i.e., the best, 1 Chron. 11. 38.
MIBSAM, sweet smell, delight, Gen. 25. 13; 1 Chron. 1. 29: 4. 25.
MIBZAR, defence, fortress, Gen. 36. 42; 1 Chron. 1. 53.
MICAH, who is like unto the Lord!
MICAIAH, who is like unto the Lord!
MICHA, who is like unto the Lord!
MICHAEL, who is like unto God! or who is as God!
MICHAL, a little stream of water.
MICHMAS, treasure, treasury, a place where treasures are kept, Ezra 2. 27; Neh. 7. 31.
MICHMETHAH, a hiding place, Josh. 16. 6; 17. 7.
MICHRI, bought of the Lord, 1 Chron. 9. 8.
MIDDIN, strife, Josh. 15. 61.
MIGDAL-EL, tower of God, i.e., a very high tower, Josh. 19. 38.
MIGDAL-GAD, tower of fortune, i.e., a tower erected in honour of Gad. Josh. 15. 37.
MIGDOL, tower, a castle, Ex. 14. 2; Num. 33. 7; Jer. 44. 1; 46. 14.
MIGRON, place of great conflict, 1 Sam. 14. 2; Isa. 10. 28.
MIKLOTH, staves, 1 Chron. 8. 32; 9. 37, 38; 27. 4.
MIKNEIAH, possession of the Lord, 1 Chron. 15. 18, 21.
MILALAI, eloquent, i.e., the promise of the Lord, Neh. 12. 36.
MILCAH, queen.
MILCOM, high king. Idol of the Ammonites.
MILETUS, refuge.
MILLO, rampart, a mound.
MINNI, part, Jer. 51, 27.
MINNITH, small, Judg. 11. 33; Ezek. 27. 17.
MIRIAM, their rebellion, or star of the sea.
MIRMA, deceit, 1 Chron. 8. 10.

MISGAB, refuge, Jer. 48. 1
MISHAEL, who (is) that which God is?
MISHAL, prayer, Josh. 19. 26; 21. 30.
MISHAM, their cleansing; one of the sons of Elpaal, 1 Chron. 8. 12.
MISHMA, hearing, Gen. 25. 14; 1 Chron. 1. 30; 4. 25, 26.
MISHMANNAH, fatness: the name of a Gadite soldier, 1 Chron 12. 10.
MISHRAITES, a slippery place.
MISPAR, number, i.e., few.
MISREPHOTH-MAIM, the burnings of waters, Josh 11. 8; 13. 6.
MITHCAH, sweetness; and probably there may have been a fountain of a pleasant water which was so denominated, Num. 33. 28, 29.
MITHNITE, strength, 1 Chron. 11. 43.
MITHREDATH, given by the sun-god, Mithras (or fire), the idol of the Persians, and others, and worshipped in caverns, Ezra 1. 8: 4. 7.
MITYLENE, last; but the derivation is very obscure. Acts 20. 14.
MIZPAH, watch-tower.
MIZRAIM, two-fold Egypt, i.e., upper and lower Egypt, Gen. 10. 6. 13; 1 Chron. 1. 8. 11.
MNASON, remembrance.
MOAB, water of a father, i.e., progeny.
MOLADAH, birthplace, Josh. 15. 26; 19. 2; 1 Chron. 4. 28; Neh. 11. 26.
MOLECH, the king. The word is always written with the article, "The King." It was the national god of the Ammonites, Canaanites, Phœnicians, and Carthaginians, and was known by the following names: Moloch, Molech, Malcom, and Milcom: his worship was always with cruel rites, and Milton makes him "king of hell" in his "Paradise Lost."
MOLID, begetting, 1 Chron. 2. 29.
MORDECAI, a little man.
MOREH, teacher, illustrious, Gen. 12. 6; Deut. 11. 30: Judg. 7. 1.
MORESHETH-GATH, possession of Gath. Micah 1. 14.
MORIAH, visible of the Lord; a hill of Jerusalem on which the Temple was built.
MOSERA, bonds, Deut. 10. 6.
MOSES, taken out of the water.
MOZA, fountain, 1 Chron. 2. 46; 8. 36, 37; 9. 42, 43.
MUPPIM, anxieties, Gen. 46. 21.
MUSHI, proved of the Lord, Ex. 6. 19; Num. 3. 20; 1 Chron. 6. 19, 47; 23. 21, 23; 24. 26, 30.
MYRA, bad waters, Acts 27. 5.
MYSIA, marsh, or swamp. The Mysians are said to have emigrated from the marshy countries about the lower Danube, called Mœsia, whence Mysia.

N.

NAAM, pleasantness, 1 Chron. 4. 15.
NAAMAH, pleasant, Gen. 4. 22; 1 Kings 14 21; 2 Chron. 12. 13; Josh. 15. 41.
NAAMAN, pleasantness. A general of the king of Syria, who came to Elisha the prophet to be cleansed of his leprosy.
NAAMATHITE, pleasantness.
NAARAI, child of the Lord, 1 Chron. 11. 37.
NAARAN, handmaid, 1 Chron. 7. 28.
NAASHON, enchanter, or serpent of the sun.
NABAL, fool, i.e., impious.
NABOTH, fruits, produce.
NACHON, smitten, 2 Sam. 6. 6.
NACHOR, burning, or noble. A son of Serug, whom Jewish tradition affirms was the founder of the idolatry of worshipping the dead, and probably he denominated this son in honour of the sun or fire. Luke 3. 34.
NADAB, volunteer.
NAGGE, shining, splendour, i.e., of the sun.
NAHALIEL, torrents of God; and so called by the Israelites when they passed over them, and called torrents of God, because seasonable and salutary, Num. 21. 19.
NAHALOL, NAHALLAL, NAHALAL, pasture, i.e., a sheep walk, or when sheep are led out, as the shepherds in the East always go before their sheep, Josh. 19. 15; 21. 35; Judg. 1. 30.

NAHAM, consolation, i.e., to his parents 1 Chron. 4. 19.
NAHAMANI, repenting, Neh. 7. 7.
NAHARAI, snorter, 2 Sam. 23. 37; 1 Chron. 11. 30.
NAHASH, serpent. The serpent was an emblem of the sun, and the name may have been given in honour of the sun.
NAHATH, letting down, Gen. 36. 13, 17; 1 Chron. 1. 37; 6. 26; 2 Chron. 31. 13.
NAHBI, hidden of the Lord, Num. 13. 14.
NAHOR, breathing hard.
NAHUM, consolation, Nah. 1. 1.
NAIN, pleasantness, pleasant to the senses.
NAIOTH, habitation, 1 Sam. 19. 18, 19, 22; 20. 1.
NAOMI, pleasantness, i.e., of the Lord.
NAPHISH, refreshment, Gen. 25. 15; 1 Chron. 1. 31; 5. 19.
NAPHTALI, my wrestling, or my twisting.
NAPHTUHIM, openings; an Egyptian people who lived on the shores of the Mediterranean, Gen. 10. 13; 1 Chron. 1. 11.
NARCISSUS, daffodil, or narcissus, Rom. 16. 11.
NATHAN, given, of God.
NATHAN-MELECH, placed or constituted of the king, 2 Kings 23. 11.
NATHANAEL, given of God, John 1. 45, 46, 47, 48, 49; 21. 2.
NAUM, consolation.
NAZARETH, diadem, or consecration.
NEAH, wandering, Josh. 19 13.
NEAPOLIS, new city. It was the sea-port of Philippi.
NEBAI, fruit of the Lord, Neh. 10. 19.
NEBAJOTH, high places, Gen. 25. 13; 28. 9; 36. 3: 1 Chron. 1. 29; Isa. 60. 7.
NEBALLAT, folly in secret, Neh. 11. 34.
NEBAT, aspect.
NEBO, Mercury, foreteller, i.e., of events, as commonly interpreted; but it is more properly the Eastern sun in the height of heaven, as identified with the Aryan Mitra.
NEBUCHADNEZZAR, Nebo is the god of fire.
NEBUSHASHBAN, Nebo will deliver, and in Dan. 6. 16, the verb occurs, "Thy God whom thou servest continually, he will deliver thee." Jer. 39. 13.
NEBUZARADAN, Mercury's lord or leader.
NECHO, the lame. He was lame, and the Targum mentions this fact. He was a successful general in the early part of his reign, but his power declined before Nebuchadnezzar, and Egypt became a province of Babylon. 2 Chron. 35. 20, 22; 36. 4.
NEDABIAH, spontaneous gift of the Lord, 1 Chron. 3. 18.
NEHELAMITE, made fat.
NEHEMIAH, comfort of the Lord. He was one of the leaders in the return of the Jews out of captivity in Babylon.
NEHUM, merciful, Neh. 7. 7.
NEHUSHTA, brass, 2 Kings 24. 8.
NEHUSHTAN, a little brazen serpent.
NEIEL, shaken of God, Josh. 19. 27.
NEKEB, cavern, Josh. 19. 33.
NEKODAH, distinguished, Ezra 2. 48, 60; Neh. 7. 50, 62.
NEMUEL, circumcision of God, Num. 26. 9, 12; 1 Chron. 4. 24.
NEPHEG, short, bud, Ex. 6. 21; 2 Sam. 5. 15; 1 Chron. 3. 7; 14. 6.
NEPHTOAH, opening. The name of a fountain near Jerusalem. Josh. 15. 9: 18. 15.
NEPHTHALIM, wrestlings, Matt. 4. 13, 15; Rev. 7. 6.
NEPHUSIM, expansions, Ezra 2. 50.
NER, lamp.
NEREUS, fluid, or flowing.
NERGAL, light rolling, or flashing, or rushing with noise.
NERGAL-SHAREZER, Nergal is the prince of fire, or Nergal is the brightness of light, 2 Kings 17 30; Jer. 39. 3, 13.
NERI, light of the Lord, Luke 3. 27.
NERIAH, light of the Lord.
NETHANEEL, given of God.
NETHANIAH, given of the Lord.
NETOPHAH, a dropping, Ezra 2. 22; Neh. 7. 26.
NEZIAH, overseer, Ezra 2. 54; Neh. 7. 50.
NEZIB, garrison, Josh. 15. 43.
NIBHAZ, lord of darkness, i.e., an evil demon. An idol of the Avites, and supposed by some to be the same as the Anubis of Egypt, 2 Kings 17. 31.
NIBSHAN, level and soft soil, Josh.

NICANOR, conqueror of men. *Greek.*

NICODEMUS, conqueror of people.

NICOLAS, conqueror of people, *Acts* 6. 5.

NICOPOLIS, city of victory. *A city of Epirus, on the gulf of Amhacia, and opposite to Actium, Titus* 3. 12.

NIMROD, rebellious, the first rebel on earth in audacity and idolatrous wickedness. *Many Assyrian scholars consider him to be the same as Merodach.*

NIMSHI, selected, drawn out.

NINEVEH, habitation of Ninus. *It is probably the oldest city of the world, and was founded by Nimrod.*

NISROCH, eagle, *i.e.,* the sun under the emblem of an eagle; and he was one of the chief idols of the Assyrians.

NO, temple, portion. *The city of Diospolis, or city of Jupiter in Egypt.*

NOADIAH, met with the Lord, *i.e.,* to whom the Lord manifested Himself.

NOAH, (1) rest, comfort; (2), motion, wandering. *The son of Lamech, of the line of Seth.*

NOB, high place.

NOBAH, a barking, a loud noise, *Num.* 32. 42; *Judg.* 8. 11.

NOD, wandering, *i.e.,* going to and fro, *Gen.* 4. 16.

NODAB, nobility, 1 *Chron.* 5. 19.

NOGAH, shining splendour, 1 *Chron.* 3. 7; 14. 16.

NOPHAH, a blast, *Num.* 21. 30.

NUN, fish.

NYMPHAS, bride. *Greek. Col.* 4. 15.

O.

OBADIAH, servant of the Lord. *Twelve persons bore this name.*

OBAL, stripped of braces, *Gen.* 10. 28.

OBED, servant, *i.e.,* of God.

OBED-EDOM, serving Edom.

OBIL, overseer of camels, 1 *Chron.* 27. 30.

OBOTH, pythones, oracular serpents, soothsayers, *Num.* 21. 10, 11; 33. 43, 44.

OCEAN, troubled.

ODED, setting up.

OG, a furrow; a king of Bashan, and of the race of the giants.

OHAD, joining together, *Gen.* 46. 10; *Ex.* 6. 15.

OHEL, tabernacle, 1 *Chron.* 3. 20.

OLYMPAS, gift of Olympus, being a contraction for *Olympodorus.*

OMAR, uppermost, *Gen.* 36. 11, 15; 1 *Chron.* 1. 36.

OMRI, servant of the Lord.

ON, sun, *i.e.,* city of the sun, and called in Greek *Heliopolis.*

ONAM, weariness, wickedness, *Gen.* 38. 4, 8, 9; 46. 12.

ONAN, iniquity.

ONESIMUS, profitable.

ONESIPHORUS, profit bearing.

ONO, strength, 1 *Chron.* 8. 12; *Ezra* 2. 33; *Neh.* 6. 2; 7. 37; 11. 35.

OPHEL, hill, activity.

OPHIR, abundance, *i.e.,* of gold.

OPHNI, mouldy (?), *Josh.* 18. 24.

OPHRAH, fawn, *Josh.* 18. 23; *Judg.* 6. 11, 24; 8. 27, 32; 9. 5; 1 *Sam.* 13. 17; 1 *Chron.* 4. 14.

OREB, raven, black

OREN, pine, *i.e.,* tall and strong, 1 *Chron.* 2. 25.

ORNAN, large pine, *i.e.,* as tall as a great pine.

ORPAH, mane, *i.e.,* neck of an animal.

OSEE, salvation, *Rom.* 9. 25.

OTHNIEL, lion of God, *i.e.,* most powerful.

OZEM, strong.

OZIAS, strength of the Lord.

OZNI, hearing, *Num.* 26. 16.

P.

PADAN-ARAM, the plain of Aram: a province between the Tigris and Euphrates.

PADON, redemption, *Ezra* 2. 44; *Neh.* 7. 47.

PAGIEL, prayer of God.

PAHATH-MOAB, governor of Moab, *Ezra* 2. 6; 8. 4; 10. 30; *Neh.* 3. 11; 7. 11; 10. 14.

PALAL, judge, *Neh.* 3. 25.

PALESTINE, the land of wanderers, *Ex.* 15. 14; *Isa.* 14. 29, 31; *Joel* 3. 4.

PALLU, separated, *Gen.* 46. 9; *Ex.* 6. 14; *Num.* 26. 5, 8; 1 *Chron.* 5. 3.

PALTI, deliverance of the Lord, *Num.* 13. 9.

PALTIEL, deliverance of God, *Num.* 34. 26; 2 *Sam.* 3. 15.

PAMPHILIA, land of every people, or region of mixed races.

PAPHOS, gate, cavity. *A city of Cyprus, which is said to have been founded by Cinyras, the father of Adonis, and a chief of the Accadians after the siege of Troy. The remains of an enormous temple to Venus are still discernible there.* Acts 13. 6, 13.

PARAH, village of heifers, *Josh.* 18. 23.

PARAN, abounding in foliage.

PARMASHTA, strong-fisted, *Esth.* 9. 9.

PARMENAS.

PARNACH, very nimble, *Num.* 34. 25.

PAROSH, a flea, *Ezra* 2. 3; 8. 3; 10. 25; *Neh.* 3. 25; 7. 8; 10. 14.

PARSHANDATHA, of noble birth, *Esth.* 9. 7.

PARTHIANS, horsemen. *Originally they were a people of Asia Minor.*

PARUAH, flourishing, 1 *Kings* 4. 17.

PARVAIM, oriental regions, 2 *Chron.* 3. 6.

PASACH, torn asunder, 1 *Chron.* 7. 33.

PAS-DAMMIN, extremity of Dammin, 1 *Chron.* 11. 13.

PASEAH, lame, 1 *Chron.* 4. 12; *Ezra* 2. 49; *Neh.* 3, 6; 7. 51.

PASHUR, most noble.

PATARA, interpretation, or oracular response. *A maritime and commercial city of Lycia.* Acts 21. 1.

PATHROS, southern region, *i.e.,* Egypt, *Isa.* 11. 11; *Jer.* 44. 1, 15; *Ezek.* 30. 14.

PATMOS, terebinth, or oak.

PATROBAS, life of the father, *Rom.* 16. 14.

PAU, bleating, crying out, *Gen.* 36. 39; 1 *Chron.* 1. 50.

PAUL, little, small. *He was also called* Saul. *2 Tim.* 4. 19.

PEDAHEL, redeemed of God, *Num.* 34. 28.

PEDAHZUR, redemption of strength, *i.e.,* God, *Num.* 1. 10; 2. 20; 7. 54, 59; 10. 23.

PEDAIAH, redemption of the Lord, 2 *Kings* 23. 36; 1 *Chron.* 3. 18, 19; 27. 20; *Neh.* 3. 25; 8. 4; 11. 7; 13. 13.

PEKAH, open-eyed.

PEKAHIAH, opening of the Lord, *i.e.,* deliverance.

PEKOD, visitation, *i.e.,* punishment, *Jer.* 50. 21; *Ezek.* 23. 23.

PELAIAH, distinguished of the Lord.

PELALIAH, judge of the Lord, *Neh.* 11. 12.

PELATIAH, deliverance.

PELEG, division, *Gen.* 10. 25; 11. 16, 17, 18, 19; 1 *Chron.* 1. 19, 25.

PELET, deliverance, 1 *Chron.* 2. 47; 12. 3.

PELETH, swiftness, *Num.* 16. 1; 1 *Chr.* 2. 33.

PELONITE, such an one, 1 *Chron.* 11. 27, 36; 27. 10.

PENINNAH, coral, 1 *Sam.* 1. 2, 4.

PENUEL, face of God.

PEOR, opening; an idol of the Moabites.

PERESH, excrement, 1 *Chron.* 7. 16.

PEREZ, breach, 1 *Chron.* 27. 33.

PEREZ-UZZAH, breach of Uzzah, 2 *Sam.* 6. 8; 1 *Chron.* 13. 11.

PERGAMOS, height, most high. *Pergamum was celebrated for its Temple of Æsculapius, whose emblem the serpent was, and who is represented on the coins of Pergamum, and is called* Pergameus Deus. *(Bishop of Lincoln's New Test.)* Rev. 2. 12.

PERGE, *valde terrestris* (Mintrat.), the metropolis of Pamphlias, and celebrated for its Temple of Diana.

PERIZITES, villagers.

PERSIA, a tract of country from Media to the Persian Gulf, embracing Susiana and Elymais.

PERSIANS, horsemen. *The founder of this race was Persis. The Persian religion consisted in the worship of the sun, moon, earth, fire, water, and the winds.*

PERSIS, one who takes by storm.

PERUDA, distinguished, *Ezra* 2. 55.

PETER, rock, or rock-like.

PETHAHIAH, loosed of the Lord, 1 *Chron.* 24. 16; *Ezra* 10. 23; *Neh.* 9. 5; 11. 24.

PETHOR, interpretation of dreams. *A city of Mesopotamia, Num.* 22. 5; *Deut.* 23. 4.

PETHUEL, ingeniousness of God, *Joel* 1. 1.

PEULTHAI, wages of the Lord, 1 *Chron.* 26. 5.

PHARAOH, the great house.

PHARAOH-HOPHRA, Pharaoh the priest of the sun.

PHARAOH-NECHOH, Pharaoh the lame.

PHARES, *vid.* Perez.

PHARPAR, most swift.

PHEBE, radiant as the moon.

PHENICE, palm, *i.e.,* abundant in palms, 26. 26.

PHICHOL, mouth of all, *Gen.* 21. 22, 32; 26. 26.

PHILADELPHIA, brotherly love.

PHILEMON, loving, friendship, *Philem.* 1.

PHINEHAS, mouth of brass.

PHILETUS, lovingly, *or* loving one's self.

PHILIP, loving.

PHILIPPI, loving horses, lover of horses.

PHILOLOGUS, lover of literature.

PHLEGON, having flaming eyes.

PHRYGIA, cold.

PHURAH, branch.

PHUVAH, mouth.

PHYGELLUS, he who flees from chains.

PI-BESETH, portion of the spouse.

PI-HAHIROTH, mouth of caverns.

PILDASH, lamp of fire, *Gen.* 22. 22.

PILEHA, servitude, *Neh.* 10. 24.

PIRAM, like a wild ass, *Josh.* 10. 3.

PIRATHON, just revenge, *Judg.* 12. 15.

PISGAH, divided rock, *or* fragment of hewn rock.

PISIDIA, damp region.

PISON, great effusion, *i.e.,* of waters.

PISPAH, dispersion, 1 *Chron.* 7. 38.

PITHOM, an enclosed place, *Ex.* 1. 11.

PITHON, great enlargement, 1 *Chron.* 8. 35; 9. 41.

POCHERETH OF ZEBAIM, retarding gazelles, *Ezra* 2. 57; *Neh.* 7. 59.

PONTIUS PILATE, *Procurator of Judea.*

PORATHA, ornament, *Esth.* 9. 8.

POTIPHAR, priest of the bull.

POTIPHERAH, priest of the sun, *in the temple of the sun, in the city of On or Heliopolis.*

PRISCA, *a shortened form for* Priscilla, 2 *Tim.* 4. 19.

PRISCILLA, ancient, old-fashioned simplicity.

PROCHORUS, leader of the choir; *one of the seven deacons,* Acts 6. 5.

PTOLEMAIS, fond of war, warlike, *Acts* 21. 7.

PUAH, splendid, light; *perhaps* joy of parents.

PUBLIUS, pertaining to the people.

PUDENS, bashful, modest.

PUHITES, a name from *Heb.* beautiful, 1 *Chron.* 2. 53.

PUL, elephant.

PUNITES, same as PHUVAH, *Num.* 26. 23.

PUNON, distraction, *Num.* 33. 42, 43.

PUT, extension.

PUTEOLI, for, pertaining to.

PUTIEL, afflicted of God, *Ex.* 6. 25.

Q.

QUARTUS, fourth, *i.e.,* child.

R

RAAMAH, thundering, *Gen.* 10. 7; 1 *Chron.* 1. 9; *Ezek.* 27. 22.

RAAMIAH, thunder of the Lord, *Neh.* 7. 7.

RAAMSES, son of the sun, (*vid.* Rameses), city of the sun, *Ex.* 1. 11.

RABBAH, great city, *i.e.,* metropolis.

RABBITH, great multitude, *Josh.* 19. 20.

RABSHAKEH, chief of the cup-bearers; an Assyrian general under Sennacherib.

RACHAL, traffic, 1 *Sam.* 30. 29.

RACHEL, an ewe; the youngest daughter of Laban, and beloved wife of Jacob.

RADDAI, subduing, 1 *Chron.* 2. 14.

RAGAU, companion, friend.

RAGUEL, friend of God, *i.e.,* a servant of God.

RAHAB, (1) insolence, fierceness; (2) spacious, *i.e.,* wide.

RAHAM, merciful, 1 *Chron.* 2. 44.

RAHEL, an ewe.

RAKKATH, a shore, *Josh.* 19. 35.

RAKKON, extreme shore, *Josh.* 19. 46.

RAM, high part.

RAMAH, lofty place.

RAMESES, son of the sun; *a city of Egypt. Gen.* 47. 11; *Ex.* 12. 37; *Num.* 33. 3, 5.

RAMIAH, placed of the Lord, *Ezra* 10. 25.

RAMOTH, heights, eminences.

RAPHA, giant, *whose descendants were called* Rephaim. *Some suppose they were the Titans.*

RAPHU, healed, *Num.* 13. 9.

REAIA, vision, 1 *Chron.* 5. 5.

REAIAH, vision of the Lord, *i.e.,* one who has seen the Lord, by faith, 1 *Chron.* 4. 2; *Ezra* 2. 47; *Neh.* 7. 50.

REBA, fourth, *Num.* 31. 8; *Josh.* 13. 21.

REBAIAH, fourth, *i.e.,* fourth son of the Lord.

REBEKAH, a rope with a noose.

RECHAB, horseman.

RECHAH, spacious, 1 *Chron.* 4. 12.

RED (SEA), the weed, or weedy sea, *Ex.* 10. 19.

REELAIAH, trembling of the Lord, *Ezra* 2. 2.

REGEM, friend, *i.e.,* of God, as from the Arabic, 1 *Chron.* 2. 47.

REGEM-MELEK, the friend of the king, *similar to the Arabic name,* Chalel Beg, friend of the king, *Zech.* 7. 2.

REHABIAH, enlarging of the Lord, 1 *Chron.* 23. 17; 24. 21; 26. 25.

REHOB, open space, *i.e.,* a street or road, *Num.* 13. 21; *Josh.* 19. 28, 30; 21. 31; *Judg.* 1. 31; 2 *Sam.* 8. 3, 12; 10. 8; 1 *Chron.* 6. 75; *Neh.* 10. 11.

REHOBOAM, enlarges the people, *i.e.,* sets at liberty.

REHOBOTH, streets, wide spaces; *one of the cities built by Nimrod.*

REHUM, merciful.

REI, friend of God, 1 *Kings* 1. 8.

REKEM, variegated, embroidered, *Num.* 31. 8; *Josh.* 13. 21; 18. 27; 1 *Chron.* 2. 43, 44.

REMALIAH, adorned of the Lord.

REMMON, pomegranate, *Josh.* 19. 7.

REPHAEL, healed of God, 1 *Chron.* 26. 7.

REPHAH, riches, 1 *Chron.* 7. 25.

REPHAIAH, healed of the Lord, 1 *Chron.* 3. 21; 4. 42; 7. 2; 9. 43; *Neh.* 3. 9.

REPHIDIM, props, supports.

RESEN, bridle, curb, *Gen.* 10. 12.

RESHEPH, sun-god, *whom the Hittites worshipped,* 1 *Chron.* 7. 25.

REU, associate, *i.e.,* of the Lord, *Gen.* 11. 18, 19, 20, 21; 1 *Chron.* 1. 25.

REUBEN, behold a son!

REUEL, friend of God, *Gen.* 36. 4, 10, 13, 17; *Ex.* 2. 18; *Num.* 2. 14; 1 *Chr.* 1. 35, 37; 9. 8.

REUMAH, exalted, *Gen.* 22. 24.

REZEPH, baking stone, 2 *Kings* 19. 12; *Isa.* 37. 12.

REZIA, delight, 1 *Chron.* 7. 39.

REZIN, firm, a king of Damascus.

REZON, prince, 1 *Kings* 11. 23.

RHEGIUM, a bursting forth.

RHESA, head first.

RHODA, a rose, *i.e., beautiful, and probably sacred to the sun.*

RHODES, *the same, famous for its Colossus.*

RIBAI, judgment of the Lord, 2 *Sam.* 23. 29; 1 *Chron.* 11. 31.

RIBLAH, multitude of people, *Num.* 34. 11; 2 *Kings* 23. 33; 25. 6, 20; *Jer.* 39. 5, 6; 52. 9, 10, 26, 27.

RIMMON, pomegranate; an Assyrian god worshipped at Damascus.

RIMMON-PAREZ, pomegranate of the breach, *Num.* 33. 19, 20.

RINNAH, a joyful cry, 1 *Chron.* 4. 20.

RIPHATH, a crusher, *i.e.,* of enemies, *Gen.* 10. 3; 1 *Chron.* 1. 6.

RISSAH, dew, *Num.* 33. 21, 22.

RITHMAH, broom, *Num.* 33. 18, 19.

RIZPAH, a baking stone.

ROGELIM, fountain of the fuller, 2 *Sam.* 17. 27; 19. 31.

ROHGAH, copious rain, 1 *Chron.* 7. 34.

ROMAMTI-EZER, I have lifted up help, 1 *Chron.* 25. 4, 31.

ROME, strong, firm.

ROSH, head, chief, *Gen.* 46. 21.

RUFUS, red.

RUMAH, high, 2 *Kings* 23. 36.

RUTH, beauty.

S.

SABTAH, breaking through, *Gen.* 10. 7; 1 *Chron.* 1. 9.

SABTECHAH, beating, *Gen.* 10. 7; 1 *Chr.* 1. 9.

SACAR, wages, 1 *Chron.* 11. 35; 26. 4.

SALAMIS, deadly serpents. *A place in the*

isle of Cyprus, famous for the worship of Aphrodite, *Acts* 13. 5.

SALCAH, firm, binding together, *Deut.* 3. 10; *Josh.* 12. 5; 13. 11; 1 *Chron.* 5. 11.

SALEM, at peace.

SALLAI, lifted up of the Lord, *Neh.* 11. 8; 12. 20.

SALMA, garment, 1 *Chron.* 2. 51, 54.

SALMON, SALMONE, shady.

SALOME, very shady.

SALU, lifted up, *Num.* 25. 14.

SAMARIA, vigilant guardian.

SAMGAR-NEBO, sword of Nebo, *Jer.* 39. 3.

SAMLAH, garment, *Gen.* 36. 36, 37; 1 *Chrôn.* 1. 47, 48.

SAMOS, lofty, very high; so called because it was situated very high. *An island in the Ionian Sea,* Acts 20. 15.

SAMOTHRACIA, Upper Thracia. *An island in the Ægean Sea,* Acts 16. 11.

SAMSON, splendid sun, *i.e.,* sun-like.

SAMUEL, heard of God.

SANBALLAT, hate in disguise.

SANSANNAH, palm branch, *Josh.* 15. 31.

SAPH, tall, 2 *Sam.* 28. 18.

SAPHIR, SAPPHIRA, beautiful.

SARAH, princess.

SARAI, my princess.

SARAPH, serpent, 1 *Chron.* 4. 22.

SARDIS, things which remain, *Rev.* 1. 11.

SAREPTA, purified, *i.e.,* in the fire, refined.

SARGON, prince of the sun. *He was king of Assyria,* B.C. 722. *He conquered Samaria, Hamuth, Arabia, Armenia, and many other places; and the late Mr. G. Smith discovered his royal seal, with his name and date, among the ruins of Konyunjik,* Isa. 20. 1.

SARID, survivor, escaped, *Josh.* 19. 10, 12.

SARON, *vid.* SHARON.

SARSECHIM, chief of the eunuchs, *Jer.* 39. 3.

SARUCH, branch. *The same as* Serug.

SATAN, the adversary, the lier in wait, the devil, who seduces men.

SAUL, asked for.

SCEVA, expectation, *or* hope of his parents.

SEBA, eminent.

SEBAT, breaking through. *The same as* Shalah, *Zech.* 1. 7.

SECACAH, enclosure, *Josh.* 15. 61.

SECHU, watch-tower, 1 *Sam.* 19. 22.

SECUNDUS, second, *Acts* 20. 4.

SEGUB, elevated, 1 *Kings* 16. 34; 1 *Chron.* 2. 21, 22.

SEIR, rough, bristly.

SELA, rock, 2 *Kings* 14. 7.

SELA-HAMMAHLEKOTH, rock of division, 1 *Sam.* 23. 28.

SELAH, rock, 2 *Kings* 14. 7; *Isa.* 16. 1.

SELED, exultation, 1 *Chron.* 2. 30.

SELEUCIA, *a city of Syria.*

SEMACHIAH, sustained of the Lord, 1 *Chron.* 26. 7.

SEMEI, heard of the Lord.

SENAAH, elevated, *Ezra* 2. 35; *Neh.* 7. 38.

SENEH, high. *A sharp rock over against* Gibeah, 1 *Sam.* 14. 4.

SENIR, coat of mail, 1 *Chron.* 5. 23; *Ezek.* 27. 5.

SENNACHERIB, sin has multiplied her brothers. *A son of Sargon, king of Assyria, who assumed the same title also as his predecessors,* Ebidu Malki, *subduer of kings. He was, like most of the Assyrian kings, a cruel tyrant.*

SENUAH, light.

SEORIM, barley.

SEPHAR, numbering. *A mountain in Arabia.*

SEPHARAD, *a place unknown.*

SEPHARVAIM, *a city in Mesopotamia.*

SERAH, SERAIAH, soldier of the Lord.

SERED, fear. *A son of Zebulon.*

SERGIUS PAULUS.

SERUG, branch.

SETH, appointed. *Third son of Adam.*

SETHER, hidden, mysterious. *This name contains the number of the Apocalyptic beast* (Rev. 13. 18) *in Hebrew letters.*

SHAALABBIN, place of foxes. *A Danite city.*

SHAAPH, balsam.

SHAARAIM, two gates.

SHAASHGAZ, servant of the beautiful, *if from the Persic,* Esth. 2. 14.

SHABBETHAI, rest of the Lord. *A Levite,* Ezra 10 15; *Neh.* 8, 7; 11. 16.

SHACHIA, captive of the Lord, 1 *Chron.* 8. 10.

SHADRACH, rejoicing in the way. *A companion of Daniel. Vid.* ABEDNEGO.

SHAGE, wandering; one of David's heroes, 1 *Chron.* 11. 34.

SHAHARAIM, two dawns, 1 *Chron.* 8. 8.

SHAHAZIMAH, lofty places. *A town of Issachar,* Josh. 19. 22.

SHALEM, peace, *Gen.* 33. 18.

SHALISHA, triangular; *a region near* Mount Ephraim.

SHALLECHETH, easting down; *a gate in the temple,* 1 Chron. 26. 16.

SHALLUM, SHALLUN, retribution.

SHALMAI, peace-offering of the Lord, *Ezra* 2. 46; *Neh.* 7. 48.

SHALMANESER, Shalman protects or helps, or likeness of Ann, *i.e.,* likeness of Noah; or worshippers of fire, *i.e.,* the sun.

SHAMA, hearing. *One of David's men of war.*

SHAMGAR, one of the judges of Israel.

SHAMIR, a sharp point; a guard, *Josh.* 15. 48; *Judg.* 10. 1, 2; 1 *Chron.* 24. 24.

SHAMMAH, astonishment. desolatiou. 1 *Chron.* 2. 28, 32, 44, 45; 4. 17

SHAMMUA, hearing of the Lord.

SHAMMERAI, brave, 1 *Chron.* 8. 26.

SHAPHAM, bare, 1 *Chron.* 5. 12.

SHAPHAN, cony, *i.e.,* cunning.

SHAPHAT, judge.

SHAPHER, beauty; *a place near where the Israelites pitched their twentieth camp in the wilderness,* Num. 33. 23, 24.

SHARAI, liberated of the Lord. *He was afterwards a captive to self-will.* Ezra 10. 40.

SHARAR, hand, stay, *i.e.,* of the family, 2 *Sam.* 23. 33.

SHAREZER, prince of fire; *or* splendour of the sun; a son of Sennacherib, who was so called in honour of the sun. *He was one of the murderers of his father, and his name does not occur in the Assyrian inscriptions.*

SHARON, a great plain, or plain country, running along the coast of the Mediterranean Sea from Joppa to Cæsarea; *and was famous for its roses, which were so beautiful that the Son of God could say of Himself,* "I am the Rose of Sharon."

SHARUHEN, a pleasant dwelling-place, *Josh.* 19. 6.

SHASHAI, habitation of the Lord, *i.e.,* he was a faithful servant of God, *Ezra* 10. 40.

SHASHAK, vehement desire, 1 *Chron.* 8. 14, 25.

SHAVEH, plain, *Gen.* 14. 17.

SHAVEH-KIRIATHAIM, plain of the double city, *Gen.* 14. 5.

SHABSHA, habitation, *i.e.,* of the Lord.

SHEAL, petition; a son of Bani, who was given in answer to prayer, *Ezra* 10. 29.

SHEALTIEL, I asked for from God.

SHEAR-JASHUB, a remnant shall return, *i.e.,* from captivity. *A prophetic name of a son of Isaiah.*

SHEARIAH, estimated of the Lord; a son of Azel, 1 *Chron.* 8. 38; 9. 44.

SHEBA, (1) man; (2) oath, *or* seven. *Number seven and an oath are often interchangeable among the Chaldeans.*

SHEBAM, sweet smell. *The same as* SIB-MAH, Num. 32. 3.

SHEBANIAH, caused to grow up of the Lord, 1 *Chron.* 15. 24; *Neh.* 9. 4, 5; 10. 4, 10, 12; 12. 14.

SHEBARIM, fracture terrors, *Josh.* 7. 5.

SHEBER, breach, singular of the preceding, 1 *Chron.* 2. 48.

SHEBNA, youth, grown up.

SHEBUEL, captive of God, 1 *Chron.* 23. 16; 25. 4; 26. 24.

SHECHANIAH, inhabited of the Lord, *i.e.,* one of the Lord's people, 1 *Chron.* 3. 21, 22; 24. 11; *Ezra* 8. 3, 5; 10 2; *Neh.* 3. 29; 6. 18; 12. 3.

SHECHEM, back; a city of Samaria. *It is now called* Nablous, *and contains about 13,000 inhabitants.*

SHEDEUR, casting forth of fire, *i.e.,* lightning, *Num.* 1. 5; 2. 10; 7. 30, 35; 10. 18.

SHEHARIAH, sought of the Lord, 1 *Chron.* 8. 26.

SHELAH, (1) prayer, request; (2) sent, shooting forth.

SHELEMIAH, repaid of the Lord.

SHELEPH, drawn out, *i.e.,* selected, *Gen.* 10. 26; 1 *Chron.* 1. 20.

SHELESH, triad, 1 *Chron.* 7. 35.

SHELOMI, my peace, *Num.* 34. 27.

SHELOMITH, retribution, *i.e.,* love of peace, *Lev.* 24. 11; 1 *Chron.* 3. 19; 23. 9, 18; 26. 25, 26, 28; 2 *Chron.* 11. 20; *Ezra* 8. 10.

SHELOMOTH, retribution, 1 *Chron.* 24. 22.

SHELUMIEL, friend of God.

SHEM, name; *i.e.*, distinguished.

SHEMA, hearing, fame, *Josh.* 15. 26; 1 *Chron.* 2. 43, 44; 5. 8; 8. 13; *Neh.* 8. 4.

SHEMAAH, hearing, fame. 1 *Chron.* 12. 3.

SHEMAIAH, heard of the Lord.

SHEMARIAH, guarded of the Lord, 1 *Chr.* 12. 5; 2 *Chr.* 11. 19; *Ezra* 10. 32, 41.

SHEMEBER, name of wing, *i.e.*, of great celebrity. *Gen.* 14. 2.

SHEMER, custody, who is in the keeping of the Lord, 1 *Kings* 16. 24.

SHEMIDA, name of knowledge, *i.e.*, famous, *Num.* 26. 32; *Josh.* 17. 2; 1 *Chron.* 7. 19.

SHEMIRAMOTH, most exalted name, 1 *Chron.* 15. 18, 20; 16. 5; 2 *Chron.* 17. 8.

SHEMUEL, asked for of God. *The same as* Samuel, *Num.* 34. 20; 1 *Chron.* 6. 33; 7. 2.

SHEN, tooth. *It was a sharp rock in shape of a tooth.* 1 Sam. 7. 12.

SHENAZAR, light of splendour, 1 *Chr.* 3. 18.

SHENIR, coat of mail.

SHEPHAM, coney, *Num.* 34. 10, 11.

SHEPHATIAH, judge of the Lord.

SHEPHI, high, *i.e.*, illustrious.

SHEPHO, high, *Gen.* 36. 23; 1 *Chron.* 1. 40.

SHEPHUPHAN, a serpent, 1 *Chron.* 8. 5.

SHERAH, consanguinity, *i.e.*, a female relation by blood, 1 *Chron.* 7. 24.

SHEREBIAH, deliverance of the Lord, *i.e.*, from captivity, *Ezra* 8. 18, 24; *Neh.* 8. 7; 9. 4, 5; 10. 12; 12. 8, 24.

SHERESH, root, *i.e.*, of a family, 1 *Chron.* 7. 16.

SHESHACH, confusion, *Jer.* 25. 26; 51. 41.

SHESHAI, whitish, *Num.* 13. 22; *Josh.* 15. 14; *Judg.* 1. 10.

SHESHAN, city. *as perhaps for Shushan,* 1 *Chron.* 2. 31, 34, 35.

SHESHBAZZAR, worshipper of fire, *i.e.*, the sun.

SHETHAR, star. *Persic.* Esth. 1. 14.

SHETHAR-BOZNAI, star of splendour, *Ezra* 5. 3, 6; 6. 6, 13.

SHEVA, habitation, 2 Sam. 20. 25; 1 *Chron.* 2. 49.

SHIBMAH, sweet smell, *Num.* 32. 38.

SHICRON, drunkenness, *Josh.* 15. 11.

SHIHON, overturning, *Josh.* 19. 19.

SHIHOR, very black, turbid; the river Nile.

SHIHOR-LIBNATH, river of glass, *Josh.* 19. 26.

SHILHI, armed, *i.e.*, of the Lord, 1 *Kings* 22. 42; 2 *Chron.* 20. 31.

SHILHIM, armed men, *i.e.*, a fortress, *Josh.* 15. 32.

SHILOAH, sent. *So called from the sending forth of the water from one source into the two pools of Bethesda and Siloam.*

SHILOH, Pacificator, the Peace-maker, Jesus Christ.

SHILONI, SHILONITE, sent, *Neh.* 11. 5.

SHILSHAH, triad, *i.e.*, third son, 1 *Chron.* 7. 37.

SHIMEA, hearing, rumour, 1 *Chron.* 8. 32.

SHIMEAH, hearing.

SHIMEAM, astonishment, 1 *Chron.* 9. 38.

SHIMEATH, hearing, fame. *An Ammonitess.* 2 *Kings* 12. 21; 2 *Chron.* 24. 26.

SHIMEATHITES, responsers, 1 *Chr.* 2. 55.

SHIMEI, famous of the Lord.

SHIMON, great desert, 1 *Chron.* 4. 20.

SHIMRATH, ward, *i.e.*, one in the hands of the Divine guardian of men, 1 *Chr.* 8. 21.

SHIMRI, ward of the Lord, 1 *Chron.* 4. 37; 11. 45; 26. 10; 2 *Chron.* 29. 13.

SHIMRITH, guarded, *i.e.*, of the Lord, 2 *Chron.* 24. 26.

SHIMRON, vigilant, guardian, *Gen.* 46. 13; *Num.* 26. 24, 1 *Chr.* 7. 1; *Josh.* 11. 1; 19. 15.

SHIMSHAI, sun of the Lord.

SHINAB, tooth of the father, *Gen.* 14. 2.

SHINAR, a casting out, or a scattering every way; *but the derivation is very uncertain.*

SHIPHI, eminent, 1 *Chron.* 4. 37.

SHIPHRAH, beauty, brightness.

SHIPHTAN, most just judge, *Num.* 34. 24.

SHISHAK, *derivation obscure.*

SHITRAI, scribe of the Lord, 1 *Chr.* 27. 29.

SHIZA, raising up, 1 *Chron.* 11. 42.

SHOBAB, backsliding, 2 Sam. 5. 14; 1 *Chron.* 2. 18; 3. 5; 14. 4.

SHOBACH, poured out, 2 Sam. 10. 16, 18.

SHOBAI, recompence of the Lord, *Ezra* 2. 42; *Neh.* 7. 45.

SHOBI, *the same*, 2 Sam. 17. 27.

SHOCHO, hedge, defence, *i.e.*, fortification, 2 *Chron.* 28. 18.

SHOCHOH, *and* SHOCO, idea, 2 *Chr.* 11. 7.

SHOMER, guarded of the Lord, 2 *Kings* 12, 21: 1 *Chron.* 7. 32.

SHUA, wealth, 1 *Chron.* 7. 32.

SHUAH, prostration.

SHUAL, fox.

SHUHAM, pit-digger, *Num.* 26. 42.

SHULAMITE, complete.

SHUNEM, two resting places, *Josh.* 19. 18; 1 Sam. 28. 4; 2 *Kings* 4. 8.

SHUNI, tranquillity, quietness, *Gen.* 46. 16; *Num.* 26. 15.

SHUPHAM, serpent, *Num.* 26. 39.

SHUPPIM, serpents, 1 *Chron.* 7. 12, 15; 26. 16.

SHUR, fort, *i.e.*, a fortified place, *Gen.* 16. 7; 20. 1; 25. 18; *Ex.* 15. 22; 1 Sam. 15. 7; 27. 8.

SHUSHAN, lily.

SHUTHELAH, crashing and rending, *Num.* 26. 35, 36; 1 *Chron.* 7. 20, 21.

SIA, council, *Neh.* 7. 47.

SIBBECHAI, thicket of the Lord, or interwoven very thickly, 2 Sam. 21. 18; 1 *Chron.* 11. 29; 20. 4; 27. 11.

SIBRAIM, two-fold hope.

SIDDIM, plains, *Gen.* 14. 3, 8, 10.

SIDON, fishing, plenty of fish.

SIHON, sweeping away, *i.e.*, a general who drives everything before him.

SILAS, a shortened form of SILVANUS.

SILOAH, SILOAM, sent.

SILVANUS, born in the wood. *See* SILAS.

SIMEON, hearing with acceptance.

SIMON, *the same.*

SIMRI, song of the Lord. *Same as* Zimri.

SIN, clay, bush. *It was called* Pelusium. *There was a moon-god among the Babylonians of this name.*

SINAI, bush of the Lord. *A very desolate region, in the midst of which rose up the Mount of Terror.*

SINIM, Pelusiots, according to Simonis, *Isa.* 49. 12.

SINITE, *the same*, *Gen.* 10. 17; 1 *Chr.* 1. 15.

SION, lifted up, *Deut.* 4. 48; *Matt.* 21. 5; *John* 12. 15; *Rom.* 9. 33; 11. 26; *Heb.* 12. 22; 1 *Pet.* 2. 6; *Rev.* 14. 1.

SIRION, breastplate. *The Sidonian name of Hermon, Deut.* 3. 9; *Ps.* 29. 6.

SISAMAI, the sun, 1 *Chron.* 2. 40.

SISERA, a field of battle.

SITNAH, accusation, hatred, *Gen.* 26. 21.

SMYRNA, *derivation obscure. This city was situated about eight miles north of Ephesus.*.

SO, lifted up.

SODI, acquaintance of God.

SODOM, flaming, burning.

SOLOMON, peaceable, *or* great peace.

◄ SOPATER, a contracted form of the following name. *Acts* 20. 4.

SOPHERETH, female scribe, *Ezra* 2. 55; *Neh.* 7. 57.

SOREK, choice vine.

SOSIPATER, wealth of the father, or servant of the father, *Rom.* 16. 21. *Vid.* SOPATER

SOSTHENES.

SOTAI, drawn back of the Lord, *Ezra* 2. 55; *Neh.* 7. 57.

SPAIN, *derivation and interpretation uncertain.*

STACHYS, ear of corn, which among the ancients was an emblem of fertility and fruitfulness.

STEPHANUS, crown. *The name of a person baptized by Paul.*

STEPHEN, crown.

SUAH, sweeping. *A son of Zophar,* 1 *Chron.* 7. 36.

SUCCOTH, booths.

SUCCOTH-BENOB, tabernacles of daughters, *i.e.*, sacristes of Venus.

SUCHATHITES, dwellers in booths. *Place unknown,* 1 *Chron.* 2. 55.

SUKKIIMS, dwellers in tents, 2 *Chron.* 12. 3.

SUR, go back, 2 *Kings* 11. 6.

SUSANCHITES, inhabitants of Susa, *Ezra* 4. 9.

SUSANNA, lily.

SUSI, horseman, *Num.* 13. 11.

SYCHAR, folly, *John* 4. 5.

SYENE, opening, key, *i.e.*, of Egypt, *Ezek.* 29. 10; 30. 6.

SYNTYCHE, good fortune, good luck, *Phil.* 4. 2.

SYRACUSE, a city of Sicily, *Acts* 28. 12.

SYRIA, *vid.* ARAM.

T.

TAANACH, wandering through, *Josh.* 12. 21; 17. 11; 21. 25; *Judg.* 1. 27; 5. 19. 1 *Kings* 4. 12; 1 *Chron.* 7. 29.

TAANATH-SHILOH, entrance to Shiloh, *Josh.* 16. 6.

TABBAOTH, rings, *Ezra* 2. 43; *Neh.* 7. 46.

TABBATH, renowned, celebrated, *Judg.* 7. 22.

TABEEL, goodness of God, *Ezra* 4. 7.

TABERAH, consuming, burning, *Num.* 11. 3.

TABITHA, gazelle, called in the Greek Testament *Dorcas,* a gazelle, *Acts* 9. 36, 40.

TABOR, stone quarry.

TABRIMON, goodness of Rimmon, 1 *Kings* 15. 18.

TACHMONITE, wisdom, 2 Sam. 23. 8.

TADMOR, Palmyrene, *or* admiration.

TAHAN, supplication, *i.e.*, of parents, 1 *Chron.* 7. 25.

TAHATH, depression, 1 *Chron.* 6. 24, 37; 7. 20.

TAHPENES, head of the age.

TAHTIM-HODSHI, under the new moon, 2 Sam. 24. 6.

TALMAI, abounding in furrows, *Num.* 13. 22; *Josh.* 15. 14; *Judg.* 1. 10; 2 Sam. 3. 3; 13. 37; 1 *Chron.* 3. 2.

TALMON, injurious, oppression, 1 *Chron.* 9. 17; *Ezra* 2. 42; *Neh.* 7. 45; 11. 19; 12. 25.

TAMAR, palm.

TAMMUZ, the sun of life.

TANACH, wandering through.

TANHUMETH, consolation, 2 *Kings* 25. 23; *Jer.* 40. 8.

TAPHATH, drop of myrrh, or stacti, *i.e.*, myrrh flowing spontaneously, 1 *Kings* 4. 11.

TAPUAH, apple, fruitful in apples, *Josh.* 12. 17; 15. 34; 16. 8; 17. 8; 1 *Chron.* 2. 43.

TARAH, delay, *Num.* 33. 27, 28.

TARALAH, reeling. *A town in the land of Benjamin,* Josh. 18. 27.

TAREA, delaying cries, 1 *Chron.* 8. 35.

TARSHISH, subjection of enemies.

TARSUS, dove.

TARTAK, the moon.

TARTAN, great increase, 2 *Kings* 18. 17; *Isa.* 20. 1.

TATNAI, gift, *Ezra* 5. 3, 6; 6. 6, 13.

TEBAH, confidence, *i.e.*, of parents, *Gen.* 22. 24.

TEBALIAH, baptized of the Lord, 1 *Chron.* 26. 11.

TEHAPHNEHES, the beginning of the age: or, the beginning of the world or earth.

TEHINNAH, grace, prayer, 1 *Chron.* 4. 12.

TEKOA, pitching, *i.e.*, of tents.

TEL-ABIB, hill of ears of corn, *Ezek.* 3. 15.

TEL-HARESHA, TEL-HARSA, hill of ploughing, *Ezra* 2. 59; *Neh.* 7. 61.

TEL-MELA, hill of salt, *Ezra* 2. 59; *Neh.* 7. 61.

TELAH, fracture 1 *Chron.* 7. 25.

TELAIM, young lambs, 1 Sam. 15. 4.

TELASSAR, hill of Assur.

TELEM, oppression. *A Levite porter,* Josh. 15. 24; *Ezra* 10. 24.

TEMA, desert. *A son of Ishmael.*

TEMAN, southern quarter.

TERAH, delay. *A son of Nahor.*

TERESH, severe, austere, *Esth.* 2. 21; 6. 2.

TERTIUS, third, *i.e.*, son.

TERTULLUS, third, diminutive.

THADDÆUS, praise of God. *The same as* Judah, *Matt.* 10. 3; *Mark* 3. 18.

THAHASH, badger. *The skin of this animal was used to cover the tabernacle, and it is rather uncertain whether it referred to the seal or badger.* Gen. 22. 24.

THAMAH, TAMAH, laughing, *i.e.*, joy of parents, *Ezra* 2. 53; *Neh.* 7. 55.

THARSHISH, vid. TARSHISH.

THEBEZ, brightness. *A town of Shechem.*

THEL SAR, giver of treasure, 2 *Kings* 19. 12; *Isa.* 37. 12.

THEOPHILUS, lover of God.

THESSALONICA, victory of Thessalos.

THEUDAS, praise. *Some suppose it a contraction of the Greek name Theodorus, the gift of God (Acts* 5. 36).

THOMAS twin, in the Hebrew, and also called *Didymus,* in the Greek, which is of the same signification.

THYATIRA.

TIBERIAS, a city built by Herod in honour of Tiberius Cæsar.

TIBERIUS, an Emperor of Rome, *Luke* 3. 1.

TIBHATH, security, *i.e.*, dwelling in safety, 1 *Chron.* 18. 8.

TIBNI, building of the Lord.

TIDAL, fear, reverence, *Gen* 14. 1, 9.

TIGLATH-PILESER, mother of the gods.

TILON, gift, 1 Chron. 4. 20.

TIMÆUS, honourable, Mark 10. 46.

TIMNA, restraint. contr. restrained, Gen. 36. 12, 22, 40; 1 Chron. 1. 36, 39, 51.

TIMNAH, portion assigned, i.e., separated, Josh. 15. 10, 57; 2 Chron. 28. 18.

TIMNATH-HERES, portion of the sun, i.e., a place dedicated to the sun, and the same as the following, Judg. 2. 9.

TIMNATH-SERAH, portion redundant. Joshua so called the portion which fell to his lot in Canaan, out of the fulness of his heart. It was an abundant portion, and a portion redundant; but as soon as he was dead, the people, in their wickedness and folly, dedicated it to the sun, and called it Timnath-Heres, Josh. 19. 50; 24. 30.

TIMON, honourable, Acts 6. 5.

TIMOTHEUS, venerating God, or worshipper of God.

TIPHSAH, passage, i.e., of the river Euphrates. 1 Kings 4. 24; 2 Kings 15. 16.

TIRAS, desire, i.e., of parents, Gen. 10. 2; 1 Chron. 1. 5.

TIRATHITES, openings, 1 Chron. 2. 55.

TIRHAKAH, exalted, 2 Kings 19. 9; Isa. 37. 9.

TIRHANAH, inhabiting of a residence, i.e., dwelling in it securely, 1 Chron. 2. 48.

TIRIA, fear. A son of Jehaleel, 1 Chron. 4. 16.

TIRZAH, pleasantness.

TITUS, honourable.

TOAH, prostration, i.e., of his mother, 1 Chron. 6. 34.

TOB, good, i.e., a good place, or fertile land, Judg. 11. 3, 5.

TOB-ADONIJAH, distinguished of the Lord. A Levite, 2 Chron. 17. 8.

TOBIAH, distinguished of the Lord.

TOCHEN, portion cut out, 1 Chron. 4. 32.

TOGARMAH, breaking bones.

TOLA, little worm.

TOLAD, generation, i.e., posterity, 1 Chron. 4. 29.

TOPHEL, insipid. A place in the desert, so called because the Israelites murmured concerning the manna, Deut. 1. 1.

TOPHET, place of burning. This place was famous for its human sacrifices made to the horrid monster, Moloch.

TOU, error. A king of Hamath.

TROAS, the name of a city in the region of the Troad.

TROGYLLIUM, cavern, Acts 20. 15.

TROPHIMUS, an Ephesian convert, Acts 20. 4; 21. 29; 2 Tim. 4. 20.

TRYPHENA, delicate. A Roman lady.

TRYPHOSA, delicate, and of gentle manners.

TUBAL, flowing forth, i.e., multiplication or diffusion of race.

TUBAL-CAIN, flowing forth of Cain, i.e., spreading and multiplication of the race of Cain, Gen. 4. 22.

TYCHICUS, fortunate, happy.

TYRANNUS, lord, prince; or a school of grammar.

TYRE, rock; a Phœnician city, situated on the eastern shore of the Mediterranean Sea.

U.

UCAL, I will prevail.

UEL, will of God, Ezra 10. 34.

ULAI, muddy water, Dan. 8. 2, 16.

ULAM, first of all, i.e., first-born, 1 Chron. 7. 16, 17; 8. 39, 40.

ULLA, yoke, 1 Chron. 7. 39.

UMMAH, union, i.e., communion of inhabitants, Josh. 19. 30.

UNNI, afflicted of the Lord, or depressed of the Lord, 1 Chron. 15. 18, 20; Neh. 12. 9.

UPHAZ, island of gold, and the same as Ophir, Jer. 10. 9; Dan. 10. 5.

UR, ligut in Hebrew; and in Chaldean the great light, i.e., the sun.

URI, URIAH, light of the Lord

URIEL, light of God, 1 Chron. 6. 24; 15, 5, 11; 2 Chron. 13. 2.

UTHAI, opposition of the Lord, 1 Chron. 9. 4; Ezra 8. 14.

UZ, counsellor.

UZAI, velocity of the Lord, Neh. 3. 25.

UZAL, going to and fro, i.e., a wanderer, Gen. 10. 27; 1 Chron. 1. 21.

UZZA, UZZAH, strength.

UZZEN-SHERAH, ear of Sherah, 1 Chron. 7. 24.

UZZI, power of the Lord, 1 Chron. 6. 5, 6, 51; 7. 2, 3, 7; 9. 8; Ezra 7. 4; Neh. 11. 22; 12. 19, 42.

UZZIA, power of the Lord, 1 Chron. 11. 44.

UZZIAH, power of the Lord.

UZZIEL, strength of God.

V.

VAJEZATHA, white, sincere, pure, Esth. 9. 9.

VANIAH, weak, Ezra 10. 36.

VASHNI, gift of God, 1 Chron. 6. 28.

VASHTI, beautiful woman.

VOPHSI, addition of the Lord, Num. 13. 14.

Z.

ZAANAN, rich in flocks, Micah 1. 11.

ZAANANNIM, enormous migration, Josh. 19. 33.

ZAAVAN, ZAVAN, great agitations, Gen. 36. 27; 1 Chron. 1. 42.

ZABAD, given, i.e., of God, 1 Chron. 2. 36, 37; 7. 21; 11. 41; 2 Chron. 24. 26; Ezra 10. 27, 33, 43.

ZABBAI, clemency of the Lord, Ezra 10. 28; Neh. 3. 20.

ZABDI, gift of the Lord, Josh. 7. 1, 17, 18; 1 Chron. 8. 19; 27. 27; Neh. 11. 17.

ZABDIEL, gift of God, 1 Chron. 27. 2; Neh. 11. 14.

ZABUD, gift bestowed, 1 Kings 4. 5.

ZACCAI, pure of the Lord, Ezra 2. 9; Neh. 7. 14.

ZACCHEUS, pure, i.e., he was just in the presence of God.

ZACCUR, mindful, Num. 13. 4; 1 Chron. 4. 26; 24. 27; 25. 2, 10; Neh. 3. 2; 10. 12; 12. 35; 13. 13.

ZACHARIAH, remembrance of the Lord.

ZACHER, remembrance, 1 Chron. 8. 31.

ZADOK, just.

ZAHAM, loathing, 2 Chron. 11. 19.

ZAIR, little, 2 Kings 8. 21.

ZALAPH, fracture, Neh. 3. 30.

ZALMON, shady, Judg. 9. 48; 2 Sam. 23. 28; Ps. 68. 14.

ZALMONAH, shady, Num. 33. 41, 42.

ZALMUNNA, shadow is withheld.

ZAMZUMMIMS, tribes making a noise; a race of giants long ago extinct, Deut. 2. 20.

ZANOAH, stinking, Josh. 15. 34, 56; 1 Chron. 4. 18; Neh. 3. 13; 11. 30.

ZAPHNATH-PAANEAH, sorrow of the age, or revealer of a secret, Gen. 41. 45.

ZAPHON, north or north wind, Josh. 13. 27.

ZAREPHATH, workshop for melting and refining metals.

ZARETAN, vid. ZARTHAN, Josh. 3. 16; 1 Kings 4. 12; 7. 46.

ZARETH-SHAHAR, splendour of the morning; i.e., a town facing the rising sun, Josh. 13. 19.

ZARTHAN, narrowness of dwelling-place; also called ZARETAN and Zartanah, Zattu, ornament, beauty, Ezra 2. 8; 10. 27; Neh. 7. 13; 10. 14.

ZAZA, Derivation unknown. 1 Chron. 2. 33.

ZEBADIAH, gift of the Lord, 1 Chron. 8. 15, 17; 12. 7; 26. 2; 27. 7; 2 Chron. 17. 8; 19. 11; Ezra 8. 8; 10. 20.

ZEBAH, sacrifice, i.e., devoted to Moloch.

ZEBEDEE, devoted to the Lord.

ZEBINAH, bought, Ezra 10. 43.

ZEBOIM, (1) gathering of troops of soldiers; (2) hyænas. A valley and town in the tribe of Benjamin.

ZEBUDAH, bestowing a gift, 2 Kings 23. 36.

ZEBUL, habitation.

ZEBULUN, wished-for habitation.

ZECHARIAH, remembrance of the Lord, 1 Chron. 5. 7; 9. 21, 37; 15. 18, 20, 24; 16. 5; 24. 25; 26. 2, 11, 14; 27. 21; 2 Chron. 17. 7; 20. 14; 21. 2; 24. 20; 26. 5; 29. 13; 34. 12; 35. 8; Ezra 5. 1; 6. 14; 8. 3, 11, 16; 10. 26; Neh. 8. 4; 11. 4, 5, 12; 12. 16, 35, 41; Isa. 8. 2; Zech. 1. 1, 7; 7. 1, 8.

ZELOPHEHAD, first rupture, i.e., first-born, Num. 26. 33.

ZELOTES, zealot, a name applied to Simon, Acts 1. 13.

ZELZAH, shade in the heat of the sun, 1 Sam. 10. 2.

ZEMARAIM, two cuttings off, Josh. 18. 22; 2 Chron. 13. 4.

ZEMIRA(H), song, i.e., joy of parents, 1 Chron. 7. 8.

ZENAN, place of flock, Josh. 15. 37.

ZEPHANIAH, bid of the Lord, 2 Kings 25. 18; 1 Chron. 6. 36; Zeph. 1. 1; Zech. 6. 10.

ZEPHATH, watch-tower, Judg. 1. 17.

ZEPHO, ZEPHI, expectation, i.e., hope of parents, Gen. 36. 11. 15; 1 Chron. 1. 36.

ZEPHTHAH, watch-tower, 2 Chron. 14. 10.

ZER, flint, Josh. 19. 35.

ZERAH, rising of light, i.e., joy of parents, Gen. 36. 13; Num. 26. 13, 20; 1 Chron. 6. 21; 2 Chron. 14. 9.

ZERAHIAH, rising of light in the Lord, 1 Chron. 6. 6; Ezra 7. 4 : 8. 4.

ZERED, luxuriant growth of trees, Num. 21. 12.

ZEREDA, cooling, 1 Kings 11. 26.

ZERESH, star of adoration, Esth. 5. 10, 14; 6. 13.

ZERETH, splendour, 1 Chron. 4. 7.

ZEROR, small bundle. 1 Sam. 9. 1.

ZERUAH, leprous, 1 Kings 11. 26.

ZERUBBABEL, born in Babylon, 1 Chron. 3. 19.

ZERUIAH, cleft, 1 Sam. 26. 6.

ZETHAM, olive, 1 Chron. 23. 8; 26. 22.

ZETHAN, olive-tree, 1 Chron. 7. 10.

ZETHAR, very great, Esth. 1. 10.

ZIA, shaking with fear, 1 Chron. 5. 13.

ZIBA, plant, 2 Sam. 9. 2.

ZIBEON, versicolour, variegated, Gen. 36. 2.

ZIBIAH, female gazelle, 2 Kings 12. 1; 1 Chron. 8, 9.

ZICHRI, remembrance of the Lord, 1 Chron. 8. 19, 23; 9. 15; 26. 25; 27. 16; 2 Chron. 17. 16; 23. 1; 28. 7; Neh. 11. 9; 12. 17.

ZIDDIM, sides, Josh. 19. 35.

ZIHA, drought, Ezra 2. 43; Neh. 11. 21.

ZIKLAG, outflowing of a fountain, Josh. 15. 31.

ZILLAH, shadow, Gen. 4. 19.

ZILPAH, dropping, Gen. 29. 24.

ZILTHAI, shadow of the Lord, 1 Chron. 8. 20; 12. 20.

ZIMA, vid. ZIZA.

ZIMMAH, wicked device, 1 Chron. 6. 20, 42; 2 Chron. 29. 12.

ZIMRAN, fine chamois, Gen. 25. 2.

ZIMRI, song of the Lord, Num. 25. 14; 1 Kings 16. 9; 1 Chron. 2. 6; 8. 36.

ZIN, a low palm-tree, Num. 13. 21; Josh. 15. 1, 3.

ZION, very dry.

ZIOR, smallness.

ZIPH, borrowed, Josh. 15. 24, 55; 1 Chr. 4. 16.

ZIPHAH, borrowed.

ZIPHION, earnest expectation, Gen. 46. 16.

ZIPHRON, sweet smell, Num. 34. 9.

ZIPPOR, little bird, Num. 22. 2.

ZIPPORAH, little bird, Ex. 2. 21.

ZITHRI, protection of the Lord, Ex. 6. 21, 22.

ZIZ, flower, 2 Chron. 20. 16.

ZIZA, abundance, 1 Chron. 4. 37; 23. 11; 2 Chron. 11. 20.

ZOAN, low region. The same as Tanis, Num. 13. 22.

ZOAR, smallness, Gen. 13. 10; 14. 2, 8; 19. 22, 23, 30; Deut. 34. 3; Isa. 15. 5; Jer. 48. 34.

ZOBA, ZOBAH, depression, 1 Sam. 14 47.

ZOBEBAH, going slowly, 1 Chron. 4. 8.

ZOHELETH, serpent 1 Kings 1. 9.

ZOHETH, 1 Chron. 4. 20.

ZOPHAH, cruse, 1 Chron. 7. 35, 36.

ZOPHAR, chirping, Job 2. 11; 11. 1; 20. 1; 42 9.

ZOPHIM, watchman, Num. 23. 14.

ZOREAH, nest of hornets, Josh. 15. 33.

ZUAR, very small, Num. 1. 8.

ZUPH, sweet, 1 Sam. 1. 1; 9. 5; 1 Chron. 6. 35.

ZUR, rock, Num. 25. 15; 1 Chron. 8. 30.

ZURIEL, rock of God, Num. 3. 35.

ZURISHADDAI, rock of the Almighty, Num. 1. 6.

ZUZIMS, commotions, Gen. 14. 5